Barron's Profiles of American Colleges

Volume 1: Descriptions of the Colleges

Thirteenth Edition

Compiled and Edited by the College Division
of Barron's Educational Series

BARRON'S EDUCATIONAL SERIES, INC.
Woodbury, New York • London • Toronto • Sydney

© Copyright 1982 by Barron's Educational Series, Inc.

Prior editions © Copyright 1980, 1978, 1976, 1974, 1973, 1972, 1971, 1970, 1968, 1967, 1966, 1965, 1964 by Barron's Educational Series, Inc.

All rights reserved.
No part of this book may be reproduced
in any form, by photostat, microfilm, xerography,
or any other means, or incorporated into any
information retrieval system, electronic or
mechanical, without the written permission
of the copyright owner.

All inquiries should be addressed to
Barron's Educational Series, Inc.
113 Crossways Park Drive
Woodbury, New York 11797

Library of Congress Catalog Card No. 82-11459

Paper Edition
International Standard Book No. 0-8120-2459-1

Cloth Edition
International Standard Book No. 0-8120-5449-0

Library of Congress Cataloging in Publication Data
  Main entry under title:
  Barron's profiles of American colleges.

  Includes bibliographies and indexes.
  Contents: v. 1. Descriptions of the colleges—
v. 2. Index of college majors.
  1. Universities and colleges—United States—
Directories.   I. Barron's Educational Series, Inc.
College Division.   II. Title: Profiles of American
colleges.
L901.B285 1982   378.73   82-11459
  ISBN 0-8120-5449-0 (v. 1)
  ISBN 0-8120-2459-1 (pbk. : v. 1)
  ISBN 0-8120-5450-4 (v. 2)
  ISBN 0-8120-2460-5 (pbk.)

PRINTED IN THE UNITED STATES OF AMERICA
2 3 4 5 004 9 8 7 6 5 4 3 2 1

CONTENTS

PREFACE TO THE THIRTEENTH EDITION   v

AN EXPLANATION OF THE BOOK   vii
The Basics
The Capsule
The General Description

COLLEGE ADMISSIONS SELECTOR   x
Most Competitive
Highly Competitive
Very Competitive
Competitive
Less Competitive
Noncompetitive
Special

CHOOSING A COLLEGE   xix
Gather Information
Determine Some Basic Preferences
Evaluate Your Record
Compare the Colleges
Investigate Sources of Financial Aid
Get More Information
Apply for Admission
Await the Replies

ADVICE FOR FOREIGN STUDENTS   xxiii
Testing and Admission
Going to the United States
Arriving on Campus
English Language and Cultural Orientation Programs
Expenses
Further Reading

COLLEGIATE TERMS   xli

FURTHER READING   xlii

KEY TO ABBREVIATIONS   xliii
Degrees
Other Abbreviations

COLLEGE-LOCATOR MAPS

PROFILES OF AMERICAN COLLEGES

Alabama	1	Nebraska	477
Alaska	16	Nevada	487
Arizona	19	New Hampshire	489
Arkansas	24	New Jersey	498
California	34	New Mexico	525
Colorado	94	New York	531
Connecticut	107	North Carolina	622
Delaware	120	North Dakota	652
District of Columbia	123	Ohio	657
Florida	132	Oklahoma	700
Georgia	150	Oregon	713
Guam	175	Pennsylvania	726
Hawaii	176	Puerto Rico	795
Idaho	179	Rhode Island	801
Illinois	184	South Carolina	808
Indiana	226	South Dakota	825
Iowa	254	Tennessee	834
Kansas	273	Texas	857
Kentucky	289	Utah	897
Louisiana	304	Vermont	901
Maine	318	Virgin Islands	911
Maryland	331	Virginia	912
Massachusetts	347	Washington	939
Michigan	390	West Virginia	951
Minnesota	416	Wisconsin	963
Mississippi	436	Wyoming	986
Missouri	446	Canada and Mexico	987
Montana	471		

COLLEGES WITH SPECIAL PROGRAMS

Religious	992
ROTC	998
Upper Division	1007

ALPHABETICAL INDEX OF COLLEGES 1009

PREFACE TO THE THIRTEENTH EDITION

The first edition of *Barron's Profiles of American Colleges,* published in 1964, was included in *Outstanding Reference Books, 1964,* compiled by the Reference Services Division of the American Library Association. Revised editions have appeared regularly since then; each not only has updated facts contained in earlier editions but also has included new kinds of information. *Barron's Profiles* has become the standard college directory used by students, parents, and guidance counselors.

The thirteenth edition anticipates the needs and concerns of college-bound students of the 1980's. This is a time when career choice is increasingly dictated by the demands of the job market, and students are selecting colleges with occupational goals in mind. *Barron's Profiles* will be an invaluable tool for this. The comprehensive information on programs of study will help students find colleges with a program in their desired major. Students will also be able to gauge the success of each school's recent graduates by comparing percentages of graduates who pursue advanced degrees; who enter medical, dental, and law schools; and who secure jobs in business and industry.

In addition, the profiles in this edition cover numerous other areas of importance. A detailed admissions section lists requirements and reveals how particular colleges arrive at admissions decisions. The financial-aid information will be especially important to many because of recent and substantial tuition increases at many schools. An expanded student-life section will help students anticipate a school's social environment.

As in the past, *Barron's Profiles of American Colleges* is the most comprehensive, easy-to-use guide available. All four-year institutions that offer bachelor's degrees are described if they are fully accredited or are recognized candidates for accreditation. The comprehensive capsule and detailed essay on each school give the reader an easy-to-absorb, complete picture of the colleges that interest him or her. And the attractive graphic design provides added readability.

The capsule of each profile lists important information for quick reference: enrollment; calendar; fall application deadline; size and salary level of the faculty; percentage of faculty members who hold doctorates; student-faculty ratio; tuition and fees; room and board costs; the number of students who applied, were accepted, and enrolled; the median SAT and/or ACT scores for 1981–82 freshmen; and finally, the College Admissions Selector Rating for the school. The essay portion of each profile includes twenty-one categories of information under seven main subheads: Environment, Student Life, Programs of Study, Admissions, Financial Aid, Foreign Students, and Admissions Contact.

Several informative chapters precede the profiles. "Choosing a College" gives readers a systematic route to follow and provides tips on interpreting the facts given in the profiles; because we feel that college-bound students should be informed consumers of educational services, we have tried to give them a basis for making an intelligent college choice. The College Admissions Selector, Barron's rating of colleges and universities by degree of admissions competitiveness, will help students assess their chances of being accepted by various schools. The chapter "Advice for Foreign Students" has been expanded since the last edition of this book, and a new section for these students has been added to each profile. Together, these give foreign students comprehensive information on special programs U.S. colleges and universities offer for them. Other features of this book include an explanation of the book, a glossary of collegiate terms, a key to abbreviations, college-locator maps, and listings of colleges with religious programs, ROTC, and upper division programs.

We are confident that the features we have added, together with those that have appeared in previous editions of *Barron's Profiles,* will make this new thirteenth edition the best guide available to the college-bound student of the 1980's.

A Word of Thanks
To all the college admissions officers, to the many participating high school advisers, to the students, parents, and other supporters of *Barron's Profiles of American Colleges,* we offer our sincere thanks.

Grateful acknowledgment is made to the late Gloria M. Barron, who inspired the editors and production personnel to create a book that would offer every possible assistance in selecting the best college.

We acknowledge, with thanks, the demanding editing task performed by Virginia Christensen and our staff of diligent writers and copy editors.

Barron's Profiles of American Colleges, Volume 2

Barron's Profiles of American Colleges, Volume 2: Index of College Majors, is a helpful aid for students who have an idea of what field they want to study but do not know what colleges offer it. This book, a companion guide to Volume 1, is organized in chart form to provide easy reference to the programs of study available at every college and university that has regional accreditation and offers a four-year bachelor's program.

Schools that offer a specific major can be found quickly by scanning the top of the chart for the major and then checking below. In addition, a capsule description of each college provides pertinent facts to give students a general idea of the type of school they are considering.

Another feature of this volume is the categorizing of colleges. Categories include single-sex schools, colleges with religious affiliations, colleges with ROTC programs, alternative-education colleges, and schools offering day-care facilities. By using these listings and the charts of college majors, students will be able to determine easily which colleges to research further in Volume 1.

AN EXPLANATION OF THE BOOK

THE BASICS

The college profiles are presented alphabetically by state, and the states are also arranged in alphabetical order. Actually, *Barron's Profiles of American Colleges* covers more than the fifty states; it also describes colleges in the District of Columbia, Guam, Puerto Rico, Canada, and Mexico.

The book includes a number of other features as well. The College Admissions Selector gives applicants an idea of the competition they will encounter when applying to a particular school. Detailed chapters give tips on choosing a college, information on interpreting facts presented about the colleges, and advice for foreign students. There are college-locator maps of each state, abbreviated profiles of schools that prepare students for religious vocations, and lists of upper division schools and schools that offer Air Force, Army, or Navy ROTC. Also included is an alphabetical index of colleges and universities in the book.

The Choice of Schools

Colleges and universities in this country may achieve recognition from a number of professional organizations, but we have based our choice of U.S. and Mexican colleges on accreditation from one of the six U.S. regional accrediting associations.

Accreditation amounts to a stamp of approval given to a college. The accreditation process evaluates institutions and programs to determine whether they meet established standards of educational quality. The regional associations listed below supervise an aspect of the accrediting procedure—the study of a detailed report submitted by the institution applying for accreditation, and then an inspection visit by members of the accrediting agency. The six agencies are members of the Council on Postsecondary Accreditation (COPA); they include:

> Middle States Association of Colleges and Schools
> New England Association of Schools and Colleges
> North Central Association of Colleges and Schools
> Northwest Association of Schools and Colleges
> Southern Association of Colleges and Schools
> Western Association of Schools and Colleges

Gaining accreditation for the first time can take a school several years. To acknowledge that schools have begun this process, the agencies accord them candidate status. Most candidates eventually are awarded full accreditation.

The U.S. and Mexican schools included in this book are fully accredited or are candidates for that status. If the latter is the case, it is indicated below the address of the school. Because the U.S. regional accrediting bodies do not officially accredit Canadian colleges and universities, and because there is no equivalent accrediting system in Canada, we have chosen to include only the larger, English-language Canadian schools—those with total full-time undergraduate enrollment of more than 10,000. It should be understood that size in no way relates to quality; there are many excellent Canadian colleges and universities with fewer than 10,000 students.

Four-Year Colleges Only

This book presents profiles for all accredited four-year colleges that grant bachelor's degrees and admit freshmen with no previous college experience. Most of these colleges also accept transfer students. Profiles of upper division schools, which offer only the junior or senior year of undergraduate study, are not included (a list of these schools and their addresses appears at the back of this book).

Consistent Entries

Each profile of a U.S. college is organized in the same way; the only profiles that vary are those of Canadian and Mexican, and religious, schools. The following discussion refers to the U.S. college profiles, but generally applies to the other profiles as well.

Every profile begins with a capsule and is followed by separate sections covering the campus environment, student life, programs of study, admissions, financial aid, information for foreign students, and the name of an admissions officer. These categories are always introduced in the same sequence, so you can find data and compare specific points easily. The following commentary will help you evaluate and interpret the information given for each college.

Data Collection

Barron's Profiles of American Colleges was first published in 1964. Since then, it has been revised almost every year; comprehensive revisions are undertaken every two years. Such frequent updating is necessary because so much information about colleges—particularly enrollment figures, costs, programs of study, and admissions standards—changes rapidly.

The facts included in this edition were gathered in early 1982 and quickly incorporated into this new thirteenth edition. You should expect all the entries in this edition to become somewhat dated, but some facts will change faster than others. Figures on tuition and room-and-board costs generally change soon after the book is published. For the most up-to-date information on such items, you should always check with the colleges. Other information—such as the basic nature of the school, its campus, and the educational goals of its students—changes less rapidly. A few new programs of study might be added or new services made available, but the basic educational offerings generally will remain constant.

THE CAPSULE

The capsule of each profile provides basic information about the college at a glance. An explanation of the standard capsule is shown in the accompanying box.

A former name is given only if the name has been changed since the twelfth edition of *Barron's Profiles*. To use the map code to the right of the college name, turn to the appropriate college-locator map just before the profile section. Wherever "n/av" is used in the capsule, it means the information was not available. The abbreviation "n/app" means not applicable.

F/T, P/T, Grad

Enrollment figures are the clearest indication of the size of a college, and show whether or not it is coeducational and what the male-female ratio is. Graduate enrollment is presented to give a better idea of the size of the entire student body; some schools have far more graduate students enrolled than undergraduates.

Year

Some of the more innovative college calendars include the *4-1-4*, *3-2-3*, *3-3-1*, and *1-3-1-4-3*. College administrators are experimenting with various intersessions or interims—special short terms—for projects, independent study, short courses, or travel programs. The early semester calendar, which allows students to finish spring semesters

---

COMPLETE NAME OF SCHOOL		MAP CODE
(Former Name, if any)		
City, State, Zip Code		Phone Number
(Accreditation Status, if a candidate)		

F/T:	Full-time undergraduate enrollment	Faculty:	Number of full-time faculty; AAUP category of school, salary-level symbol
P/T:	Part-time undergraduate enrollment		
Grad:	Graduate enrollment	Ph.D.'s:	Percentage of faculty holding them
Year:	Type of calendar, whether there is a summer session	S/F Ratio:	Student-faculty ratio
		Tuition:	Yearly tuition and fees (out-of-state tuition and fees, if different)
Appl:	Application deadline for fall admission	R and B:	Yearly room and board

Number of students who applied	Number accepted	Number enrolled
SAT: Median Verbal, Median Math	ACT: Median composite	*ADMISSIONS SELECTOR RATING*

vii

viii AN EXPLANATION OF THE BOOK

earlier than those on the traditional semester calendar, gives students a head start on finding summer jobs. A modified semester *(4-1-4)* system provides a January or winter term, approximately four weeks long, for special projects that usually earn the same credit as one, semester-long course. The trimester *(tri)* calendar divides the year into three equal parts; students may attend college during all three but generally take a vacation during any one. The quarter *(qtrs)* calendar divides the year into four equal parts; students usually attend for three quarters each year. The term *(term)* calendar is essentially the same as the quarter calendar without the summer quarter; it has three sessions between September and June. The capsule also indicates, with an "ss," schools that offer a summer session.

Appl
Indicated here is the deadline for applications for admission to the fall semester. Application deadlines for admission to other semesters are, where available, given in the admissions section of the profile.

Faculty
The first number given refers to the number of full-time faculty members at the college or university.

The Roman numeral and symbol that follow represent the salary level of faculty at the school as compared with faculty salaries nationally. This information is based on the 1980–81 salary report* published by the American Association of University Professors (AAUP). The Roman numeral refers to the AAUP category to which the particular college or university is assigned (this allows for comparison of faculty salaries at the same types of schools). *Category I* includes "institutions which offer the doctorate degree, and which conferred in the most recent three years an annual average of fifteen or more earned doctorates covering a minimum of three nonrelated disciplines." *Category IIA* includes "institutions awarding degrees above the baccalaureate, but not included in Category I." *Category IIB* includes "institutions awarding only the baccalaureate or equivalent degree." *Category IV* includes "institutions without academic ranks (with the exception of a few liberal arts colleges, this category includes mostly two-year institutions)."

The symbol that follows the Roman numeral indicates into which percentile range the average salary of professors, associate professors, assistant professors, and instructors at the school falls as compared with other schools in the same AAUP category. The symbols used in this book represent the following:

+ +$	80th percentile
+$	60th percentile
av$	40th percentile
−$	20th percentile
− −$	lower than 20th percentile

Ph.D.s
The figure here indicates the percentage of faculty who have Ph.D.s.

Student-Faculty Ratio
Student-faculty ratios may be deceptive because the faculties of many large universities include scholars and scientists who do little or no teaching. Nearly every college has some large lecture classes, usually in required or popular subjects, and many small classes in advanced or specialized fields. In general, a student-faculty ratio of 10 to 1 is very good.

Tuition
It is important to remember that tuition costs change continually and that in many cases, these changes are substantial. Particularly heavy increases have occurred very recently and continue to occur; students are therefore urged to contact individual colleges for the most current tuition figures.

The figure given here includes tuition and student fees for the school's standard academic year. If costs differ for state residents and out-of-state residents, the figure for nonresidents is given in parentheses. Where tuition costs are listed per credit hour (p/c), per course (p/course), or per unit (p/unit), student fees are not included. In some university systems, tuition is the same for all schools. However, student fees, and therefore the total tuition figure, may vary from school to school.

Room and Board
It is suggested that students check with individual schools for the most current room-and-board figures because, like tuition figures, they increase continually. The room-and-board figures given here represent annual costs. The word "none" indicates that the college does not charge for room and board; "n/app" indicates that room and board are not provided.

Applied, Accepted, Enrolled
The numbers apply to the 1981–82 freshman class.

SAT, ACT
Whenever available, the median SAT scores—both Verbal and Math—and the median ACT composite score for the 1981–82 freshman class are given. If the school has not reported median SAT or ACT scores, the capsule indicates whether the SAT or ACT is required.

Admissions Selector Rating
The College Admissions Selector (see the following section of this book) indicates the competitiveness category into which the college falls.

THE GENERAL DESCRIPTION

The Introductory Paragraph
This paragraph indicates, in general, what type of programs the college offers, when it was founded, whether it is public or private, its religious affiliation, and whether it offers an alternative education. Information on the size of the school's library collection also is provided.

In evaluating the size of the collection, you should keep in mind the difference between college and university libraries: A university's graduate and professional schools require many specialized books that would be of no value to an undergraduate. For a university, a ratio of 1 undergraduate to 500 books generally means an outstanding library, 1 to 200 an adequate library, 1 to 100 an inferior library. For a college, a ratio of 1 to 400 is outstanding, 1 to 300 superior, 1 to 200 adequate, 1 to 50 inferior.

These figures are somewhat arbitrary, because a large university with many professional schools or campuses requires more books than a smaller university. Furthermore, a recently founded college would be expected to have fewer books than an older school, since it has not inherited from the past what might be a great quantity of outdated and useless books. Most libraries can make up for their deficiencies through interlibrary loans.

The ratio of students to the number of subscriptions to periodicals is less meaningful, and again, a university requires more periodicals than a college. But for a university, subscription to more than 15,000 periodicals is outstanding and to 6000 generally more than adequate. For a college, 1500 subscriptions are exceptional, 700 very good, and 400 adequate. Subscription to fewer than 200 periodicals generally implies an inferior library with a very tight budget.

Environment
At most institutions, the existence of classrooms, administrative offices, and athletic and dining facilities may be taken for granted, and they generally are not mentioned in the entries unless they have been recently constructed or are considered exceptional. If you plan to live on campus, note the descriptions of the dormitory accommodations. Some colleges provide dormitory rooms for freshmen, but require upperclass students to make their own arrangements to live in fraternity or sorority houses, off-campus apartments, or rented rooms in private houses. Many small colleges require all students who do not live with parents or other relatives to live on campus. Some colleges have no residence halls.

This paragraph also provides information on the campus: its size, the type of area in which it is located, and its proximity to a large city. And it briefly lists any special characteristics that make the campus especially interesting.

Student Life
This section, with subdivisions that detail campus activities, sports, facilities for handicapped students, futures of graduates, and services offered to students, concentrates on the everyday life of students.

The introductory paragraph, which includes various characteristics of the student body, gives an idea of the mix of attitudes and backgrounds. It includes, where available, percentages of students from out of state and from private or public high schools, and of those who live off campus. It also indicates what percentage of the students belong to minority groups and what percentages are Protestants, Catholics, and Jews. This paragraph also tells whether campus housing is single-sex and/or coed, and whether there are visiting privileges in single-sex accommodations. Finally, it tells whether students may keep

---

*Source: "The Rocky Road Through the 1980s: Annual Report of the Economic Status of the Profession, 1980–81," *Academe: Bulletin of the AAUP*, Vol. 67, No. 4, August, 1981, pp. 210–293. (Information from this report is reprinted by permission from the American Association of University Professors.)

cars on campus and whether the school provides day-care services.

Campus organizations play a vital part in students' social lives. This subsection lists types of activities, including student government, special-interest or academic clubs, fraternities and sororities, and cultural events sponsored at the college. It also describes other cultural and recreational opportunities near the campus.

Sports are becoming increasingly important on campus again, so we indicate the extent of the athletic program by giving the number of intercollegiate and intramural sports offered for men and for women.

The colleges' own estimates of how accessible their campuses are to the physically handicapped also are provided. This information should be viewed together with the specific kinds of special facilities available. The terms *visual impairments* and *hearing impairments* refer to blindness and deafness. If a profile does not include a subsection on the handicapped, the college did not provide the information.

Data on graduates include the dropout rate and the percentages of graduates who seek advanced degrees, who go to medical, dental, and law schools, and who begin careers in business or industry. When no information is given, it has not been supplied by the school.

Services that may be available to students—free or for a fee—include job placement assistance, health care, career and psychological counseling, tutoring, and remedial instruction. Some colleges offer extensive placement services, which may include help in preparing a résumé, on-campus job interviews, and workshops on undergoing an interview.

Programs of Study
Listed here are the degrees granted, major programs, and the fields in which the most degrees are conferred. Major areas of study have been included under broader general areas (shown in capital letters in the profiles) for quicker reference; however, the general areas do not necessarily correspond to the academic divisions of the college or university.

Information on required courses or general-education distribution requirements is supplied when applicable. If the college requires students to maintain a certain grade-point average (GPA) or pass comprehensive exams to graduate, that also is shown.

Special programs are described in the subsection "Special." Students at almost every college now have the opportunity to study abroad, either through their college or through other institutions. Internships with businesses, schools, hospitals, and public agencies permit students to gain work experience as they learn. The pass/fail grading option, now quite prevalent, allows students to take courses in unfamiliar areas without threatening their academic average. Many schools offer students the opportunity to earn a combined B.A.-B.S. degree, pursue a general studies (no major) degree, or design their own major. Frequently, students may take advantage of a cooperative program (see glossary) offered by two or more universities. Such a program might be referred to, for instance, as a 3-2 engineering program; a student in this program would spend three years at one institution and two at another.

The subsection "Honors" lists or gives the number of national honor societies represented on campus. Schools also may conduct honors programs for qualified students, either university-wide or in specific major fields, and these also are listed.

Admissions
The admissions section gives detailed information on standards so you can evaluate your chances for acceptance. Where the SAT or ACT scores of the 1981-82 freshman class are broken down, you may compare your own scores. Because the role of standardized tests in the admissions process is coming under fire, more colleges are considering other factors such as recommendations from high school officials, leadership record, special talents, extracurricular activities, and advanced placement or honors courses completed. Some schools also consider education of parents, ability to pay for college, and relationship to alumni. Some give preference to state residents; others seek a geographically diverse student body.

The subsection on procedures lists what standardized tests, if any, are required; when you should take them; the application deadlines for various sessions; the application fee; and when students are notified of the admissions decision. Some schools note that their application deadlines are open; this can mean either that they will consider applications until a class is filled, or that applications are considered right up until registration for the term in which the student wishes to enroll. If a college indicates that it follows an *open admissions* policy, it is noncompetitive and generally accepts all applicants who meet certain basic requirements, such as graduation from an accredited high school. If a college follows a *rolling admissions* policy or makes admissions decisions on a *rolling basis,* it decides on each application as soon as possible after the applicant's file is complete and does not specify a notification deadline. As a general rule, it is best to submit applications as early as possible.

Some colleges offer special admissions programs for nontraditional applicants. Early admissions programs allow students to begin college either during the summer before their freshman year or during what would have been their last year of high school; in the latter case, a high school diploma is not required. These programs are designed for students who are emotionally and educationally prepared for college at an earlier age than usual.

Deferred admissions plans permit students to spend a year at another activity, such as working or traveling, before beginning college. A student who takes advantage of this option can relax during the year off, because he or she already has been accepted at a college and a space has been reserved. During the year off from study, many students become clearer about their educational goals, and they perform better when they do begin study.

Early decision plans allow students to be notified by their first-choice school during the first term of the senior year. This plan may eliminate the anxiety of deciding whether or not to send a deposit to a second-choice college that offers admission before the first-choice college responds.

The Ivy League institutions, along with the Massachusetts Institute of Technology, have adopted an early evaluation procedure under which applicants receive, between November 1 and February 15, an evaluation of their chances for admission. They are told that acceptance is likely, possible, or unlikely, or that the colleges have received insufficient evidence for evaluation. This information helps applicants decide whether to concentrate on another school. Final notification is made on a common date in April.

Information on transfer admissions is contained in a separate paragraph. Nearly every college admits some transfer students. These students may have earned associate degrees at two-year colleges and have decided to continue their education at a four-year school, or they already may be students at a four-year college who wish to attend a different school. One important thing to consider when transferring is how many credits earned at one school will be accepted at another, so entire semesters won't be spent making up lost work. Since most schools require students to spend a specified number of hours in residence to earn a degree, it is best not to wait too long to transfer if you decide to do so.

The final paragraph under "Admissions" gives information on visiting the campus. Some colleges hold special orientation programs for prospective students to give them a better idea of what the school is like. Many also will provide guides for informal visits, often allowing students to spend a night in the residence halls. You should make arrangements with the college before going.

Financial Aid
This paragraph of each profile describes the availability of financial aid. It includes the percentage of students who receive aid, the percentage who work part-time on campus, the average aid to freshmen, and the types and sources of aid available, such as scholarships, grants, loans, and work-study. Aid application deadlines and required forms are also indicated.

Foreign Students
This section begins by telling what percentage of the school's full-time students come from outside the United States. Also included in the first paragraph are special offerings for foreign students: an intensive English *course* that meets for less than 15 hours per week, an intensive English *program* that meets for more than 15 hours per week, special counseling, and/or special organizations.

The subsection "Admissions" indicates which English proficiency exam, if any, applicants must take and the minimum score required, if there is one. Any necessary college entrance exams, including ATs, are listed, as are any minimum scores required on those exams.

Admissions procedures for foreign applicants are somewhat more complicated than those for American applicants. The subsection on procedures indicates which of the following the school requires of foreign applicants: proof of good health (and what form that must take), proof of adequate funds (and what period of study those funds must cover), special fees, and/or health insurance. Also indicated are application deadlines.

Admissions Contact
This is the name of the person to whom all correspondence regarding your application should be sent.

COLLEGE ADMISSIONS SELECTOR

This index groups all the colleges listed in this book according to degree of admissions competitiveness. The *Selector* is *not* a rating of colleges by academic standards or quality of education; it is rather an attempt to describe, in general terms, the situation a prospective student will meet when he or she applies for admission.

THE CRITERIA USED

The factors used in determining the category for each college were: median entrance examination scores for the 1981-82 freshman class (the SAT score used was derived by averaging the median verbal, and the median math, scores; the ACT score used was the median composite score); percentages of 1981-82 freshmen scoring above 500 and above 600 on both the mathematical and verbal sections of the SAT; percentages of 1981-82 freshmen scoring above 21 and above 25 on the ACT; percentage of 1981-82 freshmen who ranked in the upper fifth of their high school class and percentage who ranked in the upper two-fifths; minimum class rank and grade point average *required* for admission; and percentage of applicants to the 1981-82 freshman class who were accepted. The *Selector* cannot, and does not, take into account all the other factors that each college considers when making admissions decisions. Colleges place varying degrees of emphasis on the factors that were used to delineate each of the categories.

USING THE SELECTOR

To use the *Selector* effectively, the prospective student should compare himself or herself realistically with the freshmen enrolled by the colleges in each category, as shown by the SAT or ACT scores, the quality of high school record emphasized by the colleges in each category, and the kinds of risks he or she wishes to take.

The student should also be aware of what importance a particular school places on various nonacademic factors; when available, this information is presented in the profile of the school. If a student feels that he or she has unusual qualifications that may compensate for exam scores or high school record, the student should examine the admissions policies of the colleges in the next higher category than the one that encompasses his or her score and consider those colleges that give major consideration to factors other than exam scores and high school grades. The "safety" college should usually be chosen from the next lower category, where the student can be reasonably sure that his or her scores and high school record will fall above the median scores and records of freshmen enrolled in the college.

The listing within each category is alphabetical and not in any qualitative order. State-supported institutions have been classified according to the requirements for state residents, but standards for admission of out-of-state students are usually higher. Colleges that are experimenting with the admission of students of high potential but lower achievement may appear in a less competitive category because of this fact.

A WORD OF CAUTION

The *Selector* is intended primarily for preliminary screening, to eliminate the majority of colleges that are not suitable for a particular student. Be sure to examine the admissions policies spelled out in the *Admissions* section of each profile. And remember that many colleges have to reject *qualified* students; the *Selector* will tell you what your chances are, not which college will accept you.

MOST COMPETITIVE

Even superior students will encounter a great deal of competition for admission to the colleges in this category. In general, these colleges require high school rank in the top 10% to 20% and grade averages of A to B+. Median freshman test scores at these colleges are generally between 625 and 800 on the SAT and above 27 on the ACT. In addition, many of these colleges admit only a small percentage of those who apply—usually fewer than one third.

Amherst College, *MA*
Bowdoin College, *ME*
Brown University, *RI*
Bryn Mawr College, *PA*
California Institute of Technology, *CA*
Columbia University/Columbia College, *NY*
The Cooper Union for the Advancement of Science and Art, *NY*
Cornell University, *NY*
Dartmouth College, *NH*
Duke University, *NC*
Georgetown University, *DC*
Harvard University/Harvard and Radcliffe Colleges, *MA*
Haverford College, *PA*
Johns Hopkins University, *MD*
Massachusetts Institute of Technology, *MA*
Princeton University, *NJ*
Rensselaer Polytechnic Institute, *NY*
Rice University, *TX*
Stanford University, *CA*
Swarthmore College, *PA*
United States Air Force Academy, *CO*
United States Coast Guard Academy, *CT*
United States Military Academy, *NY*
United States Naval Academy, *MD*
University of Notre Dame, *IN*
University of Pennsylvania, *PA*
Wellesley College, *MA*
Wesleyan University, *CT*
Williams College, *MA*
Yale University, *CT*

HIGHLY COMPETITIVE

Colleges in this group look for students with grade averages of B+ to B and accept most of their students from the top 20% to 35% of the high school class. Median freshman test scores at these colleges range from 575 to 625 on the SAT and from 26 to 27 on the ACT. These schools generally accept between one third and one half of their applicants.

To provide for finer distinctions within this admissions category, a plus (+) symbol has been placed before some entries. These are colleges with median freshman scores of 615 or more on the SAT *or* 27 on the ACT, and colleges that accept fewer than one quarter of their applicants.

Bates College, *ME*
Brandeis University, *MA*
Bucknell University, *PA*
+ Carleton College, *MN*
Carnegie Mellon University, *PA*
The Claremont Colleges/Claremont McKenna College, *CA*
+ The Claremont Colleges/Harvey Mudd College, *CA*
The Claremont Colleges/Pomona College, *CA*
Clarkson College of Technology, *NY*
Clark University, *MA*
Colby College, *ME*
+ Colgate University, *NY*
College of William and Mary, *VA*
+ Colorado School of Mines, *CO*
Columbia University/Barnard College, *NY*
Columbia University/School of Engineering and Applied Science, *NY*
+ Columbia University/School of General Studies, *NY*
Davidson College, *NC*
Dickinson College, *PA*
Franklin and Marshall College, *PA*
+ General Motors Institute *MI*
Georgia Institute of Technology, *GA*

+ Grinnell College, IA
Hamilton College, NY
Holy Cross College, MA
Kalamazoo College, MI
+ Kenyon College, OH
Lafayette College, PA
Lehigh University, PA
Middlebury College, VT
Mount Holyoke College, MA
New College of the University of South Florida, FL
+ Northwestern University, IL
+ Oberlin College, OH
Occidental College, CA
Polytechnic Institute of New York, NY
+ Reed College, OR
+ Rose-Hulman Institute of Technology, IN
+ St. John's College, MD
St. Olaf College, MN
Seminar College, NY
Smith College, MA
State University of New York at Binghamton, NY
Trinity College, CT
Tufts University, MA
+ Union College, NY
+ United States Merchant Marine Academy, NY
University of California/Berkeley, CA
+ The University of Chicago, IL
University of Dallas, TX
University of Illinois at Urbana-Champaign, IL
University of Michigan/Ann Arbor, MI
University of Rochester, NY
University of Virginia, VA
Vanderbilt University, TN
Vassar College, NY
Wake Forest University, NC
+ Washington University, MO
Webb Institute of Naval Architecture, NY
+ Worcester Polytechnic Institute, MA

VERY COMPETITIVE

The colleges in this category admit students whose averages are no less than B— and who rank in the top 35% to 50% of their graduating class. They report median freshman test scores in the 525 to 575 range on the SAT and in the 23 to 25 on the ACT. The schools in this category generally accept between one half and three quarters of their applicants.

The plus (+) has been placed before colleges with median freshman scores of 565 or above on the SAT or 25 on the ACT, and colleges that accept fewer than one third of their applicants.

+ Agnes Scott College, GA
Alaska Pacific University, AK
Albion College, MI
+ Albright College, PA
Alfred University, NY
Allegheny College, PA
+ Alma College, MI
Augustana College, IL
+ Babson College, MA
Bard College, NY
Baylor University, TX
+ Beloit College, WI
Bennington College, VT
+ Boston College, MA
Boston University, MA
Bryant College, RI
California College of Podiatric Medicine, CA
California State University/Long Beach, CA
+ Case Western Reserve University, OH
Catholic University of America, DC
The Claremont Colleges/Pitzer College, CA
College of Insurance, NY
College of the Atlantic, ME
Colorado College, CO
Connecticut College, CT
Depauw University, IN
DeVry Institute of Technology, TX
Drew University/College of Liberal Arts, NJ
Drexel University, PA
Earlham College, IN
+ Emory University, GA
Fairfield University, CT
+ Florida Institute of Technology, FL
Fordham University/Fordham College, NY
Furman University, SC
George Washington University, DC
Gettysburg College, PA
+ Goucher College, MD
Grove City College, PA
+ Gustavus Adolphus College, MN
Hampshire College, MA
+ Hobart and William Smith Colleges/Hobart College, NY
+ Hobart and William Smith Colleges/William Smith College, NY
Hofstra University, NY
Humboldt State University, CA
Illinois Institute of Technology, IL
Illinois Wesleyan University, IL
Indiana University of Pennsylvania, PA
James Madison University, VA
+ Knox College, IL
+ Lake Forest College, IL
+ Lawrence University, WI
+ Le Moyne College, NY
Loyola College, MD
Luther College, IA
+ Macalester College, MN
Manhattanville College, NY
Marlboro College, VT
Mary Washington College, VA
Miami University, OH
+ Michigan Technological University, MI
Millsaps College, MS
Mills College, CA
Muhlenberg College, PA
New Mexico Institute of Mining and Technology, NM
New York University, NY
Oglethorpe University, GA
Pacific Lutheran University, WA
Pennsylvania State University/University Park Campus, PA
Philadelphia College of Pharmacy and Science, PA
Providence College, RI
Randoph-Macon Woman's College, VA
Rochester Institute of Technology, NY
Rutgers University/College of Engineering, NY
Rutgers University/College of Pharmacy, NJ
Rutgers University/Cook College, NJ
Rutgers University/Newark College of Arts and Sciences, NJ
Rutgers University/Rutgers College, NJ
St. John's College, NM
Saint John's University, MN
Saint Joseph's University, PA
+ St. Lawrence University, NY
St. Louis College of Pharmacy, MO
Saint Mary's College, IN
Siena College, NY
Simon's Rock of Bard College, MA
+ Skidmore College, NY
+ Southwestern at Memphis, TN
State University of New York at Albany, NY
State University of New York at Buffalo, NY
State University of New York at Stony Brook, NY
State University of New York/College at Geneseo, NY
State University of New York/College at Oswego, NY
State University of New York/College at Potsdam, NY
State University of New York/College at Purchase, NY
+ State University of New York/Maritime College, NY
State University of New York/Upstate Medical Center, NY
Stetson University, FL
+ Stevens Institute of Technology, NJ
Syracuse University, NY
+ Thomas Aquinas College, CA
+ Trinity University, TX
+ Tulane University, LA
University of California/Davis, CA
University of California/Irvine, CA
University of California/Riverside, CA
University of California/San Diego, CA
University of California/Santa Barbara, CA
University of California/Santa Cruz, CA
+ University of Colorado at Boulder, CO
University of Connecticut, CT
University of Denver, CO
University of Florida, FL
University of Michigan/Dearborn, MI
University of Missouri/Kansas City, MO
+ University of Missouri/Rolla, MO
University of New Hampshire, NH
University of North Carolina at Chapel Hill, NC
University of Pittsburgh, PA
University of Pittsburgh at Johnstown, PA
University of Richmond, VA
University of Santa Clara, CA
University of Texas at Austin, TX
+ The University of the South, TN
University of Vermont, VT
University of Washington, WA
+ Ursinus College, PA
Villanova University, PA
Virginia Polytechnic Institute and State University, VA
Wabash College, IN
Washington and Jefferson College, PA
+ Washington and Lee University, VA
+ Wheaton College, IL
Wheaton College, MA
Whitman College, WA
William Jewell College, MO
World College West, CA
+ Yeshiva University, NY

xii COLLEGE ADMISSIONS SELECTOR

COMPETITIVE

This category is a very wide one, covering colleges that generally have median freshman test scores between 450 and 525 on the SAT and between 19 and 22 on the ACT. Some of these colleges require that students have high school averages of B− or better, although others state a minimum of C+ or C. Generally, these colleges prefer students in the top 50% to 65% of the graduating class and accept between 75% and 85% of their applicants.

Colleges with a plus (+) are those with median freshman SAT scores of 515 or more *or* median freshman ACT scores of 23, and those that admit fewer than half of their applicants.

Adelphi University, NY
Adrian College, MI
Albany College of Pharmacy, NY
Albertus Magnus College, CT
Allentown College of St. Francis DeSales, PA
Alvernia College, PA
Alverno College, WI
American University, DC
Anderson College, IN
Andrews University, MI
Anna Maria College, MA
+ Antioch College, OH
Appalachian State University, NC
Aquinas College, MI
Arizona State University, AZ
Arkansas College, AR
Armstrong College, CA
Arnold and Marie Schwartz College of Pharmacy and Health Sciences, NY
Asbury College, KY
Assumption College, MA
+ Auburn University, AL
Augsburg College, MN
+ Augustana College, SD
Aurora College, IL
Austin College, TX
+ Averett College, VA
Avila College, MO
Baker University, KS
Baldwin-Wallace College, OH
Barry University, FL
Beaver College, PA
Belhaven College, MS
Bellarmine College, KY
Bemidji State University, MN
Benedictine College, KS
+ Bentley College, MA
+ Berea College, KY
+ Berry College, GA
Bethany College, KS
Bethany College, WV
Bethel College, KS
+ Bethel College, MN
Bethel College, TN
Biola University, CA
+ Birmingham-Southern College, AL
Biscayne College, FL
Bishop College, TX
Blackburn College, IL
+ Bloomsburg State College, PA
Bluffton College, OH
Bowling Green State University, OH
+ Bradley University, IL
Brescia College, KY
Bridgewater College, VA
Bridgewater State College, MA
Brigham Young University, UT
Bryan College, TN
Buena Vista College, IA
Butler University, IN
Cabrini College, PA
California Lutheran College, CA
California Maritime Academy, CA
California Polytechnic State University, CA
California State College, PA
California State College/Bakersfield, CA
California State College/San Bernardino, CA
California State College/Stanislaus, CA
California State Polytechnic University/Pomona, CA

California State University/Chico, CA
California State University/Fresno, CA
California State University/Fullerton, CA
California State University/Hayward, CA
California State University/Los Angeles, CA
California State University/Northridge, CA
California State University/Sacramento, CA
+ Calvin College, MI
Canisius College, NY
Capital University, OH
Cardinal Newman College, MO
Cardinal Stritch College, WI
Carroll College, MT
+ Carroll College, WI
Carthage College, WI
Cedar Crest College, PA
Cedarville College, OH
Centenary College of Louisiana, LA
Central Connecticut State College, CT
Central Michigan University, MI
Central University of Iowa, IA
Central Washington University, WA
Centre College of Kentucky, KY
Chaminade University of Honolulu, HI
Chapman College, CA
Chestnut Hill College, PA
Cheyney State College, PA
+ Christian Brothers College, TN
Christian Heritage College, CA
Christopher Newport College, VA
+ The Citadel, SC
City University of New York/Bernard M. Baruch College, NY
City University of New York/Brooklyn College, NY
City University of New York/City College, NY
City University of New York/College of Staten Island, NY
City University of New York/Herbert H. Lehman College, NY
City University of New York/Hunter College, NY
City University of New York/John Jay College of Criminal Justice, NY
City University of New York/Medgar Evers College, NY
City University of New York/Queens College, NY
City University of New York/York College, NY
+ The Claremont Colleges/Scripps College, CA
Clarion State College, PA
Clarke College, IA
Clemson University, SC
+ Coe College, IA
Cogswell College, CA
Colby-Sawyer College, NH
College of Charleston, SC
+ College of Idaho, ID
College of Mount Saint Joseph on the Ohio, OH
College of Mount Saint Vincent, NY
College of New Rochelle, NY
College of Notre Dame, CA
College of Notre Dame of Maryland, MD
College of Our Lady of the Elms, MA
College of St. Benedict, MN
College of St. Catherine, MN
College of St. Francis, IL
College of St. Rose, NY

College of St. Scholastica, MN
College of St. Thomas, MN
+ College of Wooster, OH
Colorado State University, CO
Concordia College, IL
Concordia College, MI
+ Concordia College/Moorhead, MN
Concordia College/St. Paul, MN
Concordia Teachers College, NE
Converse College, SC
+ Cornell College, IA
Covenant College, TN
+ Creighton University, NE
Curry College, MA
Daemen College, NY
Dakota Wesleyan University, SD
Dana College, NE
+ Daniel Webster College, NH
David Lipscomb College, TN
The Defiance College, OH
Delaware Valley College, PA
Delta State University, MS
+ Denison University, OH
+ De Paul University, IL
Dillard University, LA
Doane College, NE
Dominican College of San Rafael, CA
Dowling College, NY
Drake University, IA
Drury College, MO
Duquesne University, PA
East Carolina University, NC
Eastern College, PA
Eastern Illinois University, IL
Eastern Mennonite College, VA
Eastern Washington University, WA
East Stroudsburg State College, PA
Eckerd College, FL
Edgewood College, WI
+ Eisenhower College of Rochester Institute of Technology, NY
Elmhurst College, IL
Elmira College, NY
Emerson College, MA
Emory and Henry College, VA
Erskine College, SC
Eureka College, IL
Fairleigh Dickinson University, NJ
Findlay College, OH
Fisk University, TN
+ Fitchburg State College, MA
Flagler College, FL
Florida Agricultural and Mechanical University, FL
Florida Southern College, FL
Florida State University, FL
Fontbonne College, MO
Fordham University/College at Lincoln Center, NY
+ Fordham University/College of Business Administration, NY
Framingham State College, MA
Francis Marion College, SC
Franklin College, IN
Fresno Pacific College, CA
Frostburg State College, MD
Gannon University, PA
Geneva College, PA
George Fox College, OR
George Mason University, VA
Georgetown College, KY
Georgian Court College, NJ

COLLEGE ADMISSIONS SELECTOR xiii

Georgia Southern College, GA
+ Georgia State University, GA
Glassboro State College, NJ
Golden Gate University, CA
Gonzaga University, WA
Gordon College, MA
+ Goshen College, IN
Grace College, IN
Grand Canyon College, AZ
Grand Valley State Colleges, MI
Greenville College, IL
+ Guilford College, NC
+ Gwynedd-Mercy College, PA
+ Hamline University, MN
+ Hampden-Sydney College, VA
Hanover College, IN
Harding University, AR
Harris-Stowe State College, MO
Hartwick College, NY
Hastings College, NE
Heidelberg College, OH
+ Hendrix College, AR
High Point College, NC
Hillsdale College, MI
Hiram College, OH
Hollins College, VA
Holy Family College, PA
Holy Names College, CA
Hood College, MD
+ Hope College, MI
+ Houghton College, NY
Houston Baptist University, TX
Howard University, DC
Huntington College, IN
Illinois Benedictine College, IL
+ Illinois College, IL
Illinois State University, IL
Immaculata College, PA
Indiana Central University, IN
Indiana Institute of Technology, IN
Indiana University/Bloomington, IN
Inter-American University of Puerto Rico/Metropolitan Campus, PR
Iona College, NY
+ Iowa State University, IA
Iowa Wesleyan College, IA
Ithaca College, NY
Jacksonville University, FL
Jamestown College, ND
+ The Jewish Theological Seminary of America, NY
+ John Carroll University, OH
+ Juniata College, PA
Kansas Wesleyan University, KS
Keene State College, NH
Kendall College, IL
Kent State University, OH
King College, TN
Kutztown State College, PA
Lake Erie College for Women, OH
Lakeland College, WI
Lake Superior State College, MI
Lambuth College, TN
La Roche College, PA
+ La Salle College, PA
Lawrence Institute of Technology, MI
Lebanon Valley College, PA
Lenoir-Rhyne College, NC
Lesley College, MA
Le Tourneau College, TX
+ Lewis and Clark College, OR
+ Lewis University, IL
+ Linfield College, OR
Lock Haven State College, PA
Long Island University/Brooklyn Center, NY
Long Island University/C.W. Post Center, NY
Long Island University/Southampton College, NY
Longwood College, VA
+ Loras College, IA

Los Angeles Baptist College, CA
Louisiana College, LA
Loyola Marymount University, CA
Loyola University/New Orleans, LA
Loyola University of Chicago, IL
Lycoming College, PA
Lynchburg College, VA
MacMurray College, IL
Maharishi International University, IA
+ Maine Maritime Academy, ME
Malone College, OH
Manhattan College, NY
Mansfield State College, PA
Marian College, IN
+ Marietta College, OH
Marion College, IN
+ Marist College, NY
+ Marquette University, WI
Mary College, ND
Marycrest College, IA
Marygrove College, MI
Marymount College of Virginia, VA
Maryville College, MO
Maryville College, TN
Marywood College, PA
Massachusetts College of Pharmacy and Allied Health Sciences, MA
+ Massachusetts Maritime Academy, MA
McKendree College, IL
McMurry College, TX
McPherson College, KS
+ Medical College of Georgia, GA
Menlo College, CA
Mercer University, GA
Meredith College, NC
Merrimack College, MA
+ Messiah College, PA
Michigan State University, MI
Midland Lutheran College, NE
Midwest College of Engineering, IL
Millersville State College, PA
Millikin University, IL
Mississippi State University, MS
Missouri Valley College, MO
Molloy College, NY
Monmouth College, IL
Monmouth College, NJ
Montana College of Mineral Science and Technology, MT
+ Montclair State College, NJ
Moorhead State University, MN
Moravian College, PA
Morningside College, IA
Mount Marty College, SD
Mount Mercy College, IA
Mount St. Mary's College, CA
Mount St. Mary's College, MD
Mount Union College, OH
Mundelein College, IL
Nasson College, ME
Nazareth College, MI
Nazareth College of Rochester, NY
+ Nebraska Wesleyan University, NE
Neumann College, PA
Newberry College, SC
New Hampshire College, NH
New Jersey Institute of Technology, NJ
New York Institute of Technology, NY
Niagara University, NY
+ Nichols College, MA
+ North Adams State College, MA
North Carolina State University, NC
+ North Central College, IL
Northeastern University, MA
Northern Arizona University, AZ
Northern Illinois University, IL
Northland College, WI
North Park College, IL
Northrop University, CA
+ North Texas State University, TX
Northwestern College, IA
Northwestern College, MN

Northwood Institute, MI
Norwich University, VT
Notre Dame College, NH
Nyack College, NY
Oakland University, MI
Ohio Dominican College, OH
Ohio Northern University, OH
Ohio University, OH
Ohio Wesleyan University, OH
Oklahoma Baptist University, OK
Oklahoma City University, OK
Oklahoma State University, OK
Old Dominion University, VA
Olivet College, MI
Oral Roberts University, OK
Oregon Institute of Technology, OR
Oregon State University, OR
Otterbein College, OH
Our Lady of the Lake University of San Antonio, TX
Pace University/College of White Plains, NY
Pace University/New York Campus, NY
Pace University/Pleasantville/Briarcliff, NY
Pacific Union College, CA
Pacific University, OR
Parks College of St. Louis University, IL
+ Pepperdine University, CA
Philadelphia College of Textiles and Science, PA
Phillips University, OK
Portland State University, OR
Pratt Institute, NY
Presbyterian College, SC
Prescott College, AZ
Principia College, IL
Purdue University/West Lafayette, IN
Queens College, NC
Quincy College, IL
+ Quinnipiac College, CT
Radford University, VA
Ramapo College of New Jersey, NJ
Randolph-Macon College, VA
Regis College, CO
Regis College, MA
Rhode Island College, RI
Rider College, NJ
+ Ripon College, WI
Rivier College, NH
Roanoke College, VA
Robert Morris College, PA
Roberts Wesleyan College, NY
+ Rockford College, IL
+ Rockhurst College, MO
Roger Williams College, RI
+ Rollins College, FL
+ Roosevelt University, IL
Rosary College, IL
Rosemont College, PA
Russell Sage College, NY
Rutgers University/Camden College of Arts and Sciences, NJ
+ Rutgers University/College of Nursing, NJ
Rutgers University/Douglass College, NJ
Rutgers University/Livingston College, NJ
Rutgers University/University College— New Brunswick, NJ
Sacred Heart University, CT
St. Ambrose College, IA
St. Andrews Presbyterian College, NC
St. Anselm College, NH
+ St. Bonaventure University, NY
St. Cloud State University, MN
Saint Francis College, IN
Saint Francis College, PA
St. John Fisher College, NY
St. John's University, NY
Saint Joseph College, CT
Saint Joseph's College, IN
Saint Joseph's College, ME
St. Joseph's College, NY
Saint Leo College, FL

+ Saint Louis University, MO
Saint Mary College, KS
Saint Mary's College, MI
Saint Mary's College, MN
Saint Mary's College of California, CA
St. Mary's College of Maryland, MD
St. Mary's University, TX
Saint Michael's College, VT
+ St. Norbert College, WI
Saint Paul's College, VA
Saint Vincent College, PA
Saint Xavier College, IL
Salem College, NC
Salem State College, MA
Salisbury State College, MD
San Diego State University, CA
San Francisco State University, CA
San Jose State University, CA
+ Sarah Lawrence College, NY
+ The School of the Ozarks, MO
+ Seattle Pacific University, WA
Seattle University, WA
Seton Hall University, NJ
Seton Hill College, PA
Shenandoah College and Conservatory of Music, VA
+ Shepherd College, WV
Shimer College, IL
+ Shippensburg State College, PA
Shorter College, GA
Simmons College, MA
Simpson College, CA
Simpson College, IA
Sioux Falls College, SD
Sonoma State University, CA
+ South Dakota School of Mines and Technology, SD
South Dakota State University, SD
Southeastern Massachusetts University, MA
Southeastern University, DC
Southern California College, CA
Southern Connecticut State College, CT
Southern Illinois University at Carbondale, IL
+ Southern Methodist University, TX
Southwest Baptist University, MO
Southwestern College, KS
+ Southwestern University, TX
Southwest Texas State University, TX
Spelman College, GA
Spring Arbor College, MI
Springfield College, MA
Spring Garden College, PA
+ Spring Hill College, AL
State University of New York/College at Brockport, NY
State University of New York/College at Buffalo, NY
State University of New York/College at Cortland, NY
+ State University of New York/College at Fredonia, NY
State University of New York/College at New Paltz, NY
+ State University of New York/College at Oneonta, NY
State University of New York/College at Plattsburgh, NY
+ State University of New York/Fashion Institute of Technology, NY
Stephen F. Austin State University, TX
Stockton State College, NJ
+ Stonehill College, MA
Suffolk University, MA
Susquehanna University, PA
Sweet Briar College, VA
Taylor University, IN

Tennessee Technological University, TN
Tennessee Wesleyan College, TN
Texas A&M University, TX
Texas Christian University, TX
Texas Lutheran College, TX
Texas Wesleyan College, TX
Thiel College, PA
Thomas College, ME
+ Thomas More College, KY
Temple University, PA
Tougaloo College, MS
Touro College, NY
Towson State University, MD
Transylvania University, KY
+ Trenton State College, NJ
Trinity Christian College, IL
Trinity College, DC
Trinity College, IL
Tri-State University, IN
Union University, TN
United States International University, CA
University of Alabama, AL
+ University of Alabama in Huntsville, AL
University of Alaska/Anchorage, AK
University of Arizona, AZ
University of Bridgeport, CT
+ University of California/Los Angeles, CA
University of Central Florida, FL
University of Cincinnati, OH
+ University of Colorado at Colorado Springs, CO
University of Colorado at Denver, CO
University of Dayton, OH
University of Delaware, DE
University of Detroit, MI
University of Dubuque, IA
University of Evansville, IN
University of Georgia, GA
University of Hartford, CT
University of Hawaii at Manoa, HI
+ University of Houston/Central Campus, TX
University of Illinois at Chicago, IL
+ University of Iowa, IA
University of Kentucky, KY
University of Louisville, KY
+ University of Lowell, MA
University of Maine at Farmington, ME
University of Maine at Orono, ME
University of Maryland/Baltimore County, MD
University of Maryland/College Park, MD
University of Maryland/Eastern Shore, MD
University of Massachusetts at Amherst, MA
University of Massachusetts at Boston, MA
University of Miami, FL
University of Michigan/Flint, MI
University of Minnesota/Morris, MN
+ University of Minnesota/Twin Cities, MN
University of Mississippi, MS
University of Missouri/Columbia, MO
University of Missouri/St. Louis, MO
University of Nevada/Reno, NV
University of New England, ME
University of North Carolina at Asheville, NC
University of North Carolina at Charlotte, NC
+ University of North Carolina at Greensboro, NC
+ University of Northern Colorado, CO
University of Northern Iowa, IA
University of Oklahoma, OK
University of Oregon, OR
University of Pittsburgh at Bradford, PA
University of Pittsburgh at Greensburg, PA
University of Portland, OR
University of Puerto Rico/Cayey University College, PR

University of Puerto Rico/Mayaguez, PR
University of Puerto Rico/Rio Piedras, PR
+ University of Puget Sound, WA
+ University of Redlands, CA
University of Rhode Island, RI
University of San Diego, CA
University of San Francisco, CA
University of Scranton, PA
+ University of South Carolina, SC
University of South Dakota, SD
University of Southern California, CA
University of Southern Maine, ME
University of South Florida, FL
University of Steubenville, OH
University of Tampa, FL
University of Tennessee/Knoxville, TN
University of Texas at Arlington, TX
University of the Pacific, CA
University of the Sacred Heart, PR
University of Toledo, OH
University of Tulsa, OK
University of Utah, UT
University of Wisconsin/Eau Claire, WI
University of Wisconsin/Green Bay, WI
+ University of Wisconsin/Madison, WI
University of Wisconsin/Milwaukee, WI
University of Wisconsin/Stout, WI
+ Upper Iowa University, IA
Upsala College, NJ
+ Utica College of Syracuse University, NY
Valparaiso University, IN
Virginia Commonwealth University, VA
Virginia Intermont College, VA
+ Virginia Military Institute, VA
Virginia Union College, VA
Virginia Wesleyan College, VA
Viterbo College, WI
Wagner College, NY
Walsh College, OH
Warren Wilson College, NC
Wartburg College, IA
Washington College, MD
Washington State University, WA
Wayne State University, MI
Webster College, MO
+ Wells College, NY
+ Wesleyan College, GA
Wesley College, DE
West Chester State College, PA
Western Connecticut State College, CT
+ Western Maryland College, MD
Western Michigan University, MI
Western New England College, MA
Western Washington University, WA
+ Westfield State College, MA
Westmar College, IA
+ Westminster College, MO
+ Westminster College, PA
Westminster College, UT
Westmont College, CA
West Virginia University, WV
Wheeling College, WV
Wheelock College, MA
+ Whittier College, CA
Whitworth College, WA
Widener College, PA
Wilberforce University, OH
Wilkes College, PA
+ Willamette University, OR
William Penn College, IA
Wilson College, PA
+ Wittenberg University, OH
Wofford College, SC
+ Woodbury University, CA
Xavier University, OH

LESS COMPETITIVE

Included in this category are colleges with median freshman test scores below 450 on the SAT and below 19 on the ACT; some colleges that require entrance examinations but do not report median scores; and colleges that admit students with averages below C who rank in the top 65% of the graduating class. These colleges usually admit 85% or more of their applicants.

Abilene Christian University, TX
Adams State College, CO
Alabama Agricultural and Mechanical University, AL
Alabama State University, AL
Albany State College, GA
Alcorn State University, MS
Alderson-Broaddus College, WV
Alliance College, PA
American International College, MA
Angelo State University, TX
Antillian College, PR
Arkansas State University, AR
Arkansas Tech University, AR
Armstrong State College, GA
Ashland College, OH
Atlantic Christian College, NC
Atlantic Union College, MA
Auburn University at Montgomery, AL
Augusta College, GA
Azusa Pacific University, CA
Ball State University, IN
Baptist College at Charleston, SC
Barat College, IL
Barber-Scotia College, NC
Barrington College, RI
Bayamon Central University, PR
Beacon College, DC
Belmont Abbey College, NC
Belmont College, TN
Benedict College, SC
Bennett College, NC
Bethany Nazarene College, OK
Bethel College, IN
Bethune-Cookman College, FL
Black Hills State College, SD
Bloomfield College, NJ
Bluefield College, VA
Blue Mountain College, MS
Boricua College, NY
Bowie State College, MD
Bradford College, MA
Brenau College, GA
Briar Cliff College, IA
Bridgeport Engineering Institute, CT
Brigham Young University/Hawaii Campus, HI
Burlington College, VT
Caldwell College, NJ
California Baptist College, CA
California State University/Dominguez Hills, CA
Calumet College, IN
Cameron University, OK
Campbellsville College, KY
Campbell University, NC
Carlow College, PA
Catawba College, NC
Catholic University of Puerto Rico, PR
Centenary College, NJ
Central Methodist College, MO
Central Missouri State University, MO
Central New England College, MA
Central State University, OK
Central Wesleyan College, SC
Chatham College, PA
Chicago State University, IL
Claflin College, SC
Clark College, GA
Cleveland State University, OH
Clinch Valley College of the University of Virginia, VA
Coker College, SC

College for Human Services, NY
College Misericordia, PA
College of Saint Elizabeth, NJ
College of St. Joseph the Provider, VT
College of Saint Mary, NE
College of Saint Teresa, MN
College of Santa Fe, NM
The College of the Ozarks, AR
College of the Southwest, NM
College of the Virgin Islands, VI
Colorado Technical College, CO
Columbia College, MO
Columbia College, SC
Columbia Union College, MD
Columbus College, GA
Concord College, WV
Concordia College, NY
Concordia College, OR
Concordia College, WI
Coppin State College, MD
Culver-Stockton College, MO
Cumberland College, KY
Dakota State College, SD
Dallas Baptist College, TX
Davis and Elkins College, WV
Delaware State College, DE
De Vry Institute of Technology, AZ
De Vry Institute of Technology, GA
De Vry Institute of Technology, IL
Dominican College of Blauvelt, NY
Dordt College, IA
D'Youville College, NY
East Central Oklahoma State University, OK
Eastern Connecticut State College, CT
Eastern Kentucky University, KY
Eastern Michigan University, MI
Eastern Nazarene College, MA
Eastern New Mexico University, NM
Eastern Oregon State College, OR
East Tennessee State University, TN
East Texas Baptist College, TX
East Texas State University, TX
Edinboro State College, PA
Edward Waters College, FL
Elizabeth City State University, NC
Elizabethtown College, PA
Elon College, NC
Emmanuel College, MA
Evangel College, MO
The Evergreen State College, WA
Fayetteville State University, NC
Felician College, NJ
Ferrum College, VA
Florida Memorial College, FL
Fort Lewis College, CO
Fort Valley State College, GA
Franklin Pierce College, NH
Freed-Hardeman College, TN
Friends University, KS
Gardner-Webb College, NC
George Williams College, IL
Georgia College, GA
Georgia Southwestern College, GA
Goldey Beacom College, DE
Graceland College, IA
Grambling State University, LA
Grand View College, IA
Green Mountain College, VT
Greensboro College, NC
Hampton Institute, VA
Hardin-Simmons University, TX
Hawaii Loa College, HI
Hawaii Pacific College, HI

Hellenic College and Holy Cross Greek Orthodox School of Theology, MA
Henderson State University, AR
Heritage College, WA
Howard Payne University, TX
Huntington College, AL
Huron College, SD
Husson College, ME
Incarnate Word College, TX
Indiana University at South Bend, IN
Indiana University Northwest, IN
Indiana University-Purdue University at Fort Wayne, IN
Indiana University-Purdue University at Indianapolis, IN
Indiana University Southeast, IN
Inter-American University of Puerto Rico/San German, PR
Jackson State University, MS
Jersey City State College, NJ
John Brown University, AR
Johnson C. Smith University, NC
Johnson State College, VT
Judson College, AL
Judson College, IL
Kansas Newman College, KS
Kean College of New Jersey, NJ
Kennesaw College, GA
Kentucky State University, KY
Kentucky Wesleyan College, KY
Keuka College, NY
The King's College, NY
King's College, PA
Knoxville College, TN
LaGrange College, GA
Lander College, SC
Lane College, TN
Langston University, OK
Lee College, TN
LeMoyne-Owen College, TN
Liberty Baptist College, VA
Limestone College, SC
Lincoln Universtiy, CA
Lincoln University, PA
The Lindenwood Colleges, MO
Livingston University, AL
Livingstone College, NC
Loma Linda University, CA
Loretto Heights College, CO
Louisiana State University and Agricultural and Mechanical College, LA
Lyndon State College, VT
Madonna College, MI
Manchester College, IN
Mankato State University, MN
Marian College of Fond du Lac, WI
Marshall University, WV
Mars Hill College, NC
Martin Center College, IN
Mary Baldwin College, VA
Marymount College, NY
Marymount College of Kansas, KS
Marymount Manhattan College, NY
Mayville State College, ND
McNeese State University, LA
Medaille College, NY
Memphis State University, TN
Mercer University in Atlanta, GA
Mercy College, MI
Mercy College, NY
Mercyhurst College, PA
Methodist College, NC
Middle Tennessee State University, TN

COLLEGE ADMISSIONS SELECTOR

Miles College, *AL*
Milligan College, *TN*
Milton College, *WI*
Milwaukee School of Engineering, *WI*
Mississippi College, *MS*
Mississippi University for Women, *MS*
Mississippi Valley State University, *MS*
Missouri Baptist College, *MO*
Missouri Institute of Technology, *MO*
Mobile College, *AL*
Morehouse College, *GA*
Morgan State University, *MD*
Morris Brown College, *GA*
Mount Mary College, *WI*
Mount St. Clare College, *IA*
Mount Saint Mary College, *NY*
Mount Senario College, *WI*
Mount Vernon College, *DC*
Mount Vernon Nazarene College, *OH*
Murray State University, *KY*
Muskingum College, *OH*
Nathaniel Hawthorne College, *NH*
National College, *SD*
National College of Education, *IL*
National University, *CA*
New England College, *NH*
New Mexico Highlands University, *NM*
New Mexico State University, *NM*
Norfolk State University, *VA*
North Carolina Agricultural and Technical State University, *NC*
North Carolina Central University, *NC*
North Carolina Wesleyan College, *NC*
North Dakota State University, *ND*
Northeastern Illinois University, *IL*
Northeastern Oklahoma State University, *OK*
Northeast Missouri State University, *MO*
Northern Michigan University, *MI*
Northern State College, *SD*
North Georgia College, *GA*
Northwest Missouri State University, *MO*
Northwest Nazarene College, *ID*
Notre Dame College of Ohio, *OH*
Oakwood College, *AL*
Ohio Institute of Technology, *OH*
Olivet Nazarene College, *IL*
Ottawa University, *KS*
Ouachita Baptist University, *AR*
Our Lady of Holy Cross College, *LA*
Paine College, *GA*
Palm Beach Atlantic College, *FL*
Park College, *MO*
Pembroke State University, *NC*
Pennsylvania State University/Behrend College, *PA*
Pfeiffer College, *NC*
Philander Smith College, *AR*
Pine Manor College, *MA*
Plymouth State College, *NH*
Point Loma College, *CA*
Point Park College, *PA*
Post College, *CT*
Prairie View A&M University, *TX*
Purdue University/Calumet, *IN*
Rockmont College, *CO*
Rocky Mountain College, *MT*
Rust College, *MS*
Rutgers University/University College — Camden, *NJ*
Rutgers University/University College — Newark, *NJ*
Sacred Heart College, *NC*

Saginaw Valley State College, *MI*
Saint Augustine's College, *NC*
St. Edward's University, *TX*
St. Francis College, *NY*
Saint Martin's College, *WA*
Saint Mary of the Plains College, *KS*
Saint Mary-of-the-Woods College, *IN*
St. Mary's Dominican College, *LA*
Saint Peter's College, *NJ*
St. Thomas Aquinas College, *NY*
Salem College, *WV*
Salve Regina — The Newport College, *RI*
Samford University, *AL*
Sam Houston State University, *TX*
Savannah State College, *GA*
Shaw University, *NC*
Sheldon Jackson College, *AK*
Siena Heights College, *MI*
Sierra Nevada College, *NV*
Silver Lake College of the Holy Family, *WI*
Slippery Rock State College, *PA*
South Carolina State College, *SC*
Southeastern Oklahoma State University, *OK*
Southeast Missouri State University, *MO*
Southern Illinois University at Edwardsville, *IL*
Southern Missionary College, *TN*
Southern Oregon State College, *OR*
Southern Technical Institute, *GA*
Southwestern Adventist College, *TX*
Southwestern Oklahoma State University, *OK*
Southwest Missouri State University, *MO*
Southwest State University, *MN*
Spalding College, *KY*
State University of New York/College at Old Westbury, *NY*
Stephens College, *MO*
Sterling College, *KS*
Stillman College, *AL*
Strayer College, *DC*
Sul Ross State University, *TX*
Talladega College, *AL*
Tarkio College, *MO*
Tarleton State University, *TX*
Tennessee State University, *TN*
Texas A&I University, *TX*
Texas A&M University at Galveston, *TX*
Texas College, *TX*
Texas Tech University, *TX*
Texas Woman's University, *TX*
Tift College, *GA*
Toccoa Falls College, *GA*
Trevecca Nazarene College, *TN*
Trinity College, *VT*
Troy State University System, *AL*
Turabo University, *PR*
Tusculum College, *TN*
Tuskegee Institute, *AL*
Union College, *KY*
Union College, *NE*
Unity College, *ME*
University of Akron, *OH*
University of Alabama in Birmingham, *AL*
University of Alaska/Fairbanks, *AK*
University of Albuquerque, *NM*
University of Arkansas at Little Rock, *AR*
University of Arkansas at Pine Bluff, *AR*
University of Central Arkansas, *AR*
University of Charleston, *WV*
University of Hawaii at Hilo, *HI*
University of La Verne, *CA*
University of Maine at Fort Kent, *ME*
University of Maine at Machias, *ME*

University of Maine at Presque Isle, *ME*
University of Mary Hardin-Baylor, *TX*
University of Minnesota/Duluth, *MN*
University of Montevallo, *AL*
University of Nevada/Las Vegas, *NV*
University of New Haven, *CT*
University of New Mexico, *NM*
University of North Alabama, *AL*
University of North Carolina at Wilmington, *NC*
University of St. Thomas, *TX*
University of Science and Arts of Oklahoma, *OK*
University of South Alabama, *AL*
University of South Carolina at Aiken, *SC*
University of South Carolina/Coastal Carolina College, *SC*
University of Southern Mississippi, *MS*
University of Tennessee at Chattanooga, *TN*
University of Tennessee at Martin, *TN*
University of Texas at El Paso, *TX*
University of Texas at San Antonio, *TX*
University of Wisconsin/La Crosse, *WI*
University of Wisconsin/Oshkosh, *WI*
University of Wisconsin/Platteville, *WI*
University of Wisconsin/River Falls, *WI*
University of Wisconsin/Stevens Point, *WI*
University of Wisconsin/Superior, *WI*
University of Wisconsin/Whitewater, *WI*
Urbana College, *OH*
Ursuline College, *OH*
Utah State University, *UT*
Valdosta State College, *GA*
Vermont College of Norwich University, *VT*
Villa Maria College, *PA*
Virginia State University, *VA*
Walla Walla College, *WA*
Warner Pacific College, *OR*
Wayland Baptist University, *TX*
Waynesburg State College, *PA*
Webber College, *FL*
Weber State College, *UT*
Wentworth Institute of Technology, *MA*
Westbrook College, *ME*
West Coast University, *CA*
Western Carolina University, *NC*
Western Illinois University, *IL*
Western New Mexico University, *NM*
Western Oregon State College, *OR*
Western State College, *CO*
West Georgia College, *GA*
West Liberty State College, *WV*
West Texas State University, *TX*
West Virginia Institute of Technology, *WV*
West Virginia State College, *WV*
West Virginia Wesleyan College, *WV*
William Carey College, *MS*
William Paterson College of New Jersey, *NJ*
William Woods College, *MO*
Wilmington College, *DE*
Wilmington College, *OH*
Wingate College, *NC*
Winona State University, *MN*
Winston-Salem State University, *NC*
Winthrop College, *SC*
Worcester State College, *MA*
Wright State University, *OH*
Xavier University of Louisiana, *LA*
Yankton College, *SD*
York College of Pennsylvania, *PA*
Youngstown State University, *OH*

COLLEGE ADMISSIONS SELECTOR xvii

NONCOMPETITIVE

The colleges in this category generally only require evidence of graduation from an accredited high school (although they may also require the completion of a certain number of high school units). Some require that entrance examinations be taken for placement purposes only, or only by graduates of unaccredited high schools or only by out-of-state students. In some cases, insufficient capacity may compel a college in this category to limit the number of students that are accepted; however, if a college accepts all its applicants, it automatically falls in this category.

Amber University, TX
Austin Peay State University, TN
Bartlesville Wesleyan College, OK
Bellevue College, NE
Bethany Bible College, CA
Bluefield State College, WV
Boise State University, ID
Capitol Institute of Technology, MD
Caribbean University College, PR
Carson-Newman College, TN
Castleton State College, VT
Central State University, OH
Chadron State College, NE
College of Great Falls, MT
De Lourdes College, IL
Dickinson State College, ND
Dyke College, OH
Eastern Montana College, MT
Embry-Riddle Aeronautical University, FL
Emporia State University, KS
Fairmont State College, WV
Ferris State College, MI
Flaming Rainbow University, OK
Fort Hays State University, KS
Franklin University, OH
Glenville State College, WV
Goddard College, VT
Huston-Tillotson College, TX
Idaho State University, ID
Indiana State University Evansville, IN
Indiana State University, IN
Indiana University at Kokomo, IN
International Institute of the Americas of World University, PR
Jacksonville State University, AL
Jarvis Christian College, TX
Kansas State University, KS
Kearney State College, NE
Lamar University, TX
Lewis-Clark State College, ID
Lincoln Memorial University, TN
Lincoln University, MO
Louisiana State University/Shreveport, LA
Louisiana Tech University, LA
Lubbock Christian College, TX
Marylhurst College for Lifelong Learning, OR
Mesa College, CO
Metropolitan State College, CO
Mid-America Nazarene College, KS
Midwestern State University, TX
Minot State College, ND
Mississippi Industrial College, MS
Missouri Southern State College, MO
Missouri Western State College, MO
Montana State University, MT
Morehead State University, KY
Morris College, SC
New College of California, CA
Nicholls State University, LA
Northeast Louisiana University, LA
Northern Kentucky University, KY
Northern Montana College, MT
Northwestern Oklahoma State University, OK
Northwestern State University, LA
Nova University, FL
Oakland City College, IN
Ohio State University, OH
Ohio State University at Lima, OH
Ohio State University at Mansfield, OH
Ohio State University at Marion, OH
Ohio State University at Newark, OH
Oklahoma Christian College, OK
Oklahoma Panhandle State University, OK
Pan American University, TX
Paul Quinn College, TX
Peru State College, NE
Piedmont College, GA
Pikeville College, KY
Pittsburgh State University, KS
Rio Grande College, OH
Shaw College at Detroit, MI
Southeastern Louisiana University, LA
Southern Arkansas University, AR
Southern University and A & M College, LA
Southern University in New Orleans, LA
Southern Utah State College, UT
Southern Vermont College, VT
Spertus College of Judaica, IL
State University of New York/Empire State College, NY
Tabor College, KS
Texas Southern University, TX
Thomas A. Edison State College, NJ
University of Alaska/Juneau, AK
University of Arkansas at Fayetteville, AR
University of Arkansas at Monticello, AR
University of Guam, Guam
University of Houston/Downtown Campus, TX
University of Idaho, ID
University of Kansas, KS
University of Montana, MT
University of Nebraska at Omaha, NE
University of Nebraska/Lincoln, NE
University of New Orleans, LA
University of North Dakota, ND
University of South Carolina at Spartanburg, SC
University of South Dakota at Springfield, SD
University of Southern Colorado, CO
University of Southwestern Louisiana, LA
University of the District of Columbia, DC
University of Wisconsin/Parkside, WI
University of Wyoming, WY
Valley City State College, ND
Voorhees College, SC
Washburn University of Topeka, KS
Washington International College, DC
Wayne State College, NE
Western International University, AZ
Western Kentucky University, KY
Western Montana College, MT
Wichita State University, KS
Wiley College, TX

SPECIAL

Listed here are colleges whose programs of study are specialized: professional schools of art, music, or theater arts. In general, the admissions requirements are not based primarily on academic criteria, but on evidence of talent or special interest in the field. Many other colleges and universities offer special-interest programs *in addition* to regular academic curricula, but such institutions have been given a regular competitive rating based on academic criteria.

Art Center College of Design, CA
Atlanta College of Art, GA
Berklee College of Music, MA
Boston Conservatory of Music, MA
Brooks Institute, CA
California College of Arts and Crafts, CA
California Institute of the Arts, CA
Center for Creative Studies, MI
Cleveland Institute of Art, OH
Cleveland Institute of Music, OH
Columbia College, IL
Columbus College of Art and Design, OH
Combs College of Music, PA
Conservatory of Music of Puerto Rico, PR
Cornish Institute, WA
Eastman School of Music, NY
Gallaudet College, DC
The Juilliard School, NY
Kansas City Art Institute, MO
Louisville School of Art, KY
Manhattan School of Music, NY
Mannes College of Music, NY
Maryland Institute/College of Art, MD
Massachusetts College of Art, MA
Memphis Academy of Arts, TN
Minneapolis College of Art and Design, MN
Moore College of Art, PA
Native American Educational Services, IL
New England Conservatory of Music, MA
New School of Music, PA
North Carolina School of the Arts, NC
Pacific Northwest College of Art, OR
Parsons School of Design, NY
Peabody Conservatory of Music, MD
Philadelphia College of Art, PA
Philadelphia College of the Performing Arts, PA
Portland School of Art, ME
Rhode Island School of Design, RI
Ringling School of Art and Design, FL
Rutgers University/Mason Gross School of the Arts, NJ
St. Louis Conservatory of Music, MO
San Francisco Art Institute, CA
San Francisco Conservatory of Music, CA
Savannah College of Art and Design, GA
School of the Art Institute of Chicago, IL
School of Visual Arts, NY
Swain School of Design, MA
Vandercook College of Music, IL
Westminster Choir College, NJ
Wisconsin Conservatory of Music, WI

CHOOSING A COLLEGE

You've decided to go to college. Perhaps you've always wanted to, or maybe you've found that it is the only way to get the training you need for the career you want. Or you may not be sure what you really want to do, and are considering college along with other options. Whatever your reason, you want to make the right decision.

Not long ago, so many students wanted to attend college that schools often rejected large numbers of applicants, including many who were qualified. Many students could not get into their first-choice college, and some found themselves at their last choice. It wasn't uncommon for a high school senior to apply to as many as five colleges at once.

Things are different now. Because of declining numbers of college-age students and the increasing availability of other options, fewer students are applying. It is now far more of a buyer's market, in which students have a much better chance of acceptance at their first-choice college. Schools may not have lowered their standards, but many are seeking students in ways they haven't before. Some accept more students on a probationary basis, offering them remedial courses, and some provide more financial aid to attract people who otherwise couldn't afford college. The most prestigious universities continue to be extremely selective.

It is important for you to consider all your options and select the college you feel will best suit your goals. Every person has different aspirations and preferences; when you choose a college, make sure you are considering your own desires, not those of your family or friends.

Selecting the right college requires two processes: setting your own goals and then determining the options open to you. If you can match the two successfully, you probably will be satisfied with your choice. In the following paragraphs, we've outlined the basic steps you need to take to make an informed decision, along with some considerations you should think about as you proceed.

GATHER INFORMATION

Get all the information available. Talk to your parents, friends, neighbors, teachers, and guidance counselor about college. Skim through this book to get a feel for what is offered. Begin gathering information on colleges, including any flyers available in the high school guidance office. Send for the catalogs of colleges you may be interested in. Look for news articles about specific colleges or higher education in general in newspapers and news magazines, and read advertisements for colleges in your vicinity. In short, become "college-aware" and watch for any news on the subject.

DETERMINE SOME BASIC PREFERENCES

Begin to think about what you want to do. You may already have some preferences—to attend a school nearby or to go away from home, to study at a college affiliated with your church, to work toward a technical degree at a specialized school. A great variety of programs and types of colleges are available.

College vs. University

One of your first decisions may be whether to attend a college (usually small) or a university (often large). A university usually has graduate programs as well as undergraduate ones, although a few colleges do offer graduate degrees and a few universities do not. A large university usually offers more courses; larger and more varied laboratory, library, and recreational facilities; and more prestigious professors. On the other hand, the nearest you may come to a famous scholar is the distance from your seat in a lecture hall to the speaker's platform. Quiz sections, laboratories, and preceptorials generally are supervised by teaching assistants—graduate students not much older or more experienced than yourself. Some of them will be excellent, because they are sincerely interested in students and in learning to become effective teachers. Others will be preoccupied with their own studies and may regard teaching as a nuisance necessary to defray their educational expenses.

The college, by way of contrast, will have fewer big names on its faculty, but it probably will have more professors primarily interested in teaching rather than research. Most classes will be smaller, there may be no graduate assistants, and close faculty-student relations may be more frequent than at a large university.

Aside from academic factors, the size of the school is important for other reasons. Some high school seniors fear they would become lost in a large school. Actually, such a concern is not always justified. Even in enormous institutions, the typical undergraduate becomes part of a small group of friends who have met in classes, in dormitories, at social functions, in clubs and fraternities, or in extracurricular activities.

Urban vs. Rural

Although three quarters of the nation's college students attend institutions in cities, the rural college is a peculiarly American invention. Such colleges frequently foster a special atmosphere, often warm and memorable. Part of the urban school's appeal is the entertainment and cultural offerings of a city. However, some cities offer few such attractions, and most good colleges attempt to schedule as many plays, concerts, films, and other events as they can afford. A city environment often is especially interesting to students of such subjects as economics, sociology, political science, and education, since it offers opportunities for direct observation and sometimes participation in their fields.

Coed vs. Single-Sex

A few years ago, with men at Vassar and women at Princeton, the one-sex college seemed to be disappearing. Recently, however, the trend toward coeducation has shown signs of slowing down, especially at all-female schools. Many such colleges have decided not to go coed, citing the opportunities for leadership and the priority on education of women as *women* rather than as members of a second and perhaps less important sex. On the other hand, many single-sex campuses are deserted on weekends, and students must seek coed social activities at other campuses.

Full-Time vs. Part-Time

There have always been part-time students on many campuses, but only in recent years, when tuition costs have really soared, have so many students chosen this route straight out of high school, or after obtaining an associate degree at a community college. These students usually take 6 to 12 credits a semester—usually while holding full-time jobs—and earn a degree only after many years of work. It is a difficult route to a degree, but, since some employers pay at least part of their employees' educational expenses, it can be a much less expensive one.

EVALUATE YOUR RECORD

Take a close look at your grades and consider, as objectively as you can, how well you have been doing in high school. What is your average? How have teachers reacted to your work? And, if you have taken the Preliminary Scholastic Aptitude Test (PSAT/NMSQT), the Scholastic Aptitude Test (SAT), or the American College Test (ACT), what were your scores?

Consider also your attitudes toward study and toward what you want from college. Make sure that college is the best thing for you to do after high school. Decide whether a less competitive school might be better for you, and keep in mind that even if your grades or test scores are poor, you generally can find a college that will accept you.

At this point, you should make a preliminary survey of the available options by comparing your academic achievements to the categories of the College Admissions Selector (see the preceding section of the book). The Admissions Selector groups colleges in six competitiveness categories that range from "Most Competitive" to "Noncompetitive." The explanation preceding each category describes the criteria by which colleges have been assigned to each group. Colleges that offer specialized programs such as music or art have been put into a seventh category if acceptance does not depend on standard academic criteria. The competitiveness category to which a college is assigned also appears in the heading of each profile.

To find your category, match your academic credentials with the criteria preceding each Selector category. Your SAT or ACT score is very important. If you have taken only the PSAT/NMSQT, you can predict your SAT scores by multiplying the two-digit PSAT/NMSQT score by 10 and adding 20 to the result. After adding your mathematical and verbal scores and dividing the results by 2, you should have an idea whether you qualify for a "Most Competitive" college or should set your sights on a less exclusive institution. Your scores should be in the top half of the range given for a category to assure probable acceptance by a college in that category.

Your guidance counselor may not be able to provide you with your

xx CHOOSING A COLLEGE

class rank until later in your senior year, but you can compute your academic average. If it is slightly below the average listed for a Selector category, but your most recent grades have been better than earlier ones, the admissions officers probably will be swayed in your favor by good SAT or ACT scores.

The percentage of applicants accepted by a college is important because it tells how closely your academic achievements should meet the college's standards. A small ratio of acceptances to applications would suggest that the only applicants who could be confident about acceptance would be those whose test scores and high school averages clearly fit the school's standards. Even so, many popular colleges have to reject well-qualified applicants for lack of space.

A rapid survey of the Selector will reveal that many colleges in your category can be immediately eliminated for reasons such as location, size, and cost. But you also will find the names of colleges you are familiar with or curious about, and these are the first whose profiles you should check.

COMPARE THE COLLEGES

When you determine your preferences and decide which category of colleges is best suited to your abilities, start comparing individual schools. The main factors you should consider are academic strengths, facilities, location of campus and size of school, and costs.

Academics

A college education is expensive, and you want to get the best value for your money. Consider first whether the school offers the program you want. Most colleges offer traditional programs in the arts and sciences; unusual, specialized, or newer disciplines usually are found in universities. To assess the strength of a given department, you should look through the college catalog; the number of faculty members and the number of courses offered in a given discipline can give you a reasonably accurate gauge of its strength. If you can, talk to seniors in, or recent graduates of, the department.

It would be difficult to find an institution without an assortment of good, mediocre, and poor teachers, but academic reputations may depend on such things as salary levels and the percentage of faculty members who hold doctoral degrees. The latter is one indication of the college's success in employing faculty members with good credentials. Remember, however, that in many technological fields, and in some social science fields such as economics and journalism, professional experience may be more important than an advanced degree. Some colleges, particularly those located in urban areas, can hire part-time instructors who also work full time in their fields. These instructors often help their departments keep abreast of new developments in the field and can provide students with practical information and contacts for future jobs.

The employment situation at the colleges today is tight. Economic pressures have caused many institutions to reduce the number of faculty members, but this usually means that a higher proportion of those who remain hold advanced degrees. At most colleges, all faculty members will have at least a master's degree, which means more and more courses are being taught by those with doctorates. Many schools also are using more part-time instructors; one disadvantage of this is that because they are on campus only for limited periods, it can be difficult to meet with them for counseling. More schools are hiring instructors on a "visiting" basis for one- or two-year appointments. Because of this, and because tenure is not granted as readily as it has been in the past, there can be a heavy turnover of faculty members that would disturb some students.

The information provided in the profiles on faculty salaries also can be useful in determining a college's academic strength. The salary ratings are based on information compiled each year by the American Association of University Professors (AAUP). The ratings are used principally by faculty members to compare pay, but they also can be used as one indicator of the quality of the teaching staff. The ratings do not consider cost-of-living differences or other benefits faculty members may receive. But they do serve as a basis of comparison among similar schools. (See an explanation of the AAUP ratings in "An Explanation of the Book"). Students should keep in mind that a professor may choose to teach at a college for a lower salary if he or she likes its atmosphere or location. Personal considerations other than salary enter into all such decisions.

Other factors also can be helpful in comparing the academic strengths of colleges. The presence of national honor societies on campus, particularly Phi Beta Kappa (liberal arts) and Sigma Xi (science), indicates that these organizations have recognized the college's academic respectability.

The breakdown in each profile of the percentage of degrees awarded in the most popular fields reflects to some extent current interests among students (such as the recent surge in business majors). But you often can assume that the programs attracting the most students are the ones the college is putting its greatest effort behind.

If you want to learn a graduate or professional degree eventually, then check the percentages of graduates who begin graduate study or enter medical, dental, or law schools. If you intend to go directly into business, note the percentage of graduates who obtain jobs in business or industry. The proportion of students who begin graduate study or find jobs in industry is an excellent indicator of the college's academic quality, because of its implication about the institution's success in attracting and producing serious students.

On the other hand, a high student dropout rate usually indicates that the college admits many students who cannot handle the work. If the percentage of entering freshmen who eventually graduate from a college is low, it may indicate either low motivation and ability on the part of many students or a high transfer rate.

Facilities

Perhaps the most important facility on campus is the library. You will use it to supplement your classroom work and to discover new ideas; if it is poor, then your education is likely to suffer. For a detailed discussion on evaluating library facilities, see the chapter "An Explanation of the Book."

Depending on your field of study, other facilities also may be of great importance. For science majors, up-to-date laboratories are essential. For business students, access to computers is valuable. For health-science majors, medical facilities for observation and practice are desirable. Select a college that offers you hands-on experience with the most advanced equipment possible.

Environment

Most students expect to spend four years at a college, so they should be happy with the physical, social, and cultural environment.

We've already discussed the differences between a college located in a rural area and one in a metropolis. And we've mentioned the differences between a coed college and a single-sex institution. But you also must decide whether you want to go away to college or to live at home and attend a school nearby. Your decision may be based largely on cost; going away to college is much more expensive because of the additional costs of room and board. For many, getting away from home is a maturing experience, although it need not be the only route to maturity. Consider your own likes and dislikes, and discuss the options with your family and friends.

Consider the other students likely to attend the college you are thinking about. The profiles in this book give some background on the student body: the percentage of state residents, the educational background of entering freshmen, how many students live on campus, and information on religious and ethnic backgrounds. There is much to be said for a diverse student body; on the same theory that "travel is broadening" a school whose students are drawn from different backgrounds can offer a broader perspective and more interesting associations than one with a homogeneous student body.

Religion is a factor for some students, and almost every campus provides some religious counselors or facilities. Some colleges with religious affiliations go further, requiring chapel attendance or prohibiting drinking or other behavior that violates religious teachings. Increasingly, religiously affiliated colleges are stating that they are open to students of all faiths. Some such schools are as secular in outlook as public institutions; in others, most students are members of the sponsoring faith. The stated purpose of the institution, its programs of study, and its requirements for worship will indicate the relative emphasis placed on its religious orientation.

The number and scope of extracurricular activities often indicate the mood of the campus and the major interests of the students. Special activities usually vary from year to year. It should not be assumed that because there is no interest in a specific activity one year, it will not appear the next.

Membership in fraternities or sororities fluctuates from generation to generation and from campus to campus. These organizations are back on the upswing, again becoming marks of social prestige on some campuses but involving a greater range of students and activities. Less secretive and exclusive than in the past, fraternities and sororities today tend to combine service projects with social activities. Membership is more open and hazing is minimal. Of course the organizations are not popular on all campuses, and membership in them generally is far from a social necessity. Whether to join or not is a decision you shouldn't make until you get to college.

Sports have their place on almost all campuses. Some schools play down intercollegiate activities and encourage intramurals. The profiles indicate the size of the intercollegiate and intramural programs. This information is apt to change, of course; new intramural sports are especially likely to be added.

Another factor that enriches college life is the variety of services offered by the college. Should you need help, the availability of health care and psychological counseling would be important. If you were to have trouble with some of your courses, you would want to know that you could obtain tutoring or remedial instruction. You would want to use the college's placement service when you graduate or if you wanted part-time or summer jobs while still in school.

Costs

Mounting tuition and room-and-board fees in a time of shrinking financial aid are making college attendance more difficult for some students. The route to a college degree may involve much sacrifice and hard work. With this edition of *Barron's Profiles of American Colleges,* we again note substantial increases in tuition as well as cuts in financial aid. When selecting a college, pick a school you feel you could afford to attend for four years; remember that the tuition fees probably will go up before you graduate.

The charges for room and board also are rising steadily to keep pace with inflation. While until a couple of years ago many students lived in off-campus apartments to save money, now college residence halls generally are regarded as less expensive. And schools are finding that looser regulations are making dormitories even more acceptable to students.

Note that the figures given in the profiles do not include personal expenses such as entertainment or travel.

INVESTIGATE SOURCES OF FINANCIAL AID

All students with extremely high grades or some financial need should consider seeking financial aid. Specific information on scholarships, grants, loans, part-time jobs, and cooperative education follows. For more information, refer to another Barron's publication, *Money for College: How to Get It,* by Donald Moore.

Scholarships and Grants

Nearly every college offers a number of scholarships and fellowships that range from partial payment of tuition to complete payment of all expenses. These grants are awarded in recognition of academic achievement and/or financial need. Special scholarships may be given to attract outstanding athletes or students with special talents in such areas as music, drama, or journalism. In addition to scholarships offered by colleges, there are many scholarship funds administered by businesses, labor unions, PTAs, veterans groups, church groups, and citizens councils.

The largest independently funded scholarship program in the United States is administered by the National Merit Scholarship Corporation and is funded by company foundations and colleges and universities. Scholarship recipients are selected on the basis of their score on the Preliminary Scholastic Aptitude Test/National Merit Scholarship Qualifying Test (PSAT/NMSQT), other academic factors, and their character. For further information, write to the National Merit Scholarship Corporation, One American Plaza, Evanston, Illinois 60201, and ask for the PSAT/NMSQT Student Bulletin.

Most states, including California, Idaho, Illinois, New Jersey, New York, and Texas, have scholarship and/or grant programs for residents.

The federal government offers Basic Educational Opportunity Grants (BEOG) and Supplemental Educational Opportunity Grants (SEOG). Recipients of these grants must show financial need, may not receive more than $2000 per academic year, and must use the funds for undergraduate study only. Federal grants are also available through the Law Enforcement Education Program and the Nursing Scholarship Program.

The Veterans Administration provides two types of funds—G.I. Bill benefits and War Orphan benefits—to veterans of all wars and to the children of deceased or entirely disabled veterans whose disability or death was service-related. There are certain time limits by which veterans must begin and terminate receipt of benefits and certain age restrictions on receipt of benefits by children of veterans; contact a local office of the Veterans Administration for details on eligibility.

Loans

Financing a college education by taking out a student loan has become commonplace in recent years. Such loans carry low interest rates and often do not have to be repaid until after graduation.

Some colleges make their own loans, but most loan money comes from federal funds provided by the National Direct Student Loan program set up by the National Defense Education Act and administered by the financial aid offices at the individual colleges and universities.

The Guaranteed Student Loan Program and the Federal Insured Student Loan Program make it possible for students to borrow money through commercial banks, savings and loan associations, and credit unions because the federal government guarantees repayment of the loan if the borrower defaults.

Many states have programs through which students may borrow from banks within the state at low interest rates. Also, some banks have instituted special loans for education; inquire about these at your local commercial bank.

Part-Time Jobs

The College Work-Study Program (CWS), federally funded in part and available to students from low-income families, allows the student to work part-time, usually in a job that relates to his or her field of study or interests; this might mean working in the college library, a laboratory, an academic department, or an administrative office.

Regular part-time jobs are available at or near most schools and are sometimes included as part of the financial aid package, as are College Work-Study jobs.

Cooperative Education

Be sure to check out schools that offer cooperative education programs, in which students alternate periods of full-time study with periods of full-time work. This type of program will allow you to earn extra money, and also will give you experience that can help you qualify for jobs after graduation. For information on such programs, write to the National Commission for Cooperative Education, 360 Huntington Avenue, Boston, Massachusetts 02115.

The information above can help you start looking for financial aid. Check the information on financial aid in each profile, then contact the colleges you are interested in for further information.

GET MORE INFORMATION

Write to the admissions directors of the colleges in which you are most interested for their latest catalogs. The catalogs will provide more specific data on course requirements, programs accredited by special or professional organizations, and other information. If you will need financial aid, be sure to indicate this in your letter; your application generally will not be discounted because of it. In effect, you are making two applications, each usually considered separately. If your application for admission is accepted, your application for financial aid may be denied, or you may be awarded anything from partial tuition to a package covering all expenses.

If possible, visit the college. Read the information in the profile on visiting procedures, and contact the school to set a time. Whether or not an interview is required for admission, it usually is worthwhile to discuss yourself and the college with an official of the institution. Ask about anything that is unclear to you. Be frank about yourself and your goals. At the end of the interview, ask about your chances for admission. The interviewer will not be able to give you a final answer, but he or she can tell you whether it would be worthwhile for you to apply in view of your test scores and academic record.

Take advantage of the informal tours offered by many colleges. They are usually conducted by undergraduates who will answer your questions from a student's point of view. You may be able to sit in on some classes or spend a night in the residence halls, both of which will give you a better idea of the college environment. Of course, it is better to visit colleges when classes are in session, but even a vacation-time visit is better than no visit at all.

APPLY FOR ADMISSION

After you have determined which colleges you would like to attend, it is time to apply. We've worked out a plan that fits a variety of situations, and should result in your being accepted to at least one college of your choice.

Follow the Three-College Plan. This will give you a chance for acceptance at a college that looks for students with credentials slightly better than yours, one whose standards you easily fit, and one that could be considered your "safety" school.

CHOOSING A COLLEGE

The Most Desirable College
This college's entrance standards may seem a cut above your qualifications. If they are too far above your test scores, high school grades, and class rank, you most likely will be wasting your time, though if you tend to underestimate your abilities it might be worth a gamble. The most sensible first choice would be limited to either a "plus" college in the Selector category corresponding to your achievements or a college in the next higher category.

Your chance for admission to a more competitive college depends on factors that are more than statistical. If a school receives a large number of applications, its admissions officers may automatically eliminate all applicants whose qualifications fall below a certain cut-off point. But this situation is becoming rarer; more schools consider applicants who do not fit their usual criteria. Bear in mind that when a freshman class has a median test score of, say, 600, as many freshmen scored below 600 as scored above. If your scores are below the median (by not much more than 100 points), a strong high school record and evidence of special talents may compensate, especially since many colleges are deemphasizing SAT and ACT scores.

Factors other than academic record that may affect chances for admission could include an unusually strong letter of recommendation, your essay or statement of purpose, the reputation of your high school, a parent who is an alumnus of that college, extracurricular activities, or even where you live, since many colleges try to make sure each freshman class includes students from across the country. The most prestigious American colleges probably could have freshman classes composed of nothing but valedictorians. They don't—and they do not want such classes.

The Next Most Desirable College
This should be a realistic choice of a college you would like to attend, whose admissions criteria correspond closely to your credentials. That does not guarantee your acceptance, for the reasons given above. For example, if ten members of your senior class applied to the same college, the admissions officers might decide that the college doesn't want ten students from the same school, even if all are highly qualified.

The "Safety" College
This is a college whose admissions policy clearly makes you acceptable, with a slight margin to spare. It may seem to be below your own potential. Choose your safety college with care—you might go there. If you should find yourself unhappy there, you could transfer after the first or second year if your grades are superior, as they should be if you are competing with students whose qualifications are inferior to yours. If you have not done well in high school, your safety college might be a junior college. Many students begin in junior college and later transfer to excellent four-year institutions.

AWAIT THE REPLIES

Waiting for responses from the colleges can be suspenseful. If you are not tense about being accepted, then you might be eager to hear whether you have been granted financial aid.

If you have been accepted by your second-choice college and it demands a deposit to ensure you a place, but you have not yet heard from your first choice, you have been caught in the "squeeze." To avoid this, when you submit your application ask for early decision from the first-choice college. If you haven't done that, you can request a delay in the deposit deadline at the second-choice college. If the colleges will not cooperate, then it is better to risk the deposit than to take a chance on missing a year of college. To avoid this squeeze, many colleges subscribe to the Candidates Reply Date Agreement (CRDA). This agreement establishes one date on which all participating colleges require prospective students to submit notification of whether they plan to attend.

When you have received all your replies and have made your final decision, send in your deposit and start planning your future. Good luck!

ADVICE FOR FOREIGN STUDENTS

More and more American colleges and universities are welcoming students from foreign countries. About 311,000 foreign students are now enrolled in U.S. institutions of higher learning, and that number is rising by 12 to 16 percent each year. There are a number of reasons why colleges seek foreign students. Those students can fill places that may otherwise go unfilled because the number of college-age Americans is declining. Education also is becoming an important American "export"; the money foreign students spend on tuition and other expenses boosts the U.S. economy. Education has long been an important supplement to the nation's foreign-aid program, giving foreign nationals skills they can use to improve life in their homelands. And colleges recognize that foreign students help educate their American counterparts by exposing them to different ideas and cultures.

The extent of special services for foreign students varies from institution to institution. Also, the increasing competition for students, both foreign and American, has led a few colleges to misrepresent the services and programs they offer. When choosing a college, as when making any major purchase, you should investigate carefully. The beginning chapters of this book give general advice on choosing a college; this chapter provides advice specifically for foreign students.

TESTING AND ADMISSION

This book provides general information on most American colleges and universities, but for the most detailed, up-to-date information you should write directly to the schools that most interest you and ask for a copy of their catalog (there may be a charge). Libraries of college catalogs also can be found at the offices of the Institute of International Education, a private, nonprofit, international educational exchange agency (located in New York, Bangkok, Hong Kong, and Mexico City), and the U. S. International Communication Agency counseling centers (generally located at U.S. embassies and at the offices of binational and Fulbright commissions).

When you are ready to apply—usually about a year before the date on which you hope to enter college—write to the schools that interest you for application materials. Include in your letters the name of your country, the field you wish to study, a brief outline of your previous education, the number of years you have studied English, and the amount of money you can spend. The college admissions officers will review this information and should let you know if the college cannot meet your needs. You should also ask the schools for information about special programs and organizations for foreign students.

Most American colleges require undergraduate applicants to submit scores on one of two standardized tests. The scores are used as an indication of your ability to do college-level work. The first of these tests, the Scholastic Aptitude Test (SAT), assesses your ability to handle English grammar and vocabulary and to do secondary-school-level mathematics. The second test, used primarily by colleges in the Midwest, is the American College Test (ACT). It is designed to test your general educational development in English, mathematics, social studies, and natural sciences. Some highly selective schools also ask applicants to take as many as three Achievement Tests (ATs), which are offered in specific subject areas such as French, physics, European history, and intermediate mathematics.

SAT/AT TEST CENTERS

This list shows some of the numerous SAT/AT test center locations throughout the world; all locations within a particular country are given.

ARGENTINA
Buenos Aires

AUSTRALIA
Alice Springs
Brisbane
Canberra
Melbourne
Perth
Sydney

BELGIUM
Brussels
Shape

BRAZIL
Belo Horizonte
Brasilia
Campinas
Ceres
Fortaleza
Recife
Rio de Janeiro
Salvador
São Paulo

CANADA
Beaconsfield
Calgary
Charlottetown
Edmonton
Grand Prairie
Halifax
Hamilton
Kingston
Lakefield
Lennoxville
London
Mill Bay
Montebello
Montreal
North Bay
Ottawa
Port Colborne
Port Hope
Prince George
Red Lake
Regina
St. Catharines
Saint John
Saskatoon
Sept-Iles
Shawnigan Lake
Stanstead
Sudbury
Thompson
Thunder Bay
Timmins
Toronto
Vancouver
Victoria
Wabash
Waterloo
Windsor
Winnipeg

CYPRUS
Nicosia

DENMARK
Copenhagen

EGYPT
Alexandria
Cairo

ENGLAND
Birmingham
Cobham
High Wycombe
Kingston-on-Thames
Lakenheath
Liverpool
London
Plymouth
Street, Somerset
Thorpe, Surrey
Totnes, Devon
Upper Heyford
Uxbridge
Woodbridge

FINLAND
Helsinki

FRANCE
Cannes
Lé Chambon-sur-Lignon
Paris
Rennes

GERMANY
Augsburg
Bad Godesberg
Baumholder
Berlin
Bitburg
Bremerhaven
Frankfurt
Hahn
Hamburg
Hanau
Heidelberg
Kaiserslautern
Kandern
Karlsruhe
Munich
Nuremberg
Stuttgart
Wiesbaden
Wurzburg
Zweibrucken

GREECE
Athens
Thessaloniki

HONG KONG
Hong Kong

INDIA
Bangalore
Bombay
Calcutta
Darjeeling
Kodaikanal
Mussoorie
New Delhi

ISRAEL
Jerusalem
Tel Aviv

ITALY
Aviano
Brindisi
Florence
Livorno
Milan
Naples
Rome
Sigonella
Torino
Vicenza

JAPAN
Camp Zama
Iwakuni
Kobe
Misawa
Nagoya
Okinawa
Tokyo
Yokohama
Yokosuka
Yokota

KOREA
Pusan
Seoul
Taegu

KUWAIT
Kuwait

MALAYSIA
Ipuh
Kuala Lumpur
Kuching, (Sarawak)
Penang

MEXICO
Guadalajara
Mexico City
Monterrey

NETHERLANDS
Amsterdam
Brunssum
The Hague

NEW ZEALAND
Auckland
Christchurch
Lower Hutt

NIGERIA
Benin City
Calabar
Enugu
Ibadan
Jos
Lagos
Port Harcourt

xxiv   ADVICE FOR FOREIGN STUDENTS

NORWAY Oslo Stavanger **SAUDI ARABIA** Jidda **SCOTLAND** Aberdeen Edinburgh	Elgin Glasgow **SINGAPORE** Singapore **SOUTH AFRICA, REPUBLIC OF** Capetown Durban	Johannesburg **SPAIN** Barcelona Las Palmas Madrid Palma de Mallorca Zaragoza **SWEDEN**	Stockholm **THAILAND** Bangkok **TRINIDAD** Port-of-Spain **VENEZUELA** Caracas	Maracaibo San Cristobal Valencia **WALES** Llantwit Major **WEST BANK** Birzeit University

ACT TEST CENTERS

This list gives some of the 173 ACT test center locations outside the United States; all locations within a particular country are given.

ARGENTINA Buenos Aires **AUSTRALIA** New South Wales **BELGIUM** Brussels Shape **BRAZIL** Belém, Pará Belo Horizonte Campinas, S.P. Fortaleza, Ceara Rio de Janeiro São Paulo **CANADA** Calgary Cardston College Heights Dawson Creek Duncan Edmonton Lethbridge Medicine Hat Mississauga Montreal Nepean, Ottawa Oshawa Red Deer Regina Saskatoon	Surrey Thunder Bay Vanderhoof Vernon Winnipeg **DENMARK** Glamsbjerg **EGYPT (UNITED ARAB REPUBLIC)** Cairo **ENGLAND** Brandon, Suffolk Cambridgeshire Cobham, Surrey High Wycombe London Northants Oxford Suffolk Uxbridge **FRANCE** St.-Cloud **GERMANY (WEST)** Augsburg Berlin Bitburg Bonn Frankfurt Hahn	Hanau/Wolfgang Heidelberg Kaiserslautern Kandem Karisruhe Ludwigsburg/Pattonville Mannheim-Kafertal Munich Nuremberg Osterholz-Scharmbeck Weisbaden-Hainerberg Wurzburg Zweibruecken **GREECE** Athens **HONG KONG** Repulse Bay **INDIA** Bombay Kodaikanal Mussoorie New Delhi Panchgani, Maharashtra **ISRAEL** Jerusalem **ITALY** Aviano Brindisi Milan	Naples Rome Tombolo Vicenza **JAPAN** Aomori-Ken Camp Zama Iwakuni Kobe Nogoya Okinawa Tokyo Yokohama **KOREA** Seoul Taegu **KUWAIT** Kuwait **MALAYSIA** Kuala Lumpur **MEXICO** Chihuahua Nuevo Leon Guadalajara Mexico City Coahuila **NETHERLANDS** Brussum	The Hague **NIGERIA** Jos **NORWAY** Stavanger **SCOTLAND** Aberdeen Dunoon, Argyll Edinburgh **SINGAPORE** Singapore **SPAIN** Aravaca, Madrid Madrid Portals Nous, Mallorca Rota **THAILAND** Bangkok **VENEZUELA** Caracas Maracaibo Tachira Valencia

TOEFL TEST CENTERS

This list shows some of the 700 TOEFL test center locations throughout the world; all locations within a particular country are given.

ARGENTINA Buenos Aires Cordoba Mendoza **AUSTRALIA** Melbourne Sydney **BELGIUM** Brussels Waterloo **BRAZIL** Belém, Pará Belo Horizonte Brasilia Campinas	Curitiba Fortaleza Natal Porto Alegre Recife Rio de Janeiro Salvador São Paulo Vicosa **CANADA** Calgary Charlottetown Edmonton Fredericton Grand Prairie Guelph Hamilton	Kapukasing Kelowna Kingston Lethbridge London Montreal Ottawa Prince George Quebec Regina St. John's Saskatoon Sherbrooke Thunder Bay Toronto Windsor Winnipeg Vancouver Victoria	**CYPRUS** Nicosia **DENMARK** Copenhagen **EGYPT** Alexandria Cairo **ENGLAND** Birmingham London Liverpool Manchester Oxford Plymouth Thorpe, Surry Uxbridge	**FINLAND** Helsinki **FRANCE** Angers Bordeaux Lille Lyon Montpellier Nancy Paris Strasbourg Toulouse **GERMANY** Berlin Frankfurt Freiburg Göttingen

ADVICE FOR FOREIGN STUDENTS xxv

Hamburg	Lucknow	Tokyo	Arnhem	Capetown
Köln	Madras	Yokahama	The Hague	Durban
Munich	Mangalore			Johannesburg
Stuttgart	Mussoorie	**KOREA**	**NEW ZEALAND**	Port Elizabeth
Tübingen	Nagpur	Kwangju	Auckland	
	Pant Nagar	Pusan	Wellington	**SPAIN**
GREECE	Patna	Seoul		Barcelona
Athens	Pilani	Taegu	**NIGERIA**	Bilbao
Thessaloniki	Pune	Taejon	Benin City	Las Palmas
	Rajkot		Calabar	Madrid
HONG KONG	Ranchi	**KUWAIT**	Enugu	Malaga
Hong Kong	Srinagar	Khaldiah	Ibadan	Sevilla
	Trivandrum	Kuwait	Jos	Valencia
	Vallabh Vidyanagar		Kaduna	
INDIA	Varanasi		Kano	**SWEDEN**
Ahmedabad	Waltair	**MALAYSIA**	Lagos	Göteborg
Aligarh		Ayer Kroh, Malacca	Owerri	Lund
Allahabad	**ISRAEL**	Ipoh, Perak	Port Harcourt	Stockholm
Bangalore	Haifa	Johore		
Baroda	Jerusalem	Kota Bharu, Kelantan		**SYRIA**
Batala	Tel Aviv	Kota Kinabalu, Sabah	**NORWAY**	Damascus
Bhopal		Kuala Lumpur	Bergen	
Bhubaneswar	**ITALY**	Kuala Trengganu	Kirstiansand	**THAILAND**
Bombay	Firenze	Kuantan, Pahang	Oslo	Bangkok
Calcutta	Milano	Kuching, Sarawak	Tromso	Chiang Mai
Chandigarh	Napoli	Penang	Trondheim	Khon Kaen
Cochin	Roma	Sandakan, Sabah		Songkhla
Coimbatore	Torino	Sibu, Sarawak	**SAUDI ARABIA**	
Darjeeling	Vicenza	Sungei Patani, Kedah	Dhahran	**TRINIDAD AND TO-**
Delhi and New Delhi			Jidda	**BAGO**
Dhanbad	**JAPAN**	**MEXICO**	Riyadh	Port-of-Spain
Dharwar	Fukuoka	Guadalajara		
Gauhati	Hiroshima	Hermosillo	**SCOTLAND**	**VENEZUELA**
Guntur	Kobe	Merida	Glasgow	Caracas
Hyderabad	Miyazaki	Mexico City		Maracaibo
Indore	Nagasaki	Monterrey	**SINGAPORE**	Valencia
Jabalpur	Nagoya	Tampico	Singapore	
Jodhpur	Naha, Okinawa			
Kanpur	Sapporo	**NETHERLANDS**	**SOUTH AFRICA,**	**WEST BANK**
Kodaikanal	Sendai	Amsterdam	**REPUBLIC OF**	Birzeit University

The SAT and ATs, which are given in English only, are part of the Admissions Testing Program. Both are administered by the Educational Testing Service for the sponsoring organization, The College Board. You can take the SAT and ATs at established test centers or may be able to arrange for a special testing location. The completed registration form for testing at test centers must be received by the Educational Testing Service about six weeks prior to the test date; requests for special locations must be received eight to ten weeks prior to the test date. (Note that you cannot take both the SAT and one or more of the ATs on the same date.) For more information, write to The College Board ATP, Box 592, Princeton, N.J. 08541, U.S.A.

The ACT, which is given in English only, is administered by the American College Testing Program. You can take the ACT at an established test center or may be able to arrange for a special testing location. You may register at a particular test center up to a week before the test is given there; requests for special locations should be directed to the American College Testing Program as soon as possible before a particular test date. For more information, write to the American College Testing Program, P.O. Box 168, Iowa City, Iowa 52243, U.S.A., and ask for the Overseas Registration Packet.

If your native language is not English, you probably will have to take a test of your ability to use English. The most widely used of these tests is the Test of English as a Foreign Language (TOEFL), given at 700 test centers throughout the world. Other English exams include the Comprehensive English Language Test, the American Language Institute of Georgetown University (ALIGU) exam, and the University of Michigan Language Institute Test.

You can take TOEFL at an established center or may be able to set up a special testing location if there is no test center in your country. Completed registration forms for testing at test centers must be received about six weeks prior to the test date. These forms must be sent to either the appropriate international TOEFL agent or the TOEFL organization in the United States, depending on where you will take the test. Requests for special testing locations, together with the application form and either the test fee or proof of fee payment, must be received by the TOEFL organization at least two months before a particular test date. For more information, write to TOEFL, Box 899, Princeton, N.J. 08541, U.S.A.

Practice TOEFL examinations are available in the books *Barron's How to Prepare for the TOEFL* and *Barron's Practice Exercises for the TOEFL*, Barron's Educational Series, Inc., 113 Crossways Park Drive, Woodbury, New York 11797, U.S.A.

When applying to a college or university, you also must submit an English translation of your transcript that is endorsed by your school and, generally, documented evidence that you can afford the college's program.

Most American students apply to more than one college, especially if they are interested in competitive schools with high admissions standards. It is recommended that you apply to more than one school, but keep in mind that most colleges charge application fees, and that filling out the application forms and forwarding transcripts and other information can be time-consuming.

GOING TO THE UNITED STATES

You should start investigating requirements for visas from the United States and from your home country (if applicable) as soon as you decide to study overseas. You cannot apply for an American visa, however, until you have been accepted by a school in the United States. You must apply for the visa at a U.S. embassy or consulate. You will need:

A passport from your own country.
A Form I-20 (Certificate of Eligibility for Non-Immigrant Student Status) from the school that has accepted you.
Evidence that you are in good health, including a recent chest X ray and, in some countries, proof that you have been vaccinated against smallpox within the past three years.
A notarized bank statement or other proof that you have enough money available and/or financial aid promised to cover your expenses for the entire term of your program. (If you have been accepted to a bachelor's degree program, for instance, the term is four years.)

Most students are admitted to the United States under an F-1 (foreign student) visa. Those who come under certain grant or scholarship programs may qualify for a J-1 (exchange visitor) visa. After you have qualified for your visa, any spouse and children of yours may be admitted

ADVICE FOR FOREIGN STUDENTS

under F-2 or J-2 visas. You must provide evidence that there is enough money to support them while you are studying.

If you would like to be met when you arrive in the United States, contact the International Student Service at 225 Park Avenue South, Suite 730, New York, New York 10003, U.S.A. (The cable address is FORSTUDENT, NEW YORK.)

You may want to consider participating in predeparture orientation programs offered by education services abroad and by the U.S. International Communication Agency. Information about these programs is available from the agency or from any U.S. embassy or consulate.

ARRIVING ON CAMPUS

As soon as you arrive on campus, you should visit the foreign-student adviser, an official who is responsible for the welfare of students from other countries. If your college has no such official, you should see the dean of students. Bring your passport and immigration documents.

Your university also will assign a faculty member to advise you on your academic program. Other services available through the school may include psychological counseling and health-care services. Although some schools provide limited health care to students at no charge, you should keep in mind that, in the United States, medical care is the responsibility of the individual, not the government. You would be wise to obtain health insurance. Many colleges offer such plans, and your foreign-student adviser can provide information on them.

Most colleges and universities offer campus orientation programs for all new students; some also hold special orientations for foreign students. The latter are generally held during the summer and may continue on after the academic year has begun. On- and off-campus tours and placement exams may be included.

ENGLISH LANGUAGE AND CULTURAL ORIENTATION PROGRAMS

Many American colleges and universities provide English language instruction, often in conjunction with courses and activities that orient foreign students to the various phases of life in the United States. Full-time English language programs generally involve at least 15 hours of intensive instruction per week and usually include orientation activities. Single courses involve fewer hours and are generally taken to help students engaged in academic courses.

You should know that your ability to speak and write English will affect your admission to most American colleges and universities. If your ability falls below that required for admission, you may be accepted conditionally, with the understanding that you will participate in an intensive English course or program. Some schools require that *all* foreign students enroll in such a course or program.

For more information, you should obtain the booklet *English Language and Orientation Programs in the United States* ($7), published by the Institute of International Education (to order, use the appropriate address given under the "Further Reading" section that follows). This publication gives detailed information on the intensive English-language courses and/or programs at many of the institutions in the accompanying chart.

EXPENSES

Most colleges will expect you to pay all fixed costs—tuition, room and board if you live and eat in college facilities, student fees—in U.S. dollars at the beginning of each academic term. Some colleges provide installment plans, under which these costs may be paid monthly over the course of the term.

Keep in mind when determining your probable expenses that personal expenses, including travel, entertainment, and textbooks, may be considerable and generally are not listed as part of a college's tuition schedule. While some colleges will provide an estimate of a typical student's personal expenses, you should generally expect to spend considerably more.

Foreign students generally are not permitted to hold jobs in the United States. Work permits are issued only when there is unexpected economic need. Part-time jobs on campus, however, are permitted and do not require government approval.

Financial aid may be available from your government; the U.S. government; cultural exchange programs; corporations; the college you attend; or religious, fraternal, or special-interest groups. For information, write for these publications:

A Guide to Scholarships, Fellowships, and Grants: A Bibliography (free), from the Institute of International Education.
Financial Planning for Studying in the United States: A Guide for Students from Other Countries (25 cents), from the College Board, Box 2815, Princeton, New Jersey 08541, U.S.A.

You also should contact a U.S. embassy or consulate and your government's ministry or department of education.

FURTHER READING

Foreign students may find the following publications useful; all are published by the Institute of International Education. If you are ordering from within the United States, publications requiring payment are available from Communications Division, Institute of International Education, 809 United Nations Plaza, New York, New York 10017; outside the United States, order publications requiring payment from UNIPUB, Box 433, Murray Hill Station, New York, New York 10016, U.S.A. Order all free publications from the Institute, whether or not you are in the United States.

The Community, Technical, and Junior College in the United States—A Guide for Foreign Students ($3.50).
Fields of Study in U.S. Colleges and Universities—A Guide for Foreign Students ($1).
A Practical Guide for Foreign Visitors ($2.50).
Study of Agriculture in the U.S.—A Guide for Foreign Students ($5).
Study in U.S. Colleges and Universities: A Selected Bibliography (single copies are free).
A Guide to Scholarships, Fellowships, and Grants: A Selected Bibliography (single copies are free).

Some of the information in this section, used by permission of the Institute of International Education, is from the booklet *A Practical Guide for Foreign Visitors* ($2.50), which is available from the Institute (to order, use the appropriate address given under the preceding "Further Reading" section).

BASIC INFORMATION FOR FOREIGN STUDENTS

The profiles in this book include comprehensive information for foreign students. In addition, basic data has been compiled in the following chart, which allows foreign students to compare, at a glance, offerings available at the various colleges and universities in the United States.

Five pieces of information are given: (Column 1) whether the school offers an intensive English *course* that meets for fewer than 15 hours per week, (Column 2) whether the school offers an intensive English *program* that meets for more than 15 hours per week, (Column 3) the percentage of full-time students who come from outside the United States, (Column 4) whether the school offers special organizations for foreign students, and (Column 5) whether the school offers special counseling for foreign students.

Colleges and universities that failed to provide information regarding foreign students have been excluded from the chart. Also, the symbol "NA" means not available, and the symbol "<" means less than.

English Course	English Program	% of Students	Organizations	Counseling	School
					ALABAMA
		10	•	•	Alabama Agricultural and Mechanical University
•		NA	•	•	Auburn University
		2	•	•	Birmingham-Southern College
		2	•	•	Huntingdon College
		2			Jacksonville State University
•		NA		•	Judson College
		2			Livingston University
•		1	•	•	Miles College
		NA			Mobile College
		18	•	•	Oakwood College
		NA			Samford University
•		<1	•	•	Spring Hill College
		NA			Talladega College
		1	•	•	Troy State University System
		11	•	•	Tuskegee Institute
•		2	•	•	University of Alabama
		1	•	•	University of Alabama in Birmingham
		2	•		University of Alabama in Huntsville
		2	•	•	University of Montevallo
		<1			University of North Alabama
		6	•	•	University of South Alabama
					ALASKA
•	•	8	•	•	Alaska Pacific University
		3			Sheldon Jackson College
		NA			University of Alaska/Anchorage
		2	•	•	University of Alaska/Fairbanks
		<1			University of Alaska/Juneau
					ARIZONA
•		3	•	•	Arizona State University
		<1			De Vry Institute of Technology
		3	•	•	Grand Canyon College
		NA	•	•	Northern Arizona University
		0	•		Prescott College
•		6	•	•	University of Arizona
		NA			Western International University
					ARKANSAS
		1			Arkansas College
		<1	•	•	Arkansas State University
		NA			Arkansas Tech University
		12	•	•	The College of the Ozarks
		4			Harding University
		1	•	•	Henderson State University
		<1			Hendrix College
		3	•		John Brown University
		15			Philander Smith College
		1	•	•	Southern Arkansas University
		4	•	•	University of Arkansas at Fayetteville
•	NA	•	•	University of Arkansas at Little Rock
		<1			University of Arkansas at Monticello
		NA			University of Arkansas at Pine Bluff
		1	•	•	University of Central Arkansas
					CALIFORNIA
•		57		•	Armstrong College
•		10		•	Art Center College of Design
•		NA	•	•	Azusa Pacific University
		3	•		Bethany Bible College
•		5	•	•	Biola University
•		15			Brooks Institute
		9			California Baptist College
		8	•	•	California College of Arts and Crafts
		5			California College of Podiatric Medicine
		8	•	•	California Institute of Technology
		8	•		California Institute of the Arts
•	•	4	•	•	California Lutheran College
		2			California Maritime Academy
•		5	•	•	California State College/Bakersfield
•		2	•	•	California State College/San Bernardino
•		5	•	•	California State College/Stanislaus
		3	•	•	California State Polytechnic University/Pomona
		10	•	•	California State University/Chico
		4	•	•	California State University/Dominguez Hills
•		8	•	•	California State University/Fresno
		2	•	•	California State University/Fullerton
		NA	•	•	California State University/Hayward
•		2	•	•	California State University/Long Beach
•		9	•	•	California State University/Los Angeles
		2	•	•	California State University/Northridge
		2	•	•	California State University/Sacramento
•		12	•	•	Chapman College
		2			Christian Heritage College
		5	•	•	The Claremont Colleges/McKenna College
		7	•	•	The Claremont Colleges/Harvey Mudd College
		6	•	•	The Claremont Colleges/Pitzer College
		5	•	•	The Claremont Colleges/Pomona College
		4	•	•	The Claremont Colleges/Scripps College
•		40	•	•	Cogswell College

xxvii

ADVICE FOR FOREIGN STUDENTS xxviii

English Course	English Program	% of Students	Organizations	Counseling	Institution
		25	•	•	College of Notre Dame
•	•	15			Dominican College of San Rafael
		8			Fresno Pacific College
	•	3	•	•	Golden Gate University
	•	NA	•	•	Holy Names College
•	•	1	•	•	Humboldt State University
	•	98			Lincoln University
•	•	8	•	•	Loma Linda University
		1			Los Angeles Baptist College
		5	•	•	Loyola Marymount University
		21	•	•	Menlo College
•	•	14	•	•	Mills College
		4	•		Mount St. Mary's College
		6		•	National University
•		11		•	New College of California
	•	50	•	•	Northrop University
		4	•		Occidental College
		4		•	Pacific Union College
•		11	•	•	Pepperdine University
		4		•	Point Loma College
	•	14	•	•	Saint Mary's College of California
	•	3	•	•	San Diego State University
		25	•	•	San Francisco Art Institute
•		11		•	San Francisco Conservatory of Music
•		NA	•		San Francisco State University
		4	•	•	San Jose State University
		2			Simpson College
•		4	•	•	Sonoma State University
		4	•	•	Southern California College
		4	•	•	Stanford University
		15			Thomas Aquinas College
	•	43		•	United States International University
•		NA	•	•	University of California/Berkeley
		5	•	•	University of California/Davis
	•	3	•	•	University of California/Irvine
		6	•	•	University of California/Los Angeles
	•	NA	•	•	University of California/Riverside
	•	7	•	•	University of California/San Diego
		NA	•	•	University of California/Santa Barbara
•	•	2	•	•	University of California/Santa Cruz
		10	•	•	University of La Verne
	•	5	•	•	University of Redlands
		NA	•	•	University of San Diego
•	•	20	•	•	University of San Francisco
		3	•	•	University of Santa Clara
•	•	13	•	•	University of Southern California
		8	•	•	University of the Pacific
	•	30	•	•	West Coast University
		2			Westmont College
	•	11			Whittier College
	•	63	•	•	Woodbury University
		2		•	World College West

COLORADO

| | | 3 | • | • | Adams State College |
| | | 3 | • | | Colorado College |

English Course	English Program	% of Students	Organizations	Counseling	Institution
		8	•	•	Colorado School of Mines
	•	2	•	•	Colorado State University
•		5		•	Colorado Technical College
		1		•	Fort Lewis College
	•	1		•	Loretto Heights College
		<1			Mesa College
		1	•	•	Metropolitan State College
		1	•	•	Regis College
		1			Rockmont College
		<1			United States Air Force Academy
	•	4	•	•	University of Colorado at Boulder
		<1			University of Colorado at Colorado Springs
		2	•	•	University of Colorado at Denver
	•	6	•	•	University of Denver
		3	•	•	University of Northern Colorado
		7	•	•	University of Southern Colorado
		1	•	•	Western State College

CONNECTICUT

		2		•	Albertus Magnus College
		2			Bridgeport Engineering Institute
		1	•	•	Central Connecticut State College
		2		•	Connecticut College
	•	3	•	•	Eastern Connecticut State College
		1		•	Fairfield University
		0			Post College
		1		•	Quinnipiac College
	•	1		•	Sacred Heart University
		1		•	Saint Joseph College
	•	NA		•	Southern Connecticut State College
		1	•	•	Trinity College
		3		•	United States Coast Guard Academy
	•	11	•	•	University of Bridgeport
		1	•	•	University of Connecticut
	•	6	•	•	University of Hartford
		9	•	•	University of New Haven
	•	1	•	•	Wesleyan University
		1	•	•	Western Connecticut State College
		6	•	•	Yale University

DELAWARE

		NA	•	•	Delaware State College
		2	•	•	Goldey Beacom College
•	•	2	•	•	University of Delaware
		1		•	Wesley College
		NA		•	Wilmington College

DISTRICT OF COLUMBIA

•	•	13	•	•	American University
		<1			Beacon College
		8	•	•	Catholic University of America
•		7	•	•	Gallaudet College
•	•	8	•	•	Georgetown University
•	•	13	•	•	George Washington University
•	•	16	•	•	Howard University
•		12	•	•	Mount Vernon College
•		NA	•	•	Southeastern University

xxix ADVICE FOR FOREIGN STUDENTS

English Course	English Program	% of Students	Organizations	Counseling	Institution
		26	•	•	Strayer College
		5	•	•	Trinity College
		9	•	•	University of the District of Columbia
•	•	6	•	•	Washington International College

FLORIDA

English Course	English Program	% of Students	Organizations	Counseling	Institution
	•	19	•	•	Barry University
		2			Bethune-Cookman College
		NA			Biscayne College
•	•	7	•	•	Eckerd College
•	•	4	•	•	Edward Waters College
•	•	8	•	•	Embry-Riddle Aeronautical University
		2	•		Flagler College
		7	•	•	Florida Agricultural and Mechanical University
	•	11	•	•	Florida Institute of Technology
		33	•	•	Florida Memorial College
		2			Florida Southern College
		4	•	•	Florida State University
	•	3	•	•	Jacksonville University
		NA			New College of the University of South Florida
•		NA	•	•	Nova University
		7	•		Palm Beach Atlantic College
		2			Ringling School of Art and Design
		5	•	•	Rollins College
		7	•	•	Saint Leo College
		2			Stetson University
		10	•	•	University of Central Florida
•		5	•	•	University of Florida
•		10	•	•	University of Miami
•	•	2	•	•	University of South Florida
•		6	•	•	University of Tampa
•	•	12	•		Webber College

GEORGIA

English Course	English Program	% of Students	Organizations	Counseling	Institution
		1	•	•	Agnes Scott College
		<1			Albany State College
		<1			Armstrong State College
•		4		•	Atlanta College of Art
		<1			Augusta College
		2	•	•	Berry College
		NA			Brenau College
		7	•	•	Clark College
		6	•	•	Columbus College
		<1			De Vry Institute of Technology
		3	•	•	Emory University
		NA			Fort Valley State College
		1	•		Georgia College
	•	8	•	•	Georgia Institute of Technology
•		1	•	•	Georgia Southern College
		<1			Georgia Southwestern College
•	•	4	•	•	Georgia State University
		1	•		Kennesaw College
•		5	•	•	LaGrange College
		1			Medical College of Georgia
		1	•		Mercer University
•		10	•	•	Mercer University in Atlanta
		2	•	•	Morehouse College

English Course	English Program	% of Students	Organizations	Counseling	Institution
		4	•	•	Morris Brown College
		<1		•	North Georgia College
•		18	•	•	Oglethorpe University
		NA		•	Paine College
		10	•	•	Piedmont College
		<3			Savannah College of Art and Design
		10	•	•	Savannah State College
		1		•	Shorter College
		<5	•		Southern Technical Institute
		2	•	•	Spelman College
		0			Tift College
		1		•	Toccoa Falls College
•		4	•	•	University of Georgia
		<1		•	Valdosta State College
		5	•		Wesleyan College
		1	•	•	West Georgia College

GUAM

English Course	English Program	% of Students	Organizations	Counseling	Institution
•		25			University of Guam

HAWAII

English Course	English Program	% of Students	Organizations	Counseling	Institution
•	•	38	•	•	Brigham Young University/Hawaii Campus
•	•	21	•	•	Chaminade University of Honolulu
•	•	20	•	•	Hawaii Loa College
•	•	28	•	•	Hawaii Pacific College
•	•	4	•	•	University of Hawaii at Hilo
		NA			University of Hawaii at Manoa

IDAHO

English Course	English Program	% of Students	Organizations	Counseling	Institution
•		1	•	•	Boise State University
		2			College of Idaho
•	•	2	•	•	Idaho State University
•		3	•	•	Lewis-Clark State College
		2		•	Northwest Nazarene College
		3	•	•	University of Idaho

ILLINOIS

English Course	English Program	% of Students	Organizations	Counseling	Institution
		<1	•	•	Augustana College
•		1		•	Aurora College
•		7	•	•	Barat College
		6	•	•	Bradley University
		1			Chicago State University
		1		•	College of St. Francis
		NA	•	•	Columbia College
		1		•	Concordia College
		1	•	•	De Paul University
		1			De Vry Institute of Technology
		2	•	•	Eastern Illinois University
		1		•	Elmhurst College
		2		•	Eureka College
		2	•	•	George Williams College
		NA	•		Greenville College
		1		•	Illinois Benedictine College
		1		•	Illinois College
		13	•	•	Illinois Institute of Technology
		1	•	•	Illinois State University
		1	•	•	Illinois Wesleyan University

ADVICE FOR FOREIGN STUDENTS

English Course	English Program	% of Students	Organizations	Counseling	Institution
		1		●	Judson College
		4	●		Kendall College
●		8	●	●	Knox College
		2	●	●	Lake Forest College
		1	●	●	Lewis University
		1		●	Loyola University of Chicago
		2	●	●	MacMurray College
		NA		●	McKendree College
		1	●	●	Millikin University
		5	●	●	Monmouth College
	●	1		●	Mundelein College
●	●	1			National College of Education
●		<1	●	●	North Central College
		2	●	●	Northeastern Illinois University
		2	●	●	Northern Illinois University
		1		●	North Park College
		<1	●	●	Northwestern University
		1	●		Olivet Nazarene College
●	●	10	●	●	Parks College of St. Louis University
		5		●	Principia College
●		4	●	●	Quincy College
		5		●	Rockford College
●	●	10	●	●	Roosevelt University
		2			Rosary College
		NA			Saint Xavier College
		7	●	●	School of the Art Institute of Chicago
●	NA		●	●	Southern Illinois University at Carbondale
		3	●	●	Southern Illinois University at Edwardsville
		14		●	Spertus College of Judaica
		3			Trinity Christian College
●		2		●	Trinity College
		2	●	●	The University of Chicago
		6	●	●	University of Illinois at Chicago
●	●	6	●	●	University of Illinois at Urbana-Champaign
●	●	4	●	●	Western Illinois University
		6	●		Wheaton College

INDIANA

English Course	English Program	% of Students	Organizations	Counseling	Institution
		NA		●	Anderson College
●	●	2	●	●	Ball State University
		2	●		Butler University
		NA			Calumet College
●		1	●	●	Depauw University
		NA	●	●	Earlham College
		1	●	●	Franklin College
●		6	●	●	Goshen College
		1		●	Grace College
		3	●	●	Hanover College
		1	●		Huntington College
		1		●	Indiana Central University
●	20	●	●		Indiana Institute of Technology
		6	●	●	Indiana State University
		1		●	Indiana State University Evansville
		1		●	Indiana University at Kokomo
		NA		●	Indiana University at South Bend
●	●	6	●	●	Indiana University/Bloomington
		<1		●	Indiana University Northwest
●		NA			Indiana University-Purdue University at Fort Wayne
●		1	●	●	Indiana University-Purdue University at Indianapolis
		<1			Indiana University Southeast
		2	●	●	Manchester College
		4			Marian College
●		1	●	●	Marion College
●		0			Martin Center College
		1		●	Oakland City College
		0			Purdue University/Calumet
●		4	●	●	Purdue University/West Lafayette
		1			Rose-Hulman Institute of Technology
		1			Saint Francis College
		1			Saint Joseph's College
	●	9	●	●	Saint Mary-of-the-Woods College
		2	●		Saint Mary's College
		<1	●	●	Taylor University
●		13		●	Tri-State University
		7	●	●	University of Evansville
●		2	●		University of Notre Dame
●		3	●	●	Valparaiso University
		1			Wabash College

IOWA

English Course	English Program	% of Students	Organizations	Counseling	Institution
		NA		●	Briar Cliff College
●		1		●	Buena Vista College
		3			Central University of Iowa
		4			Clarke College
●		10	●	●	Coe College
●		12	●	●	Cornell College
		20			Dordt College
●	●	NA	●	●	Drake University
●		NA		●	Graceland College
●		5	●	●	Grand View College
		5		●	Grinnell College
●		7	●	●	Iowa State University
		<1			Iowa Wesleyan College
		<1		●	Loras College
●	●	2	●	●	Luther College
		10	●		Maharishi International University
●		1		●	Marycrest College
		NA	●	●	Morningside College
		1	●		Mount Mercy College
●	●	1		●	Mount St. Clare College
		2	●	●	Northwestern College
●		<1	●	●	St. Ambrose College
		1	●	●	Simpson College
		7	●	●	University of Dubuque
●		3	●	●	University of Iowa
		<1	●	●	University of Northern Iowa
		5	●	●	Upper Iowa University
		7			Wartburg College
		<1		●	Westmar College
		1		●	William Penn College

xxxi ADVICE FOR FOREIGN STUDENTS

Columns: English Course | English Program | % of Students | Organizations | Counseling

KANSAS

EC	EP	%	Org	Cns	Institution
		1	•		Baker University
•		4	•	•	Benedictine College
		2	•	•	Bethany College
		4	•	•	Bethel College
	•	9	•	•	Emporia State University
•		3	•	•	Fort Hays State University
•		10	•	•	Friends University
		9	•	•	Kansas Newman College
•	•	5	•	•	Kansas State University
•	•	4	•	•	Kansas Wesleyan University
		0			Marymount College of Kansas
		3	•	•	McPherson College
•		2	•	•	Mid-America Nazarene College
		9	•	•	Ottawa University
•		NA	•	•	Pittsburg State University
•		5	•	•	Saint Mary College
		1		•	Saint Mary of the Plains College
		1	•		Southwestern College
		5			Sterling College
		NA	•	•	Tabor College
•	•	7	•	•	University of Kansas
		1			Washburn University of Topeka
	•	3	•	•	Wichita State University

KENTUCKY

EC	EP	%	Org	Cns	Institution
		2	•	•	Asbury College
		3	•	•	Bellarmine College
		6	•	•	Berea College
		4	•	•	Brescia College
		1			Campbellsville College
		1	•		Cumberland College
		<1	•	•	Eastern Kentucky University
		NA			Georgetown College
		2		•	Kentucky State University
		NA	•	•	Kentucky Wesleyan College
		0			Louisville School of Art
		2	•	•	Morehead State University
		1	•		Murray State University
•		1	•	•	Northern Kentucky University
		1			Pikeville College
•	•	2	•	•	Thomas More College
		1			Transylvania University
		2	•		Union College
		2	•	•	University of Kentucky
		1	•	•	University of Louisville
		<1	•	•	Western Kentucky University

LOUISIANA

EC	EP	%	Org	Cns	Institution
		NA	•	•	Centenary College of Louisiana
		2	•	•	Dillard University
		2	•	•	Grambling State University
		<1	•		Louisiana College
•		6	•	•	Louisiana State University and Agricultural and Mechanical College
		<1	•	•	Louisiana State University/Shreveport
•		6	•	•	Louisiana Tech University
		NA	•	•	Loyola University/New Orleans
•		1	•		McNeese State University
		1			Nicholls State University
•		2	•	•	Northeast Louisiana University
•		4	•	•	Northwestern State University
		NA	•		Our Lady of Holy Cross College
•		13	•	•	St. Mary's Dominican College
		NA	•	•	Southern University and A & M College
•		<1	•	•	Southern University in New Orleans
•		7	•	•	Tulane University
•		2	•	•	University of New Orleans
•		12	•	•	University of Southwestern Louisiana
		3		•	Xavier University of Louisiana

MAINE

EC	EP	%	Org	Cns	Institution
		2			Bates College
•		2	•		Bowdoin College
		2	•	•	Colby College
•		NA			College of the Atlantic
•		5	•	•	Husson College
		1			Maine Maritime Academy
		10	•	•	Nasson College
		<1		•	Saint Joseph's College
		1		•	Thomas College
		0			Unity College
•		<1	•	•	University of Maine at Farmington
		<1		•	University of Maine at Fort Kent
		1		•	University of Maine at Machias
		2	•	•	University of Maine at Orono
		NA	•	•	University of Maine at Presque Isle
		1			University of New England
		NA		•	University of Southern Maine
		NA	•	•	Westbrook College

MARYLAND

EC	EP	%	Org	Cns	Institution
		5	•	•	Bowie State College
		28		•	Capitol Institute of Technology
		2	•	•	College of Notre Dame of Maryland
		16	•	•	Columbia Union College
•		2	•	•	Coppin State College
		NA	•	•	Frostburg State College
•		6	•	•	Goucher College
•		<1	•	•	Hood College
		10	•	•	Johns Hopkins University
		2	•		Loyola College
•		7	•	•	Maryland Institute/College of Art
		7	•		Morgan State University
		5	•		Mount St. Mary's College
•		19	•	•	Peabody Conservatory of Music
		1			St. John's College
		1			St. Mary's College of Maryland
		<1	•		Salisbury State College
•		1	•	•	Towson State University
		<1			United States Naval Academy
		2	•		University of Maryland/Baltimore County
•	•	NA	•	•	University of Maryland/College Park
		NA	•	•	University of Maryland/Eastern Shore

ADVICE FOR FOREIGN STUDENTS xxxii

English Course	English Program	% of Students	Organizations	Counseling	Institution
		4	•	•	Washington College
•		1	•	•	Western Maryland College
					MASSACHUSETTS
		3	•	•	American International College
		2	•	•	Amherst College
		4		•	Anna Maria College
		NA	•	•	Assumption College
•		NA	•	•	Atlantic Union College
		9	•	•	Babson College
		1	•	•	Bentley College
		20		•	Berklee College of Music
		3	•	•	Boston College
		3		•	Boston Conservatory of Music
•	•	9	•	•	Boston University
•	•	14	•	•	Bradford College
		5	•	•	Brandeis University
		<1	•	•	Bridgewater State College
•		17	•	•	Central New England College
•		6	•	•	Clark University
		NA		•	College of Our Lady of the Elms
•		3	•	•	Curry College
		4		•	Eastern Nazarene College
		3	•	•	Emerson College
•		5	•	•	Emmanuel College
		<1		•	Fitchburg State College
•		<1	•	•	Framingham State College
		NA		•	Gordon College
		1		•	Hampshire College
		6	•	•	Harvard University/Harvard and Radcliffe Colleges
•		31	•	•	Hellenic College and Holy Cross Greek Orthodox School of Theology
		<1		•	Holy Cross College
		<1	•	•	Lesley College
		NA		•	Massachusetts College of Art
		17	•	•	Massachusetts College of Pharmacy and Allied Health Sciences
		6	•	•	Massachusetts Institute of Technology
		1		•	Merrimack College
•		5	•	•	Mount Holyoke College
		11	•	•	New England Conservatory of Music
		2		•	Nichols College
		<1		•	North Adams State College
•	•	5	•	•	Northeastern University
•	•	20	•	•	Pine Manor College
		2	•	•	Regis College
		1	•	•	Salem State College
		10	•	•	Simmons College
		2		•	Simon's Rock of Bard College
		7		•	Smith College
		2		•	Southeastern Massachusetts University
		2	•	•	Springfield College
		<1		•	Stonehill College
		5		•	Suffolk University
•		NA		•	Swain School of Design
		3	•	•	Tufts University

English Course	English Program	% of Students	Organizations	Counseling	Institution
		5	•	•	University of Lowell
		1	•	•	University of Massachusetts at Amherst
		3	•	•	University of Massachusetts at Boston
		5	•	•	Wellesley College
		NA	•	•	Wentworth Institute of Technology
		2		•	Western New England College
•		<1	•	•	Westfield State College
•		7	•	•	Wheaton College
		2	•	•	Wheelock College
		3	•	•	Williams College
		1	•	•	Worcester Polytechnic Institute
		6		•	Worcester State College
					MICHIGAN
		2	•	•	Adrian College
		NA	•	•	Albion College
		1	•	•	Alma College
•	•	18	•	•	Andrews University
		5	•	•	Aquinas College
•		9	•	•	Calvin College
		1	•	•	Center for Creative Studies
•		1	•	•	Central Michigan University
		6		•	Concordia College
•	•	5	•	•	Eastern Michigan University
		1	•	•	Ferris State College
		8	•	•	General Motors Institute
•		2	•	•	Grand Valley State Colleges
		3	•		Hillsdale College
•		4	•	•	Hope College
		3	•	•	Kalamazoo College
		9		•	Lake Superior State College
		3	•	•	Lawrence Institute of Technology
		1		•	Madonna College
		0	•	•	Marygrove College
		1		•	Mercy College of Detroit
•	•	3	•	•	Michigan State University
		3	•	•	Michigan Technological University
		1		•	Nazareth College
		1	•	•	Northern Michigan University
		4	•	•	Northwood Institute
		<1	•	•	Oakland University
		1		•	Olivet College
•		2		•	Saginaw Valley State College
		2		•	Saint Mary's College
		1		•	Shaw College at Detroit
•		3	•	•	Siena Heights College
		5	•	•	Spring Arbor College
•		13	•	•	University of Detroit
•	•	7	•	•	University of Michigan/Ann Arbor
		3	•	•	University of Michigan/Dearborn
		4		•	University of Michigan/Flint
•		17	•	•	Wayne State University
•	•	4	•	•	Western Michigan University
					MINNESOTA
		2	•	•	Augsburg College
		1	•	•	Bemidji State University

xxxiii ADVICE FOR FOREIGN STUDENTS

Columns: English Course | English Program | % of Students | Organizations | Counseling

EC	EP	%	Org	Cou	Institution
		1	•	•	Bethel College
		1	•	•	Carleton College
		<1	•	•	College of St. Benedict
		NA	•	•	College of St. Catherine
		1	•	•	College of St. Scholastica
•		3	•	•	College of Saint Teresa
		NA	•	•	College of St. Thomas
		2	•	•	Concordia College/Moorhead
•		4	•	•	Concordia College/St. Paul
•		2	•	•	Gustavus Adolphus College
		4	•	•	Hamline University
•		12	•	•	Macalester College
•		4	•	•	Mankato State University
		1	•	•	Minneapolis College of Art and Design
		2	•		Moorhead State University
		1	•	•	Northwestern College
•		3	•	•	St. Cloud State University
		3	•	•	Saint John's University
		1	•	•	Saint Mary's College
•		1	•	•	St. Olaf College
		2	•	•	Southwest State University
•		2	•	•	University of Minnesota/Duluth
•		<1	•	•	University of Minnesota/Morris
•	•	NA	•	•	University of Minnesota/Twin Cities
•		2	•	•	Winona State University

MISSISSIPPI

EC	EP	%	Org	Cou	Institution
•		NA			Alcorn State University
		4			Belhaven College
		NA			Blue Mountain College
		<1			Delta State University
		2	•		Jackson State University
		<1			Millsaps College
		1			Mississippi College
		NA	•		Mississippi State University
		<1			Mississippi University for Women
•		<1	•	•	Mississippi Valley State University
		NA	•	•	Rust College
		2	•	•	Tougaloo College
•		4	•	•	University of Mississippi
•		2	•	•	University of Southern Mississippi
•		NA	•	•	William Carey College

MISSOURI

EC	EP	%	Org	Cou	Institution
		1	•	•	Avila College
		3		•	Cardinal Newman College
		2	•		Central Methodist College
		2	•	•	Central Missouri State University
		9	•	•	Columbia College
		NA	•	•	Culver-Stockton College
•		2	•		Drury College
		1	•	•	Evangel College
		7	•		Fontbonne College
		1			Harris-Stowe State College
		2			Kansas City Art Institute
		7		•	Lincoln University
•		13		•	The Lindenwood Colleges

EC	EP	%	Org	Cou	Institution
	•	2	•	•	Maryville College
		1			Missouri Baptist College
		<1			Missouri Institute of Technology
		<1	•	•	Missouri Southern State College
•		2	•	•	Missouri Valley College
		1			Missouri Western State College
		2	•	•	Northeast Missouri State University
•	•	4	•	•	Northwest Missouri State University
		15	•	•	Park College
		4			Rockhurst College
		1	•	•	St. Louis College of Pharmacy
	•	6	•	•	Saint Louis University
		3	•	•	The School of the Ozarks
•		1	•	•	Southeast Missouri State University
		NA	•		Southwest Baptist University
		1	•	•	Southwest Missouri State University
		1	•	•	Stephens College
		1			Tarkio College
•	•	NA	•	•	University of Missouri/Columbia
		1	•	•	University of Missouri/Kansas City
•		7	•	•	University of Missouri/Rolla
•		1	•	•	University of Missouri/St. Louis
•		12	•	•	Washington University
•		7	•	•	Webster College
		NA	•		Westminster College
		1	•	•	William Jewell College
•		1	•	•	William Woods College

MONTANA

EC	EP	%	Org	Cou	Institution
		2	•	•	Carroll College
		5	•	•	College of Great Falls
		<1	•	•	Eastern Montana College
•		5	•	•	Montana College of Mineral Science and Technology
		NA			Montana State University
		1		•	Northern Montana College
		5			Rocky Mountain College
		2	•	•	University of Montana
		0			Western Montana College

NEBRASKA

EC	EP	%	Org	Cou	Institution
•		5			Bellevue College
		2	•	•	Chadron State College
		1			College of Saint Mary
•		3			Concordia Teachers College
•		3	•	•	Creighton University
		2			Dana College
•		NA			Doane College
		<1	•	•	Hastings College
•		NA	•	•	Kearney State College
		1		•	Midland Lutheran College
		3	•	•	Nebraska Wesleyan University
		1		•	Peru State College
		10			Union College
•	•	<1	•	•	University of Nebraska at Omaha
•		4	•	•	University of Nebraska/Lincoln
•		<1	•	•	Wayne State College

ADVICE FOR FOREIGN STUDENTS xxxiv

English Course	English Program	% of Students	Organizations	Counseling	Institution
					NEVADA
		13			Sierra Nevada College
		3	•	•	University of Nevada/Las Vegas
		3	•	•	University of Nevada/Reno
					NEW HAMPSHIRE
		2	•	•	Colby-Sawyer College
		3			Daniel Webster College
		2	•	•	Dartmouth College
		2		•	Franklin Pierce College
		<1			Keene State College
	•	10	•	•	Nathaniel Hawthorne College
•		NA	•	•	New England College
	•	1	•	•	New Hampshire College
		<1			Notre Dame College
		1	•	•	Plymouth State College
		<1			Rivier College
		<1			St. Anselm College
•		<1	•	•	University of New Hampshire
					NEW JERSEY
•		9	•	•	Bloomfield College
•	•	6	•	•	Caldwell College
		1	•	•	Centenary College
•		3	•	•	College of Saint Elizabeth
•		2	•		Drew University/College of Liberal Arts
		4	•	•	Fairleigh Dickinson University
		2	•	•	Felician College
		2			Georgian Court College
		1	•	•	Glassboro State College
•		9	•	•	Jersey City State College
•	•	5	•	•	Kean College of New Jersey
		7	•	•	Monmouth College
		2	•	•	Montclair State College
		5	•		New Jersey Institute of Technology
		5	•		Princeton University
	•	3	•	•	Ramapo College of New Jersey
		1	•	•	Rider College
•		<1		•	Rutgers University/Camden College of Arts and Sciences
•	•	4	•	•	Rutgers University/College of Engineering
•	•	<1	•	•	Rutgers University/College of Nursing
•	•	1	•	•	Rutgers University/College of Pharmacy
•	•	1	•	•	Rutgers University/Cook College
•	•	1	•	•	Rutgers University/Douglass College
•	•	1	•	•	Rutgers University/Livingston College
•	•	<1	•	•	Rutgers University/Mason Gross School of the Arts
•		1	•	•	Rutgers University/Newark College of Arts and Sciences
•	•	1	•	•	Rutgers University/Rutgers College
•		0	•	•	Rutgers University/University College—Camden
•		0	•	•	Rutgers University/University College—Newark
•	•	2	•	•	Rutgers University/University College—New Brunswick
•		3	•	•	Saint Peter's College
•		4	•	•	Seton Hall University

English Course	English Program	% of Students	Organizations	Counseling	Institution
		5	•	•	Stevens Institute of Technology
		2	•	•	Stockton State College
		0	•	•	Thomas A. Edison State College
		1	•	•	Trenton State College
		3	•		Upsala College
		7	•		Westminster Choir College
		1	•	•	William Paterson College of New Jersey
					NEW MEXICO
•		1		•	College of Santa Fe
		3	•	•	Eastern New Mexico University
		NA	•	•	New Mexico Highlands University
		5			New Mexico Institute of Mining and Technology
		<1			St. John's College
		NA	•	•	University of Albuquerque
•		3	•	•	University of New Mexico
		1		•	Western New Mexico University
					NEW YORK
•	•	NA	•	•	Adelphi University
		1			Albany College of Pharmacy
		1	•	•	Alfred University
		6	•	•	Arnold and Marie Schwartz College of Pharmacy and Health Sciences
		5	•	•	Bard College
		0			Boricua College
		<1			Canisius College
		3	•	•	City University of New York/Bernard M. Baruch College
	•	8	•	•	City University of New York/Brooklyn College
•		6	•		City University of New York/City College
•	•	<1	•	•	City University of New York/College of Staten Island
•	•	1	•	•	City University of New York/Herbert H. Lehman College
•		3	•	•	City University of New York/Hunter College
•		1	•	•	City University of New York/John Jay College of Criminal Justice
•		3	•	•	City University of New York/Medgar Evers College
•	•	NA	•	•	City University of New York/Queens College
•		3	•	•	City University of New York/York College
		<5	•	•	Clarkson College of Technology
		2	•		Colgate University
		NA	•	•	College of Insurance
		1	•		College of Mount Saint Vincent
		NA			College of New Rochelle
		<1	•		College of Saint Rose
		NA	•	•	Columbia University/Barnard College
•	•	6	•	•	Columbia University/Columbia College
•	•	8	•	•	Columbia University/School of Engineering and Applied Science
•	•	12	•	•	Columbia University/School of General Studies
		1		•	Concordia College
		2			The Cooper Union for the Advancement of Science and Art
•		NA	•	•	Cornell University
		<1			Daemen College

ADVICE FOR FOREIGN STUDENTS

English Course	English Program	% of Students	Organizations	Counseling	Institution
•		1	•		Dominican College of Blauvelt
	•	<1		•	D'Youville College
•	•	5	•	•	Eastman School of Music
	•	4	•	•	Eisenhower College of Rochester Institute of Technology
•	•	7	•	•	Elmira College
		3	•	•	Fordham University/College at Lincoln Center
		2	•	•	Fordham University/College of Business Administration
		3	•	•	Fordham University/Fordham College
		8	•	•	Hamilton College
		1		•	Hartwick College
•	•	1	•	•	Hobart and William Smith Colleges/Hobart College
		3	•	•	Hobart and William Smith Colleges/William Smith College
•		7	•	•	Hofstra University
		4	•	•	Houghton College
		NA		•	Iona College
		1	•	•	Ithaca College
•		21		•	The Juilliard School
		NA		•	Keuka College
		1		•	The King's College
		<1		•	Le Moyne College
	•	7	•	•	Long Island University/Brooklyn Center
•		2	•		Long Island University/C.W. Post Center
		1	•	•	Long Island University/Southampton College
		4	•	•	Manhattan College
•		13		•	Manhattan School of Music
•	•	12	•	•	Manhattanville College
•		20	•	•	Mannes College of Music
		2	•	•	Marist College
		7	•	•	Marymount College
		5	•	•	Marymount Manhattan College
•		1	•	•	Medaille College
•		2	•	•	Mercy College
•		2	•	•	Molloy College
		1	•		Mount Saint Mary College
		1	•	•	Nazareth College of Rochester
•		11	•	•	New York Institute of Technology
•	•	7	•	•	New York University
		1	•	•	Niagara University
		3	•		Nyack College
		2	•	•	Pace University/College of White Plains
•	•	1	•	•	Pace University/New York Campus
		1	•	•	Pace University/Pleasantville/Briarcliff
		NA	•		Parsons School of Design
		12	•	•	Polytechnic Institute of New York
		9	•	•	Pratt Institute
		3	•	•	Rensselaer Polytechnic Institute
		4	•	•	Roberts Wesleyan College
•	•	3	•	•	Rochester Institute of Technology
		NA	•	•	Russell Sage College
		1		•	St. Bonaventure University
		NA	•	•	St. Francis College
		<1	•	•	St. John Fisher College
•		7		•	St. John's University

English Course	English Program	% of Students	Organizations	Counseling	Institution
		1		•	St. Joseph's College
		2		•	St. Lawrence University
		<1		•	St. Thomas Aquinas College
		10	•	•	Sarah Lawrence College
•		3		•	School of Visual Arts
		3	•	•	Seminar College
		<1		•	Siena College
		3	•	•	Skidmore College
•	•	3	•	•	State University of New York at Albany
		3	•	•	State University of New York at Binghamton
	•	6	•	•	State University of New York at Buffalo
•		4	•	•	State University of New York at Stony Brook
•		1	•	•	State University of New York/College at Brockport
		4	•	•	State University of New York/College at Buffalo
		1	•	•	State University of New York/College at Cortland
		1	•	•	State University of New York/College at Fredonia
		1	•	•	State University of New York/College at Geneseo
•		4	•	•	State University of New York/College at New Paltz
•		3	•	•	State University of New York/College at Old Westbury
		1	•	•	State University of New York/College at Oneonta
		<1	•	•	State University of New York/College at Oswego
		2	•	•	State University of New York/College at Plattsburgh
•		1	•	•	State University of New York/College at Potsdam
•		5	•	•	State University of New York/College at Purchase
		2	•	•	State University of New York/Fashion Institute of Technology
•		4	•	•	State University of New York/Maritime College
		<1	•	•	State University of New York/Upstate Medical Center
•		10	•	•	Syracuse University
•		NA	•	•	Touro College
		<1	•	•	Union College
		4		•	United States Merchant Marine Academy
		<1	•	•	United States Military Academy
•	•	7	•	•	University of Rochester
•		<1	•	•	Utica College of Syracuse University
		5	•	•	Vassar College
•		12	•	•	Wagner College
		0		•	Webb Institute of Naval Architecture
		2	•	•	Wells College
		8	•	•	Yeshiva University

NORTH CAROLINA

English Course	English Program	% of Students	Organizations	Counseling	Institution
		<1	•	•	Appalachian State University
		1	•	•	Atlantic Christian College
		NA	•	•	Barber-Scotia College
		1	•	•	Belmont Abbey College
		5	•		Bennett College
•		3	•	•	Campbell University
		<1	•	•	Catawba College
		1	•	•	Davidson College
		NA	•	•	Duke University
		<1	•	•	East Carolina University

ADVICE FOR FOREIGN STUDENTS

English Course	English Program	% of Students	Organizations	Counseling	Institution
		NA	●	●	Elizabeth City State University
		<1			Elon College
		<1			Fayetteville State University
		NA	●	●	Gardner-Webb College
		1			Greensboro College
●		6	●	●	Guilford College
		1			High Point College
●		2	●	●	Johnson C. Smith University
		<1			Lenoir-Rhyne College
		2	●	●	Livingstone College
		<1	●	●	Mars Hill College
		1			Meredith College
●		6	●	●	Methodist College
		8	●	●	North Carolina Agricultural and Technical State University
		NA	●	●	North Carolina Central University
		2			North Carolina School of the Arts
		3	●	●	North Carolina State University
		1		●	North Carolina Wesleyan College
		1		●	Pembroke State University
		1		●	Pfeiffer College
		2	●	●	Queens College
		2			St. Andrews Presbyterian College
		16	●	●	Saint Augustine's College
		2	●	●	Salem College
●		1		●	University of North Carolina at Asheville
		2	●	●	University of North Carolina at Chapel Hill
●	●	3	●	●	University of North Carolina at Charlotte
		1		●	University of North Carolina at Greensboro
		<1	●	●	University of North Carolina at Wilmington
		1		●	Wake Forest University
		11		●	Warren Wilson College
		1	●	●	Western Carolina University
		1		●	Wingate College
		1		●	Winston-Salem State University

NORTH DAKOTA

English Course	English Program	% of Students	Organizations	Counseling	Institution
●		4		●	Jamestown College
		1			Mary College
		3		●	Mayville State College
●		2		●	Minot State College
●	●	1	●	●	North Dakota State University
		1	●	●	University of North Dakota
		1			Valley City State College

OHIO

English Course	English Program	% of Students	Organizations	Counseling	Institution
		4	●	●	Antioch College
●		4	●	●	Ashland College
		2	●	●	Baldwin-Wallace College
		4	●	●	Bluffton College
●		2		●	Bowling Green State University
		1			Capital University
●		10	●	●	Case Western Reserve University
		1		●	Cedarville College
		NA	●	●	Central State University
●		1		●	Cleveland Institute of Art
●		11	●	●	Cleveland Institute of Music

English Course	English Program	% of Students	Organizations	Counseling	Institution
●		2	●	●	Cleveland State University
		1			College of Mount Saint Joseph on the Ohio
		10	●	●	College of Wooster
		2	●	●	Columbus College of Art and Design
		2		●	The Defiance College
		2	●	●	Denison University
●		<1		●	Dyke College
●		NA	●	●	Findlay College
●		4	●	●	Franklin University
●		1		●	Heidelberg College
		1			Hiram College
●		5		●	John Carroll University
		4	●	●	Kent State University
		2	●	●	Kenyon College
●		2		●	Lake Erie College for Women
●		4	●	●	Malone College
		1	●	●	Marietta College
		1	●	●	Miami University
		2	●	●	Mount Union College
		<1			Mount Vernon Nazarene College
●		2	●	●	Muskingum College
		2		●	Notre Dame College of Ohio
		NA	●	●	Oberlin College
●	●	21	●	●	Ohio Dominican College
		1			Ohio Institute of Technology
		2	●		Ohio Northern University
		2	●	●	The Ohio State University
		0			The Ohio State University at Lima
●		0	●	●	The Ohio State University at Mansfield
		<1			The Ohio State University at Marion
		0	●	●	The Ohio State University at Newark
●		10	●	●	Ohio University
●	●	4	●	●	Ohio Wesleyan University
●	●	3	●	●	Otterbein College
●		5		●	Rio Grande College
●		5	●	●	University of Akron
		3	●	●	University of Cincinnati
●		<1	●	●	University of Dayton
		2	●		University of Steubenville
●		5	●	●	University of Toledo
●		3	●	●	Urbana College
		0			Ursuline College
●		6	●	●	Walsh College
		2	●	●	Wilberforce University
		5	●	●	Wilmington College
●		2	●	●	Wittenberg University
		2	●	●	Wright State University
●		3	●	●	Xavier University
●		2	●	●	Youngstown State University

OKLAHOMA

English Course	English Program	% of Students	Organizations	Counseling	Institution
		3			Bethany Nazarene College
		<1			Cameron University
●		7	●	●	Central State University
		<1			East Central Oklahoma State University
		0			Flaming Rainbow University

xxxvii ADVICE FOR FOREIGN STUDENTS

	English Course	English Program	% of Students	Organizations	Counseling	Institution
		17	●	●	Langston University
		1	●	●	Northeastern Oklahoma State University
●		NA	●	●	Northwestern Oklahoma State University
		2	●	●	Oklahoma Baptist University
		NA	●	●	Oklahoma Christian College
		10		●	Oklahoma City University
		2	●		Oklahoma Panhandle State University
		8	●	●	Oklahoma State University
		5	●	●	Oral Roberts University
●	●	3	●	●	Phillips University
●	●	10	●	●	Southeastern Oklahoma State University
		3	●	●	Southwestern Oklahoma State University
		7	●	●	University of Oklahoma
		4	●	●	University of Science and Arts of Oklahoma
●	●	8	●	●	University of Tulsa

OREGON

	English Course	English Program	% of Students	Organizations	Counseling	Institution
		3			Concordia College
●		3		●	Eastern Oregon State College
		1	●		George Fox College
●		6	●	●	Lewis and Clark College
●	●	4	●	●	Linfield College
		1		●	Marylhurst College for Lifelong Learning
		2	●	●	Oregon Institute of Technology
●		5	●	●	Oregon State University
●		3			Pacific Northwest College of Art
		3	●	●	Pacific University
●		10	●	●	Portland State University
		6	●	●	Reed College
●	●	2	●	●	Southern Oregon State College
		NA	●	●	University of Oregon
●		20	●	●	University of Portland
●	●	5	●	●	Warner Pacific College
		4		●	Western Oregon State College
		5	●	●	Willamette University

PENNSYLVANIA

	English Course	English Program	% of Students	Organizations	Counseling	Institution
		1	●	●	Albright College
		2	●	●	Allegheny College
		1			Allentown College of St. Francis DeSales
		NA		●	Alliance College
●		3			Alvernia College
	●	5	●	●	Beaver College
		1	●	●	Bloomsburg State College
		7	●	●	Bryn Mawr College
		7	●	●	Bucknell University
		0			Cabrini College
●	●	6	●	●	California State College
●	●	<1		●	Carlow College
		1		●	Carnegie-Mellon University
		<1		●	Cedar Crest College
		1		●	Chatham College
		NA		●	Chestnut Hill College
		4	●	●	Cheyney State College
		3			Clarion State College
		1		●	College Misericordia
●		NA			Combs College of Music

	English Course	English Program	% of Students	Organizations	Counseling	Institution
		<1	●	●	Delaware Valley College
		1	●	●	Dickinson College
		4	●	●	Drexel University
		2	●	●	Duquesne University
●		4	●	●	Eastern College
		<1	●	●	East Stroudsburg State College
●		1	●	●	Edinboro State College
		1	●	●	Elizabethtown College
		1	●	●	Franklin and Marshall College
		2	●	●	Gannon University
		2	●		Geneva College
		NA		●	Gettysburg College
		<1	●	●	Grove City College
●		7		●	Gwynedd-Mercy College
		3	●		Haverford College
		<1	●	●	Holy Family College
●		5	●	●	Immaculata College
		1	●	●	Indiana University of Pennsylvania
		1	●	●	Juniata College
●	●	2	●	●	King's College
		1	●	●	Kutztown State College
		2	●	●	Lafayette College
		1	●	●	La Roche College
●		NA	●	●	La Salle College
●		<1	●	●	Lebanon Valley College
●		1	●	●	Lehigh University
●	●	7	●	●	Lincoln University
		2		●	Lock Haven State College
		0		●	Lycoming College
●	●	<1	●	●	Mansfield State College
●	●	1	●	●	Marywood College
		1	●	●	Mercyhurst College
		2	●	●	Messiah College
		1	●	●	Millersville State College
●		2			Moore College of Art
		1	●		Moravian College
		1	●	●	Muhlenberg College
		0			Neumann College
		6		●	New School of Music
		NA	●	●	Pennsylvania State University/Behrend College
		2	●	●	Pennsylvania State University/University Park Campus
●		1			Philadelphia College of Art
●		2	●	●	Philadelphia College of Pharmacy and Science
●		11	●	●	Philadelphia College of Textiles and Science
		6			Philadelphia College of the Performing Arts
●		18	●	●	Point Park College
●		1		●	Robert Morris College
●		2		●	Rosemont College
		<1		●	Saint Francis College
●		8	●	●	Saint Joseph's University
		3	●	●	Saint Vincent College
		2	●	●	Seton Hill College
		1		●	Shippensburg State College
●		1	●	●	Slippery Rock State College
		3	●		Spring Garden College

ADVICE FOR FOREIGN STUDENTS xxxviii

English Course	English Program	% of Students	Organizations	Counseling	Institution
		<1	•	•	Susquehanna University
		7	•	•	Swarthmore College
	•	6	•	•	Temple University
		1		•	Thiel College
•	•	NA	•	•	University of Pennsylvania
•	•	7	•	•	University of Pittsburgh
		<1		•	University of Pittsburgh at Bradford
		<1			University of Pittsburgh at Greensburg
		NA			University of Pittsburgh at Johnstown
		2	•	•	University of Scranton
		2	•	•	Ursinus College
		0			Villa Maria College
		2			Villanova University
		2			Washington and Jefferson College
		1		•	Waynesburg College
•		1	•	•	West Chester State College
		1		•	Westminster College
	•	5	•	•	Widener College
•		2	•	•	Wilkes College
•		9	•		Wilson College
		1		•	York College of Pennsylvania

PUERTO RICO

English Course	English Program	% of Students	Organizations	Counseling	Institution
		14		•	Antillian College
		<1			Bayamon Central University
•	•	NA	•	•	Inter-American University of Puerto Rico/Metropolitan Campus
		1			International Institute of the Americas of World University
		15			Polytechnic University of Puerto Rico
		3			University of Puerto Rico/Humacao
		2			University of Puerto Rico/Mayaguez
		NA			University of the Sacred Heart

RHODE ISLAND

English Course	English Program	% of Students	Organizations	Counseling	Institution
		NA	•		Barrington College
		5	•	•	Brown University
		1	•	•	Bryant College
		1			Providence College
		1		•	Rhode Island College
		9	•	•	Rhode Island School of Design
•		7	•	•	Roger Williams College
		1			Salve Regina—The Newport College
		NA	•	•	University of Rhode Island

SOUTH CAROLINA

English Course	English Program	% of Students	Organizations	Counseling	Institution
•		15	•	•	Baptist College at Charleston
		3		•	Benedict College
		NA			Central Wesleyan College
		2			The Citadel
		<1			Claflin College
		1	•	•	Clemson University
•		NA			Coker College
		2	•	•	College of Charleston
		NA		•	Columbia College
		0			Converse College
		3			Erskine College
		2			Francis Marion College
		1	•	•	Furman University
		1	•	•	Lander College
		1			Limestone College
		0			Morris College
		NA			Newberry College
		<1		•	Presbyterian College
		2	•	•	South Carolina State College
	•	3	•	•	University of South Carolina
		1	•		University of South Carolina at Aiken
		2	•		University of South Carolina at Spartanburg
		1	•		University of South Carolina/Coastal Carolina College
		NA			Voorhees College
		1	•	•	Winthrop College
		1		•	Wofford College

SOUTH DAKOTA

English Course	English Program	% of Students	Organizations	Counseling	Institution
	•	1	•		Augustana College
	•	2	•	•	Black Hills State College
	•	1	•	•	Dakota State College
	•	3	•	•	Dakota Wesleyan University
		NA			Huron College
		5		•	Mount Marty College
	•	1		•	National College
		<1	•		Northern State College
		1		•	Sioux Falls College
		11	•		South Dakota School of Mines and Technology
		3	•	•	South Dakota State University
		1		•	University of South Dakota
	•	4	•	•	University of South Dakota at Springfield
		1			Yankton College

TENNESSEE

English Course	English Program	% of Students	Organizations	Counseling	Institution
	•	7	•	•	Belmont College
		<1	•	•	Bethel College
		3	•	•	Bryan College
		2	•	•	Carson-Newman College
		4	•	•	Christian Brothers College
		8			Covenant College
		<1		•	David Lipscomb College
		2	•	•	East Tennessee State University
		4		•	Fisk University
		2	•	•	Freed-Hardeman College
		8	•		King College
		8			Knoxville College
		1	•		Lambuth College
•	•	<1	•		Lane College
		NA		•	Lee College
•		2	•	•	LeMoyne-Owen College
		3	•	•	Lincoln Memorial University
•		3	•	•	Maryville College
		1			Memphis Academy of Arts
		2	•	•	Memphis State University
		2	•	•	Middle Tennessee State University
		1	•		Milligan College
•		NA		•	Southern Missionary College

xxxix ADVICE FOR FOREIGN STUDENTS

Columns: English Course | English Program | % of Students | Organizations | Counseling

EC	EP	%	Org	Cou	Institution
●		2		●	Southwestern at Memphis
		5	●	●	Tennessee State University
	●	4	●	●	Tennessee Technological University
		3		●	Tennessee Wesleyan College
●		2		●	Trevecca Nazarene College
		2			Tusculum College
		<1			Union University
●		1	●		University of Tennessee at Chattanooga
●	●	NA		●	University of Tennessee at Martin
●	●	4	●	●	University of Tennessee/Knoxville
		1		●	The University of the South
●	●	1	●	●	Vanderbilt University

TEXAS

EC	EP	%	Org	Cou	Institution
●		3	●	●	Abilene Christian University
		NA		●	Amber University
		<1	●		Angelo State University
●		2		●	Austin College
		1	●	●	Baylor University
		10	●	●	Bishop College
		5	●		Dallas Baptist College
		3			DeVry Institute of Technology
		2	●	●	East Texas Baptist College
●		2		●	East Texas State University
		<1		●	Hardin-Simmons University
●		4	●	●	Houston Baptist University
		NA			Howard Payne University
●		24	●	●	Huston-Tillotson College
●		5	●		Incarnate Word College
		NA		●	Jarvis Christian College
●	●	4	●		Lamar University
		4			Le Tourneau College
●	●	4		●	Lubbock Christian College
		1	●	●	McMurry College
		<1	●	●	Midwestern State University
●		8	●	●	North Texas State University
		6	●	●	Our Lady of the Lake University of San Antonio
●		NA	●	●	Pan American University
●		<1	●	●	Paul Quinn College
		4	●	●	Prairie View A&M University
		2			Rice University
●		16	●	●	St. Edward's University
		3	●	●	St. Mary's University
		3			Sam Houston State University
		5	●	●	Southern Methodist University
●		9	●	●	Southwestern Adventist College
		2			Southwestern University
		1	●	●	Southwest Texas State University
		1			Stephen F. Austin State University
●		3	●	●	Sul Ross State University
		9	●		Tarleton State University
		10	●	●	Texas A&I University
●	●	5	●	●	Texas A&M University
		1			Texas A&M University at Galveston
		6	●	●	Texas Christian University
		18			Texas College

EC	EP	%	Org	Cou	Institution
		<1		●	Texas Lutheran College
	●	NA	●	●	Texas Tech University
●	●	3	●	●	Texas Wesleyan College
		5	●		Texas Woman's University
		4		●	Trinity University
		5	●		University of Dallas
●	●	10	●	●	University of Houston/Central Campus
	●	8	●	●	University of Houston/Downtown Campus
	●	NA		●	University of Mary Hardin-Baylor
		7	●		University of St. Thomas
●	●	10	●	●	University of Texas at Arlington
●	●	5	●	●	University of Texas at Austin
●	●	8	●	●	University of Texas at El Paso
		<1	●	●	University of Texas at San Antonio
●		<1		●	Wayland Baptist University
		3	●	●	West Texas State University
		4	●	●	Wiley College

UTAH

EC	EP	%	Org	Cou	Institution
●		5	●	●	Brigham Young University
●		1	●	●	Southern Utah State College
		4	●	●	University of Utah
●		10	●	●	Utah State University
		4	●	●	Weber State College
	●	5	●	●	Westminster College

VERMONT

EC	EP	%	Org	Cou	Institution
●		10		●	Bennington College
		0			Burlington College
●		<1		●	Castleton State College
		1			College of St. Joseph the Provider
		NA			Goddard College
		2			Green Mountain College
●		1			Johnson State College
		<1			Lyndon State College
		3			Marlboro College
		3	●		Middlebury College
●		2			Norwich University
	●	3	●	●	Saint Michael's College
●		5	●	●	Southern Vermont College
		<1			Trinity College
		<1	●	●	University of Vermont
		1			Vermont College of Norwich University

VIRGINIA

EC	EP	%	Org	Cou	Institution
		1			Averett College
		8	●	●	Bluefield College
		1		●	Bridgewater College
		<1			Christopher Newport College
		1	●	●	Clinch Valley College of the University of Virginia
		1	●		College of William and Mary
		4	●	●	Eastern Mennonite College
		<1			Emory and Henry College
●		NA		●	Ferrum College
	●	2	●	●	George Mason University
		<1			Hampden-Sydney College
		2	●	●	Hampton Institute

ADVICE FOR FOREIGN STUDENTS xl

English Course	English Program	% of Students	Organizations	Counseling	Institution
		2	•	•	Hollins College
		<1	•	•	James Madison University
		3	•	•	Liberty Baptist College
		<1		•	Longwood College
•	NA		•	•	Lynchburg College
		2	•	•	Mary Baldwin College
•	•	15	•	•	Marymount College of Virginia
		<1		•	Mary Washington College
		4	•	•	Norfolk State University
•	•	3	•	•	Old Dominion University
•		<1	•	•	Radford University
		1		•	Randolph-Macon College
		3	•	•	Randolph-Macon Woman's College
		<1		•	Roanoke College
		3		•	Saint Paul's College
	NA			•	Shenandoah College and Conservatory of Music
		4	•	•	Sweet Briar College
		<1		•	University of Richmond
		2	•	•	University of Virginia
		9	•	•	Virginia Commonwealth University
•		4	•	•	Virginia Intermont College
		2	•	•	Virginia Military Institute
		3	•	•	Virginia Polytechnic Institute and State University
		2	•	•	Virginia State University
		5	•	•	Virginia Union University
•		4		•	Virginia Wesleyan College
		1	•	•	Washington and Lee University

VIRGIN ISLANDS

| | | 15 | | | College of the Virgin Islands |

WASHINGTON

English Course	English Program	% of Students	Organizations	Counseling	Institution
•		1	•	•	Central Washington University
		4	•	•	Cornish Institute
•	•	4	•	•	Eastern Washington University
		<1		•	The Evergreen State College
•		10	•	•	Gonzaga University
•	NA		•	•	Heritage College
		3	•	•	Pacific Lutheran University
		15	•	•	Saint Martin's College
•	•	2	•	•	Seattle Pacific University
		10	•	•	Seattle University
		2	•	•	University of Puget Sound
•	•	8	•	•	University of Washington
•		10	•	•	Walla Walla College
		6	•	•	Washington State University
		4	•	•	Western Washington University
		3	•	•	Whitman College
•	•	6	•	•	Whitworth College

WEST VIRGINIA

		2	•	•	Alderson-Broaddus College
		3	•		Bethany College
•	NA		•	•	Bluefield State College
		<1		•	Concord College
		4	•	•	Davis and Elkins College
		2	•		Fairmont State College
		1	•	•	Glenville State College
•		3	•	•	Marshall University
		1		•	Salem College
		<1	•	•	Shepherd College
		2	•	•	University of Charleston
		<1	•	•	West Liberty State College
	NA		•	•	West Virginia Institute of Technology
		<1	•	•	West Virginia State College
•		NA	•		West Virginia University
		2	•	•	West Virginia Wesleyan College
		1	•	•	Wheeling College

WISCONSIN

English Course	English Program	% of Students	Organizations	Counseling	Institution
		10			Alverno College
		3		•	Beloit College
	NA			•	Cardinal Stritch College
		1	•	•	Carroll College
		5	•	•	Carthage College
		3		•	Concordia College
		2	•	•	Edgewood College
		3	•	•	Lakeland College
		3	•	•	Lawrence University
		<1		•	Marian College of Fond Du Lac
		2	•	•	Marquette University
		3		•	Milton College
		1		•	Milwaukee School of Engineering
		4		•	Mount Mary College
•		5		•	Mount Senario College
•		3		•	Northland College
		1	•	•	Ripon College
		1		•	St. Norbert College
•		1	•	•	University of Wisconsin/Eau Claire
•		2	•	•	University of Wisconsin/Green Bay
		1	•	•	University of Wisconsin/La Crosse
•	•	7	•	•	University of Wisconsin/Madison
•		5	•		University of Wisconsin/Milwaukee
•		2	•	•	University of Wisconsin/Oshkosh
		2	•		University of Wisconsin/Parkside
		5	•	•	University of Wisconsin/Platteville
•	NA		•	•	University of Wisconsin/River Falls
•		2	•	•	University of Wisconsin/Stevens Point
		3	•	•	University of Wisconsin/Stout
•		3	•	•	University of Wisconsin/Superior
		1	•	•	University of Wisconsin/Whitewater
		3	•	•	Viterbo College
		2		•	Wisconsin Conservatory of Music

WYOMING

| | | 4 | • | • | University of Wyoming |

COLLEGIATE TERMS

accreditation Accreditation amounts to a stamp of approval given to a college. The accreditation process evaluates institutions and programs to determine whether they meet established standards of educational quality.

Achievement Tests (AT) Hour-long tests given by the College Entrance Examination Board to measure ability in specific subjects.

Advanced Placement (AP) A college may permit a freshman to skip, or even receive credit for, an introductory course if he or she demonstrates readiness for an advanced course. Many students prove their competence by enrolling in advanced placement courses in high school and then passing an Advanced Placement Examination given by the College Board. These exams are graded from 1 (low) to 5 (high), and most colleges grant advanced placement for a grade of 3 or better.

American Association of University Professors (AAUP) This professional organization publishes an annual report on faculty compensation at most colleges and universities.

American College Testing Program (ACT) This organization administers the scholastic aptitude examination known as the American College Test. The ACT is one of the two major college entrance examinations (the other is the SAT).

Candidates Reply Date Agreement (CRDA) Sponsored by the College Board, this agreement establishes a common date, May 1, that is the earliest time a subscribing college may require an accepted applicant to say whether he or she plans to attend.

Carnegie units One Carnegie unit is given for successful completion of one year's study of one college-preparatory or academic subject in a high school. Some colleges refer to these as "academic units." The name comes from the Carnegie Foundation for the Advancement of Teaching.

class rank A student's standing based on his or her academic record as compared with that of the other members of the class. In a class of 100, the best student would be No. 1; the poorest, No. 100.

college calendar The way the academic year is divided (for instance, semester, trimester, quarter, term); dates of the start of terms; or the list of holidays, vacations, examinations, etc.

College-Level Examination Program (CLEP) Run by the College Board, this program offers a series of general and subject examinations for college applicants who have gained learning in such nontraditional ways as independent reading, on-the-job training, or correspondence courses.

consortium Several colleges and universities in an area often join together in a consortium, or cooperative association, which gives students the opportunity to use the libraries of or take courses at all member institutions. Consortium members often present joint lecture programs or unusual courses.

cooperative education A program offered by a few schools for combining paid employment with study. Usually, the student alternates one or more semesters of full-time study with semesters of employment in fields related, if possible, to his or her field of concentration.

cooperative program A program of study offered by two cooperating institutions. Students usually register at one of these institutions, but may take specialized courses at the other. Or they take two or three years of general study at one institution (usually a liberal arts college) and then two or three years of specialized study such as engineering or forestry at another (usually at a large university). They eventually earn two degrees, one in liberal arts and one in the special field.

core curriculum A group of courses, in varied areas of the arts and sciences, designated by a college as one of the requirements for a degree.

credit Colleges assign a given number of credits to a particular college course based on a standard of one credit for every hour per week that the course is held. For example, a course that meets for three hours each week is generally awarded three credits. Colleges with semester calendars require fewer credits for a degree (generally between 120 and 130 for an undergraduate degree) than do colleges with quarter calendars (they generally require about 180 credits). There are many exceptions to the credit standard, particularly with courses requiring laboratory work or other extensive work outside the classroom.

deferred admission This is an admissions plan whereby a student applies to a college and is notified of acceptance during the senior year of high school. The student then may take off a year for travel, work, or other projects before attending college.

deferred tuition payment Colleges may allow students to spread out payment of tuition over the entire year.

early admissions This plan allows students to begin college work after their junior year of high school, usually without a diploma. This program usually is limited to exceptional students.

early decision Some colleges offer to notify applicants of acceptance or rejection during the first semester of their senior year. There are two types of early decision plans: the single-choice plan and the first-choice plan. In the single-choice plan, students cannot apply to other colleges until they have been notified by the early decision college. In the first-choice plan, students may apply to other colleges, but name the early decision college as the first choice and agree to enroll at that college and withdraw all other applications if accepted.

early evaluation procedure A plan under which applicants to Ivy League institutions (Brown, Columbia, Cornell, Dartmouth, Harvard, Pennsylvania, Princeton, and Yale) and the Massachusetts Institute of Technology receive between November 1 and February 15 an evaluation of their chances for acceptance. Categories used are likely, possible, unlikely, and insufficient evidence for evaluation. Final notification is made on a common date in April.

external degree program A system in which a student earns credit toward a degree through such varied means as college courses, military experience, and proficiency examinations.

Family Financial Statement (FFS) This is a summary of the finances of the family of an applicant for financial aid. The family must complete a form supplied by the American College Testing Program, which analyzes it and supplies colleges with an evaluation of the applicant's needs.

Financial Aid Form (FAF) A financial information form completed by the parents of a student seeking financial aid. The form is submitted to the College Scholarship Service, which gives the colleges to which the student applies its evaluation of his or her actual need.

General Educational Development Examination (GED) A series of tests that adults take to qualify for a high school equivalency certificate or diploma. Many colleges will accept satisfactory GED test results in place of a high school diploma.

Graduate Record Examination (GRE) A three-hour test measuring scholastic ability at the graduate level. Scores are used as the basis of admission to many graduate schools and as a factor in awarding fellowships and other aid.

guaranteed tuition A college may guarantee an entering freshman that tuition charges will not increase during the four years he or she attends. Tuition is raised only for future freshman classes.

honors program A plan of special courses, seminars, or concentrated study for superior students. Those who meet the requirements of an honors program usually graduate with "honors" degrees.

independent study A method of granting credit for study or research independent of the assignments of any specific course. Such study is often part of an honors program in the student's major and is supervised by a professor.

language proficiency examination An examination in a foreign language to determine whether a student has satisfied a college's foreign language requirement and, if not, which level of a foreign language course he or she should be placed in.

mean—median Colleges generally use the median when figuring average SAT or ACT scores. The median is determined by listing all scores and selecting the one that falls in the middle of the listing. The mean is determined by adding all the scores together and dividing that total by the number of scores. The mean is less accurate because one or two very low scores can bring the average way down.

xlii COLLEGIATE TERMS

non-matriculated student Any student enrolled in one or more college courses who is not a degree candidate.

pass-fail option Many colleges allow students to take one or more courses per year on a pass-fail basis in order to encourage good students to explore new fields they might avoid for fear of lowering their averages if the usual grades were assigned. On completion of such a course, students receive a grade of either pass or fail. This grade is not included in the overall average.

Preliminary Scholastic Aptitude Test (PSAT) This test, which has been given for several years, has replaced the former qualifying examination for the National Merit Scholarship program and is now known as the PSAT/NMSQT. It is similar to the Scholastic Aptitude Test, and is usually taken by high school students in the fall of the junior year. The score is reported in terms of the first two digits on the SAT scale (57 instead of 573).

ROTC Many colleges have units of the Reserve Officer's Training Corps that offer two- and four-year programs of military training culminating in an officer's commission. In some colleges, credits for the courses can be applied toward a degree.

rolling admissions This means that a college gives an admissions decision as soon as possible after an application is completed and does not specify a notification deadline. Usually, it is wise to apply early to such colleges, since applications are normally not accepted after the admissions quota has been reached.

Scholastic Aptitude Test (SAT) A multiple-choice test designed to measure proficiency in mathematical and verbal ability. The SAT, administered by the College Board, is used as an entrance examination by many colleges.

Single Application Method (SAM) The Associated Colleges of the Midwest have combined resources and have given students the opportunity to simplify the application process. Students planning to apply to at least two member colleges (Beloit, Carleton, Coe, Colorado, Cornell, Knox, Lawrence, Macalester, Monmouth, Ripon, and St. Olaf) may complete one application indicating their choices. This application is then considered first by the colleges indicated and then, if the student so specifies, by the remaining colleges until one offers admission.

3-2 program A program that combines three years of undergraduate study and two years of professional study. Students earn a bachelor's degree and a professional degree in five years.

transcript The official record of a student's academic performance from the time of entrance to a given institution to the end of the latest semester.

transfer student A student who has attended another college for any period from a single term to up to three years. He or she may receive *transfer credit* for all or many of the courses that have been successfully completed before transfer.

Undergraduate Program for Counseling and Evaluation (UP) A series of 35 different tests covering either general or specific knowledge in various fields and used for rating college students' progress and achievements. Results of these tests, administered by the Educational Testing Service, are often used in counseling and in awarding of nontraditional degrees.

Undergraduate Record Examination (URE) Almost identical to the Graduate Record Examination, the URE is administered to graduating seniors as an indicator of their achievement. Some colleges require the URE for graduation.

work-study program Either a combined employment and study program as described above under *Cooperative Education* or, more usually, a program whereby students are paid an hourly rate for up to 15 hours per week of employment in libraries or administrative offices to help pay their college expenses. The federal government subsidizes the College Work-Study program.

FURTHER READING

Students interested in exploring the opportunities available at junior and community colleges will find relevant information in *Barron's Guide to the Two-Year Colleges*, Volume 1, which lists all regionally accredited two-year colleges and those four-year colleges that offer associate degrees. Facts on the schools are presented in concise, easy-to-read form. Volume 2 is in chart form and shows areas of study at all schools included in Volume 1.

Further information on entrance examinations, scholarships, and other aspects of college can be found in the following Barron's publications, all of which are available from Barron's Educational Series, 113 Crossways Park Drive, Woodbury, New York 11797:

The Freshman's Friend, S. Johnson
Getting Ready for College: How to Settle Down and Make the Grade, George Weigand
Handbook of American College Financial Aid, Nicholas C. Proia and Vincent DiGaspari
How to Beat Test Anxiety and Score Higher on Your Exams, James H. Divine and David W. Kylen
How to Prepare for the American College Testing Program (ACT), Murray Shapiro, et al.
How to Prepare for College Entrance Examinations (SAT), Samuel C. Brownstein and Mitchel Weiner
How to Prepare for the Preliminary Scholastic Aptitude Test/ National Merit Scholarship Qualifying Test (PSAT-NMSQT), Samuel C. Brownstein and Mitchel Weiner
Money for College! How to Get It, Donald Moore
Strategies for Taking Tests, James and Judy Divine
Study Tactics, William Armstrong

KEY TO ABBREVIATIONS

DEGREES

A.A.—Associate of Arts
A.A.S.—Associate of Applied Science
A.B. or B.A.—Bachelor of Arts
A.B.J.—Bachelor of Arts in Journalism
A.S.—Associate of Science
B.A.A.—Bachelor of Applied Arts
B.A.A.S. or B. Applied A.S.—Bachelor of Applied Arts and Sciences
B.Ac. or B.Acc.—Bachelor of Accountancy
B.A.C.—Bachelor of Science in Air Commerce
B.A.E. or B.A.Ed.—Bachelor of Arts in Education
B.A.G.E.—Bachelor of Arts in General Education
B.Agri.—Bachelor of Agriculture
B.A.G.S.—Bachelor of Arts in General Studies
B.A.J.S.—Bachelor of Arts in Judaic Studies
B. Applied Sc.—Bachelor of Applied Science
B.Arch.—Bachelor of Architecture
B.Arch.Hist.—Bachelor of Architectural History
B.Arch.Tech.—Bachelor of Architectural Technology
B.A.S.—Bachelor of Arts and Sciences
B.A.T.—Bachelor of Arts in Teaching
B.B.A.—Bachelor of Business Administration
B.B.E.—Bachelor of Business Education
B.Bus.—Bachelor of Business
B.C. or B.Com. or B.Comm.—Bachelor of Commerce
B.C.A.—Bachelor of Creative Arts
B.C.E.—Bachelor of Civil Engineering
B.Ch. or B.Chem.—Bachelor of Chemistry
B.Ch.E.—Bachelor of Chemical Engineering
B.C.M.—Bachelor of Christian Ministries
B. Church Mus.—Bachelor of Church Music
B.C.S.—Bachelor of College Studies
B.E. or B.Ed.—Bachelor of Education
B.E.D.—Bachelor of Environmental Design
B.E.E.—Bachelor of Electrical Engineering
B.En. or B.Eng.—Bachelor of Engineering
B.E.S. or B.Eng.Sc.—Bachelor of Engineering Science
B.E.T.—Bachelor of Engineering Technology
B.F.A.—Bachelor of Fine Arts
B.G.S.—Bachelor of General Studies
B.H.S.—Bachelor of Health Science
B.I.D.—Bachelor of Industrial Design
B.I.M.—Bachelor of Industrial Management
B.Ind.Tech.—Bachelor of Industrial Technology
B.Int.Arch.—Bachelor of Interior Architecture
B.Int. Design—Bachelor of Interior Design
B.I.S.—Bachelor of Industrial Safety
B.I.S.—Bachelor of Interdisciplinary Studies
B.J.—Bachelor of Journalism
B.J.S.—Bachelor of Judaic Studies
B.L.A. or B.Lib. Arts—Bachelor of Liberal Arts
B.Land.Arch.—Bachelor in Landscape Architecture
B.L.S.—Bachelor of Liberal Studies
B.M. or B.Mus. or Mus.Bac.—Bachelor of Music
B.M.E.—Bachelor of Mechanical Engineering
B.M.E. or B.Mus.Ed.—Bachelor of Music Education
B.Med.Lab.Sc.—Bachelor of Medical Laboratory Science
B.Min.—Bachelor of Ministry
B.Mus.A.—Bachelor of Applied Music
B.M.T.—Bachelor of Music Therapy
B.O.T.—Bachelor of Occupational Therapy
B.P.A.—Bachelor of Public Administration
B.P.E.—Bachelor of Physical Education
B.Perf. Arts—Bachelor of Performing Arts
B.Ph.—Bachelor of Philosophy
B.Pharm.—Bachelor of Pharmacy
B.Phys.Hlth.Ed.—Bachelor of Physical Health Education
B.P.S.—Bachelor of Professional Studies
B.P.T.—Bachelor of Physical Therapy
B.R.T.—Bachelor of Respiratory Therapy
B.S. or B.Sc. or S.B.—Bachelor of Science
B.S.A. or B.S.Ag. or B.S.Agr.—Bachelor of Science in Agriculture
B. Sacred Mus.—Bachelor of Sacred Music
B.S.A.E. or B.S. Art Ed.—Bachelor of Science in Art Education
B.S.Ag.E.—Bachelor of Science in Agricultural Engineering
B.S.A.S.—Bachelor of Science in Administrative Sciences
B.S.B.A.—Bachelor of Science in Business Administration
B.S.Bus.—Bachelor of Science in Business
B.S.Bus.Ed.—Bachelor of Science in Business Education
B.S.C.—Bachelor of Science in Commerce
B.S.C.E. or B.S.C.I.E.—Bachelor of Science in Civil Engineering
B.S.Ch. or B.S. in Ch.—Bachelor of Science in Chemistry
B.S.Ch.E.—Bachelor of Science in Chemical Engineering
B.S.C.I.S.—Bachelor of Science in Computer Information Sciences
B.S.C.J.—Bachelor of Science in Criminal Justice
B.S.Comp.Sci.—Bachelor of Science in Computer Science
B.S.D.H.—Bachelor of Science in Dental Hygiene
B.S.E. or B.S.Ed.—Bachelor of Science in Education
B.S.E. or B.S. in E. or B.S. in Eng.—Bachelor of Science in Engineering
B.S.E.E.—Bachelor of Science in Electrical Engineering
B.S.E.H.—Bachelor of Science in Environmental Health
B.S.E.P.H.—Bachelor of Science in Environmental and Public Health
B.S.E.S.—Bachelor of Science in Engineering Science
B.S.E.T.—Bachelor of Science in Engineering Technology
B.S.F.—Bachelor of Science in Forestry
B.S.F.R.—Bachelor of Science in Forestry Resources
B.S.F.W.—Bachelor of Science in Fisheries and Wildlife
B.S.G.—Bachelor of Science in Geology
B.S.G.—Bachelor of Science in Gerontology
B.S.H.C.A.—Bachelor of Science in Health Care Administration
B.S.H.E.—Bachelor of Science in Home Economics
B.S.H.S.—Bachelor of Science in Health Sciences
B.S.I.A.—Bachelor of Science in Industrial Arts
B.S.I.E.—Bachelor of Science in Industrial Engineering
B.S.I.M.—Bachelor of Science in Industrial Management
B.S. in Biomed.Eng.—Bachelor of Science in Biomedical Engineering
B.S. in C.D.—Bachelor of Science in Communications Disorders
B.S.Ind.Ed.—Bachelor of Science in Industrial Education
B.S.Ind.Tech.—Bachelor of Science in Industrial Technology
B.S. in Elem.Ed.—Bachelor of Science in Elementary Education
B.S. in Sec.Ed.—Bachelor of Science in Secondary Education
B.S.J.—Bachelor of Science in Journalism
B.S.M.—Bachelor of Science in Music
B.S.M.E.—Bachelor of Science in Mechanical Engineering
B.S.Med.Tech. or B.S.M.T.—Bachelor of Science in Medical Technology
B.S.Met.E.—Bachelor of Science in Metallurgical Engineering
B.S.M.R.A.—Bachelor of Science in Medical Records Administration
B.S.Mus.Ed.—Bachelor of Science in Music Education
B.S.N.—Bachelor of Science in Nursing
B.S.O.A.—Bachelor of Science in Office Administration
B.S.O.E.—Bachelor of Science in Occupational Education
B.S.O.T.—Bachelor of Science in Occupational Therapy
B.S.P. or B.S.Pharm.—Bachelor of Science in Pharmacy
B.S.P.A.—Bachelor of Science in Public Administration
B.S.Pcs.—Bachelor of Science in Physics
B.S.P.E.—Bachelor of Science in Physical Education
B.S.P.T.—Bachelor of Science in Physical Therapy
B.S.Rad.Tech.—Bachelor of Science in Radiation Technology
B.S.S.—Bachelor of Special Studies
B.S.S.A.—Bachelor of Science in Systems Analysis
B.S.Soc. Work or B.S.S.W.—Bachelor of Science in Social Work
B.S.Sp.—Bachelor of Science in Speech
B.S.T. or B.S.Tech.—Bachelor of Science in Technology
B.S.V.T.E.—Bachelor of Science in Vocational Technical Education
B.S.W.—Bachelor of Social Work
B.T. or B.Tech.—Bachelor of Technology
B.Th.—Bachelor of Theology
B.U.S.—Bachelor of Urban Studies
B.Voc. Arts or B.V.A.—Bachelor of Vocational Arts
B.Voc.Ed.—Bachelor of Vocational Education
D.D.S.—Doctor of Dental Surgery
J.D.—Doctor of Jurisprudence
LL.B.—Bachelor of Laws
M.A.—Master of Arts
M.A.Ed.—Master of Arts in Education
M.A.T.—Master of Arts in Teaching
M.B.A.—Master of Business Administration
M.D.—Doctor of Medicine
M.F.A.—Master of Fine Arts
M.P.A.—Master of Public Administration
M.S.—Master of Science

KEY TO ABBREVIATIONS

Ph.D.—Doctor of Philosophy
R.N.—Registered Nurse
S.B. or B.S. or B.Sc.—Bachelor of Science

OTHER ABBREVIATIONS

ACT—American College Testing Program
ALIGU—American Language Institute of Georgetown University
AP—Advanced Placement
AT—Achievement Test
ATP—Admissions Testing Program
BEOG—Basic Educational Opportunity Grant
CAS—Certificate of Advanced Study
CEEB—College Entrance Examination Board
CELT—Comprehensive English Language Test
CLEP—College-Level Examination Program
CRDA—Candidates Reply Date Agreement
CSS—College Scholarship Service
CWS—College Work-Study
DHAT—Dental Hygiene Aptitude Test
EESL—Examination of English as a Second Language
ELS/ALA—English Language Services/American Language Academy
EOP—Equal Opportunity Program
ETS—Educational Testing Service
FAF—Financial Aid Form
FFS—Family Financial Statement
FISL—Federally Insured Student Loan
GED—General Educational Development (high school equivalency examination)
GPA—Grade Point Average
GRE—Graduate Record Examination
GSL—Guaranteed Student Loan
GSLP—Guaranteed Student Loan Program
HEOP—Higher Equal Opportunity Program
LEEP—Law Enforcement Education Program
MTELP—Michigan Test of English Language Proficiency
NDEA—National Defense Education Act
NDSL—National Direct Student Loan
PCS—Parents' Confidential Statement
PEP—Proficency Examination Program
PHEAA—Pennsylvania Higher Education Assistance Agency
PSAT/NMSQT—Preliminary Scholastic Aptitude Test/National Merit Scholarship Qualifying Test
ROTC—Reserve Officers Training Corps
RSE—Regents Scholarship Examination (New York State)
SAAC—Student Aid Application for California
SACU—Service for Admission to College and University (Canada)
SAM—Single Application Method
SAT—Scholastic Aptitude Test
SCAT—Scholastic College Aptitude Test
SCS—Students' Confidential Statement
SEOG—Supplementary Educational Opportunity Grant
TAP—Tuition Assistance Program (New York State)
TOEFL—Test of English as a Foreign Language
TTY—Talking Typewriter
UAP—Undergraduate Assessment Program
UP—Undergraduate Program (area tests)
URE, UGRE—Undergraduate Record Examination
VFAF—Virginia Financial Assistance Form
WPCT—Washington Pre-College Test

COLLEGE-LOCATOR MAPS

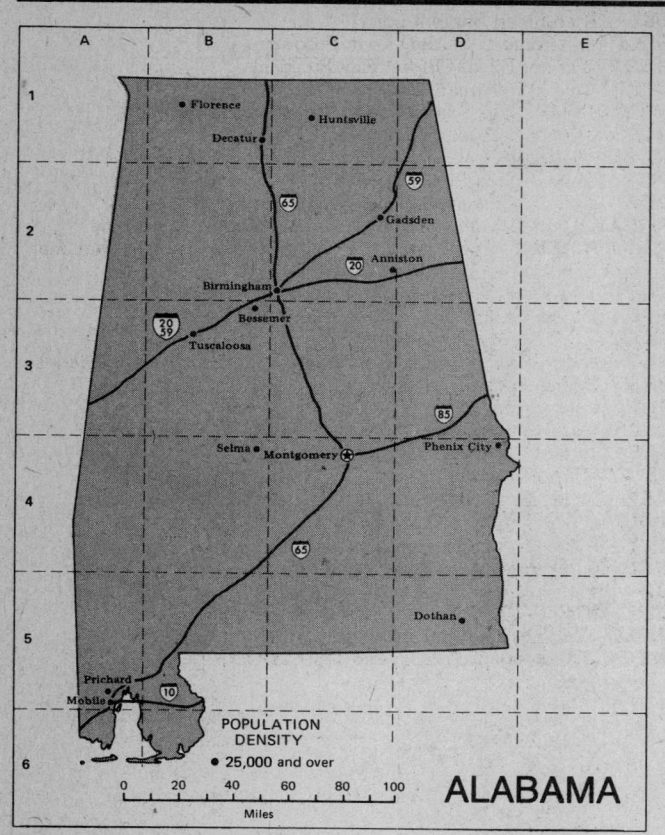

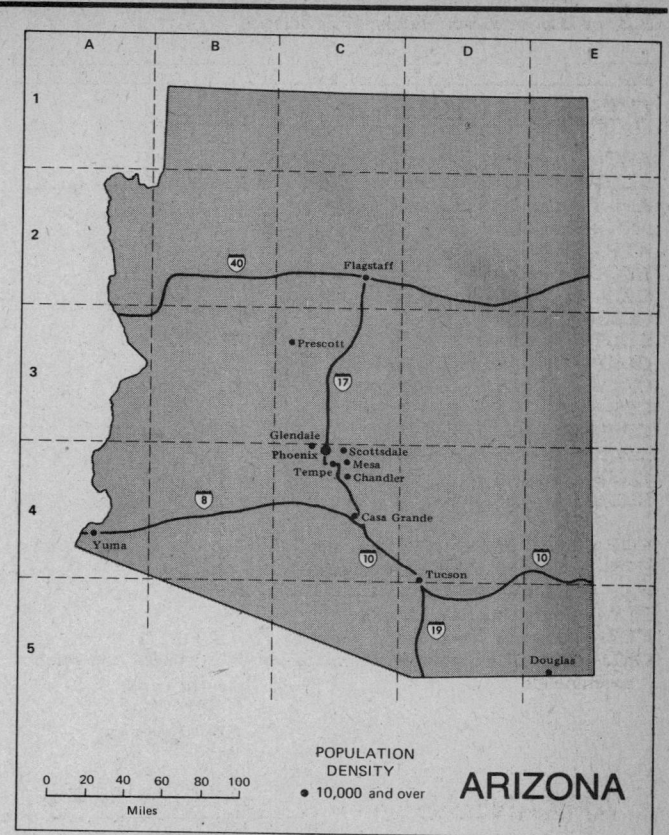

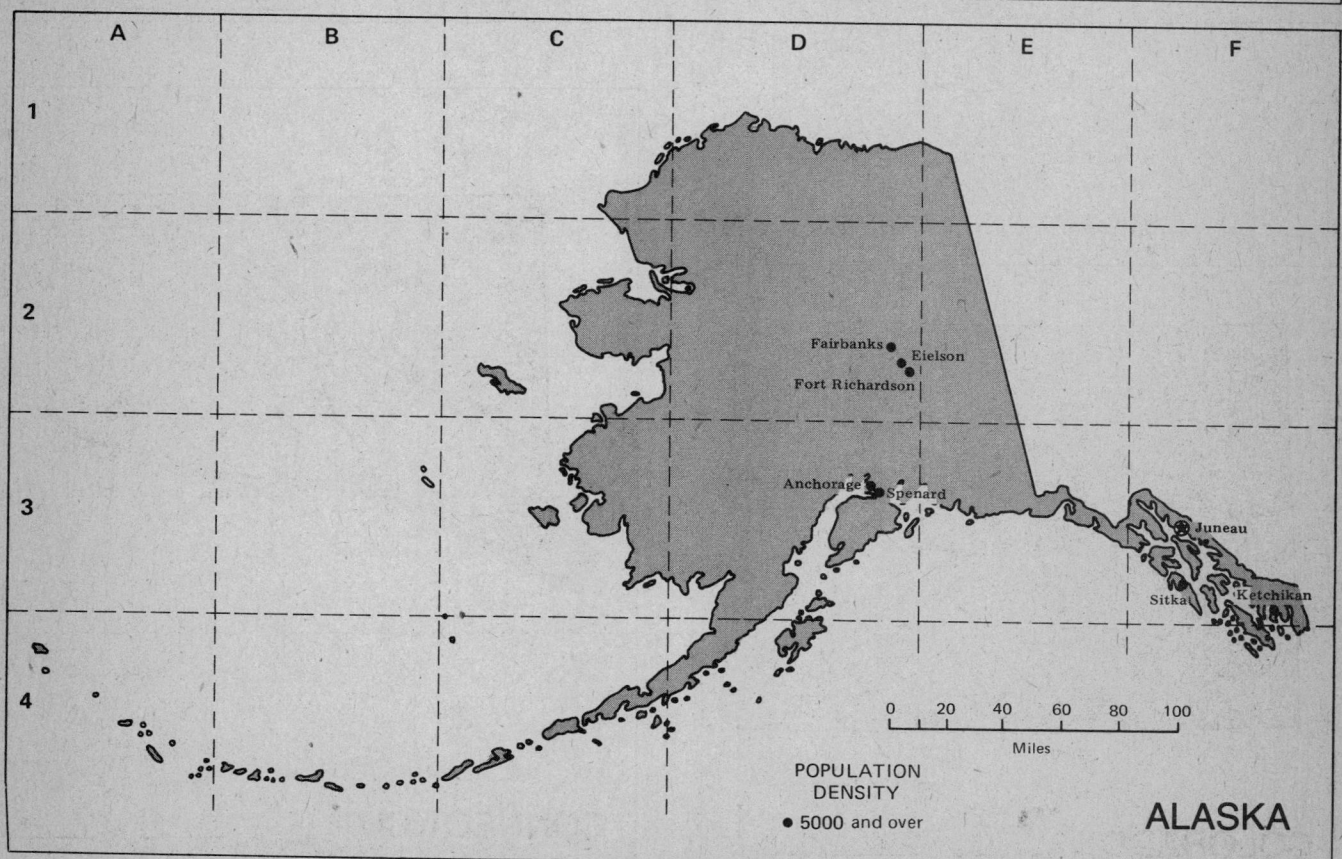

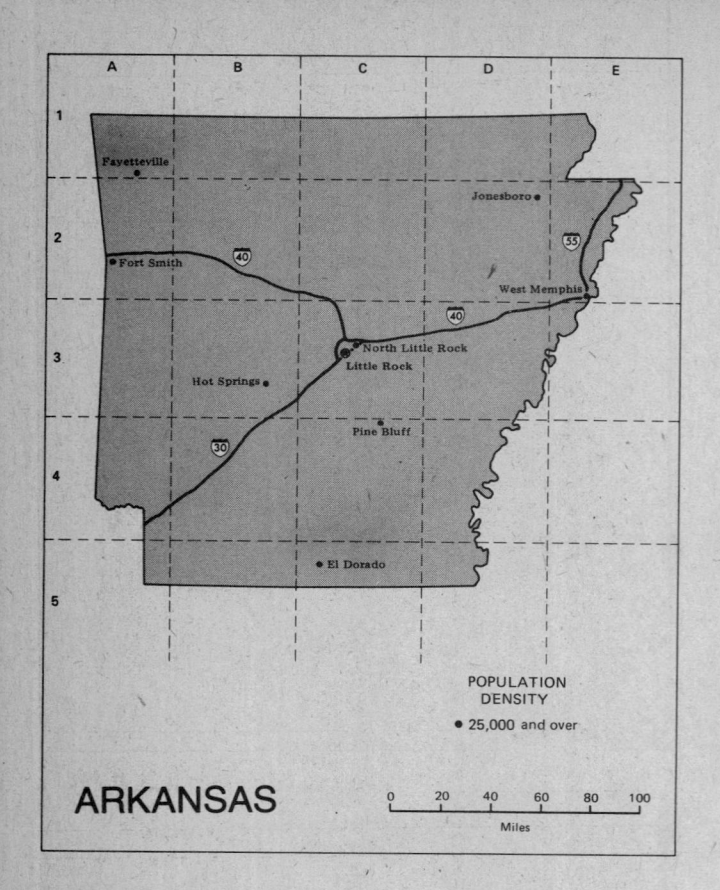

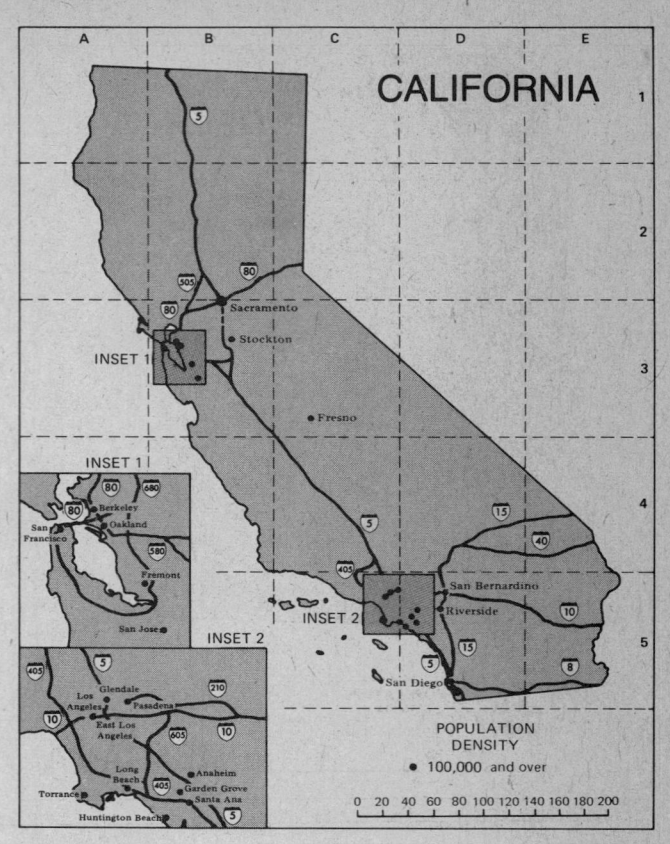

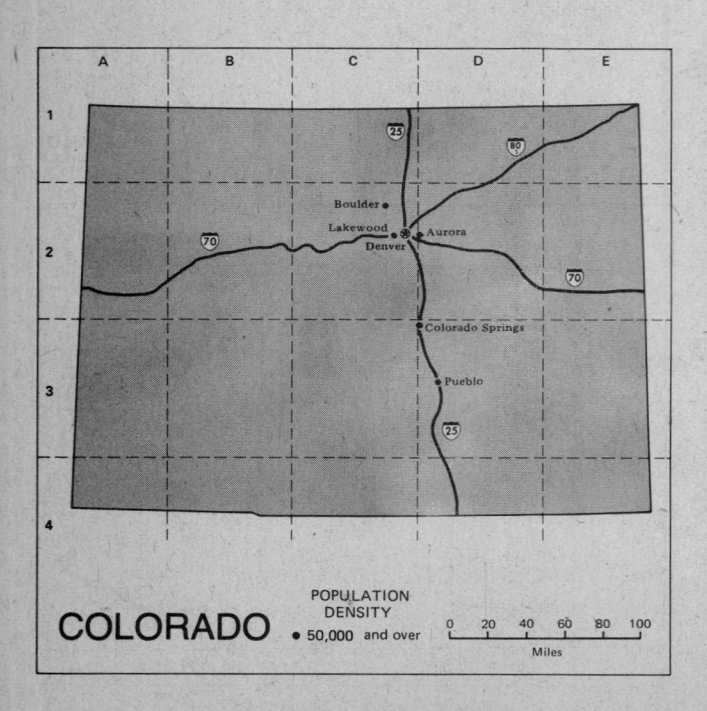

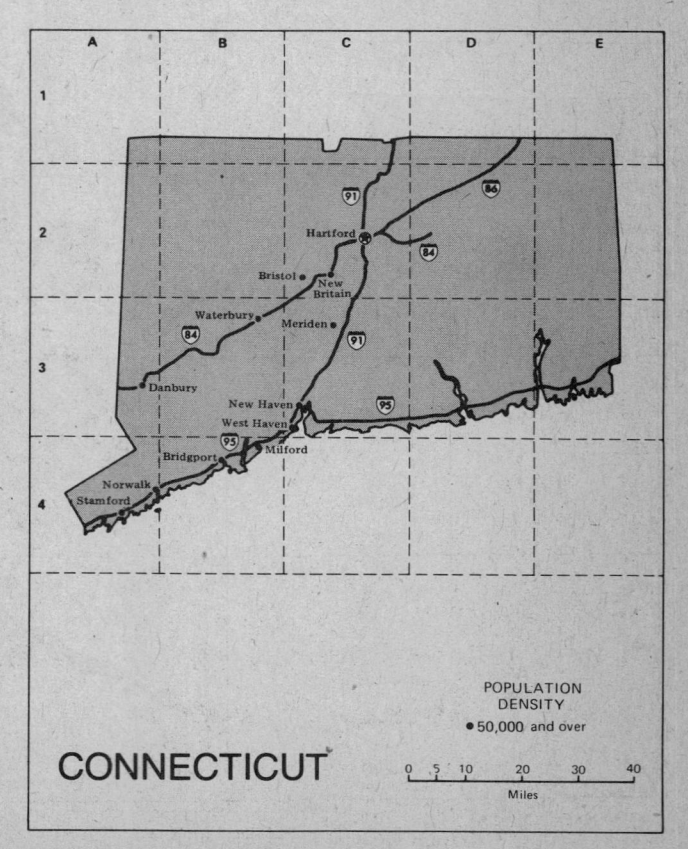

ARKANSAS

POPULATION DENSITY
• 25,000 and over

CALIFORNIA

POPULATION DENSITY
• 100,000 and over

COLORADO

POPULATION DENSITY
• 50,000 and over

CONNECTICUT

POPULATION DENSITY
• 50,000 and over

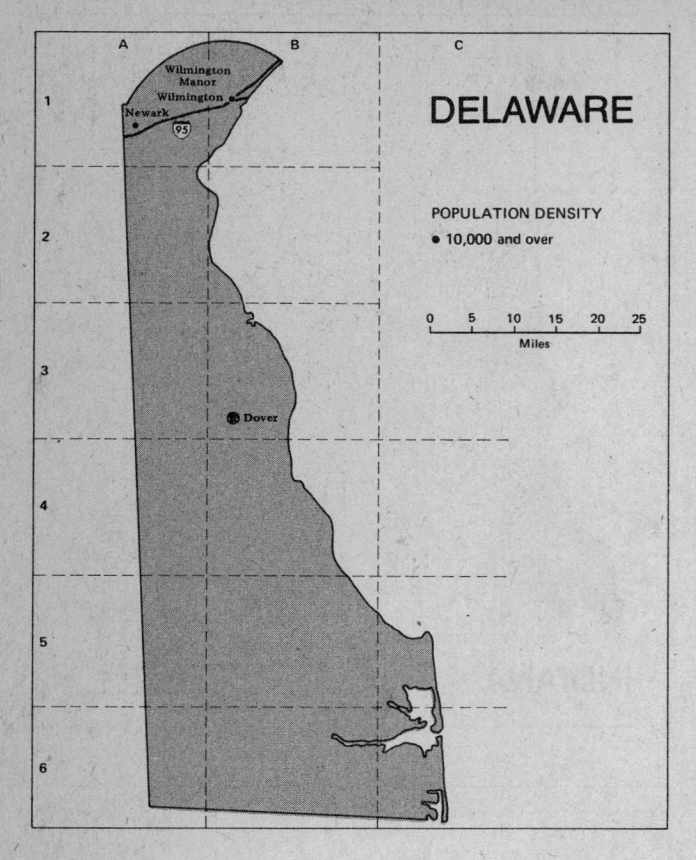

DELAWARE

POPULATION DENSITY
- 10,000 and over

DISTRICT of COLUMBIA

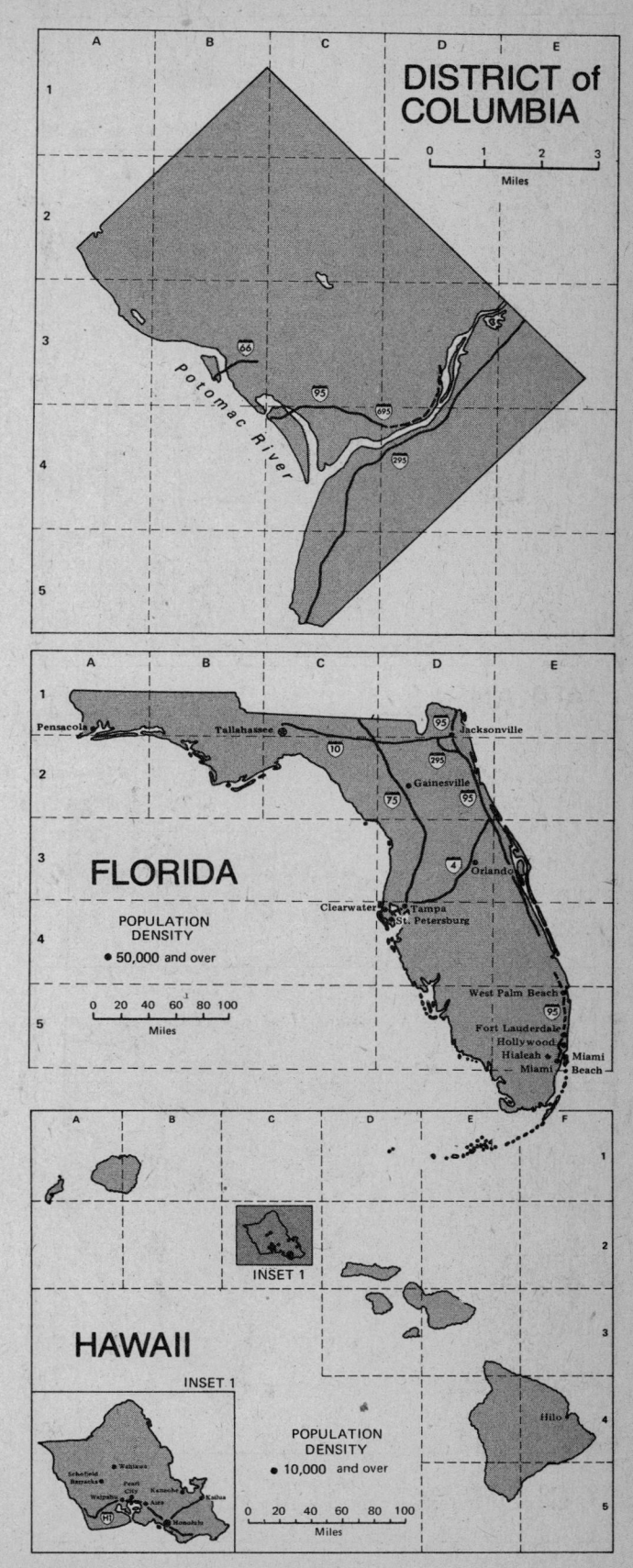

FLORIDA

POPULATION DENSITY
- 50,000 and over

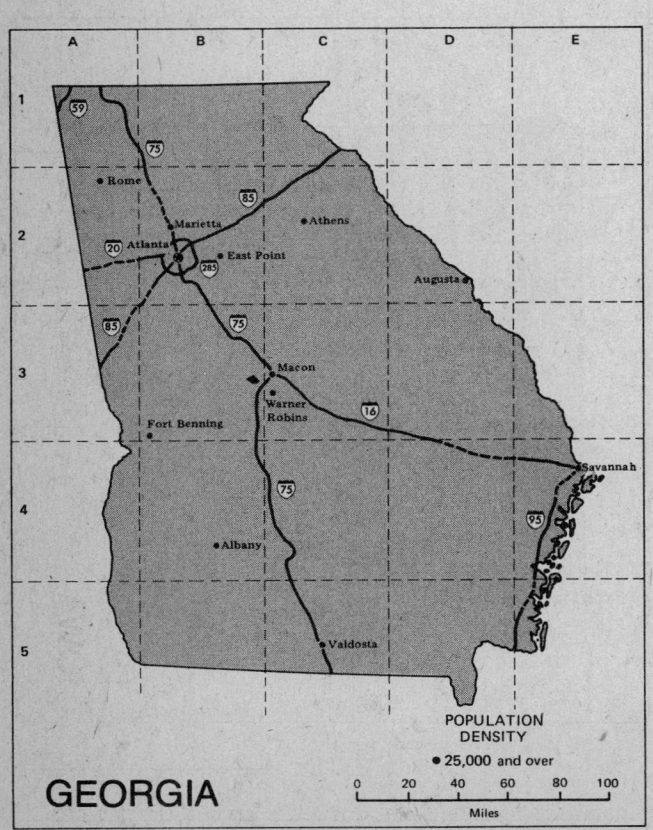

GEORGIA

POPULATION DENSITY
- 25,000 and over

HAWAII

POPULATION DENSITY
- 10,000 and over

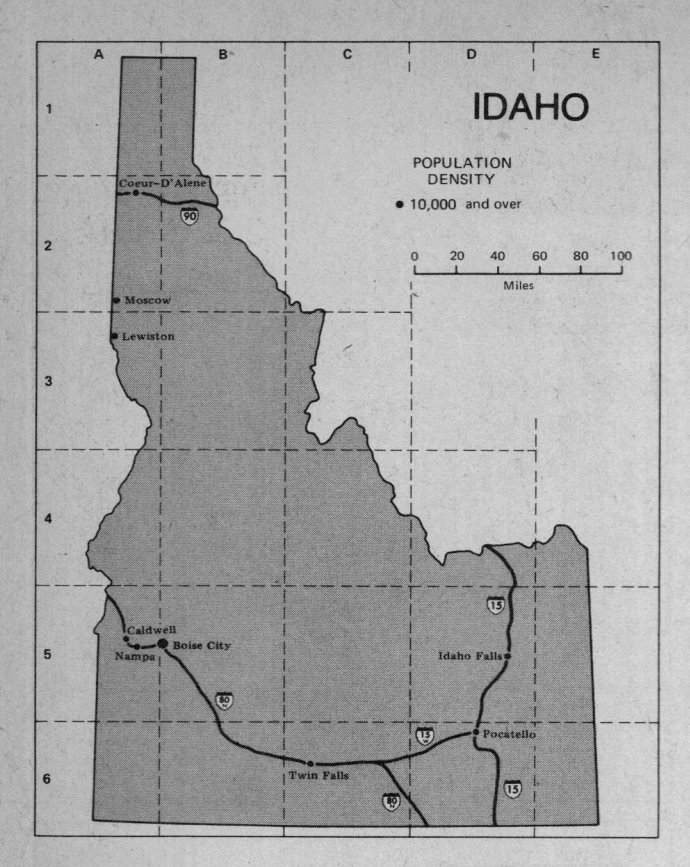

IDAHO

POPULATION DENSITY
- 10,000 and over

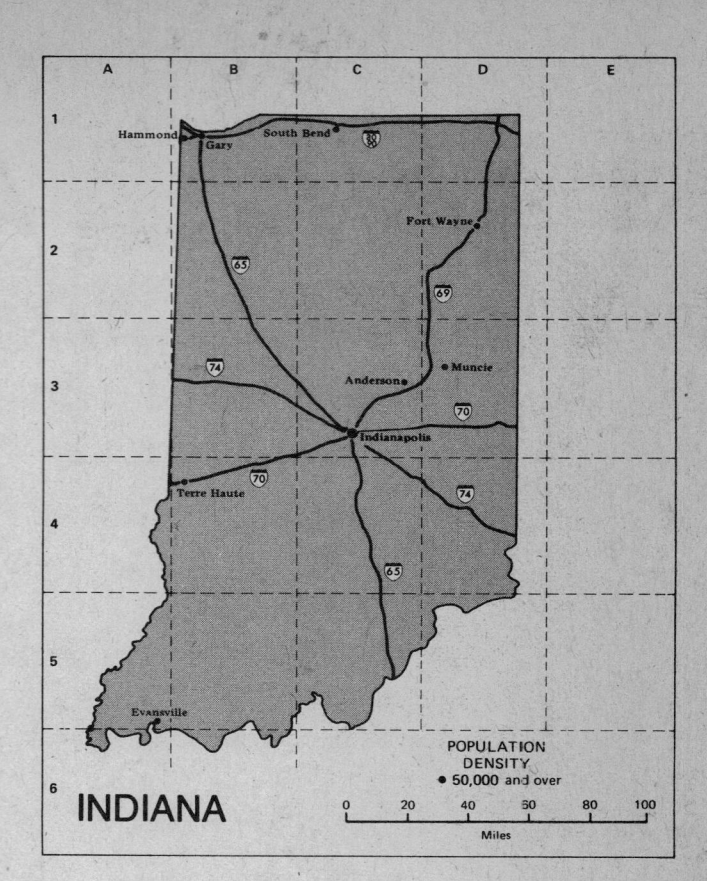

INDIANA

POPULATION DENSITY
- 50,000 and over

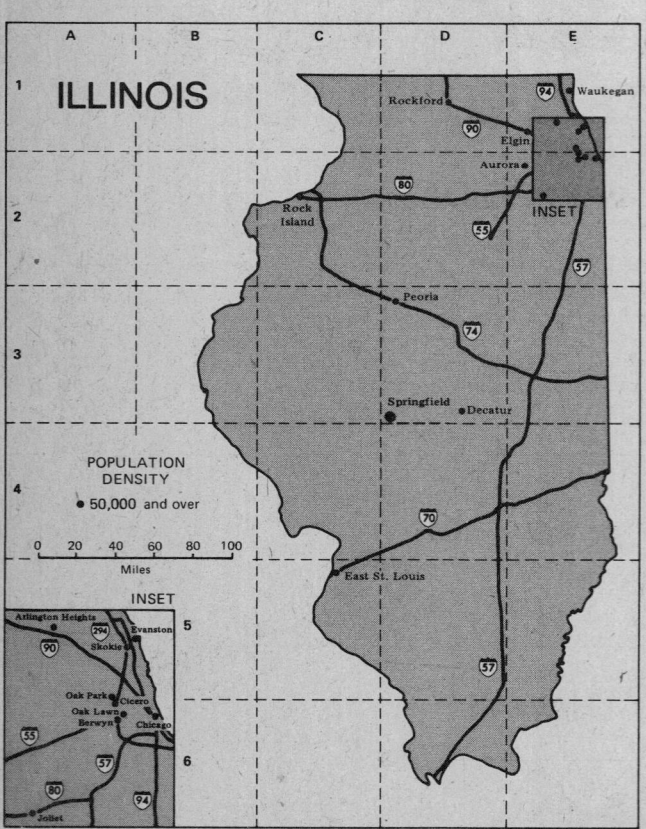

ILLINOIS

POPULATION DENSITY
- 50,000 and over

INSET

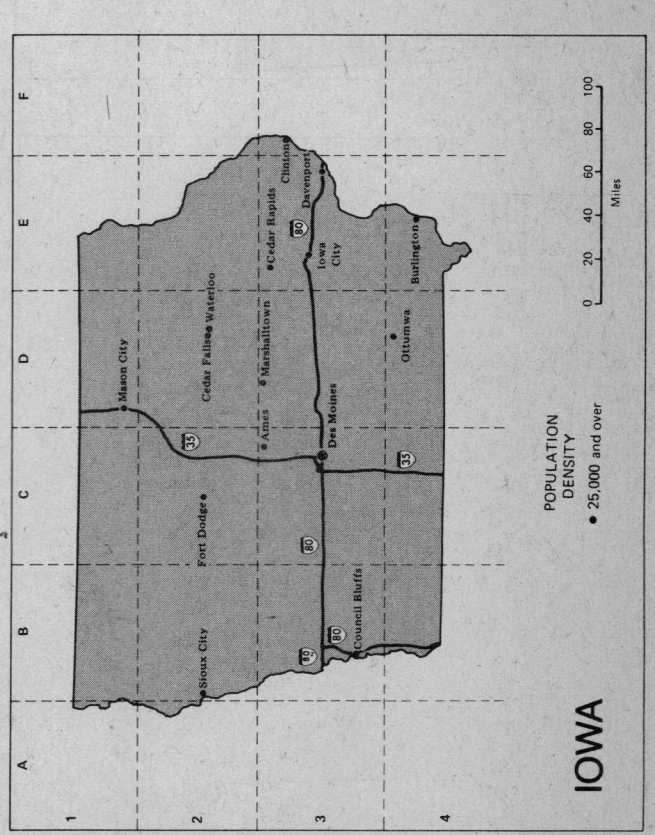

IOWA

POPULATION DENSITY
- 25,000 and over

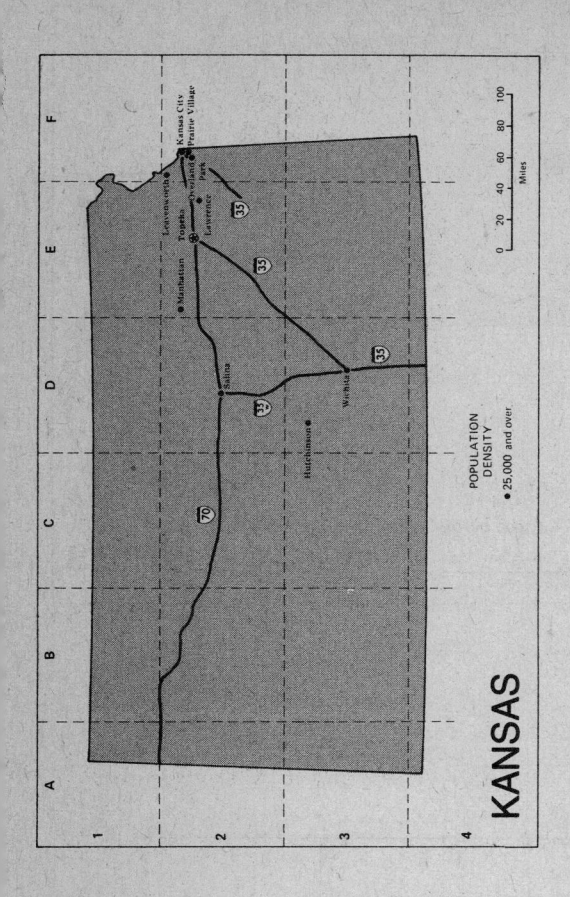

KANSAS

POPULATION DENSITY
● 25,000 and over

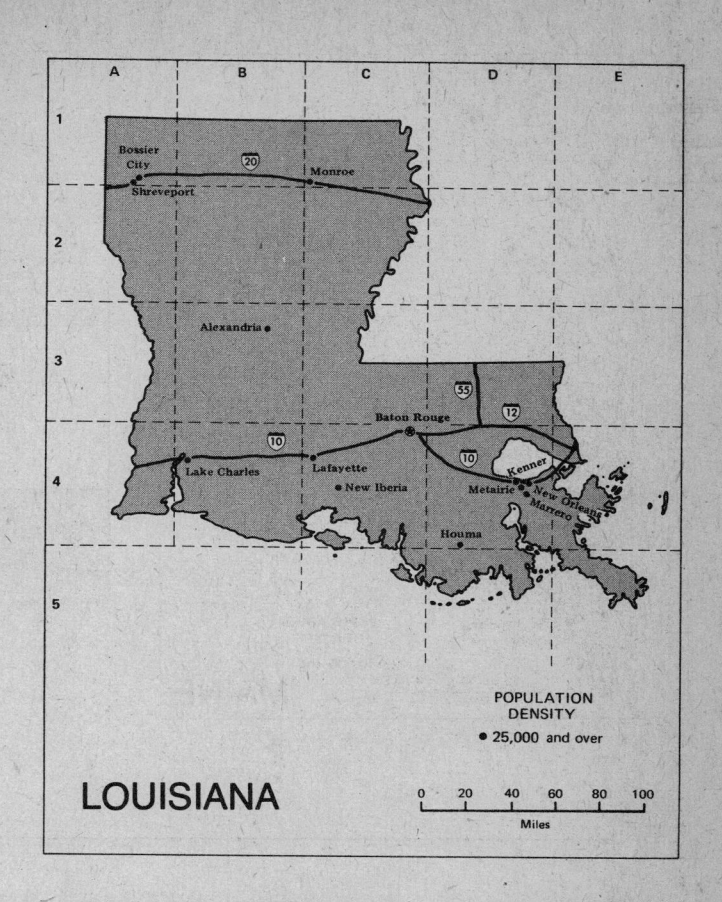

LOUISIANA

POPULATION DENSITY
● 25,000 and over

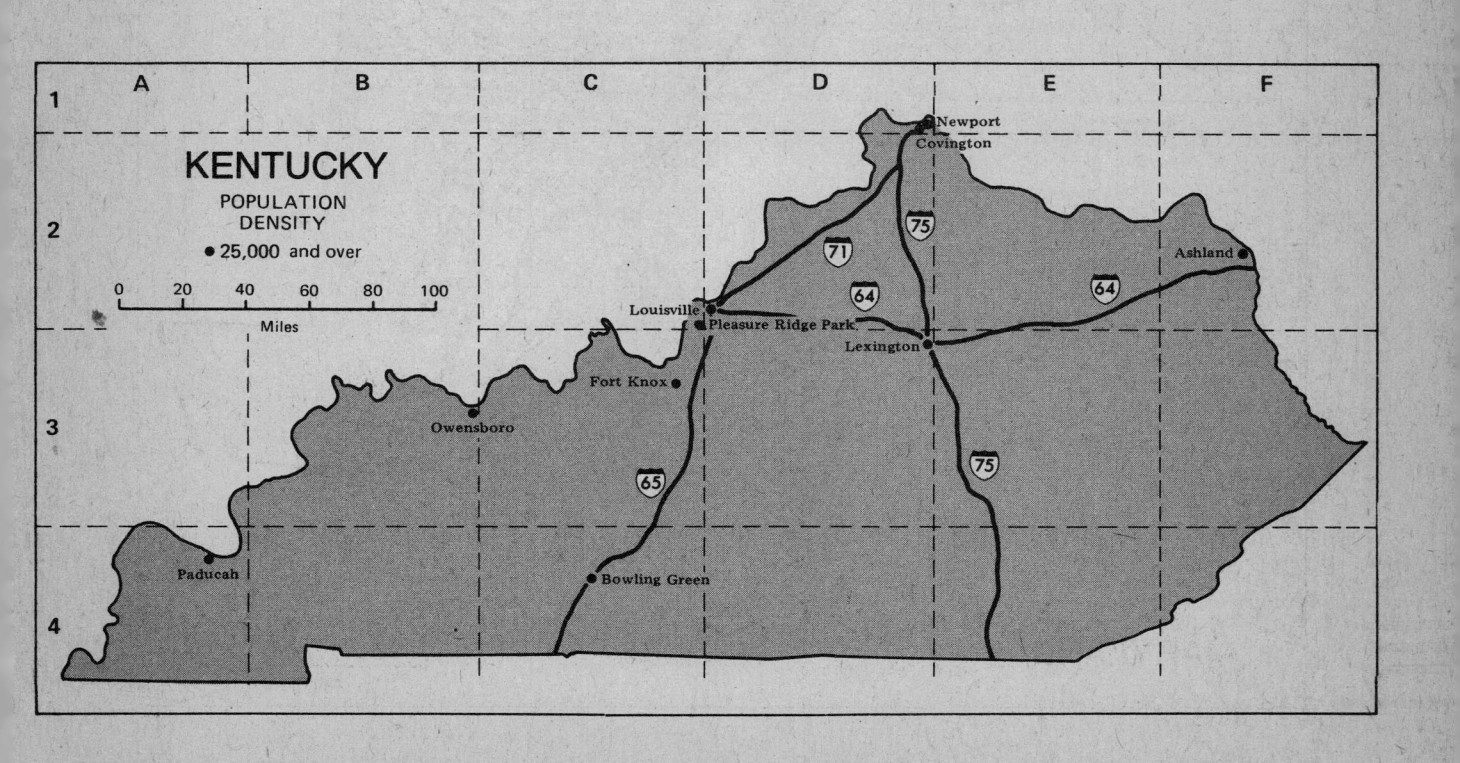

KENTUCKY

POPULATION DENSITY
● 25,000 and over

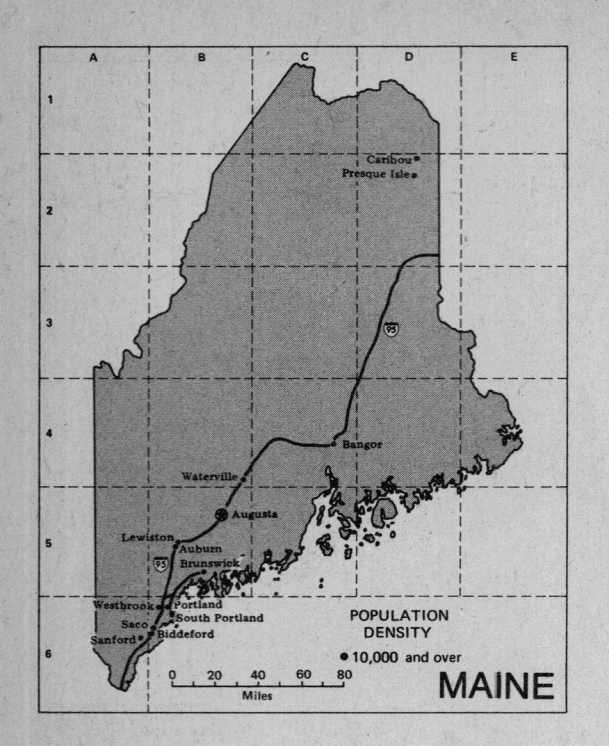

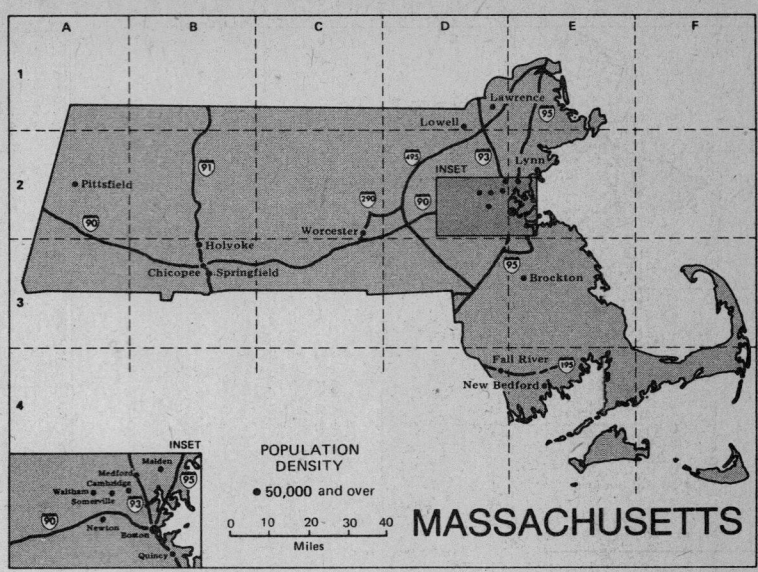

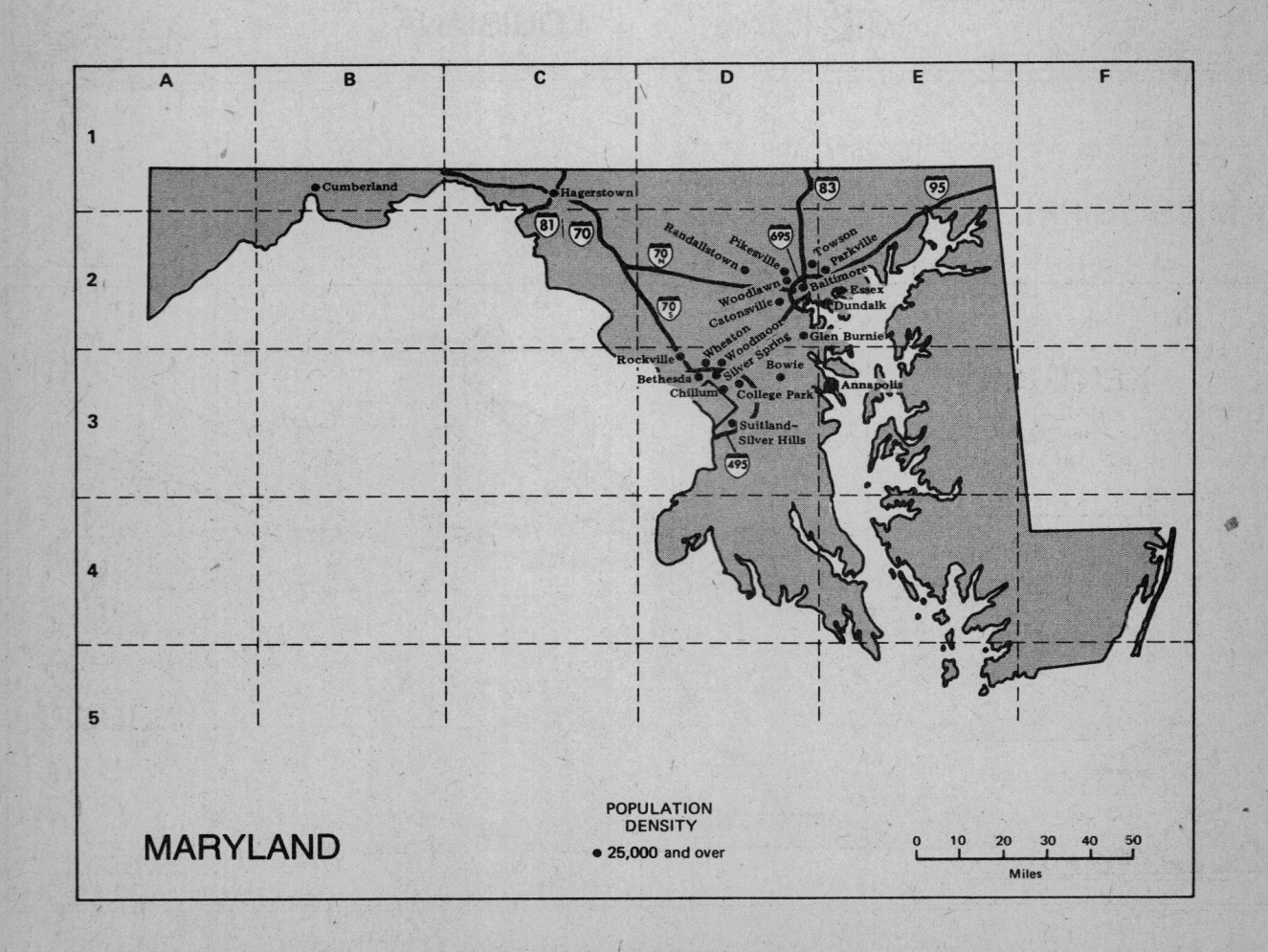

MAINE

Population Density: 10,000 and over

MASSACHUSETTS

Population Density: 50,000 and over

MARYLAND

Population Density: 25,000 and over

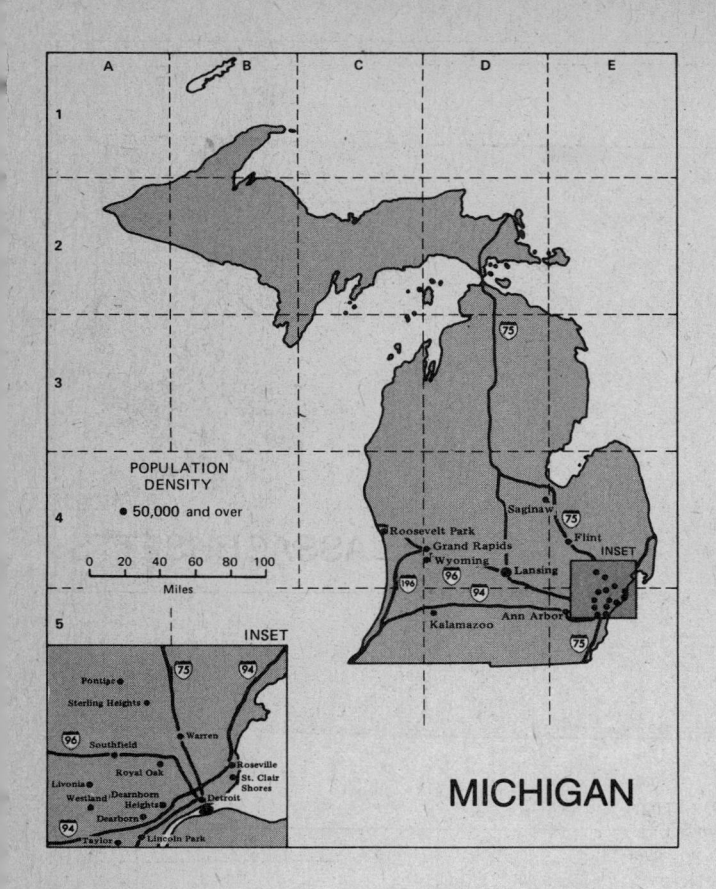

MICHIGAN

POPULATION DENSITY
• 50,000 and over

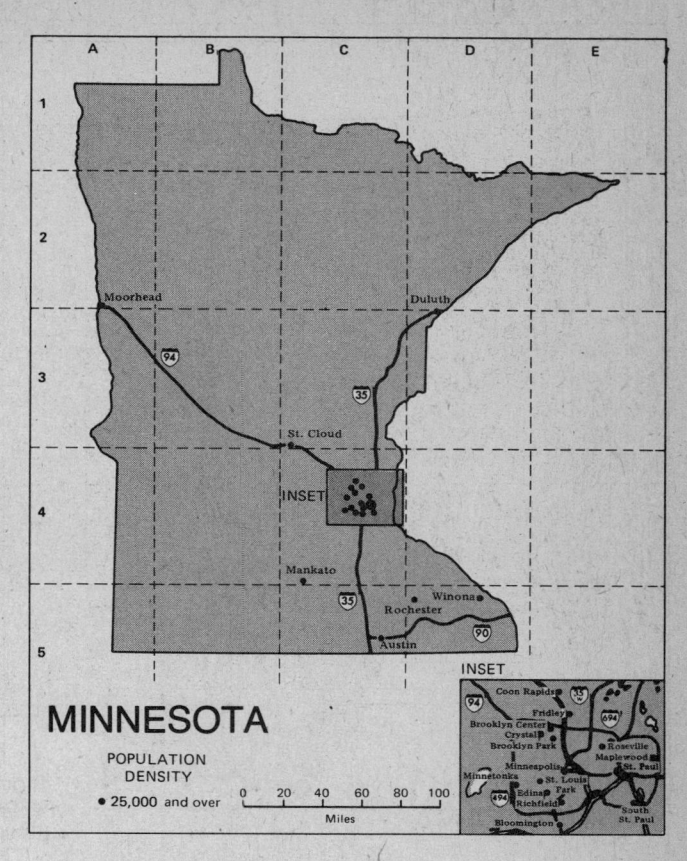

MINNESOTA

POPULATION DENSITY
• 25,000 and over

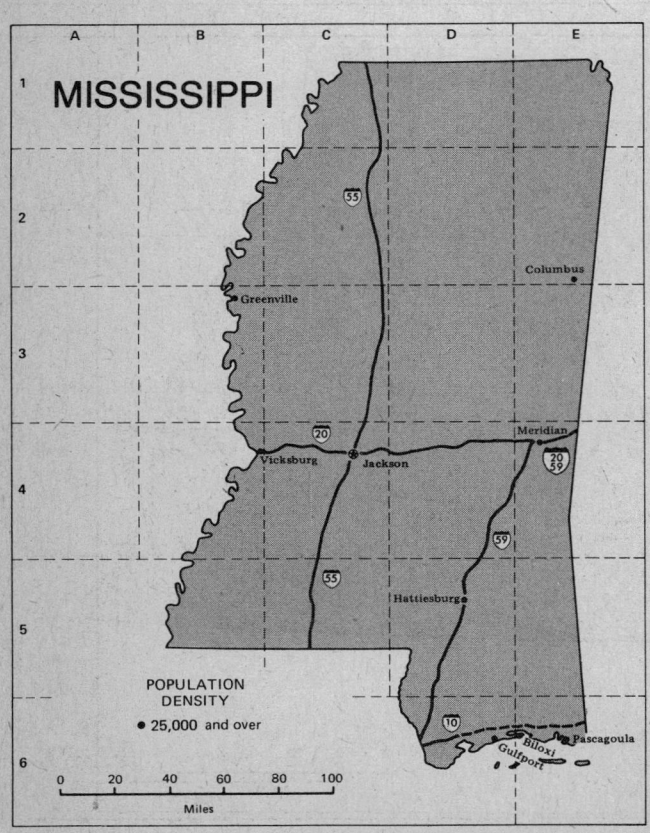

MISSISSIPPI

POPULATION DENSITY
• 25,000 and over

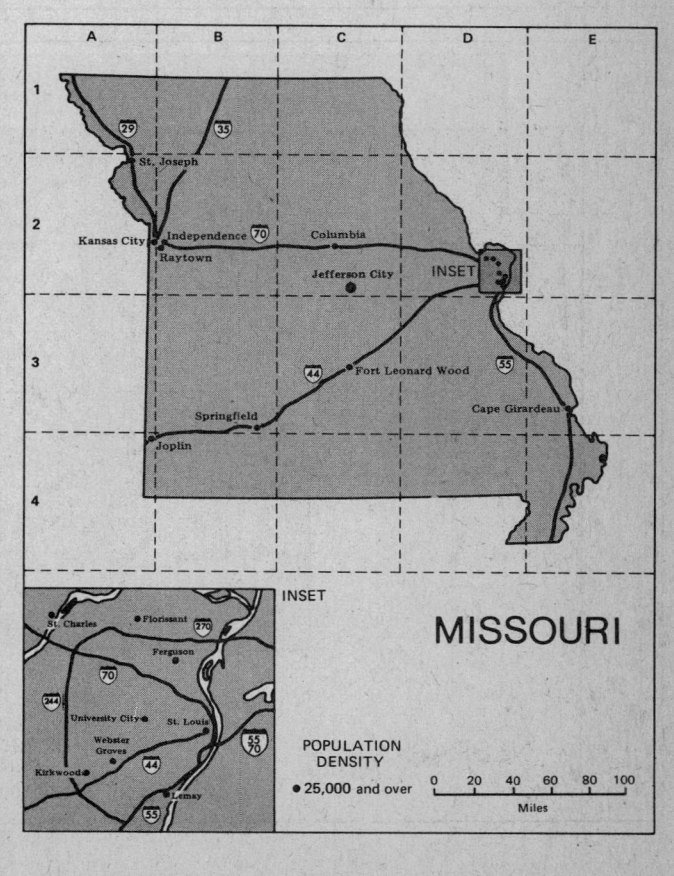

MISSOURI

POPULATION DENSITY
• 25,000 and over

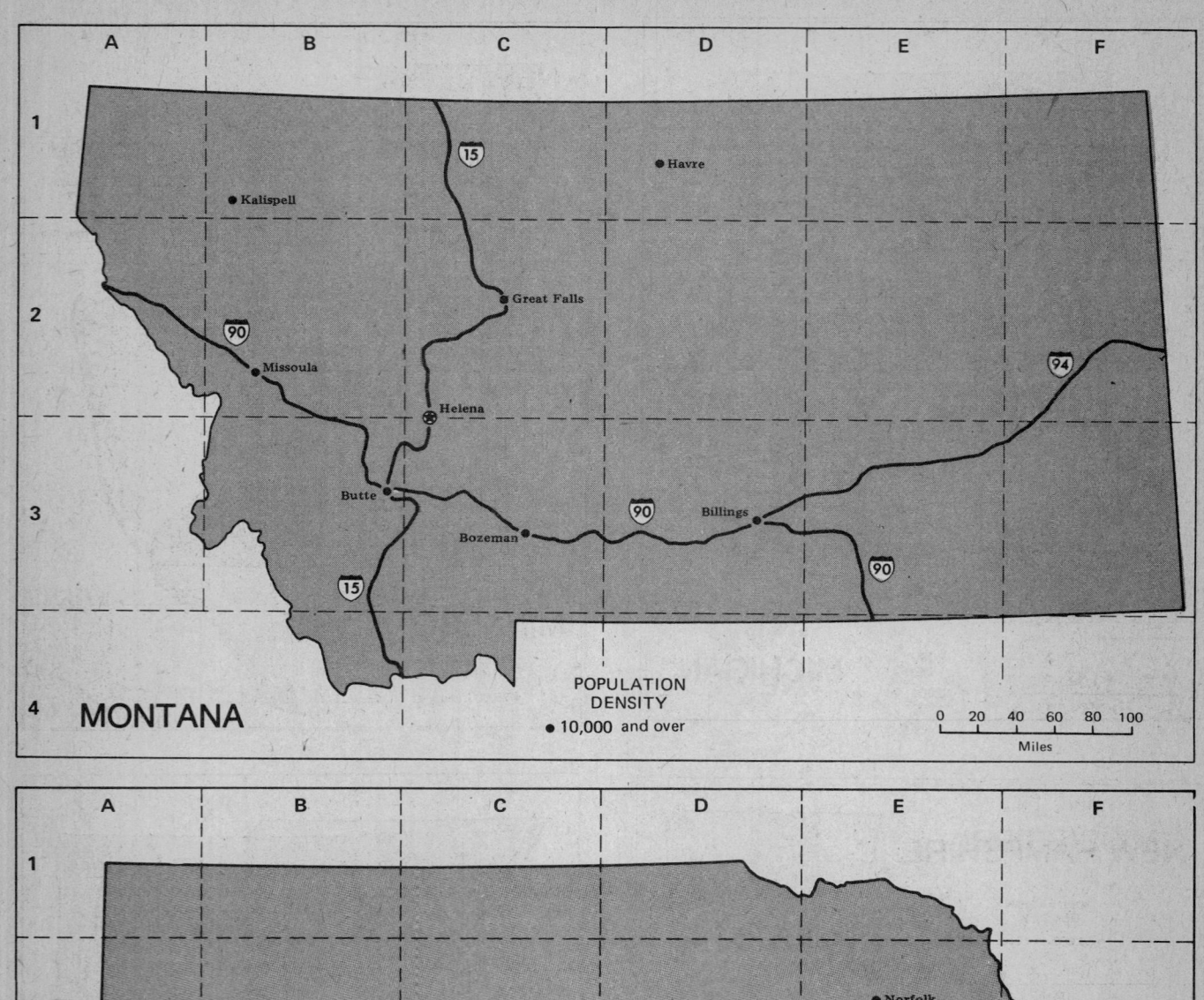

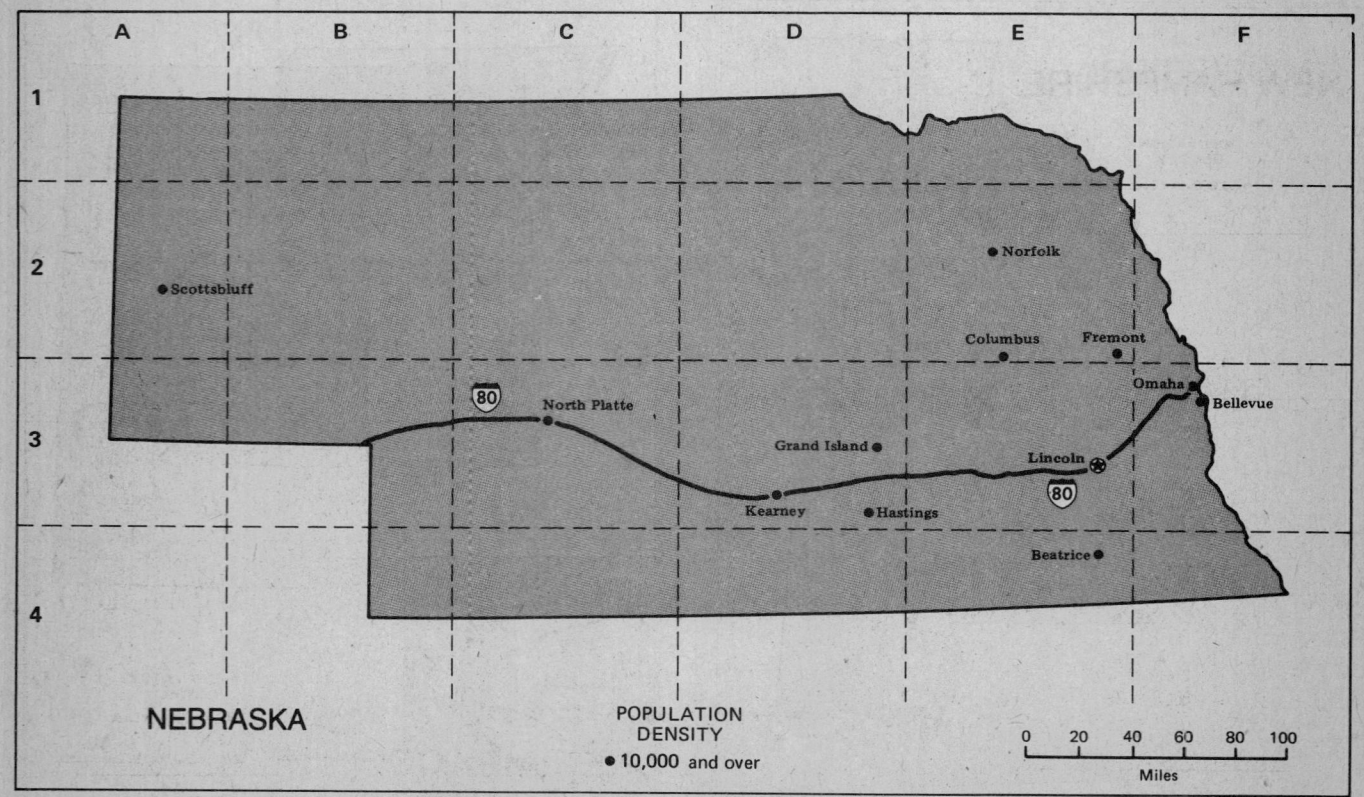

MONTANA

	A	B	C	D	E	F
1		• Kalispell	15	• Havre		
2		90 • Missoula	• Great Falls		94	
3		• Butte	⊛ Helena • Bozeman 90	• Billings 90		
4		15				

POPULATION DENSITY
• 10,000 and over

0 20 40 60 80 100 Miles

NEBRASKA

	A	B	C	D	E	F
1						
2	• Scottsbluff				• Norfolk • Columbus • Fremont	
3			80 • North Platte	• Grand Island • Kearney • Hastings	• Omaha ⊛ Lincoln 80 • Beatrice	• Bellevue
4						

POPULATION DENSITY
• 10,000 and over

0 20 40 60 80 100 Miles

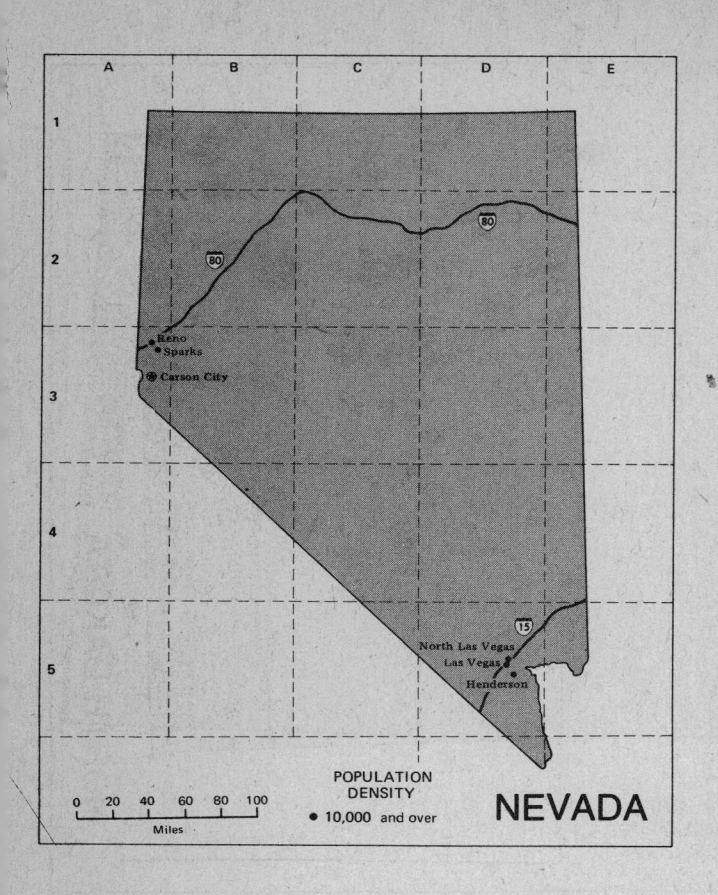

NEVADA

POPULATION DENSITY
● 10,000 and over

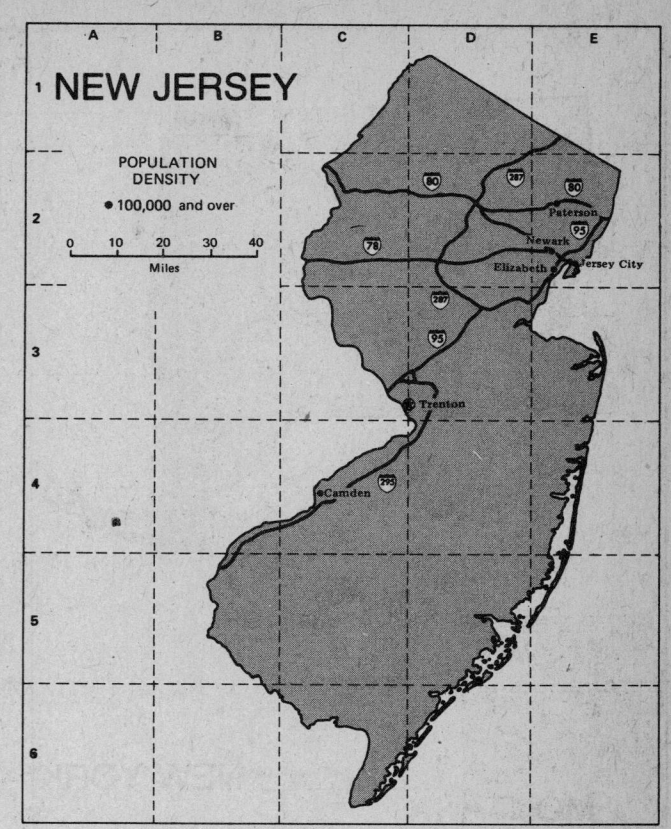

NEW JERSEY

POPULATION DENSITY
● 100,000 and over

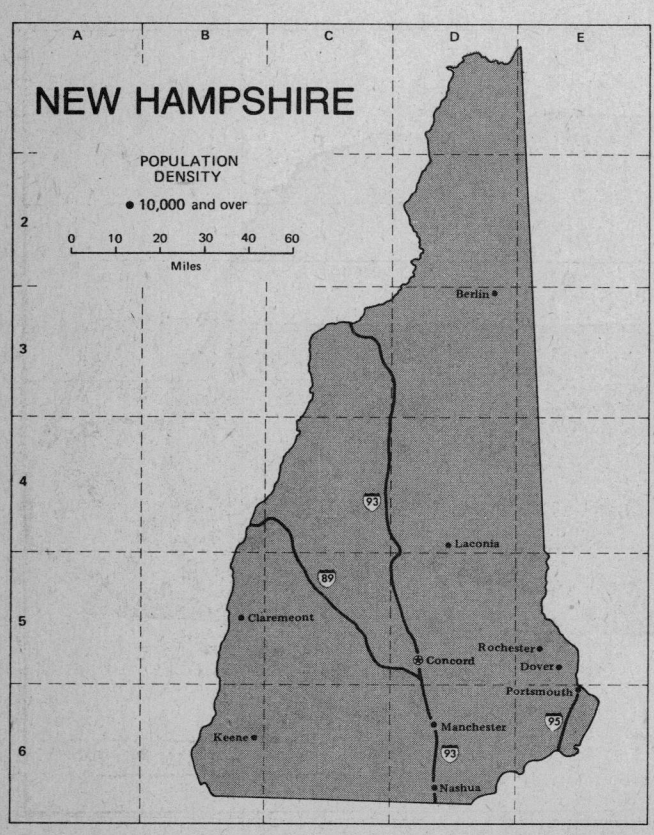

NEW HAMPSHIRE

POPULATION DENSITY
● 10,000 and over

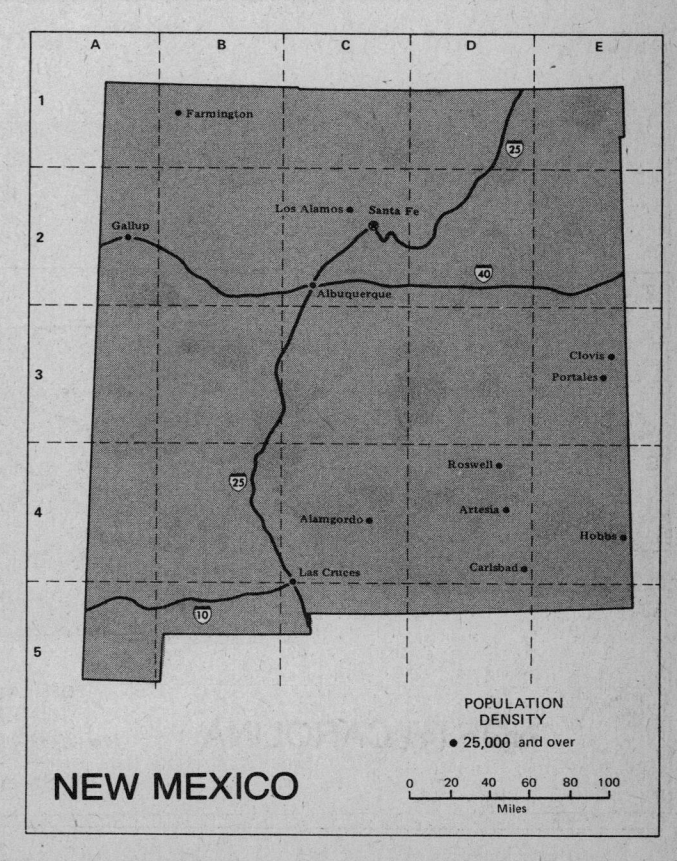

NEW MEXICO

POPULATION DENSITY
● 25,000 and over

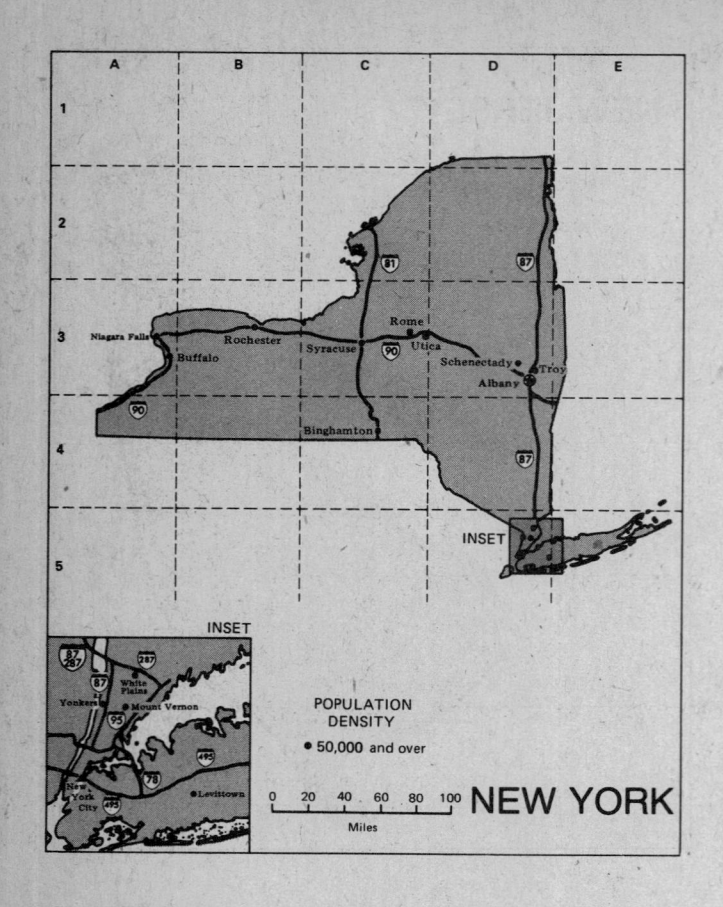

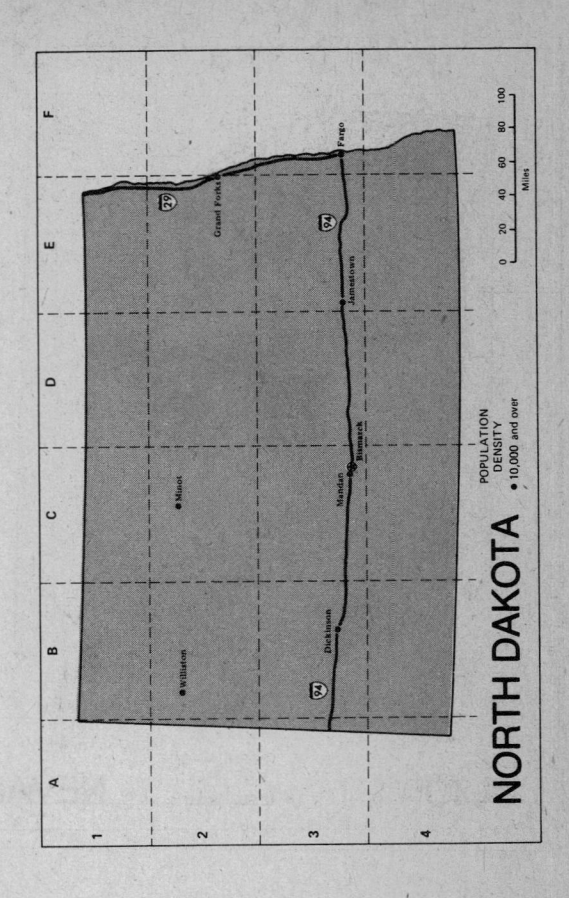

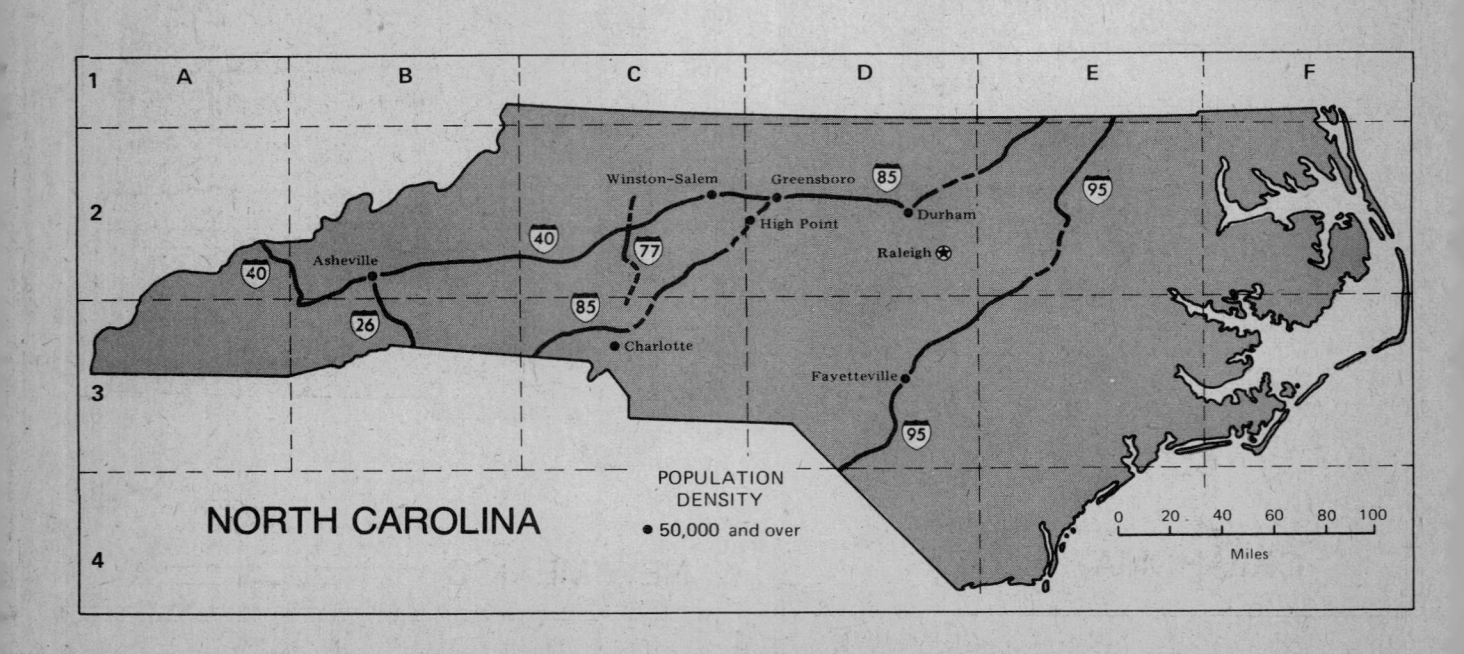

NEW YORK

POPULATION DENSITY
• 50,000 and over

NORTH DAKOTA

POPULATION DENSITY
• 10,000 and over

NORTH CAROLINA

POPULATION DENSITY
• 50,000 and over

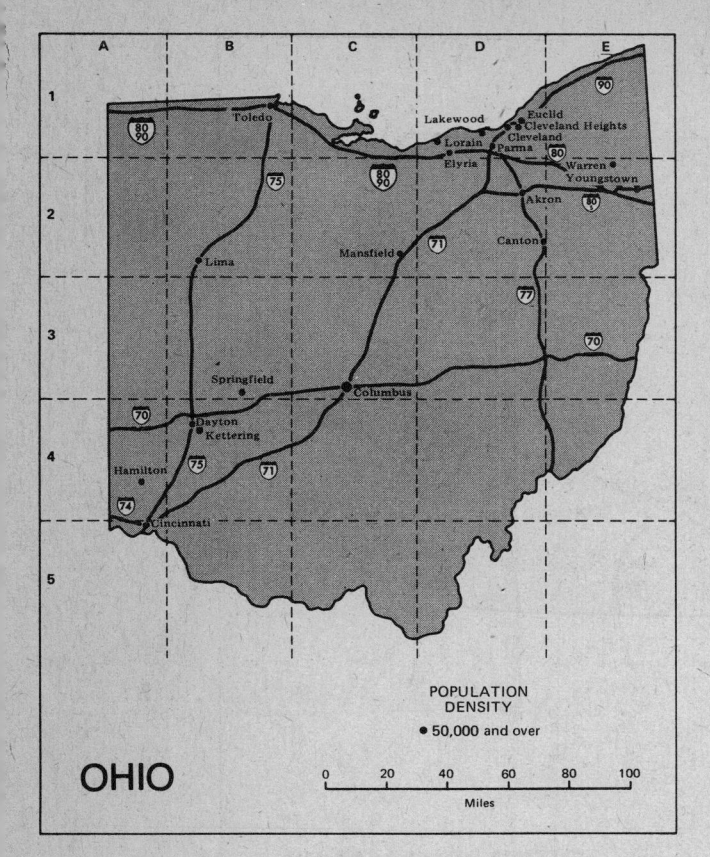

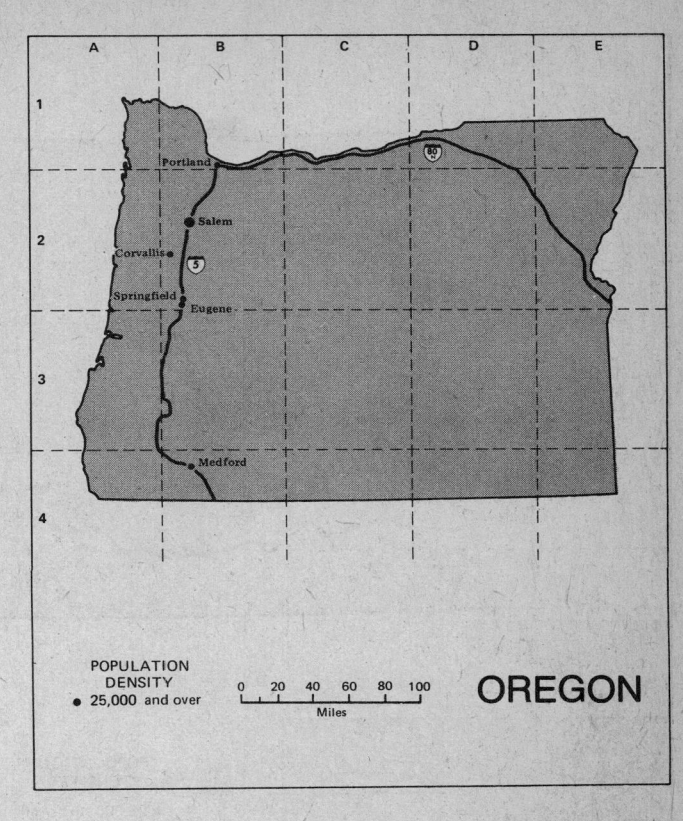

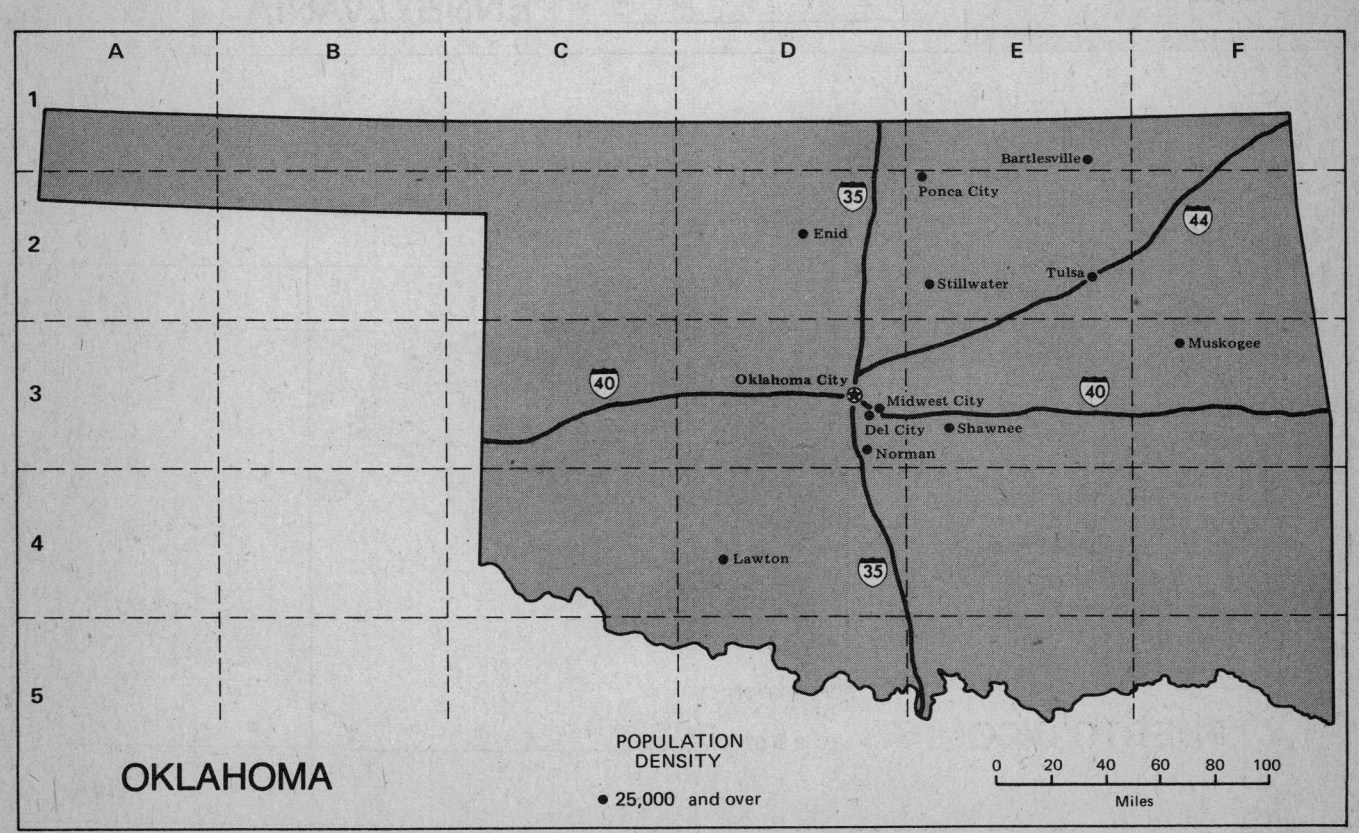

OHIO

POPULATION DENSITY
● 50,000 and over

OREGON

POPULATION DENSITY
● 25,000 and over

OKLAHOMA

POPULATION DENSITY
● 25,000 and over

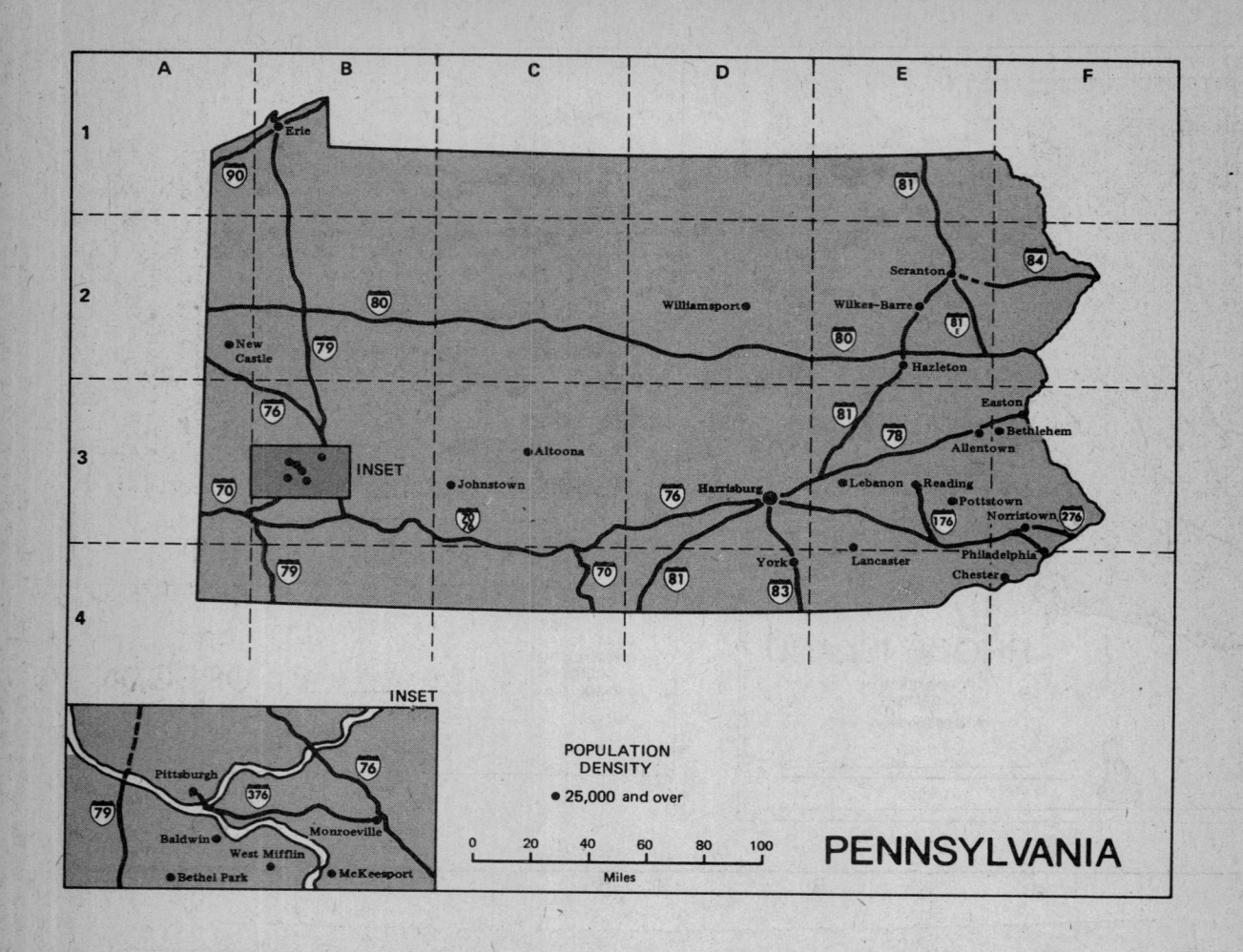

PENNSYLVANIA

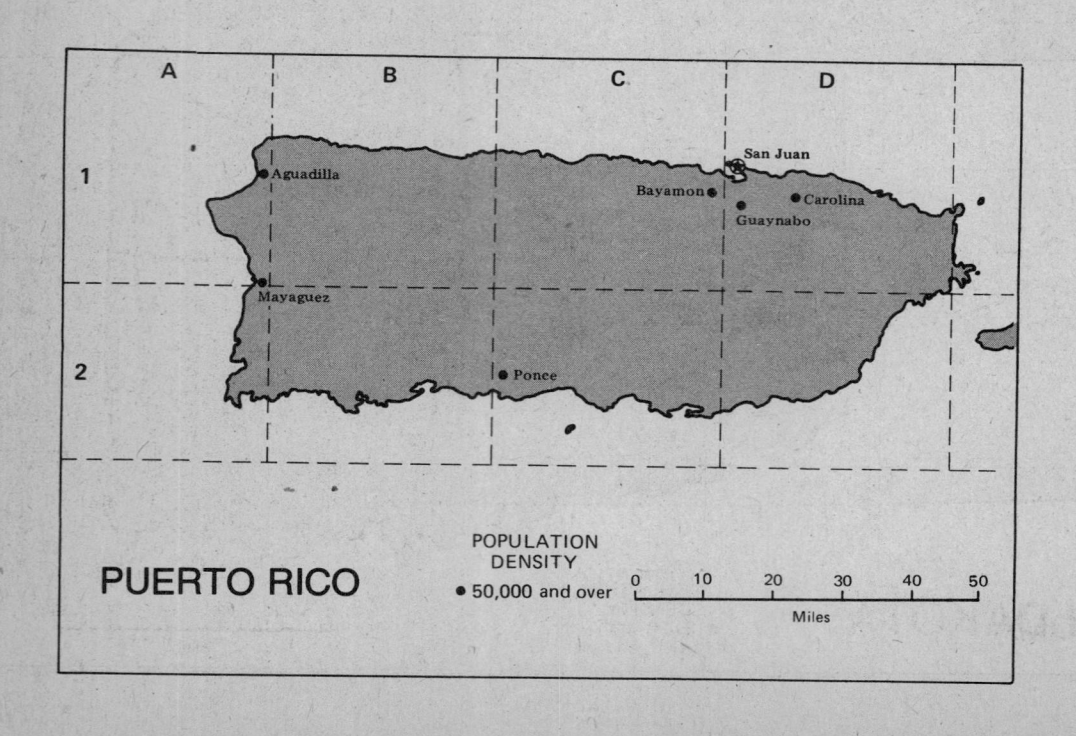

POPULATION DENSITY
- 25,000 and over

INSET

PUERTO RICO

POPULATION DENSITY
- 50,000 and over

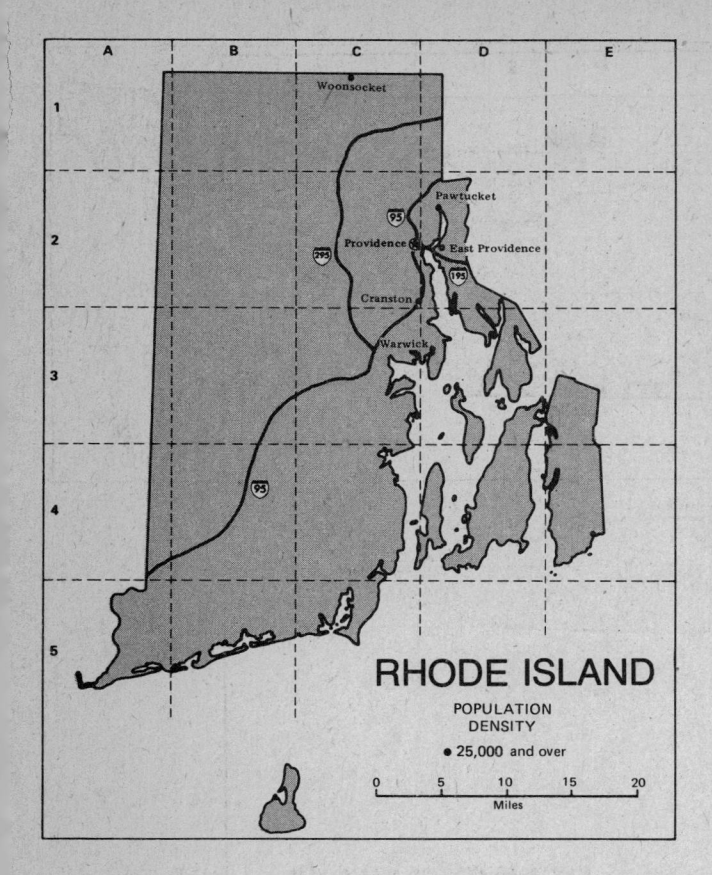

RHODE ISLAND

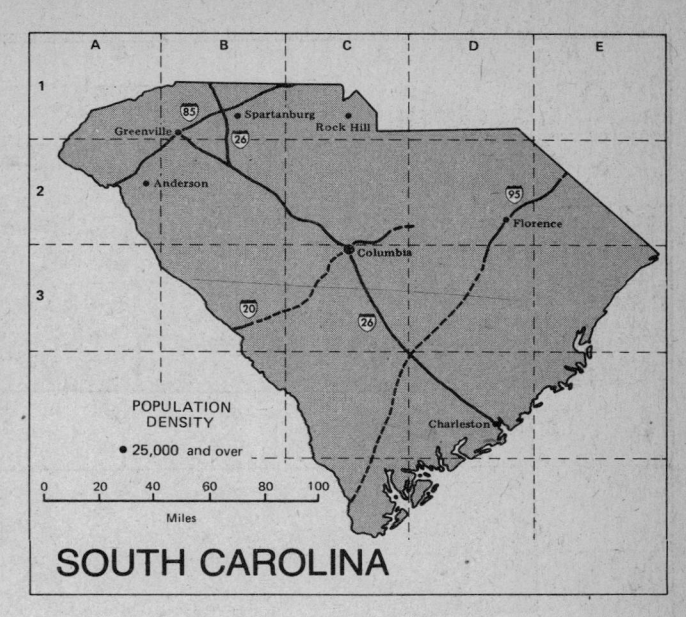

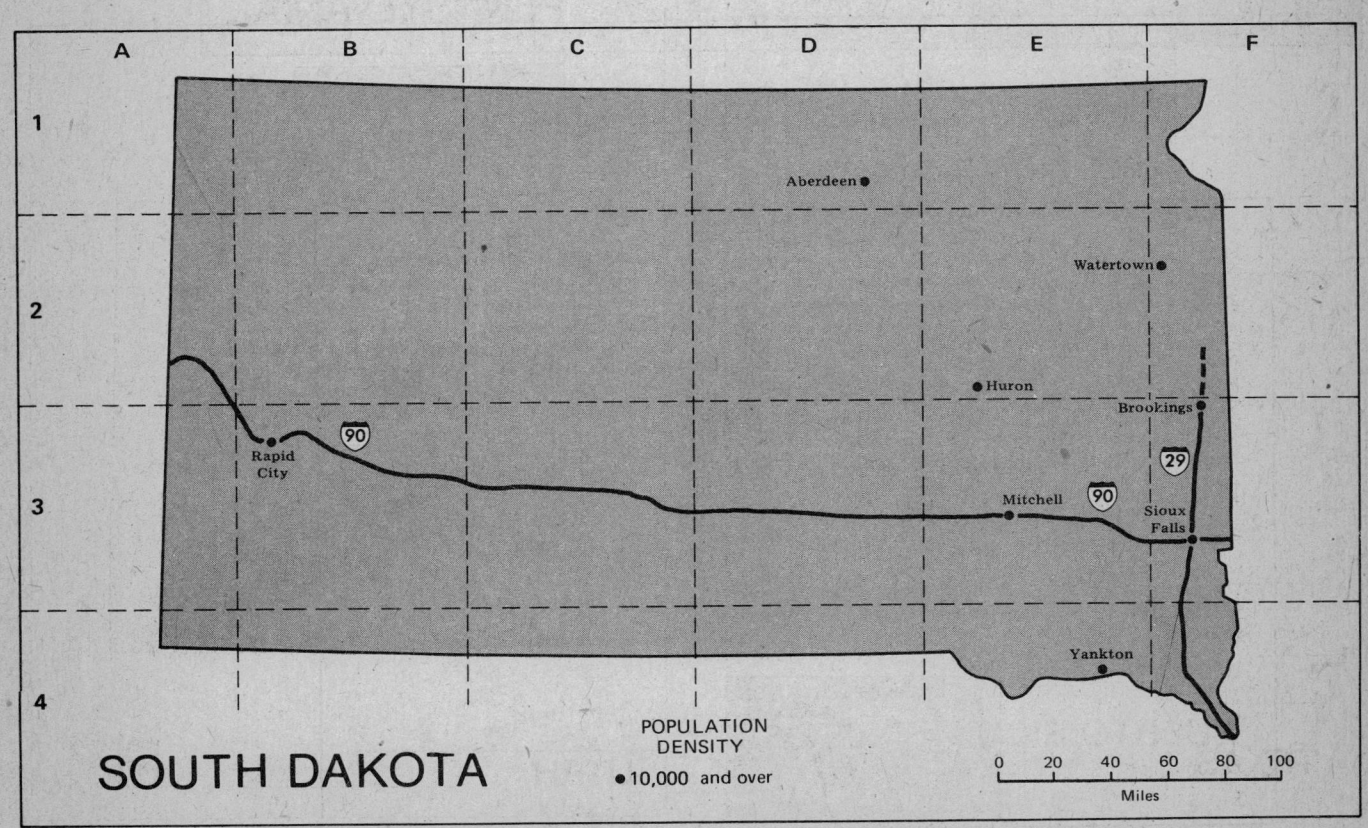

POPULATION DENSITY
- 25,000 and over

SOUTH CAROLINA

POPULATION DENSITY
- 25,000 and over

SOUTH DAKOTA

POPULATION DENSITY
- 10,000 and over

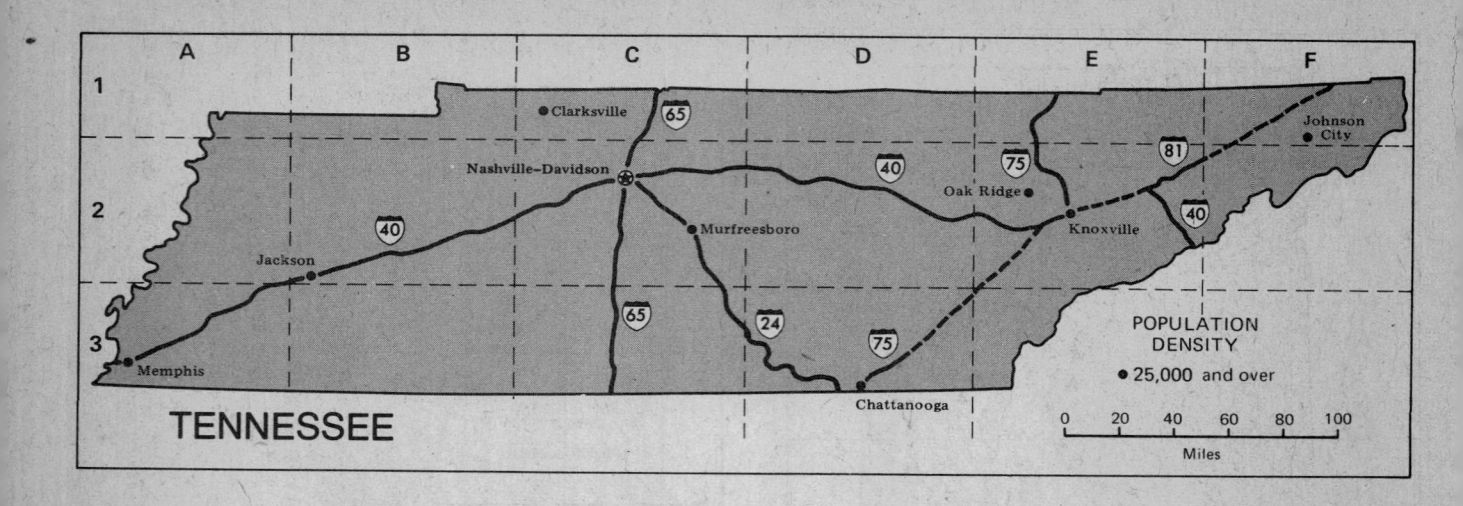

TENNESSEE

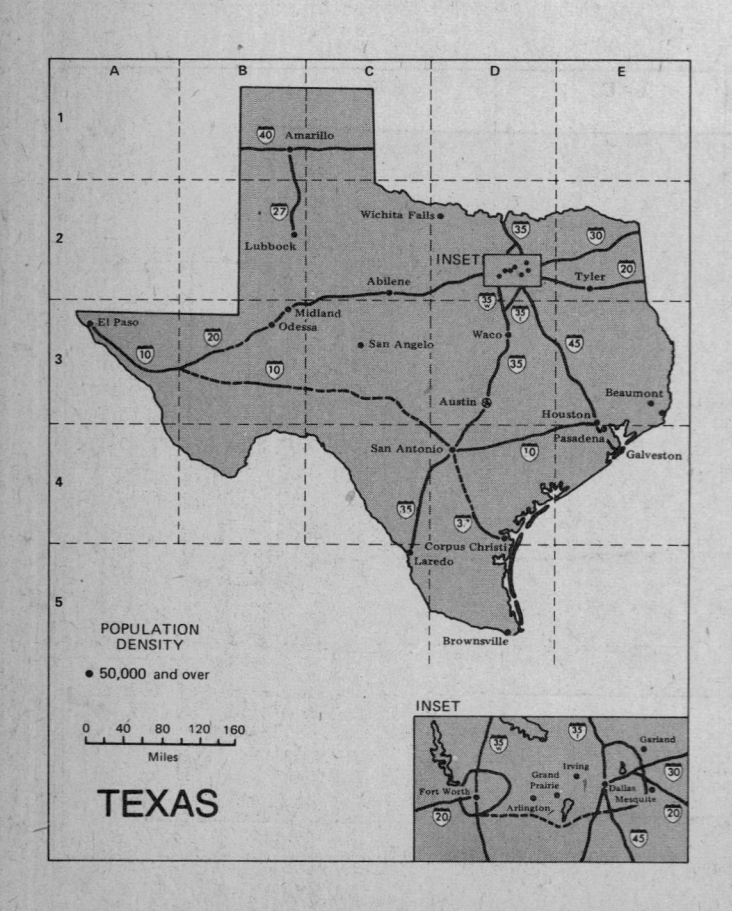

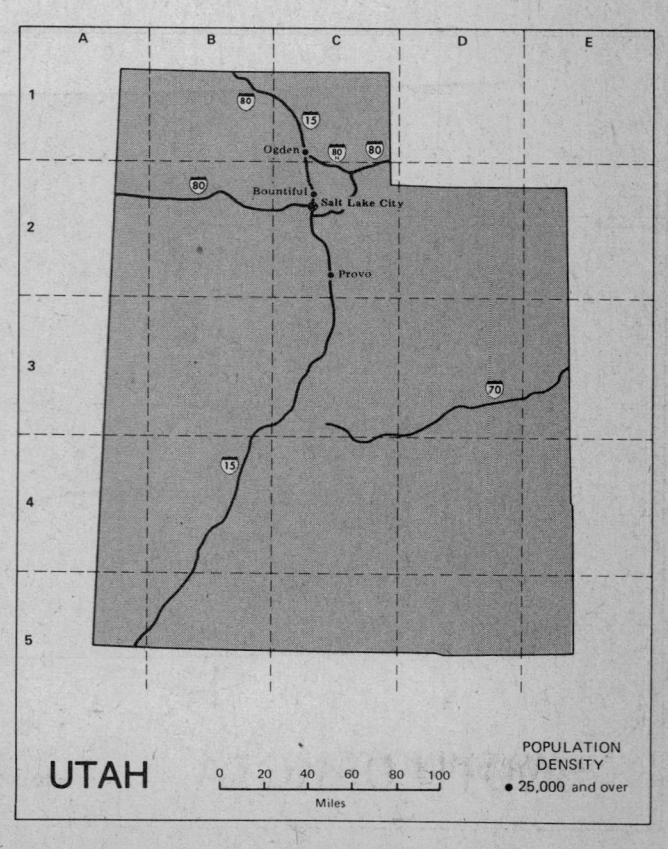

POPULATION DENSITY
● 25,000 and over

TEXAS

POPULATION DENSITY
● 50,000 and over

INSET

UTAH

POPULATION DENSITY
● 25,000 and over

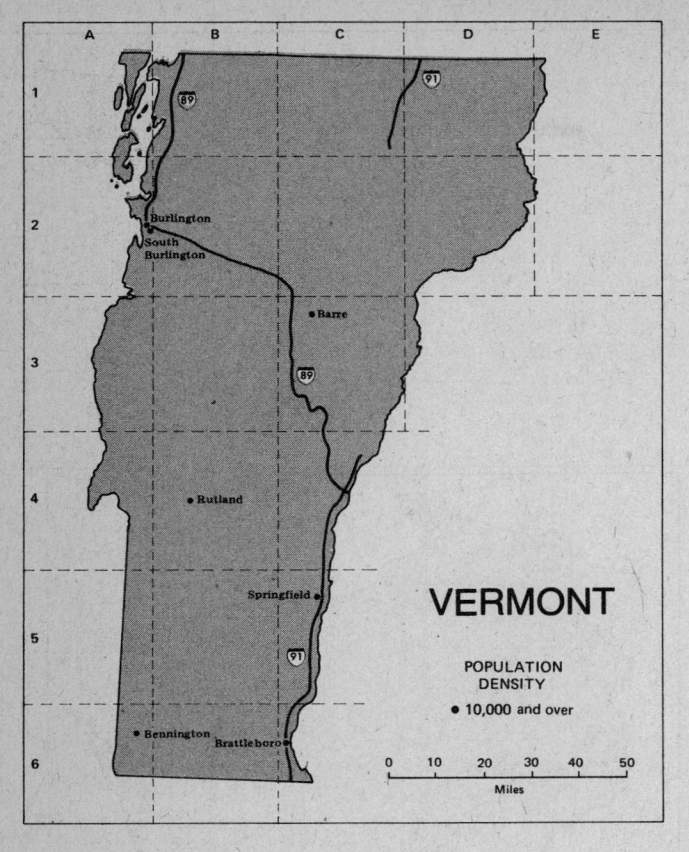

VERMONT

POPULATION DENSITY
• 10,000 and over

0 10 20 30 40 50
Miles

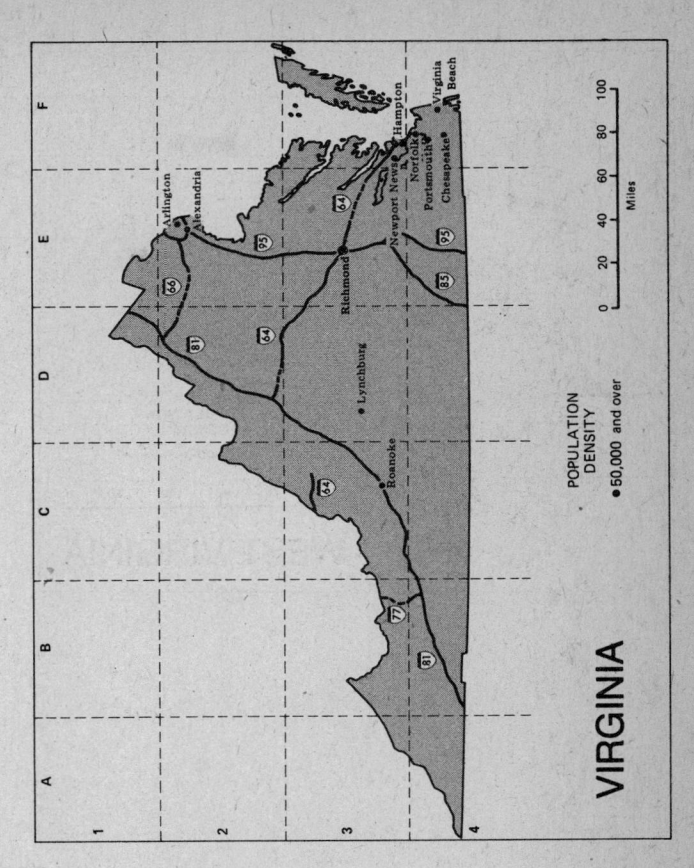

VIRGINIA

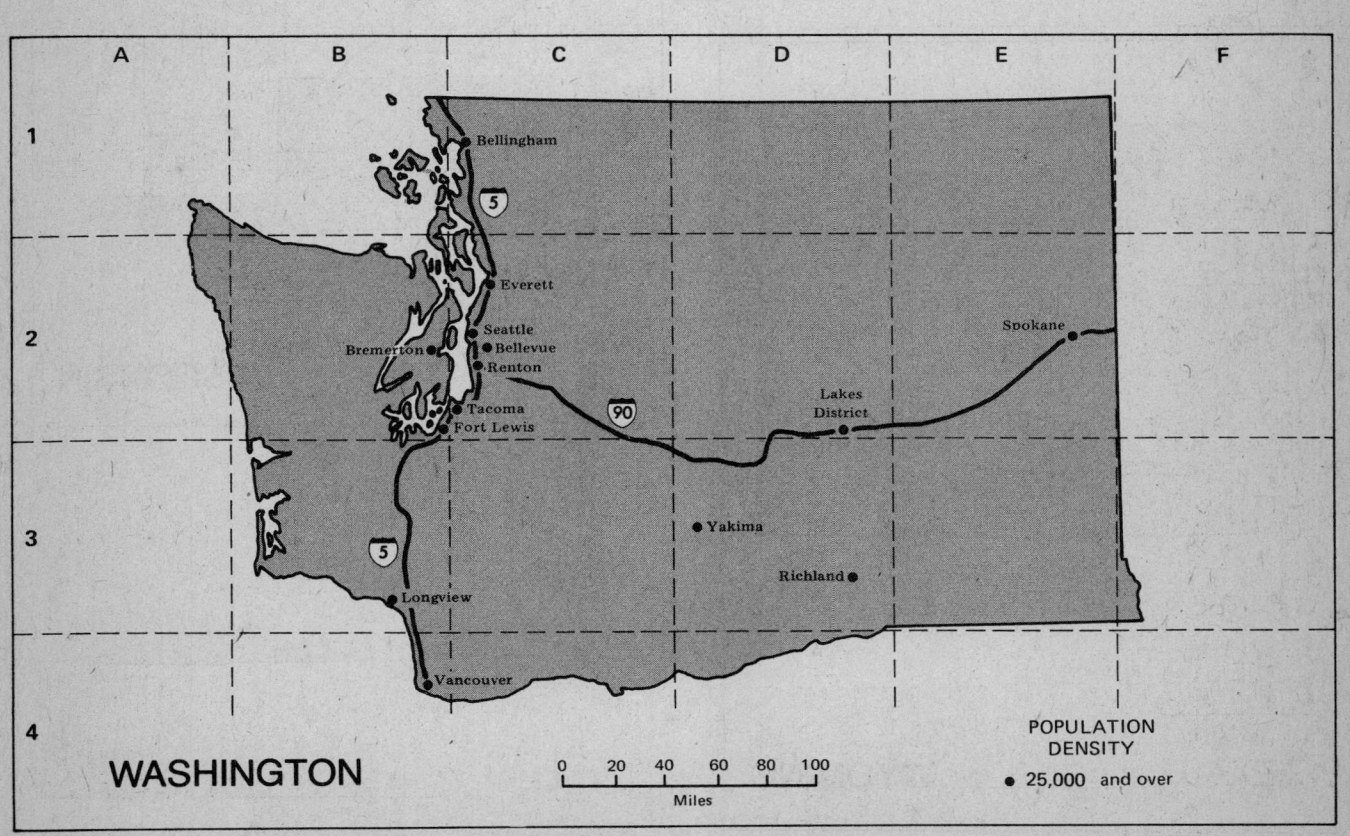

POPULATION DENSITY
• 50,000 and over

0 20 40 60 80 100
Miles

WASHINGTON

POPULATION DENSITY
• 25,000 and over

0 20 40 60 80 100
Miles

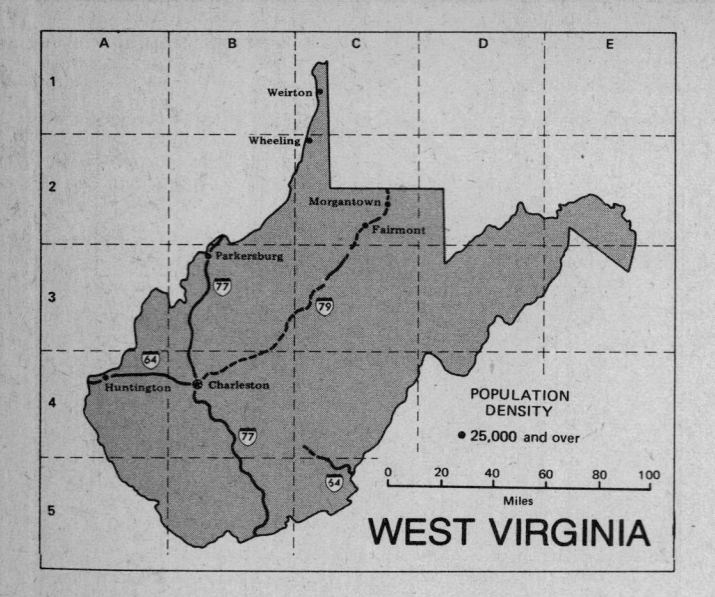

WEST VIRGINIA

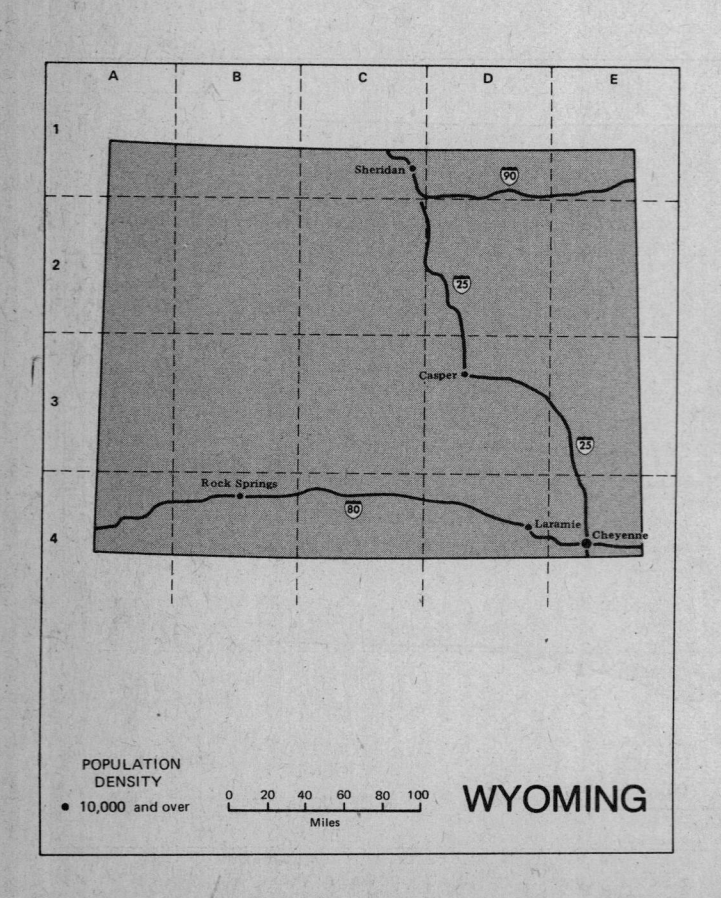

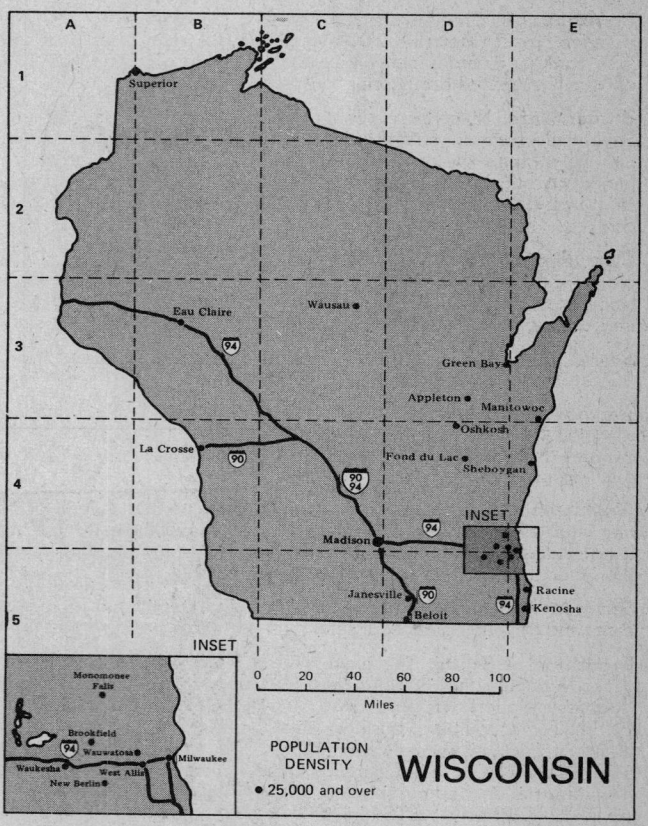

POPULATION DENSITY
- 25,000 and over

Cities: Weirton, Wheeling, Morgantown, Fairmont, Parkersburg, Huntington, Charleston

WISCONSIN

POPULATION DENSITY
- 25,000 and over

Cities: Superior, Eau Claire, Wausau, Green Bay, Appleton, Manitowoc, Oshkosh, La Crosse, Fond du Lac, Sheboygan, Madison, Janesville, Beloit, Racine, Kenosha

INSET: Menomonee Falls, Brookfield, Wauwatosa, Waukesha, West Allis, Milwaukee, New Berlin

WYOMING

POPULATION DENSITY
- 10,000 and over

Cities: Sheridan, Casper, Rock Springs, Laramie, Cheyenne

PROFILES OF AMERICAN COLLEGES
ALABAMA

ALABAMA AGRICULTURAL AND MECHANICAL UNIVERSITY
C-1

Normal, Alabama 35762 (205) 859-7468

F/T: 1829M, 1589W		Faculty:	266; IIA, −$
P/T: 24M, 23W		Ph.D.'s:	50%
Grad: 491M, 350W		S/F Ratio:	15 to 1
Year: sems, ss		Tuition:	$620 ($1180)
Appl: open		R and B:	$1380
2200 applied	2100 accepted		1159 enrolled
SAT: 300V 300M	ACT: 12		LESS COMPETITIVE

Alabama Agricultural and Mechanical University, established in 1875, is a state-supported coeducational institution. The university is organized into the School of Graduate Studies and 6 undergraduate schools: Agricultural Environmental Science and Home Economics, Arts and Sciences, Business, Education, Library Media, and Technology. The library houses 348,000 volumes and 51,000 microfilm items.

Environment: The university is located in a suburban area 2 miles from the city of Huntsville, 100 miles north of Birmingham. The 800-acre campus includes many buildings of modern architecture. The university provides dormitories for resident students.

Student Life: Ninety-six percent of the students come from Alabama. Seventy-five percent of the freshmen attended public schools. About half the students live on campus. Almost all students are members of minority groups; 92% are black. College-sponsored housing is single-sex, and there are visiting privileges. Students may keep cars on campus.

Organizations: There are 10 fraternities and 6 sororities, to which 11% of the men and 9% of the women belong. Student activities include a student government association, residence hall organizations, music and drama groups, and departmental and religious organizations.

Sports: The university provides competition in 12 intercollegiate and 12 intramural sports for both sexes.

Handicapped: Special facilities available to the handicapped include wheelchair ramps, parking areas, and elevators. About 50% of the campus is accessible to these students. Four counselors and 4 assistants are available to handicapped students.

Graduates: Ten percent of the freshmen drop out by the end of the first year. Seventy percent remain to graduate. Of the 20% of the graduates who pursue advanced degrees, 2% enter medical school, 2% enter dental school, and 3% enter law school.

Services: Placement assistance, tutoring, remedial instruction, health care, and psychological counseling are available free to students.

Programs of Study: The university confers the B.A. and B.S. degrees. Associate and master's degrees also are available. Bachelor's degrees are offered in the following subjects: AREA STUDIES (urban), BUSINESS (accounting, business administration, business education, computer science, finance, management, marketing, office administration), EDUCATION (adult, early childhood, elementary, health/physical, industrial, secondary, special), ENGLISH (English, literature), FINE AND PERFORMING ARTS (art, art education, music, radio/TV, theater/dramatics), HEALTH SCIENCES (medical technology, nursing, speech therapy), LANGUAGES (French, German, Spanish), MATH AND SCIENCES (biology, botany, chemistry, earth science, mathematics, natural sciences, physical sciences, physics, zoology), PRE-PROFESSIONAL (agriculture, dentistry, engineering, home economics, law, library science, medicine, social work, veterinary), SOCIAL SCIENCES (economics, government/political science, history, psychology, social sciences, sociology).

Required: All students must take 52 hours of general studies.

Special: The university participates in the Thirteen-College Curriculum Revision Program, an experimental program that involves students in the development of unorthodox approaches to general-education subjects. The university also awards certificates in various technical fields, particularly in the building trades.

Honors: Twenty-nine honor societies maintain chapters on campus. Departmental honors work is available in chemistry, physics and mathematics, and engineering.

Admissions: Ninety-five percent of the students who applied for admission to the 1981–82 freshman class were accepted. Of those who enrolled, 20% ranked in the upper fifth of their high school class and 80% ranked in the upper two-fifths. The university accepts all Alabama academic high school graduates with a C average in English, mathematics, science, biology, history, and social sciences. Applicants must rank in the top half of their class.

Procedure: Either the SAT or ACT is required. Freshmen are admitted to all terms. Application deadlines are open; the rolling admissions plan is used. A $5 room reservation fee, if applicable, must be submitted with the application in addition to the regular application fee of $10.

Special: Early decision and deferred admissions plans are offered. CLEP general and subject exams are accepted. A student may also earn credit through AP.

Transfer: For fall 1981, 321 transfer students applied, 301 were accepted, and 264 enrolled. Applicants must have a C average. They must complete one year and 34 semester hours on campus; the number of credits required for a degree varies with the program. Only grades of C or better transfer. Application deadlines are open.

Visiting: There are regularly scheduled orientations for prospective students. Guides are available for informal visits. Visitors may sit in on classes. To arrange such visits, contact the University Relations Office or the Office of Admissions.

Financial Aid: About 80% of the students receive financial aid in the form of scholarships, loans, work-study, or other employment. Thirteen percent of the students work part-time on campus. Aid application deadlines are April 1 (fall) and November 15 (spring). The FAF and FFS are required.

Foreign Students: About 450 students, or 10% of the university's student body, are from foreign countries. The university provides special counseling and organizations for these students.

Admissions: Foreign applicants must score 500 or better on the TOEFL. They also are required to take the ACT or SAT.

Procedure: Application deadlines for foreign students are June 1 (fall), October 1 (spring), and March 1 (summer). Students must present proof of good health and of adequate funds for 4 years of study. They must carry health insurance during the first year at the university.

Admissions Contact: A. G. Adams, Director of Admissions.

ALABAMA STATE UNIVERSITY
C-4

Montgomery, Alabama 36195 (205) 832-6072

F/T: 1450M, 1969W		Faculty:	237; IIA, −$
P/T: 254M, 361W		Ph.D.'s:	44%
Grad: 115M, 241W		S/F Ratio:	20 to 1
Year: qtrs		Tuition:	$600 ($1200)
Appl: Sept. 1		R and B:	$1200
1465 applied	1106 accepted		834 enrolled
ACT: 12			LESS COMPETITIVE

Alabama State University, founded in 1874, is a publicly controlled liberal arts and teacher education institution with a branch center in Mobile. The library contains 247,000 volumes and 10,000 microfilm items.

Environment: The university is located on an 80-acre campus in the city of Montgomery, near the State Capitol. The more than 30 campus buildings include a Learning Center. Dormitories accommodate over 1500 men and women.

Student Life: Eighty-eight percent of the students come from Alabama. About 62% commute. Almost all students are black.

Organizations: Five percent of the men and 4% of the women belong to fraternities or sororities. Extracurricular activities include student publications, campus government, special-interest clubs, service organizations, and a variety of social events.

Sports: About 12 intercollegiate and intramural sports are available.

Graduates: The freshman dropout rate is about 30%, and 55% remain to graduate. About 8% of the graduates go on to graduate study

Programs of Study: The university offers the B.A., B.S., and B.F.A. degrees. Masters degrees also are offered. Bachelor's degrees are offered in the following subjects: BUSINESS (accounting, business education, computer science, finance, management, marketing), EDUCATION (early childhood, elementary, health/physical, secondary), ENGLISH (English, journalism), FINE AND PERFORMING ARTS (art, art education, music, music education, radio/TV, studio art), HEALTH SCIENCES (medical technology), LANGUAGES (Spanish), MATH

1

2 ALABAMA

AND SCIENCES (biology, chemistry, mathematics, physics), PRE-PROFESSIONAL (child care, community services, recreation), SOCIAL SCIENCES (economics, government/political science, history, psychology, sociology).

Required: All students are required to take courses in English, mathematics, natural sciences, and social sciences.

Special: A program leading to certification in special education is offered. The university offers the B.G.S. degree.

Admissions: About 75% of those who applied were accepted for the 1981–82 freshman class. Applicants must be high school graduates and should have completed an acceptable program of high school studies.

Procedure: The SAT or ACT is required. The application deadlines are September 1 for the fall term, and 6 weeks before the beginning of the spring term. Admissions are on a rolling basis.

Special: CLEP credit is granted.

Transfer: A 2.0 GPA is required. Students must spend at least 1 year, including the final quarter, in residence to receive a degree.

Visiting: Guides are available for informal visits to the university. Visitors may sit in on classes. The best time to visit is Monday through Friday from 9 A.M. to 4 P.M. The admissions information and recruitment officer handles arrangements.

Financial Aid: Scholarships, loans, and grants based on need are all available. There is CWS in all departments, and about 25% of the students earn part of their expense money working part-time. About 90% of the students receive some form of aid. The deadline for aid applications is June 1. The FAF is required.

Admissions Contact: Henry E. Ford, Assistant Director of Admissions.

AUBURN UNIVERSITY

Auburn University was founded in 1856 as the East Alabama Male College by the Alabama Conference of the Methodist Episcopal Church (South). Donated to the state in 1872 as a land-grant state college, it became the Alabama Polytechnic Institute. Now a state-supported university, its name became Auburn University in 1960. The University consists of 2 campuses: one in Auburn and another in Montgomery. Profiles of each campus follow.

AUBURN UNIVERSITY D-3
Auburn, Alabama 36849 (205) 826-4000

F/T: 9650M, 6650W
P/T: 725M, 400W
Grad: 2000M&W
Year: qtrs, ss
Appl: see profile
6146 applied
SAT: 480V, 545M

Faculty: 1000; I, —$
Ph.D.'s: 40%
S/F Ratio: 18 to 1
Tuition: $990 ($2280)
R and B: $1635
5073 accepted   3133 enrolled
ACT: 23   COMPETITIVE+

Auburn University, a state-supported institution founded in 1856, was first known as East Alabama Male College and later as the Agricultural and Mechanical University of Alabama. It offers undergraduate and graduate degrees through the schools of Agriculture, Architecture and Fine Arts, Arts and Sciences, Business, Education, Engineering, Home Economics, Nursing, Pharmacy, and Veterinary Medicine.

Environment: The 1871-acre campus, located in Auburn (population 28,000), is 116 miles southwest of Atlanta, Georgia, and 55 miles east of Montgomery. The campus consists of 89 major buildings, including 25 residence halls as well as apartments for single and married students.

Student Life: About 90% of the students are from Alabama and other southern states, and 78% come from public schools. Less than half of the students live on campus. Three percent are members of minority groups. Dormitories are single-sex.

Organizations: There are 30 fraternities and 17 sororities on campus. Student activities include student government, publications, departmental and special-interest clubs, choral groups, drama, radio, and religious organizations.

Sports: The university fields intercollegiate teams in 12 sports. Intramural athletics are offered in 15 sports.

Handicapped: The university is working to make its campus accessible to handicapped students. Some residence halls are specially equipped.

Graduates: The freshman dropout rate is 25%. About 30% of the graduates pursue advanced degrees: 2% enter medical school, 1% enter dental school, and 1% enter law school. About 55% pursue careers in business and industry.

Services: Students receive the following services free of charge: psychological and career counseling, health care, and placement.

Programs of Study: The university confers the B.A., B.A. in Ed., B.S., B.C.E., B.E.E., B.S.I.E., B.M.E., B.S.H.E., and B.S.Pharm. degrees. Master's and doctoral programs are also available. Bachelor's degrees are offered in the following subjects: BUSINESS (accounting, agricultural business, business administration, fashion merchandising, finance, food industry management, industrial management, industrial relations, marketing, personnel management, theater management, transportation), EDUCATION (agricultural, elementary, health/physical, secondary, special, trade and industrial, vocational), ENGLISH (English, journalism, literature, speech), FINE AND PERFORMING ARTS (art, interior design, music, music education, theater/dramatics), HEALTH SCIENCES (hospital administration, medical technology, nursing, speech therapy), LANGUAGES (French, German, Spanish), MATH AND SCIENCES (applied physics, biochemistry, biology, botany, chemistry, earth sciences, entomology, geology, laboratory technology, mathematics, marine biology, microbiology, nuclear physics, physics, zoology), PHILOSOPHY (philosophy, religion), PREPROFESSIONAL (agriculture—agronomy and soils, agriculture—animal and dairy sciences, agriculture—food science, agriculture—horticulture, agriculture—poultry science, architecture, building construction, clothing and textiles, dentistry, engineering—aerospace, engineering—agricultural, engineering—aviation management, engineering—chemical, engineering—civil, engineering—electrical, engineering—industrial, engineering—materials, engineering—mechanical, engineering—textile, fisheries management, forestry, home economics, industrial design, interior design, law, landscape architecture, library science, medicine, optometry, pharmacy, social work, wildlife management, veterinary), SOCIAL SCIENCES (anthropology, criminal justice, economics, geography, government/political science, history, psychology, public administration, sociology).

Required: All students must complete the general education requirement.

Special: Special programs include study abroad, internships, an accelerated study program, and 3-2 programs.

Honors: Several honor societies have chapters on campus.

Admissions: About 82% of those who applied were accepted for the 1981–82 freshman class. Candidates must have satisfactory SAT or ACT scores and generally must have at least a C average. Advanced placement or honors courses are also important. Special consideration is given to some residents of Alabama and to children of alumni. Admissions standards are slightly higher for nonresidents.

Procedure: The ACT is preferred for state residents; out-of-state applicants may substitute the SAT. Application deadlines are open; all credentials must be submitted at least 3 weeks prior to the beginning of the quarter. Freshmen are admitted to all terms. A $15 fee must accompany the application.

Special: An early admissions plan is available. CLEP and AP credit is accepted.

Transfer: Applicants are accepted for all terms. Applicants who were eligible as freshmen should have a 2.0 GPA and be in good standing at their last school. Other applicants must have 48 quarter or 32 semester hours with a 2.0 GPA. D grades must be approved for transfer. Students generally must spend 1 year in residence to graduate. Application deadlines correspond to those of freshmen.

Visiting: Guided tours of the campus and interviews may be arranged through the admissions office.

Financial Aid: About 50% of the students receive financial aid. Scholarships, loans, and part-time jobs are available. Priority is given to those who apply by February. The FFS is required. Need is the main consideration in determining awards.

Foreign Students: About 160 foreign students are enrolled at the university. An intensive English course, special counseling, and special organizations are provided.

Admissions: Students must score 550 or better on the TOEFL and take the ACT.

Procedure: Application deadlines are the same as those for other freshmen. Students must present proof of good health and of adequate funds. Health insurance is available through the school.

Admissions Contact: Charles Reeder, Director of Admissions.

AUBURN UNIVERSITY AT MONTGOMERY C-4
Montgomery, Alabama 36193 (205) 279-9110

F/T: 2600M&W	Faculty: 126; IIA, −$
P/T: 1300M&W	Ph.D.'s: 60%
Grad: 1100M&W	S/F Ratio: 24 to 1
Year: qtrs, ss	Tuition: $585 ($1170)
Appl: see entry	R and B: $810
SAT or ACT: required	LESS COMPETITIVE

The Montgomery campus of Auburn University, founded in 1967, is primarily a commuter institution serving students in the immediate area and offering undergraduate programs in business, education, liberal arts, sciences, and nursing.

Environment: The 500-acre urban campus has 12 buildings, including 7 apartment-style units that house 48 students each.

Student Life: Almost all undergraduates are from Alabama. Seven percent live on campus. Dormitories are coed.

Organizations: Two national fraternities and 3 national sororities have chapters on campus. Since the campus primarily serves a commuting student body, there are few recreational and sports facilities. Some cultural events are offered.

Sports: The university fields intercollegiate teams in 2 sports. Several intramural sports also are offered.

Handicapped: Some special facilities, including specially equipped dorm rooms, are available for the physically handicapped.

Graduates: About 10% of the students drop out after their freshman year, and 65% remain to graduate.

Services: Students receive the following services free of charge: placement, career counseling, and psychological counseling.

Programs of Study: The university confers the B.A. and B.S. degrees. Master's programs also are offered. Bachelor's degrees are offered in the following subjects: AREA (urban), BUSINESS (accounting, business administration, business education, computer science, finance, management, marketing, personnel management), EDUCATION (early childhood, elementary, health/physical, secondary, special), ENGLISH (English, journalism, speech), FINE AND PERFORMING ARTS (art, art education, theater/dramatics), HEALTH SCIENCES (medical technology, nursing, speech therapy), MATH AND SCIENCES (biology, mathematics, physical sciences), PREPROFESSIONAL (social work), SOCIAL SCIENCES (economics, government/political science, history, justice and public safety, psychology, sociology).

Required: All students must take courses in English, history, natural sciences, and mathematics.

Special: Students may create their own majors. A general-studies degree is offered. Cooperative programs and study abroad are available. Preprofessional preparation is offered in law, medicine, dentistry, optometry, pharmacy, nursing, veterinary medicine, and engineering.

Admissions: Applicants should be graduates of an accredited high school. The GPA, high school record, and SAT or ACT scores are considered. For out-of-state students, admissions standards are somewhat higher. There are special criteria for older applicants who are not high school graduates.

Procedure: The ACT is required of Alabama residents; nonresidents may take the SAT. Admissions decisions are made on a rolling basis. The application deadline is 3 weeks prior to the beginning of the quarter in which the student wishes to enroll. Freshmen are admitted to all terms. A $10 fee must accompany the application.

Special: Early admissions and early decision plans are available. CLEP and AP credit is granted.

Transfer: Transfer applicants should have at least a C average and be in good standing at their last school. Auburn has a residency requirement of 3 quarters (45 quarter hours). D grades may transfer. Application deadlines are the same as those for freshmen.

Visiting: There are regularly scheduled orientations for prospective students. Guided tours, class visits, and interviews can be scheduled with the admissions office for Monday through Friday, 8 A.M. to 5 P.M., during the school year.

Financial Aid: Financial aid, including academic and athletic scholarships, is available through the school. Federal grants and loans also are offered. All departments participate in CWS.

Admissions Contact: Lee Davis, Director of Admissions.

ALABAMA 3

BIRMINGHAM-SOUTHERN COLLEGE C-2
Birmingham, Alabama 35254 (205) 328-5250

F/T: 703M, 661W	Faculty: n/av; IIB, +$
P/T: 60M, 110W	Ph.D.'s: 75%
Grad: none	S/F Ratio: 16 to 1
Year: 4-1-4, ss	Tuition: $3650
Appl: Aug. 15	R and B: $1800
605 applied	568 accepted	307 enrolled
SAT: 410V 525M	ACT: 23	COMPETITIVE+

Birmingham-Southern is a liberal arts college affiliated with the United Methodist Church. The library houses 115,000 volumes and subscribes to 450 periodicals.

Environment: The 200-acre campus is located in a hilly wooded area 3 miles from the business section of urban Birmingham. There are 20 modern buildings, including a theater and a planetarium. Residence facilities include dormitories accommodating 450 women and 350 men and fraternity and sorority houses. Married student housing is also available.

Student Life: About 75% of the students are from Alabama. Eighty-five percent of entering freshmen attended public schools. Eighty percent of the students live on campus. Eighty-five percent are Protestant and 8% are Catholic. Eight percent are minority-group members. Campus housing is single-sex; there are visiting privileges. Students may keep cars on campus. Although the college is affiliated with the United Methodist Church, the majority of students are not of this faith. Religious facilities exist for Catholic, Protestant, and Jewish students. Weekly attendance at convocation is not required.

Organizations: There are 5 national fraternities, 6 national sororities, and 1 local sorority on campus; 40% of the men and 40% of the women belong. Among the many extracurricular activities are the student newspaper, special-interest groups, and choir and theater productions.

Sports: There are 5 intercollegiate sports for men and 2 for women, and 4 intramural sports for men and 3 for women.

Handicapped: Special facilities for the physically handicapped include wheelchair ramps, parking areas, elevators, lowered drinking fountains, and specially equipped rest rooms. Special class scheduling can be arranged. Over 85% of the campus is accessible to the physically handicapped student. No hearing-impaired or visually impaired students are currently enrolled.

Graduates: About 8% of the freshmen drop out at the end of the year. Fifty-two percent remain to graduate, and of these, 40% go on to graduate study. Seven percent enter medical, and 6% law, schools.

Services: Students receive the following services free of charge: placement and career counseling, health care, remedial instruction, and psychological counseling. Tutoring is also available.

Programs of Study: The B.A., B.S., B.F.A., B.Mus., and B.Mus.Ed. are granted. Bachelor's degrees are offered in the following subjects: BUSINESS (accounting, business administration, computer science), EDUCATION (early childhood, elementary, health/physical), ENGLISH (English), FINE AND PERFORMING ARTS (art, art education, art history, dance, music, music education, studio art, theater/dramatics), HEALTH SCIENCES (nursing), LANGUAGES (French, German, Spanish), MATH AND SCIENCES (biology, chemistry, mathematics, physics), PHILOSOPHY (philosophy, religion), SOCIAL SCIENCES (economics, government/political science, history, psychology, sociology). Twenty-five percent of the degrees conferred are in business, 20% in math and sciences, and 20% in social sciences.

Required: Freshman English and 4 interterm (January) experiences are required.

Special: Junior year abroad, Washington Semester, and student-designed majors are permitted.

Honors: There are chapters of 15 honor or professional societies on campus, including Phi Beta Kappa.

Admissions: Ninety-four percent of those who applied were accepted for the 1981–82 freshman class. Of those, the SAT scores were as follows: Verbal—50% below 500, 35% between 500 and 599, 10% between 600 and 700, and 5% above 700; Math—45% below 500, 40% between 500 and 599, 15% between 600 and 700, and 5% above 700. On the ACT, 20% scored below 21, 25% between 21 and 23, 25% between 24 and 25, 20% between 26 and 28, and 10% above 28. Essential for admission are a C average, graduation from an accredited high school, and completion of 15 Carnegie units. The school also considers, in order of importance, recommendations by school officials, impressions made during interviews, and ability to finance the college education.

4 ALABAMA

Procedure: The college requires all applicants to take either the SAT or the ACT. Admissions are on a rolling basis, and application deadlines for freshmen are August 15 for fall, January 15 for spring, and May 15 for summer. There is a $10 application fee. A personal interview is recommended.

Special: An early admissions plan is offered. CLEP credit is available.

Transfer: The college received 145 applications for fall 1981, accepted 130, and enrolled 110 transfer students. Transfers are accepted for all classes. Applicants must have a 2.0 GPA; D grades transfer. Students must study for 2 years at the college, completing 64 semester hours, to receive a bachelor's degree. Transfer application deadlines are August 15 (fall), December 15 (winter), January 15 (spring), and May 15 (summer).

Visiting: Orientation is held during the summer for prospective students. Guided tours, class visits, and interviews can be arranged during the school year on Monday through Friday, by contacting the office of admissions.

Financial Aid: Approximately 78% of all students receive aid through the school. Those requiring assistance can apply for federal government loans, college-administered scholarships and loans, and funds from private and industrial sources. The average amount of loans or scholarship aid granted to freshmen is $2800, but with a campus job a first-year student can earn as much as $3400. Fifteen percent of the students work part-time on campus. Aid is awarded on the basis of need and academic achievement. All applicants for aid should file the FAF by March 15. The college is a member of CSS.

Foreign Students: Two percent of the students are from foreign countries. Special counseling and special organizations are available for these students.

Admissions: A minimum score of 500 on the TOEFL is required. The SAT or ACT is also necessary; on the SAT, a minimum score of 800 (400 on the verbal portion and 400 on the math portion) is required.

Procedure: Application deadlines for foreign students are April 1 for fall, November 1 for spring, and March 1 for summer. Students must submit a medical certificate completed by a doctor, and must present proof of funds adequate to cover 1 calendar year of study. Health insurance is also required, and is available through the college for a fee.

Admissions Contact: Robert D. Dortch, Vice President for Admissions Services.

HUNTINGDON COLLEGE C–4
Montgomery, Alabama 36106 (205) 834-3300

F/T: 234M, 269W	*Faculty:* 49; IIB, – – $
P/T: 48M, 140W	*Ph.D.'s:* 47%
Grad: none	*S/F Ratio:* 13 to 1
Year: sems, ss	*Tuition:* $2550
Appl: Sept. 1	*R and B:* $1950
294 applied	*232 accepted* *152 enrolled*
ACT: 20	**LESS COMPETITIVE**

Huntingdon College, founded in 1854, is a church-related liberal arts college affiliated with the United Methodist Church. The library contains over 100,000 volumes and subscribes to 450 periodicals.

Environment: The 55-acre campus is located in a residential section of the city of Montgomery and consists of 15 buildings, which include 4 dormitories housing 462 students.

Student Life: Seventy-five percent of the students come from Alabama, and 25% come from bordering states. Sixty-five percent of the students live on campus in the dorms. Eighty-five percent of the entering freshmen come from public schools. About 13% of the students are members of minority groups. Over 80% of the students are Protestant, and 7% are Catholic. Dormitories are both single-sex and coed; single-sex dorms have visiting privileges. Students may keep cars on campus.

Organizations: There are 2 sororities and 2 fraternities on campus. The college sponsors 17 extracurricular activities, the most active of which are the Huntingdon Honeys, the Scribblers Club, the Bio Club, the History Club, and various music organizations. The major social events on campus are the Miss Huntingdon Pageant and Homecoming.

Sports: Three intercollegiate programs are offered for men and women. Four intramural sports are offered for both sexes.

Handicapped: There are no facilities for handicapped students.

Graduates: Twenty percent of the freshmen drop out, and 38% remain to graduate. Thirty-nine percent of the graduates pursue advanced degrees, and 20% enter business and industry.

Services: The college provides free psychological counseling, tutoring, remedial instruction, placement aid, and career counseling.

Programs of Study: The college confers the B.A. and B.G.S. degrees. Associate degrees also are available. Bachelor's degrees are offered in the following subjects: BUSINESS (accounting, business administration, finance, management, marketing), EDUCATION (early childhood, elementary, health/physical, mental retardation, secondary, special), ENGLISH (English, speech), FINE AND PERFORMING ARTS (art, art education, church music, music, music education, theater/dramatics), HEALTH SCIENCES (medical technology), MATH AND SCIENCES (biology, chemistry, mathematics), PHILOSOPHY (Christian education, philosophy, religion), PREPROFESSIONAL (dentistry, engineering, law, medicine, ministry, pharmacy, veterinary), SOCIAL SCIENCES (economics, history, psychology, social sciences, sociology). Twenty percent of the degrees conferred are in business and 20% are in education.

Required: All undergraduate students are required to participate in the liberal arts core curriculum. A student must earn 124 credits, maintain a GPA of 2.4 or better, and attend mandatory convocations in order to graduate.

Special: The college offers a study-abroad program and a combination-degree program in engineering. Pass/fail grading is available in a few courses. Students may design their own majors.

Honors: Twelve national honor societies have chapters on campus. All departments offer honors programs.

Admissions: Seventy-nine percent of those who applied were accepted for the 1981–82 freshman class. The candidate should be a high school graduate with 15 Carnegie units. Other factors that enter into the admissions decision are advanced placement or honors courses, extracurricular activities, and leadership record.

Procedure: The SAT or ACT is required. Application deadlines are September 1 (fall), January 15 (spring), and June 1 (summer). A $10 fee must accompany the application. A rolling admissions policy is used.

Special: Early admissions, deferred admissions, and early decision plans are offered.

Transfer: For fall 1981, 84 applications were received, 55 were accepted, and 47 students enrolled. Transfers are accepted for all classes; D grades are not acceptable. Applicants should have a GPA of 2.0 or better and ACT scores of at least 18. At least 30 hours of the 124 required for a degree must be completed at the college. Application deadlines are the same as those for freshmen.

Visiting: Guides are provided for campus visitors, who may stay overnight at the school and sit in on classes. Visits can be arranged through the admissions office.

Financial Aid: Eighty-three percent of all students are receiving aid through the college. There are numerous freshman scholarships; 10% of the students have scholarships. Work contracts also are awarded to freshmen. Work-study funds are available in all departments. The average award to freshmen from all services in 1981–82 was $1755. The college is a member of the CSS. The FAF or FFS is required. The deadlines for aid applications are open.

Foreign Students: The 11 foreign students at the college represent about 2% of the student body. Special counseling and organizations are available.

Admissions: Students must score 450 or better on the TOEFL. No academic exams are required.

Procedure: Application deadlines are open; students are admitted to all terms. They must present a physician's report as proof of good health and show evidence of adequate funds for 1 year. Foreign students must carry health insurance, which is available through the school for a fee.

Admissions Contact: Jerald T. Lipscomb, Director of Admissions.

JACKSONVILLE STATE UNIVERSITY D–2
Jacksonville, Alabama 36265 (205) 435-9820

F/T: 2285M, 2515W	*Faculty:* 264; IIA, av$
P/T: 510M, 577W	*Ph.D.'s:* 55%
Grad: 319M, 303W	*S/F Ratio:* 18 to 1
Year: 4-4-1-1, ss	*Tuition:* $725 ($1075)
Appl: open	*R and B:* $1390
1588 applied	*1588 accepted* *1114 enrolled*
SAT or ACT: required	**NONCOMPETITIVE**

Jacksonville State University, founded in 1883, is a publicly supported institution of liberal arts and teacher education located in northeast Alabama. The library contains 345,000 volumes, 18,645 periodical subscriptions, and 540,142 microfilm items.

ALABAMA 5

Environment: The campus occupies 170 acres in a rural setting, 75 miles from Birmingham, Alabama. Recent additions include a coliseum with an olympic-sized pool, the Performing Arts Center housing a theatre/auditorium, and departmental buildings. The university sponsors dormitories and on- and off-campus apartments.

Student Life: About 92% of the student body comes from Alabama. The university seeks a state geographic distribution of its student body. Of the entering freshmen 95% come from public schools. About 57% of the students live off campus. Fourteen percent are minority-group members. University housing is single-sex, and there are visiting privileges. Students may keep cars on campus. Day-care facilities are available to full-time students, faculty, and staff for a fee.

Organizations: Students are encouraged to combine their academic programs with the many extracurricular activities. About 13% of men and 8% of women belong to the 9 fraternities and 6 sororities on campus.

Sports: The university fields 10 intercollegiate teams for men and 6 for women. There are 10 intramural sports for men and 7 for women.

Handicapped: About 50% of the campus is accessible to handicapped students. Fewer than 1% of the student body have visual or hearing impairments.

Graduates: At the end of their first year, about 25% of the freshmen drop out, while 40% remain to graduate.

Services: The free services available to students include placement, health care, career counseling, psychological counseling, and remedial instruction. Tutoring is available for a fee.

Programs of Study: The B.A., B.S., B.S.Ed., and master's degrees are conferred by the university. Bachelor's degrees are offered in the following subjects: BUSINESS (accounting, business administration, business education, computer science, finance, management, marketing, real estate/insurance), EDUCATION (early childhood, elementary, health/physical, secondary, special), ENGLISH (English), FINE AND PERFORMING ARTS (art, art education, music, music education, theater/dramatics), HEALTH SCIENCES (medical technology, nursing), MATH AND SCIENCES (biology, chemistry, mathematics, natural sciences, physics), SOCIAL SCIENCES (economics, geography, government/political science, history, psychology, social sciences, sociology). Thirty-three percent of undergraduate degrees conferred are in education, 29% in business, and 24% in social sciences.

Special: A B.G.S. degree is offered. Students may graduate with a bachelor's degree in 3 years by accelerating their programs.

Honors: Five national honor societies have chapters on campus. The music, English, history, and nursing departments offer honors programs.

Admissions: All applicants to the 1981–82 freshman class were accepted. Eligibility for admission depends upon graduation from an accredited high school with 15 completed high school units of work. Eleven of these must be in academic subjects, and at least 3 must be in English. No minimum grade average or class rank is required.

Procedures: The SAT or ACT is required for freshmen. There are no specific deadlines for applications, but candidates are urged to submit all credentials at least 3 months before they intend to enroll. Freshmen are admitted at midyear and in the summer. The application fee is $10.

Special: CLEP credit is granted for general and subject exams.

Transfer: For 1981–82, 752 transfer students applied, 752 were accepted, and 527 enrolled. Transfers are accepted for all classes. Depending on the overall average, some D grades may be accepted. Students must study at the university for at least one year and complete 32 of the 128 semester hours required for a bachelor's degree. As with freshman applications, a rolling decisions policy is employed.

Visiting: Guides are available for informal visits. To arrange such visits, contact the alumni office.

Financial Aid: About one-half of all students receive financial aid. The preferred deadline for aid application is April 15. The maximum amount available from campus employment is $675, and the maximum total award from all sources is $1775. The FAF is required.

Foreign Students: Two percent of the full-time students come from foreign countries.

Admissions: Foreign students must achieve a minimum TOEFL score of 500. The ACT is also required. An ACT score of 16 is required if substituted for TOEFL; otherwise there is no minimum.

Procedure: Application deadlines are the last registration day for each semester. Foreign students must present proof of funds adequate to cover 1 year of study.

Admissions Contact: Jerry D. Smith, Registrar.

JUDSON COLLEGE B–3
Marion, Alabama 36756 (205) 683-6161

F/T: 350W Faculty: 26; n/av
P/T: 154W Ph.D.'s: 40%
Grad: none S/F Ratio: 12 to 1
Year: sems Tuition: $2150–2240
Appl: Aug. 15 R and B: $1580
316 applied 253 accepted 129 enrolled
ACT: 18 LESS COMPETITIVE

Judson College, established in 1838, is a women's liberal arts college of the Alabama Baptist Church. The library contains 55,000 volumes and 1200 microfilm items, and subscribes to 315 periodicals.

Environment: The 103-acre campus is located in a suburban area 75 miles from Birmingham. Four dormitories, with singles, doubles, and suites, accommodate 305 women. Other facilities include a physical education building, a science hall, an auditorium, a fine arts building, a home economics building, and a student center.

Student Life: Eighty-two percent of the students are from Alabama. About 90% live in dormitories. Almost all the entering freshmen come from public schools. The majority of students are members of the Alabama Baptist Church; all students are required to attend weekly chapel services. There are religious organizations and counselors for all the major faiths. Students have curfews of 11 P.M. on weeknights and 12:30 A.M. or 1 A.M. on weekends, depending on class. Campus housing is single-sex; there are no visiting privileges. Students may keep cars on campus. Day-care services are available to all students, faculty, and staff.

Organizations: There are no sororities on campus, but many special interest groups, religious groups, and departmental clubs are available to students.

Sports: Three intercollegiate and 5 intramural sports are offered.

Handicapped: About 30% of the campus is accessible to physically handicapped students; wheelchair ramps and elevators are provided. Special class scheduling can be arranged. Less than 1% of the student body have hearing impairments.

Graduates: The freshman dropout rate is 25%; 45% remain to graduate. Thirty-five percent pursue graduate study after graduation; 2% enter medical school, 1% dental school, and 5% law school. Fifteen percent pursue careers in business and industry.

Services: Students receive the following services free of charge: placement, career counseling, health care, tutoring, and remedial instruction.

Programs of Study: All programs lead to the B.A. or B.S. degree. Bachelor's degrees are offered in the following subjects: BUSINESS (accounting, computer technology and management, secretarial science), EDUCATION (early childhood, clothing and textiles, elementary, health/physical, home economics, interior design, retail fashion merchandising, secondary), ENGLISH (English), FINE AND PERFORMING ARTS (art, music, music education, organ, piano, voice), HEALTH SCIENCES (medical technology, nursing), LANGUAGES (modern foreign languages, Romance languages), MATH AND SCIENCES (biology, chemistry, mathematics, natural sciences), PHILOSOPHY (religious studies), PREPROFESSIONAL (dentistry, law, medicine, pharmacy, physical therapy, veterinary), SOCIAL SCIENCES (history, psychology, social sciences, sociology). Twenty-six percent of the degrees conferred are in education, 20% in social sciences, and 15% in business.

Required: All freshmen must take history, English, religion, science, mathematics, health, physical education; some are required to take a language. In addition, all students must meet requirements in fine arts and social science.

Special: Five-year combined B.A.-B.S. degrees, cooperative programs, professional internships, special projects courses, and study abroad are offered. Air traffic control specialist is a special program unique to this state.

Honors: Chapters of 3 national honor societies are open to qualified students. Honors program participants complete a noncredit thesis, leading to a degree with distinction.

Admissions: Eighty percent of those who applied were accepted for the 1981–82 freshman class. Recommendations by school officials are required. Candidates for admission must be graduates of accredited high schools and have completed 15 high school units. No minimum class rank or grade average is required; admission depends on a predicted GPA based on a comparison of high school grades and ACT scores made by similar past students at Judson.

6 ALABAMA

Procedure: The SAT or ACT is required. Applications should be submitted by August 15 (fall), December 10 (winter), and April 15 (summer), along with a $10 fee. An interview is recommended. The college uses a rolling admissions plan.

Special: An early admissions plan is available. AP and CLEP credit is granted.

Transfer: For fall 1981, 27 transfer students applied, 23 were accepted, and 17 enrolled. A GPA of at least 2.0 and an ACT score of at least 16 are recommended. D grades are accepted if the student has an overall C average. Students must complete, at the college, 30 of the 128 credits required for a bachelor's degree. There is an 18-hour residency requirement. Application deadlines are August 15 (fall) and December 10 (winter).

Visiting: When College Days are held 3 times a year, visitors may sit in on classes, participate in special programs, and remain overnight. For informal visits, student guides can be arranged through the admissions office.

Financial Aid: About 80% of all students receive aid through the school. There are 75 freshman scholarships awarded each year from a $6200 fund. College loans and federal funds in the amount of $47,000 are also available. Aid packages are designed to fit the needs of the individual student. Average aid to freshmen is 72% of costs, with a maximum allowable scholarship of $3350, loan of $500, and employment earnings of $1000. Candidates for financial aid must file the FFS. The application deadlines are June 1 for fall, November 30 for winter, and March 30 for spring.

Foreign Students: About 1% of the students are from foreign countries. The college offers these students an intensive English course and special counseling.

Admissions: A minimum score of 450 on the TOEFL is required. The SCAT is also required.

Procedure: Application deadlines are August 15 for fall and December 10 for winter. Students must present proof of health.

Admissions Contact: Dean, Office of Admissions.

LIVINGSTON UNIVERSITY A-3
Livingston, Alabama 35470 (205) 652-9661

F/T: 466M, 472W Faculty: 82; IIA, ——$
P/T: 79M, 92W Ph.D.'s: 43%
Grad: 26M, 145W S/F Ratio: 14 to 1
Year: qtrs, ss Tuition: $296
Appl: open R and B: $1485
650 applied 450 accepted 415 enrolled
ACT: 15 LESS COMPETITIVE

Livingston University, established as Livingston Normal School in 1835, is a small, publicly controlled institution offering undergraduate and graduate instruction in liberal arts and education. The library contains 103,000 volumes and 250,000 microfilm items, and subscribes to 530 periodicals.

Environment: The 600-acre rural campus is located 38 miles from Meridian, Mississippi, and 60 miles from Tuscaloosa, Alabama, on the dividing line between cattle country and pine timberland. Residence halls can accommodate 416 women, 510 men, and 32 married students.

Student Life: About 88% of the students are from Alabama. Fifty percent live in residence halls. Eighty percent of entering freshmen come from public schools. Thirty-two percent of the students are minority-group members. University housing is single-sex; there are no visiting privileges. Students may keep cars on campus.

Organizations: About 35% of the students belong to one of the 5 national fraternities or 3 national sororities. Because the campus is located in a rural setting, there are numerous opportunities for outdoor recreational activities.

Sports: The university fields 6 intercollegiate teams for men and 3 for women. There are 5 intramural sports for men and 4 for women.

Handicapped: Special facilities for the physically handicapped include wheelchair ramps, parking, elevators, specially equipped rest rooms, and lowered drinking fountains. There are currently no visually handicapped or hearing-impaired students.

Graduates: About 45% of the freshmen drop out at the end of their first year; about 30% remain to graduate. Ten percent pursue graduate study.

Services: Students receive the following services free of charge: placement, career counseling, psychological counseling, tutoring, and remedial instruction. There are placement services available for both students and alumni.

Programs of Study: The university confers the B.A., B.S., and B.M. Ed. degrees. It also awards associate and master's degrees. Bachelor's degrees are offered in the following subjects: BUSINESS (accounting, business administration, computer science, management), EDUCATION (early childhood, elementary, health/physical, industrial, secondary), ENGLISH (English), FINE AND PERFORMING ARTS (music, music education), HEALTH SCIENCES (medical technology), MATH AND SCIENCES (biology, chemistry, ecology/environmental science, mathematics, physical sciences), SOCIAL SCIENCES (history, sociology). One-third of the degrees conferred are in education, and 30% are in business.

Honors: There are 5 honorary societies on campus.

Admissions: Sixty-nine percent of those who applied were accepted for the 1981–82 freshman class. The ACT scores of those who enrolled were as follows: 74% scored below 21, 15% between 21 and 23, 7% between 24 and 25, 3% between 26 and 28, and 1% above 28. Preference is given to applicants who have completed 15 Carnegie units at an accredited high school.

Procedure: Applicants must submit ACT or SAT scores. The application, a $10 fee, and the high school record should be submitted at least 4 weeks before the beginning of the quarter into which the applicant hopes to enroll. Livingston has a rolling admissions plan.

Special: The university has early decision, early admissions, and deferred admissions plans.

Transfer: For fall 1981, the school received 177 transfer applications; 128 students were accepted and 109 enrolled. Transfers are accepted for all classes and a 2.0 GPA guarantees admission. Transfer students must complete, at the school, 48 of 192 quarter hours necessary to receive a bachelor's degree. There is no application deadline.

Visiting: Guides are provided for informal visits, during which visitors may sit in on classes and stay overnight at the school. Visits are best made on weekdays. The director of admission services will make arrangements.

Financial Aid: Eighty-five percent of the students receive aid; 15% work part-time on campus. The application deadline is April 12. Loans are available from the university. The FFS is required. Average aid to freshmen, including funds from campus employment, is $1200.

Foreign Students: There are 22 foreign students enrolled full-time at the university.

Admissions: Foreign students must achieve a TOEFL score of 450 to be admitted to the university. They must also take either the SAT or the ACT, for which no minimum score is required.

Procedure: There are no application deadlines. Foreign students must present proof of funds adequate to cover the entire length of the program, and must deposit $1500 in an escrow account with the university. Foreign students must submit the university's student health form, and are required to carry health insurance.

Admissions Contact: Ervin L. Wood, Director of Admission Services.

MILES COLLEGE C-2
Birmingham, Alabama 35208 (205) 923-2771

F/T: 299M, 459W Faculty: 84; n/av
P/T: 74M, 77W Ph.D.'s: 33%
Grad: none S/F Ratio: 13 to 1
Year: sems, ss Tuition: $2300
Appl: July 31 R and B: $2100
648 applied 541 accepted 183 enrolled
ACT: 14 LESS COMPETITIVE

Miles College, founded in 1905, is affiliated with and controlled by the Christian Methodist Episcopal Church, and offers undergraduate programs in the liberal arts and sciences as well as business and education. The library has nearly 180,000 volumes and 850 microfilm items, and subscribes to 250 periodicals.

Environment: The 35-acre campus is located in an urban area 7 miles from downtown Birmingham. There are 17 buildings, including 2 residence halls for 300 men and women.

Student Life: Nearly 85% of the students come from Alabama. Most of the students come from public schools. Ninety-eight percent are black. About 38% reside on campus. The majority of the students are Protestants; attendance is required at chapel services at least once a week. Campus housing is single-sex, and there are visiting privileges. Alcohol is forbidden on campus; women students must observe a curfew. Students may keep cars on campus.

Organizations: The extracurricular program includes student government, clubs, publications, performing groups, and social events. There are sororities and fraternities on campus.

Sports: Intercollegiate teams are fielded in 4 sports for men and 1 for women. There are 6 intramural sports for men and 5 for women.

Graduates: The freshman dropout rate is 15%; 85% remain to graduate. About 52% of the graduates go on for further education: 2% enter medical school, 1% enter dental school, and 2% enter law school. Seventy-eight percent of each graduating class enter business and industry.

Services: The college provides free career counseling, placement, psychological counseling, tutoring, and remedial instruction to all students. Health care is available for a fee.

Programs of Study: The college confers the B.A. and B.S. degrees. Bachelor's degrees are offered in the following subjects: BUSINESS (business administration, business education), EDUCATION (early childhood, elementary, secondary), ENGLISH (English, language arts, literature), FINE AND PERFORMING ARTS (music, music education), MATH AND SCIENCES (biology, chemistry, mathematics, natural sciences), PREPROFESSIONAL (dentistry, engineering, medicine, social work), SOCIAL SCIENCES (economics, government/political science, social sciences, sociology).

Required: The general education requirement includes English, religion, world history, mathematics, natural science, social science, humanities, general psychology, and physical education.

Honors: There is a chapter of Alpha Kappa Mu on campus.

Admissions: About 84% of those who applied were accepted for the 1981-82 freshman class. The ACT scores of those who enrolled were as follows: 83% scored below 21, 15% between 21 and 23, and 2% between 24 and 25. A high school GPA of 2.0 is required.

Procedure: The ACT is required. July 31 is the fall application deadline; November 15, the spring deadline; and May 5, the summer deadline. Notification is on a rolling basis. A personal interview is recommended. There is a $15 application fee.

Transfer: For fall 1981, 103 transfer students applied, 81 were accepted, and 73 enrolled. Transfers are accepted for the second-semester-freshman, sophomore, junior, and senior classes. D grades do not transfer. Thirty-two semester hours must be completed in residence of the 148 necessary for the bachelor's degree. Application deadlines are the same as those for freshmen.

Visiting: Campus tours with student guides can be arranged. Visitors may sit in on classes.

Financial Aid: About 95% of the students receive financial aid; 89% work part-time on campus. The college, a member of CSS, participates in federal programs such as Pell Grants, NDSL, SEOG, and CWS in addition to offering other types of loans and campus employment. Academic scholarship and need, are the determining factors in the awarding of aid. The FAF or FFS is required and should be filed by April 15.

Foreign Students: About 1% of the full-time students come from foreign countries. The college offers these students an intensive English course in addition to special counseling and special organizations.

Admissions: Foreign students must achieve a score of 450 on the TOEFL. The ACT also is required.

Procedure: Application deadlines are June 31 (fall), October 12 (spring), and April 31 (summer). Proof of funds adequate to cover 4 years of study is necessary. A security deposit is also required. Foreign students must carry health insurance, which is available through the college for a fee.

Admissions Contact: Ethel M. VanBuren, Director of Admissions.

MOBILE COLLEGE   A-5
Mobile, Alabama 36613   (205) 675-5990

```
F/T:  260M, 505W           Faculty:    54; n/av
P/T:  61M, 176W            Ph.D.'s:    44%
Grad: none                 S/F Ratio:  20 to 1
Year: sems, ss             Tuition:    $93/p/c
Appl: open                 R and B:    $1860
374 applied
SAT or ACT: required                   LESS COMPETITIVE
```

Mobile College, founded in 1961, is a liberal arts institution affiliated with the Alabama Baptist State Convention. The library contains over 42,000 volumes and more than 330 periodicals.

ALABAMA 7

Environment: The 685-acre wooded campus is located in a suburban area 10 miles from downtown Mobile. The 15 buildings include residence halls that accommodate 112 single women and 120 single men. Housing for married students also is available.

Student Life: About 90% of the students come from Alabama, and 60% come from public schools. About a fourth of the students live on campus in single-sex dorms; there are no visiting privileges. Students may keep cars on campus. Drinking and dancing are prohibited on campus. Smoking is permitted in certain areas. Students are required to attend weekly religious services.

Organizations: The college sponsors choral, drama, journalism, photography, science, and service groups, and cultural events such as art shows, concerts, films, lectures, plays, recitals, and science exhibits. Several major social events are scheduled each year.

Sports: There are 6 intramural sports for men and women.

Graduates: About 15% of the freshmen drop out, and 75% remain to graduate. Ten percent of the graduates seek advanced degrees.

Programs of Study: The college awards the B.A. and B.S. degrees. Associate degrees are also conferred. Bachelor's degrees are offered in the following subjects: BUSINESS (business administration), EDUCATION (early childhood, elementary), ENGLISH (English), FINE AND PERFORMING ARTS (art, music, music education), HEALTH SCIENCES (nursing), MATH AND SCIENCES (biology, mathematics), PREPROFESSIONAL (ministry), SOCIAL SCIENCES (history, psychology, sociology).

Required: Freshmen are required to take courses in English composition, introduction to Christianity, Western civilization, physical education, mathematics, and science. All students also must take one course in public speaking, one in humanities, and 2 in social science.

Special: The college participates in an exchange program that allows students to earn credit at 2 other Mobile colleges. The college sponsors the Phonetic Reading Conference, a micro-teaching program for student teachers, and a tuition-free summer accelerated program for high school seniors in the top 10% of their class. Five-year combined degree programs are available in electrical, general, and mechanical engineering. A cooperative study-abroad program is provided.

Honors: An honors program is offered.

Admissions: Ninty-eight percent of those who applied were accepted for a recent freshman class. Candidates must be graduates of an accredited high school with at least 13 Carnegie units, and must have a 2.0 GPA. Recommendations from high school officials and friends are required.

Procedure: The ACT or SAT is required. Applications should be received at least 2 weeks before registration for the term in which the student seeks to enroll. A $10 application fee is required. Students are notified of the admissions decision soon after all credentials are received.

Special: AP credit is accepted.

Transfer: Admissions policy and application fees are the same as those for freshman applicants.

Financial Aid: About 65% of the students receive aid. Merit and need-based scholarships, BEOG, loans, and work-study jobs are available. Deadlines for the FAF or FFS and the college's aid application are open.

Foreign Students: The college accepts applications from foreign students.

Admissions: Foreign students must achieve a minimum score of 500 on the TOEFL. College entrance exams are not required.

Procedure: There is a special admissions program for foreign students. A doctor's statement of physical health is necessary. Proof of funds adequate to cover 4 years of study is required. Health insurance, although not required, is available through the college.

Admissions Contact: Janice Pittman, Assistant Director of Admissions.

OAKWOOD COLLEGE   C-1
Huntsville, Alabama 35896   (205) 873-1630

```
F/T:  608M, 686W           Faculty:    71; n/av
P/T:  43M, 58W             Ph.D.'s:    35%
Grad: none                 S/F Ratio:  18 to 1
Year: qtrs, ss             Tuition:    $3753
Appl: open                 R and B:    $1920
1404 applied      822 accepted        436 enrolled
ACT: required                         LESS COMPETITIVE
```

8 ALABAMA

Oakwood College, founded in 1896, is a private liberal arts institution affiliated with the Seventh-Day Adventist Church. The library contains more than 70,000 volumes.

Environment: The college is located in a rural community 120 miles from Birmingham. It owns 1185 acres, of which the main campus occupies 105. Five dormitories house 1033 students, and additional facilities are available for married students. Other buildings include a science hall, a dairy barn, and Moran Hall, which houses the college auditorium.

Student Life: About 20% of the students come from Alabama. Ninety-eight percent of the students are Seventh-day Adventists. The student body is primarily (98%) black; 2% belong to other minority groups. About 75% of the students live on campus; all unmarried students must do so unless they live with relatives. Campus housing is single-sex; there are visiting privileges. Students must attend daily worship services. Drinking and smoking are prohibited on campus. Students must obtain permission to leave the campus. Freshmen may not have cars.

Organizations: There are no social fraternities or sororities. Activities include special-interest, religious, and departmental clubs; Lyceum programs; the United Student Movement; and a student newspaper.

Sports: There are 9 intramural sports for men and 9 for women. The college does not participate in intercollegiate sports.

Graduates: About 52% of the freshmen drop out, and 25% remain to graduate. About 24% of the graduates seek advanced degrees.

Services: Free health care, placement, tutoring, and psychological and career counseling are provided. Remedial instruction is available for a fee.

Programs of Study: The college awards the B.A., B.G.S., and B.S. degrees. Associate degree programs are available. Bachelor's degrees are offered in the following subjects: BUSINESS (accounting, business administration, business education), EDUCATION (early childhood, elementary), ENGLISH (English), FINE AND PERFORMING ARTS (music, music education), MATH AND SCIENCES (biology, chemistry, mathematics), PREPROFESSIONAL (home economics, social work), SOCIAL SCIENCES (history, psychology, social sciences). Eighteen percent of degrees conferred are in business and management, 17% in psychology, and 10% in theology.

Required: Students must take courses in religion, physical education, humanities, social and natural sciences, and foreign language; demonstrate proficiency in English; and earn a GPA of 2.0 or better to graduate.

Special: Minors offered include black studies, corrections, political science, Biblical languages, and communications. The college offers 3-2 programs in architecture; architectural, electrical, and mechanical engineering; drafting; medical records; pre-veterinary studies; and veterinary science. Students may earn degrees in less than 4 years. Study-abroad programs and exchange programs with the University of Alabama/Huntsville and the Alabama Center for Higher Education are available. A general studies degree is offered.

Honors: The college holds an annual Honors Convocation.

Admissions: About 59% of those who applied were accepted for the 1981–82 freshman class. Applicants should be graduates of an approved secondary school with an average of 1.5 or better in at least 18 Carnegie units. Those who do not meet these requirements may be admitted on probation. Applicants also must demonstrate Christian character, good health, and motivation.

Procedure: Students should take the ACT. The college urges that applications be submitted no later than the last term of high school. There is a $5 application fee.

Special: There are early decision, early admissions, and deferred admissions plans. AP credit is available.

Transfer: Transfer applicants must follow the same procedure as freshmen applicants. D grades do not transfer. A minimum GPA of 1.5 is required (2.0 is recommended). Students must be in residence at the college for 2 quarters, completing 36 of the 192 credits necessary for the bachelor's degree. Transfer students are accepted for all classes.

Financial Aid: Seventy-five percent of the students receive aid. The college offers work assignments, denominational scholarships, state and federal loans, EOG, BEOG, and CWS. Aid is awarded on the basis of need, academic achievement, and character. The FAF is required; the college can provide additional application information.

Foreign Students: Eighteen percent of the students are from foreign countries. Special counseling and special organizations are available for these students.

Admissions: A minimum score of 500 on the TOEFL is required. College entrance exams are not required.

Procedure: The application deadline for fall entry is August 15; foreign students are admitted for the fall, winter, and spring quarters. Students must submit a medical report and proof of funds adequate to cover 1 year of study. Health insurance is also required, and is available through the college for a fee.

Admissions Contact: Roy E. Malcolm, Director of Admissions.

SAMFORD UNIVERSITY C-2
Birmingham, Alabama 35209 (205) 870-2793

F/T: 2100M&W Faculty: 267; n/av
P/T: 900M&W Ph.D.'s: 55%
Grad: 1100M&W S/F Ratio: 20 to 1
Year: 4-1-4, ss Tuition: $2784 ($2880)
Appl: see profile R and B: $1650
678 applied 621 accepted 458 enrolled
SAT: 410V 408M ACT: 22 LESS COMPETITIVE

Samford University, founded in 1841, is a private institution affiliated with the Alabama Baptist Convention. The library contains 234,500 volumes and 119,000 microforms, and subscribes to 872 periodicals.

Environment: The 400-acre campus, located in a suburban area in the mountains of Shades Valley, is less than 6 miles from Birmingham. The campus consists of 28 major buildings, 15 residence halls, and other auxiliary structures in Georgian-colonial architecture. The Leslie S. Wright Fine Arts Center includes a concert hall, a theater, and an art gallery.

Student Life: Approximately 67% of the students are from Alabama; the rest come from 41 other states and 10 foreign countries. Eighty percent of entering freshmen attended public schools. About 38% of the students live in single-sex dorms or fraternity houses. All students are required to attend convocation; 65% are Baptists.

Organizations: Four fraternities and 6 sororities have chapters on campus. Extracurricular activities include concerts, films, and lectures as well as social, religious, and professional clubs and groups. The city of Birmingham offers many cultural and recreational events at the Birmingham Art Museum, the Civic Opera, and the Botanical Gardens.

Sports: Intercollegiate sports include basketball, tennis, golf, and track. Intramural sports include softball, volleyball, and basketball.

Handicapped: The campus is accessible to physically handicapped students.

Graduates: About 16% of the freshmen drop out, and 40% remain to graduate. Approximately 45% of the graduates go on to further study.

Services: Free services include health care, tutoring or remedial instruction, career counseling, and placement.

Programs of Study: The university offers the A.B., B.S., B.S.N., B.S.B.A., B.S.Ed., B.S.Pharm., and B.Mus. degrees. Associate and master's degrees are also granted. Bachelor's degrees are offered in the following subjects: BUSINESS (accounting, business administration, finance, management, marketing, real estate/insurance), EDUCATION (church recreation, early childhood, elementary, health/physical, secondary), ENGLISH (English, speech), FINE AND PERFORMING ARTS (art, art education, music, music education, theater/dramatics), HEALTH SCIENCES (medical technology, nursing), LANGUAGES (French, German, Greek/Latin, Hebrew, Spanish), MATH AND SCIENCES (biology, chemistry, mathematics, physics), PHILOSOPHY (philosophy, religion, religious education), PREPROFESSIONAL (dentistry, foods and nutrition, home economics, interior design, law, medicine, ministry, pharmacy, social work, veterinary), SOCIAL SCIENCES (economics, history, law enforcement, psychology, public administration, social sciences, sociology). The largest percentage of degrees conferred are in health sciences; 11% are in business; and 10% are in education.

Required: Students must complete general-education requirements, which include courses in religion and physical education.

Special: Students may earn a combined 5-year B.A.-B.S. degree in engineering or forestry. A B.G.S. degree is also offered. Students may participate in the Junior-Year-Abroad program and may earn 6 hours of credit.

Honors: The university houses chapters of 39 national honor societies and offers honors programs in all departments.

Admissions: Ninety-three percent of those who applied were accepted for a recent freshman class. The SAT scores of those who enrolled were as follows: 17% were between 500 and 600 in both the verbal and mathematics sections, 9% were above 600 in verbal, and 12% were above 600 in math. On the ACT, 43% of the scores were between 20 and 26, 9% were between 26 and 28, and 7% were above

28. Applicants must have completed a minimum of 16 approved high school units, 12 of which must be academic. A minimum high school average of C is required.

Procedure: Samford has a rolling admissions policy. Applications should be filed at least 2 weeks before the beginning of a term. Freshmen may begin in any term except the January term. Candidates must take the SAT or the ACT in May of the junior year or December of the senior year, and must submit two letters of recommendation. The application fee is $25.

Special: CLEP credit is accepted.

Transfer: Transfer students may begin in any term. Applicants must have a C average and be in good standing at the last college attended. The student must complete 32 hours at Samford of the 128 required for a bachelor's degree.

Visiting: Campus visits can be scheduled 6 days a week by contacting the admissions office. Guides are available, and visitors may sit in on classes.

Financial Aid: During a recent academic year, students attending Samford received financial aid in excess of $6,000,000. In the freshman class, 81% of the students received assistance. The university participates in BEOG, SEOG, NDSL, CWS, LEEP, and GSLP. In addition, numerous academic scholarships are awarded, many on the basis of competitive campus exams. At least 75% of the students enrolled are receiving aid. The FAF and other credentials must be submitted by April 1.

Foreign Students: About 36 foreign students are enrolled at Samford.

Admissions: Foreign applicants must score 550 or better on the TOEFL. They also must take the SAT or ACT.

Procedure: Applications should be filed at least 2 weeks before the start of the term in which the student seeks to enroll. Students must present proof of good health. They also must show evidence of adequate funds for 1 year, and the college requires a $2000 deposit. Health insurance, though not required, is available through the university for a fee.

Admissions Contact: E.T. Cleveland, Dean of Admissions.

SPRING HILL COLLEGE A-5
Mobile, Alabama 36608 (205) 460-2130

F/T: 427M, 407W	Faculty: 56; IIB, av$
P/T: 20M, 44W	Ph.D.'s: 55%
Grad: none	S/F Ratio: 15 to 1
Year: sems, ss	Tuition: $4000
Appl: Aug. 15	R and B: $2290
701 applied	578 accepted 357 enrolled
SAT: 467V 481M	ACT: 23 COMPETITIVE+

Spring Hill College is a Catholic liberal arts college operated by the Jesuit Order. Founded in 1830, it is the oldest institution of higher learning in Alabama and the third-oldest Jesuit college in the United States. The library contains 150,000 volumes, 2000 current periodicals, and 3000 microfilm items.

Environment: The wooded, 500-acre campus, featuring a natural lake and an 18-hole golf course, is located in the Gulf Coast, which is noted for a mild year-round climate. Facilities range from a modern student recreation building to a quadrangle which is listed in the National Register of Historical Places. The self-contained campus is part of a suburban area 6 miles from downtown Mobile. Dormitories house 343 men and 355 women. Honors housing is available on a competitive basis.

Student Life: Thirty-five percent of the students are from Alabama; the rest are from 34 other states. About 68% of entering freshmen are graduates of parochial schools. About 75% of the students live on campus. Seventy-seven percent are Catholic and 20% Protestant. Thirteen percent are members of minority groups. Housing is single-sex, and there are visiting privileges. Students may keep cars on campus. Student life is considered highly regulated.

Organizations: About 25% of the men and 20% of the women belong to the 4 fraternities and 3 sororities. There is an active Student Government Association on campus as well as dramatic, literary, academic, service, and honorary organizations.

Sports: Spring Hill fields intercollegiate teams in 4 sports for men and 3 for women. Men can participate in 8 intramural sports, women in 7. Club sports also are available for both sexes.

Handicapped: Special facilities for the physically handicapped make the entire campus accessible. Arrangements are made for special needs.

ALABAMA 9

Graduates: Eighteen percent of the freshmen drop out by the end of the first year, and 75% remain to graduate. Fifty-three percent of the graduates pursue advanced degrees, including 7% who enter medical school, 2% who enter dental school, and 8% whho enter law school.

Services: Health care; placement, career, and psychological counseling; tutoring; and remedial instruction are available free to students. The school maintains a career counseling and development center.

Programs of Study: The college offers the B.A., B.S., and B.G.S. degrees. Bachelor's degrees are offered in the following subjects: BUSINESS (accounting, business administration, computer science, finance), EDUCATION (early childhood, elementary), ENGLISH (English), FINE AND PERFORMING ARTS (art, communication arts, radio/TV, studio art), HEALTH SCIENCES (art therapy, medical technology, respiratory therapy), MATH AND SCIENCES (biology, chemistry, mathematics), PHILOSOPHY (humanities, philosophy, theology), PRE-PROFESSIONAL (dentistry, engineering, law, legal studies, medicine), SOCIAL SCIENCES (economics, government/political science, history, psychology, sociology). Twenty-eight percent of degrees are conferred in the social sciences, 24% in business, 15% in math and science, and 14% in communication arts.

Required: All students must take courses in English, history, theology, and philosophy.

Special: It is possible to earn a combined B.A.-B.S. degree. The bachelor's degree may be earned in 3 years. Also available are a B.G.S. degree for adult students and a 3-2 engineering program. The college has a Verbal Proficiency Laboratory designed to help students deficient in English and mathematics. The college provides an opportunity for foreign travel as part of the regular curriculum during the summer, and participates in the Junior-Year-Abroad program.

Honors: There are 9 honor societies, including Lambda Tau.

Admissions: Eighty-two percent of the applicants to the 1981–82 freshman class were accepted. The SAT scores of those who enrolled broke down as follows: Verbal—60% below 500, 26% between 500 and 599, 10% between 600 and 700, and 2% above 700; Math—55% below 500, 28% between 500 and 599, 14% between 600 and 700, and 2% above 700. Of those who took the ACT, 20% scored below 21, 30% between 21 and 23, 28% between 24 and 25, 12% between 26 and 28, and 10% above 28. Applicants must have an average of C or better, rank in the upper two-thirds of their high school class, and present 16 Carnegie units, including 12 academic units. Other factors considered, in decreasing order of importance, are advanced placement or honors courses, recommendations by school officials, leadership record, impressions made during an interview, and extracurricular activities.

Procedure: The SAT or ACT is required. Applications must be received by August 15 (fall), January 5 (spring), or June 1 (summer). The application fee is $20. There is a rolling admissions plan.

Special: Early admissions and deferred admissions plans are offered.

Transfer: For fall 1981, 106 transfer students applied, 77 were accepted, and 51 enrolled. Applicants must have a GPA of 2.0 or better and minimum scores of 400 on each section of the SAT or 18 on the ACT. Grades of C or better transfer. Students must take 24 of their last 30 semester hours at Spring Hill to graduate (128 hours are required for graduation), including 50% of the coursework in their major. Application deadlines are the same as those for freshmen.

Visiting: Guides are available for informal visits, and visitors can sit in on classes. The best time to visit is during the week. Visitors can stay at the school on weekends. Contact the admissions office to arrange visits.

Financial Aid: About 68% of all students are receiving financial aid; 16% work part-time on campus. The average award to freshmen from all sources is $2059. Merit scholarships are awarded on the basis of a student's ACT or SAT scores. Application deadlines for aid are March 1 (fall), January 5 (spring), and June 1 (summer).

Foreign Students: Eighteen foreign students are enrolled at Spring Hill. An intensive English program, special counseling, and special organizations are provided for these students.

Admissions: Foreign students must score at least 500 on the TOEFL. They also must take the SAT or ACT.

Procedure: Application deadlines are May 1 (fall), September 1 (spring), and March 1 (summer). Foreign students must submit a college-prepared form signed by a doctor as proof of good health. They also must present proof of adequate funds for 1 year of study. Foreign students are required to carry health insurance, which is available through the college for a fee.

Admissions Contact: Anne M. Kennedy, Vice President for Enrollment Planning.

10 ALABAMA

STILLMAN COLLEGE
Tuscaloosa, Alabama 35403 B–3
(205) 752-2548

F/T, P/T: 622 M&W
Grad: none
Year: sems, ss
Appl: open
638 applied
SAT or ACT: required

Faculty: 34; IIB, – –$
Ph.D.'s: 41%
S/F Ratio: 17 to 1
Tuition: $1980
R and B: $1758

393 accepted   211 enrolled
LESS COMPETITIVE

Stillman College, established in 1876, is a private liberal arts institution affiliated with the Presbyterian Church. The library contains 62,000 volumes and subscribes to 350 periodicals.

Environment: The 100-acre campus is located in a city of 65,000 people 60 miles from Birmingham. Single-sex residence halls accommodate 338 men and 285 women.

Student Life: About 75% of the students are from Alabama, and 95% are graduates of public schools. About 85% of the students live on campus. The student body is predominantly black. Chapel attendance is required.

Organizations: Ten percent of the men belong to one of 4 fraternities, and 20% of the women belong to one of the 4 sororities. Religious organizations include the Westminster Fellowship, chapel, and Sunday school. Other activities include student government, a student newspaper, class and academic-area clubs, drama, choral groups, a marching band, and music ensembles.

Sports: The college competes on an intercollegiate level in basketball, baseball, golf, tennis, and track. Intramural sports for men and women also are available.

Graduates: About 36% of the freshmen drop out, and 44% eventually graduate. Twelve percent of the graduates seek advanced degrees.

Services: Health and personal counseling, tutoring, and placement services are available to students.

Programs of Study: The college awards the B.A. and B.S. degrees. Bachelor's degrees are offered in the following subjects: BUSINESS (business administration), EDUCATION (elementary, health/physical), ENGLISH (English), FINE AND PERFORMING ARTS (music), LANGUAGES (French, Spanish), MATH AND SCIENCES (biology, chemistry, mathematics, physics), SOCIAL SCIENCES (economics, history, sociology).

Required: Students must take courses in Bible, history, literature, mathematics, music, physical education, psychology, science, and writing.

Special: The college provides independent study, interdepartmental and interdisciplinary majors, courses in Afro-American history and literature, and exchange programs with the Universities of Alabama and Nebraska. In cooperation with Tuskegee Institute, the college offers a 3-2 degree in architectural science, a 3-2 degree in engineering, and a 2-4 degree in veterinary medicine. Minors are available in art, religion and philosophy, political science, and psychology.

Admissions: Sixty-two percent of those who applied were accepted for a recent freshman class. Candidates should be high school graduates with an average of C or better in 15 Carnegie units. Graduates of unaccredited high schools must have a C+ average; others may be admitted on probation. Adults or veterans with a GED also are accepted.

Procedure: The SAT or ACT is required. Application deadlines are open. New students are accepted for both semesters. There is a $10 application fee.

Transfer: Most applicants are accepted. A C average is required. D grades do not transfer. Students must spend at least 1 year in residence and earn 124 credits to graduate. Priority consideration is given to applications filed by May 1.

Financial Aid: About 85% of the students receive aid. Scholarships, loans, and work programs are available. Some awards are based on achievement or talent. The application deadline is May 1.

Admissions Contact: Evelyn Nall, Registrar.

TALLADEGA COLLEGE
Talladega, Alabama 35160   C–2
(205) 362-0206

F/T, P/T: 713 M&W
Grad: none
Year: sems, ss
Appl: open
SAT: 675 composite

Faculty: 34; IIB, –$
Ph.D.'s: 45%
S/F Ratio: 11 to 1
Tuition: $4089
R and B: $1700

ACT: 13   LESS COMPETITIVE

Talladega College, founded in 1867, is a liberal arts institution affiliated with the United Church of Christ. The library contains 56,000 volumes and subscribes to 412 periodicals.

Environment: The 50-acre campus is located in a small town about 55 miles from Birmingham. The 18 major buildings include 4 single-sex and coed dormitories that house 366 women and 205 men.

Student Life: About 81% of the students are from the South, and 80% live in the dormitories. The student body is predominantly black. Ninety-eight percent of the freshmen come from public schools.

Organizations: About 20% of the students belong to one of the 5 fraternities and 5 sororities. Extracurricular activities include special-interest and religious groups, publications, student government, theater and music groups, art shows, recitals and concerts, films, lectures, and plays. Attendance at weekly interdenominational chapel services is voluntary. Several major social events, including a Black Arts Festival, take place on campus.

Sports: The college fields intercollegiate men's and women's basketball teams. At least 7 intramural sports are offered.

Graduates: About 21% of the freshmen drop out, and 59% remain to graduate. About 31% of the graduates seek advanced degrees.

Services: Students receive free counseling, health care, and placement assistance.

Programs of Study: All programs lead to the B.A. degree. Bachelor's degrees are offered in the following subjects: BUSINESS (business administration), EDUCATION (elementary, health/physical, rehabilitation, secondary, special—early education for the handicapped), ENGLISH (English), FINE AND PERFORMING ARTS (music), LANGUAGES (French), MATH AND SCIENCES (biology, chemistry, mathematics, physics), PREPROFESSIONAL (social work), SOCIAL SCIENCES (criminal justice, economics, history, psychology, sociology).

Required: Freshmen must take courses in communications, humanities, mathematics, physical education, a laboratory science, and social sciences.

Special: Students may arrange through another institution to spend the junior year abroad. Combined 3-2 degree programs are available in engineering, physics, pharmacy, and veterinary medicine. These programs are offered in cooperation with other schools. Student research assistantships are available.

Admissions: Seventy-three percent of those who applied for a recent freshman class were accepted. The college requires that candidates have a GPA of 2.0, have 15 Carnegie units, and be high school graduates.

Procedure: The SAT or ACT is required. Application deadlines are open, and notification is made on a rolling basis. There is a $10 application fee.

Special: AP and CLEP credit is accepted.

Transfer: Transfer students should have at least a C average. They must complete the required general curriculum if they have not done so at their last school. Students must spend 2 years on campus to receive a degree.

Financial Aid: About 87% of the students receive aid. Merit and need-based scholarships, campus employment (including CWS), and loans from the federal government, local banks, and private sources are available. Tuition may be paid in installments. The FAF or FFS and the college's aid form are required.

Foreign Students: Ten full-time students are from foreign countries. Special organizations and special counseling are available for these students.

Admissions: Students must score 500 or better on the TOEFL. No other exams are required.

Procedure: Foreign students are admitted to all terms. They must take a physical and submit a health form as proof of health. They must also send one year's tuition to the college before arriving and prove they have sufficient funds to cover their complete period of study. Health insurance must be carried and is available through the college for a fee.

Admissions Contact: Robert Clayton, Director of Admissions.

TROY STATE UNIVERSITY SYSTEM C–4
Troy, Alabama 36082   (205) 566-3000

F/T: 2321M, 2333W		Faculty:	298; IIA, – $
P/T: 2342M, 1713W		Ph.D.'s:	50+%
Grad: 1183M, 793W		S/F Ratio:	22 to 1
Year: qtrs, ss		Tuition:	$840 ($1260)
Appl: open		R and B:	$1944
1307 applied	1283 accepted		885 enrolled
SAT: 440V 440M	ACT: 18	*LESS COMPETITIVE*	

Troy State University, founded in 1887, is a state-controlled liberal arts university. The major undergraduate divisions are the College of Arts and Sciences, the School of Business and Commerce, the School of Education, the School of Fine Arts, the School of Journalism, and the School of Nursing. The library contains 266,000 volumes and 106,000 microfilm items, and subscribes to 2115 periodicals.

Environment: The campus, covering 433 acres, is located in a rural area just outside Troy and 50 miles from Montgomery, the closest major city. There are 27 permanent buildings on campus. The residence facilities house more than 1900 students. Accommodations include a fraternity row, a sorority dormitory, single-sex and coed dormitories, and on-campus apartments for both singles and married couples. Recent additions include a golf course and a television and radio station.

Student Life: About 90% of the students come from the South, including 75% from Alabama. Seventy percent of entering freshmen attended public schools. About 53% of the students live on campus. Twenty-two percent are members of minority groups. There are visiting privileges in the single-sex dorms. Students may keep cars on campus. Day-care services are available.

Organizations: There are 16 fraternities and sororities. Popular activities include special-interest groups, theater and music groups, publications, concerts, plays, science exhibits, lectures, and films. The beaches of the Gulf of Mexico are only 2 hours away.

Sports: Intercollegiate teams compete in 10 sports. Nineteen intramural sports are offered.

Handicapped: Seventy-five percent of the campus is accessible to physically handicapped students. Special facilities include wheelchair ramps, parking areas, elevators, and specially equipped rest rooms. Special class scheduling can be arranged. Some facilities are available for visually impaired students. There are special counselors and assistants.

Graduates: Forty percent of the freshmen drop out by the end of the first year. Fifteen percent of graduates pursue advanced degrees, and 60% begin careers in business and industry.

Services: The following services are available free: health care, tutoring, placement aid, and psychological and career counseling. Fees are charged for health services.

Programs of Study: The university confers the B.A. and B.S. degrees. It also offers associate and master's degree programs. Bachelor's degrees are offered in the following subjects: BUSINESS (accounting, business administration, business education, computer science, finance, management, marketing), EDUCATION (adult, early childhood, elementary, health/physical, secondary, special), ENGLISH (English, journalism, speech), FINE AND PERFORMING ARTS (art, art education, art history, music education, radio/TV, theater/dramatics), HEALTH SCIENCES (medical technology, nursing), MATH AND SCIENCES (biology, chemistry, ecology/environmental science, mathematics, natural sciences, physical sciences, physics, statistics), PREPROFESSIONAL (social work), SOCIAL SCIENCES (economics, geography, government/political science, history, international relations, psychology, social sciences, sociology).

Special: Five-year combined B.A.-B.S. degrees may be earned. Independent study is offered. The B.A.S. degree is available in aviation technology, electrical technology, fire science and management, and resource management.

Honors: Honors programs are offered in the humanities and the arts. Eleven national honor societies have chapters on campus.

Admissions: Almost all those who applied for the 1981–82 freshman class were accepted. The SAT scores of an earlier class were as follows: Verbal—11% scored between 500 and 600 and 4% between 600 and 700; Math—29% scored between 500 and 600 and 2% between 600 and 700. On the ACT, 17% scored between 21 and 25, and 4% above 26. An applicant must submit a certificate of graduation from an accredited high school showing a minimum of 15 Carnegie units and a grade average of C or better.

Procedure: Students must submit either SAT or ACT scores. Application deadlines are open, and notification is sent when credentials are complete. The application fee is $10.

Special: Early decision, early admissions, and deferred admissions plans are available. CLEP credit is granted.

Transfer: Transfers are accepted for all classes. D grades will not transfer, and applicants must have a GPA of 2.0 or better. Students must study a minimum of 3 quarters at the university and earn 185 credits to receive a bachelor's degree. Application deadlines are open.

Visiting: Regularly scheduled orientations are held for prospective students. Informal visits can be arranged during school days, and guides are provided. Visitors may sit in on classes and stay overnight at the school when space is available. Arrangements can be made through the office of the dean of enrollment services.

Financial Aid: About 55% of the students receive aid. Campus employment (including CWS) and loans from the federal government, local banks, the university, and other sources are available. The university is a member of CSS and accepts the FAF. Deadlines for aid applications are open.

Foreign Students: The 64 foreign students attending full-time at the university represent 1% of the student body. Special counseling and organizations are available to them.

Admissions: Applicants must take the TOEFL.

Procedure: Application deadlines are open; students are admitted to all quarters. Students must present evidence of adequate funds for 1 year as well as proof of good health.

Admissions Contact: Rick Sandretto, Director of Enrollment Services.

TUSKEGEE INSTITUTE D–4
Tuskegee Institute, Alabama 36088   (205) 727-8580

F/T: 1615M, 1684W		Faculty:	353; IIA, – – $
P/T: 53M, 87W		Ph.D.'s:	44%
Grad: 152M, 91W		S/F Ratio:	9 to 1
Year: sems, ss		Tuition:	$2500
Appl: June 15		R and B:	$2500
2206 applied	1599 accepted		1217 enrolled
SAT: 350V 380M	ACT: 15	*LESS COMPETITIVE*	

Founded in 1881 by Booker T. Washington as a normal, or teachers', school for blacks, Tuskegee Institute today is a privately controlled professional, scientific, and technical institution. Undergraduate instruction is organized in 6 major divisions: the College of Arts and Sciences, School of Applied Sciences, School of Education, School of Engineering, School of Nursing, and School of Veterinary Medicine. The library contains 240,000 volumes and 68,000 microfilm items, and subscribes to 1000 periodicals.

Environment: The institute is located in a rural area 38 miles from Montgomery. The 5000-acre campus has 150 major buildings, including 16 single-sex dormitories and 48 apartments for married students. Off-campus housing also is available. Tuskegee Institute has been designated as a national historic site.

Student Life: The student body is almost evenly divided between Alabama and out-of-state residents. About 87% of the students are black, and most of the rest are members of other minority groups. Visiting privileges are permitted in single-sex housing. Students may keep cars on campus. Day-care services are provided for a fee.

Organizations: There are 7 national fraternities and 10 national sororities, to which 20% of the men and 20% of the women belong. Over 60 student organizations cater to extracurricular interests of many kinds.

Sports: The institute competes on the intercollegiate level in 7 sports for men and 4 for women. Three intramural sports for men are offered.

Handicapped: There are no special facilities for physically handicapped students other than designated parking areas.

Graduates: Fourteen percent of the freshmen drop out during their first year of study, and 38% remain to graduate. Eighteen percent of the graduates pursue advanced degrees; 1% enter medical school, 1% enter dental school, and 2% enter law school.

Services: Students receive the following services free of charge: placement, career counseling, tutoring, remedial instruction, and psychological counseling. Fees are charged for health-care services.

Programs of Study: The institute confers the B.A., B.S., and B.S.N. degrees. Master's and doctoral degrees also are available. Bachelor's

12 ALABAMA

degrees are offered in the following subjects: AREA STUDIES (Black/Afro-American), BUSINESS (accounting, business administration, management), EDUCATION (adult, agricultural, early childhood, elementary, health/physical, home economics, industrial, secondary, social studies, special), HEALTH SCIENCES (nursing), MATH AND SCIENCES (biology, chemistry, computer science, mathematics, physical sciences), PHILOSOPHY (philosophy), PREPROFESSIONAL (agriculture—animal and poultry sciences, agriculture—plant and soil sciences, engineering, veterinary), SOCIAL SCIENCES (economics, government/political science, history, sociology, social work). Twenty-two percent of degrees conferred are in education, 13% in health sciences, and 12% in business.

Required: All bachelor's-degree candidates must pass an examination in English proficiency and must earn an average of 2.0 or better in their major.

Special: It is possible to earn combined B.A.-B.S. degrees in various subjects. Other special programs are a cooperative program in engineering, a 3-2 program in engineering, and an exchange program with the University of Michigan.

Honors: Several honor societies, including Sigma Xi, have chapters on campus. Honors programs are available for qualified students.

Admissions: Seventy-two percent of those who applied were accepted for the 1981-82 freshman class. The SAT scores of those who enrolled were as follows: Verbal—80% below 500, 15% between 500 and 599, 5% between 600 and 700, and 0% above 700; Math—75% below 500, 20% between 500 and 599, 5% between 600 and 700, and 0% above 700. Of those who took the ACT, 85% scored below 21, 12% between 21 and 23, 3% between 24 and 25, and 0% above 25. All applicants should have completed 15 units at an accredited high school, present GPA of 2.0 or better, and rank in the top half of their high school class. Applicants to the schools of Nursing and Engineering must meet further requirements. Other factors considered are recommendations by school officials, advanced placement or honors courses, and leadership record.

Procedure: All applicants must submit SAT or ACT scores. Applications must be submitted by June 15 (fall), December 1 (spring), and May 1 (summer). Admission and notification are on a rolling basis. The application fee is $15.

Special: Early decision and early admissions plans are available. CLEP exams are accepted.

Transfer: For fall 1981, 593 transfer students applied, 379 were accepted, and 175 enrolled. Transfers are accepted for freshman, sophomore, and junior classes. D grades do not transfer. A minimum average of 2.0 is required. Students must study at the institute for at least 30 of the 120 to 130 semester hours required for a bachelor's degree. Transfer application deadlines are April 15 (fall and summer) and November 15 (spring).

Visiting: Guided tours and interviews can be scheduled Monday through Friday between September and May. Students can arrange to sit in on classes or remain overnight on campus. Arrangements will be made by the admissions office.

Financial Aid: About 86% of the students receive aid through the school. Loans, scholarships, and work opportunities are available; 22% of the students work part-time on campus. Awards are based on achievement as well as need. The aid application and the FAF must be submitted by April 15 for fall or spring entry. Notification of awards is made on a rolling basis beginning in May.

Foreign Students: The 417 foreign students enrolled full-time at Tuskegee represent 11% of the school's total enrollment. Special counseling and special organizations are provided for these students.

Admissions: Foreign applicants may have to take the institute's own test of English proficiency. All are required to take the SAT, and the school seeks minimum scores of 300 on both the verbal and mathematical sections.

Procedure: Application deadlines are May 15 (fall entry), November 1 (spring entry), and February 15 (summer entry). Students must present a record of a physical examination as proof of good health. They also must provide evidence of adequate funds for 1 year of study. They are required to carry health insurance, which is available through the college without fee.

Admissions Contact: Herbert E. Carter, Associate Dean for Admissions.

THE UNIVERSITY OF ALABAMA

The University of Alabama, established in 1831, is a state-supported university system with a total enrollment of about 37,000 students. The system has autonomous campuses at Birmingham, Huntsville, and University. Profiles of each campus follow.

UNIVERSITY OF ALABAMA B-3
University, Alabama 35486 (205) 348-5666

F/T: 6490M, 6267W Faculty: 800; I, −$
P/T: 443M, 407W Ph.D.'s: 73%
Grad: 1000M, 1260W S/F Ratio: 17 to 1
Year: tri, ss Tuition: $995 ($2120)
Appl: Aug. 1 R and B: $1925
4896 applied 3581 accepted 2493 enrolled
ACT: 21 COMPETITIVE

The university, founded in 1831, offers undergraduate and graduate degrees in the colleges of Arts and Sciences, Commerce and Business Administration, Community Health Sciences, Communication, Education, and Engineering; the schools of Communication, Home Economics, Law, and Social Work; the Capstone College of Nursing; and the Division of Continuing Education. In addition to these traditional divisions, the New College offers a less structured educational experience, including contract learning. The university library holds more than 1,100,000 books and microfilm items, and subscribes to more than 10,000 periodicals.

Environment: The 520-acre main campus is located in University, near Tuscaloosa, a town of 73,000 that is 50 miles from Birmingham. The campus contains 284 buildings, including 16 dormitories that house 2850 women and 1000 men, a coliseum that seats 15,000, and a recently constructed student center. In addition to the residence halls, the college sponsors on- and off-campus apartments, fraternity and sorority houses, and married-student housing.

Student Life: About 93% of the students are from the South, and 86% are from Alabama. Fifty-five percent live on campus. Fifteen percent of the students are members of minority groups. Housing is single-sex; there are visiting privileges. Cars are prohibited on campus; a special tram system provides transportation. Day-care services are available for a fee.

Organizations: About 30% of the women and 35% of the men belong to one of the 19 sororities or 29 fraternities on campus. Religious organizations are available for students of most major faiths. Student groups include publications; political, service, military, and special-interest organizations, and drama and music clubs.

Sports: The university sponsors teams in 9 intercollegiate sports each for men and women. Sixteen intramural sports are offered for both sexes.

Graduates: Fifteen percent of the freshmen drop out by the end of the first year. Of the 75% who remain to graduate, 15% seek advanced degrees. Of those who applied, 55% were accepted to medical school and 60% to dental school. Thirty-five percent of the graduates pursue careers in business and industry.

Services: The university provides free health care as well as career, placement, and psychological counseling. Tutoring and remedial instruction are available on a paid basis.

Programs of Study: The university awards the B.A., B.S., and B.F.A. degrees. Master's and doctoral degrees also are available. Bachelor's degrees are offered in the following subjects: AREA STUDIES (American, Latin American, Russian, urban), BUSINESS (accounting, banking, computer science, finance, general management, human resources management, industrial management, management, marketing, real estate/insurance, statistics, transportation, urban and regional management), EDUCATION (data processing, distributive, early childhood, elementary, general business, health/physical, industrial, office management, secondary, secretarial, special), ENGLISH (English, journalism), FINE AND PERFORMING ARTS (art, art education, art history, dance, film, music, music education, radio/TV, studio art, theater/dramatics), HEALTH SCIENCES (health care management, medical technology, nursing), LANGUAGES (French, German, Latin, Russian, Spanish), MATH AND SCIENCES (astronomy, biochemistry, biology, chemistry, geology, physics, statistics), PHILOSOPHY (philosophy, religion), PREPROFESSIONAL (engineering, home economics, law, library science, social work), SOCIAL SCIENCES (anthropology, economics, geography, government/political science, history, psychology, sociology).

Required: Candidates for the B.A. and B.S. must complete 12 hours of English, 6 of humanities, 6 of social science, and 8 of science. B.S. candidates also must meet a math requirement.

Special: The university participates in cooperative education and research programs with universities in Mexico and South America. Several programs involving foreign travel, including junior year abroad, are available. The university sponsors cooperative programs in engineering and mathematics, and student teaching in Alabama secondary schools.

Honors: More than 50 national honor societies, including Phi Beta Kappa, are represented on campus. Honors programs are offered by the colleges of Arts and Sciences, Communications, and Engineering, and by the departments of biology, chemistry, English, and microbiology. A computer-based honors program for freshmen also is available.

Admissions: About 73% of the applicants for the 1981–82 freshman class were accepted. The ACT scores of those who enrolled broke down as follows: 15% scored below 21, 37% between 21 and 23, 33% between 24 and 25, and 15% between 26 and 36. Applicants must have a GPA of 2.0 or better. They must be graduates of accredited high schools and have completed 16 units of work. Applicants who have not graduated from high school must be at least 19 and have a GED.

Procedure: Applicants must take the ACT, unless they graduated high school more than 4 years before projected entrance date with a GPA of 2.5 or better. Application deadlines are August 1 (fall), December 1 (spring), and May 1 (summer). The application fee is $15.

Special: A deferred admissions plan is available. AP and CLEP credit is accepted.

Transfer: For fall 1981, 1698 transfer students applied, 1278 were accepted, and 1068 enrolled. Applicants must have an average of 1.0 or better on a 3.0 scale. Grades of C or better transfer. Students may transfer no more credit than they would have been able to earn in an equivalent time at the university. Students registered at other divisions of the University of Alabama may transfer if they are eligible to continue enrollment at their current school. Students must study at the university for 1 year and earn there 64 of the 128 semester hours required for graduation.

Financial Aid: About half the students receive aid; 20% work part-time on campus. Federal and state veterans' benefits, Pell grants, SEOG, NDSL, federal and state vocational rehabilitation aid, part-time jobs, and private loans and scholarships are available. The average amount of aid granted to freshman covers 50% of costs. Aid is awarded on the basis of need. Students should submit the aid application and FFS by March 15 for fall and spring entry, March 1 for summer entry.

Foreign Students: The 350 foreign students enrolled full-time at the university make up about 2% of its student body. An intensive English program, special counseling, and special organizations are provided.

Admissions: Applicants must score 500 or better on the TOEFL or complete a course of study at the English Language Institute the university planned to open in 1982. No academic examinations are required.

Procedure: Applications from foreign students should be received in May for fall admission, in October for spring admission, and in February for summer admission. Proof of adequate funds for 1 year is required. Foreign students must carry health insurance, which is available through the college for a fee.

Admissions Contact: Lawrence B. Durham, Dean of Admissions Services.

UNIVERSITY OF ALABAMA IN BIRMINGHAM
C–2

Birmingham, Alabama 35294   (205) 934-5268

F/T: 2608M, 3628W   Faculty: 1387; I, — – $
P/T: 2071M, 2006W   Ph.D.'s: 70%
Grad: 966M, 1571W   S/F Ratio: 10 to 1
Year: qtrs, ss   Tuition: $1065 ($2091)
Appl: open   R and B: $2835
4459 applied   3998 accepted   2991 enrolled
ACT: 18   **LESS COMPETITIVE**

The university, founded in 1966, offers undergraduate and graduate degrees through the schools of Business, Education, Engineering, Humanities, Natural Science and Mathematics, and Social and Behavioral Sciences, all divisions of University College. The campus also houses a medical center, which offers degrees in medicine, optometry, dentistry, nursing, and other health-related fields, and the Graduate School. The library contains over 620,000 books and subscribes to more than 4800 periodicals.

Environment: The 170-acre campus is located about 6 blocks from downtown Birmingham. A new university union building and a new fine-arts building are planned. The university sponsors on-campus apartments.

Student Life: Almost all students are Alabama residents. Twenty-three percent are black. Campus apartments are coed. Students may keep cars on campus. A new day-care center provides services on an experimental basis.

Organizations: Eight fraternities and four sororities, all national, have chapters on campus. The university sponsors more than 75 student organizations, including a student newspaper, student government, special-interest and professional clubs, and instrumental, choral, and drama groups. The campus is close to recreational areas, and the city of Birmingham offers additional opportunities.

Sports: The university participates in 7 intercollegiate sports. There are 7 intramural sports for men and 6 for women.

Handicapped: About 90% of the campus is accessible to physically handicapped students. Facilities include wheelchair ramps, special parking, elevators, and specially equipped rest rooms. Special class scheduling and counselors (one professional and one assistant) are available.

Services: Free placement, career counseling, and remedial instruction are provided.

Programs of Study: The university awards the B.A., B.S., and B.S. in Eng. degrees. Master's and doctoral degrees also are available. Bachelor's degrees are offered in the following subjects: AREA STUDIES (urban), BUSINESS (accounting, business administration, computer science, economics, finance, management, marketing), EDUCATION (early childhood, elementary, health/physical, industrial, secondary, special), ENGLISH (English, mass communications), FINE AND PERFORMING ARTS (art history, dance, music, studio art, theater/dramatics), HEALTH SCIENCES (medical technology, nursing, occupational therapy), LANGUAGES (French, German, Greek/Latin, Russian, Spanish), MATH AND SCIENCES (biochemistry, biology, chemistry, earth science, geology, mathematics, physics), PHILOSOPHY (philosophy), PREPROFESSIONAL (dentistry, engineering, medicine, optometry, social work), SOCIAL SCIENCES (anthropology, economics, government/political science, history, psychology, sociology). About 26% of the undergraduate degrees are awarded in health sciences, 20% in education, 16% in social sciences, and 14% in business.

Required: Students must demonstrate competency in English or take freshman courses. Each student must take at least 18 hours in humanities (including 6 in freshman English), 12 in natural sciences and mathematics, and 12 in behavioral sciences.

Special: Students may design their own majors, take some courses on a pass-fail basis, and study abroad. The university offers a cooperative program with Birmingham-Southern College, Miles College, and Samford University. Cooperative education programs offering full-time or part-time work in the student's area of interest are available.

Honors: Fifteen honor societies are represented on campus. The biology department sponsors an honors program in which students participate in laboratory and field research.

Admissions: About 90% of those who applied for admission to the 1981–82 freshman class were accepted. The ACT scores of those who enrolled were: 25% below 21, 17% between 21 and 23, 8% between 24 and 25, 7% between 26 and 28, and 3% above 28. A C average is required.

Procedure: The ACT or SAT is required. There are no application deadlines; students are accepted for all quarters. The university follows a rolling admissions plan. The application fee is $15.

Special: Early decision and early admissions plans are available. AP and CLEP credit is accepted.

Transfer: For fall 1981, 2943 transfer students applied, 2611 were accepted, and 1828 enrolled. An average of 2.0 or better is generally required of transfer applicants; D grades transfer. Those with fewer than 13 semester hours or 20 quarter hours of college work also must meet freshman admission requirements. Students may transfer no more credits per term than they could have earned at the university. Transfers must complete, at the university, 32 of the 128 credits required for the bachelor's degree.

Visiting: The university schedules regular orientation programs, which include campus tours and discussions, for prospective students. Informal visits also can be arranged for weekdays—preferably Wednesdays—with the admissions office. Guides are provided.

Financial Aid: About 45% of the students receive aid; 10% work part-time on campus. Federal programs include BEOG (up to $1600 per year), FISL (up to $12,500 over 4 years), NDSL (up to $6000 over 4 years), SEOG (up to $1500 per year), and CWS. The university, a member of CSS, also offers loans and scholarships, including honors scholarships for freshmen and transfer students who have demonstrated academic excellence. Aid candidates should complete the university aid application and the FAF by April 1 for priority consideration, and in any case no later than 45 days before the beginning of the term.

Foreign Students: Foreign students comprise about 1% of the full-time enrollment. The university offers these students special counseling and special organizations.

Admissions: A score of 500 must be achieved on the TOEFL. The SAT or ACT is not required.

Procedure: Applications must be received by June for fall entry, November for winter entry, January for spring entry, and March for summer entry. Proof of funds sufficient to cover 4 years of study is required. Foreign students must register with the Student Health Service and carry health and accident insurance, which is available through the university for a fee.

Admissions Contact: Don Belcher, Assistant Dean for Admissions.

UNIVERSITY OF ALABAMA IN HUNTSVILLE C-1
Huntsville, Alabama 35899 (205) 895-6210

F/T: 1347M, 1333W	Faculty: 222; IIA, av$
P/T: 835M, 846W	Ph.D.'s: 70%
Grad: 400M, 214W	S/F Ratio: n/av
Year: terms, ss	Tuition: $966 ($1932)
Appl: Aug. 14	R and B: $2240
1620 applied	1541 accepted 1418 enrolled
ACT: 23	COMPETITIVE+

The university, part of Alabama's state university system, was founded in 1950. Its library contains 161,000 books and 136,000 microfilm items, and subscribes to 2255 periodicals.

Environment: The 337-acre suburban campus is located in Huntsville, a city of 138,000. The 15 university buildings, all constructed since 1962, include 2- and 3-bedroom apartments that house 500 students. The university also sponsors off-campus apartments and married student housing.

Student Life: About 99% of the students are from the South, and most are Alabama residents. Ninety percent of the students live off campus. Five percent of the students are minority-group members. University housing is single-sex, and there are visiting privileges. Students may keep cars on campus. Day-care services are available to all students, faculty, and staff.

Organizations: There are 4 national fraternities and 4 national sororities on campus. The university sponsors Christian religious groups; professional and special-interest clubs; arts, film, lecture, and entertainment series; a University Playhouse; a Dance Theater, 13 choral and instrumental music groups; publications; and a student government.

Sports: The university fields 4 intercollegiate teams for men and 3 for women. There are 9 intramural sports for men and 7 for women.

Handicapped: About 95% of the campus is accessible to wheelchair-bound students. Facilities include wheelchair ramps, designated parking areas, elevators, and specially equipped rest rooms. A special-student counselor works with handicapped students and makes class-scheduling and other arrangements.

Services: Free placement and career counseling and tutoring are provided to students. Alumni also may use the job placement office.

Programs of Study: The university awards the B.A., B.S., B.S.N., B.S.B.A., and B.S. in E. degrees. Master's and doctoral programs also are available. Bachelor's degrees are offered in the following subjects: AREA STUDIES (Slavic), BUSINESS (accounting, business administration, finance, management, marketing), EDUCATION (elementary, secondary), ENGLISH (English), FINE AND PERFORMING ARTS (art, music, music education), HEALTH SCIENCES (nursing), LANGUAGES (French, German), MATH AND SCIENCES (biology, chemistry, computer science, ecology/environmental science, mathematics, physics), PREPROFESSIONAL (dentistry, engineering—chemical, engineering—civil, engineering—electrical, engineering—industrial and systems, engineering—mechanical, law, medicine, pharmacy, veterinary), SOCIAL SCIENCES (economics, government/political science, history, psychology, sociology). About 37% of the undergraduate degrees are awarded in humanities and behavioral science, 19% in business, 15% in engineering, 16% in natural science, and 13% in nursing.

Required: Students must take 6 hours in each of these fields: English composition; literature; world history; economics, political science, psychology, philosophy, or sociology. Students must demonstrate competence in or take 12 hours of a foreign language. Science and mathematics distribution requirements depend on the student's major.

Special: Students may design their own majors. Juniors and seniors may take up to 12 hours of credit on a pass-fail basis. The university offers a cooperative education program. Students may arrange to study abroad through another institution.

Honors: Twenty-five national honor societies are represented on campus. Students can earn degrees with honors.

Admissions: About 95% of those who applied were accepted for the 1981–82 freshman class. The ACT scores of those who enrolled were: 48% between 21 and 23, 25% between 24 and 25, 8% between 26 and 28, and 5% above 28. Applicants must be graduates of accredited high schools and have completed 16 units of work. They should rank in the top half of their class. Applicants are judged on the basis of their high school grade averages and ACT scores. Other factors considered are recommendations by high school officials and advanced placement or honors courses.

Procedure: Applicants must take the SAT or the ACT. Applications, with a $15 fee, should be submitted by August 14 for the fall term, November 6 for the winter term, February 17 for the spring term, and May 14 for the summer term. The university has a rolling admissions plan.

Special: Early and deferred admissions plans are available. AP and CLEP credit is accepted.

Transfer: For fall 1981, 561 transfer students applied; 462 were accepted. Applicants with fewer than 18 hours of college work and either an average of 1.0 or better on a 3.0 scale or passing grades in at least half the work attempted will be considered for admission on the basis of high school grades and ACT or SAT scores. Those with 18 or more hours should have an average of C or better; those with a lower average may be admitted on probation. Applicants from other schools in the University of Alabama system may transfer to Huntsville if they are eligible to continue at their previous school. D grades transfer if the student has an average of C or better. Students must complete 25% of the degree requirements, and 12 of the last 18 credit hours, at the university to receive a bachelor's degree.

Visiting: Prospective students may arrange campus visits by contacting the office of pre-admission services. Guides are provided, and visitors may sit in on classes. Visits should be scheduled for weekdays between 9 A.M. and 3 P.M.

Financial Aid: About 30% of the students receive aid; about 5% work part-time on campus. Scholarship awards are based on need and merit; the average award to freshmen is $900. Federal and state loans and grants are available, and the university operates an emergency fund for short-term loans of $200 and below. Work-study programs also are offered. Aid applicants should submit the FFS by March 1 for priority consideration.

Foreign Students: Nearly 3% of the full-time students are from foreign countries. There are special organizations available for foreign students.

Admissions: Foreign students must take the TOEFL to be admitted to the university. The SAT or ACT is also required.

Procedure: Applications should be submitted 3 months prior to the term of entry. A $1500 deposit is required before admission is granted. Foreign students must present proof of health, and are required to carry health insurance.

Admissions Contact: Nan G. Hall, Director of Admissions and Records.

UNIVERSITY OF MONTEVALLO C-3
Montevallo, Alabama 35115 (205) 665-2521

F/T: 713M, 1288W	Faculty: 164; IIA, av$
P/T: 129M, 171W	Ph.D.'s: 52%
Grad: 71M, 180W	S/F Ratio: 19 to 1
Year: sems, ss	Tuition: $838 ($1258)
Appl: open	R and B: $1442
977 applied	911 accepted 844 enrolled
ACT: 19	LESS COMPETITIVE

The University of Montevallo is a state-supported institution offering undergraduate and graduate programs. The library contains 152,000 volumes and 239,000 microfilm items, and subscribes to 1450 periodicals.

Environment: The 500-acre urban campus, 30 miles from Birmingham, includes a 28-acre lake and a golf course. The more than 30 buildings include one of the best-equipped theaters in the South, and dormitories accommodating 900 women and 700 men. The university also sponsors fraternity houses.

Student Life: Ninety-five percent of the students are from Alabama. Thirty-five percent live on campus. Religious facilities are available for Protestant, Catholic, and Jewish students. Nine percent of the students are minority-group members. University housing is both single-sex and coed; there are visiting privileges in single-sex housing. Students may keep cars on campus.

Organizations: There are 6 national fraternities and 6 national sororities on campus. A wide variety of other groups offer social and cultural activities.

Sports: The university fields 4 intercollegiate teams for men and 3 for women. There are 14 intramural sports for men and 13 for women.

Handicapped: Approximately 95% of the campus is accessible to the physically handicapped. Facilities include wheelchair ramps, special parking, elevators, specially equipped rest rooms, and lowered drinking fountains and telephones.

Graduates: About 37% of freshmen drop out by the end of their first year; 50% remain to graduate. Forty percent of those who graduate pursue advanced degrees.

Services: Placement services, career counseling, health care, tutoring, remedial instruction, and psychological counseling are offered to students free of charge.

Programs of Study: The university confers the B.A., B.S., B.Mus., and B.Mus. Ed. degrees. Master's programs are also offered. Bachelor's degrees are offered in the following subjects: BUSINESS (accounting, business administration, business education, computer science, finance, management, marketing), EDUCATION (early childhood, elementary, health/physical, secondary, special), ENGLISH (English, speech), FINE AND PERFORMING ARTS (art, art education, art history, music, music education, radio/TV, studio art, theater/dramatics), HEALTH SCIENCES (environmental health, medical technology, speech therapy), LANGUAGES (French, Spanish), MATH AND SCIENCES (biology, chemistry, mathematics, physics, statistics), PREPROFESSIONAL (dentistry, engineering, home economics, medicine, social work), SOCIAL SCIENCES (economics, government/political science, history, international relations, psychology, social sciences, sociology).

Required: Students working toward the B.A. and B.S. degrees must fulfill the following general education requirements: 12 semester hours of English, 12 of science and/or math, 6 of world civilization and culture, 6 of social studies, 3 of art, music, or speech, 3 of psychology, philosophy, or religion, and 4 of physical education. Candidates for the B.A. must also complete 6–14 hours of a foreign language; B.S. candidates must take 6 additional hours of science and/or math.

Special: Combined B.A.-B.S. degrees are offered in all subjects. The university offers certain opportunities for foreign travel in its curriculum, but does not sponsor or permit students to take advantage of the junior year abroad program.

Honors: Eighteen national honor societies have chapters on campus. Honors programs are offered in business, fine arts, arts and sciences, and education.

Admissions: Ninety-three percent of those who applied were accepted for the 1981-82 freshman class. Of those who enrolled, the ACT scores were as follows: 66% scored below 21, 24% between 20 and 25, and 10% above 26. Candidates must be graduates of an accredited high school and have an average of C or better.

Procedure: The ACT is required. There is no formal application deadline; the university follows a rolling admissions policy. There is a $10 application fee.

Special: An early admissions plan is offered. CLEP credit is accepted.

Transfer: For fall 1981, 283 students applied, 263 were accepted, and 246 enrolled. Transfer students must take the ACT and have a GPA of 1.0 to be accepted. To receive a bachelor's degree, transfer students must earn, at the university, 30 of the 130 credits required.

Visiting: Four overnight orientation sessions are scheduled each year. Informal visits can be scheduled any time, but preferably on Saturday mornings. Guides are available; visitors may sit in on classes, with the instructor's permission. The admissions and records office should be contacted to arrange visits.

Financial Aid: Thirty-five percent of all students receive some form of financial aid; 13% work part-time on campus. Loans are available from the federal government, the university, and private sources. A fund of over $130,000 provides scholarships. Other sources of aid are part-time employment and assistantships. Aid is awarded on the basis of academic achievement; the amount is determined by need. Tuition may be paid in installments. The FSS is required. Veteran benefits and Social Security benefits are available.

Foreign Students: Two percent of the full-time students come from foreign countries. The university offers these students special counseling and special organizations.

Admissions: Foreign students must receive a score of 500 on the TOEFL to enter the university.

Procedure: Foreign students must present proof of funds adequate to cover the current term of study. They must also present proof of health, and are required to carry health insurance, which is available through the university for a fee.

ALABAMA 15

Admissions Contact: Larry A. Peevy, Director of Admissions and Records.

UNIVERSITY OF NORTH ALABAMA B-1
Florence, Alabama 35632 (205) 766-4100

F/T: 1815M, 2221W Faculty: 179; IIA, av$
P/T: 330M, 386W Ph.D.'s: 44%
Grad: 173M, 347W S/F Ratio: 23 to 1
Year: sems, ss Tuition: $790 ($1580)
Appl: see profile R and B: $1526
1025 applied 1000 accepted 902 enrolled
ACT: 17 LESS COMPETITIVE

The University of North Alabama, established in 1872, is a coeducational university of liberal arts, business, nursing, and teacher education operated under state control. The library contains over 200,000 volumes and 1000 periodicals.

Environment: The 95-acre campus, located in an urban community of 100,000, is situated 125 miles from Birmingham, Alabama. The campus is a mixture of older buildings, some listed on the historical register, and modern, high-rise residences. Married students have their own apartments.

Student Life: Ninety-one percent of the student body are from the state of Alabama; 88% of entering freshmen are from public schools. Eighty-two percent of the students live off campus. Eight percent are minority-group members. Campus housing is single-sex, with visiting privileges, and students are permitted to keep cars on campus.

Organizations: Fifteen national sororities and fraternities exist on campus. Sixteen percent of men and 8% of women belong. Extracurricular activities include numerous scholastic, departmental, professional, and religious organizations.

Sports: The University of North Alabama fields 6 intercollegiate teams for men and 5 for women. Four intramural sports are offered for men and 4 for women.

Handicapped: About 80% of the campus is accessible to handicapped students. Four special counselors are available. There are no visually or hearing impaired students.

Graduates: Of a recent class, about 10% of the students pursued graduate study after graduation. One percent entered medical school, 1% entered dental school, 1% entered law school, and 20% pursued careers in business and industry.

Services: Students receive the following services free of charge: placement, career counseling, health care, tutoring, and remedial instruction. Placement services to students include files, interviews, and assistance in making out applications.

Programs of Study: The university confers the B.A., B.S., B.S.ED., B.N., and B.S.W. degrees. Master's programs are also available. Bachelor's degrees are offered in the following subjects: BUSINESS (accounting, finance, management, management information systems, marketing, office administration), EDUCATION (early childhood, elementary, health/physical, secondary, special), ENGLISH (English, journalism, speech), FINE AND PERFORMING ARTS (art education, commercial music, commercial photography, film/photography, music, music education, radio/TV, studio art, theater-dramatics), HEALTH SCIENCES (industrial hygiene, nursing), LANGUAGES (French, German, Spanish), MATH AND SCIENCES (biology, chemistry, earth science, mathematics, physics), PREPROFESSIONAL (agriculture, architecture, dentistry, engineering, forestry, home economics, law, library science, medicine, ministry, optometry, pharmacy, podiatry, social work, veterinary), SOCIAL SCIENCES (economics, geography, government/political science, history, psychology, social sciences, sociology). Twenty-nine percent of degrees are conferred in business, and 23% in education.

Required: For the bachelor's degrees, 128 semester hours including 30 hours in residence are required. All degrees in Education require higher scholastic performances.

Special: Combination degree programs (3-1) are offered in the following preprofessional fields: engineering, dentistry, law, and medicine.

Honors: Twenty-two national honor societies have chapters on campus. Several awards are offered to students each year.

Admissions: Ninety-eight percent of all students who applied were accepted for the 1981-82 freshman class. On the ACT, 17% of the freshmen in a recent class scored 20–23, 11% scored 24–26, 4% scored 27–28, and 2% scored above 28.

Procedure: The ACT is required. Applications should be submitted at least 2 weeks before the opening of the term. There is an application

16 ALABAMA

processing fee of $15. The university maintains a rolling admission plan.

Special: GED tests are accepted for adults and veterans. CLEP subject exams are accepted.

Transfer: Transfers are accepted for all classes; D grades are acceptable with a C average overall. Good standing at a previous institution is required for transfer. Students must study at the university for at least 30 of the 128 semester hours required to receive a bachelor's degree. Application deadlines are two weeks before the beginning of each term.

Visiting: Continuous advisement and tours are available 5 days a week on request. Visitors can sit in on classes. The office of admissions will make arrangements.

Financial Aid: About 35% of all students receive financial aid. The deadline for financial aid for fall entry is April 1. The university participates in NDSL, SEOG, CWSP, LESP, and nursing loans and scholarships. The FSS is required.

Foreign Students: Fewer than 1% of the university's full-time students are from foreign countries.

Admissions: Foreign students must take the TOEFL, and must achieve a score of 55 or higher on the listening comprehension section. They must also take the ACT; no minimum score is required.

Procedure: Foreign students must present proof of funds adequate to cover 1 year of study; an additional annual fee of $1500 is required. Health insurance is not required for foreign students, but is available through the university for a fee.

Admissions Contact: J. Hollie Allen, Director of Admissions.

UNIVERSITY OF SOUTH ALABAMA   A-5
Mobile, Alabama 36688   (205) 460-6141

F/T: 2840M, 2979W	Faculty: n/av; IIA, av$
P/T: 915M, 1151W	Ph.D.'s: 79%
Grad: 290M, 524W	S/F Ratio: 18 to 1
Year: qtrs, ss	Tuition: $1125 ($1425)
Appl: Sept. 10	R and B: $1791
ACT: 21	LESS COMPETITIVE

The University of South Alabama, a state-supported institution established in 1963, offers undergraduate curricula in the arts and sciences, business, computer science, education, engineering, allied health professions, and nursing. The library houses 260,734 volumes and 350,000 microfilm items, and subscribes to 5066 periodicals.

Environment: The 1200-acre suburban campus has 34 buildings, including 14 dormitories that accommodate 500 men and 500 women. There are facilities for commuters, as well as apartments for 281 married students and more than 700 university-owned residences.

Student Life: About 65% of the students come from Alabama. Seventy-five percent are public school graduates. About 40% live on campus. About 18% of the students are minority-group members. University housing is single-sex, and there are visiting privileges. Students may keep cars on campus. Alcohol is prohibited on campus.

Organizations: There is a wide range of student-sponsored activities, including government, clubs, publications, performing groups, and social events. There are 12 fraternities and 6 sororities on campus.

Sports: The university fields 7 intercollegiate teams for men and 3 for women. There are 6 intramural sports for men and 5 for women.

Handicapped: Nearly all of the campus is accessible to handicapped students. Facilities include wheelchair ramps, parking areas, specially equipped rest rooms, lowered drinking fountains, and special dormitories.

Graduates: The freshman dropout rate is 15%; about 55% remain to graduate. About 18% of the graduates go on for further study.

Services: Offered free of charge to all students are career and psychological counseling, health care, placement, and tutoring.

Programs of Study: The B.A. and B.S. degrees are conferred. Master's and doctoral programs are also available. Bachelor's degrees are offered in the following subjects: BUSINESS (accounting, business administration, computer science, finance, management, marketing), EDUCATION, (adult, early childhood, elementary, health/physical, secondary, special), ENGLISH (English, speech), FINE AND PERFORMING ARTS (art, music), HEALTH SCIENCES (cytotechnology, medical technology, nursing, physical therapy, respiratory therapy, speech therapy), LANGUAGES (French, German, Russian, Spanish), MATH AND SCIENCES (biology, chemistry, geology, mathematics, physics), PHILOSOPHY (philosophy), PREPROFESSIONAL (dentistry, engineering, law, medicine, pharmacy, veterinary), SOCIAL SCIENCES (economics, geography, government/political science, history, international relations, psychology, sociology).

Required: There is a distribution requirement for all students.

Special: Student-designed majors are permitted. All colleges except engineering offer a 3-year degree program.

Honors: There are 8 honor societies on campus.

Admissions: About 84% of the applicants were accepted for a recent freshman class. ACT scores of enrolled students were as follows: 18% were between 23 and 26, 10% between 27 and 28, 7% above 28. A 2.0 high school GPA is required; applicants are also evaluated on the basis of ACT or SAT scores.

Procedure: The ACT is preferred, but SAT scores are accepted. The application deadlines are September 10 (fall), December 10 (winter), March 10 (spring), and June 1 (summer). Notification is on a rolling basis. There is a $10 application fee.

Special: Early decision and early admissions plans are available. CLEP credit is also available.

Transfer: Applications are accepted for all quarters and deadlines are the same as those for freshmen. A 2.0 GPA is required; D grades are not acceptable. Forty-eight of the last 64 quarter hours must be completed at the university; 192 quarter hours are required for a bachelor's degree.

Visiting: There are regularly scheduled orientations for prospective students. Informal campus tours with student guides are available. Visitors may sit in on classes but may not stay overnight at the school. Visits are best scheduled on weekdays. The admissions office should be contacted for arrangements.

Financial Aid: About 60% of the students receive financial aid. The university participates in federal programs such as BEOG, SEOG, NDSL, and CWS in addition to offering campus employment, freshman scholarships, and bank and university loan funds. The FFS is required and should be filed by April 1.

Foreign Students: Six percent of the full-time students come from foreign countries. The university offers these students special counseling and special organizations.

Admissions: Foreign students must achieve a minimum TOEFL score of 500.

Procedure: Application deadlines are the same as those for other students. Foreign students are admitted each quarter. They must present proof of adequate funds for the 4-year period of undergraduate study and must carry health insurance.

Admissions Contact: J. David Stearns, Director of Admissions and Records.

ALASKA

ALASKA PACIFIC UNIVERSITY   D-3
Anchorage, Alaska 99504   (907) 276-8181
(Recognized Candidate for Accreditation)

F/T: 77M, 73W	Faculty: 28; n/av
P/T: 41M, 139W	Ph.D.'s: 85%
Grad: 15M, 104W	S/F Ratio: 14 to 1
Year: sems, ss	Tuition: $2530
Appl: open	R and B: $3000
260 applied	78 accepted 72 enrolled
SAT: 450V 450M	ACT: 21 VERY COMPETITIVE

Alaska Pacific University, founded in 1954, is an independent institution that offers undergraduate and graduate education in business, education, and the liberal arts. The university takes a holistic approach to education, requiring a strong background in liberal arts while tailoring individual students' programs for their particular field of concentration. The core curriculum integrates understanding of the social, natural, individual, and spiritual environments. The university has no majors, departments, or divisions.

Environment: The university is located on a 270-acre campus in a suburban area about a half-mile from Anchorage. Dormitories, on-campus apartments, and married-student housing accommodate 180 students.

Student Life: About 78% of the students come from Alaska. Fifteen percent live on campus. About 18% are members of minority groups. Campus housing is coed. Students may keep cars at the university.

Organizations: Students may participate in student government, choral groups, a magazine group, the Alaskan Native and American Indian Association, and other extracurricular activities. There are no fraternities or sororities.

Sports: The university does not participate in intercollegiate sports. Eleven intramural sports are offered for both men and women.

Handicapped: About half the campus is accessible to physically handicapped students. Facilities include elevators, special parking, and specially equipped rest rooms.

Services: Free health care, psychological and career counseling, placement aid, tutoring, and remedial instruction are provided for students.

Programs of Study: The university offers the B.A. degree. Associate and master's degrees also are available. The university has no majors, but bachelor's degrees are offered in the following concentrations: AREA (Pacific studies), BUSINESS (business administration, management), EDUCATION (early childhood, elementary), ENGLISH (communications, English), FINE AND PERFORMING ARTS (art, music, theater/dramatics), HEALTH SCIENCES (medical assistant, medical assistant technology), MATH AND SCIENCE (natural sciences technologies, physical sciences), PHILOSOPHY (philosophy, religion), PREPROFESSIONAL (natural resource management), SOCIAL SCIENCES (economics, government/political science, social sciences, sociology).

Required: Students must complete a core curriculum that includes courses in the social, natural, individual, and spiritual environments. They also must pass UP exams to graduate.

Special: Students may earn a combined B.A.-B.S. degree and design their own areas of study.

Admissions: Thirty percent of the applicants were accepted for the 1981–82 freshman class. Applicants must be high school graduates with a grade average of 2.0 or better. A personal interview is required. Test scores, though used for placement purposes, are not considered in the admissions decision. Other factors considered include advanced placement or honors courses, recommendations by school officials, personality, leadership record, evidence of special talents, and ability to finance the college education.

Procedure: Application deadlines are open, and students are admitted to all terms. Admissions decisions are made on a rolling basis. The application fee is $15.

Special: An early admissions plan is offered. AP and CLEP credit is accepted.

Transfer: For fall 1981, 30 transfer students applied, and 25 were accepted and enrolled. Students must have a GPA of 2.0 or better (2.5 is preferred), scores of 450 or better on each part of the SAT, and an interview. Grades of C or better transfer. Students must complete 30 semesters at the university of the 128 required for a bachelor's degree. Application deadlines are open.

Visiting: The university schedules an open house in fall and spring. Guides are provided for informal visits anytime, and visitors may sit in on classes and arrange to stay overnight at the school. Contact the admissions office for arrangements.

Financial Aid: About 71% of the students receive aid through the school, and 15% work part-time on campus. The university offers scholarships (average $500, maximum $1000), loans (average $4000, maximum $6000), and work contracts (average $1425, maximum $2800). The average award to freshmen from all sources in 1981–82 was $3000. The FAF or FFS is required; application deadlines are open.

Foreign Students: The 34 foreign students enrolled full-time at the university make up about 8% of the student body. An intensive English course, an intensive English program, special counseling, and special organizations are offered.

Admissions: No English proficiency or academic exams are required.

Procedure: Application deadlines are open. Foreign students are admitted to all terms. Students must present proof of health and evidence of adequate funds for 1 year of study. Foreign students must pay special fees of $3750 per calendar year. They also must carry health insurance, which is available through the university for a fee.

Admissions Contact: Frank W. Schlehofer, Director of Admissions.

ALASKA 17

SHELDON JACKSON COLLEGE 3–F
Sitka, Alaska 99835 (907) 747-8290

F/T: 76M, 78W Faculty: 14; IV, –$
P/T: 15M, 30W Ph.D.'s: 7%
Grad: none S/F Ratio: 11 to 1
Year: 4-1-4 Tuition: $2850
Appl: open R and B: $2700
179 applied 155 accepted 91 enrolled
SAT, ACT: not required **LESS COMPETITIVE**

Sheldon Jackson College, established in 1878 as a training school for Tlingit Indians, is the oldest educational institution in Alaska. This private liberal arts school is associated with the United Presbyterian Church. The library houses over 50,000 volumes and 600 microfilm items, and subscribes to 330 periodicals.

Environment: The 345-acre campus is located in a small city in a rural area about 100 miles from Juneau, the state capital. Most of the buildings are in chalet-style architecture. A museum houses an outstanding collection of native artifacts. Coed and single-sex dormitories accommodate 128 students; on-campus apartments and housing for married students also are available.

Student Life: About 55% of the students are natives of Alaska. Ninety-five percent live on campus. Almost 60% of the students are members of minority groups, most of them Native Americans. Both single-sex and coed housing is available; students in single-sex housing have visiting privileges. Students may keep cars on campus.

Organizations: There are no fraternities or sororities, but professional, service, and recreational organizations serve as social groups. Extracurricular activities include chapel choir and boat trips for camping and fishing.

Sports: Men and women can participate in 6 intramural sports.

Handicapped: About 60% of the campus is accessible to physically handicapped students.

Graduates: Twelve percent of the freshmen drop out by the end of their first year, and 15% remain to graduate.

Services: Students receive the following services free of charge: health care, personal and career counseling, tutoring, and remedial instruction.

Programs of Study: A B.A. is offered in elementary education. Associate degrees also are available.

Required: All students must complete courses in English, mathematics, physical education, religion, science, and social science.

Special: Students can earn credit by examination.

Admissions: About 86% of those who applied were accepted for the 1981–82 freshman class. No specific entrance units are required for admission.

Procedure: Neither the SAT nor the ACT is required, but the Nelson-Denny Reading Test and placement examinations in English and mathematics are given. Application deadlines are open; freshmen may be admitted at the beginning of each semester. A rolling admissions plan is used. There is a $15 application fee.

Special: A deferred admissions plan is available.

Transfer: For a recent year, 12 students applied, 10 were accepted, and 8 enrolled. D grades do not transfer. Students must spend a year at the college and earn 32 of the 130 hours required for graduation in residence. There are no application deadlines.

Visiting: Informal visits with campus guides may be arranged, and visitors may stay on campus. The director of student services should be contacted for arrangements.

Financial Aid: About 90% of the students are receiving assistance from the college or the government. No academic scholarships are offered, but athletic and institutional scholarships, federal and state loans, and CWS are available. About 47% of the students receive work contracts. Tuition may be paid in installments. The FAF is required. Aid application deadlines are August 1 (fall) and January 1 (spring).

Foreign Students: Five students from foreign countries are enrolled full-time at the college.

Admissions: Students must take the college's own entrance exam.

Procedure: Application deadlines are August 15 for fall entry and January 15 for spring entry. Students must present a form completed by a doctor as proof of good health. They also must show evidence that they have adequate funds for 1 year.

Admissions Contact: Dan Etulain, Director of Recruitment.

ALASKA

UNIVERSITY OF ALASKA/ANCHORAGE   D-3
Anchorage, Alaska 99504   (907) 263-1480

F/T: 1113M, 1896W		Faculty:	129; IIA, ++$
P/T: n/a		Ph.D.'s:	65%
Grad: n/a		S/F Ratio:	17 to 1
Year: sems, ss		Tuition:	$410 ($1190)
Appl: May 1		R and B:	none
600 enrolled			
SAT or ACT: required			COMPETITIVE

The University of Alaska/Anchorage, founded in 1969, is a major unit of the University of Alaska statewide system of higher education. The university's academic and research programs are administered through the College of Arts and Sciences, the School of Business and Public Administration, the School of Education, the School of Engineering, the School of Nursing, the Justice Center, and the Center for Alcohol and Addiction Studies. Its library contains 300,000 volumes, numerous periodical subscriptions, and audiovisual and microfilm facilities.

Environment: The 424-acre wooded campus is located in Anchorage, and is convenient to the city's many facilities. There are no dormitory facilities on campus, but nearby apartments are available to students.

Student Life: About 93% of the students are from Alaska. All students live off campus in apartments or at home.

Organizations: The student government sponsors social and cultural programs for students. The city of Anchorage also offers activities.

Sports: The college competes intercollegiately in 4 sports for both men and women. Thirteen intramural sports are open to men and women.

Services: The following services are available to students free of charge: career and psychological counseling, tutoring, and remedial instruction.

Programs of Study: The university confers the B.A., B.S., B.B.A., B.Ed., B.Mus., B.F.A., B.T., and B.S.W. degrees. Master's degrees are also awarded. Bachelor's degrees are offered in the following subjects: BUSINESS (accounting, banking, economics, finance, labor relations, management, marketing, real estate/insurance), EDUCATION (elementary, health/physical, secondary), ENGLISH (communications, English, speech), FINE AND PERFORMING ARTS (art, music, theater/dramatics), HEALTH SCIENCES (medical technology, nursing), LANGUAGES (linguistics), MATH AND SCIENCES (applied statistics, biology, chemistry, computer science, mathematics, natural sciences, physics), PHILOSOPHY (humanities, philosophy), PREPROFESSIONAL (engineering—arctic, engineering—civil, engineering—engineering and science management, engineering—environmental quality, library science, social work), SOCIAL SCIENCES (anthropology, history, justice, psychology, sociology).

Special: Students can design their own majors, take graduate courses for credit, and participate in the work-study program. The B.A. or B.S. in interdisciplinary studies is also offered. CLEP credit is available.

Admissions: Candidates should have a 2.5 high school GPA.

Procedure: The SAT or ACT is required. Application deadlines are May 1 (fall), October 2 (spring), and April 3 (summer). A $10 fee should be included with the application.

Transfer: A 2.0 GPA and good standing in the previous school are required. Thirty of the last 36 credits must be taken at the university of the 130 credits required for the bachelor's degree.

Financial Aid: The university participates in all federal and state student financial aid programs. Loans, grants, scholarships, and part-time employment are available. Most aid is awarded on the basis of financial need; however, some tuition waivers and scholarships are based on academic performance and potential. Aid applicants should submit the FAF and the University of Alaska general application for financial aid no later than May 31.

Foreign Students: The university welcomes qualified students from other countries.

Admissions: The TOEFL is required of applicants from countries in which English is not the language in general use. Foreign students must also give evidence of ability to succeed in university study.

Procedure: Proof of funds adequate to cover each year of study is required. Foreign students are advised to carry their own medical insurance.

Admissions Contact: Kay Wilson, Director of Admissions and Records.

UNIVERSITY OF ALASKA/FAIRBANKS   D-2
Fairbanks, Alaska 99701   (907) 479-7521

F/T: 1273M, 1036W		Faculty:	350; I, ++$
P/T: 675M, 413W		Ph.D.'s:	80%
Grad: 242M, 176W		S/F Ratio:	8 to 1
Year: sems, ss		Tuition:	$572 ($1352)
Appl: Aug. 1		R and B:	$2080
1141 applied	996 accepted		536 enrolled
ACT: 18			LESS COMPETITIVE

The University of Alaska/Fairbanks, part of a multi-campus institution, was founded in 1917 as a territorial college and school of mines. The library contains over 900,000 volumes. Several research institutes and laboratories for study in the physical sciences are associated with the school. The museum maintains important collections of anthropological, biological, paleontological, and historical materials.

Environment: The campus is located in a suburban area 5 miles from Fairbanks, and contains dormitories, apartments, and married-student residences. A bookstore, an art gallery, a concert hall, a theater, the student union, and an ice arena are also on campus.

Student Life: Eighty percent of the students are from Alaska. Sixty percent of the students live on campus. About 10% are members of minority groups. Students may live in either coed or single-sex housing; visiting privileges are provided in single-sex housing. Students may keep cars on campus. Day-care services are provided.

Organizations: There are no social fraternities or sororities. Extracurricular activities include music and drama groups, religious groups for most Christian denominations, and social and cultural events sponsored by clubs, the university, and the student body.

Sports: The university sponsors intercollegiate teams in 5 sports for men and 5 for women. Men can compete in 12 intramural sports and women in 11.

Handicapped: About 80% of the campus is accessible to wheelchair-bound students. Special parking, ramps, and elevators are provided, and special class scheduling is possible.

Graduates: About 15% of the freshmen drop out by the end of the first year. Of the 50% who graduate, 30% pursue further study; 1% enter medical school, 1% enter dental school, and 3% enter law school. Eighty percent seek careers in business and industry.

Services: Students receive the following services free of charge: placement, career counseling, remedial instruction, and psychological counseling.

Programs of Study: The university confers the B.A., B.S., B.B.A., B.Ed., B.Mus., and B.Techn. degrees. Associate, master's, and doctoral degrees also are available. Bachelor's degrees are offered in the following subjects: AREA STUDIES (Russian), BUSINESS (accounting, business administration, business education, computer science), EDUCATION (early childhood, elementary, secondary), ENGLISH (English, speech), FINE AND PERFORMING ARTS (art, music, music education, studio art, theater/dramatics), LANGUAGES (French, German, Japanese, Russian, Spanish), MATH AND SCIENCES (biology, botany, chemistry, earth science, geology, mathematics, physics, zoology), PHILOSOPHY (philosophy), PREPROFESSIONAL (agriculture, architecture, dentistry, engineering, forestry, law, library science, medicine, ministry, pharmacy, social work, veterinary), SOCIAL SCIENCES (anthropology, economics, geography, government/political science, history, psychology, sociology). Thirty-eight percent of degrees conferred are in math and sciences, 21% are in social sciences, and 13% are in education.

Special: The university's Division of Rural Education offers both credit and noncredit educational programs to Alaska residents. Included are credit courses at military installations and other locations and correspondence courses.

Admissions: Eighty-seven percent of those who applied were accepted for the 1981-82 freshman class. Of those who enrolled, the ACT scores were as follows: 57% below 21, 19% between 21 and 23, 8% between 24 and 25, 7% between 26 and 28, and 4% above 28. Applicants must have a grade average of C or better with 15 Carnegie units, or a satisfactory grade on an entrance test. Also considered are the student's residence, the accreditation of his or her high school, AP or honor courses, school recommendations, and impressions made during the recommended personal interview.

Procedure: Applications must be received by August 1 for the fall term and by December 1 for the spring term. For the summer term, applications are accepted until the registration date. The ACT is required. There is a $10 application fee. Notification is made on a rolling basis.

Special: AP and CLEP are used.

Transfer: Transfer students must have a minimum GPA of 2.0; a 3.3 is recommended. Grades of C or better from accredited schools transfer. The ACT is required. Students must spend at least 1 year on campus, earning at least 30 of the 130 credits required for graduation. Application deadlines are the same as those for freshmen.

Visiting: Scheduled orientations are arranged for prospective students. Guided tours and interviews can be arranged; spring is the best time for a visit to the campus. Visitors may visit classes, tour facilities, and talk with faculty members and students. To arrange for a visit, contact the admissions office.

Financial Aid: About 85% of all students receive financial aid. Scholarships and loans are available, including EOG, NDSL, CWS, and state loan funds. Installment financing is possible, and many students earn a large portion of their own expenses. Fifteen percent work part-time on campus. Aid is awarded primarily on the basis of need, with some given for outstanding academic performance. Applications for financial aid must be filed before March 1 for the fall semester. The FAF is required.

Foreign Students: About 102 students from foreign countries are enrolled at the university, making up 2% of the student body. Special counseling and organizations are provided.

Admissions: Foreign applicants must score at least 550 on the TOEFL. They also must take the ACT.

Procedure: Application deadlines are the same as those for other freshmen. Students must present proof of health and evidence that they have adequate funds for 1 year of study. Health insurance is required, and students may obtain it through the university for a fee.

Admissions Contact: Ann Tremarello, Director of Admissions and Registrar.

UNIVERSITY OF ALASKA/JUNEAU   3–F
Juneau, Alaska 99801   (907) 789-2101
(Recognized Candidate for Accreditation)

F/T: 100M, 100W	Faculty: n/av; IIA, ++$
P/T: 1000M, 1200W	Ph.D.'s: 50%
Grad: 50M, 100W	S/F Ratio: 10 to 1
Year: sems, ss	Tuition: $410 (sliding scale)
Appl: open	R and B: $2600
SAT, ACT: not required	NONCOMPETITIVE

The University of Alaska/Juneau was formed by the union of Southeast Senior College and the Juneau-Douglas Community College. The state's salt-water fisheries program is located on the Juneau campus. The library contains 200,000 volumes and subscribes to 550 periodicals.

Environment: The rural 10-acre campus is located on the shores of Auke Lake and Auke Bay, 11 miles from Juneau. There are six buildings on campus and 20 small off-campus apartment units. A separate downtown campus center houses the university's business program. There are no cafeterias, dining halls, or athletic facilities.

Student Life: Ninety-eight percent of the undergraduates are from Alaska. About eight percent live in off-campus apartments, and 90% commute from home. About 20% of the students are members of minority groups. College-sponsored housing is single-sex, and there are no visiting privileges. Students may keep cars on campus. Drinking on campus is forbidden by law.

Organizations: There are no fraternities or sororities on campus, but 20 university-sponsored organizations provide extracurricular outlets for students.

Sports: There are no university-sponsored intercollegiate or intramural athletics.

Handicapped: About 90% of the campus is accessible to handicapped students. Special facilities include wheelchair ramps, special parking, elevators, and specially equipped rest rooms.

Services: The following services are available to students free of charge: placement and career counseling, psychological counseling, tutoring, and remedial instruction. Placement services are available to both graduates and undergraduates.

Programs of Study: The university confers the B.A. and B.S. degrees. Associate and master's degrees are also awarded. Bachelor's degrees are offered in the following subjects: BUSINESS (accounting, business administration, finance, management), EDUCATION (elementary, secondary), FINE AND PERFORMING ARTS (music), MATH AND SCIENCES (biology), SOCIAL SCIENCES (government/political science).

Admissions: The university has an open admissions policy. One need not apply to the university to take courses. The only standard requirement of those who do apply is graduation from an accredited high school.

Procedure: Neither the SAT nor the ACT is required. There are no application deadlines. Admissions are made on a rolling basis. There is a $10 application fee.

Special: AP and CLEP credit is available.

Transfer: Transfers are accepted for all levels. A 2.0 GPA is required for junior and senior transfers. D grades are not acceptable. Students must earn, at the university, 30 of the 130 credits necessary for a bachelor's degree. There is no deadline for transfer applications.

Visiting: There is no regular orientation program for prospective students, but guides are available for informal visits to the school. Visitors may sit in on classes, but they may not stay at the school. The best time to visit is weekdays between 9 A.M. and 7 P.M.. Contact the student services office for arrangements.

Financial Aid: About 12% of all students receive financial aid. There are currently 24 academic scholarships available to freshmen. State loans (totaling $50,000) and federal loans (totaling $6348) are also available to students. About 1% of the students also receive work contracts from the university. The total amount of aid available to freshmen is $3000; the average aid awarded to freshmen is $1500. Financial aid packages are awarded on a rolling basis. The university's policy is to attempt to award up to the maximum of financial need. There is no deadline for financial aid applications. Tuition may be paid on the installment plan. The university is a member of CSS. The FAF is required.

Foreign Students: Fewer than 1% of the full-time students come from foreign countries.

Admissions: Foreign students must take TOEFL.

Procedure: Foreign students must show proof of adequate funds. They may apply for any quarter; there are no application deadlines.

Admissions Contact: Gene Hickey, Admissions Counselor.

ARIZONA

ARIZONA STATE UNIVERSITY   C–4
Tempe, Arizona 85287   (602) 965-3255

F/T: 11,728M, 10,132W	Faculty: 1687; I, +$
P/T: 3297M, 3043W	Ph.D.'s: 80%
Grad: 4754M, 5121W	S/F Ratio: 25 to 1
Year: sems, ss	Tuition: $710 ($3250)
Appl: Aug. 1	R and B: $2500
7808 applied	6139 accepted 3439 enrolled
SAT: 427V 493M	ACT: 19 COMPETITIVE

Arizona State University, founded as a coeducational state-supported institution in 1885, consists of 9 undergraduate and several graduate divisions. The undergraduate divisions are the colleges of Architecture, Business Administration, Education, Engineering, Fine Arts, Liberal Arts, Nursing, Public Programs, and Social Work. The library houses 1,650,000 volumes and 1,000,000 microfilm items, and subscribes to 5800 periodicals.

Environment: The modern 566-acre campus contains more than 50 major buildings. It lies 10 miles from the heart of downtown Phoenix. The university also has a 320-acre experimental farm. Single-sex residence halls accommodate 4500 students. The university also sponsors fraternity houses.

Student Life: About 90% of the students are from the north central area, and 90% come from public schools. Twenty percent of the students live on campus. Nine percent are members of minority groups. Students are permitted to keep cars on campus. There are visiting privileges in the dormitories.

Organizations: Undergraduates can participate in the more than 200 student organizations. Eight percent of the men and 5% of the women belong to the 34 national fraternities and sororities. The Lyric Opera Theatre, student theater productions, and art shows are some of the cultural activities offered.

20 ARIZONA

Sports: Arizona State University competes on an intercollegiate level in 11 sports for men and 12 for women. Thirteen intramural sports are offered for men and 12 for women.

Handicapped: Ninety-five percent of the campus is accessible to wheelchair-bound students. Those with hearing problems, visual impairments, or other disabilities may obtain support services through the office for disabled student services.

Services: Students receive the following free services: psychological counseling, placement and career counseling, tutoring, and remedial instruction. Fees are charged for health-care services.

Programs of Study: The university offers the B.A., B.S., B.F.A., B.M., B.S.E., B.A.Ed., B.S.N., B.S.C.J., and B.Arch. degrees. Master's and doctoral degrees are also awarded. Bachelor's degrees are offered in the following subjects: AREA (Asian, Latin American), BUSINESS (accounting, administrative services, business administration, business education, computer science, finance, management, marketing, quantitative business analysis, real estate/insurance, transportation), EDUCATION (adult, early childhood, elementary, health/physical, industrial, secondary, special), ENGLISH (English, journalism), FINE AND PERFORMING ARTS (art, art education, art history, dance, film/photography, music, music education, radio/TV, studio art, theater/dramatics), HEALTH SCIENCES (medical technology, nursing), LANGUAGES (Chinese, French, German, Japanese, Russian, Spanish), MATH AND SCIENCES (astronomy, biochemistry, biology, botany, chemistry, earth science, geology, mathematics, physical science, physics, statistics, zoology), PHILOSOPHY (humanities, philosophy, religion), PREPROFESSIONAL (agriculture, architecture, construction, dentistry, engineering, home economics, law, medicine, pharmacy, social work, technology, veterinary), SOCIAL SCIENCES (anthropology, economics, geography, government/political science, history, international relations, psychology, social sciences, sociology). One-third of all degrees conferred are in the liberal arts.

Required: All students must take 36 semester hours in general-education courses.

Special: Students may design their own majors through the College of Education. Students may also participate in workshops, institutes, seminars, research centers, and a study-abroad program.
Interdisciplinary work in city and regional planning; environment; energy; gerontology; Asian, Latin-American, and Islamic studies; women's studies, and film is also available.

Honors: Honors programs are offered in the colleges of Liberal Arts and Business Administration. There are 26 scholastic honor societies on campus.

Admissions: Seventy-nine percent of those who applied were accepted for the 1981–82 freshman class. The SAT scores of those who enrolled were as follows: Verbal—78% scored below 500, 18% between 500 and 599, and 4% between 600 and 700; Math—64% scored below 500, 27% between 500 and 599, 8% between 600 and 700, and 1% above 700. Of those who took the ACT, 64% scored below 21, 15% between 21 and 23, 9% between 24 and 25, 7% between 26 and 28, and 5% above 28. Thirty percent of the students ranked in the upper fifth of their high school class and 48% in the upper two-fifths. Candidates must have completed 16 Carnegie units, rank in the upper half of their class, and present a GPA of 2.5 or better.

Procedure: The SAT or ACT is required. Deadlines for regular admission are August 1 (fall) and December 21 (spring). Admissions decisions are made on a rolling basis. There is a $10 application fee for nonresidents.

Special: An early decision plan is available. A special admissions program is offered for members of minority groups. CLEP and AP credit is available.

Transfer: For fall 1981, 8926 applications were received, 6886 were accepted, and 4516 students enrolled. A minimum of 12 credit hours and an average of C or better (higher for some majors) are required. D grades do not transfer. Students must study at the college for at least 30 of the 126 semester hours generally required for a degree. Transfer application deadlines are the same as those for freshmen.

Visiting: Orientations for prospective students are scheduled regularly. Weekdays are recommended for informal visits. Guides are available, and overnight accommodations can be arranged.

Financial Aid: About 80% of all students receive financial aid; 45% work part-time on campus. A fund of $2,400,000 provides undergraduate scholarships. Student loans and college-assigned jobs also are available. The average award to freshmen from all sources in 1981–82 totaled $2000. The priority deadline for financial aid applications is April 15. The FFS or SFS is required.

Foreign Students: The 1183 foreign students enrolled full-time at the university make up 3% of its enrollment. An intensive English program, special counseling, and special organizations are provided.

Admissions: Foreign applicants must score 500 or better on the TOEFL. No academic exams are required.

Procedure: Application deadlines are June 15 for fall admission and November 15 for spring admission. Students must present proof of adequate funds for 1 year of study. Foreign students are required to carry health insurance, which is available through the college for a fee.

Admissions Contact: Christine K. Wilkinson, Acting Dean of Admissions.

DE VRY INSTITUTE OF TECHNOLOGY C–4
Phoenix, Arizona 85016 (602) 957-0140
(Recognized Candidate for Accreditation)

F/T: 3379M, 271W	Faculty: 51; n/av
P/T: 104M, 7W	Ph.D.'s: n/av
Grad: none	S/F Ratio: 14 to 1
Year: tri, ss	Tuition: $3025
Appl: October	R and B: n/app
SAT or ACT: required	**LESS COMPETITIVE**

De Vry Institute of Technology, an independent institution founded in 1967, is administered by the Bell & Howell Education Group. It offers undergraduate degrees in electronics engineering technology, computer science for business, and electronics technology.

Environment: The school is located in the city of Phoenix. It has no housing facilities.

Student Life: About a third of the students are from Arizona. Twenty-three percent are members of minority groups. Students live in off-campus apartments, and the college housing office will refer students to available housing. Students may keep cars on campus.

Organizations: The 14 extracurricular activities offered include professional and honor societies, an audio recording association, a microcomputer association, a photography club, and a student activities committee. There are no fraternities or sororities.

Sports: The school does not participate in intercollegiate sports, but offers 5 intramural sports for men and women.

Handicapped: Facilities include wheelchair ramps, elevators, special parking areas, specially equipped rest rooms, and lowered drinking fountains and telephones. Special class scheduling can be arranged, and the school provides necessary tutoring or materials.

Graduates: Over 90% begin careers in business and industry.

Services: Free placement and career counseling and tutoring are available. Fees are charged for health-care services and remedial instruction.

Programs of Study: The institute offers the B.S.Comp.Sci. and the B.S.E.E. degrees. Associate degrees in electronics technology also are available. Undergraduate degrees are awarded in two subjects: BUSINESS (computer science), PREPROFESSIONAL (electronics engineering technology).

Required: Students must follow a specified curriculum and must maintain a GPA of 2.0 or better to graduate.

Honors: Tau Alpha Pi has a chapter on campus, and an honors program is offered in electronics engineering technology.

Admissions: Nineteen percent of the 1981–82 freshmen ranked in the upper fifth of their high school class, 44% in the upper two-fifths. Applicants must be high school graduates and undergo a personal interview. In addition to grades and test scores, the school considers recommendations by high school officials and impressions made during the interview.

Procedure: Applicants must take both the SAT or ACT and the Bell & Howell Education Group Entrance Exam. The application fee is $25. Applications should be submitted by October for fall admission, by March for spring admission, and by July for summer admission. Admissions notification is made on a rolling basis.

Special: A deferred admissions plan is available.

Transfer: Transfers are accepted for all classes. An interview is required. Students must complete at least 36 credits at the school of the 160 required for a bachelor's degree. Grades of C or better transfer. Application deadlines are the same as those for freshmen.

Visiting: Guides are available for informal visits, which may be scheduled for weekdays through the director of admissions.

Financial Aid: About 94% of the students receive aid through the school, and 3% work part-time on campus. Scholarships (average $3850), loans (average $2500, maximum $3000), and work contracts (average $2100, maximum $2680) are available. The FAF is required.

Foreign Students: The 17 foreign students at the school make up less than 1% of the student body.

Admissions: Foreign students must take the TOEFL or the ELS. They must score at least 450 on the TOEFL and at least 106 on the ELS. The SAT and the Bell & Howell Education Group Entrance Exam also are required.

Procedure: Application deadlines are the same as those for other freshmen. Foreign students must provide a doctor's certificate as proof of good health. Evidence of adequate funds for 1 year also is required. Students must carry health insurance, which is available through the school for a fee.

Admissions Contact: Arthur Geiger, Director of Admissions.

EMBRY-RIDDLE AERONAUTICAL UNIVERSITY
(See Embry-Riddle Aeronautical University, FL)

GRAND CANYON COLLEGE C-4
Phoenix, Arizona 85061   (602) 249-3300

F/T: 445M, 469W Faculty: 35; IIB, +$
P/T: 140M, 160W Ph.D.'s: 19%
Grad: 12M, 8W S/F Ratio: 20 to 1
Year: 4-1-4, ss Tuition: $2933
Appl: Aug. 1 R and B: $2190
327 applied 187 accepted 169 enrolled
SAT: 424V 448M ACT: 18 COMPETITIVE

Grand Canyon College, founded in 1949 by the Arizona Southern Baptist Convention, is a small, private, liberal arts college. The library houses 122,000 volumes and subscribes to 750 periodicals.

Environment: The 70-acre self-contained campus, located in northwest Phoenix, features a modern Energy Science building with "open teaching" labs. Four dormitories house 250 students.

Student Life: About 80% of the students are from Arizona, and 88% come from public schools. Twenty-five percent live on campus. Alcoholic beverages are forbidden on or off campus. Students may smoke only in their dormitory rooms. There are curfews for women students. The majority of students are Southern Baptists, and attendance is required at 2 chapel services per week. Eighteen percent of the students are minority-group members. Housing is single-sex, and there are no visiting privileges. Students may keep cars on campus.

Organizations: There are no fraternities or sororities on campus, but the college sponsors many cultural events, special-interest groups, and departmental clubs, including an International Relations Club. There is an active student government, and the dormitory councils have a strong voice in student affairs.

Sports: The college fields 4 intercollegiate teams for men and 3 for women. Men and women each may participate in 6 intramural sports.

Handicapped: About 98% of the campus is accessible to wheelchair-bound students. Wheelchair ramps, special parking, and special class scheduling are available. For the 1% of students with visual impairments, special tutoring and reading services are offered.

Graduates: The freshman dropout rate is 25%. Seventy percent of the graduates pursue advanced degrees; 1% enter medical school, 1% enter dental school, and 5% enter law school.

Services: The college provides free psychological counseling and tutoring to students. Placement aid and health care are available for a fee.

Programs of Study: The college confers the B.A., B.S., and B.S. in Nursing degrees. Bachelor's degrees are awarded in the following subjects: BUSINESS (accounting, business administration, computer science), EDUCATION (elementary, health/physical, secondary), ENGLISH (English, literature, speech), FINE AND PERFORMING ARTS (art, art education, music, music education, studio art, theater/dramatics), HEALTH SCIENCES (nursing), MATH AND SCIENCES (biology, chemistry, earth science, mathematics), SOCIAL SCIENCES (government/political science, history, psychology, social sciences, sociology).

Required: Students must complete 30 semester hours of general-studies requirements, including religion and physical education.

Special: The B.G.S. is offered. High school seniors with exceptional records may apply for the summer term preceding their senior year. The college participates in the Junior Year Abroad Program. Summer seminars for intensive study and wilderness camping programs are possible.

Honors: The college offers an interdisciplinary honors program. Five national honor societies have chapters on campus.

Admissions: Fifty-seven percent of those who applied were accepted for the 1981-82 freshman class. The ACT scores of those who enrolled in a recent freshman class were as follows: 35% between 20 and 26, 14% between 26 and 28, and 4% above 28. Candidates who scored at least 20 on the ACT, completed 16 high school units, and ranked in the upper half of their high school class are admitted unconditionally; others may be admitted on probation.

Procedure: The ACT (preferred) or the SAT is required. The deadlines for regular admission are August 1 (fall), December 1 (winter and spring), and May 1 (summer). There is a rolling admissions plan. Applications should be submitted with a $15 fee.

Special: Early decision, early admissions, and deferred admissions plans are available. AP and CLEP credit is accepted.

Transfer: For fall 1981, 364 transfer students applied, 319 were accepted, and 287 enrolled. Transfer applicants must be in good standing at their former college. An ACT score of 19 is recommended. D grades are not accepted. Students must study at the college for at least 24 of the 128 semester hours needed to receive a bachelor's degree. The transfer application deadlines are August 1 (fall), December 1 (winter), January 1 (spring), and May 1 (summer).

Visiting: Guided tours and interviews with students, faculty, and staff, as well as overnight accommodations, can be scheduled through the admissions office.

Financial Aid: About 80% of all students receive financial aid. Thirty-five percent work part-time on campus. The FAF or FFS is required. March 15 is the aid application deadline for priority consideration for fall.

Foreign Students: Twenty-five full-time students are from foreign countries. Special counseling and organizations are available to these students.

Admissions: Foreign students must achieve a TOEFL score of at least 500. No further exams are necessary.

Procedure: Application deadlines are July 15 (fall), December 15 (spring), and March 15 (summer). Foreign students must submit the results of a complete physical examination. They must also show proof of funds adequate to cover 1 year of study. Health insurance, which is required for foreign students, is available through the college for a fee.

Admissions Contact: Sam Norris, Assistant Director of Admissions.

NORTHERN ARIZONA UNIVERSITY C-2
Flagstaff, Arizona 86011   (602) 523-5511

F/T: 4478M, 4326W Faculty: 492; I, av$
P/T: 2111M&W Ph.D.'s: 78%
Grad: n/av S/F Ratio: 22 to 1
Year: sems, ss Tuition: $710 ($2650)
Appl: July 15 R and B: $1800
4312 applied 4032 accepted 1854 enrolled
ACT: 20 COMPETITIVE

Established in 1899, Northern Arizona University is a state-supported liberal arts, teacher education, and preprofessional training institution. The library contains almost 1 million volumes and subscribes to 7000 periodicals.

Environment: The 650-acre rolling campus is located in an urban area 145 miles north of Phoenix at the foot of the San Francisco Peaks. The architecture of the campus is designed to fit into the natural surroundings of mountains, desert, and forests. The campus includes a forestry center, a creative arts center, and the new Sky Dome, a 16,000-seat athletic and cultural building. Residence halls accommodate more than 5000 single and married students. The university also sponsors sorority houses and off-campus dormitories.

Student Life: About 85% of the students come from the Southwest; 75% come from Arizona. Ninety-eight percent of entering freshmen come from public schools. About 34% live off campus. About 12% of the students are minority-group members. Campus housing is both coed and single-sex; there are visiting privileges. Students are permitted to keep cars on campus.

Organizations: There are fraternities and sororities to which about 10% of the men and women belong. In addition, there are numerous musical, dramatic, literary, religious, and other organizations and activities. Among the nearby recreational areas are the Grand Canyon and Petrified Forest national parks and 11 national monuments.

Sports: There are 7 intercollegiate sports for men and 6 for women, and 17 intramural sports for men and 16 for women.

22 ARIZONA

Handicapped: About 50% of the campus is accessible to handicapped students. Special facilities include wheelchair ramps, special parking, elevators, specially equipped rest rooms, and lowered drinking fountains and telephones. Special class scheduling is also available. There are 2 counselors and 3 assistants to help handicapped students. Less than 1% of the students have hearing impairments; fewer than 1% are visually impaired.

Graduates: About 2% of the students drop out by the end of the freshman year. Eighteen percent of the graduates pursue graduate study.

Services: The following free services are provided to students: psychological counseling, placement and career counseling (for graduates as well as undergraduates), tutoring, and remedial instruction. Health care is available for a fee.

Programs of Study: The university offers the B.A., B.F.A., B.Mus., B.Mus.Ed., B.S.Ed., and B.S. degrees. Associate, master's, and doctoral degrees are also awarded. Bachelor's degrees are offered in the following subjects: AREA STUDIES (Latin American), BUSINESS (accounting, business administration, computer science, finance, management, marketing), EDUCATION (early childhood, elementary, health/physical, industrial, recreational leadership, secondary, special), ENGLISH (English, journalism, literature, speech), FINE AND PERFORMING ARTS (art, art education, art history, arts management, instrumental, jazz, music, music education, music history and literature, radio/TV, theater/dramatics, voice), HEALTH SCIENCES (dental hygiene, medical radiography, medical technology, microbiology, nursing, physical therapy, speech therapy), LANGUAGES (French, German, Spanish), MATH AND SCIENCES (astronomy, biology, botany, chemistry, earth science, ecology/environmental science, geochemistry, geology, mathematics, physical sciences, physics, zoology), PHILOSOPHY (philosophy), PREPROFESSIONAL (dentistry, engineering, forestry, law, medicine, ministry, veterinary), SOCIAL SCIENCES (anthropology, geography, government/political science, legal assistance, police science, psychology, social sciences, sociology). Twenty percent of all undergraduate degrees are conferred in education, 20% in social sciences, and 15% in business.

Special: Combined B.A.-B.S. degrees may be earned in several subjects.

Honors: There is a university-wide honors program.

Admissions: About 94% of those who applied were accepted for the 1981-82 freshman class. Graduation from an accredited high school with a 2.5 GPA and a rank in the top half is required. Students should complete 16 Carnegie units. The university considers, in order of importance, advanced placement or honors courses, high school recommendations, impressions made during an interview, and extracurricular activities.

Procedure: The SAT or ACT is required. The deadlines for admission applications are July 15 (fall) and December 15 (spring). There is a $10 application fee for nonresidents only. Admissions are granted on a rolling basis.

Special: The university has an early decision plan. AP and CLEP credit is available.

Transfer: Transfer students are considered for all classes. A 2.0 GPA is required. Minimum scores of 930 on the SAT or 21 on the ACT are recommended. D grades do not transfer. In order to receive a bachelor's degree, students must complete 125 credits. Deadlines are the same as those for freshman applicants.

Visiting: A parent-senior day is held in the spring and fall as an orientation for prospective students. The program includes reception, meeting, tour, and discussion. Guides are available for informal visits to the school. Visitors may sit in on classes, but may not stay on campus. The admissions office will make arrangements.

Financial Aid: More than $3 million in loans, scholarships, grants, and work-study funds are available to undergraduates. Thirty-five percent of the students work part-time on campus. The FAF or FFS is required. Application deadlines are April 15 (fall) and November 1 (spring). Notification is on a rolling basis.

Foreign Students: Currently, 240 foreign students are enrolled full-time at the university. Special counseling and special organizations are available for these students.

Admissions: A minimum score of 500 on the TOEFL is required; foreign students must also have completed at least 2 semesters of collegiate English. College entrance exams are not required.

Procedure: Application deadlines for foreign students are May 1 for fall, October 1 for spring, and March 1 for summer. Students must submit a doctor's statement as proof of health, and must provide proof of funds adequate to cover 1 year of study. Health insurance is not required, but is available through the university for a fee.

Admissions Contact: Margaret Cibik, Director of Admissions and New Student Programs.

PRESCOTT COLLEGE C-3
Formerly Prescott Center College
Prescott, Arizona 86301 (602) 778-2090
(Recognized Candidate for Accreditation)

F/T: 45M, 50W	Faculty:	10; IV, --$
P/T: 5M, 7W	Ph.D.'s:	75%
Grad: none	S/F Ratio:	7 to 1
Year: 4-1-4	Tuition:	$3375
Appl: July 15	R and B:	n/app
60 applied	42 accepted	39 enrolled
SAT, ACT: not required		COMPETITIVE

Prescott College offers baccalaureate study in the liberal arts and sciences. Students design their own programs and work closely with instructors. The college places heavy emphasis on experiential education.

Environment: The 2-acre campus is located in the mountains of central Arizona, 90 miles north of Phoenix. There are no residence halls.

Student Life: About 10% of the students come from Arizona. Twenty-five percent are Protestant, 20% Catholic, and 5% Jewish. Two percent are members of minority groups.

Organizations: There are no social fraternities or sororities. Extracurricular activities include sports groups, outdoor clubs, photography groups, student government, and travel clubs. Slide shows, film showings, and other events are held on campus.

Sports: Three intramural sports are offered for both sexes.

Handicapped: About 50% of the campus is accessible to students with physical handicaps. Special parking, ramps, and class scheduling are provided.

Graduates: About 10% of the freshmen withdraw by the end of their first year, and 63% remain to complete their degrees. About 24% of the graduates go on to further study: 1% enter medical school, 1% enter dental school, and 10% enter law school. Twenty percent go into business or industry.

Services: Placement, psychological, and career counseling; tutoring; and remedial instruction are available free of charge.

Programs of Study: The B.A. is offered. Students design their own majors within the framework of 5 basic programs: environment studies, outdoor leadership, humanities, Southwest studies, and human development. They may choose from traditional specializations, including AREA STUDIES (American, Asian), BUSINESS (management), EDUCATION (early childhood, elementary, secondary, special), ENGLISH (English, journalism, literature), FINE AND PERFORMING ARTS (dance, film/photography), HEALTH SCIENCES (environmental health), LANGUAGES (French, Greek/Latin, Spanish). MATH AND SCIENCES (astronomy, biology, botany, chemistry, earth science, ecology/environmental science, geology, mathematics, natural sciences, oceanography, physical sciences, physics, statistics, zoology), PHILOSOPHY (classics, humanities, philosophy, religion), PREPROFESSIONAL (agriculture, forestry, social work), SOCIAL SCIENCES (anthropology, economics, geography, government/political science, history, international relations, psychology, social sciences, sociology). About 25% of the students earn degrees in education, 25% in sciences, and 25% in social sciences.

Required: To graduate, a student must prepare a portfolio demonstrating competence in a chosen field.

Special: The average class size is 8 students. Letter grades are optional, and narrative evaluations are used. The college emphasizes "hands-on" experience such as internships. It is best known for its environmental studies and outdoor leadership programs.

Admissions: About 70% of those who applied for the 1981-82 freshman class were accepted. Applicants must rank in the upper 60% of their class and present at least a D+/C- average. Though neither the SAT nor the ACT is required, standardized test scores will be considered by admissions officers if submitted. Other factors considered, in decreasing order of importance, are personality, impressions made by the required personal essay and the recommended personal interview, evidence of special talents, recommendations by school officials, and leadership and extracurricular activities records.

Procedure: The application deadline for fall is July 15. Notification is on a rolling basis, and the college generally lets applicants know 2 weeks after all data are submitted. There is a $15 application fee.

Special: AP and CLEP credit is available.

Transfer: For fall 1981, 23 transfer students applied, 14 were accepted, and 12 enrolled. A minimum GPA of 2.0 is recommended; applicants should submit an essay and letters of recommendation in addition to their transcript and should arrange for a personal interview. Grades of C or better transfer. Students must study on campus 1 year, earning at least 45 quarter credits, to graduate. Graduation is based on competence, not solely on credits. The application deadline for fall entry is July 15.

Visiting: Formal freshman orientation is a 3½-week backpacking trip through northern Arizona. Informal campus visits may be arranged at any time with the director of admissions. Visitors may sit in on classes.

Financial Aid: Half the students receive aid through the college; 15% work part-time on campus. The college participates in all federal financial aid programs, and work/study also is available. The average award to freshmen from all sources totals $2000. Aid applicants should submit the FAF as early as possible, preferably by March 1. The college is a member of CSS. Need is the determining factor in awarding aid.

Foreign Students: Prescott College offers special organizations for foreign students.

Admissions: Foreign applicants must take the TOEFL. No other exams are required.

Procedure: Application deadlines are July 1 (fall), November 15 (winter), and December 15 (spring). Students must present proof of health and of adequate funds.

Admissions Contact: Derk Janssen, Director of Admissions.

UNIVERSITY OF ARIZONA D-4
Tucson, Arizona 85721 (602) 626-3432

F/T: 10,538M, 9360W	Faculty:	1427; I, + + $
P/T: 3870M, 3437W	Ph.D.'s:	81%
Grad: 4237M, 3764W	S/F Ratio:	22 to 1
Year: sems, ss	Tuition:	$710 ($3250)
Appl: July 1	R and B:	$2275
8859 applied	7355 accepted	4181 enrolled
ACT: 22		COMPETITIVE

The University of Arizona, which was founded in 1885 and began as a single building in the desert, now consists of 14 colleges with more than 35,000 students. The library houses 1,444,471 volumes and over a million microform items, and subscribes to more than 20,000 periodicals.

Environment: The 318-acre campus lies in the heart of Tucson, a winter resort area, and has 122 major buildings. Coed and single-sex dormitories accommodate over 5000 students. Fraternity, sorority, and married-student housing also is available.

Student Life: About 80% of the undergraduates are from Arizona. Ninety-two percent come from public schools. All states of the Union and over 100 foreign countries are represented. One-fourth of the students live on campus. Eight percent are members of minority groups. Fifteen percent identify themselves as Catholic, 13% as Protestant, and 3% as Jewish. Cars are allowed, and drinking is permitted in campus living units only. Intervisitation is permitted in single-sex housing. Campus religious facilities are available for members of all faiths.

Organizations: Over 30 social and fraternal organizations are represented on campus; 20% of the students belong. The student government owns and operates 3 bookstores, a photo service, a travel service, and other enterprises. Students run the student appropriations board and have seats on the faculty senate and most important faculty committees.

Sports: The university competes on an intercollegiate level in 9 sports for men and 10 for women. About 25 intramural sports are offered for men and 23 for women.

Handicapped: About 90% of the campus is accessible to wheelchair-bound students. There are wheelchair ramps, as well as special parking and building facilities. Special class scheduling can be arranged, and counselors are available.

Graduates: Twenty percent of the freshmen drop out by the end of the first year, and 60% remain to graduate. Thirty-five percent of the graduates pursue advanced degrees.

Services: Students receive the following free services: health care, psychological counseling, placement assistance, career counseling, tutoring, and remedial instruction.

ARIZONA 23

Programs of Study: The university grants the B.A., B.Arch., B.F.A., B.Land.Arch., B.Mus., B.S., B.S.B.A., B.S.N., B.H.E., B.Pharm., B.S.P.A., and B.S. in various fields of engineering. Master's and doctoral degrees also are available. Bachelor's degrees are offered in the following subjects: AREA STUDIES (Latin American, Mexican/American, Oriental), BUSINESS (accounting, business administration, business education, computer science, finance, management, marketing, operations management, personnel management, public administration, real estate/insurance, regional development), EDUCATION (early childhood, elementary, health/physical, secondary), ENGLISH (creative writing, English, journalism, literature, speech), FINE AND PERFORMING ARTS (art, art education, art history, dance, music, music education, radio/TV, studio art, theater/dramatics), HEALTH SCIENCES (medical technology, nursing, occupational safety and health, speech therapy), LANGUAGES (French, German, Greek/Latin, Italian, linguistics, Portuguese, Romance languages, Russian, Spanish), MATH AND SCIENCES (astronomy, biology, chemistry, earth science, ecology/environmental science, geology, geosciences, hydrology, mathematics, microbiology, physics), PHILOSOPHY (classics, philosophy, religion), PREPROFESSIONAL (agriculture, architecture, engineering—agricultural, engineering—chemical, engineering—civil, engineering—electrical, engineering—energy, engineering—geological, engineering—industrial, engineering mathematics, engineering—mechanical, engineering—mining, engineering physics, engineering—systems, home economics, landscape architecture, pharmacy), SOCIAL SCIENCES (anthropology, economics, geography, government/political science, history, psychology, social sciences, sociology). Twenty-eight percent of degrees conferred are in preprofessional studies, 12% are in education, and 20% are in business.

Required: All students must fulfill requirements in English composition and physical education.

Special: Students may spend their third year abroad. The university has an advanced-level program in addiction studies. A B.G.S. degree is available.

Honors: Honors programs are offered in all disciplines. Twenty-two national honor societies have chapters on campus, including Phi Beta Kappa.

Admissions: Eighty-three percent of those who applied were accepted for the 1981–82 freshman class. Candidates should have completed 16 Carnegie units, present at least a 2.0 average, and rank in the top half of their graduating class. The university also considers recommendations, extracurricular activities, advanced placement or honors courses, leadership potential, and evidence of special talents.

Procedure: The SAT or ACT is required, and must be taken in December or February of the senior year. Application deadlines are July 1 (fall), December 1 (spring), and May 1 (summer). Applications should be submitted with a $10 fee. Notifications are made on a rolling basis.

Special: An early admissions plan is available. CLEP and AP credit is accepted.

Transfer: For fall 1981, 4896 students applied, 3636 were accepted, and 2294 enrolled. A minimum average of C is required; D grades do not transfer. Students must complete at least 30 units on campus of the 125 or more required for a degree. Application deadlines are the same as those for freshmen.

Visiting: Guides are available for informal visits; weekdays are recommended. Arrangements can be made through the office of the dean of students.

Financial Aid: About 55% of all students receive financial aid; 13% work part-time on campus. The average amount of aid to freshmen from all sources in 1981–82 was $900. Each year, up to 1500 freshmen are awarded scholarships. The Student Assistance Financial Evaluation (SAFE) and the financial aid application must be filed by May 1.

Foreign Students: The 1454 foreign students enrolled full-time make up about 6% of the student body. An intensive English program, special counseling, and special organizations are provided for these students.

Admissions: Students must score 500 or better on the TOEFL. No academic exams are required.

Procedure: Application deadlines are May 15 (fall), September 15 (spring), and April 1 (summer). Students must present proof of adequate funds for 1 calendar year and must carry health insurance, which is available through the university for a fee.

Admissions Contact: David L. Windsor, Dean of Admissions and Records.

24 ARIZONA

WESTERN INTERNATIONAL UNIVERSITY
C-4

Phoenix, Arizona 85021   (602) 943-2311
(Recognized Candidate for Accreditation)

F/T: 72M, 75W	Faculty: 52; n/av
P/T: none	Ph.D.'s: 10%
Grad: 8M, 2W	S/F Ratio: 10 to 1
Year: tri	Tuition: $1825
Appl: open	R and B: n/app
88 applied	88 accepted
SAT or ACT: not required	NONCOMPETITIVE

Western International University, an independent institution founded in 1978, offers undergraduate and graduate degrees in business fields.

Environment: Located in the city of Phoenix, the campus is about 3 acres in size. The university does not sponsor housing facilities.

Student Life: About 17% of the students are members of minority groups. Students may have cars on campus. The university describes student life as almost free of regulation.

Organizations: Students may participate in university governance through a student advisory panel. There are no fraternities or sororities.

Sports: No intercollegiate or intramural sports programs are offered.

Handicapped: No special facilities are available for handicapped students.

Graduates: About 20% of the graduates seek advanced degrees, and 80% begin careers in business and industry.

Services: Students receive free placement and career counseling, tutoring, and remedial instruction.

Programs of Study: The university offers the B.B.A. and B.A. degrees. Master's degrees also are available. Bachelor's degrees are offered in the following subjects: BUSINESS (accounting, administrative services, data processing, hospitality management, information resources management, management, transportation, travel/tourism).

Required: Students must complete a general curriculum, maintain a GPA of 2.0 or better, and attend convocations to graduate.

Special: Monthly scheduling of courses allows students maximum flexibility. The university will assess prior experiential learning. A Personalized Educational Program leads to the B.A. degree.

Admissions: All applicants for the 1981–82 freshman class were accepted. The university considers prior academic record, recommendations from school officials, impressions made during the personal interview required of all applicants, personality, evidence of special talents, extracurricular activities, and leadership record.

Procedure: Neither the SAT nor the ACT is required, but tests may be needed for assessment of prior nonacademic learning. Application deadlines are open. New students may apply to any term. The application fee is $25.

Special: Early admissions, early decision, and deferred admissions plans are available. CLEP credit is accepted.

Transfer: Transfer students are accepted for all terms. Applicants must undergo an interview, and it is preferred that they have a GPA of 2.0 or better. D grades do not transfer. Undergraduates must take at least 12 credits at the university of the 120 required for graduation. Application deadlines are open.

Visiting: Orientations for prospective students are scheduled in May, September, and February. Guides are available for informal visits, and visitors may sit in on classes. Visits can be arranged during class hours with the registrar.

Financial Aid: About 29% of the students receive aid through the university, and 3% work part-time on campus. Loans of up to $2500 are available to freshmen; the average award from all sources is $645. Students must submit the FFS at least 2 weeks before enrollment.

Foreign Students: About 17 foreign students are enrolled at the university. Special counseling is available to them.

Admissions: It is recommended that students take the TOEFL and present a minimum score of 500. Applicants may take the college's own test of English proficiency instead. No further exams are required.

Procedure: Application deadlines are open, and new students may apply for all terms. Students must submit a health evaluation form and show evidence of adequate funds for 12 months.

Admissions Contact: Judy Beechen, Assistant Director of Admissions.

ARKANSAS

ARKANSAS COLLEGE
C-2

Batesville, Arkansas 72501   (501) 793-9813

F/T: 170M, 225W	Faculty: 27; IIB, n/av
P/T: 43M, 76W	Ph.D.'s: 56%
Grad: none	S/F Ratio: 11 to 1
Year: 4-1-4, ss	Tuition: $3300
Appl: August	R and B: $1596
286 applied	215 accepted	155 enrolled
ACT: 18	COMPETITIVE

Arkansas College, founded in 1872, is operated by the Arkansas Oklahoma Synod of the Presbyterian Church of the United States. The college is accredited by the NCATE. The library houses over 68,000 volumes and holds subscriptions to over 500 periodicals.

Environment: The 100-acre campus includes 18 buildings and is located in the White River area, 90 miles from Little Rock. A 4-acre lake is part of the college's recreational facilities.

Student Life: About 83% of the students are Arkansas residents and 99% of entering freshmen come from public schools. Dormitories accommodate 51% of the students. The majority of the students are not members of the supporting church; 94% are Protestant and 6% are Catholic. Thirteen percent are minority-group members. Campus housing is single-sex; there are visiting privileges. Permission is necessary for cars on campus; attendance is recommended at assemblies.

Organizations: There are 2 fraternities and 2 sororities to which 27% of the men and 27% of the women belong.

Sports: The school competes on an intercollegiate level in 5 sports for men and 4 for women. There are 9 intramural sports for men and 8 for women.

Handicapped: About 50% of the campus is accessible to physically handicapped students. There are no visually or hearing impaired students.

Graduates: By the end of the freshman year, 30% drop out; 30% remain to graduate, and more than 28% of the graduates pursue graduate degrees. One percent enter medical school, 2% enter dental school, and 5% enter law school.

Services: Students receive the following services free of charge: placement, career counseling, some health care services, and remedial instruction. In addition to job listings, there is a resume and application letters service.

Programs of Study: All programs lead to the B.A. degree. Bachelor's degrees are offered in the following subjects: BUSINESS (accounting, business administration, computer science, management), EDUCATION (elementary, health/physical), ENGLISH (literature), FINE AND PERFORMING ARTS (media arts, music, music education, theater/dramatics), HEALTH SCIENCES (health care administration, medical technology), MATH AND SCIENCES (biology, chemistry, mathematics), PREPROFESSIONAL (social work), SOCIAL SCIENCES (history, psychology). Twenty-nine percent of degrees conferred are in education; 19% are in business; 17% are in math and sciences; and 16% are in social sciences.

Required: A liberal arts distribution must be fulfilled by all students; physical education is also required.

Special: Professional preparation is offered to those planning to teach secondary school. The college cooperates with several other colleges across the nation in exchanging students during the January interim.

Honors: Honor students are eligible for membership in Alpha Chi.

Admissions: Seventy-five percent of those applying for the 1981–82 freshman class were accepted. The candidate should have completed 16 standard units of high school work. Although the high school academic record is the major basis for admission, other factors considered are community and school activities, demonstrated interest in studies, satisfactory performance on the SAT or ACT, and ability to finance the college education.

Procedure: The SAT or ACT is required and should be taken in December or January of the senior year. An interview with a member of the admissions staff or an alumnus will be arranged if a candidate is unable to visit the campus. The application, with a $15 fee, should be submitted well before the beginning of the semester for which the applicant wishes to enroll. The college operates a rolling admission policy.

Special: Through general and subject exams, students can get CLEP credit; credit is also granted for AP exams.

Transfer: For Fall 1981, 85 transfer students applied; 83 were accepted and enrolled. Transfer applicants must have a 2.5 GPA, a minimum ACT score of 18, and a satisfactory report from their previous school. D grades do not transfer. Transfers must complete, at the college, 24 of the 120 hours required for the bachelor's degree. A rolling admissions policy is employed.

Visiting: No formal orientations are provided, but day-long visits with a student guide can be arranged through the admissions office. Visitors may sit in on classes, and can remain overnight. The best times for campus visits are 8 to 5, Monday through Friday.

Financial Aid: About 89% of all students receive some financial aid; scholarships average $700. Forty-six percent of the students work part-time on campus. Scholarships and loans from all sources, combined with campus employment, may bring a first-year student an average of $1050 in financial aid. Prepayment of tuition may be handled on the installment plan. Application for financial aid requires the FFS and should be made by August.

Foreign Students: About 1% of the students are from foreign countries.

Admissions: Foreign students must achieve a score of 500 on the TOEFL and 18 on the ACT to qualify for admission.

Procedure: The application deadline for fall entry is August 1. Foreign students must provide proof of funds adequate to cover 1 year of study. They must also carry health insurance.

Admissions Contact: John Thompson, Director of Admissions.

ARKANSAS STATE UNIVERSITY D–2
Jonesboro, Arkansas 72467   1 (800) 382-3030 (in state)
                             1 (800) 643-0080 (out of state)

F/T: 2752M, 2892W	Faculty: n/av; IIA, –$
P/T: 412M, 747W	Ph.D.'s: 60%
Grad: 280M, 365W	S/F Ratio: 21 to 1
Year: sems, ss	Tuition: $660 ($1060)
Appl: open	R and B: $1440
1700 accepted	1637 enrolled
ACT: 17	LESS COMPETITIVE

Arkansas State University, founded in 1909, is a state-supported university. The library houses 500,000 volumes and subscribes to 3900 periodicals.

Environment: The 800-acre campus is located in a suburban area 65 miles from Memphis, Tennessee, and 136 miles from Little Rock, Arkansas. About 25% of the 42 buildings have been built or remodeled in recent years. Two high-rise dormitories accommodate 1200 women and 1100 men. The university also sponsors married-student housing.

Student Life: Eighty-nine percent of the students are from Arkansas. Ninety-eight percent attended public schools. About 30% live on campus. Ten percent are members of minority groups. Dormitories are single-sex, and there are visiting privileges. Students may keep cars on campus. Day-care services are provided.

Organizations: Ten percent of the students belong to 1 of 11 fraternities and 8 sororities. There are no fraternity or sorority houses, but the women's dormitory contains 4 sorority suites. Clubs, professional societies, special-interest groups, class organizations, and religious organizations are available.

Sports: The university participates in intercollegiate competition in 12 sports for men and 6 for women. Nine intramural sports are offered for men and 8 for women.

Handicapped: A special counselor is available for handicapped students. Facilities include wheelchair ramps, parking areas, elevators, lowered drinking fountains, and specially equipped rest rooms. Special class scheduling is also available.

Graduates: The freshman dropout rate is 34%, and 40% of the freshmen remain to graduate.

Services: The following services are available free to students: placement, career and psychological counseling, health care, and tutoring. Fees are charged for remedial instruction.

Programs of Study: The university confers the following degrees: B.A., B.F.A., B.M., B.S.E., B.S.N., B.S., B.S.Agr., B.M.E., B.S.Ed., B.S.Ag., and B.Mus.Ed. Associate and master's degrees are also awarded. Bachelor's degrees are offered in the following subjects: BUSINESS (accounting, business administration, business education, computer science, finance, management, marketing, real estate/insurance), EDUCATION (early childhood, elementary, health/physical, secondary, special), ENGLISH (English, journalism, literature, speech), FINE AND PERFORMING ARTS (art, art education, music, music education, radio/TV, theater/dramatics), HEALTH SCIENCES (medical technology, nursing, radiologic technology, speech pathology), LANGUAGES (French, Spanish), MATH AND SCIENCES (biology, botany, chemistry, mathematics, physical sciences, physics, zoology), PHILOSOPHY (philosophy), PREPROFESSIONAL (agriculture, architecture, dentistry, engineering, law, library science, medicine, optometry, pharmacy, social work, veterinary), SOCIAL SCIENCES (geography, government/political science, history, psychology, social sciences, sociology). About 26% of degrees conferred are in social sciences and in education.

Required: All students must complete a distribution of courses in general education. Men and women must take either 2 hours of ROTC or 2 hours of physical education.

Special: A 5-year program is offered for students interested in earning a combined B.S.-B.A. degree. Opportunities for foreign travel are periodically available. Work-study programs are offered.

Honors: Honor societies are open to qualified students.

Admissions: Candidates must have earned a GPA of 2.0 or better in 15 Carnegie units of work, be graduates of an accredited high school, and present recommendations from school officials. Graduates of Arkansas high schools are accepted unconditionally.

Procedure: The ACT is required (though not considered in the admissions decision, it is used for placement purposes). Applications should be submitted no later than 2 weeks after classes begin in the fall. Freshmen are admitted in fall, summer, and spring. The university uses a rolling admissions plan. There is no application fee.

Special: CLEP credit is given.

Transfer: About 80% of the transfer applicants are accepted. Transfer students must have a minimum cumulative GPA of 2.0, must present ACT scores, and must not have withdrawn from the previous school because of poor standing. D grades transfer. At least 32 of the 124 semester hours required to graduate must be earned in residence. Applications may be submitted any time before the beginning of the semester of enrollment.

Visiting: There are regularly scheduled orientations for prospective students. Guides also are available for weekday visits, which can be arranged with the admissions coordinator.

Financial Aid: Eighty-five percent of the students receive financial aid, and 25% work part-time on campus. Scholarships, loans, grants-in-aid, and work-study are available. The university awards freshman scholarships each year; the average award from all sources in 1981–82 was $1000. The FFS is required from aid applicants. Deadline for aid applications is April 1.

Foreign Students: Twenty-two foreign students are enrolled at the university. Special organizations and counseling are provided.

Admissions: Foreign applicants must score at least 500 on the TOEFL. No academic exams are required.

Procedure: Application deadlines are open. Students must present proof of adequate funds for the length of time they plan to study at the university.

Admissions Contact: Karon Sturdivant, Admissions Coordinator.

ARKANSAS TECH UNIVERSITY B–2
Russellville, Arkansas 72801   (501) 968-0343

F/T: 1600M, 1655W	Faculty: 164; IIB, +$
P/T: none	Ph.D.'s: 50%
Grad: none	S/F Ratio: 19 to 1
Year: sems, ss	Tuition: $735 ($1435)
Appl: Aug. 1	R and B: $1440
ACT: 19	LESS COMPETITIVE

Arkansas Tech University, established in 1909, is a state-supported college offering training in the liberal arts, education, and various technical fields. The library houses over 99,096 volumes and subscribes to more than 927 periodicals.

Environment: The 487-acre campus is located on the north edge of Russellville on Interstate 40. Classroom and lab buildings and the dormitories are arranged around the administration building. The out-

26 ARKANSAS

lying acreage provides space for athletic fields and part of the college farm.

Student Life: The university serves a student body drawn predominantly from Arkansas, approximately 55% of whom live on campus in the residence halls. Ninety-seven percent of entering freshmen come from public schools. The university has no requirement concerning religious attendance, but provides religious facilities for students of Catholic and Protestant faiths. Campus housing is single-sex, and there are visiting privileges. Students may keep cars on campus. Smoking is permitted everywhere but in the classrooms, and drinking is not permitted anywhere on campus.

Organizations: There are 6 local fraternities and 4 local sororities which are nationally affiliated; there are also 66 other charter organizations. The academic program is supplemented by many extracurricular activities.

Sports: Arkansas Tech University competes on an intercollegiate level in 10 sports for men and 3 for women. There are 3 intramural sports open to men and women.

Handicapped: Only 20% of the campus is accessible to physically handicapped students. No visually or hearing impaired students are enrolled.

Graduates: The freshman dropout rate is about 15%, and of the graduates, 15% pursue graduate study. One percent of those students enter medical school; 1% enter dental school; and 1% enter law school. Twenty percent pursue careers in business and industry.

Services: Students receive the following services free of charge: placement and career counseling, health care, tutoring, and remedial instruction. Placement services are available for undergraduates through the placement director.

Programs of Study: The university confers the B.A., B.F.A., and B.S. degrees. Associate and master's degrees are also awarded. Bachelor's degrees are offered in the following subjects: AREA STUDIES (American), BUSINESS (accounting, business administration, business education, computer science, finance, management, marketing), EDUCATION (elementary, health/physical, secondary), ENGLISH (English, journalism, speech), FINE AND PERFORMING ARTS (art, art education, music, music education), HEALTH SCIENCES (medical technology, nursing), LANGUAGES (French, German, Spanish), MATH AND SCIENCES (biology, chemistry, geology, mathematics, physics), PRE-PROFESSIONAL (agriculture, dentistry, engineering, forestry, law, library science, medicine, pharmacy, veterinary), SOCIAL SCIENCES (economics, government/political science, history, psychology, sociology). Twenty-five percent of degrees conferred are in business; 17% are in education; 12% are in fine and performing arts; 10% are in math and sciences.

Required: All students must take a minimum of 39 hours in specific general education courses including 2 semester hours of physical education.

Special: Independent study is available to seniors. Interdisciplinary courses are included in the general education curriculum and a general studies degree is offered.

Honors: Honor students may become eligible for membership in many departmental and honor societies, such as Tau Beta Sigma.

Admissions: For a recent freshman class, 99% of those who applied were accepted. Applicants who lack a high school degree may substitute 15 Carnegie high school units and the recommendation of the principal. Out-of-state applicants have the same entrance requirements.

Procedure: The SAT or ACT is required. Application deadlines are August 1 (fall) and December 15 (spring). Notification is on a rolling basis. No application fee is required.

Special: Early decision, early admissions, and deferred admissions are offered. There is a rolling admissions plan. CLEP general and subject exams are used.

Transfer: Transfers are accepted for the second-semester-freshman, sophomore, and junior classes. A C average is required. D grades transfer if other grades are high enough to maintain a C average. The student must study a minimum of 6 months in residence, and must complete, at the university, 30 of the 120 semester hours necessary for the bachelor's degree. Deadlines for transfer applications are the same as those for freshman applications.

Visiting: Visitors are welcome at the university. Orientation and guided tours are scheduled. Day-long visits with a student guide can also be arranged by the admissions office.

Financial Aid: About 50% of all students receive financial aid. Scholarship funds provide approximately 450 undergraduates with scholarships averaging about $720. Student loans from federal, college, and private sources average about $725. May 1 is the suggested deadline for aid applications. Tuition may be paid on the installment plan.

Foreign Students: The university accepts foreign applicants.

Admissions: Foreign students must take the TOEFL and either the SAT or ACT.

Procedure: Foreign students may apply for admission to the fall, spring, and summer terms. Application deadlines are open. All fees are payable in advance of each semester.

Admissions Contact: Dix Stallings, Director of Admissions.

THE COLLEGE OF THE OZARKS   B-2
Clarksville, Arkansas 72830   (501) 754-8715

F/T: 344M, 321W	Faculty: 40; IIB, n/av
P/T: 10M, 9W	Ph.D.'s: 44%
Grad: none	S/F Ratio: 14 to 1
Year: 4-1-4	Tuition: $1245
Appl: July 1	R and B: $1370
356 applied	288 accepted	149 enrolled
ACT: 16		LESS COMPETITIVE

The College of the Ozarks, founded in 1834, is a privately controlled, liberal arts college affiliated with the Presbyterian Church. The library contains 73,700 volumes, 2000 stereo recordings, and audiovisual equipment, and subscribes to 520 periodicals.

Environment: The 36-acre urban campus is located 100 miles from Little Rock. The physical plant includes 3 dorms (housing 150 women and 300 men), married student housing, on-campus apartments, a science center, a gymnasium with pool, a theater, and art and music buildings.

Student Life: Approximately 66% of the students are Arkansas residents. Fifty-five percent of the students live on campus. Fifty-two percent are Protestant and 11% Catholic. About 15% are members of minority groups. College housing is coed. Students may keep cars on campus.

Organizations: There are no fraternities or sororities, but extracurricular activities are numerous.

Sports: The college fields 7 intercollegiate teams for men and 3 for women. Five intramural sports are available to men and 5 to women.

Handicapped: No special facilities exist for physically handicapped students.

Graduates: Of the 55% of freshmen who remain to graduate, about 12% continue to work toward a graduate or professional degree.

Services: Students receive the following services free of charge: placement and career counseling, health care, tutoring and remedial instruction, and psychological counseling. In addition to job listings, interviewing and resume-writing workshops are available.

Programs of Study: The college confers the B.A. and B.S. degrees. Bachelor's degrees are offered in the following subjects: BUSINESS (accounting, business administration, business education, management, marketing), EDUCATION (elementary, secondary), ENGLISH (communications, English, speech), FINE AND PERFORMING ARTS (art, art education, music, music education, radio/TV, theater/dramatics), HEALTH SCIENCES (medical technology, nursing), MATH AND SCIENCES (biology, chemistry, mathematics, natural sciences, physics), PHILOSOPHY (Christian education, humanities, philosophy, religion), PREPROFESSIONAL (dentistry, engineering, forestry, law, medicine, ministry, pharmacy, social work, veterinary), SOCIAL SCIENCES (government/political science, history, psychology, social sciences, sociology). Thirty-four percent of degrees conferred are in business, 32% in education, 9% in math and science.

Required: Students are required to take 2 courses in English, one course in Bible, and 4 hours of physical education.

Special: A combined study and work experience is offered in the Mission Outreach Program. The college also offers a combination Medical Technology and Radiological Technology program. The B.G.S. degree is offered.

Honors: The college has chapters of Alpha Chi and Alpha Theta on campus.

Admissions: For the 1981-82 freshman class, 80% of applicants were accepted. In a recent freshman class, the ACT scores of those who enrolled were as follows: 51% were between 20 and 23; 2% were between 24 and 26; and 1% were between 27 and 28. Generally, students must have a C average. Advanced placement or honors courses, recommendations by high school officials, and impressions made during an interview also are considered.

Procedure: The SAT or ACT is required. The application deadlines are July 1 (fall) and January 1 (spring). The application fee is $20.

Special: Up to 30 hours of credit are available to qualifying freshmen through CLEP. The college also has early decision and admissions plans.

Transfer: Almost all transfer applicants are accepted. The minimum requirements are a C average, an ACT score of 15, and 12 credit hours. Thirty semester hours of the 128 required for a bachelor's degree must be taken in residence. The application deadlines are July 1 (fall) and January 1 (spring).

Visiting: No regular orientations are scheduled, but guided tours can be arranged on weekdays through the admissions office. Visitors may arrange to stay at the school.

Financial Aid: About 70% of all students receive aid through the school. Forty-four percent work part-time on campus. Scholarships amounting to $400 per year are available to freshmen. Federal and state government loans are available as well as those made by local banks and the college. Grants and work-study arrangements also are offered. The amount of aid granted depends upon the need. Application for financial aid should be made by June 1 (fall) and November 1 (spring).

Foreign Students: Twelve percent of the full-time students come from foreign countries. Special counseling and organizations are provided for these students.

Admissions: Foreign students must score at least 450 on the TOEFL. No other tests are required.

Procedure: Application deadlines are the same as those for other freshmen. Foreign students must present proof of adequate funding for four years and must carry health insurance, which is available at a fee through the college. They must also pay a $500 processing fee the first year.

Admissions Contacts: Greg and Cathy Blackburn, Co-Directors of Admissions.

HARDING UNIVERSITY   C-2
Searcy, Arkansas 72143   (501) 268-6161

F/T: 1336M, 1473W   Faculty: 111; IIA, --$
P/T: 112M, 115W   Ph.D.'s: 46%
Grad: 35M, 35W   S/F Ratio: 21 to 1
Year: sems, ss   Tuition: $2625
Appl: July 1   R and B: $1796
ACT: 20   COMPETITIVE

Harding University, founded in 1919, is a privately owned, liberal arts university affiliated with the Church of Christ. The library houses over 200,000 volumes and subscribes to 15,578 periodicals.

Environment: The 200-acre campus is in an urban area approximately 45 miles from Little Rock, Arkansas. The campus auditorium is the largest in the state. There are 10 dormitories with a capacity for 760 women, 720 men, and 60 married couples.

Student Life: The college seeks a national geographic distribution; only 30% of the students are from Arkansas. Eighty-six percent of the students live on campus. Most of the students are members of the Church of Christ and are required to attend chapel services daily. An emphasis is placed on religion in studies as well as in campus life. About 1% of the students are minority-group members. University housing is single-sex. Students may keep cars on campus. Day-care services are provided.

Organizations: About 85% of the students are members of the 44 social clubs. The a capella chorus, which tours each semester and presents a weekly radio program, and the yearbook, intercollegiate debating program, newspaper, plays, and operas comprise student activities. The university has a lyceum series of professional talent. Little Rock offers concerts and cultural events for off-campus entertainment.

Sports: The university fields 8 intercollegiate teams for men and 4 for women. There are 9 intramural sports for men and 8 for women.

Handicapped: Special parking and class scheduling are available for handicapped students.

Graduates: The freshman dropout rate is 30%; 60% remain to graduate. Ten percent pursue postgraduate studies.

Services: Students receive the following free services: placement, career and psychological counseling, health care, tutoring, and remedial instruction. Placement services for graduates are available.

Programs of Study: The university confers the B.A., B.S., B.B.A., B.S.N., and B.S.W. degrees as well as master's degrees. Bachelor's degrees are available in the following subjects: AREA STUDIES (American), BUSINESS (accounting, business administration, business education, computer science, management, marketing), EDUCATION (adult, early childhood, elementary, health/physical, secondary, special), ENGLISH (English, journalism, speech), FINE AND PERFORMING ARTS (art, art education, art history, music, music education, radio/TV, theater/dramatics), HEALTH SCIENCES (nursing), LANGUAGES (French, Spanish), MATH AND SCIENCES (biochemistry, biology, chemistry, mathematics, natural sciences), PHILOSOPHY (religion), PREPROFESSIONAL (dentistry, home economics, law, library science, medicine, ministry, pharmacy, social work, veterinary), SOCIAL SCIENCES (economics, government/political science, history, international relations, psychology, social sciences, sociology). Business, education, health sciences, and religion (Bible) are among the most popular fields of study.

Required: Bible courses are required.

Special: Combined B.S.-B.A. degrees can be earned.

Honors: There are 13 national honor societies.

Admissions: Ninety percent of the applications submitted for a recent year were accepted. Candidates must have a minimum C average and 15 Carnegie units, rank in the top half of their high school class, and come from an accredited high school. Important factors include recommendations, personal interviews, AP or honor courses, reputation of the applicant's high school, and whether the applicant is the son or daughter of an alumnus.

Procedure: The ACT is required. July 1 is the deadline for fall applications. The application fee is $15.

Special: CLEP credit is available through general and subject exams.

Transfer: Only transfer students with a GPA of at least 2.0 and an ACT score of 18 are accepted to the university. Three to six hours of D grades transfer. Transfer students are accepted for all semesters; the application deadline for the fall semester is July 1. The fee is the same as for freshmen. Students must earn, at the college, at least 32 of the 128 credits necessary for a bachelor's degree.

Visiting: Accommodations on campus and guided tours may be arranged. Visitors are permitted to attend classes. Two events are scheduled for prospective students. The admissions office may be contacted for details.

Financial Aid: Seventy percent of the students receive aid. Twenty-two percent work part-time on campus. A $15,000 fund provides freshman scholarships each year. Aid is available in the form of NDSL, EOG, CWS, and private loan sources. The average scholarship or loan grant given freshmen per year is between $250 and $300 for scholarships and between $350 and $500 for loans. The maximum from combined sources is $1050. The application deadline for aid for fall entry is May 1. Tuition may be paid in installments. The university is a member of CSS; the FFS is required.

Foreign Students: Forty-seven full-time students come from foreign countries.

Admissions: Foreign students must take TOEFL.

Procedure: Foreign students are admitted for fall, spring, and summer sessions. They must present proof of adequate funds, make a $2200 tuition deposit, and pay $500 to an emergency fund. The university offers health insurance for a fee but does not require that it be carried.

Admissions Contact: Durward McGaha, Director of Admissions.

HENDERSON STATE UNIVERSITY   B-4
Arkadelphia, Arkansas 71923   (501) 246-5511

F/T: 1080M, 1200W   Faculty: 160; IIA, --$
P/T: 200M, 220W   Ph.D.'s: 60%
Grad: 78M, 127W   S/F Ratio: 16 to 1
Year: sems, ss   Tuition: $760 ($1480)
Appl: open   R and B: $1400
1200 applied   1190 accepted   800 enrolled
ACT: 16   LESS COMPETITIVE

Henderson State University, founded in 1929, is a state-supported liberal arts and teachers' college offering major programs of study in 34 subject areas. The library contains 200,000 volumes, 1300 periodical subscriptions, and 34,700 microfilm items.

Environment: The 110-acre campus is located in a rural area 67 miles from Little Rock in a town of 10,000. It consists of 63 buildings, including 10 coed dormitories housing 1673 students. There are also 46 mobile homes which house 61 students.

Student Life: Most of the students are from the South. Forty-five percent live on campus. Ninety-five percent of the entering freshmen

28 ARKANSAS

come from public schools. Ninety-two percent of the students are Protestant and 4% are Catholic. Twenty-one percent are members of minority groups. Campus housing is single-sex.

Organizations: The university sponsors 25 extracurricular activities and groups. Fewer than 1% of women and men belong to fraternities or sororities.

Sports: The university fields 10 intercollegiate teams and offers 18 intramural sports.

Graduates: Forty percent of freshmen drop out by the end of the first year; 50% remain to graduate. Twenty percent of the graduates pursue graduate study; 3% enter medical school, 1% enter dental school, and 2% enter law school. Twenty percent pursue careers in business and industry.

Services: The university provides free placement services, career and psychological counseling, tutoring, and remedial instruction. Health care is available for a fee.

Programs of Study: The university confers the B.A., B.S., B.M., B.Mus.Ed., B.S.Ed., B.S.B.A., B.F.A., B.S.N., and associate's degrees. Bachelor's degrees are offered in the following subjects: BUSINESS (accounting, business education, computer science, management, marketing), EDUCATION (early childhood, elementary, health/physical, secondary, special), ENGLISH (English, journalism, speech), FINE AND PERFORMING ARTS (art, art education, music, music education, theater/dramatics), HEALTH SCIENCES (medical technology, nursing, speech therapy), LANGUAGES (French, German, Spanish), MATH AND SCIENCES (biology, chemistry, mathematics, natural sciences, physical sciences, physics), SOCIAL SCIENCES (economics, government/political science, history, psychology, social sciences, sociology). Fifty percent of degrees conferred are in education; 20% are in business.

Required: All undergraduates are required to take the general education core curriculum. The URE is required for graduation.

Special: The university offers developmental courses in English, science, and mathematics for students with inadequate academic background. Combined study and work experience programs are available in early childhood and special education. The university offers a 3-year bachelor's degree.

Honors: There are chapters of 4 national honor societies on campus.

Admissions: Ninety-nine percent of those who applied for the 1981–82 freshman class were accepted. Of those who enrolled, the ACT scores were as follows: 20% below 21, 8% between 21 and 23, 5% between 24 and 25, 2% between 26 and 28, and 1% above 28. High school graduation and 15 Carnegie units are required for admission. Out-of-state students must rank in the upper half of their high school class. Preference is given to children of alumni.

Procedure: The ACT is required and should be taken as early as possible. Application to the fall session should be prior to or at registration. Freshmen are admitted in the summer, the fall, and the spring; application deadlines are the registration dates. The university has a rolling admissions plan. A personal interview is not required, but is recommended. The interview may be held by a representative in or near the student's home town. There is no application fee.

Special: Early admission and early decision plans are available. AP and CLEP credit is available.

Transfer: For fall 1981, 280 applications were received, 210 students were accepted, and 180 students enrolled. Transfers are considered for all classes, but higher levels require higher GPAs. The ACT is required. D grades are transferable. A student must study 1 year and 30 semester hours to earn a bachelor's degree, which requires 124 credits. Deadlines for transfer applicants are the same as for freshmen.

Visiting: Guided tours and interviews can be scheduled any day of the week. Students may sit in on classes and can remain overnight on campus.

Financial Aid: About one-half of all students receive financial aid through the school. There are approximately 75 freshman scholarships. Work-study funds are available in all departments, and 20% of the students receive work contracts. Need is the main consideration in awarding financial aid. The ACT Need Analysis is used. The deadline for priority consideration is April 1.

Foreign Students: Less than 1% (31) of the full-time students come from foreign countries. The university offers these students special counseling and organizations.

Admissions: Foreign students must achieve a minimum TOEFL score of 500.

Procedure: Application deadlines are July 1 (fall), December 1 (spring), and April 1 (summer). Foreign students must present proof of funds adequate to cover one semester of study. Health insurance is available through the university, but foreign students are not required to carry such insurance.

Admissions Contact: Hershel Lucht, Registrar.

HENDRIX COLLEGE   C–3
Conway, Arkansas 72032   (501) 329-6811

F/T: 511M, 506W   Faculty: 58; IIB, +$
P/T: none   Ph.D.'s: 65%
Grad: none   S/F Ratio: 16 to 1
Year: tri   Tuition: $2760
Appl: open   R and B: $1350
621 applied   543 accepted   322 enrolled
SAT: 509V 535M   ACT: 24   COMPETITIVE+

Hendrix College, established in 1876, is a small liberal-arts institution operated by the United Methodist Church. The library contains over 130,000 volumes and subscribes to about 500 periodicals.

Environment: The college is located on 150 acres in a city of 22,000 about 30 miles from Little Rock. Seven dormitories accommodate about three-fourths of the students; another 5% live in other authorized housing.

Student Life: About 90% of the students come from the South; 85% come from Arkansas. About half the students are Methodists. Eighty-four percent come from public schools. Almost 11% of the students are minority-group members. Freshmen must live in dormitories unless their parents live in town. Campus housing is both coed and single-sex. There are visiting privileges in single-sex dorms. Students may keep cars on campus.

Organizations: The college has no fraternities or sororities, but other student organizations and activities are available. There is an active student senate, and students serve on a number of faculty committees.

Sports: The college sponsors intercollegiate teams in 7 sports for men and 4 for women. Seven intramural sports are open to men and women.

Handicapped: Special facilities for handicapped students include wheelchair ramps and specially equipped rest rooms.

Graduates: Sixty-five percent of the students pursue graduate study after graduation. About 60% of the freshmen eventually graduate from Hendrix.

Services: Free placement and career counseling services are available to students.

Programs of Study: The college awards the B.A. degree in the following subjects: BUSINESS (accounting), EDUCATION (elementary, secondary), ENGLISH (English), FINE AND PERFORMING ARTS (art, art education, music, music education, theater/dramatics), LANGUAGES (French, German, Spanish), MATH AND SCIENCES (biology, chemistry, mathematics, physics), PHILOSOPHY (humanities, philosophy, religion), PREPROFESSIONAL (dentistry, engineering, law, medicine, ministry, pharmacy, veterinary), SOCIAL SCIENCES (economics, government/political science, history, psychology, sociology).

Special: Students may spend their junior year abroad. The college offers 3-2 and 4-2 combined programs in engineering with Columbia University.

Admissions: About 87% of those who applied for a recent freshman class were accepted. Most were in the upper 40% of their high school class and had grade averages of 3.3 or higher, but the college requires no minimum rank or average. Hendrix recommends that applicants have completed 16 college-preparatory units. Admissions officers also consider test scores, extracurricular activities, athletics, and leadership. Sons or daughters of alumni are given some preference.

Procedure: Applicants must take the SAT or ACT. Applications should be submitted as early in the senior year as possible, but there is no deadline. Admissions decisions are made on a rolling basis. There is a $10 application fee.

Special: Early decision and early admissions plans are available. AP and CLEP credit is accepted.

Transfer: For fall 1981, 56 transfer students applied, 43 were accepted, and 32 enrolled. Students may not transfer for the senior year. A minimum GPA of 2.0 on previous college work is required. Thirty-six courses are required for the bachelor's degree.

Visiting: Regular orientation sessions are held for prospective students. Informal visitors may sit in on classes and stay overnight on campus. The office of admissions will handle arrangements.

Financial Aid: Direct grants, loans, and jobs are available. About 75% of all students receive aid; 27% work part-time on campus. Need is the only factor considered in awarding aid. The FFS is required. There is no deadline for applications.

Foreign Students: Less than 1% of the full-time students come from foreign countries.

Admissions: Foreign students must take the TOEFL to qualify for admission. College entrance exams are not required.

Procedure: There are no application deadlines for foreign students, who are admitted to the fall, winter, and spring terms. Proof of adequate funds is required. Health insurance is available through the college.

Admissions Contact: Rudy Pollan, Dean of Admissions.

JOHN BROWN UNIVERSITY A-1
Siloam Springs, Arkansas 72761   (501) 524-3131

F/T: 383M, 320W	Faculty: 49; IIB, +$
P/T: 25M, 24W	Ph.D.'s: 60%
Grad: none	S/F Ratio: 16 to 1
Year: sems, ss	Tuition: $2300
Appl: open	R and B: $1700
367 applied 360 accepted 307 enrolled	
ACT: 19	LESS COMPETITIVE

John Brown University is a private, Christian institution. The library contains 75,000 volumes and 407 periodical subscriptions; there are 559 volumes on microfilm.

Environment: The 350-acre campus in a rural town 90 miles from Tulsa, Oklahoma, includes 3 dormitories and married students' duplexes housing 40 couples.

Student Life: Twenty-six percent of the students come from Arkansas; the majority come from central and western states. Ninety percent of entering freshmen are from public schools. Seventy-six percent of the students reside on campus—65% in dormitories and the remainder in university-approved housing. Ninety percent are Protestant, and 1% are Catholic. Two percent of the students are minority-group members. University housing is single-sex, and there are visiting privileges. Students are encouraged to attend Sunday morning worship services and are required to attend a weekday convocation and midweek chapel services. Drinking is not allowed on campus; smoking is not allowed on campus and is discouraged off campus. Cars are permitted, but must be registered. Day-care services are provided for part-time students, faculty, and staff.

Organizations: There are no social fraternities or sororities. Extracurricular activities include chorus, orchestra, concerts, films, lectures, and plays. Major events are the annual Halloween Party, Candelight Carol Service, Bible Missionary Conference, and Christian American Heritage Seminar. Students are represented on all faculty and administrative committees.

Sports: The university fields 3 intercollegiate teams for men and 3 for women. There are 6 intramural sports for men and 5 for women.

Handicapped: About 30% of the campus is accessible to wheelchair-bound students. There are no visually or hearing impaired students.

Graduates: About 10% of the freshmen drop out at the end of their first year; 35% remain to graduate. Ten percent of the graduates pursue advanced study; 1% enter medical school and 1% enter law school. Seventy-five percent enter business and industry.

Services: Students receive the following services free of charge: placement, career, and psychological counseling, health care, tutoring, and remedial instruction.

Programs of Study: The University conferes the B.A., B.S., B.S.E., B.Mus., and B.Mus.Ed. degrees. Associate degrees are also awarded. Bachelor's degrees are offered in the following subjects: BUSINESS (business administration, business education, computer science), EDUCATION (elementary, secondary), ENGLISH (English), FINE AND PERFORMING ARTS (music, music education, radio/TV), HEALTH SCIENCES (medical technology), MATH AND SCIENCES (biology, chemistry, physics), PHILOSOPHY (religion), PREPROFESSIONAL (building construction, engineering, home economics, ministry), SOCIAL SCIENCES (history, psychology). Forty-eight percent of degrees conferred are in education.

Required: All undergraduates must complete a general education block and establish proficiency in English.

Special: It is possible to earn combined B.A.-B.S. degrees in various subjects by completing a 5-year curriculum. The B.G.S. degree is also offered.

ARKANSAS 29

Honors: Each graduate who exemplifies the ideals of the university and has a GPA of 3.25 or above for all work completed by the end of the senior year is recognized with an honor degree.

Admissions: About 98% of the applicants for the 1981–82 freshman class were accepted. The ACT scores of a recent freshman class were as follows: 27% between 20 and 23, 9% between 24 and 26, 11% between 27 and 28, and 3% above 28. The admissions candidate should be a high school graduate with a 2.0 average and rank in the top two-thirds of the class. Admissions are based on a combination of ACT score, class rank, and GPA. Recommendations, leadership record, and interview results are also considered.

Procedure: The SAT or ACT is required. Candidates are admitted to both the spring and fall terms on a rolling admissions basis. A $75 fee should accompany each application.

Special: AP and CLEP credit is granted.

Transfer: About 80 transfer students are accepted each year. Students must have a 2.0 GPA and an ACT or SAT score in the twenty-fifth percentile. Some D grades are acceptable. The number of credits necessary for a bachelor's degree are 124, of which 30 must be completed at the university. The school maintains a rolling admissions policy for transfer applicants.

Visiting: Guided tours can be scheduled at any time. Day-long visits with a student guide can be arranged by the admissions office and visitors may remain overnight at the school.

Financial Aid: About 80% of all students receive financial aid; 75% work part-time on campus. The maximum financial aid to a freshman is $4000, including a maximum $2500 yearly loan from federal or state government, or local banks, and a maximum of $1206 in campus employment. Candidates must show definite need. They must maintain a 2.0 (C) GPA for a work scholarship or loan and a 3.0 average for a Presidential Scholarship. The FFS should be filed by April 1.

Foreign Students: Twenty foreign students are enrolled full-time. The university offers these students special counseling.

Admissions: Foreign students must achieve a minimum TOEFL score of 525. No other exams are required.

Procedure: Foreign students are admitted to both semesters. The university maintains a rolling admissions policy. Foreign students must present proof of funds adequate to cover one year of study. They must also carry health insurance, which is not available through the university.

Admissions Contact: Roger Kline, Acting Director of Admissions.

OUACHITA BAPTIST UNIVERSITY B-4
Arkadelphia, Arkansas 71923   (501) 246-4531

F/T, P/T: 1450M&W	Faculty: 101; IIA, −$
	Ph.D.'s: 40%
Grad: 120M&W	S/F Ratio: 16 to 1
Year: 4-1-4, ss	Tuition: $2250
Appl: Aug. 15	R and B: $1430
ACT: 19	LESS COMPETITIVE

Ouachita Baptist University, founded in 1855, is a private, coeducational liberal-arts institution affiliated with the Arkansas Baptist Convention. The library houses 110,810 volumes and 275,000 microfilm items, and subscribes to 1000 periodicals.

Environment: The university is located 70 miles from Little Rock on the banks of the Ouachita River. The main campus is 60 acres and includes a fine-arts center. Single-sex dormitories accommodate 472 women and 446 men. Housing for married students also is available.

Student Life: Eighty-five percent of the students live in campus housing. Most students are Baptists. All students are required to attend religious services once a week.

Organizations: Fifteen percent of the men belong to one of 3 local fraternities and 18% of the women belong to one of 4 local sororities.

Sports: The university participates intercollegiately in 8 sports for men and at least 3 for women. Five intramural sports are offered.

Handicapped: Ninety percent of the campus is accessible to wheelchair-bound students. Facilities include wheelchair ramps, special parking, elevators, and specially equipped rest rooms. One percent of the students are visually impaired; another 1% are hearing-impaired. One special counselor is available.

Graduates: Eighteen percent of the freshmen drop out, and 70% remain to graduate. About 40% of the graduates pursue advanced degrees, including 1% who go to medical school and 1% who go to dental school. A fourth of the graduates enter business and industry.

30 ARKANSAS

Services: Free student services include placement, career and psychological counseling; health care; and tutoring or remedial instruction.

Programs of Study: The university confers the B.A., B.S., B.S.Ed., B.S.Mus., and B.Mus.Ed. degrees. Master's degrees also are offered. Bachelor's degrees are offered in the following subjects: BUSINESS (accounting, business administration, business education, management, office administration), EDUCATION (early childhood, elementary, health/physical, secondary, special), ENGLISH (English, journalism, speech), FINE AND PERFORMING ARTS (art, art education, art history, music, music education, theater/dramatics), HEALTH SCIENCES (speech therapy), LANGUAGES (French, Spanish), MATH AND SCIENCES (biology, botany, chemistry, mathematics, physics), PHILOSOPHY (philosophy, religion), PREPROFESSIONAL (dentistry, engineering, home economics, law, library science, medicine, ministry), SOCIAL SCIENCES (economics, government/political science, history, psychology, social sciences, sociology).

Special: Students may design their own majors. Cooperative programs in engineering and medical technology are offered.

Required: General-education requirements include ROTC and 5 hours of Bible courses.

Honors: Honor societies and an honors program are available.

Admissions: Eighty-eight percent of the applicants for a recent freshman class were accepted. All candidates must have completed 15 Carnegie units, rank in the upper 75% of their class, have a C average or better, and be recommended by high school officials.

Procedures: ACT scores, high school records, and an application must be submitted by August 15 for fall admission. A $20 application fee is required. Applications for the spring term must be submitted by January 15; for the summer term, May 15.

Special: There is an early admissions program.

Transfer: Most transfer applicants are accepted if they meet the academic requirements. Students must study at the university for 1 year to receive a degree. Application deadlines are the same as those for freshmen.

Visiting: Guided tours are available for informal visitors. Prospective students may sit in on classes and stay overnight on campus. The admissions counseling office will handle arrangements.

Financial Aid: Sixty percent of the students receive financial aid. Scholarships and loans are available from the federal government, local banks, the university, and private sources. Campus employment may be provided. Tuition may be paid in installments. The FFS is required. The deadline for financial aid applications is May 1.

Admissions Contact: Frank Taylor, Registrar and Director of Admissions.

PHILANDER SMITH COLLEGE   C-3
Little Rock, Arkansas 72203   (501) 375-9845

F/T, P/T: 600M&W	Faculty: 35; IIB, --$
Grad: none	Ph.D.'s: 30%
Year: sems, ss	S/F Ratio: 14 to 1
Appl: Aug. 15	Tuition: $1600
SAT, ACT: required	R and B: $2000
	LESS COMPETITIVE

Philander Smith College, founded in 1877, is a liberal arts college affiliated with the United Methodist Church. Its library contains about 62,000 volumes and 171 reels of microfilm, and subscribes to 365 periodicals.

Environment: The 25-acre campus is located in the heart of Arkansas' capital. The 14 buildings on campus include 2 single-sex dormitories that house 220 students. Apartments are also available for married students.

Student Life: About 82% of the students are from Arkansas. Most students are blacks. The majority of the students are Protestant, and church attendance is mandatory. Drinking on campus is forbidden.

Organizations: About 20% of the students belong to fraternities or sororities. The student government sponsors cultural and social activities.

Sports: The college fields intercollegiate teams in 2 sports and also offers intramural sports.

Graduates: About 38% of the freshmen drop out during the first year; about 31% remain to graduate. Of those, 11% seek advanced degrees.

Programs of Study: The college confers B.A. and B.S. degrees. Bachelor's degrees are offered in the following subjects: AREA STUDIES (Black/Afro-American), BUSINESS (business administration, secretarial science), EDUCATION (elementary, health/physical, special), ENGLISH (English), FINE AND PERFORMING ARTS (art, music), MATH AND SCIENCES (biology, chemistry, mathematics, physics), PHILOSOPHY (philosophy, religion), PREPROFESSIONAL (dentistry, engineering, home economics, medicine, ministry, pharmacy, social work), SOCIAL SCIENCES (economics, government/political science, psychology, social sciences, sociology).

Required: General-education requirements include courses in humanities, natural sciences and mathematics, social science, and physical education.

Special: Combination degrees in engineering and medical technology are offered. Students may study abroad, or undertake independent study. Developmental courses are available for new students. There is a cooperative work-study program and a black executive exchange program.

Honors: Two honor societies are open to qualified students.

Admissions: In a recent year, 38% of those who applied were accepted. Applicants should have 16 units of high school academic work and at least a C average. Test scores and recommendations are also considered. Applicants with less than a C average may be admitted on probation.

Procedure: The SAT is preferred, but the ACT is accepted. Applications are accepted for all terms. The fall deadline is August 15. A $5 fee is required. Admissions decisions are made on a rolling basis.

Special: An early admissions plan is available. AP credit is accepted.

Transfer: Applicants should have at least a C average. Application deadlines are the same as those for freshmen. Students must complete at least 32 hours in residence of the 124 required for a degree.

Visiting: Tours of the campus can be arranged through the admissions office.

Financial Aid: About 60% of the students receive aid. Loans, part-time jobs, and scholarships are available. Tuition may be paid in installments. The college is a member of CSS and requires the FAF. The application deadline is June 1.

Foreign Students: About 15% of the students come from foreign countries.

Admissions: Applicants must score 500 or better on the TOEFL. They also must take the ACT.

Procedure: Students are admitted to all terms. They must undergo a physical examination and present proof of adequate funds as required by immigration authorities. All students are required to carry health insurance, which is available through the college for a fee.

Admissions Contact: Mary Abrams, Assistant Director of Admissions.

SOUTHERN ARKANSAS UNIVERSITY   B-5
Magnolia, Arkansas 71753   (501) 234-5120

F/T: 787M, 880W	Faculty: 111; IIA, --$
P/T: 74M, 196W	Ph.D.'s: 47%
Grad: 30M, 70W	S/F Ratio: 18 to 1
Year: sems, ss	Tuition: $670 ($1060)
Appl: Aug. 1	R and B: $1330
491 applied	491 accepted 444 enrolled
ACT: 17	NONCOMPETITIVE

Southern Arkansas University is a state-supported liberal-arts college composed of the schools of Business Administration, Education, Liberal and Performing Arts, and Science and Technology. The library houses 102,106 volumes and 196,358 microfilm items, and subscribes to 1008 periodicals.

Environment: The campus is located in a suburban area of southwestern Arkansas, 135 miles south of Little Rock and 85 miles north of Shreveport, Louisiana. It consists of 80 acres plus a 600-acre college farm. Ten dormitories accommodate 1400 students, and 36 apartments are provided for married students.

Student Life: About 90% of the students come from Arkansas. About 47% of the students live in residence halls. About 23% are members of minority groups. Dormitories are single-sex, with visiting privileges. Students may keep cars on campus. Drinking is prohibited on campus.

Organizations: Three percent of the students belongs to a fraternity or sorority. Religious organizations are available for Protestant students.

Sports: The university fields intercollegiate teams in 8 sports for men and 5 for women. Seven intramural sports are offered for men and 6 for women.

Handicapped: Ninety percent of the campus is accessible to wheelchair-bound students. Facilities include wheelchair ramps, special parking, elevators, specially equipped rest rooms, and lowered drinking fountains and telephones. Special class scheduling is also available. One percent of the students are visually impaired; another 1% are hearing impaired.

Graduates: Thirty-five percent of the freshmen drop out, and 40% remain to graduate in 4 years. Twenty percent of the graduates pursue graduate studies: 5% enter medical school, 3% enter dental school, and 7% enter law school. Thirty-five percent enter business and industry.

Services: The following services are provided free to students: placement, career and psychological counseling; health care; tutoring; and remedial instruction. Placement services also are available to alumni.

Programs of Study: The University confers the B.A., B.A.S., B.S., B.B.A., B.S.E., and B.Mus.Ed. degrees. Master's and associate degrees also are offered. Bachelor's degrees are offered in the following subjects: BUSINESS (accounting, agricultural business, business administration, business education, computer science, economics, finance, management, marketing), EDUCATION (elementary, health/physical, industrial, secondary, special, vocational/agricultural), ENGLISH (English, speech), FINE AND PERFORMING ARTS (art, art education, mass communications, music, music education, theater/dramatics), HEALTH SCIENCES (medical technology), LANGUAGES (Spanish), MATH AND SCIENCES (biology, chemistry, general science, mathematics, physics), PREPROFESSIONAL (agriculture, dentistry, engineering, forestry, medicine, pharmacy, veterinary), SOCIAL SCIENCES (government/political science, history, psychology, regional studies, social sciences, sociology). Twenty-five percent of degrees conferred are in education, 18% in business, and 15% in math and sciences.

Special: It is possible to earn a 5-year combined B.A.-B.S. degree.

Honors: Four national honor societies—Alpha Chi, Lambda Sigma Alpha, Sigma Delta Pi, and Sigma Phi Sigma—have chapters on campus.

Admissions: All applicants for the 1981–82 freshman class were accepted. ACT scores of those who enrolled were as follows: 45% scored below 21, 25% between 21 and 23, 15% between 24 and 25, 10% between 26 and 28, and 5% above 28. Thirty percent ranked in the upper fifth of their high school class, and 40% ranked in the upper two-fifths. Applicants must be high school graduates who have completed at least 15 Carnegie units. Those without diplomas must be at least 21 years old and have a GED certificate. Out-of-state applicants must have at least a C average.

Procedure: The ACT is required. The application deadlines are August 1 (fall), January 1 (spring), and June 1 (summer). There is no application fee. Admissions decisions are made on a rolling basis.

Special: The university grants credit for CLEP exams.

Transfer: For fall 1981, 194 transfer students applied, 191 were accepted, and 172 enrolled. Applicants must be in good standing at their previous college. A 2.0 GPA is recommended. D grades can be transferred. Transfer students must earn at least 30 semester hours at the university of the 124 required for a bachelor's degree. Application deadlines are the same as those for freshmen.

Visiting: Campus housing and guides are provided for visitors, who also may sit in on classes. The admissions office should be contacted for appointments.

Financial Aid: Fifty-two percent of the students receive financial aid. Grants, scholarships, loans, and part-time jobs are available; 45% of the students work part-time on campus. BEOG, SEOG, and installment payments are other alternatives. The FFS is required. Aid applications should be submitted by July 1 (fall), December 1 (spring), or April 1 (summer).

Foreign Students: The 23 foreign students enrolled full-time at the university make up 1% of its student body. Special organizations and special counseling are offered.

Admissions: Foreign applicants must score at least 500 on the TOEFL. They also must take the ACT.

Procedure: Application deadlines are April 15 (fall), July 1 (spring), and January 1 (summer). Students must provide proof of immunization and a family medical history, as well as evidence of adequate funds for 4 years of study. They must carry health insurance, which is available through the university for a fee.

Admissions Contact: James E. Whittington, Director of Admissions.

ARKANSAS 31

UNIVERSITY OF ARKANSAS

The University of Arkansas is composed of 4 campuses at Fayetteville, Little Rock, Monticello, and Pine Bluff. The Fayetteville campus is the oldest. The Little Rock campus was formed by the merger of Little Rock University and the University of Arkansas at Little Rock. The campus at Monticello formerly was known as Arkansas Agricultural and Mechanical College. The Pine Bluff campus is the newest; it was formerly the Agricultural, Mechanical, and Normal College. The university's medical center is located at Little Rock. For descriptions of each campus, see the following entries.

UNIVERSITY OF ARKANSAS AT FAYETTEVILLE A-1
Fayetteville, Arkansas 72701   (501) 575-5346

F/T, P/T:	Faculty: 693; I, –$
7160M, 5329W	Ph.D.'s: 73%
Grad: 1632M, 1054W	S/F Ratio: 18 to 1
Year: sems, ss	Tuition: $720 ($1750)
Appl: see profile	R and B: $1695
4614 applied	4614 accepted 2630 enrolled
ACT: 19	NONCOMPETITIVE

The University of Arkansas is a land-grant institution under state control. The university was founded in 1871 as Arkansas Industrial University, and the name was changed to the current one in 1899. The campus houses the colleges of Arts and Sciences, Agriculture and Home Economics, Business Administration, Education, and Engineering; the schools of Architecture and Law; the Graduate School; the Division of General Extension; the Agricultural Experiment Station; the Bureau of Business and Economic Research, and the Engineering Experiment Station. The library contains 918,000 volumes and subscribes to 9300 periodicals.

Environment: The self-contained campus, located in a small city, covers 329 acres. The agricultural station adds another 9546 acres. The college sponsors dormitories, fraternity and sorority houses, and married-student housing.

Student Life: Nearly all the students are from the South, and 81% come from Arkansas. About 95% of the entering freshmen come from public schools. About half the students live on campus. About 8% are members of minority groups. Dormitories are both single-sex and coed; single-sex dormitories have visiting privileges. Students may keep cars on campus.

Organizations: There are 18 fraternities and 12 sororities on campus. Cultural and entertainment activities are offered. The 220 student organizations on campus include special-interest clubs, student government, and honor societies.

Sports: The university fields intercollegiate teams in 9 sports for men and 5 for women. More than 20 intramural sports are offered for both sexes. Students often visit the Buffalo National River and other nearby parks for outdoor recreation.

Handicapped: About 40% of the campus is accessible to handicapped students. Special facilities include wheelchair ramps, special parking, elevators, specially equipped rest rooms, lowered drinking fountains and telephones, and a transit system for disabled students.

Services: The following free services are provided to students: health care; psychological, placement, and career counseling; tutoring; and remedial instruction. The placement office, which sponsors on-campus interviews with corporate recruiters, may be used by graduates as well as students.

Programs of Study: The university confers 16 undergraduate degrees, including the B.A., B.S., B.Arch., B.S.Ag., B.S.B.A., B.S.E., and B.S.P.A. It also awards associate, master's, and doctoral degrees. Bachelor's degrees are offered in the following subjects: AREA (urban), BUSINESS (accounting, business administration, business education, data processing, executive secretarial, finance, management, marketing, public administration, real estate/insurance, transportation), EDUCATION (adult, agricultural, early childhood, elementary, health/physical, industrial, library-media, secondary, special), ENGLISH (English, journalism), FINE AND PERFORMING ARTS (art, art education, dance education, film/photography, music, music education, radio/TV, studio art, theater/dramatics), HEALTH SCIENCES (speech therapy), LANGUAGES (French, German, Spanish), MATH AND SCIENCES (bacteriology, botany, chemistry, computer science, earth science, ecology/environmental science, geology, mathematics, natural sciences, physics, statistics, zoology), PHILOSOPHY (classics, philosophy), PREPROFESSIONAL (agriculture, architecture, dentistry, engineering, forestry, home economics, law, library science, medicine, ministry, pharmacy, social work, veterinary), SOCIAL SCIENCES (anthropology, economics, geography, government/political science, history, psychology, sociology).

Required: All students are required to take a flexible core curriculum.

Honors: Forty-six honor societies have chapters on campus. The College of Arts and Sciences has an honors program that includes honors courses for freshmen, and honors research and thesis for juniors and seniors.

Admissions: Virtually all applicants are accepted. ACT scores for those enrolled in a recent freshman class were as follows: 25% scored between 20 and 23, 20% between 24 and 26, 10% between 27 and 28, and 7% above 28. Applicants must present 15 Carnegie units of high school work. An average of C or better is required for unconditional admission.

Procedure: The ACT is recommended. New students are admitted to the fall, midyear, and summer sessions. Applications must be submitted at least 1 week before registration. Admissions decisions are made on a rolling basis. The $15 application fee applies toward the registration fee but is otherwise nonrefundable.

Special: The university has an early admissions plan. AP and CLEP credit is accepted.

Transfer: Arkansas residents must have at least a 2.0 GPA. An ACT score of 18 is recommended. D grades transfer. Transfer students must study at the university for at least 1 year to receive a bachelor's degree, for which 124 to 132 credits are required. Application deadlines are the same as those for freshmen.

Visiting: Visits should be scheduled on weekdays. The office of admissions will handle arrangements.

Financial Aid: Scholarships are awarded to more than 1500 students. Loans and CWS part-time jobs also are available. About 65% of the students receive some form of financial aid. Applications must be filed by April 1. The FAF or FFS also must be submitted.

Foreign Students: About 530 foreign students are enrolled full-time, representing 4% of the student body. Special counseling and organizations are provided for these students.

Admissions: Foreign applicants are required to score 550 or better on the TOEFL. No further entrance examinations are required.

Procedure: Overseas applicants must file applications 2 months before registration for the term in which they wish to enroll. Foreign citizens living in the United States have until 2 weeks before registration. Students must present proof of adequate funds for 12 months. Health insurance, though not required, is available through the university for a fee.

Admissions Contact: Larry F. Matthews, Director of Admissions.

UNIVERSITY OF ARKANSAS AT LITTLE ROCK C-3
Little Rock, Arkansas 72204   (501) 569-3127

F/T: 2150M, 2350W	Faculty: 471; IIA, av$
P/T: 1800M, 2800W	Ph.D.'s: 60%
Grad: 500M, 500W	S/F Ratio: 16 to 1
Year: sems, ss	Tuition: $730 ($1560)
Appl: see profile	R and B: n/app
1466 applied	1400 accepted 1058 enrolled
ACT: 17	LESS COMPETITIVE

The Little Rock branch of the University of Arkansas was established by the merger of Little Rock University and the University of Arkansas at Little Rock. The library contains 225,000 volumes and subscribes to 3137 periodicals.

Environment: The campus is located in the city of Little Rock. No on-campus housing is provided.

Student Life: Most students are from Arkansas.

Organizations: There are 8 fraternities and 7 sororities on campus; 12% of the men and 10% of the women belong. A number of extracurricular activities are offered on campus, and Little Rock's cultural offerings are easily accessible to students.

Sports: The campus fields intercollegiate teams in 6 sports for men and 4 for women. Fourteen intramural sports are offered.

Handicapped: About 98% of the campus is accessible to handicapped students. Facilities include wheelchair ramps, special parking, elevators, specially equipped rest rooms, and lowered drinking fountains and telephones. One special counselor and 2 assistants are available. One percent of the students have visual impairments, and another 1% have hearing impairments. Tutors, readers, and guides are provided.

Graduates: Fourteen percent of the freshmen drop out by the end of the first year. About 25% of the graduates pursue careers in business and industry.

Services: The following services are available to students free: health care; psychological, placement, and career counseling; and tutoring or remedial instruction. Placement services also are open to graduates.

Programs of Study: The university awards the B.A., B.S., B.B.A., B.Bus.Ed., B.Mus., and B.Mus.Ed. degrees. Associate and master's degrees also are offered. Bachelor's degrees are offered in the following subjects: BUSINESS (accounting, administrative services, advertising, business administration, business education, computer science, finance, general business, industrial management, management, marketing, real estate/insurance), EDUCATION (adult, elementary, health/physical, secondary), ENGLISH (English, journalism, professional and technical writing, speech), FINE AND PERFORMING ARTS (art, art education, music, music education, film/photography, radio/TV, theater/dramatics), HEALTH SCIENCES (environmental health, speech therapy), LANGUAGES (French, Spanish), MATH AND SCIENCES (biology, chemistry, earth science, mathematics, physics), PHILOSOPHY (philosophy), PREPROFESSIONAL (engineering technology), SOCIAL SCIENCES (anthropology, criminal justice, economics, government/political science, history, international relations, psychology, sociology).

Special: Two-year preprofessional programs are offered in several areas. The university offers a general-studies degree. Minors are offered in library science, American studies, and several additional fields. A B.S.-M.S. program in forestry is offered in conjunction with Duke University. Independent study and research are available.

Honors: Eight national honor societies have chapters on campus. The University Scholars Program is open to students in all departments, and most departments have their own honors awards.

Admissions: About 96% of those who applied were accepted for the 1981-82 freshman class. Admissions decisions are based only on high-school records and ACT scores. Applicants must have 15 Carnegie units. Students with a GPA of less than 2.0 are admitted on academic probation.

Procedure: The SAT or ACT is required. Applications should be filed at least 30 days before the start of the term for which the student seeks to enroll. Admissions decisions are made on a rolling basis. There is a $5 application fee.

Special: The university has an early admissions plan.

Transfer: Students need a 2.0 GPA. There is a residency requirement of 1 year.

Visiting: Regular orientations are held for prospective students. Guides are also available for informal visits. Visitors may not sit in on classes or stay overnight at the school. Visits may be scheduled between 8 A.M. and 5 P.M., on any day. Appointments should be made with the director of admissions.

Financial Aid: Thirty-five percent of the students receive financial aid. About 405 scholarships are awarded, 40% on the basis of need. Loans are available. The average aid award to freshmen is $712 from all sources. Applications for aid should be submitted by May 1.

Foreign Students: About 81 foreign students are enrolled full-time at the university. An intensive English program, special counseling, and special organizations are provided.

Admissions: Students must score 500 or better on the TOEFL. No academic exams are required.

Procedure: Applications should be submitted at least 30 days before the start of the term in which the student seeks to enroll. Proof of adequate funds is required. Students must carry health insurance, which is available through the university for a fee.

Admissions Contact: Sue Pine, Director of Admissions.

UNIVERSITY OF ARKANSAS AT MONTICELLO C-4
Monticello, Arkansas 71655   (501) 367-6811

F/T: 760M, 767W	Faculty: 88; IIB, av$
P/T: 118M, 293W	Ph.D.'s: 49%
Grad: none	S/F Ratio: 21 to 1
Year: sems, ss	Tuition: $684 ($1514)
Appl: Aug. 16	R and B: $1380
700 applied	608 accepted 502 enrolled
ACT: 15	NON COMPETITIVE

Established in 1909 as Arkansas Agricultural and Mechanical College, the Monticello branch of the University of Arkansas was formed when that college merged with the university in 1971. The library contains 88,234 volumes and subscribes to 805 periodicals.

Environment: The campus is situated on 816 acres in a suburban area 3 miles from Monticello. The 44 major buildings include a cafeteria and lounge for day students, and 3 single-sex dormitories that accommodate 587 students in single and double rooms.

Student Life: Ninety-seven percent of the students are from Arkansas, 3% from other states, and less than 1% from foreign countries. Twenty-three percent are minority-group members. About 28% of the students live on campus in single-sex dormitories. There are visiting privileges. Students may keep cars on campus.

Organizations: There are 5 fraternities on campus—2 local and 3 national chapters—and 4 national sororities. Six percent of the women and 13% of the men belong to one of them. Protestant religious counselors are available on campus. Numerous extracurricular activities are offered, and there is a fine arts center on campus. Drinking is forbidden on campus.

Sports: The university sponsors intercollegiate teams in 6 sports for men and 2 for women. There are 6 intramural sports for men and 4 for women.

Handicapped: About 90% of the campus is accessible to handicapped students. Facilities include wheelchair ramps and special parking places. There are no special counselors, and no students with visual or hearing impairments.

Graduates: Forty-six percent of the full-time freshmen drop out by the end of the first year; 45% remain to graduate. Twenty percent of the graduates pursue advanced degrees.

Services: The following services are available to students free of charge: health care; psychological, placement, and career counseling; tutoring; and remedial instruction. Placement services are available to students only.

Programs of Study: The Monticello campus confers the B.A. and B.S. degrees. Associate degrees are also awarded. Bachelor's degrees are offered in the following subjects: BUSINESS (accounting, business administration, business education, management, marketing), EDUCATION (elementary, health/physical, secondary), ENGLISH (English, speech), FINE AND PERFORMING ARTS (art, art education, music), LANGUAGES (French), MATH AND SCIENCES (biochemistry, chemistry, geology, mathematics, natural sciences, physical sciences, physics), PREPROFESSIONAL (agriculture, forestry), SOCIAL SCIENCES (history, psychology, social sciences). Forty percent of all undergraduate degrees are conferred in education.

Special: The campus offers the state's only program in forestry. A Black Studies Symposium and a Black studies course are offered. A combination degree in medical technology is one of about 10 2-2 programs in health services.

Honors: The Alpha Chi honor society has a chapter on campus. A departmental honors program is also offered in English.

Admissions: Over 87% of those who applied were accepted for the 1981-82 freshman class. The ACT scores of those who enrolled were as follows: 51% below 21, 32% between 21 and 23, 9% between 24 and 25, 5% between 26 and 28, and 2% above 28. The university uses an open admissions policy.

Procedure: The ACT is required. The application deadlines are August 16 for fall admission, December 29 for spring, and May 25 for summer. Admissions decisions are made on a rolling basis. There is no application fee.

Special: CLEP credit is available.

Transfer: For fall 1981, 168 transfer students applied, 127 were accepted, and 101 enrolled. Transfers are considered for all classes. Applicants must submit a transcript from the previous college. D grades are transferable. A student must earn 30 semester hours in residence of the 124 required for the bachelor's degree. Application deadlines are the same as for freshman applicants.

Visiting: The university schedules regular orientations for prospective students. Guides are also available for informal visits. Visitors may sit in on classes and stay on campus. Visits should be scheduled on weekdays. The student affairs office will handle arrangements.

Financial Aid: The university offers loans, grants, and part-time work. Room and board may be paid in installments. About 61% of the students receive aid from the university; 17% work part-time on campus. The deadlines for aid applications are July 15 (fall), November 15 (spring), and April 15 (summer). The FFS is required.

Foreign Students: Less than 1% of the full-time students come from foreign countries.

Admissions: Foreign students must take the TOEFL to qualify for admission. The SAT and ACT are not required.

Procedure: Application deadlines are August 16 (fall) and December 29 (spring). Foreign students must present proof of funds adequate to cover their period of residence at the university. There is also a special out-of-state fee of $145 per semester. Foreign students must carry health insurance, which is available through the university for a fee.

Admissions Contact: Ernestine B. Brooks, Coordinator of Institutional Research.

UNIVERSITY OF ARKANSAS AT PINE BLUFF   C-4
Pine Bluff, Arkansas 71601   (501) 541-6558

F/T, P/T:		Faculty:	183; IIB, av$
3000M&W		Ph.D.'s:	n/av
Grad: none		S/F Ratio:	19 to 1
Year: sems, ss		Tuition:	$735 ($1690)
Appl: open		R and B:	$1358
1200 applied	1140 accepted		720 enrolled
ACT: required			LESS COMPETITIVE

The Pine Bluff branch is the most recent addition to the University of Arkansas. The institution was founded as the Arkansas Agricultural, Mechanical and Normal College. The library contains 140,000 volumes and subscribes to 1200 periodicals.

Environment: The 285-acre campus is located in a city of 60,000 about 40 miles from Little Rock. Five single-sex residence halls house 900 students. There are also apartments for married students.

Student Life: About 95% of the students are from the South; most are from Arkansas. Most students are black. All students must live on campus or in college-approved housing.

Organizations: There are 9 fraternities and 7 sororities on campus; 5% of the men and 2% of the women belong. Numerous extracurricular activities and organizations are available. Off-campus recreational and cultural facilities are easily accessible.

Sports: The university fields intercollegiate teams in 6 sports. Six intramural sports are offered.

Handicapped: There are no special facilities for physically handicapped students.

Graduates: By the end of the freshman year, about 30% of the students drop out. About 10% of the graduates pursue graduate studies; 20% enter business or industry.

Services: Students receive free placement aid and career counseling. Health care and tutoring or remedial instruction also are available.

Programs of Study: The university confers B.A. and B.S. degrees. Bachelor's degrees are offered in the following subjects: BUSINESS (accounting, business administration, business education, computer science), EDUCATION (early childhood, elementary, health/physical, industrial, special), ENGLISH (English), FINE AND PERFORMING ARTS (art, art education, music, music education), HEALTH SCIENCES (dietetics, nursing), MATH AND SCIENCES (biology, chemistry, mathematics, physics), PREPROFESSIONAL (agriculture, engineering, home economics, industrial technology, social work), SOCIAL SCIENCES (criminal justice, economics, gerontology, government/political science, history, psychology, social sciences, sociology).

Special: The university offers the B.G.S. degree. Education students may participate in workshops with the National Science Foundation, the Southern Educational Foundation, the library, the reading clinic, or the home economics department.

Admissions: About 95% of the applicants for the 1981-82 freshman class were accepted. Students must be high school graduates or hold a GED. Out-of-state applicants must have a GPA of 2.0 or better.

Procedure: Application deadlines are open. Applicants must take the ACT or the SAT. There is no application fee. Admissions decisions are made on a rolling basis.

Special: The university has an early admissions plan.

Transfer: About 90 transfer students are accepted each year. A GPA of 2.0 or better generally is required.

Visiting: The university sponsors a "Welcome Program" for prospective students that includes meetings with department heads and financial aid officers, and campus tours. Guides also are available for informal visits. Visitors may sit in on classes and stay overnight on campus. Visits should be scheduled on weekdays from 8 A.M. to 5 P.M.. The director of admissions will make arrangements.

34 ARKANSAS

Financial Aid: Over 90% of the students receive financial aid. Scholarships, student loans, and college-assigned part-time jobs are available. Aid applications should be submitted at least 6 weeks before the beginning of a term.

Foreign Students: About 100 foreign students are enrolled full-time at the university. Special counseling and organizations are provided.

Admissions: Applicants must score 500 or better on the TOEFL. No academic exams are required.

Procedure: Students are admitted to all terms; applications for fall admission should be filed by April. Students must present proof of good health and show evidence of adequate funds for at least 1 year. They also must arrange to carry health insurance.

Admissions Contact: C.N. Toney, Director of Admissions.

UNIVERSITY OF CENTRAL ARKANSAS   C-3
Conway, Arkansas 72032   (501) 450-3128

F/T: 1946M, 2945W	Faculty: 281; IIA, –$
P/T: 202M, 339W	Ph.D.'s: 60%
Grad: 210M, 340W	S/F Ratio: 19 to 1
Year: sems, ss	Tuition: $740 ($1450)
Appl: Aug. 25	R and B: $1540
1949 applied	1935 accepted 1855 enrolled
ACT: 18	LESS COMPETITIVE

The University of Central Arkansas, established in 1907 as the State Normal College of Arkansas, is a state-supported institution. The library contains 294,000 volumes and 582,244 microfilm items, and subscribes to 2577 periodicals.

Environment: The 220-acre campus is located in a rural area in the town of Conway, 27 miles from Little Rock. The more than 30 major campus buildings include the Health Science Center, Physical Education and Athletic Center, and Business Administration Center, all recently built. Residence halls accommodate 1000 men and 1000 women. The college also sponsors on- and off- campus apartments, and married student housing.

Student Life: More than 95% of the students are from Arkansas. About 35% of the students live on campus. About 15% are members of minority groups. Campus housing is single-sex, but there are visiting privileges. Students may keep cars on campus; no alcoholic beverages are permitted. Day care is available to children of all students, full-time and part-time, for a fee.

Organizations: There are 9 fraternities and 8 sororities on campus; 15% of the men and 19% of the women belong. Religious groups, professional societies, and other organizations are available on campus.

Sports: The university fields 8 intercollegiate teams for men and 8 for women. Ten intramural sports are offered for men and 9 for women. Mountain climbing and other outdoor activities also are popular.

Handicapped: About 80% of the campus is accessible to handicapped students. Facilities include wheelchair ramps, special parking, elevators, specially equipped rest rooms, and lowered drinking fountains and telephones. About 1% of the students have visual impairments. The university has some equipment for the use of visually and hearing-impaired students.

Graduates: About 40% of the students drop out by the end of the freshman year, and 60% remain to graduate. About 20% pursue advanced degrees; 2% enter medical school, 3% enter dental school, and 5% enter law school. Half the graduates enter business and industry.

Services: The following services are provided to students free of charge: health care; psychological, placement, and career counseling; tutoring; and remedial instruction. Placement services also are available to alumni.

Programs of Study: The university confers the B.A., B.B.A., B.Mus., B.S., and B.S.Ed. degrees. Associate and master's degrees also are offered. Bachelor's degrees are offered in the following subjects: BUSINESS (accounting, business administration, business education, computer science, fashion merchandising, finance, management, marketing, public administration), EDUCATION (early childhood, elementary, health/physical, industrial, secondary, special), ENGLISH (English, journalism, speech), FINE AND PERFORMING ARTS (art, art education, music, music education, radio/TV, studio art, theater/dramatics), HEALTH SCIENCES (medical technology, nursing, occupational therapy, physical therapy, radiologic technology, respiratory therapy, speech therapy), LANGUAGES (French, Spanish), MATH AND SCIENCES (biology, chemistry, mathematics, physical sciences, physics), PHILOSOPHY (philosophy), PREPROFESSIONAL (dentistry, engineering, home economics, law, medicine, pharmacy, veterinary), SOCIAL SCIENCES (economics, geography, government/political science, history, psychology, social sciences, sociology). Forty percent of all undergraduate degrees are conferred in education, 35% in business, and 10% in health sciences.

Special: There are opportunities for foreign travel.

Required: All students must take a strong liberal arts program.

Honors: There are 7 national honor societies with chapters on campus. All departments offer honors programs.

Admissions: Ninety-nine percent of those who applied for admission to the 1981–82 freshman class were accepted. Applicants should be graduates of an accredited high school or the equivalent, and have completed 15 Carnegie units of work.

Procedure: The ACT is required. Applications should be submitted by August 25 for fall, by January 12 for spring, and by June 6 for summer. There is no application fee. Decisions are made on a rolling basis.

Special: The university has an early decision plan, and early and deferred admissions plans. CLEP general and subject exams are accepted.

Transfer: For fall 1981, 630 transfer students applied, 602 were accepted, and 475 enrolled. Transfers are accepted for all classes. Transfer students must study at the university for at least 24 of the 124 semester hours needed for a bachelor's degree. Application deadlines are August 1 for fall, January 1 for spring, and June 1 for summer.

Visiting: Orientation sessions for prospective students are held every weekday from 8 A.M. to 4:45 P.M.. Visitors may sit in on classes and stay on campus. The best day to visit is Friday. The admissions office handles the orientations and all visiting arrangements.

Financial Aid: The university provides scholarships, grants, loans, and part-time employment. Loans are available from the federal government, local banks, the university, and private sources. About 200 freshman scholarships are offered each year. The average scholarship or loan given to freshmen is $710. Maximum aid, including part-time employment, is $2400. About 65% of all students receive aid. The aid application deadlines are May 1 for fall, January 1 for spring, and June 1 for summer.

Foreign Students: About 45 students enrolled full-time at the university come from foreign countries. Special counseling and organizations are provided.

Admissions: Foreign applicants must score at least 500 on the TOEFL. No further tests are required.

Procedure: Application deadlines are February 1 for fall, August 1 for spring, and January 1 for summer entry. Students must present proof of adequate funds each year. Health insurance is not required, but the college offers such insurance for a fee.

Admissions Contact: Tommy G. Smith, Director of Admissions.

CALIFORNIA

ARMSTRONG COLLEGE   B-3
Berkeley, California 94704   (415) 848-2500

F/T: 90M, 64W	Faculty: 13; n/av
P/T: 29M, 40W	Ph.D.'s: 15%
Grad: 65M, 50W	S/F Ratio: 9 to 1
Year: qtrs, ss	Tuition: $2100 ($2220)
Appl: Sept. 15	R and B: $2700
244 applied	197 accepted 77 enrolled
SAT or ACT: not required	COMPETITIVE

Armstrong College, founded in 1918, is a private business college that provides graduate and undergraduate instruction. The library contains 21,000 volumes, and subscribes to 200 periodicals.

Environment: The college has 2 campuses: a building downtown, in an urban area approximately 8 miles from San Francisco, and a 4-acre campus with 3 buildings and gymnasium in El Cerrito. There are no student residences.

Student Life: The student body is a mixture of international and domestic students. None of the students live on campus.

Organizations: There is 1 sorority on campus, but no fraternities. Student organizations include an investment club, publications, and student government.

Sports: The college is a member of the West Coast Intercollegiate Soccer Conference and competes intercollegiately in this sport. There are 3 intramural sports for men and 3 for women.

Handicapped: There are no special facilities for physically handicapped students, but the school does schedule classes conveniently for such students.

Graduates: About 15% of the students drop out at the end of the first year. Seventy-six percent remain to graduate. Eight percent of the graduates pursue advanced study, with about 2% entering law school. Ninety percent go directly into business and industry.

Services: Students receive placement and career counseling free. Health care is available for a fee.

Programs of Study: The college awards the B.B.A. and B.S. degrees. Associate and master's degree programs are also offered. Bachelor's degrees are offered in the following subjects: BUSINESS (accounting, business administration, finance, international business, management, marketing).

Required: English and mathematics are required for freshman students unless they are waived by examination. All undergraduates must take a distribution of general education and business courses.

Special: The college does allow student-designed majors in business-related areas. A data processing program is used in problem solving.

Admissions: About 81% of those who applied were accepted for the 1981-82 freshman class. Applicants must be graduates of high school or have an equivalency diploma. Students should have a minimum average of C and rank in the upper 70% of their class. Other considerations, in order of importance, are advanced placement or honor courses, recommendations, leadership record, and extracurricular activities record.

Procedure: No standardized exams are required. Applications should be submitted by September 15 for fall admission and 4 weeks prior to the beginning of the winter, spring, and summer quarters. The application fee is $15. Notification is on a rolling basis, as openings are filled.

Transfer: Recently, 45 applications were received, 40 students were accepted, and 30 enrolled. Transfers are accepted for all but the senior class; A, B, and C grades are accepted. Students must complete 150 credits at the college, of a total 186 required for the bachelor's degree. Transfer application deadlines are the same as those for freshman applicants.

Visiting: There are no regularly scheduled orientations for prospective students, but guides are available for informal visits anytime except during registration periods. Visitors may sit in on classes. Visits are arranged through the admissions office.

Financial Aid: About 40% of the students receive financial aid. One percent work part-time on campus. The school provides scholarships and loans, and loans are also available from the federal government and state government. Freshman scholarships average $450, and loans average $900. The college is a member of CSS and requires the FAF and SAAC financial statements. The deadlines for aid application are August 15 (fall), December 1 (winter), April 30 (spring), and May 1 (summer).

Foreign Students: Fifty-seven percent of the full-time students are from foreign countries. An intensive English program is available for foreign students on the El Cerrito campus. Special counseling is also offered.

Admissions: Foreign applicants are required to take Armstrong's English test. College entrance exams are not required.

Procedure: Application deadlines are open; the college uses a rolling admissions and notification procedure. The application fee is $30. Foreign students are accepted for the fall, winter, spring, and summer quarters. Foreign students must present proof of funds adequate to cover 1 year of study. There is an additional tuition fee of $120 for foreign students. They are required to carry health insurance, which is available through the college for a fee.

Admissions Contact: Kate W. Higgins, Admissions Coordinator.

CALIFORNIA 35

ART CENTER COLLEGE OF DESIGN C-5
Pasadena, California 91103 (213) 577-1700

F/T: 699M, 500W	Faculty:	45; IV, —$
P/T: none	Ph.D.'s:	7%
Grad: 3M	S/F Ratio:	11 to 1
Year: tri	Tuition:	$3580
Appl: open	R and B:	n/app
500 applied	300 accepted	250 enrolled
SAT or ACT: required		SPECIAL

Art Center College of Design, founded in 1930, is an independent, private, nonprofit college of professional arts. It prepares students for careers in art, design, photography, and film. The library has 25,000 volumes, rare art portfolios, and thousands of color slides, and subscribes to 334 periodicals.

Environment: Since 1976, the 175-acre campus has been located on a hillside in the suburban Linda Vista district of Pasadena. The college is 20 minutes from the Los Angeles Civic Center and accessible by freeway from all parts of the metropolitan basin. The 166,000 square-foot building contains a library, a 430-seat theatre auditorium, 1- and 2-story photography and film stages, film editing rooms, projection rooms, a large gallery, cafeteria, and offices. Large industrial design shops are completely equipped for building prototype models, including facilities for plastics forming, clay modeling, welding, and spray painting. There are no living facilities on campus.

Student Life: Students come equally from within and outside California; all commute daily since no residence facilities are provided. Eighty percent of entering freshmen attended public schools.

Sports: There are no organized sports programs.

Handicapped: The following facilities are available to physically handicapped students: wheelchair ramps, elevators, and specially equipped restrooms.

Graduates: The freshman dropout rate is about 10%; 60% receive an undergraduate degree, and 1% continue in graduate work.

Services: All students receive placement and counseling services free of charge. Tutoring and remedial instruction are available for a fee.

Programs of Study: The college confers the B.F.A. and B.S. degrees. Master's programs are also offered. Bachelor's degrees are offered in the following subjects: advertising design, communication design, environmental design, fashion illustration, film/photography, fine art/painting, graphic design, illustration, industrial design, product design, and transportation design.

Required: Liberal arts studies are required of all students except those who have previously completed required academic courses at an accredited college.

Admissions: About 60% of those who applied were accepted for the 1981-82 freshman class. All applicants must submit a portfolio of art, film, or photographic work. In assessing candidates, the college pays considerable attention to such factors as advanced placement or honors courses and evidence of special talents. Ninety-eight percent of entering students have previously attended an accredited liberal arts college for one or more years, and prior college experience is recommended in some cases. Applicants seeking admission directly from high school must graduate in the upper half of the class and show strong potential in the portfolio.

Procedure: The ACT or SAT is required. Freshmen are admitted at the beginning of each trimester in October, February, and June. Applications should be received several months in advance; there is a $25 application fee. A rolling admissions procedure is used.

Special: CLEP and AP credit is granted. Deferred admissions are possible.

Transfer: For fall 1981, 250 transfer students enrolled. Transfers are accepted for the freshman class. Applicants must present a portfolio and a 2.5 GPA. C grades or better transfer. There are no application deadlines. Students are advised to complete their applications 4 to 6 months in advance of their planned entry. Transfer students are admitted at each trimester.

Visiting: Informal guided tours may be arranged, but visitors are not allowed to observe classes. The best times to visit are Mondays and Wednesdays at 2 P.M. and Fridays at 10:30 A.M.

Financial Aid: Approximately 60% of all students receive financial aid. Tuition scholarships are available for the fourth and succeeding trimesters. Entering students may apply for state or federally guaranteed loans and BEOG. The college also participates in the NDSL program and students may apply for such loans for the second and succeeding trimesters. The FAF is required. Financial aid application deadlines are June (fall), November (spring), and February (summer).

36 CALIFORNIA

Foreign Students: Ten percent of the full-time students come from foreign countries. The college offers an intensive English course and special counseling.

Admissions: Foreign students must achieve a minimum score of 550 on the TOEFL, or they must have completed Level 109 at English Language School. They are not required to take the SAT or ACT.

Procedure: There are no application deadlines; admissions are on a rolling basis. Foreign candidates are advised to apply 6 months in advance of intended entry. They are admitted to the fall, spring, and summer trimesters. The college requires a doctor's examination report and proof of funds adequate to cover 1 year of study.

Admissions Contact: Rosa María Zaldívar, Director of Admissions.

AZUSA PACIFIC UNIVERSITY D-5
(Formerly Azusa Pacific College)
Azusa, California 91702 (213) 969-3434

F/T: 580M, 627W		Faculty:	94; IIA, --$
P/T: 30M, 33W		Ph.D.'s:	50%
Grad: 125M, 130W		S/F Ratio:	17 to 1
Year: 4-4-1, ss		Tuition:	$3883
Appl: Aug. 15		R and B:	$2000
320 enrolled			
SAT: 450V 450M	ACT: 19		LESS COMPETITIVE

Azusa Pacific University is a coeducational, interdenominational Christian university that emphasizes spiritual growth in its liberal arts and sciences curriculum. The library houses a collection of 80,000 volumes and 200,000 microfilm items, and subscribes to 600 periodicals.

Environment: The university has two campuses—a 40-acre campus in Azusa and a 37-acre campus in Glendale. Both are about 30 miles from Los Angeles and are located in suburban settings. Student residences include high-rise dormitories, duplex apartments, modular units, and traditional apartment buildings.

Student Life: About 80% of the students are from the West Coast, and 80% reside on campus. Virtually all of the students are Protestant. Chapel attendance is required. University housing is single-sex, and there are visiting privileges.

Organizations: Extracurricular activities include clubs, cultural groups, and opportunities for social activity. There are no fraternities or sororities.

Sports: There are 8 intercollegiate sports and 9 intramural sports.

Handicapped: All of the campus is accessible to physically handicapped students. Facilities include ramps, special parking, elevators, lowered telephones, and specially equipped rest rooms. One counselor assists handicapped students.

Graduates: The freshman dropout rate is 40%.

Services: The following services are free to all students: placement, health care, psychological counseling, career counseling, tutoring, and remedial instruction.

Programs of Study: The university confers bachelor's and master's degrees. Bachelor's degrees are offered in the following subjects: BUSINESS (accounting, business administration, management), EDUCATION (elementary, secondary), ENGLISH (English, journalism), FINE AND PERFORMING ARTS (art, music, music education, performance), HEALTH SCIENCES (nursing), LANGUAGES (Spanish), MATH AND SCIENCES (biology, chemistry, mathematics), PHILOSOPHY (Bible, philosophy, pre-ministerial, religion, theology, youth ministry), PREPROFESSIONAL (ministry, social work), SOCIAL SCIENCES (government/political science, history, psychology, social sciences, sociology).

Required: Five semesters of Christian service are required.

Special: It is possible to earn a B.G.S. degree. Students may design their own majors.

Admissions: About 75% of the students applying for a recent freshman class were accepted. The minimum class rank is the top 50%; the minimum high school GPA is 2.5. Important admissions criteria include, in order of decreasing importance, leadership record, recommendations, extracurricular activities record, advanced placement or honors courses, and personality of applicant.

Procedure: Either the SAT or the ACT is required. Applicants must also submit a $20 nonrefundable fee, 3 recommendations, 2 transcripts, and a health form. Application deadlines are August 15 (fall), December 20 (spring), and June 1 (summer). A rolling admissions policy is used.

Special: CLEP and AP are used. There is a deferred admissions plan.

Transfer: In fall 1981, 185 students enrolled. Transfer students must have a GPA of at least 2.0 and a combined SAT score of at least 800. Thirty of the 126 credits needed for a bachelor's degree must be completed in residence; D grades do not transfer. Application deadlines are the same as for freshman applicants.

Visiting: There is a formal orientation program for freshmen. Informal campus visits can be arranged. Visitors may attend classes and stay overnight in the residence halls.

Financial Aid: About 85% of the students are receiving assistance; 70% work part-time on campus. Average aid for freshmen is $400; the maximum is $1200. Scholarships, loans, and campus employment comprise the aid package. The aid application must be filed between March and July; the FAF is required. The university is a member of CSS.

Foreign Students: An intensive English course, special counseling, and organizations especially for foreign students are available.

Admissions: Foreign students must present a TOEFL score of at least 500. No college entrance exam must be taken.

Procedure: Application deadlines are August 15 (fall) and December 20 (spring). Foreign students must present proof of adequate funds, must submit an application fee of $100, and must carry health insurance, which is available through the college for a fee.

Admissions Contact: David Bixby, Director of Admissions.

BETHANY BIBLE COLLEGE B-3
Santa Cruz, California 95066 (408) 438-3800

F/T: 302M, 279W		Faculty:	38; IIB, +$
P/T: 36M, 40W		Ph.D.'s:	20%
Grad: none		S/F Ratio:	17 to 1
Year: 4-1-4, ss		Tuition:	$2480
Appl: Aug. 1		R and B:	$1730
432 applied	279 accepted		231 enrolled
ACT: required			NONCOMPETITIVE

Bethany Bible College, founded in 1919, is affiliated with the Assemblies of God. Its library holds 40,000 volumes, and subscribes to 286 periodicals.

Environment: The 45-acre campus is located in a rural area 25 miles from San Jose. Its more than 10 buildings include 2 dormitories that house 200 students.

Student Life: All students are Protestant; daily attendance at chapel is compulsory. Seventy-seven percent of the students are from California. Freshmen aged 18 or younger are required to live in the dorms, which are single-sex. Drinking on campus is forbidden. All students must observe a curfew and sign-out procedure.

Organizations: College-sponsored activities include music groups, student ministries, a school paper, a yearbook, and 1 or 2 cultural events each week. A student government has jurisdiction over student publications and activities.

Sports: Men can participate in intercollegiate basketball and softball and women in intercollegiate volleyball. Three intramural sports are offered for men and 3 for women.

Handicapped: Wheelchair ramps are provided for physically handicapped students.

Graduates: About 40% of the freshmen drop out by the end of their first year.

Services: Free placement services and psychological counseling are available.

Programs of Study: The college confers the B.A. and B.S. degrees. Bachelor's degrees are offered in the following subjects: EDUCATION (early childhood, elementary, religious), ENGLISH (English), FINE AND PERFORMING ARTS (music), PHILOSOPHY (religion), PREPROFESSIONAL (ministry), SOCIAL SCIENCES (history, psychology, social sciences).

Required: Students must earn 124 credits and maintain a GPA of 2.0 or higher to graduate.

Admissions: The college follows an open admissions policy. Applicants should have earned at least a C average in 15 Carnegie units. Admissions officers also take into account the applicant's character and personality as well as recommendations by school officials.

Procedure: The ACT is required and should be taken by June. Junior-year results are acceptable, but final senior scores must be sent upon graduation. Application deadlines are August 1 (fall) and December 15 (spring). The application fee is $20. Notification is made on a rolling basis.

Special: A deferred admissions plan is available. Credit is awarded for CLEP tests.

Transfer: In a recent year, 170 applications were received, 150 were accepted, and 117 students enrolled. Transfers are accepted for all classes. D grades do not transfer. Students must study at the college for at least one year to receive a bachelor's degree. Transfer application deadlines are the same as those for freshman applicants.

Visiting: The college schedules regular orientations for prospective students. Informal visits also can be arranged for weekdays through the admissions office. Guides are provided, and visitors may sit in on classes and stay overnight at the school.

Financial Aid: About 38% of the students receive aid through the college; 21% receive scholarships. Forty-two percent of the students receive loans. Freshman scholarships are available. Work contracts are awarded to 10% of the students, including freshmen. The college is a member of the CSS and requires aid applicants to submit the FAF. The application deadline for priority consideration is June 1. Need is the main consideration in determining awards

Foreign Students: Foreign students at the college make up about 3% of enrollment. Special organizations are available for these students.

Admissions: Applicants must score at least 500 on the TOEFL. They also must take the ACT.

Procedure: Application deadlines are the same as those for other students. Foreign students must submit a medical report and provide proof of adequate funds for 4 years. Health insurance is required, and is available through the college for a fee.

Admissions Contact: Carmine Wilson, Director of Admissions and Records.

BIOLA UNIVERSITY   D-5
(Formerly Biola College)
La Mirada, California 90639   (213) 944-0351

F/T: 818M, 1186W	Faculty: 144; IIA, —$
P/T: 128M, 156W	Ph.D.'s: 50%
Grad: 689M, 126W	S/F Ratio: 18 to 1
Year: 4-1-4, ss	Tuition: $3634
Appl: July 31	R and B: $2148
1425 applied	961 accepted 804 enrolled
SAT: 463V 487M	COMPETITIVE

Biola University, founded in 1908, is a private, interdenominational Christian university that emphasizes the arts, sciences, and theology. The library houses 180,000 volumes and 9000 microform items, and subscribes to 1100 periodicals.

Environment: The 100-acre campus is located in a suburban area 22 miles from Los Angeles. Residence halls accommodate 882 women and 492 men.

Student Life: About 70% of the students come from California. Sixty percent of the freshmen are graduates of public schools. About 60% of the students live in dormitories. About 12% are minority-group members. Students are evangelical Christians. All must attend chapel and participate in Christian service; drinking, smoking, dancing, and gambling are prohibited. Campus housing is single-sex. Day-care services are available to students and staff members. Students may keep cars on campus.

Organizations: There are no fraternities or sororities. Extracurricular activities include student government, religious organizations, student missionary union, student services clubs, academic major clubs, and guest lecturers and musical performers. The college is near Knotts Berry Farm, Disneyland, beaches, and Anaheim Stadium.

Sports: The university offers 7 intercollegiate sports for men and 3 for women. There are 10 intramural sports for men and 10 for women.

Handicapped: About 70% of the campus is accessible to physically handicapped students. Facilities include wheelchair ramps, special parking areas, and specially equipped rest rooms. About 0.5% of the students are visually impaired, and special facilities provided for them include dial-a-ride, readers, and an on-campus post office. No special counselors are available.

Graduates: Twenty percent of the freshmen drop out; 65% remain to graduate. Between 30% and 40% of the graduates seek advanced degrees.

Services: Students receive the following free services: placement, career and psychological counseling, tutoring, and remedial instruction. Health care is available for a fee.

Programs of Study: The university awards the B.A., B.S., and B.M. degrees. Master's and doctoral degrees also are available. Bachelor's degrees are offered in the following subjects: AREA STUDIES (American), BUSINESS (accounting, business administration, computer science, management, marketing), EDUCATION (adult, early childhood, elementary, health/physical, secondary), ENGLISH (English, journalism, literature, speech), FINE AND PERFORMING ARTS (art, art education, film/photography, music, music education, radio/TV, theater/dramatics), HEALTH SCIENCES (nursing, speech therapy), LANGUAGES (French, German, Greek/Latin, Hebrew, Spanish), MATH AND SCIENCES (biology, chemistry, physical sciences, physics), PHILOSOPHY (humanities, philosophy, religion), PREPROFESSIONAL (ministry, social work), SOCIAL SCIENCES (economics, government/political science, history, psychology, social sciences, sociology). Thirty percent of the undergraduate degrees are conferred in philosophy, 17% in math and sciences, and 17% in health sciences.

Required: All students must complete 30 units of Bible and Doctrine.

Special: Summer travel tours and a semester abroad are available.

Honors: Delta Epsilon Chi is represented on campus.

Admissions: About 67% of those who applied were accepted for the 1981–82 freshman class. The SAT scores of those who enrolled were as follows: Verbal—70% below 500, 24% between 500 and 599, 4% between 600 and 700, and 2% above 700; Math—61% below 500, 29% between 500 and 599, 8% between 600 and 700, and 2% above 700. On the ACT, 20% scored below 21, 28% between 21 and 23, 40% between 24 and 25, 12% between 26 and 28, and 0% above 28. All applicants must be evangelical Christians. They must demonstrate that they have a Christian character, leadership ability, and the aptitudes that indicate probable success in college. Generally, applicants must be graduates of accredited high schools, have completed 15 Carnegie units with an average of 2.5 or better, and rank in the upper half of their high school class. Admissions officers also consider recommendations by school officials, advanced placement or honors courses, and the extracurricular activities record.

Procedure: Applicants must submit SAT or ACT scores and reference forms from a pastor and the school last attended. The application fee is $25. Application deadlines are July 31 (fall), January 15 (spring), and May 15 (summer). Applicants are notified on a rolling basis.

Special: An early decision plan (with a December 1 notification date), an early admissions plan (with a November 1 application deadline), and a deferred admissions plan are offered. AP and CLEP credit (except CLEP English) is accepted.

Transfer: For fall 1981, 382 students applied, 256 were accepted, and 237 enrolled. A GPA of 2.5 and a score of at least 400 on each part of the SAT are required. D grades do not transfer. All students must complete, at the university, 30 of the 130 credits required for a bachelor's degree. Application deadlines are the same as those for freshmen.

Visiting: College Day orientations for prospective students are held once each semester. Informal visits also may be scheduled for weekdays with the admissions office. Guides are provided, and visitors may sit in on classes and remain overnight in the dorms.

Financial Aid: Sixty-six percent of the students receive aid; the average recipient gets $510 per year. About 21% of the students work part-time on campus. BEOG, scholarships (academic, athletic, music, art, and nursing), NDSL and other loans, and part-time jobs on and off campus are available. Approximately $500,000 in financial aid is distributed each year. The deadline for financial aid applications is March 1. The university is a member of CSS and requires the FAF and the Student Aid Application for California.

Foreign Students: About 5% of the full-time students come from foreign countries. An intensive English course, special counseling, and special organizations are available for these students.

Admissions: Foreign students must achieve a TOEFL score of at least 500. No college entrance exams are required.

Procedure: The application deadline is May 1; foreign students are admitted in the fall and summer terms. They must present proof of funds adequate to cover 1 year of study and must be examined by a physician. Health insurance is required and is available through the university for a fee.

Admissions Contact: Wayne Chute, Dean of Admissions and Records, or Greg Vaughan, Director of Admissions.

BROOKS INSTITUTE
Santa Barbara, California 93108   C–5
(805) 969-2291

F/T: 650M, 150W
P/T: none
Grad: none
Year: tri
Appl: open
100 applied
SAT: required

Faculty: 25; n/av
Ph.D.'s: n/av
S/F Ratio: 40 to 1
Tuition: $4060–4120
R and B: n/app

65 enrolled
SPECIAL

Brooks Institute, founded in 1945, offers degree programs in photography. The library houses 4400 volumes, and subscribes to 110 periodicals.

Environment: Brooks Institute has 3 campuses in the urban environment of Santa Barbara. No dormitories are provided.

Student Life: Students come from all over the United States as well as from foreign countries.

Sports: The institute sponsors no intercollegiate sports programs. There are 2 intramural sports for men and 1 for women.

Handicapped: There are no special facilities for handicapped students.

Graduates: Eighteen percent of the freshmen drop out by the end of the first year. Seventy percent remain to graduate. About 2% of the graduates pursue further study. About 60% to 70% work in the field of photography.

Services: Free placement services, career counseling, and psychological counseling are provided for students. Housing and part-time job information files are maintained.

Programs of Study: The institute offers bachelor's and master's degrees in photography. Bachelor's degrees are offered in cinematography/television, color technology, illustration and advertising, industrial and scientific photography, and professional portraiture.

Required: Students must complete 18 photo courses to graduate. All students who major in cinematography and television must complete 6 courses in basic and applied photography. Students also must take some general photography electives.

Special: Independent study programs may be offered to qualified students.

Admissions: Applicants should have a high school diploma or GED and a minimum GPA of 2.0. Admissions officers also consider evidence of special talents, recommendations, and advanced placement or honors courses.

Procedure: The SAT is required. Application deadlines are open, but there usually is a waiting list for admission. A new course starts 6 times per year, and each course is 7 weeks long. The registration fee is $100. Admissions decisions are made on a rolling basis.

Transfer: Transfer students are admitted 6 times a year on a rolling basis. A minimum GPA of 2.0 is required. Credits from photography courses taken elsewhere are not transferable. The institute requires that 135 of the 144 credits required for the bachelor's degree be completed at Brooks. Application deadlines are open.

Visiting: Guides are available for prospective students at 10 A.M. and 2 P.M. on weekdays. Orientations for prospective students also are scheduled regularly.

Financial Aid: Financial aid is available through the institute. Eight percent of the students work part-time on campus.

Foreign Students: Fifteen percent of the full-time students are from foreign countries. The institute offers these students an intensive English course and special counseling.

Admissions: Foreign applicants must take the English proficiency exam given by their embassy and should achieve a score of approximately 550. College entrance exams are not required.

Procedure: There are no application deadlines; applications are accepted on a rolling basis. Candidates are notified within 2 months after completion of the application.

Admissions Contact: Anita Shaw, Director of Admissions.

CALIFORNIA BAPTIST COLLEGE
Riverside, California 92504   D–5
(714) 689-5771

F/T: 259M, 280W
P/T: 69M, 48W
Grad: none
Year: 4-1-4, ss
Appl: open
167 applied   132 accepted   124 enrolled
SAT: 413V 446M   ACT: 16   LESS COMPETITIVE

Faculty: 36; IIB, av$
Ph.D.'s: n/av
S/F Ratio: 16 to 1
Tuition: $2975
R and B: $1690

California Baptist College, founded in 1950, is supported by the Southern Baptist General Convention of California. The library contains 105,000 volumes and subscribes to 600 periodicals.

Environment: The 75-acre campus, located in a city of 175,000 situated 60 miles from Los Angeles, includes single-sex dormitories with single rooms, the Book of Life Auditorium, and 96 apartments for married students.

Student Life: About 80% of the students are from California, and 80% live on campus. Most are Baptists. There are no visiting privileges in dormitories, and freshmen must live on campus unless over 21 or living with relatives. Attendance at twice-weekly chapel services is voluntary. Drinking, smoking, and dancing are prohibited on campus. Students may keep cars on campus.

Organizations: There are no fraternities or sororities. The college sponsors special-interest, departmental, and service clubs; music and drama groups; publications; a student government; and a variety of cultural and social events. Numerous universities and cultural centers near Riverside provide additional activities.

Sports: The college fields intercollegiate teams in 2 sports for men and 2 for women. Six intramural sports for men and 4 for women are offered.

Handicapped: About 95% of the campus—everything except the upper levels of dormitories and apartments—is accessible to wheelchair-bound students. Wheelchair ramps, special parking areas, elevators, specially equipped rest rooms, and lowered drinking fountains are provided. Special class scheduling can be arranged.

Services: Placement and career and psychological counseling are provided free to students. Fees are charged for health care services.

Programs of Study: The college grants the B.A., B.S., and B.M. degrees. Bachelor's degrees are offered in the following subjects: BUSINESS (business administration), EDUCATION (early childhood, elementary, secondary), ENGLISH (English), FINE AND PERFORMING ARTS (art, music, theater/dramatics), LANGUAGES (Spanish), MATH AND SCIENCES (biology, physical sciences), PHILOSOPHY (religion), PREPROFESSIONAL (criminal justice, ministry), SOCIAL SCIENCES (history, psychology, sociology). The most popular majors are religion, behavioral sciences, business administration, and education.

Required: Freshmen must complete a general education program. All undergraduates must fulfill certain liberal arts requirements.

Special: Five-year combined B.A.-B.S. degrees may be earned in life science (biology), behavioral science, physical science, psychology, and sociology. Students may design their own major or earn a general studies degree.

Honors: Qualified students may join the Alpha Chi honor society.

Admissions: Seventy-nine percent of those who applied were accepted for the 1981–82 freshman class. The combined SAT scores of those who enrolled in an earlier class were as follows: 18% between 1000 and 1200, 5% between 1200 and 1400, and 1% above 1400. Of those who took the ACT, 8% scored between 20 and 23, 8% between 24 and 26, 5% between 26 and 28, and 3% above 28. Applicants must have a high school average of 2.0 or better. Those with special ability in music, art, drama, or similar creative activities are especially welcome. Admissions officers also consider, in order of importance, financial ability, recommendations by high school officials, and advanced placement or honors courses.

Procedure: The SAT or ACT is required and should be taken by December of the senior year. Candidates must furnish evidence of good moral character and submit recommendations from the high school principal or counselor and from a pastor or other responsible person in the community. Application deadlines are open; freshmen are admitted to all terms. Notification is made on a rolling basis. Applications should be submitted with a $15 fee.

Special: CLEP credit is accepted.

Transfer: For fall 1981, all 101 transfer applicants were accepted, and 89 enrolled. Transfer students are accepted for all classes. Applicants must have an average of C or better and a combined score of at least

750 on the SAT or 16 on the ACT. Up to 6 grades of D may transfer. Students must earn 24 of the 124 credits required for a bachelor's degree at the college.

Visiting: Orientations for prospective students are scheduled regularly. Informal visits also may be arranged with the admissions office for weekdays. Visitors may sit in on classes with advance notice and stay overnight in the dormitories. Guides are provided.

Financial Aid: About 80% of the students receive aid. The average award to freshmen is 75% of college costs. California residents must apply for Cal Grants; all others must apply for the BEOG. The college also administers SEOG, NDSL, and CWS jobs. Three percent of students work part-time on campus. Valedictorians and salutatorians receive full scholarships, and scholarships equal to 35% of tuition are awarded to students with GPAs of 3.5 or better. Tuition may be paid in installments, with the final payment due by the end of the semester. Aid applications and the FAF should be filed by April 1 for priority consideration. The college is a member of CSS.

Foreign Students: Foreign students enrolled at the college make up about 9% of its student body.

Admissions: Foreign applicants must score a minimum of 500 on the TOEFL. No college entrance exams are required.

Procedure: Application deadlines are July 15 (fall), November 15 (winter), December 15 (spring), and April 15 (summer). Students must present proof of adequate funds for 4 years of study. All foreign students must carry health insurance, which is available through the college for a fee.

Admissions Contact: John E. Potter, Director of Admissions.

CALIFORNIA COLLEGE OF ARTS AND CRAFTS B–3
Oakland, California 94618 (415) 653-8118

F/T: 299M, 596W Faculty: 29; IIA, –$
P/T: 83M, 179W Ph.D.'s: 4%
Grad: 37M, 92W S/F Ratio: 15 to 1
Year: tri, ss Tuition: $4260
Appl: Aug. 1 R and B: $2700
289 applied 244 accepted 98 enrolled
SAT or ACT: not required **SPECIAL**

California College of Arts and Crafts is a privately endowed professional college and member of the Union of Independent Colleges of Art (UICA), a consortium of 8 professional colleges of art nationwide. The Meyer Library contains 27,000 volumes.

Environment: The 4½-acre campus is located in the urban environment of Oakland, 20 minutes from San Francisco. Among the 14 buildings are two of historic Victorian architecture. There is one residence hall on campus housing 72 women.

Student Life: About 96% of the students reside off campus. Out-of-state students account for 40% of the total enrollment and 12% come from foreign countries. About 33% of the students are minority-group members. College housing is single-sex during the academic year, coed during summer sessions. There are visiting privileges when the residence is single-sex.

Organizations: There are no social fraternities or sororities. The Student Association, with its elected student government, provides a means for the expression of student opinion and is responsible for many art exhibits and other functions.

Sports: There are no athletic programs.

Handicapped: Special facilities for the physically handicapped include wheelchair ramps, special parking, and elevators.

Services: The college offers students free career counseling, placement, psychological counseling, tutoring, and some remedial instruction. Placement services are also offered through the Union of Independent Colleges of Art.

Programs of Study: The college awards the B.F.A. degree. The M.F.A. and M.A.Ed. degrees are also available. Bachelor's degrees are offered in the following subjects: FINE AND PERFORMING ARTS (art, ceramics, drawing, ethnic art, film/photography, general crafts, general design, general fine arts, glass, graphic design, interior architectural design, metal arts, painting, printmaking, sculpture, studio art, textiles, wood design).

Special: A certificate program for those not seeking a degree is available as well as courses for young people under the supervision of the Department of Education. Students have the opportunity to create their own major.

Admissions: About 84% of those who applied were accepted for the 1981-82 freshman class. Applicants must rank in the top 50% of their class and be graduated from an accredited high school or its equivalent and have maintained a GPA of at least C. A college preparatory course curriculum is preferred and 2 letters of recommendation attesting to either academic or artistic potential are required.

Procedure: Admissions are on a rolling basis. The application deadlines are August 1 (fall), December 1 (spring), and May 1 (summer). ACT or SAT scores are requested. There is a $20 application fee.

Special: Deferred admissions and early decision plans are possible. CLEP or AP credit is available by petition only. Special students not working toward a degree may enroll in classes when space is available.

Transfer: For fall 1981, 422 applications were received, 345 were accepted, and 197 students enrolled. Transfers are accepted for all classes. D grades are not acceptable for advanced standing credit. A minimum average of 2.0 and 2 letters of recommendation are required for transfer. Students must study at the college for at least one year to receive a degree. A minimum of 30 semester units must be completed at the college, of the 120 semester units required for the bachelor's degree. ACT or SAT scores are requested for transfer. Application deadlines for transfers are the same as those for freshmen. Applicants are notified within 2 months.

Visiting: There are regularly scheduled orientations for prospective students. For informal visits student guides are available. For such visits the admissions office should be contacted.

Financial Aid: About 80% of the students are receiving financial aid. Twenty-five percent work part-time on campus. The average award to freshmen is $1500. Financial assistance is available to needy students in the forms of grants, work-study, and loans. Scholarships are available to students of demonstrated ability after completing one year of study. The college participates in the following federal financial aid programs: NDSL, CWSP, SEOG, BEOG, and FISL. The college is a member of CSS. The FAF and Student Aid Applications for California are required. The financial aid application deadline is February 10 for the academic year, except for loans, which may be applied for during the year.

Foreign Students: Eight percent of the full-time students come from foreign countries. The college offers these students special counseling and special organizations.

Admissions: Foreign applicants must take either the TOEFL or the University of Michigan Language Test; a minimum score of 500 is required on the former, 80 on the latter. College entrance exams are not required.

Procedure: Admission application deadlines for foreign students are July 1 (fall), November 1 (spring), and April 1 (summer). Proof of health must be presented. Proof of funds adequate to cover each year of study at the college must also be furnished.

Admissions Contact: Jean T. Thomma, Director of Admissions.

CALIFORNIA COLLEGE OF PODIATRIC MEDICINE B–3
San Francisco, California 94115 (415) 563-3444

F/T: 338M, 61W Faculty: 39; IIA, ++$
P/T: none Ph.D.'s: 100%
Grad: 10M, 4W S/F Ratio: n/av
Year: sems Tuition: $3990
Appl: April 1 R and B: n/app
SAT or ACT: required **VERY COMPETITIVE**

California College of Podiatric Medicine is an independent professional school founded in 1914. It offers both undergraduate and graduate degrees in podiatric medicine. The college maintains no student housing facilities. The undergraduate degree awarded is the Bachelor of Basic Medical Science. About 97% of the students receive financial aid; 25% work part-time on campus. Five percent of the students are from foreign countries.

Admissions Contact: Dr. Richard Stess, Director of Admissions.

CALIFORNIA INSTITUTE OF TECHNOLOGY C–5
Pasadena, California 91125 (213) 795-6341

F/T: 729M, 131W Faculty: 344; n/av
P/T: none Ph.D.'s: 99%
Grad: 789M, 99W S/F Ratio: 3 to 1
Year: qtrs Tuition: $6309
Appl: Jan. 15 R and B: $2787
1518 applied 388 accepted 217 enrolled
SAT: 670V 760M **MOST COMPETITIVE**

CALIFORNIA

The California Institute of Technology, founded in 1891, is a privately supported college of science and engineering. Its library contains 330,000 volumes, and subscribes to over 5000 periodicals.

Environment: The campus occupies 82 acres within Pasadena, in a suburban area 10 miles from Los Angeles. Seven student houses accommodate 550 men and 100 women. The college also sponsors off-campus apartments.

Student Life: About 40% of the students come from California. About 87% of entering freshman attended public schools. About 65% of the students live on campus. About 3% are members of minority groups. Dormitories are both single-sex and coed. Students may keep cars on campus. Day-care services are available to full-time students for a fee.

Organizations: There are no fraternities or sororities. The institute sponsors numerous extracurricular activities, both scientific and non-scientific. Students run the student government and student publications, and participate in curriculum decisions. There are religious organizations for students of all major faiths.

Sports: The institute fields intercollegiate teams in 15 sports for men and 11 for women. Men may participate in 10 intramural sports, women in 9. Five club sports, including sailing and water polo, also are offered.

Handicapped: About 95% of the campus is accessible to physically handicapped students. Wheelchair ramps, elevators, and specially equipped rest rooms are provided.

Graduates: The freshman dropout rate is 6%. About 72% of those who enter remain to graduate. Sixty percent of the graduates pursue advanced degrees, including 6% who enter medical school. About 35% seek careers in business and industry.

Services: Placement, career counseling, health care, psychological counseling, tutoring, and remedial instruction are free to students. Placement services also are available to graduates.

Programs of Study: The institute confers the B.S. degree. Master's and doctoral degrees also are awarded. Bachelor's degrees are offered in the following subjects: ENGLISH (literature), MATH AND SCIENCES (astronomy, biology, chemistry, geology, mathematics, physics), PREPROFESSIONAL (engineering—aeronautical, engineering—chemical, engineering—civil, engineering—electrical, engineering—energy, engineering—environmental, engineering—materials science, engineering—mechanical), SOCIAL SCIENCES (economics, history, social sciences). Sixty percent of degrees are conferred in engineering.

Required: All students must take courses in mathematics, physics, chemistry, humanities, and physical education.

Special: The institute offers exchange programs with liberal arts colleges, making possible combined B.A.-B.S. degrees. Students may design their own majors. All freshman courses are pass/fail.

Honors: All divisions of the institute offer honors programs arranged by the individual departments.

Admissions: Twenty-six percent of those who applied were accepted for the 1981-82 freshman class. The SAT scores of those who enrolled were as follows: Verbal—8% below 500, 16% between 500 and 599, 42% between 600 and 700, and 34% above 700; Math—0% below 500, 0% between 500 and 599, 8% between 600 and 700, and 92% above 700. In addition to grades and test scores, admissions officers consider, in decreasing order of importance, evidence of special talents, advanced placement or honors courses, recommendations by high school officials, extracurricular activities, impressions made during a personal interview, leadership record, personality, and commitment to and enthusiasm for science.

Procedure: Candidates must take the SAT and 3 ATs. Level II mathematics is required, and the other 2 ATs may be chosen from biology, chemistry, physics, or English composition. The ATs should be taken between May of the junior year and January of the senior year. The SAT should be taken by January of the senior year. The deadline for regular admission is January 1 for fall. Applications should be submitted with a $10 fee.

Special: Early decision, early admissions, and deferred admissions plans are available.

Transfer: For fall 1981, 123 transfer students applied, 36 were accepted, and 33 enrolled. Students may transfer only into the sophomore and junior classes, and must study two years in residence, earning half the 516 credits required for a bachelor's degree. Transfer applicants must have at least 1 year of calculus and 1 year of calculus-based physics. They must take the institute's exam in math and physics. Exams in chemistry also are required for students planning to major in chemistry or chemical engineering. A 3.0 average is required, and grades of A in science are recommended. The application deadline is April 1 for fall entry; applicants are notified by June 15.

Visiting: Guides are available for informal campus visits. Special arrangements may be made with the admissions office to sit in on classes or to stay overnight at the institute.

Financial Aid: The institute meets the financial needs of all admitted students through scholarship/self-help packages. About 76% of all students receive financial aid, and 50% work on campus. The deadline for filing the financial aid application and the FAF is February 1. The institute is a member of CSS. California residents are expected to apply for California State scholarships.

Foreign Students: The foreign students enrolled make up about 8% of the institute's student body. Special counseling and organizations are available for these students.

Admissions: Foreign applicants, like domestic applicants, must take the SAT and 3 ATs. No English proficiency exam is required.

Procedure: The application deadline is January 15. Foreign students must show some proof of adequate funds. Health insurance is not required, but is available through the institute.

Admissions Contact: Stirling L. Huntley, Director of Admissions.

CALIFORNIA INSTITUTE OF THE ARTS C-5
Valencia, California 91355 (805) 255-1050

F/T: 337M, 223W Faculty: n/av; IV, +$
P/T: 11M, 8W Ph.D.'s: n/av
Grad: 120M, 101W S/F Ratio: 7 to 1
Year: sems Tuition: $5600
Appl: Feb. 1 R and B: $3175
SAT, ACT: not required SPECIAL

California Institute of the Arts superseded the Los Angeles Conservatory of Music (founded in 1883) and the Chouinard Art Institute (founded in 1921). The Institute comprises 5 divisions: Art and Design, Dance, Film and Video, Music, and Theater. There is also a nondegree-conferring Critical Studies division. The library has 52,000 volumes and 5900 microfilm items, and subscribes to 600 periodicals.

Environment: The 60-acre campus is located in a suburban area 35 miles north of Los Angeles. The main building houses all of the major facilities; a dormitory accommodates 350 men and women. The present campus was completed in 1970.

Student Life: About 50% of the students are from California, and 85% have public school backgrounds. Fifty percent of the students live on campus in coed dormitories. Nearly 22% of the students are members of minority groups. Students may keep cars on campus.

Organizations: There are no fraternities or sororities. Popular extracurricular activities include theaters, cinemas, museums, sports arenas, and shopping centers in the vicinity.

Sports: There is no athletic program.

Handicapped: All of the campus is accessible to physically handicapped students. Facilities include ramps, elevators, and specially equipped rest rooms.

Graduates: The freshman dropout rate is 26%. About 25% of the students pursue graduate work after receiving a bachelor's degree.

Services: Placement, health care (nurse), psychological counseling, career counseling, tutoring, and remedial instruction are free to all students. Placement services include assistance in resume writing, applications for employment, and grant proposal writing.

Programs of Study: The institute grants the B.F.A. degree. Certificate and master's degree programs are also available. Bachelor's degrees are offered in the following subjects: FINE AND PERFORMING ARTS (animation, art, composition, dance, design, film/photography, instrumental performance, music, radio/TV, studio art, theater/dramatics, vocal performance).

Special: Student-designed majors are generally allowed. Humanities courses are offered in several fields. There is no fixed curriculum; students proceed at their own pace.

Honors: There is no honors program.

Admissions: About 61% of the applicants for a recent school year were accepted. Neither the SAT nor the ACT is required. Admission is based on potential and demonstrated talent.

Procedure: A portfolio should be submitted by students in the visual arts; students in the performing arts must audition. Applications for the fall semester are due February 1 with the $25 nonrefundable application fee. Notification is on a rolling basis.

Special: There is a deferred admissions plan, except in the School of Film and Video.

Transfer: Requirements are individualized and flexible. Admission is based on demonstrated talent; credits do not always transfer. There is a 1-year residency requirement.

Visiting: Informal visits may be arranged with student guides. Visitors may sit in on classes and usually may stay overnight in the dormitories.

Financial Aid: About 67% of the students are receiving assistance. The aid program includes scholarships, grants (EOG), loans (NDSL), and CWS. There are no deadlines for aid application; notification is on a rolling basis. The FAF is required. The institute is a member of CSS.

Foreign Students: About 8% of the students come from foreign countries. Special counseling is available for these students.

Admissions: Foreign students must achieve a TOEFL score of at least 525. No college entrance exams are required.

Procedure: Application deadlines are the same as those for other students. Foreign students must present proof of adequate funds. Health insurance is required and is available through the institute for a fee.

Admissions Contact: Kenneth Young, Director of Admissions.

CALIFORNIA LUTHERAN COLLEGE C–5
Thousand Oaks, California 91360   (805) 492-2411

F/T: 558M, 653W	Faculty:	81; IIA, av$
P/T: 42M, 80W	Ph.D.'s:	75%
Grad: 457M, 669W	S/F Ratio:	15 to 1
Year: 4-1-4, ss	Tuition:	$4000
Appl: Aug. 1	R and B:	$2150
1034 applied	826 accepted	467 enrolled
SAT: 431V 464M	ACT: 21	COMPETITIVE

California Lutheran College is a liberal arts institution founded in 1961 and affiliated with the American Lutheran Church and the Lutheran Church in America. The library houses 100,000 volumes.

Environment: The 285-acre campus is located in Thousand Oaks, a suburban residential community of 65,000 people 45 miles from Los Angeles. The campus is bounded on the west by the Oxnard Plains, one of the world's richest agricultural areas.

Student Life: Most students come from the West, and about 75% live in dormitories on campus. About 10% of the students are members of minority groups. Seventy-five percent are Protestant, and 15% are Catholic. Dormitories are coed, and students may keep cars on campus.

Organizations: There are no fraternities or sororities. Extracurricular activities include orchestral and choral groups, debating, language and other special-interest groups, a literary magazine, a student newspaper, a children's theater, and student government. The Pacific Ocean is 30 minutes away, ski resorts are 2 hours away, and Los Angeles and Santa Barbara each are 45 minutes away.

Sports: The college fields intercollegiate teams in 10 sports for men and 7 for women. Eleven intramural sports are offered for both sexes.

Handicapped: About 70% of the campus is accessible to wheelchair-bound students. Special facilities include wheelchair ramps, parking areas, and specially equipped rest rooms.

Graduates: Twenty-five percent of the freshmen drop out by the end of the first year, and 55% remain to graduate. Thirty percent of the graduates seek advanced degrees, including 5% who enter medical school, 1% who enter dental school, and 2% who enter law school.

Services: Students receive free placement, career and psychological counseling, health care, tutoring, and remedial instruction. Placement services also are available to graduates.

Programs of Study: The college awards the B.A. and B.S. degrees. Master's degrees also are available. Bachelor's degrees are offered in the following subjects: BUSINESS (accounting, business administration, computer science, management), EDUCATION (early childhood, elementary, secondary), ENGLISH (English), FINE AND PERFORMING ARTS (art, art education, music, music education, theater/dramatics), HEALTH SCIENCES (nursing), LANGUAGES (French, German, Spanish), MATH AND SCIENCES (biology, chemistry, geology, mathematics), PHILOSOPHY (philosophy, religion), PREPROFESSIONAL (dentistry, engineering, law, medicine, ministry, pharmacy, social work, veterinary), SOCIAL SCIENCES (administration of justice, economics, government/political science, history, psychology, sociology). Nineteen percent of the undergraduate degrees are conferred in business, 19% in education, and 10% in the social sciences.

Special: Students may design their own majors.

Admissions: About 80% of the applicants for the 1981–82 freshman class were accepted. The SAT scores of those who enrolled were as follows: Verbal—46% below 500, 32% between 500 and 599, 15% between 600 and 700, and 2% above 700; Math—53% below 500, 26% between 500 and 599, 15% between 600 and 700, and 6% above 700. Applicants should rank in the top half of their high school class and present a GPA of 2.5 or better. The basic admissions criteria are class rank, grade average, and SAT or ACT results. Other important considerations include advanced placement or honors courses, leadership record, extracurricular activities, personality, recommendations by high school officials, and leadership record.

Procedure: The SAT or ACT is required and should be taken no later than May of the senior year. Applicants are encouraged to schedule interviews. Application deadlines are August 1 (fall), February 1 (spring), and June 1 (summer). Students seeking campus housing should apply no later than May 1 for fall admission. The application fee is $15. Admissions decisions are made on a rolling basis.

Special: Early and deferred admissions and early decision plans are available. AP and CLEP credit is accepted.

Transfer: For fall 1981, 311 transfer students applied, 233 were accepted, and 135 enrolled. Applicants must have an average of 2.25 or better and have earned at least 12 credits. D grades may be transferred. At least 30 of the 128 credits required for a bachelor's degree must be earned on campus.

Visiting: Informal visits are possible on weekdays from 9 A.M. to 4 P.M. and on Saturdays by appointment. Regularly scheduled orientations include tours of the campus, an academic fair, and a financial-aid workshop. Prospective students may sit in on classes and stay overnight at the college. The admissions office will handle arrangements for visits.

Financial Aid: Eighty percent of the students receive aid, and 20% work part-time on campus. Scholarships, loans, grants, and campus jobs are available. In 1981–82, the average award to freshmen from all sources was $4100. Awards are made on the basis of need, academic record, and recommendations. Aid applications must be filed by April 1 (fall) or December 1 (spring). All applicants must file the FFS, SFS, or FAF; California residents also must submit the SAAC. The college is a member of CSS.

Foreign Students: The foreign students at the college make up 4% of its student body. An intensive English course, an intensive English program, and special counseling are provided for these students.

Admissions: Foreign applicants must score 500 or better on the TOEFL. No college entrance exams are required.

Procedure: Application deadlines are June 1 (fall) and December 1 (spring). Foreign students must present proof of good health (a College Health History) and of adequate funds for 1 year. Students are required to carry health insurance, which is available through the college for a fee.

Admissions Contact: Ronald Timmons, Director of Admissions.

CALIFORNIA MARITIME ACADEMY B–3
Vallejo, California 94590   (707) 644-5601

F/T: 475M, 25W	Faculty:	32; IIB, ++$
P/T: none	Ph.D.'s:	6%
Grad: none	S/F Ratio:	17 to 1
Year: tri	Tuition:	$1192 ($2812)
Appl: Mar. 15	R and B:	$3015
550 applied	248 accepted	170 enrolled
SAT: 490V 540M		COMPETITIVE

California Maritime Academy, founded in 1929, is a public professional college under the control of the state of California. Its purpose is to train men and women for careers in the U.S. Merchant Marine as licensed officers and for the shoreside maritime industry. The library houses 20,000 volumes, and subscribes to 250 periodicals.

Environment: The self-contained suburban campus is located in Vallejo, a small city northeast of San Francisco. It consists of 13 buildings, including two dormitories.

Student Life: About 85% of the students are from California, and 90% of entering freshmen come from public schools. Eleven percent of the students are members of minority groups. All students are required to live in dormitories. The dormitories are both single-sex and coed, and there are visiting privileges in single-sex housing. Students may keep cars on campus.

Organizations: There are no social fraternities or sororities, but the academy sponsors several extracurricular activities, including the propeller, sailing, and gun clubs. Social and cultural activities in San Francisco attract many students, and about 80% leave the campus on weekends.

Sports: The academy competes on an intercollegiate level in 7 sports. Nine intramural sports are offered.

Handicapped: Facilities include special parking, elevators, specially equipped rest rooms, and lowered drinking fountains and telephones.

Graduates: About 15% of the freshmen drop out during the first year, and 70% remain to graduate. About 1% seek advanced degrees, but most pursue careers in business and industry.

Services: Students receive the following services free of charge: placement, career counseling, tutoring, and remedial instruction.

Programs of Study: The academy confers the B.S. degree in maritime engineering technology or nautical industrial technology.

Special: A 10-week training cruise enables students to visit different foreign ports every year.

Admissions: Forty-five percent of those who applied were accepted for the 1981-82 freshman class. The SAT scores of those who enrolled were as follows: Verbal—56% below 500, 32% between 500 and 599, 11% between 600 and 700, and 2% above 700; Math—33% below 500, 48% between 500 and 599, and 19% between 600 and 700. Applicants must have completed 3 years of high school mathematics, 1 year of chemistry or physics, and 4 years of English. They must rank in the upper half of their graduating class. Other factors besides grades and test scores that enter into the admissions decision are, in order of importance, advanced placement or honors courses, extracurricular activities, leadership record, recommendations by high school officials, and impressions made during a personal interview.

Procedure: The SAT or ACT is required. Students must apply to the particular division they wish to enter: Marine Engineering Technology or Nautical Industrial Technology. There is a $20 application fee. Freshmen are admitted only in the fall. A personal interview is recommended, and may be taken with a representative in or near the applicant's hometown. Admissions notification is made on a rolling basis.

Transfer: For fall 1981, 55 students applied, 35 were accepted, and all enrolled. Transfers are accepted as sophomores only, and must complete 3 years at the academy to graduate. A total of 145 credits must be completed for the bachelor's degree. A GPA of 2.0 is required (2.5 is recommended). Grades of C or better transfer. The application deadline is March 15.

Visiting: Daily visits are possible whenever school is in session. Contact the admissions office for arrangements.

Financial Aid: About 55% of all students receive aid through the academy, and 35% work part-time on campus. Freshman scholarships, loans, or work contracts are available. The average award to freshmen from all sources totalled $2800 in 1981-82. The deadline for aid application is February 1. The FAF is required.

Foreign Students: The foreign students enrolled at the academy make up 2% of its student body. Foreign students are required to complete an intensive English course before admission.

Admissions: Students must score 500 or better on the TOEFL. No academic exams are required.

Procedure: The application deadline is March 15. Students must present proof of health. A sponsor to help prove adequate funds also is required. Health insurance, though not required, is available through the academy for a fee.

Admissions Contact: David G. Buchanan, Director of Admissions.

CALIFORNIA POLYTECHNIC STATE UNIVERSITY B-4
San Luis Obispo, California 93407   (805) 546-2311

F/T: 7514M, 5643W Faculty: n/av; IIA, ++$
P/T: 1396M, 951W   Ph.D.'s: 60%
Grad: 424M, 466W   S/F Ratio: 18 to 1
Year: qtrs, ss   Tuition: $500 ($3000)
Appl: Nov. 30   R and B: $2400
SAT: 463V 531M   COMPETITIVE

California Polytechnic State University, founded in 1901, is part of the California State University system and is a technical, occupationally centered institution that also offers programs in education and other nontechnical fields. The library contains 525,000 volumes and 350,000 microfilm items, and subscribes to 3900 periodicals.

Environment: The 5169-acre campus is located in a suburban area 200 miles northwest of Los Angeles. The 13 residence halls accommodate 1186 women and 1547 men.

Student Life: About 97% of the students come from California, and 85% have had public school educations. Eighteen percent live on campus. About 15% of the students are members of minority groups. Dormitories are coed. Students may keep cars on campus.

Organizations: Six percent of the men belong to 1 of 11 fraternities; 8% of the women belong to 1 of 7 sororities. Student activities include special-interest clubs, government, religious and service groups, publications, and social events.

Sports: The university fields intercollegiate teams in 10 sports for men and 6 for women. Six intramural sports are offered for men and 3 for women.

Handicapped: Ninety percent of the campus is accessible to handicapped students. Special facilities include wheelchair ramps, elevators, parking areas, specially equipped rest rooms, and lowered drinking fountains and telephones. Special class scheduling can be arranged.

Graduates: The freshman dropout rate is 25%, and 35% of the students remain to graduate. Of these, 25% go on for graduate study: 3% enter law school, 3% medical school, and 1% dental school. About 60% pursue careers in business and industry.

Services: Offered free to all students are health care, psychological counseling, remedial instruction, tutoring, career counseling, and placement services.

Programs of Study: B.A., B.S., and B. Arch. degrees are conferred. Master's programs also are available. Bachelor's degrees are offered in the following subjects: BUSINESS (business administration, computer science), EDUCATION (early childhood, health/physical), ENGLISH (English, journalism, speech), FINE AND PERFORMING ARTS (art), MATH AND SCIENCES (biochemistry, biology, chemistry, mathematics, physical sciences, physics, statistics), PREPROFESSIONAL (agriculture, agriculture—education, agriculture—agricultural engineering, agriculture—agricultural management, agriculture—animal science, agriculture—crop science, agriculture—dairy science, agriculture—food science, agriculture—fruit science, agriculture—natural resources management, agriculture—ornamental horticulture, agriculture—poultry science, agriculture—soil science, architecture, architecture—architectural engineering, architecture—city and regional planning, architecture—construction, architecture—landscape architecture, engineering—aeronautical, engineering—civil, engineering—electrical, engineering—electronic, engineering—engineering technology, engineering—environmental, engineering—industrial, engineering—industrial technology, engineering—mechanical, engineering—metallurgical, home economics, social work), SOCIAL SCIENCES (economics, government/political science, history, social sciences).

Required: There is a general education requirement.

Special: Combined B.A.-B.S. degrees, study abroad, internships, and independent study are offered.

Honors: There are several honor societies on campus. Honors work is offered in a number of areas.

Admissions: About 54% of those who applied were accepted for a recent freshman class. SAT scores of those who enrolled were as follows: Verbal—33% between 500 and 600, 7% between 600 and 700, and 6% above 700; Math—57% between 500 and 600, 24% between 600 and 700, and 5% above 700. Applicants must rank in the top third of their class and have at least a 2.0 GPA. The university does not encourage out-of-state applicants.

Procedure: The SAT is required. Application deadlines are November 30 (fall), June 30 (winter), August 30 (spring), and February 28 (summer). Notification is made on a rolling basis. New students are admitted to all quarters. There is a $25 application fee.

Special: AP and CLEP credit is available.

Transfer: About 67% of transfer applicants are accepted. A 2.0 GPA is required. D grades transfer. Fifty quarter credits must be completed in residence to receive a bachelor's degree.

Visiting: Visitors may sit in on classes. Visits are best scheduled on weekdays. The admissions office should be contacted for arrangements.

Financial Aid: About 40% of the students receive financial aid. About 350 scholarships are awarded yearly. The university participates in federal and state programs such as NDSL, BEOG/SEOG, and CWS. Commercial, bank, and university loans also are available. The SAAC should be filed by April 1.

Admissions Contact: Admissions Office.

CALIFORNIA STATE UNIVERSITY

The California State University system, which comprises 19 campuses and spans the state from north to south, is one of the largest systems of public higher education in the Western hemisphere. Campuses in the system are California State Colleges at Bakersfield, San Bernardino, and Stanislaus (Turlock); California State Universities at Chico, Dominguez Hills (Carson), Fresno, Fullerton, Hayward, Long Beach, Los Angeles, Northridge, and Sacramento; Humboldt State University (Arcata); San Diego State University, San Francisco State University, San Jose State University, and Sonoma State University (Rohnert Park); California State Polytechnic University/Pomona; and California Polytechnic State University.

These campuses are a unique development of the concept of tax-supported higher education for all students who qualify. California residents pay no tuition. Some fees, however, are charged, including a student services fee of $216 per academic year for full-time students. The fall 1981 total enrollment for the CSU system was 310,000 students. The full-time and part-time faculties number 17,500.

Each campus in the system has its own geographic, curricular, and academic character; all offer a basic, solid liberal arts program. Course offerings are designed to serve students' varied interests and to serve the technical and professional manpower needs of the state. Individual campuses offer programs leading to the bachelor's and master's degrees.

CALIFORNIA STATE COLLEGE/BAKERSFIELD   C-4
Bakersfield, California 93309   (805) 833-2160

F/T: 631M, 897W   Faculty: 147; IIA, ++$
P/T: 347M, 514W   Ph.D.'s: 90%
Grad: 402M, 609W   S/F Ratio: 18 to 1
Year: qtrs, ss   Tuition: $400 ($3235)
Appl: Sept. 15   R and B: $2300
497 applied   338 accepted   235 enrolled
SAT or ACT: required   COMPETITIVE

California State College/Bakersfield, founded in 1965, offers undergraduate and graduate programs in the liberal arts and sciences, business, education, and the health fields. The library contains 238,000 volumes and 269,000 microfilm items, and subscribes to 2662 periodicals.

Environment: The 375-acre campus is located in an urban area 5 miles from the center of town and 100 miles from Los Angeles. The Doré Fine Arts Theater offers modern theatrical technology in a 500-seat proscenium theater.

Student Life: Most of the students are from California. About 90% live off campus. Twenty-seven percent are members of minority groups. Dormitories are both single-sex and coed; visiting is permitted in single-sex dorms. Students may keep cars on campus. Day-care services are available to students, faculty, and staff on a sliding fee scale, based on income.

Organizations: The Associated Students Organization supports a number of student services and assists student organizations, which range from religious groups to academically related clubs. Speakers, films, dances, and other activities also are provided. Students are represented on the college council and various committees. There is 1 local fraternity and 1 national sorority.

Sports: The college fields intercollegiate teams in 6 sports for men and 4 for women. Eight intramural sports are available for both men and women.

Handicapped: Approximately 95% of the campus is accessible to the physically handicapped. Facilities include wheelchair ramps, special parking, elevators, specially equipped rest rooms, and lowered drinking fountains and telephones. Facilities for visually or hearing-impaired students include recorders, braillers, and teletype communicators; readers and interpreters are also available.

Graduates: Approximately 34% of those who graduate pursue careers in business and industry.

Services: Placement services, career counseling, health care, psychological counseling, tutoring, and remedial instruction are offered free of charge.

Programs of Study: The college awards the B.A. and B.S. degrees. It also offers master's programs. The B.A. and B.S. are offered in the following subjects: AREA STUDIES (liberal studies, special major), BUSINESS (business administration, public administration), EDUCATION (child development, health/physical), ENGLISH (English), FINE AND PERFORMING ARTS (fine arts), HEALTH SCIENCES (medical technology, nursing), LANGUAGES (French, Spanish), MATH AND SCIENCES (biology, chemistry, earth science, geology, mathematics, physical sciences), PHILOSOPHY (philosophy), SOCIAL SCIENCES (anthropology, criminal justice, economics; government/political science, history, psychology, sociology). Post-degree credential programs in education are also offered. Preprofessional coursework and advising are available in dentistry, engineering, law, medicine, and veterinary medicine. About 35% of degrees are conferred in social sciences, 19% in business, and 12% in health sciences.

Required: All students must take courses in the state college general education pattern, satisfying 13 goals among the areas of basic skills, social sciences, technology, sciences and mathematics, and humanities.

Special: Interdisciplinary minors are offered in Asian studies, Black studies, Chicano studies, environmental studies, Latin American studies, speech and theater, and women's studies. A "special major" option is provided for students with distinct interests not covered in a regular major. Study abroad and student exchange programs with other states are also available. A liberal studies (no major) degree is offered.

Honors: Three national honor societies have chapters on campus. A personalized honors program is offered to qualified freshmen.

Admissions: Approximately 68% of those who applied were accepted for the 1981–82 freshman class. Applicants must have a GPA of 2.0 or better. California residents should rank in the upper third of their high school class. Standards are somewhat higher for out-of-state applicants.

Procedure: The SAT or ACT is required. Application deadlines are September 15 (fall), January 4 (winter), and March 30 (spring). The college follows a rolling admissions policy. There is a $25 application fee.

Special: CLEP and AP credit is accepted. There are early admissions and deferred admissions plans.

Transfer: For fall 1981, 897 transfer students applied and 741 were accepted. Transfers are accepted for all classes; applicants must have a GPA of 2.0 or better and present SAT or ACT scores if transferring with fewer than 36 credits. D grades transfer. Students must take 45 units in residence of the 186 required for a bachelor's degree.

Visiting: Guides are available for informal visits on weekdays between 8 A.M. and 5 P.M. Visitors may sit in on classes. The office of school relations should be contacted to arrange visits.

Financial Aid: Approximately 40% of all students receive some form of financial aid, which is available in the form of scholarships and federal, state, local, college, and private loans. Aid packages are available. The college requires the FAF and the SAAC. The deadline for aid applications is March 1.

Foreign Students: The foreign students at the college make up 5% of its enrollment. An intensive English course, special counseling, and special organizations are provided for these students.

Admissions: Applicants must score 500 or better on the TOEFL. They also must take the SAT or ACT if they have completed fewer than 56 transferable semester units.

Procedure: Applications should be submitted by August 1 (fall), November 1 (winter), or February 1 (spring). Students must present proof of adequate funds for 1 academic year. Health insurance, though not required, is available through the college at a fee.

Admissions Contact: Homer S. Montalvo, Associate Dean, Admissions and Records.

CALIFORNIA STATE COLLEGE/   D-5
SAN BERNARDINO
San Bernardino, California 92407   (714) 887-7319

F/T: 855M, 1253W   Faculty: n/av; IIA, ++$
P/T: 583M, 707W   Ph.D.'s: 86%
Grad: 605M, 912W   S/F Ratio: 16 to 1
Year: qtrs, ss   Tuition: $340 ($4758)
Appl: Aug. 1   R and B: $2077
678 applied   418 accepted   366 enrolled
SAT: 440V 456M   ACT: 19   COMPETITIVE

California State College/San Bernardino, founded in 1960, offers undergraduate programs in the liberal arts and sciences as well as business, education, and the health fields. The library contains 340,000 volumes and 185,000 microfilm items, and subscribes to 1800 periodicals.

Environment: The 430-acre campus is located in a suburban area 5 miles from the center of town and 60 miles from Los Angeles. An

44 CALIFORNIA

Academic Village is composed of 8 residences for 400 men and women. There are also facilities for commuting students.

Student Life: About 98% of the students come from California. Five percent live on campus. Twenty-five percent are members of minority groups. Dormitories are both coed and single-sex; there are visiting privileges in single-sex dorms. Students may keep cars on campus. Day-care services are provided, with fees based on ability to pay.

Organizations: Extracurricular activities include student government and social and cultural events. There are no fraternities or sororities. Protestant and Catholic religious organizations are available.

Sports: Nine intramural sports are offered for men and women.

Handicapped: Approximately 98% of the campus is accessible to the physically handicapped. Facilities include wheelchair ramps, special parking, elevators, specially equipped rest rooms, lowered drinking fountains and telephones, and a lift for assisting handicapped students in and out of the Olympic swimming pool. The college is also readjusting showers for the handicapped. The faculty works with handicapped students through their physical therapists or doctors in rehabilitative programs.

Graduates: About 19% of the freshmen drop out during their first year, and 23% remain to graduate. Twenty-five percent of those who graduate pursue further study: 3% enter law school, 1% medical school, and 1% dental school. Fifty percent pursue careers in business and industry.

Services: Placement services, career counseling, health care, psychological counseling, tutoring, and remedial instruction are offered free to students.

Programs of Study: The college confers the B.A. degree. Master's programs also are offered. Bachelor's degrees are offered in the following subjects: AREA STUDIES (American), BUSINESS (business administration), EDUCATION (early childhood—child development, vocational), ENGLISH (English), FINE AND PERFORMING ARTS (art, art history, music, theater/dramatics), HEALTH SCIENCES (health science, nursing), LANGUAGES (French, Spanish), MATH AND SCIENCES (biology, chemistry, ecology/environmental science, mathematics, physics), PHILOSOPHY (humanities, philosophy), SOCIAL SCIENCES (anthropology, criminal justice, economics, geography, government/political science, history, human services, psychology, social sciences, sociology). About 25% of degrees are conferred in business, 24% in social sciences, and 20% in education.

Special: Study abroad and a liberal studies major are offered. Students may design their own majors.

Admissions: Approximately 62% of those who applied were accepted for the 1981–82 freshman class. The SAT scores of an earlier freshman class were as follows: Verbal—19% between 500 and 600, and 1% between 600 and 700; Math—14% between 500 and 600, and 1% between 600 and 700. On the ACT, 15% scored between 20 and 23, 5% between 24 and 26, and 1% between 27 and 28. Candidates should have a GPA of 2.0 or better. Eligibility is determined by a weighted combination of GPA and ACT or SAT scores. California residents must rank in the upper third on a scale of California high school graduates; nonresidents must rank comparably in the top sixth.

Procedure: The SAT or ACT is required. Application deadlines are August 1 (fall), December 1 (winter), and March 1 (spring). The college follows a rolling admissions policy. There is a $25 application fee.

Special: AP and CLEP credit is accepted.

Transfer: For fall 1981, the college received 1407 transfer applications and accepted 1075, and 962 students enrolled. Candidates with fewer than 56 semester units must meet the same requirements as freshman applicants; those with 56 or more units of transferable work must have a 2.0 GPA (2.4 for nonresidents). D grades transfer. Preference is given to students transferring from other colleges in the state. A student must earn 45 quarter units at the college of the 186 required for a bachelor's degree. Deadlines are the same as those for freshman applicants.

Visiting: There are no regularly scheduled orientations for prospective students. Guides are available for informal weekday visits; visitors may sit in on classes and stay overnight at the school. The office of new-student services (714/887-7608) should be contacted to arrange visits.

Financial Aid: Approximately 12% of the students receive financial aid. The college is a member of the CEEB and offers freshman scholarships. Loans are available from the federal government, local banks, and for short-term emergencies from the college loan fund. EOGs and campus employment are also available. Three percent of the students work part-time on campus. The college is a member of CSS. The FAF is required; the priority date for filing is April 1.

Foreign Students: Foreign students at the college represent about 2% of its enrollment. An intensive English course and special counseling are offered for these students.

Admissions: Applicants must score 550 or better on the TOEFL. No academic exams are required.

Procedure: Application deadlines are July 1 (fall), November 1 (winter), and January 1 (spring). Students must provide proof of health (a record of a physical examination) and of adequate funds for the period they plan to study at the college. Students are required to carry health insurance.

Admissions Contact: Cheryl E. Weese, Admissions Officer.

CALIFORNIA STATE COLLEGE/ STANISLAUS B-3
Turlock, California 95380 (209) 677-3261

F/T: 955M, 1164W Faculty: 178; IIA, ++$
P/T: 353M, 502W Ph.D.'s: 82%
Grad: 567M, 742W S/F Ratio: 17 to 1
Year: 4-1-4, ss Tuition: $485 ($2553)
Appl: Aug. R and B: $2225
644 applied 474 accepted 338 enrolled
SAT: 440V 460M ACT: 20 COMPETITIVE

California State College/Stanislaus, established in 1957, offers undergraduate degree programs in the liberal arts and sciences, education, business, and health fields. The library contains 200,000 volumes and 300,000 microfilm items, and subscribes to 3500 periodicals.

Environment: The 230-acre campus is located in a rural area in the San Joaquin Valley and is about 100 miles from San Francisco and Sacramento. There is a wide variety of housing including an on-campus coeducational residence hall.

Student Life: About 95% of the students come from California; most students are public school graduates. Five percent live on campus. About 22% are minority-group members. Campus housing is coed. Students may keep cars on campus. Day-care services are available to all students.

Organizations: There is a broad range of extracurricular activities. Social and cultural events on campus are regularly scheduled.

Sports: The college fields intercollegiate teams in 8 sports for men and 6 for women. There are 6 intramural sports for men and 6 for women.

Handicapped: Most of the campus is accessible to handicapped students. Special parking is available.

Graduates: The freshman dropout rate is about 20%; 60% remain to graduate. Thirty-five percent of the graduates go on for further study: 1% enroll in medical school, 1% in dental school, and 3% in law school. About 25% enter business and industry.

Services: The college provides tutoring, remedial instruction, psychological counseling, career counseling, and placement services free of charge. Health care may require payment.

Programs of Study: The B.A., B.S., and B.Voc.Ed. degrees are conferred. Master's programs are also offered. Bachelor's degrees are offered in the following subjects: BUSINESS (accounting, business administration, computer science, finance, management, marketing, operations administration, personnel administration), EDUCATION (bilingual, communication handicapped, elementary, learning handicapped, secondary, special), ENGLISH (English, journalism, speech), FINE AND PERFORMING ARTS (art, music, studio art, theater/dramatics), HEALTH SCIENCES (nursing, speech therapy), LANGUAGES (French, German, Spanish), MATH AND SCIENCES (biology, botany, chemistry, earth science, ecology/environmental science, marine biology, mathematics, physical sciences, physics, statistics, zoology), PREPROFESSIONAL (dentistry, laboratory technology, law, medical laboratory technology, medicine, optometry, pharmacy, veterinary), SOCIAL SCIENCES (anthropology, economics, geography, government/political science, history, international relations, psychology, social sciences, sociology).

Required: All students must take courses in English composition, physical education, American history, and a distribution of credits in 4 broad areas.

Special: A general studies degree, study abroad, a 3-year bachelor's degree, student-designed majors, and teaching certification are offered.

Admissions: About 74% of those who applied were accepted for the 1981–82 freshman class. Eligibility is determined by a weighted combination of GPA (which includes those courses taken in the last 3 years of high school) and ACT or SAT scores. California applicants must rate in the upper one-third of all California secondary school graduates; out-of-state applicants must rank comparably to the top sixth of California graduates. While no specific pattern of courses is required, the college recommends college preparatory English, a foreign language, college preparatory mathematics, laboratory science, and history and/or social science, as well as study in speech, music, art, and other subjects contributing to a general academic background.

Procedure: The SAT or ACT is required. Application deadlines are August (fall), November (winter), January (spring), and May (summer). Notification is on a rolling basis. There is a $25 application fee.

Special: There are early decision, early admissions, and deferred admissions plans. AP and CLEP credit is available.

Transfer: For fall 1981, 1397 students applied, 1184 were accepted, and 931 enrolled. A 2.0 GPA is required (2.4 for nonresidents). D grades are generally transferable. All students must complete, at the college, 30 of the 124 credits required for a bachelor's degree. Application deadlines are the same as those for freshmen.

Visiting: Campus tours with student guides may be arranged. Visitors may sit in on classes.

Financial Aid: About 21% of the students receive financial aid. Five percent work part-time on campus. The average freshman award is $2200. The college offers scholarships, grants, all types of loans, and campus employment (including CWS in most departments). The college is a member of CSS. The Student Aid Application for California should be filed by March 1 (fall) or November 15 (winter or spring).

Foreign Students: Five percent of the full-time students come from foreign countries. An intensive English program, special counseling, and special organizations are available for these students.

Admissions: Foreign students must achieve a TOEFL score of at least 500. No college entrance exams are required.

Procedure: Application deadlines are the same as those for other students. Foreign students must complete a medical form and be tested for TB. They must present proof of funds adequate to cover 1 year of study. Health insurance is required and is available through the college.

Admissions Contact: Ed Albert, Director of Admissions.

CALIFORNIA STATE POLYTECHNIC UNIVERSITY/POMONA D-5
Pomona, California 91768 (714) 598-4291

F/T: 11,031M&W	Faculty: n/av; IIA, ++$
P/T: 3584M&W	Ph.D.'s: 57%
Grad: 1310M&W	S/F Ratio: 18 to 1
Year: qtrs	Tuition: $300 ($433+ $63p/c)
Appl. Nov.	R and B: $2500
4004 applied	2762 accepted	1862 enrolled
SAT: 432V 494M	ACT: 19	COMPETITIVE

California State Polytechnic University/Pomona, founded in 1938, is a technical, occupationally oriented institution which also offers programs in teacher training and preprofessional areas. The library contains 400,000 volumes and 750,000 microfilm items, and subscribes to 2650 periodicals.

Environment: The 1100-acre campus is in a suburban community 4 miles from the center of town and 30 miles from Los Angeles. There are 43 buildings, including 6 residence halls. There are also facilities for commuting students.

Student Life: About 86% of the students come from California; most come from public schools. About 7% live on campus. Twenty-three percent are minority-group members. Campus housing is both coed and single-sex; there are visiting privileges in the single-sex housing. Students may keep cars on campus. Day-care services are available to all students.

Organizations: About 1% of the men belong to the 3 local and 4 national fraternities; 2% of the women belong to the 1 local and 2 national sororities. Student activities are traditional. There are regularly scheduled social and cultural events on campus.

Sports: There are 11 intercollegiate and 14 intramural sports.

Handicapped: The entire campus is accessible to the physically handicapped. Facilities include wheelchair ramps, special parking, elevators, specially equipped rest rooms, and lowered drinking fountains; special class scheduling is also available. Fewer than 1% of the students currently enrolled have visual or hearing impairments; facilities include a visualtek reader and a talking calculator.

Graduates: The freshman dropout rate is 28%; 35% remain to graduate. Thirteen percent of those who graduate pursue graduate study; 73% enter careers in business and industry.

Services: Placement services, career counseling, health care, psychological counseling, and remedial instruction are offered to students free of charge. Tutoring is provided for a fee.

Programs of Study: The B.A. and B.S. degrees are conferred. Master's degrees are also awarded. Bachelor's degrees are offered in the following subjects: AREA STUDIES (American), BUSINESS (accounting, business administration, data processing, hotel, restaurant, and travel management, management, marketing, real estate/insurance), ENGLISH (English), FINE AND PERFORMING ARTS (art, music, theater/dramatics), MATH AND SCIENCES (biology, botany, chemistry, computer science, earth science, geology, mathematics, microbiology, physics, zoology), PHILOSOPHY (philosophy), PREPROFESSIONAL (agriculture, architecture, engineering, home economics, social work, veterinary), SOCIAL SCIENCES (anthropology, behavioral science, economics, geography, government/political science, history, social sciences). Twenty-five percent of degrees are conferred in business, 20% in engineering, and 15% in agriculture.

Required: All students must meet general education requirements by taking courses in the natural sciences, social sciences, humanities, and basic subjects (including freshman composition).

Special: A junior year abroad program in a choice of 16 foreign countries is offered. Internship programs offering on-the-job experience are also available.

Honors: Seven national honor societies have chapters on campus.

Admissions: About 69% of those who applied were accepted for the 1981–82 freshman class. Eligibility is determined by a weighted combination of GPA (which includes those courses taken in the last 3 years of high school) and ACT or SAT scores. California applicants must rank in the upper one-third of all California secondary school graduates; out-of-state applicants must rank comparably to the top sixth of California graduates. While no specific pattern of courses is required, the university recommends college preparatory English, a foreign language, college preparatory mathematics, laboratory science, and history and/or social science, as well as study in speech, music, art, and other subjects contributing to a general academic background.

Procedure: The SAT or ACT is required. Application deadlines are November (fall), June (winter), August (spring), and February (summer). Admissions are on a rolling basis until quotas are reached. There is a $25 application fee.

Special: There is an early admissions plan.

Transfer: Over 2300 transfer students enroll annually. A 2.0 GPA is required (2.4 for nonresidents); D grades transfer. All students must complete, at the university, 50 of the 186–198 credits required for a bachelor's degree. Application deadlines are the same as those for freshmen.

Visiting: There are regularly scheduled orientations for prospective students. Guides are also available for informal visits weekdays from 9 A.M. to 3 P.M.

Financial Aid: Approximately 48% of all students receive some form of financial aid. There are scholarships, loans, and CWS. The university is a member of the CSS and requires the FAF. The deadline for financial aid applications is March 1.

Foreign Students: About 3% of the full-time students come from foreign countries. Special counseling and special organizations are available for these students.

Admissions: Foreign students must achieve a TOEFL score of at least 525. The SAT or ACT is also required.

Procedure: Application deadlines are the same as those for other students. Foreign students must present proof of adequate funds.

Admissions Contact: Arthur G. Covarrubias, Admissions Officer.

CALIFORNIA STATE UNIVERSITY/CHICO B-2
Chico, California 95929 (916) 895-6323

F/T: 2894M, 3241W	Faculty: 666, IIA, ++$
P/T: 3275M, 3131W	Ph.D.'s: 60%
Grad: 758M, 977W	S/F Ratio: 18 to 1
Year: 4-1-4, ss	Tuition: $411 ($3231)
Appl: Nov. 30	R and B: $2640
6046 applied	3836 accepted	3520 enrolled
SAT or ACT: required		COMPETITIVE

46 CALIFORNIA

California State University/Chico, founded in 1857, offers undergraduate programs in the arts and sciences, business, education, health fields, and preprofessional areas. The library contains 400,000 volumes and 250,000 microfilm items, and subscribes to 4500 periodicals.

Environment: The 115-acre campus is located in a rural community of over 40,000 inhabitants about 90 miles north of Sacramento. There are 1300 additional acres of farmland. Living facilities include dormitories and fraternity and sorority houses.

Student Life: Nearly all of the students come from California; 65% come from public schools. Seven percent live on campus. About 13% are minority-group members. Campus housing is coed. Students may not keep cars on campus. Day-care services are available to all students for a fee.

Organizations: There are 9 local and 6 national fraternities, and 6 local and 4 national sororities, with which about 6% of the students are affiliated. There are religious organizations for Catholic and Protestant students.

Sports: The university competes intercollegiately in 9 sports for men and 10 for women. There are 9 intramural sports for men and 9 for women.

Handicapped: Approximately 95% of the campus is accessible to the physically handicapped. Facilities include wheelchair ramps, special parking, elevators, specially equipped rest rooms, adaptive equipment, and lowered drinking fountains and telephones; special class scheduling is also available. Fewer than 2% of the students currently enrolled have visual or hearing impairments; facilities include talking calculators and taping equipment; readers and interpreters are also available.

Graduates: The freshman dropout rate is 5%; 65% remain to graduate. Twelve percent of those who graduate pursue advanced degrees. Fifty-five percent enter business and industry.

Services: Placement services, career counseling, health care, psychological counseling, tutoring, and remedial instruction are offered to students free of charge.

Programs of Study: The B.A. and B.S. degrees are conferred. Associate and master's degrees are also awarded. Bachelor's degrees are offered in the following subjects: AREA STUDIES (American, Asian, Black/Afro-American), BUSINESS (accounting, business administration, business education, computer science, finance, management, marketing), EDUCATION (adult, early childhood, elementary, health/physical), ENGLISH (English, speech), FINE AND PERFORMING ARTS (art, dance, music, music education, radio/TV, studio art, theater/dramatics), HEALTH SCIENCES (nursing, speech therapy), LANGUAGES (French, German, Spanish), MATH AND SCIENCES (biochemistry, biology, botany, chemistry, geology, natural sciences, physical sciences, physics, zoology), PHILOSOPHY (humanities, religion), PREPROFESSIONAL (dentistry, home economics, law, library science, medicine, ministry, pharmacy, social work, veterinary), SOCIAL SCIENCES (anthropology, economics, geography, government/political science, history, international relations, psychology, social sciences, sociology).

Special: A liberal studies major, student-designed majors, and study abroad are offered.

Admissions: Approximately 63% of those who applied were accepted for the 1981–82 freshman class. The SAT scores of those who enrolled were as follows: Verbal—76% below 500, 20% between 500 and 599, 4% between 600 and 700, and 0% above 700; Math—62% below 500, 29% between 500 and 599, 9% between 600 and 700, and 1% above 700. On the ACT, 62% scored below 21, 19% between 21 and 23, 12% between 24 and 25, 7% between 26 and 28, and 0% above 28. Candidates should have a minimum 2.0 GPA. Eligibility is determined by a weighted combination of GPA (which includes those courses taken in the last 3 years of high school) and ACT or SAT scores. California applicants must rank in the upper one-third of all California secondary school graduates; out-of-state applicants must rank comparably to the top sixth of California graduates. While no specific pattern of courses is required, the university recommends college preparatory English, a foreign language, college preparatory mathematics, laboratory science, and history and/or social science, as well as study in speech, music, art, and other subjects contributing to a general academic background. The business administration and nursing programs are restricted to California residents; applications for these programs are due in November.

Procedure: The SAT or ACT is required. November 30 is the suggested deadline for fall entry; August 30, spring entry. The university follows a rolling admissions policy. There is an application fee of $25.

Special: There is an early decision plan.

Transfer: Over 1700 transfer students enroll annually. A minimum C average is required. D grades transfer. All students must complete, at the university, 30 of the 124–132 credits required for a bachelor's degree. Application deadlines are the same as those for freshmen.

Visiting: There are regularly scheduled orientations for prospective students. Guides are also available for informal visits weekdays from 11 A.M. to 2 P.M.; visitors may sit in on classes. The admissions outreach program should be contacted to arrange visits.

Financial Aid: There are 20 freshman scholarships awarded yearly; about 150 SEOGs are available for entering freshmen. NDSL and FISL funds are also available. The university maintains a loan fund to assist students in emergency situations. Campus employment is also available. The Student Aid Application for California is required; the deadline for financial aid application is March 1.

Foreign Students: Ten percent of the full-time students come from foreign countries. Special counseling and special organizations are available for these students.

Admissions: Foreign students must achieve a TOEFL score of at least 500. No college entrance exams are required.

Procedure: Application deadlines are May 1 (fall) and October 15 (spring). Foreign students must present proof of funds adequate to cover the entire period of study. Health insurance is required and is available through the university for a fee.

Admissions Contact: Caroline Aldrich, Associate Director of Admissions and Records.

CALIFORNIA STATE UNIVERSITY/ DOMINGUEZ HILLS C–5
Carson, California 90747 (213) 515-3696

F/T: 1579M, 2094W   Faculty: 173; IIA, ++$
P/T: 884M, 1256W   Ph.D.'s: 90%
Grad: 931M, 1535W   S/F Ratio: 21 to 1
Year: qtrs, ss   Tuition: $433 ($433+ $63p/c)
Appl: Aug. 1   R and B: $1215
1021 applied   536 accepted   360 enrolled
SAT: 350V 380M   ACT: 17   LESS COMPETITIVE

California State University/Dominguez Hills, founded in 1963, offers undergraduate degree programs in the liberal arts and sciences, business, and education. The library contains 217,000 volumes and 218,000 microfilm items, and subscribes to 2000 periodicals. In addition to its traditional divisions, the university's Small College offers an interdisciplinary approach to learning. An external degree program in the humanities (bachelor's and master's) emphasizes independent study, with off-campus, teacher-guided learning.

Environment: The 350-acre campus is located in an urban area 10 miles from Los Angeles. Facilities include a gymnasium, a theater, and a humanities and fine arts building. One- and 2-bedroom self-contained on-campus apartments are available.

Student Life: More than 95% of the students come from California, and 95% have had public school educations. About 54% of the students are members of minority groups; 38% are black. The campus apartments are single-sex, with visiting privileges. Students may keep cars on campus. Day-care services are available for a fee.

Organizations: There are no fraternities or sororities. Extracurricular activities are geared for commuting students and include clubs, campus government, publications, social and cultural events, service and religious groups, and drama and other performing groups.

Sports: Eight intercollegiate sports are offered for men and 6 for women.

Handicapped: The entire campus is accessible to handicapped students. Special facilities include wheelchair ramps, parking areas, elevators, lowered drinking fountains, and specially equipped rest rooms. Special class scheduling is also available. Counselors in the disabled student services office are available to handicapped students.

Graduates: About 20% of the graduates pursue advanced degrees; 3% enter medical school, 2% dental school, and 5% law school. Sixty percent seek careers in business and industry.

Services: The university offers psychological counseling, tutoring, remedial instruction, career counseling, health care, and placement services free to students.

Programs of Study: Bachelor's and master's degree programs are offered. The B.A. or B.S. is offered in the following subjects: AREA STUDIES (Black/Afro-American, Mexican-American), BUSINESS (accounting, business administration, computer science, finance, management, marketing, public administration, real estate/insurance), EDUCATION (health/physical), ENGLISH (communications, English, journalism), FINE AND PERFORMING ARTS (art, art history, music, theater/dramatics), HEALTH SCIENCES (health science—physician's assistant, medical technology), LANGUAGES (French, Spanish), MATH AND SCIENCES (biochemistry, biology, chemistry, earth science, geology, mathematics, physics), PHILOSOPHY (humanities, philosophy), SOCIAL SCIENCES (anthropology, behavioral science, economics, geography, government/political science, history, psychology, sociology).

Required: There is a general education requirement.

Special: Study abroad and independent study programs are offered. Students may design their own majors. Teaching credentials can be earned.

Honors: There is an honors program.

Admissions: About 52% of those who applied were accepted for the 1981–82 freshman class. Students should have a 2.0 high school GPA. Eligibility is determined by a weighted combination of GPA and ACT or SAT scores. California residents must rank in the upper third on a scale of all California high school graduates. Nonresidents must rank comparably in the upper sixth. Preference is given to state residents.

Procedure: The SAT or ACT is required. Application deadlines are August 1 (fall), December 1 (winter), and March 1 (spring). Notification is made on a rolling basis. A $25 application fee must be submitted.

Special: There are early decision and early admissions plans. AP and CLEP credit is available.

Transfer: For fall 1981, 2314 transfer students applied, 1775 were accepted, and 1277 enrolled. A 2.0 GPA (2.4 for nonresidents) is required. D grades are transferable. Forty-five quarter hours of the 186 required for a bachelor's degree must be completed in residence. Application deadlines are the same as those for freshmen.

Visiting: Campus tours with student guides may be arranged. Visitors are permitted to sit in on classes. The office of school and college relations should be contacted for arrangements.

Financial Aid: About 33% of the students receive financial aid through the university; 3% work part-time on campus. The university participates in federal programs such as NDSL, BEOG/SEOG, and CWS in addition to offering state assistance, bank and university loans, and freshman scholarships. The average award to freshmen from all sources is $1463. The FAF should be filed no later than March 1 (fall), November 15 (winter), or February 15 (spring). The university is a member of CSS.

Foreign Students: The foreign students enrolled at the university represent 4% of the student body. Special counseling and special organizations are provided for these students.

Admissions: Applicants must score 550 or better on the TOEFL. No academic exams are required.

Procedure: Application deadlines are July 1 (fall), October 16 (winter), January 8 (spring). Students must present proof of adequate funds for 1 year. Health insurance, though not required, is available through the university for a fee.

Admissions Contact: Mary Auth, Admissions Counselor.

CALIFORNIA STATE UNIVERSITY/FRESNO   C–3
Fresno, California 93740   (209) 294-2192

F/T: 5255M, 5434W	Faculty:	710; IIA, + + $
P/T: 1232M, 1259W	Ph.D.'s:	75%
Grad: 1341M, 1722W	S/F Ratio:	18 to 1
Year: sems, ss	Tuition:	$426 ($95p/c + $426)
Appl: June 4	R and B:	$2250
3028 applied	2197 accepted	1552 enrolled
SAT: 420V 460M	ACT: 20	COMPETITIVE

California State University/Fresno, established in 1911, offers undergraduate preparation in the liberal arts and sciences, education, business, health fields, and preprofessional areas. The library contains 355,000 volumes and 550,000 microfilm items, and subscribes to 4500 periodicals.

Environment: The 1410-acre campus is located in a suburban area 200 miles from San Francisco and 300 miles from Los Angeles. There are 56 buildings, including 9 dormitories. Living facilities also include fraternity and sorority houses.

CALIFORNIA 47

Student Life: About 96% of the students come from California and 96% of the freshmen come from public schools. Eight percent of the students live on campus. Twenty percent are minority-group members. Campus housing is both coed and single-sex; there are visiting privileges in the single-sex housing. Students may keep cars on campus. Day-care services are available to all students for a fee.

Organizations: There are religious counselors and organizations for the 3 major faiths. Four percent of the students belong to the 9 fraternities and 5 sororities. The student activity program includes clubs, student government, publications, performing groups, dramatics, service organizations, and regularly scheduled social and cultural events.

Sports: The school competes intercollegiately in 13 sports for men and 9 for women. There are 19 intramural sports.

Handicapped: The entire campus is accessible to the physically handicapped. Special facilities include wheelchair ramps, special parking, elevators, specially equipped rest rooms, and lowered drinking fountains and telephones.

Graduates: Twenty-two percent of those who graduate go on for further study.

Services: Offered free are career counseling, placement, remedial instruction, tutoring, health care, and psychological counseling.

Programs of Study: The B.A. and B.S. are conferred. Master's degrees are also awarded. Bachelor's degrees are offered in the following subjects: BUSINESS (accounting, agribusiness, business administration, business economics, business education, computer science, decision science, distribution, finance, health care management, legal environment of business, management, marketing, personnel and industrial relations, real estate/insurance, transportation), EDUCATION (adult, early childhood, elementary, health/physical, industrial, secondary, special), ENGLISH (English, journalism, literature, speech), FINE AND PERFORMING ARTS (art, art education, art history, dance, film/photography, music, music education, radio/TV, studio art, theater/dramatics), HEALTH SCIENCES (environmental health, nursing, physical therapy, speech therapy), LANGUAGES (French, German, Russian, Spanish), MATH AND SCIENCES (biochemistry, biology, botany, chemistry, geology, mathematics, natural sciences, physical sciences, physics, statistics, zoology), PHILOSOPHY (philosophy), PREPROFESSIONAL (agriculture, dentistry, engineering, home economics, industrial arts and technology, law, library science, medicine, optometry, pharmacy, social work, veterinary), SOCIAL SCIENCES (anthropology, economics, geography, government/political science, history, psychology, social sciences, sociology). Twenty-one percent of degrees are conferred in math and sciences, 19% in business, and 18% in preprofessional areas.

Required: All students must take 54 units in general education courses.

Special: Independent study, experimental college courses, a junior year abroad, a liberal studies major, and student-designed majors are available.

Honors: Honors programs are open to qualified students.

Admissions: Approximately 73% of those who applied were accepted for the 1981–82 freshman class. Candidates should have a GPA of at least 2.0. Eligibility is determined by a weighted combination of GPA (which includes those courses taken in the last 3 years of high school) and ACT or SAT scores. California applicants must rank in the upper one-third of all California secondary school graduates; out-of-state applicants must rank comparably to the top sixth of California graduates. While no specific pattern of courses is required, the university recommends college preparatory English, a foreign language, college preparatory mathematics, laboratory science, and history and/or social science, as well as study in speech, music, art, and other subjects contributing to a general academic background.

Procedure: The SAT or ACT is required. Applications are accepted November 1 through June 4 for fall entry, and August 1 through October 23 for spring entry. The university follows a rolling admissions policy. There is a $25 application fee.

Special: AP and CLEP credit is accepted. There are early decision and early admissions plans.

Transfer: For fall 1981, 3646 students applied, 2830 were accepted, and 1959 enrolled. California residents should have a GPA of at least 2.0; others should have a GPA of at least 2.4. All students must complete, at the university, 30 of the 124 credits required for a bachelor's degree. Application deadlines are the same as those for freshmen.

Visiting: There are regularly scheduled orientations for prospective students. Guides are available for informal visits; visitors may sit in on classes. The coordinator of relations with schools should be contacted to arrange visits.

48 CALIFORNIA

Financial Aid: Approximately 55% of all students receive some form of financial aid. About 150 freshman scholarships are awarded annually. Loan funds are available from the federal government. About 20% of the students work part-time on campus. The university is a member of CSS and requires the Student Aid Application for California. March 1 (fall) and November 1 (spring) are the priority deadlines for financial aid applications.

Foreign Students: Eight percent of the full-time students come from foreign countries. An intensive English program, special counseling, and special organizations are available for these students.

Admissions: Foreign students must take either the TOEFL or the University of Michigan Language Test. On the TOEFL, a score of at least 500 is required. No college entrance exams are required.

Procedure: Application deadlines are April 15 (fall) and October 1 (spring). Foreign students must present proof of funds adequate to cover 1 year of study. Health insurance is required and is available through the university for a fee.

Admissions Contact: T. Russell Mitchell, Coordinator, Relations with Schools.

CALIFORNIA STATE UNIVERSITY/ FULLERTON D-5
Fullerton, California 92634 (714) 773-2300

F/T: 5809M, 6194W Faculty: 713; IIA, ++$
P/T: 3127M, 3318W Ph.D.'s: 78%
Grad: 2062M, 2774W S/F Ratio: 14 to 1
Year: early sems, ss Tuition: $261 ($3096)
Appl: open R and B: $3500
4382 applied 2977 accepted 2138 enrolled
SAT: 435V 485M ACT: 20 COMPETITIVE

California State University/Fullerton, established in 1957, offers undergraduate degree programs in the liberal arts and sciences, education, business, health fields, and preprofessional areas. The library contains 500,000 volumes, and subscribes to 4653 periodicals.

Environment: The 225-acre campus is set in a suburban area 30 miles southeast of Los Angeles. There are 18 buildings, including facilities for commuting students. There are no on-campus residence halls; 2 privately-run residence halls are located nearby. Fraternities and sororities also provide housing.

Student Life: Approximately 97% of the students come from California. Thirteen percent of the students are members of minority groups. Day-care services are available, with fees based on ability to pay. Students may keep cars on campus.

Organizations: There are 9 fraternities and 5 sororities as well as special-interest clubs, organizations, and cultural events on campus.

Sports: The school competes intercollegiately in 12 sports. Nine intramural sports are offered.

Handicapped: Approximately 95% of the campus is accessible to the physically handicapped. Facilities include wheelchair ramps, special parking, elevators, specially equipped rest rooms, and lowered drinking fountains and telephones. Special class scheduling and a support services program are also available. Readers, tutors, notetakers, and interpreters are available for students with visual or hearing impairments. There is a handicapped student services office with a staff of 6.

Graduates: The freshman dropout rate is 25%, and 32% remain within the CSU system to graduate. Thirty percent of those who graduate pursue advanced degrees.

Services: Placement, career and psychological counseling, tutoring, and remedial instruction are offered free of charge. Fees are charged for health care services.

Programs of Study: The university awards the B.A., B.S., and B.M. degrees. Master's programs also are available. Bachelor's degrees are offered in the following subjects: AREA STUDIES (American, Black/Afro-American, Chicano, Latin American, Russian/East European), BUSINESS (accounting, business administration, business education, computer science, economics, finance, management, marketing), EDUCATION (bilingual, elementary, reading, school administration, special), ENGLISH (English, communications, comparative literature, journalism, speech), FINE AND PERFORMING ARTS (art, art history, dance, film/photography, music, radio/TV, theater/dramatics), HEALTH SCIENCES (human services, nursing, speech therapy), LANGUAGES (French, German, Russian, Spanish), MATH AND SCIENCES (biology, chemistry, mathematics, physics, science education), PHILOSOPHY (classics, philosophy, religion), PREPROFESSIONAL (engineering), SOCIAL SCIENCES (anthropology, economics, geography, government/political science, history, psychology, sociology). Credential programs are offered in early childhood, elementary, and secondary education. About 25% of degrees are conferred in business and 15% in social sciences.

Special: A junior year abroad program, interdisciplinary studies, and a liberal studies (no major) degree are offered.

Honors: Four national honor societies have chapters on campus.

Admissions: Approximately 68% of those who applied were accepted for the 1981–82 freshman class. The SAT scores of those who enrolled were as follows: Verbal—74% below 500, 21% between 500 and 599, 5% between 600 and 700, and 0% above 700; Math—54% below 500, 34% between 500 and 599, 11% between 600 and 700, and 1% above 700. Of those who took the ACT, 55% scored below 21, 23% between 21 and 23, 14% between 24 and 25, 8% between 26 and 28, and 0% above 28. Freshman admission is determined by an applicant's placement on a scale that compares him or her with other California high school graduates. State residents must place in the upper third and nonresidents in the upper sixth. Applicants need submit only the application, SAT or ACT scores, and high school transcript.

Procedure: The SAT or ACT is required. Application deadlines are open. There is a $25 application fee.

Special: CLEP and AP credit is accepted.

Transfer: In a recent year, 5029 transfer applications were received, 4518 were accepted, and 4121 students enrolled. For students with more than 56 units, an average of C or better is necessary; students with fewer than 56 units must have an average of C or better and meet the requirements for freshman candidates. Students must complete 30 of the required 124 units at the university to receive a bachelor's degree.

Visiting: Guides are available for informal visits weekdays when classes are in session. Visitors may sit in on classes. The office of relations with schools should be contacted to arrange visits.

Financial Aid: Approximately 12% of all students receive financial aid. NDSL, long-term and short-term student loans, work-study, and a limited number of scholarships are available. The university is a member of the CSS and requires the SAAC. The deadline for aid application is March 1.

Foreign Students: Foreign students make up about 2% of the university's student body. Special counseling and organizations are offered.

Admissions: Undergraduate applicants must score 500 or better on the TOEFL; graduate applicants must score at least 550. Freshman applicants also must take the SAT or ACT.

Procedure: Application deadlines are November 30 for fall entry and August 31 for spring entry. Students must present proof of adequate funds. They are required to carry health insurance, which is available through the university for a fee.

Admissions Contact: Mildred Scott, Director of Admissions.

CALIFORNIA STATE UNIVERSITY/ HAYWARD B-3
Hayward, California 94542 (415) 881-3811

F/T: 2666M, 3331W Faculty: n/av; IIA, ++$
P/T: 1122M, 1298W Ph.D.'s: 80%
Grad: 1266M, 1800W S/F Ratio: 18 to 1
Year: qtrs, ss Tuition: $111 ($867)/qtr
Appl: Aug. 6 R and B: n/app
SAT or ACT: required COMPETITIVE

California State University/Hayward, established in 1957, offers undergraduate degree programs in the liberal arts and sciences, business, education, health fields, and preprofessional areas. The library has 470,000 volumes and 2000 microfilm items, and subscribes to over 1900 periodicals.

Environment: The 365-acre campus is located in a suburban community across the Bay from San Francisco. Facilities are available for commuting students only. There are no residence halls.

Student Life: More than 95% of the students come from California; 87% are public school graduates. All students commute.

Organizations: On-campus activities include clubs, student government, publications, performing groups, dramatics, social and cultural events, and religious and service organizations. There are no sororities or fraternities.

Sports: The university fields 13 intercollegiate teams for men and 10 for women. There are 12 intramural sports.

Handicapped: Most of the campus is accessible to handicapped students. Special facilities such as wheelchair ramps, elevators, and parking areas are provided.

Graduates: The freshman dropout rate is nearly 50%, but 34% remain to graduate. Of these, 64% eventually go on for advanced degrees.

Services: The university provides health care, psychological counseling, career counseling, placement, tutoring, and remedial instruction for all students free of charge.

Programs of Study: The B.A. and B.S. degrees are conferred. Master's degrees are also awarded. Bachelor's degrees are offered in the following subjects: AREA STUDIES (Black/Afro-American, Latin American, Mexican-American), BUSINESS (accounting, business administration, finance, management, marketing, real estate/insurance), EDUCATION (health/physical, recreation), ENGLISH (English, mass communication, speech), FINE AND PERFORMING ARTS (art, art history, music, studio art, theater/dramatics), HEALTH SCIENCES (health sciences, nursing, speech therapy), LANGUAGES (French, German, Spanish), MATH AND SCIENCES (biochemistry, biology, chemistry, computer science, earth science, mathematics, physical sciences, physics, statistics), PHILOSOPHY (philosophy), SOCIAL SCIENCES (anthropology, criminal justice administration, economics, geography, government/political science, history, human development, psychology, sociology).

Required: There is a general education requirement.

Special: A liberal studies major, study abroad, independent study, teacher certification, and student-designed majors are offered.

Honors: Departmental honors programs are available to upper-division students.

Admissions: Seventy-three percent of the applicants for the 1981–82 freshman class were accepted. Applicants need a high school diploma or GED. Eligibility is determined by a weighted combination of GPA (which includes those courses taken in the last 3 years of high school) and ACT or SAT scores. California applicants must rate in the upper one-third of all California secondary school graduates; out-of-state applicants must rank comparably to the top sixth of California graduates. While no specific pattern of courses is required, the university recommends college preparatory English, a foreign language, college preparatory mathematics, a laboratory science, and history and/or a social science, as well as study in speech, music, art, and other subjects contributing to a general academic background.

Procedure: August 6 is the application deadline for fall admission. Either the SAT or ACT is required. Notification is on a rolling basis. New students are admitted to all quarters. There is a $25 application fee.

Special: AP and CLEP credit is available.

Transfer: About 1550 transfer students are admitted each year. A 2.0 GPA (2.4 for nonresidents) is required; D grades are usually accepted. All students must complete, at the university, 45 of the 186–198 credits required for a bachelor's degree.

Visiting: Campus tours with student guides can be arranged. Visitors may sit in on classes.

Financial Aid: About 5% of the students receive financial aid. The university offers scholarships, loans (bank, university, and NDSL), grants (such as BEOG/SEOG), and work-study (CWS in most academic departments). The FAF should be filed by April 15.

Foreign Students: Special counseling is available for these students.

Admissions: Foreign students must take the TOEFL. No college entrance exams are required.

Procedure: Foreign students are admitted in the fall quarter only. They must present proof of adequate funds.

Admissions Contact: Judith L. Hirsch, Director of Admissions.

CALIFORNIA STATE UNIVERSITY/ HUMBOLDT
(See Humboldt State University)

CALIFORNIA STATE UNIVERSITY/ LONG BEACH
D-5

Long Beach, California 90840   (213) 498-4141

F/T: 7612M, 8836W	Faculty: 962; IIA, ++$
P/T: 4224M, 4228W	Ph.D.'s: 76%
Grad: 3212M, 3816W	S/F Ratio: 18 to 1
Year: early sem, ss	Tuition: $303 ($3138)
Appl: open	R and B: $2170
21,429 applied	15,149 accepted 11,244 enrolled
SAT or ACT: required	**VERY COMPETITIVE**

California State University/Long Beach, founded in 1949, offers undergraduate programs in the liberal arts and sciences, education, business, engineering, and preprofessional areas. The library contains 702,000 volumes and 508,000 microfilm items, and subscribes to more than 5200 periodicals.

Environment: The 320-acre campus, located in an urban area, has 67 buildings and 4 dormitories that house 434 women and 434 men. There are also fraternity and sorority houses as well as facilities for commuting students.

Student Life: About 97% of the students come from California. Most are public school graduates. About 3% reside on campus. Thirty-two percent of the students are members of minority groups. Housing is both single-sex and coed; there are visiting privileges in single-sex dormitories. Students may keep cars on campus. Day-care services are available, with fees based on ability to pay.

Organizations: Extracurricular activities include clubs, student government, dramatics, performing groups, social and cultural events, publications, and service and religious organizations. Three percent of the students belong to the 7 sororities and 11 fraternities.

Sports: The university fields intercollegiate teams in 15 sports for men and 13 for women. The intramural program offers 17 sports for men and 14 for women.

Handicapped: The disabled student services office provides services, programs, and activities for handicapped students.

Graduates: The freshman dropout rate is 30%. About 35% of the students remain to complete their degrees. About 19% of the graduates go on for advanced degrees.

Services: The university provides health care, psychological counseling, tutoring, career counseling, and placement services free to students.

Programs of Study: The B.A., B.S., B.S.B.A., B.S.E., B.F.A., B.M., and B.Voc.Ed. are conferred. Master's programs also are available. Bachelor's degrees are offered in the following subjects: AREA STUDIES (American, Asian, Black/Afro-American, Mexican-American), BUSINESS (accounting, administrative systems, computer science, finance, human resources management, management, marketing, operations management, quantitative methods), EDUCATION (health/physical, industrial, vocational), ENGLISH (English, comparative literature, journalism, literature, speech), FINE AND PERFORMING ARTS (art, art education, art history, dance, music, music education, radio/TV, theater/dramatics), HEALTH SCIENCES (community health, medical technology, nursing, physical therapy, school health, speech therapy), LANGUAGES (French, German, Spanish), MATH AND SCIENCES (biology, botany, chemistry, earth science, entomology, geology, marine biology, mathematics, physics, statistics, zoology), PHILOSOPHY (philosophy, religious studies), PREPROFESSIONAL (engineering, home economics, industrial technology, social work), SOCIAL SCIENCES (anthropology, economics, geography, government/political science, history, psychology, sociology).

Required: There is a general education requirement.

Special: Teacher certification, study abroad, independent study, a liberal studies major, and student-designed majors are offered.

Honors: There is a general honors program.

Admissions: About 71% of those who applied were accepted for the 1981–82 freshman class. Applicants must have an average of 2.0 or better. They must place in the top third on a scale of all California high school students; out-of-state applicants must place in the top sixth.

Procedure: The SAT or ACT is required. Applications for the fall semester should be filed in November, but are accepted until program quotas are met. Freshmen are also admitted in spring. Notification is made on a rolling basis. There is a $25 application fee.

Special: Early decision and early admissions plans are offered. AP and CLEP credit is granted.

Transfer: A 2.0 GPA is required. D grades are acceptable. Thirty credits must be completed at the university of the 124 to 132 required for a bachelor's degree.

Visiting: Campus tours with student guides may be arranged. Visitors are permitted to sit in on classes.

Financial Aid: The university offers freshman scholarships, loans (NDSL, bank, and short-term from the university), grants (including BEOG/SEOG), and part-time employment (CWS in most departments). The FAF and SAAC should be submitted by March 1.

Foreign Students: The foreign students enrolled at the university represent 2% of enrollment. The university offers these students an intensive English course, special counseling, and special organizations.

50 CALIFORNIA

Admissions: Students must score at least 500 on the TOEFL or achieve an equivalent score on the EESL. No academic exams are required.

Procedure: Contact the university for information on application deadlines. Students must present proof of health and of an adequate monthly income. Health insurance is not required, but is available through the university for a fee.

Admissions Contact: Leonard Kreutner, Director of Admissions and Records.

CALIFORNIA STATE UNIVERSITY/ LOS ANGELES   C-5
Los Angeles, California 90032 (213) 224-2171

F/T: 3940M, 4637W	Faculty: 715; IIA, ++$
P/T: 2986M, 3611W	Ph.D.'s: 75%
Grad: 2889M, 4190W	S/F Ratio: 18 to 1
Year: qtrs	Tuition: $270 ($2970)
Appl: see profile	R and B: n/app
3151 applied	1599 accepted	1164 enrolled
SAT: 420V 440M	ACT: 18	COMPETITIVE

California State University/Los Angeles, founded in 1947, offers undergraduate and graduate programs in the liberal arts and sciences, education, business, the health fields, and professional areas. The library contains 800,000 volumes and 40,000 microfilm items, and subscribes to 4800 periodicals.

Environment: The urban commuter campus includes an 8-story physical science building housing some of the most up-to-date equipment for research in physics, geology, and chemistry. Recent additions include a $7-million student union and a student health center.

Student Life: About 95% of the students are from California. Almost all students commute, though the university does sponsor fraternity and sorority houses. About 58% of the students are members of minority groups; 23% are Hispanic. Day-care services are provided for a fee.

Organizations: There are 8 fraternities and 4 sororities, to which 2% of the students belong.

Sports: The school competes intercollegiately in 11 sports for men and 8 for women. Nine intramural sports are offered for men and 8 for women.

Handicapped: Almost the entire campus is accessible to the physically handicapped. Facilities include wheelchair ramps, special parking, elevators, specially equipped rest rooms, and lowered drinking fountains and telephones. Notetaking services, recorders, and aides are available for students with visual or hearing impairments. The handicapped students' service center provides special registration and other support services.

Graduates: Approximately 15% of the freshmen drop out by the end of the first year, and 32% graduate within 7 years.

Services: Placement services, career counseling, health care, and psychological counseling are offered to students free of charge. Fees are charged for some tutoring and all remedial instruction.

Programs of Study: The university offers B.A., B.S., and B.Voc.Ed. degrees. Master's and doctoral programs are also available. Bachelor's degrees are offered in the following subjects: AREA STUDIES (American, Black/Afro-American, Latin American, liberal, Mexican-American, urban), BUSINESS (accounting, business education, computer science—information systems, entrepreneurship, finance, international business, labor relations, management, marketing, real estate/insurance, statistics, transportation), EDUCATION (health/physical, industrial, rehabilitation counseling), ENGLISH (English, journalism, speech), FINE AND PERFORMING ARTS (art, art education, art history, music, music education, radio/TV, studio art, theater/dramatics), HEALTH SCIENCES (medical technology, nursing, speech therapy), LANGUAGES (French, Japanese, Spanish), MATH AND SCIENCES (biochemistry, biology, botany, chemistry, computer science, geology, mathematics, physics, statistics), PHILOSOPHY (philosophy), PREPROFESSIONAL (aviation administration, criminal justice, engineering, fire protection administration, home economics, social work), SOCIAL SCIENCES (anthropology, economics, geography, government/political science, history, psychology, social sciences, sociology).

Required: General education requirements include 72 quarter units in the areas of social science, natural science, humanities, and basic subjects (math and oral and written communication).

Special: Cooperative education programs are offered in accounting, art, biology, business education, chemistry, engineering, English, government, home economics, industrial arts, journalism, math, music, physical education, speech, and theater arts. Students may design their own majors.

Honors: More than 20 national honor societies have chapters on campus. Honors work is offered in anthropology, chemistry, biology, and physics.

Admissions: Approximately 51% of those who applied were accepted for the 1981-82 freshman class. Applicants should have a GPA of 2.0 or better. Eligibility is determined by a weighted combination of GPA and SAT or ACT scores. California residents must rank in the upper third on a scale of all California high school graduates. Nonresidents must rank comparably in the top sixth.

Procedure: The university recommends that applications be submitted by November 30 (fall), June 30 (winter), August 31 (spring), or February 28 (summer). Applications will continue to be accepted beyond these dates if space is available. The SAT or ACT is required. The university follows a rolling admissions policy. There is a $25 application fee.

Special: AP and CLEP credit is accepted.

Transfer: For fall 1981, 3645 transfer students applied, 2671 were accepted, and 2292 enrolled. Applicants must have 56 semester units (84 quarter units) and a 2.0 GPA or meet freshman admission requirements. D grades transfer. A minimum of 45 units of the 186 to 198 required for a bachelor's degree must be completed in residence. Application deadlines are the same as those for freshmen.

Visiting: There are regularly scheduled orientations for prospective students. Guides are also available for informal visits when classes are in session. Visitors may sit in on classes. The office of school relations should be contacted to arrange visits.

Financial Aid: Approximately 32% of all students receive some form of financial aid; 5% work part-time on campus. The university requires the SAAC and 1040 form. The deadline for aid applications is June 1.

Foreign Students: The foreign students at the university make up 9% of its total enrollment. The university provides an intensive English program (through its continuing education division only) and special counseling for these students.

Admissions: Freshmen applicants must score 600 or better on the TOEFL; transfer applicants must score 550 or better. No academic exams are required.

Procedure: Application deadlines are November 30 (fall) and August 31 (spring). Students must present proof of adequate funds for 1 academic year and are required to carry health insurance.

Admissions Contact: Ronald L. Gibson, Director of Admissions.

CALIFORNIA STATE UNIVERSITY/ NORTHRIDGE   C-5
Northridge, California 91324 (213) 885-3700

F/T: 7016M, 7739W	Faculty: 901; IIA, ++$
P/T: 3667M, 4029W	Ph.D.'s: 76%
Grad: 1979M, 3599W	S/F Ratio: 19 to 1
Year: sems, ss	Tuition: $461 ($2661)
Appl: Nov. 30	R and B: $2800
5853 applied	3968 accepted	2704 enrolled
SAT: 411V 461M		COMPETITIVE

California State University/Northridge, founded in 1958, offers undergraduate degree programs in the liberal arts and sciences, education, business, and the health fields. The library contains 600,000 volumes and 1 million microfilm items, and subscribes to 4500 periodicals.

Environment: The 350-acre campus is located in a suburban area 25 miles from downtown Los Angeles, in the northwestern San Fernando Valley. On-campus apartments accommodate 600 men and women.

Student Life: Approximately 98% of the students come from California. Eighty percent come from public schools. Four percent live on campus. About 24% are minority-group members. Campus housing is coed. Students may keep cars on campus. Day-care services are available to all students for a fee.

Organizations: All registered students are members of the Associated Students. The student senate supports recreational and social functions, committee services, and cultural programs. There are 11 fraternities and 7 sororities, to which 1% of the men and women belong.

Sports: The university fields 12 intercollegiate teams for men and 10 for women. There are 13 intramural sports for men and 12 for women.

Handicapped: Approximately 95% of the campus is accessible to the physically handicapped. Facilities include wheelchair ramps, special parking, elevators, specially equipped rest rooms, and lowered drinking fountains and telephones; special class scheduling is also available. There is a national leadership training program for hearing-impaired students. The handicapped student office assists students with physical handicaps.

Graduates: Ten percent of entering freshmen drop out by the end of the first year; 50% remain to graduate.

Services: Placement services, career counseling, health care, psychological counseling, and tutoring are offered to students free of charge.

Programs of Study: The B.A., B.S., and B.M. degrees are conferred. Master's degrees are also awarded. Bachelor's degrees are offered in the following subjects: AREA STUDIES (Black/Afro-American, Mexican-American, urban), BUSINESS (accounting, business administration, business education, computer science, finance, management, marketing, office administration, production and operations management, real estate/insurance, systems analysis), EDUCATION (administration/supervision, early childhood, educational psychology, elementary, health/physical, secondary, special), ENGLISH (English, journalism, literature, speech), FINE AND PERFORMING ARTS (art, art education, art history, film/photography, music, music education, radio/TV, studio art, theater/dramatics), HEALTH SCIENCES (biostatistics and epidemiology, environmental health, health administration, health education, medical technology, physical therapy, school nursing, speech therapy), LANGUAGES (French, German, Spanish), MATH AND SCIENCES (biology, chemistry, earth science, geology, mathematics, physical sciences, physics, statistics), PHILOSOPHY (humanities, philosophy, religion), PREPROFESSIONAL (dentistry, engineering, home economics, law, library science, medicine, ministry, pharmacy, social work, veterinary), SOCIAL SCIENCES (anthropology, economics, geography, government/political science, history, international relations, psychology, sociology). A complete teacher training program is offered. About 23% of degrees are conferred in social sciences, 20% in business, and 17% in math and sciences.

Special: Student-designed majors and study abroad are offered.

Honors: Eleven national honor societies have chapters on campus. Honors work is offered in English, political science, and physics.

Admissions: Approximately 68% of those who applied were accepted for the 1981-82 freshman class. The SAT scores of a recent freshman class were as follows: Verbal—80% below 500, 17% between 500 and 599, 3% between 600 and 700, and 0% above 700; Math—62% below 500, 28% between 500 and 599, 9% between 600 and 700, and 1% above 700. Candidates should have a minimum 2.0 GPA. Eligibility is determined by a weighted combination of GPA (which includes those courses taken in the last 3 years of high school) and ACT or SAT scores. California applicants must rank in the upper one-third of all California secondary school graduates; out-of-state applicants must rank comparably to the top sixth of California graduates. While no specific pattern of courses is required, the university recommends college preparatory English, a foreign language, college preparatory mathematics, a laboratory science, and history and/or a social science, as well as study in speech, music, art, and other subjects contributing to a general academic background. Admission to majors in business administration, engineering, computer science, and physical therapy is restricted to specially selected California residents.

Procedure: The SAT or ACT is required. Application deadlines are November 30 (fall) and August 31 (spring). The university follows a rolling admissions policy. There is a $25 application fee.

Special: AP and CLEP credit is accepted. There is an early admissions plan.

Transfer: For fall 1981, 6595 students applied, 4979 were accepted, and 3142 enrolled. An average of C is required; applicants with fewer than 56 units must also meet freshman entrance criteria. Preference is given to students transferring from other California colleges. All students must complete, at the university, 30 of the 124-132 credits required for a bachelor's degree. Application deadlines are the same as those for freshmen.

Visiting: There are no regularly scheduled orientations for prospective students. Guides are available for informal visits on weekdays; visitors may sit in on classes. The office of relations with schools should be contacted to arrange visits.

Financial Aid: Approximately 25% of all students receive some form of financial aid, which is available through various federal programs such as the NDSL, GSLP, CWS, state and federal EOG, and a limited number of scholarships. About 6% of the students work part-time on campus. The average freshman award is $3100. Aid applicants are required to submit a copy of the federal income tax form and the FAF; the deadline for aid application is March 1. The university is a member of CSS.

Foreign Students: Two percent of the full-time students come from foreign countries. Special counseling and special organizations are available for these students.

Admissions: Foreign students must achieve a TOEFL score of at least 500 and must take the SAT or ACT.

Procedure: Application deadlines are the same as those for other students. Foreign students must be tested for TB and must present proof of funds adequate to cover the entire period of study. Health insurance is required and is available through the university for a fee.

Admissions Contact: Edgar Chambers, Admissions Officer.

CALIFORNIA STATE UNIVERSITY/ SACRAMENTO
B-3

Sacramento, California 95819   (916) 454-6723

F/T: 6604M, 6725W	Faculty: 800; IIA, ++$
P/T: 1979M, 2194W	Ph.D.'s: 67%
Grad: 2197M, 2963W	S/F Ratio: 19 to 1
Year: early sem, ss	Tuition: $400 ($3400)
Appl: open	R and B: $2250
2948 applied	1908 accepted	1475 enrolled
SAT: 431V 477M	ACT: 19	COMPETITIVE

California State University/Sacramento, established in 1947, offers undergraduate degree programs in the liberal arts and sciences, education, business, health fields, and preprofessional areas. The library contains over 655,000 volumes and several thousand microfilm items, and subscribes to more than 6000 periodicals.

Environment: The 288-acre urban campus is located on the banks of the American River within the city limits of the state's capital. Living facilities include dormitories, off-campus apartments, and married student housing. There are also facilities for commuting students.

Student Life: About 98% of the students come from California; most of the entering freshmen come from public schools. About 5% of the students live on campus. Campus housing is coed. Students may keep cars on campus. Day-care services are available to all students for a fee.

Organizations: The extracurricular activity program includes student government, clubs, religious and service groups, dramatic and musical groups, publications, 8 fraternities and 3 sororities (located off campus), and regularly scheduled cultural and social events.

Sports: The university fields 11 intercollegiate teams for men and 11 for women. There are 10 intramural sports for men and 11 for women.

Handicapped: Approximately 85% of the campus is accessible to the physically handicapped. Facilities include wheelchair ramps, special parking, elevators, specially equipped rest rooms, and lowered drinking fountains and telephones; pre-enrollment, priority registration, and mobility training are also available. Readers, interpreters, tutors, special arrangements for testing, classroom changes, and reader rooms are available for hearing- and visually impaired students.

Graduates: The freshman dropout rate is 20%; 40% remain to graduate. Thirty percent of those who graduate pursue advanced degrees.

Services: Placement services, career counseling, health care, psychological counseling, and tutoring are offered to students free of charge. Remedial instruction is available and may require payment.

Programs of Study: The B.A., B.S., B.Voc.Ed., and B.M. degrees are conferred. Master's degrees are also awarded. Bachelor's degrees are offered in the following subjects: AREA STUDIES (Asian, Black/Afro-American, Latin American), BUSINESS (accounting, business administration, business education, computer science, finance, international business, management, marketing, operations, production, real estate/insurance, systems management), EDUCATION (adult, early childhood, elementary, health/physical, secondary, special, vocational), ENGLISH (English, journalism, literature, speech), FINE AND PERFORMING ARTS (art, art education, art history, dance, music, music education, studio art, theater/dramatics), HEALTH SCIENCES (environmental health, medical technology, nursing, speech therapy), LANGUAGES (French, German, Spanish), MATH AND SCIENCES (biology, botany, chemistry, ecology/environmental science, geology, mathematics, natural sciences, physical sciences, physics, statistics, zoology), PHILOSOPHY (humanities, philosophy), PREPROFESSIONAL (criminal justice, engineering, home economics, social work), SOCIAL SCIENCES (anthropology, economics, geography, government/political science, history, international relations, psychology, social sciences, sociology). Twenty percent of degrees conferred are in business and 20% are in preprofessional areas such as nursing and criminal justice.

Required: There is a general education requirement.

Special: Student-designed majors, study abroad, undergraduate research, independent study, and double majors are offered.

52 CALIFORNIA

Honors: Graduation with honors and the dean's honor list are available to academically outstanding students.

Admissions: Approximately 65% of those who applied for the 1981-82 freshman class were accepted. The SAT scores of those who enrolled were as follows: Verbal—77% below 500, 19% between 500 and 599, 3% between 600 and 700, and 0% above 700; Math—58% below 500, 29% between 500 and 599, 11% between 600 and 700, and 1% above 700. Candidates should have a minimum 2.0 GPA and rank in the top third of their class. Eligibility is determined by a weighted combination of GPA (which includes those courses taken in the last 3 years of high school) and ACT or SAT scores. Out-of-state applicants must rank comparably to the top sixth of California graduates. While no specific pattern of courses is required, the university recommends college preparatory English, a foreign language, college preparatory mathematics, a laboratory science, and history and/or a social science, as well as study in speech, music, art, and other subjects contributing to a general academic background.

Procedure: The SAT or ACT is required. Deadlines are open; notification is on a rolling basis. Freshmen are admitted in the fall and spring terms. There is a $25 application fee.

Special: AP and CLEP credit is accepted. There are early decision and early admissions plans.

Transfer: For fall 1981, 6222 students applied, 4691 were accepted, and 4015 enrolled. Transfer students must have a minimum C average; students with fewer than 56 units must meet the criteria for freshman applicants. D grades transfer. All students must complete, at the university, 30 of the minimum 124 credits required for a bachelor's degree. Preference is given to students from California colleges. Deadlines are open.

Visiting: There are regularly scheduled orientations for prospective students. The School/College Relations Office should be contacted for arrangements.

Financial Aid: About 30% of all students receive some form of financial aid. Ten percent work part-time on campus. The university offers a limited number of freshman scholarships in addition to loans, grants, and part-time campus employment. Federal programs such as NDSL, BEOG/SEOG, and CWS are available. The Student Aid Application for California (SAAC) should be filed by March 1. The university is a member of CSS.

Foreign Students: Two percent of the full-time students come from foreign countries. An intensive English course, special counseling, and special organizations are available for these students.

Admissions: Foreign students must achieve a TOEFL score of at least 510. No college entrance exams are required.

Procedure: Applications are due in November for fall entry. Foreign students must have a physical examination and must present proof of funds adequate to cover 1 year of study. Health insurance is required and is available through the university for a fee.

Admissions Contact: Duane L. Anderson, Director of Admissions and Records.

CALIFORNIA STATE UNIVERSITY/ SAN DIEGO
(See San Diego State University)

CALIFORNIA STATE UNIVERSITY/ SAN FRANCISCO
(See San Francisco State University)

CALIFORNIA STATE UNIVERSITY/ SAN JOSE
(See San Jose University)

CALIFORNIA STATE UNIVERSITY/ SONOMA
(See Sonoma State University)

CHAPMAN COLLEGE
Orange, California 92666   D-5
(714) 997-6711

F/T: 526M, 540W	Faculty:	89; IIA, av$
P/T: 44M, 75W	Ph.D.'s:	65%
Grad: 125M, 190W	S/F Ratio:	12 to 1
Year: 4-1-4, ss	Tuition:	$4970
Appl: open	R and B:	$2200
1053 applied	724 accepted	285 enrolled
SAT: 420V 460M	ACT: 17	COMPETITIVE

Chapman College, established in 1861, is a coeducational liberal arts college affiliated with the Disciples of Christ. Its library houses 146,000 volumes and numerous microtexts, and subscribes to 1000 periodicals.

Environment: The 38-acre campus is located in a city of 90,000 about 32 miles southeast of Los Angeles. The environment surrounding the campus is suburban. There are 22 main buildings including dormitories, on-campus apartments, and married student housing which accommodate 582 men and women.

Student Life: About 35% of the students come from outside California. Of the entering freshmen, 79% went to public schools. Just over half of the students reside on campus. The majority of the students are Protestant. Twenty-nine percent are minority-group members. Campus housing is coed. Students may keep cars on campus. Day-care services are available to all students.

Organizations: There are 3 fraternities and 2 local sororities; 10% of men and 12% of women belong. Extracurricular activities include student publications, clubs, cultural groups and presentations, service organizations, and campus government.

Sports: Intercollegiate competition is available for men in 7 sports, for women in 3 sports. There are also 5 intramural programs for men and 5 for women.

Handicapped: Thirty percent of the campus is accessible to students with physical handicaps. Facilities include ramps, parking, elevators, and specially equipped restrooms. Special class scheduling is possible. There are readers, tutors, and transcription services for students with visual or hearing impairments.

Graduates: The freshman dropout rate is 12%. About 40% remain to graduate. Of these, 40% go on for additional education: 3% to medical school, 1% to dental school, and 5% to law school. About 35% go into business and industry.

Services: The following services are free to all students: placement (files, job listings), some psychological counseling, some health care, career counseling, tutoring, and remedial instruction.

Programs of Study: The B.A., B.S., and B.Mus. degrees are conferred. There are also programs leading to master's degrees. Bachelor's degrees are offered in the following subjects: BUSINESS (accounting, business administration, computer science, finance, management, marketing, real estate/insurance), EDUCATION (elementary, health/physical, secondary), ENGLISH (English, communications, journalism, literature), FINE AND PERFORMING ARTS (art, art education, art history, music, music education), HEALTH SCIENCES (athletic training, speech therapy, sports medicine), LANGUAGES (French, Spanish), MATH AND SCIENCES (biology, chemistry, food science and nutrition, mathematics, natural sciences), PHILOSOPHY (humanities, philosophy, religion), PREPROFESSIONAL (dentistry, law, medicine, ministry, social work, veterinary), SOCIAL SCIENCES (criminal justice, economics, government/political science, history, psychology, social sciences, sociology). Twenty-five percent of degrees conferred are in social sciences; 20% are in business.

Required: The following courses are required: humanities—12 units, social sciences—12 units, sciences—8 units, and physical education—4 units.

Special: A combined B.A.-B.S. degree is possible. Students may design their own majors.

Honors: Most departments offer honors work.

Admissions: About 69% of the applicants for the 1981–82 school year were accepted. A 2.5 high school GPA is required. The SAT scores for those who enrolled were as follows: Verbal—55% below 500, 25% between 500 and 599, 15% between 600 and 700, and 5% above 700; Math—50% below 500, 30% between 500 and 599, 15% between 600 and 700, and 5% above 700. On the ACT, 60% scored below 21, 20% between 21 and 23, 15% between 24 and 25, 5% between 26 and 28, and 0% above 28. The applicant should have completed the standard high school preparatory course.

Procedure: The SAT or ACT should be taken by July following the senior year. The application deadline is open, but for the fall semester applications should be submitted by April 1. A rolling admissions policy is used. There is an application fee of $20.

Special: There are early decision and early admissions plans. Early decision applicants are notified by November 1. The college participates in CLEP and AP programs.

Transfer: For fall 1981, 366 transfer applications were received, 272 were accepted, and 151 students enrolled. Transfers are accepted for all classes. A C average is needed. Twenty-four units must be completed in residence, of the 124 units required for the bachelor's degree. Application deadlines are open. Transfers are able to enter in the fall and spring semesters.

Visiting: There is a formal orientation program for new students but informal visits with student guides may be arranged at any time. Visitors may sit in on classes and stay overnight at the school.

Financial Aid: About 75% of all students are receiving assistance. Twenty-five percent work part-time on campus. Scholarships range from $100 yearly to full tuition; scholarships totalled $1 million in 1981–82. Campus employment can provide $1500 yearly. Additional aid is available through federal, state, and private loans and grants. The college is a member of CSS. Non-California students must submit the FAF with supplement; residents should submit the SAAC. The deadlines for aid application are March 1 (fall) and November 1 (spring).

Foreign Students: Twelve percent of the full-time students come from foreign countries. The college offers these students an intensive English course, special counseling, and special organizations.

Admissions: The TOEFL must be taken and a minimum score of 500 achieved. College entrance exams are not required.

Procedure: Foreign applicants should submit their applications by June 15 (fall and December 15 (spring). The college requires proof of funds adequate to cover 1 year of study. Foreign students must carry health insurance, which is available through the college.

Admissions Contact: Anthony Garcia, Dean of Admissions.

CHRISTIAN HERITAGE COLLEGE D–5
El Cajon, California 92021 (714) 440-3043
(Recognized Candidate for Accreditation)

F/T: 174M, 189W	Faculty: 16; n/av
P/T: 8M, 7W	Ph.D.'s: 50%
Grad: none	S/F Ratio: 22 to 1
Year: see profile	Tuition: $2750
Appl: open	R and B: $1600
215 applied	194 accepted	141 enrolled
SAT: 480V 490M		COMPETITIVE

Christian Heritage College, established in 1970, is a nonsectarian, Christian liberal arts institution. The library contains 60,000 volumes, and subscribes to 330 periodicals.

Environment: The 30-acre campus has 18 buildings and is located in a suburban setting 15 miles from San Diego. Three dormitories house 180 students.

Student Life: About 60% of the students come from California. Fifty-seven percent live on campus. All are Protestant. Chapel attendance is required 3 times weekly. Five percent of the students are minority-group members. Campus housing is single-sex; there are no visiting privileges. Students may keep cars on campus.

Organizations: There are 4 local fraternities and 4 local sororities. Drama, choral groups, newspaper, yearbook, and student government provide extracurricular activity.

Sports: The college does not compete on an intercollegiate level. There are 7 intramural sports for men and 6 for women.

Handicapped: Ninety percent of the campus is accessible to wheelchair-bound students. Special facilities include wheelchair ramps, parking areas, elevators, and specially equipped restrooms. Special class scheduling is possible.

Graduates: Twenty-five percent of the freshmen drop out. Forty-two percent of the students remain to graduate. Forty percent pursue advanced study after graduation.

Services: Students receive the following services free of charge: placement and career and psychological counseling. Health care and tutoring are available for a fee.

Programs of Study: The B.A. and B.S. degrees are awarded. Bachelor's degrees are offered in the following subjects: EDUCATION (elementary, secondary), ENGLISH (English), MATH AND SCIENCES (biology, earth science, math/physics, physics), PHILOSOPHY (Biblical studies, religion), PREPROFESSIONAL (home economics, ministry, missionary aviation, missions), SOCIAL SCIENCES (counseling psychology, history, social sciences). Fifty-four percent of degrees are conferred in preprofessional fields, 18% in education, and 18% in the social sciences.

Required: All students must complete general education requirements including Bible and apologetics.

Special: The college is affiliated with the Institute for Creation Research. The school year is modular; single courses are taken in sequence.

Admissions: Ninety percent of those who applied were accepted for the 1981–82 freshman class. The SAT scores of those who enrolled were as follows: Verbal—59% below 500, 30% between 500 and 599, 11% between 600 and 700, and 0% above 700; Math—54% below 500, 18% between 500 and 599, 24% between 600 and 700, 4% above 700. A high school diploma and GPA of 2.0 are required. The school also considers recommendations and personality.

Procedure: The SAT is required. Application deadlines are open; a rolling admissions policy is used. Freshmen are admitted to all sessions. An interview is recommended. Applications should be submitted with a $25 fee.

Transfer: For fall 1981, 61 transfer students enrolled. C grades and higher are acceptable; a C average is required. One year must be completed in residence. A minimum of 31 credits, of a total 120 required for the bachelor's degree, must be taken at the college. There are no application deadlines. Transfers are accepted for all classes on a rolling basis.

Visiting: Visitors are welcome at the college. Guided tours can be scheduled mornings, Monday through Friday, by the office of admissions.

Financial Aid: About 90% of all students receive some financial aid. Forty-four percent work part-time on campus. Scholarships and work contracts are available. Tuition may be paid in installments. The SAAC is required; need is the determining factor. Aid applications should be submitted by June 1 (fall) or December 1 (spring).

Foreign Students: Students from foreign countries represent 2% of the full-time enrollment.

Admissions: The college requires that foreign candidates take the TOEFL and achieve a minimum score of 500. College entrance exams are not required.

Procedure: There are no application deadlines; admissions are on a rolling basis. Foreign students are admitted to all terms. The college requires proof of health in the form of a physical examination certificate. Foreign students are also required to show proof of funds adequate to cover 1 year of study. They must carry health insurance, which is available through the college for a fee.

Admissions Contact: William O. Brown, Director of Admissions.

THE CLAREMONT COLLEGES

Claremont McKenna College, Harvey Mudd College, Pitzer College, Pomona College, and Scripps College are the 5 undergraduate colleges in this group of private liberal arts and technological institutions. The group plan allows each college to remain small and personal while offering the resources of a medium-sized university. It also permits greater diversity of students and faculty than normally could be found at a single institution of comparable size.

The 5 contiguous campuses are located in a small suburban town at the foot of the San Gabriel Mountains, 35 miles from Los Angeles. Mountains, deserts, and beaches are within an hour's drive.

Each college has its own educational emphasis, its own campus, its own board of trustees and faculty, and its own endowment. All cooperate in academic programs, in some extracurricular activities, and in the use of certain facilities. Each undergraduate college opens its classes at no additional charge to students in the affiliated colleges. Some courses in the graduate school are open to seniors. The combined library resources, a chaplains' office, a student health service, a counseling center, a computer center, the auditorium, and a bookstore are available to students in all the colleges. The ethnic studies centers offer all students courses in Chicano studies and black studies. Many extracurricular and cultural programs also are offered jointly by the colleges.

THE CLAREMONT COLLEGES/ D–5
CLAREMONT McKENNA COLLEGE
(Formerly The Claremont Colleges/Claremont Men's College)
Claremont, California 91711 (714) 621-8088

F/T: 621M, 206W	Faculty: 86; IIB, ++$
P/T: none	Ph.D.'s: 98%
Grad: none	S/F Ratio: 12 to 1
Year: sems	Tuition: $6400
Appl: Feb. 15	R and B: $2576
957 applied	527 accepted	275 enrolled
SAT: 550V 600M		HIGHLY COMPETITIVE

Claremont McKenna College was established in 1946. It became coed in the fall of 1976. The curriculum emphasizes economics and political science. The libraries of The Claremont Colleges contain over 1,300,000 volumes, and subscribe to over 4800 periodicals.

54 CALIFORNIA

Environment: The 40-acre campus, set in a suburban location, contains 22 buildings, including 11 residence halls, a student center, and athletic facilities.

Student Life: The college draws 60% of its students from California, and 75% are graduates of public schools. About 17% of the students are minority-group members. Ninety percent of the students live in dormitories which are both coed and single-sex. Visiting privileges are available in single-sex dorms. Students may keep cars on campus. Day-care services are offered to all students, faculty, and staff for a fee.

Organizations: There are no fraternities or sororities. Activities include publications, drama, debate, student government, and musical events. The San Gabriel Mountains, desert scenery, Pacific beaches, and the city of Los Angeles are all within an hour's drive.

Sports: Claremont McKenna College competes on an intercollegiate level in 14 sports for men (with Harvey Mudd) and 7 for women (with Harvey Mudd and Scripps). There are 5 intramural sports for both men and women.

Handicapped: About 80% of the campus is accessible to wheelchair-bound students. Special facilities include wheelchair ramps, parking areas, and elevators.

Graduates: About 10% of the freshmen drop out, and more than 70% remain to graduate. About 55% to 60% of the graduates seek higher degrees, including 5% to 7% (75% of those who apply) who enter medical school and 15% to 20% who go on to law school. About 65% to 75% of the graduates pursue careers in business and industry.

Services: The college offers the following services free to students: placement, career, and psychological counseling; health care; tutoring; and remedial instruction.

Programs of Study: The college confers the B.A. degree. Bachelor's degrees are offered in the following subjects: AREA STUDIES (American, Asian, Latin American), ENGLISH (literature), FINE AND PERFORMING ARTS (theater/dramatics), LANGUAGES (French, German, Spanish), MATH AND SCIENCES (biology, chemistry, mathematics, physics), PREPROFESSIONAL (dentistry, engineering, law, medicine, ministry, veterinary), SOCIAL SCIENCES (economics, government/political science, history, international relations, psychology). Twenty-five percent of degrees are conferred in economics, 25% in political science, and 15% in math and sciences.

Required: General requirements include courses in English, mathematics, humanities, physical education, social sciences, and natural sciences.

Special: Programs include a semester abroad in one of 40 countries in Western Europe, Africa, Asia or Latin America; a junior year at the London School of Economics; internships in industry or government; independent study; a 3-2 management-engineering program offered in conjunction with Stanford University; and pass/fail options. Students may design their own majors.

Honors: Students may be elected to the Scholastic Honor Society or to an honorary service organization. All departments offer honors programs.

Admissions: Fifty-five percent of those who applied were accepted for the 1981-82 freshman class. The SAT scores of those who enrolled were as follows: Verbal—23% below 500, 47% between 500 and 599, 25% between 600 and 700, and 4% above 700; Math—9% below 500, 39% between 500 and 599, 39% between 600 and 700, and 13% above 700. Admissions officers give serious consideration to SAT and AT scores, recommendations by high school officials, and academic achievements. Rank in class and high school average are viewed with reference to the standards of the applicant's high school. The college also considers extracurricular activities, leadership record, advanced placement or honors courses, evidence of special talents, personality, and impressions made during an interview.

Procedure: Applicants must take the SAT and are encouraged to take 3 ATs, including those in English and mathematics, for placement purposes. These tests should be taken by January of the senior year. All applicants are urged to arrange for an interview on campus. Preference is given to those who file applications by February 15 and submit complete credentials by March 15. The application deadline for spring semester is December 15. The application fee is $25.

Special: An early decision plan is available. Applicants are notified by January 10. A deferred admissions plan is also available. AP credit is accepted.

Transfer: For fall 1981, 138 transfer students applied, 67 were accepted, and 45 enrolled. Applicants must have a strong academic record. C grades or better transfer. Transfer students must study a minimum of 2 years at the college, and must complete 16 courses (one semester each) of the 32 courses required for a bachelor's degree. Application deadlines are May 1 (fall) and December 15 (spring).

Visiting: Orientations for prospective students are scheduled regularly. They include interviews, class visits, and a campus tour. Guides also are available for informal visits, and visitors may sit in on classes and stay overnight at the school. Campus visits should be arranged for weekdays or Saturday mornings anytime except holidays and in March. The admissions office handles arrangements.

Financial Aid: Between 100 and 150 freshman scholarships totaling $150,000 are awarded each year. Freshmen also may receive outside scholarships totaling more than $250,000. Scholarships range from $200 to $8500. Loans from the college and private sources also are available. About 74% of the students receive aid. Nineteen percent work part-time on campus. Tuition may be paid in installments. The FAF is required and should be filed with the CSS by February 1. March 1 is the deadline for financial aid applications. Californians should apply for state grants by early February. Aid decisions are made at the same time as admission decisions. The college encourages students from disadvantaged backgrounds who show unusual promise.

Foreign Students: About 5% of the full-time students come from foreign countries. The college offers these students special counseling and special organizations.

Admissions: The English proficiency examination required for admittance is the TOEFL. Foreign students must also take the SAT.

Procedure: Application deadlines are February 15 (fall) and December 15 (spring). Foreign students must furnish proof of adequate funds. They must also carry health insurance, which is available through the college for a fee.

Admissions Contact: Emery R. Walker Jr., Dean of Admissions.

THE CLAREMONT COLLEGES/ HARVEY MUDD COLLEGE
D–5

Claremont, California 91711   (714) 621-8088

F/T: 425M, 75W	Faculty: 40; IIB, ++$
P/T: none	Ph.D.'s: 100%
Grad: none	S/F Ratio: 8 to 1
Year: sems	Tuition: $6380
Appl: Feb. 15	R and B: $2700
565 applied 342 accepted 143 enrolled	
SAT: 600V 710M	HIGHLY COMPETITIVE+

Harvey Mudd College, established in 1955, is the member of the Claremont College system that specializes in engineering and physical science. The Claremont library contains over 1,300,000 volumes, and subscribes to over 4800 periodicals.

Environment: Its 20-acre campus, set in a suburban location, contains 4 residence halls, a campus center, 2 laboratory buildings, a classroom building, and the Claremont library, which houses a 650-seat auditorium. The gymnasium and pools are shared with Claremont McKenna College.

Student Life: About 60% of the students are from California, and 75% come from public schools. Almost a quarter of the students are minority-group members. Ninety-five percent live on campus in coed dormitories. An honor system outlines fundamental principles of conduct. Students may keep cars on campus. Day-care services are available to students, faculty, and staff for a fee.

Organizations: There are no fraternities or sororities. The college sponsors departmental, special-interest and religious organizations; music and drama groups; publications; and a student government. The San Gabriel Mountains, desert, Pacific Ocean beaches, and Los Angeles are within an hour's drive.

Sports: The college offers 15 intercollegiate sports for men and 7 for women. There are 5 intramural sports for men and women.

Handicapped: About 80% of the campus is accessible to wheelchair-bound students. Special facilities include wheelchair ramps, parking areas, and elevators.

Graduates: About 10% of the freshmen drop out, and 65% remain to graduate. Of the graduates, 60–70% seek advanced degrees, including 1% to 2% who enter medical school and 1% to 2% who enter law school. Sixty percent of the graduates pursue careers in business and industry.

Services: Student receive the following free services: placement, career, and psychological counseling; health care; and tutoring.

Programs of Study: The college awards the B.S. degree. A master's degree in engineering is also conferred. Bachelor's degrees are offered in the following subjects: MATH AND SCIENCES (chemistry, mathematics, physics), PREPROFESSIONAL (engineering). Half the degrees are conferred in engineering and 25% in physics.

Required: Students must take 2 years of physical education, and one-third of every student's program must be in a humanities or social science minor.

Special: Students may earn degrees in under 4 years. Selected students may take an aeronautics and flight training program that leads to a private pilot's license. Independent research, directed reading, and engineering and mathematics clinics are offered. The college has a 5-year program leading to the master of engineering degree; the fifth year is free.

Honors: Qualified students may join honor and professional societies such as Pi Mu Epsilon and Sigma Pi Sigma.

Admissions: Sixty percent of those who applied were accepted for the 1981-82 freshman class. The SAT scores of those who enrolled were as follows: Verbal—9% below 500, 41% between 500 and 599, 38% between 600 and 700, and 11% above 700; Math—1% between 500 and 599, 39% between 600 and 700, and 58% above 700. Eighty-one percent of the entering freshmen ranked in the top tenth of their high school class; most of the rest ranked in the second tenth. Applicants should present a full program of college preparatory work. The student's rank in class and grade average are considered important, but are examined in light of the standards of his or her high school. Admissions officers also consider recommendations by high school officials, advanced placement or honors courses, extracurricular activities, leadership record, special talents, and impressions made during an interview.

Procedure: Applicants must take the SAT and 3 ATs, including Mathematics Level II, by January of the senior year. An interview is strongly recommended. Freshmen are admitted only in the fall. Preference is given to those who apply by February 1 and file complete credentials by February 15. Applicants are notified around mid-April. The application fee is $25. The college subscribes to the CRDA.

Special: An early decision plan is available; applicants are notified by January 10. A deferred admissions plan is also available. AP credit is accepted.

Transfer: For fall 1981, 47 transfer students applied, 20 were accepted, and 11 enrolled. Students may not transfer as seniors. Applicants must have a strong academic record in math and science. Students must complete, at the college, 64 of the 128 credits required for a bachelor's degree. Application deadlines are May 1 (fall) and December 15 (spring).

Visiting: Orientations for prospective students are scheduled regularly and include a campus tour, class visits, and, if desired, meetings with faculty members. Guides also are available for informal visits, and such visitors may sit in on classes and stay overnight at the school. Arrangements should be made through the admissions office. Visits are best scheduled for weekdays and Saturday mornings, except on holidays and in March.

Financial Aid: About 74% of the students receive aid. No student should hesitate to apply for financial reasons; scholarships and loans are available. The average aid to freshmen totals more than $4000. CWS jobs are provided in all departments, and 19% of the students work part-time. A student can earn $400 to $800 per year from a part-time job. Tuition may be paid in installments. Aid candidates should file the FAF by February 21, and March 1 is the aid application deadline. Californians should file the Student Aid Application for California by early February. The college, a member of the CSS, makes decisions on aid at the same time as admissions decisions, and notification is sent with notices of acceptance. The college encourages students from disadvantaged backgrounds who show unusual promise.

Foreign Students: About 7% of the full-time students come from foreign countries. The college offers these students special counseling and special organizations.

Admissions: The English proficiency examination required for admittance is the TOEFL. Foreign students must also take the SAT and 3 ATs.

Procedure: Application deadlines are February 15 (fall) and December 15 (spring). Foreign students must furnish proof of funds adequate to cover 1 year of study. They also must undergo a complete medical examination to establish proof of health, and must carry health insurance, which is available through the college for a fee.

Admissions Contact: Emery R. Walker, Jr., Dean of Admissions.

CALIFORNIA 55

THE CLAREMONT COLLEGES/ PITZER COLLEGE D-5
Claremont, California 91711   (714) 621-8129

F/T: 317M, 346W   Faculty: 61; IIB, ++$
P/T: 31M, 76W   Ph.D.'s: 85%
Grad: none   S/F Ratio: 11 to 1
Year: 4-1-4   Tuition: $7145
Appl: open   R and B: $3643
621 applied   471 accepted   155 enrolled
SAT: 500V 550M   ACT: 24   **VERY COMPETITIVE**

Founded in 1963, Pitzer College, the newest member of the Claremont Colleges, is a liberal arts institution that concentrates on social and behavioral sciences. The library houses more than 1 million volumes, and subscribes to 7000 periodicals.

Environment: The 25-acre campus is surrounded by a suburban environment. There are 9 buildings, including Grove House, a California bungalow restored and furnished with Mission-style furniture. There are 3 coed dormitories.

Student Life: About half the students are from California, and about 5% come from foreign countries. Approximately 65% of the freshmen are graduates of public schools. Ninety percent of the students live on campus in dormitories. About 22% are members of minority groups. Campus housing is coed. Students may keep cars on campus.

Organizations: Pitzer has no fraternities or sororities. Activities include student government, religious groups, drama and music organizations, student publications, special-interest clubs, and social and cultural activities on Pitzer and other Claremont campuses.

Sports: The college competes intercollegiately in 14 sports for men and 9 sports for women. Intramural sports for men number 12; for women, 11.

Handicapped: About half the campus is accessible to physically handicapped students. Facilities include wheelchair ramps, special parking, specially equipped rest rooms, and lowered drinking fountains. Fewer than 1% of the students are visually impaired.

Graduates: About 15% of the freshmen drop out, and 50% remain to graduate. About 50% of the graduates seek advanced degrees; 1% enter medical school and 4% law school. About 38% of the graduates pursue careers in business and industry.

Services: Free placement, career and psychological counseling, health care, and tutoring are provided for students.

Programs of Study: All programs lead to the B.A. degree. Bachelor's degrees are offered in the following subjects: AREA STUDIES (American, Asian, Chicano, Latin American, women's), ENGLISH (English, literature), FINE AND PERFORMING ARTS (art, dance, music), LANGUAGES (French, German, Spanish), MATH AND SCIENCES (biology, chemistry, ecology/environmental science, mathematics, physics), PHILOSOPHY (classics, philosophy), SOCIAL SCIENCES (anthropology, economics, government/political science, history, international relations, psychology, sociology). Forty-seven percent of the degrees are awarded in social sciences and 12% in English.

Required: There are no general education (core) requirements.

Special: Students may design their own majors and study abroad, in Washington or in other areas of the United States.

Honors: There are no honor societies. Academic departments or groups award honors to students who have maintained a GPA of 3.5 or better and have completed special projects.

Admissions: About 76% of those who applied were admitted to the 1981-82 freshman class. The SAT scores of those who enrolled were as follows: Verbal—38% below 500, 42% between 500 and 599, 18% between 600 and 700, and 2% above 700; Math—29% below 500, 45% between 500 and 599, 22% between 600 and 700, and 3% above 700. About 65% of the freshmen ranked in the top fifth of their high school class. Generally, applicants should rank in the top third of their class and have an average of B or better.

Procedure: Applicants must take the SAT or ACT by January of the senior year. The application deadlines are open; admissions are on a rolling basis. Priority is given to applications received by February 1. Freshmen are admitted to the fall and spring semesters. Applicants are notified by April 15. The college subscribes to the CRDA. The application fee is $25.

Special: Early and deferred admissions plans are provided. The deadline for early decision applicants is December 15. AP credit is accepted.

Transfer: For fall 1981, 104 transfer students applied, 78 were accepted, and 52 enrolled. Transfers are accepted for the freshman,

CALIFORNIA

sophomore, and junior years. A GPA of 3.0, good SAT scores, and positive recommendations are required of all applicants. D grades do not transfer. Students must spend at least 2 years in residence. At least 64 credit hours must be taken at Pitzer, of a total 128 credit hours required for the bachelor's degree. There are no application deadlines; admissions are on a rolling basis. Transfers are accepted for both the fall and spring semesters.

Visiting: Guides are provided for informal visits by prospective students, who may sit in on classes and stay overnight in the dorms. Campus visits should be scheduled between 8 A.M. and 5 P.M. The admissions office will handle arrangements.

Financial Aid: Forty-six percent of the students receive aid through the college. Ten percent work part-time on campus. The average scholarship is $4500; the average loan is $1000; the average earnings from a campus job about $800. Total aid from all sources averages $6300. Tuition may be paid on the installment plan. The college is a member of the CSS. The FAF is required and should be filed by March 15 for the fall or December 1 for the spring.

Foreign Students: About 6% of the students come from foreign countries. The college offers special counseling and sponsors organizations for foreign students.

Admissions: The TOEFL should be taken and a minimum score of 550 attained. The SAT or ACT is not necessary.

Procedure: There are no application deadlines; admissions are on a rolling basis. Foreign students may enter in the fall or spring. Proof of health must be presented. Proof of adequate funds to cover 4 years of study must also be shown.

Admissions Contact: Martin A. Tucker, Director of Admission.

THE CLAREMONT COLLEGES/ POMONA COLLEGE   D-5
Claremont, California 91711   (714) 621-8134

F/T: 698M, 678W
P/T: 3M, 1W
Grad: none
Year: sems
Appl: Feb. 1
1572 applied
SAT: 580V 610M

Faculty: 132; IIB, + +$
Ph.D.'s: 98%
S/F Ratio: 11 to 1
Tuition: $6422
R and B: $2650
871 accepted   402 enrolled
HIGHLY COMPETITIVE

Pomona College, the oldest and the largest of the Claremont Colleges, is a coed institution established in 1887. The library holds over 1,000,000 volumes and 600,000 microfilm items, and subscribes to over 670 periodicals.

Environment: The 130-acre campus, set in a suburban community, contains more than 30 buildings. About 60% of the rooms in the 2- and 3-story residence halls are singles. One coed dormitory houses foreign-language students.

Student Life: About 54% of the students come from California, and 70% are graduates of public schools. Ninety percent of the students live on campus. Twenty-one percent of the students are minority-group members. Campus housing is both coed and single-sex. There are visiting privileges in single-sex dormitories. Students may keep cars on campus. Liquor is prohibited in public areas.

Organizations: About 20% of the men belong to one of 7 local fraternities, several of which are coed. There are no sororities. Activities include music and drama, departmental clubs, and student government. Students also enjoy swimming, camping, and backpacking at nearby mountains and beaches. Downtown Los Angeles offers numerous cultural activities.

Sports: Pomona competes on an intercollegiate level in 17 sports for men and 13 sports for women. There are 9 intramural sports for both men and women.

Handicapped: Facilities for the physically handicapped are available in some areas of the campus and are being expanded.

Graduates: About 5% of the freshmen drop out, and 70% remain to graduate. Sixty percent of the graduates seek advanced degrees, including 10% who enter medical school and 9% who enter law school. About a third of the graduates pursue careers in business and industry.

Services: The following services are available free to students: placement, career, and psychological counseling, and tutoring. Health care is available for a fee.

Programs of Study: All programs lead to the B.A. degree. Bachelor's degrees are offered in the following subjects: AREA STUDIES (American, Asian), ENGLISH (English), FINE AND PERFORMING ARTS (art, art history, film/photography, music, studio art, theater/dramatics), LANGUAGES (Chinese, French, German, Spanish), MATH AND SCIENCES (astronomy, biochemistry, biology, botany, chemistry, geology, mathematics, natural sciences, oceanography, physics, zoology), PHILOSOPHY (classics, philosophy, religion), PRE-PROFESSIONAL (law, medicine), SOCIAL SCIENCES (anthropology, economics, government/political science, history, international relations, psychology, sociology).

Required: Students must fulfill liberal-arts distribution requirements and a foreign-language requirement. They also must take physical education for 1 semester.

Special: Programs include special freshman seminars; Washington Semester; student exchanges with Fisk, Swarthmore, Colby, and Smith Colleges, a 3-2 engineering program offered in conjunction with the California Institute of Technology and Washington University (St. Louis); and opportunities for study abroad and independent study. Students may design their own majors.

Honors: Honor societies represented at the college include Mortar Board and Phi Beta Kappa. A senior honors program is available.

Admissions: About 55% of those who applied for admission to the 1981–82 freshman class were accepted. The SAT scores of those who enrolled were as follows: Verbal—13% below 500, 39% between 500 and 599, 38% between 600 and 700, and 10% above 700; Math—4% below 500, 34% between 500 and 599, 44% between 600 and 700, and 18% above 700. The high school record and recommendations from high school officials are given great weight in determining admissions. The college also considers test scores; evidence of special talent in music, drama, art, and athletics; extracurricular activities; leadership record; personality; and impressions made during an interview. Sons and daughters of alumni are given special consideration. Pomona also seeks to enroll students from disadvantaged backgrounds. In judging the admissibility of such applicants, the admissions committee may give less consideration to traditional measures of academic ability and look for other evidence of potential.

Procedure: The SAT or ACT is required and should be taken before January of the senior year. The college recommends that applicants take 3 ATs, including English Composition. There is an application fee of $25. Application deadlines are February 1 (fall) and November 15 (spring). The college subscribes to the CRDA.

Special: An early decision plan is available; the application deadline is November 15. A deferred admissions plan is also available. AP and CLEP credit is accepted.

Transfer: For fall 1981, 131 transfer students applied, 70 were accepted, and 42 enrolled. An average of B or better is required. D grades do not transfer. Students must complete at least 2 years in residence to graduate, and must complete 16 of the 32 courses required for the bachelor's degree at the college. Application deadlines are April 15 (fall) and November 15 (spring).

Visiting: The college schedules an April Admissions Day for prospective students who have been accepted. Informal visits also may be scheduled with the admissions office while school is in session. Guides are provided, and visitors may sit in on classes and stay overnight at the school.

Financial Aid: Stipends and loans from all sources amount to about $1 million and $25,000, respectively. The average freshman receiving aid is given $5300 in grants and $1300 in loans. About 48% of the students receive aid. Over 60% work part-time on campus. CWS is available in many departments; 80% of the students earn part of their expenses in summer and part-time jobs. The college is a member of CSS and requires aid applicants to file the FAF by February 15. There is no other scholarship application. All California residents seeking aid also should apply for a state scholarship. Deadlines for financial aid applications are February 1 (fall) and November 15 (spring).

Foreign Students: About 5% of the full-time students come from foreign countries. The college offers these students special counseling and special organizations.

Admissions: Foreign students must achieve a TOEFL score of at least 600 to qualify for admission. The SAT or ACT is also required.

Procedure: Application deadlines are March 1 (fall) and November 15 (spring). Foreign students must file a financial statement (Foreign FAF). They must also present Pomona's medical form as proof of health.

Admissions Contact: R. Fred Zuker, Dean of Admissions.

THE CLAREMONT COLLEGES/ SCRIPPS COLLEGE
D-5

Claremont, California 91711   (714) 621-8149

F/T: 575W	Faculty: 51; IIB, ++$
P/T: 5W	Ph.D.'s: 96%
Grad: none	S/F Ratio: 11 to 1
Year: sems	Tuition: $6285
Appl: Feb. 15	R and B: $2900
512 applied 398 accepted	151 enrolled
SAT: 530V 510M	COMPETITIVE+

Scripps College, founded in 1926, is a liberal arts institution for women. It is one of the Claremont colleges. The library houses over 87,000 volumes, and subscribes to over 125 periodicals.

Environment: The 26-acre campus, set in a suburban community, contains 13 buildings, including art, dance, and music studios and 7 residence halls that accommodate about 500 students.

Student Life: About 55% of the students come from California, and 76% are graduates of public schools. Fifteen percent of the students are minority-group members. Ninety percent live on campus. Freshmen are required to live in residence halls, which have visiting privileges. Students may keep cars on campus. Students under age 21 may not drink on campus.

Organizations: No sororities or fraternities are represented on campus. Activities offered on campus or in conjunction with other Claremont colleges include student government, publications, special-interest and departmental clubs, music, dance, and drama groups, lecture series, and dances. Students also may take advantage of cultural and recreational activities in Los Angeles, backpacking and skiing in the San Gabriel Mountains, and swimming on nearby beaches.

Sports: The college fields intercollegiate teams in 6 sports. Five intramural sports are also offered.

Handicapped: Some facilities for the physically handicapped are available.

Graduates: Twenty-two percent of the freshmen drop out, and 62% eventually graduate. About 50% of the graduates pursue further study.

Services: Career and psychological counseling are provided to students free of charge. Tutoring and health care are offered for a fee.

Programs of Study: The college awards the B.A. degree. Bachelor's degrees are offered in the following subjects: AREA STUDIES (American, Asian, Black/Afro-American, Latin American), ENGLISH (English, literature), FINE AND PERFORMING ARTS (art, art history, dance, music, studio art, theater/dramatics), LANGUAGES (French, German, Greek/Latin, Italian, Spanish), MATH AND SCIENCES (biochemistry, biology, chemistry, natural sciences, physics), PHILOSOPHY (classics, philosophy, religion), SOCIAL SCIENCES (anthropology, history, international relations, psychology, social sciences).

Required: Six courses in humanities and one in "Reading, Writing, and Thinking" are required. Students must take or demonstrate proficiency in 1 year of a laboratory science and 3 semesters of a foreign language.

Special: Students may design their own majors. Traditional grades are used. Degrees may be earned in under 4 years. Special programs include individual reading courses, independent study, a Washington Semester, and junior-year-abroad programs in France, Germany, Mexico, Spain and Italy. Five-year combined degree programs are available in government, international relations, public policy studies, and business administration.

Honors: Phi Beta Kappa has a chapter on campus.

Admissions: About 78% of those who applied for admission to the 1981-82 freshman class were accepted. The SAT scores of those who enrolled were as follows: Verbal—32% below 500, 51% between 500 and 599, 15% between 600 and 700, and 2% above 700; Math—45% below 500, 39% between 500 and 599, 14% between 600 and 700, and 2% above 700. Applicants must have completed at least 15 units from an accredited high school, present a B average or better, and rank in the upper three-fifths of their class. Fifty-two percent of those accepted rank in the top 20% of their high school class. Admissions officers also consider advanced placement or honors courses, recommendations by high school officials, evidence of special talents, extracurricular activities, and impressions made during an interview.

Procedure: Applicants are required to take the SAT and are encouraged to take ATs in English Composition and a foreign language. Application deadlines are February 15 (fall) and November 15 (spring). The application fee is $25. The college subscribes to the CRDA.

Special: Early and deferred admissions plans are available. AP credit is accepted.

Transfer: For fall 1981, 66 students applied, 32 were accepted, and 21 enrolled. An average of B is preferred. Students must spend at least 2 years in residence to graduate, and must complete, at the college, 16 of the 32 credits required for the bachelor's degree. Application deadlines are May 1 (fall) and November 15 (spring).

Visiting: Orientations for prospective students are scheduled regularly. Guides also are provided for informal visits. Visits should be scheduled with the admissions office for weekdays during the school year. Visitors may sit in on classes and stay overnight at the school.

Financial Aid: About 64% of the students receive aid; 40% work part-time on campus. Applications and the FAF are due February 1 (fall) or November 1 (spring). The college, a member of CSS, bases aid grants on financial need. Loans and part-time jobs also are available. Grants to freshmen range from $100 to $5000 per year. Tuition may be paid in installments. All California residents also must apply for a California State Scholarship by February 1.

Foreign Students: About 4% of the students come from foreign countries. The college offers these students special counseling and special organizations.

Admissions: The college recommends that foreign applicants achieve a minimum score of 550 on the TOEFL. It also suggests that students take the SAT if offered in their countries.

Procedure: Application deadlines are February 15 (fall) and November 15 (spring).

Admissions Contact: Patricia Packard, Assistant Director of Admissions.

COGSWELL COLLEGE
B-3

San Francisco, California 94108   (415) 433-5550

F/T: 374M, 71W	Faculty: 23; n/av
P/T: 58M, 9W	Ph.D.'s: n/av
Grad: none	S/F Ratio: 22 to 1
Year: qtrs, ss	Tuition: $2700
Appl: Aug. 22	R and B: n/app
300 applied 219 accepted	154 enrolled
SAT or ACT: not required	COMPETITIVE

Cogswell College is a private technological college offering associate and bachelor degrees in engineering technology, architecture, and safety management. The library contains 12,000 volumes, and subscribes to 200 periodicals.

Environment: The self-contained urban campus is located on Nob Hill in San Francisco. Dormitory facilities are not available. The college also has a campus in Seattle, Washington, which offers upper-division programs in engineering technology.

Student Life: In a recent class, 75% of the students came from public schools, 20% from private schools. About 75% are minority-group members. All students live off campus.

Organizations: There are no fraternities or sororities. Social and cultural activities can be found in San Francisco.

Sports: There are 2 intramural sports.

Handicapped: The entire campus is accessible to wheelchair-bound students. Facilities include wheelchair ramps, elevators, specially equipped rest rooms, and lowered drinking fountains. There are no students with visual or hearing impairments currently enrolled.

Graduates: About 95% of the graduates pursue careers in business and industry.

Services: Students receive the following services free of charge: placement, career counseling, tutoring, and remedial instruction.

Programs of Study: The college confers the B.S. degree. Associate degrees are also awarded. Bachelor's degrees are offered in the following subjects: PREPROFESSIONAL (architecture, engineering technology—civil/structural, engineering technology—electronics, engineering technology—mechanical, engineering technology—safety/fire protection). The B.S. in architecture is a 5-year program.

Special: It is possible to earn combined B.A.-B.S. degrees in engineering technology and architecture.

Admissions: Seventy-three percent of those who applied were accepted for the 1981-82 freshman class. All students must be high school graduates, with a 2.0 average. The school indicates that in addition to these qualifications they consider the following factors in order of importance: advanced placement or honor courses, recommendations by school officials, and evidence of special talent.

58 CALIFORNIA

Procedure: A $20 nonrefundable application fee is required. Application deadlines are August 22 (fall), December 6 (winter), March 6 (spring), and May 24 (summer). A rolling admissions policy is followed.

Special: An early decision plan is available; notification is made in February of the senior year. Deferred admission is possible. AP and CLEP credit is accepted.

Transfer: Transfer students are accepted for every quarter. A 2.0 GPA is required. All students must complete, at the college, 48 of the 194 credits required for a bachelor's degree. Application deadlines are the same as those for freshmen. C grades transfer.

Visiting: Open house is held during the year for prospective students. Informal visits may be made during the year by contacting student services or admissions. Visitors may sit in on classes.

Financial Aid: Sixty percent of all students receive some form of financial aid. Twelve percent work part-time on campus. The college participates in all federal and state financial aid programs. The deadline for financial aid applications is April 15. The college is a member of CSS and requires the FAF and the SAAC.

Foreign Students: Forty percent of the full-time students come from foreign countries. An intensive English course, special counseling, and special organizations are available for these students.

Admissions: Foreign students must achieve either a minimum score of 550 on the TOEFL or a score of at least 85 on the University of Michigan Language Test. No college entrance exams are required.

Procedure: Application deadlines are the same as those for other students. Foreign students must present proof of health and of adequate funds. There are special fees for these students.

Admissions Contact: Ginny Porter, Associate Director of Student Services.

COLLEGE OF NOTRE DAME   B-3
Belmont, California 94002   (415) 593-1601

F/T: 240M, 360W	Faculty:	88; IIA, – – $
P/T: 160M, 190W	Ph.D.'s:	68%
Grad: 200M, 300W	S/F Ratio:	15 to 1
Year: 4-1-4, ss	Tuition:	$3725
Appl: Aug. 1	R and B:	$2400
378 applied	301 accepted	150 enrolled
SAT: required		COMPETITIVE

College of Notre Dame, founded in 1851, is an independent liberal arts institution affiliated with the Roman Catholic Church and operated by the Sisters of Notre Dame of Namur. The library houses 88,500 volumes, and subscribes to 572 periodicals.

Environment: The 80-acre campus is located in a suburban area of wooded hills on a peninsula 25 miles south of San Francisco. The residence halls include apartments with a pool and recreation center, as well as more traditional dormitories. The college also has a little theater and an art studio.

Student Life: Between 65% and 70% of the students are California residents, and approximately 50% live on campus. Sixty-five percent of the freshmen are graduates of public schools. Twenty-two percent of the students are members of minority groups. Housing is both single-sex and coed; there are visiting privileges in single-sex dormitories. Students may keep cars on campus.

Organizations: There are no fraternities or sororities. Extracurricular activities include student government, career-interest organizations, drama and music programs, and a student-operated coffeehouse.

Sports: The college participates intercollegiately in 2 sports for men and 2 for women. Six intramural sports are offered for both men and women.

Handicapped: About 85% of the campus is accessible to wheelchair-bound students.

Graduates: Ten percent of the freshmen drop out by the end of their first year, and 60% remain to graduate. Forty percent of the graduates seek advanced degrees, including 1% who enter medical school and 2% who enter dental school. Half the graduates pursue careers in business and industry.

Services: Students receive free placement, career, and psychological counseling; health care; tutoring; and remedial instruction. Placement services also are available to graduates.

Programs of Study: The college offers the B.A., B.S., B.F.A., and B.Mus. degrees. Master's degrees also are available. Bachelor's degrees are offered in the following subjects: BUSINESS (business administration—accounting, business administration—finance, business administration—marketing), ENGLISH (English), FINE AND PERFORMING ARTS (art, music, theater/dramatics), LANGUAGES (French, Spanish), MATH AND SCIENCES (biochemistry, biology, chemistry, mathematics), PHILOSOPHY (philosophy, religion), PRE-PROFESSIONAL (dentistry, engineering, law, medicine, social work), SOCIAL SCIENCES (economics, government/political science, history, psychology, social sciences, sociology). Twenty-five percent of the undergraduate degrees are conferred in business, 25% in social sciences, 12% in English, and 12% in fine and performing arts.

Required: All students must take courses in English, science, philosophy, religion, behavioral science, and social science.

Special: The college offers a junior year abroad at selected European universities and conducts yearly "tours for credit" in foreign countries. Also available are an exchange program with Emmanuel College in Boston, field internships for all students, and a program that permits students to take one elective per semester on a pass-fail basis.

Honors: Honors programs are available in all academic departments. Delta Epsilon Sigma and Alpha Mu Gamma honor societies have chapters on campus.

Admissions: Eighty percent of those who applied were accepted for the 1981-82 freshman class. For an earlier class, the SAT scores were as follows: Verbal—25% between 500 and 600, and 16% above 600; Math—35% between 500 and 600, and 6% above 600. Applicants should have a solid background in traditional academic subjects and present a grade point average of at least 2.5. The high school record is the single most important factor in determining admissions. The college also considers SAT scores, extracurricular activities, leadership record, advanced placement or honors courses, evidence of special talent, personality, impressions made during an interview, and recommendations by high school officials. Special consideration is given to disadvantaged students.

Procedure: The SAT is required. Application deadlines are August 1 (fall) and December 15 (spring); deadlines for winter and summer terms are open. Admissions decisions are made on a rolling basis. The college subscribes to CRDA. The application fee is $25.

Special: Early admissions, early decision, and deferred admissions plans are available.

Transfer: For fall 1981, 158 transfer students applied, 111 were accepted, and 77 enrolled. Applicants must have a GPA of 2.0 or better, present combined SAT scores of at least 800 or an ACT composite of at least 18, and submit a letter of recommendation. A personal interview also is recommended. Grades of D or better transfer. Students must complete, at the college, 30 of the 120 credits required for a bachelor's degree. Application deadlines are the same as those for freshmen.

Visiting: Orientations for prospective students are scheduled regularly. They include campus tours, an overnight stay in the dorms, and class visits. Student guides also are available for informal visits. Such visitors may sit in on classes and spend a night in the dorms. Visits should be scheduled with the admissions office. Weekday visits are preferred, but Saturdays also are possible.

Financial Aid: Sixty percent of the students receive aid; Scholarships, NDSL, grants, EOG, guaranteed low-interest loans, and federally insured student loans are available. Scholarship awards are based on financial need, academic excellence, and leadership in high school and college. Special scholarships are offered for outstanding ability in music and art. The average award to freshmen from all sources is $2000. Regular applicants should submit the FAF, the college's aid form, and the SAAC by March 15.

Foreign Students: Foreign students at the college represent 25% of its enrollment. Special organizations and special counseling are provided for these students.

Admissions: Students must score 450 or better on the TOEFL or attain an acceptable score on the college's own English proficiency test. No academic exams are required.

Procedure: Application deadlines are August 1 (fall) and December 15 (spring). Students must present proof of adequate funds for each year of study. Foreign students also are subject to special fees.

Admissions Contact: Kris Zavoli, Director of Admissions.

DOMINICAN COLLEGE OF SAN RAFAEL   B-3
San Rafael, California 94901   (415) 457-4440

F/T: 116M, 301W	Faculty:	46; IIA, – – $
P/T: 29M, 81W	Ph.D.'s:	36%
Grad: 27M, 165W	S/F Ratio:	9 to 1
Year: sems, ss	Tuition:	$4000
Appl: open	R and B:	$2850
176 applied	155 accepted	123 enrolled
SAT: 440V 430M		COMPETITIVE

Dominican College of San Rafael, incorporated in 1890, is a small Catholic liberal arts college. The library houses 83,000 volumes, 1180 microfilm items, and subscribes to over 394 periodicals. Among the special collections are several 16th-century illuminated manuscripts.

Environment: The 80-acre campus is located in a suburban area of a small city 17 miles from San Francisco. Three residence halls accommodate 250 students.

Student Life: Most of the students are from California; 80% are from the West and Northwest. Fifty-two percent of entering freshmen come from public schools. Sixty-five percent of the students live on campus. About 8% are minority-group members. Campus housing is both coed and single-sex. There are visiting privileges in single-sex dormitories. Students may keep cars on campus.

Organizations: There are no fraternities or sororities on campus. The college offers cultural, religious, social, and political activities.

Sports: The college fields 4 intercollegiate teams for men and 4 for women. There are 3 intramural sports for both men and women.

Handicapped: About 70% of the campus is accessible to handicapped students. Facilities include wheelchair ramps, special parking, and elevators. Special class scheduling is also available.

Graduates: Ten percent of the freshmen drop out by the end of the first year; 40% remain to graduate. About 35% of the graduates pursue advanced degrees. Of these, 1% enter medical school and 2% enter law school. About 50% pursue careers in business and industry.

Services: Students receive the following services free of charge: placement, career counseling, remedial instruction, and psychological counseling. Tutoring is available for a fee.

Programs of Study: Undergraduate programs lead to the B.A., B.S., and B.M. degrees. Master's degrees are also awarded. Bachelor's degrees are offered in the following subjects: AREA STUDIES (Latin American), BUSINESS (business administration, international business), ENGLISH (English, English with a writing emphasis, literature), FINE AND PERFORMING ARTS (art, art history, dance, music, theater/dramatics), HEALTH SCIENCES (nursing), LANGUAGES (French), MATH AND SCIENCES (biology, mathematics), PHILOSOPHY (humanities), PREPROFESSIONAL (law, medicine), SOCIAL SCIENCES (government/political science, history, international relations, psychology, sociology). There is also a legal assistantship program. Thirty-five percent of degrees are conferred in social sciences.

Special: Student-designed majors are permitted. Humanities Colloquia—one-semester, in-depth analyses of specific themes, problems, or periods—are offered.

Honors: Two honor societies have chapters on campus.

Admissions: About 88% of those who applied were accepted for the 1981-82 freshman class. Of those who enrolled, the SAT scores were as follows: Verbal—85% below 500, 8% between 500 and 599, 4% between 600 and 700, and 3% above 700; Math—85% below 500, 10% between 500 and 599, 3% between 600 and 700, and 2% above 700. Candidates must have completed at least 16 units of academic work and have a high school GPA of 2.5. The school also considers the following factors in order of importance: recommendations, impressions made during an interview, advanced placement or honors courses, special talents, leadership, and extracurricular activities.

Procedure: The SAT or ACT is required. Placement tests are required in English and math. The preferred application deadline for fall is August 1; notification is on a rolling basis. There is a $20 application fee.

Special: Early decision, early admissions, and deferred admissions plans are available. The early decision notification date is December 1.

Transfer: For fall 1981, 107 transfer students applied, 90 were accepted, and 57 enrolled. A 2.0 average is required; the last 30 credits of the 124 required for the bachelor's degree must be taken at Dominican.

Visiting: Informal guided tours may be arranged. Visitors may sit in on classes and stay overnight at the school. Visits are best scheduled on weekdays. The admissions office should be contacted for arrangements.

Financial Aid: About 55% of the students receive financial aid. Thirty-five percent work part-time on campus. The deadline for financial aid applications is February 11; the FAF and SAAC are required by the college, a member of CSS.

Foreign Students: Fifteen percent of the full-time students come from foreign countries. The college offers these students an intensive English program.

Admissions: Foreign students must achieve a minimum score of 550 on the TOEFL or 85 (average) on the University of Michigan Language Test. College entrance exams are not required.

Procedure: Application deadlines are August 1 (fall), January 1 (spring), and June 1 (summer). There is a special fee of $50 for foreign students, which is payable after acceptance for processing of I-20 forms. Foreign students must present proof of funds adequate to cover 4 years of study. Proof of health is required of dormitory residents. Foreign students must also carry health insurance, which is available through the college for a fee.

Admissions Contact: Charles Lavaroni, Dean of Admissions and Financial Aid.

FRESNO PACIFIC COLLEGE   C-3
Fresno, California 93702   (209) 251-7194

F/T: 150M, 185W Faculty: 35; IV, av$
P/T: 15M, 20W   Ph.D.'s: 50%
Grad: 130M, 205W S/F Ratio: 14 to 1
Year: qtrs, ss   Tuition: $3590
Appl: Aug. 15   R and B: $2085
151 applied   132 accepted   84 enrolled
SAT: 450V 475M   COMPETITIVE

Fresno Pacific College, founded in 1944, is a church-related, liberal arts college affiliated with the Mennonite Brethren. The library contains 65,000 volumes and 850 microfilm items, and subscribes to 642 periodicals.

Environment: The 39-acre campus is located in a suburban area of Fresno, a city of 275,000, 150 miles from both San Francisco and Los Angeles. The campus comprises 10 buildings, including a cafeteria, a dining hall, a soccer field, a track, tennis and volleyball courts, and a special events center/gymnasium which seats 2000. Residence facilities include 4 dormitories housing 300 students, 18 apartments housing 36 students, and private homes housing 200 students.

Student Life: About 87% of the students are from California, 5% from bordering states, and 8% from foreign countries. Fifty percent of the students live on campus. Married students and commuters are not required to live on campus. About 13% of the students are minority-group members. Campus housing is single-sex; there are visiting privileges. Students are permitted to keep cars on campus. Drinking, drugs, and tobacco are prohibited on campus.

Organizations: There are no fraternities or sororities. Religious counselors are available for Protestant students. There are 8 college-sponsored extracurricular activities. The student government has partial jurisdiction in many areas of student life. Students are represented by voting delegates on administration and faculty committees.

Sports: Men compete intercollegiately in 2 sports; women, in 2. There are 4 intramural sports for men and 3 for women.

Handicapped: Approximately 90% of the campus is accessible to the physically handicapped. Facilities include wheelchair ramps, special parking, and specially equipped rest rooms.

Graduates: The freshman dropout rate is 15%; 25% remain to graduate. Twenty-five percent pursue advanced degrees.

Services: Placement services, tutoring, and remedial instruction are offered to students free of charge.

Programs of Study: The college confers the B.A. degree. Associate and master's programs are also offered. Bachelor's degrees are offered in the following subjects: BUSINESS (accounting, business administration), EDUCATION (elementary, secondary), ENGLISH (English, literature), FINE AND PERFORMING ARTS (music), MATH AND SCIENCES (mathematics, natural sciences), PHILOSOPHY (religion), SOCIAL SCIENCES (government/political science, history, psychology, social sciences, sociology).

Special: The college cooperates with the study-abroad program administered by Brethren Colleges Abroad. Programs are available in France, Germany, Great Britain, and Spain. The college also directly sponsors a quarter-long study tour in Europe. Concurrent enrollment programs with Fresno State College, San Joaquin College of Law, and the Mennonite Brethren Biblical Seminary are available. Students may create their own majors.

Admissions: About 87% of those who applied were accepted for the 1981-82 freshman class. Candidates should be graduates of an accredited high school, rank in the top half of their graduating class, have a minimum average of 2.5, and 15 Carnegie units. Also considered are character, personality, and intangible qualities.

Procedure: The SAT or ACT is required. The SAT may be taken in December, January, March, or May; junior year results are acceptable.

CALIFORNIA

Application deadlines are August 1 (fall), December 15 (winter), and March 15 (spring). The college follows a rolling admissions policy. A personal interview is highly recommended, and may be taken with a college representative in or near the candidate's home town. There is a $15 application fee.

Special: An early admissions plan is available; the application deadline is January 1. There is a special program concerned with recruiting minority students for admissions and aiding their college career. There are also early decision and deferred admissions plans. AP and CLEP credit is accepted.

Transfer: For fall 1981, 151 transfer students applied, 111 were accepted, and 55 enrolled. Transfers are accepted for all classes. A minimum 2.0 GPA is required. D grades transfer. There is a 1-year residency requirement. Transfers must complete, at the college, 151 of the 186 quarter units necessary for the bachelor's degree. Application deadlines are the same as those for freshmen.

Visiting: Regularly scheduled orientations for prospective students include meetings with the faculty, administration, and students, a campus tour, sitting in on classes, and a college hour. Informal visits with a student guide can be scheduled any time Monday through Friday from 8 A.M. to 5 P.M. Visitors may sit in on classes and stay overnight at the school. The admissions office should be contacted to arrange visits.

Financial Aid: Eighty percent of all students receive some form of financial aid. Forty percent work part-time on campus. The average award to freshmen from all sources is $800. Freshmen who can demonstrate academic excellence and financial need are offered academic scholarships. Federal and state aid in the form of loans, grants, and employment is available. The college is a member of CSS. Eligibility is determined by completing the SAAC for California residents or the FAF for non-California residents. The aid application deadlines are August 15 (fall), December 15 (winter), and March 15 (spring).

Foreign Students: Eight percent of the full-time students come from foreign countries.

Admissions: The TOEFL must be taken; the college requires a minimum score of 500. The SAT or ACT is also required.

Procedure: Admissions application deadlines for foreign students are July 1 (fall), November 1 (winter), and February 1 (spring). Proof of funds adequate to cover 1 year of study must be presented. Foreign students must carry health insurance, which is available through the college for a fee.

Admissions Contact: Office of Admissions.

GOLDEN GATE UNIVERSITY B-3
San Francisco, California 94105   (415) 442-7494

F/T: 262M, 213W	Faculty: 88; IIA, ++$
P/T: 1120M, 983W	Ph.D.'s: 25%
Grad: 5401M, 2781W	S/F Ratio: 11 to 1
Year: tri, ss	Tuition: $75 p/c
Appl: open	R and B: n/app
113 applied	105 accepted 67 enrolled
SAT or ACT: required	COMPETITIVE

Golden Gate University, an independent institution founded in 1901, trains students for careers in business, government, accountancy, law, and other professional fields. The library contains 250,000 volumes and 78,000 microfilm items, and subscribes to 2100 periodicals.

Environment: The university is located in the financial district of San Francisco. There are no dormitories; some students live in university-approved residence clubs.

Student Life: About 84% of the students are California residents, and most of these are from the San Francisco Bay area. The university is geared to the needs of working students, so most students are older and self-supporting. None lives on campus. About 25% are minority-group members. The college provides day-care services to all students for a fee.

Organizations: Campus activities are scheduled so working students can take advantage of them. The university sponsors a student government, professional and social clubs, and a student newspaper. There are no fraternities or sororities.

Sports: The university does not participate in intercollegiate athletics. There are 6 intramural sports for men and 6 for women.

Handicapped: The entire campus is accessible to wheelchair-bound students. Facilities include specially equipped rest rooms and braille directions in elevators. Counselors are trained to handle the needs of handicapped students. Visually impaired students may bring transcribers to class and use typewriters on examinations. Hearing-impaired students are seated in the front rows of classes and may bring interpreters.

Graduates: About 12% of the freshmen drop out, and 35% remain to graduate. Fifty-one percent of the graduates seek advanced degrees, including 16% who enter law school. Three-fourths of the graduates pursue careers in business and industry.

Services: Students receive free career and psychological counseling, placement, and tutoring. A placement center helps students and alumni find full-time, part-time, and cooperative education jobs. Health care is available for a fee.

Programs of Study: The university awards the B.A. and B.S. degrees. Associate, master's, and doctoral programs are also available. Bachelor's degrees are offered in the following subjects: BUSINESS (accounting, administrative management, business economics, finance, financial planning, hotel and restaurant management, information/computer science, insurance, management, marketing, public administration, security management, telecommunications management, transportation and physical distribution management), HEALTH SCIENCES (health services management, medical records management), PREPROFESSIONAL (law, hotel/restaurant/institutional management, security management), SOCIAL SCIENCES (administration of justice, economics, human relations, political science, public administration). Seventy percent of the undergraduate degrees conferred are in business, 20% are in social sciences, and 10% are in preprofessional studies.

Special: The Cooperative Education and Internship Program integrates classroom study with work experience at a wide range of businesses and government agencies. Undergraduate and graduate programs also are offered at 24 military installations in the United States, as well as in Los Angeles, Seattle, Monterey, and Sacramento.

Honors: Undergraduate degree candidates may earn dean's list standing and graduation with honors. There are no honor societies on campus.

Admissions: Ninety-three percent of the applicants who had no previous college credit were admitted for 1981–82. Candidates must be graduates of an accredited high school with a GPA of 2.0 or better and a satisfactory score on the SAT or ACT. Admissions officers also consider advanced placement or honors courses, recommendations by alumni and high school officials, evidence of special talent, leadership potential, and impressions made in an interview.

Procedure: Applicants are required to take the SAT or ACT. There are no application deadlines; the university follows a rolling admissions policy. The university accepts new students for all terms. The application fee is $25.

Special: Deferred admissions is possible. CLEP credit is granted.

Transfer: For the fall of 1981, 794 students applied, 534 were accepted, and 400 enrolled. Seventy-five to eighty percent of new students enter Golden Gate University with advanced standing. Transfers are accepted for all classes. Applicants must have an average of C or better at an accredited college. D grades transfer only in electives. At least 24 units, including the last 12, must be completed at the university. A total of 123 semester units are required for the bachelor's degree. There are no application deadlines.

Visiting: A day-long Open House for prospective students is scheduled each spring. Informal visits also may be arranged, preferably for 10 A.M. to 1 P.M. except during holiday periods, through the dean of students' office. Guides are provided, and visitors may sit in on classes.

Financial Aid: About 25% of the students receive aid. About 10% work part-time on campus. The average aid to undergraduates from all sources is $2000. Programs include NDSL. The SAAC and the university's aid application must be submitted by April 1 for the academic year.

Foreign Students: Three percent of the full-time students come from foreign countries. The university offers an intensive English program and special counseling. It also sponsors organizations especially for foreign students.

Admissions: The TOEFL or University of Michigan Language Test is required; a minimum score of 525 must be achieved on the former, 90 on the latter. It is recommended that the SAT or ACT be taken; a minimum composite score of 1000 is required on the SAT, 20 on the ACT.

Procedure: The university has no application deadlines. Admissions are on a rolling basis. Foreign candidates are advised to apply 3 months before the beginning of each semester. They are admitted to all semesters. Proof of funds adequate to cover 1 year must be presented.

Admissions Contact: Char Hamada, Dean of Admissions.

HOLY NAMES COLLEGE
Oakland, California 94619   B-3
(415) 436-1321

F/T: 153M, 209W	Faculty: 46; IIA, --$
P/T: 22M, 155W	Ph.D.'s: 45%
Grad: 18M, 121W	S/F Ratio: 8 to 1
Year: sems, ss	Tuition: $3870
Appl: Aug. 1	R and B: $2300
411 applied	217 accepted	152 enrolled
SAT: 425V 425M	ACT: 19	COMPETITIVE

Founded in 1880, Holy Names College is a private, coeducational, career-oriented liberal arts college affiliated with the Roman Catholic church. The library contains 91,000 volumes and 18,000 microfilm items, and subscribes to 533 periodicals.

Environment: The 65-acre campus is located in the urban environment of Oakland, California, overlooking San Francisco. There are 14 buildings in all, including 3 residence halls.

Student Life: About 75% of the students come from California, 15% from other states, and 10% from foreign countries. Students of all faiths are welcome. Forty percent of students reside on campus in dormitories and other college-authorized housing. Thirty-one percent are minority-group members. Campus housing is coed. Students may keep cars on campus.

Organizations: There are no social fraternities or sororities. The college sponsors art shows, concerts, films, lectures, operas, plays, readings, recitals, and science exhibits. Other extracurricular activities include chorus, dance, drama, journalism, orchestra, publications, and service organizations.

Sports: The college competes intercollegiately in 4 sports for men and 4 for women. There are 5 intramural sports for men and 6 for women.

Handicapped: Special facilities are available for the handicapped including wheelchair ramps, parking areas, elevators, and specially equipped restrooms.

Graduates: The freshman dropout rate is 19%. Fifty-six percent of the graduates pursue graduate or professional degrees.

Services: The following services are available on campus free of charge: placement, career counseling, and psychological counseling. Health care, tutoring, and remedial instruction are available for a fee.

Programs of Study: The college confers the B.A., B.F.A., B.M., and B.S.N. degrees. Master's degrees are also awarded. Bachelor's degrees are offered in the following subjects: AREA STUDIES (American), BUSINESS (business administration/economics), EDUCATION (liberal studies), ENGLISH (English, English studies for international students), FINE AND PERFORMING ARTS (art, music), HEALTH SCIENCES (clinical laboratory technology, nursing, speech therapy), LANGUAGES (French, Spanish), MATH AND SCIENCES (biology, chemistry, mathematics, physical sciences), PHILOSOPHY (philosophy, religion), PREPROFESSIONAL (architecture, dentistry, engineering, law, medicine, pharmacy, social work, veterinary), SOCIAL SCIENCES (government/political science, history, international relations, psychology, social sciences, sociology).

Required: A core curriculum stressing the humanities is required.

Special: It is possible to earn combined B.A.-B.S. degrees. The college allows student-designed majors. A pass-fail option can be exercised in one course outside the major each semester. Most departments provide for independent study. Students are permitted to spend the third year abroad.

Honors: The honors and independent study programs in English and history are considered outstanding. The following national honor societies have chapters on campus: Kappa Gamma Pi, Mu Phi Epsilon, Pi Delta Phi, Pi Gamma Mu, Sigma Delta Pi, and Alpha Theta Epsilon.

Admissions: Fifty-three percent of those who applied were accepted for the 1981-82 freshman class. The SAT scores of a recent freshman class were as follows: Verbal—23% scored between 500 and 599, and 7% between 600 and 700; Math—20% scored between 500 and 599, 2% between 600 and 700, and 2% above 700. Candidates must be graduates of an accredited high school with a GPA of 2.75 and must have completed 15 Carnegie high school units. The school indicates that in addition to these qualifications they consider the following factors in order of importance: advanced placement or honor courses, recommendations by school officials, evidence of special talent(s), and extracurricular activities record.

Procedure: The SAT or ACT is required. The deadlines for regular admission are August 1 for fall and January 1 for spring. New students are admitted both semesters. Applications should be submitted with a $25 fee. A rolling admissions plan is used.

Special: Early decision, early admissions, and deferred admissions plans are available. AP and CLEP are used.

Transfer: Transfers are accepted for all classes. The basic requirements are a GPA of 2.75, a minimum of 15 academic units completed, and a minimum composite SAT score of 800 or ACT of 18. D grades are acceptable. There is a one year (24 units of final 30 units) residency requirement. To earn the bachelor's degree a total of 120 units must be completed. A rolling admissions plan for transfers is in effect. Transfers may be admitted to the fall or spring semesters. Recommended deadlines for application are the same as those for freshman applicants.

Visiting: Guides are available for informal weekday visits. Visitors may sit in on classes and stay overnight at the school. The office of admissions will make arrangements.

Financial Aid: About 75% of all students receive financial aid. About one-third work part-time on campus. The average award to freshmen from all sources is $4992. Tuition may be paid in installments. The college has institutional grants and scholarships based on need, artistic ability, and merit. Packaged financial aid combining job, loan, and grant is offered depending on established need. The college is a member of the CSS, and the FAF or SAAC are required. The deadline for early decision aid applications is April 1 for fall applicants, January 15 for spring applicants.

Foreign Students: Ten percent of the full-time students come from foreign countries. The college offers special counseling and special organizations for these students.

Admissions: Either the TOEFL or the University of Michigan Language Test is required; a minimum score of 500 is necessary on the former, 80 on the latter. The SAT or ACT is also required.

Procedure: Application deadlines for foreign students are July 1 for fall and December 1 for spring. Proof of health, consisting of a complete physical exam, TB test, rubella test, urinalysis, and CBC, is required. Proof of funds adequate to cover at least 1 year of study must be presented. Foreign students must also make a $500 tuition deposit and carry health insurance. Such insurance is available through the college for a fee.

Admissions Contact: Sister Jacquelyn Slater, Director of Admissions.

HUMBOLDT STATE UNIVERSITY
Arcata, California 95521   A-1
(707) 826-3421

F/T, P/T:	Faculty: 502, IIA, ++$
3471M, 2961W	Ph.D.'s: 60%
Grad: 501M, 527W	S/F Ratio: 17 to 1
Year: qtrs, ss	Tuition: $346 ($63 p/c+ $346)
Appl: open	R and B: $2700
1905 applied	1202 accepted	730 enrolled
SAT or ACT: required	VERY COMPETITIVE

Humboldt State University is the northernmost campus of the California State University system. Founded in 1913, the university offers a curriculum based on a general education emphasis, a liberal arts core, and special degree programs in natural resources, business, nursing, teacher education, and environmental engineering. The library contains over 244,000 volumes, 100,000 microfilm items, and 250,000 government documents, and subscribes to over 2500 periodicals.

Environment: The 142-acre rural campus is in Arcata, 275 miles from San Francisco and part of the Redwood Empire. Facilities include 38 buildings, dormitory space for a total of 1100 students, an on-campus hatchery and wild game pens, and a marine laboratory in Trinidad, 20 miles north of the campus.

Student Life: Ninety-seven percent of the students are state residents and most live within easy commuting distance in the town. About 90% of entering freshmen come from public schools. Fifteen percent of the students live on campus in residence halls. Nine percent are minority-group members. Campus housing is coed. Students may keep cars on campus. Day-care services are available to full-time students.

Organizations: There are no fraternities or sororities; professional and service organizations also serve as social groups. Students participate in student government and in educational and cultural activities.

Sports: The university fields 8 intercollegiate teams for men and 7 for women. There are 15 intramural sports for both men and women.

Handicapped: Facilities for the physically handicapped include special parking, wheelchair ramps, elevators, and specially equipped rest rooms. Library and reading services are available for students with visual impairments. Counselors are available.

Graduates: The freshman dropout rate is about 35%; 65% remain to graduate. About 20% of each graduating class enter business and industry.

Services: Students receive the following services free of charge: placement, career counseling, and psychological counseling. Health care, tutoring, and remedial instruction are also available. The career development center assists with counseling, job and career information and announcements, placement file maintenance, and various workshops.

Programs of Study: Undergraduate degrees offered are the B.A. and B.S. Master's degree programs are also offered. Bachelor's degrees are offered in the following subjects: BUSINESS (accounting, business administration, computer science, finance, management, marketing), EDUCATION (early childhood, elementary, secondary), ENGLISH (English, journalism, speech), FINE AND PERFORMING ARTS (art, art history, film/photography, music, music education, studio art, theater/dramatics), HEALTH SCIENCES (medical technology, nursing, speech therapy), LANGUAGES (French, German, Spanish), MATH AND SCIENCES (biology, botany, chemistry, earth science, geology, mathematics, natural sciences, oceanography, physical sciences, physics, zoology), PHILOSOPHY (philosophy), PRE-PROFESSIONAL (environmental resources, engineering, fisheries, forestry, home economics, natural resources, range management, resources planning and interpretation, social work, wildlife management), SOCIAL SCIENCES (anthropology, economics, geography, government/political science, history, psychology, social sciences, sociology).

Required: All students must take at least 72 units in general education from the fields of basic subjects (writing, reading, communication, and mathematics), natural science, social science, and humanities.

Special: Student-designed majors are permitted. The university has a cooperative program with foreign universities for education abroad through the California State University International Program. The university also participates in the National Student Exchange Program, and has a Cooperative Education program with government agencies.

Honors: Chi Sigma Epsilon and Rho Sigma have chapters on campus.

Admissions: For the 1981-82 freshman class, the university accepted 63% of those who applied. The SAT scores of those enrolled were as follows: Verbal—63% below 500, 27% between 500 and 599, 9% between 600 and 700, and 0% above 700; Math—47% below 500, 36% between 500 and 599, 15% between 600 and 700, and 2% above 700. On the ACT, 45% scored between 18 and 23, 34% between 24 and 29, and 2% above 29. State residents who apply must rank in the top third of their class; non-residents in the top sixth.

Procedure: The ACT or SAT is required of all lower division and freshman applicants. Freshmen are admitted each quarter but not in the summer; prospective students should apply as early as possible. Applications received less than one month before the first day of classes are subject to a late fee. Some majors close immediately. A rolling admissions plan is used. The application fee is $25.

Special: An early decision plan is available. Applicants are notified by January 15. There is also an early admissions plan, with an application deadline of January 1. AP and CLEP subject matter credit is accepted.

Transfer: For fall 1981, 2285 transfer students applied, 1715 were accepted, and 1275 enrolled. Transfers may enter any class, but must take 36 units in residence. They must also complete, at the university, 45 of the 186 credits required for the B.A., and 45 of the 192 credits required for the B.S. A GPA of 2.0 is required for California undergraduate transfers; 2.4 for non-resident transfers. D grades transfer. Deadlines are the same as for freshman applicants.

Visiting: Orientation is held for prospective students. Guided tours and interviews can be scheduled when school is in session through the admissions and records office. Visitors may sit in on classes.

Financial Aid: About 50% of all students receive some form of financial aid; 30% work part-time on campus. There is limited scholarship and loan assistance. The university has work-study in all departments; 50% of the students earn part of their expenses. The application for financial aid must be obtained from the office of financial aid. The FAF is required. Applications should be filed by March 15, but an earlier date is recommended. The university is a member of CSS.

Foreign Students: Foreign students comprise about 1% of the full-time enrollment. The university offers these students an intensive English program, special counseling, and special organizations.

Admissions: Foreign students must achieve a TOEFL score of at least 550 to qualify for admission. They are also required to take the SAT or ACT.

Procedure: Application deadlines are March 1 (fall), July 1 (winter), and October 1 (spring). The fees for foreign students are the same as for non-resident applicants. Proof of funds adequate to cover 1 year of study is required. Foreign students must also provide a comprehensive medical report as proof of health, and must carry health insurance, which is available through the university for a fee.

Admissions Contact: Donald G. Clancy, Director of Admissions and Records.

LINCOLN UNIVERSITY   B-3
San Francisco, California 94118   (415) 221-1212
(Recognized Candidate for Accreditation)

F/T, P/T:	Faculty: 27; n/av
360 M&W	Ph.D.'s: 22%
Grad: 54 M&W	S/F Ratio: 13 to 1
Year: sems, ss	Tuition: $70 p/c
Appl: July 30	R and B: n/app
SAT or ACT: not required	LESS COMPETITIVE

Lincoln University, founded in 1919, is a private institution offering undergraduate and graduate programs. Most undergraduates are from foreign countries. The library contains 35,000 volumes and subscribes to 65 periodicals.

Environment: The campus is located near the heart of San Francisco. Facilities include seminar rooms, lecture halls, and a snack bar. There are no residence halls, but students may live in dormitories at the nearby University of San Francisco.

Student Life: About 98% of the students come from foreign countries. The university seeks to provide an international setting for its students.

Organizations: There are 4 fraternities and 3 sororities; about 10% of the men and 10% of the women belong. Campus activities include student government, publications, ethnic clubs, and special-interest groups. Selected students may work at a local cable television station.

Sports: The university competes intercollegiately in 1 sport. Intramural sports are available for men and women.

Graduates: The freshman dropout rate is 22%. About 35% of the graduates pursue advanced degrees.

Services: Placement and counseling services are available to students.

Programs of Study: All undergraduate programs lead to the B.A. in business administration. Master's programs are also offered. Bachelor's degrees are awarded in BUSINESS (business administration). Special concentrations or programs are available in American studies, global business operations and management, information science, communications, hotel administration, accounting, economics, and humanities.

Special: Study abroad and undergraduate research are offered.

Honors: Honors work is available.

Admissions: Fifty percent of those who applied were accepted for a recent freshman class. Candidates should be graduates of an accredited high school and have completed 15 high school units. A 2.5 GPA is required.

Procedure: Neither the SAT nor the ACT is required. Application deadlines are July 31 (fall), September 30 (spring), and May 31 (summer). An open admissions policy is used; notification is made on a rolling basis. There is a $25 application fee. Students are also admitted at midyear.

Special: An early decision plan is offered. CLEP credit is granted.

Transfer: Transfer students with good academic standing are accepted. A minimum GPA of 2.0 is required, along with high school and college transcripts. Application deadlines are open. Each student's record is evaluated individually to determine the number of transferable credits.

Visiting: Guided tours and interviews may be arranged through the admissions office.

Financial Aid: About 90% of the students receive aid. Awards are made on the basis of need. Aid application deadlines are open; the FAF is required.

Foreign Students: An intensive English program and special counseling are provided. The university actively recruits foreign students.

Admissions: Applicants must score at least 70% on the University of Michigan Language Test.

Procedure: Students must present proof of adequate funds for 4 years and must carry health insurance, which is available through the university for a fee.

Admissions Contact: Ernest Scosseria.

LOMA LINDA UNIVERSITY D-5
Riverside, California 92515 (714) 785-2118

F/T: 831M, 882W	Faculty: 150; I, — — $
P/T: 192M, 258W	Ph.D.'s: 45%
Grad: 155M, 144W	S/F Ratio: 14 to 1
Year: qtrs, ss	Tuition: $4800
Appl: Aug. 15	R and B: $2169
673 enrolled	
ACT: required	LESS COMPETITIVE

This private Seventh-day Adventist university was merged with La Sierra College in 1967. In addition to the undergraduate liberal arts programs of La Sierra, it offers professional training in several areas. The library contains 150,000 volumes and 41,219 microfilm items, and subscribes to 1200 periodicals.

Environment: The 460-acre campus is located in a suburban setting within the city of Riverside; the buildings overlook a valley famous for its citrus and walnut groves. The plant consists of 32 main buildings of similar architecture, plus a heated pool and a general store. Just off campus are the stables, dairy, and creamery of the college farm. Living facilities include dormitories, married student housing, and on- and off-campus housing.

Student Life: Between 75% and 80% of the students come from California. About 47% are minority-group members. The majority are members of the Seventh-day Adventist Church. Attendance at religious services is required. Fifty-one percent of the students live on campus. Drinking and smoking are not permitted; cars on campus are carefully regulated. Campus housing is single-sex; there are no visiting privileges. Day-care services are available to all students for a fee.

Organizations: There are no fraternities or sororities; professional and service organizations serve as social groups.

Sports: The university does not participate in intercollegiate sports. There are 8 intramural sports for men and 8 for women.

Handicapped: Facilities for physically handicapped students include special parking, some wheelchair ramps, and specially equipped rest rooms. Special class scheduling is also available. A special counselor is available for counseling and assistance.

Graduates: About 35% of entering freshmen drop out by the end of the first year; 38% remain to graduate. Thirty-three percent of the students pursue advanced study after graduation: 7% enter medical school, 6% enter dental school, and 2% enter law school. About 12% pursue careers in business and industry.

Services: Students receive the following services free of charge: placement, career counseling, health care, tutoring, remedial instruction, and psychological counseling. Placement services for undergraduates include compiling, storing and circulating individual placement files, job listings, and interviewing workshops.

Programs of Study: The university confers the B.A., B.S., B.S.W., and B.Mus. degrees. Associate, master's, and doctoral degrees are also awarded. Bachelor's degrees are offered in the following subjects: AREA STUDIES (Latin American), BUSINESS (accounting, business administration, business education, computer science, finance, management, marketing, office management, secretarial administration), EDUCATION (elementary, health/physical, industrial, recreation) ENGLISH (English, speech, writing), FINE AND PERFORMING ARTS (art, church music, film/photography, mass media, music, music education, music performance), HEALTH SCIENCES (health science, speech therapy), LANGUAGES (English as a Second Language, French, German, Spanish), MATH AND SCIENCES (biochemistry, biology, biomathematics, biophysics, chemistry, geology, mathematics, paleontology, physical sciences, physics), PHILOSOPHY (humanities, religion, Western thought), PREPROFESSIONAL (agriculture, child development, clothing and textiles, home economics, social work), SOCIAL SCIENCES (administration of justice, anthropology, government/political science, history, psychology, social sciences, sociology).

Special: A general studies (no major) degree is offered. Student-designed majors are permitted.

Admissions: Enrollment for 1981–82 totaled 673. Generally, graduates are from accredited high schools and may be admitted as regular college students upon presentation of an official transcript certifying completion of 16 units. Admissions officers also consider the applicant's leadership record and personality.

Procedure: The university requires the ACT. Math and English ATs are also required. Tests may be taken as late as May of the senior year. Applications should be filed no later than August 15 (fall), December 1 (winter), March 1 (spring), and May 1 (summer). There is a $10 application fee. Freshmen are admitted to all quarters.

Special: AP and CLEP credit is accepted.

Transfer: For fall 1981, 453 transfer students enrolled. D grades do not transfer. The requirements for transfers are the same as those for incoming freshmen. All students must complete the 190 quarter units required for a bachelor's degree. Application deadlines are the same as those for freshmen.

Visiting: There are regularly scheduled orientations for prospective students. Guided tours can be scheduled during the week through the recruitment office. Visitors may sit in on classes; overnight accommodations are available.

Financial Aid: Sixty percent of all students receive some form of financial aid. About 50% work part-time on campus. Several freshman scholarships are awarded each year and loans are available through government funds, the university, and private sources. The FAF is required. The university is a member of CSS. Applications should be submitted by May 1.

Foreign Students: Eight percent of the full-time students come from foreign countries. An intensive English course, an intensive English program, special counseling, and special organizations are available for these students.

Admissions: Foreign students must achieve a score of at least 90 on the University of Michigan Language Test. No college entrance exams are required. Achievement tests are required.

Procedure: Application deadlines are August 15 (fall), December 15 (winter), March 1 (spring), and May 1 (summer). Foreign students must have a physical exam and must present proof of funds adequate to cover 1 year of study. Health insurance is required and is available through the university.

Admissions Contact: Rick Williams, Director of Admissions and Recruitment.

LOS ANGELES BAPTIST COLLEGE C-5
Newhall, California 91322 (805) 259-3540

F/T: 185M, 164W	Faculty: 24; IIB, av$
P/T: 17M, 13W	Ph.D.'s: 42%
Grad: 2M, 5W	S/F Ratio: 15 to 1
Year: sems	Tuition: $3130
Appl: Aug. 15	R and B: $1920
219 applied	199 accepted 96 enrolled
SAT: 455V 440M	COMPETITIVE

Los Angeles Baptist College, founded in 1927, is a church-related liberal arts college affiliated with the General Association of Regular Baptist Churches. The library contains 32,000 volumes and more than 130 microfilm items, and subscribes to 150 periodicals.

Environment: The 48-acre campus is located in a suburban area, 32 miles from Los Angeles. It includes 11 buildings; a new student center is scheduled for 1982. The dormitory accommodates 150 men and 150 women.

Student Life: About 75% of the students come from California; 80% reside on campus; nearly 25% have private school backgrounds. All of the students are Protestant; attendance at daily chapel service is compulsory. Ten percent are members of minority groups. Campus housing is single-sex. Students may keep cars on campus.

Organizations: There are no fraternities or sororities on campus. Extracurricular groups include service organizations, cultural activities, and religious groups.

Sports: The college offers 4 intercollegiate sports for men and 4 for women. There are 2 intramural teams for men and 2 for women.

Handicapped: There are no special facilities for the physically handicapped.

Graduates: The freshman dropout rate is 25% at the end of the first year; about 40% of those who enter remain to graduate. About 30% of those who graduate pursue further education; 5% go directly into careers in business and industry.

Services: Students receive the following services free of charge: placement, career counseling, health care, psychological counseling, and remedial instruction. Tutoring is available for a fee.

Programs of Study: The college confers the B.A. and B.S. degrees. Associate degree programs are also available. Bachelor's degrees are offered in the following subjects: BUSINESS (business administration), EDUCATION (health/physical), ENGLISH (English), FINE AND PERFORMING ARTS (music), LANGUAGES (Greek/Latin), MATH AND SCIENCES (biology, natural sciences), PHILOSOPHY (religion), PREPROFESSIONAL (ministry), SOCIAL SCIENCES (history, psychology).

Admissions: Ninety-one percent of those who applied were accepted for the 1981-82 freshman class. Applicants should have SAT scores of 400 or better, a 2.0 GPA, and have completed 15 Carnegie units. Other considerations for admission include recommendations from pastors, the candidate's achievement in advanced placement or honors courses, the impression made during the personal interview, and extracurricular activities.

Procedure: The SAT is required; ACT scores are also accepted. The application deadline for the fall semester is August 15; for the spring semester, December 15. There is a $15 nonrefundable application fee. A rolling admissions policy is used.

Special: CLEP is used.

Transfer: For fall 1981, 89 transfer students applied, 82 were accepted, and 48 enrolled. Transfers are accepted for all classes. Applicants must score in the upper 25th percentile on standardized exams. A C average is required. D grades do not transfer. Out of a total of 122 credits required for the bachelor's degree, 24 credits must be completed at Los Angeles Baptist. Transfer deadlines are the same as those for freshman applicants.

Visiting: Regularly scheduled orientations are available for prospective students. Visitors may sit in on classes and stay overnight at the school.

Financial Aid: About 70% of all students are receiving assistance. Forty percent work part-time on campus. Federal government and local bank loans are available. The college participates in EOG; students may receive state scholarships if qualified. The average freshman scholarship is $150; the average freshman loan is $750; the average freshman campus employment income is $750. Tuition may be paid in installments. The FAF or the SAAC is required; the aid application deadline is open.

Foreign Students: Fewer than 1% of the full-time students come from foreign countries.

Admissions: The TOEFL is required; applicants should score a minimum of 450. Standardized college entrance exams are not necessary.

Procedure: Application deadlines for foreign students are April 1 for fall and September 1 for spring. Proof of funds adequate to cover the first year of study is necessary. Health insurance is required; it is available through the college for a fee.

Admissions Contact: Randy Murphy, Admissions Counsellor.

LOYOLA MARYMOUNT UNIVERSITY   C-5
Los Angeles, California 90045   (213) 642-2750

F/T: 1739M, 1977W	Faculty: 209; IIA, ++$
P/T: none	Ph.D.'s: 72%
Grad: 1450M, 1210W	S/F Ratio: 17 to 1
Year: sems, ss	Tuition: $4631
Appl: Aug. 1	R and B: $2216
2308 applied	1562 accepted	708 enrolled
SAT: 460V 490M		COMPETITIVE

Loyola Marymount University, affiliated with the Roman Catholic Church, is the direct successor of southern California's first institution of higher learning. It has 5 divisions: the colleges of Liberal Arts, Business Administration, Fine and Communication Arts, Law, and Science and Engineering. The main campus library houses 191,000 volumes, the law school library 189,000 volumes.

Environment: The modern 100-acre campus is located in a suburban area, 20 miles from the center of Los Angeles; the Law School is in downtown Los Angeles. A 4500-seat sports pavilion was completed in 1982. Residence halls and on-campus apartment complexes give students a choice of life-styles.

Student Life: About 83% of the students are from California; 13% from other states and foreign countries. Forty-five percent reside on campus. Seventy-six percent are Catholic, 9% are Protestant, and 1% are Jewish. About 30% are minority-group members. Campus housing is both single-sex and coed. There are visiting privileges in single-sex housing. Students may keep cars on campus.

Organizations: There are 7 fraternities and 3 sororities, as well as a variety of special-interest clubs and service groups. Extracurricular activities are numerous.

Sports: The university competes on an intercollegiate level in 9 sports for men, 7 for women. There are 9 intramural sports for men and 9 for women.

Handicapped: About 80% of the campus is accessible to wheelchair students. Facilities are limited, but personalized attention is given to the needs of the very small number of disabled students who attend class.

Graduates: Ten percent of the freshmen drop out. Sixty-five percent of those who enter remain to graduate. Thirty-five percent pursue advanced study after graduation.

Services: The university provides career and psychological counseling, placement, and tutorial and remedial instruction services free to all students. Health care is available for a fee.

Programs of Study: The university confers the B.A., B.S., and B.B.A. degrees, as well as master's and J.D. degrees. Bachelor's degrees are offered in the following subjects: AREA STUDIES (Black/Afro-American, urban), BUSINESS (accounting, business administration, finance, international business, management, marketing, personnel/industrial relations), EDUCATION (administrative services, counseling, elementary, secondary, reading specialist), ENGLISH (English), literature), FINE AND PERFORMING ARTS (art, art history, dance, film/photography, music education, radio/TV, studio art, theater/dramatics), LANGUAGES (French, Spanish), MATH AND SCIENCES (biology, chemistry, mathematics, natural sciences, physics), PHILOSOPHY (classics, humanities, philosophy, religion), PREPROFESSIONAL (dentistry, engineering, law, medicine, ministry, pharmacy, veterinary), SOCIAL SCIENCES (economics, government/political science, history, psychology, sociology).

Special: The Encore program is designed to assist the woman who is resuming an interrupted college education. The center for modern Greek studies and the alcohol studies program provide additional opportunities. Interdisciplinary work in women's studies and Los Angeles studies, as well as study abroad and independent study in a broad range of fields are also available. Student-designed majors are permitted. It is possible to earn the B.G.S. degree.

Honors: Loyola Marymount University offers a challenging honors program for the exceptional student. There are 3 national honor societies on campus.

Admissions: About 68% of those who applied were accepted for the 1981-82 freshman class. SAT scores for those who enrolled were as follows: Verbal—67% scored below 500, 24% between 500 and 599, 8% between 600 and 700, and 1% above 700; Math—50% scored below 500, 35% between 500 and 599, 12% between 600 and 700, and 3% above 700. The candidate should have completed 16 Carnegie high school units and have a B or better average. Other considerations in the admissions decision include advanced placement or honors courses, recommendations by school officials, and extracurricular activities record.

Procedure: Either the SAT or the ACT is required. The deadlines for regular admission are August 1 (fall) and January 1 (spring). Freshmen are admitted at midyear. A $25 application fee is charged. Rolling admissions are used.

Special: There are early decision, early admissions, and deferred admissions plans. The deadline for early decision is in December and notification is in early January; early admissions applications must be submitted by August 1. CLEP and AP credit is granted.

Transfer: For fall 1981, 1033 transfer applications were received, 575 accepted, and 391 students enrolled. Generally, a 2.5 GPA is required to apply; D grades do not transfer. A minimum of 30 academic units must be completed at Loyola Marymount, out of a total of 120-136 required for the bachelor's degree. Transfer application deadlines are the same as those for freshmen.

Visiting: Visitors are welcome at the university; weekdays are recommended. Guides are available for informal tours. Prospective students may stay at the school and are invited to take part in regularly scheduled orientations.

Financial Aid: About 68% of the students receive assistance. About 50% work part-time on campus. Average aid to freshmen is $3184. Loans and community-based work-study internships are also available. The university is a member of CSS. The SAAC is required for California students; the FAF for all others. The deadline is March 1 for fall, January 1 for spring. Tuition may be paid in installments.

Foreign Students: Five percent of the full-time students come from foreign countries. The university provides special counseling and organizations.

Admissions: The TOEFL is required; a minimum score of 500 must be achieved. The SAT or ACT is also required.

Procedure: Application deadlines for foreign students are July 1 for fall and December 1 for spring. The deadline for summer session is open. Proof of adequate funds for the upcoming academic year must be shown. The university requires that health insurance be carried; it is available through the university for a fee.

Admissions Contact: M. E. L'Heureux, Director of Admissions.

MENLO COLLEGE
B-3
Menlo Park, California 94025   (415) 323-6141

F/T: 437M, 196W	Faculty:	42; IV, +$
P/T: 5M, 3W	Ph.D.'s:	26%
Grad: none	S/F Ratio:	15 to 1
Year: 4-1-4, ss	Tuition:	$5350
Appl: open	R and B:	$2840
650 applied	429 accepted	216 enrolled
SAT: 409V 451M		COMPETITIVE

Menlo College, established in 1915, is a private, nonsectarian institution. Its School of Business Administration offers bachelor's degrees. The School of Letters and Sciences offers associate degrees in the liberal arts and sciences, and almost all its graduates transfer to 4-year colleges. The library contains 46,000 volumes and subscribes to 300 periodicals.

Environment: The 62-acre campus is located in a suburban area 30 miles from San Francisco. Five residence halls accommodate 350 men and 150 women.

Student Life: About 50% of the students are from California. Sixty percent of the freshmen are graduates of public schools. Three-fourths of the students live in campus housing; unmarried students under age 21 are required to do so unless they live with parents. About 4% of the students are minority-group members. College housing is both single-sex and coed. There are visiting privileges in single-sex housing. Students may keep cars on campus.

Organizations: There is 1 professional fraternity. Extracurricular activities include a drama group, publications, service clubs, student government, and music ensembles. The college sponsors guest speakers, films, drama and music productions, art exhibits, and an annual Spring Festival.

Sports: The college competes on an intercollegiate level in 11 sports for men and 5 for women.

Graduates: Recently, about 20% of the freshmen dropped out during their first year. Ninety-eight percent of the A.A. graduates entered 4-year programs, and 20% of the B.S. graduates pursued further study.

Services: Students receive free placement and career counseling, health services, and guidance.

Programs of Study: The college awards the B.S. degree. Associate degrees are also granted. Bachelor's degrees are offered in business administration, with concentrations in general business, accounting and finance, management, marketing, and public administration. The A.A. degree is awarded with majors in preengineering, physical sciences and mathematics, managerial sciences, biological and premedical sciences, and liberal arts.

Required: Freshmen must take English composition and 2 semesters of physical education. Other core curriculum requirements vary in each major.

Special: Internships and a January interim student exchange with cooperating colleges are offered. The School of Letters and Sciences is a two-year, lower division, transfer program that offers the A.A. degree in liberal arts, business, engineering, mathematics, science, or social sciences.

Honors: Alpha Gamma Sigma and Delta Sigma Pi have chapters on campus.

Admissions: Sixty-six percent of those who applied were accepted for the 1981–82 freshman class. The SAT scores of those who enrolled were as follows: Verbal—87% scored below 500, 11% between 500 and 599, 2% between 600 and 700, and 0% above 700; Math—69% scored below 500, 26% between 500 and 599, 4% between 600 and 700, and 1% above 700. Students must have completed at least 12 Carnegie units at an accredited high school and must present satisfactory SAT or ACT scores. A secondary school record that indicates ability to do college-level work, extracurricular activities, leadership record, and 3 recommendations are among the other important factors.

Procedure: Candidates must take the SAT or ACT by April if possible. An interview is recommended. New students are admitted to any term. Application deadlines are open. Applicants usually are notified within 2 weeks after all credentials are received. A rolling admissions plan is used. The application fee is $20.

Special: Deferred admissions and early decision plans are offered. CLEP and AP credit is accepted.

Transfer: For fall 1981, 90 students applied, 85 were accepted, and 82 enrolled. Transfer students are accepted for all classes. A 2.0 GPA is required. D grades generally transfer. There is a 1-year residency requirement. Students must earn the last 30 units at the college, out of

CALIFORNIA 65

the 124 needed to receive a bachelor's degree. Application deadlines are open.

Financial Aid: About 20% of the students receive aid. Programs include college, state, and National Merit scholarships; BEOG and SEOG; guaranteed student loans; and part-time jobs. The college is a member of CSS. The FAF is required. The college will provide further information on applying.

Foreign Students: Twenty-one percent of the full-time students come from foreign countries. The college offers these students special counseling and special organizations.

Admissions: Foreign students must score 550 on the TOEFL.

Procedure: Application deadlines are July 1 (fall) and December 15 (spring). Foreign students must submit a health examination form. They must also provide proof of funds adequate to cover a full year of study. Foreign students must pay an advance deposit of $1300. They must also carry health insurance, which is available through the college for a fee.

Admissions Contact: Douglas R. Walker, Dean of Admissions.

MILLS COLLEGE
B-3
Oakland, California 94613   (415) 430-2135

F/T: 737W	Faculty:	60; IIA, av$
P/T: 42W	Ph.D.'s:	75%
Grad: 34M, 111W	S/F Ratio:	12 to 1
Year: sems	Tuition:	$5760
Appl: Feb. 1	R and B:	$2850
459 applied	351 accepted	171 enrolled
SAT: 530V 540M		VERY COMPETITIVE

Founded in 1852, Mills College is an independent, liberal arts college for women. The library houses over 185,000 volumes and 7760 microfilm items, and subscribes to over 512 periodicals.

Environment: The 128 wooded acres of urban campus permit students to live in a rural environment while only 25 minutes from San Francisco and 15 minutes from the University of California (Berkeley). Housing for resident students is provided in 6 residence halls on the campus. The campus is a blend of Victorian and Spanish Mediterranean architecture. Notable among campus buildings are several designed by Julia Morgan, an important California architect.

Student Life: About half the students come from outside California. Thirty-two percent of all students are members of minority groups, and about 75% of the entering freshmen come from public schools. It is a requirement that all freshmen reside in college-owned apartments or residence halls, unless they live at home or receive special permission to live elsewhere. Campus housing is single-sex, and visiting privileges are available. Students may keep cars on campus. The college offers day-care services to all students, faculty, and staff for a fee.

Organizations: There are no sororities, but students participate in numerous cultural and social activities, including school newspapers, the yearbook, music and dance, and volunteer service projects.

Sports: Mills competes intercollegiately in 6 sports. Ten intramural sports are offered.

Handicapped: The college has facilities for the handicapped; 75% of the campus is accessible to these students.

Graduates: About 2% of the freshmen drop out for academic reasons; 65% remain to graduate. Sixty percent of the students pursue advanced study after graduation. About 10% enter medical school; 3% enter dental school; and 10% enter law school.

Services: The following free services are offered at the college: placement, career, and psychological counseling; tutoring; and remedial instruction. There are placement services for both undergraduates and graduates of the college. The campus-based career center also sponsors internships with corporations, publications, law firms, and research organizations in the Bay area.

Programs of Study: The college confers bachelor's and master's degrees. Bachelor's degrees are offered in the following subjects: AREA STUDIES (American, ethnic studies), BUSINESS (administration and legal processes, computer science), EDUCATION (child life-specialist, early childhood, elementary, secondary), ENGLISH (English, journalism, literature), FINE AND PERFORMING ARTS (art, art history, communications, dance, music, studio art, theater/dramatics), LANGUAGES (French, German, Spanish), MATH AND SCIENCES (biology, chemistry, mathematics, natural sciences, physical sciences, physics), PHILOSOPHY (philosophy, Western literature), PREPROFESSIONAL (engineering), SOCIAL SCIENCES (anthropology, economics, government/political science, history, international relations, psychology, social sciences, sociology, women's studies).

Required: A student takes at least one-half of all courses in fields other than her major discipline.

Special: Mills students may cross-enroll for up to 1 course per semester at the University of California at Berkeley. There are also many opportunities for students to participate in exchange programs with both domestic and foreign colleges. A 3-2 program in engineering is offered with Stanford University, the University of California at Berkeley, and Boston University. The college also allows student-designed majors.

Honors: Phi Beta Kappa Society has a chapter on campus.

Admissions: About 76% of those who applied were accepted in the 1981-82 freshman class. Freshmen applicants should rank in the upper 30% of their class. Each student should present 16 units of high school work. Other considerations include advanced placement or honors courses, recommendations by high school officials, evidence of special talents, and extracurricular activities record.

Procedure: Applicants must present the SAT and 3 ATs; English Composition is required. The college prefers students to take these tests in December or January of the senior year. It is suggested that applications be filed early in the senior year. The deadlines are February 1 for fall and November 15 for spring. Notification is made in mid-April (fall) and in December (spring). The application fee is $25.

Special: The school has an early decision plan; the notification date for early decision is December 15. Early and deferred admissions plans are also available.

Transfer: For fall 1981, 186 transfer students applied, 137 were accepted, and 95 enrolled. A 2.0 GPA is required (3.0 is recommended). D grades do not transfer. Juniors must be accepted by their major department. Three semesters of resident study are required. Transfer students must complete, at the college, 12 of the 34 semester credits required for the bachelor's degree. Application deadlines are March 1 (fall) and November 15 (spring).

Visiting: There are regularly scheduled orientations for prospective students, including 3 fall overnights for juniors and seniors, several transfer visiting days, and a day program in the spring for sophomores and juniors. There are also guides for informal visits. Visitors may sit in on classes and stay overnight at the school. The college admissions office will arrange visits.

Financial Aid: Scholarship grants are awarded for one year and are renewable. The grants range from $400 to a limited number of full-expense awards. About 55% of all students receive some financial assistance from scholarship grants and loans. Seventy percent of the students work part-time on campus; 54% in work-study programs. There is a deferred payment program. The college belongs to the CSS. Students should file the FAF no later than February 1. Decisions are based on financial need, personal and academic qualifications, and the school's recommendations.

Foreign Students: A total of 113 foreign students are enrolled at the college, which offers these students special organizations, an intensive English course, and an independent English program (ESL), housed on campus through the English Center for International Women.

Admissions: Foreign students must achieve a minimum score of 550 on the TOEFL to qualify for admission. The SAT or ACT is also required.

Procedure: Application deadlines for foreign students are February 1 (fall) and November 15 (spring). Proof of funds adequate to cover 4 years of study is required. Health insurance, while not required, is available through the college for a fee.

Admissions Contact: Gail Berson Weaver, Director of Admissions.

MOUNT ST. MARY'S COLLEGE   C-5
Los Angeles, California 90049   (213) 476-2237

F/T: 11M, 840W	Faculty:	n/av; IIA, --$
P/T: 13M, 150W	Ph.D.'s:	35%
Grad: 29M, 107W	S/F Ratio:	10 to 1
Year: 4-1-4, ss	Tuition:	$4036
Appl: Aug. 1	R and B:	$2300
287 applied	219 accepted	145 enrolled
SAT or ACT: required		COMPETITIVE

Mount St. Mary's College, founded in 1925, is a coeducational, Roman Catholic, liberal arts college conducted under the auspices of the Sisters of St. Joseph of Carondelet. The main library contains over 130,000 volumes and 600 microfilm reels, and subscribes to over 620 periodicals.

Environment: The 71-acre urban campus is divided between 2 locations. The main 4-year Chalon Campus is located in the Brentwood Hills section, and the 2-year associate degree and graduate degree Doheny Branch Campus is located in the heart of Los Angeles. There are 16 buildings including 3 residence halls accommodating 320 women.

Student Life: About 85% of the students come from California. Fifty percent are graduates of Catholic schools and 50% are from public and private schools. About 50% of undergraduates live on campus. Approximately 65% of the students are Catholic. Thirty-eight percent of the students are minority-group members. Campus housing is single-sex; there are visiting privileges. Curfew for resident students is an individual arrangement involving the parents and student. Students may keep cars on campus.

Organizations: There are 2 sororities, various clubs, and religious groups providing outside activities. The student government also provides many social and cultural activities on campus.

Sports: Intramural sports programs are offered.

Graduates: Twenty percent of the freshmen drop out by the end of the first year; 50% remain to graduate. About 20% of those who graduate become candidates for graduate degrees and/or teaching credentials.

Services: The following free services are offered by the college: placement, career and psychological counseling; tutoring; remedial instruction; and health care.

Programs of Study: The college confers the B.A., B.S., B.M., and B.F.A., as well as associate and master's degrees. Bachelor's degrees are offered in the following subjects: AREA STUDIES (American), BUSINESS (accounting, business administration, management, marketing, real estate/insurance), EDUCATION (early childhood, elementary), ENGLISH (English), FINE AND PERFORMING ARTS (art, music, music education, studio art), HEALTH SCIENCES (medical technology, nursing, physical therapy), LANGUAGES (French, Spanish), MATH AND SCIENCES (biochemistry, biology, chemistry, mathematics), PHILOSOPHY (philosophy, religion), PREPROFESSIONAL (dentistry, law, medicine), SOCIAL SCIENCES (government/political science, history, psychology, social sciences, sociology).

Required: Students seeking the B.A. must complete 27 units in general studies, as well as a foreign language, and philosophy along with 3 courses in religious studies.

Special: Qualified students may study abroad, earn credits through independent study and research, and take experience-oriented courses, including social action.

Honors: There are 8 honor societies open to qualified students as well as departmental honors programs.

Admissions: About 76% of those who applied were accepted for the 1981-82 freshman class. The candidate should have 15 Carnegie units. Advanced placement or honors courses, recommendations, impressions made during interview, and personality are also important.

Procedure: Either the SAT or ACT is required. Applications should be submitted by August 1 (fall), December 1 (winter), or January 1 (spring), along with a $25 fee. Admissions are made on a rolling basis.

Special: Early and deferred admissions plans are available. AP is used.

Transfer: For fall 1981, 512 transfer students applied, 384 were accepted, and 198 enrolled. The applicant's high school record and a minimum 2.25 GPA are required. D grades transfer. At least 30 of the 129 credits required for the bachelor's degree must be taken in residence. Application deadlines are the same as those for freshmen.

Visiting: Visits can be arranged through the admissions office.

Financial Aid: About 63% of all students receive some form of financial aid; 25% work part-time on campus. The college is a member of CSS. Scholarships and loans are available. The FAF should be filed; the application deadline for financial aid is March 1.

Foreign Students: Foreign students constitute about 4% of the student body. There are special organizations for these students.

Admissions: Foreign students must achieve a minimum score of 550 on the TOEFL. College entrance exams are not required.

Procedure: Application deadlines are June 1 (fall), November 1 (winter), and December 1 (spring). Foreign students must present proof of funds adequate to cover the entire period of study. They must also carry health insurance, which is available through the college.

Admissions Contact: Sr. Helen Oswald, Director of Admissions.

NATIONAL UNIVERSITY
San Diego, California 92108
D-5
(714) 563-7200

F/T: 1553M, 836W
P/T: 904M, 547W
Grad: 1705M, 688W
Year: qrts, ss
Appl: open
900 applied 750 accepted 590 enrolled
SAT or ACT: not required LESS COMPETITIVE
Faculty: 36; IIA, –$
Ph.D.'s: 70%
S/F Ratio: 25 to 1
Tuition: $4130
R and B: n/app

National University, founded in 1971, is a private, nonprofit institution offering higher education opportunities to career-oriented adults. The programs are offered in locations close to home or work. Both undergraduate and graduate degrees are offered. The library contains 35,000 volumes and 6000 microfiche items, and subscribes to 700 periodicals.

Environment: The 15-acre main campus is woven into an urban environment and located 2 miles from downtown San Diego. Other centers are located throughout the greater San Diego area. There are no residential facilities.

Student Life: All students commute. The average age of students is 34. About 28% of the students are minority-group members.

Organizations: There are no fraternities or sororities on campus, but 10 extracurricular activities are available to students. One or 2 cultural events take place on campus each week.

Sports: The college offers no athletic activities.

Handicapped: Special facilities are available for the handicapped and include wheelchair ramps, parking areas, elevators, lowered drinking fountains, and specially equipped rest rooms. The entire campus is accessible to wheelchair students.

Graduates: Twenty-one percent of the undergrads drop out by the end of their first year; 64% remain to graduate. Fifty-three percent go on to graduate study. Two percent enter law school. About 94% already pursue careers in business and industry.

Services: The following free services are available on campus: placement for both graduates and undergraduates and career counseling. Tutoring and remedial instruction are available on a fee basis.

Programs of Study: The university offers the B.B.A., B.A., B.P.A., and B.S. degrees. Associate and master's programs are also available. Bachelor's degrees are offered in the following subjects: BUSINESS (accounting, business administration, computer science, real estate/insurance), EDUCATION (interdisciplinary studies), HEALTH SCIENCES (nursing, occupational health and safety), SOCIAL SCIENCES (behavioral science, criminal justice). Sixty-five percent of the degrees conferred are in business.

Special: Students may earn college credit by examination.

Admissions: Eighty-three percent of those who applied were accepted for the 1981–82 class. Applicants must be high school graduates and show evidence of leadership potential and good character. National does not admit a freshman class. Special emphasis is placed on the recruitment of minority and disadvantaged students. The candidate should have a high school GPA of at least 2.0. Students who enroll generally are expected to have 5 or more years of successful work experience. A resume, vita, or similar document is helpful. A personal interview is required.

Procedure: Neither the SAT nor the ACT is required. CLEP scores, college transcripts, or other documents should be submitted. High school transcripts, GED test scores (45 average, none below 35), and state proficiency certificates should also be submitted. The application deadline is open. There is a rolling admissions plan. A half-refundable application fee of $20 must be submitted with the application.

Transfer: Most students have transferred. A 2.0 average is required. D grades do not transfer. Students must study at the university a minimum of 9 months and complete 45 of the 180 quarter hours needed to receive a bachelor's degree. Application deadlines are open.

Visiting: Guides are available for informal visits.

Financial Aid: Seventy percent of the students are receiving aid. All departments have access to federal work-study funds. Scholarships are also available. Average aid to undergraduates from all sources is $4500. Tuition may be paid on the installment plan. The university is a member of CSS. The FAF should be submitted. The deadline for aid application is open.

Foreign Students: About 6% of the full-time students come from foreign countries. The university offers these students special counseling.

CALIFORNIA 67

Admissions: Foreign students must score 450 on the TOEFL. They can substitute a personal interview and their prior U.S. college record. No college entrance examination is required.

Procedure: Application deadlines are open. Foreign students must present proof of funds adequate to cover 1 year of study. There is a special admissions fee of $100 for foreign students.

Admissions Contact: Fred Huber, Dean of Students.

NEW COLLEGE OF CALIFORNIA
San Francisco, California 94110
B-3
(415) 626-1694

F/T: 100M, 200W
P/T: 10M, 20W
Grad: 20M, 20W
Year: tri, ss
Appl: Aug. 31
200 applied 200 accepted 175 enrolled
SAT, ACT: not required NONCOMPETITIVE
Faculty: 20; n/av
Ph.D.'s: 50%
S/F Ratio: 17 to 1
Tuition: $2720
R and B: n/app

The New College of California, founded in 1971, is a private, nonsectarian liberal arts institution. Small, alternative, and unique, the college offers programs of individualized education with emphasis on independent study and active student participation in all phases of the educational process. The library contains over 6500 volumes and subscribes to over 130 periodicals.

Environment: The college, located in the city of San Francisco, is housed in a 20,000-square-foot building that contains a theater with a pipe organ, the library, and classrooms. An historic, Spanish-style building contains the law school. The college has no dormitories; students live in apartments or private homes. The college estimates room and board expenses at $4500 per year.

Student Life: About half the students are from California; the remainder come from throughout the United States and the world. Twenty-eight percent are minority-group members. Students may keep cars on campus.

Organizations: There are no fraternities or sororities. A student activity council schedules activities and sponsors campus groups. Additional cultural and recreational resources are available throughout the San Francisco Bay area. Students are encouraged to serve on all administrative committees and all school committees.

Handicapped: About half the campus is accessible to physically handicapped students. Wheelchair ramps are provided, and special class scheduling can be arranged. No students with impaired vision or hearing were registered in 1981.

Graduates: Five percent of the freshmen drop out by the end of the first year; 50% remain to graduate. About 35% of the graduates seek advanced degrees, including 2% who enter law school.

Services: Students receive free placement and career counseling, tutoring, and remedial instruction. Placement services also are available to graduates.

Programs of Study: The college confers the B.A. degree. Associate and master's degree programs are also offered. Students may study, but are not limited to, subjects in the following areas: education, English language and literature, the fine and performing arts (art, dance, music, tai chi, theater/dramatics, TV, yoga), biology and chemistry, humanities, law, medical technology, philosophy, and such social sciences as anthropology, government and political science, history, psychology, sociology, and women's studies.

Special: Students may design their own majors. Internships may be arranged in local banks, hospitals, real estate firms, drug-rehabilitation centers, prisons, city commissions, and other organizations. Courses are graded on a credit/non-credit basis, and students receive written evaluations of their work. They may request grades in specific courses. Credit for independent study and life experience is offered. College programs also include a Weekend College for Working Adults.

Admissions: All applicants for the 1981–82 freshman class were accepted. Admissions are open; no entrance exams are required. The average applicant's GPA is 3.0; the average score on the verbal portion of the SAT is 520. Admissions officers also consider impressions made during an interview, personality, evidence of special talents, recommendations by high school officials, leadership record, extracurricular activities, advanced placement or honors courses, and desire to be responsible for one's own education.

Procedure: Application deadlines are August 31 (fall), December 31 (spring), and May 20 (summer). Applications should be submitted with a $25 fee.

Special: Early decision and early and deferred admissions plans are available. AP and CLEP credit is accepted.

68 CALIFORNIA

Transfer: For fall 1981, the 58 transfer students who applied were accepted and enrolled. Applicants for transfer are evaluated by the same criteria as freshmen. Application deadlines also are the same as those for freshmen.

Visiting: Informal visits may be arranged for any time, by appointment, with the admissions office. Guides are provided, and visitors may sit in on classes.

Financial Aid: Ninety percent of the students receive aid through the college; 40% work part-time on campus. Tuition may be paid in installments. The college is a member of CSS and requires aid applicants to submit the FAF or SAAC. Awards are granted primarily on the basis of need; preference is given to women and minority students. Deadlines for financial aid applications are April 15 (fall) and November 25 (spring).

Foreign Students: Eleven percent of the students come from foreign countries. The college offers these students an intensive English course and special counseling.

Admissions: The college requires that foreign students achieve a minimum score of 500 on the TOEFL. No entrance exams are required.

Procedure: Application deadlines are the same as those for other freshmen. Foreign students must present a doctor's statement as proof of health. They must also provide proof of funds adequate to cover the first semester of study.

Admissions Contact: Mark Feldman, Director of Admissions.

NORTHROP UNIVERSITY   C-5
Inglewood, California 90306   (213) 641-3470

F/T: 1260M, 125W	Faculty: 66; IIA, — — $
P/T: 139M, 18W	Ph.D.'s: 20%
Grad: 265M, 81W	S/F Ratio: 20 to 1
Year: qtrs	Tuition: $4785
Appl: open	R and B: $3000
700 applied	600 accepted	300 enrolled
SAT: 390V 510M	ACT: 19	COMPETITIVE

Northrop University, founded in 1942, is a private, coeducational college of engineering and technology. The 3-story library contains approximately 250,000 volumes and 52,225 microfilm items, and subscribes to 289 periodicals.

Environment: The campus consists of 20 buildings on approximately 18 acres in a suburban area southwest of Los Angeles. Buildings include an 8-story residence hall accommodating 600 men and women, and a classroom and engineering laboratory building.

Student Life: Twenty percent of the students are from California, 20% are from other states, and 50% are from foreign countries. About 34% are minority-group members. This is largely a commuter school; 20% of the students live on campus in the dormitory and 1 fraternity house. Campus housing is coed. Students may keep cars on campus.

Organizations: Student life is centered around the activities in professional societies and several social and hobby clubs. About 5% of the men belong to fraternities. The university has no religious affiliation, but there are religious organizations on campus and facilities nearby for Catholic, Protestant, and Muslim students. Through the student council, the residence hall association, and student-faculty committee, undergraduates participate in student government and administration and curriculum matters.

Sports: The university does not compete on an intercollegiate level. There are 2 intramural sports for men.

Handicapped: Ninety-five percent of the campus is accessible to wheelchair students. Special parking, wheelchair ramps, elevators, and specially equipped rest rooms are available. A special counselor is assigned to handicapped students. Special class scheduling is also offered.

Graduates: The freshman dropout rate is 25%; 30% remain to graduate. Twenty percent pursue advanced study after graduation. About eighty percent of each graduating class enter business and industry.

Services: Students receive placement and career counseling free of charge. Placement services for undergraduates include resume preparation, on campus interviews, off-campus interviews, cooperative education, and international placement. Health care, tutoring, and remedial instruction are available for a fee.

Programs: The university confers the B.S. degree. Programs leading to associate, master's, and doctoral degrees are also offered. Bachelor's degrees are offered in the following subjects: BUSINESS (business administration, computer science), PREPROFESSIONAL (engineering—aerospace, engineering—aircraft maintenance, engineering—electronic, engineering—general, engineering—mechanical).

Required: There is a required core curriculum for all students.

Special: An interdisciplinary design program is offered at the senior level. There is a 40-week course offered through the Institute of Technology leading to the FCC First Class Radio Telephone License with radar endorsement; this is a license to perform the basic tasks required of an avionics technician. Also offered is a 6-week course designed for graduates of the Airframe and Powerplant program, certified A&P Technicians, or individuals having previous experience in the helicopter industry. There are modular technology programs of 6, 24, 40, 58, and 60 weeks which lead to A.A., A.S., and B.S. degree programs in aircraft technology. Northrop offers courses in English as a second language on all levels from beginning to graduate level proficiency. In addition, special courses are offered in English for aircraft technicians, English for engineers, and English for business and management.

Honors: There is an honors program in mathematics; 4 honor societies have chapters on campus.

Admissions: Eighty-six percent of those who applied were accepted for the 1981-82 freshman class. The SAT scores of those who enrolled were as follows: Verbal—94% scored below 500, 5% between 500 and 599, 1% between 600 and 700, and 0% above 700; Math—40% scored below 500, 50% between 500 and 599, 10% between 600 and 700, and 0% above 700. On the ACT, 40% scored below 21, 50% between 21 and 23, 10% between 24 and 25, and 0% above 25. Candidates must have a C average. Other considerations are advanced placement or honors courses, recommendations by school officials, and extracurricular activities record.

Procedure: The SAT or ACT is required and may be taken in May of the junior year or December of the senior year. An interview on or off campus is strongly recommended. The deadlines for filing applications are open; recommended deadlines are September 15 (fall), December 15 (winter), March 15 (spring), and June 15 (summer). Notification of acceptance is sent as soon as all credentials are complete. Admissions are on a rolling basis. There is a $25 application fee.

Special: There are early decision and early admissions plans. AP and CLEP credit is accepted.

Transfer: For fall 1981, Northrop received 65 transfer applications, accepted 58, and enrolled 30 students. Transfers are accepted to all but the senior class. A 2.0 GPA is necessary; there is a 1-year residency requirement. Transfers must complete at least 60 quarter hours at Northrop. From 136 to 196 quarter hours are required for the bachelor's degree. Deadlines are open. Transfers are admitted to the fall, winter, spring, and summer quarters.

Visiting: Although orientation is not regularly scheduled, students may visit the campus any time. Arrangements should be made through the career center. Visitors may sit in on classes and remain overnight on campus.

Financial Aid: About 25% of all students receive some form of financial aid. Twenty-five percent work part-time on campus. The university participates in the United Aid Fund, EOG, and NDSL programs. It also has its own tuition loan plan. Northrop is a member of the CSS and awards freshman scholarships each year. After acceptance for admission, the student should submit the aid application form and records. The FAF, FFS, or SFS is required, and should be filed by April 30.

Foreign Students: About 50% of the full-time students come from foreign countries. The university offers these students an intensive English program, special counseling, and special organizations.

Admissions: Foreign applicants are required to take Northrop's placement exam as evidence of English proficiency. Standardized college entrance exams are not necessary.

Procedure: There are no application deadlines; admissions are on a rolling basis. Foreign students are admitted to the fall, winter, spring, and summer quarters. The university requires that proof of health and of funds adequate to cover 1 year of study be presented. Health insurance must be carried; it is available through the university for a fee.

Admissions Contact: Judson W. Staples, Director of Admissions and Records.

OCCIDENTAL COLLEGE   C-5
Los Angeles, California 90041   (213) 259-2700

F/T: 830M, 775W	Faculty: n/av; IIA, +$
P/T: none	Ph.D.'s: 88%
Grad: 12M, 11W	S/F Ratio: 12 to 1
Year: tri, ss	Tuition: $6825
Appl: Feb. 1	R and B: $3000
1604 applied	937 accepted	420 enrolled
SAT: 570V 600M		HIGHLY COMPETITIVE

Occidental College, founded in 1887 under Presbyterian auspices, is a nonsectarian college of liberal arts and science. The library contains 450,000 volumes and 50,000 government serial publications, and subscribes to 11,000 periodicals.

Environment: This moderate-sized college occupies 120 acres in northeastern Los Angeles. Thirteen residence halls accommodate 1250 students. The campus is constructed on 4 tiers: the lowest contains athletic facilities; the second contains the main quad; the third contains administration and science buildings, and the fourth contains dormitories and Hillside Theater. In celebration of its centennial, Occidental hopes to complete approximately $20 million of campus construction by 1987. This construction includes a refurbished main classroom building, a new performing arts center, a new fine arts center, a new dormitory and parking structure, and new athletic facilities to be used in conjunction with the 1984 Olympics to be held in Los Angeles.

Student Life: Sixty percent of the students come from California; the others come from about 45 states and 35 foreign countries.

Organizations: There are 3 national fraternities and 3 local sororities to which approximately 10% of the students belong. Extracurricular activities are numerous.

Sports: Intercollegiate and intramural sports for men and women include football, basketball, baseball, track, swimming, golf, cross country, ice hockey, water polo, tennis, soccer, rugby, lacrosse, skiing and sailing. Volleyball and softball are also offered.

Handicapped: There are no facilities for the physically handicapped. One percent of the students have hearing impairments.

Graduates: The average freshman dropout rate is 5% with more than 70% remaining until graduation. Of these, between 65% and 75% go on for advanced study; about 7% enter medical school, 1% enter dental school, and 8% enter law school.

Services: Students receive the following services free of charge: placement, career counseling, health care, and psychological counseling.

Programs of Study: The college awards the B.A. degree. Master's degrees are also awarded. Bachelor's degrees are offered in the following subjects: AREA STUDIES (American, Russian, urban), EDUCATION (elementary, secondary), ENGLISH (English, literature, speech), FINE AND PERFORMING ARTS (art, art education, art history, film/photography, music, music education, radio/TV, studio art, theater/dramatics), LANGUAGES (Chinese, French, German, Japanese, Russian, Spanish), MATH AND SCIENCES (biochemistry, biology, botany, chemistry, geology, mathematics, oceanography, physics), PHILOSOPHY (philosophy, religion), PREPROFESSIONAL (dentistry, law, medicine, ministry, pharmacy, social work, veterinary), SOCIAL SCIENCES (anthropology, economics, government/political science, history, international relations, psychology, social sciences, sociology). Seventy percent of degrees conferred are in social sciences, 16% are in preprofessional studies, and 13% are in math and sciences.

Required: Students must fulfill a core curriculum which mandates course selection in 8 different areas. Proficiency in a foreign language must be demonstrated by passing a written exam and comprehensive exams in the chosen field of study must also be passed to graduate.

Special: Student-designed majors are permitted. A B.G.S. degree is offered. The college operates its own marine research vessel, the *Vantuna*. Students may participate in a 3-2 engineering program in cooperation with California Institute of Technology or Columbia University; this program leads to the B.A.-B.S. degrees, or a B.A.-M.S. combination for students who wish to accelerate. Off-campus study programs include Urban Studies, Washington, D.C. Semester, Model United Nations, Crossroads Africa, and junior year abroad. A special program for freshmen (Collegium) is a year-long course jointly taught by the faculty of all 3 academic divisions.

Honors: Phi Beta Kappa and Sigma Xi are open to students.

Admissions: Fifty-eight percent of those who applied were accepted for the 1981-82 freshman class. The candidate should be in the upper fifth of the class. The school indicates that in addition to a strong academic program and class rank, the following qualifications are considered in order of their importance: recommendations by school officials, advanced placement or honor courses, extracurricular activities record, leadership record, impressions made during an interview, and evidence of special talents.

Procedure: The college requires the SAT and suggests that the applicants take the PSAT in the junior year and the SAT in their senior year. Achievement tests are strongly recommended. Applications should be filed by February 1 for the fall term and May 1 for the summer session. Freshmen are admitted to the fall term only. The application fee is $30.

Special: Early decisions are made; candidates for early decision should file by November 15. Early and deferred admissions are possible.

Transfer: About 125 transfer students are accepted annually. A minimum GPA of 2.5 is required, although most successful candidates have 3.0 or better. D grades do transfer. All students must complete, at the college, 17 of the 35 courses required for a bachelor's degree. The deadlines are July 1 (fall), March 1 (spring), and December 1 (winter).

Visiting: Guided tours and interviews can be scheduled weekdays through the admissions office. Visitors may sit in on classes and remain overnight.

Financial Aid: About 63% of all students receive some financial aid. The average freshman award is $5600. Loans are available through the FISL program with the college acting as the lender. Loan funds are unlimited. The college is a member of the CSS and permits students to pay tuition in installments. Financial aid applications should be filed no later than February 1 for regular candidates and November 15 for early decision candidates. The FAF or Student Aid Application for California (SAAC) is required.

Foreign Students: Four percent of the full-time students come from foreign countries. Special organizations are available for these students.

Admissions: Foreign students must achieve a TOEFL score of at least 600. No college entrance exams are required.

Procedure: The application deadline for fall entry is February 1. Foreign students must present a completed medical form and proof of funds adequate to cover 1 year of study. Health insurance is required and is available through the college for a fee.

Admissions Contact: Joe S. Disbennett, Assistant Director of Admissions.

PACIFIC UNION COLLEGE B-2
Angwin, California 94508 (707) 965-6336

F/T: 841M, 860W	Faculty:	117; IIA, −−$
P/T: 111M, 150W	Ph.D.'s:	38%
Grad: 9M, 13W	S/F Ratio:	13 to 1
Year: qtrs, ss	Tuition:	$4275
Appl: open	R and B:	$2025
966 applied	741 accepted	641 enrolled
ACT: required		COMPETITIVE

Pacific Union College, an affiliate of the Seventh-Day Adventist Church, offers programs in liberal arts, business, and teacher preparation. As a church-related institution, the college places great emphasis on the role of religion in the personal lives of students. The library has 103,782 volumes and 12,903 microfilm items, and subscribes to 765 periodicals.

Environment: The college is located in a rural area, 75 miles from San Francisco. The campus consists of 1800 acres of mountainous woodland, some 200 acres of which are improved for college activities. Residence halls accommodate 773 women and 661 men. Married-student housing also is available.

Student Life: About 82% of the students are residents of California. About 68% live in the dormitories. Eighteen percent are members of minority groups. The majority of the students are members of the Seventh-day Adventist Church and all are expected to attend religious services. Dormitories are single-sex, and there are no visiting privileges. Students may keep cars on campus. Gambling, alcohol, and tobacco are prohibited. The college does not tolerate the dissemination of atheistic or disloyal ideas that undermine the religious ideals of the institution. Day-care services are provided to students for a fee.

Organizations: There are no fraternities or sororities.

Sports: Six intramural sports are offered for men and women.

Handicapped: About 10% of the campus is accessible to handicapped students. Wheelchair ramps are provided. A counselor is available to handicapped students.

Graduates: About 34% of the freshmen drop out by the end of their first year; 25% remain to graduate. Twenty-seven percent of the graduates seek advanced degrees; 9% enter medical school, 8% enter dental school, and 1% enter law school.

Services: Students receive free placement, career and psychological counseling, health care, tutoring, and remedial instruction.

Programs of Study: The B.A., B.S., B.Mus., B.B.A., B.S.Med.Tech., and B.S.W. degrees are conferred. Associate and master's degrees are also awarded. Bachelor's degrees are offered in the following subjects: BUSINESS (accounting, business administration, business education, computer science, management), EDUCATION (elementary, health/physical, industrial, secondary), ENGLISH (English, journalism, speech), FINE AND PERFORMING ARTS (advertising design, art, art

70 CALIFORNIA

education, music, music education, studio art), HEALTH SCIENCES (medical technology, nursing, speech therapy), LANGUAGES (Spanish), MATH AND SCIENCES (biochemistry, biology, botany, chemistry, ecology/environmental science, mathematics, natural sciences, physical sciences, physics, zoology), PHILOSOPHY (humanities, religion), PREPROFESSIONAL (architecture, dentistry, engineering, law, medicine, social work, veterinary), SOCIAL SCIENCES (economics, government/political science, history, psychology, social studies, sociology). Fifteen percent of degrees are conferred in business, 13% in philosophy, and 13% in social sciences.

Required: All students must take 18 hours of religion and 6 hours of health and physical education.

Special: Students may design their own majors. The college offers the B.G.S. degree. Second-year students may participate in the Adventist Colleges Abroad program, which is offered as part of the regular curriculum.

Admissions: Seventy-seven percent of those who applied were accepted for the 1981–82 freshman class. The minimum high school GPA accepted is 2.5. The school also considers previous academic performance, recommendations by school officials, ability to finance a college education, and results of a personal interview. It is advisable for candidates to arrange for an interview with a college representative, either on campus or at home.

Procedure: The ACT is required for placement purposes. Applications should be filed 3 months before enrollment, but deadlines are open. Freshmen are admitted to all quarters. There is a $10 application fee.

Special: CLEP and AP credit is accepted.

Transfer: For fall 1981, 345 transfer students applied, 266 were accepted, and 219 enrolled. Applicants should have a GPA of 2.5 or better and submit ACT scores. At least 36 of the 192 credits required for a bachelor's degree must be earned on campus. Application deadlines are the same as those for freshmen.

Visiting: Guided tours and interviews may be scheduled on weekdays. There also are regularly scheduled orientations for prospective students. Visitors may sit in on classes and stay overnight at the school. The dean of students' office or the college relations office should be contacted for arrangements.

Financial Aid: About 66% of the students receive financial aid; 62% work part-time on campus. Aid is available mainly in the form of federal loans and grants. The SAAC is required and should be filed by April 1.

Foreign Students: The 83 full-time foreign students enrolled at the college make up 4% of its enrollment. The college provides these students with a special English course and special counseling.

Admissions: Foreign applicants must score 500 or better on the TOEFL, or in the 80th percentile or higher on the University of Michigan Language Test. They also must take the ACT.

Procedure: Application deadlines are open. Students must present proof of health and of adequate funds. The college provides health insurance.

Admissions Contact: C. T. Smith, Jr., Director of Admissions.

PEPPERDINE UNIVERSITY C–5
Malibu, California 90265 (213) 456-4391

F/T: 990M, 1182W	Faculty: 94; IIA, + + $
P/T: 104M, 102W	Ph.D.'s: 85%
Grad: 44M, 39W	S/F Ratio: 21 to 1
Year: tri, ss	Tuition: $5903
Appl: Apr. 1	R and B: $2780
1850 applied	1160 accepted 623 enrolled
SAT: 478V 502M	ACT:23 COMPETITIVE+

Pepperdine University, founded in 1937, is an independent liberal arts institution affiliated with the Church of Christ. The library contains 374,500 volumes and subscribes to 2145 periodicals.

Environment: The university has 2 campuses. The 819-acre suburban campus in Malibu is the site of Seaver College, which is the undergraduate school, and of the school of law. Its 7 buildings include a chapel, a science complex, and a theater. Students live in 23 resident houses, each of which accommodates 50 persons. The second campus, in Los Angeles, houses the graduate schools of Business and Education in 21 buildings on 34 acres. Only graduate programs are offered here.

Student Life: Sixty percent of the students at the Malibu campus are from California. About 65% of the freshmen are graduates of public schools. Sixty percent of the students live on campus. Twenty-five percent of the students are Catholic, 60% Protestant, and 6% Jewish; 4% belong to other denominations; and 5% claim no religious affiliation. About 24% of the students are minority-group members. University housing is single-sex; there are visiting privileges. Students may keep cars on campus. Drinking is prohibited on campus, and smoking is permitted only in specified areas. Students must attend one chapel-convocation each week.

Organizations: Local social clubs take the place of fraternities or sororities. Extracurricular activities include religious groups, drama, music, debate, publications, and student government. The campus is 2 miles from the Malibu pier and beach.

Sports: The university fields intercollegiate teams in 7 sports for men and 3 for women. There are 14 intramural sports for men and 13 for women.

Handicapped: One hundred percent of the campus is accessible to wheelchair-bound students. Facilities include wheelchair ramps, special parking areas, elevators, and specially equipped rest rooms.

Services: Students receive the following free services: placement, career and psychological counseling and health care. Tutoring and some health care are available on a fee basis. Placement services are available to graduates.

Programs of Study: The university awards the B.A. and B.S. degrees. Master's, doctoral, and law degrees also are available. Bachelor's degrees are offered in the following subjects: BUSINESS (accounting, business administration, computer science, finance, management, marketing), EDUCATION (elementary, physical/kinesiology, recreation, secondary), ENGLISH (English, journalism, literature), FINE AND PERFORMING ARTS (art, music, radio/TV, theater/dramatics), HEALTH SCIENCES (sports medicine), LANGUAGES (French, German, Spanish), MATH AND SCIENCES (biology, chemistry, mathematics, natural sciences), PHILOSOPHY (humanities, human values, philosophy, religion), PREPROFESSIONAL (home economics, social work), SOCIAL SCIENCES (economics, government/political science, history, psychology, social sciences, sociology, youth agency administration).

Required: Undergraduates must take 4 trimesters of physical education. They also must complete the basic interdisciplinary program, which requires 4 courses in humanities, 3 in social sciences, 2 in natural sciences, 3 in communications, and 2 in religion.

Special: Sophomores, juniors, and seniors may spend a year in Heidelberg, Germany, studying European history and culture.

Honors: Six national honor societies are represented on campus.

Admissions: About 63% of those who applied were accepted for the 1981–82 freshman class. The SAT scores of those who enrolled were as follows: Verbal—60% scored below 500, 30% between 500 and 599, 9% between 600 and 700, and 1% above 700; Math—49% scored below 500, 37% between 500 and 599, 12% between 600 and 700, and 2% above 700. On the ACT, 24% scored below 21, 35% between 21 and 23, 26% between 24 and 25, 11% between 26 and 28, and 4% above 28. Applicants must have an average of B or better, graduate from high school, rank in the upper half of their graduating class, have completed 15 Carnegie units, and score at least 400 on each section of the SAT. Admissions officers also consider advanced placement or honors courses, leadership record, extracurricular activities, recommendations by high school officials, personality, impressions made during an interview, and evidence of special talents.

Procedure: Applicants should take the SAT or ACT as early as possible. Application deadlines are April 1 (fall), November 15 (winter), and March 15 (spring). The application fee is $25.

Special: An early decision plan is offered. AP and CLEP credit is accepted.

Transfer: For fall 1981, 325 students applied, 270 were accepted, and 165 enrolled. Transfers must have a GPA of at least 2.5 to be admitted. D grades do not transfer. Transfer students must spend 1 year in residence and complete the last 28 semester hours of the 128 needed to receive a bachelor's degree. Application deadlines are the same as those for freshman applicants.

Visiting: Prospective students may schedule weekday guided tours and interviews with the admissions office. Visitors may sit in on classes.

Financial Aid: Sixty percent of the students receive aid. Thirty-five percent work part-time on campus. Scholarships range from $800 to $5600. Special achievement awards of $800 to $5000 are available in art, journalism, music, speech, and physical education. The university is a member of the CSS. Aid candidates must submit the FAF. The aid application deadlines are April 1 (fall), October 15 (winter), and February 15 (spring).

Foreign Students: Eleven percent of the full-time students come from foreign countries. The university offers these students an intensive English course, special counseling, and special organizations.

Admissions: Foreign students must score 550 on the TOEFL. They must take the SAT or the ACT if attending a U.S. high school.

Procedure: Application deadlines are July 1 (fall), November 1 (winter), and March 1 (spring). Foreign students must present proof of funds adequate to cover 1 year of study and must prepay $5000 of these costs.

Admissions Contact: Robert L. Fraley, Dean of Admissions.

POINT LOMA COLLEGE D-5
San Diego, California 92120   (714) 222-6474

F/T: 618M, 864W	Faculty: n/av; IIA, –$
P/T: 55M, 44W	Ph.D.'s: 60%
Grad: 89M, 138W	S/F Ratio: 18 to 1
Year: qtrs, ss	Tuition: $3402
Appl: open	R and B: $1665
1084 applied	1013 accepted 372 enrolled
SAT: required	LESS COMPETITIVE

Point Loma College, founded in 1902 as Pasadena College, is a church-related liberal arts college affiliated with the Church of the Nazarene. Its library contains 162,000 volumes and 3217 microfilm items, and subscribes to 669 periodicals.

Environment: The 88-acre campus is woven into a suburban environment and consists of 36 buildings. Six dormitories and one apartment unit house 120 students.

Student Life: Eighty-five percent of the students are from California and 11% from bordering states. About 68% of the students live on campus and 31% at home. Ninety percent of the entering freshmen attended public schools. About 13% of the students are members of minority groups. Ninety percent are Protestant; 7% are Catholic. Dormitories are single-sex; there are no visiting privileges. Students may keep cars on campus. Attendance at chapel services is compulsory 3 days per week. Drinking on campus is forbidden. All students must observe a curfew.

Organizations: There are no social fraternities or sororities, but the college sponsors extracurricular activities. The most active are the Circle K Club, Kappa Phi Kappa, and the Viking Ski Club.

Sports: The college competes on an intercollegiate level in 7 sports for men and 6 for women. Four intramural sports are offered for men and women.

Handicapped: About 50% of the campus is accessible to wheelchair-bound students. The college provides wheelchair ramps and special parking.

Graduates: About 10% of the freshmen drop out by the end of the first year, and 35% remain to graduate. Of those, 70% become candidates for graduate or professional degrees. About 10% enter medical school and 3% enter dental school. Twenty-five percent pursue careers in business and industry.

Services: Placement and career counseling are provided free. Fees are charged for tutoring, some remedial instruction, and psychological counseling, and for all health care. Placement services also are available to graduates.

Programs of Study: The college confers the B.A. and B.S. degrees. Master's degrees also are conferred. Bachelor's degrees are offered in the following subjects: BUSINESS (accounting, business administration, business education, computer science), EDUCATION (early childhood, elementary, secondary, special), ENGLISH (English, literature, speech), FINE AND PERFORMING ARTS (art, art education, art history, music, music education, theater/dramatics), HEALTH SCIENCES (medical technology, nursing, speech therapy), LANGUAGES (French, German, Greek/Latin, Hebrew, Spanish), MATH AND SCIENCES (biochemistry, biology, chemistry, mathematics, physics), PHILOSOPHY (philosophy, religion), PREPROFESSIONAL (dentistry, engineering, home economics, law, medicine, ministry, social work), SOCIAL SCIENCES (economics, government/political science, history, psychology, sociology). Twenty-five percent of degrees conferred are in business, 25% in education, and 15% in health sciences.

Required: All undergraduates are required to take courses in English composition, literature, natural science, social science, the arts, and religion.

Special: The college offers a B.G.S. degree. Students are permitted to spend the sophomore year abroad on their own or to participate in an established study-abroad program sponsored by another college.

Admissions: Ninety-three percent of those who applied were accepted for the 1981–82 freshman class. Requirements for admission are graduation from an accredited high school with a 2.5 average and 15 Carnegie units. The school also considers personality, impressions made during an interview, advanced placement or honors courses, recommendations by school officials, leadership record, extracurricular activities, and evidence of special talents.

Procedure: The SAT is required and should be taken by July 15. The application deadlines are open. The college has a rolling admissions plan and observes the CRDA. Applications should be submitted with a $15 fee.

Special: The college has early and deferred admissions plans. AP and CLEP credit is granted.

Transfer: Transfer students are accepted for all classes. A 2.5 GPA is necessary. There is a one-year residency requirement. Students must earn, at the college, 36 credits—including half of those in their major —out of the 192 required for a bachelor's degree. Application deadlines are the same as those for freshmen.

Visiting: Guides are available for informal visits. Visitors may sit in on classes. Contact the student recruitment office for information.

Financial Aid: About 80% of all students receive financial aid. About one-third receive scholarships. The college administers a total of $350,000 in federal loan funds, and 75% of the students receive loans. Work contracts are awarded to freshmen; 18% of the students work part-time on campus. NDSLs also are awarded. CWS funds are available in all departments. Tuition may be paid in installments but is due before finals each quarter. The college is a member of CSS. The FAF is required. Applications should be filed by May for fall admission, or by December 15 (winter), March 15 (spring), and June 1 (summer).

Foreign Students: About 4% of the full-time students come from foreign countries. Special counseling is provided.

Admissions: Students must score 525 or higher on the TOEFL. No college entrance exams are required.

Procedure: Applications should be filed in May for fall admission, or by December 15 (winter entry), March 15 (spring entry), or June 1 (summer entry). Students must present proof of good health and of adequate funds for 1 academic year. All foreign students must carry health insurance, which is available through the college for a fee.

Admissions Contact: Bill Young, Director of Admissions.

SAINT MARY'S COLLEGE OF CALIFORNIA B-3
Moraga, California 94575   (415) 376-4411

F/T: 950M, 1075W	Faculty: 60; IIA, +$
P/T: 3M, 17W	Ph.D.'s: 82%
Grad: 233M, 280W	S/F Ratio: 16 to 1
Year: 4-1-4	Tuition: $5130
Appl: May 1	R and B: $2745
1500 applied	950 accepted 630 enrolled
SAT: 501V 503M	COMPETITIVE

Established in 1863, Saint Mary's is a coeducational liberal arts college affiliated with the Roman Catholic Church and conducted by the Brothers of the Christian Schools. The library contains 135,000 volumes and subscribes to 540 current periodicals.

Environment: The campus covers 420 acres in a suburban area. Its facilities include 3 classroom buildings, an administration building, a chapel, an art gallery, and 15 residence halls accommodating 913 men and women.

Student Life: Seventy-four percent of the students come from California, and 51% of all students live in the residence halls or on-campus apartments. Forty-five percent of entering freshmen come from public schools. Approximately 74% of the students are Catholic. About 21% are minority-group members. Campus housing is both single-sex and coed; there are visiting privileges in the former. Students may keep cars on campus.

Organizations: There are no fraternities or sororities but numerous special-interest clubs provide extracurricular activities.

Sports: The college participates on an intercollegiate level in 9 sports for men and 6 for women. An intramural program of 9 sports for men and 9 for women is available.

Graduates: The freshman dropout rate is 5%. Of the 80% that remain to graduate, 48% continue their studies in graduate or professional schools.

72 CALIFORNIA

Services: Placement, career and psychological counseling, outpatient care (exclusive of medication costs), tutoring, and remedial instruction are offered at no charge to the student.

Programs of Study: Studies lead to the B.A., B.S., and B.S.B.A. degrees. Associate and master's degrees are also conferred. Bachelor's degrees are offered in the following subjects: BUSINESS (accounting, business administration), EDUCATION (adult, early childhood, elementary, health/physical, secondary, special), ENGLISH (English), FINE AND PERFORMING ARTS (art), HEALTH SCIENCES (nursing), LANGUAGES (French, Greek/Latin, Spanish), MATH AND SCIENCES (biology, chemistry, mathematics), PHILOSOPHY (philosophy, religion), PREPROFESSIONAL (dentistry, law, medicine, pharmacy, veterinary), SOCIAL SCIENCES (economics, government/political science, history, psychology).

Required: Students must take 4 courses in Collegiate Seminars, an interdisciplinary Great Books Program, and 10 area studies requirements.

Special: Seminars are offered in all fields; seminar class size is limited to 18. Third-year students may receive permission to study abroad for that year, but this opportunity is not offered as part of the regular curriculum. Eight courses in the January term are offered abroad. An integral liberal arts (no major) degree is offered.

Admissions: Sixty-three percent of those who applied were accepted for the 1981-82 freshman class. Candidates must be high school graduates, have completed 15 Carnegie units with a minimum GPA of 2.5, and rank in the upper 50% of their class. Applicants must score above 400 on each section of the SAT to be seriously considered for admission. Also considered are advanced placement or honor courses, recommendations of the secondary school, extracurricular activities record, and leadership potential.

Procedure: The SAT is required; out-of-state students may substitute the ACT. Tests should be taken by January of the senior year. The deadline for application to the fall semester is May 1; to the spring semester, January 1. There is a $20 application fee. A rolling admissions procedure is used.

Special: Early admissions and deferred admissions plans are available. The early admissions application deadline is December 15. AP and CLEP credit is granted.

Transfer: For fall 1981, 375 transfer students applied, 250 were accepted, and 140 enrolled. A 2.0 GPA, a composite score of 800 on the SAT, and a high school transcript indicating a 2.5 GPA are required. A, B, and C grades transfer. Transfers are accepted for all classes. There is a residency requirement of 1 year. Nine courses, out of a total of 36 courses required for the bachelor's degree, must be taken at the college. Deadlines for application are August 1 (fall) and January 1 (spring). On-campus housing is not available for transfer students.

Financial Aid: About 60% of all students receive aid. About 15% work part-time on campus. A fund of $360,000 is allotted for scholarships each year; loans are available from the federal government and from local banks. The maximum aid package can total $5000. The average award to freshmen from all sources is about $3000. The college is a member of CSS. The SAAC is required. The deadline to apply for aid is May 1.

Foreign Students: Students from other countries represent 14% of the full-time enrollment. The college offers an intensive English program and special counseling. It also sponsors organizations for foreign students.

Admissions: The TOEFL is required; a minimum score of 500 is necessary. The SAT or ACT is not required.

Procedure: Application deadlines for foreign students are May 1 for fall entry and January 1 for spring entry. A doctor's examination is required. Foreign students must also present proof of funds adequate to cover 1 year of study. Health insurance is necessary; it is available through the college for a fee.

Admissions Contact: Peter Mohorko, Dean of Admissions.

SAN DIEGO STATE UNIVERSITY D-5
San Diego, California 92182   (714) 265-5384

F/T: 9467M, 9873W	Faculty: n/av; IIA, ++$
P/T: 3612M, 3180W	Ph.D.'s: 90%
Grad: 3118M, 4080W	S/F Ratio: 19 to 1
Year: sems, ss	Tuition: $382 ($2650)
Appl: Nov. 30	R and B: $3000
7477 applied	4728 accepted	2904 enrolled
SAT: 440V 479M	ACT: 19	COMPETITIVE

San Diego State University, established in 1897, is a liberal arts, coeducational college that is part of the California State University and Colleges system; it provides preparation for occupational goals as well as a broad liberal education. The library contains 691,000 volumes, and subscribes to 11,000 periodicals.

Environment: The 300-acre campus is located in a suburban area within 12 miles of numerous beach resorts and mountain and desert recreational sites. Facilities include classrooms, laboratories, a student union, and a student recreation center. Living facilities include dormitories and fraternity and sorority houses.

Student Life: About 95% of the students come from the West and Northwest. Only 1% live on campus. About 16% are minority-group members. Campus housing is both coed and single-sex; there are visiting privileges in the single-sex housing. Day-care services are available to all students and faculty and staff. Students may keep cars on campus.

Organizations: There are 14 fraternities and 10 sororities to which 2% of the men and 2% of the women belong. A number of clubs and organizations including religious groups and service and special-interest groups are found on campus.

Sports: The university competes on an intercollegiate level in 10 sports for men and 9 for women. There are 10 intramural sports for men and 10 for women.

Handicapped: Ninety percent of the campus is accessible to wheelchair students. Special parking, wheelchair ramps, elevators, specially equipped rest rooms, and lowered drinking fountains and telephones are available.

Graduates: About 30% of the freshmen remain to graduate; 21% of the men and 17% of the women continue on to graduate and professional schools.

Services: Students receive the following services free of charge: psychological counseling, tutoring, remedial instruction, placement, career counseling, and health care.

Programs of Study: The university confers the B.A., B.S., B.Mus., and B.Voc.Ed. degrees. Master's and doctoral programs are also offered. Bachelor's degrees are offered in the following subjects: AREA STUDIES (American, Asian, Black/Afro-American, Latin American, Russian), BUSINESS (accounting, computer science, finance, information systems, management, marketing, real estate/insurance), ENGLISH (English, journalism, literature, speech), FINE AND PERFORMING ARTS (art, music, radio/TV, theater/dramatics), HEALTH SCIENCES (nursing, speech pathology and audiology), LANGUAGES (French, German, Russian, Spanish), MATH AND SCIENCES (astronomy, biology, botany, chemistry, geology, mathematics, microbiology, physics, zoology), PHILOSOPHY (classics, philosophy, religious studies), PREPROFESSIONAL (engineering, home economics, social work), SOCIAL SCIENCES (anthropology, economics, geography, government/political science, history, psychology, social sciences, sociology). Majors leading to preprofessional degrees include dentistry, law, and medicine. Twenty-seven percent of degrees are conferred in business, 26% in preprofessional studies, and 16% in fine and performing arts.

Required: All students must take history, literature, physical education, and science.

Special: Student-designed majors are permitted. The university offers a general studies degree that consists of 3 areas of study chosen by the student in consultation with an adviser. The California State Universities offer programs of study for a full academic year at a number of distinguished universities abroad.

Honors: There are 15 honor societies on campus, including Phi Beta Kappa and Phi Kappa Phi. To be considered for enrollment, students must demonstrate superior scholarship.

Admissions: Sixty-three percent of those who applied were accepted for the 1981-82 freshman class. Candidates should be graduates of an accredited high school. California residents should rank in the top third of their graduating class; nonresidents, in the top sixth. California residents should have a minimum 2.0 GPA; nonresidents must have a 2.4 GPA.

Procedure: Students are required to take the SAT or ACT. Application deadlines are November 30 (fall) and August 31 (spring). There is a $25 application fee. A rolling admissions plan is used.

Special: CLEP and AP credit is accepted.

Transfer: For fall 1981, 9440 students applied, 5333 were accepted, and 3885 enrolled. Applicants with 56 or more units must have a GPA of 2.0 and be in good standing at the last college attended. Nonresident transfer applicants must have a GPA of 2.5. Applicants with fewer than 56 units must meet the same requirements, as well as those of incoming freshmen. All students must complete, at the university, 30 of the 124–132 credits required for a bachelor's degree. Deadlines are the same as those for freshmen.

Visiting: Guided tours and interviews can be arranged by contacting the Ambassador Program (714-265-5933). Visitors may sit in on classes and remain overnight on campus.

Financial Aid: In a recent class, 25% of all students received some form of financial aid. Students can apply for loans administered by the federal and state governments, local banks, the university, and industrial and private sources. About 25% of the students received loan funds. There are 45 academic scholarships and 15 athletic scholarships open to freshmen. The Student Aid Application for California is required from aid applicants. The university is a member of CSS. There is no formal deadline for aid applications; priority is given to applications received by February 28.

Foreign Students: Three percent of the full-time students come from foreign countries. An intensive English program, special counseling, and special organizations are available for these students.

Admissions: Foreign students must achieve a TOEFL score of at least 550. No college entrance exams are required.

Procedure: Application deadlines are the same as those for other students. Foreign students must submit results of a TB test and proof of funds adequate to cover the entire period of study. Health insurance is required and is available through the university for a fee.

Admissions Contact: Nancy C. Sprotte, Director, Admissions and Records.

SAN FRANCISCO ART INSTITUTE   B-3
San Francisco, California 94133   (415) 771-7020

F/T: 203M, 163W   Faculty: 35; IV, av$
P/T: 94M, 112W   Ph.D.'s: 1%
Grad: 51M, 49W   S/F Ratio: 8 to 1
Year: sems, ss   Tuition: $4370
Appl: open   R and B: $3060
116 applied   113 accepted   70 enrolled
SAT, ACT: not required   SPECIAL

Established in 1871, the San Francisco Art Institute is the only fully accredited degree-granting college in the United States devoted solely to the fine arts. A privately owned, independent professional school, the institute offers extensive training in the fine arts, supplemented by a humanities program. The library contains over 22,684 volumes and 20,000 slides of various artists' work, and subscribes to over 250 periodicals.

Environment: The self-contained campus is located in a residential neighborhood of San Francisco overlooking the Bay. The original 1926 main building, now expanded, is in the Spanish Colonial Revival style and was designed by Arthur Brown, Jr., architect of San Francisco's City Hall and Opera House. Other facilities include 5 studios, a large sculpture area, 2 galleries, a lecture hall, and an outdoor amphitheatre.

Student Life: The institute attracts students from across the country and internationally as well. It draws over half of its students from states other than California and about 20% from foreign countries. Seventeen percent of the students are minority-group members. The college is, however, a nonresidential institution.

Organizations: There are no social fraternities or sororities. Most recreational and cultural activities are easily accessible off campus.

Sports: The institute offers no athletic activities.

Handicapped: Plans are under way to accommodate physically handicapped students by installing wheelchair ramps and providing easy access to classrooms. At present, the school has a few students who have hearing impairments.

Graduates: Of the freshmen enrolled, 14% drop out by the end of the first year; 49% remain to receive their degree. The institute estimates that 35% of the graduates seek higher degrees. Sixty-two percent of the graduates are presently in art-related jobs, 35% in non-art-related jobs.

Services: The institute offers the following services free of charge: placement, career counseling, and psychological counseling. Health insurance is available on campus. Placement services for graduates and undergraduates include a career counselor and the newly created job locator and developer, available through the Student Life Office.

Programs of Study: The institute confers the B.F.A. degree. A master's program is also available. The B.F.A. is offered in the following subjects: FINE AND PERFORMING ARTS (art, ceramic sculpture, film/photography, painting, performance/video, printmaking, sculpture, studio art). Courses in English and the humanities supplement the fine arts program.

CALIFORNIA 73

Admissions: Ninety-seven percent of those who applied were accepted for the 1981–82 freshman class. The institute uses an open admissions policy. A high school diploma or GED is required for those under 21. Students entering directly from high school are required to submit a portfolio of 10 to 15 pieces, either slices or original work. Application and transcripts must be filed. A high school diploma is not required of a candidate over age 21. Each new student, both beginning and transfer, will be subject to an evaluation by faculty when deemed necessary before being permitted to enroll for a second year of study at the institute.

Procedure: Neither the SAT or ACT is required. The school uses a rolling admissions policy. Applications should be submitted with a $20 fee.

Special: Early decision and early and deferred admissions plans are offered.

Transfer: For fall 1981, 342 transfer students applied, all were accepted, and 300 enrolled. Transfer students must meet the same criteria as freshmen. They must complete, at the institute, 1 full year of study and 32 of the 120 semester hours required for the bachelor's degree. C grades or better transfer.

Visiting: Prospective students are welcome to visit and tour the institute. They may call ahead to arrange for a tour or drop in and a tour will be arranged for them. Visitors may sit in on classes. The best time for a visit is from Monday through Friday, 9 A.M. to 5 P.M..

Financial Aid: About 65% of all students receive financial aid; 18% work part-time on campus. Tuitition may be paid through a deferred tuition plan. The institute offers SFAI Grants-in-Aid, based on demonstrated financial need. They are available to supplement state and federal financial aid and for students who do not meet the criteria for federal grants. Financial aid may include the BEOG, CWS, state scholarships, grants, and student loans. April 1 is the priority deadline to apply for financial aid.

Foreign Students: Foreign students comprise nearly a quarter of the student body. The institute offers these students special counseling and special organizations.

Admissions: To qualify for admission, foreign students must achieve a minimum TOEFL score of 500. Entrance exams are not required.

Procedure: Foreign students must provide proof of funds adequate to cover 1 year of study. They must also carry health insurance, which is available through the institute at a fee.

Admissions Contact: Lynn Gardner Tomko, Director of Admissions and Financial Aid.

SAN FRANCISCO CONSERVATORY   B-3
OF MUSIC
San Francisco, California 94122   (415) 564-8086

F/T: 78M, 66W   Faculty: 13; IV, av$
P/T: 16M, 18W   Ph.D.'s: 25%
Grad: 18M, 23W   S/F Ratio: 10 to 1
Year: sems   Tuition: $4635
Appl: July 1   R and B: n/app
44 applied   23 accepted   16 enrolled
SAT: 470V 530M   ACT: 22   SPECIAL

The San Francisco Conservatory of Music, founded in 1917, is a private conservatory and professional college of music. The faculty includes most of the first-chair players of the San Francisco Symphony, members of the San Francisco Opera, and other outstanding musicians. The conservatory's library has 17,000 volumes and more than 6000 individual recordings and tapes, and subscribes to 56 periodicals.

Environment: The conservatory facilities are housed in a building in the Spanish Mission style with a 1975 addition. There are no student residences. A recent construction is the 345-seat Ruth and Marco Hellman Hall. The urban campus is in the heart of San Francisco.

Student Life: More than half of the students come from California. Seventy percent of the entering freshmen come from public schools. All students live off campus. Twenty percent of the students are minority-group members. Students may keep cars on campus.

Organizations: Numerous social and cultural events are scheduled each week on campus. There are no fraternities or sororities. The conservatory is near the new San Francisco Performing Arts Center.

Sports: There is no athletic program.

Handicapped: All of the campus is accessible to physically handicapped students. Facilities include special parking, elevators, lowered telephones, and specially equipped rest rooms.

74 CALIFORNIA

Graduates: Competition is described as vigorous; about 3% of the freshmen withdraw after the first year of study and 50% to 60% of the freshmen remain to graduate. Fifty-five percent of the students pursue graduate study after completion of the bachelor's degree, 1% enter law school. Five percent pursue careers in business and industry.

Services: The following services are free to all students: placement, career counseling, and psychological counseling. Job referrals are available to current students and alumni.

Programs of Study: The conservatory offers the B. Mus. degree. Master's degrees are also granted. Music is the only major offered, but students may specialize in fields such as classical guitar, composition, conducting, all orchestral instruments, all keyboard instruments, and voice.

Required: All candidates for graduation must successfully complete the yearly jury examinations, have a senior recital, and participate in ensembles and repertory classes in addition to completing academic requirements.

Honors: No program in honors work is offered.

Admissions: Fifty-two percent of the applicants to the 1981–82 class were accepted. The SAT scores of those who enrolled were as follows: Verbal—58% scored below 500, 30% between 500 and 599, 12% between 600 and 700, and 0% above 700; Math—52% scored below 500, 12% between 500 and 599, 30% between 600 and 700, and 6% above 700. On the ACT, 25% scored below 21, 25% between 21 and 23, 0% between 24 and 25, 50% between 26 and 28, and 0% above 28. A 2.0 high school GPA is needed in addition to 16 Carnegie credits of high school course work. Students' participation in high school extracurricular music activities is considered extremely important. Candidates are required to have a personal audition on a major instrument and provide recommendations from musicians.

Procedure: The SAT or ACT is required. The application is due July 1, but students are advised to apply as early as possible. New B. Mus. students are also admitted at midyear; November 15 is the application deadline. There is a rolling admissions plan in effect; CRDA is observed. A $25 nonrefundable application fee must accompany the appropriate forms. A personal interview is recommended.

Special: AP and CLEP are used. Early decision, and early and deferred admissions, plans are available.

Transfer: Applicants must meet the same criteria as incoming freshmen. For fall 1981, 90 transfer students applied, 56 were accepted, and 38 enrolled. A 2.0 GPA and a musical audition are required. Transfers must complete, at the conservatory, 28 of the 130 credits necessary for a bachelor's degree. Application deadlines are the same as those for freshmen.

Visiting: Prospective applicants may sit in on classes. There is no formal visiting student procedure.

Financial Aid: Seventy percent of the students at the conservatory are receiving some form of assistance. Twenty percent work part-time on campus. A total of $20,000 in scholarship aid is available to freshmen; the average award from all sources is $3200. Government loans, work contracts, and work-study funds are also available. Scholarships range from $300 to $5000; loans from $500 to $1500; and jobs average about $500. Tuition may be paid in installments. The FAF or the conservatory's own form is required by April 1, but students are urged to apply as early as possible. Need and talent are the determining factors.

Foreign Students: Eleven percent of the full-time students come from foreign countries. The conservatory offers these students an intensive English course.

Admissions: Foreign students must take TOEFL and the conservatory's entrance exam in the form of a musical audition.

Procedure: Foreign students are admitted in the fall and spring; the application deadlines are July 1 and November 15, respectively. They must present proof of funds adequate to cover their entire course of study.

Admissions Contact: Colleen Katzowitz, Director of Student Services.

SAN FRANCISCO STATE UNIVERSITY   B-3
San Francisco, California 94132   (415) 469-2014

F/T: 5168M, 6042W	Faculty: n/av; IIA, ++$
P/T: 2696M, 3035W	Ph.D.'s: 65%
Grad: 545M, 942W	S/F Ratio: 15 to 1
Year: sems, ss	Tuition: $206 ($1916)
Appl: Nov. 30	R and B: $2100
SAT or ACT: required	COMPETITIVE

San Francisco State University, established in 1899, is a publicly supported liberal arts college. University Extension Center programs are also offered on the university campus. The library contains 525,000 volumes, and subscribes to 3200 periodicals.

Environment: The 110-acre campus near Lake Merced in San Francisco includes dormitory accommodations for 400 men and 400 women, an 1800-seat auditorium equipped with stereophonic sound and an elevator orchestra pit, a little theater, and a theater-in-the-round.

Student Life: About 95% of the undergraduates are from California; 5% are from other states and foreign countries. The majority of the students are commuters; 10% live in campus dormitories.

Organizations: There are fraternities and sororities; professional and service organizations also serve as social groups. Extracurricular activities include religious organizations and the Associated Students (the main student government organization).

Sports: The university competes on an intercollegiate level in 12 sports. There are 6 intramural sports for men and 6 for women.

Handicapped: Facilities for physically handicapped students include wheelchair ramps, special parking, elevators, specially equipped rest rooms, and lowered drinking fountains and telephones.

Graduates: The freshman dropout rate is 10%; 60% remain to graduate. About 30% of graduates pursue advanced study.

Services: Students receive the following services free of charge: placement, career counseling, health care, tutoring, remedial instruction, and psychological counseling.

Programs of Study: The university confers the B.A., B.Mus., B.S., and B.Voc.Ed. degrees. Master's programs are also offered. Bachelor's degrees are offered in the following subjects: AREA STUDIES (American, Black/Afro-American, La Raza), BUSINESS (accounting, business administration, computer science, finance, management, marketing, real estate), EDUCATION (elementary, secondary), ENGLISH (English, journalism, literature), FINE AND PERFORMING ARTS (art, art education, art history, film/photography, music, music education, radio/TV, theater/dramatics), Health Sciences (nursing), LANGUAGES (Chinese, French, German, Italian, Japanese, Russian, Spanish), MATH AND SCIENCES (biochemistry, biology, chemistry, computer science, mathematics), PHILOSOPHY (classics, humanities, philosophy), PREPROFESSIONAL (engineering, home economics, social work), SOCIAL SCIENCES (anthropology, economics, geography, history, international relations, psychology, sociology). Twenty-two percent of degrees are conferred in business and 9% in fine and performing arts.

Required: All students must complete 48 semester units of general education courses. There are also requirements in written English, U.S. history, and California state government.

Special: Student-designed majors are permitted; a liberal studies degree is also offered. The university offers programs in independent study, experimental or exploratory courses, aerospace studies, interdisciplinary studies in the creative arts and social science, and study at distinguished universities abroad. In addition, there are accounting internships, a 3–2 engineering program with Columbia University, and field work in archeology, geology, political science, and social welfare.

Honors: Honor students on campus may become eligible for membership in Sigma Xi and Phi Beta Kappa. Numerous departmental national honor groups are also available.

Admissions: About 55% of applicants have been offered admission in recent years. Eligibility is determined by a weighted combination of GPA and ACT or SAT scores. California applicants must rank in the upper third of all California secondary school graduates; out-of-state applicants must rank comparably to the top sixth of California graduates. The following pattern of high school courses is recommended: college preparatory English, a foreign language, college preparatory mathematics, laboratory science, history and/or social science, and study in speech, music, art, and other subjects contributing to a general academic background.

Procedure: The SAT or ACT is required. Application filing periods begin November 1 (fall), June 1 (winter), August 1 (spring), and February 1 (summer), and applications are accepted until about 1 month prior to the first day of the term or until capacities are reached. There is a $25 application fee.

Transfer: Over 5000 transfer students are accepted yearly. A 2.0 GPA is required of California residents and a 2.4 GPA of out-of-state applicants. All students must complete, at the university, 30 of the 124–132 credits required for a bachelor's degree.

Visiting: Informal visits can be arranged through the University Relations Office; visitors may sit in on classes.

Financial Aid: Financial aid is awarded on the basis of need. Scholarship awards and loans are available. Campus employment, up to $900 per year, is also available. The application period is December 1 to March 1 for most types of aid. The FAF or SFS is required, and should be filed with the CSS no later than March 1.

Foreign Students: Special counseling and intensive English courses are available for students from foreign countries.

Admissions: Foreign students must take the TOEFL. No college entrance exams are required.

Procedure: The application filing period begins November 1 for the semester beginning September of the following year. Foreign students must present proof of adequate funds.

Admissions Contact: Laura Ware, Admissions Officer.

SAN JOSE STATE UNIVERSITY   B-3
San Jose, California 95192   (408) 277-3266

F/T: 6737M, 6430W	Faculty: n/av; IIA, ++$
P/T: 3467M, 3221W	Ph.D.'s: 70%
Grad: 1993M, 2899W	S/F Ratio: 18 to 1
Year: sems, ss	Tuition: $300 ($95)p/c
Appl: open	R and B: $2500
4652 applied	2470 accepted	1722 enrolled
SAT or ACT: required		COMPETITIVE

San Jose State University, founded in 1857, is part of the California State University and Colleges system. The library houses more than 700,000 volumes and 655,000 microfilm items, and subscribes to 5700 periodicals.

Environment: The 117-acre campus is located in downtown San Jose. Seven dormitories accommodate 1800 students. Married student housing and fraternity and sorority houses also are available. A nuclear-science facility contains more than $1 million worth of equipment for use by undergraduates.

Student Life: Ninety percent of the students are from California. Ten percent of the students live on campus. Dormitories are coed. Students may keep cars on campus.

Organizations: About 3% of the students belong to one of the 5 sororities and 8 fraternities on campus. The more than 140 student organizations include cultural, academic, religious, recreational, and special-interest groups.

Sports: The university fields intercollegiate teams in 12 sports for men and 10 for women. There are 10 intramurals for both men and women.

Handicapped: The entire campus is accessible to wheelchair-bound students. Special facilities include wheelchair ramps, parking areas, elevators, lowered drinking fountains and telephones, specially equipped rest rooms, readers, braille maps, an equipment repair service, talking calculators, and mobility orientation. A physical therapist, tutors, and special counselors are provided. Special class scheduling also is available.

Services: Students receive the following free services: placement, career and psychological counseling, and remedial instruction. Health care and tutoring are available both free of charge and on a fee basis. Placement services also are available to graduates.

Programs of Study: The university awards the B.A., B.S., B.F.A., and B.Mus. degrees. Master's degrees also are available. Bachelor's degrees are offered in the following subjects: AREA STUDIES (American, Black/Afro-American, Latin American), BUSINESS (accounting, computer science, finance, human resources administration, international business, management, marketing, office administration), EDUCATION (administration and higher education, counselor, early childhood, elementary, health/physical, industrial, instructional technology, secondary, special), ENGLISH (advertising, English, journalism, linguistics, speech), FINE AND PERFORMING ARTS (art, art education, art history, dance, music, music education, film/photography, radio/TV, studio art, theater/dramatics), HEALTH SCIENCES (dietetics, health science, medical technology, nursing, nutrition, occupational therapy, speech therapy), LANGUAGES (French, German, Spanish), MATH AND SCIENCES (biochemistry, biology, botany, chemistry, ecology/environmental science, entomology, geology, marine sciences, mathematics, meteorology, natural sciences, oceanography, physics, zoology), PHILOSOPHY (humanities, philosophy, religion), PREPROFESSIONAL (administration of justice, cybernetic systems, engineering, social work), SOCIAL SCIENCES (anthropology, economics, geography, government/political science, gerontology, history, psychology, recreation, social sciences, sociology).

Honors: A number of honor societies are represented on campus. Honors programs are offered in 18 majors.

Admissions: Fifty-three percent of those who applied were accepted for the 1981–82 freshman class. Applicants must have at least a 2.0 average. Admission is governed by an eligibility index based on grades for the last 3 years of high school and SAT or ACT scores.

Procedure: The SAT or ACT is required. Application deadlines are open; freshmen are admitted to the fall and spring semesters. Applications should be submitted with a $25 fee. The university follows a rolling admissions policy.

Transfer: For fall 1981, 8677 transfer students applied, 5738 were accepted, and 4350 enrolled. An average of 2.0 or better (2.4 for nonresidents) is required. Transfer students are accepted for all classes. Students must earn in residence at least 30 of the 124–140 credits required for a bachelor's degree. Application deadlines are open.

Visiting: Regularly scheduled orientations for prospective students include campus tours. Guides also are provided for informal visits on weekday afternoons. Visitors may sit in on classes. Arrangements should be made with the relations-with-schools office.

Financial Aid: About 27% of the students receive aid. Five percent work part-time on campus. Loans are available from the federal and state governments, the university, and private sources. CWS jobs also are available. The university is a member of CSS. The student aid application for California is required. Aid applications should be submitted by March 1.

Foreign Students: Four percent of the full-time students come from foreign countries. Special counseling and special organizations are available for these students.

Admissions: Applicants must score at least 500 on the TOEFL. No college entrance exams are required of students with an average of B+ or better and satisfactory TOEFL scores.

Procedure: Application deadlines are February 1 (fall) and August 30 (spring). Students must present proof of funds adequate to cover the entire program of study.

Admissions Contact: Phyllis O'Balle, Assistant Admissions Officer.

SIMPSON COLLEGE   B-3
San Francisco, California 94134   (415) 334-7400

F/T: 90M, 100W	Faculty: 15; IIB, --$
P/T: 8M, 4W	Ph.D.'s: 60%
Grad: 24M, 13W	• S/F Ratio: 13 to 1
Year: 4-1-4, ss	Tuition: $2600
Appl: Aug. 18	R and B: $1600
124 applied	102 accepted	95 enrolled
ACT: 18		COMPETITIVE

Simpson College, founded in 1921, is a church-controlled liberal arts and Bible college affiliated with the Christian and Missionary Alliance. Its library contains over 48,500 volumes and subscribes to 400 periodicals.

Environment: The 5-acre urban campus is located in the heart of San Francisco. In addition to the main building, there is a residence hall that accommodates nearly 200 men and women. Facilities are also available for commuting students.

Student Life: About 73% of the students are from California. Ninety percent have public school backgrounds. Sixty-seven percent reside on campus. Nearly all of the students are Protestant. Daily chapel service is compulsory. Christian counselors are available. About 1% of the students are minority-group members. College housing is single-sex; there are no visiting privileges. Students may keep cars on campus. Drinking and smoking are prohibited on campus.

Organizations: There are no sororities or fraternities. Social activities include picnics, parties, and banquets. There are numerous clubs, service organizations, a student newspaper, a yearbook, and religious groups.

Sports: Intercollegiate competition includes 1 sport for men and 1 for women. There are 7 intramural sports for men and 4 for women.

Handicapped: There are no special facilities for the physically handicapped. There are special readers or tutors for visually and hearing-impaired students.

Graduates: The freshman dropout rate is 7%. Recently, of those who began, about 25% remained to graduate. Fifty percent go on for further degree work. About 1% of the graduates entered careers in business and industry in a recent year.

Services: All students may receive placement, health care, psychological counseling, career counseling, tutoring, and remedial instruction free of charge.

76 CALIFORNIA

Programs of Study: The college grants the B.A. degree. Master's degrees are also offered. Bachelor's degrees are offered in the following subjects: AREA STUDIES (urban), BUSINESS (business administration), EDUCATION (elementary, secondary), ENGLISH (communication, English), PHILOSOPHY (Biblical literature, missions, religion), SOCIAL SCIENCES (history, psychology).

Special: Students may design their own majors. Study abroad can be arranged. Students also receive 2 credits for directed missionary field experience in various countries.

Admissions: About 82% of the applicants for the 1981–82 school year were accepted. The ACT scores of those who enrolled were as follows: 68% scored below 21, 12% between 21 and 23, 6% between 24 and 25, 5% between 26 and 28, and 0% above 28. There is no minimum class rank required. Recommendations, personality, and leadership record are considered important factors.

Procedure: The SAT or ACT is required, but can be taken at the college during orientation. The application deadlines are August 18 (fall) and December 1 (spring). A rolling admissions plan is used. There is a $15 nonrefundable application fee.

Special: An acceptance is valid for 2 years.

Transfer: Fifty-one transfer students enrolled in fall 1981. Most transfers are approved provided that they have a C average and good academic standing. The ACT is required of applicants with fewer than 30 credits. Students must complete, at the college, the last 15 of the 134 credits needed for a bachelor's degree. Application deadlines are the same as those for freshmen.

Visiting: There is a formal orientation program. Visitors may sit in on classes and stay overnight at the school. Contact the director of admissions to arrange informal visits.

Financial Aid: About 60% of all students receive some form of aid. Loans, grants, scholarships, and campus employment are available. Average aid to freshmen from all sources is $2500. Tuition may be paid in installments. The college is a member of CSS. The FAF and the SAAC must be submitted. Application deadlines are April 30 (fall) and October 1 (spring).

Foreign Students: Two percent of the full-time students come from foreign countries.

Admissions: Foreign students must take an English proficiency exam.

Admissions Contact: Bob Elner, Director of Admissions.

SONOMA STATE UNIVERSITY B-3
Rohnert Park, California 94928 (707) 664-2374

F/T: 1238M, 1556W	Faculty:	247; IIA, ++ $
P/T: 380M, 722W	Ph.D.'s:	75%
Grad: 608M, 910W	S/F Ratio:	16 to 1
Year: sems, ss	Tuition:	$135 ($92 p/c)
Appl: June 1	R and B:	$2706
564 applied	287 accepted	189 enrolled
SAT or ACT: required		COMPETITIVE

Established in 1961, Sonoma State University is one of the liberal arts institutions of the California State University and Colleges system. It is noted for its setting and educational innovations. The library contains over 300,000 volumes and 500,000 microfilm items, and subscribes to over 1800 periodicals.

Environment: The 200-acre campus is located in a rural community 48 miles from San Francisco. Facilities include a fine arts complex and a self-contained residential community housing 406 students.

Student Life: Over 95% of the students come from California. About half commute from home; the rest live off campus or in the residence halls. University housing is both coed and single-sex. Students may keep cars on campus. Day-care services are provided for students, faculty and staff for a fee.

Organizations: There are no fraternities or sororities; professional and service organizations serve as social groups. Religious organizations, special-interest clubs and activities are available.

Sports: The university fields 8 intercollegiate teams for men and 8 for women. There are 8 intramural sports for men and 6 for women.

Handicapped: The entire campus is accessible to wheelchair-bound students. Special parking, wheelchair ramps, elevators, specially equipped rest rooms, and lowered drinking fountains and telephones are available. Fewer than 1% of the students currently enrolled have visual or hearing impairments. There is an office for students with disabilities.

Services: Students receive the following services free of charge: placement, career counseling, health care, tutoring, remedial instruction, and psychological counseling.

Programs of Study: The university confers the B.A. and B.S. degrees. Master's degrees are also offered. Bachelor's degrees are offered in the following subjects: AREA STUDIES (Black/Afro-American, India studies, Mexican-American), BUSINESS (accounting, finance, management), EDUCATION (early childhood, elementary, secondary, special), ENGLISH (English, literature), FINE AND PERFORMING ARTS (art history, expressive arts, music, music education, studio art, theater/dramatics), HEALTH SCIENCES (nursing), LANGUAGES (French, German, Spanish), MATH AND SCIENCES (biology, chemistry, environmental studies, geology, mathematics, physics), PHILOSOPHY (philosophy), PREPROFESSIONAL (dentistry, law, library science, medicine, pharmacy, veterinary science), SOCIAL SCIENCES (anthropology, criminal justice administration, economics, geography, government/political science, history, psychology, sociology). Sixty-three percent of degrees conferred are in liberal arts, 14% are in business, and 10% are in fine and performing arts.

Required: All students must fulfill a general education requirement which includes courses in natural and social sciences, language arts, mathematics, humanities, ethnic studies, and critical thinking.

Special: Student-designed majors are permitted. The university offers students the opportunity of the junior year abroad in accordance with the California State International programs. The university considers the Hutchins School of Liberal Studies, the School of Expressive Arts, and the School of Environmental Studies and Planning noteworthy programs.

Honors: There are no honor societies on campus.

Admissions: Approximately 51% of those who applied were accepted for the 1981–82 freshman class. The SAT scores of those who enrolled were as follows: Verbal—74% below 500, 22% between 500 and 599, 4% between 600 and 700, and 0% above 700; Math—64% below 500, 30% between 500 and 599, 5% between 600 and 700, and 1% above 700. Applicants must rank in the top third of their high school class, and have a GPA of at least 2.0. Admissions decisions are based on GPA and test scores.

Procedure: The ACT or SAT is required. Application deadlines are June 1 (fall) and November 1 (spring). The application fee is $25.

Special: Early admissions is available; the deadline is November 1 for the following September. Early decision is also possible. AP and CLEP credit are available.

Transfer: For fall 1981, 3556 transfer students applied, 2639 were accepted, and 1954 enrolled. A GPA of 2.0 is required for state residents; 2.4 for non-residents. Lower-division transfers must submit SAT or ACT scores. C grades or better transfer. Transfer students must complete, at the university, 30 of the 124 credits required for the bachelor's degree. Application deadlines and fee are the same as for freshmen.

Visiting: Scheduled orientations are arranged through the school relations office. Tours can be scheduled when classes are in session. Visitors may sit in on classes with the instructor's permission. Overnight accommodations are available during the summer.

Financial Aid: Fifty percent of all students receive some form of financial aid; 15% work part-time on campus. The university, a member of CSS, has financial aid funds, and administers federal programs (NDSL, FISL, Fed Nursing Loans and Scholarships, LEEP, CWS, BEOG-BOG, SEOG, EOP, California State Scholarships) with awards based primarily on need. The SAAC is required; application for aid should be made by March 1.

Foreign Students: About 4% of the full-time students come from foreign countries. The university offers these students an intensive English course (25 hours per week), as well as special counseling and special organizations.

Admissions: Foreign undergraduate students must obtain a minimum score of 500 on the TOEFL; a score of 550 is required for graduate students. Entrance exams are not required.

Procedure: Foreign students must present proof of adequate funds to cover the entire period of study. They must also carry health insurance, which is available through the university for a fee.

Admissions Contact: Frank Tansey, Dean of Admissions and Records.

SOUTHERN CALIFORNIA COLLEGE D-5
Costa Mesa, California 92626 (714) 556-3610

F/T: 325M, 302W		Faculty:	30; IIB, ++$
P/T: 83M, 67W		Ph.D.'s:	53%
Grad: none		S/F Ratio:	17 to 1
Year: 4-1-4, ss		Tuition:	$2802
Appl: July 31		R and B:	$1970
295 applied	228 accepted		150 enrolled
SAT or ACT: required			COMPETITIVE

Southern California College, established in 1920, is a private Christian college affiliated with the Assemblies of God. It provides training in the arts, sciences, and religion. The library contains 64,000 volumes and subscribes to 345 periodicals.

Environment: The 43-acre campus is located in a suburban area, next to the city of Costa Mesa's civic center. Facilities include an administration and classroom building, chapel, library, science and music buildings, cafeteria, student union, men's and women's high-rise dormitories, apartments, and a newly acquired trailer court for married students. A soccer/track field, a baseball field, and a gymnasium are also provided.

Student Life: About 80% of the students are California residents. About 37% live on campus. Ninety-four percent are Protestant, and 2% are Catholic. Eleven percent are minority-group members. Campus housing is single-sex; there are visiting privileges. Cars may be kept on campus. Students must sign an agreement to abide by the standards of the college, which are based on Christian principles. These include abstinence from alcoholic beverages, drugs, and tobacco.

Organizations: There are no fraternities or sororities. Popular recreational activities include swimming, surfing, hiking, and skiing.

Sports: The college fields intercollegiate teams in 3 sports for men and 2 sports for women. There are 6 intramural sports for men and 2 for women.

Handicapped: Special facilities for physically handicapped students include parking areas, elevators, and specially equipped rest rooms. Sign language can be used if needed.

Graduates: About 30% of the freshmen drop out, and 25% eventually graduate from the college. About 15% of the graduates seek advanced degrees, including 2% who enter medical school and 2% who go on to law school. About a fourth of the graduates pursue careers in business and industry.

Services: The following services are free to students: placement, career and psychological counseling, health care, tutoring, and remedial instruction.

Programs of Study: The college awards the B.A. degree. Bachelor's degrees are offered in the following subjects: BUSINESS (accounting, church business management, management, marketing), EDUCATION (elementary, health/physical, secondary), ENGLISH (English, literature), FINE AND PERFORMING ARTS (radio/TV, theater/dramatics), MATH AND SCIENCES (biology, chemistry, mathematics), PHILOSOPHY (religion), PREPROFESSIONAL (law, medicine, ministry), SOCIAL SCIENCES (government/political science, history, psychology, social sciences, sociology).

Required: Students must take 16 credit hours of religion and 2 of physical education.

Special: The college offers a diversified studies major and preprofessional courses leading to elementary and secondary teaching credentials.

Admissions: Seventy-seven percent of those who applied were accepted for the 1981–82 freshman class. Applicants must present an average of 2.25, should have completed at least 12 units of college preparatory work, and should rank in the upper 70% of their high school class. An interview is encouraged. Other factors that enter into the admissions decision are personality, advanced placement or honor courses, and extracurricular activities record.

Procedure: Applicants must take the SAT or ACT. Application deadlines are July 31 (fall), December 11 (spring), and April 31 (summer). The college follows a rolling admissions policy. Applications should be submitted with a $15 fee and 2 character references, including 1 from a pastor.

Special: A deferred admissions plan is available. CLEP credit is accepted.

Transfer: For fall 1981, 219 transfer applications were received, 179 were accepted, and 125 students enrolled. Transfers are accepted for all classes. Transfer applicants must have a GPA of at least 2.25. Grades of A, B, or C transfer. Students transferring fewer than 60 semester units also must submit their high school transcripts. Students must complete their last 24 units of study in residence to graduate; a total of 124 credits are required for the bachelor's degree. Transfer application deadlines are the same as those for freshmen. They are admitted to the fall, spring, and summer sessions.

Visiting: Orientations for prospective students are scheduled regularly. Informal visits also may be arranged with the admissions office, preferably for Tuesdays, Wednesdays, or Thursdays. Guides are provided, and visitors may sit in on classes.

Financial Aid: About 80% of the students receive aid. The college is a member of CSS and permits tuition to be paid on the installment plan. The SAAC is required. Aid applications should be submitted by April 15 for priority consideration.

Foreign Students: Four percent of the full-time students come from foreign countries. The college offers these students special counseling and special organizations.

Admissions: The TOEFL is required; a minimum score of 550 is necessary. The SAT or ACT is also required.

Procedure: Application deadlines for foreign students are July 31 (fall), December 11 (spring), and April 31 (summer). Proof of health, consisting of a Medical Datamation Form, is required. Proof of adequate funds, consisting of a deposit covering 1 semester and a statement covering the full duration of studies, must be presented. Health insurance must be carried; it is available through the college for a fee.

Admissions Contact: Wes Wick, Director of Admissions.

STANFORD UNIVERSITY B-3
Stanford, California 94305 (415) 497-2091

F/T: 3726M, 2864W		Faculty:	n/av; I, ++$
P/T: none		Ph.D.'s:	100%
Grad: 4022M, 1480W		S/F Ratio:	10 to 1
Year: qtrs, ss		Tuition:	$7140
Appl: Jan. 1		R and B:	$2965
14,029 applied	2489 accepted		1549 enrolled
SAT or ACT: required			MOST COMPETITIVE

Stanford University, founded in 1885, is a privately endowed nonsectarian institution. The university's undergraduate divisions include the schools of Humanities and Sciences, Engineering, and Earth Sciences; its professional schools include the schools of Law, Medicine, Business, and Education. Stanford is one of the best-known universities in the country and provides undergraduates with extensive laboratories and research facilities. The library, one of the largest in the West, contains more than 4 million volumes and subscribes to 18,000 periodicals.

Environment: The 8000-acre campus is located in a suburban area 29 miles south of San Francisco. Students may live in coed residence halls, some of which are organized around special interests. Housing for married students, on-campus apartments, and fraternity houses also are available.

Student Life: Stanford seeks a geographically diverse student body, and students come from all parts of the country and the world. Seventy percent of the freshmen come from public schools. Eighty percent of the students live on campus, and freshmen must live in residence halls. Twenty percent of the students are members of minority groups. Students may keep cars on campus. The student honor code governs all aspects of campus life.

Organizations: Fifteen percent of the men belong to 1 of 13 national fraternities on campus; 10% of the women belong to 1 of 6 national sororities. Nondenominational services are offered in Memorial Chapel, and places of worship are available on campus for members of major faiths. Extensive activities are available in music, film, publications, and theater. San Francisco is 29 miles to the north, the Pacific Ocean 30 miles to the west.

Sports: Stanford competes on an intercollegiate level in 14 sports for men and 11 for women. Twenty-two intramural sports are offered for men and 20 for women.

Handicapped: About 80% of the campus is accessible to wheelchair-bound students. Special facilities include wheelchair ramps, special parking areas, and lowered drinking fountains and telephones. Three special counselors are available.

Graduates: Seven percent of the freshmen drop out during the first year, and 87% remain to graduate. Ninety percent of the graduates seek advanced degrees, including 20% who enter medical school, 10% who enter dental school, and 25% who enter law school. About 18% of the graduates begin careers in business and industry.

Services: Placement, career, and psychological counseling as well as health care are offered free to students. Placement services also are offered to graduates.

78 CALIFORNIA

Programs of Study: The university awards the A.B., B.S., and B.A.S. degrees. Master's and doctoral degrees also are available. Bachelor's degrees are offered in the following subjects: AREA STUDIES (American, Asian—East Asian, Black/Afro-American, Latin American, Russian), ENGLISH (English, journalism, literature), FINE AND PERFORMING ARTS (art history, music, studio art, theater/dramatics), LANGUAGES (French, German, Greek/Latin, Italian, Japanese, Russian, Spanish), MATH AND SCIENCES (biology, chemistry, earth science, geology, mathematics, physics, statistics), PHILOSOPHY (classics, humanities, philosophy, religion), PREPROFESSIONAL (engineering—chemical, engineering—civil, engineering—electrical, engineering—engineering science, engineering—industrial, engineering—materials science, engineering—mechanical, engineering—petroleum), SOCIAL SCIENCES (anthropology, economics, government/political science, history, international relations, psychology, social sciences, sociology). Thirty-eight percent of the undergraduate degrees are conferred in social science, 20% in math and sciences, 22% in engineering, and 20% in fine and performing arts.

Required: Freshmen must take a 2-quarter class in composition and a year of Western culture. All undergraduates must take at least 1 course in each of 7 academic areas.

Special: Combined B.A.-B.S. degrees may be earned in various subjects. Students may design their own majors. The grading system allows students to choose between traditional grades and credit-no credit. Programs include the Workshop on Political and Social Issues, the Undergraduate Center for Innovation and Research in Education, "theme" houses, and sequences in urban studies, technology and society, social thought, feminist studies, and international studies. The university offers study-abroad programs in conjunction with foreign universities and also operates overseas campuses for undergraduates in France and England. Approximately 40% of the students study overseas at some point.

Honors: Honor programs are offered by most departments.

Admissions: Approximately 18% of those who applied were accepted for the 1981–82 freshman class. The SAT scores of those who enrolled in a recent class were as follows: Verbal—92% scored above 500, and 14% above 700; Math—97% scored above 500, and 36% above 700. In addition to academic record and test scores, admissions officers consider advanced placement or honors courses, recommendations by high school officials, extracurricular activities, evidence of special talents, personality, and leadership record.

Procedure: Applicants must take the SAT or ACT by January of the senior year. Freshmen are accepted only for the fall term. The application deadline is January 1, and candidates are notified in early April. Stanford subscribes to the CRDA. The application fee is $30.

Special: A deferred admissions plan is available.

Transfer: For fall 1981, 1955 students applied for transfer, 225 were accepted, and 166 enrolled. Transfer students are accepted only for the junior and sophomore years. Applicants must have completed between 39 quarter units (26 semester hours) and 98 quarter units (58 semester hours) with an average of B or better. D grades do not transfer. Students must study at the university for at least 2 years to graduate, earning 90 of the 180 quarter credits required for a bachelor's degree. Application deadlines are April 1 (fall), January 15 (spring), March 15 (summer), and November 1 (winter).

Visiting: Two guided tours and information sessions at the admissions office are scheduled daily. Visitors may sit in on classes. Visits should be scheduled with the admissions office for weekdays while school is in session.

Financial Aid: About 55% of the students receive aid. Grants are based on financial need as determined through the FAF. They range from $100 to $9500 per year. Work programs and loans are included in many of the awards. Students may obtain loans from a fund of more than $1 million after the freshman year. Part-time jobs are available through the student employment office, and about 45% of the students work part-time on campus. More than half the students earn 25% or more of their college expenses during the school year. The deadline for financial aid applications is February 1.

Foreign Students: The 256 undergraduates from foreign countries make up about 4% of the student body. The university provides these students with special counseling and special organizations.

Admissions: Foreign applicants must take the TOEFL and the SAT or ACT.

Procedure: The application deadline is January 1 (fall admission only). Students must carry health insurance, which is available through the university for a fee.

Admissions Contact: John Bunnell, Associate Dean of Admissions.

THOMAS AQUINAS COLLEGE   C–5
Santa Paula, California 93060   (805) 525-4417

F/T: 60M, 50W	Faculty: 13; n/av
P/T: none	Ph.D.'s: 53%
Grad: none	S/F Ratio: 8 to 1
Year: sems	Tuition: $4290
Appl: open	R and B: $2290
75 applied	41 accepted	35 enrolled
SAT: 610V 520M	ACT: 25	VERY COMPETITIVE

Thomas Aquinas College offers a bachelor's degree program based on a traditional "Great Books" curriculum that integrates the study of mathematics, natural sciences, history, literature, language, music, philosophy, and theology. The college is affiliated with the Roman Catholic Church. The library contains 10,000 volumes and subscribes to 25 periodicals.

Environment: The college's new campus is a 137-acre ranch 20 miles from Ventura. There is a new commons building, and the college uses the existing hacienda. All other buildings, including dormitories, are temporary.

Student Life: About half the students come from California. Virtually all students live on campus. About 95% are Catholic. Three percent are minority-group members. College housing is single-sex, and there are no visiting privileges. Students may keep cars on campus.

Organizations: There are no fraternities or sororities. The college sponsors special-interest, social, and religious groups. Daily mass and regular devotions are available to students.

Sports: The college does not participate in intercollegiate sports. There are 7 intramural sports for men and 6 for women.

Handicapped: The entire campus is accessible to wheelchair-bound students. Special facilities include wheelchair ramps and specially equipped rest rooms.

Graduates: The freshman dropout rate is 15%; 75% of the freshmen remain to graduate. About 65% of the graduates seek advanced degrees, including 2% who enter medical school and 8% who enter law school. Ten percent of the graduates enter business and industry.

Services: Placement, career and psychological counseling, and tutoring are provided free to students.

Programs of Study: The B. of Arts in Liberal Arts degree is granted upon completion of a required program that stresses the Great Books, basic skills (language, logic, music, and mathematics), and the traditional interrelationships of the liberal arts, science, and philosophy. Theology courses are included in the curriculum.

Special: There are no electives, majors, minors, lectures, or textbooks. Students read original writings of Western Civilization and discuss them in groups of 15 to 20 with their teachers. Many examinations are oral.

Admissions: Fifty-five percent of those who applied were accepted for the 1981–82 freshman class. The SAT scores of those who enrolled were as follows: Verbal—18% below 500, 40% between 500 and 599, 26% between 600 and 700, and 16% above 700; Math—16% below 500, 45% between 500 and 599, 21% between 600 and 700, and 18% above 700. The ACT scores were as follows: 75% between 24 and 25 and 25% between 26 and 28. Besides test scores, high school grades, and class rank, admissions officers consider evidence of special talents, recommendations by high school officials, personality, impressions made during an interview, advanced placement or honors courses, and written responses to application questions.

Procedure: Applicants must take the SAT or ACT. There are no application deadlines, but students are advised to submit their credentials early. New students are admitted only in fall. There is no application fee. Admissions decisions are made on a rolling basis.

Special: Deferred and early admissions plans are available.

Transfer: Transfer students must begin as freshmen.

Visiting: Prospective students may visit the campus any day classes are in session. Visitors may sit in on classes and stay overnight at the school. Arrangements should be made with the director of admissions.

Financial Aid: About 60% of the students receive aid; half work part-time on campus. The college, a member of CSS, tries to meet the financial needs of all students through a program of jobs, grants, and loans. The FAF or FFS is required. Aid applications are accepted until classes begin.

Foreign Students: Fifteen percent of the students are from foreign countries.

Admissions: Foreign students must take the TOEFL and either the SAT or the ACT.

Procedures: The application deadline is May 1; foreign students are admitted in the fall only. Foreign students must file the college's health form and must carry health insurance.

Admissions Contact: Thomas J. Susanka Jr., Director of Admissions.

UNITED STATES INTERNATIONAL UNIVERSITY
D-5

San Diego, California 92131   (714) 271-4300

F/T: 537M, 254W	Faculty: 198; n/av
P/T: 62M, 38W	Ph.D.'s: 85%
Grad: 845M, 666W	S/F Ratio: 17 to 1
Year: qtrs, ss	Tuition: $4320
Appl: see profile	R and B: $2520
765 applied	382 accepted	170 enrolled
SAT: 464V 464M	ACT: 19	COMPETITIVE

United States International University is a private institution offering undergraduate and graduate programs in the liberal arts and sciences and in professional fields. It is one of 4 associated schools that compose International University. The other 3 campuses are in London, Mexico City, and Nairobi. The university libraries house more than 407,000 volumes and subscribe to 1700 periodicals.

Environment: The campus is located in a suburban setting about 20 miles from metropolitan San Diego. Residence halls are designed as apartment units rather than dormitories.

Student Life: About 52% of the students come from California. About 80% are public school graduates. There are separate apartment clusters for men and women.

Organizations: Extracurricular activities include debate, drama, publications, student government, performing groups, and social and cultural events. There are no fraternities or sororities. Alcohol is prohibited on campus.

Sports: The university fields intercollegiate teams in 10 sports for men and 7 for women. Intramural competition also is available.

Graduates: About 40% of the freshmen drop out, and 35% remain to graduate. About 42% of the graduates pursue advanced degrees.

Services: The university provides health care, psychological counseling, tutoring, remedial instruction, placement aid, and career counseling.

Programs of Study: The university awards the B.A., B.S., and B.F.A. degrees. Associate, master's, and doctoral degrees also are conferred. Bachelor's degrees are offered in the following subjects: BUSINESS (accounting, business administration, financial management, hotel/restaurant management, outdoor recreation management), EDUCATION (elementary, health/physical, secondary), ENGLISH (English), FINE AND PERFORMING ARTS (art, dance, music, theater/dramatics), MATH AND SCIENCES (mathematics, natural sciences), PREPROFESSIONAL (dentistry, engineering, medicine), SOCIAL SCIENCES (anthropology, human behavior, international relations, law and human behavior, psychology, social sciences, sociology).

Required: Students must complete general education requirements.

Special: Independent study and travel-study programs are offered.

Honors: There is an honors program.

Admissions: About 50% of those who applied were accepted for the 1981-82 freshman class. A high school GPA of at least 2.75 is required. Recommendations, advanced placement or honors courses, extracurricular activities, and leadership potential are also considered.

Procedure: The SAT or ACT should be taken by December of the senior year. Applications should be submitted at least 30 days before the start of the term in which the student seeks to enroll. Notification is made on a rolling basis. There is a $25 application fee.

Special: Early and deferred admissions plans are offered. AP and CLEP credit is granted.

Transfer: Transfer students are admitted each quarter. A 2.0 GPA is needed. D grades are not accepted. At least 45 quarter units, of the 180 required for a bachelor's degree, must be completed in residence.

Visiting: Campus tours with student guides can be arranged with the office of admissions/student development coordinator. Visitors may sit in on classes.

Financial Aid: About 45% of the students receive aid. The university offers merit scholarships for freshmen and transfer students with 3.2 GPAs. Additional aid is provided by federal, state, and university funds, and is offered in the form of scholarships, grants, loans, and part-time campus employment. The FAF or FFS should be filed; applications are accepted as long as funds are available.

Foreign Students: About 43% of the students come from foreign countries. The university offers these students an intensive English program and special counseling.

Admissions: Students must take the TOEFL (the minimum acceptable score is 500) or the university's own English proficiency exam. No college entrance exams are required.

Procedure: Application deadlines are the same as those for American students. Students must present evidence of good health and of adequate funds. They also must carry health insurance, which is available through the university for a fee.

Admissions Contact: Judith A. Lewis, Director of Admissions.

UNIVERSITY OF CALIFORNIA

The University of California was founded in 1868 at Berkeley as the land-grant institution of California. The university as a whole is governed by the Regents of the University of California, and the entire university system is administered by a single president; each individual campus has a chief administrative officer. As California has grown, the university has necessarily expanded its facilities until today it is a state-wide university system with 9 separate campuses and University Extension and Cooperative Extension (agriculture, aquaculture, nutrition and consumer) services active throughout the state. Research facilities have spread beyond the borders of California. Medical centers are located at San Francisco and Los Angeles, medical schools at Davis, Irvine, and San Diego, and graduate instruction in oceanography at San Diego, optometry at Berkeley, and veterinary medicine at Davis are offered. Undergraduate instruction is offered at 8 of the 9 campuses: Berkeley, Davis, Irvine, Los Angeles, Riverside, San Diego, Santa Barbara, and Santa Cruz.

The university's full-time faculty now numbers about 6000, the majority of the faculty on most of the campuses holding the doctoral degree or having equivalent training. Student enrollment totals over 131,000 full-time students, making it the fourth largest institution in the nation. See the individual profiles for all information on these university campuses.

UNIVERSITY OF CALIFORNIA/ BERKELEY
B-3

Berkeley, California 94720   (415) 642-0200

F/T: 11,490M, 8600W	Faculty: 1880; I, + + $
P/T: none	Ph.D.'s: 80%
Grad: 5625M, 2925W	S/F Ratio: 16 to 1
Year: qtrs, ss	Tuition: $1203 ($4073)
Appl: Nov. 30	R and B: $2575
SAT or ACT: required	HIGHLY COMPETITIVE

Berkeley, the oldest campus of the University of California system, was established in 1868. It offers undergraduate and graduate programs in the liberal arts and professional fields. The undergraduate divisions include the colleges of Chemistry, Engineering, Environmental Design, Letters and Science, and Natural Resources. There are also 9 schools for professional studies. The libraries house 6 million volumes and 1.5 million microfilm items, and subscribe to 99,000 periodicals.

Environment: The 200-acre campus, situated in a city of 113,000 facing San Francisco across the Bay, is surrounded by 1300 acres of undeveloped hillside. Over 3000 students live in 16 residence halls. In addition, there are over 1000 apartments for married students, privately operated student cooperative residence halls and apartments, and fraternities and sororities.

Student Life: About 85% of the students are from California. About 31% live on campus. Residence halls are both single-sex and coed.

Organizations: There are 36 fraternities and 14 sororities on campus; 7% of the men and 8% of the women belong. Extracurricular activities include music, drama, debate, and religious activities, as well as hundreds of special-interest and departmental clubs.

Sports: Intercollegiate and intramural sports are available for men and women.

Handicapped: About 85% of the campus is accessible to handicapped students. Facilities include wheelchair ramps, parking areas, elevators, specially equipped rest rooms, and lowered telephones and drinking fountains. Special class scheduling can be arranged. Eleven counselors are available to handicapped students.

CALIFORNIA

Graduates: The freshman dropout rate is 25%, and 60% remain to graduate.

Services: Placement, career and psychological counseling; health care; tutoring; and remedial instruction are available.

Programs of Study: The university confers the A.B. and B.S. degrees. Master's and doctoral degrees are also awarded. Bachelor's degrees are offered in the following subjects: AREA STUDIES (Asian, Asian-American, Asian—South and Southeast Asian, Black/Afro-American, Chicano, Dutch, ethnic, Latin American, Native American, Near Eastern, Slavic, women's), BUSINESS (business administration), EDUCATION (health/physical), ENGLISH (English, journalism, literature, speech), FINE AND PERFORMING ARTS (art, art history, dance, film/photography, music, theater/dramatics), HEALTH SCIENCES (health arts and science, nutrition and clinical dietetics, nutrition and food sciences), LANGUAGES (French, German, Greek/Latin, Italian, linguistics, Oriental languages, Scandinavian languages, Slavic languages and literature, Spanish), MATH AND SCIENCES (astronomy, biochemistry, bioenergetics, biology, biophysics, botany, chemistry, computer science, conservation of natural resources, earth science, ecology/environmental studies, entomology, genetics, geology, geophysics, mathematics, microbiology, molecular biology, neurobiology, paleontology, geology, physical sciences, physics, plant and soil biology, plant pathology, soil resource management, statistics, zoology), PHILOSOPHY (classics, humanities, philosophy, religion), PRE-PROFESSIONAL (agriculture, architecture, engineering—bioengineering, engineering—chemical, engineering—civil, engineering—electrical engineering and computer science, engineering—geoscience, engineering—engineering mathematics, engineering—engineering science, engineering—industrial engineering and operations research, engineering—manufacturing, engineering—materials science, engineering—mechanical, engineering—mineral, engineering—nuclear, forestry, landscape architecture, pest management, social work, wood science and technology), SOCIAL SCIENCES (anthropology, economics, geography, government/political science, history, political economics, psychology, social sciences, sociology). Students may earn elementary and secondary teaching credentials.

Required: Students must demonstrate ability in English composition and a knowledge of American history and institutions. These requirements can be fulfilled by a satisfactory score on AP exams or ATs.

Special: Combined B.A.-B.S. degrees, student-designed majors, and study abroad are offered.

Honors: Numerous honor societies, including Phi Beta Kappa, have chapters on campus.

Admissions: About 47% of those who applied for a recent freshman class were accepted. Applicants should have completed 1 year of history, 3 years of English, 2 years of mathematics, 2 years of a foreign language, and 1 year of a laboratory science. California residents with a GPA of 3.3 or higher are admitted regardless of SAT or ACT scores. For those with a GPA between 2.8 and 3.2, admission is dependent on a combination of grades and SAT or ACT scores, as weighed by the University of California Freshman Eligibility Index, which is found in the university's catalog. The lower the GPA, the higher the test scores must be. Students also may qualify by examination alone, if they score a total of 1100 on the SAT and a total of 1650 on the 3 ATs (with no less than 500 on any of the 3). GPA and test score requirements are higher for out-of-state students.

Procedure: The SAT or ACT is generally required. Students also must take 3 ATs: English Composition, Mathematics I or II, and a social studies or foreign language test. Application deadlines are November 30 (fall), July 31 (winter), and October 31 (spring). The application fee is $25. A rolling admissions plan is followed.

Special: CLEP and AP credit is granted.

Transfer: Students from other California schools are given preference. Three quarters must be taken in residence. D grades are acceptable. Application deadlines are the same as those for freshmen.

Visiting: Tours for prospective students are given daily at 1 P.M. Visitors may sit in on classes. The student union should be contacted for arrangements.

Financial Aid: About 40% of the students receive aid. Scholarships, loans, and part-time jobs are available. The FAF is required.

Foreign Students: The university provides an intensive English course, special counseling, and special organizations for these students.

Admissions: Students should contact the admissions office for information on test requirements and application deadlines.

Procedure: Health insurance is required, and is available through the university for a fee.

Admissions Contact: Robert L. Bailey, Director of Admissions.

UNIVERSITY OF CALIFORNIA/DAVIS
Davis, California 95616   (916) 752-2971   B-2

F/T: 6574M, 7206W   Faculty: 1040; I, ++$
P/T: none   Ph.D.'s: 99%
Grad: 3670M, 1734W   S/F Ratio: 19 to 1
Year: qtrs, ss   Tuition: $993 ($3873)
Appl: Nov. 30   R and B: $2245
4300 applied   3260 accepted   2881 enrolled
SAT or ACT: required   VERY COMPETITIVE

The University of California/Davis was established in 1906. It consists of the colleges of Agricultural and Environmental Sciences, Engineering, and Letters and Science; the schools of Medicine, Veterinary Medicine, and Law; and the Graduate Division. The library houses over 1.5 million volumes and 1.3 million microfilm items, and subscribes to over 42,000 periodicals.

Environment: The 3600-acre campus is located in a community of 40,000 people, 14 miles from Sacramento. There are 11 dormitories on campus accommodating 3000 students, apartments for 476 married students, and off-campus residence halls for 1000 students.

Student Life: About 94% of the students come from California. Ninety-two percent are from public schools. About a fourth of the students live on campus. University housing is both coed and single-sex. There are visiting privileges in single-sex dorms. Students may keep cars on campus. Day-care services are provided in conjunction with the early childhood education program on campus. A fee is charged for these services.

Organizations: There are 10 fraternities and 7 sororities on campus. A wide variety of special-interest, departmental, religious, and service organizations are open to students.

Sports: The university competes in 14 intercollegiate sports for men and 9 for women. There are 17 intramural sports for men and 16 for women.

Handicapped: About 90% of the campus is accessible to handicapped students. Special facilities include wheelchair ramps, parking areas, elevators, specially equipped rest rooms, lowered drinking fountains and telephones, tutors, and transportation. Special class scheduling is also available. About 1% of the students have visual impairments, 1% are hearing-impaired. Telecommunications devices and reading machines are provided for these students. Four counselors are available to handicapped students.

Graduates: The freshman dropout rate is 14%; 65% remain to graduate.

Services: Students receive the following services free of charge: placement (for students and graduates), career counseling, psychological counseling, tutoring, and remedial instruction. Health care is available for a fee.

Programs of Study: B.A. and B.S. degrees are conferred; master's and doctoral degrees are also available. Bachelor's degrees are offered in the following subjects: AREA STUDIES (American, Asian, Black/Afro-American), EDUCATION (early childhood), ENGLISH (English, comparative literature, speech), FINE AND PERFORMING ARTS (art history, music, studio art), LANGUAGES (French, German, Greek/Latin, Italian, Russian, Spanish), MATH AND SCIENCES (biology, botany, chemistry, ecology/environmental science, geology, mathematics, physics, statistics, zoology), PHILOSOPHY (classics, philosophy, religion), PREPROFESSIONAL (engineering—aerospace, engineering—agricultural, engineering—biomedical, engineering—chemical, engineering—civil, engineering—electrical, engineering—mechanical, engineering—materials science), SOCIAL SCIENCES (anthropology, economics, geography, government/political science, history, international relations, psychology, social sciences, sociology). About 25% of the degrees are conferred in agriculture, 11% in engineering.

Required: All students must demonstrate an ability in English composition and a knowledge of American history and institutions. These requirements may be satisfied by AP exams, ATs, other appropriate tests, or in the case of history, by a course in that subject.

Special: Double major degrees, student-designed majors, study abroad, and work-study are available. The Experimental College emphasizes learning outside a formal classroom atmosphere.

Honors: Honors programs are offered in 9 departments. There are 13 honor societies on campus, including a chapter of Phi Beta Kappa.

Admissions: Of those who applied for the 1981–82 freshman class, 76% were accepted. Candidates should rank in the top eighth of their high school class and have a minimum GPA of 2.0. They should have completed the following courses: 1 year of history, 4 of English, 2 of mathematics, 1 of a laboratory science, 2 of a foreign language, and 1 advanced course of either mathematics, a foreign language, or science. Eligibility is determined by a weighted combination of GPA and SAT or ACT scores. Applicants may qualify by examination alone if they achieve a score of at least 1100 on the SAT or 26 on the ACT and scores of at least 500 on each of the 3 ATs.

Procedure: Application deadlines are November 30 (fall), July 31 (winter), and October 31 (spring). The SAT or ACT is required, as are 3 ATs (English composition, social studies or foreign language, mathematics). Applicants for the fall term are notified after April 15. A rolling admissions plan is followed. The application fee is $25.

Special: There is an early and a deferred admissions plan. AP credit is granted.

Transfer: For fall 1981, 1570 transfer students applied, 1141 were accepted, and 892 enrolled. A GPA of 2.0 is required for California residents; 2.8 for out-of-state applicants. The high school record is considered if the applicant has fewer than 84 quarter units. C grades or better grades transfer. Preference is given to students transferring from an in-state school. There is a 1-year residency requirement. Students must complete a total of 180 credits for a bachelor's degree. The application deadlines are the same as for freshmen.

Visiting: There are regularly scheduled orientations for prospective students. Guides are available for informal visits. Visitors may not sit in on classes or stay overnight at the school.

Financial Aid: About 37% of the students receive financial aid. Scholarships, loans, grants, and part-time employment are available through the university, which is a member of CSS. The average aid to freshmen from all sources is $3563. The FAF is required and should be filed 1 month prior to the application deadline, which is February 10.

Foreign Students: Foreign students constitute about 5% of the full-time enrollment. The university offers these students an intensive English course, special counseling, and special organizations.

Admissions: Prior to admission, foreign students must take an English proficiency examination (TOEFL, University of Michigan Language Test, or Comprehensive English Language Test). They must also take the SAT, and, if transferring from an American school, the ATs (CEEB).

Procedure: Application deadlines are the same as those for other freshmen. Foreign students must present proof of health (medical exam and history) after admission. Health insurance, although not required, is available through the university for a fee. Proof of funds adequate to cover 1 year of study is required.

Admissions Contact: Gary Tudor, Admissions Director.

UNIVERSITY OF CALIFORNIA/ IRVINE
Irvine, California 92717   D–5
(714) 833-6701

F/T: 3890M, 3852W   Faculty: n/av; I, ++$
P/T: 396M, 347W   Ph.D.'s: 98%
Grad: 881M, 641W   S/F Ratio: 12 to 1
Year: qtrs, ss   Tuition: $816 ($3696)
Appl: Nov. 1   R and B: $2833
3720 applied   2728 accepted   1958 enrolled
SAT: 500V 550M   VERY COMPETITIVE

One of the newer campuses of the University of California system, Irvine admitted its first students in 1965. It includes the schools of Biological Sciences, Engineering, Fine Arts, Humanities, Physical Sciences, and Social Sciences; the Office of Teacher Education; the Graduate School of Management; and the College of Medicine. The library houses 1,000,000 volumes and 469,291 microfilm items, and subscribes to 15,000 periodicals.

Environment: The 1510-acre suburban campus is located 3 miles from the Pacific Ocean and 50 miles south of Los Angeles. The 200-acre San Joaquin Freshwater Marsh Reserve is adjacent to the campus. Residence halls accommodate 1550 students, and there are on-campus apartments for 800 undergraduates. There are also 562 apartment units for married and graduate students.

Student Life: About 86% of the students come from California; 30% reside on campus. About 42% are minority-group members. Campus housing is both coed and single-sex; there are visiting privileges in the single-sex housing. Students may keep cars on campus. Day-care services are available to all students for a fee. Drinking on campus is restricted.

Organizations: There are 7 fraternities and 7 sororities on campus. Numerous extracurricular activities are offered.

CALIFORNIA 81

Sports: The university competes in 9 intercollegiate sports for men and 6 for women. There are 10 intramural sports for men and 9 for women.

Handicapped: The campus is completely accessible to handicapped students. Facilities include wheelchair ramps, parking areas, elevators, specially equipped rest rooms, lowered drinking fountains, and a special rest area. Four counselors are available to handicapped students.

Graduates: Eleven percent of entering freshmen drop out by the end of the first year; 48% remain to graduate.

Services: Students receive the following services free of charge: placement (for students and graduates), health care, psychological counseling, career counseling, tutoring, and remedial instruction.

Programs of Study: B.A., B.S., and B.M. degrees are offered. Master's and doctoral degrees are also conferred. Bachelor's degrees are offered in the following subjects: AREA STUDIES (comparative cultures), ENGLISH (English, humanities, literature), FINE AND PERFORMING ARTS (art history, dance, fine arts, music, music performance, studio art, theater/dramatics), LANGUAGES (classical civilization, French, German, linguistics, Russian, Spanish), MATH AND SCIENCES (biology, chemistry, ecology/environmental science, information and computer science, mathematics, physics), PHILOSOPHY (classics, humanities, philosophy), SOCIAL SCIENCES (anthropology, economics, geography, government/political science, history, psychology, social sciences, sociology). Forty percent of undergraduate degrees are conferred in math and sciences, 20% in social sciences, 19% in social ecology.

Required: All students must demonstrate an ability in English composition and a knowledge of American history and institutions. The composition requirement may be satisfied either by a score of 3 or higher on the AP or 600 or higher on the AT.

Special: Combined B.A.-B.S. degrees, student-designed majors, study abroad, independent study through examination, computer-assisted instruction, and a 3-2 program in management are offered.

Honors: There is an honors program in political science; honors courses are offered in chemistry and math. Phi Beta Kappa has a chapter on campus.

Admissions: Seventy-three percent of those who applied were accepted for the 1981–82 freshman class. The SAT scores of those who enrolled were as follows: Verbal—48% below 500, 37% between 500 and 599, 13% between 600 and 700, and 2% above 700; Math—15% below 500, 47% between 500 and 599, 30% between 600 and 700, and 8% above 700. Applicants should have a GPA of at least 2.78 and should rank in the upper 12% of their high school class. They should have completed the following courses: 1 year of history, 4 years of college preparatory English, 2 years of mathematics, 1 year of laboratory science, 2 years of a foreign language, and 1 of the following: 1 year of advanced mathematics, 1 additional year of laboratory science, 1 additional year in the foreign language used in the requirement above, or 2 years of another foreign language. Eligibility is determined by a weighted combination of GPA and SAT or ACT scores. Applicants lacking the required high school courses may be able to qualify by examination alone if they achieve a score of at least 1100 (composite) on the SAT or 26 on the ACT and minimum scores of 500 on each of the 3 ATs (nonresidents must achieve a total score of at least 1730 on the ATs).

Procedure: The application deadlines are November 1 (fall), July 1 (winter), and October 1 (spring). The SAT or ACT and 3 ATs (English Composition, Mathematics Level 1 or 2, and a foreign language or social studies test). There is a rolling admissions plan. The application fee is $25.

Special: There are early decision, early admissions, and deferred admissions plans.

Transfer: For fall 1981, there were 2100 applications, 1429 were accepted, and 1077 students enrolled. A GPA of 2.78 is required. If the high school record is unacceptable, the GPA must be earned on at least 84 quarter units in acceptable college courses. Preference is given to students transferring from community colleges in the state. All students must complete, at the university, the last 3 quarters; 180 credits are required for a bachelor's degree. Application deadlines are the same as those for freshmen.

Visiting: There are regularly scheduled orientations for prospective students. Guides for informal visits are available. Visitors may sit in on classes and stay overnight at the school. The office of relations with schools and colleges should be contacted for arrangements.

Financial Aid: About 39% of the students receive financial aid. About 45% work part-time on campus. Scholarships, loans, and campus employment are available. The university is a member of the CSS; the Student Aid Application for California should be filed by February 12 (fall entry).

82 CALIFORNIA

Foreign Students: Three percent of the full-time students come from foreign countries. An intensive English course, an intensive English program, special counseling, and special organizations are available for these students.

Admissions: Foreign students must achieve a TOEFL score of at least 550 and must take the SAT or ACT. ATs are also required.

Procedure: Application deadlines are the same as those for other students. Foreign students must present proof of health.

Admissions Contact: James E. Dunning, Director of Admissions.

UNIVERSITY OF CALIFORNIA/ LOS ANGELES C–5
Los Angeles, California 90024 (213) 825-3101

F/T, P/T:	Faculty: n/av; I, ++$
11,202M, 11,406W	Ph.D.'s: n/av
Grad: 7199M, 4808W	S/F Ratio: 17 to 1
Year: qtrs, ss	Tuition: $1023 ($4173)
Appl: see profile	R and B: $2000–2600
8434 applied	6364 accepted 4484 enrolled
SAT: 486V 555M	COMPETITIVE+

Established in 1919, the University of California/Los Angeles (UCLA) is the largest campus in the university system, and ranks as one of the major universities in the country. The major divisions include 69 departments of instruction, 13 schools and colleges, 25 interdepartmental instruction programs, a graduate division, and 23 organized research units. The library contains over 4 million volumes and subscribes to 65,000 periodicals.

Environment: Situated within the corporate limits of Los Angeles, the 411-acre urban campus is located at the foot of the Santa Monica Mountains, 5 miles from the Pacific Ocean. The 135 buildings include the Jerry Lewis Neuromuscular Research Center, Louis Factor Health Sciences building, and Schoenberg Hall Music building addition. Facilities include dormitories, on- and off-campus apartments, fraternity and sorority houses, and married student housing.

Student Life: Most of the students come from the West and Northwest; about 90% come from public schools. Twenty percent of the students live on campus. Thirty percent of the students are minority-group members. Campus housing is coed. Limited day-care services are available to all students on a fee basis.

Organizations: There are 27 fraternities and 18 sororities on campus to which 13% of the men and 22% of the women belong. Extracurricular activities include departmental, political, religious, musical, and social groups, and publications.

Sports: The university competes in 17 intercollegiate sports for men and 11 for women. There are 15 intramural sports for men and 12 for women.

Handicapped: The campus is generally accessible to handicapped students. Special facilities include wheelchair ramps, parking areas, elevators, specially equipped rest rooms, and lowered drinking fountains and telephones. Special class scheduling is also available. The handicapped students coordinator and the office of special services assist handicapped students. There is also a handicapped students union. Services are available for visually impaired students.

Graduates: The freshman dropout rate is 19%; 55% remain to graduate.

Services: Placement, career and psychological counseling, health care, tutoring, and remedial instruction are available.

Programs of Study: The B.A. and B.S. degrees are offered. Master's and doctoral degrees are also conferred. Bachelor's degrees are offered in the following subjects: AREA STUDIES (Black/Afro-American, Chicano, East Asian, Latin American, Near Eastern), ENGLISH (communications studies, English), FINE AND PERFORMING ARTS (art education, art history, design, film/photography, music, music composition, music education, music performance, music theory, radio/TV, studio art, theater/dramatics), HEALTH SCIENCES (nursing, public health), LANGUAGES (African languages, Arabic, Chinese, French, German, Greek/Latin, Hebrew, Italian, Japanese, Portuguese, Russian, Scandinavian languages, Spanish), MATH AND SCIENCES (astronomy, atmospheric sciences, biochemistry, biology, chemistry, cybernetics, geology, kinesiology, mathematics, microbiology and immunology, physics, psychology), PHILOSOPHY (classics, philosophy, study of religion), PREPROFESSIONAL (engineering), SOCIAL SCIENCES (anthropology, business economics, economics, government/political science, history, sociology). About 39% of the degrees are conferred in social sciences, 20% in life sciences.

Required: All students must demonstrate an ability in English composition and a knowledge of American history and institutions. The composition requirement may be satisfied either by a score of 3 or higher on the AP or 600 or higher on the AT.

Special: Student-designed majors are permitted. Study abroad is available to upper division students.

Honors: There are numerous honor societies on campus.

Admissions: Of those who applied for the 1981–82 freshman class, 75% were accepted. California residents should have a GPA of at least 2.8; nonresidents, a GPA of at least 3.4. They should have completed the following courses: 1 year of history, 4 years of college preparatory English, 2 years of mathematics, 1 year of a laboratory science, 2 years of a foreign language, and 1 of the following: 1 year of advanced mathematics, 1 additional year of laboratory science, 1 additional year in the foreign language used in the requirement above, or 2 years of another foreign language. Eligibility is determined by a weighted combination of GPA and SAT or ACT scores. Applicants lacking the required high school courses may be able to qualify by examination alone if they achieve a score of at least 1100 (composite) on the SAT or 26 on the ACT and minimum scores of 500 on each of the 3 ATs (nonresidents must achieve a total score of at least 1730 on the ATs).

Procedure: Applications should be filed between November 1 and November 30 (fall entry), between July 1 and July 31 (winter entry), or between October 1 and October 31 (spring entry). The SAT or ACT and 3 ATs are required. The application fee is $25.

Special: CLEP and AP credit is given.

Transfer: For fall 1981, 5202 applications were received, 3035 were accepted, and 2127 students enrolled. California residents need a 2.0 GPA; nonresidents, a 2.8 GPA. D grades do not transfer. All students must complete, at the university, 36 of the last 48 credits; 180 credits are required for a bachelor's degree. Application deadlines are the same as those for freshmen.

Visiting: There are regularly scheduled orientations for prospective students. Guides are available for informal visits. Visitors may sit in on classes with the instructor's permission. Students may stay at the school during summer orientation programs. The office of relations with schools should be contacted for arrangements.

Financial Aid: About 48% of the students receive financial aid. About 17% work part-time on campus. The average award to undergraduates is $2437. The university is a member of CSS. Scholarships, loans, and grants are available. The Academic Advancement Program provides financial aid for disadvantaged and nontraditional students who are California residents. The financial aid application deadline is February 10; the FAF must be filed 1 month prior to this deadline.

Foreign Students: Six percent of the full-time students come from foreign countries. An intensive English course, special counseling, and special organizations are available for these students.

Admissions: Foreign students must take the university's English proficiency exam, the SAT or ACT, and ATs.

Procedure: Application deadlines are July 1 (fall), October 1 (winter), and January 1 (spring). Foreign students must present proof of health and proof of adequate funds. Health insurance is required and is available through the university for a fee.

Admissions Contact: Rae Siporin, Director, Undergraduate Admissions and Relations with Schools.

UNIVERSITY OF CALIFORNIA/ RIVERSIDE D–5
Riverside, California 92521 (714) 787-3411

F/T: 1466M, 1538W	Faculty: 323; I, ++$
P/T: 151M, 136W	Ph.D.'s: 99%
Grad: 849M, 624W	S/F Ratio: 13 to 1
Year: qtrs, ss	Tuition: $943 ($3823)
Appl: see profile	R and B: $1995
1384 applied	971 accepted 700 enrolled
SAT or ACT: required	VERY COMPETITIVE

The Riverside campus of the University of California was established in 1954. The major divisions include the College of Humanities and Social Science, the College of Natural and Agricultural Sciences, the School of Education, the Graduate School of Administration, and the Graduate Division. The library contains 1,050,134 volumes, 836,442 microfilm items, and subscribes to 14,558 periodicals.

Environment: The 1200-acre urban campus is located 2 miles from downtown Riverside and 50 miles from Los Angeles. There are several agricultural and environmental research centers on campus. Living facilities include dormitories, on-campus apartments, fraternity and sorority houses, and married student housing.

Student Life: More than 94% of the students are from California; 39% live on campus. About 25% are minority-group members. Campus housing is both coed and single-sex; there are visiting privileges in the single-sex housing. Students may keep cars on campus. Day-care services are available to all students for a fee.

Organizations: There are 5 fraternities and 5 sororities on campus; 6% of the men and 7% of the women belong to one of them. Extracurricular activities include professional, academic, social, service, and special-interest groups, as well as publications and an FM radio station.

Sports: The university competes in 9 intercollegiate sports for men and 6 for women. There are 12 intramural sports for men and 12 for women.

Handicapped: About 95% of the campus is accessible to handicapped students. Facilities include wheelchair ramps, parking areas, elevators, specially equipped rest rooms, lowered drinking fountains and telephones, and a wheelchair repair center. Three counselors are available to handicapped students.

Graduates: The freshman dropout rate is 25%; 50% remain to graduate. Fifty percent of the graduates pursue advanced degrees.

Services: Students receive the following services free of charge: placement (for students and graduates), career counseling, psychological counseling, health care, tutoring, and remedial instruction.

Programs of Study: A.B. and B.S. degrees are offered. Master's and doctoral degrees are also available. Bachelor's degrees are offered in the following subjects: AREA STUDIES (Black/Afro-American, Latin American), BUSINESS (administrative studies), EDUCATION (liberal studies), ENGLISH (English, literature), FINE AND PERFORMING ARTS (art, art history, dance, music, theater/dramatics), HEALTH SCIENCES (human development), LANGUAGES (French, German, linguistics, Spanish), MATH AND SCIENCES (biochemistry, biology, biomedical sciences, botany, chemistry, computer science, ecology/environmental science, entomology, geology, geophysics, mathematics, paleobiology, physical sciences, physics, plant science, psychobiology, soil science, statistics), PHILOSOPHY (humanities, philosophy, religion), SOCIAL SCIENCES (anthropology, economics, geography, government/political science, history, psychology, public service, sociology).

Required: Each college has a general education requirement.

Special: Combined B.A.-B.S. degrees, student-designed majors, and study abroad are offered.

Honors: There are 2 honor societies on campus.

Admissions: Of those who applied for the 1981–82 freshman class, 70% were accepted. Applicants should rank in the upper one-eighth of their high school class and should have a GPA of at least 2.78 (3.4 for nonresidents). They should have completed the following courses: 1 year of history, 1 year of a laboratory science, 2 years of a foreign language, and 1 of the following: 1 year of advanced mathematics, 1 additional year of the foreign language used in the requirement above, or 2 years of another foreign language. Eligibility is determined by a weighted combination of GPA and SAT or ACT scores. Applicants lacking the required high school courses may be able to qualify by examination alone if they achieve a score of at least 1100 (composite) on the SAT or 26 on the ACT and minimum scores of 500 on each of the 3 ATs (nonresidents must achieve a total score of at least 1730 on the ATs).

Procedure: The SAT or ACT and 3 ATs are required. Application deadlines vary; freshmen are admitted in the fall, winter, and spring quarters. There is a $25 application fee.

Transfer: For fall 1981, 510 transfer students were accepted. California residents need a 2.4 GPA; out-of-state applicants, a 2.8 GPA. All students must complete, at the university, 36 of the 180 credits required for a bachelor's degree. Application deadlines vary; transfer students are admitted in the fall, winter, and spring terms.

Visiting: There are regularly scheduled orientations for prospective students. Guides are available for informal visits. Visits are best scheduled on weekdays from 9 A.M. to 2 P.M. and on weekends from 10 A.M. to 2 P.M. Visitors may sit in on classes and stay overnight at the school.

Financial Aid: About 55% of the students receive financial aid. About 24% work part-time on campus. The university awards scholarships and grants ranging from $100 to $5850 per year. A limited number are available to out-of-state students. Loans from various sources range from $100 to $5000 per year. Part-time employment is also available. The university is a member of CSS and requires the Student Aid Application for California. Application deadlines are November 20 (fall), February 26 (winter), and May 21 (spring).

Foreign Students: An intensive English program, special counseling, and special organizations are available for these students.

Admissions: Foreign students must achieve a TOEFL score of at least 550. No college entrance exams are required.

Procedure: The application deadlines are July 1 (fall), October 1 (winter), and January 1 (spring). Foreign students must present proof of funds adequate to cover the entire period of study. Health insurance is required and is available through the university for a fee.

Admissions Contact: Robert B. Herschler, Admissions Officer.

UNIVERSITY OF CALIFORNIA/ SAN DIEGO D-5
La Jolla, California 92093 (714) 452-3160

F/T: 5414M, 4432W	Faculty: n/av; I, + +$
P/T: none	Ph.D.'s: n/av
Grad: 1779M, 694W	S/F Ratio: 19 to 1
Year: qtrs, ss	Tuition: $1005 ($3885)
Appl: Dec. 1	R and B: $2200–3390
4306 applied	3377 accepted	2100 enrolled
SAT: 510V 580M		VERY COMPETITIVE

This campus was established as a marine station in the late 1800s by Berkeley zoologists. Today, the station, the Scripps Institution of Oceanography, has expanded into the University of California at San Diego. The university consists of 4 colleges, the School of Medicine, and the Scripps Institution. The library contains 1.4 million volumes and 700,000 microfilm items, and subscribes to 26,000 periodicals.

Environment: The 1253-acre campus is located on the Pacific coast in a suburban area 12 miles north of San Diego. Residence halls and on-campus apartments house 3400 students; there are 680 apartments for married students.

Student Life: The majority of students come from California. Forty percent live on campus. About 22% are minority-group members. Campus housing is both coed and single-sex; there are visiting privileges in the single-sex housing. Students may keep cars on campus. Day-care services are available to all students.

Organizations: There are 2 sororities on campus; 1% of the women belong. Numerous extracurricular activities are available.

Sports: The university competes in 19 intercollegiate sports for men and 18 for women. There are 13 intramural sports for men and 13 for women.

Handicapped: About 98% of the campus is accessible to handicapped students. Facilities include wheelchair ramps, parking areas, elevators, specially equipped rest rooms, lowered drinking fountains and telephones, electric doors, accessible dormitories, special transportation, tutors, and interpreters. Special class scheduling is also available. Counselors are available to handicapped students.

Services: The following services are offered free of charge to all students: placement, career counseling, health care, tutoring, remedial instruction, and psychological counseling.

Programs of Study: The B.A. and B.S. degrees are granted. Master's and doctoral degrees are also conferred. Bachelor's degrees are offered in the following subjects: AREA STUDIES (Chicano, Chinese, Third World, urban), ENGLISH (English, literature, writing), FINE AND PERFORMING ARTS (art, art history, art history/criticism, music, music/humanities, studio art, theater/dramatics), LANGUAGES (Chinese, French, German, linguistics, Spanish), MATH AND SCIENCES (biochemistry, biology, chemistry, computer science, earth science, mathematics, physical sciences, physics, statistics), PHILOSOPHY (classics, philosophy), PREPROFESSIONAL (engineering), SOCIAL SCIENCES (anthropology, communications, economics, government/political science, history, psychology, sociology, urban studies and planning).

Required: Each of the 4 colleges has its own general education requirements, reflecting the different educational philosophies of the colleges.

Special: Student-designed majors are permitted.

Honors: Honors programs are offered in biology, economics, history, literature, political science, and experimental psychology. Phi Beta Kappa has a chapter on campus.

Admissions: Seventy-eight percent of those who applied were accepted for the 1981–82 freshman class. The SAT scores of those who enrolled in the 1980–81 class were as follows: Verbal—27% between 500 and 599, 12% between 600 and 700, and 3% above 700; Math —28% between 500 and 599, 24% between 600 and 700, and 7% above 700. Applicants should rank in the top one-eighth of their high school class. They should have completed the following courses: 1 year of history, 1 year of a laboratory science, 2 years of a foreign language, and 1 of the following: 1 year of advanced mathematics, 1 additional year of laboratory science, 1 additional year in the foreign language used in the requirement above, or 2 years of another foreign language. Eligibility is determined by a weighted combination of GPA and SAT or ACT scores. Applicants lacking the required high school courses may be able to qualify by examination alone if they achieve a score of at least 1100 (composite) on the SAT or 26 on the ACT and minimum scores of 500 on each of the 3 ATs (nonresidents must achieve a total score of at least 1730 on the ATs).

Procedure: The university requires the SAT or ACT and 3 ATs (English Composition, Math Level 1 or 2, and a foreign language or social studies test). Priority dates for filing applications are December 1 (fall), August 1 (winter), November 1 (spring), and July 1 (summer). A rolling admissions plan is followed. There is a $25 application fee.

Special: The university has a deferred admissions plan.

Transfer: For fall 1981, 1786 applications were received; 1137 were accepted, and 788 students enrolled. California residents must have a GPA of at least 2.0; nonresidents, a GPA of at least 2.8. All students must complete, at the university, 36 of the 180 credits required for a bachelor's degree. Deadlines are the same as those for freshmen.

Visiting: Tours are scheduled regularly for prospective students. Guides are available for informal visits. Visitors may sit in on classes but may not stay overnight at the school. The office of relations with schools should be contacted for arrangements.

Financial Aid: About 40% of the students receive financial aid. About 25% work part-time on campus. Scholarships and other forms of aid are available. The priority deadline for application for financial aid is July 1. The university is a member of CSS. The Student Aid Application for California is required.

Foreign Students: Seven percent of the full-time students come from foreign countries. An intensive English program, special counseling, and special organizations are available for these students.

Admissions: Foreign students must achieve a TOEFL score of at least 550. No college entrance exams are required.

Procedure: Application deadlines are the same as those for other students. Foreign students must present proof of health and proof of funds adequate to cover the entire period of study. Health insurance is required and is available through the university for a fee.

Admissions Contact: Ronald J. Bowker, Registrar and Admissions Officer.

UNIVERSITY OF CALIFORNIA/ SANTA BARBARA C–5

Santa Barbara, California 93106   (805) 961-2881

F/T: 13,545 M&W	Faculty: n/av; I + + $
P/T: none	Ph.D.'s: n/av
Grad: 2166 M&W	S/F Ratio: 19 to 1
Year: qtrs, ss	Tuition: $816 ($3696)
Appl: see profile	R and B: $3000
2911 enrolled	
SAT or ACT: required	**VERY COMPETITIVE**

The University of California/Santa Barbara consists of the colleges of Creative Studies, Engineering, and Letters and Science, the Graduate Division, and the Graduate School of Education. The library houses more than 1.2 million volumes and subscribes to 17,500 periodicals.

Environment: The 804-acre suburban campus is 10 miles from Santa Barbara and 100 miles northwest of Los Angeles. The campus includes a mile of beach frontage. Living facilities include dormitories, on- and off-campus apartments, fraternity and sorority houses, and married student housing.

Student Life: About 95% of the students come from the West and Northwest. Eighty percent are from public schools. Campus housing is coed.

Organizations: There are 9 fraternities and 11 sororities on campus. Extracurricular activities include musical organizations, drama groups, departmental organizations, religious groups, and student government associations.

Sports: The university competes in 10 intercollegiate sports for men and 8 for women. Over 70 intramural sports are offered.

Handicapped: Facilities for handicapped students include wheelchair ramps, parking areas, elevators, specially equipped rest rooms, and lowered drinking fountains and telephones. Special class scheduling is also available.

Graduates: About 65% of the freshmen remain to graduate; 45% of the graduates pursue advanced degrees.

Services: Students receive the following services free of charge: placement (for students and graduates), career counseling, psychological counseling, health care, and tutoring. Remedial instruction is available on a fee basis.

Programs of Study: The B.A., B.S., and B.Mus. degrees are offered. Master's and doctoral degrees are also available. Bachelor's degrees are offered in the following subjects: AREA STUDIES (Black/Afro-American, Asian, Chicano), BUSINESS (business economics, economics, economics/mathematics), EDUCATION (curriculum and instruction, education administration, education psychology, elementary, secondary, special, student personnel), ENGLISH (English, literature), FINE AND PERFORMING ARTS (art history, dance, music, studio art, theater/dramatics), HEALTH SCIENCES (speech and hearing), LANGUAGES (Chinese, French, German, Greek/Latin, Italian, Portuguese, Spanish), MATH AND SCIENCES (biochemistry and molecular biology, biology, botany, chemistry, ecology/environmental science, geology, mathematics, pharmacology, physics, physiology and cell biology, zoology), PHILOSOPHY (classics, philosophy, religious studies), PREPROFESSIONAL (engineering, law and society), SOCIAL SCIENCES (anthropology, economics, geography, government/political science, history, psychology, sociology).

Required: All students must demonstrate an ability in English composition and a knowledge of American history and institutions. The composition requirement may be satisfied by a score of 3 or higher on the AP or by an acceptable score on the AT.

Special: Student-designed majors and study abroad are available.

Honors: Honors programs are offered by the music, economics, history, French, political science, and electrical and mechanical engineering departments. There are 13 honor societies on campus.

Admissions: Applicants should have a GPA of at least 3.3. They should have completed the following courses: 1 year of history, 1 year of a laboratory science, 2 years of a foreign language, and 1 of the following: 1 year of advanced mathematics, 1 additional year of the foreign language used in the requirement above, or 2 years of another foreign language. Eligibility is determined by a weighted combination of GPA and SAT or ACT scores. Applicants lacking the required high school courses may be able to qualify by examination alone if they achieve a score of at least 1100 (composite) on the SAT or 26 on the ACT and minimum scores of 500 on each of the 3 ATs (nonresidents must achieve a total score of at least 1730 on the ATs).

Procedure: Opening dates for applications are November 1 (fall), August 1 (winter), October 1 (spring), and March 1 (summer). There is a $25 application fee. A rolling admissions plan is followed.

Special: There is a deferred admissions plan. AP credit is given.

Transfer: In-state applicants must have a 2.4 GPA; a 2.8 GPA is required for out-of-state applicants who would not have qualified as incoming freshmen. All students must complete the 180 or more credits required for a bachelor's degree. Application deadlines are the same as those for freshmen.

Visiting: Guided tours for prospective students and their parents are available at 11 A.M. and 2 P.M. during academic sessions. Visitors may sit in on classes but may not stay overnight at the school. Contact the tour coordinator, office of relations with schools, for arrangements.

Financial Aid: About 80% of the students receive financial aid. Aid is available through scholarships, loans, grants, and campus employment. The university is a member of the CSS and requires the SAAC 1 month prior to the application deadline. The deadline for financial aid applications is April 15.

Foreign Students: Special counseling and special organizations are available for these students.

Admissions: Foreign students must take the TOEFL or the University of Michigan Language Test and the SAT or ACT.

Admissions Contact: William J. Villa, Director of Admissions.

UNIVERSITY OF CALIFORNIA/ SANTA CRUZ B–3

Santa Cruz, California 95064   (408) 429-2705

F/T: 3155M, 3180W	Faculty: 294; I, + $
P/T: none	Ph.D.'s: 90%
Grad: 320M, 206W	S/F Ratio: 18 to 1
Year: qtrs, ss	Tuition: $1039 ($3919)
Appl: see profile	R and B: $2550
3074 applied	2104 accepted	1347 enrolled
SAT(mean): 517V 555M	**VERY COMPETITIVE**

The Santa Cruz campus of the University of California, established in 1965, emphasizes undergraduate education in arts and sciences. The library contains 646,643 volumes and 229,568 microfilm items, and subscribes to 10,115 periodicals.

Environment: The campus, situated on 2000 acres of forest and meadowlands, is located in a suburban area 75 miles from San Francisco and 35 miles from San Jose. Each of the 8 residential colleges on campus is a self-contained unit with its own residence halls, classrooms, dining halls, and student activities areas. University-sponsored living facilities include dormitories, on-campus apartments, and married-student quarters.

Student Life: About 82% of the students come from California, and 88% come from public schools. Half the students live on campus. About 14% are members of minority groups. Campus housing is both coed and single-sex; single-sex dormitories have visiting privileges. Students may keep cars on campus. Drinking on campus is prohibited for students under age 21. Day-care services are available.

Organizations: There are no fraternities or sororities. Extracurricular activities include student government, drama, publications, art, radio, films, crafts, and on-campus cultural events.

Sports: The university fields intercollegiate teams in 5 sports for men and 4 for women. Eight intramural sports are offered for men and 8 for women. In addition, men can participate in 9 club sports, and women in 10.

Handicapped: About 65% of the campus is accessible to handicapped students. Special facilities include wheelchair ramps, parking areas, elevators, specially equipped rest rooms, and lowered drinking fountains. Special class scheduling, registration, and transportation are also available. The office of handicapped student services will help arrange assistance.

Graduates: About 55% of the graduates pursue advanced degrees.

Services: Students receive the following services free of charge: placement, career counseling, psychological counseling, tutoring, and remedial instruction. Preventive health services and counseling are also offered without charge.

Programs of Study: The B.A. and B.S. degrees are offered. Master's and doctoral degrees are also conferred. Bachelor's degrees are offered in the following subjects: AREA STUDIES (American, Asian, French, Latin American, Medieval, Russian, urban, Western civilization, women's), BUSINESS (computer science), ENGLISH (creative writing, literature), FINE AND PERFORMING ARTS (art, art history, dance, film/photography, music, studio art, theater/dramatics), LANGUAGES (French, German, Greek/Latin, Italian, Russian, Spanish), MATH AND SCIENCES (biology, chemistry, earth science, ecology/environmental science, geology, marine science, mathematics, physics, psychobiology), PHILOSOPHY (classics, philosophy, religion), SOCIAL SCIENCES (anthropology, community studies, economics, environmental studies, government/political science, history, modern society and social thought, psychology, sociology). Of the undergraduate degrees conferred, 36% are in social sciences and 36% are in math and sciences.

Required: Three courses each in humanities, social science, and natural science are required of all students. Individual colleges may require an interdisciplinary core course for first-year students.

Special: Study-abroad programs, independent study, field study, student-taught courses, work-study programs, and community study projects are offered. The education program offers courses and student-teaching internships required for a preliminary teaching certificate. Other preprofessional programs include architecture, dentistry, engineering, forestry, law library science, medicine, pharmacy, social work, veterinary science, business administration, international relations, journalism, nursing, nutrition, public administration, and public health. Students may design their own majors.

Honors: Students may earn honors in their major field of study.

Admissions: About 68% of those who applied were accepted for the 1981-82 freshman class. The SAT scores of those who enrolled broke down as follows: Verbal—35% below 500, 38% between 500 and 599, 17% between 600 and 700, and 3% above 700; Math—30% below 500, 38% between 500 and 599, 26% between 600 and 700, and 6% above 700. California residents should rank in the top 12% of their high school class and have a B average in all required subjects taken after 9th grade. The required units are 1 of U.S. history, 4 of English, 2 of math, 1 of a laboratory science, 2 of a foreign language, and 1 or 2 advanced courses in mathematics, science, or a foreign language. Students seeking admission to science programs should present additional units in science and mathematics. Nonresidents of California should have a 3.4 average, and their academic standing must be comparable to the top 50% of eligible California residents. Advanced placement or honors courses, recommendations by school officials, and evidence of special talents may be considered in individual cases.

Procedure: Applicants must take the SAT or ACT. Three ATs also are required: English Composition, Math I or II, and either a foreign language or a social studies test. Applications for fall admission should be filed by November 30 for priority consideration, with March 30 as the final deadline. Other application deadlines are July 1 to 30 (winter), October 1 to 31 (spring), and May 1 to 31 (summer). There is a rolling admissions plan. The application fee is $25.

Special: There are early admissions and early decision plans. AP credit is given.

Transfer: For fall 1981, 1648 transfer students applied, 1007 were accepted, and 711 enrolled. California residents with at least 56 semester or 84 quarter hours should have a 2.0 to 2.4 average; nonresidents with enough hours should have a 2.8. Applicants with fewer hours should meet freshman requirements. D grades transfer. All eligible California junior college transfers are accepted. Students must earn, in residence, at least 45 of the 180 quarter hours required for a bachelor's degree. Application deadlines are the same as those for freshmen.

Visiting: There are regularly scheduled orientations for prospective students. Tour guides for informal visits are available. Visitors may sit in on classes with the permission of the instructor. The admissions office should be contacted for arrangements.

Financial Aid: About 43% of the students receive financial aid. Scholarships, loans, and part-time employment are available. Aid packages combining grants, work-study, and loans are awarded on the basis of need. The application deadline for priority consideration is February 10. The university is a member of CSS. The SAAC, California Grant Application, and university aid application are required from state residents; nonresidents may file the FAF.

Foreign Students: The foreign students at the university make up 2% of its enrollment. An intensive English course, an intensive English program, special counseling, and special organizations are provided.

Admissions: Applicants must score 550 or better on the TOEFL or 85 or better on the University of Michigan Language Test. No academic exams are required.

Procedure: Applications should be submitted between November 1 and 30 for fall entry, July 1 and 31 for winter entry, and October 1 and 31 for spring entry. Proof of good health and of adequate funds for the length of time required to earn a degree is required. Foreign students must carry health insurance, which is available through the university for a fee.

Admissions Contact: Richard Moll, Dean of Admissions.

UNIVERSITY OF LA VERNE D-5
La Verne, California 91750 (714) 593-3511

F/T: 484M, 581W	Faculty: n/av; IIA, –$
P/T: 77M, 113W	Ph.D.'s: n/av
Grad: 103M, 278W	S/F Ratio: 17 to 1
Year: 4-1-4, ss	Tuition: $4690
Appl: open	R and B: $2590
1411 applied	796 accepted 331 enrolled
SAT: 400V 410M	LESS COMPETITIVE

The University of La Verne, founded in 1891, is a small, private, liberal arts institution that emphasizes progressive programs. The library contains over 100,000 volumes.

Environment: The university is located in a suburban area near the San Gabriel Mountains, 35 miles east of Los Angeles. The campus includes the student activities center and dormitories that accommodate 523 students.

Student Life: Most students are from California. Ninety percent of entering freshmen come from public schools. Thirty-eight percent of the students live in dormitories. Thirty percent of the students are Catholic, 38% Protestant, and 9% Jewish. Forty-six percent are minority-group members. University housing is both single-sex and coed. There are visiting privileges in single-sex housing. Students may keep cars on campus. Day-care services are available to all students, faculty, and staff on a sliding fee scale.

Organizations: There are 2 fraternities and 2 sororities. Student activities include special-interest groups, a newspaper, and musical groups. Cultural and religious activities are available on campus throughout the year.

Sports: There are 10 intercollegiate sports for men and 7 for women. Both men and women participate in 7 intramural sports.

86 CALIFORNIA

Handicapped: About 75% of the campus is accessible to handicapped students. Special facilities include wheelchair ramps, elevators, parking areas, specially equipped rest rooms, and lowered drinking fountains. A counselor is available to handicapped students.

Graduates: Sixty percent of the freshmen remain to graduate. About 55% of the graduates pursue advanced degrees.

Services: The following services are available free of charge to all students: placement, career counseling, tutoring, health care, and psychological counseling.

Programs of Study: The university confers the B.A. and B.S. degrees. Master's and doctoral programs are also available. Bachelor's degrees are offered in the following subjects: AREA STUDIES (American, Armenian, Asian, Black/Afro-American, Latin American), BUSINESS (accounting, business administration, computer science, finance, management, marketing, real estate/insurance), EDUCATION (bilingual—Spanish/Armenian, early childhood, elementary, health/physical, secondary, special), ENGLISH (English, journalism, literature, speech), FINE AND PERFORMING ARTS (art, music, music education, radio/TV, theater/dramatics), HEALTH SCIENCES (environmental health, speech therapy), LANGUAGES (French, German, Spanish), MATH AND SCIENCES (biology, chemistry, ecology/environmental science, mathematics, natural sciences, physics), PHILOSOPHY (classics, humanities, philosophy, religion), PREPROFESSIONAL (dentistry, law, medicine, ministry, social work, veterinary), SOCIAL SCIENCES (economics, government/political science, history, international relations, psychology, social sciences, sociology). About half the degrees are awarded in the social sciences.

Required: Students must take at least 1 course in fine arts, humanities, social sciences, and natural sciences; they must also pass exams in math and English. UP Area Tests are required for graduation.

Special: Students are encouraged to spend at least 1 year in off-campus study, either in the United States or abroad. Students may design their own majors.

Admissions: About 56% of those who applied were accepted for the 1981–82 freshman class. The SAT scores of students enrolled in a recent year were as follows: Verbal—12% between 500 and 599; Math—16% between 500 and 599. An applicant must have at least a 2.8 high school GPA. In addition, the school considers the following factors in order of importance: advanced placement or honor courses, leadership record, recommendations, personality, impressions made during interview, and extracurricular activities.

Procedure: The SAT or ACT is required and should be taken during the fall of the senior year. Application deadlines are open. Notification is on a rolling basis. There is a $20 application fee.

Special: An early decision plan is available. AP and CLEP credit is acceptable.

Transfer: For fall 1981, 193 students applied, 126 were accepted, and 85 enrolled. Each applicant is considered on an individual basis. A 2.0 GPA, recommendations, test scores, and self-evaluation are used. D grades do not transfer. One academic year must be spent in residence. Students must complete, at the university, 36 of the 128 credits needed for a bachelor's degree. Application deadlines are open.

Visiting: Informal guided tours may be arranged. Visitors may sit in on classes and stay overnight at the school. Visits are best scheduled during the week. The admissions office should be contacted for arrangements.

Financial Aid: About 82% of the students receive financial aid. Thirty-six percent work part-time on campus. Average aid to freshmen from all sources (scholarships, loans, grants, and part-time work) is $5230. The college is a member of CSS. The SAAC or FAF should be filed by March 1.

Foreign Students: Ten percent of the full-time students come from foreign countries. The university offers these students special counseling and special organizations.

Admissions: Foreign students must score 500 on the TOEFL. No college entrance examination is required.

Procedure: The application deadlines are July 15 (fall) and December 15 (spring). Foreign students must present proof of health. They must also present proof of $9200 in funds per academic year. They must carry health insurance, which is available through the university for a fee.

Admissions Contact: Michael Welch, Director of Admissions.

UNIVERSITY OF REDLANDS D-5
Redlands, California 92373 (714) 793-2121

F/T: 592M, 608W Faculty: 107; IIA, av$
P/T: 82 M&W Ph.D.'s: 81%
Grad: 150 M&W S/F Ratio: 11 to 1
Year: 4-1-4, ss Tuition: $5650
Appl: Mar. 1 R and B: $2390
1056 applied 823 accepted 355 enrolled
SAT: 510V 525M ACT: 24 COMPETITIVE+

The University of Redlands, founded in 1907, is a private institution that offers undergraduate instruction in the liberal arts and sciences. Johnston Center for Individualized Learning, a division of the university formerly known as Johnston College, offers a nontraditional program in which students may design their own liberal arts education. The library contains more than 300,000 volumes and subscribes to about 1300 periodicals.

Environment: Located about 65 miles east of Los Angeles at the foot of snow-capped mountains, the suburban campus occupies 130 acres in a town of about 43,500 people. Its 40 buildings include the Glen Wallichs Festival Theater, a Greek theater, and 10 dormitories accommodating 700 women, 700 men, and 25 married students. Living facilities also include fraternity and sorority houses.

Student Life: About 65% of the undergraduates are from California. About 85% live on campus. Approximately 79% of the freshmen come from public schools. About 23% of the students are minority-group members. Campus housing is both coed and single-sex; there are visiting privileges in the single-sex housing. Students may keep cars on campus.

Organizations: There are 4 fraternities and 3 sororities on campus; about 16% of the students belong. Student organizations include student government, service groups, lectures, plays, social events, yearbook, theater, and dance.

Sports: Intercollegiate competition is offered in 11 sports for men and 10 for women. There are 10 intramural sports for men and 10 for women.

Graduates: About 9% of the freshmen drop out at the end of their first year; 76% remain to graduate. Forty-five percent pursue advanced degrees; 6% enter law school, 5% medical school, and 2% dental school. Forty percent pursue careers in business and industry.

Services: Students receive career counseling, health services, and placement services free of charge. Psychological counseling and tutoring are also available.

Programs of Study: The university confers the B.A., B.S., and B.Mus. degrees. Master's degree programs are also available. Bachelor's degrees are offered in a number of subjects, including: AREA STUDIES (Black/Afro-American, European, interdisciplinary, Russian, women's), BUSINESS (accounting, computer science, management), EDUCATION (early childhood, elementary, health/physical, secondary, special), ENGLISH (English, journalism, literature, speech), FINE AND PERFORMING ARTS (art, art education, art history, dance, music, music education, studio art, theater/dramatics), HEALTH SCIENCES (speech therapy), LANGUAGES (French, German, Spanish), MATH AND SCIENCES (biology, chemistry, geology, mathematics, physics), PHILOSOPHY (philosophy, religion), PREPROFESSIONAL (engineering, law, medicine), SOCIAL SCIENCES (anthropology, economics, government/political science, history, international relations, psychology, sociology).

Required: Certain departments require GRE advanced tests and AP area tests for graduation.

Special: Special programs include a credit/no credit option, independent study, a 5-year (1 year in industry) cooperative program in engineering, a semester abroad in Austria, Spain, Mexico, Hong Kong, Japan, or England, summer study in France, and Washington and U.N. semesters. Acceleration is possible. Students may graduate in 3 years and design their own majors. Johnston Center students organize, negotiate, and carry out individualized programs through a contract/review process.

Honors: Honors courses are offered; Phi Beta Kappa is represented on campus.

Admissions: Seventy-eight percent of those who applied were accepted for the 1981–82 freshman class. The SAT scores of those who enrolled were: Verbal—68% scored below 500, 24% between 500 and 599, and 8% above 600; Math—46% scored below 500, 36% between 500 and 599, and 18% above 600. The applicant must be a graduate of an accredited high school and be recommended by his or her school. The minimum acceptable average is 3.0 (B), and the applicant's class rank should be in the upper 50%. Advanced placement or honors courses, reputation of the high school, and extracurricular and athletic activities are considered important. Special consideration is given to minority or disadvantaged students. The university seeks a national geographic distribution among students.

Procedure: The SAT or ACT is required and may be taken in the junior or senior year. An interview is recommended. Application deadlines are March 1 (fall), December 1 (winter), and January 1 (spring). There is a $20 application fee. A rolling admissions policy is used.

Special: Early decision, early admissions, and deferred admissions plans are available. The early admissions application deadline is March 1. AP and CLEP credit is accepted.

Transfer: For fall 1981, 221 students applied, 180 were accepted, and 82 enrolled. A GPA of 2.5 is necessary; D grades transfer. All students must complete, at the university, 30 of the 120 credits required for a bachelor's degree. Good academic standing is required. Application deadlines are the same as those for freshman applicants.

Visiting: Guided tours, interviews, and overnight visits can be scheduled through the admissions office.

Financial Aid: About 70% of all students receive aid through the school. Sixty percent work part-time on campus. The average freshman award is $4200. The university is a member of CSS and offers scholarships, grants, and regular campus employment. It participates in EOG, NDSL, and CWS. Loans are available through the federal government and local banks. California residents must submit the SAAC; nonresidents must submit the FAF. The aid application deadline is March 15. Tuition may be paid in installments.

Foreign Students: Five percent of the full-time students come from foreign countries. An intensive English program, special counseling, and special organizations are available for these students.

Admissions: Foreign students must achieve a TOEFL score of at least 550. No college entrance exams are required.

Procedure: The application deadline is March 1 (fall entry). Foreign students must present proof of funds adequate to cover 4 years of study. Health insurance is required and is available through the university for a fee.

Admissions Contact: Steve Hankins, Dean of Admissions.

UNIVERSITY OF SAN DIEGO   D-5
San Diego, California 92110   (714) 293-4506

F/T: 1250M, 1300W		Faculty:	170; IIA, + + $
P/T: 150M, 150W		Ph.D.'s:	86%
Grad: 250M, 300W		S/F Ratio:	15 to 1
Year: 4-1-4, ss		Tuition:	$4400
Appl: Apr. 1		R and B:	$2700
2029 applied	1398 accepted		694 enrolled
SAT: 459V 497M	ACT: 21		COMPETITIVE

The University of San Diego, founded in 1949, is a coeducational institution affiliated with the Roman Catholic church. It has academic divisions of arts and sciences, business administration, education, nursing, and law. The library houses over 230,215 volumes and 1270 microfilm items, and subscribes to over 1006 periodicals.

Environment: The 175-acre urban campus has 20 buildings including 12 residence halls that house 985 students. There is also a new student sports center.

Student Life: Approximately 70% of the students come from California. About 46% of the entering freshmen come from public schools. Half of the students live off campus; 37% live on campus; and 13% live in off-campus apartments. Seventy-two percent of the students are Catholic; 14% are Protestant. The university sponsors religious counselors for its Catholic and Protestant students. Over 20% of the students are minority-group members. Campus housing is single-sex, and there are visiting privileges. Students may keep cars on campus.

Organizations: There are two dozen extracurricular groups. Major social events include dances, films, speakers, and parties. About 5% of the students belong to fraternities and sororities.

Sports: Both intercollegiate and intramural sports are offered.

Handicapped: About 80% of the campus is accessible to students with physical handicaps. Special facilities include ramps, elevators, parking, lowered telephones and drinking fountains, specially equipped rest rooms, and 12 suites in the new residence buildings. Special class scheduling is possible.

Graduates: Of those who begin, 50% complete their degrees. About half of the graduates go on for further education.

CALIFORNIA 87

Services: The following services are free of charge to all undergraduates: placement, career counseling, health care, psychological counseling, tutoring, and remedial instruction.

Programs of Study: The university confers the B.A., B.S., and B.B.A. degrees. Master's and doctoral degrees are also granted. Bachelor's degrees are offered in the following subjects: AREA STUDIES (Latin American), BUSINESS (accounting, business administration), EDUCATION (elementary, secondary), ENGLISH (English), FINE AND PERFORMING ARTS (art, music), HEALTH SCIENCES (nursing), LANGUAGES (French, Spanish), MATH AND SCIENCES (biology, chemistry, mathematics, physics), PHILOSOPHY (philosophy, religion), PREPROFESSIONAL (dentistry, engineering, law, medicine), SOCIAL SCIENCES (anthropology, economics, history, international relations, psychology, social sciences, sociology). Thirty-five percent of undergraduate degrees are awarded in business; 18% are in social sciences.

Required: All undergraduates are required to take at least 9 credits of religious studies, 6 credits of philosophy, 9 credits of humanities, 6 credits of social science, 6 credits of science/math, and the third semester of a foreign language.

Special: The B.G.S. degree is offered. Study abroad is possible at Guadalajara, Mexico and Oxford, England.

Honors: Honors work is offered in the College of Arts and Sciences. There are small honors sections of regular freshman courses. Seniors may do independent research projects. Six national honor societies have chapters on campus.

Admissions: About 69% of the applicants for the 1981-82 freshman class were accepted. The SAT scores for an earlier class were as follows: Verbal—28% between 500 and 600, and 6% above 600; Math—34% between 500 and 600, 10% between 600 and 700, and 1½% above 700. On the ACT, 32% scored between 23 and 26, 7% between 27 and 28, and 5% above 28. A 2.6 high school GPA is required, along with 16 Carnegie credits of course work. Also considered important are recommendations, advanced placement or honors courses, and evidence of special talents.

Procedure: The SAT or ACT should be taken by December of the senior year; junior year results are accepted. Application deadlines are April 1 (fall) and November 1 (spring). Notification is on a rolling basis. There is a $25 nonrefundable fee.

Special: Minority or disadvantaged students in the local area are given preference for a special admissions program. AP and CLEP are used. There is an early decision plan; notification is on a rolling basis.

Transfer: For fall 1981, 957 transfer students applied, 647 were accepted, and 427 enrolled. A 2.2 GPA is required; D grades do not transfer. Thirty-six units must be completed in residence of the 124 required for the bachelor's degree. Application deadlines are July 1 (fall) and December 1 (spring).

Visiting: There is a formal orientation program for new students. Informal campus visits may be arranged, and visitors may attend classes.

Financial Aid: About 65% of the students receive assistance. The university administers $200,000 in federal loan funds and $50,000 in private loan funds. CWS is available in 56 departments. Scholarships range from $200 to $2000; loans range from $200 to $1500; and work contracts range from $600 to $1600. BEOG and state scholarships are also available. Tuition may be paid in installments. The FAF or SAAC must be submitted by March 1. Need is the primary factor in determining aid. The university is a member of CSS.

Foreign Students: The university offers foreign students special counseling and special organizations.

Admissions: Foreign students must achieve a minimum score of 550 on the TOEFL to qualify for admission. They must also take the SAT or the ACT.

Procedure: Application deadlines are May 1 (fall) and November 1 (spring). Foreign students must furnish proof of adequate funds for study at the university.

Admissions Contact: Kathleen Walsh Estey, Director of Admissions.

UNIVERSITY OF SAN FRANCISCO   B-3
San Francisco, California 94117   (415) 666-6563

F/T: 1320M, 1497W		Faculty:	237; IIA, + + $
P/T: 171M, 166W		Ph.D.'s:	70%
Grad: 502M, 547W		S/F Ratio:	16 to 1
Year: sems, ss		Tuition:	$4465
Appl: Mar. 1		R and B:	$2606
1973 applied	1222 accepted		673 enrolled
SAT: 450V 470M			COMPETITIVE

88 CALIFORNIA

The University of San Francisco, founded in 1855, is a Roman Catholic institution operated by the Jesuits. It has undergraduate colleges of liberal arts, science, business administration, and nursing. The university library houses 500,000 volumes and 16,000 microfilm items, and subscribes to 2510 periodicals.

Environment: The 51-acre urban campus is located in the center of San Francisco. There are 14 main buildings including dormitories that house 646 men and 782 women. There are also 2 athletic fields. Lone Mountain, a 24-acre campus, was added in 1978.

Student Life: The majority of the students come from California; most have public school backgrounds. About 48% of the students reside on campus. About 47% are Catholic, 6% Protestant, and 1% Jewish. There are no religious requirements. About 50% of the students are minority-group members. Campus housing is both single-sex and coed; there are visiting privileges in the former. Students may keep cars on campus.

Organizations: There are social sororities and fraternities. Extracurricular activities include student government, publications, clubs, service organizations, music groups, a debating society, and theater.

Sports: Intercollegiate competition is offered in 6 sports for men and 6 for women. Intramural sports number more than 16 for both men and women.

Handicapped: All of the campus is accessible to students with physical handicaps. Special facilities include ramps, elevators, parking, and lowered telephones. About 1% of the students have visual impairments; 1% have hearing impairments.

Graduates: About 15% of the students drop out after the first year of study; 45% remain to complete their degrees. Sixty percent pursue advanced study after graduation.

Services: The following services are free of charge to all students: placement, psychological counseling, career counseling, tutoring, and remedial instruction. Health care is available on a fee basis.

Programs of Study: The university confers the B.A., B.S., and B.F.A. degrees. Master's and doctoral degree programs are also available. Bachelor's degrees are offered in the following subjects: BUSINESS (accounting, business administration, computer science, finance, hospitality management, industrial relations, international relations, management, marketing), ENGLISH (English), FINE AND PERFORMING ARTS (art, communication arts), HEALTH SCIENCES (nursing), LANGUAGES (French, Greek/Latin, Spanish), MATH AND SCIENCES (biochemistry, biology, chemistry, mathematics, physics), PHILOSOPHY (philosophy, religion), PREPROFESSIONAL (dentistry, engineering, law, medicine, pharmacy, veterinary), SOCIAL SCIENCES (economics, government/political science, history, psychology, sociology).

Special: The university offers a B.F.A. in cooperation with the Academy of Arts College in San Francisco. Study abroad is possible. There is a combination B.A.-J.D. degree program.

Honors: An honors program is offered.

Admissions: About 62% of the applicants for the 1981–82 school year were accepted. Of those who enrolled, the SAT scores were as follows: Verbal—72% scored below 500, 20% between 500 and 599, 7% between 600 and 700, and 1% above 700; Math—46% scored below 500, 40% between 500 and 599, 13% between 600 and 700, and 2% above 700. Minimum high school GPA is 3.0. Candidates should complete 15 Carnegie credits and achieve satisfactory scores on the SAT. Advanced placement or honors courses, recommendations, and evidence of special talents are also considered.

Procedure: The SAT should be taken by January of the senior year. Applications are due March 1 (fall) and December 15 (spring); new students are admitted both semesters. There is a $20 nonrefundable application fee. Notification is on a rolling basis.

Special: CLEP and AP credit is available.

Transfer: For fall 1981, 1394 transfer students applied, 1117 were accepted, and 579 enrolled. Transfers are accepted for all classes. Depending upon the number of units already earned at a previous institution, a 2.0 to 3.0 GPA is required. D grades and above will transfer. One year's study is residence is necessary. Twenty-four units and major requirements must be taken at the university, out of a total of 128 units required for the bachelor's degree. Application deadlines are the same as those for freshmen.

Visiting: There is a formal orientation program for new students. Informal campus visits with student guides can be arranged. Visitors may attend classes and stay overnight at the school.

Financial Aid: About 35% of the students are receiving assistance. About 23% work part-time on campus. The average award to freshmen is $3400. There are about 125 freshman scholarships in amounts totaling full tuition. Federal loans in addition to state and private loans are available. The university is a member of CSS. The deadline for the FAF statement and application is March 1.

Foreign Students: One-fifth of the full-time students come from foreign countries. The university offers these students an intensive English program, special counseling, and special organizations.

Admissions: The university requires foreign applicants to take its English proficiency test. The SAT or ACT is not necessary.

Procedure: Application deadlines for foreign students are March 1 for fall and December 15 for spring. Proof of health and of sufficient funds to cover the first year of study are required. Health insurance must be carried; it is available through the university for a fee.

Admissions Contact: Gabe Capeto, Director of Academic Services.

UNIVERSITY OF SANTA CLARA B-3
Santa Clara, California 95053 (408) 984-4288

F/T: 1805M, 1601W	Faculty: 253; IIA, + + $
P/T: 34M, 30W	Ph.D.'s: 80%
Grad: 1884M, 1671W	S/F Ratio: 18 to 1
Year: qtrs, ss	Tuition: $4593
Appl: Mar. 1	R and B: $2385
2629 applied 1668 accepted 866 enrolled
SAT: 505V 565M	**VERY COMPETITIVE**

The University of Santa Clara, founded by Jesuits in 1851, is a coeducational Catholic university open to students of all faiths. The main campus contains the College of Arts and Sciences; the schools of Business, Engineering, and Law; and the Graduate School. The library contains over 300,000 volumes and 65,000 microfilm items, and subscribes to over 70,000 periodicals.

Environment: The suburban campus is located 46 miles from San Francisco. Major buildings include dormitories that house 975 men and 910 women, an observatory, an art gallery, and the historical Mission Church. Facilities are also available for commuting students.

Student Life: The majority of students come from California; 52% have public school backgrounds. About half of the undergraduates live on campus. Sixty-nine percent of those enrolled are Catholic. Approximately 20% are minority-group members. Campus housing is both coed and single-sex. There are visiting privileges in single-sex dorms. Students may keep cars on campus. The university provides day-care services to students, faculty, and staff for a fee.

Organizations: There are 2 national sororities and 1 national fraternity; about 2% of the students belong. The university offers a varied co- and extracurricular program including service groups and clubs. Cultural activities include a film series, art exhibits, guest speakers, and dramatic productions.

Sports: Intercollegiate competition is offered in 13 sports for men and 7 for women. There are 7 intramural sports for both men and women.

Handicapped: About 70% of the campus is accessible to physically handicapped students; facilities include ramps, elevators, and special parking. Counselors and assistants are provided.

Graduates: The freshman dropout rate is 6.5%; about 75% remain to graduate. Of these, about 40% go on for further education: 3% enter medical school; 1% enter dental school; and 10% enter law school. Forty percent pursue careers in business.

Services: The following services are free to all students: placement, health care, psychological counseling, career counseling, tutoring, and remedial instruction.

Programs of Study: Programs lead to the B.A., B.S., B.S.C., and B.S. in Eng. degrees. Master's and doctoral degrees are also awarded. Bachelor's degrees are offered in the following subjects: AREA STUDIES (American), BUSINESS (accounting, computer science, economics, finance, management, marketing, quantitative methods), ENGLISH (English), FINE AND PERFORMING ARTS (art, art history, music, theater/dramatics), LANGUAGES (French, German, Italian, Spanish), MATH AND SCIENCES (biology, chemistry, combined sciences, mathematics, physics), PHILOSOPHY (classics, philosophy, religion), PREPROFESSIONAL (dentistry, engineering physics, law, medicine), SOCIAL SCIENCES (anthropology, economics, government/political science, history, psychology, sociology). Thirty-one percent of all degrees conferred are in business, 20% are in math and science, 16% are in social sciences, and 11% are in engineering.

Required: All students must take 3 courses in religious studies.

Special: Student-designed majors are possible and a B.G.S. degree is also available. There is an interdepartmental ethnic studies program. The Da Vinci Program in Engineering offers an interdisciplinary approach to humanities, science, business, and engineering.

Honors: There are 9 honor societies on campus. An interdisciplinary honors program is open to qualified students, and includes special seminars.

Admissions: About 63% of those who applied for the 1981–82 freshman class were accepted. Of those who enrolled, the SAT scores were as follows: Verbal—43% below 500, 44% between 500 and 599, 11% between 600 and 700, and 2% above 700; 50% between 500 and 599, 29% between 600 and 700, and 5% above 700. Sixteen Carnegie credits are required. In addition to high school course work and SAT scores, the admissions committee considers advanced placement or honors courses, character and personality, leadership potential, and extracurricular activities.

Procedure: The SAT is required. Application deadlines are March 1 (fall), November 15 (winter), and February 15 (spring). A rolling admissions policy is used. There is a $25 nonrefundable application fee.

Special: AP credit is possible. A deferred admissions plan is also offered.

Visiting: There is a regularly scheduled orientation program; informal campus visits may also be arranged with student guides. Visitors may attend classes and stay overnight at the school. The admissions office schedules visits.

Transfer: For fall 1981, 763 transfer students applied, 374 were accepted, and 243 enrolled. One year must be completed in residence, and students must complete, at the university, 45 quarter units of the 175 required for the bachelor's degree. Good academic standing at the last school is required; D grades do not transfer. The deadline for the fall term is July 1; the other deadlines are the same as for incoming freshmen.

Financial Aid: About 68% of all students are receiving assistance; 16% work part-time on campus. Scholarships, loans, and grants are available. CWS is offered in most academic departments. The average aid to a freshman is $3241. The FAF is required, and the aid application is due February 1. Aid is granted on the basis of need and academic potential. The university is a member of CSS.

Foreign Students: About 3% of the full-time students are from foreign countries. The university offers these students special counseling and special organizations.

Admissions: Foreign students must achieve a minimum score of 550 on the TOEFL. They must also take the SAT.

Procedure: Application deadlines are the same as for incoming freshmen. Foreign students must furnish proof of health and must carry health insurance, which is available through the university for a fee. They must also provide proof of funds adequate to cover 1 calendar year of study.

Admissions Contact: Daniel Saracino, Director of Admissions.

UNIVERSITY OF SOUTHERN CALIFORNIA C–5
Los Angeles, California 90007   (213) 743-6750

F/T: 7573M, 5549W   Faculty: 966; I, ++$
P/T: 1335M, 1037W   Ph.D.'s: 87%
Grad: 8682M, 3953W   S/F Ratio: n/av
Year: sems, ss   Tuition: $6304
Appl: May 1   R and B: $2822
10,000 applied   6788 accepted   2731 enrolled
SAT: 468V 527M   ACT: 25   COMPETITIVE

The University of Southern California is a private, nonsectarian, coeducational university established in 1880. The library contains over 2.1 million volumes and 1.1 million microfilm items, and subscribes to 30,766 periodicals.

Environment: The 150-acre urban campus is 4 miles from the downtown business area of Los Angeles. University housing accommodates 5400 students; the university sponsors dormitories, on-campus apartments, off-campus apartments, fraternity and sorority houses, and married student housing.

Student Life: About 69% of the students are from California. About 79% of the entering freshmen are from public schools. About 48% of the students live on campus. About 23% are minority-group members. Campus housing is both single-sex and coed. There are visiting privileges in the single-sex residences. Students may keep cars on campus. The university provides day-care services for a fee to full-time students, faculty, and staff.

Organizations: There are 25 national fraternities and 13 national sororities to which 22% of the men and 23% of the women belong. There is a full range of social, religious, and special-interest clubs and organizations, music and dramatic groups, and publications.

Sports: The university competes intercollegiately in 13 sports for men and 12 for women. There are 11 intramural sports for both men and women.

Handicapped: About 85% of the campus is accessible to wheelchair students. Special parking, wheelchair ramps, elevators, specially equipped rest rooms, and lowered drinking fountains and telephones are available.

Graduates: There is a freshman dropout rate of 19; 65% remain to graduate.

Services: Students receive placement and career counseling free of charge. Placement services include on-campus recruitment interviews. Health care, psychological counseling, and tutoring are available for a fee.

Programs of Study: The university confers the B.A., B.S., B.Arch., B.F.A., B.M., and B.S.N. degrees. Master's and doctoral programs are also offered. Bachelor's degrees are offered in the following subjects: AREA STUDIES (Asian, ethnic, Latin American, Spanish, urban), BUSINESS (business administration, computer science), EDUCATION (general studies, physical), ENGLISH (American literature and culture, English, communication arts and sciences, comparative literature, journalism, public relations, sports information), FINE AND PERFORMING ARTS (art, art education, art history, cinema/television, music, music composition, music education, music theory, performance, radio/TV, studio art, theater/dramatics), HEALTH SCIENCES (dental hygiene, nursing, occupational therapy), LANGUAGES (East Asian, French, German, Slavic, Spanish), MATH AND SCIENCES (astronomy, biology, chemistry, geology, mathematics, natural sciences, physical sciences, physics), PHILOSOPHY (classics, humanities, philosophy, religion), PREPROFESSIONAL (architecture, engineering—aerospace, engineering—biomedical, engineering—chemical, engineering—civil, engineering—electrical, engineering—industrial and systems, engineering—mechanical, engineering—metallurgical, engineering—petroleum, safety), SOCIAL SCIENCES (anthropology, economics, geography/planning and urban studies, gerontology, government/political science, history, international relations, psychobiology, psychology, public administration, public affairs, social sciences, sociology, women and men in society). Thirty-one percent of undergraduate degrees conferred are in business, 19% in social sciences, 7% in math and sciences, and 15% in preprofessional studies.

Required: All students must satisfy requirements in English composition.

Special: It is possible to earn combined B.A.-B.S. degrees in engineering and economics/history/math/philosophy/religion. Student-designed majors are also permitted. A 5-year curriculum and a general studies degree are offered. Study abroad in Austria, Spain, England, and other foreign countries can be arranged. Innovations include a Washington (D.C.) Semester, Sacramento Semester, Los Angeles Semester, and the Marine Biology Semester.

Honors: The university has a well-established undergraduate honors program. There are 18 national honor societies on campus.

Admissions: Sixty-eight percent of those who applied were accepted for the 1980–81 freshman class. The SAT scores of those enrolled were as follows: Verbal—61% scored below 500, 28% between 500 and 599, 10% between 600 and 700, and 1% above 700; Math—38% scored below 500, 34% between 500 and 599, 23% between 600 and 700, and 5% above 700. Applicants must furnish evidence of intellectual promise and personal qualification. Such promise will be determined by the applicant's high school academic record and satisfactory SAT or ACT scores. Candidates should have a 2.7 GPA in academic subjects for regular admissions; their combined SAT scores should equal at least 800. The school indicates that in addition to these qualifications they consider the following factors in order of importance: advanced placement or honors courses, leadership record, extracurricular activities, and evidence of special talents.

Procedure: The SAT or ACT is required. For freshman applicants, USC employs a first priority filing period, as well as a final deadline of May 1. Architecture students should apply by April 1, cinema students should apply by February 1. The first priority filing period is September 1 through December 31. Freshman applicants who have completed admissions files prior to January 1 will be notified on a rolling basis of their admission status on or before March 15. The application deadline for spring entry is December 1. There is a $35 application fee.

Special: Early admissions is available. The freshman access program allows promising students with GPAs below 2.7 and SATs below 800 (combined) to enter. CLEP and AP credit is accepted.

Transfer: For fall 1980, 4163 transfers (not including freshmen) applied, 2412 were accepted, and 1266 enrolled. Transfers are accepted to all classes, but the student must take the last 32 semester units, representing 50% of upper division major requirements, at the university to earn a degree. Generally, a total of 128 units are required for the bachelor's degree. Transfer students must have a 2.5 GPA in the last school year and a 2.0 overall GPA to be considered. A writing sample is also required. The final deadlines for transfers are May 1 (fall) and December 1 (spring).

Visiting: Informal visits can be made during the week. Hour-long walking tours are available by appointment through the admissions office.

Financial Aid: About 65% of the undergraduate students receive some form of financial aid through the school. The average award to freshmen is $5700. There are scholarships and grants totaling $25,690,000 for all undergraduates. The university is a member of CSS. The FAF, SER, and IRS 1040 are required. The final deadlines for aid application are May 1 (fall) and December 1 (spring). The priority cutoff date for fall is December 31.

Foreign Students: Thirteen percent of the full-time students are from foreign countries. The university offers these students an intensive English program, special counseling, and special organizations.

Admissions: Foreign candidates must take the TOEFL or the university's English proficiency test. The SAT or ACT is not necessary.

Procedure: International applicants should apply by April 1 for fall or summer entry and October 1 for spring entry. Proof of funds adequate to cover 1 year of study at the university must be presented. Health insurance is required; it is available through the university for a fee.

Admissions Contact: Jay V. Berger, Director of Admissions.

UNIVERSITY OF THE PACIFIC B-3
Stockton, California 95211 (209) 946-2211

F/T: 1800M, 1810W
P/T: 40M, 60W
Grad: 150M, 300W
Year: 4-1-4, ss
Appl: see profile
2350 applied
SAT: 460V 510M

Faculty: 275; IIA, ++$
Ph.D.'s: 74%
S/F Ratio: 13 to 1
Tuition: $6579
R and B: $2770
1840 accepted 750 enrolled
COMPETITIVE

The University of the Pacific, founded in 1851, is a private, nonsectarian institution. It consists of 2 liberal arts colleges—College of the Pacific and Elbert Corell College—and 7 professional schools—the schools of Education, Pharmacy, Business and Public Administration, Music, Engineering, Dentistry (in San Francisco), and Law (in Sacramento). The library houses 330,400 volumes and 280,000 microfilm items, and subscribes to 3062 periodicals.

Environment: The 150-acre campus is located in a suburban area 80 miles from San Francisco. The college has 80 buildings, including a recently constructed student center that contains student apartments; a theater; art studios; grocery, book, and record stores; a game room; and a rathskeller. Fourteen dormitories house 2000 students. Two townhouse apartment complexes accommodate another 320 students, and 4 sorority and 5 fraternity houses also offer residence facilities. There is also a new 6000-seat events center.

Student Life: The university draws 70% of its students from within the state. About 60% live on campus. Freshmen and sophomores must live on campus if they do not reside with parents or other relatives. About 27% of the students are minority-group members. The university sponsors both single-sex and coed housing; there are visitation privileges in single-sex housing. Students may keep cars on campus.

Organizations: About 15% of the students belong to one of the 5 fraternities or 6 sororities. Activities include special-interest, departmental, service, and religious groups; music and drama clubs; publications; student government; concerts; films; lectures; and debate.

Sports: The university fields 11 intercollegiate teams for men and 7 for women. There are 12 intramural sports for men and 12 for women.

Handicapped: Special facilities for physically handicapped students include wheelchair ramps, parking areas, elevators, enabling services, and specially equipped rest rooms. Special class scheduling also may be arranged. Adaptive equipment, readers, and tape recorders are provided for students with impaired vision or hearing. Two special counselors and 2 assistants are available.

Graduates: About 10% of the freshmen drop out; about 59% remain to graduate. Thirty-two percent of the graduates seek advanced degrees. Seventy percent of those who apply are accepted by medical schools and 87% of those who apply are accepted by dental schools.

Services: Students receive the following free services: placement, career, and psychological counseling; tutoring; and remedial instruction. Health care is available for a fee.

Programs of Study: The university confers the B.A., B.S., B.F.A., B.M., B.S.Pharm., and B.S. in Engineering degrees. Master's and doctoral degrees also are available. Bachelor's degrees are offered in the following subjects: AREA STUDIES (Black/Afro-American, Latin American, urban), BUSINESS (business administration, computer science, public administration), EDUCATION (elementary, secondary, special), ENGLISH (English, speech), FINE AND PERFORMING ARTS (art, art education, art history, commercial design, drawing/painting, music, music education, studio art, pre-dance therapy, theater/dramatics), HEALTH SCIENCES (medical technology, pharmacy, speech therapy), LANGUAGES (French, German, Greek/Latin, Japanese, Spanish), MATH AND SCIENCES (biology, botany, chemistry, computer science, geology, mathematics, natural sciences, physical sciences, physics, zoology), PHILOSOPHY (classics, humanities, philosophy, religion), PREPROFESSIONAL (dentistry, engineering, law, medicine, ministry, pharmacy, social work, veterinary), SOCIAL SCIENCES (economics, geography, government/political science, history, international relations, psychology, sociology). Thirteen percent of the undergraduate degrees conferred are in math and sciences, 11% are in education, and 10% are in social sciences.

Special: Students may design their own majors. The university offers study abroad, independent study, a U.N. Semester, and a Washington Semester. Elbert Covell College, one of the university's liberal arts colleges, emphasizes Spanish and Inter-American studies; almost all courses are conducted in Spanish. The School of Engineering offers a 5-year combined work-study program. The School of Pharmacy operates on a trimester schedule; students complete their professional training in 3 years after their prepharmacy studies are finished.

Honors: More than 20 national honor and professional societies, including Phi Kappa Phi, are represented on campus.

Admissions: Seventy-eight percent of those who applied were accepted for the 1981–82 freshman class. The SAT scores of a recent freshman class were as follows: Verbal—30% between 500 and 599, 9% between 600 and 700, and 2% above 700; Math—37% between 500 and 599, 21% between 600 and 700, and 3% above 700. The admissions process is very individualized and consideration is given to the applicant's essay, extracurricular activities, recommendations, SAT scores, and secondary school record. The strength of the secondary school program and the grades in academic subjects are most important. SAT scores are considered but are not of prime importance. The average high school GPA of the 1981–82 freshman class is 3.3. Eighty-five percent of the freshmen graduated in the upper quarter of their high school class.

Procedure: The SAT or ACT is required and should be taken in spring of the junior year or fall of the senior year. Application deadlines for priority consideration are March 1 (fall) and December 15 (winter and spring); freshmen also are admitted in summer. The $25 application fee may be waived for needy students. Admissions decisions are made on a rolling basis.

Special: Early and deferred admissions plans are available.

Transfer: For fall 1981, 1100 students applied, 690 were accepted, and 460 enrolled. Applicants must present an average of 2.3 or better. D grades transfer. Transfer students are accepted for all classes, but students must earn, at the university, 32 of the last 40 credits taken for the bachelor's degree; a total of between 132 and 135 credits are required for this degree. Deadlines for transfer applicants are the same as those for freshmen.

Visiting: Orientations for prospective students—including an overview of the university and its programs, campus tours, lunch, and meetings with faculty members—are scheduled regularly. Guides also are provided for informal visits. Visitors may sit in on classes and stay overnight in the school. Visits should be arranged with the admissions office for sometime during the school year.

Financial Aid: About 65% of the students receive aid; 40% work part-time on campus. University and state scholarships are offered. Athletic grants, campus jobs, and loans from the federal and state governments, local banks, and the college also are available. Tuition may be paid on the installment plan. The college is a member of CSS, and the FAF must be filed by February 10 for fall entry and by December 15 for spring entry.

Foreign Students: Eight percent of the full-time students come from foreign countries. The university offers these students an intensive English course, an intensive English program, special counseling, and special organizations.

Admissions: Applicants must either achieve a TOEFL score of 550 or take the university's English proficiency exam. Only foreign students who attend an American-type high school must take the SAT.

WEST COAST UNIVERSITY   C-5
Los Angeles, California 90020   (213) 487-4433

F/T: 372M, 93W
P/T: 300M, 35W
Grad: 466M, 95W
Year: terms, ss
Appl: open
159 applied   140 accepted   81 enrolled
SAT: recommended   LESS COMPETITIVE

Faculty: n/av
Ph.D.'s: n/av
S/F Ratio: n/av
Tuition: $2457
R and B: n/app

West Coast University, chartered in 1909, is a private coed institution that offers undergraduate and graduate training in technical and science fields. It offers evening classes only.

Environment: The university's main campus is in urban Los Angeles; another campus is located in nearby suburban Orange County. All students commute.

Student Life: Most students are from the Los Angeles metropolitan area. Eighty percent come from California. None of the students live on campus. About 18% are minority-group members.

Sports: The university does not offer any athletic activities.

Graduates: About 20% of each freshman class remain to graduate.

Programs of Study: The university confers the B.S. degree. Associate and master's degree programs are also available. Bachelor's degrees are awarded in the following subjects: BUSINESS (accounting, business administration, computer science, finance, management, marketing), PREPROFESSIONAL (engineering).

Required: The B.S. degree requires 135 units (semester hours) and can be earned in about 4½ years of part-time study.

Special: The university works closely with related industry and offers some work-study programs.

Admissions: About 88% of those who applied were accepted for 1981–82. Applicants must be high school graduates or have passed the GED tests, and they should have a minimum GPA of 2.0. The university has an open admissions policy. Exceptional applicants who do not meet admission requirements may be admitted on a provisional basis.

Procedure: Neither the SAT or the ACT is required. Students are admitted in the fall and the spring. There are no application deadlines. The university uses a rolling admissions plan. A $25 fee must accompany applications.

Special: There is a deferred admissions plan.

Transfer: For fall 1981, 372 transfer students applied, 350 were accepted, and 190 enrolled. Transfers are admitted to all classes. A minimum GPA of 2.0 is required. Full credit is given for course work substantially similar to courses offered at the university. Thirty-seven semester hours must be earned in residence, out of a total of 127 semester hours required for the bachelor's degree. There are no application deadlines. Transfers are accepted for fall, winter, spring, and summer terms.

Financial Aid: Nearly all students are fully employed engineers, technicians, or technical administrators; most receive tuition reimbursement from their employers. About 10% receive financial aid through the university. Grants, loans, and work-study are available. The university is a member of CSS. The FAF is required. Deadlines are open for the entire year.

Foreign Students: Thirty percent of the full-time students come from foreign countries. An intensive English program, special counseling, and special organizations for foreign students are available.

Admissions: Foreign candidates are required to take the university's own English proficiency test. The SAT or ACT is not required.

Procedure: Application deadlines for foreign students are June (fall), September (winter), January (spring), and March (summer). The university requires that proof of adequate funds be presented.

Admissions Contact: Maxine R. McCarty, Director of Admissions.

CALIFORNIA 91

WESTMONT COLLEGE   C-5
Santa Barbara, California 93108   (805) 969-5051

F/T: 491M, 559W
P/T: 6M, 9W
Grad: none
Year: 4-1-4, ss
Appl: open
521 applied   429 accepted   280 enrolled
SAT: 474V 506M   COMPETITIVE

Faculty: 53; IIB, ++$
Ph.D.'s: 71%
S/F Ratio: 17 to 1
Tuition: $4860
R and B: $2500

Westmont College, founded in 1940, is a coeducational, interdenominational, liberal arts college. The library contains 122,900 volumes and 5097 microfilm items, and subscribes to 600 periodicals.

Environment: The 140-acre campus is 100 miles northwest of Los Angeles and 2 miles inland from the Pacific Ocean in the foothills of the Santa Ynez Mountains. The surrounding environment is suburban. Facilities include an observatory with a 16-inch reflecting telescope and a 6-inch refracting telescope. The 2-story modular dormitories accommodate 462 women and 354 men. The college also sponsors off-campus apartments.

Student Life: Eighty-one percent of the undergraduates come from California; 95% live in dormitories. Eighty-six percent of entering freshmen come from public schools. Eighty-eight percent of the students are Protestant, 7% are Catholic; religious counselors and organizations are provided. Daily attendance at religious services is expected. Students are expected to refrain from intoxicants, smoking, gambling, drugs, and social dancing on campus. Six percent are members of minority groups. Campus housing is coed. Students may keep cars on campus.

Organizations: There are no fraternities or sororities. Extracurricular activities include art, musical groups, drama, publications, science, service organizations, and a strong student government.

Sports: The college competes on an intercollegiate level in 6 sports for men and 4 for women. Intramural sports number 17 for men and 16 for women.

Handicapped: The campus is not particularly accessible to handicapped students. Special parking is available.

Graduates: The freshman dropout rate is 10%; 58% remain to graduate. Fifty percent pursue advanced study after graduation; 1% go on to medical school.

Services: Students receive the following services free of charge: placement, career and psychological counseling, health care, and tutoring. Remedial instruction is available for a fee.

Programs of Study: All programs lead to the B.A. degree. Bachelor's degrees are offered in the following subjects: AREA STUDIES (urban), EDUCATION (elementary, secondary), ENGLISH (English, literature), FINE AND PERFORMING ARTS (fine arts, music), MATH AND SCIENCES (biology, chemistry, mathematics, natural sciences, physical sciences, physics), PHILOSOPHY (philosophy, religion), PREPROFESSIONAL (dentistry, engineering, law, medicine, ministry), SOCIAL SCIENCES (economics, government/political science, history, psychology, social sciences, sociology).

Required: All undergraduates are required to take courses in biblical studies, physical education, and a course each from a wide range of disciplines.

Special: Student-designed majors are permitted. The college offers a pass/fail option for elective courses. There is summer session travel and study all over Europe (England to Athens) in small groups; there is a fall semester in England, one in Europe, and one in San Francisco. A 3-2 combination degree program in engineering in cooperation with Stanford University is also offered. A program of practicums in sociology/psychology, under which students are accepted as full staff members in several state and local agencies, is available.

Honors: The Omicron Delta Kappa honor society is open to qualified students.

Admissions: Eighty-two percent of those who applied were accepted for the 1981–82 freshman class. The SAT scores of those enrolled were as follows: Verbal—56% scored below 500, 34% between 500 and 599, 5% between 600 and 700, fewer than 1% above 700; Math—48% scored below 500, 34% between 500 and 599, 14% between 600 and 700, and fewer than 1% above 700. Prime considerations in student selection are the results of the SAT and the English composition AT, recommendations from the applicant's high school and his or her pastor, the completion of 16 Carnegie units, and a minimum B average. The college indicates that in addition to these qualifications they consider the following factors in order of importance: recommendations by school officials, impressions made during an interview, personality, and advanced placement or honors courses.

92 CALIFORNIA

Procedure: The SAT is required. Mathematics or science majors must take the math AT (level 1 or 2). The English composition AT is recommended. Tests should be taken preferably by December of the 12th year. The student should have the interview by March. There is no application deadline, but the student is urged to file the completed form by March. The application fee is $20. Admission is on a rolling basis. Freshmen are also admitted at midyear; application must be made 30 days before the semester begins.

Special: CLEP and AP credit is accepted.

Transfer: For fall 1981, 235 applications for transfer were received, 186 were accepted, and 134 students enrolled. Transfers are accepted for all classes; students must study at the college at least 1 semester to receive a degree. Applicants must have at least a 2.3 GPA from a 2-year college or a 2.0 GPA from a 4-year college. D grades do not transfer. Out of a total of 124 credits required for the bachelor's degree, 76 credits must be completed at the college. Application must be made by March 1.

Visiting: Orientation is held in the form of 2 College Days. This includes campus tours, faculty and administration meetings, and dorm exposure. Informal visits can be arranged through the admissions office. Visitors may sit in on classes; overnight accommodations are available.

Financial Aid: Seventy-six percent of all students receive some form of financial aid. Almost half of the students work part-time on campus. The college is a member of the CSS and offers scholarships to freshmen. The average award to freshmen is $2000. A maximum aid package from all sources would total $7900. Applicants for financial aid must file the FAF by March 1. California residents must file the SAAC.

Foreign Students: About 2% of the full-time students come from foreign countries.

Admissions: The college requires foreign applicants to achieve a score of at least 500 on the TOEFL. The SAT is also required.

Procedure: There are no deadlines; admissions are on a rolling basis for both the fall and spring semesters. Proof of health and of funds adequate to cover 4 years of study are required. Foreign students must carry health insurance, which is available through the college for a fee.

Admissions Contact: Diane Horvath, Admissions Coordinator.

WHITTIER COLLEGE D-5
Whittier, California 90608 (213) 693-0771

F/T: 446M, 447W	Faculty:	80; IIA, +$
P/T: 38M, 25W	Ph.D.'s:	82%
Grad: 265M, 188W	S/F Ratio:	13 to 1
Year: 4-1-4, ss	Tuition:	$5126
Appl: Mar. 15	R and B:	$2200
705 applied	498 accepted	253 enrolled
SAT: 440V 470M	ACT: 23	COMPETITIVE+

Whittier College, founded in 1901 by the Quakers, is an institution of liberal arts and sciences. Over 20 concentrations are offered. The library houses 130,000 volumes and subscribes to 800 periodicals.

Environment: The college is located in a suburban area, 18 miles from Los Angeles, midway between the Pacific beaches and the San Gabriel Mountains. Living facilities include dormitories, fraternity houses, and sorority houses.

Student Life: Sixty-five percent of the students come from the West, Northwest, and Hawaii; 65% of the entering freshmen come from public schools. Approximately 60% of the students live on campus. Twenty-eight percent are Protestant, 37% are Catholic, and 3% are Jewish. All faiths are welcomed, and chapel attendance is voluntary. Eighty-nine percent of the students are members of various minority groups. Campus housing is both single-sex and coed, with visiting privileges in the former. Students are permitted to keep cars on campus.

Organizations: There are 4 local fraternities and 5 local sororities; 16% of the men and 24% of the women belong. Extracurricular activities are numerous. Some of the active organizations are the American Home Economics Association, Black Students Union, Choir, Christian Science Organization, Circle K, and Veterans Group.

Sports: On the intercollegiate level, there are 12 teams for men and 9 for women. On the intramural level, there are 12 teams for both men and women.

Handicapped: About 80% of the campus is accessible to wheelchair students.

Graduates: About 65% of the students who enter as freshmen graduate 4 years later, and 43% of the students who graduate go on to graduate or professional study; 5% enter medical school, 5% enter dental school, and 10% enter law school. Fifty percent pursue careers in business and industry.

Services: Students receive the following services free of charge: placement, career counseling, health care, tutoring, remedial instruction, and psychological counseling.

Programs of Study: The college confers the B.A. degree. Programs leading to the master's degree are also offered. Bachelor's degrees are offered in the following subjects: AREA STUDIES (American, Asian, Latin American, urban), BUSINESS (accounting, business administration, computer science, management), EDUCATION (early childhood, elementary, health/physical, secondary, special), ENGLISH (English, literature), FINE AND PERFORMING ARTS (art, music, music education, theater/dramatics), LANGUAGES (Chinese, French, Spanish), MATH AND SCIENCES (biology, chemistry, geology, mathematics, physics), PHILOSOPHY (classics, humanities, philosophy, religion), PREPROFESSIONAL (athletic training, dentistry, engineering, law, medicine, pharmacy, social work, veterinary), SOCIAL SCIENCES (government/political science, history, international relations, psychology, sociology).

Special: Student-designed majors are permitted. The college operates a study abroad program at an overseas campus in collaboration with the University of Copenhagen in Denmark; selected faculty members teach Whittier courses in English. Study-abroad programs are also offered in Mexico and England. A 3-year bachelor's degree program is offered, as is a 3-2 degree program in engineering. The college offers an adult learner program, for those over 25 years of age; an advanced learners program, for high school students who are capable of college-level work; and the 50/50 program, which allows those over 50 years of age to attend college for half the tuition cost.

Honors: There are over 20 honor societies on campus.

Admissions: Seventy-one percent of those who applied were accepted for the 1981-82 freshman class. Forty percent scored in the upper one-fifth of their high school graduating class. Requirements for admission to the freshman class include: graduation from an accredited high school, approval by the admissions committee, an A or B grade in 12 of the 15 standard units in a high school program, a GPA of 2.0, and satisfactory SAT or ACT scores. Other factors that enter into the admissions decision are advanced placement or honors courses, impressions made during an interview, and leadership record.

Procedure: The SAT or ACT is required. AT's may also be offered. There is a rolling admissions plan. The deadline for regular admission to the fall semester is March 15. Freshmen are also admitted to the spring semester. Applications should be submitted with a $20 fee.

Special: Early admissions and early decision plans are available. CLEP and AP credit is available.

Transfer: For fall 1981, 201 transfer applications were received, 128 were accepted, and 78 students enrolled. Transfer students are accepted for all classes. A minimum GPA of 2.0 and a composite score of at least 900 on the SAT are required. Transfers must take the last 24 units at the college, of the 120 required to earn the bachelor's degree. D grades do not transfer. There is a rolling admissions policy. The application deadline is March 15 for fall; transfers are also admitted to the spring semester.

Visiting: Orientation is scheduled for prospective students. Guided tours and interviews can be scheduled weekdays, February through April. Visitors may sit in on classes and remain on campus overnight. For further information, contact the admissions office.

Financial Aid: Seventy-eight percent of all students receive some financial aid. About 40% work part-time on campus. The average award to freshmen is $4350. The college grants scholarships on the basis of scholastic ability, need, achievement, character, and citizenship. Revolving funds are used to provide student loans. Whittier is a participant in the NDSL. The college is a member of CSS. The FAF and SAAC forms are required; applications for financial aid should be filed by March 15 (fall) and January 15 (spring).

Foreign Students: Eleven percent of the full-time students come from foreign countries. The college offers these students an intensive English program.

Admissions: The TOEFL is required and a minimum score of 500 should be achieved. The SAT is also required.

Procedure: Foreign applicants are admitted to both the fall and spring semesters. March 15 is the application deadline for the fall semester. A physical examination is necessary. Proof of funds adequate to cover 1 year of study is also required.

Admissions Contact: Barbara Lundberg, Director of Admissions.

WOODBURY UNIVERSITY
Los Angeles, California 90017
C–5
(213) 482-8491

F/T: 358M, 418W
P/T: 61M, 96W
Grad: 69M, 30W
Year: qtrs, ss
Appl: open
573 applied   248 accepted
SAT or ACT: recommended

Faculty: 36; IV, +$
Ph.D.'s: 33%
S/F Ratio: 21 to 1
Tuition: $3320
R and B: n/app
163 enrolled
COMPETITIVE+

Woodbury University, an independent, coeducational, nonsectarian institution founded in 1884, is one of the oldest universities in the West, and today offers programs in business and the professional arts. The library contains 49,000 volumes and 12,500 microfilm items, and subscribes to 500 periodicals.

Environment: The primarily commuter campus is located in the business and financial district of Los Angeles.

Student Life: At present all of the 50 states and 50 foreign countries are represented in the student body. The college does not sponsor any living facilities, but housing information is available on request. Seventy-four percent of the students are members of various minority groups. Students may keep cars on campus.

Organizations: Students belong to the Associated Student Body and participate in clubs related to their major. There are no fraternities or sororities.

Sports: The university does not field any intercollegiate teams. There is 1 intramural sport available for men.

Handicapped: The entire campus is accessible to handicapped students. Elevators, specially equipped rest rooms, and lowered drinking fountains are available.

Graduates: Seven percent of the students pursue graduate study after graduation: about 3% enter law school; 90% pursue careers in business and industry.

Services: Students receive placement and career counseling free of charge. Health care is available for a fee.

Programs of Study: The university confers the B.S. degree. Master's programs are also offered. Bachelor's degrees are offered in the following subject areas: BUSINESS (accounting, business administration, business economics, computer science, fashion merchandising, international business, management, marketing, office administration), FINE AND PERFORMING ARTS (fashion design, graphic design, interior design). Seventy-five percent of degrees conferred are in business and 25% in professional arts.

Special: An intensive English language program enables non-English-speaking students to attain language proficiency before entering a degree program.

Admissions: Forty-three percent of those who applied were accepted for the 1981–82 freshman class. Graduates of accredited secondary schools may be admitted if they give satisfactory evidence of intellectual ability to carry studies at the university level, motivation and potential for success, and good moral character. Evidence of scholastic achievement is established by the previous academic record, and by satisfactory scores on the American Council on Education Examination, the ACT, or the GED Test in the case of veterans. A GPA of 2.0 is necessary. Other factors taken into consideration in the admissions decision are advanced placement or honors courses, recommendations by school officials, and impressions made during the interview.

Procedure: Credentials for admission must include a complete record of all previous high school, college, and university work. Applications are accepted throughout the year; sufficient time must be allowed for processing prior to the quarterly registration date. A rolling admissions procedure is used. There is a $20 application fee. Freshmen are admitted to the fall, winter, spring, and summer quarters.

Special: There are early decision, early admissions, and deferred admissions plans. CLEP and AP credit are available.

Transfer: For fall 1981, 264 transfer applications were received, 156 were accepted, and 105 students were enrolled. Transfers are accepted for all classes and may enter any quarter. A minimum 2.0 GPA is required. C and above grades transfer. Two references and all transcripts must be submitted with the application. Out of a total of 188 quarter hours required for the bachelor's degree, 45 quarter hours must be taken at Woodbury. There are no deadlines for transfer; admissions are on a rolling basis. Notification is made within 1 month.

Visiting: Visits can be arranged through the admissions office, Mondays through Fridays, 8 A.M. to 4:30 P.M.

Financial Aid: About 44% of the students receive some form of financial aid. About 5% work part-time on campus. The university offers placement in part-time positions to assist those students who need help to pay their university expenses. Students are eligible for the College Work-Study, Supplemental Educational Opportunity Grant, National Direct Student Loan, Basic Opportunity Grant Program, California State Scholarship, College Opportunity Grant, the Federally Insured Student Loan Program, California Guaranteed Students Loans, veteran's benefits, and private scholarships. The average award to freshmen is $3350. The university is a member of the CSS. The FAF and SAAC must be submitted with the aid application by April 1.

Foreign Students: Foreign students represent 63% of the full-time enrollment. The university offers these students an intensive English program, special counseling, and special organizations.

Admissions: Foreign applicants must take the university's English proficiency test. The SAT or ACT is not required.

Procedure: Deadlines for foreign student applications are August 1 (fall), October 1 (winter), January 18 (spring), and April 2 (summer). Foreign students must present proof of funds sufficient to cover the 9-month academic year. Special fees include $7.50 for the English test and $250, which is applied toward tuition when the student enrolls.

Admissions Contact: Dan Angelo, Director of Admissions.

WORLD COLLEGE WEST
San Rafael, California 94912
B–3
(415) 332-4522

F/T: 29M, 32W
P/T: none
Grad: none
Year: tri
Appl: Aug. 30
53 applied   45 accepted
SAT: 540V 515M   ACT: 22

Faculty: 6; n/av
Ph.D.'s: 75%
S/F Ratio: 10 to 1
Tuition: $3250
R and B: $2400
24 enrolled
VERY COMPETITIVE

World College West, established in 1971, is a private liberal arts institution that offers nontraditional programs. The interdisciplinary, problem-oriented curriculum focuses on preparing students for an increasingly interdependent world of scarce natural resources. Classes are small and involve seminar discussion. The library houses 25,000 volumes and subscribes to 60 periodicals.

Environment: The college occupies five buildings, including student residences, 100 yards from the Pacific Ocean in the Golden Gate National Recreation Area, 3 miles north of San Francisco. The college planned to move to a permanent 200-acre campus and ecological preserve during the 1981–82 academic year.

Student Life: About half the students come from California. Three-quarters of the freshmen come from public schools. About 90% of the students live on campus. Dormitories are coed. Students may keep cars on campus.

Organizations: There are no fraternities or sororities. Some extracurricular activities are available, and students may take advantage of San Francisco's cultural offerings and enjoy hiking, fishing, swimming, and camping at nearby mountains and beaches.

Sports: Intramural sports are offered.

Graduates: About half the freshmen drop out during the first year, and 25% remain to graduate. Three-fourths of the graduates seek advanced degrees, and 25% pursue careers in business and industry.

Services: Students receive free placement, career, and psychological counseling as well as tutoring. Fees are charged for health care services.

Programs of Study: The B.A. is awarded in liberal arts, with concentrations in resource management and appropriate technology, applied environmental studies, human services, and international business and economics. Majors are offered in the following subjects: AREA STUDIES (American, Asian, Latin American), BUSINESS (international business and economics), ENGLISH (English, journalism, literature, speech), FINE AND PERFORMING ARTS (art history, studio art, theater/dramatics), LANGUAGES (Spanish), MATH AND SCIENCES (ecology/environmental science—applied environmental studies), PHILOSOPHY (classics, humanities, philosophy, religion), PRE-PROFESSIONAL (agriculture, architecture, social work), SOCIAL SCIENCES (government/political science, history, international relations, psychology, social sciences).

94 CALIFORNIA

Required: Students must complete a first-year introductory program and a second-year intercultural experience in a foreign country, or their equivalents.

Special: Students may design their own majors or earn a general-studies degree. All students hold part-time jobs related to their academic and career interests and attend life-work seminars.

Admissions: Eighty-five percent of those who applied were accepted for the 1981–82 freshman class. The SAT scores of those who enrolled were as follows: Verbal—10% below 500, 80% between 500 and 599, 10% between 600 and 700, and 0% above 700; Math—40% below 500, 60% between 500 and 599, and 0% above 599. Of those who took the ACT, 10% scored below 21, 80% between 21 and 23, 10% between 24 and 25, and 0% above 25. Applicants must have a high school diploma, present an average of 2.5 or better, and rank in the upper half of their class. Admissions officers also consider, in order of importance, evidence of special talents, recommendations by high school officials, and impressions made during an interview.

Procedure: The SAT is preferred, but the ACT is acceptable. Junior-year results may be submitted. Applications for the fall quarter should be submitted by March 30, but are accepted through August 30. Freshmen are admitted only in fall. A rolling admissions plan is in effect. An interview is recommended. The application fee is $10.

Special: A deferred admissions plan is available.

Transfer: Students must complete at least 3 terms in residence to graduate. The fall application deadline is the same as that for freshmen. Transfer students are admitted to all quarters.

Visiting: Prospective students may schedule visits with the admissions office for any time during the school year. Guides are provided, and visitors may sit in on classes and remain overnight at the school.

Financial Aid: Seventy-six percent of the students receive aid. Half work part-time on campus. Eligible students may receive BEOG, SEOG, Cal Grants, College Work Study jobs, FISL, GSL, and college scholarships. Tuition may be paid in installments. The FAF, SAAC, and 1040 tax form should be submitted as early as possible, and August 30 is the deadline. Need is the determining factor.

Foreign Students: One foreign student was enrolled in 1981–82. Special counseling is provided.

Admissions: Applicants must score 500 or better on the TOEFL. They also must take the SAT. The college recommends minimum scores of 450 on each section.

Procedure: The application deadline is July 30 for fall admission. Students must present a health form completed by a physician as proof of good health. Proof of adequate funds also is required. Health insurance is available through the college at no additional charge.

Admissions Contact: Don Snider, Director of Admissions.

COLORADO

ADAMS STATE COLLEGE C–4
Alamosa, Colorado 81102 (303) 589-7321

F/T: 687M, 803W
P/T: 50M, 112W
Grad: 78M, 144W
Year: sems, ss
Appl: Aug. 1
964 applied
ACT: 17

Faculty: n/av; IIA, +$
Ph.D.'s: n/av
S/F Ratio: 19 to 1
Tuition: $820 ($2842)
R and B: $1890
876 accepted 460 enrolled
LESS COMPETITIVE

Adams State College, established in 1921, is a state-supported college. The school functions as both a liberal arts college and a teacher-training institution. The library contains over 158,000 volumes and 37,000 microfilm items, and subscribes to over 1500 periodicals.

Environment: The 90-acre campus is in a rural environment, in a city of 8000 about 230 miles from Denver. The buildings include an observatory-planetarium, and coed and single-sex residence halls that accommodate about half the students in single rooms, double rooms, and suites. On-campus apartments and married student housing are available. The college also sponsors a museum showing the various cultures of the area.

Student Life: About 80% of all students are from Colorado. Forty percent live on the campus. Ninety-eight percent come from public schools. Almost 27% of the students are minority-group members. Visiting privileges are available in single-sex dorms. Students may keep cars on campus. The college offers day-care services to all students, faculty and staff for a fee.

Organizations: There are no fraternities or sororities on campus; however, Protestant and Catholic religious organizations provide group activities for many students. The college is nestled in a ski area, and is near many scenic spots, including Indian pueblos and other cultural sites of interest belonging to the Spanish, Indian, and Anglo people of the area.

Sports: The school competes intercollegiately in 7 sports for men and 6 for women. There are 8 intramural sports for men and 6 for women.

Handicapped: About 99% of the campus is accessible to handicapped students. Facilities include wheelchair ramps, elevators, special parking and rest rooms, and lowered drinking fountains and telephones. Less than 1% of the students currently enrolled have visual or hearing impairments. The college has no special counselors for the handicapped.

Graduates: The freshman dropout rate is 35%; 45% of the full-time freshmen remain to graduate. Between 30% and 50% of the full-time students pursue graduate study. About 30% of all graduates pursue careers in business or industry.

Student Services: The following services are offered free of charge: career counseling, tutoring, remedial instruction, and psychological counseling. Placement services are available for a fee.

Programs of Study: The college confers the B.A. and B.S. degrees. Master's and associate degrees are also offered. Bachelor's degrees are offered in the following subjects: AREA STUDIES (Chicano), BUSINESS (accounting, business administration, business education, computer science, marketing), EDUCATION (elementary, health/physical, secondary, special), ENGLISH (English, journalism, speech), FINE AND PERFORMING ARTS (art, art education, music, music education, theater/dramatics), HEALTH SCIENCES (medical technology, speech therapy), LANGUAGES (Spanish), MATH AND SCIENCES (biology, chemistry, earth science, ecology/environmental science, geology, mathematics, natural sciences, physical sciences, physics), PRE-PROFESSIONAL (architecture, dentistry, engineering, law, medicine, pharmacy, veterinary), SOCIAL SCIENCES (economics, government/political science, gerontology, history, psychology, social sciences, sociology).

Special: The college allows a general studies program and permits student-designed majors. Adams accepts credits by students who have spent their third year abroad, and gives students the chance to travel and study in several foreign countries.

Honors: The English, education, and science departments offer honors courses.

Admissions: Ninety-one percent of the students who applied were accepted for the 1981–82 freshman class. Of those who enrolled, the ACT scores were as follows: 75.6% below 21, 10.5% between 21 and 23, 7.4% between 24 and 25, 4.9% between 26 and 28, and 1.6% above 28. Candidates must be in the upper two-thirds of their high school class and have an average of C or better. Other factors include recommendations of school officials, demonstration of special talents, and advanced placement or honors courses. Students must also have completed 15 Carnegie high school units.

Procedure: Application deadlines are August 1 (fall) and December 1 (spring). The ACT is required. The application fee is $10. The college follows a rolling admissions plan.

Special: Early admissions and early decision plans are available.

Transfer: For fall 1981, 125 transfer students applied, 98 were accepted, and 55 enrolled. A 2.0 GPA is required. Some D grades transfer in elective areas only. Transfers are accepted in all classes. They must complete, at the college, 30 of the 124 semester hours required for the bachelor's degree. There is a one-year residency requirement. Applicants should have a 2.0 GPA or special admission may be granted after an interview. Deadlines are the same as those for freshmen.

Visiting: The college has regularly scheduled orientation sessions for prospective students. Guides are provided for special visits, and those wishing to may sit in on classes. Visitors may stay overnight at the school and should arrange their stay with the admissions office.

Financial Aid: The college provides financial assistance through all major federal and state aid programs, including Basic and Supplemental Grant, Colorado Student Grant, State and Federal College Work-

Study, National Direct and Guaranteed Student Loan programs. Additionally, a substantial number of academic scholarships and activity grants are awarded each year. Approximately 60% of all students receive aid; 55% work part-time on campus. The FFS is required. Applications must be received by March 1 for first priority consideration. Late applications are considered on a first-come, first-served basis.

Foreign Students: Almost 2% of the full-time students come from foreign countries. These students are actively recruited by the college, which offers them special counseling and special organizations.

Admissions: Foreign students must achieve a minimum score of 500 on the TOEFL. College entrance exams are not required.

Procedure: Applications should be submitted in June (fall), November (spring), and April (summer). Foreign students must carry health insurance, which is available through the college for a fee. They must also provide proof of funds adequate to cover the first year of study.

Admissions Contact: Robert Burk, Assistant Director for Admissions.

COLORADO COLLEGE D-3
Colorado Springs, Colorado 80903 (303) 473-2233

F/T: 925M, 925W		Faculty:	137; IIB, ++$
P/T: none		Ph.D.'s:	85%
Grad: n/av		S/F Ratio:	14 to 1
Year: see profile		Tuition:	$5500
Appl: Feb. 15		R and B:	$1800
2313 applied	1272 accepted		485 enrolled
SAT or ACT: required			VERY COMPETITIVE

Colorado College, founded in 1874, is the oldest independent liberal arts college in the Rocky Mountains. The library houses over 300,000 volumes and 30,000 microfilm items, and subscribes to over 1000 periodicals.

Environment: The 79-acre campus is situated in the suburban foothills of the Rocky Mountains in the shadow of Pike's Peak, 70 miles from Denver. The 36 buildings on campus include a 20-bed health center, the Packard Hall of Music and Art, a sports complex, a student union, and several single-sex and coed residence halls.

Student Life: About two-thirds of the students are from out-of-state, and 75% come from public schools. Seventy percent live on campus. About 8% are minority-group members. Visiting restrictions are determined by individual residence halls. Students may keep cars on campus.

Organizations: About a third of the students belong to one of 5 fraternities and 4 sororities on campus. The more than 60 student organizations include a weekly newspaper, an orchestra, religious groups, drama, debate, choir, and community volunteer groups.

Sports: The college competes on an intercollegiate level in 14 sports for men and 10 for women. There are 10 intramural sports for men and women.

Handicapped: About 75% of the campus is accessible to wheelchair-bound students. Facilities include wheelchair ramps, parking areas, elevators, lowered telephones, and specially equipped rest rooms. Special class scheduling is also available. Special equipment, materials, and instruction are available on an individual basis to the fewer than 1% of the students who have visual or hearing impairments. No special counselors are available.

Graduates: The freshman dropout rate is 12%; 68% of the entering freshmen remain to graduate. Fifty percent of the graduates seek advanced degrees. About 30% of the graduates pursue careers in business and industry.

Services: Students receive the following free services: career counseling, psychological counseling, and health care. Placement services, including preprofessional committees, departmental placement, and a campus-wide career counseling center, are available to graduates as well as students.

Programs of Study: All undergraduate programs lead to the B.A. degree. Master's degrees also are conferred. Bachelor's degrees are offered in the following subjects: AREA STUDIES (Russian), BUSINESS (business administration), EDUCATION (elementary, secondary), ENGLISH (English), FINE AND PERFORMING ARTS (art history, music, studio art, theater/dramatics), HEALTH SCIENCES (medical technology), LANGUAGES (French, German, Spanish), MATH AND SCIENCES (biology, chemistry, geology, mathematics, physics), PHILOSOPHY (classics, philosophy, religion), SOCIAL SCIENCES (anthropology, economics, government/political science, history, history—political science, history—philosophy, political economics, psychology, sociology). Forty-six percent of undergraduate degrees conferred are in social sciences, 24% are in math and sciences, 24% are in the humanities, and 15% are in business.

Required: Students must take 3 courses in each of these areas: humanities, social sciences, and natural science.

Special: Students take only one course during each of the 9 blocks of 3½ weeks that make up the academic year. Special programs include junior year abroad, student-designed majors, interdisciplinary seminars for freshmen, and concentrations in black, Asian, Latin American, and urban studies. The college is 1 of 12 members of the Associated Colleges of the Midwest, a consortium that offers programs including field studies in ecology and geology, an urban studies institute in Chicago, foreign study, research at the Argonne National Laboratory, and history seminars at Chicago's Newberry Library. The college offers 3-2 and 4-2 programs in engineering with Columbia University, Rensselaer Polytechnic Institute, and the University of Southern California; a 3-2 forestry program with Duke University; and 2-2 and 3-2 nursing programs with Rush Medical Center.

Honors: Six honor societies, including Phi Beta Kappa, are represented on campus. A Selected Student Program is available to qualified freshmen and sophomores.

Admissions: Fifty-five percent of those who applied were accepted for the 1981–82 freshman class. The SAT scores of those who enrolled were as follows: Verbal—32% below 500, 42% between 500 and 599, 13% between 600 and 700, and 1% above 700; Math—21% below 500, 39% between 500 and 599, 25% between 600 and 700, and 3% above 700. On the ACT, 7% scored below 21, 10% between 21 and 23, 6% between 24 and 25, 20% between 26 and 28, and 9% above 28. Applicants should have at least 15 academic units. The college employs no arbitrary cut-off point for test scores, class rank, or grade average. Admissions officers consider advanced placement or honors courses, extracurricular activities, evidence of special talents, personality, leadership record, and recommendations by school officials.

Procedure: The SAT or ACT should be taken in December or January of the senior year. The application, a $20 fee, test scores, and high school record should be submitted by February 15 for fall admission. Notification is made between April 1 and April 15. The college subscribes to the CRDA.

Special: AP credit is available. Requests for deferred admission and early decision are considered on a case-by-case basis.

Transfer: For fall 1981, 368 transfer students applied, 160 were accepted, and 100 enrolled. D grades do not transfer. Students must complete, at the college, 30 of the 107 semester hours required for the bachelor's degree. Applications for fall admission are due April 1; for spring, November 1.

Visiting: Orientation sessions for prospective students are held Monday through Friday at 11 A.M. and 2:15 P.M. Saturday appointments also can be made during the school year. Arrangements should be made with the admissions office.

Financial Aid: Forty percent of the students receive aid; 23% work part-time on campus. The college, a member of CSS, offers scholarships, loans, and campus jobs totaling more than $3.5 million. The maximum aid available to a student from all sources is $7500. Aid applicants must file the FAF or FFS and the college's application by February 15. Request for aid does not affect admissions decision.

Foreign Students: Foreign students comprise almost 3% of the full-time enrollment. Special organizations are available to these students.

Admissions: Foreign students must take the TOEFL. Entrance exams are not required.

Procedure: Applications must be received by February 1 for fall admission. Foreign students must present a physician's report as proof of health and must carry health insurance, which is available through the college for a fee. They must also provide proof of funds adequate to cover 1 year of study.

Admissions Contact: Richard E. Wood, Director of Admission.

COLORADO SCHOOL OF MINES C-2
Golden, Colorado 80401 (303) 279-0300

F/T: 1815M, 407W		Faculty:	195; I, +$
P/T: 63M, 14W		Ph.D.'s:	80%
Grad: 434M, 97W		S/F Ratio:	15 to 1
Year: sems, ss		Tuition:	$2048 ($5544)
Appl: Aug. 1		R and B:	$2400
1388 applied	933 accepted		506 enrolled
SAT: 540V 640M		ACT: 28	HIGHLY COMPETITIVE+

Colorado School of Mines, established in 1874, is operated by the state in close association with the mining industry. The library contains over 200,000 books and 100,000 microfilm items, and subscribes to over 140 periodicals.

Environment: The 207-acre campus is located in a suburban area 17 miles from Denver. The 21 buildings include residence halls that house 600 single men and 105 married couples. Fraternity and sorority houses are also available.

Student Life: About 70% of the students are from Colorado and 8% are from foreign countries. Six percent of the students are minority-group members. About 40% live on campus or in approved housing. Campus housing is both coed and single-sex. There are visiting privileges in single-sex dorms. Drinking is permitted in specified areas. Students may keep cars on campus.

Organizations: About 15% of the men belong to one of 6 national fraternities and 15% of the women belong to one of 2 national sororities. The area provides abundant opportunities for outdoor recreation. Extracurricular activities include publications and student government.

Sports: The school fields intercollegiate teams in 13 sports for men and 9 for women. There are 11 intramural sports for men and women.

Handicapped: About 10% of the campus is accessible to physically handicapped students. Special facilities include wheelchair ramps, parking areas, elevators, and specially equipped rest rooms. Special class scheduling also is available.

Graduates: Ten percent of the freshmen drop out, and 60% remain to graduate. About 15% of the graduates go on for further education, including 1% who go to medical school, 1% who go to dental school, and 2% who go to law school. About 85% of the graduates enter business and industry.

Services: The following services are provided free to students: placement, career, and psychological counseling; health care; tutoring; and remedial instruction. Placement services also are available to graduates.

Programs of Study: The school awards the B.S. degree. Master's and doctoral degrees also are available. Bachelor's degrees are offered in the following subjects: MATH AND SCIENCES (chemistry, mathematics, physics), PREPROFESSIONAL (engineering—geophysics, engineering—mathematics, engineering—metallurgy, engineering—mineral, engineering—mining, engineering—petroleum, engineering—chemical/petroleum/refining, engineering—physics).

Required: All freshmen must take courses in mathematics, chemistry, physics, geology, humanities, and physical education. All undergraduates must take specified courses in the social and engineering sciences.

Special: An extensive English course is available in the summer for foreign students.

Honors: One honor society is represented on campus. A humanities honors program is offered.

Admissions: About 67% of the applicants for the 1981–82 freshman class were accepted. The SAT scores of 1981–82 freshmen were as follows: Verbal—20% below 500, 65% between 500 and 599, 12% between 600 and 700, and 3% above 700; Math—0% below 500, 19% between 500 and 599, 56% between 600 and 700, and 25% above 700. The ACT scores were as follows: 0% below 21, 5% between 21 and 23, 20% between 24 and 25, 30% between 26 and 28, and 45% above 28. Applicants must rank in the top 33% of their class and present a GPA of at least 3.0. Admissions officers also consider advanced placement or honors courses, leadership record, and extracurricular activities.

Procedure: The SAT or ACT is required. There is a $10 application fee for out-of-state applicants only. Applications for fall admission are due August 1; for spring admission, December 15. Notification is made on a rolling basis.

Special: AP and CLEP credit is accepted.

Transfer: For fall 1981, 479 students applied, 210 were accepted, and 130 enrolled. Students must complete at least 1 academic year in residence to receive a degree. They must also complete, at the school, 30 of the 144–148 semester credits required for the bachelor's degree. A GPA of at least 2.5 is required for transfer. D grades do not transfer. Application deadlines are the same as those for freshmen.

Visiting: Guides are provided for prospective students during visits. Visitors may sit in on classes and stay overnight at the school. Visits should be scheduled for weekdays between 8 A.M. and 5 P.M. with the admissions office.

Financial Aid: About 60% of the students receive aid; 25% work part-time on campus. Seventy freshman scholarships are available from a fund of $60,000. Federal, state, bank, industry, and school loans are offered. The FFS and the school's aid application must be filed by March 15 (fall) or November 15 (spring).

Foreign Students: About 8% of the full-time students come from foreign countries. Special organizations are available to these students.

Admissions: Foreign students must achieve a minimum score of 500 on the TOEFL. The SAT or ACT also is required.

Procedure: The application deadline for fall entry is February 1. Foreign students must take a standard medical examination to establish proof of health and must carry health insurance, which is available through the school for a fee. They must also furnish proof of funds adequate to cover 1 year of study.

Admissions Contact: A. William Young, Director of Admissions.

COLORADO STATE UNIVERSITY   C–1
Fort Collins, Colorado 80523   (303) 491-7201

F/T: 7110M, 7308W   Faculty: 1150; I, av$
P/T: 615M, 567W   Ph.D.'s: 78%
Grad: 1970M, 1081W   S/F Ratio: 17 to 1
Year: sems, ss   Tuition: $978 ($3496)
Appl: see profile   R and B: $2160
8836 applied   6209 accepted   3257 enrolled
SAT (mean): 470V 516M   ACT: 22   COMPETITIVE

Founded in 1870 as a land-grant college, Colorado State University offers undergraduate and graduate degree programs at the main (Fort Collins) campus as well as 2 smaller campuses (Pingree Park and Foothills) and 11 research centers throughout the state. The university's library subscribes to 16,903 periodicals, and has over 1 million books and 480,000 microtexts, plus journals, manuscripts, films, and other reference items.

Environment: The 400-acre campus is located 60 miles north of Denver in a city of 75,000. The campus consists of 100 buildings including coed residence halls that accommodate 2643 men and 2626 women. University apartments are available for 666 married students. Fraternity and sorority houses also are available.

Student Life: Seventy-four percent of the students come from Colorado. About 90% have had public school education. About 65% live in campus housing or in a fraternity or sorority house. Nine percent of the students are minority-group members. Campus housing is coed. Students may keep cars on campus.

Organizations: Three percent of the men belong to 1 of 11 national fraternities; 5% of the women belong to 1 of 9 national sororities. All traditional social activities are offered. There also are special-interest clubs, a campus newspaper, a radio station, theatre and music groups, and cultural events. Nearby natural areas offer outdoor recreation.

Sports: There are 8 intercollegiate sports for men and 9 for women. Intramural competition is offered for men and women in 15 sports.

Handicapped: About 92% of the campus is accessible to students with physical handicaps. Special facilities include wheelchair ramps, parking, specially equipped rest rooms, elevators, and lowered drinking fountains. Special class scheduling is also available. The library has special audiovisual equipment to assist students with hearing or vision impairments. Three counselors are available.

Graduates: The freshman dropout rate is 7%. About 15% of the students seek further education after graduation: fewer than 2% go to medical or dental schools, fewer than 1% to law school, and 15% into business and industry.

Services: The following services are free to all students: placement, career counseling, tutoring, and psychological counseling. Health care is available for a fee. Placement services are available to undergraduates, and career placement and advising to graduates.

Programs of Study: Approximately 94 majors leading to the B.A., B.E., B.F.A., B.M., and B.S. degrees are offered by 9 colleges in the university. Master's and doctoral degrees are also conferred. Bachelor's degrees are offered in the following subjects: AREA STUDIES (Asian, criminal justice, ethnic, Latin American, religious, Russian, urban, women's), BUSINESS (accounting, business administration, business education, computer science, finance, industrial relations, information systems, management, marketing, production and operations management, real estate/insurance, records management), EDUCATION (adult, early childhood, health/physical, industrial, secondary), ENGLISH (English, journalism, literature, speech), FINE AND PERFORMING ARTS (art, art education, art history, dance, music, music education, radio/TV, studio art, theater/dramatics), HEALTH SCIENCES (environmental health, medical technology, occupational therapy, speech therapy), LANGUAGES (French, German, Spanish), MATH AND SCIENCES (biology, botany, chemistry, ecology/environmental science, entomology, geology, mathematics, natural sciences, physical sciences, physics, statistics, zoology), PHILOSOPHY (humanities, philosophy), PREPROFESSIONAL (agriculture, dentistry, engineering, forestry, home economics, law, medicine, pharmacy, social work, veterinary), SOCIAL SCIENCES (anthropology, economics, geography, government/political science, history, psychology, social sciences, sociology). Forty-one percent of undergraduate degrees are awarded in preprofessional fields, 21% in math and sciences, and 13% in business.

Required: All students must take courses in English, math, and physical education.

Special: Junior-year study abroad, a combined B.A.-B.S. degree, and a second bachelor's degree are offered.

Honors: Two honor societies have chapters on campus: Phi Beta Kappa and Phi Kappa Phi. All departments offer honors programs.

Admissions: About 70% of the applicants for the 1981-82 school year were accepted. Of those who enrolled, the SAT scores were: Verbal—31% between 500 and 600, and 10% above 600; Math—40% between 500 and 600, and 23% above 600. The ACT scores were: 16% below 21, 18% between 21 and 23, 19% between 24 and 25, 29% between 26 and 28, and 19% above 28. Graduation from an accredited high school with 15 units is required. Minimum class rank is generally the top 50%. Advanced placement or honors work, special talents, and recommendations are considered heavily in the admissions decision.

Procedure: The SAT or ACT is required along with a $15 application processing fee. Admissions close whenever enrollment projection is met. There is a rolling admissions plan.

Special: AP and CLEP credit is granted.

Transfer: For fall 1981, 3712 transfer students applied, 2292 were accepted, and 1397 enrolled. The student needs 28 credits with a 2.3 GPA or 60 credits with a 2.0 GPA. Some majors require a higher competitive GPA. Preference is given to students transferring from other colleges in the state. Thirty-two credits, of the 128 required for the bachelor's degree, must be earned in residence.

Visiting: Campus visit days are in November and February. Orientation for new students is held in July. Limited guide service is available for informal campus visits; visitors may sit in on classes.

Financial Aid: About 70% of the students receive assistance; 28% to 35% work part-time on campus. The university provides scholarships of up to $300 for Colorado residents only. Some grants (up to $1500/year) are available to nonresidents. Grants are awarded on the basis of need only. BEOG grants are available. Loans are available up to $1250/year. The FFS or FAF must be filed by April 1 for fall and summer or October 15 for spring.

Foreign Students: Two percent of the full-time students come from foreign countries. The university offers these students an intensive English program as well as special counseling and organizations.

Admissions: Foreign students must achieve a minimum score of 550 on the TOEFL. The SAT or ACT also is required and scores on these exams must be competitive with those of other students.

Procedure: Applications must be filed approximately 6 months before the beginning of the term, by March 1 for fall entry. Foreign students must present proof of health. They must also provide proof of funds adequate to cover 1 year of study. Tuition and fees are the same as for out-of-state students.

Admissions Contact: John Kennedy, Director of Admissions.

COLORADO TECHNICAL COLLEGE D-3
Colorado Springs, Colorado 80907 (303) 598-0200

F/T: 400M, 50W Faculty: n/av; IV, --$
P/T: 75M, 25W Ph.D.'s: 1%
Grad: none S/F Ratio: n/av
Year: qtrs, ss Tuition: $2570
Appl: open R and B: n/app
150 applied 148 accepted 120 enrolled
SAT or ACT: not required **LESS COMPETITIVE**

Colorado Technical College is an independent undergraduate institution offering degrees in engineering. The library holds 2377 books, and subscribes to 30 periodicals.

Environment: The 5-acre suburban campus is located in the city of Colorado Springs. There is no on-campus housing.

Student Life: About 55% of the students come from Colorado. Thirteen percent are minority-group members. Students may keep cars on campus. Drinking on campus is prohibited.

Organizations: About 5% of the men belong to a fraternity; there are no sororities. Extracurricular activities include a science-fiction club.

COLORADO 97

Students may take advantage of the social, cultural, and recreational offerings of the Colorado Springs area.

Sports: There is no intercollegiate athletic program. There are 4 intramural sports for men and 1 sport for women.

Handicapped: There are no special facilities for physically handicapped students.

Graduates: About 20% of the freshmen drop out, and 80% remain to graduate. Fewer than 1% seek advanced degrees. Virtually all graduates enter business and industry.

Services: Placement and career counseling are offered free to students. Tutoring and remedial instruction are available for a fee.

Programs of Study: The college awards the B.S. degree. Associate degrees are also awarded. Bachelor's degrees are offered in the following subjects: BUSINESS (computer science, management), PRE-PROFESSIONAL (computer science technology, engineering—biomedical, engineering—electronic, engineering—solar).

Special: Work-study programs are available in solar and electronic engineering.

Honors: One honor society is represented on campus.

Admissions: About 99% of the applicants for the 1981-82 freshman class were accepted. Applicants must have a GPA of at least 2.0 and should rank in the upper half of their high school class. Impressions made during an interview, the applicant's personality, and ability to finance a college education are also considered important.

Procedure: Neither the SAT nor the ACT is required. Application deadlines are open, but students should apply 60 days before the beginning of a quarter. New students are admitted to all quarters. Notification is made on a rolling basis. There is a $30 application fee.

Special: There are early decision, early admissions, and deferred admissions plans. AP and CLEP credit is accepted.

Transfer: For fall 1981, 75 students applied, 70 were accepted, and 50 enrolled. A GPA of at least 2.0 is required. D grades do not transfer. All students must complete, at the college, 30 of the 193 credit hours required for a bachelor's degree. Applications are due at least 2 weeks before the start of a quarter.

Visiting: Guides are provided for informal visits by prospective students. Visitors may observe classes. Visits should be scheduled on weekdays between 8 A.M. and 4 P.M. The admissions director should be contacted for arrangements.

Financial Aid: About 50% of the students receive aid. Three percent work part-time on campus. Five percent of the freshmen receive scholarships. The college administers federal loan funds totaling $85,000. Other forms of aid include CWS and SEOG. Tuition may be paid in installments. The college is a member of CSS and requires the FAF or FFS. Deadlines are open.

Foreign Students: Five percent of the full-time students come from foreign countries. An intensive English course and special counseling are available for these students.

Admissions: Foreign students must take either the TOEFL or the college's own English proficiency exam. On the TOEFL, a score of at least 500 is required. No college entrance exams are necessary.

Procedure: There are no application deadlines; foreign students are admitted in all quarters. They must present proof of funds adequate to cover 1 year of study.

Admissions Contact: Carl A. Melin, Director of Admissions.

FORT LEWIS COLLEGE B-4
Durango, Colorado 81301 (303) 247-7184

F/T: 1759M, 1382W Faculty: 175; IIB, ++$
P/T: 75M, 96W Ph.D.'s: 73%
Grad: none S/F Ratio: 22 to 1
Year: tri, ss Tuition: $724 ($2758)
Appl: Aug. 1 R and B: $1464
1500 applied 1400 accepted 1001 enrolled
ACT: 17 **LESS COMPETITIVE**

Fort Lewis College, established in 1911, is a coeducational, state-supported, 4-year college. The library contains 130,000 volumes and 20,000 microfilm items, and subscribes to 900 periodicals.

Environment: The college is located in a rural area on the top of a mesa surrounded by mountains, in the city of Durango in Southwest Colorado. Campus buildings include 13 dormitories that house 972 students, 8 fourplexes for married students, and 92 1- and 2-bedroom apartments.

COLORADO

Student Life: About 65% of the students come from Colorado, and 90% are graduates of public schools. Thirty percent of the students live on campus. Twenty-two percent are minority-group members. Campus housing is both coed and single-sex; there are visiting privileges in the single-sex housing. Students may keep cars on campus. Day-care services are available for a fee.

Organizations: There are no fraternities or sororities. Extracurricular activities and cultural events include professional and service organizations, student government, cheerleading, drama, photography, publications, art shows, concerts, films, recitals, and science exhibits. Ski resorts and other outdoor recreation areas are located nearby.

Sports: The college participates in 7 intercollegiate sports for men and 5 for women. There are 21 intramural sports for men and 21 for women.

Handicapped: About 95% of the campus is accessible to wheelchair-bound students. Special facilities include wheelchair ramps and parking areas.

Graduates: About 33% of entering freshmen drop out by the end of the first year; 42% remain to graduate. Thirty-five percent of the graduates seek advanced degrees, including 1% who enter medical school, 1% who enter dental school, and 1% who enter law school. About 20% of the graduates pursue careers in business and industry.

Services: Students receive free tutoring, placement services, career counseling, and psychological counseling. Placement services also are available to alumni. Health care is available on campus on a fee basis.

Programs of Study: The college awards the B.A. and B.S. degrees. Associate degrees also are available. Bachelor's degrees are offered in the following subjects: AREA STUDIES (American, Asian, Latin American), BUSINESS (accounting, business administration, business education, computer science), EDUCATION (elementary, secondary), ENGLISH (English, journalism), FINE AND PERFORMING ARTS (art, art education, music, music education, theater/dramatics), HEALTH SCIENCES (medical technology), LANGUAGES (French, German, Spanish), MATH AND SCIENCES (biology, chemistry, ecology/environmental science, mathematics, natural sciences, physical sciences, statistics), PHILOSOPHY (philosophy), PREPROFESSIONAL (agriculture, dentistry, engineering, forestry, law, medicine, veterinary), SOCIAL SCIENCES (anthropology, economics, government/political science, history, psychology, social sciences, sociology). Twenty-five percent of bachelor's degrees are conferred in business, 24% in math and sciences, and 21% in education.

Required: Freshmen must participate in two seminars that take the place of traditional English courses. All students must satisfy distribution requirements and complete a senior seminar or independent study program.

Special: Students may design their own majors. Electives may be taken on a pass/fail basis. An exchange program and a cooperative education program are offered. An intercultural program is available for American Indians and other bilingual students. Combination degree programs are available in medical technology and engineering.

Honors: Four honor societies are represented at the college. An honors program is available.

Admissions: Ninety-three percent of those who applied were accepted for the 1981–82 freshman class. Applicants should rank in the upper half of their high school class, present an average of at least 2.0, and have completed 15 Carnegie units. Admissions officers also consider ACT or SAT scores, advanced placement or honors courses, recommendations by school officials, and impressions made during an interview.

Procedure: Applicants must take the SAT or ACT. There is a $10 application fee. Application deadlines are August 1 (fall), December 1 (winter), and April 1 (spring). Freshmen also are admitted in summer. Admissions decisions are made on a rolling basis.

Special: Early decision and early admissions plans are available. CLEP and AP credit is accepted.

Transfer: For fall 1981, 453 students applied, 392 were accepted, and 282 enrolled. Transfer students are accepted for all classes. D grades may transfer. Applicants must have a minimum average of 2.0. All students must complete, at the college, 28 of the 128 credits required for a bachelor's degree. Application deadlines are the same as those for freshmen.

Visiting: Prospective students may schedule informal visits during the spring and summer with the admissions office. Visitors may sit in on classes and, during the summer, stay on campus overnight. Guides are provided.

Financial Aid: About 35% of the students receive aid. Fifteen percent work part-time on campus. The college requires the FFS from aid applicants. Scholarships; federal, bank, and college loans; and campus jobs are awarded to freshmen and other students on the basis of need. The deadlines for aid applications are May 1 (fall), November 15 (winter), and March 1 (summer).

Foreign Students: One percent of the full-time students come from foreign countries. Special counseling is available for these students.

Admissions: Foreign students must achieve a TOEFL score of at least 500. No college entrance exams are required.

Procedure: Application deadlines are July 1 (fall), October 1 (winter), January 1 (spring), and March 1 (summer). Foreign students must present proof of funds adequate to cover 1 year of study. Health insurance is required and is available through the college for a fee.

Admissions Contact: Harlan Steinle, Director of Admissions.

LORETTO HEIGHTS COLLEGE C–2
Denver, Colorado 80236 (303) 936-8441

F/T: 128M, 517W		Faculty:	n/av; IIB, –$
P/T: 22M, 80W		Ph.D.'s:	24%
Grad: none		S/F Ratio:	11 to 1
Year: sems, ss		Tuition:	$4345
Appl: Aug. 1		R and B:	$2400
446 applied	331 accepted		159 enrolled
SAT: 406V 414M	ACT: 18	LESS COMPETITIVE	

Loretto Heights College, established in 1918 as a Roman Catholic college for women, now is a coed, nonsectarian institution. The library contains 100,000 volumes, and subscribes to 690 periodicals.

Environment: The 105-acre campus is located at the foot of the Rockies in a suburban area 8 miles from downtown Denver. Buildings include a performing arts center, art studios, and 2 dormitories.

Student Life: About 60% of the students come from Colorado, and 90% are graduates of public schools. About 45% of the students live on campus. Fourteen percent are minority-group members. Forty percent are Catholic, 29% are Protestant, and 2% are Jewish. Campus housing is both coed and single-sex; there are visiting privileges in the single-sex housing. Students may keep cars on campus.

Organizations: Campus activities include clubs, lecture and concert series, social events, and student government. There are no sororities or fraternities. Cultural and recreational opportunities also are available in the city of Denver.

Sports: The college does not participate in intercollegiate sports. There are 8 intramural sports for men and 8 for women.

Handicapped: There are limited facilities for physically handicapped students.

Graduates: About 20% of the freshmen drop out, and 50% eventually graduate. About 20% of the graduates go on for further education, including 1% who enter medical school, 1% who enter dental school, and 1% who enter law school.

Services: Health care, psychological counseling, tutoring, remedial instruction, placement, and career counseling are provided free to students.

Programs of Study: The college confers the B.A., B.S., B.F.A., and B.S.N. degrees. Bachelor's degrees are offered in the following subjects: BUSINESS (business administration), EDUCATION (elementary, religious, secondary, special), ENGLISH (English), FINE AND PERFORMING ARTS (art, art education, dance, music, music education, theater/dramatics), HEALTH SCIENCES (medical technology, nursing), LANGUAGES (French, Spanish), MATH AND SCIENCES (biology, chemistry, mathematics, natural sciences), PHILOSOPHY (humanities, religion), PREPROFESSIONAL (law, medicine), SOCIAL SCIENCES (criminal justice, government/political science, history, international relations, psychology, social sciences, sociology). About 35% of degrees are conferred in the health sciences.

Special: Students may design their own majors. The college offers a University Without Walls program and opportunities for study abroad.

Honors: Honors programs are available.

Admissions: Seventy-four percent of the applicants for the 1981–82 freshman class were accepted. The SAT scores of those who enrolled were as follows: Verbal—85% below 500, 13% between 500 and 599, 2% between 600 and 700, and 0% above 700; Math—80% below 500, 13% between 500 and 599, 5% between 600 and 700, and 2% above 700. On the ACT, 65% scored below 21, 18% between 21 and 23, 14% between 24 and 25, 5% between 26 and 28, and 0% above 28. Applicants should present a combined score of at least 800 on the SAT or a score of at least 18 on the ACT composite, rank in the top half of their class, and have earned an average of C or better. The college prefers that students have completed at least 15 Carnegie units. Advanced placement or honors courses, impressions made during an interview, and recommendations are also considered important.

Procedure: The SAT or ACT is required. Application deadlines are August 1 (fall) and January 1 (spring). A rolling admissions policy is used. There is a $10 application fee.

Special: AP and CLEP credit is accepted.

Transfer: For fall 1981, 222 transfer students applied, 163 were accepted, and 71 enrolled. A GPA of at least 2.0 is required. All students must complete, at the college, 30 of the 128 semester hours required for a bachelor's degree. Application deadlines are the same as those for freshmen.

Visiting: Guides are provided for informal visits on weekdays while classes are in session. Prospective students may attend classes and stay overnight. Arrangements should be made with the admissions office.

Financial Aid: About 80% of the students receive aid. About 70% work part-time on campus. The average freshman award is $7000. The college offers scholarships, loans under NDSL, grants under BEOG, and CWS jobs. Aid awards are based on need and academic potential. The FFS or FAF should be filed by April 1. The college is a member of CSS.

Foreign Students: One percent of the full-time students come from foreign countries. An intensive English program is available for these students.

Admissions: Foreign students must take the TOEFL, the University of Michigan Language Test, or the Comprehensive English Language Test. On the TOEFL, a score of at least 500 is required.

Procedure: Application deadlines are August 1 (fall) and December 1 (spring). Foreign students must present proof of funds adequate to cover 1 year of study. Health insurance is required and is available through the college for a fee.

Admissions Contact: Connie Campbell, Dean of Admissions and Financial Aid.

MESA COLLEGE A-2
Grand Junction, Colorado 81501 (303) 248-1376

F/T: 1391M, 1190W	Faculty:	150; IIB, +$
P/T: 669M, 1376W	Ph.D.'s:	25%
Grad: none	S/F Ratio:	20 to 1
Year: sems, ss	Tuition:	$820 ($2826)
Appl: open	R and B:	$1874
1878 applied	1704 accepted	901 enrolled
ACT: 18		NONCOMPETITIVE

Mesa College, a state-supported institution founded in 1925, offers associate and bachelor's degree programs. The library houses 85,000 books and subscribes to 500 periodicals.

Environment: The campus is located in an urban area in the Rocky Mountains about 260 miles from Denver. Campus buildings include 4 residence halls that accommodate 630 students and an apartment complex that houses 165 students.

Student Life: About 93% of the students come from Colorado, and almost all are graduates of public schools. About 20% live on campus. About 4% are minority-group members. Students may keep cars on campus. Day-care services are available for full-time students. Campus housing is single-sex; there are visiting privileges. Women residents must follow a sign-out procedure.

Organizations: There is one sorority on campus; there are 3 fraternities. Opportunities for outdoor recreation in the area are abundant. Campus activities include about 30 clubs, a student government, and social events.

Sports: The college participates intercollegiately in 6 sports for men and 4 for women. There are 9 intramural sports for men and 8 for women.

Handicapped: About 85% of the campus is accessible to physically handicapped students. Special facilities include wheelchair ramps, parking areas, elevators, lowered drinking fountains and telephones, and specially equipped rest rooms. Special class scheduling is also available. A special counselor is available through the State Department of Rehabilitation.

Graduates: Twenty-nine percent of entering freshmen remain to graduate. About 50% of the graduates seek advanced degrees.

Services: Free placement, career counseling, health care, and remedial instruction are provided for all students. Tutoring and psychological counseling are available for a fee.

COLORADO 99

Programs of Study: The B.A., B.S., B.B.A., and B.S.N. degrees are awarded. Associate degrees also are available. Bachelor's degrees are offered in the following subjects: BUSINESS (accounting, business administration, computer science, management, marketing), EDUCATION (elementary, secondary), ENGLISH (English, journalism, literature, speech), FINE AND PERFORMING ARTS (art, music, theater/dramatics), HEALTH SCIENCES (nursing), MATH AND SCIENCES (biology, earth science, geology, mathematics), PHILOSOPHY (humanities), PREPROFESSIONAL (agriculture), SOCIAL SCIENCES (anthropology, economics, history, psychology, social sciences, sociology). About 35% of degrees are awarded in social science, 25% in business, and 17% in math and sciences.

Special: Students may design their own majors.

Honors: Two honor societies are represented on campus. Departmental honors programs are offered in English and mathematics.

Admissions: About 91% of the applicants for the 1981–82 freshman class were accepted. Applicants must have a high school diploma or GED. State residents are admitted on an open enrollment basis; nonresidents must rank in the top two-thirds of their high school class.

Procedure: Applicants must take the ACT; scores are used only for placement. There are no application deadlines; freshmen are admitted in the fall, spring, and summer terms. Notification is on a rolling basis. There is a $10 application fee.

Special: CLEP credit is accepted. There are early decision and early admissions plans.

Transfer: For fall 1981, 400 students applied, 340 were accepted, and 286 enrolled. D grades in the major do not transfer. All students must complete, at the college, 45 of the 120 credits required for a bachelor's degree. Applicants must be in good standing at their last school. There are no application deadlines; transfer students are admitted in the fall, spring, and summer terms.

Visiting: Formal orientation programs for prospective students are scheduled each summer. Guides also are available for informal visits; visitors may observe classes and, if space is available, stay overnight at the school. Arrangements should be made with the director of admissions.

Financial Aid: About 60% of the students receive aid. Twenty percent work part-time on campus. The average freshman award is $1350. The college offers loans (NDSL and FISL), grants (EOG, LEEP, and the college's own), scholarships (based primarily on academic achievement), and work-study jobs. The FFS should be filed by June 15.

Foreign Students: Fewer than 1% of the full-time students come from foreign countries.

Admissions: Foreign students must achieve a TOEFL score of at least 450 and must take the ACT.

Procedure: Application deadlines are August 1 (fall) and December 1 (summer). Foreign students must present proof of health and proof of adequate funds. Health insurance is required.

Admissions Contact: Jack Scott, Director of Admissions.

METROPOLITAN STATE COLLEGE C-2
Denver, Colorado 80204 (303) 629-3058

F/T: 3479M, 2887W	Faculty:	358; IIB, ++$
P/T: 4270M, 4800W	Ph.D.'s:	64%
Grad: none	S/F Ratio:	18 to 1
Year: sems, ss	Tuition:	$716 ($2596)
Appl: Aug. 1	R and B:	n/app
SAT or ACT: not required		NONCOMPETITIVE

Metropolitan State College, founded in 1963, is a public institution offering bachelor's programs in the arts, sciences, and applied sciences. The library contains over 628,000 volumes and 27,580 microfilm items, and subscribes to over 1700 periodicals.

Environment: Metropolitan is an urban, nonresidential college. A cafeteria, snack bar, student lounge, and lockers are available.

Student Life: Ninety-seven percent of the students come from Colorado and 1% from other states. About 14% are minority-group members. Students may keep cars on campus. Day-care services are available to all students on a fee basis.

Organizations: Student organizations include student government, minority organizations, musical concerts and theatrical productions, and the Over 25 Club for married students with families.

Sports: The college fields 8 intercollegiate teams for men and 7 for women. There are 16 intramural sports for men and 15 for women.

100 COLORADO

Handicapped: The campus is 100% accessible to wheelchair-bound students. Facilities include wheelchair ramps, elevators, specially equipped rest rooms, automatic door openers, telephones for the hearing-impaired, and lowered drinking fountains and telephones.

Services: Students receive the following services free of charge: psychological counseling, tutoring, remedial instruction, health care, placement, and career counseling.

Programs of Study: The college confers the B.A. and B.S. degrees. Bachelor's degrees are offered in the following subjects: AREA STUDIES (bilingual/Chicano, Black/Afro-American, urban), BUSINESS (accounting, business education, computer science, finance, management, marketing), EDUCATION (early childhood, elementary, health/physical, industrial, recreation), ENGLISH (communications, English, journalism, speech), FINE AND PERFORMING ARTS (art, music, music education), HEALTH SCIENCES (health care management, human services, nursing), LANGUAGES (French, German, Spanish), MATH AND SCIENCES (biology, chemistry, criminalistics, earth science, mathematics, physics), PHILOSOPHY (philosophy), PREPROFESSIONAL (aviation management, engineering technology—civil, engineering technology—electronic, engineering technology—mechanical, hospitality, meeting, and travel administration, meteorology, social work), SOCIAL SCIENCES (anthropology, economics, government/political science, history, psychology, sociology). Nineteen percent of degrees are conferred in business, 12% in social sciences, 11% in education, and 11% in health sciences.

Special: A Skills Reinforcement Center, an Urban Studies Center, and a Contract Major/Minor Program are available to the students. Student-designed majors are permitted.

Honors: There are 3 national honor societies with chapters on campus.

Admissions: The college follows an open enrollment policy. Applicants must be graduates of an accredited high school and have completed 15 Carnegie units or the GED.

Procedure: The ACT is recommended, but not required. Applications are due by August 1 (fall), December 1 (spring), or June 1 (summer). Notification is on a rolling basis. There is an application fee of $10.

Special: The college participates in the CLEP program, using the General Exam.

Transfer: For fall 1981, 2599 students applied, 2598 were accepted, and 1869 enrolled. Generally, applicants must have a 2.0 GPA. D grades do not transfer. All students must complete, at the college, 30 of the 120 credits required for a bachelor's degree. Applications are accepted until 1 week before registration for that semester.

Visiting: Visitors are permitted to sit in on classes. Guides are available for informal visits to the campus.

Financial Aid: About 11% of all students receive aid. About 62% work part-time on campus. Grants and loans are offered by the college. Federal government loans are available from a fund of about $230,000; the college administers short-term loans from a fund of $2800. The deadline for application for aid is March 15 (fall) or October 15 (spring); the FFS must be filed. The college is a member of CSS.

Foreign Students: About 1% of the full-time students come from foreign countries. Special counseling and special organizations are available for these students.

Admissions: Foreign students must achieve a TOEFL score of at least 500. No college entrance exams are required.

Procedure: The application deadline for fall entry is August 26. Foreign students must present proof of funds adequate to cover 1 year of study.

Admissions Contact: Thomas R. Gray, Director of Admissions.

REGIS COLLEGE   C-2
Denver, Colorado 80221   (303) 458-4900

F/T: 525M, 355W	Faculty: 87; IIB, av$
P/T: 70M, 45W	Ph.D.'s: 80%
Grad: 173M, 50W	S/F Ratio: 15 to 1
Year: sems, ss	Tuition: $4570
Appl: Aug. 15	R and B: $2500
750 applied	671 accepted	273 enrolled
SAT: 410V 450M	ACT: 19	COMPETITIVE

Regis College, founded in 1877, is a private Catholic liberal arts college under the direction of the Jesuit order. The library contains over 100,000 volumes and 4300 microfilm items, and subscribes to over 675 periodicals.

Environment: The 30-acre campus is in a suburban area 5 miles from Denver. There are 11 major buildings, including 3 dormitories housing 600 students.

Student Life: About 40% of the students come from Colorado. Seventy percent of the undergraduates are Roman Catholic. Half of all students live on campus. Approximately 22% of the freshmen come from public schools. Campus housing is coed. Students may keep cars on campus.

Organizations: There are 3 national fraternities and 1 sorority on campus, to which about 18% of the students belong. Student government and special-interest groups also sponsor social and cultural activities.

Sports: The college competes in 6 intercollegiate sports for men and 5 for women. There are 5 intramural sports for men and women.

Handicapped: Wheelchair ramps and special parking are available to physically handicapped students, to whom about 50% of the college is accessible. There are no hearing or visually impaired students currently enrolled.

Graduates: About 25% of the freshmen drop out during their first year; 55% remain to graduate. Of those who remain, 35% pursue graduate studies; 3% enter medical school, 3% dental school, and 10% law school. Fifty-five percent of each graduating class pursue careers in business and industry.

Services: Free tutoring, remedial instruction, career counseling, and placement services are available to students. Health care and psychological counseling are available for a fee.

Programs of Study: The college confers the B.A. and B.S. degrees. Master's programs are also offered. Bachelor's degrees are offered in the following subjects: BUSINESS (accounting, business administration), EDUCATION (elementary, secondary), ENGLISH (English), HEALTH SCIENCES (environmental studies), LANGUAGES (French, Spanish), MATH AND SCIENCES (biology, chemistry, mathematics), PHILOSOPHY (philosophy, religion), PREPROFESSIONAL (engineering), SOCIAL SCIENCES (economics, history, psychology, social sciences, sociology). About 53% of degrees are conferred in business, and 10% in the social sciences.

Required: All students must take core curriculum courses for a liberal arts degree.

Special: A junior year abroad, independent study, and internships are available. A 3-2 engineering degree is offered, and students can design their own majors.

Honors: Departmental honors programs are available to qualified students.

Admissions: About 90% of those who applied for the 1981-82 freshman class were accepted. Of those who enrolled, the SAT scores were as follows: Verbal—8% below 500, 11% between 500 and 599, 6% between 600 and 700, and 0% above 700; Math—8% below 500, 24% between 500 and 599, 4% between 600 and 700, and 0% above 700. On the ACT, 60% scored below 21, 15% between 21 and 23, 7% between 24 and 25, 8% between 26 and 28, and 5% above 28. Candidates should have completed 15 Carnegie units, have a C average, and rank in the upper 50% of their graduating class. Recommendations and interview impressions are also strongly considered before acceptance.

Procedure: Either the SAT or ACT is required. Applications for the fall should be filed by August 15; the deadline for spring entry is January 1. A $10 fee should accompany all applications. There is a rolling admissions plan.

Special: AP and CLEP credit is accepted.

Transfer: For fall 1981, 250 transfer students applied, 229 were accepted, and 120 enrolled. A minimum 2.0 GPA is required. C grades or better transfer. Students must complete, at the college, 30 of the 128 semester credits required for the bachelor's degree. Application deadlines are the same as those for freshmen.

Visiting: Tours of the campus can be arranged through the admissions office during the week. An orientation meeting is scheduled for freshmen 1 week before the beginning of the fall semester.

Financial Aid: About 55% of all students receive some form of financial assistance; 15% work part-time on campus. About 30 academic scholarships are available to freshmen, totaling $40,000. Loans and college employment are also available. The average scholarship for freshmen is $2000. The college is a member of the CSS and requires either the SFS, FAF, or FFS. Deadlines for financial applications are March 1 (fall) and November 1 (spring).

Foreign Students: Foreign students comprise about 1% of the full-time enrollment. The college offers these students special counseling and special organizations.

COLORADO 101

Admissions: Either a score of at least 550 on the TOEFL or 80 on the University of Michigan Language Test is required. College entrance exams are not required.

Procedure: Application deadlines are the same as those for freshmen. Foreign students must furnish proof of funds adequate to cover the entire period of study.

Admissions Contact: Domenic N. Teti, Director of Admissions.

ROCKMONT COLLEGE C–2
Denver, Colorado 80226 (303) 238-5386
(Recognized Candidate for Accreditation)

F/T: 101M, 125W	Faculty: 16; n/av
P/T: 24M, 27W	Ph.D.'s: 71%
Grad: none	S/F Ratio: 14 to 1
Year: qtrs, ss	Tuition: $2850
Appl: Sept. 1	R and B: $2100
135 applied	127 accepted	69 enrolled
SAT: 430V 470M	ACT: 18	LESS COMPETITIVE

Rockmont College, founded in 1914, is a small, liberal arts college associated with the Evangelical Protestant church. The library contains over 31,000 volumes, and subscribes to 210 periodicals.

Environment: The 33-acre campus is located in a suburban area 10 miles from downtown Denver. The 7 buildings on campus include a learning center and apartment-style student residences.

Student Life: Approximately 73% of the students come from Colorado; 1% come from foreign countries. Eighty-four percent of entering freshmen are from public schools. Sixty-three percent of the students live on campus. Seven percent are minority-group members. Campus housing is single-sex; there are visiting privileges. The use or possession of alcoholic beverages, tobacco, or drugs is forbidden. Students may keep cars on campus.

Organizations: There are no social fraternities or sororities, but professional and service organizations serve as social groups. Extracurricular activities include music groups, drama club, publications, and student government.

Sports: There are 4 intercollegiate sports for men and 3 for women. Two intramural sports are available to both men and women.

Handicapped: About 95% of the campus is accessible to wheelchair-bound students. Special facilities include parking areas, lowered drinking fountains, and specially equipped rest rooms. Fewer than 1% of the student body have visual impairments; no students have hearing impairments. A staff of 2 exists for special counseling and assistance.

Graduates: The freshman dropout rate is 25%; 20% remain to graduate. Twenty-five percent of the graduates pursue advanced studies. One percent enter law school. Forty-five percent pursue careers in business and industry.

Services: The following free services are offered: placement, career counseling, psychological counseling, tutoring, remedial instruction, and health care. A job listing service is provided for graduates.

Programs of Study: All programs lead to the B.A. and B.C.M. degrees. Associate degrees are also conferred. Bachelor's degrees are offered in the following subjects: BUSINESS (business administration), EDUCATION (elementary), ENGLISH (journalism, literature), FINE AND PERFORMING ARTS (art, broadcasting, music), MATH AND SCIENCES (biology), PHILOSOPHY (Christian ministries, humanities, philosophy, religion), SOCIAL SCIENCES (history, psychology, social sciences, sociology). Thirty-three percent of degrees are conferred in social sciences, 35% in philosophy, and 12% in business.

Required: All students must take Bible, communications, physical education, natural science, humanities, and social science courses to complete the general studies requirements.

Special: The Christian ministries major is unique. Students may specialize in camping, youth ministries, pastoral studies, or Christian education under this program. Rockmont has continuing education and extension programs.

Admissions: Ninety-four percent of those who applied were accepted for the 1981–82 freshman class. Of those who enrolled, the SAT scores were as follows: Verbal—73% below 500, 18% between 500 and 599, 9% between 600 and 700, and 0% above 700; Math —55% below 500, 27% between 500 and 599, 18% between 600 and 700, and 0% above 700. ACT scores were: 68% below 21, 20% between 21 and 23, 2% between 24 and 25, 10% between 26 and 28, and 0% above 28. Applicants should be in the upper 50% of their class and graduates of an accredited high school. The school also considers the following factors in order of importance: personality, impressions made during an interview, leadership record, ability to finance the college education, recommendations made by school officials, and evidence of special talents.

Procedure: The ACT or SAT is required. The application deadline for fall is September 1. There are no application deadlines for winter, spring or summer quarters. There is a $15 application fee. Notification is on a rolling basis.

Special: There are early and deferred admissions plans.

Transfer: For fall 1981, 117 transfer students applied, 111 were accepted, and 60 enrolled. Good academic standing at the previous school is required. D grades do not transfer. Forty-five quarter hours, of the 192 required for the bachelor's degree, must be earned in residence. Deadlines are the same as for freshman applicants.

Visiting: Special campus days are held in November and February for prospective students. Guided tours and interviews can be scheduled during the week. Day-long visits with a student guide can also be arranged by the admissions office. Visitors may sit in on classes and remain overnight on campus.

Financial Aid: Forty-eight percent of all students receive aid through the school. Sixteen percent work part-time on campus. A limited number of scholarships are available from the college. Need is the determining factor in awarding financial aid. Aid applications and the FFS are required by April 1.

Foreign Students: About 1% of the full-time students are from foreign countries.

Admissions: Foreign students must achieve a minimum score of 500 on the TOEFL. College entrance exams are not required.

Procedure: The application deadline for fall entry is September 1. Proof of funds adequate to cover study at the college is required. Foreign students must carry health insurance, which is available through the college for a fee.

Admissions Contact: Jack Keat, Director of Admissions.

UNITED STATES AIR FORCE ACADEMY D–3
USAF Academy, Colorado 80840 (303) 472-2640

F/T: 3954M, 548W	Faculty: 524; n/av
P/T: none	Ph.D.'s: 30%
Grad: none	S/F Ratio: 8 to 1
Year: sems, ss	Tuition: none
Appl: Jan. 31	R and B: none
8497 applied	1942 accepted	1460 enrolled
SAT: 562V 647M		MOST COMPETITIVE

The United States Air Force Academy, founded in 1954, is the newest of the United States service academies. Undergraduate instruction is offered in a variety of fields. The library contains 554,000 volumes, 13,000 microfilm items, 355,300 microfiche technical reports, and subscribes to 2220 periodicals. There is also a collection of historical aeronautical materials.

Environment: The 17,500-acre campus is located in a suburban area at the foot of the Rampart Range of the Rocky Mountains, about 50 miles from Denver. There are 11 buildings including 2 dormitories, an academic building, a cadet gymnasium, a chapel, and an administration building. In addition to athletic facilities, there is a 3500-foot airstrip to support cadet aviation programs.

Student Life: Students come from all parts of the country; about 4% come from Colorado. Seventy percent of the entering freshmen come from public schools. About 17% are minority-group members. Fifty-six percent are Protestant, and 41% are Catholic. Campus housing is coed. Juniors and seniors may keep cars on campus. All cadets are Academy residents. Graduates receive a B.S. degree and a second lieutenant's commission in the regular Air Force. The Academy is nonsectarian; religious counseling, organizations, and chapels are available to students of the 3 major faiths. Cadets must maintain a rigid daily schedule, conform to strict discipline, and develop qualities of leadership and dedication to service in the Air Force.

Organizations: Recreation is considered an important part of the cadets' daily schedule; numerous extracurricular activities are available. Cadets participate with the faculty in a number of areas of administrative affairs.

Sports: The Academy competes intercollegiately in 18 sports for men and 12 for women. There are 16 intramural sports for men and 12 for women.

Handicapped: All cadets must be in top physical shape; there are no physically handicapped students.

Graduates: The freshman dropout rate is 20%; 60% remain to complete their degrees. About 65% go on to graduate study. All cadets

102 COLORADO

enter the Air Force upon graduation and must serve a minimum of 5 years active duty.

Services: Health care, psychological counseling, tutoring, remedial instruction, placement, and career counseling are offered free of charge to all cadets.

Programs of Study: The academy confers the B.S. degree in the following subjects: BUSINESS (business administration, computer science, management), MATH AND SCIENCES (aviation sciences, basic sciences, biology, chemistry, mathematics, operations research, physical sciences, physics), PHILOSOPHY (humanities), PREPROFESSIONAL (engineering—aeronautical, engineering—astronomical, engineering—civil, engineering—electrical, engineering—mechanical, engineering sciences), SOCIAL SCIENCES (behavioral sciences, economics, geography, history, international relations, social sciences). Approximately 68% of degrees are conferred in the sciences, and 32% in the social sciences and humanities.

Required: A total of approximately 180 semester hours is required to graduate, divided among the areas of instruction as follows: academics, 138 hours; leadership and military training, 28; and physical education and athletics, 14.

Special: All cadets receive orientation flights in Air Force aircraft and take aviation science courses. There is also a 1-semester exchange program with the French Air Force Academy.

Honors: Many departments offer honors versions of core courses.

Admissions: About 23% of those who applied for the 1981-82 freshman class were accepted. The SAT scores of those who enrolled were as follows: Verbal—23% below 500, 51% between 500 and 599, 23% between 600 and 700, and 3% above 700; Math—27% between 500 and 599, 42% between 600 and 700, and 31% above 700. Candidates must be between 17 and 22 years of age, American citizens, unmarried with no dependents, and in good physical condition. They must also have leadership potential, be of sound moral character, and have a strong desire to pursue a military career. Advanced placement or honors courses and extracurricular activities are also considered important.

Procedure: The SAT or ACT must be taken no later than the senior year of high school. A physical aptitude exam and a medical exam are required. Nominations must be submitted by January 31. Applicants must obtain nominations from an official source; the majority of nominations are allotted to members of Congress. Notification is by November of the senior year. There is no application fee.

Special: There is an early decision plan.

Transfer: Few transfer students are accepted; all students must begin as freshmen. The application deadline is January 31.

Visiting: There is a formal 2-day briefing of new cadets in May. Informal visits to the Academy are also possible.

Financial Aid: All expenses are paid for by the government. A cadet is prohibited from accepting any other grant or scholarship aid unless the donor allows the cadet to use the assistance for personal expenses only.

Foreign Students: Fewer than 1% of the full-time students come from foreign countries. Foreign students are accepted only through exchange programs, which vary according to the respective country's requirements.

Admissions: Foreign students must take the SAT or ACT.

Procedure: The application deadline is December 31.

Admissions Contact: Frankie Webster, Editor, Registrar's Office.

UNIVERSITY OF COLORADO

The University of Colorado is the state's multi-campus university. It provides undergraduate and graduate instruction, research, and extension courses.

The main campus is located at Boulder. Two other campuses are at Colorado Springs and Denver. A fourth campus, the Health Sciences Center, also located in Denver, includes medical, dental, nursing, and graduate programs, and is open only to those who have completed at least 2 years of college work.

Admissions standards vary among the different campuses, but in general candidates should be graduates of accredited high schools, rank in the top half of their class, have completed 15 units of high school work, and present above-average scores on the SAT or the ACT. Tuition and expenses vary among the campuses. Detailed descriptions follow.

UNIVERSITY OF COLORADO AT BOULDER
C-2

Boulder, Colorado 80309   (303) 492-6301

F/T: 9043M, 7824W   Faculty: 945; I, +$
P/T: 741M, 657W   Ph.D.'s: 86%
Grad: 2271M, 1689W   S/F Ratio: 18 to 1
Year: sems, ss   Tuition: $980 ($3999)
Appl: open   R and B: $2174-2998
9371 applied   6843 accepted   3286 enrolled
SAT: 520V 560M   ACT: 25   VERY COMPETITIVE+

The Boulder campus is the main campus of the University of Colorado. The campus is made up of the colleges of Arts and Sciences, Business and Administration, Engineering and Applied Science, Environmental Design, and Music, the schools of Education, Journalism, Law, and Pharmacy, and the Graduate School. The library contains 1.8 million volumes and an equal number of microfilm items, and subscribes to 10,000 periodicals.

Environment: The campus occupies 600 acres in a suburban area, along the Front Range of the Rocky Mountains. Many of the campus's 160 buildings were designed in the Italian Renaissance style. Notable structures include the $3-million Student Recreation Center, University Memorial Center, the Fiske Planetarium, and the All Events/Conference Center. Dormitories accommodate 5500 single students, and apartments house 587 married students.

Student Life: About 60% of the students are from Colorado. About 25% live on campus. Eight percent are minority-group members. Campus housing is both coed and single-sex; there are visiting privileges in the single-sex housing. Students may keep cars on campus. Day-care services are available to all students, faculty, and staff for a fee. Freshmen must live on campus.

Organizations: Student organizations include fraternities and sororities, departmental and special-interest clubs, religious groups, student newspapers, and a student government. The university sponsors concerts, lectures, and exhibits.

Sports: The university participates intercollegiately in 7 sports for men and 5 for women. There are 14 intramural sports for men and 14 for women.

Handicapped: Special facilities for wheelchair-bound students include ramps, elevators, specially equipped rest rooms, and lowered drinking fountains and telephones. Special class scheduling also is available. The Office of Disabled Students has 2 counselors to assist the handicapped.

Graduates: About 23% of the freshmen drop out by the end of the first year; 40% remain to graduate. Twenty-five percent of the graduates pursue further study, including 6% who enter medical school and 5% who enter law school. About 75% enter business and industry.

Services: Students receive free tutoring, remedial instruction, and career counseling. Placement services, health care, and psychological counseling are available on a fee basis.

Programs of Study: Undergraduate degrees conferred include the B.A., B.F.A., B.S.B.A., B.S.in E., B.S.P.E., B.S. in Recreation, B.S. in Environmental Design, and B.S.Pharm. Master's and doctoral degrees also are available. Bachelor's degrees are offered in the following subjects: AREA STUDIES (American, Asian, Black/Afro-American, Latin American, Russian), BUSINESS (accounting, business administration, business education, computer science, finance, management, marketing, mineral and land management, real estate/insurance), ENGLISH (English, journalism, literature), FINE AND PERFORMING ARTS (art, art education, art history, dance, music, music education, radio/TV, studio art, theater/dramatics), HEALTH SCIENCES (medical technology, nursing, physical therapy, speech therapy), LANGUAGES (Chinese, French, German, Greek/Latin, Italian, Japanese, Portuguese, Russian, Spanish), MATH AND SCIENCES (biochemistry, biology, chemistry, ecology/environmental science, geology, mathematics, physics, statistics), PHILOSOPHY (classics, philosophy, religion), PREPROFESSIONAL (architecture, dentistry, engineering, law, medicine, pharmacy, veterinary), SOCIAL SCIENCES (anthropology, economics, geography, government/political science, history, international relations, psychology, social sciences, sociology). Seventeen percent of the undergraduate degrees are conferred in business and 15% in the social sciences.

Special: Five-year combined B.A.-B.S. degrees may be earned in various subjects, including engineering and business. Students may design their own majors. Chemical-engineering students may spend 3 months in industry under a work-study plan. The summer session includes a creative arts festival with drama, music, creative dance, fine arts, and a lecture series. The Sewell Program for freshmen and the Farrand Program for freshmen and sophomores both offer a small liberal arts college atmosphere, while taking advantage of the resources of a major university.

Honors: Phi Beta Kappa has a chapter on campus. The university conducts special honors courses in general studies.

Admissions: Seventy-three percent of those who applied were accepted for the 1981-82 freshman class. The SAT scores of those who enrolled were as follows: Verbal—49% below 500, 38% between 500 and 599, 12% between 600 and 700, and 1% above 700; Math—36% below 500, 30% between 500 and 599, 28% between 600 and 700, and 6% above 700. On the ACT, 13% scored below 21, 32% between 21 and 24, 23% between 25 and 26, 18% between 27 and 28, and 14% above 28. Applicants must have completed 15 units of high school work and rank in the top half of their class. The university restricts the number of out-of-state students, and such applicants should rank in the top 40% of their class and present a combined SAT score of at least 1050 or an ACT composite of at least 23. Advanced placement or honors courses, recommendations, and leadership qualities are also considered important.

Procedure: The SAT or the ACT should be taken by December of the senior year. Application deadlines are open; freshmen are admitted in the fall, spring, and summer terms. A $20 application fee is required. Notification is made on a rolling basis.

Special: AP and CLEP credit is offered.

Transfer: For fall 1981, 4014 students applied, 2723 were accepted, and 1535 enrolled. If less than 12 semester hours are transferred, students must have a composite score of at least 1000 on the SAT or 23 on the ACT. Colorado applicants should have a GPA of at least 2.25; out-of-state applicants must have at least a 2.5. Students must take the final 30 hours (one year) in residence to receive a degree.

Visiting: Admissions counselors are available Monday through Friday from 9 A.M. to 4:30 P.M. (8:30 A.M. to 4:00 P.M. during the summer) on a walk-in basis. Tours are conducted twice daily, Monday through Friday, at 11:00 A.M. and 2:30 P.M.

Financial Aid: The university provides scholarships, NDSL, EOC, and CWS. About 52% of the students receive aid. Fourteen percent work part-time on campus. The average freshman award is $2150. The FFS is required; the application deadline is March 1. Colorado residents also must submit the Colorado Preliminary Application for Financial Aid by March 1.

Foreign Students: Four percent of the full-time students come from foreign countries. An intensive English program, special counseling, and special organizations are available for these students.

Admissions: Foreign students must achieve a minimum score of 500 on the TOEFL or 80 on the University of Michigan Language Test and must take the SAT or ACT.

Procedure: Application deadlines are April 1 (summer or fall) and October 1 (spring). Foreign students must present proof of funds adequate to cover 1 year of study.

Admissions Contact: Norm Michaels, Director of Admissions.

UNIVERSITY OF COLORADO AT COLORADO SPRINGS D-3
Colorado Springs, Colorado 80907   (303) 593-3377

F/T: 986M, 983W   Faculty: 148; n/av
P/T: 581M, 663W   Ph.D.'s: 97%
Grad: 259M, 296W   S/F Ratio: 19 to 1
Year: sems, ss   Tuition: $693 ($2672)
Appl: July 1   R and B: n/app
788 applied   527 accepted   322 enrolled
SAT: 446V 612M   ACT: 23   COMPETITIVE+

University of Colorado at Colorado Springs, founded in 1965, is a commuter college. The library/laboratory facility contains over 115,000 volumes and 5600 microfilm items, and subscribes to over 1300 periodicals.

Environment: The 400-acre campus, located in an urban area 70 miles from Denver, has a physical plant consisting of 7 buildings.

Student Life: About 86% of the students come from Colorado; all students live off campus. Ninety percent of entering freshmen come from public schools. About 9% of the students are minority-group members. Students may keep cars on campus. Day-care services are available for a fee to all students, faculty and staff.

Organizations: Extracurricular activities sponsored by the university include academic and special-interest clubs. Students are represented on faculty and administration committees by voting delegates in the areas of student regulations, policy-making, and curriculum.

Sports: The university fields 1 intercollegiate team for men. There are 9 intramural sports for men and 8 for women.

Handicapped: The campus is 90% accessible to wheelchair students. Facilities include wheelchair ramps, elevators, and specially equipped rest rooms. One percent of the students have visual impairments; 1% have hearing impairments. There is a staff of 4 for special counseling and assistance.

Graduates: Twelve percent of those who graduate pursue careers in business or industry.

Services: The following services are available free to students: placement, career counseling, tutoring, and remedial instruction.

Programs of Study: All programs lead to the B.A. and B.S. degrees. Master's programs are also offered. Bachelor's degrees are offered in the following subjects: BUSINESS (accounting, business administration, computer science, finance, management, marketing, organizational behavior), EDUCATION (elementary, secondary), ENGLISH (English), FINE AND PERFORMING ARTS (art), LANGUAGES (Spanish), MATH AND SCIENCES (biology, chemistry, ecology/environmental science, mathematics, physics), PHILOSOPHY (philosophy), PREPROFESSIONAL (dentistry, law, medicine), SOCIAL SCIENCES (anthropology, economics, geography, government/political science, history, psychology, sociology). Thirty-one percent of degrees are conferred in social sciences, 25% in business, and 15% in math and sciences.

Special: It is possible to earn a combined B.A.-B.S. degree through the university. A general studies degree is also offered. Pass/fail options are available. Students may study abroad through the Boulder Campus Study Abroad Program.

Honors: Three national honor societies have chapters on campus. Various departments offer honors programs.

Admissions: Sixty-seven percent of those who applied were accepted for the 1981-82 freshman class. The SAT scores of those who enrolled were as follows: Verbal—63% below 500, 28% between 500 and 599, 8% between 600 and 700, and 1% above 700; Math—37% below 500, 43% between 500 and 599, 17% between 600 and 700, and 3% above 700. On the ACT, 30% scored below 21, 33% between 21 and 23, 23% between 24 and 25, 11% between 26 and 28, and 3% above 28. Applicants should have completed 15 Carnegie units, rank in the top 50% of their class, and have either a combined SAT score of 1000 or an ACT composite score of 23. Additional considerations, in order of relative importance, are: advanced placement, special talents, impressions made during an interview, and recommendations.

Procedure: Either the SAT or ACT should be taken by April of the senior year. Deadlines for application are: July 1 (fall), December 1 (spring), and May 1 (summer). There is a $10 application fee.

Special: AP and CLEP credit is accepted.

Transfer: For fall 1981, 666 transfer students applied, 560 were accepted, and 348 enrolled. Transfers are accepted in all classes. Students must complete, at the university, the final 30 semester hours of the 120-126 required for the bachelor's degree. A minimum GPA of 2.0 is required. D grades do not transfer. Deadlines for application are the same as those for freshmen.

Visiting: Guides are available for informal visits to the campus. Visitors are permitted to sit in on classes.

Financial Aid: About 25% of all students receive financial aid; 7% to 10% work part-time on campus. Scholarships, loans, and work/study programs comprise the aid sources. Tuition may be paid in installments. The deadline for applications and the FFS is April 1.

Foreign Students: Foreign students comprise less than 1% of the full-time student body.

Admissions: Foreign students must achieve a minimum score of 550 on the TOEFL. College entrance exams are not required.

Procedure: Application deadlines are July 1 (fall), November 1 (spring), and April 1 (summer). Foreign students must provide proof of funds adequate to cover 1 year of study. Although not required, health insurance is available through the university for a fee.

Admissions Contact: Douglas R. Johnson, Director of Admissions and Records.

104 COLORADO

UNIVERSITY OF COLORADO AT DENVER C-2
Denver, Colorado 80202 (303) 629-2694

F/T: 1860M, 1511W	Faculty: 203; I, --$
P/T: 2172M, 2307W	Ph.D.'s: 87%
Grad: 972M, 987W	S/F Ratio: 25 to 1
Year: sems, ss	Tuition: $765 ($2847)
Appl: Aug. 1	R and B: n/app
192 applied	92 accepted
SAT: 450V 500M	ACT: 20 COMPETITIVE

University of Colorado at Denver is a commuter college providing primarily, but not exclusively, upper division and graduate educational opportunities. The library contains over 628,000 volumes, microforms, and bound journals, and subscribes to over 1700 periodicals. A member of the Auraria Higher Educational Complex, the library has access to 3 million volumes and 400,000 periodicals and media materials, the combined total of all member schools.

Environment: The 30-acre urban campus occupies 1 square block of downtown Denver, and includes 3 buildings.

Student Life: Ninety-three percent of the students come from Colorado. All students commute. About 19% are minority-group members. Day-care services are available.

Organizations: Students are encouraged to take advantage of the cultural events available in Denver.

Sports: Intramural competition is offered in 5 sports for men and 3 for women.

Handicapped: The campus is 100% accessible to wheelchair-bound students. Facilities include wheelchair ramps, specially equipped rest rooms, lowered drinking fountains and telephones, elevators, and special parking. There is 1 special counselor for handicapped students.

Services: The following services are offered free of charge to students: psychological counseling, tutoring, remedial instruction, placement, and career counseling. Health care is provided on a fee basis.

Programs of Study: The university confers the B.A. and B.S. degrees. Master's and doctoral programs are also offered. Bachelor's degrees are offered in the following subjects: AREA STUDIES (ethnic), BUSINESS (accounting, business administration, computer science, finance, management, marketing, real estate/insurance), EDUCATION (elementary, secondary), ENGLISH (English, literature, speech), FINE AND PERFORMING ARTS (art, music, theater/dramatics), LANGUAGES (French, German, Spanish), MATH AND SCIENCES (biology, chemistry, geology, mathematics, physical sciences, physics), PHILOSOPHY (humanities, philosophy), PREPROFESSIONAL (architecture, engineering), SOCIAL SCIENCES (anthropology, economics, geography, history, psychology, social sciences, sociology, urban studies).

Special: The university offers a study skills program for freshmen, pass/fail options for certain courses, and an experiential learning program in social work and public administration. Study abroad, sponsored by the university, enables juniors to study in one of 8 countries during their third university year. Student-designed majors are permitted. Combined degree programs are offered.

Admissions: Forty-eight percent of those who applied were accepted for the 1981-82 freshman class. Of those who enrolled in a recent class, the SAT scores were as follows: Verbal—40% scored between 500 and 599, 7% between 600 and 700, and 1% over 700; Math—56% scored between 500 and 599, 21% between 600 and 700, and 1% above 700. Candidates should have completed 15 Carnegie units, score at least 500 on both the verbal and mathematical parts of the SAT or have a combined ACT score of 23, and be in the upper 50% of their graduating class. Other important considerations are advanced placement, recommendations, and impressions made during an interview.

Procedure: Either the SAT or the ACT is acceptable. Application deadlines are August 1 (fall), December 1 (spring), and May 1 (summer). Notification is on a rolling basis. A $10 fee should accompany the application.

Special: There is a deferred admissions plan. AP and CLEP credit is accepted.

Transfer: Transfers are accepted for all classes. Generally, a 2.0 GPA is required of state residents, and a 2.5 GPA of nonresidents. D grades do not transfer. All students must complete, at the university, 30 of the 120 semester hours required for a bachelor's degree. Deadlines are the same as those for entering freshmen.

Visiting: The university conducts regularly scheduled orientations prior to registration. Visitors may sit in on classes.

Financial Aid: About 26% of all students receive aid through scholarships or other forms of financial aid. Eight percent work part-time on campus. The average freshman award is $2683. The university is a member of the CSS, and requires that the FFS be filed. The deadline for filing for financial aid for the fall is March 1; for the spring, October 22.

Foreign Students: Two percent of the full-time students come from foreign countries. Special counseling and special organizations are available for these students.

Admissions: Foreign students must achieve a TOEFL score of at least 525. No college entrance exams are required.

Procedure: Application deadlines are the same as those for other students. Foreign students must present proof of health and proof of adequate funds.

Admissions Contact: Shelia Herriott, Director of Admissions.

UNIVERSITY OF DENVER C-2
Denver, Colorado 80208 (303) 753-2036

F/T: 2380M, 2313W	Faculty: 474; I, --$
P/T: 110M, 129W	Ph.D.'s: 82%
Grad: 1646M, 1648W	S/F Ratio: 13 to 1
Year: qtrs, ss	Tuition: $5130
Appl: Apr. 1	R and B: $2376
3771 applied	2699 accepted 971 enrolled
SAT: 500V 526M	ACT: 24 VERY COMPETITIVE

University of Denver, established in 1864, is a coeducational institution affiliated with the United Methodist Church. Undergraduate instruction is offered in the liberal arts and sciences, as well as education. Colorado Women's College recently merged with the university; starting in fall 1982, students from the Women's College will be taking their classes at the university. The library houses a collection of over 500,000 volumes, nearly 50,000 microfilm items, and subscribes to over 4500 periodicals.

Environment: The campus is in a suburban setting, 7 miles from downtown Denver. Apartments, residence halls, and housing for married students accommodate 2539 students. The dormitories are coeducational. Fraternity and sorority houses also are available.

Student Life: Nearly 40% of the students come from Colorado. About 74% are public school graduates. Five percent of the students commute from home; the remainder live on campus, in off-campus apartments, or in fraternity or sorority houses. Eight percent of the students are minority-group members. About 50% are Protestant, 20% Catholic, and 20% Jewish. Religious organizations and counselors are available in major denominations. University housing is coed. Students may keep cars on campus.

Organizations: Fourteen percent of the students belong to 9 national fraternities and 6 national sororities. Over 130 special-interest groups are sponsored. Campus traditions include Greek Week, Pioneer Days, Fall and Spring festivals, and a Winter Carnival. Lectures and concerts are regularly scheduled.

Sports: Intercollegiate competition is offered in 7 sports for men and 6 for women. There are 12 intramural sports available for men and 8 for women.

Handicapped: About 70% of the campus is accessible to students with physical handicaps. Facilities include wheelchair ramps, special parking, elevators, specially equipped rest rooms. Special class scheduling is also offered. One special counselor is available.

Graduates: About 70% of the students pursue advanced degrees after graduation.

Services: The following services are offered free of charge to all students: placement, career counseling, tutoring, health care, and psychological counseling.

Programs of Study: The university confers the B.A., B.S., B.F.A., B.M., B.S.N., B.M.E., B.S.Ch., B.S.E., B.S.Accounting, and B.S.B.A. degrees. Master's and doctoral programs are also offered. Bachelor's degrees are offered in the following subjects: AREA STUDIES (American, Latin American, Russian), BUSINESS (accounting, business administration, finance, hotel and restaurant management, management, marketing, real estate/insurance, statistics), EDUCATION (elementary, health/physical, secondary), ENGLISH (English, literature, speech), FINE AND PERFORMING ARTS (art, art education, art history, music, music education, studio art, theater/dramatics), HEALTH SCIENCES (nursing, speech therapy), LANGUAGES (French, German, Russian, Spanish), MATH AND SCIENCES (biology, chemistry, ecology/environmental science, mathematics, physics), PHILOSOPHY (classics, philosophy, religion), PREPROFESSIONAL (dentistry, engineering, law, medicine, veterinary), SOCIAL SCIENCES (anthropology, economics, geography, government/political science, history, psychology, public affairs, social sciences, sociology). Approximately 43% of degrees are conferred in business, 20% in social sciences, 10% in preprofessional studies, and 10% in math and sciences.

Special: Joint degree programs are offered; work-study options are available. A combination B.A.-B.S. degree is possible.

Honors: Twenty honor societies are represented on campus. All departments participate in an honors program.

Admissions: About 72% of the applicants for the 1981-82 freshman class were accepted. The SAT scores of those who enrolled were as follows: Verbal—54% below 500, 35% between 500 and 599, 10% between 600 and 700, and 1% above 700; Math—37% below 500, 44% between 500 and 599, 17% between 600 and 700, and 2% above 700. On the ACT, 10% scored below 21, 33% between 21 and 23, 25% between 24 and 25, 25% between 26 and 28, and 6% above 28. Also taken into consideration are advanced placement or honors courses, recommendations, the applicant's leadership record, impressions made during an interview, and evidence of special talents.

Procedure: Either the SAT or the ACT is required, and should be taken by March of the senior year. Application deadlines are April 1 (fall), December 1 (winter), February 15 (spring), and May 15 (summer). Notification is on a rolling basis. There is a $15 nonrefundable application fee.

Special: AP and CLEP credit is accepted. There are early and deferred admissions plans.

Transfer: For fall 1981, 1268 transfer students applied, 906 were accepted, and 544 enrolled. C grades or better transfer. Students must complete, at the university, 45 of the 183 quarter hours required for the bachelor's degree. Deadlines are the same as those for freshmen.

Visiting: There is a formal orientation program for freshmen. Informal campus visits with student guides may be arranged at any time; visitors may sit in on classes and stay overnight at the school.

Financial Aid: About 64% of all students receive financial assistance through the university, a member of CSS. Twenty percent work part-time on campus. Need and academic merit are the determining factors. Awards are made in the form of scholarships, grants, loans, and work-study. The FAF or FFS should be submitted by April 1 for the fall term.

Foreign Students: Six percent of the full-time students come from foreign countries. The university offers these students an intensive English program, special counseling, and special organizations.

Admissions: Foreign students must earn a minimum score of 500 on the TOEFL. College entrance exams are not required.

Procedure: Application deadlines are the same as those for freshmen. Foreign students must provide proof of funds adequate to cover 1 year of study. They must also carry health insurance, which is available through the university.

Admissions Contact: N. Kip Howard, Dean of Admissions and Financial Aid.

UNIVERSITY OF NORTHERN COLORADO
D-1

Greeley, Colorado 80639 (303) 351-2881

F/T, P/T:	Faculty:	464; I, — — $
3761M, 5079W	Ph.D.'s:	n/av
Grad: 566M, 896W	S/F Ratio:	17 to 1
Year: qtrs, ss	Tuition:	$879 ($3168)
Appl: Aug. 25	R and B:	$2200
4575 applied	2050 accepted	1855 enrolled
SAT: 500V 440M	ACT: 19	COMPETITIVE+

University of Northern Colorado, founded in 1890, is state-supported. The library contains 500,000 volumes and 130,009 microfilm items, and subscribes to 3801 periodicals.

Environment: The campus covers 240 acres in a suburban area, 50 miles from Denver. There are nearly 65 major buildings and recreational areas on campus. Living facilities include dormitories, married student housing, on- and off-campus apartments, and fraternity and sorority houses.

Student Life: About 80% of the students are from Colorado. Eighty percent live on campus. About 8% are minority-group members. Forty percent are Protestant, 31% are Catholic, and 2% are Jewish. Campus housing is both coed and single-sex; there are visiting privileges in single-sex housing. Students may keep cars on campus.

Organizations: In addition to fraternities and sororities, student organizations include religious groups, music organizations, publications,

COLORADO 105

forensics, and a little theater group. An excellent lecture series is sponsored by the university.

Sports: The university competes on an intercollegiate level in 11 sports for men and 7 for women. There are 11 intramural sports for men and 10 for women.

Handicapped: The campus is 100% accessible to wheelchair-bound students. Facilities include wheelchair ramps, elevators, specially equipped rest rooms, and special parking. Counselors are available to assist handicapped students.

Graduates: The freshman dropout rate is 25%; 50% remain to graduate. Forty-five percent go on to graduate study: 1% enter medical school, 5% enter law school, and 1% enter dental school. Forty percent pursue careers in business or industry.

Services: Students receive the following services free of charge: health care, tutoring, remedial instruction, psychological counseling, placement, and career counseling.

Programs of Study: The university offers the B.A., B.Mus., and B.S. degrees. There are also master's and doctoral programs. Bachelor's degrees are offered in the following subjects: AREA STUDIES (Black/Afro-American, Mexican-American, Russian), BUSINESS (accounting, business administration, business education, computer science, finance, industrial management, management, marketing, office administration, real estate/insurance, small business management), EDUCATION (audiology, early childhood, elementary, health/physical, industrial, rehabilitation, secondary, special), ENGLISH (English, journalism, speech), FINE AND PERFORMING ARTS (art, art education, music, music education, theater/dramatics), HEALTH SCIENCES (gerontology, health education, medical technology, nursing, speech therapy), LANGUAGES (French, German, Italian, Russian, Spanish), MATH AND SCIENCES (biology, botany, chemistry, earth science, ecology/environmental science, geology, mathematics, natural sciences, physical sciences, physics, zoology), PHILOSOPHY (humanities, philosophy), PREPROFESSIONAL (dentistry, engineering, home economics, law, medicine, pharmacy, social work, veterinary), SOCIAL SCIENCES (anthropology, economics, geography, government/political science, history, psychology, social sciences, sociology). Thirty-five percent of degrees are conferred in business, 41% in education, and 10% in health sciences.

Special: It is possible to earn combined B.A.-B.S. degrees. The university offers a general studies degree. Student-designed majors are permitted.

Honors: An honors program is offered by the English department.

Admissions: Forty-five percent of those who applied were accepted for the 1981-82 freshman class. The ACT scores of those who enrolled were as follows: 53% below 21, 30% between 21 and 25, and 6% above 26. Applicants should have completed 15 high school units and should rank in the top half of their class. Other factors, in order of importance, are advanced placement, recommendations, leadership record, and personality.

Procedure: The ACT or SAT is required of all candidates. The application deadline for the fall is August 25; for winter, spring, or summer entry, 1 month prior to the start of the term. Notification is on a rolling basis. There is a $15 application fee.

Special: Early admissions and early decision plans are available. CLEP and AP credit is accepted.

Transfers: For fall 1981, 1595 students applied, 1000 were accepted, and 836 enrolled. Transfers are accepted in all classes. Applicants must have a minimum 2.0 GPA. D grades do not transfer. All students must complete, at the university, 45 of the 180 credits required for a bachelor's degree. Deadlines are the same as those for freshmen.

Visiting: Guides are available for informal visits to the campus. A number of orientation sessions are held during the summer months. Contact the Visitors Center for further information.

Financial Aid: About 75% of all students receive financial aid. Forty percent work part-time on campus. Scholarships average $216 for freshmen but may reach a maximum of $480. Loans are provided through NDSL and a university fund of over $131,000. Loans to freshmen average $600 but may range from $500 to $1000 in the first year. Tuition may be paid in installments. The FFS is required. The deadline for application is March 31.

Foreign Students: About 3% of the full-time students come from foreign countries. Special counseling is available for these students.

Admissions: Foreign students must take the TOEFL or the University of Michigan Language Test. On the TOEFL, a score of at least 520 is required. No college entrance exams are required.

Procedure: The application deadline is 90 days prior to the start of the intended term of entry (fall, winter, spring, or summer). Foreign stu-

COLORADO

dents must have a physical examination and must present proof of funds adequate to cover 1 year of study. Health insurance is required and is available through the university for a fee.

Admissions Contact: James Blackburn, Director of Admissions.

UNIVERSITY OF SOUTHERN COLORADO
Pueblo, Colorado 81001   D-3   (303) 549-2461

F/T: 2189M, 1669W	Faculty: 196; IIA, +$
P/T: 285M, 405W	Ph.D.'s: 30%
Grad: 115M, 134W	S/F Ratio: 20 to 1
Year: sems, ss	Tuition: $850 ($3060)
Appl: July 21	R and B: $2124
1519 applied	1519 accepted 834 enrolled
SAT: 400V 400M	ACT: 16 NONCOMPETITIVE

University of Southern Colorado, a state-supported institution, offers 2- and 4-year liberal arts, business administration, nursing, applied science, and technology degrees. The library contains 190,000 volumes and 2060 microfilm items, and subscribes to 1368 periodicals.

Environment: The 800-acre campus is located in a suburban area 2 miles from Pueblo. The 11 buildings include a residence hall that accommodates 500 students.

Student Life: About 94% of the students come from Colorado, and almost all are graduates of public schools. Ten percent of the students live on campus. About 24% are minority-group members. Campus housing is coed. Students may keep cars on campus, and drinking 3.2 beer is permitted.

Organizations: About 1% of the students belong to 1 of 2 fraternities and 2 sororities on campus. Student organizations and activities include departmental, special-interest, service, social, and religious groups, a television station, student publications, and a student government. The university schedules many cultural and social events.

Sports: The university fields 7 intercollegiate teams for men and 5 for women. There are 6 intramural sports for men and 4 for women.

Handicapped: The entire campus is accessible to wheelchair-bound students. Special facilities include wheelchair ramps, parking areas, elevators, lowered drinking fountains and telephones, and specially equipped rest rooms, dorm rooms, and showers. Special class scheduling is also available. Facilities for students with visual and hearing impairments include braille labels in elevators and flashing lights on fire alarms. Three special counselors are available.

Graduates: The freshman dropout rate is 50%; 25% remain to graduate. Seven percent of the graduates seek advanced degrees; 1% enter medical school, 1% enter dental school, and 2% enter law school. About 77% of the graduates pursue careers in business and industry.

Services: Students receive free placement, career counseling, psychological counseling, health care, tutoring, and remedial instruction. Placement services also are available to graduates.

Programs of Study: The university awards the B.A. and B.S. degrees. Associate and master's degrees also are available. Bachelor's degrees are offered in the following subjects: BUSINESS (accounting, economics, management, marketing), EDUCATION (elementary, health/physical, industrial, secondary), ENGLISH (English, journalism, literature, speech), FINE AND PERFORMING ARTS (art, art education, art history, music, music education, photography, radio/TV, theater/dramatics), HEALTH SCIENCES (environmental health, medical technology, nursing), LANGUAGES (French, Spanish), MATH AND SCIENCES (biology, chemistry, geology, mathematics, physics), PHILOSOPHY (philosophy), PREPROFESSIONAL (agriculture, computer science technology, dentistry, engineering—civil, engineering—electrical, engineering—industrial, engineering—mechanical, engineering—metallurgical, forestry, law, medicine, pharmacy, veterinary), SOCIAL SCIENCES (anthropology, geography, government/political science, history, psychology, social sciences, social work, sociology). Thirty percent of the undergraduate degrees are conferred in business, 25% in math and sciences, and 12% in social sciences.

Required: All freshmen must take English, developmental reading, speech, and physical education. All undergraduates must take 10 hours each in humanities, behavioral sciences, and natural science.

Special: Five-year combined B.A.-B.S. degrees may be earned in any subjects. Students may design their own majors and study abroad for one semester. A work-study program combined with BEOG is available.

Honors: A number of honor societies are represented on campus.

Admissions: All of those who applied were accepted for the 1981–82 freshman class. Applicants must be graduates of an accredited high school or hold an equivalency certificate. Out-of-state applicants must rank in the upper two-thirds of their class. The university has an open-door policy for Colorado residents.

Procedure: The ACT or SAT is required. The application, high school record, test scores, and a $10 fee should be submitted no later than July 21 (fall), December 1 (spring), or May 7 (summer). Admissions decisions are made on a rolling basis.

Special: Early decision, early admissions, and deferred admissions plans are offered. CLEP credit is given.

Transfer: For fall 1981, 587 students applied, 574 were accepted, and 332 enrolled. A 2.0 GPA is required. D grades do not transfer. All students must complete, at the university, 30 of the 128 semester hours required for a bachelor's degree. Application deadlines are the same as those for freshmen.

Visiting: Orientations for prospective students are scheduled regularly. They include a campus tour, class visits, lunch, and meetings with academic advisors, admissions officers, and financial aid staff members. Informal visits can be arranged for weekdays, 9 A.M. to 5 P.M., through the admissions office.

Financial Aid: Fifty percent of the students receive aid. About 25% work part-time on campus. The university offers BEOG, work-study jobs, loans, and scholarships. Loans also are available from the federal government and local banks. The average amount of aid awarded to freshmen from all sources, including campus employment, is $1700. Aid applications must be submitted by March 15 (fall), November 1 (spring), or May 1 (summer) for priority consideration. All other applications are considered as long as funds are available. The FFS or FAF also must be filed. The university is a member of CSS.

Foreign Students: Seven percent of the full-time students come from foreign countries. Special counseling and special organizations are available for these students.

Admissions: Foreign students must achieve a minimum score of 500 on the TOEFL or 80 on the University of Michigan Language Test. No college entrance exams are required.

Procedure: Application deadlines are the same as those for other students. Foreign students must present proof of health and proof of funds adequate to cover 1 year of study.

Admissions Contact: Rudy Padilla, Director of Admissions.

WESTERN STATE COLLEGE
Gunnison, Colorado 81230   B-3   (303) 943-2119

F/T: 1659M, 1201W	Faculty: 140; IIA, av$
P/T: 133M, 152W	Ph.D.'s: 85%
Grad: 115M, 111W	S/F Ratio: 20 to 1
Year: sems, ss	Tuition: $938 ($2914)
Appl: open	R and B: $1610
1755 applied	1476 accepted 763 enrolled
ACT: 18	LESS COMPETITIVE

Western State College, a state-supported institution established in 1911, offers undergraduate training in liberal arts and sciences, business, and education. The library contains 170,000 volumes and 118,000 microfilm items, and subscribes to 1095 periodicals.

Environment: The 237-acre campus is located in a valley in a rural area 210 miles southwest of Denver. The area is noted for its natural scenery and skiing. The 32 campus buildings include residence halls and on-campus apartments for more than 1700 single students, and 18 apartments for married students.

Student Life: About 80% of the students are from Colorado, and 92% are graduates of public schools. About 45% of the students live on campus. About 14% are minority-group members. Campus housing is single-sex. Students may keep cars on campus.

Organizations: Fifteen percent of the men belong to 1 of 6 fraternities; 10% of the women belong to 1 of 2 sororities. Nearby recreational areas offer skiing and other outdoor activities. Extracurricular activities include clubs, publications, and cultural groups.

Sports: The college participates in 12 intercollegiate sports for men and 8 for women. There are 8 intramural sports.

Handicapped: Facilities for physically handicapped students include wheelchair ramps and special parking.

Graduates: About 50% of the freshmen drop out, and about 39% remain to graduate. Seven percent of the graduates seek advanced degrees.

Services: Psychological counseling, tutoring, remedial instruction, placement, and career counseling are provided free to students. Placement services also are available to graduates.

Programs of Study: The college awards the B.A. degree. Master's degrees are also conferred. Bachelor's degrees are offered in the following subjects: BUSINESS (accounting, business administration), EDUCATION (elementary, health/physical, industrial), ENGLISH (English, speech), FINE AND PERFORMING ARTS (art, art education, music education), LANGUAGES (French, Spanish), MATH AND SCIENCES (biology, chemistry, mathematics, physics), PREPROFESSIONAL (dentistry, engineering, law, medicine, pharmacy, veterinary), SOCIAL SCIENCES (anthropology, economics, government/political science, history, psychology, social sciences, sociology). About 37% of the undergraduate degrees are conferred in business, 15% in math and sciences, and 13% in the arts and humanities.

Honors: Five honor societies have chapters on campus.

Admissions: About 84% of those who applied for admission to the 1981-82 freshman class were accepted. Applicants must be graduates of accredited high schools, have completed 15 Carnegie units, and rank in the top 66% of their class. Recommendations from high school officials, evidence of special talent, and impressions made during an interview also are considered.

Procedure: Applicants must take the ACT. There are no application deadlines; freshmen are admitted to the fall, spring, and summer semesters. Notification is made on a rolling basis. There is a $10 application fee.

Special: There is an early decision plan. CLEP and AP credit is accepted.

Transfer: For fall 1981, 407 students applied, 300 were accepted, and 189 enrolled. D grades do not transfer. All students must complete, at the college, 30 of the 124 semester hours required for a bachelor's degree. Deadlines are open; transfer students are admitted to the fall, spring, and summer semesters.

Visiting: Guides are provided for informal visits while the college is in session, and prospective students may sit in on classes. Arrangements should be made with the admissions office.

Financial Aid: About half the students receive aid. About 65% work part-time on campus. The college provides NDSL for 375 students, CWS jobs for 350 students, and SEOG for 75 students. Short-term loans and other part-time jobs also are available. The FFS should be filed by April 15.

Foreign Students: One percent of the full-time students come from foreign countries. Special counseling and special organizations are available for these students.

Admissions: Foreign students must achieve a TOEFL score of at least 500 and must take the ACT.

Procedure: Application deadlines are June (fall) and December (spring). Foreign students must present proof of funds adequate to cover 1 year of study. Health insurance is required.

Admissions Contact: Stu Kaplan, Assistant Director of Admissions.

CONNECTICUT

ALBERTUS MAGNUS COLLEGE   C-3
New Haven, Connecticut 06511   (203) 865-3445

F/T: 1M, 375W	Faculty:	29; IIB, – $
P/T: 13M, 163W	Ph.D.'s:	65%
Grad: none	S/F Ratio:	13 to 1
Year: sems, ss	Tuition:	$4180
Appl: open	R and B:	$2530
266 applied	220 accepted	118 enrolled
SAT: 450V, 440M	ACT: 22	COMPETITIVE

Albertus Magnus College, founded in 1925, is a Roman Catholic institution operated by the Dominican Sisters. It offers an undergraduate degree program in the liberal arts and sciences. The library contains 92,000 books, and 4824 microfilm items, and subscribes to 475 periodicals.

Environment: The 50-acre suburban campus is in a residential section of New Haven. Residence halls are old mansions that have been converted into student housing; each building houses 25 to 30 women.

Student Life: The majority of the students are from Connecticut and have public school education. About 80% of the students are Catholic and 11% are Protestant. Places of worship are available on campus for Catholics and nearby for members of other faiths. About 14% of the students are minority-group members. Campus housing is single-sex; there are visiting privileges. Students may keep cars on campus.

Organizations: There are no sororities. Activities include a strong student government, traditional clubs, and cultural and social events.

Sports: The college fields 3 intercollegiate teams for women. There is 1 intramural sport for women.

Handicapped: There are special facilities for students with physical handicaps.

Graduates: About 12% of the students withdraw after the first year; 60% remain to graduate. About 25% continue their education: 3% go to dental school, and 3% go to law school. About 35% of the graduates go directly into business and industry.

Services: Placement, career counseling, health care, psychological counseling, and remedial instruction are free to all students.

Programs of Study: The B.A. and B.F.A. degrees are awarded. Associate degrees are also offered. Bachelor's degrees are offered in the following subjects: BUSINESS (economics), ENGLISH (English), FINE AND PERFORMING ARTS (art), LANGUAGES (classics, French, Italian, Spanish), MATH AND SCIENCES (biology, chemistry, mathematics, physical sciences), PHILOSOPHY (humanities), SOCIAL SCIENCES (economics, government/political science, history, psychology, sociology). About 40% of the degrees conferred are in social sciences; 25% are in business and economics.

Required: All students must take freshman English and satisfy distribution requirements. Catholic students must complete 2 semesters of religious studies.

Special: Study abroad, student-designed majors, independent study, and cross-registration at area colleges are all available.

Honors: There are several honor societies on campus.

Admissions: About 83% of the applicants for the 1981-82 school year were granted admission. The SAT scores of those who enrolled were as follows: Verbal—69% below 500, 22% between 500 and 599, 8% between 600 and 700, and 1% above 700; Math—74% below 500, 21% between 500 and 599, 4% between 600 and 700, and 1% above 700. Also considered important are the high school record, advanced placement or honors courses, recommendations, and impressions made during an interview.

Procedure: The SAT or ACT should be taken by December of the senior year. Application deadlines are open. Notification is on a rolling basis. New students are admitted both semesters. There is a $15 nonrefundable application fee.

Special: AP and CLEP credit is available. There are early and deferred admissions plans.

Transfer: For fall 1981, 59 transfer students applied, 40 were accepted, and 26 enrolled. A 2.0 GPA is required; D grades do not transfer. Students must complete, at the college, 30 of the 120 credits required for the bachelor's degree.

Visiting: There is an orientation program for incoming freshmen. Informal campus visits may be arranged. Visitors may stay at the school and attend classes.

Financial Aid: About 40% of the students are receiving assistance. Twenty-two percent work part-time on campus. Other aid sources include scholarships, grants, and loans. Honor scholarships are available to freshmen with high SAT scores. Awards range from $500 to $2000 and are based on need. The FAF should be filed by February 15. The college is a member of CSS.

Foreign Students: Two percent of the full-time students are from foreign countries. Special counseling is available to these students.

Admissions: Foreign students must achieve a minimum score of 500 on the TOEFL. College entrance exams are not required.

Procedure: Application deadlines for fall and spring are open. Foreign students must furnish proof of health by submitting a college health form. They must also carry health insurance, which is available through the college. Proof of funds adequate to cover 4 years of study is required.

Admissions Contact: Sister Michele Ryan, Director of Admissions.

BRIDGEPORT ENGINEERING INSTITUTE

B-4

Bridgeport, Connecticut 06606 (203) 333-4172

F/T: 860M, 35W
P/T: none
Grad: none
Year: tri, ss
Appl: Sept. 1
260 applied 245 accepted 230 enrolled
SAT, ACT: not required

Faculty: n/av
Ph.D.'s: 10%
S/F Ratio: 8 to 1
Tuition: $1625
R and B: none

LESS COMPETITIVE

Bridgeport Engineering Institute is an evening college whose students and faculty meet on a part-time basis. The institute's library has 15,000 books.

Environment: The institute is located in a suburban setting about 5 miles from downtown Bridgeport. No student housing is available.

Student Life: About 90% of the students come from Connecticut. None of the students live on campus. Cars are permitted on campus.

Organizations: There are no on-campus extracurricular groups or scheduled cultural/social events.

Sports: There is no athletic program.

Handicapped: There are no special facilities for the physically handicapped.

Graduates: Twenty percent of the freshmen drop out during the first year of study; 50% of students remain to complete their degrees. Eighteen percent of the graduates continue their education beyond the bachelor's degree. Ninety percent enter business and industry.

Services: Placement services are available to students and alumni.

Programs of Study: The B.S. is offered. Associate degrees are also offered. Bachelor's degrees are offered in PREPROFESSIONAL (engineering—electrical, engineering—mechanical).

Admissions: About 94% of the applicants for the 1981-82 freshman class were accepted. Neither the SAT nor the ACT is required. A high school diploma is required. Applicants should have 4 credits of English and 2 of mathematics. Important factors in the admissions decision include impressions made during the interview, personality, leadership record, and high school recommendations.

Procedure: The application and the high school record should be submitted as early as possible. Application deadlines are September 1 (winter), January 6 (spring), and May (summer). Freshmen are admitted each term. Notification is on a rolling basis. An interview is required. There is a $25 application fee.

Special: AP and CLEP are used.

Transfer: For fall 1981, about 100 students applied. D grades do not transfer. Students must remain at the institute for 2 years, completing 50 of the 142 credits required for a bachelor's degree. Application deadlines are open.

Visiting: There is a formal orientation program. Informal visits may be arranged. Visitors may attend classes.

Financial Aid: About 30% of the students are receiving scholarship aid and loans. All students work part-time on campus. Tuition may be paid in installments. Application deadlines are September (winter), June (spring), and May (summer).

Foreign Students: Two percent of the full-time students come from foreign countries.

Admissions: Foreign students must score at least 500 on the TOEFL. No college entrance examination is required.

Procedure: Application deadlines are September (fall), January (winter), and May (spring). Foreign students must present proof of adequate funds.

Admissions Contact: Ernest L. Greenhill, Dean of Admissions.

CENTRAL CONNECTICUT STATE COLLEGE

C-2

New Britain, Connecticut 06050 (203) 827-7548

F/T: 3449M, 3142W
P/T: 1884M, 1700W
Grad: 716M, 1516W
Year: sems, ss
Appl: see profile
4093 applied 3122 accepted 1437 enrolled
SAT(mean): 403V 442M

Faculty: 399; IIA +$
Ph.D.'s: 58%
S/F Ratio: 17 to 1
Tuition: $830 ($1770)
R and B: $2047

COMPETITIVE

Central Connecticut State College, founded in 1849, offers undergraduate instruction in the liberal arts and sciences, education, business, and preprofessional areas. The college library has a collection of 344,418 books and 48,000 microfilm items, and subscribes to 1600 periodicals.

Environment: The 140-acre suburban campus is located in a city of 81,100 people, about 8 miles from Hartford. There are 26 buildings on campus, including 2 separate clusters of high-rise dormitories that accommodate 921 women and 819 men.

Student Life: About 96% of the students come from Connecticut; 90% have had public school educations. Twenty-seven percent live on campus. Seventy percent are Catholic, and 28% are Protestant. Six percent are minority-group members. Campus housing is both coed and single-sex. Students may keep cars on campus. Day-care facilities are available to part-time students at a fee of $100 per semester (5 days per week, 2½ hours per day).

Organizations: Traditional extracurricular activities are offered. There are 3 national and 5 local fraternities to which 4% of the men belong; there are 1 national and 5 local sororities to which 3% of the women belong.

Sports: The college fields 11 intercollegiate teams for men and 9 for women. There are 12 intramural sports for men and 10 for women.

Handicapped: About 85% of the campus is accessible to individuals with physical handicaps. One assistant is available. Special facilities include wheelchair ramps, parking areas, elevators, lowered drinking fountains, and specially equipped rest rooms. Special class scheduling is possible. Special library materials are available for visually or hearing impaired students.

Graduates: About 10% of the students drop out after the first year; 60% remain to graduate. Eventually 40% go on for further education; 5% go to law school. About 75% of the students enter business and industry.

Services: Placement, career counseling, health care, and psychological counseling are offered free of charge. Tutoring and remedial instruction are available for a fee.

Programs of Study: The B.A., B.F.A., B.S., B.S.Ed., B.S.Bus., and B.S.Ind. Tech. degrees are offered. Programs which lead to master's degrees are also available. Bachelor's degrees are offered in the following subjects: AREA STUDIES (Asian), BUSINESS (accounting, business administration, business education, marketing, secretarial science), EDUCATION (early childhood, elementary, health/physical, industrial, secondary, special, vocational/technical), ENGLISH (communications, English), FINE AND PERFORMING ARTS (art education, music education, theater/dramatics), HEALTH SCIENCES (nursing), LANGUAGES (French, German, Italian, Spanish), MATH AND SCIENCES (biology, chemistry, computer science, earth science, ecology/environmental science, general sciences, mathematics, natural sciences, physical sciences, physics), PHILOSOPHY (philosophy), PREPROFESSIONAL (industrial technology), SOCIAL SCIENCES (anthropology, economics, geography, government/political science, history, psychology, social sciences, sociology). About 37% of degrees conferred are in business, 22% in education, and 17% in social sciences.

Special: Study abroad is possible. Students may design their own majors. The college offers a 5-year Cooperative Education Program leading to a bachelor's degree, in which students spend 6 months of each year in off-campus employment.

Honors: There are chapters of 11 national honor societies on campus.

Admissions: About 76% of the applicants for the 1981-82 freshman class were accepted. Applicants should be in the top 50% of their high school class. High school transcript, SAT scores, recommendations, and advanced placement or honors courses are considered important. Preference is given to state residents.

Procedure: The SAT should be taken by March of the senior year. There is a $10 nonrefundable application fee. The application is due by August 1 but should be submitted by June 1; notification is on a rolling basis. Freshmen are also admitted at midyear.

Special: AP and CLEP credit is offered.

Transfer: For fall 1981, 1375 students applied, 1063 were accepted, and 757 enrolled. A 2.0 GPA is required; D grades do not transfer unless part of an associate degree. Three semesters must be in residence. One hundred twenty credits are required for the B.A., B.S., and B.F.A. degrees, 130 credits for the B.S.Ed. Application deadlines are June 1 for fall entry and December 1 for spring entry (both can be extended).

Visiting: There is a formal orientation program for incoming freshmen. Informal campus visits may be arranged. Visitors may sit in on classes and stay at the school.

Financial Aid: About 64% of the students receive assistance. Federal and state grants, loans, and work-study opportunities are available. Twenty percent of the students work part-time on campus. Average aid to freshmen from all sources is $1500. The college is a member of CSS. The FAF and IRS tax return should be filed by March 15 for fall entry, October 15 for spring entry.

Foreign Students: Ninety-three foreign students are enrolled full-time at the college. Special counseling and special organizations are available for these students.

Admissions: Foreign students must achieve a TOEFL score of at least 500.

Procedure: Application deadlines are February 1 for fall entry and November 1 for spring entry (both can be extended). Foreign students must present proof of funds adequate to cover 1 year's study. They must also carry health insurance, which is available through the college for a fee.

Admissions Contact: Johnie Floyd, Director of Admissions.

CONNECTICUT COLLEGE E-3
New London, Connecticut 06335 (203) 447-7511

F/T: 620M, 1017W	Faculty: 141; IIA, +$
P/T: 57M, 88W	Ph.D.'s: 75%
Grad: 15M, 33W	S/F Ratio: 12 to 1
Year: sems, ss	Tuition: $6850
Appl: Feb. 1	R and B: $2450
2973 applied	439 enrolled
SAT: 540V 560M	VERY COMPETITIVE

Connecticut College, founded in 1911, is a private college offering undergraduate instruction in the liberal arts and sciences. The library has more than 352,000 volumes and 80,000 microfilm items, and subscribes to 1500 periodicals. The Greer Music Library contains 5000 books, 8400 scores, and 10,700 recordings.

Environment: The 660-acre campus is located in a suburban area 2 miles from downtown New London, midway between New York City and Boston. The 40 buildings on campus include residence halls, an art center, and several recreation facilities.

Student Life: About 30% of the students come from Connecticut, and 52% come from public schools. About 95% live on campus. Six percent of the students are minority-group members. Dormitories are coed, and students may keep cars on campus. Freshmen may not live off campus.

Organizations: There are no social fraternities or sororities. Extracurricular activities include clubs, service organizations, religious groups, student government and publications, a radio station, and social and cultural events.

Sports: The college fields 9 intercollegiate teams for men and 11 for women. There are 11 intramural sports for men and 7 for women.

Handicapped: Special facilities include ramps, elevators, and parking. Special class scheduling is also possible.

Graduates: The freshman dropout rate is less than 1%; about 85% remain to graduate. Nearly 35% of the graduates pursue advanced degrees immediately, and nearly 65% do so within 5 years of graduation. About 2% go to medical school, 1% to dental school, and 5% to law school. About 40% begin careers in business or industry.

Services: Placement, career counseling, health care, psychological counseling, tutoring, and remedial instruction are offered free to students. Placement services also are available to graduates.

Programs of Study: The college awards the B.A. degree. Master's degrees also are offered. Bachelor's degrees are offered in the following subjects: AREA STUDIES (American, Asian, Hispanic, medieval, Russian/East European, urban), EDUCATION (child development, early childhood), ENGLISH (English), FINE AND PERFORMING ARTS (art history, dance, music, studio art, theater/dramatics), LANGUAGES (Chinese, French, German, Greek/Latin, Italian, Russian), MATH AND SCIENCES (astronomy, biochemistry, botany, chemistry, ecology/environmental science, field biology, mathematical sciences, mathematics, physics, zoology), PHILOSOPHY (classics, philosophy, religion), SOCIAL SCIENCES (anthropology, economics, government/political science, history, human relations—psychology, human relations—sociology, psychology, sociology). About 44% of degrees conferred are in social sciences, and 19% are in math and sciences.

Required: All students must complete distribution requirements.

Special: Independent study, study abroad, cross-registration at other colleges, and interdepartmental majors are offered. Students may design their own majors.

CONNECTICUT 109

Honors: Phi Beta Kappa has a chapter on campus. All departments offer honors work.

Admissions: The SAT scores of 1981–82 freshmen were as follows: Verbal—23% below 500, 54% between 500 and 599, 22% between 600 and 700, and 2% above 700; Math—18% below 500, 50% between 500 and 599, 30% between 600 and 700, and 2% above 700. Applicants must have a 3.0 high-school grade average. Recommendations, advanced placement or honors courses, and the applicant's leadership record are also considered.

Procedure: The SAT or ACT and 3 ATs (including English Composition) should be taken no later than December of the senior year. There is a $30 nonrefundable application fee. The fall application deadline is February 1 and the spring deadline is December 1.

Special: AP credit is available. Early decision, early admissions, and deferred admissions programs are offered.

Transfer: For fall 1981, 261 transfer students applied, 78 were accepted, and 38 enrolled. A GPA of 3.0 or better is recommended. D grades do not transfer. Students must spend at least 2 years in residence, earning at least 64 of the 128 credits required for a bachelor's degree. Application deadlines are February 15 and May 15 (fall) and December 1 (spring).

Visiting: Informal campus visits may be arranged. Visitors may stay at the school and attend classes.

Financial Aid: About 35% of the students are receiving assistance; 46% work part-time on campus. The college offers scholarships to freshmen. Loans are available from several sources. Work contracts generally provide $700 per year. The average aid award to freshmen totaled $4539 from all sources in 1981–82. All awards are based on need. The FAF should be submitted by February 15 (fall) or December 1 (spring).

Foreign Students: Two percent of the full-time students come from foreign countries. The college offers special counseling for these students.

Admissions: Foreign students must take the TOEFL, the SAT or ACT, and 3 ATs (including English Composition).

Procedure: Application deadlines are February 1 (fall) and December 1 (spring). Foreign students must present proof of adequate funds for 4 years. Health insurance, though not required, is available through the college for a fee.

Admissions Contact: Jeanette Hersey, Dean of Admissions.

EASTERN CONNECTICUT STATE D-2
COLLEGE
Willimantic, Connecticut 06226 (203) 456-2231

F/T: 1084M, 1227W	Faculty: 110; IIA, ++$
P/T: 292M, 381W	Ph.D.'s: 60%
Grad: 54M, 211W	S/F Ratio: 16 to 1
Year: sems, ss	Tuition: $890 ($1880)
Appl: May 1	R and B: $1093
1711 applied	1530 accepted 633 enrolled
SAT: 420V 460M	LESS COMPETITIVE

Eastern Connecticut State College, founded in 1889, offers undergraduate training in the liberal arts and sciences, education, business, and preprofessional areas. The college's library has a collection of 115,000 books, periodicals, and microfilm items.

Environment: The 96-acre campus is located in a suburban town of 18,000 people about 28 miles from Hartford. The residence halls accommodate 1100 men and women.

Student Life: About 94% of the students come from Connecticut. Eighty-five percent are from public schools. Fifty percent live on campus. Seven percent of the students are minority-group members. College housing is coed. Students may keep cars on campus. Day-care services are available to full-time students.

Organizations: There are no fraternities or sororities. Traditional extracurricular activities are offered.

Sports: Intercollegiate competition is available in 7 sports for men and 5 for women. Fourteen intramural sports are offered for men and 12 for women.

Handicapped: One assistant is available to help physically handicapped students. Special class scheduling can be arranged.

Services: Placement, career counseling, health care, psychological counseling, tutoring, and remedial instruction are available free of charge.

CONNECTICUT

Programs of Study: The B.A. and B.S. are offered. Associate and master's degrees are also granted. Bachelor's degrees are offered in the following areas: AREA STUDIES (American), BUSINESS (business administration, computer science), EDUCATION (early childhood, elementary, health/physical, secondary), ENGLISH (English), FINE AND PERFORMING ARTS (art, music), HEALTH SCIENCES (medical technology), LANGUAGES (Spanish), MATH AND SCIENCES (biology, earth science, ecology/environmental science, mathematics), PRE-PROFESSIONAL (law, medicine, veterinary), SOCIAL SCIENCES (economics, government/political science, psychology, social sciences, sociology).

Special: Study abroad is possible. The college is a member of the National Student Exchange Program.

Honors: Honor societies are available for qualified students.

Admissions: Eighty-nine percent of those who applied for the 1981-82 freshman class were accepted. Applicants should be in the top 50% of their high school class. Recommendations, advanced placement or honors courses, and extracurricular activities are among the other important factors considered.

Procedure: The SAT is required. Application deadlines are May 1 (fall) and January 1 (spring). Notification is on a rolling basis. The application fee is $10.

Special: Early admissions and deferred admissions plans are available. AP and CLEP credit is offered.

Transfer: For fall 1981, 301 transfer students enrolled. A 2.0 GPA is needed. D grades do not transfer, except as part of an associate degree from Connecticut community and technical colleges. Students must complete, at the college, the last 30 of the 120 credits required for the bachelor's degree. Application deadlines are May 1 (fall) and January 1 (spring).

Visiting: There is an orientation program twice every week. Visitors are welcome Monday through Friday from 8:30 A.M. to 4:30 P.M.

Financial Aid: About 70% of the students are receiving assistance. Twenty-five percent work part-time on campus. The average award to freshmen from all sources is $1700. Federal grants, loans, and work-study programs are offered in addition to state grants. The college has a short-term loan program. The college is a member of CSS. The FAF should be filed by March 15 (fall) or November 15 (spring).

Foreign Students: Three percent of the full-time students come from foreign countries. The college offers these students an intensive English course, special counseling, and special organizations.

Admissions: Foreign students must score at least 500 on the TOEFL. No college entrance examination is required.

Procedure: Application deadlines are May 1 (fall) and January 1 (spring). Foreign students must complete the college's student health form. They must also present proof of funds adequate to cover 1 year of study. Health insurance is required, and is available through the college for a fee.

Admissions Contact: Laura Fellows-Butt, Assistant Director of Admissions.

FAIRFIELD UNIVERSITY
Fairfield, Connecticut 06430   B-4
(203) 255-5411

F/T: 1409M, 1509W   Faculty: 175; IIA +$
P/T: 410M, 864W   Ph.D.'s: 77%
Grad: 295M, 644W   S/F Ratio: 17 to 1
Year: sems, ss   Tuition: $4560
Appl. Mar. 1   R and B: $2500
4687 applied   1959 accepted   744 enrolled
SAT: 522V, 565M   **VERY COMPETITIVE**

Fairfield University, founded in 1942 by the Jesuits, is a Roman-Catholic-affiliated institution offering undergraduate programs in the liberal arts and sciences, business, education, and nursing. The library has 163,000 books and 158,000 microfilm items, and subscribes to 1400 periodicals.

Environment: The 210-acre suburban campus is located 5 miles from downtown Bridgeport and about 50 miles east of New York City. There are 21 buildings on campus, including 7 coed dormitories for 1700 students, a recreation center, and a faculty office building. On-campus apartments now under construction will house an additional 200 students.

Student Life: About 41% of the students come from Connecticut, and 48% are from public schools. Sixty percent live on campus. A majority (90%) of the students are Catholic; attendance at religious services is voluntary. Two percent of the students are minority-group members. Campus housing is coed. Students may keep cars on campus.

Organizations: There are no fraternities or sororities. Extracurricular activities include clubs, student government, publications, cultural and social groups, and service organizations. There are lectures and films.

Sports: The university competes on an intercollegiate level in 7 sports for men and 4 for women. There are 9 intramural sports for men and 9 for women.

Handicapped: The entire campus is accessible to individuals with physical handicaps. Special facilities include wheelchair ramps, parking areas, elevators, lowered drinking fountains and telephones, specially equipped rest rooms, and residence hall rooms. Special class scheduling is possible. There is 1 counselor to aid handicapped students.

Graduates: The freshman dropout rate is 13%; about 70% remain to complete their degrees. After graduation about 25% go on for further study: 3% to medical school, 1% to dental school, and 4% to law school. Seventy-five percent pursue careers in business and industry.

Services: Placement (for undergraduates and alumni), career counseling, psychological counseling, and tutoring are available free of charge. Health care is provided for a fee.

Programs of Study: The B.A. and B.S. degrees are offered. Master's degrees are also awarded. Bachelor's degrees are offered in the following subjects: AREA STUDIES (American), BUSINESS (accounting, finance, management, marketing), ENGLISH (English), FINE AND PERFORMING ARTS (art), HEALTH SCIENCES (nursing), LANGUAGES (French, German, Spanish), MATH AND SCIENCES (biology, chemistry, engineering, mathematics, physics), PHILOSOPHY (philosophy, religion), SOCIAL SCIENCES (economics, government/political science, history, psychology, sociology). About 37% of degrees conferred are in business.

Required: A core curriculum is required of all students.

Special: There is a 3-2 cooperative program in engineering with the University of Connecticut. A combination B.A.-B.S. degree is offered. Study abroad is possible. Certification for secondary teaching is possible in most arts and sciences majors.

Honors: Seven honor societies have chapters on campus. Several departments offer honors courses.

Admissions: About 42% of the applicants for the 1981-82 freshman class were accepted. The SAT scores of those who enrolled were as follows: Verbal—37% below 500, 48% between 500 and 599, 12% between 600 and 700, and 3% above 700; Math—17% below 500, 54% between 500 and 599, 27% between 600 and 700, and 2% above 700. Applicants should be in the top 40% of their high school class and have an 85 average. Also considered important are advanced placement or honors courses, the applicant's leadership record, and impressions made during the interview.

Procedure: The SAT and 3 ATs (English Composition, Language, and Mathematics I) should be taken no later than January of the senior year. March 1 is the deadline for fall applications; there is a $20 nonrefundable fee. An interview is recommended.

Special: There are early decision and deferred admissions plans. AP and CLEP credit is offered.

Transfer: For fall 1981, 492 students applied, 143 were accepted, and 74 enrolled. A 2.5 GPA is required; D grades do not transfer. Transfer students should have earned a minimum of 30 credits; an interview is also recommended. All students must complete, at the university, 60 of the 120 credits required for a bachelor's degree. The fall deadline is June 1; the spring deadline is December 1.

Visiting: There is a formal orientation program. Informal campus visits with student guides may be arranged. Visitors may attend classes.

Financial Aid: About 30% of the students are receiving assistance. Ten percent work part-time on campus. The university offers a series of achievement scholarships and grants which are based on need. The average freshman award is $3000. Federal and state grants as well as CWS are available. The university is a member of CSS. The FAF is due February 1.

Foreign Students: One percent of the full-time students come from foreign countries. Special counseling is available for these students.

Admissions: Foreign students must achieve a TOEFL score of at least 550. No college entrance exams are required.

Procedure: Application deadlines are June 1 (fall entry) and December 1 (spring entry). Foreign students must present proof of health and proof of funds adequate to cover 4 years of study. Health insurance is required and is available through the university for a fee.

Admissions Contact: David Flynn, Dean of Undergraduate Admissions.

POST COLLEGE
Waterbury, Connecticut 06708   B-3   (203) 755-0121

F/T: 324M, 543W	Faculty: 34; IIB, av$
P/T: 391M, 289W	Ph.D.'s: 24%
Grad: none	S/F Ratio: 18 to 1
Year: sems, ss	Tuition: $3500
Appl: open	R and B: $2200
646 applied	436 accepted 241 enrolled
SAT: 340V 370M	LESS COMPETITIVE

Post College is a private college that offers an undergraduate curriculum in business administration, liberal arts and sciences, and applied arts and sciences. The library has over 20,000 books, 265 periodical subscriptions, and 1800 reels of microfilm.

Environment: The 65-acre suburban campus has 11 buildings and is located 2 miles from the center of Waterbury. Single-sex dormitories house 320 men and women. There are facilities for commuter students.

Student Life: About 75% of the students come from Connecticut. Eight percent are minority-group members. Forty-nine percent reside on campus in single-sex dorms; there are visiting privileges. Students may keep cars on campus. Day-care services are available to all students, faculty, and staff for a fee.

Organizations: There are no sororities or fraternities. The college does not have religious counselors or organizations. Nine extracurricular groups include student government and clubs.

Sports: There are 5 intercollegiate sports for men and 5 for women. There is also a full intramural program consisting of 5 sports for men and 4 for women.

Handicapped: About 10% of the campus is accessible to individuals with physical handicaps. There are wheelchair ramps and parking areas. One counselor is available.

Graduates: About 15% of the students drop out after the first year of study; 75% remain to complete their degrees. About 25% of the graduates continue their education; 1% enter law school, and 67% go directly into business or industry.

Services: The following services are free to all students: placement services for undergraduates and alumni, career counseling, health care, psychological counseling, tutoring, and remedial instruction.

Programs of Study: The B.S. degree is conferred. Associate degrees are also offered. Bachelor's degrees are offered in the following subjects: BUSINESS (accounting, fashion merchandising, management, marketing, office administration).

Required: All students must take freshman English.

Special: Students may create their own majors. It is possible to earn a B.S. degree in general studies. Internships are available.

Honors: There is an honors program for academically qualified freshmen.

Admissions: About 68% of the applicants for the 1981-82 freshman class were accepted. The SAT scores of those who enrolled were: Verbal—88% below 500, 8% between 500 and 599, 2% between 600 and 700, and 2% above 700; Math—84% below 500, 11% between 500 and 599, 3% between 600 and 700, and 2% above 700. Generally, an applicant should be in the top 60% and have a C average. Other factors include recommendations, advanced placement or honors courses, leadership record, and extracurricular activities record.

Procedure: The SAT is required. New students are admitted both semesters. Notification is on a rolling basis; there are no application deadlines. A personal interview is required. There is a $15 nonrefundable application fee.

Special: AP and CLEP credit is given. There are early decision and early and deferred admissions plans.

Transfer: For fall 1981, 113 transfer students applied, 100 were accepted, and 63 enrolled. D grades generally do not transfer. An interview is required, and a 2.0 GPA is recommended. Thirty credits, of the 120 required for the bachelor's degree, must be completed in residence. There are no application deadlines.

Visiting: Informal campus visits may be arranged. Visitors may attend classes and stay at the college.

Financial Aid: About 70% of the students receive assistance. Twenty percent work part-time on campus. There are several academic and athletic scholarships for freshmen. Thirty-five percent of all students receive scholarship aid. About 80% receive loans from federal funds.

CONNECTICUT 111

CWS is offered in 15 departments. April 15 is the application deadline for the fall semester; December 15 is the deadline for spring. The FAF should be filed with CSS. Need and academic promise are the determining factors.

Foreign Students: No foreign students are enrolled.

Admissions: Foreign students must achieve a minimum score of 550 on the TOEFL. College entrance exams are not required.

Procedure: Application policies are the same as for freshman applicants. Foreign students must present a college health form signed by a physician as proof of health. They must also carry health insurance. Proof of funds adequate to cover 1 year of study is required.

Admissions Contact: Janice E. Johnston, Director of Admissions.

QUINNIPIAC COLLEGE
Hamden, Connecticut 06518   C-3   (203) 288-5251

F/T: 843M, 1493W	Faculty: 173; IIA, +$
P/T: 543M, 1014W	Ph.D.'s: 43%
Grad: 151M, 223W	S/F Ratio: 15 to 1
Year: sems, ss	Tuition: $4745
Appl: June 1	R and B: $2260
2582 applied	1575 accepted 784 enrolled
SAT: 520V 550M	COMPETITIVE+

Quinnipiac College, founded in 1929, is a private institution offering undergraduate programs in the liberal arts and sciences, business, and health sciences. The library has nearly 100,000 volumes and 9000 microfilm items, and subscribes to 727 periodicals.

Environment: The 140-acre campus has 16 buildings and is located in a suburban area 9 miles north of New Haven. Living facilities include dormitories and on-campus apartments.

Student Life: About 52% of the students come from Connecticut, and 75% come from public schools. About 59% of the students live on campus. Four percent are minority-group members. Seventy-one percent are Catholic, 21% are Protestant, and 6% are Jewish. Campus housing is both coed and single-sex; there are visiting privileges in the single-sex housing. Students may keep cars on campus. Day-care services are provided for a fee.

Organizations: There are 2 national fraternities to which 5% of the men belong; 1% of the women belong to 1 national sorority. Extracurricular activities include clubs, cultural groups, publications, a radio station, social events, and a jazz festival.

Sports: Intercollegiate competition is offered in 7 sports for men and 4 for women. There are 7 intramural sports for men and 6 for women.

Handicapped: About 95% of the campus is accessible to students with physical handicaps. Ramps, elevators, parking areas, and specially equipped rest rooms are available.

Graduates: The freshman dropout rate is 19%; about 80% remain to graduate. Thirty-five percent go on for further education: 2% go to law school. About 47% enter careers in business and industry.

Services: Placement (for undergraduates and alumni), career counseling, health care, psychological counseling, and tutoring are offered free of charge.

Programs of Study: The college confers the B.A., B.S., and B.S. in Health Science degrees. Associate and master's degrees are also awarded. Bachelor's degrees are offered in the following subjects: BUSINESS (accounting, business administration, computer science, finance, international business, management, marketing, real estate/insurance), ENGLISH (English, mass communications), FINE AND PERFORMING ARTS (studio art, theater/dramatics), HEALTH SCIENCES (environmental health, hospital and health services administration, industrial hygiene, laboratory animal technology, medical technology, nursing, occupational therapy, physical therapy, radiologic technology, respiratory therapy), MATH AND SCIENCES (biology, chemistry, mathematics), SOCIAL SCIENCES (history, legal studies, psychology, sociology). About 40% of all degrees conferred are in health sciences; 25% are in business; and 20% are in math and sciences.

Required: All students must take English composition, literature, history, and mathematics.

Special: A combination B.A.-B.S. degree is offered. Students may design their own majors. Study abroad is possible.

Honors: Several honor societies have chapters on campus.

Admissions: About 61% of the applicants for the 1981-82 freshman class were accepted. The SAT scores of those who enrolled were as follows: Verbal—38% below 500, 55% between 500 and 599, 5%

between 600 and 700, and 2% above 700; Math—34% below 500, 55% between 500 and 599, 8% between 600 and 700, and 3% above 700. Applicants should have a GPA of at least 2.5 and should rank in the upper half of their high school class. Also considered important are advanced placement or honors courses, special talents, and extracurricular activities.

Procedure: The SAT or ACT (and 3 ATs for health sciences students) should be taken by December of the senior year. Application deadlines are June 1 (fall) and December 1 (spring); notification is on a rolling basis in most areas. There is a $15 nonrefundable application fee.

Special: AP and CLEP credit is granted. There are early decision, early admissions, and deferred admissions programs.

Transfer: About 200 transfer students enroll each year. A 2.3 GPA is required; D grades do not transfer. All students must complete, at the college, 30 of the 120 (or more) credits required for a bachelor's degree. Deadlines are the same as for freshmen.

Visiting: There is no orientation program but informal campus visits may be arranged. Visitors may attend classes.

Financial Aid: About 42% of the students are receiving assistance. Seventy percent work part-time on campus. The college offers scholarships and loans; the average freshman award is $2600. Need is the determining factor; some scholarships are based solely on academic merit. The college is a member of CSS. The FAF and the application form should be submitted by March 1 (fall entry) or December 1 (spring entry).

Foreign Students: Fewer than 1% of the full-time students come from foreign countries. Special counseling is available for these students.

Admissions: Foreign students must achieve a TOEFL score of at least 500. No college entrance exams are required.

Procedure: Application deadlines are the same as those for other freshmen. Foreign students must present proof of funds adequate to cover 4 years of study and must present proof of health. They must carry health insurance, which is available through the college for a fee.

Admissions Contact: Deborah E. Wordell, Assistant Director of Admissions.

SACRED HEART UNIVERSITY B-4
Bridgeport, Connecticut 06606   (203) 371-6249

F/T: 677M, 1022W	Faculty: n/av; IIB, +$
P/T: 623M, 1554W	Ph.D.'s: n/av
Grad: 270M, 206W	S/F Ratio: 20 to 1
Year: sems, ss	Tuition: $3040
Appl: Sept. 1	R and B: none
1442 applied	875 accepted	739 enrolled
SAT: 450V 480M		COMPETITIVE

Sacred Heart University is affiliated with the Roman Catholic Church. It offers undergraduate curricula in the liberal arts and sciences, business, education, and nursing. The library has 160,000 books and 10 microfilm items, and subscribes to 1500 periodicals.

Environment: The 69-acre urban campus is located 1 mile from downtown Bridgeport and 50 miles east of New York City. There are no residence halls. Facilities are available for commuter students.

Student Life: About 96% of the students come from Connecticut; 60% come from public schools. All students commute. Fifty percent of the students are Catholic, but attendance at religious services is not compulsory. One percent are minority-group members. Students may keep cars on campus.

Organizations: There are 3 local fraternities to which 1% of the men belong; there are 4 local sororities to which 1% of the women belong. Other on-campus extracurricular activities include clubs, student government, publications, cultural and social events, and service organizations.

Sports: Intercollegiate competition is offered in 6 sports for men and 4 for women. There are 2 intramural sports for men and 1 for women.

Handicapped: About 75% of the campus is accessible to students with physical handicaps. Special facilities include wheelchair ramps, parking areas, and specially equipped rest rooms. Special class scheduling is also possible.

Graduates: The freshman dropout rate is 20%; 50% remain to graduate. Of these, 25% go on for further education; 1% to medical school and 1% to law school. Fifty percent go into careers in business and industry.

Services: Free placement, career counseling, psychological counseling, tutoring, and remedial instruction are available to students.

Programs of Study: The college confers the B.A. and B.S. degrees. Associate and master's degrees are also offered. Bachelor's degrees are offered in the following subjects: AREA STUDIES (American), BUSINESS (accounting, business administration, business education, computer science, economics, finance, management, marketing), EDUCATION (early childhood, elementary, secondary), ENGLISH (English, journalism), FINE AND PERFORMING ARTS (art, art education), HEALTH SCIENCES (medical technology, nursing), LANGUAGES (Spanish), MATH AND SCIENCES (biology, chemistry, ecology/environmental science, mathematics), PREPROFESSIONAL (social work), SOCIAL SCIENCES (economics, psychology, sociology). The majority of degrees conferred are in business.

Required: All students must complete a core curriculum.

Special: Study abroad and a 3-year bachelor's degree are possible. Students may earn combined B.A.-B.S. degrees.

Honors: There is an honors program in English.

Admissions: About 61% of the applicants for the 1981-82 freshman class were accepted. Students should be in the top 60% of the high school class and have a 2.0 GPA. An interview is required. Also considered important are recommendations, advanced placement or honors courses, and impressions made during the interview.

Procedure: The SAT should be taken by December of the senior year. Application deadlines are September 1 (fall) and January 20 (spring). Notification is on a rolling basis. Freshmen are admitted both semesters. There is a $15 nonrefundable application fee.

Special: AP and CLEP credit is available. There are early decision and deferred admissions plans.

Transfer: For fall 1981, 270 students applied, 230 were accepted, and 174 enrolled. A 2.0 GPA is required. D grades do not transfer. Thirty credits (including half of those for the major) out of the 120 required for a bachelor's degree must be completed in residence. Application deadlines are May 1 (fall) and December 1 (spring).

Visiting: There is a formal orientation program for incoming freshmen. Informal campus visits with student guides may be arranged. Visitors may sit in on classes.

Financial Aid: Sixty-three percent of the students are receiving assistance. Eighteen percent work part-time on campus. Average aid to freshmen from all sources is $1210. Scholarships, federal and state grants, loans (federal, state, and commercial), CWS, and part-time campus employment are offered. The college is a member of CSS. The FAF should be filed. Application deadlines are March 30 (fall) and October 1 (spring).

Foreign Students: One percent of the full-time students come from foreign countries. The university provides these students with an intensive English course.

Admissions: Foreign students must take the TOEFL. They must also take the university's own college entrance examination.

Procedure: Application deadlines are June 1 (fall) and November 1 (spring). Foreign students must present proof of funds adequate to cover 1 year of study. There is a special deposit of $250 payable upon acceptance.

Admissions Contact: Sharon Brennan Browne, Dean of Admissions.

SAINT JOSEPH COLLEGE C-2
West Hartford, Connecticut 06117   (203) 232-9608

F/T: 596W	Faculty: 73; IIB, av$
P/T: 164W	Ph.D.'s: 53%
Grad: 73M, 371W	S/F Ratio: 12 to 1
Year: sems, ss	Tuition: $4020
Appl: May 1	R and B: $2300
488 applied	264 accepted	155 enrolled
SAT: 460V 490M		COMPETITIVE

Saint Joseph College, affiliated with the Roman Catholic Church and operated by the Sisters of Mercy, offers undergraduate degree programs for women in the liberal arts and sciences, business, home economics, and social work. The library has 91,423 books and 4306 microfilm items, and subscribes to 558 periodicals.

Environment: The 84-acre suburban campus is located 3 miles from downtown Hartford. Four dormitories accommodate about 350 women. There are 7 other major buildings including facilities for commuter students.

Student Life: Eighty-seven percent of the students come from Connecticut. Sixty-eight percent of freshmen come from public schools. Fifty percent of the students reside on campus. Although affiliated with the Roman Catholic Church, the college is open to students of all faiths. About 5% of the students are minority-group members. Campus housing is single-sex, and there are visiting privileges. Students may keep cars on campus.

Organizations: There are no sororities. Traditional special-interest groups are offered to interested students.

Sports: There are 3 intercollegiate sports and 3 intramural sports.

Handicapped: The college is working to meet the needs of physically handicapped students. Ramps, elevators, parking areas, and specially equipped rest rooms are provided. Special class scheduling is possible.

Graduates: Four percent of the freshmen drop out by the end of the first year. Sixty-five percent remain to graduate. Nine percent of the graduates go on for further education. About 5% go into careers in business or industry.

Services: Free of charge to all students are placement services (job announcements, on-campus recruitment, career library, maintenance of a file), career counseling, health care, psychological counseling, tutoring, and remedial instruction. Alumnae are eligible for placement services.

Programs of Study: The B.A. and B.S. degrees are conferred. Master's degree programs are also offered. Bachelor's degrees are offered in the following subjects: AREA STUDIES (American, European), BUSINESS (business administration, economics), EDUCATION (early childhood, elementary, special), ENGLISH (English), FINE AND PERFORMING ARTS (art history, music, performing arts), HEALTH SCIENCES (medical technology, nursing), LANGUAGES (French, Spanish), MATH AND SCIENCES (biochemistry, biology, chemistry, mathematics, physics), PHILOSOPHY (humanities, philosophy, religion), PREPROFESSIONAL (dietetics, engineering, home economics, home economics education, social work), SOCIAL SCIENCES (government/political science, history, psychology, sociology). About 21% of degrees conferred are in education, and 40% are in health sciences.

Required: All students must take basic courses in humanities, religious studies, social sciences, and natural sciences.

Special: Students may design their own majors. Study abroad is possible. Dual degree programs are offered in conjunction with George Washington University in engineering. The Gengras Center for Exceptional Children is a teacher-training laboratory. The college is a member of the greater Hartford area consortium of colleges.

Honors: There is one honor society on campus.

Admissions: About 54% of the applicants for the 1981–82 freshman class were accepted. SAT scores of those who enrolled were as follows: Verbal—73% below 500, 22% between 500 and 599, 4% between 600 and 700, and 0% above 700; Math—54% below 500, 41% between 500 and 599, 6% between 600 and 700, and 0% above 700. The applicant should have 16 Carnegie credits. Also considered important are advanced placement or honors courses, recommendations, and impressions made during the required interview.

Procedure: The SAT should be taken by January of the senior year. Application deadlines are May 1 (fall) and December 1 (spring). Notification is on a rolling basis. There is a $15 nonrefundable application fee.

Special: AP and CLEP credit is granted. The college has early decision and early admissions plans.

Transfer: For fall 1981, 158 students applied, 89 were accepted, and 71 enrolled. A GPA of 2.7 and good academic standing at the previous institution are required. Grades of C or better transfer. Students must complete at the college, 60 out of the 120 credits required for a bachelor's degree. Application deadlines are June 1 (fall) and December 1 (spring).

Visiting: There is an orientation program for incoming freshmen. Informal campus visits with student guides can be arranged. Visitors may sit in on classes and stay overnight at the school.

Financial Aid: About 63% of the students are receiving assistance. Nineteen percent work part-time on campus. Average aid to freshmen from all sources is $2605. Aid is available in the form of scholarships, federal and/or private loans, government grants, and on-campus, part-time employment. Tuition may be paid in installments. Need and academic merit are the determining factors. The college is a member of CSS. The FAF should be filed by January 31 (fall).

Foreign Students: Fewer than 1% of the full-time students come from foreign countries.

Admissions: Foreign students must score at least 530 on the TOEFL. No college entrance examination is required.

Procedure: The application deadline is March 1 (fall). A physical examination is required upon matriculation. Foreign students must present proof of funds adequate to cover annual fees.

Admissions Contact: Mary C. Demo, Assistant Director of Admissions.

SOUTHERN CONNECTICUT STATE COLLEGE   C–3

New Haven, Connecticut 06515   (203) 397-4450

F/T, P/T: 2500M, 4400W	Faculty: n/av; IIA, ++$
Grad: n/av	Ph.D.'s: n/av
Year: sems, ss	S/F Ratio: n/av
Appl: open	Tuition: $700 ($1700)
SAT: required	R and B: $2200
	COMPETITIVE

Southern Connecticut State College, established in 1893, is a state-supported institution that provides undergraduate and graduate instruction, research, and public service. The library contains 360,000 volumes and subscribes to more than 500 periodicals.

Environment: The 150-acre campus is located in a suburban area overlooking the city of New Haven. The 22 campus buildings include 6 coed and single-sex dormitories that accommodate about 1700 men and women.

Student Life: Ninety percent of the students are from Connecticut. Twenty percent live on campus.

Organizations: Among the many student organizations are religious groups, special-interest clubs, sororities, fraternities, a campus newspaper, a band, a choir, and a debating club.

Sports: There are 11 intercollegiate teams for men and 9 for women. Intramural sports are also offered.

Graduates: About half the graduates pursue graduate or professional study. Thirty percent of the students drop out at the end of the freshman year; 45% to 50% remain to graduate.

Programs of Study: The undergraduate degrees conferred are the B.A. and B.S. Associate and master's degrees are also awarded. Bachelor's degrees are offered in the following subjects: EDUCATION (elementary, health/physical, secondary, special), ENGLISH (English, journalism, speech), FINE AND PERFORMING ARTS (art education, art history, studio art, theater/dramatics), HEALTH SCIENCES (nursing), LANGUAGES (French, German, Italian, Spanish), MATH AND SCIENCES (biochemistry, biology, botany, chemistry, earth science, marine biology, mathematics, physics, zoology), PHILOSOPHY (classics, humanities, philosophy, religion), PREPROFESSIONAL (library science, recreation, social work), SOCIAL SCIENCES (economics, geography, history, political science, psychology, social welfare, sociology).

Required: All students must take courses in fine arts, biology, literature, mathematics, physical education, physical science, social sciences, and writing/speech.

Honors: The college offers an honors program for superior students. Special placement enables these students to enroll in honors sections and interdisciplinary courses, and to carry on research in their field of special interest.

Admissions: About 55% of those who applied were accepted for a recent freshman class. Applicants must be graduates of accredited high schools, score 400 or better on the SAT, rank in the top half of their graduating class with an average of at least C, be recommended by high school authorities, and complete 16 high school units. Other considerations are the reputation of the high school, recommendations of alumni, extracurricular and athletic activities, advanced placement or honors courses, and leadership potential.

Procedure: The SAT is required and should be taken in December, January, or March of the senior year. Application deadlines are open. Freshmen are not admitted for the summer session. Notification is on a rolling basis, beginning about February 1. There is a $10 application fee.

Special: The college has a deferred admissions plan. AP credit may be earned.

Transfer: Transfer students are accepted for all classes. Applicants should have a GPA of at least 2.0. D grades are acceptable only if they are part of an associate degree. Thirty credits, of the 122 necessary for the bachelor's degree, must be completed at the college. Deadlines are the same as for freshman applications.

114 CONNECTICUT

Financial Aid: A limited amount of aid is available to students who can demonstrate financial need. Students who wish to apply for grants, loans, or campus employment must file the FAF and the aid application by April 15. The college is a member of CSS.

Foreign Students: The college offers foreign students an intensive English course and special counseling.

Admissions: Foreign students must demonstrate proficiency in the English language through satisfactory performance on either the TOEFL or the SAT, or both, as required by the admissions office.

Procedure: Applications should be submitted 90 days before the opening of the desired semester. Foreign students must submit a health record from completed by a physician, and are required to carry health insurance.

Admissions Contact: Robert Porter, Director of Admissions.

TRINITY COLLEGE C-2
Hartford, Connecticut 06106   (203) 527-3151

F/T: 850M, 791W	Faculty: 130; IIA, ++$
P/T: 66M, 89W	Ph.D.'s: 85%
Grad: 122M, 92W	S/F Ratio: 13 to 1
Year: sems	Tuition: $6580
Appl: Jan. 1	R and B: $2550
3024 applied	1287 accepted 464 enrolled
SAT: 560V 600M	HIGHLY COMPETITIVE

Trinity College, founded in 1823, is a nonsectarian liberal arts and sciences college. The library has 615,000 volumes and nearly 70,000 microfilm items, and subscribes to 1571 periodicals.

Environment: The 90-acre campus is in the southwestern section of Hartford. The main buildings are in an English-style quadrangle dominated by a Gothic-style chapel. Recent additions include a fine arts center, a life sciences center, and a math-physics building. Residence halls are of several types, and accommodate 1500 men and women. Some students live in fraternity houses.

Student Life: About 30% of the students come from Connecticut, and 60% come from public schools. Ninety percent live on campus. Five percent are members of minority groups. Dormitories are coed, and students may keep cars on campus.

Organizations: There are 6 local fraternities to which 29% of the men belong, and there are 2 sororities. Extracurricular activities include social and cultural events on campus, a radio station, publications, debating, student government, clubs, and service organizations.

Sports: The college fields intercollegiate teams in 17 sports for men and 14 for women. Eleven intramural sports are offered for men and 10 for women.

Handicapped: About 99% of the campus is accessible to students with physical handicaps. Special facilities include wheelchair ramps, parking areas, elevators, stair lifts, lowered drinking fountains and telephones, and specially equipped rest rooms. Special class scheduling is possible. One assistant is assigned to handicapped students.

Graduates: The freshman dropout rate is 2%, and about 85% of the students remain to graduate. Of these, 45% go on for additional education: 10% go to medical school, 1% to dental school, and 15% to law school. About 15% go on to careers in business and industry.

Services: The following services are offered free: placement, career counseling, health care, and psychological counseling. Fees are charged for tutoring.

Programs of Study: The B.A. and B.S. degrees are awarded. Master's degrees also are offered. Bachelor's degrees are offered in the following subjects: AREA STUDIES (American, Asian, Black/Afro-American, Latin American, urban), ENGLISH (English/literature), FINE AND PERFORMING ARTS (art history, studio art, theater/dramatics), LANGUAGES (French, German, Italian, Russian, Spanish), MATH AND SCIENCES (biochemistry, biology, chemistry, ecology/environmental science, mathematics, physics), PHILOSOPHY (classics, philosophy, religion), PREPROFESSIONAL (engineering), SOCIAL SCIENCES (economics, government/political science, history, psychology, sociology). About 41% of degrees conferred are in social sciences and 26% are in math and sciences.

Special: Emphasis is placed on independent study, relevant off-campus study, and internships. Students may design their own majors. Institutional exchanges and study abroad are available.

Honors: Four honor societies have chapters on campus.

Admissions: About 43% of the applicants for the 1981-82 freshman class were accepted. The SAT scores of those who enrolled were as follows: Verbal—17% below 500, 50% between 500 and 599, 31% between 600 and 700, and 2% above 700; Math—8% below 500, 37% between 500 and 599, 47% between 600 and 700, and 8% above 700. Besides test scores, grade average, and class rank, the college considers, in decreasing order of importance, advanced placement or honors courses, recommendations by school officials, evidence of special talents, extracurricular activities, personality, impressions made during an interview, and leadership record.

Procedure: The SAT or ACT and the AT in English Composition should be taken by December of the senior year. There is a $25 nonrefundable application fee. The deadline for fall admission, the only semester in which freshmen are admitted, is January 1.

Special: AP credit is available. There are early decision, early admissions, and deferred admissions plans.

Transfer: For fall 1981, 200 students applied, 40 were accepted, and 25 enrolled. A 3.0 GPA is recommended; D grades do not transfer. Students must spend 4 semesters in residence, completing 16 of the 36 courses required for a bachelor's degree. The fall deadline is March 1; the spring deadline is December 1.

Visiting: Informal campus visits with student guides may be arranged; visitors may sit in on classes and are generally able to stay overnight at the school.

Financial Aid: About 30% of the students are receiving aid through the college. The college offers 125 to 150 scholarships to freshmen from a fund of $500,000; awards are based on need. Federal, state, and private loans as well as government grants are also awarded. Work-study (CWS) and part-time campus employment opportunities are available, and 35% of the students take advantage of them. The maximum freshman award is $8000. The FAF or FFS is due February 1; the college is a member of CSS.

Foreign Students: Foreign students make up about 1% of the student body. Special organizations and counseling are provided.

Admissions: Foreign applicants are required to score 550 or better on the TOEFL. No academic exams are required.

Procedure: The application deadline is January 1 (fall admission only). Students must present proof of adequate funds for 4 years of study. Health insurance is not required.

Admissions Contact: Donald N. Dietrich, Director of Admissions.

UNITED STATES COAST GUARD ACADEMY E-3
New London, Connecticut 06320   (203) 444-8501

F/T: 750M, 130W	Faculty: 120; n/av
P/T: none	Ph.D.'s: 22%
Grad: none	S/F Ratio: 8 to 1
Year: sems, ss	Tuition: none
Appl: Dec. 15	R and B: none
8000 applied	700 accepted 400 enrolled
SAT: 555V 629M	MOST COMPETITIVE

The U.S. Coast Guard Academy, founded in 1876, is an Armed Forces Service Academy for men and women. Appointments to the freshman class are made solely on the basis of an annual nationwide competition. The library contains 120,000 volumes and subscribes to 800 periodicals.

Environment: The academy's 110-acre campus is located in a suburban area 100 miles from Boston and 100 miles from New York City. The 32 buildings include a dormitory that houses 890 men and women.

Student Life: Ninety percent of entering freshmen come from public schools. All cadets live on campus. Fifty-one percent are Catholic, 48% are Protestant, and 1% are Jewish. Eight percent of the students are minority-group members. All students must live on campus, and only seniors may keep cars on campus. Academy housing is coed.

Organizations: Cultural events on campus include concerts, films, lectures, professional demonstrations, and science exhibits. Major social events include the Ring Dance, Cadet Formals, Cadet Informals, Commencement Dance, and Dinner Dance. The academy sponsors organized religious discussion groups and church glee clubs. There are no social fraternities or sororities.

Sports: The academy fields 12 intercollegiate teams for women and 17 for men. There are 14 intramural sports for men and 12 for women.

Handicapped: The campus is considered inaccessible to physically handicapped students.

Graduates: The freshman dropout rate is 20%; 60% remain to graduate. Eighty percent of the graduates pursue advanced degrees during their first 5 years of active duty.

Services: Students receive the following services free of charge: career counseling, health care, tutoring, remedial instruction, and psychological counseling.

Programs of Study: The academy awards the B.S. degree; graduates are commissioned as ensigns in the United States Coast Guard. Degrees are awarded in BUSINESS (management), MATH AND SCIENCES (chemistry, marine science, mathematics, physical sciences), PREPROFESSIONAL (engineering—civil, engineering—electrical, engineering—marine, engineering—ocean), SOCIAL SCIENCES (government/political science). Fifty percent of degrees conferred are in engineering, 30% are in math and sciences, 10% are in government, and 10% are in management.

Required: All cadets must complete a core program of 26 academic courses, primarily in pre-engineering subjects.

Special: Cadets go on summer cruises to foreign ports as part of the regular curriculum.

Honors: The Academy Scholars Program is offered for cadets in their fourth year who have demonstrated outstanding scholastic abilities. Those elected are given special recognition and academic privileges that enable them to pursue individually selected projects and special research.

Admissions: Nine percent of those who applied were accepted for the 1981–82 freshman class. The SAT scores of those who enrolled were as follows: Verbal—18% below 500, 53% between 500 and 599, 27% between 600 and 700, and 1% above 700; Math—0% below 500, 28% between 500 and 599, 57% between 600 and 700, and 15% above 700. Applicants must be 17, but must not have reached the age of 22 by July 1 of the year they are to be admitted. They must be U.S. citizens at the time of entry into the academy. They must be unmarried, have no legal obligation resulting from a prior marriage, and may not marry before graduation. They must pass a qualifying medical examination and have graduated from an accredited high school by June 30 of the year of entrance. Other factors considered are leadership record, extracurricular activities, personality, and recommendations by school officials.

Procedure: The SAT or ACT is required. It may be taken in the spring of the junior year or by December of the year before entrance. Applications should be submitted by December 15. Notification begins February 15, and the final cutoff date is April 15. Cadets enter the academy at the end of June. There is no application fee.

Transfer: Transfer students are accepted, but must complete the full 4 years at the academy.

Visiting: Orientations are given every Friday at 1:15 P.M.. Guided tours and appointments for orientations can be arranged through the admissions office. Visitors may sit in on classes and may remain overnight at the academy.

Financial Aid: The federal government compensates all cadets at the rate of $5000 per year plus a daily food allowance. This is not a salary, but is intended to cover all expenses incidental to training.

Foreign Students: Three percent of the full-time students come from foreign countries. Special counseling is provided for these students.

Admission: Foreign students must score at least 500 on the TOEFL. They also must take the SAT or ACT.

Procedure: The application deadline is December 15 for summer entry. Foreign students must present proof of good health.

Admissions Contact: Captain Robert T. Getman, Director of Admissions.

UNIVERSITY OF BRIDGEPORT B–4
Bridgeport, Connecticut 06601 (203) 576-4555

F/T: 1728M, 1512W	Faculty: 285; IIA, +$
P/T: 576M, 899W	Ph.D.'s: 50%
Grad: 1173M, 845W	S/F Ratio: 13 to 1
Year: sems, ss	Tuition: $5265
Appl: Aug. 1	R and B: $2775
2993 applied	2614 accepted	808 enrolled
SAT: 423V 456M		COMPETITIVE

The University of Bridgeport, established in 1927, is a nonsectarian institution offering undergraduate programs in arts and humanities, business and public management, health sciences, science and engineering, and basic studies. The library has over 312,000 books and 402,000 microfilm items, and subscribes to over 2470 periodicals.

Environment: The 86-acre urban campus is located about 55 miles east of New York City. Residence halls accommodate 926 men and 992 women. A recreation center with an Olympic-size swimming pool was recently completed.

Student Life: About 40% of the students come from Connecticut, and 80% come from public schools. Almost 65% reside on campus in coed and single-sex dorms, which have visiting privileges. Ten percent of the students are minority-group members. Students may keep cars on campus.

Organizations: There are 3 local and 2 national fraternities to which 3% of the men belong; there are 3 local and 1 national sororities to which 3% of the women belong. Extracurricular activities are traditional and varied.

Sports: The university is active in 6 intercollegiate sports for men and 6 for women. There are 8 intramural sports for men and 7 for women.

Handicapped: Special facilities include ramps, elevators, parking, and specially equipped rest rooms in most buildings.

Graduates: The freshman dropout rate is 20%; 46% remain to graduate. About 60% of the liberal arts and 80% of the education majors go on for additional education.

Services: Placement (for undergraduates and alumni), career counseling, psychological counseling, health care, tutoring, and remedial instruction are offered free to all students.

Programs of Study: The B.A., B.S., B.Mus., B.F.A., and B.E.S. are offered. There are also programs leading to associate, master's, and doctoral degrees. Bachelor's degrees are offered in the following subjects: AREA STUDIES (American), BUSINESS (accounting, business administration, business economics, computer science, fashion merchandising, finance, international business, management, marketing), EDUCATION (early childhood, elementary, health/physical, secondary), ENGLISH (English, journalism, literature), FINE AND PERFORMING ARTS (art, art education, art history, film/photography, industrial and interior design, music, music education, studio art, theater/dramatics), HEALTH SCIENCES (dental hygiene, gerontology, human services, medical records administration, medical technology, mental health, nursing, respiratory therapy), LANGUAGES (foreign languages—general), MATH AND SCIENCES (biology, chemistry, computer science, mathematics, physics), PHILOSOPHY (philosophy), PREPROFESSIONAL (architecture, dentistry, engineering—biomedical, engineering—computer, engineering—electrical, engineering—mechanical, engineering—interdisciplinary, law, medicine, veterinary), SOCIAL SCIENCES (economics, history, political science, psychology, sociology). About 17% of degrees are conferred in health sciences, 23% in business, 18% in liberal arts, 16% in engineering, and 9% in fine and performing arts.

Special: Students may design their own majors; the B.E.S. degree is possible.

Honors: There are several honor societies; independent study is offered to an outstanding arts and sciences student in the senior year.

Admissions: About 87% of the applicants for the 1981–82 freshman class were accepted. Applicants should be in the upper 60% of their class and have at least a 2.0 high school GPA. The SAT scores of freshmen in a recent class were as follows: Verbal—17% between 500 and 600, and 1% above 600; Math—25% between 500 and 600, and 1% above 600. Other factors of importance to the admissions decision are extracurricular activities record, evidence of special talents, advanced placement or honors courses, and the applicant's leadership record.

Procedure: The SAT should be taken by January of the senior year. There is a $25 nonrefundable application fee. The deadlines are August 1 (fall), January 1 (spring), and May 1 (summer). Notification is on a rolling basis.

Special: AP and CLEP credit is offered. There is an early decision plan and early and deferred admissions plans.

Transfer: For fall 1981, 856 transfer students applied, 652 were accepted, and 341 enrolled. A C average is required; D grades do not transfer. Thirty credits, of the 120–130 required for the bachelor's degree, must be completed at the university; there is a 1-year residency requirement. Application deadlines are August 1 (fall), January 1 (spring), and May 1 (summer).

Visiting: There is a formal orientation program for incoming freshmen. Informal campus visits are also possible, and visitors may sit in on classes and stay at the school. Arrangements can be made through the admissions office.

Financial Aid: About 50% of the students are receiving assistance through the university, a member of CSS. Twenty-five percent work part-time on campus. The university provides scholarships, federal and state grants, a variety of loans, and CWS. Tuition may be paid in installments. Need and academic merit are the determining factors. The FAF should be filed by April 1.

Foreign Students: Almost 11% of the full-time students come from foreign countries. The university, which actively recruits these students, offers them an intensive English program as well as special counseling and special organizations.

Admissions: Foreign students must achieve a minimum score of 500 on the TOEFL, or 80 on the University of Michigan Language Test. College entrance exams are not required.

Procedure: Application deadlines are August 1 (fall) and December 1 (spring). Foreign students must provide a certificate signed by a physician as proof of health. They must also carry health insurance, which is available through the university for a fee. Proof of funds adequate to cover the first year of study is required.

Admissions Contact: Richard D. Huss, Associate Vice President for Enrollment Planning.

UNIVERSITY OF CONNECTICUT D-2
Storrs, Connecticut 06268 (203) 486-3137

F/T, P/T: 7874M, 7847W	Faculty: 1174; I, ++$
Grad: 2845M, 3211W	Ph.D.'s: n/av
Year: sems, ss	S/F Ratio: 14to1
Appl: Feb. 15	Tuition: $1114 ($2454)
15,012 applied 5448 accepted	R and B: $2245 3668 enrolled
SAT: 502V 554M	VERY COMPETITIVE

The University of Connecticut, founded in 1881, is Connecticut's land-grant state university. Regional campuses are maintained at Groton, Hartford, Stamford, Torrington, and Waterbury. The undergraduate divisions are the colleges of Agriculture, and Liberal Arts and Sciences; and the schools of Business Administration, Dental Medicine, Education, Engineering, Fine Arts, Home Economics, Insurance, Law, Medicine, Nursing, Pharmacy, Allied Health, and Social Work. The library contains more than 1 million volumes, has 300,000 microfilm items on file, and subscribes to 7000 periodicals.

Environment: The university's main campus is on 2000 acres in rural northeastern Connecticut. The physical plant consists of more than 100 major buildings and includes a 7-story library, a fine arts building, and a psychology building.

Student Life: Over 90% of the students are from Connecticut; the rest come mainly from New England and the middle Atlantic states. About 87% come from public schools. Seventy percent live on campus. Nine percent are minority-group members. University housing is coed. Students may keep cars on campus. Day-care services are available to all students, faculty, and staff.

Organizations: There are more than 120 student organizations, including special-interest clubs, a daily student newspaper, a radio-TV station, religious groups, and professional organizations.

Sports: There are men's intercollegiate teams in 13 sports and women's in 11. There are 11 intramural sports for both men and women.

Handicapped: Special facilities for wheelchair students include ramps, designated parking, and elevators. Special class scheduling is possible.

Services: The following services are offered at no charge to the student: psychological counseling, tutoring, remedial instruction, health care, placement, and career counseling.

Programs of Study: Undergraduate degrees granted are the B.S., B.A., B.F.A., and B.M. Master's and doctoral degrees are also awarded. Bachelor's degrees are offered in the following subjects: AREA STUDIES (Latin American, Slavic and East European, urban), BUSINESS (accounting, business administration, business education, computer science, finance, management, marketing, real estate/insurance), EDUCATION (early childhood, elementary, health/physical, rehabilitation services, secondary, special), ENGLISH (English, journalism, speech), FINE AND PERFORMING ARTS (art, art education, art history, film/photography, music, music education, studio art, theater/dramatics), HEALTH SCIENCES (clinical dietetics, medical technology, nursing, physical therapy, speech therapy), LANGUAGES (French, German, Greek/Latin, Hebrew, Italian, Portuguese, Russian, Spanish), MATH AND SCIENCES (biology, chemistry, geology, mathematics, physics, statistics), PHILOSOPHY (classics, humanities, philosophy, religion), PREPROFESSIONAL (agriculture, architecture, dentistry, engineering, home economics, law, medicine, pharmacy, social work, veterinary), SOCIAL SCIENCES (anthropology, economics, geography, government/political science, history, psychology, social sciences, sociology). Fifteen percent of the degrees conferred are in business, 12% are in health, and 11% are in math and science.

Special: Combined B.A.-B.S. degrees can be earned in a special 5-year program. Student-designed majors are permitted. Study abroad is possible.

Honors: There are 40 national honor societies with chapters on campus. There is an extensive honors program.

Admissions: Thirty-six percent of those who applied were accepted for the 1981-82 freshman class. Of those who enrolled, the SAT scores were as follows: Verbal—40% below 500, 38% between 500 and 599, 16% between 600 and 700, and 6% above 700; Math—35% below 500, 38% between 500 and 599, 17% between 600 and 700, and 11% over 700. Applicants should have completed 16 high school units and be in the upper half of their class. Certain subjects are recommended for specialized curricula. Additional factors entering into an admissions decision are advanced placement or honors courses, recommendations of school officials, and evidence of special talent.

Procedure: The SAT should be taken no later than January of the senior year. The application deadlines are February 15 (fall) and October 15 (spring). New students are admitted both semesters. There is a rolling admissions plan. Applications should be accompanied by a $20 fee.

Special: There are early and deferred admissions and early decision plans. AP and CLEP credit is accepted.

Transfer: For fall 1981, 2400 students applied, 1250 were accepted, and 800 enrolled. Preference is given to students transferring from other colleges in the state. A 2.5 GPA is required. D grades do not transfer. The last 30 credits, of the 120 required for a bachelor's degree, must be taken at the university. Application deadlines are February 15 (fall) and October 15 (spring).

Visiting: Regularly scheduled orientations are given. Informal visits are possible; the admissions office will make arrangements.

Financial Aid: Thirty-three percent of all undergraduates receive university aid. Thirty-five percent work part-time on campus. Average aid to freshmen from all sources is $2000. Special grants are available for students in nursing and health professions. The university is a member of CSS. The application and the FAF must be filed by February 15 (fall) or October 1 (spring).

Foreign Students: One percent of the full-time students come from foreign countries. The university offers these students special counseling and special organizations.

Admissions: Foreign students must score at least 550 on the TOEFL. They must also take the SAT.

Procedure: Application deadlines are March 15 (fall) and October 1 (spring). Foreign students must present proof of health. They must also submit proof of funds adequate to cover 4 years of study. They must carry health insurance, which is available through the university for a fee.

Admissions Contact: John W. Vlandis, Director of Admissions.

UNIVERSITY OF HARTFORD C-2
West Hartford, Connecticut 06117 (203) 243-4296

F/T: 2295M, 1968W	Faculty: 328; IIA, av$
P/T: 1159M, 1420W	Ph.D.'s: 54%
Grad: 1393M, 1031W	S/F Ratio: 13 to 1
Year: sems, ss	Tuition: $5500
Appl: open	R and B: $2600
5003 applied 3955 accepted	1258 enrolled
SAT: 450V 510M	COMPETITIVE

The University of Hartford, an independent, nonsectarian institution established in 1957 by the merger of 3 area colleges, offers undergraduate curricula in the liberal arts and sciences, business, education, health sciences, and the arts. The library houses 300,000 books and nearly 51,000 microtexts, and subscribes to 2257 periodicals.

Environment: The 200-acre suburban campus is located 4 miles from downtown Hartford. Six on-campus residence units and an off-campus apartment building house about 2200 students. Recent campus additions include a technologies hall, a performing arts theater, new athletic fields, and an outdoor swimming pool. A new computer center is under construction.

Student Life: About 49% of the students come from Connecticut. Eighty-two percent of the freshmen come from public schools. About 51% of the students live on campus. Forty-five percent are Catholic, 25% Jewish, and 15% Protestant. Four percent of the students are minority-group members. Campus housing is both coed and single-sex. There are visiting privileges in single-sex dorms. Students may keep cars on campus.

Organizations: Extracurricular activities and cultural/social events are varied and numerous. Several on-campus events are provided by the School of Music and the Art School. Other student activities include publications, student government, and various special-interest clubs.

Sports: Intercollegiate competition is offered in 14 sports for men and 7 for women. A full intramural program is also offered, with 7 sports for men and 8 for women.

Handicapped: All of the campus is accessible to wheelchairs. Special facilities include wheelchair ramps, parking areas, elevators, and specially equipped restrooms. One counselor is available for physically handicapped students.

Graduates: The freshman dropout rate is about 9%. About one-third of the students go on for further education. About 60% enter business careers.

Services: The following services are free to all students: placement, career counseling, tutoring, remedial instruction, health care, and psychological counseling. Placement services are offered to students and alumni, and include workshops in resume writing and job interviewing, and a full recruitment program.

Programs of Study: The B.A., B.S., B.Mus., B.Mus.Ed, B.F.A., and B.E.T. degrees are conferred. Associate, master's, and doctoral degree programs are also offered. Bachelor's degrees are offered in the following subjects: AREA STUDIES (Black/Afro-American), BUSINESS (accounting, business administration, finance, management, marketing, real estate/insurance, social systems and policy), EDUCATION (early childhood, elementary, secondary, special), ENGLISH (communications, English, journalism, linguistics, literature), FINE AND PERFORMING ARTS (art education, art history, film/photography, jazz studies, music, music education, music management and music history, musical theater, radio/TV, studio art, theater/dramatics), HEALTH SCIENCES (community health, medical technology, nursing, respiratory therapy), LANGUAGES (French, German, Italian, Russian, Spanish), MATH AND SCIENCES (biology, chemistry, computer science, mathematics, physics), PHILOSOPHY (philosophy), PREPROFESSIONAL (electronic technology, engineering), SOCIAL SCIENCES (criminal justice, economics, government/political science, history, psychology, sociology). About 29% of degrees conferred are in business, 10% are in education, 9% are in math and sciences, and 6% are in engineering.

Special: Joint majors are offered; interdisciplinary and student-designed majors are possible. Students may earn a B.A.-B.S., a 5-year B.A.-M.B.A., or a B.S. in Eng.-M.B.A. in special programs. Cross-registration at other area colleges increases study opportunities.

Honors: There are 3 honor societies on campus. Honors work is offered in several departments.

Admissions: About 79% of the applicants for the 1981–82 freshman class were offered admission. The SAT scores of those who enrolled were as follows: Verbal—71% below 500, 25% between 500 and 599, 4% above 600, and 0% above 700; Math—46% below 500, 40% between 500 and 599, 13% between 600 and 700, and 1% above 700. Other important factors include advanced placement or honors work, recommendations, and impressions made during the interview.

Procedure: The SAT or ACT should be taken by January of the senior year. Application deadlines are open (unless aid or housing is requested, then February 1 is the deadline). New students are admitted either semester. There is a $25 nonrefundable application fee. A rolling admissions plan is used.

Special: AP and CLEP credit is offered. There are early and deferred admissions plans.

Transfer: For fall 1981, 888 transfer students applied, 658 were accepted, and 333 enrolled. Thirty credits, of the 120 required for the bachelor's degree, must be completed in residence. A 2.25 GPA is required; D grades transfer only if part of an associate degree and with a 2.5 GPA. Deadlines are the same as for regular applications.

Visiting: There is a formal orientation program for freshmen and transfer students. Informal campus visits may be arranged; visitors may attend classes.

Financial Aid: About 79% of the students are receiving assistance through the university; 22% work part-time on campus. Aid is awarded in the following forms: scholarships, grants, loans, and part-time employment. Most freshman aid consists of a package; the average award is $3164. The university is a member of CSS, and the FAF is required by March 15.

Foreign Students: Foreign students comprise 6% of the full-time enrollment. The university offers these students an intensive English program and special counseling and organizations.

Admissions: A minimum score of 500 is required on the TOEFL. College entrance exams are not required.

Procedure: Application deadlines are August 1 (fall), and December 1 (spring). Foreign students must present proof of funds adequate to cover 1 year of study. They must also carry health insurance, which is available through the university for a fee.

Admissions Contact: Walter M. Bortz III, Director of Admissions.

UNIVERSITY OF NEW HAVEN C-3
West Haven, Connecticut 06516 (203) 934-6321

F/T: 1580M, 862W		Faculty:	144; IIA, +$
P/T: 1985M, 1129W		Ph.D.'s:	80%
Grad: 1684M, 783W		S/F Ratio:	17 to 1
Year: 4-1-4, ss		Tuition:	$4120
Appl: Aug. 15		R and B:	$2275
2119 applied	1777 accepted		552 enrolled
SAT: required			LESS COMPETITIVE

The University of New Haven, established in 1920, is an independent institution offering undergraduate programs in the liberal arts and sciences, business, engineering, and design. The library has 210,000 books and more than 6400 microfilm items, and subscribes to 1318 periodicals.

Environment: The 56-acre suburban campus is located 3 miles from downtown New Haven. The 13 buildings include a coed dormitory housing 200 students. The university also sponsors fraternity houses and off-campus apartments.

Student Life: About 75% of the students come from Connecticut and 85% come from public schools. About 44% live on campus. Sixteen percent of the students are minority-group members. Campus housing is both coed and single-sex; there are visiting privileges. Students may keep cars on campus.

Organizations: Extracurricular activities include mixers, a lecture and a film series, theater groups, and an arts festival. Students may participate in the campus radio station or the newspaper. There are 2 national fraternities and 2 local sororities to which 3% of the men and 7% of the women belong.

Sports: The university fields 9 intercollegiate teams for men and 5 for women. Nine intramural sports are offered for men and 8 for women.

Handicapped: About 98% of the campus is accessible to students with physical handicaps. Special facilities include wheelchair ramps, parking areas, elevators, and specially equipped restrooms. Special class scheduling is possible. The university makes special arrangements, including tutoring, for students with visual or hearing impairments.

Graduates: The freshman dropout rate is 22%; 46% remain to graduate. About 32% of the graduates go on for further education; about 9% go to law school. About 50% begin careers in business and industry.

Services: The following services are free to students: placement, career counseling, health care, psychological counseling, tutoring, and remedial instruction. Placement services also are available to alumni.

Programs of Study: The university confers the B.A. and B.S. degrees. Associate and master's degrees are also awarded. Bachelor's degrees are offered in the following subjects: BUSINESS (accounting, air transport management, business administration, communications, data processing, finance, hotel management, institutional food service, international business, management, marketing, operations management, personnel management, public administration, retailing, tourism and travel), ENGLISH (communications, English), FINE AND PERFORMING ARTS (biological illustration, art, fashion design, graphic and advertising design, interior design, music), MATH AND SCIENCES (applied math, biology, chemistry, ecology/environmental science, fire science, forensic science, mathematics, microbiology, physical sciences, physics), PREPROFESSIONAL (engineering—civil, engineering—electrical, engineering—industrial, engineering—materials, engineering—mechanical), SOCIAL SCIENCES (corrections, criminal justice, economics, government/political science, history, law enforcement science, occupational safety and health, psychology, social welfare, sociology).

Special: It is possible to earn combined B.A.-B.S. degrees.

Honors: Two honor societies are represented on campus. Honors work is offered in arts and sciences programs.

Admissions: About 84% of the applicants for the 1981–82 school year were accepted. Sixteen Carnegie credits are required. Advanced placement or honors courses and school recommendations are also considered.

Procedure: The SAT or the ACT should be taken by April of the senior year. There is a $15 nonrefundable application fee. Application deadlines are August 15 (fall) and January 15 (spring). Notification is made on a rolling basis.

Special: AP and CLEP credit is accepted. There is a deferred admissions plan.

Transfer: For fall 1981, 825 students applied, 653 were accepted, and 308 enrolled. A 2.0 GPA is required; an interview is recommended. D grades do not transfer. Thirty credits of the 120-132 credits required for a bachelor's degree must be completed in residence. The deadlines are the same as those for freshman applicants.

Visiting: Campus visits are encouraged; visitors may attend classes and tour the campus.

Financial Aid: About 65% of the students are receiving assistance. The university offers scholarships, federal and state loans, grants, and work-study. About 19% of the students work part-time on campus. The average award to freshmen from all sources was $3924 in 1981-82. Need is the main factor in determining aid. The FAF should be filed by May 1. The university is a member of CSS.

Foreign Students: About 9% of the students are from foreign countries. Special counseling and special organizations are available.

Admissions: Students must score at least 500 on the TOEFL. College entrance exams are not required.

Procedure: Applications should be submitted in July for fall entry and in November for spring entry. Students must present proof of adequate funds for 1 year. Health insurance is also required, and is available through the university for a fee.

Admissions Contact: David DuBuisson, Acting Dean of Admissions and Financial Aid.

WESLEYAN UNIVERSITY   C-3
Middletown, Connecticut 06457   (203) 347-9411

F/T: 1300M, 1210W   Faculty: 240; IIA, ++$
P/T: 5M, 5W   Ph.D.'s: 75%
Grad: 85M, 55W   S/F Ratio: 11 to 1
Year: sems   Tuition: $7350
Appl: Jan. 15   R and B: $2800
4488 applied   1479 accepted   679 enrolled
SAT: 640V 660M   MOST COMPETITIVE

Wesleyan University, founded in 1831, is a nonsectarian university offering undergraduate instruction in the liberal arts and sciences. The library has a collection of 900,000 books and 10,714 microfilm items, and subscribes to 2700 periodicals.

Environment: The 100-acre suburban campus is located 16 miles from Hartford. There are more than 80 buildings, including 24 dormitories and 10 fraternity houses, a science center, an arts complex, and recreation facilities. College housing also includes on- and off-campus apartments, and married student housing.

Student Life: About 60% of the students come from public schools. Eighty-four percent live in residence halls; 7% of the men reside in fraternity houses. Seventeen percent of the students are members of minority groups. Campus housing is both single-sex and coed, and there are visiting privileges in single-sex housing.

Organizations: Ten percent of the men belong to 1 of 3 local and 3 national fraternities; there are no sororities. Extracurricular activities are both traditional and innovative; students may participate in clubs, the university's radio stations, student government and publications, service organizations, cultural and social events held on campus, a debating society, and theatrical events.

Sports: Eighteen intercollegiate sports and 18 intramural sports are offered.

Handicapped: Special facilities for handicapped students include wheelchair ramps, parking areas, elevators, lowered drinking fountains and telephones, and specially equipped rest rooms. Special class scheduling is possible.

Graduates: The freshman dropout rate is 2%; about 91% remain to graduate. Of these, 60% go on for further education: 10% to medical school, 1% to dental school, and 18% to law school. About 20% go into business careers.

Services: Placement (undergraduates and alumni), career counseling, health care, and tutoring are offered free of charge to all students.

Programs of Study: The B.A. is awarded. Master's and doctoral programs are also offered. Bachelor's degrees are offered in the following subjects: AREA STUDIES (American, Asian, Black/Afro-American, Latin American, Russian, urban), ENGLISH (English, literature), FINE AND PERFORMING ARTS (art, art history, dance, film/photography, music, studio art, theater/dramatics), LANGUAGES (Chinese, French, German, Greek/Latin, Hebrew, Italian, Japanese, Russian, Spanish), MATH AND SCIENCES (astronomy, biochemistry, biology, chemistry, earth science, ecology/environmental science, geology, mathematics, physics), PHILOSOPHY (classics, humanities, philosophy, religion), SOCIAL SCIENCES (anthropology, economics, government/political science, history, international relations, psychology, social sciences, sociology). About 28% of degrees conferred are in math and sciences.

Special: Students may design their own majors. Independent study, study abroad, and a combination degree program in engineering with either Columbia University or California Institute of Technology are offered.

Honors: There are 2 honor societies on campus. Honors work is offered in all departments; students write an undergraduate thesis.

Admissions: About 30% of the applicants for the 1981-82 freshman class were accepted. About 87% of the current freshmen were in the upper fifth of their high school class. The SAT scores of those who enrolled were as follows: Verbal—8% scored below 500, 24% between 500 and 599, 47% between 600 and 700, and 20% above 700; Math—5% scored below 500, 20% between 500 and 599, 50% between 600 and 700, and 25% above 700. Also considered important are extracurricular activities, advanced placement or honors courses, recommendations, leadership, and personality. A personal interview is encouraged.

Procedure: The SAT and 3 ATs (including English Composition) or the ACT is required by January of the senior year. There is a $30 nonrefundable application fee. The application deadline for fall admission is January 15; notification is by the end of April. New students are admitted to all sessions.

Special: AP credit is available. There are early decision and deferred admissions plans.

Transfer: For fall 1981, 110 of the 500 transfer applicants were accepted; 80 enrolled. D grades do not transfer. Two years (4 semesters) must be taken in residence, totaling 16 course credits. Thirty-four course credits are required for the bachelor's degree. Applications for the fall semester are due March 1.

Visiting: There is a formal orientation program. Visitors may stay at the school and sit in on classes.

Financial Aid: Forty-one percent of the students receive assistance. The university offers scholarships, grants (federal and state), loans (federal, state, commercial, and short-term), and CWS. Sixty percent of students work part-time on campus. All awards are based on need. Average awards to freshmen include $4500 in scholarship, $2500 in loans, and $600 in work-study. The college is a member of CSS. The FAF should be filed by January 15.

Foreign Students: About 1% of full-time students come from foreign countries. The university offers these students an intensive English course, special counseling, and special organizations.

Admissions: Foreign students usually achieve a TOEFL score of 600. They must also take the SAT or ACT, and 3 ATs of their choice.

Procedure: Application deadlines are January 1 (fall) and November 1 (winter). Foreign students must provide proof of adequate funds. They must also carry health insurance, which is available through the university for a fee.

Admissions Contact: Karl M. Furstenberg, Dean of Admissions.

WESTERN CONNECTICUT STATE COLLEGE   A-3
Danbury, Connecticut 06810   (203) 797-4298

F/T: 1240M, 1675W   Faculty: 168; IIA, +$
P/T: 780M, 1185W   Ph.D.'s: 55%
Grad: 363M, 555W   S/F Ratio: 18 to 1
Year: sems, ss   Tuition: $766 ($1756)
Appl: Aug. 1   R and B: $1918
1833 applied   1266 accepted   673 enrolled
SAT: 430V 460M   COMPETITIVE

Western Connecticut State College, founded in 1903, offers undergraduate training in the liberal arts and sciences, education, the health professions, business, and preprofessional areas. The college's library has a collection of 115,000 books and 260,000 microforms, and subscribes to 13,000 periodicals.

Environment: The 350-acre suburban campus is located on the west side of Danbury, about 65 miles north of New York City. The Ancell School of Business is located here, along with a residence hall under construction. There are 9 buildings on the older 28-acre midtown campus. Dormitories and on-campus apartments are sponsored by the college.

Student Life: About 89% of the students come from Connecticut; 80% have had public school educations. About 57% of the students commute, 21% live in off-campus housing, and the remainder reside on campus. Campus housing is both coed and single-sex, and there are visiting privileges in single-sex housing. Students may keep cars on campus.

Organizations: Traditional extracurricular activities are offered. There is 1 fraternity, but no sororities.

Sports: The college fields 8 intercollegiate teams for men and 7 for women. There are 10 intramural sports for men and 10 for women.

Handicapped: About 85% of the campus is accessible to individuals with physical handicaps. Facilities include ramps, elevators, parking areas, and specially equipped rest rooms.

Graduates: About 25% of the freshmen drop out by the end of the first year; 49% remain to graduate. Forty percent go on for further education: 2% to medical and dental schools, and 5% to law schools. About 30% go directly into careers in business and industry.

Services: Placement, career counseling, health care, psychological counseling, tutoring, and remedial instruction are free to all students.

Programs of Study: The B.A., B.S., B.Mus., and B.B.A. are offered. Associate and master's degrees are also awarded. Bachelor's degrees are offered in the following subjects: BUSINESS (accounting, business administration, finance, management, management information systems, marketing), EDUCATION (early childhood, elementary, health/physical, music, secondary), ENGLISH (communication arts, English, speech, writing), FINE AND PERFORMING ARTS (graphic design, music, music education, theater/dramatics), HEALTH SCIENCES (medical technology, nursing), LANGUAGES (Spanish), MATH AND SCIENCES (biochemistry, biology, chemistry, earth science, earth science—biology, earth science—geology, mathematics), PREPROFESSIONAL (criminal justice, justice and law administration, law, library science, medicine, social work), SOCIAL SCIENCES (anthropology, economics, geography, government/political science, history, psychology, social sciences, social welfare, sociology). About 15% of the degrees conferred are in education.

Required: All students must complete a core curriculum.

Special: Study abroad is possible.

Honors: There are several honor societies for qualified students. The Ancell School of Business sponsors an honors program.

Admissions: About 69% of the applicants for the 1981-82 freshman class were accepted. The SAT scores of those who enrolled were as follows: Verbal—64% scored below 500, 35% between 500 and 599, and 1% between 600 and 700; Math—59% scored below 500, 40% between 500 and 599, and 1% between 600 and 700. Applicants should be in the top 70% of the high school class. Advanced placement or honor courses, leadership record, and impressions made during the interview are also considered.

Procedure: The SAT should be taken by December of the senior year. There is a $10 nonrefundable application fee. The application deadlines are August 1 for the fall and January 1 for the spring; notification is on a rolling basis.

Special: AP and CLEP credit is accepted. There are early decision, early admissions, and deferred admissions plans.

Transfer: For fall 1981, 1094 students applied, 823 were accepted, and 415 enrolled. A GPA of at least 2.0 and 12 completed credit hours are needed; D grades do not transfer unless part of an associate degree. All students must complete, at the college; 32 of the 120 credits required for a bachelor's degree. One half of the credits toward a major must be earned at the college. Application deadlines are the same as those for freshmen.

Visiting: There is a formal orientation program; informal campus visits may be arranged. Visitors may attend classes.

Financial Aid: About 65% of the students are receiving assistance. Eleven percent work part-time on campus. The average award to freshmen is $1500. Federal and state grants, loans, and work-study opportunities are available. The FAF, Institutional Application, and income tax form should be filed by April 30 for fall entry and December 1 for spring entry.

Foreign Students: One percent of the full-time students come from foreign countries. An intensive English course and special organizations are available to these students.

Admissions: Foreign students must achieve a TOEFL score of at least 500; foreign students applying as freshmen must achieve a combined score of 900 on the SAT.

Procedure: Application deadlines are June 1 (fall) and November 1 (spring). Foreign students must present proof of funds adequate to cover 1 year of study. They must also carry health insurance through the college; there is a fee.

Admissions Contact: Delmore Kinney, Jr., Director of Admissions.

CONNECTICUT 119

YALE UNIVERSITY C-3
New Haven, Connecticut 06520 (203) 436-0300

F/T: 2958M, 2170W Faculty: 1486; I, ++$
P/T: none Ph.D.'s: 100%
Grad: 2942M, 2015W S/F Ratio: n/av
Year: sems, ss Tuition: $7240
Appl: Jan. 2 R and B: $3190
11,254 applied 2186 accepted 1297 enrolled
SAT: 670V 690M MOST COMPETITIVE

Yale University, founded in 1701, is a private, independent, nonsectarian university. One of the very first colleges in the U.S., Yale is a member of the Ivy Group. All undergraduates are members of Yale College. Their studies fall into the 3 traditional liberal arts divisions: humanities, social sciences, and natural sciences. The campus library system has more than 8 million volumes and subscribes to 6000 current periodicals, and is one of the largest in the country. Sterling Memorial Library is perhaps the most important. There are also subsidiary libraries in each of the residential colleges, as well as specific professional and departmental libraries and specialized libraries for rare books and collections.

Environment: Yale has more than 675 acres of classrooms, laboratories, residential colleges, and playing fields. It occupies a substantial portion of New Haven, a city of about 140,000 people. Freshmen generally live in the Old Campus. Other undergraduates live in the 12 residential colleges.

Student Life: The students are from all sections of the country; 29% come from the middle Atlantic states, 17% from New England, 29% from the North Central, 15% from the South, 7% from the Rocky Mountain and Western area. About 60% come from public schools. About 89% live on campus. About 22% of the students are minority-group members. Campus housing is coed. Students may keep cars on campus. Day-care services are available to all students, faculty, and staff for a fee.

Organizations: Religious programs and organizations of many faiths are available on campus. All students are members of a residential college, the center of social life on campus. Students may participate in musical groups, dramatics, publications, and a variety of clubs.

Sports: There are 15 intercollegiate sports for men and 15 for women. There are 23 intramural sports for men and 20 for women.

Handicapped: Special facilities include wheelchair ramps, parking areas, elevators, lowered drinking fountains, desk telephones, and specially equipped rest rooms. Special class scheduling is also available. Fewer than 2% of students have visual or hearing impairments.

Graduates: One percent of the freshmen drop out by the end of their first year; 90% of those who begin graduate. About 50% of the graduates continue studies in graduate or professional schools; 13% enter medical school and 17% law school. About 20% pursue careers in business and industry.

Services: The following services are offered free of charge: placement, health care, psychological counseling, career counseling, and tutoring.

Programs of Study: The B.A. and B.S. degrees are offered. Master's and doctoral degrees are also awarded. Programs of study include: AREA STUDIES (American, Black/Afro-American, British, East Asian, Judaic, Latin American, Russian and East European), BUSINESS (administrative sciences, computer science), ENGLISH (English, comparative literature, literature), FINE AND PERFORMING ARTS (art, art history, music, theater/dramatics), LANGUAGES (Chinese, French, German, Greek/Latin, Italian, Japanese, Near Eastern, Portuguese, Russian, Spanish), MATH AND SCIENCES (applied mathematics, astronomy, biochemistry, biology, chemistry, geology, geophysics, mathematics, molecular biophyics, physics), PHILOSOPHY (classical civilization, classics, philosophy, religious studies), PREPROFESSIONAL (architecture, engineering), SOCIAL SCIENCES (anthropology, archeology, economics, government/political science, history, linguistics, psychology, sociology).

Required: Students must earn 36 course credits. At least 2 must be taken in each of 4 distributional groups by the end of the first 2 years, and 12 must be taken outside the distributional group that includes the major. The 4 groups are languages and literature; nonlanguage humanities; social sciences; and natural sciences, mathematics, and engineering.

Special: A Directed Studies program consists of a carefully organized combination of courses for freshmen and sophomores. A "Scholars of the House" program is available for seniors with distinguished records and ability who wish to work on approved independent projects. An Early Concentration program of small seminars is an option for freshmen. These seminars have an average of 6 students to a class. A 4-year

CONNECTICUT

B.A.-M.A. program may be undertaken by a few very talented students in certain fields. Combination majors are also available.

Honors: The numerous honor societies include Phi Beta Kappa.

Admissions: About 19% of those who applied were accepted for the 1981–82 freshman class. Of those who enrolled, the SAT scores were as follows: Verbal—4% below 500, 18% between 500 and 599, 41% between 600 and 700, and 37% above 700; Math—2% below 500, 14% between 500 and 599, 39% between 600 and 700, and 45% above 700. Yale stresses that no single factor can determine who should apply for admission. Most successful candidates rank in the top 10% of their high school class. Recommendations from academic teachers and other high school officials, high school grades, test scores, and advanced placement and honors courses are considered important by admissions officers. Students with fewer than 4 years of secondary school work may be considered, but applicants with deficiencies are at some disadvantage. Personal interviews, usually with alumni representatives near the student's home, are desirable.

Procedure: The SAT and 3 ATs are required. Students are advised to take them no later than December of their senior year. The application deadline is January 2. Notification is made in mid-April, and the CRDA is used. The application, transcript, recommendations, and test scores must be received by Yale before notification can be made. The application fee is $30.

Special: Early action, early admissions, and deferred admissions plans are available. AP credit is accepted.

Transfer: For fall 1981, 783 students applied, 99 were accepted, and 80 enrolled. Transfer students are accepted into the sophomore and junior classes only. Applicants must show acceptable grades on at least 1 full year of college work. SATs are required. Recommendations and an essay are also required. Students must complete, at the university, 18 of the 36 semester courses required for a bachelor's degree. Applications must be submitted by March 10 (fall). Spring entries are determined by the university.

Financial Aid: Thirty-seven percent of the students receive aid in the form of scholarships, long-term loans, and term-time employment. Yale assures that every student with determined financial need will receive adequate aid as long as he or she remains in good academic and personal standing. The college belongs to the CSS. The FAF should be filed and application made to the college by January 15 (fall).

Foreign Students: Six percent of the full-time students come from foreign countries. The university offers these students special counseling and special organizations.

Admissions: Foreign students must score at least 550 on the TOEFL; they must also take the SAT and any 3 ATs.

Procedure: The application deadline is January 2 (fall). Foreign students must carry health insurance, which is available through the university for a fee.

Admissions Contact: Worth David, Dean of Admissions.

DELAWARE

DELAWARE STATE COLLEGE B-3
Dover, Delaware 19901 (302) 736-4917

F/T: 719M, 900W
P/T: 207M, 211W
Grad: 35M, 56W
Year: sems, ss
Appl: June 1
1048 applied
SAT: 320V 350M

Faculty: 138; IIB, ++$
Ph.D.'s: n/av
S/F Ratio: 12 to 1
Tuition: $595 ($1495)
R and B: $1770
768 accepted   431 enrolled
LESS COMPETITIVE

Delaware State College, established in 1891, is a state-supported institution offering undergraduate programs in the arts and sciences, education, business, and a variety of other fields. The library contains 65,000 volumes and 1000 microfilm items, and subscribes to 500 periodicals.

Environment: The 300-acre campus is located in a suburban area 2 miles from Dover's business section and 45 miles from Wilmington. Five dormitories accommodate 735 men and women. There are facilities for commuting students.

Student Life: About 75% of the students come from Delaware; 95% come from public schools. About 48% of the students live on campus. About 66% are minority-group members. Campus housing is single-sex; there are visiting privileges. Students may keep cars on campus. Alcohol is not permitted on campus.

Organizations: Extracurricular activities include student government, clubs, 3 sororities and 4 fraternities (to which 5% of the students belong), and social events.

Sports: Intercollegiate competition is offered in 7 sports for men and 4 for women. There are 4 intramural sports for men and 4 for women.

Graduates: About 20–25% of entering freshmen drop out by the end of the first year; 65–70% remain to graduate.

Services: Placement, career counseling, tutoring, and remedial instruction are provided free of charge. Health care is offered on a fee basis.

Programs of Study: The college confers B.A. and B.S. degrees. Master's degrees are also awarded. Bachelor's degrees are offered in the following subjects: BUSINESS (accounting, business administration, business education, distributive education, economics, secretarial science), EDUCATION (early childhood, elementary, occupational, science), ENGLISH (English, English education), FINE AND PERFORMING ARTS (art, art education, music), HEALTH SCIENCES (nursing), LANGUAGES (French, Spanish), MATH AND SCIENCES (biology, botany, chemistry, computer science, mathematics, physics), PREPROFESSIONAL (agriculture, medicine, social work, veterinary), SOCIAL SCIENCES (history, psychology, sociology).

Required: There is a general education requirement for all students.

Special: There is a 3-2 combination degree program in engineering.

Honors: There is an honors program for outstanding students.

Admissions: About 73% of those who applied were accepted for the 1981–82 freshman class. The SAT scores of those who enrolled were as follows: Verbal—90% below 500, 10% between 500 and 599, 0% between 600 and 700, and 0% above 700; Math—90% below 500, 10% between 500 and 599, 0% between 600 and 700, and 0% above 700. Students must be graduates of accredited high schools, have at least a 2.0 average, and have completed 15 units of academic work. Residents of Delaware get preference; no more than 25% of the students may be from out of state. Advanced placement or honors courses, the applicant's personality, and recommendations are considered important.

Procedure: The SAT or ACT is required and is used for placement purposes. June 1 is the application deadline for fall admission; December 1, for spring admission. There is a $10 application fee.

Special: There is an early admissions plan. CLEP and AP credit is available.

Transfer: A 2.0 GPA is recommended; D grades do not transfer. Delaware residents are given preference. All students must complete, at the college, 30 of the 126 credits required for a bachelor's degree. Application deadlines are the same as those for freshmen.

Visiting: Campus tours with student guides may be arranged; visitors may sit in on classes.

Financial Aid: About 50% of the students receive aid. Ten percent work part-time on campus. The college offers freshman scholarships, loans (commercial and government, including NDSL), grants (such as BEOG and SEOG), and part-time campus work opportunities (including CWS in most areas). The FFS or FAF should be submitted by June 1. The college is a member of CSS.

Foreign Students: Special counseling and special organizations are available for students from foreign countries.

Admissions: Foreign students must achieve a TOEFL score of at least 400. No college entrance exams are required.

Procedure: Application deadlines are the same as those for other students. Foreign students must present proof of funds adequate to cover 4 years of study. Health insurance is required and is available through the college for a fee.

Admissions Contact: Jethro C. Williams, Director of Admissions.

GOLDEY BEACOM COLLEGE B-1
Wilmington, Delaware 19808 (302) 998-8814

F/T: 199M, 669W
P/T: 280M, 654W
Grad: none
Year: 4-1-4, ss
Appl: open
653 applied
SAT: recommended

Faculty: 21; III, –$
Ph.D.'s: 0%
S/F Ratio: 35 to 1
Tuition: $2620
R: $1500
542 accepted   434 enrolled
LESS COMPETITIVE

Goldey Beacom College, established in 1971 by the merger of Goldey College and Beacom College, is an independent coeducational institution specializing in business programs. The library contains 10,000 volumes, and subscribes to 200 periodicals.

Environment: The campus is located in Pike Creek Valley in the suburbs of Wilmington. On- and off-campus apartments are sponsored by the college.

Student Life: Twelve percent are minority-group members. About 25% of the students live on campus. Campus housing is coed; 3 apartment-style residence halls accommodate 4 students per apartment; each apartment has a kitchen. Students may keep cars on campus.

Organizations: Three fraternities and 2 sororities are represented on campus. Extracurricular activities include special-interest groups, publications, music activities, and religious groups. A college van transports resident students to local grocery stores and shopping centers on a weekly basis.

Sports: There are 5 intramural sports for men and 4 for women. No intercollegiate sports are offered.

Handicapped: Special class scheduling and special residence hall facilities are available for physically handicapped students.

Graduates: About 14% of entering freshmen drop out by the end of the first year; 80% remain to graduate. Twelve percent of the graduates pursue advanced degrees. About 76% enter business and industry.

Services: Career counseling and tutoring are available to students free of charge. Placement, health care, psychological counseling, and remedial instruction are available and may require payment.

Programs of Study: The college offers the B.S.B.A. degree. Associate degrees are also awarded. Bachelor's degrees are available in the following subjects: BUSINESS (accounting, business administration, business education, computer science, management, office administration).

Required: Students must earn a GPA of 2.0 or better to graduate.

Special: Students may work for 2 degrees at the same time.

Honors: Academic awards and prizes are available, and students may earn their degrees with honors.

Admissions: About 83% of those who applied were accepted for the 1981–82 freshman class. The SAT scores of those who enrolled were as follows: Verbal—90% below 500, 10% between 500 and 599, 0% between 600 and 700, and 0% above 700; Math—90% below 500, 10% between 500 and 599, 0% between 600 and 700, and 0% above 700. A high school diploma or GED is required. Applicants should rank in the upper 60% of their high school class and should have a GPA of at least 2.0. Recommendations are also considered important.

Procedure: Degree candidates should take the SAT. A $20 application fee is required. Deadlines are open; freshmen are admitted to all 4 semesters. Applicants will be notified of the admissions decision within 3 weeks after the high school record is received.

Special: An early admissions plan is available.

Transfer: For fall 1981, 98 students applied, 90 were accepted, and 82 enrolled. A minimum GPA of 2.0 is required. C grades or better transfer. Students must earn 31-35 of the 124-128 semester hours required for a bachelor's degree at the college. There are no application deadlines; a rolling admissions plan is used.

Visits: Campus visits can be arranged weekdays and Saturday mornings through the admissions office.

Financial Aid: About 52% of the students receive aid through the college. Six percent work part-time on campus. The average freshman award is $1184. The college is a member of CSS. Aid is available in the form of college and private scholarships, federal and state grants and loans, and campus employment. The FAF and the college application form must be filed.

Foreign Students: About 2% of the full-time students come from foreign countries. Special counseling and special organizations are available for these students.

Admissions: Foreign students must achieve a TOEFL score of at least 500 and must take a comparative guidance and placement test.

Procedure: There are no application deadlines; foreign students are admitted to all 4 terms. They must present proof of adequate funds.

Admissions Contact: Margaret Juhl, Vice President and Dean of Admissions.

DELAWARE 121

UNIVERSITY OF DELAWARE A–1
Newark, Delaware 19711 (302) 738-8123

F/T: 5441M, 6917W	Faculty: 800; I, av$
P/T: 374M, 642W	Ph.D.'s: 75%
Grad: 1020M, 940W	S/F Ratio: 17 to 1
Year: 4-1-4, ss	Tuition: $1160 ($2900)
Appl: Mar. 1	R and B: $2146 ($2246)
10,956 applied 5804 accepted	2932 enrolled
SAT: required	COMPETITIVE

University of Delaware, established in 1743, is a privately controlled, land-grant, state-supported university. Undergraduate degrees are offered by the colleges of Agricultural Sciences, Arts and Sciences, Business and Economics, Engineering, Education, Human Resources, Nursing, and Physical Education, Athletics and Recreation. The university's libraries contain 1.7 million volumes and microfilm items, and subscribe to 13,500 periodicals.

Environment: The 1565-acre campus is located in a suburban residential community 14 miles from Wilmington. The university has 130 major academic buildings and also owns a 360-acre marine-studies station in Lewes and an agricultural experimental station in Georgetown. Living facilities include dormitories, married student housing, fraternity houses, and on- and off-campus apartments.

Student Life: About 71% of the students are from Delaware. About 69% of the freshmen come from public schools. About 41% live on campus. Four percent are minority-group members. Campus housing is both coed and single-sex; there are visiting privileges in the single-sex housing.

Organizations: About 9% of the men belong to 1 of the 15 local and 15 national fraternities; 2% of the women belong to 1 of the 6 local sororities. Extracurricular activities include student government.

Sports: The university competes in 11 intercollegiate sports for men and 9 for women. There are 15 intramural sports for men and 15 for women.

Handicapped: Nearly all of the campus is accessible to physically handicapped students. Special facilities include wheelchair ramps, parking areas, elevators, lowered drinking fountains and telephones, and specially equipped rest rooms. Special class scheduling also is available.

Graduates: The freshman dropout rate is 3%; 85% of entering freshmen remain to graduate. About 32% of the graduates pursue advanced degrees, including 2% who enter medical school, 1% who enter dental school, and 3% who enter law school.

Services: Placement and career counseling services are provided free to students and graduates. Psychological counseling is available free to students, and health care, tutoring, and remedial instruction are offered on a fee basis.

Programs of Study: The university awards the B.A., B.A.S., B.S.Ag., B.F.A., B.L.S., B.S.B.A., B.S.B.E., B.S.Ed., B.C.E., B.E.E., B.E.S., B.M.E., B.S., B.S.Ch.E., B.S.N., and B.S.P.E. degrees among others. Associate, master's, and doctoral degrees also are available. Bachelor's degrees are offered in the following subjects: AREA STUDIES (American), BUSINESS (accounting, business administration, computer science, consumer economics, textile/clothing merchandising), EDUCATION (agriculture, educational studies, elementary, health/physical, secondary, special), ENGLISH (English, journalism, literature), FINE AND PERFORMING ARTS (art, art education, art history, design, music, music education, theater/dramatics), HEALTH SCIENCES (dietetics, food science, medical technology, nursing, nutritional sciences, physical therapy), LANGUAGES (French, German, Greek/Latin, Russian, Spanish), MATH AND SCIENCES (biological science, chemistry, entomology, geology, geophysics, mathematics, physics, plant science, statistics, textile/clothing technology), PHILOSOPHY (classics, philosophy), PREPROFESSIONAL (animal science, engineering—agricultural, engineering—chemical, engineering—civil, engineering—electrical, engineering—mechanical), SOCIAL SCIENCES (anthropology, communication, criminal justice, economics, economics—agricultural, economics—consumer, geography, government/political science, history, home economics, international relations, psychology, sociology). Twenty-three percent of the undergraduate degrees are conferred in business, 16% in preprofessional programs, and 14% in social sciences.

Required: All students must take freshman English.

Special: Students may design their own majors or earn five-year combined B.A.-B.S. degrees in a variety of subjects. Interdepartmental, double, and general-studies majors also are available. Undergraduates may take courses in ocean engineering, marine biology, and related fields although these are not undergraduate majors.

122 DELAWARE

Honors: Twenty-one honor societies are represented on campus. Most honors courses are offered within the College of Arts and Sciences, but students may participate regardless of their major.

Admissions: Of those who applied for admission to the 1981-82 freshman class, 53% were accepted. Applicants should have completed at least 15 Carnegie units and should have a GPA of at least 2.0. The primary factors influencing admission are an A or B average in required preparatory courses, SAT scores, and high school grades. Admissions offices also consider advanced placement or honors courses, extracurricular activities, and evidence of special talents. Out-of-state students are accepted on a competitive basis.

Procedure: The SAT should be taken in the junior year or in November or December of the senior year. Candidates are encouraged to take ATs in their areas of academic interest. The application, a $20 fee, and the high school record should be submitted by March 1 (fall) or November 15 (spring). Delaware residents applying for fall admission are notified 6 weeks after credentials are received; out-of-state residents are notified by April 15.

Special: An early admissions plan is available. AP credit is accepted.

Transfer: For fall 1981, 1604 students applied, 773 were accepted, and 509 enrolled. State residents must have at least a C average; nonresidents must have at least a B average. D grades do not transfer. All students must complete, at the university, 30 of the 124-132 credits required for a bachelor's degree. Application deadlines are the same as those for freshmen. There is an additional $10 transcript evaluation fee for transfer students.

Visiting: The university holds campus tours for prospective students. Guides also are available for informal campus visits Mondays through Fridays. Arrangements should be made with the admissions office.

Financial Aid: About 70% of the students receive aid. Twenty percent work part-time on campus. The average freshman award is $3000. In 1981-82, more than 7500 students received in excess of $14 million in scholarships, loans, grants, and university-assigned jobs. Federal programs available to students include GSL, NDSL, SEOG, CWS, BEOG, and NSL. Some students receive funds through programs sponsored by the state, private corporations, civic organizations, and the university. Most aid awards are based on financial need, but a number of grants based on academic achievement are available. The FAF and the IRS 1040 must be filed before May 1.

Foreign Students: About 2% of the full-time students come from foreign countries. An intensive English course, an intensive English program, special counseling, and special organizations are available for these students.

Admissions: Foreign students must achieve a TOEFL score of at least 500 and must take the SAT.

Procedure: Application deadlines are the same as those for other students. Foreign students must present proof of funds adequate to cover 1 year of study. Health insurance is required and is available through the university for a fee.

Admissions Contact: Douglas McConkey, Dean of Admissions.

WESLEY COLLEGE B-3
Dover, Delaware 19901 (302) 736-2438

F/T: 271M, 350W	Faculty:	48; IIB, av$
P/T: 647M, 719W	Ph.D.'s:	6%
Grad: none	S/F Ratio:	13 to 1
Year: sems, ss	Tuition:	$4640
Appl: open	R and B:	$2230
883 applied	648 accepted	348 enrolled
SAT: 440V 430M		COMPETITIVE

Wesley College, founded in 1873, is an independent institution affiliated with the United Methodist Church. The college offers 2- and 4-year degrees. The library contains more than 40,000 volumes.

Environment: The 12-acre campus is located in a suburban area of Dover, a town of 32,500 people 45 miles from Wilmington. Campus buildings include a science center, a gymnasium, and a nursing building. Students are housed in 6 residence halls, including a converted mansion.

Student Life: About 25% of the students are Delaware residents, and 25% live on campus. Full-time unmarried students under 21 generally are required to live in college dormitories, which are single-sex and have visiting privileges. Freshmen are allowed to live off campus. Students may keep cars on campus. Eight percent of the students are minority-group members.

Organizations: Extracurricular activities include publications, special-interest and religious clubs, musical activities, and student government, which schedules dances, concerts, and other social events.

Sports: The college fields intercollegiate teams in 4 sports for men and 4 for women. Intramural sports for men and women include flag football, basketball, softball, precision swimming, and volleyball.

Graduates: About 23% of the freshmen drop out, and 65% remain to graduate. Eighty percent of the graduates continue their education.

Services: The following free services are available to students: health care, tutoring, remedial instruction, career counseling, and placement.

Programs of Study: The college awards the B.S. degree. Associate degrees are also awarded. Bachelor's degrees are offered in the following subjects: BUSINESS (business administration, management, marketing), HEALTH SCIENCES (medical technology, environmental sciences).

Required: All degree candidates must complete 2 courses in physical education and at least 1 in religion. Students are expected to come to every class meeting and to attend the college convocation series regularly.

Special: The college has a direct transfer agreement with 40 other institutions: A.A. candidates are automatically accepted at one of those institutions at the recommendation of Wesley College officials. Cooperative education and developmental academic skills programs are available.

Honors: A number of honor societies are represented on campus. Students may earn degrees with honors.

Admissions: About 73% of those who applied were accepted for the 1981-82 freshman class. Candidates must have completed 16 units of high school work. The high school record, impressions made during an interview, and recommendations by high school officials are considered important.

Procedure: Applicants must take the SAT. An interview is recommended. There is a $15 application fee. Notification is made on a rolling basis. Applications for fall admission should be submitted by July 1, but may be accepted after that date. Early decision candidates should apply by November 1 and are notified by December 1.

Special: Early decision, early admissions and deferred admissions plans are available. CLEP and AP credit is accepted.

Transfer: For fall 1981, 60 transfer students applied, 48 were accepted, and 28 enrolled. A 2.0 GPA is required. D grades do not transfer. Applicants must present a letter of honorable dismissal from their last college. Transfers must complete, at the college, 30 of the 127 credits required for a bachelor's degree. Application deadlines are the same as those for freshmen.

Visiting: Prospective students should schedule visits through the admissions office. Visits may be arranged for Mondays through Saturdays.

Financial Aid: About 58% of the students receive aid in the form of scholarships, loans, grants, or campus jobs. Thirty-five percent work part-time on campus. Honor scholarships are available. The average award to freshmen from all sources is $1400. Aid applications should be submitted by April 15. The college is a member of CSS. The FAF or SFS is required.

Foreign Students: One percent of the full-time students come from foreign countries. The college offers these students special counseling.

Admissions: Foreign students must achieve a minimum score of 450 on the TOEFL. College entrance exams are not required.

Procedure: Application deadlines are May 15 (fall) and November 15 (winter). Foreign students must present proof of health and carry health insurance.

Admissions Contact: Maija S. Mason, Dean of Admissions.

WILMINGTON COLLEGE B-1
New Castle, Delaware 19720 (302) 328-9401

F/T: 325 M&W	Faculty:	n/av; IIA, n/av
P/T: 550 M&W	Ph.D.'s:	29%
Grad: 100 M&W	S/F Ratio:	14 to 1
Year: 4-1-4, ss	Tuition:	$2900
Appl: open	R:	$1200
313 applied	295 accepted	176 enrolled
SAT or ACT: not required		LESS COMPETITIVE

Wilmington College, founded in 1967, is a private liberal arts institution. The library contains 60,000 volumes and 800 microfilm items, and subscribes to 260 periodicals.

Environment: The 15-acre campus is located in a small, suburban town 6 miles from Wilmington. The college has 15 buildings and some athletic facilities including basketball courts and soccer fields. A limited amount of on-campus housing is available.

Student Life: The Student Affairs Office helps students find off-campus housing; there are modern apartments within walking distance of campus. Students who wish to apply for on-campus housing should notify the Student Affairs Office as soon as possible.

Organizations: There are professional fraternities and sororities. The college sponsors extracurricular events and activities, the most popular of which are the Aviation Club, the Communication Arts Society, the student newspaper, and student government.

Sports: The college fields 2 intercollegiate teams for men and 1 team for women. There are 4 intramural sports for men and 4 for women.

Handicapped: The entire campus is accessible to handicapped students. Facilities include wheelchair ramps and special parking areas. Fewer than 1% of the students have visual impairments. No special counselors are available.

Graduates: About 25% of the freshmen drop out. Of those who graduate, about 25% pursue advanced degrees, including about 5% who enter law school. About 50% of the graduates pursue careers in business and industry.

Services: Placement, career counseling, tutoring, and remedial instruction are provided free to students.

Programs of Study: The college confers the B.A., B.S., and B.B.A. degrees. Associate and master's degrees also are available. Bachelor's degrees are offered in the following subjects: BUSINESS (accounting, advertising production, aviation management, business administration, hotel/motel management, management), EDUCATION (early childhood, parenting), ENGLISH (communication arts), FINE AND PERFORMING ARTS (film/photography, radio/TV), PREPROFESSIONAL (social work), SOCIAL SCIENCES (criminal justice, psychology, sociology). Sixty percent of the undergraduate degrees are conferred in business, 30% in social sciences, and 10% in fine and performing arts.

Required: All undergraduates must take courses in mathematics, English, science, behavioral science, history, and humanities.

Special: The college offers supportive services for students with an inadequate academic background in English and/or mathematics. The Applied Professions program is designed for students graduating with technical degrees from community colleges. The Professional Arts program is for nurses with their R.N. license who wish to continue their education in the areas of behavioral science, business administration, or supervisory management.

Admissions: Ninety-four percent of those who applied were accepted for the 1981–82 freshman class. Candidates must be graduates of an accredited high school. Recommendations by high school officials also are considered important.

Procedure: Applications are accepted through final registration. Freshmen are admitted to the fall, winter, spring, and summer sessions. There is an application fee of $20.

Special: AP and CLEP credit is accepted. Credits may be earned for experiential learning when evaluated by the college.

Transfer: About 275 transfer students enroll each year. A GPA of at least 2.0 is necessary. All students must complete, at the college, 45 of the 120 credits required for a bachelor's degree.

Visiting: Guides are provided for informal visits by prospective students. Appointments should be made with the admissions office.

Financial Aid: Recently, about 40% of the students received aid. Most departments have CWS funds, and various partial and full scholarships are available. The college is a member of the CSS. Aid applicants should submit the FAF or FFS and contact the college's financial aid office for further information.

Foreign Students: Special counseling is available for students from foreign countries.

Admissions: Foreign students must take the TOEFL and the SAT or ACT.

Procedure: There are no application deadlines. Foreign students must present proof of adequate funds.

Admissions Contact: Arthur E. Landgren, Director of Admissions.

DISTRICT OF COLUMBIA

AMERICAN UNIVERSITY   A-2
Washington, D.C. 20016   (202) 686-2211

F/T: 2072M, 2455W	Faculty:	373; I, +$
P/T: 502M, 631W	Ph.D.'s:	69%
Grad: 3651M, 5321W	S/F Ratio:	12 to 1
Year: sems, ss	Tuition:	$5310
Appl: Feb. 1	R and B:	$2670
3876 applied	2527 accepted	807 enrolled
SAT or ACT: required		COMPETITIVE

American University, founded in 1893, is a private institution affiliated with the United Methodist Church. Its divisions are the colleges of Arts and Sciences, Public and International Affairs, and Business Administration; the School of Nursing; and the Washington College of Law. The library contains 510,960 volumes and 111,312 microfilm items, and subscribes to 6000 periodicals.

Environment: The 74-acre suburban campus is located 5 miles from downtown Washington. Living facilities include dormitories and off-campus apartments.

Student Life: About 76% of the students come from the Middle Atlantic states, and most are graduates of public schools. Fifty percent of the undergraduate students live on campus. About 16% are minority-group members. Campus housing is both coed and single-sex; there are visiting privileges in the single-sex housing. Day-care services are available to all students for a fee. Seniors, juniors, sophomores, and commuting freshmen may obtain parking permits.

Organizations: About 6% of the students belong to 1 of 11 fraternities and sororities. Student organizations include theater groups, a choir, an orchestra, special-interest clubs, a newspaper, and student government. Recreational and cultural facilities in the Washington area are easy to reach.

Sports: The university fields intercollegiate teams in 7 sports for men and 5 for women. There are 7 intramural sports for men and 6 for women.

Handicapped: Special facilities available for physically handicapped students include wheelchair ramps, special parking, elevators, and lowered drinking fountains and telephones. About 65 handicapped students were enrolled in 1981–82. A special counselor is provided for such students.

Graduates: About 52% of entering freshmen remain to graduate.

Services: The following services are available free to students: tutoring; remedial instruction; health care; and psychological, career, and placement counseling.

Programs of Study: The university awards the B.A. and B.S. degrees. Associate, master's, and doctoral degrees also are available. Bachelor's degrees are offered in the following subjects: AREA STUDIES (American, Latin American, Russian, urban, West European), BUSINESS (accounting, business economics, computer science, finance, international business, management, marketing, real estate/insurance), EDUCATION (early childhood, elementary, secondary, special), ENGLISH (cinema studies, journalism, literature), FINE AND PERFORMING ARTS (art, art education, art history, dance, design, music, music education, studio art, theater/dramatics), HEALTH SCIENCES (medical technology, nursing), LANGUAGES (French, German, Russian, Spanish), MATH AND SCIENCES (biology, chemistry, computer science, mathematics, physics, statistics), PHILOSOPHY (philosophy, religion), PREPROFESSIONAL (dentistry, law, medicine), SOCIAL SCIENCES (anthropology, economics, government/political science, history, justice, law and society, psychology, sociology). A preprofessional program in engineering is available only as a second major. The most popular fields of study are international studies, business, social sciences, and communication.

Required: All students are required to take English composition and reading or an approved substitute.

Special: There is a pass/fail option program for courses outside the major. An independent study program, interdisciplinary studies, and opportunities for foreign study are available. A general studies degree is offered. Students may design their own majors. Combined B.S.-M.A. programs are offered in mathematics, applied mathematics, mathematics and statistics, and psychology. Combined B.S.-M.S. programs are offered in computer science, mathematics, and political science and public administration. A B.A.-M.A. degree is offered in anthropology.

DISTRICT OF COLUMBIA

Honors: The College of Arts and Sciences offers an honors curriculum. Departments with honors programs include history, government, chemistry, music, and communications. About 10 honor societies are represented on campus.

Admissions: About 65% of those who applied were accepted for the 1981–82 freshman class. The SAT scores of those who enrolled were as follows: Verbal—70% below 500, 14% between 500 and 599, 10% between 600 and 700, and 2% above 700; Math—48% below 500, 39% between 500 and 599, 12% between 600 and 700, and 1% above 700. Applicants should rank in the upper half of their graduating class, present an average of at least 2.0, and have completed at least 15 Carnegie units. Admissions officers also consider recommendations from high school officials, test results, and pattern of academic performance.

Procedure: The SAT or ACT is required and should be taken in May of the junior year or in December or January of the senior year. The English composition AT also is required, and mathematics and foreign language ATs are recommended. The application, a $20 fee (which may be waived in cases of financial need when requested by a high school counselor), high school record, and test scores should be submitted by February 1 (fall), December 1 (spring), or April 15 (summer). Applicants are notified on a rolling basis, and those who plan to attend must reply by May 1.

Special: Early decision, early admissions, and deferred admissions plans are available. CLEP credit is accepted.

Transfer: For fall 1981, 1507 applications were received, 1156 were accepted, and 596 students enrolled. Applicants must have a GPA of at least 2.0. Those with an associate degree may transfer up to 75 hours; those without a degree may transfer grades of C or better up to 60 hours. All students must complete, at the university, 30 of the 120 credits required for a bachelor's degree. Application deadlines are March 1 (fall), November 1 (spring), and March 1 (summer).

Visiting: Guides are provided for informal visits. Visitors may sit in on classes and might be able to spend the night on campus. Arrangements should be made through the admissions office.

Financial Aid: About 60% of the students receive aid through the university. The university provides scholarships, loans, and part-time employment. The university participates in all federal loan, grant, and work-study programs. Tuition may be paid in installments. Aid is awarded on the basis of financial need and academic record. Aid applications and the FAF must be filed by March 1 (summer or fall) or November 1 (spring). The university is a member of CSS.

Foreign Students: Thirteen percent of the full-time students come from foreign countries. An intensive English course, an intensive English program, special counseling, and special organizations are available for these students.

Admissions: Foreign students must achieve a TOEFL score of at least 600 and must take the university's own English proficiency exam. The SAT is required if the student's education is similar to that of U.S. students.

Procedure: Application deadlines are June 1 (fall), October 15 (spring), and March 15 (summer). Foreign students must submit a physician's health report and must present proof of funds adequate to cover the entire period of study. Health insurance is required and is available through the university for a fee.

Admissions Contact: Jennifer Hantho, Director of Admissions.

BEACON COLLEGE
Washington, D.C. 20009   (202) 797-9270

F/T: 17M, 19W   Faculty: 0; n/av
P/T: 3M, 1W   Ph.D.'s: n/app
Grad: 42M, 85W   S/F Ratio: n/app
Year: terms   Tuition: $2450
Appl: open   R and B: n/app
190 applied   145 accepted   127 enrolled
SAT or ACT: not required   **LESS COMPETITIVE**

Beacon College, founded in 1971, is an independent, liberal arts institution that offers a unique program of individualized education.

Environment: The college has no traditional campus; no living facilities are sponsored.

Student Life: Thirty-three percent of the students are minority-group members.

Handicapped: There are no services for the handicapped.

Graduates: Sixty-five percent of the full-time students pursue advanced study after graduation.

Programs of Study: The college confers the bachelor's degree. Associate and master's degrees are also awarded. Bachelor's degrees are offered in the following subjects: AREA STUDIES (American, Black/Afro-American), BUSINESS (business education, management), EDUCATION (adult, early childhood), ENGLISH (English, journalism), FINE AND PERFORMING ARTS (art education, art history), HEALTH SCIENCES (environmental health), PHILOSOPHY (humanities).

Special: All students design their own curriculum plan and work closely with a program adviser. Students use the community for instruction and resource materials. Study-abroad programs are available.

Admissions: Seventy-six percent of those who applied were accepted for the 1981–82 freshman class. Factors that enter into the admissions decision include leadership record, personality, recommendations by school officials, extracurricular activities record, and advanced placement or honor courses.

Procedure: Entrance exams are not required. Students are admitted to the fall, winter, spring, and summer terms; a rolling admissions policy is used. There is a $50 application fee.

Transfer: For fall 1981, 25 transfer students applied, all were accepted, and 21 enrolled. Transfers must submit a writing sample, schedule an interview, and be approved by a program adviser. C– grades or better transfer. A minimum of 30 of 124 credits required for a bachelor's degree must be completed at the college. Transfers are considered for all classes. Junior status is automatically granted if the applicant has an associate degree. Application deadlines are open.

Visiting: No regularly scheduled orientations are available. Call the admissions director for information.

Financial Aid: Eighty-nine percent of the students receive aid through the college; 21% hold part-time employment. The FAF or FFS is required. Deadlines for financial aid application are August (fall), September (winter), March 15 (spring), and May 31 (summer).

Foreign Students: Fewer than 1% of the full-time students come from foreign countries.

Admissions: English proficiency exams and college entrance exams are not required.

Procedure: Application deadlines are open; a rolling admissions policy is followed. Foreign students are admitted to all terms. Proof of funds adequate to cover study at the college is required.

Admissions Contact: Ursula Poetzschke, Admissions Director.

CATHOLIC UNIVERSITY OF AMERICA   C-2
Washington, D.C. 20064   (202) 635-5305

F/T: 1294M, 1397W   Faculty: 400; I, – – $
P/T: 92M, 118W   Ph.D.'s: 90%
Grad: 2441M, 2256W   S/F Ratio: 7 to 1
Year: sems, ss   Tuition: $5005
Appl: Aug. 1   R and B: $2800
3620 applied   1800 accepted   700 enrolled
SAT: 520V 550M   **VERY COMPETITIVE**

Catholic University of America, founded in 1887, is the national university of the Catholic Church in America. The university is composed of the schools of Arts and Sciences, Education, Engineering and Architecture, Law, Library Information and Science, Music, Nursing, Philosophy, Religious Studies, and Social Service, and University College. The library contains more than 1 million volumes.

Environment: The 190-acre campus is located in a suburban area of northeast Washington. Its 62 buildings include 14 dormitories. Off-campus apartments are also available.

Student Life: About 30% of the students are from the Washington area; others are from 40 states and 50 foreign countries. About 80% of the students live on campus. Twelve percent of the students are minority-group members. About 89% are Catholic and 9% are Protestant. Campus housing is both coed and single-sex. There are visiting privileges in single-sex dorms. Students may keep cars on campus.

Organizations: About 30% of the students belong to 1 of 6 fraternities and 3 sororities. The student government and some of the more than 60 social and professional groups on campus sponsor social and cultural programs. Many activities are available in the city of Washington.

Sports: The university competes in 8 intercollegiate sports for men and 8 for women. There are 6 intramural sports for men and 6 for women.

Handicapped: Facilities for physically handicapped students include wheelchair ramps, elevators, special parking, and special class scheduling.

Graduates: Five percent of the freshmen drop out by the end of the first year; 80% remain to graduate. About 60% of the graduates seek advanced degrees; 4% enter medical school, 1% dental school, and 10% law school. About 25% enter business and industry.

Services: Free health care, tutoring, remedial instruction, placement, and psychological and career counseling are available to students.

Programs of Study: The university awards the B.A., B.S., B.S.N., B.Arch., B.E.E., B.F.A., B.C.E., B.M.E., B.S. in Eng., and B.Mus. degrees. Master's and doctoral programs are also offered. Bachelor's degrees are offered in the following subjects: AREA STUDIES (American, Latin American, urban), BUSINESS (accounting, business administration, computer science, finance, human resource management, management, marketing, quantitative management), EDUCATION (early childhood, elementary, secondary, special), ENGLISH (English, literature, speech), FINE AND PERFORMING ARTS (art, music, music composition, music education—choral, music education—combined general choral and instrumental, music education—instrumental, music performance, music therapy, studio art, theater/dramatics), HEALTH SCIENCES (medical technology, nursing), LANGUAGES (French, German, Greek/Latin, Italian, Semitic, Spanish), MATH AND SCIENCES (biochemistry, biology, chemical physics, chemistry, ecology/environmental chemistry, mathematics, oceanography, physics), PHILOSOPHY (classics, humanities, philosophy, religion), PREPROFESSIONAL (architecture, bioengineering, dentistry, engineering—chemical, engineering—civil, engineering—electrical, engineering—mechanical, engineering—nuclear, law, library science, medicine, ministry, social work, veterinary), SOCIAL SCIENCES (anthropology, economics, government/political science, history, international relations, medieval/Renaissance studies, psychology, sociology). About 57% of the degrees are conferred in arts and sciences, 6% in fine and performing arts, 16% in health sciences, and 21% in engineering and architecture.

Required: All students in arts and sciences must take classes in English, humanities, language and literature, mathematics and natural science, social and behavioral science, philosophy, and religion.

Special: Independent study and combination degree programs are available. Students may design their own majors or earn bachelor's degrees in 3 years. Gifted students may obtain B.A.-M.A. degrees in 4 years and B.A.-J.D. degrees in 6 years.

Honors: Sixteen honor societies are represented on campus. The School of Philosophy also offers an honors program.

Admissions: About 50% of those who applied for the 1981-82 freshman class were accepted. Of those who enrolled the SAT scores were: Verbal—37% below 500, 45% between 500 and 599, 16% between 600 and 700, and 2% above 700; Math—26% below 500, 48% between 500 and 599, 21% between 600 and 700, and 6% above 700. Candidates must have completed at least 15 Carnegie units and present at least a 2.5 GPA. It is preferred that they rank in or near the upper third of their class. Admissions officers also consider education of parents, financial situation, special talents, and results of an interview.

Procedure: The SAT or ACT is required. The English Composition AT is also required. Applicants who will need university housing should submit their forms by February 1; the rest have until August 1. Notification is made on a rolling basis. There is a $20 application fee.

Special: A deferred admissions plan is available. AP and CLEP credit is accepted.

Transfer: For fall 1981, 729 transfer students applied, 576 were accepted, and 190 enrolled. A GPA of at least 2.5 is required; students must also have minimum SAT scores of 500 on the verbal and 500 on the math. There is a 1-year residency requirement, and transfer students must complete, at the university, the last 30 of the 120 hours required for the bachelor's degree. Application deadlines are the same as for freshmen.

Visiting: Five orientations for prospective students and their parents are scheduled each year. Informal visits also may be arranged with the admissions office for 10 A.M. to 3:30 P.M. on weekdays. Guides are provided, and students may sit in on classes and remain overnight on campus.

Financial Aid: About 40% of the students receive aid; 20% work part-time on campus. Scholarships, loans, and grants from the university and the federal government are available. There are 30 full-tuition Diocesan scholarships available each year, 5 scholarships of $1000 each from the Knights of Columbus for members or relatives of living or deceased members, and 1 more $1000 scholarship for entering freshmen who are junior members of the Knights. Other scholarships include National Merit, Mullen, Cardinal Gibbons, and Music School scholarships. Work-study programs and loans from local banks also are available. The average award to freshmen from all sources is $1500. The university is a member of CSS. Aid applications and the FAF must be submitted by February 1.

Foreign Students: Nine percent of the full-time students come from foreign countries. The university offers these students special counseling and special organizations.

Admissions: Foreign students must achieve a minimum score of 500 on the TOEFL. College entrance exams are not required.

Procedure: Application deadlines are June 1 (fall) and November 1 (spring). Foreign students must present a completed medical form as proof of health. They must also carry health insurance, which is available through the university for a fee. Proof of funds adequate for 1 year of study is required.

Admissions Contact: Robert J. Talbot, Director, Admissions and Financial Aid.

GALLAUDET COLLEGE C-3
Washington, D.C. 20002 (202) 651-5114

F/T: 528M, 634W	Faculty: 226; IIA, +$
P/T: 34M, 46W	Ph.D.'s: 40%
Grad: 63M, 211W	S/F Ratio: 10 to 1
Year: sems, ss	Tuition: $1070
Appl: June 30	R and B: $2026
960 applied	484 accepted	294 enrolled
SAT or ACT: not required		SPECIAL

Gallaudet College, founded in 1864, is the world's only private liberal arts college for the deaf. The library has over 140,000 volumes, 500 periodical subscriptions, and 3500 microfilm items.

Environment: The 92-acre campus, located in northeastern Washington, D.C., consists of 34 buildings, including 6 dormitories housing over 800 students. In addition, there are acres of outdoor courts and playing fields as well as a swimming pool, a theater, gymnasiums, and bowling alleys.

Student Life: The student population is national in scope. About 85% of the students live on campus in coed dormitories. All but freshmen may keep cars on campus.

Organizations: The college sponsors religious organizations for its Protestant, Catholic, and Jewish students. It also sponsors 20 extracurricular activities, the most active of which are the student government, the 4 fraternities and 4 sororities, and the Junior National Association of the Deaf. Twenty percent of the men belong to a fraternity, and 20% of the women belong to a sorority. Each week 2 to 5 cultural events take place on campus. The student government has partial control over student discipline, dorm regulations, and student publications.

Sports: The college fields 7 intercollegiate teams for men and 5 for women. There are 11 intramural sports for men and 8 for women.

Handicapped: Since Gallaudet is specifically a college for the hearing impaired there are many programs and classes designed for these students, who constitute 90% of the student body. There are also some visually impaired students. Facilities for the physically handicapped include wheelchair ramps, parking areas, elevators, and lowered telephones. Special class scheduling is also available.

Graduates: Academic competition at the college is considered moderate; 33% of the freshmen drop out while 50% remain to graduate. Twenty-five percent of graduates pursue graduate study.

Services: The following services are provided free of charge: career and psychological counseling, placement, tutoring, remedial instruction, and health care.

Programs of Study: The college confers the B.A. and B.S. degrees. Associate, master's, and doctoral degrees are also awarded. Bachelor's degrees are offered in the following subjects: BUSINESS (business administration, computer science), ENGLISH (English), FINE AND PERFORMING ARTS (art, art education, theater/dramatics), LANGUAGES (French, German, Russian, Spanish), MATH AND SCIENCES (biology, chemistry, mathematics, physics), PHILOSOPHY (humanities), SOCIAL SCIENCES (economics, government/political science, history, psychology, sociology). Thirty-three percent of the degrees are conferred in social sciences, 20% in business, and 20% in preprofessional.

Required: Undergraduates are required to take courses in English, social studies, science, a foreign language, physical education, and communication arts.

Special: The college was one of the first to establish a precollege remedial program; all students who are accepted with deficiencies are expected to spend their first year in this intensive program, which concentrates on English and mathematics. In addition to deaf students, Gallaudet enrolls selected non-deaf juniors and seniors from other colleges. An A.A. program in interpreting is available to select students with normal hearing. Study abroad is also available.

Admissions: About 50% of those who applied were accepted for the 1981-82 freshman class. The college gives applicants its own entrance and placement tests, which allow the applicant full opportunity to demonstrate his or her talents. However, high scores on either the SAT or ACT may exempt an applicant from the college's tests. Other factors that enter into the admissions decision include recommendations, advanced placement or honor courses, evidence of special talent, leadership record, and extracurricular activities.

Procedure: The application deadline for the fall session is June 30. Entrance tests are generally given in February. Freshmen are admitted in the fall or spring (deadline, December 1). Notification date for those applying for fall admission is April 2. A personal interview is not required but recommended. There is no application fee.

Special: The college has an early decision plan. CLEP and AP are used, but no credit is earned through AP exams.

Transfer: For fall 1981, 80 transfer students applied, 61 were accepted, and 43 enrolled. C grades or better transfer. At least 1 year must be spent at the college to earn a degree. Transfers must also complete half of their major in residence. A total of 124 credits is necessary for a bachelor's degree. Application deadlines are the same as those for freshmen.

Visiting: The best times for campus visits are weekdays. Guides are available for informal visits. Prospective students should contact the Visitors Center for details.

Financial Aid: Ninety percent of the students receive financial aid. Ten percent work part-time on campus. Because the college's students are handicapped persons, they are entitled to receive support from their state vocational rehabilitation agency. This aid varies from full to partial assistance and can be supplemented by grants-in-aid from the college, which is a member of CSS. The FAF is required.

Foreign Students: Seven percent of the full-time students come from foreign countries. The college offers them an intensive English course, special counseling, and special organizations.

Admissions: Foreign students must achieve an above average score on both the college's entrance exam and the Comprehensive English Language Test.

Procedure: The application deadline for fall is December 1. Foreign students must present proof of funds adequate to cover 5 years of study. They must also carry health insurance, which is included in the standard fees.

Admissions Contact: Jerald M. Jordan, Director of Admissions and Records.

GEORGETOWN UNIVERSITY   B-3
Washington, D.C. 20057   (202) 625-3051

F/T: 2553M, 2877W   Faculty: 384; I, av$
P/T: none   Ph.D.'s: 70%
Grad: 3942M, 1790W   S/F Ratio: 14 to 1
Year: sems   Tuition: $5750
Appl: Jan. 15   R and B: $2600
8322 applied   2425 accepted   1164 enrolled
SAT: 620V 635M   MOST COMPETITIVE

Georgetown University, founded in 1789, is the oldest Roman Catholic institution of higher learning in the country and is conducted by the Jesuit Fathers. The university offers programs leading to undergraduate, graduate, and professional degrees. The library contains 1.5 million volumes, subscribes to 12,500 periodicals, and houses 558,000 microfilm items.

Environment: The 110-acre main campus is on a hilltop overlooking the Potomac River in the Georgetown section of Washington, D.C. The Law Center and Research Center are located in the downtown section of Washington, D.C. There are 35 major buildings, including a recreational center with swimming pool, indoor track, sauna, weight rooms, and multipurpose and specialized courts. Living facilities include dormitories, married student housing, and on- and off-campus apartments.

Student Life: Most students are from out of state and many foreign countries; only 9% are from Washington, D.C. Forty-eight percent of entering freshmen come from public schools. About 65% of the students live on campus. All freshmen are guaranteed housing on campus. Eighteen percent of the students are minority-group members. Sixty percent are Catholic, 22% are Protestant, and 6% are Jewish. Campus housing is both coed and single-sex; there are visiting privileges in single-sex housing. Students may keep cars on campus.

Organizations: There are many student organizations, including special interest clubs, religious groups for the 3 major faiths, theater, glee club, choir groups, band, debate, and public speaking groups, a literary magazine, and 2 weekly publications. Student government has several levels and branches and is concerned with many aspects of student life.

Sports: There are teams in 13 intercollegiate sports for men and 12 for women. There are 13 intramural sports for men and 10 for women.

Handicapped: About 80% of the campus is wheelchair accessible. Facilities on campus include a reading room for visually impaired students, wheelchair ramps, elevators, and special parking and rest rooms. There are no special counselors for handicapped students.

Graduates: There is a freshman dropout rate of 10%; 75% remain to graduate. Recently, about 90% of graduating students indicated that they planned to attend graduate school some time in the future; 60% did so immediately: 20% entered law school, 8% entered medical school, and 2% entered dental school. Fifty percent of graduates pursue careers in business and industry.

Services: The university provides free career counseling, placement service, health care, and remedial instruction. Tutoring and psychological counseling are available on a fee basis.

Programs of Study: The university confers B.A. and B.S. degrees. Master's and doctoral programs are also offered. Bachelor's degrees are offered in the following subjects: AREA STUDIES (American, Arab, Asian, Latin American, Russian), BUSINESS (accounting, business administration, finance, international management, management, marketing), ENGLISH (English), FINE AND PERFORMING ARTS (art history, studio art, theater/dramatics), HEALTH SCIENCES (nursing), LANGUAGES (Arabic, Chinese, French, German, Greek/Latin, Italian, Japanese, linguistics, Portuguese, Russian, Spanish), MATH AND SCIENCES (biology, chemistry, mathematics, physics), PHILOSOPHY (classics, philosophy, religion), PREPROFESSIONAL (dentistry, law, medicine, pharmacy, veterinary), SOCIAL SCIENCES (economics, government/political science, history, international relations, psychology, sociology). Forty-two percent of degrees conferred are in social sciences.

Required: Required courses vary according to the program.

Special: The university offers 13 study abroad programs and offers credit for foreign study as a part of its regular curriculum. There is a liberal arts seminar, and seniors who are accounting majors can participate in an internship program. Public administration, international affairs, and international economics majors also have an elective internship program available. Student-designed majors are permitted.

Honors: The university honors program is conducted by department. There are also 8 national honor societies on campus.

Admissions: About 29% of those who applied were accepted for the 1981-82 freshman class. The SAT scores of those who enrolled were as follows: Verbal—5% below 500, 31% between 500 and 599, 47% between 600 and 700, and 17% above 700; Math—4% below 500, 24% between 500 and 599, 51% between 600 and 700, and 21% above 700. Candidates should be graduates of accredited high schools. In addition, the following factors are considered in order of importance: advanced placement or honor courses, extracurricular activities, and evidence of special talent. Children of former students receive some preference.

Procedure: The SAT or ACT should be taken by January of the senior year. All applicants are encouraged to take ATs—1 in English composition and 2 in areas related to the course of study the student intends to pursue. The application, a $30 fee, test scores, and high school record should be submitted by January 15. Notification is by April 15, and the CRDA is used.

Special: Early decision applicants should take the SAT during their junior year. The application must be submitted by November 1 of the senior year; notification is by December 15. Students accepting must pay the deposit by May 1. Only the most gifted students are accepted under this plan. There are also early admissions and deferred admissions plans. AP credit is accepted.

Transfer: For fall 1981, 1622 transfer students applied, 504 were accepted, and 308 enrolled. Transfer students are accepted only in the sophomore and junior classes. It is recommended that applicants have a GPA of about 3.0 or better; D grades do not transfer. All students must complete, at the university, 60 of the 120 credits required for a bachelor's degree. Deadline for applications is March 1.

Visiting: Interviews, group information sessions, and campus tours are available on a regular basis. The undergraduate admissions office should be contacted weekdays from 9 A.M. to 5 P.M. for details and arrangements. Prospective students can also arrange to stay at the university.

Financial Aid: The university provides scholarships, NDSL, EOG, and CWS to freshmen in financial need. The university is a member of CSS and awards freshmen scholarships totaling $1.2 million and initial SEOGs of about $300,000. The average freshman award is over

$5000. About 45% of students receive some form of financial aid. Thirty percent work part-time on campus. Tuition may not be paid in installments except by special arrangement. Aid is based on financial need and academic and disciplinary records. Awards are granted on a semester basis and renewal depends on continued need and satisfactory academic performance. Application must be made by January 15; the FAF is required. Aid applicants are notified on or before April 15.

Foreign Students: Eight percent of the full-time students come from foreign countries. An intensive English course, an intensive English program, special counseling, and special organizations are available for these students.

Admissions: Foreign students must achieve a TOEFL score of at least 550 and must take the SAT or ACT. They must also take 3 ATs (1 in English composition and 2 others related to the student's area of interest).

Procedure: The application deadline is January 15. Foreign students must present proof of funds adequate to cover 4 years of study and must carry health insurance, which is available through the university for a fee.

Admissions Contact: Charles A. Deacon, Director of Admissions.

GEORGE WASHINGTON UNIVERSITY B-3
Washington, D.C. 20052 (202) 676-6040

F/T: 2768M, 2443W   Faculty: 1102; I, +$
P/T: 515M, 660W   Ph.D.'s: 87%
Grad: 5035M, 3667W   S/F Ratio: 14 to 1
Year: sems, ss   Tuition: $4900
Appl: Mar. 1   R and B: $3400
4871 applied   3642 accepted   1171 enrolled
SAT: 520V 550M   ACT: 23   VERY COMPETITIVE

George Washington University, established in 1821, is a private, coeducational, nonsectarian institution that provides undergraduate and graduate education as well as adult continuing education. The libraries contain 1,120,000 volumes, and subscribe to 11,900 periodicals. In addition to its traditional schools and divisions, the university has a Division of Experimental Programs that helps develop new courses and programs involving interdisciplinary study or utilizing the educational resources of the Washington, D.C., area.

Environment: The university's campus occupies 20 blocks in downtown Washington, near the White House. The physical plant includes 9 major classroom buildings, a university center, an athletic center, and residences that accommodate 2400 men and women. Living facilities include high-rise dormitories, on-campus apartments, and fraternity and sorority houses. The university is building an academic cluster that will contain the music and art departments, classrooms, and offices.

Student Life: Eighty-five percent of the students come from outside the District of Columbia metropolitan area. Students come from every state and 120 foreign countries. Eighty percent of entering freshmen come from public schools. Eleven percent are members of minority groups. About 35% of students reside in dormitories, 35% live in apartments, and 30% commute from home. Campus housing is both coed and single-sex. There are visiting privileges in single-sex dorms. Cars are permitted on campus, but parking is limited.

Organizations: There are more than 150 student organizations. Students may enjoy the varied social life of Washington, D.C., and the cultural opportunities offered by the Kennedy Center, the National Gallery of Art, the National Theater, the Smithsonian Institution, and many other facilities. There are fraternities and sororities.

Sports: The university fields intercollegiate teams in 8 sports for men and 10 for women. Thirteen intramural sports are offered for both men and women.

Handicapped: Mobility throughout the campus is made easier for handicapped students by level terrain and by architectural and environmental modifications. Support services for visually and hearing-impaired students include readers, sign-language interpreters, a reading room with tape recorders and Visual-Tek, and registration assistance. Other help can be arranged through the office of services for students with disabilities.

Graduates: Fifty-five percent of entering freshmen remain to graduate. About 55% of the graduates seek advanced degrees; 40% to 50% of applicants are accepted to medical school.

Services: The Career Services Office offers free career counseling and placement services. Health care, tutoring, and psychological counseling also are available; fees are charged for some services.

DISTRICT OF COLUMBIA 127

Programs of Study: Undergraduate degrees offered are the B.A., B.B.A., and B.S. Associate, master's, and doctoral programs are also available. Bachelor's degrees are offered in the following subjects: AREA STUDIES (American, Asian, early modern European, Latin American, Middle Eastern, urban), BUSINESS (accounting, economics and public policy, finance, information processing, management, marketing), EDUCATION (early childhood, elementary, human services, health/physical, middle school, secondary, special), ENGLISH (English, journalism, literature—American, literature—English, speech), FINE AND PERFORMING ARTS (art history, dance, dance education, music, radio/TV, studio art, theater/dramatics), HEALTH SCIENCES (medical technology, nursing, physician's assistant, radiologic sciences and administration, speech therapy), LANGUAGES (Chinese, French, German, Russian, Spanish, Spanish-American literature), MATH AND SCIENCES (biology, botany, chemistry, ecology/environmental science, geology, mathematics, physics, statistics, zoology), PHILOSOPHY (classics—classical archaeology and anthropology, classics—classical archaeology and classics, general curriculum in the liberal arts, humanities, Judaic studies, philosophy, religion), PREPROFESSIONAL (dentistry, engineering, law, medicine, ministry, operations research and computational science, veterinary), SOCIAL SCIENCES (anthropology, economics, geography, government/political science, history, international relations, psychology, public affairs, sociology).

Required: All students are required to take English composition and complete a "meaningful initiation" in the humanities, social sciences, and science or mathematics.

Special: A limited number of pass/fail courses, a sophomore-year-in-Paris option, and internship programs are available. Students may study abroad, create their own majors, select double majors, obtain academic credits for work in Washington, and participate in the programs of the consortium of D.C. universities. A general studies degree is available.

Honors: Honors programs include a 90-hour degree program and a college program for secondary school students. There are numerous honor societies on campus, including Phi Beta Kappa and Omicron Delta Kappa.

Admissions: About 75% of those who applied were accepted for the 1981–82 freshman class. The SAT scores of those who enrolled were as follows: Verbal—37% below 500, 48% between 500 and 599, 13% between 600 and 700, and 2% above 700; Math—21% below 500, 52% between 500 and 599, 23% between 600 and 700, and 4% above 700. Forty-one percent ranked in the top fifth of their high school class, 78% in the top two-fifths. Candidates must be graduates of accredited high schools and have completed 4 years of English and 2 years each of mathematics, science, social studies, and a foreign language. In addition, students should rank in the upper two-fifths of their graduating class and have a B average or better. The most important factors are an applicant's academic record, class rank, and test scores. Other factors considered are advanced placement or honors courses and evidence of special talent.

Procedure: The SAT or ACT should be taken in the spring of the junior year or the fall of the senior year. It is recommended that applicants present 3 ATs. The application, a $20 fee (waived in financial-need cases if certified by a high school counselor), test scores, and high school record should be submitted early in the senior year. Deadlines are March 1 (fall), November 1 (spring), and March 1 (summer). The university follows a rolling admissions policy.

Special: An early admissions plan is offered. AP and CLEP credit is accepted.

Transfer: For fall 1981, 2171 students applied, 1395 were accepted, and 713 enrolled. Transfer students need a GPA of at least 2.0 (a 2.5 is recommended) from an accredited school. Individual interviews are provided but not required. D grades do not transfer. Transfer students must complete at least 30 semester hours at the university of the 120 required for a degree. Deadlines are June 1 (fall), November 1 (spring), and April 1 (summer).

Visiting: Personal interviews are not used in the freshman selection process; instead, there are daily group information sessions and tours of the campus. Prospective students are urged to visit the campus. The admissions office should be contacted for information.

Financial Aid: Twenty-three percent of the students receive aid through the university, which provides scholarships, grants, loans, and work-study. Many students earn some part of their expenses in part-time employment. Financial aid is based on need and academic performance. However, there is a limited number of scholarships (half-tuition per academic year) based solely on academic performance. Renewal of need-based awards is contingent on continued need and satisfactory academic performance. Application must be made by February 1 for freshman enrollment and by November 1 for spring semes-

128 DISTRICT OF COLUMBIA

ter enrollment. The university is a member of CSS. The FAF must be filed. Request for aid does not influence the admissions decision.

Foreign Students: The 663 undergraduate foreign students enrolled at the university make up nearly 13% of its student body. The university provides an intensive English course, an intensive English program, special counseling, and special organizations.

Admissions: Foreign applicants must take the TOEFL, and some programs require a minimum score of 550. Applicants also may take the university's own English proficiency test. No academic entrance exams are required.

Procedure: Application deadlines are the same as those for other freshmen. Students must present proof of adequate funds for 1 year. Health insurance, though not required, is available through the college for a fee.

Admissions Contact: Joseph Y. Ruth, Director of Admissions.

HOWARD UNIVERSITY   C–3
Washington, D.C. 20059   (202) 636-6100

F/T: 2651M, 3273W   Faculty: 1250; I, av$
P/T: 1171M, 1163W   Ph.D.'s: 65%
Grad: 2013M, 1586W   S/F Ratio: 10 to 1
Year: sems, ss   Tuition: $2165
Appl: Apr. 1   R and B: $2116
SAT: required   COMPETITIVE

Howard University, founded in 1867, is a private, nonsectarian university. While students have always been admitted without regard to race, sex, creed, or national origin, the university has a special obligation to make comprehensive educational opportunities available to the black people. Divisions include the colleges of Fine Arts, Liberal Arts, Allied Health Sciences, Human Ecology, and Pharmacy; and the schools of Engineering, Architecture and City Planning, Business and Public Administration, Nursing, Education, and Communication. The library contains 1,058,514 volumes and over 802,548 microfilm items, and subscribes to 9427 periodicals. Additional underground library facilities are now under construction.

Environment: The university's urban main campus occupies more than 72 acres in the northeast section of Washington, D.C. There are 60 major buildings on the campus including the Armour J. Blackburn University Center. Living facilities include dormitories and off-campus apartments.

Student Life: Twenty-two percent of the students are from Washington, D.C. Eighty-one percent come from public schools. Twenty percent live on campus. Virtually all students are minority-group members. Campus housing is both coed and single-sex; there are visiting privileges in the single-sex housing. Students may keep cars on campus.

Organizations: Three percent of the women belong to 1 of 4 sororities, and 2% of the men belong to 1 of 4 fraternities. Other student organizations include religious groups for the 3 major faiths and Bahai, special-interest clubs, band, chorus, debating groups, publications, radio and television, gospel chorus, a string ensemble, and service clubs. The university offers a full and varied cultural and social program. Student government is concerned with most aspects of student life. Students participate in the University Senate, the Board of Trustees, and faculty meetings.

Sports: There are intercollegiate teams in 10 sports for men and 7 for women. There are 13 intramural sports for men and 11 for women.

Handicapped: About 90% of the campus is wheelchair accessible. The student body generally includes 1 or 2 visually or hearing impaired students. Counselors are available to assist handicapped students in obtaining all services needed. Facilities for the physically handicapped include wheelchair ramps, special parking, elevators, and specially equipped rest rooms; special class scheduling is available.

Services: The university offers a full placement program that includes career fairs, counseling, and interview scheduling. Other services available to students free of charge include psychological and career counseling, tutoring, and remedial instruction. Health care is offered on a fee basis.

Programs of Study: The university offers the B.A., B. Arch., B.F.A., B.Mus., B.Mus.Ed., B.B.A., B.S.N., B.S. Pharm., B.S.W., B. of City Planning, B.S.Ch.E., B.S.C.E., B.S.E.E., B.S.M.E., and B.S. degrees. Master's and doctoral programs are also available. Bachelor's degrees are offered in the following subjects: AREA STUDIES (American, Asian, Black/Afro-American, Latin American, Russian, urban), BUSINESS (accounting, business administration, computer science, finance, international business, management, marketing, real estate/insurance), ED-UCATION (adult, early childhood, elementary, secondary, special), ENGLISH (English, journalism, literature, speech), FINE AND PERFORMING ARTS (art, art education, art history, dance, film/photography, music, music education, radio/TV, theater/dramatics), HEALTH SCIENCES (medical technology, nursing, occupational therapy, physical therapy, speech therapy), LANGUAGES (French, German, Portuguese, Spanish), MATH AND SCIENCES (astronomy, biochemistry, biology, botany, chemistry, earth science, ecology/environmental science, geology, mathematics, natural sciences, physical sciences, physics, statistics, zoology), PHILOSOPHY (classics, humanities, philosophy), PREPROFESSIONAL (architecture, dentistry, engineering—chemical, engineering—civil, engineering—electrical, engineering—mechanical, home economics, law, medicine, ministry, pharmacy, social work), SOCIAL SCIENCES (anthropology, economics, geography, government/political science, history, human development, international relations, psychology, sociology). Twenty-two percent of degrees conferred are in math and sciences; 17% are in the health sciences.

Required: Course requirements vary, depending on the particular school or college.

Special: The university is a member of the Consortium of Universities, which by cooperative arrangement among the 5 universities in the District of Columbia enables advanced undergraduates and graduate students in 1 university to enroll in courses of the others. The university has many special institutes and centers extending research and service into areas affecting the public interest.

Honors: Also offered are honors and departmental honors programs for students of exceptional ability.

Admissions: Applicants must be graduates of accredited high schools and present acceptable secondary school records, including transcripts, SAT scores, and recommendations from school officials. Applicants should rank in the upper half of their graduating class and have a GPA of at least 2.0. Other factors considered are advanced placement or honor courses and recommendations.

Procedure: The SAT is required for all students except those applying to the schools of Business and Public Administration and Engineering; these students must take the ACT. The School of Engineering also requires ATs in English composition and mathematics. Applicants to the College of Liberal Arts who have studied a foreign language for 2 years and intend to continue that study must take ATs in that language as well. The application, a $25 fee, test scores, and high school record should be submitted by April 1 (fall), November 1 (spring), and April 15 (summer). Notification on a rolling basis begins about 1 month after all credentials are received.

Special: There is an early admissions plan. Gifted and mature students may be admitted at the end of the junior year of high school. AP and CLEP credit is acceptable.

Transfer: Transfers are accepted for all but the senior class. A GPA of at least 2.0 is required. D grades do not transfer. All students must complete, at the university, 30 of the 124 or more credits required for a bachelor's degree. Application deadlines are April 1 (fall), November 1 (spring), and March 1 (summer).

Visiting: Prior to registration there is a 1-week orientation available. Guides are available for informal visits. Contact the director of recruitment for information.

Financial Aid: Sixty percent of the students receive aid through the university. About 30% work part-time on campus. The university has designed its financial aid program to assist the maximum number of students. It includes scholarships, loans, grants, and part-time employment. The amount of financial aid granted a student is determined by the availability of funds, the extent of the student's need, and his or her academic performance or promise. Renewal is contingent upon continued need and academic accomplishment. The university is a member of CSS and requires the FAF. Aid application deadlines are April 1 (fall), November 1 (spring), and April 15 (summer).

Foreign Students: Sixteen percent of the full-time students come from foreign countries. Special counseling and special organizations are available for these students.

Admissions: Foreign students must achieve a TOEFL score of at least 500. Foreign students applying to the schools of Engineering and Business and Public Administration must take the ACT; all others must take the SAT. Engineering majors must take the AT in mathematics.

Procedure: Application deadlines are March 1 (fall), August 1 (spring), and February 1 (summer). Foreign students must present a physician's report and proof of funds adequate to cover 1 year of study.

Admissions Contact: Adrienne McMurdock, Director of Admissions.

MOUNT VERNON COLLEGE
B–3
Washington, D.C. 20007 (202) 331-3444

F/T: 450W		Faculty:	26; IIB, +$
P/T: 83W		Ph.D.'s:	65%
Grad: none		S/F Ratio:	18 to 1
Year: tri, ss		Tuition:	$4200
Appl: open		R and B:	$3000
386 applied	283 accepted		150 enrolled
SAT: 383V 390M			LESS COMPETITIVE

Mount Vernon College, founded in 1875, is an independent, liberal arts college for women that offers students the opportunity to plan their own programs. The library contains 30,000 volumes and 2920 microfilm items, and subscribes to 275 periodicals.

Environment: The urban campus is located on 26 acres in a residential area of northwest Washington. Facilities include a chapel and 8 dormitories with space for more than 500 students.

Student Life: More than 80% of the students come from outside Washington. Fifty-one percent of the freshmen are graduates of public schools. About 70% of the students live on campus. Ten percent are minority-group members. There are visiting privileges in the dorms. Students may keep cars on campus. All noncommuting freshmen and sophomores must live in dorms. Freshmen are subject to curfews. About half the students leave campus on weekends.

Organizations: Extracurricular activities include performing arts groups, 3 student publications, and social service organizations. There are no sororities.

Sports: There are 5 intercollegiate sports and 7 intramural sports.

Handicapped: Facilities include wheelchair ramps and special parking. One counselor is available to handicapped students.

Graduates: About 30% of entering freshmen drop out by the end of the first year. Eight percent of graduates undertake advanced study; 3% enter law school. About 12% pursue careers in business and industry.

Services: The following services are available free to students: health care, placement, and career counseling. Tutoring is offered on a fee basis. Placement services may be used by graduates as well as students.

Programs of Study: The college confers the B.A. degree. Associate degrees are also awarded. Bachelor's degrees are offered in the following subjects: BUSINESS (business administration), EDUCATION (early childhood, elementary), ENGLISH (communications), FINE AND PERFORMING ARTS (art), PREPROFESSIONAL (interior design), SOCIAL SCIENCES (government/political science, human development, public affairs). Majors in languages (French, Italian, Russian, Spanish), math and sciences, and philoscphy are available through a consortium with other area colleges and universities. About 24% of degrees are conferred in business and 14% in social sciences.

Special: Students may design their own majors. The college also offers internships, study abroad, and independent study. The academic calendar consists of 3 terms of 10 weeks each, and students take 3 or 4 courses per term.

Honors: The honor society Alpha Chi has a chapter on campus.

Admissions: About 73% of those who applied were accepted for the 1981–82 freshman class. Applicants must have completed 16 high school units and should present at least a C average. The following factors also are considered: recommendations by high school officials, extracurricular activities, personality, and impressions made during an interview.

Procedure: The SAT or ACT is required. Students are encouraged to arrange an interview. Notification is made on a rolling basis. Students are admitted to all terms. There are no application deadlines. The application fee is $20.

Special: AP and CLEP credit is accepted.

Transfer: For fall 1981, 81 students applied, 55 were accepted, and 25 enrolled. Students should present evidence of above-average performance in their major. D grades do not transfer. All students must complete, at the college, 30 of the 120 credits required for a bachelor's degree. Deadlines are open; transfer students are admitted to all 3 semesters.

Visiting: Orientations are scheduled regularly for prospective students. They include meetings with students and faculty members, class visits, and a night in the dormitories. Guides also are provided for informal visits, which should be arranged with the admissions office for Mondays through Fridays from 9 A.M. to 5 P.M.. Visitors may sit in on classes and spend the night.

DISTRICT OF COLUMBIA 129

Financial Aid: About 20% of the students receive financial aid. About 21% work part-time on campus. The average freshman award is $5245. The college is a member of the CSS. Aid awards are based on need. Scholarships, federal loans, and CWS are available. Aid applications and the FAF must be submitted by March 1.

Foreign Students: About 12% of the full-time students come from foreign countries. An intensive English course, special counseling, and special organizations are available for these students.

Admissions: Foreign students must achieve a TOEFL score of at least 450. No college entrance exams are required.

Procedure: There are no application deadlines; foreign students are admitted to all 3 semesters. They must complete a health form and present proof of funds adequate to cover 1 year of study.

Admissions Contact: Elaine Liles, Director of Admissions.

SOUTHEASTERN UNIVERSITY
D–4
Washington, D.C. 20024 (202) 488-8162

F/T: 460M, 260W		Faculty:	175; n/av
P/T: 150M, 300W		Ph.D.'s:	n/av
Grad: 440M, 200W		S/F Ratio:	20 to 1
Year: tri, ss		Tuition:	$3000
Appl: open		R and B:	n/app
550 applied	400 accepted		250 enrolled
SAT: required			COMPETITIVE

Southeastern University, founded in 1879, is a private school that offers undergraduate programs in business administration and accounting. The library contains 15,000 volumes, and subscribes to 220 periodicals.

Environment: The one-acre self-contained campus is located in an urban environment. The university is entirely a commuter school.

Student Life: About 50% of the students come from the District of Columbia; 25% come from Maryland and Virginia; and the remainder come from foreign countries. About 20% of the students are minority-group members.

Organizations: Ten percent of the men belong to 1 of 2 fraternities; 10% of the women belong to the 1 sorority. Extracurricular activities are limited by the school's evening hours. There are special-interest clubs, service groups, and publications. Students have jurisdiction in all campus social activities, as well as voting privileges on most university committees.

Sports: The university fields 3 intercollegiate teams for men. There is no intramural program.

Handicapped: There are no facilities for the handicapped.

Graduates: There is a freshman dropout rate of 10%; 40% remain to graduate. About 15% of graduates go on for graduate study.

Services: Job placement and career counseling, as well as tutoring, are available to students free of charge. Remedial instruction is available on a fee basis.

Programs of Study: The College of Administrative Sciences confers the B.S. degree. Master's and associate programs are also available. Bachelor's degrees are offered in the following subjects: BUSINESS (accounting, business administration, computer science, economics, finance, information systems management, management, marketing, public administration).

Required: A core curriculum of 48 hours of liberal arts and social sciences is required.

Special: An accelerated bachelor's degree is possible.

Honors: Honor societies are available for eligible students.

Admissions: About 73% of those who applied were accepted for the 1981–82 freshman class. A high school diploma (or GED) is required. Applicants should rank in the upper 50% of their high school class. In addition, the following factors are considered: advanced placement or honors work, recommendations, and impressions made during an interview, which is recommended. Preference is given to children of alumni. The school seeks a geographic distribution.

Procedure: The SAT is required. Applications for the fall semester, with a $25 fee, should be filed; there is no application deadline. The university follows a rolling admissions policy.

Special: There is a deferred admissions plan. AP and CLEP credit is accepted.

Transfer: Transfers are admitted to all but the senior class. An average of at least 2.0 is necessary. Grades of C or above transfer. Thirty credits must be completed in residence; 120 credits are required to earn the bachelor's degree. Application deadlines are open.

Visiting: There are no regularly scheduled orientations for prospective students. Those who are interested in visiting the campus should contact the dean for information and arrangements.

Financial Aid: Thirty-two scholarships (academic and athletic) are available to freshmen; 50% of the students receive scholarship aid. Loans are available from the federal government and the government of the District of Columbia; 20% of the students receive loan aid. CWS is available; 5% of the students work part-time on campus. Tuition may be paid in installments. The university is a member of CSS and requires the FAF or the FSF. There is no application deadline.

Foreign Students: The university offers these students an intensive English course, special counseling, and special organizations.

Admissions: Foreign students must achieve a minimum TOEFL score of 550; they must also take the university's own English proficiency and entrance exams.

Procedure: Application deadlines are 7 weeks before the start of each semester. Foreign students must present proof of funds adequate to cover 1 year of study.

Admissions Contact: John C. Carter, Director of University Relations.

STRAYER COLLEGE C–3
Washington, D.C. 20005 (202) 783-5180

F/T: 526M, 907W Faculty: 42; IIB, — – $
P/T: 139M, 482W Ph.D.'s: 12%
Grad: none S/F Ratio: 34 to 1
Year: qtrs, ss Tuition: $2670
Appl: open R and B: n/app
1240 applied 986 accepted 735 enrolled
SAT or ACT: not required LESS COMPETITIVE

Strayer College, founded in 1904, offers business–education programs leading to associate and bachelor's degrees. The library contains 16,500 volumes, and subscribes to 120 periodicals.

Environment: The college occupies one building in the District of Columbia and one building in Arlington, Virginia. There are no dormitories.

Student Life: About 30% of the students come from the District of Columbia, 44% from Maryland and Virginia, and 26% from foreign countries. Seventy-two percent of the students are black and 19% are members of other minorities.

Organizations: There are 15 extracurricular groups, including a student government. Students have voting rights on several faculty and administration committees. There are no fraternities or sororities.

Sports: There are no intramural or intercollegiate sports available.

Handicapped: The campus is totally accessible to physically handicapped students. Special facilities include elevators.

Graduates: The freshman dropout rate is 30%; 60% remain to graduate. Twenty-five percent of the graduates seek advanced degrees. Virtually all pursue careers in business, industry, or government.

Services: Career counseling, placement, and tutoring are available free of charge to students. The placement office may be used by graduates as well as students. Remedial instruction is available on a fee basis.

Programs of Study: The college confers the B.S. degree. Associate degrees are also awarded. Bachelor's degrees are offered in the following subjects: BUSINESS (accounting, business administration, data processing, government administration), HEALTH SCIENCES (hospital and health care administration).

Required: All students must complete a core curriculum.

Admissions: About 80% of those who applied were accepted for the 1981–82 freshman class. Applicants must have graduated from high school after completing 16 Carnegie units.

Procedure: Neither the SAT nor the ACT is required. The college administers its own entrance/placement examination. There are no application deadlines; applications are accepted up to registration. New students are admitted to any term. An interview is recommended. The $25 application fee is refundable if the student is rejected.

Transfer: Transfers are accepted for all classes. Grades of C or above transfer. Students must complete, at the college, 48 of the 188 to 192 quarter hours required to earn a bachelor's degree. Application deadlines are open.

Visiting: Guides are provided for informal visits from 9 A.M. to 5 P.M. on weekdays. Prospective students also may sit in on classes. Arrangements should be made with the director of admissions.

Financial Aid: Eighteen freshman scholarships are available as well as federal and state loans, grants, and work programs. About 80% of the students receive financial assistance; 2% work part-time on campus. Need is the primary determining factor. The average award to freshmen from all sources is $2100. Tuition may be paid in installments. The college is a member of CSS; the FAF must be submitted by May 15.

Foreign Students: About 26% of the students are from foreign countries. The college offers these students an intensive English program, special counseling, and special organizations.

Admissions: Foreign students must achieve a minimum TOEFL score of 475; they must also take the college's own entrance exam.

Procedure: Application deadlines are 6 weeks prior to the beginning of each quarter. Foreign students must present proof of health as well as proof of funds adequate to cover 1 year of study. They must also carry health insurance, which is available through the college for a fee.

Admissions Contact: Phillip M. Ramsey, Director of Marketing and Admissions.

TRINITY COLLEGE C–2
Washington, D.C. 20017 (202) 269-2201

F/T: 800W Faculty: n/av; IIA, — – $
P/T: 55W Ph.D.'s: 50%
Grad: 100 M&W S/F Ratio: 12 to 1
Year: sems, ss Tuition: $4700
Appl: open R and B: $2900
700 applied 420 accepted 197 enrolled
SAT: 500V 500M COMPETITIVE

Trinity College, founded in 1897, is a private women's college. The college is operated by the Sisters of Notre Dame de Namur. The library contains 180,000 volumes and 5526 microfilm items, and subscribes to 700 periodicals.

Environment: The campus is located on 34 acres of woodland about 2½ miles from downtown Washington. The 7 main buildings include a chapel, a science building, and 4 dormitories that accommodate 850 students.

Student Life: Ninety percent of the students are from outside the District of Columbia. About 50% of the freshmen come from public schools. Most students are Catholic. About 11% of the students are minority-group members. Ninety percent live on campus. There are visiting privileges in the dorms. Cars are permitted, and there are no curfews after October of the freshman year. Day-care services are available to all students, faculty, and staff.

Organizations: Student activities include publications, political and special-interest groups, a glee club, and student government.

Sports: The college fields 4 intercollegiate teams. There are 2 intramural sports.

Handicapped: Special facilities include wheelchair ramps, parking areas, elevators, specially equipped rest rooms, and specially equipped dormitories.

Graduates: There is a freshman dropout rate of 12%, and 80% of the freshmen remain to graduate. Sixty-five percent of graduates pursue advanced degrees.

Services: The following services are offered free to students: career counseling, placement, health care, psychological counseling, tutoring, and remedial instruction.

Programs of Study: The college confers the B.A., B.S., and B.F.A. degrees. Master's degrees also are available. Bachelor's degrees are offered in the following subjects: AREA STUDIES (American), EDUCATION (early childhood, elementary, special), ENGLISH (English), FINE AND PERFORMING ARTS (art, art history, music), HEALTH SCIENCES (medical technology), LANGUAGES (French, Spanish), MATH AND SCIENCES (biochemistry, biology, chemistry, mathematics), PHILOSOPHY (philosophy), SOCIAL SCIENCES (economics, government/political science, history, psychology, sociology).

Required: A third of the student's courses are required by the general program. These include a freshman world literature and world history sequence, courses in math and science, a theology course, and a foreign language or logic course.

Special: For second-year students majoring in English or history, Trinity sponsors a year at Oxford, England. Students also may participate in the junior year abroad programs of other institutions, or Trinity's junior-year program in France. Independent study also is available, and students may design their own majors.

Honors: An honors program and honor societies are available.

Admissions: About 60% of those who applied were accepted for the 1981-82 freshman class. Applicants should rank in the upper half of their class, present an average of at least 2.5, and have completed 16 units of high school work. The following factors also are considered: advanced placement or honor courses, recommendations by school officials, leadership record, and extracurricular activities record. Daughters of alumnae are given preference.

Procedure: The SAT or ACT should be taken in October of the senior year. The application, a $25 fee, high school record, and test scores should be submitted by March 15 for the fall semester, although applications are accepted until the class is filled. Students are notified after February 1 on a rolling basis.

Special: Early decision, early admissions, and deferred admissions plans are available. Students may earn credit through AP exams.

Transfer: For a recent year, the college received 105 applications, accepted 75, and enrolled 35 students. Transfers are considered for all classes. Applicants must present a letter of good standing from the registrar or academic dean of the college last attended, and transcripts from all colleges attended. A 3.0 GPA is required. Grades of C or above transfer. All students must complete 32 hours at the college to receive a degree; the bachelor's degree requires 128 credits. Admissions decisions are made on a rolling basis; there are no formal application deadlines.

Visiting: Visits are arranged on an individual basis. Guides are available and prospective students may stay at the college. Visits should be scheduled for September through November or February through May. Arrangements should be made with the admissions office.

Financial Aid: The college provides scholarships, grants, loans, and CWS. About 30% of the students work part-time on campus, and about half receive some type of aid. Aid is awarded on the basis of financial need and academic record. It is renewed annually if need continues and academic record is maintained. The average award to freshmen from all sources is $4500. The college is a member of CSS; the FAF and aid application should be submitted by April 15.

Foreign Students: About 5% of the full-time students come from foreign countries. The college offers these students an intensive English course, special counseling, and special organizations.

Admissions: Foreign students must take the TOEFL and the college's placement exams.

Procedure: Application deadlines for fall and spring are open. Foreign students must present proof of health as well as proof of funds adequate to cover 4 years of study. They must also carry health insurance, which is available through the college.

Admissions Contact: Susanne Nolan, Director of Admissions.

UNIVERSITY OF THE DISTRICT OF COLUMBIA
C-2, D-3
Washington, D.C. 20004 (202) 727-2270

F/T: 2073M, 2091W Faculty: 884; IIA, ++$
P/T: 4451M, 6239W Ph.D.'s: 23%
Grad: 164M, 225W S/F Ratio: n/av
Year: sems, ss Tuition: $374 ($1614)
Appl: Aug. 1 R and B: n/app
2240 applied 2130 accepted 1524 enrolled
SAT or ACT: not required NONCOMPETITIVE

University of the District of Columbia was formed in 1977 by the merger of District of Columbia Teachers College, Federal City College, and Washington Technical College. The publicly controlled university offers a wide range of programs in liberal arts, teacher education, and technical fields. Its divisions are the colleges of Business and Public Management; Education and Human Ecology; Liberal and Fine Arts; Life Sciences; and Physical Science, Engineering and Technology. The library contains over 400,000 volumes and 400,000 microfilm items, and subscribes to 3000 periodicals.

Environment: The university has 3 campuses: Georgia-Harvard, Mount Vernon Square, and Van Ness. The main campus (Van Ness) is being expanded, and development will begin in the near future on the new Mount Vernon Square campus. There are no dormitory facilities.

Student Life: About 91% of the students come from the District of Columbia. About 84% are black.

Organizations: There are 4 fraternities and 4 sororities on campus. Other campus organizations include traditional extracurricular clubs and service groups.

Sports: The university fields intercollegiate teams in 10 sports. Intramural sports for men and women also are available.

Handicapped: About 40% of the campus is accessible to handicapped students. Facilities include special parking areas and elevators. Special counselors are available.

Services: The university provides the following services free to students: health care, career and psychological counseling, tutoring, remedial instruction, and placement aid.

Programs of Study: The university awards B.A., B.S., B.B.A., B.Mus.Ed., and B.F.A. degrees. Associate and master's degrees also are conferred. Bachelor's degrees are offered in the following subjects: AREA STUDIES (urban), BUSINESS (accounting, business administration, business education, computer science, finance, management, marketing, office administration, printing management, procurement and public contracting), EDUCATION (early childhood, elementary, family living and child development, health/physical, industrial, secondary, special), ENGLISH (English, journalism), FINE AND PERFORMING ARTS (art education, film/photography, music education, radio/TV, studio art, theater/dramatics), LANGUAGES (French, German, Spanish), HEALTH SCIENCES (food and nutrition, food science, nursing, speech therapy), MATH AND SCIENCES (biology, chemistry, ecology/environmental science, geoscience, mathematics, physics), PHILOSOPHY (philosophy), PREPROFESSIONAL (clothing and textiles, construction management technology, engineering—civil, engineering—electrical, engineering—mechanical, forestry, home economics, library science, ornamental horticulture, social work, veterinary, wildlife management), SOCIAL SCIENCES (anthropology, fire science administration, geography, government/political science, history, psychology, public management, sociology).

Required: Students must complete a core curriculum.

Honors: There are 2 honor societies on campus, and the university offers an honors program.

Admissions: About 95% of those who applied were accepted for the 1981-82 freshman class. A high school diploma or GED is required. The university maintains an open admissions policy.

Procedure: Application deadlines are August 1 (fall), December 1 (spring), and May 1 (summer). The application fee is $10. The university follows a rolling admissions plan.

Special: A deferred admissions plan is available.

Transfer: Applicants should have a GPA of 2.0 or better and be in good academic standing at their last school. Those with lower GPAs may be admitted on probation. D grades do not transfer. Students must earn, in residence, at least 30 semester hours of the 120 required for a bachelor's degree.

Financial Aid: About 35% of the students receive aid. Scholarships, CWS jobs, and federal grants are available. Tuition may be paid in installments. The FAF or FFS is required; the FFS is preferred. The application deadline is April 15.

Foreign Students: Nine percent of the student body are from foreign countries. Special counseling and special organizations are provided for these students.

Admissions: Foreign applicants must score at least 500 on the TOEFL. No college entrance exams are required.

Procedure: Application deadlines are May 1 (fall) and September 15 (spring). Students must show evidence of adequate funds for 4 years of study.

Admissions Contact: Rick L. Winston, Associate Director of Admissions.

WASHINGTON INTERNATIONAL COLLEGE
B-2
Washington, D.C. 20006 (202) 466-7220
(Recognized Candidate for Accreditation)

F/T: 177M, 196W Faculty: 250; n/av
P/T: 72M, 137W Ph.D.'s: 40%
Grad: none S/F Ratio: 2 to 1
Year: modular Tuition: $40 p/c
Appl: open R and B: n/app
307 accepted
SAT or ACT: not required NONCOMPETITIVE

Washington International College, founded in 1970, is a private liberal arts college. An extension program is available to students in other parts of the country. Students structure their own learning process, using independent study, study abroad, and internships. The college makes use of the learning facilities in the community, which range from the Library of Congress to the various government departments.

Environment: The college consists solely of an administrative building.

Student Life: Almost all local students are from the District of Columbia, Maryland, or Virginia. No college housing is available. Sixty percent of the students are black.

Organizations: The college sponsors few extracurricular activities but encourages participation in the varied activities of Washington, D.C. Students have voting representation on all major college committees.

Sports: There is no sports program.

Handicapped: There are no facilities for handicapped students.

Services: The college provides individualized academic counseling and tutoring.

Programs of Study: The college grants B.A. degrees in virtually any field of concentration. Associate degrees are also conferred. Bachelor's degrees are offered in the following subjects: AREA STUDIES (American, Asian, Black/Afro-American, Latin American, urban), BUSINESS (accounting, business administration, business education, computer science, finance, management, marketing), EDUCATION (adult, early childhood, elementary, secondary), ENGLISH (English, journalism, literature, speech), FINE AND PERFORMING ARTS (art, art education, art history, dance, film/photography, music, radio/TV, studio art, theater/dramatics), HEALTH SCIENCES (environmental health), LANGUAGES (Chinese, French, German, Greek/Latin, Hebrew, Italian, Japanese, Portuguese, Russian, Spanish), PHILOSOPHY (classics, humanities, philosophy, religion), PREPROFESSIONAL (home economics, social work), SOCIAL SCIENCES (anthropology, economics, geography, government/political science, history, international relations, psychology, social sciences, sociology).

Required: All students must take part in the Career-Life Planning Seminar.

Special: The extension program makes use of an extensive telecommunications service. Students may design their own majors or earn a general studies degree. The college offers a Basic Skills Program for students who need additional instruction in communication and math skills.

Admissions: The college follows an open-admissions policy. A high school diploma or GED is required.

Procedure: The college's own entrance exam is required. An interview is recommended. A $15 application fee is required. Application deadlines are open. Freshmen are admitted throughout the academic year.

Special: CLEP credit is accepted.

Transfer: Almost all transfer applicants are admitted. D grades do not transfer. Students must complete at least 30 credit hours through the college; life-learning and transfer credits also may be accepted.

Visiting: The best times for campus visits are 9 A.M. through 6 P.M. on weekdays. The admissions director should be contacted for arrangements.

Financial Aid: Federal and state grants, loans, and work-study are available. Aid is awarded on the basis of need. Tuition may be paid in installments. Aid applications are accepted throughout the year.

Foreign Students: The 35 students from foreign countries make up about 6% of enrollment. The college offers these students special counseling, an intensive English course, and an intensive English program.

Admissions: Applicants must score at least 500 on the TOEFL. Another English-proficiency exam may be taken instead.

Procedure: Application deadlines are open; freshmen may start at any time. Foreign students must present proof of adequate funds for 1 year.

Admissions Contact: Director of Admissions.

FLORIDA

BARRY UNIVERSITY E-5
(Formerly Barry College)
Miami Shores, Florida 33161 (305) 758-3392

F/T: 215M, 704W   Faculty: 51; IIA, —$
P/T: 325M, 446W   Ph.D.'s: 45%
Grad: 128M, 348W   S/F Ratio: 13 to 1
Year: sems, ss   Tuition: $4110
Appl: Aug. 15   R and B: $1850–2750
584 applied   366 accepted   191 enrolled
SAT(mean): 460V 488M   COMPETITIVE

Barry University, founded in 1940, is a private liberal arts university affiliated with the Roman Catholic Church. The library contains over 123,000 volumes, and subscribes to over 1500 periodicals.

Environment: The 83-acre campus is located in a suburban area 12 miles north of Miami. The 15 Spanish-style buildings, built around a center mall, include 6 dormitories that house 350 men and women; the university also sponsors off-campus apartments.

Student Life: Seventy percent of the students are from Florida. About 45% of the students come from public schools, and 30% live on campus. Sixty percent are Catholic, 19% are Protestant, and 11% are Jewish. Almost a quarter of the students are minority-group members. University housing is single-sex, and there are visiting privileges. Students may keep cars on campus.

Organizations: There are no fraternities or sororities; professional and service organizations also serve as social groups. Activities include special-interest, business, and professional clubs; chorus; drama; publications; and Catholic religious organizations. Campus cultural events include art shows, concerts, films, lectures, plays, recitals, and informal mixers. Beaches are 20 minutes away.

Sports: The university fields 2 intercollegiate teams for men and 2 for women. There are 6 intramural sports for men and 4 for women.

Handicapped: Special facilities for physically handicapped students include wheelchair ramps, parking areas, elevators, lowered drinking fountains, and specially equipped rest rooms. Special class scheduling is also available. No special counselors are available.

Graduates: The freshman dropout rate is 18%, and 65% of the freshmen remain to graduate. Eighty percent of the graduates seek advanced degrees; 5% enter medical school, 1% dental school, and 7% law school. Another 45% pursue careers in business and industry.

Services: Students receive the following services free of charge: placement, career, and psychological counseling and health care. Tutoring services are available on a fee basis. Placement services also are available to alumni.

Programs of Study: The university awards the B.A., B.S., B.F.A., B.Mus., B.S.W., and B.S.N. degrees. Master's degrees also are available. Bachelor's degrees are offered in the following subjects: BUSINESS (accounting, business administration, computer science, economics, finance, management, marketing), EDUCATION (early childhood, elementary, secondary, special), ENGLISH (English), FINE AND PERFORMING ARTS (art, art education, music, music education, theater/dramatics), HEALTH SCIENCES (cytotechnology, diagnostic medical ultrasound technology, medical technology, nuclear medical technology, nursing), LANGUAGES (Spanish), MATH AND SCIENCES (biology, chemistry, mathematics), PHILOSOPHY (religion), PREPROFESSIONAL (dentistry, law, medicine, social work, veterinary), SOCIAL SCIENCES (government/political science, history, international relations, psychology), Eighteen percent of degrees are conferred in business, another 18% in health sciences, 15% in math and sciences, and 9% in education.

Required: All students must take 9 hours of philosophy and/or religion plus 6 hours of communication arts.

Special: Students who have completed 3 semesters of foreign language may spend a spring semester abroad. The program, based at The University of Neuchâtel, Switzerland, includes study at Neuchâtel, Konstanz, and Madrid and travel to other major European cities. A 3–2 B.S.W.-M.S.W. program and bilingual programs are available. A general studies degree is offered. Independent study is offered in all areas.

Honors: Seven honor societies have chapters on campus. No other programs are available.

Admissions: About 63% of those who applied were accepted for the 1981–82 freshman class. The SAT scores of those who enrolled were as follows: Verbal—58% below 500, 19% between 500 and 599, 1% between 600 and 700, and 0% above 700; Math—54% below 500, 23% between 500 and 599, 4% between 600 and 700, and 0% above 700. Applicants must rank in the upper two-fifths of their high school class and must have a grade point average of at least 3.0.

Procedure: The SAT or ACT should be taken in May of the junior year or in November, December, or January of the senior year. The application, $20 fee, test scores, and high school record should be submitted by August 15 for the fall term, January 1 for the spring term, and May 1 for the first summer session, and June 15 for the second summer session. Notification on a rolling basis begins about 2 weeks after all credentials are received. The university subscribes to the CRDA.

Special: Early and deferred admissions plans and an early decision plan are available. AP and CLEP credit is accepted.

Transfer: For fall 1981, 291 students applied, 142 were accepted, and 90 enrolled. Transfer students need a GPA of at least 2.0, a completed reference form, and 15 completed credit hours. Grades of D do not transfer. Students must earn, at the college, at least 30 of the 120 credits necessary for a bachelor's degree. Deadlines for applications are the same as those for freshmen.

Visiting: Orientations for prospective students are scheduled regularly. Guided tours also are provided for informal visits while classes are in session. Students may sit in on classes and, if convenient, stay overnight in the dormitories. Arrangements should be made through the admissions office.

Financial Aid: Sixty-five percent of the students receive aid; 80% work part-time on campus. The university provides scholarships—including 18 freshman awards from a $24,000 fund—loans, and campus employment. Loans also are available from the federal and state governments, local banks, and private sources. Freshman scholarships range from $1400 to $1800, and loans average $700 with a maximum of $2500. The average award to freshmen from all sources is $3600. The university packages aid awards under CSS procedures. Awards are made on the basis of financial need and academic record. Applications and the FAF should be submitted by April 1. Applicants are notified by April 30.

Foreign Students: Nineteen percent of the full-time students come from foreign countries. The university offers these students an intensive English program, special counseling, and special organizations.

Admissions: Foreign students must achieve a minimum TOEFL score of 450 to enter the university's Cross-Cultural Program and at least 550 for the regular academic program.

Procedure: Application deadlines are August 1 (fall), December 1 (spring), and May 1 and June 1 (summer sessions). Foreign students must present proof of funds adequate to cover 1 year of study. They must also carry health insurance, which is available through the university for a fee.

Admissions Contact: Deborah J. Iacono, Director of Freshman Admissions.

BETHUNE-COOKMAN COLLEGE D-2
Daytona Beach, Florida 32015 (904) 255-1401

F/T: 700M, 1050W		Faculty:	127; IIB, −$
P/T: 30M, 50W		Ph.D.'s:	38%
Grad: none		S/F Ratio:	17 to 1
Year: 4-1-4, ss		Tuition:	$3162
Appl: July 30		R and B:	$2150
SAT or ACT: required			**LESS COMPETITIVE**

Bethune-Cookman College, founded in 1904, is a small, private, liberal arts college related to the Methodist Church. The library houses 93,777 volumes and 4700 microfilm items, and subscribes to 506 periodicals.

Environment: The 58-acre campus is located in a city of 60,000 people, 50 miles north of Cape Canaveral. Six dormitories house over 1000 men and women. The school is close to business centers and ocean beaches.

Student Life: About 90% of the students are from Florida. The student body is predominantly black. About 60% of the students live in the dormitories, which are single-sex. There are curfews for women residents.

Organizations: About half the students belong to the 10 sororities and 10 fraternities. Other organizations include band, choir, orchestra, theater, and religious and social groups.

Sports: Teams compete in 4 intercollegiate sports. Intramural programs also are offered for men and women.

Handicapped: Over 60% of the campus is accessible to handicapped students. Special facilities recently installed or under construction include ramps, parking areas, and specially equipped rest rooms.

Graduates: About 10% of the freshmen drop out, and 80% remain to graduate. About 20% of the graduates seek advanced degrees; 1% go to medical school, 1% to dental school, and 2% to law school.

Services: Free health care, tutoring, remedial instruction, placement aid, and career counseling are available to students.

Programs of Study: The college awards the B.A. and B.S. degrees. Certificate programs also are available. Bachelor's degrees are offered in the following subjects: BUSINESS (business administration, business education), EDUCATION (elementary, health/physical, recreation, secondary, special), ENGLISH (English, speech), FINE AND PERFORMING ARTS (music, music education), HEALTH SCIENCES (nursing), MATH AND SCIENCES (biology, chemistry, mathematics), PHILOSOPHY (philosophy, religion), SOCIAL SCIENCES (government/political science, history, psychology, sociology).

Required: All students must complete the general-education program, which includes English, mathematics/science, religion and philosophy, black history, and physical education.

Special: Engineering degrees are offered in cooperation with Tuskegee Institute and the University of Florida. A medical-technology degree is offered with Meharry Medical College or the University of Florida. Minors are offered in accounting, finance, management, marketing, secretarial administration, French, Spanish, and law enforcement and corrections. Internships and field experiences are available. Juniors may participate in study-abroad programs.

Honors: There is a freshman honors program. Four national honor societies have chapters on campus.

Admissions: About 57% of those who applied were accepted for a recent freshman class. Of those who enrolled, 1% scored above 500 on the mathematics portion of the SAT and 2% scored above 500 on the verbal portion. One percent scored between 20 and 23 points on the ACT. Median SAT scores were 295 V and 321 M; the median ACT score was 12. Applicants should have completed 15 Carnegie units with at least a C average. Non-high-school graduates must be 25 years old and have a GED diploma. The following factors also are weighed: financial ability, high school recommendations, and evidence of special talents.

Procedure: The SAT or ACT is required. The deadlines for regular admission are July 30 (fall) and November 30 (spring). The application fee is $15.

Special: An early admissions plan is offered. AP and CLEP credit is accepted.

Transfer: A 2.0 GPA is required. D grades do not transfer. Students must spend at least 1 year in residence, earning 30 of the 124 credits required for a bachelor's degree. Application deadlines are the same as those for freshmen.

Visiting: Visits can be arranged through the director of student personnel.

Financial Aid: The college offers scholarships and campus jobs to freshmen. About 90% of all students receive aid. CWS is available. The FAF must be filed; the financial aid deadline is March 1.

Foreign Students: About 2% of the students come from foreign countries.

Admissions: Students must meet regular freshman requirements and demonstrate proficiency in English.

Admissions Contact: James C. Wymes, Registrar/Director of Admissions.

BISCAYNE COLLEGE E-5
Miami, Florida 33054 (305) 625-6000

F/T: 1000M, 600W	Faculty:	80; IIA, n/av
P/T: 250M, 200W	Ph.D.'s:	58%
Grad: 140M, 100W	S/F Ratio:	17 to 1
Year: sems, ss	Tuition:	$3850
Appl: Aug. 15	R and B:	$2400
1200 applied	700 accepted	300 enrolled
SAT: 440V 460M	ACT: 20	**COMPETITIVE**

Biscayne College, founded in 1962, is a small, private liberal arts college related to the Roman Catholic Church. The college provides undergraduate and graduate instruction conducted by the Augustinian Order. The library contains over 100,000 volumes and 4140 microfilm items, and subscribes to over 550 periodicals.

Environment: The 130-acre campus is located in a suburban area north of Miami. There are 13 buildings on campus, including 3 dormitories accommodating 250 students. A student lounge and cafeteria are available to day students.

Student Life: Sixty-five percent of the students are from Florida. Fifty percent of entering freshmen come from public schools. Over 35% of the students live on campus. Sixty percent are Catholic and 38% are

134 FLORIDA

Protestant. Over a quarter of the students are minority-group members. College housing is single-sex, and there are visiting privileges. Students may keep cars on campus.

Organizations: Student organizations include a fraternity, a dramatic society, Circle K, a newspaper, a literary magazine, and a yearbook.

Sports: The college fields 7 intercollegiate teams for men and 4 for women. There are 6 intramural sports for both men and women.

Handicapped: The campus is accessible to wheelchair-bound students. Facilities for the handicapped include wheelchair ramps, special parking and rest rooms, and special class scheduling. No students with hearing or visual impairments are currently enrolled.

Graduates: At the end of the freshman year 20% drop out; 50% remain to graduate. Forty percent pursue advanced study after graduation; 2% enter medical school, 1% dental school, and 4% law school. Fifty percent pursue careers in business and industry.

Services: Students receive the following services free of charge: placement, career counseling, health care, psychological counseling, tutoring, and remedial instruction.

Programs of Study: The college confers the B.A. and B.S. degrees. Associate and master's degree programs are also offered. Bachelor's degrees are offered in the following subjects: AREA STUDIES (American), BUSINESS (accounting, business administration, computer science, finance, management, marketing), EDUCATION (early childhood, elementary, secondary), ENGLISH (English), LANGUAGES (Spanish), MATH AND SCIENCES (biology, chemistry, mathematics), PHILOSOPHY (humanities, religion), PREPROFESSIONAL (dentistry, law, medicine), SOCIAL SCIENCES (government/political science, history, international relations, psychology, social sciences, sociology).

Required: All students must take 9 hours each of theology and philosophy.

Admissions: About 60% of those who applied were accepted for the 1981–82 freshman class. The SAT scores of those who enrolled were as follows: Verbal—55% below 500, 20% between 500 and 599, 20% between 600 and 700, and 5% above 700; Math—55% below 500, 20% between 500 and 599, 20% between 600 and 700, and 5% above 700. On the ACT, 66% scored below 21, 20% between 21 and 23, 10% between 24 and 25, 2% between 26 and 28, and 2% above 28. Applicants must graduate from an accredited high school with a B average or better, rank in at least the upper 50% of the class, score a minimum of 400 on each part of the SAT, and have completed 15 Carnegie units. The school also considers the following factors in order of importance: recommendations by school officials, advanced placement or honor courses, and impressions made during an interview.

Procedure: The SAT or ACT should be taken in December of the senior year. The application, a $20 fee, scholastic records, and SAT scores should be submitted by August 15 (fall), December 31 (spring), and May 1 (summer).

Special: Early decision, early admissions, and deferred admissions plans are available. CLEP and AP credit is accepted.

Transfer: About 150 transfer students are accepted each year. A 2.0 GPA is required. Some D grades transfer. Thirty credits of the 120 credits required for the bachelor's degree must be completed at the college. Deadlines are the same as for freshman applicants.

Visiting: Orientation is held for prospective students. Guided tours and interviews can be scheduled Monday through Friday during school sessions; visitors may sit in on classes and remain overnight. Visits can be arranged through the admissions office.

Financial Aid: About 70% of all students receive aid through the college, which is a member of CSS. Five percent of the students work part-time on campus. Aid applicants should submit a financial statement (FAF, FFS, or SFS) and the aid application by May 15.

Foreign Students: The college actively recruits foreign students.

Admissions: Foreign students must achieve a minimum score of 500 on TOEFL. No other exams are required.

Procedure: Application deadlines are August 15 (fall) and December 31 (spring). Foreign students must present proof of funds adequate to cover 1 year of study. They must also furnish a doctor's certificate as proof of health.

Admissions Contact: Rev. Robert M. Burke, Assistant Director of Admissions.

ECKERD COLLEGE D-4
St. Petersburg, Florida 33733 (813) 867-1166

F/T: 543M, 531W Faculty: 75; IIB, ++$
P/T: 10M, 10W Ph.D.'s: 90%
Grad: none S/F Ratio: 15 to 1
Year: 4-1-4, ss Tuition: $5095
Appl: open R and B: $2150
924 applied 716 accepted 276 enrolled
SAT: 467V 502M ACT: 22 COMPETITIVE

Eckerd College is a coeducational, liberal arts institution affiliated with the Presbyterian Church. Interdisciplinary courses and studies are an important part of the curriculum. The library contains 150,000 volumes, and subscribes to 1100 periodicals.

Environment: The 280-acre waterfront campus is located in a suburban area 3 miles from the city of St. Petersburg. The 55 major buildings include a chapel, music and fine-arts centers, and dormitory complexes.

Student Life: Eighty percent of the students live on campus. Ten percent are minority-group members. About 45% are Protestant, 31% Catholic, and 2% Jewish. Campus housing is both coed and single-sex; there are visiting privileges in the single-sex housing. Students may keep cars on campus.

Organizations: There are no fraternities or sororities on campus; professional and service organizations serve as social groups. The student government operates a coffeehouse, newspaper, literary magazine, yearbook, and radio station. It sponsors films, concerts, dances, and special-interest clubs, including a ski team and a forensic club. Additional cultural opportunities are available in nearby St. Petersburg, Tampa, and Sarasota.

Sports: The college participates intercollegiately in 8 sports for men and 7 for women. There are 10 intramural sports for men and 8 for women.

Handicapped: Ninety percent of the campus is accessible to wheelchair-bound students. Special facilities include wheelchair ramps, parking areas, and specially equipped rest rooms. Special class scheduling is also available. No special counselors are provided. Two students with visual or hearing impairments were enrolled in 1981–82.

Graduates: About 15% of the freshmen drop out, and 60% remain to graduate. Sixty percent of the graduates pursue advanced degrees; 10% enter medical school, 2% dental school, and 10% law school. Thirty percent of the graduates begin careers in business and industry.

Services: Students receive the following services free of charge: placement, career counseling, psychological counseling, health care, tutoring, and remedial instruction.

Programs of Study: The college awards the B.A. and B.S. degrees. Bachelor's degrees are offered in the following subjects: AREA STUDIES (American, Russian), BUSINESS (business administration, management), EDUCATION (early childhood, elementary, secondary), ENGLISH (comparative literature, creative writing, English, literature), FINE AND PERFORMING ARTS (art, music, theater/dramatics), LANGUAGES (French, German, modern languages, Russian, Spanish), MATH AND SCIENCES (biology, chemistry, ecology/environmental science, mathematics, physics), PHILOSOPHY (humanities, philosophy, religion), PREPROFESSIONAL (dentistry, engineering, law, medicine, ministry, veterinary), SOCIAL SCIENCES (anthropology, economics, government/political science, history, human resources, international relations, psychology, sociology).

Required: All freshmen complete a year-long course in Western heritage. Sophomores and juniors complete 4 courses in the following subjects: the aesthetic perspective, the cross-cultural perspective, the environmental perspective, and the social relations perspective. Seniors complete 1 seminar in the Judeo-Christian perspective and 1 seminar in the major. Graduation requirements also include the equivalent of 1 year of foreign language study, 1 college-level course in a quantitative field (math, computer science, logic), satisfaction of writing competency, and a comprehensive examination in the major field.

Special: Student-designed majors are permitted. Students may spend a winter term, semester, or full year abroad. Degrees may be earned in fewer than 4 years. Independent study is available in freshman through senior years. The faculty is organized by divisions rather than traditional departments to encourage interdisciplinary study.

Honors: All departments invite qualified students to participate in an honors thesis program.

Admissions: Seventy-seven percent of those who applied were accepted for the 1981–82 freshman class. The SAT scores of those who enrolled were as follows: Verbal—66% below 500, 23% between 500 and 599, 9% between 600 and 700, and 2% above 700; Math—50%

below 500, 35% between 500 and 599, 14% between 600 and 700, and 1% above 700. On the ACT, 32% scored below 21, 38% between 21 and 23, 8% between 24 and 25, 11% between 26 and 28, and 11% above 28. Besides grades, class rank, and test scores, admissions officers also consider, in order of importance, advanced placement or honors courses, leadership record, extracurricular activities, recommendations by school officials, and special talents.

Procedure: The SAT or ACT is required and should be taken in May of the junior year or November of the senior year. While ATs are not required, applicants are encouraged to take them in English and Level I or II Mathematics. An interview is recommended. The application, a $15 fee, high school record, and recommendations should be submitted at the end of the junior year or early in the senior year. There are no application deadlines. Freshmen are admitted in the fall, winter, and spring terms. Notification is made on a rolling basis beginning October 1.

Special: There is a deferred admissions plan.

Transfer: For fall 1981, 205 transfer students applied, 158 were accepted, and 94 enrolled. Applicants must be in good standing at their last school. D grades do not transfer. All students must complete, at the college, 16 of the 32 credits required for a bachelor's degree. There is no application deadline; transfer students are admitted in the fall, winter, and spring terms.

Visiting: Regularly scheduled orientations for prospective students include a night in the dorms, interviews with faculty members, admissions interviews, and class visits. Informal visits may be arranged with the dean of admissions for any time college is in session. Guides are provided, and visitors may sit in on classes and stay overnight on campus.

Financial Aid: Seventy-five percent of the students receive aid. The college provides scholarships, loans, and part-time jobs. About 50% of the students work part-time on campus. The average freshman award is $1500. Scholarships range from $500 to $5000, and 208 of the 1981–82 freshmen were awarded scholarships totaling $360,000. Installment and deferred payment plans are available. Aid is awarded on the basis of financial need and academic record. The application deadlines for priority consideration are April 1 (fall), December 1 (winter), and January 1 (spring). The college is a member of CSS. The FAF or FFS must be filed.

Foreign Students: Seven percent of the full-time students come from foreign countries. An intensive English course, an intensive English program, special counseling, and special organizations are available for these students.

Admissions: Foreign students must achieve a TOEFL score of at least 550 or must have completed the final level (109) of the ELS program. No college entrance exams are required.

Procedure: Application deadlines are July 1 (fall), December 1 (winter), and January 1 (spring). Foreign students must submit a medical form completed by a physician and must present proof of funds adequate to cover 1 year of study. Health insurance is required and is available through the college for a fee.

Admissions Contact: Richard Hallin, Dean of Admissions and Records.

EDWARD WATERS COLLEGE   D-1
Jacksonville, Florida 32209   (904) 355-3030

F/T: 260M, 544W	Faculty: 37; IIB, --$
P/T: 14M, 49W	Ph.D.'s: n/av
Grad: 112M&W	S/F Ratio: 21 to 1
Year: sems, ss	Tuition: $1100
Appl: Aug. 1	R and B: $1100
250 applied	200 accepted	177 enrolled
SAT or ACT: not required	LESS COMPETITIVE

Edward Waters College, founded in 1866, is the state's first institution of higher learning for black students. Affiliated with the African Methodist Episcopal Church, the college offers undergraduate programs in the arts and sciences, business, and education. Its library has 65,000 books and 25,000 microfilm items, and subscribes to 5000 periodicals.

Environment: The 20-acre campus is in an urban setting and consists of 9 buildings, including 1 residence hall for 200 men and women.

Student Life: About 95% of the students come from Florida. Nearly all attended public schools. About 96% are minority-group members. About 23% live on campus. Weekly chapel service attendance is required. Campus housing is single-sex; there are visiting privileges. Students may keep cars on campus.

Organizations: About 20% of the students belong to fraternities and sororities.

Sports: The college fields 2 intercollegiate teams for men and 2 for women. There are 6 intramural sports for men and 6 for women.

Services: Psychological counseling, tutoring, and remedial instruction are offered to students free of charge.

Programs of Study: B.A. and B.S. degrees are conferred. Bachelor's degrees are offered in the following subjects: BUSINESS (business administration), EDUCATION (early childhood, elementary, health/physical), ENGLISH (English), MATH AND SCIENCES (biology, chemistry, mathematics), PHILOSOPHY (philosophy, religion), PRE-PROFESSIONAL (social work), SOCIAL SCIENCES (criminology, government/political science, social sciences, sociology).

Admissions: About 80% of the 1981–82 applicants were accepted. A high school diploma or GED is required; applicants must have a 2.0 minimum GPA. Advanced placement or honors courses, ability to finance a college education, and recommendations are also considered important.

Procedure: The California Achievement Test is required. Application deadlines are August 1 (fall), December 30 (spring), and May 1 (summer). There is a $10 application fee.

Special: CLEP and AP credit is granted.

Transfer: For fall 1981, 198 students applied, 189 were accepted, and 76 enrolled. A GPA of at least 1.5 is required. D grades do not transfer. All students must complete the 124 credits required for a bachelor's degree. Application deadlines are the same as those for freshmen.

Financial Aid: About 95% of the students are receiving assistance. About 15% work part-time on campus. The average freshman award is $1210. The college is a member of CSS. Various government and commercial loan programs, federal grants such as BEOG, and campus employment opportunities (including CWS) are available. The FFS should be filed by April 15.

Foreign Students: Three percent of the full-time students come from foreign countries. An intensive English course, an intensive English program, special counseling, and special organizations are available for these students.

Admissions: Foreign students must take the TOEFL and the California Achievement Test.

Procedure: Application deadlines are the same as those for other students. Foreign students must have a complete medical examination, including a chest X-ray, and must present proof of funds adequate to cover 1 year of study. Health insurance must be carried and is available through the college for a fee.

Admissions Contact: Willie B. Jackson, Admission Counselor.

EMBRY-RIDDLE AERONAUTICAL UNIVERSITY   D-2
Daytona Beach, Florida 32014   (800) 874-9912
Prescott, Arizona 86301

F/T: 5324M, 377W	Faculty: 323; IIA, --$
P/T: 219M, 42W	Ph.D.'s: 13%
Grad: 97M, 9W	S/F Ratio: 20 to 1
Year: tri, ss	Tuition: $2650
Appl: open	R and B: $1950
1313 enrolled	
SAT or ACT: required	NONCOMPETITIVE

Embry-Riddle Aeronautical University, founded in 1926, is an independent institution offering undergraduate degree programs in aviation education including engineering, management, aircraft maintenance, and pilot training. In addition to the Daytona Beach campus, Embry-Riddle has a second campus in Prescott, Arizona. The library has 45,000 volumes and 3500 microfilm items, and subscribes to more than 350 periodicals.

Environment: The 85-acre suburban campus is located at Daytona Beach Regional Airport. Facilities include an aeronautical science and flight complex, academic complex, and university center. Housing is available on campus for 766 students; official housing off campus accommodates another 405 students. The 510-acre Prescott, Arizona, campus includes dormitory facilities.

Student Life: About 20% of the students come from Florida; 70% have had public school educations. About 20% live on the main campus. Campus housing is coed. Students may keep cars on campus.

FLORIDA

Organizations: Twelve percent of the men belong to fraternities. Student government, special-interest clubs, and social activities are offered.

Sports: At the main campus, there are 4 intramural sports for men and 4 for women. There are 7 intramural sports for men and 5 for women at the Arizona campus.

Graduates: The freshman dropout rate is 15%. About 98% of the graduates enter business and industry.

Services: The university provides free health care, career counseling, placement, and remedial instruction.

Programs of Study: The B.S. and B.S. of Professional Aeronautics degrees are conferred. Associate and master's degrees are also awarded. Bachelor's degrees are offered in the following subjects: BUSINESS (aviation administration, aviation management, computer science), MATH AND SCIENCES (aeronautical science, aeronautical studies), PREPROFESSIONAL (aviation maintenance management, aviation technology, engineering—aeronautical, engineering technology—aircraft, professional aeronautics). The Arizona campus offers all these degree programs except aircraft engineering technology, aviation maintenance management, and aviation technology.

Required: All students must complete courses in humanities/social sciences, mathematics/physical sciences, economics, and computer technology.

Special: There are cooperative work-study programs.

Honors: Honor societies are open to qualified students.

Admissions: A high school diploma or GED is required.

Procedure: The SAT or ACT is required for placement purposes only. Deadlines are open; freshmen are admitted in the fall, spring, and summer terms. Notification is on a rolling basis. There is a $25 application fee.

Special: There are early decision, early admissions, and deferred admissions plans. AP and CLEP credit is available.

Transfer: For fall 1981, 656 transfer students enrolled. Good academic standing and SAT or ACT scores are required; D grades do not transfer. All students must complete, at the university, 30 of the minimum 129 credits required for a bachelor's degree; 2 trimesters of study must be taken in residence. There are no application deadlines.

Visiting: Campus tours with student guides may be arranged.

Financial Aid: About 80% of the students receive financial aid. Twenty percent work part-time on campus. The university offers federal programs such as BEOG/SEOG and NDSL. Other loan programs and scholarships are available. The average award to freshmen from all sources is 30% of expenses. Tuition may be paid in installments. The FAF is required and should be filed by January (fall), April (spring), or August (summer). The university is a member of CSS.

Foreign Students: Eleven percent of the full-time students come from foreign countries. An intensive English course, an intensive English program, special counseling, and special organizations are available for these students.

Admissions: Foreign students must achieve a minimum score of 500 on the TOEFL or 85 on the University of Michigan Language Test. No college entrance exams are required.

Procedure: Deadlines are open; foreign students are admitted in the fall, spring, and summer terms. The application fee is $50. They must complete the university's medical report form and must present proof of funds adequate to cover 1 year of study. There is a $50 special fee per trimester for educational services for foreign students.

Admissions Contact: Peter D. Brooker, Dean of Admissions.

FLAGLER COLLEGE D-2
St. Augustine, Florida 32084 (904) 829-6481

F/T: 350M, 500W	Faculty:	35; n/av
P/T: 20M, 25W	Ph.D.'s:	54%
Grad: none	S/F Ratio:	20 to 1
Year: sems, ss	Tuition:	$2450
Appl: June 1	R and B:	$1540
843 applied	538 accepted	265 enrolled
SAT: 430V 450M		COMPETITIVE

Flagler College, founded in 1968, is an independent, private liberal arts college. The library contains 71,000 volumes and 5800 microfilm items, and subscribes to 436 periodicals.

Environment: Only 35 miles from Jacksonville and 50 miles from Daytona Beach, the 30-acre campus is located in the urban environment of St. Augustine. The focal point of the campus is the former Ponce de Leon Hotel, built in 1888 by Henry M. Flagler and listed in the *National Register of Historic Places*. Students are housed in the hotel rooms. The campus consists of 10 buildings, an Olympic-sized swimming pool, and an athletic field complex located 2 miles away.

Student Life: Forty-six percent of the students come from Florida, 4% from bordering states, and 2% from foreign countries. Fifty-five percent live on campus. Three percent are minority-group members. Campus housing is single-sex; there are no visiting privileges. Students may keep cars on campus.

Organizations: The largest student group on campus is the Student Government Association. The many social events on campus include beach parties, poolside parties, Parents' Weekend, and dances. The college does not sponsor any religious counselors or organizations for the students. There are no social fraternities or sororities on campus.

Sports: Intercollegiate sports for men number 6; for women, 4. There are 7 intramural sports for both men and women.

Handicapped: There are no special facilities for the physically handicapped.

Graduates: About 20% of the students continue on to graduate schools; less than 2% enter law school. Thirty-five percent pursue careers in business and industry.

Services: The following services are available to the students free of charge: placement, health care, career counseling, and tutoring. Remedial instruction is available for a fee.

Programs of Study: The college confers the B.A. degree. Bachelor's degrees are offered in the following subjects: AREA STUDIES (Latin American), BUSINESS (business administration), EDUCATION (elementary, physical, recreation, secondary, special/deaf), ENGLISH (English), FINE AND PERFORMING ARTS (art, art education, commercial art, studio art, theater/dramatics), LANGUAGES (Spanish), PHILOSOPHY (philosophy/religion), PREPROFESSIONAL (law, youth ministry), SOCIAL SCIENCES (history, psychology, social sciences). Of the degrees conferred, 41% are in education, 22% in social sciences, and 13% in business.

Required: All students are required to take the following: 2 semesters of English composition (may be waived for students with advanced placement), 2 semesters of humanities, 2 semesters of social sciences, 2 semesters of natural sciences/mathematics, and 2 additional semesters from any one of the 3 broad areas mentioned above.

Special: Student-designed majors are permitted. A writing/composition laboratory is available to freshmen. Beginning in the sophomore year, students majoring in deaf education can work directly with students at the Florida State School for the Deaf. Special education concentrations are offered in deaf education, mental retardation, and special learning disabilities. Students are permitted to spend their junior year abroad. Students majoring in Spanish and Latin American studies are encouraged to study abroad for a semester. Flagler has an established study abroad program in Guanajuato, Mexico. Study abroad in Costa Rica, Argentina, and Bolivia can also be arranged.

Honors: Alpha Chi, a national honor society, has a chapter on campus.

Admissions: Approximately 64% of those who applied were accepted for the 1981–82 class. The candidate must have graduated from high school with at least 16 units and a 2.0 GPA. Other factors considered, in the order of importance, are: recommendations by school officials, impressions made during an interview, and advanced placement or honors courses. A personal interview is not required but is recommended, and may be taken with a representative in or near the student's hometown.

Procedure: The SAT or ACT is required, but no minimum score has been established. Junior year results are acceptable. Application deadlines are June 1 (fall) and January 1 (spring). There is a rolling admissions policy; priority is given to applications received before May 1. A $15 fee should accompany the application.

Special: Early and deferred admissions are available. AP and CLEP credit is also available.

Transfer: The college has a quota of 100 transfer students accepted each year. A 2.0 GPA is required, with a minimum of 24 semester hours of credit. If the student has earned fewer than 24 semester hours, a high school transcript and a secondary school recommendation form must be submitted. Transfer students planning to major in education must have scores in the upper 40th percentile on the SAT or ACT. D grades generally do not transfer; 9 semester hours of D credit will be accepted with the A.A. degree. Transfers are accepted for all but the senior year. Thirty credits must be taken at the college, of a total 120 credits required for the bachelor's degree. Deadlines are the same as for entering freshmen.

Visiting: Campus visits can be made any time during the semester while classes are in session. Guides are provided for informal visits, and arrangements can be made to stay at the school by contacting the office of admissions.

Financial Aid: About 80% of all students are receiving aid through the college. About 30% work part-time on campus. There are 30 athletic merit awards and 25 freshman honor scholarships; the college has $190,000 in scholarship aid available to freshmen and upperclassmen and administers $459,163 in loan funds from the federally insured loan program. Work grants are available up to $1000 per year. Last year, students received more than $90,000 in work-study assistance. Assistance is also available through various federal programs such as NDSL, SEOG, and CWSP. Additional grants are awarded on the basis of academic achievement or special merit. Grants-in-aid range from $200 to $3650; loans range from $200 to $2500; and work contracts range from $600 to $1000. The college is a member of CSS. The FAF is required from aid applicants in addition to the college's own institutional form. Need and academic potential are the principal considerations. The deadlines for aid applications are April 1 (fall) and December 1 (spring).

Foreign Students: Two percent of the students come from foreign countries. Special counseling and special organizations are available.

Admissions: A minimum score of 500 must be achieved on the TOEFL. The SAT or ACT is also required.

Procedure: Foreign students should apply by April 1 for fall entry. They must present proof of adequate funds to cover 1 academic year. Health insurance is available through the college for a fee.

Admissions Contact: William T. Abare, Jr., Director of Admissions and Enrollment Planning.

FLORIDA AGRICULTURAL AND MECHANICAL UNIVERSITY C–1
Tallahassee, Florida 32307 (904) 599-3796

F/T: 2077M, 2047W	Faculty:	348; n/av
P/T: 400M, 358W	Ph.D.'s:	55%
Grad: 208M, 185W	S/F Ratio:	28 to 1
Year: 4-1-4, ss	Tuition:	$970 ($3015)
Appl: July 1	R and B:	$2530
1900 applied	1100 accepted	700 enrolled
SAT or ACT: required		COMPETITIVE

Florida Agricultural and Mechanical University, chartered in 1887, is a state-supported, historically black university and land-grant college. The library contains 320,000 volumes and 25,000 microfilm items, and subscribes to 3000 periodicals.

Environment: The 418-acre campus is located in an urban environment, about a mile from the center of Tallahassee. The library houses a black archive listed in the *National Register.* Residence halls house 835 men and 932 women. Students also are housed in mobile units, and 116 apartments are available to married students.

Student Life: Most students are from Florida, and 90% come from public schools. Sixty-five percent live on campus. Eighty-eight percent of the students are black, 3% are Hispanic, 2% are Oriental, and 7% are members of other minority groups. Campus housing is single-sex; there are no visiting privileges. Students may keep cars on campus.

Organizations: About 7% of the students belong to 1 of 5 fraternities or 5 sororities. Campus activities include religious and departmental clubs, student government, and publications.

Sports: The university fields 6 intercollegiate teams for men and 6 for women. There are 4 intramural sports for men and 3 for women.

Handicapped: About 80% of the campus is accessible to physically handicapped students. Facilities include wheelchair ramps, special parking, elevators, special class scheduling, lowered telephones, and specially equipped rest rooms.

Graduates: Of entering freshmen, 15% drop out by the end of the first year and 40% remain to graduate. Thirty percent of the graduates pursue further study; 2% enter medical school, 2% dental school, and 3% law school. Thirty percent begin careers in business or industry.

Services: Students receive the following services free of charge: psychological, placement, and career counseling and tutoring. Health care is available for a fee.

Programs of Study: The university awards the B.A., B.S., and B.T. degrees. Master's degrees also are available. Bachelor's degrees are offered in the following subjects: AREA STUDIES (Black/Afro-American), BUSINESS (accounting, business administration, business education, computer science, finance, management, marketing), EDUCATION (early childhood, elementary, health/physical, secondary), ENGLISH (English, journalism), FINE AND PERFORMING ARTS (art, art education, music, music education, theater/dramatics), HEALTH SCIENCES (hospital and health care administration, medical record administration, nursing, physical therapy, respiratory therapy), MATH AND SCIENCES (biology, chemistry, mathematics, physics), PHILOSOPHY (philosophy, religion), PREPROFESSIONAL (agriculture, architecture, pharmacy, social work, veterinary), SOCIAL SCIENCES (economics, government/political science, history, psychology, sociology).

Required: Students must take courses in English, humanities, mathematics, natural sciences, physical education, and social sciences. Veterans may waive the physical education requirement.

Special: Programs are available in general studies and environmental studies. A 3–2 degree in civil engineering is offered in conjunction with the University of Florida.

Honors: Five honor societies have chapters on campus. The university also offers an honors program.

Admissions: About 58% of those who applied were accepted for the 1981–82 freshman class. Applicants must be high school graduates who have completed 16 units of work and must present an average of at least 2.0. Other factors weighed, in order of importance, are advanced placement or honors courses, ability to finance a college education, recommendations by school officials, and leadership record.

Procedure: Students must take the SAT or ACT. The application, a $15 fee, test scores, and scholastic records should be submitted by July 1 (fall), December 1 (spring), and April 1 (summer). Notification is made on a rolling basis.

Special: CLEP credit is accepted.

Transfer: For fall 1981, 488 students applied, 365 were accepted, and 310 enrolled. Applicants must have at least a C average from an accredited junior college, with a minimum of 60 credits earned. A, B, and C grades transfer. Preference is given to applicants from state community colleges and universities. Students must take 12 months' work at the university; at least 30 hours must be completed at the university, of a total 120 hours required for the bachelor's degree. Application deadlines are the same as those for freshmen.

Visiting: Orientations for prospective students are scheduled regularly. They include campus tours and meetings with university officials. Informal visits also may be arranged with the admissions office. Appointments are required, and guides are provided.

Financial Aid: About 80% of the students receive aid. About 15% work part-time on campus. The average award to freshmen is $1200. The university provides scholarships as well as long- and short-term loans. The FAF or FFS is required, and applications should be submitted by April 1.

Foreign Students: Students from foreign countries represent 7% of the enrollment. Special counseling is available, and there are organizations especially for foreign students.

Admissions: Foreign applicants are required to score at least 500 on the TOEFL. The SAT or ACT must also be taken; the minimum required (composite) score is 800 on the SAT or 17 on the ACT.

Procedure: Foreign students should apply 6 months prior to each semester. They are admitted to the fall, spring, and summer sessions. Proof of health, in the form of a doctor's certification, is required. Proof of adequate funds to cover 1 year is also necessary. Health insurance must be carried while in attendance.

Admissions Contact: Daisy O. Young, Assistant Director of Admissions.

FLORIDA INSTITUTE OF TECHNOLOGY E–3
Melbourne, Florida 32901 (305) 723-3701

F/T: 2369M, 790W	Faculty:	209; I, – – $
P/T: 387M, 129W	Ph.D.'s:	85%
Grad: 267M, 89W	S/F Ratio:	20 to 1
Year: qtrs, ss	Tuition:	$3452
Appl: June 30	R and B:	$2040
4000 applied	2600 accepted	1000 enrolled
SAT: 480V 552M	ACT: 25	VERY COMPETITIVE+

Florida Institute of Technology is a private university specializing in engineering and science. The library contains more than 103,000 volumes, and subscribes to 895 periodicals.

Environment: The 146-acre campus is located in a suburban environment, about a mile from the town of Melbourne and 28 miles south of Cape Canaveral. Sixteen residence halls house 1800 men and women. Types of living facilities sponsored by the institute include, dormitories, on-campus apartments, and fraternity houses.

138 FLORIDA

Student Life: Twenty-five percent of the students are residents of Florida. Eighty percent of the freshmen are from public schools. Sixty percent live on campus. About 6% are minority-group members. Campus housing is both single-sex and coed; in the single-sex residences, there are visiting privileges. Students may keep cars on campus.

Organizations: There are 8 fraternities and 1 sorority. Extracurricular activities include publications, student government, technical clubs, and a campus ministry center.

Sports: The college competes on an intercollegiate level in 12 sports for men and 10 for women. Intramural sports for both men and women number 9.

Handicapped: Ninety-five percent of the campus is accessible to wheelchair-bound students. Special facilities include wheelchair ramps, parking areas, elevators, and specially equipped rest rooms. Special class scheduling is also available. No special counselors are provided.

Graduates: Thirty percent drop out by the end of the first year. About 50% of each entering class graduate in four years, and 20% of the graduates pursue advanced degrees. Eighty percent begin careers in business and industry.

Services: Students receive the following services free of charge: placement, career, and psychological counseling, health care, tutoring, and remedial instruction.

Programs of Study: The college awards the B.S. degree. Associate, master's, and doctoral degrees also are available. Bachelor's degrees are offered in the following subjects: BUSINESS (accounting, air commerce flight technology, air commerce, transportation technology, computer science, finance, management, marketing), EDUCATION (secondary/science), ENGLISH (business communications, technical communications), FINE AND PERFORMING ARTS (film/photography), HEALTH SCIENCES (medical technology), MATH AND SCIENCES (biochemistry/molecular biology, biology, chemistry, ecology/environmental science, marine biology, mathematics, oceanography, physics, space science), PHILOSOPHY (humanities), PREPROFESSIONAL (dentistry, engineering—chemical, engineering—civil, engineering—computer, engineering—electrical, engineering—environmental, engineering—mechanical, engineering—ocean, medicine, veterinary). Forty percent of bachelor's degrees are conferred in preprofessional studies.

Required: All students must take courses in math, chemistry, physics, English, history, and computer science.

Special: The institute offers a Bachelor of Air Commerce degree. Other special programs include the Junior Engineers and Scientists Summer Institute, the Annual College-Preparation Summer Institute, and the Summer Workshop in Oceanography. The institute's School of Applied Technology offers programs in aeronautics and underwater technology.

Honors: A number of honor societies have chapters on campus.

Admissions: Sixty-five percent of those who applied were accepted for the 1981–82 freshman class. SAT scores of entering freshmen were as follows: Verbal—45% below 500, 45% between 500 and 599, 5% between 600 and 700, 5% above 700; Math—30% below 500, 50% between 500 and 599, 15% between 600 and 700, 5% above 700. On the ACT, 10% scored below 21, 15% between 21 and 23, 30% between 24 and 25, 30% between 26 and 28, and 15% above 28. Applicants should have a minimum GPA of 2.5 and should rank in the upper 40% of their class. Other factors that enter into the admissions decision include advanced placement or honors courses, recommendations by school officials, and impressions made during an interview.

Procedure: The SAT or ACT is required. The fall application deadline is June 30; all other application deadlines are open. Candidates are notified within 3 weeks after their credentials are received. There is a $20 application fee. Freshmen are admitted to the fall and winter quarters. Admissions are on a rolling basis.

Special: Early decision and early and deferred admissions plans are available. The early admissions application deadline is January of the junior year. CLEP and AP credit is granted.

Transfer: About 200 transfers enrolled for fall 1981. Applicants must have taken college preparatory courses in high school. A minimum GPA of 3.0 is recommended as well as minimum SAT scores of 450 on the verbal and 550 on the math or a composite score of at least 25 on the ACT. Only C grades or better transfer. Students must complete 45 quarter hours in residence to receive a degree. Transfers are accepted to all classes. They are also admitted to all quarters. The transfer application deadlines are the same as for freshman applicants.

Visiting: Guided tours and interviews can be scheduled with the admissions office for Monday through Friday, at 10 A.M. or 2 P.M. Guides are provided, and students may sit in on classes and spend the night on campus.

Financial Aid: Eighty percent of the students receive aid. About 13% work part-time on campus. The average award to freshmen is $1800. Institute-administered aid includes NDSL, EOG, CWS, and a limited number of scholarships. The institute is a member of CSS. Aid applications and the FAF must be submitted by March 15.

Foreign Students: Of the full-time student body, 11% come from foreign countries. The institute offers an intensive English program, special counseling, and organizations especially for foreign students.

Admissions: Foreign candidates must take the institute's English proficiency test. They are not required to take the SAT or ACT.

Procedure: Foreign candidates should apply by July 1 (fall), October 1 (winter), January 1 (spring), and March 15 (summer). A health form must be completed. Proof of adequate funds must be shown and a $200 emergency deposit made. It is necessary to carry health insurance, which is available through the institute for a fee.

Admissions Contact: Monica M. Rudzik, Assistant Director of Admissions.

FLORIDA MEMORIAL COLLEGE E-5
Miami, Florida 33054 (305) 625-4141

F/T: 419M, 508W Faculty: 44; IIB, ——$
P/T: 31M, 55W Ph.D.'s: 75%
Grad: none S/F Ratio: 22 to 1
Year: sems, ss Tuition: $2340
Appl: see profile R and B: $1620
1087 applied 427 accepted 370 enrolled
SAT or ACT: not required LESS COMPETITIVE

Florida Memorial College, founded in 1879, is a private, coeducational college of liberal arts affiliated with the American Baptist Church. The library contains more than 72,000 volumes, and subscribes to 400 periodicals.

Environment: The urban campus, located in Miami, has 12 buildings constructed in the Spanish style. Living facilities include dormitories and off-campus apartments.

Student Life: The college seeks a national student body. All students are graduates of public schools. About 33% live on campus. Almost 100% are minority-group members. Campus housing is coed. Students may keep cars on campus. Day-care services are available to full-time students for a fee.

Organizations: Several fraternities and sororities are represented on campus. The college sponsors concerts, lectures, movies, and drama productions. Religious activities include Sunday services and various student organizations. The college has also developed a Center for Community Change; this center sponsors national figures that provide input on new community developments.

Sports: The college fields intercollegiate teams in 3 sports. There are 5 intramural sports.

Graduates: About 38% of entering freshmen drop out by the end of the first year; 25% remain to graduate. About 10% of the graduates pursue advanced degrees. Thirty-five percent enter business and industry.

Services: Career counseling, placement, health care, psychological counseling, tutoring, and remedial instruction are provided free of charge.

Programs of Study: The college awards the B.A. and B.S. degrees. Bachelor's degrees are offered in the following subjects: AREA STUDIES (urban), BUSINESS (accounting, business administration, business education, management), EDUCATION (adult, elementary), ENGLISH (English), FINE AND PERFORMING ARTS (art, art education, music, music education), HEALTH SCIENCES (environmental health), LANGUAGES (French, Greek/Latin, Hebrew, Spanish), MATH AND SCIENCES (biology, chemistry, mathematics), PHILOSOPHY (religion), SOCIAL SCIENCES (clinical psychology, criminal justice, economics, public administration, social sciences, urban planning, urban services and community).

Required: Core requirements must be satisfied for graduation.

Admissions: About 39% of those who applied were accepted for the 1981–82 freshman class. Candidates must have a GED or high school diploma.

Procedure: Applicants are encouraged, but not required, to take the SAT or ACT. Applications are due 1 month prior to the beginning of the fall or spring term, or 2 weeks prior to the beginning of the summer term. There is a $15 application fee. Three personal recommendations and a health certificate also are required.

Transfer: D grades do not transfer. A satisfactory recommendation from the last school attended is required. All students must complete the 124 credits required for a bachelor's degree. Application deadlines are the same as those for freshmen.

Financial Aid: About 98% of the students receive aid through the college. Scholarships, grants, loans, and part-time jobs are available. Applications for scholarships must be submitted by June 15. Applications for other types of aid should be submitted by December 1. The FAF is required.

Foreign Students: About 33% of the full-time students come from foreign countries. An intensive English course, special counseling, and special organizations are available for these students.

Admissions: Foreign students must take the college's English proficiency test. No college entrance exams are required.

Procedure: Applications are due 6 months prior to the starting date of either semester. Foreign students must present a physician's statement certifying health and must present proof of funds adequate to cover 1 year of study. Health insurance is available through the college for a fee.

Admissions Contact: Robert Branch, Director of Admissions.

FLORIDA SOUTHERN COLLEGE D-4
Lakeland, Florida 33802 (813) 683-5521

F/T: 817M, 1005W	Faculty:	94; IIB, –$
P/T: 35M, 65W	Ph.D.'s:	54%
Grad: 72M, 44W	S/F Ratio:	19 to 1
Year: sems, ss	Tuition:	$3022
Appl: Aug. 1	R and B:	$1990
1117 applied	729 accepted	469 enrolled
SAT: 470V 500M	ACT: 21	COMPETITIVE

Florida Southern College, founded in 1885, is a liberal arts college affiliated with the Methodist Church. The library contains 160,000 volumes and 8220 microfilm items, and subscribes to 767 periodicals.

Environment: The campus was designed by Frank Lloyd Wright. It is situated on 67 acres in a suburban community of 65,000 people. The communications building was opened in January 1980. Living facilities include dormitories and fraternity and sorority houses.

Student Life: The student body consists of 65% state residents. Eighty-two percent of the students live on campus. About 5% are minority-group members. Seventy percent are Protestant, and 21% are Catholic. Campus housing is single-sex; there are no visiting privileges. Students may keep cars on campus. Drinking is prohibited.

Organizations: There are 6 sororities and 9 fraternities on campus; about 50% of men and women belong. There are numerous scholastic and professional societies open to qualified students.

Sports: The college fields 7 intercollegiate teams for men and 5 for women. There are 9 intramural sports for men and 9 for women.

Handicapped: Almost the entire campus is accessible to physically handicapped students. Facilities include ramps, special parking, and specially equipped rest rooms. Special class scheduling is possible.

Graduates: Five percent of entering freshmen drop out by the end of the first year; 60% remain to graduate.

Services: Placement, career counseling, and psychological counseling are available free to all students. Some tutoring services require payment. Health care is provided on a fee basis.

Programs of Study: The college offers B.A. and B.S. degrees. Master's degrees are also awarded. Bachelor's degrees are offered in the following subjects: BUSINESS (accounting, business administration), EDUCATION (early childhood, elementary, health/physical, secondary, special), ENGLISH (communications, English), FINE AND PERFORMING ARTS (art, art education, music, music education, radio/TV, sacred music, theater/dramatics), LANGUAGES (French, German, Spanish), MATH AND SCIENCES (biology, chemistry, citrus and horticulture, mathematics, physics), PHILOSOPHY (religion), SOCIAL SCIENCES (economics, government/political science, history, psychology, sociology). Over 30% of degrees are conferred in the business areas.

Required: All students are required to take English, science, mathematics, fine arts, history, social science, physical education, and religious courses. UP Field Tests must be taken before graduation.

Special: The program in special education meets requirements for teacher certification. AP or CLEP credit is accepted. A year-abroad program is open to all students. Other special areas of study are a Washington, D.C., Semester and United Nations Semester.

FLORIDA 139

Honors: There are 18 national and local honor societies on campus.

Admissions: About 65% of those who applied were accepted for the 1981–82 freshman class. Candidates should have completed 13 Carnegie units and should rank in the upper half of their class with a GPA of at least 2.5. In addition to these qualifications, the school considers the following factors important: advanced placement or honors courses, recommendations by school officials, and leadership record.

Procedure: Either the SAT or ACT is required. The deadline for regular admission is August 1; freshmen are admitted in the fall, spring, and summer terms. There is a rolling admissions policy. Applications should be submitted with a $20 fee.

Special: There are early admissions and deferred admissions plans.

Transfer: For fall 1981, 460 students applied, 287 were accepted, and 215 enrolled. A 2.0 average and a school recommendation are required. D grades for acceptable courses do transfer. All students must complete, at the college, 30 of the 124 credits required for a bachelor's degree and one-half of the credits needed for the major. The deadlines are the same as for entering freshmen.

Visiting: The campus is open all year and there are guides available; arrangements should be made through the admissions office.

Financial Aid: About 72% of all students receive aid. Ten percent work part-time on campus. The average freshman award is $1000. The college is a member of CSS. The FAF must be filed along with a financial aid application by April 1 (fall) or November 15 (spring).

Foreign Students: About 2% of the full-time students come from foreign countries. Special counseling is available for these students.

Admissions: Foreign students must achieve a TOEFL score of at least 550. No college entrance exams are required.

Procedure: The application deadline is August 1; foreign students are admitted in the fall, spring, and summer terms. They must submit a medical form completed by a physician, and they must present proof of funds adequate to cover 1 year of study. Health insurance is required and is available through the college for a fee.

Admissions Contact: William B. Stephens, Jr., Director of Admissions.

FLORIDA STATE UNIVERSITY C-1
Tallahassee, Florida 32306 (904) 644-6200

F/T: 7852M, 9120W	Faculty:	n/av; I, +$
P/T: 1411M, 1692W	Ph.D.'s:	85%
Grad: 4287M, 1535W	S/F Ratio:	23 to 1
Year: sems, ss	Tuition:	$840 ($2030)
Appl: see profile	R and B:	$1960
8000 applied	5500 accepted	2520 enrolled
SAT: 460V 498M	ACT: 22	COMPETITIVE

Florida State University, chartered in 1851, is a state-supported university with 14 undergraduate divisions. The library houses 1,253,427 volumes and 1,796,217 microfilm items, and subscribes to 13,543 periodicals.

Environment: The 332-acre campus is located in a suburban area of Tallahassee, a city of 100,000 people. The many buildings on the campus include a biological science building and 14 dormitories that accommodate 1433 men, 2871 women, and 450 married students. Other living facilities include on-campus apartments, fraternity houses, and sorority houses.

Student Life: About 91% of the students are from Florida. Approximately 25% live on campus. Fourteen percent are minority-group members. Campus housing is both single-sex and coed; there are visiting privileges in the former. Students may keep cars on campus.

Organizations: There are 23 fraternities and 21 sororities on campus. There are also many student organizations, including special clubs and religious groups.

Sports: The university competes intercollegiately in 9 sports for men and 9 for women. There are 10 intramural sports for men and 11 for women.

Handicapped: The campus is about 75% accessible to wheelchair-bound students. Ramps, special parking, elevators, and lowered telephones and drinking fountains are among the special facilities. Reading machines and special tutors are available to visually impaired students.

Services: Career counseling and placement services are available free of charge to students. Health care and tutoring are available for a fee. Psychological counseling may require a fee.

Programs of Study: The university confers the B.A., B.F.A., B.M., B.M.Ed., and B.S. degrees. Associate, master's, and doctoral programs are also offered. Bachelor's degrees are offered in the following subjects: AREA STUDIES (American, Asian), BUSINESS (accounting, business administration, computer science, finance, hotel/restaurant administration, management, marketing, real estate/insurance), EDUCATION (adult, early childhood, elementary, health/physical, secondary, special), ENGLISH (English, literature, speech), FINE AND PERFORMING ARTS (art, art education, art history, dance, music, music education, radio/TV, studio art, theater/dramatics), HEALTH SCIENCES (medical technology, nursing, speech therapy), LANGUAGES (French, German, Spanish), MATH AND SCIENCES (biology, chemistry, geology, mathematics, natural sciences, physical sciences, physics, statistics), PHILOSOPHY (classics, humanities, philosophy, religion), PREPROFESSIONAL (dentistry, law, library science, medicine, ministry, pharmacy, social work, veterinary), SOCIAL SCIENCES (anthropology, economics, geography, government/political science, history, international relations, psychology, social sciences, sociology).

Special: The university offers summer travel and study abroad.

Honors: Honors programs are available in most areas of study.

Admissions: About 69% of those who applied were accepted for the 1981–82 freshman class. Graduation from an accredited high school or the equivalent is required. Applicants must have at least 2 units of high school English, 2 units of mathematics (Algebra I or higher), and 3 additional units from the disciplines of English, mathematics, social science, natural science, and/or foreign languages. Additional requirements are as follows: Florida residents—a combined SAT score of 840 (or a composite ACT score of 17) and a 2.0 GPA; nonresidents—a combined SAT score of 1000 (or a composite ACT score of 23) and a 3.0 GPA.

Procedure: The SAT or ACT is required. Freshmen are admitted to the fall, spring, and summer sessions. It is recommended that application for fall term be made at the beginning of the senior year. The deadlines are 30 days prior to the start of the term; however, quotas may be reached earlier. Applications should be submitted with a $15 application fee. Admissions are on a rolling basis.

Special: Early admissions and early decision plans are available. AP and CLEP credit is accepted.

Transfer: About 5300 transfer students are accepted annually. They are accepted for all classes, and they are admitted to all terms. Residents must have a 2.0 GPA and nonresidents need a 2.5 GPA; these minimum GPAs are not required of students with 52 semester hours or more of credit. D grades transfer. Thirty semester hours must be taken at the university, of a total 120 semester hours required for the bachelor's degree. Applications are accepted until 1 month before the start of the term.

Visiting: Guides are available for informal visits; sitting in on classes is permitted.

Financial Aid: Forty-eight percent of the students receive aid through the college. About 25% work part-time on campus. The university offers scholarships, grants, loans, and CWS programs to students on the basis of need and academic performance. The university is a member of CSS. The FAF or FFS (preferred) statement is required; the aid application must be filed by March 1.

Foreign Students: Four percent of the full-time students come from foreign countries. The university offers special counseling and organizations especially for foreign students.

Admissions: The university requires that foreign applicants take the TOEFL and either the SAT or ACT.

Procedure: Foreign students are admitted to the fall, spring, and summer sessions. Deadlines are open; admissions are on a rolling basis. Foreign students must present proof of adequate funds.

Admissions Contact: Peter F. Metarko, Director of Admissions.

FLORIDA TECHNOLOGICAL UNIVERSITY
(See University of Central Florida)

JACKSONVILLE UNIVERSITY
Jacksonville, Florida 32211   D-1
(904) 744-3950

F/T: 1195M, 879W	Faculty:	113; IIA, ——$
P/T: 94M, 112W	Ph.D.'s:	75%
Grad: 115M, 201W	S/F Ratio:	18 to 1
Year: see profile	Tuition:	$3540
Appl: Aug. 1	R and B:	$2140
1632 applied	1089 accepted	535 enrolled
SAT: 450V 488M	ACT: 21	COMPETITIVE

Jacksonville University, founded in 1934, is a private liberal arts institution providing graduate and undergraduate instruction. The library contains 265,000 volumes, and subscribes to 685 periodicals.

Environment: The university's 273-acre campus is located 3 miles from the city in a suburban area adjacent to the St. John's River. The 26 buildings include 8 dormitories. The campus also has a 9-hole golf course and an Olympic-size pool.

Student Life: Fifty-three percent of the students are from Florida. Most students come from public schools. About half the students live in dormitories. Thirty-seven percent are Catholic, 35% Protestant, and 8% Jewish. About 17% are members of various minority groups. Campus housing is single-sex; there are visiting privileges. Students may keep cars on campus.

Organizations: About 17% of the men belong to 1 of the 6 fraternities on campus, and 16% of the women belong to 1 of 4 sororities. Extracurricular activities include academic, service, and social clubs; a weekly paper; a student government; religious groups; a chorus; an orchestra; and drama. Cultural and sports facilities also are available in the city of Jacksonville. Beaches are 17 miles from campus.

Sports: Jacksonville competes in 7 intercollegiate sports for men and 4 for women. Intramural sports number 14 for men and 12 for women.

Handicapped: About 85% of the campus is accessible to wheel-chair-bound students. Special facilities include wheelchair ramps, parking areas, elevators, and specially equipped rest rooms. Special class scheduling is also available. A special service program and counselors are available for qualified freshman and sophomore students who are in need of such assistance.

Graduates: Thirty-two percent of the freshmen drop out; 47% remain to graduate. Thirty-six percent of the graduates pursue advanced degrees. About 44% of the graduates enter business and industry.

Services: Students receive free placement, career and psychological counseling, and remedial instruction. Health care and tutoring are available for a fee.

Programs of Study: The university offers the B.A., B.A.E., B.F.A., B.M., B.M.E., and B.S. degrees. Master's degrees also are available. Bachelor's degrees are offered in the following subjects: AREA STUDIES (urban), BUSINESS (accounting, business administration, computer science, management, marketing, public management), EDUCATION (early childhood, elementary, health/physical, secondary, special), ENGLISH (communications, English), FINE AND PERFORMING ARTS (art education, art history, commercial art, dance, music, music education, music theater, speech/theatre, studio art, theater/dramatics), HEALTH SCIENCES (medical technology), LANGUAGES (French, German, Spanish), MATH AND SCIENCES (biology, chemistry, marine science, mathematics, physics), PHILOSOPHY (humanities, philosophy), PREPROFESSIONAL (dentistry, engineering—electrical, engineering—mechanical, law, medicine, veterinary), SOCIAL SCIENCES (economics, geography, government/political science, history, international relations, psychology, social sciences, sociology).

Required: All students must take courses in English, social sciences, mathematics, science, humanities, and physical education. All except B.S. candidates must take a foreign language.

Special: An urban studies program and a 3-2 engineering program with Columbia University, the University of Florida, and Georgia Institute of Technology are offered. The university also offers a 4-year, dual degree engineering program with the Florida Institute of Technology. Students may spend their junior year abroad and design their own majors with university approval. The university operates on a modified trimester system, with optional spring and summer sessions.

Honors: Honors programs are available for students with at least a 3.5 average in their major who complete a thesis or creative production. One honor society, Phi Kappa Phi, is represented on campus.

Admissions: About 67% of those who applied were accepted for the 1981–82 freshman class. The SAT scores of those who enrolled were as follows: Verbal—75% below 500, 18% between 500 and 599, 6% between 600 and 700, and fewer than 1% above 700; Math—57% below 500, 33% between 500 and 599, 9% between 600 and 700, and 1% above 700. Applicants must be graduates of an accredited high school and must have completed 14 Carnegie units. The university prefers that applicants rank in the top half of their class and present an average of at least C. Besides high school record, recommendations, and test scores, admissions officers consider advanced placement or honors courses, leadership record, evidence of special talents, and impressions made during an interview.

Procedure: The SAT or ACT is required. The SAT should be taken in May of the junior year or December of the senior year. The application fee is $20. Application deadlines are August 1 (fall), December 1 (winter), April 1 (spring), and June 1 (summer). An interview is recommended. Notification is made on a rolling basis.

Special: Early and deferred admissions plans are available. CLEP credit is accepted.

Transfer: For fall 1981, 458 students applied, 394 were accepted, and 229 enrolled. Transfer students are accepted for all classes and for all sessions. They must have a minimum GPA of 2.0. Transfers must earn at least 32 semester hours at the university to receive a degree; depending upon the major, 128 to 160 semester hours are required for the bachelor's degree. D grades do not transfer. Transfer application deadlines are the same as those for freshmen.

Visiting: Informal visits can be arranged through the admissions office during fall and winter semesters. Guides are provided. Visitors may sit in on classes and, if space is available, remain overnight on campus.

Financial Aid: About 68% of all students receive aid. Forty-one percent work part-time on campus. The average award to freshmen is $2900. The university provides scholarships, loans under NDSL, grants under EOG, and CWS jobs. Aid is awarded on the basis of academic record and financial need. Students usually must maintain an average of B or better to continue receiving aid. The FAF and the school's aid application must be filed by March 15 for fall entry. Aid is limited for the winter, spring, and summer entrance dates.

Foreign Students: Students from other countries represent 3% of the full-time enrollment. The university offers these students an intensive English program, special counseling, and special organizations.

Admissions: The TOEFL is required and a minimum score of 500 is necessary. The SAT is required only when the foreign applicant has been unable to take the TOEFL; in this case, a verbal SAT score below 400 is considered marginal.

Procedure: Foreign candidates should apply by July 1 (fall), November 1 (winter), March 1 (spring), and May 1 (summer). Proof of health, consisting of the university's health insurance application, is required. Proof of funds adequate to cover 1 calendar year is necessary. Health insurance must be carried; it is available through the university for a fee.

Admissions Contact: J. Bradford Sargent III, Director of Admissions.

NEW COLLEGE OF THE UNIVERSITY OF SOUTH FLORIDA D-4
Sarasota, Florida 33580 (813) 355-7671

F/T: 240M, 260W Faculty: 43; n/av
P/T: none Ph.D.'s: 90%
Grad: none S/F Ratio: 11 to 1
Year: 4-1-4 Tuition: $876 ($2350)
Appl: open R and B: $1850
300 applied 179 accepted 110 enrolled
SAT: 600V 600M HIGHLY COMPETITIVE

New College was founded in 1960 as a private liberal arts college and became affiliated with the University of South Florida in 1975. New College provides students with the freedom to take responsibility for the course of their own education and with the resources to pursue individual goals within a liberal arts curriculum. The library contains 145,000 volumes and 9090 microfilm items, and subscribes to 1046 periodicals.

Environment: The 129-acre campus is in a suburban area overlooking Sarasota Bay, and is 50 miles from Tampa. It consists of 22 buildings and adjoins the Ringling Art Museum and the Asolo Theatre. The building, now used as a library, was the home of the former circus magnate, Charles E. Ringling. Residence halls house approximately 270 students.

Student Life: Fifty percent of the students are from Florida and 50% are from other states; about half live on campus. Approximately 65% of the freshmen are from public schools. Eleven percent are minority-group members. Campus housing is coed. Students may keep cars on campus.

Organizations: Student organizations include drama, orchestra, photography, publications, and religious groups. The college sponsors art shows, concerts, films, lectures, readings, and recitals.

Sports: There are 7 intramural sports for men and 7 for women.

Handicapped: Seventy percent of the campus is accessible to the physically handicapped. Special parking, wheelchair ramps, and specially equipped rest rooms are provided.

Graduates: The freshman dropout rate is 20%. Forty percent of the graduates continue on to graduate schools; about 3% enter medical school and 7% law school.

Services: Students receive the following services free of charge: psychological counseling, career counseling, and placement. Health care is provided on a fee basis.

Programs of Study: All programs lead to the B.A. degree. Bachelor's degrees are offered in the following subjects: AREA STUDIES (American, Asian, Black/Afro-American, environmental, European, Latin American, medieval, Russian, urban), ENGLISH (English, literature), FINE AND PERFORMING ARTS (art, art history, music, studio art), LANGUAGES (French, German, Greek/Latin, Russian, Spanish), MATH AND SCIENCES (biochemistry, biology, botany, chemistry, earth science, ecology/environmental science, mathematics, natural sciences, physical sciences, physics, psychobiology), PHILOSOPHY (classics, humanities, philosophy, religion), PREPROFESSIONAL (dentistry, law, medicine), SOCIAL SCIENCES (anthropology, economics, government/political science, history, international relations, psychology, social sciences, sociology).

Required: Independent studies are required.

Special: Student-designed majors are encouraged. Written evaluations are used in place of grades. Small classes, tutorials, independent study, fieldwork, internships, and off-campus study are offered.

Honors: The entire program is classified as an honors program.

Admissions: Approximately 60% of the applications received were accepted for the 1981–82 freshman class. The SAT scores of those who enrolled were as follows: Verbal—13% below 500, 37% between 500 and 599, 40% between 600 and 700, and 10% above 700; Math—9% below 500, 38% between 500 and 599, 41% between 600 and 700, and 12% above 700. Other considerations for admission include advanced placement or honors courses, evidence of special talent, recommendations by school officials, leadership potential, extracurricular activities, and personality.

Procedure: The SAT or ACT is required. The SAT should be taken in May of the junior year or August or September of the senior year. The college uses a rolling admissions plan.

Special: There are early admissions, early decision, and deferred admissions programs.

Transfer: Transfers are accepted for all but the senior class. A 3.0 average is recommended. Since the college does not use a course-credit system, individual transcripts must be evaluated in order to determine current academic status. D grades do not transfer. Two years must be spent in residence. A rolling admissions plan is used.

Visiting: Campus visits are on an informal basis and are welcomed any time after September 15. Visitors may sit in on classes and are permitted to stay at the school. The director of admissions should be contacted to make arrangements.

Financial Aid: Seventy-five percent of all students receive some financial aid. The average freshman award is $2500. Awards are based on need. Scholarships, loans, and jobs are available. The FAF or FFS form should be returned by February 1. The college is a member of CSS.

Foreign Students: The college admits foreign applicants.

Admissions: Foreign students must take the TOEFL and the SAT or ACT.

Procedure: A rolling admissions plan is used. Foreign students must present proof of funds adequate to cover 1 year of study.

Admissions Contact: Roberto Noya, Director of Admissions.

NOVA UNIVERSITY E-5
Fort Lauderdale, Florida 33314 (305) 475-7340

F/T: 383M, 202W Faculty: n/av; I, +$
P/T: 429M, 213W Ph.D.'s: n/av
Grad: 3296M, 2659W S/F Ratio: n/av
Year: terms, ss Tuition: $2330
Appl: open R and B: $1380
600 accepted 554 enrolled
SAT or ACT: required NONCOMPETITIVE

Although Nova University is primarily an institution of higher learning that offers various master's and doctoral degrees, it also confers bachelor's degrees in 5 fields of study.

Environment: The 200-acre campus is located in suburban Davie, a small town west of Fort Lauderdale, about 10 miles inland from the Atlantic Ocean. There are 3 permanent buildings and several temporary structures. A number of other buildings are under construction. On-campus apartments are available.

142 FLORIDA

Student Life: Five percent of the students lives on campus. Campus housing is both coed and single-sex. Students may keep cars on campus.

Sports: There are 7 intramural sports for men and 7 for women.

Programs of Study: The university confers the B.A. and B.S. degrees. Master's and doctoral degrees are also awarded. Bachelor's degrees are offered in the following subjects: BUSINESS (business administration, computer science, management), EDUCATION (early childhood, elementary, secondary, special), MATH AND SCIENCES (mathematics), PREPROFESSIONAL (law), SOCIAL SCIENCES (sociology).

Admissions: Admissions requirements vary according to program and degree sought.

Procedure: The SAT or ACT is required. There are no application deadlines; freshmen are admitted to all 4 terms. Notification is on a rolling basis. There is a $20 application fee for bachelor's degree programs.

Special: There is an early admissions plan.

Transfer: All students must complete, at the university, 30–45 of the 120–135 credits required for a bachelor's degree. There are no application deadlines; transfer students are admitted to all 4 terms and to all classes. An interview is required.

Financial Aid: Various forms of aid are available to undergraduates. The average freshman award is $600. The university is a member of CSS and requires the FAF. Aid applications are due June 1.

Foreign Students: An intensive English program, special counseling, and special organizations are available for foreign students.

Admissions: Foreign students must achieve a TOEFL score of at least 500 or must take the university's own English proficiency exam. No college entrance exams are required.

Procedure: Foreign students are admitted to all 4 terms. They must present proof of funds adequate to cover 1 year of study.

Admissions Contact: Undergraduate Admissions.

PALM BEACH ATLANTIC COLLEGE E-5
West Palm Beach, Florida 33401 (305) 833-8592

F/T: 233M, 265W	Faculty: 30; IIB, −$
P/T: 33M, 36W	Ph.D.'s: 70%
Grad: none	S/F Ratio: 17 to 1
Year: sems, ss	Tuition: $1350 ($2100)
Appl: open	R and B: $1850
510 applied 420 accepted 216 enrolled	
SAT: 440V 420M ACT: 17 LESS COMPETITIVE	

Palm Beach Atlantic College, founded in 1968, is a liberal arts institution affiliated with the Southern Baptist Convention. The library contains more than 60,000 volumes, and subscribes to 220 periodicals.

Environment: The campus, located in the city of West Palm Beach, is surrounded by a suburban environment. There are 34 buildings, including 6 dormitories that house 160 single women, 120 single men, and 4 married couples. A new $2.5 million student services center is scheduled to open in fall 1982.

Student Life: About 70% of the students are from Florida and 7% are from foreign countries. Eighty percent of the freshmen come from public schools. Fifty percent of the students live in dormitories. Most students are Baptists, and all must attend weekly chapel services. About 10% are minority-group members. Campus housing is single-sex; there are no visiting privileges. Students may keep cars on campus. Drinking is prohibited on campus, and students must observe curfew and dress regulations. About 40% of the students leave campus on weekends.

Organizations: There are no social fraternities or sororities on campus. Extracurricular activities include publications, orchestra, drama, academic fraternities, and service organizations. Cultural activities are available in the city.

Sports: The college participates in 3 intercollegiate sports for men and 3 for women. There are 6 intramural sports for both men and women.

Graduates: About 40% of the freshmen drop out; 15% remain to graduate. Forty percent pursue advanced study after graduation. Thirty percent enter business and industry.

Services: Students receive the following services free of charge: placement, career counseling, health care, tutoring, and remedial instruction.

Programs of Study: The college confers the B.A. and B.S. degrees. Bachelor's degrees are offered in the following subjects: BUSINESS (accounting, business administration), EDUCATION (early childhood, elementary), ENGLISH (English, speech), FINE AND PERFORMING ARTS (music, music education), HEALTH SCIENCES (nursing), MATH AND SCIENCES (biology, mathematics), PHILOSOPHY (religion), PREPROFESSIONAL (ministry), SOCIAL SCIENCES (history, psychology).

Required: All students must complete 9 hours of communications, 9 hours of humanities, 6 hours of religion, and 9 hours of social sciences. Science, mathematics, and language requirements vary with each major.

Special: All students participate in a program of workship for 50 hours per semester in community service.

Admissions: Eighty-two percent of those who applied were accepted for the 1981–82 freshman class. Candidates must be high school graduates, and should rank in the upper 75% of their class and present at least a C average. Admissions officers also consider advanced placement or honor courses, impressions made during an interview, and leadership record.

Procedure: The ACT or SAT is required. Application deadlines are open. Freshmen are admitted to both semesters. There is a rolling admissions policy. The application fee is $15.

Special: CLEP credit is accepted.

Transfer: Transfers are accepted to all classes. Applicants must present at least a C average and a composite score of 800 or 17 on the SAT or ACT, respectively. Up to 67 hours may be transferred from a junior college. A, B, and C grades transfer. Students must spend 1 year at the college to receive a degree. Thirty-two credits, of a total 128 required for the bachelor's degree, must be taken at the college. Application deadlines are open; admissions are on a rolling basis. Transfers are admitted to both semesters.

Visiting: Guided tours can be arranged for weekdays from 9 A.M. to 4 P.M. through the admissions office. Visitors also may sit in on classes.

Financial Aid: About 45% of the students receive aid. About 22% work part-time on campus. The average award to freshmen is $1200. Scholarships are available to students who rank in the top 10% of their class, intend to become ministers, or demonstrate ability in the arts. Other programs include NDSL, SEOG, and CWS. The state of Florida offers grants and loans, including a $750 tuition voucher. The college is a member of CSS. The FFS or FAF should be filed by May 1.

Foreign Students: Seven percent of the full-time students come from foreign countries. There are organizations on campus especially for them.

Admissions: The college requires that foreign applicants take the TOEFL and achieve a score 500. College entrance exams are not required.

Procedure: There are no deadlines for admissions application. Foreign students may enter either semester. A health form must be completed. Proof of funds adequate to cover 1 year of study must be presented. Students must carry health insurance; it is available through the college for a fee.

Admissions Contact: Don Harp, Director of Admissions.

RINGLING SCHOOL OF ART AND DESIGN D-4
(Formerly Ringling School of Art)
Sarasota, Florida 33580 (813) 355-9771

F/T: 220M, 250W	Faculty: 21; IV, −$
P/T: none	Ph.D.'s: none
Grad: none	S/F Ratio: 22 to 1
Year: sems	Tuition: $2900
Appl: open	R and B: $1870
SAT or ACT: not required	SPECIAL

Ringling School of Art and Design is a private, 3-year professional art college. The library contains 10,000 volumes, and subscribes to 90 periodicals.

Environment: The campus is located in Sarasota and is surrounded by an urban environment. Dormitories accommodate 30% of the students; the school also sponsors off-campus apartments. A new library/studio complex is being used for the first time.

Student Life: Most entering freshmen come from other post-secondary schools. Sixteen percent are minority-group members. Campus housing is single-sex; there are visiting privileges. Students may keep cars on campus.

Organizations: Students attend events at Van Wezel Performing Arts Hall; the state museum and state theater are located nearby.

Handicapped: Facilities available for the physically handicapped include elevators and specially equipped rest rooms. The campus is 100% accessible to handicapped students, although there is no housing for these students.

Services: Students receive placement and career counseling services free of charge.

Programs of Study: Students may obtain a B.F.A. degree by completing 3 years of specialized art training at Ringling and 1 academic year at another institution. Bachelor's degrees are offered in the following subjects: FINE AND PERFORMING ARTS (fine art, graphic design, illustration, interior design and space planning).

Admissions: Candidates must have a high school diploma or the equivalent. A portfolio and statement of purpose are required. Admission is also based on evidence of special talent, advanced placement or honor courses, personality, leadership, and recommendations.

Procedure: Neither the SAT nor the ACT is required. There are no application deadlines; the priority date, however, is March 1. Freshmen are admitted to the fall semester only. Applications must be accompanied by a $25 fee. A rolling admissions plan is used.

Transfer: Ninety-four transfer students enrolled for the fall semester in 1981. Transfer applications are accepted for the freshman and sophomore years only. Transfer students are admitted to both semesters. Fifty percent of the freshmen are transfers. Transfers should have a C average and must submit a portfolio and statement of purpose. Only C and higher grades transfer. The last 3 semesters must be completed at Ringling; at least 60 semester hours, out of a total of 123 semester hours required for the bachelor's degree, must also be taken at the school. There are no application deadlines. Applicants are notified within 1 month.

Visiting: Guided tours can be scheduled through the admissions office.

Financial Aid: About 62% of all students receive aid through the school. About 10% work part-time on campus. The school participates in BEOG, SEOG, CWS, scholarship, and guaranteed loan programs. The FAF must be filed by March 1 (fall) and December 1 (spring).

Foreign Students: About 3% of the full-time students come from foreign countries.

Admissions: Foreign candidates should take the TOEFL; a minimum score of 500 is necessary. The SAT or ACT is not required.

Procedure: There are no application deadlines. Foreign students are admitted to the fall semester. They must have the school's standard health statement completed by a physician. They must also show proof of funds adequate to cover 1 academic year.

Admissions Contact: Lisa Redling Kaplan, Director of Admissions and Registrar.

ROLLINS COLLEGE
Winter Park, Florida 32789

D-3

(305) 646-2161

F/T: 675M, 675W
P/T: none
Grad: 300M, 200W
Year: 4-1-4
Appl: Mar. 1
1600 applied
SAT: 490V 530M

Faculty: 100, IIA, +$
Ph.D.'s: 92%
S/F Ratio: 13 to 1
Tuition: $5230
R and B: $2410
900 accepted
ACT: 25

400 enrolled
COMPETITIVE+

Rollins College, founded in 1885, is a private liberal arts institution. The library contains 200,000 volumes, and subscribes to 1000 periodicals.

Environment: The 65-acre campus is located on the shore of a lake, in a suburban area outside Orlando. Buildings include 11 dormitories, music and fine-arts centers, and a well-equipped science center. The college also sponsors fraternity and sorority houses.

Student Life: Forty percent of the students are Florida residents, and 72% come from public schools. Approximately 80% of the students live on campus. All students may have cars, but freshmen must park off campus. About 40% of the students are Catholic, 30% are Protestant, and 10% are Jewish. About 8% of the students are minority-group members. Campus housing is coed and single-sex; there are visiting privileges.

Organizations: About 42% of the students belong to 1 of 6 fraternities and 6 sororities. Extracurricular activities are available on campus, and beaches, Disney World, and the Orlando area provide other recreational and cultural offerings.

Sports: The college fields 8 intercollegiate teams for men and 8 for women. There are 8 intramural sports for men and 8 for women.

Handicapped: Seventy-five percent of the campus is accessible to wheelchair-bound students. Special facilities include wheelchair ramps, parking areas, elevators, and specially equipped rest rooms. Special class scheduling is also available. A few students with visual or hearing impairments were enrolled in 1981-82.

Graduates: About 10% of the freshmen drop out, and 65% remain to graduate. Thirty-five percent of the graduates pursue advanced degrees, including 5% who enter medical school, 8% who enter law school, and 2% who enter dental school. Another 50% begin careers in business and industry.

Services: Students receive the following services free of charge: placement, career, and psychological counseling, health care, and tutoring. Placement services also are available to graduates.

Programs of Study: The college confers the B.A. degree. Master's degrees are also awarded. Bachelor's degrees are offered in the following subjects: AREA STUDIES (American, Latin American), EDUCATION (elementary, secondary), ENGLISH (English), FINE AND PERFORMING ARTS (art, music, theater/dramatics), LANGUAGES (French, German, Spanish), MATH AND SCIENCES (biology, chemistry, mathematics, physics), PHILOSOPHY (philosophy), PREPROFESSIONAL (dentistry, engineering, forestry, law, medicine, veterinary), SOCIAL SCIENCES (anthropology, economics, government/political science, history, international relations, psychology, sociology).

Required: A core curriculum is required of all students, including basic skill levels in math, English, and foreign languages and distribution courses to meet cognitive and affective requirements.

Special: Students may spend their junior year in Europe; a summer in Madrid, Spain, or Tours, France; or a fall term in Ireland or Australia. There are 3-2 degree programs in forestry, with Duke University, and in engineering, with Columbia, Washington, and Georgia technological universities. Student-designed majors are permitted.

Honors: A special honors program offers honors courses, individual advisement, and special research and thesis papers. All honors students are given a tuition grant for their fourth year.

Admissions: Fifty-six percent of those who applied were accepted for the 1981-82 freshman class. The SAT scores of those who enrolled were as follows: Verbal—57% below 500, 33% between 500 and 599, 8% between 600 and 700, and 2% above 700; Math—33% below 500, 47% between 500 and 599, 18% between 600 and 700, and 2% above 700. The college prefers that applicants rank in the top 40% of their class and present an average of B or better. Admissions officers also consider recommendations of high school officials, extracurricular activities, leadership potential, and impressions made during a personal interview.

Procedure: All applicants must take the SAT or ACT, preferably in May of the junior year for early decision candidates and in December of the senior year for others. Application deadlines are March 1 (fall) and December 1 (spring). Early decision applicants must apply by December 1. Applicants are notified on a rolling basis. The college subscribes to the CRDA. The application fee is $20.

Special: Early decision, early admissions, and deferred admissions plans are available. CLEP and AP credit is accepted.

Transfer: For fall 1981, 250 transfer students applied, 120 were accepted, and 60 enrolled. Applicants should present at least a 2.5 average, SAT or ACT scores, and an acceptable high school record. Grades of C— or better transfer. Students must spend at least 1 year at the college to receive a degree. Deadlines for applications are April 15 (fall) and December 1 (spring).

Visiting: Orientations for prospective students are scheduled regularly. Informal visits also may be arranged. Visitors may sit in on classes and remain overnight on campus. Guides are provided. Arrangements should be made through the admissions office.

Financial Aid: About 46% of all students receive aid; about 33% work part-time on campus. About 145 freshman scholarships are available each year. Students may apply for federal loans and loans administered by the college. The college is a member of CSS; the FAF and college aid application are required. Applications for aid must be received by March 1 (fall) and December 1 (spring).

Foreign Students: About 5% of the students come from foreign countries. The college offers these students special counseling and special organizations.

Admissions: Foreign students must achieve a minimum TOEFL score of 550; they must also take the SAT or ACT.

Procedure: Application deadlines are March 1 (fall) and December 1 (spring). Foreign students must submit the college's health form as well

SAINT LEO COLLEGE
St. Leo, Florida 33574

D-3

(904) 588-8283

F/T: 598M, 508W
P/T: 20M, 26W
Grad: none
Year: sems, ss
Appl: May
900 applied
SAT: 425V 427M

Faculty: 50; IIB, --$
Ph.D.'s: 60%
S/F Ratio: 17 to 1
Tuition: $3621
R and B: $1740
750 accepted   364 enrolled
                   COMPETITIVE

Saint Leo College, chartered in 1889, is a coeducational liberal arts institution. Once affiliated with the Catholic Church, the college is now private. The library contains 85,000 volumes and subscribes to 700 periodicals.

Environment: The 54-acre campus is located in a rural area 30 miles from Tampa. The 27 major buildings include 9 dormitories that house 500 women and 600 men.

Student Life: About 45% of the students are from Florida. Half the students come from public schools. Most students are Roman Catholic. Eighty-five percent live in dormitories. College housing is single-sex, and there are visiting privileges. Students may keep cars on campus.

Organizations: About 30% of the men belong to 1 of 4 local fraternities, and 25% of the women belong to 1 of 4 local sororities. Student activities include Catholic religious groups, student government, special-interest clubs, publications, a chorus, an orchestra, and a debating team. The college sponsors art shows, concerts, films, lectures, plays, professional demonstrations, readings, and recitals.

Sports: The college participates intercollegiately in 6 sports for men and 5 sports for women. There are 16 intramural sports for men and 14 for women.

Handicapped: Special facilities available to wheelchair-bound students include wheelchair ramps and specially equipped rest rooms.

Graduates: About 25% of the freshmen drop out, and 45% remain to graduate. Forty percent of the graduates seek advanced degrees, including 5% who enter law school. Another 40% pursue careers in business and industry.

Services: Students receive the following services free of charge: tutoring, remedial instruction, and placement, career, and psychological counseling. Health care is available on campus.

Programs of Study: The college awards the B.A. and B.S. (medical technology only) degrees. Associate degrees also are conferred. Bachelor's degrees are offered in the following subjects: BUSINESS (accounting, business education, human resources, management, marketing, real estate/insurance, secretarial science), EDUCATION (early childhood, elementary, health/physical, religious, secondary, special), ENGLISH (English), FINE AND PERFORMING ARTS (art, art management, dance, music, theater/dramatics), MATH AND SCIENCES (biology, medical technology), PHILOSOPHY (religion), PREPROFESSIONAL (dentistry, law, medicine, pharmacy, veterinary), SOCIAL SCIENCES (criminal justice, criminology, government/political science, history, psychology, social work, sociology).

Required: All students must complete basic studies programs.

Special: The college offers independent study as well as a junior year abroad under the auspices of the Central College European Studies Program.

Admissions: Eighty-three percent of those who applied were accepted for the 1981-82 freshman class. Applicants must be graduates of accredited high schools with an average of at least 2.5 in 16 Carnegie units. Applicants are assured of acceptance in the fall of their senior year if they are enrolled in a college preparatory course, present at least a B average, rank in the upper half of their class, have outstanding SAT scores, and are recommended by their counselor. Applicants are assured of acceptance after receipt of their first senior-year grades if they are enrolled in a college preparatory course, present at least a C average, have good SAT scores, and are recommended by their counselor. The school also considers impressions made during an interview and advanced placement or honors courses.

Procedure: The SAT should be taken in the junior or senior year. The application, a $15 fee, test scores, and high school record should be submitted by May for fall admission and by September for spring admission. Notification is made on a rolling basis.

Special: Early decision, and early and deferred admissions, plans are available. CLEP and AP credit is accepted.

Transfer: For fall 1981, 234 transfer students applied, 200 were accepted, and 100 enrolled. Applicants must have at least a C average. D grades transfer if the student has a GPA of at least 2.5. Students must complete a minimum of 1 year at the college to receive a degree. Of the 124 credits required for the bachelor's degree, 30 must be completed at the college. Application deadlines are the same as those for freshmen.

Visiting: Orientation interviews and tours are scheduled regularly for prospective students. Visits may be scheduled Monday through Friday with the admissions office. Guides are provided, and visitors may sit in on classes.

Financial Aid: The college, a member of CSS, provides scholarships, loans, and campus employment. Aid applications must be submitted by March 1 for fall entry, and the FAF also must be filed.

Foreign Students: Approximately 7% of the full-time students come from foreign countries. The college offers these students special counseling and special organizations.

Admissions: Foreign students must achieve a TOEFL score of at least 550 to enter the academic program and, if possible, should take the SAT, obtaining a minimum score of 425V and 425M.

Procedure: Application deadlines are April 1 (fall) and September 1 (spring). Foreign students must undergo a medical examination prior to arrival for registration, and must carry health insurance, which is available through the college for a fee. They also must present proof of funds adequate to cover 1 year of study. A special fee of $20 must accompany the usual $15 application fee.

Admissions Contact: Rev. J. Dennis Murphy, Director of Admissions.

STETSON UNIVERSITY
De Land, Florida 32720

D-2

(904) 734-4121

F/T: 1020M, 910W
P/T: 234M, 410W
Grad: 700M&W
Year: 4-1-4, ss
Appl: Mar. 15
1372 applied
SAT: 500V 500M

Faculty: n/av; IIA, av$
Ph.D.'s: 72%
S/F Ratio: 17 to 1
Tuition: $3875
R and B: $1760
902 accepted   503 enrolled
ACT: 24   VERY COMPETITIVE

Stetson University, founded in 1883, is a private liberal arts university affiliated with churches of the Florida Baptist Convention. It provides undergraduate and graduate instruction and research. The College of Law is located in St. Petersburg. The library contains 286,000 volumes and 13,000 microfilm items, and subscribes to 1200 periodicals.

Environment: The university's main campus is on 100 acres in a suburban town of 25,000, 20 miles from Daytona Beach. There are 30 buildings including a science center, the School of Business Administration, and the School of Music. Sixteen residence halls accommodate 750 women and 800 men; the university also sponsors on-campus apartments, fraternity houses, and married student housing.

Student Life: Sixty-five percent of the students are from Florida. Seventy percent of the entering freshmen come from public schools. Thirty percent live on campus. Protestant students comprise 60% of the student body, Catholic students 25%, and Jewish students 3%. Five percent are members of minority groups. Campus housing is single-sex; there are visiting privileges. Students may keep cars on campus.

Organizations: There are 7 national fraternities and 7 national sororities to which about 40% of the students belong. Student organizations include special-interest groups, religious groups, and a newspaper. Student government has several levels and branches and is concerned with most aspects of student life.

Sports: The university fields 5 intercollegiate teams for men and 4 for women. There are 11 intramural sports for men and 8 for women.

Handicapped: Eighty percent of the campus is accessible to wheelchair-bound students. Facilities for handicapped students include wheelchair ramps, elevators, and special parking and rest rooms; special class scheduling is also available. Less than 1% of the students have visual or hearing impairments.

Graduates: The freshman dropout rate is 13%; of those who remain, 50% pursue graduate study. Five percent enter medical school, 12% law school, and 2% dental school. Thirty percent pursue careers in business and industry.

Services: Students receive the following services free of charge: psychological counseling, health care, and placement and career counseling. Tutoring is available for a fee.

Programs of Study: The university offers the B.A., B.B.A., B.S., B.S.Mus., and B.S.Mus.Ed. degrees. Master's degrees and a doctoral degree in law are also offered. Bachelor's degrees are offered in the following subjects: AREA STUDIES (American), BUSINESS (accounting, business administration, finance, management, marketing), EDUCATION (early childhood, elementary, health/physical, special), ENGLISH (English, speech), FINE AND PERFORMING ARTS (art, art education, music, music education, theater/dramatics), HEALTH SCIENCES (medical technology), LANGUAGES (French, German, Spanish), MATH AND SCIENCES (biology, chemistry, mathematics, physics), PHILOSOPHY (philosophy, religion), PREPROFESSIONAL (dentistry, engineering, forestry, law, medicine, ministry, veterinary), SOCIAL SCIENCES (economics, geography, government/political science, history, psychology, sociology). Thirty percent of degrees are conferred in business, 15% in education, 10% in math and sciences, and 10% in social sciences.

Required: All students are required to take communications, humanities, religion and philosophy, and physical education. Students in liberal arts must also take mathematics, science, and social studies, and B.A. candidates must take a foreign language.

Special: The university offers independent study and research; Washington, D.C., and U.N. semesters; a marine biology research laboratory; a 3-year bachelor's degree program; a pass/fail program; and provisions for a junior year abroad. A 3-2 combination degree program in engineering is offered with the following schools: University of Florida, University of Central Florida, and Washington University, and, in forestry, with Duke University. A minor in computer science and business is also available. Student-designed majors are permitted.

Honors: There are 23 honor societies on campus. An honors program is also offered.

Admissions: Sixty-six percent of those who applied were accepted for the 1981–82 freshman class. The SAT scores of those who enrolled were as follows: Verbal—44% below 500, 40% between 500 and 599, 14% between 600 and 700, and 2% above 700; Math—29% below 500, 48% between 500 and 599, 21% between 600 and 700, and 2% above 700. Applicants should be graduates of accredited schools. It is recommended that they rank in the upper two-fifths of their graduating class, have a B— average or better, and score a minimum of 500 on the verbal and 500 on the mathematical portions of the SAT. The school indicates that in addition to these qualifications they consider, in order of importance, leadership record, evidence of special talents, advanced placement or honors courses, recommendations by school officials, and extracurricular activities record.

Procedure: The SAT or ACT is required and should be taken between March of the junior year and January of the senior year. ATs in English composition and mathematics, levels I or II, are recommended. The application, a $20 fee, test scores, and high school record should be submitted by March 15 for the fall term, December 1 for the winter term, January 1 for the spring term, and May 1 for the summer session. Notification begins after January of the senior year.

Special: An early decision plan is available for those who are certain that they want to attend Stetson. These students must apply prior to November 15 of their senior year. Notification will be made by December 1. Early admissions and deferred admissions are available. CLEP and AP credit is accepted.

Transfer: For fall 1981, 374 transfer students applied, 242 were accepted, and 166 enrolled. Applicants must be in good standing at their previous schools, have a minimum GPA of 2.8, and show acceptable SAT (minimum 900 V&M combined) or ACT scores. All students must complete 32 credits at the university of the 128 credits required for the bachelor's degree. In some cases D grades may transfer. Applications for transfer are accepted throughout the year. Aid application deadlines are the same for transfer applicants as for freshman applicants.

Visiting: Day-long visits can be arranged through the admissions office. Visitors can sit in on classes and remain overnight on campus.

Financial Aid: About 48% of all students receive aid through the school. Forty-five percent work part-time on campus. The university provides scholarships, loans, and campus employment. The average aid to freshmen from all sources available through the university is $2200. Aid is awarded on the basis of financial need and academic record. Special consideration is given to economically deprived students. The university is a member of the CSS. Application must be made by April 1; either the FAF or the FFS must also be filed. The deadline for aid applications for all terms is April 1.

Foreign Students: Approximately 2% of the full-time students come from foreign countries.

Admissions: Foreign students must take the TOEFL and either the SAT or ACT. While a minimum score of 500 is required on the TOEFL, no minimum score is required on the SAT or ACT.

Procedure: Foreign students are accepted for the fall semester only; the application deadline is March 15. Proof of adequate funds and a standing deposit of $500 are required. Students must take a physical examination and present a completed health form as proof of health.

Admissions Contact: Gary A. Meadows, Director of Admissions.

UNIVERSITY OF CENTRAL FLORIDA D–3
Orlando, Florida 32816 (305) 275-2511

F/T: 3672M, 3249W	Faculty: 364; IIA, +$
P/T: 2496M, 2358W	Ph.D.'s: 76%
Grad: 606M, 716W	S/F Ratio: 19 to 1
Year: sems, ss	Tuition: $876 ($2766)
Appl: June 14	R and B: $1898
2841 applied	2272 accepted	1134 enrolled
SAT: 448V 501M	ACT: 19	COMPETITIVE

University of Central Florida, a state-supported institution, offers degree programs in 5 academic divisions. The library contains 513,948 volumes and 266,867 microfilm items, and subscribes to 5219 periodicals.

Environment: The 1227-acre campus is located in a rural area 10 miles from Orlando. The university has about 25 major buildings, including 8 dormitories that house 864 students.

Student Life: About 97% of the students are Florida natives, and 90% come from public schools. About 6% of the students live on campus; of those who live off-campus, about half live at home. Eleven percent are minority-group members. Campus housing is single-sex; dormitory residents determine daily intervisiting hours. Almost all students leave campus on weekends. Students may keep cars on campus. The university provides day-care services to all students, faculty, and staff for a fee.

Organizations: Six sororities and 12 fraternities are represented on campus. Numerous religious and special-interest organizations are available. There is a student government, and student representatives vote on faculty and administration committees. Cultural activities are available in Orlando and other central Florida communities.

Sports: The university competes on an intercollegiate level in 8 sports for men and 6 for women. There are 13 intramural sports for men and 12 for women.

Handicapped: The whole campus is accessible to physically handicapped students. Special facilities include wheelchair ramps, parking areas, elevators, lowered drinking fountains and telephones, and specially equipped rest rooms.

Graduates: Forty percent of the freshmen drop out; 40% remain to graduate. Eleven percent pursue advanced study after graduation.

Services: Health care, psychological counseling, career counseling, tutoring, placement, and remedial instruction are available free of charge.

Programs of Study: The university awards the B.A., B.S., B.F.A., B.S.E., and B.E.T. degrees. Associate, master's, and doctoral degree programs also are offered. Bachelor's degrees are offered in the following subjects: BUSINESS (accounting, business administration, business education, computer science, finance, management, marketing), EDUCATION (education media specialist, elementary, health/physical, secondary, science, social science, special, speech), ENGLISH (English, journalism, speech), FINE AND PERFORMING ARTS (art, film/photography, music, radio/TV, theater/dramatics), HEALTH SCIENCES (medical record administration, medical technology, nursing, radiologic sciences, respiratory therapy, speech therapy), LANGUAGES (French, Spanish), MATH AND SCIENCES (biology, botany, chemistry, forensic science, limnology, mathematics, microbiology, physics, statistics, zoology), PHILOSOPHY (humanities, philosophy), PREPROFESSIONAL (engineering), SOCIAL SCIENCES (anthropology, economics, government/political science, history, psychology, sociology). About 45% of the undergraduate degrees are conferred in arts and sciences, 24% in business, 13% in engineering and education, and 5% in health.

Required: All students must take courses in English and speech, humanities or history, mathematics and science, and social and behavioral sciences.

Special: Combined B.A.-B.S. degrees may be earned in 4 years. A liberal studies degree is available. Students may design their own majors.

Honors: Ten honor societies are represented on campus.

Admissions: The university accepted 80% of those who applied for admission to the 1981–82 freshman class. The SAT scores of those who enrolled were as follows: Verbal—73% below 500, 23% between

500 and 599, 4% between 600 and 700, and 0% above 700; Math—48% below 500, 38% between 500 and 599, 13% between 600 and 700, and 1% above 700. On the ACT, scores were as follows: 57% below 21, 18% between 21 and 23, 10% between 24 and 25, 11% between 26 and 28, and 4% above 28. Applicants should have earned at least 12 Carnegie units with a GPA of 2.5 or better and should rank in the upper 35% of their graduating class. They should score at least 400 on each part of the SAT or at least 17 on the ACT. Admissions officers also consider advanced placement or honors courses and recommendations by school officials.

Procedure: The SAT or ACT is required. Applications are due June 14 (fall), mid-October (spring), and mid-March (summer). Applications should be submitted with a $15 fee. Notification is made on a rolling basis.

Special: Early decision, early admissions, and deferred admissions plans are available. AP and CLEP credit is accepted.

Transfer: For fall 1981, 2943 transfer students applied, 2117 were accepted, and 1540 enrolled. Transfers are accepted for all classes. Applicants should have at least a 2.5 GPA, and a combined score of 850 on the SAT or 19 on the ACT. D grades transfer. Students must earn 30 semester hours at the university, of a total 120 semester hours required for the bachelor's degree. Application deadlines are the same as those for freshmen. Transfers are admitted to the fall, spring, and summer sessions.

Visiting: Orientations for prospective students are scheduled regularly. Informal visits also can be arranged through the dean of students for weekdays between 8 A.M. and 4 P.M.. Students may sit in on classes, and guides are provided.

Financial Aid: About 75% of the students receive financial aid. Twenty percent work part-time on campus. The average award to freshmen from all sources is $2100. Academic and athletic scholarships, tuition waivers, loans, and part-time jobs are available. The university is a member of CSS. Aid applicants should file the FAF or FFS by April 1.

Foreign Students: Ten percent of the full-time students come from foreign countries. The university offers these students special counseling and special organizations.

Admissions: The university requires that the TOEFL be taken; applicants should score a minimum of 550. The SAT or ACT is also required; the minimum combined score needed on the SAT is 850.

Procedure: Foreign applicants should complete their applications 3 months prior to the start of the term. They are admitted to the fall, spring, and summer terms. They must complete the standard health form required of all students and present proof of funds adequate to cover the current school year. Health insurance is required; it is available through the university for a fee.

Admissions Contact: Ralph C. Boston, Director of Admissions.

UNIVERSITY OF FLORIDA   D–2
Gainesville, Florida 32611   (904) 392-1365

F/T: 13,018M, 9789W   Faculty: 2945; I, av$
P/T: 2377M, 1873W   Ph.D.'s: 83%
Grad: 4283M, 2432W   S/F Ratio: 8 to 1
Year: sems, ss   Tuition: $23 ($57)p/c
Appl. Mar. 1   R and B: $2400
11,552 applied   5711 accepted   2890 enrolled
SAT(mean): 508V 562M   **VERY COMPETITIVE**

University of Florida, established in 1853, is a combined state university and land-grant college. Divisions include the colleges of Agriculture, Architecture, Business Administration, Dentistry, Education, Engineering, Fine Arts, Health-Related Professions, Journalism and Communications, Law, Liberal Arts and Sciences, Medicine, Nursing, Pharmacy, Physical Education, Health, and Recreation; and the schools of Forest Resources and Conservation, Accounting, and Building Construction. The library contains 3 million volumes and subscribes to more than 20,000 periodicals.

Environment: The main campus takes up 2000 acres in a suburban area of Gainesville, a city of 80,000. There are over 500 buildings on campus, including 19 sorority houses, 29 fraternity houses, 6 cafeterias, and a student services center. The 23 dormitories accommodate 3300 single men, 3000 single women, and 860 married students.

Student Life: Most students are from Florida. About 20% live on campus. About 11% are minority-group members. Students may keep cars on campus. Campus housing is both single-sex and coed; there are visiting privileges in the single-sex dormitories. The university provides day-care services for full-time men and women students.

Organizations: The more than 300 student organizations include a marching band, theater groups, an orchestra, a daily newspaper, religious groups, and dance groups.

Sports: The university participates in 9 intercollegiate sports for men and 8 for women. There are 10 intramural sports for men and 9 for women.

Handicapped: The college is working formally on barrier-free compliance.

Graduates: About 50% of the freshmen remain to graduate, and about 30% of the graduates go on to professional or graduate schools.

Services: Students receive the following services free of charge: placement, tutoring, and psychological and career counseling. Health care is available for a fee.

Programs of Study: The university awards over 30 undergraduate degrees. Master's and doctoral degrees also are conferred. Bachelor's degrees are offered in the following subjects: AREA STUDIES (American, Asian), BUSINESS (accounting, business administration, computer science, finance, management, marketing, real estate/insurance), EDUCATION (agricultural extension, early childhood, elementary, English, foreign language, health/physical, math, recreation, science, secondary, social studies, special), ENGLISH (English, journalism, speech), FINE AND PERFORMING ARTS (art, art education, art history, graphic arts, music, music education, theater/dramatics), HEALTH SCIENCES (medical technology, nursing, occupational therpay, physical therapy), LANGUAGES (French, German, Russian, Spanish), MATH AND SCIENCES (astronomy, botany, chemistry, geology, mathematics, physics, statistics, zoology), PHILOSOPHY (classics, philosophy, religion), PREPROFESSIONAL (agriculture, architecture, dentistry, engineering, forestry, law, medicine, pharmacy, veterinary), SOCIAL SCIENCES (anthropology, economics, geography, government/political science, history, psychology, sociology).

Required: Freshmen and sophomores must take courses in American institutions, behavioral science, English, mathematics, physical sciences, biological sciences, humanities, and physical education.

Special: Independent study is offered. Interdisciplinary programs are available in numerous areas. The university sponsors study abroad. A cooperative program in engineering is available.

Honors: An honors program is available.

Admissions: Forty-nine percent of those who applied were accepted for the 1981–1982 freshman class. The SAT scores of those who enrolled were as follows: Verbal—48% below 500, 39% between 500 and 599, 12% between 600 and 700, and 1% above 700; Math—21% below 500, 49% between 500 and 599, 26% between 600 and 700, and 5% above 700. Applicants must have graduated from an accredited high school with at least a C average in 15 units of work. Out-of-state applicants should have at least a B average and score a minimum of 500 in each part of the SAT. The university also considers advanced placement or honors courses, recommendations by school officials, and evidence of special talents.

Procedure: The SAT or ACT is required and should be taken in December or January of the senior year. Application deadlines are March 1 (fall), November 1 (spring), and March 1 (summer). There is a rolling admissions plan. The application fee is $15.

Special: Students with a 3.5 average and junior-year scores of at least 600 on each section of the SAT may apply for early decision; they are notified by December 1. An early admissions plan also is available. AP and CLEP credit is accepted.

Transfer: For fall 1981, 7636 transfer applications were received, 3188 were accepted, and 2612 were enrolled. Transfer applicants should have a minimum GPA of 2.0. Preference is given to A.A. graduates of Florida public community college. D grades transfer. Students must take at least 30 semester hours in residence to receive a bachelor's degree. The application deadline for fall admission is June 15; other deadlines are the same as those for freshmen.

Financial Aid: In 1981–82, about 70% of the students received aid. About 20% worked part-time on campus. The average scholarship to freshmen was $1200; the average loan was $2100. The university offers aid in the form of scholarships, grants, loans, and part-time jobs. The university is a member of CSS. Applicants must submit the FAF and the University of Florida Financial Aid Supplement by March 1.

Foreign Students: Five percent of the student body come from foreign countries. The university offers these students an intensive English program, special counseling, and organizations especially for foreign students.

Admissions: Foreign students must achieve a minimum TOEFL score of 550. No other exams are required.

UNIVERSITY OF MIAMI
Coral Gables, Florida 33124
E-5
(305) 284-4323

F/T: 4951M, 3786W
P/T: 763M, 1032W
Grad: 2513M, 1599W
Year: sems, ss
Appl: open
6087 applied
SAT: 460V 508M

Faculty: 739; I, av$
Ph.D.'s: 75%
S/F Ratio: 18 to 1
Tuition: $5192
R and B: $2200
4606 accepted   1683 enrolled
COMPETITIVE

University of Miami, established in 1925, is a private, nonsectarian university that offers undergraduate and graduate degrees in numerous fields of study. It conducts interdisciplinary research in biochemistry, cell physiology, ocean engineering, ocean law, and biological sciences. The university also has centers for theoretical research in physics, advanced international studies, studies in law and economics, and molecular and cellular research. Its libraries contain more than 1.3 million volumes, subscriptions to 13,000 periodicals, and 1 million microfilm items.

Environment: The 260-acre main campus, located in the suburban environment of Coral Gables, consists of 119 buildings with air-conditioned classrooms. The coed and single-sex residence halls accommodate 2561 single men, 1853 single women, and 372 married students. The School of Marine and Atmospheric Science occupies a separate 7-acre campus on Virginia Key, about 9 miles from the main campus.

Student Life: About 59% of the students are from Florida. Twenty-five percent live on campus. Campus housing is coed. Students may keep cars on campus. The university provides day-care services.

Organizations: Eight percent of the men belong to 1 of 13 national fraternities on campus; 8% of the women belong to 1 of the 10 national sororities. Numerous extracurricular activities and regularly scheduled social and cultural events take place. The more than 200 student organizations include special-interest groups and a semiweekly newspaper. There are 6 religious centers.

Sports: The university competes on an intercollegiate level in 10 sports for men and 9 for women. There are 19 intramural sports for men and 17 for women.

Handicapped: About 90% of the campus is accessible to students with physical handicaps. Special facilities include wheelchair ramps, parking areas, elevators, lowered drinking fountains and telephones, and specially equipped rest rooms. Special class scheduling is also available. Fewer than 2% of the students have visual or hearing impairments.

Graduates: About 32% of the freshmen drop out at the end of the first year and about 40% remain to graduate.

Services: Career counseling and placement services are provided free of charge. Health care is available for a fee.

Programs of Study: Undergraduate degrees offered are the B.A., B.S., B.B.A., B.C.S., B.F.A., B.M., B.Arch, B.S.N., B.S.Ed., and B.G.S. Master's and doctoral degrees also are available. Bachelor's degrees are offered in numerous subjects, including the following: AREA STUDIES (American, Russian), BUSINESS (accounting, business administration, computer science, finance, management, marketing, systems analysis), EDUCATION (early childhood, elementary, health/physical, human services, secondary, special, speech), ENGLISH (communication, English), FINE AND PERFORMING ARTS (art, art education, dance, music, music education, radio/TV, theater/dramatics), HEALTH SCIENCES (medical technology, nursing, physical therapy, speech therapy), LANGUAGES (French, German, Russian, Spanish), MATH AND SCIENCES (biochemistry, biology, chemistry, geology, information systems, mathematics, microbiology, oceanography, physics), PHILOSOPHY (philosophy, religion), PREPROFESSIONAL (architecture, engineering, law, medicine), SOCIAL SCIENCES (anthropology, economics, geography, government/political science, history, psychology, sociology). Twenty-five percent of undergraduate degrees are awarded in business, 15% in social sciences, and 14% in math and sciences.

Required: All students must complete 24 credits in English composition, fine arts, history, humanities, natural sciences, and social sciences.

Special: The university offers the B.G.S. degree and a 5-year combined B.A.-B.S. degree. Students may spend their junior year abroad. Individualized majors may be arranged.

Procedure: Application deadlines are March 1 (fall), July 1 (spring), and January 1 (summer). Foreign students must present a health certificate. They must present proof of adequate funds to cover the proposed period of stay. The university also requires that foreign students carry health insurance, which is available through the university.

Admissions Contact: James B. Parrish, Director of Admissions.

Honors: Thirty honor societies have chapters on campus. Eleven departments offer honors programs.

Admissions: About 76% of those who applied for the 1981–82 freshman class were accepted. The SAT scores of those who enrolled were as follows: Verbal—65% below 500, 24% between 500 and 599, 9% between 600 and 700, and 2% above 700; Math—44% below 500, 35% between 500 and 599, 16% between 600 and 700, and 5% above 700. Applicants must be in the top half of their high school class. Advanced placement or honors courses, special talents, and recommendations are also considered important.

Procedure: The SAT or ACT is required. There are no application deadlines; notification is on a rolling basis. A $30 fee must accompany applications.

Special: There are early decision, early admissions, and deferred admissions plans. The early admissions deadline is July 15 for fall. AP and CLEP credit is accepted.

Transfer: For fall 1981, 2744 transfer students applied, 1919 were accepted, and 1065 enrolled. Transfers are accepted for all but the senior year. A 2.0 GPA from a regionally accredited institution is required. C or higher grades are accepted in academic courses. At least 30 credits must be completed in residence, of a total 120 credits required for the bachelor's degree. Application deadlines are open; transfers are admitted to all terms. Notification is given within 1 month.

Visiting: Two orientation programs are held each summer for entering freshmen. Attendance is voluntary. Guides are available for informal visits. Visitors may sit in on classes but may not stay overnight at the school. Visits are best scheduled for weekdays during school sessions. The admissions office will make arrangements.

Financial Aid: Sixty-three percent of all students receive financial aid. Twenty percent work part-time on campus. The average award to freshmen from all sources available through the university is $6000. The university is a member of CSS. The FAF is required. The deadline for aid applications is March 15 for all students.

Foreign Students: Ten percent of the full-time students are from foreign countries. The university offers these students an intensive English program, special counseling, and special organizations.

Admissions: The TOEFL is required; a minimum score of 550 must be achieved. The SAT or ACT is not required.

Procedure: Suggested guidelines for application by foreign students are May 1 (fall), November 1 (spring), and March 1 (summer). Proof of funds adequate to cover 12 months of study must be presented.

Admissions Contact: Emilio F. Garcia, Assistant Director of Admissions.

UNIVERSITY OF SOUTH FLORIDA
Tampa, Florida 33620
D-4
(813) 974-4030

F/T: 6192M, 6148W
P/T: 2816M, 2861W
Grad: 1511M, 1881W
Year: sems, ss
Appl: see profile
5517 applied
SAT: 440V 490M

Faculty: 1052; I, –$
Ph.D.'s: 73%
S/F Ratio: 18 to 1
Tuition: $796 ($2026)
R and B: $1879
3695 accepted   2067 enrolled
ACT: 20   COMPETITIVE

Established in 1956, University of South Florida, a unit of the state university system, offers undergraduate and graduate programs in its colleges of Arts and Letters, Business Administration, Education, Engineering, Fine Arts, Medicine, Natural Sciences, Nursing, and Social and Behavioral Sciences. The library houses 584,000 volumes and 200,000 microfilm items, and subscribes to 5460 periodicals.

Environment: The 1700-acre main campus is located in a suburban area 10 miles from downtown Tampa. Living facilities include dormitories and on-campus apartments. The university also has campuses in St. Petersburg, Sarasota, and Fort Myers.

Student Life: Over 85% of the students come from Florida. About 15% live on campus. Nine percent are minority-group members. Campus housing is single-sex; there are visiting privileges. Students may keep cars on campus. Day-care facilities are available to all students for a fee.

Organizations: There are chapters of 17 national fraternities and 9 national sororities. Popular student activities include publications, music groups, theater, special-interest clubs, concerts, and major social events such as Homecoming.

Sports: The university fields 8 intercollegiate teams for men and 7 for women. There are 15 intramural sports for men and 14 for women.

148 FLORIDA

Handicapped: Special facilities for the physically handicapped include wheelchair ramps, parking areas, elevators, lowered drinking fountains and telephones, and specially equipped rest rooms. Special class scheduling can be arranged with the assistance of the handicapped student adviser. The entire campus is accessible to the handicapped.

Graduates: Of those who enter, 50% remain to graduate.

Services: Career and psychological counseling, tutoring, remedial instruction, and placement services are available free of charge to all students. Health care is provided on a fee basis.

Programs of Study: The university confers the B.A., B.S., B.I.S., B.F.A., B.S.W., B.S.E.S., B.S. in Eng., and B.E.T. degrees. Master's and doctoral degrees are also awarded. Bachelor's degrees are offered in the following subjects: AREA STUDIES (American, Black/Afro-American), BUSINESS (accounting, business administration, business education, computer science, economics, finance, management, marketing), EDUCATION (early childhood, elementary, health/physical, industrial, secondary, special), ENGLISH (creative writing, English, journalism, literature, mass communications, speech), FINE AND PERFORMING ARTS (art, art education, art history, dance, film/photography, music, music education, radio/TV, studio art, theater/dramatics), HEALTH SCIENCES (medical technology, nursing, speech therapy), LANGUAGES (French, German, Greek/Latin, Italian, Russian, Spanish), MATH AND SCIENCES (biology, botany, chemistry, chemistry—clinical, geology, mathematics, microbiology, natural sciences, physics, zoology), PHILOSOPHY (classics, humanities, liberal studies, philosophy, religion), PREPROFESSIONAL (dentistry, engineering science, engineering technology, forestry, law, medicine, pharmacy, social work, veterinary), SOCIAL SCIENCES (anthropology, criminal justice, economics, geography, government/political science, history, international relations, psychology, social sciences, sociology). About 22% of the degrees are conferred in social sciences, 22% in business, and 20% in education.

Required: All undergraduates must complete 40 semester hours of general distribution with at least 6 semester hours in each of the following areas: English composition, fine arts and humanities, mathematics and quantitative methods, natural sciences, and social and behavioral sciences.

Special: There are dual degree programs, opportunities for independent study and study abroad, and cooperative work-study programs.

Honors: Honors work is possible.

Admissions: About 67% of the 1981–82 freshman applicants were accepted. The SAT scores of those who enrolled were as follows: Verbal—74% below 500, 20% between 500 and 599, 5% between 600 and 700, and 0% above 700; Math—51% below 500, 37% between 500 and 599, 12% between 600 and 700, and 1% above 700. On the ACT, 54% scored below 21, 22% between 21 and 23, 13% between 24 and 25, 7% between 26 and 28, and 4% above 28. A 2.0 high school GPA is required. An 850 SAT score or an 18 ACT score is required of applicants with a GPA of less than 3.0. Recommendations, advanced placement or honors courses, and special talents are also considered important.

Procedure: Either the SAT or the ACT is required. The application deadline is 8 weeks prior to the beginning of the fall, spring, or summer term. Notification is on a rolling basis. There is a $15 application fee.

Special: AP and CLEP credit is granted. There is an early admissions plan.

Transfer: For fall 1981, 5826 students applied, 4429 were accepted, and 3013 enrolled. A 2.0 GPA is required; D grades are accepted. All students must complete, at the university, 30 of the 120 credits required for a bachelor's degree. Application deadlines are the same as those for freshmen.

Visiting: There is a prospective student orientation program. Appointments for pre-admission counseling may be arranged through the admissions office. The best times for visits are from 9 A.M. to 5 P.M., Monday through Friday. A self-guided cassette tour is available.

Financial Aid: About 50% of the students are receiving aid. About 15% work part-time on campus. The average freshman award is $2000. CWSP, grants, and various loans (federal, state, and university) are available. There are both merit and need-based scholarships. The FAF and the Institutional Financial Aid Application are due February 1. The university is a member of CSS.

Foreign Students: Two percent of the full-time students come from foreign countries. An intensive English course, an intensive English program, special counseling, and special organizations are available for these students.

Admissions: Foreign students must achieve a TOEFL score of at least 550 and either an SAT combined score of 850 or an ACT score of 18.

Procedure: The application deadline is 6 months prior to the start of the intended term of entry; foreign students are admitted in the fall, spring, and summer terms. Foreign students must present proof of funds adequate to cover 1 year of study.

Admissions Contact: Linda Erickson, Director of Admissions.

UNIVERSITY OF TAMPA D-4
Tampa, Florida 33606 (813) 253-8861

F/T: 837M, 770W	Faculty: 87; IIA, −$
P/T: 72M, 65W	Ph.D.'s: 79%
Grad: 130M, 49W	S/F Ratio: 18 to 1
Year: 2-2-2-2-1, ss	Tuition: $4496
Appl: open	R and B: $2030
2100 applied	1551 accepted	532 enrolled
SAT: 450V 490M	ACT: 21	COMPETITIVE

University of Tampa, established in 1931, is a private, nonsectarian, liberal arts institution. The library contains 190,000 volumes and subscribes to 601 periodicals.

Environment: The university's 68-acre urban campus, a 5-minute walk from downtown Tampa, overlooks the Hillsborough River. Buildings include a theater, an art building, an auditorium, and a student center. Living facilities include dormitories, on-campus apartments, and fraternity houses.

Student Life: Thirty percent of the students are from Florida. Sixty-five percent of the freshmen come from public schools. About 70% live on campus. Twenty-four percent are minority-group members. About 42% are Catholic, 35% are Protestant, and 18% are Jewish. Campus housing is both coed and single-sex; there are visiting privileges in the single-sex housing. Students may keep cars on campus.

Organizations: Student organizations include subject-area clubs, publications, and religious and fraternal groups. About 15% of the men belong to 1 of 9 fraternities, and 4% of the women belong to a sorority. The university sponsors artists' performances, films, and recitals.

Sports: The university fields 9 intercollegiate teams for men and 8 for women. There are 12 intramural sports for men and 12 for women.

Handicapped: Ninety percent of the campus is accessible to wheelchair-bound students. Special facilities include wheelchair ramps, parking areas, elevators, and specially equipped rest rooms.

Graduates: About 48% of entering freshmen drop out by the end of the first year; 35% remain to graduate. About 48% of the graduates week advanced degrees (3% in medicine, 1% in dentistry, and 6% in law). Sixty percent enter business and industry.

Services: Placement, career counseling, psychological counseling, and health care are provided free to students. Placement services also are available to graduates. Tutoring is provided on a fee basis.

Programs of Study: The university awards the B.A., B.S., B.F.A., and B.Mus. degrees. Associate and master's degrees also are available. Bachelor's degrees are offered in the following subjects: BUSINESS (accounting, business administration, computer science, finance, management), EDUCATION (elementary, secondary), ENGLISH (English), FINE AND PERFORMING ARTS (art, art education, music, music education), HEALTH SCIENCES (medical technology), LANGUAGES (French, Spanish), MATH AND SCIENCES (biology, chemistry, mathematics, oceanography), PHILOSOPHY (philosophy), PREPROFESSIONAL (dentistry, engineering, law, medicine, veterinary), SOCIAL SCIENCES (economics, government/political science, history, psychology, social work, sociology, urban affairs). Thirty-four percent of degrees conferred are in business, 22% are in math and sciences, and 22% are in social sciences.

Required: All students must take English, 3 courses in humanities, 3 in social sciences, and 3 in science, math and/or logic.

Special: The university offers independent study in some majors. Third-year students may study abroad. A 3-2 combination degree program is offered in conjunction with Gerogia Institute of Technology and Auburn University. Instruction is on a seminar/tutorial basis. Under the bimester calendar (2-2-2-2-1), students usually take 2 courses at a time. Each course lasts 7 weeks and meets 2 to 3 times per day, 4 days per week.

Honors: Seven honor societies are represented on campus.

Admissions: Seventy-four percent of those who applied were accepted for the 1981–82 freshman class. The SAT scores of those who enrolled were as follows: Verbal—70% below 500, 15% between 500 and 599, 10% between 600 and 700, and 5% above 700; Math—59% below 500, 20% between 500 and 599, 15% between 600 and 700, and 6% above 700. On the ACT, 45% scored below 21, 31% between 21 and 23, 14% between 24 and 25, 6% between 26 and 28, and 4% above 28. Applicants must have graduated from an accredited high school with an average of C or better and a class rank in the upper 50%, score a minimum total of 900 on the SAT or 20 on the ACT, and present 15 Carnegie units. Admissions officers also consider advanced placement or honors courses, recommendations by school officials, and extracurricular activities.

Procedure: The SAT or ACT is required and should be taken early in the senior year. The application, a $30 fee, high school records, and test scores should be submitted. There are no application deadlines; freshmen are admitted in the fall, winter, spring, and summer terms. Notification begins January 1. The university subscribes to the CRDA.

Special: Early and deferred admissions plans are available. CLEP credit is awarded.

Transfer: For fall 1981, 644 students applied, 406 were accepted, and 161 enrolled. Applicants must have at least a 2.0 average and be in good standing at their last school. D grades do not transfer. Students must complete, at the university, 30 of the 120 credits required for a bachelor's degree. There are no application deadlines; transfer students are admitted in all terms.

Visiting: Informal visits may be arranged through the admissions office for spring semester. Guides are provided, and visitors may sit in on classes.

Financial Aid: About 61% of the students receive aid. Forty percent work part-time on campus. The average freshman award is $4400. The university provides scholarships, loans, and campus employment. Scholarships range from $500 to $3500, loans from $600 to $1200, and earnings from campus employment from $400 to $1200. Aid is awarded on the basis of financial need and academic record. The aid application and the FAF or FFS should be submitted by March 12 (fall) or October 15 (winter). The university is a member of CSS.

Foreign Students: About 6% of the full-time students come from foreign countries. An intensive English course, special counseling, and special organizations are available for these students.

Admissions: Foreign students must achieve a TOEFL score of at least 550. No college entrance exams are required.

Procedure: Application deadlines are May 1 (fall) and October 15 (winter). Foreign students must present proof of health and proof of funds adequate to cover 1 year of study.

Admissions Contact: Robert W. Cook, Associate Director of Admissions.

WEBBER COLLEGE
Babson Park, Florida 33827

D-3
(813) 638-1431

F/T: 75M, 100W
P/T: 20M, 30W
Grad: none
Year: sems, ss
Appl: open
200 applied
SAT: 430V 440M

Faculty: 20; n/av
Ph.D.'s: 75%
S/F Ratio: 12 to 1
Tuition: $2890
R and B: $1941
150 accepted   82 enrolled
ACT: 18   LESS COMPETITIVE

Webber College, founded in 1927, is an independent institution offering undergraduate degrees in business fields.

Environment: The 110-acre campus is located in a rural area 14 miles from Winter Haven and 50 miles from Orlando. Dormitories house 100 men and 100 women.

Student Life: About 55% of the students are from Florida, and 70% are graduates of public schools. Forty-eight percent live on campus. Seventeen percent are members of minority groups. Campus housing is single-sex, with visiting privileges. Students may keep cars on campus.

Organizations: About 10% of the men belong to the 1 national fraternity on campus, and 10% of the women belong to the 1 national sorority. The 25 activities and organizations available to students include an international club and a student activities board.

Sports: The college fields intercollegiate teams in 3 sports for men and 4 for women. Eleven intramural sports for men and 10 for women also are offered.

Handicapped: Ninety-five percent of the campus is accessible to physically handicapped students. Facilities include wheelchair ramps, special parking areas, and specially equipped rest rooms. Special class scheduling can be arranged.

Graduates: About 24% of the freshmen drop out during their first year; 70% remain to graduate. Twenty percent of the graduates seek advanced degrees, and 90% eventually begin careers in business and industry.

Services: Students are provided with free placement aid, health care, psychological counseling, career counseling, tutoring, and remedial instruction.

Programs of Study: The college awards the B.S.Bus. degree. Associate degrees also are available. Bachelor's degrees are offered in the following subjects: BUSINESS (accounting, business administration, computer science, finance, hotel and restaurant management, management, marketing, real estate/insurance, retail management, travel/tourism).

Required: Special freshmen programs, a core curriculum, and physical education courses are required. Students must maintain a GPA of 2.0 or better to graduate.

Special: Study-abroad programs are available. Students may earn a general studies degree.

Admissions: Seventy-five percent of those who applied were accepted for the 1981–82 freshman class. The SAT scores of those who enrolled were as follows: Verbal—80% below 500, 15% between 500 and 599, 5% between 600 and 700, and 0% above 700; Math—70% below 500, 20% between 500 and 599, 10% between 600 and 700, and 0% above 700. Of those who took the ACT, 80% scored below 21, 5% between 21 and 23, 3% between 24 and 25, 2% between 26 and 28, and 0% above 28. Applicants must be high school graduates, rank in the top 60% of their class, and present a GPA of 2.5 or better. Other considerations include evidence of special talents, impressions made during an interview, leadership record, recommendations by school officials, and advanced placement or honors courses.

Procedure: Students must take the SAT or the ACT. Freshmen are admitted to all terms; application deadlines are open. Admissions decisions are made on a rolling basis. The application fee is $20.

Special: Early and deferred admissions plans are offered. CLEP credit is accepted.

Transfer: For fall 1981, 12 transfer students applied, 10 were accepted, and 8 enrolled. Students must have a GPA of 2.5 or better. C grades or better transfer. Students must complete the last 24 credits in residence, of the 130 required for a bachelor's degree. Application deadlines are open.

Visiting: Informal visits may be scheduled with the director of admissions for Mondays through Fridays, 9 A.M. to 4 P.M. Guides are provided, and prospective students may sit in on classes and remain overnight at the college.

Financial Aid: About 70% of the students receive aid through the college; 30% work part-time on campus. Scholarships (average $500, maximum $2810), loans (average $600, maximum $1000), and work contracts (average $500, maximum $800) are available to freshmen; the average aid award from all sources totaled $800. The college is a member of CSS and requires students to file the FAF or FFS. Aid application deadlines are July 15 (fall), December 15 (spring), and May 15 (summer).

Foreign Students: The 30 students from foreign countries represent 12% of the full-time enrollment. The college offers these students an English course, an intensive English program, and special organizations.

Admissions: Applicants must score 500 or better on the TOEFL. No college entrance exams are required.

Procedure: Application deadlines are July 15 (fall), December 15 (spring), and May 15 (summer). Students must present a physician's report of a physical examination and must show evidence of adequate funds for 1 year. They must also carry health insurance, which is available through the college for a fee.

Admissions Contact: Thomas D. Creola, Director of Admissions.

GEORGIA

AGNES SCOTT COLLEGE
Decatur, Georgia 30030   B-2
(404) 373-2571

F/T: 525W   Faculty: 68; IIB, +$
P/T: 34W   Ph.D.'s: 84%
Grad: none   S/F Ratio: 8 to 1
Year: qtrs   Tuition: $4375
Appl: Sept. 1   R and B: $1700
405 applied   285 accepted   162 enrolled
SAT: 530V 540M   ACT: 25   **VERY COMPETITIVE+**

Agnes Scott College, founded in 1889, is a private liberal arts college for women. The college, although founded by Presbyterians, is nonsectarian. The library contains 165,500 volumes, subscribes to 760 periodicals, has 4340 microfilm items on file, and has 3377 recordings.

Environment: The college's 100-acre suburban campus is located 6 miles from downtown Atlanta. The physical plant consists of 16 major buildings of neo-Gothic architecture, including 6 dormitories that accommodate 600 women. The college also sponsors housing for married students.

Student Life: Forty-seven percent of the students are from Georgia. Seventy-four percent of entering freshmen come from public schools. About 93% reside in the dormitories. Ninety-one percent are Protestant. Seven percent are minority-group members. College housing is single-sex, and there are visiting privileges. Students may keep cars on campus.

Organizations: There are no sororities on campus. Student organizations and activities include special interest clubs, a weekly newspaper, a yearbook, religious groups, debate, theater, and concert and lecture series. Museums, a symphony orchestra, and Broadway shows are among the attractions to be found in nearby Atlanta.

Sports: The college fields 3 intercollegiate teams and offers 13 sports either on an intramural basis or through the physical education program.

Handicapped: Special facilities for handicapped students include designated parking, elevators, special stairway handrails, lowered drinking fountains and telephones, and specially equipped rest rooms. No visually impaired or hearing-impaired students are currently enrolled.

Graduates: The freshman dropout rate is 5%. Of the 60% who remain to graduate, 25% enter graduate study: about 3% enter medical school and about 3% enter law school. Fifty-five percent of the graduates pursue careers in business or industry.

Services: The following services are offered at no charge to the student: career counseling and placement services. Health care is covered by student fees. Psychological counseling is available. Tutoring is available in group sessions in certain departments.

Programs of Study: The college offers the B.A. degree in the following subjects: ENGLISH (creative writing, English), FINE AND PERFORMING ARTS (art, art history-English literature, fine arts, music, theater), LANGUAGES (French, German, Greek/Latin, Spanish), MATH AND SCIENCES (biology, chemistry, mathematics, mathematics-physics, physics, physics-astronomy), PHILOSOPHY (classics, philosophy, religion), SOCIAL SCIENCES (economics, history, history-English literature, international relations, political science, psychology, sociology). Of the degrees conferred, 45% are in social sciences, 16% in the arts, 16% in English, and 13% in math and sciences.

Required: Unless exempted, all students must take courses in Biblical literature, English, foreign language, physical education, science-mathematics, social sciences, history, classics or philosophy, and fine arts.

Special: Junior-year-abroad and summer-abroad programs are offered for students with sound academic records. The college has a reciprocal arrangement with other colleges and universities in the area for library services, exchange of instructors, research grants, lectures, and various conferences. Independent study for juniors and seniors, a legislative internship in political science, student-designed majors, and a 5-year dual-degree program in engineering, information and computer science, industrial management, or management sciences with Georgia Tech are available. A student exchange program exists with Mills College in Oakland, California.

Honors: Phi Beta Kappa and Mortar Board have chapters on campus.

Admissions: Seventy percent of those who applied were accepted for the 1981-82 freshman class. Of those who enrolled, the SAT scores were as follows: Verbal—30% scored below 500, 46% between 500 and 599, 20% between 600 and 700, and 4% above 700; Math—25% scored below 500, 55% between 500 and 599, and 22% between 600 and 700. On the ACT, 9% scored below 20, 13% between 20 and 23, 29% between 24 and 25, 33% between 26 and 28, and 16% above 28. In addition to academic record and test scores, other factors of importance are advanced placement or honors courses, impressions made during an interview, and recommendations by school officials.

Procedure: The ACT or SAT and 3 ATs, including English Composition and Math Level I, should be taken by and/or in the senior year. Admissions are on a rolling basis. Application with all supporting credentials must be in by September 1 for fall quarter, December 29 for winter quarter. There is a $25 application fee. The college subscribes to the CRDA.

Special: Early and deferred admissions plans are offered. AP credit is granted.

Transfer: Of the 32 transfer applications received for fall 1981, 19 were accepted and 8 students enrolled. Transfers are accepted in the freshman, sophomore, and junior years. D grades are not acceptable. Good academic standing and a professor's recommendation are required; students must also take the SAT or ACT. Students must study for 6 quarters at the college to receive a bachelor's degree.

Visiting: A prospective-student weekend is held in the fall, and an applicants' weekend is held in the spring. Guides are available for informal visits to the campus when the college is in session and by appointment during the summer. Visitors are permitted to sit in on classes and stay overnight in the dorms. To arrange a visit at the school, the admissions office should be contacted a week in advance.

Financial Aid: Forty-nine percent of all students receive aid. Forty percent work part-time on campus. The college provides scholarships, grants-in-aid, loans, and on-campus jobs. Freshman awards range from $100 to full tuition; the average award is $4281. Aid is based on need; academic scholarships are available. The FAF is preferred, but the FFS is accepted. The preferred filing date is February 15.

Foreign Students: Eight foreign students are enrolled at the college. The college offers counseling and special organizations for these students.

Admissions: Foreign students must achieve a TOEFL score of at least 600 and must take the SAT.

Procedure: Application deadlines are February 1 (fall) and October 15 (winter). Foreign students must file the college's health form. They must also present proof of funds adequate to cover a year of study. Financial aid recipients must have $1000 on deposit in the U.S. for personal expenses. Foreign students must carry health insurance, which is available through the college for a fee.

Admissions Contact: Judith Maguire Tindel, Director of Admissions.

ALBANY STATE COLLEGE
Albany, Georgia 31705   B-4
(912) 439-4336

F/T, P/T: Faculty: 125; IIB, +$
   1571M&W   Ph.D.'s: 44%
Grad: none   S/F Ratio: 18 to 1
Year: qtrs, ss   Tuition: $681 ($1170)
Appl: Sept. 1   R and B: $1665
1362 applied   680 accepted   383 enrolled
SAT: 350V 330M   **LESS COMPETITIVE**

Albany State College, established in 1903, is a state-supported liberal arts and teacher-education college. The library contains 150,000 volumes and 309,527 microfilm items, and subscribes to 1000 periodicals.

Environment: The 202-acre campus is located just outside Albany, a city of 100,000 people 175 miles south of Atlanta. Six dormitories accommodate 360 men and 622 women.

Student Life: Ninety percent of the students are from Georgia. The student body is predominantly black. About 40% of the students live in the dormitories, which are single-sex. Alcohol is prohibited on campus. Freshmen are required to attend regular assemblies.

Organizations: Four fraternities and 4 sororities have chapters at the college. Campus activities include Lyceum programs, assembly and vesper programs, departmental clubs, drama, choir, band, a debating team, student government, publications, and Sunday school.

Sports: The college competes on an intercollegiate level in 7 sports for men and 5 for women. Intramural sports for men and women also are offered.

Graduates: About 70% of the entering freshmen remain to graduate. Ten percent of the graduates seek advanced degrees.

Services: Students receive free counseling and health care.

Programs of Study: The college confers the B.A., B.S., B.S.N., and B.B.A. degrees. Master's degrees also are awarded. Bachelor's degrees are offered in the following subjects: BUSINESS (business administration, business education, computer science, office administration), EDUCATION (early childhood, health/physical, middle grades, secondary, special), ENGLISH (English, speech), FINE AND PERFORMING ARTS (art, music, music education, theater/dramatics), HEALTH SCIENCES (nursing), LANGUAGES (French, Spanish), MATH AND SCIENCES (biology, chemistry, computer science, mathematics), SOCIAL SCIENCES (criminal justice, government/political science, history, psychology, sociology).

Required: Students must complete a general-education program during their freshman and sophomore years. It requires 20 hours in humanities, 20 in mathematics and sciences, 20 in social sciences, and 30 appropriate to the major. Students also must take 6 hours of physical education. Participation in the cooperative-education program, which places students in off-campus jobs, is required.

Special: A 3-2 program in engineering is offered in conjunction with Georgia Institute of Technology. The sociology department offers work-experience opportunities: a gerontology training program and the Georgia Intern Program, which places students in public agencies. Language majors are urged to participate in at least one of the college's study-abroad programs. Preprofessional programs are offered in medicine, medical technology, pharmacy, and law.

Honors: Five honor societies are represented on campus.

Admissions: Fifty percent of those who applied were accepted for the 1981–82 freshman class. Applicants must be graduates of an accredited high school and have completed 16 academic units. State high school equivalency certificates and GED diplomas also are accepted. Admissions officers also consider the reputation of the high school, recommendations from high school officials, and impressions made during a personal interview. Preference is given to Georgia residents.

Procedure: The SAT is required and should be taken in December of the senior year. The application, test scores, and high school records should be submitted by September 1 (fall), December 4 (winter), March 1 (spring), or May 15 (summer). Applicants are notified on a rolling basis. There is no application fee.

Special: An early admsissions plan is available. AP and CLEP credit is accepted.

Transfer: Applicants should have a GPA of at least 2.0. D grades do not transfer. Students must spend at least 3 quarters at the college, earning 45 of the 186 quarter credits required for a bachelor's degree. Application deadlines are the same as those for freshmen.

Financial Aid: Eighty-seven percent of the students receive aid through the school. Scholarships, loans, and jobs are available. Programs include BEOG, Georgia Incentive Scholarship, NDSL, Guaranteed Student Loan, and CWS. Aid is awarded on the basis of financial need and academic promise. The average award to freshmen is $1336. The FAF and aid application must be submitted by April 15.

Foreign Students: Two students from foreign countries were enrolled in 1981–82.

Admissions: Applicants must take the TOEFL.

Admissions Contact: Dorothy B. Hubbard, Director of Admissions.

ARMSTRONG STATE COLLEGE E–4
Savannah, Georgia 31406 (912) 927-5275

F/T: 980M, 1350W	Faculty: 128; IIA, av$
P/T: 250M, 400W	Ph.D.'s: 60%
Grad: 40M, 70W	S/F Ratio: 22 to 1
Year: qtrs, ss	Tuition: $700 ($1800)
Appl: Sept. 1	R and B: $1800
790 applied	750 accepted 600 enrolled
SAT: 420V 400M	LESS COMPETITIVE

Armstrong State College, founded in 1935, is a state-controlled liberal arts college. The library contains over 115,000 volumes and 240,000 microfilm items, and subscribes to over 1100 periodicals.

Environment: The 200-acre suburban campus consists of 14 buildings, including a new human services building with the latest medical equipment in the University System of Georgia. Limited college-sponsored housing is available in off-campus apartments.

Student Life: About 82% of the students are from Georgia. Eighteen percent are minority-group members. College-sponsored housing is single-sex, and there are visiting privileges. Students may keep cars on campus.

Organizations: Four fraternities and 3 sororities attract as members 15% of the men and 10% of the women. Other student activities include publications, religious organizations, drama and music groups, a concert-lecture series, and a concert-dance series.

Sports: There are intercollegiate teams in 5 sports for men and 3 for women. Seven intramural sports are offered to both sexes.

Handicapped: The campus is estimated to be 50% accessible to the handicapped student. Special facilities include specially designed rest rooms, ramps, and designated handicapped parking. Special class scheduling can be arranged. Less than 1% of the student body have visual impairments.

Graduates: The freshman dropout rate is 25%; 60% remain to graduate. Thirty-three percent of graduating students pursue further study.

Services: The following services are offered at no charge to the student: psychological counseling, tutoring, health care, placement, and career counseling. A fee is charged for remedial instruction.

Programs of Study: The college offers the B.A. and B.S. degrees and also has associate and master's degree programs. Bachelor's degrees are offered in the following subjects: EDUCATION (elementary, health/physical, secondary), ENGLISH (English), FINE AND PERFORMING ARTS (art, art education), HEALTH SCIENCES (medical technology, nursing, speech therapy), LANGUAGES (French, German, Spanish), MATH AND SCIENCES (biology, chemistry, mathematics), PREPROFESSIONAL (social work), SOCIAL SCIENCES (government/political science, history, psychology, sociology). Of the degrees conferred, 60% are in health sciences, 14% are in education, and 10% are in social sciences.

Required: All students are required to take courses in English, mathematics, laboratory science, physical education, social sciences, and western civilization.

Special: A 3-2 degree program is offered in conjunction with Georgia Tech.

Honors: Five national honor societies have chapters on campus.

Admissions: Ninety-five percent of those who applied were accepted for the 1981–82 freshman class. The SAT scores of those who enrolled were as follows: Verbal—70% below 500, 10% between 500 and 599, 0.2% between 600 and 700, and 0.2% above 700; Math—70% below 500, 10% between 500 and 599, 0.2% between 600 and 700, and 0.2% above 700. Applicants must be graduates of accredited high schools with 16 units of academic work and a minimum GPA of 1.8. Admission is determined by a combination of SAT scores and high school average.

Procedure: The SAT is required. Application deadlines for any quarter are 20 days prior to the beginning of that quarter (September 1 for the fall term). There is a rolling admissions plan. The application fee is $10.

Special: Early decision and early and deferred admissions plans are available. AP and CLEP credit is granted.

Transfer: For fall 1981, 480 transfer students applied, 450 were accepted, and 410 enrolled. Applicants must be in good standing at their previous institutions. A minimum GPA of 1.8 is required for admission; C grades or better transfer. Forty-five quarter hours must be taken in residence out of the 191 hours required for the bachelor's degree. Deadlines are the same as for freshman applications.

Visiting: Guides are availble for informal visits to the campus. Midquarter is the recommended time for such visits. For further information, the admissions office should be contacted.

Financial Aid: About 60% of all students receive aid. The college provides scholarships, loans, and campus employment as financial aids. Application must be made 6 weeks prior to the beginning of the quarter. The FAF must be filed with the CSS. Notification is made by August 15.

Foreign Students: Foreign students comprise less than 1% of the full-time enrollment.

Admissions: Foreign students must achieve a TOEFL score of at least 500. A minimum SAT score of 750 (combined) also is required.

GEORGIA

Procedure: Application deadlines for any quarter are 6 weeks prior to the beginning of that quarter. Foreign students must furnish proof of funds adequate to cover 4 years of study. They also must carry health insurance.

Admissions Contact: Thomas P. Miller, Director of Admissions.

ATLANTA COLLEGE OF ART   B–2
Atlanta, Georgia 30309   (404) 892-3600

F/T: 140M, 151W	Faculty:	38; IV, –$
P/T: 175M, 190W	Ph.D.'s:	10%
Grad: none	S/F Ratio:	11 to 1
Year: sems, ss	Tuition:	$3850
Appl: June 1	R and B:	$2000
250 applied	175 accepted	105 enrolled
SAT: 350V		SPECIAL

The Atlanta College of Art, founded in 1928, is a private, independent, professional college controlled by the Atlanta Arts Alliance. The library contains 35,000 volumes and 30,000 microfilm items, and subscribes to 152 periodicals.

Environment: The college occupies the third and fourth floors of the Atlanta Memorial Art Center, which also houses the Atlanta Symphony Orchestra, the Alliance Theater Company, and the High Museum of Art. A college-owned apartment building nearby is available to students.

Student Life: Fifty-eight percent of the students come from Georgia. Ninety percent attended public schools. A third live in the student apartment building, which is coed.

Organizations: Students have access to symphony, theater, and museum offerings in the college building and to social and cultural opportunities in the Atlanta area. There are no fraternities or sororities.

Sports: Coed intramural sports are offered.

Handicapped: The entire campus is accessible to handicapped students. Special facilities include ramps, specially equipped rest rooms, designated parking areas, elevators, and lowered drinking fountains and telephones.

Graduates: Thirty-five percent of the freshmen remain to graduate. Of those, 26% pursue graduate study while 15% begin careers in business and industry.

Services: Health care, placement services, and career counseling are offered free to students.

Programs of Study: The college confers the B.F.A. degree in 7 majors: drawing, painting, photography, printmaking, sculpture, video imagery, and visual communications.

Required: The first year is devoted to core courses in design and drawing. A third of the bachelor's degree program consists of general studies courses, primarily in the humanities.

Special: A 4-week summer foundation workshop is offered for preregistered freshmen. Students may spend their junior year abroad and design their own majors.

Admissions: Seventy percent of those who applied were accepted for the 1981–82 freshman class. The college considers only the verbal score on the SAT. Applicants should be graduates of an accredited high school, have a C+ average, and rank in the upper 50% of their class. Other factors considered are the student's portfolio, impressions made during an interview, advanced placement or honors courses, and a written statement of purpose.

Procedure: The SAT or ACT is required. Freshmen are accepted only in the fall; the application deadline is June 1. Applications should be submitted with a $15 fee. The rolling admissions plan is used. Notification is given within 2 weeks. An interview is recommended, and students must submit a portfolio with at least 12 pieces of work.

Special: Early decision, early admissions, and deferred admissions plans are offered.

Transfer: Applicants must meet the same requirements as entering freshmen, and must show greater proficiency in their portfolio. D grades do not transfer. Students generally must spend 2 years in residence (although the requirement may be waived) and earn a total of 144 credits for a bachelor's degree.

Visiting: Guides are available for informal visits to the campus; visits should be scheduled during business hours, Monday through Friday. Visitors may sit in on classes. Contact the admissions office for arrangements.

Financial Aid: About 70% of all students receive aid. Freshman scholarships, NDSL, CWS, SEOG, BEOG, and Georgia State Grants are available. The average award to freshmen is $2500. The college is a member of the CSS and requires the FAF. Aid applications should be submitted by April 1 for priority consideration.

Foreign Students: The 6 students from foreign countries represent nearly 4% of full-time enrollment. An intensive English course and special counseling are provided for these students.

Admissions: Applicants must score at least 500 on the TOEFL. They also must take the SAT.

Procedure: The application deadline is June 1 for fall admission. Students must present proof of adequate funds for 1 year. Health insurance is included in tuition fees.

Admissions Contact: William Linthicum, Director of Admissions.

AUGUSTA COLLEGE   D–2
Augusta, Georgia 30910   (404) 828-3301

F/T: 934M, 1150W	Faculty:	152; IIA, av$
P/T: 588M, 842W	Ph.D.'s:	60%
Grad: 122M, 200W	S/F Ratio:	14 to 1
Year: qtrs, ss	Tuition:	$636 ($1686)
Appl: Aug. 13	R and B:	n/app
933 applied	757 accepted	612 enrolled
SAT: 407V 426M		LESS COMPETITIVE

Augusta College is an arts and sciences commuter college offering associate, baccalaureate, and master's degrees as a senior unit of the University System of Georgia. The library has holdings of 234,961 volumes and 212,491 microform items, and subscribes to 1594 periodicals.

Environment: The college's 72-acre campus is in an urban environment, 140 miles east of Atlanta. There are 30 major buildings on campus. No dormitory facilities are available.

Student Life: About 90% of the students are from Georgia. Eighty-nine percent of entering freshmen attended public schools. All students commute. About 16% of the students are minority-group members. Day-care services are available to all students, faculty, and staff for a fee.

Organizations: Thirty-five percent of the men and 4% of the women belong to the 3 fraternities and 5 sororities on campus. Other student organizations include service societies, religious associations, student publications, cultural activities, and special-interest clubs.

Sports: The college fields 8 intercollegiate teams for men and 4 for women. There are 5 intramural sports for men and 3 for women.

Handicapped: Special facilities for the handicapped student include wheelchair ramps, elevators, and designated handicapped parking. The Office to Promote the Independence of Disabled Students is staffed by students and coordinates services and individualized assistance for disabled students on campus.

Graduates: The freshman dropout rate is 20%; about 30% remain to graduate. Fifteen percent of the graduates go on to further study; 2% enter medical school, 2% law school, and 2% dental school. Thirty-five percent enter careers in business and industry.

Services: Psychological counseling, placement, career counseling, tutoring, and remedial instruction are offered at no charge to the student. Placement services for students and alumni include on-campus recruiting, credentials files, employment listings, and co-op programs.

Programs of Study: The college confers the B.A., B.S., B.B.A., B.F.A., B.S.Ed., B.S.Med.Tech., and B.M. degrees. Associate and master's degree programs are also offered. Bachelor's degrees are offered in the following subjects: BUSINESS (accounting, business administration, business education, economics, executive secretarial, finance, management, marketing, real estate/insurance), EDUCATION (elementary, special), ENGLISH (English), FINE AND PERFORMING ARTS (art, art education, music education, music performance, studio art), HEALTH SCIENCES (medical technology), MATH AND SCIENCES (biology, chemistry, computer science, mathematics, physical sciences, physics), SOCIAL SCIENCES (government/political science, history, psychology, sociology). Of the degrees conferred, 29% were in business, 27% in social sciences, and 12% in math and sciences.

Required: All students must complete 186 quarter hours, including 6 hours of physical education.

Special: Study abroad may be arranged with other institutions.

Honors: There are 2 national honor societies with chapters on campus. The college does not have an honors program.

Admissions: Eighty-one percent of those who applied were accepted for the 1981-82 freshman class. Applicants must be graduates of an accredited high school or its equivalent and have completed 16 units of high school work.

Procedure: The SAT is required. Applications should be submitted, along with a $10 application fee by August 13 (fall), December 3 (winter), February 25 (spring), and May 20 (summer). Admission is on a rolling basis.

Special: Early and deferred admissions plans are offered. Applications for early admissions should be received 30 days prior to the quarter. CLEP general and subject exams are accepted.

Transfer: For fall 1981, 405 transfer students applied, 313 were accepted, and 225 enrolled. Transfers are accepted for all classes. The requirements are a minimum GPA of 2.0, minimum SAT scores of 410 on the verbal and 410 on the math (required only if less than 30 quarter hours have been earned), and good standing at the previous school. Grades of C or above transfer. Students must study at the college for at least 45 of a minimum 180 quarter hours to receive a bachelor's degree; there is a 1 year residency requirement. Application deadlines are the same as those for freshmen.

Visiting: There are no regularly scheduled orientations for prospective students. Guides are available for informal visits to the campus. Visitors may sit in on classes. The director of admissions will make the arrangements.

Financial Aid: About 24% of all students receive aid; 9% work part-time on campus. The college provides scholarships, grants, loans, and work-study (available in all departments) to aid students. The average award to freshmen from all sources is $2608. The college is a member of CSS; the FAF is required. Applications completed 90 days prior to the start of the quarter will be given priority.

Foreign Students: About 1% of the full-time students come from foreign countries.

Admissions: Foreign students must achieve a minimum TOEFL score of 550; they must also score at least 410 on the verbal portion of the SAT and 410 on the math.

Procedure: Application deadlines are May 13 (fall), September 13 (winter), November 13 (spring), and February 20 (summer). Foreign students must present proof of funds adequate to cover 1 year of study. They must also carry health insurance, which is available through the college for a fee.

Admissions Contact: Donald L. Smith, Assistant Dean of Students and Director of Admissions.

BERRY COLLEGE A-2
Mount Berry, Georgia 30149 (404) 235-4494

F/T: 572M, 805W	Faculty: 86; IIA, av$
P/T: 36M, 53W	Ph.D.'s: 65%
Grad: 53M, 67W	S/F Ratio: 16 to 1
Year: qtrs, ss	Tuition: $2985
Appl: open	R and B: $1320
1100 applied	519 accepted	472 enrolled
SAT: 475V 506M	ACT: 24	COMPETITIVE+

Berry College, established in 1902, is a private liberal arts college. The library houses 120,000 volumes and 216,000 microfiche items, and subscribes to 1097 periodicals.

Environment: The 600-acre campus, which is located in a suburban area 60 miles from Atlanta, comprises 30 major buildings, including dormitories.

Student Life: About 79% of the students are from Georgia. Eighty-six percent of entering freshmen attended public schools. Approximately 70% of the students live in residence halls. About 6% of the students are minority-group members. Campus housing is single-sex; there are visiting privileges. Students may keep cars on campus.

Organizations: There are no fraternities or sororities on campus. Student activities include special-interest clubs, publications, music and drama organizations, guest artist and distinguished lecturer series, and religious groups. Snow skiing is available in Tennessee and North Carolina. Theater, concerts, sports, and other recreational opportunities are offered in Atlanta.

Sports: The college fields 5 intercollegiate teams for men and 4 for women. There are 2 intramural sports for men and 2 for women.

Handicapped: Special facilities for the handicapped student include wheelchair ramps, designated parking, and elevators.

GEORGIA 153

Graduates: By the end of the freshman year 25% drop out; 54% remain to graduate. Thirty-five percent of the graduates go on to graduate or professional schools.

Services: The following services are offered free of charge to the student: psychological counseling, health care, tutoring, placement, and career counseling.

Programs of Study: The college confers the B.A., B.F.A., B.Mus., and B.S. degrees. Associate and master's degree programs are also offered. Bachelor's degrees are offered in the following subjects: BUSINESS (accounting, business administration, business education), EDUCATION (early childhood, elementary, health/physical, home economics, industrial, secondary), ENGLISH (English, speech), FINE AND PERFORMING ARTS (art), LANGUAGES (French, German, Spanish), MATH AND SCIENCES (biology, chemistry, mathematics, oceanography/marine biology, physics), PHILOSOPHY (philosophy and religion), PREPROFESSIONAL (dentistry, engineering, home economics, law, medicine, ministry, pharmacy, social work, veterinary), SOCIAL SCIENCES (economics, government/political science, history, psychology, social sciences, sociology).

Required: A sequence of 74 (of a total 192) quarter hours required of all students is a flexible grouping from the behavioral sciences, humanities, mathematics and natural sciences, and physical education.

Special: The college offers independent study, a 3-year bachelor's degree, and a 3-2 combination degree program in engineering with Georgia Tech. Student-designed majors and study abroad are possible.

Admissions: Forty-seven percent of those who applied were accepted for the 1981-82 freshman class. Applicants should rank in the upper 50% of their high school class, have a C+ average or better, bring college-qualifying recommendations from the high school, and present 16 Carnegie units. Other influencing factors are test scores, advanced placement or honors courses, personality, and leadership record.

Procedure: The SAT or ACT is required and should be taken by December of the senior year. Freshmen are admitted to any term. Application deadlines are open. There is a $15 application fee. Admission and notification are on a rolling basis.

Special: There are early decision, early admissions, and deferred admissions plans. The application deadline for early admissions is August 1. CLEP general and subject exams are accepted. Students may also earn credit through AP.

Transfer: Transfers are considered for all classes. Applicants must have a GPA of 2.0; a GPA of 2.5 is recommended. Grades of C or above transfer. There is a residency requirement of 3 quarters; 45 of the 192 credits needed for a bachelor's degree must be completed at the college. Application deadlines are the same as those for freshmen.

Visiting: There are no regularly scheduled orientations for prospective students. Guides are available for informal visits to the campus. Visitors may sit in on classes. To arrange an overnight stay at the campus, the admissions office should be contacted.

Financial Aid: About 80% of all students receive aid, which is awarded on the basis of financial need and academic record. About 60% of the students work part-time on campus. Scholarships, loans (federal government and college), and jobs are available. Between 20% and 100% of the expenses can be obtained through aid or employment; the average freshman award is 25% of expenses. The college is a member of CSS; the FAF is required. The recommended filing date for aid applications is February 1.

Foreign Students: About 2% of the full-time students come from foreign countries. The college offers these students an intensive English course, special counseling, and special organizations.

Admissions: Foreign students must achieve a minimum score of 550 on the TOEFL or an equally acceptable score on the University of Michigan Language Test or the ALIGU exam. No college entrance exams are required.

Procedure: There are no application deadlines; a rolling admissions plan is used. Foreign students must present proof of funds adequate to cover 1 year of study. They must also carry health insurance, which is available through the college for a fee.

Admissions Contact: Thomas C. Glover, Dean of Admissions.

154 GEORGIA

BRENAU COLLEGE
Gainesville, Georgia 30501 B-2
(404) 534-6299

F/T, P/T: 821W
Grad: 125M&W
Year: qtrs, ss
Appl: open
SAT: required
Faculty: 60; n/av
Ph.D.'s: 55%
S/F Ratio: 15 to 1
Tuition, R and B: $5800

LESS COMPETITIVE

Brenau College, founded in 1878, is a private liberal arts institution primarily for women. The library contains about 50,000 volumes and subscribes to 450 periodicals.

Environment: The 43-acre campus is located in Gainesville, a metropolitan area of 50,000 people 50 miles from Atlanta. The 52 buildings include 8 dormitories that house 300 women, 8 sorority houses, and a recreation building.

Student Life: About 88% of the students are from the South; 60% are from Georgia. Seventy percent of the freshmen come from public schools. Students must live on campus unless they are residing with parents. An honor code governs student conduct.

Organizations: About 68% of the students belong to the 7 sororities on campus. Extracurricular activities include chorus, dance, drama, orchestra, student government, religious groups, and publications. The college sponsors concerts, lectures, plays, recitals, and sorority functions.

Sports: The college sponsors intercollegiate teams in 3 sports. There are 4 intramural sports.

Graduates: About 30% of the freshmen drop out, and 60% remain to graduate. More than one-third of the graduates pursue advanced degrees.

Programs of Study: The college awards the B.A., B.S., B.S.N., and B.Mus. degrees. Master's programs also are available. Bachelor's degrees are offered in the following subjects: BUSINESS (accounting, business administration, fashion merchandising), EDUCATION (early childhood, health/physical, home economics, middle-school, special), ENGLISH (English, journalism), FINE AND PERFORMING ARTS (art, church music, commercial art, crafts, dance, interior design, music, music education, piano, radio/TV, theater/dramatics, voice), HEALTH SCIENCES (medical technology, nursing), MATH AND SCIENCES (biology), PREPROFESSIONAL (law, medicine), SOCIAL SCIENCES (criminal justice, government/political science, history, psychology, social services). Twenty percent of the undergraduate degrees are conferred in education and 19% in business.

Required: Students must take courses in English, psychology, biology, fine arts, mathematics, behavioral science, social science, and physical education. Nursing students must earn a GPA of 2.5 or better to graduate; students majoring in other fields must earn a GPA of at least 2.0 in all academic work not related to the major and a GPA of at least 2.25 in courses in the major field.

Special: The college offers independent study and tours to Europe, Mexico, and places of interest in the United States. Bachelor's degrees may be earned in 3 years. Combination degree programs are available. Students may design their own majors. A 4-year academic and career advisement program is available.

Honors: An honors program is offered.

Admissions: Ninety-two percent of those who applied were accepted for a recent freshman class. Applicants should have completed 16 Carnegie units at an accredited high school. Admissions officers also consider advanced placement or honors courses and leadership potential.

Procedure: The SAT or ACT is required. Application deadlines are open; notification is made within 2 weeks after all credentials are received. Freshmen are admitted to all sessions. The application fee is $15.

Special: Early admission, early decision, and deferred admission programs are available. AP and CLEP credit is accepted. Joint enrollment with Brenau Academy is possible.

Transfer: Applicants should have a GPA of 2.0 or better. D grades transfer, except in Englsh composition. All graduates of accredited junior colleges will be admitted as juniors or seniors, and all grades received will be assigned the same credit as those awarded by Brenau. Students must take 45 hours of work at the college to graduate.

Financial Aid: About 40% of the students receive aid. Georgia residents may receive state tuition grants. The college offers scholarships for needy students and for those who show academic achievement or special talent in swimming, tennis, journalism, drama, and music. Other aid, awarded on the basis of need, is available through federal NDSL, CWS, BEOG, and SEOG programs. The college is a member of the CSS and the FAS; the FAF should be filed by June 1.

Admissions Contact: Deborah S. Fennell, Director of Admissions.

CLARK COLLEGE
Atlanta, Georgia 30314 B-2
(404) 681-3080

F/T: 660M, 1353W
P/T: 4M, 14W
Grad: none
Year: sems
Appl: open
1177 applied
SAT: 400V 400M
Faculty: 129; IIB, −$
Ph.D.'s: 46%
S/F Ratio: 16 to 1
Tuition: $3115
R and B: $1600
965 accepted 521 enrolled

LESS COMPETITIVE

Clark College, established in 1869, is a private liberal arts institution affiliated with the United Methodist Church. The library contains 68,000 books and subscribes to 429 periodicals.

Environment: The 20-acre urban campus is located 2 miles from downtown. The 8 major buildings include dormitories that house about 600 men and women; there are off-campus apartments as well. A health and physical education center houses the gymnasium, a swimming pool, and practice areas.

Student Life: About 60% of the students are from Georgia, and 60% live on campus. The student body is predominantly black; virtually all students are minority-group members. Ninety percent of the students are Protestant. Campus housing is both coed and single-sex; there are visiting privileges in the single-sex housing. Students may keep cars on campus.

Organizations: Student activities include publications, religious and special-interest clubs, student government, band, choir, drama, debate, a monthly newspaper, 6 fraternities, and 6 sororities. The city of Atlanta offers abundant cultural and recreational opportunities.

Sports: The college fields intercollegiate teams in 4 sports for men and 3 for women. Intramural competition is offered in 7 sports for men and 7 for women.

Handicapped: No special facilities are provided for handicapped students.

Graduates: About 20% of the freshmen drop out by the end of the first year, and 40% remain to graduate. Ten percent of the graduates go on for additional study. Thirty percent enter business and industry.

Services: Free career counseling, placement, tutoring, remedial instruction, and psychological counseling are provided. Health care is available on a fee basis.

Programs of Study: The college awards the B.A., B.S., and B.S.Med.Tech. degrees. Bachelor's degrees are offered in the following subjects: BUSINESS (accounting, business administration, business education, computer science, finance, management, marketing, office management/secretarial studies, real estate/insurance), EDUCATION (early childhood, elementary, health/physical, secondary), ENGLISH (English, journalism), FINE AND PERFORMING ARTS (art, music, radio/TV, theater/dramatics), HEALTH SCIENCES (clinical dietetics, medical illustration, medical records administration, medical technology, physical therapy), LANGUAGES (French, German, Spanish), MATH AND SCIENCES (biology, chemistry, computer science, mathematics, physics), PHILOSOPHY (philosophy, religion), PREPROFESSIONAL (engineering, home economics, social work), SOCIAL SCIENCES (economics, government/political science, history, psychology, social sciences, sociology). About 25% of the degrees are conferred in business, 20% in education, 17% in social sciences, and 17% in mass communications (journalism and radio/TV).

Required: Students must take courses in art, biology, education, English, a foreign language, history, mathematics, physics, psychology, social science, and speech and drama. Seniors must take the GRE.

Special: The college offers a general studies degree, a 5-year dual degree program in engineering (with Georgia Tech), a cooperative work-study program, exchange programs with other Southern universities, and study-abroad programs.

Honors: Five honor societies are represented on campus. There is a college-wide honors program.

Admissions: About 82% of those who applied were accepted for the 1981-82 freshman class. The SAT scores of those who enrolled were as follows: Verbal—85% below 500, 10% between 500 and 599, 4% between 600 and 700, and 1% above 700; Math—86% below 500, 9% between 500 and 599, 4% between 600 and 700, and 1% above 700. Applicants must have graduated from an accredited high school with an average of 2.0 or better in 15 Carnegie units, and should rank in the upper half of their high school class. Admissions officers also consider advanced placement or honors courses, special talents, recommendations by high school officials, leadership record, and extracurricular activities.

Procedure: The SAT or ACT is required. Application deadlines are open, and freshmen are admitted to both semesters. An interview is required. Notification is made on a rolling basis. There is a $20 application fee.

Special: An early admissions plan is available.

Transfer: Applicants must have a GPA of 2.0 or better, achieve an SAT composite score of at least 700, and be in good standing at their last school. D grades do not transfer. All students must complete, at the college, 30 of the 120 credits required for a bachelor's degree. Deadlines are open.

Visiting: Orientations for prospective students are scheduled regularly. Informal visits to campus also may be arranged for weekdays with the admissions office. Guides are provided, and students may sit in on classes.

Financial Aid: About 94% of the students receive aid. Twenty-seven percent work part-time on campus. The college provides scholarships, academic grants, grants-in-aid, loans, and CWS. Loans also are available from the federal government and the Methodist Church. Aid is awarded on the basis of financial need and academic promise. Tuition may be paid in installments. The FAF and the aid application should be filed by April 30 (fall) or October 1 (summer). The college is a member of CSS.

Foreign Students: Seven percent of the full-time students come from foreign countries. An intensive English course, special counseling, and special organizations are available for these students.

Admissions: Foreign students must achieve a TOEFL score of at least 490. No college entrance exams are required.

Procedure: Application deadlines are August 1 (fall) and December 1 (spring). Foreign students must present proof of health and proof of adequate funds. Health insurance is required and is available through the college for a fee.

Admissions Contact: Clifton B. Rawles, Director of Admissions.

COLUMBUS COLLEGE A-3
Columbus, Georgia 31993 (404) 568-2237

F/T: 1081M, 1321W		Faculty:	196; IIA, av$
P/T: 699M, 881W		Ph.D.'s:	52%
Grad: 174M, 328W		S/F Ratio:	15 to 1
Year: qtrs, ss		Tuition:	$650 ($1700)
Appl: Aug. 27		R and B:	n/app
798 applied	725 accepted		622 enrolled
SAT: 417V 430M			LESS COMPETITIVE

Columbus College, founded in 1958, is a state-supported liberal arts institution that primarily serves commuters from the local community. The library contains 163,723 books and 305,722 microfilm items, and subscribes to 1358 periodicals.

Environment: The 132-acre campus is located in a suburban area, in a town of 175,000 people. The college has 14 buildings. There are no dormitories.

Student Life: About 87% of the students are Georgia residents. Twenty percent are members of minority groups. Students may keep cars on campus. Day-care services are provided for a fee.

Organizations: Extracurricular activities include a student newspaper, student government, drama and choral groups, and religious organizations. Ten percent of the men belong to the 7 fraternities; 10% of the women to the 5 sororities.

Sports: The college fields intercollegiate teams in 6 sports for men and 4 for women. Three intramural sports are offered for both sexes.

Handicapped: The entire campus is accessible to physically handicapped students. Special class scheduling can be arranged, and special facilities include wheelchair ramps, transportation between classes, elevators, parking areas, specially equipped restrooms, and lowered drinking fountains and telephones.

Graduates: About 40% of the freshmen drop out during the first year, and 25% remain to graduate.

Services: Free psychological counseling, health care, and tutoring are available. Career counseling and placement services are provided free to students and alumni. Fees are charged for remedial instruction.

Programs of Study: The college awards the B.A., B.S., B.Mus., B.B.A., and B.S.Ed. degrees. Master's and associate degrees also are available. Bachelor's degrees are offered in the following subjects: BUSINESS (accounting, business administration, finance, management, marketing), EDUCATION (early childhood, elementary, health/physical, middle grades, recreation, secondary, special), ENGLISH (English, speech), FINE AND PERFORMING ARTS (art, art education, music, music education, theater/dramatics), HEALTH SCIENCES (medical technology, speech therapy—communicative disorders), LANGUAGES (German), MATH AND SCIENCES (biology, chemistry, earth science, mathematics), SOCIAL SCIENCES (criminal justice, economics, government/political science, history, psychology, sociology). About 31% of the undergraduate degrees are conferred in business, 15% in social sciences, and 12% in education.

Required: Students must complete a core curriculum.

Special: A general studies degree is available. A 3-2 engineering program is offered with Georgia Tech. The college sponsors study-abroad programs, internships, and cooperative education.

Honors: Two national honor societies are represented on campus.

Admissions: Ninety-one percent of those who applied were admitted to the 1981-82 freshman class. The SAT scores of those who enrolled were as follows: Verbal—82% below 500, 13% between 500 and 599, 4% between 600 and 700, and 1% above 700; Math—76% below 500, 19% between 500 and 599, 5% between 600 and 700, and 0% above 700. Applicants must have graduated from an accredited high school or obtained a GED certificate. Those who do not present a combined SAT score of at least 700 must have a GPA of 1.8 or better.

Procedure: The SAT is required. Application deadlines are August 27 (fall), December 3 (winter), February 25 (spring), and May 20 (summer). Notification is made on a rolling basis. There is a $10 application fee.

Special: A deferred admissions plan is available. AP and CLEP credit is accepted.

Transfer: For fall 1981, 347 students applied, 297 were accepted, and 230 enrolled. No minimum GPA is required. Credit usually is given for grades of 2.0 or better. Students must earn at least 45 credits at the college of the 192 required for a degree. Deadlines are the same as those for freshmen.

Visiting: Prospective students may schedule informal visits for mornings while classes are in session by contacting the admissions office. Guides are provided, and visitors may sit in on classes.

Financial Aid: A third of the students receive aid. Most awards are based on need, but some academic scholarships are available. Federal loans and grants and campus jobs are also offered. The average award to freshmen from all sources is $1013. The FAF and college aid application must be filed by July 1 (fall), December 1 (winter), February 1 (spring), or March 15 (summer).

Foreign Students: The foreign students enrolled at the college make up about 6% of the student body. Special counseling and organizations are provided for these students.

Admissions: Foreign applicants must score at least 480 on the TOEFL or 70 on the University of Michigan Language Test. They also must take the SAT, scoring a combined total of 700 or better. Verbal and math scores must be at least 330.

Procedure: Deadlines are the same as those for other freshman applicants. Students must provide proof of adequate funds for 1 year and must arrange for health insurance.

Admissions Contact: Sharon Jamison, Admissions Counselor.

DE VRY INSTITUTE OF TECHNOLOGY B-2
Atlanta, Georgia 30341 (404) 452-0045
(Recognized Candidate for Accreditation)

F/T: 1737M, 229W	Faculty:	35; n/av
P/T: 103M, 11W	Ph.D.'s:	n/av
Grad: none	S/F Ratio:	17 to 1
Year: tri, ss	Tuition:	$3025
Appl: October	R and B:	n/app
SAT or ACT: required		LESS COMPETITIVE

De Vry Institute of Technology, an independent institution founded in 1969, is administered by the Bell & Howell Education Group. It offers undergraduate degrees in electronics engineering technology, computer science for business, and electronics technology.

Environment: The school is located in the city of Atlanta. It has no housing facilities.

Student Life: About 41% of the students come from Georgia. Forty percent are members of minority groups. The institute's housing office helps students find off-campus housing. Students are permitted to keep cars on campus.

156 GEORGIA

Organizations: The 7 extracurricular activities sponsored by the school include a student newspaper, a scuba club, an audio-visual club, a photography club, and professional organizations. There are no fraternities or sororities.

Sports: The institute does not participate in intercollegiate sports but offers 3 intramural sports for men and women.

Handicapped: All programs are accessible to the handicapped. Facilities include wheelchair ramps, elevators, special parking, specially equipped rest rooms, and lowered drinking fountains and telephones. Special class scheduling can be arranged, as can additional tutoring or materials.

Graduates: Over 90% begin careers in business and industry.

Services: Placement aid, career counseling, and tutoring are provided free to students. Fees are charged for health care services and remedial instruction.

Programs of Study: The institute awards the B.S.E.E. and B.S.Comp.Sci. degrees. Associate degrees in electronics technology also are available. Bachelor's degrees are offered in: BUSINESS (computer science), PREPROFESSIONAL (electronics engineering technology).

Required: Students must follow a specified curriculum and maintain a GPA of 2.0 or better to graduate.

Honors: Tau Alpha Phi has a chapter on campus, and an honors program is offered in electronics engineering technology.

Admissions: Eighteen percent of the 1981–82 freshmen ranked in the upper fifth of their high school class, and 41% ranked in the top two-fifths. Applicants must be high school graduates or have earned a GED. In addition to grades and test scores, admissions officers consider impressions made during the required personal interview and recommendations from high school officials.

Procedure: Applicants must take both the SAT or ACT and the Bell & Howell Education Group Entrance Exam. Applications should be submitted by October for fall admission, March for spring admission, or July for summer admission. The application fee is $25. Admissions decisions are made on a rolling basis.

Special: A deferred admissions plan is available.

Transfer: Transfer students are accepted for all programs. Applicants must undergo a personal interview. Grades of C or better transfer. Students must earn at the institute at least 36 credits of the 160 required for a bachelor's degree.

Visiting: Guides are provided for informal visits, which may be scheduled for weekdays with the director of admissions.

Financial Aid: Eighty-five percent of the students receive aid through the school, which offers scholarships averaging $3845 and loans averaging $2000. The FAF is required.

Foreign Students: The foreign students enrolled full-time make up less than 1% of the student body.

Admissions: Foreign applicants must score at least 450 on the TOEFL or 106 on the ELS. They also must take both the SAT and the Bell & Howell Education Group Entrance Exam.

Procedure: Application deadlines are the same as those for other freshmen. Students must provide a physician's certificate as proof of good health and also must show evidence of adequate funds for 1 year. Foreign students are required to carry health insurance, which is available through the institute for a fee.

Admissions Contact: Marjory Coffing, Director of Admissions.

EMORY UNIVERSITY
Atlanta, Georgia 30322   B–2
(404) 329-6036

F/T: 1562M, 1487W
P/T: 23M, 12W
Grad: 2300M, 1700W
Year: sems, ss
Appl: Feb. 15
3912 applied   2344 accepted   882 enrolled
SAT: 550V 600M   ACT: 26   VERY COMPETITIVE+

Faculty: 935; I, +$
Ph.D.'s: 98%
S/F Ratio: 12 to 1
Tuition: $5400
R and B: $2372

Emory University, founded in 1836, is a privately controlled university affiliated with the Methodist Church. In addition to Emory College (arts and sciences), the schools of Allied Health Professions, Dentistry, Medicine, Law, Theology, Nursing, and Business Administration are located on the Atlanta campus. A 2-year branch campus is located 40 miles away at Oxford. The main library contains 1.5 million volumes and 774,000 microfilm items, and subscribes to 14,000 periodicals. It is one of 9 libraries on campus.

Environment: There are 67 major buildings on the 550-acre campus, which is located in a suburban area. The 15 dormitories accommodate 2130 students. Fraternity housing, sorority housing (officers only), and married student housing are also available.

Student Life: About 20% of the students are from Georgia; 30% are from other southern states. About 67% live on campus. About 32% of the students are Protestant, 24% are Jewish, and 12% are Catholic. Seven percent are minority-group members. Campus housing is coed and single-sex; freshman residence halls are single-sex only. There are visiting privileges in single-sex housing. Students may keep cars on campus.

Organizations: There are 106 extracurricular organizations and activities available on campus, as well as a variety of social and cultural opportunities in the city of Atlanta. Fourteen fraternities and 10 sororities have chapters on campus, to which 50% of the men and 45% of the women belong.

Sports: The university fields 9 intercollegiate teams for men and 6 for women. There are 13 intramural sports for men and 10 for women.

Handicapped: The following facilities are available to the handicapped student: wheelchair ramps, specially equipped rest rooms, designated handicapped parking, elevators, and lowered drinking fountains and telephones. If a building in which a particular program is given is inaccessible, special arrangements will be made. Examples of special facilities for visually and hearing-impaired students are raised numbers in the elevators and a visible fire alarm. Two special counselors and an assistant dean provide counseling and assistance.

Graduates: About 12% of the freshmen do not return for their second year; 80% remain to graduate. Seventy-five percent of those who graduate pursue further study; 22% enter medical school, 16% law school, and 5% dental school. Fourteen percent pursue careers in business or industry.

Services: The following services are offered at no charge to the student: psychological counseling, health care, placement, and career counseling.

Programs of Study: The university confers the undergraduate degrees of B.A., B.S., B.S.N., and B.B.A. Master's and doctoral programs are also offered. Bachelor's degrees are offered in the following subjects: AREA STUDIES (Black/Afro-American, French, Hispanic-Latin American, international, Judaic), BUSINESS (accounting, business economics, computer science/mathematics, finance, management, marketing), EDUCATION (elementary, educational studies, secondary), ENGLISH (English, literature), FINE AND PERFORMING ARTS (art history, music, theater/dramatics), HEALTH SCIENCES (nursing), LANGUAGES (French, German, Greek/Latin, Russian, Spanish), MATH AND SCIENCES (biology, chemistry, geology, mathematics, mathematics/computer science, physics), PHILOSOPHY (classical civilization, humanities, philosophy, religion), PREPROFESSIONAL (dentistry, law, library science, medicine, ministry, social work, veterinary), SOCIAL SCIENCES (anthropology, economics, government/political science, history, psychology, sociology). Of the degrees conferred, 46% were in social sciences, 35% in math and sciences, and 15% in business.

Required: All students must take 2 years of physical education.

Special: Four-year B.A.-M.A. programs are offered in 6 major fields of study; B.S.-M.S. programs are offered in 3 major fields. There are several summer study-abroad programs, as well as exchange programs with 4 local colleges and universities. Students may design their own majors.

Honors: There are 6 national honor societies, including Phi Beta Kappa, with chapters on campus. Honors programs are available in all departments.

Admissions: Sixty percent of those who applied were accepted for the 1981–82 freshman class. The SAT scores of those who enrolled were as follows: Verbal—24% below 500, 54% between 500 and 599, 17% between 600 and 700, and 3% above 700; Math—8% below 500, 47% between 500 and 599, 37% between 600 and 700, and 8% above 700. Candidates should have graduated from an accredited high school, be highly recommended by their school, and have completed 16 Carnegie units. Other important considerations are recommendations by school officials, advanced placement or honors courses, and impressions made during an interview.

Procedure: The SAT or ACT is required and should be taken by the beginning of the senior year. The application deadlines are February 15 (fall), December 10 (winter), and May 10 (summer). Applications should be submitted with a $25 fee. There is a modified rolling admissions plan.

Special: There are an early decision plan (notification by December 1), an early admissions plan, and a deferred admissions plan. AP and CLEP credit is granted.

Transfer: For fall 1981, 288 transfer students applied, 164 were accepted, and 91 enrolled. High school as well as college grades and SAT scores are considered. A 2.0 GPA is required; a 3.0 GPA is recommended. Grades of C and above transfer. Four semesters of credit of the 130 credits required for a bachelor's degree must be completed at the university. The application deadlines are July 1 (fall), December 1 (winter), and May 1 (summer).

Visiting: A regularly scheduled orientation weekend is conducted each spring for admitted students; students stay on campus, visit classes, and meet with professors. Guides are available for informal visits to the campus. Interviews are available daily by appointment. Visitors may sit in on classes. Overnight stays can be arranged, as space permits, through the admissions office, given at least 1 week's notice.

Financial Aid: For fall 1981, about 49% of freshmen received aid. Scholarships, loans, and work-study jobs are awarded to students on the basis of financial need. Numerous merit scholarships are available also. Loans are available from federal and state governments, local banks, the university, and private sources. The deadline for filing financial aid applications is April 1. The university is a member of CSS; the FAF is required. Tuition may be paid on the installment plan.

Foreign Students: About 3% of the full-time students come from foreign countries. The university offers these students special counseling and special organizations.

Admissions: It is recommended that foreign students achieve a minimum TOEFL score of 550; it is also recommended that they take the SAT, in addition to the required TOEFL.

Procedure: Application deadlines are February 15 (fall) and December 1 (winter). Foreign students must submit a medical form as well as proof of funds adequate to cover 1 year of study.

Admissions Contact: Judith V. Sullivan, Admissions Counselor.

FORT VALLEY STATE COLLEGE B-3
Fort Valley, Georgia 31030 (912) 825-6307

F/T: 713M, 825W Faculty: 141; IIA, av$
P/T: 116M, 49W Ph.D.'s: 40%
Grad: 130M&W S/F Ratio: 9 to 1
Year: qtrs, ss Tuition: $756 ($1806)
Appl: see profile R and B: $1500
SAT: 270V 300M *LESS COMPETITIVE*

Fort Valley State College, established in 1895, is a state-controlled college offering undergraduate and graduate programs in liberal arts and teacher education. The library contains over 137,000 volumes and subscribes to 1400 periodicals.

Environment: The 630-acre campus is located in a community of 11,000 people 100 miles south of Atlanta. The 45 buildings include a gymnasium, a student center, and an infirmary. Residence halls house 368 men and 768 women. Much of the campus is covered by experimental agricultural plots.

Student Life: About 84% of the students are from Georgia. About 65% live on campus in single-sex dorms. Out-of-town students must receive permission to live off campus. The student body is predominantly black.

Organizations: Extracurricular activities include student government, a student newspaper, religious and departmental clubs, drama, choral groups, dance, yearbook, and music ensembles. Four fraternities and 4 sororities have chapters on campus.

Sports: The college competes on an intercollegiate level in 5 sports for men and 2 for women. Intramural sports also are available.

Handicapped: Structural modifications are being made to make the campus accessible to handicapped students.

Graduates: About 64% of the freshmen drop out, and 20% remain to graduate. A third of the graduates go on for further study.

Services: The college offers career, placement, and psychological counseling as well as health care.

Programs of Study: The college awards the B.S., B.A., B.S.Ed., B.S.Bus.Ed., B.S.Mus.Ed., B.S.E.E., B.S.Agr., B.S.H.E., and B.B.A. degrees. Associate and master's degrees also are available. Bachelor's degrees are offered in the following subjects: BUSINESS (accounting, accounting and data processing, business administration, business education, management, marketing, office administration), EDUCATION (agricultural, early childhood, elementary, health/physical, secondary), ENGLISH (English), FINE AND PERFORMING ARTS (music education), LANGUAGES (French), MATH AND SCIENCES (chemistry, mathematics, zoology), PREPROFESSIONAL (agriculture—animal science, agriculture—plant science, engineering—electronics, food and nutrition, home economics, infant and child development), SOCIAL SCIENCES (criminal justice, economics, government/political science, psychology, social welfare, sociology).

Required: Students must take 20 hours of humanities, 20 of mathematics and natural sciences, and 20 of social science. To graduate, students must earn a cumulative GPA of 2.0 or better, receive no grade below C in any courses in their major, and pass a comprehensive exam.

Special: A cooperative work-study program and study-abroad programs are offered.

Honors: Six honor societies are represented on campus.

Admissions: Two-thirds of those who applied for admission to a recent freshman class were accepted. Applicants must have graduated from an accredited high school and have completed at least 16 units of high school work. The college accepts students over age 21 who hold a high school equivalency certificate.

Procedure: The SAT is required. The application, test scores, and high school record should be submitted at least 20 days before registration for the term in which the student wishes to enroll. Notification is made within 2 weeks. There is no application fee.

Special: An early admissions plan is available.

Transfer: Transfer applicants must meet freshman requirements. D grades do not transfer from colleges outside the University of Georgia system. Students must earn at least 45 quarter credits in residence of the 180 or more required for a bachelor's degree.

Financial Aid: About 90% of the students receive aid. Programs include part-time jobs; federal, state, and private loans; and ROTC, college, and state scholarships. Students should contact the college's financial aid office for information on applying. The college is a member of the CSS.

Admissions Contact: Delia W. Taylor, Director of Admissions.

GEORGIA COLLEGE C-3
Milledgeville, Georgia 31061 (912) 453-4558

F/T: 821M, 1306W Faculty: n/av; IIA, av$
P/T: 345M, 323W Ph.D.'s: n/av
Grad: 326M, 301W S/F Ratio: n/av
Year: qtrs, ss Tuition: $687 ($1737)
Appl: Sept. 1 R and B: $1380
SAT: required *LESS COMPETITIVE*

Georgia College, established in 1889, is a publicly controlled liberal arts institution. The library contains 140,409 volumes, subscribes to 1350 periodicals, and has 238,734 microforms.

Environment: The 43-acre urban campus is located 30 miles from Macon and 98 miles from Atlanta. A physical education and recreational area occupies an additional 700 acres. There are more than 35 buildings on campus, including 2-story residence halls that accommodate 300 men and 800 women.

Student Life: Only 5% of the students come from out of state. About 85% of the students attended public schools. Thirty percent reside on campus. Eighteen percent are minority-group members. Campus housing is single-sex; there are visiting privileges. Students may keep cars on campus.

Organizations: Twenty percent of the men and 25% of the women belong to one of 5 fraternities or 5 sororities. Other student organizations include religious and music groups, special-interest clubs, and a newspaper. Facilities for tennis and other sports may be found at a nearby park.

Sports: The college fields 4 intercollegiate teams for men and 3 for women. There are 8 intramural sports for men and 8 for women.

Handicapped: The college estimates the campus to be 50% accessible to the handicapped student. Wheelchair ramps are available, and special class scheduling can be arranged. There are no visually impaired or hearing-impaired students currently enrolled.

Graduates: Twenty-eight percent of freshmen drop out by the end of the first year; 40% remain to graduate. Twenty percent of the graduates pursue further study.

Services: Placement and career counseling are offered at no charge to the student.

Programs of Study: The college confers the B.A., B.B.A., B.M., B.Mus.Ed., B.S., B.S.H.E., B.S.N., and B.S.Ed. Associate and master's programs are also offered. Bachelor's degrees are offered in the following subjects: BUSINESS (accounting, business administration, business education, computer science, finance, management, marketing),

158 GEORGIA

EDUCATION (early childhood, health/physical, secondary, special), ENGLISH (English), FINE AND PERFORMING ARTS (art education, music, music education), HEALTH SCIENCES (nursing), LANGUAGES (French, Spanish), MATH AND SCIENCES (biology, chemistry, mathematics), PREPROFESSIONAL (dentistry, engineering, home economics, medicine, ministry, pharmacy, veterinary), SOCIAL SCIENCES (economics, government/political science, history, psychology, sociology). Of the degrees conferred, 34% are in business, 17% in education, and 17% in social sciences.

Required: All students must take courses in English composition, English literature, mathematics and science, social studies, western civilization, fine arts, and physical education. All B.A. candidates and some B.S. candidates are also required to take a language.

Special: Students may participate in summer study-abroad programs of the University System of Georgia. There is a combination degree program with the Georgia Institute of Technology.

Honors: Two national honor societies have chapters on campus.

Admissions: Ninety-two percent of those who applied were accepted for a recent freshman class. Of those who enrolled, the SAT scores were as follows: Verbal—5% between 500 and 600; Math—5% between 500 and 600. Applicants must be graduates of accredited high schools (or have a GED diploma), have a combined SAT score of at least 750, and have completed 16 Carnegie units with a minimum average of C. The academic record and the school's recommendations are also considered in the admissions decision.

Procedure: The SAT should be taken by January of the senior year. The application deadlines are September 1 (fall), December 15 (winter), March 1 (spring), and June 1 (summer). There is a $10 application fee. Acceptance and notification are on a rolling basis. The college subscribes to the CRDA.

Special: An early admissions plan is offered. AP and CLEP credit is granted.

Transfer: Of the 430 applications received for a recent year, 385 were accepted, and 296 students enrolled. An average of at least 1.8 is required; D grades may be credited. Transfers are not accepted for the senior class. Students must spend 4 quarters in residence, completing at least 60 of the 186 quarter hours required for the bachelor's degree.

Visiting: Regularly scheduled orientations for prospective students are conducted by the college. Guides are available for informal visits. Visitors may sit in on classes or stay overnight on campus. To arrange a visit, the secretary at the office of admissions should be contacted.

Financial Aid: About 40% of all students receive aid. The college provides scholarships, loans, and campus employment as financial aids. State government scholarships and various loan funds (from federal, college, and private sources) are available. Aid is awarded on the basis of need and academic record. The aid application deadline is March 1. The FAF is required.

Foreign Students: One percent of the full-time students are from outside the United States. There are special organizations for these students.

Admissions: Foreign students must achieve a TOEFL score of at least 535. No college entrance exams are required.

Procedure: Application deadlines are September 1 (fall), December 15 (winter), March 1 (spring), and June 1 (summer). Foreign students must present proof of funds adequate to cover 1 year of study, and they must carry health insurance. Out-of-state resident fees apply.

Admissions Contact: R. Linton Cox, Jr., Director of Admissions.

GEORGIA INSTITUTE OF TECHNOLOGY
Atlanta, Georgia 30332   B-2
(404) 894-4154

F/T: 6890M, 1791W   Faculty: 516; I, + +$
P/T: 389M, 92W   Ph.D.'s: 84%
Grad: 1659M, 338W   S/F Ratio: 17 to 1
Year: qtrs, ss   Tuition: $975 ($2790)
Appl: see profile   R and B: $2400
6584 applied   3882 accepted   1724 enrolled
SAT: 530V 628M   HIGHLY COMPETITIVE

Founded in 1888, Georgia Institute of Technology is a land-grant college and technological institution offering programs in architecture, management, engineering, and science. The library contains 1 million volumes, 12,000 serials, 1,365,000 microtexts, and 235,000 other bibliographic units.

Environment: Located next to downtown Atlanta, the 300-acre urban campus has 135 buildings, including 22 dormitories with a capacity of 700 women and 3000 men. There are also 220 apartments for married students. Fraternity and sorority houses also accommodate students. There are many notable buildings, such as the $1.1 million architecture building.

Student Life: Only 55% of the students come from Georgia. About 83% are from public schools. Forty-five percent live on campus. Fifty-two percent are Protestant, 23% Catholic, and 3% Jewish. Nine percent are minority-group members. Campus housing is single-sex, and there are visiting privileges. Students may keep cars on campus.

Organizations: In addition to the 28 fraternities and 4 sororities to which 35% of the men and 25% of the women belong, there are also numerous clubs and activities, publications, music and drama groups, and social and cultural opportunities on campus and in Atlanta.

Sports: The institute fields 17 intercollegiate teams for men and 10 for women. There are 5 intramural sports for men and 5 for women.

Handicapped: Special facilities for the wheelchair-bound student are ramps, elevators, lowered telephones, and designated parking. Less than 1% of the students are visually or hearing-impaired. A special counselor is provided. Instructors work out suitable alternate lab requirements for these students.

Graduates: The freshman dropout rate is 16%; 66% of the entering freshmen remain to graduate, and 25% go on to graduate or professional studies (4% to medical school, 1% to dental school, and 2% to law school). Seventy-five percent pursue careers in business or industry.

Services: The following services are offered at no charge to students: psychological counseling, health care, tutoring, remedial instruction, placement, and career counseling.

Programs of Study: The institute confers the B.S. and many specialized bachelor's degrees in technical and engineering fields. There are also master's and doctoral programs. Bachelor's degrees are offered in the following subjects: BUSINESS (computer science, management), MATH AND SCIENCES (biology, chemistry, mathematics, physics), PREPROFESSIONAL (architecture, dentistry, engineering—aerospace, engineering—ceramic, engineering—chemical, engineering—civil, engineering—electrical, engineering—engineering science, engineering—health physics, engineering—health systems, engineering—industrial, engineering—mechanical, engineering—mechanics, engineering—nuclear, engineering—textile, law, medicine, veterinary), SOCIAL SCIENCES (economics, psychology).

Required: All freshmen must take English, calculus, chemistry, social science, graphics, and physical training.

Special: A cooperative work-study plan is offered in engineering, chemistry, computer science, physics, and management. In addition, there is a 3-2 cooperative engineering program with about 100 liberal arts colleges and universities in the eastern United States. Student-designed majors are permitted.

Honors: Six national honor societies have chapters on campus. Honors programs are offered in chemistry and mathematics to qualified students.

Admissions: Fifty-nine percent of those who applied were accepted for the 1981–82 freshman class. Of those who enrolled, the SAT scores were as follows: Verbal—34% below 500, 44% between 500 and 599, 19% between 600 and 700, and 3% above 700; Math—8% below 500, 24% between 500 and 599, 50% between 600 and 700, and 18% above 700. The institute has no set minimum for rank in class, high school average, or SAT scores. However, the average candidate ranks in the top 10% and has a 3.5 average. The admissions committee also considers advanced placement or honors courses, extracurricular activities, leadership record, and recommendations by school officials. Some preference is given to children of alumni.

Procedure: The SAT is required and should be taken by November of the senior year. The deadline for application to the fall quarter is January 1 (nonresidents) or April 1 (residents). Freshmen are also admitted to the winter, spring, and summer terms (deadlines, respectively, are December 1, March 1, and January 1). Admission and notification are on a rolling basis. There is a $15 application fee.

Special: There are early decision, early admissions, and deferred admissions plans. The deadline for filing for early admission is the same as for conventional application. AP credit is granted.

Transfer: For fall 1981, 1199 applications were received, 523 were accepted, and 368 students actually enrolled. Transfers are not accepted for the senior class; D grades are not acceptable. A minimum average of 2.5 for residents, 2.7 for nonresidents, and SAT scores are required for transfer. Students must complete, at the institute, at least 50 of the approximately 200 credits necessary to receive a bachelor's degree. Application deadlines are the same as those for freshmen.

Visiting: There are no regularly scheduled orientations for prospective students. Guides are available for informal visits to the campus on weekdays during the school year. Visitors may sit in on classes. For further information, the admissions office should be contacted.

Financial Aid: About 20% of all students receive aid. The institute is a member of CSS and awards 250 freshman scholarships annually. Ten percent of students work part-time on campus. Loans from the federal government and from local banks are also available. Most aid offers are in the form of a "package." There is CWS in all departments. The FAF and the institute's own aid application are required. The deadline for aid application is February 15; notification is sent by May 1. Tuition may be paid on the installment plan.

Foreign Students: Eight percent of the full-time students come from foreign countries. The institute offers an intensive English program, special counseling, and special organizations.

Admissions: Foreign students must achieve a TOEFL score of at least 550 and must take the SAT.

Procedure: The application deadline for foreign students is January 1 for both the fall and summer terms. Foreign students must present proof of health (chest X-ray, PPD skin test for tuberculin). They must also present proof of funds adequate to cover the period of study anticipated. They must carry health insurance, which is available through the college for a fee.

Admissions Contact: Jerry L. Hitt, Director of Admissions.

GEORGIA SOUTHERN COLLEGE   D-3
Statesboro, Georgia 30460   (912) 681-5531

F/T: 2498M, 2780W	Faculty: 375; IIA, av$
P/T: 246M, 205W	Ph.D.'s: 59%
Grad: 264M, 610W	S/F Ratio: 18 to 1
Year: qtrs, ss	Tuition: $738 ($1788)
Appl: Sept. 2	R and B: $1530
3345 applied	2528 accepted 1380 enrolled
SAT: 424V 459M	COMPETITIVE

Georgia Southern College, founded in 1906, is a publicly controlled college under the direction of the University System of Georgia. The library contains 240,000 volumes and 260,000 microfilm items, and subscribes to 2300 periodicals.

Environment: Located in a rural environment 60 miles from Savannah, the 457-acre campus includes 35 major buildings, among them a full-service infirmary and 18 dormitories that accommodate 3500 students. The college also sponsors on-campus apartments.

Student Life: About 92% of the students are from Georgia. In a recent freshman class, 88% had attended public schools. Fifty-three percent of the students reside on campus. About 80% of the students are Protestant and 11% are Catholic. Almost 10% of the students are minority-group members. Campus housing is single-sex; there are visiting privileges. Students may keep cars on campus.

Organizations: Twenty-six percent of the men and 20% of the women belong to one of 14 fraternities and 9 sororities. Other student activities include religious groups, weekly publications, special-interest clubs, drama and music organizations, and lecture and concert series.

Sports: The college fields 8 intercollegiate teams for men and 4 for women. There are 13 intramural sports for men and 11 for women.

Handicapped: The campus is 85% accessible to the handicapped student. Special facilities include wheelchair ramps, specially equipped rest rooms, elevators, and designated handicapped parking. Special class scheduling can be arranged. Readers, tape recorders, and counseling and guidance facilities are provided for the visually impaired or hearing-impaired student.

Graduates: The freshman dropout rate is 38%; about 36% remain to graduate, and 29% of those go on for further study. Forty-three percent of the graduates begin careers in business and industry.

Services: The following services are offered at no charge to the student: psychological counseling, tutoring, placement, and career counseling. Placement services to both students and alumni include job recruitment and placement folders. Health care and remedial instruction are available on a fee basis.

Programs of Study: The college confers the A.B., B.S., B.S. in Bio., B.S. in Chem., B.S. in C.J., B.S. in Home Ec., B.S. in Math, B.S. in M.T., B.B.A., and B.S.Ed. degrees. Master's and associate programs are also offered. Bachelor's degrees are offered in the following subjects: BUSINESS (accounting, business administration, business education, computer science, economics, finance, management, marketing, office administration, real estate/insurance), EDUCATION (adult, early childhood, elementary, health/physical, industrial, secondary, special), ENGLISH (English, journalism, speech), FINE AND PERFORMING ARTS (art, art education, music, music education), HEALTH SCIENCES (medical technology, nursing), LANGUAGES (French, German), MATH AND SCIENCES (biology, chemistry, earth science, geology, mathematics, physics), PREPROFESSIONAL (agriculture, dentistry, engineering, forestry, home economics, law, library science, medicine, pharmacy, social work, veterinary), SOCIAL SCIENCES (economics, government/political science, history, psychology, social sciences, sociology). Of the degrees conferred, 25% were in education, 24% in business, and 6% in social sciences.

Required: All students are required to take courses in mathematics, natural sciences, and social sciences.

Special: It is possible to earn a 5-year combined B.A.-B.S. degree. Students may study abroad for a quarter in France, Germany, or Mexico.

Honors: There are 2 national honor societies with chapters on campus.

Admissions: Seventy-six percent of those who applied were accepted for the 1981-82 freshman class. The SAT scores of those who enrolled were as follows: Verbal—86% below 500, 12% between 500 and 599, 1% between 600 and 700, and fewer than 1% above 700; Math—77% below 500, 19% between 500 and 599, 4% between 600 and 700, and fewer than 1% above 700. Applicants must have a high school average of C or better and must have completed 16 academic units. The SAT scores are also a determining factor. For non-high school graduates, a GED diploma is acceptable. Advanced placement or honors courses and recommendations by school officials are also considered.

Procedure: It is recommended that the SAT be taken by December of the senior year. Applications must be submitted by September 2 (fall), December 13 (winter), March 6 (spring), and May 25 (summer). Notification is on a rolling basis. There is no application fee.

Special: There is an early admissions plan. AP and CLEP credit is given.

Transfer: For fall 1981, 1145 transfer students applied, 785 were accepted, and 547 enrolled. Applicants must have at least a C average and minimum SAT scores of 350 on both the verbal and math sections. Grades of C or above transfer. At least 45 of the 190 quarter hours required for a bachelor's degree must be taken in residence. Application deadlines are the same as those for freshmen.

Visiting: Regularly scheduled orientations for prospective students include campus tours and interviews with admissions representatives and faculty advisers. Visitors may sit in on classes and stay overnight at the school. To arrange a visit, Diane Dickey, assistant director of admissions, should be contacted. The college recommends 8 A.M. to 5 P.M. weekdays during the school year as the best time to visit.

Financial Aid: About 45% of all students receive aid; 18% work part-time on campus. The college provides scholarships, loans, and part-time jobs as sources of financial aid. The average award to freshmen from all sources is $950. The college is a member of CSS. Award of aid is based on need and academic record. The college application, SAT scores, transcript, and FAF should be filed by March 1 for financial aid.

Foreign Students: About 1% of the full-time students come from foreign countries. The college offers these students an intensive English course, special counseling, and special organizations.

Admissions: Foreign students must achieve a minimum TOEFL score of 500 or an equally acceptable score on the University of Michigan Language Test. No college entrance exams are required.

Procedure: Application deadlines are March 22 (fall), July 5 (winter), September 28 (spring), and December 16 (summer). Foreign students must present proof of health as well as proof of funds adequate to cover 1 year of study. They must also carry health insurance, which is available through the college for a fee.

Admissions Contact: Don Coleman, Registrar and Director of Admissions.

GEORGIA SOUTHWESTERN COLLEGE   B-4
Americus, Georgia 31709   (912) 928-1273

F/T: 620M, 1006W	Faculty: 111; IIA, av$
P/T: 94M, 188W	Ph.D.'s: n/av
Grad: 57M, 256W	S/F Ratio: 14 to 1
Year: qtrs, ss	Tuition: $693 ($1743)
Appl: Sept. 1	R and B: $1600
691 applied	648 accepted 452 enrolled
SAT: 417V 437M	LESS COMPETITIVE

GEORGIA

Georgia Southwestern College, founded in 1906, is a state-supported liberal arts and teacher education college. The library contains 124,708 volumes and 211,662 microfilm items, and subscribes to 973 periodicals.

Environment: Located in a rural area 35 miles from Albany, Georgia, the 187-acre campus has 27 buildings, including 9 dormitories with a capacity for 600 women and 558 men. The college also sponsors fraternity houses.

Student Life: About 98% of the students are from Georgia. Forty-three percent reside in dormitories and 3% in fraternity houses. About 22% of the students are minority-group members. Campus housing is single-sex; there are visiting privileges. Students may keep cars on campus.

Organizations: Five percent of the students belong to 1 of 5 fraternities or 4 sororities. Other student activities include a weekly newspaper, religious organizations, a theater group, choir, concert band, and a popular and cultural concert series.

Sports: The college fields 4 intercollegiate teams. There are 9 intramural sports.

Handicapped: The college estimates the campus to be 95% accessible to the handicapped student. Special facilities include wheelchair ramps, specially equipped rest rooms, designated handicapped parking, lowered drinking fountains, and elevators. Special class scheduling can be arranged.

Graduates: The freshman dropout rate is 35%; 30% remain to graduate. Twenty-five percent of those who graduate pursue further study: 1% enter medical school, 1% law school, and 1% dental school. Forty percent pursue careers in business and industry.

Services: Placement, career counseling, and psychological counseling are offered at no charge to the student. Health care, tutoring, and remedial instruction are available for a fee.

Programs of Study: The college confers the B.A., B.S., B.S.Ed., and B.B.A. degrees. Associate and master's degree programs are also offered. Bachelor's degrees are offered in the following subjects: BUSINESS (accounting, agribusiness, business administration, business education, computer science, finance, management, marketing), EDUCATION (early childhood, early grades, health/physical, middle grades, secondary), ENGLISH (English, speech), FINE AND PERFORMING ARTS (art, art education, music education), HEALTH SCIENCES (nursing), LANGUAGES (French, Spanish), MATH AND SCIENCES (biology, chemistry, earth science, geology, mathematics, natural sciences, physical sciences, physics), PREPROFESSIONAL (dentistry, engineering, law, medicine, pharmacy, veterinary), SOCIAL SCIENCES (government/political science, history, psychology, social sciences, sociology). Of the degrees conferred, 40% were in arts and sciences, 28% in education, and 22% in business.

Required: All students are required to take courses in biology, English, humanities, mathematics, physical education, physical sciences, and social sciences.

Special: Study abroad programs in Spanish and French are offered. Cooperative education and internship programs are available.

Honors: There are 5 national honor societies with chapters on campus. Three honors programs are offered in the core curriculum.

Admissions: Ninety-four percent of those who applied were accepted for the 1981-82 freshman class. The SAT scores of those who enrolled were as follows: Verbal—81% below 500, 18% between 500 and 599, 1% between 600 and 700, and 0% above 700; Math—69% below 500, 25% between 500 and 599, 6% between 600 and 700, and 0% above 700. Applicants must be high school graduates with at least a C average and should have a minimum combined SAT score of 700.

Procedure: The SAT is required and should be taken by January of the senior year. Application deadlines are September 1 (fall), December 1 (winter), March 1 (spring), and June 1 (summer). A rolling admissions plan is in effect. Applicants are notified 2 to 3 weeks after all credentials are received. There is a $15 application deposit.

Special: AP and CLEP credit is offered.

Transfer: For fall 1981, 296 transfer students applied, 249 were accepted, and 198 enrolled. Students must be eligible to return to their last college attended. C grades or better transfer. Forty of the final 60 quarter hours must be taken in residence; at least 180 quarter hours are required for a bachelor's degree. Application deadlines are the same as those for freshmen.

Visiting: Regularly scheduled orientations are conducted by the college. Guides are available for informal visits. Visitors may sit in on classes and stay overnight at the school. To arrange a visit, the admissions office should be contacted.

Financial Aid: About 65% of all students receive aid; 40% work part-time on campus. The college provides scholarships, loans and campus employment. Loans are also available from federal and state governments and private sources. Aid is awarded on the basis of financial need and academic record. Special consideration is given to economically deprived students. The college is a member of CSS; the FAF is required. Aid application deadlines are open; the college recommends filing 60 days prior to the start of the quarter.

Foreign Students: Fewer than 1% of the full-time students come from foreign countries.

Admissions: Foreign students must achieve a minimum TOEFL score of 500; they must also take the SAT.

Procedure: Application deadlines are the same as those for freshmen. Foreign students must pass a physical examination and present proof of funds adequate to cover 1 year of study. They must also carry health insurance.

Admissions Contact: Ronald J. deValinger, Director of Admissions.

GEORGIA STATE UNIVERSITY   B-2
Atlanta, Georgia 30303   (404) 658-4044

F/T: 6233M&W	Faculty: 831; I, +$
P/T: 8043M&W	Ph.D.'s: 74%
Grad: 6733M&W	S/F Ratio: 10 to 1
Year: qtrs, ss	Tuition: $803 ($2569)
Appl: Aug. 14	R and B: n/app
2485 applied	1668 accepted 1223 enrolled
SAT: 465V 497M	COMPETITIVE+

Georgia State University, founded in 1913, is a state-controlled institution that offers undergraduate and graduate degrees through the colleges of Arts and Sciences, Business Administration, Education, General Studies, Health Sciences, and Public and Urban Affairs. The library contains 678,000 books and 738,000 microfilm items, and subscribes to 5000 periodicals.

Environment: The 20-acre main campus in the heart of Atlanta contains classroom buildings, an urban life complex, and a student center. There are no residence halls. The university also owns 200 acres in a nearby suburban area for research, athletic, and recreational facilities.

Student Life: About 93% of the students come from Georgia. About 20% are members of minority groups. Day-care services are available on a fee basis to all students, faculty, and staff.

Organizations: There are over 100 student organizations including professional, service, honor, and social groups. There are 8 social sororities and 12 social fraternities. Social events include Homecoming, Mardi Gras, Spring Festival, and Greek Week. Abundant cultural and recreational activities are available in the metropolitan area.

Sports: The university fields 7 intercollegiate sports for men and 6 for women. There are 15 intramural sports for men and 13 for women.

Handicapped: Virtually the entire campus is accessible to wheelchair-bound students. Facilities include wheelchair ramps, special parking, elevators, specially equipped rest rooms, and lowered drinking fountains and telephones. Provisions have also been made for students who have impaired vision or hearing; readers, library assistance, hearing-booster phones, braille tabs, and visual fire alarms are provided. Special counselors are available.

Services: Psychological, career, and placement counseling; tutoring; remedial instruction; and health care are offered free to students. Placement services also are available to graduates.

Programs of Study: The university confers the B.A., B.I.S., B.M., B.S., B.V.A., B.B.A., B.S.Ed., and B.S.W. degrees. Master's and doctoral degree programs also are available. Bachelor's degrees are offered in the following subjects: BUSINESS (accounting, actuarial science, business administration, computer science, economics, finance, information systems, management, marketing, real estate/insurance, urban affairs), EDUCATION (adult, business, early childhood, elementary, health/physical, industrial, secondary, special), ENGLISH (English, journalism, literature, speech), FINE AND PERFORMING ARTS (art, art education, art history, film/photography, music, music education, radio/TV, studio art, theater/dramatics), HEALTH SCIENCES (community health nutrition, medical technology, mental health, nursing, physical therapy, respiratory therapy, speech therapy), LANGUAGES (French, German, Greek/Latin, Hebrew, Italian, Japanese, Russian, Spanish), MATH AND SCIENCES (astronomy, biochemistry, biology, botany, chemistry, earth science, geology, mathematics, physical sciences, physics, zoology), PHILOSOPHY (philosophy), PREPROFESSIONAL (dentistry, medicine, social work, veterinary), SOCIAL SCIENCES (anthropology, economics, geography, government/political science, history, international relations, psychology, social sciences, sociology). About 42% of the undergraduate degrees are conferred in business, 11% in health sciences, 9% in education, 27% in arts and sciences, and 11% in public and urban affairs.

Required: All students must take courses in English, literature, math, social science, and laboratory science.

Special: The Division of Developmental Studies offers remedial programs. The university sponsors junior-year-abroad and summer-study-in-Europe programs. It is developing a program to allow students to design their own majors.

Honors: Fifteen honor societies are represented on campus. Honors programs are offered by the College of Arts and Sciences and the departments of art, anthropology, biology, chemistry, English, foreign languages, history, journalism, math, philosophy, political science, and speech and drama.

Admissions: About 67% of those who applied were accepted for the 1981–82 freshman class. The SAT scores of those who enrolled were as follows: Verbal—65% below 500, 28% between 500 and 599, 6% between 600 and 700, and 1% above 700; Math—49% below 500, 40% between 500 and 599, 10% between 600 and 700, and 1% above 700. Applicants must have completed at least 14 Carnegie units with an average of 2.0 or better. Generally, only those ranking in the upper half of their class are admitted. Besides high school record and SAT scores, admissions officers consider advanced placement or honors courses, recommendations by high school officials, extracurricular activities, special talents, and impressions made during an interview.

Procedure: The SAT is required. Application deadlines are August 14 (fall), December 4 (winter), February 19 (spring), and May 14 (summer). The application fee is $10. Candidates are notified about 3 weeks after applications are received.

Special: AP and CLEP credit is accepted.

Transfer: For fall 1981, 3862 transfer students applied, 2928 were accepted, and 2296 enrolled. Applicants must have a GPA of 2.0 or better and be in good standing at their last school. A limited number of D's transfer. Students must earn at least 45 hours of the 180–225 hours required for a bachelor's degree in residence to graduate. Application deadlines are the same as those for freshmen.

Visiting: Prospective students may schedule informal weekday visits by contacting the public information office. Guides are provided.

Financial Aid: About 20% of the students receive aid. Twenty percent work part-time on campus. The university participates in the NDSL, BEOG, SEOG, and CWS programs. Bonafide undergraduate residents of Georgia may apply for state grants of up to $450 per academic year. Approximately 75 scholarships, ranging from $200 to $1000 per academic year, are available from institutional sources. The Guaranteed Student Loan Program is the major source of assistance. The average award to freshmen from all sources is $865. The university is a member of CSS; the FAF must be filed. The deadline for accepting financial aid applications is April 1.

Foreign Students: About 4% of the full-time students come from foreign countries. The university offers these students an intensive English course, an intensive English program, special counseling, and special organizations.

Admissions: Foreign students must achieve a minimum TOEFL score of 525, or they must take the Georgia State University Test of English Proficiency. The SAT is required, with minimum scores of 400 Math for non-natives of English and 400V/400M for natives of English.

Procedure: Application deadlines are 60 days prior to the beginning of each quarter. Foreign students must present proof of funds adequate to cover 1 year of study. They must also carry health insurance, which is available through the university for a fee.

Admissions Contact: George W. Stansbury, Director of Admissions.

KENNESAW COLLEGE B–2
Marietta, Georgia 30061 (404) 422-8770

F/T: 963M, 1123W Faculty: n/av; III, +$
P/T: 805M, 1311W Ph.D.'s: 51%
Grad: none S/F Ratio: 30 to 1
Year: qtrs, ss Tuition: $600 ($1650)
Appl: Sept. 1 R and B: n/app
2186 applied 1873 accepted 1618 enrolled
SAT: 405V 419M LESS COMPETITIVE

Kennesaw College, established in 1966, is a state-controlled commuter institution offering undergraduate programs in the liberal arts and sciences and in education. Its library has 91,995 books and 11,776 microfilm items, and subscribes to 900 periodicals.

Environment: The 153-acre campus is located in a suburban area 9 miles from Marietta and 25 miles from Atlanta. There are 14 buildings on campus. No residence facilities are offered.

Student Life: About 90% of the students come from Georgia. Most have had public school educations. All students commute. About 4% of the students are minority-group members. Students may keep cars on campus.

Organizations: There are no fraternities or sororities. Extracurricular activities are traditional—special-interest clubs, student government, and publications. On-campus social and cultural events, such as dances and concerts, are regularly scheduled. The Atlanta area offers extensive recreational and cultural facilities.

Sports: There is no intercollegiate athletics program. There are 9 intramural sports.

Handicapped: Special facilities for the physically handicapped include wheelchair ramps, parking areas, elevators, lowered drinking fountains, and specially equipped rest rooms. Special class scheduling can be arranged. About 80% of the campus is accessible to these students. Three special counselors are provided.

Services: Remedial instruction, career counseling, psychological counseling, and placement services are offered free of charge. Limited health care service is available. Tutoring is available on a fee basis.

Programs of Study: Kennesaw confers the B.A. and B.S. degrees. Associate degree programs are also offered. Bachelor's degrees are offered in the following subjects: AREA STUDIES (American, Asian, Latin American), BUSINESS (accounting, business administration, business education, computer science, economics, secretarial science), EDUCATION (early childhood, elementary, secondary), ENGLISH (English), FINE AND PERFORMING ARTS (music), LANGUAGES (French, German, Spanish), MATH AND SCIENCES (biology, chemistry, mathematics), SOCIAL SCIENCES (government/political science, history, psychology). Forty percent of the degrees are granted in business, 30% in education, and 15% in sciences.

Required: All students must take a core curriculum and satisfy physical education requirements.

Special: Study abroad is possible.

Honors: There is an annual Honors Day program.

Admissions: About 86% of the 1981–82 freshman applicants were accepted. The SAT scores of those who enrolled were as follows: Verbal—81% below 500, 13% between 500 and 599, 5% between 600 and 700, and 1% above 700; Math—82% below 500, 13% between 500 and 599, 4% between 600 and 700, and 1% above 700. Candidates must be graduates of an accredited high school and have completed 16 Carnegie units. A minimum GPA of 1.8 is required.

Procedure: The SAT is required. September 1 is the fall application deadline. New students are admitted each term. Admission and notification are on a rolling basis. There is no application fee.

Special: CLEP is used. A special studies program offers remedial work in English, reading, and mathematics to freshmen who scored below the recommended minimums on the SAT (430V, 430M). There is an early admissions plan.

Transfer: Transfers are accepted for freshman, sophomore, junior, and senior years. A 1.8 GPA is required; some D grades (in nonmajor courses) may transfer. Forty-five of a minimum 185 quarter credits required for a bachelor's degree must be completed in residence. Applications are due 20 days before the start of the quarter.

Visiting: The orientation program for prospective applicants includes campus tours and talks with faculty and admissions personnel. Informal tours with student guides can be arranged when school is in session. Visitors may sit in on classes. To arrange such visits, the director of admissions should be contacted.

Financial Aid: About 11% of the students are receiving assistance; 10% work part-time on campus. The college offers 50 freshman scholarships as well as various loans (government and commercial), grants (including BEOG), and part-time campus work opportunities. The average award to freshmen from all sources is $750. CWS is offered in 4 departments. The college is a member of CSS; the FAF should be filed by April 15.

Foreign Students: About 1% of the full-time students come from foreign countries. The college offers special organizations for these students.

Admissions: Foreign students must achieve a minimum TOEFL score of 500, or they must take the Georgia State University Test of English Proficiency. They must also take the SAT and achieve minimum scores of 250 on the verbal and 280 on the math.

GEORGIA

Procedure: Application deadlines are 20 days before the beginning of the quarter. Foreign students must present proof of funds adequate to cover 1 year of study. Health insurance is not required but is available through the college for a fee.

Admissions Contact: Thomas H. Rogers, Registrar and Director of Admissions.

LaGRANGE COLLEGE A-3
LaGrange, Georgia 30240 (404) 882-2911

F/T: 271M, 416W		Faculty:	52; IIA, --$
P/T: 99M, 157W		Ph.D.'s:	50%
Grad: 24M, 29W		S/F Ratio:	16 to 1
Year: qtrs, ss		Tuition:	$2205
Appl: Aug. 1		R and B:	$1335
321 applied	282 accepted		184 enrolled
SAT: 420V 430M			LESS COMPETITIVE

LaGrange College, established in 1831, is a private liberal arts college affiliated with the United Methodist Church. The library contains over 65,000 volumes and 1778 microfilm items, and subscribes to over 347 periodicals.

Environment: The college campus is on 30 acres in a small town 70 miles southwest of Atlanta. The physical plant consists of 17 buildings, including 4 dormitories accommodating 244 women and 151 men.

Student Life: About 83% of the students are from Georgia. Fifty percent reside on campus. About 35% of the students are Methodist; 98% are Protestant. Ten percent are minority-group members. College housing is single-sex; visiting privileges are not available. Freshman women living in dorms observe a curfew. Students may keep cars on campus.

Organizations: There are 3 fraternities and 3 sororities on campus, to which 25% of the students belong. Other activities include drama and vocal groups, religious groups, enrichment programs, fine arts exhibits, and concerts.

Sports: There are 4 intercollegiate teams for men and 2 for women. An intramural program of 4 sports for men and 3 for women is offered.

Graduates: The freshman dropout rate is 30%; 50% remain to graduate. Forty percent of the graduates go on to graduate or professional schools.

Programs of Study: The college confers the B.A. and B.B.A. degrees. Associate and master's degrees are also awarded. The B.A. degree is offered in the following subjects: BUSINESS (accounting, business administration), EDUCATION (early childhood, elementary, health/physical, secondary, special), ENGLISH (English), FINE AND PERFORMING ARTS (art, art education, theater/dramatics), HEALTH SCIENCES (nursing), LANGUAGES (Spanish), MATH AND SCIENCES (biology, chemistry, earth science, ecology/environmental science, mathematics), PHILOSOPHY (religion), PREPROFESSIONAL (dentistry, engineering, law, medicine, ministry, pharmacy, social work), SOCIAL SCIENCES (economics, government/political science, history, psychology).

Required: All students are required to take 60 quarter hours in English, fine arts, foreign language, history, laboratory science, mathematics, physical education, religion, and social sciences.

Special: The college offers independent study. There are combination degree programs in conjunction with Georgia Institute of Technology and Auburn University.

Admissions: Eighty-eight percent of those who applied were accepted for the 1981-82 freshman class. Applicants must have at least a 2.0 GPA in 15 high school units. Other considerations are advanced placement or honors courses, extracurricular activities record, and impressions made during an interview. A GED diploma may be accepted in lieu of a high school diploma.

Procedure: The SAT is required (ACT may be substituted) and should be taken by January of the senior year. The deadlines for application are August 1 (fall), December 1 (winter), March 1 (spring), and May 1 (summer). Admission and notification are on a rolling basis. There is a $10 application fee.

Special: An early admissions plan is available.

Transfer: For fall 1981, 146 transfer students applied, 124 were accepted, and 114 enrolled. Applicants must be in good academic standing at their previous school; C grades or better may transfer. Sixty quarter-hours, of the 185 required for the bachelor's degree, must be taken in residence. Deadlines are the same as those for freshmen.

Visiting: There are no regularly scheduled orientations for prospective students. Guides are available for informal tours of the campus. Visitors may sit in on classes and stay overnight at the school. To arrange such visits, the admissions office should be contacted.

Financial Aid: About 50% of all students receive aid; 20% work part-time on campus. Scholarships, loans, and campus employment are available. The FAF is the only application required and must be filed with CSS by June 1. Notification is sent by July 15. Aid is awarded on the basis of financial need.

Foreign Students: Five percent of the full-time students are from foreign countries. The college offers these students an intensive English course and special counseling.

Admissions: A minimum score of 450 on the TOEFL is necessary for admission. College entrance exams are not required.

Procedure: Foreign students are admitted for the fall, winter, spring, and summer quarters. A completed physical examination form is required as proof of health. Health insurance, though not required, is available through the college. Foreign students must furnish proof of adequate funds.

Admissions Contact: Tom Helton, Director of Admissions.

MEDICAL COLLEGE OF GEORGIA D-2
Augusta, Georgia 30912 (404) 828-2725

F/T: 104M, 705W		Faculty:	583; n/av
P/T: n/av		Ph.D.'s:	n/av
Grad: 1191M&W		S/F Ratio:	n/av
Year: qtrs		Tuition:	$927 ($2376)
Appl: see entry		R:	$540
307 applied	137 accepted		114 enrolled
SAT or ACT: required			COMPETITIVE+

The Medical College of Georgia is a state-supported college, founded in 1828. The library houses 117,700 volumes and subscribes to more than 1600 periodicals.

Environment: The college's campus is on 78 acres in an urban area. There are 59 buildings on the campus, including 4 dormitories that house 350 women, 104 men, and 64 married students. On-campus apartments also are available. The Eugene Talmadge Memorial Hospital, an integral part of the college, offers teaching and clinical research facilities.

Student Life: About 96% of the students are from Georgia. Forty percent live on campus. Ten percent are members of minority groups. Dormitories are both single-sex and coed; visiting privileges are provided in single-sex dorms. Students may keep cars on campus.

Organizations: The Christian Medical Society is the religious organization on campus. There are also special-interest clubs. The nearby Clark Hill Reservoir provides facilities for water skiing, swimming, boat racing, camping, and other outdoor recreational activities. Two national fraternities have chapters on campus.

Sports: The college offers some intercollegiate and intramural sports.

Handicapped: Special facilities for the handicapped student include wheelchair ramps, designated parking areas, elevators, lowered drinking fountains, and specially equipped rest rooms.

Services: Psychological, placement, and career counseling are offered free. Health care is available for a fee.

Programs of Study: The college confers the B.S. degree as well as associate, master's, and doctoral degrees. Bachelor's degrees are offered in the following subjects: HEALTH SCIENCES (dental hygiene, medical records administration, medical technology, nuclear medicine technology, nursing, occupational therapy, physical therapy, physician's assistant, radiologic technology, respiratory therapy).

Honors: Four national honor societies have chapters on campus.

Admissions: Forty-five percent of those who applied were accepted for the 1981-82 freshman class. Applicants must be high school graduates or have a GED, and must have completed 16 units of secondary school work with a 2.0 or better average. Other factors that enter into the admissions decision include impressions made during an interview, personality, recommendations by school officials, advanced placement or honors courses, and leadership record. SAT scores of around 400 on each part are acceptable.

Procedure: The SAT or ACT is required. Some departments also require pre-entrance tests. There is no application fee. Deadlines for application vary with the program to which entrance is sought. New students enter only in fall; most start at the junior level.

Transfer: A minimum GPA of 2.0 and scores of 410 on each part of the SAT are required. Students must earn, at the college, 90 of the 180 quarter hours required for a bachelor's degree. There is a 1-year residency requirement.

Visiting: To arrange a group visit, contact Julie Weber.

Financial Aid: About 60% of all students receive aid. The FAF is required. Priority is given to applications received by April 1.

Foreign Students: The foreign students enrolled full-time make up about 1% of the student body. No special services are provided.

Admissions: Foreign applicants must score 500 or better on the TOEFL. They also must score at least 410 on each part of the SAT.

Procedure: Application deadlines vary with the program. Students must show proof of good health and of adequate funds. All students must carry health insurance, which is available through the college at no extra charge.

Admissions Contact: Elizabeth Griffin, Coordinator of Academic Admissions.

MERCER UNIVERSITY

Mercer University, established in 1833, is a private liberal arts institution affiliated with the Georgia Baptist Convention. The university provides undergraduate and graduate instruction at its main campus in Macon and its branch campus in Atlanta, which was formed by the merger of Atlanta Baptist College with Mercer in 1972. The university also operates a school of law and a school of pharmacy. Profiles of the 2 campuses follow.

MERCER UNIVERSITY C-3
Macon, Georgia 31207   (912) 744-2650

F/T: 1181M, 1178W	Faculty: n/av; IIA, av$
P/T: n/av	Ph.D.'s: 70%
Grad: n/av	S/F Ratio: 18 to 1
Year: qtrs, ss	Tuition: $3669
Appl: open	R and B: $1785
1563 applied 1233 accepted 560 enrolled	
SAT: 500V 500M	COMPETITIVE

Mercer University, affiliated with the Southern Baptist Convention, offers business, education, health science, liberal arts, and preprofessional programs. The library contains 250,000 volumes and 40,000 microfilm items, and subscribes to 1600 periodicals.

Environment: The 140-acre campus is located in the urban environment of western Macon. The 25 buildings include 7 dormitories that accommodate 597 women and 572 men, 36 housing units for married students, and 2 gymnasiums. The university also sponsors on- and off-campus apartments.

Student Life: About 52% of the students come from Georgia. Eighty percent live in dormitories; freshmen are required to do so. Fifteen percent of the students leave campus on weekends. Drinking on campus is forbidden. About 83% of the students are Protestant, 10% are Catholic, and 2% are Jewish. About 12% of the students are minority-group members. Campus housing is single-sex; there are visiting privileges. Students may keep cars on campus.

Organizations: Forty percent of the students belong to 1 of the 11 fraternities and 6 sororities. Extracurricular activities include special-interest, religious, and service groups; student government; drama; publications; and music and choral groups. The university sponsors 5 to 10 cultural events each week.

Sports: The university fields 5 intercollegiate teams for men and 2 for women. There are 9 intramural sports for men and 6 for women.

Handicapped: The entire campus is accessible to physically handicapped students. Facilities include wheelchair ramps, special parking areas, elevators, specially equipped rest rooms, and lowered telephones. Special class scheduling and one special counselor are provided.

Graduates: About 38% of the graduates go on for further study; 13% enter medical school, 6% dental school, and 11% law school. Nine percent begin careers in business and industry.

Services: Psychological, placement, and career counseling; tutoring; and remedial instruction are provided free to students. Placement services also are available to alumni. Health care is available on a fee basis.

Programs of Study: The university awards the B.A., B.S., and B.B.A. degrees. Master's and doctoral degrees also are available. Bachelor's degrees are offered in the following subjects: AREA STUDIES (Black/Afro-American), BUSINESS (accounting, business, business administration, computer science, economics, finance, management, marketing), EDUCATION (early childhood, elementary, health/physical, mental retardation, secondary, special), ENGLISH (English, dramatic arts, journalism, speech), FINE AND PERFORMING ARTS (art, art education, art history, music, music education, studio art, theater/dramatics), HEALTH SCIENCES (medical technology), LANGUAGES (French, German, Greek/Latin, Spanish), MATH AND SCIENCES (biochemistry, biology, botany, chemistry, mathematics, natural sciences, physical sciences, physics), PHILOSOPHY (philosophy, religion), PRE-PROFESSIONAL (dentistry, engineering, forestry, law, medicine, ministry, pharmacy, social work), SOCIAL SCIENCES (economics, government/political science, history, psychology, social sciences, sociology). Twenty percent of the undergraduate degrees are conferred in business, 20% in health sciences, 20% in preprofessional areas, 10% in education, and 10% in English.

Required: Students must take freshman English and 12 courses chosen from general education grouping. To graduate, students must pass a Senior Comprehensive Exam.

Special: Minors are offered in anthropology, broadcasting and film studies, criminal justice, Greek, and journalism. Students may design their own majors. First-year students may take one freshman seminar, an interdisciplinary study of current events, each quarter to exempt themselves from general education requirements. The Human Services Program provides 9-month internships in areas dealing with services to people. Independent study and summer travel programs are available.

Honors: Fourteen honor societies are represented on campus.

Admissions: About 79% of the applicants for the 1981–82 freshman class were accepted. The minimum high school GPA required is 2.5. Applicants should have completed 15 Carnegie units and should rank in the upper half of their high school class.

Procedure: Applicants must take the SAT or ACT. Applications are accepted up to one week before a quarter starts; freshmen are admitted to all quarters. Notification is made on a rolling basis. The application fee is $10.

Special: AP and CLEP credit is accepted. An early admissions plan is available.

Transfer: For fall 1981, 250 transfer students applied, 200 were accepted, and 163 enrolled. Applicants must present evidence of satisfactory work at and honorable dismissal from last school attended. A GPA of at least 2.5 and a minimum combined SAT score of 1000 are recommended. Students must complete at least 45 of the 180 quarter hours required for a bachelor's degree at the university. C grades or better transfer. Applications are due 2 weeks before the start of a quarter.

Visiting: Prospective students should notify the admissions office at least a week before they plan to visit. Guides are provided, and students may sit in on classes and stay overnight in the dormitories. The university recommends scheduling Thursday-to-Friday overnight visits.

Financial Aid: About 60% of the students receive aid; about 45% work part-time on campus. Ten freshman and 25 athletic scholarships are awarded each year. Federal and university loans are available. The university participates in CWS and awards work contracts to freshmen. The average award to freshmen from all sources is $3800. Need is the primary consideration in awarding aid. The university is a member of the CSS, and candidates should submit the university aid application and the FAF by May 1.

Foreign Students: About 1% of the students come from foreign countries. The university offers these students special counseling.

Admissions: Foreign students must achieve a minimum TOEFL score of 500; in addition, they must also take the SAT or ACT.

Procedure: Application deadlines are May 1 (fall), November 10 (winter), and February 9 (spring). Foreign students must present proof of health and proof of adequate funds. A $500 deposit is required. Foreign students must also carry health insurance, which is available through the university for a fee.

Admissions Contact: Joseph S. McDaniel, Director of Admissions.

MERCER UNIVERSITY IN ATLANTA B-2
Atlanta, Georgia 30341   (404) 458-5904

F/T: 388M, 455W	Faculty: 50; IIB, – $
P/T: 265M, 205W	Ph.D.'s: 85%
Grad: 238M, 167W	S/F Ratio: 17 to 1
Year: qtrs, ss	Tuition: $2700
Appl: Sept. 5	R and B: n/app
394 applied 280 accepted 266 enrolled	
SAT: 400V 400M	LESS COMPETITIVE

GEORGIA

Mercer University in Atlanta, affiliated with the Southern Baptist Convention, is a commuter school with business, education, and liberal arts and sciences programs. The library contains 75,000 books and nearly 140,000 microfilm items, and subscribes to 578 periodicals.

Environment: The campus is located in a suburban area 12 miles from the center of Atlanta. The university has no residence halls.

Student Life: Nearly all students are from Georgia. All students commute.

Organizations: The university sponsors special-interest clubs and service groups. There are no fraternities or sororities.

Sports: The university fields 2 intercollegiate teams for men and 3 for women. There are 9 intramural sports for men and 8 for women.

Handicapped: About 87% of the campus is accessible to physically handicapped students. Facilities include wheelchair ramps, special parking areas, elevators, specially equipped rest rooms, and lowered drinking fountains and telephones. Special class scheduling and student assistance can be arranged.

Services: Career counseling and limited placement services are provided free to students.

Programs of Study: The university awards the B.A., B.S., B.M., and B.B.A. degrees. Master's programs also are available. Bachelor's degrees are offered in the following subjects: BUSINESS (accounting, business, finance, management, marketing), EDUCATION (elementary, health/physical, social science), ENGLISH (English, communications), FINE AND PERFORMING ARTS (art, church music, fine arts, music, theater/dramatics), MATH AND SCIENCES (biochemistry, biology, chemistry, mathematics), PHILOSOPHY (humanities, philosophy, religion), SOCIAL SCIENCES (economics, government/political science, history, human services, psychology, sociology). About 32% of the undergraduate degrees are conferred in social sciences, 22% in business, and 19% in education.

Required: The university has some distribution requirements.

Special: Students may design their own majors. Study abroad and independent study are available.

Honors: There are no honor societies on campus.

Admissions: About 71% of the applicants for the 1981–82 freshman class were accepted. Applicants must have earned a high school diploma and completed 15 Carnegie units with a GPA of 2.0 or better.

Procedure: The SAT or the ACT is required. New students are admitted each quarter. Applications for fall admission are due September 5. Notification is made on a rolling basis. There is a $10 application fee.

Special: AP and CLEP credit is accepted.

Transfer: For fall 1981, 506 transfer students applied and 428 were accepted. Transfer students must submit SAT or ACT scores and transcripts of previous college work. A 2.0 GPA is recommended. C grades or better transfer. Students must complete 45 quarter hours, of the 180 quarter hours required, to earn a bachelor's degree. Application deadlines are the same as those for freshmen.

Visiting: The university schedules orientations for prospective students that include campus tours, class visits, and information sessions. Informal visits also may be scheduled, preferably for weekday mornings, by contacting the admissions office. Visitors may sit in on classes, and guides are provided.

Financial Aid: About 35% of the students receive aid; 10% of the students work part-time on campus. Scholarships, grants, loans, and CWS jobs are available. The average award is 75% of school expenses. Aid applications should be filed by May 1 (fall) or April 1 (summer). The university is a member of CSS; the FAF and income tax statements must be filed.

Foreign Students: About 10% of the full-time students come from foreign countries. The university offers these students an intensive English course, special counseling, and special organizations.

Admissions: Foreign students must achieve an acceptable score on the TOEFL or the Georgia State University Test of English Proficiency. No college entrance exams are required.

Procedure: Foreign students are admitted to all terms. A completed health form and proof of funds adequate to cover 3 quarters of study must be presented. Health insurance is required and is available through the university for a fee.

Admissions Contact: Richard V. Swindle, Director of Admissions.

MOREHOUSE COLLEGE   B-2
Atlanta, Georgia 30314   (404) 681-2800

F/T: 1769M	Faculty: 104; IIB, −$
P/T: 72M	Ph.D.'s: 64%
Grad: none	S/F Ratio: 16 to 1
Year: sems	Tuition: $3026
Appl: Apr. 15	R and B: $1890
1250 applied	1025 accepted 525 enrolled
SAT: 368V 403M	LESS COMPETITIVE

Morehouse College, founded in 1867, is a private, four-year college for men. It is proud to count the late Rev. Martin Luther King, Jr., among its notable alumni. The library contains over 250,000 volumes.

Environment: The 40-acre campus is located in an urban area about 1½ miles from downtown Atlanta. Facilities include 10 buildings which have been constructed since 1967. Most notable is the M. L. King Chapel, which seats 2500.

Student Life: About 30% of the students are from Georgia. The student body is composed predominantly of blacks. About 90% of the entering freshmen come from public schools. About 50% of the students reside in college dormitories. The college also sponsors fraternity houses. About 75% of the students are Protestant and 15% are Catholic. Students may keep cars on campus.

Organizations: There are 5 fraternities. Extracurricular activities are numerous and include publications, the student government association, a business club, a jazz club, and theater groups. Religious clubs and activities are also offered.

Sports: The college fields 5 intercollegiate teams. There are 4 intramural sports.

Graduates: The freshman dropout rate is 15%; 50% remain to graduate. About 45% pursue graduate study after graduation; 5% enter medical school, 3% law school, and 1% dental school. About 55% enter business and industry.

Services: Students receive the following services free of charge: career counseling, placement, psychological counseling, health care, tutoring, and remedial instruction. The Office of Career Counseling and Placement secures and arranges interviews for graduating seniors, holds individual sessions for counseling, and maintains a current career library with catalogs and job information.

Programs of Study: Undergraduate programs lead to the B.A. and B.S. degrees. Bachelor's degrees are offered in the following subjects: BUSINESS (accounting, banking and finance, business administration, insurance, management), EDUCATION (elementary, secondary), ENGLISH (English, journalism), FINE AND PERFORMING ARTS (art, music, theater/dramatics), LANGUAGES (French, German, Spanish), MATH AND SCIENCES (biology, chemistry, computer science, mathematics, physics), PHILOSOPHY (philosophy, religion), PREPROFESSIONAL (dentistry, engineering, law, medicine, ministry, social work, veterinary), SOCIAL SCIENCES (economics, government/political science, history, international studies, psychology, sociology, urban studies).

Required: All students must take courses in English, a modern foreign language, humanities, mathematics, religion, philosophy, physics, social science, and speech.

Special: The college allows selected students to spend their third year abroad. Combination degrees in engineering are offered in cooperation with Georgia Institute of Technology.

Honors: There is a well-established undergraduate honors program; requirements for departmental honors vary with each department and involve comprehensive written and oral reports, research, and independent study. National honor societies and departmental honor societies are available.

Admissions: Eighty-two percent of those who applied were accepted for the 1981–82 freshman class. The SAT scores of those who enrolled were as follows: Verbal—93% below 500, 6% between 500 and 599, 1% between 600 and 700, and 0% above 700; Math—89% below 500, 10% between 500 and 599, 1% between 600 and 700, and 0% above 700. Applicants should rank in the upper half of their high school class and have a 2.0 GPA. The recommendation of an accredited high school is required. Counselor recommendation, extracurricular activities, and leadership record are considered.

Procedure: Candidates should take the SAT in May of the junior year or December or January of the senior year. Candidates are accepted at midyear. Applications, accompanied by a $15 fee, should be submitted by April 15 (fall) and December 1 (spring). Acceptance notification is on a rolling basis.

Special: Early admission is possible. AP and CLEP credit is offered.

Transfer: For fall 1981, 132 transfer students applied, 87 were accepted, and 45 enrolled. Transfer students must be in good academic standing with the school last attended. A 2.0 GPA is required. Those with fewer than 15 semester hours must present SAT scores. The last 30 semester hours of the 128 required for a bachelor's degree must be taken in residence. C grades or better transfer. Application deadlines are the same as those for freshmen.

Visiting: Guided tours and interviews may be scheduled through the admissions office.

Financial Aid: Financial aid is granted to about 70% of the students; 25% of the students work part-time on campus. Financial aid is based upon need; aid is given in the form of scholarships, loans, and grants. Tuition may be paid in installments. The deadline to apply for financial aid is April 15 (fall) and December 1 (spring). The college is a member of CSS; the FAF is required.

Foreign Students: About 2% of the full-time students come from foreign countries. The college offers these students special counseling.

Admissions: Foreign students must achieve a score of at least 450 on the TOEFL. They must also receive a minimum combined score of 700 on the SAT.

Procedure: Application deadlines are the same as those for other students. Foreign students must present proof of health as well as proof of adequate funds.

Admissions Contact: Robert E. Miller, Director of Admissions.

MORRIS BROWN COLLEGE B-2
Atlanta, Georgia 30314 (404) 525-7831

F/T: 647M, 879W	Faculty:	142; IIB, − −$
P/T: 34M&W	Ph.D.'s:	47%
Grad: none	S/F Ratio:	16 to 1
Year: sems, ss	Tuition:	$2770
Appl: open	R and B:	$2300
1077 applied	948 accepted	417 enrolled
SAT or ACT: required		LESS COMPETITIVE

Morris Brown College, founded in 1881, is a private liberal arts institution affiliated with the African Methodist Episcopal Church. The library contains 56,900 volumes and subscribes to 401 periodicals.

Environment: The campus occupies 21 acres in the Atlanta University Center, which also includes Atlanta University; Morehouse, Spelman, and Clark Colleges; and the Interdenominational Theological Center. Facilities include a student center and residence halls that accommodate 225 men, 230 women, and 8 families.

Student Life: About 85% of the students are from Georgia, and about half live on campus in the single-sex dormitories. The student body is predominantly black.

Organizations: About 5% of the students belong to the 5 fraternities and 5 sororities on campus. Extracurricular activities include publications, student government, special-interest clubs, a debate team, and a drama league.

Sports: Intramural and intercollegiate sports are available.

Graduates: About 35% of the freshmen drop out during their first year, and half remain to graduate. About 1% of the graduates immediately pursue advanced degrees.

Services: Students receive free health care, tutoring, remedial instruction, and placement, career, and psychological counseling.

Programs of Study: The college awards the B.A., B.S., and B.S. in E. degrees. Bachelor's degrees are offered in the following subjects: AREA STUDIES (urban), BUSINESS (accounting, business administration, business education, management, office administration, restaurant and institutional management), EDUCATION (early childhood, health/physical, middle school, secondary, special), ENGLISH (English, mass communications, speech), FINE AND PERFORMING ARTS (art, music, theater/dramatics), HEALTH SCIENCES (allied health, therapeutic recreation), LANGUAGES (French, German, Spanish), MATH AND SCIENCES (biology, chemistry, computer science, mathematics), PHILOSOPHY (philosophy, religion), PREPROFESSIONAL (engineering, fashion design, food and nutrition, home economics), SOCIAL SCIENCES (child development, criminal justice, economics, family studies, geography, government/political science, history, psychology, sociology).

Required: Students must take a total of 50 hours in communications, speech, mathematics, humanities, social science, natural science, foreign languages, and physical education.

Special: Programs include cooperative education, independent study, internships, study abroad, and cross-registration with other colleges in the Atlanta University Center. A developmental skills program is available for freshmen.

Admissions: About 88% of the applicants for the 1981–82 freshman class were accepted. Candidates must have completed 15 units of work at an accredited high school and present at least a C average.

Procedure: The SAT or ACT is required, as are recommendations from high school officials. There is a $20 application fee. Application deadlines are open.

Special: An early admissions plan is available. CLEP and AP credit is accepted.

Transfer: Students may transfer up to 92 hours of work in which grades of C or better were received. They must spend at least 1 year in residence and earn a total of 124 credits for a bachelor's degree.

Financial Aid: About 95% of the students receive aid. Programs include NDSL; EOG; CWS; the Morris Brown Work-Aid Program; and athletic, academic, band, choir, and need scholarships. The average award to freshmen from all sources is $4675. Tuition may be paid in installments. The college will provide application information.

Foreign Students: The foreign students enrolled full-time make up about 4% of the student body. The college provides these students with an intensive English course, special counseling, and special organizations.

Admissions: Applicants must score at least 425 on the TOEFL. No college entrance exams are required.

Procedure: Application deadlines are open; students are admitted to the fall and spring semesters. Students must submit proof of adequate funds for their entire period of study and must carry health insurance, which is available through the college for a fee.

Admissions Contact: Lucille S. Williams, Director of Admissions.

NORTH GEORGIA COLLEGE B-1
Dahlonega, Georgia 30597 (404) 864-3391

F/T: 657M, 766W	Faculty:	105; IIB, + +$
P/T: 104M, 159W	Ph.D.'s:	51%
Grad: 59M, 205W	S/F Ratio:	19 to 1
Year: qtrs, ss	Tuition:	$699 ($1749)
Appl: Sept. 1	R and B:	$1335
843 applied	644 accepted	451 enrolled
SAT: required		LESS COMPETITIVE

North Georgia College, established in 1873, is a state-supported liberal arts and military college. The library contains 120,000 volumes and over 95,000 microfilm items, and subscribes to 1000 periodicals.

Environment: The 200-acre rural campus, which lies 72 miles north of Atlanta, includes 18 major buildings, a large athletic field and a drill area, and dormitories that house about 1190 students.

Student Life: About 95% of the students are from Georgia. About four-fifths of the students reside in residence halls. About 4% are minority-group members. Campus housing is single-sex; there are no visiting privileges. Students may keep cars on campus.

Organizations: Student organizations include special-interest clubs, dramatics, officers' club, noncommissioned officers' club, religious groups, band, 4 fraternities, and 2 sororities.

Sports: The college fields 4 intercollegiate teams for men and 5 for women. There are 4 intramural sports for men and 3 for women.

Handicapped: The college estimates the campus to be 75% accessible to the handicapped student. There are no special facilities.

Graduates: The freshman dropout rate is 25%; 65% remain to graduate. Of the latter, 20% pursue graduate study: 1% enter medical school, 1% dental school, and 1% law school. Seventy percent of the graduates pursue careers in business or industry.

Services: The following services are offered at no charge to the student: psychological counseling, placement, career counseling, and remedial instruction. Health care and tutoring are available for a fee.

Programs of Study: The college offers the B.A., B.B.A., B.S., and B.S.W. degrees. It also has associate and master's programs. Bachelor's degrees are offered in the following subjects: BUSINESS (accounting, business education, economics, finance, management, marketing), EDUCATION (early childhood, health/physical, secondary, special), ENGLISH (English), FINE AND PERFORMING ARTS (art education, music education), LANGUAGES (French), MATH AND SCIENCES (biology, chemistry, mathematics, physics), SOCIAL SCIENCES (economics, government/political science, history, psychology, social sciences, sociology). Of the degrees conferred, 30% are in education, 29% in social sciences, and 22% in business.

Required: All students are required to take courses in English, humanities, mathematics, science, social sciences, and physical education. All resident male students must participate in the military.

Special: A special studies program is offered. Students may participate in study abroad programs sponsored by other institutions.

Admissions: Seventy-six percent of those who applied were accepted for the 1981-82 freshman class. Forty percent of those who enrolled ranked in the upper two-fifths of their high school class. Applicants must be graduates of accredited high schools and have completed 16 Carnegie units. Recommendations by school officials and leadership potential are also considered.

Procedure: The SAT is required and should be taken by March of the senior year. Applications should be submitted by September 1 for fall entry, December 1 for winter entry, March 1 for spring entry, and June 1 for summer entry. There is a $10 application fee.

Special: An early admissions plan is offered; the application deadline is September 1. Credit for some AP and CLEP exams is granted.

Transfer: For fall 1981, 156 transfer students applied, 123 were accepted, and 119 enrolled. An average of C, with no disciplinary problems, is required of applicants. All students must complete 45 quarter hours at the college out of a total of 185 quarter hours required for the bachelor's degree. Application deadlines are the same as those for freshman applicants.

Visiting: Regularly scheduled orientations, providing a total overview of the college, are conducted for prospective students. Guides are available for informal visits to the campus. Visitors may sit in on classes. To arrange an overnight campus visit, the admissions department should be contacted. Fridays or Saturdays during the school year are the recommended days for visits.

Financial Aid: About 60% of all students receive aid. Fifteen percent work part-time on campus. Scholarships, loans, grants, work-study, and ROTC are sources of aid. The college is a member of the CSS. The FAF is required. The aid application deadline for fall is July 1.

Foreign Students: Less than 1% of the students come from foreign countries. The college offers special counseling to these students.

Admissions: Foreign students must take the SAT and TOEFL; a minimum score of 500 is required on the TOEFL.

Procedure: Application deadlines for foreign students are the same as those for freshman applicants. The college requires proof of adequate funds to cover 4 years.

Admissions Contact: Gary R. Steffey, Director of Admissions.

OGLETHORPE UNIVERSITY   B-2
Atlanta, Georgia 30319   (404) 261-1441

F/T: 431M, 418W	Faculty: 48; IIA, av$
P/T: 134M, 311W	Ph.D.'s: 89%
Grad: 7M, 54W	S/F Ratio: 18 to 1
Year: sems, ss	Tuition: $3550
Appl: Aug. 1	R and B: $1950
668 applied	474 accepted	306 enrolled
SAT: 487V 519M	ACT: 23	VERY COMPETITIVE

Oglethorpe University, founded in 1835 as Oglethorpe College, is a private liberal arts college. The library contains 80,000 volumes and 150,000 microfilm items, and subscribes to 400 periodicals.

Environment: The 160-acre campus is located in a suburban community 10 miles from downtown Atlanta. The physical plant consists of 7 major academic buildings, 5 men's dormitories arranged in a quad, a women's dormitory complex, and a newly expanded science facility, mainly in neo-Gothic architecture. The university also sponsors fraternity and sorority houses.

Student Life: About 48% of the students are from Georgia, 19% from Florida, and 22% from the northeast and middle Atlantic states. About 60% reside on campus. About 50% of the students are Protestant, 21% are Catholic, and 7% are Jewish. About 13% are minority-group members. Campus housing is single-sex; there are visiting privileges. Students may keep cars on campus.

Organizations: Student activities on campus include 3 national fraternities and 2 national sororities, religious groups, a weekly newspaper, a drama group, special-interest clubs, concerts, dances, and social affairs. Atlanta offers many cultural and social opportunities.

Sports: The university fields 5 intercollegiate teams for men and 4 for women. There are 5 intramural sports for men and 6 for women.

Handicapped: The university estimates the campus to be 60% accessible to the wheelchair-bound student. Special class scheduling can be arranged, and specially equipped rest rooms, elevators, and ramps are available.

Graduates: The freshman dropout rate is 15%; 65% remain to graduate, and 55% of these pursue graduate study: 10% enter medical school, 6% enter law school, and 4% enter dental school. Fifty-five percent pursue careers in business or industry.

Services: Psychological and career counseling, placement services, and health care are offered at no charge to the student. Placement services for both students and alumni include on-campus interviews, files of job openings, and career seminars. Tutoring is available on a fee basis.

Programs of Study: The university awards the B.A., B.S., B.B.A., and B.S.Med.Tech. degrees, as well as master's degrees. Bachelor's degrees are offered in the following subjects: AREA STUDIES (American, general), BUSINESS (accounting, business administration), EDUCATION (early childhood, elementary, secondary), ENGLISH (English), FINE AND PERFORMING ARTS (art), HEALTH SCIENCES (medical technology), MATH AND SCIENCES (biology, chemistry, mathematics, physics), PHILOSOPHY (philosophy), PREPROFESSIONAL (dentistry, engineering, law, medicine, ministry, nursing, pharmacy, social work, veterinary), SOCIAL SCIENCES (economics, government/political science, history, international relations, psychology, sociology). Of the degrees conferred, 35% are in business, 15% are in preprofessional studies, and 12% are in social sciences.

Required: All students must take a core curriculum, including various liberal arts courses.

Special: A general studies degree program is offered. Double majors are available. Travel abroad is offered. Dual-degree programs in engineering and art are available. Academic internships are available in all majors.

Honors: Two national honor societies have chapters on campus. Honors programs are offered in social studies, science, and business.

Admissions: Seventy-one percent of those who applied were accepted for the 1981-82 freshman class. Applicants must have completed 15 Carnegie units and have a 2.3 GPA. Other factors entering into an admissions decision are advanced placement or honors courses, recommendations by school officials, and leadership record.

Procedure: The SAT or ACT is required and should be taken early in the senior year. Application deadlines are August 1 (fall), January 1 (spring), and May 15 (summer). A rolling admissions plan is used. Applications should be submitted with a $20 application fee.

Special: There are early decision, early admissions, and deferred admissions plans. CLEP and AP credit is granted.

Transfer: For fall 1981, 140 transfer students applied, 125 were accepted, and 91 enrolled. Transfers are accepted for all classes except the senior class. Grades of C or above transfer. A 2.3 GPA is required plus a letter of good standing from the dean or registrar. There is a residency requirement of 60 semester hours (2 years); 120 semester hours are required to earn the bachelor's degree. Application deadlines are the same as those for freshmen.

Visiting: The university conducts regularly scheduled orientations for prospective students. Visitors may sit in on classes and stay overnight at the school. To arrange a visit, the admissions office manager should be contacted.

Financial Aid: About 80% of all students receive aid; 40% work part-time on campus. The university provides scholarships and loans as sources of financial aid. There are numerous Oglethorpe Merit Awards for scholarship. Loans are available from the federal government. The average award to freshmen from all sources is $1180. The college is a member of CSS; the FAF is required. Application must be made by May 1 for fall or summer entry; the winter deadline is December 1. Notification is within 1 month.

Foreign Students: About 18% of the students come from foreign countries. The university offers these students an intensive English course, special counseling, and special organizations.

Admissions: Foreign students must achieve a minimum TOEFL score of 500; no further exams are required.

Procedure: Application deadlines are August 1 for fall, December 15 for winter, and May 15 for summer. Foreign students must present proof of adequate funds.

Admissions Contact: T. Randolph Smith, Assistant Director of Admissions.

PAINE COLLEGE
Augusta, Georgia 30910
D-2
(404) 722-4471

F/T: 230M, 533W
P/T: 38M, 41W
Grad: none
Year: qtrs, ss
Appl: Sept. 1
419 applied   325 accepted   207 enrolled
SAT or ACT: required   LESS COMPETITIVE
Faculty: 50; IIB, −−$
Ph.D.'s: 46%
S/F Ratio: 15 to 1
Tuition: $2445
R and B: $1370

Paine College, founded in 1882, is affiliated with the United Methodist and Christian Methodist Episcopal churches. It offers undergraduate degrees in arts and sciences, education, and business. The library contains 75,000 books and 3500 microfilm items, and subscribes to 2750 periodicals.

Environment: The 43-acre campus includes dormitories that house 148 men and 256 women. Other facilities include a gymnasium, athletic fields, and an administration building. The college also sponsors fraternity houses and on-campus apartments.

Student Life: About 85% of the students come from Georgia, and 95% are graduates of public schools. Most students are not members of the supporting church, but all must attend assembly services once a week. The student body is predominantly (95%) black. Drinking is prohibited on campus, and women residents must observe a curfew. About 98% of the students are Protestant. Campus housing is single-sex. Students may keep cars on campus.

Organizations: The college sponsors a student government, drama club, choir, Lyceum programs, Honors Day, and other groups and programs. Fourteen percent of the men belong to one of 8 fraternities, and 20% of the women belong to one of 8 sororities.

Sports: The college fields 1 intercollegiate team for men and 1 for women. There are 6 intramural sports for men and 6 for women.

Handicapped: About 16% of the campus is accessible to physically handicapped students. Facilities include wheelchair ramps, special parking, elevators, and specially equipped rest rooms.

Graduates: Twenty percent of the freshmen drop out, and 50% remain to graduate. Three percent of the graduates go on for further education.

Services: Tutoring, remedial instruction, placement, career counseling, and psychological counseling are offered free to students. Health care is available on campus at a fee.

Programs of Study: The college confers the B.A., B.S., and B.B.A. degrees. Bachelor's degrees are offered in the following subjects: BUSINESS (accounting, business administration, management), EDUCATION (early childhood, elementary, secondary), ENGLISH (English, journalism), FINE AND PERFORMING ARTS (art, music, music education, studio art), HEALTH SCIENCES (environmental health, nursing, occupational therapy, physical therapy), MATH AND SCIENCES (biology, chemistry, mathematics, natural sciences, physics), PHILOSOPHY (philosophy/religion), PREPROFESSIONAL (dentistry, engineering, medicine, ministry, pharmacy), SOCIAL SCIENCES (history, psychology, social sciences, sociology). About 28% of the degrees are conferred in elementary education, 25% in business, and 20% in history or sociology.

Required: Students must take courses in fine arts, physical education, psychology, natural science, social science, language, composition and speech, and philosophy and religion.

Special: Certification is awarded in secondary education. The journalism major is offered in cooperation with Clark College in Atlanta. Other programs include Senate internships, cooperative education, and internships in family and children's services.

Admissions: About 78% of the applicants for the 1981–82 freshman class were accepted. Applicants should have an average of 2.0 or better; those with a lower average may be admitted conditionally. Candidates also should have completed 15 Carnegie units and should be recommended for college by their high school counselor. The college seeks a geographically diverse student body.

Procedure: Applicants should take the SAT or ACT in December of the senior year. Application deadlines are September 1 (fall), December 1 (winter), March 15 (spring), and June 1 (summer). There is no application fee. Applicants are notified on a rolling basis.

Special: Early decision and early admissions plans are available. AP credit is accepted.

Transfer: For fall 1981, 83 transfer students applied, 47 were accepted, and 45 enrolled. An average of C or better is necessary. Grades of C or better transfer. Students must spend at least 1 year in residence to graduate. The bachelor's degree requires the completion of 180 quarter hours.

Visiting: Prospective students may contact the director of admissions to arrange informal visits to campus. Visitors may attend classes and stay overnight in the residence halls. Guides are provided.

Financial Aid: About 95% of the students receive aid; about 60% work part-time on campus. Scholarships, loans, and CWS jobs are available. The average scholarship granted to a freshman is $600 and the maximum is $1875. The average award to freshmen from all sources is $3500. Federal loans may range as high as $2500 per year. Earnings from part-time jobs average $150 per month; the maximum is $360. Awards are based on need and academic achievement. The college is a member of the CSS; the FAF must be filed by March 15. Tuition may be paid in installments.

Foreign Students: The college offers foreign students special counseling.

Admissions: Foreign students must take the TOEFL; a score of between 450 and 500 is required. In addition, they must also take the SAT or ACT, as well as the college's own exam.

Procedure: The application deadline is September 1 for fall. Foreign students must present proof of health as well as proof of funds adequate to cover 1 year of study.

Admissions Contact: Edythe G. Dimond, Coordinator of Admissions.

PIEDMONT COLLEGE
Demorest, Georgia 30535
C-1
(404) 778-8033

F/T: 321M&W
P/T: 82M&W
Grad: none
Year: qtrs, ss
Appl: Aug. 31
SAT: required   NONCOMPETITIVE
Faculty: 25; IIB, −−$
Ph.D.'s: 40%
S/F Ratio: 15 to 1
Tuition: $1665
R and B: $2340

Piedmont College, a liberal arts institution established in 1897, is privately controlled and affiliated with the Congregational Christian Churches. The library houses 75,000 volumes and subscribes to 150 periodicals.

Environment: The 50-acre campus is situated in a small community 85 miles northeast of Atlanta. Among its 16 buildings are dormitories that house 425 men and 150 women. Housing for married students also is available.

Student Life: Forty-nine percent of the students are from the South. Almost all attended public schools. About 45% live on campus in the single-sex dorms; unmarried students not living with relatives are required to do so. Chapel attendance is required twice weekly. A dress code is enforced. Alcohol is prohibited. Women residents must obtain permission to stay out late on weekends or spend a night away from campus.

Organizations: Student government, music and drama groups, publications, and religious and special-interest clubs provide extracurricular activities. There are no sororities or fraternities.

Sports: The college fields intercollegiate teams in 5 sports. Intramural sports also are available.

Handicapped: About 70% of the campus is accessible to wheelchair-bound students. Facilities include ramps and designated parking areas.

Graduates: Twenty-five percent of the graduates seek advanced degrees.

Services: Tutoring, placement aid, and career counseling are offered free to students.

Programs of Study: The college confers the B.A. and B.S. degrees. Bachelor's degrees are offered in the following subjects: BUSINESS (accounting, business administration), EDUCATION (early childhood, elementary, secondary), ENGLISH (English), FINE AND PERFORMING ARTS (art, art education), LANGUAGES (Spanish), MATH AND SCIENCES (biology, chemistry, mathematics), PREPROFESSIONAL (social work), SOCIAL SCIENCES (history, psychology, sociology).

Required: Students must complete distribution requirements, including foreign-language courses.

Special: A degree may be earned in 3 years. Additional minors are available in computer science, criminal justice, economics, music, physical education, speech and drama, and religion. Preprofessional programs are available in medicine, dentistry, nursing, pharmacy, medical technology, optometry, forestry, and veterinary medicine.

168 GEORGIA

Honors: The national honor society Alpha Chi has a chapter on campus.

Admissions: A high school diploma or GED is required.

Procedure: The SAT is required. Application deadlines are August 31 (fall), December 31 (winter), March 15 (spring), and May 25 (summer). Freshmen are admitted to all sessions. Admissions decisions are made on a rolling basis. There is a $10 application fee.

Special: An early admissions plan is offered. CLEP credit is accepted.

Transfer: Transfer applicants must have a 2.0 GPA and present a letter of honorable dismissal from the previous college. Only 20% of D grades are transferable. Students must study at least 1 year at the college and earn 180 quarter credits to receive a bachelor's degree. Application deadlines are the same as those for freshmen.

Visiting: Visitors' Day is held during the spring quarter. Guides also are available for informal visits. Visitors may sit in on classes and stay overnight at the school. Contact the registrar's office for arrangements.

Financial Aid: About 60% of all students receive aid, which includes scholarships, loans, and work-study jobs. Scholarships are awarded for academic achievement, athletics, and talent in such areas as music. The deadline for aid application is August 15. The FAF is required.

Foreign Students: The full-time students from foreign countries represent about 10% of enrollment. The college offers these students special counseling and special organizations.

Admissions: Applicants must score at least 425 on the TOEFL. No college entrance exams are required.

Procedure: Application deadlines are the same as those for American students. Foreign students must submit a completed medical form as proof of good health and show evidence of adequate funds for 1 year. There is a special $200 admission fee for foreign students. Health insurance is required, and is available through the college for a fee.

Admissions Contact: Nolan Nix, Registrar and Director of Admissions.

THE SAVANNAH COLLEGE OF ART AND DESIGN E-4
Savannah, Georgia 31401 (912) 236-7458
(Recognized Candidate for Accreditation)

F/T: 130M, 180W	Faculty: 34; n/av
P/T: 30M, 44W	Ph.D.'s: 86%
Grad: none	S/F Ratio: 9 to 1
Year: qtrs, ss	Tuition: $2320 ($2995)
Appl: Sept. 1	R and B: $1500
370 applied	123 accepted	113 enrolled
SAT: 530V 480M	ACT: 21	SPECIAL

The Savannah College of Art and Design, founded in 1978, is an independent undergraduate and professional school offering programs in fine and commercial art.

Environment: The 3-acre campus is located in the city of Savannah. On-campus apartments house 250 men and 250 women.

Student Life: About 38% of the students come from Georgia, and 64% are graduates of public schools. About 90% live on campus. Eleven percent are members of minority groups. Campus housing is single-sex, with visiting privileges. Students may keep cars on campus.

Organizations: The 9 extracurricular activities available to students include a film society, a travel club, and a chorale.

Sports: The college sponsors intercollegiate teams in 3 sports for men and 2 for women.

Handicapped: The entire campus is accessible to handicapped students. Special class scheduling can be arranged.

Graduates: About 10% of the freshmen drop out, and 70% remain to graduate. Virtually all of the graduates begin careers in business and industry.

Services: Free placement aid, career counseling, psychological counseling, and remedial instruction are provided. Fees are charged for health care and tutoring.

Programs of Study: The college awards the B.F.A. degree in FINE AND PERFORMING ARTS (art, film/photography, graphic design, historic preservation, illustration, interior design, painting, photography, studio art).

Required: Students must complete a core curriculum and maintain a 2.0 average to graduate.

Special: Students are given the opportunity to study abroad. Major programs are career-oriented.

Admissions: About 33% of those who applied were accepted for the 1981-82 freshman class. The SAT scores of those who enrolled were as follows: Verbal—20% below 500, 50% between 500 and 599, 28% between 600 and 700, and 2% above 700; Math—30% below 500, 50% between 500 and 599, 19% between 600 and 700, and 1% above 700. Applicants must be high school graduates with a GPA of 2.0 or better. Also considered are evidence of special talents, recommendations by school officials, advanced placement or honors courses, extracurricular activities, and personality.

Procedure: Applicants must take the SAT or the ACT. Application deadlines are September 1 (fall), December 1 (winter), March 1 (spring), and June 1 (summer). Admissions decisions are made on a rolling basis. The application fee is $25.

Special: AP and CLEP credit is accepted.

Transfer: For fall 1981, 56 transfer students applied, 32 were accepted, and all 32 enrolled. Transfers are accepted for all classes. Students must have a GPA of 2.0 or better and SAT scores of at least 450 on each part. Grades of C or better transfer. Students must complete in residence at least 90 of the 180 hours required for a bachelor's degree. Application deadlines are the same as those for freshmen.

Visiting: Informal visits may be arranged for any time when school is in session by contacting the dean of admissions. Guides are provided, and visitors may sit in on classes.

Financial Aid: Twenty percent of the students receive aid through the school; 10% work part-time on campus. Scholarships of $1000, loans of $2500, and work contracts of $2100 are available to freshmen; the average aid award is $1500. The college is a member of CSS, and students must file the FAF. Aid application deadlines are the same as those for admissions applications.

Foreign Students: The foreign students enrolled make up 3% of the student body.

Admissions: Students must take the TOEFL, the University of Michigan Language Test, or the Comprehensive English Language Test. The SAT or the ACT also is required.

Procedure: Application deadlines are the same as those for American students. Foreign applicants must present proof of adequate funds for 1 year. Health insurance, though not required, is available through the college for a fee.

Admissions Contact: May Poetter, Dean of Admissions.

SAVANNAH STATE COLLEGE E-4
Savannah, Georgia 31404 (912) 356-2181

F/T: 750M, 950W	Faculty: 135; IIA, av$
P/T: 150M, 150W	Ph.D.'s: n/av
Grad: 75M&W	S/F Ratio: 20 to 1
Year: qtrs, ss	Tuition: $756 ($1059)
Appl: see profile	R and B: $1455
2307 applied	1250 accepted	600 enrolled
SAT: 425V 400M		LESS COMPETITIVE

Savannah State College, founded in 1892, is a state-controlled college offering programs in arts and sciences, teacher education, and technological fields. The library contains more than 100,000 volumes and 175,000 microfilm items, and subscribes to 900 periodicals.

Environment: The 136-acre campus is located in the city of Savannah. The 43 buildings include residence halls for 390 men and 423 women. Accommodations for married students also are available. The campus also includes a student center, a stadium, and a laboratory nursery school and kindergarten.

Student Life: About 90% of the undergraduates are from the South. The student body is predominantly black. Half the students come from public schools. About half live on campus in the single-sex dorms. All out-of-town students must live in the residence halls as long as space is available.

Organizations: Six fraternities and 4 sororities have chapters on campus. Other student activities include drama, choir, marching and concert bands, publications, special-interest clubs, debate, public-affairs programs, lecture and concert series, and the student government association.

Sports: The college competes on an intercollegiate level in 7 sports. Eleven intramural sports also are offered.

Graduates: Forty percent of the graduates seek advanced degrees.

Services: Counseling, health care, and placement services are provided.

Programs of Study: The college confers the B.A., B.B.A., B.S., and B.S.W. degrees. Associate and master's degrees also are awarded. Bachelor's degrees are offered in the following subjects: BUSINESS (accounting, business administration, computer science, finance, management, marketing, office administration), ENGLISH (English, literature), FINE AND PERFORMING ARTS (music), MATH AND SCIENCES (biology, chemistry, ecology/environmental studies, mathematics, oceanography), PREPROFESSIONAL (dietetics and institutional management, engineering—civil engineering technology, engineering—electronics engineering technology, engineering—mechanical engineering technology, social work, textiles and clothing), SOCIAL SCIENCES (criminal justice, economics, government/political science, history, social sciences, sociology). Preprofessional programs are offered in medical technology, nursing, physical therapy, medical illustration, medical social work, engineering, law, medicine, veterinary medicine, dentistry, and pharmacy.

Required: All students must take physical education, 20 hours of humanities, 20 of mathematics and natural science, and 20 of social science. To graduate, students must demonstrate competency in English, pass a comprehensive exam in their major, and earn no grade below C in a prescribed number of courses.

Special: The college offers special workshops in driver education, journalism, and mathematics; science institutes; seminars in business; continuing education programs; and summer trial programs for students who do not qualify for regular admission. The college has a Special Studies Program for academically deficient students. The college cooperates with 2 other state-supported institutions in offering a general-education program. Students may participate in study-abroad programs sponsored by other institutions and in the Georgia Legislative Intern Program. Available minors include hotel management, restaurant management, real estate, mass communications, religion and philosophical studies, French, Spanish, German, art, electronics/physics, air traffic control, information systems, computer science, naval science, Black/Afro-American studies, child development, disadvantaged and handicapped families, and gerontology.

Honors: Four honor societies are represented on campus.

Admissions: About 54% of those who applied were accepted for the 1981–82 freshman class. Applicants must be graduates of accredited high schools and have completed at least 16 units of work with a GPA of 2.0 or better.

Procedure: The SAT is required. The application fee is $10. Students should apply as early as possible during the senior year, but no later than 20 days before the start of the term in which they wish to enroll.

Special: AP and CLEP credit is accepted. An early admissions plan is offered.

Transfer: Applicants must meet freshman entrance standards and have an average of C or better in college work. D grades do not transfer. Students must study at the college for at least 1 year and earn at least 185 quarter credits to receive a bachelor's degree.

Financial Aid: About 90% of the students receive aid. Programs include CWS, NDSL, SEOG, BEOG, guaranteed student loans, Pickett and Hatcher Educational Fund scholarships, and Law Enforcement Education Program loans and grants. The college will provide application information.

Foreign Students: The foreign students enrolled full-time make up about 10% of the student body. The college provides special counseling and special organizations for these students.

Admissions: Applicants must score 500 or better on the TOEFL. They also must take the SAT.

Procedure: Foreign students are admitted to all quarters and should submit applications at least 60 days before the start of the term in which they seek to enroll. Students must submit a completed health form and show evidence of adequate funds for 1 year. They also must arrange to carry health insurance.

Admission Contact: David E. Foye, Director of Admissions.

SHORTER COLLEGE
Rome, Georgia 30161

A-2
(404) 291-2121

F/T: 298M, 475W
P/T: 21M, 18W
Grad: none
Year: sems, ss
Appl: open
525 applied
SAT or ACT: required

Faculty: 50; n/av
Ph.D.'s: 60%
S/F Ratio: 15 to 1
Tuition: $2350
R and B: $1500

475 accepted
325 enrolled
COMPETITIVE

Shorter College is a privately endowed college affiliated with the Georgia Baptist Convention. The library houses more than 100,000 volumes and subscribes to 747 periodicals.

Environment: The campus is urban, located 2 miles from Rome's business center, and is within easy driving distance of Atlanta and Chattanooga (both 70 miles away). Its physical plant includes dormitory facilities and library and fine arts buildings.

Student Life: Eighty-five percent of the students are from Georgia. About 65% live in the residence halls. About 95% of the students are Protestants. Minority-group members comprise about 5% of the student body. Campus housing is single-sex; there are no visiting privileges. Students may keep cars on campus.

Organizations: There is a full range of activities, including 3 local fraternities and 3 local sororities to which 60% of the students belong.

Sports: The college fields 4 intercollegiate teams for men and 3 for women. Five intramural sports are offered for both men and women.

Graduates: The freshman dropout rate is 10%. About 60% remain to graduate, and 40% of the graduates pursue further study: 2% enter medical school, 2% dental school, and 5% law school. Fifteen percent of the graduates pursue careers in business or industry.

Services: The following services are offered at no charge to the student: placement, health care, psychological and career counseling, tutoring, and remedial instruction.

Programs of Study: The college confers the B.A., B., Church Mus., B.F.A., B.Mus., B.Mus.Ed., B.S. in Elem.Ed., and B.S.Med.Tech. degrees. Bachelor's degrees are offered in the following subjects: BUSINESS (accounting, business administration, finance, management, marketing), EDUCATION (early childhood, elementary, secondary), ENGLISH (English), FINE AND PERFORMING ARTS (art, art education, music, music education, radio/TV, studio art, theater/dramatics), HEALTH SCIENCES (medical technology), LANGUAGES (French, German, Italian, Spanish), MATH AND SCIENCES (biology, chemistry, earth science, ecology/environmental science, mathematics, natural sciences), PHILOSOPHY (philosophy, religion), PREPROFESSIONAL (dentistry, forestry, law, medicine, ministry, pharmacy, social work, veterinary), SOCIAL SCIENCES (economics, government/political science, history, psychology, recreation management, social sciences, sociology).

Required: The college requires satisfactory scores on the UAP area tests for graduation.

Special: A general studies degree is also available.

Admissions: Ninety percent of those who applied were accepted for the 1981–82 freshman class. A candidate must be a graduate of an accredited high school with a minimum of 16 units of credit and at least a 2.0 GPA. An applicant must also rank in the upper half of his/her high school class. Other important considerations are test scores, advanced placement or honors courses, recommendations by school officials, and evidence of special talent.

Procedure: The SAT or ACT is required and should be taken by December of the senior year. There are no application deadlines. A $10 application fee must be included. Admission is on a rolling basis.

Special: There are early and deferred admissions plans. CLEP general and subject exams receive credit.

Transfer: For fall 1981, 100 transfer students applied, 95 were accepted, and 84 enrolled. Transfers are accepted for all classes. Students must be eligible to return to their previous school. D grades transfer if the student's overall average is at least a C. Shorter has a 1-year residency requirement. The college also requires that 30 of the 128 semester hours required for the bachelor's degree be taken at Shorter. Transfer application deadlines are the same as those for freshman applicants.

Visiting: Regularly scheduled orientations are conducted for prospective students. Guides are available for informal visits to the campus. Visitors may attend classes and stay overnight on campus. For arrangements, the admissions office should be contacted.

Financial Aid: About 60% of all students receive aid. About 10% work part-time on campus. The average award to freshmen from all sources is $850. Students in the upper 15% of their high school class are awarded academic scholarships. Loans are available from the federal government (including NDSL), the state government, the college, and private sources. The college is a member of the CSS. The FAF or the FFS is required. Applications for aid are accepted throughout the year. Students also have the option of paying tuition in installments.

Foreign Students: One percent of the students come from foreign countries. There are special organizations for foreign students.

170 GEORGIA

Admissions: Foreign students are required to take the SAT and TOEFL.

Procedure: Admissions are on a rolling basis; foreign students may apply at any time for either the fall or spring semester. They must take a medical examination as proof of health. The college also requires proof of adequate funds to cover 1 academic year. Health insurance is included in the tuition.

Admissions Contact: Patricia Hart, Director of Admissions.

SOUTHERN TECHNICAL INSTITUTE   B–2
Marietta, Georgia 30060   (404) 424-7281

F/T: 1774M, 202W	Faculty: 97; IIB, ++$
P/T: 880M, 108W	Ph.D.'s: 38%
Grad: none	S/F Ratio: 20 to 1
Year: qtrs, ss	Tuition: $660 ($1710)
Appl: see profile	R and B: $1860
890 applied	682 accepted 452 enrolled
SAT: 400V 420M	LESS COMPETITIVE

Southern Technical Institute, part of the University System of Georgia, was founded in 1948. It is a 4-year technical college that offers majors in a variety of engineering technologies.

Environment: The 180-acre campus is located in a suburban area 15 miles from Atlanta. Dormitories accommodate 477 men and women.

Student Life: About 89% of the students come from Georgia. Fifteen percent live on campus. Eight percent are members of minority groups. Dormitories are single-sex, with visiting privileges. Students may keep cars on campus.

Organizations: About 11% of the men belong to the 7 national fraternities represented on campus, and 30% of the women belong to the 2 sororities, 1 local and 1 national. About 32 organizations, including a student newspaper, are available to students.

Sports: The institute fields teams in 4 intercollegiate sports for men. Three intramural activities are offered for both sexes.

Handicapped: Some of the campus is accessible to physically handicapped students. Facilities include wheelchair ramps and special parking areas.

Graduates: About 98% of the graduates begin careers in business and industry.

Services: The institute provides free placement aid, career counseling, health care, psychological counseling, and tutoring. Fees are charged for remedial instruction.

Programs of Study: The institute awards bachelor's and associate degrees in engineering technology. Bachelor's degrees are offered in apparel engineering technology, architectural engineering technology, civil engineering technology, electrical engineering technology, industrial engineering technology, mechanical engineering technology, and textile engineering technology.

Required: Students must complete a core curriculum and maintain a GPA of 2.0 or better to graduate.

Admissions: About 77% of those who applied were accepted for the 1981–82 freshman class. Applicants should be high school graduates with a GPA of 2.0 or better and satisfactory SAT scores.

Procedure: Applicants must take the SAT. New students are admitted to all 4 quarters, and applications must be submitted at least 20 working days before the start of the quarter in which the student wishes to enroll. There is no application fee. The institute uses a rolling admissions plan.

Special: Early decision and early admissions plans are offered. CLEP credit is accepted.

Transfer: For fall 1981, 790 transfer students applied, 511 were accepted, and 343 enrolled. Transfers are accepted for all classes. SAT scores of at least 300V and 320M are required; scores of at least 380V and 440M and a GPA of 2.0 or better are preferred. Grades of C or better transfer. Students must earn at least 45 credits in residence of the approximately 200 required for a bachelor's degree. Application deadlines are the same as those for freshmen.

Visiting: Prospective students may schedule visits with the director of admissions for a time when classes are in session. Guides are provided, and visitors may sit in on some classes.

Financial Aid: About 25% of the students receive aid through the institute; 3% work part-time on campus. Scholarships averaging $750, loans averaging $900, and work contracts averaging $900 (but going up to $4000) are available to freshmen; the average award from all sources is $1800. The institute is a member of the CSS and requires students to file the FAF. The aid application deadline for all terms is April 1.

Foreign Students: The foreign students at the institute make up nearly 5% of enrollment. The institute provides special organizations for these students.

Admissions: Applicants must score at least 500 on the TOEFL. They also must take the SAT.

Procedure: Students are admitted to all 4 quarters; applications must be filed at least 60 working days before registration. Students must present proof of adequate funds for 1 year and arrange for health insurance.

Admissions Contact: Gini Smith, Director of Admissions.

SPELMAN COLLEGE   B–2
Atlanta, Georgia 30314   (404) 681-3643

F/T: 1450W	Faculty: 101; IIB, av$
P/T: n/av	Ph.D.'s: 53%
Grad: none	S/F Ratio: 14 to 1
Year: sems	Tuition: $2950
Appl: Mar. 1	R and B: $2035
1108 applied	819 accepted 458 enrolled
SAT or ACT: required	COMPETITIVE

Spelman College, established in 1881, is a private liberal arts college for women. The library contains over 41,000 volumes and subscribes to about 250 periodicals. Spelman students also use the Atlanta University library, which has 250,000 volumes and a microfilm depository.

Environment: The campus has an urban setting. The college is a member of the Atlanta University Center and therefore shares facilities and resources with 6 other institutions in the Atlanta area. Dormitory facilities are available for 850 women. The college also sponsors off-campus housing.

Student Life: Twenty-six percent of the students come from Georgia. Over 50% of the students reside on campus. All students are black. Campus housing is single-sex; there are visiting privileges. The college provides day-care services to students, faculty, and staff for a fee.

Organizations: All students belong to the student government. Extracurricular activities include newspaper, yearbook, radio, dance, drama, and orchestra. Social events are arranged with the 5 other colleges of the Atlanta University Center.

Sports: The college fields 3 intercollegiate teams and offers 10 intramural sports.

Graduates: The freshman dropout rate is 10%; about 70% remain to graduate. Of the most recent graduating class, 14% entered medical or dental schools and 5% entered law schools.

Services: Students receive the following services free of charge from the college: health care, career and psychological counseling, placement, tutoring, and remedial instruction.

Programs of Study: The college confers the B.A., B.S., and B.S.E. degrees. Bachelor's degrees are offered in the following subjects: AREA STUDIES (urban, urban/environmental), BUSINESS (computer science), EDUCATION (early childhood, elementary, health/physical, reading, secondary, special), ENGLISH (English, journalism), FINE AND PERFORMING ARTS (art, art education, music, theater/dramatics), LANGUAGES (French, German, Spanish), MATH AND SCIENCES (biochemistry, biology, chemistry, mathematics, nutrition, physics), PHILOSOPHY (philosophy, religion), PREPROFESSIONAL (medicine), SOCIAL SCIENCES (economics, government/political science, history, psychology, social sciences, sociology).

Required: All students must take courses in English composition, reading, mathematics, and foreign language unless exempted by placement examinations.

Special: Special academic programs include an accelerated program, cooperative education, and independent study. A 3-2 liberal arts and engineering degree is offered in combination with Georgia Institute of Technology or Boston University. A dual degree program in engineering is also available in combination with Atlanta University. Through the Atlanta University Consortium students may take courses not available at Spelman.

Honors: Honors programs are available.

Admissions: About 74% of those who applied were accepted for the 1981–82 freshman class. Applicants should have a 2.0 GPA. SAT or ACT scores, advanced placement or honors courses, recommendations by high school officials, extracurricular activities, and leadership record are considered important.

Procedure: The SAT or ACT is required; tests should be taken in October, November, or December of the senior year and no later than January for fall entry. All credentials should be filed by March 1 for the fall semester and by November 15 for the spring semester. There is a rolling admissions plan. The $20 application fee may be waived for applicants with financial need.

Special: There is a deferred admissions plan. CLEP general and subject exams are accepted. Students may also earn credit through AP exams.

Transfer: For fall 1981, 162 transfer students applied, 99 were accepted, and 57 enrolled. Transfers are accepted for all classes; D grades are not accepted. Applicants must present a 2.0 GPA and a recommendation from the dean of the former institution. Students must study at Spelman for at least 1 year to receive a degree. They must also take 30 of the 124 credit hours required for the bachelor's degree at Spelman. Transfer application deadlines are March 1 for the fall and November 1 for the spring.

Visiting: Guided tours and interviews can be scheduled through the admissions office.

Financial Aid: About 22% of all students receive financial aid from the college itself. Twenty-five percent work part-time on campus. The average aid to freshmen from all sources is $2053. The college is a member of the CSS. The FAF and Spelman College Application for Financial Aid are required. The deadlines for aid application are April 1 for fall and November 1 for spring.

Foreign Students: Two percent of the students come from foreign countries. Special counseling and special organizations for foreign students are available.

Admissions: Foreign students are required to take the TOEFL. No other exams are required.

Procedure: Application deadlines are March 1 for fall entry and November 1 for spring entry. Foreign applicants must present proof of health. They must also present proof of adequate funds each year for 4 years and maintain a $1000 deposit in the school account. Foreign students are not required to carry health insurance, but it is available through the college for a fee.

Admissions Contact: Juanita W. Wallace, Director of Admissions.

TIFT COLLEGE B-3
Forsyth, Georgia 31029 (912) 994-6594

F/T: 400W Faculty: 36; IIB, +$
P/T: n/av Ph.D.'s: 50%
Grad: none S/F Ratio: 15 to 1
Year: qtrs, ss Tuition: $2325
Appl: open R and B: $1995
278 applied 255 accepted 115 enrolled
SAT: 890 V&M LESS COMPETITIVE

Tift College, founded in 1847, is a private liberal arts college for women affiliated with the Georgia Baptist Convention. The library contains 59,000 volumes and subscribes to 460 periodicals.

Environment: The college's 275-acre campus is in a rural environment 20 miles from Macon. The physical plant includes a 3-story academic building, an auditorium, and 5 dormitories to accommodate 400 women. Ponder Hall, a pre-Civil War structure, was recently restored and houses the departments of Education and Natural Sciences.

Student Life: Sixty-five percent of the students are from Georgia. Seventy-five percent reside on campus. Ninety-five percent of the students are Protestant, 1% are Catholic. All students must attend chapel services once a month. There is a dormitory curfew of midnight on weeknights and 2 A.M. on weekends. Ten percent of the students are minority-group members. Campus housing is single-sex; there are visiting privileges. Students may keep cars on campus.

Organizations: Student organizations include departmental clubs, religious groups, and publications. There are no sororities. Only 60 miles away, the city of Atlanta offers numerous cultural and recreational opportunities.

Sports: Three intercollegiate sports and 5 intramural sports are offered.

Handicapped: The college estimates the campus to be 20% accessible to the physically handicapped student, with a limited number of wheelchair ramps available. No students with visual or hearing impairments are currently enrolled.

Graduates: The freshman dropout rate is 15%; 50% remain to graduate. Of the latter, 35% pursue graduate study. Forty percent of each graduating class enter business and industry.

Services: The following services are available on campus: placement, health care, tutoring, remedial instruction, and career and psychological counseling.

Programs of Study: The college confers the B.A. and B.S. degrees. Bachelor's degrees are offered in the following subjects: BUSINESS (business administration), EDUCATION (early childhood, elementary, health/physical, secondary, special), ENGLISH (English, journalism), FINE AND PERFORMING ARTS (art, music, music education, theater/dramatics), LANGUAGES (Spanish), MATH AND SCIENCES (biology, chemistry, mathematics), PHILOSOPHY (religion), PREPROFESSIONAL (dentistry, law, medicine, pharmacy, social work), SOCIAL SCIENCES (history, psychology, social sciences).

Required: All students are required to take courses in English, religious studies, mathematics-science, and history.

Special: A general studies degree program is offered. Students may arrange to study abroad for 1 year.

Honors: There are honor societies and an honor council on campus.

Admissions: Ninety-two percent of those who applied were accepted for the 1981–82 freshman class. Their average combined SAT score was 890. On both the Verbal and Math parts of the SAT, 80% scored below 500, and 20% scored between 500 and 599. Applicants must be graduates of accredited high schools with a C average and 16 Carnegie units. Other factors entering into an admissions decision are recommendations by school officials, impressions made during an interview, and advanced placement or honors courses.

Procedure: The SAT or the ACT is required. Application deadlines are 10 days prior to the start of the quarter. Freshmen may enter in any quarter. There is a $10 application fee. A rolling admissions plan is used.

Special: An early admissions plan is available; application deadlines are the same as for regular admission. Early decision and deferred admissions plans are also available. The CLEP general exam is acceptable; students can also earn credit with AP exams.

Transfer: For fall 1981, 47 transfer students applied, 45 were accepted, and 35 enrolled. Transfers are accepted for all classes. Good standing at the previous institution is required. A minimum GPA of 2.0 is required. C and higher grades transfer. Tift has a residency requirement of 45 quarter hours, out of a total of 190 quarter hours required for the bachelor's degree. Transfers are admitted to all quarters. Transfer application deadlines are the same as those for freshmen.

Visiting: Guides are available for informal visits to the campus. Prospective applicants may sit in on classes and stay overnight at the school, or may participate in one of the regularly scheduled orientations held each quarter. For further information, the Admissions Office should be contacted.

Financial Aid: About 85% of all students receive aid. About 75% work part-time on campus. The college provides scholarships, loans, and campus employment. The college is a member of CSS. Application for aid must include the FAF. There are no deadlines for aid application.

Foreign Students: Presently there are no foreign students at Tift.

Admissions: The TOEFL is required; a minimum score of 500 is necessary. The SAT or ACT is also required; the minimum composite score for the SAT is 700, for the ACT, 14.

Procedure: Foreign applicants should submit their applications 10 days prior to the beginning of the quarter. A physical examination is required. A special deposit and proof of adequate funds to cover 1 year are also necessary.

Admissions Contact: Adele West, Director of Admissions.

TOCCOA FALLS COLLEGE C-1
Toccoa Falls, Georgia 30598 (404) 886-6831
(Recognized Candidate for Accreditation)

F/T: 300M, 270W Faculty: 36; IV, --$
P/T: 24M, 67W Ph.D.'s: 28%
Grad: none S/F Ratio: 16 to 1
Year: 4-1-4, ss Tuition: $1135
Appl: open R and B: $840
459 applied 350 accepted 303 enrolled
SAT: 400V 400M ACT: 18 LESS COMPETITIVE

Toccoa Falls College, an independent Bible college founded in 1907, offers undergraduate programs in theology, education, general studies, and music.

Environment: The 1100-acre campus is located in a rural area about 100 miles from Atlanta. Dormitories, on-campus apartments, and married-student housing accommodate 220 men and 250 women.

Student Life: About 15% of the students come from Georgia, and 60% are graduates of public schools. About 80% live on campus. Five percent are members of minority groups. All are Protestant. Dormitories are single-sex, and students may keep cars on campus.

Organizations: The 15 student organizations include a student senate, a foreign missions fellowship, a married-students' association, and a student wives' fellowship.

Sports: The college fields intercollegiate teams in 4 sports for men and 3 for women. Five intramural sports are offered for men and women.

Handicapped: Special parking is provided for handicapped students. Special class scheduling also can be arranged, and 1 special counselor is available.

Graduates: About 25% of the freshmen drop out by the end of their first year, and 50% remain to graduate. About half of the graduates seek advanced degrees, and 10% begin careers in business and industry.

Services: The following services are provided free to students: placement aid, career counseling, health care, psychological counseling, tutoring, and remedial instruction.

Programs of Study: The college awards the B.A., B.S., and B.Th. degrees. Associate degrees also are available. Bachelor's degrees are offered in the following subjects: EDUCATION (early childhood, middle grades), FINE AND PERFORMING ARTS (music, music education), PHILOSOPHY (religion—counseling, religion—humanities, religion—pastoral ministries), SOCIAL SCIENCES (missiology).

Required: Students must complete a core curriculum and take 30 credits in Bible/Theology and Christian service.

Special: A general-studies degree is available.

Admissions: About 76% of the applicants for the 1981–82 freshman class were accepted. Applicants must be high school graduates with averages of 1.6 or better. Other factors considered include test scores, impressions made during an interview, leadership record, recommendations by school officials, and personality.

Procedure: Applicants must take the SAT or ACT. Application deadlines are open; students are admitted in fall, winter, and spring. Admissions decisions are made on a rolling basis. The application fee is $20.

Special: Early admissions, early decision, and deferred admissions programs are available. CLEP and AP credit is accepted.

Transfer: Transfer students are accepted for all classes. Applicants should have at least a 2.2 GPA and either SAT scores of 800 or better or an ACT composite of 18. Christian testimony and 3 personal references are required. Students must earn at least 30 credits in residence of the 130 required for a bachelor's degree.

Visiting: Guides are provided for informal visits by prospective students. Visitors may sit in on classes and remain overnight at the school. Visits should be arranged through the admissions office for Monday through Friday, 9 A.M. to 5 P.M.

Financial Aid: About 75% of the students receive aid through the college; 40% work part-time on campus. The college is a member of CSS, and aid applicants must submit the FAF, FFS, or SFS by August 15 (fall) or January 15 (spring).

Foreign Students: The foreign students at the college make up about 1% of enrollment. The college offers these students special counseling.

Admissions: Applicants must score at least 500 on the TOEFL. No college entrance exams are required.

Procedure: Application deadlines are open; students are admitted in fall and spring. Students must present proof of adequate funds for 1 year and must carry health insurance.

Admissions Contact: D. Murry Evans, Admissions Counselor.

UNIVERSITY OF GEORGIA
Athens, Georgia 30602

C-2
(404) 542-2112

F/T: 8120M, 8640W
P/T: 1579M, 1489W
Grad: 3126M, 2708W
Year: qtrs, ss
Appl: see profile
7494 applied   5906 accepted   3449 enrolled
SAT: 470V 521M
Faculty: 1418; I, +$
Ph.D.'s: 78%
S/F Ratio: 12 to 1
Tuition: $954 ($2433)
R and B: $1716
COMPETITIVE

The University of Georgia, a state-supported institution founded in 1785, offers undergraduate and graduate degrees through the colleges of Arts and Sciences, Agriculture, Education, Business Administration, Home Economics, and Veterinary Medicine; the schools of Law, Forest Resources, Journalism and Mass Communications, Pharmacy, Social Work, and Environmental Design; and the Graduate School. Three libraries contain a total of 2,062,499 books and 2,040,318 microforms, and subscribe to 12,946 periodicals.

Environment: The 3500-acre campus is located in Athens, a city of 60,000 people about 70 miles from Atlanta. A suburban environment surrounds the campus. The North Campus is the older section of the university, distinguished by traditional architecture; the South Campus houses most of the newer buildings. A six-building Science Center contains biology, chemistry, physics, geography and geology, food-science, and animal-science laboratories. Seventeen residence halls, including 2 for graduate students, accommodate 6300 men and women. Other living facilities include housing for married students and fraternity and sorority houses.

Student Life: Most students are Georgia residents, and 94% are from the South. About 85% of the freshmen are graduates of public schools. About 33% of the undergraduates live on campus. Fifty-one percent are Protestant, 11% are Catholic, and 4% are Jewish. About 6% are members of various minority groups. Campus housing is both single-sex and coed; there are visiting privileges in the single-sex housing. Students may keep cars on campus.

Organizations: About a fourth of the students belong to one of the 30 national fraternities or 16 national sororities on campus. Extracurricular activities include choral and instrumental music groups, the University Theatre, art exhibits, debates, a student newspaper, an FM radio station, religious organizations for most major faiths, special-interest clubs, and student government.

Sports: The university fields intercollegiate teams in 11 sports for men and 10 for women. There are 24 intramural sports for men and 23 for women.

Handicapped: Special facilities for physically handicapped students include wheelchair ramps, special parking areas, elevators, specially equipped rest rooms, and special transportation. Special class scheduling and counseling also are available. Fewer than 1% of the students have impaired vision or hearing.

Graduates: About 22% of the freshmen drop out, and 56% remain to graduate. About 35% of the graduates pursue advanced degrees, including 2% who enter medical school, 1% who enter dental school, and 3% who enter law school. Twenty-five percent of the graduates begin careers in business and industry.

Services: Placement, career counseling, tutoring, remedial instruction, and some health care and psychological counseling are provided free of charge. Extensive health care and psychological counseling are available for a fee.

Programs of Study: The university awards these undergraduate degrees: A.B., B.S., B.B.A., A.B.J., B.S.A., B.S.A.E., B.F.A., B.S.Ed., B.S.Chem., B.S.H.E., B.Mus., B.S.F.R., B.S.E.H., B.L.A., B.S.Phar., B.S.W., and B.S.Pcs. degrees. Master's and doctoral degrees also are available. Bachelor's degrees are offered in the following subjects: AREA STUDIES (Black/Afro-American, French, German, global, Latin American, Medieval, women's), BUSINESS (accounting, advertising, agricultural economics, business administration, business administration/industrial geography, business education, business systems, computer science, finance, industrial relations, international business, management, marketing, real estate/insurance), EDUCATION (agricultural, agricultural extension, distributive, early childhood, elementary, health/physical, industrial, recreation and leisure studies, secondary, special/mental retardation), ENGLISH (English, journalism, literature, speech), FINE AND PERFORMING ARTS (art, art education, dance education, music, music education, film/photography, radio/TV, studio art, theater/dramatics), HEALTH SCIENCES (environmental health, speech pathology/audiology), LANGUAGES (French, German, Greek/Latin, Spanish), MATH AND SCIENCES (agricultural technology, agronomy, animal science, biochemistry, biology, botany, chemistry, dairy science, entomology, food science, genetics, geology, horticulture, mathematics, microbiology, physical sciences, physics, poultry science, statistics, zoology), PHILOSOPHY (classics, philosophy, religion), PREPROFESSIONAL (agriculture, agricultural engineering, dentistry, engineering, forestry, home economics, landscape architecture, law, medicine, ministry, pharmacy, social work, veterinary), SOCIAL SCIENCES (anthropology, criminal justice, economics, geography, government/political science, history, international relations, psychology, public relations, social sciences, sociology). About 21% of the undergraduate degrees are conferred in business and 15% in education.

Required: All students must take courses in physical education and English.

Special: Five-year combined B.A.-B.S. degrees may be earned in all areas. Students with SAT scores totaling 1300 or above may earn combined bachelor's and master's degrees in four years. A 5-year B.S. in engineering is offered in conjunction with the Georgia Institute of Technology. Students may design their own majors or pursue a general studies degree. The College of Agriculture offers work-study programs. The university provides opportunities for study abroad.

Honors: A number of national honor societies have chapters on campus. Honors programs of various types are offered by the colleges and schools of arts and sciences, agriculture, business administration, education, environmental design, forest resources, home economics, journalism, pharmacy, and veterinary medicine.

Admissions: About 79% of the applicants for the freshman class of 1981-82 were accepted. The SAT scores of those who enrolled were: Verbal—62% below 500, 30% between 500 and 599, 7% between 600 and 700, and 1% above 700; Math—39% below 500, 45% between 500 and 599, 14% between 600 and 700, and 2% above 700. Applicants must have completed at least 16 Carnegie units. Both high school GPA and SAT scores are important criteria in the admissions decision, but there are no cutoffs.

Procedure: All applicants must take the SAT. Students who have studied a foreign language for 2 years or more must take the appropriate AT. Applications must be submitted at least 20 days before the first day of classes each quarter; the freshman class, however, usually is filled by May 1. Freshmen are admitted to all quarters. Admissions decisions are made on a rolling basis. The application fee is $15.

Special: Early and deferred admissions plans are available. Students may earn credit with CLEP and AP exams and ATs.

Transfer: For fall 1981, 3879 transfer students applied, 2950 were accepted, and 2052 enrolled. Transfers are accepted for all classes. Applicants should present an average of 2.0 or better (2.9 for business) to be assured of admission. They also must be in good standing at their previous school. A limited number of D grades transfer, and no more than 105 quarter hours from a junior college or 150 from a four-year college will be accepted. Students must earn at least 90 quarter hours at the university to graduate, out of a total of 195 quarter hours required for the bachelor's degree. Transfer students are admitted to all quarters. Application deadlines are the same as those for freshmen. The fall deadline is August 25.

Visiting: Prospective students may arrange weekday tours by contacting the admissions office. Visitors may sit in on classes.

Financial Aid: About 41% of the students receive aid. Twenty-six percent work part-time on campus. The average award to freshmen is $1700. Scholarships, grants, loans, and part-time jobs are awarded singly or in packages. Some gift scholarships are available, most only to Georgia residents. Interested students should contact the college or academic department in which they wish to study. The university is a CSS member. The FAF should be filed by April 1 (fall), November 1 (winter), or February 1 (spring).

Foreign Students: About 4% of the students come from foreign countries. The university offers an intensive English course and special counseling, and there are organizations on campus especially for foreign students.

Admissions: The TOEFL is required; 500 is the minimum score for consideration. The SAT is also required. An AT is only required if the student is planning to study a language other than his or her native language.

Procedure: Applications are due 20 days prior to the first day of classes each quarter. A certificate of health and immunizations is required. Proof of adequate funds to cover each year of study must be shown. Health insurance is required; it is available through the university for a fee.

Admissions Contact: M. O. Phelps, Director of Admissions.

VALDOSTA STATE COLLEGE C-5
Valdosta, Georgia 31601 (912) 247-3233

F/T: 1200M, 1700W Faculty: 240; IIA, av$
P/T: 500M, 700W Ph.D.'s: 50%
Grad: 75M, 125W S/F Ratio: 15 to 1
Year: qtrs, ss Tuition: $680 ($1625)
Appl: see profile R and B: $1500
2000 applied 1650 accepted 950 enrolled
SAT: 430V 420M LESS COMPETITIVE

Valdosta State College, a state-supported institution founded in 1906, offers undergraduate and graduate programs in the arts and sciences, education, business, nursing, and fine arts. Its library holds 200,000 books and 300,000 microfilm items, and subscribes to 2000 periodicals.

GEORGIA 173

Environment: The 141-acre campus, located in a suburban area a half-mile from Valdosta, has residence halls and apartments that house 1158 women and 638 men.

Student Life: About 90% of the students come from Georgia, and 33% live in campus housing, which is single-sex.

Organizations: Fourteen fraternities and 12 sororities have chapters on campus. Extracurricular activities include special-interest clubs, publications, student government, entertainment planned by the student union board, and programs sponsored by off-campus religious groups.

Sports: The college fields intercollegiate teams in 6 sports for men and 3 for women. Intramural sports also are available for both sexes.

Handicapped: The entire campus is accessible to physically handicapped students. Facilities include wheelchair ramps, special parking, elevators, and specially equipped rest rooms. One special counselor is available.

Graduates: Ten percent of the graduates go on for further study, including 1% who enter medical school. Eighty percent pursue careers in industry or business.

Services: Psychological counseling, tutoring, remedial instruction, and placement and career counseling are offered free to students. Placement services also are available to graduates.

Programs of Study: The college awards the B.A., B.S., B.B.A., B.S.Ed., B.S.C.J., B.Mus., B.F.A.; and B.S.N. degrees. Associate and master's programs also are available. Bachelor's degrees are offered in the following subjects: AREA STUDIES (American), BUSINESS (accounting, business education, finance, management, marketing, secretarial administration), EDUCATION (early childhood, elementary, health/physical, industrial, secondary, special), ENGLISH (English, speech), FINE AND PERFORMING ARTS (art, art education, music, music education, theater/dramatics), HEALTH SCIENCES (nursing), LANGUAGES (French, Spanish), MATH AND SCIENCES (applied mathematics, astronomy, biology, chemistry, mathematics, physics), PHILOSOPHY (philosophy), SOCIAL SCIENCES (anthropology, criminal justice, economics, government/political science, history, psychology, social sciences, sociology).

Required: All students must take courses in English, mathematics, a laboratory science, health, and the history and constitutions of the United States and Georgia.

Special: Independent study and study abroad are available. Five-year dual degrees in areas such as engineering and industrial management are offered in conjunction with Georgia Institute of Technology. Preprofessional preparation is available in law, medicine, dentistry, veterinary medicine, ministry, and other professional fields.

Honors: Six honor societies are represented on campus. The English department and the speech and drama department offer honors programs.

Admissions: About 82% of those who applied were accepted for the 1981-82 freshman class. Sixty-five percent of those who enrolled ranked in the upper fifth of their high school class, and 85% ranked in the upper two-fifths. Applicants must have completed 16 high school units.

Procedure: The SAT is required and should be taken between March of the junior year and July of the senior year. New students are admitted each quarter; applications should be filed at least 20 days before registration. There is a $10 application fee.

Special: CLEP credit is accepted. An early admissions plan is available.

Transfer: D grades may transfer as long as the student's GPA stays at 2.0 or better. Students must earn at least 45 quarter hours in residence of the 183 or more required for a bachelor's degree. Preference is given to students transferring from other Georgia colleges.

Visiting: An Open Campus Day is held every February. Prospective students also may contact the admissions office to schedule informal visits. Visitors may sit in on classes and spend a night in the residence halls, and guides are provided. Visits are best scheduled for Saturday mornings.

Financial Aid: About 45% of the students receive aid. State scholarships, CWS jobs, NDSL, and EOG are available. The FAF should be filed by April 15.

Foreign Students: Foreign students make up less than 1% of the student body. The college offers these students special counseling.

Admissions: Applicants must take the TOEFL and the SAT. A minimum score of 500 is required on the TOEFL.

174 GEORGIA

Procedure: Application deadlines are the same as those for American students. Foreign students must present a completed medical form and show evidence of adequate funds for 1 year.

Admissions Contact: Gary L. Bass, Director of Admissions.

WESLEYAN COLLEGE C–3
Macon, Georgia 31297 (912) 477-0115

F/T: 318W		Faculty:	42; IIB, –$
P/T: 74W		Ph.D.'s:	48%
Grad: none		S/F Ratio:	9 to 1
Year: sems + May term, ss		Tuition:	$2920 ($3720)
Appl: open		R and B:	$1800
273 applied	223 accepted		85 enrolled
SAT: 483V 498M	ACT: 26		COMPETITIVE+

Wesleyan College was founded in 1836. It is privately endowed and affiliated with the United Methodist Church. The library contains 113,000 volumes and 5000 microfilm items, and subscribes to 560 periodicals.

Environment: The 240-acre suburban campus, which is 75 miles from Atlanta, contains 17 buildings of Georgian architecture, including dormitory facilities to accommodate 500 women.

Student Life: Fifty percent of the student body is from Georgia. Sixty-four percent of the students reside on campus. Fifteen percent are minority-group members. Seventy-two percent are Protestant; 13% are Catholic. Campus housing is single-sex; there are visiting privileges. Day-care services are available to all students for a fee. Students may keep cars on campus.

Organizations: There are no sororities on campus. Among the extracurricular activities offered are special interest groups and publications, including a biweekly newspaper and a quarterly literary magazine. Also available on campus are a lake for boating, woodland jogging trails, and tennis courts.

Sports: The college fields 2 intercollegiate teams. There are 8 intramural sports.

Handicapped: There are no special facilities or counselors for handicapped students. Currently, there are no students with visual or hearing impairments enrolled.

Graduates: The freshman dropout rate is 28%. Of the graduates, about 22% enter graduate study: 2% enter medical school, 2% dental school, and 4% law school. Ten percent of the graduates pursue careers in business or industry.

Services: Students are offered the following services free of charge: psychological counseling, placement, and career counseling. Tutoring and health care are available for a fee.

Programs of Study: The college confers the B.A., B.B.A., B.S.Med. Tech., B.F.A., and B.Mus. degrees. Bachelor's degrees are offered in the following subjects: AREA STUDIES (American), BUSINESS (accounting, business administration, management, marketing), EDUCATION (early childhood, elementary, health/physical, secondary, special), ENGLISH (English, speech/communications), FINE AND PERFORMING ARTS (art, art education, music, music education, studio art, theater/dramatics), HEALTH SCIENCES (medical technology), LANGUAGES (French, Spanish), MATH AND SCIENCES (biology, chemistry, mathematics), PHILOSOPHY (philosophy, religion), PRE-PROFESSIONAL (dentistry, law, medicine, social work, veterinary), SOCIAL SCIENCES (government/political science, history, international relations, psychology, sociology). Of the degrees conferred, 20% are in business, 20% in education, and 20% in social sciences.

Required: Students are required to take 10 basic education courses, 2 from each of the following divisions of the college: fine arts, natural sciences, humanities, and social sciences. Candidates for the B.F.A. degree must meet additional general requirements.

Special: The college has a medical technology program with field studies in all areas. Students may study abroad, but they do so independently. An internship program is offered in all fields.

Honors: There are 9 national honor societies with chapters on campus.

Admissions: Eighty-two percent of those who applied were accepted for the 1981–82 freshman class. In a recent freshman class, the SAT scores were as follows: Verbal—25% scored between 500 and 599, 12% between 600 and 700, and 3% over 700; Math—30% scored between 500 and 599, and 10% between 600 and 700. The college recommends that candidates complete 12 Carnegie units at an accredited high school. Other important considerations are the grade average (minimum, 2.0), class rank (applicants should rank in the top half of their high school class), advanced placement or honors courses, and recommendations by school officials.

Procedure: Either the ACT or the SAT is required and should be taken between March of the junior year and May of the senior year. The college uses the rolling admissions plan. There is a $15 application fee.

Special: Students may be considered for early admission or deferred admission. AP and CLEP credit is available.

Transfer: In 1981–82, 48 students applied, 38 were accepted, and 17 enrolled. Good academic standing, an interview, and a 2.0 average are necessary. D grades do not transfer. Applicants for a major in applied music must pass a placement exam. All students must complete, at the college, the last 30 of the 120 credits required for a bachelor's degree.

Visiting: A regularly scheduled orientation conducted by the college includes tours, class visits, a financial aid presentation, and a night in the dorm. Guides are available for informal visits to the campus during the week. Visitors may attend classes and stay at the school. To make arrangements, the admissions office should be contacted.

Financial Aid: About 77% of all students receive aid. Nineteen percent work part-time on campus. The average aid to freshmen from all sources is $3000. Tuition may be paid in installments. The college is a member of the CSS. The FAF and Institutional Application are required. Deadlines for aid applications are April 1 (fall), September 15 (spring), and March 15 (summer).

Foreign Students: Five percent of the full-time students come from foreign countries. There are special organizations available to these students.

Admissions: Foreign students must achieve a TOEFL score of at least 500. No college entrance exams are required.

Procedure: Foreign students are admitted for the fall and spring terms. They must present proof of health and proof of funds. They must also carry health insurance, which is available through the college for a fee. There are no application deadlines.

Admissions Contact: Herbert C. Mudie, Dean of Admissions.

WEST GEORGIA COLLEGE A–2
Carrollton, Georgia 30118 (404) 834-1290

F/T: 1773M, 2097W		Faculty:	237; IIA, av$
P/T: 339M, 392W		Ph.D.'s:	64%
Grad: 255M, 768W		S/F Ratio:	16 to 1
Year: qtrs, ss		Tuition:	$750 ($1800)
Appl: Sept. 1		R and B:	$1416
2690 applied	2071 accepted		1498 enrolled
SAT: 372V 399M			LESS COMPETITIVE

West Georgia College, established in 1933, is a state-supported institution that offers graduate and undergraduate instruction in liberal arts and sciences, business, and education. The library contains 250,700 books and 635,000 microfilm items, and subscribes to 1500 periodicals.

Environment: The 398-acre campus is located in a town of 16,000 people, about 50 miles from Atlanta. A rural environment surrounds the campus. The college has more than 30 buildings, including dormitories that house 1700 men and women.

Student Life: Almost all students are from the South, and most are from Georgia. About 89% of the freshmen are graduates of public schools. Fifty percent of the students live on campus; freshmen and sophomores must do so unless they live at home. About 15% are members of various minority groups. Campus housing is both single-sex and coed; there are visiting privileges in the single-sex dorms. Cars are permitted on campus. Day-care services are available to all students, faculty, and staff for a fee.

Organizations: About 23% of the students belong to one of 11 fraternities, and 17% of the women belong to one of 8 sororities. Campus activities include student government, a weekly newspaper, drama, religious groups, a choir, a debating club, and a campus radio station.

Sports: The college participates in 8 intercollegiate sports for men and 6 for women. There are 10 intramural teams for men and 10 for women.

Handicapped: About 75% of the campus is accessible to wheelchair-bound students. Special facilities include ramps, special parking areas, elevators, specially equipped rest rooms, and special class scheduling. Fewer than 1% of the students have impaired vision or hearing.

Services: Students may obtain free psychological and career counseling, placement, and tutoring. Health care and remedial instruction are available for a fee.

Programs of Study: The college awards the B.A., B.S., B.M., B.B.A., and B.S.Ed. degrees. Associate and master's programs also are available. Bachelor's degrees are offered in the following subjects: BUSINESS (accounting, business administration, business education, computer science, economics, finance, management, marketing), EDUCATION (early childhood, elementary, health/physical, middle grades, secondary, special), ENGLISH (English, speech), FINE AND PERFORMING ARTS (art, art education, music, music education, studio art, theater/dramatics), LANGUAGES (French, German, Spanish), MATH AND SCIENCES (biology, earth science, geology, mathematics, physics), PHILOSOPHY (philosophy), PREPROFESSIONAL (agriculture, dentistry, engineering, forestry, law, library science, medicine, pharmacy, social work, veterinary), SOCIAL SCIENCES (anthropology, economics, geography, government/political science, history, psychology, social sciences, sociology). About 27% of the undergraduate degrees are conferred in business, 23% in social sciences, and 19% in education.

Required: Students must take 20 quarter hours of humanities, science and mathematics, and social sciences.

Special: Study abroad and interdisciplinary courses are offered.

Honors: Eleven national honor societies are represented on campus. All departments offer honors programs.

Admissions: About 77% of the applicants for the 1981-82 freshman class were accepted. The SAT scores of those who enrolled were: Verbal—91% below 500, 8% between 500 and 599, 1% between 600 and 700, and 0% above 700; Math—85% below 500, 13% between 500 and 599, 2% between 600 and 700, and 0% above 700. Applicants must have completed 18 units of high school work with a GPA of 2.5 or better. Admissions officers also consider advanced placement or honors courses and recommendations by high school officials.

Procedure: The SAT is required. The application deadline for the fall is September 1; deadlines are open for all other quarters. Applicants are notified on a rolling basis. The application fee is $10.

Special: An early admissions plan is available. CLEP and AP credit is accepted.

Transfer: For fall 1981, 683 transfer students applied, 525 were accepted, and 332 enrolled. Transfer students are accepted for all classes. A minimum GPA of 1.8 and 30 completed credit hours are required. C and better grades transfer. Transfer students must take at least 50 quarter hours in residence to graduate (190 credits are required to earn the bachelor's degree). Preference is given to students transferring within the state. Transfers are admitted to all quarters. Application deadlines are the same as those for freshmen.

Visiting: Orientations for prospective students are scheduled at the start of each quarter. Students also can arrange informal visits, preferably on weekdays before 3 P.M., by contacting the admissions office. Guides are provided, and visitors may sit in on classes. Prospective students may spend a night in the dormitories.

Financial Aid: About 41% of the students receive aid. Fourteen percent work part-time on campus. The average award to freshmen is $1526. The college provides scholarships, grants, loans, and part-time jobs. Awards are based on financial need and academic achievement. The college is a CSS member. The FAF and the aid application must be filed by April 1 (fall), November 1 (winter), February 1 (spring), or April 15 (summer).

Foreign Students: Fewer than 1% of the students are from foreign countries. The college offers special counseling and sponsors organizations especially for these students.

Admissions: The TOEFL is required; a minimum score of 500 is necessary for consideration. The SAT is also required.

Procedure: The application deadline for the fall quarter is September 1; for all other quarters, the deadlines are open. A medical questionnaire must be completed. Proof of adequate funds to cover 1 year must be presented, and a special deposit of $1500 is required. Health insurance is also required; it is available through the college for a fee.

Admissions Contact: Doyle Bickers, Director of Admissions.

GUAM

UNIVERSITY OF GUAM
Mangilao, Guam 96913   734-3450

F/T: 704M, 875W	Faculty: 182; IIA, +$
P/T: 325M, 408W	Ph.D.'s: 50%
Grad: 141M, 207W	S/F Ratio: 18 to 1
Year: sems, ss	Tuition: $15 ($34) p/c
Appl: Aug. 3	R and B: $2200
704 applied 704 accepted 537 enrolled	
SAT or ACT: not required	NONCOMPETITIVE

The University of Guam, founded in 1952, is a public liberal arts institution situated on the island of Guam. The university provides the opportunity for higher education on Guam and in Micronesia. The library has over 300,000 volumes, periodical subscriptions, and microfilm items.

Environment: The 100-acre campus overlooks Pago Bay, 5 miles from Agana. Located in a suburban area, the campus consists of 15 buildings, including 3 dormitories housing 300 students. A $4 million athletic complex is now under construction.

Student Life: Forty percent of the students come from Guam, 35% from mainland United States, and 25% from foreign countries. About 30% of entering freshmen come from public schools. About 60% reside at home, 10% on campus, and the rest off campus in apartments and the military base. Fifty percent of the students are Catholic; 10% are Protestant. Seven percent are minority-group members. University housing is both coed and single-sex. Students may keep cars on campus. Drinking is forbidden. The university provides day-care services to full- and part-time students for a monthly fee.

Organizations: There are no fraternities or sororities on campus, but the university sponsors several extracurricular activities.

Sports: The university fields no intercollegiate teams, but offers 5 intramural sports.

Handicapped: About 25% of the campus is accessible to handicapped students. Special facilities include wheelchair ramps, parking areas, specially equipped rest rooms, and lowered telephones. Special class scheduling is also available.

Graduates: About 72% of the students drop out by the end of the freshman year; 19% remain to graduate. About 20% of the graduates pursue advanced degrees.

Services: Free placement, career counseling, and tutoring are available to all students on campus. Health care is available for a fee.

Programs of Study: The university confers the B.A., B.A. in Ed., B.B.A., B.S., and B.S.W. degrees. Associate and master's degrees are also awarded. Bachelor's degrees are offered in the following subjects: BUSINESS (accounting, business administration, finance, management, marketing), EDUCATION (early childhood, elementary, secondary, special), ENGLISH (literature, speech), FINE AND PERFORMING ARTS (art, art education), MATH AND SCIENCES (biology, chemistry, mathematics), PREPROFESSIONAL (agriculture), SOCIAL SCIENCES (history, psychology, social sciences, sociology). Thirty-seven percent of degrees conferred are in education, 33% in business.

Required: All students seeking a B.A. degree are required to take courses in English, mathematics, social science, natural science, and behavioral science.

Special: The English Language Institute is for students who have difficulty with basic English. The Micronesian Area Research Center provides opportunity for research into Micronesian history and development.

Admissions: All students who applied were accepted for the 1981-82 freshman class. The university has instituted an open admissions policy. Students who have graduated from high school are admitted as regular students. Students 18 years or older who do not meet these requirements are admitted as special students. Through the Upward Bound program, disadvantaged students who show potential are contacted by the university and their expenses are paid by various groups.

Procedure: Neither the SAT nor the ACT is required. The application deadlines are August 3 (fall), December 14 (spring), and May 7 (summer). A personal interview is recommended. A $10 fee must accompany the application.

Special: CLEP general exams are used.

Transfer: For fall 1981, 221 transfer students applied, all were accepted, and 157 enrolled. Transfers are accepted for all classes. Good academic standing is required; D grades do not transfer. Students must complete at least 32 semester hours in residence of the 124 required for the bachelor's degree. Deadlines are the same as for freshman applicants.

176 GUAM

Visiting: Prospective students will find weekdays the best time to visit the campus. Visitors may sit in on classes with the consent of faculty members and may stay overnight at the school. Contact the director of housing for arrangements.

Financial Aid: About 13% of the students receive financial aid, 12% receive scholarship aid, and 6% work part-time on campus. There are 100 freshman scholarships. CWS funds are available in all departments. Tuition may be paid in installments. Aid applications should be submitted by June 15 for fall.

Foreign Students: Twenty-five of the full-time students are from foreign countries. The college provides the English Language Institute.

Admissions: Foreign students must take the TOEFL as well as English, math, and speech placement examinations.

Procedure: Application deadlines are July 2 (fall), November 13 (spring), and April 12 (summer). Foreign students must take a complete physical examination to establish proof of health. They must also provide proof of funds adequate to cover 1 year of study.

Admissions Contact: Forrest Gene Rogers, Director of Admissions and Registration.

HAWAII

BRIGHAM YOUNG UNIVERSITY/ HAWAII CAMPUS   C–2
Laie, Hawaii 96762   (808) 293-3743

F/T: 865M, 1080W	Faculty: 78; n/av
P/T: 58M, 51W	Ph.D.'s: 58%
Grad: none	S/F Ratio: 25 to 1
Year: tri, ss	Tuition: $950 ($1424)
Appl: Aug. 15	R and B: $1650
580 applied	560 accepted	420 enrolled
SAT or ACT: required		LESS COMPETITIVE

Brigham Young University/Hawaii Campus, founded in 1955, is a 4-year liberal arts and teachers' college established by the Church of Jesus Christ of Latter-day Saints. The library contains 116,000 volumes, 10,000 microfilm items, and subscribes to 1000 periodicals.

Environment: The campus occupies 60 acres in an urban area south of the Mormon Hawaiian Temple. It consists of 22 buildings, including 13 connected covered walks. The new activity center has a seating capacity of 4500 for sports and conventions. Six dormitories house 1130 single students. Married student apartments house 250 families.

Student Life: Twenty-seven percent of the students are from Hawaii. Sixty-five percent reside on campus. Ninety-five percent are Mormons. Church activity is strongly encouraged. Assemblies are presented weekly and attendance is expected of all students. About 48% of the students are members of various minority groups. Campus housing is single-sex. Students may keep cars on campus. The university provides day-care services for full-time students, faculty, and staff for a fee.

Organizations: Under the direction of the college, organized student social activity is encouraged. There are no fraternities or sororities.

Sports: The university fields 4 intercollegiate teams for men and 2 for women. There are 19 intramural sports for men and 17 for women.

Handicapped: The campus is accessible to physically handicapped students. Ramps, specially equipped rest rooms, and elevators are incorporated in the campus structures.

Services: Health care, placement, and career counseling are available to students free of charge. Tutoring is obtainable for a fee.

Programs of Study: The university awards the B.A., B.S., and B.S.W. degrees. Associate degree programs are also offered. Bachelor's degrees are offered in the following subjects: BUSINESS (accounting, business administration, business education, hotel management, management, restaurant management, travel management), EDUCATION (elementary, health/physical, industrial, secondary, teaching English as a second language (TESL)), ENGLISH (English), FINE AND PERFORMING ARTS (art, music), MATH AND SCIENCES (biology, mathematics, physical sciences), PREPROFESSIONAL (social work), SOCIAL SCIENCES (government/political science, history, psychology).

Required: All students must complete a core curriculum.

Admissions: Ninety-seven percent of those who applied for the 1981–82 freshman class were accepted. Applicants must file an official application form, 2 recommending reference forms, and 1 official copy of the high school transcript. They must give evidence of graduation from an approved high school and completion of 15 academic units with a GPA of no less than 2.0. Additional factors entering into an admissions decision are impressions made during an interview and recommendations.

Procedure: All candidates must present SAT or ACT scores. Freshmen are admitted to fall, winter, and spring sessions. August 15 is the application deadline for fall, December 15 for winter, and April 15 for spring. The application fee is $10.

Special: Early admissions are possible; students should apply by August 15. CLEP subject exams are accepted.

Transfer: For fall 1981, 269 transfer students enrolled. Transfers are accepted for all classes. Good academic standing is necessary; applicants should have a GPA of at least 2.0. D grades do not transfer. Application deadlines are August 14 (fall), December 14 (winter), April 12 (spring), and June 21 (summer).

Visiting: Guided tours are available for informal visits to the college. For further information or to arrange a visit contact H. Nolan Reed in the Office of Pre-Admission.

Financial Aid: Financial Aid is administered to about 90% of the students. Scholarships, church-sponsored loans, and part-time employment are limited and based on financial need. The college is a member of CSS and requires the FAF of aid applicants. Applications for aid must be submitted by July 1 (fall), November 1 (winter), and March 1 (spring).

Foreign Students: Foreign students represent 38% of the full-time enrollment. The university offers an intensive English program, special counseling, and special organizations for foreign students.

Admissions: Either the TOEFL or University of Michigan Language Test is required. On the TOEFL, the minimum required score is 450; on the Michigan, 65. The SAT or ACT is also required.

Procedure: Foreign applicants should apply by July 1 (fall) or November 2 (winter). A complete physical examination is required. Proof of adequate funds must be presented. The university requires health insurance; it is available through the university for a fee.

Admissions Contact: Charles W. H. Goo, Director of Admissions and Registrar.

CHAMINADE UNIVERSITY OF HONOLULU   C–2
Honolulu, Hawaii 96816   (808) 735-4735

F/T: 419M, 421W	Faculty: 51; IIB, –$
P/T: 65M, 54W	Ph.D.'s: 40%
Grad: 108M, 24W	S/F Ratio: 17 to 1
Year: sems, ss	Tuition: $2660
Appl: Aug. 1	R and B: $2360
380 applied	309 accepted	208 enrolled
SAT: 387V 441M	ACT: 20	COMPETITIVE

Chaminade University of Honolulu, founded in 1955, is a small, Roman Catholic, liberal arts college. The library contains 50,000 volumes, holds subscriptions to 450 periodicals, and stores 3075 microfilm items.

Environment: The 7-acre campus, located 4 miles from Honolulu, is located in a suburban environment. It consists of classrooms, a gymnasium, a communications arts center, a cafeteria, the student union, a bookstore complex, a chapel, 3 resident dormitories, and on-campus apartments.

Student Life: About 60% of the students are from Hawaii, 20% are from the mainland, and 20% are from foreign countries. Thirty percent reside on campus. About 48% are members of the Catholic Church. Campus housing is single-sex; there are visiting privileges. Students may keep cars on campus.

Organizations: Student organizations and activities include a religious group, special-interest clubs, a campus newspaper, a yearbook, and a literary magazine. Students own and operate an on-campus business enterprise that affords them an opportunity to gain managerial/work experience while still in school. There are no fraternities or sororities.

Sports: Chaminade competes intercollegiately in 4 sports for men and 3 for women. There are 6 intramural sports for men and 6 for women.

Handicapped: The campus is 85% accessible to physically handicapped students. Special facilities include parking, ramps, lowered drinking fountains, and special class scheduling.

Graduates: About 38% of the students pursue advanced study following graduation: 1% enter medical school; 2% law school. Seventy percent of the graduates pursue careers in business or industry.

Services: The following free services are available to the student: placement and career counseling, tutoring, remedial instruction, health care, and psychological counseling.

Programs of Study: The university confers the B.A., B.B.A., B.F.A., B.S., and B.G.S. degrees. Associate and master's degrees are also granted. Bachelor's degrees are offered in the following subjects: AREA STUDIES (American, Asian), BUSINESS (accounting, business administration, computer science, management, marketing), EDUCATION (adult, early childhood, elementary, secondary), ENGLISH (English), FINE AND PERFORMING ARTS (art, studio art), MATH AND SCIENCES (biology, chemistry, mathematics), PHILOSOPHY (humanities, philosophy, religion), PREPROFESSIONAL (dentistry, law, medicine, veterinary), SOCIAL SCIENCES (behavioral sciences, economics, government/political science, history, international relations, psychology, sociology). Forty-nine percent of degrees are conferred in business; 36% in social science.

Special: Evening classes and an accelerated 10-week semester are offered.

Honors: Although there are no departmental honors programs, there are 4 honor societies on campus.

Admissions: Eighty-one percent of those who applied for entrance in the 1981-82 freshman class were accepted. Applicants must rank in the upper 50% of the graduating class and have completed 15 Carnegie units of high school work. Of prime consideration is the GPA; the minimum GPA is 2.0. In addition to this, and in their order of importance, are impressions made during an interview, recommendations, advanced placement or honor courses, personality, leadership record, and extracurricular activities.

Procedure: The SAT or ACT should be taken in November or December of the senior year. Test scores and high school record should be submitted by August 1 (fall), January 1 (spring), and May 15 (summer). Notification is made within 2 weeks. There is a $20 application fee. A rolling admissions plan is used.

Special: There is a large early admissions program; the application deadlines are August 1 and January 1. Early decision candidates may apply after the 6th semester. Deferred admissions are also possible. CLEP general and subject exams are accepted for those studying for the B.G.S. degree. All students may earn credit through AP exams.

Transfer: For fall 1981, 358 transfer students applied, 304 were accepted, and 158 enrolled. Transfers are accepted for all classes. Applicants must have a 2.0 minimum GPA and a composite score of 800 on the SAT or 18 on the ACT. D grades do not transfer. All students must complete at least 30 hours at the college, of a total 124 hours required for the bachelor's degree. Application deadlines are the same as those for freshmen.

Visiting: Guides are available for informal visits to the campus. Regularly scheduled orientations are arranged by the office of admissions.

Financial Aid: About 43% of students receive financial aid. Fifteen percent work part-time on campus. The university provides scholarships, loans, and part-time employment. Tuition is reduced if 2 or more students are from the same family. The university is a CSS member. The FAF or 1040 tax form must be filed. Application must be made by March 15.

Foreign Students: About 20% of the full-time students come from foreign countries. The university offers these students an intensive English program, special counseling, and special organizations.

Admissions: The TOEFL is required; a minimum score of 450 must be achieved. The SAT is also required.

Procedure: Deadlines for foreign applications are August 1 (fall), December 1 (winter), January 1 (spring), and May 1 (summer). The application fee is $25. Notification is made within 1 month. A physical examination and TB clearance are required. Students must also present proof of funds adequate to cover 1 to 4 years of study.

Admissions Contact: William F. Murray, Director of Admissions.

HAWAII 177

HAWAII LOA COLLEGE C-2
Kaneohe, Hawaii 96744 (808) 235-3641

F/T: 180M, 180W	Faculty: 31; IIB, av$
P/T: 10M, 20W	Ph.D.'s: 60%
Grad: none	S/F Ratio: 15 to 1
Year: 4-1-4, ss	Tuition: $2850
Appl: see profile	R and B: $2600
SAT or ACT: required	**LESS COMPETITIVE**

Hawaii Loa College was founded in 1963 by 4 local Protestant denominations: the United Methodist Church, the Episcopal Church, the United Church of Christ, and the United Presbyterian Church. The college offers the B.A. degree in 4 major divisions: Communication Arts, Humanities, Natural Science and Mathematics, and Social Sciences. The library contains 37,000 volumes, and subscribes to more than 200 periodicals.

Environment: The college occupies a 135-acre campus on Oahu, approximately 8 miles from Honolulu. Six dormitories surround a dining commons that serves the entire college community.

Student Life: The racial and ethnic make-up of the college reflects the diversity to be found in Hawaii. Forty percent of the students are state residents, 40% come from the mainland, and 20% come from foreign countries (particularly Asia and the Pacific Islands). About half the students live in the coed dormitories.

Organizations: Students may participate in student government, a student newspaper, an International Student Association, and special-interest groups. There are no fraternities or sororities.

Sports: Athletics are limited to intramural competition.

Handicapped: The entire campus is accessible to physically handicapped students. Ramps, special parking, elevators, and specially equipped rest rooms and dormitory facilities are available. A special counselor is provided.

Graduates: About 40% of the graduates pursue advanced degrees.

Services: The following services are offered free: remedial instruction, tutoring, career and placement counseling, and psychological counseling.

Programs of Study: The college grants the B.A. degree. Bachelor's degrees are offered in the following subjects: AREA STUDIES (American, Asian—East Asian), BUSINESS (business administration, international business, marine business), ENGLISH (English—English composition, literature), FINE AND PERFORMING ARTS (art, art history, music, theater/dramatics), MATH AND SCIENCES (biology, chemistry, computer science, mathematics, oceanography, physics), PHILOSOPHY (philosophy, religion), PREPROFESSIONAL (biomedical sciences, dentistry, food and nutrition sciences, law, medicine, ministry, pharmacy, public health, veterinary), SOCIAL SCIENCES (anthropology, economics, government/political science, history, psychology). Thirty percent of degrees are conferred in math and sciences, 30% in social sciences, and 20% in humanities.

Required: The required liberal arts core program includes freshman and senior seminars as well as distribution requirements.

Special: The college offers an interdisciplinary curriculum emphasizing intercultural studies of East and West, particularly with respect to contemporary problems. A dual-degree engineering program is offered in conjunction with Washington University in St. Louis. Students may study abroad.

Admissions: Seventy-five percent of those who applied were accepted for a recent freshman class. A normal college preparatory program of 16 high school units is recommended. The college also recommends that students have a high school grade average of B or better and either a combined SAT score of at least 900 or an ACT composite of at least 19. Other factors considered include advanced placement or honors courses, extracurricular activities, impressions made during an interview, recommendations by school officials, leadership record, and personality.

Procedure: The SAT (preferred) or the ACT is required of all students. These tests should be taken early in the senior year. Application deadlines for fall are April 15 (priority consideration) and August 15 (final); deadlines for spring are October 15 (priority) and January 15 (final). Decisions will be made within 2 weeks after the applicant's file is complete. There is a $20 application fee.

Special: Early decision, deferred admissions, and early admissions plans are possible. CLEP and AP credit is accepted.

Transfer: In a recent year, 35 transfer students enrolled. Transfers are considered for all classes; applicants must have at least a C average. D grades do not transfer. All students must study at the college for at

HAWAII

least 1 year, completing 8 of the 32 courses required for a bachelor's degree. Application deadlines are the same as those for freshmen.

Visiting: Guides are available for informal visits to the campus. For information on orientations and overnight accommodations, contact the director of admissions.

Financial Aid: About 65% of all students receive aid. EOG grants and NDSL are available, as well as college-funded loans. There are a limited number of scholarships from church and community sources. Part-time work is available on campus, and the college participates in CWS. The college is a member of CSS and requires the FAF. The recommended deadline for aid applications is April 15.

Foreign Students: Twenty percent of the full-time students come from foreign countries. The college offers special organizations and several English as a Second Language courses for these students.

Admissions: Applicants must take the TOEFL.

Procedure: Application deadlines are the same as those for other students. Foreign applicants must complete special application forms available from the college. There is a special $25 application fee.

Admissions Contact: Janie Bossert, Director of Admissions.

HAWAII PACIFIC COLLEGE   C–2
Honolulu, Hawaii 96813   (808) 521-8061

F/T: 413M, 297W	Faculty: 24; IIB, –$
P/T: 552M, 216W	Ph.D.'s: 90%
Grad: none	S/F Ratio: 16 to 1
Year: sems, ss	Tuition: $2340
Appl: Sept. 7	R and B: n/app
385 accepted	289 enrolled
SAT: 400V 430M	LESS COMPETITIVE

Hawaii Pacific College, founded in 1966, is a private, nonprofit institution that has schools of Liberal Arts and Business Administration. The library contains more than 23,000 volumes and subscribes to about 600 periodicals.

Environment: The campus environment is urban. The college occupies 3 floors of the Sun-Life of Canada Building and the second floor of the Grosvenor Building in downtown Honolulu. There are no living facilities for students.

Student Life: Seventy percent of the students are from Hawaii, and about 80% come from public schools. All of the students are members of various minority groups; 80% are of Asian-American origin.

Organizations: There are no fraternities or sororities. Students may join art, drama, publications, service groups, student council, and ethnic organizations. The city also offers opportunities for entertainment.

Sports: The college competes intercollegiately in 2 sports for men and 1 for women. There are 4 intramural sports for both men and women.

Services: The college provides tutoring, career counseling, placement, and remedial instruction free of charge. Health care and psychological counseling are available for a fee.

Programs of Study: The college confers the B.A. and B.S. degrees. Associate degree programs are also available. Bachelor's degrees are offered in the following subjects: AREA STUDIES (American, Asian), BUSINESS (accounting, business administration, computer science, finance, management, marketing, real estate/insurance, travel industry management), EDUCATION (teaching English as a second language), ENGLISH (English), PHILOSOPHY (humanities), SOCIAL SCIENCES (economics, government/political science, history, social sciences). The college also confers a B.A. in liberal arts.

Required: Freshmen must take courses in English, humanities and social studies, and mathematics and sciences.

Special: Cooperative work-study, accelerated study, study-abroad programs, and an English foundations program are offered.

Admissions: Candidates should be graduates of accredited high schools. Standardized test scores are used in the admissions decision, as are impressions made during an interview, advanced placement or honors courses, and recommendations by school officials.

Procedure: The SAT or ACT are recommended. The application deadlines are September 7 (fall), January 17 (spring), and May 16 (summer). A rolling admissions procedure is used. A $30 fee is required, as well as a health certificate.

Special: Early decision and early and deferred admissions plans are offered. CLEP credit is given.

Transfer: The college accepts transfer students for all classes. Applicants must have a 2.0 GPA; D grades do not transfer. All students must take 30 credit hours at the college, of a total 120 required for the bachelor's degree. Transfer deadlines are August 23 (fall), January 3 (spring), and May 9 (summer).

Financial Aid: About 25% of the students receive aid. Seven percent work part-time on campus. The average award to freshmen is $2382. Scholarships, grants, and loans are available to students. The college participates in BEOG, SEOG, NDSL, and CWSP. The college is a member of CSS and requires the FAF. Deadlines for aid applications are August 23 (fall), January 3 (spring), and May 9 (summer).

Foreign Students: Twenty-eight percent of the full-time students come from foreign countries. The college offers these students an intensive English program, special counseling, and special organizations.

Admissions: Foreign candidates must take the college's English proficiency test and entrance exam.

Procedure: Application deadlines for foreign applicants are August 23 (fall), January 3 (spring), and May 9 (summer). Foreign students must show proof of TB clearance. They must also present proof of funds adequate to cover 1 to 4 years of study.

Admissions Contact: Howard Markowitz, Director of Admissions.

UNIVERSITY OF HAWAII

University of Hawaii, founded in 1907, is a state-supported university which provides undergraduate and graduate instruction, research, and extension courses. The university operates campuses at Manoa and Hilo as well as 7 community colleges throughout the state.

UNIVERSITY OF HAWAII AT HILO   F–4
Hilo, Hawaii 96720   (808) 961-9325

F/T: 1336M, 1324W	Faculty: n/av; IIB, ++$
P/T: 336M, 471W	Ph.D.'s: 39%
Grad: none	S/F Ratio: 15 to 1
Year: sems, ss	Tuition: $80–$330 ($930)
Appl: July 1	R and B: $3320
760 enrolled	
SAT: 411V 460M	LESS COMPETITIVE

University of Hawaii at Hilo, established in 1970, offers undergraduate programs in the liberal arts and sciences, business administration, and agriculture. The library houses 150,000 books and 25,000 microfilm items, and subscribes to 1500 periodicals.

Environment: The 78-acre campus is located in a rural area 200 miles from Honolulu. Dormitories and on-campus apartments are available. Buildings include a learning resources center, a media center, and an academic complex.

Student Life: About 85% of the students come from Hawaii; the majority have had public school educations. Fifteen percent live on campus. About 90% are members of various minority groups; 32% are of Asian-American origin. Campus housing is both single-sex and coed; there are visiting privileges in the single-sex housing. Students may keep cars on campus.

Organizations: There are no fraternities or sororities. Campus extracurricular activities include student government, publications, clubs, and social and cultural events.

Sports: The college competes intercollegiately in 3 sports for men and 2 for women. There are 8 intramural teams for men and 8 for women.

Handicapped: About 50% of the campus is currently accessible to students with physical handicaps. Special facilities include wheelchair ramps, parking areas, elevators, lowered drinking fountains and telephones, and specially equipped rest rooms. Special class scheduling is also available.

Graduates: About 20% of the freshmen remain to graduate. About 8% of the graduates go on for additional education; 12% begin careers in business.

Services: Career counseling, placement, health care, psychological counseling, and tutoring are offered without charge. Remedial instruction is available for a fee.

Programs of Study: The B.A., B.S., and B.B.A. degrees are awarded. Associate degrees are also available. Bachelor's degrees are offered in the following subjects: BUSINESS (business administration), ENGLISH (English, speech), FINE AND PERFORMING ARTS (music), MATH AND SCIENCES (biology, chemistry, mathematics, physics), PHILOSOPHY (philosophy), PREPROFESSIONAL (agriculture), SOCIAL SCIENCES (anthropology, economics, geography, government/political science, history, psychology, social sciences, sociology).

Special: Student-designed majors, cooperative work-study, and study abroad are offered. Certificates and A.A. or A.S. degrees are available in liberal arts, business education, technical and vocational shop programs, nursing, and public services.

Honors: One honor society has a chapter on campus.

Admissions: For the 1981–82 class, 760 students were enrolled. An applicant must have a C average and be in the top 50% of the high school class.

Procedure: The SAT is required. One recommendation is requested. The application and a $10 application fee should be submitted by July 1 for fall admission, by December 1 for spring entry. Notification is on a rolling basis.

Special: There is an early admissions plan. AP and CLEP are used.

Transfer: Transfers are accepted for all classes. An average of C and a minimum score of 400 on both parts of the SAT are required. One year must be completed in residence. Transfers must complete 30 credits at the university, of a total 120 to 123 credits required for the bachelor's degree. July 1 is the fall application deadline; December 1 is the spring deadline.

Visiting: Prospective applicants may arrange for a guided tour of the campus, including attendance of classes. There is an orientation program for new students.

Financial Aid: About 39% of the students are receiving assistance. About 35% work part-time on campus. The school offers grants (federal and state), loans, merit scholarships, need-based scholarships, and part-time work. The university is a member of CSS. The FAF should be submitted by March 1.

Foreign Students: About 4% of the full-time students come from foreign countries. The university offers these students an intensive English program, special counseling, and special organizations.

Admissions: Foreign applicants must achieve a score of 450 on the TOEFL. The SAT is also required; applicants should score a minimum of 400 on each part.

Procedure: Application deadlines are July 1 (fall) and December 1 (spring). Proof of health and of adequate funds must be presented to the university. Health insurance is required; it is available through the university for a fee.

Admissions Contact: Peggy Yorita, Admissions Coordinator.

UNIVERSITY OF HAWAII AT MANOA   C–2
Honolulu, Hawaii 96822   (808) 948-8975

F/T: 6000M, 6300W	Faculty: n/av; I, +$
P/T: 1300M, 1300W	Ph.D.'s: n/av
Grad: 2800M, 2700W	S/F Ratio: n/av
Year: sems, ss	Tuition: $480 ($1155)
Appl: May 1	R and B: $2965
SAT: required	COMPETITIVE

University of Hawaii at Manoa, founded in 1907, is part of the University of Hawaii system. Its library contains almost 1.5 million volumes and 41,700 microfilm items, and subscribes to more than 25,000 periodicals.

Environment: The 300-acre campus is located in the verdant Manoa Valley, 2 miles from the center of Honolulu. The university has more than 200 major buildings. Dormitories accommodate about 2000 students.

Student Life: Most students are from Hawaii; a limited number are accepted from out of state. Fewer than 10% live on campus. Both coed and single-sex dorms are available.

Organizations: The more than 100 student organizations include special-interest clubs, fraternities and sororities, religious groups, and a student newspaper.

Sports: The university fields intercollegiate teams in numerous sports. An intramural program also is offered.

Handicapped: The university is working on barrier-free compliance.

Programs of Study: The university confers the B.A. and B.S. degrees. Master's and doctoral degrees also are awarded. Bachelor's degrees are offered in the following subjects: AREA STUDIES (American, Asian, Hawaiian, Pacific Island), BUSINESS (accounting, business administration, computer science, fashion design and merchandising, finance, international business, management, management information systems, marketing, personnel and industrial relations, real estate/insurance, travel industry management), EDUCATION (early childhood, elementary, health/physical, industrial, secondary, vocational—agricultural, vocational—home economics), ENGLISH (communications, English, journalism, speech), FINE AND PERFORMING ARTS (art, art education, dance, music, music education, studio art, theater/dramatics), HEALTH SCIENCES (medical technology, nursing, speech therapy), LANGUAGES (Chinese, French, German, Greek/Latin, Hawaiian, Japanese, Russian, Spanish), MATH AND SCIENCES (agronomy and soil sciences, animal science, biology, botany, chemistry, earth science, food and nutritional sciences, geology, mathematics, math education, mechanical agricultural production, meteorology, microbiology, physics, science education, tropical horticulture, zoology), PHILOSOPHY (classics, philosophy, religion), PRE-PROFESSIONAL (agriculture—agricultural economics, agriculture—agricultural technology, architecture, engineering—civil, engineering—electrical, engineering—mechanical, environmental design, home economics, social work), SOCIAL SCIENCES (anthropology, economics, geography, government/political science, history, human development, psychology, recreation, sociology). Twenty-six percent of degrees are conferred in business, 26% in social sciences, and 12% in math and sciences.

Special: The university offers a selected studies program. Students may design their own majors.

Honors: An honors program is offered by the university, and a number of national honor societies are represented on campus.

Admissions: Seventy percent of those who applied were accepted for a recent freshman class. The SAT scores of those who enrolled were as follows: Verbal—19% between 500 and 599, 4% between 600 and 700, and 1% above 700; Math—38% between 500 and 599, 18% between 600 and 700, and 3% above 700. High school graduates from 4-year programs must present 15 units of high school work. Graduates of 3-year high schools must present 12 units of high school work. Applicants should rank in the upper 40% of their graduating class. The minimum acceptable GPA is 3.0. Recommendations received from school officials are also considered.

Procedure: The SAT should be taken by December of the senior year. The application, test scores, and high school record should be submitted by May 1 (fall) or November 1 (spring). The university uses a rolling admissions plan. There is a $10 application fee for nonresidents.

Special: An early admissions plan is available. AP and CLEP credit is accepted.

Transfer: Transfers are considered for all years. D grades do not transfer. Preference is given to Hawaii residents. Students must earn at least 30 semester credits at the university to receive a degree. Application deadlines are the same as those for freshmen.

Visiting: Visitors may sit in on classes with the permission of the instructor.

Admissions Contact: Director of Admissions.

IDAHO

BOISE STATE UNIVERSITY   B–5
Boise, Idaho 83725   (208) 385-1177

F/T: 3117M, 3513W	Faculty: 348; IIA, av$
P/T: 1737M, 1959W	Ph.D.'s: 60%
Grad: 572M, 646W	S/F Ratio: 19 to 1
Year: sems, ss	Tuition: $689 ($2389)
Appl: Aug. 19	R and B: $1900
2986 applied	2900 accepted 1951 enrolled
SAT: 440V 460M	ACT: 18 NONCOMPETITIVE

Boise State University, founded in 1932, is a liberal arts and vocational studies college that is part of the Idaho state system. The library contains 230,000 volumes and 17,451 microfilm items, and subscribes to 2000 periodicals.

Environment: The 134-acre campus is located in an urban area, near the center of the city. The 47 major buildings on campus include a 7-story education building, a science education building, and 4 dormitories that accommodate 740 single students and 85 married couples.

Student Life: About 98% of the entering freshmen come from public schools. About 10% live on campus. Six percent are minority-group members. Campus housing is both single-sex and coed; there are visiting privileges in the single-sex dorms. Cars may be kept on campus. The university provides day-care services to all students, faculty, and staff for a fee.

Organizations: There are 3 national fraternities and 4 national sororities on campus, to which about 2% of the men and about 2% of the women belong. Student government and special-interest clubs provide social and cultural activities.

Sports: The university completes intercollegiately in 7 sports for men and 7 for women. Intramural sports for both men and women number 3.

Handicapped: About 95% of the campus is accessible to physically handicapped students. Special facilities include wheelchair ramps, special parking, elevators, specially equipped rest rooms, and lowered drinking fountains and telephones. Special class scheduling is also available. There are fewer than 1% visually impaired or hearing-impaired students currently enrolled. There are 2 special counselors and 2 assistants.

Graduates: The freshman dropout rate is 21%; 30% of the freshmen remain to graduate. About 3% of the graduates go on to advanced study; 35% pursue careers in business and industry.

Services: Free health care, tutoring, remedial instruction, psychological counseling, and career counseling services are available to full-time students. Placement services, which include on-campus job interviews and referrals, are available for a fee.

Programs of Study: The university confers the B.A., B.M., B.S., B.B.A., and B.F.A. degrees. Associate and master's programs are also offered. Bachelor's degrees are offered in the following subjects: BUSINESS (accounting, business administration, business education, computer science, finance, industrial business, management, marketing, office administration, real estate/insurance), EDUCATION (elementary, special), ENGLISH (communications, English), FINE AND PERFORMING ARTS (art, music, music education, theater/dramatics), HEALTH SCIENCES (environmental health, health science, medical technology, nursing, radiologic technology, respiratory therapy), LANGUAGES (German, Spanish), MATH AND SCIENCES (biology, chemistry, earth science, geology, mathematics, physics), PREPROFESSIONAL (dentistry, law, medicine, veterinary), SOCIAL SCIENCES (economics, government/political science, history, psychology, social sciences, sociology). About 37% of degrees conferred are in business, and 20% in math and sciences.

Special: An aviation management program, work-study programs, independent study, and study abroad are available.

Honors: Honor societies are open to qualified students; most departments have honors programs.

Admissions: Approximately 97% of those who applied were accepted for the 1981–82 freshman class. The SAT scores of those who enrolled were as follows: Verbal—73% below 500, 24% between 500 and 599, 3% between 600 and 700, and 0% above 700; Math—57% below 500, 37% between 500 and 599, 6% between 600 and 700, and 0% above 700. On the ACT, 68% scored below 21, 17% scored between 21 and 23, 7% between 24 and 25, 7% between 26 and 28, and 1% above 28. Admissions are open to graduates of an accredited high school.

Procedure: The SAT or ACT is required. Applications should be submitted before August 19 (fall), January 4 (spring), and June 4 (summer). A record of a physical exam must also accompany the application, along with a $10 fee. Admissions are on a rolling basis.

Special: CLEP and AP credit is accepted.

Transfer: For fall 1981, 1450 transfer students applied, 1200 were accepted, and 800 enrolled. Transfers are accepted for all classes. Students must have a 2.0 GPA and be in good standing at their former school; D grades transfer. All students must earn at least 30 semester hours in residence to receive a bachelor's degree (128 semester hours). There is a residency requirement of 2 semesters. Deadlines for transfers are the same as those for freshmen.

Visiting: There are regularly scheduled orientations for prospective students. Guides are also available for informal visits; visitors may sit in on classes and stay at the school. Jerry Davis (385-1401) should be contacted to arrange visits.

Financial Aid: About 30% of all students receive financial aid. About 13% work part-time on campus. The average aid to freshmen is $1870. The university offers scholarships, loans, and campus employment. The university is a CSS member. Either the FAF, Pell SER, or IRS 1040 (if requested) is required; the application deadline is prior to April 1.

Foreign Students: One percent of the full-time students are from foreign countries. The university offers these students an intensive English course, special counseling, and special organizations.

Admissions: The TOEFL and University of Michigan Language Test are required, the latter for placement purposes. For admissions purposes, the applicant must score at least 500 on the TOEFL.

Procedure: There are no admissions deadlines for foreign students. They may enter the fall, spring, or summer session. A special fee of $50 per semester, proof of adequate funds for 1 year, and an affadavit of support for the entire duration of studies are required. The university requires health insurance; the fee for insurance is included in the general registration fee.

Admissions Contact: Guy Hunt, Dean of Admissions.

COLLEGE OF IDAHO
Caldwell, Idaho 83605

A-5
(208) 459-5305

F/T: 250M, 210W
P/T: 29M, 43W
Grad: 111M, 191W
Year: 4-1-4
Appl: Sept. 1
500 applied
SAT: 435V 440M

Faculty: n/av; IIA, – –$
Ph.D.'s: 80%
S/F Ratio: 13 to 1
Tuition: $4224
R and B: $1910
250 accepted
ACT: 23

194 enrolled
COMPETITIVE+

College of Idaho, established in 1891, is a private liberal arts college affiliated with the Presbyterian Church. A School of Business will soon be added. The library contains 185,000 volumes and subscribes to 700 periodicals.

Environment: The 50-acre campus, located in a town of 18,000 people about 25 miles west of Boise, is surrounded by a rural, agricultural environment. The physical plant consists of 18 major buildings, including a 900-seat chapel-auditorium, a science center, and 4 dormitories that accommodate 640 men and women.

Student Life: Fifty-three percent of the students come from Idaho. About 95% come from public schools. Twenty percent commute to the campus. Eighty percent live on campus. Four percent are minority-group members. Campus housing is both single-sex and coed; there are visiting privileges in the single-sex dorms. Students may keep cars on campus.

Organizations: There are 4 sororities, 2 fraternities, and 1 national fraternity. The college frequently invites guest lecturers to the campus to provide students with first-hand information about various fields of interest. A number of religious organizations are available.

Sports: There are intercollegiate teams for men in 2 sports, and for women in 2.

Graduates: At the end of the freshman year, about 30% of the students drop out; 50% remain to graduate. Forty-five percent of the graduates go on to graduate or professional school.

Programs of Study: The college confers the B.A. and B.S. degrees. Master's programs are also offered. Bachelor's degrees are offered in the following subjects: AREA STUDIES (American), BUSINESS (accounting, business administration, finance, management, marketing), EDUCATION (elementary, health/physical, secondary), ENGLISH (English, literature), FINE AND PERFORMING ARTS (art, music, music education), HEALTH SCIENCES (medical technology, recreation), MATH AND SCIENCES (biology, botany, chemistry, human ecology, mathematics, mathematics/computer science, zoology), PHILOSOPHY (philosophy, religion), PREPROFESSIONAL (dentistry, engineering, law, medicine, veterinary), SOCIAL SCIENCES (economics, government/political science, history, human services, psychology, sociology). Half of all degrees conferred are in the sciences.

Special: Field trips ranging from 1 to 13 weeks are available. Some are international, with destinations such as Europe, Asia, Africa, Australia, Canada, and Mexico. The college offers 3-2 and 4-2 programs in engineering and medical technology with Columbia University, Stanford University, and the University of Idaho. Seminars, independent research, tutorial programs, and student-designed majors are all offered.

Honors: Several honors programs are offered at the college.

Admissions: About 50% of those who applied were accepted for the 1981–82 freshman class. Applicants must be high school graduates with at least a 2.0 GPA in secondary courses. Adults who present satisfactory scores on the GED test may be admitted. Other considerations are the student's promise of success as indicated by his academic record, extracurricular activities, special talents, secondary school recommendations, the reputation of the high school, and ACT or SAT scores. Children of graduates are given preference among equally qualified applicants.

Procedure: The ACT or SAT is required. Application deadlines are September 1 (fall), January 4 (winter), March 1 (spring), and June 1 (summer). There is a $15 application fee. Admissions are on a rolling basis.

Special: The college has a deferred admissions plan. CLEP and AP credit is accepted.

Transfer: For fall 1981, 4 transfer students applied, 4 were accepted, and none enrolled. Transfers are considered for all classes. Applicants must present a 2.0 GPA and references from their former school. D grades transfer. All students must earn at least 30 semester hours of credit at the college, of a total 124 semester hours required for the bachelor's degree. Deadlines for applications are the same as those for freshmen.

Financial Aid: Eighty-six percent of the students receive financial aid. About 25% work part-time on campus. The college provides scholarships, loans, and campus employment as sources of financial aid. Between 90 and 100 freshman scholarships are offered each year. Loans are available from the federal government, local banks, the college, and private sources. The average aid from all these sources granted to freshmen is $3500; the maximum, including part-time employment, is $5000. The college is a member of CSS. The FAF or FFS are required. Filing deadlines for financial aid are April 1 (fall), December 1 (winter), March 1 (spring), and June 1 (summer).

Foreign Students: About 2% of the full-time students are from foreign countries.

Admissions: The TOEFL is required; a minimum score of 500 is necessary. The SAT or ACT is also required.

Procedure: Application deadlines for foreign students are September 1 (fall), January 4 (winter), March 1 (spring), and June 1 (summer). The college requires proof of funds adequate to cover 1 year. Health insurance must be carried; it is available through the college.

Admissions Contact: Eleanor Montgomery, Director of Admissions.

IDAHO STATE UNIVERSITY D-6
Pocatello, Idaho 83209 (208) 236-0211

F/T: 1732M, 1637W	Faculty: 356; I, - -$
P/T: 365M, 544W	Ph.D.'s: 55%
Grad: 376M, 342W	S/F Ratio: 14 to 1
Year: sems, ss	Tuition: $680 ($2380)
Appl: Aug. 15	R and B: $1875
1400 applied	1000 accepted 950 enrolled
ACT: required	NONCOMPETITIVE

Idaho State University, established in 1901, is a state-supported institution providing undergraduate, graduate, extension, and vocational programs. The library contains over 285,000 volumes and 651,800 microfilm items, and subscribes to 4000 periodicals.

Environment: The 317-acre campus is located in a residential section of Pocatello, Idaho's second-largest city. The 49 major buildings include 12 dormitories that house over 1200 men and women. Apartments are available for 150 married students. A cafeteria, 2 dining halls, a student lounge, and lockers serve day students.

Student Life: About 90% of the students are from Idaho. Ninety-six percent come from public schools. Twenty-two percent live in the dormitories, which are single-sex. Regulations prohibit drinking on campus.

Organizations: About 5% of the women and 5% of the men belong to sororities and fraternities. The student government is responsible for managing extracurricular activities.

Sports: The university fields intercollegiate teams in 10 sports. Intramural sports also are offered.

Handicapped: Special facilities for handicapped students include wheelchair ramps, handrails, elevators, electric doors, specially equipped rest rooms, and special parking. Many elevators have braille pushbuttons. Housing for handicapped and visually impaired students is available in a centrally located residence hall.

Graduates: Thirty percent of the freshmen drop out by the end of their first year, and 50% remain to graduate. About 20% of the graduates seek advanced degrees.

Services: The following services are available free to students: health care, psychological counseling, placement aid, and career counseling. Placement services also are available to graduates.

Programs of Study: The university confers the B.A., B.S., B.F.A., B.B.A., B.Pharm., B.Mus., and B.Mus.Ed. degrees. Associate, master's, and doctoral degrees also are awarded. Bachelor's degrees are offered in the following subjects: AREA STUDIES (American), BUSINESS (accounting, business administration, business education, computer science, finance, management, marketing), EDUCATION (early childhood, elementary, health/physical, industrial, secondary), ENGLISH (English, journalism, speech), FINE AND PERFORMING ARTS (art, film/photography, music, music education, radio/TV, theater/dramatics), HEALTH SCIENCES (dental hygiene, dietetics, health care administration, medical technology, nursing, radiography, speech therapy), LANGUAGES (French, German, Spanish), MATH AND SCIENCES (biochemistry, biology, botany, chemistry, ecology/environmental science, geology, mathematics, microbiology, physics, zoology), PHILOSOPHY (philosophy), PREPROFESSIONAL (architecture, engineering, home economics, park and recreation management, pharmacy, social work), SOCIAL SCIENCES (anthropology, economics, government/political science, history, psychology, sociology).

Required: All students must take 30 hours of general-education courses.

Special: A 3-1 dual degree in medical technology is offered. Cooperative programs are offered in dentistry, medicine, and veterinary medicine. The university also has a school of vocational and technical education with over 20 programs in various fields. Nonmajor preprofessional programs are offered in law and in medicine and other health fields.

Honors: Several honor societies have chapters on campus.

Admissions: About 71% of those who applied were accepted for the 1981-82 freshman class. The university accepts all Idaho residents who are graduates of accredited high schools. Nonresidents must have at least a 2.0 GPA.

Procedure: The ACT is required of freshman applicants under 20 years of age, and those over 20 who have fewer than 25 semester hours of acceptable college credit. Application deadlines are August 15 (fall) and December 15 (spring). Admissions are granted on a rolling basis. There is no application fee.

Special: CLEP and AP credit is accepted.

Transfer: Transfers are accepted for all classes. Applicants must have at least a 2.0 GPA or an A.A. degree. D grades sometimes transfer. Students must earn at least 32 semester hours at the university of the 128 or more required for a bachelor's degree. Application deadlines are the same as those for freshmen.

Financial Aid: About 60% of all students receive aid. The university provides scholarships, loans, and campus employment. The FAF or FFS is required. Application deadlines are April 1 and November 1.

Foreign Students: The 165 foreign students at the university represent 2% of the full-time enrollment. An American Language Academy is located on campus, and special counseling and special organizations also are provided.

Admissions: Applicants must score at least 500 on the TOEFL. No college entrance exams are required.

Procedure: Application deadlines are March 1 (fall), August 1 (spring), and October 15 (summer). Students must present proof of adequate funds for 1 year. A special fee ($50 in 1981-82) is levied to cover the cost of correspondence and health insurance.

Admissions Contact: Tim Hayhurst, Director of Admissions.

LEWIS-CLARK STATE COLLEGE A-3
Lewiston, Idaho 83501 (208) 746-2341

F/T: 588M, 571W	Faculty: 88; IIB, +$
P/T: 260M, 532W	Ph.D.'s: n/av
Grad: none	S/F Ratio: 15 to 1
Year: sems, ss	Tuition: $600 ($2300)
Appl: open	R and B: $1900
ACT: required	NONCOMPETITIVE

Lewis-Clark State College, founded in 1893, offers undergraduate programs in the liberal arts and sciences, nursing, education, business, and the applied sciences. The library contains 91,786 volumes and 16,496 microfilm items, and subscribes to 7,456 periodicals.

Environment: The 44-acre small town campus is located in a rural area about 100 miles from Spokane, Washington. The physical plant includes a winterized indoor tennis facility, a baseball field with a seating capacity of 3200, and 2 residence halls that accommodate 150 students.

Student Life: About 73% of the students are from Idaho; 8% live on campus. Six percent are minority-group members. Campus housing is single-sex; there are visiting privileges. Students may keep cars on campus. The college provides day-care services to all students, faculty, and staff for a fee.

IDAHO

Organizations: There are no fraternities or sororities. Student government, service clubs, publications, and special-interest clubs are among the extracurricular activities.

Sports: The college competes intercollegiately in 3 sports for men and 3 for women. Intramural sports for both men and women number 4.

Handicapped: About 60% of the campus is accessible to the physically handicapped. Facilities include wheelchair ramps, special parking, elevators, specially equipped rest rooms, and lowered drinking fountains and telephones. Special class scheduling is also available. Handicapped students are counseled through the college's counseling service.

Graduates: Twenty-five percent of the freshmen drop out by the end of the first year; 20% remain to graduate. Thirty-three percent of the graduates pursue advanced study after graduation.

Services: Health care, career counseling, tutoring, remedial instruction, and psychological counseling are offered free of charge to students. Placement services are available for a fee.

Programs of Study: The college confers the B.A. and B.S. degrees. Associate degree programs are also available. Bachelor's degrees are offered in the following subjects: BUSINESS (business administration, industrial management technology), EDUCATION (elementary, special, vocational), ENGLISH (English, speech), FINE AND PERFORMING ARTS (art, drama/speech), HEALTH SCIENCES (nursing), MATH AND SCIENCES (chemistry, earth science, mathematics, natural sciences), SOCIAL SCIENCES (criminal justice, history, social sciences). Approximately 50% of the degrees are conferred in vocational education, 15% in business, 15% in nursing, and 10% in education.

Required: All students must complete a core curriculum.

Special: Vocational education includes programs of study in business, mechanics, welding, drafting, electronics, and graphics.

Honors: Two national honor societies have chapters on campus. The honors program offers special opportunities to students with extraordinary ability and motivation.

Admissions: For a recent freshman class, 503 applications were received and 373 students enrolled. The college adheres to an open admissions policy.

Procedure: The ACT is required; junior results are acceptable. Deadlines are open. The college follows a rolling admissions policy. There is no application fee. Freshmen may enroll in the fall, spring, or summer session.

Special: There is an early admissions plan. Credits are granted for life and work experiences.

Transfer: Admissions are open. Applicants are accepted into all classes. D grades transfer. There is a 1-year residency requirement. Transfer students must earn at least 32 semester credits at the college, of a total 128 semester credits required for the bachelor's degree. There are no transfer deadlines.

Visiting: Students are encouraged to visit the college on an individual basis. Guides are available for informal visits; visitors may sit in on classes and stay at the school. The admissions office should be contacted to arrange visits.

Financial Aid: About 65% of all students receive some form of financial aid. Ten percent work part-time on campus. The average award to freshmen is $650. Sixty-five freshman scholarships are available from a fund of $20,278. Federal loan funds total $100,000. CWS is available. The FAF is required; deadline for aid application is April 1. Need is the determining factor.

Foreign Students: About 2% of the full-time students come from foreign countries. The college offers an intensive English program, special counseling, and organizations for foreign students.

Admissions: The TOEFL is required; the minimum score is 500. College entrance exams are not necessary.

Procedure: Application deadlines are open.

Admissions Contact: P. Reid Bailey, Director of Admissions.

NORTHWEST NAZARENE COLLEGE A-5
Nampa, Idaho 83651   (208) 467-8496

F/T: 584M, 668W Faculty: 62; III, −$
P/T: 33M, 53W   Ph.D.'s: 45%
Grad: 2M, 12W   S/F Ratio: 18 to 1
Year: qtrs, ss   Tuition: $3165
Appl: open   R and B: $1695
494 applied   465 accepted   361 enrolled
ACT: 20   LESS COMPETITIVE

Northwest Nazarene College, established in 1913, is a liberal arts college operated by the Church of the Nazarene. The library contains 80,000 volumes and over 200,000 microfilm items, and subscribes to 450 periodicals.

Environment: The 62-acre campus is located in a city of about 30,000 people, 20 miles west of Boise. The environment surrounding the campus is rural. The buildings include 7 residence halls that accommodate 530 women and 452 men, a dining hall, and recreational facilities. The college also sponsors on-campus apartments and married student housing.

Student Life: About 32% of the students come from Idaho, 67% come from other states, and 2% come from foreign countries. Ninety-eight percent of the freshmen come from public schools. Seventy-two percent live in the campus residence halls. Seventy-three percent of the students are members of the supporting church. The use of tobacco and alcoholic beverages is forbidden. Campus housing is single-sex; there are visiting privileges in the dorms only during open house. Students may keep cars on campus.

Organizations: There are no fraternities or sororities; professional and service organizations also serve as social groups.

Sports: Intercollegiate athletic competition is available in 7 sports for men and 4 for women. Intramural sports for both men and women number 13.

Handicapped: About 75% of the campus is accessible to wheelchair-bound students. Facilities include wheelchair ramps and special parking; special class scheduling is also available. Less than 1% of the students currently enrolled have visual impairments.

Graduates: The freshman dropout rate is 30%; 29% remain to graduate. Twenty percent pursue graduate study after graduation. Twenty-five percent enter careers in business and industry.

Services: Students receive the following services free of charge: placement, career counseling, health care, tutoring, remedial instruction, and psychological counseling.

Programs of Study: The college confers the B.A. and B.S. degrees. Associate and master's programs are also offered. Bachelor's degrees are offered in the following subjects: BUSINESS (accounting, business administration), EDUCATION (elementary, health/physical, secondary, special), ENGLISH (English), FINE AND PERFORMING ARTS (art, art education), HEALTH SCIENCES (speech therapy), MATH AND SCIENCES (biology, chemistry, mathematics, physics), PHILOSOPHY (philosophy, religion), PREPROFESSIONAL (agriculture, architecture, dentistry, engineering, forestry, law, medicine, ministry, pharmacy, social work, veterinary), SOCIAL SCIENCES (history, psychology). Twenty percent of degrees are conferred in business, 20% in education, and 20% in philosophy and religion.

Required: Physical education is required. All students must also complete 4 courses in philosophy and religion. The URE must be taken by all candidates for graduation.

Special: It is possible to earn combined B.A.-B.S. degrees in various subjects. Student-designed majors are permitted. The college offers a general studies (no major) degree.

Honors: Phi Delta Lambda and Alpha Delta Sigma have chapters on campus.

Admissions: Ninety-four percent of those who applied were accepted for the 1981-82 freshman class. Of those who enrolled, the ACT scores were as follows: 54% scored below 21, 23% between 21 and 23, 14% between 24 and 25, 6% between 26 and 28, and 3% above 28. Students must be graduates of an accredited high school and have an average of at least C for admission with regular standing. Some provisional students (those with a below-C average) are also accepted. Recommendations by school officials, leadership record, and personality are important factors in evaluating candidates for admission.

Procedure: The ACT is required. There are no application deadlines. Freshmen are admitted to every quarter. There is a $10 application fee. A rolling admissions plan is used.

Special: CLEP and AP credit is accepted.

Transfer: For fall 1981, 171 transfer students applied, 155 were accepted, and 114 enrolled. Transfers are admitted to all classes. D grades transfer. Of a total 188 quarter credits required for the bachelor's degree, transfers must complete 47 quarter credits at the college. At least 1 year must be completed in residence. There is a rolling admissions policy; application deadlines are open. Transfers may enroll in any quarter.

Visiting: A Junior-Senior Day is held for prospective students. Informal visits may be made to the campus any time during the year; arrangements can be made through the admissions office. Visitors may sit in on classes and remain on campus overnight.

Financial Aid: About 73% of all students receive some form of financial aid. Twenty-five percent work part-time on campus. The average award to freshmen is $2180. The college is a member of CSS. The FAF is required, and the college prefers that applications for financial aid be filed by May 1. Loans are available from the federal government.

Foreign Students: About 2% of the full-time students are from foreign countries. The college offers these students special counseling.

Admissions: The TOEFL is required; a minimum score of 500 must be achieved. The SAT or ACT is not required.

Procedure: There are no application deadlines. Foreign candidates may apply for entry to the fall, winter, spring, or summer quarter. Proof of health, consisting of a health history questionnaire and T.B. test, must be presented. Proof of funds adequate to cover the intended period of study is required.

Admissions Contact: Bruce Webb, Director of Admissions.

UNIVERSITY OF IDAHO A-2
Moscow, Idaho 83843   (208) 885-6326

F/T: 3806M, 2300W	Faculty: 501; I, – –$
P/T: 669M, 539W	Ph.D.'s: 70%
Grad: 1178M, 506W	S/F Ratio: 18 to 1
Year: early sems, ss	Tuition: $701 ($2501)
Appl: Aug. 1	R and B: $1822
1800 applied	1676 accepted 1167 enrolled
SAT: 444V 478M	ACT: 21 NONCOMPETITIVE

University of Idaho, established in 1889 as a land-grant institution, is composed of 9 colleges—Letters and Sciences, Agriculture, Engineering, Law, Mines and Earth Resources, Forestry, Wildlife and Range Sciences, Education, Art and Architecture, and Business and Economics—and the Graduate School. The library contains 1,031,475 volumes and 153,319 microfilm items, subscribes to 12,086 periodicals, and is the regional depository for U.S. government documents.

Environment: Located in a town surrounded by mountains 90 miles southeast of Spokane, Washington, the rural main campus and farms constitute 1400 acres. In addition, the university has a 12,200-acre forest and its branch stations occupy 1800 acres. There are a total of 23 dormitories for 2300 students and apartments for married couples. Additional housing is available in 18 fraternity and 9 sorority houses.

Student Life: Out-of-state enrollment is limited to 20% of the student body; 40% of all students live on campus. Three percent are minority-group members. Campus housing is both single-sex and coed; there are visiting privileges in the single-sex housing. Students may keep cars on campus. Day-care services are available to all students.

Organizations: There are 18 fraternities and 9 sororities on campus, to which 21% of the men and 18% of the women belong. An active student government participates in administrative and curricular matters, and plans social and cultural events. There are special-interest clubs and a campus radio station.

Sports: The university fields 8 intercollegiate teams for men and 8 for women. There are 25 intramural sports for men and 18 for women.

Handicapped: About 50% of the campus is accessible to the physically handicapped. Facilities include wheelchair ramps, special parking, elevators, specially equipped rest rooms, and lowered drinking fountains. Fewer than 1% of the students currently enrolled have visual or hearing impairments. A counselor and an assistant are available to assist handicapped students.

Graduates: The freshman drop-out rate is 33%. Almost 40% of those who graduate pursue graduate study: 1% enter medical school, 1% dental school, and 4% law school. About 65% of graduates pursue careers in business and industry.

Services: Free tutoring, remedial instruction, psychological counseling, placement, and career counseling are available free of charge.

Programs of Study: The university confers 49 different bachelor's degrees, including the B.A., B.S., B.F.A., B.Arch., B.Land.Arch., and B.Physics. Master's and doctoral degrees are also awarded. Bachelor's degrees are offered in the following subjects: AREA STUDIES (American, Latin American), BUSINESS (accounting, business administration, business education, computer science, finance, management, marketing), EDUCATION (early childhood, elementary, health/physical, industrial, secondary, special), ENGLISH (English, journalism, literature, speech), FINE AND PERFORMING ARTS (art, art education, art history, dance, film/photography, music, music education, radio/TV, studio art, theater/dramatics), HEALTH SCIENCES (medical technology), LANGUAGES (French, German, Greek/Latin, Spanish), MATH AND SCIENCES (bacteriology, biochemistry, biology, botany, chemistry, earth science, ecology/environmental science, geology, mathematics, natural sciences, physical sciences, physics, statistics, zoology), PHILOSOPHY (classics, philosophy), PREPROFESSIONAL (agriculture, architecture, cartography, dentistry, engineering, forestry, home economics, law, medicine, veterinary), SOCIAL SCIENCES (anthropology, economics, geography, government/political science, history, psychology, sociology). Thirty-two percent of the degrees are conferred in the liberal arts, 14% in business, and 13% each in engineering and forestry.

Required: All students must take courses in English and physical education, spend the senior year in residence, and have an overall GPA of 2.0. In addition, students must meet requirements which vary with the college in which they are enrolled.

Special: The university offers accelerated courses, which cover a full semester's work in half the time, and a general studies division for students who have not decided on their major. Qualified students may study abroad and engineering students may participate in work-study programs with major industries. The university also participates in the National Student Exchange Program.

Honors: There are 26 honor societies on campus; departmental honors programs are also offered.

Admissions: Approximately 90% of those who applied were accepted for the 1981–82 freshman class. The SAT scores of those who enrolled were as follows: Verbal—71% below 500, 23% between 500 and 599, 4% between 600 and 700, and 2% above 700; Math—57% below 500, 25% between 500 and 599, 13% between 600 and 700, and 5% above 700. On the ACT, 52% scored below 21, 21% between 21 and 23, 13% between 24 and 25, 8% between 26 and 28, and 6% above 28. The admissions decision is based on the applicant's academic record. Standardized test scores are used for placement purposes only. Candidates must be graduates of an accredited high school and have completed 15 high school units. There is open admission for Idaho residents; out-of-state applicants must have an average of at least C and rank in the top half of their graduating class.

Procedure: Either the SAT or ACT is required. Application deadlines are August 1 (fall), December 1 (spring), and May 15 (summer). A $10 fee should accompany all applications. Notification is on a rolling basis.

Special: There are early decision, early admissions, and deferred admissions plans. AP and CLEP credit is accepted.

Transfer: For fall 1981, 2250 students applied, 1818 were accepted, and 1125 enrolled. Transfer students need a 2.0 GPA and must take the SAT or ACT if transferring with less than 26 credits. Students must reside at the university for at least 1 year and must complete, at the university, 32 of the last 40 credits (128 credits are required for a bachelor's degree). Application deadlines are the same as those for freshmen.

Visiting: There are regularly scheduled orientations for prospective students. Guides are also available for informal visits; visitors may sit in on classes and stay at the school. The office of high school and junior college relations should be contacted to arrange visits (208-885-6163).

Financial Aid: The university annually awards 400–500 scholarships to freshmen from a fund of $200,000. Other financial aid is available from BEOG, SEOG, NDSL, CWS, Pell, and SSIG. The average award to freshmen from all sources is $2200. About 50% of all students receive some form of aid. Thirty-five percent work part-time on campus. The FAF is required; the deadline for financial aid application is March 11.

Foreign Students: Three percent of the full-time students come from foreign countries. Special counseling and special organizations are available to these students.

Admissions: Foreign students must achieve a TOEFL score of at least 500. No college entrance exams are required.

Procedure: Application deadlines are April 15 (fall), September 15 (spring), and March 15 (summer). Foreign students must present proof of funds. There is a special $50-per-semester fee for these students. Health insurance is optional; it is available through the university for a fee.

Admissions Contact: Matt E. Telin, Director of Admissions and Registrar.

ILLINOIS

AUGUSTANA COLLEGE   C-2
Rock Island, Illinois 61201   (309) 794-7341

F/T: 1065M, 1200W	Faculty: 115; IIB, ++$
P/T: 80M, 79W	Ph.D.'s: 81%
Grad: 6M, 3W	S/F Ratio: 17 to 1
Year: qtrs, ss	Tuition: $4065
Appl: open	R and B: $1932
1480 applied	1243 accepted 600 enrolled
ACT: 24	VERY COMPETITIVE

Augustana College is a liberal arts institution chartered in 1860 and affiliated with the Lutheran Church. The library contains 220,000 volumes and 104 microfilm items, and subscribes to 1876 periodicals.

Environment: The 110-acre urban campus is located in the heart of the Quad-Cities, 180 miles from Chicago. The campus has 20 buildngs. College housing includes dormitories and on-campus and off-campus apartments.

Student Life: About 85% of the students come from Illinois, and 90% come from public schools. About 65% live on campus. About 61% are Protestant, and 26% are Catholic; attendance at chapel services is voluntary. Seven percent of the students are minority-group members. Campus housing is single-sex; there are visiting privileges. Students may keep cars on campus. Alcohol is prohibited on campus.

Organizations: There are 6 fraternities and 5 sororities on campus; about 15% of the men and 15% of the women belong to one of them. A variety of student organizations is available.

Sports: Augustana offers intercollegiate competition in 10 sports for men and 7 for women. There are 11 intramural sports for men and 11 for women.

Handicapped: Facilities for handicapped students include elevators and lowered drinking fountains.

Graduates: About 12% of the students drop out after the first year; 70% remain to graduate. Of the graduates, 40% pursue advanced degrees: 3% in medicine, 3% in dentistry, and 5% in law. About 36% pursue careers in business and industry.

Services: Students receive the following services free of charge: placement and career counseling, health care, tutoring, remedial instruction, and psychological counseling.

Programs of Study: The college confers the B.A., B.Mus., and B.Mus.Ed. degrees. Master's degrees are also awarded. Bachelor's degrees are offered in the following subjects: AREA STUDIES (Asian, urban), BUSINESS (accounting, business administration, computer science, public administration), EDUCATION (elementary, health/physical, secondary), ENGLISH (English, journalism, speech), FINE AND PERFORMING ARTS (art, art education, art history, mass communications, music, music education), HEALTH SCIENCES (medical technology, speech therapy), LANGUAGES (French, German, Greek/Latin, Scandinavian, Spanish), MATH AND SCIENCES (biology, chemistry, earth science, ecology/environmental science, geology, mathematics, physics), PHILOSOPHY (Christian education, classics, humanities, philosophy, religion), PREPROFESSIONAL (dentistry, engineering, environmental management, forestry, law, library science, medicine, ministry, pharmacy, physical therapy, social work, veterinary), SOCIAL SCIENCES (economics, geography, government/political science, history, psychology, social sciences, sociology). About 30% of the degrees are conferred in business.

Required: All students must take English, foreign language, speech, religion, philosophy, physical education, laboratory science, fine arts, and social science.

Special: Student-designed majors, foreign travel, interdepartmental majors, and 3-2 dual degree programs in engineering and in forestry or environmental management are offered.

Honors: There are 16 honor societies on campus, including a chapter of Phi Beta Kappa.

Admissions: Eighty-four percent of those who applied were accepted for the 1981-82 freshman class. The ACT scores of those who enrolled were as follows: 19% below 21, 26% between 21 and 23, 21% between 24 and 25, 22% between 26 and 28, and 12% above 28. Applicants should have completed 15 Carnegie units and should rank in the upper half of their class. Other considerations are impressions made during the interview, leadership, advanced placement or honor courses, and extracurricular activities.

Procedure: The SAT or ACT should be taken no later than January of the senior year. There are no application deadlines. A $15 fee is required. Notification is on a rolling basis.

Special: Early decision and deferred admissions programs are available. Students may earn credit through AP exams.

Transfer: For fall 1981, 220 students applied, 170 were accepted, and 111 enrolled. Transfer applicants are considered for all classes; students must have a 2.0 GPA. D grades transfer. Students must earn 186 quarter credits to receive a bachelor's degree.

Visiting: There are regularly scheduled orientations for prospective students. Guides are available for informal visits; visitors may sit in on classes and stay overnight at the school. Visits are best scheduled on weekdays. The admissions office should be contacted for arrangements.

Financial Aid: About 81% of the students receive financial aid. Fifty-nine percent work part-time on campus. The college provides scholarships, loans, and campus employment. The average scholarship or loan given to freshmen is $2300, but the maximum grants combined with campus employment can go as high as $5250. The FAF is required. There are no application deadlines. The college is a member of CSS.

Foreign Students: Fewer than 1 percent of the full-time students come from foreign countries. Special counseling and special organizations are available for these students.

Admissions: Foreign students must achieve a TOEFL score of at least 500. No college entrance exams are required.

Procedure: There are no application deadlines; foreign students are admitted in all quarters. They must present proof of health and proof of funds adequate to cover 1 year of study. Health insurance is not required, but it is available through the college.

Admissions Contact: Ralph E. Starenko, Vice-President for Admissions and Financial Aid.

AURORA COLLEGE   E-2
Aurora, Illinois 60507   (312) 896-1975

F/T: 307M, 387W	Faculty: 64; n/av
P/T: 352M, 203W	Ph.D.'s: n/av
Grad: 70M, 14W	S/F Ratio: 11 to 1
Year: terms, ss	Tuition: $3675
Appl: open	R and B: $2100
315 applied	257 accepted 155 enrolled
ACT: 20	COMPETITIVE

Aurora College, founded in 1893 by the Advent Christian Church, is a small liberal arts college. The library contains 94,915 volumes, 106 microfilm items, and subscribes to 385 periodicals.

Environment: The 26-acre suburban campus is located in a residential neighborhood 40 miles from Chicago. The 14 buildings include 4 dormitories (2 for women, 1 for men, and 1 coed) that house 427 students. The 5000-square foot nursing building houses multi-purpose teaching facilities, offices, and hospital and clinical mockups. There is a new dining hall that seats 225, and a banquet room for 400.

Student Life: About 89% of the students are from Illinois; 89% of the freshmen come from public schools. About half of the students live on campus. Drinking on campus is prohibited and smoking is permitted only in designated areas. Attendance at religious services is not required. Fifteen percent of the students are minority-group members. Thirty-eight percent are Protestant, 30% are Catholic, and 30% claim no religious affiliation. Campus housing is both coed and single-sex; there are visiting privileges in the single-sex housing. Students may keep cars on campus.

Organizations: There are 2 fraternities and 1 sorority, to which 12% of the men and 8% of the women belong. Student organizations and the town offer social and cultural entertainment for students.

Sports: The college fields 7 intercollegiate teams for men and 6 for women. There are 7 intramural sports for men and 6 for women.

Handicapped: There are no special facilities for physically handicapped students, but 80% of the campus is accessible to them. There are no hearing or visually impaired students currently enrolled.

Graduates: About 25% of the students who graduate pursue advanced degrees; 30% pursue careers in business and industry.

Services: Free tutoring, remedial instruction, career counseling, job placement services, psychological counseling, and health care are available to students.

Programs of Study: The college confers the B.A., B.S., and B.S.N. degrees. Master's degrees are also awarded. Bachelor's degrees are offered in the following subjects: BUSINESS (accounting, business administration, computer science), EDUCATION (elementary, health/physical, secondary), ENGLISH (English, literature), FINE AND PERFORMING ARTS (art, theater/dramatics), HEALTH SCIENCES (medical technology, nursing), LANGUAGES (French), MATH AND SCIENCES (biology, chemistry, ecology/environmental science, mathematics), PHILOSOPHY (humanities, philosophy, religion), PRE-PROFESSIONAL (dentistry, engineering, law, medicine), SOCIAL SCIENCES (economics, government/political science, history, psychology, social sciences, sociology).

Required: Satisfactory completion of 40 courses is required. The distribution includes 4 courses from each of the 3 major divisions (humanities, social and behavioral science, and natural science and mathematics). An upper-level colloquium is also required; the colloquium is a dialog confrontation approach to Christian values in society, as well as their application to the classroom.

Special: Internships are offered in all academic areas. Student-designed majors and study abroad are also available.

Admissions: Approximately 82% of those who applied were accepted for the 1981–82 freshman class. The ACT scores of those who enrolled were as follows: 53% scored below 21, 20% between 21 and 23, 14% between 24 and 25, 10% between 26 and 28, and 3% above 28. Candidates should have a high school diploma or the equivalent and rank in the top 60% of their class. Other factors influencing the admissions decision are recommendations, impressions made during the interview, advanced placement or honors courses, and the student's extracurricular activities record.

Procedure: The ACT or SAT is required and should be taken by May of the senior year. An English placement exam and a campus interview are required. There are no application deadlines; notification is on a rolling basis. There is a $15 fee.

Special: AP and CLEP credit is accepted.

Transfer: For fall 1981, 204 students applied, 178 were accepted, and 108 enrolled. Transfer students are not accepted in the senior year. A minimum GPA of 2.0 and 15 credit hours are needed to transfer. All students must complete, at the college, 36 of the 120 credits required for a bachelor's degree. There are no application deadlines; notification is given within 1 month after receipt of the application.

Visiting: Open House meetings are held once a month for prospective students. Arrangements for informal visits can be made through the admissions office.

Financial Aid: As a member of the CSS, the college requires the FAF, FFS, or SFS (FAF is preferred). A typical freshman aid package consists of a $3600 grant and scholarship, and a $1000 loan. About 83% of all students receive some form of financial assistance. Forty percent work part-time on campus. There are no application deadlines, but early application is encouraged.

Foreign Students: One percent of the full-time students come from foreign countries. The college offers an intensive English course and special counseling for these students.

Admissions: Students must achieve a TOEFL score of at least 550. No college entrance exams are required.

Procedure: Foreign students are admitted in all 4 terms; there are no application deadlines. They must present proof of health (the college provides a form to be filled out by a doctor) and must present proof of funds adequate to cover 1 year of study. They must carry health insurance, which is available through the college for a fee.

Admissions Contact: John Seveland, Director of Admissions.

BARAT COLLEGE
Lake Forest, Illinois 60045

E-1

(312) 234-3000

F/T: 2M, 338W	Faculty: 38; IIB, –$
P/T: 10M, 302W	Ph.D.'s: 62%
Grad: none	S/F Ratio: 13 to 1
Year: sems, ss	Tuition: $4200
Appl: open	R and B: $2100
197 applied	160 accepted	102 enrolled
SAT: 410V 380M	ACT: 17	LESS COMPETITIVE

Barat College, founded in 1919, is a private liberal arts college for women affiliated with the Roman Catholic Church. The library houses 81,000 volumes and 1350 microfilm items, and subscribes to 495 periodicals.

Environment: The 40-acre campus, located in a suburban area of the Lake Michigan shoreline 25 miles from Chicago, has 8 major buildings, including 2 theaters and 2 dance studios. Two dormitories house 450 women.

Student Life: Eighty-eight percent of the students are from Illinois. About 30% live on campus. There are visiting privileges in the dormitories. Students may keep cars on campus. Day-care services are available, for a fee, to all students, faculty, and staff.

Organizations: There are no sororities. Extracurricular activities include special-interest clubs, music and drama groups, publications, concerts, films, lectures, art shows, and social mixers.

Sports: The college competes on an intercollegiate level in 2 sports. Three intramural sports are offered for women.

Handicapped: The entire campus is accessible to wheelchair-bound students. Facilities include wheelchair ramps, special parking, and elevators.

Graduates: About 25% of the freshmen drop out during the first year, and 40% remain to graduate. About 48% of the graduates seek advanced degrees; 1% enter medical school and 3% enter law school. About 80% pursue careers in business and industry.

Services: Students receive the following free services: health care, psychological counseling, career counseling, placement services, tutoring, and remedial instruction.

Programs of Study: The college confers the B.A. and B.F.A. degrees. Bachelor's degrees are offered in the following subjects: AREA STUDIES (American), BUSINESS (accounting, banking and finance, computer science, international business, labor relations and personnel, management, marketing), EDUCATION (secondary), ENGLISH (English), FINE AND PERFORMING ARTS (art, art and dance therapy, art history, dance, music, studio art, theater/dramatics), LANGUAGES (French, Spanish), MATH AND SCIENCES (biology, chemistry, mathematics/computer studies), PHILOSOPHY (humanities, philosophy, religion), SOCIAL SCIENCES (economics, history, human sciences and services, international relations, psychology, social sciences, sociology). Twenty-eight percent of degrees conferred are in social sciences, 21% in fine and performing arts, and 18% in business.

Special: A degree completion program is offered in health studies (for registered nurses only). Programs are also offered in learning disabilities, educable mentally handicapped, and women's studies. Cross-registration with Lake Forest College is available. Students may design their own majors. Work-study internships and study abroad offer additional opportunities.

Honors: The college offers honors courses in all departments. Two national honor societies are represented on campus.

Admissions: Eighty-one percent of those who applied were accepted for the 1981–82 freshman class. The SAT scores of those who enrolled were as follows: Verbal—83% below 500, 16% between 500 and 599, and 0% above 600; Math—80% below 500, 9% between 500 and 599, 2% between 600 and 700, and 0% above 700. Of those who took the ACT, 70% scored below 20, 13% between 21 and 23, 8% between 24 and 25, 3% between 26 and 28, and 2% above 28. Candidates must be graduates of an accredited high school, be recommended by school authorities, and have a GPA of 2.0 or better. The college also considers evidence of special talents and impressions made during an interview.

Procedure: The SAT or ACT is required. The SAT should be taken in March of the junior year or January of the senior year; the ACT in May of the junior year or January of the senior year. Application deadlines are open; new students are admitted to fall and spring semesters. There is a $15 application fee. Notification is made on a rolling basis.

Special: CLEP and AP credit is accepted.

Transfer: For fall 1981, 220 applications were received, 202 were accepted, and 168 students enrolled. Transfers are considered for all classes and must have a GPA of 2.0 or better. An ACT score of 17 or combined SAT scores of 800 are recommended. Students must complete, in residence, at least 30 of the 120 semester hours required for a bachelor's degree.

Visiting: Informal visits to the college may be made 5 days a week; guides are available. Overnight accommodations can be arranged through the admissions office. Open-house orientations for prospective students are held twice a year.

Financial Aid: About 58% of all students receive aid in the form of scholarships, grants, and campus employment. Twenty-one percent work part-time on campus. Awards are based on financial need and academic record. Tuition may be paid in installments. The recom-

ILLINOIS

mended deadline for financial aid applications is May 1. The FFS or (preferably) the FAF must be filed. The college is a member of the CSS.

Foreign Students: Foreign students enrolled full-time at the college represent about 7% of enrollment. An intensive English course, special counseling, and special organizations are provided for these students.

Admissions: Applicants must score 480 or better on the TOEFL. No academic exams are required.

Procedure: Application deadlines are open; new students are admitted to all terms. Students must present proof of good health and of adequate funds. A fee of about $35 for evaluation of credits may be required. Foreign students must carry health insurance, which is available through the college for a fee.

Admissions Contact: Carol L. McCart, Director of Admissions.

BLACKBURN COLLEGE C-4
Carlinville, Illinois 62626 (217) 854-3231

F/T: 205M, 281W	Faculty:	n/av; IV, av$
P/T: 18M, 38W	Ph.D.'s:	75%
Grad: none	S/F Ratio:	12 to 1
Year: sems	Tuition:	$3025
Appl: open	R and B:	$1075
SAT or ACT: required		**COMPETITIVE**

Blackburn College, founded in 1857, is a small, private liberal arts college affiliated with the Presbyterian Church. The college is noted for its work program, staffed by resident students who are responsible for the operation of the entire physical plant of the college. The library contains 69,500 volumes and subscribes to 375 periodicals.

Environment: The 8-acre rural campus is located on the outskirts of a small town about 70 miles from St. Louis, Missouri. Nine of the 15 buildings on campus were constructed entirely by student labor through the work program. Six dormitories accommodate 509 men and women.

Student Life: The majority of students are from Illinois. About 91% attended public schools. Over 90% live on campus. Most students are not Presbyterian, and the student religious organization is interdenominational. Campus housing is both coed and single-sex; there are visiting privileges in single-sex dorms. Students may keep cars on campus.

Organizations: There are no fraternities or sororities. Extracurricular activities include a student newspaper, choir, theater, and religious groups; and special-interest clubs. Nearby lakes offer opportunities for water sports.

Sports: The college fields intercollegiate teams in 5 sports for men and 5 for women. There are 6 intramural sports for men and 5 for women.

Handicapped: Special arrangements for handicapped students include parking privileges and special class scheduling.

Graduates: By the end of freshman year, 20% of the students drop out; about 65% remain to graduate. About 30% of the graduates pursue advanced degrees, with 2% entering law school, 1% entering dental school, and 2% entering medical school. Twenty percent of the graduates pursue careers in business or industry.

Services: The following services are available free to students: psychological counseling, placement and career counseling, tutoring, and remedial instruction. Placement services, including resume service, interviews, and counseling, are open to alumni as well as undergraduates.

Programs of Study: All programs lead to the B.A. degree. Bachelor's degrees are offered in the following subjects: EDUCATION (elementary, secondary, special), ENGLISH (English, literature), FINE AND PERFORMING ARTS (art, art history, music, studio art, theater/dramatics), LANGUAGES (Spanish), MATH AND SCIENCES (biology, chemistry, mathematics), SOCIAL SCIENCES (business administration, economics, government/political science, history, psychology, sociology).

Required: Unless waived by proficiency examination, courses in foreign language, philosophy/religion, and written English are required of all students. A Cultural Studies option to the foreign-language requirement is available.

Special: Under the work program, all resident students are required to work 15 hours per week at some campus job. Students run the dining hall, kitchen, student center, and bookstore; work on new construction and campus maintenance; and serve as janitors and faculty assistants. Internships are available to qualified juniors and seniors in most fields of study. Students may spend a semester at the University of Mexico or at American University in Washington, D.C. Students may design their own majors.

Honors: Three national honor socieites have chapters on campus.

Admissions: About 83% of those who applied for admission were accepted for a recent freshman class. Applicants should rank in or near the upper quarter of their high school class and have at least a B average. The applicant's stability, maturity, and willingness to assume responsibility also are considered.

Procedure: The SAT or ACT is required. Application, high school record, and test scores may be submitted beginning in October. Application deadlines are open. Students are admitted at midyear as well as in the fall. Notification is made on a rolling basis and usually begins 2 weeks after all credentials are received. There is no application fee.

Special: The college has a deferred admissions plan. AP and some CLEP examinations are acceptable for credit.

Transfer: D grades may not be accepted for credit. Students must spend at least 1 year at the college to receive a bachelor's degree. There is a rolling admissions policy.

Visiting: A regular orientation program is available for prospective students. Guides are also available for informal visits. Visitors may sit in on classes and stay overnight on campus. The best time to visit is during the school year, from August to May. Arrangements may be made through the admissions office.

Financial Aid: About 63% of all students receive aid. About 70% of entering freshmen receive scholarships, either from the college or, for Illinois residents, from the state. Loans are also available from the college. The mandatory 15 hours of part-time work per week substantially reduces the room and board costs of resident students. Aid is awarded on the basis of financial need. Economically deprived students are given special consideration. The FAF or FFS is required.

Admissions Contact: Donald J. Gix, Director of Admissions and Records.

BRADLEY UNIVERSITY D-3
Peoria, Illinois 61625 (309) 676-7611

F/T: 2627M, 1964W	Faculty:	n/av; IIA, +$
P/T: 332M, 260W	Ph.D.'s:	75%
Grad: 222M, 253W	S/F Ratio:	16 to 1
Year: sems, ss	Tuition:	$4080
Appl: open	R and B:	$1960
SAT: 460V 510M ACT: 23		**COMPETITIVE+**

Bradley University, founded in 1897, is a private nonsectarian university that provides undergraduate instruction in the liberal arts and sciences, business, education, engineering, fine arts and communication, health sciences, and international studies. It also offers graduate programs. The library houses over 310,000 volumes and 200,000 microfilm items, and subscribes to over 1600 periodicals.

Environment: The self-contained, 63-acre campus is in a suburban section of Peoria. The 32 major buildings include a sports and recreation center, a performing arts center, a 100-unit apartment complex, and 13 dormitories housing 974 women and 1162 men. There are 18 fraternity houses and 9 sorority houses 1 block from campus.

Student Life: About 78% of the students are from Illinois and 21% are from out of state. Ninety percent live in campus dormitories, fraternity or sorority houses, or on-campus apartments. Eight percent of the students are members of minority groups. Campus housing is both coed and single-sex. There are visiting privileges in single-sex dorms. Students may keep cars on campus.

Organizations: Thirty-five percent of the men and 35% of the women belong to 1 of 18 national fraternities or 9 national sororities. There are numerous extracurricular activities, including theater, chorale, instrumental ensembles, and a nationally ranked forensics team. There are religious organizations and counselors for students of all major faiths.

Sports: The university fields intercollegiate teams in 11 sports for men and 10 for women. There are 15 intramural sports for men and 14 for women.

Handicapped: About 75% of the campus is accessible to wheelchair-bound students. Special parking and specially equipped rest rooms are available, as are wheelchair ramps, elevators, and some lowered drinking fountains. Special class scheduling is available. One percent of the students have visual or hearing impairments.

Graduates: Sixteen percent of the freshmen drop out at the end of their first year; 66% remain to graduate. About 30% of the graduates pursue advanced degrees; 50% pursue careers in business and industry.

Services: Students receive the following services free of charge: psychological counseling, placement, health care, career counseling, tutoring, and remedial instruction.

Programs of Study: Bradley confers the following undergraduate degrees: B.A., B.S., B.F.A., B.Mus., B.S.E., B.S.M.E., and B.S.Tech. Master's degrees are also awarded. Bachelor's degrees are offered in the following subjects: BUSINESS (accounting, business administration, computer science, economics, finance, management, marketing), EDUCATION (early childhood, elementary, secondary, special), ENGLISH (English, journalism, speech), FINE AND PERFORMING ARTS (art, art education, art history, film/photography, music, music education, radio/TV, studio art, theater/dramatics), HEALTH SCIENCES (medical technology, nursing), LANGUAGES (French, German, Spanish), MATH AND SCIENCES (biology, chemistry, ecology/environmental science, geology, mathematics, physics), PHILOSOPHY philosophy, religion), PREPROFESSIONAL (engineering, home economics, social work), SOCIAL SCIENCES (economics, geography, government/political science, history, international relations, psychology, social sciences, sociology). Thirty-one percent of the undergraduate degrees conferred are in preprofessional fields and 22% are in business.

Special: Student-designed majors and study abroad are available.

Honors: The university does not maintain traditional honors programs.

Admissions: About 78% of those who applied were accepted for the 1981–82 freshman class. In addition to scholastic record, the admissions committee considers special talent, recommendations, extracurricular activities, advanced placement or honors work, leadership abilities, and impressions made during a personal interview. Applicants should be graduates of an accredited high school with 16 Carnegie units and should rank in the upper half of their high school class.

Procedure: The ACT or SAT is required. Suggested application deeadlines are August 1 (fall), January 10 (spring), and June 1 (summer). Notification is on a rolling basis. There is a $20 application fee.

Special: AP and CLEP credit is accepted. There is an early decision plan with notification 2 weeks from date of application.

Transfer: For fall 1981, 994 transfer students applied, 712 were accepted, and 496 enrolled. Applicants to the College of Engineering must have a 2.75 GPA; applicants to the College of Business, a 2.5 GPA; and all other applicants, a 2.0 GPA. Transfer students must complete in residence 30 of the 124–136 hours required for the bachelor's degree.

Visiting: There is an orientation program for prospective students that includes a campus tour and an admissions interview. Informal guided tours of the campus can be arranged. Visitors may sit in on classes and stay overnight at the school. Visits are best made on weekdays. The admissions office will make arrangements.

Financial Aid: Seventy percent of all students receive financial assistance; 50% work part-time on campus. The aid application deadline is April 1. Among the programs available are BEOG, NDSL, Illinois State Grant, Illinois Guaranteed Loans, and CWS. The FAF is required.

Foreign Students: Foreign students constitute about 6% of the full-time enrollment. The university offers these students special counseling and special organizations.

Admissions: Either a score of 500 on the TOEFL or 80 on the University of Michigan Language Test is necessary for admission. College entrance exams are not required.

Procedure: Application deadlines are February 1 (fall and summer) and September 1 (spring). Foreign students must present proof of funds adequate to cover 4 years of study. Health insurance is available through the university for a fee.

Admissions Contact: Robert Voss, Director of Freshman Admissions.

CHICAGO STATE UNIVERSITY   E–2
Chicago, Illinois 60628   (312) 995-2513

F/T: 1173M, 2090W	Faculty: 118; IIA, av$
P/T: 794M, 1407W	Ph.D.'s: 60%
Grad: 618M, 1359W	S/F Ratio: 12 to 1
Year: tri, ss	Tuition: $788 ($2168)
Appl: Aug. 2	R and B: n/app
2379 applied	1010 accepted 663 enrolled
ACT: 13	LESS COMPETITIVE

Chicago State University, founded in 1869, is a member of the State of Illinois University system; it is controlled by the state board of governors. The undergraduate divisions include the School of Education, the School of Arts and Sciences, the School of Nursing, the College of Allied Health, and the School of Business Administration. The library contains 250,000 volumes and 120,000 microfilm items, and subscribes to 2300 periodicals.

Environment: The 160-acre urban campus is 12 miles south of the Chicago Loop. A commuter school, the university provides a cafeteria, lounge, and locker facilities. A recent addition to the 10-building campus is a Science Center containing research labs, a surgery complex, an electron microscopy lab, a plant growth room, an animal room, and a weather station.

Student Life: All but 1% of the students are residents of the Chicago metropolitan area; 85% of the entering freshmen come from public schools. All students live off campus. About 79% are minority-group members. About 56% are Catholic, and 24% are Protestant. Students may keep cars on campus. Day-care services are available to all students, faculty, and staff for a fee.

Organizations: A variety of student-operated activities includes the student government, student publications, choir, orchestra, 3 sororities, 3 fraternities, special interest groups, and honorary societies. Religious organizations are available to students of the 3 major faiths.

Sports: The university fields 7 intercollegiate teams for men and 5 for women. There are 3 intramural sports for men and 1 for women.

Handicapped: Approximately 90% of the campus is accessible to the physically handicapped. Facilities include wheelchair ramps, special parking, elevators, specially equipped rest rooms, and lowered drinking fountains and telephones; special class scheduling is also available. Fewer than 1% of the students currently enrolled have visual or hearing impairments. Counselors are assigned according to individual need.

Graduates: At the end of the freshman year, 35% drop out; 25% remain to graduate, with 20% of the graduates pursuing graduate study; 1% enter medical school and 1% enter law school. About 30% of graduates pursue careers in business and industry.

Services: Placement, career counseling, health care, tutoring, remedial instruction, and psychological counseling are offered to students free of charge.

Programs of Study: The university confers the B.A., B.S., and B.S.Ed. degrees. Master's programs are also offered. Bachelor's degrees are offered in the following subjects: AREA STUDIES (Black/Afro-American), BUSINESS (accounting, business education, computer science, finance, information systems, management, marketing), EDUCATION (early childhood, elementary, health and safety, health/physical, home economics, industrial, secondary, special), ENGLISH (English, linguistics, literature), FINE AND PERFORMING ARTS (art, art education, art history, music, music education, radio/TV, studio art), HEALTH SCIENCES (dietetics, medical technology, nursing, occupational therapy, radiation therapy technology), LANGUAGES (Spanish/secondary teaching), MATH AND SCIENCES (biology, chemistry, preprofessional), PREPROFESSIONAL (dentistry, law, medicine, pharmacy, veterinary), SOCIAL SCIENCES (anthropology, corrections, economics, geography, government/political science, history, psychology, sociology). Thirty percent of degrees conferred are in education, 21% in business, and 7% in math and sciences.

Required: All students are required to take 18 hours each in humanities, social science, natural science, and English composition. Students in the Education Option must complete 19 hours of professional education and 3 hours of physical education.

Special: It is possible to earn combined B.A.-B.S. degrees in all majors, in a 5-year program. Individualized curriculum, the University Without Walls program, and the Board of Governors B.A. program are also offered. Life experience credits are offered in the last 2 programs.

Honors: There are 2 honor societies on campus, Kappa Delta Pi for education, and Kappa Mu Epsilon for mathematics. A departmental honors award is given to an outstanding student in each department; 4 other students receive departmental certificates of achievement.

Admissions: Of those who applied for the 1981–82 freshman class, 42% were accepted. The ACT scores of those who enrolled were as follows: 95% below 21, 2% between 21 and 23, 1% between 24 and 25, and 2% between 26 and 28. Candidates must have completed 16 Carnegie units of high school work, be graduates of accredited high schools, and rank in the top 25% of their graduating class, or have compensatory ACT scores. The school indicates that in addition to these qualifications they consider the following factors in order of importance: evidence of special talents, recommendations by school officials, advanced placement or honors courses, and impressions made during the interview.

Procedure: The ACT is required and should be taken between April of the junior year and February of the senior year. The application, ACT scores, and high school transcript should be submitted as soon as possible after September 15 of the senior year. Application deadlines are August 2 (fall), December 1 (winter), March 5 (spring), and May 31 (summer). Notification is on a rolling basis. There is no application fee.

ILLINOIS

Special: There is an early decision plan with notification given 2 weeks following receipt of credentials. There are also early and deferred admissions plans. CLEP and AP credit is accepted.

Transfer: For fall 1981, 2645 students applied, 1404 were accepted, and 1127 enrolled. Transfers are considered for all classes; students must have a minimum C average and an ACT score of at least 14 if transferring with less than 30 semester credits from their former school. All students must complete, at the university, 30 of the 120 credits required for a bachelor's degree. D grades transfer in non-major courses only. Transfer application deadlines are the same as those for freshmen.

Visiting: There are no regularly scheduled orientations for prospective students. Guides are available for informal visits; visitors may sit in on classes. The admissions office should be contacted to arrange visits.

Financial Aid: Approximately 3% of all students receive aid through the university. Six percent work part-time on campus. Scholarships, grants, loans, and employment are offered. Deadlines for financial aid applications are July 9 (fall), October 29 (winter), March 15 (spring), and May 24 (summer); the FFS is required.

Foreign Students: One percent of the full-time students come from foreign countries.

Admissions: Foreign students must achieve a TOEFL score of at least 500 and must take the English Qualifying Exam. They must also have completed 30 semester hours in a U.S. college. No college entrance exams are required.

Procedure: Application deadlines for foreign students are July 1 (summer), November 1 (winter), March 1 (spring), and June 1 (summer). Foreign students must complete the university's health report and must present proof of funds adequate to cover 1 year of study. Health insurance is not required, but it is available through the university.

Admissions Contact: B. J. Holloway, Director of Admissions.

COLLEGE OF ST. FRANCIS
Joliet, Illinois 60435   E-2
(815) 740-3400

F/T: 280M, 360W
P/T: 90M, 140W
Grad: 100M, 220W
Year: sems, ss
Appl: July 30
250 applied
ACT: 21

Faculty: 45; IIB, av$
Ph.D.'s: 30%
S/F Ratio: 12 to 1
Tuition: $3390
R and B: $1920
180 accepted
140 enrolled
COMPETITIVE

The College of Saint Francis, founded in 1925, is a private liberal arts and professional college affiliated with the Roman Catholic Church. The library contains over 110,000 volumes and 100 microfilm items, and subscribes to over 500 periodicals.

Environment: The 15-acre campus is located in a suburban area 40 miles from Chicago. The physical plant consists of 5 major buildings; 2 dormitories accommodate 400 students.

Student Life: Ninety-five percent of the students are from Illinois; 50% of the entering freshmen come from parochial schools. About 50% of the students reside on campus. Seventy percent are Catholic, 25% are Protestant, and 3% are Jewish. Minority-group members comprise about 6% of the student body. Campus housing is coed. Students may keep cars on campus.

Organizations: Student organizations include religious groups, special-interest clubs, publications, and musical groups.

Sports: An intercollegiate athletic program is available, fielding 5 teams each for men and women. There are 4 intramural sports for both men and women.

Handicapped: About 80% of the campus is accessible to handicapped students. Facilities include wheelchair ramps, special parking, and elevators.

Graduates: At the end of the freshman year, 10% drop out; 60% remain to graduate. About 20% of the graduates pursue advanced degrees; 1% enter medical school, 1% enter dental school, and 3% enter law school. Twenty-five percent pursue careers in business and industry.

Services: Students receive the following services free of charge: placement and career counseling, health care, and psychological counseling. Tutoring is available for a fee.

Programs of Study: The college offers the B.A., B.B.A., and B.S. degrees. Bachelor's degrees are offered in the following subjects: BUSINESS (accounting, business administration, management, marketing), EDUCATION (elementary), ENGLISH (English, journalism), FINE AND PERFORMING ARTS (creative arts, radio/TV), HEALTH SCIENCES (cytotechnology, medical technology, nuclear medicine technology, recreational therapy), MATH AND SCIENCES (biology, mathematics), PHILOSOPHY (religion), PREPROFESSIONAL (dentistry, law, library science, medicine, social work, veterinary), SOCIAL SCIENCES (government/political science, history, psychology). Twenty-five percent of the degrees are conferred in business.

Special: Student-designed majors are permitted.

Honors: There are 2 honor societies on campus.

Admissions: Seventy-two percent of those who applied were accepted for the 1981-82 freshman class. Of those who enrolled, the ACT scores were as follows: 35% below 21, 40% between 21 and 23, 10% between 24 and 25, 10% between 26 and 28, and 5% above 28. Applicants must be high school graduates, rank in the upper half of their class, and have completed 15 academic units. The minimum GPA accepted is 2.5. Other considerations include recommendations, extracurricular activities, leadership, and impressions made during an interview.

Procedure: Either the ACT or SAT is required. The application, a $15 fee, test scores, and high school record should be submitted by July 30 (fall), December 30 (spring), or June 15 (summer). Notification is on a rolling basis.

Special: Early and deferred admissions plans are available. CLEP and AP credit is accepted.

Transfer: For fall 1981, 150 transfer students applied, 130 were accepted, and 110 enrolled. Transfers are considered for all classes; students must have a 2.0 GPA. D grades do not transfer. All students must complete, at the college, 32 of the 128 semester hours required for the bachelor's degree. The residency requirement is 1 year. Application deadlines are August 15 (fall) and January 10 (spring).

Visiting: Informal guided tours of the campus are available. Visitors may sit in on classes but may not stay overnight at the school. Campus visits may be scheduled throughout the academic year. The admissions office should be contacted for arrangements.

Financial Aid: About 86% of the students receive financial aid. Scholarships, loans, and part-time employment are available. Freshman aid from all sources, including campus employment, averages $2600 but may go as high as $5000. The deadlines for aid application are June 1 (fall) and January 1 (spring). The FAF must be filled.

Foreign Students: Foreign students account for about 1% of the full-time enrollment. The college offers special counseling to these students.

Admissions: Foreign students must achieve a minimum TOEFL score of 550. Entrance requirements include an SAT score of at least 900 (combined Verbal and Math); an ACT score of 20 also is acceptable.

Procedure: Application deadlines are April 1 (fall) and October 1 (spring). Foreign students must furnish proof of adequate funds to cover 1 year of study. They must establish proof of health through a physician's examination, and carry health insurance, which is available through the college for a fee.

Admissions Contact: Charles Beutel, Director of Admissions.

COLUMBIA COLLEGE
Chicago, Illinois 60605   E-2
(312) 663-1600

F/T: 1369M, 1171W
P/T: 656M, 768W
Grad: 31M, 43W
Year: sems, ss
Appl: open
1534 applied
SAT, ACT: not required

Faculty: 69; IV, +$
Ph.D.'s: 12%
S/F Ratio: 10 to 1
Tuition: $3055
R and B: n/app
1366 accepted
814 enrolled
SPECIAL

Columbia College, founded in 1890, is a private liberal arts institution that, in an unstructured, noncompetitive atmosphere, seeks to educate students for creative occupation in the arts. The college combines general liberal arts training with vocational preparation that offers professional apprenticeships and experience with modern technical equipment. The library contains 40,000 volumes and subscribes to 250 periodicals.

Environment: The college is a commuter institution; its main branch is located in a downtown Chicago office building. The college also maintains a dance center and a theater center in other parts of the city. Columbia has extensive motion-picture, arts, graphics, photography, and television facilities. There are no dormitories.

Student Life: Ninety-seven percent of the students are from Illinois, and the remainder are from bordering states. Forty-two percent are minority-group members. All students live off campus.

Organizations: There are no fraternities, sororities, or other organized, college-sponsored groups besides a student-run radio station, a student government, and a newspaper. Students arrange their own activities. More than 10 cultural events take place on campus each week.

Sports: There are 3 intramural sports for men and 2 for women.

Handicapped: The entire campus is accessible to handicapped students. Facilities include elevators, specially equipped rest rooms, and lowered drinking fountains.

Graduates: About 25% of the freshmen drop out. Forty to 50% of the graduates go on for further study. Sixty percent pursue careers in business and industry.

Services: Free psychological and career counseling, tutoring, and remedial instruction are provided. A placement office helps students obtain internships while in school and full-time jobs on graduation.

Programs of Study: The college confers the B.A. degree. Master's degrees are also awarded. Bachelor's degrees are offered in the following subjects: ENGLISH (creative writing), FINE AND PERFORMING ARTS (art, dance, film/photography, music, radio/TV, studio art, theater/dramatics). Eighty percent of all degrees are conferred in the arts.

Required: Students must complete 48 hours in general studies, including courses in writing, literature, contemporary studies, science, and the humanities.

Special: Study abroad may be arranged, and independent study is encouraged. Cooperative plans and internships are available with cultural and educational institutions around Chicago. Past programs for credit have included a sailing course, a raft trip, exploration of the Everglades, and a wilderness canoe trip. Students may design their own majors or earn a general studies degree.

Admissions: About 89% of those who applied were accepted for the 1981–82 freshman class. Applicants must be high school graduates or hold a GED certificate. Admissions are fairly open, but students must demonstrate potential in an interview or in correspondence. Admissions officers also consider special talents, impressions made during the interview, and extracurricular activities.

Procedure: The SAT or ACT is recommended but not required. There are no application deadlines. Admissions decisions are made on a rolling basis. The application fee is $20 for full-time students, $5 for part-time students.

Special: There are early decision, early admissions, and deferred admissions plans. CLEP credit may be earned.

Transfer: For fall 1981, 1612 students applied, 1261 were accepted, and 935 enrolled. Transfer applicants are considered for all classes. Some D grades transfer. Students must reside at the college for at least 1 year. They must complete, at the college, 36 of the 124 credits required for a bachelor's degree. There are no application deadlines.

Visiting: The college schedules regular orientations for prospective students that include a campus tour and visits with faculty members. Students also may contact the director of admissions to arrange informal visits. Visitors may sit in on classes, and guides may be available. Visits should be scheduled for Mondays through Thursdays, 10 A.M. to 3 P.M.

Financial Aid: Federal, state, and college aid programs are available, including BEOG, CWS, SEOG, the Illinois Guaranteed Loan Program, and the Columbia College Work Aid Plan. Seventy percent of the students receive aid. Applications should be filed 8 weeks before the beginning of the term. The college is a member of CSS; no financial statements are required.

Foreign Students: Special counseling is available to foreign students.

Admissions: Foreign students must achieve a TOEFL score of at least 500. No college entrance exams are required.

Procedure: There are no application deadlines; students are admitted in the fall, spring, and summer. Foreign students must present proof of funds adequate to cover 1 year of study.

Admissions Contact: Donald Warzeka, Director of Admissions.

CONCORDIA COLLEGE E-1
River Forest, Illinois 60305 (312) 771-8300

F/T: 368M, 724W	Faculty: 96; IIA, –$
P/T: 13M, 30W	Ph.D.'s: 55%
Grad: 59M, 123W	S/F Ratio: 11 to 1
Year: qtrs, ss	Tuition: $2709
Appl. Sept. 1	R and B: $1809
391 applied	337 accepted 224 enrolled
ACT: 21	COMPETITIVE

Concordia College, founded in 1864, is a liberal arts school owned and operated by the Lutheran Church, Missouri Synod. Although a full liberal arts program is offered, the school's main thrust is to prepare professional personnel for elementary, high school, college, and special educational programs of the Lutheran Church. The library houses 129,000 volumes and 188,000 microfilm items.

Environment: The 40-acre campus is in a suburban setting 10 miles from the Chicago Loop. Among its 12 buildings are a new worship and performing arts center. Dormitories are provided.

Student Life: Sixty-six percent of the students come from Illinois. The student body is 10% Catholic and 90% Protestant, with the majority of students Lutheran. About 2% are minority-group members. Eighty-five percent reside on campus; the remainder commute from home. Campus housing is single-sex, and there are visiting privileges. Students may keep cars on campus.

Organizations: There are no fraternities or sororities on campus, but there is a wide variety of extracurricular activities and cultural and social events available to students. The Chicago Loop, with all its cultural and recreational facilities, is just 10 miles away.

Sports: Concordia College competes on an intercollegiate level in 7 men's and 6 women's sports. There are 5 intramural sports for men and 5 for women.

Handicapped: The campus is equipped with wheelchair ramps for the benefit of handicapped students. Currently, no students with visual or hearing impairments are enrolled at Concordia. The college has no special counselors for handicapped students.

Graduates: At the end of freshman year, 25% drop out, and 55% of the students remain to graduate. Of those, 25% pursue advanced study after graduation.

Services: Students receive the following services free of charge: health care, psychological counseling, tutoring, placement, and career counseling.

Programs of Study: Concordia confers the B.A., B.Mus., and B.Mus.Ed. degrees, as well as master's degrees. Bachelor's degrees are offered in the following subjects: BUSINESS (computer science, management), EDUCATION (early childhood, elementary, secondary), ENGLISH (English), FINE AND PERFORMING ARTS (art education, music, music education), HEALTH SCIENCES (nursing), LANGUAGES (German), MATH AND SCIENCES (biology, chemistry, earth science, mathematics, natural sciences), PHILOSOPHY (religion), PREPROFESSIONAL (law, medicine, ministry, social work), SOCIAL SCIENCES (geography, government/political science, history, psychology, sociology). Eighty-five percent of all degrees are conferred in education, 5% in the arts, and 5% in the social sciences.

Required: All undergraduates are required to take 2 years of liberal arts.

Special: Student-designed majors are permitted.

Admissions: Eighty-six percent of those who applied were accepted for the 1981–82 freshman class. On the ACT, 43% scored below 21, 17% between 21 and 23, 16% between 24 and 25, 4% between 26 and 28, and 20% above 28. Recommendation by a student's pastor is required, as are a minimum 2.0 GPA and rank in the upper half of the high school class. Recommendations by the candidate's school and the school's accreditation and reputation are also important.

Procedure: The ACT is required. The rolling admissions plan is used; applicants are notified of their acceptance within 2 weeks of their completed applications. Freshmen are admitted in any session. The deadlines for admission are September 1 (fall), December 15 (winter), February 15 (spring), and June 15 (summer). There is no application fee.

Special: A deferred admissions plan is available. AP and CLEP credit is offered.

Transfer: For fall 1981, 168 transfer students applied, 138 were accepted, and 95 enrolled. A minimum 2.0 GPA is required. D grades transfer. Forty-eight quarter hours and half the major requirements must be completed in residence. Deadlines are the same as those for freshmen.

Visiting: There are regularly scheduled orientations for prospective students, during which tours, financial aid seminars, and meetings with faculty are available. Guides are available for informal visits to the campus. Visitors may sit in on classes and may also stay overnight at the school. The best time to visit is when classes are in session. Arrangements may be made through the admissions office.

Financial Aid: About 85% of all students receive financial aid. The college, a member of CSS, awards about 30 scholarships to freshmen each year. The FAF is required. Federal and state government, local bank, and college loans are available. Aid packages may include

190 ILLINOIS

work, loan, grant, and/or scholarship arrangements. The school's policy is to attempt to meet 100% of demonstrated financial need. The deadline for aid applications is July 15.

Foreign Students: Foreign students comprise less than 1% of the total enrollment. Special organizations are available for these students.

Admissions: Students must take either the TOEFL (minimum score, 525) or the University of Michigan Language Test (minimum score, 90) to qualify for admission. No college entrance exams are required if the student ranks in the upper half of the high school class.

Procedure: Application deadlines are August 1 (fall), December 1 (winter), February 1 (spring), and May 1 (summer). Foreign students must provide proof of funds adequate to cover 1 year of study. Health insurance, although not mandatory, is available through the college for a fee.

Admissions Contact: Robert A. Preloger, Director of Admissions.

DE LOURDES COLLEGE
E-1
Des Plaines, Illinois 60016 (312) 298-6942
(Recognized Candidate for Accreditation)

F/T, P/T: 170W	Faculty: n/av
Grad: none	Ph.D's: n/av
Year: sems, ss	S/F Ratio: n/av
Appl: open	Tuition: $35 p/c
SAT or ACT: not required	R and B: n/app
	LESS COMPETITIVE

De Lourdes College, founded in 1927, is an undergraduate college for women that is affiliated with the Catholic Church. The college accepts only mature women, not recent high school graduates.

Environment: The suburban campus is located in a city of 45,000 about 30 miles from Chicago. The school provides no student housing.

Student Life: All students are Illinois residents.

Programs of Study: The college offers bachelor's degrees in education, liberal arts/humanities, and social sciences.

Admissions: Most applicants are accepted. The only requirement is a high school diploma. The college is interested in mature women who are returning to college.

Procedure: A personal interview is required. Application deadlines are open; new students are admitted in spring and fall. The college follows a rolling admissions plan.

Admissions Contact: Sr. Mary Canisa, President and Dean.

DE PAUL UNIVERSITY
E-2
Chicago, Illinois 60604 (312) 321-7600

F/T: 2599M, 2567W	Faculty: 380; IIA, ++$
P/T: 1170M, 1994W	Ph.D's: 68%
Grad: 3057M, 1913W	S/F Ratio: 20 to 1
Year: qtrs, ss	Tuition: $3603
Appl: May 1	R and B: $2964
2579 applied	1538 accepted 946 enrolled
SAT: 480V 510M	ACT: 23 COMPETITIVE+

De Paul University, established in 1898 by the Vincentian Fathers, is a private Catholic university providing graduate and undergraduate instruction. The library contains 428,173 volumes and 90,790 microfilm items, and subscribes to 2192 periodicals.

Environment: The university's facilities include the Frank J. Lewis Downtown Center in the Chicago Loop and the Lincoln Park campus in the Near North section of the city. Single-sex dormitories accommodate 654 students. The university also sponsors married-student housing.

Student Life: The majority of the students are from the Chicago area. Only 5% of the students live in dormitories. Fifty-eight percent of the students are Catholic. Eighteen percent are minority-group members. Campus housing is single-sex, and there are visiting privileges. Students may keep cars on campus.

Organizations: There are 62 organizations on campus, including fraternities and sororities; 70% of the students are active in 1 or more of them. Extracurricular activities include religious groups, special-interest groups, music groups, and publications.

Sports: The university competes in 5 intercollegiate sports for men and 4 for women. There are 6 intramural sports for men and 3 for women.

Handicapped: About 80% of the campus is accessible to handicapped students. Facilities include parking areas, elevators, lowered drinking fountains and telephones, and specially equipped rest rooms. Special class scheduling is also available. A counselor and 6 assistants are provided for handicapped students.

Graduates: About 8% of the freshmen drop out by the end of the first year, and 60% remain to graduate. Of those, 40% enter graduate or professional schools.

Services: The following services are available free to students: psychological counseling, placement, career counseling, tutoring, and remedial instruction. Health care is available for a fee.

Programs of Study: The university offers the B.A., B.S., B.M., and B.F.A. degrees. Master's and doctoral degrees also are conferred. Bachelor's degrees are awarded in the following subjects: AREA STUDIES (American, Jewish, Latin American, urban), BUSINESS (accounting, business administration, business education, computer science, economics, finance, management, marketing), EDUCATION (bilingual, early childhood, elementary, health/physical, secondary, special), ENGLISH (communications, English, literature), FINE AND PERFORMING ARTS (art, art history, music, music education, studio art, theater/dramatics), HEALTH SCIENCES (medical technology, nursing, radiologic technology), LANGUAGES (French, German, Spanish), MATH AND SCIENCES (biochemistry, biology, chemistry, ecology/environmental science, mathematics, physics, statistics), PHILOSOPHY (philosophy, religion, religious studies), PREPROFESSIONAL (dentistry, engineering, law, medicine, pharmacy), SOCIAL SCIENCES (economics, geography, government/political science, history, psychology, social sciences, sociology). About 50% of degrees are conferred in business.

Required: Required courses vary according to the student's major.

Special: Independent study, research, and study-abroad programs are offered. A combination degree in engineering and a 3-year bachelor's degree are available. The university's School for New Learning offers students over the age of 24 a nontraditional, competency-based approach to education.

Honors: Thirteen honor societies are represented on campus. The honors program offers interdisciplinary courses for outstanding students.

Admissions: About 60% of those who applied were accepted for the 1981–82 freshman class. Candidates should have completed 16 Carnegie units and rank in the upper half of their graduating class. The university also considers advanced placement or honors courses and recommendations.

Procedure: The SAT or ACT should be taken by March of the senior year. The application deadlines are May 1 for fall, November 1 for winter, February 1 for spring, and May 1 for summer. There is a $20 application fee. Notification is made on a rolling basis.

Special: Early and deferred admissions plans are available. AP and CLEP credit is given.

Transfer: For fall 1981, 1503 transfer applications were received, 887 were accepted, and 589 students enrolled. Applicants must have a C+ average, and should have a minimum of 16 quarter hours earned. D grades transfer, but grades of C or better are required in the student's major. To receive a bachelor's degree, which requires 184 quarter hours, students must complete at least 48 quarter hours and half the work in the major field at De Paul. Application deadlines are the same as those for freshmen.

Visiting: There are regularly scheduled orientations for prospective students. Guides are available for informal visits. Visitors may sit in on classes and stay overnight at the school. The admissions office should be contacted for arrangements.

Financial Aid: About 50% of the students receive aid. The university awards scholarships. Federal grants, state and federal loans, and jobs are also available; about 4% of the students work part-time on campus. Applications for scholarships should be made by February 15; other aid applications should be submitted by May 1. The FAF and the university's aid application are required. The university is a member of CSS.

Foreign Students: About 115 of the full-time students are from foreign countries. Special counseling and special organizations are available.

Admissions: Students must achieve a minimum score of 525 on the TOEFL. No college entrance exam is required.

Procedure: Application deadlines are May 1 (fall), September 1 (winter), December 1 (spring), and March 1 (summer). Proof of health and evidence of adequate funds for 1 academic year are required. Health insurance, though not required, is available through the university for a fee.

Admissions Contact: Nancy Iszard, Director of Admissions.

DE VRY INSTITUTE OF TECHNOLOGY E-2
Chicago, Illinois 60618 (321) 929-6550
(Recognized Candidate for Accreditation

F/T: 3724M, 540W	Faculty: 69; n/av
P/T: 719M, 145W	Ph.D.'s: n/av
Grad: none	S/F Ratio: 16 to 1
Year: tri, ss	Tuition: $3025
Appl: October	R and B: n/app
SAT or ACT: required	LESS COMPETITIVE

De Vry Institute of Technology, an independent institution founded in 1931, is administered by the Bell & Howell Education Group. It offers undergraduate degrees in electronics engineering technology, computer science for business, and electronics technology.

Environment: The school is located in an urban setting. It has no housing facilities.

Student Life: About 92% of the students come from Illinois. About 42% are members of minority groups. The school's housing office helps students find off-campus apartments. Students may keep cars on campus.

Organizations: The 20 extracurricular activities available include professional organizations, a ham club, an audio-visual club, and a camera club. There are no fraternities or sororities.

Sports: The school does not participate in intercollegiate sports, but offers 3 intramural sports for men and 2 for women.

Handicapped: Facilities include wheelchair ramps, special parking, elevators, specially equipped rest rooms, and lowered drinking fountains and telephones. Special class scheduling can be arranged, and the school provides tutoring and materials as needed.

Graduates: Over 90% of the graduates begin careers in business and industry.

Services: Placement aid, career counseling, and tutoring are free. Fees are charged for health care and remedial instruction.

Programs of Study: The school awards the B.S.E.E. and B.S.Comp.-Sci. degrees. Associated degrees in electronics technology also are available. Bachelor's degrees are awarded in the following areas of study: BUSINESS (computer science), PREPROFESSIONAL (electronics engineering technology).

Required: Students must follow a specified curriculum and must maintain a GPA of 2.0 or better to graduate.

Honors: An honors program is offered in electronics engineering technology.

Admissions: Twenty-three percent of the 1981–82 freshmen ranked in the top fifth of their high school class, 49% in the top two-fifths. Applicants must be high school graduates or have GED. Besides grades and test scores, admissions officers consider impressions made during the required personal interview and recommendations by high school officials.

Procedure: Applicants must take both the SAT or ACT and the Bell & Howell Education Group Entrance Exam. Applications should be submitted by October for fall admission, by March for spring admission, and by July for summer admission. The application fee is $25. Admissions decisions are made on a rolling basis.

Special: A deferred admissions plan is available.

Transfer: Transfers are accepted for all classes. Applicants must have a personal interview. D grades do not transfer. Students must earn at least 36 credits on campus of the 160 required for a bachelor's degree. Application deadlines are the same as those for freshmen.

Visiting: Guides are available for informal visits, which may be scheduled for weekdays with the director of admissions.

Financial Aid: About 80% of the students receive aid through the school, and 4% work part-time on campus. The school offers scholarships (average $465 per term, maximum $556), loans (average $833 per term), and work contracts (average $1000 per term). Students must submit the FAF.

Foreign Students: Foreign students enrolled full-time represent 1% of the student body.

Admissions: Students must score at least 450 on the TOEFL or at least 106 on the ELS. They also must take the SAT and the Bell & Howell Education Group Entrance Exam.

Procedure: Application deadlines are the same as those for freshmen. Students must present a doctor's certificate as proof of good health and must show evidence of adequate funds for 1 year. They must carry health insurance, which is available through the school for a fee.

Admissions Contact: Lawrence E. McHugh, Director of Admissions.

EASTERN ILLINOIS UNIVERSITY E-4
Charleston, Illinois 61920 (217) 581-2223

F/T: 3910M, 4869W	Faculty: 481; IIA, av$
P/T: 110M, 214W	Ph.D.'s: 67%
Grad: 403M, 510W	S/F Ratio: 21 to 1
Year: sems, ss	Tuition: $1019 ($2399)
Appl: see profile	R and B: $1771
4517 applied	3832 accepted	1735 enrolled
ACT: 20		COMPETITIVE

Eastern Illinois University, a state-supported school, was founded in 1895. Its divisions include the College of Letters and Science, the Graduate School, and the schools of Business, Teaching, Health and Physical Education, Industrial Arts, and Music. The library contains 427,000 volumes and 810,000 microfilm items, and subscribes to 3810 periodicals.

Environment: The self-contained 314-acre campus is located in Charleston, a rural town of 18,500 people 18 miles from Chicago. The 41 major buildings include residence halls in a variety of styles from high-rise to single-level. The university sponsors housing for married students. Fraternities and sororities provide off-campus housing for members.

Student Life: Ninety-eight percent of the students are from the Midwest. Fifty-five percent of the students live in residence halls. About 11% are minority-group members. University housing is coed and single-sex; students in single-sex housing have visiting privileges. Juniors, seniors, and graduate students may keep cars on campus.

Organizations: About 10% of the men belong to one of 2 local or 13 national fraternities; 8% of the women belong to one of 11 national sororities. Students participate in student government, departmental clubs, religious organizations, and music and drama groups.

Sports: The university fields 11 intercollegiate teams for men and 10 for women. There are 16 intramural sports.

Handicapped: About 25% of the campus is accessible to wheelchair students. Facilities include wheelchair ramps, special parking, elevators, and specially equipped rest rooms. Special class scheduling is also available. The university provides audio-visual equipment and a limited collection of braille library books for students with visual or hearing impairments. It also employs 1 special counselor.

Graduates: The freshman dropout rate is 8%; 58% of the freshmen remain to graduate. Twenty percent of the graduates seek advanced degrees. Fifty percent pursue careers in business and industry.

Services: Free career counseling, psychological counseling, tutoring, and remedial instruction are provided. Free job placement services for undergraduates and graduates include a monthly newsletter and a service that sends records to potential employers. Health care is available for a fee.

Programs of Study: The university confers the B.A., B.S., and B.S.Ed., and B.S.M. degrees. Master's degrees are also offered. Bachelor's degrees are offered in the following subjects: AREA STUDIES (Black/Afro-American), BUSINESS (accounting, business education, computer science, environmental management, finance, management, marketing), EDUCATION (early childhood, elementary, health/physical, industrial, secondary, special), ENGLISH (English, journalism, speech), FINE AND PERFORMING ARTS (art, art education, music, music education, theater/dramatics), HEALTH SCIENCES (environmental biology, medical technology, prenursing, speech pathology and audiology), LANGUAGES (French, German, Spanish), MATH AND SCIENCES (botany, chemistry, earth science, geography, geology, mathematics, physics, zoology), PHILOSOPHY (philosophy), PREPROFESSIONAL (dentistry, engineering, law, medicine, pharmacy, veterinary), SOCIAL SCIENCES (economics, government/political science, history, psychology, social sciences, sociology). Twenty-nine percent of degrees are conferred in business and 28% in education.

Special: Students may sign up for study in Europe. The university offers combination degree programs in medicine (with the University of Illinois) and medical technology. Student-designed majors are permitted, and a general studies program is available. The Board of Governors (BOG) program gives college credit for work and life experiences applicable to a degree.

Honors: National honor and scholastic societies are open to qualified students.

ILLINOIS

Admissions: The university accepted 85% of the applicants for the 1981-82 freshman class. Twenty-one percent of those who enrolled scored below 21 on the ACT, 37% between 21 and 26, and 11% above 26. Applicants must rank in the top half of their high school class.

Procedure: The ACT is strongly recommended. Applications are accepted up to 1 year in advance and as late as 10 days before the start of a semester. Applications, high school transcripts, and test scores should be submitted as soon as 6th-semester transcripts are available. Under rolling admissions, applicants are notified as soon as possible after all credentials are received. There is no application fee.

Special: An early admissions plan is offered. AP and CLEP credit is accepted.

Transfer: For fall 1981, 1924 students applied, 1483 were accepted, and 1034 enrolled. Transfer students need a GPA of at least 2.0 and 15 completed credit hours. Grades of D transfer if the student's overall GPA exceeds 2.0. Students must complete, at the university, 42 of the 120 credits required for a bachelor's degree. Deadlines for applications are the same as those for freshmen.

Visiting: The university schedules regular orientation sessions at which prospective students talk with faculty members, learn about student services, and are shown the campus and residence halls. Individual visits are possible any time; guides are provided and during the spring semester prospective students may stay overnight on campus. The admissions office handles arrangements.

Financial Aid: Seventy percent of the students receive aid. Thirty percent work part-time on campus. The university, a member of CSS, distributes aid through scholarship programs, loans, grants, and work-study programs. Either the FSS or FAF is required with aid applications, which are accepted through April 1.

Foreign Students: Two percent of the full-time students come from foreign countries. The university offers these students special counseling and special organizations.

Admissions: Foreign students must achieve a TOEFL score of 550. No college entrance exam must be taken.

Procedure: Application deadlines are the same as those for freshmen. Foreign students must present both a self-completed medical form as proof of health and proof of funds adequate to cover one calendar year. They must also carry health insurance, which is available through the university for a fee.

Admissions Contact: John E. Beacon, Director of Admissions.

ELMHURST COLLEGE E-2
Elmhurst, Illinois 60126 (312) 279-4100

F/T: 900M, 1150W	Faculty:	100; IIB, +$
P/T: 485M, 930W	Ph.D.'s:	50%
Grad: none	S/F Ratio:	18 to 1
Year: 4-1-4, ss	Tuition:	$3988
Appl: Aug. 15	R and B:	$2050
706 applied	577 accepted	313 enrolled
SAT: 410V 440M	ACT: 20	COMPETITIVE

Elmhurst College, established in 1871, is a private liberal arts college affiliated with the United Church of Christ. The library houses 145,000 volumes and 3400 microfilm items, and subscribes to 800 periodicals.

Environment: The 35-acre campus, located in a suburban area 16 miles from downtown Chicago, has 23 buildings, including the college union with dining facilities, game rooms, and lounges. There are 4 dormitories that house 650 students. The college also sponsors off-campus apartments.

Student Life: About 94% of the students are from Illinois. Eighty percent come from public schools. Forty percent of the students live in dormitories; off-campus housing must be approved by the dean of students. Forty-five percent of the students are Protestant and 33% are Catholic; there is no requirement to attend services at the college's supporting church. Fewer than 14% of the students are minority-group members. College housing is coed and single-sex. Students in single-sex housing have visiting privileges; women residents establish their own curfew hours. Students may keep cars on campus. Day-care facilities are available for a fee to all full-time and part-time students, faculty, and staff.

Organizations: Twenty percent of the men and women belong to the 3 national fraternities and 2 sororities. Students participate with faculty on committees planning special events programs. In addition to numerous service and social organizations, a radio station, theater, singing groups, the Women's Union, Campus Christian Fellowship, concerts, and lectures, students have access to all the cultural and recreational opportunities of Chicago.

Sports: The college fields 10 intercollegiate teams for men and 4 for women. There are 4 intramural sports for men and 4 for women.

Handicapped: Wheelchair students would have convenient access to very little of the campus. Special parking and special class scheduling are provided for handicapped students.

Graduates: The freshman dropout rate is 20%, and 48% of the freshmen remain to graduate. Twenty percent of those who remain go on to graduate study; 5% enter medical school, 5% enter dental school, and 10% enter law school. Another 50% pursue careers in business and industry.

Services: The following services are offered to students free of charge: health care, psychological counseling, career counseling, placement services, and tutoring.

Programs of Study: The college confers the B.A., B.S., and B. Mus. degrees. Bachelor's degrees are offered in the following subjects: AREA STUDIES (Latin American, urban), BUSINESS (accounting, business administration, finance, health and hospital service management, human resources management, information systems, international business, management, marketing), EDUCATION (early childhood, elementary, health/physical, recreation management, secondary, special), ENGLISH (English, oral and written communication, speech, teaching English as a second language), FINE AND PERFORMING ARTS (art, art education, music, music/business, music education, piano pedagogy, theater/dramatics), HEALTH SCIENCES (nursing, speech pathology), LANGUAGES (French, German, Spanish), MATH AND SCIENCES (biology, chemistry, chemistry/business, computer science, management sciences, mathematics, physics), PHILOSOPHY (philosophy, religion), SOCIAL SCIENCES (economics, geography, government/political science, history, psychology, sociology). Thirty-nine percent of degrees conferred are in business, 17% in social sciences, and 13% in health sciences.

Required: All students must take courses in the fine arts, language and thought, literature, natural sciences, philosophy, physical education, social sciences, and theology.

Special: Independent study in 22 fields is available. Opportunities for study abroad are also provided.

Honors: The college has interdisciplinary honor programs open by invitation to outstanding students in all departments. There are 12 national honor societies on campus.

Admissions: Eighty-two percent of those who applied were accepted for the 1981-82 freshman class. Of those who enrolled, the ACT scores were as follows: 50% below 21, 25% between 21 and 23, and 25% above 23. Candidates should have completed 16 Carnegie high school units, rank in the top half of their class, and have a minimum C average. Other considerations include advanced placement or honors courses, recommendations by school officials, and impressions made during an interview.

Procedure: Either the SAT or ACT is required (ACT preferred) and should be taken by June of the senior year. The deadlines for regular admission are August 15 (fall) and January 15 (spring). Notification is on a rolling basis. Applications should be submitted with a $15 fee (waived in case of hardship).

Special: A deferred admissions plan is available. CLEP and AP credit is accepted for certain academic subjects.

Transfer: For fall 1981, 670 students applied, 590 were accepted, and 350 enrolled. Transfers in good standing, with a minimum 2.0 GPA, are considered for all classes. Grades of D do not transfer in business and nursing. Students must complete, at the college, the last 32 semester hours and must earn 32 of the 132 credits required for a bachelor's degree there. Application deadlines are the same as those for freshmen.

Visiting: Open house orientations for prospective students are held 3 times a year. Guides are available for informal visits; October/November and March/April are the recommended times. Overnight accommodations can be arranged by contacting the assistant director of admissions.

Financial Aid: Seventy-five percent of the students receive financial aid. Fifteen percent work part-time on campus. Average aid to freshmen is $2500; the average loan is $500. The college, a member of CSS, provides scholarships and NDSL loans and allows students to pay tuition in installments. Applications and the FAF should be submitted by March 1 for fall and November 1 for spring.

Foreign Students: One percent of the full-time students come from foreign countries. The college offers these students special counseling.

Admissions: Foreign students must achieve a TOEFL score of 550. No college entrance exam must be taken.

EUREKA COLLEGE
Eureka, Illinois 61530

D–3

(309) 467-3721

F/T: 250M, 240W
P/T: 2M, 8W
Grad: none
Year: qtrs, ss
Appl: open
475 applied
ACT: 19

Faculty: 38; IIB, –$
Ph.D.'s: 50%
S/F Ratio: 12 to 1
Tuition: $4050
R and B: $2450
347 accepted
103 enrolled
COMPETITIVE

Eureka College, founded in 1855, is a small, private, liberal arts college affiliated with the Disciples of Christ. The library houses 125,000 volumes and 1500 microfilm items, and subscribes to 400 periodicals.

Environment: The 112-acre campus, located in a rural setting 18 miles from Peoria, has 23 buildings, including 2 historical landmarks. Other campus features are the Lilac Arboretum and Rinker Open-Air Theater. Eleven single-sex dormitories accommodate 445 students.

Student Life: The majority of students are from Illinois; approximately 15% belong to the Christian Church. All students must live on campus unless they receive permission to live off campus. Cars are permitted.

Organizations: Thirty-five percent of the men and 35% of the women belong to the 7 fraternities and sororities on campus. Extracurricular activities include a biweekly student paper, clubs, student government, choir, drama, and lecture and artist series.

Sports: The college fields intercollegiate teams in 6 sports for men and 6 for women. Intramural sports also are available.

Handicapped: About 50% of the campus is accessible to wheelchair-bound students. Facilities include wheelchair ramps.

Graduates: The freshman dropout rate is 13%, and 45% remain to graduate. Thirty percent of the graduates seek advanced degrees and 30% pursue careers in business or industry.

Services: Students receive the following free services: health care, psychological counseling, career counseling, and placement aid.

Programs of Study: The college confers the B.A. and B.S. degrees. Bachelor's degrees are offered in the following subjects: BUSINESS (accounting, arts management, business administration, computer science, finance management, marketing), EDUCATION (athletic trainer, elementary, health/physical, secondary), ENGLISH (English, journalism, speech), FINE AND PERFORMING ARTS (art, art therapy, communications, music, theater/dramatics), HEALTH SCIENCES (medical technology), MATH AND SCIENCES (biology, chemistry, mathematics, physical sciences, physics), PHILOSOPHY (philosophy, religion), PREPROFESSIONAL (dentistry, engineering, law, medicine, ministry, pharmacy, social work, veterinary), SOCIAL SCIENCES (criminal justice, economics, history, psychology, social sciences).

Required: All students must take English composition, biological and physical sciences, general studies, speech, physical education, math, 3 courses in the humanities, and 3 courses in the social sciences.

Special: The college offers an intensive study plan under which students take fewer courses and receive more individualized attention. Combined B.A.-B.S. degrees may be earned in all areas, and students may design their own majors. There is a cooperative program with Illinois State University to share courses, libraries, and technical resources. Internship programs, independent study, and study abroad are also available.

Admissions: About 73% of those who applied were accepted for the 1981–82 freshman class. Of those who enrolled, the ACT scores were as follows: 60% below 21, 15% between 21 and 23, 15% between 24 and 25, 10% between 26 and 28, and 0% above 28. Candidates should have completed at least 12 units in academic subjects, and rank in the top half of their graduating class. Other factors considered are advanced placement or honors courses, and recommendations.

Procedure: The ACT is required and should be taken by December of the senior year. There is a rolling admissions plan; candidates must accept within 1 month after admission is offered. There is no application fee.

Special: An early decision plan is available. CLEP credit is accepted.

Transfer: A 2.0 grade point average is required to apply. D grades transfer. Students must complete, at the college, at least 30 of the 120 semester hours required for a bachelor's degree. Application deadlines are open.

Procedure: Application deadlines are July 1 (fall) and December 1 (spring). Foreign students must pay in advance 50% of first-term costs.

Admissions Contact: Michael E. Dessimoz, Director of Admissions.

Visiting: There are regularly scheduled orientations for prospective students. Overnight accommodations must be prearranged through the office of admissions. Guides are available for informal visits.

Financial Aid: About 80% of all students receive aid. Scholarships, loans, and campus jobs are available through federal and institutional aid programs. Deadlines for aid applications are open. The FFS must be filed.

Foreign Students: Foreign students enrolled full-time at the college represent about 2% of the student body. Special counseling is provided.

Admissions: Foreign students must take the TOEFL. No further exams are required.

Procedure: Applications should be received by the college before March 1; new students are admitted to all quarters. Students must present proof of adequate funds for 4 years. Health insurance, though not required, is available through the college for a fee.

Admissions Contact: George Hearne, Dean of College Relations.

GEORGE WILLIAMS COLLEGE
Downers Grove, Illinois 60515

E–2

(312) 964-3113

F/T: 157M, 280W
P/T: 30M, 69W
Grad: 207M, 350W
Year: qtrs, ss
Appl: Sept. 1
197 applied
ACT: 15

Faculty: 62; IIA, –$
Ph.D.'s: 61%
S/F Ratio: 12 to 1
Tuition: $4265
R and B: $1866
160 accepted
89 enrolled
LESS COMPETITIVE

George Williams College, founded in 1890 as a training institute for YMCA professionals, is an independent, nonsectarian college that aims to prepare students for service careers such as counseling, teaching, social work, and social science research. The library contains 90,000 volumes and subscribes to 600 periodicals.

Environment: The 200-acre campus is located in a suburban community 10 miles west of Chicago. The 14 modern buildings include dormitories that accommodate 360 single students, an apartment complex for married students, a college theater, and computer and science laboratories. The college also has a campus at Williams Bay, Wisconsin.

Student Life: Eighty percent of the students come from Illinois. About 80% of the freshmen come from public schools. About half the students live on campus. About a third of the undergraduates are over age 21. Thirty percent are minority-group members. Campus housing is coed. Students may keep cars on campus.

Organizations: About 70 students belong to the 3 fraternities and 3 sororities. Student activities include special-interest clubs, student government, a newspaper, a magazine, a yearbook, drama, choral groups, musical theater, and dance. Additional activities and cultural events can be found in Chicago.

Sports: The college competes on an intercollegiate level in 6 sports for men and 6 for women. There are 8 intramural sports for men and 7 for women.

Graduates: About 25% of the freshmen drop out, and 40% remain to graduate. About 15% of the graduates pursue advanced degrees.

Services: Students receive free health care, psychological counseling, tutoring, placement, and career counseling. Remedial instruction is available for a fee. A learning center offers special learning materials and tutorial services.

Programs of Study: The college confers the B.A., B.S., and B.S.W. degrees. Master's degrees also are available. Bachelor's degrees or concentrations are offered in the following subjects: AREA STUDIES (Latin American), BUSINESS (management), EDUCATION (health/-physical), ENGLISH (literature), FINE AND PERFORMING ARTS (art, music, theater/dramatics), HEALTH SCIENCES (medical technology, occupational therapy, physical therapy), LANGUAGES (French, Spanish), MATH AND SCIENCES (biology, ecology/environmental science, natural sciences), PHILOSOPHY (humanities, philosophy, religion), PREPROFESSIONAL (dentistry, law, medicine, ministry, social work, veterinary), SOCIAL SCIENCES (anthropology, economics, government/political science, history, international relations, psychology, social sciences, sociology). Fifty-six percent of the undergraduate degrees conferred are in public affairs and services, 21% are in social sciences, and 9% are in education.

Required: Students must take half their courses in a general education curriculum that includes Western civilization, cross-cultural studies, math, humanities, social sciences, and natural sciences. To graduate, students must demonstrate proficiency in writing.

194 ILLINOIS

Special: Students may study abroad and participate in model United Nations teams. Independent study and student-designed majors are encouraged. Most programs include supervised internships or microcourses in businesses or public and private agencies. Courses offered at the Wisconsin campus include outdoor education, social work, concentrated language study, and inner-city experience. Students may take courses at 5 other area colleges.

Honors: An honors program is offered.

Admissions: Eighty-one percent of those applied were accepted for the 1981-82 freshman class. The ACT scores of those who enrolled were as follows: 76% below 21, 6% between 21 and 23, 4% between 24 and 25, 3% between 26 and 28, and 1% over 28. Candidates must have graduated from an accredited high school or hold a GED diploma. Students should rank in the upper half of their graduating class and/or present an average of C or better. The college also considers letters of recommendation, leadership potential, extracurricular activities, and character.

Procedure: The SAT or ACT is required. Application deadlines are September 1 (fall), December 1 (winter), March 1 (spring), and May 1 (summer). The application fee is $15. Notification is made on a rolling basis.

Special: Early and deferred admissions plans are offered. CLEP and AP credit may be earned.

Transfer: For fall 1981, 198 students applied, 170 were accepted, and 112 enrolled. Transfer students are accepted for all classes. Applicants must have a GPA of at least 2.0 in at least 16 quarter hours of work. D grades transfer if not in the major. Students must complete, at the college, 48 of the 192 quarter credits required for a bachelor's degree. An interview is recommended. Application deadlines are the same as those for freshmen.

Financial Aid: About 81% of the students receive aid; 40% work part-time on campus. Awards average $4300 per recipient; 65% of the average package is gift aid and the rest subsidized loans and part-time jobs. Programs include state, federal, and college scholarships; NDSL; work-study employment; and guaranteed student loans. Candidates must submit the FAF and the college's aid application by July 15. The college is a member of CSS.

Foreign Students: About 1% of the full-time students come from foreign countries. The college offers these students special counseling and special organizations.

Admissions: Foreign students must achieve a TOEFL score of at least 450. The SAT or ACT is required.

Procedure: The application deadline for fall entry is August 15. Foreign students are admitted in all terms. They must present proof of health (the college provides a form to be completed and signed by a doctor). They must also present proof of funds adequate to cover 1 year of study. The college requires submission of $3000 plus a statement of financial support. Foreign students must carry health insurance, which is available through the college for a fee.

Admissions Contact: Donald Weiss, Director of Admissions.

GREENVILLE COLLEGE   D-4
Greenville, Illinois 62246   (618) 664-1840

F/T: 314M, 407W   Faculty: 46; IIB, av$
P/T: 37M, 77W   Ph.D.'s: 57%
Grad: none   S/F Ratio: 16 to 1
Year: 4-1-4, ss   Tuition: $3861
Appl: open   R and B: $1892
455 applied   389 accepted
ACT: 20   COMPETITIVE

Greenville College, founded in 1892, is a private liberal arts college affiliated with the Free Methodist Church. The library contains 96,300 volumes and 297 microfilm items, and subscribes to 439 periodicals.

Environment: The rural 8-acre main campus, in a small town 50 miles from St. Louis, Missouri, has 16 major buildings. The college also has a 14-acre athletic field and 13 acres of wooded land adjacent to the main campus. Six single-sex dormitories with single and double rooms accommodate 300 men and 300 women. A dining hall and a student lounge are available for day students.

Student Life: Sixty-two percent of the students are from Illinois and 36% from other states. Ninety-eight percent of entering freshmen come from public schools. Eighty-two percent live in the campus dormitories. Seven percent are minority-group members. Campus housing is single-sex; there are visiting privileges. Students may keep cars on campus. Student regulations prohibit drinking, smoking, dancing, and gambling. Students are required to attend chapel 3 times a week.

Organizations: There are no fraternities or sororities. Students may join a variety of religion groups, special-interest clubs, student music ensembles, and publications.

Sports: The college fields 7 intercollegiate teams for men and 5 for women. There are 6 intramural sports for men and 5 for women.

Handicapped: There are no special facilities for the physically handicapped.

Graduates: The freshman dropout rate is 18%; 55% remain to graduate. About 25% of those who receive degrees go on to graduate or professional school.

Services: The following services are available to all students free of charge: placement, career counseling, tutoring, and psychological counseling.

Programs of Study: The college offers the B.A., B.S., and B.Mus.Ed. degrees. Bachelor's degrees are offered in the following subjects: BUSINESS (accounting, business administration, computer science), EDUCATION (elementary, secondary, special), ENGLISH (English, speech), FINE AND PERFORMING ARTS (art, music, music education), HEALTH SCIENCES (environmental health, medical technology, occupational therapy, physical therapy, speech therapy), LANGUAGES (French, Spanish), MATH AND SCIENCES (biology, chemistry, mathematics, physics), PHILOSOPHY (philosophy, religion), PREPROFESSIONAL (dentistry, engineering, law, medicine, ministry, social work), SOCIAL SCIENCES (economics, government/political science, history, psychology, sociology). Thirty-three percent of degrees conferred are in education.

Required: All students are required to take courses in English composition, fine arts, literature, philosophy, physical education, religion, science/mathematics, social science, and speech. B.A. candidates must also take a foreign language.

Special: It is possible to earn combined B.A.-B.S. degrees in engineering and medical technology. A general studies (no major) degree is also awarded. Students may design their own majors. The college offers a European study tour, a junior year abroad, and a summer program in Santiago, Dominican Republic. Work-study programs are available, as are an individually tailored education program and opportunities for independent study or cooperative education.

Honors: An honors program is offered for qualified students.

Admissions: Eighty-five percent of those who applied for admission to the 1981-82 freshman class were accepted. Applicants must have completed 16 units of high school work with a minimum C average and rank in the top half of their high school class. In addition to these qualifications, the following factors, in order of importance, affect admission: recommendations, advanced placement or honors courses, leadership, and impressions made during the interview.

Procedure: The SAT or ACT is required. There are no application deadlines; notification is on a rolling basis. Freshmen are admitted to the fall, spring, and summer terms. There is a $10 application fee.

Special: CLEP and AP credit is accepted. There is an early admissions plan.

Transfer: For fall 1981, 74 applications were received and 70 students were accepted. Transfers are accepted for all classes. A minimum average of C and good standing are required for transfer. Students must study at the college for at least 1 year to receive a degree. All students must complete, at the college, 40 of the 132 credits required for a bachelor's degree. There are no application deadlines; notification is on a rolling basis.

Visiting: Informal guided visits during the week are available. Visitors may sit in on classes and stay overnight on campus. Arrangements can be made through Dale Stewart.

Financial Aid: Seventy percent of all students receive financial aid in the form of scholarships, grants, loans, or campus employment. Thirty-five percent work part-time on campus. The average award to freshmen from all sources is $1975. The FAF must be filed with CSS when applying for aid. It is recommended that applications be received by June 1 for fall entry and 30 days before the term begins for spring entry.

Foreign Students: Special organizations are available for foreign students.

Admissions: Foreign students must achieve a TOEFL score of at least 500. No college entrance exams are required.

Procedure: There are no application deadlines. Foreign students are admitted to the fall, spring, and summer terms. Notification is on a rolling basis. Foreign students must present proof of funds adequate to cover 4 years of study.

Admissions Contact: Thomas D. Morgan, Director of Admissions.

ILLINOIS BENEDICTINE COLLEGE E-2
Lisle, Illinois 60532 (312) 968-7270

F/T: 622M, 485W	Faculty:	66; IIB, av$
P/T: 462M, 372W	Ph.D.'s:	52%
Grad: 321M, 153W	S/F Ratio:	16 to 1
Year: sems, ss	Tuition:	$3900
Appl: Aug. 1	R and B:	$2250
550 applied	444 accepted	273 enrolled
ACT: 21		COMPETITIVE

Illinois Benedictine College, founded in 1887, is a private Roman Catholic liberal arts and sciences college conducted by the Benedictine Monks. The library contains 175,000 volumes and 8000 microfilm items, and subscribes to 835 periodicals.

Environment: The 100-acre campus is located in a suburban area 25 miles from Chicago. There are 10 buildings on campus. The 3 men's dormitories house 455 men, and the women's dormitory houses 180 women.

Student Life: About 97% of the students are from Illinois. Sixty percent live on campus. About 90% are Roman Catholic, 5% are Protestant, and 1% are Jewish. About 5% are members of minority groups. Campus housing is single-sex, with visiting privileges. Students may keep cars on campus. Day-care services are available for a fee.

Organizations: The student government and a variety of special-interest groups sponsor social and cultural events. There are no fraternities or sororities.

Sports: The college competes in 10 intercollegiate sports for men and 6 for women. There are 7 intramural programs for men and 7 for women.

Handicapped: The college is expanding its facilities for the physically handicapped. Currently, about 95% of the campus is accessible. Elevators, wheelchair ramps, specially equipped rest rooms, and residence-hall facilities, and special parking are available.

Graduates: The freshman dropout rate is 33%; 39% remain to graduate. Of those who graduate, 40% pursue advanced study: 9% enter medical school, 5% enter dental school, and 2% enter law school. About 60% of graduates pursue careers in business and industry.

Services: Free health care, psychological counseling, tutoring, and remedial instruction are available. The college also offers free placement and career counseling through the Student Development Center.

Programs of Study: The college confers the B.A., B.Mus., and B.S. degrees. Master's degrees are also awarded. Bachelor's degrees are offered in the following subjects: BUSINESS (accounting, business and economics, international business and economics), EDUCATION (elementary, health/physical), ENGLISH (communications and literature), FINE AND PERFORMING ARTS (music), HEALTH SCIENCES (health science, medical technology, nursing, nutrition), MATH AND SCIENCES (biochemistry, biology, chemistry, computer science, mathematics, physics), PHILOSOPHY (philosophy, religious studies), PRE-PROFESSIONAL (dentistry, engineering, law, medicine, nursing, optometry, pharmacy, podiatry, veterinary), SOCIAL SCIENCES (economics, government/political science, history, psychology, social sciences, sociology).

Required: All students must take courses in English, mathematics, science, philosophy, religious studies, and social science.

Special: Students in the upper-division science program work at Argonne National Laboratories, the Fermi National Accelerator Lab, and several local industries.

Honors: Six honor societies are represented on campus.

Admissions: About 81% of the students who applied for admission to the 1981-82 freshman class were accepted. Candidates should have completed 16 Carnegie units, have a C average or better, and rank in the top half of their class. Impressions made during interview, personality, and leadership record are also considered.

Procedure: Students should take either the SAT or the ACT by January of the senior year. The application deadlines are August 1 for fall and December 1 for spring; a $10 fee is required.

Special: AP and CLEP credit is accepted.

Transfer: For fall 1981, 354 applications were received, 306 were accepted, and 227 students enrolled. A minimum GPA of 2.0 and a minimum ACT score of 20 are required (the ACT may be waived if more than 20 credits have been earned). D grades do not transfer. At least 45 hours of the 120 required, must be taken in residence to earn a bachelor's degree. Application deadlines are May 1 for fall and October 1 for spring.

Visiting: Tours of the campus can be arranged for weekdays through the admissions office. Orientation sessions are scheduled before the fall and spring semesters.

Financial Aid: Scholarships, grants, loans, and campus jobs are available to qualified students. The average award to 1981-82 freshmen was $3600. About 93% of all students receive aid; 39% work part-time on campus. Applications must be made by April 15; the FAF or FFS should be filed with CSS.

Foreign Students: Fewer than 1% of the full-time students are from foreign countries.

Admissions: Minimum scores of 500 on the TOEFL and 900 on the SAT are required.

Procedure: Application deadlines are May 1 for fall and October 1 for spring. Students must submit a completed health form and proof of adequate funds for their entire period of study. Health insurance is required, and is available through the college for a fee.

Admissions Contact: Thomas F. Rich, Director of Admissions.

ILLINOIS COLLEGE C-3
Jacksonville, Illinois 62650 (217) 245-7126

F/T: 408M, 340W	Faculty:	48; IIB, +$
P/T: 6M, 10W	Ph.D.'s:	70%
Grad: none	S/F Ratio:	16 to 1
Year: sems	Tuition:	$2820
Appl: Aug. 15	R and B:	$1730
437 applied	405 accepted	232 enrolled
SAT: 550V 550M	ACT: 23	COMPETITIVE+

Illinois College, founded in 1829, is a liberal arts college affiliated with the Presbyterian Church and the United Church of Christ. The library contains 90,000 volumes and 2500 microfilm items, and subscribes to 700 periodicals.

Environment: The 60-acre rural campus, 90 miles from St. Louis, has 23 buildings. Nine dormitories house 603 students. The college also sponsors on-campus apartments (suites).

Student Life: Eighty-five percent of the students are from Illinois, and 87% come from public schools. Fifty-five percent of the students are Protestant and 40% are Catholic. Four percent are minority-group members. Campus housing is single-sex, with visiting privileges. About 85% live on campus. Cars are permitted on campus; drinking is prohibited. Study hours are observed, and students must attend convocation.

Organizations: Extracurricular activities include clubs, orchestra, choir, debating, publications, art shows, concerts, films, lectures, and plays. There are 7 Greek literary social societies on campus, 4 for men and 3 for women.

Sports: The college competes on an intercollegiate level in 7 sports for men and 5 for women. There are 5 intramural sports for men and 5 for women.

Handicapped: The entire campus is accessible to wheelchair-bound students. Facilities include wheelchair ramps, elevators, special parking, specially equipped rest rooms, and lowered drinking fountains.

Graduates: The freshman dropout rate is 5%. Thirty percent of the graduates pursue advanced degrees; 3% enter medical school, 3% enter dental school, and 5% enter law school. Thirty percent pursue careers in business and industry.

Services: Students receive the following free services: health care, career counseling, and placement aid.

Programs of Study: The college confers the B.A. and B.S. degrees. Bachelor's degrees are offered in the following subjects: BUSINESS (accounting, business administration, economics), EDUCATION (elementary, secondary), ENGLISH (English), FINE AND PERFORMING ARTS (art, theater/dramatics), LANGUAGES (French, German, Spanish), MATH AND SCIENCES (biology, chemistry, mathematics, physics), PHILOSOPHY (philosophy, religion), PREPROFESSIONAL (dentistry, engineering, home economics, law, medicine, ministry, pharmacy, veterinary), SOCIAL SCIENCES (economics, government/political science, history, psychology, sociology).

Required: All students must take English, a laboratory science, social studies, and religious studies. Freshmen are required to take an interdisciplinary course, Man in Change.

Special: Students may earn a combined B.A.-B.S. degree or design their own majors. Interdisciplinary study is offered in social studies. Study-abroad programs are available. There is a 3-2 program in engineering and home economics.

Honors: A number of honor societies, including Phi Beta Kappa, have chapters on campus.

Admissions: About 93% of those who applied were accepted for the 1981–82 freshman class. The SAT scores of those who enrolled were as follows: Verbal—40% between 500 and 599, 9% between 600 and 700, and 3% above 700; Math—33% between 500 and 599, 7% between 600 and 700, and 3% above 700. Of those who took the ACT, 5% scored below 21, 32% between 21 and 23, 27% between 24 and 25, 20% between 26 and 28, and 16% above 28. Candidates should have completed 15 high school units, have at least a 3.0 average, and rank in the top half of their class. Other factors entering into the admissions decision are recommendations from high school officials and extracurricular activities.

Procedure: The SAT or ACT is required and should be taken during the junior or senior year. Application deadlines are August 15 (fall) and January 12 (spring). Notification is made on a rolling basis. Applications should be submitted with a $10 fee.

Special: CLEP and AP credit is accepted.

Transfer: For fall 1981, 64 transfer students applied, 52 were accepted, and 34 enrolled. A minimum GPA of 3.0, an ACT score of at least 18 or an SAT score of at least 850, and an interview are recommended. Grades of C or better transfer. Students must complete, at the college, at least the last 30 of the 120 credit hours necessary for the bachelor's degree. Application deadlines are the same as those for freshmen.

Visiting: Four orientations are scheduled in spring and fall for prospective students. Visitors may sit in on classes; guides are available. Overnight visits should be arranged through the admissions office.

Financial Aid: About 60% of all students receive aid, including scholarships, loans, and campus jobs. Aid is provided on the basis of financial need. About 15% of the students work part-time on campus. The average award to freshmen from all sources in 1981–82 was 30% of college costs. The FAF or FFS should be filed with CSS by June 1 for winter or October 30 for spring.

Foreign Students: About 1% of the full-time students are from foreign countries.

Admissions: A minimum score of 430 on the TOEFL is required. The SAT (minimum score, 850) or the ACT (minimum score, 18) must be taken if the TOEFL is not submitted.

Procedure: Students must complete a college health form and present proof of adequate funds for their entire period of study.

Admissions Contact: Martha V. Clark, Director of Admissions.

ILLINOIS INSTITUTE OF TECHNOLOGY E-2
Chicago, Illinois 60616 (312) 567-3025

F/T: 2299M, 494W	Faculty:	269; I, av$
P/T: 996M, 248W	Ph.D.'s:	70%
Grad: 2267M, 829W	S/F Ratio:	12 to 1
Year: sems, ss	Tuition:	$4970
Appl: Aug. 1	R and B:	$2376
2008 applied	1265 accepted	1106 enrolled
SAT: 468V 570M	ACT: 24	VERY COMPETITIVE

The Illinois Institute of Technology was formed in 1940 by the merger of 2 Chicago institutions: Armour Institute of Technology, founded in 1892, and Lewis Institute, founded in 1896. A private college of science, engineering, architecture and planning, design, liberal arts, and management, the institute offers graduate and undergraduate programs. The library contains 1.4 million volumes.

Environment: The 120-acre urban campus is located 3 miles from downtown Chicago. The master plans of the campus and many of the more than 50 buildings were designed by the well-known architect, Mies van der Rohe. Six dormitories accommodate 840 men and 140 women. Fraternity houses and high-rise apartments are also available.

Student Life: Seventy percent of the students are from Illinois. About 68% come from public schools. Forty percent of the students live on campus. Forty-one percent of the students are minority-group members. Institute housing is both single-sex and coed. There are visiting privileges in single-sex housing. Students may keep cars on campus.

Organizations: There are 9 fraternities on campus and 2 sororities; about one-third of the students belong to them. There are many student organizations, including religious groups, departmental clubs, publications, a campus radio station, and special interest clubs. The cultural and recreational facilities of Chicago's Loop are easily accessible to students.

Sports: There are 7 intercollegiate sports for men and 4 for women. There are 12 intramural sports for men and 4 for women.

Handicapped: Special facilities for handicapped persons include wheelchair ramps, elevators, and specially equipped rest rooms.

Graduates: Seventeen percent of the freshmen drop out by the end of the first year. Sixty-five percent remain to graduate. Eighty-five percent of graduates enter business and industry.

Services: The following services are available free to students: health care, psychological counseling, placement and career counseling (for graduates as well as undergraduates), and tutoring.

Programs of Study: The institute offers the B.S., B.Arch., and B.B.A. degrees. Master's and doctoral degrees are also awarded. Bachelor's degrees are offered in the following subjects: BUSINESS (business administration), HEALTH SCIENCES (medical technology, nursing), MATH AND SCIENCES (biology, chemistry, mathematics, physics), PREPROFESSIONAL (architecture, city and regional planning, dentistry, design—photography, design—visual communications, design—product design, engineering, law, medicine), SOCIAL SCIENCES (psychology).

Required: All students must take a core of courses outside their areas of concentration.

Special: The institute offers a cooperative work-study program and selective exchange study overseas. Students may earn a B.S.-M.B.A. in 5 years, or a B.S.-J.D. in 6 years.

Honors: The institute offers a variety of honors opportunities. There are chapters of national honor and professional societies on campus.

Admissions: About 63% of those who applied were accepted for the 1981–82 freshman class. The SAT scores of those who enrolled were as follows: Verbal—59% below 500, 30% between 500 and 599, 10% between 600 and 700, and 1% above 700; Math—19% below 500, 42% between 500 and 599, 29% between 600 and 700, and 10% above 700. On the ACT, 24% scored below 21, 24% between 21 and 23, 16% between 24 and 25, 21% between 26 and 28, and 15% above 28. Applicants must be within the top half of their high school class. They should generally have at least a 2.5 grade average. Grades, test scores, and recommendations from the high school are part of the criteria used by the admissions committee in making its decisions. Advanced placement or honors courses are especially important.

Procedure: The SAT or ACT is required. Application deadlines are August 1 (fall) and December 1 (spring). Admission is on a rolling basis; notification usually is made within 6 weeks of receipt of all credentials. There is a $20 application fee.

Special: AP credit is accepted.

Transfer: For fall 1981, 976 students applied, 491 were accepted, and 259 enrolled. Transfers are considered for all classes except senior. Students must meet the regular entrance requirements of the institute and be in good standing at their former school with at least a 2.5 GPA. D grades do not transfer. All students must complete, at the institute, at least 45 of the 128–171 credit hours required in order to receive a bachelor's degree. Application deadlines are August 1 (fall) and December 1 (spring).

Visiting: Guides are available for informal visits to the school. Visitors may sit in on classes and in some cases may stay overnight at the school. The admissions office handles arrangements.

Financial Aid: Sixty-five percent of all students receive aid in the form of scholarships, loans, or jobs. Aid is awarded on the basis of financial need and academic accomplishment. The institute has a program of cooperative education (work-study) for qualified students, beginning with the sophomore year. The institute is a member of CSS. The FAF is required. Aid applications should be in by February 1. Notification is made by April 15.

Foreign Students: Thirteen percent of the full-time students come from foreign countries. The institute offers these students special counseling and special organizations.

Admissions: Foreign students must score at least 550 on the TOEFL. They must also take the SAT or the ACT.

Procedure: Application deadlines are July 1 (fall) and October 1 (spring). Foreign students must present proof of funds adequate for 1 year of study.

Admissions Contact: Ron R. Koger, Director of Admissions.

ILLINOIS STATE UNIVERSITY   D-3
Normal, Illinois 61761   (309) 438-2181

F/T: 7055M, 9028W		Faculty:	955; I, --$
P/T: 581M, 728W		Ph.D.'s:	66%
Grad: 937M, 1150W		S/F Ratio:	17 to 1
Year: sems, ss		Tuition:	$967 ($2327)
Appl: see entry		R and B:	$1998
10,127 applied	5094 accepted		3518 enrolled
SAT or ACT: required			COMPETITIVE

Illinois State University, founded in 1857, is the oldest state university in Illinois offering programs leading to graduate and undergraduate degrees. The library contains 1,136,000 volumes and 970,233 microfilm items, and subscribes to 4922 periodicals.

Environment: The 740-acre campus is located in a rural area 130 miles from Chicago. There are 55 buildings on campus. Single-sex and coed residence halls accommodate 7788 men and women. In addition, there are 292 family-student apartments.

Student Life: About 97% of the students are from Illinois, and 39% live on campus. Nine percent are members of minority groups. There are visiting privileges in single-sex dorms. Students may keep cars on campus. Day care is available, for a fee, to all students.

Organizations: Thirteen fraternities and 12 sororities have chapters on campus. Extracurricular activities include religious organizations as well as departmental and campus clubs.

Sports: The university offers 11 intercollegiate sports for men and 11 for women. Fifteen intramural programs are available for men and women.

Handicapped: Facilities include wheelchair ramps, parking areas, elevators, lowered drinking fountains and telephones, and dormitories that have been adapted for use by handicapped students. Special class scheduling is also available. About 1% of the students have visual impairments and 1% have hearing problems. A counselor is available to handicapped students.

Graduates: About 31% of the graduates pursue careers in business and industry.

Services: Students receive free placement aid, career counseling, tutoring, remedial instruction, and psychological counseling. Health-care costs are included in full-time students' fees.

Programs of Study: The university awards B.A., B.S., B.M., B.F.A., B.M.Ed., and B.S.Ed. degrees. Master's and doctoral degrees also are conferred. Bachelor's degrees are offered in the following subjects: AREA STUDIES (Russian), BUSINESS (accounting, agricultural business, business administration, business education, computer science, finance, management, marketing, office administration), EDUCATION (early childhood, elementary, health/physical, industrial, junior high/middle school education, special), ENGLISH (English, mass communications, speech), FINE AND PERFORMING ARTS (art, dance, music, music education, theater/dramatics), HEALTH SCIENCES (environmental health, health education, medical records administration, medical technology, speech pathology and audiology), LANGUAGES (French, German, Spanish), MATH AND SCIENCES (biology, chemistry, geology, mathematics, physics), PHILOSOPHY (philosophy), PRE-PROFESSIONAL (agriculture, home economics, industrial technology, library science, recreation and park administration, safety, social work), SOCIAL SCIENCES (anthropology, corrections, economics, geography, government/political science, history, psychology, social sciences, sociology). Twenty-five percent of degrees are conferred in education and 20% in business.

Special: A variety of off-campus educational experiences, study abroad, and a 3-2 engineering program are offered. Students may design their own majors. The High Potential Students Program provides financial and academic assistance to economically, culturally, or educationally deprived students.

Honors: Qualified students are eligible for membership in 28 national honor societies. A university honors program permits superior students to participate in special sections of a number of courses.

Admissions: About half of those who applied were accepted for the 1981-82 freshman class. Applicants must be graduates of an approved high school. Students generally must rank in the upper half of their high school class.

Procedure: Either the SAT or ACT is required; scores should be submitted any time after October 1. The application deadline is 21 days prior to the beginning of the semester in which the student seeks to enroll. A rolling admissions plan is followed. There is no application fee.

Special: An early admissions plan is available. CLEP and AP credit is accepted.

Transfer: For fall 1981, 3250 transfer students applied, 1697 were accepted, and 1292 enrolled. Transfers are considered for all classes. Students must be in good standing and have an overall C average. They must complete, at the university, at least 30 hours of the 120 hours required for a bachelor's degree. There are no formal application deadlines.

Visiting: Guided tours are available. Visitors may sit in on classes if they make arrangements with the instructor. The office of admissions and records should be contacted for visiting arrangements.

Financial Aid: About 80% of the students receive aid. A scholarship program is provided for Illinois residents. Federal, state, and college loans are available. The average aid to freshmen from all sources is $1800; the maximum is $3840. The university aid application should be filed by March 1.

Foreign Students: About 122 foreign students are enrolled full-time at the university, which provides special counseling and organizations for them.

Admissions: Foreign applicants must score 550 or better on the TOEFL. No academic exams are required.

Procedure: Students should apply at least 2 months before the start of the term in which they seek to enroll. They must present proof of adequate funds for 1 year. They are required to carry health insurance, which is available from the university for a fee.

Admissions Contact: Wilbur Venerable, Director of Admissions.

ILLINOIS WESLEYAN UNIVERSITY   D-3
Bloomington, Illinois 61701   (309) 556-3031

F/T: 729M, 954W		Faculty:	130; IIB, +$
P/T: 14M, 29W		Ph.D.'s:	75%
Grad: none		S/F Ratio:	13 to 1
Year: 4-1-4, ss		Tuition:	$4942
Appl: open		R and B:	$2100
1611 applied	1127 accepted		516 enrolled
ACT: 24			VERY COMPETITIVE

Illinois Wesleyan University, founded in 1850, is affiliated with the United Methodist Church. The university includes the College of Liberal Arts; the College of Fine Arts with schools of music, art, and drama; and the Collegiate School of Nursing. The library contains 140,000 volumes, 5500 microfilm items, and subscribes to 1200 periodicals.

Environment: The 47-acre campus is located in a suburban area, 140 miles from Chicago. The physical plant consists of 36 major buildings, including 10 dormitories which accommodate 1100 students. Fraternity and sorority houses are also available. Facilities are available for commuters.

Student Life: About 93% of the students are from Illinois; 80% of entering freshmen come from public schools. The majority of students (85%) live on campus (freshmen must live on campus). Sixty-two percent of the students are Protestant, 25% are Catholic, and 1% are Jewish. Nearly 8% are members of minority groups. Campus housing is both coed and single-sex; there are visiting privileges in single-sex dorms. Students are permitted to keep cars on campus.

Organizations: There are 7 fraternities and 6 sororities on campus; 38% of the men and 30% of the women belong to one of them. Student organizations include religious groups, publications, and special interest clubs. Numerous cultural events are scheduled.

Sports: The university fields 8 intercollegiate teams for men and 5 for women. There are 8 intramural sports for men and 5 for women.

Handicapped: There are parking areas for handicapped students.

Graduates: About 15% of freshmen drop out by the end of the first year; 66% remain to graduate, and 21% of the graduates pursue advanced degrees. Four percent enter medical school, 1% dental school, and 4% law school. Thirty-six percent pursue careers in business and industry.

Services: Students receive the following services free of charge: placement, career counseling, health care, tutoring, and psychological counseling.

Programs of Study: The university offers the B.A., B.F.A., B.Mus., B.SacredMus., B.S., B.Mus.Ed., and B.S.N. degrees. Bachelor's degrees are offered in the following subjects: AREA STUDIES (American), BUSINESS (accounting, business administration, computer science, finance, real estate/insurance), EDUCATION (elementary, secondary), ENGLISH (English), FINE AND PERFORMING ARTS (art, art education, music, music education, theater/dramatics), HEALTH

198 ILLINOIS

SCIENCES (medical technology, nursing), LANGUAGES (French, German, Spanish), MATH AND SCIENCES (biology, chemistry, mathematics, physics), PHILOSOPHY (philosophy, religion), PREPROFESSIONAL (dentistry, engineering, forestry, law, medicine, ministry, pharmacy, social work, veterinary), SOCIAL SCIENCES (economics, government/political science, history, psychology, sociology). Twenty-five percent of the degrees are conferred in business.

Required: All students must take 1 course in English and 2 courses in physical education.

Special: Student-designed majors, study abroad, internships, and 3-2 programs in engineering and medical technology are offered.

Honors: The university offers honors programs in art, music, and drama. There are 30 honor societies on campus.

Admissions: Seventy percent of those who applied were accepted for the 1981–82 freshman class. Of those, the ACT scores were as follows: 26% below 21, 27% between 21 and 23, 18% between 24 and 25, 15% between 26 and 28, and 14% above 28. Applicants should have completed 15 high school units and rank in the upper 40% of their class. Advanced placement or honors courses, interview impressions, extracurricular activities, and leadership record are also considered.

Procedure: Either the SAT or ACT should be taken by December of the senior year. The application, test scores, and high school record are accepted until housing facilities are filled; applications should be received before June 1. There is no application fee. Notification is on a rolling basis.

Special: There is an early admissions plan. CLEP and AP credit is also offered.

Transfer: For fall 1981, 222 applications were received, 76 were accepted, and 39 students enrolled. Transfers are considered for all classes. Good academic standing and a 2.0 GPA are required. Grades of C or better may be transferred. Students must spend a year and a half in residence, completing 45.5 of the 120 semester hours required for a bachelor's degree.

Visiting: Guides are available for informal visits; visitors may sit in on classes and stay overnight at the school. The admissions office should be contacted for arrangements.

Financial Aid: About 75% of the students receive financial aid. Scholarships, loans, grants, and campus employment are offered. Thirty percent of the students work part-time on campus. The application and the FAF must be filed by March 1 for fall entry or December 1 for winter entry. The average award to freshmen from all sources available through the university is $4800. The university is a member of CSS.

Foreign Students: Fewer than 1% of the full-time students are from foreign countries. Special counseling is available for these students.

Admissions: Foreign students must achieve a TOEFL score of at least 550. College entrance exams are not required.

Procedure: Admission is on a rolling basis; foreign students are admitted to the fall, winter, and spring terms. Foreign students must present proof of funds adequate to cover 4 years of study. They must also complete a university health form and are required to carry health insurance, which is available from the university for a fee.

Admissions Contact: Jim Ruoti, Director of Admissions.

JUDSON COLLEGE
Elgin, Illinois 60120   E–1
(312) 695-2500

F/T: 191M, 208W	Faculty: 25; IIB, av$
P/T: 17M, 10W	Ph.D.'s: 44%
Grad: none	S/F Ratio: n/av
Year: tri	Tuition: $3255
Appl: Aug. 15	R and B: $2865
191 applied	162 accepted	103 enrolled
ACT: 19		LESS COMPETITIVE

Judson College, founded in 1963, is a church-related liberal arts college affiliated with the American Baptist Church. The library contains 75,000 volumes and 20,000 microfilm items, and subscribes to 300 periodicals.

Environment: The 75-acre suburban campus includes 13 buildings, and is 40 miles from Chicago. The 3 two-story dormitories house 326 students. On-campus apartments are also available.

Student Life: About 60% of the students come from Illinois, 37% are from bordering states, and the rest from other states in the country. About 92% of entering freshmen come from public schools. Approximately 82% live on campus. In a recent year, 94% of the students were Protestant and 3% were Catholic. Chapel attendance is required 3 times a week. About 7% of the students are minority-group members. Housing is single-sex; there are visiting privileges. Students may keep cars on campus.

Organizations: There are no sororities or fraternities. Religious organizations are sponsored for Protestant students. The college sponsors 15 extracurricular activities, the most active of which are the K, Reach Out teams, and the Student Senate.

Sports: The college competes on an intercollegiate level in 5 sports for men and 2 for women. There are three intramural sports for men and 1 for women.

Handicapped: The campus is accessible to physically handicapped students via wheelchair ramps. None of the present students have visual or hearing impairments; there are no special counselors available for handicapped students.

Graduates: The freshman dropout rate is 38%. About 41% remain to graduate. After graduation, 40% become candidates for graduate or professional degrees. Fewer than 1% enter medical school; 1% enter law school. Fifty percent pursue careers in business and industry.

Services: Students receive the following services free of charge: placement, career counseling, and health care. Tutoring, remedial instruction, and psychological counseling are available on a fee basis.

Programs of Study: The college confers the B.A. degree. Bachelor's degrees are offered in the following subjects: AREA STUDIES (American, urban), BUSINESS (business administration, computer science), EDUCATION (health/physical), ENGLISH (communications arts, linguistics, literature, mass media, speech, theater), FINE AND PERFORMING ARTS (art, music, theater/dramatics), MATH AND SCIENCES (chemistry, physical sciences, physics), PHILOSOPHY (philosophy, religion), PREPROFESSIONAL (law, medicine), SOCIAL SCIENCES (economics, history). Forty-eight percent of degrees conferred are in social sciences, 15% in fine and performing arts, and 12% in philosophy.

Required: All undergraduates are required to take physical education, 1 religion course, and 3 courses called Cognizance and Awareness (core curriculum).

Special: Students may elect to earn a general studies (no major) degree. Independent study is available for superior students. Juniors may spend the year abroad on their own or participate in an established study-abroad program offered by another college.

Honors: All divisions have honors programs for superior students.

Admissions: Eighty-five percent of those who applied were accepted for the 1981–82 freshman class. Of those who enrolled in a recent year, the ACT scores were as follows: 26% between 20 and 23, 25% between 24 and 26, 24% between 27 and 28, and 12% above 28. Candidates need a minimum C average, should be in the top half of their class, and should have 15 Carnegie units. The student's character, personality, and recommendations are also important in the admissions decision. Special preference is given to disadvantaged students.

Procedure: The ACT or SAT is required and should be taken by July. Junior year results are acceptable. Application deadlines are August 15 (fall), November 15 (winter), and March 1 (spring). The college follows a rolling admissions plan. A $15 nonrefundable fee must accompany the application.

Transfer: For fall 1981, 84 students applied, 68 were accepted, and 47 enrolled. Transfers are considered for all classes. Students must be in good standing at their former school. A C average is needed to transfer. Students must complete, at the college, 30 semester hours out of the 123 needed to earn a bachelor's degree. Deadlines are the same as for freshman applicants.

Visiting: Tours, testing, and social activities can be arranged through the admissions office. There are also regularly scheduled orientations for prospective students. Visitors may sit in on classes and stay overnight at the school.

Financial Aid: Eighty-nine percent of all students receive some form of financial aid. Forty-nine percent work part-time on campus. The average award to freshmen from all sources is $3986. There are 30 freshman scholarships and 12 athletic scholarships. Federal work-study funds are available in all departments. Tuition may be paid in installments. Most financial aid is packaged. The college is a member of the CSS. The FAF is required; financial need is a main consideration for eligibility. There is no specific application deadline. Aid is awarded on a first-come, first-served basis.

Foreign Students: About 1% of the full-time students come from foreign countries. The college offers these students special counseling.

Admissions: Students must score 500 on the TOEFL. No college entrance examination is required.

Procedure: Application deadlines are open. Foreign students must present a completed health form. They must also present proof of funds adequate to cover 1 year of study.

Admissions Contact: M. Richard Mitchell, Director of Enrollment Services.

KENDALL COLLEGE E-1
Evanston, Illinois 60201 (312) 866-1305

F/T: 132M, 213W	Faculty: 20; III, −$
P/T: 30M, 42W	Ph.D.'s: 25%
Grad: none	S/F Ratio: 17 to 1
Year: 4-1-4, ss	Tuition: $3468
Appl: open	R and B: $2060
179 applied	116 accepted	87 enrolled
ACT: 17		COMPETITIVE

Kendall College is a privately supported institution affiliated with the United Methodist Church. The library contains 36,000 volumes.

Environment: The college is located less than 2 blocks from Lake Michigan in a residential section of Evanston, a Chicago suburb. Dormitories house 122 men and 124 women.

Student Life: About 97% of the undergraduates are from Illinois. Thirty percent of the students live on campus. Twelve percent are Catholic, 6% are Jewish, and 2% are Protestant; 66% claim no religious affiliation. About 27% of the students are minority-group members. College housing is coed and single-sex; there are visiting privileges in single-sex dorms. Students may keep cars on campus.

Sports: There are 3 intramural sports for men and 1 for women.

Graduates: The freshmen dropout rate is 12%, and 84% of the freshmen remain to graduate.

Services: Free career counseling and remedial instruction are provided.

Programs of Study: The college awards the B.A. and B.S. degrees. Associate degrees are also awarded. Bachelor's degrees are offered in the following subjects: AREA STUDIES (American), BUSINESS (accounting, business administration, computer science, finance, management, marketing), EDUCATION (early childhood), HEALTH SCIENCES (nursing), PREPROFESSIONAL (social work).

Special: Special academic programs include exchange programs with Evanston Art Center and Stuart Rodgers School of Photography.

Admissions: About 65% of those who applied were accepted for the 1981–82 freshman class. Students must have graduated from an accredited high school or hold an equivalency certificate. High school graduates should have completed 16 Carnegie units. Other considerations include recommendations by school officials, personality, and impressions made during an interview.

Procedure: The SAT or ACT is required. Application deadlines are open; the college follows a rolling admissions policy. New students are admitted at midyear as well as in fall. There is a $15 application fee.

Special: A deferred admissions plan is available. AP credit is granted.

Transfer: For fall 1981, 166 students applied, 81 were accepted, and 57 enrolled. Transfer students must present a GPA of at least 2.0 and transcripts of high school and college work; an ACT score of 20 and an interview are recommended. Grades of D do not transfer. Students must spend at least 1 year in residence and complete 30 of the 120 credits required for a bachelor's degree. Application deadlines are open.

Financial Aid: Forty-five percent of the students receive aid. Seventeen percent work part-time on campus. Need-based scholarships, BEOG, and loans are available. The college is a member of CSS. The FAF should be submitted with the college application form by August 1 for the fall term or January 1 for the spring term.

Foreign Students: Four percent of the full-time students come from foreign countries. The university offers these students special organizations.

Admissions: Foreign students must achieve a TOEFL score of 500. No college entrance exam must be taken.

Procedure: Application deadlines are open. Foreign students must present proof of health and proof of adequate funds. Health insurance is not required but is available through the college.

Admissions Contact: Michael J. Alexander, Director of Admissions and Financial Aid.

ILLINOIS 199

KNOX COLLEGE C-2
Galesburg, Illinois 61401 (309) 343-0112

F/T, P/T:	Faculty: 86; IIB, ++$
976 M&W	Ph.D.'s: 90%
Grad: none	S/F Ratio: 10 to 1
Year: see profile	Tuition: $5550–$5580
Appl: open	R and B: $910–$1160
700 applied	561 accepted	286 enrolled
SAT: 520V 550M	ACT: 25	VERY COMPETITIVE+

Knox College, established in 1837, is a private, nonsectarian, liberal arts college. The library contains more than 200,000 volumes and subscribes to 625 periodicals.

Environment: The 60-acre suburban campus is located in a community of 38,000 people about 180 miles from Chicago. There is a 760-acre biological field station near the campus. The 35 campus buildings include student residence halls, grouped in quads, that accommodate about 1050 students. About 125 students live in fraternity houses.

Student Life: Seventy-nine percent of the students are from Illinois, and 70% come from public schools. About 80% live in residence halls and 10% in fraternity houses; all students must live on campus unless living at home. Dormitories are both single-sex and coed, with visiting privileges in the single-sex halls.

Organizations: Twenty to twenty-five percent of the students belong to the 5 fraternities and 3 sororities. Religious organizations and counselors are available for Catholic, Jewish, and Protestant students. Additional social organizations and activities include the student union, special-interest clubs, music and drama groups, and publications.

Sports: The college fields intercollegiate teams in 10 sports, including 7 teams for women. Intramural sports also are available.

Handicapped: Approximately 50% to 75% of the campus is accessible to physically handicapped students. Some wheelchair ramps, special parking facilities, elevators, and specially equipped rest rooms are provided.

Graduates: Ten percent of the freshmen drop out by the end of the first year, and 66% remain to graduate. About 50% of the men and 35% of the women who graduate seek advanced degrees; 5% to 8% enter medical school, and 10% to 12% enter law school. Thirty-three percent pursue careers in business and industry.

Services: The following free services are available: placement, career counseling, health care, tutoring, remedial instruction, and psychological counseling.

Programs of Study: The college offers the B.A. degree. Bachelor's degrees are offered in the following subjects: AREA STUDIES (American, German, Russian), BUSINESS (business administration), EDUCATION (elementary, secondary), ENGLISH (English, literature, writing), FINE AND PERFORMING ARTS (art, art education, art history, music, music education, studio art, theater/dramatics), LANGUAGES (French, German, Greek/Latin, modern languages, Russian, Spanish), MATH AND SCIENCES (biology, chemistry, computer science, geology, mathematics, physics), PHILOSOPHY (classics, philosophy), SOCIAL SCIENCES (anthropology, economics, government/political science, history, international relations, psychology, sociology).

Required: All students must select 2 courses from each of the following areas: humanities, social sciences, and math/science or psychology.

Special: The academic year consists of 3 terms of 10 weeks each, with an optional miniterm between Thanksgiving and Christmas. The normal academic load is 3 coarses per term. Cooperative programs with other universities are offered in law, medicine, forestry, nursing, medical technology, engineering, and social work. Students may design their own majors. Interdisciplinary or interdepartmental majors also are offered. Satellite programs with a term of intensive study of community communications and a farm term for credit are available. Several off-campus study programs, including study abroad and a Washington semester, are offered.

Honors: Most departments offer honors programs involving independent research and a thesis. Five national honor societies maintain campus chapters.

Admissions: Eighty percent of those who applied were accepted for the 1981–82 freshman class. The SAT scores for an earlier class were as follows: Verbal—40% between 500 and 599, 20% between 600 and 700, and 1% above 700; Math—45% between 500 and 599, 40% between 600 and 700, and 3% above 700. On the ACT, 10% scored between 20 and 23, 35% between 24 and 26, 45% between 27 and 28, and 10% above 28. Candidates must be high school graduates and have completed at least 15 units. A rank in the top 30% of the class is generally required. Other considerations for acceptance are advanced placement or honors courses, recommendations, personality, leadership record, and extracurricular activities.

Procedure: The SAT or ACT is required. Application deadlines are open; new students are admitted to all terms. Notification is made on a rolling basis. The application fee is $15.

Special: Early and deferred admissions plans are available. CLEP and AP credit is accepted.

Transfer: Transfer students are accepted for the freshman, sophomore, and junior classes. Candidates must be in good standing at their former school and have a GPA of 2.5 or better. D grades do not transfer. All transfer students must complete, in residence, at least 14 of the 36 term course credits required for a bachelor's degree. Application deadlines are open.

Visiting: The college schedules periodic orientation tours and conferences for prospective students. Informal guided tours are also provided on weekdays when school is in session. Visitors may sit in on classes and stay overnight on campus. The admissions office should be contacted to arrange visits.

Financial Aid: About 65% of all students receive aid in the form of scholarships, loans, grants, and jobs. Loans are available through NDSL, grants through EOG, and employment through CWS programs. The average award to 1981–82 freshmen from all sources was $5945. Aid is awarded on the basis of need; renewal is contingent upon continued need. The FAF is required; the aid application deadline is February 1.

Foreign Students: Full-time foreign students at the college represent about 8% of the student body. The college offers these students an intensive English course, special counseling, and special organizations.

Admissions: Foreign applicants must score 550 or better on the TOEFL. No academic exams are required.

Procedure: The application deadline is April 1 for the fall term, the only one to which foreign students are admitted. Students must present proof of adequate funds for their entire period of study. They also must carry health insurance, which is available through the college for a fee.

Admissions Contact: David Tilley, Director of Admissions.

LAKE FOREST COLLEGE   E-1
Lake Forest, Illinois 60045   (312) 234-3100

F/T: 516M, 525W	Faculty: 80; IIB, ++$
P/T: 25M, 50W	Ph.D.'s: 96%
Grad: 2M, 26W	S/F Ratio: 13 to 1
Year: early sems, ss	Tuition: $6165
Appl: see profile	R and B: $2050
910 applied	589 accepted	278 enrolled
SAT: 520V 540M	ACT: 25	VERY COMPETITIVE+

Lake Forest College, chartered in 1857, is a private liberal arts college affiliated with the Presbyterian Church. The library contains 200,000 volumes and 15,000 microfilm items, and subscribes to 950 periodicals.

Environment: The campus is located on 100 wooded acres in a suburban town 25 miles from Chicago. Special facilities include science and sports centers, a student union, a dining hall, and dormitories that house 424 women and 430 men.

Student Life: Thirty-five percent of the students are from Illinois. About 85% live in campus dormitories; students may live off campus only with the approval of the dean of the college. Ten percent of the students are minority-group members. Campus housing is both coed and single-sex; there are visiting privileges in single-sex dorms. Freshmen may not keep cars on campus.

Organizations: Ten percent of the men belong to the 2 fraternities. Student organizations include special-interest clubs, a radio station, a student theater, newspaper, and various religious and service groups.

Sports: There are 11 intercollegiate sports for men and 8 for women, and 9 intramural sports each for men and women.

Handicapped: The campus has wheelchair ramps.

Graduates: The freshman dropout rate is approximately 8%; 62% of the students remain to graduate. Twenty-seven percent of them go on to graduate or professional study: 2–3% enter medical school, 1–2% enter dental school, and 8–10% enter law school. Another 60–65% pursue careers in business and industry.

Services: All students are offered the following free services: placement, career counseling, health care, tutoring, and psychological counseling.

Programs of Study: The college confers the B.A. degree. Bachelor's degrees are offered in the following subjects: AREA STUDIES (American, urban), BUSINESS (finance, general business, management), EDUCATION (elementary, secondary), ENGLISH (English, literature, writing), FINE AND PERFORMING ARTS (art history, music—history and theory), LANGUAGES (French, German, Spanish), MATH AND SCIENCES (biology, chemistry, computer studies, ecology/environmental science, mathematics, physics), PHILOSOPHY (philosophy), SOCIAL SCIENCES (anthropology, economics, government/political science, history, international relations, psychology, social sciences, sociology). Certification programs are offered in elementary and secondary education.

Special: A 5-year program leading to a combined B.A.-B.S. degree in engineering is offered in cooperation with Washington University. A cooperative program with Rush University offers courses in nursing and medical technology. The college also offers, in cooperation with the University of Chicago, 5-year combined B.A.-M.A. programs in public policy and social service administration. Students may design their own majors; emphasis is placed on individually designed programs with an extremely close faculty adviser system. The college offers foreign study and independent study. The Robert E. Wood Institute provides an opportunity for the study of local and regional problems. In addition, internships during the flexible second semester give students an opportunity to work with local businesses and agencies.

Honors: There is an honors program and a campus chapter of Phi Beta Kappa.

Admissions: Sixty-five percent of the applicants for the 1981–82 freshman class were accepted. Of those who enrolled, the SAT scores were as follows: Verbal—32% below 500, 57% between 500 and 599, 9% between 600 and 700, and 2% above 700; Math—38% below 500, 41% between 500 and 599, 16% between 600 and 700, and 5% above 700. Of those who took the ACT, 5% scored below 21, 32% between 21 and 23, 30% between 24 and 25, 24% between 26 and 28, and 9% above 28. Although test scores are required, the college places greater emphasis on the depth and breadth of high school preparation, with particular concern for the senior-year program. Other factors influencing the admission decision are advanced placement or honors courses, special talents, and extracurricular activities.

Procedure: The SAT or ACT is required. The recommended application deadlines are March 1 for fall and December 1 for spring. Notification is made according to the CRDA. A $15 fee must accompany the application.

Special: Early decision, early admissions, and deferred admissions plans are offered. Students may earn credit through AP exams.

Transfer: For fall, 1981, 234 transfer students applied, 123 were accepted, and 92 enrolled. Students should have a GPA of at least 2.0. An associate degree and an interview are recommended. D grades do not transfer. There is a 1½-year residency requirement, and students must complete 12 courses at the college of the 32 required for a bachelor's degree. Application deadlines are July 1 for fall and December 15 for spring.

Visiting: Guides are available for informal visits Monday through Friday and Saturday mornings during the academic year. Visitors may sit in on classes and stay overnight at the school. The office of admissions should be contacted to arrange such visits.

Financial Aid: Fifty-four percent of all students receive aid. The college provides grants, loans, and campus jobs. About 55–60% of the students work part-time on campus. Loans are also available from the federal government and local banks. Aid is awarded on the basis of need; renewal is contingent upon continued need and a satisfactory academic record. The average award to freshmen from all sources was $6644 in 1981–82. The college's aid application must be submitted by March 1 for fall or December 1 for spring. The college is a member of CSS.

Foreign Students: Two percent of the full-time students are from foreign countries. Special counseling and special organizations are available.

Admissions: Foreign students must take the TOEFL (minimum score, 525) or the University of Michigan Language Test, or complete the ELS/ALA program. College entrance exams may also be required.

Procedure: Application deadlines are March 1 for fall and December 1 for spring. Students must present proof of adequate funds for 1 year. Health insurance is required, and is available through the college for a fee.

Admissions Contact: Francis B. Gummere, Jr., Director of Admissions.

LEWIS UNIVERSITY   E-2
Romeoville, Illinois 60441   (815) 838-0500

F/T: 997M, 641W
P/T: 266M, 463W
Grad: 297M, 112W
Year: sems, ss
Appl: Aug. 27
1151 applied   502 accepted   444 enrolled
ACT: 18   COMPETITIVE+

Faculty: 104; IIB, av$
Ph.D.'s: 36%
S/F Ratio: 18 to 1
Tuition: $3960
R and B: $1870

Lewis University, founded in 1930, is Roman Catholic in origin and tradition and has had a long association with the Christian Brothers religious order. Now administered by a lay president under an independent board of religious and lay trustees, the university is composed of the College of Arts and Sciences, the College of Nursing, and the College of Business. The library houses 110,334 volumes and 92,000 microfilm items, and subscribes to 650 periodicals.

Environment: The 250-acre campus is located in a suburban town about 35 miles southwest of downtown Chicago. Among the more than 15 buildings on campus are dormitories housing about 650 students and the 40,000-square foot aviation training center. An airport operated by the university adjoins the campus.

Student Life: Most students are from the Chicago area and 25% live on campus. Seventy-five percent of the students are Catholic, 25% are Protestant. Fourteen percent are minority-group members. Campus housing is both single-sex and coed. There are visiting privileges in single-sex housing. Students may keep cars on campus.

Organizations: There are 11 fraternities and 7 sororities on campus; about 10% of the men and 10% of the women belong to them. Extracurricular activities include student government, musical groups, theater, publications, and an FM radio station.

Sports: Men participate in 6 intercollegiate sports and women in 4. There are 9 intramural sports for men and 9 for women.

Handicapped: Fewer than 1% of the students have visual impairments and fewer than 1% have hearing problems. A counselor is available to handicapped students.

Graduates: Fifteen percent of freshmen drop out of the end of the first year; 60% remain to graduate. Sixteen percent of the graduates pursue advanced degrees. Of these, 1% enter medical school, 1% enter dental school, and 1% enter law school. Fifty percent enter business and industry.

Services: Students receive the following services free of charge: psychological and career counseling, health care, placement, tutoring, and remedial instruction.

Programs of Study: The university confers the B.A., B.E.S., B.S., and B.S.N. degrees. Associate and master's degrees are also granted. Bachelor's degrees are offered in the following subjects: BUSINESS (accounting, aviation maintenance management, business administration, computer science, finance, fire science management, management, marketing, public administration), EDUCATION (elementary, health/physical, secondary), ENGLISH (English, journalism), FINE AND PERFORMING ARTS (art, music, music merchandising, speech/drama), HEALTH SCIENCES (medical technology, nursing), MATH AND SCIENCES (biology, chemistry, mathematics, physics), PHILOSOPHY (philosophy, religious studies), PREPROFESSIONAL (dentistry, engineering, law, medicine, pharmacy, veterinary), SOCIAL SCIENCES (economics, elected studies, government/political science, history, psychology, social justice, social work, sociology). Thirty-seven percent of degrees are conferred in business, 33% in social sciences.

Special: A general education B.A. program is available; student-designed majors are permitted.

Honors: All departments offer honors programs and seminars. There are 7 national honor societies on campus.

Admissions: Forty-four percent of those who applied were accepted for the 1981-82 freshman class. Among freshmen, ACT scores were as follows: 71% below 21, 14% between 21 and 23, 7% between 24 and 25, 6% between 26 and 28, and 2% above 28. Candidates must have graduated from a certified high school with 15 units of academic credit. A rank in the upper two-thirds of the graduating class and a C average are required.

Procedure: The SAT or ACT is required. The application, high school record, and test scores should be submitted to the admissions office. Application deadlines are August 27 (fall), January 1 (spring), and May 31 (summer). Notification is on a rolling basis. There is no application fee.

Special: Early admissions, early decision, and deferred admissions plans are available. CLEP and AP is accepted.

Transfer: For fall 1981, 589 students applied, 466 were accepted, and 322 enrolled. Transfers are accepted for all classes. A minimum GPA of 2.0 is required. D grades are not acceptable. Students must complete, at the university, at least 32 of the 128 semester hours necessary to receive a bachelor's degree. Application deadlines are the same as for freshman applicants.

Visiting: There are regularly scheduled orientations for prospective students. Guides are available for informal visits. Visitors may sit in on classes and stay overnight at the school. Visits are best scheduled on weekdays. The admissions office should be contacted for arrangements.

Financial Aid: About 85% of the students receive financial aid. A full range of scholarships, loans, and work-study opportunities are available. The FAF should be filed by March 15.

Foreign Students: Fewer than 1% of the full-time students come from foreign countries. The university offers these students special counseling and special organizations.

Admissions: Foreign students must score at least 500 on the TOEFL. No college entrance examination is required.

Procedure: Application deadlines are August 27 (fall), January 1 (spring), and May 31 (summer). Foreign students must present proof of funds adequate for 1 year of study. They must also carry health insurance.

Admissions Contact Ralph Miller, Director of Admissions.

LOYOLA UNIVERSITY OF CHICAGO   E-2
Chicago, Illinois 60611   (312) 670-3000

F/T: 2951M, 3690W
P/T: 887M, 1255W
Grad: 2521M, 2400W
Year: sems, ss
Appl: Aug. 15
4591 applied   3407 accepted   1988 enrolled
SAT: 460V 483M   ACT: 22   COMPETITIVE

Faculty: 700; I, —$
Ph.D.'s: 87%
S/F Ratio: 9 to 1
Tuition: $3780
R and B: $2230-2640

Loyola University, founded in 1870, is a private Roman Catholic university providing undergraduate and graduate instruction, an evening school, and extension courses. The library contains 754,738 volumes and 504,321 microfilm items, and subscribes to 5813 periodicals.

Environment: The university is composed of 4 urban campuses. The 3 undergraduate campuses are the Water Tower in downtown Chicago, the Lake Shore in a residential area on the shores of Lake Michigan, and the Rome Center in Rome, Italy. The Water Tower Campus includes law school and library buildings, a chapel, a student center, and a swimming pool and gymnasium. The 25-acre Lake Shore campus includes a 19-story student center, residence hall, and theater; an art gallery; a chapel; and a gymnasium with a swimming pool and complete weight room, exercise, and sauna facilities. The university sponsors dormitories and on-campus apartments.

Student Life: About 90% of the students are from Illinois. Sixty-four percent are Catholic, 14% are Protestant, and 5% are Jewish. Seventeen percent are minority-group members. About 44% live on campus. Campus housing is both single-sex and coed; there are visiting privileges in the single-sex housing. Students may keep cars on campus.

Organizations: Student organizations and activities include cultural, political, religious, and social clubs, a weekly newspaper, an FM radio station, and student government. About 15% of the men and women belong to one of the 12 fraternities and 4 sororities. Cultural, recreational, and shopping opportunities are as large as the city of Chicago.

Sports: The university fields intercollegiate men's teams in 9 sports and intercollegiate women's teams in 5 sports. There are 10 intramural sports for men and 10 for women.

Handicapped: About 95% of the campus is accessible to wheelchair students. Facilities include wheelchair ramps, specially equipped rest rooms, and lowered drinking fountains and telephones.

Graduates: About 5% of the students drop out after the freshman year; 72% remain to graduate. In a recent year, 41% of the graduates went on to graduate study.

Services: The university provides students with free placement, health care, tutoring, and psychological and career counseling. Free placement services for graduates and undergraduates include scheduling of on- and off-campus interviews.

Programs of Study: The university confers the undergraduate degrees of B.A., B.B.A., B.S., B.S.Ed., and B.S.N. It also awards master's and doctoral degrees. Bachelor's degrees are offered in the following subjects: BUSINESS (accounting, business administration, computer science, economics, finance, management, marketing, personnel man-

202 ILLINOIS

agement), EDUCATION (elementary, special), ENGLISH (communication arts, English), FINE AND PERFORMING ARTS (art, theater/dramatics), HEALTH SCIENCES (dental hygiene, nursing), LANGUAGES (French, German, Greek/Latin, Italian, linguistics, Spanish), MATH AND SCIENCES (biology, chemistry, computer science, mathematics, physics), PHILOSOPHY (philosophy, religion), PREPROFESSIONAL (criminal justice, dentistry, engineering, law, medicine, pharmacy, public administration, social work, veterinary), SOCIAL SCIENCES (anthropology, economics, government/political science, history, psychology, sociology). Nineteen percent of degrees conferred are in business, 18% are in sciences, 15% are in social sciences, and 13% are in nursing and dental hygiene.

Required: Core requirements vary depending on the student's curriculum; they generally include experience in the behavioral sciences, expressive and communicative arts, literature, history, social sciences, math or science, theology, and philosophy.

Special: The university offers a sophomore or junior year abroad. Academically or financially disadvantaged students can enroll in an Educational Opportunity Program. Students may earn combined B.A.-B.S. degrees.

Honors: Honors programs are available to students taking any major in the College of Arts and Sciences. They must take honors sections of courses in the core curriculum and their major fields.

Admissions: The university accepted 74% of those who applied for the 1981–82 freshman class. The SAT scores of those who enrolled were as follows: Verbal—65% below 500, 26% between 500 and 599, 9% between 600 and 700, and 1% above 700; Math—57% below 500, 29% between 500 and 599, 12% between 600 and 700, and 2% above 700. On the ACT, 29% scored below 21, 33% between 21 and 23, 17% between 24 and 25, 16% between 26 and 28, and 4% above 28. Applicants must have graduated from an accredited high school with at least 15 units. Applicants also must rank in or near the top half of their high school class. Admissions officers also consider, in descending order of importance, advanced placement or honors courses, recommendations from high school officials, and extracurricular activities.

Procedure: Applicants should take the SAT or ACT as early as possible, normally in December or January of the senior year. Freshmen are admitted for the fall and spring semesters. The application, a $15 fee, test scores, and high school records should be submitted after October 1, but no later than December 31 for the spring semester or August 15 for the fall semester. Applicants are notified within 3 weeks after all credentials are received.

Special: Credit can be earned through AP and CLEP tests.

Transfers: Almost all transfer applications are accepted. About 650 such students enroll each year. Applicants must have a minimum C average; D grades do not transfer. Transfer students must take at least 32 credits in residence. The high school transcript is required.

Visiting: The university schedules open houses in the fall. Individual visits also are welcome; prospective students are shown the campus and may sit in on classes. Those interested should call (312) 274-3000, ext. 121.

Financial Aid: About 80% of the students receive financial aid, which is awarded on the basis of need and academic record. The university has a $320,000 scholarship fund, and also provides loans, grants, and work aid. Loans are available from NDSL, grants from EOG, and employment through CWS. The FAF is required; the deadline for financial aid application is June 1.

Foreign Students: Seventy-three foreign students are enrolled full-time at the university; special counseling and special organizations are available for these students.

Admissions: Foreign students must achieve a TOEFL score of at least 500 and must take the SAT or ACT.

Procedure: Application deadlines are May 1 for fall entry and November 1 for spring entry. Foreign students must present proof of funds adequate to cover 1 year of study. They must also carry health insurance, which is available through the university for a fee.

Admissions Contact: John W. Christian, Director of Admissions Counseling.

MacMURRAY COLLEGE   C-3
Jacksonville, Illinois 62650   (217) 245-6151

F/T: 221M, 397W		Faculty:	54; IIB, av$
P/T: 23M, 45W		Ph.D.'s:	64%
Grad: none		S/F Ratio:	12 to 1
Year: 4-1-4, ss		Tuition:	$3990
Appl: open		R and B:	$1800
361 applied	325 accepted		168 enrolled
ACT: 20			COMPETITIVE

MacMurray College, founded in 1846, is a private coeducational liberal arts institution affiliated with the United Methodist Church. The library contains 145,000 volumes and subscribes to 800 periodicals.

Environment: The 60-acre campus is located in a medium-sized rural town 75 miles north of St. Louis, Missouri. There are 17 buildings on campus, including dormitories that house 683 students.

Student Life: About 87% of the students are from Illinois. About 87% of the freshmen come from public schools. Seventy-five percent of the students live on campus. Twenty-nine percent of the students are Catholic, 58% are Protestant, and 1% are Jewish. About 11% are minority-group members. Campus housing is both single-sex and coed. There are visiting privileges in single-sex housing. Students may keep cars on campus.

Organizations: There are no fraternities or sororities on campus. Student organizations sponsor social and cultural entertainment, as well as performing services on campus and in the community.

Sports: The college competes in 9 intercollegiate sports for men and 8 for women. It offers 10 intramural sports for men and 11 for women.

Graduates: Twenty-five percent of the freshmen drop out by the end of the first year. Fifty percent remain to graduate; 12% of those who graduate pursue advanced degrees. Twenty percent enter business and industry.

Services: Free psychological and career counseling, job placement, health care, and tutoring services are available to students.

Programs of Study: The college confers the B.A., B.Mus.Ed., and B.S. degrees. Associate degrees are also granted. Bachelor's degrees are offered in the following subjects: AREA STUDIES (Russian, urban), BUSINESS (accounting, business administration, computer science, marketing, personnel and labor relations), EDUCATION (elementary, health/physical, secondary, special), ENGLISH (English, journalism), FINE AND PERFORMING ARTS (art, art education, art history, music, music education, theater/dramatics), HEALTH SCIENCES (nursing), LANGUAGES (French, German, Spanish), MATH AND SCIENCES (biology, chemistry, mathematics, physics), PHILOSOPHY (philosophy, religion), PREPROFESSIONAL (dentistry, engineering, law, medicine, pharmacy, veterinary), SOCIAL SCIENCES (economics, government/political science, history, psychology, social work, sociology).

Required: All students must demonstrate competence in 11 areas spanning the liberal arts and sciences.

Special: Students may take examinations to earn credit. Independent study and study abroad programs are offered.

Honors: Several honor societies have chapters on campus.

Admissions: Ninety percent of those who applied were accepted for the 1981–82 freshman class. The ACT scores of those who enrolled were as follows: 45% below 21, 20% between 21 and 23, 15% between 24 and 25, 10% between 26 and 28, and 10% above 28. Students must rank in the upper 60% of their class. Advanced placement or honors courses, recommendations, personality, and impressions made during the interview are among the considerations taken into account.

Procedure: The SAT or ACT is required, and an interview is strongly recommended. Application deadlines are open. There are rolling admissions. The application fee is $10.

Special: AP and CLEP subject exam credit is accepted.

Transfer: For fall 1981, 108 students applied, 84 were accepted, and 48 enrolled. Students may transfer in any year. Good academic standing is necessary; D grades are accepted only if the student has a 2.0 GPA. Students must complete, at the college, 32 of the 128 credits required for a bachelor's degree.

Visiting: Tours of the campus can be arranged through the admissions office during the week and on Saturday mornings. Open houses are scheduled for prospective students.

Financial Aid: About 80% of all students receive some form of aid. Forty-one percent work part-time on campus. The average award to freshmen from all sources is $3650. The college offers scholarships, grants, Illinois State Monetary Awards, EOG funds, NDSL, CWS, and campus employment. The FAF or the FFS is required. Deadlines are open; notification is on a rolling basis.

Foreign Students: About 1% of full-time students come from foreign countries. The college offers these students special counseling and special organizations.

Admissions: Foreign students must take the TOEFL. They must also take the SAT or ACT.

Procedure: Application deadlines are June 1 (fall) and November 1 (spring). Foreign students must present a completed physical examina-

McKENDREE COLLEGE C-5
Lebanon, Illinois 62254 (618) 537-4481

F/T: 250M, 250W	Faculty: 30; IIB, av$
P/T: 80M, 125W	Ph.D.'s: 47%
Grad: none	S/F Ratio: 13 to 1
Year: sems, ss	Tuition: $3595
Appl: see profile	R and B: $1800
150 applied	90 accepted	72 enrolled
ACT: 18		COMPETITIVE

McKendree College, founded in 1828, is a private college affiliated with the United Methodist Church offering liberal arts and teacher education programs. The library houses 145,000 volumes and 2700 microfilm items, and subscribes to 400 periodicals.

Environment: The 23-acre rural campus, 23 miles from St. Louis, Missouri, is a blend of the old and new and includes 16 buildings, several of historical interest. Four dormitories house approximately 280 students.

Student Life: About 77% of the students are from Illinois; 88% of entering freshmen come from public schools. Ninety percent live on campus. Sixty percent are Catholic and 25% are Protestant; attendance is not required at chapel services. College housing is single-sex, and there are visiting privileges and no curfew. Drinking on campus is prohibited. Students may keep cars on campus.

Organizations: Thirty-eight percent of the women and 48% of the men belong to the 3 local sororities and 5 local fraternities. Many social and cultural activities are offered, and students participate on all school committees.

Sports: The college fields 4 intercollegiate teams for men and 3 for women. There are 7 intramural sports for men and 7 for women.

Handicapped: About 50% of the campus is accessible to wheelchair students. Facilities include wheelchair ramps and special parking; special class scheduling is also available. A special counselor is available to assist students who have hearing or visual impairments or other disabilities.

Graduates: The freshman dropout rate is 9%, and 60% of the freshmen remain to graduate. Twenty percent of the graduates seek advanced degrees. Another 50% pursue careers in business and industry.

Services: Students receive the following services free of charge: health care, tutoring, career counseling, and placement. The school will also assist students in finding jobs and internships.

Programs of Study: The college confers the B.A., B.B.A., B.F.A., B.S.Ed., B.S.N., and B.S. degrees. Master's degrees are also awarded. Bachelor's degrees are offered in the following subjects: BUSINESS (accounting, business administration, business/chemistry, management, marketing), EDUCATION (elementary, health/physical, secondary), ENGLISH (English, speech, speech/communication), FINE AND PERFORMING ARTS (art, art education, music), HEALTH SCIENCES (medical technology, nursing), MATH AND SCIENCES (biology, chemistry, mathematics), PHILOSOPHY (Christian education, philosophy, religion), PREPROFESSIONAL (dentistry, law, medicine, ministry, optometry, pharmacy, social work, veterinary), SOCIAL SCIENCES (anthropology, criminal justice, government/political science, history, international relations, psychology, public administration, sociology). Thirty-five percent of degrees conferred are in business.

Special: It is possible to earn a combined B.A.-B.S. degree in various subjects. Student-designed majors are also permitted. The bachelor's degree program in nursing is open to registered nurses only. Students may choose a minor in computer science.

Honors: Honors programs are offered in all departments. Honorary societies on campus include Alpha Psi Omega, Sigma Zeta, Sigma Tau Delta, and Phi Beta Lambda.

Admissions: Sixty percent of those who applied were accepted for the 1981–82 freshman class. The ACT scores of those who enrolled were as follows: 30% below 21, 50% between 21 and 23, 10% between 24 and 25, 5% between 26 and 28, and 5% above 28. Candidates must have a minimum 2.0 average and rank in the top half of their class. Other factors influencing the admissions decision are advanced placement or honors courses, ability to finance education, and recommendations.

Procedure: The ACT is required. An interview is recommended. Application deadlines are open for the fall and summer sessions, but there is a deadline of December 15 for the spring term. Notification is on a rolling basis. The application fee is $15.

Special: Early admissions, deferred admissions, and early decision plans are available. CLEP and AP credit is accepted.

Transfer: For fall 1981, 134 students applied, 103 were accepted, and 75 enrolled. Tranfer students need a GPA of at least 2.0, a minimum ACT score of 18, and 70 completed credit hours; an interview is also required. Students must complete, at the college, the last 28 of the 128 credits required for a bachelor's degree. There are no application deadlines.

Visiting: For prospective students there are regularly scheduled orientations. Guides are available for informal visits; overnight accommodations can be arranged through the admissions office.

Financial Aid: Eighty-five percent of all students receive some form of financial aid. Fifty percent work part-time on campus. The total amount of scholarship aid available is $125,000. Loans are also available from several sources. Average aid to freshmen is $3800. The college is a member of CSS. Either the FAF or FFS should be submitted with applications by March for the fall term or December for the spring term.

Foreign Students: Twenty-seven foreign students are enrolled full-time. The college offers these students special counseling.

Admissions: Foreign students must achieve a TOEFL score of 500. No college entrance exam must be taken.

Procedure: Application deadlines are January (fall) and September (spring). Foreign students must present both a completed institutional medical form as proof of health and proof of funds adequate to cover 1 year of study.

Admissions Contact: Steve Jackson, Director of Admissions.

MIDWEST COLLEGE OF ENGINEERING E-2
Lombard, Illinois 60148 (312) 627-6850

F/T, P/T:	Faculty: 55; n/av
180 M&W	Ph.D.'s: 40%
Grad: 54 M&W	S/F Ratio: 10 to 1
Year: qtrs, ss	Tuition: $3960
Appl: July 15	R and B: n/app
12 applied	10 accepted	7 enrolled
ACT: 22		COMPETITIVE

The Midwest College of Engineering was established to provide students interested in engineering a place for serious vocational study. Its library contains 5600 volumes and subscribes to 100 periodicals.

Environment: The 5-acre campus, which includes 4 buildings, is located in a suburban area 20 miles from Chicago. The college has no student housing.

Student Life: About 99% of the students are from Illinois. More than half attend part-time, and most have been out of high school for several years.

Organizations: The only college-sponsored organization is the student association.

Sports: No sports programs are offered.

Handicapped: About half of the campus is accessible to the physically handicapped. Facilities include special parking.

Graduates: About 5% of the freshmen drop out by the end of the first year, and 85% remain to graduate. About 15% of the graduates pursue advanced degrees, and almost all the others begin careers in business and industry.

Services: Job placement and career counseling are available free of charge.

Programs of Study: The college awards the B.S. degree. Master's programs are also available. Bachelor's degrees are offered in the following subjects: PREPROFESSIONAL (engineering—chemical, engineering—civil, engineering—electrical, engineering—industrial, engineering—mechanical). About 37% of the degrees conferred are in electrical engineering, 29% in mechanical engineering, 18% in civil engineering, and 8% in chemical engineering.

Required: All students must complete a core curriculum.

Admissions: About 83% of those who applied for the 1981–82 freshman class were accepted. The ACT scores of those who enrolled were as follows: 0% below 21, 60% between 21 and 23, 40% between 24 and 25, and 0% above 26. Candidates should be graduates of an accredited high school and rank in the upper 50% of their class. Admission is based on academic record.

ILLINOIS

Procedure: The ACT is required of applicants who are right out of high school. The college follows a rolling admissions plan. The application deadline for fall admission is July 15. There is a $20 application fee.

Transfer: Almost all transfer applicants are accepted. A GPA of at least 2.5 is required. D grades do not transfer. Applicants must spend at least a year at the college to receive a degree.

Visiting: Orientations for prospective students are held the first Saturday of every month. Informal visits are best made on Saturday mornings. Guides are available. The admissions office will make arrangements.

Financial Aid: About 10% of the students receive aid. Loans and scholarships are available. Aid application deadlines are open.

Admissions Contact: Marie C. Piet, Registrar.

MILLIKIN UNIVERSITY D-3
Decatur, Illinois 62522 (217) 424-6210

F/T: 731M, 768W	Faculty: 112; IIB, +$
P/T: 51M, 78W	Ph.D.'s: 50%
Grad: none	S/F Ratio: 14 to 1
Year: 4-1-4, ss	Tuition: $4382
Appl: open	R and B: $1900
846 applied	734 accepted	433 enrolled
SAT (mean): 431V 489M ACT: 21	COMPETITIVE

Millikin University, founded in 1901, is a private university affiliated with the United Presbyterian Church. It consists of 4 schools and colleges: the College of Arts and Science, the School of Business and Industrial Management, the School of Music, and the School of Nursing. The library houses 154,000 volumes and 1505 microfilm items, and subscribes to 776 periodicals.

Environment: The 40-acre urban campus, 125 miles from St. Louis, Missouri, has 15 major buildings, including a student center, fine arts center, and gymnasium. Five dormitories house 700 students.

Student Life: About 92% of the students are from Illinois; 89% of entering freshmen come from public schools. All full-time freshmen who are not living at home or with close relatives are required to live on campus. Campus housing is single-sex; there are visiting privileges. Smoking is permitted in designated areas; cars are permitted on campus for upperclassmen only.

Organizations: Forty-two percent of the men and 39% of the women belong to the 6 national fraternities and 5 sororities. Extracurricular activities include a newspaper, literary magazine, fine arts series, radio station, religious groups, clubs, and forensic and music activities.

Sports: The university fields 9 intercollegiate teams for men and 4 for women. There are 4 intramural sports for men and 4 for women.

Handicapped: About 50% of the campus is accessible to wheelchair students. Facilities include elevators and specially equipped rest rooms.

Graduates: The freshman dropout rate is 25%; 57% remain to graduate, and 18% of these go on to graduate study.

Services: Students receive the following services free of charge: health care, psychological counseling, career counseling, placement services, tutoring, and remedial instruction.

Programs of Study: The college confers the B.A., B.F.A., B.S., B.S.N., and B.M. degrees. Bachelor's degrees are offered in the following subjects: AREA STUDIES (American), BUSINESS (accounting, business administration, business data processing, finance, management, marketing), EDUCATION (elementary, health/physical, secondary), ENGLISH (communications, English), FINE AND PERFORMING ARTS (applied music, art, art education, art management, art therapy, church music, commercial music, music, music education, theater/dramatics), HEALTH SCIENCES (medical technology, nursing, occupational therapy, physical therapy), LANGUAGES (French, German, Spanish), MATH AND SCIENCES (biology, chemistry, ecology/environmental science, mathematics, physics), PHILOSOPHY (philosophy, religion), PREPROFESSIONAL (dentistry, engineering—industrial, engineering—welding, law, medicine, veterinary), SOCIAL SCIENCES (history, psychology, sociology). Thirty-one percent of degrees conferred are in business, 25% in math and sciences, and 19% in education.

Required: All students are required to take courses in general education, which includes communication skills, humanities, natural science, and social sciences.

Special: Interdisciplinary majors are offered, as well as combined B.A.-B.S. degrees in numerous subjects. A liberal arts general studies degree is available. Students may also choose from among such valuable options as the Washington Semester, Drew Semester, and study abroad programs.

Honors: The university recognizes academic achievement with a wide-ranging honors program. There are 10 national honor societies on campus.

Admissions: Eighty-seven percent of those who applied were accepted for the 1981–82 freshman class. The SAT scores of those who enrolled were as follows: Verbal—82% below 500, 11% between 500 and 599, 6% between 600 and 700, and 1% above 700; Math—51% below 500, 31% between 500 and 599, 15% between 600 and 700, and 3% above 700. On the ACT, 44% scored between 18 and 23, 30% between 24 and 29, and 2% above 30. Applicants should rank in the top 75% of their class and have completed 15 (preferably 16) high school units. Other factors entering into the admissions decision are recommendations, advanced placement or honors courses, evidence of special talents, and impressions made during an interview.

Procedure: The SAT and/or the ACT is required and should be taken by the end of the junior year and no later than January of the senior year. Application deadlines are open; notification is on a rolling basis. Applications should be submitted with a $15 fee.

Special: Auditions are required for admission to the School of Music. Early decision, early admissions, and deferred admissions plans are available. AP credit is accepted.

Transfer: For fall 1981, 212 students applied, 171 were accepted, and 118 enrolled. Transfers in good standing, with a minimum C average and 12 credit hours earned, are considered for all classes. All students must complete, at the college, 32 of the 128 credits required for a bachelor's degree. There are no application deadlines.

Visiting: Visitors are welcome at the university weekdays from 9 A.M. to 3 P.M.; guides are available for informal visits. There are regularly scheduled orientations for prospective students.

Financial Aid: About 72% of all students receive financial aid in the form of scholarships, grants, loans, and part-time employment. Eighty percent of all students qualify for financial aid. The average award from all sources to incoming freshmen is $1200. Campus employment may add an additional $550 yearly; 45% of the students work part-time on campus. Deadlines for financial aid applications are open, but early application is encouraged. The FAF must also be filed at the same time.

Foreign Students: Fewer than 1% of full-time students come from foreign countries. The university offers these students special counseling and special organizations.

Admissions: Foreign students must achieve a TOEFL score of at least 500. No college entrance exams are required.

Procedure: Application deadlines are May 1 (fall), November 1 (spring), and January 1 (summer). Foreign students must present proof of health (they must pass a physical exam by a doctor) and must present proof of funds adequate to cover 4 years of study. They must carry health insurance, which is available through the university for a fee.

Admissions Contact: Jack C. Allen, Dean of Admissions and Records.

MONMOUTH COLLEGE C-2
Monmouth, Illinois 61462 (309) 457-2131

F/T: 350M, 325W	Faculty: 51; IIB, +$
P/T: 10M, 10W	Ph.D.'s: 90%
Grad: none	S/F Ratio: 11 to 1
Year: terms, ss	Tuition: $4545
Appl: open	R and B: $2070
540 applied	400 accepted	182 enrolled
ACT: 22	COMPETITIVE

Monmouth College, founded in 1853, is an independent liberal arts college affiliated with the Presbyterian Church. The library contains 185,000 volumes and 18,000 microfilm items, and subscribes to 800 periodicals.

Environment: The 30-acre rural campus is located in a residential area 17 miles west of Galesburg and 190 miles from Chicago. The 30 campus buildings include dormitories with single, double, and triple rooms and suites. There are also fraternity houses on campus.

Student Life: Eighty-five percent of the students are from Illinois; the rest are from 20 other states and 6 foreign countries. Ninety percent come from public schools. About 95% live on campus; students must live in the dormitories if they do not live with their parents. Fifty-five percent of the students are Protestant (20% are Presbyterian), 20% are Catholic, and 1% are Jewish. Seven percent are minority-group members. Attendance at weekly convocation is required. Campus housing is single-sex, with visiting privileges. Students may keep cars on campus.

Organizations: Fifty percent of the men and 50% of the women belong to a Greek-letter society. Other student organizations and activities include student government, a weekly newspaper, special-interest clubs, music groups, a radio station, religious organizations, and concert and lecture series.

Sports: The college participates in 10 intercollegiate sports for men and 9 for women. There are 10 intramural sports for men and 9 for women.

Graduates: About 15% of the freshmen drop out by the end of the first year, and 60% remain to graduate. About 30% of the graduates seek advanced degrees.

Services: Placement, career counseling, health care, tutoring, and remedial instruction are available free to students. Placement counselors help with resumes and arrange job interviews on campus.

Programs of Study: The B.A. degree is conferred in the following subjects: BUSINESS (accounting, business administration, computer science), EDUCATION (elementary, health/physical, secondary, special—learning disabilities), ENGLISH (English, speech), FINE AND PERFORMING ARTS (art, art education, music, music education, theater/dramatics), HEALTH SCIENCES (medical technology, nursing), LANGUAGES (French, German, Greek/Latin, Spanish), MATH AND SCIENCES (biology, chemistry, geology, mathematics, natural sciences, physics), PHILOSOPHY (classics, humanities, philosophy, religion), PREPROFESSIONAL (dentistry, engineering, law, medicine, ministry, pharmacy, social work, veterinary), SOCIAL SCIENCES (economics, government/political science, history, psychology, sociology). Twenty percent of the degrees conferred are in business, 13% in math and sciences, 12% in education, and 10% in social sciences.

Special: It is possible to earn a combined B.A.-B.S. degree in nursing, medical technology, or engineering. Students may design their own majors. There are 17 special programs, most of them off campus. The college offers 3-2 engineering programs with the University of Illinois, Washington University, and Case-Western Reserve; 2-2 nursing and medical technology programs with Rush University; and a 3-1 program in medical technology with several hospital schools.

Honors: Departmental honors are awarded at graduation. Thirteen national honor societies, including Blue Key, Mortar Board, and National Collegiate Players, have chapters on campus.

Admissions: Seventy-four percent of those who applied were accepted for the 1981–82 freshman class. The ACT scores of those who enrolled were: 35% below 21, 30% between 21 and 23, 10% between 24 and 25, 15% between 26 and 28, and 10% above 28. Applicants should be high school graduates who have completed 15 academic units. They should have ACT scores of at least 20 and rank in the upper half of their high school class. The minimum GPA accepted is 2.0. Other considerations in the admissions process are recommendations, personality, advanced placement or honors courses, impressions made during an interview, extracurricular activities, and leadership record.

Procedure: The ACT is preferred, but the SAT also is accepted. Students are admitted to all terms; there are no application deadlines. Admissions are made on a rolling basis. The application fee is $15.

Special: There is a deferred admissions plan. CLEP and AP credit is accepted.

Transfer: Eighty transfer students applied for fall 1981, 70 were accepted, and 35 enrolled. Applicants must have a GPA of at least 2.0 and be in good standing at the previous college. An interview is recommended. D grades do not transfer for credit but may be used to meet distribution requirements. Students must complete, at the college, 9 of the 36 credits required for the bachelor's degree. There are no application deadlines.

Visiting: Regularly scheduled orientations include admissions and financial aid interviews, classroom visits, and individual discussions with faculty. Informal campus visits are best made between 9 A.M. and 4 P.M. Monday through Friday. The admissions office will make arrangements.

Financial Aid: Seventy percent of the students receive aid from the college. Aid programs include Monmouth College Awards, Monmouth College Honor Scholarships, BEOG, SEOG, NDSL, and Guaranteed Loans. Forty-six percent of the students work part-time on campus. Illinois residents must file for the Illinois State Scholarship Commission Monetary Award. Tuition may be paid on a monthly payment plan. The average award to 1981–82 freshmen was $4400. The FAF, FFS, or SFS must be submitted. There are no deadlines for aid applications. The college is a member of CSS.

Foreign Students: Five percent of the full-time students are from foreign countries. Special counseling and special organizations are available.

Admissions: Students must achieve a minimum score of 550 on the TOEFL. No college entrance exams are required.

Procedure: Application deadlines are June 1 for fall, November 1 for winter, and February 1 for spring. Before enrolling, students must submit a standard health form completed by a physician, and must also present proof of adequate funds. Health insurance is required, and is available through the college for a fee.

Admissions Contact: John M. Fettig, Director of Admissions.

MUNDELEIN COLLEGE   E–2
Chicago, Illinois 60660   (312) 989-5406

F/T: 20M, 633W	Faculty: 86; IIA, – –$
P/T: 57M, 644W	Ph.D.'s: 44%
Grad: 25M, 55W	S/F Ratio: 12 to 1
Year: 3 terms, ss	Tuition: $3855
Appl: Sept. 1	R and B: $1980
158 applied   110 accepted   85 enrolled
ACT: 18	COMPETITIVE

Mundelein College, established in 1929, is a Roman Catholic liberal arts college administered by a board of trustees composed primarily of laymen. The multimillion-dollar Learning Resources Center contains 123,000 volumes and 42 microfilm items, and subscribes to 673 periodicals.

Environment: The one-acre lakeside campus, in a residential suburb north of Chicago, includes a modern 15-story skyscraper that houses offices, laboratories, classrooms, art studios, dining facilities, a gymnasium, and a swimming pool. Dormitories house 550 students.

Student Life: The majority of students are from Illinois; 59% of entering freshmen come from parochial schools. About 20% of the students live in campus residence halls. Housing is single-sex, and there are visiting privileges. Regulations permit seniors and/or students over 21 to live off campus. Students may keep cars on campus.

Organizations: There are no fraternities or sororities. Extracurricular activities include a commuter council, an international student club, a black student organization, theater, choir, and concert and lecture series.

Sports: The college offers 2 intramural sports for women.

Handicapped: Facilities for the physically handicapped include wheelchair ramps, special parking, elevators, specially equipped rest rooms, and lowered drinking fountains and telephones. Special class scheduling and residence arrangements are also available.

Graduates: The freshman dropout rate is 8%; 85% remain to graduate, and 15% of those who remain go on to graduate study.

Services: The following services are offered free to all students: health care, psychological counseling, career counseling and placement, tutoring, and remedial instruction.

Programs of Study: The college confers the B.A., B.F.A., and B.S. degrees. A master's program is offered in religious studies. Bachelor's degrees are offered in the following subjects: AREA STUDIES (Asian, bilingual-bicultural studies), BUSINESS (accounting, finance, management, marketing), EDUCATION (early childhood), ENGLISH (English, literature), FINE AND PERFORMING ARTS (art, art education, music, music education), HEALTH SCIENCES (medical technology, speech therapy), LANGUAGES (French, German, Japanese, Spanish), MATH AND SCIENCES (biology, chemistry, mathematics, physics), PHILOSOPHY (humanities, philosophy, religion), PREPROFESSIONAL (home economics, interior architecture and design, social work), SOCIAL SCIENCES (economics, government/political science, history, psychology, social sciences, sociology). Twenty-five percent of degrees conferred are in social sciences, 21% in business, and 15% in preprofessional studies.

Required: There is a core requirement of 2 courses in each of 6 areas of the liberal arts for a total of 12 courses.

Special: It is possible to earn a combined B.A.-B.S. degree in science and mathematics. There is also a combination degree program in engineering with Georgia Institute of Technology. General studies majors and student-designed majors are permitted; independent study and study abroad are encouraged. Certificate programs are offered in elementary, secondary, special, and bilingual/bicultural education. In addition to major concentrations, programs are also available in premedical, prepharmacy, predental, and preoptometry. The Weekend College offers adults a degree completion program during weekend hours. There are four majors: English/Communications, Management, Community Studies, and Personal Universe.

ILLINOIS

Honors: There are 7 national honor societies on campus.

Admissions: Seventy percent of those who applied were accepted for the 1981-82 freshman class. The SAT scores of those who enrolled were as follows: Verbal—88% below 500, 6% between 500 and 599, 6% between 600 and 700, and 0% above 700; Math—75% below 500, 19% between 500 and 599, 6% between 600 and 700, and 0% above 700. On the ACT, 79% scored below 21, 14% between 21 and 23, 6% between 24 and 25, 1% between 26 and 28, and 0% above 28. Candidates must have a minimum average of 2.5 and class rank in the top 50%. While admission is based on high school record, test scores, and recommendations, each applicant is given individual consideration.

Procedure: The SAT or ACT is required. September 1 is the application deadline for the fall term, December 10 for the winter term, and March 10 for the spring term. Admission is on a rolling basis. Applications should be submitted with a $15 fee (waived in case of hardship).

Special: Deferred admissions are available. CLEP and AP credit is given.

Transfer: For fall 1981, 485 students applied, 460 were accepted, and 220 enrolled. Transfers are considered for all classes. Students must have a minimum GPA of 2.0; D grades do not transfer. At least 1 year must be spent at the college, and students must complete at least 30 of the 120 semester hours required to receive a bachelor's degree. Application deadlines are September 1 for the fall term, December 10 for the winter term, and March 15 for the spring term.

Visiting: Guided tours and interviews can be scheduled 6 days a week. Overnight accommodations must be prearranged through the admissions office. Open house orientations are held 3 times a year for prospective students.

Financial Aid: Seventy-three percent of all students receive some form of financial aid. Twenty percent work part-time on campus. Aid, in the form of scholarships, grants, loans, and work-study, is awarded on the basis of need, academic achievement, or artistic talent. The college is a member of CSS. Illinois residents should file the ISSC; all students should file the FAF. The deadline for aid applications is September 1 for the fall term, December 1 for the winter term, and March 1 for the spring term.

Foreign Students: One percent of full-time students come from foreign countries. The college offers these students an intensive English program and special counseling.

Admissions: Foreign students must achieve a TOEFL score of at least 500. No college entrance test is required.

Procedure: There is a rolling admissions policy for foreign students. Foreign students are admitted to any term. They must present proof of funds adequate to cover at least 1 year of study. They must also carry health insurance, which is available through the college for a fee.

Admissions Contact: Betty Miller, Director, Admissions Office.

NATIONAL COLLEGE OF EDUCATION E-1
Evanston, Illinois 60201   (312) 256-5150
Chicago, Illinois 60603   (312) 621-9658
Lombard, Illinois 60148   (312) 629-5077

F/T: 300M, 750W		Faculty:	n/av
P/T: 20M, 50W		Ph.D.'s:	40%
Grad: 200M, 3000W		S/F Ratio:	8 to 1
Year: qtrs, ss		Tuition:	$4665 (Evanston) $3795 (Chicago, Lombard)
Appl: Sept. 1		R and B:	$2445
90 applied	80 accepted		55 enrolled
SAT: 440V 450M	ACT: 19		LESS COMPETITIVE

The National College of Education is a private, independent, liberal arts and teacher-education institution, founded in 1886. In 1978, the college initiated a program that trains students for careers as human-service professionals. The Evanston campus library holds 100,000 volumes and 1000 microfilm items, and subscribes to 500 periodicals. The Chicago campus library contains over 20,000 volumes and subscribes to 110 periodicals.

Environment: The 7-acre suburban Evanston campus is 12 miles from Chicago. Its 7 buildings include a laboratory school and 1 dormitory that accommodates 400 students. There are no dormitory facilities at the 1-acre downtown Chicago campus or at the suburban campus in Lombard. The Lombard campus is upper division only.

Student Life: About 40% of the students are local, and 25% are from out of state. Approximately 50% of the students live on campus. Twenty-three percent of the students are minority-group members. Campus housing is both coed and single-sex; there are no visiting privileges in the single-sex dorms. Students may keep cars on campus.

Organizations: There are no sororities or fraternities, but a number of other activities are open to students. Youth groups for various religious denominations are available. Students also take advantage of cultural and recreational activities in Chicago.

Sports: The college fields 2 intercollegiate teams for women. There are 6 intramural sports for men and 7 for women.

Handicapped: About 95% of the campus is accessible to wheelchair-bound students. Facilities include special parking, elevators, and specially equipped rest rooms.

Graduates: The freshman dropout rate is 15%; nearly 45% remain to graduate. About 80% of the graduates pursue advanced degrees, and 30% begin careers in business and industry.

Services: The following free services are available to students: placement, health care, psychological and career counseling, tutoring, and remedial instruction.

Programs of Study: The college confers the B.A. degree. Master's programs are also offered. Bachelor's degrees are offered in the following subjects: EDUCATION (early childhood, elementary, special), FINE AND PERFORMING ARTS (art education), HEALTH SCIENCES (radiation therapy technology), SOCIAL SCIENCES (applied behavioral sciences, human services). A minor is also offered in legal assistant studies. Ninety percent of degrees conferred are in education.

Required: All students in teacher education must take 3 courses in English, 11 in education, 1 in fine arts, 1 in philosophy, 3 in psychology, 5 in math and sciences, and 4 in social sciences. Human-services students take liberal arts courses, 10 human-services courses, and a 4-course specialization sequence. In addition, they participate in 3 terms of practical experience.

Special: The teacher education curriculum includes 4 years of contact with children in practice teaching: students observe and participate in their freshman and sophomore years, and do a full term of student teaching in each of the junior and senior years. Students may choose a general-studies (no major) degree. The college allows students to design their own majors. A Ford Foundation grant provides closed-circuit TV for additional studies. A study-abroad program is open to all students. The college also offers a field experience program in applied behavioral sciences.

Honors: Kappa Delta Pi has a chapter on campus.

Admissions: Eighty-eight percent of those who applied were accepted for the 1981-82 freshman class. The SAT scores of those who enrolled were as follows: Verbal—70% below 500, 30% between 500 and 599, and 0% above 600; Math—70% below 500, 30% between 500 and 599, and 0% above 600. Of those who took the ACT, 50% scored below 21, 25% between 21 and 23, 20% between 24 and 25, and 3% between 26 and 28. Students should have at least a C average and rank in the top half of their class. If the SAT is taken, a minimum score of 400 is required on each part. A personal interview is necessary. The school also considers impressions made during the interview, personality, extracurricular activities, and recommendations.

Procedure: Applicants must take the SAT or ACT by July of the senior year. Applications should be filed by September 1 (fall), December 15 (winter), April 1 (spring), and June 1 (summer). Notification is made within 2 weeks after all credentials have been received. A $15 fee must accompany the application.

Special: CLEP subject exams are accepted; students can also earn credit with AP exams. There is a deferred admissions plan.

Transfer: For fall 1981, 750 transfer students applied, 725 were accepted, and 600 enrolled. A 2.0 GPA and 2 letters of recommendation are required. An interview is also recommended. D grades do not transfer. To receive a degree, students must study at the college 1 year for liberal arts, and 2 years for teacher education and human services; 184 quarter hours are required for the bachelor's degree. Transfer application deadlines are the same as for freshman applicants.

Visiting: Regularly scheduled orientations for prospective students include tours, a financial seminar, an interview, and a meeting with students and faculty. For informal visits, guided tours can be arranged for weekdays through the admissions office. Visitors may sit in on classes and stay overnight at the school.

Financial Aid: About 80% of all students receive scholarships (including EOG), loans (including NDSL), or campus jobs (including CWS). Fifty-five percent of the students work part-time on campus. Honors scholarships and grants-in-aid are also available. The college, a CSS member, requires the FAF form. The application deadlines for financial aid are August 1 (fall), December 1 (winter), February 1 (spring), and April 1 (summer).

Foreign Students: Fewer than 1% of the students are from foreign countries. The college offers these students an intensive English course or program.

Admissions: The University of Michigan Language Test is required. No college entrance exams are necessary.

Procedure: Application deadlines are September 1 (fall), December 1 (winter), February 1 (spring), and April 1 (summer). Proof of adequate funds for 1 year is required. Health insurance is not required, but is available through the college.

Admissions Contact: Gail Kligerman Straus, Director of Admissions.

NATIVE AMERICAN EDUCATIONAL SERVICES E-2
Chicago, Illinois 60640 (312) 728-1662
(Recognized Candidate for Accreditation)

F/T: 13M, 25W	Faculty: 5; n/av
P/T: 7M, 10W	Ph.D.'s: 20%
Grad: none	S/F Ratio: 7 to 1
Year: tri, ss	Tuition: $3350
Appl: open	R and B: n/app
SAT, ACT: not required	SPECIAL

The Native American Educational Service Inc. was established in 1974 as an independent Indian educational agency. The adult-degree-completion program is for native American adults 24 years and older who are working in Indian communities.

Environment: Instruction is given in 4 separate Indian communities. The central offices are located in Chicago.

Student Life: Nearly all students (95%) are members of the Indian community, where they live and work.

Graduates: Eleven percent of freshmen drop out in the first year. Of those who graduate, 20% pursue advanced study, and 7% enter careers in business and industry. All others assume professional positions in the Indian community.

Services: Free career counseling, placement services, tutoring, and remedial instruction are available.

Programs of Study: The school offers an academic program leading to the B.A. through Antioch College in Ohio. The core area of study is community studies.

Special: Students can earn a 3-year bachelor's degree and, to a certain extent, design their own majors.

Admissions: Applicants must be 24 years old or over. All students must work in an Indian-agency program. Qualified students need only a high school degree or G.E.D. Factors that enter into the admissions decision include impressions made during an interview, ability to finance a college education, and personality.

Procedure: There is immediate notification. An interview is required. There are no deadlines, and no application fee is required.

Transfer: Applicants must be in good standing at their last school and meet regular admission requirements. Students must spend at least 3 trimesters in the program, completing at least 39 of the 120 credits necessary to receive a bachelor's degree.

Visiting: Visits can be arranged through any of the faculty members or students.

Financial Aid: About 93% of all students receive scholarship aid; 8% work part-time for the school. The Bureau of Indian Affairs and federal programs provide financial aid. The FAF and the school's application are required; the application deadline for winter is January 3; for spring, April 18; and for summer, July 30.

Admissions Contact: Faith Smith, President.

NORTH CENTRAL COLLEGE E-2
Naperville, Illinois 60566 (312) 420-3414

F/T: 510M, 456W	Faculty: 60; IIB, +$
P/T: 175M, 188W	Ph.D.'s: 65%
Grad: none	S/F Ratio: 15 to 1
Year: tri, ss	Tuition: $4284
Appl: open	R and B: $2115
589 applied	480 accepted 250 enrolled
ACT: 23	COMPETITIVE+

North Central College, founded in 1861, is a private liberal arts college affiliated with the United Methodist Church. The library contains 100,000 volumes and 1300 microfilm items, and subscribes to 700 periodicals.

Environment: The 55-acre suburban campus is located in Naperville, a city of 43,000 28 miles west of Chicago. The 15 buildings include a science center, academic buildings, and recreational facilities. The college sponsors dormitories and on-campus and off-campus apartments.

Student Life: Ninety-five percent of the students are from Illinois. Sixty-five percent of entering freshmen come from public schools. About 45% of the students live on campus. Seven percent are minority-group members. Thirty-two percent are Catholic and 27% are Protestant. Campus housing is both coed and single-sex; there are visiting privileges in the single-sex housing. Students may keep cars on campus.

Organizations: There are religious groups on campus, but no fraternities or sororities. Student activities include speech and drama, music, a weekly newspaper, the college radio station, and college-sponsored trips to musical, theatrical, and sports events in Chicago. Students have a voice in college affairs through a college senate and a student union activities board.

Sports: The college competes intercollegiately in 11 men's sports and 9 women's sports. There are 4 intramural sports for men and 5 for women.

Handicapped: No special facilities are available for students with physical handicaps or visual or hearing impairments.

Graduates: About 7% of the students drop out after freshman year. Seventeen percent of those who remain go on to graduate school: 2% enter law school. Sixty-four percent of graduates pursue careers in business and industry.

Services: Students receive free career and psychological counseling, health care, tutoring, and remedial instruction. Free job placement services are available to undergraduates and graduates.

Programs of Study: The college offers the B.A. degree through day and evening programs. Bachelor's degrees are offered in the following subjects: AREA STUDIES (American, environmental studies, urban), BUSINESS (accounting, business administration, computer science, management, marketing), EDUCATION (elementary, health/physical, recreation, secondary), ENGLISH (English, speech), FINE AND PERFORMING ARTS (music, theater/dramatics), HEALTH SCIENCES (medical technology), LANGUAGES (French, German, Greek/Latin, Spanish), MATH AND SCIENCES (biology, chemistry, computer science, general science, mathematics, natural sciences, physical sciences, physics), PHILOSOPHY (classics, humanities, philosophy, religion), PREPROFESSIONAL (dentistry, engineering, law, medicine, veterinary), SOCIAL SCIENCES (anthropology, government/political science, psychology, sociology). Thirty-two percent of degrees conferred are in business, 13% in education, 16% in social sciences, 14% in math and sciences, and 12% in preprofessional programs.

Special: The college offers Washington and United Nations semesters, independent study, and a junior year abroad. It is affiliated with the Illinois Institute of Technology, allowing students to pursue a special 2-2 engineering program. The college also offers a 2-2 nursing program with Rush University. Other off-campus programs include computer science and an urban term. Student-designed majors are permitted.

Honors: An honors program is available to qualified students.

Admissions: The college accepted 81% of those who applied for the 1981–82 freshman class. The ACT scores of those who enrolled were as follows: 47% below 21, 34% between 21 and 25, and 19% between 26 and 36. Applicants must have a minimum C average, be in the top half of their high school class, and have completed 15 high school units. In most cases applicants must have scored at least 400 on each section of the SAT or at least 18 on the ACT composite, but a high class rank may counteract a low test score. Admissions officers also consider, in descending order of importance, leadership record, recommendations by school officials, and advanced placement or honors courses.

Procedure: Applicants must take the ACT. There are no application deadlines; notification is on a rolling basis. There is a $15 application fee.

Special: Early decision, early admissions, and deferred admissions plans are available. Students may earn credit through CLEP general and subject exams or AP exams.

Transfer: For fall 1981, the college received 280 transfer applications and accepted 242; 164 students enrolled. Transfers are considered for all classes. Applicants must be in good standing, have an ACT score of at least 18, and have a minimum C average. All students must complete, at the college, 9 of the 36 course units required for a bache-

ILLINOIS

lor's degree. There are no application deadlines; transfer students are admitted to all 4 terms.

Visiting: The college holds open houses in the fall, winter, and spring. It also welcomes prospective students for individual visits. The admissions office can arrange for guides, class visits, and overnight accommodations on campus. The best times for campus visits are 9 A.M. to 4 P.M. on Mondays, Tuesdays, Thursdays and Fridays.

Financial Aid: Eighty-six percent of the students receive financial aid. Seventeen percent work part-time on campus. The college offers loans, work aid, and $500,000 in scholarships. The average loan is $700. Incoming freshmen with ACT composites of at least 24 who are in the top 25% of their class are eligible for "no-need scholarships" of $750 to $4200. Financial aid applications must be received by September; the FFS must also be filed. Applicants are notified about 1 month after their credentials are received. The college is a CSS member.

Foreign Students: Fewer than 1 percent of the full-time students come from foreign countries. The college offers these students an intensive English course, special counseling, and special organizations.

Admissions: Foreign students must achieve a TOEFL score of at least 500. No college entrance exams are required.

Procedure: The application deadline is May 30 for fall entry. Foreign students must present proof of funds adequate to cover 1 year of study. They must pass a physical exam and must carry health insurance, which is available through the college.

Admissions Contact: Rick Spencer, Director of Admissions.

NORTHEASTERN ILLINOIS UNIVERSITY   E-2
Chicago, Illinois 60625   (312) 583-4050

F/T: 2025M, 2650W   Faculty: 354; IIA, av$
P/T: 1450M, 1724W   Ph.D.'s: 67%
Grad: 678M, 1518W   S/F Ratio: 22 to 1
Year: tri, ss   Tuition: $824 ($2204)
Appl: Aug. 1   R and B: n/app
2264 applied   1678 accepted   1044 enrolled
ACT: 14   LESS COMPETITIVE

Northeastern Illinois University was founded in 1961 as a teachers' college. Now a public liberal arts university, it includes colleges of of Education and of Liberal Arts and Science. The library contains approximately 381,000 volumes and 427,000 microfilm items, and subscribes to over 4600 periodicals.

Environment: The 67-acre campus is located in the city of Chicago and consists of 11 buildings. There are no dormitory facilities.

Student Life: About 99% of the students come from Illinois. Fifty-one percent attended public schools. About 39% of the students are minority-group members. Day-care services are available.

Organizations: There are 2 sororities and 1 fraternity on campus; about 1% of the students belong. The university sponsors 70 different activities and groups, the most active of which are the Stage Players, the Football Club, the Society for the Advancement of Management, and Collegium Musicum. Each week, 5 cultural events take place on campus, including concerts and plays.

Sports: The university sponsors intercollegiate teams in 6 sports for men and 5 for women. There are 6 intramural sports each for women and men.

Handicapped: Special facilities for handicapped students include wheelchair ramps, special parking, and specially equipped rest rooms.

Graduates: About 40% of the students drop out by the end of freshman year; 30% remain to graduate.

Services: The following services are provided free to students: health care, placement aid, and career counseling (for alumni as well as students).

Programs of Study: Undergraduate programs lead to the B.A. or B.S. degree. Master's programs are also offered. Bachelor's degrees are offered in the following subjects: BUSINESS (business education, management), EDUCATION (early childhood, elementary, health/physical, secondary, special), ENGLISH (English, literature), FINE AND PERFORMING ARTS (art, art education, music, music education, theater/dramatics), HEALTH SCIENCES (medical technology), LANGUAGES (French, Spanish), MATH AND SCIENCES (biology, chemistry, earth science, ecology/environmental science, geology, mathematics, natural science, physics), PHILOSOPHY (philosophy), PREPROFESSIONAL (dentistry, law, medicine), SOCIAL SCIENCES (anthropology, economics, government/political science, history, psychology, social sciences, sociology). Thirty percent of the undergraduate degrees are conferred in the social sciences, 18% in education, and 32% in business and information science.

Required: All students are required to pass the Comparative Political Systems course or a test on the Constitution. The university also imposes 30 semester hours of distribution requirements.

Special: Experimental programs include the Board of Governors Degree Program and the University Without Walls, in which students receive credit for life and work experience; the Kaskaskia Plan, in which undergraduates design their own curriculum; and the Center for Program Development, in which programs that permit greater freedom in academic techniques and procedure are created.

Admissions: About 74% of those who applied were accepted for the 1981–82 freshman class. The ACT scores of those who enrolled were as follows: 85% below 21, 9% between 21 and 23, 4% between 24 and 25, and 3% between 26 and 28. Freshman students are admitted if they are in the upper half of their high school graduating class or have an ACT score of 23. Other factors entering into the admissions decision are school recommendations, advanced placement or honors courses, and personal qualities.

Procedure: The ACT is required; junior-year results are acceptable. Application deadlines are August 1 (fall), December 1 (winter), April 1 (spring), and June 1 (summer). Admissions are granted on a rolling basis. There is no application fee.

Special: There are three special programs for disadvantaged students, which accept 300 students yearly without regard to academic record or test scores. CLEP and AP credit is available.

Transfer: For fall 1981, 1870 students applied, 1230 were accepted, and 951 enrolled. Transfers are accepted for all classes. Good standing at the last school attended and a C average are required. D grades transfer. The university has a residency requirement of 30 semester hours of the 120 necessary to receive a bachelor's degree. Transfer application deadlines are the same as for freshmen.

Visiting: Guides are available for informal visits. Visitors may sit in on classes. The best time to visit is Monday through Friday from 9 A.M. to 4 P.M. by arrangement with the admissions and records office.

Financial Aid: About 50% of all students receive aid. For 1981–82, undergraduates received $2,734,660 in federal aid, $2,705,648 from state plans, $863,627 from institutional programs, and $56,336 from other sources. During 1981–82, 150 undergraduate tuition, talent, and athletic scholarships were awarded. Loan amounts ranged from $100 to $5000, and college work-study awards up to $3000. About 6% of the students work part-time on campus. The average award to 1981–82 freshmen from all sources was $4995. Students who show significant need will receive a combination aid package. The university is a member of CSS and requires the FFS as well as an institutional aid application. Deadlines for financial aid applications are October 16 (fall), February 1 (winter), March 1 (spring), and July (summer). May 1 is the deadline for priority consideration.

Foreign Students: About 2% of the students are from foreign countries. Special counseling and special organizations are available.

Admissions: A minimum score of 500 on the TOEFL is necessary. No college entrance exams are required.

Procedure: Application deadlines are July 1 for fall, November 1 for winter, March 1 for spring, and May 1 for summer. Students must submit proof of adequate funds for their entire period of study. Health insurance is not required, but is available through the university.

Admissions Contact: Eric B. Moch, Director of Admissions and Records.

NORTHERN ILLINOIS UNIVERSITY   D-2
De Kalb, Illinois 60115   (815) 753-0446

F/T: 7670M, 9188W   Faculty: 1060; I, – $
P/T: 631M, 859W   Ph.D.'s: 62%
Grad: 3008M, 4072W   S/F Ratio: 16 to 1
Year: sems, ss   Tuition: $997 ($2357)
Appl: Aug. 6   R and B: $2000
9813 applied   7207 accepted   3377 enrolled
ACT: 21   COMPETITIVE

Northern Illinois University, a state-assisted coeducational institution, was founded in 1895 as a state teachers' college. Besides the College of Education, it now includes the Graduate School and the colleges of Business, Visual and Performing Arts, Continuing Education, Professional Studies, Liberal Arts and Sciences, and Law. The university also has a branch campus in Oregon, Illinois, 40 miles west of De Kalb. The library contains 1,054,517 volumes and 1,459,050 microform items, and subscribes to 14,764 periodicals.

Environment: The 449-acre main campus in the city of De Kalb, in a suburban area 65 miles west of Chicago, features a lagoon and wooded area. High- and low-rise dorms accommodate 7600 students; married student housing also is available.

Student Life: More than 90% of the students come from Illinois. About 82% of entering freshmen come from public schools. Forty-five percent of the undergraduates live in dorms; the university requires unmarried freshmen under 21 who do not live with parents or legal guardians to stay in the residence halls if space is available. About 50% of the students are Catholic, 21% are Protestant, and 5% are Jewish. Eight percent are minority-group members. University housing is both single-sex and coed, and there are visiting privileges. All students may have cars on campus but must pay a registration fee for parking. Day-care services are available for a fee. First priority is given to full-time students, but day-care is also available to part-time students and faculty and staff.

Organizations: About 7% of the men belong to the 13 national fraternities and 4 Black Greek Councils; 7% of the women belong to the 12 national sororities and 4 Black Greek Councils. Religious clubs exist for students of all major faiths. Many scholastic and professional societies have campus chapters. Activities include lectures, films, workshops, concerts and recitals, theater and dance performances, an artist series, and art galleries.

Sports: The university fields 12 intercollegiate teams for men and 12 for women. There are 12 intramural teams for men and 12 for women.

Handicapped: Facilities for physically handicapped students include wheelchair ramps, special parking, elevators, specially equipped rest rooms, and lowered drinking fountains and telephones. Special class scheduling is also available. The university provides a special reading room for students with visual impairments and interpreters for those with hearing impairments. Special counselors also are available.

Graduates: About 20% of the freshmen leave school after the first year. Fifty-five percent remain to graduate. Of those, 12% immediately enter graduate school on a full-time basis. Seventy percent of graduates pursue careers in business and industry.

Services: The university provides free career and psychological counseling, health care, and remedial instruction. Tutoring and health care services are available on a fee basis. Free placement services available to undergraduates and graduates include a credential service and on-campus interviewing with prospective employers.

Programs of Study: The university confers the B.A., B.S., B.F.A., B.G.S., B.M., and B.S.Ed. degrees. Master's and doctoral programs are also offered. Bachelor's degrees are offered in the following subjects: BUSINESS (accounting, business administration, business education, computer science, finance, management, marketing), EDUCATION (elementary, health/physical, secondary, special), ENGLISH (English, journalism, speech), FINE AND PERFORMING ARTS (art, art education, art history, music, music education, studio art, theater/dramatics), HEALTH SCIENCES (communication disorders, community health, medical technology, nursing, physical therapy), LANGUAGES (French, German, Russian, Spanish), MATH AND SCIENCES (biology, chemistry, geology, mathematics, meterology, physics), PHILOSOPHY (philosophy), PREPROFESSIONAL (child development and family relations, dietetics/nutrition/food science, home economics, textiles/clothing), SOCIAL SCIENCES (anthropology, economics, geography, government/political science, history, industry and technology, psychology, social sciences, sociology). Twenty-three percent of degrees conferred are in business, 24% in education, 9% in math and sciences, and 9% in social sciences.

Required: All students must take courses in English, math, and speech. Fulfillment of general education requirements in the areas of humanities, science, social sciences, and a special-interest area is also required. Requirements in some areas may be met by examination scores.

Special: Students may arrange to spend a year abroad. The Lorado Taft Field Campus offers an outdoor education program and serves as a laboratory for elementary and physical education teachers. Students may design their own majors; a general studies program is available.

Honors: Students enrolled in the honors program must earn an A or B in 27 hours of honors courses, including 12 outside their major, and must have a cumulative GPA of at least 3.2 on graduation. Over 30 national honor societies have chapters on campus.

Admissions: The university accepted 73% of those who applied for the 1981-82 freshman class. The ACT scores of those who enrolled were as follows: 43% below 21, 28% between 21 and 23, 15% between 24 and 25, 12% between 26 and 28, and 2% above 28. Students in the top half of their class must score at least 17 on the ACT; students ranking in the upper two-thirds but below the top half must score at least 22.

Procedure: The ACT is required and should be taken by December of the senior year. The application deadlines are August 6 (fall), December 17 (spring), and May 7 (summer). There is no application fee. Students who apply before February and who rank in the upper third of their class and score at least 21 on the ACT will be notified as their applications are completed. Those who apply after February will be evaluated and notified after April 15.

Special: The university offers special consideration and restricted admission to high school graduates who do not meet regular admission standards but have the potential to do college work. Those interested should inquire about the following programs: Complete Help and Assistance Necessary for a College Education and Sponsored Admission by the Academic Departments. The university accepts CLEP and AP credit and proficiency credit.

Transfer: For fall 1981, 4467 transfer students applied, 3623 were accepted, and 2116 enrolled. Applicants with at least 30 transferable semester hours must have a minimum C average and be in good standing at the last school attended. Those with more than 12 but fewer than 30 semester hours and an average of C from all colleges attended must be in good standing at the last college and meet freshman entrance requirements. All students must complete, at the university, at least 30 of the 124 semester hours required for a bachelor's degree. Application deadlines are the same as those for freshmen applicants.

Visiting: The university schedules orientation sessions for prospective students. Sessions include campus tours, academic advising, placement tests, and registration. Individual visits are possible on weekdays and Saturdays when classes are in session; guides are provided and visitors may sit in on classes with the instructor's consent. The admissions and orientation offices should be contacted to arrange visits.

Financial Aid: About 67% of all students receive a total of more than $18.5 million in financial aid. The average aid package is about $1000. Sources of aid are scholarships, grants, loans, and employment, including BEOG, CWS, and Illinois State Grants. Awards are made on the basis of academic record and financial need. Applicants must submit the financial aid application and the FAF. Application deadlines are April 1 (fall) and November 1 (spring). The university is a member of CSS.

Foreign Students: Two percent of the full-time students are from foreign countries. The university offers these students special counseling and organizations.

Admissions: Foreign students must achieve a minimum TOEFL score of 500. No college entrance exams are required.

Procedure: Application deadlines are May 1 (fall) and October 1 (spring). Foreign students must present proof of funds adequate to cover the term for which they are enrolled. They must also carry health insurance, which is available through the university for a fee.

Admissions Contact: Daniel S. Oborn, Director of Admissions.

NORTH PARK COLLEGE E-2
Chicago, Illinois 60625 (312) 583-2700

F/T: 498M, 580W		Faculty:	77; n/av
P/T: 66M, 109W		Ph.D.'s:	36%
Grad: none		S/F Ratio:	14 to 1
Year: qtrs, ss		Tuition:	$4122
Appl: open		R and B:	$2031
527 applied	403 accepted		275 enrolled
SAT: 470V 510M	ACT: 20		COMPETITIVE

North Park College, established in 1891 and affiliated with the Evangelical Covenant Church of America, offers undergraduate programs in liberal arts and sciences, education, business, and religion. The library holds 115,000 books and 2500 microfilm items, and subscribes to more than 600 periodicals.

Environment: The 25-acre campus is located in an urban area of northwest Chicago. The 25 buildings include 4 residence halls that house 60% of the students. Freshmen have their own dormitories. The college also sponsors on-campus apartments.

Student Life: About 65% of the students come from Illinois, the rest from 40 other states and foreign countries. Sixty percent live on campus. Seventy percent are Protestant, 18% are Catholic, and 1% are Jewish. Voluntary chapel services are held twice a week. Fourteen percent of the students are minority-group members. College housing is single-sex, and there are visiting privileges. Smoking and drinking are prohibited. Students may keep cars on campus.

Organizations: Student activities include religious groups, special-interest clubs, student government, publications, drama, instrumental and vocal music groups, social and cultural events, and service organizations.

Sports: The college fields 9 intercollegiate teams for men and 5 for women. There are 3 intramural sports for men and 2 for women.

Graduates: About 28% of the freshmen drop out; 40% remain to graduate. About 40% of the graduates go on for further education.

Services: The college provides free health care and psychological, placement, and career counseling. Most tutoring and remedial instruction is for a fee.

Programs of Study: The college awards the B.A., B.S., and B.Mus. degrees. Bachelor's degrees are offered in the following subjects: AREA STUDIES (urban), BUSINESS (accounting, business administration, computer science), EDUCATION (early childhood, elementary, health/physical, secondary), ENGLISH (English, speech), FINE AND PERFORMING ARTS (art, art education, music, music education, theater/dramatics), HEALTH SCIENCES (medical technology, nursing), LANGUAGES (French, German, Spanish, Swedish), MATH AND SCIENCES (biology, chemistry, mathematics, natural sciences, physics), PHILOSOPHY (philosophy, religion), PREPROFESSIONAL (dentistry, engineering, law, medicine, ministry, social work), SOCIAL SCIENCES (anthropology, economics, government/political science, history, international relations, psychology, social sciences, sociology). About 30% of the degrees are awarded in education, 20% in management, 14% in social science, 11% in biology, and 10% in English.

Required: Students must take a 14- or 15-course general education program that includes fine arts, English composition, foreign language, science, math, social sciences, religion, and physical education. These requirements are somewhat flexible.

Special: Independent study is encouraged for superior students. Internship programs and non-credit courses in such areas as painting, shorthand, calligraphy, religion, and conversational Swedish are available. A 3-week project period offers opportunities for such programs as United Nations and Washington semesters, study courses abroad and in other sections of the United States, and special courses. Students may study at institutions in Sweden, Heidelberg, London, Madrid, Paris, and Strasbourg.

Admissions: About 76% of those who applied for admission to the 1981-82 freshman class were accepted. The SAT scores of those who enrolled were as follows: Verbal—60% below 500, 35% between 500 and 599, 4% between 600 and 700, and 1% above 700; Math—46% below 500, 31% between 500 and 599, 18% between 600 and 700, and 5% above 700. On the ACT, 50% scored below 21. A high school diploma and acceptable SAT or ACT scores are required. Applicants generally should rank in the top half of their class and must have a grade average of at least 2.0. Other considerations include impressions made during an interview and advanced placement or honors courses.

Procedure: The SAT or ACT and personal references are required. Freshmen are admitted to all quarters. Application deadlines are open, but applications should be filed early in the senior year. Notification is made on a rolling basis. There is a $20 application fee.

Special: An early admission plan is available. CLEP and AP are used.

Transfer: In fall 1981, 268 students applied, 240 were accepted, and 202 enrolled. Transfer students need a GPA of at least 2.0. Grades of D transfer. Students must complete, at the college, the last 45 of the 180 quarter hours required for a bachelor's degree. Application deadlines are open.

Visiting: Prospective students from outside the Chicago area must make reservations for visits, preferably scheduling them for weekends between October and May. Housing and meals are provided at nominal cost for groups, and may be provided free for individuals. Students from the Chicago area may visit any time, but appointments and class visits should be arranged in advance.

Financial Aid: About 80% of the students receive aid. Thirty-three percent work part-time on campus. Average aid to freshmen is $2400. The college participates in federal programs such as NDSL, BEOG/SEOG, and CWS. Scholarships and grants for outstanding scholastic ability or other special talent are available. Loans are available from local banks and the college. Tuition remissions are offered to sons and daughters of clergy. The college is a member of CSS. Either the FAF or FFS should be filed. Application deadlines are open.

Foreign Students: Fewer than 1% of the full-time students come from foreign countries.

Admissions: Foreign students must achieve a TOEFL score of at least 550 and take either the SAT or ACT.

Procedure: Application deadlines are open. Foreign students must present both a doctor's report of physical examination as proof of health, and proof of funds adequate to cover 1 year of study. They must also carry health insurance.

Admissions Contact: James Lundeen, Director of Admissions.

NORTHWESTERN UNIVERSITY E-1
Evanston, Illinois 60201 (312) 492-7271

F/T: 3754M, 3137W Faculty: 1305; I, ++$
P/T: 33M, 35W Ph.D.'s: 90%
Grad: 2059M, 1372W S/F Ratio: 8 to 1
Year: qtrs, ss Tuition: $6885
Appl: Feb. 15 R and B: $2680
7457 applied 3885 accepted 1806 enrolled
SAT: 590V 630M ACT: 29 HIGHLY COMPETITIVE+

Northwestern University, established in 1851, is a privately endowed university. It consists of 6 undergraduate and several graduate schools. The combined university libraries hold more than 2,800,000 volumes and 1,094,000 microfilm items, and subscribe to over 31,000 periodicals.

Environment: The 230-acre Evanston campus, on the wooded shores of Lake Michigan, has about 150 buildings that house the 6 undergraduate schools, the Graduate School, and the Kellogg Graduate School of Management. On-campus housing accommodates approximately 5400 undergraduates. The university provides dormitories, fraternity and sorority houses, and on- and off-campus apartments for graduate students. The Chicago campus, on an urban lakefront site, includes the professional schools of dentistry, law, medicine, and the Division of Continuing Education.

Student Life: About 31% of the students are from Illinois. Sixty-seven percent of the men and 77% of the women live in campus residence halls. Thirty-seven percent of the students are Protestant, 30% are Catholic, and 22% are Jewish. About 15% are minority-group members. Campus housing is both single-sex and coed; there are visiting privileges in single-sex housing. Students are permitted to keep cars on campus.

Organizations: Thirty percent of the men and 30% of the women belong to the 23 national fraternities and 14 national sororities at the university. In a recent year, more than 600 musical and 60 theatrical events took place on campus. In addition to campus activities, students have access to all the cultural and recreational opportunities of Chicago, 30 minutes away by rapid transit.

Sports: The university competes on an intercollegiate level in 15 sports, and offers 24 intramural sports, with equal emphasis for men and women.

Handicapped: Almost 90% of the campus is accessible to wheelchair-bound students. Facilities include wheelchair ramps, special parking, elevators, specially equipped rest rooms, and lowered drinking fountains and telephones. Special class scheduling is also available. Those with hearing impairments may use one of the communicative-disorders clinics.

Graduates: The freshman dropout rate is 9%; 80% remain to graduate. Eighty percent of the graduates seek advanced degrees, with a 90% rate of acceptance for applicants to medical, dental, and law schools. Forty-three percent of the graduates enter careers in business and industry.

Services: Students receive the following free services: health care, psychological counseling, career counseling, placement services, and tutoring.

Programs of Study: The university confers the B.A., B.S., B.M., B.Mus.Ed., B.S.Ed., and B.S.J. degrees. Master's and doctoral programs are also offered. Bachelor's degrees are offered in the following subjects: AREA STUDIES (American, Asian, Russian, urban), EDUCATION (human development and social policy, secondary), ENGLISH (English, journalism, literature, speech), FINE AND PERFORMING ARTS (art, art history, dance, film/photography, interpretation, music, music education, radio/TV, studio art, theater/dramatics), HEALTH SCIENCES (dental hygiene, medical technology, nursing, occupational therapy, physical therapy, speech therapy), LANGUAGES (French, German, Greek/Latin, Italian, Portuguese, Russian, Slavic, Spanish), MATH AND SCIENCES (astronomy, biochemistry, biology, botany, chemistry, computer science, earth science, ecology/environmental science, geology, mathematics, natural sciences, physical sciences, physics, statistics, zoology), PHILOSOPHY (classics, humanities, philosophy, religion), PREPROFESSIONAL (engineering), SOCIAL SCIENCES (anthropology, economics, geography, government/political science, history, international relations, psychology, social sciences, sociology).

Required: Undergraduates must fulfill general-education requirements.

Special: The university offers a voluntary tutorial system, advanced placement, independent study, and a pass/no credit option. Students may design their own majors. The College of Arts and Sciences offers a 3-year bachelor's degree program, as well as special programs in integrated science, math methods in the social sciences, and the humanities. Together with the School of Speech and the Technological Institute, the College of Arts and Sciences also offers 4-year master's programs in 35 departments. There are 5-year master's programs in management, transportation, and urban and regional planning.

Honors: The university has an honors program in the College of Arts and Sciences and in the Technological Institute. Each year, 60 entering students are selected for this 6-year program, which admits them as freshmen to the Medical School.

Admissions: Fifty-two percent of those who applied were accepted for the 1981-82 freshman class. The SAT scores of those who enrolled were as follows: Verbal—16% below 500, 44% between 500 and 599, 35% between 600 and 700, and 5% above 700; Math—7% below 500, 30% between 500 and 599, 48% between 600 and 700, and 15% above 700. Of those who took the ACT, 2% scored below 21, 7% between 21 and 23, 10% between 24 and 25, 34% between 26 and 28, and 45% above 28. Candidates should have completed 16 high school units and have at least a B+ average. Alumni relationship receives consideration, but the principal basis for admission is demonstrated intellectual commitment, plus academic and extracurricular success within the secondary school environment. School recommendations are also considered.

Procedure: The SAT or ACT is required, and 3 ATs, including English Composition, are strongly recommended. All tests should be taken by December or January of the senior year. For entrance to the Technical Institute, the ATs should be in English composition, math, and either physics or chemistry. For the honors medical program and the integrated science program, the ATs should be English Composition, Math II, and Chemistry. Deadlines for regular admission are February 15 (fall), November 1 (winter), February 1 (spring), and May 1 (summer). Notification is made on a rolling basis. Freshmen are rarely admitted at midyear, but are admitted in the summer. Applications should be submitted with a $25 fee.

Special: For admission to the School of Music, an audition is required. Early and deferred admissions plans are available. AP credit is accepted.

Transfer: For fall 1981, 742 transfer students applied, 190 were accepted, and 145 enrolled. Transfers are considered for the sophomore and junior classes. A GPA of at least 3.0 is recommended. A high school transcript and the university's dean's reference form are required. An interview is also recommended. D grades do not transfer. Students must complete, at the university, 24 of the 45-48 course units required for the bachelor's degree. The fall application deadline is June 1; other deadlines are the same as those for freshmen.

Visiting: There are regularly scheduled orientations for prospective students. Visitors may sit in on classes; guides are available for informal visits. Overnight accommodations can be arranged through the office of admission.

Financial Aid: About 52% of all undergraduates receive aid in the form of scholarships, loans, and grants. Seventy-five percent of the students work part-time on campus. The average award to freshmen from all sources in 1981-82 was 57% of college costs. The CWS program is available. The FAF must be filed by February 15 (fall), November 1 (winter), February 1 (spring), or May 1 (summer).

Foreign Students: The 65 undergraduates from foreign countries make up less than 1% of the student body. Special counseling and special organizations are available.

Admissions: Students must achieve a minimum score of 550 on the TOEFL. The SAT or the ACT is also required.

Procedure: The application deadline for fall is February 1. Students must provide proof of adequate funds for 4 years of study and carry health insurance, which is available through the university for a fee.

Admissions Contact: Roger Campbell, Director of Undergraduate Admissions.

OLIVET NAZARENE COLLEGE   E-2
Kankakee, Illinois 60901   (815) 939-5011

F/T: 752M, 1001W	Faculty: 88; IIA, ——$
P/T: 99M, 135W	Ph.D.'s: 38%
Grad: 49M, 23W	S/F Ratio: 19 to 1
Year: 4-1-4, ss	Tuition: $2920
Appl: Aug. 1	R and B: $1716
912 applied	768 accepted 492 enrolled
ACT: 18	*LESS COMPETITIVE*

Olivet Nazarene College, founded in 1907, is a liberal arts college operated by the Church of the Nazarene. It provides graduate and undergraduate instruction and seeks to promote a well-rounded education in an atmosphere of Christian culture. The library contains 127,000 volumes and 30,000 microfilm items, and subscribes to 900 periodicals.

Environment: The 160-acre campus is located in a residential suburban area 60 miles south of Chicago. There are 26 buildings on campus, including 10 dormitories that accommodate 1500 students.

Student Life: About 45% of the students are from Illinois; 95% of entering freshmen come from public schools. Approximately 75% live on campus. Ninety-seven percent of the students are Protestant. The majority of students are members of the affiliated church. Three percent are Catholic. Five percent are minority-group members. College housing is single-sex. There are no visiting privileges. Students may keep cars on campus. All students are required to attend chapel services. Drinking and smoking are forbidden.

Organizations: There are no fraternities or sororities. Student organizations sponsor social and cultural events on campus.

Sports: The college competes in 7 intercollegiate sports for men and 4 for women. It also offers 9 intramural programs for men and 5 for women.

Handicapped: Approximately 90% of the campus is accessible to the physically handicapped. Facilities include wheelchair ramps, special parking, elevators, specially equipped rest rooms, and lowered drinking fountains and telephones. Fewer than 1% of the students currently enrolled have visual or hearing impairments.

Graduates: There is a freshman dropout rate of 30%; 40% remain to graduate. Of those who remain, 15% go on to graduate or professional school; 1% enter medical school, 1% dental school, and 1% law school. Fifteen percent pursue careers in business and industry.

Services: Free health care, placement services, career counseling, psychological counseling, tutoring, and remedial instruction are offered.

Programs of Study: The college confers the B.A., B.S., and B.Th. degrees. Associate and master's degrees are also offered. Bachelor's degrees are offered in the following subjects: BUSINESS (accounting, business administration, business education, computer science, economics, finance, management, marketing, secretarial), EDUCATION (early childhood, elementary, health/physical, secondary), ENGLISH (English, speech), FINE AND PERFORMING ARTS (art, art education, church music, music, music education, music performance), HEALTH SCIENCES (medical technology, nursing, physical therapy), LANGUAGES (romance languages), MATH AND SCIENCES (biochemistry, biology, botany, chemistry, earth science, mathematics, physical sciences, physics, zoology), PHILOSOPHY (biblical literature, Christian education, philosophy, religion), PREPROFESSIONAL (dentistry, engineering, home economics, law, medicine, ministry, pharmacy, social work, veterinary), SOCIAL SCIENCES (anthropology, economics, government/political science, history, psychology, sociology). About 20% of degrees conferred are in education and 19% in health sciences.

Special: A 3-2 engineering degree and a 2-2 program with an A.A. from Olivet and a B.S. from the University of Illinois are available. European tours for credit are also offered.

Honors: Phi Delta Lambda and the National Nazarene Honor Society honors programs are available.

Admissions: About 84% of those who applied were accepted for the 1981-82 freshman class. The ACT scores of those who enrolled were as follows: 64% below 21, 15% between 21 and 23, 8% between 24 and 25, 10% between 26 and 28, and 3% above 28. Candidates should have completed 15 Carnegie units, rank in the top 75% of their class, and have a minimum C average. Recommendations are also considered.

Procedure: The ACT is required. Application deadlines are August 1 (fall), January 1 (spring), and May 1 (summer). There is no application fee.

Special: AP and CLEP credit is accepted.

Transfer: For fall 1981, 275 applications were received, 228 were accepted, and 165 students enrolled. Students should have a minimum C average at their former school. D grades do not transfer. At least 1 year must be spent in residence, and students must complete, at the college, 30 of the 128 semester hours required to earn a bachelor's degree.

Visiting: Informal tours of the campus can be arranged through the admissions office. Regular orientations are scheduled for prospective students.

212 ILLINOIS

Financial Aid: About 70% of all students receive some form of financial aid; 40% work part-time on campus. The average award to freshmen from all sources is $1000. The college participates in most of the federal education aid programs. Loans are also available. The college is a member of CSS. The FAF must be filed. Application deadlines are at least one month before each semester. Earlier applications receive preference.

Foreign Students: One percent of the full-time students come from foreign countries. The college offers these students special organizations.

Admissions: Foreign students must score 500 on the TOEFL. No college entrance examination is required.

Procedure: Application deadlines are August 1 (fall), December 1 (winter), January 1 (spring), and May 1 (summer). Foreign students must present proof of adequate funds.

Admissions Contact: Rev. Roy F. Quanstrom, Director of Admissions.

PARKS COLLEGE OF ST. LOUIS UNIVERSITY C-5
Cahokia, Illinois 62206   (618) 337-7500

F/T: 1000M, 78W		Faculty:	50; n/av
P/T: none		Ph.D.'s:	25%
Grad: none		S/F Ratio:	22 to 1
Year: tri, ss		Tuition:	$2920
Appl: Aug. 1		R and B:	$2000
1056 applied	901 accepted		350 enrolled
SAT: 447V 531M	ACT: 21		COMPETITIVE

Parks College, part of St. Louis University, offers undergraduate programs in aerospace engineering, aeronautical technology, aeronautical administration, pilot training, meteorology, and travel, tourism, and transportation. The library contains 32,000 volumes and 1100 microfilm items, and subscribes to 260 periodicals.

Environment: The 113-acre campus is located in a small suburban town (pop. 20,000) 15 minutes from St. Louis. The 16 buildings include meteorology, physics, electrical, and chemical structures and aerodynamics laboratories. Two dormitories house 450 students.

Student Life: About 35% of the students are from Illinois, 25% are from Missouri, and 25% are from 35 other states. Sixty percent of entering freshmen come from public schools. Twenty-five percent of the students commute. Although this is a Jesuit institution, attendance at religious services is not compulsory. Forty-five percent of the students are Catholic, and 45% are Protestant. Eight percent of the students belong to minority groups. University housing is single-sex, and there are visiting privileges. Students may keep cars on campus.

Organizations: Approximately 25% of the men belong to the 5 fraternities; 25% of the women belong to the 1 sorority. Students have a vote on faculty committees in regard to regulations and discipline and are represented in a nonvoting capacity at departmental meetings. Social activities on campus include dances, a coffeehouse, and various cultural events.

Sports: The college competes intercollegiately in 4 men's sports. There are 7 intramural sports for men and 2 for women.

Handicapped: There are no special facilities for the physically handicapped.

Graduates: The freshman dropout rate is 20%; 65% remain to graduate. Fifteen percent of those who remain pursue graduate study; 85% enter careers in business and industry.

Services: Placement, health care, psychological counseling, career counseling, tutoring, and remedial instruction are offered to students free of charge.

Programs of Study: The B.S. degree is conferred. Associate degrees are also awarded. Bachelor's degrees are offered in the following subjects: BUSINESS (business administration), MATH AND SCIENCES (meteorology), PREPROFESSIONAL (engineering—aeromaintenance, engineering—aerospace, pilot training), SOCIAL SCIENCES (transportation, travel, and tourism). Ninety-five percent of degrees conferred are in preprofessional studies and 5% in business.

Required: Required courses for all students include English, mathematics, science (chemistry, physics and/or physical science), and computer science.

Special: The college concentrates almost exclusively on aeronautics and offers a special program in aeronautical maintenance.

Honors: There are 3 national honor societies on campus.

Admissions: Eighty-five percent of those who applied were accepted for the 1981–82 freshman class. The SAT scores of those who enrolled in a recent freshman class were as follows: Verbal—40% between 500 and 600, and 10% between 600 and 700. On the ACT, 65% scored between 20 and 23, 25% between 24 and 26, 5% between 27 and 28, and 5% above 28. Factors influencing the admissions decision are high school major, advanced placement or honors courses, recommendations, and impressions made during an interview.

Procedure: Either the SAT or ACT is required; junior year results are acceptable. Application deadlines are August 1 for fall entry, December 1 for winter entry, and April 1 for spring entry. The college follows a rolling admissions policy. There is a $25 application fee. Freshmen are admitted to any term.

Special: Early decision, early admissions, and deferred admissions plans are available. AP and CLEP credit is accepted.

Transfer: In the fall of 1981, 142 transfer students applied, 130 were accepted, and 102 enrolled. Transfers are considered for the freshman, sophomore, and junior classes. Students must have a minimum average of C at their former school. All students must complete 136 credits for a bachelor's degree; the final 30 semester hours must be earned at Parks. Preparation in mathematics/science or in programs similar to those offered by the college is recommended. Application deadlines are the same as for freshman applicants.

Visiting: There are no regularly scheduled orientations for prospective students. Guides are available for informal visits Monday through Friday; visitors may sit in on classes and stay overnight at the school. The admissions office should be contacted to arrange visits.

Financial Aid: About 65% of all students receive some form of financial aid. According to demonstrated need, the college awards aid packages of EOG, BEOG, NDSL. Work-study is also available in almost all departments; 33% of all students work part-time on campus. There are no academic or athletic scholarships, but 8% of the students receive Air Force ROTC scholarships. Federal loans are also available. The college is a member of CSS. The FAF is required. Financial aid application deadlines are July 1 (fall), December 1 (winter), and April 1 (spring). Tuition may be paid in installments.

Foreign Students: Ten percent of the full-time students come from foreign countries. St. Louis University offers an intensive English course and an intensive English program, as well as special counseling and special organizations.

Admissions: Foreign students must score at least 500 on the TOEFL or 75 on the University of Michigan Language Test. Foreign students are not required to take the SAT or ACT, but may take either in place of the TOEFL.

Procedure: Application deadlines are the same as for other students. Foreign students must present proof of funds adequate for their total program of study.

Admissions Contact: John Wilbur, Director of Admissions.

PRINCIPIA COLLEGE C-4
Elsah, Illinois 62028   (618) 374-2131

F/T: 365M, 424W		Faculty:	70; IIB, +$
P/T: none		Ph.D.'s:	67%
Grad: none		S/F Ratio:	13 to 1
Year: qtrs		Tuition:	$5103
Appl: see profile		R and B:	$2664
221 applied	203 accepted		168 enrolled
SAT: 482V 521M			COMPETITIVE

Principia College, founded in 1910, is a private liberal arts college for Christian Scientists. The library contains 135,000 volumes and 5000 microfilm items, and subscribes to 1284 periodicals.

Environment: The 3000-acre campus is located in a rural area and stretches for 4 miles along the Mississippi River. It consists of some 49 buildings, including 8 men's and 6 women's dormitories with a capacity for 750 students. St. Louis, Missouri, the nearest major city, is 40 miles away.

Student Life: About 13% of the students are from Illinois; the majority are from out of state. Three-quarters of the entering freshmen come from public schools. About 99% reside on campus in dormitories. All of the students are Christian Scientists and are expected to attend religious services. Two percent are minority-group members. Campus housing is single-sex; there are visiting privileges. Students may keep cars on campus.

Organizations: There are no social fraternities or sororities, but professional and service organizations serve as social groups. Student organizations include special-interest clubs, a radio station, theater, a weekly newspaper, and a concert and lecture series.

Sports: The college fields 10 intercollegiate teams for men and 9 for women. There are 3 intramural sports for men and 3 for women.

Handicapped: There are no facilities for the handicapped.

Graduates: The freshman dropout rate is 5%; 85% remain to graduate, and 25% go on to graduate school. Ten percent of the graduates enter law school, and 25% pursue careers in business and industry.

Services: Students receive free career counseling and placement services. Tutoring and remedial instruction are provided for a fee.

Programs of Study: All programs lead to the B.A. or B.S. degree in the following subjects: AREA STUDIES (German, Russian), BUSINESS (business administration), EDUCATION (elementary, secondary), ENGLISH (English, literature), FINE AND PERFORMING ARTS (art, art history, music, studio art, theater/dramatics), LANGUAGES (French, Spanish), MATH AND SCIENCES (biology, chemistry, earth science, mathematics, physics), PHILOSOPHY (philosophy, religion), SOCIAL SCIENCES (economics, government/political science, history, sociology).

Required: All students are required to take courses in fine arts, history, literature, natural or physical science, physical education, religion or philosophy, and social science.

Special: Off-campus study is offered as part of the regular curriculum. Students may arrange to spend one quarter in places such as Europe, Australia, the Far East, Washington, D.C., or Mexico studying with Principia professors. A Special Studies Program and the Special Major Program allows qualified students to plan their own liberal arts degree program outside of the structured degree curriculum and regulations. It is also possible to earn a combined B.A.-B.S. degree.

Admissions: Ninety-two percent of those who applied were accepted for the 1981–82 freshman class. The SAT scores of those who enrolled were as follows: Verbal—58% below 500, 25% between 500 and 599, 10% between 600 and 700, and 2% above 700; Math—43% below 500, 35% between 500 and 599, 16% between 600 and 700, and 6% above 700. Applicants should be high school graduates with at least a 2.0 GPA. They must have completed 15 Carnegie high school units and should rank in the upper half of their class. Other considerations are advanced placement or honors courses, recommendations, the extracurricular activities record, and a commitment to Christian Science teaching.

Procedure: The SAT or ACT is required and should be taken in the spring of the junior year and January of the senior year. Applications should be submitted with a $25 fee. Notification is on a rolling basis. The application deadline is 1 week before the quarter begins for fall entry, December 30 for winter entry, and March 27 for spring entry.

Special: An early admissions plan is available.

Transfer: For fall 1981, the college received 90 transfer applications; 83 were accepted; 71 students enrolled. Transfers are considered for all classes. Students must have a C average and SAT scores of at least 500 on each part. D grades do not transfer. All students must reside at least 4 consecutive quarters at the college and must complete, at the college, 16 of the 36 course credits required for a bachelor's degree.

Visiting: The college sponsors a visiting program in which prospective students spend a 3-day weekend at the college. They stay in a dorm, eat in the college dining room, and take classes, all free of charge. Arrangements can be made through the Hospitality Office.

Financial Aid: About 50% of the students receive financial aid through the school. About 85% work part-time on campus. Freshman loans and grants average $2000, and campus employment may earn the student an additional $150 to $600 per quarter. The college is a member of CSS. The FAF and the application are due August 30 (fall), December 30 (winter), or March 30 (spring). Tuition may be paid in installments.

Foreign Students: Five percent of the full-time students come from foreign countries. Special counseling is available for these students.

Admissions: Foreign students must achieve a TOEFL score of at least 500. Students whose native language is English must achieve SAT scores of at least 500 on each part.

Procedure: The application deadline for foreign students is March 1 (fall entry). They must present proof of funds adequate to cover 9–12 months of study.

Admissions Contact: Martha Green Quirk, Director of Admissions.

ILLINOIS 213

QUINCY COLLEGE
Quincy, Illinois 62301

B–3
(217) 222-8020

F/T: 604M, 661W
P/T: 266M, 409W
Grad: none
Year: sems, ss
Appl: Aug. 20
556 applied
SAT: 490V 530M

Faculty: 80; IIB, –$
Ph.D.'s: 32%
S/F Ratio: 16 to 1
Tuition: $3664 ($4064)
R and B: $1800 ($1900)
497 accepted   219 enrolled
ACT: 21   COMPETITIVE

Quincy College, founded in 1859, is a Roman Catholic college of liberal arts and education conducted by the Franciscan Friars. Our Lady of Angels Franciscan Seminary is affiliated with the college and exists as an independent organization within the academic framework. The library houses 210,000 volumes and 58,097 microfilm items, and subscribes to 981 periodicals.

Environment: The college occupies a 28-acre campus within Quincy (pop. 48,000), a suburban town about 1½ miles from the Mississippi River. There is also an 80-acre field station for biology research. There are more than 20 buildings, including 5 dormitories, which accommodate about 800 students, and lounge facilities for day students.

Student Life: About 70% of the men and 80% of the women are from Illinois. Sixty percent of the students live on campus, either in the dormitories or in other authorized housing. Sixty percent of the students are Catholic, 39% are Protestant, and fewer than 1% are Jewish. About 7% are minority-group members. University housing is both single-sex and coed; students in single-sex housing have visiting privileges. First semester freshmen observe a curfew for 6 weeks. There is also married-student housing. Students may keep cars on campus.

Organizations: About 33% of the students belong to 1 of the 2 fraternities or the 1 sorority. There are also choirs, a band, an orchestra, student publications, an FM radio station, a theater club, Circle-K, student government, religious organizations, and academic clubs.

Sports: The athletic program features 5 intercollegiate sports for men and 5 for women. There are also 4 intramural sports for men and 3 for women.

Handicapped: About 40% of the campus is accessible to wheelchair students. Special facilities include wheelchair ramps and elevators.

Graduates: Of the entering freshmen 8% drop out by the end of the first year, 57% remain to graduate, and 12% of those go on to graduate schools. Three percent of the graduates enter medical school, about 1% dental school, and 2% law school. Thirty-three percent pursue careers in business and industry.

Services: Students receive the following services free of charge: psychological counseling, tutoring, remedial instruction, placement, and career counseling. There is a full-time placement office for undergraduates and graduates.

Programs of Study: The college confers the degrees of B.A., B.S., B.F.A., B.S.Med.Tech., and B.S.Mus.Ed. Bachelor's degrees are offered in the following subjects: AREA STUDIES (Japanese), BUSINESS (accounting, computer science, international business, management, marketing, personnel management), EDUCATION (elementary, health/physical, learning disabilities, secondary), ENGLISH (English), FINE AND PERFORMING ARTS (art, art education, art history, communications, music, music and business studies, music education, studio art), HEALTH SCIENCES (medical technology, nuclear medical technology, nursing), LANGUAGES (Japanese), MATH AND SCIENCES (biochemistry, biology, chemistry, ecology/environmental science, mathematics), PHILOSOPHY (humanities, philosophy, religion, religious education), PREPROFESSIONAL (dentistry, engineering, law, medicine, pharmacy, veterinary), SOCIAL SCIENCES (alcohol education, economics, government/political science, history, psychology, sociology, social work). Thirty-two percent of degrees conferred are in business; 17% are in social sciences; and 14% are in math and sciences.

Required: All students must take 2 physical education activities as well as a distribution of courses in 5 areas of study. Two courses in theology and 2 courses in philosophy are required.

Special: Student-designed majors are permitted. Study abroad is possible.

Admissions: Eighty-nine percent of those who applied for the 1981–82 freshman class were accepted. Of those who enrolled the SAT scores were as follows: Verbal—68% below 500, 30% between 500 and 599, 2% between 600 and 700, and 0% above 700; Math—58% below 500, 28% between 500 and 599, 14% between 600 and 700, and 0% above 700. On the ACT, 43% scored below 21, 25% from 21 to 23, 12% from 24 to 25, 15% from 26 to 28, and

5% above 28. Candidates must be high school graduates, have at least a C average, and should be enrolled in a college preparatory curriculum. In addition, the admissions officers consider the reputation of the school from which the student is applying, the recommendations of that school, advanced placement or honors courses, and the personal impressions made during an interview. An interview is not required.

Procedure: All candidates must take the SAT or the ACT. Applications must be submitted by August 20 for the fall semester, January 18 for the spring semester, or June 7 for the summer session. There is no application fee. A recommendation, official transcripts, and test scores must also be forwarded. Notification is made on a rolling basis, as soon as all of the credentials are received.

Transfer: For fall 1981, 154 transfer students applied, 149 were accepted, and 108 enrolled. Transfer students must have a C average. No more than 9 hours of D grades will transfer unless part of a conferred associate degree. No more than 64 semester hours of community college credit will transfer. Students must complete, at the college, at least 30 of the 120 credits required for a bachelor's degree. Application deadlines are August 20 for the fall semester, January 18 for the winter semester, and June 7 for the summer session.

Visiting: Guides are available for informal visits during school sessions. Visitors can sit in on classes and stay at the school. The admissions office will make arrangements.

Financial Aid: Ninety percent of students receive financial aid. Sixty percent work part-time on campus. The average award is $3620. Students receive aid from these sources: grants (including EOG), loans (including NDSL), and campus employment (including CWS). Quincy College scholarship aid, which is based on academic performance and ACT or SAT scores, is also available. The college is a member of CSS. The FAF or FFS is required. Application deadlines are August 1 for the fall semester, January 1 for the winter semester, and May 15 for the summer session.

Foreign Students: Four percent of full-time students come from foreign countries. The college offers these students an intensive English course, special counseling, and special organizations.

Admissions: Foreign students must take either the TOEFL or the SAT. They must score at least 500 on the TOEFL.

Procedure: Applications deadlines are July 1 for the fall semester, November 1 for the winter semester, and April 1 for the summer session. Foreign students must present proof of funds adequate for 4 years of study. They must also carry health insurance, which is available through the college for a fee.

Admissions Contact: Richard J. Smith, Director of Admissions.

ROCKFORD COLLEGE   D-1
Rockford, Illinois 61101   (815) 226-4050

F/T: 310M, 400W	Faculty:	62; IIB, +$
P/T: 250M, 450W	Ph.D.'s:	70%
Grad: 50M, 125W	S/F Ratio:	15 to 1
Year: 4-1-4, ss	Tuition:	$3990
Appl: open	R and B:	$1875
609 applied	432 accepted	208 enrolled
SAT: 460V 460M	ACT: 23	COMPETITIVE+

Rockford College, established in 1847, is a private, nonsectarian liberal arts school. It provides graduate and undergraduate instruction and an evening division. The library houses 120,000 volumes and 1350 microfilm items, and subscribes to 800 periodicals.

Environment: The 304-acre self-contained campus, in a suburban town 90 miles from Chicago, has 26 modern buildings, including 15 residence halls.

Student Life: About 90% of the students are from the Midwest. Sixty percent live on campus. Thirty-five percent of the students are Catholic, 63% are Protestant, and 2% are Jewish. Six percent are minority-group members. Campus housing is both single-sex and coed; there are visiting privileges in single-sex housing. Students may keep cars on campus.

Organizations: There are no fraternities or sororities. Students participate in faculty and administrative committees. Extracurricular activities include modern dance, chorus, publications, a radio station, and many special-interest clubs.

Sports: Rockford College fields intercollegiate teams in 8 sports for men and 6 for women. It offers 11 intramural sports for men and 6 for women.

Handicapped: About 90% of the campus is accessible to wheelchair students. Facilities include wheelchair ramps, special parking, elevators, and specially equipped rest rooms. One percent of the students have visual impairments; 1% have hearing impairments. For these students there are tapes, tape players, and braille equipment.

Graduates: Ten percent of freshmen drop out by the end of the first year. Fifty percent remain to graduate. Twenty percent of students pursue graduate study after graduation.

Services: Students receive the following services free of charge: health care, psychological counseling, career counseling, placement services, tutoring, and remedial instruction.

Programs of Study: The college confers the B.A., B.S., B.F.A., and B.S.N. degrees. Only the B.S. degree is awarded to part-time students in the evening division. Master's programs are also offered. Bachelor's degrees are offered in the following subjects: BUSINESS (accounting, business administration, computer science), EDUCATION (early childhood, elementary, health/physical, secondary), ENGLISH (English), FINE AND PERFORMING ARTS (art, art history, dance, music, studio art, theater/dramatics), HEALTH SCIENCES (medical technology, nursing), LANGUAGES (French, German, Greek/Latin, Spanish), MATH AND SCIENCES (biology, botany, chemistry, mathematics, natural sciences, zoology), PHILOSOPHY (classics, humanities, philosophy, religion), PREPROFESSIONAL (dentistry, engineering, law, medicine, ministry, optometry, pharmacy, social work, veterinary), SOCIAL SCIENCES (anthropology, economics, government/political science, history, psychology, social sciences, sociology).

Required: All students are required to take orientation for physical education for 2 semesters. Two semesters of English composition and rhetoric are also required. Two courses must be completed in each of the following areas: arts, humanities, social sciences, and math and sciences.

Special: Work-study, internships, junior year abroad, the Washington Semester, the U.N. Semester, and independent study are some of the special options available. Student-designed majors are also permitted; 3-2 programs are offered in dentistry, engineering, law, medicine, optometry, physical therapy, medical technology, and veterinary.

Honors: The college offers an honors program in humanities. There is a Phi Beta Kappa chapter on campus.

Admissions: Seventy-one percent of those who applied were accepted for the 1981-82 freshman class. Of those who enrolled in a recent class, the SAT scores were as follows: Verbal—60% between 500 and 599, 30% between 600 and 700, and 10% above 700; Math—50% between 500 and 599, 40% between 600 and 700, and 10% above 700. Candidates should rank in the top half of their class, present minimum combined SAT scores of 975, and have a minimum C average. Advanced placement or honors courses, recommendations, and impressions made during an interview are also considered.

Procedure: Either the SAT or ACT is required and should be taken in November of the senior year. Application deadlines are open. Notification is on a rolling basis. Applications must be submitted with a $15 fee.

Special: Early decision, early admissions, and deferred admissions are available; an interview is required. CLEP and AP credit is accepted.

Transfer: For fall 1981, 503 transfer applications were received, 375 were accepted, and 120 students enrolled. Students must have a 2.0 GPA and should submit recommendations from their former school; D grades do not transfer. Thirty semester hours, of the 128 needed for a bachelor's degree, must be completed at the college. Application deadlines are open.

Visiting: There are regularly scheduled orientations for prospective students. Guides are also available for informal visits. Overnight accommodations can be arranged through the office of admissions.

Financial Aid: Eighty-three percent of the students receive some form of financial aid. Fifty percent work part-time on campus. Scholarships have ranged from $100 to $3100. The median award for entering freshmen is $2000. Special consideration is given to economically deprived students. The college is a member of CSS. The FAF or FFS must be filed. Deadline for financial aid application is August 1.

Foreign Students: Five percent of the full-time students come from foreign countries. The college offers these students special counseling and special organizations.

Admissions: Foreign students must achieve a TOEFL score of at least 550. No college entrance examination is required.

Procedure: Application deadlines are June 1 for the fall and December 1 for the spring. Foreign students must present proof of a health examination. They must also present proof of funds adequate to cover 1 year of study. There is also a $1000 special deposit payable at the time of admission. Foreign students must carry health insurance, which is available through the college for a fee.

Admissions Contact: Charles B. Wharton, Dean of Enrollment Planning.

ROOSEVELT UNIVERSITY E-2
Chicago, Illinois 60605 (312) 341-3515

F/T: 740M, 995W	Faculty:	185; IIA, av$
P/T: 1176M, 1540W	Ph.D.'s:	61%
Grad:1181M, 1023W	S/F Ratio:	16 to 1
Year: sem, ss	Tuition:	$3502
Appl: Aug. 15	R and B:	$2480
674 applied	240 accepted	180 enrolled
ACT: 22		COMPETITIVE+

Roosevelt University, founded in 1945, is a private liberal arts university. The library houses 336,000 volumes and 110,004 microforms, and subscribes to 3232 periodicals.

Environment: The university is located in downtown Chicago in the famous Auditorium Building, a 10-story structure that was declared a National Historic Landmark in 1975. There is an ongoing program of restoration. Adjacent to the Auditorium Building is the only dormitory, Herman Crown Center, which houses 360 students.

Student Life: About 83% of the students are from Illinois; 7% are from out of state. Approximately 80% of the entering freshmen come from public schools. The majority of students commute and only 5% live in the dormitory. About 48% of the students are minority-group members. Campus housing is coed. Students may keep cars on campus.

Organizations: Student activities are varied and include ethnic groups, an International Student Union, special-interest clubs, concerts, and lectures. There are no fraternities or sororities.

Sports: There are 5 intercollegiate sports for men and 4 for women. There are also 5 intramural sports for men and 2 for women.

Handicapped: Elevators, lowered drinking fountains, and lowered telephones are available.

Graduates: The freshman dropout rate is 8%; 60% remain to graduate. Twenty-five percent pursue graduate study after graduation. Fifty percent go on to careers in business and industry.

Services: Students receive placement and career counseling, health care, psychological counseling, tutoring, and remedial instruction free of charge. A placement service offers undergraduates and graduates total career planning.

Programs of Study: Roosevelt University confers the following degrees: B.A., B.S., B.M., B.S.B.A., B.A.Ed., B.F.A., and B.G.S. Master's degrees are also awarded. Bachelor's degrees are offered in the following subjects: AREA STUDIES (African, American, Black/Afro-American, Jewish, urban, women's), BUSINESS (accounting, advertising, business education, business law, computer science, computing and information science, data processing, finance, management, marketing), EDUCATION (early childhood, elementary, music, science, special), ENGLISH (English, journalism, literature, speech), FINE AND PERFORMING ARTS (art history, fine arts, fine arts in music, fine arts in theater, music, music history, music literature, music theory, theater/dramatics), HEALTH SCIENCES (cytotechnology, medical technology, nuclear medicine technology, podiatric science), LANGUAGES (comparative literature, French, German, Russian, Spanish), MATH AND SCIENCES (actuarial science, allied health, biology, chemistry, mathematics, physics, urban environmental management), PHILOSOPHY (philosophy), PREPROFESSIONAL (dentistry, engineering—industrial, law, medicine, pharmacy), SOCIAL SCIENCES (anthropology, economics, geography, gerontology, government/political science, history, labor relations, labor studies, psychology, public administration, sociology, social work). Forty-two percent of degrees conferred are in business, 26% in social sciences, and 15% in math and sciences.

Required: All liberal arts and sciences students are required to take 12 semester hours in each of the following three areas: natural science and mathematics, social sciences, and the humanities. Business administration majors are required to complete a minimum 48 semester hours in the liberal arts and sciences. All students must take English.

Special: Independent study is available. The Bachelor of General Studies degree program for adults over the age of 25 offers 27 fields of concentration.

Honors: The honors program enables students to work more closely with faculty and to explore various fields of study within the college curriculum in depth. The national honor society, Beta Gamma Sigma, has a chapter on campus.

Admissions: Thirty-five percent of those who applied were accepted for the 1981–82 freshman class. The ACT scores of those who enrolled were as follows: 34% below 21, 24% between 21 and 23, 13% between 24 and 25, 11% between 26 and 28, and 8% above 28. Requirements for admission are as follows: graduation from an accredited high school or a high school transcript that shows a minimum of 3 years of completed work, a C average, rank in the upper 75% of the class, and completion of 15 Carnegie units.

Procedure: Either the ACT or SAT should be taken in the spring of the junior year or during the senior year. However, students may choose to take the university's entrance examination in place of the ACT or SAT. The deadlines for applications are August 15 (fall), December 15 (spring), and just before the beginning of each summer session. Students who are also applying for housing should apply as early as possible. Notification is made as soon as all credentials are received. A $20 fee must accompany the application.

Special: Early admissions and deferred admissions are available. CLEP and AP credit is possible.

Transfer: For fall 1981, the university received 1508 transfer applications; 1244 were accepted; 985 students actually enrolled. Transfers are considered for all classes. Students must have a C average for all previous college work. D grades in one's major field do not transfer. All students must complete, at the university, 30 or more semester hours, depending on their program of study, out of the 120 needed to receive a bachelor's degree. Application deadlines are the same as those for freshman applicants.

Visiting: There are guides available for informal visits on weekdays, and visitors can sit in on classes. The undergraduate admissions office will make arrangements.

Financial Aid: Fifty-five percent of students receive financial aid. The university provides scholarships, loans, grants, and work as sources of financial aid. A total of $1,500,000 in scholarships is available. Loans are received from NDSL, the state government, local banks, the university, and private sources. Scholarships range in amount from $200 to $2850, loans from $500 to $2500. Campus employment may earn a student $1000 to $2000. Tuition may be paid on the installment plan. The university is a member of the CSS. The FAF is required of aid applicants. Scholarships are awarded on the basis of academic record. Special consideration is given to economically deprived students. Application must be made by May 1.

Foreign Students: Ten percent of the full-time students come from foreign countries. The university offers these students an intensive English course, an intensive English program, special counseling, and special organizations.

Admissions: Foreign students must take the university's own English proficiency examination. No college entrance examinations are required.

Procedure: Application deadlines are June 1 for the fall, October 1 for the spring, and March 1 for the summer. Foreign students must present proof of funds adequate for their entire period of study. It is strongly recommended that they carry health insurance, which is available through the university for a fee.

Admissions Contact: Lily S. Rose, Director of Undergraduate Admissions.

ROSARY COLLEGE E-2
River Forest, Illinois 60305 (312) 366-9189

F/T: 130M, 556W	Faculty:	n/av; IIA, −$
P/T: 57M, 274W	Ph.D.'s:	70%
Grad: 244M, 431W	S/F Ratio:	10 to 1
Year: sems, ss	Tuition:	$4350
Appl: open	R and B:	$2300
355 applied	257 accepted	158 enrolled
ACT: 22		COMPETITIVE

Rosary College is a Catholic liberal arts college providing both graduate and undergraduate instruction. The library contains 230,000 volumes and 50,000 microfilm items, and subscribes to 1100 periodicals.

Environment: The 30-acre campus is located in a suburban area 10 miles from downtown Chicago. The 7 modern Gothic buildings include an auditorium, recital hall, and 2 dormitories.

Student Life: About 95% of the students are from Illinois; 50% of entering freshmen come from public schools. About 70% of the students live on campus. Twelve percent are minority-group members. About 65% are Catholic, and 30% are Protestant. Campus housing is both coed and single-sex; there are visiting privileges in the single-sex housing. Day-care services are available to all students for a fee. Students may keep cars on campus.

216 ILLINOIS

Organizations: Student organizations include government activity, musical and religious groups, as well as several publications.

Sports: The college fields 3 intercollegiate teams for men and 4 for women. There are 10 intramural sports for men and 9 for women.

Handicapped: Facilities for handicapped students include special parking, elevators, and specially equipped rest rooms. Three counselors are available for handicapped students.

Graduates: At the end of the freshman year about 20% of the students drop out, and about 50% remain to graduate. About 65% of the graduates pursue advanced study.

Services: Students receive placement services and career counseling free of charge. Health care is provided for a fee.

Programs of Study: The college confers the B.A., B.Mus., and B.Mus.Ed. degrees. Master's degrees are also awarded. Bachelor's degrees are offered in the following subjects: AREA STUDIES (American), BUSINESS (accounting, business administration, computer science, computer science/mathematics, international business), EDUCATION (secondary, special), ENGLISH (English, literature), FINE AND PERFORMING ARTS (art, communication arts and sciences, fine art, music, music education), LANGUAGES (French, German, Italian, modern foreign languages, Spanish), MATH AND SCIENCES (biochemistry, biology, chemistry, gerontology, mathematics, natural sciences), PHILOSOPHY (philosophy, religion), PREPROFESSIONAL (fashion design, fashion merchandising, food and nutrition, home economics, home economics education), SOCIAL SCIENCES (British studies, economics, government/political science, history, psychology, social sciences, sociology, women's studies). Twenty-four percent of the degrees are conferred in business.

Required: All students must take a freshman seminar.

Special: Student-designed majors and study abroad are permitted. The college has divisional majors in biology-chemistry, fine arts, modern languages, and social sciences.

Honors: There are 9 honor societies on campus. The college offers an honors degree program and a 4-year B.A.-M.A. program in English, French, and history.

Admissions: Seventy-two percent of those who applied were accepted for the 1981-82 freshman class. The ACT scores of those who enrolled were as follows: 30% below 21, 25% between 21 and 23, 20% between 24 and 25, 15% between 26 and 28, and 10% above 28. Applicants should rank in the upper half of their high school class, have a 2.0 GPA or better, and be high school graduates with 16 Carnegie units of academic work. Recommendations, leadership qualities, and extracurricular activities are also considered important.

Procedure: Either the SAT or ACT is required. Applicants for the 4-year B.A.-M.A. program must take 2 ATs. There are no application deadlines. Freshmen are admitted for the fall, midyear, and summer sessions. A personal interview on campus should be arranged. The application, a $15 free, high school record, and test scores should be submitted early in the senior year. Notification is on a rolling basis.

Special: The college offers both early admissions and early decision plans. CLEP and AP credit is available.

Transfer: For fall 1981, 204 transfer applications were received, 168 were accepted, and 105 students enrolled. D grades do not transfer. Applicants should have a 2.0 GPA or better. All students must complete, at the college, the first 90 or the last 34 of the 124 credits required for a bachelor's degree. There are no application deadlines.

Visiting: There are regularly scheduled orientations for prospective students. Informal guided tours are available; visitors may sit in on classes and stay overnight at the school. The admissions office should be contacted for arrangements.

Financial Aid: About 70% of the students receive financial aid. Fifteen percent work part-time on campus. The average award to freshmen is $2500. Academic scholarships are available to freshmen. The college also participates in NDSL, BEOG/SEOG, and CWS. The college is a member of CSS. The FAF should be filed by February 15.

Foreign Students: Two percent of the full-time students come from foreign countries.

Admissions: Foreign students must take the TOEFL.

Procedure: Foreign students must present proof of adequate funds.

Admissions Contact: John Ballheim, Dean of Admissions.

SAINT XAVIER COLLEGE
Chicago, Illinois 60655

E-2
(312) 779-3300

F/T: 408M, 983W	Faculty: 132; IIA, – $
P/T: 209M, 532W	Ph.D.'s: n/av
Grad: 18M, 161W	S/F Ratio: 12 to 1
Year: 4-1-4, ss	Tuition: $3660
Appl: Aug. 15	R and B: $2350
519 applied	433 accepted	314 enrolled
ACT: 20		COMPETITIVE

Saint Xavier College, founded in 1847 by the Sisters of Mercy, is a liberal arts college affiliated with the Roman Catholic Church. The library contains more than 60,000 volumes and subscribes to 500 periodicals.

Environment: The 40-acre campus is located in a residential, urban area of southwest Chicago, 30 minutes from downtown. The nine major buildings include a coed residence hall that houses 180 students. Recreational facilities include outdoor tennis and basketball courts, a baseball field, and a small lake.

Student Life: The college is primarily a commuter school; 96% of the students come from the Chicago area. Ten percent live on campus. Ten percent are minority-group members. College-sponsored housing is coed. Students may keep cars on campus. Day-care services are available to all students, faculty, and staff for a fee.

Organizations: Student activities include a coffeehouse, chorus, choir, orchestra, and social events. Students are represented on the Faculty Senate.

Sports: The college fields 3 intercollegiate teams for men and 3 for women.

Graduates: About 10% of the freshmen drop out, and 65% remain to graduate. Forty percent of the graduates seek advanced degrees.

Services: Offered free of charge are placement, health care, and psychological and career counseling. Tutoring and remedial instruction are available for a fee.

Programs of Study: The college awards the B.A. and B.S. degrees. Master's programs also are available. Bachelor's degrees are offered in the following subjects: BUSINESS (business administration), EDUCATION (early childhood, elementary, secondary), ENGLISH (English, speech), FINE AND PERFORMING ARTS (art, art education, mass communication), HEALTH SCIENCES (nursing, speech therapy), LANGUAGES (French, Spanish), MATH AND SCIENCES (biology, chemistry, mathematics, natural sciences), PHILOSOPHY (philosophy, religion), PREPROFESSIONAL (dentistry, law, medicine, pharmacy, veterinary), SOCIAL SCIENCES (government/political science, history, international business, psychology, sociology). About 28% of the undergraduate degrees are awarded in health professions, 22% in education, and 17% in social sciences.

Required: All students must complete a 38-hour core curriculum that includes courses in critical thinking, humanities and fine arts, natural sciences, philosophy, social sciences, and religion.

Special: The 4-week January term is a period of intensive short courses, independent study, off-campus field courses, and opportunities for community involvement. Students may design their own majors and spend their junior year abroad.

Admissions: Eighty-three percent of the applicants for 1981-82 were accepted. Applicants must be high school graduates with at least 16 academic units. They must rank in the upper half of their high school class, and should have at least a 2.0 GPA.

Procedure: The SAT or ACT should be taken late in the junior year or in November or December of the senior year. The application, a $15 fee, test scores, and high school records should be submitted by August 15 (fall) or January 15 (spring). Notification is made on a rolling basis.

Special: CLEP and AP credit is accepted.

Transfer: For fall 1981, 253 transfer students applied, 207 were accepted, and 166 enrolled. Transfer students are accepted for all classes. Students must have a GPA of at least 2.0 and must submit college and high school transcripts. A minimum ACT score of 18 is required. D grades do not transfer. Students must complete, at the college, at least 30 of the 120 semester hours required for a bachelor's degree. The application deadlines are the same as those for freshmen.

Financial Aid: Seventy-eight percent of the students receive aid. Programs include Illinois state awards, BEOG, SEOG, college scholarships and grants, nursing loans, NDSL, Illinois-guaranteed student loans, CWS, merit scholarships, and residence hall scholarships. The college is a member of the CSS. Students should contact the financial aid office for application information. The deadline for financial aid application is August 20.

Foreign Students: Foreign students are accepted.

Admissions: Foreign students must achieve a minimum TOEFL score of 500. No college entrance exam is required.

Procedure: Application deadlines are July 15 (fall) and December 15 (spring). Foreign students must present proof of funds adequate to cover 1 year of study. There is a special $25 application fee.

Admissions Contact: Robert J. Schwendau, Director of Admissions.

SCHOOL OF THE ART INSTITUTE OF CHICAGO E-2
Chicago, Illinois 60603   (312) 443-3717

F/T: 304M, 407W	Faculty:	72; IIA, −$
P/T: 77M, 170W	Ph.D.'s:	12%
Grad: 81M, 104W	S/F Ratio:	10 to 1
Year: sems, ss	Tuition:	$4365
Appl: July 15	R and B:	n/app
226 applied	169 accepted	106 enrolled
SAT or ACT: required		SPECIAL

The School of the Art Institute of Chicago is a private, nonsectarian professional art school directly attached to the Art Institute of Chicago. The library contains 15,455 volumes, 908 exhibition catalogs, 576 pamphlets, 209 artists' books, 649 audio tapes, 420 records, 266 films, and 450 videotapes, and subscribes to 188 periodicals.

Environment: Located within the city of Chicago, the school is a nonresident institution. As such, it has no housing facilities but recommends downtown residences. Lockers and a cafeteria are available.

Student Life: In a recent freshman class, 90% came from public schools, 5% from private schools. About 20% of the students are minority-group members. Students may keep cars on campus.

Organizations: The student union represents the student body and holds special events such as film series and exhibitions. Other organizations include the Multi-Cultural Organization and the Committee for Alternative Artistic Education. The Midwest Film Center is located at the school, and the museum offers art lectures and films.

Handicapped: Approximately 95% of the campus is accessible to the physically handicapped. Facilities include wheelchair ramps, special parking, elevators, specially equipped rest rooms, and lowered drinking fountains and telephones; special class scheduling is also available.

Sports: The school fields 1 intercollegiate team for men and 1 for women. There are no intramural sports.

Graduates: Seventy percent of entering freshmen remain to graduate.

Services: Placement services, career counseling, health care, tutoring, and remedial instruction are offered to students free of charge. There is sometimes a fee for psychological counseling. Co-op education and internships are also available.

Programs of Study: The school confers the B.F.A. degree. Master's degrees are also awarded. Studio concentrations are available in the following subjects: ceramics, fashion design, fiber/fabric, filmmaking, generative systems, interior architecture, painting and drawing, performance, photography, printmaking, sculpture, video, and visual communication. Courses are also offered in art history/aesthetics, art education/art therapy, fundamentals, liberal arts, and sound/music. There are also special interdepartmental courses. A program of study for the preparation of teachers in the visual and other arts for all levels of instruction is offered by the department of art education.

Special: Study abroad, student-designed majors, independent external credit projects, and independent research are offered.

Admissions: Seventy-five percent of those who applied were accepted for the 1981–82 freshman class. Admission is by portfolio; each applicant's portfolio is judged by a committee of faculty. Since the committee feels that the recommendation and portfolio say more about a student's chance of success at a professional art school than any other single factor, there are no requirements as to class rank or GPA.

Procedure: Applicants are asked to submit SAT or ACT scores unless they have completed 2 full years of college or have been out of high school for over 5 years. An application, a $15 fee, high school and college transcripts, and 1 letter of recommendation should be filed with the admissions office. A compact portfolio, preferably consisting of slides but in any case no larger than 22" by 28", should be sent, containing 10 to 15 pieces of the applicant's best work. No 3-dimensional work may be submitted. The deadline for fall admission is July 15; the spring deadline is November 1. The school follows a rolling admissions policy.

Special: There is a deferred admissions plan. CLEP and AP credit is accepted, with the exception of the Studio Art AP.

Transfer: For fall 1981, 332 students applied, 279 were accepted, and 200 enrolled. Transfers are accepted for the freshman, sophomore, and junior classes. Students must submit a statement of purpose, a letter of recommendation, and a portfolio in addition to the regular requirements; D grades do not transfer. There is a 1-year residency requirement. Students must complete, at the school, 36 of the 144 credits required for a bachelor's degree. Application deadlines are July 15 (fall) and November 1 (winter).

Visiting: Guided tours can be scheduled by the admissions office 5 days a week. There are also regularly scheduled orientations for prospective students.

Financial Aid: About 75% of all students receive some form of financial aid. About 27% work part-time on campus. Aid is available from the following sources: scholarships, grants (including EOG), loans (including NDSL), and work-study programs (including CWS). No-need awards are also available. Renewal of need-based awards is based on academic record and continued financial need. The FAF, SFS, or FFS should be filed. The school is a member of CSS. There is no application deadline.

Foreign Students: Seven percent of the full-time students come from foreign countries. An intensive English course, special counseling, and special organizations are available for these students.

Admissions: Foreign students must take either the TOEFL, the University of Michigan Language Test, or the Comprehensive English Language Test if English is not their native language. On the TOEFL, a minimum score of 500 is required. No college entrance exams are required.

Procedure: Application deadlines are May 1 (fall) and November 1 (winter). Foreign students must present proof of funds and must carry health insurance, which is available through the school for a fee.

Admissions Contact: Nicole Rae Brown, Director of Admissions.

SHIMER COLLEGE C-1
Waukegan, Illinois 60085   (312) 623-8400
(Recognized Candidate for Accreditation)

F/T, P/T:	Faculty:	15; n/av
80M&W	Ph.D.'s:	n/av
Grad: none	S/F Ratio:	7 to 1
Year: sems, ss	Tuition:	$3500
Appl: open	R and B:	$2300
25 applied	15 accepted	15 enrolled
ACT: 19		COMPETITIVE

Shimer College, founded in 1853, is an independent, undergraduate college of liberal arts and sciences. The college uses the "great books" approach in seminar-sized classes. The library holds 35,000 books and 650 microfilm items, and subscribes to 200 periodicals.

Environment: The 85-acre suburban campus is located in a small city 40 miles north of Chicago.

Student Life: About 60% of the students come from Illinois. Most students live in the coed dormitories.

Organizations: College activities include student government, publications, clubs, drama, dance, an orchestra, a radio station, and regularly scheduled social and cultural events. There are no fraternities or sororities.

Sports: The college fields intercollegiate teams in soccer and basketball. Seven intramural sports are available.

Handicapped: No special facilities are provided for handicapped students.

Graduates: About 25% of the freshmen drop out, and 55% remain to graduate. About 73% of the graduates go on for further education, including 6% who enter medical school and 29% who enter law school.

Services: Free placement aid, health care, psychological counseling, remedial instruction, and tutoring are provided.

Programs of Study: The college awards the B.A. in the following subjects: ENGLISH (English, literature), FINE AND PERFORMING ARTS (art), LANGUAGES (foreign language), MATH AND SCIENCES (biology, mathematics, physical sciences, physics), PHILOSOPHY (classics, philosophy), SOCIAL SCIENCES (history, psychology, social sciences, sociology).

218 ILLINOIS

Required: Eighty of the 120 hours required for graduation are composed of a core curriculum that includes courses in foreign language, history, humanities, mathematics, natural sciences, philosophy, and social sciences. Students must pass 4 comprehensive examinations.

Special: The college offers an optional year at Oxford College in England, where students take two-thirds of their programs with Shimer faculty members and one-third with Oxford tutors. Pass-fail options are available. The college awards a general studies degree, and students may design their own majors. A teacher-preparation program is available.

Honors: The college offers an honors program.

Admissions: About 60% of those who applied were accepted for the 1981-82 freshman class. For an earlier class, the SAT scores were: Verbal—60% between 500 and 599, 31% between 600 and 700, and 8% above 700; Math—14% between 500 and 599, 3% between 600 and 700, and 3% above 700. Of those who took the ACT, 40% scored between 20 and 23, 30% between 24 and 26, 8% between 27 and 28, and 12% above 28. Admissions officers also consider an applicant's admission essay, advanced placement or honors courses, academic interests, and recommendations by high school officials.

Procedure: Applicants must take the SAT or ACT. Application deadlines are open. Students are notified within 3 weeks after their credentials are received. There is no application fee. An interview is recommended.

Special: AP and CLEP credit is accepted.

Transfer: For a recent year, 5 students applied, 4 were accepted, and all 4 enrolled. Students must complete at least 2 years in residence to receive a degree.

Visiting: Prospective students should contact the admissions office to arrange campus visits. Visitors may attend classes and stay overnight in the residence halls. Guides are provided.

Financial Aid: More than half the students receive aid. The college provides scholarships, grants, loans, and a limited number of half-tuition scholarships based on academic excellence. Campus jobs are available. Loans are available from federal and state governments, banks, and the college itself. Aid is awarded on the basis of need and academic achievement. The FAF or SFS is required; application deadlines are open.

Admissions Contact: Pat Dwyer, Director of Admissions.

SOUTHERN ILLINOIS UNIVERSITY

Southern Illinois University has 2 major campuses at Carbondale and at Edwardsville. Together, the campuses comprise a university with a full-time enrollment of about 32,000 students. Chartered in 1868, the university has grown to a multi-campus institution offering both undergraduate and graduate degrees. Descriptions of both campuses follow.

SOUTHERN ILLINOIS UNIVERSITY AT CARBONDALE   D-5

Carbondale, Illinois 62901   (618) 453-4381

F/T: 11,935M, 6546W   *Faculty:* 1235; I, — — $
P/T: 1049M, 731W   *Ph.D.'s:* 65%
Grad: 2098M, 1632W   *S/F Ratio:* 16 to 1
Year: sems, ss   *Tuition:* $1050 ($2456)
Appl: Aug. 1   *R and B:* $2000
8590 applied   6733 accepted   3057 enrolled
ACT: 21   COMPETITIVE

Southern Illinois University at Carbondale offers programs leading to associate, baccalaureate, master's, doctoral, and professional degrees. The library contains 1.7 million volumes, more than 1 million microfilm items, and subscribes to more than 10,000 periodicals.

Environment: The rural Carbondale campus includes the School of Technical Careers, Southern Illinois Airport and training facilities, and a recreation and outdoor education center on Little Grassy Lake. On-campus housing facilities include dormitories, on-campus apartments, apartments for married students, and fraternities and sororities.

Student Life: Most of the students are from Illinois; about 25% live on campus. Twelve percent are minority-group members. Campus housing is both coed and single-sex; there are visiting privileges in the single-sex housing. Upper division students may keep cars on campus. Day-care services are available to all students for a fee.

Organizations: There are 13 fraternities and 9 sororities on campus. Extracurricular activities include student government and special interest groups.

Sports: The university fields 11 intercollegiate teams for men and 11 for women. There are 4 intramural sports for men and 4 for women.

Handicapped: About 90% of the campus is accessible to handicapped students. Facilities include wheelchair ramps, parking areas, elevators, specially equipped rest rooms, and lowered drinking fountains and telephones. Special class scheduling is also available. Two counselors are available to handicapped students.

Graduates: About 26% of the full-time students drop out by the end of their freshman year; 45% remain to graduate.

Services: The following services are available to students free of charge: health care, tutoring, psychological and career counseling, and placement.

Programs of Study: The university confers the B.A., B.Mus., B.Mus.Ed., and B.S. degrees. Associate, master's, and doctoral programs are also available. Bachelor's degrees are offered in the following subjects: BUSINESS (accounting, business administration, business education, clothing and textiles, computer science, family economics management, finance, management, marketing), EDUCATION (early childhood, elementary, health/physical, industrial, secondary, special), ENGLISH (English, journalism, linguistics, speech), FINE AND PERFORMING ARTS (art, art education, art history, design, film/photography, interior design, music, music education, radio/TV, studio art, theater/dramatics), HEALTH SCIENCES (food and nutrition, speech therapy), LANGUAGES (French, German, Russian, Spanish), MATH AND SCIENCES (biology, botany, chemistry, geology, mathematics, physics, zoology), PHILOSOPHY (classics, philosophy, religion), PREPROFESSIONAL (agriculture, engineering, forestry, home economics, plant and soil science, social work), SOCIAL SCIENCES (anthropology, economics, geography, government/political science, history, psychology, sociology).

Special: Student-designed majors, a B.G.S. degree, a special major program, Black American studies, university studies, and an extensive foreign study program are offered. The School of Technical Careers offers a broad range of career-oriented programs. Students in these programs also have access to all programs and services in the baccalaureate-oriented programs.

Honors: There are 50 honor societies on campus. All schools and colleges offer honors programs.

Admissions: About 78% of those who applied were accepted for the 1981-82 freshman class. In a recent class, the ACT scores of enrolled students were as follows: 16% between 20 and 23, 15% between 24 and 26, 13% between 27 and 28, and 12% above 28. Candidates should be high school graduates; both class rank and test scores are considered.

Procedure: The ACT is required. Applications should be submitted by August 1 for fall, December 15 for spring, or June 1 for summer. Notification is on a rolling basis. There is no application fee.

Special: An early admissions plan is available. AP and CLEP credit is given.

Transfer: For fall 1981, 5470 students applied, 4021 were accepted, and 2690 enrolled. Transfers are considered for all classes. Students should have an overall C average. All students must complete, at the university, from 30 to 60 of the 120 credits required for a bachelor's degree. Application deadlines are the same as those for freshmen. There is no application fee.

Visiting: There are regularly scheduled orientations for prospective students. Guides are available for informal visits. Visitors may sit in on classes but may not stay overnight at the school. Visits are best scheduled on weekdays. The admissions office should be contacted for arrangements.

Financial Aid: About 80% of the students receive financial aid. Fourteen percent work part-time on campus. The aid program includes scholarships, awards, grants-in-aid, loans, and part-time work. The average award to freshmen from all sources is $1700. The FFS is required; applications for financial aid should be submitted by April 1 (fall), September 1 (spring), or January 1 (summer).

Foreign Students: The university offers foreign students an intensive English program, special counseling, and special organizations.

Admissions: Foreign students must achieve a TOEFL score of at least 525. No college entrance exams are required.

Procedure: Application deadlines for foreign students are July 1 (fall), December 1 (spring), and May 1 (summer). Foreign students must present proof of funds adequate to cover 1 year of study.

Admissions Contact: Jerre C. Pfaff, Associate Director of Admissions.

SOUTHERN ILLINOIS UNIVERSITY AT EDWARDSVILLE
C-4

Edwardsville, Illinois 62026   (618) 692-2720

F/T: 3076M, 3192W	Faculty: n/av; IIA, +$
P/T: 881M, 982W	Ph.D.'s: 63%
Grad: 1069M, 1005W	S/F Ratio: 14 to 1
Year: qtrs, ss	Tuition: $952 ($2338)
Appl: open	R and B: $2100
2834 applied	2445 accepted 1272 enrolled
ACT: 18	LESS COMPETITIVE

Southern Illinois University at Edwardsville offers undergraduate and graduate instruction. The library contains 750,000 volumes, 400,000 microfilm items, and 13,000 phonograph records, and subscribes to 4950 periodicals.

Environment: The 2679-acre campus is located in a rural setting along the Mississippi River Bluffs, 20 miles from St. Louis, Missouri. The 109 buildings on campus include housing facilities for 1200 single and 248 married students.

Student Life: About 90% of the students are from Illinois; 85% of the entering freshmen come from public schools. Fifteen percent of the students live on campus. Eighteen percent are minority-group members. Campus housing is coed. Students may keep cars on campus. Day-care services are available to all students.

Organizations: There are 11 fraternities and 7 sororities to which 10% of the men and 10% of the women belong. The student government and special-interest groups sponsor social and cultural events.

Sports: The university competes in 8 intercollegiate sports for men and 7 for women. It offers 15 intramural sports for men and 14 for women.

Handicapped: Approximately 95% of the campus is accessible to the physically handicapped. Facilities include wheelchair ramps, special parking, elevators, and lowered drinking fountains and telephones; special class scheduling is also available.

Services: Free tutoring, remedial instruction, psychological and career counseling, and placement services are available to all students. Health care is offered on a fee basis.

Programs of Study: The university offers the B.A., B.S., B.F.A., B.S. in Eng., B.Mus., Bachelor of Liberal Studies, and B.S. in Accountancy degrees. Master's and doctoral programs are also available. Bachelor's degrees are offered in the following subjects: AREA STUDIES (American), BUSINESS (accounting, business administration, business education, computer science, finance, management, marketing), EDUCATION (early childhood, elementary, health/physical, secondary, special), ENGLISH (English, journalism, speech), FINE AND PERFORMING ARTS (art, art education, art history, dance, music, music education, radio/TV, studio art, theater/dramatics), HEALTH SCIENCES (medical technology, nursing, speech therapy), LANGUAGES (French, German, Spanish), MATH AND SCIENCES (biology, chemistry, earth science, ecology/environmental science, mathematics, physics, statistics), PHILOSOPHY (classics, philosophy), PREPROFESSIONAL (dentistry, engineering, law, medicine, veterinary), SOCIAL SCIENCES (anthropology, economics, geography, government/political science, history, psychology, social sciences, social work, sociology).

Special: A 3-year bachelor's degree, student-designed majors, and work-study programs are available. Arrangements can be made to travel and study abroad.

Honors: There are 12 honor societies represented on campus. The Humanities Department and the Dean's College offer honors programs.

Admissions: Approximately 86% of those who applied were accepted for the 1981–82 freshman class. The ACT scores of those who enrolled were as follows: 56% below 21, 28% between 21 and 23, 8% between 24 and 25, 5% between 26 and 28, and 3% above 28. Candidates should have a high school or GED diploma and rank in the top half of their class. Recommendations from school officials also enter into the admissions decision. Students with ACT scores below 18, or who do not meet the other requirements, may enter conditionally in the summer, winter, or spring.

Procedure: The ACT is required and should be taken by winter of the senior year. Application deadlines are open. There is a rolling admissions plan. There is no application fee.

Special: Early admission is available. CLEP credit is accepted.

Transfer: For fall 1981, 1566 students applied, 1305 were accepted, and 863 enrolled. A GPA of 3.0 (on 5.0) is required. D grades transfer if they are no more than one-third of total marks. Students must earn, at the university, at least 48 of the 192 quarter hours required for a bachelor's degree. Application deadlines are open.

Visiting: Tours of the campus can be arranged through the university information center. Freshman orientations are scheduled for students before classes begin.

Financial Aid: Forty-five percent of all students receive some form of financial assistance. Twenty percent work part-time on campus. The average aid to freshmen from all sources is $800. Federal, state, and private loans and work-study contracts are available. The university is a member of CSS. The FFS should be filed with the ACT. Deadlines for financial aid applications are May 1 (fall), October 1 (winter), January 1 (spring), and April 1 (summer).

Foreign Students: About 3% of the full-time students come from foreign countries. The university offers these students special counseling and special organizations.

Admissions: Foreign students must score at least 500 on the TOEFL. No college entrance examination is required.

Procedure: Application deadlines are July 1 (fall), October 1 (winter), January 1 (spring), and April 1 (summer). Foreign students must present proof of funds adequate to cover at least 1 year of study.

Admissions Contact: Victoria Staples, Coordinator of School/University Relations.

SPERTUS COLLEGE OF JUDAICA
E-2

Chicago, Illinois 60605   (312) 922-9012

F/T: 10M, 34W	Faculty: 12; IIA, +$
P/T: 34M, 124W	Ph.D.'s: 80%
Grad: 9M, 23W	S/F Ratio: 5 to 1
Year: qtrs, ss	Tuition: $3290
Appl: open	R and B: n/app
40 applied	40 accepted 32 enrolled
SAT or ACT: not required	NONCOMPETITIVE

Spertus College of Judaica, an independent institution founded in 1925, offers undergraduate and graduate programs in Judaic studies, Jewish communal service, and Jewish education.

Environment: The 5-acre campus is located in the city of Chicago. The school provides no housing facilities.

Student Life: All undergraduates are from Illinois. About 5% are members of minority groups.

Organizations: The college sponsors no extracurricular activities.

Sports: No sports programs are available.

Handicapped: Elevators and specially equipped rest rooms are available for handicapped students.

Graduates: About 15% of the freshmen drop out during the first year, and 60% remain to graduate. Eighty percent of the graduates seek advanced degrees

Services: Placement and career counseling are available free to students. Fees are charged for tutoring and remedial instruction.

Programs of Study: The college offers the B.J.S. and the B.A.J.S. degrees. Master's degrees also are available. The college offers bachelor's degrees in: AREA STUDIES (Judaic).

Required: All students must complete a core curriculum in Judaic studies. They must maintain an average of C or better to graduate.

Special: Students may study abroad and design their own majors.

Admissions: All applicants for the 1981–82 freshman class were accepted. Applicants must be high school graduates.

Procedure: Students are admitted to all quarters; application deadlines are open. Admissions decisions are made on a rolling basis. The application fee is $20.

Special: Early decision, early admissions, and deferred admissions plans are available. CLEP and AP credit is accepted.

Transfer: Transfer students are admitted to all classes. D grades do not transfer. Students must complete, at the college, at least 45 of the 180 quarter hours required for a bachelor's degree. Application deadlines are September 15 (fall), December 31 (winter), March 20 (spring), and June 7 (summer).

Visiting: Informal visits can be arranged with the admissions office for Mondays through Thursdays. Visitors may sit in on classes, and guides are provided.

Financial Aid: About 65% of the students receive aid, and 5% work part-time on campus. Scholarships, loans, and work contracts are avail-

220 ILLINOIS

able to freshmen. Students must submit the application by September 20 (fall), January 20 (winter), March 20 (spring), or June 15 (summer).

Foreign Students: The foreign students enrolled full-time at the college make up 14% of the student body. Special counseling is provided for these students.

Admissions: No English proficiency or academic exams are required.

Procedure: Application deadlines are September 15 (fall), December 31 (winter), March 20 (spring), and June 7 (summer).

Admissions Contact: Sheldon L. Siegel, Director of Admissions.

TRINITY CHRISTIAN COLLEGE E-2
Palos Heights, Illinois 60463 (312) 597-3000

F/T: 166M, 196W	Faculty: 28; IIB, +$
P/T: 23M, 44W	Ph.D.'s: 53%
Grad: none	S/F Ratio: 13 to 1
Year: 4-1-4	Tuition: $3350
Appl: Aug. 15	R and B: $1925
226 applied	219 accepted	166 enrolled
ACT: 21		COMPETITIVE

Trinity Christian College, founded in 1959, is a privately controlled liberal arts college. The library contains 43,000 volumes and 20,000 microfilm items, and subscribes to 300 periodicals.

Environment: The campus occupies 50 acres in a suburban setting 25 miles from Chicago. Among the 13 buildings are 3 dormitories that accommodate 250 students, and a physical education building.

Student Life: About 70% of the students come from Illinois; 60% of entering freshmen are from parochial schools. At Trinity Christian College, with its Reformed Christian background, 60% of the students live on campus in single-sex dorms; there are visiting privileges. Ninety percent of the students are Protestant and 5% are Catholic. About 4% are minority-group members. Regulations prohibit the consumption of alcoholic beverages on campus. There is no curfew, and students may have cars.

Organizations: There are no sororities or fraternities on campus, but students can enjoy numerous extracurricular and cultural activities. All the college's regular committees are open to undergraduates. They can participate in administration, student government, curriculum matters, and publications.

Sports: The college fields 3 intercollegiate teams for men and 3 for women. There are 7 intramural sports for men and 6 for women.

Handicapped: About 90% of the campus is accessible to physically handicapped students. Facilities include elevators and specially equipped rest rooms.

Graduates: At the end of the freshman year, 20% of the undergraduates drop out; 60% go on to graduate. Fifteen percent pursue graduate study after graduation: 4% enter law school, 3% enter medical school, and 1% enter dental school. Twenty percent pursue careers in business and industry.

Services: Placement and career counseling are provided free of charge. Health care, tutoring, and psychological counseling are available on a fee basis.

Programs of Study: The college confers the B.A., B.S., and B.S.N. degrees. Bachelor's degrees are offered in the following subjects: BUSINESS (accounting, business administration, business education, computer science, management, marketing), EDUCATION (business, elementary, health/physical, home economics, industrial, secondary), ENGLISH (English), FINE AND PERFORMING ARTS (art, art education, music, music education), HEALTH SCIENCES (medical technology, nursing), LANGUAGES (German), MATH AND SCIENCES (biology, chemistry, mathematics), PHILOSOPHY (philosophy, theology), PREPROFESSIONAL (dentistry, home economics, law, medicine, ministry, veterinary), SOCIAL SCIENCES (history, psychology, sociology). Twenty-five percent of degrees conferred are in business, 17% in education, and 15% in health sciences.

Required: All students are required to take philosophy, theology, English, physical education, and history.

Special: The college sponsors transcultural programs in Mexico, Spain, and Holland. Work done during this period may be applied toward graduation requirements. A full semester's internship is available in all major areas of study via a metropolitan studies or major department program.

Admissions: About 97% of the freshman applicants for 1981-82 were accepted. The ACT scores of those who enrolled were as follows: 30% below 21, 20% between 21 and 23, 22% between 24 and 25, 25% between 26 and 28, and 3% above 28. Candidates need 16 Carnegie units of high school work, a minimum C average, and a class rank in the top third of their class. Other qualifications the college considers include advanced placement or honors courses, extracurricular activities, and recommendations.

Procedure: Applicants should take the ACT in May of the junior year or December of the senior year; the SAT is also acceptable. Application deadlines are August 15 (fall) and January 5 (spring); notification is on a rolling basis. There is no application fee.

Special: Early and deferred admissions plans are available. The early admissions deadline is the spring of junior year. CLEP subject exams are accepted; students may also earn credit through AP exams.

Transfer: For fall 1981, the college received 47 transfer applications; 46 students were accepted and 34 enrolled. Transfers are considered for all classes. Students must have an ACT of 19 (or SAT of 900) and a minimum C average at their former school; D grades do not transfer. Students must complete, at the college, 30 of the 125 credits required for a bachelor's degree. Application deadlines are the same as for freshman applicants.

Visiting: The admissions office can arrange for guides any weekday, or evenings and weekends by appointment. During these informal visits, prospective students may sit in on classes and stay overnight at the school.

Financial Aid: About 85% of all students receive some form of financial aid. Loans are available through the federal and state governments and local banks. Trinity awards aid on the basis of a student's financial need, usually in a "package" combining loan, grant, and/or employment. The average grant awarded to a freshman is $1727 ($4300 maximum, including federal and state programs); freshman loans average $700 ($1000 maximum); campus employment averages $600 ($1000 maximum). Thirty-five percent of the students work part-time on campus. The average freshman award from all sources of aid is $3173, with a maximum of $5800. The FAF is required. June 1 is the fall deadline; November 1, the spring.

Foreign Students: Three percent of the full-time students come from foreign countries.

Admissions: Foreign students must achieve a TOEFL score over 500. They must also take the college's own English proficiency exam, and must have an ACT score of at least 18. The SAT is also accepted.

Procedure: Application deadlines are August 15 (fall) and January 5 (spring). Foreign students must present proof of funds adequate to cover 1 year of study, and must pay a transcript evaluation fee of $50. Students must submit a physician's statement as proof of good health, and are required to carry health insurance, which is available through the college for a fee.

Admissions Contact: Keith Uander Pol, Director of Admissions.

TRINITY COLLEGE E-1
Deerfield, Illinois 60015 (312) 948-8980

F/T: 269M, 329W	Faculty: 43; IIB, av$
P/T: 29M, 31W	Ph.D.'s: 50%
Grad: none	S/F Ratio: 14 to 1
Year: sems, ss	Tuition: $3950
Appl: open	R and B: $2000
521 applied	433 accepted	315 enrolled
ACT: 20		COMPETITIVE

Trinity College, founded in 1897, is an independent Christian college that offers undergraduate programs in liberal arts and sciences, education, and religion. A new library has been built and now holds approximately 80,000 books and 25,000 microfilm items, and subscribes to 375 periodicals.

Environment: The 80-acre campus is located in a suburban area 20 miles north of Chicago. The 8 buildings include 2 single-sex dormitories that house 207 men and 252 women. Recreational facilities include a student center, a gymnasium, 6 tennis courts, 2 soccer fields, a baseball field, and an indoor ice-hockey rink.

Student Life: About 64% of the students come from Illinois. The rest come from 31 states and 5 foreign countries. Seventy-one percent live on campus. Students must attend chapel 2 days a week, and drinking, smoking, and dancing are prohibited. Three percent of the students are Catholic and 80% are Protestant. Five percent are minority-group members. Campus housing is single-sex, and there are visiting privileges. Students may keep cars on campus.

Organizations: Student activities include religious groups, music and drama, publications, clubs, and student government. There are no fraternities or sororities. The college sponsors lectures, monthly convocations, a Fine Arts Series, and other special events.

Sports: Intercollegiate teams are sponsored in 7 sports for men and 4 for women. There are 5 intramural sports for men and 5 for women.

Graduates: About 20% of the freshmen leave the college and 47% remain to graduate. Nearly half the graduates go on for further study.

Services: The college provides free health care, psychological and career counseling, tutoring, and remedial instruction. Placement services are on a fee basis.

Programs of Study: The B.A. is offered in the following subjects: AREA STUDIES (American), BUSINESS (accounting, computer science, economics/management, human resources/organizational development), EDUCATION (elementary, health/physical, secondary), ENGLISH (English), FINE AND PERFORMING ARTS (music, music education), HEALTH SCIENCES (medical technology), MATH AND SCIENCES (biology, chemistry, computer and information sciences, mathematics, natural sciences), PHILOSOPHY (philosophy), PRE-PROFESSIONAL (dentistry, law, medicine, ministry), SOCIAL SCIENCES (economics, psychology, social sciences, sociology). About 28% of degrees are conferred in letters, 27% in education, 16% in biology, and 14% in social sciences.

Required: All students must complete 12 hours of religion courses and another 36 hours in religion, humanities, natural sciences, and social sciences. To graduate, students must earn a GPA of 2.0 or better, complete 4 units of off-campus Christian service, demonstrate competence in English, and, in some majors, pass a comprehensive exam.

Special: Students may pursue a general studies degree or a divisional major in social science, humanities, or natural science. The college provides a 2-year prenursing program and a 3-1 medical technology program. Other programs include summer study tours, an Oregon Extension in which students and faculty members live in community on the site of an old Cascade Mountains logging camp, an American Studies program that offers study in Washington and internships, a 9-week summer program in San Francisco, opportunities to study in Europe and Israel, and evangelical studies.

Admissions: About 83% of those who applied were accepted for the 1981-82 freshman class. Applicants must be graduates of accredited high schools with a C+ average in at least 15 units of work and must be within the top 50% of their high school class. Recommendations, advanced placement or honor courses, impressions made during the interview, and evidence of special talents are also important.

Procedure: Students should take the ACT, but the SAT also is accepted. New students are admitted each semester. Application deadlines are open, but prospective freshmen are urged to apply after completing the junior year of high school. There is a $15 application fee.

Special: AP credit is granted.

Transfer: For fall 1981, 191 students applied, 161 were accepted, and 102 enrolled. Transfer credit is given for courses in which a C or better is earned. GPA scores of at least 2.0 are recommended. Transcripts from all schools and 2 recommendations are required. Students must complete 30 of the last 45 credits in residence to graduate, and must complete 126 credits in all for a bachelor's degree.

Visiting: Prospective students may arrange to visit the campus by contacting the admissions office. Overnight Friday-Saturday visits are recommended. Campus tours with student guides can be arranged. Visitors may sit in on classes, attend chapel, talk with admissions officers, and tour the campus.

Financial Aid: Over 80% of the students receive aid. Programs include college, state, and federal scholarships, grants, loans, and part-time jobs. Twenty-seven percent of students work part-time on campus. Scholarships of up to $700 per year are offered for academic achievement or talent in fields such as music, athletics, and journalism. Tuition may be paid in installments. The FAF should be filed as early as possible. May 15 is the financial aid application deadline for fall entry.

Foreign Students: Two percent of full-time students are from foreign countries. The college offers these students an intensive English course and special counseling.

Admissions: Foreign students must score at least 500 on the TOEFL to enter.

Procedure: Application deadlines are the same as for all students. Foreign students must present proof of funds adequate for 1 academic year. They must also carry health insurance, which is available through the college.

Admissions Contact: Edward Bozaan, Admissions Counselor.

ILLINOIS 221

THE UNIVERSITY OF CHICAGO E-2
Chicago, Illinois 60637 (312) 962-8662

F/T: 1870M, 986W
P/T: 100M&W
Grad: 2938M, 1453W
Year: qtrs, ss
Appl: Jan. 15
4216 applied
SAT: 620V 645M

Faculty: 1040; I, ++$
Ph.D.'s: 99%
S/F Ratio: 6 to 1
Tuition: $6015
R and B: $3180
1939 accepted 748 enrolled
ACT: 28 HIGHLY COMPETITIVE+

The University of Chicago was founded in 1890 as a private, independent institution, and was the first major university to accept women as students on an equal basis with men. The undergraduate college offers instruction in 5 divisions: Humanities, Physical Sciences, Biological Sciences, Social Sciences, and the New Collegiate Division, which is devoted to independent work in interdisciplinary studies. Undergraduates may apply at the end of their junior year to the university's Business School, Law School, Library School, or School of Social Service Administration. The Joseph Regenstein Library contains over 3.5 million volumes and subscribes to 42,000 periodicals.

Environment: The college is located on the main campus of the university, on a 165-acre site on Lake Michigan, 7 miles from downtown Chicago. The campus has over 100 buildings, including several historic landmarks. The dormitories house about 1800 students, and students are assured housing for their undergraduate years. Fraternity houses, on-campus apartments, and married student housing are also available.

Student Life: Thirty percent of the students are from Illinois and 35% are from the East Coast. About 70% come from public schools. Sixty-seven percent live on campus. Sixteen percent of the students are minority-group members. Campus housing is both coed and single-sex; there are visiting privileges. Students are permitted to keep cars on campus.

Organizations: Five fraternities have chapters on campus, some of which are coed, and 6% of the students are members. More than 100 recognized student organizations exist, including orchestral, choral, dramatic, religious, and literary groups.

Sports: The university sponsors intercollegiate teams in 11 sports for men and 9 for women. There are 18 intramural sports for men and 16 for women.

Handicapped: There are some special facilities for handicapped students.

Graduates: Nine percent of freshmen drop out by the end of the first year, and 70% remain to graduate. Seventy percent of the graduates pursue advanced degrees; 12% enter medical school and 8% enter law school.

Services: The following services are free to students: health care, psychological and career counseling, placement, and tutoring.

Programs of Study: The college confers the B.A. and B.S. degrees. Master's and doctoral degrees also are awarded. Bachelor's degrees are offered in the following subjects: AREA STUDIES (American, Asian—Far Eastern, Asian—South Asian, Latin American, Russian), ENGLISH (creative writing, dramatic literature, English, literature), FINE AND PERFORMING ARTS (art, art and design, art history, music), LANGUAGES (Chinese, French, German, Greek/Latin, Italian, Japanese, linguistics, Near Eastern languages, Portuguese, Russian, South Asian languages, Spanish), MATH AND SCIENCES (astronomy, biochemistry, biology, botany, chemistry, earth science, geology, mathematics, natural sciences, physical sciences, physics, statistics, zoology), PHILOSOPHY (classics, early Christian literature, humanities, ideas and methods, philosophy, religion, religion and literature), SOCIAL SCIENCES (anthropology, economics, education, geography, government/political science, history, international relations, political science, psychology, public affairs, social sciences, sociology).

Required: All students take a year-long core course in the biological, physical, and social sciences, and humanities. Further general-education courses are required, depending on the major.

Special: Students may design their own majors. A general-studies-in-humanities major is offered. Study abroad, independent study, and research may be arranged. Professional options are available leading to an M.B.A., J.D., M.L.S., or M.A. in Social Work degree. Students in the New Collegiate Division perform independent study in an established or self-designed program under the supervision of faculty members. These students write extensive research papers in problem areas common to several fields of knowledge.

222 ILLINOIS

Honors: All departments allow students to complete honors projects. Phi Beta Kappa and Sigma Xi have chapters on campus.

Admissions: Forty-six percent of those who applied were accepted for the 1981-82 freshman class. The SAT scores of those who enrolled were as follows: Verbal—3% below 500, 36% between 500 and 599, 40% between 600 and 700, and 21% above 700; Math—2% below 500, 31% between 500 and 599, 41% between 600 and 700, and 25% above 700. Most applicants have at least a B average, rank in the upper 20% of their graduating class, and have completed 15 Carnegie units. The school also considers advanced placement or honors courses, recommendations, leadership record, extracurricular activities, and evidence of special talents.

Procedure: Either the SAT or ACT is required and should be taken by January of the senior year. The application, a $20 fee, test scores, and high school record must be submitted by January 15 for fall admission, or two months before the beginning of the winter, spring, or summer quarter. Notification is in early April.

Special: Early decision and early admissions plans are available. AP credit is given in some areas.

Transfer: For fall 1981, 222 transfer students applied, 160 were accepted, and 104 enrolled. Transfers are accepted for the sophomore and junior years. High school and college recommendations are required; a GPA of 3.0 or better and an interview are recommended. D grades do not transfer. Students must study at the college for at least 2 years, completing 18 of the 42 quarter courses necessary for a bachelor's degree. The application deadline for fall is July 1; applications for other quarters should be submitted 2 months before the beginning of the term.

Visiting: Guides are available for informal visits during the academic year. Visitors may sit in on classes and stay overnight at the school. The office of college admissions should be contacted for arrangements.

Financial Aid: About 90% of the students receive aid. The college provides scholarships, loans, and some campus jobs; 60% of the students work part-time on campus. The average award to freshmen from all sources was $5350 in 1981-82. Aid is awarded on the basis of need; a few honors scholarships are awarded for academic and extracurricular achievement. Application must be made by January 15 or 2 months before the beginning of the term. The FAF must also be filed with CSS.

Foreign Students: Thirty-five full-time students are from foreign countries. Special counseling and special organizations are available.

Admissions: Students must achieve a minimum score of 600 on the TOEFL. The SAT or the ACT is also required.

Procedure: The application deadline for fall is January 15. Proof of adequate funds for 1 year is necessary. Health insurance is also required.

Admissions Contact: Dan Hall, Dean of College Admissions and Aid.

UNIVERSITY OF ILLINOIS

The University of Illinois, a comprehensive state university, has grown from a land-grant college founded more than 100 years ago into one of the nation's leading centers for graduate education and research.

The university has 2 campuses—1 in Urbana-Champaign and 1 in Chicago—and extension centers throughout the state. More than 55,000 students are enrolled on the campuses. Ninety-two percent of undergraduates come from Illinois; an equivalent percentage successfully complete their freshman year. The university employs about 20,200 faculty and nonacademic staff members.

The university library—the third largest among American universities and fourth among world universities—divides more than 5.8 million volumes among the 3 campuses. The university offers the most complete instruction, therapy, and athletic program for physically handicapped students of any such institution in the world.

The Urbana-Champaign campus, which opened in 1868, is the foundation of the university. The Chicago campus was formed in 1982 as a result of the merger of the Chicago Circle and the Medical Center campuses.

Descriptions of the Urbana-Champaign and Chicago campuses follow.

UNIVERSITY OF ILLINOIS AT CHICAGO
(Formerly University of Illinois/Chicago Circle)

Chicago, Illinois 60680   (312) 996-0998

E-2

F/T: 7798M, 5926W   Faculty: 1056; I, +$
P/T: 1751M, 1518W   Ph.D.'s: 72%
Grad: 1834M, 1773W   S/F Ratio: 16 to 1
Year: qtrs, ss   Tuition: $1080 ($2574)
Appl: July 30   R and B: n/app
6262 applied   4230 accepted   2988 enrolled
SAT or ACT: required   COMPETITIVE

The Chicago campus of the University of Illinois opened in 1965 as the successor to the Chicago undergraduate division at Navy Pier. The library holds 1,120,335 volumes and 680,725 microfilm items, and subscribes to 8187 periodicals.

Environment: The 118-acre urban campus is located southwest of Chicago's Loop. It consists of low-rise classroom and laboratory buildings situated around a Great Court, and high-rise buildings containing offices and seminar rooms just off the center of campus. There are no student housing facilities. A new sports pavilion was to have been completed in 1982.

Student Life: Eighty percent of the undergraduates are Cook County residents. About 36% of the students are minority-group members. Day-care services are available for a fee.

Organizations: The university sponsors approximately 150 student organizations, including 11 fraternities and 6 sororities. The resources of the Chicago area complement campus offerings; several museums, the Art Institute, and cultural and recreational areas are nearby.

Sports: The university fields intercollegiate teams in 12 sports for men and 10 for women. Fifteen intramural sports are offered for men and 14 for women.

Handicapped: Most areas of the campus are accessible to handicapped students. Facilities include wheelchair ramps, special parking, elevators, specially equipped rest rooms, and lowered drinking fountains and telephones. Special class scheduling is also available. There are two specialized counselors for handicapped students.

Graduates: Thirty percent of the graduates pursue advanced degrees. About 80% enter business and industry.

Services: Students may obtain free health care, career and psychological counseling, tutoring, and remedial instruction. Free placement services are offered to alumni as well as students.

Programs of Study: The campus confers the B.A., B.S., B.Arch., and B.S.W. degrees. Master's and doctoral degrees also are awarded. Bachelor's degrees are offered in the following subjects: AREA STUDIES (Black/Afro-American, Latin American), BUSINESS (accounting, finance, management, marketing, quantitative methods), EDUCATION (elementary, health/physical, secondary), ENGLISH (English, literature), FINE AND PERFORMING ARTS (art education, art history, film/photography, industrial design, music, music education, radio/TV, studio art, theater/dramatics), LANGUAGES (French, French commercial studies, German, Greek/Latin, Italian, Judaic studies, Polish, Russian, Spanish), MATH AND SCIENCES (bioengineering, biology, botany, chemistry, earth science, geology, mathematics and computer science, physics, statistics), PHILOSOPHY (philosophy), PREPROFESSIONAL (architecture, dentistry, engineering, law, medicine, pharmacy, social work, veterinary), SOCIAL SCIENCES (anthropology, criminalistics, criminal justice, economics, geography, government/political science, history, psychology, sociology). Twenty-eight percent of degrees are awarded in business, 16% in social sciences, and 6% in math and sciences.

Special: Special programs are offered to meet the needs of a student body with diverse social, economic, cultural, and educational backgrounds. Academically talented students may apply to the university's honors program. The Educational Assistance Program offers support services for disadvantaged students. Programs for study abroad are offered, and students may design their own majors.

Honors: Six honor societies, including Phi Beta Kappa, have chapters on campus. Honors programs are available.

Admissions: Sixty-eight percent of those who applied were accepted for the 1981-82 freshman class. Candidates must be graduates of an accredited high school or the equivalent, be at least 16 years old, present 16 units of high school work, and rank in the upper half of their high school class. The university is making special efforts to recruit minority students, and applicants to special programs may not be required to meet established test scores. Out-of-state applicants are admitted on the same basis as residents if space is available.

Procedure: The university prefers that applicants take the ACT, but the SAT also is acceptable. Tests should be taken by the summer following the junior year. The application deadline for fall is July 30. Tentative deadlines for the remaining quarters are November 25 (winter), February 26 (spring), and May 28 (summer). The application fee is $20. The university follows a rolling admissions policy.

Special: CLEP and AP credit is available.

Transfer: For fall 1981, 5906 transfer students applied, 3847 were accepted, and 3259 enrolled. Admissions requirements vary according to the student's major. D grades transfer. All students must complete, at the university, at least 90 of the 180 quarter hours required for a bachelor's degree. Applications are accepted as long as space is available.

Visiting: Visits are best scheduled between 9 A.M. and 4:30 P.M. on Mondays, Tuesdays, and Thursdays. Visitors may sit in on classes. The college relations office should be contacted for information.

Financial Aid: About 57% of the students receive aid; 12% work part-time on campus. Scholarships, grants, and loans are available. The university requires the FFS as well as its own aid application. Application deadlines are October 1 (fall), December 1 (winter), and February 1 (spring and summer). May 1 is the deadline for priority consideration. Applicants are urged to apply as early as possible.

Foreign Students: More than 1000 students are from foreign countries, making up 6% of enrollment. The university offers these students an intensive English program, special counseling, and special organizations.

Admissions: Students must score at least 480 on the TOEFL or 80 on the University of Michigan Language Test. No college entrance exams are required.

Procedure: Application deadlines are the same as those for other freshmen. Students must present proof of good health and carry health insurance, which is available through the university.

Admissions Contact: Dennis Morgan, Pre-admissions Counselor.

UNIVERSITY OF ILLINOIS AT URBANA-CHAMPAIGN
E-3

Urbana, Illinois 61801 (217) 333-0302

F/T: 14,495M, 10,914W
P/T: 557M, 631W
Grad: 5373M, 3182W
Year: sems, ss

Faculty: 2796; I, ++$
Ph.D.'s: 83%
S/F Ratio: 13 to 1
Tuition: $1075–1125 ($2571–2721)
R and B: $2426

Appl: see profile
13,480 applied 9541 accepted 5786 enrolled
ACT: 26 **HIGHLY COMPETITIVE**

The Urbana-Champaign campus is the oldest and largest of the 3 University of Illinois campuses. The library contains 5.9 million volumes and 1.3 million microfilm items, and subscribes to 23,990 periodicals.

Environment: The 703-acre urban campus is located in the twin cities of Urbana-Champaign (population 100,000), 130 miles south of Chicago. The university also owns 1900 acres of agricultural experiment fields nearby and another 3000 acres of farmland elsewhere in the state. The campus has 179 major buildings, including the Speech and Hearing Science building, considered one of the finest facilities of its kind in the world, and Assembly Hall, one of the nation's largest arenas. Residence halls house 10,500 single and 300 married undergraduates.

Student Life: Ninety-seven percent of the undergraduates are Illinois residents. Single undergraduates who are under 21 and have completed fewer than 60 semester hours must live in university-approved housing. About 71% of the students live off campus. Seven percent of the students are minority-group members. Campus housing is both coed and single-sex; there are visiting privileges in the single-sex housing. Students may keep cars on campus.

Organizations: About 12% of the men belong to one of the 48 fraternities on campus; 9% of the women belong to one of 24 sororities. Students may choose from about 300 professional, social, religious, student government, scholastic, and special interest organizations. Students can use Robert Allerton Park, the university's 1768-acre conference and nature center at nearby Monticello.

Sports: The university fields 12 intercollegiate teams for men and 9 for women. There are 26 intramural sports for men and 25 for women.

Handicapped: The entire campus is accessible to handicapped students. Facilities include wheelchair ramps, special parking, elevators, specially equipped rest rooms, lowered drinking fountains and telephones, an elevator-equipped campus bus system, and sports programs for men and women. Special class scheduling is also available. For students with impaired hearing or vision, the campus has a braille library and a rehabilitation center. A number of professionals on campus are available to handicapped students.

Graduates: Four percent of the freshmen drop out by the end of the first year; 62% remain to graduate.

Services: Students may obtain free career and psychological counseling, placement, and remedial instruction. Tutoring sometimes involves a fee, and health care is provided for a fee.

Programs of Study: The school confers the B.A., B.S., B.F.A., B.Mus., B.Land.Arch., B.S.W., and B.Urban Planning. Master's and doctoral programs also are offered. Bachelor's degrees are offered in the following subjects: AREA STUDIES (American, Asian, Russian, urban), BUSINESS (accounting, business administration, business education, computer science, economics, finance, marketing), EDUCATION (business, early childhood, elementary, health/physical, industrial, secondary, special), ENGLISH (English, journalism, literature, rhetoric and composition, speech), FINE AND PERFORMING ARTS (art, art education, art history, dance, music, music education, radio/TV, theater/dramatics), HEALTH SCIENCES (nursing, speech therapy), LANGUAGES (French, German, Greek/Latin, Italian, Portuguese, Russian, Spanish), MATH AND SCIENCES (astronomy, biochemistry, biology, botany, chemistry, ecology/environmental science, entomology, geology, mathematics, microbiology, physical sciences, physics, statistics, zoology), PHILOSOPHY (classics, humanities, philosophy, religion), PREPROFESSIONAL (agriculture, architecture, dentistry, engineering, forestry, home economics, landscape architecture, law, library science, medicine, pharmacy, social work, veterinary), SOCIAL SCIENCES (anthropology, economics, geography, government/political science, history, medieval civilization, psychology, sociology). There is also a program in advertising. Twenty-three percent of degrees are awarded in engineering, 18% in business, and 11% in math and sciences.

Required: All students must meet the rhetoric requirement for graduation.

Special: Special programs include foreign study, a combined 5-year engineering/liberal arts program, a 5-year agricultural science/agricultural engineering program, cooperative work-study programs in industrial education and engineering, student-designed majors, and independent study.

Honors: There are 41 honor societies on campus, including a chapter of Phi Beta Kappa. All colleges and departments offer honors programs.

Admissions: Seventy-one percent of those who applied were accepted for the 1981–82 freshman class. The ACT scores of those who enrolled were as follows: 4% below 18, 22% between 18 and 23, 61% between 24 and 29, and 13% above 29. Candidates must be at least 16 years old, be graduates of an accredited high school, and have completed at least 15 Carnegie units. Admission is determined on the basis of ACT or SAT scores and class rank.

Procedure: Candidates should take the ACT or SAT in the spring of their junior year and apply between September 25 and November 15. Applications are accepted up to 2 weeks before fall registration. Freshmen may be admitted to either semester or to the summer session. There is a $20 application fee.

Special: Early decision, early admissions, and deferred admissions plans are available. AP and CLEP credit is acceptable.

Transfer: For fall 1981, the university received 3683 transfer applications and accepted 1811; 1473 students enrolled. Applicants must have a GPA of 3.25 or higher. Preference is given to those with an associate degree or at least 60 hours of college work. D grades transfer. Students must complete, at the university, the last 30 of the 120–130 credits required for a bachelor's degree. Students should apply by March 15 (fall), November 1 (spring), or March 15 (summer), although applications are considered if submitted no later than 2 weeks before registration.

Visiting: There are regularly scheduled orientations for prospective students. Guides are available for informal visits. Visitors may sit in on classes. The office of admissions and records should be contacted for arrangements.

Financial Aid: About 50% of the students receive financial aid. About 30% work part-time on campus. In a recent year about 13,000 grants, scholarships, and tuition waivers valued at almost $12 million were awarded. Cash awards and grants ranged from $100 to $1800; the average was $1000. Loans are available from the federal govern-

224 ILLINOIS

ment or the university. Tuition, fees, and residence hall charges may be paid in installments. The university is a member of CSS; the FAF or FFS is required in addition to the university aid application. Illinois residents must apply for an ISSC. Application deadlines are March 14 (fall or spring entry) and April 1 (summer entry).

Foreign Students: Six percent of the full-time students come from foreign countries. An intensive English course, an intensive English program, special counseling, and special organizations are available for these students.

Admissions: Foreign students must achieve a TOEFL score of at least 520 or a University of Michigan Language Test score of at least 84. No college entrance exams are required.

Procedure: Foreign students should apply between September 25 and November 15 for fall, spring, or summer entry. They must take a tuberculin test and must present proof of funds adequate to cover the entire period of study. They must also carry health insurance, which is available through the university for a fee.

Admissions Contact: Gary R. Engelgau, Director of Admissions and Records.

VANDERCOOK COLLEGE OF MUSIC   E-2
Chicago, Illinois 60616   (312) 225-6288

F/T, P/T:	Faculty: n/av
72M, 26W	Ph.D.'s: 20%
Grad: 14 M&W	S/F Ratio: 11 to 1
Year: sems, ss	Tuition: $3069
Appl: Aug. 1	R and B: $2376
60 applied	53 accepted 36 enrolled
SAT or ACT: required	SPECIAL

VanderCook College of Music, founded in 1909, is an independent institution that prepares undergraduates to teach music in elementary and secondary schools. The library contains 18,000 books and 4000 reels of microfilm, and subscribes to 85 periodicals.

Environment: The 2-acre campus has 3 buildings. Students may live in dormitories at the Illinois Institute of Technology nearby.

Student Life: About 75% of the students come from Illinois, and more than half live in dormitories. Drinking is prohibited on campus.

Organizations: No extracurricular activities are scheduled on campus, but students attend cultural events at the Illinois Institute of Technology and use that school's athletic facilities. Students also take advantage of cultural facilities in the city of Chicago. There is a student government.

Handicapped: Most of the campus is accessible to physically handicapped students.

Graduates: About 18% of the freshmen drop out, and 85% remain to graduate. Five percent of the graduates go on to further study.

Services: The college provides free health care, psychological and career counseling, tutoring, remedial instruction, and placement services.

Programs of Study: The college awards the B.Mus.Ed. degree in music education. Master's degrees also are available.

Required: Students must complete a core curriculum and earn a GPA of 2.0 or better to graduate.

Special: Degrees may be earned in less than 4 years.

Honors: Two honor band fraternities are represented on campus.

Admissions: About 88% of the applicants for the 1981–82 freshman class were accepted. An audition is required. An applicant must present a high school diploma or GED and recommendations from high school officials.

Procedure: The SAT or the ACT should be taken by July. Applications for fall semester are due August 1; notification is made on a rolling basis. New students also are admitted at midyear. There is a $25 application fee.

Special: AP credit is accepted.

Transfer: Applicants must present an average of 2.0 or better and meet freshman admissions standards. Students must complete 2 years in residence to graduate.

Financial Aid: Federal grants such as BEOG and Illinois State Scholarship Commission funds are available. About half the students receive such aid. In addition, the college awards tuition waivers to outstanding freshmen.

Admissions Contact: Anthony G. Gunia, Director of Admissions.

WESTERN ILLINOIS UNIVERSITY   C-3
Macomb, Illinois 61455   (309) 298-1891

F/T: 5395M, 4925W	Faculty: 620; IIA, av$
P/T: 522M, 457W	Ph.D.'s: 65%
Grad: 835M, 1163W	S/F Ratio: 17 to 1
Year: sems, ss	Tuition: $967 ($2347)
Appl: see profile	R and B: $1798
7204 applied 5993 accepted	2521 enrolled
ACT: 19	LESS COMPETITIVE

Western Illinois University, founded in 1899, is a state institution composed of 6 undergraduate colleges and a school of graduate studies. The library contains over 500,000 volumes and 150,000 microfilm items and subscribes to 14,000 periodicals.

Environment: The 1056-acre campus, in a suburban setting 80 miles from Peoria, includes a field campus, a life science station on the Mississippi River, and a 9-hole golf course. Notable among its more than 50 buildings is the 2000-seat library, one of the largest libraries in the U.S. for nondoctoral degree-granting universities. Thirteen residence halls and 7 married-student units house approximately 6750 students.

Student Life: Over 96% of the students are from Illinois. Fifty-five percent live on campus, fewer than 5% in fraternity or sorority houses. About 10% of the students are minority-group members. University housing is both single-sex and coed; there are visiting privileges in single-sex housing. Students may keep cars on campus.

Organizations: Seventeen percent of the men and 11% of the women belong to one of the 19 fraternities and 10 sororities. Students may choose from a wide variety of on-campus extracurricular activities, cultural events, and social gatherings, as well as from numerous outdoor recreational opportunities at Argyle State Park, 8 miles away.

Sports: The university competes on an intercollegiate level in 11 sports for men and 11 for women. There are 20 intramural sports for men and 20 for women.

Handicapped: About 90% of the campus is accessible to wheelchair students. Facilities include wheelchair ramps, special parking, elevators, specially equipped rest rooms, and lowered drinking fountains. Special class scheduling is also available.

Graduates: The freshman dropout rate is 15%; 65% remain to graduate. Fifteen percent of graduates go on to advanced study; about 1% enter medical school, 1% dental school, and 1% law school. About 56% pursue careers in business and industry.

Services: Students receive the following services free of charge: health care, psychological counseling, career counseling, placement services, and tutoring. Tutoring is also offered on a fee basis.

Programs of Study: The university confers the B.A., B.S., B.S.Ed., and B.Bus. degrees. Master's programs are also offered. Bachelor's degrees are offered in the following subjects: BUSINESS (accounting, administrative office management, business administration, business education, computer science, finance, management, marketing, operations management, personnel administration and industrial relations, transportation and physical distribution), EDUCATION (bilingual/bicultural, corrections, early childhood, elementary, health/physical, industrial, learning resources, secondary, special), ENGLISH (English, mass communications, speech), FINE AND PERFORMING ARTS (art education, art history, music, music education, studio art, theater/dramatics), HEALTH SCIENCES (health science, medical technology, speech therapy), LANGUAGES (French, German, Spanish), MATH AND SCIENCES (biology, chemistry, earth science, geology, industrial education and technology, mathematics, physics), PHILOSOPHY (philosophy), PREPROFESSIONAL (agriculture, architecture, dentistry, engineering, forestry, home economics, law, medicine, nursing, optometry, pharmacy, veterinary), SOCIAL SCIENCES (anthropology, economics, geography, government/political science, history, law enforcement administration, psychology, recreation and parks administration, sociology). Twenty-eight percent of degrees conferred are in business, 16% in education, and 7% in math and sciences.

Required: All undergraduates are expected to take 44 semester hours in the fields of basic skills, well being, natural science and mathematics, historical and social foundations, and humanities.

Special: The university offers student-designed majors, independent study, and study abroad.

Honors: All departments within the College of Arts and Sciences provide honors work. There are 30 national honor societies on campus.

Admissions: Approximately 83% of those who applied were accepted for the 1981–82 freshman class. The ACT scores of those who enrolled were as follows: 63% below 21, 20% between 21 and 23, 9% between 24 and 25, 7% between 26 and 28, and 1% above 28. Applicants should rank in the top two-thirds of their class or achieve a minimum ACT score of 19 or SAT combined score of 850 for an immediate admissions decision.

Procedure: The SAT or ACT is required and should be taken no later than April of the senior year. Junior year results are acceptable. Freshmen are admitted to all terms. Application deadlines are 2 weeks prior to the beginning of each term. A rolling admissions policy is followed; there is no application fee.

Special: CLEP and AP credit is accepted. Academic Services is a multicultural recruitment and supportive admissions program for selected students who do not meet freshman or transfer requirements.

Transfer: For fall 1981, 2122 transfer students applied for admission, 1146 were accepted, and 1027 enrolled. Transfer students must have a 2.0 GPA, have an ACT score of 19 if transferring less than 24 semester credits or 36 quarter credits, and be in good standing at their last school. Grades of D and better transfer. A high school transcript or GED certificate is required if transfer work is less than 24 semester or 36 quarter hours. Transfer students must complete, at the university, 30 of the 120 semester hours required for a bachelor's degree. Application deadlines are the same as for freshman admissions.

Visiting: Informal visits to the college can be made during all times that school is in session. Guided tours and overnight accommodations can be arranged through the admissions office. The admissions office is open for interviews Monday through Friday. There are regularly scheduled orientations for prospective students.

Financial Aid: About 93% of all students receive aid in the form of scholarships, federal, state, and university loans. Forty percent work part-time on campus. The average aid awarded from all sources is $1829. The FFS is required. There are no deadlines for financial aid applications.

Foreign Students: Four percent of the full-time students come from foreign countries. The university offers these students an intensive English course, an intensive English program, special counseling, and special organizations.

Admissions: Foreign students must take the TOEFL, the University of Michigan Language Test, or the university's own language test. They must score at least 550 on the TOEFL. No college entrance examination is required.

Procedure: Application deadlines are 1 month before the beginning of each semester or summer session. Foreign students must present a completed university health form. They must also present proof of funds adequate to cover 1 year of study. They must carry health insurance, which is available through the university for a fee.

Admissions Contact: Frederick E. Fess, Dean of Admissions and Records.

WHEATON COLLEGE E-2
Wheaton, Illinois 60187 (312) 260-5011

F/T: 990M, 1033W	Faculty: 140; IIB, ++$
P/T: 9M, 4W	Ph.D.'s: 70%
Grad: 223M, 140W	S/F Ratio: 14 to 1
Year: sems, ss	Tuition: $4234
Appl: Feb. 15	R and B: $2358
1165 applied	749 accepted 528 enrolled
SAT: 544V 594M	ACT: 26 VERY COMPETITIVE+

Wheaton College, established in 1860, is a private liberal arts college dedicated to providing students with a Christian education. It is supported by a number of evangelical denominations. The library houses 250,000 books and 7500 microtexts, and subscribes to 1030 periodicals.

Environment: The 70-acre campus is located in a suburban area 25 miles from Chicago. The 25 buildings on campus include 7 dormitories that accommodate about 1600 men and women. The college also sponsors off-campus apartments and married-student housing.

Student Life: About 30% of the students are from Illinois. Seventy-five percent live on campus; freshmen are required to do so. Ninety-nine percent of the students are Protestant, and 1% are Catholic; daily attendance at chapel services is required. Six percent of the students are minority-group members. College housing is single-sex, and there are visiting privileges. Students may keep cars on campus.

Organizations: There are no fraternities or sororities. Student activities include music groups, professional and service organizations, religious organizations, a debate group, a drama group, a radio station, films, and artist and lecture series. There is an active student government.

Sports: The college fields intercollegiate teams in 11 sports for men and 8 for women. There are 3 intramural sports for men and 3 for women.

Handicapped: About 75% of the campus is accessible to wheelchair-bound students. Wheelchair ramps, special parking, and lowered drinking fountains and telephones are available.

Graduates: The freshman dropout rate is about 4%, and 68% remain to graduate.

Services: The following services are provided free of charge: health care, psychological counseling, and career counseling.

Programs of Study: The college confers the B.A., B.M., B.Mus. Ed., or B.S. degrees. Master's degrees also are awarded. Bachelor's degrees are offered in the following subjects: EDUCATION (Christian, elementary, secondary), ENGLISH (literature, speech), FINE AND PERFORMING ARTS (art, music, music education, music performance), LANGUAGES (French, German, Spanish), MATH AND SCIENCES (biology, chemistry, mathematics, natural resources, physics), PHILOSOPHY (Biblical studies, philosophy), PREPROFESSIONAL (engineering, medicine), SOCIAL SCIENCES (economics, government/political science, history, psychology, social sciences, sociology).

Required: All students must take courses in Bible, fine arts, foreign language, a laboratory science, literature, philosophy, physical education, social science, speech, and writing.

Special: The college offers an independent study program for upperclassmen. Part of the senior year may be spent in off-campus professional in-service study-training. Combined degree programs are offered in liberal arts/education and liberal arts/engineering.

Honors: Honors courses are offered in various departments, and include classes in ancient language studies, physics, philosophy, and speech. Membership in the Scholastic Honor Society is based on scholarship. Eight honor societies have chapters on campus.

Admissions: Sixty-four percent of applicants for admission to the college in 1981–82 were accepted. Of those who enrolled, the SAT scores were as follows: Verbal—20% scored below 500, 38% between 500 and 599, 55% between 600 and 700, and 1% above 700; Math—11% scored below 500, 25% between 500 and 599, 66% between 600 and 700, and 9% above 700. Of those who took the ACT, 4% scored below 21, 16% between 21 and 23, 26% between 24 and 25, 42% between 26 and 28, and 12% above 28. Applicants must rank in the upper half of their graduating class and have completed 16 Carnegie units of high school work with an average of 2.0 or better. The college also considers recommendations by school officials, personality, leadership record, impressions made during an interview, extracurricular activities, advanced placement or honors courses, and evidence of special talents.

Procedure: An interview is required. The SAT is also required, and should be taken in November or December of the senior year. The ACT may be submitted instead. ATs in English, math, and language are strongly recommended. The application, a $20 fee, test scores, and the high school record should be submitted by February 15 (fall or summer) or November 1 (spring). The college has a rolling admissions plan; notification is made as soon as all credentials are received.

Special: Early decision and early admissions plans are offered. Credit is available through AP and CLEP exams.

Transfer: For fall 1981, 351 students applied and 184 were accepted. Applicants must have a 2.0 GPA and either a combined SAT score of 1000 or an ACT composite of 21. D grades do not transfer. The deadlines are April 1 (fall and summer) and November 1 (spring). A bachelor's degree requires 124 credits, 60 of which must be taken at Wheaton.

Visiting: The college provides regularly scheduled orientations for prospective students. The admissions center will make arrangements for visits.

Financial Aid: About 40% of the students receive aid. The college provides scholarships and loans. Loans from federal and private sources are also granted. The average aid award to a freshman in 1981–82 was $1000. Aid is awarded on the basis of financial need. The college is a member of CSS, and the FAF is required. Applications must be filed by February 1.

Foreign Students: The 128 full-time students from foreign countries make up 6% of enrollment. Special organizations are available to these students.

Admissions: Foreign students must score at least 550 on the TOEFL. They also must take the college entrance test of their country of origin, and the SAT or ACT are recommended.

Procedure: Application deadlines are February 15 (fall and summer) and November 1 (spring). Foreign students must present proof of adequate funds for 1 year. They also must submit a completed health questionnaire.

Admissions Contact: Stuart O. Michael, Director of Admissions.

INDIANA

ANDERSON COLLEGE C-3
Anderson, Indiana 46011 (317) 649-9071

F/T: 767M, 930W	Faculty: n/av; IIA, —$
P/T: 50M, 111W	Ph.D.'s: 58%
Grad: 144M, 36W	S/F Ratio: 17 to 1
Year: sems, ss	Tuition: $3840
Appl: Aug. 15	R and B: $1540
1075 applied	946 accepted	620 enrolled
SAT: 450V 450M	ACT: 21	COMPETITIVE

Anderson College, founded in 1917, is a liberal arts college affiliated with the Church of God. It provides both graduate and undergraduate instruction. The library's holdings include 145,000 volumes, 10,200 microfilm items, and 6700 units of audio visual equipment; it subscribes to 942 periodicals.

Environment: The 77-acre campus is near the edge of Anderson, a city of 75,000, 40 miles from Indianapolis. There are 22 main buildings on campus, including 7 academic buildings, a fine arts center, a gymnasium, an auditorium, a natatorium, and a church. There are 8 residence halls with single, double, and triple rooms and suites, as well as 97 apartments for married students and faculty members. A cafeteria, student lounge, and lockers are available for day students.

Student Life: About 40% of the students are from Indiana and 55% are from other states. About 96% of entering freshmen come from public schools. Seventy-five percent reside on campus, and about 65% belong to the Church of God. Students must attend chapel convocations twice a week as part of their regular class schedules. Students may keep cars on campus. Smoking and drinking are prohibited.

Organizations: There are no fraternities or sororities. Organizations and activities include religious groups, musical groups, theater, debate groups, social clubs, special-interest clubs, student government, and publications. The college sponsors art shows, concerts, films, lectures, operas, plays, professional demonstrations, and recitals.

Sports: The college fields 13 intercollegiate teams. There are 12 intramural sports for men and 12 for women.

Handicapped: About 75% of the campus is accessible to physically handicapped students, including 1 of the 8 residence halls. Special facilities include wheelchair ramps, parking areas, elevators, and lowered drinking fountains. Special class scheduling is possible. There is a special counselor to assist handicapped students.

Graduates: The freshman dropout rate is 17%, and 53% remain to graduate. Fifty percent of the graduates seek advanced degrees; 2% enter medical school, 1% enter dental school, and 3% enter law school. About 75% pursue careers in business and industry.

Services: Students receive the following services free of charge: health care, psychological counseling, tutoring, remedial instruction, placement, and career counseling. Placement services for undergraduates include workshops on resume writing and interviewing techniques.

Programs of Study: Undergraduate programs lead to the B.A. degree. Associate and master's degree programs are also offered. Bachelor's degrees are offered in the following subjects: AREA STUDIES (American), BUSINESS (accounting, business education, computer science—business, computer science—math, management, marketing), EDUCATION (bi-lingual [Spanish/English], elementary, health/physical, secondary), ENGLISH (English, mass communications, speech—broadcasting, speech—drama), FINE AND PERFORMING ARTS (art, band and orchestra instruments, graphic design, museology and museography, music, music education, music industry, radio/TV, sacred music, theater/dramatics), HEALTH SCIENCES (athletic training, medical technology, nursing), LANGUAGES (French, German, Spanish), MATH AND SCIENCES (biology, chemistry, ecology/environmental science, mathematics, physics), PHILOSOPHY (Bible, Christian education, philosophy, religion), PREPROFESSIONAL (dentistry, engineering, law, medicine, ministry, social work, veterinary), SOCIAL SCIENCES (administration of criminal justice, economics, government/political science, history, international studies, marriage and family relations, psychology, social studies, social work, sociology). About 25% of degrees conferred are in business, 20% are in social sciences, and 15% are in preprofessional studies.

Special: Student-designed majors are permitted. The Center for Public Service prepares students for careers in public service. Pass/fail options, off-campus study, and study abroad are offered.

Honors: Honors programs include advanced placement, advanced standing with credit, special sections, certain reading courses, tutorials, seminars, and individual study. Ten national honor societies have chapters on campus.

Admissions: Eighty-eight percent of those who applied were accepted for a recent freshman class. The SAT scores of those who enrolled were as follows: Verbal—20% between 500 and 599, and 4% above 600; Math—23% between 500 and 599, 11% above 600, and 1% above 700. Applicants must be graduates of accredited high schools, have completed 15 Carnegie high school units, and rank in the upper half of their class with a GPA of C or better. Recommendations by spiritual leaders and school officials, evidence of special talent, leadership record, and advanced placement or honors courses are, in that order, among the factors which enter into admissions decisions.

Procedure: The SAT or ACT should be taken in May of the junior year, or in December, January, or April of the senior year. New students are admitted in the fall, winter, spring, and summer. The application, the high school record, and test scores must be submitted by August 15 (fall) or January 1 (winter). Notification is on a rolling basis, beginning when all credentials are received. There is a $10 application fee.

Special: Early and deferred admissions plans and an early decision plan are available. CLEP and subject exams are accepted; AP credit is also given.

Transfers: Transfers are accepted for all classes; D grades are not acceptable. Students must study at the college for at least 30 of the 124 semester hours necessary to receive a bachelor's degree. Application deadlines are open.

Visiting: Orientation programs are scheduled for prospective students, and include general campus tours, as well as opportunities to sit in on classes, talk with professors, attend home sports events, and have breakfast and lunch with students. Visits may be made on a weekday or over a weekend; visitors may stay overnight at the school.

Financial Aid: Over 80% of the students receive financial aid. The college provides scholarships, loans, and part-time employment; the aid package granted to freshmen from these sources varies according to financial need, academic record, and convenience. Awards are renewable. The college is a member of the CSS. The FAF and an aid application should be filed by March 1. After March 1, applicants are placed on a waiting list and are considered for available funds. Notification is made after admissions acceptance.

Foreign Students: The college's degree programs are open to citizens of other countries. Special counseling is available to these students.

Admissions: Foreign students must present TOEFL or University of Michigan Language Test scores. The SAT is also required.

Procedure: The application deadline for fall entry is June 1. Foreign students must present proof of health and proof of adequate funds.

Admissions Contact: George Nalywaiko, Director of Admissions.

BALL STATE UNIVERSITY D-3
Muncie, Indiana 47306 (317) 285-8282

F/T: 6337M, 8010W	Faculty: 870; I, —$
P/T: 774M, 978W	Ph.D.'s: 65%
Grad: 1104M, 1248W	S/F Ratio: 20 to 1
Year: qtrs, ss	Tuition: $1116 ($2460)
Appl: see profile	R and B: $1719
6069 applied	4092 accepted	3752 enrolled
SAT: 403V 436M		LESS COMPETITIVE

Ball State University, founded in 1918, is a state-assisted university which provides opportunities in both graduate and undergraduate education. Programs are offered in business, education and the liberal arts. Preprofessional training is also available in a wide range of areas. The library houses 855,172 volumes and 151,734 microfilm items and subscribes to 5502 periodicals.

Environment: The 905-acre campus is located in a suburban area 56 miles from Indianapolis. There are 57 buildings on campus including low- and high-rise residence halls in groups of three. There are also fraternity houses and married student housing.

Student Life: About 93% of the students are residents of Indiana; 98% of entering freshmen come from public schools. Fifty-nine percent of the students live on campus. Six percent are minority-group members. Campus housing is both coed and single-sex; there are visiting privileges in the single-sex housing. Students may keep cars on campus.

Organizations: There are 31 national Greek letter organizations, to which 12% of the men and 15% of the women belong. In addition there are numerous religious groups for the major faiths, and extracurricular activities including 26 departmental clubs and 11 student government organizations.

Sports: The University fields 13 intercollegiate teams for men and 13 for women. There are 16 intramural sports for men and 13 for women.

Handicapped: Ninety percent of the campus is accessible to wheelchair students. Special facilities include wheelchair ramps, parking areas, elevators, lowered drinking fountains and telephones, specially equipped rest rooms, and modified transportation. Special class scheduling is also possible. There is a small percentage of visually and hearing-impaired students for which there are classroom adaptation booklets, a resources and equipment room in the library, paid reader services, and assistance in ordering tapes and locating interpreters.

Graduates: Over 11% of the students go on to graduate school. About 72% of the students pursue careers in business and industry.

Services: Placement, health care, tutoring, remedial instruction, and psychological and career counseling services are provided free of charge to all students.

Programs of Study: The university awards the B.A., B.S., and B.F.A. degrees. Associate, master's, and doctoral degrees are also awarded. Bachelor's degrees are offered in the following subjects: AREA STUDIES (Latin American), BUSINESS (accounting, business administration, business education, computer science, distributive education, finance, management, marketing, office systems administration), EDUCATION (elementary, health/physical, industrial, secondary, special), ENGLISH (English, journalism, speech), FINE AND PERFORMING ARTS (art, art education, art history, dance, film/photography, music, music education, radio/TV, studio art, theater/dramatics), HEALTH SCIENCES (medical technology, nursing, physical therapy), LANGUAGES (French, German, Greek/Latin, Spanish), MATH AND SCIENCES (actuarial science, biology, chemistry, earth science, geology, mathematics, natural resources, physical sciences, physics), PHILOSOPHY (philosophy, religion), PREPROFESSIONAL (architecture, home economics, landscape architecture, social work), SOCIAL SCIENCES (anthropology, criminal justice and corrections, economics, geography, government/political science, history, psychology, sociology). About 23% of degrees conferred are in education, 20% are in business, and 9% are in health sciences.

Required: All students are required to take the general education program during the first two years which includes courses in the natural sciences, humanities, and social and behavioral sciences.

Special: It is possible to earn a B.G.S. degree.

Honors: There are 34 national honor societies that have chapters on campus. Although there are no specific departmental honors programs, the Honors College core curriculum may be taken by students regardless of their major or minor.

Admissions: About 67% of those who applied were accepted for the 1981-82 freshman class. The SAT scores of those who enrolled were as follows: Verbal—84% below 500, 14% between 500 and 599, 1% between 600 and 700, and 0% above 700; Math—73% below 500, 21% between 500 and 599, 6% between 600 and 700, and 1% above 700. An applicant should have a verbal SAT score of at least 400, and must be a graduate of a commissioned secondary school or its equivalent. Indiana residents should rank in the upper 75% of their class; others should rank in the top half. Other considerations include recommendations from school officials, honors courses, and evidence of special talent.

Procedure: The SAT or ACT is required and should be taken in spring of the junior year. Application, transcript, test scores, and a $15 application fee should be submitted 30 days prior to the beginning of the fall, winter, or spring terms and 2 weeks prior to the beginning of the summer quarter. Notification is on a rolling basis.

Special: There are early admissions and deferred admissions plans. Credit is awarded for CLEP examinations.

Transfer: For fall 1981, 602 transfer students enrolled. A GPA of at least 1.8 and minimum scores of 310 on the verbal part of the SAT or 13 on the ACT are required. D grades do not transfer. Application deadlines are the same as those for freshmen. Students must complete, at the university, 45 of the last 60 credits (186 are required for a bachelor's degree).

Visiting: Ball State welcomes visitors, on both an informal and planned basis. The best times for campus visits are when classes are in session. Guides are available, and hotel rooms may be arranged for a nominal fee in the Student Center. Visitors should contact the Campus Visit House or Office of Admissions.

Financial Aid: About 79% of all students receive financial aid. About 17% work part-time on campus. The average award to freshmen is $1544. The university is a member of CSS. The FAF and the financial aid application should be submitted by March 1 for the fall, winter, and spring quarters, and by April for the summer quarter.

Foreign Students: Two percent of the full-time students come from foreign countries. An intensive English program, an intensive English course, special counseling, and special organizations are available for these students.

Admissions: Foreign students must achieve a TOEFL score of at least 425 to enter the intensive English program and 550 to enter most other programs. They must also take the university's English proficiency exam. No college entrance exams are required.

Procedure: Application deadlines are March 1 (fall), July 1 (winter), and November 1 (spring). Foreign students must present proof of funds adequate to cover 1 year of study and must carry health insurance, which is available through the university for a fee.

Admissions Contact: Charles E. Kaufman, Director, Pre-Admission Services.

BETHEL COLLEGE C-1
Mishawaka, Indiana 46544 (219) 259-8511

F/T: 176M, 185W		Faculty:	n/av; IIB, —$
P/T: 38M, 32W		Ph.D.'s:	30%
Grad: 7 M&W		S/F Ratio:	14 to 1
Year: 4-1-4, ss		Tuition:	$3255
Appl: open		R and B:	$1900
249 applied	199 accepted		180 enrolled
SAT: 414V 443M	ACT: 19		LESS COMPETITIVE

Bethel College, founded in 1947, is affiliated with the Missionary Church and offers a liberal arts program. The library houses 55,000 volumes and 200 microfilm items, and subscribes to 350 periodicals.

Environment: The 60-acre campus is located in a suburban area 90 miles from Chicago. There are 2 dormitories and a student center.

Student Life: Ninety percent of entering freshmen come from public schools. About 91% are Protestant, 9% Catholic. Forty percent belong to the Missionary Church, and daily church attendance is compulsory. Fifty-five percent of the students reside on campus. Drinking and smoking are not permitted; curfew hours are 11:30 P.M. weekdays, and 12:30 A.M. weekends. Cars are permitted with parental consent.

Organizations: There are no sororities or fraternities on campus, but a number of extracurricular and on-campus cultural events are offered.

Sports: The college fields 5 intercollegiate teams for men and 3 for women. Intramural sports for men and women include volleyball, basketball, and numerous other events.

Handicapped: About 75% of the campus is accessible for the physically handicapped.

Graduates: Twenty-five percent of students pursue graduate study after graduation; 19% enter law school. About 33% pursue careers in business and industry.

Services: Students receive health care and career counseling. There are placement services available for undergraduate students, and for graduates there is a career and life planning office.

Programs of Study: The college awards the B.A. degree. Associate and master's degrees are also awarded. Bachelor's degrees are offered in the following subjects: BUSINESS (accounting, business administration, computer science), EDUCATION (elementary, secondary), ENGLISH (English), FINE AND PERFORMING ARTS (art education, music, music education), HEALTH SCIENCES (medical technology, nursing), MATH AND SCIENCES (biology, chemistry, mathematics, natural sciences), PHILOSOPHY (religion), PREPROFESSIONAL (dentistry, engineering, law, medicine, ministry, social work, veterinary), SOCIAL SCIENCES (history, psychology, social sciences, sociology). Twenty percent of degrees conferred are in education and 20% are in business.

Special: There is a combination degree in medical technology. Students may study abroad in England, Brazil, Nigeria, and Mexico. It is possible to earn a B.G.S. degree.

Admissions: Eighty percent of those who applied were accepted for the 1981-82 freshman class. The SAT scores of those who enrolled were as follows: Verbal—10% scored between 500 and 599, and 0% above 600; Math—23% between 500 and 599, 6% between 600 and 700, and 0% above 700. Candidates should have completed 12 Carnegie units and be in the upper two-thirds of their class. A minimum GPA of 2.0 is required. Other factors are recommendations by school officials, personality, intangible qualities, and impressions made during an interview.

228 INDIANA

Procedure: Either the SAT or ACT is required, as well as transcripts of high school and personal references. There is no deadline for applying for the fall session. A $15 fee is required. Admissions ae on a rolling basis.

Special: There are early decision and deferred admissions plans. Credit is awarded for CLEP exams.

Transfer: Almost all transfer applicants are accepted, provided they meet the same requirements as high school seniors. All students must complete, at the college, 30 of the 124 credits required for a bachelor's degree. At least 6 credits must be earned in the major.

Visiting: Guided tours and interviews can be scheduled on weekdays. Overnight accommodations are available and can be arranged by contacting the admissions office.

Financial Aid: About 75% of students receive aid through the school. Scholarships are available in amounts of $500 each. Students in the top 15% of their high school class and who have a total of 950 SAT or 21 ACT receive scholarships without regard to financial need. Loans from federal and state government are available. Campus employment is also possible. The FAF or FFS is required. The application deadline is April 1.

Admissions Contact: Robert L. Beyer, Director of Admissions/Financial Aid.

BUTLER UNIVERSITY   C-3
Indianapolis, Indiana 46208   (317) 283-9310

F/T, P/T:	Faculty:	249; IIA, —$
2676 M&W	Ph.D.'s:	70%
Grad: 1360 M&W	S/F Ratio:	16 to 1
Year: sems, ss	Tuition:	$3850
Appl: open	R and B:	$1850
1143 applied	953 accepted	567 enrolled
SAT: 500V 520M		COMPETITIVE

Butler University, a coeducational, nonsectarian institution, was one of the first colleges in the nation to admit women and men on an equal basis when it opened in 1855. The library contains 146,925 volumes and 16,001 microfilm items, and subscribes to more than 700 periodicals.

Environment: The 152-acre suburban campus contains 17 buildings, including a research building; a planetarium and observatory; Clowes Memorial Hall, the home of the Indianapolis Symphony; and an outdoor theater. The university is 5 miles from downtown Indianapolis.

Student Life: Most students are from Indiana, and more than half live in the 3 residence halls or the 15 sorority or fraternity houses on campus.

Organizations: Eight national fraternities have campus chapters, and 37% of the men belong. Seven sororities with chapters on campus enroll 38% of the women. There are about 70 student organizations and clubs on campus, including a student newspaper and an FM radio station.

Sports: The university competes on an intercollegiate level in 8 sports for men and 4 for women. Numerous intramural sports are offered for men and women.

Handicapped: About 50% of the campus is accessible to students in wheelchairs. Special facilities include wheelchair ramps, parking areas, and elevators. Special class scheduling can be arranged.

Services: The university provides placement, career counseling, and health care free of charge.

Programs of Study: The university confers the B.A. and B.S. degrees. Associate and master's degrees also are awarded. Bachelor's degrees are offered in the following subjects: AREA STUDIES (American), BUSINESS (accounting, actuarial science, business administration, business education, computer science, public and corporate communication, secretarial science), EDUCATION (elementary, health/physical, secondary), ENGLISH (English, journalism, speech), FINE AND PERFORMING ARTS (dance, music, music education, radio/TV, theater/dramatics), LANGUAGES (French, German, Greek/Latin, Spanish), MATH AND SCIENCES (biology, botany, chemistry, ecology/environmental science, mathematics, physics, zoology), PHILOSOPHY (classics, philosophy, religion), PREPROFESSIONAL (home economics, pharmacy), SOCIAL SCIENCES (economics, geography, government/political science, history, psychology, sociology).

Required: All students must complete a core curriculum of courses in humanities, social science, and natural science. Freshman English and physical education are also required.

Special: Preprofessional programs are offered in medicine, dentistry, nursing, medical technology, engineering, forestry, law, ministry, and dietetics.

Honors: Each department has its own honors programs, and 10 honor societies have chapters on campus.

Admissions: About 83% of those who applied were accepted for the 1981–82 freshman class. About 58% ranked in the top fifth of their high school class, and 90% ranked in the top two-fifths. The SAT scores for an earlier class were as follows: Verbal—29% between 500 and 600, 12% between 600 and 700, and 2% above 700; Math—34% between 500 and 600, 18% between 600 and 700, and 5% above 700. Candidates should have a college preparatory background that includes 4 years of English and at least 2 years each of mathematics, social sciences, foreign languages, and laboratory science. They must rank in the top half of their class and have at least a C+ average. The school also considers advanced placement or honors courses, impressions made during an interview, extracurricular activities, special talents, and recommendations.

Procedure: There are no application deadlines. Notification is made on a rolling basis. The SAT or ACT is required. The application fee is $15.

Special: Early and deferred admissions plans are available.

Transfer: Transfer applicants must have a C average or better. Students must spend at least 1 year in residence; 124 credits are required for a bachelor's degree.

Visiting: Guides are available for informal visits. Visitors may sit in on classes and stay overnight at the university. Weekday visits are recommended. Visits can be arranged through the admissions office.

Financial Aid: About 85% of all students receive aid. Grants-in-aid are given to freshmen who show promise in some area of intercollegiate competition, such as athletics or debate. There are also awards for music and dance, and for assistance given academic departments or campus organizations. BEOG, SEOG, NDSL, and work-study are available. Students are encouraged to file the aid application by March 1.

Foreign Students: The foreign students enrolled full-time at the university make up about 2% of the student body. Special organizations are provided for these students.

Admissions: Applicants must score 550 or better on the TOEFL. They also must take the SAT.

Procedure: Students are admitted to all terms and should submit application forms at least 60 days before the start of any term. Students must present proof of adequate funds for 1 year and must carry health insurance, which is available through the university for a fee.

Admissions Contact: Joseph L. Collier, Associate Dean of Admissions.

CALUMET COLLEGE   B-1
Whiting, Indiana 46394   (219) 473-4215

F/T: 230M, 270W	Faculty:	n/av; IIB, av$
P/T: 450M, 550W	Ph.D.'s:	n/av
Grad: none	S/F Ratio:	20 to 1
Year: sems, ss	Tuition:	$1860
Appl: Sept. 10	R and B:	n/app
SAT or ACT: required		LESS COMPETITIVE

Calumet College is a commuter institution established in 1951. It is affiliated with the Catholic Church, and provides a liberal arts education in a Christian environment. The college offers a programming schedule that allows students to complete a degree in as little as 32 months. The library houses 98,000 books and 2600 microfilm items, and subscribes to 850 periodicals.

Environment: The campus, located in an urban environment 15 miles from Chicago's Loop, covers 255 acres and includes an administration building, science building, student center, and library. There are no residence halls.

Student Life: Sixty-eight percent of the students are from Indiana; the rest come from other states. About 65% are Roman Catholic. Ninety percent of the entering freshmen come from public schools.

Organizations: There are 2 fraternities and 1 sorority on campus: about 1% of the students belong to each. Other organizations include the student council and the commerce, Spanish, biology, science, and humanities clubs. Fine arts and theater are among activities offered.

Sports: There are 3 intramural sports for men and 1 for women.

Handicapped: The entire campus is accessible to students in wheelchairs. Special facilities include wheelchair ramps, parking areas, elevators, and specially equipped rest rooms.

Services: Students receive tutoring, remedial instruction, placement, career counseling, and psychological counseling free of charge. Employment officers visit the college to interview prospective employees.

Programs of Study: The college offers the B.A. and B.S. degrees. Associate degrees are also awarded. Bachelor's degrees are offered in the following subjects: BUSINESS (accounting, business administration, business education, management), EDUCATION (elementary, secondary), ENGLISH (English, journalism, speech), FINE AND PERFORMING ARTS (art, art education, radio/TV, theater/dramatics), HEALTH SCIENCES (medical technology), LANGUAGES (French, Spanish), MATH AND SCIENCES (biology, chemistry, general science), PHILOSOPHY (philosophy, religion), PREPROFESSIONAL (dentistry, law, medicine, social work), SOCIAL SCIENCES (criminal justice, economics, government/political science, history, psychology, social sciences, sociology). Sixty-five percent of the degrees conferred are in business; 15% are in preprofessional studies.

Required: Successful completion of UP Area Tests and the URE is required for graduation.

Special: Student-designed majors and general studies degrees are offered. Students are permitted to spend the junior year abroad, although the college does not sponsor such a program.

Honors: All major areas offer honors programs. Honors candidates must have a 3.25 GPA in the major sequence for admission into a program. There is 1 honor society on campus.

Admissions: About 82% of those who applied were accepted for the 1981–82 freshman class. Applicants must be in the upper three-fourths of the high school graduating class, and hold at least a 1.5 GPA.

Procedure: The SAT or ACT should be taken in May of the junior year or during the first semester of the senior year. The application, a $15 fee, high school records, and test scores must be filed by September 10 for the fall session, and January 10 for the spring session. Freshmen are admitted for the fall, spring, and summer sessions. Admissions are on a rolling basis.

Special: There are programs for early decisions, early admissions, and deferred admissions. CLEP is accepted.

Transfer: Recently, 166 of 189 transfer applications were approved. Good academic standing at the previous school is the prime consideration; D grades are acceptable. There is a 1-year residency requirement. Students must complete 124 credits to receive a bachelor's degree. There is a rolling admissions policy.

Visiting: There are regularly scheduled 2-day orientation programs for prospective students, during which meetings are held with students and academic advisers. There are also guides for informal visits, and visitors may sit in on classes. Arrangements for visits can be made through the admissions office.

Financial Aid: Fifty-five percent of all students receive financial aid. The college provides scholarships; loans from NDSL, grants from BEOG, and CWS funds are also available. The FAF is required. There is no deadline for applying for financial aid, and applications are accepted until classes begin if funds are still available. The college is a member of the CSS and participates in the Cooperative Education Program.

Foreign Students: The college is authorized to enroll nonimmigrant alien students. Interested students should contact the admissions office for foreign student admissions guidelines.

Admission Contact: Sandra Trilli, Assistant Director of Admissions.

DEPAUW UNIVERSITY B-3
Greencastle, Indiana 46135 (317) 658-4006

F/T: 1050M, 1280W	Faculty:	152; IIB, ++$
P/T: 25M, 25W	Ph.D.'s:	75%
Grad: 25M, 25W	S/F Ratio:	15 to 1
Year: 4-1-4	Tuition:	$5482
Appl: see profile	R and B:	$2300
2031 applied	1501 accepted	650 enrolled
SAT: 510V 550M	ACT: 24	VERY COMPETITIVE

DePauw University, founded in 1834, is a private nonsectarian university affiliated with the Methodist Church. The university is composed of the Asbury College of Liberal Arts, the School of Music, and the School of Nursing. It offers graduate and undergraduate instruction. The library houses 360,000 volumes, 6000 microfilms, 5806 microtexts, and 1833 microfiche items, and subscribes to 1100 periodicals.

Environment: The 115-acre campus is located in a rural area 40 miles from Indianapolis. There are 32 buildings including 7 residence houses and a newly completed Physical Education and Recreation Center. There is a freshman quad with the remaining residences interspersed throughout the campus. Living facilities also include fraternity and sorority houses. The East College, built in 1877, has been entered in the register of historic places.

Student Life: About 41% of the students are from Indiana, 1% from foreign countries, and the rest from 44 other states. About 95% of the students reside on campus. Five percent of the students are minority-group members. Sixty percent are Protestant, 22% are Catholic, and 1% are Jewish. Campus housing is both coed and single-sex; there are visiting privileges in the single-sex dorms. Students may keep cars on campus.

Organizations: There are 13 national fraternities and 9 national sororities and 70 to 75% of the students are members. Extracurricular activities are numerous and include choir, band, orchestra, concerts, plays, lecture series, a biweekly newspaper, religious groups, special-interest groups, radio and television, speech and dramatics, oratory and debating.

Sports: The university fields 11 intercollegiate teams for men and 9 for women. There are 7 intramural sports for men and 8 for women.

Handicapped: Facilities for the physically handicapped are limited to wheelchair ramps and elevators.

Graduates: The freshman dropout rate is 10%; 70% of the entering freshmen remain to graduate. About 33% pursue advanced study after graduation: 3% in medicine, 2% in dentistry, and 5% in law. About 29% of the graduates enter business and industry.

Services: Students receive the following free of charge: tutoring, remedial instruction, psychological counseling, health care, placement, and career counseling.

Programs of Study: The university confers the B.A., B.S.N., and B.Mus. degrees. Master's degrees are also awarded. Bachelor's degrees are offered in the following subjects: AREA STUDIES (American, Asian, Black/Afro-American, Latin American, Russian, urban), BUSINESS (computer science, economics and management), EDUCATION (elementary, health/physical, secondary), ENGLISH (composition, English, journalism, literature), FINE AND PERFORMING ARTS (area performance, art, art education, art history, communication arts and sciences, music, music/business, music composition, music education, performance, radio/TV, studio art, theater/dramatics), HEALTH SCIENCES (medical technology, nursing), LANGUAGES (French, German, Greek/Latin, Romance languages, Russian, Spanish), MATH AND SCIENCES (bacteriology, botany, chemistry, computational mathematics, earth science, mathematics, physics, zoology), PHILOSOPHY (classics, philosophy, religion), PREPROFESSIONAL (dentistry, engineering, law, medicine, ministry, speech language pathology and audiology, veterinary), SOCIAL SCIENCES (anthropology, economics, geography, government/political science, history, psychology, sociology). Twenty-five percent of degrees conferred are in social sciences, 13% in math and sciences, and 12% in business.

Special: It is possible to earn a combined B.A.-B.S. degree in pre-engineering. Student-designed majors are permitted. DePauw is a member of the Great Lakes College Association, through which off-campus study opportunities all over the world are offered.

Honors: DePauw has a well-established honors scholar program involving all departments. There are 8 national honor societies that have chapters on campus.

Admissions: Seventy-four percent of students who applied were accepted for the 1981–82 freshman class. The SAT scores of those who enrolled were as follows: Verbal—40% below 500, 47% between 500 and 599, 12% between 600 and 700, and 1% above 700; Math—21% below 500, 47% between 500 and 599, 27% between 600 and 700, and 5% above 700. On the ACT, 8% scored below 21, 22% between 21 and 23, 22% between 24 and 25, 33% between 26 and 28, and 15% above 28. The candidate should rank in the upper half of the class. Other considerations are extracurricular activities, athletics, honors courses, leadership activities, and personality.

Procedure: The SAT or ACT should be taken in the junior year or by December of the senior year. The deadline dates are December 1, February 1, or March 1. Notification is sent by the middle of the month selected by the applicant. Freshmen are admitted in the fall and spring terms. A fee of $20 must be submitted.

Special: Early admissions, early decision, and deferred admissions plans are available. AP credit is given.

Transfer: For fall 1981, 107 students applied, 69 were accepted, and 44 enrolled. D grades do not transfer. A GPA of 3.0 or above is recommended. Six of the last 8 courses must be taken in residence. At least 32 courses are required for a bachelor's degree. Application deadlines are April 1 (fall) and December 1 (spring).

230 INDIANA

Visiting: There are regularly scheduled orientations for prospective students. Campus tours, meetings with faculty, and general meetings are included. Visitors may stay at the university.

Financial Aid: About 76% of students receive some financial aid. The university provides scholarships of $1.7 million, loans totalling $358,000 and grants of $912,000. Students also receive $2.9 million in loans and $1 million in scholarships and/or grants from outside agencies. Part-time employment is available. Twenty-five percent work to earn part of expenses. The FAF must be submitted by CSS by March 1 for need-based aid. A number of honor awards not requiring a FAF are given for academic excellence or unusual talent.

Foreign Students: One percent of the full-time students come from foreign countries. An intensive English course, special counseling, and special organizations are available for these students.

Admissions: Foreign students must achieve a TOEFL score of at least 500–550 and must take the university's English proficiency exam. A minimum composite score of 1000 on the SAT is required.

Procedure: Application deadlines are the same as those for other students. Foreign students must present proof of adequate funds and proof of health. Health insurance is required and is available through the university.

Admissions Contact: Anne Seed, Admissions Counselor.

EARLHAM COLLEGE D-3
Richmond, Indiana 47374 (317) 962-6561

F/T: 487M, 608W		Faculty:	78; IIB, +$
P/T: 9M, 14W		Ph.D.'s:	70%
Grad: 40M, 35W		S/F Ratio:	12 to 1
Year: 3-3-3		Tuition:	$5835
Appl: Mar. 15		R and B:	$1950
752 applied	579 accepted		284 enrolled
SAT: 520V 540M			VERY COMPETITIVE

Earlham College, established in 1847, is a small liberal arts college which is operated by the Society of Friends but is nonsectarian in policy and practice. Quaker values, such as respect for the individual, importance of the community, and intercultural and international awareness, are stressed. The library contains 260,000 volumes and 7000 microfilm items, and subscribes to 1300 periodicals.

Environment: The 120-acre main campus is located in a rural area on the west edge of Richmond, a city of 45,000. There are 15 buildings on the campus, including a student center and dormitories. Living facilities also include married-student housing and off-campus apartments. The college owns 650 acres of adjoining farm and wooded land, the Conner Prairie Museum, and the Pioneer Settlement near Noblesville.

Student Life: About 50% of the students come from the Midwest, and 80% are graduates of public schools. Ninety percent of the students live on campus. Nine percent are minority-group members. About 53% are Protestant, 8% are Catholic, and 7% are Jewish. Twenty percent are members of the Society of Friends. Attendance at convocations is voluntary. Campus housing is both coed and single-sex; there are visiting privileges in the single-sex dorms. Freshmen may not keep cars on campus.

Organizations: There are no fraternities or sororities. Student organizations include musical groups, service organizations, religious groups, and radio station, newspaper, and yearbook staffs.

Sports: The college fields 10 intercollegiate teams for men and 9 for women. There are 12 intramural sports for men and 12 for women.

Handicapped: About 70% of the campus is accessible to handicapped students. Facilities include wheelchair ramps, parking areas, elevators, lowered telephones, and specially equipped rest rooms.

Graduates: At the end of the freshman year, 10% drop out; 60% remain to graduate, and 60% of the graduates eventually go on to graduate or professional schools. About 5% enter medical school, 1% go on to dental school, and 3% enter law school. Sixty percent of the graduates enter business and industry.

Services: Students receive the following services free of charge: career counseling, placement (for students and graduates), health care, tutoring, and psychological counseling.

Programs of Study: The college offers the B.A. degree. Bachelor's degrees are offered in the following subjects: AREA STUDIES (Black/Afro-American), EDUCATION (elementary, health/physical, outdoor, secondary), ENGLISH (literature), FINE AND PERFORMING ARTS (music), LANGUAGES (French, German, Japanese, Spanish), MATH AND SCIENCES (astronomy, biology, chemistry, ecology/environmental science, geology, mathematics, physics), PHILOSOPHY (philosophy, religion), PREPROFESSIONAL (engineering, law, medicine), SOCIAL SCIENCES (African/African American studies, anthropology, economics, government/political science, history, international relations, Japanese studies, peace and conflict studies, psychology, sociology). About 36% of degrees conferred are in social sciences; 32% are in math and sciences.

Required: All students are required to take courses in the humanities, philosophy or religion, psychology or sociology, political science or economics, biological or physical sciences, creative arts, foreign language, literature, history of world civilization, and mathematics or logic. Some departments require the URE.

Special: Independent study programs are available, and the colloquium concept has been incorporated into several major fields. An optional work term provides an opportunity to earn money while gaining practical experience on the job. The Wilderness Program offers training in outdoor skills combined with related academic instruction. The college has a 3-2 program in engineering with several engineering schools. Domestic off-campus study is also available in various cities. Foreign study is offered in Europe, Latin America, and Asia.

Honors: There is a chapter of Phi Beta Kappa on campus.

Admissions: Seventy-seven percent of those who applied were accepted for the 1981–82 freshman class. The SAT scores of those who enrolled were as follows: Verbal—30% below 500, 30% between 500 and 599, 21% between 600 and 700, and 3% above 700; Math—20% below 500, 40% between 500 and 599, 25% between 600 and 700, and 3% above 700. Applicants should have completed 15 academic units and have a GPA of at least 2.0. The college also considers the following factors in the admissions decision: advanced placement or honor courses, recommendations by school officials, personality, and extracurricular activities. Relatives of alumni, Quakers or minorities may receive preference. An interview is recommended.

Procedure: The SAT or ACT is required; the SAT is preferred. The high school record and test scores should be submitted by March 15 (fall), December 1 (winter), or March 1 (spring). Notification is made on a rolling basis. There is a $15 application fee.

Special: Early admissions, deferred admissions, and early decision plans are available. AP and CLEP credit is acceptable.

Transfer: For fall 1981, 29 transfer students enrolled. Applicants wishing to transfer should have at least a 2.0 average and 3 credit hours; test scores, a dean's report, and the financial aid transcript should be submitted by April 15 (fall), November 15 (winter), or February 15 (spring). D grades do not transfer. There is a 1-year residency requirement. Students must complete, at the college, 9 of the 36 credits required for a bachelor's degree.

Visiting: Regularly scheduled orientations are available for prospective students. Guides are available for informal visits at any time. During the school year, visitors may sit in on classes and stay overnight at the school. The admissions office should be contacted for arrangements.

Financial Aid: About 70% of the students receive financial aid. Sixty-five percent work part-time on campus. The average award to freshmen is $4600. The college provides scholarships, loans, and jobs. Aid is awarded on the basis of financial need, and renewal is contingent upon continued need. Financial aid applications should be submitted with applications for admission by February 15 (fall), December 1 (winter), or March 1 (spring). The college is a member of CSS and requires the FAF.

Foreign Students: Two percent of the full-time students come from foreign countries. Special counseling and special organizations are available for these students.

Admissions: Foreign students must take either the TOEFL (minimum score 500) or the University of Michigan Language Test. No college entrance exams are required.

Procedure: Application deadlines are the same as those for other freshmen. Foreign students must present proof of funds adequate to cover 4 years of study. Health insurance is required and is available through the college.

Admissions Contact: Lynette Robinson-Weening, Dean of Admissions.

FRANKLIN COLLEGE C-4
Franklin, Indiana 46131 (317) 736-8441

F/T: 275M, 276W		Faculty:	55; IIB, −$
P/T: 17M, 34W		Ph.D.'s:	61%
Grad: none		S/F Ratio:	13 to 1
Year: 4-1-4, ss		Tuition:	$4400
Appl: Aug. 1		R and B:	$1930
636 applied	532 accepted		204 enrolled
SAT: 426V 476M	ACT: 21		COMPETITIVE

Franklin College is a small, private, liberal arts school, established in 1834 by Baptist pioneers. It is affiliated with the American Baptist Convention. The library houses 95,000 volumes, 800 maps and 1100 reels of microfilm, and subscribes to 575 periodicals.

Environment: The campus occupies 74 acres in a rural town 20 miles south of Indianapolis. There are 16 buildings, including a computer center, 2 physical education buildings, a chapel, a science building, a campus center, and 2 buildings that are registered as historical landmarks. There are 4 residence halls, 2 for men, 2 for women.

Student Life: About 80% of the students are from Indiana, and 19% are from other states. About 90% of entering freshmen come from public schools. The residence halls accommodate 67% of the students, while 15% reside in fraternity houses adjacent to the campus. Fourteen percent of the students are Catholic. One percent are minority-group members. College housing is single-sex; and there are visiting privileges. Students may keep cars on campus.

Organizations: Four national fraternities attract 40% of the men; 44% of the women belong to 4 national sororities. Students also participate in the Student Congress, departmental clubs, a concert choir, vocal ensembles, religious groups, forensics, a radio station, and a weekly newspaper. The Student Entertainment Board plans concerts, dances, and films on campus.

Sports: The college's men compete on an intercollegiate level in 8 sports and women in 8. There are 2 intramural sports for men and women.

Handicapped: About 30% of the campus is accessible to wheelchair students. Special facilities include wheelchair ramps, parking areas, elevators, and specially equipped rest rooms. Special class scheduling is possible.

Graduates: The freshman dropout rate is 20%; 55% remain to graduate, and 25% continue their studies after graduation. Five percent enter medical school, 2% dental school, and 5% law school. Careers in business and industry attract 13%.

Services: Students receive the following services free of charge: health care, tutoring, remedial instruction, career counseling, and placement. There is also a full-time career planning and placement counselor.

Programs of Study: The college offers the B.A. degree. Bachelor's degrees are offered in the following subjects: AREA STUDIES (American), BUSINESS (accounting, business administration), EDUCATION (early childhood, elementary, health/physical, secondary, special), ENGLISH (English, journalism, literature), FINE AND PERFORMING ARTS (art, art education, studio art), HEALTH SCIENCES (medical technology, nursing), LANGUAGES (French, Spanish), MATH AND SCIENCES (biology, chemistry, mathematics, physics), PHILOSOPHY (philosophy, religion), PREPROFESSIONAL (dentistry, engineering, forestry, law, medicine, ministry, pharmacy, veterinary), SOCIAL SCIENCES (economics, government/political science, history, psychology, sociology). The forestry degree is awarded through a cooperative program with Duke University. The medical technology and engineering degrees are also awarded through cooperative programs.

Required: A 6-course transdisciplinary sequence, in which courses are selected from a variety of departments, is required of all students.

Special: Students may take advantage of special programs, which include the Junior Year Abroad; Washington, D.C. semester; and United Nations semester.

Honors: The junior-senior honors program and the Franklin Scholars Program are available in all major areas to students who maintain a 3.5 GPA. These programs permit advanced independent study. Three national honor societies have chapters on campus: Blue Key, Chi Beta Phi, and Women in Communications.

Admissions: The college accepted about 84% of the applicants to its 1981-82 freshman class. The SAT scores of those who enrolled were as follows: Verbal—78% below 500, 19% between 500 and 599, 3% between 600 and 700, and 0% above 700; Math—63% below 500, 31% between 500 and 599, 6% between 600 and 700, and fewer than 1% above 700. Applicants must have completed 15 Carnegie units, be graduates of accredited high schools, rank in the upper half of their graduating class, and have a minimum C average. In addition, the school considers the following factors, in order of significance, in its admissions decisions: extracurricular activities record, leadership record, impressions made during an interview, recommendations by high school officials, and advanced placement or honors courses.

Procedure: The SAT or ACT should be taken in April of the junior year and no later than December of the senior year. The application deadlines are August 1 (fall), December 1 (winter), January 1 (spring), and May 15 (summer). Applicants are accepted on a rolling basis. New students are accepted all terms. There is no application fee.

Special: Early decisions will be made on applications received by November 1. Early admissions are possible; applications must be filed by June 1. Deferred admissions are also possible. CLEP and AP credit is also granted.

Transfer: Recently, 38 applications were received, 35 were accepted, and 21 students enrolled. Transfers are accepted for all classes. GPAs required are 1.45 (freshman), 1.7 (sophomore), 1.9 (junior), and 2.0 (senior). D grades do not transfer. Applicants must not be on academic probation at their current colleges. Students must complete 138 credit hours to receive a bachelor's degree. Application deadlines are the same as for freshman applicants.

Visiting: Visits to the campus may be made Monday through Friday and Saturday by appointment. Visitors may sit in on classes and stay overnight at the school. Four-day orientations for prospective students are regularly scheduled on weekends by the admissions office.

Financial Aid: About 85% of the students are receiving financial aid; 70% work part-time on campus. The average award to freshmen from all sources is $1000. The college provides scholarships, grants, loans, and employment. About 120 institutional scholarships are awarded to freshmen each year. Loans are available from the federal government, local banks, the college, and private sources. Aid is awarded on the basis of financial need and academic achievement. The college is a member of CSS. The FAF should be filed. The deadline for application is March 1, but awards are made on a rolling basis.

Foreign Students: One percent of the full-time students come from foreign countries. The college offers these students an intensive English course, special counseling, and special organizations.

Admissions: Foreign students must score at least 550 on the TOEFL. No college entrance examination is required.

Procedure: The application deadline is May 15 (fall). Foreign students must present proof of health. They must also present proof of adequate funds. There is a special fee of $2330 for foreign students that covers an 11-month period, including the summer session. Foreign students must also carry health insurance.

Admissions Contact: Marcia Martin, Assistant Director of Admissions.

GOSHEN COLLEGE C-1
Goshen, Indiana 46526 (219) 533-3161

F/T: 454M, 626W	Faculty:	84; IIB, av$
P/T: 41M, 87W	Ph.D.'s:	76%
Grad: none	S/F Ratio:	14 to 1
Year: tri, ss	Tuition:	$3790
Appl: open	R and B:	$1760
388 applied	370 accepted	227 enrolled
SAT: 528V 534M		COMPETITIVE

Goshen College, established in 1894, is a private liberal arts college affiliated with the Mennonite Church. The library contains 105,365 volumes and subscribes to 705 periodicals.

Environment: The campus is situated on 135 acres in the town of Goshen, located in a rural area 90 miles east of Chicago and 35 miles from South Bend. The college has about 20 major buildings, including the recently built Umble Center for the Performing Arts. The library also houses a special Mennonite historical collection. Seven dormitories accommodate 466 women and 347 men.

Student Life: Over 50% of the students are from the Midwest. About 83% come from public schools. About 68% live on campus. About 70% of the students are affiliated with the Mennonite Church; most of the rest belong to other Protestant denominations, and 3% are Catholic. About 13% are members of minority groups. College-sponsored housing is both single-sex and coed; visiting privileges are offered in single-sex housing. Students may keep cars on campus. Attendance at chapel is compulsory. Drinking and smoking are not approved.

Organizations: The college has no fraternities or sororities. Student organizations and activities include religious groups; choral, dramatic and literary groups; academic and departmental clubs; a symphony orchestra; publications; and other cultural activities. The Artist Series brings nationally known artists to campus. Three off-campus recreation areas are available to students.

Sports: The college offers 7 intercollegiate sports for men and 5 for women. Men and women each may participate in 3 intramural sports.

Handicapped: Facilities for handicapped students include wheelchair ramps and elevators. Special class scheduling is also available. Sign language courses and interpreters are available for hearing-impaired students.

Graduates: About 15% of entering students drop out by the end of their freshman year, and 60% remain to graduate. Twenty-two percent of the graduates pursue advanced degrees, including 6% who enter medical school, 5% who enter law school, and 2% who enter dental school. About 15% of the graduates seek careers in business and industry.

Services: The following services are provided to students free of charge: health care, psychological counseling, placement and career counseling, tutoring, and remedial instruction.

Programs of Study: The college confers the B.A. and B.S.N. degrees. Bachelor's degrees are offered in the following subjects: BUSINESS (accounting, business administration, business education), EDUCATION (early childhood, elementary, health/physical, secondary), ENGLISH (English, journalism, literature, speech), FINE AND PERFORMING ARTS (art, art education, music, music education, theater/dramatics), HEALTH SCIENCES (nursing), LANGUAGES (French, German, Spanish), MATH AND SCIENCES (biology, chemistry, mathematics, natural sciences, physics), PHILOSOPHY (religion), PRE-PROFESSIONAL (engineering, home economics, medicine, ministry, pharmacy, social work), SOCIAL SCIENCES (economics, government/political science, history, psychology, sociology). Twenty percent of all degrees are conferred in health sciences, 14% in math and science, and 11% in social sciences.

Required: All students are required to take courses in Bible and religion, English, fine arts, international studies, natural sciences, and social sciences.

Special: In the Study and Work Program, the college helps students obtain employment in the community. A cooperative engineering program with Purdue University is offered. The college offers Mennonite tours in Europe every summer and a junior year abroad program in France, Spain, and Germany. Study-Service Trimester in Haiti, Belize, Costa Rica, Germany, or China is a regular part of the general education program; all students may enroll in it for college credit at no additional cost.

Admissions: About 95% of those who applied were accepted for the 1981–82 freshman class. The SAT scores among freshmen were as follows: Verbal—33% below 500, 34% between 500 and 599, 17% between 600 and 700, and 6% above 700; Math—34% below 500, 29% between 500 and 599, 21% between 600 and 700, and 6% above 700.

Procedure: The SAT or ACT is required and should be taken in either the junior or senior year. The application, $10 fee (which may be waived in cases of extreme financial hardship), the high school record, and test scores should be submitted by August 15 for fall admission. Freshmen are also admitted in the summer and at midyear. Admissions decisions are made on a rolling basis.

Special: The college has early and deferred admissions plans. AP and CLEP credit is offered.

Transfer: For fall 1981, all 184 transfer students who applied were accepted, and 94 enrolled. Good academic standing at the previous institution is required, and a C average is recommended. Thirty hours, of the 120 required for a bachelor's degree, must be taken in residence. Transfers are admitted in all semesters.

Visiting: Usually, 2 or 3 orientation sessions are held each trimester for prospective students. Guides are also available for informal visits. Visitors may sit in on classes and may also stay overnight at the school. Visits are best scheduled Monday through Friday. The office of admissions should be contacted for arrangements.

Financial Aid: Scholarships, grants, loans, and work-study arrangements are available. Eighty percent of the students receive aid through the college; 65% work part-time on campus. The average award to freshmen is $2977. The college is a member of CSS; the FAF must be filed. Aid application deadlines are open.

Foreign Students: Six percent of the full-time students at Goshen are from foreign countries. The college offers an intensive English course, special counseling, and special organizations for these students.

Admissions: A minimum score of 500 on the TOEFL is required. No other tests must be taken.

Procedure: Application deadlines are April 1 for fall entry and October 1 for spring entry. Proof of adequate funds for 1 year is required. Foreign students must carry health insurance, which is available through the college for a fee.

Admissions Contact: Dennis Koehn, Director of Admissions.

GRACE COLLEGE C-2
Winona Lake, Indiana 46590 (219) 267-8191

F/T: 359M, 453W Faculty: n/av; IIA, ––$
P/T: 64M, 55W Ph.D.'s: 50%
Grad: none S/F Ratio: 17 to 1
Year: sems, ss Tuition: $3200
Appl: Aug. 1 R and B: $2000
378 applied 329 accepted 243 enrolled
ACT: 19 COMPETITIVE

Founded in 1948, Grace College is affiliated with the Fellowship of Grace Brethren Churches, and is related to the Grace Theological Seminary. It offers a liberal arts program. The library has 120,000 volumes and 27,000 microfilm items, and subscribes to 650 periodicals.

Environment: The 150-acre campus has 18 buildings and is located in a small-town setting about 40 miles from Fort Wayne. Nine dormitories house 681 students. Facilities include a gymnasium, an athletic field, a YMCA swimming pool, a science building, and 6 tennis courts.

Student Life: About 37% of the students come from Indiana, and 27% come from bordering states. About 70% of the freshmen come from public schools. Seventy-two percent live on campus. Almost all students are Protestant, and most are members of the affiliated church. About 1% of the students are members of minority groups. Dormitories are single-sex; there are no visiting privileges. Daily chapel attendance is mandatory. Drinking is forbidden on campus. All students observe a curfew and sign-out procedure. Students may keep cars on campus.

Organizations: Extracurricular activities include special-interest clubs, service groups, and student government. There are no fraternities or sororities on campus. The Student Activities Board plans weekly activities.

Sports: The college competes intercollegiately in 6 sports for men and 5 for women. Men can compete in 4 intramural sports and women in 3.

Handicapped: About 95% of the campus is accessible to handicapped students. Facilities include wheelchair ramps, special parking, elevators, lowered drinking fountains, and specially equipped rest rooms. Special class scheduling is also available.

Graduates: The freshman dropout rate is 21%, and 48% of the entering students remain to graduate. Fourteen percent of the graduates pursue graduate studies. About 15% seek careers in business and industry.

Services: The following services are available to students free of charge: placement, psychological, and career counseling; health care, tutoring, and remedial instruction.

Programs of Study: The college confers B.A. and B.S. degrees. Associate degrees are offered in nursing. Bachelor's degrees are offered in the following subjects: BUSINESS (accounting, business administration), EDUCATION (elementary, health/physical, secondary), ENGLISH (English, speech), FINE AND PERFORMING ARTS (applied music, art, art education, church music, music, music education, music management), HEALTH SCIENCES (nursing), LANGUAGES (French, Greek/Latin, Spanish), MATH AND SCIENCES (biology, chemistry, general science, mathematics), PHILOSOPHY (Biblical studies, Christian ministries), PREPROFESSIONAL (home economics, ministry, social work), SOCIAL SCIENCES (history, psychology, social sciences, sociology). Thirty percent of the degrees are conferred in education, 28% in business.

Required: Students must complete a core curriculum. The URE is also required.

Special: Combination degree programs are offered in nursing and home economics. Study abroad is possible in Canada, France, Spain, and Mexico.

Honors: There is a chapter of Alpha Chi on campus.

Admissions: Eighty-seven percent of those who applied were accepted for the 1981–82 freshman class. The ACT scores of those who enrolled were as follows: 27% between 20 and 23, 10% between 24 and 26, 7% between 27 and 28, and 2% above 28. Applicants should have a high school diploma, 16 Carnegie units, a GPA of at least 2.5, and rank in the upper half of their graduating class. In addition, the school considers the following factors in order of importance: recommendations by school officials, leadership record, advanced placement or honors courses, personality, evidence of special talents, and extracurricular activities.

Procedure: The ACT must be taken. August 1 is the application deadline for the fall semester, December 1 is the deadline for spring. A rolling admissions plan is used. The application fee is $10.

Special: Early decision, early admissions, and deferred admissions plans are available.

Transfer: For fall 1981, 113 transfer students applied, 111 were accepted, and 68 enrolled. Applicants must be in good academic standing and have at least a 2.0 average. A 2.5 is preferred. D grades do not transfer. Thirty semester hours must be earned in residence.

Visiting: There are regularly scheduled orientations for prospective students. Guides are available for informal visits. Visitors may sit in on classes and stay overnight at the school. The director of admissions should be contacted for arrangements.

Financial Aid: Financial aid is available in the form of scholarships, grants, CWS, federal loans, and part-time jobs. About 80% of the students receive aid. The FAF is required. The deadline for financial aid applications is June 1.

Foreign Students: Fewer than 1% of the full-time students are from foreign countries. The college provides special counseling for these students.

Admissions: An English proficiency exam is not required, but foreign applicants must take the ACT.

Procedure: Admissions deadlines are open. Applicants must provide a medical report indicating they are healthy. They also must present proof of adequate funds for one year, with an indication that they will have funds for the remaining years of their education.

Admissions Contact: Ron Henry, Director of Admissions.

HANOVER COLLEGE D-5
Hanover, Indiana 47243 (812) 866-2151

F/T: 520M, 470W		Faculty:	74; n/av
P/T: 4M, 6W		Ph.D.'s:	70%
Grad: none		S/F Ratio:	13 to 1
Year: 4-4-1		Tuition:	$3250
Appl: Mar. 15		R and B:	$1690
875 applied	680 accepted		335 enrolled
SAT: 500V 510M	ACT: 22		COMPETITIVE

Hanover College, founded in 1827, is an independent liberal arts college affiliated with the Presbyterian Church. The library houses 215,000 volumes and 25,000 microfilm items, and subscribes to 1200 periodicals.

Environment: The 600-acre campus is located in a rural setting 40 miles from Louisville, Kentucky. A center for the fine arts is a major feature. Dormitories accommodate most undergraduates. The college also sponsors fraternity and sorority houses.

Student Life: About 55% of the students are from Indiana; the rest come from 30 other states. About 95% of the students live on campus. Thirty percent of the students are Catholic, 60% are Protestant, and 1% are Jewish. Five percent are minority-group members. College housing is single-sex, with visiting privileges. Students may keep cars on campus.

Organizations: Activities include science clubs, a drama group, publications, weekend programs, movies, dances, music groups, a religious group, and cultural events. Five national fraternities and 4 national sororities are represented on campus.

Sports: The college sponsors intercollegiate teams in 8 sports for men and 6 for women. There are 8 intramural sports for men and 8 for women.

Handicapped: About 60% of the campus is accessible to physically handicapped students. Special facilities include wheelchair ramps and parking areas. Special class scheduling is possible.

Graduates: Ten percent of the freshmen drop out by the end of the first year, and 55% remain to graduate. About 45% of the graduates pursue graduate study; 5% enter medical school, 2% enter dental school, and 5% enter law school. Twenty percent pursue careers in business and industry.

Services: Placement and career counseling are available free to students. Tutoring, remedial instruction, and health care are available on a fee basis.

Programs of Study: The college offers the B.A. degree in the following subjects: AREA STUDIES (Asian), BUSINESS (business administration), EDUCATION (elementary, secondary), ENGLISH (English, speech), FINE AND PERFORMING ARTS (art, radio/TV, theater/dramatics), LANGUAGES (French, German, Spanish), MATH AND SCIENCES (biology, chemistry, geology, mathematics, physics), PHILOSOPHY (philosophy, religion), PREPROFESSIONAL (dentistry, engineering, law, medicine, ministry, social work), SOCIAL SCIENCES (economics, government/political science, history, psychology, sociology).

Required: Required courses include English, fine arts, foreign language, Hebrew-Christian thought, independent study, literature, natural science, non-Western studies, philosophy, physical education, social sciences, and speech.

Special: The college sponsors a Junior Year Abroad program; a Washington, D.C., semester; and the Merrill-Palmer Institute. A program in marine science is offered in conjunction with Duke University. Hanover is a member of a 9-college consortium giving students the opportunity to enroll in off-campus courses.

Honors: Eight honor societies have chapters at the college. Honors courses are given, and the departments choose honor scholars based on a GPA of 3.5 in the major area and a 3.2 in overall course work.

Admissions: About 78% of those who applied were accepted for the 1981–82 freshman class. The SAT scores of those who enrolled were: Verbal—22% scored below 500, 51% between 500 and 599, 25% between 600 and 700, and 2% above 700; Math—15% scored below 500, 50% between 500 and 599, 30% between 600 and 700, and 5% above 700. Applicants must have completed 16 Carnegie units, rank in the upper half of their graduating class, have at least a C average, and be recommended by their secondary schools. Other considerations are the reputation and accreditation of the high school, academic achievements, extracurricular activities, leadership record, advanced placement or honors courses, and SAT scores.

Procedure: All candidates are required to take the SAT and an AT in a foreign language. These tests should be taken in April of the junior year or in December or January of the senior year. The application, a transcript, and test scores should be submitted by March 15 (fall) and December 15 (spring). New students are admitted in the fall and midyear. There is a rolling admission plan. The application fee is $10.

Special: AP credit is offered.

Transfer: For fall 1981, 50 students applied, 40 were accepted, and 30 enrolled. Applicants must have a GPA of 2.0 or better. D grades do not transfer. There is a one-year residency requirement. Application deadlines are March 15 (fall) and December 15 (winter).

Visiting: Informal weekday visits may be arranged through the office of admissions. Visitors may sit in on classes and stay overnight at the school.

Financial Aid: Sixty percent of the students receive financial aid. Thirty percent work part-time on campus. The average award to freshmen from all sources was $1000 in 1981–82. The college provides scholarships, loans, and employment. Aid is awarded on the basis of academic achievement, good character, and financial need. Special consideration is given to economically deprived students. The college is a member of CSS. The FAF must be filed. Applications for financial aid are due by April 15 (fall) and December 1 (winter).

Foreign Students: Thirty students come from foreign countries, making up 3% of enrollment. The college provides these students with special counseling and special organizations.

Admissions: Foreign students must score at least 500 on the TOEFL. No college entrance examination is required.

Procedure: Application deadlines are March 15 (fall) and November 15 (winter). Foreign students must present a completed college health form. They must also provide proof of adequate funds for 4 years. Students must carry health insurance, which is available through the college for a fee.

Admissions Contact: C. Eugene McLemore, Director of Admissions.

HUNTINGTON COLLEGE D-2
Huntington, Indiana 46750 (219) 356-6000

F/T: 192M, 211W		Faculty:	33; IIB, −$
P/T: 19M, 34W		Ph.D.'s:	60%
Grad: 44M, 1W		S/F Ratio:	17 to 1
Year: 4-1-4, ss		Tuition:	$3750
Appl: open		R and B:	$1820
184 applied	160 accepted		107 enrolled
SAT: 450V 500M			COMPETITIVE

Huntington College, established in 1897, is a liberal arts college owned and operated by the Church of the United Brethren in Christ. It provides graduate and undergraduate instruction. The library houses 60,000 volumes.

Environment: The college campus is located on 120 acres in a rural area 20 miles from Ft. Wayne. The 10 major buildings include the student union; residence halls, including a new $1-million dormitory, and the Merrilat Physical Education Center, which has 2 gyms, an indoor pool, a sauna, and weight-lifting equipment. The college sponsors off-campus apartments as well as dorms.

234 INDIANA

Student Life: Most of the students are from Indiana; 32 other states and 7 foreign countries are also represented. Forty percent of the students live on campus. Eighty percent of the students are Protestant (25% belong to the supporting denomination) and 10% are Catholic. Two percent are members of minority groups. Students may keep cars on campus. All students are required to attend chapel and convocation 3 times a week. All students under 21 must reside on campus or in college-approved housing.

Organizations: Student organizations and activities include a band, a concert and lecture series, and a choir. There is 1 national sorority and 1 national fraternity; 10% of the students belong. Numerous clubs, social groups, a bimonthly newspaper and various recreational activities also are available.

Sports: The college participates in 7 intercollegiate sports for men and 4 for women. Men may participate in 6 intramural sports, women in 4.

Handicapped: There are no facilities for the physically handicapped.

Graduates: About 5% of entering freshmen drop out by the end of the first year. Sixty percent remain to graduate. Of those, 30% pursue advanced degrees, including 5% who enter law school and 5% who enter medical school. About 25% of the graduates seek careers in business and industry.

Services: Students receive the following services free: psychological counseling, health care, placement, and career counseling. Tutoring and remedial instruction also are offered; fees are charged.

Programs of Study: The college awards the B.A. and B.S. degrees. Master's and associate degrees also are available. Bachelor's degrees are offered in the following subjects: AREA STUDIES (American), BUSINESS (accounting, business administration, business education), EDUCATION (elementary, health/physical, secondary, special), ENGLISH (English, speech), FINE AND PERFORMING ARTS (music, music education), HEALTH SCIENCES (medical technology), MATH AND SCIENCES (biology, chemistry, mathematics), PHILOSOPHY (philosophy, religion), PREPROFESSIONAL (law, medicine), SOCIAL SCIENCES (economics, history, psychology, sociology). Thirty percent of the degrees conferred are in business, 30% in education, and 15% in math and sciences.

Required: All students must take 15 general education courses for the B.S. degree and 18 courses for the B.A. degree. The courses are in the humanities, fine arts, social and natural sciences, and religion.

Special: It is possible to earn a combined B.A.-B.S. degree.

Honors: A chapter of the national honor society Alpha Chi is located on campus. The English department has an honors program.

Admissions: About 87% of those who applied for admission to the 1981–82 freshman class were accepted. The SAT scores of those who enrolled were as follows: Verbal—45% below 500, 40% between 500 and 599, 10% between 600 and 700, and 5% above 700; Math—45% below 500, 40% between 500 and 599, 10% between 600 and 700, and 5% above 700. Applicants must rank in the top half of their class, have a GPA of 2.0 or better, and have completed a college preparatory program of at least 10 academic units. Admissions officers also consider extracurricular activities, recommendations by school officials, leadership record, and evidence of special talents.

Procedure: The SAT or ACT is required. An application fee of $15, the high school record, and test scores should be submitted. Application deadlines are open, and there is a rolling admissions plan. Notification is made about 2 weeks after all the credentials have been received. New students are admitted to all terms.

Special: There is an early admissions plan. AP and CLEP credit is offered.

Transfer: For fall 1981, 40 transfer students applied and 27 were accepted. A 2.0 average and minimum combined SAT scores of 700 are recommended. D grades do not transfer. Five courses must be taken in residence. Admissions deadlines are open.

Visiting: Orientations for prospective students are scheduled regularly, and visitors are welcome on the campus 5 days a week. Guided tours, overnight stays, and class visits can be arranged through the admissions office.

Financial Aid: The college offers scholarships, loans, and grants (including grants based not on financial need but on academic performance). Eighty-five percent of the students receive some financial aid. Twenty-five percent work part-time on campus. The FAF must be filed. Aid application deadlines are open. The college is a member of CSS.

Foreign Students: One percent of the students are from foreign countries. The college provides special organizations for these students.

Admissions: Foreign applicants must score at least 450 on the TOEFL. No other entrance exams are required.

Procedure: Application deadlines are open. Students must present proof of adequate funds. Though students are not required to carry health insurance, insurance is available through the college for a fee.

Admissions Contact: John Schafer, Director of Admissions.

INDIANA CENTRAL UNIVERSITY C–3
Indianapolis, Indiana 46227 (317) 788-3216

F/T: 430M, 828W	Faculty: 110; IIA, – $
P/T: 453M, 1337W	Ph.D.'s: 30%
Grad: 206M, 98W	S/F Ratio: 13 to 1
Year: 4-4-X, ss	Tuition: $3660
Appl: Aug. 15	R and B: $1850
775 applied	752 accepted	346 enrolled
SAT: 413V 452M	ACT: 21	COMPETITIVE

Indiana Central University is a small, private, liberal arts university, established in 1902 and affiliated with the United Methodist Church. It provides graduate and undergraduate studies and has an evening division. The library contains 98,000 volumes and subscribes to 600 periodicals.

Environment: The 60-acre campus is located in a suburban area 5 miles from downtown Indianapolis. It is near major interstate highways and an international airport. There are 3 classroom buildings, a student center, a gymnasium, 6 dormitories that house about 820 students, and 28 apartments for married students.

Student Life: Approximately 96% of the students come from Indiana. About 58% live on campus. Thirty percent are Catholic; 30%, Protestant. About 15% are minority-group members. Campus housing is single-sex and coed, and there are visiting privileges. Students may keep cars on campus. Alcohol is not permitted on campus.

Organizations: There are no fraternities or sororities on campus. Activities include religious groups, student publications, departmental clubs, music groups, debating, and service clubs.

Sports: The university fields 9 intercollegiate teams for men and 5 for women. There are 3 intramural sports for men and 3 for women.

Handicapped: About 95% of the campus is accessible to handicapped students. Facilities include wheelchair ramps, parking areas, elevators, lowered drinking fountains and telephones, specially equipped rest rooms, and a special residence hall. Special class scheduling is also available. Two counselors are available to handicapped students.

Graduates: About 15% of the freshmen drop out by the end of the first year, and 70% remain to graduate. Twenty-five percent of the graduates pursue graduate study. About 1% enter medical school; 1%, dental school; and 1%, law school. Thirty percent pursue careers in business and industry.

Services: Free services include placement aid, career counseling, health care, tutoring, remedial instruction, and psychological counseling.

Programs of Study: The university confers the B.A., B.S., and B.S.N. degrees. Associate and master's programs are also available. Bachelor's degrees are offered in the following subjects: BUSINESS (accounting, business administration, business education, economics, management), EDUCATION (elementary, health/physical, secondary), ENGLISH (English, literature), FINE AND PERFORMING ARTS (art, art education, art therapy, music, music education, music performance, theater/dramatics), HEALTH SCIENCES (medical technology, nursing, physical therapy), LANGUAGES (French, German, Spanish), MATH AND SCIENCES (biology, chemistry, earth science, general science, mathematics, mortuary science, physics), PHILOSOPHY (philosophy, religion), PREPROFESSIONAL (dentistry, engineering, forestry, law, medicine, veterinary), SOCIAL SCIENCES (corrections, economics, government/political science, history, law enforcement, psychology, social sciences, sociology, youth agency administration). Thirty percent of undergraduate degrees conferred are in business, and 25% in health sciences.

Required: All students must take courses in art or music, religion, classics, English composition and literature, a foreign language (for the B.A. only), history of Western civilization, a laboratory science, physical education, speech, and world literature.

Special: Combined B.A.-B.S. degrees are offered. Students may design their own majors. Cooperative programs are available in engineering, forestry, medical technology, and mortuary science.

Honors: The university sponsors an interdisciplinary honors program. Several national honor societies have chapters on campus.

Admissions: Ninety-seven percent of those who applied were accepted for the 1981–82 freshman class. About 27% ranked in the top fifth of their high school class, and 47% in the top two-fifths. For an earlier class, the SAT scores were as follows: Verbal—10% between 500 and 599 and 5% above 600; Math—15% between 500 and 599 and 10% above 600. Applicants must be graduates of accredited high schools, and it is recommended that they rank in the upper half of their class and have at least a C average. They also should have completed 16 units of high school work, with a minimum of 12 in academic areas. Electives in academic subjects are preferred.

Procedure: Either the SAT or ACT is required. The application deadline for fall admission is August 15; students also are admitted in spring and summer. The university uses a rolling admissions plan. The application fee is $10.

Special: An early admissions plan is offered to high school seniors who rank in the top 25% of their class. There is also a deferred admissions plan. AP and CLEP credit is available.

Transfer: For fall 1981, 187 students applied, 181 were accepted, and 64 enrolled. A GPA of 2.0 is required, and the SAT or ACT plus an interview are recommended. D grades do not transfer. Students must take 45 semester hours in residence of the total required for a bachelor's degree. The application deadlines are the same as those for freshmen.

Visiting: The university holds an annual High School Day in the fall. Guides also conduct informal tours; visitors may sit in on classes and stay overnight at the school. Visits are best scheduled on weekdays. The admissions office should be contacted for arrangements.

Financial Aid: About 90% of the students receive aid. The deadline for aid applications is March 1. The university is a member of the CSS. The FAF is required.

Foreign Students: The full-time students from foreign countries represent 1% of enrollment.

Admissions: A minimum TOEFL score of 500 is required. Students must also take the SAT or ACT.

Procedure: The application deadline for fall is August 15; students also are admitted to other terms. The university recommends that applications be filed 1 year in advance. Foreign students must present proof of adequate funds for 1 year.

Admissions Contact: Terry L. Taylor, Assistant Director of Admissions.

INDIANA INSTITUTE OF TECHNOLOGY D–2
Fort Wayne, Indiana 46803   (219) 422-5561

F/T: 375M, 125W	Faculty: 26; n/av
P/T: 65M, 35W	Ph.D.'s: 65%
Grad: none	S/F Ratio: 20 to 1
Year: sems, ss	Tuition: $3240
Appl: open	R and B: $2175
650 applied 500 accepted 200 enrolled	
SAT: 500V 600M	COMPETITIVE

Indiana Institute of Technology, established in 1930, is an independent institution offering undergraduate curricula in engineering, science, business, and leisure studies. The library contains 50,000 volumes and subscribes to 325 periodicals.

Environment: The 25-acre urban campus is located in a city of 200,000 inhabitants. Dormitory facilities accommodate 400 students. The college also sponsors fraternity houses.

Student Life: Most of the students come from the Midwest and the East, and 90% are public-school graduates. About 50% live on campus. Thirteen percent are minority-group members. College housing is coed. Students may keep cars on campus.

Organizations: Extracurricular activities include student government, special-interest clubs, fraternities, and social events.

Sports: The school fields intercollegiate teams in 2 sports for men and 1 for women. There are 7 intramural sports for men and 7 for women.

Graduates: Ten percent of the freshmen drop out by the end of the first year, and 25% remain to graduate. Ten percent of the graduates pursue advanced degrees, and 90% begin careers in business and industry.

Services: The institute provides free placement, psychological counseling, tutoring, remedial instruction, and career counseling. Health care is available on a fee basis.

Programs of Study: The institute confers the B.S. degree. Associate degrees are also offered. The B.S. is offered in the following subjects: BUSINESS (accounting, business administration, computer science, data processing), PREPROFESSIONAL (engineering—aerospace, engineering—chemical, engineering—civil, engineering—computer, engineering—electrical, engineering—mechanical, engineering—management).

Required: All students must complete a core curriculum in the social sciences and humanities.

Special: There are cooperative programs, internships, and work-study options. The institute also offers a program in leisure studies.

Honors: An engineering honor society is represented on campus.

Admissions: About 77% of those who applied were accepted for the 1981–82 freshman class. The SAT scores of those who enrolled were as follows: Verbal—20% were below 500, 75% between 500 and 599, 5% between 600 and 700, and 0% over 700; Math—0% were below 500, 85% between 500 and 599, 20% between 600 and 700, and 5% above 700. A high school average of at least 2.5 and rank in the top half of the graduating class are required, although students not meeting these requirements may be admitted provisionally. Impressions made during an interview, evidence of special talents, and recommendations are also considered.

Procedure: All applicants must submit SAT scores. New students are admitted each term; application deadlines are open. Notification is made on a rolling basis. There is a $25 application fee.

Special: Early decision and early admissions plans are available. CLEP credit is accepted.

Transfer: For fall 1981, 30 students applied, 25 were accepted, and 20 enrolled. A 2.0 GPA is required. D grades do not transfer. One year must be completed in residence as well as half of the 120 to 134 credits required for the bachelor's degree. Application deadlines are the same as those for freshman applicants.

Visiting: Campus tours with student guides may be arranged.

Financial Aid: Seventy percent of the students receive aid. Twenty-five percent work part-time on campus. The average award to freshmen from all sources covered 55% of costs in 1981–82. The institute offers merit and need-based scholarships, BEOG/SEOG, and various loans, including NDSL. The institute is a member of CSS. The FAF and copies of income-tax returns are required and should be filed by April for fall entry.

Foreign Students: Twenty percent of the full-time students come from foreign countries. The institute offers these students an intensive English program, special counseling, and special organizations.

Admissions: Foreign students should score at least 500 on the TOEFL. No college entrance examination is required.

Procedure: Application deadlines are open. Foreign students must present immunization records and proof of adequate funds for 1 year. A special $35 application fee and a $500 tuition deposit are required. Foreign students must carry health insurance.

Admissions Contact: Lance C. Andrews, Director of Admissions.

INDIANA STATE UNIVERSITY

Indiana State University has 2 campuses. The main one, at Terre Haute, is residential, and the newer campus at Evansville is for commuter students.

INDIANA STATE UNIVERSITY B–4
Terre Haute, Indiana 47809   (812) 232-6311

F/T: 5261M, 5232W	Faculty: 636; I, — —$
P/T: 5M, 8W	Ph.D.'s: 65%
Grad: 726M, 859W	S/F Ratio: 16 to 1
Year: sems, ss	Tuition: $1147 ($2635)
Appl: Aug. 15	R and B: $1587
4006 applied 3886 accepted 2454 enrolled	
SAT: 367V 400M ACT: 19	NONCOMPETITIVE

Indiana State University, established in 1865, is a publicly supported institution offering undergraduate and graduate study. It has a College of Arts and Sciences, and schools of Business, Health, Physical Education and Recreation, Education, Nursing, and Industrial Technology. The library contains 801,000 volumes and 339,000 microfilm items, and subscribes to 4667 periodicals.

Environment: The 91-acre campus is located in an urban area. It includes 46 major buildings and physical-education fields. Dormitories, married-student housing, and fraternity houses are provided. There are no sorority houses; sororities have meeting rooms and living suites in the residence halls.

236 INDIANA

Student Life: Eighty-one percent of the students come from Indiana. Fifty-two percent live on campus. Campus housing is both single-sex and coed, and there are visiting privileges. Students under 20 who have not earned 62 hours and do not return to their homes each evening must live in university housing. Students may keep cars on campus. Day-care services are available for a fee.

Organizations: Six percent of men belong to 1 of the 15 national fraternities with chapters on campus; 6% of women belong to 1 of the 14 national sororities. Extracurricular activities include religious organizations for all major faiths and an active student government.

Sports: The university sponsors 12 intercollegiate teams for men and 11 for women. Intramural sports number 7 for men and 6 for women.

Handicapped: About 75% of the campus is accessible to wheelchair-bound students. Adapted residential facilities are available. Other facilities include wheelchair ramps, parking areas, elevators, lowered drinking fountains and telephones, and specially equipped rest rooms. Special class scheduling is possible. About 1% of the students are visually impaired; 15 hours of reading each week is provided free for them.

Graduates: The freshman dropout rate is 25%, and 50% remain to graduate. Nineteen percent of the graduates pursue graduate study; 2% enter medical school. About 77% pursue careers in business and industry.

Services: Students receive the following free services: placement aid, health care, psychological counseling, career counseling, tutoring, and remedial instruction.

Programs of Study: The university grants the B.A. and B.S. degrees. Associate, master's, and doctoral degrees are also awarded. Bachelor's degrees are offered in the following subjects: AREA STUDIES (American, Black/Afro-American, Latin American, urban), BUSINESS (accounting, business administration, business education, computer science, finance, management, marketing, office administration), EDUCATION (early childhood, elementary, health/physical, industrial, secondary, special), ENGLISH (English, journalism, speech), FINE AND PERFORMING ARTS (art, art education, art history, film/photography, music, music education, radio/TV, studio art, theater/dramatics), HEALTH SCIENCES (environmental health, medical technology, nursing, speech therapy), LANGUAGES (French, German, Greek/Latin, Russian, Spanish), MATH AND SCIENCES (biology, chemistry, earth science, ecology/environmental science, geology, mathematics, natural sciences, physical sciences, physics), PHILOSOPHY (humanities, philosophy, religion), PREPROFESSIONAL (aerospace, electronics and computer technology, home-economics, industrial and mechanical technology, industrial technology education, manufacturing and construction technology, social work), SOCIAL SCIENCES (anthropology, economics, geography, government/political science, history, psychology, public administration, social sciences, sociology).

Required: All students must take 6 hours of English, 2 hours of speech, 2 hours of physical education, 11 hours of philosophy and arts, 11 hours of science and mathematics, 11 hours of social and behavioral sciences, and 7 additional hours of supplementary courses.

Special: Students may design their own majors. The college offers a B.G.S. degree. Students may earn a bachelor's degree in 3 years, summer sessions included.

Honors: The history, mathematics, and physics departments offer honors programs. There are 22 national honor societies on campus.

Admissions: Ninety-seven percent of those who applied were accepted for the 1981-82 freshman class. The SAT scores of those who enrolled were as follows: Verbal—33% scored below 500, 11% between 500 and 599, 2% between 600 and 700, Math—35% scored below 500, 23% between 500 and 599, and 5% between 600 and 700. Students must be graduates of accredited high schools and have completed 16 academic units of work. The minimum high school class rank for out-of-state applicants is 50%; in-state students are granted open admission. Students granted conditional admission will be asked to enroll in the freshman opportunity program.

Procedure: The SAT or ACT is required and should be taken by December of the senior year. Applications should be filed with a $10 fee by August 15 (fall), December 15 (spring), May 15 for the first summer session, and June 15 for the second summer session. New students are admitted to all sessions. There is a rolling admissions plan.

Special: Early and deferred admissions plans and an early decision plan are available. AP and CLEP credit is accepted.

Transfer: Almost all transfer applications are approved. The basic requirement is a GPA of 2.0 or better. Grades of C and higher are accepted for credit. Thirty of the 124 hours required for a bachelor's degree must be taken in residence. The deadlines are August 1 (fall), January 1 (spring), and May 15 (summer).

Visiting: Regularly scheduled orientations are held for prospective students. Informal visits, including guided tours, can be arranged with the office of admissions.

Financial Aid: About 45% of all undergraduates receive financial aid; 13% work part-time on campus. The average award to freshmen from all sources was $950 in 1981-82. Loans are available from the federal government, local banks, the university, and private funds, based both on talent and aptitude and on need. Automatic awards to high school valedictorians and salutatorians are given. The university is a member of CSS. The FAF must accompany applications for aid, and the application must be repeated each year by March 1. The application deadline is March 1.

Foreign Students: Six percent of the full-time students come from foreign countries. The university actively recruits foreign students and offers them special counseling and organizations.

Admissions: Foreign undergraduates must score at least 500 on the TOEFL or 75-80 on the University of Michigan Language Test; graduate students must score 550 on the TOEFL or 80-85 on the Michigan Test. The university's own exam also may be used. The GMAT and GRE are required for graduate study. No college entrance exams are required for undergraduates.

Procedure: Application deadlines are August 1 (fall) and December 1 (winter); for the first summer session, applications must be filed 3 weeks in advance, and for the last two summer sessions, 5 weeks in advance. Foreign students must present a Home Health Certificate and show proof of adequate funds for at least 1 semester. They must carry health insurance, which is available through the university for a fee.

Admissions Contact: John F. Bush, Director of Admissions.

INDIANA STATE UNIVERSITY EVANSVILLE A-5
Evansville, Indiana 47712   (812) 464-1765

F/T: 1065M, 1105W	Faculty: 104; IIB, ++$
P/T: 694M, 727W	Ph.D.'s: 80%
Grad: none	S/F Ratio: 21 to 1
Year: sems, ss	Tuition: $992 ($2248)
Appl: Aug. 15	R and B: n/app
1160 applied	1150 accepted 780 enrolled
SAT: 396V 435M	ACT:19 NONCOMPETITIVE

The Evansville campus of Indiana State University was founded in 1965. The library holds 116,000 volumes and 16,700 microfilm items, and subscribes to 580 periodicals.

Environment: The 300-acre campus, located in a suburban area, consists of 12 buildings, including a science center, a university center with conference wing, a medical center, a day-care center, an engineering technology building, an art colony, and a health, physical education, and recreation building. There are no housing facilities. A cafeteria is provided.

Student Life: Almost 90% of the students come from Indiana. About 75% of the entering freshmen come from public schools. Five percent are minority-group members. Students may keep cars on campus. Day-care facilities are available for a fee. Alcohol is forbidden on campus.

Organizations: About 10% of the men belong to 5 fraternities; 10% of the women belong to 4 sororities. Student organizations include the student government, the science club, Alpha Kappa Psi, and other academically related groups. The major social events are the Spring Formal, Homecoming, Spring Week, and Greek Week.

Sports: The university fields 5 intercollegiate teams for men and 4 for women. There are 2 intramural sports for men and 1 for women.

Handicapped: The entire campus is accessible to handicapped students. Facilities include wheelchair ramps, parking areas, elevators, lowered drinking fountains and telephones, and specially equipped rest rooms. About 1% of the students have visual or hearing impairments. There are readers for the visually impaired. A counselor is available to handicapped students.

Graduates: Twenty-five percent of the graduates pursue graduate studies. Two percent enter medical school; 2%, dental school; and 2%, law school. About 30% pursue careers in business and industry.

Services: Students receive the following services free of charge: placement, health care, psychological counseling, career counseling, and tutoring. Remedial instruction is available for a fee.

Programs of Study: The university confers the B.A. and B.S. degrees. Associate degrees are also awarded. Bachelor's degrees are offered in the following subjects: BUSINESS (accounting, business administration, business education, finance, management, marketing),

EDUCATION (elementary), ENGLISH (English), FINE AND PERFORMING ARTS (art, art education), HEALTH SCIENCES (medical technology), LANGUAGES (Spanish), MATH AND SCIENCES (biology, chemistry, mathematics), PHILOSOPHY (philosophy), PREPROFESSIONAL (dentistry, engineering, forestry, law, medicine, pharmacy, veterinary), SOCIAL SCIENCES (economics, government/political science, history, psychology, social sciences, sociology).

Required: All students must take English, speech, and physical-education courses.

Special: Combined B.A.-B.S. degrees may be earned in all four-year programs.

Honors: Six national honor societies have chapters on campus.

Admissions: Ninety-nine percent of those who applied were accepted for the 1981–82 freshman class. Applicants must have a GPA of 2.0 or better. Other factors considered are SAT or ACT scores, rank in high school class, recommendations, and extracurricular and leadership records. Indiana residents are given preference.

Procedure: Either the SAT or the ACT is required. A personal interview is recommended. The application deadlines are August 15 (fall), January 1 (spring), and June 1 and July 1 (summer sessions). Notification is made on a rolling basis. There is no application fee.

Special: Early admissions and early decision plans are offered. A special summer program for minority and disadvantaged students from the Evansville area is held every year by the local office of the Neighborhood Youth Corps. AP and CLEP credit is available.

Transfer: For fall 1981, 455 transfer students applied, 448 were accepted, and 316 enrolled. Applicants must be in good academic standing. A GPA of 2.0 or better is recommended. If the GPA is 2.0 or higher, D grades are transferable. Thirty of the 124 hours required for a bachelor's degree must be taken in residence. Application deadlines are the same as those for freshmen.

Visiting: Regularly scheduled orientations are held for prospective students. Informal visits and guided tours can be arranged any weekday. Visitors may sit in on classes. The admissions office should be contacted for arrangements.

Financial Aid: About 75% of the students receive financial aid. Thirty-three percent work part-time on campus. Academic and athletic scholarships are available to freshmen, as are loans and work contracts. The university is a member of the CSS; either the FAF or the SFS should be filed. Applications completed by March 1 are awarded maximum aid if sufficiently funded by HEW. Secondary consideration is given to applications received after this date.

Foreign Students: One percent of the full-time students are from foreign countries.

Admissions: Foreign students must score a minimum of 500 on the TOEFL. They also must take the SAT.

Procedure: Application deadlines are open; foreign students are admitted to the fall semester only. They must present proof of adequate funds for 1 year. Health insurance, though not required, is available through the university for a fee.

Admissions Contact: Tim Buecher, Director of Admissions.

INDIANA UNIVERSITY

Indiana University, founded in 1820, is one of the oldest state universities in the country. Its philosophy is based on the state's 1816 constitution, which made it the duty of the General Assembly "to provide by law for a general system of education, ascending in a regular gradation from township schools to a state university, wherein tuition shall be gratis and equally open to all." As research and public services have been added to its responsibilities, the University has continued to keep outstanding teaching by a distinguished faculty as its chief objective.

The university has 8 campuses: the main residential campus is at Bloomington; 6 commuter campuses are located at Gary, Kokomo, New Albany, Richmond, and South Bend; the Indianapolis and Fort Wayne campuses are shared with Purdue University.

INDIANA UNIVERSITY AT KOKOMO   C-2
Kokomo, Indiana 46901   (317) 453-2000

F/T, P/T:	Faculty: 65; IIB, ++$
1900 M&W	Ph.D.'s: 75%
Grad: 240 M&W	S/F Ratio: n/av
Year: sems, ss	Tuition: $1250 ($2555)
Appl: July 1	R and B: n/app
500 applied	500 accepted
SAT: 398V 441M	NONCOMPETITIVE

Indiana University at Kokomo, founded in 1945, is a community college for north-central Indiana as well as a 4-year university. The 2-year degree programs are mostly in vocational fields. The library contains about 80,000 volumes and subscribes to about 800 periodicals.

Environment: The 24-acre campus is located in a city of 45,000 people, 45 miles from Indianapolis. One building houses all university activities. There are no dormitories.

Student Life: About 99% of the students come from Indiana. Ninety-eight percent come from public schools. Drinking is prohibited on campus.

Organizations: Student groups include the Black Student Union, the Carriage House Theater, the Nursing and Education Associations, the student senate, drama and choral groups, special-interest clubs, and professional organizations.

Sports: The university has an intramural sports program.

Graduates: About 8% to 10% of the freshmen drop out.

Services: The university provides free career counseling, psychological counseling, and tutoring.

Programs of Study: The university confers the B.A., B.S.Bus., B.S. in Elem.Ed., and B.S.Med.Tech. Associate degrees also are awarded. Bachelor's degrees are offered in the following subjects: BUSINESS (accounting, business administration labor studies), EDUCATION (elementary, kindergarten, junior high), HEALTH SCIENCES (medical technology), MATH AND SCIENCES (biology, physical sciences), PHILOSOPHY (humanities), SOCIAL SCIENCES (social sciences). Two-year degrees are available in banking, criminal justice, engineering technology, finance, fire science, operator supervision technology, nursing, and radiologic technology. A non-degree program in secretarial studies also is offered.

Special: Students may arrange to study abroad through another institution and design their own majors. General studies degrees are available. The university provides the Venture Program for students with special educational needs.

Admissions: All who applied for admission to the 1981–82 freshman class were accepted. Applicants should be high school graduates with above-average scores on the SAT. They should have completed at least 13 high school units and rank in the top half of their class. Candidates applying to all 2-year programs except nursing and engineering technology need only a high school diploma or GED to qualify for admission.

Procedure: The SAT or ACT is required. Candidates planning to continue studying a foreign language or chemistry should take the appropriate ATs. Application deadlines are July 1 (fall) and December 1 (spring). Admissions decisions are made on a rolling basis. There is a $15 application fee.

Special: An early decision plan is available. CLEP and AP credit is accepted.

Transfer: Transfer students are accepted for all classes. D grades do not transfer. Applicants who are Indiana residents must have a GPA of at least 2.0 and a record of good conduct. Out-of-state applicants must have a 3.0 or better. Students must earn at least 30 credit hours at the university of the 120 required for a bachelor's degree. Application deadlines are the same as those for freshmen.

Financial Aid: Academic scholarships, federal grants, and work contracts are available. About 55% of the students receive aid; 25% receive scholarships. Need is the primary consideration in awarding aid. The university is a member of the CSS, and the FAF or FFS must be filed. The deadline for aid applications is February 15.

Foreign Students: Fewer than 1% of the full-time students are from foreign countries.

Admissions: Foreign applicants must take the TOEFL and the SAT.

Procedure: Application deadlines are March 15 for fall admission and October 15 for spring admission. Students must present proof of adequate funds for 1 year.

Admissions Contact: Lois Hathaway, Admissions Counselor.

INDIANA UNIVERSITY AT SOUTH BEND   C-1
South Bend, Indiana 46634   (219) 237-4455

F/T: 725M, 968W	Faculty: 154; IIA, av$
P/T: 886M, 1342W	Ph.D.'s: 83%
Grad: 514M, 744W	S/F Ratio: 15 to 1
Year: sems, ss	Tuition: $987 ($2292)
Appl: see profile	R and B: n/app
865 applied	694 accepted 578 enrolled
SAT: 430V 440M	ACT: 20 LESS COMPETITIVE

238 INDIANA

Indiana University at South Bend is a commuter college offering a broad range of undergraduate programs and a limited range of graduate studies. The library contains 160,000 volumes and subscribes to 1500 periodicals.

Environment: The self-contained urban campus is located in a town of 125,000, 90 miles from Chicago. The physical plant consists of 4 buildings, a food service area with cafeteria, and recreational facilities. There are no student residences.

Student Life: Ninety-seven percent of the students come from Indiana. Ninety percent come from public schools. Thirteen percent are minority-group members. Day-care services are available for a fee. Students may keep cars on campus.

Organizations: There is 1 fraternity and 1 sorority at the university; 10% of the men and 10% of the women belong. Student government and other extracurricular activities are available.

Sports: There are some intercollegiate sports. Five intramural sports for men and 5 for women are offered.

Handicapped: About 95% of the campus is accessible to handicapped students. Facilities include wheelchair ramps, special parking, elevators, specially equipped rest rooms, and lowered drinking fountains and telephones. Special class scheduling is also available. The Office of Disabled Student Services provides assistance to handicapped students. The university has a visual-aid resource center and adaptive equipment to aid hearing-impaired students.

Graduates: Between 30% and 40% of the students pursue graduate study after graduation.

Services: The following services are provided free to students: psychological counseling, placement, and career counseling, and tutoring or remedial instruction.

Programs of Study: The university confers the B.A. and B.S. degrees. Associate and master's degrees are also awarded. Bachelor's degrees are offered in the following subjects: BUSINESS (accounting, business administration, finance, management, marketing, operations and systems management, personnel and industrial relations, quantitative methods), EDUCATION (elementary, secondary, special), ENGLISH (English), FINE AND PERFORMING ARTS (art, music, music education, theater/dramatics), HEALTH SCIENCES (nursing), LANGUAGES (French, German, Spanish), MATH AND SCIENCES (biology, chemistry, mathematics, physics), PHILOSOPHY (philosophy), PREPROFESSIONAL (dentistry, medicine), SOCIAL SCIENCES (economics, government/political science, history, psychology, social sciences).

Special: Summer tours to Europe sponsored by the history, English, and modern language departments are available for variable credit. Work-study is offered in the Law Enforcement Technician program, in which South Bend police department cadets are full-time students and half-time police officers. Combined B.A.-B.S. degrees may be earned in business and arts and sciences. A B.G.S. is offered.

Honors: The university has a general honors program with courses available in a number of subjects within arts and sciences.

Admissions: About 80% of the applicants were accepted for the 1981–82 freshman class. Candidates should have completed 13 Carnegie units, be high school graduates, and rank in the upper half of their class. Other factors influencing the admissions decision are advanced placement or honors courses, recommendations, and leadership record. Admissions criteria are more stringent for out-of-state candidates.

Procedure: Either the SAT or the ACT is acceptable. Priority deadlines for applications are July 15 (fall), April 15 (summer), and December 1 (spring). Notification is made on a rolling basis. There is a $20 application fee.

Special: Qualified minority students who have experienced academic difficulty may be admitted on the recommendation of the university's special services department. AP and CLEP credit is available.

Transfer: Transfer students should rank in the upper half of their high school class and should have completed a college-preparatory curriculum. Grades below C do not transfer. All students must complete, at the university, at least 30 of the 122 credits required for a bachelor's degree. Application deadlines are the same as those for freshmen.

Visiting: Guides are available for informal visits. Visitors may sit in on classes with prior permission. Visits are best scheduled on weekdays. The admissions office should be contacted for arrangements.

Financial Aid: Package aid consists of one-third gift, one-third loan, and one-third work. About 40% of the students receive aid through the university. About 23% work part-time on campus. The average freshman aid award in 1981–82 was $700. The school is a member of CSS; the FAF is required. The deadline for aid applications is February 15 for incoming freshmen and March 1 for upperclassmen and graduate students.

Foreign Students: The university admits foreign students.

Admissions: Applicants must take the TOEFL and the SAT or ACT.

Procedure: Application deadlines are May 1 (fall), October 15 (spring), and March 15 (summer). Foreign students must present proof of adequate funds for 1 year.

Admissions Contact: Connie Horton-Neville, Director of Admissions.

INDIANA UNIVERSITY/BLOOMINGTON C-4
Bloomington, Indiana 47401 (812) 337-0661

F/T: 10,871M, 11,423W Faculty: 1380; I, +$
P/T: 751M, 840W Ph.D.'s: 87%
Grad: 4062M, 3088W S/F Ratio: 16 to 1
Year: sems, ss Tuition: $1193 ($3224)
Appl: July 15 R and B: $1819
11,856 applied 9530 accepted 5434 enrolled
SAT: 460V 507M COMPETITIVE

Indiana University/Bloomington, part of the Indiana University System, was founded in 1820 and provides undergraduate and graduate instruction in the liberal arts, sciences, and professional areas. The campus library contains over 4 million volumes; the rare-book collections are among the finest in the country.

Environment: The 2000-acre woodland campus is located in a suburban setting 50 miles from Indianapolis. The 250 buildings on campus include dormitory facilities for 10,900 single, 1452 married, and 1423 graduate students. The university also sponsors fraternity and sorority houses.

Student Life: About 70% of the students are residents of Indiana, and over 90% come from public schools. Fifty-five percent live on campus. About 13% of the students are minority-group members. Campus housing is both single-sex and coed; there are visiting privileges in single-sex housing. Students may keep cars on campus only after their junior year. Day-care services are available to all students, faculty, and staff for a fee.

Organizations: There are 32 fraternities and 21 sororities on campus; 10% of the men and 8% of the women belong. Extracurricular activities include special-interest clubs, departmental organizations, and publications.

Sports: The university competes in 12 intercollegiate sports for men and 11 for women. There are 22 intramural sports for both men and women.

Handicapped: About 80% of the campus is accessible to handicapped students. Facilities include wheelchair ramps, parking areas, elevators, lowered drinking fountains and telephones, and specially equipped rest rooms. Special class scheduling is also available. A counselor is available to handicapped students.

Graduates: Eighteen percent of the freshmen drop out by the end of the first year, and 52% remain to graduate after 5 years.

Services: Tutoring, remedial instruction, career and psychological counseling, and placement services are available free to students. Health care and psychological counseling are also available on a fee basis.

Programs of Study: The university confers the B.A., B.S., B.F.A., B.Mus., and B.Mus.Ed. degrees. It also offers associate, master's, and doctoral degrees. Bachelor's degrees are offered in the following subjects: AREA STUDIES (Asian, Black/Afro-American, Russian, urban), BUSINESS (accounting, business administration, business education, computer science, finance, management, marketing, real estate/insurance), EDUCATION (adult, early childhood, elementary, health/physical, secondary, special), ENGLISH (English, journalism, literature, speech), FINE AND PERFORMING ARTS (art, art education, art history, dance, film/photography, music, music education, radio/TV, studio art, theater/dramatics), HEALTH SCIENCES (environmental health, medical technology, nursing, occupational therapy, physical therapy, speech therapy), LANGUAGES (Chinese, French, German, Greek/Latin, Hungarian, Italian, Japanese, Portuguese, Russian, Spanish), MATH AND SCIENCES (astronomy, biochemistry, biology, botany, chemistry, earth science, ecology/environmental science, geology, mathematics, natural sciences, physical sciences, physics, statistics, zoology), PHILOSOPHY (classics, humanities, philosophy, religion), PREPROFESSIONAL (dentistry, home economics, law, library science, medicine, pharmacy, social work, veterinary), SOCIAL SCIENCES (anthropology, economics, government/political science, history, psychology, social sciences, sociology).

Required: All students must take English composition and complete a core curriculum.

Special: Study abroad is offered. Students may design their own majors.

Honors: Eight honor societies have chapters on campus. The university offers an honors program.

Admissions: About 80% of those who applied were accepted for the 1981-82 freshman class. The SAT scores of those who enrolled were as follows: Verbal—66% scored below 500, 25% between 500 and 599, 8% between 600 and 700, and 1% above 700; Math—44% scored below 500, 38% between 500 and 599, 16% between 600 and 700, and 2% above 700. Indiana residents should have completed 13 Carnegie units and rank in the upper half of their graduating class. Out-of-state students should rank in the top third of their class. Advanced placement or honors courses, evidence of special talent, and recommendations are also considered.

Procedure: The SAT or ACT is required and should be taken by March of the senior year. Application deadlines are July 15 (fall), December 1 (spring), April 1 (first summer session), and April 15 (second summer session). The university follows a rolling admissions plan. There is a $20 application fee.

Special: Early admissions and deferred admissions plans are available. AP and CLEP credit is accepted.

Transfer: For fall 1981, 1058 students enrolled. Indiana residents need at least a 2.0 GPA, out-of-state students a 2.5. At least 12 months and 62 credit hours must be taken in residence out of the 122 or more credit hours needed for a bachelor's degree. Application deadlines are the same as those for freshman applicants.

Visiting: The university offers regular orientations for prospective students. Guides are available for informal visits. Visitors may sit in on classes. Visits are best scheduled for weekdays. The admissions office should be contacted for arrangements.

Financial Aid: Fifty percent of the students receive aid. Thirty-three percent work part-time on campus. The university awards grants-in-aid, scholarships, loans, CWS jobs, and nursing loans and scholarships. The FAF is required. The application deadline is February 15.

Foreign Students: Six percent of the full-time students come from foreign countries. The university offers these students an intensive English course, an intensive English program, special counseling, and special organizations.

Admissions: Foreign students must score at least 500 to 550 on the TOEFL, depending on their major. The University of Michigan Language Test or the ALIGU may be taken instead. No college entrance examination is required.

Procedure: Application deadlines are May 1 (fall), October 15 (spring), and March 15 (summer). Foreign students must present proof of adequate funds for 1 year.

Admissions Contact: Robert S. Magee, Director of Admissions.

INDIANA UNIVERSITY NORTHWEST B-1
Gary, Indiana 46408 (219) 980-6821

F/T: 543M, 1119W Faculty: 181; IIA, +$
P/T: 779M, 1548W Ph.D.'s: 70%
Grad: 294M, 290W S/F Ratio: 9 to 1
Year: sems, ss Tuition: $987 ($2286)
Appl: July 15 R and B: n/app
1728 applied 1478 accepted 1111 enrolled
SAT: 377V 397M **LESS COMPETITIVE**

Indiana University Northwest, founded in 1959, is a commuter college offering liberal arts and professional programs. Its library contains 102,425 volumes and 4750 reels of microfilm.

Environment: The 27-acre urban campus has 19 buildings, including an $8-million library/conference center. There is no student housing.

Student Life: About 94% of the students are Indiana residents. About 36% of the students are minority-group members. Students may keep cars on campus. Drinking is forbidden on campus.

Organizations: Eight percent of the students belong to the 2 fraternities and 2 sororities on campus. Extracurricular activities include 13 organizations, student government, and various special-interest groups.

Sports: The college offers 5 sports for men and women on an intramural level.

Handicapped: About 38% of the campus is accessible to handicapped students. Facilities, located primarily in 2 newer buildings, include wheelchair ramps, parking areas, elevators, lowered drinking fountains and telephones, and specially equipped rest rooms. Special class scheduling is also available. Special tutoring, readers, and 3 counselors are available to students with physical, visual, or hearing disabilities.

Graduates: Forty-two percent of the freshmen drop out by the end of their first year. About 20% of the graduates continue their education; 1% enter medical school, 1% enter dental school, and 1% enter law school.

Services: Free tutoring, psychological and career counseling, and job placement services are offered to all students. Remedial instruction is available on a fee basis.

Programs of Study: The university confers the B.A. and B.S. degrees. Associate and master's programs are also available. Bachelor's degrees are offered in the following subjects: AREA STUDIES (Black/Afro-American), BUSINESS (accounting, business administration, finance, management, marketing), EDUCATION (elementary, secondary), ENGLISH (English, organizational communication), FINE AND PERFORMING ARTS (art, theater/dramatics), HEALTH SCIENCES (medical technology, nursing), LANGUAGES (French, Spanish), MATH AND SCIENCES (biology, chemistry, geology, mathematics), PHILOSOPHY (humanities), PREPROFESSIONAL (law, medicine, social work), SOCIAL SCIENCES (economics, government/political science, history, psychology, social sciences, sociology).

Special: Courses may be taken on a pass/fail basis. The Special Services Program offers disadvantaged students remedial work during the summer session and tutoring and counseling throughout their college careers. Study abroad and a general-studies degree are available. Students may earn a combined B.A.-B.S. degree in geology under a 5-year program.

Honors: The Arts and Sciences division offers special classes for students with a 3.5 GPA or better.

Admissions: About 86% of those who applied for the 1981-82 freshman class were accepted. In a recent entering class, the SAT scores were as follows: Verbal—16% between 500 and 599, and 5% above 600; Math—25% between 500 and 599, and 6% above 600. Candidates should have completed 13 Carnegie units, have a C average, and rank in the upper 50% of their graduating class. Advanced placement or honors courses and recommendations are also considered.

Procedure: The SAT or ACT is required and should be taken by July of the senior year. Nursing and allied-health students should make an additional application to the appropriate division. The deadlines for applications are July 15 (fall), December 15 (spring), April 15 (first summer session), and May 15 (second summer session). Notification is made on a rolling basis. There is a $20 fee.

Special: Early decision and early admissions plans are available. AP and CLEP credit is given.

Transfer: For fall 1981, 298 students applied, 258 were accepted, and 232 enrolled. A 2.0 GPA is required. D grades do not transfer. Students must spend at least 1 year at the university, earning at least 30 credits of the 120 required for a bachelor's degree. Application deadlines are the same as those for freshmen.

Visiting: Formal orientations are scheduled for prospective students, and special arrangements for informal visits can be made through the admissions office. Visitors may sit in on classes but may not stay overnight at the school.

Financial Aid: Thirty percent of students receive aid. Five percent work part-time on campus. Average aid to freshmen from all sources in 1981-82 was $1500. Scholarship grants, loans, and work contracts are available. The university is a member of the CSS. The FAF should be filed. The application deadline is February 15.

Foreign Students: Fewer than 1% of the full-time students come from foreign countries.

Admissions: Foreign students must take the TOEFL. No college entrance examination is required.

Procedure: Application deadlines are May 1 (fall), October 15 (spring), and March 15 (summer). Students must present proof of adequate funds. There are special fees for foreign students. Health insurance, though not required, is available through the university.

Admissions Contact: William D. Lee, Director of Admissions.

240 INDIANA

INDIANA UNIVERSITY–PURDUE UNIVERSITY AT FORT WAYNE
Fort Wayne, Indiana 46805   D-2
(219) 485-5626

F/T: 2009M, 2035W
P/T: 2278M, 2923W
Grad: 483M, 655W
Year: sems, ss
Appl: Aug. 1
1512 applied   1330 accepted   890 enrolled
SAT: 417V 464M

Faculty: 306; IIA, av$
Ph.D.'s: 65%
S/F Ratio: 13 to 1
Tuition: $1050 ($2000)
R and B: $2600

LESS COMPETITIVE

Indiana University at Fort Wayne was founded in 1917; Purdue University at Fort Wayne, in 1964. The combined school is a state-controlled institution offering programs in the liberal arts and sciences, business, education, and health sciences. The library contains 130,000 volumes and 3000 microfilm items, and subscribes to 1590 periodicals.

Environment: The 410-acre campus is located in a suburban area 5 miles from Fort Wayne. A new classroom building and a gymnasium were recently constructed. The university sponsors no housing facilities, but dormitories are available at a nearby college.

Student Life: Almost all students are from Indiana. Drinking is forbidden on campus. Eight percent of the students are minority-group members. Students may have cars on campus. Day-care services are available to all students for a fee.

Organizations: Fewer than 1% of the students belong to 1 fraternity and 2 sororities on campus. Extracurricular activities include student government and special-interest groups.

Sports: The university fields 7 intercollegiate teams for men and 4 for women. There are 9 intramural sports for men and 9 for women.

Handicapped: The entire campus is accessible to handicapped students. Special facilities include wheelchair ramps, parking areas, elevators, lowered drinking fountains and telephones, and specially equipped rest rooms. Although fewer than 1% of the students have visual or hearing impairments, special readers, tapes, and interpreters are available. A counselor is available to handicapped students.

Services: The following services are available free to students: tutoring, remedial instruction, health care, psychological counseling, and placement. Career counseling sometimes involves a fee.

Programs of Study: The university offers the B.A., B.S., B.S.Ed., B.S.C., B.F.A., B.Mus.Ed., and B.Mus. degrees. Associate and master's degrees are also awarded. Bachelor's degrees are offered in the following subjects: BUSINESS (accounting, business administration, computer science, finance, management, marketing), EDUCATION (elementary, secondary), ENGLISH (English, journalism, literature, speech), FINE AND PERFORMING ARTS (art, music, music education, radio/TV, studio art, theater/dramatics), HEALTH SCIENCES (medical technology, nursing), LANGUAGES (French, German, Spanish), MATH AND SCIENCES (biology, chemistry, earth science—earth science education, geology, mathematics, physics), PHILOSOPHY (philosophy), PREPROFESSIONAL (dentistry, engineering, forestry, law, library science, medicine, ministry, pharmacy, veterinary), SOCIAL SCIENCES (anthropology, economics, government/political science, history, psychology, sociology). American studies is offered as a certificate program. About 17% of the degrees conferred are in health sciences, and 14% are in business.

Required: All students must take English composition.

Special: Study abroad and continuing education programs are offered. Five-year combined B.A.-B.S. degrees may be earned in languages, history, political science, and education. The university also offers the B.G.S. degree.

Honors: Honors programs are available.

Admissions: About 88% of those who applied were accepted for the 1981–82 freshman class. Twenty-nine percent of those who enrolled ranked in the top fifth of their high school class, and 70% ranked in the top half. Candidates should have completed 15 Carnegie units and rank in the upper two-thirds of their class.

Procedure: Either the SAT or the ACT must be taken. Application deadlines are August 1 (fall), December 15 (spring), and May 1 (summer). Notification is made on a rolling basis. There is a $20 application fee.

Special: AP and CLEP credit is given in some departments.

Transfer: For fall 1981, 590 students applied, all were accepted, and 450 enrolled. A 2.0 GPA is required. D grades do not transfer. Application deadlines are the same as those for freshmen.

Visiting: Guides are available for informal visits, and self-guided walking tours are available. Visitors may sit in on classes. Campus visits may be scheduled anytime during school hours; prior notification is requested. The admissions office should be contacted for arrangements.

Financial Aid: About 28% of the students receive aid. Three percent work part-time on campus. Scholarships, federal loans, and work contracts are available. The average award to freshmen was $1400 in 1981–82. The university is a member of CSS. The FAF is required, and applications should be filed by March 1.

Foreign Students: An intensive English course is available.

Admissions: Foreign students applying to Indiana University must apply through the admissions office at the university's Bloomington campus, and those applying to Purdue must apply through the admissions office at Purdue's West Lafayette campus.

Admissions Contact: Phillip A. Kennell, Director of Admissions.

INDIANA UNIVERSITY–PURDUE UNIVERSITY AT INDIANAPOLIS
Indianapolis, Indiana 46202   C-3
(317) 264-4591

F/T: 4231M, 4967W
P/T: 6507M, 7639W
Grad: 6909M&W
Year: sems, ss
Appl: open
3986 applied   3689 accepted   2951 enrolled
SAT: 411V 455M

Faculty: 1171; I, – –$
Ph.D.'s: 45%
S/F Ratio: 8 to 1
Tuition: $1035 ($2550)
R and B: $1445

LESS COMPETITIVE

The Indianapolis campus, founded in 1946, has offered undergraduate and graduate instruction under the auspices of both Purdue and Indiana University since 1969. The library contains 585,805 volumes and over 500,000 microfilm items, and subscribes to 10,601 periodicals.

Environment: The 300-acre urban campus has 30 buildings. There is also an 85-acre medical center. Student housing is limited, since the university is primarily a commuter college. There are, however, some dormitories, on-campus apartments, and married-student housing.

Student Life: About 95% of the students are residents of Indiana. About 3% live on campus. Ten percent are minority-group members. Campus housing is both coed and single-sex; there are visiting privileges in the single-sex housing. Students may keep cars on campus. Day-care services are available to all students for a fee. Alcohol is prohibited on campus.

Organizations: Extracurricular activities include special-interest groups, student publications, student government, and theater. There are no fraternities or sororities.

Sports: The university offers 3 intercollegiate sports for men and 3 for women.

Handicapped: The entire campus is accessible to handicapped students. Facilities include wheelchair ramps, parking areas, elevators, lowered drinking fountains and telephones, and specially equipped rest rooms. Special class scheduling and 2 special counselors also are available.

Graduates: The freshman dropout rate is 40%. About 75% of the graduates enter business and industry.

Services: Free placement and career counseling are available. Fees are charged for some psychological counseling, tutoring, and remedial instruction, and for all health care.

Programs of Study: The university confers the B.A., B.S., B.S.E.E., B.S.M.E., and B.F.A. degrees. Associate, master's, and doctoral degrees are also conferred. Bachelor's degrees are offered in the following subjects: AREA STUDIES (urban), BUSINESS (accounting, business administration, finance, management, marketing), EDUCATION (early childhood, elementary, health/physical, secondary), ENGLISH (English, journalism, speech), FINE AND PERFORMING ARTS (art, art education, art history, radio/TV, theater/dramatics), HEALTH SCIENCES (medical technology, nursing, occupational therapy, physical therapy), LANGUAGES (French, German, Spanish), MATH AND SCIENCES (biology, chemistry, geology, mathematics, physics), PHILOSOPHY (philosophy, religion), PREPROFESSIONAL (agriculture, dentistry, engineering, forestry, law, medicine, ministry, pharmacy, social work, veterinary), SOCIAL SCIENCES (anthropology, economics, government/political science, history, psychology, sociology).

Special: The B.G.S. degree is offered, as are combined B.A.-B.S. degrees. The university's Herron School of Art and its programs in general engineering, and philosophy all have national reputations. Study abroad is available. The university offers a metropolitan studies program for career work in the city.

INDIANA 241

Admissions: About 93% of those who applied were accepted for the 1981–82 freshman class. The SAT scores of those who enrolled were as follows: Verbal—75% scored below 500, 18% between 500 and 599, 6% between 600 and 700, and 1% above 700; Math—54% scored below 500, 30% between 500 and 599, 14% between 600 and 700, and 2% above 700. Candidates should have an average of at least C, be graduates of an accredited high school or have a GED diploma, and rank in the top half of their graduating class (applicants to the schools of technology and agriculture should rank in the top two-thirds). Advanced placement or honors courses and recommendations are also considered.

Procedure: The SAT or ACT is required. Admission is on a rolling basis; freshmen are admitted in the fall, spring, and summer. There is a $20 application fee.

Special: AP and CLEP credit is given. There are early decision, early admissions, and deferred admissions plans.

Transfer: For fall 1981, 2710 students applied, 2241 were accepted, and 1793 enrolled. A GPA of at least 2.0 and good academic standing are required. D grades do not transfer. All students must complete, at the university, at least 30 of the 122–126 credits required for a bachelor's degree. There are no application deadlines; transfer students are admitted to all terms.

Visiting: Orientations are regularly scheduled for prospective students. Guides are available for informal visits. Visitors may sit in on classes. Visits are best scheduled on Fridays. The assistant director of admissions should be contacted for arrangements.

Financial Aid: About 56% of the students receive some form of aid. Twelve percent work part-time on campus. The average award to freshmen in 1981–82 was $1400. The university is a member of CSS. The FAF, SFS, or FFS should be filed. The priority deadline for aid applications is February 15.

Foreign Students: One percent of the full-time students come from foreign countries. An intensive English course, special counseling, and special organizations are available.

Admissions: Foreign students must achieve a TOEFL score of at least 550 and must take the university's English proficiency test. No college entrance exams are required.

Procedure: Foreign students must present proof of adequate funds for 1 year. Health insurance is required and is available through the university for a fee.

Admissions Contact: John C. Krivacs, Director of Admissions.

INDIANA UNIVERSITY SOUTHEAST C-5
New Albany, Indiana 47150   (812) 945-2731

F/T: 839M, 998W		Faculty:	200; IIA, av$
P/T: 989M, 1257W		Ph.D.'s:	80%
Grad: 90M, 218W		S/F Ratio:	28 to 1
Year: sems, ss		Tuition:	$32.50 p/c ($76 p/c)
Appl: open		R and B:	n/app
1150 applied	1130 accepted		980 enrolled
SAT or ACT: required			LESS COMPETITIVE

Indiana University Southeast, one of the 8 campuses of the Indiana University System, was founded in 1941. The library contains 113,000 volumes and 14,500 microfilm items, and subscribes to 600 periodicals.

Environment: The 180-acre campus, located in a suburban area 10 miles from Louisville, Kentucky, includes 4 classroom buildings, a University Center, and an activities building. There are no residence halls.

Student Life: About 97% of the students are residents of Indiana. Approximately 90% come from public schools. Alcohol is forbidden on campus.

Organizations: Three fraternities and 3 sororities have chapters on campus. Extracurricular activities include the student government and special-interest clubs.

Sports: Intercollegiate and intramural sports are offered for men and women.

Handicapped: The entire campus is accessible to handicapped students. Facilities include wheelchair ramps, special parking, elevators, specially equipped rest rooms, and lowered drinking fountains and telephones. A counselor is available.

Services: Free career and psychological counseling and placement services are available.

Programs of Study: The university confers the B.A. and B.S. degrees. Associate and master's programs are also available. Bachelor's degrees are offered in the following subjects: BUSINESS (accounting, business administration, management), EDUCATION (elementary, secondary, special), ENGLISH (English), FINE AND PERFORMING ARTS (art, theater/dramatics), HEALTH SCIENCES (medical technology, nursing), MATH AND SCIENCES (biology, chemistry, mathematics), SOCIAL SCIENCES (economics, government/political science, history, psychology, sociology).

Required: All students must complete a core curriculum.

Special: The university offers associate degrees, the B.G.S. degree, and interdepartmental majors. A certificate is available in women's studies.

Honors: Honor societies are open to qualified students.

Admissions: About 98% of the applicants were accepted for the 1981–82 freshman class. Candidates should have completed 26 Carnegie units. Indiana residents should rank in the upper half of their graduating class; out-of-state applicants in the upper third.

Procedure: Either the SAT or the ACT is acceptable. Application deadlines are open; students are admitted in fall and spring. There is a $15 application fee. The university follows a rolling admissions policy.

Special: Early decision and early admissions plans are available. AP and CLEP credit is given.

Transfer: Applicants must have a 2.0 GPA and must complete at least 1 year in residence, earning at least 26 of the 120 credits required for a bachelor's degree.

Visiting: There are regularly scheduled orientation sessions for prospective students. Guides are available for informal tours. Visitors may sit in on classes. The admissions office should be contacted for arrangements.

Financial Aid: Freshman scholarships, federal loans and work contracts are available. Tuition may be paid in installments. The university is a member of the CSS; the FAF should be filed. About 34% of all students receive aid. The deadline for priority consideration of freshman aid applications is February 15.

Foreign Students: Fewer than 1% of the full-time students are from foreign countries.

Admissions: Foreign students must score at least 500 to 550 on the TOEFL, depending on their major. No college entrance examinations are required.

Procedure: Application deadlines are open; students are admitted in the fall, spring, and summer.

Admissions Contact: Kela O. Adams, Director of Admissions and Marketing Services.

MANCHESTER COLLEGE C-2
North Manchester, Indiana 46962   (219) 982-2141

F/T: 577M, 612W		Faculty:	70; IIB, av$
P/T: 21M, 32W		Ph.D.'s:	70%
Grad: 6M, 5W		S/F Ratio:	15 to 1
Year: 4-1-4, ss		Tuition:	$3600
Appl: open		R and B:	$1710
667 applied	575 accepted		314 enrolled
SAT: 416V 466M			LESS COMPETITIVE

Manchester College, established in 1889, is a liberal arts college affiliated with the Church of the Brethren and serving the central region of Ohio, Indiana, Illinois, Michigan, and Wisconsin. The library houses 154,000 volumes and 7000 microfilm items, and subscribes to 750 periodicals.

Environment: The 200-acre campus, located in a rural area on the edge of a small town, is 35 miles from Fort Wayne. It has 34 buildings, including 6 residence halls that house more than 1200 men and women, a devotional chapel, and a college union. There is a 1300-seat auditorium as well as a new gymnasium. Married-student housing is available.

Student Life: About 70% of the students are from Indiana. Ninety percent live on campus. Fourteen percent are Catholic, and 80% Protestant. Five percent are members of minority groups. Campus housing is both coed and single-sex, and there are visiting privileges. Smoking is permitted in designated areas; alcohol is prohibited on campus.

Organizations: There are no fraternities or sororities.

242 INDIANA

Sports: The college competes on the intercollegiate level in 8 sports for men and 7 for women. Intramural sports number 6 for men and 6 for women.

Handicapped: About 20% of the campus is accessible to handicapped students. Facilities include wheelchair ramps and lowered drinking fountains. Special class scheduling is also available.

Graduates: About 29% of the freshmen drop out by the end of the first year, and 50% remain to graduate. About 40% of the graduates receive their master's degrees within 4 years of graduation. Two percent enter medical school, and 1% enter law school.

Services: Free services include placement, career counseling, tutoring, health care, and psychological counseling. Placement services are also available to graduates.

Programs of Study: The college offers the B.A. and B.S. degrees. Associate and master's programs are also available. Bachelor's degrees are offered in the following subjects: AREA STUDIES (peace studies), BUSINESS (accounting, business administration, business education, computer science), EDUCATION (early childhood, elementary, health/physical, secondary, special), ENGLISH (English, journalism), FINE AND PERFORMING ARTS (art, art education, music, music education, radio/TV, theater/dramatics), HEALTH SCIENCES (medical technology, pre-nursing), LANGUAGES (French, German, Spanish), MATH AND SCIENCES (biochemistry, biology, chemistry, ecology/environmental science, mathematics, physics), PHILOSOPHY (philosophy, religion), PREPROFESSIONAL (dentistry, home economics, law, medicine, social work, veterinary), SOCIAL SCIENCES (economics, government/political science, history, psychology, sociology).

Required: Basic skills, non-Western culture, Western culture/heritage, natural sciences, and social sciences courses are required.

Special: Students may spend their junior year abroad under the Brethren Colleges Abroad program.

Admissions: Eighty-six percent of those who applied were accepted for the 1981–82 freshman class. The SAT scores for those who enrolled were as follows: Verbal—82% scored below 500, 14% between 500 and 599, 4% between 600 and 700, and 1% above 700; Math—60% scored below 500, 28% between 500 and 599, 9% between 600 and 700, and 3% above 700. Applicants should rank in the top 60% of their graduating class, be graduates of accredited high schools, and have acceptable SAT or ACT scores and satisfactory personal references.

Procedure: The SAT (preferred) or the ACT is required. There are no application deadlines. The college follows a rolling admissions plan. The application fee is $10.

Special: AP and CLEP credit is available.

Transfer: For fall 1981, 80 transfer students applied, 51 were accepted, and 34 enrolled. Transfers must have good academic standing at their previous institution. Grades of C or better transfer. There is a 1-year residency requirement; 32 of the 128 semester hours required for a bachelor's degree must be taken at the university.

Visiting: Regularly scheduled orientations are held for prospective students. Guides are provided for informal visits. Visitors may sit in on classes and stay overnight at the school. Visits are best scheduled on weekdays. The admissions office should be contacted for arrangements.

Financial Aid: About 85% of the students receive financial aid; 60% work part-time on campus. Scholarships, NDSL, BEOG, SEOG, and CWS are available on the basis of need and scholarship. Students may also apply for loans from local banks, the college, and other sources. The university is a member of CSS. The FAF is required; applications for aid should be filed by March 1.

Foreign Students: Two percent of the full-time students are from foreign countries. The college offers special organizations and counseling for these students.

Admissions: A minimum TOEFL score of 350 is required. No academic exams are required.

Procedure: The application deadline is August 1 for the fall semester, the only one to which foreign students are admitted. Students must present a completed college-supplied physician's form. They also must present proof of adequate funds for 1 year. They must carry health insurance, which is included in the college's general activity fee.

Admissions Contact: Doraleen Scheetz Hollar, Director of Admissions.

MARIAN COLLEGE   C–3
Indianapolis, Indiana 46200   (317) 924-3291

F/T: 178M, 390W	Faculty: 53; IIB, – – $
P/T: 92M, 226W	Ph.D.'s: 40%
Grad: none	S/F Ratio: 11 to 1
Year: sems, ss	Tuition: $3015
Appl: open	R and B: $1620
500 applied 410 accepted	187 enrolled
SAT or ACT: required	COMPETITIVE

Marian College, founded in 1851 by the Sisters of St. Francis, provides an undergraduate liberal arts education. The library houses 100,000 volumes and subscribes to 588 periodicals.

Environment: The 115-acre campus is located in a suburban area on the northwest side of Indianapolis and has 22 major buildings. Living facilities include dormitories, on-campus apartments, and married-student housing.

Student Life: Ninety percent of the students are from Indiana. Fifty percent reside on campus. Seventy percent come from public schools. Eight percent of the students are minority-group members. Sixty percent are Catholic, and 40% are Protestant. Campus housing is single-sex. Students may keep cars on campus.

Organizations: Student activities include departmental clubs, religious groups, drama, and publications. There are no sororities or fraternities.

Sports: The college fields 4 intercollegiate teams for men and 5 for women. There are 13 intramural sports for men and 10 for women.

Handicapped: Wheelchair ramps, special parking, elevators, and special class scheduling are available. The campus is totally accessible to handicapped students.

Graduates: The freshman dropout rate is 9%, and 55% remain to graduate. Ten percent of the graduates pursue graduate study: 2% enter medical school, 1% enter dental school, and 3% enter law school. Fifty percent enter careers in business and industry.

Services: Fees are charged for health care, placement services, tutoring, and psychological and career counseling.

Programs of Study: The college confers the B.A. and B.S. degrees. Associate degrees are also awarded. Bachelor's degrees are offered in the following subjects: BUSINESS (accounting, business administration, finance, management), EDUCATION (early childhood, elementary, secondary, special), ENGLISH (English, speech), FINE AND PERFORMING ARTS (art, art education, art therapy, music, music education, theater/dramatics), HEALTH SCIENCES (medical technology, nursing), LANGUAGES (French, German, Spanish), MATH AND SCIENCES (biology, chemistry, mathematics, physics), PHILOSOPHY (classics, religion), PREPROFESSIONAL (dentistry, engineering, home economics, law, medicine, veterinary), SOCIAL SCIENCES (economics, history, psychology, sociology). Forty percent of the degrees are conferred in business, 27% in education, and 14% in math and sciences.

Required: All students must take courses in English, theology/philosophy, literature/fine arts, non-Western studies, social sciences, and natural sciences. Students must have completed 128 credits and have at least a 2.0 GPA to graduate.

Special: Four courses outside the college requirements and the student's major may be taken pass/fail. Students in highly technical areas of study can draw on resources of neighboring institutions with a full transfer of credits and grades. Study abroad is available during the junior year. The Division of Business offers a cooperative program for juniors and seniors.

Admissions: Eighty-two percent of those who applied were accepted for the 1981–82 freshman class. For an earlier class, the SAT scores were as follows: Verbal—18% scored between 500 and 600, 4% between 600 and 700, and 1% above 700; Math—27% scored between 500 and 600 and 8% between 600 and 700. On the ACT, 50% scored between 20 and 23, 30% between 24 and 26, and 20% between 27 and 28. Candidates should have completed 16 Carnegie units, rank in the upper half of their class, and have at least a 2.0 GPA.

Procedure: The SAT or ACT is required and should be taken by December of the senior year. There are no application deadlines; freshmen are admitted in the fall, spring, and summer terms. The rolling admissions plan is used. The application should be accompanied by a $15 fee.

Special: AP and CLEP credit is granted.

Transfer: A minimum GPA of 2.0 and a minimum composite score of 800 on the SAT are recommended. There are no application deadlines; transfer students are admitted in the fall, spring, and summer.

Visiting: Visits are best scheduled for weekday afternoons. Guides are provided. Visitors may sit in on classes and stay overnight at the school. Arrangements can be made through the admissions office.

Financial Aid: Eighty percent of all the students are receiving scholarships, grants, loans, or work-study. Nine percent work part-time on campus. College scholarships are awarded solely on the academic record; other awards are based on need. The average award to freshmen in 1981–82 was $1868. The college is a member of CSS. The FAF must be filed. The deadline for submitting the aid application is March 1.

Foreign Students: Four percent of the full-time students come from foreign countries.

Admissions: Foreign students must achieve a TOEFL score of at least 500. No college entrance exams are required.

Procedure: The application deadline is June 1 for fall or winter entry. Foreign students must present proof of adequate funds.

Admissions Contact: Donald R. French, Director of Admissions.

MARION COLLEGE C-2
Marion, Indiana 46952 (317) 674-6901

F/T, P/T:	Faculty: 94; IIB, — — $
1071 M&W	Ph.D.'s: 45%
Grad: 26 M&W	S/F Ratio: 14 to 1
Year: 4-1-4, ss	Tuition: $3560
Appl: open	R and B: $1830
385 applied	325 accepted 254 enrolled
SAT: 410V 435M	COMPETITIVE

Marion College, founded in 1920, is a private liberal arts college affiliated with the Wesleyan Church. The library houses 84,567 volumes and subscribes to 520 periodicals.

Environment: The 38-acre campus, located in a suburban area of Marion, includes 15 buildings, several small homes that are used as residence halls, and larger dormitories.

Student Life: About 60% of the students are from Indiana and 25% are from other Midwestern states. Single-sex dormitories accommodate 50% of the students. Approximately 95% of the students are Protestant; all students are required to attend chapel services 3 times a week.

Organizations: Student organizations include religious groups, publications, and departmental clubs. Musicians, lecturers, and artists are invited to the campus each year. Twice-a-week convocations feature educational and cultural programs. There are no sororities or fraternities.

Sports: The college fields 7 intercollegiate teams for men and 4 for women. Intramural sports also are available.

Handicapped: Ninety percent of the college is accessible to wheelchair-bound students. There are elevators and wheelchair ramps.

Graduates: About 16% of the freshmen drop out by the end of the first year, and 70% remain to graduate. About 40% of the graduates go on to further study.

Services: Students are provided with the following free services: health care, tutoring, remedial instruction, placement and psychological counseling, and career counseling.

Programs of Study: The college offers the B.A. and B.S. degrees. Associate and master's degrees also are conferred. Bachelor's degrees are offered in the following subjects: BUSINESS (accounting, business administration), EDUCATION (Christian, elementary, health/physical, secondary), ENGLISH (English, journalism), FINE AND PERFORMING ARTS (art, art education, church music, music, music education), HEALTH SCIENCES (medical technology, nursing), LANGUAGES (Spanish), MATH AND SCIENCES (biology, chemistry, general science, mathematics), PHILOSOPHY (philosophy, religion), PREPROFESSIONAL (ministry, social work), SOCIAL SCIENCES (criminal justice, economics, government/political science, history, psychology, social sciences, sociology).

Required: Basic courses in education, psychology, fine arts, a modern language, literature, natural sciences, mathematics, religion, philosophy, and social studies are required.

Special: A senior seminar, study abroad, an intersession, and cooperative programs with various agencies in the city are all offered. Combination degree programs are available in medical technology.

Honors: The journalism, religion, and English departments offer honors programs. Pi Gamma Mu and Sigma Zeta have chapters on campus. An honors course is offered for upperclassmen.

Admissions: About 84% of those who applied were accepted for the 1981–82 freshman class. The SAT scores of those who enrolled were as follows: Verbal—60% below 500, 17% between 500 and 599, 15% between 600 and 700, and 15% above 700; Math—65% below 500, 15% between 500 and 599, 15% between 600 and 700, and 15% above 700. Applicants should have ranked in the top half of their high school class, have completed an approved 4-year college preparatory course, and have earned at least a C average. Honors courses and recommendations by school officials are also considered.

Procedure: The SAT or ACT is required. Application deadlines are open; students are admitted to all terms. Admissions decisions are made on a rolling basis.

Special: Early decision, early admissions, and deferred admissions plans are available. CLEP and AP credit is accepted.

Transfer: A minimum GPA of 2.0 is required for transfer. Students must earn, at the college, at least 30 of the 124 semester hours required for a bachelor's degree.

Visiting: There are regularly scheduled orientations for prospective students. Informal visits also can be arranged with the admissions office. The best times are Monday, Wednesday, or Friday, when it is possible to sit in on classes. Visitors also may stay overnight at the school.

Financial Aid: About 80% of the students receive aid. The college provides scholarships, loans, grants, and part-time jobs. The average total award to a freshman from all sources was $3200 in 1981–82. Aid is awarded on the basis of financial need and academic record. Aid applications and the FAF should be submitted by March 1; the final deadline is May 1.

Foreign Students: The foreign students enrolled full-time represent about 1% of the student body. The college provides an intensive English course, special counseling, and special organizations for these students.

Admissions: Foreign applicants must score 550 or better on the TOEFL. They also must take the SAT.

Procedure: Application deadlines are May 1 for fall entry, September 1 for spring entry, and February 1 for summer entry. Students must provide a completed health form and submit proof of adequate funds for 4 years. Health insurance is included in student fees.

Admissions Contact: James C. Blackburn, Director of Admissions.

MARTIN CENTER COLLEGE C-3
Indianapolis, Indiana 46205 (317) 923-5349
(Recognized Candidate for Accreditation)

F/T: 28M, 42W	Faculty: see profile; n/av
P/T: 5M, 5W	Ph.D.'s: n/av
Grad: none	S/F Ratio: n/app
Year: see profile	Tuition: $2275
Appl: see profile	R and B: n/app
26 applied 23 accepted 21 enrolled
SAT or ACT: not required LESS COMPETITIVE

Martin Center College, founded in 1977, is an independent institution offering undergraduate training in business, human services, theology, and communications.

Environment: The 2-acre campus is located in the city of Indianapolis. No housing is provided.

Student Life: Most students are state residents, and all are graduates of public schools. About 75% are black. Students may keep cars on campus.

Organizations: The college offers non-credit seminars. There are no fraternities or sororities.

Sports: The college has no intramural or intercollegiate sports programs.

Handicapped: About half the campus is accessible to physically handicapped students. Facilities include special parking areas and specially equipped rest rooms. Special class scheduling also can be arranged.

Graduates: About 20% of the freshmen drop out by the end of the first year, and 30% remain to graduate. Almost all graduates begin careers in business and industry.

Services: Free placement, career counseling, tutoring, and remedial instruction are available to students.

Programs of Study: The college awards the B.S. degree in AREA STUDIES (Black/Afro-American), BUSINESS (accounting, business administration, computer science, management, marketing), EN-

GLISH (English, journalism, literature, speech), HEALTH SCIENCES (environmental health), MATH AND SCIENCES (mathematics), PHILOSOPHY (humanities, religion), PREPROFESSIONAL (ministry), SOCIAL SCIENCES (government/political science, history, social sciences, sociology). About half the degrees are conferred in business and 25% in the social sciences.

Required: Students must complete 10 general-education units and maintain a 2.0 average to graduate.

Special: Students may design their own majors. The college operates on a rolling-quarter calendar, so students may start at the beginning of any month. All faculty members are part-time. Accelerated programs are available, and credit may be given for prior learning.

Admissions: About 88% of the applicants were accepted for the 1981-82 freshman class. Applicants must be high school graduates and must undergo a personal interview.

Procedure: Students must take Iowa tests for placement purposes. Applications should be submitted at least 15 days before the beginning of the quarter in which the student seeks to enroll. The application fee is $25. Admissions decisions are made on a rolling basis.

Special: Early decision, early admissions, and deferred admissions programs are offered. AP and CLEP credit is accepted.

Transfer: For fall 1981, 25 transfer students applied, 18 were accepted, and 13 enrolled. Applicants must have a GPA of 2.0 or better and at least 3 completed credit hours. An interview is required. D grades do not transfer. Students must complete at least 3 quarters in residence, earning 9 or more of the 36 units required for a bachelor's degree. Application deadlines are August 15 (fall), November 15 (winter), February 15 (spring), and May 15 (summer).

Visiting: Guides are available for informal visits, and visitors may sit in on classes. Visits should be arranged with the academic dean.

Financial Aid: About 25% of the students receive aid through the school; 10% work part-time on campus. Scholarships are available (the average amount is $300 per year; the maximum, $600). The average aid award to a freshman from all sources is $450. Students must submit the FAF by August 15 (fall), November 15 (winter), February 15 (spring), or May 15 (summer).

Foreign Students: No foreign students were enrolled in 1981-82. The college offers an intensive English course. There are no special requirements or fees for foreign students.

Admissions Contact: Stephen D. Wall, Director of Admissions.

OAKLAND CITY COLLEGE A-5
Oakland City, Indiana 47660 (812) 749-4781

F/T: 366M, 227W	Faculty: 28; IIB, --$
P/T: 19M, 40W	Ph.D.'s: 36%
Grad: none	S/F Ratio: 21 to 1
Year: qtrs, ss	Tuition: $3072
Appl: Sept. 1	R and B: $1542
713 applied	713 accepted	338 enrolled
SAT: 374V 426M	ACT: 18	NONCOMPETITIVE

Oakland City College, founded in 1885 as Oakland Institute, is a coeducational, church-related liberal arts college with programs in teacher education, business, ministry, and technical studies. The library houses 63,555 volumes and subscribes to 286 periodicals.

Environment: The 25-acre campus, located 30 miles from Evansville in a rural town of 4000, has an administration building, 6 classroom buildings, a gym, and a chapel. Four dormitories, 3 for men and 1 for women, are all in the campus vicinity. There is also a limited amount of married-student housing.

Student Life: Most students are from Indiana and commute daily. Thirty-five percent reside in campus dormitories. Thirteen percent of the students are Catholic, and 76% are Protestant, of which about 25% are General Baptists. Campus housing is single-sex, and there are visiting privileges. Students may keep cars on campus. Drinking is prohibited on campus.

Organizations: There are no social fraternities or sororities. Extracurricular activities include a choir, a music fraternity, an art guild, an association for childhood education, a dramatics club, a student educational association, several religious organizations, and various sports clubs. The students handle all discipline problems; there is a student judicial court with an attorney. The dean of students works with the student court.

Sports: The college competes intercollegiately in 3 sports for men and 3 for women. Intramural sports include 10 for men and 10 for women.

Handicapped: Although there are no special facilities for physically handicapped students, 100% of the campus is accessible to them. There are no visually impaired or hearing-impaired students, nor are there special counselors.

Graduates: The freshman dropout rate is 20%; 60% remain to graduate. Ten percent of the graduates pursue graduate study. Fifty percent enter careers in business and industry.

Services: Students receive the following services free: personal counseling, health care, tutoring, remedial instruction, and placement and career counseling. In addition to participating in on-campus interviews and career assessment, the student can maintain a placement file.

Programs of Study: The college confers the B.A. and B.S. degrees. Associate degrees are also awarded. Bachelor's degrees are offered in the following subjects: AREA STUDIES (humanities), BUSINESS (accounting, business administration, business education), EDUCATION (elementary, health/physical, secondary), ENGLISH (English), FINE AND PERFORMING ARTS (art, art education, music, music education), MATH AND SCIENCES (biology, chemistry), PHILOSOPHY (humanities, religion), PREPROFESSIONAL (dentistry, law, medicine, ministry, nursing). Twenty-five percent of the bachelor's degrees conferred are in business, 19% are in education, and 11% are in philosophy.

Required: All liberal arts students must take a general studies core component.

Special: The college offers a developmental mathematics and English program for freshmen needing these services, and has a Special Services Program offering developmental assistance. Students may earn a bachelor's degree in 3 years.

Honors: The college has 2 national honor society chapters on campus—Alpha Psi Omega, an honorary dramatic fraternity, and Alpha Phi Gamma, a society for collegiate journalists.

Admissions: The college has an open admissions policy. One-hundred percent of those who applied were accepted for the 1981-82 freshman class. Of those who enrolled, the SAT scores were as follows: Verbal—83% below 500, 14% between 500 and 599, and 4% between 600 and 700; Math—73% below 500, 22% between 500 and 599, 3% between 600 and 700, and 2% above 700. Candidates generally graduate from an accredited or commissioned high school with a C average.

Procedure: The SAT or ACT is required. Application deadlines are September 1 for the fall, and at least 1 week before the beginning of the other sessions. There is a $25 nonrefundable application fee.

Special: There is an early decision plan; candidates should apply in the summer preceding their senior year. Early admission is available, for which a personal interview is required. The college accepts AP and CLEP credit.

Transfer: For the 1981-82 school year, 67 students applied for transfer, all were accepted, and 42 enrolled. Applicants must meet the basic freshman requirements. D grades will transfer if the GPA is at least 2.0. The last 3 academic quarters and 45 quarter hours must be taken in residence. A minimum of 180 quarter hours is required for the bachelor's degree. Application deadlines are the same as for entering freshmen.

Visits: Orientations for prospective students are usually scheduled to coincide with major campus events. Visits are best made during such orientations or on weekdays. Arrangements for guides can be made through the admissions counselors.

Financial Aid: Eighty percent of the students receive financial aid. Eighteen percent work part-time on campus. NDSL and GSL loans are available. The total yearly amount set aside is $1,134,000. The average award to freshmen through the college is $2925. Tuition may be paid in installments. The college is a member of the CSS. The FAF is required. The deadline for filing aid applications is April 1 for fall entry and 4 weeks prior to the beginning of other quarters.

Foreign Students: One percent of full-time students come from foreign countries. Special counseling is available for these students.

Admissions: Foreign students must score a minimum of 500 on the TOEFL and must take the SAT or the ACT.

Procedure: The application deadlines are September 1 for the fall quarter and one week before the beginning of the winter, spring, and summer quarters. Foreign students must present proof of funds adequate to cover 1 year of study. Health insurance is available to foreign students through the college, although they are not required to carry such insurance.

Admissions Contacts: Don Brown, Director of Admissions, and David Masterson, Associate Director of Admissions.

PURDUE UNIVERSITY

Purdue University, established in 1869, is a publicly supported institution the land-grant college of Indiana. It is composed of a number of schools and colleges offering training on both the undergraduate and the graduate level in a wide variety of fields. The University comprises 5 campuses: the main campus at West Lafayette; a regional campus with baccalaureate programs at Calumet; a 2-year campus at Westville (North Central); and 2 campuses (at Indianapolis and Fort Wayne) operated jointly with Indiana University. Descriptions of the West Lafayette and Calumet campuses follow. Profiles of the Indianapolis and Fort Wayne campuses can be found in the book following the Indiana University entries.

PURDUE UNIVERSITY/CALUMET B-1
Hammond, Indiana 46323 (219) 844-0520

F/T: 1511M, 1271W	Faculty: 360; IIA, av$
P/T: 2182M, 2033W	Ph.D.'s: 31%
Grad: 283M, 488W	S/F Ratio: 22 to 1
Year: sems, ss	Tuition: $1250 ($3000)
Appl: open	R and B: n/app
4500 applied	4200 accepted 3830 enrolled
SAT: 400V 420M	LESS COMPETITIVE

Purdue University's Calumet campus, established in 1951, offers undergraduate degrees in the liberal arts and sciences, business, education, nursing and health fields, and technological areas. The library has 125,000 volumes and 6000 microfilm items, and subscribes to 1200 periodicals.

Environment: The 167-acre campus is located in a city of 110,000. There are no residence halls. Facilities include a cafeteria, student lounge, and a physical-education building.

Student Life: About 75% of the students come from Indiana; most of the rest are from neighboring Illinois and Michigan. Almost all come from public schools. Seventeen percent are minority-group members. The university provides day-care services for a fee.

Organizations: There are 4 fraternities to which 2% of the men belong; 1% of the women belong to the 4 sororities. Extracurricular activities include service groups, special-interest clubs, and publications.

Sports: There are 2 intercollegiate sports for men and 2 for women, and 2 intramural sports for men and women.

Handicapped: The entire campus is accessible to handicapped students. Special facilities include wheelchair ramps, parking areas, elevators, lowered drinking fountains and telephones, and specially equipped rest rooms. Three counselors are available.

Graduates: About 36% of the graduates go on for advanced degrees; 60% pursue careers in business and industry.

Services: Health care, placement, psychological and career counseling, tutoring, and remedial instruction are offered free to students.

Programs of Study: The university confers the B.A., B.S., and B.P.E. degrees. Associate and master's degrees are also granted. Bachelor's degrees are offered in the following subjects: BUSINESS (management), EDUCATION (elementary, health/physical, industrial, secondary, technological—architecture, technological—electrical, technological—mechanical), ENGLISH (English), FINE AND PERFORMING ARTS (radio/TV), HEALTH SCIENCES (medical technology), LANGUAGES (French, German, Spanish), MATH AND SCIENCES (biology, chemistry, mathematics, physics), PREPROFESSIONAL (engineering), SOCIAL SCIENCES (history, psychology, sociology).

Honors: Two national honor societies have chapters on campus.

Admissions: About 93% of those who applied were accepted for the 1981-82 freshman class. SAT scores for an earlier class were as follows: Verbal—9% between 500 and 599, 6% between 600 and 700, and 1% above 700; Math—13% between 500 and 599, 9% between 600 and 700, and 3% above 700. Students should have completed 15 Carnegie units, rank in the upper three-quarters of their graduating class, and have at least a C average.

Procedure: The SAT or ACT is required. Application deadlines are open; new students are admitted each semester. Notification is on a rolling basis. There is no application fee.

Special: AP and CLEP credit is available.

Transfer: For fall 1981, 700 students applied, 650 were accepted, and 500 enrolled. Indiana residents need at least a C average; non-residents need a C+. Students must spend at least 1 year in residence, earning at least 33 of the 126 credits required for a bachelor's degree.

INDIANA 245

Visiting: There are regularly scheduled orientations for prospective students. Guides are available for informal campus tours. Students may sit in on classes. The admissions office should be contacted for arrangements.

Financial Aid: Thirty percent of the students receive financial aid. Thirty percent work part-time on campus. The university offers scholarships, loans, grants, and CWS. The university is a member of CSS. The FAF is required. The aid application deadline is March 3.

Foreign Students: Foreign students must apply through the West Lafayette campus.

Admissions Contact: John P. Fruth, Director of Admissions and Financial Aid.

PURDUE UNIVERSITY/WEST LAFAYETTE B-3
West Lafayette, Indiana 47907 (317) 494-1776

F/T: 15,513M, 10,950W	Faculty: 1800; I, +$
P/T: 577M, 572W	Ph.D.'s: 98%
Grad: 3354M, 1831W	S/F Ratio: 9 to 1
Year: sems, ss	Tuition: $1158 ($3118)
Appl: Nov. 15	R and B: $2050
16,900 applied	13,667 accepted 6321 enrolled
SAT: 456V 531M	COMPETITIVE

Purdue University's main campus, established in 1869, is a publicly supported institution offering undergraduate and graduate degree programs in a wide range of disciplines. The university's library has a collection of 1.5 million volumes and 700,000 microtexts, and subscribes to 15,000 periodicals.

Environment: The 1556-acre suburban campus is located in a community of 70,000, about 70 miles from Indianapolis. Facilities include the Life Science Building and the Potter Engineering Center. Residence halls accommodate 13,000 students. Married-student housing is also provided, and facilities are available for commuting students.

Student Life: About 75% of the students come from Indiana, and 90% come from public schools. Forty-five percent live on campus. Eleven percent of the students are minority-group members. University housing is both single-sex and coed; there are visiting privileges in single-sex housing. Only juniors and seniors may keep cars on campus.

Organizations: Eighteen percent of the men belong to the 45 fraternities, and the 16 sororities attract 22% of the women. Extracurricular activities include student government, special-interest groups, publications, departmental organizations, and religious groups.

Sports: Intercollegiate and intramural programs are provided for men and women.

Handicapped: About 60% of the campus is accessible to handicapped students. Special facilities include wheelchair ramps, parking areas, elevators, lowered drinking fountains and telephones, and specially equipped rest rooms. Special class scheduling is also available.

Graduates: Four percent of the freshmen drop out by the end of their first year. Seventy-two percent remain to graduate. About 30% of the graduates go on to graduate or professional schools; 70% enter careers in business and industry.

Services: Offered free to students are career counseling, placement, tutoring, remedial instruction, psychological counseling, and outpatient health care. Tutoring is also available on a fee basis.

Programs of Study: The university confers the B.A., B.S., B.F.A., and B.P.E. degrees. Associate, master's, and doctoral degrees are also granted. Bachelor's degrees are offered in the following subjects: AREA STUDIES (American, Black/Afro-American, medieval), BUSINESS (accounting, business administration, computer science, finance, management, marketing), EDUCATION (early childhood, elementary, health/physical, industrial, secondary, special), ENGLISH (English, journalism, literature, speech), FINE AND PERFORMING ARTS (art, art education, art history, film/photography, interior design, radio/TV, studio art, theater/dramatics, visual design), HEALTH SCIENCES (environmental health, medical technology, nursing, speech therapy), LANGUAGES (French, German, Russian, Spanish), MATH AND SCIENCES (biochemistry, biology, botany, chemistry, earth science, ecology/environmental science, geology, mathematics, natural sciences, physical sciences, physics, statistics, zoology), PHILOSOPHY (philosophy), PREPROFESSIONAL (agriculture, engineering, forestry, home economics, library science, pharmacy, technologies, veterinary), SOCIAL SCIENCES (anthropology, economics, government/political science, history, international relations, psychology, social sciences, sociology). About 51% of the degrees are awarded in preprofessional areas.

246 INDIANA

Required: In most majors, students must take courses in English, mathematics, science, and social science.

Special: Students may design their own majors. Independent study and study abroad are offered. Combined B.A.-B.S. degrees may be earned in education. Cooperative work/study 5-year programs in technical and scientific areas are also available.

Honors: Phi Beta Kappa has a chapter on campus, and most departments offer honors programs.

Admissions: About 81% of those who applied were accepted for the 1981-82 freshman class. The SAT scores of those who enrolled were as follows: Verbal—50% below 500, 35% between 500 and 599, 14% between 600 and 700, and 1% above 700; Math—38% below 500, 35% between 500 and 599, 37% between 600 and 700, and 5% above 700. Applicants must be graduates of accredited high schools, have completed 15 academic units with a C+ average or better, and rank in the top half of their graduating class. Preference is given to state residents; standards are higher for out-of-state applicants.

Procedure: Either the SAT or the ACT is required. Application deadlines are November 15 (fall), December 15 (spring), and May 15 (summer). Notification is made on a rolling basis. There is no application fee.

Special: AP and CLEP credit is available. There is an early admissions plan.

Transfer: For fall 1981, 2432 students applied, 1942 were accepted, and 961 enrolled. A 2.5 average is required; D grades do not transfer. Students must spend at least 1 year at the university, completing at least 32 of the 128 hours required for a bachelor's degree. Application deadlines are the same as those for freshman applicants.

Visiting: There are regularly scheduled orientation programs for prospective applicants. Informal campus tours may be arranged; students may sit in on classes. Visits are best scheduled on weekdays. The admissions office should be contacted for arrangements.

Financial Aid: Fifty-four percent of the students receive financial aid. The university offers scholarships, loans, grants, and employment. The university is a member of CSS. The FAF should be submitted by February 15.

Foreign Students: About 4% of the full-time students come from foreign countries. The university offers these students an intensive English course, special counseling, and special organizations.

Admissions: Foreign students must score at least 550 on the TOEFL. No college entrance examination is required.

Procedure: Application deadlines are January 1 (fall) and October 1 (spring). Foreign students must present a written explanation of any health problems. They also must present proof of adequate funds for 1 year. They must carry health insurance, which is available through the university for a fee.

Admissions Contact: James R. Kraynak, Director of Admissions.

ROSE-HULMAN INSTITUTE OF TECHNOLOGY
B-4

Terre Haute, Indiana 47803   (812) 877-1511

```
F/T: 1250M            Faculty:    85; IIB, ++$
P/T: none             Ph.D.'s:    82%
Grad: 15M             S/F Ratio:  16 to 1
Year: qtrs            Tuition:    $4140
Appl: open            R and B:    $1995
2200 applied      1300 accepted         356 enrolled
SAT: 540V 670M    ACT: 31  HIGHLY COMPETITIVE+
```

Founded in 1874, Rose-Hulman Institute of Technology is a private, independent professional college for men. It provides both graduate and undergraduate instruction in the fields of science and engineering. The library houses 50,000 volumes and subscribes to 300 periodicals.

Environment: The 125-acre campus is located in a rural area 2 miles from Terre Haute. The 9 buildings on campus include a student center and a field house. Living facilities include 7 dormitories, fraternity houses, and on-campus apartments.

Student Life: About 60% of the students are from Indiana. About 75% come from public schools. Ninety percent live on campus. Two percent are minority-group members. College housing is single-sex, and there are visiting privileges. Students may keep cars on campus.

Organizations: There are 7 fraternities on campus, and 43% of the students are members. Activities include special-interest clubs, publications, a band, and a dance group. Cultural offerings include art shows, concerts, and plays.

Sports: The institute fields 10 intercollegiate teams. There are 9 intramural sports.

Handicapped: There are no special facilities for handicapped students.

Graduates: Seven percent of the freshmen drop out by the end of the first year, and 75% remain to graduate. Fifteen percent of the graduates go on to graduate schools. About 85% pursue careers in business and industry.

Services: The following services are available free to students: placement, career counseling, health care, psychological counseling, tutoring, and remedial instruction.

Programs of Study: The institute offers the B.S. degree. Master's degrees are also conferred. Bachelor's degrees are offered in the following subjects: BUSINESS (computer science, mathematical economics), MATH AND SCIENCES (chemistry, mathematics, physics), PREPROFESSIONAL (engineering—chemical, engineering—civil, engineering—electrical, engineering—mechanical). Eighty-five percent of undergraduate degrees are awarded in engineering.

Required: Freshmen are required to take courses in calculus, chemistry, graphics, humanities, physics, and ROTC.

Special: Rose-Hulman offers independent study, a maximum of 15 hours a week in work-study programs, and a liberal approach to engineering education. Students also may earn a Technical Translator's Certificate in Russian and German.

Honors: Honors programs are offered in chemistry and mathematics. Blue Key and Tau Beta Pi have chapters on campus.

Admissions: About 59% of those who applied were accepted for the 1981-82 freshman class. The SAT scores of those who enrolled were as follows: Verbal—30% scored below 500, 46% between 500 and 599, 21% between 600 and 700, and 3% above 700; Math—0% scored below 500, 17% between 500 and 599, 50% between 600 and 700, and 33% above 700. Applicants must be high school graduates, rank in the upper third of their high school class and have completed 16 units of high school work. Other factors considered are extracurricular activities, recommendations by school officials, leadership record, and impressions made during an interview.

Procedure: The SAT or ACT should be taken no later than December of the senior year. Application deadlines are open; students are admitted only in fall. Notification is made on a rolling basis beginning about 2 weeks after all credentials are received. A $20 fee must be submitted with the application, high school record, and test scores.

Special: CLEP credit is available on a limited basis.

Transfer: For fall 1981, 20 students enrolled. Transfer students need a GPA of at least 2.5 and must present either SAT or ACT scores. An interview is recommended. D grades are not acceptable. Application deadlines are open.

Visiting: Orientations for prospective students are held regularly. Visitors may sit in on classes and stay overnight at the school. Visits are best scheduled on weekdays. The admissions office should be contacted for arrangements.

Financial Aid: Eighty-five percent of the students receive financial aid. Fifty percent work part-time on campus. Average aid to freshmen in 1981-82 was $3800. The institute provides scholarships and loans, and is a member of CSS. Aid is awarded on the basis of financial need and academic record. The FAF must be filed with the aid application, which is due by February 15.

Foreign Students: Fewer than 1 percent of the full-time students come from foreign countries.

Admissions: Foreign students must achieve a TOEFL score of at least 550 and a combined SAT score of at least 1000.

Procedure: Application deadlines are open; students are admitted only in fall. Foreign students must present proof of adequate funds.

Admissions Contact: Charles G. Howard, Director of Admissions.

SAINT FRANCIS COLLEGE
D-2

Fort Wayne, Indiana 46808   (219) 432-3551

```
F/T: 109M, 254W       Faculty:    36; IIA, --$
P/T: 132M, 308W       Ph.D.'s:    50%
Grad: 254M, 169W      S/F Ratio:  11 to 1
Year: sems, ss        Tuition:    $2794
Appl: open            R and B:    $1900
371 applied       289 accepted         200 enrolled
SAT: 425V 470M    ACT: 20              COMPETITIVE
```

Saint Francis College is a Roman Catholic liberal arts college operated by the Sisters of St. Francis. It provides graduate and undergraduate instruction. The library houses 71,210 volumes and 274,514 microfilm items, and subscribes to 565 periodicals.

Environment: The campus covers more than 71 acres in suburban Fort Wayne. Dormitories are provided.

Student Life: About 75% of the students are from Indiana. Twenty-three percent reside on campus; all single men and women under 21 must do so unless living with relatives. About 50% of the students are Catholic; 30% are Protestant. Three percent are members of minority groups. College housing is single-sex, and there are no visiting privileges. Students may keep cars on campus.

Organizations: Ten percent of the men belong to the 1 local fraternity, and 3% of the women belong to the 1 local sorority. Extracurricular activities include the student council, religious groups, a weekly newspaper, and special-interest clubs. The Student Government Association sponsors Homecoming, Winter Derby, and Little Regatta.

Sports: The college competes on an intercollegiate level in 6 sports for men and 4 for women. There are 3 intramural sports for men and 3 for women.

Handicapped: About 75% of the campus is accessible to the physically handicapped. There are special parking areas, elevators, and specially equipped restrooms.

Graduates: Forty percent of the freshmen drop out by the end of the first year, and 37% remain to graduate. Fifteen percent of the graduates pursue graduate study; 1% enter medical school, 1% dental school, and 2% law school. Twenty percent pursue careers in business and industry.

Services: Students receive free placement, health care, psychological counseling, career counseling, tutoring, and remedial instruction. Placement services also are available for graduates.

Programs of Study: The college offers the B.A., B.S., B.S.W., and B.S.Ed. degrees. Associate and master's programs are also available. Bachelor's degrees are offered in the following subjects: AREA STUDIES (American), BUSINESS (accounting, business administration, business education), EDUCATION (elementary, health/physical, secondary, special), ENGLISH (English), FINE AND PERFORMING ARTS (art, art education), HEALTH SCIENCES (medical technology, nursing), MATH AND SCIENCES (biology, chemistry, general science), PREPROFESSIONAL (dentistry, law, medicine, social work), SOCIAL SCIENCES (psychology, social sciences).

Required: All students are required to take English, fine arts, mathematics and science, philosophy, psychology, social science, and religious studies. Candidates for graduation must pass the U.R.E.

Special: The college offers independent study.

Honors: Delta Epsilon Sigma has a chapter on campus.

Admissions: Seventy-eight percent of the students who applied were accepted for the 1981-82 freshman class. The SAT scores of those who enrolled were as follows: Verbal—72% scored below 500, 23% between 500 and 599, 4% between 600 and 700, and none above 700; Math—61% scored below 500, 31% between 500 and 599, 6% between 600 and 700, and 1% above 700. Of those who took the ACT, 57% scored below 21, 21% between 21 and 23, 7% between 24 and 25, 7% between 26 and 28, and 7% above 28. Applicants must have completed 16 academic units of secondary school work and rank in the upper half of their graduating class. An interview is recommended.

Procedure: Either the ACT or the SAT is required. The SAT should be taken during the first semester of the senior year. There are no application deadlines; students are admitted to all terms. Notification is usually made within 2 weeks after the application is received. There is a rolling admissions plan. The application fee is $20.

Special: Students from nonaccredited high schools are given special consideration. There is a deferred admissions plan. CLEP credit is given.

Transfer: For fall 1981, 54 transfer students applied, 45 were accepted, and 27 enrolled. A minimum GPA of 2.0 is required. D grades may be acceptable in some cases. Thirty-two of the 128 semester hours required for a bachelor's degree must be taken in residence. A rolling admissions policy is employed. The application fee is $23. There are no application deadlines.

Visiting: Guided tours and interviews can be scheduled for any weekday. Overnight accommodations are available. All arrangements should be through the admissions office.

Financial Aid: About 80% of all students receive aid; 18% work part-time on campus. The average award to freshmen from all sources was $2500 in 1931-82. The college offers its own scholarships and work-study programs. NDSL, Pell, CWS, and federally insured student loan funds also are available. Special consideration is given to economically deprived students. The college is a member of CSS. The FAF is required. The deadlines for aid applications are March 1 (fall) and December 1 (spring).

Foreign Students: Six foreign students were enrolled in 1981-82.

Admissions: A minimum TOEFL score of 500 is required. No college entrance exams are necessary.

Procedure: Application deadlines are June 1 (fall) and October 1 (spring). Foreign students must present proof of adequate funds for 1 year. Health insurance, though not required, is available through the college for a fee.

Admissions Contact: V. Peter Pitts, Director of Admissions.

SAINT JOSEPH'S COLLEGE B-2
Rensselaer, Indiana 47978 (219) 866-7111

F/T: 620M, 380W Faculty: 62; IIB, +$
P/T: 10M, 10W Ph.D.'s: 65%
Grad: 100M, 100W S/F Ratio: 16 to 1
Year: sems, ss Tuition: $3660
Appl: Aug. 1 R and B: $1900
1040 applied 743 accepted 326 enrolled
SAT: 453V 482M ACT: 21 COMPETITIVE

Saint Joseph's College, affiliated with the Roman Catholic Church, is a coeducational liberal arts college offering programs in teaching and business. The library contains 175,000 volumes and 60,000 microfilm items, and subscribes to 1500 periodicals.

Environment: The 160-acre campus is located on in a rural area, 75 miles from Chicago. There are 9 residence halls, 2 for women and 7 for men. Among the 23 buildings that are located on campus is Drexel Hall, built in 1889, a state historic landmark.

Student Life: About 50% of the students come from Indiana. Ninety-five percent live on campus. Seventy-eight percent are Catholic, 21% are Protestant, and 1% are Jewish. Nine percent are members of minority groups. Dormitories are single-sex; there are visiting privileges. Students may keep cars on campus.

Organizations: Although no Greek letter organizations have chapters on campus, there are various recreational groups, clubs, and activities.

Sports: The college participates in 8 intercollegiate sports for men and 6 for women. Fifteen intramural sports are offered for men and 13 for women.

Handicapped: About 50% of the campus is accessible to wheelchair-bound students. Special class scheduling and special rest room facilities are available.

Graduates: Twenty-two percent of the freshmen drop out during the first year, and 56% remain to graduate. About 28% of the graduates seek advanced degrees. Approximately 1% enter medical school and 3% enter law school. About 62% pursue careers in business and industry.

Services: Students receive free placement and career counseling. Health care, remedial instruction, tutoring, and psychological counseling are available on a fee basis. Placement services include on-campus interviews and credential files.

Programs of Study: The college awards the B.A., B.B.A. and B.S. degrees. Master's degrees also are available. Bachelor's degrees are offered in the following subjects: AREA STUDIES (international studies), BUSINESS (accounting, business administration, computer science, finance, management, marketing), EDUCATION (elementary, health/physical, secondary), ENGLISH (English), FINE AND PERFORMING ARTS (communications/theater arts, music, music education), HEALTH SCIENCES (medical technology), MATH AND SCIENCES (biology, chemistry, earth science, ecology/environmental science, geology, mathematics, physics), PHILOSOPHY (philosophy, religion), PREPROFESSIONAL (agriculture, dentistry, engineering, law, medicine), SOCIAL SCIENCES (economics, government/political science, history, psychology, sociology). Forty percent of degrees conferred are in business, 23% are in the social sciences, and 14% are in preprofessional programs.

Required: All students are required to take a core of interdisciplinary courses in the contemporary world, the modern world, Western heritage, non-Western studies, science, Christianity, and the human situation.

Special: Students may earn a combined B.A.-B.S. degree in agriculture and engineering. Independent study is possible in most fields. Preprofessional programs and combination degree programs in medical technology are offered in affiliation with other universities. There is a pass/fail option in elective courses, and a junior year abroad may be arranged.

Honors: The Blue Key National Honorary Society has a chapter on campus.

Admissions: About 71% of those who applied were accepted for the 1981-82 freshman class. The SAT scores of those who enrolled were as follows: Verbal—39% below 500, 37% between 500 and 599, 21% between 600 and 700, and 3% above 700; Math—34% below 500, 41% between 500 and 599, 21% between 600 and 700, and 4% above 700. Applicants must be graduates of an accredited, reputable high school, have a C average or better, and have completed 15 Carnegie units. Other factors besides test scores include, in decreasing order of importance, leadership record, personality, evidence of special talents, impressions made during an interview, recommendations by school officials, extracurricular activities record, and advanced placement or honors courses.

Procedure: The SAT should be taken in May of the junior year or in December or January of the senior year. The ACT also is acceptable. The application, a $10 fee, test scores, and high school record should be submitted by August 1 for fall admission or December 1 for spring. Notification will be made on a rolling basis. The college subscribes to the CRDA.

Special: Early admissions, early decision, and deferred admissions plans are offered. AP and CLEP credit is available.

Transfer: For fall 1981, 106 students applied for transfer, 78 were accepted, and 44 enrolled. A GPA of 2.0 is required. The last 30 hours must be taken in residence. Application deadlines are the same as those for freshmen.

Visiting: There is a 4-day orientation program in August, a 2-day program in January, and a summer preview in July to acquaint prospective students with the college. Informal weekday visits may be arranged. Visitors may sit in on classes and stay overnight at the school.

Financial Aid: Freshman scholarships total $116,000. Aid is also available through a federal loan fund, local banks, and private sources. The Trustee Scholarship, which pays half of tuition costs, is awarded to students in the top 15% of their class with combined SAT scores of at least 1000. Twenty-three percent of the students work part-time on campus. Between 60% to 70% of all students receive aid, which is most often based on need and academic record. The average freshman scholarship is $1700. Priority application deadlines are May 1 for fall admission and November 1 for spring admission. The FAF or FFS must be filed; the college is a member of CSS.

Foreign Students: One percent of the full-time students are from foreign countries.

Admissions: Foreign applicants must take the TOEFL. No minimum score or further entrance exams are required.

Procedure: Application deadlines are the same as those for other prospective students. Applicants from foreign countries must present proof of adequate funds for 1 year. Foreign students are required to carry health insurance, which is available from the college for a fee.

Admissions Contact: William T. Craig, Director of Admissions.

SAINT MARY-OF-THE-WOODS COLLEGE B-4
Saint Mary-of-the-Woods, Indiana 47876   (812) 535-4141

F/T: 380W	Faculty:	52; n/av
P/T: 310W	Ph.D.'s:	50%
Grad: none	S/F Ratio:	9 to 1
Year: sems	Tuition:	$3611
Appl: open	R and B:	$1802
199 applied	184 accepted	105 enrolled
SAT: 410V 410M	ACT: 19	LESS COMPETITIVE

Saint Mary-of-the-Woods College, founded in 1840, is a private liberal arts college for women conducted by the Sisters of Providence. The library houses 132,000 volumes and 800 microfilm items, and subscribes to over 400 periodicals.

Environment: The 67-acre campus is located in a rural area 4 miles from Terre Haute. The 10 buildings on campus include 2 residence halls that accommodate 475 students.

Student Life: Fifty percent of the students are from Indiana. The majority attended public schools. Nineteen percent are minority-group members. There are visiting privileges in college housing. Students may keep cars on campus. Forty percent of the students leave campus on weekends.

Organizations: Fifteen percent of the students belong to 1 of the 3 national sororities on campus. Extracurricular activities include religious groups and special-interest clubs. Cultural events include art shows, concerts, films, plays, and recitals. Major social events are scheduled by the student senate.

Sports: The college fields 5 intercollegiate teams. There are 5 intramural sports.

Handicapped: There are no special facilities for the handicapped. A few visually or hearing-impaired students are enrolled.

Graduates: The freshmen dropout rate is 30%, and 45% of the freshmen remain to graduate. Thirty-three percent pursue graduate study after graduation; 2% enter medical school, and 2% enter law school. More than 50% pursue careers in business and industry.

Services: Students receive the following free services: health care, tutoring, remedial instruction, placement, and career counseling.

Programs of Study: The college awards the B.A. and B.S. degrees. Associate degrees are also offered. Bachelor's degrees are awarded in the following subjects: BUSINESS (accounting, business administration, business education, management, marketing), EDUCATION (early childhood, elementary, secondary, special), ENGLISH (English, journalism), FINE AND PERFORMING ARTS (art, art education, music, music education, studio art, theater/dramatics), HEALTH SCIENCES (medical technology), LANGUAGES (French, Spanish, translator training), MATH AND SCIENCES (biology, chemistry, general science, mathematics), PHILOSOPHY (humanities, religion), PREPROFESSIONAL (home economics, law, medicine, social work), SOCIAL SCIENCES (history, psychology).

Required: All students must take English composition, humanities, physical education, science-mathematics, sociology-psychology, speech, and theology-religion.

Special: Combined B.A.-B.S. degrees may be earned. Students may design their own majors and spend their junior year abroad. There is a consortium with Indiana State University, the Rose-Hulman Institute of Technology, Wabash College, Depauw University, and Indiana Vocational Technical College. The WED (Women's External Degree) program provides educational opportunities to women over 22 years of age. Nineteen majors are available in this program; students study mostly at home, spending 2 to 3 days at the college every 6 months. The English Language Institute, a program offering intensive study in English language and American culture, is offered twice for a 4-month duration or once for a 3-month duration each year.

Admissions: Ninety-two percent of those who applied were accepted for the 1981-82 freshman class. The SAT scores of those who enrolled were as follows: Verbal—66% scored below 500, 26% between 500 and 599, 7% between 600 and 700, and 1% above 700; Math—69% scored below 500, 25% between 500 and 599, 5% between 600 and 700, and 1% above 700. Of those who took the ACT, 48% scored below 21, 37% between 21 and 23, 7% between 24 and 25, 7% between 26 and 28, and 1% above 28. Applicants should have completed 16 high school units, rank in the upper half of their class, and have a GPA of at least 2.0 and a minimum combined SAT score of 850. The college considers the following factors important: impressions made during an interview, personality, advanced placement or honors courses, and leadership record.

Procedure: The SAT should be taken in December or January of the senior year. The ACT may be substituted. Application deadlines are open; new students are admitted to all terms. Notification is made 2 weeks after the complete application is received. Application, test scores, and high school record should be submitted with a $20 fee.

Special: An early decision plan is available. CLEP subject exams are accepted, and AP credit is also given.

Transfer: For fall 1981, 28 students applied, 26 were accepted, and 15 enrolled. Transfers are accepted for all classes. Good standing at previous institution is required; transfer students also need a GPA of at least 2.0. D grades are not acceptable. Students must earn in residence at least 30 of the 122 credits necessary for a bachelor's degree. Application deadlines are open.

Visiting: Orientations are scheduled 3 or 4 times a year for prospective students. Informal guided tours and overnight accommodations are available during the school year or in the summer. Arrangements should be made through the admissions office.

Financial Aid: Sixty-eight percent of all students receive aid; 50% work part-time on campus. About 50 to 60 grants or scholarships are awarded to freshmen every year from a fund of $50,000. Average aid to freshmen in 1981-82 was $5400 from scholarships, loans, and campus jobs. Loans are available from the federal government, local banks, and private sources. The college is a member of CSS. Either the FAF or the FFS must be filed by February 15 for in-state students.

Foreign Students: About 9% of the full-time students are from foreign countries. The college offers these students an intensive English program, special counseling, and special organizations.

Admissions: Foreign students must achieve a TOEFL score of at least 500 or a University of Michigan score of at least 60. No college entrance exams are required.

Procedure: Application deadlines are open; students are admitted to all terms. Foreign students must present a report of a physical exam and proof of adequate funds for 1 year. The college can help foreign students obtain health insurance.

Admissions Contact: Terri Grasso, S.P., Dean of Admissions.

SAINT MARY'S COLLEGE
Notre Dame, Indiana 46556   C-1
(219) 284-4305

F/T: 17M, 1802W	Faculty: 117; IIB, +$
P/T: 3M, 31W	Ph.D.'s: 70%
Grad: none	S/F Ratio: 13 to 1
Year: sems	Tuition: $4700
Appl: Mar. 1	R and B: $2337
1093 applied	769 accepted 489 enrolled
SAT: 493V 521M	ACT: 24 VERY COMPETITIVE

Saint Mary's College is a Roman Catholic liberal arts college operated by the Sisters of the Holy Cross. The library contains 154,000 volumes and subscribes to 778 periodicals.

Environment: The campus, which includes an auditorium, academic buildings and an athletic center, adjoins 288 acres of gardens, fields, woods, and walks along the St. Joseph River. Dormitories accommodate 1560 students. The college is 90 miles from Chicago in a suburban area.

Student Life: About 15% of the students are from Indiana. About 90% of the students live in dormitories on campus. About 96% of the students are members of the Roman Catholic Church, and about 3% are Protestant. Fewer than 4% are members of minority groups. Campus housing is single-sex, and there are visiting privileges on weekends. Upperclassmen may keep cars on campus. Day-care services are available to all students, faculty, and staff for a fee.

Organizations: There are no fraternities or sororities on campus. Extracurricular activities are numerous, and cultural programs offer symphonies, jazz and rock concerts, ballet, films, opera, plays, and a wide variety of art.

Sports: The college competes on an intercollegiate level in 15 sports for women. Intramural sports for women number 6.

Handicapped: About 75% of the campus is accessible to wheelchair students, and special facilities include ramps, parking areas, and elevators.

Graduates: The freshman dropout rate is 9%; 76–80% remain to graduate. About 16–17% of the graduates enter graduate or professional schools; 2% go to medical school and 4% go to law school. Sixty-four percent pursue careers in business and industry.

Services: Students receive placement, limited remedial instruction, some tutoring, career counseling, and psychological counseling free of charge. Health care is available for a fee. The college has a Career Resources Library, on-campus interviewing, a job vacancy newsletter, and a variety of academic and career planning workshops.

Programs of Study: The college offers the B.A., B.B.A., B.F.A., B.Mus., and B.S. degrees. Bachelor's degrees are offered in the following subjects: BUSINESS (business administration), EDUCATION (elementary, secondary), ENGLISH (communications, literature, writing), FINE AND PERFORMING ARTS (art, art education, music, music education, studio art, theater/dramatics), HEALTH SCIENCES (medical technology, nursing), LANGUAGES (French, Spanish), MATH AND SCIENCES (biology, chemistry, mathematics) PHILOSOPHY (philosophy, religious studies), SOCIAL SCIENCES (economics, government/political science, history, psychology, sociology). About 25% of degrees are conferred in business administration, 20% in social sciences, 18% in letters and humanities, and 11% in fine arts.

Required: All students are required to exhibit proficiency in English composition and a foreign language, and to meet the requirements in science, social science, and liberal arts.

Special: Students may spend their sophmore year in Rome or Ireland. There is an exchange program with the University of Notre Dame; the drama departments have merged, and the religious studies department is coordinated with the theology department at Notre Dame. Students may attend classes at either campus. Recently, a 3-2 liberal arts and engineering combination program was established with Notre Dame. It is possible to earn combined B.A.-B.S. degrees.

Honors: There are honor societies in chemistry, history, and psychology, along with a society of Catholic college women.

INDIANA 249

Admissions: Seventy percent of those who applied were accepted for the 1981–82 class. The SAT scores of those who enrolled were as follows: Verbal—52% below 500, 41% between 500 and 599, 7% between 600 and 700, and 0% above 700; Math—40% below 500, 48% between 500 and 599, 12% between 600 and 700, and less than 1% above 700. For those submitting ACT scores, 6% scored below 19, 54% between 19 and 24, 39% between 25 and 30, and less than 1% above 30. The candidate must have completed 16 units of college preparatory work, have a B average, and rank in the top quarter of the high school graduating class. The college indicates that in addition to these qualifications it considers advanced placement or honors courses, recommendations, special talents, extracurricular activities, and leadership.

Procedure: The SAT or ACT is required and should be taken in May or July of the junior year or in November or December of the senior year. The AT is required in English composition, the foreign language to be continued in college, and mathematics or science. The application, test scores, high school record, recommendations, and a $25 fee (refundable until May 1) should be submitted by March 1 (fall) or November 15 (spring). Later applications are accepted if space is available. Notification is made on a rolling basis. New students are admitted to both semesters.

Special: Deferred admissions are available. AP and CLEP credit is given.

Transfer: For fall 1981, 113 transfer students applied, 47 were accepted, and 36 enrolled. A GPA of 3.0 is strongly recommended. Minimum SAT scores of 500 Verbal and 550 Math and an ACT score of 25 or higher are required. D grades are not accepted. Sixty of the 128 credit hours necessary for the bachelor's degree must be taken at the college. A rolling admissions policy is used. The application deadlines are May 15 (fall) and November 15 (spring).

Visiting: Guides are available for informal visits to the college. Visitors are allowed to sit in on classes and may stay overnight at the school. Weekday and Saturday morning visits can be arranged through the admissions office.

Financial Aid: Sixty-two percent of all students receive financial aid. Twenty-seven percent work part-time on campus. The average aid to freshmen is more than $4500. The college offers scholarships, loans, grants, and work assistance, and participates in the federal NDSL, EOG, and CWS programs. Aid is awarded on the basis of financial need and academic promise. The college is a member of CSS. The FAF is required. The deadline for financial aid application is March 1.

Foreign Students: Two percent of the full-time students are from foreign countries. The college offers special organizations for foreign students.

Admission: A minimum TOEFL score of approximately 600 (on both Verbal and Math) is required. The SAT or ACT may also be taken. Foreign students must take the same ATs as required for regular admissions.

Procedure: Application deadlines are March 1 (fall) and November 15 (spring). Foreign students must produce proof of health in the form of a general physical examination. They must also present proof of funds adequate to cover 4 years of study.

Admissions Contact: Mary Ann Rowan, Director of Admissions.

TAYLOR UNIVERSITY
Upland, Indiana 46989   D-3
(317) 998-2751

F/T: 682M, 826W	Faculty: 84; IIB, +$
P/T: 36M, 47W	Ph.D.'s: 54%
Grad: none	S/F Ratio: 17 to 1
Year: 4-1-4, ss	Tuition: $4175
Appl: open	R and B: $1925
819 applied	676 accepted 485 enrolled
SAT: 462V 497M	COMPETITIVE

Taylor University, a nonsectarian Christian institution, offers programs in business, education, and the liberal arts. The library contains 119,000 volumes and 3400 microfilm items, and subscribes to 709 periodicals.

Environment: The 240-acre campus is located in the town of Upland, 60 miles from Indianapolis. The rural setting includes an 8-acre lake. Residence halls are built around the perimeter of the campus. The university also sponsors off-campus apartments and married-student housing.

Student Life: About 41% of the students come from Indiana, and 92% come from public schools. About 85% live on campus, 80% in the residence halls. Nearly all the students are Protestant. Chapel services are held 3 times a week, and all students are expected to

250 INDIANA

attend. About 2% of the students are minority-group members. University housing is single-sex, and there are no visiting privileges. Students may keep cars on campus.

Organizations: Special-interest clubs, religious groups, musical organizations, a weekly newspaper, lectures, art exhibits, and drama productions are available to students. There are no fraternities or sororities.

Sports: The university fields 8 intercollegiate teams for men and 6 for women. There are 7 intramural sports for men and 6 for women.

Handicapped: Special facilities for handicapped students include wheelchair ramps, special parking, elevators, lowered drinking fountains and telephones, and specially equipped rest rooms. Special class scheduling is also available.

Graduates: Sixty-five percent of the freshmen remain to graduate. Fifty percent of the graduates seek advanced degrees; 3% enter medical school, 3% enter dental school, and 3% enter law school. Another 50% pursue careers in business and industry.

Services: The following services are provided free to students: psychological and career counseling, tutoring, remedial instruction, and placement aid. Fees are charged for health-care services.

Programs of Study: The university confers the B.A., B.S., B.Mus., and B.S.W. degrees. Associate degrees are also awarded. Bachelor's degrees are offered in the following subjects: BUSINESS (accounting, business administration, computer science), EDUCATION (early childhood, elementary, health/physical, secondary, special), ENGLISH (English), FINE AND PERFORMING ARTS (art, art education, music, music education, radio/TV, theater/dramatics), HEALTH SCIENCES (medical technology, nursing), LANGUAGES (French, Spanish), MATH AND SCIENCES (biology, chemistry, mathematics, natural sciences, physics), PHILOSOPHY (philosophy, religion), PREPROFESSIONAL (dentistry, engineering, law, medicine, ministry, social work), SOCIAL SCIENCES (economics, government/political science, history, psychology, sociology). Nineteen percent of degrees conferred are in business, 14% in education.

Required: All students must take courses in English, fine arts, history, science or mathematics, literature, philosophy, physical education, and religion.

Special: Students may earn combined B.A.-B.S. degrees and design their own majors. Also available are off-campus experiences during the January interterm, a junior-year-abroad program, a 4-year nursing program with Ball State University, and a combination-degree program in engineering.

Honors: Honors programs are offered. Chi Alpha has a chapter on campus.

Admissions: About 83% of those who applied were accepted for the 1981–82 freshman class. The SAT scores of those who enrolled were as follows: Verbal—27% scored between 500 and 599, and 6% between 600 and 700; Math—33% scored between 500 and 599, and 15% between 600 and 700. Applicants must be graduates of an accredited high school, rank in the upper half of their class, and submit acceptable scores on either the SAT or ACT. Other considerations are advanced placement or honors courses, extracurricular activities, and recommendations from school officials and the applicant's pastor.

Procedure: The SAT or ACT is required. Test scores and high school record should be submitted at least 15 days before the beginning of any term; applications are accepted as long as space is available. The university follows a rolling admissions plan. There is a $15 application fee.

Special: AP and CLEP credit is available.

Transfer: For fall 1981, 180 students applied for transfer, 92 were accepted, and 91 enrolled. A minimum GPA of 2.0, acceptable scores on the SAT or ACT, and recommendations from the student's previous college are required; an interview is recommended. D grades do not transfer. Students must spend at least 1 year in residence, completing at least 30 of the 128 credits required for a bachelor's degree. Application deadlines are open.

Visiting: Orientations for prospective students are held in the spring and the summer. Guides are available for informal visits. Visitors may sit in on classes and stay overnight at the school. The admissions office should be contacted for arrangements.

Financial Aid: Half the students receive aid; 40% work part-time on campus. Average aid to freshmen covered 50% of costs in 1981–82. The university, a member of CSS, provides scholarships, grants, and loans. The FAF must be filed. The deadline for aid applications is April 1.

Foreign Students: Fewer than 1 percent of the full-time students come from foreign countries. The university offers these students special counseling and special organizations.

Admissions: Foreign students must achieve a TOEFL score of at least 550. The SAT is also required.

Procedure: Application deadlines are open; students are admitted to all terms. Foreign students must present proof of adequate funds and arrange for health insurance.

Admissions Contact: Ron Keller, Dean of Admissions and Institutional Research.

TRI-STATE UNIVERSITY D–1
Angola, Indiana 46703 (219) 665-3141

F/T: 830M, 207W		Faculty:	72; IIB, av$
P/T: 61M, 12W		Ph.D.'s:	48%
Grad: none		S/F Ratio:	16 to 1
Year: qtrs, ss		Tuition:	$3420
Appl: July 1		R and B:	$1710
978 applied	692 accepted		328 enrolled
SAT: 427V 518M	ACT: 21		COMPETITIVE

Tri-State University, founded in 1884, is an independent college offering programs in liberal arts, technical fields, and teacher training. The library contains 86,000 volumes and 2700 microfilm items, and subscribes to 809 periodicals.

Environment: The 400-acre campus is located in a small town in a rural area 45 miles from Fort Wayne. The campus consists of 24 buildings. Campus housing includes dormitories and fraternity houses. There is an outdoor track and an 18-hole golf course.

Student Life: Forty percent of the students come from Indiana. Sixty-five percent come from public schools. About 35% live on campus. Two percent are minority-group members. Campus housing is single-sex, with visiting privileges. Students may keep cars on campus.

Organizations: There are 8 national fraternities on campus to which 20% of the men belong. Fourteen percent of the women belong to the 1 national sorority. Extracurricular activities include the student senate and professional societies.

Sports: Intercollegiate competition is offered in 7 sports for men and 5 for women. There are 4 intramural sports for men and 4 for women.

Handicapped: About 20% of the campus is accessible to wheelchair-bound students. There are few special facilities for the handicapped. Special class scheduling is possible.

Graduates: The freshman dropout rate is about 11%; 31% remain to graduate. Ten percent of the graduates pursue graduate study. Most pursue careers in business and industry.

Services: Students receive placement, psychological, and career counseling free of charge. Tutoring and remedial instruction are provided for a fee.

Programs of Study: The university confers the B.A. and B.S. degrees. Associate degrees are also awarded. Bachelor's degrees are offered in the following subjects: BUSINESS (accounting, business administration, business education, computer science, management, marketing), EDUCATION (elementary, health/physical, secondary), ENGLISH (English), MATH AND SCIENCES (biology, chemistry, mathematics, physical sciences), PREPROFESSIONAL (engineering), SOCIAL SCIENCES (economics, history, social sciences). About 51% of the degrees conferred are in preprofessional studies and 33% are in business.

Required: All undergraduates must take English composition and physical education.

Special: Prep courses are offered for freshmen who have not completed the high school courses normally required for admission. Cooperative education programs offer industrial and business work experience.

Honors: Eight honor societies have chapters on campus.

Admissions: Seventy-one percent of those who applied were accepted for the 1981–82 freshman class. The SAT scores of those who enrolled were as follows: Verbal—19% scored below 500, 55% between 500 and 599, 24% between 600 and 700, and 2% above 700; Math—20% scored below 500, 59% between 500 and 599, 20% between 600 and 700, and 1% above 700. Of those who took the ACT, 26% scored below 21, 45% between 21 and 23, 17% between 24 and 25, 11% between 26 and 28, and 1% above 28. Applicants should rank in the upper half of their high school class, should have a GPA of at least 2.0, and should have completed a minimum of 15 Carnegie high school units. Advanced placement or honors courses, extracurricular activities, leadership record, recommendations by school officials, and personality also are considered.

Procedure: The SAT or ACT is required. Junior-year results are acceptable. Freshmen must apply to the academic division in which they are interested. The deadlines are July 1 (fall), November 1 (winter), and February 1 (spring). There is a rolling admissions plan. A personal interview is recommended. A $15 application fee is required.

Special: There are early decision and early admissions plans. CLEP and AP credit is available.

Transfer: For fall 1981, there were 102 transfer applicants; 84 were accepted and 47 enrolled. Transfer students are not accepted in the senior class. Students must complete 45 quarter hours in residence of the 186–206 required for a bachelor's degree. A 2.0 average and a 900 composite score on the ACT are necessary; D grades do not transfer. Application deadlines are the same as for entering freshmen.

Visiting: Orientations for prospective students are held regularly, and visitors may sit in on classes. Visits are arranged by the admissions office.

Financial Aid: About 45% of all students receive aid. Twenty percent work part-time on campus. The average freshman aid award in 1981–82 was $2500. Federal work-study funds are available in all departments. Scholarships and loans also are awarded. The university is a member of the CSS. The FAF is required of aid applicants. Need is the principal consideration in determining awards. The deadline for filing for financial aid is March 1.

Foreign Students: Thirteen percent of the full-time students come from foreign countries. An intensive English program, special counseling, and special organizations are available for these students.

Admissions: Foreign students must achieve a TOEFL score of at least 550. No college entrance exams are required.

Procedure: Application deadlines are January 1 (fall) and March 1 (winter). Foreign students must present proof of adequate funds for 1 year. There are special orientation and application fees. Students must carry health insurance, which is available through the university for a fee.

Admissions Contact: Milton F. Woody, Director for Enrollment Services.

UNIVERSITY OF EVANSVILLE A-5
Evansville, Indiana 47702 (812) 479-2468

F/T: 1242M, 1698W	Faculty: 201; IIA, –$
P/T: 472M, 893W	Ph.D.'s: 50%
Grad: 253M, 350W	S/F Ratio: 15 to 1
Year: qtrs, ss	Tuition: $3795
Appl: open	R and B: $1935
1593 applied	1389 accepted	690 enrolled
SAT: 449V 490M		COMPETITIVE

The University of Evansville, established in 1854, is a private coeducational university affiliated with the United Methodist Church. It offers a curriculum that combines liberal arts and professional training. The library houses 250,000 volumes and subscribes to 1200 periodicals.

Environment: The 75-acre campus is located in a suburban area in eastern residential Evansville, 150 miles from Indianapolis. There are 12 classroom buildings, science facilities, an engineering building, and a student union. Five university-owned residence halls, 5 fraternity houses, and 2 apartment buildings are all on, or close to, campus.

Student Life: The majority of the students are from Indiana; 25% come from other states. Ninety percent of the entering freshmen come from public schools. Fifty percent live in college dormitories. A wide variety of religious denominations are represented on campus. About 30% of the students are Catholic, 60% are Protestant, and 1% are Jewish. About 7% are minority-group members. Campus housing is both single-sex and coed, and there are visiting privileges. Students may keep cars on campus. Day-care facilities are provided for all students, faculty, and staff for a fee.

Organizations: Approximately 30% of the students belong to fraternities or sororities. Student organizations include student government, religious groups, a newspaper, an FM radio station, musical activities, debate groups, and various cultural activities and professional organizations.

Sports: The university has teams in 10 intercollegiate sports for men and 8 for women. There are 13 intramural sports for men and 10 for women.

Handicapped: About 40% of the campus is accessible to physically handicapped students. Special parking, wheelchair ramps, specially equipped rest rooms, and some elevators are available. Facilities available to visually impaired students include readers, a tape service, and a summer "prep" program. There is also a special counselor.

Graduates: The freshman dropout rate is 29%; 41% of the freshmen remain to graduate. Twelve percent of the students pursue graduate study after graduation: 1% enter medical school, 1% dental school, and 1% law school. Thirty percent pursue careers in business and industry.

Services: Students receive the following services free of charge: placement, health care, psychological counseling, career counseling, tutoring, and remedial instruction. In addition to job listings and on-campus interviews, there are employer information files and job search seminars.

Programs of Study: The university offers the B.A., B.F.A., B.L.S., B.S.M., B.S.Mus.Ed., and B.S. degrees. Associate and master's degrees are also awarded. Bachelor's degrees are offered in the following subjects: AREA STUDIES (environmental, urban), BUSINESS (accounting, business administration, business education, computer science, finance, international business, management, marketing, office administration), EDUCATION (early childhood, elementary, health/physical, secondary, special), ENGLISH (advertising, composition, English, journalism, literature, speech), FINE AND PERFORMING ARTS (art, art education, art therapy, commercial art, music, music education, music therapy, music management, radio/TV, theater/dramatics, theater management), HEALTH SCIENCES (medical technology, nursing, occupational therapy, physical therapy, radiological technology), LANGUAGES (French, German, Spanish), MATH AND SCIENCES (biology, chemistry, ecology/environmental science, mathematics, physics), PHILOSOPHY (philosophy, religion), PRE-PROFESSIONAL (dentistry, law, medicine, ministry, optometry, pharmacy, social work, veterinary), SOCIAL SCIENCES (economics, government/political science, history, psychobiology, psychology, sociology, social work). Thirty percent of the degrees conferred are in the health sciences; 18% are in business; and 16% are in education.

Required: All students are required to take courses in English composition, humanities, natural science, physical education, social science, and fine arts.

Special: The university has an overseas campus, Harlaxton College in England. All students, including incoming freshmen, are eligible to participate.

Honors: There is a university honors program, and all departments have enriched courses available to exceptional students. There are many national honor societies on campus.

Admissions: Eighty-seven percent of those who applied for the 1981–82 freshman class were accepted. The SAT scores of those who enrolled were as follows: Verbal—72% below 500, 22% between 500 and 599, 5% between 600 and 700, and 1% above 700; Math—56% below 500, 29% between 500 and 599, 13% between 600 and 700, and 2% above 700. Also considered are the following factors in order of importance: advanced placement or honors courses, recommendations by school officials, evidence of special talent, and leadership.

Procedure: The SAT or ACT is required. Application deadlines are open. Notification is on a rolling basis and begins when all the credentials are received. New students are admitted to all sessions. The application fee is $15.

Special: Early admissions are possible. Gifted students may be admitted at the end of the junior year. There is a deferred admissions plan. The notification date for the early decision plan is May 1. AP and CLEP credit is available.

Transfer: For fall 1981, 408 transfer applications were received, 315 were accepted, and 212 students enrolled. A C average is necessary. Transfer students should have a minimum of 16 credit hours earned. An 800 SAT composite score is recommended. Some D grades are acceptable. Forty-five of the 192 quarter hours needed for the bachelor's degree must be taken in residence.

Visiting: Visitors may stay at the university. Guided tours can be arranged through the admissions office. Scheduled orientations are held for prospective students.

Financial Aid: About 80% of the students receive some financial aid; 25% work part-time on campus. The university provides scholarships, loans, and campus employment and participates in the following federal financial aid programs: NDSL, EOG, CWS, and the Nursing Student Loan Program. The average aid awarded to a freshman is $3275. There are work-study programs in 26 departments. Aid is awarded on the basis of financial need and academic record. The university is a member of CSS. The FAF or FFS must be filed and is due by February 1. Application deadline for financial aid is March 1.

Foreign Students: About 7% of the full-time students are from foreign countries. The university actively recruits foreign students and offers them special counseling and organizations.

Admissions: A minimum TOEFL score of 500 is required. No college entrance exams are necessary.

252 INDIANA

Procedure: Deadlines for application are July 1 (fall), October 23 (winter), January 25 (spring), and April 15 (summer). Proof of funds adequate to cover 1 academic year is required. Foreign students must also carry health insurance, which is available through the university for a fee.

Admissions Contact: Stephen Grissom, Director of Admissions.

UNIVERSITY OF NOTRE DAME C-1
Notre Dame, Indiana 46556 (219) 239-7505

F/T: 5279M, 1885W	Faculty: 695; I, +$
P/T: none	Ph.D.'s: 81%
Grad: 1274M, 560W	S/F Ratio: 12 to 1
Year: sems, ss	Tuition: $5270
Appl: Mar. 1	R and B: $1865
7728 applied	2820 accepted 1753 enrolled
SAT: 570V 640M	MOST COMPETITIVE

The University of Notre Dame, established in 1842, is affiliated with the Roman Catholic Church. The undergraduate divisions are the College of Arts and Letters, the College of Science, and the College of Business Administration. The university's library is one of the largest in the world, with holdings of 1.4 million volumes (exclusive of the Law Library), subscriptions to 12,800 periodicals, and 600,000 microfilm items.

Environment: The university is located in an urban area on a 1250-acre, wooded campus, 1 mile from South Bend and 90 miles from Chicago. Its 90 buildings include 24 residence halls, accommodating over 5300 students, that are grouped into 2 quadrangles and 2 high-rise towers. In addition, there is a residence for nuns and graduate women, and an apartment complex for married students housing 102 families. The oldest parts of the campus have been designated a National Historical District.

Student Life: About 8% of the undergraduates are from Indiana, 2% from abroad, and the rest from the other 49 states. The largest number of students are from the Midwest and Northeast, particularly New York, New Jersey, Pennsylvania, and the New England states. Increasing numbers of students are coming from Sunbelt states such as California and Texas. About 50% of entering freshmen come from public schools. About 80% of the students live on campus; freshmen are required to do so. Ninety-two percent of the students are Catholic, and most of the rest are Protestant. Nine percent are members of minority groups. Housing is single-sex; there are visiting privileges. All students but freshmen may have cars. Attendance at religious services is not required.

Organizations: There are no social fraternities or sororities at Notre Dame. Social and athletic facilities on campus include the Athletic and Convocation Center, which is a regional center for concerts and sports events.

Sports: Notre Dame fields intercollegiate or intercollegiate club teams in 18 sports for men and 15 for women. Men can participate in 15 intramural sports and women in 13.

Handicapped: About 90% of the campus is accessible to the physically handicapped. Special facilities include wheelchair ramps, parking areas, elevators, lowered drinking fountains and telephones, and specially equipped rest rooms. Special class scheduling is possible. For students with visual impairments, the elevators are marked in braille and a campus map in braille is available. There is a University Committee for the Handicapped, and a special counselor to provide assistance.

Graduates: Fewer than 2% of the students drop out during the freshman year, 90% remain to graduate, and 50% of the graduates become candidates for advanced degrees. Ten percent enter medical school, 3% dental school, and 15% law school. Careers in business and industry are chosen by 45%.

Services: The following services are available free to all students: health care, psychological counseling, tutoring (for freshmen), and placement and career counseling. In addition, there are Catholic counselors on campus.

Programs of Study: The university awards the following undergraduate degrees: B. Arch., B.A., B.B.A., B.F.A., B. Mus., B.S., B.S. in Eng. Master's and doctoral degrees also are available. Bachelor's degrees are offered in the following subjects: AREA STUDIES (American, Black/Afro-American), BUSINESS (accounting, business administration, finance, management, marketing), ENGLISH (comparative literature, English), FINE AND PERFORMING ARTS (art, music, studio art), LANGUAGES (Chinese, French, German, Greek/Latin, Italian, Japanese, Russian, Spanish), MATH AND SCIENCES (biology, chemistry, earth science, geology, mathematics, physics), PHILOSOPHY (classics, humanities, philosophy, religion), PREPROFESSIONAL (architecture, dentistry, engineering, law, medicine, ministry, pharmacy), SOCIAL SCIENCES (anthropology, economics, government/political science, history, international relations, psychology, social sciences, sociology). Business students receive 30% of the total undergraduate degrees conferred, preprofessional students 28%, social sciences students 19%, and math and sciences students 10%.

Required: All students must take courses in English, mathematics, science, social science, physical education, philosophy, and theology.

Special: It is possible to earn a combined 3-2 Engineering/Arts and Letters degree in a 5-year program; a 5-year civil engineering/earth science program is also available. The sophomore year may be spent abroad. Architecture students spend their third year in Rome. There is a General Program of Liberal Studies centered on the discussion of great books. Teaching certification is available through neighboring Saint Mary's College.

Honors: Fifteen national honor societies, including Phi Beta Kappa, have chapters on campus. The Program of the Collegiate Scholars is open to seniors for advanced independent study and writing under committee supervision. The Committee on Academic Progress is an honors program for exceptional students in the College of Arts and Letters.

Admissions: Notre Dame accepted 36% of those who applied in 1981-82. The SAT scores of those who enrolled were as follows: Verbal—17% below 500, 48% between 500 and 599, 30% between 600 and 700, and 5% above 700; Math—5% below 500, 23% between 500 and 599, 53% between 600 and 700, and 19% above 700. Most students ranked in the top 7% of their high school class, and A− is a typical grade average. Applicants should be graduates of an accredited high school and should have completed the credit requirements for the college in which they want to enroll. Other factors influencing admission are advanced placement or honors courses, extracurricular activities, recommendations by school officials, personality, leadership record, and evidence of special talents.

Procedure: The SAT is required, and should be taken in the spring of the junior year or the fall of the senior year. Freshmen are admitted in the fall only; the deadline for applications is March 1. There is a $25 application fee. Admissions decisions are made on a rolling basis.

Special: AP credit is granted.

Transfer: For fall 1981, 706 transfer students applied, 364 were accepted, and 259 enrolled. Transfers are considered for sophomore and junior classes. Applicants must have a 3.0 average and 30 completed credit hours. D grades are not transferable. A student must complete, at Notre Dame, 60 of the 120-128 credits necessary to receive a bachelor's degree. Deadlines for applications are April 1 for the fall term and October 15 for the spring term.

Visiting: Prospective students may participate in regularly scheduled group information sessions, followed by individual interviews. Guides are available for informal visits, and visitors may sit in on classes and stay at the school. The admissions office should be contacted for arrangements; 2 weeks' notice is requested.

Financial Aid: About 50% of all students are receiving financial aid. Three hundred freshman scholarships are granted each year from endowment fund income. The average award to freshmen is $2300 from all sources. Qualified students may receive aid from NDSL and GSLP. Campus employment is also available; 27% of the students work part-time on campus. Awards are made on the basis of financial need. Students should complete and submit the FAF, including the supplement, by March 1. The university is a member of the CSS.

Foreign Students: About 100 students from foreign countries are enrolled full-time at Notre Dame. An intensive English course and special organizations are provided for these students.

Admissions: Foreign applicants generally must score 550 or better on the TOEFL. They also must take the SAT.

Procedure: The application deadline is March 1. Students must present proof of adequate funds for 4 years. Health insurance is not required.

Admissions Contact: John T. Goldrick, Director of Admissions.

VALPARAISO UNIVERSITY B-1
Valparaiso, Indiana 46383 (219) 464-2387

F/T: 1537M, 1881W	Faculty: 285; IIA, −$
P/T: 66M, 107W	Ph.D.'s: 53%
Grad: 276M, 239W	S/F Ratio: 13 to 1
Year: sems, ss	Tuition: $4222
Appl: open	R and B: $1880-2090
2034 applied	1787 accepted 931 enrolled
SAT: 490V 530M	COMPETITIVE

Valparaiso University, founded in 1859, is a private university affiliated with the Lutheran Church. It provides both graduate and undergraduate instruction. Christ College, an innovative division, offers an individualized honors program. The library contains 340,000 volumes and 30,000 microfilm items, and subscribes to 1350 periodicals.

Environment: The 310-acre campus is located in a suburban area 45 miles from Chicago. There are 45 buildings on campus. The Chapel of Resurrection is the largest collegiate chapel in the world. Living facilities include dormitories, on-campus and off-campus apartments, and fraternity houses.

Student Life: Thirty percent of the students are from Indiana and 70% are from out of state. About 85% of the entering freshmen come from public schools. Eighty percent of the students reside on campus. Five percent are minority-group members. About 77% are Protestant, 18% are Catholic, and 1% are Jewish. Campus housing is both coed and single-sex; there are visiting privileges in the single-sex housing. Students may keep cars on campus.

Organizations: There are 14 fraternities and 8 sororities on campus; 36% of the men and 37% of the women belong to one of them. Student organizations include special and academic interest clubs, religious groups, publications, and musical groups. Cultural and social events are sponsored by the university.

Sports: The university fields intercollegiate teams in 12 sports for men and 7 sports for women. There are also 14 intramural sports for men and 12 for women.

Handicapped: About 50% of the campus is accessible to handicapped students. Special facilities include wheelchair ramps, parking areas, and elevators.

Graduates: At the end of the freshman year, 10% of the students drop out, and 70% remain to graduate. Sixty percent of the students pursue graduate study after graduation. Of these, 2% enter medical school; 1% enter dental school; and 3% enter law school.

Services: The university offers the following services free of charge to all students: placement, career counseling, health care, tutoring, and psychological counseling.

Programs of Study: The university offers the B.A., B.Mus., B.Mus.Ed., B.S.N., B.S.W., and B.S. degrees. Associate, master's, and doctoral degrees are also awarded. Bachelor's degrees are offered in the following subjects: AREA STUDIES (American, Asian, British, Latin American, urban), BUSINESS (accounting, business administration, computer science, economics, finance, management, marketing, personnel), EDUCATION (elementary, secondary, special), ENGLISH (English, journalism, literature, speech), FINE AND PERFORMING ARTS (art, art education, art history, music, music education, studio art, theater/dramatics), HEALTH SCIENCES (medical technology, nursing, speech therapy), LANGUAGES (French, German, Greek/Latin, Hebrew, Spanish), MATH AND SCIENCES (biology, chemistry, earth science, geology, mathematics, natural sciences, physical sciences, physics, zoology), PHILOSOPHY (classics, humanities, philosophy, religion), PREPROFESSIONAL (dentistry, engineering, home economics, law, medicine, ministry, social work), SOCIAL SCIENCES (economics, geography, government/political science, history, international relations, psychology, social sciences, sociology). Eighteen percent of degrees conferred are in business; 12% are in social sciences.

Required: All students must take English composition, literature, physical education, science or mathematics, social studies, and theology; certain programs require a foreign language.

Special: It is possible to earn combined B.A.-B.S. degrees in the sciences and in art. Students may also design their own majors. A semester of study may be taken at the university's extensions in Cambridge, England; and Reutlingen, Germany. The university offers professional degree programs in home economics and social work. Christ College offers an unconventional honors program which emphasizes scholarship, creativity, and independent study.

Honors: Six national honor societies have chapters on campus. All departments offer honors programs.

Admissions: Eighty-eight percent of those who applied were accepted for the 1981-82 freshman class. Applicants should be graduates of accredited high schools. The university does not specify a minimum high school rank or a minimum grade average. The school considers the following factors in order of importance: advanced placement or honors courses, leadership record, extracurricular activities, recommendations by school officials, personality, and impressions made during an interview.

Procedure: The SAT is required and should be taken by January of the senior year. Notification is on a rolling basis. The application fee is $15. Freshmen are admitted in all terms.

Special: There are early decision, early admissions, and deferred admissions plans. AP and CLEP credit is offered.

Transfer: Recently, 354 transfer applications were received, 301 were accepted, and 173 students enrolled. A minimum GPA of 2.0 as well as good academic standing are required. D grades are usually accepted. Students must reside at the university for at least 1 year and must complete, at the university, at least 30 of the 124 credits required for a bachelor's degree.

Visiting: Regularly scheduled orientations for prospective students are available. There are guides for informal visits; visitors may sit in on classes and stay overnight at the school. Visits are best scheduled on Fridays and Saturdays, September through November and February through April. The admissions office should be contacted for arrangements.

Financial Aid: About 62% of the students receive financial aid. Forty percent work part-time on campus. The university provides scholarships, grants, loans, and campus employment. The average award to freshmen from all sources is $3500. About 1500 scholarships and grants are awarded to students each year from a fund of $3.8 million. Loans of up to $1500 each are available from the federal government and the school. Campus employment may earn a student $1000 a year. Application for aid is made after admission is granted; the FAF should be filed by March 1. The university is a member of CSS.

Foreign Students: Three percent of the full-time students come from foreign countries. The university offers these students an intensive English course, special counseling, and special organizations.

Admissions: Foreign students must achieve a TOEFL score of at least 500. College entrance exams are sometimes required.

Procedure: There are no application deadlines; foreign students are admitted in the fall, spring, and summer terms. Foreign students must present proof of health and proof of adequate funds. They must also carry health insurance, which is available through the university for a fee.

Admissions Contact: Warren W. Muller, Dean of Admissions and Financial Aid.

WABASH COLLEGE   B-3
Crawfordsville, Indiana 47933   (317) 362-1400

F/T: 800M Faculty: 70; IIB, ++$
P/T: none Ph.D.'s: 90%
Grad: none S/F Ratio: 11 to 1
Year: sems Tuition: $4780
Appl. Mar. 15 R and B: $2125
545 applied 424 accepted 225 enrolled
SAT: 500V 580M VERY COMPETITIVE

Wabash College, founded in 1832, is a private, independent, liberal arts men's college. It is strongly preprofessional in its training and purpose. The library contains 225,000 volumes and 5738 microfilm items, and subscribes to 770 periodicals.

Environment: The 50-acre campus is located in a rural setting 45 miles from Indianapolis. Among the 32 buildings are a humanities center, a theater, biological and ecological laboratories, a gymnasium, a pool, and indoor tennis courts. Three dormitories accommodate 160 men. Fraternity houses provide additional residence facilities.

Student Life: About 75% of the students come from Indiana, 24% are from other states, and 2% are from abroad. About 90% reside on campus; 30% in dormitories and 60% in fraternity houses. Six percent of the students are minority-group members. Sixty percent are Protestant, 35% are Catholic, and 1% are Jewish. There are visiting privileges in the campus housing. Students may keep cars on campus.

Organizations: Nine national fraternities attract 75% of the students. Students participate in student government and publications. There are numerous extracurricular activities, social events, and cultural offerings on campus.

Sports: The college competes in 13 intercollegiate sports. There are 13 intramural sports.

Handicapped: There are no special facilities or counselors for the handicapped.

Graduates: The freshman dropout rate is 5-10%; about 75% remain to graduate, and 50-55% go on to graduate or professional schools. Ten percent enter medical school, 4% dental school, and 15% law school. About 30% pursue careers in business and industry.

Services: Students receive the following services free of charge: health care, psychological counseling, tutoring, placement, and career counseling. The Office of Career Services provides early counseling

254 INDIANA

to help students find jobs. Religious counseling for all 3 major faiths is available.

Programs of Study: The college awards the B.A. degree. Bachelor's degrees are offered in the following subjects: AREA STUDIES (Black/Afro-American), EDUCATION (secondary), ENGLISH (English, speech), FINE AND PERFORMING ARTS (music, theater/dramatics), LANGUAGES (French, German, Greek/Latin, Spanish), MATH AND SCIENCES (biology, chemistry, mathematics, physics), PHILOSOPHY (classics, philosophy, religion), PREPROFESSIONAL (dentistry, engineering, law, medicine, veterinary), SOCIAL SCIENCES (economics, government/political science, history, psychology). The highest percentages of undergraduate enrollments are in political science and biology.

Required: All undergraduates must take a freshman tutorial, cultures and traditions, 1 year of lab science, a major distribution, and demonstrate proficiency in English.

Special: Student-designed majors are allowed. The junior year, and sometimes the sophomore year, may be spent abroad. Pass/fail options are offered. There is a 3-2 combination degree program in engineering with Columbia and with Washington University (St. Louis), and there is a 3-3 program in law with Columbia. Internships are available in the community for experience in business or community relations.

Honors: There are 8 national honorary, scholastic, and professional societies open to undergraduates.

Admissions: Wabash accepted 78% of those who applied for entrance in 1981-82. The SAT scores of those who enrolled were as follows: Verbal—45% below 500, 33% between 500 and 599, 17% between 600 and 700, and 1% above 700; Math—16% below 500, 42% between 500 and 599, 33% between 600 and 700, and 5% above 700. Recommendation by an accredited high school and 15 Carnegie units are required. Rank in the top quarter of class is preferred; candidates from the top half will be considered. An A or B average is preferred, but students with C averages will be considered.

Procedure: The PSAT should be taken in March of the junior year, and the SAT in May of the junior year, or in August or December of the senior year. Application deadlines are March 15 for fall and December 1 for spring. There is a $15 application fee. New students are admitted to both terms. Admissions are on a rolling basis.

Special: AP credit is granted.

Transfer: Recently 15 students applied for transfer, 11 were accepted, and 8 enrolled. Prime consideration is a good overall high school and college background. D grades are not acceptable. There is a 2-year residency requirement. Students must complete, at the college, 17 of the 34 courses required for a bachelor's degree.

Visiting: Guides are available for informal weekday visits to the campus. Visitors may sit in on classes, and may stay overnight at the school. The admissions office makes arrangements.

Financial Aid: About 76% of all students receive aid. About 30% work part-time on campus. The average award to freshmen is $4675. Federal government, local bank, and college-administered loans are also available. Financial need, scholastic promise, and academic ability determine the amount of aid. Tuition may be paid in installments. The college is a member of the CSS. The FAF is required. The deadline for financial aid application is March 15 (fall) or December 1 (spring).

Foreign Students: One percent of the full-time students come from foreign countries.

Admissions: Foreign students must take the TOEFL. No college entrance exams are required.

Procedure: Application deadlines are March 15 (fall) and December 1 (spring). Foreign students must present proof of funds adequate to cover the intended period of study and must present proof of health. Health insurance is required and is available through the college for a fee.

Admissions Contact: Paul M. Garman, Director of Admissions.

IOWA

BRIAR CLIFF COLLEGE
Sioux City, Iowa 51104

B-2
(712) 279-5422

F/T: 900M&W
P/T: 400M&W
Grad: none
Year: see entry
Appl: open
360 applied
ACT: 21

Faculty: n/av; IIB, av$
Ph.D.'s: 31%
S/F Ratio: 16 to 1
Tuition: $3150
R and B: $1600
340 accepted   220 enrolled
LESS COMPETITIVE

Briar Cliff College, founded in 1930, is a coeducational, liberal arts institution associated with the Roman Catholic Church. The library contains 85,000 volumes and 15,000 microfilm items, and subscribes to 490 periodicals.

Environment: The 70-acre campus is located 3 miles from downtown Sioux City, on the crest of wooded hills overlooking the city. The 8 campus buildings include 3 single-sex dormitories.

Student Life: About 70% of the students are from Iowa, and 60% come from public schools. About 45% of the students live on campus; unmarried students under 21 who are not seniors generally must do so. Most students are Catholic.

Organizations: There are no fraternities or sororities, but student organizations include special-interest and service groups, a chorus, and publications. Cultural and recreational activities also are available in the Sioux City area.

Sports: Briar Cliff College competes in 4 intercollegiate sports for men and 5 for women. Eight intramural sports are offered for men and women.

Handicapped: The entire campus is accessible to physically handicapped students. Special facilities include wheelchair ramps, parking areas, and elevators. Special class scheduling also is available.

Graduates: About 20% of the freshmen drop out, and 65% remain to graduate. Twenty percent of the graduates continue their studies. About half pursue careers in business and industry.

Services: Free psychological counseling, placement aid, career counseling, and tutoring or remedial instruction are available. Health care is available on campus. Alumni as well as students may use the placement services.

Programs of Study: The college awards the B.A., B.S., and B.S.Med.Tech. degrees. Bachelor's degrees are offered in the following subjects: BUSINESS (accounting, business administration), EDUCATION (health/physical, religious), ENGLISH (English, mass communication), FINE AND PERFORMING ARTS (art, music), HEALTH SCIENCES (medical technology, nursing, radiologic technology), LANGUAGES (Spanish), MATH AND SCIENCES (biology, chemistry, mathematics, natural sciences), PHILOSOPHY (philosophy, religion), PREPROFESSIONAL (engineering, social work), SOCIAL SCIENCES (history, psychology, sociology). Preprofessional programs also are offered in dentistry, law, medicine, pharmacy, physical therapy, and veterinary medicine.

Special: The academic year is divided into 3 terms of 10 weeks each. Combination degree programs are offered in engineering, medical technology, physical therapy, and nursing. Students may design their own majors and earn their degree in 3 years. Minors are offered in computer science, elementary and secondary education, physics, political science, and speech and theater. Psychology and sociology majors may spend a special term at the State Mental Health Institute working with experts in their fields. Internships are offered in business administration, accounting, psychology, elementary and secondary education, sociology, mass communications, religious education, and social work. Students may study abroad.

Admissions: The college accepted nearly all applicants for the 1981-82 freshman class. About 28% ranked in the top fifth of their high school class; 56% ranked in the top two-fifths. The ACT scores of an earlier freshman class were as follows: 22% between 20 and 23, 15% between 24 and 26, 10% between 27 and 28, and 2% above 28. Applicants should have completed 16 Carnegie units, present an average of C or better, rank in the upper three-quarters of their high school class, and show satisfactory test scores. Others may be accepted on probation.

Procedure: Applicants must take the ACT. Application deadlines are open, and freshmen are admitted to all terms. The application fee is $10. Admissions decisions are made on a rolling basis.

Special: An early admissions plan is available. AP and CLEP credit is accepted.

Transfer: In a recent year, 94 students applied, 90 were accepted, and 75 enrolled. Applicants must be in good standing at their last school. D grades do not transfer. Students must take at least 30 hours at the college to receive a degree. Application deadlines are open.

Visiting: Informal visits may be arranged with the director of admissions for weekdays from 8 A.M. to 4:30 P.M. while school is in session. Guides are provided, and visitors may sit in on classes and stay overnight at the school.

Financial Aid: About 83% of the students receive aid. Scholarships, grants, loans, and part-time jobs are awarded on the basis of need. The average award to 1981-82 freshmen from all sources totaled $2050. The college is a member of CSS. Aid applicants must file the FAF or, preferably, the FFS. Applications should be filed by April 1 for priority consideration.

Foreign Students: About 17 foreign students are enrolled. Special counseling is available for these students.

Admissions: Students must score 500 or above on the TOEFL. No academic exams are required.

Procedure: Application deadlines are open; students are admitted to all terms. Students must undergo a physical examination and present proof of adequate funds for 4 years. Health insurance, though not required, is available through the college for a fee.

Admissions Contact: James J. Hoffman, Director of Admissions.

BUENA VISTA COLLEGE B-2
Storm Lake, Iowa 50588 (712) 749-2235

F/T: 482M, 422W	Faculty:	51; IIB, +$
P/T: 11M, 37W	Ph.D.'s:	55%
Grad: none	S/F Ratio:	18 to 1
Year: 4-1-4, ss	Tuition:	$4270
Appl: open	R and B:	$1690
538 applied	496 accepted	275 enrolled
ACT: 22		COMPETITIVE

Buena Vista, founded in 1891, is a private, coeducational college of liberal arts, affiliated with the United Presbyterian Church. The library contains 84,000 volumes and 2000 microfilm items, and subscribes to 484 periodicals.

Environment: Located in a rural community on the shore of Storm Lake, the 40-acre campus is near the Great Lakes region of north central Iowa, and is 160 miles from Des Moines. The dormitories accommodate 750 students.

Student Life: About 92% of the students are from Iowa. Ninety percent come from public schools. The majority of the students live on campus. Seventy-two percent of the students are Protestant and 20% are Catholic. Fewer than 5% of the students are minority-group members. Campus housing is both single-sex and coed, and there are visiting privileges in single-sex housing. Cars are permitted on campus.

Organizations: Student organizations sponsor musical, dramatic, political, social, and cultural programs.

Sports: The college fields 10 intercollegiate teams for men and 8 for women. There are 8 intramural sports for men and 8 for women.

Handicapped: There is special parking for handicapped students. However, a very small percentage of the campus is accessible to these students.

Graduates: About 58% of the entering freshmen remain to graduate, and 18% of the graduates continue their studies. Of these, 1% enter medical school, 1% enter dental school, and 2% enter law school. Twenty-eight percent of the graduates pursue careers in business and industry.

Services: The following services are available free of charge: health care, tutoring, remedial instruction, career counseling, and placement.

Programs of Study: Programs lead to the B.A. and B.S. degrees. Bachelor's degrees are offered in the following subjects: BUSINESS (accounting, business administration, business education, computer science, corporate communications, finance, management), EDUCATION (elementary, health/physical, secondary, special), ENGLISH (English, journalism, speech), FINE AND PERFORMING ARTS (art, art education, music, music education, radio/TV, theater/dramatics), HEALTH SCIENCES (medical technology, physical therapy), LANGUAGES (German, Spanish), MATH AND SCIENCES (biology, chemistry, mathematics, natural sciences, physics), PHILOSOPHY (philosophy, religion), PREPROFESSIONAL (dentistry, engineering, law, library science, medicine, ministry, social work, veterinary), SOCIAL SCIENCES (economics, government/political science, history, psychology, social sciences, sociology). The majority of degrees are granted in business, education, and the sciences.

Required: All students must take 2 courses in each of 5 basic core areas.

Special: Numerous preprofessional programs are offered. Students may also design their own majors.

Honors: Three national honor societies are open to qualified students. All departments offer honors programs.

Admissions: About 92% of those who applied were accepted for the 1981-82 freshman class. The ACT scores of those who enrolled were as follows: 20% scored below 21, 30% between 21 and 23, 25% between 24 and 25, 15% between 26 and 28, and 10% above 28. Applicants should have completed 15 Carnegie units of high school work, including 4 years of English, and 2 years each of mathematics, social studies, and science. Applicants should rank in the top 50% of their class, and should have a high school grade average of 2.0. The college also considers advanced placement or honor courses, extracurricular activities, leadership record, recommendations, and personality.

Procedure: Either the SAT or the ACT is required. An interview is recommended. Applications should be submitted early in the senior year; priority consideration will be given to applications received by April 1. The college uses a rolling admissions policy. There is a $15 application fee.

Special: Early admissions, deferred admissions, and early decision plans are available.

Transfer: Of the 141 applications received for the 1981-82 school year, 131 were accepted, and 82 students enrolled. Transfer students must have a GPA of 2.0. Grades of C and above are acceptable. Students must earn, at the college, at least 30 of the 128 credit hours required to receive a bachelor's degree. The application deadline for fall entry is June 1.

Visiting: Guides are available for informal visits. Visitors may sit in on classes and stay overnight at the school. The admissions office should be contacted for arrangements.

Financial Aid: A fund of $290,000 is available for scholarships and grants. About 85% of the students receive some form of aid; 40% work part-time on campus. The average award to freshmen from all sources is $3480. The FFS, FAF, or SFS is required. It is recommended that students apply for financial aid by March 1. About 30% of the students earn 25% or more of their expenses.

Foreign Students: Fewer than 1% of the students come from foreign countries. The college actively recruits foreign students, and offers them an intensive English course and special counseling.

Admissions: A TOEFL score of 500 is required for admission. It is recommended, but not required, that foreign students take the SAT or the ACT.

Procedure: The application deadline for fall entry is June 1. Foreign students must present proof of funds adequate to cover their period of attendance at the college.

Admissions Contact: Kent McElvania, Director of Admissions.

CENTRAL UNIVERSITY OF IOWA D-3
(Formerly Central College)
Pella, Iowa 50219 (515) 628-5286

F/T: 612M, 657W	Faculty:	72; n/av
P/T: 18M, 21W	Ph.D.'s:	60%
Grad: none	S/F Ratio:	17 to 1
Year: 3-3 term	Tuition:	$4214
Appl: open	R and B:	$1709
778 applied	741 accepted	413 enrolled
SAT: 460V 500M	ACT: 22	COMPETITIVE

Central University of Iowa, founded in 1853 as Central College, is a private liberal arts college affiliated with the Reformed Church in America. The library contains 120,000 volumes and subscribes to 800 periodicals.

Environment: The 66-acre rural campus is located 43 miles from Des Moines. Facilities include the Vermeer Science Center and an outdoor recreation area. The dormitories accommodate over 1100 students. The university sponsors on-campus and off-campus apartments, fraternity and sorority houses, and married student housing.

Student Life: About 76% of the students are from Iowa; 97% come from public schools; and 86% live in dormitories (freshmen must live on campus). Campus housing is single-sex. About 15% of the students belong to the Reformed Church, and places of worship are available in the surrounding community for students of other faiths. Alcohol is prohibited on campus. Students may keep cars on campus.

Organizations: There are 3 local fraternities and 2 local sororities on campus; about 12% of the men and 7% of the women join one of these. The Student Union Activities Board plans a wide range of social and cultural events on campus. Other student groups include departmental and service organizations, publications, a radio station, and musical groups.

256 IOWA

Sports: The university fields 8 intercollegiate teams for men and 8 for women.

Handicapped: About 35% of the campus is accessible to handicapped students. Facilities include wheelchair ramps, special parking, elevators, and lowered drinking fountains.

Graduates: The freshman dropout rate is 33%; 50% remain to graduate, and 13% pursue advanced degrees after graduation. Of these, about 2% enter medical school, 1% dental school, and 1% law school. About 57% pursue careers in business and industry.

Services: Free health care, tutoring, remedial instruction, and placement, career, and psychological counseling are available to all students.

Programs of Study: All programs lead to the B.A. degree. Bachelor's degrees are offered in the following subjects: AREA STUDIES (Black/Afro-American, Latin American, urban), BUSINESS (accounting, business administration, business education, computer science, finance, international business, management, marketing), EDUCATION (early childhood, elementary, health/physical, secondary, special), ENGLISH (English, journalism, literature, speech), FINE AND PERFORMING ARTS (art, art education, art history, music, music education, studio art, theater/dramatics), LANGUAGES (French, German, Spanish), MATH AND SCIENCES (biology, chemistry, mathematics, physical sciences, physics), PHILOSOPHY (philosophy, religion), PRE-PROFESSIONAL (dentistry, home economics, law, medicine, ministry, social work), SOCIAL SCIENCES (anthropology, economics, government/political science, history, international relations, psychology, social sciences, sociology). About 30% of the degrees are conferred in education, 26% in business, and 7% in languages.

Required: All students must take 9 courses in general education, including 1 course in religion.

Special: The college offers a B.G.S. degree. Interdisciplinary majors, independent study, and an achievement creativity term are available. An accelerated program is possible, and students may spend a year abroad. Teacher training programs lead to appropriate certification.

Honors: Alpha Zeta Mu has a chapter on campus.

Admissions: Over 95% of those who applied were accepted for the 1981–82 freshman class. Candidates must have completed 15 Carnegie units, and should rank in the upper half of their graduating class. Advanced placement or honors courses, recommendations, evidence of special talents, and leadership record are also considered important.

Procedure: Candidates must take the SAT or ACT; a personal interview is recommended. There are no application deadlines. A $20 fee must accompany the application. The college follows a rolling admissions policy.

Special: The university has a deferred admissions plan. AP credit is available.

Transfer: For fall 1981, 108 students applied, 102 were accepted, and 60 enrolled. A GPA of at least 2.0 is recommended. Students must complete, at the university, 9 of the 36 courses required for a bachelor's degree. D grades do not transfer. There are no application deadlines.

Visiting: Guides are available for informal visits. Visitors may sit in on classes and stay overnight at the school. The admissions office should be contacted for arrangements.

Financial Aid: Eighty-five percent of the students receive some form of financial aid. The average award in scholarships, grants, and loans is $3100. CWS is available in most departments. Either the FAF or FFS should be filed; there are no application deadlines. The university is a member of CSS.

Foreign Students: Over 3% of the full-time students come from foreign countries.

Procedure: There is no deadline for admission.

Admissions Contact: Garrett Knoth, Director of Admissions.

CLARKE COLLEGE
Dubuque, Iowa 52001 E–2
(319) 588-6316

F/T: 73M, 488W	Faculty:	54; IIA, – –$
P/T: 75M, 187W	Ph.D.'s:	50%
Grad: 6M, 19W	S/F Ratio:	10 to 1
Year: sems, ss	Tuition:	$3510
Appl: open	R and B:	$1695
267 applied	240 accepted	167 enrolled
SAT: 457V 496M	ACT: 21	COMPETITIVE

Clarke College, founded in 1843, is a private liberal arts institution affiliated with the Roman Catholic Church. The library contains 100,000 volumes and 3000 microfilm items, and subscribes to 525 periodicals.

Environment: The 120-acre campus is located in a suburban area of Dubuque, a city 180 miles from Chicago. Campus buildings include a student union and an intramural gym with swimming pool and indoor track. Residence halls accommodate 640 students.

Student Life: About half the students come from Iowa. More than half come from private schools. About 93% of the students are Catholic and 7% are Protestant; attendance at services is not compulsory. Twenty-two percent are members of minority groups. There are visiting privileges in the single-sex dorms. Students may keep cars on campus.

Organizations: There are no sororities or fraternities. Campus activities include drama, service groups, publications, student government, art shows, debates, and plays. Students share social and cultural activities with undergraduates from nearby Loras College and the University of Dubuque. Social, cultural, and recreational activities also are available around the city.

Sports: The college fields intercollegiate teams in 3 sports for women. Five intramural sports are offered for men and women.

Handicapped: About half the campus is accessible to wheelchair-bound students. One percent of the students have visual impairments.

Graduates: About 15% to 20% of the freshmen drop out, and 55% remain to graduate. Twenty percent of the graduates pursue further study, including 2% who enter medical school and 1% who enter dental school. Another 50% of the graduates begin careers in business or industry.

Services: Students receive free psychological, placement, and career counseling; health care; and remedial instruction. Fees are charged for tutoring.

Programs of Study: The college awards the B.A., B.S., and B.F.A. degrees. Master's and associate degrees also are available. Bachelor's degrees are offered in the following subjects: BUSINESS (accounting, business administration, computer science), EDUCATION (early childhood, elementary, secondary, special), ENGLISH (English), FINE AND PERFORMING ARTS (art, art education, music, music education, theater/dramatics), HEALTH SCIENCES (medical technology, nursing, physical therapy), LANGUAGES (French, Spanish), MATH AND SCIENCES (biology, chemistry, mathematics), PHILOSOPHY (philosophy, religion), PREPROFESSIONAL (dentistry, law, medicine, social work), SOCIAL SCIENCES (history, psychology, sociology). About 25% of undergraduate degrees are conferred in fine and performing arts, 15% in business, and 10% in health sciences.

Required: All students must demonstrate proficiency in English and in a foreign language, and take 6 hours of theology.

Special: Third-year students may arrange to study abroad through another institution. Degrees may be earned in 3 years. A combination degree program offering a B.A. in human biology and an R.N. certificate is available. Students may design their own majors.

Honors: A number of honor societies are open to qualified students.

Admissions: Ninety percent of those who applied were accepted for the 1981–82 freshman class. The SAT scores of those who enrolled were as follows: Verbal—64% scored below 500, 27% between 500 and 599, 9% between 600 and 700, and 0 above 700; Math—36% scored below 500, 46% between 500 and 599, 18% between 600 and 700 and 0% above 700. Of those who took the ACT, 33% scored below 21, 23% between 21 and 23, 16% between 24 and 25, 14% between 26 and 28, and 12% above 28. Applicants must rank in the upper half of their class, present an average of C or better, and have graduated from an accredited high school with 16 Carnegie units. The minimum acceptable score on each part of the SAT is 400; the minimum score on the ACT is 18. Other factors considered are impressions made during an interview and recommendations by school officials.

Procedure: Candidates must take the SAT or the ACT, preferably by January of the senior year. Students who want to waive the foreign-language requirement should take an AT in a language. Application deadlines are open. Acceptance is on a rolling basis. A $15 application fee is required.

Special: Early and deferred admissions plans and an early decision plan are available. AP and CLEP credit is accepted.

Transfer: For fall 1981, 53 students applied, 47 were accepted, and 37 enrolled. Applicants with an average of C or better usually are accepted. Students must earn at least 30 credits in residence of the 120 required for a bachelor's degree. Application deadlines are open.

Visiting: Guides are available for informal visits. Visitors may sit in on classes and stay overnight. Arrangements should be made with the director of admissions.

Financial Aid: About 60% of the students receive aid. Nearly 100 scholarships are granted to undergraduates. Loans also are available. Applicants should submit the admissions application, the FAF, FFS, or SFS, and the aid application by August 15 (fall) or December 15 (spring).

Foreign Students: Foreign students enrolled at the college represent about 4% of the student body.

Admissions: Applicants must take the TOEFL. No academic exams are required.

Procedure: Application deadlines are open; students are admitted in fall and spring. Students must submit a completed health form as proof of good health and must show evidence of adequate funds for at least 1 year. Health insurance is not required.

Admissions Contact: Edwin B. Reger, Director of Admissions.

COE COLLEGE   E-3
Cedar Rapids, Iowa 52402   (319) 399-8500

F/T: 552M, 535W		Faculty:	91; IIB,+$
P/T: 41M, 121W		Ph.D.'s:	80%
Grad: none		S/F Ratio:	14 to 1
Year: 4-1-4, ss		Tuition:	$4600
Appl: May 1		R and B:	$1650
706 applied	640 accepted		274 enrolled
SAT: 460V 520M	ACT: 23		COMPETITIVE+

Founded in 1851, Coe is an independent Christian liberal arts college affiliated with the United Presbyterian Church. Its library contains 180,000 volumes and subscribes to over 560 periodicals.

Environment: The 31-acre campus is located 10 blocks from downtown Cedar Rapids. The dormitories house 850 students. Off-campus apartments are available.

Student Life: About 55% of the students come from Iowa; 75% of the freshmen are graduates of public schools. Two percent are minority-group members. All single students not living with their families are required to live on campus. Campus housing is both coed and single-sex. There are visiting privileges in single-sex dorms. Students may keep cars on campus.

Organizations: There are 5 national fraternities and 3 national sororities represented; about 25% of the students belong. Activities include student government, student publications, musical and dramatic performances, debates, and a fine arts festival.

Sports: The college competes in 11 intercollegiate sports for men and 9 for women. There are 9 intramural sports for men and women.

Handicapped: There are no special facilities for the physically handicapped.

Graduates: About 16% of the freshmen drop out after the first year; 60% remain to graduate and of these 17% go on to graduate schools. Almost 4% enter medical school, 5% dental school, and 6% law schools. Over 45% of the students pursue careers in business and industry.

Services: Free remedial instruction, psychological counseling, and career counseling are offered to students. Some free health care and tutoring services are available; others require payment.

Programs of Study: All programs lead to the B.A., B.S.N., and B.Mus. degrees. Bachelor's degrees are offered in the following subjects: AREA STUDIES (American, Black/Afro-American), BUSINESS (accounting, business administration, computer science), EDUCATION (elementary, health/physical, secondary), ENGLISH (English, literature, speech), FINE AND PERFORMING ARTS (art, art education, music, music education, theater/dramatics), HEALTH SCIENCES (nursing), LANGUAGES (French, German, Spanish), MATH AND SCIENCES (biology, biosocial science, chemistry, ecology/environmental science, mathematics, natural sciences, physics), PHILOSOPHY (humanities, philosophy, religion), PREPROFESSIONAL (dentistry, engineering, law, medicine, ministry, social work), SOCIAL SCIENCES (economics, government/political science, history, psychology, sociology). Most degrees are awarded in business administration and the social sciences.

Special: Students may earn a combined B.A.-B.S. degree in engineering. Off-campus studies and cooperative programs with other nearby colleges are available as well as internships.

Honors: There are 4 national honor societies on campus, along with the college's own honor program.

Admissions: Ninety-one percent of those who applied were accepted for the 1981–82 freshman class. The SAT scores of those who enrolled were as follows: Verbal—68% scored below 500, 25% between 500 and 599, 6% between 600 and 700, and 1% above 700; Math—41% scored below 500, 34% between 500 and 599, 21% between 600 and 700, and 4% above 700. On the ACT, 14% scored below 21, 23% between 20 and 23, 25% between 24 and 26, 12% between 27 and 29, and 6% above 29. Applicants must rank in the upper 50% of their class with a C+ average or better. Personality, special talents, and extracurricular activities record are also considered.

Procedure: Either the SAT or ACT is required. The SAT should be taken in December, January, or March of the senior year. The college uses a modified rolling admissions policy, with the closing date determined by available dormitory space. Applications should be submitted with a $15 fee by May 1 (fall), January 1 (spring) and June 6 (summer).

Special: Early decision, early admissions, and deferred admissions plans are offered. Early admission applications should be in by December 1. AP and CLEP credit is accepted.

Transfer: For fall 1981, 241 applications were received, 167 accepted, and 70 students enrolled. A 2.0 GPA is necessary, D grades do not transfer. There is a 30-hour residency requirement. Students must also complete, at the college, 9 of the 36 credits necessary for the bachelor's degree. Deadlines are the same as for freshman applicants.

Visiting: Visitors are welcome and visits can be arranged weekdays through the admissions office.

Financial Aid: The college makes $1,400,000 available for scholarships and about 77% of the students receive some form of financial aid. Sixty-five percent of the students work part-time on campus. Students can earn up to $700 from campus employment. The college is a member of CSS and the FAF or FFS must be filed. Financial aid applications must be in by June 30.

Foreign Students: Foreign students comprise about 10% of the full-time enrollment. The college, which actively recruits these students, offers them an intensive English program as well as special counseling and special organizations.

Admissions: Foreign students must achieve a score of 500 on the TOEFL. The SAT and ACT are not required.

Procedure: Application deadlines are June (fall), November (winter and spring), and April (summer). A health certificate or physician's report is required as proof of health. Foreign students must furnish proof of funds adequate to cover all periods of study. They must also carry health insurance, which is available through the college.

Admissions Contact: Peter D. Feickert, Dean of Admissions.

CORNELL COLLEGE   E-3
Mount Vernon, Iowa 52314   (319) 895-8811

F/T: 476M, 431W	Faculty:	70; IIB, ++$
P/T: 4M, 2W	Ph.D.'s:	75%
Grad: none	S/F Ratio:	12 to 1
Year: see profile	Tuition:	$5112
Appl: open	R and B:	$1866
890 applied		302 enrolled
SAT: 501V 510M	ACT: 24	COMPETITIVE+

Cornell College, founded in 1853, is a privately endowed, liberal arts college related to the United Methodist Church. The library contains 172,000 volumes and 13,000 microfilm items, and subscribes to 900 periodicals.

Environment: The 100-acre campus is located 15 miles from Cedar Rapids. The 30 buildings include a student union and 9 dormitories.

Student Life: About 26% of the students are from Iowa. The other 74% are from out of state, including 12% from foreign countries. Almost all students reside on campus. College housing is both coed and single-sex.

Organizations: There are a number of fraternities and sororities at the college. Cultural, athletic, and social events, as well as student activities, are centered on campus.

Sports: The college fields 10 intercollegiate teams for men and 7 for women. There are 18 intramural sports for men and 18 for women.

Handicapped: There are no special facilities for the handicapped.

Graduates: The freshman dropout rate is 20%; 50% to 60% remain to graduate. About 50% to 60% of the graduates seek advanced degrees.

Services: The following services are available to students free of charge: placement, career, and psychological counseling; and tutoring or remedial instruction. Health care is provided for a fee.

Programs of Study: The college confers the degrees of B.A., B.Mus., B.Ph., and B.S.S. Bachelor's degrees are offered in the following subjects: AREA STUDIES (American, Russian), BUSINESS (business administration), EDUCATION (elementary, health/physical, secondary), ENGLISH (English, literature, speech), FINE AND PERFORMING ARTS (art, music, music education, studio art, theater/dramatics), HEALTH SCIENCES (medical technology), LANGUAGES (French, German, Greek/Latin, Russian, Spanish), MATH AND SCIENCES (biology, chemistry, ecology/environmental science, geology, mathematics, physics), PHILOSOPHY (classics, humanities, philosophy, religion), PREPROFESSIONAL (dentistry, engineering, forestry, law, medicine, ministry, social work, veterinary), SOCIAL SCIENCES (economics, government/political science, history, psychology, sociology).

Special: All students take 1 course at a time; the school year is divided into 9 terms of 3½ weeks each. A 3-2 program in forestry is offered in cooperation with Duke University, a 3-2 program in social work is available with the University of Chicago, and a 3-2 program in hospital and health administration is available with the University of Iowa. Study abroad and an independent study program are also offered. Students may design their own majors.

Honors: Eight honor societies, including Phi Beta Kappa, have chapters on campus. All departments offer honors programs.

Admissions: About 88% of those who applied were accepted for the 1981-82 freshman class. Applicants should rank in the top third of their graduating class. The college also considers recommendations from school officials and evidence of special talents.

Procedure: Either the SAT or the ACT is required. A personal interview is recommended. Application deadlines are open; students are admitted at the beginning of each of 9 terms. The college uses a rolling admissions policy. All applications should be submitted with a $15 fee.

Special: Early admissions, early decision, and deferred admissions plans are offered. AP and CLEP credit is available.

Transfer: About 30 students transfer yearly. Most transfer applicants are accepted; good academic standing is required. D grades do not transfer. There is a 1-year residency requirement.

Visiting: Guides are available for informal visits. Visitors may sit in on classes and stay overnight at the school during the week. The admissions office must be contacted for arrangements.

Financial Aid: The college is a member of the CSS. Scholarships ranging from $1000 to full tuition are awarded to 65% of the freshmen. Tuition may be paid under a deferred payment plan. CWS is available. The FAF or FFS is required.

Foreign Students: Twelve percent of the students come from foreign countries. Intensive English courses, special counseling, and special organizations are available for these students.

Admissions: Foreign students must take oral and written tests in English at the college before registration.

Procedure: Interested students should contact the college's foreign student services office.

Admissions Contact: Frank G. Krivo, Dean of Admissions.

DORDT COLLEGE B-1
Sioux Center, Iowa 51250 (712) 722-6080

F/T: 499M, 587W	Faculty: 64; IIB, av$
P/T: 4M, 6W	Ph.D.'s: 37%
Grad: none	S/F Ratio: 17 to 1
Year: sems	Tuition: $3400
Appl: Aug. 31	R and B: $1410
463 applied	460 accepted 371 enrolled
ACT: 22	**LESS COMPETITIVE**

Dordt College, founded in 1955, is a private liberal arts college, affiliated with the Christian Reformed Church. Its library contains 110,000 volumes and 150 reels of microfilms, and subscribes to 740 periodicals.

Environment: The 45-acre rural campus is located in a small town, 42 miles from Sioux City. In addition to dormitories, the college also sponsors on- and off-campus apartments and married student housing.

Student Life: Only 32% of the students come from Iowa, and 68% come from bordering states. About 70% of the freshmen attended private schools. All the students are Protestant. Chapel attendance is required twice a week. About 75% of the students live on campus and must observe a curfew with a sign-out procedure. Campus housing is single-sex; there are visiting privileges. Students may keep cars on campus.

Organizations: There are no fraternities or sororities on campus. A strong student government has jurisdiction in many areas and provides social and cultural events on campus.

Sports: The college fields 9 intercollegiate teams for men and 7 for women. There are 10 intramural sports for men and 10 for women.

Handicapped: Special facilities for the handicapped are minimal.

Graduates: About 26% of the freshmen drop out after the first year; 60% remain to graduate. About 2% of graduates go to medical school, 1% to dental school, and 2% to law school. Twenty-eight percent enter business and industry.

Services: The college offers free career counseling, tutoring, and remedial instruction. Placement services are available on a fee basis.

Programs of Study: The B.A. degree is offered in the following subjects: BUSINESS (accounting, agribusiness, business administration), EDUCATION (elementary, secondary), ENGLISH (English), FINE AND PERFORMING ARTS (art, art education, music, music education, theater/dramatics), HEALTH SCIENCES (medical technology), LANGUAGES (German), MATH AND SCIENCES (biology, chemistry, mathematics, natural sciences, physics), PREPROFESSIONAL (agriculture, dentistry, engineering, forestry, law, medicine, ministry, pharmacy, social work), SOCIAL SCIENCES (government/political science, history, psychology, social sciences, sociology).

Required: All undergraduates are required to take courses in physical education, English, science, theology, and a foreign language.

Special: Students are permitted to participate in study-abroad programs. Combination degrees are offered in engineering and medical technology.

Admissions: Over 99% of those who applied were accepted for the 1981-82 freshman class. The ACT scores of those who enrolled were as follows: 17% below 21, 40% between 21 and 23, 30% between 24 and 25, 10% between 26 and 28, and 3% above 28. Candidates should have completed 12 Carnegie units and should have a GPA of 1.86.

Procedure: The ACT is required and should be taken by September. Deadlines for applications are August 31 (fall) and January 14 (winter). A $10 fee should accompany the application. There is a rolling admissions plan.

Transfer: For fall 1981, 75 students applied and were accepted, and 65 enrolled. Applicants must have passing grades; D grades transfer. A minimum GPA of 1.86 is required; 2.0 is recommended. There is a 1-year residency requirement, and students must complete, at the college, 30 of the 120 credits required for the bachelor's degree. Application deadlines are the same as those for freshmen.

Visiting: Visitors are welcome and tours can be arranged in advance through the admissions office.

Financial Aid: About 90% of the students receive some form of financial aid. The average award to freshmen from all sources available through the college is $1500. Federal work-study funds are available in certain departments; work contracts are awarded to 55% of the students. Federal and private loans are also available. The college is a member of the CSS. Either the FAF or the FFS is acceptable. The deadline for financial aid applications is May 15 (fall) or December 15 (winter).

Foreign Students: Twenty percent of the students come from foreign countries. The college offers these students individual tutoring if needed.

Admissions: Foreign students must take the ACT.

Procedure: Application deadlines are the same as those for other freshmen. Students must present proof of funds adequate to cover 1 year of study. Health insurance, while not required, is available through the college for a fee.

Admissions Contact: Howard J. Hall, Director of Admissions.

DRAKE UNIVERSITY C-3
Des Moines, Iowa 50311 (515) 271-3181

F/T, P/T:	Faculty: 387; IIA, +$
4900M&W	Ph.D.'s: 64%
Grad: 1500M&W	S/F Ratio: 12 to 1
Year: sems, ss	Tuition: $4590
Appl: Aug. 15	R and B: $2120
2512 applied	1989 accepted 1976 enrolled
ACT: 22	**COMPETITIVE**

Drake University is an independent, nonsectarian university consisting of the undergraduate colleges of Liberal Arts, Business Administration,

Education, Fine Arts, and Pharmacy; the School of Journalism; the Law School; the Graduate Division; and the College for Continuing Education. The Cowles Library contains over 400,000 volumes and 225,000 microfilm items, and subscribes to 2000 periodicals. There is also the Law School Library, the Curriculum Library, and the Pharmacy Reading Room.

Environment: The 75-acre campus is located in a suburban area of Des Moines. Students live in coed dormitories and fraternity housing.

Student Life: About 42% of the students are from Iowa. Half live on campus. The majority of the students are Protestants, but most major religious denominations are represented on campus.

Organizations: There are 11 fraternities and 9 sororities; 20% of the men and 20% of the women belong. Student organizations provide social activities, and the city of Des Moines also offers cultural opportunities.

Sports: Intercollegiate and intramural sports are available for men and women.

Handicapped: Facilities for handicapped students include wheelchair ramps, special parking, elevators, specially equipped rest rooms, lowered drinking fountains, and lowered telephones. Special class scheduling is also available. A counselor is available to handicapped students.

Graduates: The freshman dropout rate is 24%, and 43% remain to graduate. About 23% of the graduates pursue advanced degrees, and about 63% pursue careers in business and industry.

Services: The following services are available free to students: health care, and placement, psychological, and career counseling.

Programs of Study: Drake confers the B.A., B.S., B.S.Pharm., B.S.B.A., B.S.Ed., B.F.A., B.Mus., B.Mus.Ed., and B.A.Journ. degrees. Master's and doctoral degrees also are awarded. Bachelor's degrees are offered in the following subjects: BUSINESS (accounting, advertising, business administration, computer science, finance, management, marketing, real estate/insurance), EDUCATION (early childhood, elementary, health/physical, secondary, special), ENGLISH (English, journalism, literature, speech), FINE AND PERFORMING ARTS (art, art education, art history, music, music education, radio/TV, theater/dramatics), HEALTH SCIENCES (medical technology), LANGUAGES (French, German, Spanish), MATH AND SCIENCES (astronomy, biology, botany, chemistry, earth science, geology, marine biology, mathematics, natural sciences, physical sciences, physics, statistics), PHILOSOPHY (humanities, philosophy, religion), PREPROFESSIONAL (dentistry, law, medicine, pharmacy), SOCIAL SCIENCES (criminal justice, economics, geography, government/political science, history, international relations, psychology, public administration, social sciences, sociology).

Special: It is possible to earn a combined B.A.-B.S. degree or a B.G.S. degree. Students may design their own majors. The university offers a junior year abroad; Washington, United Nations, and Appalachian semesters; and a cooperative education program.

Honors: About 37 honor and professional societies have chapters on campus.

Admissions: About 79% of those who applied were accepted for the 1981-82 freshman class. For an earlier class, the SAT scores were as follows: Verbal—30% between 500 and 600, 12% above 600; Math —24% between 500 and 600, 31% between 600 and 700. On the ACT, 14% were between 20 and 23, 21% between 24 and 26, 19% between 27 and 28, and 8% above 28. Applicants should rank in the top half of their high school class and generally should have at least a B average. The university also considers advanced placement or honors courses, impressions made during an interview, leadership record, and extracurricular activities.

Procedure: The ACT is required. Application deadlines are August 15 (fall) and December 15 (spring). A $20 fee must accompany all applications. The university uses a rolling admissions policy.

Special: Early decision, early admissions, and deferred admissions plans are offered. AP and CLEP credit is available.

Transfer: A GPA of 2.0 or better and good academic standing at the last college are required. There is a 30-hour residency requirement.

Visiting: Guides are available for informal visits, which are best scheduled weekdays from 9 A.M. to 3 P.M.. Visitors may sit in on classes. The admissions office should be contacted for arrangements.

Financial Aid: About 55% of the students receive aid. The university is a member of the CSS and awards scholarships, grants, loans, and work. The FAF is required. The deadline for financial aid applications is March 1.

Foreign Students: About 120 foreign students are enrolled full-time at the university. An intensive English course, an intensive English program, special organizations, and special counseling all are available.

Admissions: Students must score 500 or better on the TOEFL. No academic exams are required.

Procedure: Applications should be filed at least 3 months before the beginning of the semester in which the student seeks to enroll. Students must present a completed health certificate and proof of adequate funds for 1 year. They must carry health insurance, which is available through the university for a fee.

Admissions Contact: Everett E. Hadley, Executive Director of Admissions.

GRACELAND COLLEGE   C–4
Lamoni, Iowa 50140   (515) 784-3311

F/T: 553M, 597W   Faculty: 91; IIB, –$
P/T: 35M, 111W   Ph.D.'s: 36%
Grad: none   S/F Ratio: 12 to 1
Year: 4-1-4, ss   Tuition: $4060
Appl: open   R and B: $1710
SAT or ACT: required   **LESS COMPETITIVE**

Graceland College, founded in 1895, is an independent, coeducational institution sponsored by the Reorganized Church of Jesus Christ of the Latter-day Saints. The library contains more than 85,000 volumes and subscribes to 600 periodicals.

Environment: The 175-acre campus is located in a rural community about 80 miles from Des Moines. The 18 major buildings include dormitories that accommodate 335 women and 358 men; there is limited housing for married students.

Student Life: Seventy-five percent of the students come from out of state. About 75% live on campus. Campus housing is single-sex. Most of the students are members of the Reorganized Church of Jesus Christ of the Latter-day Saints. Attendance at religious services is not required. Drinking and smoking are prohibited on campus. Freshmen and sophomores who do not live with parents or guardians must live in college-approved housing.

Organizations: The college has no fraternities or sororities, but other social groups and extracurricular activities are available.

Sports: The college participates in 10 intercollegiate sports for men and 8 for women. At least 6 intramural sports are available for men and women.

Graduates: Ten percent of the freshmen drop out. About 10% of the graduates pursue further study.

Programs of Study: All programs lead to the B.A. or B.S. degree. Bachelor's degrees are offered in the following subjects: BUSINESS (business administration, business education, computer engineering, computer science), EDUCATION (elementary, health/physical, secondary), ENGLISH (English, speech), FINE AND PERFORMING ARTS (art, music, music education, theater/dramatics), HEALTH SCIENCES (medical technology, nursing), LANGUAGES (German, modern foreign language, Spanish), MATH AND SCIENCES (biology, chemistry, mathematics, science), PHILOSOPHY (religion), PREPROFESSIONAL (law, medicine), SOCIAL SCIENCES (economics, government/political science, history, international studies, psychology, social sciences, sociology).

Required: Students must take courses in English, speech, physical education, and 6 of the following 9 areas: biological science, physical science, mathematics, fine arts, foreign language, literature, history or political science, religion or philosophy, and social science.

Special: Students may spend their junior year abroad. An interdepartmental major in social welfare and a combination degree program in special education with Drake University are available. Students may design their own majors.

Admissions: Applicants must have at least a C average in 15 or more Carnegie units. Other factors considered include recommendations from high school officials, class rank, extracurricular activities, and leadership potential. Recommendations from friends and alumni also may help.

Procedure: The ACT or SAT is required and should be taken by December of the senior year. Applications should be filed in the summer before desired entrance, although deadlines are open. There is a $20 application fee.

Special: Early admissions and early decision plans are offered. AP and CLEP are used.

Transfer: A GPA of at least 2.0 is required. Students must complete at least 24 of the final 32 credits in residence; 128 credits are required for a bachelor's degree.

IOWA

Financial Aid: Federal loans, loans from the college, scholarships, grants, and campus jobs are available. Deadlines for financial-aid applications are open. The FAF or FFS is required.

Foreign Students: The college offers foreign students intensive English courses and special counseling.

Admissions: The TOEFL exam is recommended.

Procedure: Applications from foreign countries are handled on an individual basis. The college requires foreign students to fill out a special information form before an application for admissions is supplied. Interested students should contact the office of international student affairs.

Admissions Contact: Robert L. Watts, Director of Admissions.

GRAND VIEW COLLEGE C–3
Des Moines, Iowa 50316 (515) 263-2810

F/T: 450M, 515W Faculty: 52; IIB, av$
P/T: 92M, 239W Ph.D.'s: 20%
Grad: none S/F Ratio: 16 to 1
Year: 4-4-1, ss Tuition: $2904
Appl: open R and B: $1700
750 applied 749 accepted 353 enrolled
ACT: 19 LESS COMPETITIVE

Grand View College, founded in 1896, is a small, liberal arts college affiliated with the Lutheran Church. The library holds 60,000 volumes and subscribes to 450 periodicals.

Environment: The 25-acre campus is located in the city of Des Moines. The 10 buildings on campus include 2 dormitories that house 225 students. Five apartments also are available on campus for upper-division students.

Student Life: About 90% of the students come from Iowa, and almost all attended public schools. Fifteen percent live on campus. Seventy percent of the students are Protestant and 23% are Catholic. Nine percent are minority-group members. Campus housing is single-sex. Students may keep cars on campus.

Organizations: There are no fraternities or sororities. Extracurricular activities include various special-interest groups.

Sports: The college fields 4 intercollegiate sports for men and 5 for women. There are 6 intramural sports for men and 5 for women.

Handicapped: About 50% of the campus is accessible to the handicapped. Special facilities include wheelchair ramps, parking areas, and elevators. Special class scheduling is possible.

Graduates: Seven percent of freshmen drop out by the end of the first year; 62% remain to graduate.

Services: The college provides free career counseling for undergraduates. Health care, tutoring, and remedial instruction are also available.

Programs of Study: The college confers the B.A. and B.S.N. degrees. Associate degrees also are offered. Bachelor's degrees are offered in the following subjects: AREA STUDIES (American), BUSINESS (business administration, computer science), ENGLISH (English, journalism), FINE AND PERFORMING ARTS (art, commercial art, radio/TV), HEALTH SCIENCES (nursing), PHILOSOPHY (humanities, religion), PREPROFESSIONAL (dentistry, law, medicine, ministry, social work, veterinary), SOCIAL SCIENCES (social sciences).

Admissions: Nearly all those who applied for the 1981–82 freshman class were accepted. The candidate should have completed 15 Carnegie units and have a C average.

Procedure: Either the SAT or the ACT is required. There are no application deadlines. There is a rolling admissions plan. The application fee is $15.

Special: AP and CLEP credit is available.

Transfer: For fall 1981, all 246 transfer students who applied were accepted and 118 enrolled. A GPA of 2.0 is recommended; all passing grades transfer. Students must complete, at the college, the last 30 of the 124 to 130 credits necessary for a bachelor's degree. There are no application deadlines.

Visiting: Visitors are welcome between 9 A.M. and 2 P.M. daily, and visits can be arranged through the admissions office.

Financial Aid: About 62% of all students receive some form of financial aid; the average award is $1800. Ten percent of the students work part-time on campus. The college is a member of CSS. The FAF should be filed by March 1 for fall entry. Tuition may be paid in installments.

Foreign Students: Five percent of the students are from foreign countries. The college offers these students an intensive English course, special counseling, and special organizations.

Admissions: Foreign students are required to take the TOEFL. No college entrance exam is required.

Procedure: The application deadlines are June 1 for fall entry and November 1 for spring entry. Foreign students must undergo a physical and submit a health history form. Proof of adequate funds for 1 academic year is required. Health insurance is not required.

Admissions Contact: Jerry Slater, Director of Admissions.

GRINNELL COLLEGE D–3
Grinnell, Iowa 50112 (515) 236-7545

F/T: 657M, 573W Faculty: 105; IIB, ++$
P/T: none Ph.D.'s: 82%
Grad: none S/F Ratio: 11 to 1
Year: sems Tuition: $5950
Appl: Feb. 15 R and B: $1765
1161 applied 837 accepted 353 enrolled
SAT: 580V 600M ACT: 27 HIGHLY COMPETITIVE+

Grinnell is a privately endowed, nonsectarian liberal arts college that was founded by Congregationalists in 1846. Its library contains 250,000 volumes and 4000 microfilm items, and subscribes to 1500 periodicals. A two-story addition to the library under construction in 1981–82 was to increase capacity to 550,000 volumes.

Environment: The wooded campus, covering 90 acres, is located in the small residential community of Grinnell, 55 miles from Des Moines. The college also has a 365-acre environmental research area near Grinnell.

Student Life: Only 11% are Iowa residents; the rest of the students come from 47 states and 35 other nations. About 82% attended public schools. Ninety-two percent of the students live on campus. About 9% of the students are minority-group members. Campus housing is both single-sex and coed; there are visiting privileges for single-sex housing. Students may keep cars on campus. Day-care services are available to faculty and staff.

Organizations: There are no fraternities or sororities on campus. The student government organizes and sponsors many events. More than 100 student-organized, student-run groups and clubs are active on campus. There is an extensive cultural program.

Sports: The college fields 14 intercollegiate teams for men and 12 for women. There are 19 intramural sports for men and 19 for women.

Handicapped: About 50% of the campus is accessible to the handicapped. Special facilities include wheelchair ramps, elevators, and specially equipped restrooms. Special class scheduling and tutoring are provided.

Graduates: About 3% of the freshmen drop out and 78% remain to graduate. About 65% of the graduates pursue further studies. Of these, 9% enter medical school, 2% enter dental school, and 8% enter law school. About 35% pursue careers in business and industry.

Services: Students receive free health care, tutoring, psychological counseling, placement aid, and career counseling.

Programs of Study: All programs lead to the B.A. degree. Bachelor's degrees are offered in the following subjects: AREA STUDIES (American, Black/Afro-American, Latin American, Russian, urban, Western European), EDUCATION (elementary, secondary), ENGLISH (English, general literary studies), FINE AND PERFORMING ARTS (art, music, theater/dramatics), LANGUAGES (French, German, Greek/Latin, Russian, Spanish), MATH AND SCIENCES (biology, chemistry, computer studies, ecology/environmental science, general science, mathematics, physics), PHILOSOPHY (classics, humanities, philosophy, religion), SOCIAL SCIENCES (anthropology, economics, government/political science, history, international relations, psychology, social sciences, sociology). Preprofessional studies, although not major programs, are available. Thirty percent of degrees are conferred in math and sciences, 39% in social sciences, and 31% in humanities.

Required: A freshman tutorial seminar is required.

Special: Students may design their own majors. Over 50 off-campus study programs are available both abroad and in the U.S. A wide range of nonmajor preprofessional programs is offered.

Honors: Phi Beta Kappa and Sigma Delta Chi are represented on campus.

Admissions: Seventy-two percent of those who applied were accepted for the 1981–82 freshman class. The SAT scores of those who enrolled were as follows: Verbal—16% scored below 500, 44% between 500 and 599, 30% between 600 and 700, and 10% above 700; Math—9% scored below 500, 36% between 500 and 599, 41% between 600 and 700, and 14% above 700. Candidates should have completed 16 Carnegie units and have at least a B average. The college also considers advanced placement or honors courses, recommendations by counselors and teachers, an application essay, an interview (recommended, but not required), evidence of special talents, and extracurricular activities.

Procedure: Either the SAT or ACT should be taken by December or January of the senior year. The deadline for fall entry is February 15 and for spring entry November 1. Applications should be accompanied by a $20 fee.

Special: Early and deferred admissions plans are available. AP credit is given. Early decisions are possible on applications received by December 15 for students whose first-choice college is Grinnell.

Transfer: For fall 1981, 72 of 112 applicants were accepted, and 41 enrolled. Four semesters must be taken in residence. D grades do not transfer. Students must complete, at the college, 62 of the 124 credits necessary for a bachelor's degree. The deadlines to apply are June 1 for fall and December 15 for spring, but preference will be given to early applications.

Visiting: Orientations for new students are scheduled regularly, and informal visits can be arranged through the admissions office. Visitors may sit in on classes and stay overnight at the school.

Financial Aid: The college has more than $3 million available for scholarships, grants, and loans. Sixty-nine percent of all students receive some form of financial aid; 40% work part-time on campus. The average financial aid package is $4903; the average scholarship is $3583. Applicants for aid should file the FAF with CSS at least 4 weeks prior to the decision notification deadline.

Foreign Students: The college actively recruits foreign students; nearly 5% of the full-time students are from foreign countries. Special counseling and special organizations are offered.

Admissions: Foreign students must receive a minimum score of 550 on the TOEFL. The SAT or ACT is also required.

Procedure: Application deadlines are February 15 for fall and November 1 for spring. Students must complete the college's health form, and must present proof of adequate funds for 1 academic year. Health insurance is required and is available through the college for a fee.

Admissions Contact: John R. Hopkins, Director of Admissions and Student Financial Aid.

IOWA STATE UNIVERSITY C–3
Ames, Iowa 50011 (515) 294-5836

F/T: 11,822M, 7445W	Faculty: 1833; n/av
P/T: 797M, 737W	Ph.D.'s: 62%
Grad: 2195M, 1206W	S/F Ratio: 19 to 1
Year: early sems, ss	Tuition: $950 ($2350)
Appl: open	R and B: $1640
8059 applied	7223 accepted	4107 enrolled
ACT: 24		COMPETITIVE+

Iowa State University was established in 1858 as a public nonsectarian university. The library contains 1,450,000 volumes, 1,300,000 microfilm items, and subscribes to over 18,000 periodicals.

Environment: The 1000-acre urban campus is located 30 miles north of Des Moines. The 75 buildings include a spacious student union, a music building, and residence halls accommodating nearly 50% of the student body. The Energy Research and Development Commission also maintains a research installation on the campus.

Student Life: Over 75% of the students are from Iowa; 50% of the women and 40% of the men reside on campus. Three percent are minority-group members. Campus housing is both coed and single-sex. There are visiting privileges in single-sex dorms. Students may keep cars on campus. The university provides day-care services to all students, faculty, and staff for a fee.

Organizations: There are 16 national sororities and 32 national fraternities. The Iowa State Theatre and the Brunnier Gallery provide cultural activities on campus.

Sports: The university belongs to the Big 8 Conference. It fields 11 intercollegiate teams for men and 10 for women. There are 13 intramural sports for both men and women.

Handicapped: About half the campus is accessible to the physically handicapped. Special facilities include transportation, wheelchair ramps, parking areas, elevators, lowered drinking fountains and telephones, and specially equipped restrooms. Special class scheduling is possible. There is an equipment repair service as well. For students with visual impairments there are braille computers. Special counseling is provided for handicapped students.

Graduates: About 20% of freshmen drop out after the first year; 57% remain to graduate. Of these, 15% pursue further studies after graduation.

Services: Students receive free psychological counseling, placement and career planning services.

Programs of Study: The university confers the B.A., B.Arch., B.B.A., B.F.A., B.L.A., B.Land. Arch., B.Mus., and B.S. degrees. Master's and doctoral degrees are also possible. Bachelor's degrees are offered in the following subjects: BUSINESS (accounting, agri-business, business administration, computer science, finance, institution management, management, marketing, transportation/logistics), EDUCATION (agricultural, early childhood, elementary, health/physical, home economics, industrial, leisure studies, secondary), ENGLISH (English, journalism, speech), FINE AND PERFORMING ARTS (art, art education, craft design, dance, graphic design, interior design, music, music education), HEALTH SCIENCES (food and nutrition), LANGUAGES (French, German, Russian, Spanish), MATH AND SCIENCES (agricultural biochemistry, biochemistry, biology, biometry, biophysics, botany, chemistry, earth science, entomology, food technology, geology, horticulture, mathematics, metallurgy, meteorology, microbiology, physics, plant pathology, statistics, wildlife biology, zoology), PHILOSOPHY (philosophy), PREPROFESSIONAL (law, medicine, veterinary), SOCIAL SCIENCES (anthropology, economics, government/political science, history, international studies, psychology, sociology). Over 32% of degrees conferred are in sciences and humanities, 20% in agriculture and 18% in engineering.

Special: General studies degrees and student-designed majors are allowed. International service programs are also offered.

Honors: There are 32 honor societies as well as varied honors programs.

Admissions: About 90% of those who applied were accepted for the 1981-82 freshman class. Of those who enrolled, the ACT scores were as follows: 26% scored below 21, 21% between 21 and 23, 17% between 24 and 25, 24% between 26 and 28, and 12% above 28. Applicants must be graduated from an accredited high school and rank in the upper half of their class for unconditional admission. Nonresidents must rank in the top 50% of their class. Impressions made during interview and recommendations by school officials are also considered important.

Procedure: The SAT or ACT is required and should be taken by July of the senior year. There is a rolling admissions plan. Applications should be accompanied by a $10 fee.

Special: AP and CLEP credit is accepted. There are also deferred and early admissions plans.

Transfer: Transfer students are admitted in fall, spring, and summer; there are no application deadlines. Students must have a 2.0 GPA; D grades do transfer. Students must complete, at the university, the last 32 semester hours of the 124.5 required for the bachelor's degree.

Visiting: There is a summer orientation for prospective students. Campus tours are given twice a day when school is in session. Visitors may sit in on classes.

Financial Aid: About 53% of all students receive some form of financial aid; 25% work part-time on campus. The FAF or FFS must be filed and financial aid applications should be made by March 1.

Foreign Students: Almost 7% of the full-time students come from foreign countries. The university offers these students an intensive English program and special counseling and organizations.

Admissions: Foreign students must achieve a score of 500 on the TOEFL. The SAT and ACT are not required.

Procedure: Admission deadlines are July 25 (fall), December 19 (spring), and May 1 (summer). Foreign students must furnish proof of funds sufficient to cover the entire program of study. Health insurance is available through the university for a fee.

Admissions Contact: Karsten Smedal, Director of Admissions.

IOWA WESLEYAN COLLEGE E–4
Mt. Pleasant, Iowa 52641 (319) 385-4614

F/T: 242M, 373W	Faculty: 60; IIB, –$
P/T: 144M, 72W	Ph.D.'s: 31%
Grad: none	S/F Ratio: 11 to 1
Year: 4-1-4, ss	Tuition: $4060
Appl: Aug. 15	R and B: $1520
357 applied	282 accepted	136 enrolled
SAT or ACT: required		COMPETITIVE

IOWA

Iowa Wesleyan is a small, private liberal arts college affiliated with the Methodist Church. Its library contains over 89,170 volumes, subscriptions to more than 820 periodicals, and over 2100 reels of microfilm.

Environment: The 60-acre rural campus is located 28 miles from Burlington, and consists of 13 major buildings of varied architecture. The dormitories accommodate 800 men and women.

Student Life: About 60% of the students are from Iowa and Illinois; 90% of entering freshmen come from public schools. Almost 75% of students live on campus. Seven percent are minority-group members. Eighty percent of the students are Protestant, 18% are Catholic, and 1% are Jewish. Although the majority of students are Methodist, there are religious facilities for 31 other denominations. Campus housing is single-sex. There are visiting privileges. Students may keep cars on campus.

Organizations: There are 2 national fraternities with 17% membership and 3 national sororities with 24% membership on campus. There is a very active student government; students also belong to departmental clubs and special interest groups. All noncommuters must live in college-approved housing.

Sports: The college competes in 7 intercollegiate sports for men and 8 for women. There are 6 intramural sports for both men and women.

Handicapped: About 80% of the campus is accessible to the physically handicapped; special facilities include ramps and elevators.

Graduates: The freshman dropout rate is 10%; 60% remain to graduate. Of these, 15% continue their studies; 2% enter medical, 1% dental, and 3% law school. Over 25% pursue careers in business and industry.

Services: Free remedial instruction, placement, and career counseling are available. Both graduates and undergraduates can use placement services which include resume and interview workshops.

Programs of Study: The college awards the B.A., B.G.S., B.Mus.Ed., B.S., and B.S.N. degrees. Bachelor's degrees are offered in the following subjects: AREA STUDIES (American), BUSINESS (accounting, business administration, business education, computer science, industrial psychology/personnel administration), EDUCATION (early childhood, chemistry, elementary, health/physical, home economics, math, secondary, special), ENGLISH (English, speech), FINE AND PERFORMING ARTS (art, music, music education, studio art, theater/dramatics), HEALTH SCIENCES (medical technology, nursing, physical therapy), MATH AND SCIENCES (biology, chemistry, ecology/environmental science, mathematics, natural sciences, physical sciences), PHILOSOPHY (philosophy, religion), PREPROFESSIONAL (dentistry, engineering, forestry, law, medicine, ministry, pharmacy, veterinary), SOCIAL SCIENCES (government/political science, history, psychology, social sciences, social work, sociology). The majority of degrees are granted in education and business.

Required: Composition and rhetoric, required of all freshmen, may be satisfied by AP or CLEP examinations.

Special: There is a 3-2 forestry program, a 3-1 medical technology program, and a 3-2 engineering program. Students may create their own majors. The college allows a B.G.S. degree for students over 24.

Admissions: Almost 80% of those who applied were accepted for the 1981-82 freshman class. The ACT scores of those who enrolled were: 24% scored below 21, 45% between 21 and 23, 22% between 24 and 25, 6% between 26 and 28, and 1% above 28. The candidates were required to have taken either the SAT or ACT tests, have 15 Carnegie units, and graduate in the top half of their high school class. Advanced placement or honor courses and recommendations from school officials are also considered important.

Procedure: The SAT or ACT should be taken in August, December, or January of the senior year. The college uses the rolling admissions procedure. Application deadlines are August 15 (fall), January 1 (winter), February 1 (spring), and May 15 (summer). New students are admitted to all sessions. Applications should be accompanied by a $15 fee.

Special: There are early and deferred admissions plans. AP and CLEP credit is available.

Transfer: For fall 1981, 76 transfer students applied, 54 were accepted, and 50 enrolled. The basic requirement is a 2.0 GPA. Thirty hours, of the 124 necessary for the bachelor's degree, must be taken in residence. A rolling admissions policy is employed.

Visiting: Weekday tours of the college can be arranged through the office of admissions. Visitors may sit in on classes and stay overnight at the school.

Financial Aid: About 70% of all students receive some form of financial aid; 74% work part-time on campus. The FAF or FFS is required; the college is a member of the CSS. Tuition may be paid in installments. The deadline for state residents to apply for state grants is March 1. The college participates in NDSL, SEOG, and CWS.

Foreign Students: About 1% of the full-time students come from foreign countries.

Admissions: Foreign students must score in the 60th percentile on the TOEFL. The SAT, ACT, or GCE is also required.

Procedure: Foreign students may apply for fall entry. Proof of funds adequate to cover 1 year of study is necessary. Foreign students must also carry health insurance.

Admissions Contact: Laurie A. Wolf, Director of Admissions.

LORAS COLLEGE   E-2
Dubuque, Iowa 52001   (319) 588-7236

F/T: 1275M, 700W   Faculty: 106; IIA, —$
P/T: 200M, 125W   Ph.D.'s: 75%
Grad: 80M, 45W   S/F Ratio: 17 to 1
Year: sems, ss   Tuition: $4500
Appl: May 1   R and B: $1750
1200 applied   825 accepted   610 enrolled
ACT: 23   COMPETITIVE+

Loras, a Roman Catholic liberal arts college, was founded in 1839. Its library contains 240,000 volumes and subscribes to 1100 periodicals.

Environment: The 60-acre urban campus is located on one of the highest hills in Dubuque, within easy access of the city's business district. The campus consists of 14 buildings, including residence halls that house over 1900 students.

Student Life: About 35% of the students come from outside Iowa. Thirty-five percent attended public schools. Seventy percent of the students live in residence halls; freshmen are required to live on campus. About 99% of the students are Catholics. Two percent of the students are minority-group members. Campus housing is both single-sex and coed, with visiting privileges in single-sex housing. Students may keep cars on campus.

Organizations: There are chapters of 6 fraternities and 4 sororities, to which 55% of the men and 35% of the women belong. Social and cultural events are sponsored on campus.

Sports: The college participates in 14 intercollegiate sports for men and 11 for women. There are 13 intramural sports for men, 12 for women.

Handicapped: Special facilities for the physically handicapped include wheelchair ramps, parking areas, elevators, and specially equipped rest rooms. Special class scheduling can be arranged. The entire campus is accessible to the handicapped.

Graduates: About 15% of the freshmen drop out during the first year; 55% remain to graduate. Of these, 45% continue their studies; 5% enter medical school, 5% enter dental school, and 5% enter law school. Another 45% pursue careers in business and industry.

Services: Free health care, tutoring, remedial instruction, career and psychological counseling, and placement services are available.

Programs of Study: The college confers the B.A., B.S., and B.Mus.Ed. degrees. Associate and master's degrees are also awarded. Bachelor's degrees are offered in the following subjects: BUSINESS (accounting, business administration, computer science, finance, management, marketing), EDUCATION (adult, early childhood, elementary, health/physical, secondary, special), ENGLISH (English, journalism, speech), FINE AND PERFORMING ARTS (art, art education, music, music education, radio/TV), HEALTH SCIENCES (medical technology), LANGUAGES (French, German, Greek/Latin, Russian, Spanish), MATH AND SCIENCES (biology, chemistry, mathematics, physics), PHILOSOPHY (philosophy, religion), PREPROFESSIONAL (architecture, dentistry, engineering, forestry, law, medicine, ministry, pharmacy, social work, veterinary), SOCIAL SCIENCES (economics, government/political science, history, psychology, sociology). Most undergraduate degrees are conferred in the social sciences and business.

Required: Freshmen must demonstrate competency in English, speech, and logic.

Special: Preprofessional and 3-2 cooperative programs are available. Students may spend their junior year abroad and design their own majors. There is also a secondary teacher training program. A 3-year bachelor's degree program is available.

Honors: There are honor societies as well as departmental honors programs on campus.

Admissions: About 69% of those who applied were accepted for the 1981-82 freshman class. The candidate should be a graduate of an accredited high school, have completed 15 Carnegie units, have a 2.0 GPA or better, and rank in the upper two-thirds of his or her class. Recommendations, extracurricular activities, and honors courses are also considered important. Children of alumni are given preference.

Procedure: Either the ACT or SAT is required and should be taken by May of the senior year. Application deadlines are May 1 (fall) and January 1 (spring). Admission is on a rolling basis. Applications should be accompanied by a $15 fee. Freshmen are also admitted to the summer session.

Special: There is an early decision plan (notification in junior year) and an early admissions plan. AP and CLEP credit is available.

Transfer: For fall 1981, 130 transfer students applied, 98 were accepted, and 85 enrolled. The college requires a minimum GPA of 2.0 and an ACT score of 18 or higher. D grades transfer. Students must complete, at the college, 30 of the 128 credits required for a bachelor's degree. The deadlines are August 1 (fall), January 1 (spring), and June 1 (summer).

Visiting: Regularly scheduled orientations for prospective students include campus tours and discussions with financial-aid officers. Guides are provided for informal visits, and visitors may sit in on classes and stay overnight at the school. Weekday visits can be arranged through the admissions director.

Financial Aid: About 59% of the students receive some form of aid. Freshman scholarships and loans from private funds are available. The average freshman award is $700. EOGs are also available. About 65% of the students work part-time on campus. Tuition may be paid in installments. The college is a member of CSS, and either the FAF, FFS, or SFS must be filed. Application deadlines are February 1 for academic scholarships and March 1 for general scholarships.

Foreign Students: The college actively recruits foreign students, who represent less than 1% of the student body. Special counseling is available for these students.

Admissions: A minimum score of 550 on the TOEFL is required.

Procedure: There are no application deadlines; students are admitted to all terms. Proof of funds adequate for 4 years is required.

Admissions Contact: Dan Conry, Dean of Admissions.

LUTHER COLLEGE   E-1
Decorah, Iowa 52101   (319) 387-1287

F/T: 901M, 1129W   Faculty: 130; IIB, +$
P/T: 31M, 49W   Ph.D.'s: 65%
Grad: none   S/F Ratio: 15 to 1
Year: 4-1-4, ss   Tuition: $5225
Appl: June 1   R and B: $1675
1100 applied   900 accepted   600 enrolled
SAT: 520V 550M   ACT: 24   VERY COMPETITIVE

Luther College, founded in 1861, is a liberal arts institution affiliated with the American Lutheran Church. Its library holds 250,000 volumes and 10,000 microfilm reels, and subscribes to 2100 periodicals.

Environment: The 800-acre campus is located in a rural setting in the rugged bluff country of northeast Iowa, 70 miles from Rochester, Minnesota. The 21 modern buildings include 7 coed and single-sex dormitories. The college also sponsors married student housing.

Student Life: Fifty percent of the students come from Iowa. About 97% are from public schools. Most students (93%) live in residence halls. Freshmen must live on campus. Eighty-seven percent of the students are Protestant, 10% are Catholic. Minority-group members comprise 5% of the student body. Housing is both coed and single-sex, with visiting privileges in single-sex dorms. Students may keep cars on campus.

Organizations: There are 11 local fraternities and 6 local sororities on campus to which 50% of the men and 35% of the women belong. Other extracurricular activities include special-interest and service clubs, music groups, "pop" concerts, plays, films, dances, and lectures. Religious clubs include the Luther College Student Congregation.

Sports: The college participates in 13 intercollegiate programs for men and 10 for women. There are 19 intramural events for men and 18 for women.

Handicapped: Special facilities for the physically handicapped include wheelchair ramps, parking areas, elevators, lowered drinking fountains, and specially equipped rest rooms. About 98% of the campus is accessible to the handicapped.

Graduates: The freshman dropout rate is 12%, and 75% remain to graduate. Of these, 27% go on to graduate schools. Four percent of the graduates enter medical school; another 25% pursue careers in business and industry.

Services: Free health care, tutoring, remedial instruction, placement services, and career and psychological counseling are available to undergraduates.

Programs of Study: All programs lead to the B.A. degree. Bachelor's degrees are offered in the following subjects: AREA STUDIES (Black/Afro-American), BUSINESS (accounting, business administration, computer science, management), EDUCATION (early childhood, elementary, health/physical, secondary, special), ENGLISH (English, speech), FINE AND PERFORMING ARTS (art, art education, music, music education, theater/dramatics), HEALTH SCIENCES (medical technology, nursing, physical therapy), LANGUAGES (French, German, Greek/Latin, Hebrew, Norwegian, Spanish), MATH AND SCIENCES (biochemistry, biology, chemistry, earth science, ecology/environmental science, mathematics, natural sciences, physics), PHILOSOPHY (classics, philosophy, religion), PREPROFESSIONAL (dentistry, engineering, forestry, law, library science, medicine, ministry, pharmacy, social work, veterinary), SOCIAL SCIENCES (anthropology, economics, government/political science, history, international relations, psychology, social sciences, sociology). Most degrees are granted in natural sciences, education, and business-related fields.

Required: Freshmen are required to take an interdisciplinary introduction to the liberal arts.

Special: Independent study, study abroad, and a Washington semester are offered. Students may design their own majors.

Honors: The college offers departmental honors programs.

Admissions: Eighty-two percent of the applicants were accepted for the 1981-82 freshman class. The SAT scores of those who enrolled were as follows: Verbal—40% scored below 500, 41% between 500 and 599, 15% between 600 and 700, and 4% above 700; Math—18% scored below 500, 34% between 500 and 599, 35% between 600 and 700, and 13% above 700. Of those who took the ACT, 25% scored below 21, 23% between 21 and 23, 21% between 24 and 25, 23% between 26 and 28, and 8% above 28. Applicants should have completed 15 Carnegie units and must rank in the top 50% of their graduating class. Advanced placement or honors courses, school recommendations, leadership potential, and extracurricular activities are also considered.

Procedure: The SAT or ACT is required. The application deadlines are June 1 for fall and January 1 for spring. There is a rolling admissions policy. Applications should be accompanied by a $20 fee. An interview is recommended.

Special: Application for early admission must be made by March 1. There is also a deferred admissions plan. AP and CLEP credit is available.

Transfer: For fall 1981, 153 students applied, 145 were accepted, and 108 enrolled. A 2.5 GPA is required. D grades are not transferable. Students must complete, at the school, at least 32 of the 128 credits necessary for a bachelor's degree. Application deadlines are June 1 (fall) and January 1 (spring).

Visiting: The college holds regularly scheduled orientations for prospective students. Guides are provided for informal visits, and visitors may sit in on classes and stay overnight at the school. The best time for visiting is weekdays during the school year. Arrangements can be made through the admissions office.

Financial Aid: About 75% of the students receive some form of financial aid; 56% work part-time on campus. Federal and state loans and freshman scholarships are available. The average award to freshmen from all sources in 1981-82 was $4510. Tuition may be paid in installments. The college is a member of CSS. The FAF or FFS should be filed; the aid application deadline is June 1. Notification of award is sent 2 weeks after the FAF or FFS information has been received and the student accepted for admission.

Foreign Students: Two percent of the students are from foreign countries. The college offers these students an intensive English course and program, special counseling, and special organizations.

Admissions: A TOEFL score of at least 550 is required. College entrance exams are not required.

Procedure: The application deadline is June 1 for fall admission. Students must submit the college's standardized health form, and must present proof of adequate funds for 1 academic year. Health insurance is required, and is available through the college for a fee.

Admissions Contact: Dennis R. Johnson, Director of Admissions.

MAHARISHI INTERNATIONAL UNIVERSITY

E-4

Fairfield, Iowa 52556   (515) 472-2565

F/T: 314M, 196W	Faculty: 65; n/av
P/T: 21M, 16W	Ph.D.'s: 45%
Grad: 46M, 34W	S/F Ratio: 8 to 1
Year: sems	Tuition: $4320
Appl: open	R and B: $2160
256 applied	208 accepted 131 enrolled
SAT or ACT: required	COMPETITIVE

Maharishi International University adheres to the principles of the Science of Creative Intelligence and the Transcendental Meditation and TM-Sidhi program. The library contains 51,000 volumes and subscribes to 300 periodicals.

Environment: The 185-acre campus is located in a rural area 60 miles from Iowa City and 110 miles from Des Moines. The 70 buildings include research laboratories, a video production studio, and a geodesic dome. Students are grouped in residence halls by year and, if possible, by major. Married-student housing and on-campus apartments also are available.

Student Life: Almost all students (96%) live on campus. Five percent are members of minority groups. Dormitories are single-sex, with no visiting privileges. Students may keep cars on campus.

Organizations: There are no fraternities or sororities. Traditional extracurricular activities are available. Cultural activities, including films, concerts, and lectures, are scheduled each weekend. More cultural opportunities can be found in Iowa City, about 50 minutes away.

Sports: The university fields intercollegiate teams in 5 sports for men and 2 for women. Six intramural sports are offered for men and women.

Handicapped: Wheelchair ramps and special parking areas are available for physically handicapped students.

Graduates: About 46% of the graduates seek advanced degrees.

Services: Free remedial instruction, career counseling, and placement services are available. Placement facilities also are available to graduates. Fees are charged for health-care services.

Programs of Study: The university confers the B.A., B.S., and B.F.A. degrees. It also offers master's programs. Bachelor's degrees are available in the following subjects: BUSINESS (business administration, computer science), EDUCATION (secondary), ENGLISH (literature), FINE AND PERFORMING ARTS (art), MATH AND SCIENCES (biology, mathematics, physics), PHILOSOPHY (philosophy), SOCIAL SCIENCES (law, government and public affairs, psychology).

Required: There is a core curriculum for the first 2 years.

Special: Four-year combined B.A.-B.S. degrees and a general studies degree are available.

Admissions: About 81% of those who applied were accepted for the 1981-82 freshman class. The SAT scores of an earlier freshman class were as follows: Verbal—53% above 500 and 20% above 600; Math—49% above 500 and 17% above 600. Before they can be admitted, students must take personal instruction in Transcendental Meditation and complete the introductory course in the Science of Creative Intelligence. Both courses may be taken at a local Age of Enlightenment Center or at the central campus in Fairfield. Applicants must be high school graduates, but the university has an open admissions policy with regard to previous academic background.

Procedure: The SAT or ACT is required of applicants who have not completed 60 semester or 90 quarter hours of college work. The application, 2 letters of recommendation (one from a teacher of Transcendental Meditation), official transcripts, and an essay stating the reasons for choosing the university must be submitted. Application deadlines are open. There is a $15 application fee ($10 for veterans). Admissions decisions are made on a rolling basis.

Transfer: The SAT or ACT is required of applicants who have not completed at least 60 semester or 90 quarter hours of college credit. Admissions are open.

Visiting: Tours of the campus can be arranged through the admissions office for Mondays through Saturdays while school is in session. Guides are provided, and visitors may sit in on classes and stay overnight at the school.

Financial Aid: Financial aid programs include FISL, BEOG, SEOG, CWS, and NDSL. About 85% of all students receive aid; 70% work part-time on campus. The average award to 1981-82 freshmen from all sources totaled $4756. The FAF is required. Application deadlines are open.

Foreign Students: Foreign students at the university make up about 10% of the student body. Special organizations are provided for these students.

Admissions: Students must score 500 or better on the TOEFL and take the SAT or ACT.

Procedure: Application deadlines are open; students are admitted to all terms. Students must present proof of adequate funds for 9 months. Health insurance, though not required, is available through the university.

Admissions Contact: Richard M. Johnsen, Director of Admissions.

MARYCREST COLLEGE

E-3

Davenport, Iowa 52804   (319) 326-9226

F/T: 98M, 343W	Faculty: 50; IIB, —$
P/T: 89M, 356W	Ph.D.'s: 34%
Grad: 410 M&W	S/F Ratio: 12 to 1
Year: sems, ss	Tuition: $3720
Appl: open	R and B: $1740
384 applied	317 accepted 207 enrolled
ACT: 19	COMPETITIVE

Established in 1939, Marycrest College is an independent institution affiliated with the Roman Catholic Church. It is organized in 6 divisions: Education, Library Science, and Psychology; Fine Arts and Communication; Humanities; Natural Science and Mathematics; Nursing; and Vocations for Human Needs. Its library has 150,000 books and 850 microfilms, and subscribes to 175 periodicals.

Environment: The 20-acre campus is located in a suburban area of Davenport (population 100,000), on a bluff overlooking the Mississippi River. Des Moines and Chicago are about 150 miles away. There are 10 major buildings, including a nursing education facility and a student activities center. There are four residence halls.

Student Life: Seventy percent of the students come from Iowa. About 76% attended public schools. Thirty-six percent live on campus. Campus housing is both coed and single-sex; there are visiting privileges in the single-sex housing. Students may keep cars on campus.

Organizations: Extracurricular activities include religious and service groups, clubs, student government, publications, performing groups, and social events.

Sports: Marycrest fields intercollegiate teams in 4 sports for men and 4 for women. There are 5 intramural sports for men and 5 for women.

Graduates: The freshman dropout rate is 20%; about 50% remain to graduate.

Services: Placement, health care, and career and psychological counseling are available free of charge.

Programs of Study: Marycrest offers the B.A., B.S., B.S.N., and B.A. in Special Studies degrees. Associate and master's degrees are also awarded. Bachelor's degrees are offered in the following subjects: AREA STUDIES (special studies), BUSINESS (accounting, business administration, food service management), EDUCATION (early childhood, elementary, pre-school handicapped), ENGLISH (English, journalism), FINE AND PERFORMING ARTS (art, computer/graphics, music, radio/TV, theater/dramatics), HEALTH SCIENCES (medical technology, nursing), LANGUAGES (Spanish), MATH AND SCIENCES (biology, chemistry/biology, computer/chemistry, natural sciences), PHILOSOPHY (humanities), PREPROFESSIONAL (dentistry, fashion merchandising, foods and nutrition, home economics, law, library science, medicine), SOCIAL SCIENCES (history, social work). Most degrees are granted in education, health sciences, and nursing.

Required: General education requirements must be met in these areas: written and oral communication, philosophy and religious studies, language and literature, natural science and math, social and behavioral sciences, and the arts. These requirements may be fulfilled by CLEP or AP exams.

Special: Student-designed majors and study abroad are offered. There is a combination degree program in medical technology.

Honors: There are chapters of 3 national honorary societies on campus. Honors work is offered.

Admissions: About 83% of the 1981-82 freshman applicants were accepted. The ACT scores of those who enrolled were as follows: 41% below 21, 34% between 21 and 23, 11% between 24 and 25, 13% between 26 and 28, and 1% above 28. Candidates should be graduates of accredited high schools or the equivalent, with 15 Carnegie units completed. A 2.0 high school GPA is required; class rank should be in the upper 60%. Advanced placement or honors courses, extracurricular activities, and school recommendations are also considered in the admissions decision.

Procedure: Either the SAT or the ACT is required. Deadlines are open; new students are admitted in the fall and spring. Admissions decisions are made on a rolling basis; notification is sent 10 days after the credentials file is complete. An interview is recommended. There is a $15 application fee.

Special: AP and CLEP credit is granted.

Transfer: For fall 1981, 208 students applied, 170 were accepted, and 126 enrolled. Transfer students must have a GPA of at least 2.0 and an ACT score of at least 16, and should have ranked in the upper 60% of their high school class. D grades do not transfer. All students must complete, at the college, 30 of the 120 credits required for a bachelor's degree. There are no application deadlines.

Visiting: An orientation program for prospective students is offered each July. Informal guided campus tours and meetings with faculty and admissions personnel can be arranged through the admissions office.

Financial Aid: About 68% of the students are receiving a financial aid package. Twenty percent work part-time on campus. CWS, NDSL, BEOG/SEOG, and National Nursing Loans are available to qualified students. There are freshman scholarships and other loan funds. The FAF or FFS is required; April 15 is the deadline for completing all admissions and financial aid requirements for fall entrance. The spring deadline is December 15. Tuition may be paid in installments. The college is a member of CSS.

Foreign Students: One percent of the students come from foreign countries. An intensive English program and special counseling are available for these students.

Admissions: Foreign students must achieve a TOEFL score of at least 550. No college entrance exams are required.

Procedure: There are no application deadlines; foreign students are admitted in the fall and spring. They must submit a medical examination form and must present proof of funds adequate to cover 1 year of study.

Admissions Contact: Sr. Rae Elwood, Dean of Admissions and Financial Aid.

MORNINGSIDE COLLEGE B–2
Sioux City, Iowa 51106 (712) 274-5000

F/T, P/T:	Faculty: n/av, IIA, – – $
1470 M&W	Ph.D.'s: 50%
Grad: 50M&W	S/F Ratio: 16 to 1
Year: sems, ss	Tuition: $4200
Appl: open	R and B: $1470
	269 enrolled
ACT: 21	COMPETITIVE

Morningside College, founded in 1894, is a private liberal arts college affiliated with the United Methodist Church. Its library contains 130,000 volumes and subscribes to 802 periodicals.

Environment: The 27-acre campus with its 15 buildings and student commons is located in a suburban area 90 miles from Omaha. The 3 single-sex dormitories house almost 800 students. Married students are given separate accommodations on campus.

Student Life: About 75% of the students are from Iowa. Almost all come from public schools. About 65% live on campus. Religious facilities are available on campus for Protestant students; attendance at services is not required.

Organizations: Three national fraternities and 3 national sororities have chapters on campus. About 15% of men and 15% of women are members. The student government helps plan and coordinate social affairs and works closely with the faculty and administration. On-campus cultural activities include the Community Theatre and the Sioux City Symphony performances.

Sports: The college sponsors intercollegiate teams in 8 sports for men and 6 for women. Numerous intramural sports are offered.

Handicapped: There are limited facilities for wheelchair-bound students.

Graduates: The freshman dropout rate is 28%, and 50% remain to graduate. About 22% of the graduates pursue further studies; 3% enter medical school, 2% enter dental school, and 5% enter law school. About 35% begin careers in business and industry.

Services: The college offers free health care, psychological counseling, tutoring or remedial instruction, placement aid, and career counseling. Graduates as well as undergraduates may use placement services.

Programs of Study: The college offers the B.A., B.S., B.Mus., B.S.N., and B.Mus.Ed. degrees. Master's degrees also are available. Bachelor's degrees are offered in the following subjects: BUSINESS (accounting, agribusiness, business administration, business education, office administration), EDUCATION (early childhood, elementary, health/physical, secondary, special), ENGLISH (English, literature, speech), FINE AND PERFORMING ARTS (art, mass communications, music, music education, theater/dramatics), HEALTH SCIENCES (nursing), LANGUAGES (French, German, Spanish), MATH AND SCIENCES (biology, biopsychology, chemistry, mathematics, physics), PHILOSOPHY (philosophy, religion), PREPROFESSIONAL (engineering, library science, social work), SOCIAL SCIENCES (criminal justice, economics, government/political science, history, psychology, sociology, tribal management).

Required: All students must take 27 hours of core requirements, including 2 hours of physical education, in the 124-hour degree program.

Special: Students may take courses at other universities and spend the junior year abroad. Students may design their own majors. A minor in Indian studies and preprofessional programs in computer science, home economics, law, medical technology, medicine, pharmacy, and ministry are available.

Honors: Interdepartmental seminars and team teaching in interdisciplinary studies are offered.

Admissions: Over 90% of those who applied were accepted for a recent freshman class. Candidates are required to have completed 15 Carnegie high school units and generally must rank in the upper 50% of their graduating class. They also should have at least a C average and an ACT score of 13 or better.

Procedure: The ACT is required. Application deadlines are open. New students are admitted to all terms. There is no application fee.

Special: There are early and deferred admissions and early decision plans. AP and CLEP credit is available.

Transfer: Over 100 transfer students are enrolled annually. A 2.0 GPA is requested. At least 30 hours must be taken in residence.

Visiting: Weekday visits can be arranged through the director of admissions. Visitors may sit in on classes and stay overnight at the school.

Financial Aid: About 80% of all students receive aid. About $800,000 is available for scholarships and grants. Campus employment is also available. Tuition may be paid in installments. Either the FFS or FAF should be filed. Applications should be submitted by June 1.

Foreign Students: Twelve foreign students are enrolled at the college, which provides them with special counseling and special organizations.

Admissions: Students must take the TOEFL.

Procedure: Application deadlines are open. Students must present proof of adequate funds for their entire term of study. They must register for health insurance, which is available through the college for a fee.

Admissions Contact: Fred Erbes, Director of Admissions.

MOUNT MERCY COLLEGE E–3
Cedar Rapids, Iowa 52402 (319) 363-8213

F/T: 147M, 594W	Faculty: 83; IIB, – $
P/T: 160M, 220W	Ph.D.'s: 30%
Grad: none	S/F Ratio: 13 to 1
Year: 4-1-4, ss	Tuition: $3515
Appl: Aug. 15	R and B: $1670
253 applied	246 accepted 185 enrolled
SAT: 450V 513M	ACT: 20 COMPETITIVE

Mount Mercy College is a Catholic liberal arts college with a liberal foundation. The library contains 75,000 volumes and 1700 periodicals.

Environment: The 30-acre urban campus is located 2 miles from downtown Cedar Rapids. Its buildings include 3 dormitories that house 400 students. The college also sponsors on-campus apartments.

Student Life: Almost 90% of the students come from Iowa, and 40% live on campus. At least 75% of students come from public schools. Fifty percent of the students are Catholic; 40% are Protestant. About 4% are minority-group members. Campus housing is both single-sex and coed; single-sex dorms have visiting privileges. Students may keep cars on campus.

Organizations: There are no fraternities or sororities. The college offers a variety of social and extracurricular activities.

Sports: The college participates in 3 intercollegiate sports for men and 3 for women. It offers 4 intramural sports for men and 4 for women.

Handicapped: The entire campus is accessible to the handicapped students. Special facilities include wheelchair ramps, elevators, and parking areas.

Graduates: The freshman dropout rate is 30%; 50% remain to graduate. About 8% of the graduates seek advanced degrees. Of these, 2% enter medical school and 5% enter law school. Twenty-five percent of the graduates pursue careers in business and industry.

Services: Free health care, psychological counseling, tutoring, remedial instruction, placement assistance, and career counseling are available.

Programs of Study: The college offers the B.A., B.S., and B.S.N. degrees. Bachelor's degrees are offered in the following subjects: BUSINESS (accounting, business administration, business education, computer science), EDUCATION (elementary), ENGLISH (English, public relations), FINE AND PERFORMING ARTS (art, art education, music, music education, theater/dramatics), HEALTH SCIENCES (medical technology, nursing), MATH AND SCIENCES (biology, mathematics), PHILOSOPHY (religion), PREPROFESSIONAL (agriculture, architecture, dentistry, forestry, home economics, law, medicine, ministry, pharmacy, social work, veterinary), SOCIAL SCIENCES (government/political science, history, psychology, sociology). Almost 40% of degrees conferred are in health sciences and 29% in business.

Required: All undergraduates are required to complete 12 general-education courses.

Special: A combination degree program is offered in medical technology. Seminars and independent study are offered by most departments.

Admissions: About 97% of those who applied were accepted for the 1981–82 freshman class. The ACT scores of those who enrolled were as follows: 31% scored below 21, 46% between 21 and 23, 10% between 24 and 25, 8% between 26 and 28, and 5% above 28. Candidates should have completed 16 Carnegie units, rank in the upper 60% of their class, and have a minimum GPA of 2.0. Recommendations by school officials and the student's academic record are also considered.

Procedure: Either the SAT or ACT is required. The deadlines for regular admission are August 15 (fall), December 20 (winter), January 15 (spring), and May 25 (summer). Decisions are made on a rolling basis. A $10 fee should accompany all applications.

Special: Early and deferred admissions plans are available. AP and CLEP credit is accepted.

Transfer: For fall 1981, 351 students applied, 340 were accepted, and 275 enrolled. A minimum ACT score of 17 and a 2.0 GPA are required. D grades do not transfer. One year must be taken in residence. Students must earn, at the college, at least 30 of the 123 credits required for a bachelor's degree. Application deadlines are the same as those for freshmen.

Visiting: Orientations are scheduled regularly. Informal visits can be arranged through the admissions office. Visitors may sit in on classes and stay overnight at the school.

Financial Aid: About 85% of all students are receiving aid; 50% work part-time on campus. Freshman scholarships are available. The average award to freshmen from all sources was $3200 from all sources in 1981–82. The FAF, FFS, or SFS is required of aid applicants. The college is a member of CSS. Deadline for aid application is March 1 for fall entry, December 20 for winter entry, January 15 for spring entry, and May 20 for summer entry.

Foreign Students: One percent of the students are from foreign countries. There are special organizations for these students.

Admissions: A minimum score of 480 on the TOEFL is required. If applicants have not taken the TOEFL, the ACT (minimum score 17) or SAT (minimum score 800) is necessary.

Procedure: Application deadlines are June 1 for fall, September 1 for winter, October 1 for spring, and April 1 for summer. Students must undergo a physical as proof of health. Evidence of adequate funds for 4 years is required.

Admissions Contact: Don McCormick, Director of Admissions.

MOUNT ST. CLARE COLLEGE F-3
Clinton, Iowa 52732 (319) 242-4023

F/T: 99M, 201W Faculty: n/av; IV, av$
P/T: 40M, 53W Ph.D.'s: 11%
Grad: none S/F Ratio: 17 to 1
Year: sems, ss Tuition: $1900
Appl: Aug. 1 R and B: $2000
242 applied 220 accepted 176 enrolled
ACT: 19 **LESS COMPETITIVE**

Mount St. Clare College, an undergraduate institution affiliated with the Roman Catholic church, offers programs in the liberal arts, education, and business. Its library has 22,000 books and subscribes to 180 periodicals.

Environment: The 136-acre urban campus is located in a town about 135 miles from Chicago. There are 7 buildings, including 2 residence halls that accommodate 175 students.

Student Life: About 60% of the students come from Iowa. Forty percent live on campus. Fifty percent of the students are Catholic, 50% are Protestant. Campus housing is single-sex; there are visiting privileges. Students are permitted to keep cars on campus.

Organizations: There are no sororities or fraternities. There are religious organizations for Catholic and Protestant students. Extracurricular activities include student government and campus ministry; major social events include Homecoming and the prom.

Sports: The college fields 1 intercollegiate team for men and 1 for women. One intramural sport is offered for men and 1 for women.

Handicapped: About 80% of the campus is accessible to students with physical handicaps. Ramps, elevators, specially equipped rest rooms, and parking areas are offered. One percent of the students have hearing impairments; there are no visually impaired students currently enrolled.

Graduates: The freshman dropout rate is 8%; about 65% of the class remain to graduate. Eighty percent of the graduates seek advanced degrees.

Services: Career counseling and placement services are offered free of charge to all students.

Programs of Study: The college confers the B.A. degree. Associate degrees are also awarded. The bachelor's degree is offered in only 1 major field: BUSINESS (business administration).

Special: Work-study programs are available.

Honors: There are chapters of 4 honor societies on campus. Honors work is offered in the art, business, and science departments.

Admissions: About 92% of the 1981–82 freshman applicants were accepted. Applicants should be graduates of an accredited high school. Class rank should be in the top 75%; the high school GPA should be at least 2.0. The minimum ACT score accepted is 18. Preference is given to children of alumni.

Procedure: The ACT or the SAT is required. Application deadlines are August 1 for fall, January 10 for spring, and June 1 for summer; the college follows the rolling admissions procedure. An interview is recommended. There is a $15 application fee.

Special: CLEP is used.

Transfer: Transfer students must have a GPA of at least 2.0 and an ACT score of at least 18. D grades do not transfer. Application deadlines are the same as those for freshmen; notification is made within 1 month of receipt of the application.

Visiting: There is an orientation program for prospective applicants. Informal guided campus tours can be arranged during school days. Visitors may attend classes and stay overnight at the school. Arrangements can be made through the admissions office.

Financial Aid: About 80% of the students are getting aid through the college. The college offers 59 freshman scholarships (average $600, maximum $3000). There are also work opportunities, including CWS in all departments; 30% of students work part-time on campus. The college is a member of the CSS. The FAF or FFS should be filed no later than March 1 for priority consideration.

Foreign Students: One percent of the students are from foreign countries. An intensive English course and program and special counseling are available for these students.

Admissions: No English proficiency exam is required, nor is a college entrance exam.

Procedure: The application deadlines are May 1 for fall and October 1 for spring. Students must present proof of health and proof of funds adequate to cover 1 year of study.

Admissions Contact: Sister Evelyn McKenna, Dean of Admissions and Financial Aid.

NORTHWESTERN COLLEGE B-2
Orange City, Iowa 51041 (712) 737-4821

F/T:	410M, 461W	Faculty:	53; IIB, +$
P/T:	12M, 20W	Ph.D.'s:	55%
Grad:	none	S/F Ratio:	16 to 1
Year:	sems, ss	Tuition:	$3645
Appl:	Aug. 15	R and B:	$1505

385 applied 370 accepted 293 enrolled
ACT: 20 COMPETITIVE

Founded in 1882, Northwestern is a private college affiliated with the Reformed Church in America. It offers liberal arts and teacher education from a Christian perspective. The library contains 85,000 volumes, 9000 microfilm items, and 18,000 government documents. It subscribes to 500 periodicals.

Environment: The 55-acre campus is located in a rural setting, 45 miles from Sioux City. There are 14 major buildings, including a student center and 4 dormitories that accommodate 560 students. On-campus apartments and married-student housing are also available.

Student Life: Approximately 65% of the students are from Iowa. Ninety percent attended public schools. More than half of the students live on campus. The majority of students (95%) are Protestant; 3% are Catholic. Minority-group members comprise 2% of the student body. Campus housing is single-sex, with visiting privileges. Students may keep cars on campus. Drinking is prohibited on campus, and smoking is allowed only in designated areas.

Organizations: There are no fraternities or sororities. Students participate in special-interest and service clubs, music and drama groups, and a variety of other activities. The student government sponsors social and cultural events, including a winter carnival, a fine arts festival, and a homecoming.

Sports: The college participates in 9 intercollegiate sports for men and 8 for women. Ten intramural sports are offered for men and 10 for women.

Handicapped: Special facilities for the physically handicapped include elevators and wheelchair ramps.

Graduates: About 5% of the freshmen drop out during their first year; 50% remain to graduate. About 20% of the graduates continue their studies; 2% enter medical school and 2% enter law school. Another 23% pursue careers in business and industry.

Services: Free tutoring, remedial instruction, career counseling, and psychological counseling are available. Free placement services are offered to students and alumni.

Programs of Study: All programs lead to the B.A. degree. Bachelor's degrees are offered in the following subjects: BUSINESS (business administration, business education), EDUCATION (elementary, secondary, special), ENGLISH (English, literature, speech), FINE AND PERFORMING ARTS (art, art education, music, music education, theater/dramatics), HEALTH SCIENCES (medical technology), LANGUAGES (French, Spanish), MATH AND SCIENCES (biology, chemistry, mathematics, natural sciences), PHILOSOPHY (humanities, philosophy, religion), SOCIAL SCIENCES (history, psychology, social sciences, sociology).

Required: Freshmen must take core courses in Western civilization and the Bible, and 2 hours of physical education.

Special: Combination degree programs in medical technology and physical therapy are offered. Students may study a year abroad. Internships are also available.

Honors: Honor societies represented on campus include Phi Beta Lambda and Pi Kappa Delta.

Admissions: About 96% of those who applied were accepted for the 1981-82 freshman class. The ACT scores of those who enrolled were as follows: 20% scored below 21, 33% between 21 and 23, 29% between 24 and 25, 15% between 26 and 28, and 3% above 28. Candidates should have completed 15 Carnegie units in an accredited high school and rank in the upper two-thirds of their graduating class. Recommendations by school officials, personality, and evidence of special talents are also considered.

Procedure: The ACT or SAT is required. Applications must be submitted by August 15 for the fall term and January 1 for the winter term.

A $15 fee should accompany all applications. A rolling admissions plan is in effect; notification is sent 10 days after applications are complete.

Special: Credit is available through CLEP subject exams.

Transfer: For fall 1981, 81 students applied, 64 were accepted, and 53 enrolled. A GPA of at least 2.0 is required. D grades transfer. Students must complete, at the college, 30 of the 126 credits required for the bachelor's degree. Application deadlines are the same as those for freshmen.

Visiting: Focus Weekend in the fall offers orientation for prospective students. Informal guided tours also can be arranged through the admissions office. Visitors may sit in on classes and stay overnight at the school.

Financial Aid: Over 86% of the students receive some form of aid, usually in the form of a package. Freshman academic scholarships, loans from federal and state governments, local banks, and the college itself, and campus employment are available; 55% of students work part-time on campus. The average award to freshmen from all sources was $2800 in 1981-82. The aid application deadlines are June 1 for fall and January 1 for winter; the FAF or FFS is required.

Foreign Students: Two percent of the students are from foreign countries. Special counseling and special organizations are available for these students.

Admissions: Foreign students must achieve a minimum score of 500 on the TOEFL. College entrance exams are not required.

Procedure: Application deadlines are August 15 for fall and January 1 for winter. Students must submit proof of funds adequate for 1 academic year. Health insurance is not required, but is available through the college for a fee.

Admissions Contact: Ronald K. DeJong, Admissions Director.

ST. AMBROSE COLLEGE E-3
Davenport, Iowa 52803 (319) 383-8888

F/T:	653M, 500W	Faculty:	126; IIB, +$
P/T:	312M, 365W	Ph.D.'s:	70%
Grad:	179M, 51W	S/F Ratio:	16 to 1
Year:	sems, ss	Tuition:	$3810
Appl:	open	R and B:	$1700

662 applied 536 accepted 343 enrolled
ACT: 18 COMPETITIVE

St. Ambrose is a private, coeducational, Roman Catholic College of liberal arts. The library contains 100,000 volumes and 2000 microfilm items, and subscribes to 750 periodicals.

Environment: Located in an urban residential area of north-central Davenport, 180 miles from Chicago, the campus has several buildings in both traditional and modern styles. Ambrose Hall has been designated as an historical landmark. Dormitories are available for students.

Student Life: About 63% of the students come from Iowa, and 60% are graduates of public schools. About 40% of the students live on campus. About 70% are Catholic and 30% are Protestant. Minority-group members comprise 3% of the student body. Campus housing is single-sex, with visiting privileges. Students may keep cars on campus. Day-care services are available to all students.

Organizations: There are no social fraternities or sororities. A wide variety of clubs provide social and extracurricular activities.

Sports: The college fields intercollegiate teams in 7 sports for men and 4 for women. Six intramural sports are offered for men and 5 for women.

Handicapped: Special facilities include wheelchair ramps and elevators. Three counselors are available to handicapped students.

Graduates: The freshman dropout rate is 25%; 60% remain to graduate. Thirty percent of the graduates seek advanced degrees; 10% enter medical school, 10% enter dental school, and 5% enter law school. About 60% pursue careers in business and industry.

Services: The following services are available to students free of charge: health care, tutoring, remedial instruction, placement, career counseling, and psychological counseling.

Programs of Study: The college confers the B.A., B.M., B.Mus.Ed., B.S., and B.S.S. degrees. Master's programs are also available. Bachelor's degrees are offered in the following subjects: BUSINESS (accounting, business administration, computer science), EDUCATION (elementary, health/physical, secondary), ENGLISH (English, speech), FINE AND PERFORMING ARTS (art, art education, music, music education, radio/TV, theater/dramatics), LANGUAGES (French, German,

Greek/Latin, Italian, Russian, Spanish), MATH AND SCIENCES (biology, chemistry, mathematics, natural sciences, physics), PHILOSOPHY (philosophy, theology), PREPROFESSIONAL (dentistry, engineering, law, medicine, veterinary), SOCIAL SCIENCES (criminal justice and law enforcement, economics, government/political science, history, psychology, sociology). About 40% of the degrees conferred are in business and 35% in social sciences.

Special: Combined B.A.-B.S. degrees may be earned. The college offers the B.G.S. degree, and students may design their own majors. Study abroad is available.

Honors: There are 4 honor societies on campus, and departmental honors programs also are available.

Admissions: About 81% of those who applied were accepted for the 1981-82 freshman class. Applicants should have completed 15 units of work, rank in the upper half of their class, and have at least a 2.0 average.

Procedure: The SAT or ACT is required. Students are admitted for the fall, spring, and summer terms. There are no application deadlines. Notification is on a rolling basis. An interview is recommended, and the application fee is $15.

Special: CLEP credit is available.

Transfer: For fall 1981, 387 transfer students applied, 380 were accepted, and 317 enrolled. Transfer students must score a minimum of 18 on the ACT and have a GPA of at least 2.0 (2.5+ recommended). D grades transfer. Students must complete, at the college, 30 of the 120 credits required for a bachelor's degree. There are no application deadlines.

Visiting: Orientations are available for prospective students, and guides are provided for informal visits. Visitors may sit in on classes and stay overnight at the school. The admissions office should be contacted for arrangements.

Financial Aid: About 70% of the students receive some form of financial aid; 65% work part-time on campus. The FAF, FFS, or SFS must be filed; the deadline for financial aid applications is February 15. The college is a member of CSS.

Foreign Students: Nearly 2% of the students are from foreign countries. The college offers these students an intensive English course, special counseling, and special organizations.

Admissions: The TOEFL is required.

Procedure: Application deadlines are open. Proof of adequate funds for 12 months is required.

Admissions Contact: James T. Barry, Dean of Admissions.

SIMPSON COLLEGE C-3
Indianola, Iowa 50125 (515) 961-6251

F/T: 457M, 387W	Faculty:	58; IIB, av$
P/T: 67M, 89W	Ph.D.'s:	70%
Grad: 524M, 476W	S/F Ratio:	13 to 1
Year: 4-1-4, ss	Tuition:	$4535
Appl: Aug. 15	R and B:	$1630
617 applied	586 accepted	218 enrolled
ACT: 21		COMPETITIVE

Simpson College, founded in 1860, is an independent liberal arts college, which is historically related to the Methodist Church. The library contains 110,000 volumes and 3119 microfilm items, and subscribes to 550 periodicals.

Environment: The 55-acre campus is located in a suburban area 12 miles from Des Moines and has 26 buildings, including a recreation center with an Olympic-sized pool, a theater, and 4 dormitories accommodating 500 students. The college also sponsors fraternity and sorority houses, off-campus apartments, and married student housing.

Student Life: About 75% of the students are from Iowa. Ninety percent of entering freshmen come from public schools. Seventy percent of all students live on campus. Thirteen percent of the students are Catholic, 9% are Protestant, and 1% are Jewish. Four percent of the students are minority-group members. Campus housing is both single-sex and coed; there are visiting privileges in single-sex housing. Students may keep cars on campus.

Organizations: There are 4 national fraternities, 3 national sororities, and 1 local fraternity on campus; 35% of the men and 25% of the women belong to 1 of them.

Sports: The college competes in 8 intercollegiate sports for men and 7 for women, and offers 16 intramural programs for men and 13 for women.

Handicapped: About 85% of the campus is accessible to handicapped students. Special facilities include wheelchair ramps, parking areas, elevators, and specially equipped rest rooms. Special class scheduling is also available. Fewer than 1% of the students are visually impaired or hearing-impaired.

Graduates: About 15% of the freshmen drop out at the end of the first year, and 60% remain to graduate. About 30% of the graduates pursue advanced degrees. Four percent enter medical school, 2% dental school, and 7% law school. Fifty-eight percent pursue careers in business and industry.

Services: The college offers free health care, tutoring, remedial instruction, placement, and career and psychological counseling to students.

Programs of Study: The college confers the B.A. or the B.Mus. degree in the following subjects: BUSINESS (accounting, agricultural resource management, computer science, economics, management), EDUCATION (early childhood, elementary, health/physical, secondary, special), ENGLISH (English, speech), FINE AND PERFORMING ARTS (art, art education, music, music education, theater/dramatics), HEALTH SCIENCES (medical technology), LANGUAGES (French, German, international management, Spanish), MATH AND SCIENCES (biology, chemistry, computer science/accounting, computer science/management, health administration, mathematics, natural science/management), PHILOSOPHY (philosophy, religion), PREPROFESSIONAL (agriculture, architecture, dentistry, engineering, forestry, law, library science, medicine, ministry, pharmacy, pre-nursing, social work, veterinary), SOCIAL SCIENCES (criminal justice/corrections, government/political science, history, international relations, psychology, social sciences, sociology). About 20% of the degrees conferred are in education, 18% in business, and 15% in fine and performing arts.

Required: B.A. students must complete at least 34 or 35 courses from 6 areas and the Senior Colloquium of an additional 3 hours. B.Mus. students must complete at least 18 hours from 5 of 6 required areas.

Special: Students may create their own majors, study abroad, and take either a Washington, D.C., or United Nations semester. The college offers a 5-year combined B.A.-B.S. degree.

Honors: Five honor societies have chapters on campus. Departmental honors are also available.

Admissions: About 95% of all applicants were accepted for the 1981-82 freshman class. The ACT scores of those who enrolled were as follows: 24% scored below 21, 31% between 21 and 23, 23% between 24 and 25, 14% between 26 and 28, and 8% above 28. Candidates should have completed 15 Carnegie units and graduated in the top 60% of their class. Advanced placement or honor courses, impressions made during the personal interview, and leadership potential are also considered very important.

Procedure: The SAT or ACT is required. The SAT should be taken in May of the junior year or August of the senior year. Application deadlines are August 15 (fall), November 15 (winter), January 15 (spring), and May 15 (summer). The college has a rolling admissions plan. There is no application fee.

Special: A deferred admissions plan is available. AP and CLEP credit is offered.

Transfer: For fall 1981, 124 transfer students applied, 119 were accepted, and 63 enrolled. A 2.0 GPA and an ACT score of at least 18 are recommended. Grades of C or better transfer. Students must complete, at the college, 32 of the 128 credits required for a bachelor's degree. Application deadlines are the same as those for freshmen.

Visiting: Orientations are held for prospective students. Guides are available for informal visits. Visitors may sit in on classes and stay overnight at the school. Visits are best scheduled for weekdays. The admissions office should be contacted for arrangements.

Financial Aid: Over 85% of the students receive some form of financial aid; 73% work part-time on campus. The average scholarship ranges from $50 to $2690, and loans are available. The average award to students from all sources is 16% of college costs. Either the FAF or FFS should be filed; a rolling financial aid program and an installment plan are available. The college is a member of CSS. Application deadlines for financial aid are September 15 (fall), November 15 (winter), December 15 (spring), and May 15 (summer).

Foreign Students: Fewer than 1% of the students are from foreign countries. Special counseling and special organizations are available.

Admissions: A minimum score of 550 on the TOEFL is required for admission to the college; college entrance exams are not required.

Procedure: Application deadlines are August 15 (fall), November 15 (winter), January 15 (spring), and May 15 (summer). Students must present proof of adequate funds. Health insurance is required, and is available through the college for a fee.

Admissions Contact: John Kellogg, Director of Admissions.

UNIVERSITY OF DUBUQUE
Dubuque, Iowa 52001

E-2
(319) 589-3200

F/T: 424M, 235W	Faculty:	50; IIA, −$
P/T: 125M, 280W	Ph.D.'s:	44%
Grad: none	S/F Ratio:	15 to 1
Year: sems, ss	Tuition:	$3650
Appl: Sept. 1	R and B:	$1550
773 applied	710 accepted	402 enrolled
ACT: 19		COMPETITIVE

The University of Dubuque was established in 1852 and is affiliated with the United Presbyterian Church. The library holds 71,000 volumes and 25,000 microfilm items, and subscribes to 500 periodicals.

Environment: The 58-acre suburban campus has 21 buildings and is located in the residential section of Dubuque, on the west bank of the Mississippi River. The 4 single-sex dormitories house 500 students.

Student Life: About 71% of the students come from Iowa, and 65% come from public schools. About 36% of the students are Catholic and 31% are Protestant. About 8% of the students are minority-group members. Forty-five percent of students live on campus. There are visiting privileges in the dormitories. Students may keep cars on campus.

Organizations: Four fraternities and 3 sororities have campus chapters. Student government and political and departmental clubs are open to all students.

Sports: The university competes in 8 intercollegiate sports for men and 7 for women, and has 10 intramural programs for men and 7 for women.

Handicapped: Half the campus is accessible to handicapped students. There are few special facilities.

Graduates: The freshman dropout rate is 12%; 40% remain to graduate. About 27% of the graduates continue their studies; 1% enter medical school, 2% enter dental school, and 3% enter law school. Over 20% pursue careers in business and industry.

Services: Free health care, placement, tutoring, remedial instruction, and career and psychological counseling are offered.

Programs of Study: The university offers the B.A., B.S., B.Mus., and B.S.B.A. degrees. Associate degrees are also awarded. Bachelor's degrees are offered in the following subjects: BUSINESS (accounting, business administration, business education, computer science, finance, management, marketing, real estate/insurance), EDUCATION (early childhood, elementary, health/physical, industrial, secondary, special), ENGLISH (English), FINE AND PERFORMING ARTS (art, art education, music, music education), HEALTH SCIENCES (medical technology, nursing), LANGUAGES (French, German, Spanish), MATH AND SCIENCES (biology, chemistry, earth science, ecology/environmental science, mathematics, physics), PHILOSOPHY (philosophy, religion), PREPROFESSIONAL (aviation and pilot training, dentistry, engineering, law, medicine, ministry, social work), SOCIAL SCIENCES (economics, government/political science, history, psychology, social sciences, sociology). About 21% of degrees conferred are in social sciences and 17% in business.

Required: Students must complete up to 36 hours of core requirements.

Special: A 3-year B.A., a 3-1 medical-technology program, a cooperative engineering program with other schools, and a junior year abroad are offered. Students may design their own majors. Teacher-training programs lead to certification. Students may cross-register at Clarke and Loras Colleges.

Honors: An honors semester is offered.

Admissions: For the 1981-82 freshman class, 92% of those who applied were accepted. The ACT scores of the students who enrolled were as follows: 59% scored below 21, 17% between 21 and 23, 13% between 24 and 25, 9% between 26 and 28, and 2% above 28. Applicants must have completed 15 Carnegie units, rank in the upper 50% of their class, and present acceptable test scores. Recommendations by high school officials, evidence of special talents, and the student's personality are also considered.

Procedure: The SAT or ACT is required. The SAT should be taken in May of the junior year or by March of the senior year. Applications must be in by September 1 (fall) or January 1 (spring). New students are admitted to the fall, spring, and summer sessions. A $15 fee should accompany all applications.

Special: Early decision and early and deferred admissions plans are available. AP and CLEP credit is given.

Transfer: For fall 1981, 149 transfer students were accepted. A minimum GPA of 2.0 is required. Thirty-six credit hours, of the 124 required for the bachelor's degree, must be taken at the university. The deadlines are August 15 (fall) and January 1 (spring).

Visiting: Visitors are welcome. Tours can be arranged for weekdays through the admissions office.

Financial Aid: About 41% of the students receive aid. The average award to freshmen from all sources was about $1000 in 1981-82. Scholarships and campus employment are also available, and 40% of students work part-time on campus. The university participates in SEOG and CWS. The FAF is required. Deadlines for filing are August 15 (fall) and December 15 (spring).

Foreign Students: Seven percent of the students are from foreign countries. Special counseling and special organizations are available.

Admissions: Foreign students must take the TOEFL (a minimum score of 500 is required) or the University of Michigan Language Test. Academic exams are not required.

Procedure: Applications should be submitted in March or April for fall entry and in November for spring entry. Students must present proof of good health in the form of a physician's statement, and must submit proof of adequate funds for 1 year. Health insurance is also required, and is available through the university for a fee.

Admissions Contact: Clifford D. Bunting, Director of Student Services.

UNIVERSITY OF IOWA
Iowa City, Iowa 52242

E-3
(319) 353-3361

F/T: 9337M, 9381W	Faculty:	1500; I, +$
P/T: n/av	Ph.D.'s:	50%
Grad: 4497M, 3249W	S/F Ratio:	20 to 1
Year: sems, ss	Tuition:	$1040 ($2580)
Appl: Aug. 15	R and B:	$1834
6500 applied	5600 accepted	3810 enrolled
ACT: 23		COMPETITIVE+

The University of Iowa, a publicly controlled institution established in 1847, is composed of 5 undergraduate and 5 graduate and professional colleges. It offers training in the liberal arts and sciences, in professional and technological programs, and in the field of education. Its library contains 2,300,000 volumes and 60,000 microfilm items, and subscribes to 4000 periodicals.

Environment: Located in a rural area on the Iowa River 20 miles from Cedar Rapids, the 900-acre campus contains 60 primary buildings, including the original state capitol. The 9 dormitories accommodate 5500 students and contain 800 apartments for married couples. The university also sponsors fraternity and sorority houses.

Student Life: Seventy percent of the students are from Iowa. About 95% come from public schools. Thirty percent live on campus. Nearly 5% of the students are minority-group members. Housing is both single-sex and coed, with visiting privileges for single-sex housing. Students may keep cars on campus.

Organizations: There are 20 fraternities and 19 sororities on campus, and 10% of the students belong. Social and cultural activities—including clubs, ballets, concerts, drama productions, and films—are also sponsored by the student government.

Sports: The college participates in 11 intercollegiate sports for men and 11 for women, and offers 12 intramural sports for men and 11 for women.

Handicapped: Ninety-five percent of the campus is accessible to handicapped students. Special facilities include wheelchair ramps, elevators, a bionic bus system, and specially equipped rest rooms. Three special counselors and their 2 assistants can arrange special class scheduling and other help. Student readers and audio training sets are provided for visually impaired or hearing-impaired students.

Graduates: The freshman dropout rate is 20%, and 60% remain to graduate.

Services: Free health care, psychological and career counseling, placement services, and remedial instruction are available to students. Tutoring is available for a fee. Interviewing workshops and resume-writing clinics are offered, as are bulletins of job openings.

270 IOWA

Programs of Study: The university confers the B.A., B.B.A., B.S., B.F.A., B.M., B.S.N., B.S.Pharm., B.S. in Biomed.Eng., B.S.Ch.E., B.S.M.E., B.S.E.E., and B.S.I.E. Master's and doctoral degrees are also conferred. Bachelor's degrees are offered in the following subjects: AREA STUDIES (American, Asian, Black/Afro-American), BUSINESS (accounting, business administration, computer science, finance, management, marketing), EDUCATION (early childhood, elementary, health/physical, recreation, secondary, special), ENGLISH (English, journalism, literature, speech), FINE AND PERFORMING ARTS (art, art education, art history, dance, film/photography, music, music education, radio/TV, studio art, theater/dramatics), HEALTH SCIENCES (dental hygiene, medical technology, nursing, physical therapy, physician's assistant, speech therapy), LANGUAGES (Chinese, French, German, Greek/Latin, Italian, Japanese, Portuguese, Russian, Spanish), MATH AND SCIENCES (astronomy, biochemistry, biology, botany, chemistry, general science, geology, mathematics, physics, statistics, zoology), PHILOSOPHY (classics, philosophy, religion), PREPROFESSIONAL (dentistry, engineering, home economics, law, medicine, pharmacy, social work), SOCIAL SCIENCES (anthropology, economics, geography, government/political science, history, psychology, social sciences, sociology). About 20% of the degrees are conferred in health sciences, 20% in business, and 15% in math and sciences.

Required: Freshmen are required to take rhetoric. All students must take science, history, social science, foreign language, and literature requirements if not fulfilled by secondary-school study.

Special: There is a 3-2 combination degree program in engineering and liberal arts. Students may design their own majors and arrange to study in Austria.

Honors: Sixty-six scholastic and professional honor societies, including Phi Beta Kappa, are represented on campus. Most honors programs are offered in the College of Liberal Arts.

Admissions: About 86% of those who applied were accepted for the 1981–82 freshman class. The ACT scores of those who enrolled were as follows: 27% scored below 21, 24% between 21 and 23, 18% between 24 and 25, 22% between 26 and 28, and 9% above 28. Forty-five percent of the freshmen graduated in the top fifth of their high school class. Candidates should have completed 15 Carnegie units, score at least 21 (residents) or 22 (out-of-state students) on the ACT, and must rank in the upper half (residents) or upper 40% (out-of-state students) of the graduating class. The university gives preference to Iowa residents. It also considers the accreditation and reputation of the high school.

Procedure: All candidates must take the ACT. Applications must be received by August 15 for fall, January 5 for spring, and May 20 for summer. A $10 fee must accompany the application. The university uses a rolling admissions plan.

Special: AP and CLEP credit is available. A deferred admissions plan is offered.

Transfer: For fall 1981, 3051 transfer applications were received, 2372 were accepted, and 1779 students enrolled. Transfer students should have an ACT score of at least 21 and a minimum of 12 credit hours. A minimum GPA of 2.0 is required for liberal arts and pharmacy students; requirements are higher for the other colleges. D grades transfer. Thirty semester hours of the 124 required for a bachelor's degree must be taken at the university. Application deadlines are August 15 (fall), January 5 (spring), and May 20 (summer).

Visiting: Eight 2-day orientation programs for prospective students are held in July. Informal guided tours can be arranged weekdays (8:30 A.M. to 4:30 P.M.) through the admissions office.

Financial Aid: About 2600 undergraduate scholarships are awarded each year. About 65% of all students receive some form of financial aid; the average award is $2200. Campus employment and loans are available, and tuition may be paid in installments. Half the students work part-time on campus. The college is a member of CSS; the FAF or FFS is required. Application deadlines for financial aid are March 1 (fall), December 1 (spring), and May 1 (summer).

Foreign Students: The university has 1200 foreign students. An intensive English program, special counseling, and special organizations are available.

Admissions: A minimum score of 480 on the TOEFL is required; students scoring below 550 must also take the university's own English proficiency exam. The ACT is required if the TOEFL is not submitted.

Procedure: Application deadlines are April 15 for fall, October 1 for spring, and March 1 for summer. Students must present proof of adequate funds for 1 year of study.

Admissions Contact: John E. Moore, Director of Admissions.

UNIVERSITY OF NORTHERN IOWA   D–2
Cedar Falls, Iowa 50614   (319) 273-2281

F/T: 3585M, 4624W   Faculty: 553; IIA, av$
P/T: 594M, 934W   Ph.D.'s: 66%
Grad: 527M, 690W   S/F Ratio: 16 to 1
Year: sems, ss   Tuition: $990 ($2040)
Appl: Aug. 15   R and B: $1528
2482 applied   2259 accepted   1998 enrolled
ACT: 21   COMPETITIVE

The University of Northern Iowa, established in 1876, is a publicly supported institution offering education in the liberal arts and preparation for teaching. Its library holds more than 500,000 volumes and 288,676 microfilm items, and subscribes to 3044 periodicals.

Environment: The 723-acre campus is located in a rural area 8 miles from Waterloo and 100 miles from Des Moines. The residence halls accommodate more than 5000 students. The university also sponsors fraternity and sorority houses and family housing for married students.

Student Life: About 97% of the students are from Iowa. Forty-five percent live on campus. About 2% of the students are minority-group members. Campus housing is both coed and single-sex; there are visiting privileges in single-sex housing. Students are permitted to keep cars on campus. Day-care services are available, for a fee, to all students.

Organizations: Six national fraternities and 5 national sororities have chapters on campus; 7% of the men and 5% of the women belong. Other university and community activities include student government, music groups, clubs, lectures, concerts, theater, an artists' series, and religious organizations.

Sports: The university participates in 12 intercollegiate sports for men and 10 for women, and in 10 intramural sports for men and 12 for women.

Handicapped: Special facilities include wheelchair ramps, parking areas, elevators, lowered drinking fountains and telephones, and specially equipped rest rooms. Special class scheduling is also available.

Graduates: About 15% of the freshmen drop out after the first year, and 41% remain to graduate. Of these, 12% continue their studies. Another 45% pursue careers in business and industry.

Services: Free health care, tutoring, remedial instruction, and psychological, career, and placement counseling are available. Students may also use placement services and receive job-search training.

Programs of Study: Graduates receive the B.A., B.A.Ed., B.F.A., B.L.A., B.Mus., and B.T. degrees. Master's and doctoral degrees are also available. Bachelor's degrees are offered in the following subjects: AREA STUDIES (American, Asian, Latin American, Russian), BUSINESS (accounting, business education, computer science, finance, management, marketing), EDUCATION (early childhood, elementary, health/physical, industrial, secondary, special), ENGLISH (English, speech), FINE AND PERFORMING ARTS (art, art education, art history, music, music education, radio/TV, studio art, theater /dramatics), HEALTH SCIENCES (health administration, recreation therapy, speech therapy), LANGUAGES (French, German, Spanish), MATH AND SCIENCES (biology, chemistry, earth science, ecology/ environmental science, geology, mathematics, natural sciences, physical sciences, physics), PHILOSOPHY (humanities, philosophy, religion), PREPROFESSIONAL (architecture, dentistry, engineering, law, library science, medicine, pharmacy, veterinary), SOCIAL SCIENCES (anthropology, economics, geography, government/political science, history, psychology, public administration, social sciences, sociology). Almost 30% of the degrees are conferred in education, 23% in business, and 11% in preprofessional studies.

Required: General-education requirements are satisfied by completion of the 2-year A.A. or A.S. degree.

Special: The university offers special, experimental, and individual study programs, as well as workshops, conferences, and opportunities for research. Juniors may spend a year abroad. Combination degree programs are offered in physical therapy, medical technology, medicine, and dentistry. Students may design their own majors.

Honors: Eighteen honor societies are represented on campus, and many departments offer honors programs.

Admissions: About 91% of those who applied were accepted for the 1981–82 freshman class. The ACT scores of those who enrolled were as follows: 49% scored below 21, 23% between 21 and 23, 12% between 24 and 25, 21% between 26 and 28, and 5% above 28. Candidates should rank in the top 75% of their high school class. The college also considers advanced placement or honors courses, impressions made during an interview, special talents, and recommendations. About 35% of the freshmen graduated in the top fifth of their high school class. Candidates must come from an accredited high school.

Procedure: The SAT or ACT must be taken. Applications should be in by August 15 for fall or January 3 for winter/spring. The application fee is $10. The university has a rolling admissions policy.

Special: AP and CLEP credit is accepted. The university has a deferred admissions plan.

Transfer: For fall 1981, 1239 students applied, 1127 were accepted, and 832 enrolled. A GPA of at least 2.0 is usually necessary, and an ACT score of 17 or better is recommended. Transfer students should have a minimum of 12 credit hours earned. D grades transfer. Students must complete, at the college, 32 of the 124–133 credit hours required for a bachelor's degree. Application deadlines are the same as those for freshmen.

Visiting: Tours can be arranged weekdays from 8 A.M. to 3 P.M. Guides are available for informal visits. Visitors may attend classes and, in some cases, stay overnight at the school. Regularly scheduled 1½-day orientation programs are held in June and July. The admissions office should be contacted for arrangements.

Financial Aid: About 50% of the students receive aid; 20% work part-time on campus. The average award to freshmen was $2000 in 1981–82. Either the FAF or FFS must be filed with CSS. The aid application deadline is March 1 for fall and December for spring.

Foreign Students: Fewer than 1% of the students are from foreign countries. The university offers these students an intensive English course, special counseling, and special organizations.

Admissions: The TOEFL (minimum score 550) or the University of Michigan Language Test is required. College entrance exams are not required.

Procedure: Application deadlines are May 1 for fall, November 1 for spring, and March 1 for summer. Foreign students must present proof of adequate funds for the time they plan to study at the university. Health insurance is required, and is available through the university for a fee.

Admissions Contact: Jack L. Wielenga, Director of Admissions.

UPPER IOWA UNIVERSITY E–2
Fayette, Iowa 52142 (319) 425-4015

F/T: 250M, 200W	Faculty:	29; IIB, – –$
P/T: 15M, 28W	Ph.D.'s:	38%
Grad: none	S/F Ratio:	12 to 1
Year: sems, ss	Tuition:	$4140
Appl: open	R and B:	$1860
458 applied	205 accepted	110 enrolled
ACT: 18		COMPETITIVE+

Upper Iowa University, founded in 1857, is an independent, nonsectarian liberal arts institution. Its library has 97,500 volumes and 1172 microfilm items, and subscribes to 444 periodicals.

Environment: The 20-acre campus is located in a rural area 50 miles from Waterloo. The 5 dormitories have single and double rooms and accommodate 930 students. Additional students are housed in approved private homes. The university also sponsors married-student housing.

Student Life: Fifty percent of the students come from Iowa. About 70% live on campus. Ninety percent attended public schools. About 13% of the students are minority-group members. Campus housing is single-sex, with visiting privileges. Students may keep cars on campus. Day-care services are available for a fee.

Organizations: Ten percent of the men belong to the 2 fraternities on campus. The chorus, band, drama group, publications, and other special-interest groups are available. Social and cultural events on campus include an artist series, dances, debates, and lectures. The outdoor recreation facilities, especially for cross-country skiing, are excellent.

Sports: Eight intercollegiate sports are offered for men and 6 for women. Men may participate in 8 intramural activities and women in 6.

Handicapped: No special facilities are available. About 10% of the campus is accessible to handicapped students.

Graduates: Forty percent of the freshmen drop out by the end of the first year, and about 30% remain to graduate. About 25% of the graduates begin graduate study; 2% enter medical school, 2% enter dental school, and 2% enter law school. About 75% of the graduates begin careers in business and industry.

Services: The university offers free health care, career counseling, placement, tutoring, and remedial instruction.

IOWA 271

Programs of Study: The university confers the B.A., B.A.S., B.G.S., B.S., and B.S.N. degrees. Bachelor's degrees are offered in the following subjects: BUSINESS (accounting, business administration, business education, computer science), EDUCATION (early childhood, elementary, health/physical, secondary, special), ENGLISH (English, speech), FINE AND PERFORMING ARTS (art, art education, music, music education, theater/dramatics), HEALTH SCIENCES (medical technology, nursing), LANGUAGES (French, German), MATH AND SCIENCES (biology, chemistry, ecology/environmental science, mathematics), PREPROFESSIONAL (agriculture, chiropractic, dentistry, law, medicine, pharmacy, physical therapy, podiatry, veterinary), SOCIAL SCIENCES (economics, history, psychology, sociology). The most popular majors are physical education and business administration.

Required: Freshmen must take English I and II. All undergraduates must complete 38 semester hours of general-education requirements.

Special: A work-study program is available to laboratory assistants. Other special programs include a combined B.A.-B.S. degree (5 years) and a 3-year bachelor's degree. Students may design their own majors.

Honors: All departments offer honors programs.

Admissions: Forty-five percent of those who applied were accepted for the 1981–82 freshman class. The SAT scores of those who enrolled were as follows: Verbal—80% below 500, 10% between 500 and 599, 10% between 600 and 700, and 0% above 700; Math—80% below 500, 10% between 500 and 599, 10% between 600 and 700, and 0% above 700. Of those who took the ACT, 50% scored below 21, 20% between 21 and 23, 20% between 24 and 25, 5% between 26 and 28, and 5% above 28. Students must be graduates of accredited high schools, must have completed 16 academic units of work, must rank in the upper half of their graduating class, and should have at least a C+ average. The university also considers advanced placement or honors courses, extracurricular activities, recommendations by school officials, personality, leadership record, impressions made during an interview, and special talents.

Procedure: The SAT or ACT is required. There are no deadlines; admission is on a rolling basis. The application fee is $25.

Special: Early decision, early admissions, and deferred admissions plans are available. CLEP subject exams are accepted; AP credit is also given.

Transfer: For fall 1981, 42 transfer students applied, 30 were accepted, and 22 enrolled. Transfer students must have a minimum GPA of 2.25 and an ACT score of at least 19 or combined SAT scores of at least 875. D grades are accepted. Students must study, at the university, at least 30 of the 124 semester hours required for a bachelor's degree. There are no application deadlines.

Visiting: Orientations are scheduled regularly for prospective students, and guides are available for informal visits. The best time to visit is when school is in session. Visitors may sit in on classes and stay overnight at the school. For further information, contact the director of admissions.

Financial Aid: Eighty percent of the students receive aid; 75% work part-time on campus. The university awards approximately 25 freshman scholarships each year. Aid is also available from a loan fund administered by the university. The average award to freshmen was $600 in 1981–82. Tuition may be paid in installments. The university is a member of the CSS and requires the FAF or the FFS. The deadlines for financial aid applications are March (fall) and December (spring).

Foreign Students: Five percent of the students are from foreign countries. An intensive English course and special organizations are available for these students.

Admissions: Applicants should have a minimum score of 550 on the TOEFL. College entrance exams are not required.

Procedure: Application deadlines are open; students are admitted to the fall, winter, and summer sessions. A medical exam report is required, and students must present proof of adequate funds for 4 years of study. Health insurance is available through the university at no cost.

Admissions Contact: Paul H. Jones, Director of Admissions.

WARTBURG COLLEGE D–2
Waverly, Iowa 50677 (319) 352-1200

F/T: 500M, 500W	Faculty:	68; IIB, av$
P/T: 15M, 15W	Ph.D.'s:	70%
Grad: none	S/F Ratio:	15 to 1
Year: 4-4-1, ss	Tuition:	$4700
Appl: open	R and B:	$1800
620 applied	552 accepted	300 enrolled
SAT: 500V 510M	ACT: 22	COMPETITIVE

272 IOWA

Wartburg College, founded in 1852, is a private, liberal arts institution affiliated with the American Lutheran Church. The Engelbrecht Library contains 125,000 volumes, subscribes to 900 periodicals, and has an audio-visual center.

Environment: The 83-acre, wooded campus is located in the small, rural community of Waverly, 100 miles northeast of Des Moines. The residence halls accommodate over 900 students. The college also sponsors on-campus apartments.

Student Life: About 65% of the students come from Iowa, and 95% of the students live on campus. Seventy percent of the students are Protestant and 12% are Catholic. Minority-group members make up 11% of the student body. Campus housing is both coed and single-sex; there are visiting privileges in single-sex dorms. Students may keep cars on campus.

Organizations: There are no fraternities or sororities. A student senate provides social and cultural programs. In addition, there are many special-interest groups.

Sports: The college competes in 10 intercollegiate sports for men and 8 for women. There are 6 intramural sports for men and 6 for women.

Handicapped: There are no facilities for handicapped students.

Graduates: The dropout rate for freshmen is 10%; 70% remain to graduate. Fifteen percent of the graduates pursue further studies. Five percent of graduates enter medical school, 5% enter dental school, and 5% enter law school. About 25% pursue careers in business and industry.

Services: Students receive free health care, tutoring, remedial instruction, placement aid, and career and psychological counseling.

Programs of Study: The college confers the B.A., B.M., and B.Mus.Ed. degrees. Bachelor's degrees are offered in the following subjects: BUSINESS (accounting, business administration, business education, computer science), EDUCATION (early childhood, elementary, health/physical, secondary, special), ENGLISH (communication arts, English, journalism), FINE AND PERFORMING ARTS (art, art education, music, music education, radio/TV, theater/dramatics), HEALTH SCIENCES (medical technology, occupational therapy, physical therapy), LANGUAGES (French, German, Spanish), MATH AND SCIENCES (biology, chemistry, mathematics, physics), PHILOSOPHY (philosophy, religion), PREPROFESSIONAL (architecture, dentistry, engineering, law, medicine, ministry, pharmacy, social work, veterinary), SOCIAL SCIENCES (economics, government/political science, history, psychology, social sciences, sociology). Most degrees are conferred in education, business, and the arts.

Special: It is possible to take a 5-year program leading to a combined B.A.-B.S. degree in engineering. Overseas language study is possible. The college offers a B.G.S. degree. A Corporation Education program is offered for business majors.

Honors: Eight honor societies have chapters on campus, and a 4-year honors program is offered.

Admissions: About 89% of those who applied were accepted for the 1981–82 freshman class. The SAT scores of those who enrolled were as follows: Verbal—40% below 500, 40% between 500 and 599, 20% between 600 and 700, and 0% above 700; Math—40% below 500, 40% between 500 and 599, 20% between 600 and 700, and 0% above 700. Of those who took the ACT, 20% scored below 21, 60% between 21 and 23, 10% between 24 and 25, 5% between 26 and 28, and 5% above 28. The candidate should have completed 15 Carnegie units and rank in the upper half of the graduating class. Recommendations and advanced placement or honors courses are also considered.

Procedure: Either the SAT or ACT is required and should be taken during the junior year or early in the senior year. The application should be submitted along with a $15 fee. An interview is recommended. Application deadlines are open. There is a rolling admissions policy.

Special: Early decision, early admissions, and deferred admissions plans are offered. AP and CLEP credit is available.

Transfer: For fall 1981, 120 transfer applications were received, 95 were approved, and 56 students enrolled. A 2.0 GPA is required, and there is a 1-year residency requirement.

Visiting: Visits can be arranged for weekdays through the admissions office. Visitors may sit in on classes and stay overnight at the school.

Financial Aid: About 89% of the students receive aid. Fifty percent work part-time. Most aid awards are based on need. The average award to freshmen in 1981–82 was $3500. The college is a member of CSS; either the FAF, the FFS, or the SFS must be filed. Applications for scholarships should be submitted by March 1, but aid is awarded as long as it is available.

Foreign Students: More than 7% of the students are from foreign countries.

Admissions: A minimum score of 550 on the TOEFL is required. College entrance exams are not necessary.

Procedure: Application deadlines are open.

Admissions Contact: Drew R. Boster, Director of Admissions.

WESTMAR COLLEGE B-2
Le Mars, Iowa 51031 (712) 546-7081

F/T: 325M, 275W Faculty: 48; IIB, −$
P/T: 32M, 23W Ph.D.'s: 47%
Grad: none S/F Ratio: 15 to 1
Year: sems, ss Tuition: $3700
Appl: see entry R and B: $1720
332 applied 291 accepted 160 enrolled
ACT: 19 COMPETITIVE

Westmar College, operated by the United Methodist Church, is a private liberal arts college offering professional and preprofessional programs. Its library contains more than 84,000 volumes and 5000 microfilm items, and subscribes to 411 periodicals.

Environment: The 82-acre campus is located in a rural area 25 miles from Sioux City. Four coed and single-sex dormitories accommodate 700 students. Apartments are available for married students.

Student Life: Ninety-three percent of the students are from the North Central region. About 75% live on campus. Ninety percent of the students are Protestant, and 40% belong to the supporting denomination. Eight percent are Catholic. About 2% are members of minority groups. The single-sex dormitories have visiting privileges; there are also coed dorms. Students may keep cars on campus. All students must attend a weekly encounter.

Organizations: There are no fraternities or sororities. The Guthrie Theatre and the Dakota Dome are nearby recreational facilities.

Sports: The college offers 7 intercollegiate sports for men and 5 for women. Eight intramural sports are offered for men and 7 for women.

Handicapped: There are no special facilities for handicapped students.

Graduates: Thirty-five percent of the freshmen drop out by the end of the first year, and 38% remain to graduate. Eleven percent of the graduates seek advanced degrees.

Services: Students receive placement services, health care, and psychological and career counseling without charge. Fees are charged for tutoring and remedial instruction.

Programs of Study: The college awards the B.A. and B.Mus.Ed. degrees. Bachelor's degrees are offered in the following subjects: BUSINESS (accounting, business administration, computer science), EDUCATION (elementary, industrial, secondary), ENGLISH (English), FINE AND PERFORMING ARTS (art, music, music education, radio/TV), HEALTH SCIENCES (physical therapy), LANGUAGES (German, Spanish), MATH AND SCIENCES (biology, chemistry, mathematics, natural sciences), PHILOSOPHY (religion), PREPROFESSIONAL (engineering, home economics, law, medicine, ministry, social work), SOCIAL SCIENCES (economics, government/political science, history, psychology, social sciences, sociology). Twenty percent of degrees conferred are in education and 20% in social sciences.

Required: All students must complete a general education program.

Special: Students may spend their junior year abroad.

Honors: Two national honor societies have chapters on campus. Honor students are selected to serve as department fellows.

Admissions: Eighty-eight percent of the applicants were accepted for the 1981–82 freshman class. The ACT scores of those who enrolled were as follows: 19% scored below 21, 38% between 21 and 23, 32% between 24 and 28, and 11% above 28. Six percent ranked in the upper fifth of their high school class, 24% in the upper two-fifths. Candidates must be graduates of accredited high schools, have completed 15 Carnegie units with a grade average of C or better, and rank in the upper half of their graduating class. The college also considers the following factors: recommendations by school officials, evidence of special talents, leadership record, ability to finance college education, extracurricular activities, and advanced placement or honors courses.

Procedure: The ACT is required. There is a $10 application fee. Freshmen are admitted to any term. Applications may be submitted until the first week of classes. The college uses a rolling admissions plan.

Special: There is an early admissions plan. CLEP and AP credit is accepted.

Transfer: For fall 1981, 77 transfer students applied, 62 were accepted, and 34 enrolled. Applicants must have a GPA of 2.0 or better and an ACT composite score of 16 or better. Good standing also is required. Students must study at the college for at least 30 semester hours of the 128 required for a bachelor's degree. Applications may be submitted until the first week of classes.

Visiting: Orientations for prospective students are scheduled regularly on visitation weekend and on special career days. There are guides for informal visits, and guests may sit in on classes and stay overnight at the school. The academic year is the best time for visits, which can be arranged through the admissions director.

Financial Aid: Scholarships and loans are available from the federal government and from the college. About 85% of all students receive aid, and 45% work part-time on campus. The FAF should be submitted by March 1 for fall admission. The college is a member of CSS.

Foreign Students: Ten foreign students are enrolled at the college, which provides special counseling for them.

Admissions: Applicants must score 500 or better on the TOEFL. No academic exams are required.

Procedure: Applications are accepted until the first week of classes, and freshmen are admitted to all terms. Foreign students must present proof of adequate funds for 1 year of study. Health insurance is not required.

Admissions Contact: Valda Embree, Director of Admissions.

WILLIAM PENN COLLEGE D–3
Oskaloosa, Iowa 52577 (515) 673-8311

F/T, P/T:	Faculty:	n/av; IIB, –$
580 M&W	Ph.D.'s:	42%
Grad: none	S/F Ratio:	14 to 1
Year: sems, ss	Tuition:	$4715
Appl: Aug. 15	R and B:	$1420
550 applied	400 accepted	135 enrolled
ACT: 17		COMPETITIVE

William Penn College, founded in 1873, is a liberal arts and sciences college affiliated with the Society of Friends (Quakers). The library has a capacity of 100,000 volumes.

Environment: The 40-acre campus is located in a small town 58 miles from Des Moines. Facilities include a fine-arts center, a student union, and a chapel. Four single-sex and coed dormitories accommodate 350 women and 551 men.

Student Life: About 52% of the students come from Iowa, and 85% come from public schools. About 51% live in dormitories and 34% in other college-approved housing. Alcohol is not permitted on campus. Attendance at convocations is compulsory; chapel attendance is not required.

Organizations: There are 3 sororities and 5 fraternities. Extracurricular activities include religious groups, departmental clubs, publications, student government, and performing groups.

Sports: The college fields intercollegiate teams in 10 sports. Intramural competition is available in 8 sports.

Graduates: About 25% of the freshmen drop out by the end of the first year, and 50% remain to graduate. Of these, 20% go on for further education.

Services: Career counseling and placement aid are provided.

Programs of Study: The B.A. is offered in the following subjects: BUSINESS (accounting, business administration, business education), EDUCATION (elementary, health/physical, secondary), ENGLISH (communication arts, English), FINE AND PERFORMING ARTS (music), MATH AND SCIENCES (biology, chemistry, ecology/environmental science, mathematics), PHILOSOPHY (religion), PRE-PROFESSIONAL (home economics, industrial arts), SOCIAL SCIENCES (economics, history, psychology, social sciences, sociology).

Required: Two semesters of physical education and 4 hours of religion are required.

Special: Work-study, study abroad, and internships are offered. Elementary and secondary teacher training programs lead to certification.

Admissions: About 73% of those who applied were accepted for the 1981–82 freshman class. The ACT scores of those who enrolled were as follows: 70% below 21, 10% between 21 and 23, 6% between 24 and 25, 2% between 26 and 28, and 12% above 28. Twenty percent ranked in the top fifth of their high school class, and 55% ranked in the top two-fifths. A high school GPA of 2.0 or better and 15 academic units are required. The admissions committee also considers the applicant's academic record, including advanced placement or honors courses, extracurricular activities, leadership record, and impressions made during an interview. Sons and daughters of alumni receive preference.

Procedure: The SAT, PSAT, or ACT is required. New students are admitted each semester. August 15 is the application deadline for the fall semester, January 1 the deadline for spring. Notification is on a rolling basis. There is a $10 application fee.

Special: An early admissions plan is offered. CLEP credit is available.

Transfer: Transfer students must be in good standing at their last school. D grades transfer only if the applicant has an associate degree. One semester must be completed in residence.

Visiting: Campus tours may be arranged.

Financial Aid: About 90% of the students receive financial aid. The college participates in federal programs such as NDSL and BEOG/SEOG. Bank loans and campus jobs are available. Tuition may be paid in installments. The FAF is required. Applications should be submitted by July 15 (fall) or December 15 (spring).

Foreign Students: About 5 foreign students were enrolled in 1981–82. Special counseling is provided.

Admissions: Applicants must score 500 or better on the TOEFL.

Procedure: Application deadlines are the same as those for other students. Proof of adequate funds for 4 years and good health is required. Students must carry health insurance, which is available through the college for a fee.

Admissions Contact: Eric Otto, Director of Admissions.

KANSAS

BAKER UNIVERSITY E–2
Baldwin City, Kansas 66006 (913) 594-6644

F/T: 397M, 437W	Faculty:	60; IIB, –$
P/T: 9M, 18W	Ph.D.'s:	50%
Grad: 33M, 41W	S/F Ratio:	14 to 1
Year: 4-1-4, ss	Tuition:	$3375
Appl: open	R and B:	$1990
359 applied	319 accepted	224 enrolled
SAT or ACT: required		COMPETITIVE

Founded in 1858, Baker University is a liberal arts institution affiliated with the Methodist Church. The library contains more than 75,000 volumes, subscribes to 340 periodicals, and houses the Quayle Rare Bible Collection and the United Methodist Historical Society Collection.

Environment: The 26-acre campus, located in Baldwin, is surrounded by a rural environment, but is only 45 miles from Kansas City. Among the 27 buildings on campus are a music arts building, a student union, and 4 dormitories that accommodate 246 women and 292 men. There are also fraternity and sorority houses.

Student Life: About 64% of the students are from Kansas, 13% from Missouri, and the rest from 1 of 24 other states and 8 foreign countries. Seventy-one percent of the students live on campus. Sixty-one percent of the students are Protestant; 36% are members of the Methodist Church. Eleven percent are members of various minority groups. Campus housing is single-sex; there are visiting privileges. Students may keep cars on campus. Drinking on campus is prohibited.

Organizations: About 50% of the women and 40% of the men belong to a fraternity or sorority. There is a full schedule of extracurricular and cultural events on campus. Students participate in administrative and curricular matters and sit on the Student Affairs Committee of the Board of Trustees.

Sports: The college fields intercollegiate teams in 8 sports for men and 7 for women. Intramural sports number 8 for men and 5 for women.

Graduates: About 25% of the students drop out by the end of their freshman year; 45% remain to graduate. Thirty-five percent of the graduates pursue advanced degrees.

Services: Students receive placement, health care, career and psychological counseling, and tutoring services free of charge.

Programs of Study: The university awards the B.A., B.S., and B.Mus.Ed. degrees. Master's programs are also available. Bachelor's degrees are offered in the following subjects: BUSINESS (accounting, business administration, computer science), EDUCATION (elementary, health/physical, secondary), ENGLISH (English, journalism, speech), FINE AND PERFORMING ARTS (art, art education, music, music education, theater/dramatics), HEALTH SCIENCES (medical technology, nursing, physical therapy), LANGUAGES (French, German, Spanish), MATH AND SCIENCES (biology, chemistry, mathematics, physics), PHILOSOPHY (philosophy, religion), PREPROFESSIONAL (dentistry, engineering, forestry, home economics, law, medicine, pharmacy, veterinary), SOCIAL SCIENCES (economics, government/political science, history, psychology, sociology).

Required: All undergraduates must take 36 hours of a general education curriculum and 4 semesters of physical education. B.A. candidates must take a foreign language.

Special: The January Interterm is used for guided study with heavy emphasis on independent work. Interterms range from study abroad to work-study jobs on campus. Study abroad programs may also be taken during the junior year.

Admissions: About 89% of the applicants for the 1981–82 freshmen class were accepted. A C average and a minimum high school rank in the upper 50% of the graduating class are required. In evaluating applicants, Baker considers their high school record, SAT or ACT scores, and recommendations concerning their potential.

Procedure: The ACT or SAT is required. Students are admitted to both semesters and the summer session. There are no application deadlines, but applications should be submitted as early as possible. There is a $15 application fee. The university uses a rolling admissions procedure.

Special: Early decision, early admissions, and deferred admissions plans are available. AP and CLEP credit is granted.

Transfer: For fall 1981, 67 transfer students applied, 58 were accepted, and 49 enrolled. Transfers are accepted for all classes. A 2.0 GPA is required. D grades transfer. Students must complete 31 credits, including the final 27, at Baker. For the bachelor's degree, a total of 124 credits and 3 Interterms must be completed. Application deadlines are open. The university uses a rolling admissions procedure.

Financial Aid: Financial aid recipients represent 84% of the student body. About 35% of the students work part-time on campus. The average award to freshmen is $933. Scholarships and loans are available from the university and other sources. Campus employment (including CWS) can provide students with up to $600 a year. Tuition may be paid in installments. The university is a CSS member. Applicants should submit the FAF or FSS. The financial aid application deadlines are March 1 (fall) and January 15 (spring).

Foreign Students: One percent of the full-time students come from foreign countries. The university sponsors special organizations for these students.

Admissions: The university requires the TOEFL; a minimum score of 500 must be achieved. College entrance exams are not required.

Procedure: There are no application deadlines. Foreign applicants may enter the fall, spring, or summer session. Proof of health, in the form of a completed health form, is necessary. Proof of funds adequate to cover 1 year of study must be presented. Health insurance is required; it is available through the university for a fee.

Admissions Contact: Ken Snow, Dean of Admissions.

BENEDICTINE COLLEGE E–1
Atchison, Kansas 66002 (913) 367-5340

F/T: 482M, 497W	Faculty:	61; IIB, –$
P/T: 24M, 42W	Ph.D.'s:	40%
Grad: none	S/F Ratio:	14 to 1
Year: 4-1-4, ss	Tuition:	$3247
Appl: Aug. 1	R and B:	$1730
792 applied	618 accepted	333 enrolled
ACT: 22		COMPETITIVE

Benedictine College is a Roman Catholic liberal arts college established in 1971 by the merger of St. Benedict's College (founded in 1858) and Mount St. Scholastica College (founded in 1924). The college is run by members of the Benedictine Order. The two libraries, one on each of the two campuses, contain a total of 284,000 volumes, and subscribe to a total of 1000 periodicals.

Environment: The two campuses are located 16 blocks apart in Atchison, a town of 13,000 people 45 miles from Kansas City. The environment surrounding the campus is rural. The combined area of the campuses is 225 acres, and they contain a total of 22 buildings. Seven dormitories accommodate 1046 students.

Student Life: Forty percent of the students come from Kansas and 4% from foreign countries. Ninety-five percent of the students live on campus. All freshmen must observe a curfew. Sixty-five percent of entering freshmen come from parochial schools. Eighty-seven percent of the students are Catholic and 13% are Protestant. Ten percent are minority-group members. Campus housing is single-sex; there are visiting privileges. Students may keep cars on campus.

Organizations: Fraternities and sororities are associated with academic areas. Major social events include the Homecoming and Winter Weekends. There is a student government, and voting student delegates sit on some faculty and administration committees. The college sponsors religious organizations for students.

Sports: Intercollegiate programs are available for 6 men's and 5 women's sports. There are 7 intramural sports for men and 7 for women.

Handicapped: About 80% of the campus is accessible to handicapped students. Facilities include wheelchair ramps, special parking, elevators, and special class scheduling. Some dormitories have special facilities. Very small numbers of students have impaired vision or hearing. Readers are available, and faculty members are cooperative in administering exams and in other areas.

Graduates: About 32% of the freshmen drop out; 48% remain to graduate. Thirty-five percent of the graduates pursue advanced degrees immediately after graduation.

Services: The following services are available to students free of charge: health care; psychological, placement, and career counseling; tutoring; and remedial instruction.

Programs of Study: The college offers the B.A., B.M., and B.Mus.Ed. degrees. Associate degree programs are also available. Bachelor's degrees are offered in the following subjects: BUSINESS (accounting, business administration), EDUCATION (day-care/preschool administration, early childhood, elementary, secondary), ENGLISH (English, journalism), FINE AND PERFORMING ARTS (art, music, music education, theater/dramatics), LANGUAGES (French, Greek/Latin, Spanish), MATH AND SCIENCES (biology, chemistry, mathematics, physics), PHILOSOPHY (classics, philosophy, religion), SOCIAL SCIENCES (economics, government/political science, history, psychology, social sciences, sociology). Twenty-nine percent of degrees are conferred in business and 28% in social sciences.

Required: Students must complete 55 hours of general education courses. They must pass URE exams to graduate.

Special: Students may travel and study abroad. There are 3-2 combination degree programs in engineering and medical technology. Combined B.A.-B.S. degrees are also available in other subjects. The college offers a general studies major. Student-designed majors are permitted.

Honors: Departmental honors programs are offered in math, history, and logic. The programs require considerable independent study.

Admissions: Seventy-eight percent of those who applied were accepted for the 1981–82 freshman class. Freshman ACT scores were as follows: 35% below 21, 22% between 21 and 23, 19% between 24 and 25, and 24% above 26. Applicants must have a C average and graduate in the top half of their high school class with 16 Carnegie units. Admissions officers also consider recommendations by high school officials, advanced placement or honors courses, and impressions made during an interview.

Procedure: The SAT or ACT is required; the ACT is preferred. The ACT should be taken before the July following graduation from high school. Junior year results are acceptable. A personal interview is recommended. Application deadlines are August 1 (fall), December 1 (spring), and June 1 (summer). Freshmen are admitted to all terms. The college has a rolling admissions policy. There is a $10 application fee.

Special: The college has a deferred admissions plan. CLEP and AP credit is accepted.

Transfer: For fall 1981, 77 transfer students applied, 56 were accepted, and 42 enrolled. Transfers are accepted for all but the senior class. A GPA of at least 2.0 and an ACT score of at least 16 are necessary. C and above grades transfer. Students must take at least 30 semester hours in residence, of 122 semester hours required for the bachelor's degree. Application deadlines are the same as those for freshmen.

Visiting: The college holds orientation sessions for prospective students during the summer in nearby cities, including St. Louis and Kansas City. Guides also are available for informal visits to the college. Visitors may sit in on classes and stay overnight on campus. Visits should be scheduled for weekdays. The admissions office will handle arrangements.

Financial Aid: About 85% of the students receive financial aid; 60% work part-time on campus. The average award to freshmen is $3000. A $70,000 fund provides freshman scholarships ranging from $500 to $1800. The college divides $325,000 in federal loan funds among 35% of the students. Work contracts range from $450 to $750, loans from $800 to $1000. Federal work-study funds are available. Tuition may be paid in installments. The college is a member of CSS. Either the FAF or the FFS is acceptable; the FFS is preferred. Applications should be filed by July 1 (fall), November 1 (spring), and May 1 (summer).

Foreign Students: Four percent of the full-time students are from foreign countries. The college offers these students an intensive English course, special counseling, and special organizations.

Admissions: Foreign candidates must take the TOEFL and score a minimum of 500. College entrance exams are not necessary.

Procedure: Applications are due August 1 (fall), November 30 (spring), and May 1 (summer). Proof of funds adequate to cover 1 academic year must be presented.

Admissions Contact: Ronald W. Lehmann, Director of Admissions.

BETHANY COLLEGE D-2
Lindsborg, Kansas 67456 (913) 227-3311

F/T: 388M, 395W		Faculty:	56; IIB, –$
P/T: 8M, 16W		Ph.D.'s:	40%
Grad: none		S/F Ratio:	14 to 1
Year: 4-1-4, ss		Tuition:	$3090
Appl: open		R and B:	$1985
701 applied	639 accepted		310 enrolled
ACT: 20			COMPETITIVE

Bethany College, founded in 1881, is a small, coeducational, liberal arts college affiliated with the Lutheran Church. The library houses 95,000 volumes, and subscribes to 340 periodicals.

Environment: The 60-acre campus is located in a rural area 20 miles from Salina. Stroble-Gibson Centennial Center was recently completed. Dormitories accommodate 300 women and 315 men.

Student Life: Three-fourths of the students live on campus. Eighty-one percent are Protestant; 13% are Catholic. Five percent are minority-group members. Campus housing is both single-sex and coed; there are visiting privileges in the former. Students may keep cars on campus.

Organizations: Ten percent of the students belong to 1 of 3 fraternities and 3 sororities on campus. Student activities include drama, concerts, lecture series, and art shows.

Sports: The college sponsors intercollegiate teams in 8 sports for men and 7 for women. Intramural sports for both men and women number 12.

Handicapped: The entire campus is accessible to handicapped students. Facilities include wheelchair ramps, special parking, elevators, and specially equipped rest rooms. Two counselors and 2 assistants work with handicapped students.

Graduates: Approximately 10% of the students drop out at the end of their freshman year; 60% remain to graduate. Four percent enter medical school, 1% dental school, and 3% law school. Twenty-eight percent enter business and industry. Fifteen percent of the graduates pursue advanced degrees.

Services: The following services are provided to students free of charge: health care, psychological and career counseling, placement, and remedial instruction. Tutoring services are available for a fee.

Programs of Study: All programs lead to the B.A. degree. Bachelor's degrees are offered in the following subjects: BUSINESS (accounting, business administration, management), EDUCATION (elementary, health/physical, secondary, special), ENGLISH (English), FINE AND PERFORMING ARTS (art, art education, music, music education), MATH AND SCIENCES (biology, chemistry), PREPROFESSIONAL (dentistry, law, medicine, ministry, social work), SOCIAL SCIENCES (behavioral science, economics, history/political science, psychology, social sciences, sociology).

Special: Independent study and student-designed majors are permitted. The experience-based education program allows underclassmen an opportunity to work and receive college credit at the same time.

Honors: Several honor societies are open to qualified students.

Admissions: Ninety-one percent of those who applied were accepted for the 1981–82 freshman class. The college prefers applicants who rank in the upper half of their class and have a B average. The minimum GPA is 2.0. Other factors considered are advanced placement or honors courses, recommendations by high school officials, and extracurricular activities. The college seeks a geographically diverse student body.

Procedure: The ACT or SAT is required. Tests should be taken by December of the senior year. A personal interview, on or off campus, is strongly recommended. Applications, accompanied by a $10 fee, should be filed in the fall of the senior year, although there is no deadline. Admission is granted on a rolling basis. Freshmen are accepted to the fall or spring semester.

Special: The college offers early decision and early admissions plans. AP and CLEP credit are available.

Transfer: For fall 1981, 101 transfer students applied, 97 were accepted, and 59 enrolled. Transfers are accepted for all classes. A minimum GPA of 2.0 is necessary. Nine out of 35 credits required for the B.A. must be taken at the college. Application deadlines are open. Transfers may enter the fall, spring, or summer session.

Visiting: Regular orientations held for prospective students include visits with faculty members, students, financial aid advisers, and admissions staff members. Guides also are available for informal visits. Visitors may sit in on classes and spend the night on campus. Visits are best scheduled in October, November, March, or April. The admissions office should be contacted for arrangements.

Financial Aid: About 85% of all students receive some form of financial aid. About 26% work part-time on campus, many in CWS jobs. The average award to freshmen is $2700. Grants, scholarships, and loans are available. Applications for financial aid must include the FFS, FAF, or SFS. The deadline for scholarship applications is February 1. Notification is made on a rolling basis. Need is the determining factor.

Foreign Students: Two percent of the student body are foreign students. The college offers these students special counseling and special organizations.

Admissions: The college requires that foreign applicants take the TOEFL and score a minimum of 500. The SAT or ACT is not required.

Procedure: Application deadlines are open. Foreign students may enter the fall or spring semester. A physical examination and a completed health form are required. Proof of funds adequate to cover the entire period of study must be presented.

Admissions Contact: Leon Burch, Dean of Admissions.

BETHEL COLLEGE D-3
North Newton, Kansas 67117 (316) 283-2500

F/T: 282M, 337W		Faculty:	23; IIB, –$
P/T: 64M, 65W		Ph.D.'s:	n/av
Grad: none		S/F Ratio:	14 to 1
Year: 4-1-4, ss		Tuition:	$3122
Appl: Aug. 15		R and B:	$1794
215 applied	201 accepted		162 enrolled
ACT: 22			COMPETITIVE

Bethel College, founded in 1887, is a Christian liberal arts school affiliated with the Mennonite Church. The library contains 51,749 volumes, and subscribes to 340 periodicals.

Environment: The 40-acre campus is located in a suburban area 22 miles from Wichita. Campus buildings include a gymnasium and student center and an administration building, built in 1888 out of Kansas limestone, that is a national landmark. Dormitories accommodate 600 students in double rooms. The college also sponsors off-campus apartments and married student housing.

Student Life: Sixty-five percent of the students come from Kansas, and 66% live on campus. Two-thirds of the students are Mennonites. Attendance at the twice-a-week convocation series is compulsory. Twenty-one percent of the students are minority-group members. Campus housing is both single-sex and coed; there are visiting privileges in the former. Students may keep cars on campus. Drinking is prohibited on campus.

Organizations: The college has no fraternities or sororities. Activities include student government, publications, music groups, debating, special-interest clubs, a drama society, and a radio station.

Sports: The college participates intercollegiately in 7 sports for men and 5 for women. There are 8 intramural sports for both men and women.

Handicapped: About 75% of the campus is accessible to handicapped students. Facilities include wheelchair ramps, special parking, and specially equipped rest rooms.

Graduates: Twenty-five percent of the freshmen drop out at the end of the first year; 50% remain to graduate. About 20% of the graduates pursue advanced degrees; 5% enter medical school and 2% law school. More than 50% of the graduates enter business and industry.

Services: The following services are provided to students free of charge: health care, psychological and career counseling, tutoring, and remedial instruction. Placement services are available only for education majors.

Programs of Study: The college awards the B.A. and B.S. degrees. Associate degree programs are also available. Bachelor's degrees are offered in the following subjects: BUSINESS (business administration, computer science), EDUCATION (early childhood, elementary, health/physical, industrial, secondary), ENGLISH (English, speech), FINE AND PERFORMING ARTS (art, art education, music, music education, theater/dramatics), HEALTH SCIENCES (medical technology, nursing, physical therapy), LANGUAGES (German), MATH AND SCIENCES (biology, chemistry, ecology/environmental science, mathematics, natural sciences, physics), PHILOSOPHY (philosophy, religion), PREPROFESSIONAL (agriculture, dentistry, home economics, law, medicine, ministry, social work), SOCIAL SCIENCES (economics, history, psychology, sociology). Sixteen percent of all bachelor's degrees are conferred in math and sciences, 12% in business, and 11% in the arts.

Required: Two credits of health and physical education are required, as are 8 hours of Bible and religion.

Special: Students may spend their junior year studying abroad. Cooperative education programs are offered with Kansas State University in agriculture, engineering, and home economics. Seminars in non-Western studies are offered jointly with 5 other colleges. Combination degree programs are available. Independent study and student-designed majors are permitted. The college offers a general studies degree.

Honors: Honor societies are available in speech, forensics, drama, and home economics. The mathematics and chemistry departments offer honors programs.

Admissions: Ninety-three percent of those who applied were accepted for the 1981-82 freshman class. Freshman ACT scores were as follows: 42% below 21, 15% between 21 and 23, 18% between 24 and 25, 21% between 26 and 28, and 4% above 28. Applicants should rank in the upper half of their class and have completed 17 Carnegie units with an average of at least 2.0. A recommendation from the high school is required. Admissions officers also consider an applicant's character and personality.

Procedure: The ACT or SAT is required, the ACT preferred. The test should be taken by March of the senior year. Candidates are urged to apply as early as possible, up to a year before entrance. A personal interview is recommended. The application deadlines are August 15 (fall), December 15 (winter), January 15 (spring), and May 15 (summer). There is a $10 application fee. Admissions decisions are made on a rolling basis.

Special: The college has a deferred admissions plan. CLEP and AP credit are accepted.

Transfer: For fall 1981, 109 transfer students applied, 102 were accepted, and 60 enrolled. Transfer applicants are considered for all classes. Applicants must have a GPA of at least 2.0 and be in good standing at their last college. Students must earn a minimum of 30 semester hours at Bethel, of a total 124 hours required for the bachelor's degree. Application deadlines are the same as those for freshmen.

Visiting: Guides are available for informal visits. Visitors may sit in on classes and stay at the school. Visits are best scheduled during fall or spring visitation weekends. The admissions office will handle arrangements.

Financial Aid: Ninety percent of the students receive aid. Fifty-five percent work part-time on campus. Scholarships of $75 to $1200 per year and loans of $100 to $2500 per year are available. Aid awards to freshmen vary between $100 and $4000. The average award to freshmen is $2800. The FAF or FFS should be filed, preferably the FFS. The deadlines for aid applications are April 1 (fall) and October 1 (spring). The priority date is April 1.

Foreign Students: About 4% of the full-time students come from foreign countries. Special counseling and organizations especially for foreign students are available.

Admissions: The college requires the TOEFL and a minimum score of 500. The SAT or ACT is not required.

Procedure: Applications are due April 1 (fall), and September 1 (spring). Proof of funds adequate to cover the entire period of study must be shown. Health insurance is required; it is available through the college for a fee.

Admissions Contact: Diana Torline, Director of Admissions.

EMPORIA STATE UNIVERSITY E-2
Emporia, Kansas 66801   (316) 343-1200

F/T: 1727M, 2085W   Faculty: 245; IIA, av$
P/T: 254M, 397W   Ph.D.'s: 55%
Grad: 588M, 971W   S/F Ratio: 20 to 1
Year: sems, ss   Tuition: $718 ($1512)
Appl: see profile   R and B: $1730
1598 applied   1598 accepted   882 enrolled
ACT: 18   NONCOMPETITIVE

Emporia State University, founded in 1863, is a state-supported institution offering liberal arts, teacher education, and vocational programs. The library houses 620,000 volumes and 140,000 microfilm items, and subscribes to 2674 periodicals.

Environment: The 200-acre campus, in a rural area 110 miles from Kansas City, features an education and psychology building. Residence halls accommodate 1400 students. Fraternity and sorority houses also provide living facilities.

Student Life: About 87% of the students are from Kansas. Almost all come from public school. About 26% live on campus: 23% in dormitories and the rest in fraternity or sorority houses. About 7% of the students are members of minority groups. Campus housing is both single-sex and coed; there are visiting privileges in the former. Students may keep cars on campus. The university provides day-care services to all students, faculty, and staff for a fee.

Organizations: Six percent of the women and 5% of the men belong to 1 of the 8 sororities or 8 fraternities with chapters on campus. Extracurricular activities include religious clubs for all major faiths.

Sports: Emporia State University competes intercollegiately in 7 sports for men and 9 for women. Intramural sports for both men and women number 14.

Handicapped: About 95% of the campus is accessible to wheelchair-bound students. Special facilities include wheelchair ramps, special parking, elevators, special class scheduling, specially equipped rest rooms, and lowered drinking fountains and telephones. The 1% of students who are visually impaired and the 1% who are hearing impaired may use audiovisual equipment, raised room numbers, and guide service. Two special counselors are available, as is a rehabilitation program for the physically handicapped.

Graduates: About 40% of the freshmen drop out, and about 50% remain to graduate. Fifteen percent of the graduates pursue advanced degrees: 1% enter medical school, 1% dental school, and 1% law school. About 35% of the graduates pursue careers in business and industry.

Services: Students receive the following free services: psychological, career, and placement counseling, and remedial instruction. Health care and tutoring are available for a fee.

Programs of Study: The university awards the B.A., B.F.A., B.G.S., B.S., B.S.Ed., B.S.Bus., B.Mus., B.Mus.Ed., and B.S.Med.Tech. degrees. Associate and master's degree programs also are available. Bachelor's degrees are offered in the following subjects: BUSINESS (accounting, business administration, business education, management, marketing, secretarial studies), EDUCATION (elementary, health/physical, industrial, rehabilitation counseling), ENGLISH (English, speech), FINE AND PERFORMING ARTS (art, music, music education, music merchandising, theater/dramatics), HEALTH SCIENCES (medical technology), LANGUAGES (foreign languages—general), MATH AND SCIENCES (biology, chemistry, earth science, mathematics, physical sciences, physics), PHILOSOPHY (philosophy), PREPROFESSIONAL (home economics), SOCIAL SCIENCES (anthropology, economics, geography, government/political science, history, public affairs, psychology, social sciences, sociology). Forty-five percent of degrees are conferred in education, 28% in business, and 10% in social sciences.

Special: Combined B.A.-B.S. degrees are available in several subjects. A general studies degree is also available.

Honors: A number of honor societies have chapters on campus.

Admissions: All applicants were accepted for the 1981–82 freshman class. The ACT scores of those who enrolled were as follows: 66% below 21, 17% between 21 and 23, 8% between 24 and 25, 7% between 26 and 28, and 2% above 28. All graduates of accredited Kansas high schools are admitted. Nonresidents must have at least a C average and an ACT score of 17.8 or better, and must rank in the upper half of their high school class.

Procedure: The ACT is required. Applications should be received at least 10 days before registration. New students are admitted to the fall, spring, or summer session. Admissiosn decisions are made on a rolling basis. There is no application fee.

Special: Early decision, early admissions, and deferred admissions plans are available. CLEP and AP credit are accepted.

Transfer: For fall 1981, 2290 transfer students enrolled. Transfers are admitted to all classes. Applicants must be high school graduates or GED recipients. D grades are transferable. Transfer students must earn 30 credits at the university, of a total 124 required for the bachelor's degree. Applications must be in at least 10 days before registration. Transfers are admitted to the fall, spring, or summer session.

Visiting: Orientations are scheduled regularly for prospective students. Guides are available for informal visits; visitors may sit in on classes and stay in the dormitories. The admissions office will handle arrangements.

Financial Aid: About 60% of the students receive aid from the school in the form of scholarships, grants, NDSL loans, and/or campus employment. About 35% of the students work part-time on campus. The amount of aid for entering freshman from all sources covers about 45% of costs. EOG is available for those who need it. The university is a member of the CSS. The FFS must be filed. The application deadline is open.

Foreign Students: Students from other countries represent 9% of the student body. The university offers an intensive English program, special counseling, and organizations especially for foreign students.

Admissions: Foreign applicants must take either the TOEFL, University of Michigan Language Test, or the university's own test. The minimum TOEFL score is 400. The SAT or ACT is not required.

Procedure: Candidates from foreign countries should apply by June 1 (fall) November 1 (spring), or April 1 (summer). The university's health form must be completed. Proof of funds adequate to cover at least 1 year must be shown. Health insurance must be carried; the fee for such insurance is included in regular ESU fees.

Admissions Contact: Jan Jantzen, Director of Admissions.

FORT HAYS STATE UNIVERSITY C–2
Hays, Kansas 67601 (913) 628-4222

F/T: 1769M, 1828W	Faculty: 243; IIA, –$
P/T: 178M, 414W	Ph.D.'s: 48%
Grad: 517M, 901W	S/F Ratio: 15 to 1
Year: sems, ss	Tuition: $795 ($1590)
Appl: Aug. 15	R and B: $1764–1860
1395 applied	1367 accepted 864 enrolled
ACT: 19	NONCOMPETITIVE

Fort Hays State University, founded in 1902, is a state institution for liberal arts, applied arts, and teacher education. The library houses 500,000 volumes and 120,000 microfilm items, and subscribes to 1300 periodicals.

Environment: The 4160 acres owned by the university occupy about half the old Fort Hays Military Reservation, in a rural area 250 miles from Kansas City and 300 miles from Denver. The campus proper consists of 280 acres. Nearly all university buildings are constructed of native limestone. A physical education and athletic facility, a humanities building, a media center, and a nursing school were recently constructed. Housing facilities accommodate 800 men and 900 women, and 84 apartments are available for married students. In addition, there are fraternity and sorority houses and off-campus apartments.

Student Life: Most students are from Kansas. Ninety-two percent of entering freshmen come from public schools. About 34% of the students live in dormitories. Six percent of the students are minority-group members. Campus housing is both single-sex and coed; there are visiting privileges in the former. Students may keep cars on campus. The university provides day-care services for a fee; all students, faculty, and staff are eligible.

Organizations: Ten percent of the students belong to 1 of 5 fraternities or 4 sororities on campus. The university sponsors a number of social groups, scholastic organizations, and religious clubs for members of the major faiths. Religious facilities are available for Protestant and Catholic students.

Sports: The university participates intercollegiately in 10 sports for men and 8 for women. Intramural sports for both men and women number 17.

Handicapped: About 90% of the campus is accessible to handicapped students. Facilities include wheelchair ramps, special parking, elevators, and special class scheduling. There are no special counselors for handicapped students, but special arrangements are made for them as needed. About 1% of the students are visually impaired, and 1% hearing-impaired. Tutoring is available for these students, and instructors make special arrangements for exams and other classwork.

Graduates: About 60% of the students drop out at the end of the freshman year; 40% remain to graduate. About 22% of the graduates pursue advanced degrees. About 3% enter law school. Sixty-five percent of the graduates begin careers in business and industry.

Services: The following free services are provided: health care; psychological, placement, and career counseling; tutoring; and remedial instruction.

Programs of Study: The university confers the B.A., B.S., B.F.A., B.G.S., B.M., B.S.N., B.S.Ag., B.S.Bus., B.S.Ed., B.S.H.E., B.S.Ind.Ed., and B.S.P.E. degrees. Associate and master's degrees also are available. Bachelor's degrees are offered in the following subjects: BUSINESS (accounting, business administration, business education, data processing, finance, management, marketing, office administration), EDUCATION (early childhood, elementary, health/physical, industrial, secondary, special, speech pathology/audiology), ENGLISH (English, speech), FINE AND PERFORMING ARTS (art, art education, communication, music, music education, studio art), HEALTH SCIENCES (medical technology, nursing), LANGUAGES (French, German, Spanish), MATH AND SCIENCES (biology, botany, chemistry, general science, geology, mathematics, physics, zoology), PHILOSOPHY (humanities, philosophy), PREPROFESSIONAL (agri-business, dentistry, engineering, forestry, law, medicine, pharmacy, theology, veterinary), SOCIAL SCIENCES (economics, government/political science, history, psychology, sociology). Twenty-four percent of undergraduate degrees are conferred in education, 32% in business, and 9% in social sciences.

Special: A general studies degree is offered. Pass/no credit grading options are available.

Honors: Seventeen honor societies have chapters on campus.

Admissions: Ninety-eight percent of those who applied were accepted for the 1981–82 freshman class. ACT scores for freshmen were as follows: 57% below 21, 17% between 21 and 23, 10% between 24 and 25, 7% between 26 and 28, and 3% above 28. The university admits all graduates of accredited Kansas high schools who have never attended college. Out-of-state applicants must have at least a C average. Leadership record, recommendations, and advanced placement or honors courses are other factors that enter into admissions decisions.

Procedure: Candidates are required to take the ACT or SAT. Application deadlines are August 15 (fall), December 30 (spring), and May 15 (summer). There is no application fee. The university follows a rolling admissions policy.

Special: Early decision, early admissions, and deferred admissions plans are offered. AP and CLEP credit are accepted.

Transfer: For fall 1981, 655 transfer students applied, 627 were accepted, and 459 enrolled. Transfers are accepted for all classes. A C average is required. D grades transfer. Transfer students must complete at least 30 credits at the university, of a total 124 credits required for the bachelor's degree. Application deadlines are the same as those for freshmen.

Visiting: Orientation sessions including tours, visits with faculty members, and descriptions of special services are scheduled for prospective students. Guides also are available for informal visits. Visitors may sit in on classes and stay at the school. Visits should be scheduled on weekdays. The director of admissions counseling should be contacted for arrangements.

Financial Aid: A $70,000 fund provides 200 to 225 scholarships for freshmen. The university participates in the following financial-aid programs: NDSL, Nursing Student Loan, Guaranteed Student Loan, BEOG, Nursing Scholarship, and CWS. The state finances about 600 part-time jobs. Aid granted to a freshman generally ranges from $2000 to $2500. In addition, a full-time student may earn up to $1600 a year from a campus job. About 74% of the students receive aid. About 18% work part-time on campus. The FFS or other financial statement must be submitted. Deadline for scholarship aid is March 1. Applications for all other types of aid must be submitted by July 1.

KANSAS

Foreign Students: Three percent of the full-time students come from foreign countries. An intensive English course, special counseling, and special organizations are available to these students.

Admissions: The TOEFL is required; applicants should score at least 500. College entrance exams are not required.

Procedure: Foreign candidates should apply by June 15 (fall), November 15 (spring), or April 1 (summer). A personal health history form must be completed. Proof of funds adequate to cover 1 year must be presented. Students must carry health insurance; it is available through the university.

Admissions Contact: James V. Kellerman, Registrar and Director of Admissions.

FRIENDS UNIVERSITY   D-3
Wichita, Kansas 67213   (316) 261-5842

F/T: 366M, 313W	Faculty: 54; IIB, –$
P/T: 102M, 110W	Ph.D.'s: 43%
Grad: none	S/F Ratio: 14 to 1
Year: sems, ss	Tuition: $3260
Appl: Aug. 1	R and B: $1540
287 applied	
ACT: 17	LESS COMPETITIVE

Friends University, founded in 1898, is a private liberal arts institution affiliated with the Society of Friends. The library contains 86,762 volumes and 1244 microfilm items, and subscribes to 505 periodicals.

Environment: The 25-acre campus is located in the city of Wichita. Dormitories accommodate about 200 students. Other living facilities sponsored by the university include off-campus apartments and married student housing.

Student Life: About 87% of the students are from Kansas. About 95% come from public schools. Only 15% live on campus. Dancing, drinking, and smoking are prohibited on campus. Sixty percent of the students are Protestant; 10% are Catholic. About 11% are minority-group members. Campus housing is single-sex; there are no visiting privileges. Students may keep cars on campus.

Organizations: Students may join fraternities or sororities. A student government, service groups, publications, and special-interest groups also are available.

Sports: The university participates in intercollegiate sports for men and 5 for women. Intramural sports number 3 for men, 2 for women.

Graduates: About 27% of the freshmen drop out after the first year; 40% remain to graduate. Thirty percent pursue advanced study after graduation; 1% enter medical school and 1% law school.

Services: Health care, tutoring, remedial instruction, career counseling, and job placement services are available free of charge on campus. Psychological counseling is available for a fee.

Programs of Study: The college confers the B.A., B.S., B.Mus., and B.Th. degrees. Associate degree programs are also available. Bachelor's degrees are offered in the following subjects: BUSINESS (accounting, business administration, data processing, secretarial science), EDUCATION (early childhood, elementary, health/physical, secondary), ENGLISH (communications, English), FINE AND PERFORMING ARTS (art, music, music education, theater/dramatics, visual communications), HEALTH SCIENCES (medical technology, nurse anesthesia), LANGUAGES (Spanish), MATH AND SCIENCES (biology, chemistry, ecology/environmental science, mathematics, natural sciences), PHILOSOPHY (philosophy, religion), PREPROFESSIONAL (agriculture, dentistry, engineering, home economics, medicine, veterinary), SOCIAL SCIENCES (economics, government/political science, history, human services, sociology). Most students major in education, business, or fine arts.

Required: All students must take 6 hours of religion courses.

Special: A cooperative program between Friends University and Kansas Newman College allows students from each to attend classes and use facilities of the other. Students may participate in work-study semester programs in their major field.

Honors: Departmental honors programs are available.

Admissions: Candidates should have at least a C average and be graduates of an accredited high school. The ACT and impressions made during a personal interview also are considered.

Procedure: The ACT or SAT is required. The application deadline for fall is August 1; there are no application deadlines for the spring and summer sessions. A $10 fee is required.

Special: An early admissions plan is available. CLEP credit is given.

Transfer: For fall 1981, 156 transfer students applied. Transfers may apply for entrance to any class. A minimum GPA of 2.0 is required, and SAT or ACT scores must be submitted. The last 30 hours must be completed at the university, of the 124 hours required for the bachelor's degree. Application deadlines are the same as those for freshmen.

Financial Aid: About 79% of the students receive aid; 5% work part-time on campus. Scholarships, loans, and work-study programs are available to qualified students. The university also participates in the BEOG, SEOG, and NDSL programs. The university requires the FFS. Deadline for application is March 1.

Foreign Students: About 10% of the full-time students come from foreign countries. The university offers these students an intensive English course, special counseling, and special organizations.

Admissions: The university requires the University of Michigan Language Test. Foreign applicants should score 80 for full admission, 76 for provisional admission (limit, 14 hours). College entrance exams are not required.

Procedure: Applications are due June 1 (fall), November 1 (spring), and March 1 (summer). A health form must be completed. Proof of funds adequate to cover tuition for 2 semesters must be presented. Foreign students must carry health insurance; it is available through the university for a fee.

Admissions Contact: George Potts, Dean of Admissions.

KANSAS NEWMAN COLLEGE   D-3
Wichita, Kansas 67213   (316) 261-5800

F/T: 242M, 231W	Faculty: 65; IIB, n/av
P/T: 113M, 109W	Ph.D.'s: 48%
Grad: none	S/F Ratio: 14 to 1
Year: sems, ss	Tuition: $2800
Appl: open	R and B: $1540
550 applied	430 accepted	260 enrolled
ACT: 17	LESS COMPETITIVE

Kansas Newman College is a private liberal arts institution affiliated with the Roman Catholic Church. The library houses 68,300 volumes, and subscribes to 437 periodicals.

Environment: The 55-acre campus is located in a suburban area of Wichita. The 10 major buildings include a chapel and 2 dormitories that accommodate 276 students.

Student Life: Ninety-one percent of the students come from Kansas. Twenty percent live on campus in single-sex or coed residence halls. Mass is celebrated daily, but attendance is optional. Student conduct is regulated by an honor system.

Organizations: The college has no fraternities or sororities. Activities include clubs, music and drama productions, lectures, and art shows. Retreats and other spiritual opportunities are offered.

Sports: The college fields intercollegiate teams in 4 sports for men and 3 for women. Six intramural sports also are available.

Handicapped: About 80% of the campus is accessible to handicapped students. Facilities include wheelchair ramps, special parking, elevators, and lowered telephones.

Graduates: About 30% of the freshmen drop out by the end of the first year, and 39% remain to graduate. Nineteen percent of the graduates pursue advanced degrees; 2% enter medical school, 1% law school, and 1% dental school. Eleven percent begin careers in business and industry.

Services: Health care, placement aid, and career counseling are available free to students.

Programs of Study: The college awards the B.A. and B.S. degrees. Associate degrees also are conferred. Bachelor's degrees are offered in the following subjects: AREA STUDIES (American), BUSINESS (accounting, business administration, industrial management, management), EDUCATION (bilingual/bicultural, elementary, health/physical, secondary), ENGLISH (English, speech), FINE AND PERFORMING ARTS (art, art education, art therapy, music, music education, theater/dramatics), HEALTH SCIENCES (cytotechnology, medical technology, nuclear medicine technology, nurse anesthesia), MATH AND SCIENCES (biology, chemistry, human biology, mathematics), SOCIAL SCIENCES (government/political science, history, psychology, sociology). Thirty-five percent of all degrees are conferred in business, 20% in social sciences, 15% in math and sciences, 14% in health sciences, and 13% in education.

Required: UP Area Tests are required for graduation.

Special: A cooperative program with a neighboring university is available. Five-year combined B.A.-B.S. degrees may be earned in art therapy and American studies. Minors are offered in journalism, philosophy, theology, computer science, and library science.

Honors: Four national honor societies have chapters on campus.

Admissions: Seventy-eight percent of those who applied were accepted for the 1981-82 freshman class. About 54% of those who enrolled scored above 21 on the ACT. Candidates should have a GPA of at least 2.0.

Procedure: The ACT is required and should be taken in the junior or senior year. An interview is recommended. Application deadlines are open. Admission is on a rolling basis. There is a $15 application fee.

Special: The college has an early admissions plan. CLEP credit is accepted.

Transfer: For a recent year, 180 applications were received, 108 were accepted, and 96 students enrolled. Transfers are accepted for all classes. D grades transfer if the student has earned an A.A. degree. Applicants must have an average of at least 2.0. Students must study at the college for at least 30 semester hours to receive a degree.

Visiting: Regular orientation sessions are held for prospective students. They include visits to classes and departments, campus tours, and financial aid discussions. Guides are also available for informal visits. Visitors may sit in on classes and stay overnight on campus. Visits are best scheduled on Mondays, Wednesdays, or Fridays from October to December. The director of admissions should be contacted for arrangements.

Financial Aid: About 78% of the students receive aid; 79% work part-time. Scholarships, loans, and grants are available. The average aid award to freshmen in 1981-82 was $1000. Applications for aid should be submitted by March 1 for priority consideration. The FFS also must be filed. Tuition may be paid in installments.

Foreign Students: The 82 students from foreign countries represent about 9% of enrollment. The college offers these students special counseling and special organizations.

Admissions: Applicants must score 500 or better on the TOEFL. No college entrance exams are required.

Procedure: Application deadlines are June 1 (fall), November 1 (spring), and March 1 (summer). Students must present a health certificate and show evidence of adequate funds for 1 year. Health insurance is required, and is available through the college.

Admissions Contact: James M. Perez, Director of Admissions.

KANSAS STATE UNIVERSITY E-2
Manhattan, Kansas 66506 (913) 532-6250

F/T: 8636M, 6470W	Faculty: n/av; I, −$
P/T: 1148M, 1009W	Ph.D.'s: 52%
Grad: 1300M, 1012W	S/F Ratio: 19 to 1
Year: sems, ss	Tuition: $898 ($2214)
Appl: Aug. 15	R and B: $1560
5718 applied 5548 accepted 3260 enrolled	
ACT: 22	NONCOMPETITIVE

Kansas State University, founded in 1863, is a state-administered university with colleges of Agriculture, Architecture and Design, Arts and Sciences, Business Administration, Education, Engineering, and Home Economics. The library contains 900,000 volumes and 60,000 microfilm items.

Environment: The 153-acre campus is located in the town of Manhattan, 120 miles from Kansas City and 50 miles from Topeka. The environment surrounding the campus is suburban. Beyond the campus are 3853 acres of university land used for agricultural experimentation. In addition, 5 branches of the Agricultural Experimental Station are located on 4485 acres in several outlying fields. The campus has more than 90 buildings, including residence halls accommodating 4500 students. Living facilities include dormitories, on-campus apartments, off-campus apartments, fraternity and sorority houses, and married student housing.

Student Life: Most students are from Kansas; about 15% are from other states and 5% are from foreign countries. About 25% of the students live on campus. About eight percent are minority-group members. Campus housing is both single-sex and coed; there are visiting privileges in the former. Upperclass students may keep cars on campus. Alcohol may not be used at university functions, and smoking is permitted in designated areas only. Day-care services are provided for all students, faculty, and staff.

Organizations: There are 24 fraternities and 11 sororities on campus; 22% of the men and 27% of the women belong to 1 of them. Other student groups include departmental organizations, student government, professional groups, scholastic societies, and religious groups. The 20-mile-long Tuttle Creek Lake, 5 miles from the campus, provides off-campus recreational facilities.

Sports: The university fields intercollegiate teams in 7 sports for men and 7 for women. Intramural sports number 15 for men and 11 for women.

Handicapped: About 50% of the campus is accessible to handicapped students. Facilities include wheelchair ramps, special parking, elevators, specially equipped rest rooms, and lowered drinking fountains and telephones. Special class scheduling is also available. Three counselors are available to handicapped students.

Graduates: About 18% of the freshmen drop out at the end of the first year, and nearly 65% remain to graduate. About 33% of the graduates pursue advanced degrees.

Services: The following services are available to students free of charge: psychological, placement, and career counseling; and tutoring. Health care and remedial instruction are available for a fee.

Programs of Study: Degrees offered are the B.A., B.Arch., B.Mus., B.Int.Arch., B.Land.Arch., B.F.A., B.S., and B.S.Ed. Associate, master's, and doctoral degrees also are available. Bachelor's degrees are offered in the following subjects: BUSINESS (accounting, business administration, business education, computer science, finance, labor relations, management, marketing, office administration), EDUCATION (adult, early childhood, elementary, health/physical, secondary, special), ENGLISH (English, journalism, literature, speech), FINE AND PERFORMING ARTS (art, art education, dance, music, music education, radio/TV, studio art, theater/dramatics), HEALTH SCIENCES (medical technology, speech therapy), LANGUAGES (French, German, Spanish), MATH AND SCIENCES (biochemistry, biology, chemistry, geology, mathematics, physics, statistics), PHILOSOPHY (philosophy), PREPROFESSIONAL (agriculture, architecture, dentistry, engineering, forestry, home economics, law, medicine, pharmacy, social work, veterinary), SOCIAL SCIENCES (anthropology, economics, geography, government/political science, history, psychology, sociology). Thirteen percent of undergraduate degrees are awarded in business.

Special: Five-year combined B.A.-B.S. degrees may be earned in all subjects. The university also offers the B.G.S. degree.

Honors: Six honor societies have chapters on campus. The colleges of Agriculture, Arts and Sciences, Engineering, and Home Economics offer honors programs.

Admissions: Ninety-seven percent of those who applied were accepted for the 1981-82 freshman class. The university admits any Kansas resident who is a high school graduate. Out-of-state applicants must rank in the top half of their class, score well on the ACT, and have an average of at least 2.0.

Procedure: The ACT is required. Applicants should apply early in the senior year of high school. The application, high school record, and ACT scores must be submitted to the admissions office by August 15 for fall admission. Other application deadlines are January 10 (spring) and June 1 (summer). New students are admitted to all terms. There is no application fee.

Special: The university has a deferred admissions plan. AP and CLEP credit is accepted.

Transfer: More than 1500 transfer students enroll each year. Transfers are accepted for all classes. A GPA of at least 2.0 is generally required. D grades may transfer, depending upon the college entered. The last 30 hours must be taken at the university. The total number of credits required for the bachelor's degree depends upon the program. Application deadlines are the same for transfers as they are for freshmen. Transfers may enter all terms.

Visiting: Orientations are available to prospective students any weekday from 8 A.M. to 5 P.M. Guides are available for informal visits. Visitors may sit in on classes but may not stay overnight at the school. Visits are best scheduled in the spring. The admissions office should be contacted for arrangements.

Financial Aid: About 66% of the students receive aid; 42% work part-time on campus. Scholarships and loans are available from the university. Loans also are available from the federal government and local banks. The university is a member of CSS. The FFS and the Kansas Student Data Form are required, and the deadline for financial aid applications is March 15.

Foreign Students: Five percent of the full-time students come from foreign countries. An intensive English program, special counseling, and organizations especially for foreign students are available.

Admissions: The TOEFL must be taken and a score of at least 550 achieved. College entrance exams are not required.

280 KANSAS

Procedure: Deadlines for foreign student application are June 1 (fall), October 1 (spring), and March 1 (summer). Proof of health must be presented. Proof of funds adequate to cover the full course of study must also be furnished. Health insurance is required; it is available through the university for a fee.

Admissions Contact: Richard N. Elkins, Director of Admissions.

KANSAS WESLEYAN UNIVERSITY D-2
Salina, Kansas 67401 (913) 827-5541

F/T: 180M, 156W	Faculty: 37; IIB, — — $
P/T: 24M, 67W	Ph.D.'s: n/av
Grad: none	S/F Ratio: 9 to 1
Year: 4-1-4, ss	Tuition: $3372
Appl: see profile	R and B: $1738
500 applied 250 accepted	107 enrolled
SAT or ACT: required	COMPETITIVE

Kansas Wesleyan University, founded in 1886, is a Methodist-affiliated institution which offers programs in the liberal arts and teacher education. Its library contains 72,000 volumes, and subscribes to 600 periodicals.

Environment: The 25-acre campus is located in a suburban environment 90 miles from Wichita. Living facilities accommodate almost 500 students; these include dormitories, on-campus apartments, and married student housing.

Student Life: About 83% of the students are from Kansas; 95% of the students come from public schools. Attendance at religious services is not required. No alcoholic beverages are allowed on campus. Forty-three percent of the students live on campus. Sixty-one percent are Protestant; 13% are Catholic. Sixteen percent are members of various minority groups. Campus housing is both single-sex and coed; there are visiting privileges in the former. Students may keep cars on campus.

Organizations: There are 2 sororities and numerous departmental clubs on campus to which about 50% of the students belong. The university sponsors social and cultural activities.

Sports: The university competes on an intercollegiate level in 4 sports for men and 5 for women. There are 8 intramural teams for men and 6 for women.

Graduates: About 30% of the freshmen drop out. Seven percent of the graduates pursue advanced study. About 3 percent enter medical school and 3% enter law school.

Programs of Study: The college confers the B.A. and B.S. degrees. Associate degree programs are also offered. Bachelor's degrees are offered in the following subjects: BUSINESS (accounting, business administration, computer science), EDUCATION (elementary, health/physical, secondary, special), ENGLISH (English, literature, speech), FINE AND PERFORMING ARTS (art, music, music education, theater/dramatics), HEALTH SCIENCES (nursing), LANGUAGES (Spanish), MATH AND SCIENCES (biology, chemistry, mathematics, physical sciences), PHILOSOPHY (religion), PREPROFESSIONAL (dentistry, engineering, home economics, law, medicine, ministry, pharmacy), SOCIAL SCIENCES (economics, history, psychology, sociology). Recently, most degrees were granted in education, social sciences, and business.

Required: All students are required to take 4 hours of religious studies.

Special: The college offers a 3-2 engineering program, Washington, D.C., and UN semesters, and study-abroad programs.

Honors: There are 4 honor societies on campus to which qualified students belong.

Admissions: About 50% of those who applied for the 1981–82 freshman class were accepted. Candidates should have a 2.5 high school average from an accredited school. Test scores and class rank are also important. Other factors that enter into the admissions decision are recommendations by school officials, leadership record, and personality.

Procedure: The ACT or SAT is required and an interview is recommended. The deadline for applications is 4 weeks before the start of any semester. There is no fee. Admissions are on a rolling basis.

Special: Early decision is available. CLEP credit is given.

Transfer: For fall 1981, 70 transfer students applied, 50 were accepted, and 35 enrolled. Transfers are accepted for all classes. A 2.0 GPA is recommended. D grades transfer. The last 12 semester hours in the major and 24 of the last 33 hours must be taken in residence. A total of 123 credits must be earned for the bachelor's degree. Application deadlines are the same for transfers as they are for freshmen. Transfers may enter any term.

Visiting: Tours of the campus can be arranged through the admissions office.

Financial Aid: Ninety-three percent of the students receive aid; 30% work part-time on campus. The average award to freshmen is $3700. The university is a CSS member. The FAF, FFS, or SFS must be submitted with aid applications. There is no deadline.

Foreign Students: Four percent of the full-time students are from foreign countries. The university has an intensive English program, special counseling, and organizations especially for foreign students.

Admissions: The TOEFL is required; the minimum acceptable score is 550. College entrance exams are not required.

Procedure: There are no admissions deadlines; foreign students are admitted to the fall, winter, spring, and summer sessions. Proof of funds adequate to cover 1 year must be presented. There is a special fee, consisting of 15% of tuition, to cover advising assistance. Health insurance is required; it is available through the university for a fee.

Admissiosn Contact: Jack Ropp, Director of Admissions.

MARYMOUNT COLLEGE OF KANSAS D-2
Salina, Kansas 67401 (913) 825-2101

F/T: 227M, 392W	Faculty: 50; IIB, — — $
P/T: 43M, 129W	Ph.D.'s: 34%
Grad: none	S/F Ratio: 12 to 1
Year: sems, ss	Tuition: $2970
Appl: open	R and B: $1640
205 accepted	123 enrolled
ACT: 19	LESS COMPETITIVE

Marymount College of Kansas, founded in 1922 as a women's college but now coeducational, is the oldest Catholic liberal arts college in Kansas. The library contains 60,000 volumes, and subscribes to more than 500 periodicals.

Environment: The 30-acre campus, 90 miles from Wichita, is located in a suburban environment. It has 5 major buildings, including 3 dormitories that house 350 students.

Student Life: About 80% of the students are from Kansas. About 65% come from public schools. Thirty percent live on campus. Approximately 66% are Catholic; about 21% are Protestant. About 6% are minority-group members. Fewer than 20% of the students leave campus on weekends. Campus housing is single-sex; there are visiting privileges. Students may keep cars on campus.

Organizations: There are no fraternities or sororities, but other social and extracurricular activities are offered. The Marymount College Artist Series brings cultural events to campus, and additional recreational opportunities are available in Salina, which has 8 major parks and a new 8,500-seat special-events arena.

Sports: Marymount College competes on an intercollegiate level in 5 sports for men and 5 for women. Intramural sports for both men and women number 6.

Handicapped: About 90% of the campus is accessible to wheelchair-bound students. Facilities include special class scheduling, special parking, elevators, and specially equipped rest rooms.

Graduates: Thirty percent of the freshmen drop out, and 40% remain to graduate. Of these, 7% go on to graduate or professional school, including 2% who enter medical school and 1% who enter law school. About 40% pursue careers in business and industry.

Services: Students receive the following free services: health care, psychological counseling, career counseling, religious counseling, and tutoring. Placement services are available for a fee.

Programs of Study: The college offers the B.A., B.S., B.Mus., B.Mus.Ed., and B.S.N. degrees. Associate degrees are also available. Bachelor's degrees are offered in the following subjects: BUSINESS (accounting, business administration), EDUCATION (elementary, secondary), ENGLISH (English), FINE AND PERFORMING ARTS (art, art education, film/photography, music, music education, studio art, theater/dramatics), HEALTH SCIENCES (medical technology, nursing), LANGUAGES (French), MATH AND SCIENCES (biology, chemistry, mathematics), PREPROFESSIONAL (dentistry, law, medicine, pharmacy, veterinary), SOCIAL SCIENCES (history, psychology). Thirty-five percent of degrees are conferred in business, 33% in health sciences, and 20% in social sciences.

Required: All undergraduates must take 2 courses in English, philosophy, mathematics, and/or science, and 1 course each in history and fine arts. Two semesters of freshman English also are required.

Special: Combined B.A.–B.S. degrees may be earned in most subjects.

Admissions: Sixty-five percent of those who applied were accepted for the 1981–82 freshman class. On the ACT, 64% of the freshmen scored below 21, 24% between 21 and 25, and 13% above 26. Candidates must have completed 15 high school units, score well on the ACT, and be recommended by their high school.

Procedure: The ACT or SAT is required. Application deadlines are open. New students may be admitted to fall, spring, or summer sessions. The application fee is $10.

Special: CLEP credit is accepted.

Transfer: For fall 1981, 122 transfers were accepted and 88 enrolled. Transfer students are accepted for all classes. A minimum GPA of 2.0 is required. Some D grades are transferable with departmental approval. Students must spend at least 1 year in residence to receive a degree. At least 30 hours must be completed at the college, of a total 124 semester hours required for the bachelor's degree. There are no application deadlines. Transfers are admitted to the fall, spring, and summer sessions.

Visiting: Visits can be scheduled Monday through Friday, from 8 A.M. to 3 P.M., in October, November, February, March, and April. Guides are available and overnight accommodations can be arranged by Sam Rowdon of the admissions office.

Financial Aid: About 85% of all students receive aid through the school, and about 17% work part-time on campus. The average award to freshmen covers about 80% of costs. Approximately 100 freshman scholarships are available each year. The college is a member of CSS. The FAF, SFS, or FFS must be filed. There is no application deadline.

Foreign Students: There are no foreign students presently enrolled at Marymount, although the college will accept qualified foreign applicants.

Admissions: The TOEFL is required; a minimum score of 500 is necessary for admission. The ACT is also required.

Procedure: There are no application deadlines. Foreign students are accepted to the fall, spring, and summer sessions. A physical examination is necessary. A school health form must also be completed. Proof of funds adequate to cover 1 year must be presented. Health insurance is required; it is available through the college for a fee.

Admissions Contact: Sr. Marilyn Stahl, Director of Admissions.

McPHERSON COLLEGE   D-2
McPherson, Kansas 67460   (316) 241-0731

F/T, P/T:	Faculty:	35; IIB, — –$
236M, 230W	Ph.D.'s:	51%
Grad: none	S/F Ratio:	15 to 1
Year: 4-1-4	Tuition:	$3110
Appl: open	R and B:	$1110
214 applied	180 accepted	90 enrolled
ACT: 19		COMPETITIVE

McPherson College, founded in 1887, is affiliated with the Church of the Brethren. The library contains about 64,000 volumes, and subscribes to 412 periodicals.

Environment: The self-contained campus is located in McPherson, a town of about 13,000 people, 50 miles north of Wichita. The area surrounding the campus is rural. Dormitories house 180 women and 348 men; apartments are available for 32 married students.

Student Life: About 55% of the students are from Kansas and 35% from surrounding states. Sixty-eight percent live in campus housing. About 23% are Protestant; 9% are Catholic. About 7% are members of minority groups. Campus housing is both single-sex and coed. Students may keep cars on campus. Gambling and drinking are prohibited on campus; smoking is permitted in designated areas.

Organizations: There are no fraternities or sororities on campus. A variety of clubs are available, including Alpha Psi Omega, Phi Alpha Theta, Minority Student Council, Fellowship of Christian Athletes, and departmental clubs.

Sports: The college fields 7 intercollegiate teams for men and 5 for women. Intramural sports number 3 for men and 3 for women.

Graduates: About 48% of the entering freshmen graduate. One-fifth of the men and one-tenth of the women begin full-time graduate study immediately after graduation.

Programs of Study: The college awards the B.A. and B.S. degrees. Associate degree programs are also available. Bachelor's degrees are offered in the following subjects: BUSINESS (accounting, business administration, computer science), EDUCATION (early childhood, elementary, health/physical, industrial), ENGLISH (English, speech), FINE AND PERFORMING ARTS (art, audiovisual, music, music education), HEALTH SCIENCES (medical technology), LANGUAGES (German, Spanish), MATH AND SCIENCES (biology, chemistry, ecology/environmental science, mathematics, physical sciences), PHILOSOPHY (philosophy/religion), PREPROFESSIONAL (home economics), SOCIAL SCIENCES (economics, history, psychology, sociology). Most undergraduate degrees are conferred in elementary education and business.

Required: Forty-eight credits of general education courses from 5 divisions are required.

Special: The college offers a junior year abroad, in countries including France, Germany, England, and Spain. During the 4-week interim in January, students may take field trips to points across the United States and abroad, or enroll in courses at any of the 5 other colleges within 35 miles of McPherson. Student-designed majors are permitted. A 1- or 2-year auto-restoration major is offered in industrial education.

Admissions: Eighty-four percent of those who applied were accepted for the 1981–82 freshman class. Candidates must have graduated from an approved secondary school, must have acceptable ACT scores, satisfactory grades (2.0 GPA), and character recommendations.

Procedure: The ACT is required and should be taken during the senior year of high school. Students from states in which the ACT is not regularly administered can take the test at McPherson during the opening days of school. SAT scores can be used for admittance, but students must also take the ACT. The application deadlines are open. Admissions decisions are made on a rolling basis. There is a $15 application fee.

Special: Deferred admissions are possible. CLEP and AP credit is accepted.

Transfer: For fall 1981, 97 transfer students applied, 67 were accepted, and 51 enrolled. Transfer students are accepted for all classes. A minimum GPA of 2.0 and a minimum ACT score of 15 are required. D grades do not transfer. Students must take 62 hours in residence, of a total 124 hours required for the bachelor's degree. Deadlines are the same as those for freshmen. Transfers are admitted to the fall or spring semester.

Visiting: An orientation program that includes a campus tour, class visits, and meetings with faculty members is available for prospective students. Guides also are provided for informal visits. Visitors may sit in on classes and stay overnight at the school. Visits should be scheduled from September through December or February through May. The admissions office should be contacted for arrangements.

Financial Aid: About 80% of the students receive financial aid. About 40% work part-time on campus. The average award to freshmen is $1300. Scholarships, loans, and grants are awarded through a committee. Music awards are available for music majors or participants in music groups. Limited athletic aid is available. The college employs student assistants for clerical and similar tasks. Students may also find part-time jobs in town. The college participates in Pell Grants, Work-Study, BEOG and SEOG. The college is a CSS member. The FAF or FFS should be submitted. The deadline for aid applications is March 15.

Foreign Students: Students from foreign countries represent 3% of the student body. The college offers special counseling and organizations especially for foreign students.

Admissions: The TOEFL is required; a minimum score of 500 is necessary. College entrance exams are not required.

Procedure: There are no application deadlines. Foreign students may enter the fall or spring semester. They must complete the health form, and they must present proof of funds adequate to cover 4 years of study. Health insurance is required.

Admissions Contact: Connie Andes Weddle, Director of Admissions.

MID-AMERICA NAZARENE COLLEGE   F-2
Olathe, Kansas 66062   (913) 782-3750

F/T: 548M, 592W	Faculty:	59; n/av
P/T: 140M, 96W	Ph.D.'s:	35%
Grad: none	S/F Ratio:	19 to 1
Year: 4-1-4, ss	Tuition:	$2236
Appl: see profile	R and B:	$1840
441 enrolled		
ACT: 18		NONCOMPETITIVE

Mid-America Nazarene College, founded in 1966, is a liberal arts institution affiliated with the Church of the Nazarene. The library contains 82,000 volumes, and subscribes to 300 periodicals.

Environment: The 105-acre, self-contained campus is located in a suburban setting about 20 miles outside of Kansas City, Missouri. The 16 major buildings include a career center and an athletic facility. Living facilities consist of dormitories and off-campus apartments.

Student Life: About 50% percent of the students are from Kansas. About 94% of the entering freshmen come from public schools. Seventy percent of the students live on campus. Two percent are minority-group members. Ninety-eight percent are Protestant, and 1% are Catholic. Campus housing is single-sex; there are no visiting privileges. Students may keep cars on campus. Chapel attendance is required twice a week. Drinking is forbidden. Resident students must observe a curfew.

Organizations: The college has no fraternities or sororities. The most popular extracurricular activities are the drama club, Circle "K," and the Campus Government Association. Each week 1 or 2 cultural or social events take place on campus. The campus government has jurisdiction over student publications and student activities. Students are represented on some faculty committees by voting delegates.

Sports: The college fields intercollegiate teams in 5 men's and 5 women's sports. There are 6 intramural sports for men and 3 for women.

Handicapped: About 80% of the campus is accessible to handicapped students. Facilities include wheelchair ramps, special parking, and lowered drinking fountains. Special class scheduling is also available. There are no special counselors for handicapped students. Fewer than 1% of the students are visually impaired.

Graduates: Thirty-nine percent of entering freshmen drop out by the end of the first year; 25% remain to graduate.

Services: Students receive the following services free of charge: psychological counseling, career counseling, and tutoring. Health care, placement services, and remedial instruction are available on a fee basis.

Programs of Study: The college awards the B.A. and B.S.N. degrees. Bachelor's degrees are offered in the following subjects: BUSINESS (business administration, business education, computer science, marketing), EDUCATION (elementary, health/physical, secondary, special), ENGLISH (English), FINE AND PERFORMING ARTS (music, music education, church music, music performance), HEALTH SCIENCES (nursing), LANGUAGES (French, Spanish), MATH AND SCIENCES (biology, chemistry, mathematics), PHILOSOPHY (philosophy, religion, religious education), PREPROFESSIONAL (agriculture, home economics, ministry), SOCIAL SCIENCES (history, psychology, social sciences, sociology).

Required: Students must meet core curriculum requirements in humanities-communications, natural sciences-mathematics, social sciences, and religion-philosophy. In order to graduate, the student must maintain a GPA of 2.0.

Special: The college offers a remedial program for those who need it. Combined B.A.-B.S. degrees may be earned in home economics and agriculture.

Honors: An honors program is available.

Admissions: The college follows an "open door" admissions policy. The ACT scores of those who enrolled in the 1981–82 freshman class were: 59% below 21, 16% between 21 and 23, 11% between 24 and 25, 8% between 26 and 28, and 4% above 28.

Procedure: The SAT or ACT is required; the ACT is preferred. Application deadlines are August 31–September 10 (fall), January 6 (winter), February 12 (spring), and May 31–June 2 (summer). Notification is made on a rolling basis. There is a $20 application fee.

Special: The college has a special admissions program with remedial work in mathematics, reading, and English for educationally disadvantaged students. AP and CLEP credit is available.

Transfers: For fall 1981, 95 transfer students enrolled. All transfer applications are approved if the student is in good academic standing. All students must complete, at the college, 9 of the 36 courses required for a bachelor's degree. Application deadlines are the same as those for freshmen.

Visiting: Three-day orientation visits are scheduled for prospective students. Guides also are available for informal visits. Visitors may sit in on classes and stay overnight on campus. Visits should be scheduled on weekdays. The director of recruitment should be contacted for arrangements.

Financial Aid: About 93% of all students receive aid through the college. About 38% work part-time on campus. The average freshman award is $1800. The college is a member of CSS. Federal CWS funds are available in all departments. Tuition may be paid in installments. Aid is awarded on the basis of financial need and academic potential. The FFS or FAF is required.

Foreign Students: Two percent of the full-time students come from foreign countries. An intensive English course, special counseling, and special organizations are available for these students.

Admissions: Foreign students must achieve a TOEFL score of at least 500. No college entrance exams are required.

Procedure: Application deadlines are the same as those for other students. Foreign students must present proof of funds adequate to cover 4 years of study.

Admissions Contact: Barth Smith, Director of Admissions.

OTTAWA UNIVERSITY   E–2
Ottawa, Kansas 66067   (913) 242-6445

F/T: 248M, 179W   Faculty: 36; IIB, – – $
P/T: 10M, 18W   Ph.D.'s: 53%
Grad: none   S/F Ratio: 16 to 1
Year: sems, ss   Tuition: $3429
Appl: open   R and B: $1924
203 applied   180 accepted   109 enrolled
SAT: 410V 430M   ACT: 20   LESS COMPETITIVE

Ottawa University, founded in 1865, is an independent liberal arts school affiliated with the American Baptist Churches. The library contains 86,304 volumes, and subscribes to 454 periodicals.

Environment: The college occupies 60 acres in a town of 12,500 people located in a rural area 45 miles from Kansas City. It also owns 100 acres of recreational land and 35 acres of woodlands. There is a physical education center. Dormitories accommodate 300 women and 400 men.

Student Life: About half the students are Kansas residents. About 95% of the students come from public schools. Eighty-five percent of the students live on campus. Thirty-four percent are Baptists; 57% are Protestants; 9% are Catholics. Thirty-three percent of the students are minority-group members. Campus housing is single-sex; there are visiting privileges. Students may keep cars on campus.

Organizations: Fifteen local social clubs operate as nonaffiliated fraternities and sororities. Religious organizations are available on campus and places of worship are located nearby for Catholic and Protestant students and 40 miles away for Jewish students. Students have a voice in campus government through a student manager system and joint student-faculty-administration committees.

Sports: Six intercollegiate sports are offered for men and 3 for women. There is no intramural program.

Handicapped: About 40% of the campus is accessible to handicapped students. Special facilities include wheelchair ramps and special parking. Three counselors are available to assist handicapped students.

Graduates: Twenty-five percent of the students drop out by the end of the freshman year. Thirty-seven percent remain to graduate. About half the graduates pursue advanced degrees; 1% enter medical school and 2% law school. About 30% of the graduates enter careers in business and industry.

Services: The university provides the following free services: health care; psychological, placement, and career counseling; tutoring; and remedial instruction.

Programs of Study: All programs lead to the B.A. degree. Bachelor's degrees are offered in the following subjects: AREA STUDIES (American), BUSINESS (accounting, business administration, computer science, finance, management/arts/health facilities, marketing, personnel administration, public relations), EDUCATION (Christian education, elementary, health/physical, secondary) ENGLISH (communications, English, literature, speech), FINE AND PERFORMING ARTS (art, art education, music, music education, radio/TV), LANGUAGES (French), MATH AND SCIENCES (biology, botany, chemistry, mathematics, natural sciences, physical sciences, zoology), PHILOSOPHY (humanities, philosophy, religion), PREPROFESSIONAL (agriculture, allied health, dentistry, engineering, forestry, home economics, law, library science, medicine, ministry, pharmacy, social work), SOCIAL SCIENCES (economics, government/political science, history, human services, psychology, social sciences, sociology).

Special: Special programs include independent study, interdisciplinary majors, and study abroad. Cooperative programs are offered in nursing, pre-engineering, forestry, home economics, and agriculture. A general studies degree is offered and student-designed majors are encouraged.

Honors: Seven honor societies, 5 national and 2 local, have chapters on campus. Special honors programs are available.

Admissions: Eighty-nine percent of those who applied were accepted for the 1981-82 freshman class. ACT scores of the freshmen were as follows: 25% below 21, 19% between 21 and 23, 21% between 24 and 25, 19% between 26 and 28, and 10% above 28. The SAT scores were as follows: Verbal—60% below 500, 28% between 500 and 599, 12% between 600 and 700, and 0% above 700; Math —60% below 500, 14% between 500 and 599, 21% between 600 and 700, and 5% above 700. Applicants must rank in the upper 60% of their graduating class, have a 2.4 GPA or better, be recommended by their high schools, and have completed 15 Carnegie units. Admissions officers also consider advanced placement or honors courses, recommendations, extracurricular activities, and personality.

Procedure: Applicants must take the SAT or ACT, preferably by December of the senior year. An interview is recommended. Application deadlines are open. Notification is made on a rolling basis. There is a $15 application fee.

Special: Early decision and early and deferred admissions plans are available. AP and CLEP are accepted.

Transfer: For fall 1981, 52 transfers applied, 36 were accepted, and 26 enrolled. Transfers are accepted to all classes. A GPA of at least 2.0 is required. C or above grades transfer. Students must take at least 1 year (30 hours) in residence, of a total 124 semester hours required for the bachelor's degree. Deadlines are open; admissions are rolling.

Visiting: Orientation sessions for prospective students are scheduled regularly. They include a campus tour, an overnight visit with a student host or hostess, an admissions interview, class visits, and meetings with faculty members. Guides also are available for informal visits. Visitors may sit in on classes and stay at the school. Weekdays are the best times to visit. The admission office should be contacted for arrangements.

Financial Aid: Ninety-five percent of the students receive aid. Fifty percent work part-time on campus. The average award to freshmen is $3300. Loans are available from the federal government, local banks, the university, and private sources. The university is a member of CSS. The FAF, FFS, or SFS must be filed with the application. Applications should be filed by February 1.

Foreign Students: Nine percent of the full-time students are from foreign countries. The university offers an intensive English program, special counseling, and organizations especially for foreign students.

Admissions: The TOEFL and an impromptu composition are required; a minimum score of 450 is necessary on the TOEFL. College entrance exams are not required.

Procedure: There are no official deadlines, but foreign students should file applications 1 month prior to the date of entry. They may enter the fall, spring, or summer session. The university health form must be filled out by the student and a physician. Proof of adequate funds to cover the full period of study must be presented. Health insurance is required; it is available through the university for a fee.

Admissions Contact: Dan Baker, Director of Admissions.

PITTSBURG STATE UNIVERSITY F-3
Pittsburg, Kansas 66762 (316) 231-7000

F/T: 1755M, 1563W	Faculty: 132; n/av
P/T: 314M, 317W	Ph.D.'s: 63%
Grad: 459M, 723W	S/F Ratio: 20 to 1
Year: sems, ss	Tuition: $696 ($1490)
Appl: open	R and B: $1588-2096
1137 applied	1106 accepted 618 enrolled
ACT: 18	NONCOMPETITIVE

Pittsburg State University, a state-supported institution established in 1903, offers undergraduate degrees through the schools of Arts and Sciences, Business and Economics, Education, and Technology and Applied Science. The library contains 450,000 volumes and 125,000 microfilm items, and subscribes to 1400 periodicals.

Environment: The 110-acre campus is located in a rural area 125 miles from Kansas City, Kansas. The more than 30 major campus buildings include a library and science labs. Campus housing accommodates 800 women, 789 men, and 203 married students in dormitories, fraternity and sorority houses, and married student housing.

Student Life: Ninety-five percent of the students are from Kansas. About 80% of the students live on campus. About 4% of the freshmen are minority-group members. Campus housing is both single-sex and coed; there are visiting privileges in the former. Students may keep cars on campus.

Organizations: About 4% of the students belong to 1 of 8 fraternities or 3 sororities on campus. The Ozark Mountains and several wildlife and recreational areas are within driving distance.

Sports: The university fields teams in 5 intercollegiate sports for men and 4 for women. There are 16 intramural sports for men and 12 for women.

Handicapped: About 10% of the campus is accessible to handicapped students. Facilities include wheelchair ramps, special parking, elevators, special class scheduling, specially equipped rest rooms, and lowered drinking fountains and telephones. No special counselors are available.

Graduates: Twenty-five percent of the graduates pursue advanced degrees.

Services: The following services are available free to students: psychological, placement, and career counseling, tutoring, remedial instruction, and limited health care.

Programs of Study: The university confers the B.A., B.S., B.F.A., B.G.S., B.S.B.A., B.S.Ed., B.Mus., B.Mus.Ed., B.S.N., B.S.Tech., and B.S.Voc.Tech.Ed. degrees. Associate and master's degree programs also are offered. Bachelor's degrees are offered in the following subjects: BUSINESS (accounting, business administration, business education, computer science, finance, management, marketing), EDUCATION (elementary, health/physical, industrial, secondary, special), ENGLISH (English, journalism, literature, speech), FINE AND PERFORMING ARTS (art, art education, music, music education, radio/TV, studio art, theater/dramatics), HEALTH SCIENCES (medical technology, nursing), LANGUAGES (French, German, Spanish), MATH AND SCIENCES (biochemistry, biology, chemistry, earth science, ecology/environmental science, mathematics, natural sciences, physical sciences, physics), PREPROFESSIONAL (agriculture, architecture, dentistry, engineering, forestry, home economics, law, library science, medicine, ministry, pharmacy, social work, veterinary), SOCIAL SCIENCES (economics, geography, government/political science, history, psychology, social sciences, sociology).

Required: All students must take 30 hours of general education courses.

Special: Combined B.A.-B.S. degrees may be earned. A general studies degree is offered. Students may design their own majors.

Honors: More than 20 honor societies have chapters on campus.

Admissions: About 97% of those who applied were accepted for the 1981-82 freshman class. Freshmen ACT scores were as follows: 62% below 21, 23% between 21 and 23, 10% between 24 and 25, 4% between 26 and 28, and 1% above 28. All residents of Kansas who have graduated from an accredited state high school are admitted. Out-of-state applicants should rank in the top half of their graduating class and have at least a C average. Other factors considered are accreditation of the high school, advanced placement or honors courses, recommendations by high school officials, and impressions made during an interview.

Procedure: The ACT is required. The application, high school record, and ACT scores should be submitted before registration for the fall session. Admissions decisions are made on a rolling basis. There is no application fee.

Special: AP and CLEP credit are accepted.

Transfer: For fall 1981, 888 transfer students applied, 881 were accepted, and 594 enrolled. Transfers are accepted for all classes. A GPA of at least 2.0 is required for out-of-state students. At least 30 hours must be taken in residence. There is a time residency requirement of 1 year. There are no deadlines for application. Transfers may enter any term, including summer.

Visiting: Guides are available for informal visits. Visitors may sit in on classes and stay overnight on campus. Visits are best scheduled Monday through Friday. The admissions office should be contacted for arrangements.

Financial Aid: About 75% of the students receive financial aid. Scholarships, loans, and campus employment are available. About 80 scholarships ranging from $100 to $500 a year are offered to freshmen. CWS is available in all departments. The FFS must be submitted. The deadline for scholarship applications is March 15.

Foreign Students: The university offers an intensive English program, special counseling, and organizations especially for foreign students.

Admissions: The TOEFL is required; a minimum score of 520 is necessary. College entrance exams are not required.

Procedure: Foreign candidates should apply at least 1 month prior to the start of the semester. They may enter any term. Foreign students must pay special out-of-state fees.

Admissions Contact: James E. Parker, Director of Admissions.

SAINT MARY COLLEGE F-2
Leavenworth, Kansas 66048 (913) 682-5151

F/T: 70M, 294W	Faculty: 33; IIB, n/av
P/T: 180M, 280W	Ph.D.'s: 39%
Grad: none	S/F Ratio: 11 to 1
Year: sems, ss	Tuition: $2510
Appl: open	R and B: $1540
123 applied	110 accepted	86 enrolled
ACT: 21		COMPETITIVE

Saint Mary College is a liberal arts college affiliated with the Roman Catholic Church and operated by the Sisters of Charity of Leavenworth. The library contains 110,188 volumes, and subscribes to 493 periodicals.

Environment: The 240-acre campus is located in a suburban area 26 miles from Kansas City. Campus facilities include a library, a student center, and dormitories.

Student Life: About 60% of the students come from states other than Kansas. Forty-four percent are Catholic, 34% are Protestant, and 1% are Jewish. Attendance at daily Mass is not required. Twenty-one percent of the students live on campus. Twenty-eight percent are minority-group members. Campus housing is single-sex; there are no visiting privileges. Students may keep cars on campus. The college provides day-care services to students, faculty, and staff.

Organizations: There are no fraternities or sororities at the college. Student organizations include the Student Government Association and special-interest clubs. Activities center around student-directed social events and church events. Leavenworth, the oldest town in Kansas, features many historical sites; Kansas City offers many cultural opportunities.

Sports: The college fields 1 intercollegiate team for women. Intramural sports for women number 8.

Handicapped: About 90% of the campus is accessible to handicapped students. Facilities include wheelchair ramps, special parking, elevators, special class scheduling, and special showers. Assistance to handicapped students is provided by arrangement. Fewer than 1% of the students have visual impairments.

Graduates: About 30% of the freshmen generally drop out by the end of the year; 40% remain to graduate. About 12% of the graduates pursue advanced degrees. Twelve percent enter careers in business or industry.

Services: The following services are provided to students free of charge: psychological, placement, and career counseling and remedial instruction. Health care is available for a fee.

Programs of Study: The college confers the B.A., B.S., B.Mus., B.Mus.Ed., and B.S.N. degrees. Associate degrees are also awarded. Bachelor's degrees are offered in the following subjects: BUSINESS (accounting, business administration, computer science), EDUCATION (early childhood, elementary), ENGLISH (English), FINE AND PERFORMING ARTS (art, music, music education, theater/dramatics), HEALTH SCIENCES (medical technology, nursing), LANGUAGES (Spanish), MATH AND SCIENCES (biology, chemistry, mathematics), PHILOSOPHY (religion), PREPROFESSIONAL (dietetics, home economics, medicine, law), SOCIAL SCIENCES (history, psychology, sociology). Twenty-six percent of all degrees are conferred in education, 13% in math and sciences, and 10% each in English, the arts, social sciences, and preprofessional subjects.

Special: A junior year abroad and exchange programs with area colleges are offered.

Honors: Three national honor societies have chapters on campus. All departments offer honors programs to qualified students.

Admissions: Eighty-nine percent of those who applied were accepted for the 1981–82 freshman class. Freshmen ACT scores were as follows: 40% below 21, 38% between 21 and 23, 14% between 24 and 25, 5% between 26 and 28, and 2% above 28. Applicants should be graduates of accredited high schools, and should have completed 16 high school units with at least a C+ average. Recommendations of high school officials are also considered important.

Procedure: The ACT is required and an interview on or off campus is strongly recommended. Applications should be submitted as early as possible in the senior year, but there is no deadline. The college makes admissions decisions on a rolling basis. There is a $10 application fee.

Special: The college has early decision, early admissions, and deferred admissions plans. AP and CLEP credit are available.

Transfer: Transfer students are accepted for all classes. D grades do not transfer. An average of C or better is required for transfer. Students must study at the college for at least 30 semester hours to receive a degree. Application deadlines are September 1 (fall), January 1 (spring), and June 1 (summer).

Visiting: Regular orientations are held in the fall and spring for prospective students. They include an overnight stay, meetings with faculty, visits to classes, and financial aid and college information discussions. Guides also are available for informal visits, and visitors may stay overnight at the school. Advance notice is requested. The office of admissions will handle arrangements.

Financial Aid: Forty-four percent of the students receive aid through the college. Fourteen percent work part-time on campus. The college awards about 60 freshmen scholarships each year, and loans are available from the federal government and the college. The average scholarship or grant is $300 to $1000 per year. Aid from all sources, including campus employment, can reach a maximum of $2000 during the freshman year, depending on need. Tuition may be paid in installments. The FFS form must accompany the application for aid. Application deadlines are open.

Foreign Students: Students from foreign countries comprise 5% of the student body. The college offers an intensive English course, special counseling, and organizations especially for foreign students.

Admissions: The TOEFL is required. College entrance exams are not necessary.

Procedure: There are no application deadlines for foreign students. They may enter the fall or spring semester. Proof of adequate funds to cover 4 years of study must be presented.

Admissions Contact: Sr. Susan Rieke, Director of Admissions.

SAINT MARY OF THE PLAINS COLLEGE C-3
Dodge City, Kansas 67801 (316) 225-0108

F/T: 192M, 397W	Faculty: 57; IIB, – – $
P/T: 8M, 30W	Ph.D.'s: 21%
Grad: none	S/F Ratio: 10 to 1
Year: 4-1-4, ss	Tuition: $3110
Appl: Aug. 15	R and B: $2000
ACT: 17	LESS COMPETITIVE

Saint Mary of the Plains College, a Roman Catholic liberal arts college founded in 1952, is run by the Sisters of Saint Joseph of Wichita. The library contains 45,203 volumes, and subscribes to 425 periodicals.

Environment: The 60-acre campus is located in a rural setting at the edge of historic Dodge City, 150 miles from Wichita. Campus buildings include 3 residence halls that house 270 women and 240 men. The campus also includes the Joan Challons Wildlife Sanctuary.

Student Life: Seventy-two percent of the students are from Kansas. About 58% live in dormitories. Campus housing is single-sex; there are no visiting privileges. Students may keep cars on campus. Alcohol is prohibited on campus, and smoking is confined to certain areas.

Organizations: The college has no fraternities or sororities. Activities include special-interest and departmental clubs, a student council, concerts, dances, plays, and films. Major social events include the Blue-White Ball and Homecoming.

Sports: The college participates intercollegiately in 3 sports for men and 3 for women. Intramural sports for both men and women number 3.

Handicapped: About 95% of the campus is accessible to handicapped students. Special facilities include elevators and lowered telephones. One special counselor works with handicapped students. Four percent of the students are visually impaired; the college has no special facilities for them.

Graduates: Forty percent of the students drop out at the end of the freshman year, and 32% remain to graduate. Eight percent of the graduates pursue advanced degrees. Twenty percent of each graduating class enter business and industry.

Services: Students may obtain the following free services: career and psychological counseling, placement, tutoring, and remedial instruction.

Programs of Study: The college offers the B.A., B.S., B.S.W., B.Mus.Ed., B.S.N., and Bachelor of Respiratory Therapy degrees. Bachelor's degrees are offered in the following subjects: BUSINESS (agribusiness, business administration, business education), EDUCATION (elementary, secondary), ENGLISH (English), FINE AND PERFORMING ARTS (music, music education, theater/dramatics), HEALTH SCIENCES (medical technology, nursing, respiratory therapy), LANGUAGES (Spanish), MATH AND SCIENCES (biology, chemistry, mathematics), PHILOSOPHY (religion), PREPROFESSIONAL (law, medicine, social work), SOCIAL SCIENCES (government/political science, history, psychology, sociology). Thirty percent of all undergraduate degrees are conferred in education, 30% in business, and 25% in health sciences.

Special: Combined B.A.-B.S. degrees may be earned in chemistry and biology. The college offers a general studies degree. Interdisciplinary studies, individual study, and student-designed majors are permitted.

Honors: Two national honor societies have chapters on campus.

Admissions: Almost all those who applied were accepted for a recent freshman class. Freshman ACT scores broke down as follows: 25% below 21, 30% between 21 and 23, 22% between 24 and 25, 21% between 26 and 28, and 2% above 28. Freshman SAT scores were: Verbal—30% below 500, 45% between 500 and 599, 20% bewteen 600 and 700, and 5% above 700; Math—35% below 500, 35% beween 500 and 599, 15% between 600 and 700, and 5% above 700. Applicants should be graduates of an accredited high school or the equivalent (GED) and have a minimum grade average of 2.0. Besides grades and test scores, admissions officers consider the applicant's recommendations, personality, leadership record, and advanced placement or honor courses.

Procedure: The ACT or SAT is required. The high school transcript, test scores, and 3 recommendations should be submitted. The deadline for fall application is August 15. Admissions decisions are made on a rolling basis. There is a $20 application fee. New students are admitted to the fall, winter, spring, and summer terms.

Special: AP and CLEP credit are accepted.

Transfer: For fall 1981, 60 transfer students applied, 60 were accepted, and 38 enrolled. Transfers are admitted to all classes. D grades do not transfer. Students must take 24 of the last 30 hours in residence; 124 hours are required for the bachelor's degree. Application deadlines for transfers are August 1 (fall), January 25 (spring), and June 1 (summer).

Visiting: Regular orientation sessions are held for prospective students. They include campus tours and visits with academic and financial-aid advisors. Guides also are available for informal visits. Visitors may sit in on class and stay overnight on campus. Visits should be scheduled while classes are in session. Contact the dean of admissions for arrangements.

Financial Aid: About 87% of the students receive aid. About 7% work part-time on campus. Scholarships, loans, and grants are available. Loans may be secured from the federal or state governments, local banks, and the college. The average award to freshmen from all sources is $3400. Charges may be paid in installments through a private company. The college is a member of the CSS and requires aid applicants to submit the FFS. There is no deadline for aid applications, but the priority date is April 1.

Foreign Students: About 1% of the full-time students come from foreign countries. The college offers these students special counseling.

Admissions: The TOEFL is required. The ACT is also required; a minimum score of 17 is needed.

Procedure: Foreign candidates should apply by August 15 (fall), January 1 (spring), and June 1 (summer). Proof of health and of adequate funds must be presented.

Admissions Contact: Maurice Werner, Dean of Admissions.

SOUTHWESTERN COLLEGE D-3
Winfield, Kansas 67156 (316) 221-4150

F/T: 306M, 248W	Faculty:	43; IIB, −$
P/T: 13M, 25W	Ph.D.'s:	44%
Grad: none	S/F Ratio:	12 to 1
Year: 4-1-4, ss	Tuition:	$2740
Appl: Aug. 31	R and B:	$1725
368 applied	295 accepted	200 enrolled
ACT: 21		COMPETITIVE

Southwestern College, founded in 1885, is a private liberal arts college affiliated with the United Methodist Church. The library holds 100,000 volumes, and subscribes to 500 periodicals.

Environment: The 70-acre campus, located in a small city 45 miles from Wichita, is surrounded by a rural environment. It has 12 buildings, including science laboratories and an Olympic-size indoor swimming pool. Six dormitories house approximately 560 students.

Student Life: Eighty-five percent of the students come from Kansas. Sixty-three percent live on campus. About 9% are minority-group members. Campus housing is both single-sex and coed; there are visiting privileges in single-sex dorms. Students may keep cars on campus. Drinking on campus is prohibited.

Organizations: Twenty percent of the men belong to 1 of 3 fraternities; 10% of the women belong to the 1 sorority on campus. Religious clubs include Methodist, Campus Y, and pre-ministerial. Other special-interest clubs and a student variety show fill out the rest of campus extracurricular life. The Walnut Valley Bluegrass Festival takes place locally every fall.

Sports: Southwestern College competes intercollegiately in 6 sports for men and 4 for women. Intramural sports for both men and women' number 7.

Handicapped: About 65% of the campus is accessible to wheelchair-bound students. Facilities include special class scheduling, wheelchair ramps, special parking, and specially equipped rest rooms. A Social Rehabilitation Services Department is available, and most handicapped students are given an assistant.

Graduates: The freshman dropout rate is 30%. Forty-seven percent of the students remain to graduate. Of these, 17% go on to graduate study, including 1% who enter medical school, 1% who enter dental school, and 1% who enter law school. Thirty percent of the graduates pursue careers in business and industry.

Services: Students receive the following services free of charge: health care, career counseling, tutoring, and remedial instruction.

Programs of Study: The college awards the B.A., B.S., B.Mus., B.B.A., and B.Ph. degrees. Bachelor's degrees are offered in the following subjects: BUSINESS (accounting, business administration, business education, computer science, international business, management), EDUCATION (early childhood, elementary, health/physical, home economics, secondary), ENGLISH (communications, English, literature, speech), FINE AND PERFORMING ARTS (art, art education, music, music education, theater/dramatics), HEALTH SCIENCES (medical technology), LANGUAGES (French, German, Spanish), MATH AND SCIENCES (biology, chemistry, mathematics, physics), PHILOSOPHY (humanities, philosophy, religion), PREPROFESSIONAL (agriculture, dentistry, forestry, home economics, law, medicine, ministry, social work, veterinary), SOCIAL SCIENCES (anthropology, economics, government/political science, history, psychology, sociology). Twenty-five percent of degrees are conferred in business, 25% in education, and 22% in health sciences.

Special: Combined B.A.-B.S. degrees and a general studies degree are offered. Students may design their own majors. There is an accelerated program through which students may earn the B.A. in 3 years. A double major is also possible. A work-study program at a state institution for the retarded is available for psychology majors. There is a cross-registration policy with St. John's College in Winfield, Kansas.

Honors: Honors work is available in the humanities department. Four honor societies have chapters on campus.

Admissions: Eighty percent of those who applied were accepted for the 1981–82 freshman class. ACT scores for those who enrolled were as follows: 34% below 21, 13% between 21 and 23, 21% between 24 and 25, 21% between 26 and 28, and 6% above 28. Applicants must have at least a C average.

Procedure: Applicants must take the ACT or the SAT. Application deadlines are August 31 (fall), January 26 (spring), and June 7 (summer). New students are admitted to all 3 terms. Admissions decisions are made on a rolling basis. The application fee is $10.

Special: Early and deferred admissions plans are available. Non-high-school graduates may be admitted on the basis of their GED tests. Students with special problems are admitted by approval of the dean. CLEP exam credit is accepted.

Transfer: For fall 1981, 98 transfer students applied, 77 were accepted, and 64 enrolled. Transfers are accepted for all classes. An average of C or better is required. All passing grades transfer for credit. Students must study at the college at least 30 semester hours, of a total 124 semester hours required for the bachelor's degree. Transfer application deadlines are the same as those for freshmen.

Visiting: The college schedules regular orientations at which prospective students may tour the campus, meet faculty members, and obtain financial aid information. Informal visits also may be scheduled weekdays in the fall and spring. Guides are provided and visitors may sit in on classes and stay overnight on campus. The admissions office should be contacted for arrangements.

Financial Aid: About 92% of all students receive aid through the school. About 25% work part-time on campus. The average award to freshmen covers 56% of costs. Financial aid can be in the form of scholarships, loans, or campus employment. Tuition may be paid in installments. The college is a CSS member. The FAF or FFS must be filed. Deadlines for aid applications are open.

KANSAS

Foreign Students: One percent of the full-time students come from foreign countries. There are organizations on campus especially for foreign students.

Admissions: The TOEFL is required and a minimum score of 450 is necessary. The ACT or SAT is not required.

Procedure: Foreign candidates should apply by August 31 (fall) and January 26 (spring). Proof of adequate funds to cover the duration of the program must be presented. Health insurance is required; it is available through the college and is included in the general student fees.

Admissions Contact: Carl Pagles, Admissions Director.

STERLING COLLEGE D-2
Sterling, Kansas 67579 (316) 278-2173

F/T: 187M, 209W	Faculty: 40; IIB, –$
P/T: 12M, 19W	Ph.D.'s: 48%
Grad: none	S/F Ratio: 11 to 1
Year: 4-1-4, ss	Tuition: $3350
Appl: open	R and B: $1850
183 applied	180 accepted	88 enrolled
ACT: 19		LESS COMPETITIVE

Sterling College, founded in 1887, is a private liberal arts college affiliated with the United Presbyterian Church. The library contains 82,000 volumes and 1200 microfilm items, and subscribes to 400 periodicals.

Environment: The 43-acre campus is situated in a rural area 70 miles from Wichita in the heart of wheat-farming country. Its several modern buildings include a gymnasium with an Olympic-size swimming pool. Dormitories house 550 students.

Student Life: About half the students are from Kansas. About 85% of the students come from public schools. Eighty percent live in residence halls. About 43% of the students are Presbyterians. Eighty-five percent are Protestant; 15% are Catholic. Campus housing is single-sex; there are visiting privileges. Drinking and smoking are forbidden on campus. Cars are permitted.

Organizations: There are no fraternities or sororities. Activities include drama, forensics, band, and religious clubs. The student union maintains its own bowling alley. Other cultural and recreational opportunities are available 20 miles away in Hutchinson.

Sports: The college fields teams in 3 intercollegiate sports for men and 3 for women. Intramural sports for both men and women number 2.

Handicapped: About 40% of the campus is accessible to wheelchair-bound students. Facilities include wheelchair ramps, special parking, special class scheduling, and lowered telephones. A special counselor is available to assist the handicapped.

Graduates: About 20% of the freshmen drop out; 35% remain to graduate. Twenty percent of the graduates pursue advanced degrees: 5% enter medical school and 5% enter law school. Ten percent enter business and industry.

Services: Students receive free career counseling, tutoring, and remedial instruction. The education department has a placement service for prospective teachers.

Programs of Study: All programs lead to the B.A. or B.S. degree. Bachelor's degrees are offered in the following subjects: BUSINESS (accounting, computer science, management), EDUCATION (elementary, secondary), ENGLISH (English), FINE AND PERFORMING ARTS (art, art education, theater/dramatics), MATH AND SCIENCES (mathematics), PHILOSOPHY (philosophy, religion), PREPROFESSIONAL (dentistry, engineering, law, medicine, ministry, pharmacy, veterinary), SOCIAL SCIENCES (history, sociology). Most degrees are granted in the social sciences.

Required: All students must take the equivalent of 6 hours of Bible study.

Special: Computer science may be taken as a minor. A nursing program is offered in conjunction with Wesley Medical Center in Wichita and with Kansas University. Seminars in non-Western studies are offered in cooperation with Bethany, Bethel, and McPherson Colleges and with Kansas Wesleyan. Pass/fail grades are permitted in some courses. Three-year degree programs may be arranged for preprofessional students, and study abroad is an option.

Honors: The college offers an honors program with independent study and auditing privileges for upperclassmen, and pre-honors work for sophomores.

Admissions: Ninety-eight percent of those who applied were accepted for the 1981–82 freshman class. ACT scores of a recent entering freshman class were as follows: 15% between 21 and 23, 20% between 24 and 26, and 34% above 26. Applicants should rank in the upper half of their high school class, have completed 17 high school units, and have at least a C average.

Procedure: The ACT is required. There are no deadlines for admission. Freshmen are admitted for all 3 sessions. There is a rolling admissions plan. The application fee is $10.

Special: CLEP and AP credit are accepted.

Transfer: For fall 1981, 37 transfer students applied, all were accepted, and all enrolled. Transfer students are accepted for all classes. Recommendations and an average of at least C are required. D grades transfer. Students must earn at least 30 credits at the college, of a total 124 credits required for the bachelor's degree. There are no application deadlines. Transfers are admitted to the fall, winter, and spring sessions on a rolling basis.

Visiting: Weekend orientations for prospective students are scheduled regularly. Informal visits during the week also are possible when school is in session. Guides are provided, and visitors may sit in on classes and stay overnight at the school. The admissions office should be contacted for arrangements.

Financial Aid: About 83% of all students receive financial aid. Three hundred scholarships with a total value of $120,000 and college-administered federal loans totaling $138,000 were available for a recent year. The maximum aid to incoming freshmen from all sources, including campus employment, is $4200. The average award to freshmen is $2700. Tuition may be paid in installments. The FFS must be filed. The application deadline for financial aid is April 1.

Foreign Students: Students from foreign countries represent 5% of the student body.

Admissions: The TOEFL is required. The ACT or SAT is not necessary.

Procedure: There are no application deadlines. Admissions are on a rolling basis. Foreign students may enter the fall, winter, or spring session. Proof of adequate funds must be presented. Health insurance must be carried; it is available through the college for a fee.

Admissions Contact: Bob Bethell, Director of Admissions.

TABOR COLLEGE D-2
Hillsboro, Kansas 67063 (316) 947-2266

F/T: 184M, 200W	Faculty: 65; IIB, –$
P/T: 20M, 34W	Ph.D.'s: 21%
Grad: none	S/F Ratio: 13 to 1
Year: 4-1-4	Tuition: $2854
Appl: July 1	R and B: $1800
196 applied	196 accepted	139 enrolled
ACT: 20		NONCOMPETITIVE

Tabor College, founded in 1908, is a private college of liberal arts and teacher education affiliated with the Mennonite Brethren Church. The library contains 57,000 volumes, and subscribes to 450 periodicals.

Environment: The 26-acre campus is located in a small town in the wheat and dairy area of central Kansas, 50 miles from Wichita. The environment surrounding the campus is rural. The campus has 21 buildings, including a fitness center and 10 dormitories that accommodate 300 students.

Student Life: Fifty-four percent of the students come from Kansas. About 88% of the freshmen come from public schools. Students are encouraged, but not required, to attend chapel services. Smoking and drinking are prohibited on campus. Sixty-eight percent of the students are Protestant. Four percent are minority-group members. Campus housing is single-sex; there are visiting privileges. Students may keep cars on campus.

Organizations: The college has no fraternities or sororities. However, other extracurricular activities are available.

Sports: The college fields intercollegiate teams in 6 sports for men and 5 for women. There are 5 intramural programs for both men and women.

Handicapped: About 88% of the campus is accessible to handicapped students. Special parking is available. No visually or hearing-impaired students were enrolled in 1981–82.

Graduates: About 29% of the freshmen drop out at the end of the first year; 32% remain to graduate. Thirty percent of the graduates pursue advanced degrees. About 1% enter medical school.

Services: The following free services are available: health care; psychological, placement, and career counseling; tutoring; and remedial instruction.

Programs of Study: All 4-year programs lead to the B.A. degree. There are also associate degree programs. Bachelor's degrees are offered in the following subjects: BUSINESS (business administration, business education, computer science), EDUCATION (early childhood, elementary, health/physical, secondary, special), ENGLISH (English), FINE AND PERFORMING ARTS (art, music, music education), HEALTH SCIENCES (environmental health, medical technology), MATH AND SCIENCES (biology, chemistry, earth science, mathematics, natural sciences, physical sciences), PHILOSOPHY (humanities, religion), PREPROFESSIONAL (agriculture, dentistry, engineering, law, medicine, ministry, social work), SOCIAL SCIENCES (government/political science, history, psychology, social sciences, sociology). Twenty-three percent of degrees are conferred in education, 17% in social sciences, and 17% in business.

Required: All students must take general education courses, including 12 hours in Bible and philosophy.

Special: Students may study abroad by special arrangement. A combination degree program in medical technology is offered. Students may design their own majors.

Honors: Honor societies on campus include Pi Kappa Delta.

Admissions: All applicants for the 1981–82 freshman class were accepted. Candidates must be graduates of an accredited high school with 15 Carnegie units and the high school's recommendation. They should have an average of at least C and rank in the top half of their class. Other factors considered by the college are personality, leadership, extracurricular activities, special talents, and ability to finance a college education.

Procedure: The ACT or SAT is required. Applications and a $16 fee should be submitted by July 1 for fall admission. Freshmen are admitted to the fall semester only. Admissions decisions are made on a rolling basis.

Special: AP and CLEP credit are accepted.

Transfer: For fall 1981, 30 transfers applied, all were accepted, and 20 enrolled. Transfers are accepted for all but the senior class. Those with a GPA of less than 2.0 are admitted on academic probation. All students must complete at least 1 year at the college to receive a degree. For the bachelor's degree, a total of 124 credits must be earned. Application deadlines are the same as those for freshmen.

Visiting: Guides are available for informal visits. Visitors may sit in on classes and stay overnight on campus. The college suggests scheduling visits on Monday through Thursday mornings. The director of admissions should be contacted for arrangements.

Financial Aid: About 80% of the students receive financial aid; nearly half the students work part-time. Scholarships, grants, and loans are available. The FAF or FFS must be filed, but the FFS is preferred. The deadline for financial aid applications is May 1.

Foreign Students: The college offers special counseling and organizations especially for foreign students.

Admissions: The TOEFL is required. College entrance exams are not necessary.

Procedure: Foreign students should apply by June 1 for the fall semester. There are no deadlines for the winter and spring terms to which foreign students are also admitted. A medical report from a physician must be submitted. Proof of adequate funds to cover 4 years of study must be presented. Health insurance is required; it is available through the college for a fee.

Admissions Contact: Barry W. Jackson, Director of Admissions.

UNIVERSITY OF KANSAS E-2
Lawrence, Kansas 66045   (913) 864-3911

F/T: 8223M, 7046W	Faculty: 1295; I, av$
P/T: 1105M, 1410W	Ph.D.'s: 90%
Grad: 3141M, 3065W	S/F Ratio: 13 to 1
Year: sems, ss	Tuition: $918 ($2234)
Appl: open	R and B: $1662–1773
6267 applied	4939 accepted 2941 enrolled
ACT: 23	NONCOMPETITIVE

University of Kansas, founded in 1866, is a large state university with schools of Education, Journalism, Liberal Arts and Sciences, Fine Arts, Engineering, Business, Architecture, Law, Medicine, Allied Health and Nursing, Pharmacy, and Social Welfare. The library contains more than 1.8 million volumes, and subscribes to 22,000 periodicals.

Environment: The 960-acre urban campus is located in Lawrence, a city of 50,000 people 40 miles from Kansas City, Missouri. The campus has 81 buildings, including a law school and a visual arts school. Eight dormitories, 8 scholarship residence halls, and married students' apartment units house a total of 2800 students. There are also living facilities in fraternity and sorority houses. The Medical Center is located on another campus in Kansas City, Kansas.

Student Life: Three-fourths of the students are from Kansas. Eighty-eight percent come from public schools. About 22% live on campus. About 9% are minority-group members. Campus housing is both single-sex and coed; there are visiting privileges in single-sex dorms. Students may keep cars on campus, but because of limited parking, use of cars on campus is discouraged. The university provides day-care services to students, faculty, staff, and community members for a fee.

Oragnizations: Twenty percent of the men and 13% of the women belong to 1 of 23 fraternities and 13 sororities on campus. Cultural and extracurricular activities include special-interest and departmental clubs, music and drama groups, AM and FM radio stations, and religious organizations. The university has its own art and natural history museums.

Sports: The university competes intercollegiately in 9 sports for men and 9 for women. Intramural sports for both men and women number 22.

Handicapped: About 90% of the campus is accessible to wheelchair-bound students. Facilities include special class scheduling, wheelchair ramps, special parking, elevators, specially equipped rest rooms, lowered drinking fountains and telephones, and lift-van transportation. An audio reader for visually impaired students is available. Academic aides are also available.

Graduates: The freshman dropout rate is 11%. Three-fourths of the students remain to graduate, and 60% go on to graduate study.

Services: Students receive free psychological and career counseling and remedial instruction. Extensive free placement counseling for students and alumni is available in liberal arts, fine arts, business, law, and journalism. Health care is available on campus with insurance or at a fee.

Programs of Study: The university awards the B.A., B.S., and B.G.S. degrees. Master's and doctoral degrees also are available. Bachelor's degrees are offered in the following subjects: AREA STUDIES (American, Asian, Black/Afro-American, Latin American, Russian), BUSINESS (accounting, business administration, computer science, management), EDUCATION (counseling, early childhood, elementary, health/physical, secondary, special), ENGLISH (English, journalism, speech), FINE AND PERFORMING ARTS (art, art education, art history, film/photography, music, music education, radio/TV, studio art, theater/dramatics), HEALTH SCIENCES (medical technology, nursing, occupational therapy, physical therapy, speech therapy), LANGUAGES (Chinese, French, German, Greek/Latin, Italian, Japanese, Portuguese, Russian, Serbo-Croatian, Spanish), MATH AND SCIENCES (astronomy, biochemistry, biology, botany, chemistry, ecology/environmental science, geology, human biology, mathematics, physics), PHILOSOPHY (classics, humanities, philosophy, religion), PREPROFESSIONAL (architecture, dentistry, engineering, law, medicine, pharmacy, social work, veterinary), SOCIAL SCIENCES (anthropology, economics, geography, government/political science, history, psychology, social sciences, sociology).

Required: All freshmen must take courses in composition and literature.

Special: The university offers combined B.A.-B.S. degrees in many subjects, a general studies degree, and independent study. Students may design their own majors. Options for study abroad include summer language institutes in 7 foreign countries. Extensive field trips are available in archeology, entomology, and natural history. The university maintains a summer geology camp in Colorado.

Honors: Twenty honor societies have chapters on campus.

Admissions: Seventy-nine percent of those who applied were accepted for the 1981–82 freshman class. On the ACT, freshmen scored as follows: 35% below 21, 21% between 21 and 23, 15% between 24 and 25, 19% between 26 and 28, and 10% above 28. Applicants from Kansas must have graduated from an accredited state high school and have completed 17 high school units. Nonresident candidates must have at least a C average or rank in the upper 50% of their class. State residents are given preference.

Procedure: The ACT is required. Application deadlines are open. Freshmen are accepted in fall, spring, or summer terms. Admissions decisions are made on a rolling basis. There is no application fee.

Special: An early decision plan is offered. AP exam credit is accepted.

Transfer: For fall 1981, 3353 transfer students applied, 2715 were accepted, and 2107 enrolled. Transfer students with a GPA of at least 2.0 and a minimum ACT score of 23 are accepted for all classes. A,

288 KANSAS

B, C, and D grades transfer. Students must study at the university for their last 30 semester hours to receive a degree. The bachelor's degree requires the completion of 124 semester hours. There are no application deadlines. Transfers are admitted to all terms.

Visiting: Orientations for prospective students are scheduled regularly. Informal visits may be scheduled weekdays from 8:30 A.M. to 5 P.M. Guides are available. For arrangements, in-state visitors should call 800-332-6332; out-of-state visitors should call 800-255-6322.

Financial Aid: A third of the students receive aid through the university. About 16% work part-time on campus. The average award to freshmen through the university is $1050. The school is a member of CSS. The FFS is required. The deadlines for aid applications are March 1 (fall) and November 15 (spring).

Foreign Students: Seven percent of the full-time students come from foreign countries. An intensive English program, special counseling, and organizations are available.

Admissions: The TOEFL, the University of Michigan Language Test, or the university's own test must be taken. A minimum TOEFL score of 550 is required. College entrance exams are not required.

Procedure: Deadlines for foreign applicants are June (fall), November (spring), and March (summer). Proof of funds adequate to cover each calendar year in attendance must be presented.

Admissions Contact: Linda Thompson, Director of Admissions.

WASHBURN UNIVERSITY OF TOPEKA E-2
Topeka, Kansas 66621 (913) 295-6574

F/T: 1300M, 1300W *Faculty:* 200; IIA, av$
P/T: 1000M, 1450W *Ph.D.'s:* 60%
Grad: 500M, 150W *S/F Ratio:* 25 to 1
Year: sems, ss *Tuition:* $31 p/c ($62 p/c)
Appl: see profile *R and B:* $1600
SAT or ACT: not required **NONCOMPETITIVE**

Washburn University, a coeducational, nonsectarian, municipal institution, was founded in 1865 as a liberal arts college. The library contains 210,000 volumes, and subscribes to 1500 periodicals.

Environment: The 150-acre campus is located in a residential area of downtown Topeka, a city of 145,000 people. Many of the 15 campus buildings are less than 20 years old. Dormitories accommodate more than 300 unmarried students, and there are 48 campus apartments for married students. Fraternity and sorority housing also is available.

Student Life: About 84% of the students are from Kansas. About 12% live on campus. Ninety percent are from public schools. Drinking is prohibited on campus. Dormitories are both single-sex and coed.

Organizations: About 10% of the students belong to 1 of the 5 fraternities or 5 sororities on campus. Activities include a weekly newspaper, a band, a choir, debates, drama, music, an educational TV station, the student council, and many professional, special-interest, and departmental clubs. There are religious clubs on campus for Catholic and Protestant students.

Sports: The university fields intercollegiate teams in 6 sports for men and 6 for women. A variety of intramural sports is offered.

Handicapped: Ninety-five percent of the campus is accessible to handicapped students. Facilities include wheelchair ramps, special parking, elevators, specially equipped rest rooms, and lowered drinking fountains. Special class scheduling can be arranged. Special counselors are available to assist handicapped students.

Graduates: About 40% of the freshmen drop out during their first year, and 55% remain to graduate. A fourth of the graduates pursue advanced degrees; 10% enter law school and 2% medical school. About 50% of the students begin careers in business and industry.

Services: The following free services are provided: health care, psychological counseling, placement, and career counseling. Placement services also may be used by graduates.

Programs of Study: The university confers the B.A., B.B.A., B.F.A., B.S., B.Ed., and B.Mus. degrees. Associate, master's, and doctoral degrees also are available. Bachelor's degrees are offered in the following subjects: BUSINESS (accounting, business administration, finance, management, marketing, merchandising and retailing), EDUCATION (elementary, health/physical, secondary), ENGLISH (communication arts, English), FINE AND PERFORMING ARTS (art, music, music education, studio art, theater/dramatics), HEALTH SCIENCES (medical technology, nursing), LANGUAGES (French, German, Spanish), MATH AND SCIENCES (biology, chemistry, computer science, mathematics, physics), PHILOSOPHY (philosophy), PREPROFESSIONAL (engineering, home economics, recreation, social work), SOCIAL SCIENCES (economics, corrections, criminal justice, government/political science, history, psychology, sociology). About 30% of undergraduate degrees are conferred in business, 20% in social sciences, and 15% in health sciences.

Required: All freshmen must take physical education.

Special: The university offers cooperative engineering programs with Kansas State University, the University of Kansas, and Wichita State University; a joint 4-year program in medical technology with Topeka Medical Technology School; and a spring semester in Copenhagen. Five-year combined B.A.-B.S. degrees may be earned in any combination of subjects. The university offers a general studies degree. Preprofessional programs (nonmajor) are available in aviation technology, dentistry, engineering, law, medicine, pharmacy, and theology.

Honors: Two national honor societies, Phi Kappa Phi and Kappa Mu Epsilon, have chapters on campus.

Admissions: Ninety-eight percent of those who applied were accepted for a recent freshman class. Kansas applicants must be graduates of accredited high schools; otherwise, admission is open. Out-of-state residents must have a GPA of at least 2.0.

Procedure: The ACT is recommended and should be taken before registration. Applications should be filed during the final semester of the senior year, but are accepted up to 15 days before registration. Notification is sent as soon as credentials are complete. Freshmen are admitted to the fall, spring and summer sessions. There is no application fee.

Special: AP and CLEP credit is given.

Transfer: About 1200 transfer students enroll each year. A 2.0 GPA is necessary. Students must earn 30 semester hours in residence of the 124 generally required for a bachelor's degree.

Visiting: Guides are available for informal visits during the school year. Visitors may sit in on classes and stay overnight on campus. Visits can be scheduled by contacting the dean of students.

Financial Aid: About 50% of the students receive aid. Two hundred freshman scholarships are available. Loans from the federal government and local banks also are offered, as is campus employment. The university is a member of CSS. The deadline for scholarship applications is March 15. The FAF or FFS must be filed.

Foreign Students: There are 50 foreign students currently enrolled at Washburn.

Admissions: Applicants must score 500 or better on the TOEFL. No college entrance exams are required.

Procedure: Foreign students are admitted to all terms, and should submit applications at least 2 months before the start of the term. Students must provide evidence of adequate funds for 4 years of study.

Admissions Contact: John E. Triggs, Registrar and Director of Admissions.

WICHITA STATE UNIVERSITY D-3
Wichita, Kansas 67208 (316) 689-3085

F/T: 3444M, 3156W *Faculty:* 575; IIA, av$
P/T: 3360M, 3504W *Ph.D.'s:* 62%
Grad: 1554M, 1936W *S/F Ratio:* 18 to 1
Year: sems, ss *Tuition:* $912 ($2228)
Appl: Aug. 1 *R and B:* $1700-2000
3712 applied 3564 accepted 1995 enrolled
ACT: 18 **NONCOMPETITIVE**

Wichita State University, a state-supported coeducational institution, was founded as Fairmount College in 1895. The library houses 1.5 million items and 75,000 bound periodicals.

Environment: The 320-acre Wichita State campus is surrounded by an urban environment. It has 50 major buildings. Four residence halls accommodate 1000 students. Other university-sponsored living facilities include off-campus apartments, fraternity houses, and sorority houses.

Student Life: Ninety-four percent of the undergraduates are from Kansas. Ninety percent of the students live in residence halls or university-approved housing. About 14% are members of minority groups. Campus housing is both single-sex and coed; there are visiting privileges in single-sex dorms. Students may keep cars on campus. The university provides day-care services to students, faculty, and staff for a fee.

Organizations: There are 5 sororities and 7 fraternities at the university, and 6% of the women and 10% of the men belong to 1 of them. Numerous organizations and cultural activities are available.

Sports: Wichita State competes intercollegiately in 8 sports for men and 7 for women. An intramural program offers 7 sports for men and 7 for women.

Graduates: The freshman drop out at a rate of 20%. Fifty-six percent of the freshmen remain to graduate. Forty-four percent of the graduates go on to advanced study.

Services: Students receive the following free services: placement, health care, career and psychological counseling, tutoring, and remedial instruction.

Programs of Study: The university confers the B.A., B.ArtEd., B.B.A., B.Mus., B.F.A., B.Mus.Ed., B.S., B.S.A.E., B.S.E.E., B.S.I.E., and B.S.N. degrees. Associate, master's, and doctoral degree programs are also available. Bachelor's degrees are offered in more than 180 fields, including: AREA STUDIES (American, Black/Afro-American, Latin American, minority, urban, women's), BUSINESS (accounting, aviation management, business administration, business education, computer science, finance, management, marketing, real estate/insurance), EDUCATION (early childhood, elementary, health/physical, industrial, secondary, special), ENGLISH (English, journalism, literature, speech), FINE AND PERFORMING ARTS (art, art education, art history, music education, radio/TV, studio art, theater), HEALTH SCIENCES (hospital administration, medical records, medical technology, nursing, physical therapy), LANGUAGES (French, German, Greek/Latin, Spanish), MATH AND SCIENCES (biochemistry, biology, chemistry, geology, mathematics, natural sciences, physics), PHILOSOPHY (classics, philosophy, religion), PREPROFESSIONAL (dentistry, engineering, law, medicine, optometry, pharmacy, social work, veterinary), SOCIAL SCIENCES (administration of justice, economics, history, international studies, psychology, sociology).

Required: Students must take 2 English courses and 1 speech course the first year.

Special: A major in communicative disorders is offered, and an Institute of Logopedics is located near campus. Also available is a 3-1 program in medical technology.

Honors: There is an honors program based on past performance and test scores.

Admissions: Ninety-six percent of those who applied for admission to the 1981-82 freshman class were accepted. All Kansas high school graduates who apply are accepted. Applicants from out of state should rank in the upper half of their class.

Procedure: The ACT is required and should be taken as early as possible during the senior year. A campus visit and interview are recommended. The suggested application deadlines are August 1 (fall), January 1 (spring), and May 1 (summer). There is no application fee. Admissions are on a rolling basis.

Special: There are early decision and early admissiosn plans. CLEP credit is accepted.

Transfer: Most transfer applications are accepted. For fall 1981, 1687 transfer students applied, 1651 were accepted, and 1201 enrolled. Transfers are accepted for all classes. Applicants must have a minimum GPA of 2.0. A, B, C, and D grades transfer. The last 30 hours for a transfer student from a 4-year college, or the last 60 hours for a transfer student from a 2-year community college, must be taken at the university. A total of 124 semester hours must be completed to receive a bachelor's degree. The suggested application deadlines are August 1 (fall), January 1 (spring), and May 1 (summer).

Financial Aid: About 30% of all students receive financial aid. About 5% work part-time on campus. The university makes 300 scholarships available to freshmen each year. The total amount of aid for freshmen is $580,000. Loans administered by the university total $1 million; those administered by the NDSL, $1 million. The average aid to qualified freshmen from all sources is $750. The FFS must be filed. The recommended deadline for aid applications is March 15.

Foreign Students: About 3% of the full-time students come from foreign countries. An intensive English program, special counseling, and organizations especially for foreign students are available.

Admissions: The TOEFL is required; a minimum score of 500 is necessary. College entrance exams are not required.

Procedure: Foreign students in the country should apply 30 days prior to enrollment; those not in the country, 60 days prior to enrollment. For those students out of the country, deadlines are June 1 (fall), November 1 (spring), and April 1 (summer). The university's health form must be completed by the student's physician. Proof of adequate funds to cover a 9-month academic year must be shown. Health insurance is required; it is available through the university for a fee.

Admissions Contact: Stanley E. Henderson, Director of Admissions.

KENTUCKY

ASBURY COLLEGE
Wilmore, Kentucky 40390

D-3
(606) 858-3511

F/T: 558M, 646W
P/T: 3M, 5W
Grad: none
Year: qtrs, ss
Appl: Aug. 15
566 applied
ACT: 21

Faculty: 92; IIB, av$
Ph.D.'s: 40%
S/F Ratio: 16 to 1
Tuition: $3294
R and B: $1963

540 accepted

370 enrolled
COMPETITIVE

Asbury College is a private liberal arts institution emphasizing Christian education. The library contains 96,000 volumes and subscribes to 658 periodicals.

Environment: The 60-acre campus is located in a rural area 17 miles from Lexington. There are 21 main buildings. Living facilities include dormitories, on-campus and off-campus apartments, and married student housing.

Student Life: The majority of students come from states other than Kentucky; 16% are residents of Kentucky and 2% come from foreign countries. About 89% of entering freshmen come from public schools. About 85% of the students live on campus. Three percent are minority-group members. Ninety-five percent are Protestant. Campus housing is single-sex; there are no visiting privileges. Freshmen may not keep cars on campus. Although the college is an independent institution, it follows the Methodist doctrine. All students are required to attend religious services 3 times a week.

Organizations: Religious clubs include Methodist and Foreign Mission Fellowship.

Sports: The college fields 5 intercollegiate teams for men and 4 for women. There are 3 intramural sports for men and 3 for women.

Handicapped: Special facilities for the physically handicapped include wheelchair ramps and elevators. Special class scheduling is possible. About 10% of the campus is accessible to handicapped students.

Graduates: Only 10% of the students fail to return after the first year; 55% remain to graduate. About 60% of the students pursue graduate study after graduation; 2% enter medical school and 1% enter law school. Ten percent of the graduates enter business and industry.

Services: Students receive the following services free of charge: placement and career counseling, health care, tutoring, remedial instruction, and psychological counseling.

Programs of Study: The college confers the A.B. and B.S.Ed. degrees. Bachelor's degrees are offered in the following subjects: BUSINESS (accounting, computer science, management), EDUCATION (elementary, secondary), ENGLISH (English, speech), FINE AND PERFORMING ARTS (art, church music, music, music education), HEALTH SCIENCES (medical technology), LANGUAGES (Biblical languages, French, Spanish), MATH AND SCIENCES (applied mathematics, biology, chemistry, mathematics), PHILOSOPHY (Bible studies, Christian ministries, philosophy, religion), PREPROFESSIONAL (law, medicine, ministry, social work), SOCIAL SCIENCES (history, psychology, sociology). About 25% of all degrees conferred are in social sciences, 29% are in education, and 10% are in math and science.

Required: Twelve quarter hours of religion are required of all students.

Special: It is possible to earn combined B.A.-B.S. degrees in education. The college offers study abroad in France and Germany, a 3-1 program in medical technology with an accredited hospital, and a "Credits in Escrow" program for high school juniors.

290 KENTUCKY

Honors: There are 2 national honor societies on campus. The departments of Spanish and history offer honors programs.

Admissions: Approximately 95% of those who applied were accepted for the 1981–82 freshman class. Of those who enrolled, the ACT scores were as follows: 29% below 21, 50% between 21 and 23, 15% between 24 and 25, 5% between 26 and 28, and 1% above 28. Candidates must be graduates of accredited high schools, have at least a C average, have completed 15 academic units of high school work, and rank in the top half of their class. Advanced placement or honors courses and the extracurricular activities record are also considered. Freshmen are admitted for all terms.

Procedure: The ACT is required. The deadlines for regular admissions are August 15 (fall), December 1 (winter), March 1 (spring), and May 1 (summer). There is a $25 application fee. Admissions are on a rolling basis.

Special: There is an early admissions plan; students must apply by January 1. Deferred admissions are also possible. AP and CLEP credit is available.

Transfer: For fall 1981, 150 applications were received, 130 were accepted, and 120 students enrolled. Applicants should have a C average and a minimum composite score of 18 on the ACT. D grades do not transfer. There is a one-year residency requirement. Fifty percent of the credits in the major must be earned at Asbury; 192 credits are required for a bachelor's degree. The fall deadline is August 1; winter, spring, and summer deadlines are the same as for regular admissions.

Visiting: There are regularly scheduled orientations for prospective students. Informal guided tours and classroom visits can also be arranged. Visits are best scheduled during the months of October, February, and April. Inquiries should be addressed to the director of admissions.

Financial Aid: About 55% of all students receive financial aid. Fifty percent work part-time on campus. The average award to freshmen is $600. Scholarships, loans, NDSL, SEOG, and BEOG are available. The college is a member of CSS; the FAF and the application should be submitted by May 1 (summer or fall), December 1 (winter), or March 1 (spring).

Foreign Students: Two percent of the full-time students come from foreign countries. Special counseling and special organizations are available for these students.

Admissions: Foreign students must achieve a TOEFL score of at least 540. No college entrance exams are required.

Procedure: Application deadlines are August 1 (fall), December 1 (winter), March 1 (spring), and May 1 (summer). Foreign students must have a medical exam and must present proof of funds adequate to cover 4 years of study. Health insurance is required and is available through the college for a fee.

Admissions Contact: William E. Eddy, Director of Admissions.

BELLARMINE COLLEGE D-2
Louisville, Kentucky 40205 (502) 452-8131

F/T: 561M, 566W Faculty: 91; IIB, av$
P/T: 262M, 835W Ph.D.'s: 80%
Grad: 248M, 113W S/F Ratio: 18 to 1
Year: sems, ss Tuition: $2850
Appl: Aug. 15 R and B: $1650
601 applied 550 accepted 335 enrolled
SAT: 500V 480M ACT: 22 COMPETITIVE

Bellarmine College, founded in 1950, is a Catholic, liberal arts institution. The library contains 90,000 volumes and 2700 microfilm items, and subscribes to 585 periodicals.

Environment: The college's 115-acre suburban campus is located only 15 minutes from downtown Louisville. The physical plant consists of 9 main buildings including an indoor/outdoor tennis center. There are 2 dormitories.

Student Life: About 75% of the undergraduates are from Kentucky; 25% reside on campus. Nine percent are minority-group members. About 70% are Catholic, 25% are Protestant, and 5% are Jewish. Campus housing is single-sex; there are visiting privileges. Students may keep cars on campus. Although Bellarmine is a Catholic college, participation in any of the varied religious activities is completely voluntary.

Organizations: There is 1 national fraternity at Bellarmine. In addition, more than 20 clubs and social and preprofessional groups are active on campus.

Sports: The college competes on an intercollegiate level in 7 sports for men and 6 for women. There are 5 intramural sports for men and 5 for women.

Handicapped: Special facilities for the physically handicapped include wheelchair ramps, elevators, and lowered drinking fountains. About 80% of the campus is accessible. Special class scheduling is possible.

Graduates: The freshman dropout rate is 15%; 70% remain to graduate. Forty percent pursue graduate study after graduation: 5% enter medical school; 2% dental school; and 5% law school. Approximately 60% pursue careers in business and industry.

Services: Students receive the following services free of charge: placement and career counseling, health care, remedial instruction, and psychological counseling. Tutoring is available for a fee.

Programs of Study: The college offers B.A., B.S., B.S.N., and B.S.C. degrees. Associate and master's degrees are also awarded. Bachelor's degrees are offered in the following subjects: BUSINESS (accounting, business administration, computer science), EDUCATION (elementary, secondary, special), ENGLISH (English), FINE AND PERFORMING ARTS (art, art education, music, music education), HEALTH SCIENCES (medical technology, nursing), MATH AND SCIENCES (biology, chemistry, mathematics), PHILOSOPHY (philosophy, religion), PREPROFESSIONAL (dentistry, engineering, law, medicine, pharmacy, veterinary), SOCIAL SCIENCES (economics, government/political science, history, psychology, sociology). About 50% of all degrees conferred are in business.

Required: Nine credit hours of theology are required of all students. Non-Catholic students may fulfill these requirements with courses in Protestant and Jewish thought and development. All candidates for graduation must successfully complete either the GRE Aptitude Tests or the Senior Level Aptitude Test.

Special: A combination degree program exists in engineering. It is possible to earn a B.G.S. degree. A combined B.A.-B.S. degree is also offered. The college is a member of the Kentuckiana Metroversity, a consortium of 6 local colleges and universities.

Admissions: About 92% of those who applied were accepted for the 1981–82 freshman class. The SAT scores of those who enrolled were as follows: Verbal—20% below 500, 70% between 500 and 599, 10% between 600 and 700, and 0% above 700; Math—30% below 500, 60% between 500 and 599, 10% between 600 and 700, and 0% above 700. On the ACT, 30% scored below 21, 41% between 21 and 23, 10% between 24 and 25, 10% between 26 and 28, and 9% above 28. The college prefers that students rank in the upper half of their graduating classes and have averages of at least C in college preparatory programs. Each applicant must present 15 Carnegie units of high school work. The college also considers the following factors in order of importance: advanced placement or honor courses, extracurricular activities, and leadership record.

Procedure: Applicants should take the SAT or ACT in the fall of the senior year. Application deadlines are August 15 (fall), January 4 (spring), and June 1 (summer). Notification is on a rolling basis.

Special: Early admissions, deferred admissions, and early decision plans are available. CLEP and AP credit is available.

Transfer: For fall 1981, 160 students applied, 123 were accepted, and 87 enrolled. An average of 2.0 and minimum composite scores of 18 on the ACT and 820 on the SAT are required; D grades are accepted. All students must complete, at the college, 36 of the 126 credits required for a bachelor's degree. Application deadlines are the same as those for freshmen.

Visiting: There are regularly scheduled orientations for prospective students. It is possible to sit in on classes and stay overnight at the school. Arrangements can be made through the admissions office.

Financial Aid: About 70% of the students receive financial aid. About 35% work part-time on campus. The average award to freshmen is $800. Recently, the college awarded $240,000 in academic scholarships, and $110,000 in loans. The FAF is required; the deadline for financial aid application is May 1 (fall) or November 1 (spring). The college is a member of CSS.

Foreign Students: Three percent of the full-time students come from foreign countries. Special counseling and special organizations are available for these students.

Admissions: Foreign students must achieve a TOEFL score of at least 500. No college entrance exams are required.

Procedure: Application deadlines are August 1 (fall), December 1 (spring), and June 1 (summer). Foreign students must present proof of adequate funds.

Admissions Contact: Robert G. Pfaadt, Director of Admissions and Educational Services.

BEREA COLLEGE
Berea, Kentucky 40404   D-3
(606) 986-9341

F/T: 685M, 825W	Faculty: 112; IIB, +$
P/T: 30M, 48W	Ph.D.'s: 60%
Grad: none	S/F Ratio: 13 to 1
Year: 4-1-4, ss	Tuition: $113
Appl: Aug. 1	R and B: $1575
1133 applied	539 accepted 404 enrolled
SAT: 448V 467M	ACT: 19 COMPETITIVE+

Berea College, founded in 1855, is a privately endowed, nonsectarian liberal arts college. The library contains 230,000 volumes and subscribes to 1000 periodicals. Berea has a commitment to the Christian faith and ethic, and its programs are constructed within that context.

Environment: The 140-acre campus is located in a rural area in the foothills of the Cumberland Mountains, 40 miles from Lexington. In addition to the campus, the college property consists of 50 acres of gardens, 1100 acres of farmlands, and 6000 acres of forest. There are more than 100 college buildings. Living facilities include dormitories and married student housing.

Student Life: While 60% of the students come from outside of Kentucky, 80% are residents of the Southern Appalachian Mountain region. About 95% come from public schools. Approximately 84% of the students live on campus. Thirteen percent are minority-group members. Campus housing is single-sex; there are visiting privileges. Only seniors may keep cars on campus.

Organizations: Campus life is characterized by a strong student government and active participation in a number of student organizations.

Sports: The college competes on an intercollegiate level in 8 sports for men and 9 sports for women. There are 10 intramural sports for men and 10 for women.

Handicapped: Special facilities for the physically handicapped include wheelchair ramps, specially equipped rest rooms, and lowered drinking fountains. Special class scheduling is possible.

Graduates: The freshman dropout rate is 27%; 55% remain to graduate. About 56% of the graduates eventually pursue graduate study: 4% enter medical school; 3% enter dental school; and 3% enter law school. Approximately 15% pursue careers in business and industry.

Services: Students receive the following services free of charge: placement, career counseling, tutoring, remedial instruction, and psychological counseling. Health care is provided for a fee.

Programs of Study: The college confers the B.A., B.S.Ag, B.S.B.A., B.S.H.E., B.S.I.A., and B.S.N. degrees. Bachelor's degrees are offered in the following subjects: BUSINESS (business administration, business education, management), EDUCATION (elementary, health/physical, industrial, secondary), ENGLISH (English), FINE AND PERFORMING ARTS (art, art education, music, music education), HEALTH SCIENCES (nursing), LANGUAGES (French, German, Spanish), MATH AND SCIENCES (biology, chemistry, mathematics, physics), PHILOSOPHY (philosophy, religion), PREPROFESSIONAL (agriculture, home economics), SOCIAL SCIENCES (economics, government/political science, history, psychology, sociology). The degree program in nursing places special emphasis on rural public health, with field experience in the senior year. About 25% of the degrees conferred are in preprofessional studies; 16% are in business.

Required: Three terms of physical education and 1 term of health are required. In addition to a year's course in religious and historical perspectives, all students must take a senior course whose essential orientation is the Christian faith in the modern world. UP and URE exams are required.

Special: Student-designed majors are available. Independent study and interdepartmental majors are also offered.

Honors: There are 13 honor societies on campus.

Admissions: About 48% of those who applied were accepted for the 1981-82 freshman class. The SAT scores of those who enrolled were as follows: Verbal—68% below 500, 26% between 500 and 599, 5% between 600 and 700, and 1% above 700; Math—64% below 500, 26% between 500 and 599, 10% between 600 and 700, and 0% above 700. On the ACT, 62% scored below 21, 25% between 21 and 23, 6% between 24 and 25, 4% between 26 and 28, and 3% above 28. Enrollment is limited to persons who are well qualified, but who have little money for college. The leading criterion for evaluating a student's qualifications is the recommendation from his or her high school. Applicants should rank in the top 40% of their class and have a 2.0 average. Consideration is also given to recommendations from alumni, advanced placement or honors courses, and personality. Some preference is given to children of alumni.

Procedure: Either the SAT or the ACT is required and should be taken by December or January of the senior year. Students should apply by August 1 (fall), January 1 (spring), or May 15 (summer). Notification is on a rolling basis. A $2 application fee is required.

Special: The college has an early admissions program; the application deadline is August 1. CLEP credit is available.

Transfer: For fall 1981, 339 students applied, 75 were accepted, and 57 enrolled. A 2.0 average as well as a modest income are required. D grades do not transfer. There is a residency requirement of 1 year. All students must complete, at the college, 32 of the 132 credits required for a bachelor's degree. Application deadlines are the same as those for freshmen.

Visiting: Informal guided tours and classroom visits can be arranged by the admissions office. Visitors can stay overnight at the school.

Financial Aid: All of the students receive financial aid covering the educational cost of $5100 per student each year. A variety of scholarships and loans are available. A substantial form of financial aid is the Labor Program, in which all students participate by working at least 10 hours per week, enabling them to earn from one-third to one-half of their school costs. One of the basic policies of the college is that qualified students shall not be prevented from attending school because of lack of money. All applicants must submit either the FAF or the FFS. The deadline for financial aid application is August 1 (fall) or January 1 (spring). The college is a member of CSS.

Foreign Students: Six percent of the full-time students come from foreign countries. Special counseling and special organizations are available for these students.

Admissions: Foreign students must achieve a TOEFL score of at least 500 (the University of Michigan Language Test is also accepted). No college entrance exams are required.

Procedure: The application deadline is December 31 for fall entry. There is a special fee for foreign students for the first year's room and board. Health insurance is required and is available through the college for a fee.

Admissions Contact: John S. Cook, Director of Admissions.

BRESCIA COLLEGE
Owensboro, Kentucky 42301   B-3
(502) 685-3131

F/T: 182M, 306W	Faculty: 54; IIB, -$
P/T: 170M, 232W	Ph.D.'s: 30%
Grad: none	S/F Ratio: 9 to 1
Year: sems, ss	Tuition: $80 p/c
Appl: open	R and B: $1620
409 applied	306 accepted
ACT: 20	COMPETITIVE

Brescia College, founded in 1950, is a small, 4-year, liberal arts college owned by and affiliated with the Roman Catholic Church. The library contains 90,000 volumes, has 107,000 microfilm items on file, and subscribes to 500 periodicals.

Environment: The 6-acre urban campus is located within 200 miles of Louisville, Kentucky; Nashville, Tennessee; Cincinnati, Ohio; and Indianapolis, Indiana; and is 45 miles from Evansville, Indiana. Campus housing includes dormitories and apartments.

Student Life: About 75% of the students are residents of Kentucky and bordering states; 20% reside on campus. Six percent are minority-group members. About 60% are Catholic, and 40% are Protestant. Attendance at religious services is not required. Campus housing is single-sex; there are visiting privileges. Students may keep cars on campus.

Organizations: There are numerous extracurricular activities on campus. Religious organizations include Young Christian Students.

Sports: The college participates on an intercollegiate level in 1 sport (tennis). There are 5 intramural sports.

Handicapped: About 90% of the campus is accessible to wheelchairs. Ramps, elevators, special parking, class scheduling, and specially equipped rest rooms are provided.

Graduates: The freshman dropout rate is 17%; 38% remain to graduate.

Services: Students receive the following services free of charge: psychological counseling, career counseling, and tutoring.

Programs of Study: The college grants the B.A., B.S., B.Mus., and B.Mus.Ed. degrees. Associate degrees are also awarded. Bachelor's

292 KENTUCKY

degrees are offered in the following subjects: BUSINESS (accounting, business administration, business education), EDUCATION (elementary, special), ENGLISH (English), FINE AND PERFORMING ARTS (art, art education, music, music education), LANGUAGES (French), MATH AND SCIENCES (biology, chemistry, mathematics), SOCIAL SCIENCES (history, psychology, social sciences, sociology).

Required: All undergraduates must take 6 hours of religious studies and 45 hours of liberal arts courses.

Special: The college offers a B.G.S. degree. Student-designed majors are permitted.

Honors: Two national honor societies are represented on campus.

Admissions: About 75% of those who applied were accepted for the 1981-82 freshman class. The ACT scores of those who enrolled were as follows: 30% below 21, 40% between 21 and 23, 15% between 24 and 25, 12% between 26 and 28, and 3% above 28. Applicants should rank in the upper half of their class and have a C average or better. Impressions made during the interview, personality, and the extracurricular activities record are also considered important.

Procedure: Either the SAT or the ACT is acceptable and should be taken by March of the senior year. There are no application deadlines; freshmen are admitted in the fall, spring, and summer. Applications should be submitted with a $15 fee. Admissions are on a rolling basis.

Special: AP and CLEP credit is accepted.

Transfer: For fall 1981, 63 students applied, 58 were accepted, and 49 enrolled. A GPA of at least 2.0 and a minimum composite score of 15 on the ACT or 900 on the SAT are required. D grades do not transfer. All students must complete, at the college, 32 of the 128 credits required for a bachelor's degree. There are no application deadlines; transfer students are admitted in the fall, spring, and summer.

Visiting: The college conducts open door tours each Wednesday which include lunch and class visits. Arrangements to stay overnight at the college should be made with the admissions office.

Financial Aid: About 68% of all students receive aid. Twelve percent work part-time on campus. The average award to freshmen is $2100. The college participates in all federal and state financial aid programs. Grants, jobs, and loans are available. In addition, no-need scholarships are provided. March 31 is the preferred date by which to apply for fall entry, December 1 is the deadline for spring entry. The FAF is required.

Foreign Students: Four percent of the full-time students come from foreign countries. Special counseling and special organizations are available for these students.

Admissions: Foreign students must achieve a TOEFL score of at least 500. No college entrance exams are required.

Procedure: There are no application deadlines; foreign students are admitted in the fall, spring, and summer. They must present a doctor's statement and proof of funds adequate to cover 1 year of study.

Admissions Contact: Annalita Lancaster, Dean of Admissions.

CAMPBELLSVILLE COLLEGE D-3
Campbellsville, Kentucky 42718 (502) 465-8158

F/T: 282M, 331W
P/T: 22M 46W
Grad: none
Year: sems, ss
Appl: open
403 applied
ACT: required

Faculty: 44; IIB, --$
Ph.D.'s: 40%
S/F Ratio: 15 to 1
Tuition: $2440
R and B: $1770
362 accepted 292 enrolled
LESS COMPETITIVE

Campbellsville College, founded in 1906, is a church-related liberal arts college affiliated with the Kentucky Baptist Convention. The library houses 90,000 volumes and subscribes to 650 periodicals.

Environment: The 30-acre campus is located in a rural area 85 miles from Louisville. There are 15 campus buildings including dormitories and married student housing.

Student Life: Seventy percent of the students are from Kentucky, 27% are from bordering states, and 1% are from foreign countries. Fifty percent live on campus. Campus housing is single-sex. Students may keep cars on campus. Convocation attendance is required.

Organizations: There are no fraternities or sororities. The college sponsors 32 extracurricular groups, the most active of which are the Harlequins (drama), Circle K (civics), the student government, and the Pep Club. The college sponsors religious counselors and organizations for Protestant and Catholic students.

Sports: The college fields 4 intercollegiate teams for men and 3 for women. There are 7 intramural sports for men and 6 for women.

Graduates: Thirty-five percent of the freshmen drop out at the end of the year; 60% remain to graduate. About 30% of the students pursue graduate studies after graduation.

Services: The college provides free placement services, health care, career counseling, and psychological counseling. Tutoring and remedial instruction are provided for a fee.

Programs of Study: The college confers the B.A., B.S., and B.M. degrees. Associate degrees are also awarded. Bachelor's degrees are offered in the following subjects: BUSINESS (accounting, business administration, business education), EDUCATION (elementary), ENGLISH (English), FINE AND PERFORMING ARTS (art, art education), MATH AND SCIENCES (biology, chemistry, mathematics), PRE-PROFESSIONAL (dentistry, law, medicine, ministry, pharmacy, social work), SOCIAL SCIENCES (economics, government/political science, history, psychology, social work, sociology). Degrees in church music and church recreation are also offered.

Required: All undergraduates are required to take 48 credits of general education. There are distribution requirements as well. All seniors are required to take the GRE.

Special: The college offers a remedial English-math orientation counseling program once a week for the first semester. There is an internship program in state government offices for political science majors. A 3-2 dual degree in engineering is offered in conjunction with the Georgia Institute of Technology.

Honors: There are 5 honor society chapters on campus.

Admissions: Ninety percent of those who applied were accepted for the 1981-82 freshman class. The ACT scores of those who enrolled were as follows: 60% below 21, 20% between 21 and 23, 8% between 24 and 25, 7% between 26 and 28, and 5% above 28. A minimum average of 2.0 or a composite score of 16 on the ACT is required. Eight Carnegie units from an accredited high school are recommended for admission. School recommendations and personality are also considered.

Procedure: The ACT and high school recommendations are required. Junior year test scores are accepted tentatively pending receipt of final high school transcript. There are no application deadlines; freshmen are admitted in the fall, spring, and summer. The college has a rolling admissions plan. There is a $20 application fee. The college has a special admissions program for disadvantaged students whereby the normal application fees are waived and tutors are provided through the work-study program. Interviews are recommended, but not required.

Special: Up to 36 credit hours are available through CLEP subject tests.

Transfer: Transfer students must have a GPA of at least 2.0 and an ACT composite score of at least 16. All students must complete, at the college, 30 of the 128 credits required for a bachelor's degree. One-third of the credits required for the major or minor must be completed at Campbellsville. There are no application deadlines; transfer students are admitted in the fall, spring, and summer.

Visiting: There are no regular orientations for prospective students. Guides are available for informal weekday visits to the campus. Visitors may sit in on classes and may stay at the school. The admissions office will make arrangements.

Financial Aid: About 80% of the students receive aid. About 35% work part-time on campus. The average aid package is $2400. A total of $1.6 million comes through 5 federally funded programs (Pell grants, SEOG, state grants, work study, NDSL), and the college's own scholarships and grants. Students may receive scholarships for academic achievement and performance grants for their skills in art, drama, music, and athletics. Many students also receive aid through church-related scholarships and grants. The FAF is required of all applicants and the preferred application date is March 15. Late applications will also be considered.

Foreign Students: One percent of the students come from foreign countries.

Admissions: Foreign students must achieve a TOEFL score of at least 500 and must take the ACT.

Procedure: Application deadlines are April 1 (fall) and December 1 (spring). Foreign students must present proof of health and proof of funds adequate to cover 1 year of study. Health insurance is required.

Admissions Contact: James C. Coates, Director of Admissions.

CENTRE COLLEGE OF KENTUCKY D-3
Danville, Kentucky 40422 (606) 236-5211

F/T, P/T: 450M, 325W	Faculty: 65; IIB, +$
Grad: none	Ph.D.'s: 80%
Year: 4-2-4	S/F Ratio: 12 to 1
Appl: May 1	Tuition: $4750
SAT or ACT: required	R and B: $2100
	COMPETITIVE

Centre College, founded in 1819, is an independent liberal arts college. The library contains 125,000 volumes and subscribes to 750 periodicals.

Environment: The 75-acre campus is located in a rural community 35 miles from Lexington and consists of 23 buildings, including 9 dormitories for men and 7 dormitories for women.

Student Life: Sixty percent of the students are from Kentucky. Seventy percent come from public schools. About 95% of the students live on campus.

Organizations: There are 6 national fraternities to which 55% of the men belong. There are no sororities. On-campus events include the performing-arts series and concerts.

Sports: The college participates in 9 intercollegiate sports for men and 5 for women, and sponsors 4 coed teams. Eight intramural sports are offered for men and 9 for women.

Handicapped: About 50% of the campus is accessible to wheelchair-bound students. Special facilities include wheelchair ramps, parking areas, elevators, and specially equipped rest rooms. Special class scheduling is possible.

Graduates: The freshman dropout rate is 5%; 60% remain to graduate. Fifty percent of the graduates pursue further study; 8% to 10% enter medical school, 5% enter dental school, and 10% to 15% enter law school. Up to 25% pursue careers in business and industry.

Services: Students receive the following free services: placement and career counseling, health care, and psychological counseling.

Programs of Study: All programs lead to the B.A. and B.S. degrees. Bachelor's degrees are offered in the following subjects: BUSINESS (management), EDUCATION (elementary, secondary), ENGLISH (English), FINE AND PERFORMING ARTS (art, music, theater/dramatics), LANGUAGES (French, German, Spanish), MATH AND SCIENCES (biochemistry, biology, chemical physics, chemistry, ecology/environmental science, mathematics, physics, psychobiology), PHILOSOPHY (philosophy, religion), SOCIAL SCIENCES (economics, government/political science, history, psychology). Thirty-five percent of degrees conferred are in math and science, 20% are in social sciences, 15% are in economics and management, and 10% are in English.

Special: Students may design their own majors. The 6½-week winter term provides time for independent and special studies in a student's major in the junior and senior years. The winter term is also used for off-campus study and travel in the U.S. and abroad.

Honors: Seven honor societies are represented on campus, including Phi Beta Kappa.

Admissions: Eighty-five percent of those who applied were accepted for a recent freshman class. Of those who enrolled, the SAT scores were as follows: Verbal—40% between 500 and 599, 20% between 600 and 700, and 3% above 700; Math—44% between 500 and 599, 24% between 600 and 700, and 3% above 700. On the ACT, 19% scored between 20 and 23, 44% between 24 and 26, 27% between 27 and 28, and 10% above 28. Graduation from an accredited high school is required along with 16 Carnegie units. The school also considers advanced placement or honors courses, recommendations by school officials, extracurricular activities, leadership record, impressions made during an interview, and evidence of special talents.

Procedure: The SAT or ACT is required and should be taken by March. Applications for fall admission should be submitted before May 1 for priority consideration. Freshmen also are admitted at midyear. The CRDA is observed. A $15 fee must accompany the application.

Special: An early admissions plan and a deferred admissions plan are available. AP and CLEP credit is accepted.

Transfer: Good academic standing and the basic freshman requirements are necessary. D grades are unacceptable. There is a 1½-year residency requirement.

Visiting: Visits are recommended. Guided tours can be scheduled with the admissions office during the school year. Visitors may sit in on classes and remain overnight on campus.

Financial Aid: Forty percent of all students receive aid through the school. The college makes available grants, loans, and work contracts. About 40% of the students work part-time. The college is a member of CSS. Need is the main consideration in determining awards. The FAF is required. The deadline for aid application is March 15.

Admissions Contact: Hal Smith, Dean of Admissions.

CUMBERLAND COLLEGE E-4
Williamsburg, Kentucky 40769 (606) 549-2200

F/T: 658M, 903W	Faculty: 107; n/av
P/T: 145M, 211W	Ph.D.'s: 40%
Grad: none	S/F Ratio: 16 to 1
Year: sems, ss	Tuition: $2124
Appl: Aug. 1	R and B: $1408
SAT: 419V 441M ACT: 16	LESS COMPETITIVE

Cumberland College, established in 1889, is a small, coeducational liberal arts college, controlled by the Southern Baptist Church. It offers liberal arts and science, general education, and preprofessional and professional programs. The library contains 97,000 volumes and 11,000 microfilm items, and subscribes to 820 periodicals.

Environment: The 30-acre campus is located in a rural area 105 miles from Lexington. The 22 main buildings include 7 single-sex dormitories that accommodate 600 men and 600 women.

Student Life: About 70% of the students come from Kentucky. About 70% reside on campus. Five percent are members of minority groups. The majority of students are Baptists. Chapel attendance once a week is compulsory. Students may keep cars on campus. Freshman women must observe a weeknight curfew.

Organizations: In addition to special-interest and service clubs, the college has music and drama groups and sponsors films, lectures, art shows, and debates. There are no fraternities or sororities.

Sports: The college competes on an intercollegiate level in 6 sports for men and 4 for women. Five intramural sports are offered for men and women.

Handicapped: There are no facilities for physically handicapped students.

Graduates: Approximately 20% of the freshmen drop out by the end of the first year, and 40% remain to graduate. About 65% of graduates go on to graduate or professional study; 3% enter medical school, 3% enter dental school, and 2% enter law school. Twenty percent pursue careers in business and industry.

Services: Students receive free health care, placement assistance, career counseling, tutoring, remedial instruction, and psychological counseling.

Programs of Study: The college confers the B.A. and B.S. degrees. Associate degrees also are available. Bachelor's degrees are offered in the following subjects: BUSINESS (accounting, business administration, computer science), EDUCATION (early childhood, elementary, health/physical, secondary, special), ENGLISH (English), FINE AND PERFORMING ARTS (art, art education, music, music education), HEALTH SCIENCES (medical technology, nursing), MATH AND SCIENCES (biology, chemistry, mathematics), PHILOSOPHY (religion), PREPROFESSIONAL (dentistry, engineering, law, medicine, ministry, pharmacy, social work, veterinary), SOCIAL SCIENCES (government/political science, history, psychology, sociology). About 35% of the degrees conferred are in education, and 30% are in business.

Required: All students are required to take 18 hours of personal development, 13 hours of symbolics/communication, and 18 hours of natural and social sciences.

Special: A 3-year bachelor's degree is available. Combination degree programs are offered in medical technology and in engineering.

Honors: Special honors programs are available. Two national honor societies have chapters on campus.

Admissions: The SAT scores of those who enrolled in a recent class were as follows: Verbal—18% scored between 500 and 600, 3% between 600 and 700, and 1% above 700; Math—22% scored between 500 and 600, 5% between 600 and 700, and 3% above 700. On the ACT, 19% scored between 20 and 23, 8% between 24 and 26, 2% between 27 and 28, and 1% above 28. Candidates should have a GPA of 2.0 or better and an ACT score of 16, rank in the upper three-fourths of their graduating class, and have completed 15 Carnegie units of work.

Procedure: The SAT or ACT is required. There is a $5 application fee. The application deadlines are August 1 (fall), January 1 (spring), and June 1 (summer). Admission is on a rolling basis.

294 KENTUCKY

Special: Early decision and early admissions plans are available. CLEP and AP credit is accepted.

Transfer: For fall 1981, 125 transfer students applied, 115 were accepted, and 93 enrolled. Transfers are accepted for all classes. D grades are transferable. Students must earn, at the college, at least 30 of the 128 credits required for a bachelor's degree. Transfer application deadlines are the same as those for freshmen.

Visiting: Informal guided tours and classroom visits are encouraged. Tours can be scheduled 6 days a week. Inquiries on campus visits and lodging should be addressed to the admissions office.

Financial Aid: About 90% of all students receive financial aid; 40% work part-time on campus. The college awards 150 scholarships to freshmen. Loans are available from the federal government, local banks, the college, and other sources. The average award to freshmen from all sources in 1981-82 was $3000. The application deadlines for financial aid are April 1 (fall), January 1 (spring), and June 1 (summer); the FAF or FFS is required. The college is a member of CSS.

Foreign Students: Foreign students enrolled full-time at the college represent about 1% of the student body. Special organizations are provided for these students.

Admissions: Students must score 500 or better on the TOEFL. No academic exams are required.

Procedure: Application deadlines are August 1 (fall), January 1 (spring), and June 1 (summer). Students must submit a completed school medical form as proof of good health. The cost of health insurance is included in their school fees.

Admissions Contact: Topper Criscillis, Director of Admissions.

EASTERN KENTUCKY UNIVERSITY E-3
Richmond, Kentucky 40475 (606) 622-2106

F/T: 4479M, 5589W	Faculty: n/av; IIA, av$
P/T: 767M, 901W	Ph.D.'s: 55%
Grad: 539M, 1119W	S/F Ratio: 15 to 1
Year: sems, ss	Tuition: $626 ($1780)
Appl: open	R and B: $1350
5593 applied	5106 accepted 3524 enrolled
ACT: required	LESS COMPETITIVE

Eastern Kentucky University, founded in 1906, is a state-controlled coeducational institution that offers graduate and undergraduate training. The library contains 553,270 volumes and 470,000 microfilm items, and subscribes to 3400 periodicals.

Environment: The 325-acre campus is located in a rural area 26 miles from Lexington. The 14 dormitories accommodate 2026 women and 2454 men, and apartments or trailers are available for married students.

Student Life: About 85% of the students come from Kentucky, and 77% live on campus. Seven percent are members of minority groups. Dormitories are single-sex; there are no visiting privileges. Students may have cars on campus.

Organizations: There are 16 fraternities and 18 sororities; about 5% of the men and 5% of the women belong. Among the 89 special-interest groups are various religious clubs. Many cultural and social events are sponsored by the university and the student government.

Sports: The university competes on an intercollegiate level in 13 sports. Twelve intramural sports are offered.

Handicapped: Facilities for the physically handicapped include wheelchair ramps, special parking, elevators, specially equipped rest rooms, and lowered drinking fountains and telephones. About 20% of the campus is accessible. Special class scheduling is possible. There is one counselor for handicapped students.

Graduates: The freshman dropout rate is 30%, and 30% remain to graduate. Forty percent of those who graduate seek advanced degrees.

Services: The following services are available free to students: placement and career counseling, health care, tutoring, remedial instruction, and psychological counseling. Graduates also may use placement services.

Programs of Study: The university confers B.A. and B.S. degrees. Associate, master's, and doctoral degrees also are available. Bachelor's degrees are offered in the following subjects: AREA STUDIES (urban), BUSINESS (accounting, coal-mining administration), EDUCATION (early childhood, elementary, health/physical, industrial, secondary, special), ENGLISH (English, journalism, speech), FINE AND PERFORMING ARTS (art, art education, music, music education, radio/TV, studio art, theater/dramatics), HEALTH SCIENCES (environmental health, medical technology, nursing, occupational therapy, speech therapy), LANGUAGES (French, German, Russian, Spanish), MATH AND SCIENCES (biology, chemistry, earth science, ecology/environmental science, geology, mathematics, physics, statistics), PHILOSOPHY (philosophy, religion), PREPROFESSIONAL (dentistry, engineering, forestry, law, medicine, pharmacy, veterinary), SOCIAL SCIENCES (anthropology, economics, geography, government/political science, history, psychology, sociology, transportation).

Special: Students may design their own majors. The university has a College of Law Enforcement. It is possible to earn combined B.A.-B.S. degrees in a 5-year program. The B.G.S. degree is also offered.

Honors: Four national honor societies have chapters on campus. The English department offers an honors program for entering students who score above 26 on the ACT.

Admissions: About 91% of those who applied were accepted for the 1981-82 freshman class. Candidates must be graduates of an approved high school. Out-of-state residents must rank in the upper half of their high school class. Admissions officials also consider recommendations by high school officials, personality, and impressions made during an interview.

Procedure: The ACT is required. Application deadlines are open, and admission is on a rolling basis. Freshmen are admitted to all terms. There is no application fee.

Special: Early and deferred admissions and early decision plans are available.

Transfer: For fall 1981, 1107 students applied, 1008 were accepted, and 624 enrolled. An average of C or better and ACT scores are required. Students must earn, at the university, at least 30 of the 128 credits generally required for a bachelor's degree.

Visiting: Campus visits can be arranged with the admissions office.

Financial Aid: About 80% of the students receive aid; 12% work part-time on campus. A variety of scholarships, loans, and employment programs are available. The average award to 1981-82 freshmen from all sources was $850. Applications should be submitted by April 15 (fall), November 15 (spring), or March 15 (summer). The FAF is required; the university is a member of CSS.

Foreign Students: About 167 foreign students are enrolled full-time at the university, which provides special counseling and organizations for them.

Admissions: Applicants must score 550 or better on the University of Michigan Language Test. They also must take the ACT.

Procedure: Applications must be submitted at least 30 days before the start of the semester in which the student seeks to enroll. Students must present a certificate of good health and show evidence of adequate funds for 1 year. Health insurance is available through the university for a fee.

Admissions Contact: Charles Ambrose, Dean of Admissions.

GEORGETOWN COLLEGE D-2
Georgetown, Kentucky 40324 (502) 863-8493

F/T: 475M, 519W	Faculty: 63; IIB, av$
P/T: 21M, 44W	Ph.D.'s: 55%
Grad: 34M, 170W	S/F Ratio: 14 to 1
Year: sems, ss	Tuition: $3101 ($3110)
Appl: July. 1	R and B: $1950
573 applied	503 accepted 325 enrolled
SAT: 450V 470M	ACT: 20 COMPETITIVE

Georgetown College, founded in 1829, is a liberal arts college affiliated with the Kentucky Baptist Convention. It has a graduate as well as an undergraduate division. The library contains 120,000 volumes and 16,000 microfilm items, and subscribes to 670 periodicals.

Environment: The 52-acre suburban campus is located in the heart of the bluegrass section of Kentucky in a city of 10,500. Among the 29 major buildings is Giddings Hall, a Greek Revival structure dating back to 1840. 14 single-sex dormitories accommodate 550 women and 525 men. The college also sponsors fraternity and sorority houses.

Student Life: Approximately 65% of the students come from Kentucky, and 95% of entering freshmen come from public schools. About 90% of the students live on campus—72% in the dormitories and the rest in sorority and fraternity houses. Eighty-five percent of the students are Protestant and 10% are Catholic. Sixty percent of the students are members of the supporting church. Four percent are members of minority groups. There are no visiting privileges in the dormitories. Students may keep cars on campus.

Organizations: Five fraternities and 3 sororities have chapters on campus, and about 35% of the men and 30% of the women belong. Student organizations sponsor dramatic, musical, and social activities.

Sports: The college competes on an intercollegiate level in 7 sports for men and 4 for women. Eight intramural sports are offered for men and 6 for women.

Handicapped: Special facilities for the physically handicapped include wheelchair ramps, special parking, and elevators. About half the campus is accessible to wheelchairs.

Graduates: The freshman dropout rate is 20%, and 55% remain to graduate. About 50% of the graduates pursue advanced degrees; 6% enter medical school, 1% enter dental school, and 8% enter law school. Thirty percent begin careers in business and industry.

Services: Students receive free placement aid, career counseling, and health care.

Programs of Study: The college confers the B.A., B.S., B.Mus.Ed., and B.S.Med.Tech. degrees. Master's degrees are also offered. Bachelor's degrees are offered in the following subjects: AREA STUDIES (American), BUSINESS (accounting, business administration, secretarial science), EDUCATION (elementary), ENGLISH (English, speech), FINE AND PERFORMING ARTS (art, art education, theater/dramatics), HEALTH SCIENCES (medical technology), LANGUAGES (French, German, Spanish), MATH AND SCIENCES (biology, chemistry, ecology/environmental science, mathematics, physics), PHILOSOPHY (philosophy, religion), PREPROFESSIONAL (home economics, social work), SOCIAL SCIENCES (economics, government/political science, history, psychology, sociology). About 22% of the degrees conferred are in business, and 20% are in education.

Required: All students must take 56 semester hours in liberal arts and sciences, including 2 courses in religion.

Special: Students may design their own majors. A combination degree program is offered in engineering and industrial management.

Honors: Fifteen national honor societies have chapters on campus. Most departments offer honors programs.

Admissions: About 88% of those who applied were accepted for the 1981–82 freshman class. The ACT scores of those who enrolled were as follows: 47% below 21, 28% between 21 and 23, 9% between 24 and 25, 10% between 26 and 28, and 2% above 28. An applicant must be a graduate of an accredited high school with 18 units of work, rank in the upper 50% of his or her class, and have earned a grade point average of 2.6 or better. Admissions officers also consider recommendations by high school officials, extracurricular activities, and leadership record.

Procedure: The ACT or SAT is required. There is a $15 application fee. Application deadlines are July 1 (fall), December 15 (spring), and May 1 (summer). Admissions are on a rolling basis.

Special: CLEP and AP credit is accepted.

Transfer: For fall 1981, 88 applications were received, 78 were accepted, and 58 students enrolled. Transfers are accepted for freshman, sophomore, and junior classes; D grades are not acceptable. An average of 2.0 or better is required. Students must earn 30 of the last 36 semester hours at the college, with 128 hours required for a bachelor's degree. Transfer application deadlines are the same as those for freshmen.

Visiting: Orientations for prospective students are scheduled regularly. Informal guided tours and classroom visits can be arranged 6 days a week with the admissions office.

Financial Aid: About 75% of all students receive aid; 20% work part-time on campus. The average award to 1981–82 freshmen from loans, scholarships, and work contracts totaled $2000. The deadlines for aid applications are April 1 (fall), December 15 (spring), and May 1 (summer). The FAF must be filed; the college is a member of CSS.

Foreign Students: Foreign students are accepted.

Admissions: Students must score 487 or better on the TOEFL. No academic exams are required.

Procedure: Application deadlines are June 1 (fall), November 1 (spring), and March 1 (summer). Students must present proof of good health and of adequate funds. They must carry health insurance, which is available through the college for a fee.

Admissions Contact: Don De Borde, Director of Admissions.

KENTUCKY 295

KENTUCKY STATE UNIVERSITY D–2
Frankfort, Kentucky 40601 (502) 564-5813

F/T: 614M, 561W Faculty: 110; IIA, –$
P/T: 384M, 693W Ph.D.'s: 44%
Grad: 79M, 54W S/F Ratio: 21 to 1
Year: sems, ss Tuition: $660 ($1814)
Appl: open R and B: $1390
978 applied 723 accepted 702 enrolled
ACT: 16 **LESS COMPETITIVE**

Kentucky State University, founded in 1886, is a state-supported liberal arts institution. It was founded as a college for blacks. Today, the enrollment is about 56% white. The library contains over 135,248 volumes and 8852 microfilm items, and subscribes to more than 1081 periodicals.

Environment: The 344-acre campus is situated on a hill overlooking the city of Frankfort, about 25 miles from Lexington. Among the new or revamped facilities are a football stadium, a baseball diamond, 2 renovated women's dormitories, and a new academic services building. Dormitories house about one-third of the students.

Student Life: About 60% of the students are from the South, 25% from the Midwest, and 15% from the North. Ninety-nine percent of the entering freshmen come from public schools. Twenty-nine percent of the students live on campus. Almost 55% are minority-group members. Campus housing is both coed and single-sex. There are visiting privileges in single-sex dorms. Students may keep cars on campus. The university provides day-care services to all students, faculty, and staff for a fee.

Organizations: There are 5 fraternities and 4 sororities on campus; 15% of the men and 20% of the women belong to 1 of them. Plays, lectures, small concerts, talent shows, and other student activities are popular.

Sports: There are intercollegiate teams in 6 sports for men and 5 for women. There are 4 intramural sports for both men and women.

Handicapped: About 80% of the campus is accessible to handicapped students. Special facilities include wheelchair ramps and parking. There are no students with visual or hearing impairments currently enrolled.

Graduates: About 15% of the graduates pursue graduate or professional study; 1% enter medical school, 1% dental school, and 1% law school. Forty percent pursue careers in business or industry. At the end of the freshman year, 30% of the students drop out; 35% remain to graduate.

Services: The following services are available to students free of charge: health care, placement, career and psychological counseling, and tutoring.

Programs of Study: The university confers the B.A. and B.S. degrees. Master's and associate degree programs are also available. Bachelor's degrees are offered in the following subjects: BUSINESS (accounting, business administration, business education, computer science, management, marketing), EDUCATION (early childhood, elementary, health/physical, industrial), ENGLISH (English), FINE AND PERFORMING ARTS (art, art education, music, music education), HEALTH SCIENCES (medical technology), MATH AND SCIENCES (biology, chemistry, mathematics), PREPROFESSIONAL (home economics), SOCIAL SCIENCES (government/political science, history, social sciences, sociology). Twenty-eight percent of all undergraduate degrees conferred are in education, 35% in business, and 14% in social sciences.

Admissions: About 74% of those who applied were accepted for the 1981–82 freshman class. The ACT scores of those who enrolled were: 94% below 21, 2% between 21 and 23, 0.4% between 24 and 25, 0.4% between 26 and 28, and 0% above 28. For Kentucky residents, there is no minimum class rank or GPA required. Out-of-state residents should rank in the top half of their graduating class, have an ACT score of at least 18, and have an average of at least 2.0. All students must be graduates of accredited high schools and have completed 17 Carnegie units.

Procedure: The ACT is required. There is no application deadline for in-state applicants. Out-of-state applicants must apply at least 2 weeks before registration. Admissions are granted on a rolling basis. There is no application fee.

Special: The university has an early admissions plan for which there is no application deadline. AP and CLEP credit is accepted.

Transfer: For fall 1981, 148 transfer students enrolled. Good standing at the applicant's previous college or university is required. C grades or better transfer. Students must complete, at the university, the last 32 semester hours of the 128 or more required for the bachelor's degree.

296 KENTUCKY

Visiting: There are regular orientation programs for prospective students. Guides are available for informal visits to the university. Visitors may sit in on classes, but may not stay overnight at the school. The admissions office handles arrangements.

Financial Aid: Scholarships, work-study, and loans are available. The aid application deadline is July 1. About 75% of all students receive financial aid; 30% work part-time on campus. The university, a member of CSS, requires the FAF, KSU, or FAA.

Foreign Students: Two percent of the full-time students come from foreign countries. Special counseling is available to these students.

Admissions: Foreign students must achieve a score of 525 on the TOEFL. The ACT is also required.

Procedure: There is no application deadline for foreign students, who are admitted to the fall, spring, and summer terms. Foreign students must take a medical examination and carry health insurance, which is available through the university for a fee. Proof of funds adequate to cover the proposed course of study is required, as is a $1000 deposit to guarantee payment of fees.

Admissions Contact: Fred D. Williams, Director of Admissions.

KENTUCKY WESLEYAN COLLEGE B-3
Owensboro, Kentucky 42301 (502) 926-3111

F/T: 305M, 392W Faculty: 51; IIB, +$
P/T: 80M, 161W Ph.D.'s: 44%
Grad: none S/F Ratio: 14 to 1
Year: 4-1-4, ss Tuition: $2880
Appl: open R and B: $1630
ACT: 20 **LESS COMPETITIVE**

Kentucky Wesleyan College, founded in 1858, is a liberal arts college affiliated with the United Methodist Church. Almost half the graduates go into the educational field. The library houses 93,000 books and subscribes to 500 periodicals.

Environment: The 60-acre, self-contained campus is located in the city of Owensboro (population 61,000), 115 miles from Louisville. The Georgian-style buildings include 4 dormitories, 3 of them grouped around a main quad area with the library and the student union.

Student Life: Eighty percent of the students are from Kentucky. Ninety percent come from public schools. Fifty-five percent live on campus. Ten percent are members of minority groups. Dormitories are single-sex, with visiting privileges. Students may keep cars on campus. Day care is available.

Organizations: There are 3 fraternities and 2 sororities, to which 25% of the men and 20% of the women belong. Cultural events include on-campus theater productions.

Sports: Six intercollegiate sports are offered for men and 4 for women. Eight intramural sports are offered.

Handicapped: Sixty percent of the campus is accessible to handicapped students. Special facilities include wheelchair ramps, parking areas, elevators, specially equipped rest rooms, and lowered drinking fountains and telephones. Special class scheduling is also possible.

Graduates: The freshman dropout rate is 15%, and 75% remain to graduate. About 45% of the graduates seek advanced degrees; 5% enter medical school, 3% enter dental school, and 5% enter law school. About 50% pursue careers in business and industry.

Services: The following services are available free to students: psychological counseling, career counseling, tutoring, and remedial instruction. Fees are charged for health-care services.

Programs of Study: The college awards the B.A. and B.S. degrees. Associate degrees also are available. Bachelor's degrees are offered in the following subjects: BUSINESS (accounting, business administration, management), EDUCATION (elementary, health/physical, secondary, special), ENGLISH (English), FINE AND PERFORMING ARTS (art, art education, art history, commercial illustration, music, music education, radio/TV, sacred music, theater/dramatics), HEALTH SCIENCES (medical technology, physical therapy), LANGUAGES (French, German, Spanish), MATH AND SCIENCES (biology, chemistry, mathematics, physics), PHILOSOPHY (religion), PREPROFESSIONAL (dentistry, engineering, law, library science, medicine, ministry, optometry, pharmacy, veterinary), SOCIAL SCIENCES (government/political science, history, psychology, sociology). Twenty-one percent of all degrees are conferred in health sciences, 16% in the arts, 14% in social sciences, 12% in business, 11% in education, and 11% in preprofessional subjects.

Required: Freshmen are required to take a writing workshop. All undergraduates must satisfy distribution requirements.

Special: The English department offers a creative writing program. Students may take the junior year abroad. Students may design their own majors.

Honors: Five honor societies have chapters on campus.

Admissions: In a recent freshman class, the ACT scores were as follows: 12% between 20 and 23, 6% from 24 to 26, 6% from 27 to 28, and 4% above 28. ACT scores should be at least 17. If the SAT is taken, scores should total at least 800. Applicants for admission should have completed 12 Carnegie high school units, including 4 years of English. They should rank in the top half of their graduating class and have at least a C average.

Procedure: Either the SAT or the ACT should be taken. The exams should be taken in May of the junior year, or in December of the senior year. Application deadlines are open. New students are accepted for all terms. There is a $15 application fee. Admissions decisions are made on a rolling basis.

Special: The college offers early decision, early admissions, and deferred admissions plans. CLEP and AP credit is available.

Transfer: Transfers are accepted for all classes. A GPA of 2.0 is required; D grades are not acceptable. Students must complete, at the college, at least 30 semester hours of the 128 required for a bachelor's degree.

Visiting: Regular "get-acquainted" activities are held for prospective students. Guides are available for informal visits to the campus. Visitors may sit in on classes and stay overnight on campus.

Financial Aid: About 70 scholarships are available to freshmen. Those applying for aid should submit the FAF. About 80% of all students receive aid. The deadline for aid applications is early May, although the college prefers that they be sent in by March 15. Tuition may be paid in installments.

Foreign Students: About 2% of the students are from foreign countries. Special counseling and organizations are provided for these students.

Admissions: Students must score 590 or better on the TOEFL. No academic exams are required.

Procedure: Application deadlines are open; students are admitted in fall, spring, and summer. Students must present a completed university medical form as proof of good health and also must show evidence of adequate funds for 1 year. They must carry health insurance, which is available through the college for a fee.

Admissions Contact: Richard Button, Director of Admissions.

LOUISVILLE SCHOOL OF ART D-2
Anchorage, Kentucky 40204 (502) 589-5867

F/T: 29M, 39W Faculty: 7; IIB, n/av
P/T: 27M, 32W Ph.D.'s: none
Grad: none S/F Ratio: 13 to 1
Year: sems, ss Tuition: $2180
Appl: open R and B: n/app
28 applied 28 accepted 28 enrolled
SAT, ACT: not required **SPECIAL**

The Louisville School of Art, founded in 1909, was created to promote art and art education. Its library and resource center contains 75,000 volumes, more than 6000 monographs, and 11,000 visual aids, and subscribes to 63 periodicals.

Environment: The school is located in a historic section of Louisville, 1 mile from the center of the city. A recently purchased building is listed in the National Historical Register. The school has no housing facilities.

Student Life: About 85% of the students are from Kentucky. Twelve percent are members of minority groups. Students may have cars on campus.

Organizations: There are no fraternities or sororities. The city of Louisville offers cultural and social entertainment.

Sports: Intercollegiate touch football is offered for men and women.

Handicapped: There are no special facilities for the handicapped.

Graduates: Eight percent of the freshmen drop out during the first year, and 40% remain to graduate. About 30% of the graduates seek advanced degrees.

Services: Free placement aid, career counseling, and health care are available.

Programs of Study: The school awards the B.F.A. degree in various art and fine arts programs. About 30% of the degrees are conferred in painting, 20% in sculpture, 10% in metalsmithing, and 10% in textiles.

Required: All students must take basic foundation courses.

Admissions: All students who applied for admission in 1981-82 were accepted. Applicants should have completed a full high school curriculum with an average of 2.0 or better. Admission depends on a review of the students' portfolio, grades, and impressions made during the required personal interview.

Procedure: Applicants must submit a portfolio of their work. Applications for full-time study must be submitted with a $15 fee. Application deadlines are open. The school follows a rolling admissions policy.

Special: CLEP credit is offered.

Transfer: All 10 transfer students who applied for fall 1981 admission were accepted and enrolled. Transfers are accepted for all classes. Students must be in good standing, with a 2.0 or better average. D grades transfer. Students must earn 129 credits for a bachelor's degree.

Visiting: Visits can be arranged through the office of admissions.

Financial Aid: Forty percent of the students receive aid through the school. There are federal, state, and other loans and grants. CWS is available, and 20% of the students participate. The average amount of aid to 1981-82 freshmen from all sources totaled $2500. The application deadline is April 1. The FAF is required.

Admissions Contact: Linda A. Probus, Director of Admissions.

MOREHEAD STATE UNIVERSITY E-2
Morehead, Kentucky 40351 (606) 783-2186

F/T: 2084M, 2341W
P/T: 296M, 389W
Grad: 584M, 1045W
Year: sems, ss
Appl: open
3761 applied
ACT: 16

Faculty: 283; IIA, av$
Ph.D.'s: 49%
S/F Ratio: 16 to 1
Tuition: $606 ($1760)
R and B: $1700
3388 accepted   2277 enrolled
NONCOMPETITIVE

Morehead State University, founded in 1922, offers undergraduate programs in the liberal arts and sciences, education, and vocational areas. The library contains 400,000 volumes and 270,607 microtexts, and subscribes to 2154 periodicals.

Environment: The 412-acre campus is located in a rural community of 7200 inhabitants, midway between Lexington and Ashland. The 100 buildings include single-sex dormitories and apartments for men and women. The university also sponsors off-campus mobile homes and married-student housing.

Student Life: About 80% of the students come from Kentucky. Most have had public school educations. About 60% live on campus. About 4% are members of minority groups. Dormitories are single-sex, with visiting privileges. Students may keep cars on campus.

Organizations: Fraternities, sororities, clubs, publications, performing groups, student government, and regular social and cultural events are sponsored by the university.

Sports: The athletic program includes intercollegiate competition in 8 sports for men and 8 for women, as well as 17 intramural sports for men and 15 for women.

Graduates: About 44% of the freshmen drop out by the end of the first year, and 29% remain to graduate.

Services: The university provides free health care, psychological counseling, tutoring, remedial instruction, career counseling, and placement aid.

Programs of Study: Undergraduate degrees conferred are the B.A., B.S., B.B.A., B.U.S., B.S.W., B.M., and B.Mus.Ed. Associate and master's degrees also are available. Bachelor's degrees are offered in the following subjects: BUSINESS (accounting, business administration, business education, computer science, data processing, finance, industrial economics, management, marketing, office administration, real estate/insurance, secretarial studies), EDUCATION (adult, early childhood, elementary, health/physical, industrial, secondary, special), ENGLISH (English, journalism, speech), FINE AND PERFORMING ARTS (art, music, music education, radio/TV, theater/dramatics), HEALTH SCIENCES (dietetics, health education, medical laboratory technology, medical technology, nursing), LANGUAGES (French, German, Spanish), MATH AND SCIENCES (biology, chemistry, earth science, ecology/environmental science, geology, mathematics, physics), PHILOSOPHY (philosophy, religion), PREPROFESSIONAL (agriculture, agriculture education, clothing and textiles, dentistry, engineering, food service technology, home economics, interior design,

law, legal assistant, medicine, mining technology, social work, veterinary), SOCIAL SCIENCES (corrections, economics, geography, government/political science, history, parks and recreation, psychology, public administration, social sciences, sociology).Over half of the degrees are conferred in education and the social sciences.

Required: The general education requirement includes courses in communications and humanities, science and mathematics, social sciences, and health.

Special: A general university studies degree is offered.

Honors: Honors work is possible. Eleven honor societies have chapters on campus.

Admissions: About 90% of those who applied were accepted for the 1981-82 freshman class. The ACT scores of those who enrolled were as follows: 76% below 21, 14% between 21 and 23, 6% between 24 and 25, 4% between 26 and 28, and 1% above 28. Graduates of accredited Kentucky high schools are admitted without examination. Out-of-state applicants must rank in the upper half of their graduating class. Students should have completed 15 Carnegie units.

Procedure: The ACT is required for placement purposes. Deadlines are open. New students are admitted in fall, at midyear, and in summer. Notification is made on a rolling basis. There is no application fee.

Special: CLEP credit is accepted.

Transfer: At least 300 transfer students enroll each fall. A 2.0 average is needed. D grades do not transfer. Students must study at the university for at least 1 year, completing at least 32 of the 128 semester hours required for a bachelor's degree.

Visiting: Campus tours with student guides can be arranged. Visitors may sit in on classes.

Financial Aid: About 60% of the students receive aid; 20% work part-time on campus. The university participates in federal programs such as NDSL, BEOG/SEOG, and CWS. Other loan programs, state aid, and part-time campus jobs are available. Freshman scholarships also are available. Financial aid applications and the FAF should be filed by April 30 (fall), November 1 (spring), and April 30 (summer).

Foreign Students: About 100 foreign students are enrolled full-time at the university. Special counseling and organizations are provided.

Admissions: Students must score 550 or better on the TOEFL, and take the ACT.

Procedure: Applications should be submitted at least 30 days before the beginning of the term in which the student seeks to enroll. Students must submit a completed medical form as proof of health and show a certified bank statement as evidence of adequate funds for 1 year.

Admissions Contact: Rondal Hart, Director of Admissions.

MURRAY STATE UNIVERSITY B-4
Murray, Kentucky 42071 (502) 762-3741

F/T: 2667M, 2904W
P/T: 326M, 411W
Grad: 563M, 851W
Year: sems, ss
Appl: Aug. 1
2500 applied
ACT: 18

Faculty: 350; IIA, av$
Ph.D.'s: 65%
S/F Ratio: 18 to 1
Tuition: $626 ($1780)
R and B: $1460
2250 accepted   1501 enrolled
LESS COMPETITIVE

Murray State University, established in 1922, is a publicly controlled institution. The library contains 500,000 volumes and 19,000 microtexts, and subscribes to 2200 periodicals.

Environment: The 200-acre campus is located in a rural area, 120 miles from Nashville, Tennessee. The residence halls accommodate 1850 men and 1850 women. Fraternity houses and married-student housing also are available. The university maintains a 350-acre farm.

Student Life: About 80% of the students are from Kentucky. Half of the students live on campus. Seven percent are members of minority groups. Both single-sex and coed dorms are available; there are visiting privileges in the single-sex dorms. Students may keep cars on campus.

Organizations: About 15% of the men and 10% of the women belong to one of the 12 national fraternities and 8 national sororities on campus.

Sports: The university offers 9 intercollegiate sports for men and 7 for women. Six intramural sports are offered for men and 5 for women.

Handicapped: About 90% of the campus is accessible to handicapped students. Special facilities for the physically handicapped include wheelchair ramps, special parking, elevators, and lowered telephones.

298 KENTUCKY

Graduates: The freshman dropout rate is 35%, and 60% remain to graduate. Approximately 25% of the graduates pursue advanced degrees, including 1% each who enter medical, dental, and law school.

Services: Students receive free placement aid, career counseling, tutoring, remedial instruction, and psychological counseling. Fees are charged for health-care services. Placement services are also available to graduates.

Programs of Study: The university offers the B.A., B.F.A., B.Mus., B.Mus.Ed., B.S., B.S.Agr., B.S.H.E., B.S.N., B.S.B., and B.S.V.T.E. degrees. Associate and master's degrees also are available. Bachelor's degrees are offered in the following subjects: BUSINESS (accounting, business administration, business education, computer science, finance, management, marketing, real estate/insurance), EDUCATION (early childhood, elementary, health/physical, industrial, secondary), ENGLISH (English, journalism, literature, speech), FINE AND PERFORMING ARTS (art, art education, music, music education, radio/TV, studio art, theater/dramatics), HEALTH SCIENCES (medical technology, nursing, speech therapy), LANGUAGES (French, German, Spanish), MATH AND SCIENCES (biology, chemistry, earth science, mathematics, physics), PHILOSOPHY (philosophy), PREPROFESSIONAL (agriculture, architecture, dentistry, engineering, forestry, home economics, law, library science, medicine, ministry, pharmacy, social work, veterinary), SOCIAL SCIENCES (economics, geography, government/political science, history, psychology, sociology).

Required: All students must complete 9 semesters of English, 9 of humanities, 12 of science and math, and 12 of social science.

Special: Combined degree programs are offered in medical technology and engineering.

Honors: Fifteen national honor societies have chapters on campus.

Admissions: About 90% of those who applied were accepted for the 1981–82 freshman class. The ACT scores of those who enrolled were as follows: 75% below 21, 10% between 21 and 23, 8% between 24 and 25, 6% between 26 and 28, and 3% above 28. Candidates must have graduated from an accredited high school. Out-of-state applicants must rank in the upper third of their high school class and score at least 20 on the ACT. Advanced placement or honors courses, and the leadership and extracurricular activities record are also considered.

Procedure: All candidates must take the ACT. A rolling admissions policy is used. Application deadlines are August 1 (fall), December 1 (winter), and May 1 (summer). There is no application fee.

Special: A deferred admissions plan is available. CLEP and AP credit is accepted.

Transfer: For fall 1981, 900 transfer students applied, 800 were accepted, and 530 enrolled. Candidates must present a GPA of 2.0 or better. Students must earn, at the university, 32 of the 128 semester hours required for a bachelor's degree. Application deadlines are the same as those for freshmen.

Visiting: Informal guided tours and classroom visits can be arranged with the director of school relations.

Financial Aid: About 60% of the students receive financial aid; 22% work part-time on campus. Scholarships and loans are available from the university. Additional loan funds may be obtained through federal sources. The average award to freshmen from all sources in 1981–82 was $2000. The FAF or FFS is required. The deadlines for financial aid applications are April 1 (fall), October 15 (spring), and March 1 (summer).

Foreign Students: The foreign students enrolled full-time at the university make up about 1% of the student body. Special counseling and organizations are provided.

Admissions: Applicants must score 500 or better on the TOEFL. No academic exams are required.

Procedure: Application deadlines are January 1 (fall) and July 1 (spring). Students must present a completed medical record as proof of good health and must show evidence of adequate funds for 1 year. Health insurance is not required, but is available through the university for a fee.

Admissions Contact: Wilson Gantt, Dean of Admissions.

NORTHERN KENTUCKY UNIVERSITY D–1
Highland Heights, Kentucky 41076   (606) 572-5220

F/T: 2203M, 2074W	Faculty: 265; IIA, av$
P/T: 1393M, 2085W	Ph.D.'s: 70%
Grad: 574M, 524W	S/F Ratio: 25 to 1
Year: sems, ss	Tuition: $626 ($11780
Appl: open	R: $550
2183 applied	2183 accepted 1711 enrolled
ACT: required	NONCOMPETITIVE

Northern Kentucky University, founded in 1968, is a publicly controlled institution offering programs in liberal arts, preprofessional and technical training, business, and education. The library contains 169,000 volumes and subscribes to 1865 periodicals.

Environment: The 300-acre campus at Highland Heights is located in a suburban area 7 miles from Cincinnati, Ohio. There are dormitories, which are equipped for the handicapped.

Student Life: Out-of-state enrollment is limited to 20%, and 10% of the students are from outside the state. About 5% of the students live on campus. Four percent are members of minority groups. Dormitories are single-sex, with visiting privileges. Students may keep cars on campus. Day-care services are available to all students, faculty, and staff.

Organizations: Four fraternities and 3 sororities have chapters on campus; about 200 men and 100 women belong. Campus activities include student government, publications, political clubs, dances, a coffeehouse, and cultural events.

Sports: Intercollegiate competition is offered in 3 sports for men and 3 for women. Ten intramural sports are offered for men and women.

Handicapped: The campus is completely accessible to handicapped students. Special facilities include wheelchair ramps, parking areas, elevators, and specially equipped rest rooms.

Services: The following services are available free to students: health care, psychological counseling, placement aid, career counseling, tutoring, and remedial instruction. The career services office also is open to graduates.

Programs of Study: The university confers the B.A., B.F.A., B.Mus., B.Mus.Ed., B.S.N., B.S.W., and B.S. degrees. Associate, master's, and law degrees also are available. Bachelor's degrees are offered in the following subjects: AREA STUDIES (international, urban), BUSINESS (accounting, business education, computer science, management, marketing), EDUCATION (elementary, health/physical, industrial), ENGLISH (English, speech), FINE AND PERFORMING ARTS (art, art education, art history, commercial art, music, music education, radio/TV, studio art, theater/dramatics), HEALTH SCIENCES (medical technology, nursing), MATH AND SCIENCES (biology, chemistry, geology, mathematics, physics), PHILOSOPHY (philosophy), PREPROFESSIONAL (social work), SOCIAL SCIENCES (anthropology, economics, government/political science, history, psychology, public administration, sociology).

Required: Required general studies courses make up about 25% of a student's baccalaureate program.

Special: Students may design their own majors.

Admissions: The university has an open admissions policy and accepts almost all applications received. The GED is accepted in lieu of a high school diploma. Students seeking admission to the nursing, human services, and radiologic technology programs should contact the admissions office concerning applications requirements and deadlines.

Procedure: The ACT is required for placement purposes and must be taken by July 15. Junior-year scores also may be submitted. Applications may be submitted through the first week of classes of the term in which the student seeks to enroll. Admissions decisions are made on a rolling basis. There is no application fee.

Special: The university has an early admissions plan. AP and CLEP credit is accepted.

Transfer: Good academic standing and a GPA of 2.0 or better are required. Students must earn, in residence, at least 30 semester hours of the 128 required for a bachelor's degree.

Visiting: Regular orientations are held for prospective students. Guides are also available for informal weekday visits. The admissions office will make arrangements.

Financial Aid: About 40% of the students receive aid. Scholarships, grants, jobs, and loans are available. Applicants for financial aid must file the FAF. The priority deadline for aid applications is April 1. The university is a member of CSS.

Foreign Students: One percent of the full-time students are from foreign countries. The university offers these students an intensive English course, special counseling, and special organizations.

Admissions: Applicants must take the TOEFL (minimum score 500), the University of Michigan Language Test, or the college's own test of English proficiency. The ACT also is required.

Procedure: Application deadlines are June 20 (fall) and November 15 (spring). Students must submit a completed health form as proof of good health and provide evidence of adequate funds to complete their degree program. Students are required to carry health insurance, which is available through the university for a fee.

Admissions Contact: James L. Alford, Director of Admissions.

PIKEVILLE COLLEGE   F-3
Pikeville, Kentucky 41501   (606) 432-9332

F/T: 239M, 275W	Faculty:	55; IIB, −$
P/T: 34M, 68W	Ph.D.'s:	35%
Grad: none	S/F Ratio:	12 to 1
Year: 4-1-4, ss	Tuition:	$2550
Appl: Sept. 10	R and B:	$1920
460 applied	460 accepted	297 enrolled
ACT: 18		NONCOMPETITIVE

Pikeville College, established in 1889, is a small, private liberal arts college affiliated with the United Presbyterian Church. Its emphasis is on preparing elementary and secondary teachers, but it also offers education in the liberal arts, preprofessional fields, and technological fields. The library holds 65,000 volumes and subscribes to 123 periodicals.

Environment: The 27-acre campus is located in a rural area of eastern Kentucky, 20 miles from the Virginia border. The 10 buildings on campus include 4 dormitories and on-campus apartments.

Student Life: Most students are residents of Kentucky. Almost all come from public schools. About 40% live on campus. Four percent are members of minority groups. Dormitories are single-sex, with visiting privileges. Students may keep cars on campus. Alcoholic beverages are not permitted on campus.

Organizations: There are no fraternities or sororities. Among the many organizations on campus are religious, music, drama, and special-interest groups.

Sports: The college competes in 4 intercollegiate sports for men and 2 for women. Seven intramural sports are offered for men and women. Two nearby state parks offer hiking, horseback riding, and water sports.

Handicapped: There are no special facilities for physically handicapped students, and only 10% of the campus is accessible.

Graduates: About 35% of the freshmen drop out during their first year, and 42% remain to graduate. Of those, 28% continue their studies; 3% enter medical school, 1% enter dental school, and 5% enter law school. About 40% pursue careers in business and industry.

Services: Free health care, tutoring, remedial instruction, career counseling, and placement services are offered.

Programs of Study: The college confers the B.A., B.S., and B.B.A. degrees. Associate degrees also are available. Bachelor's degrees are offered in the following subjects: BUSINESS (accounting, business administration, business education, management, marketing), EDUCATION (elementary, health/physical, secondary, special), ENGLISH (English), FINE AND PERFORMING ARTS (art, art education, music, music education), HEALTH SCIENCES (medical technology), MATH AND SCIENCES (biology, chemistry, mathematics), PHILOSOPHY (religion), SOCIAL SCIENCES (economics, government/political science, history, psychology, sociology). Associate degrees are granted in early childhood education and in nursing. About 35% of the bachelor's degrees are granted in education and 25% in preprofessional fields.

Required: Four semester hours of physical education and 6 semester hours of Bible study are required.

Special: A 3-1 program in medical technology with Methodist Hospital leads to the B.S. degree and certification. Special freshman studies and independent study are also offered.

Honors: Departmental honors programs in English and humanities are offered.

Admissions: All applicants for the 1981-82 freshman class were accepted. Candidates should have completed 16 high school units and have an average of at least C. Non-high-school graduates must have a GED with a total score of 250.

Procedure: Either the SAT or ACT is required and should be taken by the end of the first semester at college. Applications should be submitted with a $10 fee by September 10 (fall), January 1 (winter), January 25 (spring), or May 20 (summer). An interview is recommended. There is a rolling admissions plan.

Special: AP credit is available.

Transfer: A 2.0 GPA is recommended. Students must earn, at the college, at least 30 of the 128 semester hours required for a bachelor's degree.

Visiting: At orientation meetings, prospective students are given a tour and talk to academic, financial aid, and admissions personnel. Informal visits, during which visitors may sit in on classes, can be arranged through the admissions office for weekdays.

Financial Aid: About 78% of the students receive aid; 12% work part-time on campus. The college awards several scholarships each year. Students may also apply for college and federal loans. Tuition may be paid in installments. Aid applications submitted by March 31 will be given priority. The FAF is required; the college is a member of CSS.

Foreign Students: Fewer than 1% of the full-time students are from foreign countries. Special counseling is provided.

Admissions: Students must score at least 500 on the TOEFL or take the ELS. No academic exams are required.

Procedure: Application deadlines are May 15 (fall) and October 15 (spring). Students must submit a completed institutional form as proof of health and should present evidence of adequate funds for 1 year. There is a special application fee for foreign students. Health insurance, though not required, is available through the college for a fee.

Admissions Contact: William R. Little, Dean of Admissions.

SPALDING COLLEGE   D-2
Louisville, Kentucky 40203   (502) 585-9911

F/T: 25M, 400W	Faculty:	94; IIA, n/av
P/T: 50M, 280W	Ph.D.'s:	40%
Grad: 220 M&W	S/F Ratio:	15 to 1
Year: sems, ss	Tuition:	$2700
Appl: Aug. 15	R and B:	$1730
SAT: 450V 400M	ACT: 19	LESS COMPETITIVE

Spalding College, founded in 1920, is an independent liberal arts college affiliated with the Roman Catholic Church. The library contains 106,000 volumes and subscribes to 620 periodicals.

Environment: The campus occupies two blocks in the heart of Louisville. The college is built around the post-Civil War mansion that was its first home. The mansion is listed on the National Register of Historic Places. Two dormitories house 300 men and women.

Student Life: Eighty-six percent of the students are from Kentucky, and 15% live on campus. About 78% come from public schools. Three-fourths of the students are Catholic, but chapel attendance is not required. Single, out-of-town, full-time freshmen and sophomores must live in the dormitories.

Organizations: Extracurricular activities include chorus, drama, art, publications, and special-interest clubs. The college also sponsors concerts, films, lectures, plays, and the Holly Ball. There are religious organizations on campus. The college has no fraternities or sororities.

Sports: At least 3 intramural sports are offered.

Handicapped: Special facilities for handicapped students include wheelchair ramps, parking areas, elevators, and lowered telephones. Special class scheduling is possible.

Graduates: About 12% to 15% of the graduates seek advanced degrees.

Services: The following services are available free to students: health care, psychological counseling, placement and career counseling, and tutoring or remedial instruction. Placement services also are available to alumni.

Programs of Study: Undergraduate programs lead to the B.A. or B.S. degree. Master's degrees are also granted. Bachelor's degrees are offered in the following subjects: BUSINESS (business administration), EDUCATION (early childhood, elementary, secondary), ENGLISH (English), FINE AND PERFORMING ARTS (art, radio/TV, theater/dramatics), HEALTH SCIENCES (medical technology, nursing, speech therapy), LANGUAGES (Spanish), MATH AND SCIENCES (biology, chemistry, mathematics), PHILOSOPHY (humanities, philosophy, religion), PREPROFESSIONAL (home economics, library science, social work), SOCIAL SCIENCES (history, psychology, sociology). Fifty-seven percent of undergraduate degrees are conferred in health sciences and 14% in preprofessional subjects.

Special: The college is a member of the Kentuckiana Metroversity, a 6-member consortium enabling students to take courses at any of the member colleges. Students are permitted to study abroad for 1 year. Combined B.A.-B.S. degrees are possible. The college confers the B.G.S. degree. Students may design their own majors.

KENTUCKY

Honors: Two national honor societies have chapters on campus.

Admissions: Seventy-four percent of those who applied were accepted for a recent freshman class. The ACT scores of those who enrolled were as follows: 23% scored between 20 and 23, 5% between 24 and 26, 7% between 27 and 28, and 2% above 28. The college prefers applicants who are graduates of accredited high schools, rank in the upper half of their class, have at least a C average, and have completed 16 Carnegie units. The admissions committee also considers extracurricular activities, leadership record, and advanced placement or honors courses.

Procedure: Either the SAT or the ACT should be taken in May. Deadlines for applications are August 15 (fall), January 2 (winter), and May 15 (summer). Notification is made within 3 weeks after all credentials are submitted. There is a $10 application fee. Freshmen are admitted to all sessions.

Special: AP and CLEP credit is available.

Transfer: Most applicants are accepted; about 75 enroll each year. D grades do not transfer. Students must spend at least 1 academic year in residence.

Visiting: Guides are available for informal weekday visits to the campus. Visitors may sit in on classes and stay overnight at the school. Contact the admissions office for arrangements.

Financial Aid: About 77% of the students receive aid. The college awards several scholarships to freshmen each year. Loans are available from the federal government, local banks, and the college itself. Spalding also participates in the SEOG and nursing scholarship programs. Every student offered financial aid must be willing to accept a package that may consist of grants, loans, and a job offer. Tuition may be paid on the installment plan. Need is the primary consideration in determining financial aid awards. The college is a member of the CSS. The FAF is required. The priority deadline for aid applications is March 15.

Admissions Contact: Mary Pat Nolan, Director of Admissions.

THOMAS MORE COLLEGE   D-1
Fort Mitchell, Kentucky 41017   (606) 341-5800

F/T: 402M, 344W   Faculty: 54; IIB, — $
P/T: 176M, 377W   Ph.D.'s: 48%
Grad: none   S/F Ratio: 20 to 1
Year: sems, ss   Tuition: $3338
Appl: Aug. 15   R and B: $2080
411 applied   405 accepted   242 enrolled
SAT: 450V 550M   ACT: 23   COMPETITIVE+

Thomas More College, founded in 1921 as Villa Madonna College, is a Catholic college of liberal arts and sciences. The library contains 80,000 volumes and subscribes to 625 periodicals.

Environment: The 310-acre campus is located in Fort Mitchell, in a suburban area about 10 miles from Cincinnati, Ohio. The two main buildings contain 9 academic wings, a student union, and administration offices. Three dormitories house 235 students.

Student Life: About 63% of the students are from Kentucky. Fifteen percent live on campus. About 4% are members of minority groups. Seventy-eight percent are Catholic, 20% are Protestant. Dormitories are single-sex, with visiting privileges. Students may keep cars on campus.

Organizations: There is 1 national fraternity, 1 local fraternity, and 1 local sorority. The college offers many student groups. Popular campus events include the spring hot-air balloon race; a fall arts and crafts fair; and plays, dances, and other student-initiated activities.

Sports: The college fields intercollegiate teams in 4 sports for men and 3 for women. Seven intramural sports are offered for men and 5 for women.

Handicapped: About 90% of the campus is accessible to handicapped students. Special facilities include wheelchair ramps, parking areas, elevators, and specially equipped rest rooms.

Graduates: Thirty percent of the freshmen drop out by the end of the first year, and 50% remain to graduate. About 30% of the graduates pursue advanced degrees; 3% enter medical school, 2% enter dental school, and 6% enter law school.

Services: The following services are available free to students: psychological counseling, career counseling, and tutoring.

Programs of Study: The college confers the B.A. and B.S.N. degrees. Associate degrees also are available. Bachelor's degrees are offered in the following subjects: BUSINESS (accounting, banking, business administration, computer science, real estate/insurance), EDUCATION (elementary, secondary), ENGLISH (English), FINE AND PERFORMING ARTS (art, theater/dramatics), HEALTH SCIENCES (medical technology, nursing), MATH AND SCIENCES (biology, chemistry, mathematics, physics), PHILOSOPHY (philosophy, religion), PREPROFESSIONAL (social work), SOCIAL SCIENCES (economics, history, psychology). Thirty-eight percent of the undergraduate degrees are conferred in business, 17% in math and sciences, and 15% in social sciences.

Special: The general requirements are flexible, and the college encourages double majors. There are 3-2 and 3-3 combination degree programs in engineering, and a 3-1 program in medical technology. A B.G.S. degree is offered, and students may design their own majors. Additional majors are available through a consortium of 10 area colleges. A cooperative education program is available in 13 major fields.

Honors: Two honor societies have chapters on campus.

Admissions: Almost all applicants (98%) were accepted for the 1981-82 freshman class. The SAT scores of those who enrolled were as follows: Verbal—48% below 500, 51% between 500 and 599, 1% between 600 and 700, and 0% above 700; Math—16% below 500, 43% between 500 and 599, 32% between 600 and 700, and 9% above 700. Of those who took the ACT, 14% scored below 21, 41% between 21 and 25, and 16% above 26. SAT scores should be above 450, the ACT composite score above 18. Students must have a C average or better, be graduates of accredited high schools, and rank in the top half of their class. If the student is graduating from a Catholic school, 2 years of religion are also required. The college also considers advanced placement or honors courses, recommendations by school officials, and special talents.

Procedure: The SAT or ACT is required. The application, high school records, test scores, and recommendations from a high school counselor should be submitted by August 15 (fall), December 30 (spring), or April 30 (summer). There is a $25 application fee. Admissions decisions are made on a rolling basis.

Special: Early and deferred admissions plans are available. AP and CLEP credit is offered.

Transfer: Transfer applicants are accepted for all classes. Students must complete, at the college, at least 38 of the 128 credits required for a bachelor's degree. Application deadlines are the same as those for freshmen.

Visiting: A slide show, financial aid discussion, tour, class visits, and faculty interviews are all available for prospective students. Guides are available for informal weekday visits. Visitors may stay overnight at the school. Contact the admissions office for arrangements.

Financial Aid: About 68% of the students receive aid through the school. A freshman scholarship fund is available, as are federal loans and part-time jobs. Aid applications and the FAF should be submitted by March 1. Tuition may be paid in installments. The college is a member of CSS.

Foreign Students: Foreign students enrolled full-time make up about 2% of the total enrollment. The college provides an intensive English course and program, special counseling, and special organizations.

Admissions: Foreign students must take the TOEFL. No academic exams are required.

Procedure: Application deadlines are the same as those for other freshmen. Students must undergo a college physical and show evidence of adequate funds for at least 1 year of study. They also must carry health insurance, which is available through the college for a fee.

Admissions Contact: Catherine M. Grady, Director of Admissions.

TRANSYLVANIA UNIVERSITY   D-3
Lexington, Kentucky 40508   (606) 233-8242

F/T: 343M, 371W   Faculty: 54; IIB, +$
P/T: 18M, 18W   Ph.D.'s: 67%
Grad: none   S/F Ratio: 14 to 1
Year: 4-4-1, ss   Tuition: $4800
Appl: open   R and B: $2100
460 applied   415 accepted   222 enrolled
SAT: 440V 467M   ACT: 21   COMPETITIVE

Transylvania University, established in 1780, is a private, coeducational school that seeks to provide a liberal arts education within a Christian environment. The library contains 100,000 volumes and subscribes to 500 periodicals.

Environment: The 27-acre campus is located in the city of Lexington. The 10 main campus buildings include Old Morrison, a national historical landmark built in 1833, and 3 dormitories.

Student Life: About 80% of the students are from Kentucky, and 72% of the freshmen come from public schools. Eighty percent of the students live on campus. Seven percent are members of minority groups. Dormitories are single-sex, with visiting privileges. Students may keep cars on campus.

Organizations: Four fraternities and 4 sororities have chapters on campus, and about 55% of the men and women belong. These groups do not maintain housing facilities. Campus cultural activities include theater, glee club, films, lectures, band, and publications. Various religious organizations are available, and places of worship for the 3 major faiths are nearby.

Sports: The school sponsors intercollegiate teams in 6 sports for men and 6 for women. Intramural sports also are available.

Handicapped: With the exception of elevators, there are no special facilities for handicapped students. The university will provide assistance to students if necessary.

Graduates: About 20% of the freshmen drop out by the end of the first year, and 60% remain to graduate. Fifty-five percent of the graduates pursue advanced degrees; 10% enter medical school, 10% enter dental school, and 10% enter law school.

Services: The following services are provided free to students: health care, placement aid, career counseling, and tutoring.

Programs of Study: All programs lead to the B.A. degree. Bachelor's degrees are offered in the following subjects: BUSINESS (accounting, business administration, computer science, hotel/restaurant administration, management), EDUCATION (elementary, health/physical, secondary), ENGLISH (English), FINE AND PERFORMING ARTS (art, art education, music, music education), HEALTH SCIENCES (medical technology), MATH AND SCIENCES (biology, chemistry, mathematics, physics), PHILOSOPHY (philosophy, religion), PREPROFESSIONAL (dentistry, engineering, medicine, pharmacy, veterinary), SOCIAL SCIENCES (anthropology, government/political science, history, psychology, sociology). Most degrees are conferred in health sciences and business.

Required: A core curriculum in humanities, social sciences, natural sciences, foreign language, and mathematics is required.

Special: Students may spend their junior year abroad. A 2-2 program in physical therapy is offered. Students may design their own majors.

Honors: Eight honor societies have chapters on campus. An honors program is available in English.

Admissions: Ninety percent of those who applied were accepted for the 1981-82 freshman class. The recommendation of the high school is the prime consideration in selecting applicants. Applicants must have an average of 2.0 or better. Preference is given to applicants who rank in the top half of their high school classes, have a B average, scored at least 450 on each part of the SAT, and have completed 12 Carnegie units at an accredited high school. Also considered are impressions made during an interview and special talents. The university seeks a national distribution of its student body.

Procedure: Students must take the SAT or the ACT, preferably in December of the senior year. An interview is recommended. Application deadlines are open; students are admitted to all terms. Applicants are notified on a rolling basis. There is a $15 application fee, which may be waived for applicants with financial need.

Special: Early and deferred admissions plans are offered. AP and CLEP credit is available.

Transfer: A C average and a score of 800 on the SAT or 18 on the ACT are required. About 75% of transfer applicants are accepted, and 20 to 25 enroll annually. D grades do not transfer. Students must complete 36 course units for a bachelor's degree.

Visiting: Guides are available for informal weekday visits. Visitors may sit in on classes and stay overnight at the school. Contact the admissions office for arrangements.

Financial Aid: About 45% of the students receive aid through the school, and 29% work part-time on campus. The university is a member of CSS and offers scholarships, NDSL loans, and campus employment. The average award to freshmen from all sources in 1981-82 was $4360. Tuition reductions are available for children of ordained ministers. Tuition may be paid in installments. Applicants for aid should file the FAF, FFS, or SFS by April 1 (fall) or November 1 (winter).

Foreign Students: One percent of the full-time students are from foreign countries.

Admissions: Applicants must score 550 or better on the TOEFL. No academic exams are required.

Procedure: Applications should be submitted at least 1 week before the start of the term in which the student wishes to enroll. Students must show evidence of adequate funds for 1 year.

Admissions Contact: Wendy Warner, Director of Admissions.

UNION COLLEGE E-4
Barbourville, Kentucky 40906 (606) 546-4151

F/T: 183M, 233W	Faculty: 42; IIA, n/av
P/T: 80M, 152W	Ph.D.'s: 55%
Grad: 129M, 253W	S/F Ratio: 24 to 1
Year: sems, ss	Tuition: $3050
Appl: open	R and B: $1640
394 applied	367 accepted	164 enrolled
SAT or ACT: required	LESS COMPETITIVE

Union College, established in 1879, is a private, liberal arts institution related to the Methodist Church. The library contains 74,431 volumes and 1684 microfilm items, and subscribes to 568 periodicals.

Environment: The 100-acre campus is located in a rural area about 100 miles from Lexington, Kentucky. Living facilities include dormitories and married student housing.

Student Life: About 81% of the undergraduates come from Kentucky; 85% of entering freshmen come from public schools. Approximately 52% reside on campus. Chapel services are voluntary. About 82% of the students are Protestant, and 4% are Catholic. Six percent are minority-group members. Campus housing is single-sex; there are visiting privileges. Students may keep cars on campus.

Organizations: Campus organizations include 1 local fraternity and 1 local sorority. In addition, there are Catholic and Protestant organizations, professional societies, and social and special interest groups.

Sports: The college competes on an intercollegiate level in 9 sports for men and 8 for women. There are 6 intramural sports for men and 4 for women.

Handicapped: Union College is in the process of complying with Section 504 of the Rehabilitation Act of 1973.

Graduates: The freshman dropout rate is 25%; 46% remain to graduate. About 43% of the students pursue graduate study after graduation: 13% enter medical school, 3% dental school, and 17% law school. Approximately 40% pursue careers in business and industry.

Services: Students receive the following services free of charge: placement, career counseling, tutoring, and remedial instruction. Placement services are available to graduates as well as to undergraduates.

Programs of Study: The college confers the B.A., B.S., and B.Mus.Ed. degrees. Associate and master's degrees are also awarded. Bachelor's degrees are offered in the following subjects: BUSINESS (accounting, business administration, business education, music/business, office administration), EDUCATION (elementary, health/physical, secondary), ENGLISH (English, journalism, speech), FINE AND PERFORMING ARTS (music, music education, theater/dramatics), MATH AND SCIENCES (biology, mathematics), PHILOSOPHY (Christian education, religion), PREPROFESSIONAL (dentistry, engineering, law, medicine, ministry, optometry, pharmacy, physical therapy, science education, veterinary), SOCIAL SCIENCES (history, psychology, social work, sociology). About 10% of the degrees are conferred in education, 18% in business.

Required: The only specific course required is English composition.

Special: Student-designed majors are permitted. Special programs include independent study, a Washington semester, a 3-2 engineering program with the University of Kentucky, and 3-1 programs in both medicine and medical technology.

Honors: There are several honor societies including Alpha Psi Omega.

Admissions: About 93% of those who applied were accepted for the 1981-82 freshman class. Consideration is also given to recommendations, extracurricular activities, and personality.

Procedure: Either the SAT or ACT is required. It is suggested that all tests be taken by January of the senior year. There are no application deadlines. There is a $15 application fee. The college has a rolling admissions policy; notification is sent promptly after all credentials are received. Freshmen are admitted to all terms.

Special: Early decision, early admissions, and deferred admissions plans are available. CLEP general and subject exams are accepted.

Transfer: For fall 1981, 90 students applied and 40 enrolled. Applicants must take the SAT or ACT. D grades do not transfer. All students

302 KENTUCKY

must complete, at the college, 30 of the 128 credits required for a bachelor's degree. There are no application deadlines; transfer students are accepted for all classes.

Visiting: Campus tours and classroom visits can be arranged by the admissions office. Visits are best scheduled on Fridays.

Financial Aid: About 74% of all students receive financial aid. About 36% work part-time on campus. Scholarships and loans are available. Applications for honors scholarships should be filed by April 1. The deadline for financial aid applications is August 15. The college is a member of CSS. The FAF is required.

Foreign Students: Two percent of the full-time students come from foreign countries. Special organizations are available for these students.

Admissions: Foreign students must achieve a TOEFL score of at least 500 and must take the SAT or ACT.

Procedure: There are no application deadlines; foreign students are admitted in all terms. They must present proof of funds adequate to cover 4 years of study.

Admissions Contact: James Garner, Director of Admissions.

UNIVERSITY OF KENTUCKY   D-3
Lexington, Kentucky 40506   (606) 257-1606

F/T: 8335M, 7068W	Faculty:	n/av; I, av$
P/T: 1257M, 1650W	Ph.D.'s:	95%
Grad: 2562M, 2235W	S/F Ratio:	16 to 1
Year: sems, ss	Tuition:	$740 ($2318)
Appl: June 1	R and B:	$2090
7741 applied	6588 accepted	3251 enrolled
ACT: 20		COMPETITIVE

The University of Kentucky is a state-controlled land-grant institution founded in 1865. Sixteen colleges and schools confer undergraduate, graduate, and professional degrees. The library contains more than 1.75 million volumes and 1.86 million microforms, and subscribes to 25,000 periodicals.

Environment: The 350-acre main campus is located in Lexington, a city of more than 200,000. The 100 main buildings include a fine arts center and the Sanders-Brown Center for the Study of Aging. Residence facilities include a complex housing 2300 men and women in 23-story twin towers. On-campus apartments, fraternity and sorority houses, and married-student housing also are available. The university also contains a medical center, an agricultural science center (home of the National Tobacco Research Laboratory), and farms and research stations throughout the state with more than 24,000 acres devoted to agricultural research.

Student Life: About 86% of the students are from Kentucky. About 25% live on campus. Six percent are members of minority groups. Dormitories are both single-sex and coed, and there are visiting privileges in single-sex dorms. Drinking on campus is forbidden. Women resident students follow a sign-out procedure. Students may have cars on campus.

Organizations: There are 24 fraternities and 16 sororities on campus to which about 15% of the men and 15% of the women belong. The university sponsors many extracurricular activities, both social and cultural. There are religious organizations on campus for the 3 major faiths.

Sports: The university fields intercollegiate teams in 9 sports for men and 7 for women. Men can compete in 6 club and 7 intramural sports, women in 6 club and 6 intramural sports.

Handicapped: Special facilities for the handicapped include wheelchair ramps, parking areas, elevators, specially equipped rest rooms, and lowered drinking fountains and telephones. Visually impaired students use recorded textbooks and other academic materials in braille. Special class scheduling can be arranged. A director of handicapped student services heads a staff of several volunteer assistants.

Graduates: About 24% of the freshmen drop out by the end of the first year, and 30% remain to graduate. About 35% of the graduates seek advanced degrees, and 50% enter careers in business and industry.

Services: The following services are available free to students: psychological counseling, placement aid, career counseling, and some tutoring. Fees are charged for health care. Placement services also are available to graduates.

Programs of Study: The university grants the B.A., B.S., B.S.Ag., B.S.Med.Tech., B.Arch., B.S.N., B.B.A., B.F.A., B.A.Ed., B.S.C.E., B.S.E.E., B.S.M.E., B.S.Met.E., B.S.Ch.E., B.S.Agr.E., B.Mus., B.S.H.E., and B.S.Pharm. Master's and doctoral degrees also are awarded. Bachelor's degrees are offered in the following subjects: AREA STUDIES (Latin American, Russian), BUSINESS (accounting, business administration, business education, computer science, finance, industrial administration, management, marketing), EDUCATION (early childhood, elementary, health/physical, home economics, industrial, school media, secondary, special), ENGLISH (comparative literature, English, journalism, literature, speech), FINE AND PERFORMING ARTS (art, art education, art history, music, music education, radio/TV, studio art, theater/dramatics), HEALTH SCIENCES (medical technology, nursing, physical therapy), LANGUAGES (French, German, Greek/Latin, Italian, Russian, Spanish), MATH AND SCIENCE (astronomy, biology, botany, chemistry, geology, horticulture, mathematics, physics, zoology), PHILOSOPHY (classics, philosophy), PREPROFESSIONAL (architecture, engineering—agricultural, engineering—chemical, engineering—civil, engineering—electrical, engineering—mechanical, engineering—mining, engineering—metallurgical, forestry, home economics, pharmacy, social work, veterinary), SOCIAL SCIENCES (anthropology, economics, geography, government/political science, history, psychology, rural sociology, sociology).

Required: All freshmen are required to complete 2 semesters of English composition.

Special: A 3-2 engineering program is offered in conjunction with other schools. The university offers a work-study, 5-year program which is on a voluntary basis. There is a general-studies major, and students may design their own majors.

Honors: Nineteen honor societies have chapters on campus, and a university-wide honors program is available to qualified students.

Admissions: Eighty-five percent of those who applied were accepted for the 1981–82 freshman class. The ACT scores of those who enrolled were as follows: 49% below 21, 21% between 21 and 23, 12% between 24 and 25, 14% between 26 and 28, and 4% above 28. Applicants must be graduates of accredited high schools and have at least a 2.0 average. The high school transcript is not required. The admissions criteria were being revised in 1982 to make the school more selective.

Procedure: The ACT is required and should be taken by April of the senior year. High school seniors who list the University of Kentucky as their first choice on the ACT Profile need not submit an application form. The deadlines for applications are June 1 (fall), October 15 (spring), and April 15 (summer). There is no application fee. The university uses a rolling admissions plan. An interview is recommended but not required.

Special: The university offers an early admissions plan. AP and CLEP credit (for subject examinations) is available.

Transfer: For fall 1981, 2660 students applied, 2031 were accepted, and 1549 enrolled. A 2.0 GPA is required. D grades transfer. Students must complete 30 of the last 36 semester hours at the university; a total of 120 or more semester hours is required for a bachelor's degree. Application deadlines are the same as those for freshmen.

Visiting: Campus tours by bus are available to prospective students and other visitors Monday through Friday. Visitors may sit in on classes. Contact the admissions office for arrangements.

Financial Aid: The university administers NDSL, EOG, and CWS as well as its own aid programs. About 40% of the students receive aid; 12% hold campus jobs. The average award to freshmen in 1981–82 totaled $1400 from all sources. About $120,000 is available for scholarships in engineering. The FAF is required, and applications should be in before the March 15 priority date.

Foreign Students: The foreign students enrolled full-time at the university represent 2% of enrollment. Special counseling and organizations are available.

Admissions: Applicants must score 550 or better on the TOEFL and must take the ACT.

Procedure: Deadlines for students outside the United States are January 30 (fall) and August 30 (spring). For those inside the United States, deadlines are June 1 (fall), October 1 (spring), and April 1 (summer). Students must present proof of health, show evidence of adequate funds, and obtain health insurance, which is available through the university for a fee.

Admissions Contact: Elbert W. Ockerman, Dean of Admissions and Registrar.

KENTUCKY 303

UNIVERSITY OF LOUISVILLE D-2
Louisville, Kentucky 40292 (502) 588-6531

F/T: 4725M, 4163W	Faculty:	n/av; I, −$
P/T: 2833M, 3162W	Ph.D.'s:	78%
Grad: 2635M, 2541W	S/F Ratio:	8 to 1
Year: sems, ss	Tuition:	$852 ($2476)
Appl: July 1	R and B:	$1840
4293 applied	3204 accepted	2386 enrolled
SAT: 449V 490M	ACT: 18	COMPETITIVE

The University of Louisville, established in 1798, is a liberal arts university controlled by the Commonwealth of Kentucky. The university administers 13 individual schools. The library contains 988,749 volumes and 368,128 microfilm items, and subscribes to 6032 periodicals.

Environment: The campus occupies 140 acres near downtown Louisville and 238 acres in suburban Jefferson County. Recent additions to the campus include a new main library and an observatory. Coed residence halls accommodate 821 men and 526 women. On-campus apartments also are available for graduate and married students.

Student Life: About 90% of the students are from Kentucky; all 49 other states and 36 foreign countries are also represented. Ten percent of the students live on campus.

Organizations: There are 12 fraternities and 8 sororities on campus to which about 8% of the students belong. Extracurricular activities include student government, publications, music and drama groups, service organizations, a campus radio station, and special-interest clubs. There are religious organizations for students of all major faiths.

Sports: The university fields 8 intercollegiate teams for men, 7 for women, and a coed swim team. More than 40 intramural, club, and recreational sports are available.

Handicapped: Special facilities include wheelchair ramps, parking areas, elevators, specially equipped rest rooms, and lowered drinking fountains and telephones. About 400 handicapped students are enrolled, including 18 visually impaired students. Counselors are available, and special class scheduling can be arranged.

Graduates: About 50% of the students pursue graduate study after graduation; 40% pursue careers in business and industry.

Services: The following services are available free to students: health care, psychological counseling, placement and career counseling, and tutoring or remedial instruction.

Programs of Study: The undergraduate degrees conferred by the university are the B.A., B.S., B.Mus., B.Mus.Ed., B.S.B.A., B.S.Med.-Tech., and engineering degrees. Master's and doctoral programs are also offered. Bachelor's degrees are offered in the following subjects: AREA STUDIES (American, Asian, Black/Afro-American, Latin American, Russian, urban), BUSINESS (accounting, business administration, business economics, computer science, finance, management, marketing, office administration), EDUCATION (counseling and guidance, early childhood, elementary, health/physical, industrial, special), ENGLISH (English, journalism, linguistics, speech), FINE AND PERFORMING ARTS (art, art education, art history, interior design, music, music education, music history, studio art, theater/dramatics), HEALTH SCIENCES (dental hygiene, medical technology, nursing, physical therapy), LANGUAGES (French, German, Greek/Latin, Russian, Spanish), MATH AND SCIENCES (applied mathematics, biology, botany, chemistry, geology, mathematics, physics, zoology), PHILOSOPHY (humanities, philosophy), PREPROFESSIONAL (dentistry, engineering, food and nutrition, medicine, social work), SOCIAL SCIENCES (anthropology, economics, geography, government/political science, history, justice administration, psychology, sociology). Twenty-nine percent of all undergraduate degrees are conferred in business, 18% in social sciences, 11% in engineering, and 10% in math and sciences.

Required: Courses in English, foreign language, history, humanities, natural science, physical education or ROTC, and social science are required of all students in the College of Arts and Sciences. Freshman requirements may be met by enrollment in the interdisciplinary Freshman Symposium.

Special: Combined B.A.-B.S. degrees may be earned in various subjects. The university offers a general-studies degree and allows students to design their own majors. The university's engineering program is based on cooperative work, with the student receiving employment experience in addition to academic work.

Honors: Professional and honor societies in each of the general academic areas recognize scholastic achievement.

Admissions: About 75% of those who applied were accepted for the 1981-82 freshman class. Candidates must rank in the upper half of their graduating class at an accredited high school. They must have a GPA of at least C and an ACT composite score of 19. Applicants must have at least 12 academic high school credits.

Procedure: The ACT is required and the PSAT is recommended. The PSAT should be taken in May of the junior year. Applications are accepted for the fall term up to August 1, although March 1 is the priority date for most programs. Most health programs have earlier deadlines. The deadline for spring is November 15; for summer, May 1. Notification is made on a rolling basis. There is no application fee.

Special: The university has an early admissions plan. AP and CLEP credit is available.

Transfer: A 2.0 GPA is recommended. D grades are not transferable. Thirty hours must be taken in residence. Deadlines are the same as those for freshmen.

Visiting: Guides are available for informal visits. The best time to visit is a weekday. The admissions office will make arrangements.

Financial Aid: Financial aid is awarded on the basis of need and academic potential. Forty-five percent of all students receive aid. Freshmen are encouraged to apply before February 1, although applications are accepted until April 1. The FAF is required.

Foreign Students: Foreign students enrolled full-time at the university make up a little more than 1% of the student body. Special counseling and special organizations are provided.

Admissions: Foreign applicants must score 550 or better on the TOEFL. They also must take the ACT.

Procedure: Application deadlines are July 15 for fall admission, November 15 for spring admission, and April 15 for summer admission. Students must present proof of adequate funds for 1 year and must carry health insurance, which is available through the university for a fee.

Admissions Contact: Ray A. Stines, Director of Admissions.

WESTERN KENTUCKY UNIVERSITY C-4
Bowling Green, Kentucky 42101 (502) 745-2551

F/T: 4343M, 4118W	Faculty:	n/av; IIA, av$
P/T: 819M, 997W	Ph.D.'s:	44%
Grad: 1089M, 1998W	S/F Ratio:	17 to 1
Year: sems, ss	Tuition:	$626 ($1780)
Appl: see profile	R and B:	$1700
4500 applied	4254 accepted	2870 enrolled
ACT: 18		NONCOMPETITIVE

Western Kentucky University, established in 1906, is a state university that offers training on both the graduate and undergraduate levels. The library contains 700,000 volumes and 350,000 microfilm items, and subscribes to 6100 periodicals.

Environment: The 200-acre campus is located in a small town 120 miles from Louisville. The 65 major buildings include 16 single-sex dormitories that accommodate 2998 women and 2050 men. Apartments for married students also are available.

Student Life: About 80% of the students are from Kentucky. Approximately 55% of the undergraduates live in dormitories.

Organizations: Sixteen local fraternities and 11 local sororities have chapters on campus. Student organizations include religious and professional societies.

Sports: The university competes in 8 intercollegiate sports. About 22 intramural sports and 16 club sports are available.

Handicapped: Special facilities for the physically handicapped include parking areas, elevators, and specially equipped rest rooms.

Services: Students receive the following free services: placement, career counseling, tutoring or remedial instruction, and psychological counseling. Health care is also available. Placement services may be used by graduates.

Programs of Study: The university confers the B.A., B.S., B.F.A., B.M., and B.S.N. degrees. Associate and master's degrees also are available. Bachelor's degrees are offered in the following subjects: BUSINESS (accounting, advertising, business administration, business education, computer science, finance, hotel/motel management, information systems, management, marketing, office administration, public relations, restaurant management), EDUCATION (elementary, secondary, health/physical, industrial, special), ENGLISH (English, journalism, speech), FINE AND PERFORMING ARTS (art, art education, dance, music, music education, film/photography, radio/TV, theater/dramatics), HEALTH SCIENCES (environmental health, health and safety, health care administration, medical technology, nursing), LAN-

304 KENTUCKY

GUAGES (French, German, Russian, Spanish), MATH AND SCIENCES (astronomy, biochemistry, biology, chemistry, earth science, geology, geophysics, mathematics, physics), PHILOSOPHY (philosophy, religion), PREPROFESSIONAL (agriculture, engineering, home economics, industrial technology, interior design, library science, medicine, optometry, pharmacy, social work), SOCIAL SCIENCES (anthropology, economics, geography, government/political science, history, psychology, sociology).

Required: All students must take 53 to 54 hours of general-education courses.

Special: The university offers certificate programs in secretarial science and real estate. It is possible to earn a combined B.A.-B.S. degree in 5 years. The B.G.S. degree is given. Preprofessional programs are available in chiropractic, dentistry, forestry, engineering, law, medicine, optometry, pharmacy, physical therapy, speech pathology, theology, and veterinary medicine.

Honors: Honors courses are available in several departments for students who have demonstrated superior ability. Sixteen honor societies have chapters on campus.

Admissions: About 95% of those who applied were admitted to the 1981–82 freshman class. Applicants must be graduates of accredited high schools. Out-of-state applicants must have a GPA of 2.0 or better and rank in the top half of their high school class. Consideration is also given to recommendations, ACT scores, class rank, and personal qualifications. Non-high-school graduates must present a GED diploma and receive individual approval.

Procedure: The ACT is required. The deadlines for Kentucky residents are August 1 (fall), January 1 (spring), and May 15 (summer). Deadlines for nonresidents are June 1 (fall), December 1 (spring), and May 1 (summer). There is a rolling admissions plan.

Special: Early and deferred admissions and early decision plans are available. AP and CLEP credit is given.

Transfer: In a recent year, 902 students applied, 842 were accepted, and 777 enrolled. A 2.0 GPA is required. D grades usually transfer. Students must earn at least 32 semester hours in residence of the 128 generally required for a bachelor's degree.

Visiting: There are regularly scheduled orientations for prospective students. Informal guided tours and classroom visits can be arranged weekdays with the office of university relations.

Financial Aid: About 50% of all students receive aid. Scholarships, loans, grants, and employment programs are available. The deadlines for priority consideration of aid applications are May 1 (fall), November 1 (spring), and April 1 (summer).

Foreign Students: Foreign students enrolled full-time at the university make up about 1% of the student body. Special counseling and special organizations are available for these students.

Admissions: Foreign applicants must score 500 or better on the TOEFL. No college entrance exams are required.

Procedure: Application deadlines are April 1 for fall entry, September 1 for spring entry, and March 1 for summer entry. Students must submit a medical history as well as proof of adequate funds for the length of their stay at the university. Health insurance is required, and is available through the university for a fee.

LOUISIANA

CENTENARY COLLEGE OF LOUISIANA A-1
Shreveport, Louisiana 71104 (318) 869-5131

F/T: 379M, 382W	Faculty: 57; IIB, av$
P/T: 109M, 110W	Ph.D.'s: 66%
Grad: 95M, 168W	S/F Ratio: 14 to 1
Year: 4-1-4, ss	Tuition: $2820
Appl: open	R and B: $1900
277 applied	200 enrolled
ACT: 21	COMPETITIVE

Centenary College of Louisiana, established in 1825, is a private liberal arts college affiliated with the Louisiana Conference of The United Methodist Church. The library houses 120,000 volumes, and subscribes to 729 periodicals.

Environment: The 65-acre campus, located in a suburban area, contains 26 buildings including dormitories accommodating 600 students.

Student Life: Two-thirds of the students are from Louisiana; more than 50% reside on campus. Sixty percent of entering freshmen come from public schools. About 70% of the students are Protestant, 11% are Catholic, and 1% are Jewish. About 13% are minority-group members. Campus housing is single-sex; there are visiting privileges. Students may keep cars on campus.

Organizations: Student activities include a Lyceum series, a student fair, student forums, movies, and numerous campus organizations. There are 4 national fraternities and 2 national sororities with chapters on campus.

Sports: The college fields 6 intercollegiate teams for men and 4 for women. There are 6 intramural sports for men and 3 for women.

Graduates: The college estimates that 45% of its graduates become candidates for higher degrees.

Services: Placement, career counseling, and psychological counseling are offered at no charge to the student.

Programs of Study: The college awards the B.A. and B.S. degrees. Associate and master's degrees are also conferred. Bachelor's degrees are offered in the following subjects: BUSINESS (accounting, business administration), EDUCATION (adult, early childhood, elementary, health/physical, secondary), ENGLISH (English), FINE AND PERFORMING ARTS (art, music, music education, theater/dramatics), LANGUAGES (French, German, Spanish), MATH AND SCIENCES (biology, chemistry, geology, mathematics, physics), PHILOSOPHY (philosophy), PREPROFESSIONAL (dentistry, engineering, forestry, law, medical technology, medicine, ministry), SOCIAL SCIENCES (economics, geography, government/political science, history, psychology, sociology). Forty percent of the degrees conferred are in business.

Special: There are combination degree programs in computer science, dance, journalism, medicine, medical technology, forestry, public administration, and engineering. The BGS degree is offered.

Honors: There are 10 national honor societies with chapters on campus. Honors programs are conducted by many departments of the college.

Admissions: Eighty-four percent of those who applied were accepted for a recent freshman class. Prospective students should be graduates of an accredited high school, having completed 15 Carnegie units with a C or better average. Veterans with GED are given special admissions status.

Procedure: The SAT or the ACT is required. The college uses a rolling admissions system. Students are encouraged to apply by May. There is a $10 application fee.

Special: An early admissions plan is offered; the deadline for application is April 15. AP and CLEP credit is offered.

Transfer: For fall 1981, 247 transfer students applied, 203 were accepted, and 137 enrolled. A GPA of 2.0 is necessary; grades of C or above transfer. Thirty hours must be taken in residence; 124 credits are required to earn the bachelor's degree. Admissions are on a rolling basis.

Visiting: Appointments to visit the campus can be made by contacting the admissions office.

Financial Aid: About 86% of all students receive aid. The college awards scholarships and grants-in-aid totaling $1,072,000 each year. Other aid sources include EOG, NDSL, and CWS. The college is a member of CSS; either the FAF or FFS is required. The application deadline for aid is registration.

Foreign Students: The college offers foreign students special counseling and special organizations.

Admissions: Foreign students must achieve a minimum TOEFL score of 500; no college entrance exams are required.

Procedure: Application deadlines are August 1 (fall), December 1 (winter and spring), and May 1 (summer). Foreign students must complete the college's health form and present proof of funds adequate to cover 1 year of study. They must also carry health insurance, which is available through the college.

Admissions Contact: John L. Lambert, Director of Admissions and Financial Aid.

DILLARD UNIVERSITY

New Orleans, Louisiana 70122   D-4   (504) 283-8822

F/T: 329M, 891W   Faculty: 96; IIB, −$
P/T: 4M, 12W   Ph.D.'s: 61%
Grad: none   S/F Ratio: 12 to 1
Year: sems, ss   Tuition: $2600
Appl: July 15   R and B: $1900
910 applied   622 accepted   480 enrolled
SAT or ACT: required   COMPETITIVE

Dillard University is a private liberal arts institution affiliated with the United Church of Christ and the Methodist Church. It was established in 1930 by the merger of New Orleans University and Straight College, both founded in 1869. The library contains 132,000 volumes, and subscribes to 687 periodicals.

Environment: The 62-acre campus is located in the city of New Orleans. Residence halls accommodate 122 men and 217 women.

Student Life: About 44% of the students are residents of New Orleans, and 13% come from other parts of Louisiana. Most students are black. More than 80% are graduates of public schools. About 52% of the students live in dormitories. About 60% are Protestant and 40% are Catholic. Campus housing is single-sex; there are no visiting privileges. Students may keep cars on campus.

Organizations: About 25% of the men belong to 1 of 5 fraternities, and about 33% of the women belong to 1 of 5 sororities. Campus activities include student government, publications, religious organizations, special-interest clubs, artist and lecture series, convocations, dances, movies, and drama.

Sports: The university fields 2 intercollegiate teams for men and 1 for women. There are 8 intramural sports for men and 6 for women.

Handicapped: Special parking is provided for the physically handicapped. No students with visual or hearing impairments were enrolled in a recent class.

Graduates: About 28% of the freshmen drop out; 45% remain to graduate. Twenty-two percent of the graduates seek advanced degrees, including 3% who enter medical school, 2% who enter law school, and 1% who enter dental school. Approximately 48% of the graduates pursue careers in business and industry.

Services: Students receive free placement and career counseling, health care, tutoring, and remedial instruction. Placement services also are available to graduates.

Programs of Study: The university confers the B.A., B.S., and B.S.N. degrees. Bachelor's degrees are offered in the following subjects: BUSINESS (accounting, business administration), EDUCATION (early childhood, elementary, health/physical, secondary, special), ENGLISH (English), FINE AND PERFORMING ARTS (art, art education, music, music education, speech and drama), HEALTH SCIENCES (nursing), LANGUAGES (French, German, Spanish), MATH AND SCIENCES (biology, chemistry, mathematics, physical sciences, physics), PHILOSOPHY (philosophy, religion), PREPROFESSIONAL (dentistry, engineering, law, medicine, ministry, pharmacy, social work), SOCIAL SCIENCES (government/political science, history, psychology, social welfare, sociology).

Honors: Honors programs are offered in social sciences and in natural sciences. Six national honor societies are represented on campus.

Admissions: About 68% of those who applied were admitted to the 1981-82 freshman class. Applicants must have completed 16 units of high school work and present an average of at least C. The university prefers that applicants rank in the upper half of their class. Admissions officers also consider advanced placement or honors courses, leadership record, recommendations by high school officials, extracurricular activities, personality, and evidence of special talents.

Procedure: The SAT or ACT is required. Application deadlines are July 15 (fall) and December 1 (spring). Freshmen also are admitted in summer. Applicants for fall admission are urged to apply early in the senior year. Admissions decisions are made on a rolling basis. A $5 application fee is required.

Special: Students with an average of B or better and above-average test scores after 3 years of high school may apply for early admission. The deadline is June 1. AP credit is accepted.

Transfer: For fall 1981, 53 transfer students applied, 33 were accepted, and 28 enrolled. Transfer students are accepted for the second-semester freshman and the sophomore classes. Applicants must have at least a C average and be in good standing at the previous institution. A 2.5 GPA is recommended. No more than 60 hours may transfer. Students must earn at least 62 hours at the university to receive a degree; 124 credits are required to earn the bachelor's degree. Application deadlines are the same as those for freshmen.

Visiting: Informal visits may be scheduled with the director of admissions. Guides are provided, and prospective students may sit in on classes and stay overnight in the residence halls.

Financial Aid: About 85% of the students receive aid; 58% work part-time on campus. Scholarships and loans are available. About a third of the students earn at least 25% of their expenses. The university is a member of CSS. The deadlines for aid applications are June 1 (fall), October 15 (spring), and April 15 (summer).

Foreign Students: About 2% of the full-time students come from foreign countries. The university offers these students special counseling and special organizations.

Admissions: Foreign students must take the TOEFL; no college entrance exams are required.

Procedure: Application deadlines are June 1 (fall) and November 1 (spring). Foreign students must submit a health form completed by a physician. They must also carry health insurance, which is available through the university for a fee.

Admissions Contact: Vernese B. O'Neal, Director of Admissions.

GRAMBLING STATE UNIVERSITY

Grambling, Louisiana 71245   B-1   (318) 247-6941

F/T: 1600M, 1700W   Faculty: 254; IIA, − −$
P/T: 100M, 200W   Ph.D.'s: 33%
Grad: 196M, 204W   S/F Ratio: 12 to 1
Year: sems, ss   Tuition: $650 ($1280)
Appl: July 1   R and B: $1375
1461 applied   1217 accepted   899 enrolled
SAT ot ACT: required   LESS COMPETITIVE

Grambling State University, founded in 1901, is a state-controlled liberal arts and teachers' college. The library contains 177,962 volumes and 161,000 microfilm items, and subscribes to 1217 periodicals.

Environment: The 340-acre campus is located in a town of 3000 people, 35 miles from Monroe and 60 miles from Shreveport. The university's 50 buildings include a stadium, farm facilities, and 15 dormitories that house 2659 students.

Student Life: About 84% of the students come from Louisiana, and 81% live on campus. Almost all students are black. Dormitories are single-sex. Drinking is prohibited on campus. Women students must observe a curfew and follow a sign-out procedure. Freshmen and sophomores may not have cars on campus.

Organizations: About 8% of the women belong to 1 of the 16 sororities on campus, and 4% of the men belong to 1 of the 16 fraternities. Extracurricular activities include religious groups, a choir, a band, drama, and student government.

Sports: Grambling competes in 5 intercollegiate sports. Intramural sports are offered for men and women.

Handicapped: About 20% of the campus is accessible to the physically handicapped. Facilities include special parking, elevators, and specially equipped rest rooms.

Graduates: About 30% of the entering freshmen remain to graduate. Twenty percent of the graduates seek advanced degrees, including 4% who enter medical school, 1% who enter dental school, and 4% who enter law school. About 35% of the graduates pursue careers in business and industry.

Services: Students receive free placement, career, and psychological counseling; health care; tutoring; and remedial instruction. Placement services also are offered to graduates.

Programs of Study: The college confers the B.A., B.S., and B.P.A. degrees. Associate and master's degrees also are available. Bachelor's degrees are offered in the following subjects: AREA STUDIES (Asian, Black/Afro-American, Latin American, urban), BUSINESS (accounting, business education, computer science, finance, management, marketing, real estate/insurance), EDUCATION (early childhood, elementary, health/physical, industrial, secondary, special), ENGLISH (English, journalism, speech), FINE AND PERFORMING ARTS, (art, art education, music, music education, radio/TV, theater/dramatics), HEALTH SCIENCES (pre-nursing, speech therapy), LANGUAGES (French, German, Spanish), MATH AND SCIENCES (biology, chemistry, mathematics, physics, statistics), PREPROFESSIONAL (dentistry, home economics, law, medicine, social work), SOCIAL SCIENCES (anthropology, criminal justice, economics, geography, government/political science, history, psychology, social sciences, sociology).

306 LOUISIANA

Required: Students must take basic courses in English, biology and physical science, social science, and physical education.

Special: Combined B.A.-B.S. degrees may be earned in various subjects. The college sponsors Project Rescue for disadvantaged students. Work-study programs also are available.

Honors: Fifteen national honor societies are represented on campus.

Admissions: About 83% of those who applied were accepted for the 1981-82 freshman class. Applicants must be graduates of an accredited high school and have completed 18 Carnegie units. Out-of-state applicants should rank in the upper half of their class.

Procedure: Applicants must take the SAT or the ACT. Deadlines for applications are July 1 (fall) and December 15 (spring). The university follows a rolling admissions policy. A $5 application fee is required.

Special: Early admissions and early decision plans are offered.

Transfer: Most transfer applicants are accepted. An average of C or better is required. Preference is given to applicants seeking to transfer from other Louisiana schools. D grades do not transfer. Students must spend at least a year in residence to graduate.

Visiting: Prospective students may arrange weekday visits to campus with the director of high school relations. Guides are provided, and visitors may sit in on classes and spend the night in the dormitories.

Financial Aid: About 98% of the students receive aid. A total of 308 academic and athletic scholarships are awarded to freshmen. Loans from federal and state governments also are available, as are work contracts. The neediest students receive aid packages that include an EOG and a part-time job; others may borrow as part of their package. Tuition may be paid in installments. The university's aid application and the FFS must be filed by June 15 (fall), November 15 (spring), or April 15 (summer).

Foreign Students: The 92 foreign students enrolled at the university make up about 2% of the student body. Special counseling and special organizations are provided.

Admissions: Applicants must score 450 or better on the TOEFL. They also should take the SAT or the ACT.

Procedure: Application deadlines are the same as those for American students. Foreign students must provide evidence of adequate funds for 4 years. Health insurance is included in their general fees. There is a special $15 application fee.

Admissions Contact: Irene S. A. Thomas, Director of Admissions.

LOUISIANA COLLEGE
Pineville, Louisiana 71360   B-3
                                              (318) 487-7386

F/T, P/T:	Faculty:	81; IIB, -$
1321M&W	Ph.D.'s:	60%
Grad: none	S/F Ratio:	16 to 1
Year: sems, ss	Tuition:	$1440
Appl: open	R and B:	$1410
700 applied	555 accepted	240 enrolled
ACT: 20		COMPETITIVE

Louisiana College, established in 1906, is a private liberal arts college affiliated with the Southern Baptist Churches of Louisiana. The library contains 90,000 volumes, and subscribes to 500 periodicals.

Environment: The 81-acre campus is located in a small town near Alexandria. Five dormitories, including an "English Student Village" complex, house 580 men and women. Fraternity and sorority housing also is available, as is married-student housing.

Student Life: Eighty-two percent of the students come from Louisiana. Half the students live on campus. Dormitories are single-sex. Drinking is prohibited on campus. All first-semester freshmen living in dormitories must observe a curfew. Chapel attendance is required.

Organizations: There are 2 fraternities and 2 sororities, all local, as well as a student government and other social, music, and drama groups. Kisatchie National Forest and other nearby game areas provide outdoor recreation.

Sports: The college participates in 3 intercollegiate sports. Intramural sports also are available.

Handicapped: About 90% of the campus is accessible to wheelchair-bound students. Facilities include ramps, designated parking areas, and elevators. Special class scheduling can be arranged.

Graduates: About 3% of the freshmen drop out, and 35% remain to graduate. Forty percent of the graduates pursue further study.

Services: Health care and psychological, placement, and career counseling are offered free to students. Tutoring and remedial instruction also are available.

Programs of Study: The college confers the B.A., B.S., and B.M. degrees. Associate degrees also are available. Bachelor's degrees are offered in the following subjects: BUSINESS (accounting, business education, finance, management, office administration), EDUCATION (early childhood, elementary, health/physical, religious, secondary, special), ENGLISH (English, journalism, speech), FINE AND PERFORMING ARTS (art, art education, church music, media communications, music, music education), HEALTH SCIENCES (medical technology), LANGUAGES (French), MATH AND SCIENCES (biology, chemistry, mathematics), PHILOSOPHY (philosophy, religion), PREPROFESSIONAL (dentistry, law, medicine, ministry, social work), SOCIAL SCIENCES (criminal justice, economics, history, psychology, public administration, sociology).

Required: Students must complete 9 semester hours of religion and 4 of physical education.

Special: A 3-1 cooperative program in medical technology leads to a B.S.Med.Tech. A general studies degree is offered. Students may design their own majors.

Honors: A college-wide honors program gives qualified upperclassmen an opportunity for independent study and research. Nine national honor societies have chapters on campus.

Admissions: Seventy-nine percent of those who applied were accepted for the 1981-82 freshman class. Candidates must have graduated from an accredited high school with at least 17 academic units. They should rank in the upper half of their class, present an average of C or better, score above 18 on the ACT, or score 800 or better (combined) on the SAT. Admissions officers also consider AP or honors courses, leadership record, and impressions made during an interview.

Procedure: The SAT or the ACT is required. Notification is made on a rolling basis. There are no application fees or deadlines. Freshmen are admitted to all terms.

Special: An early admissions plan is available. The college has its own AP program.

Transfer: Transfer students are accepted for all classes. D grades transfer if the student's GPA is 2.0 or better. Students must earn the last 30 semester hours in residence of the 127 or more required for a bachelor's degree.

Visiting: The college holds a Fall College Preview on the last Monday in October and a Spring College Preview on the first Saturday in March. Prospective students also may schedule informal visits for weekdays. Guides are provided, and visitors may sit in on classes and spend the night in the dormitories. The admissions office handles arrangements.

Financial Aid: About 63% of the students receive aid. Freshman scholarships and loans are available, and the college participates in NDSL, BEOG, SEOG, and CWS. The average aid award to freshmen in 1981-82 totaled $1600. Tuition may be paid in installments. Aid applications and the FAF should be filed by May 1 (fall) or October 15 (spring).

Foreign Students: Fewer than 1% of the full-time students come from foreign countries. Special counseling and special organizations are offered for these students.

Admissions: Applicants must score at least 540 on the TOEFL. They also must take the ACT.

Procedure: Application deadlines are open. Students must submit a completed health form and evidence of adequate funds. Health insurance, though not required, is available through the college.

Admissions Contact: Wayne Ryan, Director of Admissions and Financial Aid.

LOUISIANA STATE UNIVERSITY SYSTEM

The Louisiana State University System is composed of the Agricultural and Mechanical College at Baton Rouge; the state universities at Alexandria, Eunice, and Shreveport; the University of New Orleans, which has 2 campuses—Lakefront and an evening program called the Metropolitan College downtown; The Paul M. Hebert Law Center; the Medical Center, which has 2 campuses in New Orleans and 1 in Shreveport; and the Center for Agricultural Sciences and Rural Development. The Agricultural and Mechanical College and the universities at Shreveport and New Orleans award bachelor's and graduate degrees; the universities at Alexandria and Eunice offer associate degrees and college transfer credit only. The Baton Rouge campus operates both a graduate and undergraduate resident center at the

Alexandria campus offering limited bachelor's and master's degrees and a graduate resident center on the Eunice campus. The Medical Center includes the schools of Medicine, Nursing, Dentistry, and Allied Health, and the Graduate School; all require 1 year or more of college work for admission. In addition, the Center for Agricultural Sciences and Rural Development operates 18 agricultural research centers in various parts of the state and a Cooperative Extension Service in each of the state's 64 parishes. Detailed profiles of the schools that offer bachelor's degrees follow.

LOUISIANA STATE UNIVERSITY AND AGRICULTURAL AND MECHANICAL COLLEGE

C-4

Baton Rouge, Louisiana 70803   (504) 388-1175

F/T: 11,202M, 9736W	Faculty: 1088; I, av$
P/T: 1335M, 1777W	Ph.D.'s: 72%
Grad: 2296M, 2327W	S/F Ratio: 18 to 1
Year: sems, ss	Tuition: $662 ($1692)
Appl: July 1	R and B: $1890
6700 applied	6200 accepted 4926 enrolled
ACT: required	LESS COMPETITIVE

Louisiana State University and Agricultural and Mechanical College, established in 1860, offers undergraduate programs in agriculture, arts and sciences, business, chemistry and physics, education, engineering, and environmental design and music. The library contains about 1.5 million volumes, and subscribes to almost 14,000 periodicals.

Environment: The 300-acre campus is located on the outskirts of Baton Rouge, 80 miles from New Orleans. Among the 350 buildings are 30 dormitories that house 3785 single women, 3410 single men, and 578 married couples; a Greek theater; a student union; 6 museums; a 267,800-square-foot Center for Engineering and Business Administration; and a planetarium.

Student Life: About 85% of the students are Louisiana residents, and 31% live on campus. About 13% are minority-group members. Campus housing is single-sex; there are visiting privileges. All single, full-time undergraduates who have completed fewer than 30 semester hours must live on campus unless they live with relatives, have worked full-time or served in the military for at least 18 months before enrolling in the university, or have severe financial problems. Alcohol may be served at registered university parties. Women residents must obey curfews. Students may keep cars on campus.

Organizations: About 14% of the men belong to 1 of the 23 national fraternities on campus, and 17% of the women belong to 1 of the 19 national sororities. Extracurricular activities include special-interest, departmental, and service clubs; publications; choral, band, and drama groups; and student government. Religious groups and places of worship are available for all major faiths. On-campus cultural events include debates, lectures, films, and concerts. The university's theaters bring plays, acts, and concerts to the Baton Rouge area. The city itself offers a number of recreational and cultural activities.

Sports: The university fields 11 intercollegiate teams for men and 8 for women. There are 21 intramural sports for men and 17 for women.

Handicapped: About 80% of the campus and 30% of its buildings are accessible to physically handicapped students. Facilities include wheelchair ramps, special parking areas, elevators, specially equipped rest rooms, and lowered drinking fountains and telephones. Special class scheduling can be arranged. For students with impaired vision or hearing, the university provides student readers and signers. Two special counselors in the Junior (freshman) Division specialize in the problems of handicapped students.

Services: Placement and career counseling, some tutoring, and remedial instruction are provided free to students. Health care and psychological counseling are available on campus; fees are charged. Placement services may be used by graduates as well as students.

Programs of Study: The university awards these undergraduate degrees: B.A., B.S., B.Arch., B.E.T., B.C.T., Bachelor of Law Enforcement, B.F.A., B.Land. Arch., B.Mus., and B.Mus.Ed. Master's and doctoral degrees also are available. Bachelor's degrees are available in the following subjects: AREA STUDIES (Latin American, Russian), BUSINESS (accounting, business administration, business education, commercial banking, computer science, finance, international trade and finance, management, marketing, merchandising, office administration, real estate/insurance, transportation), EDUCATION (elementary, health/physical, home economics, industrial, secondary, special), ENGLISH (English, journalism, speech), FINE AND PERFORMING ARTS (art education, art history, ceramics, crafts, dance, design technology, glass, graphic arts, music, music education, music history and literature, music performance, music theory, instrumental, organ, sacred music, voice, painting, radio/TV, sculpture, studio art), HEALTH SCIENCES (cytotechnology, dietetics, environmental health, food and nutrition, food science, medical technology), LANGUAGES (French, German, Greek/Latin, Italian, Russian, Spanish), MATH AND SCIENCES (astronomy, biochemistry, botany, chemistry, entomology, geology, mathematics, microbiology, physics, statistics, zoology), PHILOSOPHY (classics, philosophy), PREPROFESSIONAL (agriculture—animal science, agriculture—business, agriculture—crop production and soil management, agriculture—crop science, agriculture—dairy manufacturing/management, agriculture—dairy manufacturing science, agriculture—dairy production/commerce, agriculture—dairy production/science, agriculture—economics, agriculture—horticultural science, agriculture—horticultural technology, agriculture—international, agriculture—mechanization, agriculture—plant and animal protection, agriculture—poultry science, agriculture—soil science, dentistry, engineering—agricultural, engineering—aerospace, engineering—basic engineering-design technology, engineering—chemical, engineering—civil, engineering—electrical, engineering—engineering science, engineering—industrial, engineering—mechanical, engineering—petrochemical, engineering—petroleum, engineering—sugar, forestry, industrial technology, law, medicine), SOCIAL SCIENCES (anthropology, criminal justice, economics, family life and environment, geography, government/political science, history, psychology, public administration, sociology). Twenty-one percent of the undergraduate degrees conferred are in business, 15% in engineering, 14% in math and sciences, and 11% in education.

Required: All freshmen enroll in the Junior Division for one year, then choose a college in which to complete the undergraduate program. Freshmen who have decided on a major should follow the first-year course of study prescribed by that college. Others must take certain prescribed courses and electives.

Special: The university offers a general studies degree. Combined curricula are available in arts and sciences/medicine, arts and sciences/law, business administration/law, and English/business administration. Engineering students may participate in a cooperative work-study program.

Honors: About 30 honor societies are represented on campus. Honors programs are available for qualified students.

Admissions: About 93% of those who applied were accepted for the 1981–82 freshman class. The ACT scores of those who enrolled were as follows: 26% between 20 and 23, 16% between 24 and 26, 7% between 27 and 28, and 4% above 28. Louisiana residents should submit high school transcripts as soon as possible after completion of high school studies. Out-of-state applicants should submit transcripts as soon as 7th-semester grades are available. Exceptionally well-qualified applicants may submit transcripts at the end of their junior year. Residents whose high school records or test scores indicate that they may have difficulty with college work may be required to come to the campus for an interview. Residents who have graduated from high schools that are not state-approved may apply for admission by entrance examinations. Residents who have not graduated from high school must be at least 21 years old and present satisfactory evidence of education, training, and experience. Out-of-state applicants are accepted only if their academic work is clearly above average.

Procedure: All applicants must take the ACT; for state residents who have graduated from accredited high schools, it is used only for placement. Application deadlines are July 1 (fall), December 1 (spring), and May 1 (summer). Admissions decisions are made on a rolling basis. The application fee is $10.

Special: An early admissions program is available; high-school juniors applying for it must have completed at least 15 Carnegie units, present an average of 3.0 or better, and score at least 27 on the ACT. CLEP credit is accepted.

Transfer: For fall 1981, 2986 transfer students applied, 2725 were accepted, and 1520 enrolled. Out-of-state applicants must have a GPA of 2.0 or better. Louisiana residents with fewer than 12 semester hours must meet freshman admission requirements; those with 12 to 55 hours must have an average of 1.75 or better (if not, they may be allowed to enroll in remedial courses); those with more than 55 hours must have an average of at least 2.0. Residency requirements vary according to the particular program selected; 128–170 semester hours are needed to receive a bachelor's degree. Application deadlines are the same as those for freshmen.

Visiting: Informal visits may be scheduled for weekdays from 8 A.M. to 4:30 P.M. Guides are provided, and prospective students may sit in on classes and, if space is available, spend a night in the dormitories. The Junior Division handles arrangements for visits.

Financial Aid: About 59% of the students receive aid; 19% work part-time on campus. Five hundred freshman scholarships are awarded each year. Loans are available from federal and state governments, the university, and local banks. The university fills about 1800 part-time jobs each year. Tuition may be paid in installments. The university is a member of CSS; the FAF or FFS must be submitted. Aid applications must be filed by July 1.

Foreign Students: Six percent of the full-time students come from foreign countries. The university offers these students an intensive English program, special counseling, and special organizations.

Admissions: Foreign students must achieve a minimum TOEFL score of 500. They must also take the SAT or ACT.

Procedure: Application deadlines are July 1 (fall), December 1 (spring), and May 1 (summer). Foreign students must submit the general health service form and present proof of funds adequate to cover at least 1 year of study. They must also carry health insurance, which is available through the university for a fee.

Admissions Contact: Ordell Griffith, Director of Admissions.

LOUISIANA STATE UNIVERSITY/ SHREVEPORT A-1
Shreveport, Louisiana 71115 (318) 797-5061

F/T: 976M, 1035W	Faculty: 142; IIB, ++$
P/T: 715M, 1005W	Ph.D.'s: 66%
Grad: 146M, 299W	S/F Ratio: 14 to 1
Year: sems, ss	Tuition: $480 ($1410)
Appl: see profile	R and B: n/app
885 applied	883 accepted 653 enrolled
ACT: 17	NONCOMPETITIVE

Louisiana State University/Shreveport, founded in 1965, is a state-controlled liberal arts and teacher-education institution. The library contains 131,526 volumes, and subscribes to 1779 periodicals.

Environment: The 200-acre campus, located in a suburban area of a city of 200,000 people, consists of 5 buildings, including a recently constructed Business/Education Building housing the Computer Center. There are no dormitories.

Student Life: Virtually all students come from Louisiana. About 10% are minority-group members. Students may keep cars on campus. Drinking is restricted on campus.

Organizations: About 10% of the students belong to 1 of 3 fraternities or 3 sororities. Extracurricular activities include special-interest clubs and service groups, as well as university-sponsored entertainment and social events. Art galleries, theater, concerts, thoroughbred racing, and water skiing are available in the Shreveport area.

Sports: The university does not participate in intercollegiate sports. There are 7 intramural sports.

Handicapped: About 95% of the campus is accessible to wheelchair-bound students. Special class scheduling is available, and structural adaptations include wheelchair ramps, elevators, designated parking areas, specially equipped rest rooms, and lowered drinking fountains and telephones.

Graduates: The freshman dropout rate is 30%; 60% remain to graduate. About 10% of the graduates seek advanced degrees, including 6% who enter medical school, 1% who enter dental school, and 4% who enter law school. Thirty percent of the graduates pursue careers in business or industry.

Services: Free tutoring, remedial instruction, and placement, career, and psychological counseling, are provided. Placement services also are available to graduates.

Programs of Study: The university grants the B.A., B.S., and B.G.S. degrees. Master's and associate degrees also are available. Bachelor's degrees are offered in the following subjects: BUSINESS (accounting, business administration, business education, computer science, economics, finance, management, marketing, office administration, real estate/insurance), EDUCATION (elementary, secondary, special), ENGLISH (English, journalism, speech), FINE AND PERFORMING ARTS (art education), HEALTH SCIENCES (medical technology, occupational therapy, physical therapy, speech therapy), LANGUAGES (French, German, Spanish), MATH AND SCIENCES (biology, mathematics, physical sciences), PREPROFESSIONAL (criminal justice, public administration, public relations), SOCIAL SCIENCES (economics, psychology, social sciences). Of the undergraduate degrees conferred, 34% are in area studies, 23% in business, and 21% in education.

Special: Students may design their own majors. A general studies degree is available.

Honors: Alpha Sigma Omicron has a chapter on campus.

Admissions: Almost all those who applied were accepted for the 1981–82 freshman class. The ACT scores of those who enrolled were as follows: 30% below 21, 23% between 21 and 23, 23% between 24 and 25, 18% between 26 and 28, and 6% above 28. A high school diploma or GED is required. Out-of-state applicants must be academically superior to be admitted.

Procedure: Applicants must take the ACT; junior-year results are acceptable. Applications should be submitted 30 days before registration for the term the applicant wants to enter. There is no application fee.

Special: An early admissions plan is available. AP and CLEP credit is accepted.

Transfer: Almost all transfer applicants are accepted. D grades transfer. Transfers are accepted for all classes. Students must complete at least 30 of the last 40 semester hours in residence to graduate. Application deadlines are the same as those for freshmen.

Visiting: Informal visits may be scheduled for weekdays from 8:30 A.M. to 4:00 P.M. Visitors may sit in on classes, and guides are provided.

Financial Aid: About 30% of the students receive aid; 15% work part-time on campus. Federal loans and grants (NDSL), part-time jobs, and a limited number of scholarships are available. Applications should be filed by April 1 for priority consideration.

Foreign Students: Fewer than 1% of the full-time students come from foreign countries. The university offers these students special counseling.

Admissions: Foreign students must achieve a minimum TOEFL score of 500; no college entrance exams are required.

Procedure: Application deadlines are August 1 (fall), January (spring), and June (summer).

Admissions Contact: Sylvia Booras, Staff Assistant.

LOUISIANA STATE UNIVERSITY/UNIVERSITY OF NEW ORLEANS
(See University of New Orleans)

LOUISIANA TECH UNIVERSITY B-1
Ruston, Louisiana 71272 (318) 257-2238

F/T: 4478M, 2969W	Faculty: 439; IIA, av$
P/T: 1257M, 718W	Ph.D.'s: 60%
Grad: 568M, 1029W	S/F Ratio: 25 to 1
Year: qtrs, ss	Tuition: $651 ($1251)
Appl: Aug. 15	R and B: $1782
1936 enrolled	
ACT: 19	NONCOMPETITIVE

Louisiana Tech University, established in 1894, is a public, state-supported institution that offers undergraduate programs in arts and sciences, life sciences, business, education, engineering, and home economics. The library contains 935,000 volumes and 260,000 microfilm items.

Environment: The 235-acre campus is located in a rural area in northern Louisiana, 70 miles from Shreveport. The university also operates a 275-acre demonstration farm nearby. Four dormitories accommodate 2258 men and 2033 women, and institutional apartments house 141 married couples. The university also sponsors fraternity houses.

Student Life: About 87% of the students come from Louisiana. Three-fourths of the freshmen are graduates of public schools. About 42% of the students live in campus housing. Unmarried freshmen under 21 must live on campus if they do not live with parents or other relatives. About 50% of the students are Protestant and 12% are Catholic. About 11% are minority-group members. Students may keep cars on campus.

Organizations: About 16% of the men belong to 12 national fraternities, and 12% of the women belong to the 10 national sororities on campus. University activities include the Louisiana Tech Concert Association.

Sports: The university fields 8 intercollegiate teams for men and 3 for women. There are 10 intramural sports for men and 10 for women.

Handicapped: Facilities for the physically handicapped include wheelchair ramps, parking areas, elevators, special class scheduling, specially equipped rest rooms, and lowered drinking fountains and telephones.

Graduates: About 30% of the freshmen drop out, while 45% remain to graduate.

Services: Students receive free placement, career counseling, and tutoring. Health care is available on a fee basis. Placement services also are available to graduates.

Programs of Study: The university confers the B.A., B.S., B.F.A., and B.Arch. degrees. Associate, master's, and doctoral degrees also are available. Bachelor's degrees are offered in the following subjects: BUSINESS (accounting, business administration, business education, computer science, finance, management, marketing), EDUCATION (adult, early childhood, elementary, health/physical, industrial, secondary, special), ENGLISH (English, journalism, speech), FINE AND PERFORMING ARTS (art, film/photography, music, music education, studio art), HEALTH SCIENCES (medical records administration, medical technology, nursing), LANGUAGES (French, Spanish), MATH AND SCIENCES (botany, chemistry, geology, mathematics, physics, statistics, zoology), PREPROFESSIONAL (agriculture, architecture, dentistry, engineering—biomedical, engineering—chemical, engineering—civil, engineering—industrial, engineering—mechanical, engineering—petroleum, forestry, home economics, library science), SOCIAL SCIENCES (economics, geography, government/political science, history, psychology, sociology). About 23% of the undergraduate degrees are conferred in education, 22% in engineering, and 17% in math and sciences.

Special: Research is sponsored in chemistry, zoology, and engineering. Also available are an opera workshop, summer music and debate camps, and a summer program in Rome.

Honors: Twenty honor societies are represented on campus. Honors programs in English and mathematics are offered.

Admissions: The university has an open admissions policy for Louisiana high school graduates. Out-of-state applicants must score 20 or above on the ACT. Applicants must have graduated from an accredited high school with 15 units of work. Students should rank in the top half of their class, present acceptable ACT scores, and be recommended for college by their high school.

Procedure: The ACT is required. Applications should be submitted no later than 1 month before registration (the fall deadline is August 15). Freshmen are admitted to all quarters. Admissions decisions are made on a rolling basis. The application fee is $5.

Special: An early admissions plan is available. AP and CLEP credit is accepted.

Transfer: For fall 1981, 720 transfer students enrolled. A GPA of at least 2.0 is required. Students must earn the last 30 hours in residence to graduate; the bachelor's degree requires between 126 and 140 credits. Grades of C and above transfer. Application deadlines are the same as those for freshmen.

Visiting: Orientations are scheduled regularly for prospective students. Informal visits, for which guides are provided, also may be arranged with the dean of admissions.

Financial Aid: Over 50% of the students receive aid; about 10% work part-time on campus. The deadline for financial aid applications is May 1. Scholarships and loans are available. Tuition may be paid in installments. The FFS must be submitted.

Foreign Students: About 6% of the full-time students come from foreign countries. The university offers these students an intensive English program, special counseling, and special organizations.

Admissions: Foreign students must achieve a minimum TOEFL score of 500; no college entrance exams are required.

Procedure: Application deadlines are August 15 (fall), November 15 (winter), February 15 (spring), and May 15 (summer). Out-of-state tuition rates apply.

Admissions Contact: Patsy Lewis, Dean of Admissions, Orientation, Basic, and Career Studies.

LOYOLA UNIVERSITY/NEW ORLEANS D-4
New Orleans, Louisiana 70118 (504) 865-3240

F/T: 1072M, 1374W	Faculty: n/av; IIA, av$
P/T: 256M, 362W	Ph.D.'s: 65%
Grad: 760M, 465W	S/F Ratio: 16 to 1
Year: sems, ss	Tuition: $3200
Appl: Aug. 1	R and B: $2100–2500
1653 applied	1410 accepted 631 enrolled
ACT: 21	COMPETITIVE

Loyola University/New Orleans, founded in 1912, is a private, coeducational institution operated by the Society of Jesus. The undergraduate divisions are the colleges of Arts and Sciences, Business Administration, and Music, and City College, which offers evening programs. The library contains 280,700 volumes and 21,800 microfilm items, and subscribes to 1200 periodicals.

Environment: The university occupies 7 square blocks in a residential section of New Orleans. The surrounding environment is urban. Facilities include a humanities center, a science building, a student center, and high-rise residence halls that accommodate 840 men and women.

Student Life: About 64% of the freshmen are graduates of parochial schools. Ten percent of the men and 15% of the women live in the residence halls. About 60% of the students are Catholic. Attendance at daily Mass is voluntary. About 21% of the students are minority-group members. Campus housing is single-sex.

Organizations: Twenty percent of the students belong to the 4 fraternities and 5 sororities on campus. The university sponsors professional organizations, campus radio and TV stations, music and drama groups, publications, student government, films, and lecture series. Religious organizations are available for members of the major faiths, and there is a resident chaplain. The city of New Orleans offers many other activities.

Sports: The university does not participate in intercollegiate sports. Intramural sports include soccer, volleyball, and wrestling.

Handicapped: About 60% of the campus is accessible to physically handicapped students. Facilities include wheelchair ramps, elevators, and lowered drinking fountains. The residence halls are nearly barrier-free, and alterations to rest rooms are scheduled. Members of the university's Community Action Program help handicapped students get around campus and provide library and study assistance for visually impaired students.

Graduates: Sixty percent of the freshmen eventually graduate, and 65% of the graduates seek advanced degrees. Of those who apply, 90% are admitted to medical school, 70% to dental school, and 65% to law school.

Services: Students are offered the following free services: tutoring, remedial instruction; health care; and placement, career, and psychological counseling. Placement services also are available to graduates.

Programs of Study: The university offers the B.A., B.S., B.B.A., and B.P.A. degrees. Associate, master's, and law degrees also are available. Bachelor's degrees are offered in the following subjects: BUSINESS (accounting, business administration, computer science, finance, management, marketing), EDUCATION (elementary, health/physical, secondary), ENGLISH (communications, English), FINE AND PERFORMING ARTS (dance, music, music education, radio/TV, theater/dramatics), HEALTH SCIENCES (dental hygiene, medical technology, nursing), LANGUAGES (French, German, Greek/Latin, Italian, Russian, Spanish), MATH AND SCIENCES (biology, chemistry, geology, mathematics, physics), PHILOSOPHY (philosophy, religion), PREPROFESSIONAL (architecture, dentistry, engineering, law, medicine, ministry, pharmacy, social work, veterinary), SOCIAL SCIENCES (economics, government/political science, history, psychology, public administration, sociology). Of the undergraduate degrees conferred, 54% are in arts and sciences, 28% in business, 8% in preprofessional studies, and 7% in music.

Required: Students must complete a core curriculum that includes courses in philosophy, English, mathematics, religion, and, in most majors, science and social science.

Special: Programs include a junior year in Rome, a summer session in Mexico City, institutes in politics and human relations, and an opera workshop. Loyola participates with neighboring St. Mary's Dominican College and Xavier University in the New Orleans Consortium. An exchange program with Tulane University allows Loyola students to enroll in courses in aerospace, anthropology, geology, theater, and architecture.

Honors: A number of honor societies have chapters on campus.

Admissions: Eighty-five percent of those who applied were accepted for the 1981–82 freshman class. The ACT average composite of those who enrolled was 21; the SAT average composite was 1000. Applicants must be graduates of an accredited high school, be recommended for college by a high school counselor, and present an average of 2.0 or better. Admissions officers also consider advanced placement or honors courses, evidence of special talent, impressions made during an interview, leadership record, and extracurricular activities. Special consideration is given to children of alumni and to disadvantaged students.

Procedure: The SAT or ACT is required and should be taken between March of the junior year and May of the senior year. Application deadlines are August 1 (fall) and January 5 (spring). Freshmen also are admitted in summer. There is a $15 application fee. Admissions decisions are made on a rolling basis.

LOUISIANA

Special: An early decision plan and an early admissions plan are available. AP and CLEP credit is accepted in specific areas.

Transfer: For fall 1981, 871 transfer students applied, 785 were accepted, and 571 enrolled. A GPA of at least 2.0 is required. D grades transfer. Students must earn at least 30 credits in residence to graduate. The bachelor's degree requires between 129 and 136 credits. Application deadlines are the same as those for freshmen.

Visiting: Prospective students may contact the admissions office to make appointments for informal visits to the campus. Guides are provided, and visitors may sit in on classes and spend a night in the residence halls if space is available.

Financial Aid: About 54% of the students receive aid; 10% work part-time on campus. Scholarships, grants, CWS, and loans, including EOG and NDSL, are available. Aid applications should be filed as early as possible since funds are limited. The university is a member of CSS; either the FAF, FFS, or BEOG is required. The application deadline for aid is April 30.

Foreign Students: The university offers these students special counseling and special organizations.

Admissions: Foreign students must achieve a minimum TOEFL score of 500; in lieu of the TOEFL, students may take the SAT or ACT.

Procedure: Application deadlines are 5 weeks before registration for each semester. Foreign students must present proof of health as well as proof of funds adequate to cover 1 semester of study. They must also carry health insurance, which is available through the university.

Admission Contact: Susan Williams, Associate Director of Admissions for Recruitment.

McNEESE STATE UNIVERSITY B-4
Lake Charles, Louisiana 70609 (318) 477-2520

F/T: 1983M, 2363W	Faculty: 219; I, --$
P/T: 431M, 684W	Ph.D.'s: 50%
Grad: 519M, 1037W	S/F Ratio: 20 to 1
Year: sems, ss	Tuition: $554 ($1184)
Appl: July 15	R and B: $1704
1482 applied	1440 accepted	1381 enrolled
ACT: 15	LESS COMPETITIVE

McNeese State University, founded in 1939, is a state-controlled institution offering graduate and undergraduate programs. The library contains 197,800 volumes and 275,750 microfilm items, and subscribes to 1369 periodicals.

Environment: The 407-acre campus, which includes a 280-acre farm, is located in a city of 78,000 people 150 miles from Houston, Texas. The surrounding environment is suburban. The 60 campus buildings include 6 dormitories that accommodate 1434 students in double rooms and suites. The university also sponsors married student housing.

Student Life: About 97% of the students are Louisiana residents, and 22% live on campus. Eighty percent of the students leave campus on weekends. About 17% of the students are minority-group members. Campus housing is single-sex. Students may keep cars on campus.

Organizations: About 13% of the students belong to 1 of 8 national fraternities or 6 national sororities. The university sponsors about 50 extracurricular activities and groups for undergraduates. There is a student government. Major social events include Homecoming, LaBelle Contest, and Greek Week.

Sports: The university fields 8 intercollegiate teams for men and 4 for women. There are 11 intramural sports for men and 11 for women.

Handicapped: About 90% of the campus is accessible to the physically handicapped. Facilities include wheelchair ramps, special parking, elevators, and lowered drinking fountains. No special counselors are available.

Graduates: About 35% of the freshmen drop out; 50% remain to graduate. Approximately 2% of the graduates seek advanced degrees, and 34% pursue careers in business and industry.

Services: Students receive free placement and career counseling, health care, and psychological counseling. Placement services also are available to graduates. Tutoring and remedial instruction are available for a fee.

Programs of Study: The university confers the B.A., B.Mus., B.Mus.Ed., and B.S. degrees. Associate and master's degrees also are available. Bachelor's degrees are offered in the following subjects: BUSINESS (accounting, business administration, business education, computer science, finance, management, marketing), EDUCATION (early childhood, elementary, health/physical, secondary, special), ENGLISH (English, speech), FINE AND PERFORMING ARTS (art education, music, music education, radio/TV, studio art, theater/dramatics), HEALTH SCIENCES (medical technology, nursing), LANGUAGES (French, Spanish), MATH AND SCIENCES (biology, chemistry, ecology/environmental science, mathematics, physics, statistics, zoology), PREPROFESSIONAL (agriculture, dentistry, engineering, forestry, home economics, medicine), SOCIAL SCIENCES (criminal justice, economics, government/political science, history, psychology, sociology). About 33% of the undergraduate degrees are conferred in business, 26% in education, 11% in health sciences, and 11% in social sciences.

Honors: Fifteen national honor societies have chapters on campus. Honors programs are available in languages and mathematics; eligibility is based on ACT scores.

Admissions: About 97% of those who applied were accepted for the 1981–82 freshman class. The ACT scores of those who enrolled were as follows: 77% below 21, 11% between 21 and 23, 4% between 24 and 25, 5% between 26 and 28, and fewer than 1% above 28. Applicants must be graduates of an accredited high school. Out-of-state applicants must rank in the upper half of their class and present a 2.5 or better average. Admissions officers also consider recommendations by high school officials, extracurricular activities, special talents, and advanced placement or honors courses.

Procedure: The ACT is required. Admissions decisions are made on a rolling basis. Application deadlines are July 15 (fall), December 5 (spring), and May 1 (summer). A $5 application fee is required. The university subscribes to the CRDA.

Special: An early admissions plan is available; the application deadline is 30 days before the beginning of the semester.

Transfer: Transfer students are accepted for all classes. A 2.5 GPA is recommended. D grades transfer. Students must complete 30 credits at the university to receive a degree; 130 credits are required to earn a bachelor's degree. Application deadlines are the same as those for freshmen.

Visiting: A 2-day orientation for prospective students is scheduled each summer. Informal visits may be arranged with the director of high school relations. Guides are provided, and visitors may sit in on classes (with the instructor's permission) and spend the night in the residence halls.

Financial Aid: About 48% of the students receive aid; 10% work part-time on campus. The application deadline is May 1. Fifty academic and 20 athletic scholarships are awarded to freshmen each year. The average award to freshmen from all sources is $2200. CWS jobs are available in all departments. Loans also are provided. Need is the primary criterion for awards. The university is a member of CSS; the FFS must be filed.

Foreign Students: About 1% of the full-time students come from foreign countries. The university offers these students an intensive English course and special organizations.

Admissions: Foreign students must achieve a minimum TOEFL score of 450. They must also take the ACT.

Procedure: Application deadlines are May 1 (fall), October 1 (spring), and March 1 (summer). Foreign students must present proof of funds adequate to cover at least 1 year of study. Non-resident fees are applicable. They must also carry health insurance, which is available through the university for a fee.

Admissions Contact: Barbara Breedlove, Admissions Counselor.

NICHOLLS STATE UNIVERSITY D-4
Thibodaux, Louisiana 70310 (504) 446-8111

F/T: 2318M, 2364W	Faculty: 252; IIA, +$
P/T: 440M, 702W	Ph.D.'s: 50%
Grad: 442M, 982W	S/F Ratio: 19 to 1
Year: sems, ss	Tuition: $547 ($1177)
Appl: Aug. 15	R and B: $1440
1600 applied	1575 accepted	1375 enrolled
ACT: 15	NONCOMPETITIVE

Founded in 1948, Nicholls State University is a state-supported, comprehensive institution. The library contains 184,708 volumes, and subscribes to 1520 periodicals.

Environment: The 175-acre suburban campus was once part of the historic Acadia Plantation. The university fronts on Bayou Lafourche, which forms the eastern limit of the city of Thibodaux, located about 60 miles from New Orleans. Living facilities include dormitories, married student housing, and fraternity and sorority houses.

Student Life: Almost all students are from Louisiana. Ninety percent of the freshmen come from public schools. About 20% of the students live on campus. About 18% are minority-group members. Sixty percent are Catholic, 2% are Protestant, and 1% are Jewish. Campus housing is both coed and single-sex; there are visiting privileges in the single-sex housing. Students may keep cars on campus. Day-care services are available to all students for a fee.

Organizations: About 12% of the students belong to 1 of 7 fraternities and 5 sororities. The student government sponsors films, freshman orientation programs, intramural sports, and dances. The university offers arts and lecture series, science fairs, a literary rally, and other cultural and recreational events. Several Christian organizations have chapters on campus.

Sports: Intercollegiate teams are sponsored in 8 sports for men and 4 for women. There are 4 intramural sports for men and 4 for women.

Handicapped: About 90% of the campus is accessible to physically handicapped students. Special facilities include wheelchair ramps, designated parking, and specially equipped rest rooms. Special class scheduling is available. Fewer than 1% of the students have visual or hearing impairments. Readers are available for visually impaired students.

Graduates: About 44% of the freshmen drop out, and 56% remain to graduate. Eighty percent of the graduates enter business and industry.

Services: The following services are provided free to students: placement, career counseling, tutoring, and health care. Placement services also are available to alumni.

Programs of Study: The university confers the B.A., B.S., B.Mus., and B.Mus.Ed. degrees. Associate and master's degrees also are available. Bachelor's degrees are offered in the following subjects: BUSINESS (accounting, business administration, business education, computer science, finance, marketing, personnel administration), EDUCATION (early childhood, elementary, health/physical), ENGLISH (English, journalism, speech), FINE AND PERFORMING ARTS (art, art education, music, music education, theater/dramatics), HEALTH SCIENCES (medical technology, nursing, physical therapy, speech therapy), LANGUAGES (French), MATH AND SCIENCES (biology, chemistry, geology, mathematics, physics), PREPROFESSIONAL (dentistry, engineering, medicine, pharmacy), SOCIAL SCIENCES (economics, government/political science, history, psychology, sociology). Thirty-nine percent of the undergraduate degrees are conferred in education, 27% in business, and 18% in health sciences.

Special: The university offers a general studies degree.

Honors: Fifteen honor societies have chapters on campus. The English department offers honors courses.

Admissions: Ninety-eight percent of those who applied were accepted for the 1981–82 freshman class. The ACT scores of those who enrolled were as follows: 58% below 21, 20% between 21 and 23, 2% between 24 and 25, 2% between 26 and 28, and 2% above 28. Applicants must be graduates of accredited high schools. The university has an open admissions policy.

Procedure: The ACT is required. Application deadlines are August 15 (fall), December 15 (spring), and May 15 (summer). There is a $5 application fee.

Special: The university offers an early admissions plan. CLEP credit is accepted.

Transfer: For fall 1981, 430 students applied, 420 were accepted, and 407 enrolled. A GPA of 1.5 is required. Applicants must be in good standing at the last school they attended. D grades transfer. All students must complete, at the university, 24 of the 130 credits required for a bachelor's degree. Application deadlines are August 15 (fall), January 15 (spring), and June 7 (summer).

Visiting: Orientation sessions are scheduled regularly for prospective students. Informal campus tours also may be scheduled with the assistant vice president for student affairs for anytime classes are in session.

Financial Aid: Merit scholarships, BEOG, work-study jobs, and loans are available. About 19% of the students receive aid. About 10% work part-time on campus. The FFS is required. Aid application deadlines are June 1 (fall), November 1 (spring), and April 1 (summer).

Foreign Students: One percent of the full-time students come from foreign countries.

Admissions: Foreign students must achieve a TOEFL score of at least 500 and must take the ACT.

Procedure: Application deadlines are June 1 (fall), November 1 (spring), and April 1 (summer). Foreign students must present proof of funds adequate to cover 4 years of study and must pay a $15 application fee.

Admissions Contact: S. Dan Montz, Jr., Dean of Admissions and Registrar.

NORTHEAST LOUISIANA UNIVERSITY C–1
Monroe, Louisiana 71201 (318) 342-4170

F/T: 3532M, 4112W	Faculty: 367; I, – – $
P/T: 301M, 880W	Ph.D.'s: 55%
Grad: 713M, 1315W	S/F Ratio: 21 to 1
Year: sems, ss	Tuition: $527 ($1157)
Appl: see profile	R and B: $1564
2373 applied	2365 accepted 2349 enrolled
ACT: required	NONCOMPETITIVE

Northeast Louisiana University, established in 1931, is a state-supported institution offering undergraduate and graduate programs. The library contains 412,666 volumes and 305,161 microfilm items, and subscribes to 3520 periodicals.

Environment: The 190-acre campus is located in the city of Monroe, 100 miles from Shreveport. The university's recreational facilities include an indoor Olympic-size pool. The residence halls accommodate more than 3000 men and women.

Student Life: About 93% of the students are from Louisiana, and 33% live on campus. About 24% are minority-group members. Campus housing is coed and single-sex; there are visiting privileges in single-sex dorms. Students may keep cars on campus.

Organizations: About 8% of the students belong to 1 of 9 national fraternities or 7 national sororities. Religious facilities are provided for students of various faiths. The university sponsors publications, music groups, and drama societies. Abundant cultural and recreational facilities can be found in the Monroe area.

Sports: The university fields 13 intercollegiate teams for men and 6 for women. There are 12 intramural sports for men and 12 for women.

Handicapped: The entire campus is accessible to wheelchair-bound students. Facilities for the physically handicapped include wheelchair ramps, special parking, elevators, special class scheduling, specially equipped rest rooms and dormitory rooms, and lowered drinking fountains and telephones. One counselor is available.

Graduates: Forty-four percent of the freshmen drop out, and 40% remain to graduate. Two percent of the graduates enter medical school and 1% enter dental school.

Services: The following services are offered free to students: placement and career counseling, tutoring, and remedial instruction. Placement services also are available to graduates. Health care is available on a fee basis.

Programs of Study: The university confers the B.A., B.B.A., B.M., B.M.E., and B.S. degrees. Associate, master's, and doctoral degrees also are available. Bachelor's degrees are offered in the following subjects: BUSINESS (accounting, business administration, business education, computer science, finance, management, marketing, real estate/insurance), EDUCATION (early childhood, elementary, health/physical, secondary, special), ENGLISH (English, journalism, speech), FINE AND PERFORMING ARTS (art, art education, film/photography, music, music education, radio/TV), HEALTH SCIENCES (medical technology, nursing, occupational therapy, speech therapy, toxicology), LANGUAGES (French, German, Spanish), MATH AND SCIENCES (biology, chemistry, computer science, geology, mathematics, natural sciences, physics, zoology), PREPROFESSIONAL (agriculture, home economics, law, medicine, pharmacy, social work), SOCIAL SCIENCES (corrections, economics, geography, government/political science, history, law enforcement, psychology, social sciences, sociology). About 28% of the undergraduate degrees are conferred in health sciences, 18% in education, and 19% in business.

Special: The university offers a general studies degree.

Honors: Five national honor societies have chapters on campus.

Admissions: The university follows an open admissions policy. Almost all those who applied were accepted for the 1981–82 freshman class. The ACT scores of those who enrolled were as follows: 76% below 21, 12% between 21 and 23, 6% between 24 and 25, 4% between 26 and 28, and 1% above 28. Candidates must be graduates of accredited high schools.

Procedure: All applicants must take the ACT, which is used for placement. Applications are due 30 days before registration for the session in which the student hopes to enroll. A $5 application fee is required.

Special: CLEP credit is accepted.

Transfer: For fall 1981, 800 transfer students enrolled. D grades transfer. Students must earn at least 30 hours in residence to receive a

312 LOUISIANA

degree; 128 credits are required to earn the bachelor's degree. Application deadlines are the same as those for freshmen.

Visiting: Informal visits may be scheduled weekdays when school is in session. Guides are provided, and prospective students may sit in on classes and arrange to spend a night in the residence halls. The director of school services can provide further information.

Financial Aid: About 50% of the students receive aid; 15% work part-time on campus. There is no application deadline. Scholarships, including 400 freshman awards loans, and student employment programs are available.

Foreign Students: Almost 2% of the full-time students come from foreign countries. The university offers these students an intensive English course, special counseling, and special organizations.

Admissions: Foreign students must achieve a score of 85 on the University of Michigan Language Test or 600 on the TOEFL to be exempted from the English requirement. In addition, students must take the ACT.

Procedure: Application deadlines are July 1 (fall), November 1 (spring), and April 1 (summer). Foreign students must present proof of health as well as proof of funds adequate to cover 1 year of study. They are required to pay out-of-state fees. They must also carry health insurance, which is available through the university for a fee.

Admissions Contact: David J. Settle, Director of Admissions.

NORTHWESTERN STATE UNIVERSITY B-2
Natchitoches, Louisiana 71457 (318) 357-4503

F/T: 1250M, 1762W	Faculty: 361; I, --$
P/T: 891M, 794W	Ph.D.'s: 47%
Grad: 205M, 1820W	S/F Ratio: 9 to 1
Year: sems, ss	Tuition: $746 ($1376)
Appl: open	R and B: $1590
916 applied	916 accepted 886 enrolled
ACT: 16	NONCOMPETITIVE

Northwestern State University, founded in 1884, is a state-controlled institution that offers undergraduate programs in business, education, liberal arts, science and technology, and nursing. The library contains 240,000 volumes, and subscribes to 2500 periodicals.

Environment: The 900-acre campus is located in a small town 70 miles from Shreveport. Its 92 buildings include 18 dormitories that house 1691 women, 1767 men, and 59 married couples.

Student Life: Ninety-four percent of the students come from Louisiana, and 61% live on campus. Dormitories are single-sex.

Organizations: More than 20% of the students belong to 1 of the 9 fraternities and 7 sororities on campus. The college sponsors professional societies, a student government, organizations for Catholic and Protestant students, and special-interest, departmental, and service groups. Outdoor recreation areas nearby offer hunting, fishing, skiing, and boating.

Sports: The university participates on an intercollegiate level in 7 sports. Intramural sports also are available.

Handicapped: The entire campus is accessible to wheelchair-bound students. Facilities include wheelchair ramps, special parking areas, and elevators. Special class scheduling can be arranged. Three counselors are on hand.

Graduates: About 43% of the freshmen drop out, and 33% remain to graduate.

Services: The following services are offered free to students: psychological, placement, and career counseling; tutoring; remedial instruction; and health care. Placement services also are available to graduates.

Programs of Study: The university confers the B.A., B.S., B.Mus.Ed., B.Mus., and B.S.N. degrees. Associate, master's and doctoral degrees also are available. Bachelor's degrees are offered in the following subjects: BUSINESS (accounting, agribusiness, business administration, business education, computer science, secretarial administration), EDUCATION (early childhood, elementary, health/physical, industrial, secondary, special), ENGLISH (English, journalism, speech), FINE AND PERFORMING ARTS (advertising design, art, art education, dance, music, music education, radio/TV, theater/dramatics), HEALTH SCIENCES (medical technology, nursing, pre-physical therapy, radiologic technology, speech therapy), LANGUAGES (French, German, Spanish), MATH AND SCIENCES (biochemistry, biology, botany, chemistry, geology, mathematics, microbiology, physics, zoology), PREPROFESSIONAL (agriculture, architecture, aviation, engineering, home economics, industrial technology, interior design, library science, social work, veterinary, wildlife management), SO-CIAL SCIENCES (anthropology, economics, geography, government/political science, history, psychology, recreation, social sciences, sociology).

Required: All students must take freshman orientation and courses in English, mathematics, science, social science, and physical education.

Special: The university offers summer tours of Europe and various regions of the United States. Combined work-study programs are offered in industrial technology-electronics and industrial technology-machine tools. Students may design their own majors. A general studies degree is offered. Nonmajor preprofessional programs are offered in law, ministry, and medicine and other health professions.

Honors: A number of honor societies are represented on campus. The English and mathematics departments offer honors programs.

Admissions: All applicants were accepted for the 1981-82 freshman class. The ACT scores of those who enrolled were as follows: 52% below 21, 18% between 21 and 23, 6% between 24 and 25, 2% between 26 and 28, and 1% above 28. Applicants must have graduated from an accredited high school with at least 15 Carnegie units. Admissions officers also consider advanced placement or honors courses and place of residence.

Procedure: The ACT is required. Application deadlines are open. There is a $5 application fee. Admissions decisions are made on a rolling basis.

Special: An early admissions plan is available. AP and CLEP credit is accepted.

Transfer: Almost all transfer applicants are accepted. They should have an average of at least 2.0 and plan to complete at least 30 semester hours on campus.

Visiting: Guides are available for informal visits arranged with the director of admissions. Visitors may sit in on classes.

Financial Aid: About 49% of the students receive aid. Loans may be secured from the federal and state governments and from local banks. Campus jobs are available. The university awards about 350 freshman scholarships each year. Aid usually is awarded in a package that may include a CWS job, EOG, NDSL, and a scholarship. The average aid package for a freshman in 1981-82 was $612. Application deadlines are open.

Foreign Students: The 116 foreign students make up about 4% of enrollment. The university offers these students an intensive English program, special counseling, and special organizations.

Admissions: Applicants must take the TOEFL or the University of Michigan Language Test. The minimum acceptable score on the TOEFL is 500. Students also must take the ACT.

Procedure: Foreign students are accepted for all terms; applications should be submitted at least 30 days before registration. Students must present a completed health form and show evidence of adequate funds for 1 year. Health insurance is included in the registration fee.

Admissions Contact: Curtis B. Wester, Director of Admissions.

OUR LADY OF HOLY CROSS COLLEGE D-4
New Orleans, Louisiana 70114 (504) 394-7744

F/T: 69M, 185W	Faculty: n/av; IIB, --$
P/T: 153M, 359W	Ph.D.'s: 30%
Grad: none	S/F Ratio: 14 to 1
Year: sems, ss	Tuition: $2250
Appl: Aug. 15	R and B: n/app
70 enrolled	
ACT: required	LESS COMPETITIVE

Our Lady of Holy Cross College, founded in 1916, is affiliated with the Roman Catholic Church. The library contains 36,900 volumes, and subscribes to 450 periodicals.

Environment: The 40-acre urban campus, 2½ miles from the center of New Orleans, consists of 2 buildings surrounded by landscaped patios. There are no dormitory facilities.

Student Life: Most students come from Louisiana. About 65% are Catholic. All students commute; students may keep cars on campus.

Organizations: Because the college is a commuter school, there are few social or other extracurricular activities on campus. Those that exist include publications and student government.

Sports: There are 5 intramural sports for men and 5 for women.

Handicapped: Special facilities for the physically handicapped include wheelchair ramps, elevators, special class scheduling, and specially equipped rest rooms. About 1% of the students are visually impaired, and 1% are hearing-impaired.

LOUISIANA 313

Graduates: Ninety percent of those who enter a degree program graduate. About 21% of the graduates seek advanced degrees, including 1% who enter dental school and 2% who enter law school. About 4% of the graduates pursue careers in business and industry.

Services: Students receive free placement and career counseling. Health care, tutoring, and remedial instruction are available on a fee basis.

Programs of Study: The college confers the B.A. and B.S. degrees. Bachelor's degrees are offered in the following subjects: BUSINESS (accounting, business administration, business education, management, marketing), EDUCATION (elementary, health/physical, secondary, special), ENGLISH (English), FINE AND PERFORMING ARTS (art, art education, music, music education, theater/dramatics), HEALTH SCIENCES (pre-radiologic technology, pre-dental hygiene), LANGUAGES (French, Spanish), MATH AND SCIENCES (astronomy, biology, chemistry, earth science, natural sciences), PHILOSOPHY (humanities), SOCIAL SCIENCES (criminal justice, geography, government/political sciences, history, international relations, psychology, social sciences, sociology).

Special: Students may spend their junior year abroad or participate in a study-abroad program sponsored by another institution. The college offers a general studies degree.

Honors: The Blue Key honor society is represented on campus.

Admissions: Applicants must be graduates of an accredited high school, present an average of C or better, rank in the upper two-thirds of their class, and have completed at least 12 Carnegie units.

Procedure: Applicants must take the ACT by August 15, the application deadline for fall admission. Freshmen also are admitted at midyear (application deadline, December 15) and in the summer (May 15). The college offers provisional admission (45 days into the semester) for students who cannot meet these deadlines. A $15 fee must accompany the application.

Special: An early admissions plan is available. AP and CLEP credit is accepted.

Transfer: All transfer applicants with a C average or better are accepted. D grades do not transfer. All students must complete, at the college, 30 of the 130 credits required for a bachelor's degree. Application deadlines are the same as those for freshmen.

Visiting: Prospective students may arrange guided tours and class visits with the director of admissions.

Financial Aid: About a third of the students receive aid. The application deadline is June 1. The college administers NDSL, BEOG, SEOG, CWS, jobs, state grants and loans, veteran's programs, and its own scholarships. Tuition may be paid in installments.

Foreign Students: Special counseling is available for students from foreign countries.

Admissions: Foreign students must take the TOEFL and the ACT or SAT.

Procedure: Application deadlines are the same as those for other students. Foreign students must present proof of adequate funds.

Admissions Contact: Marianne Terrebonne Kerner, Director of Admissions.

ST. MARY'S DOMINICAN COLLEGE D-4
New Orleans, Louisiana 70118 (504) 865-7761

F/T: 10M, 490W	Faculty: 45; IIB, − −$
P/T: 100M, 300W	Ph.D.'s: 40%
Grad: none	S/F Ratio: 10 to 1
Year: sems, ss	Tuition: $3490
Appl: open	R and B: $2120
165 applied	150 accepted	86 enrolled
SAT: 430V 446M	ACT: 20	LESS COMPETITIVE

St. Mary's Dominican College is a private liberal arts college affiliated with the Roman Catholic Church. The library contains 75,000 volumes and 6100 microfilm items, and subscribes to 550 periodicals.

Environment: The 12-acre campus is located in the historic university section of New Orleans. College buildings include a science complex, a student center, and a dormitory that houses 300 students.

Student Life: Sixty percent of the students are from Louisiana. About 60% are graduates of private schools. Forty percent live on campus. Seventy-five percent of the students are Catholic, 22% Protestant, and 3% Jewish. About 37% are minority-group members. College housing is single-sex; there are visiting privileges. Students may keep cars on campus. Attendance at daily Mass is voluntary. Smoking is prohibited in classrooms and dormitory bedrooms. Curfews are in effect for freshmen.

Organizations: Extracurricular activities include clubs, publications, sororities, and student government. Cultural and social events on campus include art shows, lectures, spring fiesta, and the Mardi Gras ball. Other activities include Founders Week, Spring Formal, and monthly student-sponsored theme parties. In addition, students may enjoy theater, opera, and other cultural and recreational offerings of New Orleans.

Sports: There are 5 intramural sports for women.

Handicapped: About 95% of the campus is accessible to wheelchair-bound students. Classrooms and offices recently were relocated to make them totally accessible. Facilities include ramps, elevators, and designated parking areas.

Graduates: About 4% of the freshmen drop out, and 42% remain to graduate. Twenty-five percent of the graduates seek advanced degrees, including 2% who enter medical school and 4% who enter law school. Forty percent of the graduates pursue careers in business and industry.

Services: Health care, tutoring, remedial instruction, placement, and career counseling are offered free to students.

Programs of Study: The college awards the B.A., B.S., and B.F.A. degrees. Associate degrees are also conferred. Bachelor's degrees are offered in the following subjects: BUSINESS (accounting, business administration, business education, management), EDUCATION (deaf, early childhood, elementary, health/physical, secondary, special, speech pathology), ENGLISH (English), FINE AND PERFORMING ARTS (art, art education), HEALTH SCIENCES (medical technology, speech therapy), LANGUAGES (French), MATH AND SCIENCES (biology, chemistry, mathematics), PREPROFESSIONAL (home economics, law, medicine, social work), SOCIAL SCIENCES (history, psychology). Of the degrees conferred, 25% are in business, 25% in education, and 15% in math and sciences.

Special: Juniors may spend a year studying in such cities as London, Madrid, Paris, Rome, and Vienna through cooperative programs with other colleges.

Admissions: Ninety-one percent of those who applied were accepted for the 1981–82 freshman class. The SAT scores of those who enrolled were as follows: Verbal—70% below 500, 20% between 500 and 599, 8% between 600 and 700, and 2% above 700; Math—65% below 500, 27% between 500 and 599, 7% between 600 and 700, and 1% above 700. On the ACT, 65% scored below 21, 15% between 21 and 23, 10% between 24 and 25, 5% between 26 and 28, and 5% above 28. Candidates should complete at least 16 Carnegie units, rank in the upper half of their class, have an average of C or better, be recommended for college by high school officials, and present SAT scores above 400 on each section or an ACT composite of 18 or better. The college seeks a geographically diverse student body.

Procedure: The SAT or ACT is required and should be taken in May of the junior year or December of the senior year. An interview is recommended. Application deadlines are open. Students may enter in the fall, spring, and summer. Admissions decisions are made on a rolling basis. There is a $15 application fee.

Special: A Weekend College is open to adults. Education Access is available to those who score under 18 on the ACT, 800 on the SAT, or those who have below a 2.0 GPA. CLEP or AP credit is accepted.

Transfer: For fall 1981, 160 students applied, 140 were accepted, and 99 enrolled. D grades do not transfer. Applicants must have an average of 2.0 or better and satisfactory SAT or ACT scores. Students must study at the college for at least 30 semester hours of the 128 needed to receive a bachelor's degree. Application deadlines are open.

Visiting: Guides are available for informal visits to the campus. Visitors may sit in on classes and stay overnight in the residence halls.

Financial Aid: About 60% of the students receive aid. Thirty percent work part-time on campus. Average aid to freshmen from all sources totals $3000. The college awards $200,000 in scholarships each year. Loans are available from federal and state governments, local banks, and other sources. Campus jobs also are provided. The college is a member of CSS. Aid candidates must file the FAF and apply for admission before March 15 (fall) and November 15 (spring).

Foreign Students: Thirteen percent of the full-time students come from foreign countries. The college offers these students an intensive English program, special counseling, and special organizations.

Admissions: Foreign students must score at least 500 on the TOEFL. They must also take the SAT, ACT, or the college's own test.

314 LOUISIANA

Procedure: Application deadlines are August 1 (fall), January 1 (spring), and May 1 (summer).

Admissions Contact: Laurie Leftwich, Director of Admissions.

SOUTHEASTERN LOUISIANA UNIVERSITY
D-3

Hammond, Louisiana 70402   (504) 549-2187

F/T: 3513M, 5348W	Faculty: 286; IIA, +$
P/T: 335M, 487W	Ph.D.'s: 50%
Grad: 540M, 1460W	S/F Ratio: 23 to 1
Year: sems, ss	Tuition: $634 ($1248)
Appl: May 1	R and B: $1356
2355 applied	2350 accepted 1754 enrolled
ACT: 15	NONCOMPETITIVE

Southeastern Louisiana University is a state-supported institution that offers graduate and undergraduate instruction. The library contains 210,000 volumes, and subscribes to 1700 periodicals.

Environment: The 375-acre campus is located on the north side of Hammond, about 50 miles from Baton Rouge. The university's 30 buildings include 8 residence halls for women and 4 for men, 102 apartments for married students, a football stadium, and a coliseum. The residence halls accommodate 2768 men and women. Some students live in fraternity and sorority houses. The university also owns a 700-acre agricultural area on the east side of Hammond.

Student Life: About 90% of the students are from Louisiana. Eighty-eight percent are graduates of public schools. More than 60% of the students live on campus. Dormitories are single-sex.

Organizations: About 17% of the students belong to 1 of the 9 fraternities and 7 sororities on campus. The university sponsors a student government, departmental clubs, and Catholic and Protestant religious organizations.

Sports: The university participates in a number of intercollegiate sports. Intramural sports also are offered.

Handicapped: Facilities for wheelchair-bound students include ramps and elevators. One special counselor is available.

Graduates: About 20% of the freshmen drop out, and 40% remain to graduate.

Services: The following services are offered free to students: psychological, placement, and career counseling; health care; tutoring; and remedial instruction. Placement services also are available to graduates.

Programs of Study: The university awards the B.A., B.S., B.Mus., and B.Mus.Ed. degrees. Associate and master's degrees also are available. Bachelor's degrees are offered in the following subjects: BUSINESS (accounting, business administration, business education, marketing, office administration), EDUCATION (early childhood, elementary, health/physical, industrial, secondary), ENGLISH (English, journalism, speech), FINE AND PERFORMING ARTS (art, art education, dance, music, music education, theater/dramatics), HEALTH SCIENCES (medical technology, nursing, occupational safety), LANGUAGES (French, Spanish), MATH AND SCIENCES (biology, botany, chemistry, earth science, mathematics, physics, zoology), PREPROFESSIONAL (agriculture, home economics, social work, veterinary), SOCIAL SCIENCES (criminal justice, economics, government/political science, history, psychology, social sciences, social welfare, sociology). Thirty percent of the undergraduate degrees are awarded in education, 15% in preprofessional subjects, and 12% in math and sciences.

Honors: Phi Kappa Phi and Kappa Delta Pi have chapters on campus.

Admissions: Almost all the applicants for the 1981–82 freshman class were accepted. For an earlier freshman class, the ACT scores were as follows: 50% between 20 and 23, 35% between 24 and 26, 11% between 27 and 28, and 4% above 28. Applicants must be graduates of an approved high school.

Procedure: The ACT is required. Application deadlines are May 1 (fall and summer) and December 12 (spring). There is a $5 application fee. Admissions decisions are made on a rolling basis.

Special: An early admissions plan is offered. CLEP and AP credit is granted.

Transfer: Transfer students are accepted for all classes. D grades transfer. Students must study at the university for at least 36 weeks and earn at least 30 semester hours to graduate. Application deadlines are the same as those for freshmen.

Visiting: Orientations for prospective students are scheduled twice each semester and 3 times in the summer. Informal visits may be arranged by appointment with the director of high school relations. Guides are provided, and visitors may sit in on classes and stay overnight in the residence halls.

Financial Aid: About half the students receive aid. Freshman scholarships are available to Louisiana residents. Work-study jobs and loans from the federal government and the college are available. The deadline for aid applications is June 1.

Admissions Contact: Iris Wiggins, Director of Admissions.

SOUTHERN UNIVERSITY

Southern University is a public institution with campuses in Baton Rouge, New Orleans, and Shreveport. The Shreveport campus offers only associate-degree programs. Separate profiles follow for the Baton Rouge and New Orleans campuses.

SOUTHERN UNIVERSITY AND A & M COLLEGE
C-4

Baton Rouge, Louisiana 70813   (504) 771-2430

F/T, P/T:	Faculty: 475; IIA, −$
7400M&W	Ph.D.'s: 34%
Grad: 1200M&W	S/F Ratio: 21 to 1
Year: sems, ss	Tuition: $538 ($630)
Appl: open	R and B: $1169
4500 applied	4500 accepted 2078 enrolled
ACT: 12	NONCOMPETITIVE

Southern University and A & M College, founded in 1880, is a publicly supported, nonsectarian, land-grant institution that offers undergraduate programs in agriculture, arts and humanities, business, education, engineering, home economics, and sciences. Graduate programs also are provided. The library contains 260,000 volumes, and subscribes to 2000 periodicals.

Environment: The 800-acre campus is located in a suburban area of Baton Rouge. Twenty-two dormitories accommodate 1885 women and 1367 men, and 80 units are available for married students. The university has branches in New Orleans and Shreveport.

Student Life: About 81% of the undergraduates are from Louisiana. The student body is primarily black. About 37% of the students live in the dormitories, which are single-sex. Drinking on campus is forbidden. Freshmen are required to live on campus.

Organizations: About 3% of the women and 8% of the men belong to the 4 fraternities and 4 sororities on campus. Religious facilities are provided for Catholic and Protestant students. Extracurricular activities include student government, spiritual programs, assemblies, and social activities.

Sports: The university fields intercollegiate teams in 7 sports for men and 3 for women. Intramural sports also are offered.

Graduates: About 18% of the freshmen drop out, and 60% remain to graduate. Twenty percent of the graduates go on for further study.

Services: Students receive free counseling, health care, and placement aid.

Programs of Study: The university awards the B.A. and B.S. degrees. Associate and master's degrees also are available. Bachelor's degrees are offered in the following subjects: BUSINESS (accounting, business administration, computer science, management, marketing, office management), EDUCATION (early childhood, elementary, health/physical, industrial, recreation, secondary), ENGLISH (communication, English, journalism, speech), FINE AND PERFORMING ARTS (art, art education, art history, dance, music, music education, studio art, theater/dramatics), HEALTH SCIENCES (medical technology, nutrition, speech pathology and audiology, speech therapy), LANGUAGES (French, German, Spanish), MATH AND SCIENCES (bacteriology, biology, botany, chemistry, mathematics, microbiology, natural sciences, physics, zoology), PHILOSOPHY (philosophy), PREPROFESSIONAL (agriculture, architecture, engineering, home economics, interior design, law, library science, marriage and family counseling, medicine, social work, textiles and clothing, veterinary), SOCIAL SCIENCES (child care and family studies, child psychology, economics, geography, government/political science, history, psychology, social sciences, sociology).

Special: Students may design their own majors or earn a general studies degree. Special academic programs include accelerated degrees, cooperative education, study abroad, internships, and an exchange program with Louisiana State University.

Honors: Nine honor societies are represented on campus, and the university offers an honors program.

Admissions: All who applied were accepted for the 1981–82 freshman class. Applicants must be high-school graduates with at least 15 Carnegie units or must present a GED diploma or an equivalency certificate. The university prefers that applicants rank in the top half of their high school class, and that they have a GPA of at least 1.4.

Procedure: The ACT is required. Applications should be submitted at least 2 weeks before registration for the term in which the student wishes to enroll. There is no application fee.

Special: Early and deferred admissions plans are available. CLEP credit is accepted.

Transfer: Transfer students are accepted for all classes. D grades do not transfer. Students must study at the university for at least 1 year to receive a degree.

Financial Aid: Eighty percent of the students receive aid. Scholarships usually are awarded only to state residents. Loans are available from the university and the federal government, and campus jobs also are provided. The average award to 1981–82 freshmen was $716. The FAF or FFS is required. The university will provide further information on aid application procedures.

Foreign Students: About 1000 foreign students are currently enrolled at the university, which offers them special counseling and special organizations.

Admissions: Applicants must score at least 450 on the TOEFL. No college entrance exams are required.

Procedure: Applications should be filed at least 3 months before registration for the term. Students must provide a physician's statement as evidence of good health and must show proof of adequate funds for 4 years. Health insurance, though not required, is available through the university.

Admissions Contact: Colonel Johnson, Director of Admissions.

SOUTHERN UNIVERSITY IN NEW ORLEANS
New Orleans, Louisiana 70126   (504) 282-4401   D-4

F/T, P/T: Faculty: 104; IIB, +$
2600M&W   Ph.D.'s: 55%
Grad: none   S/F Ratio: 23 to 1
Year: sems, ss   Tuition: $490 ($1220)
Appl: Aug. 1   R and B: n/app
1100 applied   600 enrolled
ACT: 12   **NONCOMPETITIVE**

Southern University's campus in New Orleans, established in 1956, is a state-supported liberal arts institution. The library contains more than 135,000 volumes.

Environment: The 22-acre campus, located in a suburban area of New Orleans, has 8 buildings. There are no dormitories.

Student Life: Nearly all students are from the New Orleans area. Most students are black. Ninety percent of the freshmen come from public schools.

Organizations: About 2% of the students belong to the 4 fraternities and 5 sororities at the university. Extracurricular activities, geared to serve commuting students, include special-interest and service groups, a cultural series, student government, a student newspaper, drama clubs, and a musical theater.

Sports: The university fields intercollegiate teams in 4 sports for men and 2 for women. Intramural sports also are available.

Graduates: About 58% of the freshmen drop out, and 20% remain to graduate. Ten percent of the graduates seek advanced degrees.

Services: Health care and placement services are provided.

Programs of Study: The university awards the B.A. and B.S. degrees. Associate degrees also are conferred. Bachelor's degrees are offered in the following subjects: BUSINESS (accounting, business administration, management, office management), EDUCATION (elementary, health/physical, secondary), ENGLISH (English), FINE AND PERFORMING ARTS (art), HEALTH SCIENCES (speech pathology and audiology), LANGUAGES (French, Spanish), MATH AND SCIENCES (biology, mathematics, physics), PREPROFESSIONAL (social work), SOCIAL SCIENCES (history, sociology).

Special: Programs include cooperative education, internships, an exchange program with other schools, and study abroad.

Admissions: Almost all applicants for admission are accepted under the open admissions program. Ninety-nine percent of those who enrolled in 1981–82 scored below 21 on the ACT. Applicants must be graduates of accredited high schools and present at least 15 Carnegie units.

Procedure: The ACT is required. There is no application fee. Application deadlines are August 1 (fall), December 15 (spring), and April 15 (summer). Applicants are notified on a rolling basis.

Special: Early and deferred admissions plans are available.

Transfer: Transfer students must spend at least 1 year on campus to receive a bachelor's degree.

Financial Aid: About 75% of the students receive aid, including state scholarships, merit scholarships, NSDL, BEOG, SEOG, short-term loans, and campus jobs. The average award to 1981–82 freshmen totaled $300. Aid applicants must file the FFS and contact the university for information about application deadlines.

Foreign Students: The 50 students from foreign countries represent about 2% of enrollment. The university offers these students an intensive English course, special counseling, and special organizations.

Admissions: Applicants must score at least 500 on the TOEFL. They also must take the SAT.

Procedure: Students must file applications at least 90 days before the start of the term. They must submit a completed medical form and provide proof of adequate funds for 4 years.

Admissions Contact: Director of Admissions.

TULANE UNIVERSITY
New Orleans, Louisiana 70118   (504) 865-5731   D-4

F/T: 3433M, 2064W   Faculty: 467; I, −$
P/T: 482M, 481W   Ph.D.'s: 90%
Grad: 2512M, 1349W   S/F Ratio: 13 to 1
Year: sems, ss   Tuition: $5656
Appl: Feb. 1   R and B: $2545
5205 applied   3841 accepted   1478 enrolled
SAT: 530V 580M   ACT: 25   **VERY COMPETITIVE+**

Tulane University, established in 1834, is a private, nonsectarian institution that offers undergraduate and graduate degrees in 11 colleges and professional schools. A freshman enters one of 5 undergraduate divisions: Newcomb College, the liberal arts division for women; the College of Arts and Sciences for men; the schools of Architecture or Engineering; or the University College, for physical education majors. The library contains 1,350,000 volumes and 740,000 microfilm items, and subscribes to 11,000 periodicals.

Environment: The main campus consists of 100 acres in the uptown residential section of New Orleans. All university divisions are located there except the School of Medicine and the School of Health and Tropical Medicine, which are 3 miles away. All of the residence halls, which house 1200 women and 1453 men, have been built or remodeled in the past 10 years. Other university buildings include a student center with an indoor swimming pool, an auditorium that seats 2000, a 30-bed infirmary, and a 191-unit apartment building for married and graduate students.

Student Life: About 25% of the students are from Louisiana, another 25% come from other Southern states, and the rest come from all over the country. About 55% of the undergraduates come from public schools. Fifty percent live on campus; 22% of the undergraduate men live in fraternity houses. Freshmen from outside metropolitan New Orleans must live in the residence halls. Twenty-eight percent of the students are Catholic, 22% Protestant, and 27% Jewish. Ten percent of the students are minority-group members. University housing is both single-sex and coed. There are visiting privileges in single-sex housing. Students may keep cars on campus. Day-care services are available to all students, faculty, and staff for a fee.

Organizations: More than 175 student organizations and activities are available, including religious groups representing 11 faiths. About 40% of the men belong to 1 of 18 national fraternities; 45% of the women belong to 1 of 7 national sororities. In addition, the resources of the city—including the French Quarter, the Superdome, and the New Orleans Museum of Art—attract many students.

Sports: The university competes in 11 intercollegiate sports for men and 5 for women. There are 14 intramural sports for men and 10 for women.

Handicapped: The university is in the process of making the campus accessible to the physically handicapped. All programs are accessible now. Facilities include special parking and special class scheduling.

Graduates: Ten percent of the freshmen drop out by the end of their first year. Seventy-five percent remain to graduate. About 70% of the

316 LOUISIANA

graduates seek advanced degrees, including 8% who enter medical school, 5% dental school, and 10% law school. Twenty percent pursue careers in business and industry.

Services: Students receive free placement, career and psychological counseling, health care, tutoring, and remedial instruction. Placement services also are available to graduates.

Programs of Study: The university confers the B.A., B.S., B.F.A., B.Arch., and B.S.E. degrees. Master's and doctoral degrees also are available. Bachelor's degrees are offered in the following subjects: AREA STUDIES (American, Asian, Latin American), BUSINESS (management), EDUCATION (elementary, secondary), ENGLISH (English, speech), FINE AND PERFORMING ARTS (art history, music, studio art, theater/dramatics), LANGUAGES (French, German, Italian, Portuguese, Russian, Spanish), MATH AND SCIENCES (biochemistry, biology, chemistry, earth science, geology, mathematics, physics), PHILOSOPHY (philosophy), PREPROFESSIONAL (architecture, engineering), SOCIAL SCIENCES (anthropology, economics, government/political science, history, psychology, sociology).

Required: Students must take physical education or ROTC as well as English. Each undergraduate college has additional distribution requirements.

Special: Students may design their own majors or pursue a general studies major. Combined B.A.-B.S. degrees may be earned in engineering and liberal arts. Students may work toward a B.S. in management through the Graduate School of Business Administration. Nonmajor programs are available qualifying students for teacher certification. Special opportunities for superior students include junior year abroad, individual studies programs, a chance to take graduate courses, Washington semester, and internships.

Honors: All departments offer honors programs. More than 40 national honor societies are represented on campus.

Admissions: About 74% of those who applied were accepted for the 1981-82 freshman class. The SAT scores of those who enrolled were as follows: Verbal—39% below 500, 40% between 500 and 599, 18% between 600 and 700, and 3% above 700; Math—20% below 500, 45% between 500 and 599, 29% between 600 and 700, and 6% above 700. Admissions decisions are based on academic achievement as indicated by ACT or SAT scores, class rank, and high school average. Other important factors include advanced placement or honors courses, special talents, leadership record, extracurricular activities, and recommendations by high school officials. Special consideration is given to sons and daughters of alumni and to disadvantaged students.

Procedure: Applicants must take the SAT or ACT by January of their senior year. An interview is recommended. Application deadlines are February 1 (fall) and December 1 (spring). Freshmen also are admitted in summer. There is a $25 application fee.

Special: Early decision and early and deferred admissions plans are available. CLEP and AP credit is accepted.

Transfer: For fall 1981, 487 students applied, 325 were accepted, and 155 enrolled. Transfer applicants are considered for all classes. They must present an average of C+ or better and be in good standing at their last school. D grades do not transfer. Students must complete, at the university, 32 of the 128 semester hours required for the bachelor's degree. Transfer applications should be submitted by March 1 (fall) and December 1 (spring). Transfers are accepted for all classes.

Visiting: Prospective students may schedule informal visits with the admissions office for Monday through Thursday. Guides are provided. Visitors may sit in on classes and stay in the residence halls for 1 night.

Financial Aid: About 25% of the students receive aid. Twenty percent work part-time on campus. Average aid to freshmen from all sources is $2500. Scholarships, loans, and campus jobs, including CWS in all departments, are available. The university is a member of CSS. The FAF and the aid application must be filed by March 1.

Foreign Students: Seven percent of the full-time students come from foreign countries. The university offers these students an intensive English program, special counseling, and special organizations.

Admissions: Foreign students must score at least 550 on the TOEFL. They must also take the SAT or the ACT.

Procedure: Application deadlines are February 1 (fall) and October 1 (spring). Foreign students must present proof of funds adequate for at least 1 academic year. They must also carry health insurance, which is available through the university.

Admissions Contact: Jillinda Jonker, Acting Director of Admissions.

UNIVERSITY OF NEW ORLEANS D-4
New Orleans, Louisiana 70148 (504) 286-0595

F/T: 4051M, 3894W Faculty: 532; IIA, +$
P/T: 2192M, 2932W Ph.D.'s: 67%
Grad: 884M, 1642W S/F Ratio: 20 to 1
Year: sems, ss Tuition: $624 ($1654)
Appl: July 1 R and B: $1674
4800 applied 4500 accepted 2400 enrolled
ACT: required NONCOMPETITIVE

University of New Orleans, established in 1958, is a state-controlled, coed institution. The library contains 420,000 volumes, and subscribes to 117,784 periodicals.

Environment: The 295-acre campus is located in the city of New Orleans, 15 minutes from downtown and the French Quarter. One dormitory accommodates 260 women and 340 men. A lounge and lockers are available for commuters.

Student Life: About 95% of the students are from Louisiana. Sixty-eight percent are graduates of public schools. About 5% of the students live on campus. Twenty-four percent are minority-group members. University housing is single-sex; there are visiting privileges. Students may keep cars on campus.

Organizations: About 2% of the students belong to 5 national fraternities and 6 national sororities. The university sponsors a student government, extracurricular activities, social events, and religious organizations.

Sports: The university competes on an intercollegiate level in 6 sports for men and 4 for women. There are 14 intramural sports for men and 11 for women.

Handicapped: About 98% of the campus is accessible to the physically handicapped. Facilities include wheelchair ramps, special parking, and elevators. Special counselors are available.

Graduates: About 40% of the freshmen drop out by the end of their first year; 45% remain to graduate.

Services: Students receive free placement, career counseling and psychological counseling, health care, tutoring, and remedial instruction. Placement services also are available to graduates.

Programs of Study: The university grants the B.A. and B.S. degrees. Associate, master's and doctoral degrees also are available. Bachelor's degrees are offered in the following subjects: BUSINESS (accounting, business education, computer science, finance, management, marketing), EDUCATION (elementary, health/physical, secondary, special), ENGLISH (English), FINE AND PERFORMING ARTS (music, music education, studio art), HEALTH SCIENCES (medical technology), LANGUAGES (French, German, Spanish), MATH AND SCIENCES (biology, chemistry, cytotechnology, earth science, mathematics, physics), PHILOSOPHY (philosophy), PREPROFESSIONAL (engineering—civil, engineering—electrical, engineering—mechanical), SOCIAL SCIENCES (anthropology, economics, geography, government/political science, history, psychology, social sciences, sociology).

Special: Combination degrees may be earned in preprofessional areas such as law, medicine, and dentistry. A general studies degree is available.

Honors: Ten national honor societies have chapters on campus.

Admissions: About 94% of those who applied were accepted for the 1981-82 freshman class. The ACT scores of those who enrolled were as follows: 55% below 21, 31% between 21 and 23, 11% between 24 and 25, 1% between 26 and 28, and 0% above 28. All Louisiana residents who are graduates of state-approved high schools and who have not attended college are eligible for admission. Those whose high school records or test scores indicate the probability of academic difficulty may be required to come to the university for an interview. Residents who are not graduates of state-approved high schools may apply but must take entrance examinations. Out-of-state applicants must meet more stringent admissions standards and are considered on the basis of academic achievement and aptitude.

Procedure: The ACT is required; for state residents, the results are used only for placement. Application deadlines are July 1 (fall), November 15 (spring), and May 1 (summer). Notification is made on a rolling basis. There is a $10 application fee.

Special: There is an early admissions plan. AP and CLEP credit is accepted.

Transfer: For fall 1981, 3400 students applied, 2777 were accepted, and 1707 enrolled. Those with fewer than 55 semester hours must present a GPA of at least 1.7; students with more than 55 semester hours need at least a 2.0. D grades transfer. Students must complete the last 30 hours in residence, of the 128 needed for a bachelor's degree. Application deadlines are the same as those for freshmen.

Visiting: Orientations for prospective students are scheduled regularly. Informal visits also may be arranged with the admissions office for weekdays. Guides are provided. Visitors may sit in on classes. Appointments are necessary.

Financial Aid: About 60% of the students receive aid. Thirty percent work part-time on campus. Average aid to freshmen from all sources is $464. The university awards about 20 freshman scholarships each year, and loans from the federal and state governments, local banks, and the school are available. The FAF is required. Aid application deadlines are May 1 (fall), December 1 (spring), and April 1 (summer).

Foreign Students: Two percent of the full-time students come from foreign countries. The university offers these students an intensive English course, an intensive English program, special counseling, and special organizations.

Admissions: Foreign students must score at least 500 on the TOEFL. No college entrance examination is required.

Procedure: Application deadlines are June 1 (fall), October 15 (spring), and March 1 (summer). Foreign students must present proof of funds adequate to cover their entire period of study. They must also pay out-of-state tuition fees. They must carry health insurance, which is available through the university for a fee.

Admissions Contact: Stanley P. Orvis, Associate Director of Admissions.

UNIVERSITY OF SOUTHWESTERN LOUISIANA C-4
Lafayette, Louisiana 70504 (318) 231-6474

F/T: 5058M, 4859W Faculty: 594; IIA, +$
P/T: 988M, 1165W Ph.D.'s: 50%
Grad: 292M, 979W S/F Ratio: 21 to 1
Year: sems, ss Tuition: $558 ($1181)
Appl: see profile R and B: $1524
2500 applied 2500 accepted 2300 enrolled
ACT: 15 NONCOMPETITIVE

University of Southwestern Louisiana is a state-supported institution that awards undergraduate and graduate degrees. The library contains 460,000 volumes and 783,500 microfilm items, and subscribes to 5300 periodicals.

Environment: The 736-acre campus is located in Lafayette, in the French-Acadian section of Louisiana, about 50 miles from Baton Rouge. University buildings include a student union complex on the shore of Cypress Lake, an art museum, a coliseum that seats more than 9000, an athletic field that seats 23,000, and residence halls for 1850 women, 1775 men, and 150 married couples.

Student Life: About 90% of the students come from Louisiana. About 20% live on campus. Unmarried full-time freshmen and sophomores must live on campus if space is available. Dormitories are single-sex.

Organizations: About 12% of the men belong to 1 of 16 fraternities, and 10% of the women belong to 1 of 10 sororities.

Sports: The university competes on an intercollegiate level in 8 sports for men and 3 for women. Intramural sports for men and women also are available.

Handicapped: About 60% of the campus is accessible to wheelchair-bound students. Facilities include ramps, parking areas, and elevators. Special class scheduling can be arranged. About 1% of the students have visual impairments and another 1% have hearing impairments. Tutoring, special test conditions, and other accommodations are provided for them. One special counselor is available.

Services: Students are provided with free psychological, placement and career counseling, tutoring, and remedial instruction. A small fee is charged for health care. Placement services also are available to graduates.

Programs of Study: The university awards the B.A., B.Arch., B.Mus., B.Mus.Ed., B.S.N., B.S.Ag., B.S.H.E., B.S., and several engineering degrees. Associate, master's, and doctoral degrees also are available. Bachelor's degrees are offered in the following subjects: AREA STUDIES (French), BUSINESS (accounting, business communication, business education, computer science, executive secretary, finance, management, marketing, merchandising, personnel, production management, public relations, restaurant administration), EDUCATION (agricultural, distributive, elementary, health/physical, industrial, secondary, special), ENGLISH (English, journalism, mass communication, speech), FINE AND PERFORMING ARTS (art, art education, dance, music, music education, music history and literature, radio/TV, theater/dramatics), HEALTH SCIENCES (dietetics, medical records, pre-medical technology, nursing, pre-physical therapy, speech and hearing therapy), LANGUAGES (French, German, Spanish), MATH AND SCIENCES (aquatic and fishery biology, biology, botany, chemistry, geology, mathematics, microbiology, physics, statistics, zoology), PHILOSOPHY (philosophy), PREPROFESSIONAL (agriculture, architecture, dentistry, engineering, engineering—chemical, engineering—civil, engineering—electrical, engineering—mechanical, engineering—petroleum, forestry, home economics, horticulture, interior architecture, law, medicine, optometry, veterinary, wildlife management), SOCIAL SCIENCES (anthropology, city and regional planning, criminal justice, economics, geography, government/political science, history, psychology, sociology).

Special: Students may design their own majors. A general studies degree is available.

Honors: Twenty-five national honor societies have chapters on campus. Honors programs are offered by the departments of biology, chemistry, computer science, English, history, mathematics, philosophy, political science, and psychology.

Admissions: All those who applied were accepted for the 1981–82 freshman class. Louisiana residents must be graduates of accredited high schools. Out-of-state applicants must have at least a 2.0 GPA.

Procedure: The ACT is required. Applications should be submitted at least 30 days before the start of the semester. The application fee is $5. Admissions decisions are made on a rolling basis.

Special: Early admissions and early decision plans are available. AP and CLEP credit is accepted.

Transfer: Most transfer applications are approved. A GPA of at least 2.0 is required. Students must earn in residence at least 30 of the 124 credits generally required for a bachelor's degree.

Visiting: Prospective students may arrange informal visits to the campus with the admissions office. Visitors may sit in on classes with the instructor's consent and stay overnight in the residence halls if space is available. Visits should be scheduled for weekdays during office hours.

Financial Aid: About 45% of the students receive aid in the form of scholarships, grants, loans, and part-time jobs. The average award to 1981–82 freshmen was $500. For priority consideration, aid applications should be submitted by February 15 (fall), October 1 (spring), and February 1 (summer).

Foreign Students: The 1700 foreign students at the university represent 12% of enrollment. An intensive English program, special counseling, and special organizations are offered.

Admissions: Foreign applicants must take the University of Michigan Language Test. No college entrance exams are required.

Procedure: Foreign students are admitted to all terms, and should file applications at least 90 days before the start of the term. Students must present evidence of adequate funds for 1 year. Health insurance, though not required, is available through the university for a fee.

Admissions Contact: Leroy Brusard, Director of Admissions.

XAVIER UNIVERSITY OF LOUISIANA D-4
New Orleans, Louisiana 70125 (504) 486-7411

F/T: 685M, 1120W Faculty: 119; IIA, – – $
P/T: 36M, 68W Ph.D.'s: 50%
Grad: 26M, 280W S/F Ratio: 15 to 1
Year: sems, ss Tuition: $2600
Appl: Aug. 1 R and B: $1850
1256 applied 875 accepted 469 enrolled
SAT: 390V 400M ACT: 15 LESS COMPETITIVE

Xavier University of Louisiana is a liberal arts institution affiliated with the Roman Catholic Church. The library contains 100,000 volumes and 10,000 microfilm items, and subscribes to 660 periodicals.

Environment: The 23-acre campus is located in the city of New Orleans. Dormitories house 496 students.

Student Life: Students come from 36 states; 82% are from the South. About 63% of the freshmen are graduates of public schools. Fifty-one percent of the students are Catholic. About 92% of the students are minority-group members. University housing is single-sex; there are no visiting privileges. Students may keep cars on campus.

Organizations: About 40% of the men belong to 3 national fraternities, and 25% of the women belong to 3 national sororities. Campus activities include movies, discos, and coffeehouses. The city of New Orleans offers other cultural and recreational activities.

318 LOUISIANA

Sports: The university participates in 1 intercollegiate sport for men and women. There are 9 intramural sports for men and 8 for women.

Handicapped: The university has no special facilities for the physically handicapped.

Graduates: Twenty-eight percent of the freshmen drop out by the end of their first year; 54% eventually graduate. About 22% of the graduates seek advanced degrees; 7% enter medical school, 1% dental school, and 2% law school. Fifty-six percent of the graduates pursue careers in business and industry.

Services: Students receive the following free services: placement, career, and psychological counseling, tutoring, and remedial instruction. Placement services also are available to graduates. Health care is available on a fee basis.

Programs of Study: The university confers the B.A., B.S., B.S.Pharm., B.F.A., and B.M. degrees. Master's degrees also are available. Bachelor's degrees are offered in the following subjects: BUSINESS (accounting, business administration, marketing), EDUCATION (early childhood, elementary, health/physical, secondary), ENGLISH (English, speech), FINE AND PERFORMING ARTS (art, art education, music, music education, music performance, radio/TV, studio art, therapeutic arts), HEALTH SCIENCES (medical technology, speech therapy), LANGUAGES (French, German, Greek/Latin, Russian, Spanish), MATH AND SCIENCES (biochemistry, biology, chemistry, mathematics, mathematics/computer science, microbiology, physics), PHILOSOPHY (philosophy), PREPROFESSIONAL (dentistry, engineering, medicine, pharmacy, social work), SOCIAL SCIENCES (economics, government/political science, history, psychology, sociology).

Required: Undergraduates must take 9 hours of English; 6 hours each of world history, social science, and natural science; and 3 hours of arts. Students must pass the URE to graduate.

Special: Combined B.A.-B.S. degrees may be earned in preengineering. Language majors are offered through the New Orleans Consortium of colleges.

Honors: The English and history departments offer honors programs. Two national honor societies are represented on campus.

Admissions: About 70% of those who applied were accepted for the 1981-82 freshman class. Of those who enrolled, the SAT scores were as follows: Verbal—87% below 500, 12% between 500 and 599, 1% between 600 and 700, and 0% above 700; Math—82% below 500, 12% between 500 and 599, 6% between 600 and 700, and 0% above 700. On the ACT, 82% scored below 21, 10% between 21 and 23, 5% between 24 and 25, 3% between 26 and 28, and 0% above 28. Applicants must be high school graduates, present an average of C or better, rank in the upper half of their class, have the recommendation of their high school, and have completed 16 Carnegie units. Admissions officers also consider ability to finance a college education, education of the parents, and leadership record.

Procedure: Applicants must take the ACT or the SAT. Application deadlines are August 1 (fall), December 15 (spring), and May 1 (summer). The university follows a rolling admissions policy. A $10 fee must accompany the application.

Special: Early decision and early admissions plans are available. AP credit is accepted.

Transfer: For fall 1981, 303 students applied, 152 were accepted, and 82 enrolled. A 2.0 GPA or better and a statement of honorable status from the last school attended are required. Students must spend at least 1 year in residence and must complete 30 of the 128 credits needed for a bachelor's degree. Application deadlines are the same as those for freshmen.

Visiting: Prospective students may schedule informal visits to campus with the admissions office. Guides are provided, and visitors may sit in on classes and spend a night in the residence halls if space is available. The best months for visits are October, November, February, March, and April.

Financial Aid: About 90% of the students receive aid. Forty-five percent work part-time on campus. Average aid to freshmen from all sources is $3000. Scholarships, federal loans, EOG, and CWS are available. Need is the primary consideration in determining awards. Tuition may be paid in installments. The university is a member of CSS. The FAF, FFS, or SFS must be submitted. The application deadlines are May 15 (fall), December 1 (spring), and May 1 (summer).

Foreign Students: About 3% of the full-time students come from foreign countries. The university offers these students special counseling.

Admissions: Foreign students must score at least 550 on the TOEFL. No college entrance examination is required.

Procedure: Application deadlines are August 1 (fall), December 1 (spring), and May 1 (summer). Foreign students must present a medical evaluation, as well as results of serological and tuberculin tests. They must also present proof of funds adequate to cover 1 year of study. They must carry health insurance, which is available through the university for a fee.

Admissions Contact: Sheila Hamilton, Coordinator of Admissions.

MAINE

BATES COLLEGE
Lewiston, Maine 04240

B-5
(207) 784-0181

F/T: 715M, 715W	Faculty: 130; IIB, +$
P/T: 10M, 10W	Ph.D.'s: 85%
Grad: none	S/F Ratio: 13 to 1
Year: 4-4-1	Tuition: $6960
Appl: Feb. 1	R and B: $2040
2337 applied	1015 accepted 410 enrolled
SAT: 560V 590M	HIGHLY COMPETITIVE

Bates College, founded in 1864, is a nonsectarian, private liberal arts college. The library houses 310,000 volumes and 30,000 microfilm items, and subscribes to 1470 periodicals.

Environment: The suburban campus occupies 125 wooded acres just outside Lewiston-Auburn, a community of about 70,000 people 30 miles from Portland. The 50 buildings on campus include a recently constructed recreational-athletic facility and a computer center. Eight brick dormitories house between 50 and 130 students each, and 24 converted Victorian houses accommodate between 15 and 30 students each.

Student Life: About 12% of the students come from Maine. About 67% are graduates of public schools. All but 3% of the students live on campus. About 6% are members of minority groups. The dormitories are both single-sex and coed; single-sex dorms have visiting privileges. Students may keep cars on campus.

Organizations: Bates has no fraternities or sororities. Extracurricular activities include publications; student government; special-interest, departmental, religious, and social-action groups; music and drama clubs; debating, and an outing club that explores the Maine countryside.

Sports: The college fields intercollegiate teams in 23 sports. About 24 intramural sports are offered, many on a coed basis.

Handicapped: About 40% of the campus is accessible to handicapped students. Special facilities include wheelchair ramps, parking areas, elevators, special class scheduling, and specially equipped rest rooms. The college has talking books available.

Graduates: About 5% of the freshmen drop out, and 80% remain to graduate. Fifty percent of the graduates pursue advanced degrees: 4% to 8% enter medical school, 1% enter dental school, and 6% to 8% go on to law school. About one-third of the graduates begin careers in business and industry.

Services: The following services are available free to students: health care; psychological, placement, and career counseling; and tutoring. Placement services also are available to graduates.

Programs of Study: The college awards the B.A. and B.S. degrees. Bachelor's degrees are offered in the following subjects: ENGLISH (rhetoric), FINE AND PERFORMING ARTS (art, music, theater/dramatics), LANGUAGES (French, German, Russian, Spanish), MATH AND SCIENCES (astronomy, biology, chemistry, geology, mathematics, physics), PHILOSOPHY (philosophy, religion), SOCIAL SCIENCES (anthropology, economics, government/political science, history, psychology, sociology). Fifty-two percent of all degrees are conferred in the social sciences, 29% in math and sciences, and 10% in English and theater.

Required: Students must take 5 courses in humanities, 3 in natural sciences, 3 in social sciences, and 1 of quantitative work.

Special: The 5-week "short term" from late April through early June allows time for special, independent, and cooperative programs. Virtually every department offers special on- and off-campus study opportunities. Students may graduate in 4 years by taking 32 courses and 2 short terms, or in 3 years by taking 30 courses and 3 short terms. Bates offers a junior year abroad, as well as nonmajor programs in uncommonly taught languages. Four-year combined B.A.-B.S. degrees are available in all fields, and students may design their own majors.

Honors: Phi Beta Kappa and several departmental honor societies have chapters on campus. All departments offer honors work. Degrees may be awarded with honors, high honors, and highest honors.

Admissions: About 43% of the applicants were accepted for the 1981-82 freshman class. SAT scores for those who enrolled in an earlier class were as follows: Verbal—52% between 500 and 600, 23% between 600 and 700, and 2% above 700; Math—42% between 500 and 600, 38% between 600 and 700, and 7% above 700. Eighty percent of the 1981-82 freshmen ranked in the top fifth of their high school class; 95% in the upper two-fifths. A student's high school record is the single most important factor considered by admissions officers. Other important considerations are test scores, advanced placement or honors courses, recommendations by high school officials, extracurricular activities, leadership record, evidence of special talents, impressions made during an interview, and personality.

Procedure: Applicants must take the SAT and 3 ATs. The SAT should be taken in May of the junior year or in November, December, or January of the senior year. A personal interview is strongly recommended. Applications should be submitted early in the senior year. The deadline is February 1 (freshmen are admitted only in fall). Notification is sent in April. There is a $25 application fee.

Special: Early and deferred admissions and early decision plans are available. AP credit is accepted.

Transfer: For fall 1981, 150 transfer students applied, 50 were accepted, and 30 enrolled. Applicants must have completed at least 4 college courses and must submit 3 recommendations. Other requirements are flexible, but a 3.2 GPA is recommended, as is a personal interview. Students must study at the college for at least 2 years, completing at least half of the 32 credits required for a bachelor's degree. D grades do not transfer. The application deadline is March 1.

Visiting: Prospective students may arrange overnight visits from September 15 through December 1 or January 5 to April 1. Guides are provided, and visitors may sit in on classes. The admissions office should be contacted for arrangements.

Financial Aid: Forty percent of the students receive aid through the college, and almost all of them work part-time on campus. The college is a member of CSS and grants approximately 125 freshman scholarships totaling $500,000. The average freshman financial-aid package totals about $4000. The total fund for all forms of aid is $3 million. The FAF must be submitted by February 1. Notification is sent at the same time as the admissions decision.

Foreign Students: Foreign students make up about 2% of the student body.

Admissions: Foreign applicants must take the TOEFL. No academic exams are required.

Procedure: The application deadline is February 1. Students must present proof of funds adequate for 1 academic year. Health insurance is not required.

Admissions Contact: William C. Hiss, Dean of Admissions and Financial Aid.

BOWDOIN COLLEGE B-5
Brunswick, Maine 04011 (207) 725-8731

F/T: 780M, 600W   Faculty: n/av; IIB, ++$
P/T: none   Ph.D.'s: 85%
Grad: none   S/F Ratio: 12 to 1
Year: sems   Tuition: $6865
Appl: Jan. 15   R and B: $2520
3017 applied   763 accepted   367 enrolled
SAT or ACT: not required   MOST COMPETITIVE

Bowdoin College, founded in 1794, is a coeducational, private liberal arts college. It is Maine's oldest institution of higher learning. The library houses 580,000 volumes and subscribes to 1757 periodicals.

Environment: The 110-acre campus is located in a rural area, in a town of 18,000 people, 26 miles from Portland. The 55 campus buildings include Massachusetts Hall, the original college, a registered national historic landmark. Residential buildings of various styles—small houses accommodating 9 to 30 people, dormitories housing 60 to 75, a residential tower with space for 200, garden apartments, and fraternity houses—accommodate 90% of the students.

Student Life: About 81% of the students are from out of state. Seventy-five percent of the students live in dormitories and 15% live in Greek-letter houses. Six percent of the students are members of minority groups. Housing is both coed and single-sex; the single-sex dormitories have visiting privileges. Freshmen must live in dormitories. Students may keep cars on campus.

Organizations: About 45% of the men and women belong to 1 of 6 local and 4 national fraternities on campus for part of their 4 years at college. There are no sororities. Campus activities include publications, music and drama groups, a radio station, special-interest and religious groups, films, lectures, and an orchestra. About 30% of the students participate in community service, including work with the elderly, the mentally and physically handicapped, and the young. Places of worship are available nearby for all faiths. The Atlantic Ocean is 10 minutes from campus, and ski areas and other recreational sites are within driving distance.

Sports: The college fields intercollegiate teams in 16 sports for men and 12 for women. Nine intramural sports are offered for men and 5 for women.

Handicapped: Special facilities for physically handicapped students include wheelchair ramps and elevators. About 1% of the students have impaired vision or hearing.

Graduates: About 2% of the freshmen drop out, and 95% remain to graduate. Seventy-five percent of the graduates pursue further study. Between 8% and 10% go to medical school, 1% enter dental school, and 8% to 10% go to law school.

Services: The following services are available free to students: psychological, placement and career counseling; tutoring; and remedial instruction. Placement services also may be used by graduates.

Programs of Study: All programs lead to the A.B. degree. Bachelor's degrees are offered in the following subjects: AREA STUDIES (Black/Afro-American), ENGLISH (English), FINE AND PERFORMING ARTS (art history, music, studio art), LANGUAGES (French, German, Greek/Latin, Italian, Russian, Spanish), MATH AND SCIENCES (biochemistry, biology, chemistry, geology, mathematics, physics), PHILOSOPHY (classics, philosophy, religion), PREPROFESSIONAL (engineering, law, medicine), SOCIAL SCIENCES (anthropology, economics, government/political science, history, psychology, sociology). A preprofessional program also is offered in education.

Special: The college participates in an exchange program with Amherst, Williams, Dartmouth, Trinity, Mt. Holyoke, Smith, Wellesley, Wheaton, Vassar, Wesleyan, and Connecticut colleges. A five-year combined B.A.-B.S. degree in engineering may be earned in conjunction with an approved college of engineering. A 6-year combined B.A.-LL.D. law program is offered with Columbia University. Off-campus study at other universities and a junior year abroad arranged through other institutions are available. Independent study is offered, and students may design their own majors.

Honors: Phi Beta Kappa has a chapter on campus. All departments have honors programs that emphasize independent study.

Admissions: Twenty-five percent of those who applied were accepted for the 1981-82 freshman class. Candidates should have completed 16 Carnegie units with an average of B or better and rank in the top 10% of their high school class. Admissions officers also consider advanced placement or honors courses, recommendations by school officials, evidence of special talents, extracurricular activities, impressions made during a personal interview, personality, and leadership record.

Procedure: Applicants are encouraged, but not required, to take the SAT. An interview is recommended. Freshmen are admitted only in fall. Application deadlines are January 15 for fall entry and November 15 for spring entry. Applicants are notified by April 1. There is a $25 application fee. The college observes the CRDA.

Special: Informal early and deferred admissions plans and an early decision plan are available. The deadline for early decision is December 15. AP credit is accepted.

Transfer: For fall 1981, the college received 92 applications, accepted 19, and enrolled 15 students. A GPA of 3.0 or better is required; a 3.5 is recommended. Students must spend at least 2 years in residence, earning 16 of the 32 credits required for a bachelor's degree. The application deadlines are January 15 (fall) and November 15 (spring).

Visiting: Guides are available for informal visits. Visitors may sit in on classes and stay overnight at the school. The admissions office should be contacted for arrangements.

Financial Aid: About 40% of the students receive aid, and 35% work part-time on campus. Scholarships, grants (including SEOG), loans (including NDSL), and campus employment (including CWS) are available. In 1981-82, 34% of the freshmen were offered a total of $1,203,450 in grants and $305,200 in loans. The average award was $6662 per student. All aid is awarded on the basis of academic ability and personal promise, and the amount is based on financial need. Special aid is given to students from disadvantaged backgrounds and minority groups. The college is a member of CSS. The FAF and the aid application must be filed by March 1.

Foreign Students: The 30 foreign students at Bowdoin make up about 2% of the student body. The college offers these students an intensive English course and special organizations.

Admissions: Foreign applicants must take the TOEFL. No academic exams are required.

Procedure: The application deadline is January 15. Students are required to carry health insurance, which is available through the college at no extra charge.

Admissions Contact: A. W. Wohltman, Admissions Fellow.

COLBY COLLEGE   B-4
Waterville, Maine 04901   (207) 873-1131

F/T: 875M, 800W	Faculty: 115; IIB, ++$
P/T: 14M, 25W	Ph.D.'s: 75%
Grad: none	S/F Ratio: 14 to 1
Year: 4-1-4	Tuition: $6540
Appl: Feb. 1	R and B: $2550
2974 applied	1309 accepted	450 enrolled
SAT: 570V 610M	HIGHLY COMPETITIVE

Colby College, founded in 1813, is a private, nonsectarian liberal arts institution. The library contains 365,000 volumes and 63,000 microfilm items, and subscribes to 1300 periodicals.

Environment: The 900-acre rural campus is situated on Mayflower Hill, 2 miles outside the city of Waterville and 190 miles from Boston. Most of the 42 buildings, including the science center, are of Georgian architecture. Other buildings include an art museum; a performing arts center; a physical education center with a pool, hockey rink, and indoor track; and dormitories that accommodate 733 women and 800 men. The college also sponsors fraternity houses.

Student Life: About 13% of the students are from Maine, and 71% are from New England. Seventy percent are from public schools. Ninety-one percent of the students live on campus. Four percent are minority-group members. Campus housing is both single-sex and coed. There are visiting privileges in single-sex housing. Only upperclassmen with permission may live off campus. Students may keep cars on campus.

Organizations: Nine national fraternities and 2 national sororities have chapters on campus, and 35% of the men and 15% of the women belong to one of them. Extracurricular activities include a weekly newspaper, student government, music groups, a drama society, special-interest and service clubs, and such cultural events as concerts, lectures, and plays. The Sugarloaf Ski Area and Belgrade Lakes are nearby.

Sports: The college sponsors intercollegiate teams in 15 sports for men and 14 for women. There are 10 intramural sports for men and 10 for women.

Handicapped: About 90% of the campus is accessible to physically handicapped students. Wheelchair ramps, special parking, elevators, and special class scheduling are available. There are no special counselors for handicapped students.

Graduates: Three percent of the freshmen drop out by the end of their first year; and 75% remain to graduate. Seventy percent of the graduates seek advanced degrees, including 2% who enter medical school, 10% who enter law school, and 1% who enter dental school. Twenty percent of the graduates pursue careers in business and industry.

Services: Students receive the following services free of charge: health care; psychological, placement, and career counseling; tutoring, and remedial instruction. Placement services including career workshops, preprofessional advisory programs, and on-campus interviews are available to graduates as well as students.

Programs of Study: All undergraduate programs lead to the A.B. degree. Bachelor's degrees are offered in the following subjects: AREA STUDIES (American, Asian, Western Civilization), BUSINESS (administrative science), ENGLISH (English), FINE AND PERFORMING ARTS (art, music), LANGUAGES (French, German, Spanish), MATH AND SCIENCES (biochemistry, biology, chemistry, geology, mathematics, physics), PHILOSOPHY (classics, philosophy, religion), SOCIAL SCIENCES (economics, government/political science, history, psychology, sociology). Forty-nine percent of undergraduate degrees are conferred in social sciences, 22% in math and sciences, 21% in humanities, and 8% in area studies.

Required: Students must demonstrate competency in English, a foreign language, and physical education; complete 3 of 4 January independent study programs; and meet distribution requirements in 3 academic divisions. Some departments require majors to pass the GRE before graduation.

Special: Programs include junior year abroad; a 3-2 engineering program, leading to a combined B.A.-B.S. degree, with the University of Rochester and Case Western Reserve University; an exchange program with Fisk University and Pomona and Pitzer Colleges; Washington Semester Program with American University; affiliation with Manchester College, Oxford, England; study programs in France at the University of Caen and in Japan at Doshisha University; and the January Program for Independent Study. Certification in secondary education is available. Students may design their own majors.

Honors: Five national honor societies have chapters on campus. A Senior Scholar Program is available.

Admissions: About 44% of those who applied were accepted for the 1981-82 freshman class. The SAT scores of those who enrolled were as follows: Verbal—9% below 500, 52% between 500 and 599, 34% between 600 and 700, and 4% above 700; Math—7% below 500, 35% between 500 and 599, 47% between 600 and 700, and 10% above 700. Applicants must have completed 16 Carnegie units and be recommended by high school officials. Successful candidates generally rank in the top 20% of their class and have at least a B average. Most can present advanced placement or honors courses and come from well-regarded high schools. The college also considers the student's extracurricular and athletic activities as well as leadership ability. Special consideration is given to disadvantaged students and children of alumni. Colby seeks a geographically diverse student body.

Procedure: Candidates must take the SAT and 3 ATs, including English Composition. The SAT should be taken by December of the senior year and the ATs by January of that year. ACTs are accepted in lieu of SATs and ATs, but the latter are preferred. An interview is recommended. An English teacher's recommendation and a guidance counselor's recommendation are required. The deadline for fall applications is February 1. Early decision candidates must apply by January 1 and are notified 4 weeks after all credentials are received, starting December 15. Others are notified by mid-April. New students are admitted to the fall and spring terms. There is a $30 application fee.

Special: Early decision and deferred admissions plans are available. The CRDA is observed. AP credit is accepted.

Transfer: For fall 1981, 51 students applied, 22 were accepted, and 12 enrolled. A B average and a satisfactory personal record are required. D grades do not transfer. Students must spend at least 2 years in residence and complete 60 of the 120 credits required to receive a bachelor's degree. Application deadlines are March 15 (fall) and December 15 (spring).

Visiting: Guides are available for informal visits. Visitors may sit in on classes and stay overnight at the college. Visitors may schedule an appointment to speak with a staff member during weekdays from May 1 to January 31 and on Saturday mornings from August through January.

Financial Aid: Thirty-five percent of the students receive financial aid. Thirty-two percent work part-time on campus. The college awards about 130 freshman scholarships each year from a fund of $2,000,000. The average award to freshmen from all sources is $6150. Students may apply for federal (NDSL) and state-guaranteed loans. The college is a member of CSS. The FCS, for upperclassmen, and the FAF are required. Application deadlines are February 1 (fall) and November 1 (spring).

Foreign Students: Two percent of the full-time students come from foreign countries. The college offers these students special counseling and special organizations.

Admissions: Foreign students must take the TOEFL. They must also take the SAT and ATs, including the EN or ES, and 2 others.

Procedure: Application deadlines are February 1 (fall) and December 1 (spring). Foreign students must present proof of a medical examination. They must also present proof of funds adequate to cover 4 years of study, and are required to carry health insurance, which is available through the college without charge.

Admissions Contact: Robert McArthur, Acting Dean of Admissions.

COLLEGE OF THE ATLANTIC   D-5
Bar Harbor, Maine 04609   (207) 288-5015

F/T: 85M, 94W	Faculty: 15; IV, av$
P/T: 4M, 5W	Ph.D.'s: n/a
Grad: none	S/F Ratio: 8 to 1
Year: tri, ss	Tuition: $4350
Appl: May 1	R and B: $1825
170 applied	118 accepted	74 enrolled
SAT: 540V 560M	VERY COMPETITIVE

The College of the Atlantic, founded in 1969, is an independent college devoted to the study of human ecology. The library houses 13,500 volumes and subscribes to 220 periodicals.

Environment: The 25-acre rural campus is located on a renovated estate on Frenchman Bay, within walking distance of Acadia National Park and the Atlantic Ocean. The college is 150 miles from Portland. A number of small houses and a converted oceanfront mansion house 45 students. Other facilities include laboratories, a solar woodworking shop, and a solar greenhouse. The college also sponsors on- and off-campus apartments and married student housing.

Student Life: Most students come from the northeastern United States, although more than 20 states are represented. About 40% live in campus housing. Five percent are members of minority groups. Residence facilities are coed. Students may keep cars on campus. Day-care services are available to all students, faculty, and staff.

Organizations: There are no fraternities or sororities. Extracurricular activities include chorus, chamber music, a film series, dances, and concerts.

Sports: The college does not participate in intercollegiate sports. Three intramural sports are offered for men and women.

Handicapped: About 75% of the campus is accessible to handicapped students. A ride service is available.

Graduates: About 8% of the freshmen drop out during the first year, and 75% remain to graduate. Twenty-five percent of the graduates pursue advanced degrees.

Services: Students receive the following free services: psychological and career counseling and placement aid. Fees are charged for health care and tutoring. The placement officer also assists graduates.

Programs of Study: The college grants the B.A. degree in human ecology. Students design their own programs from one or more of the following resource areas: environmental design, environmental science, public policy, and human studies.

Required: All students must participate in a workshop, independent study, internship, and senior project.

Honors: There are no honor societies or programs.

Admissions: About 70% of those who applied were accepted for the 1981–82 freshman class. Eighty percent of those who enrolled ranked in the upper fifth of their high school class, 90% in the upper two-fifths. The applicant's academic record should show evidence of high motivation and ability. The college seeks active, self-directed students who understand and are committed to human ecology. Special attention is paid to recommendations by school officials, evidence of special talents, personality, impressions made during an interview, advanced placement or honors courses, leadership record, and extracurricular activities.

Procedure: Applicants are encouraged, but not required, to take the SAT. An interview is required. The application fee is $20. The deadlines for applications are May 1 (fall), December 1 (winter), December 10 (spring), and May 30 (summer). Notification is made on a rolling basis.

Special: A deferred admissions plan is available. AP credit is accepted.

Transfer: About half the students who enter each year are transfers. The college prefers applicants to have a GPA of 3.0 or better and minimum scores of 500 on each part of the SAT. D grades are not transferable. Students must complete at least 2 years in residence, earning at least 54 of the 108 credit hours required for a bachelor's degree. Application deadlines are the same as those for freshmen.

Visiting: Visits may be scheduled through the admissions office, preferably for Mondays, Tuesdays, or Thursdays. Guides are provided, and visitors may sit in on classes and spend the night at the school.

Financial Aid: Grants, federal and college loans, and work-study jobs are available. About 45% of the students receive aid, and 36% work part-time on campus. Awards are determined on the basis of need. The average award to freshmen from all sources in 1981–82 was $2666. Application deadlines are March 1 (fall), December 1 (winter), and February 1 (spring). The FAF and a copy of the federal income tax return must be submitted. The college is a member of CSS.

Foreign Students: The college offers an intensive English course for foreign students.

Admissions: Applicants must take the TOEFL, the University of Michigan Language Test, or the Comprehensive English Language Test. No academic exams are required.

Procedure: Application deadlines are the same as those for other freshmen. Students must present proof of good health and evidence of adequate funds for 1 year of study. They are required to carry health insurance, which is available through the college for a fee.

Admissions Contact: Jim Frick, Director of Admissions.

HUSSON COLLEGE   C-4
Bangor, Maine 04401   (207) 947-1121

F/T: 306M, 345W   Faculty: 35; IIB, av$
P/T: 389M, 427W   Ph.D.'s: 37%
Grad: 50M, 40W   S/F Ratio: 20 to 1
Year: sems, ss   Tuition: $3825
Appl: open   R and B: $2240
748 applied   730 accepted   327 enrolled
SAT: 420V 440M   LESS COMPETITIVE

Husson College, founded in 1898, is a private institution offering teacher training, professional, and technical programs. The library contains 27,000 volumes and subscribes to 300 periodicals.

Environment: The 350-acre campus is located in a suburban area 1 mile from downtown Bangor. Facilities include 3 dormitories housing 580 students and a physical education center that contains an Olympic-size pool.

Student Life: About 65% of the undergraduates are from Maine. About 75% live on campus. Ninety percent of the freshmen come from public schools. Four percent are members of minority groups. Dormitories are single-sex, with visiting privileges. Students may keep cars on campus.

Organizations: About 30% of the students belong to 1 of 5 fraternities or 3 sororities on campus. About 30 campus organizations are available. Religious groups and counselors are provided for Catholic, Jewish, and Protestant students. The Maine coast, Acadia National Park, and several ski areas are nearby.

Sports: Four intercollegiate sports are offered for men and 3 for women. Seven intramural sports are offered for men and women.

Handicapped: The entire campus is accessible to handicapped students. Facilities include wheelchair ramps, special parking, elevators, special class scheduling, tutorial and remedial programs, and specially equipped rest rooms. Tape recorders and special testing, tutorial, and counseling services are available for students with impaired hearing or vision.

Graduates: About 16% of the freshmen drop out, and 70% remain to graduate. Ten percent of the graduates pursue advanced degrees, and 95% begin careers in business and industry.

Services: The following services are available free to students: psychological, placement, and career counseling; tutoring; remedial instruction; and health care. Placement services, including on-campus interviews and resume preparation, are available to graduates as well.

Programs of Study: The college awards the B.S. degree. Associate and master's degrees also are available. Bachelor's degrees are offered in the following subjects: BUSINESS (accounting, business administration, business education, computer science, court and conference reporting, finance, marketing, office administration, personnel management, real estate insurance, small business administration). Ninety percent of the undergraduate degrees are conferred in business and 10% in education.

Special: The accounting program has won recognition from the National Board of C.P.A. Examiners. Most commercial teachers in Maine are graduates of the business education program. The educational programs lead to certification.

Honors: Qualified students may join Kappa Phi Kappa.

Admissions: Ninety-seven percent of those who applied were accepted for the 1981–82 freshman class. The SAT scores of those who enrolled were as follows: Verbal—91% below 500, 9% between 500 and 599, 0% between 600 and 700, and 0% above 700; Math—76% below 500, 19% between 500 and 599, 4% between 600 and 700, and 0% above 700. A recommendation from the applicant's high school is required. Other factors considered by the admissions committee include advanced placement or honors courses, impressions made during an interview, extracurricular activities, special talents, personality, and leadership record.

Procedure: Neither the SAT nor the ACT is required. Application deadlines are open. Admissions decisions are made on a rolling basis. There is a $10 application fee.

Special: Early and deferred admissions and early decision plans are available. AP and CLEP credit is accepted.

Transfer: For fall 1981, all 60 transfer applications were accepted, and 42 students enrolled. Requirements are flexible, but applicants

322 MAINE

should have a GPA of 2.0 or better. D grades do not transfer. There is a 1-year residency requirement; students must earn at least 30 of the 120 credits required for a bachelor's degree.

Visiting: Regularly scheduled orientations for prospective students include classroom visits, an overnight stay, a campus tour, and visits with faculty members and students. Guides also are available for informal visits while school is in session. Visitors may sit in on classes and stay overnight at the school. The admissions office should be contacted for arrangements.

Financial Aid: About 70% of the students receive aid, and 50% work part-time on campus. Award packages consist of grants, CWS jobs, and low-interest loans. The average award is $2100. The FAF and the aid application are required; application deadlines are open.

Foreign Students: The foreign students at the college represent 5% of total enrollment. The college offers an intensive English program, special counseling, and special organizations.

Admissions: Foreign applicants must score 500 or better on the TOEFL. No academic exams are required.

Procedure: Application deadlines are open. Students must present proof of adequate funds for 1 year and must carry health insurance, which is available through the college for a fee.

Admissions Contact: Paul E. Husson, Director of Admissions.

MAINE MARITIME ACADEMY   C-5
Castine, Maine 04421   (207) 326-4311

F/T: 625M, 20W	Faculty: 50; IIB, +$
P/T: none	Ph.D.'s: 17%
Grad: none	S/F Ratio: 13 to 1
Year: tri, ss	Tuition: $2195 ($3725)
Appl: May 15	R and B: $2485
869 applied	257 accepted	184 enrolled
SAT: 442V 532M		COMPETITIVE+

The Maine Maritime Academy, founded in 1941, is a state-supported institution that qualifies students for a license in the U.S. Merchant Marine and a B.S. degree. The library contains 50,000 volumes and subscribes to 1000 periodicals.

Environment: The campus is located in a rural area 40 miles from Bangor. Buildings include waterfront laboratories and machine shops, a gymnasium, a fieldhouse with a swimming pool, a student union, coed dormitories, and a learning resource center.

Student Life: About 70% of the students come from Maine. Almost all freshmen are from public schools. Two percent are members of minority groups. All students must live on campus. Standard military academy regulations and curfews apply. Drinking is prohibited on campus. Only upperclassmen may keep cars on campus, and cars may be used only on weekends.

Organizations: There are no fraternities. A chapter of Alpha Phi Omega, a national service fraternity, is active. Religious organizations and counselors for Catholic and Protestant students are available.

Sports: The academy fields intercollegiate teams in 5 sports for men and 1 for women. Eleven intramural sports are offered for men and 8 for women.

Handicapped: Special facilities for physically handicapped students include wheelchair ramps, special parking, and elevators.

Graduates: Fifteen percent of the freshmen drop out, and 70% remain to graduate. About 1% of the graduates pursue advanced degrees; all begin careers in business and industry, primarily in the maritime field.

Services: The following services are available free to students: psychological, placement, and career counseling; tutoring; and remedial instruction. Fees are charged for health-care services.

Programs of Study: The program leads to the B.S. degree and a license in the Merchant Marine. Major programs are offered in nautical sciences and marine engineering. A minor program is recommended for all students. They may choose from a variety of technical and scientific fields and from traditional academic subjects.

Required: Students must apply for and accept, if offered, commissions in the U.S. Naval Reserve or U.S. Coast Guard Reserve.

Admissions: Thirty percent of those who applied were accepted for the 1981-82 freshman class. The SAT scores of those who enrolled were as follows: Verbal—77% below 500, 19% between 500 and 599, 4% between 600 and 700, and 0% above 700; Math—30% below 500, 57% between 500 and 599, 12% between 600 and 700, and 1% above 700. Applicants must have completed 15 Carnegie units and be recommended by the secondary school. They should present at least a C average and rank in the top half of their class. Personality, financial ability, leadership record, advanced placement or honors courses, recommendations, extracurricular activities, and impressions made during an interview also are considered. Residents of Maine are given preference, and standards are higher for out-of-state residents.

Procedure: Applicants should take the SAT in March of the junior year or November of the senior year. The ACT also is acceptable. An interview is strongly recommended. The application deadline for fall admission is May 15. Notification is made on a rolling basis. There is a $20 application fee.

Special: AP credit is accepted.

Transfer: A limited number of transfer students are accepted. Students may transfer only before the junior year. Requirements include an interview, a GPA of 2.0 or better, and a college program equivalent to that of the academy. Applicants must spend 3 years in residence, earning all 140 credit hours required for a bachelor's degree.

Visiting: Regularly scheduled orientations for prospective students include guided tours, meals, and interviews. Guides are not available for informal visits, but such visitors may sit in on classes by prior arrangement and stay overnight at the school. Visits are best scheduled from 9 A.M. to noon on weekdays. The admissions office should be contacted for arrangements.

Financial Aid: Forty percent of the students receive aid through the college, and 28% work part-time on campus. Students accepted as cadets in the U.S. Maritime Service receive a federal subsidy of approximately $100 a month, which is applied to their fees. Loans are available from the federal government ($50,000), local banks ($440,000), and the academy ($50,000). The average scholarship is $400 (maximum $500); the average loan is $800 (maximum $1000 per semester). Students may earn up to $1000 a year from campus employment. Total aid from all sources averages $2500. The FAF and aid application must be filed by May 15. The academy is a member of the CSS. Tuition may be paid on the installment plan.

Foreign Students: About 1% of the students are from foreign countries.

Admissions: Applicants must take the TOEFL. No academic exams are required.

Procedure: The application deadline is May 15. Students must meet the physical requirements for a license as established by the U.S. Coast Guard. They also must provide evidence of adequate funds for 1 year. Students are required to carry health insurance, which is available through the academy for a fee.

Admissions Contact: Cmdr. Leonard H. Tyler, Director of Admissions and Financial Aid.

NASSON COLLEGE   A-6
Springvale, Maine 04083   (207) 324-5340

F/T: 352M, 248W	Faculty: 51; IIB, -$
P/T: none	Ph.D.'s: 55%
Grad: none	S/F Ratio: 11 to 1
Year: sems, ss	Tuition: $4680
Appl: open	R and B: $2220
561 applied	431 accepted	201 enrolled
SAT: 460V 480M		COMPETITIVE

Nasson College, established in 1912, is a private, nonsectarian institution. Its library contains 140,000 volumes and subscribes to 1200 periodicals.

Environment: The 280-acre campus is located in rural Springvale, 35 miles southwest of Portland and 82 miles from Boston. Springvale lies virtually at the gateway to Maine's famous vacation areas. The college's 33 buildings include 14 single-sex and coed residence halls that accommodate 90% of the students.

Student Life: Most students come from the Northeast, with 80% from New England and 10% from Maine. Two percent are members of minority groups. Single students not staying with their immediate families must live in dormitories. All students may have cars on campus. Single-sex dormitories have visiting privileges.

Organizations: There are no fraternities or sororities. Extracurricular activities include a radio station, campus publications, an outing club, social service groups, music, theater, and student government.

Sports: Nasson sponsors intercollegiate teams in 5 sports. Four intramural sports also are offered.

Handicapped: About 50% of the campus is accessible to handicapped students. Facilities include wheelchair ramps and special parking.

Graduates: Approximately 10% of the freshmen drop out, and 60% remain to graduate. Between 35% and 40% of the graduates pursue advanced degrees. Five percent go to medical school, 2% to dental school, and 8% to law school. Another 35% of the graduates begin careers in business and industry.

Services: The following services are available to students free of charge: health care; psychological, placement and career counseling; tutoring; and remedial instruction.

Programs of Study: The college awards B.A. and B.S. degrees. Associate degrees also are available. Bachelor's degrees are offered in the following subjects: BUSINESS (accounting, business administration, finance, management, marketing), ENGLISH (English communications/journalism), FINE AND PERFORMING ARTS (art, radio/TV, studio art, theater/dramatics), HEALTH SCIENCES (medical technology), MATH AND SCIENCES (biology, chemistry, earth science, ecology/environmental science, natural sciences, physical sciences, water technology), PREPROFESSIONAL (dentistry, engineering, law, veterinary), SOCIAL SCIENCES (government/political science, history, public administration, psychology, sociology). Thirty percent of the degrees are conferred in math and sciences, 30% in business, and 25% in social sciences.

Special: Internships are available to students majoring in environmental studies, human services, art, theater, and public administration. Students in good standing may study in Italy for six months. Four-year combined B.A.-B.S. degrees are offered in all subjects. A general studies degree is available, and students may design their own majors.

Honors: All departments offer honors programs.

Admissions: Seventy-seven percent of those who applied were accepted for the 1981-82 freshman class. The SAT scores of those who enrolled were as follows: Verbal—30% between 500 and 599, 10% between 600 and 700, and 5% above 700; Math—32% between 500 and 599, 8% between 600 and 700, and 1% above 700. Applicants should rank in the top 75% of their high school class, present an average of 2.0 or better, be graduates of a high school college-prep program, have recommendations from high school officials, and show evidence of contributions to school or community activities. Admissions officers also consider advanced placement or honors courses, personality, evidence of special talents, and impressions made during a personal interview.

Procedure: Applications for fall admission should be submitted in the fall of the senior year and are accepted until the class is filled. Students also are admitted to spring and summer terms. The SAT or ACT is required, and an interview is recommended. Notification is made on a rolling basis. There is a $20 application fee.

Special: Early decision and deferred admissions plans are available. AP and CLEP credit is accepted.

Transfer: For fall 1981, all 40 transfer applicants were accepted, and 30 enrolled. Applicants must have a GPA of 2.0 or better and at least 16 credits; a C+ average and a combined SAT score of 1000 are recommended. Students must spend at least 3 semesters in residence, earning at least 45 of the 120 credits required for a bachelor's degree. Students should apply in August for fall entry and in December for spring entry.

Visiting: Guides are available for informal visits. Visitors may sit in on classes. Visits should be scheduled during the school year with the admissions office.

Financial Aid: About 47% of the students receive aid. The college has $350,000 available for scholarships, $50,825 for loans, and $65,000 for campus jobs. Scholarship-and-loan packages average $2680 per year, and students can earn an additional $600 from campus employment. Financial aid applications and the FAF should be filed by March 1 for fall admission and December 15 for spring admission. The college is a member of CSS.

Foreign Students: Foreign students represent about 10% of the student body. The college provides special counseling and special organizations.

Admissions: Foreign applicants must take the TOEFL. No academic exams are required.

Procedure: Applications should be submitted by August for fall entry and by January for spring entry. Students must present a medical report as proof of health and also must show evidence of adequate funds. Health insurance is available through the college for a fee.

Admissions Contact: Richard Lolatte, Director of Admissions.

MAINE 323

PORTLAND SCHOOL OF ART   B-6
Portland, Maine 04101   (207) 775-3052

F/T: 99M, 165W	Faculty: 16; IV, −$
P/T: 3W	Ph.D.'s: n/av
Grad: none	S/F Ratio: 13 to 1
Year: sem, ss	Tuition: $3720
Appl: Apr. 1	R and B: n/app
384 applied	134 accepted	112 enrolled
SAT: 560V 500M	ACT: 17	SPECIAL

The Portland School of Art, established in 1882, is a division of the Portland Society of Art. The school offers day and evening art classes. Its library contains 12,000 volumes and 35,000 slides, and subscribes to 50 periodicals.

Environment: The school is located in the city of Portland and is housed in 4 historic buildings. One of the buildings, constructed in 1832, is listed in the National Register of Historic Places. There are no on-campus living facilities.

Student Life: Students come from 23 states and 1 foreign country. Two percent are members of minority groups. Most evening students are commuters.

Graduates: Nineteen percent of the freshmen drop out during the first year, and 58% remain to graduate. Five percent of the graduates pursue advanced degrees.

Services: Placement, career, and psychological counseling are available without charge. Fees are charged for health-care services.

Programs of Study: All programs lead to the B.F.A. degree. Degrees are offered in FINE AND PERFORMING ARTS (ceramics and pottery, fine arts, graphic design/commercial art, painting, photography, printmaking, sculpture, silversmithing and jewelry, studio art).

Admissions: Thirty-five percent of those who applied were accepted for the 1981-82 freshman class. Admissions decisions are based primarily on a student's past performance and talent. Applicants must have earned a high school diploma or the equivalent and must present a portfolio. They should rank in the upper half of their class. The school also considers evidence of special talents, recommendations by school officials, and impressions made during an interview.

Procedure: Applicants are encouraged, but not required, to take the SAT or ACT. Applications should be submitted by April 1 for priority consideration. Students are admitted only in the fall. A $20 fee is required. The school follows a rolling admissions policy.

Transfer: For fall 1981, 12 transfer students applied, 6 were accepted, and all 6 enrolled. Students must complete 2 years in residence, and must complete 120 credits to receive a bachelor's degree. Application deadlines are April 1 (fall) and December 1 (spring).

Visiting: Guides are available for informal visits, and visitors may sit in on classes. Arrangements should be made with the registrar.

Financial Aid: Fifty percent of the students receive financial aid. Applications should be submitted by April 1 for priority consideration.

Admissions Contact: Leslie Bowman, Director of Admissions.

SAINT JOSEPH'S COLLEGE   A-6
North Windham, Maine 04062   (207) 892-6766

F/T: 155M, 345W	Faculty: 36; IIB, −−$
P/T: 35M, 67W	Ph.D.'s: 65%
Grad: none	S/F Ratio: 12 to 1
Year: sems, ss	Tuition: $3425
Appl: July 1	R and B: $1700
597 applied	425 accepted	180 enrolled
SAT: 440V 465M		COMPETITIVE

St. Joseph's College, the Catholic college of Maine, was chartered in 1912 and is operated by the Sisters of Mercy. The library contains 76,000 volumes and subscribes to 470 periodicals.

Environment: The 115-acre campus is located in a rural setting on the shore of Sebago Lake, 16 miles from Portland. Students live in single-sex residence halls and townhouse facilities.

Student Life: About 57% of the students come from public schools, and 70% live on campus. Two percent are members of minority groups. There are no dormitory visiting privileges. All students may have cars on campus.

Organizations: There are no fraternities or sororities. Extracurricular activities include a newspaper, a drama club, and student government. An academic council, composed equally of faculty and students, formulates policy and sponsors programs. Cultural and recreational centers near campus include Portland Symphony Hall, Cumberland County Civic Center, a major 4-season recreational area, and Maine's best ski slopes.

Sports: The college fields intercollegiate teams in 3 sports for men and 4 for women. Eight intramural sports are offered for men and women.

Handicapped: There are no special facilities for physically handicapped students.

Graduates: About 15% of the freshmen drop out, and 70% remain to graduate. Forty percent of the graduates pursue advanced degrees, including 2% who go to law school, 1% who go to dental school, and 1% who go to medical school. About 20% of the graduates begin careers in business and industry.

Services: The following services are provided to students free of charge: health care; psychological, placement, and career counseling; tutoring; and remedial instruction. Graduates also may use the career placement center.

Programs of Study: The college awards the B.A., B.S., B.S.B.A., B.S.P.A., and B.S.N. degrees. Bachelor's degrees are offered in the following subjects: AREA STUDIES (American), BUSINESS (accounting, business administration, management, marketing), EDUCATION (elementary, secondary), ENGLISH (English), FINE AND PERFORMING ARTS (Communications/broadcasting), HEALTH SCIENCES (nursing), LANGUAGES (French), MATH AND SCIENCES (biology, ecology/environmental science, mathematics, natural sciences), PRE-PROFESSIONAL (dentistry, law, medicine, veterinary), SOCIAL SCIENCES (history, sociology). Forty percent of the degrees are conferred in health sciences, 24% in education, and 20% in business.

Required: All students must take 6 hours of religious studies.

Special: The college offers independent study and internships. Social-sciences majors spend an 8-week field period with the State Division of Child Welfare. Third- and fourth-year students may make arrangements through other institutions to spend a year abroad.

Honors: Delta Epsilon Sigma and Beta Omicron have chapters on campus.

Admissions: Seventy-one percent of those who applied were accepted for the 1981–82 freshman class. The SAT scores of those who enrolled were as follows: Verbal—72% below 500, 22% between 500 and 599, 6% between 600 and 700, and 0% above 700; Math—64% below 500, 27% between 500 and 599, 9% between 600 and 700, and 0% above 700. Applicants should rank in the top 70% of their class. Sixteen high school units are required. Applicants whose SAT scores are lower than the college's median should present a strong recommendation from a guidance counselor or principal. Advanced placement or honors courses, personality, extracurricular activities, and results of an interview also are considered important.

Procedure: The SAT is required and should be taken by January of the senior year. Applications for fall admissions should be filed during the senior year. Application deadlines are July 1 (fall) and December 1 (winter). Notification is made on a rolling basis beginning in December. There is a $20 application fee.

Special: A deferred admissions plan is available. AP and CLEP credit is accepted.

Transfer: For fall 1981, 67 students applied, 51 were accepted, and 38 enrolled. A C average is recommended. D grades do not transfer. Students must spend at least 1 year in residence, earning at least 32 of the 128 credits required for a bachelor's degree.

Visiting: Guides are available for informal visits. Visitors may sit in on classes and stay overnight on campus by prior arrangement. Visits should be scheduled with the admissions office for a weekday from 9 A.M. to 5 P.M..

Financial Aid: Partial and full scholarships are awarded on the basis of academic achievement and financial need. The college participates in the NDSL, EOG, and CWS programs. About 65% of the students work part-time; about 72% receive some form of aid. The average aid package in 1981–82 was $2800. A deferred payment plan is available. Applications for scholarships must be filed, along with the FAF, by April 1. Loan applications must be filed by July 1.

Foreign Students: One foreign student was enrolled in 1981–82.

Admissions: Students must score 500 or better on the TOEFL. They also must take the SAT.

Procedure: Application deadlines are March 1 (fall) and September 1 (winter). Students must submit a signed statement from a physician as proof of health and also must provide evidence of adequate funds for 4 years. Students are required to carry health insurance.

Admissions Contact: Frederic V. Stone, Admissions Counselor.

THOMAS COLLEGE B-4
Waterville, Maine 04901 (207) 873-0771

F/T: 179M, 225W Faculty: 22; IIA, – – $
P/T: 110M, 277W Ph.D.'s: 38%
Grad: 73M, 10W S/F Ratio: 18 to 1
Year: sems, ss Tuition: $4070
Appl: open R and B: $2200
552 applied 507 accepted 170 enrolled
SAT: 383V 460M COMPETITIVE

Thomas College is a private college founded in 1894 to give young men and women a business and professional education with a liberal arts foundation. The library houses 18,000 volumes and subscribes to 185 periodicals.

Environment: The college is located in a rural setting on a 70-acre campus 2 miles from the town of Waterville. Four coed dormitories house 103 women and 140 men. A student village houses 82 upperclassmen, and a townhouse built in 1977 houses 18 upperclassmen.

Student Life: Seventy percent of the students come from Maine. Three-fourths of the freshmen come from public schools. Seventy-seven percent of the students live on campus. None were members of minority groups in 1981–82. Students may keep cars on campus.

Organizations: Thirty percent of the students belong to 1 of 3 fraternities or 3 sororities on campus. Activities include service clubs; art, music, journalism, and photography groups; student government; cultural events such as lectures, films, and plays; major social events such as Winter Carnival and Spring Weekend; and Catholic and Protestant religious organizations.

Sports: The college participates in 5 intercollegiate sports for men and 3 for women. Nine intramural sports are offered for men and 8 for women.

Handicapped: About 90% of the campus is accessible to physically handicapped students. No special facilities or counselors are available.

Graduates: About 1% of the freshmen drop out, and 53% remain to graduate. Ten percent of the graduates pursue advanced degrees.

Services: The following services are available free to students: health care; placement, career, and psychological counseling; and tutoring. Placement services, including on-campus job interviews, also may be used by graduates.

Programs of Study: The college offers the B.S. degree as well as master's and associate degrees. Bachelor's degrees are offered in business (accounting, business administration, business education, computer science, management, marketing, retail management).

Required: Freshmen must take courses in English, humanities, mathematics, and basic accounting.

Special: Two-year programs are offered in liberal arts, retail merchandising, banking, business, real estate, and secretarial science (executive, legal, and medical). Independent study also is available.

Honors: The Alpha Chi national honor society is represented on campus.

Admissions: Ninety-two percent of those who applied were accepted for the 1981–82 freshman class. The SAT scores of those who enrolled were as follows: Verbal—99% below 500 and 1% between 500 and 599; Math—68% below 500, 31% between 500 and 599, and 1% between 600 and 700. Applicants must complete 15 Carnegie units, rank in the top half of their class, present an average of at least 75, and score at least 400 on each part of the SAT. Other important factors include advanced placement or honors courses; recommendations by school officials, friends, or alumni; an interview; and extracurricular activities.

Procedure: The SAT is required and should be taken in May of the junior year or in December or January of the senior year. An interview is recommended. Application deadlines are May 1 (fall), December 15 (spring), and June 15 (summer). There is a $10 application fee. Notification is made on a rolling basis.

Special: Deferred and early admissions and early decision plans are available. CLEP and AP credit is accepted.

Transfer: For fall 1981, 66 students applied, 60 were accepted, and 27 enrolled. Transfer students are accepted for the freshman, sophomore, and junior classes. D grades do not transfer. A minimum average of 2.0, scores of 400 or better on each section of the SAT, and a C or better in each course if the applicant has no A.S. degree are required. Students must study at the college for at least 1 year, earning at least 30 of the 120 credits required to receive a bachelor's degree. Application deadlines are open.

Visiting: Visiting prospective students are individually interviewed by an admissions officer and then tour the campus with student guides. Visitors may sit in on classes and stay overnight at the college. Visits should be scheduled when classes are in session. The admissions office should be contacted for arrangements.

Financial Aid: The college awards financial aid to 70% of the entering freshmen, and 25% of the students work part-time on campus. It is a member of the CSS. Loans from the federal government and local banks are available. The average scholarship is $3300; the average loan, $1000. Students may earn up to $1400 a year from campus employment. The deadlines for applications and the FAF are May 1 (fall) and October 31 (spring).

Foreign Students: Four foreign students, representing 1% of the student body, are enrolled at the college, which provides special counseling for them.

Admissions: Students must take either the TOEFL or the SAT. A minimum score of 450 is required on the TOEFL.

Procedure: Application deadlines are July 1 (fall), November 1 (spring), and May 1 (summer). Students must present proof of health and evidence of adequate funds for the term of study. They may be subject to special fees during vacation periods. Health insurance, though not required, is available through the college for a fee.

Admissions Contact: L. Lincoln Brown, Jr., Dean of Admissions.

UNITY COLLEGE   C-4
Unity, Maine 04988   (207) 948-3131

F/T: 200M, 100W		Faculty:	23; IIB, --$
P/T: none		Ph.D.'s:	50%
Grad: none		S/F Ratio:	12 to 1
Year: see entry		Tuition:	$4020
Appl: open		R and B:	$2200
364 applied	312 accepted		128 enrolled
SAT: 390V 410M			LESS COMPETITIVE

Unity College, founded in 1965, is a private, nonsectarian college of liberal arts and environmental science. The library contains 38,000 volumes and subscribes to 450 periodicals.

Environment: The 185-acre campus is located in a rural area 20 miles east of Waterville. The 14 buildings include a new library and coed dormitories that accommodate 240 students. The college also sponsors off-campus apartments.

Student Life: About one-sixth of the students are from Maine, and about half live on campus. Two percent are members of minority groups. Students may keep cars on campus. Day-care services are provided, for a fee, to all students, faculty, and staff.

Organizations: There are no fraternities or sororities. About 40% of the students leave the campus on weekends, some with college organizations such as the outing club. The Maine coast, Acadia National Park, and ski resorts are within a 2-hour drive.

Sports: The college sponsors intercollegiate teams in 4 sports for men and 2 for women. Six intramural sports are offered for men and 4 for women.

Handicapped: There are no special facilities or counselors for handicapped students.

Graduates: About 20% of the freshmen drop out, and 60% remain to graduate. Ten percent of the graduates seek advanced degrees. Sixty-five percent begin careers in business or industry.

Services: The following services are available free to students: psychological, placement, and career counseling; tutoring; and remedial instruction. Fees are charged for health care. The placement center also is open to graduates.

Programs of Study: The college offers B.A. and B.S. degrees. Associate degrees also are available. Bachelor's degrees are offered in the following subjects: FINE AND PERFORMING ARTS (environmental photography, visual studies), MATH AND SCIENCES (aquatic biology, ecology/environmental science), PREPROFESSIONAL (fisheries, forestry, outdoor recreation, wildlife). Associate degrees are available in conservation, law enforcement, forest technology, general studies, and wildlife and fisheries technology. Those degrees are transferable to 4-year degree programs. Eighty-five percent of all undergraduate degrees are conferred in sciences.

Special: A 3-year bachelor's degree program is available. Students may design their own majors. A general studies degree is offered. The college operates on a semester basis with 2 3-week terms, 1 in January and 1 in May.

Admissions: Eighty-six percent of those who applied were accepted for the 1981-82 freshman class. The SAT scores of those who enrolled were as follows: Verbal—80% below 500, 15% between 500 and 599, 5% between 600 and 700, and 0% above 700; Math—80% below 500, 15% between 500 and 599, 5% between 600 and 700, and 0% above 700. Applicants must have graduated from high school or have earned a high school equivalency certificate. High school graduates must rank in the top 60% of their class and present an average of 2.0 or better. Admissions decisions are based on a student's interest and motivation, rather than on past academic or extracurricular achievements. Recommendations from school officials, personality, impressions made during a personal interview, leadership record, and evidence of special talents also are considered.

Procedure: Neither the SAT nor the ACT is required. A copy of the high-school transcript must be submitted. Recommended application deadlines are August 30 (fall) and January 1 (spring). There is a $15 application fee. Notification is on a rolling basis.

Special: Early and deferred admissions and early decision plans are available. CLEP general and subject exams are accepted.

Transfer: For fall 1981, all 21 transfer applicants were accepted, and 20 enrolled. Transfer students are accepted for all classes. A minimum average of C is required; a 2.6 is preferred. D grades do not transfer. Students must earn at least 60 semester hours at the college of the 120 required to receive a bachelor's degree. Application deadlines are August 15 (fall) and January 15 (spring).

Visiting: All applicants who live within a reasonable distance are encouraged to visit the campus for a tour and interview before an admissions decision is made. Visitors may sit in on classes and stay overnight at the school. The best time to visit is when classes are in session. The admissions office should be contacted for arrangements.

Financial Aid: Grants, loans, and jobs are available. The average award is more than $3000. About 80% of the students receive aid; 60% work part-time on campus. The FAF and the college's aid application must be submitted by August 1.

Foreign Students: No foreign students were enrolled in 1981-82, but the college welcomes their applications.

Admissions: It is recommended that applicants take the TOEFL. They also must take the college's own entrance exam.

Procedure: Application deadlines are open; students are admitted to all terms. Students must present proof of adequate funds and carry health insurance, which is available through the college for a fee.

Admissions Contact: Ed Hinkley, Director of Admissions.

UNIVERSITY OF MAINE

The University of Maine is a 7-campus university system. The 4-year comprehensive campuses are located at Farmington, Southern Maine (Portland/Gorham), Orono, Fort Kent, Machias, and Presque Isle. Graduate programs are offered at the Orono and Southern Maine campuses. A two-year community college is located at Augusta. Separate profiles for each of the 4-year campuses follow.

UNIVERSITY OF MAINE AT   B-4
FARMINGTON
Farmington, Maine 04938   (207) 778-9521

F/T: 406M, 138W		Faculty:	81; IIB, +$
P/T: 136M, 306W		Ph.D.'s:	58%
Grad: none		S/F Ratio:	16 to 1
Year: sems, ss		Tuition:	$1235 ($3335)
Appl: open		R and B:	$2110
900 applied	687 accepted		437 enrolled
SAT: 424V 451M			COMPETITIVE

The University of Maine at Farmington, a campus of the University of Maine system, offers bachelor's and associate degrees. The library contains 90,000 volumes and 17,800 microfilm items, and subscribes to 749 periodicals.

Environment: The 32-acre campus is located in a rural village of 5000 people, 30 miles from Augusta. The 19 buildings include a student center and dormitories that house 850 students.

Student Life: About 80% of the students are from Maine, and 91% come from public schools. About 61% of the students live in residence halls. Two percent are members of minority groups. Dormitories are both single-sex and coed; there are visiting privileges in single-sex dorms. Students may keep cars on campus. Day care is available, for a fee, to all students.

326 MAINE

Organizations: Ten percent of the students belong to one of 2 fraternities and 2 sororities. Ski facilities are available nearby at Sugarloaf USA. Religious facilities are available for Catholic and Protestant students.

Sports: The university competes on an intercollegiate level in 5 sports for men and 5 for women. Four intramural sports are offered for men and 3 for women.

Handicapped: Eighty percent of the campus is accessible to physically handicapped students. Special facilities include wheelchair ramps, elevators, and specially equipped rest rooms. About 1% of the students are visually impaired.

Graduates: About 15% of the freshmen drop out, and 60% remain to graduate. About 1% of the graduates pursue advanced degrees, and 20% begin careers in business and industry.

Services: Students receive the following services free of charge: health care; tutoring; remedial instruction; and psychological, placement, and career counseling. Placement services also are available to graduates.

Programs of Study: The university confers the B.A., B.S., and B.G.S. degrees. Associate degrees also are awarded. Bachelor's degrees are offered in the following subjects: BUSINESS (business administration), EDUCATION (early childhood, elementary, secondary, special), ENGLISH (English), HEALTH SCIENCES (environmental health, speech therapy), MATH AND SCIENCES (biology, chemistry, ecology/environmental science, mathematics), PREPROFESSIONAL (dentistry, home economics, law, medicine, social work), SOCIAL SCIENCES (economics, geography, government/political science, history, psychology, social sciences). Associate degrees are offered in early childhood education, education of the trainable mentally retarded, land planning, instructional media technology, and dietetic technology.

Special: Students may design their own majors.

Admissions: Seventy-six percent of those who applied were accepted for the 1981-82 freshman class. The SAT scores of those who enrolled were as follows: Verbal—84% below 500, 13% between 500 and 599, 2% between 600 and 700, and 1% above 700; Math—66% below 500, 31% between 500 and 599, 3% between 600 and 700, and 0% above 700. Applicants must have completed 16 Carnegie units, present a grade average of at least 83, and rank in the upper half of their class. Other factors considered include recommendations by school officials, advanced placement or honors courses, personality, and extracurricular activities.

Procedure: The SAT is required. Application deadlines are open; new students are admitted to fall and spring semesters. Interviews are required of students who plan to major in special education, elementary education, or a 2-year program. A $10 application fee is required. Admissions decisions are made on a rolling basis.

Special: Early decision and deferred admissions plans are available. CLEP and AP credit is accepted.

Transfer: For fall 1981, 258 transfer students applied, 168 were accepted, and 129 enrolled. Transfers are accepted for all classes. D grades do not transfer. Applicants must present a GPA of 2.0 or better and undergo a personal interview. Students must earn, at the university, at least 30 of the 120-122 credits required for a bachelor's degree. Application deadlines are open.

Visiting: Guides are available for informal visits, and visitors may sit in on classes.

Financial Aid: About 65% of the students receive aid through the school; 24% work part-time on campus. Scholarships are available, as are loans from the federal government, local banks, and the university. The average award to freshmen from all sources in 1981-82 was $1600. Aid applications, the FAF, and a copy of the federal tax return must be submitted by March 15. The university is a member of the CSS.

Foreign Students: About 5 foreign students are enrolled at the university. Special counseling is provided, as is an intensive English course.

Admissions: Foreign applicants must take the TOEFL and the SAT.

Procedure: Application deadlines are open; new students are admitted in the fall and spring. Students must submit a completed health questionnaire as proof of good health and must show evidence of adequate funds for 1 academic year. Health insurance, though not required, is available through the university for a fee.

Admissions Contact: James Collins, Assistant Director of Admissions.

UNIVERSITY OF MAINE AT FORT KENT D-1
Fort Kent, Maine 04743 (207) 834-3162

F/T: 135M, 135W Faculty: 22; IIB, av$
P/T: 135M, 160W Ph.D.'s: 55%
Grad: none S/F Ratio: 12 to 1
Year: sems, ss Tuition: $1200 ($3300)
Appl: Aug. 1 R and B: $2250
327 applied 321 accepted 175 enrolled
SAT: 406V 430M **LESS COMPETITIVE**

The University of Maine at Fort Kent, founded in 1878, is a state-supported 4-year campus of the University of Maine system. The library contains 40,000 volumes and 3250 microfilm items, and subscribes to 178 periodicals.

Environment: The university occupies 52 acres on the Fish River in a rural area on the Canadian border, 40 miles from Caribou and 215 from Bangor. Dormitories house 153 students. The university is located in a bilingual region where French is dominant.

Student Life: Eighty-five percent of the students are from Maine. About 43% live on campus. About 1% are members of minority groups. Sixty-five percent are Catholic. Dormitories are coed. Students may keep cars on campus.

Organizations: About 7% of the students belong to the 1 fraternity or 1 sorority on campus. Campus groups include the environmental studies club, a literary magazine, a radio station, and the ski club. A ski slope and cross-country trails are adjacent to campus.

Sports: The university competes on an intercollegiate level in 3 sports for men and 2 for women. Fourteen intramural sports are offered for men and women.

Handicapped: About 30% of the campus is accessible to physically handicapped students. Wheelchair ramps, specially equipped rest rooms, and lowered telephones are provided. Special class scheduling may be arranged.

Graduates: About 42% of the freshmen drop out, and 19% remain to graduate. Ten percent of the graduates pursue further study, including 1% who enter medical school, 1% who enter dental school, and 1% who enter law school. Forty percent begin careers in business and industry.

Services: Students receive the following free services: tutoring, remedial instruction, placement aid, and career counseling.

Programs of Study: The university confers the B.A., B.S., B.S.N., B.S. in Environmental Studies, and Bachelor of University Studies degrees. Associate degrees also are available. Bachelor's degrees are offered in the following subjects: AREA STUDIES (bilingual/bicultural), EDUCATION (elementary, junior high), ENGLISH (English), HEALTH SCIENCES (nursing), LANGUAGES (French), MATH AND SCIENCES (biology, ecology/environmental science, math/science), SOCIAL SCIENCES (history, social sciences).

Special: Five-year combined B.A.-B.S. degrees may be earned in English, French, history, biology, and environmental science. Students may design their own majors. The university offers a general studies degree. Sophomores may study for 1 year in Canada, Mexico, or Europe.

Admissions: Almost all those who applied were accepted for the 1981-82 freshman class. The SAT scores of those who enrolled were as follows: Verbal—65% below 500, 35% between 500 and 599, and 0% above 600; Math—65% below 500, 35% between 500 and 599, and 0% above 600. Admissions for those seeking B. U. S. or A.A. degrees are open. Other candidates should have completed 16 Carnegie units. The university also considers such factors as interview impressions, school recommendations, and advanced placement or honors courses.

Procedure: Applicants for bachelor's degrees should take the SAT before March of the senior year. An interview is recommended. The application deadlines are August 1 (fall) and January 1 (spring). Applications should be submitted with a $10 fee. A rolling admissions plan is used.

Special: Early and deferred admissions plans are available. June 1 is the application deadline for early admission.

Transfer: Transfer students are accepted for all classes and admitted to fall and spring semesters. Grades of D or better transfer. A GPA of 2.0 and SAT scores of 400 on each part are recommended. Students must earn, at the university, at least 30 credits of the 120 required for a bachelor's degree.

Visiting: The university schedules orientations for prospective students. Guides also are available for informal visits while school is in session. Visitors may sit in on classes and stay overnight on campus. Arrangements should be made with the director of admissions.

Financial Aid: About 67% of the students receive aid; 25% work part-time on campus. Packages of grants, loans, and work-study jobs are available. The average award to freshmen in 1981-82 totaled $1538. The deadline for freshman aid applications is April 1. The FAF and an income-tax form are required. The university is a member of CSS.

Foreign Students: Fewer than 1% of the students are from foreign countries.

Admissions: Applicants must take the TOEFL or the SAT. A minimum score of 400 on each section of the SAT is recommended.

Procedure: Application deadlines are June 1 (fall), December 1 (spring), and June 1 (summer). Students must present proof of funds adequate for 1 year. Health insurance, though not required, is available through the university for a fee.

Admissions Contact: Glenys Sayward, Director of Admissions.

UNIVERSITY OF MAINE AT MACHIAS E-4
Machias, Maine 04654 (207) 255-3313

F/T: 201M, 275W	Faculty: 32; IIB, +$
P/T: 97M, 149W	Ph.D.'s: 38%
Grad: 4M, 25W	S/F Ratio: 13 to 1
Year: sems, ss	Tuition: $1245 ($3345)
Appl: open	R and B: $2250
430 applied	360 accepted 220 enrolled
SAT: 390V 460M	LESS COMPETITIVE

The University of Maine at Machias was founded in 1909 as the Washington State Normal School. The library contains 60,000 volumes and 2193 microfilm items, and subscribes to 300 periodicals.

Environment: The 47-acre rural campus is located in a small coastal town 90 miles from Bangor. The 10 buildings include 3 single-sex residence halls that house 380 students.

Student Life: About 85% of the students are from Maine, and 60% live on campus. About half the students leave campus on weekends. Three percent of the students are members of minority groups. Visiting is permitted in the dorms. Students may keep cars on campus.

Organizations: Student organizations include religious and professional groups, the Campus Recreation Association, the concert choir, and the student senate. About 20% of the students belong to 1 of 3 fraternities and 3 sororities. Outdoor recreation areas are nearby.

Sports: The university competes on an intercollegiate level in 2 sports for men and 2 for women. Ten intramural or club sports are offered for men and 8 for women.

Handicapped: About 75% of the campus is accessible to wheelchair-bound students. Special facilities include parking areas and specially equipped rest rooms.

Graduates: About 15% of the freshmen drop out and 50% remain to graduate. Ten percent of the graduates pursue advanced degrees, and 40% begin careers in business or industry.

Services: Students receive free health care, tutoring, and placement and career counseling. Placement services also are available to graduates.

Programs of Study: The university awards the B.A. and B.S. degrees. Associate degrees are also awarded. Bachelor's degrees are offered in the following subjects: BUSINESS (accounting, business administration, business education, management, marketing, recreation management), EDUCATION (early childhood, elementary, secondary—junior high), ENGLISH (English), MATH AND SCIENCES (biology, ecology/environmental science), SOCIAL SCIENCES (history). Thirty percent of the degrees conferred are in education, 30% in business, and 15% in math and sciences.

Required: Students must complete physical education and general education requirements.

Special: Students may design their own majors.

Honors: The university submits names of qualified students for listing in *Who's Who in American Universities and Colleges.*

Admissions: Eighty-four percent of those who applied were accepted for the 1981-82 freshman class. All candidates must have graduated from an accredited high school or have earned an equivalency certificate, rank in the upper 50% of their class, and present an average of C or better. Admissions officers also consider recommendations by school officials.

Procedure: The SAT or ACT is required. There are no application deadlines. Freshmen are admitted to all sessions. A $10 application fee is required. The university uses a rolling admissions plan.

Special: An early admissions plan is available. AP and CLEP credit is accepted.

Transfer: A GPA of 2.0 is required. D grades do not transfer. Students must spend 1 year in residence, earning at least 30 of the 120 credits required to receive a bachelor's degree.

Visiting: Guides are available for informal visits. Visitors may sit in on classes and stay overnight on campus. Visits should be scheduled for weekdays with the admissions office.

Financial Aid: About 75% of the students receive aid. Aid is available to needy students through federal and state governments and through CWS. Thirty-five percent of the students, including freshmen, receive work contracts. Tuition may be paid on the installment plan. Aid decisions are based on need. The college is a member of CSS. The FAF and aid application must be filed by May 1 (fall) or December 1 (spring).

Foreign Students: Foreign students make up about 1% of the student body.

Admissions: Applicants must take the TOEFL, University of Michigan Language Test, or Comprehensive English Language Test. The SAT or ACT also is required.

Procedure: Application deadlines are open. Students must present proof of adequate funds. Health insurance is available through the university.

Admissions Contact: Issy M. Bucklin, Assistant Director of Admissions.

UNIVERSITY OF MAINE AT ORONO C-4
Orono, Maine 04469 (207) 581-7568

F/T: 4936M, 3778W	Faculty: 621, I, — — $
P/T: 695M, 1135W	Ph.D.'s: 69%
Grad: 437M, 334W	S/F Ratio: 15 to 1
Year: sems, ss	Tuition: $1330 ($3640)
Appl: Mar. 1	R and B: $2530
5457 applied	4659 accepted 2555 enrolled
SAT: 474V 527M	COMPETITIVE

The University of Maine, established in 1865, is a state-supported institution offering training in liberal arts and sciences, business, education, life sciences and agriculture, and technology on both the undergraduate and graduate levels. The library at the Orono campus includes over 550,000 volumes and subscribes to over 4000 periodicals.

Environment: The 1100-acre campus is located in a rural area 8 miles north of Bangor. The university sponsors dormitories, on-campus apartments, fraternity houses, and married-student housing. Housing is available for 2487 men, 2419 women, and 120 married students.

Student Life: About 75% of the students come from Maine, 85% come from public schools, 70% live on campus. Dormitories are both single-sex and coed; there are visiting privileges in the single-sex dorms. Students may keep cars on campus. Day-care services are available, for a fee, to all full-time students, faculty, and staff.

Organizations: The university sponsors a wide variety of extracurricular activities and social events. About 20% of the students are members of the 16 fraternities and 8 sororities.

Sports: The university fields intercollegiate teams in 11 sports for men and 10 for women. Men can participate in a choice of 21 intramural sports, women in 19.

Graduates: About 20% of the freshmen drop out during the first year, and 60% remain to graduate. Of the graduates, 15% go on for further study.

Services: Psychological counseling, tutoring, career counseling, and placement assistance are provided free. Fees are charged for health care and remedial instruction.

Programs of Study: The university awards the B.A., B.S., and B.M. degrees. Associate and master's programs also are offered. Bachelor's degrees are offered in the following subjects: BUSINESS (business administration, finance, management, marketing), EDUCATION (child development, elementary, health/physical, home economics, secondary), ENGLISH (English, journalism, speech), FINE AND PERFORMING ARTS (art, art education, music, music education, radio/TV, theater/dramatics), HEALTH SCIENCES (medical technology),

328 MAINE

LANGUAGES (French, German, Greek/Latin, modern languages, romance languages, Spanish), MATH AND SCIENCES (biochemistry, biology, botany, chemistry, entomology, geology, mathematics, microbiology, plant and soil sciences, physics, zoology), PHILOSOPHY (philosophy), PREPROFESSIONAL (agriculture, dentistry, engineering, forestry, home economics, law, medicine, recreation and parks management, social work, veterinary, wildlife management), SOCIAL SCIENCES (anthropology, economics, government/political science, history, international relations, psychology, sociology).

Required: Each of the undergraduate colleges has its own requirements.

Special: Study abroad and a Washington semester are offered.

Honors: A number of honor societies have chapters on campus. An honors program also is offered.

Admissions: About 85% of those who applied were accepted for the 1981–82 freshman class. The SAT scores of those who enrolled were as follows: Verbal—61% below 500, 33% between 500 and 599, 6% between 600 and 700, and 0% above 700; Math—34% below 500, 46% between 500 and 599, 18% between 600 and 700, and 2% above 700. Applicants should have completed 16 units of academic work. Preference is given to residents of Maine. Advanced placement or honors courses, school recommendations, and the student's extracurricular activities record are also considered.

Procedure: The SAT and 2 ATs (English Composition for all applicants, and Mathematics Level I for engineering and science applicants) should be taken by March of the senior year. Application deadlines are March 1 (fall) and November 1 (spring). Notification is made on a rolling basis. There is a $10 application fee.

Special: An early admissions plan is available; the application deadline is March 1. AP and CLEP credit is available.

Transfer: For fall 1981, 1200 transfer students applied, 900 were accepted, and 600 enrolled. The university prefers that applicants have a GPA of 2.5 or better and an associate degree. Students must spend at least 1 year in residence, earning at least 30 of the 120 credit hours required for a bachelor's degree. Application deadlines are April 1 (fall) and November 1 (spring).

Visiting: Campus tours with student guides can be arranged. Visitors may sit in on classes.

Financial Aid: About 70% of the students receive aid; half work part-time on campus. The university offers various loans (NDSL included), federal/state grants (BEOG/SEOG included), and part-time campus employment (CWS included). About 1200 scholarships are awarded yearly. The average award to freshmen from all sources in 1981–82 totaled $2380. Tuition may be paid in installments. The FAF should be filed by March 1. The university is a member of CSS.

Foreign Students: The 118 foreign students enrolled at the university make up about 2% of the student body. The university provides special organizations and counseling for these students.

Admissions: Foreign applicants are required to score 550 or better on the TOEFL. No academic exams are required.

Procedure: Application deadlines are the same as those for other freshmen; students are encouraged to apply for fall admission only. Students must present proof of adequate funds for 1 year and must carry health insurance, which is available through the university for a fee.

Admissions Contact: William J. Munsey, Director of Admissions.

UNIVERSITY OF MAINE AT PRESQUE ISLE   D-2

Presque Isle, Maine 04769   (207) 764-0311

F/T, P/T: 1400M&W	Faculty:	76; IIB, av$
Grad: 15M&W	Ph.D.'s:	51%
Year: sems, ss	S/F Ratio:	18 to 1
Appl: open	Tuition:	$1170 ($3270)
761 applied	R and B:	$2187
SAT: 405V 425M	675 accepted	445 enrolled
		LESS COMPETITIVE

The University of Maine at Presque Isle, founded in 1903, is one of 8 campuses in the University of Maine system. The library contains 70,000 volumes and more than 4150 microfilm items, and subscribes to 600 periodicals.

Environment: The 150-acre campus is located on a hillside at the edge of Presque Isle, a town of 14,000 people 150 miles from Bangor. There are 15 buildings, including 2 single-sex and 2 coed residence halls and a recently built library.

Student Life: About 88% of the students are from Maine, 95% come from public schools, and 45% live on campus.

Organizations: About 10% of the students belong to 1 of 3 fraternities and 3 sororities on campus. University groups include outing, skiing, and mountain-climbing clubs; a geology club; music and drama associations; and Catholic and Protestant organizations. Social highlights include a winter carnival. Several outdoor recreation areas are located nearby.

Sports: The university competes on an intercollegiate level in 5 sports for men and 4 for women. Intramural sports for one or both sexes include football, softball, and basketball.

Handicapped: About 75% of the campus is accessible to wheelchair-bound students. Facilities include wheelchair ramps, special parking, specially equipped rest rooms, and lowered drinking fountains and telephones. Special tutoring and counseling are available for students with impaired vision or hearing.

Graduates: Thirty percent of the graduates pursue advanced degrees, including 1% who enter law school and 1% who enter dental school. Twenty-five percent begin careers in business or industry.

Services: Students receive the following free services: health care; tutoring or remedial instruction; and psychological, placement, and career counseling. Placement services also are available to alumni.

Programs of Study: The university awards the B.A., B.S., B.S.Sec. Ed., and B.S. in Environmental Studies degrees. Associate and master's degrees also are available. Bachelor's degrees are offered in the following subjects: BUSINESS (business administration, management), EDUCATION (elementary, health/physical, recreation, secondary), ENGLISH (English, speech), FINE AND PERFORMING ARTS (art, theater/dramatics), LANGUAGES (French), MATH AND SCIENCES (biology, ecology/environmental science, geo-ecology, mathematics, physical sciences), PHILOSOPHY (humanities), SOCIAL SCIENCES (behavioral science, government/political science, history, psychology, social sciences).

Special: Five-year combined B.A.-B.S. degrees in electrical engineering technology are available. Transfer programs are available in engineering, geology, nursing, medical technology, agricultural specialties, child development, food and nutrition, forestry specialties, and health and family life. Additional minors are available in economics, music, sociology, Soviet studies, and special education. The university also offers a general studies degree.

Admissions: Eighty-nine percent of those who applied were accepted for the 1981–82 freshman class. The SAT scores of those who enrolled were as follows: Verbal—93% below 500 and 7% above 500; Math—84% below 500, 14% between 500 and 600, 2% between 600 and 700, and 0% above 700. The most important criterion for admission is the high school transcript. Admissions officers also consider test scores, advanced placement or honors courses, leadership record, recommendations by school officials, impressions made during an interview, personality, and special talents. Special consideration is given to veterans and older adults.

Procedure: The SAT or ACT and 2 ATs, including English Composition, are required. Application deadlines for all terms are open. A $10 application fee is required.

Special: Early and deferred admissions plans are available. AP and CLEP credit is accepted.

Transfer: For a recent year, 174 applications were received, 162 were accepted, and 124 students enrolled. Transfers are accepted for all classes. D grades do not transfer. A minimum average of 2.0 is required.

Visiting: The university schedules orientations for prospective students. Guides also are available for informal visits, and visitors may sit in on classes. Visits should be scheduled with the admissions office for a time when classes are in session.

Financial Aid: About 75% of the students receive aid. Programs include EOG, NDSL, United Student Aid Loan Funds, Law Enforcement Education Grants, nursing scholarships, university scholarships, CWS, public benefit programs, and private scholarships. Guaranteed loans and campus jobs also are available. The average aid package in 1981–82 was $2200. Tuition may be paid in installments. The FAF and the university's aid application must be submitted as early as possible.

Foreign Students: About 10 foreign students are enrolled full-time. Special counseling and special organizations are provided.

Admissions: Applicants must score 450 or better on the TOEFL. The SAT is optional, and can be taken instead of the TOEFL.

Procedure: Application deadlines are open; new students are admitted to all terms. Students must present proof of adequate funds for 1

UNIVERSITY OF NEW ENGLAND A–6
Biddeford, Maine 04005 (207) 283-0171

F/T: 177M, 191W	Faculty: 25; n/av
P/T: 10M, 53W	Ph.D's: 80%
Grad: 191M, 39W	S/F Ratio: 15 to 1
Year: 4-1-4	Tuition: $4300
Appl: open	R and B: $2420
540 applied	370 accepted 183 enrolled
SAT: 430V 450M	COMPETITIVE

The University of New England, founded in 1953 as St. Francis College, is a private, nonsectarian college offering undergraduate and professional instruction. The library contains 65,000 volumes and subscribes to more than 500 periodicals.

Environment: The 122-acre oceanfront campus is located in a rural town of 20,000 people on the coast of southern Maine, 16 miles from Portland and 90 miles from Boston. The 10 buildings include 5 dormitories that accommodate 480 students.

Student Life: Twenty-seven percent of the undergraduates are from Massachusetts. About 85% live on campus. About 70% come from public schools. Three percent are minority-group members. All students may keep cars on campus. Campus housing is both coed and single-sex; there are no visiting privileges. Day-care services are available for a fee.

Organizations: There are no fraternities or sororities; professional and service organizations serve as social groups. Extracurricular activities include the radio station, student government, a ski club, and political, social service, and religious groups.

Sports: The university fields intercollegiate teams in 8 sports for men and 5 for women. There are 7 intramural sports for men and 6 for women.

Handicapped: About 60% of the campus is accessible to wheelchair-bound students. Special class scheduling is available.

Graduates: About 15% of the freshmen drop out, and 50% remain to graduate. Twenty-five percent of the graduates pursue further study, including 8% who enter medical school and 1% who enter dental school. Twenty percent begin careers in business and industry.

Services: Students receive the following services free of charge: placement, career, and psychological counseling; health care; tutoring; and remedial instruction. Placement services may be used by graduates as well as students.

Programs of Study: All programs lead to B.A. or B.S. degrees. Doctoral programs are also offered. Bachelor's degrees are offered in the following subjects: BUSINESS (business administration), EDUCATION (elementary), HEALTH SCIENCES (occupational therapy, physical therapy), MATH AND SCIENCES (biology, chemistry, ecology/environmental science, marine biology, medical biology), SOCIAL SCIENCES (human services). Sixty percent of degrees conferred are in the sciences.

Required: All students must take English composition and psychology. Students must earn an average of at least 2.0 to graduate.

Special: Work-study programs are available in all majors. Study abroad can be arranged through other institutions. A liberal studies degree is offered.

Admissions: Sixty-nine percent of those who applied were accepted for the 1981–82 freshman class. The SAT scores of those who enrolled in an earlier class were as follows: Verbal—36% between 500 and 600, 9% between 600 and 700, and 5% above 700; Math—37% between 500 and 600, 9% between 600 and 700, and 7% above 700. Applicants should have a high school average of at least C, rank in the top 50% of their graduating class, score at least 400 on each section of the SAT, and be high school graduates. Admissions officers also consider recommendations by high school officials, personality, extracurricular activities, leadership record, advanced placement or honors courses, and impressions made during an interview.

Procedure: The SAT is required and should be taken by the spring. Notification is made on a rolling basis. An interview is recommended. Applications must be submitted with a $15 fee. There are no application deadlines.

Special: Early decision and early and deferred admissions plans are available. CLEP and AP credit is accepted.

year. Health insurance, though not required, is available through the college for a fee.

Admissions Contact: Steve Crouse, Director of Admissions.

Transfer: For fall 1981, 100 applications were received, 50 were accepted, and 20 students enrolled. A GPA of at least 2.0, SAT scores of at least 400 on each part, and 2 recommendations are required. An interview is recommended. Students must spend at least 1 year in residence, completing at least 9 of the 34 course credits required, in order to receive a bachelor's degree.

Visiting: Guided tours for informal visits on weekdays, 9 A.M. to 4 P.M. while school is in session, can be arranged through the admissions office. Visitors may sit in on classes and stay overnight on campus.

Financial Aid: Sixty percent of the students receive aid. Seventy academic scholarships are awarded. Loans also may be obtained through the state and federal governments. Work contracts are awarded to about 45% of the students, including freshmen. The average aid granted to freshmen from all sources in 1981–82 was $2600. Tuition may be paid on the installment plan. The college is a member of CSS; the FAF must be submitted. There are no application deadlines.

Foreign Students: About 1% of the students are from foreign countries.

Admissions: A minimum score of 550 on the TOEFL is required. Students must also take the university's entrance exam for placement purposes.

Procedure: Foreign students are admitted for the fall, winter, and spring semesters; there are no application deadlines. Students must present proof of adequate funds, and are required to carry health insurance, which is available through the university.

Admissions Contact: Judith Evrard, Director of Admissions.

UNIVERSITY OF SOUTHERN MAINE B–6
Portland, Maine 04032 (207) 780-5215
Gorham, Maine 04038

F/T: 1724M, 2252W	Faculty: n/av; IIA, av$
P/T: 1399M, 2019W	Ph.D.'s: 51%
Grad: 520M, 540W	S/F Ratio: 13 to 1
Year: sems, ss	Tuition: $1319 ($3629)
Appl: June 1	R and B: $2210
2107 applied	1895 accepted 1208 enrolled
SAT: 485V 512M	COMPETITIVE

The University of Southern Maine has 2 campuses, one in Portland and one in Gorham. The university is composed of the College of Arts and Sciences and the schools of Business and Economics, Education, and Nursing. The library contains 250,000 volumes and subscribes to 1600 periodicals.

Environment: The Portland campus is located in that city, the Gorham campus in a rural town 10 miles away. The Gorham campus covers 125 acres and includes 15 buildings. McLellan House, built in 1773 and believed to be the oldest brick house in Maine, is used as a residence hall on the Gorham campus. Single-sex and coed dorms there accommodate 1000 students in single and double rooms. Fraternity houses also are available. There is no housing on the Portland campus. The two campuses are linked by a special bus service.

Student Life: About 99% of the students are from New England, about 84% from Maine. About 88% of the students come from public schools. About 4% are members of minority groups. Twenty percent of the students live in dormitories on the Gorham campus. Freshman residents may not use cars on campus. Day-care services are available to full-time students, faculty, and staff.

Organizations: About 10% of the men and 4% of the women belong to 1 of 5 fraternities and 3 sororities on campus. Campus organizations include student government, departmental and special-interest clubs, choir, band, chorus, glee club, publications, and religious groups for Catholic and Protestant students. Campus cultural activities include concerts, lectures, and plays. Portland has a civic center and symphony, and ski resorts, Sebago Lake, and Casco Bay are nearby.

Sports: The university fields intercollegiate teams in 6 sports for men and 6 for women. Ten intramural sports are offered for men and women.

Handicapped: About 95% of the campus is accessible to physically handicapped students. Facilities include wheelchair ramps, special parking, elevators, specially equipped rest rooms and residence halls, and lowered drinking fountains and telephones. Special class scheduling also is available. A full-time coordinator of handicapped services is available.

Graduates: About 25% of the freshmen drop out, and 75% remain to graduate. About 18% of the graduates pursue further studies immediately after graduation; 4% each enter medical, law, and dental schools. About 60% of the graduates begin careers in business or industry.

330 MAINE

Services: Students receive the following free services: health care; psychological, placement, and career counseling; tutoring; and remedial instruction. Placement services—including counseling, advice on resume writing and interview techniques, and placement folders—are available to graduates as well as students.

Programs of Study: The university confers B.A. and B.S. degrees. Associate, master's, doctoral, and law degrees also are available. Bachelor's degrees are offered in the following subjects: AREA STUDIES (American), BUSINESS (accounting, business administration, computer science, management), EDUCATION (early childhood, elementary, industrial, secondary), ENGLISH (English), FINE AND PERFORMING ARTS (art, art education, music, music education, studio art, theater/dramatics), HEALTH SCIENCES (nursing, therapeutic recreation), LANGUAGES (French), MATH AND SCIENCES (biology, chemistry, earth science, geology, mathematics), PHILOSOPHY (philosophy), PREPROFESSIONAL (law, social work), SOCIAL SCIENCES (anthropology, criminal justice, economics, geography, government/political science, history, psychology, social sciences, social welfare, sociology). Non-major preprofessional programs are available in dentistry, medicine, and veterinary medicine. Twenty-seven percent of all undergraduate degrees are conferred in education, 25% in business, and 25% in social sciences.

Special: Two-year and four-year degree programs in therapeutic recreation are offered. Five-year combined B.A.-B.S. degrees may be earned in business, education, and arts and sciences. The university offers a general studies degree, and students may design their own majors. Independent study, pass/fail options, and study abroad are available. The university participates in the National Student Exchange program.

Required: All students must take courses in composition and literature, fine arts, mathematics, humanities, science, and social sciences.

Honors: Three national honor societies are represented on campus.

Admissions: About 90% of those who applied were accepted for the 1981–82 freshman class. The SAT scores of those who enrolled in an earlier class were as follows: Verbal—27% between 500 and 600, 7% between 600 and 700, and 1% above 700; Math—40% between 500 and 600, 13% between 600 and 700, and 2% above 700. All candidates should have completed 15 high school units, present at least a C average, and rank in the top half of their class. Other important considerations include recommendations by school officials, advanced placement or honors courses, leadership record, extracurricular activities, and special talents. Residents of Maine are given preference.

Procedure: Applicants must take the SAT or the ACT. Exams should be taken between May of the junior year and January of the senior year. Interviews are required for candidates planning to major in industrial arts or music. The deadlines for applications are June 1 (fall) and December 1 (spring). Notification is made on a rolling basis. There is a $10 application fee.

Special: Early and deferred admissions plans are available. The deadline for early admission is April 15. CLEP credit is accepted.

Transfer: In 1981–82, 1231 applications were received, 1058 were accepted, and 790 students enrolled. Transfer students are accepted for all classes. D grades do not transfer. A minimum average of 2.0 is required for transfer. Preference is given to students transferring from within the University of Maine system. Students must earn at least 30 semester hours at the university, at least 30 semester hours of the 120 required for a bachelor's degree. Transfer application deadlines are the same as those for freshmen.

Visiting: Orientations for prospective students are scheduled regularly. Guides also are available for informal visits during the academic year. Visitors may sit in on classes and stay overnight at the school. Visits are best scheduled from October 1 to mid-December or from February 1 to May 1. The admissions office should be contacted for arrangements.

Financial Aid: About 65% of the students receive aid. Loans are provided through the federal and state governments and local banks. Scholarships, including EOG, and jobs, including CWS, are available. Students are awarded combinations of scholarships, jobs, and loans. The average award is $2300 a year. All financial aid is awarded on the basis of need. The university is a member of the CSS and requires aid applicants to submit the FAF. An institutional form also is required of transfer students. Application deadlines are June 1 (fall) and December 1 (spring).

Foreign Students: About 50 foreign students are enrolled at the university. Special counseling is provided.

Admissions: Foreign applicants must score 500 or better on the TOEFL. No academic exams are required.

Procedure: The application deadline is April 15 for fall entry. Students must present proof of health and evidence of adequate funds for 4 years of study. Students are required to carry health insurance, which is available through the university for a fee.

Admissions Contact: Dennis J. Farrell, Director of Admissions.

WESTBROOK COLLEGE B-6
Portland, Maine 04103 (207) 797-7261

F/T: 76M, 570W Faculty: 44; IV, −$
P/T: 98M, 268W Ph.D.'s: n/av
Grad: none S/F Ratio: 14 to 1
Year: sems, ss Tuition: $4475
Appl: open R and B: $2370
852 applied 562 accepted 321 enrolled
SAT: 410V 420M **LESS COMPETITIVE**

Westbrook College, founded in 1831, offers liberal arts and career preparation. It is a private 2-year college with 4-year extensions. The library subscribes to over 250 periodicals and contains more than 30,000 volumes and 200 microfilm items.

Environment: The 40-acre suburban campus is located 100 miles north of Boston. The 18 buildings include a science and nursing center, a library, and 6 dormitories, which house 330 students.

Student Life: Fifty-five percent of the students are from Maine, and the remainder are primarily from the northeastern states. Fifty-five percent live on campus. Ninety percent of the freshmen are graduates of public high schools. College housing is single-sex, and there are visiting privileges. Students may keep cars on campus. Day-care services are provided to all students, faculty, and staff for a fee.

Organizations: There are no sororities or fraternities at this school. Students may attend the Westbrook Cultural Affairs Series and participate in other extracurricular activities on campus. They may also enjoy sailing or skiing.

Sports: The college participates in 1 intercollegiate sport for women. There are 4 intramural sports for both men and women.

Handicapped: Special facilities for the handicapped include parking areas, specially equipped restrooms, wheelchair ramps, and lowered drinking foundations.

Graduates: The freshman dropout rate is 17%. Seventy-five percent of those who enter remain to graduate. Thirty percent of graduates enter careers in business and industry; 62% enter occupations in health-related fields.

Services: Free psychological counseling, career counseling, and tutoring are available to all students. Health care is also available. Free placement services for undergraduates include on-campus recruiting, interviewing, resume preparation, and the maintaining of a placement file.

Programs of Study: The college confers the B.S. degree and associate degrees. Bachelor's degrees are offered in the following areas: BUSINESS (accounting, business administration, management), HEALTH SCIENCES (medical technology, nursing). Sixty percent of the degrees conferred are in medical fields, 30% in business.

Required: All undergraduates must take courses in English.

Special: Study abroad at approved institutions is permitted. Most of the career programs offer some work experience during the academic year. A combined A.A.-B.S. degree is offered in business administration and medical technology.

Admissions: Sixty-six percent of those who applied for the 1981–82 freshman class were accepted. High school graduation is required. About 80% of the freshmen were in the top half of their high school class. In addition to the academic record, other factors that enter into the admissions decision, in order of importance, are recommendations by school officials, personality, leadership and activities record, and impressions made during interviews.

Procedure: Neither the SAT or ACT is required, and there is no deadline for fall admission applications. Students must apply to a particular academic curriculum division of the college. A $25 application fee is required. The college has a rolling admissions plan. The CRDA is observed. A personal interview is recommended.

Special: An early admissions plan, a deferred admissions plan, and an early decision plan with a notification date of December 1 are other features of the admissions program.

Transfer: For fall 1981, 31 transfer students were accepted. Transfers are considered for second freshman semester and senior year. Students must have a C− or better average; D grades do not transfer. Transfer students must complete, at the college, 30 credits for the associate degree, and 60 of the 120 credits necessary for the bachelor's degree. Transfer admission is handled on a rolling basis.

Visiting: Regularly scheduled orientations allow prospective students to visit classes, meet students and faculty, and talk to admissions and financial aid personnel. Guides are provided for informal visits, and visitors may stay overnight at the school. It is recommended that visits be made when classes are in session. Arrangements may be made through the director of admissions.

Financial Aid: Eighty percent of all students are receiving financial aid, totaling more than $2,000,000, from a variety of sources. Forty percent work part-time on campus. The financial aid package usually consists of a scholarship (ranging in amount from $200 to $1500), a loan (from $500 to $1500), and a work contract (from $300 to $1000). The college is a member of the CSS. The FAF or FFS are the only aid application forms required. Need is the main consideration. There is no application deadline, but March 31 is preferred. Tuition may be paid in installments.

Foreign Students: The college accepts foreign applicants.

Admissions: Neither an English proficiency exam, nor the SAT or ACT is required.

Procedure: Foreign students must provide proof of funds adequate to cover 1 full year of study.

Admissions Contact: Ruth Ann Brooks, Director of Admissions.

MARYLAND

BOWIE STATE COLLEGE D-3
Bowie, Maryland 20715 (301) 464-3211

F/T: 548M, 661W	Faculty: n/av; IIA, ++$
P/T: 242M, 407W	Ph.D.'s: 55%
Grad: 230M, 431W	S/F Ratio: 17 to 1
Year: sems, ss	Tuition: $1125 ($2075)
Appl: June 1	R and B: $2140
806 applied	634 accepted	384 enrolled
SAT: required		LESS COMPETITIVE

Bowie State College, founded in 1865, is a state-supported liberal arts institution. The library houses 151,421 volumes and 317,751 microfilm items, and subscribes to 1220 periodicals.

Environment: The 287-acre campus is located in a suburban area 17 miles from Washington, D.C. The college's 18 buildings include residence halls that house 600 students in double rooms.

Student Life: All but 15% of the students come from Maryland, and 44% of the full-time undergraduates live on campus. About 80% of the students are Protestant, and 20% are Catholic. About 72% are minority-group members. Campus housing is both coed and single-sex; there are visiting privileges in the single-sex housing. Students may keep cars on campus.

Organizations: About 10% of the students belong to 1 of 4 sororities or 6 fraternities. Extracurricular activities and cultural programs are available on campus.

Sports: The college competes intercollegiately in 4 sports for men and 1 sport for women. There are 4 intramural sports for men and 2 for women.

Handicapped: Special facilities for wheelchair-bound students include elevators, special parking, wheelchair ramps, and specially equipped rest rooms. Two percent of the students have impaired vision or hearing. Special counseling is provided as needed.

Graduates: Thirty percent of the graduates pursue further study, and 45% begin careers in business and industry.

Services: The following services are provided free of charge: psychological counseling, health care, tutoring, remedial instruction, placement, and career counseling. Placement services also are available to graduates.

Programs of Study: The college awards the B.A., B.S., B.S.N., and B.S. in E. degrees. Master's degrees also are available. Bachelor's degrees are offered in the following subjects: BUSINESS (business administration), EDUCATION (early childhood, elementary, science education), ENGLISH (English, journalism), FINE AND PERFORMING ARTS (art, art education, music, music education, theater/dramatics), HEALTH SCIENCES (nursing), MATH AND SCIENCES (biology, mathematics), PREPROFESSIONAL (engineering, social work), SOCIAL SCIENCES (anthropology, government/political science, history, psychology, public administration, sociology). About 34% of the undergraduate degrees are awarded in education and 27% in business.

Required: Students must take freshman orientation, physical education, and courses in the humanities, social sciences, science, math, English, and speech.

Special: A dual-degree program in engineering is offered.

Honors: Nine honor societies are represented on campus.

Admissions: Seventy-nine percent of those who applied were accepted for the 1981–82 freshman class. Applicants must be graduates of accredited high schools, present an average of C or better, and have completed 16 high school units. Admissions officers also consider advanced placement or honors courses, recommendations by school officials, evidence of special talent, impressions made during an interview, and extracurricular activities. Maryland residents are given some preference.

Procedure: Applicants must file an application, a $10 application fee, an official high school transcript, and SAT scores. Application deadlines are June 1 (fall), December 15 (spring), and April 30 (summer). Admissions decisions are made on a rolling basis.

Special: An early decision plan and a deferred admissions plan are available. AP and CLEP credit is given.

Transfer: For fall 1981, 391 students applied, 252 were accepted, and 162 enrolled. A GPA of at least 2.0 is required. D grades do not transfer. All students must complete, at the college, 30 of the 120 credits required for a bachelor's degree. Application deadlines are the same as those for freshmen.

Visiting: At least 30 high school tours are conducted each year. Guides also are available for informal visits while classes are in session. Visits may be scheduled with the director of admissions, overnight stays with the director of housing.

Financial Aid: About 65% of the students receive aid. Forty percent work part-time on campus. The average freshman award is $1100. Loans and grants are available from federal and state agencies. The college participates in BEOG, SEOG, CWS, and the guaranteed student loan programs at 3% and 7% interest. Special state funds are available for residents and/or minorities. The application and the FAF must be submitted by June 1 (fall), December 15 (spring), or April 30 (summer). The college is a member of CSS.

Foreign Students: Five percent of the full-time students come from foreign countries. Special counseling and special organizations are available for these students.

Admissions: Foreign students must achieve a TOEFL score of at least 500 and a composite SAT score of at least 700.

Procedure: Application deadlines are June 1 (fall), December 15 (spring), and April 30 (summer). Foreign students must present a health certificate and proof of funds adequate to cover 1 year of study. Health insurance is required.

Admissions Contact: Patricia A. Wilson, Director of Admissions.

CAPITOL INSTITUTE OF TECHNOLOGY D-3
Kensington, Maryland 20895 (301) 933-3300

F/T: 436M, 63W	Faculty: 12; IIB, av$
P/T: 275M, 29W	Ph.D.'s: n/av
Grad: 114M, 9W	S/F Ratio: 24 to 1
Year: qtrs, ss	Tuition: $2628
Appl: see profile	R and B: n/app
176 applied	168 accepted	97 enrolled
SAT or ACT: not required		NONCOMPETITIVE

Capitol Institute of Technology, an independent technical college, was founded in 1932. The library contains 9000 volumes and subscribes to 93 periodicals.

Environment: The 1-acre campus is located in a suburban area 10 miles from Washington, D.C. The institute's 2 buildings house lecture rooms, labs, and a student center. There are no dormitories.

Student Life: About 68% of the students come from Maryland. About 72% are minority-group members. All students commute.

Organizations: Since this is a commuter campus, the number of extracurricular activities is limited. A student government and special-interest clubs are available.

332 MARYLAND

Sports: The institute does not participate in intercollegiate sports. There are 3 intramural sports for men and 3 for women.

Handicapped: There are no special facilities for physically handicapped students.

Graduates: The freshman dropout rate is 30%. Twenty percent of the graduates pursue advanced study after graduation. All graduates pursue careers in business and industry.

Services: Students receive free placement services, career counseling, and psychological counseling. Tutoring is provided on a fee basis.

Programs of Study: The institute offers the B.S. degree in electronic engineering technology. Associate degrees are also awarded. The curriculum prepares students for employment upon graduation. Those planning graduate study in engineering, mathematics, or science may have to take additional undergraduate courses to qualify.

Required: All students must take a distribution of courses, including electives in humanities and social studies.

Special: Degrees may be earned in day or evening programs.

Honors: The Tau Alpha Pi honor society has a chapter on campus.

Admissions: Ninety-five percent of those who applied were accepted for the 1981–82 freshman class. Applicants should be high school graduates or hold a GED equivalent. There are no minimum requirements for grades, class standing, or test scores; the institute practices an open admissions-selective retention policy. Admissions officers consider the applicant's preparation, competence in the institute's type of academic program, and motivation.

Procedure: All candidates should submit the application and high school transcripts as early as possible. Applications are accepted until 2 weeks before registration. New students are admitted to all quarters. A rolling admissions policy is used.

Special: Early decision and deferred admissions plans are available.

Transfer: Transfer students are admitted each quarter. D grades do not transfer. Applicants must be in good academic standing at their previous institution. All students must complete, at the institute, 45 of the 186 quarter hour credits required for a bachelor's degree. There are no application deadlines.

Visiting: Orientations for prospective students are scheduled regularly. Informal visits also may be scheduled for Mondays through Fridays, 9 A.M. to 4 P.M.. Guides are provided, and visitors may sit in on classes.

Financial Aid: About 64% of the students receive aid. Eight percent work part-time on campus. The institute offers scholarships to qualified freshmen. Federal and state loans are available. Work-study jobs can be arranged both on and off campus. Tuition may be paid in installments. All aid awards are based on financial need. The FAF is required. Preferred deadlines are April 15 (summer or fall entry), September 15 (winter entry), and January 1 (spring entry).

Foreign Students: Twenty-eight percent of the full-time students come from foreign countries. Special counseling is available for these students.

Admissions: Foreign students must achieve a TOEFL score of at least 500. No college entrance exams are required.

Procedure: Application deadlines are June 15 (fall), September 15 (winter), January 7 (spring), and March 15 (summer). Foreign students must present proof of funds adequate to cover 9 months of study. There is a special $75 application fee for foreign students. Health insurance is required and is available through the institute for a fee.

Admissions Contact: Timothy McCormick, Assistant Director of Admissions.

COLLEGE OF NOTRE DAME OF MARYLAND
Baltimore, Maryland 21210 D–2
(301) 435-0100

F/T: 565W	Faculty: 90; IIB, av$
P/T: 30M, 820W	Ph.D.'s: 60%
Grad: none	S/F Ratio: 9 to 1
Year: 4-1-4	Tuition: $3450
Appl: July 1	R and B: $2300
440 applied	270 accepted	175 enrolled
SAT: 510V 470M		COMPETITIVE

College of Notre Dame of Maryland is a private liberal arts college for women. Its library contains 185,000 volumes and subscribes to 1000 periodicals.

Environment: The 58-acre campus is located in a suburban area of Baltimore. Two dormitories house 400 women. The Knott Science Center contains a planetarium and a science theater.

Student Life: About 60% of the students are Maryland residents. Approximately 52% of the freshmen come from public schools. Forty percent of the students live on campus. Twenty-two percent are minority-group members. About 85% are Catholic, 10% are Protestant, and 3% are Jewish. Campus housing is single-sex; there are visiting privileges. Students may keep cars on campus.

Organizations: There are no sororities on campus. The Kymry Club plans social programs for students. Other extracurricular activities include student government, a student newspaper, special-interest clubs, a student theater, concerts, lectures, and performing arts series. The campus ministry office serves students of all faiths. Cultural and recreational activities also are available in the city of Baltimore.

Sports: The college competes in 6 intercollegiate sports. There are 3 intramural sports.

Handicapped: About 80% of the campus is accessible to physically handicapped students. Specially equipped rest rooms, parking areas, wheelchair ramps, lowered drinking fountains, and elevators are provided. Fewer than 1% of the students have visual or hearing impairments.

Graduates: About 7% of the freshmen drop out, and 80% remain to graduate. Thirty percent of the graduates continue their education, including 3% who enter medical school, 5% who enter dental school, and 8% who enter law school. Fifty percent enter business and industry.

Services: Tutoring, remedial instruction, health care, career and psychological counseling, and job placement services are provided free to students. Placement services also are available to graduates.

Programs of Study: The college awards the B.A. degree. Bachelor's degrees are offered in the following subjects: BUSINESS (accounting, business administration, management), EDUCATION (elementary, secondary), FINE AND PERFORMING ARTS (art, art education, art history, communications arts, film/photography, music, music education, radio/TV), HEALTH SCIENCES (prenursing), LANGUAGES (French, Greek/Latin, Italian, Spanish), MATH AND SCIENCES (biology, chemistry, mathematics, physics), PHILOSOPHY (classics, humanities, philosophy, religion), SOCIAL SCIENCES (economics, government/political science, history, international relations, psychology, social sciences). About 24% of the degrees are conferred in math and sciences, 17% in the social sciences and 12% in business.

Required: All students must take courses in English, social science, fine arts, natural science, language, philosophy, physical education, and religion.

Special: There is cross-registration with Loyola College, and there are cooperative programs with Johns Hopkins, Towson State, Morgan State, and Goucher. The college offers a five-year B.A.-B.S. degree in engineering. Junior-year-abroad and independent study programs are available. Students may earn degrees in 3 years and design their own majors.

Honors: Eleven national honor societies are represented on campus. The college also offers an honors program.

Admissions: About 61% of those who applied for the 1981–82 freshman class were accepted. The SAT scores of those who enrolled were as follows: Verbal—58% below 500, 32% between 500 and 599, 8% between 600 and 700, and 2% above 700; Math—60% below 500, 30% between 500 and 599, 9% between 600 and 700, and 1% above 700. Candidates generally should have completed 18 Carnegie units, present a GPA of 2.5 or better, rank in the upper half of their graduating class, and score at least 450 on each section of the SAT. Admissions officers also consider advanced placement or honors courses, leadership record, recommendations by school officials, impressions made during an interview, and evidence of special talent. Children of alumnae and applicants from disadvantaged backgrounds are given special consideration.

Procedure: The SAT is required and should be taken in November, December, or January of the senior year. An interview is recommended. Application deadlines are July 1 (fall) and January 15 (spring). The college follows a rolling admissions policy. The application fee is $15.

Special: Early decision, early admissions, and deferred admissions plans are available. AP credit is accepted.

Transfer: For fall 1981, 48 students applied, 43 were accepted, and 36 enrolled. Applicants must have an average of at least 2.5 and be in good academic standing at their last institution. D grades do not transfer. All students must complete, at the college, 60 of the 120 credits required for a bachelor's degree. Application deadlines are July 1 (fall) and January 15 (spring).

Visiting: Informal weekday visits may be scheduled with the director of admissions. Guides are provided, and visitors may sit in on classes and stay overnight in the dormitories.

Financial Aid: About 75% of the students receive aid. Twenty percent work part-time on campus. The average freshman award is $1200. Loans are available from the state and federal governments, local banks, and the college. Scholarships and part-time jobs also are provided. The college is a member of CSS. Aid applicants should file the FAF and the admissions and aid applications by February 15 (fall entry) or January 15 (spring entry).

Foreign Students: Two percent of the full-time students come from foreign countries. Special counseling and special organizations are available for these students.

Admissions: Foreign students must achieve a TOEFL score of at least 500. No college entrance exams are required.

Procedure: Application deadlines are May 1 (fall) and November 1 (spring). Foreign students must complete a college medical report after acceptance and must present proof of funds adequate to cover 1 year of study. Health insurance is required and is available through the college.

Admissions Contact: Michael L. Mahoney, Dean of Admissions.

COLUMBIA UNION COLLEGE   D-3
Takoma Park, Maryland 20912   (301) 891-4118

F/T: 200M, 337W	Faculty: n/av; IIB, – $
P/T: 100M, 194W	Ph.D.'s: 31%
Grad: none	S/F Ratio: 10 to 1
Year: sems, ss	Tuition: $1988
Appl: Aug. 1	R and B: $1095
262 applied	200 accepted	140 enrolled
SAT or ACT: required		LESS COMPETITIVE

Columbia Union College, founded in 1904, is a liberal arts and teacher education college affiliated with the Seventh-day Adventist Church. The library contains 96,500 volumes and subscribes to 473 periodicals.

Environment: The 2-acre campus, located in a suburb 10 miles from Washington, D.C., consists of 11 buildings, including a 4-story campus center. Living facilities include dormitories and off-campus apartments.

Student Life: The student body is geographically diverse; 44% come from states other than Maryland. About 65% of the freshmen are graduates of parochial schools. About 39% live on campus. About 43% are minority-group members. Ninety-five percent are Protestant. Most students are Seventh-day Adventists, and weekly attendance at religious services is required. Alcohol and smoking are prohibited on campus. There is an 11 P.M. curfew. Campus housing is single-sex; there are visiting privileges in the lobby only. Students may keep cars on campus.

Organizations: There are no fraternities or sororities. Student representatives have a voice in administrative and curricular decisions. The cultural and recreational offerings of Washington, D.C., are close by.

Sports: The college does not participate in intercollegiate sports. There are 13 intramural sports for men and 12 for women.

Services: Students receive free placement, career counseling, tutoring, and remedial instruction. Health care is available on a fee basis, and psychological counseling sometimes requires payment. Placement services also may be used by graduates.

Programs of Study: The college awards the B.A., B.S., and B.S.W. degrees. Associate degrees are also awarded. Bachelor's degrees are offered in the following subjects: BUSINESS (accounting, computer science, management), EDUCATION (early childhood, elementary, secondary), ENGLISH (English), FINE AND PERFORMING ARTS (music, music education), HEALTH SCIENCES (health science, medical technology, nursing, respiratory therapy), MATH AND SCIENCES (biochemistry, biology, chemistry, mathematics, physics), PHILOSOPHY (religion), PREPROFESSIONAL (dentistry, engineering, law, library science, medicine, ministry, pharmacy, social work, veterinary), SOCIAL SCIENCES (history, psychology, sociology). Forty percent of degrees are conferred in health sciences, 15% in math and sciences, 15% in social sciences, and 15% in business.

Required: Students must take courses in English, religion, physical education, history, language, science, and mathematics. All students must pass the URE to graduate.

Special: External degree programs and a general studies major are available. Selected students may study for one year at a university in France, Spain, Austria, England, or Germany.

Admissions: Seventy-six percent of those who applied were accepted for the 1981–82 freshman class. Applicants should be graduates of an approved high school and present a grade average of at least 2.0. Recommendations from school officials also are considered important.

Procedure: The SAT or ACT is required. Application deadlines are August 1 (fall), December 1 (winter), and April 1 (summer). Applicants are notified within 4 weeks of the time their files are complete. There is a $15 application fee.

Special: There are early decision and early admissions plans. AP and CLEP credit is accepted.

Transfer: For fall 1981, the college received 210 applications, accepted 143, and 61 students enrolled. An average of C or better is necessary. D grades transfer. All students must complete, at the college, 30 of the 128 semester hours required for a bachelor's degree. Application deadlines are the same as those for freshmen.

Visiting: Informal visits can be scheduled for regular school days through the college affairs office. Prospective students may sit in on classes and stay overnight on campus. Guides are provided.

Financial Aid: Loans are available from the federal and state governments, local banks, and the college. If grants can be matched with earnings from part-time employment, the college reduces the loans. The FAF or FFS and the aid application must be filed by June 1.

Foreign Students: Sixteen percent of the full-time students come from foreign countries. Special counseling and special organizations are available for these students.

Admissions: Foreign students must achieve either a minimum score of 550 on the TOEFL or minimum scores of 80 (aural) and 90 (vocabulary) on the University of Michigan Language Test. No college entrance exams are required.

Procedure: Application deadlines are March 1 (fall), July 1 (winter), and November 1 (summer). Foreign students must be examined by a physician and must present proof of funds adequate to cover the entire period of study. Health insurance is required and is available through the college for a fee. There is a special fee for foreign students.

Admissions Contact: Connie Hovanic, Director of Admissions.

COPPIN STATE COLLEGE   D-2
Baltimore, Maryland 21216   (301) 383-5990

F/T: 367M, 1112W	Faculty: n/av; IIA, av$
P/T: 84M, 248W	Ph.D.'s: 41%
Grad: 39M, 88W	S/F Ratio: 14 to 1
Year: sems, ss	Tuition: $1045 ($1995)
Appl: July 31	R and B: n/app
925 applied	618 accepted	406 enrolled
SAT: 350V 360M		LESS COMPETITIVE

Coppin State, founded in 1900, is a coeducational institution providing instruction in the arts and sciences and teacher training. The library contains 78,000 volumes and subscribes to 800 periodicals.

Environment: The campus covers 29 acres in the city of Baltimore. The 10 buildings include a multipurpose college center. There are no dormitories.

Student Life: About 90% of the students come from Maryland. None of the students live on campus. Ninety-six percent of the students are minority-group members. Students may keep cars on campus.

Organizations: About 10% of the men belong to 5 fraternities, and 8% of the women belong to 4 sororities. The college schedules lectures and performing arts programs.

Sports: The college participates in 2 intercollegiate sports for men. There are 2 intramural sports for both men and women.

Handicapped: The entire campus is accessible to wheelchair-bound students. Special facilities include wheelchair ramps, parking areas, elevators, lowered drinking fountains and telephones, and specially equipped rest rooms. No students with visual impairments or hearing problems are enrolled.

Graduates: Forty-five percent of the freshmen drop out during their first year. Of the graduates, 25% pursue advanced degrees.

Services: Students receive the following free services: placement, career counseling, tutoring, remedial instruction, and psychological counseling.

Programs of Study: The college awards the B.A. and B.S. degrees. Master's degrees also are available. Bachelor's degrees are offered in the following subjects: BUSINESS (management), EDUCATION (early childhood, elementary, health/physical, industrial, secondary, special), ENGLISH (English), HEALTH SCIENCES (nursing), MATH AND SCIENCES (biology, chemistry, mathematics), PREPROFESSIONAL (dentistry, engineering, law, medicine, pharmacy), SOCIAL SCIENCES (psychology, social sciences).

Special: Project Mission is a cooperative program that develops teachers for inner-city schools. Project Talent Search encourages young people from rural areas and students with financial problems to attend college.

Honors: Four honor societies have chapters on campus.

Admissions: About 67% of those who applied were accepted for the 1981-82 freshman class. The SAT scores of those who enrolled in a recent freshman class were as follows: Verbal—4% above 500; Math—4% above 500. Applicants must have graduated from an accredited high school with an average of C or better. They usually rank in the upper half of their class. Other important factors are test scores, recommendations by high school officials, extracurricular activities, and impressions made during an interview.

Procedure: The SAT is required. The candidate's high school transcript should accompany the application. Application deadlines are July 31 (fall) and December 31 (spring). Admissions decisions are made on a rolling basis. There is a $10 application fee.

Special: An early admissions plan is available. CLEP credit is accepted.

Transfer: For fall 1981, 337 students applied, 238 were accepted, and 169 enrolled. Transfer students are accepted for all classes. D grades transfer with a minimum average of 2.0 or an A.A. degree. Students must study at the college for at least 1 year. They must also complete, at the college, 30 of the 128 credits needed to receive a bachelor's degree. Transfer applications must be submitted by July 30 (fall) or December 30 (spring).

Visiting: Fall Open House and Spring Personal Decision Day are scheduled for prospective students. Informal visits also can be arranged for Mondays, Wednesdays, and Fridays with the admissions office. Visitors may sit in on classes. Guides are provided.

Financial Aid: Ninety percent of the students receive aid. Sixty percent work part-time on campus. Loans are made on the basis of academic promise and financial need. An emergency loan fund also is available to students who have completed at least 1 semester's work. Scholarships and grants also are provided. The college is a member of CSS. Applications for aid, accompanied by the FAF, must be filed by June 30 (fall) and December 30 (winter).

Foreign Students: Two percent of the full-time students come from foreign countries. The college offers these students an intensive English program and special counseling.

Admissions: Foreign students must score at least 500 on the TOEFL. They must also take the SAT.

Procedure: Application deadlines are June 30 (fall) and November 30 (spring). Foreign students must present proof of health. They must also present proof of adequate funds.

Admissions Contact: Clyde W. Hatcher, Director of Admissions.

FROSTBURG STATE COLLEGE   B-1
Frostburg, Maryland 21532   (301) 689-4201

F/T: 1430M, 1482W	Faculty:	155; IIA, +$
P/T: 127M, 140W	Ph.D.'s:	60%
Grad: 317M, 239W	S/F Ratio:	17 to 1
Year: sems, ss	Tuition:	$1142 ($2092)
Appl: open	R and B:	$1850
1722 applied	1148 accepted	696 enrolled
SAT: 420V 452M		COMPETITIVE

Frostburg State College, founded in 1898, is a state-supported institution that offers liberal arts and teacher education programs. The library houses 300,000 volumes and 57,600 microfilm items, and subscribes to 875 periodicals.

Environment: The 222-acre campus, located in a rural setting 175 miles from Baltimore and from Washington, D.C., contains 30 buildings. Eleven dormitories accommodate 1500 students.

Student Life: Ninety percent of the undergraduates are from Maryland. Eighty percent live on campus. Almost all freshmen come from public schools. Eight percent of the students are minority-group members. College housing is both single-sex and coed. Students may keep cars on campus.

Organizations: Six sororities and 7 fraternities are represented on campus. Numerous extracurricular activities, including a student government, and cultural and social events are available on campus. Parks and skiing areas are located nearby.

Sports: The college participates intercollegiately in 9 sports for men and 7 for women. There are 3 intramural sports for men and 3 for women.

Handicapped: There are no facilities for handicapped students.

Graduates: About 5% of the freshmen drop out; and 65% remain to graduate. Eighty percent of the graduates seek advanced degrees, including 2% who enter medical school, 3% dental school, and 3% law school. About 70% of the graduates pursue careers in business and industry.

Services: Students receive the following free services: placement, career counseling, health care, tutoring, remedial instruction, and psychological counseling.

Programs of Study: The college awards the B.A. and B.S. degrees. Master's and doctoral degrees also are available. Bachelor's degrees are offered in the following subjects: AREA STUDIES (urban), BUSINESS (accounting, business administration), EDUCATION (early childhood, elementary, health/physical, secondary), ENGLISH (English, speech), FINE AND PERFORMING ARTS (art, art education, music, music education, theater/dramatics), LANGUAGES (French, German, Russian, Spanish), MATH AND SCIENCES (biology, chemistry, earth science, mathematics, physics, reclamation, wildlife and fisheries), PHILOSOPHY (philosophy), PREPROFESSIONAL (dentistry, engineering, law, medicine, ministry, pharmacy, social work, veterinary), SOCIAL SCIENCES (economics, geography, government/political science, history, psychology, social sciences, sociology). Thirty-one percent of degrees are conferred in business, 23% in education, and 22% in social sciences.

Required: Students must complete 2 English courses and the general studies program. A cumulative average of 2.0 is required for graduation.

Special: The college offers pass/fail options and internship programs in 9 academic areas. A combination degree program is available in engineering. Students may arrange to study abroad through another institution.

Honors: Ten honor societies are represented on campus.

Admissions: About 67% of those who applied were accepted for the 1981-82 freshman class. The SAT scores of those who enrolled were as follows: Verbal—60% below 500, 35% between 500 and 599, 4% between 600 and 700, and 1% above 700; Math—68% below 500, 30% between 500 and 599, 1% between 600 and 700, and 1% above 700. The applicant must be a graduate of an accredited high school, rank in the upper half of his or her class, and present an average of C or better. Admissions officers also consider recommendations by high-school officials and impressions made during an interview.

Procedure: The SAT is required and must be taken by January of the senior year. Results from the junior year are acceptable. The college uses the rolling admissions plan. Application deadlines are open, and freshmen are admitted in fall and spring. A personal interview is recommended. The application fee is $20.

Special: CLEP credit is accepted.

Transfer: For fall 1981, 447 students applied, 364 were accepted, and 282 enrolled. A GPA of at least 2.0 is required. D grades transfer. Students must earn, at the college, the last 30 credits of the 120 needed to receive a bachelor's degree. Application deadlines are open.

Visiting: Six orientation sessions for prospective students are held on Saturdays in the fall. Informal visits also can be arranged for weekdays from 9 A.M. to 3 P.M. Guides are available. Visitors may sit in on classes and stay overnight on campus. Visits should be arranged through the admissions office.

Financial Aid: Seventy-three percent of the students receive aid. Fifty percent work part-time on campus. The college has no scholarship funds but participates in EOG, NDSL, and CWS programs. Work-study jobs are available in all departments. All financial aid is packaged, and each package includes grants, loans, and jobs. The FAF is required, and the deadline for aid applications is May 30.

Foreign Students: The college offers foreign students special counseling.

Admissions: Foreign students must take the TOEFL. They must score at least 57 on each of 3 parts. They must also take the SAT.

Procedure: Foreign students are admitted to all semesters. They must present proof of health and of adequate funds.

Admissions Contact: David L. Sanford, Dean of Admissions.

GOUCHER COLLEGE
Towson, Maryland 21204   D–2
(301) 337-6100

F/T: 847W	Faculty: 74; IIB, ++$
P/T: 138W	Ph.D.'s: n/av
Grad: 6M, 59W	S/F Ratio: 10 to 1
Year: sems	Tuition: $5515
Appl: Mar. 1	R and B: $2900
589 applied	459 accepted 218 enrolled
SAT: 500V 520M	ACT: 25 VERY COMPETITIVE+

Goucher College, founded in 1885, is an independent liberal arts institution for women. The library houses 190,000 volumes and subscribes to 900 periodicals.

Environment: The 330-acre suburban campus, located 8 miles from Baltimore, includes a modern gymnasium, an interdenominational chapel, and the accoustically renowned Kraushaar Auditorium. Four residence halls, each made up of 3 to 5 houses with 45 to 60 students in each, accommodate 750 students.

Student Life: About 39% of the students are from Maryland. About 70% of the freshmen come from public schools. About 69% of the students live on campus. About 14% of the students are minority-group members. Campus housing is single-sex. Students may keep cars on campus.

Organizations: There are no sororities. Extracurricular activities include religious, departmental, music, and drama groups; publications; a student government; and social events. The campus is 20 minutes from downtown Baltimore and 1 hour from Washington, D.C.

Sports: The college competes in 10 intercollegiate sports. There are 8 intramural sports.

Handicapped: The entire campus is accessible to wheelchair-bound students. Special facilities include wheelchair ramps, parking areas, and specially equipped rest rooms. Special class scheduling also is available. About 1% of students have visual impairments and 1% have hearing impairments.

Graduates: About 18% of the freshmen drop out during their first year. Sixty-nine percent remain to graduate. Nineteen percent of the graduates pursue further study; 4% enter medical school, 2% dental school, and 2% law school.

Services: Students receive free career counseling and placement services including a career library, newsletter, and on-campus interviews. Special programs and workshops are available free to students and graduates. Health care and tutoring are available on a fee basis.

Programs of Study: All programs lead to the B.A. degree. Master's degrees are also granted. Bachelor's degrees are offered in the following subjects: AREA STUDIES (American, European, French, German, Hispanic, Russian), BUSINESS (computer science, finance, management), EDUCATION (elementary, secondary, special), ENGLISH (English, journalism, literature), FINE AND PERFORMING ARTS (art, art education, art history, dance, music, music education, studio art, theater/dramatics), LANGUAGES (French, Russian, Spanish), MATH AND SCIENCES (biochemistry, biology, botany, chemistry, computer science, mathematics, premedical studies, public health, statistics, zoology), PHILOSOPHY (philosophy, religion), PREPROFESSIONAL (law, medicine, ministry, social work, veterinary), SOCIAL SCIENCES (anthropology, economics, government/political science, historic preservation, history, international relations, psychology, social sciences, sociology). The most popular majors are biology, chemistry, economics, psychology, English, sociology, and education.

Required: Students must complete at least 1 course in each of the following areas: abstract reasoning, fine and performing arts, history, literature, natural science, philosophy, and social science. In addition, students must complete 3 units of physical education, must take 1 computer course, and must demonstrate proficiency in 1 foreign language and in English composition and grammar.

Special: Courses in Hebrew and German are offered. Double majors, student-designed majors, independent study, and a junior-year-abroad program are permitted. Goucher shares a number of programs with Johns Hopkins University, Loyola College, Towson State University, Morgan State College, Essex Community College, Baltimore Hebrew College, and the Maryland Institute/College of Art. Internships are available.

Honors: Phi Beta Kappa is represented on campus.

Admissions: Seventy-eight percent of those who applied were accepted for the 1981–82 freshman class. The SAT scores of those who enrolled in a recent freshman class were as follows: Verbal—45% between 500 and 599 and 15% between 600 and 700; Math—40% between 500 and 599, and 20% between 600 and 700. Applicants should have completed 16 units of high school work and have an average of at least B–. The high school record and recommendations by high school officials are considered extremely important.

Procedure: Applicants must take the SAT or the ACT by January of the senior year. An interview is required. Applications should be filed by March 1 (fall) for priority consideration, but may be accepted after that date. Admissions decisions are made on a rolling basis. The application fee is $25.

Special: Early decision and early admissions plans are available. AP credit is accepted.

Transfer: For fall 1981, 81 students applied, 58 were accepted, and 41 enrolled. A 2.0 GPA is required. D grades do not transfer. Students are not accepted into the senior class. Students must complete 60 semester hours, in residence, of the 120 needed to receive a bachelor's degree. Applications filed by April 1 are given priority, but they may be accepted after that date. Applications for spring admission must be filed by December 10.

Visiting: Two Open Campus days are scheduled each fall. Students attend classes, tour the campus, meet faculty members, and attend information sessions on student life and financial aid. Informal visits also may be arranged with the admissions office for Mondays through Saturdays while classes are in session and Mondays through Fridays in summer. Guides are provided. Visitors may sit in on classes and stay overnight on campus.

Financial Aid: About 54% of all students receive aid. Thirty-five percent work part-time on campus. An aid package usually includes a grant, loan, and part-time campus job. Scholarships are awarded on the basis of need. The college is a member of CSS. Aid applications and the FAF must be filed by May 15 (fall) or December 15 (spring) for priority.

Foreign Students: Six percent of the full-time students come from foreign countries. The college offers these students an intensive English course and special counseling.

Admissions: Foreign students must take the TOEFL.

Procedure: The application deadlines are March 1 (fall) and December 10 (spring) for priority admissions. Foreign students must present proof of funds adequate to cover 1 academic year. They must also carry health insurance, which is available through the college.

Admissions Contact: Janis L. Boster, Director of Admissions.

HOOD COLLEGE
Frederick, Maryland 21701   C–2
(301) 663-3131

F/T: 20M, 830W	Faculty: 87; IIA, –$
P/T: 70M, 205W	Ph.D.'s: 55%
Grad: 249M, 449W	S/F Ratio: 11 to 1
Year: sems, ss	Tuition: $4825
Appl: March 31	R and B: $2445
550 applied	450 accepted 275 enrolled
SAT: 460V 463M	COMPETITIVE

Hood College is an independent liberal arts college for women. Men living within a reasonable distance are permitted to enroll as commuting students. The library contains 140,000 volumes and 123,300 microform items, and subscribes to 1000 periodicals.

Environment: The 100-acre campus, surrounded by the foothills of the Blue Ridge Mountains, is located in a city 45 miles from Baltimore and from Washington, D.C. The 26 buildings include an astronomical observatory, a science building, a laboratory nursery school, 7 dormitories, and a health center.

Student Life: Fifty-six percent of the students come from Maryland, and about 70% are graduates of public schools. Seventy-three percent of the students live on campus. Special French, Spanish, and German houses are available for resident students interested in those languages. There is an Honor Code. About 25% of the students are Catholic, about 55% Protestant, and 1% Jewish. About 6% of the students are minority-group members. College housing is single-sex; there are visiting privileges. Hood has a nursery school staffed by faculty and students in the Department of Education; day-care services are available to faculty, staff, and members of the community.

Organizations: Religious organizations are available on campus for Catholic, Protestant, and Jewish students. There are no fraternities or sororities. Extracurricular and cultural activities include riding, publications, music and drama groups, student government, concerts, films, and special-interest clubs. The cultural facilities of Washington, D.C., are within easy access. Several state and national parks and Civil War battle sites are nearby.

Sports: The college competes intercollegiately in 6 sports. There are 10 intramural sports for women.

MARYLAND

Handicapped: Fifteen percent of the campus is accessible to wheelchair-bound students. Special facilities include wheelchair ramps, parking areas, elevators, lowered drinking fountains and telephones, and specially equipped rest rooms. Special class scheduling is also available. The college makes an effort to accommodate individual students' needs. Fewer than 1% of the students have impaired vision or hearing. One counseling assistant is available to handicapped students.

Graduates: The freshman dropout rate is 15%, and 60% of the freshmen remain to graduate. Fifty percent of the graduates seek advanced degrees; fewer than 1% enter medical and dental schools, and 6% enter law school. Fifty percent enter careers in business and industry.

Services: Students receive the following free services: placement, career, and psychological counseling; health care; tutoring, and remedial instruction. Placement services also are available to graduates.

Programs of Study: The college awards the B.A. and B.S. degrees. Master's degrees also are available. Bachelor's degrees are offered in the following subjects: AREA STUDIES (Latin American), BUSINESS (business administration, computer science, management), EDUCATION (early childhood, elementary, secondary, special), ENGLISH (communications, English), FINE AND PERFORMING ARTS (art, art education, art history, art therapy, music, studio art, visual communications/applied art), HEALTH SCIENCES (medical technology, radiologic technology), LANGUAGES (French, German, Spanish), MATH AND SCIENCES (biochemistry, biology, chemistry, ecology/environmental science, mathematics, psychobiology), PHILOSOPHY (church music, philosophy, religion, youth work/religious education), PREPROFESSIONAL (dentistry, engineering, home economics, law, medicine, social work, veterinary), SOCIAL SCIENCES (economics, government/political science, history, law and society, psychology, recreation and leisure studies, sociology).

Required: Students must fulfill the requirements of the core curriculum.

Special: A 5-year combined B.A.-B.S. degree can be earned in math and engineering. Students may design their own majors. An extensive program of internships, a junior year abroad, and independent study are offered. Field trips to Washington, Baltimore, and other metropolitan areas complement classroom instruction. Self-scheduling of examinations and a pass/fail program are available.

Honors: Seven honor societies are represented on campus. Honors programs are available in all departments; qualified students are invited to participate in the middle of their junior year.

Admissions: About 82% of those who applied were accepted for the 1981–82 freshman class. Applicants should rank in the top 50% of their high school class, have at least a 2.0 GPA, and be enrolled in a college-preparatory curriculum. The college bases admissions decisions primarily on high school record, accreditation and reputation of the high school, recommendations by school officials, and SAT or ACT results. Advanced placement or honors courses, impressions made during an interview, and personality also are considered. The college seeks a geographically diverse student body.

Procedure: The SAT or ACT is required and should be taken by December of the senior year. The application deadlines are March 31 (fall), December 31 (spring), and June 15 (summer). An interview is strongly recommended. The $20 application fee is waived for needy applicants.

Special: An early reply and early and deferred admissions plans are available. AP credit is granted in some cases.

Transfer: About 80% of the applications are approved. A GPA of at least 2.5 is required. D grades do not transfer. Students must earn at least 30 hours, in residence, of the 120 needed to receive a bachelor's degree. The application deadlines are March 31 (fall) and December 31 (spring).

Visiting: Orientations for prospective students are scheduled regularly. Informal visits also can be arranged through the admissions office. The best time to visit is when classes are in session. Guides are provided. Visitors may sit in on classes and spend the night on campus.

Financial Aid: About 50% of all students receive aid. Forty-five percent work part-time on campus. Average aid to freshmen from all sources is $4750. Scholarships, loans, grants, and work-study jobs are available. The college is a member of CSS. The aid application, the FAF, and the federal 1040 form of parents' income must be filed by March 31 (fall) or January 1 (winter).

Foreign Students: Fewer than 1% of the full-time students come from foreign countries. The college offers these students an intensive English course and special counseling.

Admissions: Foreign students must score at least 550 on the TOEFL. No college entrance examination is required.

Procedure: Application deadlines are March 31 (fall) and December 31 (spring). Foreign students must submit a college health form signed by a physician. They must also present proof of adequate funds.

Admissions Contact: Diane R. Wilson, Director of Admissions and Financial Aid.

JOHNS HOPKINS UNIVERSITY D-2
Baltimore, Maryland 21218   (301) 338-8171

F/T: 1546M, 690W   Faculty: 289; I, ++$
P/T: none   Ph.D.'s: 99%
Grad: 559M, 290W   S/F Ratio: 10 to 1
Year: 4-1-4, ss   Tuition: $6050
Appl: Jan. 15   R and B: $2800
3914 applied   1704 accepted   571 enrolled
SAT or ACT: required   MOST COMPETITIVE

Johns Hopkins University is a private, nonsectarian institution of international renown. The Milton Eisenhower Library contains 1.8 million volumes and 826,000 microfilm items, and subscribes to 10,000 periodicals.

Environment: The wooded 140-acre campus is located in the city of Baltimore, 40 miles from Washington, D.C. Buildings are of American Georgian architecture and include a center for biological studies and a new Center for Earth and Planetary Sciences. Dorms accommodate more than 600 students, and an additional 400 live in university-owned apartments. The university has other facilities in East Baltimore, Washington, D.C., and Bologna, Italy.

Student Life: Students come from all states; 27% are residents of Maryland. About 64% come from public schools. A code of ethics governs student conduct. About 12% of the students are minority-group members. University housing is both single-sex and coed. There are visiting privileges in single-sex housing. Freshmen must live in dormitories unless they are Baltimore residents. All students may keep cars on campus.

Organizations: Twenty percent of the men belong to the 11 national fraternities on campus. There are 2 sororities. Extracurricular activities include publications, music groups, special-interest clubs, religious organizations for the major faiths, and a radio station. The university schedules a program of lectures, concerts, and social and intellectual activities. Students also have access to the cultural and recreational opportunities of Baltimore and Washington.

Sports: The university competes in 14 intercollegiate sports for men and 10 for women. There are 11 intramural offerings for men and 1 for women.

Handicapped: The university attempts to make all programs accessible to wheelchair-bound students. Special facilities include wheelchair ramps, parking areas, elevators, lowered drinking fountains and telephones, and specially equipped rest rooms. Special class scheduling is available. About 1% of the students have impaired vision or hearing; large-print reading materials, tapes, interpreters, and escort services are provided. Extensive counseling and psychiatric services are available. Each academic division has a specially assigned staff member responsible for program accessibility, and managers in the physical plant department are trained to make facilities accessible. Two professors counsel visually impaired students. A compliance coordinator is in charge of services for the handicapped.

Graduates: About 3% of the freshmen drop out, and 85% remain to graduate. Eighty percent of the graduates seek advanced degrees: 20% enter law school, and 33% enter medical school. Twenty percent of the graduates pursue careers in business and industry.

Services: Students receive free health care, career counseling, placement, psychological counseling, and tutoring. Placement services may be used by alumni.

Programs of Study: The university awards the B.A. and B.E.S. degrees. Master's and doctoral degrees also are available. Bachelor's degrees are offered in the following subjects: AREA STUDIES (Near Eastern, urban), BUSINESS (computer science), ENGLISH (English, literature), FINE AND PERFORMING ARTS (art history), LANGUAGES (French, German, Greek/Latin, Italian, Portuguese, Russian, Spanish), MATH AND SCIENCES (biology, chemistry, earth and planetary science, ecology/environmental science, mathematics, natural sciences, physics, statistics), PHILOSOPHY (classics, humanities, philosophy), PREPROFESSIONAL (engineering), SOCIAL SCIENCES (anthropology, economics, geography, government/political science, history, international relations, psychology, social sciences, sociology). Forty-five percent of the undergraduate degrees conferred are in math and sciences, 25% in social sciences, and 15% in engineering.

MARYLAND 337

Required: For the B.A. most students must take one year beyond the elementary course in a foreign language. This requirement may be satisfied by AP, AT, or departmental exams.

Special: Nonmajor preprofessional programs are offered in many fields, including medicine, law, and foreign service. Seminars in social relations, Oriental studies, and writing are available. Many departments allow early entrance into independent research or advanced-level courses. Combination degree programs are available in international studies and humanities and in medicine and human biology. Students may study abroad and design their own majors.

Honors: An honors program is offered in humanistic studies. Thirteen honor societies, including Phi Beta Kappa, are represented on campus.

Admissions: About 44% of those who applied were accepted for the 1981-82 freshman class. The SAT scores of those who enrolled were as follows: Verbal—7% below 500, 22% between 500 and 599, 54% between 600 and 700, and 17% above 700; Math—2% below 500, 12% between 500 and 599, 41% between 600 and 700, and 46% above 700. The most likely applicants to be accepted are those who present a B average or better and rank in the top 10% of their class. Children of alumni are given some preference. The university also seeks a geographically diverse student body. Admissions officers also consider advanced placement or honors courses, leadership record, extracurricular activities, recommendations by school officials, impressions made during an interview, and personality.

Procedure: Applicants must take either the SAT or the ACT and 3 ATs (English Composition with or without the essay is required). The application deadline for fall admission is January 15. Applicants are notified by April 15. A fee of $30 must accompany the application. An interview is recommended.

Special: Early decision and early and deferred admissions plans are available. AP credit is accepted.

Transfer: For fall 1981, 146 students applied, 50 were accepted, and 35 enrolled. Transfer applicants are considered for sophomore and junior classes. D grades do not transfer. Applicants should have a 3.0 GPA or better and must submit a transcript and SAT scores. D grades do not transfer. Students must study at the university for at least 60 semester hours of the 120 needed to receive a bachelor's degree. Application deadlines are July 1 (fall, March 15 preferred) and November 15 (spring).

Visiting: Orientations for prospective students are scheduled at 11 A.M., 1 P.M., and 3 P.M. on Mondays through Fridays during the school year. Informal visits also may be made between 9 A.M. and 4 P.M. on Mondays through Fridays. Guides are provided. Visitors may sit in on classes and spend the night at the school. Arrangements should be made through the admissions office.

Financial Aid: Sixty-four percent of the students receive aid. The average aid to freshmen is $6800. About 50% of the students work part-time on campus. Students from needy families may receive enough aid to cover all college expenses. The university is a member of CSS. The FAF and the aid application must be filed by February 1.

Foreign Students: About 10% of the full-time students come from foreign countries. The university offers these students special counseling and special organizations.

Admissions: Foreign students must score at least 560 on the TOEFL. They must also take the SAT or the ACT. Three ATs are required (English Composition is recommended).

Procedure: The application deadline is December 1 (fall). Foreign students must present proof of funds adequate to cover their entire period of study. They must also carry health insurance, which is available through the university for a fee.

Admissions Contact: Jerome Schnydman, Director of Admissions.

LOYOLA COLLEGE D-2
Baltimore, Maryland 21210   (301) 323-1010

F/T: 1400M, 1200W   Faculty: 127; IIA, av$
P/T: 438M, 330W   Ph.D.'s: 69%
Grad: 1640M, 1193W   S/F Ratio: 18 to 1
Year: 4-1-4, ss   Tuition: $3365
Appl: open   R and B: $1975
2000 applied 1300 accepted 700 enrolled
SAT: 507V 547M   VERY COMPETITIVE

Loyola College, established in 1852, is a private liberal arts college in the Jesuit, Mercy tradition. The library contains 190,000 volumes and 185,000 microfilm items, and subscribes to 2000 periodicals.

Environment: The 53-acre campus is located in a residential area of Baltimore. The 16 buildings include dormitories and apartments that house 1000 students.

Student Life: About 70% of the students are from Maryland. About 24% come from public schools. Forty percent of the students live on campus. Seventy percent are Catholic, 20% Protestant, and 5% Jewish. Ten percent of the students are minority-group members. College housing is single-sex; there are visiting privileges. Freshman dormitory residents may not have cars on campus.

Organizations: There are no fraternities or sororities. Religious organizations and counseling are available for Catholic, Protestant, and Jewish students. Extracurricular activities include academic and political clubs, a weekly newspaper, cultural activities, a student government, a music club, and social events.

Sports: The college fields intercollegiate teams in 10 sports. There are 5 intramural sports.

Handicapped: About 95% of the campus is accessible to wheelchair-bound students. Special facilities include wheelchair ramps, elevators, and specially equipped rest rooms. Special class scheduling is also available. The office of the dean of freshmen helps make necessary arrangements. No students with visual or hearing impairments are enrolled.

Graduates: About 17% of the freshmen drop out by the end of their first year. Seventy percent remain to graduate. About 23% of the graduates seek advanced degrees; 5% enter medical school, 2% dental school, and 5% law school. Seventy percent enter careers in business and industry.

Services: Students receive the following free services: placement, career, and psychological counseling, and tutoring. Placement services also are available to alumni.

Programs of Study: The college awards the B.A. and B.S. degrees. Master's degrees also are available. Bachelor's degrees are offered in the following subjects: BUSINESS (accounting, business administration, computer science), EDUCATION (elementary, secondary), ENGLISH (English, literature), HEALTH SCIENCES (medical technology, speech therapy), LANGUAGES (French, German, Greek/Latin, Spanish), MATH AND SCIENCES (biology, chemistry, engineering science, mathematics, physics), PHILOSOPHY (philosophy, religion), PRE-PROFESSIONAL (dentistry, engineering, law, medicine, veterinary), SOCIAL SCIENCES (economics, government/political science, history, psychology, sociology).

Required: Students must take courses in English, ethics, history, language, mathematics, philosophy, social sciences, theology, and science.

Special: Four-year combined B.A.-B.S. degrees may be earned in various subjects. Students may design their own majors. The college offers independent study and, in cooperation with Loyola University of Chicago, a foreign study program.

Honors: A number of honor societies are represented on campus. The college offers an honors program for superior students.

Admissions: Sixty-five percent of those who applied were accepted for the 1981–82 freshman class. The SAT scores of those who enrolled were as follows: Verbal—45% below 500, 43% between 500 and 599, 10% between 600 and 700, and 2% above 700; Math—23% below 500, 49% between 500 and 599, 23% between 600 and 700, and 3% above 700. Applicants should rank in the upper half of their high school class and have completed 16 units of high school work. Also important are SAT scores, recommendations from high school officials, advanced placement or honors courses, and extracurricular activities.

Procedure: The SAT is required and should be taken in April of the junior year or in November or December of the senior year. Application deadlines are open, and freshmen are admitted to all terms. Students are notified of acceptance on a rolling basis. A $15 application fee is required.

Special: Early and deferred admissions plans are available. AP and CLEP credit is accepted.

Transfer: For fall 1981, 312 students applied, 250 were accepted, and 125 enrolled. A GPA of at least 2.5 is required. D grades do not transfer. There is a 2-year residency requirement. At least 60 credit hours of the 120 needed for a bachelor's degree must be taken in residence. Application deadlines are open.

Visiting: Orientations, scheduled regularly for prospective students, include campus tours, talks by faculty members, and information sessions. Informal visits can be scheduled for Monday through Friday, 9 A.M. to 5 P.M., with the admissions office. Guides are provided. Visitors may sit in on classes.

Financial Aid: Sixty percent of the students receive aid, which is awarded primarily in packages consisting of loans, scholarships, and campus jobs. Five percent of the students work part-time on campus. Average aid to freshmen from all sources is $1500. Most awards are made on the basis of financial need and academic ability, and are renewed if students maintain a good academic record and need continues. Some scholarships are awarded solely on the basis of athletic or academic achievement. The college is a member of CSS. The FAF also is required. Applications must be filed by March 1.

Foreign Students: Two percent of the full-time students come from foreign countries. The college offers these students special organizations.

Admissions: Foreign students must score at least 600 on the TOEFL. They must also take the SAT.

Procedure: Application deadlines are December (fall), May (winter), August (spring), and December (summer). Foreign students must present the I-20 form. They must also present proof of funds adequate to cover 4 years of study.

Admissions Contact: Martha Gagnon, Director of Admissions.

MARYLAND INSTITUTE/COLLEGE OF ART D-2
Baltimore, Maryland 21217   (301) 669-9200

F/T: 860M&W	Faculty: 43; n/av
P/T: 150M&W	Ph.D.'s: n/av
Grad: 86M&W	S/F Ratio: 16 to 1
Year: sems, ss	Tuition: $4200
Appl: June 1	R and B: n/app
600 applied	350 accepted 200 enrolled
SAT or ACT: not required	SPECIAL

Maryland Institute/College of Art, founded in 1826, is a private, nonsectarian institution that offers training in fine arts, crafts, design, and photography. The library contains 40,000 volumes and 70,000 slides, and subscribes to 200 periodicals.

Environment: The campus is located in the city of Baltimore. The institute has 41 buildings. The college has no dormitories; students may live in those of the Peabody Conservatory of Music nearby, but most live in apartments in the area.

Student Life: About 54% of the students are Maryland residents, and 86% come from public schools.

Organizations: The college sponsors publications, lectures, dances, film festivals, appearances by visiting artists, a student-operated gallery, and dances. There are no fraternities, sororities, or religious groups.

Sports: The institute sponsors no sports programs.

Handicapped: About 25% of the campus is accessible to physically handicapped students. Special class scheduling can be arranged. Elevators, specially equipped rest rooms, and lowered telephones are available.

Graduates: About 15% of the freshmen drop out, and 50% remain to graduate. Of those, 25% continue their education.

Services: Health care, tutoring, remedial instruction, career and psychological counseling, and placement services are provided free to students. Placement services also are available to graduates.

Programs of Study: The college awards the B.F.A. degree with majors in art education (elementary and secondary), ceramics, crafts, drawing, fine arts, graphic design/illustration, interior design, painting, photography, printmaking, and sculpture. Diplomas and master's degrees also are available.

Required: All freshmen must complete the Foundation Studio Program, which includes courses in English and history as well as fundamental drawing and painting. All undergraduates must take 18 credits in art history, 40 in fine arts, 40 in their major, and 24 in liberal arts.

Special: Qualified juniors and seniors may take graduate-level liberal arts courses and progress at their own rate. Students may select oral or written exams in many liberal arts courses, and may spend their junior year abroad.

Honors: Painting, drawing, and senior honors programs are available. They include individual studio space and independent study.

Admissions: About 58% of those who applied were accepted for the 1981–82 freshman class. Applicants must be high school graduates and should, but are not required to, present at least a C average and rank in the upper 50% of their class. Advanced placement or honors courses and quality of the applicant's portfolio also are considered.

Procedure: Applicants must submit a portfolio of 8 to 12 pieces of work. If the applicant is able to visit the college, he or she should schedule an interview and portfolio review session. Applications and a $20 fee must be submitted by June 1 (fall), December 15 (spring), or June 10 (summer). Notification is made on a rolling basis.

Special: Early and deferred admissions plans are available. AP and CLEP credit is given.

Transfer: A GPA of at least 2.0 and a portfolio of at least 15 works are required. At least 2 years (60 credits) must be taken in residence to receive a bachelor's degree, for which at least 120 credits are required. Application deadlines are the same as those for freshmen.

Visiting: Visits can be arranged through the admissions office for January through June. Visitors may sit in on classes, and guides are provided.

Financial Aid: About half the students receive aid. Freshman aid packages usually are made up of one-half SEOG or merit scholarship, one-quarter part-time job, and one-quarter NDSL. State loans also are available. The institute is a member of the CSS. The aid application and the FAF must be submitted by March 1.

Foreign Students: The 60 students from foreign countries make up 7% of enrollment. The institute offers these students an intensive English course, special counseling, and special organizations.

Admissions: Applicants must score 500 or better on the TOEFL. No college entrance exams are required.

Procedure: Application deadlines are open; foreign students are admitted to all terms. Students must present proof of adequate funds for 1 year. Health insurance is provided through the institute at no additional charge.

Admissions Contact: Theresa M. Lynch, Director of Admissions.

MORGAN STATE UNIVERSITY D-2
Baltimore, Maryland 21239   (301) 444-3000

F/T: 1613M, 2107W	Faculty: 286; IIA, +$
P/T: 325M, 801W	Ph.D.'s: 45%
Grad: 254M, 224W	S/F Ratio: 15 to 1
Year: sems, ss	Tuition: $1112 ($2147)
Appl: open	R and B: $1275
2321 applied	1695 accepted
SAT: 350V 325M	LESS COMPETITIVE

Morgan State University, founded in 1867, is a state-supported liberal arts institution. The library contains 170,000 volumes and subscribes to more than 13,000 periodicals.

Environment: The 130-acre suburban campus, 5 miles from downtown Baltimore, has residence halls that house more than 700 students.

Student Life: About 70% of the students are residents of Maryland. Fifteen percent of the students live on campus. Nearly 100% of the students are minority-group members. University housing is single-sex; there are visiting privileges. Students may keep cars on campus.

Organizations: Two percent of the men belong to the 15 fraternities; and 2% of the women belong to the 15 sororities that serve the campus. Fraternities and sororities do not provide housing. Special-interest groups, clubs, organizations, and publications are among the extracurricular activities. Religious facilities are provided for Catholics, Protestants, and Jews. Students also have access to the cultural and recreational opportunities of Baltimore.

Sports: The university competes on an intercollegiate level in 5 sports for men and 3 for women. Six intramural sports are offered for both men and women.

Handicapped: Sixty-five percent of the campus is accessible to wheelchair-bound students. Special facilities include wheelchair ramps, parking areas, elevators, lowered drinking fountains and telephones, and specially equipped rest rooms. One special counselor is available.

Graduates: Forty percent of the freshmen remain to graduate. About 15% of the graduates seek advanced degrees; 3% enter medical school, 3% dental school, and 5% law school. Seventy-five percent of the graduates pursue careers in business and industry.

Services: Students receive the following free services: health care, psychological and career counseling, placement, tutoring, and remedial instruction. Placement services also are available to alumni.

Programs of Study: The university awards the B.A. and B.S. degrees. Master's and doctoral degrees also are available. Bachelor's degrees are offered in the following subjects: BUSINESS (accounting, business administration, business education, economics, secretarial science), EDUCATION (elementary, health/physical, secondary), EN-

GLISH (English, journalism, speech), FINE AND PERFORMING ARTS (art, art education, music, music education, radio/TV, theater/dramatics), HEALTH SCIENCES (medical technology), LANGUAGES (French, German, Spanish), MATH AND SCIENCES (biology, chemistry, mathematics, physical sciences, physics), PHILOSOPHY (philosophy, religion), PREPROFESSIONAL (home economics, ministry, social work), SOCIAL SCIENCES (economics, geography, government/political science, history, international relations, mental health, psychology, social sciences, sociology).

Required: Students must take 50 hours of general courses and pass proficiency exams in speech and writing.

Special: Five-year combined B.A.-B.S. degrees are available. Students may design their own majors. A cooperative 3-2 engineering program, a cooperative teacher training project for inner-city schools, and a 3-4 premedical program in cooperation with the University of Maryland Medical School are offered.

Honors: An honors program is offered in mathematics. A number of honor societies are represented on campus.

Admissions: Seventy-three percent of those who applied were accepted for the 1981–82 freshman class. The SAT scores of those who enrolled were as follows: Verbal—95% below 500, 5% between 500 and 599, 0% between 600 and 700, and 0% above 700. Candidates should have completed 18 high school units, present a C average or better, and rank in the upper 75% of their class. State residents are given preference, although the college seeks a geographically diverse student body.

Procedure: The SAT is required. The application deadlines are open. The application, transcript, and test scores must be forwarded; a completed health form is required upon acceptance. The college follows a rolling admissions policy. There is a $20 application fee.

Special: Early decision and early and deferred admissions plans are available. CLEP credit is accepted.

Transfer: For a recent year, 520 applications were received, 333 were accepted, and 215 students enrolled. Applicants must be in good standing and present a 2.0 GPA or better. Transfer students are admitted to all but the senior class; in-state applicants are given preference. Students must complete at least 30 credit hours at the university, of the 120 needed to receive a bachelor's degree. The application deadline is open.

Visiting: Orientations for prospective students are scheduled regularly. Participants tour the campus and meet students and faculty members. Informal visits also may be arranged with the admissions office. Visitors may sit in on classes. Guides are provided. The best day for campus visits is Friday.

Financial Aid: Seventy-three percent of all students receive aid in the form of scholarships, loans, and campus jobs. Sixteen percent of the students work part-time on campus. The university awards 25 scholarships on the basis of financial need. Federal loan funds are available. The university is a member of CSS. The FAF should be submitted. The aid application deadline is May 1.

Foreign Students: Seven percent of the full-time students come from foreign countries. The university offers these students special organizations.

Admissions: Foreign students must score at least 550 on the TOEFL. No college entrance examination is required.

Procedure: Application deadlines are June 1 (fall) and November 1 (spring). Foreign students must present the results of a physical examination. They must also present proof of funds adequate to cover each year of study. They must pay out-of-state tuition fees. Foreign students must also carry health insurance, which is available through the university.

Admissions Contact: Chelseia Harold, Director of Admissions.

MOUNT ST. MARY'S COLLEGE D–1
Emmitsburg, Maryland 21727 (301) 447-6122

F/T: 800M, 700W	Faculty:	72; IIB, av$
P/T: 30M, 25W	Ph.D.'s:	64%
Grad: 145M, 20W	S/F Ratio:	20 to 1
Year: 4-1-4	Tuition:	$4300
Appl: Mar. 1	R and B:	$2200
1196 applied	631 accepted	332 enrolled
SAT: 440V 470M		COMPETITIVE

Mount St. Mary's College, established in 1808, is a private liberal arts institution and the oldest independent Catholic college in the nation. The library contains 135,000 volumes and 6000 reels of microfilm, and subscribes to 675 periodicals.

Environment: The 1400-acre wooded campus is located in a rural area in the foothills of the Blue Ridge Mountains, 12 miles south of historic Gettysburg, Pennsylvania, and about 65 miles from Baltimore and Washington, D.C. Traditional dormitories for freshmen, sophomores, and juniors, and apartment-style dorms for juniors and seniors, accommodate 1200 students.

Student Life: About 85% of the students are from the Middle Atlantic states. Approximately 40% come from public schools. About 96% live on campus. Eighty-five percent of the students are Catholic and 12% are Protestant. Four percent are minority-group members. College housing is coed. Students may keep cars on campus.

Organizations: The college sponsors about 50 clubs and organizations, including a newspaper, radio and TV stations, student government, and special-interest, departmental, and religious groups. There are no fraternities or sororities. Cultural and outdoor recreation facilities are found in the area.

Sports: The college competes intercollegiately in 10 sports for men and 9 for women. There are 8 intramural sports for men and 7 for women.

Handicapped: Special parking areas and dormitory facilities are available for physically handicapped students. No students with impaired vision or hearing are currently enrolled.

Graduates: Eight percent of the freshmen drop out during their first year; and 79% remain to graduate. About 25% of the graduates continue their studies; 7% enter medical school, 5% dental school, and 7% law school. Forty-two percent pursue careers in business and industry.

Services: Free health care, tutoring, remedial instruction, career and psychological counseling, and job placement services are offered to students. Placement services also are available to graduates.

Programs of Study: The college awards the B.A. and B.S. degrees. Master's degrees are also offered. Bachelor's degrees are offered in the following subjects: BUSINESS (accounting, business administration), EDUCATION (elementary, secondary), ENGLISH (English), FINE AND PERFORMING ARTS (art, music, theater/dramatics), HEALTH SCIENCES (medical technology), LANGUAGES (French, general foreign languages, Spanish), MATH AND SCIENCES (biology, chemistry, mathematics), PHILOSOPHY (philosophy), PRE-PROFESSIONAL (dentistry, law, medicine), SOCIAL SCIENCES (criminal justice, economics, government/political science, history, psychology, sociology). About 40% of the undergraduate degrees are conferred in business and 35% in the social sciences.

Required: Students must fulfill a core curriculum consisting of 51 credit hours of liberal arts classes.

Special: Study abroad, internships, and cooperative education programs are available in all majors.

Honors: Nine honor societies are represented on campus.

Admissions: About 53% of those who applied were accepted for the 1981–82 freshman class. The SAT scores of those who enrolled were as follows: Verbal—75% below 500, 19% between 500 and 599, 6% between 600 and 700, and 0% above 700; Math—58% below 500, 32% between 500 and 599, 9% between 600 and 700, and 1% above 700. Candidates should have completed 16 Carnegie units, rank in the top half of their class, and have a combined score of 900 or more on the SAT. Admissions officers also consider recommendations, advanced placement or honors courses, and extracurricular activities, and strongly recommend campus tours with an interview.

Procedure: The SAT or ACT is required and should be taken by December of the senior year. The application deadlines are March 1 (fall) and January 1 (spring). Admissions decisions are made on a rolling basis. The application fee is $15.

Special: Early decision and early and deferred admissions plans are offered. AP and CLEP credit is accepted.

Transfer: For fall 1981, 236 students applied, 165 were accepted, and 112 enrolled. A 2.5 GPA is required. D grades do not transfer. There is a two-semester residency requirement for the senior year. Students must complete 30 credits at the college, of the 120 needed for a bachelor's degree. Application deadlines are March 1 (fall) and November 1 (spring).

Visiting: Orientations for prospective students are scheduled regularly. Participants meet professors and current students, and attend information sessions on admissions and financial aid. Interviews also may be scheduled with the admissions office for weekdays between 10 A.M. and 3:30 P.M.. Guides are provided. Visitors may sit in on classes and arrange, on their own, to stay overnight in a student's dorm room.

Financial Aid: Including student loans, about 85% of the students receive some financial aid. Work-study programs are available, and

340 MARYLAND

about 15% of the students work part-time on campus. A fund of $175,000 is available for scholarships, including freshman Presidential Merit Scholarships of $2250 each, renewable over 4 years. The average scholarship is about $1500. The FAF should be submitted. Applications for aid should be submitted by April 1.

Foreign Students: Five percent of the full-time students come from foreign countries. The college offers these students special counseling.

Admissions: Foreign students must score at least 500 on the TOEFL. No college entrance examination is required.

Procedure: Application deadlines are March 1 (fall) and November 1 (spring). Foreign students must present proof of funds adequate to cover each academic year. They must also carry health insurance, which is available through the college for a fee.

Admissions Contact: Lawrence J. Riordan, Director of Admissions.

PEABODY CONSERVATORY OF MUSIC D-2
Baltimore, Maryland 21202 (301) 659-8110

F/T, P/T:
259 M&W
Grad: 161 M&W
Year: sems, ss
Appl: see profile
120 enrolled
SAT: 450V 450M

Faculty: 103; n/av
Ph.D.'s: 22%
S/F Ratio: 5 to 1
Tuition: $4950
R and B: $2500

SPECIAL

Peabody Conservatory of Music, founded in 1857, is a private institution affiliated with the Peabody Institute of Baltimore and Johns Hopkins University. The Peabody-Pratt Library contains 300,000 volumes, including a 69,000-volume music collection, and 14,000 records.

Environment: The campus covers one city block and consists of 4 buildings: the main conservatory, a practice building, and 2 dormitories housing 170 students.

Student Life: Forty percent of the students are from Maryland. Almost all are graduates of public schools. About 40% of the students live in the dormitories, which are single-sex. Freshmen are required to do so. Visitation hours are determined by residents of each dormitory.

Organizations: Two fraternities and 2 sororities have chapters on campus. The student government has jurisdiction over student publications and activities. Each week, 10 to 15 cultural events take place on campus. Off-campus activities include the Baltimore Symphony, the Opera Society, and the Maryland Ballet.

Sports: The conservatory has no sports program.

Handicapped: There are no special facilities for handicapped students.

Services: Students receive free health care and psychological, career, and placement counseling. Placement services also are available to graduates.

Programs of Study: The conservatory confers the B.Mus. degree in composition and music education, keyboard instruments, percussion instruments, stringed instruments, voice, and wind instruments. Master's and doctoral degrees also are available.

Special: Students are evaluated on the basis of performances and examinations. They must pass a graduation recital to qualify for a degree.

Admissions: Twenty percent of those who applied were accepted for a recent freshman class. The SAT scores of those who enrolled were as follows: Verbal—55% above 500 and 18% above 600; Math—53% above 500 and 18% above 600. Candidates must have graduated from an accredited high school with 16 Carnegie units and at least a B average. The single most important factor influencing admission is an audition, which is required. Recommendations by high school officials also are important.

Procedure: Applicants must take the SAT or the ACT. The audition can be taken up to a year before the time the student wishes to enter. An admissions committee travels to other parts of the country to hear auditions, and, under special circumstances, a tape-recording may be submitted. The application deadline for fall admission is May 1. Students also are admitted in spring. Scholarship applicants should apply by January 15 for fall admission. There is a rolling admissions plan. Applications should be submitted with a $25 fee.

Special: Early decision and early admissions plans are available.

Transfer: In a recent year, 17 transfer students were admitted. An audition is required. Students must spend at least 2 years in residence, earning at least 60 of the 122 credits required for a bachelor's degree. Application deadlines are the same as those for freshmen.

Visitors: Informal visits may be arranged with the admissions office for a time when classes are in session. Visitors may sit in on classes, guides are available, and overnight accommodations can be arranged.

Financial Aid: About 78% of all students receive aid. Tuition may be paid in installments. The conservatory is a member of the CSS. Performance at the audition is the main consideration in awarding aid. The aid application and the FAF must be filed by January 15.

Foreign Students: The 81 students from foreign countries make up about 19% of enrollment. The conservatory offers these students an intensive English course, special counseling, and special organizations.

Admissions: Applicants must score 500 or better on the TOEFL. College entrance exams are not required.

Procedure: Application deadlines are the same as those for American students. Students must present a physician's statement as proof of good health and provide evidence of adequate funds for 1 year. Health insurance is required and is available through the conservatory for a fee.

Admissions Contact: Edward J. Weaver, Director of Admissions.

ST. JOHN'S COLLEGE E-3
Annapolis, Maryland 21404 (301) 263-2371

F/T: 209M, 162W
P/T: none
Grad: none
Year: sems
Appl: open
220 applied
SAT: 650V 590M

Faculty: 60; IV, +$
Ph.D.'s: 50%
S/F Ratio: 8 to 1
Tuition: $6050
R and B: $2400

170 accepted 105 enrolled
HIGHLY COMPETITIVE+

St. John's College, founded in 1696, is the third-oldest college in the United States. This private, nonsectarian institution offers a liberal arts program with no academic majors or electives, but instead based on rigorous study of language, science, mathematics, music, literature, philosophy, and theology. The library contains 72,000 volumes and subscribes to 97 periodicals.

Environment: The 36-acre campus is located in the seaport town of Annapolis, 35 miles from Washington, D.C. The college's 16 buildings include 6 dormitories that house 180 women and 200 men.

Student Life: About 16% of the students are from Maryland. Seventy-four percent of the freshmen come from public schools. Eighty percent of the students live on campus. About 4% are minority-group members. College housing is both single-sex and coed. There are visiting privileges in single-sex housing. Students may keep cars on campus.

Organizations: There are no fraternities or sororities. Student activities include drama, publications, chorus, organic gardening, woodworking, community service, and professional and special-interest groups. Cultural and social events on campus include art exhibits, concerts, debates, films, lectures, dances, and Senior Prank Day.

Sports: The college does not participate in intercollegiate sports. There are 11 intramural sports for men and 10 for women.

Handicapped: There are no special facilities for handicapped students.

Graduates: About 10% of the freshmen drop out by the end of their first year; 65% remain to graduate. Sixty percent of the graduates seek advanced degrees; 2% enter medical school and 19% law school. About 2% of the graduates pursue careers in business and industry.

Services: Students receive the following free services: placement, career counseling, health care, tutoring, and psychological counseling.

Programs of Study: All students follow a common course of study leading to a B.A. in liberal arts. The program is built around twice-weekly seminars of up to 21 students each on the Great Books of Western tradition, from the ancient Greeks to the 20th century. Students also take tutorials of up to 16 students each in foreign languages (2 years of Greek and 2 years of French), mathematics (4 years), music (2 years), and laboratory science (3 years). During the winter, junior and senior seminars are replaced by 8-week preceptorials, in which groups of 6 to 8 students engage in intensive study of one book or subject. Students are evaluated by papers and individual, oral final exams. Grades are not reported, but students are given periodic judgments of their progress.

Admission: Seventy-seven percent of those who applied were accepted for the 1981–82 freshman class. The SAT scores of those who enrolled were as follows: Verbal—3% below 500, 21% between 500 and 599, 55% between 600 and 700, and 21% above 700; Math—12% below 500, 39% between 500 and 599, 32% between 600 and

700, and 17% above 700. Generally, an applicant must be a graduate of an accredited high school. The college does not require a minimum class rank or grade average, but most St. John's students ranked in the top fifth of their class and earned a high school average of B or better. Of prime importance is the 2000-to-3000-word essay each applicant is required to submit. Admissions officers also consider impressions made in an interview, recommendations of high school officials, evidence of special talents, and personality.

Procedure: The SAT or ACT are not required. Application deadlines are open, but the freshman class usually is filled by May. An interview and 3-day campus visit are recommended. Notification is made on a rolling basis. There is no application fee.

Special: A deferred admissions plan is available.

Transfer: For fall 1981, 20 transfer students enrolled. New students must enroll as freshmen. Credits from other colleges do not transfer. About 25% of the students in each class have attended other colleges.

Visiting: Regularly scheduled 2-day orientations for prospective students consist of class observation and interviews by admissions officers. Students are housed and fed on campus. Informal visits also may be arranged for fall and spring through the admissions office. Guides are provided. Students may sit in on classes and stay overnight on campus.

Financial Aid: About 50% of the students receive aid. Thirty-six percent work part-time on campus. Average aid to freshmen from all sources is $6420. Aid is awarded only on the basis of need. The college is a member of CSS. The FAF must be filed with the college's form at the same time the application for admission is submitted. Application deadlines are open.

Foreign Students: One percent of the full-time students come from foreign countries.

Admissions: Foreign students must take the TOEFL. No college entrance examination is required.

Procedure: Application deadlines are open. Foreign students must present the results of a physical examination. They must also present proof of funds adequate to cover each academic year.

Admissions Contact: John Christensen, Director of Admissions.

ST. MARY'S COLLEGE OF MARYLAND E-4
St. Mary's City, Maryland 20686   (301) 863-7100

F/T: 503M, 619W	Faculty: 66; IIB, ++$
P/T: 102M, 124W	Ph.D.'s: 76%
Grad: none	S/F Ratio: 17 to 1
Year: sems, ss	Tuition: $1125 ($2075)
Appl: see profile	R and B: $2550
735 applied	563 accepted	364 enrolled
SAT: 456V 478M		COMPETITIVE

St. Mary's College, founded in 1839, is a state-supported liberal arts institution. The library houses 100,615 volumes and 2403 microfilm items, and subscribes to 702 periodicals.

Environment: The 265-acre campus is located in a rural area 68 miles from Washington, D.C. The 22 buildings include a fine-arts center and 5 dormitories that house nearly 800 students in double rooms.

Student Life: More than 90% of the students come from Maryland. Seventy percent of the freshmen come from public schools. Seventy-one percent of the students live on campus. About 13% are minority-group members. College housing is both single-sex and coed. There are visiting privileges in single-sex housing. Students may keep cars on campus.

Organizations: There are no fraternities, sororities, or religious organizations. College-sponsored extracurricular activities are related to academic programs. Among the most active are the jazz ensemble, the wind ensemble, the chorale, and field learning in the community (educational and tutorial). There is a student government. Cultural and social events on campus include films, pop concerts, dances, lectures, and art exhibits.

Sports: The college fields intercollegiate teams in 7 sports for men and 7 for women. There are 15 intramural sports for both men and women.

Handicapped: Eighty percent of the campus is accessible to physically handicapped students. Special parking areas, elevators, wheelchair ramps, specially equipped rest rooms, and lowered drinking fountains and telephones are provided. Special class scheduling is offered. No students with impaired vision or hearing are enrolled. No special counselors are provided.

Graduates: About 20% of the freshmen drop out by the end of their first year. About 35% remain to graduate. Twenty-five percent of the graduates seek advanced degrees.

Services: Students receive the following free services: placement, career, and psychological counseling, tutoring, and remedial instruction. Health care is provided through the mandatory health fee.

Programs of Study: The college awards the B.A. and B.S. degrees. Bachelor's degrees are offered in the following subjects: ENGLISH (English), FINE AND PERFORMING ARTS (art, music, theater/dramatics), MATH AND SCIENCES (biology, mathematics, natural sciences), SOCIAL SCIENCES (anthropology, economics, government/political science, history, human development, social sciences, sociology). Forty-seven percent of degrees are conferred in social sciences, 28% in math and sciences, and 25% in English and in fine and performing arts.

Required: Students must complete 12 credit hours in the Arts and Letters Division, 8 credit hours in both human development and history, and 4 in science, mathematics, and social science.

Special: Some independent study is offered. A 3-2 dual degree program is available in engineering. A secondary teaching certificate may be earned. The St. Mary's City Commission offers a summer archeology program of on-site work. Students may travel or study abroad and may design their own natural-science majors.

Honors: There are no honor societies on campus. All divisions offer honors programs.

Admissions: About 77% of those who applied were accepted for the 1981–82 freshman class. The SAT scores of those who enrolled were as follows: Verbal—71% below 500, 22% between 500 and 599, 7% between 600 and 700, and fewer than 1% above 700; Math—62% below 500, 28% between 500 and 599, 9% between 600 and 700, and 1% above 700. Candidates for admission must have a GED certificate or be graduates of an accredited high school with 16 Carnegie units and an average of C or better. The college prefers that applicants score at least 400 on each section of the SAT. Admissions officers also consider recommendations by high school officials, evidence of special talents, advanced placement or honors courses, impressions made in an interview, extracurricular activities, and leadership record. No more than 15% of the students may be from outside Maryland.

Procedure: The SAT is required and should be taken by January of the senior year; junior-year results are acceptable. There are no application deadlines, but preference is given to applications received by April 15 (fall) and October 15 (spring). Campus housing for the fall semester usually is filled by mid-spring. Applicants are notified on a rolling basis. The application fee is $20. An interview is recommended.

Special: Early decision and early and deferred admissions plans are available. An Academic Assistance Program aids those deficient in basic academic skills. AP and CLEP credit is accepted.

Transfer: For fall 1981, 174 students applied, 147 were accepted, and 98 enrolled. Transfer students are accepted in the freshman, sophomore, and junior classes. A 2.0 GPA or better is required. D grades are assessed individually. Students must earn at least 30 semester hours of the final 36 at the college, of the 128 needed to receive a bachelor's degree. Application deadlines are the same as those for freshman applicants.

Visiting: Orientation sessions for prospective students are scheduled regularly. They include campus tours, meetings with faculty members and students, and information sessions. Open-house programs also are held on several Saturdays. Informal visits can be arranged for weekdays from 8:30 A.M. to 4:30 P.M. through the admissions office. Visitors may sit in on classes with permission of the instructor.

Financial Aid: About 47% of the students receive aid. Loans may be secured from the federal and state governments and local banks. Work contracts are awarded to 13% of the students, including freshmen. CWS jobs are offered in all departments. The average scholarship is $547; the average loan, $1196; the average earnings from a work contract, $1097. Tuition may be paid in installments. Aid awards are based on financial need. The college is a member of CSS. The FAF must be submitted. Priority consideration is given to aid applications filed by April 1.

Foreign Students: Fewer than 1% of the full-time students come from foreign countries. The college offers these students special counseling.

Admissions: Foreign students must score at least 450 on the TOEFL. A college entrance examination is sometimes required.

Procedure: The application deadlines are open through the beginning of each semester. Foreign students must present a certificate of health from their physician. They must also present proof of adequate funds. They must carry health insurance, which is available through the college and included in the regular tuition fees.

Admissions Contact: Nancy Blanks, Director of Admissions.

SALISBURY STATE COLLEGE   F-4
Salisbury, Maryland 21801   (301) 546-3261

F/T: 1289M, 1623W	Faculty:	188; IIA, +$
P/T: 360M, 508W	Ph.D.'s:	70%
Grad: 186M, 387W	S/F Ratio:	16 to 1
Year: sems, ss	Tuition:	$1070 ($2070)
Appl: open	R and B:	$2140
1533 applied	1114 accepted	700 enrolled
SAT: 425V 460M		COMPETITIVE

Salisbury State College, founded in 1925, is a state-supported institution of liberal arts. The library contains 260,000 volumes and 160,000 microfilm items, and subscribes to 1900 periodicals.

Environment: The 140-acre campus, in a rural area 110 miles from Baltimore, has 16 buildings, including a physical activities center. Dorms house 1200 students.

Student Life: About 85% of the students are Maryland residents. Ninety percent come from public schools. Fifty percent of the students live on campus. Nine percent are minority-group members. College housing is both single-sex and coed. There are visiting privileges in single-sex housing. Freshmen may not own or operate automobiles on campus; other students may have cars.

Organizations: Fifteen percent of the men belong to 4 fraternities and 10% of the women to 4 sororities. Extracurricular activities include special-interest clubs, a chorus, drama, symphony and ballet performances, publications, and literature readings. Downtown Salisbury, a few blocks from the college, provides additional recreation.

Sports: The college competes on an intercollegiate level in 12 sports for men and 11 for women. There are 6 intramural sports for both sexes.

Handicapped: The entire campus is accessible to wheelchair-bound students. Special facilities include wheelchair ramps, parking areas, elevators, and specially equipped rest rooms. Special class scheduling and 1 counselor also are available.

Graduates: Twenty-eight percent of the freshmen drop out by the end of their first year. Fifty-six percent remain to graduate. Twenty-five percent of the graduates pursue further study; 1% enter medical school, 1% dental school, and 23% law school. Another 35% of the graduates begin careers in business and industry.

Services: Students receive the following services free: health care, placement, psychological and career counseling, tutoring, and remedial instruction. Placement services are available also to graduates.

Programs of Study: The college awards the B.A., B.S., B.S.W., and B.S.N. degrees. Master's degrees are also available. Bachelor's degrees are offered in the following subjects: BUSINESS (accounting, business administration, computer science, finance, management, marketing), EDUCATION (early childhood, elementary, secondary), ENGLISH (English, literature, speech), FINE AND PERFORMING ARTS (art, art education, music, music education, radio/TV, studio art, theater/dramatics), HEALTH SCIENCES (medical technology, nursing), LANGUAGES (French, Spanish), MATH AND SCIENCES (biology, chemistry, mathematics, natural sciences, physical sciences), PHILOSOPHY (philosophy), PREPROFESSIONAL (dentistry, engineering, law, medicine, pharmacy, veterinary), SOCIAL SCIENCES (economics, geography, history, psychology, social sciences, sociology). About 30% of the undergraduate degrees are conferred in education, 35% in business, and 15% in social sciences.

Required: Students must meet general education requirements.

Special: A general studies major is offered. Students may design their own majors.

Honors: Phi Alpha Theta and Omicron Delta Kappa have chapters on campus.

Admissions: Seventy-three percent of those who applied were accepted for the 1981-82 freshman class. The SAT scores of those who enrolled were as follows: Verbal—75% below 500, 18% between 500 and 599, 7% between 600 and 700, and fewer than 1% above 700; Math—65% below 500, 25% between 500 and 599, 8% between 600 and 700, and 1% above 700. Applicants should have at least a C average and be graduates of accredited high schools. Academic record and SAT scores are also considered.

Procedure: The SAT is required. Application deadlines are open. Admissions decisions are made on a rolling basis. Applications should be submitted with a $15 fee.

Special: An early admissions plan is available. CLEP and AP credit is accepted.

Transfer: Transfer students with a GPA of 2.0 or better are accepted for all classes. D grades do not transfer. Students must earn at least 30 semester hours on campus, of the 120 needed to receive a bachelor's degree. Application deadlines are open.

Visiting: Weekend orientation programs for prospective students are scheduled regularly. Informal visits also may be arranged with the director of admissions for weekdays. Guides are provided. Visitors may sit in on classes.

Financial Aid: About 35% of the students receive financial aid. Forty-five percent work part-time on campus. Average aid to freshmen from all sources is $2400. The college is a member of CSS. The FAF and aid application must be filed by November 15.

Foreign Students: Fewer than 1% of the full-time students come from foreign countries. The college offers these students special organizations.

Admissions: Foreign students must score at least 550 on the TOEFL. No college entrance examinations are required.

Procedure: The application deadlines are April 1 (fall) and August 1 (spring). Foreign students must present proof of funds adequate to cover their entire period of study. They must also carry health insurance, which is available through the college for a fee.

Admissions Contact: M.P. Minton, III, Director of Admissions.

TOWSON STATE UNIVERSITY   D-2
Towson, Maryland 21204   (301) 321-2112

F/T: 4163M, 5246W	Faculty:	453; IIA, ++$
P/T: 1814M, 2559W	Ph.D.'s:	63%
Grad: 334M, 991W	S/F Ratio:	21 to 1
Year: 4-1-4, ss	Tuition:	$1097 ($2047)
Appl: June 1	R and B:	$1160
4080 applied	2847 accepted	1998 enrolled
SAT: 430V 461M		COMPETITIVE

Towson State University, founded in 1866, offers undergraduate programs in the liberal arts and sciences, business, education, health, and preprofessional areas. Its library contains 340,579 books and subscribes to 2192 periodicals.

Environment: The 324-acre campus is located in a suburban area 5 miles from downtown Baltimore. Dorms accommodate 1265 students. Education and psychology buildings were recently constructed.

Student Life: Nearly all students come from Maryland and are graduates of public schools. About 13% of the students live on campus. Fifteen percent are minority-group members. University housing is both single-sex and coed. There are visiting privileges in single-sex housing. Students may keep cars on campus. Day-care services are available to all students, faculty, and staff on a sliding fee scale.

Organizations: There are 10 local fraternities and 6 local sororities. Extracurricular activities include clubs, student government, music and drama groups, and publications.

Sports: The college fields intercollegiate teams in 12 sports for men and 10 for women. There are 8 intramural sports for men and 7 for women.

Handicapped: About 95% of the campus is accessible to students with physical handicaps. Special facilities include wheelchair ramps, parking areas, elevators, and lowered drinking fountains and telephones. Facilities for students with impaired vision or hearing include special course registration, parking permits, reader services, specially marked elevator buttons, and railings.

Graduates: About 35% of the freshmen drop out by the end of their first year. Fifty percent remain to graduate. Thirty percent of the graduates go on to further education. Forty-six percent enter careers in business and industry.

Services: Psychological counseling, health care, tutoring, remedial instruction, placement services, and career counseling are offered free to students. Placement services also are available to graduates.

Programs of Study: The college awards the B.A., B.S., B.S.N., B.M., B.B.A., and B.F.A. degrees. Master's degrees also are available. Bachelor's degrees are offered in the following subjects: BUSINESS (accounting, business administration), EDUCATION (early childhood, elementary, general, health/physical, instructional technology, secondary), ENGLISH (English, speech), FINE AND PERFORMING ARTS (art, art education, mass communications, music, music education, theater/dramatics), HEALTH SCIENCES (health, health records administration, medical technology, nursing, occupational therapy, speech therapy), LANGUAGES (French, German, Spanish), MATH AND SCIENCES (biology, chemistry, mathematics, natural sciences, physics), PHILOSOPHY (philosophy), SOCIAL SCIENCES (anthropology, economics, general studies, geography, government/political science, history, international relations, psychology, social sciences, sociology). About 37% of the undergraduate degrees are awarded in business, 19% in education, and 12% in social sciences.

Required: Students must fulfill general education requirements, which are divided among 4 general areas: arts and humanities, science and mathematics, social science, and health and physical education.

Special: Students may design their own majors or pursue a general studies degree. Education programs include Urban Education, a work-study program that prepares teachers to work in the inner city. A cooperative exchange program allows students to study at other institutions in Maryland and in the Domestic Student Exchange Program. Study abroad also is available.

Honors: A number of honor societies are represented on campus. The history, art, English, biology, psychology, physics, and sociology departments offer honors programs.

Admissions: About 70% of those who applied for admission to the 1981–82 freshman class were accepted. The SAT scores of those who enrolled were: Verbal—80% below 500, 17% between 500 and 599, 3% between 600 and 700, and fewer than 1% above 700; Math—68% below 500, 24% between 500 and 599, 6% between 600 and 700, and 1% above 700. Applicants should present an average of at least 2.5. Completion of a college-preparatory program in high school is not required.

Procedure: Applicants must take the SAT between March of the junior year and December of the senior year. The application deadline for fall admission is June 1. New students are admitted to all terms. Admissions decisions are made on a rolling basis. The application fee is $20.

Special: Early decision and early and deferred admissions plans are available. AP and CLEP credit is accepted.

Transfer: For fall 1981, 1868 students applied, 1494 were accepted, and 1016 enrolled. A 2.0 GPA is required. D grades transfer except in freshman composition. Transfer students are accepted for all classes, but must earn at least 30 credits at Towson, of the 120 needed to receive a bachelor's degree. Application deadlines are the same as those for freshmen.

Visiting: Open house days for prospective students are scheduled Wednesdays during the fall semester. Guides also are available for informal visits. The best times for such visits are January and June.

Financial Aid: About 63% of the students receive aid. Thirteen percent work part-time on campus. The university offers grants, loans, and CWS jobs. The university is a member of CSS. The FAF and the university application should be submitted by April 1. January 15 is the preferred deadline.

Foreign Students: One percent of the full-time students come from foreign countries. The university offers these students an intensive English course, special counseling, and special organizations.

Admissions: Foreign students must score at least 500 on the TOEFL. They must also take the SAT and score at least 400 on both the verbal and math tests.

Procedure: The application deadline is June 1 (fall). Foreign students must present proof of funds adequate to cover 1 academic year. They must pay out-of-state tuition fees.

Admissions Contact: Linda J. Collins, Director of Admissions.

UNITED STATES NAVAL ACADEMY E-3
Annapolis, Maryland 21402 (301) 267-4361

F/T: 4226M, 299W		Faculty:	532; IIB, ++$
P/T: none		Ph.D.'s:	34%
Grad: none		S/F Ratio:	9 to 1
Year: sems, ss		Tuition:	none
Appl: Jan. 31		R and B:	none
11,897 applied	1647 accepted		1328 enrolled
SAT: 572V 656M			MOST COMPETITIVE

U.S. Naval Academy, founded in 1845 as one of the nation's service schools, is a 4-year, coeducational undergraduate college. Graduates are awarded the B.S. degree and a commission in the Navy or Marine Corps. The library contains 470,000 volumes and subscribes to 1900 periodicals.

Environment: The 329-acre campus is located in Annapolis on the Chesapeake Bay, 35 miles from Washington, D.C., and 25 miles from Baltimore. Facilities include a dormitory that accommodates all students in double and triple rooms. The domed chapel is used for Protestant and Catholic services. Other facilities include a computer center, gymnasiums, a golf course, swimming pools, a student union with an indoor ice rink, and a sailing center.

Student Life: Students come from all 50 states, the District of Columbia, the Philippines, Puerto Rico, the Virgin Islands, Guam, American Samoa, and other American territories. As a service school, the academy has many military regulations, including regulated liberty time and designated study hours, that are not common to civilian institutions. About 12% of the students are minority-group members. Academy housing is coed. Alcohol is restricted on campus, and smoking is permitted in the dormitory and other specified areas. Seniors may keep cars on campus. There is an honor system.

Organizations: Qualified students may join such national societies as the AIAA, the Marine Technological Society, and Sigma Pi Sigma. Extracurricular activities for midshipmen include a glee club, concert and dance bands, a drum and bugle corps, publications, special-interest clubs, concerts, lectures, and plays. The major social events are Commissioning Week and Homecoming. The academy encourages students to attend religious services. Jewish, Greek Orthodox, and some Protestant services are available in the Annapolis area. The academy sponsors Catholic and Protestant clubs and choirs, a Bible study group, and an annual retreat. The student government consists of selected seniors who direct the Brigade of Midshipmen, or student body. The seniors are primarily responsible for the military indoctrination of freshmen.

Sports: The academy fields intercollegiate teams in 20 sports for men and in 5 for women. In addition, midshipmen may participate in 26 intramural sports for men and 12 for women.

Graduates: About 10% of the students drop out during the freshman year; 73% remain to graduate.

Services: The Academy provides the following services free of charge: placement, health care, psychological counseling, career counseling, tutoring, and remedial instruction.

Programs of Study: The academy awards the B.S. degree in the following subjects: ENGLISH (English), MATH AND SCIENCES (chemistry, mathematics, oceanography, physical sciences, physics), PREPROFESSIONAL (engineering—aerospace, engineering—electrical, engineering—general, engineering—marine, engineering—mechanical, engineering—naval architecture, engineering—ocean, engineering—systems), SOCIAL SCIENCES (economics, government/political science, history). The academy requires that at least 80% of the students major in engineering, math, science, or resources management. Students must have their choices of major approved; all but a few receive their first choice.

Required: All students must satisfy distribution requirements in the humanities, social sciences, mathematics, science, and a modern language. Students also receive thorough training in seamanship, navigation, engineering, and weaponry during the academic year and required summer sessions. A student may omit some core courses, giving him or her time to pursue advanced work, independent study, or a double major, by validating previous college-level work. Students must earn an average of at least 2.0 and meet required standards of military performance, conduct, honor, and physical education to graduate. Graduates must serve at least 5 years on active duty as commissioned officers.

Special: Seniors selected for the Trident Scholar program pursue independent research and study programs, supervised by faculty advisers. The Immediate Graduate Education Program enables qualified graduates to study for their M.A. at the Navy's Postgraduate School in Monterey, California, immediately after graduation.

Honors: A number of honor societies have chapters on campus.

Admissions: About 14% of those who applied were accepted for the 1981–82 freshman (plebe) class. The SAT scores of those who enrolled were as follows: Verbal—9% below 500, 36% between 500 and 599, 41% between 600 and 700, and 14% above 700; Math—1% below 500, 8% between 500 and 599, 68% between 600 and 700, and 23% above 700. Every applicant must meet basic eligibility requirements; obtain a nomination; qualify academically, medically, and physically; and be selected for appointment. To be eligible, a candidate must be a U.S. citizen of good moral character, between 17 and 21 years old, have a sound secondary-school background, be unmarried, and have no children. To be considered for appointment, candidates must obtain a nomination from their U.S. senator, representative, delegate to Congress, or territorial commissioner; the vice president; or an honor naval or military school. Candidates also may be nominated after at least 1 year of service in the regular Navy or Marine Corps or their reserve components. Children of active, retired, or deceased military personnel are eligible to compete for presidential appointments.

344 MARYLAND

Procedure: Applicants must take the SAT or ACT. The deadline for applications is January 31. There is a rolling admissions plan.

Special: An early admissions plan is available. AP credit is given after a series of placement tests are administered at the beginning of the first year.

Transfer: One in 12 entering midshipmen has at least 1 semester of college. All must enter as freshmen and complete 4 years of study at the academy.

Financial Aid: Tuition, room, board, and medical and dental care are provided by the government. Midshipmen receive a monthly salary of over $450 for uniforms, books, and personal needs.

Foreign Students: Fewer than 1% of the full-time students come from foreign countries.

Admissions: Foreign students must take the TOEFL. They must also take the SAT or the ACT.

Procedure: The application deadline is January 31 (fall).

Admissions Contact: Candidate Guidance Office.

UNIVERSITY OF MARYLAND/ BALTIMORE COUNTY
D-2

Baltimore, Maryland 21228   (301) 455-2291

F/T: 2257M, 2617W	Faculty: 259; I, – $
P/T: 680M, 772W	Ph.D.'s: 96%
Grad: 211M, 216W	S/F Ratio: 19 to 1
Year: 4-1-4, ss	Tuition: $1028 ($2952)
Appl: Aug. 1	R and B: $2280
2866 applied	2250 accepted 1404 enrolled
SAT: required	COMPETITIVE

University of Maryland's Baltimore County campus was established in 1966. It offers programs in the liberal arts and sciences. The library houses 283,000 volumes and over 700 microfilm items, and subscribes to 3200 periodicals.

Environment: Located 5 miles from Baltimore in a suburban area adjacent to the Baltimore Beltway, the campus occupies 476 acres. The 28 buildings include 3 new dormitories. On-campus apartments also are available.

Student Life: Most students are from Maryland, many from the Baltimore area. Eighty percent are public school graduates. About a third of the students live on campus. Twenty-six percent are members of minority groups. Dormitories are both single-sex and coed. Students may keep cars on campus.

Organizations: Ten percent of the men belong to the 3 national fraternities on campus, and 5% of the women are members of the 3 national sororities. Many social, cultural, and recreational facilities are available in the Baltimore-Washington area.

Sports: The university fields intercollegiate teams in 7 sports for men and 8 for women. The 2 gymnasiums also provide facilities for intramural sports.

Handicapped: About 95% of the campus is accessible to physically handicapped students. Special parking areas, specially equipped rest rooms, wheelchair ramps, elevators, and lowered telephones are provided.

Graduates: About 42% of the entering freshmen remain to graduate. Forty percent of the graduates pursue advanced degrees, and 18% begin careers in business and industry.

Services: Psychological counseling, career counseling, tutoring, remedial instruction, and placement services are available free. Placement services also are offered to alumni.

Programs of Study: The university confers the B.A. and B.S. degrees. Master's and doctoral degrees also are awarded. Bachelor's degrees are offered in the following subjects: AREA STUDIES (American, Black/Afro-American), BUSINESS (computer science), EDUCATION (early childhood, elementary, secondary, special), ENGLISH (English), FINE AND PERFORMING ARTS (art, art education, art history, dance, film/photography, music, music education, studio art, theater/dramatics), HEALTH SCIENCES (emergency health services, nursing), LANGUAGES (French, German, Spanish), MATH AND SCIENCES (biochemistry, biology, chemistry, mathematics, physics), PHILOSOPHY (classics, philosophy), PREPROFESSIONAL (social work), SOCIAL SCIENCES (economics, geography, government/political science, history, psychology, sociology).

Required: One year of physical education is required.

Special: Combined-degree programs are offered in nursing, pharmacy, dental hygiene, physical therapy, medical technology, medicine, dentistry, and radiologic technology. Students may design their own majors.

Honors: Two national honor societies have chapters on campus.

Admissions: Seventy-nine percent of those who applied for admission to the 1981–82 freshman class were accepted. For a recent class, the SAT scores were as follows: Math—42% between 500 and 599, 13% between 600 and 700, and 2% above 700; Verbal—35% between 500 and 599, 12% between 600 and 700, and 1% above 700. Maryland residents should have at least a C average and rank in the top 40% of their high school class. Admission is generally determined by a combination of SAT scores and GPA, as shown in a table contained in the university catalog. Special factors such as leadership potential, special talents, and personal circumstances also may be considered. Preference is given to Maryland residents; the number of nonresidents admitted is limited.

Procedure: The SAT must be taken. Application deadlines are August 1 (fall), December 1 (winter), January 5 (spring), and May 13 and June 24 (summer sessions). There is a rolling admissions plan. A fee of $15 must accompany the application.

Special: Early and deferred admissions plans are available. AP and CLEP credit is granted.

Transfer: For fall 1981, 1219 transfer students applied, 1005 were accepted, and 656 enrolled. Maryland residents must have a 2.0 GPA; out-of-state applicants must have a 2.5. Preference is given to students transferring from schools in Maryland. Students must complete at least 30 hours in residence of the 120 required for a bachelor's degree. Application deadlines are the same as those for freshmen.

Visiting: Regularly scheduled orientations are held for prospective students. Visitors are provided with guides and may sit in on classes and stay overnight at the school. The best times for visits are weekdays between 8:30 A.M. and 4:30 P.M.. The admissions office may be contacted for further information.

Financial Aid: Fifty percent of all students receive aid. Scholarships, loans, and CWS and other campus jobs are available. The university is a member of CSS. The FAF must be filed by March 1.

Foreign Students: The 100 students from foreign countries make up about 2 percent of enrollment. The university offers these students an intensive English course and special organizations.

Admissions: Applicants must score at least 500 on the TOEFL. No college entrance exams are required.

Procedure: Application deadlines are March 1 (fall) and August 1 (spring). Students must present proof of adequate funds for 1 year. Health insurance is available through the university for a fee.

Admissions Contact: Barbara Shahpazian, Associate Director of Admissions.

UNIVERSITY OF MARYLAND/ COLLEGE PARK
D-3

College Park, Maryland 20742   (301) 454-5550

F/T: 13,263M, 11,559W	Faculty: 1837; I, av$
P/T: 2640M, 2540W	Ph.D.'s: n/av
Grad: 3681M, 3845W	S/F Ratio: 14 to 1
Year: sems, ss	Tuition: $1073 ($2998)
Appl: May 1	R and B: $2650
13,253 applied	9635 accepted 4679 enrolled
SAT: 457V 513M	COMPETITIVE

University of Maryland/College Park is composed of 5 academic divisions: Agricultural and Life Sciences, Arts and Humanities, Human and Community Resources, Behavioral and Social Sciences, and Mathematical and Physical Sciences and Engineering. These divisions include the undergraduate colleges of Agriculture; Architecture; Journalism; Human Ecology; Physical Education, Recreation, and Health; Education; Business and Management; and Engineering. The university also operates overseas centers in cooperation with the armed forces. The library contains 1,231,500 volumes and 1,076,900 microfilm items, and subscribes to 15,847 periodicals. The library also houses an extensive Maryland collection, as well as the Katherine Anne Porter, Rare Book, East Asian, and Health Sciences Historical Collections.

Environment: The 750-acre suburban campus is located about 9 miles from Washington, D.C. High-rise and low-rise dormitories, Greek letter houses, and married-student apartments accommodate about 8100 men and women.

Student Life: About 83% of the students are from Maryland. Twenty-five percent live on campus. About 14% of the students are minority-group members. University housing is both single-sex and coed. There are visiting privileges in single-sex housing. Students may keep cars on campus.

Organizations: About 16% of the men belong to 29 fraternities; 13% of the women belong to 22 sororities. The university sponsors a variety of events and activities, including religious groups. The Student Union houses a pub, restaurant, ballroom, movie theater, and bowling alley.

Sports: The University fields intercollegiate teams in 10 sports. Intramural sports also are available for both men and women.

Handicapped: Special facilities for physically handicapped students include wheelchair ramps, special parking, elevators, special class scheduling, specially equipped rest rooms, and lowered telephones. Exam readers and access guides are available for students with impaired vision or hearing. Special counselors are provided.

Graduates: Thirty-six percent of the freshmen drop out by the end of their first year. Twenty-six percent remain to graduate.

Services: Psychological counseling is offered to students free of charge. Health care is available on a fee basis.

Programs of Study: The university confers the B.A., B.S., and B.Mus. degrees. Master's and doctoral degrees also are available. Bachelor's degrees are offered in the following subjects: AREA STUDIES (American, Russian, urban), BUSINESS (accounting, business administration, business education, computer science, finance, management, marketing), EDUCATION (adult, early childhood, elementary, health/physical, industrial, secondary, special), ENGLISH (English, journalism, speech), FINE AND PERFORMING ARTS (art, art education, art history, dance, music, music education, radio/TV, studio art, theater/dramatics), LANGUAGES (French, German, Greek/Latin, Hebrew, Portuguese, Russian, Spanish), MATH AND SCIENCES (astronomy, biochemistry, biology, botany, chemistry, ecology/environmental science, geology, mathematics, physical sciences, physics, zoology), PHILOSOPHY (philosophy), PREPROFESSIONAL (dentistry, engineering—aerospace, engineering—agricultural, engineering—chemical, engineering—civil, engineering—electrical, engineering—mechanical, forestry, law, medicine, pharmacy, social work, veterinary), SOCIAL SCIENCES (anthropology, economics, geography, government/political science, history, psychology, social sciences, sociology).

Special: The Law Enforcement Institute and Cultural Studies Center offer special programs. A general studies major is offered. Combination degrees can be earned in veterinary medicine, law, and pharmacy. Students may design their own majors.

Honors: About 38 honor societies have chapters on campus. The university has a general honors program. Some departments offer individual programs.

Admissions: About 73% of those who applied were accepted for the 1981-82 freshman class. The SAT scores of those who enrolled were as follows: Verbal—67% below 500, 25% between 500 and 599, 6% between 600 and 700, and 1% above 700; Math—45% below 500, 35% between 500 and 599, 17% between 600 and 700, and 3% above 700. Applicants should be graduates of accredited high schools. An average of C or better is required for Maryland residents who rank in the top 40% of their class; out-of-state residents must meet higher standards. Out-of-state admissions are limited.

Procedure: The SAT is required for placement and counseling purposes and should be taken before the end of the fall of the senior year. Applications for admission must be submitted by May 1 (fall) and December 1 (spring). Freshmen are admitted to the spring semester, except in the professional schools. There is a $15 application fee.

Special: The university has early decision and early admissions plans. AP and CLEP credit is granted.

Transfer: More than 3000 transfer students are accepted each year. Maryland residents, who receive preference, must have a GPA of at least 2.0. D grades transfer for Maryland residents. Out-of-state applicants should present a higher average. Students must complete the final 30 semester hours in residence, of the 120 needed to receive a bachelor's degree. Application deadlines are July 30 (fall) and December 1 (spring).

Visiting: Orientations for prospective students, which include group interviews and campus tours, are scheduled regularly. Informal visits also may be arranged for weekday afternoons and specified Saturdays. Guides are provided. Visitors may sit in on classes. Interested students should contact the office of undergraduate admissions.

Financial Aid: Fifty percent of the students receive financial aid. Eight percent work part-time on campus. Average aid to freshmen from all sources is $2200. Scholarships, grants, and loans are available. The university is a member of CSS. The FAF must be filed. The deadline for aid applications is February 15.

Foreign Students: The university offers foreign students an intensive English course, an intensive English program, special counseling, and special organizations.

Admissions: Foreign students must take the TOEFL.

Procedure: The application deadlines are March 1 (fall) and July 31 (spring). Proof of funds adequate to cover study at the university is required.

Admissions Contact: Jon Boome, Director, Undergraduate Admissions.

UNIVERSITY OF MARYLAND/ EASTERN SHORE   F-4
Princess Anne, Maryland 21853   (301) 651-2200

F/T: 515M, 554W Faculty: n/av; IIB, ++$
P/T: n/av Ph.D.'s: 56%
Grad: 20M, 40W S/F Ratio: 13 to 1
Year: sems, ss Tuition: $859 ($2448)
Appl: Aug. 15 R and B: $2176
1142 applied 741 accepted 430 enrolled
SAT: required COMPETITIVE

University of Maryland/Eastern Shore is a state-supported land-grant university founded in 1866. The library contains 106,050 volumes and 143,200 microfilm items, and subscribes to 853 periodicals.

Environment: The 300-acre campus is located in Princess Anne, in a rural area on the Eastern Shore of Maryland. Most campus buildings are concentrated in a 30-acre area. These include a performing arts center, a gymnasium-auditorium, and dormitories.

Student Life: Most students are residents of Maryland. Ninety percent of the freshmen come from public schools. Forty percent of the students live on campus. Seventy-one percent of the students are minority-group members. University housing is both single-sex and coed. There are visiting privileges in single-sex housing. Students may keep cars on campus.

Organizations: Fraternities and sororities, special-interest clubs, and a student government are available.

Sports: The university participates intercollegiately in 7 sports for men and 4 for women. There are 5 intramural sports for men and 4 for women.

Handicapped: Facilities for handicapped students include special parking areas and specially equipped rest rooms.

Services: The following services are provided free to students: health care, placement, psychological and career counseling, tutoring, and remedial instruction.

Programs of Study: The university awards the B.A. and B.S. degrees. Master's and doctoral degrees also are available. Bachelor's degrees are offered in the following subjects: BUSINESS (business administration, business education, computer science), EDUCATION (elementary, secondary, special), ENGLISH (English), FINE AND PERFORMING ARTS (art, art education), HEALTH SCIENCES (physical therapy), MATH AND SCIENCES (biology, chemistry, ecology/environmental science, mathematics), SOCIAL SCIENCES (social sciences, sociology).

Special: Bachelor's degree programs in nursing, physical therapy, radiologic technology, dental hygiene, and pharmacy are offered in cooperation with the Baltimore City Campus of the University of Maryland. Four-year combined B.A.-B.S. degrees may be earned in some subjects.

Honors: The honors program has been designed with the professional schools of the Baltimore City Campus for students in these preprofessional programs: medicine, law, pharmacy, nursing, and social work and community planning.

Admissions: About 65% of those who applied were accepted for the 1981-82 freshman class. Graduates of accredited high schools who present at least a C average and rank in the upper half of their graduating class are admitted as regular students. Other applicants may be admitted to the Academic Development Program.

Procedure: The SAT is required. Application deadlines are August 15 (fall) and January 7 (spring). Admissions decisions are made on a rolling basis. There is a $15 application fee.

Special: Early decision, early admissions, and deferred admissions plans are available. AP and CLEP credit is accepted.

346 MARYLAND

Transfer: For fall 1981, 150 students applied, 121 were accepted, and 63 enrolled. Transfer students are accepted for all classes. A 2.0 GPA is required. D grades do not transfer. Students must earn at least 30 semester hours at the university, of the 120 needed to receive a bachelor's degree. Application deadlines are August 15 (fall) and January 7 (spring).

Visiting: Orientation programs for prospective students are held in fall and spring. Guides also are available for informal visits on Mondays through Fridays, 8:30 A.M. to 4:30 P.M.. Visitors may sit in on classes and stay overnight on campus. Arrangements should be made with the director of admissions and registration.

Financial Aid: Eighty percent of the students receive financial aid. Forty-five percent work part-time on campus. Scholarships and loan grants are available. The state of Maryland awards Legislative Scholarships and special grants. The university is a member of CSS. The FAF and BEOG are required. The deadline for applications is April 15.

Foreign Students: The university offers foreign students special counseling and special organizations.

Admissions: Foreign students must score at least 600 on the TOEFL. No college entrance examination is required.

Procedure: The application deadlines are June (fall) and December (spring). Foreign students must submit a completed health form. They must also present proof of funds adequate to cover 1 year of study.

Admissions Contact: James B. Ewers, Director of Admissions and Registration.

WASHINGTON COLLEGE E-2
Chestertown, Maryland 21620 (301) 778-2800

F/T: 344M, 325W Faculty: 57; IIB, +$
P/T: 12M, 8W Ph.D.'s: 75%
Grad: 31M, 54W S/F Ratio: 12 to 1
Year: sems Tuition: $4014
Appl: open R and B: $2050
633 applied 443 accepted 177 enrolled
SAT: 492V 509M ACT: 22 COMPETITIVE

Washington College, founded in 1782, is an independent college of liberal arts and sciences. The library houses 175,000 volumes and 9000 microfilm items, and subscribes to 605 periodicals.

Environment: The 100-acre campus is located on Maryland's rural Eastern Shore, within 2 hours of Wilmington, Baltimore, Philadelphia, and Washington, D.C. Buildings include a fine arts center, drama and music studios, and 12 dormitories that house 650 students. Three of the men's dormitories have been listed in the *National Register of Historic Places.*

Student Life: About 58% of the students come from Maryland. Sixty-eight percent are graduates of public schools. Ninety-five percent of the students live on campus. About 3% are minority-group members. College housing is both single-sex and coed. There are visiting privileges in single-sex housing. Students may keep cars on campus.

Organizations: There are 4 fraternities and 3 sororities on campus; 25% of the men and 30% of the women belong to them. Extracurricular activities include publications, music and drama groups, a variety of clubs, and student government.

Sports: The college participates in 8 intercollegiate sports for men and 6 for women. There are 9 intramural sports for men and 6 for women.

Handicapped: The college has no special facilities for handicapped students.

Graduates: About 25% of the freshmen drop out by the end of their first year; about 60% remain to graduate. Recently, about 40% of the graduates sought advanced degrees. Sixty-five percent of the graduates began careers in business and industry.

Services: Students receive the following services free of charge: placement, career, and psychological counseling; health care; tutoring, and remedial instruction.

Programs of Study: The college awards the B.A. and B.S. degrees. Master's degrees also are available. Bachelor's degrees are offered in the following subjects: AREA STUDIES (American), BUSINESS (business administration, computer science), EDUCATION (secondary), ENGLISH (English, journalism, literature), FINE AND PERFORMING ARTS (art, art education, art history, dance, music, music education, studio art, theater/dramatics), LANGUAGES (French, German, Spanish), MATH AND SCIENCES (biology, chemistry, mathematics, physics, statistics), PHILOSOPHY (classics, humanities, philosophy, religion), PREPROFESSIONAL (dentistry, law, medicine, pharmacy, social work, veterinary), SOCIAL SCIENCES (economics, government/political science, history, international relations, psychology, social sciences, sociology).

Required: Most students carry 4 courses per semester. Students must complete 12 courses from 3 of the following areas: social science, natural science, humanities, and formal studies. Seniors must demonstrate competency in their major.

Special: Four-year combined B.A.-B.S. degrees may be earned in most subjects. Students may design their own majors. Special programs include a Washington semester at American University, an exchange program with the University of Warwick in England, and a year at Manchester College of Oxford University. Pass-fail options are available. The college prepares students for certification in secondary education in most majors.

Honors: All majors offer honors programs. Several honor societies have chapters on campus.

Admissions: Seventy percent of those who applied were accepted for the 1981-82 freshman class. The SAT scores of those who enrolled were as follows: Verbal—55% below 500, 30% between 500 and 599, 12% between 600 and 700, and 3% above 700; Math—47% below 500, 37% between 500 and 599, 16% between 600 and 700, and 0% above 700. Candidates must be graduates of an accredited high school and be recommended for college by their school. Sixteen Carnegie units usually are required. Admissions officers also consider the reputation of the high school, recommendations by school officials, advanced placement or honors courses, impressions made during an interview, leadership record, extracurricular activities, and personality. The college seeks a geographically diverse student body.

Procedure: The SAT or ACT is required and should be taken between March of the junior year and January of the senior year. Applicants are encouraged to arrange a personal interview. Applications should be filed early in the senior year. There are no deadlines; decisions are made on a rolling basis. The application fee is $15.

Special: Early decision and early admissions plans are available. Minority students or those from disadvantaged backgrounds are encouraged to apply. CLEP and AP credit is accepted.

Transfer: For a recent year, 150 applications were received, 125 were accepted, and 87 students enrolled. Transfer students are accepted for all but the senior class. A minimum average of 2.5 is required. D grades transfer. Students must spend at least 1 year on campus to earn a degree. Application deadlines are open.

Visiting: Two orientation days for prospective students are scheduled in the spring. Informal visits also may be scheduled with the admissions department all year round, from 8:30 A.M. to 4:30 P.M. on weekdays and 9 A.M. to noon on Saturdays. Guides are provided. Visitors may sit in on classes.

Financial Aid: Thirty percent of the students receive aid. Forty percent work part-time on campus. Average aid to freshmen from all sources is $3000. The college offers grants-in-aid, scholarships, loans, and part-time jobs. State scholarships also are awarded to entering students. Loans are available from local banks and private sources. Tuition may be paid in installments. The college is a member of CSS. The FAF and admissions application must be filed before February 15 (fall) and November 1 (spring).

Foreign Students: Four percent of the full-time students come from foreign countries. The college offers these students special counseling and special organizations.

Admissions: Foreign students must take the TOEFL. No college entrance examination is required.

Procedure: Application deadlines are open. Foreign students must present proof of health and of adequate funds. They must also carry health insurance, which is available through the college for a fee.

Admissions Contact: A.M. DiMaggio, Director of Admissions.

WESTERN MARYLAND COLLEGE D-1
Westminster, Maryland 21157 (301) 848-7000

F/T: 600M, 758W Faculty: 82; IIB, ++$
P/T: 13M, 16W Ph.D.'s: 76%
Grad: 152M, 357W S/F Ratio: 14 to 1
Year: 4-1-5, ss Tuition: $4500
Appl: see profile R and B: $1925
1050 applied 879 accepted 433 enrolled
SAT: 500V 530M COMPETITIVE+

Western Maryland College, established in 1867, is a private college of liberal arts and sciences. The library contains 120,000 volumes and 138,000 microfilm items, and subscribes to 951 periodicals.

Environment: The college is located on an 160-acre campus in a rural area 28 miles from Baltimore and 58 miles from Washington, D.C. Campus facilities include several dormitories, 2 chapels, a music building, 2 gymnasiums, a student center, a concert hall, a fine-arts building, a football stadium, a golf course, and parks and picnic areas.

Student Life: About 71% of the students come from Maryland. Seventy-five percent are from public schools. Ninety-three percent of the students live in college housing. Thirty-seven percent are Catholic, 50% Protestant, and 7% Jewish. About 8% are minority-group members. College housing is both single-sex and coed. There are visiting privileges in single-sex housing. Students may keep cars on campus. An honor system covers all academic matters.

Organizations: Thirty percent of the men belong to the 4 fraternities, and 22% of the women belong to the 4 sororities. Extracurricular activities include academic and social-service organizations, music and drama groups, and concert and lecture series.

Sports: The college participates in 12 intercollegiate sports for men and 11 for women. There are 20 intramural sports for men and 18 for women.

Handicapped: About 30% of the campus is accessible to wheelchair-bound students. Special facilities include wheelchair ramps, parking areas, elevators, lowered drinking fountains and telephones, and specially equipped rest rooms. Special class scheduling is also available. Fewer than 1% of the students are visually impaired; about 1% are hearing-impaired. Mobility training is provided for visually impaired students. Special housing, TTYs, interpreters, and class notetakers are provided for the hearing-impaired. Special assistance from library workers and counselors is also available.

Graduates: About 9% of the freshmen drop out by the end of their first year; 65% remain to graduate. Sixty percent of the graduates seek advanced degrees; 5% enter medical school, 2% dental school, and 5% law school. Fifty percent of the graduates pursue careers in business and industry.

Services: Students receive the following free services: placement, career counseling, health care, tutoring, and psychological counseling. Placement services, which include job listings, on-campus interviews, symposia, and internships, are available also to alumni.

Programs of Study: All undergraduate programs lead to the B.A. degree. Master's degrees also are available. Bachelor's degrees are offered in the following subjects: AREA STUDIES (American), BUSINESS (business administration, computer science), EDUCATION (health/physical), ENGLISH (English, comparative literature), FINE AND PERFORMING ARTS (art, art education, art history, music, music education, studio art, theater/dramatics), LANGUAGES (French, German, Spanish), MATH AND SCIENCES (biology, chemistry, mathematics, physics), PHILOSOPHY (philosophy, religion), PREPROFESSIONAL (social work), SOCIAL SCIENCES (economics, government/political science, history, psychobiology, psychology, sociology). Preprofessional programs, which are not majors, are available in dentistry, engineering, forestry, law, medicine, ministry, and veterinary medicine. Thirty-six percent of degrees are conferred in social sciences, 18% in math and sciences, and 9% in English.

Required: Each student must fulfill distribution requirements, which include basic liberal arts courses. Students also must meet proficiency requirements in the following areas: English composition, foreign language (1 year), and physical education.

Special: Students may design their own majors. Special programs include independent study, study abroad, and other off-campus programs. Elementary and secondary education courses lead to NASDTEC certification, recognized in 38 states.

Honors: Nine honor societies, including Phi Beta Kappa, have chapters on campus. Honors programs are available in every major.

Admissions: About 84% of those who applied were accepted for the 1981-82 freshman class. The SAT scores of those who enrolled were as follows: Verbal—58% below 500, 35% between 500 and 599, 5% between 600 and 700, and 1% above 700; Math—38% below 500, 44% between 500 and 599, 17% between 600 and 700, and 1% above 700. The college seeks students from accredited secondary schools who have completed 16 Carnegie units. Admissions decisions are based on high school record, SAT results, recommendations, and extracurricular activities.

Procedure: The SAT is required and should be taken at the end of the junior year. Three ATs, including a foreign language, math, and English, are recommended. The college uses a rolling admissions policy, with applications accepted until 1 month before the beginning of a term. Freshmen are admitted to fall, winter, spring, and summer terms. A $15 fee should accompany the application.

Special: A deferred admissions plan is available. CLEP and AP credit is accepted.

Transfer: For fall 1981, 121 applications were received, 95 were accepted, and 58 students enrolled. Transfer students are accepted for all classes. A minimum average of 2.0 is required. D grades do not transfer. Students must earn a minimum of 30 semester hours on campus, of the 120 needed to receive a bachelor's degree. Application deadlines are the same as those for freshman applicants.

Visiting: Orientations for prospective students are scheduled regularly. They include campus tours, visits to academic departments, and information sessions on student organizations, admissions, and financial aid. Informal visits also may be scheduled for weekdays, 9:30 A.M. to 3:30 P.M., while school is in session. Guides are provided. Visitors may sit in on classes and remain overnight on campus. Visits can be arranged through the admissions office.

Financial Aid: About 45% of the students receive aid. Forty percent work part-time on campus. Average aid to freshmen from all sources is $2000. Approximately 500 scholarships are awarded each year. Federal loans are available to freshmen. The college is a member of CSS. The FAF should be filed by March 15.

Foreign Students: One percent of the full-time students come from foreign countries. The college offers these students an intensive English course and special counseling.

Admissions: Foreign students must score at least 550 on the TOEFL. No college entrance examination is required.

Procedure: The application deadline is February 15 (fall). Foreign students must present proof of health and of funds adequate to cover each academic year.

Admissions Contact: L. Leslie Bennett, Jr., Director of Admissions and Financial Aid.

MASSACHUSETTS

AMERICAN INTERNATIONAL COLLEGE B-3
Springfield, Massachusetts 01009 (413) 737-7000

F/T: 908M, 697W	Faculty: 101; IIA, ——$
P/T: 50M, 81W	Ph.D.'s: 58%
Grad: 315M, 295W	S/F Ratio: 17 to 1
Year: sems, ss	Tuition: $4041
Appl: open	R and B: $2116
1951 applied	1713 accepted 540 enrolled
SAT: 425V 452M	LESS COMPETITIVE

American International is a coeducational college of liberal arts, business administration, education, and nursing. Originally chartered as a French-Protestant college in 1885, it is privately controlled and nonsectarian. The library contains over 100,000 volumes and 4700 microfilm items, and subscribes to more than 650 periodicals.

Environment: The campus, located in a city of 166,000, occupies 46 acres and has 26 buildings. The 5 dormitories with single and double rooms accommodate 700 students. Fraternity houses are also available.

Student Life: About 60% of the students come from Massachusetts. Fifty-five percent live on campus. Forty-two percent of the students are Catholic, 45% are Protestant, and 7% are Jewish. Four percent are minority-group members. Campus housing is both coed and single-sex. There are visiting privileges in single-sex dorms. Students may keep cars on campus.

Organizations: About 10% of the men belong to 1 of 4 fraternities; 7% of the women belong to 1 of 3 sororities. Extracurricular activities and cultural events include special-interest clubs, service groups, art shows, films, lectures, and plays. There are religious counselors and organizations representing the 3 major faiths. About 35% of the resident students leave the campus on weekends.

Sports: The college participates in 8 intercollegiate sports for men and 6 for women. Seven intramural sports are available for both men and women.

Handicapped: About 40% of the campus is accessible to physically handicapped students. Special facilities for the handicapped include wheelchair ramps, parking areas, elevators, and specially equipped rest rooms. In addition, special class scheduling can be arranged. Less

348 MASSACHUSETTS

than 1% of the student body have visual or hearing impairments; there are no special facilities for these students.

Graduates: At the end of the freshman year about 10% of the students drop out; 80% of those who enter remain to graduate, and, of these, 33% immediately go on to graduate school. Fifty-three percent earn graduate degrees within 5 years of graduation. Seventy-five percent of each graduating class enters business and industry.

Services: Students receive the following services free of charge: placement, psychological counseling, career counseling, tutoring, and remedial instruction. Health care is available for a fee.

Programs of Study: The college confers the B.A., B.S., B.S.B.A., and B.S.N. degrees. Master's degrees are also awarded. Bachelor's degrees are offered in the following subjects: AREA STUDIES (American), BUSINESS (accounting, business education, finance, information systems, management, marketing), EDUCATION (elementary, secondary, special), HEALTH SCIENCES (nursing), LANGUAGES (French, Spanish), MATH AND SCIENCES (biochemistry, biology, chemistry, mathematics), PHILOSOPHY (philosophy), PREPROFESSIONAL (dentistry, law, medicine, veterinary), SOCIAL SCIENCES (economics, government/political science, history, psychology, sociology).

Required: All students must fulfill requirements in English, social sciences, humanities, and laboratory science.

Special: It is possible to earn combined B.A.-B.S. degrees in business and liberal arts. A general studies degree is also available. The college has no study-abroad program but will assist a student in planning his or her own year abroad. A supportive services program is also available for learning disabled students.

Honors: Honors programs are available in certain departments, and interdepartmental honors seminars are conducted. Two national honor societies have chapters on campus.

Admissions: Eighty-eight percent of those who applied were accepted for the 1981–82 freshman class. Applicants should have completed 18 units of high school work. In evaluating candidates, emphasis is placed on the secondary school record, recommendations, and SAT scores. The reputation of the high school is also important, as are extracurricular activities, evidence of leadership potential, and advanced placement and honors courses.

Procedure: The SAT or ACT is required and should be taken in May of the junior year or December or January of the senior year; transfer students should take the test in March. A fee of $15 must accompany the application. The deadline for applying to the fall session is open. The college follows a rolling admissions policy.

Special: Early decision is available, with a notification date of December 1. Early admissions and deferred admissions are also available. CLEP general and subject exams are accepted; AP credit is given.

Transfer: For fall 1981, 362 transfer students applied, 323 were accepted, and 188 enrolled. Transfers are accepted for any year. A minimum average of 2.0 is required for transfer; D grades do transfer with a 2-year degree. Students must complete a minimum of 30 semester hours of study, out of the 120 required for the bachelor's degree, on campus. Application is on a rolling basis.

Visiting: There are regularly scheduled orientations for prospective students. Guided tours can be arranged on weekdays by arrangement with the admissions office. Visitors can sit in on classes and can arrange to stay overnight at the school.

Financial Aid: About 70% of all students receive financial aid. Thirty percent work part-time on campus. A fund of approximately $60,000 is available for freshman academic scholarships, and about 35 are awarded each year; the average scholarship grant is $2650. Loans to freshmen average $250, with a maximum of $600. The college is a member of CSS; the FAF is required. The deadline for aid application is April 1.

Foreign Students: Three percent of the full-time students come from foreign countries. The college offers these students special counseling and special organizations.

Admissions: Foreign students must achieve a minimum score of 450 on the TOEFL. The SAT or ACT is not required.

Procedure: Application deadlines are open; foreign students are admitted to the fall and spring semesters, as well as to the summer session. Proof of funds adequate to cover 4 years of study is required. Foreign students must carry health insurance, which is available through the college for a fee.

Admissions Contact: John H. DeBonville, Director of Admissions.

AMHERST COLLEGE B–2
Amherst, Massachusetts 01002 (413) 542-2328

F/T: 941M, 613W Faculty: 159; IIB, ++$
P/T: 4M, 3W Ph.D.'s: 85%
Grad: none S/F Ratio: 10 to 1
Year: 4-0-4 Tuition: $7345
Appl: Jan. 15 R and B: $2550
3891 applied 695 accepted 391 enrolled
SAT or ACT: required **MOST COMPETITIVE**

Amherst College, founded in 1821, is an independent liberal arts college for men and women concerned almost entirely with undergraduate education. The library contains 562,442 volumes and 119,107 microfilm items, and subscribes to 1538 periodicals.

Environment: The 700-acre campus is situated on a hill overlooking the Connecticut River Valley 25 miles from Springfield, Massachusetts. Dormitories with single, double, and triple rooms and suites accommodate 1150 students.

Student Life: The college is almost 95% residential; freshmen are required to live on campus. About 23% of a recent freshman class came from New York, 18% from Massachusetts, 17% from the middle states, 11% from other New England states, and 31% from other states and foreign countries. The school has no religious affiliation and requires no attendance at religious or chapel services. Ten percent of the students are minority-group members. Campus housing is coed. Students may keep cars on campus.

Organizations: Four local and 5 national fraternities are represented on campus. All are coeducational. There are no sororities on campus. Student activities include special-interest and departmental clubs, photography, musical and dramatic organizations, debating, radio, and student publications.

Sports: The college participates in 16 intercollegiate sports for men and 12 for women. There are 9 intramural sports for men and 8 for women.

Handicapped: A large portion of the campus is accessible to the handicapped. Facilities include wheelchair ramps, elevators, and special parking and rest rooms. Fewer than 1% of the students are visually handicapped. There are no hearing-impaired students currently enrolled.

Graduates: Less than 2% of all students drop out their first year; about 85% remain to graduate. About 70% of those who graduate pursue graduate study: 12% enter medical school, 1% dental school, and 16% law school. Twenty-five percent of each graduating class enter business and industry.

Services: The following services are available free of charge to all students: placement and career counseling, some health care, psychological counseling, tutoring, and remedial instruction. There are placement services at the college for undergraduates.

Programs of Study: The college confers the B.A. degree. Bachelor's degrees are offered in the following subjects: AREA STUDIES (American, Asian, Black/Afro-American), ENGLISH (English), FINE AND PERFORMING ARTS (art, music, theater/dramatics), LANGUAGES (French, German, Greek/Latin, Russian, Spanish), MATH AND SCIENCES (astronomy, biology, chemistry, geology, mathematics, neuroscience, physics), PHILOSOPHY (classics, philosophy, religion), SOCIAL SCIENCES (anthropology, economics, government/political science, history, psychology, sociology). About 36% of degrees are conferred in social sciences, 18% in math and sciences, 18% in English, and 9% in area studies.

Required: Each student must complete 32 full semester courses, 2 years of residence, and the courses and comprehensive examination required in his major field.

Special: The college allows student-designed majors. Through a 5-college cooperative program, students may take courses at Hampshire College, Mount Holyoke College, Smith College, and the University of Massachusetts. During 1980–81 there were over 1091 incoming enrollments for courses at Amherst and 878 outgoing enrollments under this program. Some departments also sponsor seminars with Smith and Mount Holyoke. Each semester students may elect 1 independent reading course with a sponsoring professor, which allows them to pursue any topic of special interest to them. The field study program allows a student to leave Amherst for any type of approved "field work." This permits a student to do research, work in an area of special interest, or pursue any unusual opportunity that could not be followed up in the college community. Amherst also offers programs of study abroad. Students may arrange study at a foreign or domestic institution for a semester or a year.

Honors: Phi Beta Kappa and Sigma Xi honorary societies have chapters on campus. A few juniors and seniors are selected by the faculty each year as independent scholars; they are freed from course obligations and become responsible only to a faculty tutor. Projects range from completion of a detailed academic paper to production of a play or film.

Admissions: Eighteen percent of those who applied for the 1981-82 freshman class were accepted. Of those who enrolled, the SAT scores were as follows: Verbal—5% below 500, 32% between 500 and 599, 44% between 600 and 700, and 19% above 700; Math—3% below 500, 21% between 500 and 599, 47% between 600 and 700, and 29% above 700. Candidates should have a solid college preparatory record. Other important considerations are recommendations from the student's high school, a good extracurricular record, character, and intellectual interests.

Procedure: The SAT or ACT and 3 ATs are required of all applicants and should be taken no later than January of the senior year. (Applicants from New York State must submit results from the Regents Examinations.) All credentials should be filed by January 15. Freshmen are admitted only in the fall. Notification is made on April 15. There is a $30 application fee.

Special: An early decision plan is available; and students receive notification by December 15. There is an early admissions plan as well as a deferred admissions plan.

Transfer: For fall 1981, 227 applications were received, 21 were accepted, and 11 enrolled. Transfers are accepted in the freshman, sophomore, and junior years. A minimum average of B is required for transfer with preference given to A.A. degree holders and veterans. D grades do not transfer. Preference is given to Massachusetts college graduates. A minimum of 2 years' study on campus is required for a degree. Transfers must also complete, at the college, 16 of the 32 courses required for the bachelor's degree. Application deadlines are March 1 for September entrance and December 1 for February entrance.

Visiting: There are no regularly scheduled orientations for prospective students; however, guides are provided by the college for informal visits. Visitors may sit in on classes. The best time for campus visits is July through January. Visitors may stay overnight at the school and should contact the admissions office to arrange such visits.

Financial Aid: About 31% of all students receive financial aid; 80% work part-time on campus. The deadline for financial aid application is January 15. In a recent year scholarships ranging from $100 to $6500 were awarded to 479 students, 127 of whom were freshmen. The average freshman aid award was $2575. Awards are made on the basis of financial need as determined from information supplied to CSS. They usually take the form of packages, of which the first $800 is supplied through a job, the next $1500 by means of a loan, and the remainder as a scholarship grant. The FCS must be filed. In addition, a separate Amherst College Financial Aid Application is required. Early decision candidates should file aid application forms by November 15. The college is a member of CSS. Notification of awards is made by April 15 for regular applicants and December 15 for early decision candidates.

Foreign Students: Two percent of the full-time students come from foreign countries. Special counseling and special organizations are available to these students.

Admissions: Foreign students must take the TOEFL. College entrance exams are not required.

Procedure: The application deadline for fall entry is January 15. Foreign students must carry health insurance, which is available through the college for a fee.

Admissions Contact: Edward B. Wall, Dean of Admission.

ANNA MARIA COLLEGE   C-2
Paxton, Massachusetts 01612   (617) 757-4586

F/T: 80M, 317W
P/T: 21M, 156W
Grad: 688M, 347W
Year: 4-1-4, ss
Appl: May 1
300 applied   210 accepted   120 enrolled
SAT: 435V 445M   COMPETITIVE

Faculty: 30; IIB, av$
Ph.D.'s: 38%
S/F Ratio: 15 to 1
Tuition: $3850
R and B: $2360

Anna Maria College, founded in 1946, is a liberal arts college under the auspices of the Roman Catholic Church. Undergraduate degree programs are also offered in the business, education, and health fields. The library contains over 50,000 volumes and subscribes to more than 300 periodicals.

Environment: The 180-acre suburban campus is located 8 miles from Worcester. Dormitories accommodate 300 students. There are facilities for commuting students as well.

Student Life: About 93% of the students come from New England; 72% come from public schools; 60% live on campus. Sixty percent are Catholic; there are no religious requirements. Thirty percent of the students are minority-group members. Campus housing is coed. Students may have cars on campus.

Organizations: There are no fraternities or sororities. Clubs, concerts, a lecture program, publications, dramatics, and student government are available.

Sports: The college fields 4 intercollegiate teams for men and 4 for women. There is intramural competition for men and women in 1 sport.

Handicapped: Special facilities (wheelchair ramps, special parking) and class scheduling are provided for students with physical handicaps.

Graduates: Ten percent drop out after the first year; 75% remain to graduate. About 35% go on to graduate study.

Services: Placement, career counseling, and psychological counseling are provided to students free of charge. Health care and tutoring are available for a fee.

Programs of Study: The college confers the B.A., B.B.A., B.S., B.S.N., and B.M. degrees. Associate and master's degrees are also awarded. Bachelor's degrees are offered in the following subjects: BUSINESS (accounting, business administration, computer science, finance, management, marketing), EDUCATION (elementary), ENGLISH (English), FINE AND PERFORMING ARTS (art, art education, art therapy, music, music education, music performance, music therapy), HEALTH SCIENCES (medical technology, nuclear medicine technology, nursing), LANGUAGES (French, Spanish), MATH AND SCIENCES (biology, chemistry), PREPROFESSIONAL (dentistry, law, medicine, social work), SOCIAL SCIENCES (psychology, social relations). Twenty-five percent of degrees conferred are in the arts, 20% are in health sciences, and 15% are in preprofessional areas.

Required: All students must take course work in religious studies and demonstrate competency in the liberal arts.

Special: A general studies major is possible. Independent study, study abroad, field work/internships, a 3-2 engineering program, and a 3-year bachelor's degree are offered.

Admissions: About 70% of the 1981-82 applicants were accepted. Freshmen should rank in the top half of their high school class and have a B average. Other factors of importance in the admissions decision are impressions made during an interview, recommendations by school officials, and advanced placement or honors courses.

Procedure: Application deadlines are May 1 (fall) and December 15 (winter); notification is on a rolling basis. There is a $15 application fee. The SAT is required; 3 ATs are recommended.

Special: AP and CLEP credit is accepted. There are early decision and early and deferred admissions plans.

Transfer: For fall 1981, 89 transfer students applied, 70 were accepted, and 40 enrolled. A 2.0 GPA is required; D grades transfer only if part of an associate degree. There is a 1-year residency rule. Transfers must complete, at the college, 30 of the 120 credits required for the bachelor's degree. Application deadlines are the same as those for freshmen.

Visiting: There is an open house each October. Informal campus tours can be arranged; visitors may sit in on classes.

Financial Aid: About 45% of all students receive financial aid; 35% work part-time on campus. The college, a member of CSS, offers freshman scholarships, federal/state/bank loans, grants, and short-term loans from the college itself. CWS is offered. The FAF is due February 15 (fall) or December 15 (winter).

Foreign Students: Four percent of the full-time students come from foreign countries.

Admissions: Foreign students must achieve a minimum score of 450 on the TOEFL. The SAT or ACT is also required. On the SAT, students must achieve a minimum score of 450V, 450M.

Procedure: Application deadlines are June 15 (fall) and December 1 (winter). Proof of funds adequate to cover study at the college is required. Foreign students must carry health insurance, which is available through the college for a fee.

Admissions Contact: Paul J. Lynskey, Director of Admissions.

350 MASSACHUSETTS

ASSUMPTION COLLEGE C-2
Worcester, Massachusetts 01609 (617) 752-5615

F/T: 694M, 764W	Faculty: 120; IIA, −$
P/T: 14M, 25W	Ph.D.'s: 75%
Grad: 153M, 249W	S/F Ratio: 15 to 1
Year: 4-1-4, ss	Tuition: $4450
Appl: Mar. 1	R and B: $2350
1550 applied 1050 accepted 420 enrolled	
SAT: 460V 490M	COMPETITIVE

Assumption College, conducted by the Assumption Order, is a Roman Catholic liberal arts institution. Its library contains more than 150,000 volumes and 2993 reels of microfilm, and subscribes to over 826 periodicals.

Environment: The 96-acre campus is located in the residential section of Worcester, 40 miles west of Boston. Its 21 buildings include 9 dorms that accommodate 1000 students. On-campus apartments are also available.

Student Life: About 80% of the students are from New England and 53% are from Massachusetts. Sixty percent attended public schools. Most of the students are Catholic, but attendance at services is voluntary. Four percent are minority-group members. Campus housing is single-sex, and there are visiting privileges. Students may keep cars on campus.

Organizations: There are no fraternities or sororities on campus. The student government and special-interest groups provide social and cultural entertainment. The cities of Worcester and Boston offer a variety of leisure activities.

Sports: The college competes in 11 intercollegiate sports for men and 9 for women. There are 6 intramural sports for men and 5 for women.

Handicapped: About 75% of the campus is accessible to physically handicapped students. Special facilities include wheelchair ramps, parking areas, elevators, and specially equipped rest rooms. Special class scheduling can be arranged. There are 1% hearing-impaired and 1% visually impaired students enrolled. Assumption's social and rehabilitation major offers handicapped students many resources as well as educational preparation for careers.

Graduates: The freshman dropout rate is 5%; 80% remain to graduate. Of these, 65% continue their studies; 3% enter medical, 1% dental, and 5% law schools.

Services: Free health care, tutoring, remedial instruction, career and psychological counseling, and job placement services are offered to students.

Programs of Study: All undergraduate programs lead to the B.A. degree. Master's degrees in some fields are also offered. Bachelor's degrees are offered in the following subjects: BUSINESS (accounting, business administration, finance, management), ENGLISH (English), HEALTH SCIENCES (medical technology), LANGUAGES (French, Spanish), MATH AND SCIENCES (biology, chemistry, mathematics, natural sciences), PHILOSOPHY (classics, philosophy, religion), PRE-PROFESSIONAL (dentistry, law, medicine, ministry, social work, veterinary), SOCIAL SCIENCES (economics, government/political science, history, international relations, psychology, social and rehabilitation services, social sciences, sociology). Certification programs are available in elementary education. About 46% of all degrees are conferred in social sciences, 17% in math and sciences, and 25% in business.

Special: A 3-2 combination liberal arts/engineering program is offered with Worcester Polytechnic Institute. Junior year abroad, a general studies degree, and student-designed majors are also offered.

Honors: Three national honor societies have chapters on campus. Each department has its own honors program for the above average student.

Admissions: About 68% of those who applied were accepted for the 1981-82 freshman class. The SAT scores of those who enrolled were as follows: Verbal—74% below 500, 22% between 500 and 599, 4% between 600 and 700, and 0% above 700; Math—62% below 500, 31% between 500 and 599, 7% between 600 and 700, and 0% above 700. Candidates should have completed 15 Carnegie units in an accredited high school, maintain a B average, and rank in the upper 50% of their graduating class. Recommendations, advanced placement and honors courses, and leadership and extracurricular activities record are also strongly considered.

Procedure: The SAT or ACT is required and should be taken by May of the junior year or December of the senior year. ATs are recommended for placement purposes. An interview is also recommended. Applications should be filed by March 1 for fall or December 1 for spring, along with a $20 fee. Rolling admissions is used.

Special: Early admissions deadline is March 1. The notification date for early decision is December 15; deferred admissions is also available. AP and CLEP credit is given.

Transfer: For fall 1981, 100 transfer students applied, 50 were accepted, and 20 enrolled. Transfers are accepted for all but the senior year. A minimum C grade average is required; D grades do not transfer. Students must complete, at the college, 60 of the 120 credits required for the bachelor's degree. Fall application deadlines are May 1 for residents and August 1 for non-residents.

Visiting: Guided tours can be arranged weekdays, from 8:30 A.M. to 4:30 P.M., through the office of admissions. Visitors may sit in on classes and lunch with the students. Interviews with a counselor will be arranged if desired.

Financial Aid: About 55% of all students receive some form of aid; 30% work part-time on campus. There is a $120,000 scholarship fund available to freshmen. The college is a member of CSS. The FAF must be filed. February 1 is the deadline for financial applications.

Foreign Students: The college accepts applications from foreign students and offers them special counseling.

Admissions: Foreign students must take the TOEFL. The SAT or ACT is also required.

Procedure: Application deadlines are the same as those for other freshmen. Students must present a medical report completed by a physician as proof of health. Proof of funds adequate to cover 4 years of study is also required. Foreign students must carry health insurance, which is available through the college for a fee.

Admissions Contact: Thomas E. Dunn, Dean of Admissions and Financial Aid.

ATLANTIC UNION COLLEGE C-2
South Lancaster, Massachusetts 01561 (617) 365-4561

F/T: 288M, 312W	Faculty: n/av; IIB, −$
P/T: 100	Ph.D.'s: 33%
Grad: none	S/F Ratio: 12 to 1
Year: sems, ss	Tuition: $4596
Appl: Sept. 1	R and B: $2050
350 applied 290 accepted 180 enrolled	
ACT: required	LESS COMPETITIVE

Atlantic Union College, established in 1882, is affiliated with the Seventh-day Adventist Church. It offers undergraduate programs in the liberal arts and sciences, business, and nursing. The library contains over 91,000 volumes and subscribes to 590 periodicals.

Environment: The 350-acre campus is 15 miles from Worcester. There are 55 buildings including dormitories accommodating 300 men and 300 women.

Student Life: About 35% of the students come from Massachusetts; 45% come from public schools. Fifty percent live on campus in single-sex dorms. The majority of the students are members of the supporting church; chapel service attendance is mandatory. Smoking and drinking on campus are prohibited. Students may keep cars on campus. A registration fee is charged.

Organizations: There are no sororities or fraternities. On-campus activities include social and cultural events.

Sports: Intramural competition is offered in 8 sports.

Handicapped: Special facilities include wheelchair ramps and special rest rooms; class scheduling is arranged for students with physical handicaps.

Graduates: The freshman dropout rate is 15%; 30% remain to graduate. About 19% go on to graduate work (5% to medical school and 2% to dental school); 6% pursue careers in business and industry.

Services: Health care, psychological counseling, career counseling, and placement services are available free of charge to all students.

Programs of Study: The college confers the B.A., B.M., and B.S. degrees. An associate degree in science is also awarded. Bachelor's degrees are offered in the following subjects: BUSINESS (accounting, business administration, business education, computer science), EDUCATION (elementary, health/physical), ENGLISH (English), FINE AND PERFORMING ARTS (art, interior design, music, music education, performance), HEALTH SCIENCES (health science, medical technology, nursing), LANGUAGES (French, Spanish), MATH AND SCIENCES (biology, chemistry, mathematics), PHILOSOPHY (religion, theology), PREPROFESSIONAL (engineering, foods and nutrition, home economics, personal ministries, social work), SOCIAL SCIENCES (history, psychology).

Special: Study abroad is offered.

Honors: There is an honors core program for high school seniors with a minimum GPA of 3.2.

Admissions: About 83% of those who applied were accepted for a recent freshman class. A 2.0 high school GPA is required. Also considered important are the applicant's ability to finance a college education, impressions made during an interview, and recommendations.

Procedure: The ACT is required. September is the fall semester application deadline; notification is on a rolling basis. New students are admitted at midyear; December 15 is the application deadline. There is a $15 application fee.

Special: AP and CLEP credit is accepted. There are early decision, early admissions, and deferred admissions plans.

Transfer: About 50 transfer students are admitted annually. D grades transfer except in the student's major field. Thirty-six credits, of the 128 credits required for the bachelor's degree, must be earned in residence.

Visiting: There is an orientation program. Informal campus tours with student guides may be arranged. Visitors may sit in on classes and stay overnight at the school.

Financial Aid: About 50% of all students receive financial aid. Merit scholarships are available to freshmen. Loans from a variety of sources as well as part-time employment are offered. The FAF should be submitted by June 1.

Foreign Students: The college welcomes foreign applicants, and offers these students special counseling as well as an intensive English program through the English Language Institute.

Admissions: Students whose native language is not English must achieve a minimum score of 480 on the TOEFL, or score above the 80th percentile on the Comprehensive English Language Test. Those scoring below these levels must enroll in the English Language Institute.

Procedure: Application deadlines and general requirements are the same as those for other freshmen. Proof of funds adequate to cover the entire period of study at the college is required, as is an advance deposit of $1900. Foreign students must carry accident and health insurance, which is available through the college for a fee.

Admissions Contact: Ronna R. Archbold, Director of Admissions/College Relations.

BABSON COLLEGE   D-2
Babson Park (Wellesley),   (617) 235-1200
Massachusetts 02157

F/T: 913M, 470W   Faculty: 93; IIA, ++$
P/T: none   Ph.D.'s: 87%
Grad: 1102M, 597W   S/F Ratio: 22 to 1
Year: sems, ss   Tuition: $5539
Appl: Feb. 1   R and B: $2300–3180
2243 applied   712 accepted   323 enrolled
SAT: 490V 580M   VERY COMPETITIVE+

Babson College, established in 1919, is an independent institution offering undergraduate and graduate programs in management education. The library contains over 170,000 volumes and 21,280 microfilm items, and subscribes to more than 1500 periodicals.

Environment: The 450-acre campus is located in a suburban setting 12 miles from Boston. Facilities include a management laboratory, computer center, and auditorium. Campus housing is available for 965 students.

Student Life: Babson students come from more than 31 states and 37 foreign countries; 70% live on campus. Fewer than 1% are minority-group members. Campus housing is both coed and single-sex. There are visiting privileges in single-sex dorms. Students may keep cars on campus.

Organizations: There are 2 sororities and 4 fraternities on campus. Extracurricular activities include student government newspaper, Judicial Court, yearbook, student business, and a film series.

Sports: The college participates in 13 intercollegiate sports for men and 11 for women. There are 10 intramurals for men and 7 for women.

Handicapped: Special facilities for handicapped students include wheelchair ramps, parking areas, elevators, and specially equipped rest rooms. Counselors are available to handicapped students.

Graduates: Five percent of the freshmen drop out by the end of the first year; 95% remain to graduate. Eleven percent of the graduates pursue advanced degrees; about 85% enter careers in industry and business.

Services: Health care, psychological counseling, tutoring, placement, and career counseling are available free of charge to all students.

Programs of Study: There are bachelor's and master's programs. The B.S. degree is offered in the following subjects: AREA STUDIES (American, society and technology), BUSINESS (accounting, communications, entrepreneurial studies, finance, investments, management, marketing, organizational behavior), MATH AND SCIENCES (quantitative methods), PREPROFESSIONAL (law), SOCIAL SCIENCES (economics). Dual majors are offered in quantitative methods/economics, quantitative methods/finance, quantitative methods/investments, and quantitative methods/marketing.

Special: Student-designed majors, an accelerated 3-year B.S. degree, and a junior year abroad program are offered.

Honors: Two honor societies have chapters on campus; all departments offer honors work.

Admissions: About 32% of those who applied were accepted for the 1981–82 freshman class. The SAT scores of those who enrolled were as follows: Verbal—50% below 500, 44% between 500 and 599, 5% between 600 and 700, and 1% above 700; Math—8% below 500, 52% between 500 and 600, 38% between 600 and 700, and 2% above 700. About 91% of the freshmen graduate in the top 40% of their high school class. In addition to the academic record, recommendations are considered important.

Procedure: The SAT is required and should be taken by January of the senior year; ACT scores are accepted. An interview is strongly recommended. February 1 is the application deadline for fall admission; November 1 for spring admission. There is a $25 application fee.

Special: AP and CLEP credit is available. There are early decision and deferred admissions plans.

Transfer: For fall 1981, 508 applications were received, 134 were accepted, and 73 students enrolled. An average of at least C is needed; D grades do not transfer. Two years must be completed in residence. Transfers must earn, at the college, 64 of the 128 credits necessary for the bachelor's degree. April 1 (fall) and November 1 (spring) are the application deadlines.

Visiting: Informal campus tours with student guides may be arranged. Visitors may sit in on classes (with advance notice) and may stay overnight at the college. Visits are best scheduled on weekdays. The admissions office should be contacted for arrangements.

Financial Aid: About 34% of the students receive aid. The college offers various loans (including NDSL), grants (BEOG, SEOG), and part-time campus employment (including CWS). Eighteen percent of the students work part-time on campus. Need is the determining factor. The college is a member of CSS. The FAF and the Babson College Financial Aid Form should be filed by February 15.

Foreign Students: Almost 9% of the full-time students come from foreign countries. Babson actively recruits these students and offers them special counseling and special organizations.

Admissions: The college recommends that foreign students achieve a minimum score of 550 on the TOEFL. After matriculation, students must take the college's own English proficiency exam. The SAT or ACT is also required.

Procedure: Application deadlines are the same as those for other freshmen. Proof of funds sufficient to cover a full year of study is required. Foreign students must carry health insurance, which is available through the college for a fee.

Admissions Contact: Joseph B. Carver, Director of Admission.

BENTLEY COLLEGE   D-2
Waltham, Massachusetts 02254   (617) 891-2244

F/T: 2070M, 1588W   Faculty: 165; IIA, +$
P/T: 1276M, 1517W   Ph.D.'s: 59%
Grad: 909M, 291W   S/F Ratio: 22 to 1
Year: sems, ss   Tuition: $4550
Appl: Mar. 10   R and B: $2525
4019 applied   1999 accepted   859 enrolled
SAT: 460V 540M   COMPETITIVE+

Bentley College, founded in 1917, is a private liberal arts and business college. The library contains over 100,000 volumes and 3915 microfilm items, and subscribes to more than 820 periodicals.

Environment: The 104-acre campus is located in a suburban area 9 miles west of Boston and consists of 32 buildings, including 16 dormitory and apartment residences.

MASSACHUSETTS

Student Life: Sixty-two percent of the students come from Massachusetts. About 59% reside on campus in the dormitories. Almost 2% of the students are minority-group members. Campus housing is coed. Students may have cars on campus.

Organizations: The college sponsors many extracurricular activities such as forums, service and special-interest clubs, mixers, folk concerts, film festivals, and talent shows. About 25% of the students leave campus on weekends. About 20% of the men belong to 1 of 2 local and 4 national fraternities; 12% of the women belong to 1 of 3 local sororities.

Sports: The college participates in 9 intercollegiate sports for men and 5 for women. There are 4 intramural sports for both men and women.

Handicapped: About 95% of the campus is accessible to physically handicapped students. Wheelchair ramps, special parking, and elevators are provided. Less than 1% of the students have visual or hearing impairments; there are no special facilities for these students.

Graduates: Approximately 10% of the students drop out by the end of the freshman year. Of those who enter, 60% remain to graduate, and 10% of the graduates pursue advanced degrees after graduation. Eighty-five percent of each graduating class enter business and industry.

Services: All students receive the following services free of charge: placement, health care (on campus), psychological counseling, career counseling, tutoring, and remedial instruction.

Programs of Study: The college confers the B.S. degree. Associate and master's degrees are also awarded. Bachelor's degrees are offered in the following subjects: BUSINESS (accounting, business administration, business communications, computer science, finance, management, marketing, public administration), MATH AND SCIENCES (quantitative analysis), PREPROFESSIONAL (law), SOCIAL SCIENCES (economics, government/political science, history, psychology, social sciences). About 40% of the students are enrolled in the accounting program.

Required: All students must take a prescribed distribution of core courses.

Special: Under the direct study program, a student of superior academic ability may choose a course not in the curriculum as a substitute for an elective course, then find a faculty member who is willing to supervise his or her project, and obtain approval for it. The college has internships in public administration, accounting, economics/finance, and computer information systems. A 3-year bachelor's degree is also available. Students may design their own majors.

Honors: Two national honor societies have chapters on campus. All college departments offer honors programs.

Admissions: Fifty percent of those who applied were accepted for the 1981-82 freshman class. Of those, the SAT scores were as follows: Verbal—75% below 500, 21% between 500 and 599, 2% between 600 and 700, and 0.4% above 700; Math—29% below 500, 49% between 500 and 599, 17% between 600 and 700, and 2% above 700. Requirements for admission are as follows: graduation from an accredited high school with a B average, counselor recommendations, completion of 16 Carnegie units, and satisfactory test scores. Class rank (top 40%) and a successful interview are also considered in the admissions decision.

Procedure: Either the SAT or the ACT is acceptable and should be taken by January of the senior year. A personal interview is not required but is considered important. A $25 application fee must accompany the application. The application deadlines are March 10 (fall), December 1 (spring), and May 10 (summer).

Special: An early decision plan is available to students for whom Bentley is the first choice; the application deadline is December 1, with notification by December 15. There is an early admissions plan for qualified high school juniors. Deferred admissions are also available. CLEP general and subject exams are accepted; AP credit is also given.

Transfer: For fall 1981, 949 applications were received, 497 were accepted, and 300 students actually enrolled. Transfers are accepted in all but the senior year. A minimum average of 2.5 is required for transfer; D grades do not transfer. A minimum of 10 courses completed on campus is required. Transfers must earn, at the college, 30 of the 120 credits necessary for the bachelor's degree. Application deadlines are May 1 for fall and December 1 for spring.

Visiting: Regularly scheduled orientations for prospective students include open house general sessions followed by sessions in major areas of study. Informal visits and guided tours can be arranged on weekdays through the Office of Day Admissions throughout the school year.

Financial Aid: About 65% of all students receive financial aid; 20% work part-time on campus. A total of $267,000 in scholarship aid is available to freshmen and there are 125 freshman scholarships. There are also 100 awards of $1000 each, which are not based on need. Loans are available from the federal and state governments, local banks, the college, and industrial and private sources. Scholarships range in amount from $500 to $3500, loans from $200 to $1250, and work contracts from $400 to $1800. The college is a member of CSS. Either the FAF or FFS is required from aid applicants. Need and academic record are the main considerations in determining award of financial aid. The deadline for aid application is March 1.

Foreign Students: About 1% of the full-time students come from foreign countries. Bentley actively recruits these students and offers them special counseling and special organizations.

Admissions: Foreign students must achieve a minimum score of 500 on the TOEFL. The SAT is also required.

Procedure: The application deadline for fall entry is March 10. Foreign students must complete a report of medical history and must carry health insurance, which is available through the college for a fee. Proof of funds adequate to cover all years of study is required.

Admissions Contact: Edward M. Gillis, Director of Admissions.

BERKLEE COLLEGE OF MUSIC E-2
Boston, Massachusetts 02215 (617) 266-1400

F/T: 2252M, 375W Faculty: n/av; IV, --$
P/T: none Ph.D.'s: n/av
Grad: none S/F Ratio: 13 to 1
Year: sems, ss Tuition: $3510
Appl: open R and B: $2490
1958 applied 1502 accepted 910 enrolled
SAT or ACT: required SPECIAL

Primarily a professional school of music, Berklee offers undergraduate preparation in music study. Its library contains 35,705 volumes, subscribes to over 70 periodicals, and houses 3000 microfilm items.

Environment: Located in downtown Boston, the college maintains 2 coed dormitories. The school also has facilities for commuting students.

Student Life: Campus housing is coed; about 25% of the students live on campus. Cars are not permitted on campus.

Organizations: Concerts by students and faculty are regularly scheduled. There are no fraternities or sororities, nor is there an athletic program.

Services: Tutoring, career counseling, and placement services are provided free of charge. Health care and psychological counseling are available for a fee.

Programs of Study: The B. Mus. is offered in the following fields of specialization: arranging, audio recording, composition, electronic music, film scoring, music education, and music performance.

Special: Students may design their own majors. A 5-year dual major is also available.

Admissions: About 77% of the 1981-82 applicants were accepted. The SAT or ACT is required. Interviews are encouraged. Two years of previous music experience are also required. Freshmen are admitted to all sessions; deadlines are open; notification is on a rolling basis. There is a $25 application fee.

Special: There is a deferred admissions plan. AP credit is accepted.

Transfer: For fall 1981, 348 transfer students enrolled. The requirements are the same as for freshmen. D grades do not transfer. Two years must be completed in residence. Transfers must earn, at the college, 70 of the 134 credits necessary for the bachelor's degree. Application deadlines are open.

Visiting: Visitors to the campus are encouraged.

Financial Aid: About 14% of all students receive financial aid; 8% work part-time on campus. The school offers all standard government assistance programs. The average award to freshmen from all sources is $4300. The FAF or FFS should be submitted by March 31; the college is a member of CSS.

Foreign Students: About 20% of the full-time students come from foreign countries. Berklee actively recruits these students and offers them special counseling.

Admissions: Foreign students must submit either the TOEFL or a statement regarding English proficiency. The SAT or ACT is not required.

Procedure: There are no application deadlines; students are admitted in the fall, spring, and summer. Proof of funds adequate to cover 1 academic year is required.

Admissions Contact: Steven Lipman, Director of Admissions.

BOSTON COLLEGE E-2
Chestnut Hill, Massachusetts 02167 (617) 969-0100

F/T: 3666M, 4923W		Faculty:	558; I, +$
P/T: 805M, 1253W		Ph.D.'s:	79%
Grad: 1542M, 1977W		S/F Ratio:	16 to 1
Year: sems, ss		Tuition:	$5354
Appl: Feb. 1		R and B:	$2784
12,748 applied	4227 accepted		1968 enrolled
SAT: 507V 555M			VERY COMPETITIVE+

Boston College, founded in 1863, is one of the oldest Jesuit-sponsored universities in America. It consists of 10 schools, colleges, and institutes. The undergraduate divisions are the College of Arts and Sciences, the School of Management, the School of Nursing, the School of Education, and the Evening College of Arts, Sciences, and Business Administration. The library houses over 971,605 volumes and 508,000 microfilm items, and subscribes to more than 6106 periodicals.

Environment: The 200-acre suburban campus includes 40 buildings in English Collegiate Gothic architecture as well as several modern buildings. The campus, built on 3 levels of a hillside, overlooks Boston, 6 miles away. Dormitories and modular suites accommodate 4800 students. Newton Campus provides additional facilities on a 40-acre area. The college also sponsors on- and off-campus apartments.

Student Life: About 50% of the undergraduates are from Massachusetts; 66% of entering freshmen come from public schools. Forty-nine percent of the students live on campus. The majority of students are Roman Catholic but there is no requirement to attend services. Almost 8% of the students are minority-group members. Campus housing is both coed and single-sex. There are visiting privileges in single-sex dorms. Students may keep cars on campus.

Organizations: There are no social fraternities or sororities, but professional and service organizations also serve as social groups. Extracurricular activities are numerous. There are political and professional organizations, religious groups, and sports clubs. On-campus cultural events include a Humanities Series, a Younger Poets Series, and the Loyola Lecture Series. Museums, the Boston Garden, and a variety of attractions in the Boston area offer opportunities for cultural and recreational activities.

Sports: Boston College competes on an intercollegiate level in 17 sports for men and 16 sports for women. There are 11 intramural sports for men and 9 for women.

Handicapped: Special facilities for the physically handicapped include wheelchair ramps, parking areas, elevators, library services, housing, transportation, and specially equipped rest rooms. Special class scheduling can be arranged. About 80% of the campus is accessible to wheelchair students. Fewer than 1% of the students have visual or hearing impairments; for these students there are readers, tape recorders, special books, and speech clinics. A staff of 9 offers special counseling and assistance.

Graduates: The freshman dropout rate is about 7%; 80% remain to graduate. Sixty percent pursue advanced study after graduation: 3% enter medical school; 1% dental school; and 5% law school. Thirty-five percent pursue careers in business and industry.

Services: Students receive the following services free of charge: psychological counseling, tutoring, remedial instruction, and placement and career counseling. In addition to job listings, there are interviewing and resume-writing workshops. Health care is available for a fee.

Programs of Study: All undergraduate programs lead to the B.A. or B.S. degrees. The college also has master's and doctoral programs. Bachelor's degrees are offered in the following subjects: AREA STUDIES (Russian), BUSINESS (accounting, business administration, computer science, finance, management, marketing), EDUCATION (early childhood, elementary, secondary, special), ENGLISH (English, speech), FINE AND PERFORMING ARTS (studio art, theater/dramatics), HEALTH SCIENCES (nursing), LANGUAGES (Chinese, French, German, Greek/Latin, Italian, Portuguese, Russian, Spanish), MATH AND SCIENCES (biology, chemistry, geology, mathematics, physics), PHILOSOPHY (philosophy, religion), PREPROFESSIONAL (dentistry, law, medicine), SOCIAL SCIENCES (economics, history, psychology, sociology). Thirty-two percent of the degrees conferred are in social sciences, 21% are in business, and 16% are in preprofessional studies.

Special: It is possible to earn combined B.A.-B.S. degrees in various subjects. Student-designed majors and independent research are permitted. Junior-year study abroad and a work-study program offer valuable opportunities. A "Free University" with ungraded seminars and courses is conducted by faculty members and undergraduate and graduate students. Some cross-disciplinary programs are also available.

MASSACHUSETTS 353

Honors: Boston College has a well-established undergraduate honors program; the College of Arts and Sciences honors program is highly selective. There are chapters of 11 national honor societies on campus.

Admissions: Thirty-three percent of those who applied were accepted for the 1981-82 freshman class. Of those who enrolled, the SAT scores were as follows: Verbal—43% below 500, 41% between 500 and 599, and 16% between 600 and 800; Math—23% below 500, 45% between 500 and 599, and 32% between 600 and 800. The candidate should have completed 15 Carnegie units at an accredited high school, and have at least a B+ average. The school also considers the following factors: advanced placement or honors courses, interview impressions, recommendations, extracurricular activities, and personality. Qualified children of alumni receive preference.

Procedure: The SAT is required and should be taken by December of the senior year. The deadline for regular admission is February 1 for fall, November 15 for spring. Applications should be submitted with a $30 fee.

Special: For early decision the fall deadline is November 15, with a notification date of December 5. Early admissions and deferred admissions plans are available. CLEP and AP credit is granted.

Transfer: For fall 1981, 1800 transfer applications were received, 525 were accepted, and 315 students enrolled. Transfers are not accepted to the nursing program or for less than 1 year's study in any other program. A minimum average of 2.5 is required to apply and D grades do not transfer. Two years must be spent in residence to qualify for a degree. Students must complete, at the college, 18 of the 38 courses required for the bachelor's degree. Application deadlines are May 15 (fall) and November 15 (spring).

Visiting: Guided tours and interviews can be scheduled 6 days a week. Day-long visits with a student guide can also be arranged by contacting the admissions office 3 weeks in advance. Visitors may sit in on classes.

Financial Aid: About 55% of all students receive aid; 28% work part-time on campus. The university provides scholarships for freshmen; the total amount of such aid exceeds $1 million. The average award to freshmen is $3400. More than $1 million is available in loans. Awards are based on need and academic performance. The FAF and a xerox copy of the family's 1040 income tax form are required of aid applicants. Deadline for financial aid application is February 1 for fall, November 1 for spring; the FAF should be filed with CSS by February 1.

Foreign Students: About 3% of the full-time students come from foreign countries. The college, which actively recruits these students, offers them special counseling and special organizations.

Admissions: Foreign students must achieve a minimum score of 550 on the TOEFL. The SAT or ACT is also required.

Procedure: Application deadlines are the same as those for other freshmen. Proof of health must be established. Proof of funds adequate to cover study at the college is also required.

Admissions Contact: Charles S. Nolan, Director of Admissions.

BOSTON CONSERVATORY OF MUSIC E-2
Boston, Massachusetts 02215 (617) 536-6340

F/T: 131M, 277W		Faculty:	18; IV, --$
P/T: 5M, 5W		Ph.D.'s:	n/av
Grad: 8M, 6W		S/F Ratio:	23 to 1
Year: sems		Tuition:	$3930
Appl: Apr. 15		R and B:	$2475
395 applied	211 accepted		166 enrolled
SAT or ACT: required			SPECIAL

The Boston Conservatory of Music, founded in 1867 to provide training in music, drama, and dance, is a private professional college. Its library contains over 32,000 volumes and subscribes to 59 periodicals.

Environment: Located in an urban area, the conservatory's facilities include 5 dormitories accommodating 160 students.

Student Life: About 41% of the students come from Massachusetts. About 32% live on campus. Dormitories are coed and single-sex; there are visiting privileges in the single-sex dormitories. Students may keep cars on campus.

Organizations: There are 2 fraternities and 2 sororities on campus. The Conservatory takes advantage of the heavy performance schedule of Boston for most of its cultural and social life.

Handicapped: Special facilities are being built for handicapped students, and about 80% of the campus is accessible to the physically handicapped. There are no hearing-impaired or visually impaired students currently enrolled.

Graduates: The freshman dropout rate is 15%; 44% remain to graduate. About 45% of the graduates go on to graduate or professional study.

Services: Free psychological counseling is available. Tutoring and remedial instruction are provided on a fee basis. Notices of auditions and teaching openings are accessible to students.

Programs of Study: The Conservatory confers the B.Mus., B.Mus.Ed., and B.F.A. degrees. Master's programs are also offered. Bachelor's degrees are offered in these major fields: FINE AND PERFORMING ARTS (applied music, dance, music, music/composition, music education, theater/dramatics).

Special: The conservatory offers diploma programs for a limited number of very talented but academically ineligible candidates.

Honors: Three honor societies have chapters on campus.

Admissions: About 53% of those who applied were accepted for the 1981-82 freshman class. The candidate should have 16 Carnegie units. Auditions, entrance examinations, impressions made during the interview, and recommendations are considered very important in the admissions decision. Children of alumni are given preference.

Procedure: The SAT or ACT is required and should be taken in May of the junior year or by December of the senior year. The conservatory administers an elementary theory test in music and auditions in music, drama, and dance. These on-campus audition-interviews are extremely important. Freshmen are only admitted in the fall; applications are accepted from October to April. The final deadline is April 15. Admission is on a rolling basis. The application fee is $45.

Special: There is a deferred admissions plan. AP credit is given.

Transfer: Transfers are accepted in sophomore and junior years. A 2.0 GPA is required. D grades do not transfer. All students must complete, at the Conservatory, 57 of the 132 credits required for a bachelor's degree. Application deadlines are April 15 for fall and October 15 for spring.

Visiting: Guided tours can be arranged for weekday mornings through the director of admissions.

Financial Aid: About 78% of all students receive some form of aid. Twenty-three percent work part-time on campus. A variable number of scholarships are available to freshmen. Loans are available from the state, local banks, and other industrial and private sources. The conservatory is a member of CSS and requires the FAF. Application deadline is April 15.

Foreign Students: Three percent of the students come from foreign countries.

Admissions: Foreign students must achieve a TOEFL score of at least 500. No college entrance exams are required.

Procedure: The application deadline is April 15 for fall entry. Foreign students must present proof of funds adequate to cover 1 year of study.

Admissions Contact: Margaret M. Haley, Director of Admissions.

BOSTON STATE COLLEGE
(See University of Massachusetts at Boston)

BOSTON UNIVERSITY
Boston, Massachusetts 02215   E-2
(617) 353-2310

F/T: 6127M, 6876W
P/T: 100M, 160W
Grad: 4495M, 4836W
Year: sems, ss
Appl: Feb. 1
17,203 applied
SAT: 539V 576M

Faculty: 1507; I, +$
Ph.D.'s: 70%
S/F Ratio: 14 to 1
Tuition: $6390
R and B: $2970
10,784 accepted   3611 enrolled
VERY COMPETITIVE

Boston University, established in 1869, is an independent nonsectarian institution offering a wide variety of undergraduate and graduate programs in the liberal arts and sciences, health fields, education, business, engineering, communications, and the arts. There are 16 colleges and schools within the university. The library has 1.3 million books and 1.5 million microtexts, and subscribes to 23,000 periodicals.

Environment: The 65-acre urban campus along the Charles River includes dormitories, fraternity houses, and on-campus apartments. There are also off-campus apartments. The dormitories range in style from brick row houses to high-rise buildings.

Student Life: Eighty percent of the students are from the Northeast and middle Atlantic states. About 80% come from public schools. About 43% of the students reside on campus. Nine percent are minority-group members. Thirty percent are Catholic, 20% are Protestant, and 19% are Jewish. Campus housing is both coed and single-sex; there are visiting privileges in the single-sex housing. Students may not keep cars on campus.

Organizations: There are fraternities and sororities, to which 4% of the students belong. Extracurricular activities and cultural/social events are varied and numerous. More than 200 activities are sponsored by the university.

Sports: The university fields 9 intercollegiate teams for men and 7 for women. There are 11 intramural sports for men and 10 for women.

Handicapped: Special facilities for the physically handicapped include wheelchair ramps, parking areas, elevators, lowered drinking fountains and telephones, and specially equipped rest rooms.

Graduates: Ten percent of the entering freshmen drop out by the end of the first year; 50% remain to graduate. About 23% of the graduates pursue advanced study.

Services: Placement services and career counseling are offered free of charge. Health care, psychological counseling, tutoring, and remedial instruction are provided on a fee basis.

Programs of Study: Undergraduate degrees conferred are the B.A., B.S., B.F.A., B.M., B.S.Ed., B.A.S., B.L.S., B.A.A., and B.S.B.A. Master's and doctoral programs are also available. Bachelor's degrees are offered in numerous subjects, including: AREA STUDIES (Russian, urban), BUSINESS (accounting, business administration, business education, computer science, finance, management, marketing), EDUCATION (early childhood, elementary, special), ENGLISH (English, journalism), FINE AND PERFORMING ARTS (art education, art history, film/photography, music, music education, radio/TV), HEALTH SCIENCES (nursing, occupational therapy, physical therapy), LANGUAGES (French, German, Greek/Latin, Russian, Spanish), MATH AND SCIENCES (astronomy, biology, chemistry, earth science, geology, mathematics, physics), PHILOSOPHY (classics, humanities, philosophy, religion), PREPROFESSIONAL (dentistry, engineering, law, medicine, ministry, social work), SOCIAL SCIENCES (anthropology, economics, geography, government/political science, history, psychology, sociology). Most degrees conferred are in liberal arts, business, and engineering.

Special: Study abroad, a 3-year bachelor's degree, a 4-year master's degree, a B.A.-J.D., and student-designed majors are offered, as well as a 6-year liberal arts medical education and a 7-year liberal arts dental education.

Honors: National honor societies represented on campus include Phi Beta Kappa.

Admissions: About 63% of the 1981-82 freshman applicants were accepted. The SAT scores of those who enrolled were as follows: Verbal—31% below 500, 42% between 500 and 599, 23% between 600 and 700, and 3% above 700; Math—15% below 500, 45% between 500 and 599, 34% between 600 and 700, and 6% above 700. A secondary school diploma or equivalency certificate and a GPA of at least 2.5 are required. The admissions decision is based on the academic record, recommendations from school officials, test scores, and leadership record.

Procedure: The deadline for fall entry is February 1, new students are also admitted in the spring. Notification is on a rolling basis. There is a $25 application fee. The SAT or ACT is required and should be taken by January of the senior year. ATs are required of applicants to accelerated medical programs and to the School of Public Communications.

Special: There are early decision, early admissions, and deferred admissions plans. AP and CLEP credit is granted.

Transfer: Recently, 2937 applications were received, and 852 transfer students enrolled. A GPA of at least 3.0 and a combined SAT score of at least 1000 are required; D grades do not transfer. All students must complete, at the university, 64 of the 128 credits required for a bachelor's degree. Application deadlines are 60 days prior to each semester.

Visiting: There is an orientation program for prospective applicants. Informal guided campus tours, including class attendance, can be arranged through the admissions office. The university suggests 10 A.M. to 3 P.M. weekdays as the best times for visits.

Financial Aid: About 80% of the students receive aid. About 66% work part-time on campus. The average award to freshmen is $3515. The university offers freshman scholarships, and a variety of loans, grants, and campus employment (including CWS) are available. Tuition may be paid in installments. Need and academic merit are the determining factors. There is a special minority group aid program.

The university is a member of CSS and requires the FAF, FFS, or SFS. Priority is given to applications received before March 1.

Foreign Students: Nine percent of the full-time students come from foreign countries. Intensive English courses, intensive English programs, special counseling, and special organizations are available for these students.

Admissions: Foreign students must take the TOEFL, the University of Michigan Language Test, or the Comprehensive English Language Test. On the TOEFL, a score of at least 550 is required. The SAT is also required.

Procedure: Application deadlines are May 1 (fall) and November 1 (spring). Foreign students must present proof of funds adequate to cover 1 year of study and must carry health insurance, which is available through the university for a fee.

Admissions Contact: Anthony T. G. Pallett, Executive Director of Admissions.

BRADFORD COLLEGE   D-1
Bradford, Massachusetts 01830   (617) 372-7161

F/T: 121M, 191W	Faculty: 28; IV, –$
P/T: 16M, 40W	Ph.D.'s: 43%
Grad: none	S/F Ratio: 13 to 1
Year: sems	Tuition: $5800
Appl: open	R and B: $3150
663 applied	507 accepted 127 enrolled
SAT: 400V 420M	LESS COMPETITIVE

Bradford College, founded in 1803, is an independent liberal arts college that offers interdisciplinary programs of study leading to associate and bachelor's degrees. The library houses over 50,000 books and 2773 microfilm items, and subscribes to over 200 periodicals.

Environment: The suburban 70-acre campus is located near a city of 45,000, about 30 miles north of Boston. There are 12 buildings on campus, including 4 dormitories that house 300 students. Limited apartment housing is available for upperclassmen.

Student Life: Thirty percent of the students come from Massachusetts. Over 85% reside on campus. Ten percent of the students are minority-group members. Campus housing is coed. Students may keep cars on campus.

Organizations: There are no sororities or fraternities on campus. In addition to clubs and service groups, there are films, exhibits, informal parties, and Spring Weekend. Students are within easy access of Boston's varied cultural activities, major New England ski areas, and the Atlantic Ocean.

Sports: Bradford participates on an intercollegiate level in 1 sport for men and 1 for women. There are 5 intramural sports for men and 5 for women.

Handicapped: About 68% of the campus is accessible to physically handicapped students. Special parking and elevators are available.

Graduates: The freshman dropout rate is 30%; 60% remain to graduate. About 50% of the students pursue graduate study after graduation: 3% enter law school. About 70% enter business and industry.

Services: Students receive the following services free of charge: placement, health care, career counseling, and tutoring. Psychological counseling and remedial instruction are provided on a fee basis.

Programs of Study: The college confers the B.A. degree. Associate degrees are also awarded. Concentrations are offered in the following subjects: AREA STUDIES (American), BUSINESS (administration and management), ENGLISH (creative writing, English, expository writing, literature), FINE AND PERFORMING ARTS (art history, art theory, creative arts, dance, music, studio art, theater/dramatics), PHILOSOPHY (humanities, philosophy), SOCIAL SCIENCES (government/political science, human studies, international relations, psychology, sociology).

Special: All programs of study are interdisciplinary. Independent study, internships, and individually created majors are available. An accelerated bachelor's degree is possible.

Honors: All departments offer honors programs, which are open only to sophomores, juniors, and seniors on the cumulative high honors list by vote of the department concerned.

Admissions: Seventy-six percent of those who applied were accepted for the 1981–82 freshman class. The SAT scores of those who enrolled were as follows: Verbal—76% below 500, 22% between 500 and 599, 2% between 600 and 700, and 0% above 700; Math—92% below 500, 5% between 500 and 599, 3% between 600 and 700, and 0% above 700. A high school diploma is required; the minimum grade average acceptable is C. Applicants should rank in the upper 70% of their class. The college also considers AP or honors work and recommendations.

Procedure: Applicants must take either the SAT or the ACT. The college seeks geographic distribution. An interview is recommended. A rolling admissions plan is employed. The application fee is $25; deadlines are open. Freshmen are admitted in the fall and spring terms.

Special: Early admissions and deferred admissions plans are available. There is an early decision plan with a notification date of December 15. AP credit is available.

Transfer: Recently 45 applications were received, 23 were accepted, and 9 students enrolled. A 2.0 GPA is required. The college will not accept D grades. There is a 1-year residency rule. All students must complete, at Bradford, 30 of the 120 credits required for a bachelor's degree. Deadlines are open; transfer students are admitted in the fall and spring terms.

Visiting: Bradford Days, a 2-day orientation program, usually occurs 3 times a year (fall, winter, and spring). Campus tours and personal admissions interviews are scheduled on weekdays throughout the year with advance notice. Student visitors may arrange to stay overnight at the school. The admissions office should be contacted for arrangements.

Financial Aid: About 40% of the students receive assistance. About 50% work part-time on campus. Financial aid is granted on the basis of need and academic achievement, and includes outright grants, honor awards, NDSL, SEOG, Pell grants, state scholarships, and campus employment. CWS is available. The average freshman award is $5600. The college is a member of CSS and requires the application and the FAF by March 15 (fall entry) or December 15 (spring entry).

Foreign Students: Fourteen percent of the full-time students come from foreign countries. An intensive English course, an intensive English program, special counseling, and special organizations are available for these students.

Admissions: Foreign students must achieve a TOEFL score of at least 500. No college entrance exams are required.

Procedure: Application deadlines are open; foreign students are admitted in the fall and spring terms. They must complete the college's health form and must present proof of funds adequate to cover 4 years of study. Health insurance is required and is available through the college for a fee.

Admissions Contact: Dianne V. Louis, Director of Admissions.

BRANDEIS UNIVERSITY   D-2
Waltham, Massachusetts 02254   (617) 647-2880

F/T: 1449M, 1338W	Faculty: 359; I, ++$
P/T: 4M, 15W	Ph.D.'s: 87%
Grad: 569 M&W	S/F Ratio: 10 to 1
Year: sems, ss	Tuition: $6849
Appl: Feb. 1	R and B: $2975
3769 applied	2224 accepted 748 enrolled
SAT: 580V 620M	HIGHLY COMPETITIVE

Brandeis University, founded in 1948 under Jewish auspices, is an independent liberal arts and science university. Its library contains over 770,000 volumes and 145,000 microtexts, and subscribes to 3500 periodicals.

Environment: The 300-acre suburban campus is located 10 miles from Boston. There are 70 major buildings, including dormitories, on-campus apartments, and married student housing.

Student Life: Only 27% of the students are from Massachusetts; the rest are from 45 other states and 41 foreign countries. About 81% come from public schools. Approximately 80% reside on campus. Eleven percent of the students are minority-group members. Campus housing is coed. Students may keep cars on campus. Day-care services are available to all students for a fee.

Organizations: There are no sororities or fraternities. Extracurricular activities are varied and numerous (there are 97 clubs and organizations). Students are near enough to Boston to take advantage of its social and cultural offerings.

Sports: The university fields 12 intercollegiate teams for men and 11 for women. There are 10 intramural sports for men and 10 for women.

Handicapped: The hilly campus is not readily accessible to nonambulatory students, although some wheelchair ramps, elevators, and special parking areas are provided.

Graduates: The freshman dropout rate is about 8%; 90% remain to graduate. About 48% go on for further education directly after graduation, 6% to medical school, 2% to dental school, and 11% to law school.

356 MASSACHUSETTS

Services: Psychological counseling, tutoring, career counseling, and health care are offered without charge to all students. Remedial instruction is provided for a fee.

Programs of Study: The university confers the B.A. degree. Master's and doctoral degrees are also awarded. The B.A. is offered in the following subjects: AREA STUDIES (American, Black/Afro-American, classical/oriental, Judaic, Latin American, legal, medieval, Russian, urban, women's), BUSINESS (computer science), EDUCATION (elementary, secondary), ENGLISH (creative writing, English, literature, poetry writing), FINE AND PERFORMING ARTS (art, art history, music, studio art, theater/dramatics), LANGUAGES (French, German, Greek/Latin, Hebrew, Italian, Russian, Spanish, Yiddish), MATH AND SCIENCES (biochemistry, biology, chemistry, mathematics, physics), PHILOSOPHY (classics, humanities, Near Eastern and Judaic studies, philosophy), SOCIAL SCIENCES (anthropology, economics, government/political science, history, international relations, psychology, sociology, women's studies).

Required: All students must complete course work in English composition, a foreign language, and general studies requirements.

Special: Study abroad and student-designed majors are offered.

Admissions: About 59% of the 1981-82 freshman applicants were accepted. The SAT scores of those who enrolled were as follows: Verbal—10% below 500, 52% between 500 and 599, 34% between 600 and 700, and 4% above 700; Math—7% below 500, 34% between 500 and 599, 46% between 600 and 700, and 13% above 700. Factors in the admissions decision include advanced placement or honors courses, recommendations, SAT scores, rank in class, and special talent.

Procedure: The SAT and 3 ATs (English Composition, math or science, and preferably a foreign language) should be taken by February of the senior year. February 1 is the fall semester application deadline; December 1, the spring. Freshmen are not admitted in the summer. The university subscribes to the CRDA. There is a $25 fee.

Special: There are early decision, early admissions, and deferred admissions plans. The early admissions application deadline is February 1. AP credit is given.

Transfer: For fall 1981, 304 students applied, 184 were accepted, and 98 enrolled. Transfer students are accepted in freshman, sophomore, and junior years. SAT scores, transcripts, and evaluations are required. D grades do not transfer. There is a 2-year residency requirement; 32 courses are required for a bachelor's degree. April 1 (fall) and December 1 (spring) are the application deadlines.

Visiting: There is an orientation program for prospective students, which includes scheduled personal interviews and tours. Informal campus tours are conducted Monday through Friday during the school year at 10:30 A.M., 1 P.M., and 3 P.M.. Visitors may sit in on classes and stay overnight at the university. For further information, the admissions office should be contacted.

Financial Aid: About 46% of the students are receiving aid; 90% of the applicants for aid received aid. About 68% work part-time on campus. The average freshman award from university grant funds is $3800. The university also offers freshman scholarships. Other aid forms include federal/state grants, CWS, and various loans. The average freshman aid package is above $5000. The university aid application and the FAF should be filed by February 1 (fall) or December 1 (spring). The university is a member of CSS.

Foreign Students: Five percent of the full-time students come from foreign countries. Special organizations and special counseling are available for these students.

Admissions: Foreign students must achieve a TOEFL score of at least 550. It is strongly recommended that they also take the SAT.

Procedure: Application deadlines are the same as for other freshmen. Foreign students must fill out a health form and must present proof of funds adequate to cover 1 year of study. Health insurance is required and is available through the university for a fee.

Admissions Contact: David Gould, Dean of Admissions.

BRIDGEWATER STATE COLLEGE E-3
Bridgewater, Massachusetts 02324   (617) 697-8321

F/T: 1627M, 2529W   Faculty: 224; IIA, +$
P/T: 76M, 234W   Ph.D.'s: 63%
Grad: 406M, 649W   S/F Ratio: 19 to 1
Year: sems, ss   Tuition: $975 ($2788)
Appl: Mar. 1   R and B: $1830-2130
5916 applied   4000 accepted   1251 enrolled
SAT: 440V 480M   COMPETITIVE

Bridgewater, established in 1840, is a state-supported college of liberal arts and education. The library contains 183,000 volumes and 283,000 microfilm items, and subscribes to 1448 periodicals.

Environment: The suburban campus occupies 176 acres in the center of Bridgewater, a town of 17,202 population 30 miles from Boston. The 22 campus buildings include a laboratory school and modern townhouse apartments. Residence halls accommodate 1147 students.

Student Life: Most of the students are from New England, primarily from Massachusetts. About 34% live on campus. Two percent are minority-group members. About 62% are Catholic, 35% are Protestant, and 1% are Jewish. Campus housing is both coed and single-sex; there are visiting privileges in single-sex housing. Students may keep cars on campus. Day-care services are provided to all students for a fee.

Organizations: The college has 1 fraternity and 2 sororities; approximately 1% of the students are members. There are many cultural and recreational activities on campus as well as in Boston. Cape Cod and Providence, Rhode Island, are within easy driving distance.

Sports: The college fields 10 intercollegiate teams for men and 10 for women. There are 9 intramural sports for men and 7 for women.

Handicapped: About 40% of the campus is accessible to physically handicapped students. Special facilities include wheelchair ramps, special parking areas, and elevators. Special class scheduling can be arranged. There are 3 special counselors to assist handicapped students. Less than 1% of the students are hearing or visually impaired. There are no special facilities on campus for these students.

Graduates: About 16% of the students drop out at the end of freshman year; 36% remain to graduate. Fifteen percent of the students pursue advanced study after graduation. Twenty-four percent enter careers in business and industry.

Services: The following services are provided to students free of charge: health care, psychological counseling, career counseling, tutoring, and remedial instruction. There is a fee for the use of placement services.

Programs of Study: The college confers the B.A., B.S., and B.S.Ed. degrees. Master's and doctoral degrees are also awarded. Bachelor's degrees are offered in the following subjects: BUSINESS (aviation management, computer science, management), EDUCATION (early childhood, elementary, health/physical, secondary, special), ENGLISH (English, speech), FINE AND PERFORMING ARTS (art, art education, radio/TV, studio art, theater/dramatics), HEALTH SCIENCES (speech therapy), LANGUAGES (French, Spanish), MATH AND SCIENCES (biology, chemistry, chemistry/geology, earth science, mathematics, physics), PHILOSOPHY (philosophy), PRE-PROFESSIONAL (dentistry, law, medicine, social work), SOCIAL SCIENCES (anthropology, government/political science, history, psychology, sociology). Almost half of all the undergraduate degrees conferred by the college are in education, 27% are in social sciences, and 10% are in math and sciences.

Honors: Two national honor societies, Phi Beta Kappa and Kappa Delta Pi, have chapters on campus. Honors programs are offered in several departments.

Admissions: About 68% of those who applied were accepted for the 1981-82 freshman class. The SAT scores of those who enrolled were as follows: Verbal—85% scored below 500, 10% between 500 and 599, 5% between 600 and 700, and 0% above 700; Math—70% scored below 500, 20% between 500 and 599, 10% between 600 and 700, and 7% above 700. Students should be graduates of an accredited high school, have at least a 2.0 GPA, and rank in the upper 60% of their graduating class. Advanced placement or honors courses, recommendations, special talents, and extracurricular activities are also considered important.

Procedure: The SAT is required. The deadlines for applications are March 1 (fall) and December 1 (spring). Freshmen are not admitted in the summer. Admissions are granted on a rolling basis; the CRDA is observed. There is an $18 application fee.

Special: The college has an early admissions plan with a rolling deadline, and a deferred admissions plan as well. CLEP and AP credit is given.

Transfer: For fall 1981, 1273 students applied, 971 were accepted, and 510 enrolled. Transfer students are accepted in freshman, sophomore, and junior classes; D grades are not acceptable. A 2.0 GPA is required. All students must complete, at the college, 30 of the 120 semester hours required for a bachelor's degree. Application deadlines are May 1 (fall) and December 1 (spring).

Visiting: Regular tours are held for prospective students from Monday through Friday at 11 A.M. and 3 P.M. Interviews are an optional part of the orientation process. Guides are available for informal visits. Visitors may sit in on classes with the instructor's permission but may not stay on campus. The best time to visit is when school is in session. The Office of Undergraduate Admissions handles arrangements.

Financial Aid: About 80% of the students receive financial aid from the following sources: grants (including BEOG), loans (including NDSL), and campus employment (including CWS). Twenty-two percent of the students work part-time on campus. The average freshman award is $1800. The college is a member of CSS. Loans are available from the federal government, local banks, and college-administered funds. The FAF must be filed. The deadline for aid applications is April 15 (fall) or November 15 (spring).

Foreign Students: Fewer than 1% of the full-time students come from foreign countries. Special counseling and special organizations are available for these students.

Admissions: Foreign students must take the TOEFL. No college entrance exams are required.

Procedure: Application deadlines are January 1 (fall) and May 1 (spring). Foreign students must complete a health form and present proof of funds adequate to cover 4 years of study.

Admissions Contact: James F. Plotner, Jr., Director of Admissions.

CENTRAL NEW ENGLAND COLLEGE C-2
(Formerly Central New England College of Technology)
Worcester, Massachusetts 01610 (617) 755-4314

F/T: 517M, 164W Faculty: 18; n/av
P/T: 959M, 183W Ph.D.'s: 30%
Grad: none S/F Ratio: 20 to 1
Year: tri, ss Tuition: $3400
Appl: Sept. 8 R: n/app
800 applied 700 accepted 680 enrolled
SAT, ACT: not required **LESS COMPETITIVE**

Founded in 1971, Central New England College is an independent institution offering undergraduate training in management and technology.

Environment: The college has a 5-acre urban campus. There are facilities for commuters.

Student Life: About 60% of the students come from Massachusetts; most have had public school educations. Only 1% live on campus. Students may keep cars on campus.

Organizations: Extracurricular activities are varied. There are no fraternities or sororities.

Sports: The college has no intercollegiate sports. There are 5 intramural sports for both men and women.

Handicapped: Most of the campus is accessible to handicapped students.

Graduates: Fifteen percent of entering freshmen drop out; 60% remain to graduate.

Services: The college provides career counseling and placement services free of charge. Psychological counseling, tutoring, and remedial instruction are offered on a fee basis.

Programs of Study: The B.E.T. and B.S. in Engineering Technology degrees are conferred. Associate degrees are also awarded. Bachelor's degrees are offered in the following subjects: BUSINESS (computer science, marketing), MATH AND SCIENCES (engineering).

Required: The bachelor's programs require specific courses for graduation.

Special: The college offers a cooperative education program, the English Language Institute for international students, and a weekend program for part-time students.

Admissions: About 88% of those who applied were accepted for the 1981–82 freshman class. An interview is recommended. Impressions made during the interview, recommendations, and the applicant's personality are considered important.

Procedure: Deadlines are September 8 (fall), September 25 (winter), May 15 (spring), and May 15, June 19, or July 24 (summer sessions). Notification is on a rolling basis. There is no application fee.

Special: An early decision plan is available and, depending on the high school, an early admissions plan is possible. CLEP credit is acceptable.

Transfer: Transfers are accepted for all classes. Good academic standing and a 2.0 GPA are required; D grades do not transfer. At least 1 year must be completed in residence for a bachelor's degree. Application deadlines are the same as those for freshmen.

MASSACHUSETTS 357

Visiting: Campus tours with student guides can be arranged. Visitors may sit in on classes.

Financial Aid: About 89% of the students receive financial aid. About 11% work part-time on campus. The college offers various loans (including NDSL), grants (including BEOG), and campus employment opportunities. The college is a member of CSS. The FAF is required; aid application deadlines are open.

Foreign Students: Seventeen percent of the full-time students come from foreign countries. An intensive English program and special counseling are available for these students.

Admissions: Foreign students must achieve a score of at least 450 on the TOEFL and must take the college's own English proficiency test and entrance exam.

Procedure: There are no application deadlines; foreign students are admitted to all terms. They must present proof of funds adequate to cover 1 semester of study. There is a special $100 processing fee for foreign students. Health insurance is required and is available through the college for a fee.

Admissions Contact: Heather C. Smith, Associate Director of Admissions.

CLARK UNIVERSITY C-2
Worcester, Massachusetts 01610 (617) 793-7431

F/T: 953M, 1077W Faculty: 130; I, av$
P/T: 14M, 13W Ph.D.'s: 98%
Grad: 320M, 252W S/F Ratio: 14 to 1
Year: sems Tuition: $6496
Appl: Feb. 15 R and B: $2290
2695 applied 1425 accepted 545 enrolled
SAT: 554V 580M **HIGHLY COMPETITIVE**

Clark University, established in 1887, is an independent institution that offers undergraduate degree programs in the liberal arts and sciences, business, and education. The library contains 400,000 volumes and 50,000 microfilm items, and subscribes to 2500 periodicals.

Environment: The 35-acre urban campus is located in a residential section of Worcester, 45 miles from Boston. There are 26 major buildings, including dormitories, on-campus apartments, and facilities for commuting students. Off-campus apartments are also available.

Student Life: The majority of students come from New England and metropolitan New York; 10% commute; about 70% come from public schools. Eighty percent live on campus. Eight percent are minority-group members. Campus housing is both coed and single-sex; there are visiting privileges in the single-sex housing. Students may keep cars on campus.

Organizations: There is 1 fraternity, to which 2% of the men belong; there are no sororities. Clubs, religious and service groups, student government, publications, dramatics and performing groups, and a regularly scheduled social and cultural program are offered.

Sports: The university fields 12 intercollegiate teams for men and 11 for women. There are 13 intramural sports for men and 12 for women.

Handicapped: About 75% of the campus is accessible to students with physical handicaps. Special facilities (wheelchair ramps, elevators, special parking and rest rooms, and lowered drinking fountains and telephones) and class scheduling are offered; there are 3 counselors and 3 assistants for handicapped students.

Graduates: The freshman dropout rate is 9%; about 78% remain to graduate. About 50% go on to graduate study: 8% to medical school, 3% to dental school, and 11% to law school. Eighteen percent pursue careers in business and industry.

Services: Tutoring, remedial instruction, psychological counseling, career counseling, and placement are offered free of charge to all students. Health care is available on a fee basis.

Programs of Study: The B.A. and B.F.A. degrees are conferred. Master's and doctoral degrees are also awarded. Bachelor's degrees are offered in the following subjects: AREA STUDIES (American, urban), BUSINESS (business administration, computer science, management), EDUCATION (early childhood, elementary, secondary, special), ENGLISH (English, literature), FINE AND PERFORMING ARTS (art, art education, art history, film/photography, music, music education, studio art, theater/dramatics), LANGUAGES (French, German, Hebrew, Russian, Spanish), MATH AND SCIENCES (biochemistry, biology, botany, chemistry, ecology/environmental science, mathematics, natural sciences, physical sciences, physics, zoology), PHILOSOPHY (classics, philosophy), PREPROFESSIONAL (dentistry, law, medicine, social work, veterinary), SOCIAL SCIENCES (geography, government/political science, history, international relations, psychology, sociology). About 38% of degrees conferred are in social sciences and 23% in math/sciences.

Special: Student-designed majors, study abroad, a Washington semester, a large internship program, and interdisciplinary programs are offered. The university is a member of the 10-college Worcester Consortium.

Honors: There are 2 honor societies; most departments offer senior honors programs.

Admissions: About 53% of those who applied were accepted for the 1981-82 freshman class. The SAT scores of those who enrolled were as follows: Verbal—23% scored below 500, 52% between 500 and 599, 22% between 600 and 700, and 3% above 700; Math—15% scored below 500, 43% between 500 and 599, 36% between 600 and 700, and 6% above 700. Advanced placement/honors work, recommendations, and leadership are also important factors.

Procedure: The SAT or ACT and 3 ATs should be taken by January of the senior year. The fall semester application deadline is February 15. There is a $25 application fee. An interview is recommended.

Special: AP credit is accepted. There are early decision and deferred admissions plans.

Transfer: For fall 1981, 225 students applied, 110 were accepted, and 50 enrolled. Good academic standing is required; D grades do not transfer. May 1 is the fall deadline; the deadline for spring entry is December 1. All students must complete, at the university, 16 of the 32 units required for a bachelor's degree.

Visiting: Informal campus tours with student guides can be arranged. Visitors may stay at the school and sit in on classes.

Financial Aid: About 48% of all students receive financial aid. About 51% work part-time on campus. The college offers scholarships, various loans, grants, and campus employment (including CWS). The average freshman aid package is $3300; the maximum, $5200. The FAF should be filed by February 15. Need and academic merit are the determining factors. The university is a member of CSS.

Foreign Students: Six percent of the full-time students come from foreign countries. An intensive English program, special counseling, and special organizations are available for these students.

Admissions: Foreign students must achieve a TOEFL score of at least 550. No college entrance exams are required.

Procedure: The application deadline for fall entry is February 15. Foreign students must present proof of health and proof of adequate funds.

Admissions Contact: Gary S. Poor, Director of Admissions.

COLLEGE OF THE HOLY CROSS
(See Holy Cross College)

COLLEGE OF OUR LADY OF THE ELMS   B-3
Chicopee, Massachusetts 01013   (413) 598-8351

F/T: 530W	Faculty:	45; IIB, av$
P/T: 85W	Ph.D.'s:	38%
Grad: none	S/F Ratio:	10 to 1
Year: sems, ss	Tuition:	$3650
Appl: open	R and B:	$2050
320 applied	255 accepted	146 enrolled
SAT: 426V 430M		COMPETITIVE

The College of Our Lady of the Elms is a liberal arts college for women affiliated with the Roman Catholic Church. The library contains 58,834 volumes and 1211 microfilm items, and subscribes to 522 periodicals.

Environment: The 32-acre suburban campus is 2 miles north of Springfield. Dormitories accommodate 70% of the students; facilities are available for commuting students.

Student Life: About 76% of the students come from Massachusetts; 65% are public school graduates. Three percent are minority-group members. Eighty percent are Catholic, 18% are Protestant, and 2% are Jewish. There are weekend visiting privileges in the single-sex dormitories. Students may keep cars on campus.

Organizations: There are no sororities. Student activities include musical organizations, religious groups, clubs, and publications.

Sports: The college fields 2 intercollegiate teams. There are 6 intramural sports.

Handicapped: About 50% of the campus is accessible to students with physical handicaps. Wheelchair ramps, elevators, and special parking and rest rooms are provided. About 2% of the students currently enrolled have hearing impairments. There are 2 special counselors.

Graduates: The freshman dropout rate is 13%; 65% remain to graduate. Twenty percent of those who remain go on to graduate study (5% to law school) and 15% pursue careers in business and industry.

Services: Health care, psychological counseling, tutoring, remedial instruction, career counseling, and placement are offered free of charge to all students.

Programs of Study: The B.A., B.S., and B.S.N. degrees are conferred. Bachelor's degrees are offered in the following subjects: AREA STUDIES (American), BUSINESS (management), EDUCATION (elementary, secondary), ENGLISH (English), FINE AND PERFORMING ARTS (art, art education), HEALTH SCIENCES (medical technology, nursing, speech therapy), LANGUAGES (French, Spanish), MATH AND SCIENCES (biology, chemistry, mathematics), PREPROFESSIONAL (law, social work), SOCIAL SCIENCES (history, social sciences, sociology).

Required: There is a distribution requirement that includes English composition.

Special: Students may design their own majors.

Admissions: About 80% of those who applied were accepted for the 1981-82 freshman class. Applicants need a class rank in the top 60% and a 2.3 high school GPA. Advanced placement or honors courses, recommendations, and impressions made during interview are considered important. An interview is recommended.

Procedure: The SAT should be taken by January of the senior year. Deadlines are open; notification is on a rolling basis. Freshmen are admitted in the fall and spring terms. There is a $15 application fee.

Special: There is a deferred admissions plan.

Transfer: For fall 1981, 68 students applied, 60 were accepted, and 40 enrolled. A 2.0 GPA is required. D grades do not transfer. All students must complete, at the college, 60 of the 120 credits required for a bachelor's degree. There are no application deadlines; transfer students are admitted in the fall and spring terms.

Visiting: There is an orientation program for prospective students. Informal campus tours with student guides may be arranged. Visitors may stay at the school and sit in on classes.

Financial Aid: About 60% of all students receive financial aid. Thirty percent work part-time on campus. The average freshman award is $1500. The college offers scholarships, loans (NDSL), grants (BEOG), and campus employment (CWS). April 1 (fall) and December 1 (spring) are the aid application deadlines; the FAF should be submitted. The college is a member of CSS.

Foreign Students: Fewer than 1% of the full-time students come from foreign countries. Special counseling is available for these students.

Admissions: Foreign students must take the TOEFL. No college entrance exams are required.

Procedure: Application deadlines are August 1 (fall) and December 1 (spring).

Admissions Contact: Peter J. Miller, Director of Admissions.

CURRY COLLEGE   E-2
Milton, Massachusetts 02186   (617) 333-0441

F/T: 430M, 445W	Faculty:	59; IIB, −$
P/T: 68M, 302W	Ph.D.'s:	49%
Grad: none	S/F Ratio:	13 to 1
Year: sems, ss	Tuition:	$4950
Appl: open	R and B:	$2900
1500 applied	1150 accepted	385 enrolled
SAT: 450V 465M		COMPETITIVE

Curry College, founded in 1879, is a private liberal arts institution. The library contains 100,000 volumes and 450 microfilm items, subscribes to 637 periodicals, and is a designated depository for U.S. government documents.

Environment: The 120-acre campus is located in a suburban area 7 miles from Boston. The 11 major campus buildings include 10 dormitories that accommodate 575 students in single, double, and triple rooms.

Student Life: Forty-seven percent of the students are from Massachusetts, and 65% are graduates of public schools. About 60% live on campus. Unmarried students who do not live with parents or guardians must live on campus unless they obtain special permission from the dean of students. Six percent of the students are minority-group members. Dormitories are both coed and single-sex; there are visiting privileges in the single-sex dorms. Students may keep cars on campus.

Organizations: Cultural activities sponsored by the college include a drama group, choral and instrumental ensembles, lecture series, and a dance company. Other student organizations include a student-operated FM radio station, a student newspaper, and an arts journal. There are no fraternities or sororities.

Sports: The college fields 6 intercollegiate teams for men and 4 for women. There are 5 intramural sports for men and 5 for women.

Graduates: About 10% of the freshmen drop out, and 50% remain to graduate. About 30% of the graduates seek advanced degrees, and 60% enter business and industry.

Services: Psychological, placement, and career counseling are provided free to students. Health care is available on campus; visits by the college physician outside regular office hours are at the student's own expense. Tutoring and remedial instruction also are offered on a fee basis, and the college provides a special program for dyslexic students.

Programs of Study: The college confers the B.A. and B.S.N. degrees. Bachelor's degrees are offered in the following subjects: BUSINESS (management), EDUCATION (elementary, preschool, special), ENGLISH (English, literature), FINE AND PERFORMING ARTS (art, music, radio/TV, studio art), HEALTH SCIENCES (nursing), MATH AND SCIENCES (biology, chemistry, physics), PHILOSOPHY (philosophy), SOCIAL SCIENCES (government/political science, history, international relations, psychology, sociology).

Required: Students for whom English is a foreign language must demonstrate competency in it. The Central Liberal Arts Curriculum (CLAC), required of all students, incorporates a variety of academic disciplines into every student's plan of study.

Special: A student may supplement the career potential of standard majors by completing a special program such as human services, moderate special needs education, preschool education, management-communication, radio broadcasting, and computer science (minor). Students are permitted to design their own majors, spend their sophomore or junior year abroad, graduate in fewer than 4 years, and take one course each semester on a pass-fail basis. Field experience courses, structured for individual students, allow them to connect classroom learning with work experience. Under an exchange program, students may spend up to 2 semesters during their sophomore or junior years at Johnston College of the University of Redlands in California. Curry is also affiliated with the Washington Center for Learning Alternatives. Students in any major may participate in a full-semester, 15-credit internship with either a government agency or a private firm in Washington, D.C.

Honors: The college has an honor society, and students may earn degrees cum laude, magna cum laude, or summa cum laude.

Admissions: About 77% of those who applied were accepted for the 1981–82 freshman class. The SAT scores of those who enrolled were as follows: Verbal—55% scored below 500, 35% between 500 and 599, 10% between 600 and 700, and 0% above 700; Math—50% scored below 500, 40% between 500 and 599, 10% between 600 and 700, and 0% above 700. Applicants must present an average of at least C, rank in the top 50% of their class, have completed 16 Carnegie units, and be recommended for college by their high school. Admissions officers also consider reputation of the high school, SAT or ACT scores, advanced placement or honors courses, the candidate's readiness for college, recommendations, and extracurricular activities. The college seeks a geographically diverse student body.

Procedure: The SAT or ACT is required and should be taken in May of the junior year or in December or January of the senior year. Applications for fall admission should be submitted early in the fall or winter of the year preceding intended entry; those for spring admission by December. Admissions decisions are made on a rolling basis. There is a $25 application fee.

Special: The college offers early decision, early admissions, and deferred admissions plans. AP and CLEP credit may be earned.

Transfer: For fall 1981, 400 students applied, 300 were accepted, and 55 enrolled. Applicants must have an average of at least 2.0. D grades sometimes transfer. All students must complete, at Curry, 30 of the 120–121 credits required for a bachelor's degree. There are no application deadlines; transfer students are admitted in the fall and spring terms.

Financial Aid: About 70% of the students receive aid. The average aid package is $2225. The college awards grants-in-aid of up to $1000 each. Loans are available from the federal and state governments, local banks, and the college. Students may earn up to $800 per year from campus jobs. The college belongs to CSS. The FAF is required. The application deadline is April 1 (fall) or December 1 (spring).

Foreign Students: Three percent of the full-time students come from foreign countries. An intensive English course is available for these students.

Admissions: Foreign students must achieve a TOEFL score of at least 500 and must take the SAT.

Procedure: Application deadlines are April 1 (fall) and December 1 (spring). Foreign students must have a physical exam and must present proof of funds adequate to cover 4 years of study.

Admissions Contact: Dana K. Denault, Director of Admissions.

EASTERN NAZARENE COLLEGE E–2
Quincy, Massachusetts 02170 (617) 773-2317

F/T: 315M, 405W	Faculty: 51; IIA, — —$
P/T: 35M, 64W	Ph.D.'s: 43%
Grad: 25M, 58W	S/F Ratio: 16 to 1
Year: 4-1-4, ss	Tuition: $3326
Appl: Aug. 1	R and B: $2050
491 applied	432 accepted	286 enrolled
SAT: 417V 456M		LESS COMPETITIVE

Eastern Nazarene College, founded in 1900, is a liberal arts institution affiliated with the Church of Nazarene. The library contains 91,000 volumes and 25,000 reels of microfilm, and subscribes to 467 periodicals.

Environment: The 15-acre suburban campus is located in Quincy, about 7 miles from Boston. Living facilities include dormitories and married student housing.

Student Life: About 32% of the students are residents of Massachusetts. Almost all entering freshmen come from public schools. About 36% of the students live on campus. Eight percent are minority-group members. Eighty percent are Protestant, and 8% are Catholic. The majority of students are members of the supporting church; all students are required to attend chapel 3 times a week. Smoking, drinking, dancing, and attendance at theaters are forbidden for all students living on campus or who move to town for the express purpose of attending the college. Dormitories are single-sex; there are visiting privileges. Women's dormitories usually close at 11 P.M. A student must be 21 or a sophomore to have a car unless he or she has special permission.

Organizations: There are no fraternities or sororities on campus. A variety of extracurricular activities are offered. Recreational facilities are provided by the college. The greater Boston area affords many cultural and recreational opportunities.

Sports: The college fields 5 intercollegiate teams for men and 4 for women. There are 4 intramural sports for men and 2 for women.

Handicapped: Wheelchair ramps and elevators are available to physically handicapped students. About half the campus is accessible to them. There are no hearing-impaired or visually impaired students enrolled.

Graduates: About 30% of the freshmen drop out after their first year. Fifty percent of those who graduate continue their education.

Services: Free health care, career counseling, and job placement are offered.

Programs of Study: The college offers the B.A. and B.S. degrees. Associate and master's degrees are also awarded. Bachelor's degrees are offered in the following subjects: BUSINESS (business administration, economics), EDUCATION (Christian, early childhood, elementary, health/physical, special), ENGLISH (English), LANGUAGES (modern languages, Spanish), MATH AND SCIENCES (biology, chemistry, computer science, general science, mathematics, physics), PHILOSOPHY (philosophy), PREPROFESSIONAL (dentistry, engineering, law, medicine, nursing, secondary education, veterinary), SOCIAL SCIENCES (economics, history, psychology, religion, social studies, social work, sociology). About 10% of the degrees are conferred in the social sciences, 11% in education, and 12% in business.

Special: Cooperative programs in pre-nursing, pre-medicine, pre-veterinary, pre-dental, pre-law, and pharmacy are offered. A 5-year combined B.A.-B.S. degree is available in engineering. Students may elect a general studies degree or design their own majors.

Honors: The Phi Delta honor society is represented on campus.

Admissions: About 88% of those who applied were accepted for the 1981–82 freshman class. The SAT scores of those who enrolled were as follows: Verbal—78% scored below 500, 15% between 500 and 599, 7% between 600 and 700, and 0% above 700; Math—67% scored below 500, 22% between 500 and 599, 9% between 600 and 700, and 2% above 700. Preference is given to those with a B average who are graduates of accredited, well-reputed high schools and show

MASSACHUSETTS

qualities of leadership. Recommendations and impressions made during interview are also considered important.

Procedure: The SAT or ACT is required and should be taken by December of the senior year or no later than March. Application deadlines are August 1 for fall and February 2 for spring entry. Admission is on a rolling basis. There is a $20 application fee.

Special: Early decision and early admissions plans are available. AP and CLEP credit is given.

Transfer: For fall 1981, 65 students applied and 51 enrolled. All students must complete, at the college, 32 of the 130 credits required for a bachelor's degree. D grades do not transfer. Application deadlines are August 1 (fall) and February 2 (spring).

Visiting: There are regularly scheduled orientations for prospective students. Guides are provided for informal visits. Visitors can sit in on classes and stay at the school. Arrangements can be made through the admissions office.

Financial Aid: About 80% of the students receive some form of financial assistance. Forty-three percent work part-time on campus. The average award to freshmen is $1500. About 30 scholarships are awarded each year to freshmen. Loans from federal, state, and local sources, and the college are available. The college is a member of CSS and requires the FAF. Application deadlines are March 1 (fall) and January 1 (spring).

Foreign Students: Four percent of the full-time students come from foreign countries. Special counseling is available for these students.

Admissions: Foreign students must achieve a TOEFL score of at least 500 and must take the SAT or ACT.

Procedure: Application deadlines are May 31 (fall) and October 31 (spring). Foreign students must complete a health form and must present proof of funds adequate to cover 4 years of study. Health insurance is required.

Admissions Contact: Donald A. Yerxa, Director of Admissions.

EMERSON COLLEGE   E–2
Boston, Massachusetts 02116   (617) 262-2010

F/T: 670M, 847W		Faculty:	88; n/av
P/T: 37M, 35W		Ph.D.'s:	45%
Grad: 63M, 129W		S/F Ratio:	15 to 1
Year: sems, ss		Tuition:	$5190
Appl: open		R and B:	$3250
SAT or ACT: required			COMPETITIVE

Emerson College, established in 1880, is a private institution offering undergraduate programs in communication and performing arts. In addition, the Emerson curriculum includes humanities, social sciences, and sciences. The library maintains 83,000 volumes, 11,000 microfilms, and 4,000 records and tapes, subscribes to 418 journals, and is affiliated with the Fenway Consortium, which includes 10 colleges and universities in the Boston area.

Environment: The 2-acre urban campus has 5 dormitories that accommodate 726 students. Other facilities include a new theater complex, a television studio, a speech clinic, and a nursery for preschool hearing-impaired children.

Student Life: About 54% of the students come from Massachusetts and about 50% live on campus. Eight percent are minority-group members. Campus housing is coed. Students may not keep cars on campus.

Organizations: There are 5 fraternities and 2 sororities. Extracurricular activities include religious and service groups, clubs, student government, theater and communication companies, and cultural and social events.

Sports: The college fields 5 intercollegiate teams for men and 3 for women. There are 5 intramural sports for men and 3 for women.

Handicapped: Special class scheduling, an advisor, and private tutors are available for physically handicapped students.

Graduates: About 55% of entering freshmen remain to graduate. Forty percent go on to graduate study.

Services: Career counseling, placement, psychological counseling, health care, tutoring, and remedial instruction are offered free of charge to all students.

Programs of Study: The college offers the B.A., B.S., B.F.A., B.L.I., B.S.Sp., and B. Mus. degrees. Master's programs are also available. Bachelor's degrees are offered in the following subjects: BUSINESS (advertising/public relations, business communication), EDUCATION (speech education, theater education), ENGLISH (creative writing, journalism, literature, mass communication, speech), FINE AND PERFORMING ARTS (dance, film/photography, music, radio/TV, theater/dramatics), HEALTH SCIENCES (speech therapy), PREPROFESSIONAL (law), SOCIAL SCIENCES (communication, politics and law).

Required: There is a distribution requirement that includes course work in English composition, liberal arts, and speech.

Special: Student-designed majors, interdisciplinary majors, study abroad, and cooperative degree programs in art and music are offered.

Admissions: About 78% of the applicants for the 1981–82 school year were accepted. The SAT scores of those who enrolled were as follows: Verbal—63% below 500, 26% between 500 and 599, 9% between 600 and 700, and 1% above 700; Math—67% below 500, 26% between 500 and 599, 6% between 600 and 700, and 1% above 700. Applicants should rank in the upper 50% of their high school class.

Procedure: There are no application deadlines; freshmen are admitted in the fall and spring terms. Notification is on a rolling basis. There is a $25 application fee. The SAT or ACT is required and should be taken by December.

Special: AP and CLEP credit is accepted. There are early admissions and deferred admissions plans.

Transfer: About 200 students transfer annually. D grades do not transfer. A 2.5 GPA is required. One year must be completed in residence; 128 credits are required for a bachelor's degree. There are no application deadlines.

Visiting: There is an orientation program for prospective applicants. Informal campus tours may be arranged. Visitors may sit in on classes and stay at the college. Arrangements should be made through the Admissions Office.

Financial Aid: About 34% of all students receive financial aid. About 23% work part-time on campus. The college offers grants, loans, scholarships, and work-study funds. All students must also apply for the PELL grant. The FAF is due January 15. Emerson is a member of CSS.

Foreign Students: Three percent of the full-time students come from foreign countries. Special counseling and special organizations are available for these students.

Admissions: Foreign students must take the TOEFL and, depending on their background, may be required to take a college entrance exam.

Procedure: Application deadlines are April 15 (fall) and December 15 (spring). Foreign students must have a health form completed by a physician and must present proof of funds adequate to cover 4 years of study. Health insurance is required and is available through the college for a fee.

Admissions Contact: Anne Heller, Director of Admissions.

EMMANUEL COLLEGE   E–2
Boston, Massachusetts 02115   (617) 277-9340

F/T: 6M, 687W		Faculty:	68; IIA, – – $
P/T: 9M, 314W		Ph.D.'s:	80%
Grad: 3M, 46W		S/F Ratio:	13 to 1
Year: sems, ss		Tuition:	$4950
Appl: open		R and B:	$2600
460 applied	394 accepted		160 enrolled
SAT: 425V 442M			LESS COMPETITIVE

Emmanuel College, established in 1919, is a Roman Catholic institution offering undergraduate degree programs in business and the liberal arts and sciences. The library contains 121,600 volumes and nearly 950 microfilm items, and subscribes to 490 periodicals.

Environment: The small urban campus has 7 major buildings, including 3 dormitories. Facilities are available for commuting students.

Student Life: About 74% of the students come from Massachusetts; 75% come from public schools. About 70% live on campus. Seventy-two percent of the students are Catholic, 10% are Protestant, and 4% are Jewish; attendance at religious services is voluntary. Eleven percent of the students are minority-group members. Dormitories are single-sex; there are visiting privileges. Students may keep cars on campus.

Organizations: There are no sororities. Extracurricular activities include clubs, religious and service groups, student government, and cultural and social events.

Sports: The college fields 4 intercollegiate teams for women. There are 6 intramural sports for women.

Handicapped: About 30% of the campus is accessible to physically handicapped students. Special facilities include parking, wheelchair ramps, and elevators. Less than 1% of the students currently enrolled have visual or hearing impairments.

Graduates: The freshman dropout rate is 20%; about 60% remain to graduate. Ten percent pursue graduate study.

Services: Placement, career counseling, tutoring, remedial instruction, health care, and psychological counseling are offered free of charge to all students.

Programs of Study: B.A., B.S., B.F.A., and B.S.N. degrees are conferred. Associate degrees are also awarded. Bachelor's degrees are offered in the following subjects: BUSINESS (management), EDUCATION (elementary, secondary), ENGLISH (communication arts, English), FINE AND PERFORMING ARTS (art, art education, art history, music, music education), LANGUAGES (French, Spanish), MATH AND SCIENCES (biochemistry, biology, chemistry, mathematics, physics), PHILOSOPHY (philosophy, religion), PREPROFESSIONAL (engineering), SOCIAL SCIENCES (economics, government/political science, history, psychology, sociology).

Required: There is a distribution requirement that includes course work in English composition, mathematics, and computer literacy.

Special: Study abroad, cooperative programs in health fields, a 3-2 engineering program, and a Washington semester are offered.

Honors: Eight honor societies have chapters on campus.

Admissions: About 86% of the applicants for the 1981-82 freshman class were accepted. The SAT scores of those who enrolled were as follows: Verbal—79% scored below 500, 18% between 500 and 599, 3% between 600 and 700, and 0% above 700; Math—72% scored below 500, 23% between 500 and 599, 4% between 600 and 700, and 1% above 700. Also considered important are advanced placement or honors courses, leadership record, and recommendations. Applicants should have a 2.0 GPA and should rank in the upper half of their class.

Procedure: The SAT and an interview are required; ATs are recommended. Deadlines are open; notification is on a rolling basis. New students are admitted to both semesters. There is a $20 application fee.

Special: There are early decision, early admissions, and deferred admissions plans. AP credit is accepted.

Transfer: For fall 1981, 36 students applied, 25 were accepted, and 25 enrolled. D grades do not transfer. Two years must be completed in residence. All students must complete, at the college, 64 of the 132 credits required for a bachelor's degree. Deadlines are open; transfer students are admitted to both semesters.

Visiting: There is an open house every November. Informal campus tours can be arranged. Visitors may sit in on classes and stay at the school.

Financial Aid: About 65% of all students receive financial aid. Twenty-three percent work part-time on campus. The college offers scholarships, federal grants (PELL), federal loans (NDSL), and work-study (CWS). Need is the determining factor. The FAF should be filed by February 15. The college belongs to CSS.

Foreign Students: Five percent of the full-time students come from foreign countries. An intensive English course, special counseling, and special organizations are available for these students.

Admissions: Foreign students must achieve a TOEFL score of at least 500 and must take the college's English proficiency exam. No college entrance exams are required.

Procedure: Application deadlines are 6 months prior to the beginning of either semester. Foreign students must complete a health form and must present proof of funds adequate to cover 1 year of study. Health insurance is required and is available through the college for a fee.

Admissions Contact: Tina Segalla, Director of Admissions.

FITCHBURG STATE COLLEGE C-2
Fitchburg, Massachusetts 01420 (617) 345-2151

F/T: 1396M, 2260W	Faculty: 225; IIA, av$
P/T: 1470M, 1242W	Ph.D.'s: 60%
Grad: 310M, 574W	S/F Ratio: 16 to 1
Year: sems, ss	Tuition: $910 ($2683)
Appl: Mar. 1	R and B: $1928
8243 applied	3986 accepted	913 enrolled
SAT: 426V 463M		COMPETITIVE+

Fitchburg State College, founded in 1894, is a state-supported institution offering degree programs in the liberal arts and sciences, business, education, nursing and the health professions, and social work. The library contains 150,000 volumes and 110,000 microfilm items, and subscribes to 2200 periodicals.

Environment: The 90-acre urban campus is 45 miles from Boston. There are 3 residence halls; 33 off-campus apartments are also available.

Student Life: About 98% of the students come from Massachusetts; two-thirds of the students commute. Thirty percent live on campus. Eight percent are minority-group members. Campus housing is both coed and single-sex; there are visiting privileges in the single-sex housing. Students may keep cars on campus.

Organizations: Extracurricular activities include clubs, publications, campus government, religious and service groups, and social and cultural events.

Sports: The college fields 8 intercollegiate teams for men and 5 for women. There are 2 intramural sports for men and 1 for women.

Handicapped: The campus is 80% accessible to students with physical handicaps. Wheelchair ramps, elevators, special parking and rest rooms, lowered drinking fountains and telephones, and special class scheduling are offered. Less than 1% of the students currently enrolled have hearing or visual impairments.

Graduates: Ten percent of the freshmen drop out; 60% remain to graduate. Twenty-five percent go on to graduate study: 1% to medical school, 1% to dental school, and 2% to law school. Ten percent enter business and industry.

Services: Career counseling and remedial instruction are offered without charge. Health care, placement, and tutoring are provided on a fee basis.

Programs of Study: The B.A., B.S., and B.S.Ed. degrees are conferred. Master's degrees are also awarded. Bachelor's degrees are offered in the following subjects: BUSINESS (accounting, labor relations, management, marketing), EDUCATION (early childhood, elementary, industrial, secondary, special), ENGLISH (English, journalism), HEALTH SCIENCES (medical technology, nursing), MATH AND SCIENCES (biology, chemistry, ecology/environmental science, mathematics), PREPROFESSIONAL (law, medicine, social work, veterinary), SOCIAL SCIENCES (geography, history, psychology, sociology). About 40% of degrees conferred are in education and 18% in the health sciences.

Required: There is a distribution requirement that includes course work in English composition.

Honors: There are 4 honorary societies on campus.

Admissions: Forty-eight percent of those who applied were accepted for the 1981-82 freshman class. The SAT scores of those who enrolled were as follows: Verbal—81% scored below 500, 18% between 500 and 599, 0% between 600 and 700, and 0% above 700; Math—63% scored below 500, 31% between 500 and 599, 6% between 600 and 700, and 0% above 700. Applicants should rank in the upper half of their class and have a GPA of at least 2.0. Advanced placement or honors courses, special talent, and recommendations are also considered important.

Procedure: The SAT or ACT is required. The application deadline is March 1; notification is on a rolling basis. Freshmen are admitted to both semesters. There is an $18 fee.

Special: CLEP and AP credit is accepted.

Transfer: About 280 transfer students enroll each year. A 2.0 GPA is required. All students must complete, at the college, 30 of the 120-128 credits required for a bachelor's degree. The application deadlines are April 1 (fall) and December 1 (spring).

Visiting: There is an orientation program for prospective applicants. Informal campus tours may be arranged; visitors may sit in on classes.

Financial Aid: About 60% of all students receive financial aid. Eighteen percent work part-time on campus. The average freshman award is $1273. The college offers federal/state grants (BEOG, SEOG), loans (NDSL and bank), local scholarships, CWS, and part-time employment. Aid is determined by need and academic merit. The FAF should be filed by April 15 (fall entry) or December 1 (spring entry). The college is a member of CSS.

Foreign Students: Fewer than 1% of the full-time students come from foreign countries.

Admissions: Foreign students must achieve a score of at least 500 on the TOEFL and must take the SAT.

Procedure: The application deadline is March 1 for fall entry. Foreign students must complete a college health form and must present proof

MASSACHUSETTS

of funds adequate to cover 4 years of study. Out-of-state tuition rates apply. Health insurance is available through the college for a fee.

Admissions Contact: Joseph A. Angelini, Director of Admissions.

FRAMINGHAM STATE COLLEGE D-2
Framingham, Massachusetts 01701 (617) 620-1220

F/T: 1026M, 2019W	Faculty: 157; IIA, av$
P/T: 128, 330W	Ph.D.'s: 70%
Grad: 150M, 376W	S/F Ratio: 20 to 1
Year: sems	Tuition: $975 ($2788)
Appl: Mar. 1	R and B: $1517
5633 applied 3826 accepted 888 enrolled	
SAT: 423V 455M	COMPETITIVE

Framingham State College, established in 1839, is a state-supported institution offering undergraduate degree programs in the liberal arts and sciences, business, education, and home economics. The library contains 200,000 volumes and 70,000 microfilm items, and subscribes to 962 periodicals.

Environment: The 40-acre suburban campus is 20 miles from Boston. There are 16 buildings, including 6 dormitories housing 1450 students. Facilities are also available for commuting students.

Student Life: About 98% of the students come from Massachusetts; 45% live on campus. Four percent are minority-group members. Campus housing is both coed and single-sex. Students may keep cars on campus. Day-care services are available to all students for a fee.

Organizations: There are no fraternities or sororities. About 40 extracurricular activities are sponsored by the college. Student government, dramatics, publications, and the campus radio station are the most popular.

Sports: The college fields 5 intercollegiate teams for men and 5 for women. There are 6 intramural sports for men and 5 for women.

Handicapped: The campus is about 60% accessible to physically handicapped students. Special facilities include wheelchair ramps, elevators, and special parking and rest rooms.

Graduates: About 50% of the entering freshmen remain to graduate. Of these, 30% go on to graduate study (1% enter law school) and 40% pursue careers in business and industry.

Services: Career counseling, tutoring, remedial instruction, psychological counseling, health care, and placement are offered free of charge.

Programs of Study: The B.A., B.S., and B.S.Ed. degrees are conferred. Master's degrees are also awarded. Bachelor's degrees are offered in the following subjects: BUSINESS (computer science), EDUCATION (early childhood, elementary), ENGLISH (English), FINE AND PERFORMING ARTS (art history, media communications, studio art), HEALTH SCIENCES (dietetics, food and nutrition, medical technology), LANGUAGES (French, Spanish), MATH AND SCIENCES (biology, chemistry, earth science, food science, mathematics), PHILOSOPHY (liberal studies, philosophy), PREPROFESSIONAL (clothing and textiles, home economics), SOCIAL SCIENCES (economics, geography, government/political science, history, psychology, sociology). About 30% of degrees conferred are in preprofessional programs, 27% in social sciences, and 20% in education.

Required: There is a general education requirement of 12 courses.

Special: Independent study, study abroad, internships, and student-designed majors are offered. The Alternative for Individual Development (AID) program offers an opportunity for a college degree to students who are culturally, educationally, or economically disadvantaged.

Honors: There are 7 honor societies; an honors program is also offered.

Admissions: About 68% of those who applied were accepted for the 1981–82 freshman class. The SAT scores of those who enrolled were as follows: Verbal—88% scored below 500, 11% between 500 and 599, 1% between 600 and 700, and 0% above 700; Math—73% scored below 500, 23% between 500 and 599, 4% between 600 and 700, and 0% above 700. Applicants should rank in the upper half of their class and should have a GPA of at least 2.0. Advanced placement or honors courses, recommendations, and leadership record are also considered important.

Procedure: Deadlines for applications are March 1 (fall) and December 1 (spring). Notification is on a rolling basis. There is an $18 application fee. All students must take the SAT.

Special: There are early admissions and deferred admissions plans. AP and CLEP credit is accepted.

Transfer: For fall 1981, 1188 students applied, 672 were accepted, and 339 enrolled. A 2.0 GPA and good academic standing at the previous institution are required; D grades do not transfer. All students must complete, at the college, 8 of the 32 credits required for a bachelor's degree. Application deadlines are April 1 (fall) and December 1 (spring).

Visiting: Informal campus tours with student guides may be arranged; visitors may sit in on classes. Information sessions followed by a tour of the campus are held Fridays at 10 A.M. in the fall.

Financial Aid: About 47% of all students receive financial aid. Twelve percent work part-time on campus. The college offers some freshman scholarships. There are federal (NDSL) loans, government grants, and work contracts (CWS). The average freshman award is $1600. Aid is determined according to need. The FAF must be filed by April 15 (fall) or November 15 (spring). The college is a member of CSS.

Foreign Students: Fewer than 1% of the full-time students come from foreign countries. An intensive English course and special counseling are available for these students.

Admissions: Foreign students must take the TOEFL and the SAT.

Procedure: The application deadline for fall entry is March 1. Foreign students must present proof of health and of adequate funds. Health insurance is required and is available through the college for a fee.

Admissions Contact: Philip M. Dooher, Director of Admissions.

GORDON COLLEGE E-2
Wenham, Massachusetts 01984 (617) 927-2300

F/T: 492M, 601W	Faculty: 53; IIB, +$
P/T: 18M, 14W	Ph.D.'s: 85%
Grad: none	S/F Ratio: 18 to 1
Year: tri	Tuition: $4605
Appl: open	R and B: $2175
960 applied 720 accepted 300 enrolled	
SAT or ACT: required	COMPETITIVE

Gordon College, founded in 1889, is a private liberal arts institution committed to the evangelical Protestant position and offering a distinctively Christian education. Its library has 153,000 books and 17,000 microtexts, and subscribes to 637 periodicals.

Environment: The 800-acre suburban campus on historic Cape Ann is 25 miles northeast of Boston. There are 22 major buildings, including dormitories for 770 men and women.

Student Life: About 56% of the students are from New England; 32% are from the Mid-Atlantic region. Ninety percent come from public schools. Seventy-five percent live on campus. Almost all students are Protestant; chapel service is mandatory 3 times a week. Four percent of the students are minority-group members. Dormitories are both coed and single-sex; there are visiting privileges in the single-sex dorms. Students may keep cars on campus.

Organizations: There are no sororities or fraternities. Religious organizations, clubs, student government, publications, and cultural/social events are offered. The campus is within easy access of Boston and its resources and of the recreational opportunities offered by nearby ski areas and the Atlantic Ocean.

Sports: The college fields 5 intercollegiate teams for men and 5 for women. There are 5 intramural sports for men and 5 for women.

Handicapped: About 50% of the campus is accessible to the physically handicapped. Wheelchair ramps are provided. Special class scheduling can be arranged. At present, there are no students with visual or hearing impairments.

Services: Placement services, career counseling, tutoring, health care, and psychological counseling are provided at no additional charge.

Programs of Study: The B.A., B.S., B.Mus., and B.Mus.Ed. degrees are conferred. Bachelor's degrees are offered in the following subjects: AREA STUDIES (American), BUSINESS (business administration, economics), EDUCATION (early childhood, elementary), ENGLISH (English), FINE AND PERFORMING ARTS (music, music education), LANGUAGES (French, German, Spanish), MATH AND SCIENCES (mathematics), PHILOSOPHY (philosophy), PREPROFESSIONAL (law, medicine, ministry), SOCIAL SCIENCES (government/political science, history, psychology, sociology).

Required: A core curriculum includes course work in the Bible.

Special: Special programs include the Institute of Holy Land Studies, a Washington internship, a 10-week European seminar, and a 3-2 engineering program with Worcester Polytechnic Institute.

MASSACHUSETTS 363

Honors: There are chapters of 3 national honor societies on campus. Honors work is offered in all departments.

Admissions: About 75% of the 1981-82 freshman applicants were accepted. A high school diploma is required. Fifteen units of high school work are necessary for admission. Christian experience and academic records are the most important admissions factors.

Procedure: The SAT or ACT should be taken by March of the senior year. There are no application deadlines; freshmen are admitted to the fall, winter, and spring terms. Admission and notification are on a rolling basis. There is a $25 application fee.

Special: AP and CLEP credit is granted. There are early decision, early admissions, and deferred admissions plans. The notification date for early decision is February 1.

Transfer: Over 100 students are admitted each year. A minimum average of C is necessary; D grades do not transfer. Forty-eight credits are required for a bachelor's degree. Deadlines are open; transfer students are admitted to the fall, winter, and spring terms.

Visiting: There is an orientation program for prospective students. Informal guided campus visits may be arranged. Students can attend classes and stay at the school. For further information, the admissions office should be contacted.

Financial Aid: About 80% of the students receive aid in the form of scholarships, grants, loans, and campus employment (including CWS). About 75% work part-time on campus. Need is the determining factor. The aid application, the financial aid transcript from the previous school, and the FAF or FFS should be filed by March 15.

Foreign Students: The college accepts applications from foreign students. No special services are available for these students.

Admissions: Foreign students must take the TOEFL; no college entrance exams are required.

Procedure: There are no application deadlines; foreign students are admitted to the fall, winter, and spring terms. They must present proof of health and of adequate funds.

Admissions Contact: David Macmillan, Dean of Admissions and Financial Aid.

HAMPSHIRE COLLEGE
Amherst, Massachusetts 01002   B-2   (413) 549-4600

F/T: 558M, 682W
P/T: none
Grad: none
Year: 4-1-4
Appl: Feb. 15
868 applied
SAT: 556V 542M

Faculty: 105; IIB, ++$
Ph.D.'s: 71%
S/F Ratio: 14 to 1
Tuition: $7450
R and B: $2425
665 accepted   315 enrolled
VERY COMPETITIVE

Hampshire College, founded in 1965, is an independent liberal arts college that offers an innovative undergraduate curriculum. Its library has 65,000 books and 3400 microtexts, subscribes to 575 periodicals, and is a member of the Five-College Consortium, giving students access to a total of 3.2 million volumes.

Environment: The 550-acre campus is located in a rural area 20 miles from Springfield. There are 28 buildings, including 2 dormitories and 3 apartment complexes.

Student Life: About 35% of the students are from New England, and 38% are from the Middle Atlantic states. Ninety percent live on campus. About 73% come from public schools. Eight percent are minority-group members. Campus housing is both coed and single-sex; there are visiting privileges in the single-sex housing. Students may keep cars on campus. Day-care services are available to students for a fee.

Organizations: There are no sororities or fraternities. Extracurricular activities are numerous and traditional; there is a full social and cultural calendar, including shared events with other members of a five-college consortium. The college sponsors an Outdoors Program and a program of recreational athletics as alternatives to compulsory physical education and to intercollegiate competition. The Outdoors Program sponsors activities such as kayaking, rock-climbing, and wilderness trips.

Sports: There are no intercollegiate sports. There are 13 intramural sports for men and 13 for women.

Handicapped: Special facilities for physically handicapped students include wheelchair ramps, parking areas, elevators, lowered telephones, and specially equipped rest rooms. Guides are available for the visually impaired, interpreters for the hearing-impaired.

Graduates: About 10% of entering freshmen drop out by the end of the first year; 55% remain to graduate. About 65% of the graduates pursue further education: 5% go to medical school and 5% to law school. About 20% enter business and industry.

Services: Career counseling, tutoring, and remedial instruction are provided without charge. An Options Office informs students of job and internship opportunities but does not offer placement service. Health care and psychological counseling are available for a fee.

Programs of Study: The college confers the B.A. degree. Students design individualized "areas of concentration" from subject areas offered through the 4 interdisciplinary schools: Humanities and Arts (American studies, art, cultural history, dance, design, film, Hispanic-American literature, history, literature, music, philosophy, philosophy of religion, photography, studio arts, theater arts, writing), Language and Communication (anthropology, communications, communication technology, computer science, education, journalism, linguistics, mass communications, mathematics, philosophy, psychology, television), Natural Science (agriculture, astronomy, biology, botany, chemistry, geology, history and philosophy of science, mathematics, physics, science and public policy, science education, statistics, zoology), Social Science (anthropology, economics, education, history, law, political science, psychology, sociology), and Cross-School programs (American studies, Black studies, development and underdevelopment—African, Latin American, and Asian studies, education and child studies, environmental studies, health care and society, mathematics, statistics and computer science, philosophy, psychology, women's studies).

Required: Students must complete 3 divisions in order to graduate: Division I tests learning competence in each of the 4 schools (Humanities and Arts, Language and Communication, Natural Science, and Social Science); Division II emphasizes the student's area of concentration; Division III requires an independent study project on the scale of a thesis.

Special: Neither students nor faculty at Hampshire are organized along strict departmental and disciplinary lines. Students pursue individually designed interdisciplinary concentrations. There are no specific course requirements. No grades are given; written evaluations are provided upon request. Since Hampshire is a member of the Five-College Consortium (with Amherst, Mount Holyoke, Smith, and the University of Massachusetts), its students may take courses, without additional cost, at any other institution in the consortium.

Admissions: About 77% of those who applied were accepted for the 1981-82 freshman class. The SAT scores of those who enrolled were as follows: Verbal—26% below 500, 38% between 500 and 599, 27% between 600 and 700, and 9% above 700; Math—30% below 500, 40% between 500 and 599, 24% between 600 and 700, and 6% above 700. There are no formal admission requirements. Important factors include the applicant's personality, impressions made during an interview, and special talents.

Procedure: February 15 is the fall semester application deadline; December 1, the spring. The SAT or ACT is optional. The CRDA is observed. There is a $30 application fee, which is waived for financial aid applicants.

Special: There are early decision (notification date, December 15), early admissions (application deadline, February 15), and deferred admissions plans.

Transfer: About 100 transfer students enroll each year. Previously earned credits do not transfer directly; rather, transfer students submit tangible evidence of their learning competence for Division I examinations, and incorporate appropriate previous learning in their Division II concentrations. Application deadlines are the same as those for freshmen.

Visiting: Regularly scheduled orientations for prospective students include interviews and tours. Guides are provided for informal visits on Monday through Friday, and Saturday mornings when school is in session. Visitors may sit in on classes and stay overnight at the college. For further information, the admissions office should be contacted.

Financial Aid: About 35% of the students receive aid through the college. About 40% work part-time on campus. The average freshman award is $6900. The college is a member of CSS. The FAF should be submitted by February 15 (fall) or December 1 (spring).

Foreign Students: About 1% of the students come from foreign countries. Special counseling is available for these students.

Admissions: Foreign students must take an English proficiency exam. No college entrance exams are required.

Procedure: Application deadlines are the same as those for other students. Foreign students must present proof of funds adequate to cover the entire period of study and must carry health insurance, which is available through the college for a fee.

Admissions Contact: Robert de Veer, Director of Admissions.

HARVARD UNIVERSITY/HARVARD AND RADCLIFFE COLLEGES

D-2

Cambridge, Massachusetts 02138   (617) 495-1551

F/T: 4062M, 2434W	Faculty: 568; I, ++$
P/T: 2746M, 4882W	Ph.D.'s: 100%
Grad: 5949M, 3166W	S/F Ratio: 11 to 1
Year: sems, ss	Tuition: $7490
Appl: Jan. 1	R and B: $3050
13,513 applied 2164 accepted 1597 enrolled	
SAT: 650V 650M	**MOST COMPETITIVE**

Harvard University, an independent institution founded in 1636, is one of the world's most prestigious universities. It is made up of the undergraduate colleges, Harvard and Radcliffe; 10 professional schools of business administration, dentistry, design, divinity, education, law, medicine, public administration, and public health; and the Graduate School of Arts and Sciences. The university library system, the largest in the world, contains 10.2 million volumes and 2 million microform items, and subscribes to 100,000 periodicals. Each undergraduate house has a library of about 12,000 volumes. Hilles and Lamont (the undergraduate libraries) contain 363,739 volumes.

Environment: The campus is located just across the Charles River from Boston. Its architecture spans 3 centuries from Puritan New England to 20th-century modernism. A number of buildings are listed in the "National Register of Historic Places." Harvard's famous museums include the Fogg Museum of Art, the Busch-Reisinger Museum of Scandinavian and Germanic Art, and the Botanical Museum. There are 40 acres of athletic fields, and recently constructed facilities include a pool, a hockey center, and a track and tennis building. The university also owns an experimental forest in New York State, a center for the study of the Italian Renaissance in Italy, and a center for Byzantine studies in Washington, D.C. Living facilities include dormitories (for freshmen), married student housing, and the "House Plan" for upperclassmen.

Student Life: Harvard enrolls students from every state and territory and from 45 foreign countries. The diversity is not only geographical; students represent every race and major religious group; every social, economic, and occupational background; farm, small town, city, and suburb. About 69% of the 1981–82 freshmen were graduates of public schools. About 94% of the students live on campus. Nineteen percent are minority-group members. Campus housing is coed. Cars are permitted on campus.

Students live according to a House Plan that is Harvard's way of securing the advantages of a small college within a large university. All freshmen live together as a class in the dormitories. As sophomores, they move into one of the 13 Houses, each of which is a self-contained community of about 350 students and faculty members. Classroom instruction and some extracurricular activities cut across House lines, but for the last 3 years each student lives, eats, works, and is tutored in the House. All Houses and almost all campus and academic activities are coeducational.

Organizations: The House is the center of most undergraduate social, athletic, and extracurricular life. There are no fraternities or sororities. Extracurricular activities include music, drama, debating, and publications. Places of worship for all faiths are available on campus and in Cambridge. Students participate in university government through the Freshman Council and joint student-faculty-administration committees. The cultural and recreational offerings of Boston are 8 minutes away by subway.

Sports: The university fields teams in 20 intercollegiate sports for men and 18 for women. There are 24 intramural sports for men and 22 for women.

Handicapped: All essential buildings are accessible to physically handicapped students. Special facilities include wheelchair ramps, parking areas, elevators, specially equipped rest rooms, lowered drinking fountains, amplified emergency telephones, transportation, and an equipment repair service. For students with impaired vision or hearing, the university provides readers, tutors, speech therapy, a transcription service, videotapes, mobility orientation, interpreters, and total communication classes. Every school or academic division has a coordinator for handicapped services. Special academic and psychological counseling also are available, and 2 coordinators are attached to the university president's office.

Graduates: Fewer than 1% of entering freshmen drop out by the end of the first year; over 98% remain to graduate. Ninety-five percent of the graduates pursue advanced degrees: 14% in medicine and 19% in law. Eighteen percent enter business and industry.

Services: Placement and career and psychological counseling are provided free of charge. Health care, tutoring, and remedial instruction are provided on a fee basis. Placement services also are available to alumni, and the university has a special student employment office for those seeking term-time employment.

Programs of Study: The university awards the A.B. and S.B. degrees. Master's and doctoral degrees also are available. Bachelor's degrees are offered in the following subjects: AREA STUDIES (American, Asian, Black/Afro-American, general European, Middle Eastern, Russian), ENGLISH (classics, creative writing, English, folklore and mythology, linguistics, literature), FINE AND PERFORMING ARTS (art, art history, music, musicology), LANGUAGES (Chinese, French, German, Greek/Latin, Hebrew, Italian, Japanese, Portuguese, Russian, Spanish), MATH AND SCIENCES (applied mathematics, astronomy, biochemistry, bioelectricity, biology, chemistry, engineering science, geology, geophysics, mathematics, physical sciences, physics, statistics), PHILOSOPHY (classics, humanities, philosophy, religion), PRE-PROFESSIONAL (engineering), SOCIAL SCIENCES (anthropology, economics, government/political science, history, psychology, social sciences, sociology). Fifty-four percent of the undergraduate degrees are conferred in social sciences and 26% in math and sciences.

Required: The basic unit of study is a half-course, and 32 or more are required for graduation. Students must take 1 half-course in expository writing; 2 each (including 4 core courses) from the natural science, social science, and humanities areas; and 4 more from outside the major. Students also must meet a mathematics requirement. The foreign language requirement may be met by earning a score of at least 560 on an AT or by passing a college course at the required level.

Special: The university is adding to its core curriculum, which currently includes nearly 100 courses. The courses deal with central themes and modes of thought deemed essential to a liberal education. The courses, which are interdisciplinary, fall into 5 major areas: literature and the arts, historical study, social analysis and moral reasoning, science, and foreign cultures.

Freshmen may take small-group laboratory workshops or seminars with senior faculty members. Students may register for part or all of their studies in terms of time rather than formal courses, giving them greater freedom for individual work. Students may design their own majors and spend a year abroad. The university emphasizes independent study, individual tutorials, and honors programs. All undergraduates are assigned an adviser.

Honors: Qualified students may join Phi Beta Kappa. Departmental honors programs are offered in history and literature, history and science, social studies, comparative religion, chemistry and physics, and applied mathematics.

Admissions: Sixteen percent of those who applied for the 1981–82 freshman class were accepted. Admissions officers give great weight to factors such as special talents, recommendations by school officials, personality, and advanced placement or honors courses. Rank in class and SAT scores are not considered too important, but about 80% of those admitted score 600 or higher on each part, and most successful applicants rank in the top 10% of their class. The university strives to enroll a class with diverse geographical and personal backgrounds.

Procedure: Students must take the SAT and 3 ATs, preferably in December or January of their senior year. Early Action Program (early decision) candidates should apply by November 1 for fall admission; regular candidates by January 1. Applicants are notified in mid-April, and the university subscribes to the CRDA. Candidates are interviewed in their home states by Harvard or Radcliffe graduates working with admissions officers. The application fee is $25.

Transfer: A very limited number of transfer students are admitted each year. Applicants must have outstanding academic credentials. The SAT is required. Students must study at the university for at least 2 years; 128 credits are required for a bachelor's degree. The application deadline is February 15 for fall entry.

Visiting: Group information sessions for prospective students are scheduled at 10 A.M. and 2 P.M. on weekdays and at 9:30 A.M. and 11:30 A.M. on Saturdays from October through mid-December. Tours also are given twice a day on weekdays and once a day on Saturdays (October to mid-December only). Visitors may sit in on classes, and high school seniors may be overnight guests of students. Visits should be scheduled for October through April when school is in session. Summer schedules differ. The undergraduate admissions council should be contacted through the admissions office for arrangements.

Financial Aid: About 40% of the college students receive scholarships. About 75% work part-time on campus. The average freshman award is $4890. The Admissions and Scholarships Committee follows CSS policies in making awards. If need continues, scholarships are renewed annually. Loans of up to $1500 per year (more in exceptional cases) are available from the university, NDSL, and local banks. The loans remain interest-free until the student graduates. About $1,421,460 in college funds was lent to undergraduates in 1980–81. Sixty-five percent of the freshmen have term-time jobs and earn an average of $750 per year. Jobs and loans are not restricted to scholarship holders,

HELLENIC COLLEGE AND HOLY CROSS GREEK ORTHODOX SCHOOL OF THEOLOGY

D-2

Brookline, Massachusetts 02146   (617) 731-3500

F/T: 93M, 56W   Faculty: 23; n/av
P/T: 5M, 5W   Ph.D.'s: 65%
Grad: 93M, 6W   S/F Ratio: 11 to 1
Year: sems, ss   Tuition: $3025
Appl: May 1   R and B: $1700
64 applied   53 accepted   30 enrolled
SAT: 399V 423M   **LESS COMPETITIVE**

Hellenic College, founded in 1937 as Holy Cross Greek Orthodox School of Theology, is a liberal arts and professional college. It is the only Orthodox Christian college and school of theology in the western hemisphere. Its library contains 80,000 volumes and subscribes to 430 periodicals.

Environment: The 52-acre campus is located in a suburb of Boston. There are 10 main buildings, including a new 6-unit dormitory complex and the Maliotis Cultural Center, with its 400-seat auditorium.

Student Life: About 51% of the students are from out of state. Twenty-two percent of entering freshmen attended public schools. Approximately 95% live on campus. The majority of students are Greek Orthodox; daily chapel attendance is required of them. Dormitories are single-sex; there are no visiting privileges. Only upperclassmen may have cars.

Organizations: No fraternities or sororities are represented on campus. An active student government provides social and cultural entertainment on campus. There are several religious organizations. Boston, Cape Cod, and nearby ski areas offer a wealth of leisure activities.

Sports: The college fields 3 intercollegiate teams for men and 2 for women. There are 6 intramural sports for men and 5 for women.

Handicapped: There are no facilities for the handicapped, and there are none enrolled.

Graduates: About 8% of the freshmen drop out after the first year; 55% remain to graduate. Of these, 65% continue their education.

Services: Free tutoring, career counseling, and psychological counseling are available to students. Health care is provided on a fee basis.

Programs of Study: All undergraduate programs lead to the B.A. degree. Master's degrees are also offered. Bachelor's degrees are offered in the following subjects: AREA STUDIES (Greek), BUSINESS (management), EDUCATION (education and parish service), ENGLISH (communication), LANGUAGES (Greek/Latin), PHILOSOPHY (philosophy, religion), SOCIAL SCIENCES (human development).

Admissions: About 83% of those who applied for the 1981-82 freshman class were accepted. The candidate should have completed 15 Carnegie units in an accredited high school and have at least a C average. The reputation of the high school is important. Recommendations, advanced placement and honors courses, personality, and impressions made during the interview are also important criteria. Children of alumni are given some preference.

Procedure: The SAT or ACT is required and should be taken in December of the senior year. An interview is required. Application deadlines are May 1 for fall and December 1 for spring terms. There is a $25 application fee.

Transfer: For fall 1981, 22 students applied, 14 were accepted, and 14 enrolled. D grades do not transfer. A C average is necessary. Two years must be taken in residence. All students must complete, at the college, 65 of the 125 credits required for a bachelor's degree. Application deadlines are the same as those for freshmen.

Visiting: Guides are provided for informal visits. Visitors may observe classes and arrange to stay overnight at the school. The best time for such visits is in the fall. For further information, the admissions office should be contacted.

Financial Aid: About 90% of the students receive some form of financial aid. About 20% work part-time on campus. Federal and local bank loans are available. The deadline for financial aid applications is March 1. Tuition may be paid in installments. The college is a member of CSS and requires the FAF or FFS.

Foreign Students: About 31% of the full-time students come from foreign countries. An intensive English course, special counseling, and special organizations are available for these students.

Admissions: Foreign students must take the TOEFL. No college entrance exams are required.

Procedure: Application deadlines are the same as those for other students. Foreign students must complete a health form and must present proof of funds adequate to cover 4 years of study. Health insurance is required and is available through the college for a fee.

Admissions Contact: Reverend Athanasios Demos, Dean of Admissions.

HOLY CROSS COLLEGE

C-2

(Formerly College of the Holy Cross)
Worcester, Massachusetts 01610   (617) 793-2443

F/T: 1312M, 1182W   Faculty: 174; IIA, av$
P/T: 105M, 18W   Ph.D.'s: 81%
Grad: 3M, 1W   S/F Ratio: 14 to 1
Year: sems   Tuition: $5530
Appl: Feb. 1   R and B: $2650
4305 applied   1300 accepted   610 enrolled
SAT: 560V 600M   **HIGHLY COMPETITIVE**

Holy Cross College, established in 1843 and operated by the Jesuits of the Roman Catholic Church, offers undergraduate programs in the liberal arts and sciences and in business. Its library has 383,000 volumes and 2020 microfilm items, and subscribes to 2145 periodicals.

Environment: The 174-acre suburban campus is located 1 mile from downtown Worcester and 45 miles from Boston. There are 21 buildings, including 9 dormitories.

Student Life: About 48% of the students come from Massachusetts; 44% are from public schools. Seventy-three percent of the students reside on campus. Fewer than 1% are minority-group members. Dormitories are coed. Students may keep cars on campus. Religious-service attendance is not required.

Organizations: There are no sororities or fraternities. Religious groups, publications, dramatics, a film and lecture series, clubs, student government, and music groups are offered. Through a consortium arrangement, the facilities of 11 area colleges are available to Holy Cross students.

Sports: The college fields 15 intercollegiate teams for men and 15 for women. There are 6 intramural sports for men and 4 for women.

Handicapped: Special facilities for the physically handicapped include wheelchair ramps, parking areas, elevators, lowered drinking fountains and telephones, and specially equipped rest rooms. Special class scheduling can be arranged.

Graduates: The freshman dropout rate is 3%; about 80% remain to graduate. Of these, 84% go on for further education (5% to medical school, 1% to dental school, and 8% to law school), and 30% go into business and industry.

Services: Services available to students free of charge include placement, career counseling, and psychological counseling. Health care is provided on a fee basis.

Programs of Study: The B.A. is offered. Master's degrees are also awarded. Bachelor's degrees are offered in the following subjects: BUSINESS (accounting), ENGLISH (English), FINE AND PERFORMING ARTS (art history, music, studio art), LANGUAGES (French, German, Greek/Latin, Russian, Spanish), MATH AND SCIENCES (biology, chemistry, mathematics, physics), PHILOSOPHY (classics, humanities, philosophy, religion), PREPROFESSIONAL (dentistry, law, medicine), SOCIAL SCIENCES (economics, history, psychology, sociology). About 58% of the degrees are conferred in social sciences, 20% in math and sciences, and 12% in English.

MASSACHUSETTS

Special: There is a 3-2 engineering program with Worcester Polytechnic Institute. Study abroad is offered.

Honors: Four honor societies, including Phi Beta Kappa, have chapters on campus. Honors work is offered in all departments.

Admissions: About 30% of the 1981-82 freshman applicants were accepted. The SAT scores of those who enrolled were as follows: Verbal—22% scored below 500, 51% between 500 and 599, 24% between 600 and 700, and 3% above 700; Math—11% scored below 500, 46% between 500 and 599, 38% between 600 and 700, and 5% above 700. Candidates must be graduates of accredited high schools and present superior academic records and college-qualifying recommendations from school officials. Also considered important are advanced placement or honors courses, personality, and extracurricular activities.

Procedure: The SAT and 3 ATs (including English Composition) should be taken by January of the senior year. Freshmen are admitted only in the fall. The application deadline is February 1; admission and notification are on a rolling basis. There is a $25 application fee. An interview is recommended.

Special: AP credit is granted. There are early decision (notification date, December 15), early admissions (application deadline, February 1), and deferred admissions plans.

Transfer: For fall 1981, 172 applications were received, 42 were accepted, and 41 transfer students enrolled. Transfers are accepted for sophomore and junior classes. A 3.0 GPA is required; D grades are not accepted. There is a residency requirement of 2 years, including the senior year. Students must complete, at the college, 16 of the 32 semester courses required for a bachelor's degree. The application deadlines are May 1 (fall) and December 1 (spring).

Visiting: There are Saturday morning orientation programs for prospective students. Informal guided campus tours can be arranged. Visitors may sit in on classes and stay in the dormitories. To make arrangements, the admissions office should be contacted.

Financial Aid: About 71% of the students receive aid; 28% work part-time on campus. The college awards freshman scholarships each year from a fund of $240,000. Other aid is available in the form of federal and state loans and grants, and campus employment (including CWS). The average freshman award is $3180. Need, academic promise, and the applicant's character are the determining factors. The college's aid application and the FAF should be filed by February 1. Notification is given at the time of acceptance.

Foreign Students: Fewer than 1% of the full-time students come from foreign countries.

Admissions: Foreign students must take the TOEFL, the SAT, and 3 ATs (English Composition and 2 others).

Procedure: The application deadline for fall entry is February 1. Foreign students must present proof of funds adequate to cover 4 years of study.

Admissions Contact: James R. Halpin, Director of Admissions.

LESLEY COLLEGE   D-2
Cambridge, Massachusetts 02238   (617) 868-9600

F/T: 780W	Faculty:	63; n/av
P/T: none	Ph.D.'s:	30%
Grad: 300W, 2000M	S/F Ratio:	21 to 1
Year: sems	Tuition:	$4840
Appl: Mar. 1	R and B:	$2830
440 applied	325 accepted	170 enrolled
SAT: required		COMPETITIVE

Established in 1909, Lesley College is a private college offering undergraduate programs in education. The library contains 72,189 volumes and subscribes to 263 periodicals.

Environment: The 7-acre suburban campus is located 4 miles from Boston. There are 22 buildings on campus, including 4 independently operated private schools. Dormitories house 82% of the students.

Student Life: About 50% of the students come from Massachusetts; most have public school backgrounds. Eight percent are minority-group members. Eighty-two percent live on campus. Dormitories are single-sex; there are visiting privileges.

Organizations: There are no sororities. The college sees itself as a "laboratory for learning" and emphasizes student involvement in the community. Social and cultural events are regularly held on campus.

Sports: The college fields 2 intercollegiate teams for women. There are 3 intramural sports available to women.

Handicapped: About 75% of the campus is accessible to physically handicapped students. One counselor is assigned to these students. Special facilities (wheelchair ramps, elevators, special parking) and class scheduling are available.

Graduates: About 22% of freshmen drop out after the first year; 70% remain to graduate. Seven percent go on to graduate study.

Services: Career counseling, placement, tutoring, remedial instruction, and psychological counseling are provided free of charge. Health care is provided on a fee basis.

Programs of Study: The B.S.Ed. and B.S. in Elem. Ed. degrees are conferred. Master's degrees are also awarded. Bachelor's degrees are offered in the following subjects: EDUCATION (early childhood, elementary, middle school, special), SOCIAL SCIENCES (child and community).

Required: A core curriculum is required of all students.

Honors: Honors work is offered in 3 broad areas.

Admissions: About 74% of those who applied were accepted for the 1981-82 freshman class. An average of C is required. Impressions made during an interview, the applicant's personality, recommendations, and advanced placement or honors courses are also taken into consideration.

Procedure: The SAT and the AT in English are required. All students must have an interview. March 1 is the fall deadline; December 15, the spring deadline. Notification is on a rolling basis. There is a $25 application fee.

Special: AP and CLEP credit is accepted. There is a deferred admissions plan.

Transfer: For fall 1981, 120 students applied, 85 were accepted, and 58 enrolled. A GPA of at least 2.0 is required; D grades may transfer. There is a 2-year residency rule. All students must complete, at the college, 63 of the 128 credits required for a bachelor's degree. May 1 is the fall deadline; December 15, the spring deadline.

Visiting: Informal campus tours with student guides may be arranged. Visitors may sit in on classes.

Financial Aid: About 52% of all students receive financial aid. The college offers scholarships, loans, and campus employment, and participates in federal aid programs such as NDSL, SEOG, and CWS. The average freshman award is $2400. The college is a member of CSS. The FAF and supplement should be submitted by March 1.

Foreign Students: Fewer than 1% of the full-time students come from foreign countries. Special counseling and special organizations are available for these students.

Admissions: Foreign students must achieve a TOEFL score of at least 480 and must take the SAT.

Procedure: Application deadlines are March 1 (fall) and December 15 (spring). Foreign students must present proof of adequate funds.

Admissions Contact: Martha B. Ackerson, Director of Admissions.

MASSACHUSETTS COLLEGE OF ART   E-2
Boston, Massachusetts 02215   (617) 731-2340

F/T: 379M, 681W	Faculty:	46; IIA, av$
P/T: 13M, 25W	Ph.D.'s:	5%
Grad: 21M, 50W	S/F Ratio:	16 to 1
Year: sems, ss	Tuition:	$975 ($2608)
Appl: Apr. 15	R and B:	n/app
828 applied	249 accepted	144 enrolled
SAT: required		SPECIAL

The Massachusetts College of Art, organized in 1873, is a professional institution supported by the Commonwealth of Massachusetts. Its library has 60,000 books and over 1300 microfilm items, and subscribes to 350 periodicals.

Environment: The 2-building urban campus is located in the Back Bay section of Boston. There is no campus housing.

Student Life: About 80% of the students are from Massachusetts. All students commute. Most of the freshmen come from public schools. Six percent of the students are minority-group members.

Organizations: There are no fraternities or sororities; there is a small extracurricular program. Extensive cultural and recreational opportunities exist in the Boston area.

Sports: The college has no athletic program.

Handicapped: About 50% of the campus is accessible to students with physical handicaps. Special parking areas and elevators are provided. A signage tutor is provided for the hearing-impaired student.

Graduates: Ten percent of the entering freshmen drop out; 80% remain to graduate. Twelve percent go on for additional study, and 55% to 60% enter careers in business and industry.

Services: Career counseling, health care, tutoring, remedial instruction, and psychological counseling are available free of charge. Placement services are provided on a fee basis.

Programs of Study: The B.F.A. degree is conferred. Master's degrees are also awarded. Bachelor's degrees are offered in these major fields: FINE AND PERFORMING ARTS (art, art education, art history, film/photography, studio art), PREPROFESSIONAL (architecture).

Admissions: About 30% of the 1981–82 freshman applicants were accepted. The SAT scores of those who enrolled were as follows: Verbal—73% scored below 500, 20% between 500 and 599, 6% between 600 and 700, and 1% above 700; Math—72% scored below 500, 23% between 500 and 599, 5% between 600 and 700, and 1% above 700. The most important admissions criterion is the applicant's portfolio. Applicants must be high school graduates or have a GED diploma. The admissions committee also evaluates the student's potential as evidenced by the high school record, SAT scores, and the required essay. Preference is given to Massachusetts residents.

Procedure: The SAT is required. Freshmen are only admitted in the fall; April 15 is the application deadline. Admission and notification are on a rolling basis. The application fee is $28 for Massachusetts residents, $35 for others. The Massachusetts State College Application form is required. The art portfolio submitted should have at least 15 pieces of work.

Special: There is a deferred admissions plan. AP and CLEP credit is granted.

Transfer: For fall 1981, 569 applications were received, 270 were accepted, and 179 transfer students enrolled. D grades are not accepted. A portfolio must be submitted. State residents are given preference. Four semesters must be completed in residence. All students must complete, at the college, 64 of the 132 credits required for a bachelor's degree. April 15 is the fall deadline; November 15, the spring.

Visiting: There is an orientation program for prospective students. Guides are provided for informal campus visits, which may be arranged through the admissions office. The best times for such visits are October through December and February through May.

Financial Aid: About 38% of the applicants receive aid. Federal/state loans and grants are offered; no scholarships are available to freshmen. The FAF should be filed by May 1.

Foreign Students: No special services are available for these students.

Admissions: Foreign students must achieve a TOEFL score of at least 530 and must take the SAT.

Procedure: The application deadline for fall entry is March 1. Foreign students must present proof of funds adequate to cover 4 years of study. Health insurance is required and is available through the college.

Admissions Contact: K. Ransdell, Director of Admissions.

MASSACHUSETTS COLLEGE OF PHARMACY AND ALLIED HEALTH SCIENCES

E-2

Boston, Massachusetts 02115   (617) 732-2850

F/T: 553M, 451W   Faculty: n/av; IIB, +$
P/T: 46M, 20W   Ph.D.'s: 70%
Grad: 98M, 35W   S/F Ratio: 14 to 1
Year: qtrs, ss   Tuition: $4320
Appl: June 1   R and B: $3600
420 applied   371 accepted   160 enrolled
SAT: 430V 490M   COMPETITIVE

The Massachusetts College of Pharmacy and Allied Health Sciences was established in 1823 and today offers undergraduate and graduate preparation in pharmaceutical work and research as well as health fields. The library has 52,000 books and 150 microfilm items; it subscribes to 600 periodicals.

Environment: The 2-acre urban campus is located 1 mile from the center of Boston. Students are housed in dormitory facilities at nearby Emmanuel College. The college also has another campus at Springfield, Massachusetts.

Student Life: About 70% of the students come from Massachusetts, and 24% from other New England states. About 85% of the students commute. The dormitories are both coed and single-sex; there are visiting privileges in the single-sex dorms.

Organizations: Ten percent of the men and women belong to fraternities and sororities. Extracurricular activities include special interest clubs, service organizations, and various social and cultural events both on and off campus.

Sports: There are no intercollegiate teams. There are 4 intramural sports for men and 1 sport for women.

Handicapped: About 90% of the campus is accessible to students with physical handicaps. There are special facilities such as wheelchair ramps, parking areas, elevators, specially equipped rest rooms, and lowered telephones and drinking fountains. At present there are no visually impaired or hearing-impaired students.

Graduates: The freshman dropout rate is 20%; about 75% remain for the five years to complete the degree. Ten percent go on for further study: 2% enter medical school, 1% enter dental school, and 1% enter law school.

Services: Psychological counseling, health care, tutoring, career counseling, and placement services are offered without charge.

Programs of Study: The college confers the B.S.Pharm. and B.S. in C. degrees. Master's and doctoral degrees are also awarded. Bachelor's degrees are offered in the following subjects: MATH AND SCIENCES (chemistry), PREPROFESSIONAL (pharmacy). The B.S. in Pharmacy is a 5-year curriculum, including 2 preprofessional and 3 professional years.

Honors: There is one honor society on campus.

Admissions: About 88% of the 1981–82 applicants were accepted. A high school diploma with 15 Carnegie units and a C average is required. Recommendations are considered important. An interview is recommended.

Procedure: The SAT or ACT must be taken. June 1 is the fall term deadline; admission and notification are on a rolling basis. Freshmen are admitted in the winter and spring terms also. There is a $20 application fee.

Special: There are early decision, early admissions, and deferred admissions plans. CLEP subject exams and AP are used.

Transfer: For fall 1981, 254 students applied, 208 were accepted, and 124 enrolled. A cumulative C average is required; D grades do not transfer. Three years must be completed in residence.

Visiting: There is an orientation program for prospective applicants. Guides are provided for informal campus tours; visitors may sit in on classes. The best times to visit the school are Monday through Friday from 9 A.M. to 3 P.M. Arrangements can be made through the admissions office.

Financial Aid: About 48% of the students are receiving assistance in the form of scholarships, federal loans and grants, work contracts, or CWS. The average freshman award is $3700. Need is the determining factor. The FAF must be filed. The aid application is due March 1. The college is a member of CSS.

Foreign Students: Seventeen percent of the full-time students come from foreign countries. Special counseling and special organizations are available for these students.

Admissions: Foreign students must achieve a TOEFL score of at least 500 or, if English is their native language, must take the SAT.

Procedure: Application deadlines are June 1 (fall), September 1 (winter), and January 1 (spring). Foreign students must have a complete physical exam and must present proof of funds adequate to cover 1 year of study. Health insurance is required and is available through the college for a fee.

Admissions Contact: Ben Hershenson, Dean of Admissions.

MASSACHUSETTS INSTITUTE OF TECHNOLOGY

D-2

Cambridge, Massachusetts 02139   (617) 253-4791

F/T: 3549M, 951W   Faculty: 1294; I, ++$
P/T: 31M, 29W   Ph.D.'s: 90%
Grad: 3857M, 812W   S/F Ratio: 4 to 1
Year: 4-1-4, ss   Tuition: $7568
Appl: Jan. 1   R and B: $3200
5921 applied   1898 accepted   1031 enrolled
SAT: required   MOST COMPETITIVE

The Massachusetts Institute of Technology, founded in 1861, is a private, independent university and technical institution. Its library contains over 1.6 million volumes and an extensive microfilm collection, and subscribes to 18,000 periodicals.

Environment: The 125-acre urban campus is located 2 miles from downtown Boston and extends for more than a mile along the bank of the Charles River. Living facilities include dormitories, fraternity and sorority houses, on-campus and off-campus apartments, and housing for married students.

Student Life: About 81% of the students come from states outside New England, and 6% are from foreign countries. Most of the entering freshmen attended public schools. Eighty-five percent of the students live on campus. Twenty-eight percent are minority-group members. Campus housing is both coed and single-sex; there are visiting privileges in the single-sex housing. Students may keep cars on campus. Day-care services are available to all students on a fee basis.

Organizations: There are 31 independent living groups on campus and about 120 student-run activities; in addition, most students take advantage of Boston's social and cultural offerings.

Sports: The institute competes in 21 intercollegiate events for men and 11 for women. There are 21 intramural sports for men and 21 for women.

Graduates: Only 2% of the freshmen drop out after the first year. About 85% remain to graduate, and 57% of those enter graduate school immediately after graduation. About 8% enter medical schools, 5% law schools. Thirty-one percent enter business and industry.

Services: Free career counseling, placement services, tutoring, and remedial instruction are available to students. Health care is offered for a fee. Psychological counseling is available and sometimes requires payment.

Programs of Study: The B.S. degree is offered in 39 major fields. Master's and doctoral programs are also offered. Among the major fields in which bachelor's degrees are offered are the following: AREA STUDIES (urban), BUSINESS (management), MATH AND SCIENCES (biology, chemistry, earth science, life sciences, mathematics, planetary science, physics), PHILOSOPHY (humanities, philosophy), PRE-PROFESSIONAL (architecture, engineering—aeronautics and astronautics, engineering—chemical, engineering—civil, engineering—electrical engineering and computer science, engineering—materials, engineering—mechanical, engineering—nuclear, engineering—ocean, engineering—naval architecture and marine), SOCIAL SCIENCES (economics, government/political science). Almost half the degrees conferred are in engineering; 25% are in the sciences.

Required: All undergraduates must complete a core curriculum, of which 27% is in mathematics and physical or biological sciences and 20% in the humanities and social sciences. The freshman year is entirely pass/fail.

Special: Students may study abroad during their junior year. Work-study programs are available in engineering fields and in political science. Students may participate in research through the Undergrad Research Opportunities Program or may design their own majors. The ESG program provides an opportunity for self-paced study, and the Concourse program presents the entire curriculum in a unified manner.

Honors: There are chapters of professional and honor societies on campus. A departmental honors program is offered.

Admissions: Only 32% of those who applied were accepted for the 1981-82 freshman class. The SAT scores of those who enrolled were as follows: Verbal—6% scored below 500, 22% between 500 and 599, 52% between 600 and 699, and 20% at or above 700; Math—0% scored below 500, 3% between 500 and 599, 22% between 600 and 699, and 75% at or above 700. The candidate should have completed 16 Carnegie units at an accredited high school. The majority of students at MIT were in the top 10% of their high school class. Each applicant is studied as an individual case. Serious attention is given to the secondary school's evaluation of the candidate. Evidence of energy and leadership in curricular and extracurricular areas is also important.

Procedure: The SAT is required. Required ATs are (1) Math I or Math II, (2) English Composition or American or European History, and (3) Physics, Chemistry, or Biology. These tests should be taken in the junior year or by January of the senior year. Freshmen are admitted only to the fall session. Applications should be in by January 1 along with a $30 fee. The CRDA is observed. A personal interview is required.

Special: There is an early action plan; January 1 is the notification date. Early admissions applications must be filed by November 1. There is also a deferred admissions plan. AP credit is given.

Transfer: For fall 1981, 425 applications were received, 118 were accepted, and 82 transfer students enrolled. Transfers are accepted for the sophomore and junior years. D grades do not transfer. An 18-month residency rule is in effect. The institute requires 360 credits for a bachelor's degree. Application deadlines are April 1 (fall) and November 15 (winter).

Visiting: There are regularly scheduled orientations for prospective students. Tours are scheduled on weekdays at 10 A.M. or 2 P.M. Visitors can sit in on classes. For further information, the admissions office should be contacted.

Financial Aid: Almost 50% of the students receive some form of financial aid. Thirty percent of the undergraduates work part-time on campus. Part-time employment, scholarship aid, and loans (from federal government, the institute, and local bank funds) are available on the basis of need. The average amount given to freshmen is $5100. The aid application deadline is January 1; the FAF and the IRS 1040 form must also be submitted. The institute is a member of CSS.

Foreign Students: Six percent of the full-time students come from foreign countries. Special counseling and special organizations are available for these students.

Admissions: Foreign students must achieve a TOEFL score of at least 550 and must take a college entrance exam. They must also take 3 ATs (Math Level I or II and any 2 of the following: Biology, Chemistry, English, History, and Physics).

Procedure: The preliminary application is due November 15 and the final application is due January 1 for entry in the fall. Health insurance is required and is available through the institute for a fee.

Admissions Contact: Brenda L. Hambleton, Admissions Officer.

MASSACHUSETTS MARITIME ACADEMY E-4
Buzzards Bay, Massachusetts 02532   (617) 759-5761

F/T: 850M, 30W   Faculty: n/av; IIB, +$
P/T: none   Ph.D.'s: 14%
Grad: none   S/F Ratio: 15 to 1
Year: sems, ss   Tuition: $725
Appl: Mar. 1   R and B: $1987
1439 applied   314 accepted   250 enrolled
SAT: 449V 530M   COMPETITIVE+

The Massachusetts Maritime Academy, founded in 1891, is a state-controlled professional college that provides the necessary academic and professional background so that its graduates can qualify as officers in the U.S. Merchant Marine, the U.S. Coast Guard, or the U.S. Naval Reserve. The library contains over 42,000 volumes, 10,000 reels of microfilm, and 250 nautical charts, and subscribes to 330 periodicals.

Environment: The 55-acre campus is located in a small town, 60 miles from Boston. It is comprised of 7 buildings, including a dormitory for 876 students, and a training ship.

Student Life: About 85% of the students are from Massachusetts. All students are required to live on campus and subscribe to military discipline. Drinking on campus is forbidden; all students observe a curfew and follow a sign-out procedure.

Organizations: There are no fraternities or sororities on campus. The Academy sponsors several extracurricular activities, including special-interest clubs, service groups, and music organizations. The Cape Cod area offers a variety of cultural and recreational opportunities.

Sports: There are 9 intercollegiate teams and 15 intramural programs for men and 13 for women.

Handicapped: About 90% of the campus is accessible to the physically handicapped. Special facilities include lowered telephones and drinking fountains and specially equipped rest rooms. There are no hearing-impaired or visually impaired students enrolled.

Graduates: About 25% of entering freshmen drop out after the first year; 65% remain to graduate. Of these, 5% enter graduate schools and 95% pursue careers in business and industry.

Services: Free health care, tutoring, remedial instruction, career counseling, psychological counseling, and placement services are available to students. A full-time placement director assists undergraduates and alumni.

Programs of Study: The Academy confers the B.S. degree in marine engineering and in marine transportation.

Required: All undergraduates must take physical education, a freshman core curriculum, and NROTC.

Special: The Academy offers courses in oceanography, ocean engineering, and fisheries science. One quarter term (10 weeks) is spent each year at sea aboard the Academy's training ship, Bay State, cruising to foreign and domestic ports.

Admissions: Only 22% of those who applied were accepted for the 1981-82 freshman class. The minimum SAT scores acceptable are 400 verbal and 400 math. The candidates should have completed 16 Carnegie units at an accredited high school, with a minimum 2.0 GPA. Other important criteria include advanced placement or honors courses, leadership record, personality, and extracurricular activities record. The admissions quota for out-of-state students is 10% of the freshman class.

Procedure: The SAT is required and should be taken by December of the senior year. Freshmen are only admitted in the fall; the application deadline is March 1. Notification is sent by April. A personal interview is recommended. All applicants must have a physical examination. There is an $18 application fee. A rolling admissions plan is used.

Special: The Academy has an early admissions plan. AP and CLEP credit is granted.

Transfer: A limited number of transfers are accepted; only about 6 enroll annually. A 2.0 GPA is required. There is a 4-year residency requirement.

Visiting: Informal guided tours can be arranged during school hours through the director of admissions. Visitors may sit in on classes. During Open House week, formal guided tours are part of the agenda for prospective students.

Financial Aid: Eligible cadets may be awarded a $1200 per annum federal subsidy. About 75% of all cadets receive financial aid. Scholarship and need are the determining factors in awards. Tuition may be paid in installments. The Academy is a member of CSS and requires the FAF by June 1.

Admissions Contact: Commander Thomas S. Lee, Director of Admissions.

MERRIMACK COLLEGE   E-2
North Andover, Massachusetts 01845   (617) 683-7111

F/T: 1238M, 967W   Faculty: 122; IIB, +$
P/T: 734M, 926W   Ph.D.'s: 48%
Grad: none   S/F Ratio: 16 to 1
Year: sems, ss   Tuition: $4410
Appl: See profile   R and B: $2700
2400 applied   1300 accepted   515 enrolled
SAT: 465V 510M   COMPETITIVE

Merrimack College, established in 1947 by the Augustinian Fathers, is affiliated with the Roman Catholic Church. The major divisions are Humanities, Social Sciences, Science and Engineering, Business Administration, and Continuing Education. The library holds 91,300 volumes and 40 microfilm items, and subscribes to 900 periodicals.

Environment: The 220-acre campus is located in a suburban area 25 miles northwest of Boston, situated on a hill overlooking the countryside. The 16 major buildings include a chapel, a physical education center, a student union, and an infirmary. Dormitories house 650 students in double rooms and suites, and 14 townhouses accommodate 12 students each.

Student Life: About 90% of the students are Catholic, 8% are Protestant, and 1% are Jewish. The college exists primarily to train Catholic youth and follows Catholic principles in its educational policy. Seventy percent of the students come from Massachusetts. Fifty percent live on campus. Two percent are minority-group members. College housing is both single-sex and coed. There are visiting privileges in single-sex housing. Students may keep cars on campus.

Organizations: About 40% of the men belong to 1 of 6 local fraternities. Fifty women belong to a local sorority. Campus activities include orchestra, publications, drama, concerts, films, and lecture series. There are religious and community service activities for students of all faiths. Boston is within a half-hour drive, and several coastal and historic towns and New Hampshire's lakes and mountains also are within easy driving range.

Sports: The college fields varsity teams in 7 sports for men and 4 sports for women. There are 11 intramural sports for men and 7 for women.

Handicapped: About 90% of the campus is accessible to physically handicapped students. Special facilities include wheelchair ramps, parking areas, and elevators. Special class scheduling can be arranged. The college provides a counselor for the handicapped, with 2 assistants. At present, there are no students with visual or hearing impairments.

Graduates: About 7% of the students drop out by the end of freshman year; 75% remain to graduate. After graduation, 23% of the graduates pursue advanced degrees.

Services: The college offers its students free career, religious, and psychological counseling, health care, and tutoring. Free placement services are available to students and alumni.

Programs of Study: The college awards the B.A. and B.S. degrees. Associate degrees are also granted. Bachelor's degrees are offered in the following subjects: AREA STUDIES (American), BUSINESS (accounting, business economics, computer science, finance, management, marketing), EDUCATION (secondary), ENGLISH (English), HEALTH SCIENCES (health science, medical technology), MATH AND SCIENCES (biochemistry, biology, chemistry, mathematics), PHILOSOPHY (philosophy, religion), PREPROFESSIONAL (dentistry, engineering, law, medicine), SOCIAL SCIENCES (economics, government/political science, history, psychology, sociology). Thirty-nine percent of the degrees are granted in business, 26% in the social sciences, and 25% in math and sciences.

Required: All students must take courses in religious studies in addition to a general education curriculum.

Special: Students may earn 5-year combined B.A.-B.S. degrees in all major fields. The college also has 5-year cooperative degree programs in business administration, computer science, and civil or electrical engineering. The 4-year medical technology program includes 1 year of internship. Students may design their own majors and may study abroad.

Honors: Honors programs are available, and honor students may be elected to Phi Beta Kappa.

Admissions: The college accepted 54% of those who sought admission to the 1981-82 freshman class. The SAT scores of those who enrolled were as follows: Verbal—62% scored below 500, 33% between 500 and 599, 5% between 600 and 700, and 0% above 700; Math—46% scored below 500, 42% between 500 and 599, 11% between 600 and 700, and 1% above 700. Applicants must be graduates of accredited high schools and have completed 16 Carnegie units. They should rank in the top half of their high-school class and have a grade average of 2.0 or higher. Admissions officers also consider, in descending order, advanced placement or honors courses, extracurricular activities, recommendations by school officials, leadership potential, impressions made during a personal interview, and evidence of special talents. Children of alumni may receive some preference.

Procedure: All applicants must take the SAT or ACT by January of the senior year. Three ATs in English Composition, Mathematics, and an optional field are recommended. Application deadlines for the fall term are March 1 for students who plan to live on campus and June 3 for those who plan to commute. The application deadline for the spring term is December 15. The college uses the rolling admissions plan. Applicants are notified beginning February 15. New students are not admitted to the summer session. The application fee is $20.

Special: Early decision, early admissions, and deferred admissions plans are available. AP credit is granted.

Transfer: For fall 1981, 250 transfer students applied, 170 were accepted, and 95 enrolled. Transfers are accepted in sophomore and junior classes. A minimum average of 2.0 is required. D grades are not acceptable. Students must study at Merrimack at least 3 semesters. They must also complete, at the college, 45 of the 120 credits required for the bachelor's degree. The application deadlines are August 15 (fall) and December 15 (spring).

Visiting: An open house at which prospective students can meet with faculty members, financial aid officials, and current students is scheduled in November. Students are encouraged to visit the campus for an interview. Juniors may visit during the summer before the senior year; seniors in October, November, early December, and February through May. The admissions office should be contacted to arrange guides, class observation, and a place to stay on campus.

Financial Aid: Sixty percent of the students receive financial aid. Twenty-five percent work part-time on campus. The average aid to a freshman, from all sources, is $2000. The college awards a total of more than $1 million in scholarships and loans. Work-study aid also is available. Tuition remission is granted to children of faculty members, depending on tenure, and to members of various religious orders. There are 60 academic, 100 athletic, and 60 miscellaneous scholarships. The college is a member of CSS. The FAF and the college financial aid application should be filed. The application deadline is March 1 (fall). Applicants are notified of awards by April 30.

Foreign Students: One percent of the full-time students come from foreign countries.

370 MASSACHUSETTS

Admissions: Foreign students must score 500 on the TOEFL. No college entrance examination is required.

Procedure: The application deadlines are March 1 (fall) and December 15 (spring). Foreign students must present proof of health. They must also provide proof of adequate funds.

Admissions Contact: E. Joseph Lee, Dean of Admissions and Financial Aid.

MOUNT HOLYOKE COLLEGE B-3
South Hadley, Massachusetts 01075   (413) 538-2246

F/T: 1921W	Faculty: 171; IIB, ++$
P/T: 5W	Ph.D.'s: 80%
Grad: 13W	S/F Ratio: 11 to 1
Year: 4-1-4	Tuition: $6530
Appl: Feb. 1	R and B: $2870
2273 applied	1221 accepted 534 enrolled
SAT: 590V 590M	**HIGHLY COMPETITIVE**

Mount Holyoke College, an independent, nonsectarian liberal arts college and the oldest continuing institution of higher education for women in the United States, was founded in 1837. The library contains 461,000 volumes and 7869 microfilm items, and subscribes to 1720 periodicals.

Environment: The college is located in the Connecticut River Valley of western Massachusetts in a suburban setting 90 miles west of Boston. It is part of a consortium of 4 colleges and a university (Amherst, Hampshire, and Smith Colleges, and the University of Massachusetts) that share academic offerings and social and cultural events. About 30,000 students live and study within a radius of 10 miles. The 800-acre campus contains more than 40 major buildings, including 19 dormitories, each with a dining hall.

Student Life: About 23% of the students are from Massachusetts. About 75% attended public schools. Ninety-five percent of the students live on campus. Twenty-five percent are Catholic, 60% Protestant, and 10% Jewish; 5% belong to other denominations. Fifteen percent of the students are minority-group members. College housing is single-sex; there are visiting privileges. Students may keep cars on campus.

Organizations: Residence halls are the primary center of social activity on campus. Campus organizations sponsor popular concerts, craft fairs, and social functions. Student organizations include a variety of service and special-interest groups. Many cultural events are available at the college: lectures, concerts, art exhibitions, and dance programs. Two lakes, a golf course, riding trails, and tennis courts offer recreational opportunities on campus.

Sports: The college participates in 12 intercollegiate sports and offers 10 intramural sports.

Handicapped: Special facilities for the physically handicapped include wheelchair ramps, parking areas, elevators, specially equipped rest rooms, and curb cuts for wheelchairs. At present, fewer than 1% of the students have hearing impairments, and there are no students with visual impairments. There are no special counselors for handicapped students.

Graduates: No more than 3% of the students fail to return after the first year; 78% remain to graduate. Over 30% pursue graduate study. Six percent enter medical and dental schools; 7%, law schools. Over thirty-five percent pursue careers in business and industry.

Services: Students receive the following services free of charge: placement, psychological counseling, and career counseling. Health care, tutoring, and remedial instruction are also available. In addition to interviewing, there are on-campus recruiting, job notifications, and resume-writing and job-hunting workshops.

Programs of Study: The college confers the B.A. degree. In addition, master's degrees and a cooperative Ph.D. are offered through the Consortium. Bachelor's degrees are offered in the following subjects: AREA STUDIES (American, Asian, Black/Afro-American, Latin American, urban), ENGLISH (English, literature), FINE AND PERFORMING ARTS (art, art history, dance, music, studio art, theater/dramatics), LANGUAGES (French, German, Greek/Latin, Italian, Russian, Spanish), MATH AND SCIENCES (astronomy, biochemistry, biology, botany, chemistry, earth science, geology, mathematics, natural sciences, physical sciences, physics), PHILOSOPHY (classics, humanities, philosophy, religion), SOCIAL SCIENCES (anthropology, economics, geography, government/political science, history, international relations, psychology, sociology). Twenty-eight percent of the degrees conferred are in social sciences, 21% are in math and science, and 12% are in English.

Required: Undergraduates must fulfill distribution requirements (unless exempted by the departments concerned) and are required to take a foreign language and physical education, and to complete two winter terms.

Special: Examinations are self-scheduled. The college offers independent study, student-designed majors, and interdepartmental courses and majors. A noteworthy program offers a political science summer internship with federal and international agencies. Students may take courses on the other campuses of the Five-College Consortium. Qualified students may spend a semester or a year abroad or participate in an exchange program with 1 of 11 other colleges in the Twelve-College Exchange Program.

Honors: All majors and special majors offer honors programs. Two national honor societies, Phi Beta Kappa and Sigma Xi, have chapters on campus.

Admissions: Fifty-four percent of those who applied were accepted for the 1981-82 freshman class. The SAT scores of those who enrolled were as follows: Verbal—17% scored below 500, 43% between 500 and 599, 34% between 600 and 700, and 5% above 700; Math—11% scored below 500, 55% between 500 and 599, 31% between 600 and 700, and 2% above 700. Of those accepted, 86% ranked in the top 20% of their graduating class. High school records, the results of the SAT and ATs, and the recommendations of the secondary school authorities all figure prominently in the evaluation; indications of academic interest and motivation are especially important. No minimum class rank or grade average is specified.

Procedure: Required tests are the SAT and 3 ATs, including English composition. Tests may be taken in the junior year or through January of the senior year. An interview at the college is expected for those within 200 miles, or with alumnae for those who live farther away. The application should be sent in the fall of the senior year, and no later than February 1. Candidates are notified in mid-April. The application fee is $25.

Special: There is an early decision plan, with notification in mid-December. Early admissions and deferred admissions are available. The deadline to apply for early admission is February 1. CRDA is used. AP credit is granted.

Transfer: For Fall 1981, 119 students applied, 33 were accepted, and 5 enrolled. Transfer students should submit a transcript and have a 3.0 GPA. D grades do not transfer. They should also have SAT scores of 550 on both the Verbal and Math tests. Transfer students must have completed at least 32 credits at their last school and must earn, at the college, 64 of the 128 credits needed for a bachelor's degree. The application deadline is February 15 (fall).

Visiting: There are no regularly scheduled orientations for prospective students. Informal visits and guided tours during the academic year are available through arrangement with the admissions office. Visitors can sit in on classes and arrange to stay at the college.

Financial Aid: About 62% of the students receive financial aid. Sixty percent work part-time on campus. Average aid to freshmen from all sources is $5850. Thirty-three percent of the students hold Mount Holyoke scholarships. Loans, including federal funds, are awarded without academic restriction. Aid to freshmen is usually given as a scholarship, a small loan, and a campus job. The college is a member of CSS. The Parent Loan Plan is available. An aid application should be filed with the college along with the FAF and a copy of the parents' income tax return. The application deadline is February 1. Notification is in mid-April.

Foreign Students: Five percent of the full-time students come from foreign countries. The college offers these students an intensive English course, special counseling, and special organizations.

Admissions: Foreign students must take the TOEFL, the SAT, and 3 ATs, including English composition and 2 others. The university entrance examination of the foreign country may be substituted if successfully completed.

Procedure: The application deadline is February 1 (fall). Foreign students must present a report of their medical history signed by the student, the parents, or the guardians. They must also submit a health evaluation signed by a physician. They must present proof of funds adequate to cover the first year as well as projected support for the next 3 years. They must also carry health insurance, which is available through the college for a fee.

Admissions Contact: Susan P. Staggers, Director of Admissions.

NEW ENGLAND CONSERVATORY OF MUSIC
Boston, Massachusetts 02115   (617) 262-1120   E-2

F/T: 263M, 198W	Faculty: n/av; IV, av$
P/T: 13M, 8W	Ph.D.'s: n/app
Grad: 131M, 137W	S/F Ratio: 10 to 1
Year: sems, ss	Tuition: $5675
Appl: Feb. 15	R and B: $3125
745 applied 329 accepted	167 enrolled
SAT: 512V 524M	SPECIAL

The New England Conservatory is the oldest independent school of its kind in the United States. Founded in 1867, the conservatory has long provided a training environment for talented young musicians. The library consists of more than 40,000 books and scores, and 12,200 records and tapes. In addition, the conservatory subscribes to 165 periodicals.

Environment: The conservatory is located in the Back Bay section of Boston. Dormitories accommodate 175 students.

Student Life: About 33% of the students are from Massachusetts. Seventy-five percent of entering freshmen come from public schools. Twenty-one percent live on campus. Fifteen percent of the students are minority-group members. Conservatory housing is coed, and students may keep cars on campus.

Organizations: Professional societies, among them Pi Kappa Lambda, are open to students. The city of Boston offers students innumerable cultural and recreational activities.

Handicapped: The conservatory is currently redesigning its facilities to accommodate the handicapped. Elevators are available. There are a minimal number of visually impaired students. A staff of 2 offers special counseling and assistance, including special class scheduling.

Graduates: Approximately 10% of the degree candidates drop out by the end of the freshman year; 85% remain to graduate. Sixty-five percent pursue advanced study after graduation.

Services: Students receive the following services free of charge: placement and career counseling. Tutoring, remedial instruction, health care, and psychological counseling are available on a fee basis.

Programs of Study: Undergraduate programs lead to the Bachelor of Music degree. Master's degrees are also granted. Bachelor's degrees are awarded in the following areas: FINE AND PERFORMING ARTS (applied voice and instrumental music, composition, jazz studies, music education, music history, performance of early music, theory, Third Stream studies). The overall conservatory curriculum includes the preceding areas but with the greater breadth of a coordinated interdepartmental program in the humanities.

Required: All students must take courses in theory, English and literature, music literature, and foreign language. In addition, each student must participate in one of the performing groups each semester in residence.

Special: It is possible to earn a combined B.A.-B.S. degree in liberal arts and sciences plus music; this is a 5-year program in conjunction with Tufts University. Students may design their own majors.

Honors: There are 2 national honor society chapters on campus.

Admissions: Forty-four percent of those who applied were accepted for the 1981-82 freshman class. Of those, 50% scored above 500 on both the verbal and mathematical aptitude tests of the SAT. Preparation must include 4 years of English. Candidates should have a B average in their secondary school work, make a favorable personal impression, have participated significantly in extracurricular activities in the field of music, present advanced placement or honor courses, and be graduates of accredited secondary schools. The most important criteria for admission are the personal audition, the high school record, recommendations, and SAT scores, in that order.

Procedure: The conservatory requires that all candidates present the SAT and give an audition. Freshmen are admitted only in the fall. The application deadline is February 15. There is an application/audition fee of $35.

Transfer: Recently, 175 applications were received, 82 were accepted, and 62 students actually enrolled. Transfers are accepted for freshman, sophomore, and junior classes. Transfer requirements are the same as for freshman students. D grades are not acceptable. Students must study at the conservatory for at least 2 years and must have completed a total of 120 to 126 credits to receive a bachelor's degree. The transfer application deadline is February 15.

Visiting: Orientations for prospective students take place Monday through Friday at 11 A.M. Guides are provided for informal visits. Visitors can sit in on classes. For information, the office of admissions should be contacted.

Financial Aid: Sixty percent of all students receive financial aid. Thirty-two percent work part-time on campus. Average aid to freshmen from all sources covers 65% of costs. Aid is available in the form of scholarships and loans. Loans are provided by federal and state government funds, local banks, and private sources. The conservatory is a member of CSS. The FAF is required. The deadline for applying for financial aid is February 15.

Foreign Students: Eleven percent of the full-time students come from foreign countries. The conservatory offers these students an intensive English course, special counseling, and special organizations.

Admissions: Foreign students must score 450 on the TOEFL. They must also take the SAT.

Procedure: The application deadlines are February 15 (fall) and November 15 (spring). Foreign students must present proof of funds on a yearly basis.

Admissions Contact: Lawrence Eric Murphy, Director of Admissions.

NICHOLS COLLEGE
Dudley, Massachusetts 01570   (617) 943-2055   C-3

F/T: 560M, 240W	Faculty: 41; n/av
P/T: 125M, 75W	Ph.D.'s: 66%
Grad: 175M, 50W	S/F Ratio: 22 to 1
Year: sems, ss	Tuition: $4010
Appl: open	R and B: $2300
900 applied 678 accepted	281 enrolled
SAT: 400V 472M ACT: 23	COMPETITIVE+

Nichols College, a private institution for men founded in 1815, became coeducational in 1971. Its library contains 65,000 volumes and 93 microform items, and subscribes to 433 periodicals.

Environment: The rural 200-acre campus is located 18 miles from Worcester and 45 miles from Boston. Its 41 buildings include 10 dormitories and 4 houses accommodating 650 students.

Student Life: About 55% of the students are from Massachusetts; 75% of entering freshmen come from public schools. About 75% of the students reside on campus. Three percent of the students are minority-group members. Campus housing is single-sex; there are visiting privileges. Students may keep cars on campus.

Organizations: There are no fraternities or sororities on campus. The student government and special-interest clubs provide social and cultural entertainment.

Sports: The college competes in 9 intercollegiate sports for men and 3 for women. There are 4 intramural sports for men and 3 for women.

Handicapped: About 50% of the campus is accessible to the physically handicapped. Special facilities include wheelchair ramps, parking areas, and specially equipped rest rooms. There are no hearing-impaired or visually impaired students currently enrolled.

Graduates: About 20% of the freshmen drop out during the first year; 66% remain to graduate. Of those, 20% go on to graduate studies; 2% enter law school. Eighty percent pursue careers in business and industry.

Services: Free career and psychological counseling, tutoring, remedial instruction, and placement services are available on campus. Health care is on a fee basis.

Programs of Study: The college awards the B.A., B.S.B.A., and B.S.P.A. degrees. Master's degrees are also offered. Bachelor's degrees are offered in the following subjects: BUSINESS (accounting, business administration, economics, finance, management, management information systems, marketing) EDUCATION (secondary), SOCIAL SCIENCES (history, psychology, public administration, social services). About 85% of the degrees conferred are in business, and 15% in the social sciences.

Honors: There are 5 professional honor societies with chapters on campus.

Admissions: About 75% of those who applied were accepted for the 1981-82 freshman class. The SAT scores of those who enrolled were as follows: Verbal—80% scored below 500, 18% between 500 and 599, 2% between 600 and 700, and 0% above 700; Math—60% scored below 500, 30% between 500 and 599, 9% between 600 and 700, and 1% above 700. On the ACT, 70% scored below 21, 20% between 21 and 23, 8% between 24 and 25, 2% between 26 and 28, and 0% above 28. The candidate should have completed 16 Carnegie units, have at least a C average, and rank in the upper 70% of the graduating class. SAT scores, advanced placement and honor courses, personality, and leadership record are also important.

Procedure: The SAT or ACT is required and may be taken in May of the junior year or in December or January of the senior year. Application deadlines are open. Freshmen are also admitted to the summer session. The rolling admissions plan is used. A $15 fee should accompany all applications.

Special: Early decision, early admissions, and deferred admissions plans are available. AP and CLEP credits are offered.

Transfer: For fall 1981, 105 transfer applications were received, 94 were accepted, and 72 students enrolled. Transfers are accepted for all classes. A 2.0 GPA is required. D grades are not acceptable. At least 30 credits must be taken in residence of the 122 needed for a bachelor's degree. Application deadlines are the same as those for freshmen.

Visiting: Informal guided tours are available weekdays and Saturday mornings. Visitors may sit in on classes and arrange to stay at the school. For further information, the admissions office should be contacted.

Financial Aid: About 30% of all students receive some form of financial aid. Twenty percent work part-time on campus. The average aid award to freshmen is $1900. Freshman scholarships and federal loan funds are available. The college is a member of the CSS and requires the FAF. The deadline for financial aid applications is March 1 (fall) and November 1 (winter).

Foreign Students: Two percent of the full-time students come from foreign countries. The college offers these students special counseling.

Admissions: Foreign students must score 450 on the TOEFL. No college entrance examination is required.

Procedure: Application deadlines are open. Foreign students are admitted to the fall and spring semesters. They must present proof of adequate funds and carry health insurance, which is available through the college for a fee.

Admissions Contact: Thomas J. McGinn III, Director of Admissions.

NORTH ADAMS STATE COLLEGE A-1
North Adams, Massachusetts 01247   (413) 664-4511

F/T: 1034M, 1208W	Faculty: 98; IIA, —$
P/T: 60M, 106W	Ph.D.'s: 60%
Grad: 124M, 172W	S/F Ratio: 21 to 1
Year: 4-1-4, ss	Tuition: $975 ($2788)
Appl: Mar. 1	R and B: $1828
4937 applied	2366 accepted	1806 enrolled
SAT: 421V 464M		COMPETITIVE+

North Adams State College, established in 1894, offers undergraduate degree programs in the liberal arts and sciences, business, and education. The library contains 110,000 volumes, 6500 microfilm items, and subscribes to 870 periodicals.

Environment: The 13-acre campus is located in a town of 16,000 inhabitants 130 miles west of Boston. There are 9 major buildings, including 3 residence halls that accommodate 1201 students. Facilities are available for commuting students.

Student Life: About 98% of the students come from Massachusetts; 75% come from public schools; 75% live on campus. One percent of the students are minority-group members. College housing is both single-sex and coed. There are visiting privileges in single-sex housing. Juniors and seniors may keep cars on campus. Day-care services are available to all students, faculty, and staff for a fee.

Organizations: There are 3 fraternities and 3 sororities. On-campus activities include student government, clubs, publications, and regularly scheduled social events.

Sports: The college competes intercollegiately in 8 sports for men and 7 for women. There is intramural competition for men in 9 sports and in 8 for women.

Handicapped: About 50% of the campus is accessible to physically handicapped students. Facilities include wheelchair ramps, special parking, and elevators. Special class scheduling can be arranged.

Graduates: The freshman dropout rate is 13%; about 58% remain to graduate. Eight percent go on to graduate study.

Services: Placement, career counseling, remedial instruction, and psychological counseling are available free of charge. Health care and tutoring are available on a fee basis.

Programs of Study: The B.A., B.S., B.S.Ed., or B.S.Med. degree is offered. Master's degrees are also awarded. There are bachelor's programs in the following subjects: BUSINESS (business administration, computer science), EDUCATION (early childhood, elementary), ENGLISH (English), HEALTH SCIENCES (medical technology), MATH AND SCIENCES (biology, chemistry, mathematics, physics), PHILOSOPHY (philosophy), SOCIAL SCIENCES (history, psychology, sociology). Forty percent of degrees conferred are in business and 20% are in math/sciences.

Special: There are co-op and winter study programs.

Honors: There is 1 honor society.

Admissions: About 48% of the 1981-82 applicants were accepted. The SAT scores of those who enrolled in a recent year were as follows: Verbal—25% scored between 500 and 599, 5% between 600 and 700; Math—25% scored between 500 and 599, 5% between 600 and 700. A 2.8 GPA and rank in the top 33% are required. Advanced placement/honors courses, extracurricular activities, and impressions made during an interview are also taken into consideration.

Procedure: The SAT is required; ATs are recommended. Deadlines are March 1 (fall) and December 1 (spring). Notification is on a rolling basis. There is an $18 fee.

Special: There are early and deferred admissions plans. CLEP credit is accepted.

Transfer: For fall 1981, 812 students applied, 463 were accepted, and 231 enrolled. A 2.0 GPA is required. D grades transfer. Thirty credits must be completed in residence of the 120 needed for a bachelor's degree. The deadlines for application are the same as those for freshmen.

Visiting: There is an orientation program for prospective applicants. Informal campus tours may be arranged. Visitors may sit in on classes.

Financial Aid: About 70% of all students receive financial aid. Fifteen percent work part-time on campus. The average aid awarded to freshmen from all sources is $2000. The college offers some freshman scholarships in addition to government and commercial loans, grants (BEOG, SEOG), and work-study (CWS). There are several college-assigned jobs available. The college is a member of CSS. The FAF and the college's aid application are due May 1 (fall) and December 1 (spring).

Foreign Students: Fewer than 1% of the full-time students come from foreign countries.

Admissions: Foreign students must score 500 on the TOEFL. No college entrance examination is required.

Procedure: Application deadlines are March 1 (fall) and December 1 (spring). Foreign students must complete the college's own physical examination form. They must also provide proof of funds adequate to cover 4 years of study.

Admissions Contact: William T. West, Jr., Director of Admissions.

NORTHEASTERN UNIVERSITY E-2
Boston, Massachusetts 02115   (617) 437-2200

F/T: 11,548M, 6891W	Faculty: 832; I, —$
P/T: 7850M, 8214W	Ph.D.'s: 68%
Grad: 3315M, 1910W	S/F Ratio: 22 to 1
Year: qtrs, ss	Tuition: $4238
Appl: May. 1	R and B: $3000
SAT or ACT: required	COMPETITIVE

Northeastern University, an independent institution founded in 1898, is the largest cooperative-plan university in the nation, with over 90% of its upperclass students employed by more than 2500 U.S. firms. The campus library system has 435,000 books and 560,000 microtexts, and subscribes to 3717 periodicals.

Environment: The 52-acre urban campus is situated in the cultural center of Boston. It includes residence halls that accommodate 3300 undergraduates and 12 fraternity houses that accommodate 3% of the male upperclassmen. West Hall is a 400-student upperclass apartment complex. Boston Arena, the oldest indoor ice arena in the nation, was recently acquired by the university. Meserve Hall has been completely renovated and now houses the university's College of Arts and Sciences. A new classroom building and Law School addition are now under construction.

Student Life: Most of the students are from the Northeast. Fifty-four percent reside on campus. University housing is both single-sex and coed. There are visiting privileges in single-sex housing. Students may keep cars on campus. Day-care services are available to all full-time students, faculty, and staff for a fee.

Organizations: There are 6 local and 6 national fraternities as well as 3 national sororities. On-campus activities include clubs, religious and service organizations, student government, publications, and social/cultural events.

Sports: There are 12 intercollegiate sports for men and 13 for women. Intramural competition is offered in 13 sports for men and in 12 for women.

Handicapped: Special facilities include wheelchair ramps, parking areas, elevators, lowered drinking fountains and telephones, specially equipped rest rooms, electromagnetic doors, and outside ramps and railway. Special class scheduling is also available. For the hearing-impaired there are interpreters and note-takers; for the visually impaired there are braille maps, adaptive equipment, readers, taped textbooks, and mobility orientation to the campus. One special counselor and 1 assistant aid handicapped students.

Graduates: In a recent year, 15% of the freshmen dropped out; about 65% of those who graduated sought graduate or professional degrees.

Services: Career and psychological counseling, placement, tutoring, and remedial instruction are offered without charge to all students. Health care is on a fee basis.

Programs of Study: The university offers the B.A. and B.S. degrees. There are also associate, master's, and doctoral programs. The bachelor's degree is offered in the following subjects: AREA STUDIES (Black/Afro-American), BUSINESS (accounting, business administration, computer science, finance, management, marketing, real estate/insurance), EDUCATION (adult, early childhood, elementary, health/physical, secondary, special), ENGLISH (English, journalism, literature, speech), FINE AND PERFORMING ARTS (art, art history), HEALTH SCIENCES (medical technology, nursing, physical therapy, speech therapy), LANGUAGES (French, German, Italian, Russian, Spanish), MATH AND SCIENCES (biology, chemistry, earth science, geology, mathematics, physics, statistics), PHILOSOPHY (philosophy), PREPROFESSIONAL (engineering, pharmacy), SOCIAL SCIENCES (economics, government/political science, history, psychology, sociology).

Required: Freshman requirements vary according to college.

Special: Internships, student-designed majors, study abroad, and a general studies major are offered.

Honors: There are 22 honor societies on campus. Honors work is offered in arts and sciences.

Admissions: About 79% of the applicants were accepted in a recent year. Admissions officers weigh heavily such factors as class rank, school record, and meaningful life experiences. It is expected that the applicant will have shown particular strength in the subjects that will be important to his or her course of study at the university.

Procedure: The SAT or ACT and 3 ATs (including English Composition) are required. These test scores are for counseling purposes only. Application deadlines are May 1 (fall), September 1 (winter), January 1 (spring), and April 1 (summer). Decisions are made on a rolling basis. There is a $25 application fee.

Special: There are early admissions and deferred admissions plans. AP and CLEP credit is accepted.

Transfer: About 900 transfer students are admitted each year. Good academic standing is required. One year must be completed in residence, as well as 50% of the 176 quarter hours needed for a bachelor's degree. Application deadlines are open; a rolling admissions plan is followed.

Visiting: There is an orientation program. Informal campus tours with student guides can be arranged through the admissions office.

Financial Aid: About 54% of the students receive aid. Twenty-five percent work part-time on campus. The university offers, on the average, $3800 in freshman assistance awarded in packages that consist of scholarships, loans, grants, and part-time campus employment. Need and academic merit are the determining factors. The university is a member of CSS. The FAF, FFS, or SFS forms are required. Application deadlines are February 15 (fall), October 15 (winter), November 15 (spring), and January 15 (summer).

Foreign Students: Five percent of the full-time students come from foreign countries. The university offers these students an intensive English course, an intensive English program, special counseling, and special organizations.

Admissions: Foreign students must score 450 on the TOEFL. They must also take the university's own English proficiency test. The SAT or the ACT and 3 ATs, including English Composition, are also required.

Procedure: The deadlines for application are May 1 (fall), September 1 (winter), January 1 (spring), and April 1 (summer). Foreign students must present the university's own health questionnaire after acceptance. They must also present proof of funds adequate to cover 1 year of study and pay a special fee of $200 for additional services. Foreign students must carry health insurance, which is available through the university for a fee.

Admissions Contact: Philip R. McCabe, Dean of Admissions.

PINE MANOR COLLEGE
Chestnut Hill, Massachusetts 02167

E-2
(617) 731-7104

F/T: 530W
P/T: none
Grad: none
Year: sems, ss
Appl: open
586 applied
SAT: 400V 400M

Faculty: 29; IV, +$
Ph.D.'s: 25%
S/F Ratio: 18 to 1
Tuition: $6270
R and B: $3500

542 accepted   246 enrolled
LESS COMPETITIVE

Pine Manor College, established in 1911, is a private liberal arts college for women. The library contains 32,000 volumes and 1700 microfilm items, and subscribes to 250 periodicals.

Environment: The 79-acre suburban campus is located 5 miles from Boston. There are 32 buildings, including 17 dormitories that can house 520 women.

Student Life: About 20% of the students come from Massachusetts; 98% live on campus. College housing is single-sex; there are visiting privileges. Students may keep cars on campus. Day-care services are available for a fee.

Organizations: There are no sororities. Student government is a popular extracurricular activity.

Sports: Intercollegiate teams compete in 5 sports. There are 9 intramural athletics.

Handicapped: There are no special facilities for the physically handicapped.

Graduates: Of those freshmen who enter, 5% drop out by the end of their first year. About 75% complete their degrees. Fifty percent pursue graduate degrees; 1% enter law school. Fifty percent enter careers in business and industry.

Services: Career counseling, placement, tutoring, remedial instruction, and psychological counseling are offered to students free of charge. Health care is on a fee basis.

Programs of Study: The B.A. degree is offered. Associate degrees are also awarded. The college confers the bachelor's degree in the following subjects: AREA STUDIES (American), BUSINESS (business administration, management), ENGLISH (English, literature), FINE AND PERFORMING ARTS (art history, visual arts), LANGUAGES (French), SOCIAL SCIENCES (biological psychology, developmental psychology).

Required: All students must take course work in communication skills.

Special: Study abroad and internship opportunities are available. There is also cross-registration with Boston College and Babson College.

Honors: There is no honors program.

Admissions: Ninety-two percent of those who applied were accepted for the 1981-82 freshman class. The SAT scores of those who enrolled were as follows: Verbal—89% scored below 500, 10% between 500 and 599, 1% between 600 and 700, and 0% above 700; Math—85% scored below 500, 13% between 500 and 599, 2% between 600 and 700, and 0% above 700. High school record, recommendations, impressions made during the interview, and extracurricular activities are among the important criteria for admission. Special consideration is given to children of alumnae.

Procedure: Either the SAT or the ACT is required. Application deadlines are open. Notification is on a rolling basis. There is a $15 application fee. Freshmen are admitted at midyear. An interview is recommended.

Special: There are early decision, early admissions, and deferred admissions plans. AP and CLEP credit is accepted.

Transfer: For fall 1981, 10 students applied. Transfer students must take the SAT or ACT and must have earned at least 16 college preparatory units. D grades do not transfer. Students must complete 64 credits for an associate degree and 128 for a bachelor's degree. Deadlines are the same as those for freshman applicants.

Visiting: There is an orientation program for prospective applicants. Campus tours can also be arranged. Visitors may stay at the school and sit in on classes.

MASSACHUSETTS

Financial Aid: About 20% of all students receive financial aid; 20% work part-time on campus. Average aid to freshmen from all sources is $3000. Work contracts and loans are available. There are several freshman scholarships. Tuition may be paid in installments. Need is the determining factor. The college is a member of CSS. The FAF is due March 15.

Foreign Students: Twenty percent of the full-time students come from foreign countries. The college offers these students an intensive English course, an intensive English program, special counseling, and special organizations.

Admissions: Foreign students must score at least 450 on the TOEFL or the equivalent on the University of Michigan Language Test. No college entrance examination is required.

Procedure: There is a rolling admissions policy; foreign students are admitted to all terms. They must complete the college's own health form. They must also present proof of funds adequate to cover 1 year of study. Health insurance is not required, but is strongly recommended.

Admissions Contact: Dorothy Clift, Acting Director of Admissions.

REGIS COLLEGE   D-2
Weston, Massachusetts 02193   (617) 893-1820

F/T: 923W	Faculty: 49; IIB, av$
P/T: 239W	Ph.D.'s: 67%
Grad: 9M, 79W	S/F Ratio: 14 to 1
Year: 4-1-4, ss	Tuition: $4270
Appl: open	R and B: $2630
610 applied	520 accepted	278 enrolled
SAT: 430V 434M		COMPETITIVE

Regis College is a private liberal arts college for women affiliated with the Roman Catholic Church. The library contains 123,000 volumes and subscribes to 900 periodicals.

Environment: The 168-acre suburban campus is 12 miles from Boston. There are 14 buildings, including a new athletic/recreation center and residence halls that accommodate 78% of the students. Facilities are available for commuting students.

Student Life: About 80% of the students come from Massachusetts; 42% come from public schools. Seventy-eight percent of the students live on campus. Eighty-eight percent are Catholic, 7% Protestant, and 2% Jewish. About 5% of the students are minority-group members. College housing is single-sex; there are visiting privileges. Students may keep cars on campus.

Organizations: There are no sororities. On-campus activities include clubs, student government, publications, performing groups, service and religious organizations, and theater.

Sports: In addition to 8 intercollegiate athletics, there is intramural competition in 12 sports.

Handicapped: There are currently no special facilities for physically handicapped students.

Graduates: Sixteen percent of the freshmen drop out by the end of their first year. Seventy percent remain to graduate. Fifteen percent go on to graduate study; fewer than 1% go to medical school and 1% to law school. Twenty-six percent enter careers in business and industry.

Services: Tutoring, remedial instruction, career counseling, placement, health care, and psychological counseling are offered free of charge to all students.

Programs of Study: The college confers the B.A. and B.S. degrees. There are also master's programs. Bachelor's degrees are offered in the following subjects: EDUCATION (elementary, secondary), FINE AND PERFORMING ARTS (art, music), HEALTH SCIENCES (medical technology), LANGUAGES (French, German, Spanish), MATH AND SCIENCES (biology, chemistry, mathematics), PHILOSOPHY (classics), SOCIAL SCIENCES (economics, government/political science, history, psychology, sociology). About 41% of degrees conferred are in social sciences, 21% in math/sciences, and 15% in the arts.

Special: Student-designed majors, study abroad, independent study, and combination degree programs in technical areas are offered.

Honors: There are several honor societies on campus. Honors work is possible.

Admissions: Eighty-five percent of the applicants for the 1981-82 freshman class were accepted. The SAT scores of those who enrolled were as follows: Verbal—76% scored below 500, 19% between 500 and 599, 4% between 600 and 700, and 1% above 700; Math—75% scored below 500, 21% between 500 and 599, 4% between 600 and 700, and 0% above 700. The college considers advanced placement/honors courses, recommendations, and impressions made during an interview as important factors for admission.

Procedure: The SAT is required; it should be taken by January of the senior year. ATs are suggested for placement, especially in modern languages. Deadlines are open; new students are admitted each semester. Notification is on a rolling basis. There is a $20 application fee.

Special: There are early admissions and deferred admissions plans.

Transfer: For fall 1981, 90 students applied, 63 were accepted, and 35 enrolled. Transfer students should have a 2.0 GPA. D grades do not transfer. Eighteen courses must be completed in residence of the 36 required for a bachelor's degree. Application deadlines are open. An interview and recommendations are required.

Visiting: There is an orientation program for new students. Informal campus tours may be arranged. Visitors may sit in on classes and stay at the school.

Financial Aid: About 78% of all students receive financial aid. About 28% work part-time on campus. Average aid to freshmen from all sources is $3049. The college offers scholarships, federal/state grants (BEOG, SEOG), federal loans (including NDSL), and CWS. It is a member of CSS. The FAF should be filed along with the FAF Supplement and a copy of the parents' federal tax return no later than February 1.

Foreign Students: About 2% of the full-time students come from foreign countries. The college offers these students special counseling and special organizations.

Admissions: Foreign students must score 500 on the TOEFL. They must also score about 450 on each part of the SAT. Two ATs are required for placement purposes: English Composition and a foreign language.

Procedure: Application deadlines are open for the fall. December 15 is the spring deadline. Foreign students must present the college's own health form completed by a physician. They must also carry health insurance, which is available through the college.

Admissions Contact: Paul F. Eaton, Director of Admissions and Financial Aid.

SALEM STATE COLLEGE   E-2
Salem, Massachusetts 01970   (617) 745-0556

F/T: 2078M, 3205W	Faculty: n/av; IIA, av$
P/T: 262M, 552W	Ph.D.'s: 44%
Grad: 44M, 102W	S/F Ratio: 20 to 1
Year: sems, ss	Tuition: $914 ($2702)
Appl: Mar. 1	R and B: $1885
8886 applied	5465 accepted	1428 enrolled
SAT: required		COMPETITIVE

Founded in 1854, Salem is a state-supported institution whose offerings include programs in the liberal arts, business, education, and nursing. The library houses 180,000 volumes and 207,083 microfilm items, and subscribes to 1085 periodicals.

Environment: The 27-acre campus is set in a suburban environment 15 miles from Boston. Campus buildings include a large sports complex and a new library. There are housing facilities for 640 students.

Student Life: Approximately 80% of the students commute. Ninety-five percent are residents of Massachusetts. Twelve percent of the students live on campus. Four percent are minority-group members. College housing is both single-sex and coed. There are visiting privileges in single-sex housing. Students may keep cars on campus. Day-care services are available to all students, faculty, and staff.

Organizations: Extracurricular activities include the usual range of clubs and organizations. The school is a block from the Atlantic Ocean and 15 miles from Boston, giving Salem students access to a wide variety of cultural and recreational activities.

Sports: The college offers 10 intercollegiate sports for men and 10 for women. There are 18 intramural sports for men and 17 for women.

Handicapped: Special facilities for the physically handicapped include wheelchair ramps, parking areas, elevators, lowered drinking fountains, and specially equipped rest rooms. About 75% of the campus is accessible to these students. Fewer than 1% of all students are visually handicapped, and fewer than 1% are hearing impaired. A special counselor is available to work with the handicapped.

Graduates: Forty-seven percent of the freshmen remain to graduate.

Services: Placement, psychological counseling, career counseling, health care, and tutoring are offered for a fee.

Programs of Study: The college confers the B.A. and B.S. degrees. Master's degrees are also offered. Bachelor's degrees are offered in the following subjects: BUSINESS (accounting, business administration, business education, computer science, finance, management, marketing), EDUCATION (early childhood, elementary, health/physical), ENGLISH (English, journalism, literature), FINE AND PERFORMING ARTS (art), HEALTH SCIENCES (medical technology, nursing), MATH AND SCIENCES (biology, chemistry, earth science, geology, mathematics), PREPROFESSIONAL (dentistry, engineering, law, medicine, social work), SOCIAL SCIENCES (economics, geography, government/political science, history, psychology, sociology).

Required: Every degree program includes 2 years of general education with courses in the humanities, sciences, social sciences, and (for the B.A. candidate) foreign language.

Special: An experiential education program offers the opportunity for on-the-job training. Other options include study abroad or at another state college. There are interdisciplinary and interdepartmental majors, individually designed majors, and also a combined B.S.-B.A. degree.

Honors: The school has chapters of 5 honor societies. Honors programs are offered.

Admissions: About 62% of the students who applied were admitted to the 1981–82 freshman class. Of those who enrolled in a recent class, the SAT scores were as follows: Verbal—15% scored between 500 and 600, 2% between 600 and 700, and fewer than 1% above 700; Math—25% scored between 500 and 600, 4% between 600 and 700, and fewer than 1% above 700. Candidates must have completed 16 Carnegie units with a grade average of C or better and should rank in the top quarter of the graduating class. Other factors taken into consideration are advanced placement or honors courses, special talents, and recommendations by high-school officials.

Procedure: The SAT is required and should be taken by December of the senior year. The deadlines for regular admission are March 1 (fall) and December 1 (winter). There is a rolling admissions plan. An application fee of $18 is required.

Special: The school provides a deferred admissions plan. CLEP and AP credit is granted.

Transfer: A 2.0 GPA is required. Transfer students are accepted regularly. Salem has a 1-year residency requirement. Students must complete 30 credits, in residence, of the 127 generally needed for a bachelor's degree. Application deadlines are April 1 (fall) and December 1 (winter).

Visiting: Regularly scheduled orientations for prospective students include a Saturday morning tour and a talk by school officials. As a general rule, visitors may not sit in on classes. To arrange a visit, the prospective student should contact the director of admissions.

Financial Aid: About 56% of all students receive financial aid. Thirty percent of the students work part-time on campus. Average aid to freshmen from all sources is $2000. Most aid is in the form of loans, grants, and work/study. The college is a member of CSS. The FAF is required. Application deadlines are open.

Foreign Students: One percent of the full-time students come from foreign countries. The college provides these students with special counseling and special organizations.

Admissions: Foreign students must score 500 on the TOEFL. No college entrance examination is required.

Procedure: The application deadlines are March 1 (fall) and December 1 (winter). Foreign students must present proof of funds adequate to cover 1 year of study.

Admissions Contact: David A. Sartwell, Director of Admissions.

SIMMONS COLLEGE E–2
Boston, Massachusetts 02115 (617) 738-2107

F/T: 1706W	Faculty:	167; n/av
P/T: 205W	Ph.D.'s:	56%
Grad: 808 M&W	S/F Ratio:	12 to 1
Year: sems, ss	Tuition:	$5856
Appl: Mar. 15	R and B:	$2806
1562 applied	1213 accepted	433 enrolled
SAT: 480V 490M		COMPETITIVE

Simmons College, founded in 1899, is a private college for women offering a liberal arts education. The library contains 189,000 volumes and 5000 microfilm items, and subscribes to 1300 periodicals.

Environment: The 10-acre urban campus is located in the Back Bay section of Boston. There are 11 buildings, including 9 residence halls.

Student Life: About 75% of the students come from New England; 62% live on campus. Eight percent of the students are minority-group members. College housing is single-sex; there are visiting privileges.

Organizations: There are no sororities. There is a wide range of extracurricular activities and social/cultural events. Student government is a popular activity.

Sports: The college sponsors intercollegiate teams in 6 sports. Intramural activities are offered in 2 sports.

Handicapped: About 70% of the campus is accessible to students with physical handicaps. Facilities include wheelchair ramps, elevators, special parking and rest rooms, and lowered drinking fountains and telephones. Special class scheduling is also available.

Graduates: Three percent of the freshmen drop out by the end of their first year. About 75% of all freshmen remain to graduate. Twenty-five percent go on to graduate study, and 40% pursue business careers.

Services: Placement, career counseling, tutoring, remedial instruction, and psychological counseling are offered free of charge. Health care is available on a fee basis.

Programs of Study: The B.A. or B.S. degree is offered. There are also master's and doctoral programs. The bachelor's degree is conferred in the following subjects: AREA STUDIES (American, Black/Afro-American), BUSINESS (finance, management, retail management), EDUCATION (early childhood, elementary, human services, secondary), ENGLISH (literature), FINE AND PERFORMING ARTS (art, music), HEALTH SCIENCES (medical technology, nursing, physical therapy), LANGUAGES (French, Spanish), MATH AND SCIENCES (applied computer science, biology, chemistry, mathematics, nutrition, physics), PREPROFESSIONAL (engineering), SOCIAL SCIENCES (communications, economics, government/political science, history, international relations, psychology, sociology, women's studies). About 19% of degrees conferred are in health sciences, 17% in social sciences, and 14% in communications.

Special: Student-designed majors, a general studies major, a B.A.-B.S. degree in chemistry/pharmacy, study abroad, a Washington semester, 3-2 engineering programs with Dartmouth College and Boston University, interdepartmental programs, and independent study are offered.

Admissions: About 78% of those who applied for the 1981–82 freshman class were accepted. The SAT scores of those who enrolled were as follows: Verbal—70% scored below 500, 25% between 500 and 599, 4% between 600 and 700, and 1% above 700; Math—59% scored below 500, 32% between 500 and 599, 8% between 600 and 700, and 1% above 700. Advanced placement/honors work, special talents, and leadership are also considered important factors.

Procedure: The SAT (or the ACT) and 3 ATs are required by January of the senior year. One AT must be English Composition. Application deadlines are March 15 (fall) and December 1 (spring). Notification is on a rolling basis. There is a $25 fee.

Special: There are early admissions and deferred admissions plans. AP credit is accepted.

Transfer: For fall 1981, 389 students applied, 263 were accepted, and 162 enrolled. Transfer students must have a 2.5 GPA. D grades do not transfer. They must complete, at the college, 3 semesters and a minimum of 48 credits of the 128 needed for a bachelor's degree. Application deadlines are June 1 (fall) and December 1 (spring).

Visiting: There is an orientation program for prospective students. Informal campus tours with student guides may be arranged. Visitors may stay at the school and sit in on classes.

Financial Aid: About 38% of all students receive financial aid. Eighty percent work part-time on campus. Average aid to freshmen from all sources is $3500. The college offers scholarships, loans, and part-time employment (including CWS). It is a member of CSS. The FAF and the college's own form are due March 1.

Foreign Students: Ten percent of the full-time students come from foreign countries. The college offers these students special counseling and special organizations.

Admissions: Foreign students must score 500 on the TOEFL. They can also take the SAT instead of the TOEFL. They must take 3 ATs, including English Composition, Math, and 1 of their choice.

Procedure: The application deadlines are March 15 (fall) and December 1 (spring). Foreign students must submit a completed health form. They must also provide proof of funds adequate to cover 1 year of study. They must carry health insurance, which is available through the college for a fee.

Admissions Contact: Linda Cox Maguire, Director of Admissions.

MASSACHUSETTS

SIMON'S ROCK OF BARD COLLEGE A-2
Great Barrington, Massachusetts 01230 (413) 528-0771

F/T: 132M, 161W
P/T: 1M, 2W
Grad: none
Year: 4-4-1
Appl: open
270 applied
SAT: 565V 560M

Faculty: 26; IV, –$
Ph.D.'s: 60%
S/F Ratio: 9 to 1
Tuition: $6665
R and B: $2300
163 accepted 135 enrolled
VERY COMPETITIVE

Simon's Rock of Bard College, founded in 1964, is a private liberal arts institution designed to offer collegiate studies to people of high school age. The college fosters community involvement as well as academic development. Simon's Rock has been a part of Bard College since 1979. The library contains 45,000 volumes and subscribes to 360 periodicals.

Environment: The 275-acre small-town campus has over 20 buildings; it is located in a rural area 135 miles from Boston and 125 miles from New York City. Living facilities include dormitories and on-campus apartments. A gymnasium and 4 other buildings were purchased in 1981.

Student Life: About 25% of the students are from Massachusetts. About 93% live on campus. Seventy-five percent have public school backgrounds. Five percent of the students are minority-group members. Campus housing is both coed and single-sex; there are visiting privileges in the single-sex housing. Freshmen may not keep cars on campus.

Organizations: There are no fraternities or sororities. There are about 10 extracurricular groups.

Sports: The college competes intercollegiately in 2 sports for men and 2 for women. There are 7 intramural sports for men and 7 for women.

Handicapped: There are no special facilities for the physically handicapped.

Graduates: Ten percent of entering freshmen drop out by the end of the first year; 85% remain to graduate with an A.A.; 25% graduate with a B.A. Fifty percent go on to graduate study (13% enter medical school, and 12% enter law school).

Services: Free to all students are career counseling, health care, and psychological counseling.

Programs of Study: The B.A. is offered in 7 interdisciplinary majors: arts and aesthetics, environmental studies, intercultural studies, literary studies, premedicine, quantitative studies, and social sciences.

Special: Independent study, internships, and study abroad are offered.

Admissions: About 60% of those who applied were accepted for the 1981–82 freshman class. The SAT scores of those who enrolled were as follows: Verbal—26% below 500, 34% between 500 and 599, 29% between 600 and 700, and 11% above 700; Math—24% below 500, 39% between 500 and 599, 32% between 600 and 700, and 5% above 700. Impressions made during the interview, recommendations, and special talent are also considered important.

Procedure: The SAT or ACT is required. There are no application deadlines; freshmen are admitted in the fall and winter terms. Notification is on a rolling basis. There is a $25 application fee. All students must have interviews.

Special: There is a deferred admissions plan.

Transfer: Since Simon's Rock is an early college, the number of transfer students is negligible. All students must complete, at the college, 72 of the 132 credits required for a bachelor's degree.

Visiting: There is an orientation program for prospective students. Informal campus tours can be arranged. Visitors may stay overnight at the school and sit in on classes.

Financial Aid: About 55% of all students receive financial aid. About 52% work part-time on campus. The average freshman award is $2600. Scholarships, federal/state loans, and CWS are offered. Tuition may be paid in installments. Need is the determining factor. The college is a member of CSS. The FAF is due by June 15.

Foreign Students: Two percent of the students come from foreign countries.

Admissions: Foreign students must take the TOEFL and the SAT.

Procedure: There are no application deadlines; foreign students are admitted in the fall and winter terms. They must complete a health form and must present proof of funds adequate to cover 1 year of study.

Health insurance is required and is available through the college for a fee.

Admissions Contact: Sharon K. Pinkerton, Director of Admissions.

SMITH COLLEGE B-2
Northampton, Massachusetts 01060 (413) 584-0515

F/T: 2600W
P/T: 54W
Grad: 89W
Year: 4-1-4
Appl: Feb. 1
2443 applied
SAT: 600V 600M

Faculty: 248; IIA, ++$
Ph.D.'s: 90%
S/F Ratio: 10 to 1
Tuition: $9500
R and B: $2700
1342 accepted 664 enrolled
HIGHLY COMPETITIVE

Smith College is an independent institution offering a liberal arts education. It was founded in 1871. The library contains 865,000 volumes and subscribes to 2425 periodicals.

Environment: The 204-acre campus is located in a community of 30,000 inhabitants, about 85 miles from Boston. All students live in "houses."

Student Life: About 15% of the students come from Massachusetts; 66% come from public schools; 99% live on campus. Twelve percent of the full-time students are minority-group members. College housing is single-sex; there are visiting privileges. Students may keep cars on campus. Day-care services are available to all faculty and staff; there are limited facilities for students.

Organizations: There are no sororities. The extracurricular program is rich and varied and includes clubs, religious and service organizations, performing groups, and student government. There are regularly scheduled on-campus cultural and social events.

Sports: In addition to 16 intercollegiate athletics, there is a full intramural program of 23 sports.

Handicapped: About 90% of the campus is accessible. Ramps, elevators, parking areas, and specially equipped rest rooms are provided for physically handicapped students.

Graduates: Five percent of the freshmen drop out by the end of their first year. Eighty-five percent remain to graduate. About 75% of graduates go on for further education; 12% go to medical school and 10% to law school.

Services: Career counseling, placement, psychological counseling, health care, and tutoring are offered without additional charge to all students.

Programs of Study: The college offers the B.A. degree. There are also master's and doctoral programs. The bachelor's degree is offered in the following subjects: AREA STUDIES (American, Asian, Black/Afro-American, Latin American, Russian), BUSINESS (computer science), EDUCATION (early childhood, elementary, secondary), ENGLISH (English, literature), FINE AND PERFORMING ARTS (art, art education, art history, dance, music, music education, studio art, theater/dramatics), LANGUAGES (Chinese, French, German, Greek/Latin, Hebrew, Italian, Japanese, Portuguese, Russian, Spanish), MATH AND SCIENCES (astronomy, biochemistry, biology, botany, chemistry, computer science, geology, mathematics, natural sciences, physics, psychology, zoology), PHILOSOPHY (classics, philosophy, religion), SOCIAL SCIENCES (anthropology, economics, government/political science, history, international relations, medieval studies, social sciences, sociology). About 19% of the degrees are offered in math and sciences and 16% in fine and performing arts.

Special: Student-designed majors, combination degree programs, study abroad, exchange programs, and a Washington, D.C. semester are offered.

Honors: There are 2 national honor societies. All departments offer honors work.

Admissions: About 55% of the 1981–82 applicants were accepted. The SAT scores of those who enrolled were as follows: Verbal—12% scored below 500, 42% between 500 and 599, 36% between 600 and 700, and 9% above 700; Math—11% scored below 500, 41% between 500 and 599, 43% between 600 and 700, and 4% above 700. Advanced placement or honors work, recommendations, and extracurricular activities are important factors in the admissions decision.

Procedure: The SAT and 3 ATs (including English Composition) should be taken by January of the senior year. February 1 (fall) and November 15 (winter) are the application deadlines. There is a $25 application fee.

Special: There is an early decision plan. AP credit is given.

Transfer: For fall 1981, 181 students applied, 96 were accepted, and 71 enrolled. Good academic standing is needed. A 3.0 GPA is recommended. Grades are considered on an individual basis. Two years must be completed in residence. Students must complete, at the college, 64 of the 128 semester hours needed for a bachelor's degree. February 1 (fall) and November 15 (spring) are the deadlines.

Visiting: There is an orientation program for prospective applicants. Informal campus tours with student guides can be arranged. Visitors may sit in on classes and stay at the college.

Financial Aid: About 40% of the students receive assistance through the college. Sixty-three percent work part-time on campus. The average award to freshmen from all sources is $3596. The college, a member of CSS, offers loans and part-time campus employment. February 1 is the date the FAF must be filed.

Foreign Students: About 7% of the full-time students come from foreign countries.

Admissions: Foreign students must take the TOEFL and the SAT.

Procedure: The application deadline is February 1 (fall). Foreign students must present proof of health and of funds upon admission. They must carry health insurance, which is available through the college as part of general fees.

Admissions Contact: Jane H. Percy, Associate Director of Admission.

SOUTHEASTERN MASSACHUSETTS UNIVERSITY E-4
North Dartmouth, Massachusetts 02747   (617) 999-8605

F/T: 2433M, 2493W   Faculty: 297; IIA, +$
P/T: 250M, 188W   Ph.D.'s: 75%
Grad: 53M, 30W   S/F Ratio: 15 to 1
Year: sems   Tuition: $998 ($3004)
Appl: open   R and B: $2989
5859 applied   3218 accepted   1636 enrolled
SAT: 450V 500M   COMPETITIVE

Southeastern Massachusetts University, established in 1964, is a state-supported institution offering undergraduate programs in business, the medical/health fields, the arts and sciences, and engineering. The library contains 225,000 volumes, houses 86,500 microfilm items, and subscribes to 1700 periodicals.

Environment: The 730-acre suburban campus is located in a town of 20,000 people about 50 miles south of Boston. The university provides residence facilities. There are also facilities for commuters.

Student Life: About 95% of the students come from the New England area. About 35% live on campus. Five percent of the students are minority-group members. University housing is coed. Students may keep cars on campus. Day-care services are available to all students, faculty, and staff for a fee.

Organizations: There are 2 fraternities and 1 sorority. Extracurricular activities include dramatics, a folk festival, a cultural affairs series, a lecture series, clubs, student government, and social events.

Sports: The university competes intercollegiately in 10 sports for men and 10 for women. There are 6 intramural sports for men and 5 for women.

Handicapped: About 70% of the campus is accessible to students with physical handicaps. Special facilities include wheelchair ramps, elevators, special parking and rest rooms, and lowered drinking fountains and telephones. Special class scheduling and personnel (2 counselors and 15 assistants) are provided. About 1% of the students have visual or hearing impairments.

Graduates: Recently, about 60% of the students remained to graduate; 10% went on to graduate study.

Services: Psychological counseling, health care, remedial instruction, tutoring, placement, and career counseling are offered free of charge.

Programs of Study: The B.A., B.S., and B.F.A. are offered. There are also master's programs. Bachelor's degrees are offered in the following subjects: BUSINESS (accounting, finance, human resources management, management, marketing), ENGLISH (English), FINE AND PERFORMING ARTS (art education, art history, design, fine arts, music, textile design), HEALTH SCIENCES (medical technology, nursing), LANGUAGES (French, German, Portuguese, Spanish), MATH AND SCIENCES (biology, chemistry, computer science, mathematics, physics), PHILOSOPHY (philosophy), PREPROFESSIONAL (engineering), SOCIAL SCIENCES (economics, government/political science). About 28% of degrees conferred are in business and 26% in social sciences.

Required: All students must take English composition.

Special: Students may design their own majors.

Honors: There are 2 honor societies on campus. Five departments offer honors programs.

Admissions: About 55% of the 1981–82 freshman applicants were accepted. The SAT scores of those who enrolled were as follows: Verbal—48% scored below 500, 21% between 500 and 599, 3% between 600 and 700, and 0% above 700; Math—38% scored below 500, 38% between 500 and 599, 11% between 600 and 700, and 1% above 700. Applicants must be in the 70th percentile. Advanced placement/honors work, recommendations, and extracurricular activities are also taken into consideration.

Procedure: The SAT should be taken by March of the senior year. There are no application deadlines. Notification is on a rolling basis. The fee is $18 for residents and $25 for nonresidents.

Special: There is an early admissions plan. AP and CLEP credit is accepted.

Transfer: For fall 1981, 1474 students applied, 800 were accepted, and 583 enrolled. Good academic standing is required; a 2.0 GPA is needed. D grades do not transfer. Sixty credits must be taken, in residence, out of the 120 minimum needed for a bachelor's degree. Application deadlines are open.

Visiting: There is an orientation program for prospective applicants. Informal campus tours, including attendance of classes, may be arranged.

Financial Aid: About 64% of all students receive financial aid. Twenty percent work part-time on campus. The school offers scholarships (private and industrial endowments), grants (EOG), loans (including NDSL), and campus employment (CWS and other types). Need and academic merit determine the amount of aid awarded. The university is a member of CSS. The FAF should be submitted by May 1 for priority consideration.

Foreign Students: About 2% of the full-time students come from foreign countries. The university offers these students special counseling.

Admissions: Foreign students must take the TOEFL and the SAT.

Procedure: The application deadline is February 1 (fall). Foreign students must present proof of funds adequate to cover 1 year of study. Out-of-state tuition fees apply. They must also carry health insurance, which is available through the university for a fee.

Admissions Contact: Geraldine M. Sullivan, Assistant Director of Admissions.

SPRINGFIELD COLLEGE B-3
Springfield, Massachusetts 01109   (413) 788-3136

F/T: 928M, 1077W   Faculty: n/av; IIA, −$
P/T: 23M, 17W   Ph.D.'s: 49%
Grad: 95M, 72W   S/F Ratio: 20 to 1
Year: sems, ss   Tuition: $4093
Appl: Apr. 1   R and B: $2150
1803 applied   1210 accepted   524 enrolled
SAT: 410V 450M   COMPETITIVE

Springfield College is an independent, nonsectarian college of the liberal arts. Its library has a collection of 117,000 books and 280,000 microfilm items, and subscribes to 840 periodicals.

Environment: The 90-acre suburban campus is located on a lake 2 miles from the center of Springfield. There are 27 major buildings, including 7 residence halls.

Student Life: About 34% of the students are from Massachusetts. Eighty-one percent come from public schools. Eighty-eight percent of the students live on campus. Thirteen percent are minority-group members. College housing is both single-sex and coed. There are visiting privileges in single-sex housing. Only juniors and seniors may keep cars on campus.

Organizations: There are no sororities or fraternities. Extracurricular activities include student government, religious and service groups, clubs, social and cultural events, and publications.

Sports: Men's intercollegiate teams compete in 13 sports, women's teams in 12 sports. Intramural competition for both men and women includes 13 sports.

Handicapped: The campus is 85% accessible. Special facilities for the physically handicapped include wheelchair ramps, parking areas, elevators, and some specially equipped rest rooms. Special class scheduling can be arranged. There are 3 counselors to assist students with

378 MASSACHUSETTS

physical handicaps. At present, there are no students with visual or hearing impairments.

Graduates: The freshman dropout rate is 10%; about 75% remain to graduate. Thirty percent go on for further education; 10% enter careers in industry or business.

Services: All students receive free psychological counseling, tutoring, remedial instruction, career counseling, and placement services. Health care is available on a fee basis.

Programs of Study: The college confers the B.A., B.S., and B.P.E. degrees. There are also master's and doctoral programs. Bachelor's degrees are offered in the following subjects: BUSINESS (management), EDUCATION (early childhood, elementary, health/physical, secondary), ENGLISH (English), FINE AND PERFORMING ARTS (art), HEALTH SCIENCES (medical technology), MATH AND SCIENCES (biology, chemistry, ecology/environmental science, mathematics), PREPROFESSIONAL (dentistry, law, medicine, ministry, veterinary), SOCIAL SCIENCES (government/political science, history, psychology, sociology). About 47% of the degrees are offered in education, 41% in social sciences, and 8% in math and sciences.

Required: All students must complete a distribution requirement in 5 broad areas of study.

Special: Study abroad and a general studies major are offered. Springfield is one of 2 colleges in the country that prepares students specifically for the YMCA.

Honors: There is 1 honor society. Honors work is offered in psychology.

Admissions: About 67% of the 1981-82 freshman applicants were accepted. Of those who enrolled, the SAT scores were as follows: Verbal—80% scored below 500, 15% between 500 and 599, 4% between 600 and 700, and 1% above 700; Math—75% scored below 500, 20% between 500 and 599, 4% between 600 and 700, and 1% above 700. Candidates must have a high school diploma or the equivalent and should have completed 16 high school units. The academic record is of extreme importance. Advanced placement or honors work, recommendations, leadership ability, and extracurricular record are also considered important.

Procedure: The SAT should be taken by January of the senior year. An interview is required. Freshmen are admitted in the fall term only. The application deadline is April 1. Admission and notification are on a rolling basis. There is a $20 application fee.

Special: There is a deferred admissions plan. AP and CLEP subject exams are used.

Transfer: For fall 1981, 311 students applied, 184 were accepted, and 127 enrolled. Transfers are accepted in the sophomore and junior years. An interview is required. The college will not accept D grades. The final 48 credits must be completed, in residence, out of the 130 needed for a bachelor's degree. The deadlines are June 1 (fall), September 1 (winter), and December 1 (spring).

Visiting: There are no regularly scheduled orientations. Informal guided campus tours may be arranged. Visitors may sit in on classes and stay at the school. The best times for visits are 8:30 A.M. to 4:30 P.M., Monday through Friday. To make arrangements, the admissions office should be contacted.

Financial Aid: About 41% of the students are receiving aid in the form of college or federal/state grants (SEOG), loans (including NDSL), and campus employment (including CWS). The average aid awarded to freshmen from all sources is $2000. Need and the academic record are the determining factors. The college is a member of CSS. The college's aid application and the FAF are due April 1. Notification is usually given upon acceptance to the college.

Foreign Students: Two percent of the full-time students come from foreign countries. The college offers these students special counseling and special organizations.

Admissions: Foreign students must score 500 on the TOEFL. No college entrance examination is required.

Procedure: The application deadlines are April 1 (fall) and December 1 (spring). Foreign students must present proof of funds adequate to cover 1 year of study. They must also carry health insurance, which is available through the college for a fee.

Admissions Contact: Robert B. Palmer, Dean of Admissions.

STONEHILL COLLEGE E-3
North Easton, Massachusetts 02356 (617) 238-1081

F/T: 808M, 914W Faculty: 85; IIB, +$
P/T: 5M, 10W Ph.D.'s: 73%
Grad: none S/F Ratio: 17 to 1
Year: sems, ss Tuition: $4360
Appl: see profile R and B: $2500
2739 applied 1248 accepted 464 enrolled
SAT: 475V 525M COMPETITIVE+

Stonehill College, established in 1948, is a liberal arts college affiliated with the Roman Catholic Church. The library holds 110,000 volumes and 12,503 microfilm items, and subscribes to 963 periodicals.

Environment: The self-contained, wooded campus occupies 618 acres in a suburban area 25 miles from Boston. Major buildings include a renovated and expanded science center, a classroom building, a gymnasium, a student activity building, dormitories with double rooms housing 500 students, and 24 townhouse-style units accommodating 480 upperclassmen.

Student Life: About 84% of the students are from New England. Sixty percent have graduated from public schools. About 65% of the students live on campus. Upperclassmen are permitted to live off campus. Eighty-eight percent of the students are Catholic, 7% are Protestant, and fewer than 1% are Jewish; about 2% are members of other denominations; and 3% claim no religious affiliation. About 1% are minority-group members. College housing is both single-sex and coed. There are visiting privileges in single-sex housing. Students may keep cars on campus.

Organizations: There are no sororities or fraternities. Campus activities include a glee club, publications, films, lecture series, a radio station, and a debate team. Students work in the community with retarded and handicapped children, juvenile delinquents, and disadvantaged students. The campus is located 25 minutes from Boston and an hour from Cape Cod.

Sports: The college competes in 10 intercollegiate sports for men and 9 for women. There are 5 intramural sports for both men and women.

Handicapped: Facilities for physically handicapped students include wheelchair ramps, special parking areas, and specially equipped rest rooms. Special class scheduling can be arranged. Fewer than 1% of the students are visually impaired or hearing impaired. The college has no special counselors for the handicapped.

Graduates: Approximately 15% of the students drop out during freshman year. Of the 75% who go on to graduate, 23% have sought advanced degrees, and 30% have entered business and industry.

Services: Free placement services, career and psychological counseling and remedial instruction are available to students. The placement office serves students and graduates by maintaining job listings and bringing recruiters to campus. Health care is available on a fee basis.

Programs of Study: The college awards the B.A., B.S., and B.S.B.A. degrees. Bachelor's degrees are offered in the following subjects: AREA STUDIES (American), BUSINESS (accounting, business administration, finance, human resource management, management, marketing), EDUCATION (early childhood, elementary), ENGLISH (English), HEALTH SCIENCES (health care administration, medical technology), LANGUAGES (French, Spanish), MATH AND SCIENCES (biology, chemistry, mathematics), PHILOSOPHY (philosophy, religion), PREPROFESSIONAL (dentistry, engineering, law, medicine), SOCIAL SCIENCES (criminal justice, economics, government/political science, history, international relations, psychology, public administration, sociology). Forty-one percent of the degrees are conferred in the social science fields, 26% in business, and 12% in education.

Special: Programs include a junior year abroad, independent study for upperclassmen, and pass-fail options. A 3-2 program leading to a combined B.A.-B.S. degree in engineering is offered in conjunction with the University of Notre Dame. The training program for elementary school teachers uses the clinical professor approach, in which students train under outstanding teachers in their subject field. Students may design their own majors. There is also a general liberal arts degree.

Honors: An honors program is available. Honor societies with chapters on campus include Delta Mu Delta, Phi Alpha Theta, and Sigma Zeta.

Admissions: Stonehill accepted 46% of those who sought admission to the 1981-82 freshman class. The SAT scores of those who enrolled were as follows: Verbal—62% scored below 500, 32% between 500 and 599, 6% between 600 and 700, and 0% above 700; Math—37% scored below 500, 50% between 500 and 599, 12% between 600 and 700, and 0% above 700. About 40% of the freshmen were in the top fifth of their high-school class. Applicants must have completed 16 Carnegie units. Admissions officers also consider advanced placement or honors courses, extracurricular activities, recommendations by school officials, personality, leadership record, evidence of special talents, and impressions made during an interview at the college. Disadvantaged students are given special consideration.

Procedure: Applicants must take the SAT or ACT, preferably in May of the junior year or November or December of the senior year. Candidates are urged to apply early in the senior year. The application deadlines are March 1 (fall) for residents, and May 1 (fall) and December 1 (spring) for nonresidents. Admission and notification are on a rolling basis. The $20 application fee may be waived for applicants demonstrating financial need.

Special: Students applying for early decision are notified by December 1. Applicants interested in early admission should apply by March 1 of the junior year. A deferred admissions plan also is available. Students may earn credit through CLEP or AP exams.

Transfer: For fall 1981, 417 students applied, 130 were accepted, and 79 enrolled. Transfers are accepted in the freshman, sophomore, and junior classes. A 2.0 GPA is required. D grades do not transfer. Transfer students must spend at least 2 years at Stonehill and must complete 60 of the 120 credits needed to receive a bachelor's degree. Application deadlines are the same as for freshman applicants.

Visiting: Prospective students are advised to make an appointment for an interview and tour by calling the college. Group orientations are scheduled, and individual visits also are welcome when classes are in session (September through December and February through May). Guides are provided. Visitors can sit in on classes.

Financial Aid: Thirty-five percent of the students receive financial aid. Eighteen percent work part-time on campus. Average aid awarded to freshmen from all sources is $3500. Ninety-two academic scholarships are available to freshmen each year. Students also may apply for federal government loans and loans from local banks. The college is a member of CSS. Aid applicants should file the FAF. The application deadline is March 1.

Foreign Students: Fewer than 1% of the full-time students come from foreign countries.

Admissions: Foreign students must score 550 on the TOEFL. The SAT or ACT is not required.

Procedure: Applications should be submitted 8 to 12 months prior to enrollment. Foreign students must present proof of health. They must also present proof of funds adequate to cover their entire period of study. Health insurance, which is available through the college for a fee, is required.

Admissions Contact: Brian P. Murphy, Director of Admissions and Enrollment.

SUFFOLK UNIVERSITY E-2
Boston, Massachusetts 02108 (617) 723-4700

F/T: 1080M, 1050W	Faculty: 145; IIA, +$
P/T: 323M, 492W	Ph.D.'s: 72%
Grad: 665M, 431W	S/F Ratio: 22 to 1
Year: sems, ss	Tuition: $3275
Appl: May 1	R and B: n/app
1489 applied	1192 accepted	518 enrolled
SAT: 440V 450M		COMPETITIVE

Suffolk University, established in 1906, is a private, independent, nonresidential institution offering liberal arts and science, business, education, and preprofessional programs on both the graduate and undergraduate levels. The library has 90,000 books and 24,000 microtexts, and subscribes to 193 periodicals.

Environment: The campus consists of 5 classroom buildings located in downtown Boston. There are no university-owned dormitories.

Student Life: About 85% of the students are from New England; 65% come from public schools. All students commute.

Organizations: There are 4 fraternities to which 5% of the men belong; 4% of the women belong to 3 sororities. On-campus activities are geared toward commuting students. Many of the social and cultural activities take place in Boston and its environs.

Sports: The university competes in 6 sports for men and 4 for women on the intercollegiate level. Intramural competition is available in 10 sports for men and 8 for women.

Handicapped: Special facilities for the physically handicapped include wheelchair ramps, parking areas, elevators, lowered drinking fountains and telephones, and specially equipped rest rooms. Special class scheduling can be arranged. There is 1 counselor for handicapped students. Fewer than 1% of the students have visual or hearing impairments.

Graduates: The average freshman dropout rate is 20%; about 50% of the students remain to graduate. Twenty-five percent go on for further study. Thirty-five percent enter careers in business and industry.

Services: Health care, psychological counseling, tutoring, remedial instruction, career counseling, and placement services are provided free of charge. Placement services include workshops on resume writing and interviewing techniques.

Programs of Study: The university confers the B.A., B.S., B.S.B.A., and B.S.J. degrees. Master's degrees are also awarded. Bachelor's degrees are offered in the following subjects: BUSINESS (accounting, business education, computer science, finance, management, marketing), EDUCATION (business, elementary), ENGLISH (English, journalism, dramatic arts, speech), FINE AND PERFORMING ARTS (radio/TV), HEALTH SCIENCES (medical technology), LANGUAGES (French, Spanish), MATH AND SCIENCES (biochemistry, biology, chemistry, mathematics, physics), PHILOSOPHY (humanities, philosophy), PREPROFESSIONAL (dentistry, law, medicine, social work, veterinary), SOCIAL SCIENCES (economics, government/political science, history, psychology, sociology). About 45% of the degrees are conferred in business, 28% in the social sciences, and 14% in math and sciences.

Required: All students must take English composition, history, a humanities option, a social science option, and a communications option. AP exams may be used to fulfill these requirements.

Special: A general studies degree, student-designed majors, and a combination degree program in law are offered.

Honors: There are 5 honor societies represented on campus. Honors programs are offered in several areas.

Admissions: About 80% of the applicants for the 1981–82 freshman class were accepted. The SAT scores of those who enrolled were as follows: Verbal—82% scored below 500, 14% between 500 and 599, 4% between 600 and 700, and 0% above 700; Math—73% scored below 500, 23% between 500 and 599, 4% between 600 and 700, and 0% above 700. Candidates must be graduates of an accredited high school. Class rank should be in the top 60%; a C average is necessary. Other factors considered important are special talents, extracurricular activities, recommendations by high-school officials, and advanced placement or honors courses.

Procedure: The SAT should be taken by January of the senior year. The English AT is also required. Application deadlines are May 1 (fall), December 1 (spring), and April 1 (summer). Admission and notification are on a rolling basis. There is a $15 application fee.

Special: There are early decision, early admissions, and deferred admissions plans. The notification date for early decision is December 15; the application deadline for early admission is June 1. CLEP and AP credit is granted.

Transfer: For fall 1981, 578 applications were received, 440 were accepted, and 266 transfer students enrolled. Students must have a 2.0 GPA. Required courses may be waived with D grades. Thirty hours must be completed in residence of the 122 needed for a bachelor's degree. Application deadlines are June 1 (fall) and December 1 (spring).

Visiting: There are no regularly scheduled orientations for prospective students. Informal campus tours with student guides may be arranged. Wednesdays are the suggested days for such visits. Visitors may sit in on classes. For further information, the director of admissions should be contacted.

Financial Aid: Sixty-four percent of the students receive financial aid. Twenty-two percent work part-time on campus. The average award to freshmen from all sources covers 70% of costs. Aid is available in the form of scholarships, loans, grants, and part-time employment. Federal programs include EOG, NDSL, and CWS. The university is a member of CSS. The aid application and the FAF are due March 1.

Foreign Students: Five percent of the full-time students come from foreign countries. Special organizations are available to these students.

Admissions: Foreign students must score 500 on the TOEFL. No college entrance examination is required.

Procedure: The application deadlines are April 1 (fall) and October 1 (spring). Foreign students must present proof of funds adequate to cover 4 years of study. They must also carry health insurance, which is available through the university for a fee.

Admissions Contact: William F. Coughlin, Director of Admissions.

380 MASSACHUSETTS

SWAIN SCHOOL OF DESIGN E-4
New Bedford, Massachusetts 02740 (617) 997-7831
(Recognized Candidate for Accreditation)

F/T: 83M, 88W Faculty: 17; IIB, – – $
P/T: 4M, 5W Ph.D.'s: 6%
Grad: none S/F Ratio: 10 to 1
Year: sems Tuition: $3500
Appl: open R and B: n/app
230 applied 129 accepted 76 enrolled
SAT: 350V 380M SPECIAL

The Swain School of Design, a private college established in 1881, offers four-year programs in design and fine arts. The library contains more than 12,000 volumes and 12,000 slides.

Environment: The 3-acre campus is located in a residential section of New Bedford, a few blocks from downtown and the docks. The school's 7 buildings include the William Crapo Gallery, opened in 1925, which displays original works of art and provides studio space. The school maintains no housing facilities.

Student Life: About half the students are Massachusetts residents. Most are over age 21. Ninety-five percent are graduates of public schools.

Organizations: Extracurricular activities vary each year depending on student interests. They generally include informal music groups, a student-sponsored film series, and theatrical productions. The school sponsors lectures and exhibitions by prominent artists and designers, and bus trips to museums and galleries in New York City and Boston. There is a student council, and students are represented on the planning, academic affairs, and student affairs committees.

Sports: There is no formal athletic program.

Handicapped: About 30% of the campus is accessible to physically handicapped students. Special facilities include wheelchair ramps.

Graduates: About 25% of the freshmen drop out, and 60% of the graduates pursue further study.

Services: Placement and career counseling are provided free. A housing service compiles a list of rooms and apartments available near the school.

Programs of Study: The school grants the B.F.A. degree for a standard program of study and a four-year diploma for a program made up almost entirely of studio courses. The first two years of the B.F.A. program are devoted to numerous studio electives and to required courses in art history, two- and three-dimensional design, drawing, printmaking, English, and Western civilization. In the final two years, students major in design, painting, printmaking, and sculpture. Electives are offered in literature, social studies, the humanities, and visual studies. Students may take courses at Southeastern Massachusetts University at no extra charge.

Admissions: About 56% of those who applied were admitted for the 1981–82 freshman class. Applicants are admitted primarily on the basis of their portfolio and, when possible, an interview. High school records and SAT scores also are considered.

Procedure: The SAT is required. The application, high school records, one letter of recommendation (from a teacher, counselor, or employer), and a $15 application fee should be sent to the admissions office. After Swain receives this material, the applicant should schedule a portfolio interview through the admissions secretary. Applicants who would have difficulty coming to campus may ask to be considered without the interview. Application deadlines are open.

Special: The school offers a deferred admissions plan.

Transfer: Transfer applicants must follow the same procedure as freshman applicants. Their portfolios must include work that substantiates their request for advanced standing. D grades do not transfer.

Visiting: Guides are available for informal visits, and prospective students may sit in on classes. Visits are best scheduled for Tuesdays, Thursdays, and Fridays from 9 A.M. to 3 P.M. The admissions secretary handles arrangements.

Financial Aid: About 80% of the students receive aid. A number of programs are available, including BEOG, SEOG, NDSL, GSL, CWS, state scholarships and loans, and school scholarships. Aid awards are based solely on financial need. The deadline for priority consideration of aid applications is March 15.

Foreign Students: Four foreign students are enrolled at the school. An intensive English course is provided.

Admissions: No English proficiency or college entrance exams are required. Applicants must submit a portfolio of their work.

Procedure: Application deadlines are open; students are admitted to both semesters. Foreign students must submit a medical certificate and proof of adequate funds for 1 year.

Admissions Contact: Peter W. Newport, Director of Admissions.

TUFTS UNIVERSITY D-2
Medford, Massachusetts 02155 (617) 628-5000

F/T: 2162M, 2152W Faculty: 313; I, +$
P/T: none Ph.D.'s: 93%
Grad: 1319M, 877W S/F Ratio: 14 to 1
Year: sems, ss Tuition: $6801
Appl: Jan. 15 R and B: $3485
9493 applied 3198 accepted 1231 enrolled
SAT: 580V 630M HIGHLY COMPETITIVE

Tufts University, a private, nonsectarian institution established in 1852, offers undergraduate and graduate programs in the liberal arts and sciences, engineering, health, and education. The College of Liberal Arts for Men and Jackson College for Women maintain separate names because of tradition but are in every way coeducational. These 2 liberal arts colleges and the College of Engineering share faculty, resources, and activities on the Medford campus. The schools of Medicine, Dental Medicine, and Veterinarian Medicine are located on the Boston campus at the Tufts New England Medical Center. The library houses a collection of 584,000 volumes and nearly 14,000 microfilm items, and subscribes to 4300 periodicals.

Environment: The university occupies a 150-acre suburban campus about 6 miles from Boston. There are 125 buildings, including dormitories, fraternity houses, and co-op and language houses that accommodate more than 3100 students.

Student Life: About 45% of the students are from New England. Sixty-eight percent come from public schools. Seventy-five percent live on campus. Twelve percent of the students are minority-group members. University housing is both single-sex and coed. There are visiting privileges in single-sex housing. Upperclassmen may keep cars on campus. Day-care services are available to all students, faculty, and staff for a fee.

Organizations: There are 8 national fraternities, which attract 10% of the men, and 3 national sororities, to which 1% of the women belong. The extracurricular program is extensive and varied. Clubs, a film series, musical groups, and radio and television stations are among the 170 student organizations.

Sports: Intercollegiate teams are fielded in 13 sports for men and 13 for women. The intramural program includes competition in 23 sports for men and 21 for women.

Handicapped: Special facilities for the physically handicapped include wheelchair ramps, parking areas, elevators, and specially equipped rest rooms. Special class scheduling and counselors (4) are provided. Fewer than 1% of the students have visual or hearing impairments.

Graduates: The freshman dropout rate is 1%; about 90% remain to graduate. Fifty-five percent of the students go on for further education; 7% to medical school, 2% to dental school, and 6% to law school.

Services: Career counseling, placement services, tutoring, and psychological counseling are offered without charge. Health care is available under an insurance program.

Programs of Study: The B.A., B.S., B.S.C.E., B.S.Ch.E., B.S.E.E., B.S.E.S., and B.S.M.E. degrees are offered. There are also master's and doctoral programs. The bachelor's degree is granted in the following subjects: AREA STUDIES (American, Russian), EDUCATION (early childhood, elementary, secondary, special), ENGLISH (English), FINE AND PERFORMING ARTS (art, art history, music, theater/dramatics), HEALTH SCIENCES (community health, mental health, occupational therapy), LANGUAGES (Chinese, French, German, Greek/Latin, Italian, Russian, Spanish), MATH AND SCIENCES (astronomy, biochemistry, biology, chemistry, computer science, ecology/environmental science, geology, mathematics, physics), PHILOSOPHY (classics, philosophy, religion), PREPROFESSIONAL (engineering), SOCIAL SCIENCES (anthropology, economics, government/political science, history, international relations, sociology). About 18% of the degrees are conferred in engineering, 14% in math or sciences, and 11% in English.

Required: A general education requirement in Liberal Arts includes course work in English and a foreign language. Engineering students must complete 8 courses in social studies or the humanities. Students in the occupational therapy program must complete a 9-month hospital internship.

Special: Student-designed majors, study abroad, and 5-year combined degrees (B.A.-B.S., B.A.-B.F.A., B.A.-B.M.) are offered. The Experimental College offers interdepartmental courses and courses that are outside all other departments.

Honors: There are 3 honor societies represented on campus, including Phi Beta Kappa. All departments offer honors programs, usually involving the completion of an undergraduate thesis.

Admissions: About 34% of the 1981-82 applicants were accepted. The SAT scores of those who enrolled were as follows: Verbal—17% scored below 500, 44% between 500 and 599, 34% between 600 and 700, and 5% above 700; Math—6% scored below 500, 29% between 500 and 599, 48% between 600 and 700, and 16% above 700. There is no cutoff point for either class rank or grade average: half the current freshman class came from the first decile; most of the students presented A or B records. Candidates are not required to have any specific secondary school preparation. Important factors in addition to academic ability include special talents, recommendations, and extracurricular activities.

Procedure: The SAT (or ACT) and 3 ATs should be taken by January of the senior year. Liberal Arts applicants should take an English AT and 2 others; engineering applicants should take an English AT, the Math Level I or II AT, and a science AT. Application deadlines are January 15 (fall), and November 15 (spring). Freshmen are not admitted in the summer. There is a $30 application fee.

Special: There are early decision, early admissions, and deferred admissions plans. The notification date for early decision is within 4 weeks of the completion of credentials. The application deadline for both early decision and early admission is January 15. AP credit is granted.

Transfer: For fall 1981, 757 students applied, 173 were accepted, and 89 enrolled. Outstanding academic credentials are necessary. D grades do not transfer. Four semesters must be completed in residence. Seventeen courses must be completed out of the 34 required in Liberal Arts and 38 in Engineering to receive a bachelor's degree. March 1 (fall) and November 15 (spring) are the application deadlines.

Visiting: Informal guided campus tours may be arranged on Mondays through Fridays during the school year. Visitors may sit in on classes.

Financial Aid: About 39% of the students receive assistance. Twenty-three percent work part-time on campus. Average aid awarded to freshmen from all sources is $5505. The university offers scholarships for freshmen in addition to federal/state programs (EOG, NDSL, CWS) and private loans. Need is the determining factor. The university is a member of CSS. The aid application and the FAF should be filed. Application deadlines are February 1 (fall) and November 15 (spring). Notification is usually by April 15.

Foreign Students: Three percent of the full-time students come from foreign countries. The university offers these students special counseling and special organizations.

Admissions: Foreign students must take the TOEFL and the SAT or ACT. ATs are recommended.

Procedure: The application deadlines are January 15 (fall) and November 15 (spring). Foreign students must present proof of health. They must also present proof of adequate funds on a yearly basis. They must carry health insurance, which is available from the university for a fee.

Admissions Contact: Isabel B. Abbott, Assistant Director of Admissions.

UNIVERSITY OF LOWELL D-1
Lowell, Massachusetts 01854 (617) 452-5000

F/T: 4900M, 2756W	Faculty: 419; n/av
P/T: 155M, 215W	Ph.D.'s: 58%
Grad: 1019M, 533W	S/F Ratio: 18 to 1
Year: sems, ss	Tuition: $1035 ($3140)
Appl: Apr. 1	R and B: $2144
6326 applied	2968 accepted 2122 enrolled
SAT: 473V 544M	COMPETITIVE+

The University of Lowell, a merger of Lowell State College and Lowell Technological Institute, is composed of 7 colleges. The library contains more than 300,000 volumes and 11,000 microfilm items, and subscribes to 2000 periodicals.

Environment: The university has 2 campuses, totaling 100 acres, in the city of Lowell, 30 miles northwest of Boston. Lowell is an historic textile manufacturing city on the Merrimack River; it was the first city to be designated a National Historical Park. There are 40 buildings on campus, including a wide variety of dorm life-styles—from high-rise to small dorms.

Student Life: Over 90% of the students are from Massachusetts; 65% of the entering freshmen come from public schools. The majority of students commute. About 5% of the students are minority-group members. University housing is both single-sex and coed. Students may keep cars on campus.

Organizations: There are 7 fraternities and 4 sororities on campus, to which 3% of the men and 3% of the women belong. Student clubs are available, as well as an on-campus cultural series. The cities of Lowell and Boston provide additional recreational and cultural opportunities.

Sports: The university competes on an intercollegiate level in 17 sports for men and 11 for women. There are 15 intramural sports for men and 13 for women.

Handicapped: About 65% of the campus is accessible to wheelchair students. Special facilities for the physically handicapped include wheelchair ramps, parking areas, elevators, and specially equipped rest rooms. Special class scheduling can be arranged. A dormitory wing with highly specialized facilities is available. Fewer than 1% of the student body are visually or hearing impaired. One counselor is available, and readers or interpreters can be provided.

Graduates: Twenty percent of the freshmen drop out by the end of the first year. Sixty percent remain to graduate. About 25% of the students pursue advanced study after graduation; 1% enter medical school, and about 2% law school. Sixty-five percent of the graduates pursue careers in business and industry.

Services: Placement services, career counseling, and remedial instruction for graduates and undergraduates are available on campus free of charge.

Programs of Study: The university grants the B.A., B.S., B.Mus., and B.Mus.Ed. degrees. Associate, master's, and doctoral degrees are also awarded. Bachelor's degrees are offered in the following subjects: AREA STUDIES (American), BUSINESS (business administration, industrial management), ENGLISH (English), FINE AND PERFORMING ARTS (art, music, music education), HEALTH SCIENCES (health education, health services administration, medical technology, nursing, physical therapy), LANGUAGES (French, modern languages, Spanish), MATH AND SCIENCES (biology, chemistry, computer science, earth science, mathematics, meteorology, physics, radiological health physics), PHILOSOPHY (philosophy), PREPROFESSIONAL (engineering—chemical, engineering—civil, engineering—electrical, engineering—mechanical, engineering—nuclear, engineering—plastics, engineering—industrial technology, law and justice), SOCIAL SCIENCES (economics, government/political science, history, psychology, sociology). Twenty-nine percent of the degrees conferred are in preprofessional studies, 22% in business, and 13% in social sciences.

Special: The university offers a general studies degree.

Honors: There are a number of honor and professional societies on campus.

Admissions: Forty-seven percent of those who applied were accepted for the 1981-82 freshman class. Of those who enrolled in a recent year, the SAT scores were as follows: Verbal—26% scored between 500 and 600, 4% between 600 and 700, and 1% above 700; Math—45% scored between 500 and 600, 19% between 600 and 700, and 3% above 700. The candidate should have at least a C+ grade average and rank in the upper half of the class. Applicants should submit 16 Carnegie units of high school work. Other qualifications considered, in order of importance, are advanced placement or honors courses, recommendations by school officials, and personal characteristics.

Procedure: All candidates are required to take the SAT and the English Composition AT. Applications for the fall term should be filed early in the senior year. Application deadlines are April 1 (fall) and November 1 (spring). The rolling admissions plan is followed. The application fee is $18 for state residents and $25 for out-of-state applicants.

Special: Early decision and early admissions plans are available. CLEP general and subject exams are accepted, and AP exams are considered.

Transfer: For fall 1981, 1681 students applied, 772 were admitted, and 681 enrolled. A minimum average of 2.5 is required for transfer. D grades do not transfer. To earn a degree, students must study at the university at least 1 year and earn 30 of the 120 minimum credits required for a bachelor's degree. Application deadlines are April 1 (fall) and November 1 (spring).

Visiting: There are regularly scheduled orientations for prospective students on selected Saturdays during the year and a 2-day freshman orientation in June. Informal visits are possible weekdays from 9 A.M. to 2 P.M. Visitors can sit in on classes if arrangements are made beforehand through the admissions office.

MASSACHUSETTS

Financial Aid: About 50% to 60% of the students receive financial aid. About 10% work part-time on campus. Average aid to freshmen from all sources is $700. Aid is available through loans and scholarships. The university participates in BEOG, CWS, NDSL, and SEOG. The university is a member of CSS. The FAF is required. Applications for financial aid must be filed by April 1 (fall) and November 1 (spring).

Foreign Students: Fewer than 1% of the full-time students come from foreign countries. The university offers these students an intensive English course, special counseling, and special organizations.

Admissions: Foreign students must score 500 on the TOEFL. They must also take the SAT.

Procedure: The application deadlines are April 1 (fall) and November 1 (spring). Foreign students are advised to apply early to facilitate processing the visa and appropriate immigration papers. They must present proof of adequate funds and carry health insurance, which is available through the university.

Admissions Contact: Lawrence R. Martin, Director of Admissions.

UNIVERSITY OF MASSACHUSETTS

The University of Massachusetts is a state university of the Commonwealth, founded in 1863 under provisions of the Morrill Land Grant Act. Campuses are located in Amherst and Boston; additional schools are the Medical School in Worcester and the School of Agriculture in Amherst.

Admissions are controlled at each campus. Separate profiles of the Amherst and Boston campuses follow. The Worcester Medical School enrolled its first class in the fall of 1970. The Stockbridge School of Agriculture is a 2-year school at Amherst. It is considered an integral part of the College of Agriculture at the Amherst campus.

UNIVERSITY OF MASSACHUSETTS AT AMHERST   B-2

Amherst, Massachusetts 01003   (413) 545-0222

F/T: 9901M, 9048W	Faculty: 1230; I, +$
P/T: 30M, 64W	Ph.D.'s: 80%
Grad: 2800M, 2400W	S/F Ratio: 18 to 1
Year: sems, ss	Tuition: $1452 ($3850)
Appl: Mar. 1	R and B: $2500
13,464 applied 9860 accepted 4109 enrolled	
SAT: 458V 510M	COMPETITIVE

The campus at Amherst occupies the original site of the University of Massachusetts and is today the system's largest and central branch. The undergraduate schools at the university are the College of Arts and Sciences and the Schools of Agriculture, Business Administration, Education, Engineering, Food and Natural Resources, Health Science, Physical Education, and Nursing. The library contains 2.4 million volumes and 680,000 microfilm items, and subscribes to 10,000 periodicals.

Environment: The 1100-acre campus is situated in a town of 15,000, about 90 miles west of Boston, in the Connecticut Valley, one of the most picturesque sections of the state. Included among the over 150 buildings are a variety of residence facilities, from high-rise dormitories to suites, quads, and Greek letter houses.

Student Life: All but 15% of the students are residents of the state. About 65% live on campus, 65% in residence halls and 5% in fraternity or sorority houses. Eight percent of the students are minority-group members. University housing is both single-sex and coed. There are visiting privileges in single-sex housing. Students may keep cars on campus. Day-care services are available to all full-time students, faculty, and staff on a sliding fee scale.

Organizations: There are 14 fraternities and 9 sororities at the university, to which about 9% of the students belong. A wide spectrum of campus activities is offered, including publications, communications, music and drama groups, religious organizations, and over 500 special-interest groups. The university participates with 4 other area colleges in sponsoring a full schedule of cooperative cultural events.

Sports: The university participates in intercollegiate activity in 14 sports for men and 13 for women. In addition, there are 17 intramural sports for men and 16 for women.

Handicapped: About 75% of the campus is accessible to handicapped students. Special facilities include wheelchair ramps, special parking areas, elevators, specially equipped rest rooms, lowered drinking fountains and telephones, and a transportation system. Special class scheduling can be arranged. There are 3 counselors to assist handicapped students. About 5% of the students are hearing impaired, and 1% visually impaired. Special facilities for these students include interpreting and note taking, and a reading machine and readers.

Graduates: Twenty-five percent of the freshmen drop out by the end of their first year. Sixty percent remain for the full 4 years and receive their degrees. About 25% of the students go on to graduate study.

Services: The following services are available to students free of charge: psychological counseling, placement and career counseling (for graduates as well as undergraduates), and remedial instruction. Tutoring is available both free and on a fee basis. Health care is available on a fee basis.

Programs of Study: Undergraduate degrees offered by the various schools of the university are the B.A., B.S., and B.F.A. Associate, master's and doctoral degrees are also conferred. Bachelor's degrees are offered in the following subjects: AREA STUDIES (Asian, Black/Afro-American, Russian, urban), BUSINESS (accounting, business administration, computer science, finance, management, marketing), EDUCATION (early childhood, elementary, secondary, special), ENGLISH (English, journalism, literature), FINE AND PERFORMING ARTS (art, art education, art history, dance, music, music education, radio/TV, studio art, theater/dramatics), HEALTH SCIENCES (communication disorders, environmental health, medical technology, nursing, speech therapy), LANGUAGES (Chinese, French, German, Italian, Japanese, Portuguese, Russian, Spanish), MATH AND SCIENCES (astronomy, biochemistry, botany, chemistry, ecology/environmental science, geology, geography, mathematics, microbiology, physics, statistics, zoology), PHILOSOPHY (classics, philosophy), PREPROFESSIONAL (agriculture, dentistry, engineering, forestry, home economics, law, medicine, social work, veterinary), SOCIAL SCIENCES (anthropology, economics, geography, government/political science, history, psychology, social thought and political economy, sociology).

Required: All students must take general education distribution requirements, including courses in rhetoric and 9 other liberal arts areas.

Special: Special programs include honors, study abroad, and independent study. The Residential College program emphasizes a complete living-learning environment for small groups of students. Student-designed majors are permitted. The university shares some facilities with nearby Amherst, Hampshire, Mount Holyoke, and Smith Colleges. Qualified students are permitted to earn academic credit in various subjects at the other colleges. A special Inquiry Program, designed for freshmen and sophomores, offers an alternative and personalized approach to lower-division study.

Honors: There is a school-wide University Honors Program. In addition, most departments have their own honors systems.

Admissions: About 73% of those who applied were accepted for the 1981–82 freshman class. SAT scores among enrolled freshmen were as follows: Verbal—66% scored below 500, 26% between 500 and 599, 6% between 600 and 700, and 1% above 700; Math—45% scored below 500, 36% between 500 and 599, 16% between 600 and 700, and 2% above 700. Applicants must have completed a 4-year high school course or its equivalent and should rank in the top 40% of their graduating class. Other factors considered important are advanced placement or honors courses, recommendations, special talents, and extracurricular activities. Residents of Massachusetts receive preference. Admissions for nonresidents is very competitive.

Procedure: The SAT is required, and 3 ATs are recommended. December testing dates are preferred. Completed applications from in-state students must be received no later than March 1 (fall) and October 15 (spring). A campus visit is recommended, but personal interviews are not required. Admissions are rolling, and candidates are notified by April 15. There is an $18 in-state application fee ($25 for out-of-state).

Special: The university has early and deferred admissions plans. AP and CLEP are accepted within certain limitations.

Transfer: For fall 1981, 3724 students applied, 2205 were accepted, and 1331 enrolled. About 45% of the upperclassmen are transfer students. The minimum standard (for state residents) is a 2.5 GPA in all course work. D grades do not transfer. Students applying with fewer than 30 credits must submit high school and SAT credentials. Transfer admission for nonresidents is limited. Transfer students must complete, at the university, 45 of the 120 credits needed for a bachelor's degree. Application deadlines are April 1 (fall) and October 15 (spring).

Visiting: An orientation program held for prospective students on Saturday mornings during the fall includes a tour of the campus. Guides are also available for informal visits to the school. Visitors may sit in on classes and may also stay on campus. The Admissions Office handles arrangements.

Financial Aid: About 80% of all students receive some form of aid. Seventy-five percent work part-time on campus. Average aid to freshmen from all sources is $1000. Aid is awarded on the basis of financial need. All major federal aid programs are available, as well as a variety of state and institutional funds for which residents of Massachusetts are eligible. All students must maintain satisfactory academic progress to remain eligible for financial assistance. The university is a member of CSS. The FAF is required. The deadlines for aid applications are March 1 (fall) and September 1 (spring).

Foreign Students: About 1% of the full-time students come from foreign countries. The university offers these students an intensive English program, special counseling, and special organizations.

Admissions: Foreign students must score 550 on the TOEFL. They must also take the SAT. A score of 500 on each test is recommended.

Procedure: The deadline for application is February 1 (fall). Foreign students must present the results of a physical examination. They must also present proof of funds adequate for an entire calendar year before their visa qualification. They must carry health insurance, which is available through the university for a fee.

Admissions Contact: David Taggart, Director of Admissions.

UNIVERSITY OF MASSACHUSETTS AT BOSTON E-2
Boston, Massachusetts 02125   (617) 287-1900

F/T: 6313 M&W   Faculty: 440; IIA, ++$
P/T: 590 M&W   Ph.D.'s: n/av
Grad: 85 M&W   S/F Ratio: n/av
Year: sems, ss   Tuition: $1135 ($3533)
Appl: July 1   R and B: n/app
3500 applied   2000 accepted   1200 enrolled
SAT: 462V 493M   COMPETITIVE

The University of Massachusetts at Boston, established in 1965, is a state-supported campus that offers undergraduate study in its 3 colleges: Arts and Sciences, Management and Professional Studies, and Public and Community Service. Its library has over 325,000 books and subscribes to 3000 periodicals. Boston State College recently merged with this university.

Environment: The College of Public and Community Service is housed in the original downtown Boston campus; the other 2 colleges are located at the new Harbor Campus on Columbia Bay. The university provides no housing facilities. A physical-education complex has recently been completed.

Student Life: About 96% of the students come from Massachusetts, most from the Boston area. About 85% attended public schools.

Organizations: Student activities include 70 clubs and organizations, publications, a student radio station, community action programs, and numerous social and cultural events. In addition, the many cultural, educational, recreational, and social advantages of the Boston area are available to students.

Sports: The university campus at Boston competes in 3 intercollegiate sports. Several intramural sports also are available.

Handicapped: All university buildings have been remodeled to make them totally accessible to wheelchair-bound students. The Handicapped Center provides reading and instruction services in braille and sign language and has tape and braille libraries and braille typewriters.

Graduates: About 20% of the graduates go on for further education.

Services: Career, personal, peer-support, and psychological counseling are provided. Health care services are available. Placement and career planning services are provided for students and alumni.

Programs of Study: The university confers the B.A. and B.S. degrees. Master's degrees also are awarded. Bachelor's degrees are offered in the following subjects: AREA STUDIES (Black/Afro-American, East Asian, Irish, Latin American), BUSINESS (accounting, computer science, human resources management, management, management information systems, marketing, operations management, public management), ENGLISH (English), FINE AND PERFORMING ARTS (art, music, theater/dramatics), HEALTH SCIENCES (health services administration), LANGUAGES (French, German, Greek/Latin, Italian, Russian, Spanish), MATH AND SCIENCES (biology, chemistry, mathematics, physics), PHILOSOPHY (classics, philosophy), PREPROFESSIONAL (engineering—chemical, engineering—civil, engineering—electrical, engineering—industrial, engineering—mechanical), SOCIAL SCIENCES (anthropology, economics, government/political science, history, psychology, sociology). A teaching certification program is offered.

Required: All students take a freshman writing (which can be waived by examination) and 12 courses from the following 7 areas: art, historical and cultural studies, philosophical and humanistic studies, social and behavioral sciences, natural sciences, mathematics and computer languages, and foreign languages.

Special: Individually designed majors, study abroad, student exchange programs, independent research, field work and internships, and interdisciplinary majors are offered. Special programs are available in creative writing, labor studies, women's studies, urban studies, New England history and archaeology, Armenian studies, Japanese studies, Polish, and Portuguese studies. The Developmental Studies program, a 6-week summer program, helps academically deficient students make a successful start in college.

Honors: Honors work is possible in most fields.

Admissions: About 57% of the applicants for the 1981-82 freshman class were accepted. The SAT scores of those who enrolled were as follows: Verbal—42% below 500, 27% between 500 and 599, 15% between 600 and 700, and 2% above 700; Math—52% below 500, 36% between 500 and 599, 8% between 600 and 700, and 3% above 700. Applicants must rank in the top three-fifths of their high school class and have at least a C average. High school graduation is not required. Recommendations, talents, extracurricular activities, advanced placement and honors courses, and personal qualities also are considered.

Procedure: The SAT is required and should be taken as early as possible in the senior year. Older students who have been out of school for several years may have this requirement waived. Application deadlines are July 1 (fall) and December 1 (spring). Freshman applicants are advised to submit completed credentials as soon as possible after the first marking period of the senior year. Notification is usually sent 2 to 3 weeks after the file is complete. The application fee is $10 for Massachusetts residents and $25 for out-of-state students.

Special: AP and CLEP credit is given. Early decision and deferred admissions plans are offered.

Transfer: Transfer students are accepted for all classes; preference is given to Massachusetts residents. A 2.0 GPA is recommended. D grades do not transfer. Students must complete at least 45 credits at the university of the 128 required for a bachelor's degree.

Visiting: Prospective applicants may visit the campus, sit in on classes, chat with students or faculty, and meet with an admissions counselor. The admissions office offers tours of the Harbor Campus on Tuesdays, Thursdays, and Fridays from 10 A.M. to 4 P.M. by appointment.

Financial Aid: About 63% of the students receive aid. Federal and commercial bank loans, grants (such as BEOG), scholarships, and campus jobs (including CWS) are available. Commonwealth scholarships also are offered to state residents only. All awards are based on need. The FAF and the university aid application should be filed by March 31 for priority consideration.

Foreign Students: Foreign students make up 3% of enrollment. The university offers these students an intensive summer English program, special counseling, and special organizations.

Admissions: Applicants must score at least 500 on the TOEFL. No college entrance exams are required.

Procedure: The application deadline for the fall semester, the only one to which foreign students are admitted, is January 1. Students must present proof of adequate funds for 4 years of study.

Admissions Contact: Douglas Hartnagel, Dean of Admissions.

WELLESLEY COLLEGE D-2
Wellesley, Massachusetts 02181   (617) 235-0320

F/T: 2060W   Faculty: 224; IIB, ++$
P/T: 160W   Ph.D.'s: 81%
Grad: none   S/F Ratio: 11 to 1
Year: sems   Tuition: $6530
Appl: Feb. 1   R and B: $3180
2294 applied   1106 accepted   585 enrolled
SAT: 610V 610M   MOST COMPETITIVE

Wellesley College, established in 1870, is an independent liberal arts college for women. Its library has a collection of 600,000 books and 16,000 microtexts, and subscribes to 2672 periodicals.

Environment: The 500-acre suburban campus is located 12 miles west of Boston. There are 64 buildings, including 14 residence halls that accommodate 1970 women.

Student Life: Students come from all 50 states. About 70% are from public schools. Ninety-four percent live on campus. About 22% of the students are minority-group members. College housing is single-sex; there are visiting privileges. Students may keep cars on campus.

MASSACHUSETTS

Organizations: There are no sororities. The college sponsors a traditional extracurricular program, including more than 50 organizations and clubs. Regularly scheduled social and cultural events take place on campus, and nearby Boston offers a wealth of cultural facilities.

Sports: In addition to 11 intercollegiate athletics, there is intramural competition in 14 sports.

Handicapped: About 70% of the campus is accessible to the handicapped. Special facilities include wheelchair ramps, parking areas, elevators, lowered drinking fountains and telephones, and some specially equipped rest rooms. Special class scheduling can be arranged. A counselor is provided to aid students with special needs. At present, there are at least 2 visually impaired students attending classes.

Graduates: The freshman dropout rate is less than 1%; 85% of the students remain to graduate. About 28% continue their educations directly after graduation: 11% at medical school and 15% at law school. About 40% enter careers in business and industry.

Services: Psychological counseling, health care, remedial instruction, tutoring, career counseling, and placement services are offered without charge. The career placement service provides counseling and information about occupations, graduate and professional training, internships, fellowships, and awards.

Programs of Study: The B.A. is offered in the following subjects: AREA STUDIES (American, Black/Afro-American, Chinese, East Asian, French, Italian, language, Latin American, urban, women's), EDUCATION (secondary), ENGLISH (English, literature), FINE AND PERFORMING ARTS (art, art history, music, studio art, theater/dramatics), LANGUAGES (Chinese, French, German, Greek/Latin, Italian, Russian, Spanish), MATH AND SCIENCES (astronomy, biology, chemistry, geology, mathematics, molecular biology, physics), PHILOSOPHY (classical and Near Eastern archeology, classical civilization, humanities, medieval/renaissance studies, philosophy, religion), SOCIAL SCIENCES (anthropology, economics, government/political science, history, international relations, psychobiology, psychology, sociology). About 42% of the degrees are conferred in the social sciences, 22% in math and sciences, and 9% in English.

Required: Unless exempted, students must elect 3 units from each of the following 3 groups: (1) literature, foreign languages, art, and music; (2) social science, religion and biblical studies, and philosophy; and (3) science and mathematics.

Special: Student-designed majors, study abroad, independent study/research, exchange programs, and summer internships are offered.

Honors: All departments offer honors work for highly qualified students. Two honor societies, Phi Beta Kappa and Sigma Xi, have chapters on campus.

Admissions: About 48% of the 1981-82 freshman applicants were accepted. The SAT scores of those who enrolled were as follows: Verbal—10% scored below 500, 31% between 500 and 599, 47% between 600 and 700, and 12% above 700; Math—9% scored below 500, 28% between 500 and 599, 51% between 600 and 700, and 12% above 700. In addition to the academic record, the admissions committee considers advanced placement or honors work, recommendations, and special talents important.

Procedure: The SAT and 3 ATs (including English Composition) must be taken by January of the senior year. The ACT may be substituted for the SAT. February 1 is the application deadline for fall entry. Notification is made by the middle of April. A personal interview is required. There is a $25 application fee.

Special: There are early decision, early admissions, and deferred admissions plans. Candidates wishing early evaluation of their chances for admission must submit completed applications by January 1. AP credit is given.

Transfer: For fall 1981, 184 transfer students applied, 77 were accepted, and 50 enrolled. An excellent academic record is necessary. D grades do not transfer. To receive a degree, 2 years must be completed at Wellesley, along with 16 of the 32 course credits needed for a bachelor's degree. February 1 (fall) and November 15 (spring) are the application deadlines.

Visiting: There is an orientation program for prospective students. Guided campus tours and group chats can be arranged. Visitors can attend classes and stay at the college. The fall of the senior year is recommended for visits. Appointments should be made well in advance with the admissions office.

Financial Aid: About 40% of the students are receiving aid. Thirty-eight percent work part-time on campus. Average aid to freshmen from all sources is $5906. Aid is based on need and comes from college, federal, and state funds and in combinations of grants, loans, and work opportunities. Grants from other sources and state-guaranteed loans are also available. Awards vary in size according to individual need and may amount to or exceed the full fee. The Financial Aid Office assists students in finding paid jobs. The college is a member of CSS. The FAF, the college's aid application, and a copy of the federal income tax form should be filed by February 1 for those seeking regular admission, November 1 for early decision.

Foreign Students: More than 5% of the full-time students come from foreign countries. The college offers these students special counseling and special organizations.

Admissions: Foreign students must take the SAT and 3 ATs, including English Composition and 2 others of the student's choice, except the student's native language.

Procedure: The application deadline is February 1 for the fall. Foreign students must present the standard health forms. They must also present proof of funds adequate to cover 4 years of study. They must carry health insurance, which is available through the college for a fee.

Admissions Contact: Mary Ellen Ames, Director of Admission.

WENTWORTH INSTITUTE OF TECHNOLOGY
E-2

Boston, Massachusetts 02115   (617) 442-9010

F/T: 2782M, 250W   Faculty: 150; n/av
P/T: none   Ph.D.'s: n/av
Grad: none   S/F Ratio: 17 to 1
Year: sems, ss   Tuition: $3580
Appl: Sept. 1   R and B: $2550
3066 applied   2759 accepted   1475 enrolled
SAT: 372V 441M   **LESS COMPETITIVE**

Wentworth Institute of Technology is a private undergraduate college offering programs in engineering technologies. The library contains 50,000 volumes and 75 microfilm items, and subscribes to 250 periodicals.

Environment: The 9-acre urban campus has 18 buildings; 1 dormitory and 4 apartment-style residences are available.

Student Life: About 80% of the students come from Massachusetts; 25% live on campus. Twelve percent are minority-group members. Institute housing is single-sex. Students may keep cars on campus.

Organizations: There are no fraternities or sororities. About 16 clubs and activities are offered on campus.

Sports: The school competes intercollegiately in 5 sports. Two intramural athletics are also available.

Handicapped: Special facilities for physically handicapped students include wheelchair ramps and elevators.

Graduates: Twenty percent of the freshmen drop out by the end of their first year. About 75% remain to graduate. Twenty-five percent of the graduates pursue advanced study. Ninety-five percent enter careers in industry and business.

Services: Health care, placement, career counseling, psychological counseling, and remedial instruction are offered free of charge to all students. Tutoring is on a fee basis.

Programs of Study: The B.S. in Engineering Technology is offered. Associate degrees are also awarded. The bachelor's degree is offered in the following areas: PREPROFESSIONAL (engineering—architectural, engineering—civil, engineering—computer science, engineering—electronic, engineering—management, engineering—mechanical).

Honors: There is 1 honor society on campus.

Admissions: Ninety percent of the applicants for the 1981-82 freshman class were admitted. A high-school diploma is required. Students should have a C average. Admissions are based largely on specific math and science units from the high school.

Procedure: The SAT is recommended. September 1 is the fall semester deadline. Notification is on a rolling basis. There is a $25 application fee. An interview is strongly recommended.

Special: AP and CLEP credit is accepted.

Transfer: About 50 transfer students enroll yearly. Transfers are accepted for all classes. A C average is required. D grades do not transfer. Students must complete the last 2 semesters at the institute to receive a bachelor's degree. Application deadlines are the same as those for freshmen.

Visiting: There is an orientation program for prospective students. Informal campus tours may be arranged. Visitors may sit in on classes.

Financial Aid: About 85% of all students receive financial aid. Twenty percent work part-time on campus. Federal loans and CWS are offered. There are no scholarships for freshmen. The institute is a member of CSS. The FAF should be submitted by May 1.

Foreign Students: About 8% of the full-time students come from foreign countries. The institute offers these students special counseling and special organizations.

Admissions: Foreign students must score 490 on the TOEFL or 80 on the University of Michigan Language Test. No college entrance examination is required.

Procedure: The deadline for application is September 1 (fall). Foreign students must present a completed health form. They must also present proof of adequate funds. There is a $100 surcharge. Foreign students must carry health insurance, which is available through the institute for a fee.

Admissions Contact: Charles P. Uppvall, Dean of Admissions.

WESTERN NEW ENGLAND COLLEGE   B-3
Springfield, Massachusetts 01119   (413) 782-3111

F/T: 1378M, 793W	Faculty:	107; IIA, +$
P/T: 540M, 331W	Ph.D.'s:	52%
Grad: 617M, 283W	S/F Ratio:	20 to 1
Year: sems, ss	Tuition:	$3588
Appl: open	R and B:	$2130
2037 applied	1574 accepted	641 enrolled
SAT: 420V 500M		COMPETITIVE

Western New England College, established in 1919, is a private institution, offering a blend of liberal and professional education. Degrees are awarded in the arts and sciences, social work, engineering, and business. The library contains 90,000 volumes and 13,000 microfilm items, and subscribes to 876 periodicals.

Environment: The 94-acre campus, located in a suburban area 3 miles from Springfield, contains 16 Georgian and colonial buildings, plus 11 houses adjacent to the main campus for offices and the dispensary. There are 9 residence facilities, housing approximately 1000 students in a variety of living styles.

Student Life: About 64% of the students come from Massachusetts. The majority of the remainder come from New England, New York, and New Jersey. Seventy percent are from public schools. Fifty-four percent of the students are Catholic, 18% Protestant, and 2% Jewish; 26% belong to other denominations. About 7% of the students are minority-group members. College housing is both single-sex and coed. There are visiting privileges in single-sex housing. Students may keep cars on campus.

Organizations: There are a wide variety of recreational and cultural activities on campus, such as concerts, lectures, dances, homecoming, and films. Nearby cities in the area have many attractions, including the Springfield Symphony, museums, and the Springfield Civic Center.

Sports: The college competes in 11 intercollegiate sports for men and 6 for women. Intramural sports are offered in 5 sports for men and 4 for women.

Handicapped: Forty percent of the campus is accessible to handicapped students. Special parking and specially equipped rest rooms are available. The college provides counselors for these students.

Graduates: About 19% of the freshmen drop out during their first year. Forty-eight percent go on to graduate. Five percent pursue advanced study after graduation. Fewer than 1% enter medical school, 2% enter law school, and another 85% enter careers in business and industry.

Student Services: The following free services are offered on campus: placement and career counseling, health care, tutoring, and psychological counseling.

Programs of Study: The B.A., B.S., B.S.B.A., B.S. in E., B.S.E.E., B.S.I.E., B.S.M.E., and B.S.W. degrees are conferred. The college also offers master's programs. Bachelor's degrees are offered in the following subjects: BUSINESS (accounting, business administration, computer systems, finance, general business, human resource management, management, marketing, quantitative methods, technical business), ENGLISH (English), MATH AND SCIENCES (biology, chemistry, computer science, mathematics), PHILOSOPHY (philosophy), PREPROFESSIONAL (engineering, social work), SOCIAL SCIENCES (economics, government/political science, history, psychology, sociology). About 53% of all students receive degrees in business, 28% in arts and sciences, and 19% in engineering.

Required: Courses in English studies and physical education are required of all students.

Special: The college participates in the Cooperative Colleges Plan of Greater Springfield with 7 other colleges. Washington Semester and study abroad are available. Independent study and a major in integrated liberal studies are offered. A student may design his or her own major.

Honors: Four national honor societies have chapters on campus. Each school has special honors seminars for qualified students.

Admissions: About 77% of all those who applied were admitted into the 1981–82 freshman class. The SAT scores of those who enrolled were as follows: Verbal—76% scored below 500, 18% between 500 and 599, 3% between 600 and 700, and fewer than 1% above 700; Math—46% scored below 500, 36% between 500 and 599, 13% between 600 and 700, and fewer than 1% above 700. Fifteen Carnegie units should have been completed. Academic and background requirements vary according to program. Other important factors in the admissions decision are advanced placement or honors courses, recommendations by high school officials, and impressions made during an interview.

Procedure: The SAT or ACT is required. A high school transcript and letter of recommendation should be sent with the application. The deadline for admission is open. The school has a rolling admissions plan. There is a $20 application fee.

Special: The school has an early decision plan and a deferred admissions plan.

Transfer: For fall 1981, 378 applications were received, 277 were accepted, and 147 transfer students enrolled. Transfers are accepted for all classes. D grades are acceptable in certain cases. A minimum average of 2.0 is required for transfer. Students must study at the college for at least 30 semester hours out of the 120 needed to receive a bachelor's degree. Application deadlines are the same as for freshmen.

Visiting: There are no regularly scheduled orientations for prospective students. However, visitors are encouraged to visit during the school week from 8:30 A.M. to 4:30 P.M.. For informal visits, guides are provided. Visitors may sit in on classes by arrangement. To arrange such visits, the Dean of Admissions should be contacted.

Financial Aid: About 75% of all students now receive financial aid. Seventeen percent work part-time on campus. The college awards some scholarships based on both academic performance and need. Other programs include CWS, NDSL, SEOG, BEOG, guaranteed insured loans, and state scholarships. The college is a member of CSS. The FAF is required. Application for financial aid should be made no later than April 1 for priority consideration.

Foreign Students: About 2% of the full-time students come from foreign countries. The college offers these students special organizations.

Admissions: Foreign students must score 500 on the TOEFL. No college entrance examination is required.

Procedure: Application deadlines are open. Foreign students are admitted to all terms. Proof of funds adequate for 4 years of study is required.

Admissions Contact: Rae J. Malcolm, Dean of Admissions.

WESTFIELD STATE COLLEGE   B-3
Westfield, Massachusetts 01086   (413) 568-3311

F/T: 2700 M&W	Faculty:	160; n/av
P/T: 805 M&W	Ph.D.'s:	60%
Grad: 659 M&W	S/F Ratio:	19 to 1
Year: sems, ss	Tuition:	$875 ($2675)
Appl: Apr. 1	R and B:	$1800
5000 applied	2327 accepted	800 enrolled
SAT: 430V 460M		COMPETITIVE+

Founded in 1839, Westfield State College offers undergraduate and graduate degree programs in the liberal arts and sciences and education. Its library contains 126,000 books and subscribes to 698 periodicals.

Environment: The 288-acre suburban campus is located 10 miles west of Springfield. Living facilities include dormitories and off-campus apartments.

Student Life: About 98% of the students are from Massachusetts. Almost all come from public schools. About 65% live on campus. Six percent are minority-group members. About 70% are Catholic, 27% are Protestant, and 2% are Jewish. Campus housing is both coed and

MASSACHUSETTS 385

MASSACHUSETTS

single-sex; there are visiting privileges in the single-sex housing. Students may keep cars on campus.

Organizations: There are no fraternities or sororities. Extracurricular activities include clubs, social and cultural events, student government, publications, and religious and service groups. Nearby ski areas are popular with the students.

Sports: Fourteen sports are offered on an intercollegiate level. There are over 20 intramural sports.

Handicapped: About 75% of the campus is accessible to students with physical handicaps. Special dormitory rooms are also available.

Graduates: The freshman dropout rate is 9%; about 50% remain to graduate. Seven percent of the graduates continue their studies, and 77% go into business and industry.

Services: Placement, career counseling, tutoring, remedial instruction, and psychological counseling are offered free of charge. Health care is provided on a fee basis. A special program offers support to students who come from disadvantaged backgrounds.

Programs of Study: The college grants the B.A. and B.S. degrees. Master's degrees are also awarded. Bachelor's degrees are offered in the following subjects: BUSINESS (business administration), EDUCATION (early childhood, elementary, secondary, special), ENGLISH (English, media systems and management), FINE AND PERFORMING ARTS (art, art education, music, music education), LANGUAGES (French, Spanish), MATH AND SCIENCES (computer science, mathematics), PREPROFESSIONAL (social work), SOCIAL SCIENCES (economics, government/political science, history, psychology, social sciences). Forty-four percent of the degrees conferred are in the social sciences; 28% are in education.

Required: Core requirements include course work in English composition, natural science, humanities, mathematics, and social science.

Special: A degree in general studies is offered. Exchange programs with several other colleges and study abroad are possible.

Honors: There are honors programs for qualified students.

Admissions: About 47% of the 1981–82 applicants were accepted. Applicants must have graduated from high school, should have a 2.0 GPA, and should rank in the upper half of their class. No specific high school units are required. The most important considerations are advanced placement or honors courses, extracurricular activities, and leadership record. There is a 5% quota for admission of out-of-state residents.

Procedure: The SAT is required. April 1 is the fall application deadline; December 1, the spring. Admission and notification are on a rolling basis. There is an $18 application fee.

Special: There is a deferred admissions plan. CLEP and AP credit is granted.

Transfer: For fall 1981, 800 applications were received, 500 students were accepted, and 300 transfers enrolled. A 2.0 GPA is required; D grades are usually accepted. The SAT is required. All students must complete, at the college, 30 of the 120 credits required for a bachelor's degree. Preference is given to students transferring from instate colleges. The deadline for application is April 1; transfer students are admitted in the fall and spring terms.

Visiting: Informal campus tours may be arranged during the school year; guides will be provided. Visitors can sit in on classes. For further information, the director of admissions should be contacted.

Financial Aid: About 70% of the students are receiving aid. Fifty percent work part-time on campus. The average freshman award is $1200. Aid is available in the form of scholarships, loans, grants (federal and state), and work opportunities (including CWS). Need is the principal determining factor. The aid application and the FAF should be submitted by March 1. The college is a member of CSS.

Foreign Students: Fewer than 1% of the full-time students come from foreign countries. An intensive English course and special counseling are available for these students.

Admissions: Foreign students must achieve a TOEFL score of at least 550 and must take the SAT.

Procedure: The application deadline for fall entry is March 1. Foreign students must present proof of funds adequate to cover 1 year of study. There is a $25 application fee.

Admissions Contact: William E. Crean, Director of Admissions.

WHEATON COLLEGE D–3
Norton, Massachusetts 02766 (617) 285-7722

F/T: 1218W Faculty: 89; IIB, + +$
P/T: 28W Ph.D.'s: 93%
Grad: none S/F Ratio: 13 to 1
Year: sems Tuition: $7010
Appl: Feb. 1 R and B: $2850
1314 applied 931 accepted 407 enrolled
SAT: 530V 540M **VERY COMPETITIVE**

Wheaton College is a private, nonsectarian liberal arts college for women. The library collection contains 220,000 volumes, over 17,000 microfilm items, and subscribes to 1200 periodicals.

Environment: The 300-acre campus is located in a rural setting 15 miles north of Providence and 35 miles south of Boston. Daily bus service links the campus to Boston. There are more than 25 buildings, including 18 dormitories and commuter facilities.

Student Life: About 25% of the students come from Massachusetts; 68% come from public schools; 98% live on campus. About 8% of the students are minority-group members. College housing is single-sex; there are visiting privileges. Students may keep cars on campus. Massachusetts law regulates the use of alcohol on campus.

Organizations: There are no sororities, but there are numerous clubs for various academic and extracurricular interests, including student government, the newspaper, radio station, dance company, and theater arts society. On-campus activities include regularly scheduled cultural and social events.

Sports: The college fields 9 intercollegiate teams. There is intramural competition in 15 sports.

Handicapped: About 75% of the campus is accessible to handicapped students. Special facilities include wheelchair ramps, parking areas, and specially equipped rest rooms. Special class scheduling is also available.

Graduates: Fourteen percent of the students drop out during the freshman year; 70% remain to graduate. About 30% go on to graduate and professional schools; 3% to medical and dental schools, and 4% to law school. Fifty percent enter careers in business and industry.

Services: Career counseling, health care, psychological counseling, and tutoring are offered free of charge to all students. Remedial instruction is available on a fee basis.

Programs of Study: Programs lead to the B.A. degree. Bachelor's degrees are offered in the following subjects: AREA STUDIES (American, Asian, classical civilizations, Italian, Russian), ENGLISH (English), FINE AND PERFORMING ARTS (art history, music, studio art), LANGUAGES (French, German, Greek/Latin, Russian, Spanish), MATH AND SCIENCES (biochemistry, biology, chemistry, mathematics, physics, psychobiology), PHILOSOPHY (philosophy, religion), SOCIAL SCIENCES (anthropology, economics, government/political science, history, mathematics and economics, psychology, sociology). About 37% of the degrees are conferred in social sciences and 16% in math and sciences.

Required: All students must complete 2 semester courses in each of 5 areas, plus 2 semesters of physical education.

Special: Student-designed majors, study abroad, exchange programs, dual degree programs, preprofessional preparation, independent study/field work, and teacher certification are offered.

Honors: Five honor societies have chapters at the college. Many departments offer honors programs.

Admissions: About 71% of those who applied were accepted for the 1981–82 freshman class. SAT scores of enrolled students were as follows: Verbal—33% scored below 500, 52% between 500 and 599, 13% between 600 and 700, and 2% above 700; Math—33% scored below 500, 51% between 500 and 599, 14% between 600 and 700, and 2% above 700. Students are expected to have a strong, well-balanced academic program. Advanced placement or honor courses, recommendations, and extracurricular activities are also considered important.

Procedure: The SAT or ACT and 2 ATs (including English composition) are required and should be taken by January of the senior year. An interview is recommended. February 1 is the application deadline for fall admission and December 15 for spring. There is a $25 application fee.

Special: There are early decision, early admissions, and deferred admissions plans. AP credit is available.

Transfer: For fall 1981, 95 students applied, 45 were accepted, and 27 enrolled. Good academic standing is required. D grades do not transfer. Four semesters must be completed in residence, as well as 16 of the 32 course credits needed for a bachelor's degree. The application deadlines are March 1 (fall) and December 15 (spring).

Visiting: There are regularly scheduled orientations for prospective applicants. Informal campus tours with guides can be arranged. Visitors may sit in on classes and stay overnight at the school. The admissions office should be contacted for arrangements.

Financial Aid: About 32% of the students receive aid through the college. Seventy-seven percent work part-time on campus. Average aid awarded to freshmen from all sources is $5712. The college offers loans, grants, and campus employment. Most aid is awarded solely on the basis of financial need. The college is a member of CSS. The FAF should be submitted. Aid application deadlines are February 15 (fall) and December 15 (spring).

Foreign Students: About 7% of the full-time students come from foreign countries. The college offers these students an intensive English course, special counseling, and special organizations.

Admissions: Foreign students must score 560 on the TOEFL. They must also take the SAT or the ACT, as well as the English composition AT and one other of their choice.

Procedure: The application deadlines are February 1 (fall) and December 1 (spring). Foreign students must present proof of funds adequate to cover 4 years of study. They must carry health insurance, which is available through the college for a fee.

Admissions Contact: Niki Janus, Director of Admissions.

WHEELOCK COLLEGE   E-2
Boston, Massachusetts 02215   (617) 734-5200

F/T: 8M, 535W	Faculty: 57; IIA, −$
P/T: 4W	Ph.D.'s: 61%
Grad: 12M, 212W	S/F Ratio: 12 to 1
Year: sems	Tuition: $5050
Appl: see profile	R and B: $2700
334 applied	251 accepted	125 enrolled
SAT: 425V 450M		COMPETITIVE

Wheelock College, founded in 1888, is a nonsectarian college specializing in early childhood education. The curriculum integrates studies in the liberal arts and professional education. Its library contains 65,000 volumes and 2237 microfilm reels, and subscribes to 500 periodicals. Wheelock is a member of a 10-library consortium, which extends to students full privileges at all member libraries.

Environment: The 4½-acre urban campus includes 6 dormitories. A Resource Center collects curriculum materials and devices used in teaching.

Student Life: About 40% of the students are from Massachusetts. Sixty-eight percent come from public schools. About 70% of the students reside on campus. College housing is both single-sex and coed. There are visiting privileges in single-sex housing. Cars are permitted on campus only during student-teaching terms.

Organizations: There are no sororities or fraternities on campus, but special-interest clubs and organizations are available. The Boston area offers many cultural and social opportunities.

Sports: The college participates in 2 intercollegiate sports for women. Intramural programs include 4 sports for both men and women.

Handicapped: About half the campus is accessible to physically handicapped students, and some special facilities (wheelchair ramps and elevators) are available. There are no hearing-impaired or visually impaired students currently registered.

Graduates: About 24% of the freshmen drop out by the end of their first year. Seventy-six percent remain to graduate. Four percent pursue advanced study after graduation. Most of them enter the field of early childhood and human services.

Services: Free career and psychological counseling, placement services, and tutoring are offered to students. Health care is available both free of charge and for a fee.

Programs of Study: The college confers the B.S.Ed. degree. Master's degrees are also available. The college offers bachelor's degrees in the following subjects: EDUCATION (children in health care settings, early childhood, elementary, social services, special). Also offered are programs in day care, learning disorders, children in hospitals, therapeutic tutoring, infant and toddler care, and education in museums and music.

Required: Forty-two credits are required in the liberal arts in addition to core professional requirements in each of the majors.

Special: The college has a student-teaching program arrangement with many schools and health-care facilities in the Boston area. A combined 5-year B.A.-B.S. degree in education is possible.

Admissions: About 75% of those who applied were accepted for the 1981-82 freshman class. Of those who enrolled, the SAT scores were as follows: Verbal—60% scored below 500, 28% between 500 and 599, 2% between 600 and 700, and 0% above 700; Math—60% scored below 500, 21% between 500 and 599, 5% between 600 and 700, and 0% above 700. The candidate should have completed 16 Carnegie units at an accredited high school and must show a potential for working with young children. Recommendations and personality are also very important. High school average and class rank requirements are flexible.

Procedure: The SAT or ACT is required and should be taken in November or December of the senior year. A personal interview is required. Application deadlines are December 15 (fall) for education students, February 15 (fall), and December 15 (winter). A rolling admissions policy is observed. A $20 fee should accompany all application forms.

Special: Early decision and deferred admissions are available. The college subscribes to the CRDA. AP credit is given.

Transfer: For fall 1981, 106 applications were received, 80 accepted, and 56 transfer students enrolled. Transfers are accepted for sophomore and junior classes. A 2.0 GPA is needed. D grades are not acceptable. Students must earn at least 64 credits in residence, of the 128 needed for a bachelor's degree. Application deadlines are April 15 (fall) and December 15 (winter).

Visiting: Informal guided tours can be arranged on weekdays from 9 A.M. to 4 P.M. through the admissions office. Visitors can sit in on classes and stay at the school. The fall orientation session for prospective students includes an interview and tour.

Financial Aid: About 39% of all students receive some form of financial aid. Thirty-eight percent work part-time on campus. Freshman financial aid packages average $3200 and usually include an NDSL loan, a scholarship, and a campus job. The college is a member of CSS. The FAF is required. Applications for financial aid should be in by March 1 (fall) and December 15 (spring).

Foreign Students: Two percent of the full-time students come from foreign countries. The college offers these students special organizations.

Admissions: Foreign students must score 500 on the TOEFL. No college entrance examination is required.

Procedure: The application deadlines are February 15 (fall) and December 15 (winter). Foreign students must complete the college's own health certificate. They must also present proof of adequate funds. They must carry health insurance, which is available through the college.

Admissions Contact: Joan Wexler, Dean of Admissions.

WILLIAMS COLLEGE   A-1
Williamstown, Massachusetts 01267   (413) 597-2211

F/T: 1081M, 841W	Faculty: 154; IIB, ++$
P/T: none	Ph.D.'s: 85%
Grad: 23M, 19W	S/F Ratio: 12 to 1
Year: 4-1-4	Tuition: $7016
Appl: Jan. 15	R and B: $2660
4214 applied	993 accepted	508 enrolled
SAT: 630V 660M	ACT: 29	MOST COMPETITIVE

Williams College, founded in 1793, is a private institution offering undergraduate degree programs in the liberal arts and sciences. The library contains 480,000 volumes, and 70,000 microfilm items, and subscribes to 2800 periodicals. It also houses a rare book collection as well as a music collection.

Environment: The 450-acre rural campus is located in the Berkshire Mountains 140 miles from Boston and 160 miles from New York City. Seven freshman and 15 upperclass residences accommodate 95% of the students.

Student Life: About 26% of the students come from New England; 60% come from public schools. Ninety-four percent of the students live on campus. Eleven percent are minority-group members. College housing is both single-sex and coed. There are visiting privileges in single-sex housing. Students may keep cars on campus.

Organizations: There are no fraternities or sororities. There are religious organizations, student government, nearby art and music opportunities, clubs, and regularly scheduled on-campus social and cultural events, including films, theater, debates, concerts, and a lecture series.

MASSACHUSETTS

Sports: In addition to 19 intercollegiate athletics for men and 17 for women, the college sponsors intramural competition in 15 sports for men and 13 for women.

Handicapped: About 25% of the campus is accessible to the physically handicapped. The college provides counselors, special facilities, and special class scheduling to handicapped students.

Graduates: The freshman dropout rate is less than 1%; about 93% remain to graduate. About 90% go on to graduate study; 11% to medical school, 2% to dental school, and 17% to law school. About 40% enter careers in business or industry.

Services: Health care, psychological counseling, tutoring, remedial instruction, career counseling, and placement are available to students free of charge.

Programs of Study: The college confers the B.A. degree. There are also master's programs. The bachelor's degree is offered in the following subjects: AREA STUDIES (American), BUSINESS (computer science), ENGLISH (comparative literature, English), FINE AND PERFORMING ARTS (art history, music, studio art, theater/dramatics), LANGUAGES (French, German, Russian, Spanish), MATH AND SCIENCES (astronomy, biology, chemistry, geology, mathematics, physics), PHILOSOPHY (classics, philosophy, religion), SOCIAL SCIENCES (economics, government/political science, history, history of ideas, political economy, psychology, sociology). About 27% of degrees conferred are in social sciences and about 24% in math/sciences.

Required: Physical education is required.

Special: Student-designed majors, study abroad, independent study, a semester exchange program with 14 other colleges, a combination degree program in engineering, and interdepartmental majors in area studies are offered. Williams offers a semester-long maritime studies program at Mystic Seaport, Connecticut. Students may complete a special program in environmental studies using the college's 2000-acre Hopkins Experimental Forest.

Honors: Phi Beta Kappa has a chapter on campus. Honors work is offered in all degree-granting departments.

Admissions: About 24% of those who applied were accepted for the 1981-82 freshman class. The SAT scores of those who enrolled were as follows: Verbal—8% scored below 500, 28% between 500 and 599, 45% between 600 and 700, and 19% above 700; Math—3% scored below 500, 19% between 500 and 599, 47% between 600 and 700, and 31% above 700. Also taken into consideration are recommendations, advanced placement/honors work, and special talents.

Procedure: The SAT or ACT is required before January of the senior year; ATs are recommended. January 15 is the application deadline for the fall semester. There is a $30 fee.

Special: There are early decision, early admissions, and deferred admissions plans.

Transfer: For fall 1981, 250 applications were received, 50 were accepted, and 36 students enrolled. An outstanding academic record is required. D grades do not transfer. Transfer students must complete, at the college, 2 years (4 consecutive semesters) and at least 2 Winter Study Credits of the 8 full semesters needed for a bachelor's degree. March 1 (fall) and December 1 (spring) are the application deadlines.

Visiting: There are daily, informal campus tours led by student guides. Interviews are available either on campus or nation-wide through alumni. Visitors may sit in on classes and stay at the college.

Financial Aid: About 35% of all students receive financial aid. Sixty percent work part-time on campus. Average aid to freshmen from all sources is $6472. The college offers scholarships, loans (federal, state, commercial, and from the college itself), campus employment, and CWS. Williams is a member of CSS. The college's own financial aid form and the FAF are due January 15 (fall) or December 1 (spring).

Foreign Students: Three percent of the full-time students come from foreign countries. The college offers these students special counseling and special organizations.

Admissions: Foreign students must score 600 on the TOEFL. They must also take the SAT.

Procedure: The application deadline is January 15 (fall). Foreign students must carry health insurance, which is available through the college for a fee.

Admissions Contact: Mike Reed and Karen Fisher, Assistant Directors of Admissions.

WORCESTER POLYTECHNIC INSTITUTE   C-2
Worcester, Massachusetts 01609   (617) 793-5286

F/T: 1950M, 450W   Faculty: 201; IIA, ++$
P/T: 49 M&W   Ph.D.'s: 80%
Grad: 925 M&W   S/F Ratio: 12 to 1
Year: qtrs, ss   Tuition: $6044
Appl: Feb. 15   R and B: $2410
2500 applied   1100 accepted   600 enrolled
SAT: 550V 650M   ACT: 28   HIGHLY COMPETITIVE+

Worcester Polytechnic, founded in 1865, is one of the nation's oldest science and engineering colleges. It is nonsectarian and privately endowed. Its library contains 175,000 volumes and 600,000 microfiche items, and subscribes to over 1200 periodicals.

Environment: The 55-acre, self-contained campus, situated on a hilltop and bordered on 2 sides by parks, is located in a suburban section of Worcester, a city of 170,000. Boston is 45 miles away. There are 26 buildings on campus, including 8 dormitories, fraternity housing, and other institute-owned housing that accommodate 1100 students. The institute also has a 10-building, 250-acre research center.

Student Life: About 52% of the students are from Massachusetts. Eighty percent graduated from public schools. About 75% live on campus. Noncommuting freshmen are guaranteed space in residence halls. About 7% of the full-time students are minority-group members. Institute housing is both single-sex and coed. There are visiting privileges in single-sex housing. Upperclassmen may keep cars on campus.

Organizations: About a third of the men belong to 1 of 12 national fraternities. Three sororities also have campus chapters. Activities include music, drama, publications, special-interest clubs, and religious organizations. Worcester's cultural offerings include museums and the nation's oldest music festival.

Sports: The college participates in 23 intercollegiate sports. There are 8 intramural sports.

Handicapped: Special facilities for physically handicapped students include wheelchair ramps, parking areas, elevators, lowered drinking fountains, and specially equipped rest rooms. Fewer than 1% of the students have impaired vision or hearing. The college has 6 Braille computer terminals.

Graduates: Ninety-two percent of the freshmen complete their first year successfully, and 70% remain to graduate. About 25% enter graduate school immediately after graduating; 60% ultimately earn graduate degrees. Seventy-five percent enter business and industry.

Services: Free psychological and career counseling, health care, tutoring, and remedial instruction are available to students. The college offers free placement services to students and alumni. In a recent year, more than 350 companies conducted more than 350 interviews on campus, an average of 10 to 12 for each graduating senior.

Programs of Study: The college awards the B.S. degree. Master's and doctoral degrees are also granted. Bachelor's degrees are offered in the following subjects: BUSINESS (business administration, computer science), MATH AND SCIENCES (biochemistry, biology, chemistry, mathematics, natural sciences, physics), PREPROFESSIONAL (dentistry, engineering—aerospace, engineering—biomedical, engineering—chemical, engineering—civil, engineering—electrical, engineering—environmental, engineering—management, engineering—mechanical, engineering—nuclear systems, medicine, veterinary), SOCIAL SCIENCES (economics, history of technology). Three-fourths of the degrees are granted in preprofessional subjects, the rest in math and sciences.

Required: There are no required courses. Each student must complete 2 tutorial study projects, undergo a competency evaluation, and complete a minor in an area of the humanities.

Special: All students design their own majors. Under the WPI Plan, degrees are awarded on the basis of competency rather than credit hours, so that students can graduate in less than 4 years. The plan balances classroom work with varied off-campus experiences and is highly project-oriented. Students may earn 5-year combined B.A.-B.S. degrees in a 3-2 program with 8 liberal arts colleges. Through the Worcester Consortium for Higher Education, students may take courses at other colleges in the city. Students may study abroad for 1 year.

Honors: Any student is eligible to graduate with honors or high honors according to performance on 4 WPI degree requirements. Ten honor societies, including Tau Beta Pi and Sigma Xi, have chapters on campus.

Admissions: The college accepted 44% of those who sought admission to the 1981-82 freshman class. SAT scores of those who enrolled in a recent freshman class were as follows: Verbal—47% scored between 500 and 599, 20% between 600 and 700, and 3% above 700; Math—20% scored between 500 and 599, 56% between 600 and 700, and 20% above 700. Applicants must have completed 15 Carnegie units. Those who rank in the top quarter of their class and have an average of at least 85 have a good chance of admission. Admissions officers also consider advanced placement or honors courses, recommendations by school officials, personality, leadership record, evidence of special talents, and impressions made during interviews.

Procedure: All applicants must take the SAT or ACT and 3 ATs in English Composition, Mathematics I or II, and Chemistry or Physics, between May of the junior year and January of the senior year. Application deadlines are February 15 (fall), November 25 (winter), and April 30 (summer). The application fee is $25.

Special: The institute offers early and deferred admissions and early decision plans. Students may earn credit through AP or CLEP tests.

Transfer: For fall 1981, 200 transfer students applied, 75 were accepted, and 50 enrolled. Transfers are accepted for the freshman and sophomore classes. D grades are not acceptable. A campus interview is required. Students must study at the institute 2 years and must complete 72 of the 136 credits needed to receive a bachelor's degree. The application deadline is April 15.

Visiting: Admissions officers strongly encourage applicants to visit the campus for individual interviews. Group orientations for prospective students are scheduled, and individual visits are welcome when classes are in session. The admissions office should be contacted to make arrangements.

Financial Aid: Sixty-five percent of the students receive financial aid based on need and achievement. Forty percent work part-time on campus. Average aid to freshmen from all sources is $2400. Aid is packaged, when possible, in the form of scholarships, loans, and employment. Loans are available from federal and state governments, local banks, and the institute itself. Tuition may be paid in installments through private agencies. Worcester participates in the CSS and requires aid applicants to submit the FAF and the institute's own form. The application deadlines are March 15 (fall), December 15 (winter), and April 15 (summer).

Foreign Students: Six percent of the full-time students come from foreign countries. The institute offers these students an intensive English course, special counseling, and special organizations.

Admissions: Foreign students must score 550 on the TOEFL. They must also take the SAT or ACT as well as 3 ATs: Math, English Composition, Chemistry, or Physics.

Procedure: The application deadlines are February 15 (fall), November 25 (winter), and April 1 (summer). Foreign students must present proof of health. They are not eligible for financial aid. Health insurance, which is available through the institute for a fee, is required.

Admissions Contact: Roy A. Seaberg, Director of Admissions.

WORCESTER STATE COLLEGE C-2
Worcester, Massachusetts 01602   (617) 793-8000

F/T: 1101M, 1634W   Faculty: 180; IIA, av$
P/T: 492M, 678W   Ph.D.'s: 49%
Grad: 735M, 1225W   S/F Ratio: 16 to 1
Year: sems, ss   Tuition: $882 ($2632)
Appl: May 1   R and B: $1790
3201 applied   2419 accepted   782 enrolled
SAT: 396V 427M   LESS COMPETITIVE

Worcester State College, founded in 1874, is 1 of 8 general studies institutions supported by the Commonwealth of Massachusetts. The library houses 149,662 volumes and 94,950 microfilm items, and subscribes to 883 periodicals.

Environment: The 55-acre urban campus is located 2 miles from the center of Worcester and 40 miles from Boston. On campus are a gymnasium, an administration building, a science building, a learning resources center, and a student center. Dormitories with single, double, and triple rooms accommodate 500 students.

Student Life: About 98% of the students are from Massachusetts. Eighty-six percent of entering freshmen come from public schools. The college is primarily a commuter school; 15% of the students live on campus. Two percent are minority-group members. College housing is single-sex; there are visiting privileges. Students may keep cars on campus. Day-care services are available to all students, faculty, and staff.

Organizations: There are no sororities or fraternities at Worcester, but the college sponsors a variety of clubs, a weekly newspaper, an orchestra, and a chorus. The proximity of Boston affords students a wide choice of cultural and recreational activities.

Sports: The college participates in 8 intercollegiate sports for men and 6 for women. Intramural competition includes 3 sports for men and 2 for women.

Handicapped: About 75% of the campus is accessible to handicapped students. Special facilities include wheelchair ramps, parking areas, elevators, and specially equipped rest rooms. At present, there are no hearing-impaired or visually handicapped students at the college.

Graduates: By the end of freshman year approximately 15% of the students drop out; 40% remain to graduate. About 10% go on to graduate study.

Services: Career counseling, psychological counseling, health care, tutorial services, and remedial instruction are available without charge. Placement is available to students for a fee.

Programs of Study: The college offers the B.A. and B.S. degrees. Master's programs are also available. Bachelor's degrees are offered in the following subjects: AREA STUDIES (urban), BUSINESS (management), EDUCATION (early childhood, elementary, health/physical), ENGLISH (English), FINE AND PERFORMING ARTS (media), HEALTH SCIENCES (nursing, speech therapy), LANGUAGES (French, Spanish), MATH AND SCIENCES (biology, chemistry, mathematics, natural sciences, physics), SOCIAL SCIENCES (economics, geography, history, psychology, sociology). About 32% of the students received degrees in the social sciences, 15% in education, 13% in management, and 11% in math and sciences.

Required: Students must take English, 2 years of physical education, and a course in state and national constitution.

Special: Under the Consortium program, students may take courses in any of the other 5 participating city colleges. There also is a 1-year nursing program in cooperation with local hospitals.

Honors: A national honor society has a chapter on campus. All departments offer honors classes to qualified students.

Admissions: About 76% of all those who applied for the 1981-82 freshman class were accepted. Of those who enrolled, the SAT scores were as follows: Verbal—78% scored below 500, 20% between 500 and 599, 2% between 600 and 700, and 0% above 700; Math—69% scored below 500, 26% between 500 and 599, 4% between 600 and 700, and 1% above 700. Candidates must be graduates of accredited high schools or the equivalent and should have a C average or better. Recommendations by high school officials are important. Preference is given to residents of Massachusetts.

Procedure: The SAT is required and should be taken in May of the junior year or December of the senior year. The application deadlines are May 1 (fall) and December 1 (spring). A rolling admissions plan is used. An application fee of $18 is required.

Special: CLEP general and subject exams are accepted. AP credit is also given.

Transfer: For fall 1981, 1003 students applied, 776 were accepted, and 452 enrolled. Transfers are accepted for all classes. Only D grades from Massachusetts state schools transfer. Preference is given to state residents. To receive a bachelor's degree, students must study at the college for at least a year, and must complete 30 of the 128 credits needed. Application deadlines are the same as for freshmen.

Visiting: The regularly scheduled orientation sessions for prospective students include campus tours and talks by department heads. Guides are supplied for informal visits. Students may sit in on classes but may not stay at the school. To arrange a visit, the director of admissions should be contacted.

Financial Aid: About 50% of all students receive financial aid. Fifteen percent work part-time on campus. Average aid to freshmen from all sources is $1100. The college awards a number of freshman scholarships each year. State scholarships are also offered. Loans are available from federal sources and the local banks. The college is a member of CSS. The FAF is required. Application for aid must be made by May 1 (fall) or December 15 (spring).

Foreign Students: One percent of the full-time students come from foreign countries.

Admissions: Foreign students must take the SAT and must score 350 on both the Verbal and Math examinations.

Procedure: The application deadlines are May 1 (fall) and December 15 (spring). Foreign students must present a certificate of good health completed by a U.S. physician.

Admissions Contact: Joseph P. Scannell, Director of Admissions.

MICHIGAN

ADRIAN COLLEGE
Adrian, Michigan 49221   E-5
(517) 265-5161

F/T: 544M, 517W
P/T: 21M, 60W
Grad: none
Year: sems, ss
Appl: Aug. 15
1136 applied
SAT: 500V 500M

Faculty: 66; IIA, av$
Ph.D.'s: 79%
S/F Ratio: 11 to 1
Tuition: $4686
R and B: $2000
977 accepted   350 enrolled
ACT: 21   COMPETITIVE

Adrian College, founded in 1845, is a liberal arts institution affiliated with the United Methodist Church. The library contains 108,000 volumes and 3000 microfilm items, and subscribes to 865 periodicals.

Environment: The 230-acre campus is located in a suburban area about 34 miles from Toledo, Ohio. There are 30 buildings on campus, including a solar greenhouse, 8 dormitories, 5 fraternity houses, and 5 sorority houses. Facilities are available for commuting students.

Student Life: About 75% of the students come from Michigan. Seventy-five percent come from public schools. Ninety percent of the students live on campus. Fifty-nine percent are Protestant, and 25% are Catholic. Five percent of the students are minority-group members. College housing is coed and single-sex; students in single-sex housing have visiting privileges. Students may keep cars on campus.

Organizations: Twenty-five percent of the students belong to fraternities and sororities. On-campus activities include student government, clubs, dramatics, publications, radio, and musical groups.

Sports: The college fields 9 intercollegiate teams for men and 8 for women. There are 5 intramural sports for men and 4 for women.

Handicapped: About one third of the campus is accessible to handicapped students. Facilities include wheelchair ramps and parking areas. Three counselors are available to handicapped students.

Graduates: The freshman dropout rate is 33%, and about 42% of the freshmen remain to graduate. Twenty-five percent go on for further education.

Services: Career counseling, placement, tutoring, remedial instruction, and health care are provided without charge to all students.

Programs of Study: The college awards the B.A., B.S., B.B.A., B.M., B.M.E., and B.F.A. degrees. Associate degrees are also conferred. Bachelor's degrees are offered in the following subjects: BUSINESS (accounting, business administration), EDUCATION (elementary, health/physical, secondary), ENGLISH (English), FINE AND PERFORMING ARTS (art, art education, music, music education, radio/TV, theater/dramatics), LANGUAGES (French, Spanish), MATH AND SCIENCES (biology, chemistry, earth science, mathematics, physics)/PHILOSOPHY (philosophy, religion), PREPROFESSIONAL (dentistry, engineering, law, medicine, ministry), SOCIAL SCIENCES (economics, government/political science, history, psychology, sociology). About 30% of degrees are awarded in business, 10% in education, and 11% in the health sciences.

Required: Freshman English is required of all students.

Special: Students may design their own majors. Independent study and study abroad are offered. Five-year combined B.A.-B.S. degrees are available in biology, chemistry, psychology, and mathematics.

Honors: There are 12 honor societies on campus.

Admissions: About 86% of those who applied were accepted for the 1981-82 freshman class. Students should be high school graduates, have completed 15 Carnegie units, rank in the top half of their class, and have a C+ average. The college also considers impressions made during an interview, extracurricular activities record, and advanced placement or honor courses.

Procedure: Either the SAT or ACT is required. Application deadlines are August 15 (fall) and December 15 (winter). Notification is on a rolling basis. There is a $15 application fee.

Special: CLEP and AP credit is given.

Transfer: For fall 1981, 55 students applied, 48 were accepted, and 42 enrolled. A 2.0 average, standardized exam scores, and recommendations are required; an interview is recommended. D grades do not transfer. Students must earn, at the college, at least 34 of the 124 credits necessary for a bachelor's degree. Application deadlines are the same as those for freshmen.

Visiting: There are regularly scheduled orientations for prospective students. Informal campus visits with student guides may be arranged; visitors may sit in on classes and stay overnight at the school. Visits are best scheduled on weekdays. The admissions office should be contacted for arrangements.

Financial Aid: About 87% of the students receive financial aid. Twenty-seven percent work part-time on campus. The average aid award to freshmen from all sources (including campus employment) is $4055. Aid is available in the form of 322 scholarships totaling $500,000 and loans from several sources. The college is a member of CSS and requires the FAF or FFS. Application deadlines are March 15 (fall) and December 1 (winter).

Foreign Students: Two percent of the full-time students come from foreign countries. The college offers these students an intensive English course, special counseling, and special organizations.

Admissions: Foreign students must achieve a minimum TOEFL score of 500 or a University of Michigan Language Test score of at least 75. No college entrance exam must be taken.

Procedure: Application deadlines are July 1 (fall) and November 1 (winter). Foreign students must present a health survey report processed through the college, proof of funds adequate to cover 1 year of study, and a special orientation fee of $110. They must also carry health insurance, which is available through the college.

Admissions Contact: Richard D. Paul, Director of Admissions.

ALBION COLLEGE
Albion, Michigan 49224   D-5
(517) 629-5511

F/T: 982M, 934W
P/T: none
Grad: none
Year: sems, ss
Appl: open
1617 applied
SAT: 530V 580M

Faculty: 120; IIB, ++$
Ph.D.'s: 75%
S/F Ratio: 15 to 1
Tuition: $5080
R and B: $2272
1430 accepted   537 enrolled
ACT: 24   VERY COMPETITIVE

Albion College, chartered in 1835, offers undergraduate programs in the liberal arts and sciences, business, and preprofessional fields. The library contains 200,000 volumes, and subscribes to 1200 periodicals.

Environment: The 90-acre campus, located in a rural area 90 miles from Detroit, has 50 buildings. In addition to dormitories, the college sponsors fraternity houses and off-campus apartments.

Student Life: About 85% of the students come from Michigan; 82% have had public school educations. Eighty-nine percent of the students live on campus. Sixty percent are Protestant, 20% are Catholic, and 1% are Jewish. About 2% of the students are minority-group members. College housing is single-sex, and there are visiting privileges. Upperclassmen may keep cars on campus. Alcohol is prohibited.

Organizations: There are 6 fraternities to which 60% of the men belong and 6 sororities to which 40% of the women belong. The extracurricular program is varied and extensive.

Sports: The college fields 9 intercollegiate teams for men and 7 for women. There are 11 intramural sports for men and 8 for women.

Handicapped: Special facilities include wheelchair ramps, parking areas, elevators, and specially equipped rest rooms. Special class scheduling is also available.

Graduates: The freshman dropout rate is 11%, and about 65% of the students remain to graduate. Of these, 16% pursue graduate study; 9% enter medical school, and 5% law school. Another 53% enter careers in business and industry.

Services: Offered free of charge to all students are placement, career counseling, health care, and psychological counseling. Tutoring is available for a fee.

Programs of Study: The A.B. or B.F.A. degree is offered in the following subjects: AREA STUDIES (American, urban), BUSINESS (business administration, management), EDUCATION (elementary, secondary), ENGLISH (English, speech), FINE AND PERFORMING ARTS (art, music), LANGUAGES (French, German, Spanish), MATH AND SCIENCES (biology, chemistry, geology, mathematics, physics), PHILOSOPHY (philosophy, religion), PREPROFESSIONAL (dentistry, engineering, forestry, home economics, law, medicine, ministry, social work, veterinary), SOCIAL SCIENCES (anthropology, economics, government/political science, history, psychology, sociology).

Required: All students must complete a distribution requirement and a major program of study.

Special: Study abroad, independent research, combination degree programs, and student-designed majors are offered.

Honors: A campus-wide honors program is available. There are 17 honor societies on campus, including Phi Beta Kappa.

Admissions: About 88% of those who applied were accepted for the 1981-82 freshman class. A 2.75 high school GPA and 15 Carnegie credits are required. The SAT scores of those who enrolled were as follows: Verbal—37% below 500, 49% between 500 and 599, 13% between 600 and 700, and 1% above 700; Math—21% below 500, 41% between 500 and 599, 34% between 600 and 700, and 4% above 700. Applicants must rank in the upper third of their high school class. The college also considers recommendations, advanced placement or honor courses, and extracurricular activities.

Procedure: The SAT or ACT is required. There are no application deadlines; new students are admitted each semester. Notification is on a rolling basis. There is a $15 application fee.

Special: There are early and deferred admissions plans. AP and CLEP credit is acceptable.

Transfer: For fall 1981, 112 students applied, 84 were accepted, and 50 enrolled. A 2.0 GPA and a recommendation are required; D grades are accepted only with an associate degree. Students must spend 1½ years in residence and complete at least 64 of the 124 semester hours necessary for a bachelor's degree. Application deadlines are open.

Visiting: There is an orientation program for prospective students. Informal campus tours with student guides may be arranged; visitors may sit in on classes and stay overnight at the school. Visits are best scheduled on weekdays. The admissions office should be contacted for arrangements.

Financial Aid: About 92% of the students received financial aid. Forty percent work part-time on campus. Average aid to freshmen is $3000. The college awards scholarships, grants, and loans on the basis of need, academic promise, and personal merit. The college is a member of CSS and requires either the FAF or the FFS. Application deadlines are March 15 (fall) and November 15 (spring).

Foreign Students: Eighteen of the full-time students come from foreign countries. The college offers these students special counseling.

Admissions: Foreign students must achieve a minimum TOEFL score of 500 or a Comprehensive English Language Test score of at least 85. No college entrance exam must be taken.

Procedure: Application deadlines are open.

Admissions Contact: Frank Bonta, Dean of Admissions.

ALMA COLLEGE D-4
Alma, Michigan 48801   (517) 463-7139

F/T: 560M, 590W		Faculty:	75; IIB, ++$
P/T: 15M, 10W		Ph.D.'s:	61%
Grad: none		S/F Ratio:	16 to 1
Year: 4-4-1		Tuition:	$4979
Appl: Mar. 1		R and B:	$2201
852 applied	749 accepted		357 enrolled
SAT: 541V 591M	ACT: 24	VERY COMPETITIVE+	

Alma College, founded in 1886, is a liberal arts institution affiliated with the Presbyterian Church. The library contains nearly 140,000 volumes and 7500 microfilm items, and subscribes to 939 periodicals.

Environment: The campus is located in a rural area 45 miles from Lansing. Facilities include the Swanson Academic Center and Eddy Music Center. The 9 dormitories accommodate 1200 men and women; the college also sponsors fraternity and sorority houses. Facilities are available for commuting students.

Student Life: About 84% of the students come from Michigan; 75% come from public schools. Ninety-six percent of the students live on campus. Sixty-five percent are Protestant, 27% are Catholic, and 1% are Jewish; attendance at religious services is voluntary. Five percent of the students are minority-group members. College housing is coed and single-sex; students in single-sex housing have visiting privileges. Students may keep cars on campus.

Organizations: There are 5 fraternities and 4 sororities; about 33% of the men and 33% of the women belong to 1 of them. On-campus activities include religious groups, service organizations, clubs, student government, publications, radio and TV stations, and social and cultural events.

Sports: The college fields 11 intercollegiate teams for men and 9 for women. There are 11 intramural sports for men and 8 for women.

Handicapped: About 75% of the campus is accessible to handicapped students. Special facilities include wheelchair ramps, parking areas, elevators, and specially equipped rest rooms.

Graduates: The freshman dropout rate is 16%, and 65% of the freshmen remain to graduate. Of these, 35% go on for graduate study; 5% enter medical school, 2% dental school, and 5% law school. About 36% pursue careers in business and industry.

Services: Placement, career counseling, tutoring, health care, and psychological counseling are offered to all students free of charge.

Programs of Study: The college awards the B.A., B.S., B.S.W., B.F.A., and B.M. degrees. Bachelor's degrees are offered in the following subjects: BUSINESS (business administration, international business), EDUCATION (bilingual, elementary, secondary), ENGLISH (English, speech), FINE AND PERFORMING ARTS (art, art education, dance, music, music education, studio art, theater/dramatics), LANGUAGES (French, German, Spanish), MATH AND SCIENCES (biology, chemistry, computer science, mathematics, physics), PHILOSOPHY (philosophy, religion), PREPROFESSIONAL (dentistry, engineering, forestry, law, library science, medicine, ministry, social work, veterinary), SOCIAL SCIENCES (economics, foreign service, government/political science, history, psychology, sociology). About 28% of the degrees are conferred in math and sciences, 20% in business, and 29% in social sciences.

Required: Freshman English is required.

Special: Student-designed majors, study abroad and interdivisional courses are possible. Combination degree programs in engineering, medical technology, and natural resources are offered in conjunction with the University of Michigan.

Honors: Ten departments offer honors programs. Phi Beta Kappa and 14 other honor societies have chapters on campus.

Admissions: About 88% of those who applied were accepted for the 1981-82 freshman class. The SAT scores of those who enrolled were as follows: Verbal—24% below 500, 58% between 500 and 599, 12% between 600 and 700, and 6% above 700; Math—5% below 500, 32% between 500 and 599, 47% between 600 and 700, and 16% above 700. On the ACT, 22% scored below 21, 22% between 21 and 23, 21% between 24 and 25, 17% between 26 and 28, and 18% above 28. Candidates should rank in the top 25% of their class and have at least a 3.0 GPA. Also considered important are personality, recommendations, and impressions made during an interview.

Procedure: The SAT or ACT should be taken by December of the senior year. Application deadlines are March 1 (fall), December 1 (winter), and April 1 (spring). Notification is on a rolling basis. There is a $10 application fee.

Special: There are early and deferred admissions plans. AP and CLEP credit is available.

Transfer: For fall 1981, 51 students applied, 40 were accepted, and 27 enrolled. A 3.0 GPA, a minimum score of 20 on the ACT, high school transcripts, and a transfer recommendation form are required; an interview and 30 completed credit hours are recommended. D grades are not accepted. Students must complete, at the college, at least 34 of the 136 credits necessary for a bachelor's degree. Application deadlines are the same as those for freshmen.

Visiting: There is an orientation program for prospective students. Informal campus tours with guides are possible; students may sit in on classes and stay overnight in the dorms. Visits are best scheduled on weekdays. The admissions office should be contacted for arrangements.

Financial Aid: About 71% of the students receive financial aid. Fifty-eight percent work part-time on campus. The average award to freshmen from all sources is $2841. The college offers 282 freshman scholarships, ranging from $100 to $2000, from a fund of $300,000. The average loan is $800 per year. The maximum aid award from all sources is $6245. The college is a member of CSS and requires either the FAF or the FFS. Application deadlines are April 1 (fall and spring) and December 1 (winter).

Foreign Students: One percent of the full-time students come from foreign countries. The college offers these students special counseling and special organizations.

Admissions: Foreign students must achieve a minimum TOEFL score of 525. No college entrance exam must be taken.

Procedure: Application deadlines are March 1 (fall), December 1 (winter), and April 1 (spring). Foreign students must present proof of adequate funds. They must also carry health insurance, which is available through the college for a fee.

Admissions Contact: Ted Rowland, Director of Admissions.

ANDREWS UNIVERSITY
Berrien Springs, Michigan 49104
C-5
(616) 471-3303

F/T: 791M, 823W	Faculty: 216; n/av
P/T: 135M, 214W	Ph.D.'s: 58%
Grad: 817M, 303W	S/F Ratio: 14 to 1
Year: qtrs, ss	Tuition: $1504 p/qtr
Appl: open	R and B: $790 p/qtr
978 applied	740 accepted	353 enrolled
ACT: 19		COMPETITIVE

Andrews University, established in 1874, is a liberal arts university affiliated with the Seventh-day Adventist Church. The library contains 379,493 volumes and 196,269 microfilm items, and subscribes to 2916 periodicals.

Environment: Situated on the banks of the St. Joseph River, the 1000-acre campus is located in an urban area 25 miles from South Bend, Indiana. Three dormitories accommodate 1246 students. The college also sponsors on-campus and off-campus apartments and married student housing.

Student Life: About 34% of the students come from Michigan and 43% from other states. About 22% of the freshmen come from public schools. The majority are members of the Seventh-day Adventist Church; dormitory students are required to attend daily chapel. University housing is single-sex, and there are no visiting privileges. Students may keep cars on campus. Drinking and smoking are forbidden.

Organizations: There are no fraternities or sororities. Extracurricular activities include student government, publications, clubs, and formal parties.

Sports: No intercollegiate sports are offered. There are 14 intramural sports for men and 12 for women.

Handicapped: About 10% of the campus is accessible to handicapped students. Special facilities include wheelchair ramps, parking areas, and elevators. A counselor is available to handicapped students.

Graduates: In a recent year, about 33% of the freshmen dropped out. About 18% of the graduates pursued advanced degrees, and another 3% entered careers in business and industry.

Services: Students receive placement and career counseling services free of charge. Tutoring, remedial instruction, psychological counseling, and health care are available for a fee.

Programs of Study: The university offers the B.A., B.S., B.F.A., B.M., B.B.A., B.E.T., B.Arch. Tech., and B.Ind.Tech. degrees. Associate, master's, and doctoral degrees are also awarded. Bachelor's degrees are offered in the following subjects: BUSINESS (accounting, business administration, business education, computer science, management), EDUCATION (early childhood, elementary, secondary, special), ENGLISH (English, journalism), FINE AND PERFORMING ARTS (art, art education, art history, music, music education), HEALTH SCIENCES (medical technology, nursing, occupational therapy, physical therapy, speech therapy), LANGUAGES (French, German, Spanish), MATH AND SCIENCES (biology, botany, chemistry, mathematics, physics, zoology), PHILOSOPHY (religion), PREPROFESSIONAL (dentistry, law, medicine, veterinary), SOCIAL SCIENCES (geography, history, psychology, sociology).

Required: All students must take courses in contemporary issues and philosophy, English language and literature, fine arts, communications skills, modern language (for most programs), religion, social studies, and world civilizations.

Special: Study abroad, cooperative programs with Loma Linda University, and a 2-2 engineering program with Walla Walla College are available.

Honors: Seven honor societies have chapters on campus.

Admissions: About 76% of those who applied were accepted for the 1981–82 freshman class. The ACT scores of those who enrolled were as follows: 56% below 21, 18% between 21 and 23, 10% between 24 and 25, 13% between 26 and 28, and 3% above 28. Applicants should present 10 units of academic work and have at least a 2.0 grade average. Other important factors considered include recommendations and advanced placement or honors courses.

Procedure: The ACT is required. Application deadlines are open. Notification is on a rolling basis. There is a $15 application fee.

Special: AP and CLEP credit is given.

Transfer: For fall 1981, 375 students applied, 259 were accepted, and 170 enrolled. Standardized exam scores, recommendations, and medical records are required; a minimum GPA of 2.0 is recommended. D grades do not transfer. Students must complete, at the university, at least 45 of the 190 quarter credits necessary for a bachelor's degree. Application deadlines are open.

Visiting: There are regularly scheduled orientations for prospective students. Guides are available for informal visits. Visitors may sit in on classes and stay overnight at the school. The admissions office should be contacted for arrangements.

Financial Aid: About 80% of the students receive financial aid. Fifty percent work part-time on campus. Scholarships and loans are available. The FAF should be filed by June 1.

Foreign Students: Eighteen percent of the full-time students come from foreign countries. The university offers these students an intensive English course and program, special counseling, and special organizations.

Admissions: Foreign students must take either the TOEFL or the Comprehensive English Language Test.

Procedure: Application deadlines are open. Foreign students must present a medical report signed by a physician, proof of funds adequate to cover 1 year of study, and an advance deposit of $1500. They must also carry health insurance, which is available through the university for a fee.

Admissions Contact: Douglas K. Brown, Director of Admissions and Records.

AQUINAS COLLEGE
Grand Rapids, Michigan 49506
D-4
(616) 459-8281

F/T: 605M, 683W	Faculty: 80; IIB, +$
P/T: 440M, 632W	Ph.D.'s: 45%
Grad: 260M, 133W	S/F Ratio: 15 to 1
Year: sems, ss	Tuition: $4016
Appl: Aug. 1	R and B: $2100
630 applied	508 accepted	275 enrolled
ACT: 22		COMPETITIVE

Aquinas College, established in 1887, is a Roman Catholic institution offering undergraduate programs in the liberal arts and sciences, business, education, and graphic arts. The library contains 110,000 volumes and 16,000 microfilm items, and subscribes to 700 periodicals.

Environment: The 70-acre campus is located in a suburban area. The 10 buildings include 2 dormitories that house 462 students.

Student Life: About 89% of the students come from Michigan; 50% come from public schools. Thirty-seven percent reside on campus. About 88% of the students are Catholic, and 12% are Protestant; there are no compulsory religious services. Eight percent of the students are minority-group members. College housing is coed. Students may keep cars on campus.

Organizations: There are no sororities or fraternities. A full program of extracurricular activities includes musical groups, drama, debating, service clubs, and publications.

Sports: The college fields 7 intercollegiate teams for men and 6 for women. There are 10 intramural sports for men and 8 for women.

Handicapped: About 95% of the campus is accessible to handicapped students. Facilities include wheelchair ramps, parking areas, elevators, lowered drinking fountains and telephones, and dormitory rooms. There is a counselor for handicapped students.

Graduates: About 25% of the students drop out after the first year; 49% remain to graduate. Of these, 25% pursue advanced degrees: 10% enter medical school, 1% dental school, and 5% law school. Forty percent pursue careers in business and industry.

Services: Psychological counseling, tutoring, placement, and career counseling are offered to all students free of charge. Health care is available for a fee.

Programs of Study: The college confers the B.A., B.S., B.F.A., B.M., B.Mus.Ed., B.A.G.E., and B.B.A. degrees. Associate and master's degrees are also awarded. Bachelor's degrees are offered in the following subjects: AREA STUDIES (urban), BUSINESS (accounting, business administration, computer science), EDUCATION (elementary, health/physical, secondary), ENGLISH (English, speech), FINE AND PERFORMING ARTS (art, art education, music, music education), HEALTH SCIENCES (medical technology), LANGUAGES (French, German, Spanish), MATH AND SCIENCES (biology, chemistry, earth science, ecology/environmental science, mathematics), PHILOSOPHY (philosophy, religion), PREPROFESSIONAL (dentistry, engineering, law, medicine, veterinary), SOCIAL SCIENCES (economics, geography, government/political science, history, international relations, psychology, social sciences, sociology). Thirty-one percent of the degrees are conferred in business and 13% in English.

Required: English composition and a liberal education program are required.

Special: Special programs include the B.A.G.E. degree, student-designed majors, combined B.A.-B.S. degrees, study abroad, and a 3-year bachelor's degree.

Honors: There are 6 honor societies on campus.

Admissions: About 81% of those who applied were accepted for the 1981-82 freshman class. ACT scores of enrolled students were as follows: 40% below 21, 12% between 21 and 23, 9% between 24 and 25, 12% between 26 and 28, and 3% above 28. Candidates should have completed 15 Carnegie units and have at least a 2.5 grade average. Also considered important are special talents, leadership, personality, and extracurricular activities.

Procedure: The ACT or SAT should be taken by December of the senior year. Application deadlines are August 1 (fall) and January 1 (winter). Notification is on a rolling basis. There is a $15 application fee.

Special: There are early and deferred admissions plans. AP and CLEP credit is available.

Transfer: For fall 1981, 222 students applied, 192 were accepted, and 150 enrolled. Transfers are not accepted for the senior year. A minimum GPA of 2.0 is required. An associate degree fulfills the general education requirements. Students must earn, at the college, at least 28 of the 124 credits necessary for a bachelor's degree. Application deadlines are August 15 (fall), December 15 (winter), and April 15 (summer).

Visiting: There is an orientation program for prospective students. Informal campus tours with guides are available. Visitors may sit in on classes and stay overnight at the school. Visits are best scheduled on weekdays during the fall or winter.

Financial Aid: About 87% of the students receive financial aid. Thirty percent work part-time on campus. Average aid to freshmen is $3000. The college offers scholarships and federal, bank, and private loans. Need and academic promise are the determining factors in the award of aid. Tuition may be paid in installments. The college is a member of CSS and requires the FAF. Application deadlines are March 31 (fall) and October 31 (winter).

Foreign Students: Five percent of the full-time students come from foreign countries. The college offers these students special counseling and special organizations.

Admissions: Foreign students must score in the upper 75% of the TOEFL or the University of Michigan Language Test. They also must take either the SAT or the ACT.

Procedure: The application deadline is April 1 for fall entry. Foreign students must present a health certificate from either a government or personal physician and proof of funds adequate to cover 4 years of study. They must also carry health insurance.

Admissions Contact: James L. Schultz, Dean of Admissions.

CALVIN COLLEGE
Grand Rapids, Michigan 49506

D-4

(616) 949-4000

F/T: 1900M, 1850W
P/T: 100M, 50W
Grad: 30M, 20W
Year: 4-1-4, ss
Appl: open
1468 applied   1440 accepted
ACT: 23

Faculty: 210; IIB, ++$
Ph.D.'s: 70%
S/F Ratio: 19 to 1
Tuition: $3480
R and B: $1720
1050 enrolled
COMPETITIVE+

Calvin College, established in 1876, is a liberal arts institution affiliated with the Christian Reformed Church. The library houses 330,000 volumes and 17,000 microfilm items, and subscribes to 2060 periodicals.

Environment: The 166-acre suburban campus is located 6 miles from downtown Grand Rapids. Residence halls accommodate 1800 students. On-campus apartments also are provided. Facilities are available for commuting students.

Student Life: About 57% of the students come from Michigan. Eighty percent are members of the supporting church. About 50% live on campus; freshmen and sophomores under age 21 are required to do so unless living at home.

Organizations: Extracurricular activities include student government, publications, special-interest clubs, service organizations, performing groups, and a debating society. There are no fraternities or sororities.

Sports: The college fields intercollegiate teams in 11 sports for men and 8 for women. Intramural sports also are offered for men and women.

Handicapped: Nearly all of the campus is accessible to handicapped students. Facilities include wheelchair ramps, elevators, parking areas, specially equipped rest rooms, specially designed dorm rooms, and lowered drinking fountains and telephones. Special class scheduling can be arranged. Three counselors assist handicapped students.

Graduates: About 15% of the freshmen drop out, and 55% remain to graduate. About 25% of the graduates pursue advanced degrees; 3% enter medical school and 1% dental school. About 30% begin careers in business and industry.

Services: The following services are available to students: placement, career, and psychological counseling; health care; tutoring; and remedial instruction.

Programs of Study: The college confers the B.A., B.F.A., and B.S. degrees. Master's degrees are also available. Bachelor's degrees are offered in the following subjects: BUSINESS (accounting, business administration), EDUCATION (bilingual, elementary, middle school, health/physical, secondary, special), ENGLISH (English, speech), FINE AND PERFORMING ARTS (art, art education, music, music education), HEALTH SCIENCES (medical technology, nursing), LANGUAGES (classical languages, Dutch, French, German, Greek/Latin, Spanish), MATH AND SCIENCES (biology, chemistry, computer science, geology, mathematics, physics), PHILOSOPHY (classics, philosophy, religion), PREPROFESSIONAL (agriculture, architecture, dentistry, engineering, forestry, law, medicine, ministry, natural resources, pharmacy, social work), SOCIAL SCIENCES (economics, government/political science, history, psychology, sociology).

Required: All students must satisfy requirements in English, religion and theology, and physical education. Students also must complete a distribution of credits in several broad areas.

Special: Study abroad and combined B.A.-B.S. degrees are offered.

Honors: All departments offer honors programs. A general program also is available.

Admissions: About 98% of those who applied were accepted for the 1981-82 freshman class. Of those who enrolled, 40% scored below 21 on the ACT and 16% scored above 28. Students should have at least a C+ average, have completed 15 Carnegie units, and rank in the upper half of their high school class. They should score 16 or higher on the ACT or at least 370V and 390M on the SAT. Those with lower grades on test scores may be admitted conditionally.

Procedure: Applicants should take the SAT or the ACT by January of the senior year. Application deadlines are open, but applications received after July 1 (for fall admission) must be accompanied by a $10 fee. Notification is on a rolling basis. New students are admitted to both semesters and in the summer.

Special: AP and CLEP credit is granted.

Transfer: About 275 transfer students enroll each year. Transfers are accepted for all classes. A 2.0 GPA is required. D grades are generally accepted. One year must be completed in residence to receive a bachelor's degree.

Visiting: An orientation program is conducted for prospective students. Informal guided campus tours are available. Visitors may sit in on classes and stay overnight at the college. Visits are best scheduled on Fridays. The admissions office should be contacted for arrangements.

Financial Aid: About 70% of the students receive aid. The college offers 300 freshman scholarships, loans, and campus employment, including CWS. Federal loans also are available. The average award to freshmen in 1981-82 totaled $2000. The FAF should be submitted by February 1 for priority consideration.

Foreign Students: The 375 students from foreign countries make up 9% of enrollment. The college offers these students an intensive English course, special counseling, and special organizations.

Admissions: Applicants must score 500 or better on the TOEFL. Canadian students also must take the SAT.

Procedure: Application deadlines are June 1 (fall) and November 1 (spring). Students must present proof of adequate funds for 4 years and must carry health insurance, which is available through the college for a fee.

Admissions Contact: Donald Lautenbach, Director of Admissions.

394 MICHIGAN

CENTER FOR CREATIVE STUDIES E-5
Detroit, Michigan 48202 (313) 872-3118

F/T: 320M, 253W	Faculty: 41; IIB, ++$
P/T: 217M, 313W	Ph.D.'s: 7%
Grad: none	S/F Ratio: 12 to 1
Year: sems, ss	Tuition: $3900
Appl: June 15	R and B: $1450
430 applied	246 accepted	152 enrolled
SAT: 440V 420M	ACT: 18	SPECIAL

Center for Creative Studies, established in 1926, is an independent professional art college. The library contains 12,000 volumes and 24,000 slides, and subscribes to 100 periodicals.

Environment: The campus is located in an urban area within 2 blocks of 90% of the cultural institutions in Detroit, including the Institute of Arts. The school utilizes 4 dormitories in the area for housing and places students in apartments located within walking distance of the college.

Student Life: About 88% of the students come from Michigan. Fourteen percent are minority-group members. Students may keep cars on campus.

Organizations: There are no sororities or fraternities. Extracurricular activities on campus are limited. Students may participate in campus governance and student art exhibits.

Sports: There is no athletic program.

Handicapped: All facilities are accessible to students with physical handicaps.

Graduates: Recently, the overall student dropout rate was 21%. About 25% of the graduates pursue advanced study.

Services: Career counseling, placement, psychological counseling, and remedial instruction are provided free of charge.

Programs of Study: The B.F.A. is granted with majors in advertising design, art direction, ceramics, fabric design, glass, illustration, industrial design, metal and jewelry, painting, photography, printmaking, and sculpture.

Special: There are work-study programs in all majors.

Honors: There is no honors program.

Admissions: About 57% of the applicants for the 1981-82 freshman class were accepted. For a recent freshman class, the SAT scores of those who enrolled were as follows: Verbal—8% between 500 and 599, 3% between 600 and 700, and 1% above 700; Math—6% between 500 and 599, 1% between 600 and 700, and 1% above 700. On the ACT, 21% scored between 21 and 23, 15% between 24 and 26, 9% between 27 and 28, and 6% above 28. Candidates should have a 2.5 GPA and must present a portfolio. An interview is required for Michigan residents and recommended for out-of-state students.

Procedure: The SAT or ACT is required. Application deadlines are June 15 (fall) and December 1 (winter). Notification is on a rolling basis. There is a $15 application fee.

Special: A deferred admissions plan is available. AP and CLEP credit is accepted.

Transfer: For fall 1981, 195 students applied, 160 were accepted, and 134 enrolled. A 2.5 GPA, standardized exam scores, previous college transcripts, and a portfolio are required. D grades do not transfer. Students must spend 2 years in residence and complete at least 72 of the 144 credits necessary for a bachelor's degree. Application deadlines are the same as those for freshmen.

Visiting: There is a regularly scheduled orientation program for new students. Informal campus tours, including sitting in on classes, can be arranged through the admissions office.

Financial Aid: About 71% of all students receive some form of financial aid. Fifteen percent work part-time on campus. Average aid to freshmen is $2500. The school offers scholarships, and tuition may be paid in installments. The school is a member of CSS and requires either the FAF or the FFS. Application deadlines are March 1 (fall), October 31 (winter), and May 1 (summer).

Foreign Students: Fewer than 1% of the full-time students come from foreign countries. The school offers these students special counseling and special organizations.

Admissions: Foreign students must achieve a minimum TOEFL score of 450. No college entrance exam must be taken.

Procedure: Application deadlines are June 15 (fall) and December 1 (spring). Foreign students must present proof of funds adequate to cover 1 year of study.

Admissions Contact: Janice Bergstrom, Director of Admissions.

CENTRAL MICHIGAN UNIVERSITY D-4
Mount Pleasant, Michigan 48859 (517) 774-3076

F/T: 6137M, 7828W	Faculty: 600; IIA, ++$
P/T: 433M, 575W	Ph.D.'s: 80%
Grad: 741M, 763W	S/F Ratio: 23 to 1
Year: sems, ss	Tuition: $1215 ($3010)
Appl: open	R and B: $2000
10,355 applied	8103 accepted	3338 enrolled
ACT: 20		COMPETITIVE

Central Michigan University, established in 1892, is a publicly supported institution that offers undergraduate programs in the liberal arts and sciences, business, education, and preprofessional areas. The library contains 650,000 volumes and nearly 550,000 microfilm items, and subscribes to 4824 periodicals.

Environment: The 872-acre campus is located in a rural area 45 miles from Saginaw. Living facilities include dormitories and married student housing.

Student Life: Nearly all of the students are from Michigan. Forty percent live on campus. About 4% are minority-group members. Twenty-three percent are Catholic, 22% are Protestant, and 1% are Jewish. Campus housing is both coed and single-sex; there are visiting privileges in the single-sex housing. Students may keep cars on campus.

Organizations: There are 12 national fraternities and 10 national sororities, to which 5% of the men and 5% of the women belong. Campus life is full and diversified; many extracurricular activities are offered. There are religious organizations in the 3 major faiths.

Sports: The university competes intercollegiately in 9 sports for men and 8 for women. There are 11 intramural sports for men and 10 for women.

Handicapped: Facilities for the physically handicapped include wheelchair ramps, special parking, elevators, specially equipped rest rooms, and lowered drinking fountains and telephones.

Graduates: There is a freshman dropout rate of 10%; 45% remain to graduate. Thirty percent of those who graduate pursue advanced degrees.

Services: Placement services, career counseling, psychological counseling, and tutoring are offered to students free of charge. Health care and remedial instruction are provided on a fee basis.

Programs of Study: The university confers the B.A., B.S., B.M., B.Mus.Ed., B.S.Ed., B.F.A., B.S.B.A., B.S.W., B.A.A., and B. of Individualized Studies degrees. Master's and doctoral degrees are also awarded. Bachelor's degrees are offered in the following subjects: AREA STUDIES (American), BUSINESS (accounting, business administration, business education, computer science, finance, management, marketing), EDUCATION (early childhood, elementary, health/physical, industrial, secondary), ENGLISH (English, journalism, speech), FINE AND PERFORMING ARTS (art, art education, film/photography, music, music education, radio/TV, studio art, theater/dramatics), HEALTH SCIENCES (medical technology), LANGUAGES (French, German, Spanish), MATH AND SCIENCES (biology, chemistry, earth science, geology, mathematics, physics), PHILOSOPHY (philosophy, religion), PREPROFESSIONAL (home economics, social work), SOCIAL SCIENCES (anthropology, economics, geography, government/political science, history, psychology, sociology). Twenty-five percent of degrees are conferred in business and 25% in education.

Special: Student-designed majors and a general studies (no major) degree are offered.

Honors: Ten national honor societies have chapters on campus. Honors programs are offered in natural sciences, humanities, and social sciences.

Admissions: Approximately 78% of those who applied were accepted for the 1981-82 freshman class. The ACT scores of those who enrolled were as follows: 50% below 21; 24% between 21 and 23, 12% between 24 and 25, 12% between 26 and 28, and 2% above 28. Candidates must be graduates of an accredited high school and must rank in the upper half of their high school class. Other factors influencing the admissions decision are advanced placement or honors courses, evidence of special talents, recommendations, leadership record, and the ability to finance a college education.

Procedure: The ACT is required. Application deadlines are open; the university follows a rolling admissions policy. There is no application fee.

Special: AP and CLEP credit is accepted.

Transfer: For fall 1981, 2192 students applied, 1857 were accepted, and 1117 enrolled. Transfers are accepted for all classes; D grades sometimes transfer. A minimum C average is required. Preference is given to students transferring from Michigan colleges. All students must complete, at the university, 30 of the 124 or more credits required for a bachelor's degree.

Visiting: There are regularly scheduled orientations for prospective students. Guides are also available for informal visits; visitors may arrange to stay at the school. The housing office should be contacted to arrange overnight visits.

Financial Aid: Approximately 80% of all students receive some form of financial aid. Twenty-five percent work part-time on campus. Scholarships, loans, and grants are available, as is work-study in all departments. The university is a member of the CSS; the deadlines for aid applications are February 1 (fall), October 1 (winter), and April 1 (summer). The FAF or FFS is required.

Foreign Students: One percent of the full-time students come from foreign countries. An intensive English course, special counseling, and special organizations are available for these students.

Admissions: Foreign students must take either the TOEFL or the University of Michigan Language Test. On the TOEFL, a score of at least 525 is required.

Procedure: Deadlines are open; foreign students are admitted to all terms. They must present proof of funds adequate to cover the entire period of study. Health insurance is required and is available through the university.

Admissions Contact: Michael A. Owens, Director of Admissions.

CONCORDIA COLLEGE
Ann Arbor, Michigan 48105

E-5

(313) 665-3691

F/T: 254M, 239W	Faculty:	58; IIB, −$
P/T: 43 M&W	Ph.D.'s:	30%
Grad: none	S/F Ratio:	11 to 1
Year: sems, ss	Tuition:	$2409
Appl: open	R and B:	$1830
220 applied	211 accepted	160 enrolled
ACT: 21		COMPETITIVE

Concordia College, founded in 1963, is maintained by the Lutheran Church and offers career programs in teaching, social work, ministry, and parish services. The library has 100,000 volumes.

Environment: The 234-acre suburban campus has 28 buildings and is located about 45 miles from Detroit. Sixteen dormitories house 512 men and women.

Student Life: Sixty percent of the students are from Michigan and 97% are Protestant. Dormitories are single-sex. Full-time freshmen and sophomores under age 21 must live on campus unless living at home. Drinking on campus is forbidden.

Organizations: There are no fraternities or sororities. Student government and traditional extracurricular groups are available.

Sports: The college fields intercollegiate teams in 7 sports for men and 4 for women. Intramural sports for men and women also are available.

Handicapped: About 75% of the campus is accessible to students with physical handicaps. Facilities include wheelchair ramps, special parking, and elevators. Special class scheduling is also available.

Graduates: About 5% of the freshmen drop out, and 90% remain to graduate. About 85% of graduates pursue advanced study.

Services: Health care and career counseling are provided free. Tutoring and remedial instruction is also available.

Programs of Study: The college confers the B.A. degree. Associate degrees are also awarded. Bachelor's degrees are offered in the following subjects: AREA STUDIES (Hebrew), EDUCATION (elementary, religious, secondary), ENGLISH (English, speech), FINE AND PERFORMING ARTS (art, music), LANGUAGES (Greek/Latin), MATH AND SCIENCES (biology, earth science, general science, mathematics), PHILOSOPHY (classics, humanities, philosophy, religion), PREPROFESSIONAL (ministry), SOCIAL SCIENCES (history/political science, psychology, psychology/sociology, sociology).

Required: All students must complete a liberal arts core curriculum, including physical education, and pass the GRE to graduate.

Special: Additional minors are offered in business administration, history, German, and physical education. The college also offers a 2-year pre-social-work program. Study abroad is available.

Admissions: About 96% of the 1981–82 applicants were accepted. The ACT scores of those who enrolled were as follows: 50% below 21, 38% between 21 and 23, 8% between 24 and 25, 2% between 26 and 28, and 2% above 28. Applicants must rank in the upper 40% of their high school class and have a GPA of at least 2.5. Recommendations, evidence of special talents, and the ability to finance a college education also are considered.

Procedure: The SAT or ACT is required. Application deadlines are open. Notification is made on a rolling basis. There is no application fee.

Special: AP and CLEP credit is accepted. There is a deferred admissions plan.

Transfer: In a recent year, 27 transfer students enrolled. D grades do not transfer. Students must earn at least 30 hours in residence of the 128 required for a bachelor's degree. Applications should be submitted 2 weeks before the beginning of the semester.

Visiting: An orientation program is conducted for prospective students. Informal campus tours may be arranged; visitors may stay at the school and sit in on classes.

Financial Aid: About 73% of all students receive aid. The college offers 30 academic scholarships for freshmen. In addition, government loans and CWS are available. The FAF should be submitted by May 31 for priority consideration. Need is the determining factor.

Foreign Students: The 30 students from foreign countries make up about 6% of the student body.

Admissions: Applicants must score 550 or better on the TOEFL. Another English-proficiency test may be substituted; contact the college for its preference. No college entrance exams are required.

Procedure: Application deadlines are open. Students must present proof of adequate funds for 1 year. Special tuition fees are charged; the fee in 1981–82 was $1000.

Admissions Contact: Timothy E. Winter, Director of Admissions.

EASTERN MICHIGAN UNIVERSITY
Ypsilanti, Michigan 48197

E-5

(313) 487-3060

F/T: 4414M, 5622W	Faculty:	624; IIA, ++$
P/T: 1963M, 2500W	Ph.D.'s:	67%
Grad: 1955M, 2852W	S/F Ratio:	20 to 1
Year: sems, ss	Tuition:	$1136 ($2741)
Appl: see profile	R and B:	$2020
7040 applied	5495 accepted	2380 enrolled
SAT or ACT: required		LESS COMPETITIVE

Eastern Michigan University, founded in 1849, is a state-supported, multi-purpose university made up of the colleges of Arts and Sciences, Business, Education, Human Services, and Technology, as well as a graduate school. The library contains 551,000 volumes and 372,000 microfilm items, and subscribes to 7200 periodicals.

Environment: The 460-acre campus is located in a suburban area 35 miles from Detroit. The 112 buildings include a new music building, a physical education/recreation facility scheduled for completion by fall 1982, and 12 dormitories that accommodate more than 4000 students. The university also sponsors fraternity and sorority houses, on-campus and off-campus apartments, and married student housing.

Student Life: About 91% of the students are from Michigan. Approximately 48% of the students live on campus. About 12% are minority-group members. University housing is coed and single-sex; students in single-sex housing have visiting privileges. Students may keep cars on campus. Day-care facilities are available for a fee to full-time and part-time students, faculty, and staff.

Organizations: There are 13 fraternities and 10 sororities. Extracurricular, special-interest, and religious groups sponsor social and cultural events.

Sports: The college fields 15 intercollegiate teams for men and 12 for women. There are 21 intramural sports for men and 18 for women.

Handicapped: Facilities for the physically handicapped include wheelchair ramps, special parking, elevators, specially equipped rest rooms, and lowered drinking fountains and telephones.

Graduates: The freshman dropout rate is 34%, and 35% of the freshmen remain to graduate. Thirty-five percent of those who graduate pursue advanced degrees.

Services: Free tutoring, remedial instruction, career and psychological counseling, and job placement services are offered to all students. Health care is available for a fee.

Programs of Study: The university confers the B.A., B.S., B.B.A., B.F.A., B.S.N., B.Mus.Ed., B. of Music Performance, B. of Music Therapy, and B. of Art Education degrees. Master's programs are also available. Bachelor's degrees are offered in the following subjects: AREA STUDIES (African, Asian, Latin American, Middle Eastern, Russian), BUSINESS (accounting, business administration, business education, computer science, finance, management, marketing, real estate/insurance), EDUCATION (early childhood, elementary, health/physical, industrial, recreation, secondary, special), ENGLISH (English, linguistics, literature, speech), FINE AND PERFORMING ARTS (art, art education, arts management, dance, music, music education, music therapy, radio/TV, theater/dramatics), HEALTH SCIENCES (dietetics, health administration, medical technology, nursing, occupational therapy), LANGUAGES (French, German, Spanish), MATH AND SCIENCES (biochemistry, biology, chemistry, earth science, geology, mathematics, metallurgy, physical sciences, physics), PHILOSOPHY (philosophy), PREPROFESSIONAL (computer aided design, construction technology, forestry, home economics, industrial technology, library science, manufacturing technology, social work), SOCIAL SCIENCES (anthropology, criminology, economics, geography, government/political science, history, labor studies, land use analysis, psychology, social sciences, social work, sociology). About 25% of the degrees are conferred in business, 21% in arts and sciences, 13% in education, 13% in human services, and 4% in technology.

Required: A basic studies requirement must be met by all students before graduation, but this varies with the student's major. Some academic departments require that designated courses be completed before admission to that program is granted.

Special: Study abroad, cooperative education experiences, and student-designed majors are available.

Honors: Departmental honors programs are offered in chemistry, English, political science, and music. There are 11 national honor societies represented on campus.

Admissions: About 78% of those who applied for the 1981-82 freshman class were accepted. Candidates should have completed 15 Carnegie units and have a 2.5 average. Recommendations are also considered.

Procedure: Either the SAT or ACT is required and should be taken by December of the senior year. Applications are accepted until the last day of registration. Notification is on a rolling basis. There is no application fee.

Special: AP and CLEP credit is accepted.

Transfer: For fall 1981, 2751 students applied, 2102 were accepted, and 1518 enrolled. Transfers are accepted for all classes. A minimum GPA of 2.0 and 12 completed credit hours are required. D grades transfer. Students must complete, at the university, at least 30 of the 124 semester hours necessary for a bachelor's degree. Application deadlines are the same as those for freshmen.

Visiting: Campus tours, offered on a daily basis, include a comprehensive look at the campus and an opportunity to meet with faculty and staff. Arrangements for an informal visit can be made by calling the Admissions on Campus Program Center at (313) 487-1111.

Financial Aid: Sixty-five percent of the students receive financial aid. Twenty-three percent work part-time on campus. Average aid to freshmen is $1900. Aid is available in the form of scholarships, grants, and loans. The university is a member of CSS and requires either the FAF or the FFS. Application deadlines are April 1 (fall and winter) and March 1 (spring and summer).

Foreign Students: Five percent of the full-time students come from foreign countries. The university offers these students an intensive English course and program, special counseling, and special organizations.

Admissions: Foreign students must achieve a minimum TOEFL score of 500 or a University of Michigan Language Test score of at least 80. No college entrance exam must be taken.

Procedure: Application deadlines are August 1 (fall), December 1 (winter), April 1 (spring), and May 1 (summer). Foreign students must present proof of funds adequate to cover the first year of study.

Admissions Contact: Don Kajcienski, Director of Admissions.

FERRIS STATE COLLEGE
Big Rapids, Michigan 49307

D-4
(616) 796-0461

F/T: 6342M, 4381W
P/T: 221M, 191W
Grad: 102M, 24W
Year: qtrs, ss
Appl: Aug. 1
5070 accepted
ACT: 17

Faculty: 471; IIA, av$
Ph.D.'s: 35%
S/F Ratio: 19 to 1
Tuition: $1164 ($2730)
R and B: $2067

2890 enrolled
NONCOMPETITIVE

Ferris State College, founded in 1884, offers undergraduate programs in applied sciences, business, education, and the health fields. The library contains 210,000 volumes and 800 microfilm items, and subscribes to 1500 periodicals.

Environment: The 485-acre campus is located in a town of 12,000 inhabitants about 55 miles from Grand Rapids. Twenty-two residence halls accommodate 424 married and more than 5000 single students.

Student Life: Nearly all of the students come from Michigan. Sixty percent live on campus. Five percent of the students are minority-group members. College housing is coed and single-sex; students in single-sex housing have visiting privileges. Students may keep cars on campus.

Organizations: There are 15 national fraternities and 10 national sororities. Extracurricular activities include recreation in the vicinity, on-campus social and cultural events, and traditional organizations and groups.

Sports: The college fields 12 intercollegiate teams for men and 9 for women. There are 13 intramural sports for men and 12 for women.

Handicapped: The entire campus is accessible to the physically handicapped. Facilities include wheelchair ramps, special parking, elevators, specially equipped rest rooms, lowered drinking fountains and telephones, and a van with a lift.

Graduates: The freshman dropout rate is 35%. Five percent of those who remain to graduate pursue advanced study, and 65% enter careers in business and industry.

Services: Placement services, career counseling, psychological counseling, health care, tutoring, and remedial instruction are offered to students free of charge.

Programs of Study: The college offers the B.S. and B. Applied Arts degrees. Associate and doctoral degrees are also awarded. Bachelor's degrees are offered in the following subjects: BUSINESS (accounting, business administration, business education, computer science, finance, hospitality management, management, marketing, professional golf management, quantitative business analysis, real estate/insurance), EDUCATION (allied health, community education, industrial, secondary), FINE AND PERFORMING ARTS (radio/TV), HEALTH SCIENCES (environmental health, medical records administration, medical technology, nuclear medicine technology, occupational therapy, physical therapy), MATH AND SCIENCES (applied biology, applied mathematics), PREPROFESSIONAL (auto and heavy equipment, broadcasting technology, engineering, manufacturing technology, pharmacy, printing, social work, surveying), SOCIAL SCIENCES (public administration).

Special: The B.S. in pharmacy is a 5-year program; the optometry curriculum is a 6-year program leading to the O.D. degree.

Honors: There are 14 professional and honor societies on campus.

Admissions: The ACT scores of those who enrolled for the 1981-82 freshman class were as follows: 18% between 21 and 23, 10% between 24 and 25, 3% between 26 and 28, and 1% above 28. Candidates should have a minimum 2.0 GPA.

Procedure: The ACT is required. Deadlines for application are August 1 (fall), November 1 (winter), February 1 (spring), and May 1 (summer). Notification is on a rolling basis. There is a $15 application fee.

Special: AP and CLEP credit is accepted.

Transfer: For fall 1981, 1577 of the applicants were accepted and 1016 enrolled. A minimum 2.0 GPA is required. D grades do not transfer. Students generally are required to spend 1 year in residence and complete at least 45 of the approximately 200 credits necessary for a bachelor's degree. Application deadlines are the same as those for freshmen.

Visiting: There are orientation sessions for new students prior to the beginning of each quarter. There is a 2-day orientation for prospective students and their parents during the summer. Informal campus visits allow visitors to sit in on classes and stay at the school. These visits are best scheduled for weekdays from 8 A.M. to 4 P.M.. The admissions office should be contacted for arrangements.

Financial Aid: Approximately 60% of all students receive some form of financial aid. Forty-five percent work part-time on campus. Aid is available in the form of scholarships, grants, and loans. The college is a member of CSS and requires the FAF. The deadline for aid applications is at least 30 days before the beginning of each quarter; it is best to file in April for the fall quarter.

Foreign Students: One percent of the full-time students come from foreign countries. The college offers these students special counseling and special organizations.

Admissions: Foreign students must achieve a minimum TOEFL score of 500 and are required to take the ACT.

Procedure: Application deadlines are the same as those for freshman applicants. Foreign students must present proof of health and proof of adequate funds. They must also pay out-of-state tuition and carry health insurance.

Admissions Contact: Karl S. Walker, Director of Admissions, Records, and Registration.

GENERAL MOTORS INSTITUTE E-4
Flint, Michigan 48502 (313) 762-7865

F/T: 1614M, 775W	Faculty: 142; n/av
P/T: none	Ph.D.'s: 35%
Grad: none	S/F Ratio: 15 to 1
Year: sems	Tuition: $1408
Appl: Jan. 2	R and B: $1210
2672 applied	573 accepted	573 enrolled
SAT: 550V 655M	ACT: 27 HIGHLY COMPETITIVE+

General Motors Institute, established in 1919 by the General Motors Corporation, is a college of engineering and management operating on the cooperative plan of education. The library contains 90,000 volumes and 7842 microfilm items, and subscribes to 800 periodicals.

Environment: The 49-acre campus is located in an urban area on the Flint River. Over 30% of the total floor space of the academic building is devoted to laboratories. The campus residence hall houses 450 students. The institute also sponsors 12 fraternity and 2 sorority houses.

Student Life: Approximately 44% of the students come from Michigan; 87% come from public schools. Nineteen percent of the students live on campus; all unmarried freshmen are required to live in the campus residence hall. Forty-two percent of the students are Catholic, 17% are Protestant, and 1% are Jewish; religious counseling is available. About 18% are minority-group members. Campus housing is coed and single-sex; students in single-sex housing have visiting privileges. Students may keep cars on campus.

Organizations: There are 15 fraternities and 4 sororities on campus. The institute sponsors lectures and concerts.

Sports: There is no intercollegiate program. There are 17 intramural sports for men and 17 for women.

Graduates: The freshman dropout rate is 8%, and 75% of the freshmen remain to graduate. Thirty-five percent of the graduates pursue advanced degrees. Nearly all the graduates enter careers in business and industry.

Services: Health care, psychological counseling, tutoring, and academic counseling are offered to students free of charge.

Programs of Study: The institute confers the Bachelor of Mechanical Engineering, Bachelor of Industrial Engineering, Bachelor of Electrical Engineering, and Bachelor of Industrial Administration degrees. The programs extend over 5 years; the first 4½ years operate on the cooperative plan, with students spending alternating 12-week periods at the institute and in their sponsoring units for a total of 24 weeks in intensive study and a maximum of 24 weeks in related, directed work experience each year. Upon completion of the cooperative phase, students continue to work for the degree under the thesis plan, which requires the preparation of a thesis.

Special: College credit may be given for college-level secondary work on the basis of records and test scores.

Honors: Eleven professional and honor societies have chapters on campus.

Admissions: Approximately 21% of those who applied were accepted for the 1981-82 freshman class. The SAT scores of those who enrolled were as follows: Verbal—25% below 500, 56% between 500 and 599, 17% between 600 and 700, and 2% above 700; Math—2% below 500, 19% between 500 and 599, 59% between 600 and 700, and 20% above 700. On the ACT, 1% scored below 21, 3% between 21 and 23, 12% between 24 and 25, 53% between 26 and 28, and 31% above 28. High school graduation must include these 16 units of college preparatory work: 2.0 units algebra, 1.0 unit geometry, 0.5 unit trigonometry, 3.0 units English, 2.0 units lab science, and 7.5 units engineering drawing. A high scholastic standing is essential. Applicants are judged on their educational record, test scores, class rank, recommendations, and evidence of talent, ability, and interest. The evaluation and selection of applicants is a joint activity of the institute and the participating sponsoring units.

Procedure: The SAT or ACT is required and should be taken as early as possible in the senior year. Also strongly recommended are ATs in mathematics, English, and either chemistry or physics. The deadline for fall application is January 2. There is a $10 application fee.

Special: Early admissions and early decision plans are available. AP credit is accepted for math, physics, and chemistry.

Transfer: For fall 1981, 38 of the applicants were accepted and all enrolled. Transfers must have completed at least one academic year or the equivalent, with courses comparable to those required at GMI in the applicant's chosen curriculum. A GPA of at least 3.0 is also required. Students must study at the institute for at least 5 semesters (including the senior year) and complete at least 105 of the 180 credits necessary for a bachelor's degree. Deadlines are the same as those for freshmen.

Financial Aid: Students are paid during their work periods by their sponsoring unit; entering students earn approximately $6500 per year before deductions for income tax and social security. A limited amount of part-time work is available to students during their school period. The General Motors Institute Student Loan Fund insures that no student performing acceptably in the cooperative phase of the program will be forced to discontinue his or her education because of financial difficulties arising out of emergency situations. The institute does not award scholarships; earnings under the cooperative plan are more substantial than most scholarships. Students are encouraged to apply for the Pell Grant. The FAF is required of all students. Application deadlines are open.

Foreign Students: Eight percent of the full-time students come from foreign countries. The institute offers these students special counseling and special organizations.

Admissions: Foreign students are not required to take either an English proficiency exam or a college entrance exam.

Procedure: The application deadline for fall entry is January 1. Foreign students must present proof of a physical examination.

Admissions Contact: Fern R. Ramirez, Associate Dean of Admissions, Records, and Financial Aid.

GRAND VALLEY STATE COLLEGES D-4
Allendale, Michigan 49401 (616) 895-6611

F/T: 1512M, 1639W	Faculty: 236; IIA, ++$
P/T: 1188M, 1288W	Ph.D.'s: 75%
Grad: 515M, 557W	S/F Ratio: 19 to 1
Year: sems, ss	Tuition: $1200 ($2760)
Appl: Aug. 1	R and B: $2120
2086 applied	1735 accepted	1071 enrolled
ACT: 20		COMPETITIVE

Grand Valley State Colleges, a state-supported institution founded in 1960, consists of a federation of 4 colleges on 1 campus: the College of Arts and Sciences, William James College, Kirkhof College, and the F.E. Seidman Graduate College of Business and Administration. William James College offers an individualized, interdisciplinary curriculum. The library contains 275,000 volumes and 12,000 microfilm items, and subscribes to 1750 periodicals.

Environment: The 876-acre campus, located in a rural area 12 miles from Grand Rapids, includes 21 modern, air-conditioned buildings. Living facilities include dormitories and on- and off-campus apartments.

Student Life: About 97% of the students come from Michigan; almost all come from public schools. About 25% live on campus. Eight percent are minority-group members. Campus housing is single-sex; there are visiting privileges. Students may keep cars on campus. Daycare services are available to all students for a fee.

Organizations: There are 2 national fraternities and 2 national sororities, to which 1% of the men and 1% of the women belong. Extracurricular activities are varied, numerous, and traditional. Regularly scheduled social and cultural events include concerts, films, and theater.

398 MICHIGAN

Sports: The colleges field 6 intercollegiate teams for men and 4 for women. There are 6 intramural sports for men and 5 for women.

Handicapped: Approximately 60% of the campus is accessible to the physically handicapped. Facilities include wheelchair ramps, special parking, elevators, specially equipped rest rooms, and lowered telephones; special class scheduling is also available. Special tutoring is offered to students with visual or hearing impairments.

Graduates: The freshman dropout rate is 33%; 40% remain to graduate. Twenty-five percent of those who graduate pursue advanced degrees (2% in medicine, 1% in dentistry, and 1% in law). Ten percent pursue careers in business and industry.

Services: Placement services, career counseling, tutoring, and psychological counseling are offered to students free of charge. Health care and remedial instruction are provided on a fee basis.

Programs of Study: The B.A., B.S., B.F.A., B.B.A., B.M., B.M.E., B.S.W., and B.A.S. degrees are offered. Master's degrees are also awarded. Bachelor's degrees are offered in the following subjects: AREA STUDIES (Latin American), BUSINESS (accounting, business administration, computer science, finance, management, marketing, real estate/insurance), EDUCATION (early childhood, elementary, health/physical, secondary, special), ENGLISH (English, journalism), FINE AND PERFORMING ARTS (art, film/photography, music, radio/TV, theater/dramatics), HEALTH SCIENCES (environmental health, medical technology, nursing), LANGUAGES (French, German, Spanish), MATH AND SCIENCES (biology, chemistry, earth science, ecology/environmental science, geology, mathematics, natural sciences, physics), PHILOSOPHY (philosophy), PREPROFESSIONAL (dentistry, law, medicine, social work), SOCIAL SCIENCES (anthropology, economics, government/political science, history, psychology, social sciences, sociology). About 15% of the degrees are offered in business, 15% in education, 15% in fine and performing arts, and 15% in social sciences.

Required: All students in the College of Arts and Sciences, Seidman College of Business Administration, and Kirkhof College must fulfill requirements in the humanities, the arts, social studies, and combined math-science courses.

Special: A general studies (no major) degree and student-designed majors are offered; internships, pass/fail options, study abroad, and learning modules are also available. Combination degrees are possible in engineering, medical technology, and forestry, wildlife, and fisheries. William James College offers a practically oriented liberal arts program in which students design their own majors, participate in internships, and conduct independent studies.

Honors: Phi Kappa Phi has a chapter on campus; a cross-college honors program is also offered.

Admissions: Approximately 83% of those who applied were accepted for the 1981-82 freshman class. The ACT scores of those who enrolled were as follows: 47% below 21, 32% between 21 and 23, 10% between 24 and 25, 8% between 26 and 28, and 3% above 28. Candidates should have a 2.5 GPA. Other factors entering into the admissions decision are advanced placement or honors courses, recommendations, extracurricular activities, and the applicant's leadership record.

Procedure: The ACT is required. A personal interview is required only of borderline applicants. Deadlines are August 1 (fall) and December 15 (winter); notification is on a rolling basis. There is a $15 application fee.

Special: AP and CLEP credit is accepted. There are early admissions and deferred admissions plans.

Transfer: For fall 1981, 1214 transfer applications were received, 1049 were accepted, and 779 students enrolled. D grades do not transfer. A minimum 2.0 GPA and high school transcripts are required. All students must complete, at the colleges, 30 of the 120 hours required for a bachelor's degree. Deadlines are the same as those for freshman applicants.

Visiting: There are regularly scheduled orientations for prospective students. Guides are also available for informal visits Monday through Friday from 9 A.M. to 4 P.M. and Saturday from 9:30 A.M. to 12 noon; visitors may sit in on classes and stay at the school.

Financial Aid: Approximately 70% of all students receive some form of financial aid. Sixty percent work part-time on campus. The average freshman award is $2000. Loans are available from the federal and state governments. CWS is available in all departments. Need is the determining factor. The FAF, FFS, or SFS is required. The deadline for aid application is March 1 (fall) or December 1 (spring). The colleges are members of CSS.

Foreign Students: Two percent of the full-time students come from foreign countries. An intensive English course and special counseling are available for these students.

Admissions: Foreign students must achieve a TOEFL score of at least 550 or an MTELP score of at least 82. No college entrance exams are required.

Procedure: Application deadlines are April 1 (fall), November 1 (winter), and March 1 (summer). Foreign students must have a TB test and must present proof of funds adequate to cover 1 year of study. Health insurance is required and is available through the colleges for a fee.

Admissions Contact: Carl Wallman, Admissions Director.

HILLSDALE COLLEGE D-5
Hillsdale, Michigan 49242 (517) 437-7341

F/T: 540M, 510W	Faculty:	72; IIB, ++$
P/T: 10M, 10W	Ph.D.'s:	70%
Grad: none	S/F Ratio:	14 to 1
Year: sems, ss	Tuition:	$4870
Appl: July 1	R and B:	$2380
910 applied	640 accepted	340 enrolled
SAT: 475V 510M	ACT: 21	COMPETITIVE

Hillsdale College, a small, privately controlled institution founded in 1844, offers undergraduate programs in the liberal arts and sciences, business, and preprofessional areas. The library contains 100,000 volumes and 1100 microfilm items, and subscribes to 290 periodicals.

Environment: The 150-acre campus is located in a suburban area 90 miles from Detroit. The college has an extensive conference center, an arboretum, and a private nursery school. Dormitories accommodate 790 men and women. The college also sponsors fraternity and sorority houses.

Student Life: About 50% of the students come from Michigan; 85% come from public schools. Eighty-five percent of the students live on campus; juniors and seniors may live in private housing. Sixty-four percent of the students are Protestant, 35% are Catholic, and 1% are Jewish. About 7% are minority-group members. College housing is single-sex, and there are visiting privileges. Students may keep cars on campus. Drinking on college property is forbidden.

Organizations: About 50% of the men belong to the 6 national fraternities; 45% of the women belong to the 3 national sororities. Special activities include a leadership workshop, art exhibitions, lecture and concert series, plays, and musical productions.

Sports: The college fields 7 intercollegiate teams for men and 8 for women. There are 12 intramural sports for men and 9 for women.

Handicapped: There are no special facilities for students with physical handicaps.

Graduates: The freshman dropout rate is 15%; 60% remain to graduate. Of these, 52% go on for further study; 5% enter medical school, 2% dental school, and 10% law school. Thirty-five percent pursue careers in business and industry.

Services: Placement, career counseling, and health care are provided free of charge. Psychological counseling is available for a fee.

Programs of Study: The B.A., B.S., or B. of Liberal Studies is offered in the following subjects: AREA STUDIES (American, European), BUSINESS (accounting, business administration), EDUCATION (early childhood, elementary, health/physical, secondary), ENGLISH (English, speech), FINE AND PERFORMING ARTS (art, music, music education, theater/dramatics), LANGUAGES (French, German, Spanish), MATH AND SCIENCES (biology, chemistry, mathematics, physics), PHILOSOPHY (philosophy, religion), PREPROFESSIONAL (dentistry, engineering, forestry, law, medicine, pharmacy, social work, veterinary), SOCIAL SCIENCES (economics, history, international business, political economy, psychology, sociology). About 25% of degrees are conferred in business and 25% in preprofessional areas.

Special: Independent study, foreign travel and study tours, a 5-year B.A.-B.S. program in engineering, a Washington semester, and a 3-year bachelor's degree are offered.

Honors: The honors program is open to majors from any field. Twelve national honor societies have chapters on campus.

Admissions: Approximately 70% of those who applied were accepted for the 1981-82 freshman class. The SAT scores of those who enrolled were as follows: Verbal—51% below 500, 39% between 500 and 599, 8% between 600 and 700, and 2% above 700; Math—46% below 500, 42% between 500 and 599, 9% between 600 and 700, and 3% above 700. On the ACT, 43% scored below 21, 28% between 21 and 23, 17% between 24 and 25, 9% between 26 and 28, and 3% above 28. Applicants should rank in the top half of their class and have at least a 2.5 GPA. The most important factors in evaluating a candidate are grades, the strength of the college preparatory program, the total testing pattern, and the remarks of counselors. The college seeks a national geographic distribution; veterans are given special consideration.

Procedure: The SAT or ACT is required and should be taken in the junior year or early in the senior year; ATs are recommended but not required. Application deadlines are July 1 (fall) and December 1 (spring). Notification is on a rolling basis. There is a $15 application fee.

Special: There are early and deferred admissions plans. AP and CLEP credit is accepted.

Transfer: For fall 1981, 75 students applied, 60 were accepted, and 40 enrolled. Transfers are not accepted for the senior year. Applicants are judged on individual merit, but a minimum 2.5 GPA and an interview are recommended. D grades do not transfer. Students must spend at least the senior year in full-time residence toward completion of the 124 credits necessary for a bachelor's degree. Application deadlines are July 1 (fall) and December 1 (spring).

Visiting: There is a 2-day orientation for new students and their parents in May. Informal visits allow visitors to sit in on classes and stay at the school. These visits are best scheduled for weekdays from 9 A.M. to 4 P.M.. The admissions office should be contacted for arrangements.

Financial Aid: Approximately 55% of all students receive some form of financial aid. Thirty-five percent work part-time on campus. The average award to freshmen from all sources is $1800; loans are available. The college is a member of CSS and requires the FAF. Deadlines for aid application are March 15 (fall) and November 15 (spring).

Foreign Students: Three percent of the full-time students come from foreign countries. The college offers these students special organizations.

Admissions: Foreign students must achieve a minimum TOEFL score of 500 or a University of Michigan Language Test score of at least 75. No college entrance exam must be taken.

Procedure: Application deadlines are March 15 (fall) and December 1 (spring). Foreign students must present proof of funds adequate to cover 1 year of study.

Admissions Contact: Russell L. Nichols, Director of Admissions.

HOPE COLLEGE   C-4
Holland, Michigan 49423   (616) 392-5111

F/T: 1077M, 1119W	Faculty:	148; IIB, ++$
P/T: 106M, 156W	Ph.D.'s:	78%
Grad: none	S/F Ratio:	15 to 1
Year: sems, ss	Tuition:	$4520
Appl: open	R and B:	$2080
1221 applied	1080 accepted	587 enrolled
SAT: 496V 542M	ACT: 23	COMPETITIVE+

Hope College is a coeducational liberal arts and sciences college associated with the Reformed Church in America. The library contains 192,000 volumes and nearly 25,000 microfilm items, and subscribes to 1150 periodicals.

Environment: The 45-acre campus, 5 miles from the shores of Lake Michigan, is located in an urban area 150 miles from both Detroit and Chicago. Residence halls house 75% of the students. There are also fraternity and sorority houses and on-campus apartments.

Student Life: About 75% of the students come from Michigan; the majority are public school graduates. Seventy-five percent of the students live on campus; all non-commuting students are required to do so. Sixty-eight percent are Protestant, 8% are Catholic, and 0% are Jewish; attendance at daily chapel services is voluntary. Eight percent of the students are minority-group members. College housing is coed and single-sex; students in single-sex housing have visiting privileges. Students may keep cars on campus.

Organizations: Five local fraternities and 5 local sororities attract 25% of the men and 25% of the women. Extracurricular activities include student government, publications, performing groups, clubs, a campus radio station, religious organizations, and informal Bible studies. Outdoor recreation areas are in the vicinity.

Sports: The college fields 13 intercollegiate teams for men and 10 for women. There are 10 intramural sports for men and 8 for women.

Handicapped: About 80% of the campus is accessible to students with physical handicaps. Facilities include wheelchair ramps, special parking, and specially equipped rest rooms.

MICHIGAN 399

Graduates: The freshman dropout rate is 5%, and 55% of the freshmen remain to graduate. About 40% of the graduates go on for further study; 5% enter medical school, 2% dental school, and 3% law school. About 35% pursue careers in business and industry.

Services: Placement and career counseling are offered to students free of charge. Health care, psychological counseling, and tutoring sometimes require a fee.

Programs of Study: The B.A., B.S., B.S.N., and B.M. degrees are offered in the following subjects: AREA STUDIES (Spanish), BUSINESS (accounting, business administration, computer science, economics), EDUCATION (elementary, health/physical, secondary, special), ENGLISH (English, literature), FINE AND PERFORMING ARTS (art, art education, art history, music, music education, studio art, theater/dramatics), HEALTH SCIENCES (environmental health, medical technology, nursing, physical therapy), LANGUAGES (French, German, Greek/Latin, Spanish), MATH AND SCIENCES (biochemistry, biology, chemistry, geology, mathematics, natural sciences, physics), PHILOSOPHY (philosophy, religion), PREPROFESSIONAL (dentistry, engineering, law, medicine, ministry, social work, veterinary), SOCIAL SCIENCES (economics, government/political science, history, international relations, psychology, sociology). About 25% of the degrees are conferred in social sciences and 22% in math and sciences.

Required: There is a required core curriculum.

Special: Opportunities are available for students to major in general studies, design their own majors, study abroad, and study in Washington, D.C. and other U.S. cities.

Honors: There are 18 honor societies on campus.

Admissions: About 88% of those who applied were accepted for the 1981–82 freshman class. The SAT scores of those who enrolled were as follows: Verbal—52% below 500, 31% between 500 and 599, 14% between 600 and 700, and 3% above 700; Math—34% below 500, 34% between 500 and 599, 26% between 600 and 700, and 6% above 700. On the ACT, 28% scored below 18, 40% between 18 and 23, 29% between 24 and 29, and 3% above 29. Applicants must rank in the top half of their high school class and should have a good grade average. Also considered important are standardized exam scores, advanced placement or honor courses, and recommendations by school officials.

Procedure: Either the SAT or ACT is required; the ACT is preferred. Application deadlines are open. Notification is on a rolling basis. There is a $15 application fee.

Special: Deferred admissions and early decision plans are available. AP and CLEP credit is accepted. The FOCUS program allows students to enroll on a probationary basis to demonstrate that admission to the regular degree programs should be granted.

Transfer: For fall 1981, 194 students applied, 170 were accepted, and 115 enrolled. Standardized exam scores and both high school and college transcripts are required; a 2.0 GPA is recommended. D grades transfer only with an overall GPA of 2.0 or better. Students must complete, at the college, at least 30 of the 126 semester hours necessary for a bachelor's degree. Application deadlines are open.

Visiting: There is an orientation program for prospective students. Informal campus tours may be arranged; visitors may sit in on classes and stay at the school.

Financial Aid: About 89% of all students receive some form of financial assistance. Forty-four percent work part-time on campus. Average aid to freshmen is $3101. There are 30 freshman academic scholarships, in addition to grants and loans. The college is a member of CSS and requires the FAF. Application deadlines are January 31 for Michigan residents and March 1 for out-of-state students.

Foreign Students: Four percent of the full-time students come from foreign countries. The college offers these students an intensive English course, special counseling, and special organizations.

Admissions: Foreign students must take either the TOEFL, the University of Michigan Language Test, or the Comprehensive English Language Test, but the TOEFL is preferred with a minimum score of 500 required. No college entrance exam must be taken.

Procedure: Application deadlines are May 1 (fall) and December 1 (spring). Foreign students must present a certificate of health from a physician and proof of funds adequate to cover 4 years of study.

Admissions Contact: Robert T. Pocock, Associate Director of Admissions.

KALAMAZOO COLLEGE

Kalamazoo, Michigan 49007   (616) 383-8408   D-5

F/T: 713M, 654W	Faculty: 75; IIB, ++$
P/T: none	Ph.D.'s: 75%
Grad: none	S/F Ratio: 17 to 1
Year: qtrs, ss	Tuition: $5529
Appl: May 1	R and B: $2169
1150 applied 850 accepted 400 enrolled	
SAT: 550V 595M ACT: 26 HIGHLY COMPETITIVE	

Kalamazoo College, founded in 1833, is a private, coeducational liberal arts college affiliated with the American Baptist Church. The library contains 230,000 volumes, and subscribes to 900 periodicals.

Environment: The 52-acre campus is located in a suburban area about 150 miles from both Detroit and Chicago. There are 23 buildings, including 6 dormitories. The college also sponsors on-campus apartments.

Student Life: About 70% of the students come from Michigan; 80% come from public schools. Ninety percent live on campus. Forty percent of the students are Protestant, 30% are Catholic, and 8% are Jewish; there are no religious requirements. Five percent of the students are minority-group members. College housing is coed and single-sex; students in single-sex housing have visiting privileges. Freshmen may not keep cars on campus.

Organizations: There are no fraternities or sororities. Extracurricular activities include campus governance, student publications, clubs, service groups, performing groups, religious organizations, and social and cultural events.

Sports: The college fields 12 intercollegiate teams for men and 11 for women. There are 8 intramural sports for men and 6 for women.

Graduates: There is a freshman dropout rate of 13%; 70% remain to graduate. Of those who remain, over 80% eventually pursue graduate study; 7% enter medical school, 3% dental school, and 10% law school. About 40% pursue careers in business and industry.

Services: Health care, psychological counseling, career counseling, and placement are provided free of charge to all students.

Programs of Study: The B.A. degree is offered in the following subjects: BUSINESS (business administration), EDUCATION (secondary), ENGLISH (English), FINE AND PERFORMING ARTS (art, art history, music, theater/dramatics), HEALTH SCIENCES (health sciences), LANGUAGES (French, German, Spanish), MATH AND SCIENCES (biology, chemistry, mathematics, physics), PHILOSOPHY (philosophy, religion), PREPROFESSIONAL (dentistry, engineering, law, medicine), SOCIAL SCIENCES (anthropology, economics, government/political science, history, psychology, sociology).

Required: All undergraduates must take courses in each of the 4 academic divisions of the college.

Special: The "Kalamazoo Plan" gives all students the opportunity to integrate a career internship, an extended foreign study experience, and a senior independent project into the traditional liberal arts curriculum. The foreign study programs, subsidized heavily by the college, offer learning experiences in Europe, Africa, Asia, and South America. Also available to students are 3-2 engineering programs with the University of Michigan, Georgia Tech, and Washington University (St. Louis).

Admissions: Approximately 74% of those who applied were accepted for the 1981-82 freshman class. The SAT scores of those who accepted were as follows: Verbal—20% below 500, 40% between 500 and 599, 30% between 600 and 700, and 10% above 700; Math—16% below 500, 30% between 500 and 599, 44% between 600 and 700, and 10% above 700. On the ACT, 1% scored below 21, 12% between 21 and 23, 28% between 24 and 25, 34% between 26 and 28, and 25% above 28. Applicants should have completed 16 Carnegie high school units; preference is given to those in the top 25% of their class. An interview is recommended. Other factors entering into the admissions decision are advanced placement or honors courses, extracurricular activities record, leadership record, and recommendations by school officials.

Procedure: Either the SAT or ACT is required. Application deadlines are May 1 (fall), December 1 (winter), March 1 (spring), and June 1 (summer). Notification is on a rolling basis. There is a $20 application fee.

Special: There is a deferred admissions plan. AP credit is accepted.

Transfer: Recently, 80 applications were received, 50 were accepted, and 45 students enrolled. An interview, a minimum GPA of 3.0, and scores of 1000 on the SAT or 23 on the ACT are strongly recommended. Students must spend 1 year in residence and complete at least 8 courses toward the 35 credits required for a bachelor's degree. Application deadlines are the same as those for freshmen.

Visiting: Campus visits are strongly encouraged. A typical visit will include a campus tour with a student guide and an admissions interview. Visitors may sit in on classes and stay overnight. The admissions office should be contacted for arrangements.

Financial Aid: Approximately 50% of all students receive some form of need-based financial aid. About 40% work part-time on campus. Average aid to freshmen is $4350. The college offers scholarships, grants, and loans. A limited number of no-need academic scholarships are awarded each year. The college is a member of CSS. Either the FAF or the FFS is required and should be filed by January 31; deadlines for aid application are May 1 (fall), December 1 (winter), March 1 (spring), and June 1 (summer).

Foreign Students: Three percent of the full-time students come from foreign countries. The college offers these students special counseling and special organizations.

Admissions: Foreign students must achieve a minimum TOEFL score of 550 or a University of Michigan Language Test score of at least 80. No college entrance exam must be taken.

Procedure: Application deadlines are May 1 (fall), November 1 (winter), February 1 (spring), and April 1 (summer). Foreign students must present a medical survey form and proof of funds adequate to cover the first year of study. They must also carry health insurance, which is available through the college for a fee.

Admissions Contact: David M. Borus, Director of Admissions.

LAKE SUPERIOR STATE COLLEGE

Sault Sainte Marie, Michigan 49783   (906) 632-6841   D-2

F/T: 1104M, 879W	Faculty: n/av; IIB, ++$
P/T: 297M, 279W	Ph.D.'s: 38%
Grad: 1401M, 1158W	S/F Ratio: 19 to 1
Year: qtrs, ss	Tuition: $1203 ($2211)
Appl: see profile	R and B: $2085
ACT: 19	COMPETITIVE

Lake Superior State College, founded in 1946, is a state-assisted college offering undergraduate programs in the liberal arts and sciences, business, and the health fields. The library contains 107,000 volumes and 4500 microfilm items, and subscribes to 700 periodicals.

Environment: The 121-acre campus is located in a suburban town of 15,000 inhabitants, 360 miles north of Detroit. Dormitories accommodate 450 men and 450 women; apartments house 74 married students. The college also sponsors fraternity and sorority houses.

Student Life: Ninety percent of the students are Michigan residents; 90% come from public schools. Fifty percent live on campus. College housing is coed and single-sex; students in single-sex housing have visiting privileges. Students may keep cars on campus. Day-care facilities are available to full-time and part-time students, faculty, and staff.

Organizations: There is 1 local fraternity, to which 2% of the men belong, and there are 2 local sororities, to which 3% of the women belong. Student government, religious and service organizations, clubs, performing groups, and publications make up part of the extracurricular life.

Sports: The college fields 8 intercollegiate teams for men and 6 for women. There are 7 intramural sports for men and 5 for women.

Handicapped: About 90% of the campus is accessible to the physically handicapped. Facilities include wheelchair ramps, special parking, elevators, and specially equipped rest rooms.

Graduates: The freshman dropout rate is 20%.

Services: Placement, career counseling, health care, tutoring, and psychological counseling are offered free of charge. Remedial instruction is available for a fee.

Programs of Study: The B.A., B.S., B.B.A., and B.E.T. degrees are conferred. Associate and master's degrees are also awarded. Bachelor's degrees are offered in the following subjects: BUSINESS (accounting, business administration, finance, management, marketing), ENGLISH (English language and literature), HEALTH SCIENCES (medical technology, nursing), MATH AND SCIENCES (biology, chemistry, earth science, ecology/environmental science, geology, mathematics), PREPROFESSIONAL (engineering technology), SOCIAL SCIENCES (economics, government/political science, history, psychology, social sciences, sociology). About 31% of the degrees are conferred in social sciences, 23% in business, and 19% in math and sciences.

Required: All students are required to take a distribution of core courses in the liberal arts and sciences.

Honors: There is 1 national honor society on campus.

Admissions: About 93% of the applicants for a recent freshman class were accepted. The ACT scores of those who enrolled for the 1981–82 freshman class were as follows: 14% between 24 and 25, and 22% scored above 28. A 2.0 high school GPA is required. Other factors considered in the admissions decision include personality and advanced placement or honors courses.

Procedure: The ACT is required. Students with an average of C− may be required to take the college's own series of entrance examinations. New students are admitted each quarter; applications are due 1 week before the term begins. Notification is on a rolling basis. There is a $15 application fee.

Special: A deferred admissions plan is available. AP and CLEP credit is accepted.

Transfer: For fall 1981, 9 students applied. Transfers are accepted for all classes. A 2.0 GPA is required; D grades transfer. Students must spend 6 months in residence and complete at least 48 of the 189 quarter hours necessary for a bachelor's degree. Application deadlines are the same as those for freshmen.

Visiting: There is an orientation program for freshmen. Informal campus tours may be arranged; visitors may sit in on classes and stay overnight at the school. The admissions office should be contacted to arrange visits.

Financial Aid: About 75% of all students receive some form of financial aid. Twenty percent work part-time on campus. The college offers grants and loans; 90 freshman scholarships are generally available. Either the FAF or the FFS is required. Applications must be received by April 1.

Foreign Students: Nine percent of the full-time students come from foreign countries. The college offers these students special counseling.

Admissions: Foreign students must achieve a minimum TOEFL score of 550. No college entrance exam must be taken.

Procedure: Applications must be submitted 6 months before the intended term of entry. Foreign students must complete a health record form and present proof of adequate funds. They must also carry health insurance, which is available through the college for a fee.

Admissions Contact: James E. Honkanen, Dean of Admissions.

LAWRENCE INSTITUTE OF TECHNOLOGY
Southfield, Michigan 48075   (313) 356-0200   E-5

F/T: 2862M, 548W   Faculty: 66; IIB, ++$
P/T: 1788M, 457W   Ph.D.'s: 18%
Grad: 45M, 3W   S/F Ratio: 52 to 1
Year: qtrs, ss   Tuition: $1890
Appl: open   R and B: $2200
2221 applied   1932 accepted   1306 enrolled
SAT: 414V 534M   ACT: 20   COMPETITIVE

Lawrence Institute of Technology, founded in 1932, is an independent, coeducational college composed of the schools of Architecture, Engineering, Arts and Science, Management, and Associate Studies. The library contains 60,000 volumes and 20,000 microfilm items, and subscribes to 475 periodicals.

Environment: The 85-acre campus is in a suburban area 10 miles from Detroit. New additions include a management building. A student activities building is under construction. There is a 142-unit apartment building on campus; fraternities provide off-campus housing.

Student Life: Approximately 93% of the students come from Michigan. Eight percent live on campus. About 8% are minority-group members. Campus housing is coed. Students may keep cars on campus.

Organizations: There are 2 national fraternities and 1 local fraternity, to which 2% of the men belong; 5% of the women belong to the 2 local sororities. Major social events on campus include the open house and various other student-sponsored activities.

Sports: The college fields 1 intercollegiate team for men and 1 for women. There are 5 intramural sports for men and 5 for women.

Handicapped: Approximately 95% of the campus is accessible to the physically handicapped. Facilities include wheelchair ramps, special parking, and elevators; special class scheduling is also available.

Graduates: There is a freshman dropout rate of 35%; 35% remain to graduate. Of those who remain, 20% pursue graduate study; 80% enter careers in business and industry.

Services: Placement services, career counseling, and tutoring are offered to students free of charge. Remedial instruction is available for a fee.

Programs of Study: The B.S. and B.Arch. degrees are conferred. Associate degrees are also awarded. Bachelor's degrees are offered in the following subjects: BUSINESS (accounting/finance, business administration, computer/business systems, human resources, industrial management, industrial studies, manufacturing, marketing), MATH AND SCIENCES (chemistry, mathematics, mathematics/computer science, physics/computer science), PHILOSOPHY (humanities), PREPROFESSIONAL (architecture, engineering, interior architecture). Fifty-nine percent of degrees are conferred in preprofessional studies and 26% in business.

Required: All freshmen are required to take courses in English, mathematics, and science. All undergraduates are expected to gain some exposure to the humanities and social sciences.

Special: Students may design their own majors; independent research is also possible. Five-year professional programs are offered.

Honors: Three national honor societies have chapters on campus.

Admissions: Approximately 87% of those who applied were accepted for the 1981–82 freshman class. The SAT scores of those who enrolled were as follows: Verbal—77% below 500, 19% between 500 and 599, 4% between 600 and 700, and 0% above 700; Math—43% below 500, 35% between 500 and 599, 18% between 600 and 700, and 4% above 700. On the ACT, 50% scored below 21, 27% between 21 and 23, 12% between 24 and 25, 8% between 26 and 28, and 3% above 28. Applicants should be graduates of accredited high schools, have completed 16 Carnegie units, and present a minimum GPA of 2.0.

Procedure: The SAT or ACT is recommended but not required. Freshmen are admitted in the fall, at midyear, and in the summer; application deadlines are open. Notification is on a rolling basis. There is a $15 application fee.

Special: Early and deferred admissions plans and an early decision plan are available. AP and CLEP credit is accepted.

Transfer: For fall 1981, 1206 students applied, 1163 were accepted, and 859 enrolled. A minimum 2.0 GPA is required in each of the following: language and literature, mathematics, natural sciences, and language and literature/social sciences. D grades do not transfer. Students must complete, at the institute, at least 42 of the minimum 180 credit hours necessary for a bachelor's degree. Application deadlines are open.

Visiting: There are no regularly scheduled orientations for prospective students. Guides are available for informal visits; visitors may sit in on classes. The admissions office should be contacted to arrange visits.

Financial Aid: Approximately 85% of all students receive some form of financial aid. Ten percent work part-time on campus. Average aid to freshmen is $900; need is the determining factor. The institute provides 35 scholarships each year; the total amount of scholarship aid available to freshmen is $54,900. Loans are available from a variety of sources up to a maximum of $2500 per year. Students are eligible for private college tuition grants from the Michigan Higher Education Authority; they may also receive the Michigan Tuition Differential Grant in amounts up to $600. The institute is a member of the CSS and the ACT. The FAF, FFS, or SFS is required. Deadlines for aid application are June 1 (fall), October 1 (winter), February 1 (spring), and May 1 (summer).

Foreign Students: Three percent of the full-time students come from foreign countries. The institute offers these students special counseling and special organizations.

Admissions: Foreign students must achieve a minimum TOEFL score of 550 or a University of Michigan Language Test score of at least 85. No college entrance exam must be taken.

Procedure: Application deadlines are open. Foreign students must present proof of funds adequate to cover 1 year of study.

Admissions Contact: Stan Harris, Director of Admissions.

MADONNA COLLEGE
Livonia, Michigan 48150   (313) 591-5052   E-5

F/T: 277M, 1091W   Faculty: n/av; IIB, −$
P/T: 527M, 1490W   Ph.D.'s: n/av
Grad: none   S/F Ratio: n/av
Year: sems, ss   Tuition: $1748
Appl: open   R and B: $1860
486 applied   463 accepted   361 enrolled
ACT: 18   LESS COMPETITIVE

402 MICHIGAN

Madonna College is a coeducational Catholic liberal arts institution operated by the Felician Sisters. The college consists of 3 divisions: Humanities, Natural Sciences, and Social Sciences. The library contains 94,600 volumes and 16,000 microfilm items, and subscribes to 500 periodicals.

Environment: The 50-acre suburban campus, 14 miles from Detroit, has 1 dormitory that accommodates 220 men and women, a cafeteria accommodating 450, and a student lounge.

Student Life: About 97% of the students come from Michigan. Five percent live on campus. About 13% are minority-group members. Fifty percent are Catholic, and 50% are Protestant. Campus housing is single-sex. Students may keep cars on campus.

Organizations: There are no fraternities or sororities. Extracurricular activities include student government, plays, lecture series, chorale, and special-interest clubs.

Sports: The college fields 1 intercollegiate team for men and 1 for women. There are 7 intramural sports for men and 7 for women.

Handicapped: The entire campus is accessible to the physically handicapped. Facilities include wheelchair ramps, special parking, elevators, and lowered drinking fountains and telephones. Special class scheduling is also available. Approximately 2% of the students currently enrolled have hearing impairments; interpreters, note-takers, and modifications in residence halls are provided.

Graduates: Forty-five percent of those who graduate pursue graduate study.

Services: Placement services and career counseling are offered to students free of charge. Health care, psychological counseling, tutoring, and remedial instruction are provided on a fee basis.

Programs of Study: The B.A., B.S., B.S.W., and B.S.N. degrees are conferred. Associate degrees are also awarded. Bachelor's degrees are offered in the following subjects: BUSINESS (accounting, business administration, computer science, management, marketing), EDUCATION (early childhood, elementary, secondary, special), ENGLISH (English, journalism), FINE AND PERFORMING ARTS (art, art education, music, music education), HEALTH SCIENCES (emergency medical technology, medical technology, nursing, radiologic technology), LANGUAGES (American sign language, French, Spanish), MATH AND SCIENCES (biology, chemistry, mathematics, natural sciences), PREPROFESSIONAL (dentistry, engineering, home economics, law, medicine, social work), SOCIAL SCIENCES (history, psychology, social sciences, sociology). Thirty percent of degrees are conferred in social sciences, 26% in health sciences, and 20% in math and sciences.

Required: All students must take 4 hours of religious studies for the associate degree, and 8 semester hours for the bachelor's degree.

Special: Cooperative work experiences, student-designed majors, and study abroad are offered.

Honors: Two national honor societies have chapters on campus; an honors program is open to exceptional students.

Admissions: Approximately 95% of those who applied were accepted for the 1981-82 freshman class. Candidates should be graduates of an accredited high school and have a minimum GPA of 2.0.

Procedure: The ACT is required. Nursing applicants are accepted only in September; all other applications are considered on a rolling basis for any term. There is a $15 application fee. A personal interview is recommended.

Special: There are early admissions and deferred admissions plans. AP and CLEP credit is accepted. Experiential learning is evaluated.

Transfer: For fall 1981, 878 students applied, 670 were accepted, and 582 enrolled. D grades do not transfer. A GPA of at least 2.0 and the ACT score are required. Admission to sophomore-level nursing is competitive. All students must complete, at the college, 30 of the 120 semester hours required for a bachelor's degree. There are no application deadlines.

Visiting: There are no regularly scheduled orientations for prospective students. Guides are available for informal visits; visitors may sit in on classes and stay at the school. The admissions office should be contacted to arrange visits.

Financial Aid: Approximately 63% of all students receive some form of financial aid. Fewer than 1% work part-time on campus. All students who are state residents are eligible for scholarship and tuition grants from the state of Michigan; the maximum award from the state is $1200. Federal aid is also available. The FAF is required and should be submitted by March 1 (fall), September 1 (winter), or January 1 (spring or summer). The college is a member of CSS.

Foreign Students: One percent of the full-time students come from foreign countries. Special counseling is available for these students.

Admissions: Foreign students must take either the TOEFL or the University of Michigan Language Test. On the TOEFL, a score of at least 510 is required. No college entrance exams are required.

Procedure: Applications are due 1 year prior to the intended date of entry. Foreign students must have a physical exam and must present proof of funds adequate to cover 1 year of study. Health insurance is required.

Admissions Contact: Louis E. Brohl, III, Director of Admissions.

MARYGROVE COLLEGE E-5
Detroit, Michigan 48221 (313) 862-8000

F/T: 126M, 590W Faculty: 53; IIA, — — $
P/T: 47M, 205W Ph.D.'s: 49%
Grad: 23M, 144W S/F Ratio: 18 to 1
Year: sems, ss Tuition: $3425
Appl: Aug. 15 R and B: $1950
640 accepted 365 enrolled
SAT or ACT: required COMPETITIVE

Marygrove College, founded in 1910, is a private Catholic coeducational liberal arts college. The library contains 171,000 volumes and 15,700 microfilm items, and subscribes to 825 periodicals.

Environment: The 68-acre campus is located in an urban area about 11 miles from downtown Detroit. There are 7 major campus buildings, including the Tudor Gothic Liberal Arts Building and Madame Cadillac Hall. The 1 residence hall accommodates 250 men and women students.

Student Life: About 85% of the students are from the north central states. Fourteen percent of the students live on campus; the remainder commute. About 25% are Catholic. Sixty-five percent are minority-group members. College housing is coed and single-sex; students in single-sex housing have visiting privileges. Students may keep cars on campus.

Organizations: There are no fraternities or sororities. There are numerous extracurricular activities and organizations.

Sports: There are 2 intramural sports for men and 2 for women.

Handicapped: There are no special facilities for handicapped students.

Graduates: Twenty-four percent of the graduates pursue advanced degrees.

Services: The following services are available to students free of charge: health care, psychological counseling, placement, career counseling, tutoring, and remedial instruction.

Programs of Study: The college awards the B.A., B.F.A., B.S., B.S.W., and B.M. degrees. Associate and master's programs are also offered. Bachelor's degrees are offered in the following subjects: AREA STUDIES (urban), BUSINESS (accounting, business administration, business education, computer science, management), EDUCATION (early childhood, elementary, emotionally impaired, emotionally disturbed, mentally impaired, secondary, special), ENGLISH (English), FINE AND PERFORMING ARTS (art, art education, art history, dance, music, music education), LANGUAGES (French, German, Spanish, translation), MATH AND SCIENCES (biology, chemistry, natural sciences), PHILOSOPHY (humanities, philosophy, religion), PREPROFESSIONAL (dentistry, engineering, home economics, medicine, social work), SOCIAL SCIENCES (economics, government/political science, history, psychology, social sciences, sociology). Seventeen percent of degrees are conferred in business and 11% in computer science.

Required: There is a core program from which students must select courses in the humanities, natural sciences or mathematics, social science, philosophy, and religious studies.

Special: Foreign language majors may spend their junior year abroad; students spend 7 months in Europe. The program combines instruction provided by Marygrove professors with participation in regular classes of the cooperating university. Under a consortium program among the University of Detroit, Mercy College of Detroit, and Madonna College, students may enroll in classes at any of these institutions without additional cost.

Honors: A foreign language honors program is offered by the college. There are 4 honor societies with chapters on campus.

Admissions: About 63% of those who applied were accepted for the 1981-82 freshman class. Applicants must be graduates of accredited high schools and should have at least a 2.7 GPA. An interview is recommended. The student's average, class rank, test scores, recommendations, and special talents are important factors in evaluating an application for admission.

Procedure: The SAT or ACT is required and may be taken in May of the junior year or at any time during the senior year. The PSAT should be taken in March of the junior year. Application deadlines are August 15 (fall) and December 15 (winter). Notification is on a rolling basis. There is a $15 application fee.

Special: Early and deferred admissions plans and an early decision plan are available. AP and CLEP credit is accepted. Students may acquire credit for knowledge and skills obtained outside an academic context by documenting their achievement in portfolio form.

Transfer: For fall 1981, 497 students applied, 287 students were accepted, and 188 enrolled. A GPA of at least 2.0 is required; an interview, an associate degree, and 24 completed credit hours are recommended. D grades do not transfer. Students must earn, at the college, at least 30 of the minimum 128 credits necessary for a bachelor's degree. Application deadlines are August 1 (fall), December 1 (winter), and May 1 (spring and summer).

Visiting: The college provides a general orientation and campus tour for prospective students. Guides are available for informal visits as well. Visitors may sit in on classes with permission and stay overnight at the school. The best time to visit is weekdays. The admissions office should be contacted to arrange visits.

Financial Aid: Eighty-five percent of all students receive some form of financial aid. Average aid to freshmen is $3000. About 150 scholarships ranging from $100 to $2700 per year are available to incoming freshmen. Some scholarships are awarded on the basis of need, others are based on academic excellence. Loan funds are available from many sources. Aid recipients must maintain a 2.0 minimum average. The college is a member of CSS and requires the FAF. The application deadline is March 15.

Foreign Students: No foreign students are currently enrolled at Marygrove, but the college does accept foreign applicants and offers them special counseling and special organizations.

Admissions: Foreign students must achieve a minimum TOEFL score of 550. No college entrance exam must be taken.

Procedure: Application deadlines are July 15 (fall) and November 15 (winter). Foreign students must complete a standard medical form and present proof of funds adequate to cover 1 year of study. They must also carry health insurance, which is available through the college.

Admissions Contact: Kathy Tkach, Amber Patterson, Assistant Directors of Admissions.

MERCY COLLEGE OF DETROIT   E-5
Detroit, Michigan 48219   (313) 592-6030

F/T: 181M, 1089W		Faculty:	76; IIB, av$
P/T: 170M, 707W		Ph.D.'s:	n/av
Grad: 2M, 14W		S/F Ratio:	15 to 1
Year: sems, ss		Tuition:	$2940
Appl: Aug. 15		R and B:	$1530
659 applied	575 accepted		230 enrolled
ACT: 18			LESS COMPETITIVE

Mercy College of Detroit, founded in 1941, is a 4-year, coeducational liberal arts college conducted by the Religious Sisters of Mercy. The library contains 100,000 volumes and 4000 microfilm items, and subscribes to 700 periodicals.

Environment: The 40-acre campus, located in the urban setting of northwestern Detroit, has 10 buildings. One dormitory accommodates 300 women.

Student Life: About 95% of the students come from Michigan; 64% come from public schools. Thirty-four percent live on campus. Forty-seven percent of the students are Catholic, 28% are Protestant, and 1% are Jewish; attendance at religious services is voluntary. About 35% are minority-group members. College housing is single-sex, and there are visiting privileges. Students may keep cars on campus.

Organizations: There are no fraternities or sororities. Extracurricular activities include a variety of musical performances, a film series, student government, sodality, and special-interest clubs.

Sports: The college fields 1 intercollegiate team for men and 1 for women. There is 1 intramural sport for men and 3 for women.

Handicapped: Approximately 75% of the campus is accessible to the physically handicapped. Facilities include wheelchair ramps, special parking, elevators, specially equipped rest rooms, and lowered drinking fountains and telephones. Special class scheduling is also available.

Graduates: The freshman dropout rate is 25%; 15% of graduates pursue advanced study, and twenty-five percent enter careers in business and industry.

MICHIGAN 403

Services: Placement services, career counseling, health care, tutoring, remedial instruction, and psychological counseling are offered to students free of charge.

Programs of Study: The college confers the B.A., B.S., and B.S.N. degrees. Associate and master's degrees are also awarded. Bachelor's degrees are offered in the following subjects: BUSINESS (business administration), EDUCATION (early childhood, elementary, secondary), ENGLISH (English), FINE AND PERFORMING ARTS (art, theater/dramatics), HEALTH SCIENCES (anesthesia, health services, medical record science, medical technology, nursing, physician's assistant, respiratory care), LANGUAGES (French, Spanish), MATH AND SCIENCES (biology, chemistry, forensic science, mathematics), PHILOSOPHY (philosophy, religion), PREPROFESSIONAL (dentistry, engineering, law, medicine), SOCIAL SCIENCES (government/political science, history, psychology, social work, sociology). About 40% of degrees are conferred in the health sciences and 15% in business.

Required: There is a general curriculum of required courses.

Special: Cross-registration at 4 other Catholic institutions in Detroit is possible.

Honors: There is an honors program for qualified students.

Admissions: Approximately 87% of those who applied were accepted for the 1981–82 freshman class. The ACT scores of those who enrolled were as follows: 52% below 21, 25% between 21 and 23, 15% between 24 and 25, 5% between 26 and 28, and 3% above 28. Candidates must be graduates of an accredited high school and have a GPA of at least 2.5. Other factors entering into the admissions decision are advanced placement or honors courses, recommendations by school officials, impressions made during an interview, and personality.

Procedure: The SAT or ACT is required, but the ACT is preferred for entrance into health programs. Application deadlines are August 15 (fall), December 15 (spring), and April 15 (summer). Notification is on a rolling basis. There is a $15 application fee.

Special: There is an early decision plan. AP and CLEP credit is accepted.

Transfer: For fall 1981, 712 students applied, 653 were accepted, and 310 enrolled. A minimum GPA of 2.0 and 25 completed credit hours are required. D grades do not transfer. Students must earn, at the college, at least 30 of the 120 semester credits necessary for a bachelor's degree. Application deadlines are the same as those for freshmen.

Visiting: There are regularly scheduled orientations for prospective students. Guides are also available for informal visits; visitors may sit in on classes and stay at the school. The admissions office should be contacted to arrange visits.

Financial Aid: About 83% of all students receive some form of financial aid. Ten percent work part-time on campus. The college offers scholarships, grants, and loans. Tuition may be paid in installments. The college is a member of CSS; it requires the FAF but will accept the FFS. Application deadlines are June 1 (fall), December 1 (winter), and April 1 (summer).

Foreign Students: One percent of the full-time students come from foreign countries.

Admissions: The college requires a minimum score of 500 on the TOEFL, but will accept University of Michigan Language Test scores. No college entrance exam must be taken.

Procedure: Foreign students are advised to apply 1 semester prior to the intended entry date. They are required to present proof of funds adequate to cover the duration of study.

Admissions Contact: Jeanne Umholtz, Director of Admissions.

MICHIGAN STATE UNIVERSITY   D-4
East Lansing, Michigan 48824   (517) 355-6532

F/T: 15,253M, 15,428W		Faculty:	2517; I, +$
P/T: 1845M, 1831W		Ph.D.'s:	76%
Grad: 4459M, 3278W		S/F Ratio:	12 to 1
Year: qtrs, ss		Tuition:	$1515 ($3293)
Appl: see profile		R and B:	$2134
14,890 applied	11,515 accepted		6067 enrolled
SAT: 453V 515M	ACT: 22		COMPETITIVE

Michigan State University, the pioneer land-grant college, was founded in 1855 and today is one of the largest universities in the United States. Its 16 colleges and more than 100 departments offer 200 undergraduate and more than 500 graduate fields of study. The library contains 2.6 million volumes and 3.8 million microfilm items, and subscribes to 22,000 periodicals.

404 MICHIGAN

Environment: The 5000-acre campus is located in a suburban area 85 miles from Detroit. Dormitories accommodate 18,500 students, and there are 2280 apartments for married students. The college also sponsors fraternity and sorority houses.

Student Life: About 86% of the students come from Michigan; 85% come from public schools. Forty-eight percent of the students live on campus. Eight percent are minority-group members. University housing is coed and single-sex; students in single-sex housing have visiting privileges. Upperclassmen may keep cars on campus.

Organizations: There are 26 national fraternities, to which 8% of the men belong; 7% of the women are members of 15 national sororities. Numerous and varied social and cultural events are scheduled regularly on campus. All types of extracurricular activities are available.

Sports: The college fields 15 intercollegiate teams for men and 11 for women. There are 24 intramural sports for men and women.

Handicapped: Over 50% of the campus is accessible to the physically handicapped. An increasing number of campus buildings are becoming accessible through reconstruction and/or rescheduling methods of accommodation. Equipment for the visually impaired includes tape recorders, talking calculators, TV magnifiers, and large print duplicators. Interpreter and note-taker programs are available. Additional services are offered through the Handicapper Services Program.

Graduates: The freshman dropout rate is 18, and 65% of the freshmen remain to graduate. Seventeen percent of the graduates pursue advanced degrees. Another 30% enter careers in business and industry.

Services: Placement, career counseling, tutoring, and remedial instruction are provided free of charge. Health care and psychological counseling are available for a fee.

Programs of Study: The B.A., B.S., B.F.A., B.Mus., and B.Land. Arch. degrees are conferred. Master's and doctoral degrees are also awarded. Bachelor's degrees are offered in the following subjects: AREA STUDIES (American, urban), BUSINESS (accounting, business administration, business education, computer science, finance, hotel and restaurant management, management, marketing, real estate/insurance, travel and tourism management), EDUCATION (early childhood, elementary, health/physical, recreation and youth leadership, special), ENGLISH (English, journalism, linguistics, speech/communication), FINE AND PERFORMING ARTS (art history, dance, music, studio art, telecommunication, theater/dramatics), HEALTH SCIENCES (environmental health, medical technology, music therapy, nursing, speech therapy/audiology and speech sciences), LANGUAGES (Chinese, French, German, Greek/Latin, Russian, Spanish), MATH AND SCIENCES (astronomy/astrophysics, biochemistry, biology, botany, chemistry, earth science, entomology, geology, mathematics, microbiology, physical chemistry, physical sciences, physics, physiology, statistics, zoology), PHILOSOPHY (humanities, philosophy, religion), PREPROFESSIONAL (dentistry, law, medicine, veterinary), SOCIAL SCIENCES (anthropology, economics, geography, government/political science, history, psychology, social sciences, sociology). About 15% of degrees are conferred in social sciences, 19% in business, and 6% in education.

Required: A core curriculum that includes courses in American thought and language, natural science, social science, and the humanities is required of all students.

Special: Student-designed majors, study abroad, off-campus internships, and B.A.-B.S. degrees in engineering are offered.

Honors: Honors programs are offered in all departments. There are 30 honor societies on campus.

Admissions: Approximately 77% of those who applied were accepted for the 1981-82 freshman class. The SAT scores of those who enrolled were as follows: Verbal—65% below 500, 24% between 500 and 599, 9% between 600 and 700, and 1% above 700; Math—41% below 500, 37% between 500 and 599, 19% between 600 and 700, and 3% above 700. On the ACT, 26% scored below 21, 33% between 21 and 23, 16% between 24 and 25, 18% between 26 and 28, and 7% above 28. Most resident candidates rank in the upper quarter of their high school class and must present a recommendation from their principal or high school counselor. Nonresidents should present an average of B or better and a total score of 950 on the SAT or 22 on the ACT for an immediate decision. A strong college preparatory program is suggested for all prospective applicants. Also considered in the admissions decision are leadership, personality, and impressions made during an interview.

Procedure: The SAT or ACT is required. New students are accepted in the fall and at midyear. Application deadlines are 1 month prior to the beginning of the term; however, admission for any term is subject to earlier closing without notice. Notification is on a rolling basis. There is a nonrefundable application fee of $20.

Special: Deferred admissions and early decision plans are available. AP and CLEP credit is accepted.

Transfer: For fall 1981, 4908 students applied, 2860 were accepted, and 2043 enrolled. Transfers are accepted for the sophomore, junior, and senior classes. A minimum GPA of 2.0 and 36 completed quarter credits are required. D grades sometimes transfer. Students must earn, at the university, at least the final 45 of the 180 quarter credits necessary for a bachelor's degree. Application deadlines are the same as those for freshmen.

Visiting: There are 16 regularly scheduled summer orientation programs for prospective freshmen and 5 for transfer students. Guides are available for informal visits; visitors may sit in on classes. The office of admissions and scholarships should be contacted to arrange visits.

Financial Aid: About 60% of all students receive some form of financial aid. Forty-two percent work part-time on campus. The average aid to freshmen is $1390. Loans are available from many sources. The university is a member of CSS. The FAF or FFS is required, and should be submitted 60 days prior to the beginning of any term or within 30 days of the date of admission.

Foreign Students: Three percent of the full-time students come from foreign countries. The university offers these students an intensive English course and program, special counseling, and special organizations.

Admissions: Foreign students must take the TOEFL, the University of Michigan Language Test, or the university's own English proficiency exam; a minimum score of 450 is required on the TOEFL. Students must also take the SAT, the ACT, or the university's own entrance exam.

Procedure: Applications must be submitted 90 days prior to the beginning term. Foreign students must present a self-reported health form after admission and proof of funds adequate to cover 1 year of study. They must also carry health insurance, which is available through the university for a fee.

Admissions Contact: Charles F. Seeley, Director of Admissions and Scholarships.

MICHIGAN TECHNOLOGICAL UNIVERSITY
Houghton, Michigan 49931   (906) 487-1885   B-1

F/T: 5617M, 1647W   Faculty: 410; IIA, ++$
P/T: 126M, 81W   Ph.D.'s: 65%
Grad: 267M, 41W   S/F Ratio: 19 to 1
Year: qtrs, ss   Tuition: $1272 ($3006)
Appl: see profile   R and B: $2073
3349 applied   2773 accepted   1627 enrolled
SAT: 480V 590M   ACT: 25   **VERY COMPETITIVE**

Michigan Technological University, established in 1885, is a state-supported institution of engineering and science. The library contains 507,607 volumes and 50,847 microfilm items, and subscribes to 2066 periodicals.

Environment: The 240-acre campus is located in a rural area of Michigan's upper peninsula, 450 miles north of Chicago and 600 miles from Detroit. A 4100-acre forestry center is located 40 miles south of the main campus, in Alberta. A new $19.5 million student activities center was completed in 1980. Three residence halls accommodate 300 women and 2050 men; there are also 352 apartment units. The university also sponsors fraternity and sorority houses and married student housing.

Student Life: Approximately 86% of the students come from Michigan; 94% come from public schools. Forty-six percent live on campus. About 2% of the students are minority-group members. University housing is coed and single-sex; students in single-sex housing have visiting privileges. Students may keep cars on campus. Day-care facilities are available for a fee to full-time and part-time students, faculty, and staff.

Organizations: There are 2 local and 10 national fraternities, to which 6% of the men belong; 4% of the women belong to the 1 local and 2 national sororities. Extracurricular activities include music, drama, and special-interest clubs.

Sports: The university fields 7 intercollegiate teams for men and 4 for women. There are 16 intramural sports for men and 9 for women.

Handicapped: Approximately 50% of the campus is accessible to the physically handicapped. Facilities include wheelchair ramps, special parking, elevators, specially equipped rest rooms, and lowered drinking fountains and telephones; special class scheduling is also available. Tape recorders and assistants are provided for visually and hearing-impaired students.

Graduates: The freshman dropout rate is 18%, and 50% of the freshmen remain to graduate. Of those who remain, 21% pursue graduate study. Sixty-nine percent enter careers in business and industry.

Services: Placement, career counseling, psychological counseling, tutoring, and remedial instruction are offered free of charge. Health care is available for a fee.

Programs of Study: Associate, bachelor's, master's, and doctoral programs are offered. The college confers the B.A. degree in liberal arts; the B.S. degree is offered in the following subjects: BUSINESS (business administration, computer science, engineering administration), EDUCATION (secondary science), HEALTH SCIENCES (medical technology), MATH AND SCIENCES (applied geophysics, applied physics, biology, chemistry, geology, mathematics, physics, wood and fiber utilization), PREPROFESSIONAL (dentistry, engineering—chemical, engineering—civil, engineering—electrical, engineering—geological, engineering—mechanical, engineering—metallurgical, engineering—mining, forestry, land surveying, law, medicine, veterinary), SOCIAL SCIENCES (history, social sciences). Seventy-two percent of degrees are conferred in preprofessional fields, 10% in business, and 16% in math and sciences.

Special: The university offers a cooperative program in most fields of engineering, as well as in forestry, wood and fiber utilization, land surveying, computer science, and business administration. Dual degree programs in engineering and forestry with several other colleges are available. A general studies major and student-designed majors are also offered.

Honors: Sixteen honor societies have chapters on campus.

Admissions: Approximately 83% of those who applied were accepted for the 1981–82 freshman class. The SAT scores of those who enrolled were as follows: Verbal—58% below 500, 30% between 500 and 599, 11% between 600 and 700, and 19% above 700; Math—15% below 500, 41% between 500 and 599, 37% between 600 and 700, and 7% above 700. On the ACT, 10% scored below 21, 29% between 21 and 23, 21% between 24 and 25, 28% between 26 and 28, and 12% above 28. Candidates should have completed 15 Carnegie units, rank in the top half of their class, and have an average of at least 2.5. An interview is recommended. Other factors entering into the admissions decision are standardized test scores and advanced placement or honors courses.

Procedure: The ACT is required for placement purposes. Freshmen are admitted each quarter; applications should be filed no later than 30 days before the beginning of the session. Notification is on a rolling basis. There is $20 application fee.

Special: There is a deferred admissions plan. CLEP and AP credit is accepted.

Transfer: For fall 1981, 1019 students applied, 574 were accepted, and 325 enrolled. A minimum GPA of 2.5 is required; 3.0 is recommended for engineering applicants. An associate degree and an interview are also recommended for transfers. D grades do not transfer. Students must spend 1 year at the university and complete at least one-fourth of the minimum 186 credits necessary for a bachelor's degree. Deadlines for application are the same as those for freshmen.

Visiting: There are no regularly scheduled orientations. Guides are available for informal visits; visitors may sit in on classes. Prospective students only may stay overnight at the school if space is available. The admissions office should be contacted to arrange visits.

Financial Aid: Approximately 75% of all students receive some form of financial aid. Twenty-six percent work part-time on campus. The average aid to freshmen is $1498; the maximum, including job earnings on campus, is $3475. A fund of $1.6 million provides scholarships each year; loans are available from federal, state, and university sources. The university is a member of CSS and requires the FAF. The application deadline is March 1.

Foreign Students: Three percent of the full-time students come from foreign countries. The university offers these students special counseling and special organizations.

Admissions: Foreign students must achieve a TOEFL score of at least 500. No college entrance exam must be taken.

Procedure: The application deadline for fall entry is July 1. Foreign students must present proof of funds adequate to cover the entire course of study. They must also carry health insurance, which is available through the university for a fee.

Admissions Contact: Ernest R. Griff, Director of Admissions and School Services.

MICHIGAN 405

NAZARETH COLLEGE   D–5
Nazareth, Michigan 49074   (616) 349-7783

F/T: 53M, 287W	Faculty: 30; IIB, – – $
P/T: 36M, 169W	Ph.D.'s: 37%
Grad: none	S/F Ratio: 11 to 1
Year: sems	Tuition: $4240
Appl: Aug. 15	R and B: $2120
412 applied 288 accepted 123 enrolled	
ACT(mean): 19	COMPETITIVE

Nazareth College, founded in 1924, is an independent Catholic college for men and women offering programs in the human service professions.

Environment: The 55-acre campus is located in a suburban setting on the eastern perimeter of Kalamazoo, a city with a population of 120,000. The 2 residence halls, with a combined capacity for 480 students, are connected by Albers Hall, an activities building with dining and recreational facilities.

Student Life: Approximately 95% of the students come from Michigan. Thirty-five percent live on campus in residence halls. Fifty-four percent of the students are Catholic. Eleven percent are minority-group members. College housing is single-sex, and there are visiting privileges. Students may keep cars on campus.

Organizations: There are no fraternities or sororities.

Sports: The college fields 2 intercollegiate teams for men and 2 for women. There are 5 intramural sports for men and 4 for women.

Handicapped: Approximately 80% of the campus is accessible to the physically handicapped. Facilities include wheelchair ramps, special parking, and elevators. The administration building and the other campus buildings are connected by an underground concourse that can be easily maneuvered by handicapped students.

Graduates: There is a freshman dropout rate of 45% and an overall dropout rate of 27%. Of those who remain to graduate, 6% pursue advanced study. Most graduates enter careers in business and industry or nursing.

Services: Placement services, career counseling, health care, and psychological counseling are offered to students free of charge. Tutoring and remedial instruction are available for a fee.

Programs of Study: The B.A., B.S., B.S.N., B.B.A., and B.S.W. degrees are offered in the following subjects: AREA STUDIES (American), BUSINESS (accounting, business administration, management, management of health care facilities), EDUCATION (early, childhood, elementary, learning disabilities), ENGLISH (applied writing), FINE AND PERFORMING ARTS (fine arts—interdisciplinary), HEALTH SCIENCES (medical technology, nursing), MATH AND SCIENCES (natural sciences), PHILOSOPHY (humanities), PREPROFESSIONAL (dentistry, law, medicine, veterinary), SOCIAL SCIENCES (criminal justice, social work). About 61% of the degrees are conferred in the health sciences, 21% in the social sciences, and 9% in education.

Required: There are no specific general education requirements, but students must demonstrate that they can meet basic liberal arts and science expectations before graduating.

Special: Individually designed majors are possible.

Admissions: Approximately 70% of those who applied were accepted for the 1981–82 freshman class. The ACT scores of those who enrolled were as follows: 36% below 21, 29% between 21 and 25, and 3% above 25. Candidates should rank in the top half of their class and have a minimum GPA of 2.5. Other factors entering into the admissions decision include advanced placement or honors courses, recommendations by school officials, and impressions made during an interview.

Procedure: The SAT or ACT is required. Students are encouraged to apply by June 1 for the fall; deadlines for application are August 15 (fall) and December 15 (winter). Notification is on a rolling basis. There is a $10 application fee.

Special: An early decision plan is available. AP and CLEP credit is accepted.

Transfer: Recently, 79 transfer students enrolled; transfers are accepted for all classes. A minimum GPA of 2.5 and an ACT score of 18 are required; an interview is recommended. Grades of C or better transfer. Students must complete, at the college, at least 30 of the 120 semester hours necessary for a bachelor's degree; beyond the first 60 hours, all credits should be at the advanced level. Application deadlines are the same as those for freshmen.

Visiting: Guides are available for informal visits; visitors may sit in on classes and stay overnight at the school. The admissions office should be contacted to arrange visits.

406 MICHIGAN

Financial Aid: About 85% of all students receive some form of financial aid. Seventy-five percent work part-time on campus. Average aid to freshmen is $2968. The college offers scholarships averaging $1000. Participation in the NDSL, BEOG, EOG and other programs enables the granting of awards on the basis of financial need and achievement. The college is a member of CSS and requires the FAF or the FFS. Application deadlines are March (fall) and October (winter).

Foreign Students: One percent of the full-time students come from foreign countries. The university offers these students special counseling.

Admissions: Students must achieve a minimum TOEFL score of 550 or take the University of Michigan Language Test. No college entrance exam must be taken.

Procedure: Application deadlines are April (fall) and September (winter). Foreign students must present a completed datamation form as proof of health as well as proof of funds adequate to cover 1 year of study.

Admissions Contact: Dr. Virginia Jones, SSJ, Director of Admissions.

NORTHERN MICHIGAN UNIVERSITY   C-2
Marquette, Michigan 49855   (906) 227-2650

F/T: 3855M, 3476W   Faculty: 387; IIA, +$
P/T: 387M, 415W   Ph.D.'s: 61%
Grad: 401M, 512W   S/F Ratio: 18 to 1
Year: sems, ss   Tuition: $1219 ($2771)
Appl: Aug. 15   R and B: $2071
5151 applied   5042 accepted   2210 enrolled
ACT: 18   LESS COMPETITIVE

Northern Michigan University, established in 1899, offers undergraduate training in the liberal arts and sciences, business, education, health fields, and preprofessional areas. It is a publicly supported institution. The library contains 362,658 volumes and 333,214 microfilm items, and subscribes to 2388 periodicals.

Environment: The 300-acre campus is located in an urban area. The 50 buildings include 12 residence halls and 196 apartments for married students. A 160-acre woodland tract 4 miles from the campus is used for recreation.

Student Life: Most students are Michigan residents. About 50% live on campus. University housing is coed and single-sex; students in single-sex housing have visiting privileges. Students may keep cars on campus. Day-care facilities are available to full-time and part-time students, faculty, and staff.

Organizations: There are 6 national fraternities on campus, to which 1% of the men belong; fewer than 1% of the women belong to the 5 national sororities. The extensive extracurricular activities include clubs, music, drama, and special-interest groups.

Sports: The university fields 7 intercollegiate teams for men and 5 for women. There are 10 intramural sports for men and 9 for women.

Handicapped: Approximately 70% of the campus is accessible to the physically handicapped. Facilities include wheelchair ramps, special parking, elevators, specially equipped rest rooms, and lowered drinking fountains and telephones; special class scheduling is also available. There are 2 special counselors.

Graduates: The freshman dropout rate is 40%, and 52% of the freshmen remain to graduate. Approximately 8% of those who graduate pursue advanced degrees: 1% enter medical school, 1% dental school, and 1% law school. Fifty-six percent pursue careers in business and industry.

Services: Career and psychological counseling are offered to students free of charge. Health care and remedial instruction are available for a fee; some tutoring also requires a fee.

Programs of Study: The university confers the B.A., B.S., B.Mus.Ed., B.S.N., B.S.W., and B.F.A. degrees. Associate, master's, and Education Specialist degrees are also awarded. Bachelor's degrees are offered in the following subjects: BUSINESS (accounting, business education, computer science, finance, management, marketing, office administration), EDUCATION (early childhood, elementary, health/physical, industrial, secondary, special), ENGLISH (English, journalism, literature, mass communications, speech), FINE AND PERFORMING ARTS (art, art education, film/photography, music, music education, radio/TV, studio art, theater/dramatics), HEALTH SCIENCES (medical technology, nursing, speech therapy), LANGUAGES (French, German, Spanish), MATH AND SCIENCES (biochemistry, biology, botany, chemistry, computing, data processing, earth science, ecology/environmental science, mathematics, natural sciences, oceanography, physical sciences, physics, statistics, water science, zoology), PHILOSOPHY (philosophy), PREPROFESSIONAL (architecture, dentistry, engineering, law, medicine), SOCIAL SCIENCES (economics, geography, government/political science, history, psychology, public administration, social work, sociology). Twenty-seven percent of degrees are conferred in the social sciences, 23% in education, and 20% in business.

Required: All undergraduates must complete a liberal studies core of approximately 36 semester credits.

Special: A 5-year program leading to a combined B.A.-B.S. degree is offered in many subjects; students may also design their own majors. Special programs are offered in business (1 and 2 years), practical nursing (1 year), art (2 years), home economics (2 years), industrial education (2 years), and medical laboratory technology (2 years).

Honors: Ten national honor societies have chapters on campus.

Admissions: Approximately 98% of those who applied were accepted for the 1981-82 freshman class. The ACT scores of those who enrolled were as follows: 70% below 21, 15% between 21 and 23, 6% between 24 and 25, 5% between 26 and 28, and 4% above 28. Applicants should have completed 15 Carnegie high school units, and have a GPA of at least 2.0. Other factors influencing the admissions decision are evidence of the applicant's intellectual capacity to do university work, maturity, character, recommendations from school officials, evidence of special talents, and extracurricular activities record.

Procedure: The ACT is required; the university also administers its own mathematics placement test and English proficiency tests. Students may be admitted to any term. Deadlines for application are August 15 (fall), December 15 (winter), April 15 (spring), and May 15 (summer). Notification is on a rolling basis. There is a $15 application fee.

Special: Early and deferred admissions plans and an early decision plan are available. AP and CLEP credit is accepted.

Transfer: For fall 1981, 938 students applied, 871 were accepted, and 535 enrolled. A minimum GPA of 2.0 and a completed transfer questionnaire are required. All passing grades transfer. Students must spend 1 year in residence and complete at least 32 of the minimum 124 semester credits necessary for a bachelor's degree. Application deadlines are the same as those for freshmen.

Visiting: There are regularly scheduled orientations for prospective students. Guides are also available for informal visits; visitors may sit in on classes and stay overnight at the school. The admissions office should be contacted to arrange visits.

Financial Aid: Approximately 67% of all students receive some form of financial aid. Twenty-five percent work part-time on campus. Average aid to freshmen is $1200. The university awards 1500 Board of Control scholarships on the basis of academic achievement. Substantial NMU merit awards are available for students who are National Merit semi-finalists or have an ACT composite score of 30 or more. Grants and loans are also available. The university is a member of CSS and requires either the FAF or FFS. Deadlines for financial aid applications are February 1 (fall), December 1 (winter), April 1 (spring), and May 1 (summer).

Foreign Students: One percent of the full-time students come from foreign countries. The university offers these students special counseling and special organizations.

Admissions: Foreign students must achieve a minimum TOEFL score of 500. No college entrance exam must be taken.

Procedure: Applications must be submitted 1 year prior to enrollment; deadlines are August 15 (fall), December 15 (winter), April 15 (spring), and May 15 (summer). Foreign students must present proof of funds adequate to cover the length of the program. They must also carry health insurance, which is available through the university for a fee.

Admissions Contact: Martin L. Dolan, Assistant Director of Admissions.

NORTHWOOD INSTITUTE   D-4
Midland, Michigan 48640   (517) 631-1600

F/T: 950M, 830W   Faculty: 38; IIB, - -$
P/T: 90M, 70W   Ph.D.'s: 10%
Grad: none   S/F Ratio: 30 to 1
Year: qtrs, ss   Tuition: $3330
Appl: open   R and B: $1935
1450 applied   1131 accepted   781 enrolled
ACT: 19   COMPETITIVE

Northwood Institute, founded in 1959, is an independent college offering undergraduate programs in business, designed to turn out professionals ready to enter the business world without additional training. The library contains 50,000 volumes, and subscribes to 500 periodicals.

Environment: The 280-acre campus is located in a suburban area 125 miles from Detroit. There are 18 major buildings, including 10 dormitories that house 1000 students. On-campus apartments are also maintained. The institute maintains a branch campus at West Baden, Indiana. Facilities include a sports center with basketball and indoor tennis courts and a 75-meter indoor pool.

Student Life: Fifty percent of the students come from Michigan. About 60% live on campus. Forty-three percent of the students are Catholic, 41% are Protestant, and 5% are Jewish. Thirteen percent are minority-group members. Campus housing is single-sex, and there are visiting privileges. Students may keep cars on campus.

Organizations: There are 4 local and 3 national fraternities, to which 60% of the men belong; 50% of the women belong to the 3 national sororities on campus. Extracurricular activities include an active student government, films, and numerous social and cultural events.

Sports: The college fields 6 intercollegiate teams for men and 4 for women. There are 11 intramural sports for men and 9 for women.

Handicapped: The entire campus is accessible to the physically handicapped. Facilities include wheelchair ramps, special parking, and elevators; special class scheduling is also available.

Graduates: Seventy-five percent of the freshmen remain to graduate. Of those, 7% pursue graduate study. Nearly all of the graduates enter careers in business and industry.

Services: Placement services and career counseling are offered free of charge. The institute has a 90% job placement record.

Programs of Study: Associate degrees are awarded in addition to the B.B.A., which is offered in the following subjects: BUSINESS (accounting, business administration, finance, management, marketing).

Required: All students are required to take English composition.

Special: Students may design their own majors. There are industry-sponsored programs in automobile marketing, truck marketing, automotive replacement management, and interior marketing and merchandising. Students majoring in fashion merchandising have the opportunity to study in Paris during the fall term of their sophomore year. The institute also offers an external degree program.

Admissions: Seventy-eight percent of those who applied were accepted for the 1981-82 freshman class. Of those who enrolled, the ACT scores were as follows: 51% below 21, 22% between 21 and 23, 11% between 24 and 25, 9% between 26 and 28, and 7% above 28. Applicants should have a minimum GPA of 2.0. Other factors influencing the admissions decision are advanced placement or honors courses, recommendations by school officials, and extracurricular activities record.

Procedure: The ACT is required. Application deadlines are open. Notification is on a rolling basis. There is a $15 application fee.

Special: AP and CLEP credit is accepted.

Transfer: For fall 1981, 112 students applied, 104 were accepted, and 101 enrolled. A minimum 2.0 GPA is required for transfer; an interview is recommended. D grades do not transfer. Freshman transfers must live on campus until they have completed 45 credit hours; 180 credits are necessary for a bachelor's degree. Application deadlines are open.

Visiting: There are regularly scheduled orientations for prospective students. Guides are also available for informal visits; visitors may sit in on classes and stay at the school. The admissions office should be contacted to arrange visits.

Financial Aid: About 65% of all students receive some form of financial aid. Twelve percent work part-time on campus. Average aid to freshmen covers 60% of costs. The institute offers academic and athletic scholarships, grants, and loans. Veterans may pay tuition in installments. The institute is a member of CSS. The FAF or FFS is due January 31 for certain Michigan aid and grant programs.

Foreign Students: Four percent of the full-time students come from foreign countries. The institute offers these students special counseling and special organizations.

Admissions: Foreign students must achieve a minimum TOEFL score of 550 and are required to take the ACT.

Procedure: Application deadlines are open. Foreign students must present proof of a complete physical exam by a qualified physician and proof of funds adequate to cover an entire year of study. They must also carry health insurance, which is available through the institute for a fee.

Admissions Contact: Jack S. King, Dean of Admissions; Anne M. Blitz, Thomas R. Gibbons, Assistant Directors of Admissions.

OAKLAND UNIVERSITY E-4
Rochester, Michigan 48063 (313) 377-3360

F/T: 2700M, 3500W	Faculty: n/av; IIA, +$
P/T: 1390M, 2200W	Ph.D.'s: 80%
Grad: 585M, 1814W	S/F Ratio: 20 to 1
Year: sems, ss	Tuition: $1245 ($3074)
Appl: open	R and B: $2135
2475 accepted	1550 enrolled
ACT: 21	COMPETITIVE

Oakland University, founded in 1957, is a state-supported liberal arts and professional university. The library contains 285,761 volumes and 350,071 microfilm items, and subscribes to 1981 periodicals.

Environment: The 2000-acre campus, which is in a suburban area 30 miles from Detroit, includes rolling hills, woods, and farmland. Among its 22 buildings is a new classroom/office facility. The 7 dormitories accommodate 800 men and 825 women.

Student Life: Approximately 95% of the students are from Michigan; 90% come from public schools. Twenty percent live on campus. Eleven percent of the students are minority-group members. University housing is coed and single-sex; students in single-sex housing have visiting privileges. Students may keep cars on campus. Day-care facilities are available for a fee to full-time students, faculty, and staff.

Organizations: There is 1 local fraternity, to which fewer than 1% of the men belong; fewer than 1% of the women belong to the 1 local sorority. Extracurricular activities include theater, musical performances, clubs, and student government.

Sports: The university fields 8 intercollegiate teams for men and 5 for women. There are 7 intramural sports for men and 7 for women.

Handicapped: Approximately 90% of the campus is accessible to the physically handicapped. Facilities include wheelchair ramps, special parking, elevators, specially equipped rest rooms, and lowered telephones. Special class scheduling is also available. Readers are provided for visually impaired students. Special counseling is available.

Graduates: The freshman dropout rate is 8%; 45% remain to graduate. Of those who remain, 20% pursue advanced degrees; 5% enter medical school, 3% dental school, and 8% law school. About 40% pursue careers in business and industry.

Services: Placement, career counseling, tutoring, and remedial instruction are offered free of charge. Health care and psychological counseling are available for a fee.

Programs of Study: The B.A. and B.S. degrees are awarded. Master's and doctoral degrees are also conferred. Bachelor's degrees are offered in the following subjects: AREA STUDIES (American, Asian, Black/Afro-American, Latin American, Slavic), BUSINESS (accounting, computer science, finance, human resource management, international management, management, marketing, public management), EDUCATION (early childhood, elementary, human resource development, secondary), ENGLISH (English, journalism, literature, speech), FINE AND PERFORMING ARTS (art history, dance, music, music education, theater/dramatics), HEALTH SCIENCES (environmental health, industrial health and safety, medical physics, medical technology, nursing, physical therapy), LANGUAGES (Chinese, French, German, Russian, Spanish), MATH AND SCIENCES (biochemistry, biology, chemistry, ecology/environmental science, mathematics, physics), PHILOSOPHY (philosophy), PREPROFESSIONAL (dentistry, engineering, law, medicine, ministry, social work, veterinary), SOCIAL SCIENCES (anthropology, economics, government/political science, history, psychology, social sciences, sociology). About 27% of degrees conferred are in business, 15% in social sciences, and 13% in health sciences.

Required: There is a general education requirement.

Special: A general studies major, student-designed majors, study abroad, independent study, and a combination degree program in medical technology are offered.

Honors: The honors program is intradepartmental. There are 7 honor societies on campus.

Admissions: About 80% of the applicants were accepted for a recent freshman class. Candidates should have completed 15 Carnegie units and have a 2.75 high school grade average. Other factors include advanced placement or honor courses, recommendations, and the applicant's personality.

Procedure: The ACT is recommended and should be taken by April of the senior year. New students are admitted every term; application deadlines are open. Notification is on a rolling basis. There is a $15 application fee.

Special: Early and deferred admissions plans and an early decision plan are available. CLEP and AP credit is accepted.

Transfer: For fall 1981, 2450 students applied, 1950 were accepted, and 1395 enrolled. A 2.0 GPA and 62 completed credit hours are required. D grades do not transfer. Students must earn, at the university, 32 of the 128 credits necessary for a bachelor's degree. Application deadlines are open.

Visiting: There is an orientation program for incoming freshmen. Informal campus tours are possible; visitors may sit in on classes and stay at the school. The admissions office should be contacted to arrange visits.

Financial Aid: About 40% of all students receive some form of financial aid. Ten percent work part-time on campus. The university awards scholarships ($100 to $2550), federal and state grants, and various loans (averaging $500 per year). The university is a member of CSS and requires the FAF. The application deadline for fall entry is March 1.

Foreign Students: Fewer than 1% of the full-time students come from foreign countries. The university offers these students special counseling and special organizations.

Admissions: Foreign students must achieve a minimum TOEFL score of 550 or take the University of Michigan Language Test. No college entrance exam must be taken.

Procedure: Application deadlines are open; foreign students are admitted in fall and winter. They must present proof of health, proof of funds adequate to cover 1 year of study, and a special fee of $8400. They must also carry health insurance, which is available through the university.

Admissions Contact: Jerry W. Rose, Director of Admissions.

OLIVET COLLEGE D–4
Olivet, Michigan 49076 (616) 749-7635

F/T: 371M, 238W	Faculty:	n/av; IIA, — — $
P/T: 7M, 21W	Ph.D.'s:	60%
Grad: 1M	S/F Ratio:	13 to 1
Year: sems	Tuition:	$4570
Appl: May 15	R and B:	$2150
501 applied	457 accepted	256 enrolled
SAT: 424V 460M	ACT: 19	COMPETITIVE

Olivet College is an independent liberal arts institution affiliated with the United Church of Christ and the Congregational Christian Church. The library contains 82,000 volumes and 2000 microfilm items, and subscribes to 20,000 periodicals.

Environment: The 44-acre campus is located in a rural area 18 miles from Battle Creek and 30 miles from Lansing. Facilities include a $1.7 million natatorium and a sports arena. There are 3 dormitories that accommodate 260 women and 352 men. The college also sponsors fraternity and sorority houses and on-campus apartments.

Student Life: Most of the students are from Michigan; 80% come from public schools. All of the students live on campus. Fifty-six percent are Catholic, 35% are Protestant, and 2% are Jewish. About 9% are minority-group members. College housing is coed and single-sex; students in single-sex housing have visiting privileges. Students may keep cars on campus. Day-care facilities are available.

Organizations: There are 3 local fraternities and 3 local sororities to which about 13% of the men and 14% of the women belong. On-campus activities include a theater, radio station, visiting poets series, music groups, opera, and special-interest clubs.

Sports: The college fields 9 intercollegiate teams for men and 5 for women. There are 6 intramural sports for men and 6 for women.

Handicapped: About 85% of the campus is accessible to students with physical handicaps. Special parking, elevators, and housing facilities are provided.

Graduates: The freshman dropout rate is 15%, and about 53% of the freshmen remain to graduate. Of these, 29% pursue advanced study; 2% enter dental school, and 4% enter law school. About 28% pursue careers in business and industry.

Services: Health care, psychological counseling, remedial instruction, tutoring, career counseling, and placement are offered free of charge.

Programs of Study: The college awards the B.A., B.M., and B.Mus. Ed. degrees. Master's degrees are also conferred. Bachelor's degrees are offered in the following subjects: BUSINESS (accounting, business administration, management, marketing, real estate/insurance), EDUCATION (elementary, secondary), ENGLISH (journalism), FINE AND PERFORMING ARTS (art, art history, music, music education, radio/TV, theater/dramatics), MATH AND SCIENCES (biochemistry, biology, chemistry, mathematics), PREPROFESSIONAL (dentistry, engineering, medicine, social work), SOCIAL SCIENCES (anthropology, economics, government/political science, history, psychology, social sciences, sociology). About 68% of degrees are conferred in arts and sciences, 13% in business, and 13% in education.

Special: Students may design their own majors, choose a general studies degree program, study abroad, and follow a professional semester program.

Honors: Honors programs are offered by 6 departments. Nine honor societies have chapters on campus.

Admissions: Approximately 91% of those who applied were accepted for the 1981–82 freshman class. The ACT scores of those who enrolled were as follows: 64% below 21, 17% between 21 and 23, 11% between 24 and 25, 5% between 26 and 28, and 3% above 28. Applicants should have completed 15 Carnegie units, rank in the upper half of their high school class, and have a minimum 2.5 grade average. Other factors entering into the admissions decision are the student's extracurricular activities record, advanced placement or honors courses, and recommendations by school officials.

Procedure: The SAT or ACT is required. Application deadlines are May 15 (fall) and December 15 (spring). Notification is on a rolling basis. There is a $10 application fee.

Special: There is a deferred admissions plan.

Transfer: For fall 1981, 39 students applied, 32 were accepted, and 25 enrolled. A GPA of 2.0, an ACT score of 19, and an interview are required. D grades do not transfer. Students must earn, at the college, at least 58 of the 120 credits necessary for a bachelor's degree. Application deadlines are the same as those for freshmen.

Visiting: There are regularly scheduled orientations for prospective students. Guides are also available for informal visits; visitors may sit in on classes and stay overnight at the school.

Financial Aid: About 84% of all students receive some form of financial aid. Sixty percent work part-time on campus. Average aid to freshmen is $3200. The college offers scholarships and loans. The college participates in the CSS and ACT. Either the FAF or the FFS is required. Aid application deadlines are January 31 (fall) and October (spring).

Foreign Students: One percent of the full-time students come from foreign countries. The college offers these students special counseling.

Admissions: Foreign students must achieve a minimum TOEFL score of 500. No college entrance exam must be taken.

Procedure: Application deadlines are May 15 (fall) and December 15 (spring). Foreign students must present proof of health and proof of funds adequate to cover 1 year of study.

Admissions Contact: Ron E. Lynch, Dean of Admissions.

SAGINAW VALLEY STATE COLLEGE D–4
University Center, Michigan 48710 (517) 790-4200

F/T: 942M, 1058W	Faculty:	120; IIA, av$
P/T: 768M, 986W	Ph.D.'s:	80%
Grad: 210M, 359W	S/F Ratio:	16 to 1
Year: tri, ss	Tuition:	$1364 ($2728)
Appl: Aug. 25	R and B:	$2126
1759 applied	1562 accepted	1363 enrolled
SAT or ACT: required		LESS COMPETITIVE

Saginaw Valley State College, founded in 1963, offers programs in the arts; behavioral sciences; business; education; science, engineering, and technology; and health fields. The library contains 88,529 volumes and 4000 microfilm items, and subscribes to 572 periodicals.

Environment: The 780-acre campus is located in a rural area 5 miles from Saginaw. There are 13 buildings, including 7 apartment-like dormitories that accommodate 500 students. Facilities are available for commuting students.

Student Life: About 99% of the students come from Michigan. Twelve percent live on campus. Thirteen percent of the students are minority-group members. College housing is single-sex, and there are visiting privileges. Students may keep cars on campus. Day-care facilities are available for a fee to full-time and part-time students, faculty, and staff.

Organizations: There are 3 national fraternities and 4 national sororities, to which 4% of the men and 4% of the women belong. There is a wide variety of extracurricular activities, including volunteer work, political clubs, and theater groups.

Sports: The college fields 8 intercollegiate teams for men and 6 for women. There are 5 intramural sports for men and 4 for women.

Handicapped: Approximately 55% of the campus is accessible to the physically handicapped. Facilities include wheelchair ramps, special parking, elevators, specially equipped rest rooms, and lowered drinking fountains. Special class scheduling is also available. Tape recorders, readers, and magnifying equipment are available for visually impaired students.

Graduates: There is a freshman dropout rate of 14%, and 35% of the freshmen remain to graduate. Sixteen percent of the graduates pursue advanced degrees; 1% enter medical school, 1% dental school, and 2% law school. About 22% pursue careers in business and industry.

Services: The following services are offered to students free of charge: placement, career counseling, health care, tutoring, remedial instruction, and psychological counseling.

Programs of Study: The B.A., B.S., B.B.A., and B.S.N. degrees are conferred. Master's degrees are also awarded. Bachelor's degrees are offered in the following subjects: BUSINESS (accounting, data processing, finance, management, marketing), EDUCATION (elementary, health/physical, secondary), ENGLISH (English, speech), FINE AND PERFORMING ARTS (art, art education, music, music education, theater/dramatics), HEALTH SCIENCES (medical technology, nursing), LANGUAGES (French, Spanish), MATH AND SCIENCES (biochemistry, biology, chemistry, computer math, computer physics, mathematics, physics), PREPROFESSIONAL (dentistry, law, medicine, social work, theology), SOCIAL SCIENCES (economics, government/political science, history, psychology, sociology). About 28% of degrees are conferred in social sciences, 22% in business, and 18% in math and sciences.

Special: Student-designed majors and cooperative education programs are offered.

Honors: There is an interdepartmental honors program.

Admissions: About 89% of the students who applied for the 1981–82 freshman class were accepted. The ACT scores of those who enrolled were as follows: 70% below 21, 15% between 21 and 23, 6% between 24 and 25, 8% between 26 and 28, and 1% above 28. A 2.0 high school average in academic courses is required.

Procedure: The ACT or SAT should be taken by January of the senior year. Application deadlines are August 25 (fall), December 15 (winter), April 15 (spring), and June 15 (summer). Notification is on a rolling basis. There is no application fee.

Special: There is a special admissions program for students who do not meet normal admissions requirements. AP and CLEP credit is accepted.

Transfer: For fall 1981, 793 students applied, 659 were accepted, and 494 enrolled. A 2.0 GPA is required; an interview is recommended. D grades are not accepted. Students must complete, at the college, at least 31 of the 124 credits necessary for a bachelor's degree. Deadlines are the same as those for freshman applicants.

Visiting: Informal campus tours with student guides may be arranged; visitors may sit in on classes and stay at the school. The admissions office should be contacted to arrange visits.

Financial Aid: About 80% of all students receive some form of financial aid. Ten percent work part-time on campus. Loan funds from several sources are available. There are 50 freshman scholarships from a fund of $29,000 yearly. The college is a member of CSS and requires either the FAF or the FSS. Application deadlines are April 15 (fall), October 15 (winter), and March 15 (spring and summer).

Foreign Students: Two percent of the full-time students come from foreign countries. The college offers these students an intensive English course and special counseling.

Admissions: Foreign students must achieve a minimum TOEFL score of 500 or take the University of Michigan Language Test. No college entrance exam must be taken.

Procedure: Application deadlines are June 1 (fall), October 1 (winter), February 1 (spring), and April 1 (summer). Foreign students must present proof of funds adequate to cover the entire period of study. They must also carry health insurance, which is available through the college for a fee.

Admissions Contact: Richard P. Thompson, Director of Admissions.

SAINT MARY'S COLLEGE   E–4
Orchard Lake, Michigan 48033   (313) 682-1885

F/T: 82M, 49W		Faculty:	25; n/av
P/T: 44M, 67W		Ph.D.'s:	50%
Grad: none		S/F Ratio:	6 to 1
Year: sems, ss		Tuition:	$1950
Appl: Aug. 15		R and B:	$1600
74 applied	68 accepted		58 enrolled
ACT: 20			COMPETITIVE

Saint Mary's College, founded in 1885, is the only college founded to serve Polish and Catholic persons in the United States. The Roman Catholic institution offers undergraduate programs in the liberal arts and sciences. The library contains 46,000 volumes, and subscribes to 450 periodicals.

Environment: The 130-acre campus is located in a suburban area 17 miles from Detroit. The 13 buildings include 2 dormitories.

Student Life: A majority of the students come from Michigan. Forty percent live on campus. Seventy-five percent of the students are Catholic, and 20% are Protestant; attendance at religious services is not compulsory. Nine percent are minority-group members. College housing is single-sex, and there are visiting privileges. Students may keep cars on campus.

Organizations: About 20% of the men belong to 1 national fraternity; there is 1 sorority. Much of the extracurricular activity on campus is service-centered.

Sports: The college fields 1 intercollegiate team for men. There are 3 intramural sports for men and 3 for women.

Handicapped: There are no special facilities for the physically handicapped.

Graduates: The freshman dropout rate is 30%, and 40% of the freshmen remain to graduate. About 55% of the graduates pursue advanced study; 5% enter medical school, and 10% enter law school. About 50% pursue careers in business and industry.

Services: Placement and career counseling are offered free of charge.

Programs of Study: The college awards the B.A., B.B.A., and B.S. degrees. Associate degrees are also conferred. Bachelor's degrees are offered in the following subjects: AREA STUDIES (Polish), BUSINESS (business administration), ENGLISH (English, literature), FINE AND PERFORMING ARTS (communication arts), HEALTH SCIENCES (radiologic technology), LANGUAGES (Polish), MATH AND SCIENCES (biology, chemistry), PHILOSOPHY (philosophy, religious education, theology), SOCIAL SCIENCES (social sciences). About 50% of degrees are conferred in philosophy, 10% in business, 10% in the fine and performing arts, and 10% in the health sciences.

Required: Courses in theology are required.

Special: The college's program in Polish is a distinguishing factor. Study-abroad programs are available.

Admissions: Approximately 92% of those who applied were accepted for the 1981–82 freshman class. The ACT scores of those who enrolled were as follows: 25% below 21, 50% between 21 and 23, 10% between 24 and 25, 10% between 26 and 28, and 5% above 28. Applicants should be in the top half of their class and have a minimum GPA of 2.0. Also considered in the admissions decision are advanced placement or honors courses.

Procedure: The ACT is required. Application deadlines are August 15 (fall), December 15 (winter), and April 15 (spring). Notification is on a rolling basis. There is a $10 application fee.

Special: Early admissions and early decision plans are available. CLEP credit is accepted.

Transfer: For fall 1981, 25 students applied, 20 were accepted, and 14 enrolled. The college accepts transfer students for the second semester freshman, sophomore, and junior classes. A GPA of at least 2.0 is required; ACT scores are also required unless the candidate is classified as a nontraditional student. D grades do not transfer. Students must earn, at the college, 30 of the 120 credits necessary for a bachelor's degree. Application deadlines are August 15 (fall), December 15 (winter), and March 15 (spring).

Visiting: There are regularly scheduled orientations for prospective students. Guides are also available for informal visits; visitors may sit in on classes and stay overnight at the school. The admissions office should be contacted to arrange visits.

Financial Aid: Approximately 60% of all students receive some form of financial aid. Ten percent work part-time on campus. Average aid to freshmen is $1200. There is a $300 per year tuition discount for students who take courses in Polish language or culture. Aid is available through traditional loan programs as well as a number of institutional scholarships. The college is a member of CSS and requires the FAF. Application deadlines are July 15 (fall), November 15 (winter), and March 15 (spring).

Foreign Students: Two percent of the full-time students come from foreign countries.

Admissions: Foreign students must achieve a minimum TOEFL score of 500. They must also take either the SAT or the ACT.

Procedure: Application deadlines are July 15 (fall), November 15 (winter), and March 15 (spring). Foreign students must present proof of health and proof of funds adequate to cover 1 year of study.

Admissions Contact: Randall J. Berd, Director of Admissions.

SHAW COLLEGE AT DETROIT   E-5
Detroit, Michigan 48202   (313) 873-7920
(Recognized Candidate for Accreditation)

F/T: 203M, 339W	Faculty: 30; IIB, — —$
P/T: 29M, 84W	Ph.D.'s: 35%
Grad: none	S/F Ratio: 16 to 1
Year: sems, ss	Tuition: $2100
Appl: open	R and B: n/app
350 applied	347 accepted	294 enrolled
SAT or ACT: not required	NONCOMPETITIVE

Shaw College at Detroit, founded in 1936, is a 4-year liberal arts college, and one of the few predominantly black colleges in a major northern city. The library contains 88,618 volumes and 26,500 microfilm items, and subscribes to 350 periodicals.

Environment: The campus is located in the New Center Area of Detroit, an urban setting. There are 4 main buildings. Dental and medical courses are given in the Allied Health Building about 5 miles away. Shaw is a commuter college; there are no dormitories.

Student Life: Ninety-eight percent of the students come from Michigan, mainly from the Detroit area; almost all come from public schools. Ninety-eight percent of the students are minority-group members. Students may keep cars on campus.

Organizations: There are no fraternities or sororities. Extracurricular activities include numerous special-interest clubs, the college choir, the pep club, the yearbook, and student government.

Sports: The college fields 2 intercollegiate teams for men and 2 for women. There are 2 intramural sports for men and 1 for women.

Handicapped: There are no special facilities for handicapped students.

Graduates: The freshman dropout rate is 10%, and 34% of the freshmen remain to graduate. About 60% of the graduates pursue advanced study; 1% enter medical school, and 2% enter law school. About 50% pursue careers in business or industry.

Services: The following services are available to students free of charge: psychological counseling, placement, career counseling, and tutoring. Remedial instruction is available for a fee.

Programs of Study: The college confers the B.A. and B.S. degrees. Associate degrees are also awarded. Bachelor's degrees are offered in the following subjects: BUSINESS (accounting, business administration), ENGLISH (English), MATH AND SCIENCES (biology, chemistry, mathematics, natural sciences), PHILOSOPHY (humanities), SOCIAL SCIENCES (government/political science, history, psychology, social sciences, sociology). Fifty percent of degrees are conferred in business, 45% in social sciences, 4% in natural science, and 1% in humanities.

Special: A dual degree in engineering is offered in cooperation with the University of Detroit.

Admissions: About 99% of those who applied were accepted for the 1981-82 freshman class. Admissions are open: the college accepts all qualified applicants who have obtained a high school diploma or its equivalent.

Procedure: Neither the SAT nor the ACT is required. The deadline for applications is open. Notification is on a rolling basis. There is a $10 application fee.

Transfer: For fall 1981, all of the 69 applicants were accepted, and 54 enrolled. A minimum GPA of 2.0 is recommended. D grades do not transfer. Students must spend 1 year in residence and complete at least 24 of the 124 credits necessary for a bachelor's degree. Application deadlines are open.

Visiting: Guides are available for informal visits; visitors may sit in on classes but may not stay on campus. The office of admissions should be contacted to arrange visits.

Financial Aid: Ninety percent of all students receive some form of aid. Sixty percent work part-time on campus. Average aid to freshmen is $5700. Aid is available from a number of sources, including college and state grants, SEOG, BEOG, NDSL and other loans, and various scholarships. The college is a member of CSS and requires the FAF. There is no application deadline.

Foreign Students: Fewer than 1% of the full-time students come from foreign countries. The college offers these students special counseling.

Admissions: Foreign students must achieve a minimum TOEFL score of 500. No college entrance exam must be taken.

Procedure: Application deadlines are July (fall), October (winter), March (spring and summer). Foreign students must present proof of funds adequate to cover the entire period of study.

Admissions Contact: Doris G. Davis, Registrar/Director of Admissions.

SIENA HEIGHTS COLLEGE   E-5
Adrian, Michigan 49221   (517) 263-0731

F/T: 304M, 417W	Faculty: 51; IIA, — —$
P/T: 126M, 257W	Ph.D.'s: 35%
Grad: 25M, 70W	S/F Ratio: 15 to 1
Year: sems, ss	Tuition: $2940
Appl: Sept. 1	R and B: $1900
433 applied	415 accepted	195 enrolled
SAT or ACT: required	LESS COMPETITIVE

Siena Heights College, founded in 1919, is an independent coeducational institution emphasizing career programs based on the liberal arts. The library contains 81,567 volumes and 22,013 microfilm items, and subscribes to 400 periodicals.

Environment: The 140-acre campus is located in Adrian, a city of 20,000 people, 30 miles from Toledo, Ohio, and 65 miles from Detroit. The campus is made up of 10 buildings including the Siena Activities Center, a 57,000-square foot athletic, recreational, and special events facility. Two dormitories house 450 students.

Student Life: About 82% of the students are from Michigan. Thirty-six percent live on campus in dormitories; the remainder commute from home. Nine percent of the students are minority-group members. College housing is coed and single-sex; students in single-sex housing have visiting privileges. Students may keep cars on campus.

Organizations: There are no fraternities or sororities. The major social events on campus are the Aquinas Forum lecture series, theater performances, film series, alumni weekends, mixers, formal dances, concerts, and family weekends. The college also sponsors many extracurricular activities and groups, the most active of which is the student government.

Sports: The college fields 6 intercollegiate teams for men and 6 for women. There are 4 intramural sports for men and 2 for women.

Handicapped: About 75% of the campus is accessible to handicapped students. Facilities include wheelchair ramps, special parking, elevators, and specially equipped rest rooms.

Graduates: About 20% of the students pursue advanced study after graduation. Fifty-three percent enter careers in business and industry.

Services: The following services are available to students free of charge: placement, tutoring, remedial instruction, career counseling, health care, and psychological counseling. Placement services, including workshops, credential services, alumni services, on-campus interviews, career courses, and counseling, are available to graduates as well as undergraduates.

Programs of Study: The college confers the B.A., B.S., B.F.A., and B. Applied Sc. degrees. Associate and master's programs are also awarded. Bachelor's degrees are offered in the following subjects: AREA STUDIES (American), BUSINESS (accounting, banking and finance, business administration, business education, computer science, fashion merchandising, food service/lodging and institutional management, management, office administration), EDUCATION (elementary, home economics), ENGLISH (English/communications), FINE AND PERFORMING ARTS (art, music, theater and speech communication), MATH AND SCIENCES (biology, mathematics, natural sciences), PHILOSOPHY (humanities, philosophy, religious studies), PREPROFESSIONAL (home economics, law, medicine, social work), SOCIAL SCIENCES (criminal justice, history, psychology, public administration, social sciences). Sixteen percent of degrees are conferred in business/management, 16% in social sciences and human services, and 9% in the fine and performing arts.

Special: The art department has taken a large group of students to Italy, where they studied under the college's auspices and received credit from the college. There is a directed student teaching program for education majors. Contractual learning is available. A general studies degree is offered. Three-year bachelor's degrees may be earned. Student-designed majors are permitted. Flexible learning formats include evening courses, weekend courses, two-month class cycles, and extended weekend courses for out-of-town and out-of-state students.

Honors: The Phi Sigma Tau honor society has a chapter on campus.

Admissions: About 96% of those who applied were accepted for the 1981–82 freshman class. The requirements for admission are graduation from an accredited high school and a 2.0 GPA. A personal interview is recommended.

Procedure: Either the SAT or the ACT is required. Application deadlines are September 1 (fall), January 5 (spring), and June 3 (summer). Notification is on a rolling basis. There is a $15 application fee.

Special: A deferred admissions plan is available. AP and CLEP credit is accepted.

Transfer: For fall 1981, 104 full-time students applied, 100 were accepted, and 67 enrolled. Transfers are accepted for all classes. A minimum average of 2.0 and an associate degree are required. D grades transfer only with an associate degree. Students must complete, at the college, at least 24 of the 120 semester hours necessary for a bachelor's degree. Application deadlines are the same as those for freshmen.

Visiting: The college holds orientation sessions regularly for prospective students. Guides are also available for informal visits; visitors may sit in on classes and stay overnight at the school. Visitors are welcome any time. The admissions office should be contacted to arrange visits.

Financial Aid: About 85% of all students receive some form of financial aid. Fifteen percent work part-time on campus. Average aid to freshmen covers 43% of costs; need and academic proficiency are the main criteria for determining awards. Aid includes BEOG and SEOG. State awards include scholarships and tuition grants, plus state differential grants for freshmen and sophomores. Loans are available to eligible aid applicants. Institutional awards include scholarships and grants; awards range from $200 to $5000. The college is a member of CSS and requires the FAF. Application deadlines are September 1 (fall), January 5 (spring), and June 3 (summer).

Foreign Students: Three percent of the full-time students come from foreign countries. The college offers these students an intensive English program, special counseling, and special organizations.

Admissions: Foreign students must achieve a minimum TOEFL score of 480 or a University of Michigan Language Test score of at least 80. They must also take either the SAT or the ACT.

Procedure: Application deadlines are September 1 (fall), January 5 (spring), and June 3 (summer). Foreign students must present a completed college medical form and proof of funds adequate to cover 1 year of study. They must also carry health insurance, which is available through the college for a fee.

Admissions Contact: Sister Anne Marie Brown, Director of Admissions.

SPRING ARBOR COLLEGE D–5
Spring Arbor, Michigan 49283 (517) 750-1200

F/T: 302M, 373W	Faculty:	38; IIB, –$
P/T: 55M, 71W	Ph.D.'s:	39%
Grad: none	S/F Ratio:	18 to 1
Year: 4-1-4, ss	Tuition:	$4050
Appl: July 1	R and B:	$1700
373 applied	307 accepted	189 enrolled
ACT: 18		COMPETITIVE

Spring Arbor College, founded in 1873, is a private liberal arts institution affiliated with the Free Methodist Church. The library contains 69,832 volumes and 178 microfilm items, and subscribes to 329 periodicals.

Environment: The 70-acre campus is located in a rural town of 2000 inhabitants 8 miles from Jackson and 70 miles from Detroit. There are 30 buildings on campus, including a physical education center containing an indoor track and an Olympic-size swimming pool. Living facilities include 2 residence halls, a 4-winged dormitory complex, 1 house, and college apartments; married students are accommodated.

Student Life: About 84% of the students come from Michigan. Eighty percent live on campus. Students not commuting from home or living in approved off-campus housing are expected to live in dormitories. Ninety-two percent of the students are Protestant, and 2% are Catholic; attendance at chapel twice weekly is compulsory. About 8% are minority-group members. College housing is single-sex, and there are visiting privileges. Students may keep cars on campus. Drinking and smoking are prohibited.

Organizations: There are no fraternities or sororities. Extracurricular activities include special-interest and service clubs, publications, music and drama groups, and religious organizations for Protestant students.

Sports: The college fields 6 intercollegiate teams for men and 5 for women. There are 6 intramural sports for men and 5 for women. Wrestling is a club sport for men.

Handicapped: Approximately 25% of the campus is accessible to the physically handicapped. Facilities include wheelchair ramps, special parking, elevators, specially equipped rest rooms, and lowered drinking fountains and telephones. There are 2 special counselors to assist handicapped students.

Graduates: The freshman dropout rate is 35%, and 39% of the freshmen remain to graduate. Of those who remain, 17% pursue graduate study; 1% enter medical school, 1% dental school, and 1% law school. About 40% pursue careers in business and industry.

Services: Placement, career counseling, health care, and psychological counseling are offered free of charge. Tutoring and remedial instruction are available for a fee.

Programs of Study: Associate degrees are awarded in addition to the B.A. degree, which is offered in the following subjects: BUSINESS (business administration), EDUCATION (elementary, health/physical, secondary), ENGLISH (English, English/speech), FINE AND PERFORMING ARTS (art, art education, music, music education), LANGUAGES (French, Spanish), MATH AND SCIENCES (biology, chemistry, mathematics, physics, physics/mathematics), PHILOSOPHY (contemporary ministries, philosophy, philosophy/religion, religion), PREPROFESSIONAL (social work), SOCIAL SCIENCES (business administration, economics/business administration, history, psychology, social sciences, sociology). About 36% of the degrees are awarded in social sciences, 22% in math and sciences, and 13% in business.

Required: All students must take 3 courses related to the Christian perspective in the liberal arts, a physical education course, and introductory courses in the liberal arts, speech, and English.

Special: Students may design their own majors. The college offers study abroad, an urban semester in Chicago, an environment-oriented educational semester at the Au Sable Trails Institute of Environmental Studies, and travel options during the January interim.

Honors: Honors work is available in 4 departments. There is 1 honor society.

Admissions: About 82% of those who applied for the 1981–82 freshman class were accepted. The ACT scores of those who enrolled were as follows: 59% below 21, 30% between 21 and 25, and 5% above 26. A minimum 2.6 GPA is suggested. Also considered in the admissions decision are extracurricular activities, impressions made during an interview, and evidence of special talents.

Procedure: The ACT is preferred and should be taken by the fall of the senior year, but SAT scores will be accepted. The application deadlines are July 1 for fall, December 1 for January interim, and January 1 for spring. Notification is on a rolling basis. There is a $15 application fee.

Special: There is an early admissions plan. AP and CLEP credit is accepted.

Transfer: For fall 1981, 133 students applied, 111 were accepted, and 61 enrolled. A 2.0 GPA is required; only transferring freshmen must take the ACT, with a minimum score of 18 recommended. Courses in the major must average at least 2.2 to transfer, while other courses must average 2.0. Students must complete, at the college, at least 30 of the 124 semester hours necessary for a bachelor's degree. Application deadlines are the same as those for freshmen.

Visiting: Special days are set aside each semester for prospective students to visit, but individual campus visits are also encouraged. Visitors may stay overnight at the school and sit in on classes. The admissions office should be contacted to arrange visits.

Financial Aid: About 95% of all students receive some form of aid. Seventy-five percent work part-time on campus. Average aid to freshmen is $2000. The college offers scholarships, grants, and loans. The college is a member of CSS and requires the FAF. Application deadlines are January 31 (fall), October 1 (January interim), and November 1 (spring).

Foreign Students: Five percent of the full-time students come from foreign countries. The college offers these students special counseling and special organizations.

Admissions: Foreign students must achieve a minimum TOEFL score of 550 or a University of Michigan Language Test score of at least 90. No college entrance exam must be taken.

Procedure: Application deadlines are May 1 (fall), October 1 (January interim), November 1 (spring), and March 1 (summer). Foreign students must present a medical and health evaluation report and proof of funds adequate to cover the entire period of study. They must also carry health insurance, which is available through the college for a fee.

Admissions Contact: Richard H. Bailey, Coordinator of Enrollment and College Relations.

UNIVERSITY OF DETROIT E-5
Detroit, Michigan 48221 (313) 927-1245

F/T: 1337M, 957W	Faculty: 244; I, +$
P/T: 817M, 509W	Ph.D.'s: 78%
Grad: 1693M, 1062W	S/F Ratio: 13 to 1
Year: tri, ss	Tuition: $4230
Appl: Aug. 15	R and B: $2050
1444 applied	1093 accepted	522 enrolled
SAT: 440V 490M	ACT: 21	COMPETITIVE

University of Detroit is an independent institution sponsored by the Jesuits, offering undergraduate and graduate instruction in the liberal arts and sciences, architecture, engineering, the health fields, law, dentistry, business, and education. The library contains 503,205 volumes and 131,657 microfilm items, and subscribes to 3451 periodicals.

Environment: The 70-acre campus is located in an urban area. Facilities include a television studio, a student union, an administrative center, 6 classroom buildings, and a field house. In addition to high-rise dormitories and quads, the university sponsors fraternity and sorority houses and married student housing.

Student Life: About 70% of the students come from Michigan; 49% come from public schools. Ten percent live on campus. Fifty-five percent of the students are Catholic, 15% are Protestant, and 1% are Jewish; attendance at religious services is voluntary. Eighteen percent of the students are minority-group members. University housing is coed and single-sex; students in single-sex housing have visiting privileges. Students may keep cars on campus.

Organizations: Approximately 4% of the men belong to the 5 national fraternities; 4% of the women belong to the 1 local and 2 national sororities. Extracurricular activities and social and cultural events are numerous and varied.

Sports: The university fields 7 intercollegiate teams for men and 4 for women. There are 15 intramural sports for men and 11 for women.

Handicapped: Approximately 60% of the campus is accessible to the physically handicapped. Facilities include wheelchair ramps, special parking, elevators, and lowered drinking fountains. Special class scheduling is also available.

Graduates: Approximately 52% of those who graduate pursue advanced degrees, and twenty-five percent enter careers in business and industry.

Services: Placement services, career counseling, psychological counseling, health care, and tutoring are offered to students free of charge.

Programs of Study: The university awards the B.A., B.S., B.S.Ed., B.B.A., B.F.A., B.Arch., B.M., B.S.C.E., B.S.Ch.E., B.S.E.E., B.S.M.E., and B.S. in E. degrees. Master's and doctoral degrees are also conferred. Bachelor's degrees are offered in the following subjects: AREA STUDIES (Asian), BUSINESS (accounting, business administration, computer science, finance, management, marketing, personnel administration), EDUCATION (elementary, health/physical, secondary, special), ENGLISH (English, journalism, literature, speech), FINE AND PERFORMING ARTS (radio/TV, theater/dramatics), HEALTH SCIENCES (medical technology, nuclear medicine technology, respiratory therapy), LANGUAGES (French, German, Greek/Latin, Spanish), MATH AND SCIENCES (biology, chemistry, chemistry-business, computer science, mathematics, statistics), PHILOSOPHY (classics, humanities, philosophy, religion), PREPROFESSIONAL (architecture, dentistry, engineering—chemical, engineering—civil, engineering—electrical, engineering—mechanical, engineering—polymer, law, medicine, social work), SOCIAL SCIENCES (economics, government/political science, history, psychology, sociology). About 30% of degrees are conferred in business, 24% in social sciences, and 19% in preprofessional areas.

Special: Cooperative education is a mandatory feature of the 5-year architecture program and the 4-year engineering programs. Optional cooperative education programs are available in the colleges of Business and Administration, Liberal Arts, and Education and Human Services. Students may study abroad in Ireland, Tokyo, or Rome.

Honors: An honors program is open to superior students. Ten national honor societies have chapters on campus.

Admissions: Approximately 76% of those who applied were accepted for the 1981–82 freshman class. The SAT scores of those who enrolled were as follows: Verbal—68% below 500, 19% between 500 and 599, 12% between 600 and 700, and 1% above 700; Math—50% below 500, 23% between 500 and 599, 20% between 600 and 700, and 7% above 700. On the ACT, 48% scored below 21, 15% between 21 and 23, 12% between 24 and 25, 18% between 26 and 28, and 7% above 28. Applicants should be in the top half of their class and have a minimum GPA of 2.75.

Procedure: The SAT or ACT is required and should be taken by December of the senior year. The deadline for fall application is August 15. Notification is on a rolling basis. There is a $20 application fee.

Special: Project 100 is designed to help underachieving, academically disadvantaged students from the metro-Detroit area. AP and CLEP credit is accepted.

Transfer: For fall 1981, 578 students applied, 432 were accepted, and 191 enrolled. Transfers are considered for all classes. Applicants should have a minimum 2.0 GPA based on 24 semester hours of college work; those with less hours must submit a high school transcript. D grades do not transfer. Students must complete, at the university, at least 32 of the 128 semester hours necessary for a bachelor's degree. Application deadlines are the same as those for freshmen.

Visiting: There are regularly scheduled orientations for prospective students. Guides are also available for informal visits; visitors may sit in on classes and stay at the school. The admissions office should be contacted to arrange visits.

Financial Aid: Approximately 70% of all students receive some form of financial aid. Average aid to freshmen is $3500. Aid is available in the form of scholarships, grants, and loans and is usually awarded on the basis of need and ability. The university participates in the CSS and the ACT. The FAF is required; the aid application deadline is April 1.

Foreign Students: Thirteen percent of the full-time students come from foreign countries. The university offers these students an intensive English program, special counseling, and special organizations.

Admissions: All non-native English speakers are tested on arrival; they must achieve a minimum score of 80 on the University of Michigan Language Test or take the TOEFL. No college entrance exam must be taken.

Procedure: Application deadlines are open. Foreign students must present a completed university medical form as proof of a physical examination, proof of funds adequate to cover the entire course of study, and a special application fee of $35. They must also carry health insurance, which is available through the university for a fee.

Admissions Contact: James M. Masuga, Director of Admissions.

UNIVERSITY OF MICHIGAN

University of Michigan, founded in 1817, offers high-quality education commensurate with the diverse components of a great state-controlled university of 18 separate schools and colleges. The main campus is located at Ann Arbor. There are also university campuses at Dearborn and Flint. Separate profiles for each follow.

UNIVERSITY OF MICHIGAN/ ANN ARBOR E-5
Ann Arbor, Michigan 48109 (313) 764-2573

F/T: 11,081M, 9439W	Faculty: 2660; I, ++$
P/T: 910M, 883W	Ph.D.'s: 90%
Grad: 7874M, 5035W	S/F Ratio: 15 to 1
Year: tri, ss	Tuition: $1759 ($5011)
Appl: Mar. 1	R and B: $2281
13,307 applied	8073 accepted	4322 enrolled
SAT: 540V 600M	ACT: 26	HIGHLY COMPETITIVE

University of Michigan/Ann Arbor, the site of the main campus of the University of Michigan, offers a wide range of undergraduate and graduate degree programs. The university has an innovative division, Residential College, which offers interdisciplinary programs in the humanities, natural sciences, and social sciences. The library contains nearly 5.5 million volumes and 2 million microfilm items, and subscribes to 42,708 periodicals.

Environment: There are 198 buildings on the suburban campus, which is 40 miles from Detroit. Living facilities include dormitories, married student housing, on- and off-campus apartments, and fraternity and sorority houses.

Student Life: About 75% of the students come from Michigan; the majority come from public schools. Thirty-five percent live on campus. Fifteen percent are minority-group members. Campus housing is both coed and single-sex; there are visiting privileges in the single-sex housing. Students may keep cars on campus.

Organizations: There are 36 national fraternities, to which 10% of the men belong; 13% of the women are members of the 19 national sororities. Religious counselors are available. There is a large variety of extracurricular activities and on-campus social and cultural events. About 225 acres of the campus are devoted to recreational and athletic use.

Sports: The university fields 12 intercollegiate teams for men and 11 for women. There are 22 intramural sports for men and 19 for women.

Handicapped: Approximately 80% of the campus is accessible to the physically handicapped. Facilities include wheelchair ramps, special parking, elevators, specially equipped rest rooms, and lowered drinking fountains and telephones. Special class scheduling is also available. Fewer than 1% of the students currently enrolled have visual or hearing impairments. The library has special equipment for visually impaired students; a note service and an interpreter referral service are provided for students with hearing impairments.

Graduates: The freshman dropout rate is 9%; over 70% remain to graduate. Of those, about 80% pursue graduate study.

Services: Placement services, career counseling, and psychological counseling are offered free of charge to all students. Health care is provided on a fee basis.

Programs of Study: The B.A., B.S., B.B.A., B.M., B.S.N., and B.Arch. degrees are conferred. Master's and doctoral degrees are also awarded. Bachelor's degrees are offered in the following subjects: AREA STUDIES (American, Asian, Black/Afro-American, Eastern European, Near Eastern/North African, Russian, urban), BUSINESS (accounting, business administration, business education, finance, management, marketing), EDUCATION (adult, early childhood, elementary, health/physical, industrial, secondary, special), ENGLISH (creative writing, English, journalism, linguistics, literature, speech), FINE AND PERFORMING ARTS (art, art education, art history, dance, film/photography, music, music education, radio/TV, studio art, theater/dramatics), HEALTH SCIENCES (environmental health, medical technology, nursing, physical therapy, speech therapy), LANGUAGES (Arabic, Chinese, French, German, Greek/Latin, Hebrew, Italian, Japanese, Portuguese, Russian, Slavic languages, Spanish), MATH AND SCIENCES (applied mathematics, astronomy, atmospheric sciences and meteorology, biology, botany, cell biology, chemistry, earth science, ecology/environmental science, geology, marine biology, mathematics, microbiology, molecular biology, natural sciences, oceanography, pharmacology, physical sciences, physics, statistics, zoology), PHILOSOPHY (classics, humanities, philosophy, religion), PREPROFESSIONAL (architecture, dentistry, engineering, forestry, law, library science, medicine, ministry, pharmacy, social work, veterinary), SOCIAL SCIENCES (anthropology, economics, government/political science, history, international relations, psychology, social sciences, sociology, women's studies). About 13% of degrees are conferred in social sciences, 9% in health sciences, and 7% in education.

Special: There is a junior year abroad program; students may design their own majors. Residential College students may undertake independent studies, fieldwork, and tutorials.

Honors: Twenty-six honor societies have chapters on campus; honors work is offered in nearly all academic areas.

Admissions: Approximately 61% of those who applied were accepted for the 1981–82 freshman class. The SAT scores of those who enrolled were as follows: Verbal—29% below 500, 47% between 500 and 599, 21% between 600 and 700, and 4% above 700; Math—11% below 500, 35% between 500 and 599, 38% between 600 and 700, and 16% above 700. On the ACT, 6% scored below 21, 21% between 21 and 23, 20% between 24 and 25, 25% between 26 and 28, and 28% above 700. Applicants should be graduates of an accredited high school, have completed 15 Carnegie units, rank in the top 20% of their class, and have an average of 3.3 or better. Advanced placement or honors courses are also considered important. Within the limits of its resources, the university admits all of the qualified applicants who are Michigan residents. Out-of-state applicants must be very highly qualified; among out-of-state applicants, some preference is given to qualified applicants who are children of alumni.

Procedure: The SAT or ACT is required, and must be taken by January of the senior year. Application deadlines are March 1 (spring, summer, or fall) and December 1 (winter). Notification is on a rolling basis. There is a $20 application fee.

Special: AP credit is accepted. There are early admissions and deferred admissions plans.

Transfer: For fall 1981, 2632 students applied, 1561 were accepted, and 1139 enrolled. A GPA of at least 2.5 is required. D grades do not transfer. All students must complete, at the university, 60 of the 120 credits required for a bachelor's degree. Application deadlines are the same as those for freshmen. Preference is given to Michigan residents.

Visiting: There are regularly scheduled orientations for prospective students. Guides are also available for informal visits; visitors may sit in on classes and stay overnight at the school. The admissions office should be contacted to arrange visits.

Financial Aid: Approximately 62% of all students receive some form of financial aid. Fifty percent work part-time on campus. The office of financial aid offers all federal aid programs: EOG, NDSL, CWS, and the health professions aid programs. Grants and loans are also available. Institutional gift aid is very limited for out-of-state freshmen. Need is the determining factor. The FFS, FAF, or SFS is required; the deadline for aid applications is March 1 (spring, summer, or fall) or December 1 (winter). The university is a member of CSS.

Foreign Students: Seven percent of the full-time students come from foreign countries. An intensive English course, an intensive English program, special counseling, and special organizations are available for these students.

Admissions: Foreign students must take either the TOEFL or the University of Michigan Language Test. The SAT or ACT is also required.

Procedure: Application deadlines are March 1 (spring, summer, or fall) and October 1 (winter). Foreign students must present proof of funds adequate to cover 4 years of study and must carry health insurance, which is available through the university for a fee.

Admissions Contact: Cliff Sjogren, Director of Admissions.

UNIVERSITY OF MICHIGAN/ DEARBORN   E–5
Dearborn, Michigan 48185   (313) 593-5100

F/T: 1924M, 1597W	Faculty: n/av; IIA, +$
P/T: 1509M, 1545W	Ph.D.'s: n/av
Grad: 254M, 215W	S/F Ratio: n/av
Year: tri, ss	Tuition: $1328 ($4080)
Appl: Mar. 1	R: $116/month
1774 applied	1205 accepted 747 enrolled
SAT: 460V 540M	ACT: 23 VERY COMPETITIVE

University of Michigan/Dearborn provides undergraduate and graduate instruction in the liberal arts and sciences, engineering, business, and education. The library contains 225,000 volumes and 5061 microfilm items, and subscribes to 1592 periodicals.

Environment: The 210-acre suburban campus is 10 miles from Detroit. There are 8 buildings, including a new university mall and library and learning and resource center. The campus is commuter-oriented; the limited amount of housing includes on-campus apartments and married student housing.

Student Life: Almost all of the students come from Michigan; most come from public schools. Almost all students commute; 1% live on campus. The limited amount of campus housing is both coed and single-sex. Students may keep cars on campus. Day-care services are available to all students.

Organizations: There are no fraternities or sororities. Over 20 student organizations reflect a wide variety of interests.

Sports: The university fields 3 intercollegiate teams for men and 2 for women. There are 3 intramural sports for men and 3 for women.

Handicapped: Approximately 99% of the campus is accessible to the physically handicapped. Facilities include wheelchair ramps, special parking, elevators, specially equipped rest rooms, and lowered drinking fountains and telephones; special class scheduling is also available. Fewer than 1% of the students currently enrolled have visual or hearing impairments; readers, cassette tapes, and interpreters are provided.

Services: Psychological counseling, remedial instruction, career counseling, and placement services are offered to students free of charge. Health care and tutoring are provided on a fee basis.

Programs of Study: The B.A., B.S., B.B.A., B.S.E., B.S.A., and B.G.S. degrees are conferred. Master's degrees are also awarded. Bachelor's degrees are offered in the following subjects: AREA STUDIES (American, environmental, international), BUSINESS (accounting, business administration, finance, management, marketing), EDUCATION (early childhood, elementary, secondary), ENGLISH (English), FINE AND PERFORMING ARTS (art history, music history), MATH AND SCIENCES (biochemistry, biology, chemistry, ecology/environmental science, mathematics, microbiology, natural sciences, physics), PHI-

414 MICHIGAN

LOSOPHY (humanities, philosophy), PREPROFESSIONAL (dentistry, engineering, law, medicine), SOCIAL SCIENCES (anthropology, economics, government/political science, history, psychology, sociology). About 35% of degrees are conferred in preprofessional areas, 30% in business, and 25% in math and sciences.

Required: The university requires a core curriculum of general education credits.

Special: There are cooperative internship programs in engineering, business, and the arts, sciences, and letters. A general studies degree is offered.

Honors: Honors programs are offered in psychology and the liberal arts.

Admissions: Approximately 68% of those who applied were accepted for the 1981-82 freshman class. The SAT scores of those who enrolled were as follows: Verbal—71% below 500, 25% between 500 and 599, 3% between 600 and 700, and 1% above 700; Math—31% below 500, 45% between 500 and 599, 20% between 600 and 700, and 4% above 700. On the ACT, 12% scored below 19, 53% between 19 and 24, 24% between 25 and 27, 9% between 28 and 30, and 1% above 30. Students should have a high school GPA of at least 2.9 and should rank in the upper 20% of their class. Other factors entering into the admissions decision are advanced placement or honors courses, recommendations by school officials, extracurricular activities, and impressions made during an interview.

Procedure: The SAT or ACT is required. Deadlines for application are March 1 (fall), November 15 (winter), March 15 (spring), and April 15 (summer). The university follows a rolling admissions policy. There is a $20 application fee.

Special: AP and CLEP credit is accepted.

Transfer: For fall 1981, 1306 students applied, 869 were accepted, and 671 enrolled. Transfers are accepted for the freshman, sophomore, and junior classes. A minimum GPA of 2.5 is required; D grades do not transfer. Preference is given to students from Michigan colleges. All students must complete, at the university, the last 30 of the 120-128 credits required for a bachelor's degree. Application deadlines are August 1 (fall), December 1 (winter), March 1 (spring), and June 1 (summer).

Visiting: There are regularly scheduled orientations for prospective students. Guides are available for informal visits; visitors may sit in on classes. The office of university relations should be contacted to arrange visits.

Financial Aid: Approximately 30% of all students receive some form of financial aid. About 4% work part-time on campus. The average freshman award is $1900. Tuition may be paid in installments. The university is a member of the CSS and requires the FFS or FAF. The deadlines for aid application are March 1 (fall) and November 1 (winter). For equal consideration, aid applications should be filed by December 31.

Foreign Students: Three percent of the full-time students come from foreign countries. An intensive English course, special counseling, and special organizations are available for these students.

Admissions: Foreign students must achieve a TOEFL score of at least 550 or must take the University of Michigan Language Test. No college entrance exams are required.

Procedure: The application deadline is March 1 for fall entry. Foreign students already living in the U.S. may apply for winter entry; the deadline is September 1. Foreign students must present proof of funds adequate to cover 4 years of study.

Admissions Contact: Edward J. Bagale, Director of Admissions.

UNIVERSITY OF MICHIGAN/FLINT
E-4

Flint, Michigan 48503   (313) 762-3300

F/T: 1129M, 1246W	Faculty: 129; IIA, +$
P/T: 850M, 1214W	Ph.D.'s: 80%
Grad: 105M, 65W	S/F Ratio: 18 to 1
Year: sems, ss	Tuition: $1180 ($3820)
Appl: Aug. 19	R and B: n/app
1094 applied	896 accepted 653 enrolled
SAT: 451V 514M	ACT: 21 COMPETITIVE

University of Michigan/Flint, established in 1956, is a state-supported, primarily undergraduate institution offering programs in the liberal arts and sciences, business, education, the health fields, and engineering. Master's degree programs are offered in business, public administration, and liberal studies. The library contains 124,895 volumes and 201,159 microfilm items, and subscribes to 957 periodicals.

Environment: The riverfront urban campus is 60 miles from Detroit. The University Center includes a cafeteria, bookstore, student lounges, and a swimming pool. A physical education building is scheduled to open soon, and a new science building is being planned. There is no on-campus housing.

Student Life: About 99% of the students come from Michigan; 94% come from public schools. All students live off campus. Fifteen percent are minority-group members. Students may keep cars on campus.

Organizations: There are 3 local and 2 national fraternities to which 1% of the men belong; 1% of the women are members of the 3 local and 2 national sororities. Extracurricular activities are commuter oriented.

Sports: The school competes intercollegiately in several sports. There are 7 intramural sports for men and 4 for women.

Handicapped: Approximately 96% of the campus is accessible to the physically handicapped. Facilities include wheelchair ramps, special parking, elevators, specially equipped rest rooms, and lowered drinking fountains and telephones.

Graduates: The freshman dropout rate is 20%; 40% remain to graduate. Of those who graduate, 13% pursue advanced study.

Services: The following services are offered to students free of charge: placement, career counseling, health care, tutoring, remedial instruction, and psychological counseling. Placement services for undergraduates include job referrals, career planning, job counseling, and resume writing.

Programs of Study: The B.A., B.S., B.S.N., B.B.A., B.G.S., B. Applied Sc., and B.M.Ed. degrees are conferred. Master's degrees are also awarded. Bachelor's degrees are offered in the following subjects: AREA STUDIES (Black/Afro-American), BUSINESS (accounting, business administration, computer science), EDUCATION (early childhood, elementary, secondary, vocational), ENGLISH (English), FINE AND PERFORMING ARTS (music, music education, theater/dramatics), HEALTH SCIENCES (anesthesiology, health care, medical technology, nursing, physical therapy), LANGUAGES (French, German, Spanish), MATH AND SCIENCES (applied science, biology, botany, chemistry, mathematics, physical sciences, physics, zoology), PHILOSOPHY (philosophy, philosophy and psychology), PREPROFESSIONAL (dentistry, engineering, engineering and physical science, law, medicine, pharmacy), SOCIAL SCIENCES (anthropology, economics, government/political science, history, psychology, public administration, resource planning, social sciences, sociology, urban development). About 28% of degrees are conferred in social sciences, 27% in business, and 16% in education.

Required: All students must take courses in English composition, laboratory science, social sciences, and a foreign language if the major requires it.

Special: Independent study is offered.

Honors: There is an honors program for qualified students. Five honor societies have chapters on campus.

Admissions: About 82% of those who applied were accepted for the 1981-82 freshman class. The SAT scores of those who enrolled were as follows: Verbal—70% below 500, 19% between 500 and 599, 9% between 600 and 700, and 2% above 700; Math—49% below 500, 37% between 500 and 599, 9% between 600 and 700, and 5% above 700. On the ACT, 42% scored below 21, 20% between 21 and 23, 20% between 24 and 25, 13% between 26 and 28, and 5% above 28. A GPA of at least 2.7 is required. Advanced placement or honors courses, recommendations, and impressions made during an interview are also taken into consideration.

Procedure: The SAT or ACT is required. An interview is recommended, but not required. Application deadlines are August 19 (fall), December 21 (winter), March 30 (spring), and May 24 (summer). Notification is on a rolling basis. There is a $20 application fee.

Special: AP credit is accepted.

Transfer: For fall 1981, 848 transfer students applied, 757 were accepted, and 562 enrolled. Transfers are accepted for all classes except the senior year; D grades do not transfer. All students must complete at the university, approximately 60 of the 120-124 credits required for a bachelor's degree. Application deadlines are the same as those for freshman applicants.

Visiting: Freshman orientations are held weekly in July and August. Guides are available for informal visits; visitors may sit in on classes. The admissions office should be contacted to arrange visits.

Financial Aid: Approximately 30% of all students receive some form of financial aid. Ten percent work part-time on campus. Some freshman scholarships are offered by the university; the total amount of freshman scholarship aid available varies. Loans may be secured from the federal and state governments, local banks, the university, and other sources. The average freshman award is $1000. The FFS or FAF is required. Aid application deadlines are April 1 (spring or fall), November 1 (winter), and April 15 (summer); notification begins in mid-April for freshmen.

Foreign Students: Four percent of the full-time students come from foreign countries.

Admissions: Foreign students must achieve a TOEFL score of at least 550 or a University of Michigan Language Test score of at least 85. The ACT or SAT is required.

Procedure: Application deadlines are the same as those for other students. Foreign students must present proof of adequate funds.

Admissions Contact: Charles Rickard, Director of Admissions.

WAYNE STATE UNIVERSITY   E–5
Detroit, Michigan 48202   (313) 577-3581

F/T: 6025M, 6560W	Faculty: 1500; I, +$
P/T: 4499M, 4859W	Ph.D.'s: 85%
Grad: 4592M, 4987W	S/F Ratio: 18 to 1
Year: sems, ss	Tuition: $1670 ($3590)
Appl: Aug. 15	R and B: n/app
3956 accepted	2198 enrolled
SAT: 440V 490M ACT: 21	COMPETITIVE

Wayne State University, founded in 1868, is a state-supported university offering programs in 10 schools and colleges in the liberal arts and sciences, business, health fields, education, the arts, engineering and technological areas, and preprofessional areas. The library contains over 1.5 million volumes and nearly 300,000 microfilm items, and subscribes to 12,000 periodicals.

Environment: The 180-acre urban campus contains 107 buildings. There are a limited number of on-campus apartments.

Student Life: About 96% of the students come from Michigan; 80% come from public schools. Only about 1% live on campus. About 28% are minority-group members. Nine percent are Catholic, 9% are Protestant, and 1% are Jewish. The limited campus housing is both coed and single-sex; there are visiting privileges in the single-sex housing. Students may keep cars on campus. Day-care services are available to all students.

Organizations: Extracurricular activities are geared toward commuting students. There are 9 local fraternities and 10 local sororities. Clubs, service groups, performing groups, religious organizations, student government, and publications are some of the organizations.

Sports: The university fields 11 intercollegiate teams for men and 6 for women. There are 10 intramural sports for men and 5 for women.

Handicapped: About 85% of the campus is accessible to the physically handicapped. Facilities include wheelchair ramps, special parking, elevators, specially equipped rest rooms, lowered drinking fountains and telephones, special transportation, and specially designed housing. Special class scheduling is also available.

Graduates: About 63% of the graduates pursue advanced degrees, and 60% enter business and industry.

Services: The following services are offered to students free of charge: placement, career counseling, psychological counseling, and remedial instruction. Health care is available on a fee basis.

Programs of Study: The B.A., B.S., B.G.S., and B.F.A. degrees are conferred. Master's and doctoral degrees are also awarded. Bachelor's degrees are offered in the following subjects: AREA STUDIES (American, Asian), BUSINESS (business administration, computer science), EDUCATION (adult, early childhood, elementary, health/physical, industrial, secondary, special), ENGLISH (English, journalism, speech), FINE AND PERFORMING ARTS (art, art education, art history, film/photography, music, music education, radio/TV, studio art, theater/dramatics), LANGUAGES (French, German), MATH AND SCIENCES (biology, chemistry, geology, mathematics, physics), PHILOSOPHY (philosophy), PREPROFESSIONAL (dentistry, engineering, law, medicine, optometry, osteopathy, pharmacy, social work, veterinary), SOCIAL SCIENCES (anthropology, economics, geography, government/political science, history, psychology, public administration, sociology).

Required: All students must take courses in English and U.S. government.

Special: There are several study abroad options.

Honors: Several honor societies have chapters on campus; there are several honors programs for qualified students.

Admissions: The SAT scores of those who enrolled in the 1981–82 freshman class were as follows: Verbal—71% below 500, 20% between 500 and 599, 6% between 600 and 700, and 0% above 700; Math—48% below 500, 30% between 500 and 599, 16% between 600 and 700, and 1% above 700. On the ACT, 43% scored below 21, 23% between 21 and 23, 15% between 24 and 25, 16% between 26 and 28, and 2% above 28. Candidates should be graduates of accredited high schools, have a minimum GPA of 2.75, and have completed 15 Carnegie units. Other factors that enter into the admissions decision are the student's latest trend in grades, advanced placement or honors courses, evidence of special talents, extracurricular activities record, recommendations by school officials, and leadership record.

Procedure: The SAT or ACT is required. Application deadlines are August 15 (fall), December 15 (winter), and April 15 (spring and summer). Notification is on a rolling basis. There is a $15 application fee.

Special: There are early decision and early admissions plans. AP and CLEP credit is accepted.

Transfer: For fall 1981, 4082 students applied, 3162 were accepted, and 2187 enrolled. A 2.0 GPA is required; D grades do not transfer. All students must complete, at the university, 30 of the 120–136 credits required for a bachelor's degree. Application deadlines are the same as those for freshmen.

Visiting: There is an orientation program for prospective students. Visitors may tour the campus and sit in on classes.

Financial Aid: About 86% of all students receive some form of financial assistance. About 25% work part-time on campus. The university administers loans, grants, and CWS funds. The university is a member of the CSS; the FAF or SFS is required. The aid application deadline is April 1 (fall, spring, or summer) or September 1 (winter).

Foreign Students: About 17% of the full-time students come from foreign countries. An intensive English program, special counseling, and special organizations are available for these students.

Admissions: Foreign students must take the TOEFL. No college entrance exams are required.

Procedure: Application deadlines are May 1 (fall), October 1 (winter), and February 1 (spring or summer). Foreign students must present proof of funds adequate to cover 4 years of study. Health insurance is required and is available through the university for a fee.

Admissions Contact: Ronald C. Hughes, Director of Admissions.

WESTERN MICHIGAN UNIVERSITY   D–5
Kalamazoo, Michigan 49008   (616) 383-1950

F/T: 7311M, 6694W	Faculty: 840; I, –$
P/T: 1420M, 1414W	Ph.D.'s: 60%
Grad: 1600M, 1830W	S/F Ratio: 17 to 1
Year: split third term, ss	Tuition: $1195 ($2769)
Appl: open	R and B: $1900
7236 applied 5415 accepted	2793 enrolled
ACT: 20	COMPETITIVE

Western Michigan University, founded in 1903, is a state-supported institution offering undergraduate and graduate degree programs in the liberal arts and sciences, business, education, the health fields, and preprofessional areas. The library contains 1,186,919 volumes and 475,000 microfilm items, and subscribes to 11,000 periodicals.

Environment: The 830-acre campus is located in an urban area 140 miles from Detroit. There are 27 residence halls that accommodate 3600 women and 3200 men; apartments are available for 487 married students. The college also sponsors fraternity and sorority houses.

Student Life: About 90% of the students come from Michigan; 89% come from public schools. Thirty-five percent live on campus. Thirty-five percent of the students are Catholic, 32% are Protestant, and 2% are Jewish. About 6% are minority-group members. University housing is coed and single-sex; students in single-sex housing have visiting privileges. Students may keep cars on campus.

Organizations: There are 2 local and 15 national fraternities, to which 7% of the men belong; 7% of the women belong to 10 national sororities. On-campus groups include social, religious, political, and cultural organizations. Extracurricular activities are varied, numerous, and traditional.

Sports: The college fields 14 intercollegiate teams for men and 11 for women. There are 19 intramural sports for men and 15 for women.

Handicapped: Over 50% of the campus is accessible to the physically handicapped. Facilities include wheelchair ramps, special parking, elevators, specially equipped rest rooms, lowered drinking fountains

416 MICHIGAN

and telephones, braille-numbered elevators, curb cuts, and a van-wheelchair lift. Special class scheduling is also available. Two percent of the students currently enrolled have visual impairments. There are readers and books on tape for hearing-impaired students. Two counselors and 1 assistant are available to assist handicapped students.

Graduates: The freshman dropout rate is 30%, and 42% of the freshmen remain to graduate.

Services: The following services are offered to students free of charge: placement, career counseling, tutoring, and remedial instruction. Health care and psychological counseling are available for a combined fee per semester.

Programs of Study: The B.A., B.S., B.B.A., B.F.A., B.M., B.S. in E., B.S.W., and B.S. in Medicine degrees are awarded. Master's and doctoral degrees are also conferred. Bachelor's degrees are offered in the following subjects: AREA STUDIES (American, Asian, Black/Afro-American, European, Latin American, Medieval), BUSINESS (accounting, business administration, business education, computer science, finance, international business, management, marketing, operations research, real estate/insurance, retailing, secretarial studies, statistics, transportation), EDUCATION (adult, early childhood, elementary, health/physical, home economics, industrial, secondary, special), ENGLISH (communications, English, linguistics), FINE AND PERFORMING ARTS (art, art education, art history, dance, dance education, multi-media, music, music education, music history, music jazz, music performing, music theater, music theory and composition, music therapy, studio art, textile design, theater/dramatics, theater education), HEALTH SCIENCES (health care administration, medical technology, occupational therapy, physician's assistant, social work, speech therapy), LANGUAGES (French, German, Greek/Latin, Russian, Spanish), MATH AND SCIENCES (biochemistry, biology, chemistry, earth science, ecology/environmental science, geology, geophysics, mathematics, natural sciences, physical sciences, physics, science education, statistics), PHILOSOPHY (philosophy, religion), PRE-PROFESSIONAL (agriculture, architecture, dentistry, engineering, law, library science, medicine), SOCIAL SCIENCES (anthropology, criminology, economics, geography, government/political science, history, international relations, psychology, social sciences, sociology, tourism and travel). About 23% of degrees are conferred in business and 18% in education.

Special: Student-designed majors and cooperative degree programs are offered.

Honors: Honors work is offered in 11 departments and includes independent study with a senior year project. There are 9 honor societies on campus.

Admissions: About 75% of those who applied for the 1981–82 freshman class were accepted. The ACT scores of those who enrolled were as follows: 59% below 21, 20% between 21 and 23, 10% between 24 and 25, 9% between 26 and 28, and 2% above 28. A 2.5 high school GPA is required. Other factors considered in the admissions decision are advanced placement or honors courses and recommendations by school officials.

Procedure: The ACT is required. New students are admitted each term; application deadlines are open. Notification is on a rolling basis. There is a $15 application fee.

Special: AP and CLEP credit is accepted.

Transfer: For fall 1981, 3706 students applied, 2723 were accepted, and 1902 enrolled. A 2.0 GPA is required; standardized exam scores are recommended. D grades transfer if the applicant's overall GPA is 2.0 or better. Students must complete, at the university, at least 60 of the 122 credits necessary for a bachelor's degree. Applications are accepted until the final day of fall registration.

Visiting: There are regularly scheduled orientations for prospective students. Informal campus tours may be arranged; visitors may sit in on classes and stay overnight at the school. The tour coordinator in the undergraduate admissions office should be contacted to arrange visits.

Financial Aid: About 74% of all students receive some form of financial assistance. Fifty-two percent work part-time on campus. The university awards loans and grants. There are several freshman scholarships averaging $500 from a fund of $150,000. Loans are available from a federal government fund of $1.3 million, from a university fund, and from private sources. The college is a member of CSS and requires either the FAF or the FFS. The deadline for aid application is July 15 for fall entry; if there are remaining funds, additional deadlines are mid-December (winter), mid-March (spring) and mid-June (summer).

Foreign Students: Four percent of the full-time students come from foreign countries. The university offers these students an intensive English course and program, special counseling, and special organizations.

Admissions: Foreign students must achieve a minimum TOEFL score of 555 or a University of Michigan Language Test score of at least 85. No college entrance exam must be taken.

Procedure: Application deadlines for out-of-country students are June 15 (fall) and September 15 (winter); for in-country students, July 15 (fall) and October 15 (winter). Foreign students must present proof of funds adequate to cover their entire educational needs. They must also carry health insurance, which is available through the university for a fee.

Admissions Contact: David A. Morris, Associate Director.

MINNESOTA

AUGSBURG COLLEGE   C–4
Minneapolis, Minnesota 55454   (612) 330-1001

F/T: 653M, 771W   Faculty: 90; IIB, +$
P/T: 27M, 109W   Ph.D.'s: 57%
Grad: none   S/F Ratio: 13 to 1
Year: 4-1-4, ss   Tuition: $4300
Appl: Aug. 1   R and B: $2077
716 applied   624 accepted   365 enrolled
SAT: 420V 490M   ACT: 22   COMPETITIVE

Augsburg College, founded in 1869, is a private liberal arts college affiliated with the American Lutheran Church. Its library contains 160,000 volumes and subscribes to 750 periodicals.

Environment: The 22-acre campus is located in the center of the city and consists of 17 buildings, including high-rise dormitories and apartments. Off-campus apartments are also available. The University of Minnesota adjoins the college's campus.

Student Life: About 85% of the students come from Minnesota, and 90% come from public schools. About 70% live on campus. Five percent are members of minority groups. Sixty-six percent are Protestant (52% are Lutheran) and 15% are Catholic. Dormitories are both single-sex and coed; single-sex dorms have visiting privileges. Cars are permitted on campus.

Organizations: Extracurricular activities include special interest clubs, choir, concert band, orchestra, debating society, drama club, and political and religious organizations. Most of the social and cultural activities are sponsored by the student government.

Sports: The college sponsors intercollegiate teams in 9 sports for men and 5 for women. Two intramural sports are offered for men and 1 for women.

Handicapped: The entire campus is accessible to handicapped students. Facilities include wheelchair ramps, elevators, parking areas, and specially equipped rest rooms.

Graduates: About 25% of the freshmen drop out. Nine percent of the graduates continue their studies; 2% enter medical school, 1% enter law school, and 1% enter dental school.

Services: Free health care, tutoring, career counseling, and placement assistance are available.

Programs of Study: The college confers the B.A. and B.S. degrees. Bachelor's degrees are offered in the following subjects: AREA STUDIES (Asian, Russian, urban), BUSINESS (accounting, business administration, finance, international business, management, marketing), EDUCATION (early childhood, elementary, health/physical, secondary), ENGLISH (English), FINE AND PERFORMING ARTS (art, art education, art history, music, music education, studio art, theater/dramatics), HEALTH SCIENCES (corrective therapy, medical technology, music therapy, nursing), LANGUAGES (French, German, Norwegian, Spanish), MATH AND SCIENCES (biology, chemistry, mathematics, natural sciences, physics), PHILOSOPHY (philosophy, religion), PREPROFESSIONAL (social work), SOCIAL SCIENCES (economics, government/political science, history, international relations, psychology, social sciences, sociology).

Required: All undergraduates must take courses in English, history, religion, sociology, physical education, art or music, philosophy, a foreign language, natural science or mathematics, political science or economics, and speech or literature.

Special: Students may participate in numerous programs for overseas study and design their own majors.

Honors: Two honor societies have chapters on campus, and all departments offer honors programs.

Admissions: About 87% of all applicants were accepted for the 1981-82 freshman class. The SAT scores of those who enrolled were as follows: Verbal—61% below 500, 23% between 500 and 599, 14% between 600 and 700, and 2% above 700; Math—54% below 500, 29% between 500 and 599, 15% between 600 and 700, and 2% above 700. Of those who took the ACT, 54% scored below 21, 30% between 21 and 25, and 17% above 25. Applicants should have completed 15 Carnegie units and rank in the upper half of their graduating class. Advanced placement and honors courses, recommendations, impressions made during an interview, extracurricular activities, special talents, and personality are also considered.

Procedure: The PSAT, SAT, or ACT is required and should be taken by March. The fall application deadline is August 1. All applications should be accompanied by a $15 fee. Decisions are made on a rolling basis.

Special: Early decision and early admissions plans are available. AP and CLEP credit is accepted.

Transfer: For fall 1981, 222 applications were received, 200 were accepted, and 117 students enrolled. A GPA of 2.0 or better is required, and SAT scores of 450 on each part or an ACT composite of 21 is recommended. Students must complete the senior year in residence; 37 credits are required for a bachelor's degree.

Visiting: Visits can be arranged weekdays through the admissions office. Visitors may sit in on classes and stay overnight at the school.

Financial Aid: About 82% of all students are receiving aid; 34% work part-time on campus. The average award to freshmen from all sources in 1981-82 was $4000. The college is a member of CSS. The FAF or FFS is required. The deadline for applications is April 23.

Foreign Students: Foreign students enrolled full-time represent about 2% of the student body. Special counseling and special organizations are provided.

Admissions: Students must take the TOEFL, the University of Michigan Language Test, or the Comprehensive English Language Test. A minimum score of 520 on the TOEFL is required. No academic exams need be taken.

Procedure: Application deadlines are July 15 (fall) and December 15 (spring). Students must submit a completed college health form and provide evidence of adequate funds for 1 year. They must also carry health insurance, which is available through the college for a fee.

Admissions Contact: John Hjelmeland, Director of Admissions.

BEMIDJI STATE UNIVERSITY B-2
Bemidji, Minnesota 56601 (218) 755-2040

F/T: 2098M, 1938W	Faculty: 243; IIA, +$
P/T: 99M, 133W	Ph.D.'s: 44%
Grad: 63M, 87W	S/F Ratio: 16 to 1
Year: qtrs, ss	Tuition: $817 ($1465)
Appl: Aug. 15	R and B: $1365
1512 applied	1233 accepted	980 enrolled
ACT: 21		COMPETITIVE

Bemidji State University, founded in 1919, is a multi-purpose institution with programs in the liberal arts and teacher education. Its library contains 204,511 volumes and 440,614 reels of microfilm and subscribes to 854 periodicals.

Environment: The 89-acre campus is located in a rural area on the shores of Lake Bemidji, 230 miles north of Minneapolis. The dormitories accommodate 2000 students.

Student Life: About 90% of the students are from Minnesota; almost all come from public schools. About 52% of the students live on campus. Seven percent are minority-group members. University-sponsored housing is coed. Students may keep cars on campus.

Organizations: There are 4 fraternities and 5 sororities on campus, to which 7% of the students belong. The student government provides social and cultural entertainment on campus. There are religious organizations for Catholic and Protestant students.

Sports: The university fields 12 intercollegiate teams for men and 8 for women. It offers 12 intramural sports for men and 11 for women.

Handicapped: The entire campus is accessible to physically handicapped students, and facilities include wheelchair ramps, special parking, elevators, and specially equipped rest rooms. There are Opticon Readers, special tutoring and classes, and a speech pathologist for hearing-impaired students; taped text books are available for visually impaired students.

Graduates: The freshman dropout rate is 34%. Thirty-seven percent of freshmen remain to graduate. Nine percent of those who graduate continue their studies; 18% pursue careers in business and industry.

Services: Students receive free career and psychological counseling; health care, tutoring, and placement services are available for a fee.

Programs of Study: The university offers the B.A. and B.S. degrees. Associate and master's degrees are also available. Bachelor's degrees are offered in the following subjects: AREA STUDIES (American, Indian), BUSINESS (accounting, business administration, business education, computer science, office administration), EDUCATION (early childhood, elementary, health/physical, industrial, secondary), ENGLISH (English, journalism, speech), FINE AND PERFORMING ARTS (art, art education, music, music education, radio/TV, theater/dramatics), HEALTH SCIENCES (medical technology), LANGUAGES (French, German, Ojibwe, Spanish), MATH AND SCIENCES (biology, chemistry, earth science, ecology/environmental science, geology, mathematics, natural sciences, aquatic biology, physics), PHILOSOPHY (philosophy), PREPROFESSIONAL (agriculture, dentistry, engineering, fisheries and wildlife management, forestry, home economics, law, optometry, pharmacy, physical therapy, veterinary), SOCIAL SCIENCES (economics, geography, government/political science, history, psychology, social sciences, sociology). About 35% of the degrees are conferred in education.

Required: All students must fulfill requirements in freshman English.

Special: It is possible to earn a B.G.S. degree. Students can spend a year studying abroad.

Honors: The university has a full departmental honors program.

Admissions: Eighty-two percent of those who applied were accepted for the 1981-82 freshman class. The ACT scores of those who enrolled were as follows: 49% were below 21, 24% were between 21 and 23, 14% were between 24 and 25, 9% were between 26 and 28, and 4% were above 28. The candidates should have completed 15 Carnegie units and rank in the upper half of their graduating class. Out-of-state students must rank in the upper 40%. Qualities of leadership and recommendations may also be considered.

Procedure: The ACT, SAT, or PSAT is required. Application deadlines are August 15 (fall), November 1 (winter), February 7 (spring), and May 9 (summer). Freshmen are admitted for all quarters. A $10 fee should accompany the application form. A rolling admissions policy is used.

Special: There is a deferred admissions plan. AP and CLEP credit is offered. Early decisions are possible upon special request.

Transfer: For fall 1981, 555 applications were received, 467 were accepted, and 300 students enrolled. The minimum recommended GPA is 2.0 (1.75 is required for the first year; 1.9 for the second year; 2.0 for any work completed past the second year). D grades do not transfer. A student must take 45 quarter hours in residence for a bachelor's degree, which requires a total of 180 quarter hours. The application deadlines are the same as those for freshman applicants.

Visiting: A formal orientation program is held for new students. Prospective students can visit and stay at the school; arrangements are made by the admissions office.

Financial Aid: Ninety percent of the students receive aid; 32% work part-time on campus. The university awards about $65,000 in scholarships and grants each year. The average award to freshmen from all sources is $2346. The FAF or FFS should be filed. The aid application deadline for fall entry is April 23 (for priority consideration); for the other quarters, the deadlines are 60 days prior to the beginning of the quarter.

Foreign Students: About 1% of the full-time students come from foreign countries. The university offers these students special counseling and organizations.

Admissions: Foreign students must achieve a minimum TOEFL score of 550. No other exams are required.

Procedure: The university recommends that foreign students apply several months in advance of the quarter to which they seek admission. Foreign students must present proof of funds adequate to cover one year of study. They must also carry health insurance, which is available through the university for a fee.

Admissions Contact: Jon Quistgaard, Director of Admissions.

418 MINNESOTA

BETHEL COLLEGE   C-4
St. Paul, Minnesota 55112   (612) 638-6242

F/T: 932M, 1155W	Faculty: 100; IIB, +$
P/T: 32M, 61W	Ph.D.'s: 70%
Grad: none	S/F Ratio: 21 to 1
Year: 4-1-4, ss	Tuition: $4035
Appl: July 1	R and B: $1925
979 applied	811 accepted	642 enrolled
ACT: 23		COMPETITIVE+

Bethel College is a liberal arts institution operated by the Baptist Church. The college has a close identity with a theological seminary sharing the same general administration and board. The library contains 115,000 volumes and subscribes to 640 periodicals.

Environment: The college's campus is located in a suburban area, 10 miles from Minneapolis. Freshmen are housed in dorm units. Upperclassmen are accommodated in 2 townhouse quadrangles or in college-owned off-campus apartments.

Student Life: About 59% of the students come from Minnesota; 40% are from other states. About 90% of the students are Protestant, 2% are Catholic, and 8% claim no religious affiliation. Although the majority of students are members of the Baptist Church, there is no requirement to attend services. The college prohibits drinking and smoking, and asks students to refrain from social dancing. About 1% of the students are minority-group members. College housing is single-sex, and there are visiting privileges. Students may keep cars on campus.

Organizations: A student association functions through a series of councils and provides most extracurricular activities, including a wide range of special-interest clubs in addition to the school-sponsored convocation series, lectures, and special missionary and religious emphasis weeks.

Sports: The college fields 12 intercollegiate teams and offers 4 intramural sports.

Handicapped: Special facilities for the physically handicapped include wheelchair ramps, special parking, elevators, specially equipped rest rooms, lowered drinking fountains, and lowered telephones.

Graduates: Sixty percent of entering freshmen remain to graduate. About 30% of the students seek higher degrees after graduation. In addition, many pursue careers in business and industry.

Services: Students receive the following services free of charge: placement and career counseling, health care, tutoring, and psychological counseling. Remedial instruction is available for a fee.

Programs of Study: The college offers the B.A. degree. Associate degrees are also awarded. Bachelor's degrees are offered in the following subjects: BUSINESS (accounting, business administration, computer science, management), EDUCATION (early childhood, elementary, health/physical, secondary), ENGLISH (English, journalism, literature, speech), FINE AND PERFORMING ARTS (art, art education, music, music education, theater/dramatics), HEALTH SCIENCES (nursing), LANGUAGES (French, German, Greek, Hebrew, Spanish), MATH AND SCIENCES (biology, chemistry, mathematics, natural sciences, physics), PHILOSOPHY (philosophy, religion), PREPROFESSIONAL (agriculture, dentistry, engineering, law, medicine, ministry, social work, veterinary), SOCIAL SCIENCES (anthropology, economics, government/political science, history, psychology, sociology). About 23% of the degrees awarded are in social sciences.

Required: All students must satisfy requirements in a broad distribution of liberal studies courses; physical education and Bible are also required.

Special: Student-designed majors are allowed. Third-year students may receive permission to study abroad. A 3-2 program in engineering is offered in conjunction with other schools.

Admissions: About 83% of those who applied were accepted for the 1981-82 freshman class. Of those who enrolled, about 10% had ACT scores below 21, about 30% between 21 and 23, 30% between 24 and 25, 20% between 26 and 28, and 10% above 28. Candidates must rank in the upper half of their graduating class and present strong recommendations from pastors and high school officials. Other factors that may be considered are advanced placement or honor courses, extracurricular activities, and leadership potential. Each student must also submit a statement of faith in Jesus Christ.

Procedure: Candidates must take the SAT, PSAT, or ACT by January of the senior year. The deadlines for application are July 1 (fall), December 1 (interim-winter), and January 1 (spring). There is a rolling admissions plan. A $10 application fee must be paid.

Special: AP credit is accepted.

Transfer: For fall 1981, 301 transfer students applied for admission; 260 were accepted, and 176 enrolled. A C average (minimum GPA of 2.0) is required. A minimum ACT score of 19 is necessary for admission, and an interview is recommended. Grades of 2.0 and above transfer. There is a 1-year residency requirement. Thirty-two of the 136 semester hours required for the bachelor's degree must be completed at the college.

Visiting: There are regularly scheduled orientations for prospective students. Informal guided tours and classroom visits can also be arranged. Prospective students should contact the campus-visit secretary in the admissions office for further information.

Financial Aid: About 85% of the students receive aid. Thirty percent work part-time on campus. The college requires the FFS or FAF. March 1 is the priority-consideration deadline for fall, winter, spring, and summer entry.

Foreign Students: Ten of the full-time students are from foreign countries. The college offers students special organizations and counseling.

Admissions: The TOEFL is required, as well as the SAT. The minimum SAT score accepted is 825 (total Verbal and Math).

Procedure: Application deadlines for foreign students are July 1 (fall), December 1 (winter), and January 1 (spring). Foreign students are also admitted for the summer sessions. Foreign students must present proof of adequate funds for one year of study. They must also carry health insurance, which is available through the college for a fee.

Admissions Contact: Philip Kimball, Director of Admissions.

CARLETON COLLEGE   C-4
Northfield, Minnesota 55057   (507) 663-4190

F/T: 931M, 919W	Faculty: 133; IIB, ++$
P/T: 9M, 10W	Ph.D.'s: 85%
Grad: none	S/F Ratio: 12 to 1
Year: 3-3-3	Tuition: $5755
Appl: Feb. 1	R and B: $2225
2003 applied	1021 accepted	480 enrolled
SAT: 600V 630M	ACT: 28	HIGHLY COMPETITIVE+

Carleton College was originally established by the Congregational Church in 1866, but is now privately owned and nonsectarian. Its library contains over 300,000 volumes and 46,000 reels of microfilm, and subscribes to over 1100 periodicals.

Environment: The 1000-acre campus is located in a rural setting 35 miles from Minneapolis and contains 8 academic buildings and 9 dormitories. There are also off-campus college-owned houses.

Student Life: About 70% of the students are from outside Minnesota, and 85% come from public schools. About 95% of the students live on campus. About 10% of the students are minority-group members. Campus housing is both single-sex and coed. There are visiting privileges in single-sex housing. Students are not permitted to keep cars on campus.

Organizations: There are no fraternities or sororities represented on campus, but student organizations sponsor social and cultural entertainment.

Sports: The college competes in 14 intercollegiate sports for men and 12 for women. It also offers 6 intramural programs for men and 5 for women.

Handicapped: Facilities available for handicapped students include wheelchair ramps, elevators, specially equipped rest rooms, and special class scheduling, but a large percentage of the campus is inaccessible to wheelchair students.

Graduates: Six percent of freshmen drop out by the end of the first year. About 75% remain to graduate. Between 65% and 75% of the graduates pursue studies on the graduate level. Of these, 8% enter medical school, about 1% enter dental school, and 6% enter law school. Another 20% pursue careers in business and industry.

Services: Free health care, tutoring, psychological and career counseling, and placement are available to students. Summer work and lifetime placement services are offered to graduates.

Programs of Study: All programs lead to the B.A. degree. Bachelor's degrees are offered in the following subjects: AREA STUDIES (American, Asian, Black/Afro-American, Latin American, Russian, urban), ENGLISH (English), FINE AND PERFORMING ARTS (art history, film/photography, music, studio art), LANGUAGES (French, German, Greek/Latin, Russian, Spanish), MATH AND SCIENCES (biology, chemistry, ecology/environmental science, geology, mathematics, physics), PHILOSOPHY (classics, philosophy, religion), SOCIAL SCIENCES (economics, government/political science, history, international relations, psychology, sociology/anthropology). About 36% of degrees conferred are in math and sciences, and 35% are in social sciences.

Required: Each student must demonstrate proficiency in writing and a foreign language, and is required to take 12 credits in humanities, 18 credits in math and science, 18 credits in social sciences, and 12 credits in history, philosophy, or religion. A senior integrative exercise is required.

Special: The college offers 3-2 programs in engineering and nursing, and a 3-3 program in law. A Junior Year Abroad program and independent study are available. Students can also design their own majors. The Morgan Fellows Program gives students the opportunity to follow an unconventional, individualized program, which may or may not include distribution requirements. Students may also do a concentration within a standard major in science, technology, and public policy or in computer science.

Honors: Phi Beta Kappa and Sigma Xi honor societies are represented on campus.

Admissions: Fifty-one percent of those who applied were accepted for the 1981–82 freshman class. The SAT scores of those who enrolled were as follows: Verbal—7% below 500, 30% between 500 and 599, 41% between 600 and 700, and 12% above 700; Math—6% below 500, 25% between 500 and 599, 43% between 600 and 700, and 18% above 700. The candidates should have completed 15 Carnegie units, rank in the upper 20% of their graduating class, and have a B average. Advanced placement or honors courses, recommendations, leadership record, and special talents also play a major part in consideration.

Procedure: The SAT or ACT should be taken by February of the senior year. Three ATs are recommended, including English Composition. Applications for the fall term should be filed by February 1, along with a $25 fee.

Special: Early and deferred admissions are available. Candidates for an early decision must apply by December 1 of their senior year (fall option) or February 2 (winter option). AP credit is available.

Transfer: For fall 1981, 89 students applied, 19 were accepted, and 16 enrolled. Good academic standing and a B average are required; D grades do not transfer. The SAT or ACT is required. A minimum GPA of 3.0 and an interview are recommended. Two years of study must be taken in residence, and students must complete, at the college, 102 of the 204 credits required for a bachelor's degree. Application deadlines are April 15 (fall), November 15 (winter), and March 1 (spring).

Visiting: Visits are possible during the academic year. Guides are provided for informal tours; visitors may sit in on classes. Arrangements can be made to stay at the school.

Financial Aid: Forty-eight percent of the students receive some form of financial aid from the college. Seventy-one percent work part-time on campus. The average award to freshmen is $4477. The college is a member of CSS. The FFS (for Minnesota residents) or FAF must be filed. Applications for financial aid should be filed by February 15 for the fall.

Foreign Students: One percent of the full-time students come from foreign countries. The college offers these students special counseling and special organizations.

Admissions: Foreign students must take the TOEFL. They may take the SAT in lieu of the TOEFL. No minimum scores are required.

Procedure: The application deadline is February 1 for the fall. Foreign students must present the college's own health form completed by a physician. They must also present proof of funds adequate for 1 year of study.

Admissions Contact: Richard Steele, Dean of Admissions.

COLLEGE OF ST. BENEDICT
C–3
Saint Joseph, Minnesota 56374 (612) 363-5308

F/T: 1700W	Faculty: 90; n/av
P/T: none	Ph.D.'s: 49%
Grad: none	S/F Ratio: 17 to 1
Year: 4-1-4	Tuition: $3690
Appl: Apr. 1	R and B: $1610
991 applied	910 accepted 592 enrolled
SAT: 500V 500M	ACT: 22 COMPETITIVE

The College of St. Benedict, founded in 1913, is a Roman Catholic liberal arts institution for women. Its library contains 140,000 volumes and subscribes to 700 periodicals.

Environment: The 700-acre campus is located in a rural area 65 miles from Minneapolis. There are 7 dormitories and 2 apartment complexes for the students who live on campus. The college also sponsors off-campus apartments.

Student Life: About 85% of the students come from Minnesota; 75% of entering freshmen come from public schools. Ninety percent of the students live on campus. Eighty-five percent of the students are Catholic; 15% are Protestant. Fewer than 1% are minority-group members. There are visiting privileges in college housing. Students may keep cars on campus.

Organizations: There are no social sororities, but students may participate in student government. Special-interest clubs offer social and cultural activities.

Sports: The college participates in 6 intercollegiate sports; 10 intramural programs are offered.

Handicapped: About 90% of the campus is accessible to the physically handicapped and there are special facilities for them including wheelchair ramps, elevators, special parking, specially equipped rest rooms, and special class scheduling.

Graduates: Twenty-four percent of the freshmen drop out by the end of the first year; 55% remain to graduate. About 10% of the graduates go on to graduate school; 3% enter medical school; 3%, dental school; and 3%, law school. Forty percent of the graduates enter business and industry.

Services: The school provides free placement, psychological and career counseling, tutoring, and remedial instruction. Health care is available for a fee. Placement services, which include internships, resume workshops, and job files, are also available to alumnae.

Programs of Study: The B.A., B.S., and B.Mus. degrees are offered. Associate degrees are also awarded. Bachelor's degrees are offered in the following subjects: AREA STUDIES (family studies, liberal studies), BUSINESS (accounting, business administration, computer science), EDUCATION (early childhood, elementary, family life, religious, secondary), ENGLISH (English), FINE AND PERFORMING ARTS (art, art education, art history, liturgical music, music, music education, theater/dramatics), HEALTH SCIENCES (medical technology, nursing, physical therapy), LANGUAGES (French, German, Greek/Latin, Spanish), MATH AND SCIENCES (biology, chemistry, mathematics, natural sciences, physics), PHILOSOPHY (humanities, philosophy, theology), PREPROFESSIONAL (dentistry, engineering, forestry, home economics, home maker rehabilitation, law, medicine, pharmacy, social work, veterinary), SOCIAL SCIENCES (economics, government-political science, history, psychology, social sciences, sociology). Over 20% of the degrees conferred recently were in education, and 14% were in health sciences.

Required: The college operates on a competency-based system of general educational requirements.

Special: Students are allowed to design their own majors, work on projects, do independent study, and travel. The college has a cooperative program with a nearby men's college. Students may earn a B.G.S. or a combined B.A.-B.S. degree.

Honors: Delta Epsilon Sigma is represented on campus, and an honors program exists for exceptional students.

Admissions: Ninety-two percent of those who applied were accepted for the 1981–82 freshman class. Of those who enrolled, the ACT scores were as follows: 26% below 21, 22% between 21 and 23, 27% between 24 and 25, 19% between 26 and 28, and 6% above 28. The candidate should have completed 15 Carnegie units, have a C+ average, and rank in the upper half of her graduating class. Advanced placement or honor courses and recommendations, as well as leadership and extracurricular activities records, are also important.

Procedure: Either the ACT or SAT is required and should be taken in May or August of the junior year or December of the senior year. The application deadlines are April 1 (fall) and November 15 (spring). All applications should be accompanied by a $10 fee. There is a rolling admissions plan.

Special: Deferred admission is possible. AP and CLEP credit is available.

Transfer: For fall 1981, 131 transfer students applied, 128 were accepted, and 93 enrolled. Almost all applications are accepted as long as students have an overall C average or better. D grades transfer if the GPA is 2.0 or above. A minimum of 30 of the 124 credits required for the bachelor's degree must be taken in residence. Application deadlines for transfer students are March 1 (fall) and November 15 (spring). A $15 fee must accompany the application.

Visiting: Visits to the school can be arranged through the office of admissions while school is in session.

420 MINNESOTA

Financial Aid: Eighty-eight percent of the students receive financial aid in the form of scholarships, grants, loans, and CWS. Forty percent of the students work part-time on campus. The average award to freshmen from all sources is $3625. The college is a member of CSS and requires the FFS or FAF. The deadlines for financial aid applications are March 1 (fall) and November 15 (spring).

Foreign Students: Thirty-eight foreign students are enrolled at the college. The college offers foreign students special counseling and organizations.

Admissions: The TOEFL is required; the minimum score accepted is 500. Foreign students must also take the SAT or the ACT. Minimum scores required are 500 Verbal and 500 Math on the SAT and 22 on the ACT.

Procedure: Application deadlines for foreign students are March 1 (fall) and November 15 (spring). Foreign students must present proof of health in the form of a physical exam. They must also give proof of funds adequate to cover their entire stay at the college. In addition, they must carry health insurance, which is available through the college for a fee.

Admissions Contact: Mary Milbert, Admissions Counselor.

COLLEGE OF ST. CATHERINE C-4
St. Paul, Minnesota 55105 (612) 690-6506

F/T: 1816W	Faculty:	148; IIB, +$
P/T: 551W	Ph.D.'s:	32%
Grad: 2498W	S/F Ratio:	15 to 1
Year: 4-1-4, ss	Tuition:	$3815
Appl: open	R and B:	$1900
765 applied	697 accepted	450 enrolled
SAT: 500V 510M	ACT: 22	COMPETITIVE

The College of St. Catherine, founded in 1905, is a Catholic liberal arts institution conducted by the Sisters of St. Joseph of Carondelet. The library contains 200,000 volumes and several thousand microfilm items, and subscribes to 1000 periodicals.

Environment: The 110-acre campus is located in an urban residential area, midway between St. Paul and Minneapolis. There are 15 buildings including a fine arts complex that contains an 1800-seat auditorium, an experimental theater, and a recital hall. Eight residence halls and 2 on-campus apartment buildings offer a variety of living situations.

Student Life: About 80% of the students come from Minnesota; nearly 50% of all students live on campus. The majority (80%) of students are Catholic; attendance at services, however, is not required. About 3% of the students are minority-group members. College-sponsored housing is single-sex, and there are visiting privileges. Students may keep cars on campus. Day-care facilities are available to all students, faculty, and staff for a fee.

Organizations: Student government is an important part of college life, and all students are members of the student association. Many extracurricular activities are offered. Off-campus cultural attractions include the Tyrone Guthrie Theater and the St. Paul Chamber Orchestra.

Sports: The college competes on an intercollegiate level in 8 sports. There are 7 intramural sports.

Handicapped: The campus is almost completely accessible to the physically handicapped. Special facilities include wheelchair ramps, parking, elevators, special class scheduling, and specially equipped rest rooms. A counselor is also available.

Graduates: The freshman dropout rate is 19%. Sixty percent of entering freshmen remain to graduate. About 25% of the students go on for further study: 2% enter medical school, 1% enter dental school, and 3% enter law school. Approximately 12% pursue careers in business and industry.

Services: Students receive the following services free of charge: placement and career counseling, health care, tutoring, and psychological counseling. Placement and career counseling services are also available to alumnae.

Programs of Study: The college awards the B.A. degree. Bachelor's degrees are offered in the following subjects: AREA STUDIES (Russian), BUSINESS (accounting, business administration, business education, computer science, finance, management, marketing), EDUCATION (early childhood, elementary, health/physical, secondary), ENGLISH (English, journalism, literature, speech), FINE AND PERFORMING ARTS (art, art education, dance, music, music education, radio/TV, theater/dramatics), HEALTH SCIENCES (medical technology, nursing, occupational therapy), LANGUAGES (French, German, Greek/Latin, Japanese, Russian, Spanish), MATH AND SCIENCES (biology, chemistry, geology, mathematics, physics), PHILOSOPHY (classics, humanities, philosophy, religion), PREPROFESSIONAL (dentistry, engineering, home economics, law, library science, medicine, pharmacy, social work, veterinary), SOCIAL SCIENCES (economics, government/political science, history, international relations, psychology, social sciences, sociology). About 21% of the degrees conferred are in health sciences; 12% are in business.

Required: Courses in history/social science, fine arts/literature, foreign language through the intermediate level (not required of junior transfer students), mathematics/laboratory science, philosophy/theology, and physical education are required of all students.

Special: Student-designed majors are allowed. An exchange program exists with the College of St. Thomas, Augsburg College, Hamline University, and Macalester College. There are also many opportunities for foreign travel. Students may participate in a 3-2 engineering program with Washington University in St. Louis. The Weekend College division offers a special program of studies.

Honors: There are 13 national honor societies on campus. Many departments offer honors programs.

Admissions: Ninety-one percent of those who applied were accepted for the 1981–82 freshman class. Of those who enrolled, the SAT scores were as follows: Verbal—60% scored below 500, 33% between 500 and 599, 9% between 600 and 700, and 2% above 700; Math—60% scored below 500, 31% between 500 and 599, 10% between 600 and 700, and none above 700. On the ACT, 26% scored below 21, 20% between 21 and 23, 15% between 24 and 25, 29% between 26 and 28, and 3% above 28. Applicants are expected to have followed a college preparatory program in high school and should have a minimum GPA of 2.0. They should be in the upper half of their class. Other important factors are advanced placement or honor courses, recommendations, leadership record, and impressions made during interview.

Procedure: Either the SAT, PSAT, or ACT should be taken by December of the senior year. Students are encouraged to apply by January of their senior year for fall admission. There is a $15 application fee. Day students are accepted through the month of August. The college has a rolling admissions plan.

Special: Early decision, early admissions, and deferred admissions plans are available.

Transfer: For fall 1981, 306 transfer students applied for admission; 152 enrolled. A GPA of 2.0 is required. D grades transfer. Four semesters must be taken in residence. The fall semester application deadline is April 1; the spring semester deadline is December 31.

Visiting: Regularly scheduled orientations are held for prospective students. Guided tours and classroom visits can also be arranged. Applicants should contact the admissions office for further information.

Financial Aid: About 58% of the students receive financial aid. Seventy percent work part-time on campus. Scholarships, loans, and campus employment are available. Scholarships range from $100 to $1900; loans range from $100 to $1500. The FAF or FFS is required. The aid application deadline is February 15.

Foreign Students: The college actively recruits foreign students. It offers them special counseling and organizations.

Admissions: The TOEFL is required, and the minimum score accepted is 400–450. No other examinations are required.

Procedure: Foreign students are admitted for the fall and spring semesters. They must present proof of adequate funds for study at the college. They must also carry health insurance, which is available for free through the college.

Admissions Contact: Darcy M. Welch, Admissions Counselor.

COLLEGE OF ST. SCHOLASTICA D-3
Duluth, Minnesota 55811 (218) 723-6046

F/T: 187M, 720W	Faculty:	70; IIB, −$
P/T: 20M, 121W	Ph.D.'s:	34%
Grad: 6W	S/F Ratio:	13 to 1
Year: qtrs, ss	Tuition:	$3730
Appl: Sept. 1	R and B:	$1890
462 applied	448 accepted	211 enrolled
SAT or ACT: required		COMPETITIVE

The College of St. Scholastica, founded in 1912 as a women's junior college, became coeducational in 1969. It is affiliated with the Roman Catholic Church. The curriculum particularly emphasizes health careers and teacher education. Its library contains 87,000 volumes and subscribes to 619 periodicals.

Environment: The 160-acre campus is located in a suburban area 10 minutes from Duluth and contains 5 academic buildings as well as dormitories. There are also on-campus apartments. Nearby, St. Mary's Hospital offers facilities for majors in nursing, medical technology, and medical record science.

Student Life: About 85% of the students are from Minnesota; 45% of all students live on campus. About one-half of the students are Catholic; 25% are Protestant. Church attendance is not compulsory. State laws govern drinking; smoking is permitted in designated areas. Students may keep cars on campus. The college provides day-care services to students, faculty, and staff.

Organizations: There are no fraternities or sororities on campus. An active student government provides social and cultural programs. Other social and political organizations are also represented on campus.

Sports: The college fields 5 intercollegiate teams for men and 4 for women. There are 6 intramural sports for men and 6 for women.

Handicapped: Ninety percent of the campus is accessible to handicapped students, and facilities include wheelchair ramps, special parking, elevators, and specially equipped rest rooms. Special class scheduling is also available.

Graduates: The freshman dropout rate is 28%; 48% remain to graduate, and 11% pursue studies on a higher level. Of the latter, 4% enter medical school, 1% enter dental school, and 3% enter law school. Another 19% pursue careers in business and industry.

Services: Free placement, career and psychological counseling, tutoring, and remedial instruction are available to students. Health care is available for a fee.

Programs of Study: The college awards the B.A. degree. Master's degrees are also offered. Bachelor's degrees are offered in the following subjects: AREA STUDIES (American Indian), BUSINESS (computer science, management), EDUCATION (early childhood, elementary, secondary), ENGLISH (English, literature), FINE AND PERFORMING ARTS (film/photography, music, music education, radio/TV), HEALTH SCIENCES (dietetics, medical records administration, medical technology, nursing, physical therapy), MATH AND SCIENCES (actuarial science, biology, chemistry, mathematics, natural sciences), PHILOSOPHY (humanities, religion), PREPROFESSIONAL (dentistry, engineering, home economics, law, medicine, pharmacy, social work), SOCIAL SCIENCES (history, psychology, social sciences, sociology). About 60% of degrees conferred are in health sciences.

Special: A combination degree in engineering is possible, as is a B.G.S. degree. Students may create their own majors.

Honors: The Alpha Chi and Kappa Gamma Pi honor societies are represented on campus. There are also departmental honors programs.

Admissions: Ninety-seven percent of those who applied for the 1981-82 freshman class were accepted. Of those who enrolled and took the ACT, scores were as follows: 52% scored below 21, 16% between 21 and 23, 14% between 24 and 25, 11% between 26 and 28, and 7% above 28. Candidates should have completed 15 Carnegie units and rank in the upper half of their graduating class. Recommendations by school officials, advanced placement or honors courses, and impressions made during the interview are also considered.

Procedure: Either the ACT, PSAT, or SAT should be taken. Application deadlines are September 1 (fall), November 20 (winter), March 1 (spring), and May 15 (summer). All applications should be accompanied by a $10 fee. There is a rolling admissions plan.

Special: There is a deferred admissions plan. AP and CLEP credit is offered.

Transfer: For fall 1981, 238 transfer students applied; 163 were accepted, and 99 enrolled. A 2.0 GPA is required, and D grades do not transfer. For those with a GPA below 2.0, a second-chance program is available. There is a 1-year residency requirement; 48 of the 192 quarter hours required for a bachelor's degree must be taken at the college. Application deadlines are the same as for freshmen. Special transfer programs are offered for nursing and physical therapy students.

Visiting: Visits can be arranged through the admissions office and are best made during school sessions. Guides are available for informal tours. Visitors can sit in on classes and may stay at the school.

Financial Aid: Eighty-one percent of the students receive aid. Twenty-five percent work part-time on campus. The college is a member of CSS and awards scholarships from a fund totaling $150,000 each year. The average freshman award from all sources available through the college is $4062. The FAF or FFS (preferred) is required, along with the Institutional Data form. The deadline for aid application is April 23.

Foreign Students: Eight students from foreign countries are enrolled full-time. The college offers foreign students special counseling.

Admissions: The TOEFL or the University of Michigan Language Test is required. The minimum scores accepted are 550 on the TOEFL and an average of 85 on the University of Michigan Language Test.

Procedure: The application deadline is August 1 for fall entry. Foreign students must present proof of funds adequate for 1 year of study. They must also carry health insurance, which is available through the college for a fee.

Admissions Contact: James R. Buxton, Director of Admissions.

COLLEGE OF SAINT TERESA D-5
Winona, Minnesota 55987 (507) 454-2930

F/T: 10M, 600W Faculty: 65; IIB, −$
P/T: 5M, 120W Ph.D.'s: 35%
Grad: none S/F Ratio: 10 to 1
Year: qtrs Tuition: $4041
Appl: open R and B: $1800
355 applied 320 accepted 160 enrolled
SAT: 420V 430M ACT: 21 LESS COMPETITIVE

The College of Saint Teresa, established in 1907, is a private, church-related women's college for the liberal arts and the professions under the auspices of the Sisters of Saint Francis. The library houses 250,000 volumes and subscribes to 638 periodicals.

Environment: The 75-acre rural campus is located in the small town of Winona, 150 miles southeast of Minneapolis-St. Paul. Four residence halls accommodate 950 women.

Student Life: About 50% of the students are from Minnesota, and 95% live on campus. Eighty-five percent of the students are Catholic and 15% are Protestant. About 7% are minority-group members. Campus housing is single-sex; there are visiting privileges. Students are permitted to keep cars on campus. Day-care services are available.

Organizations: There are no fraternities or sororities. Extracurricular activities are organized by the student government, which also channels student action and opinion.

Sports: The college competes in 5 intercollegiate sports for women and offers 7 intramural programs for women.

Handicapped: The entire campus is accessible, and special facilities include ramps and elevators.

Graduates: The freshman dropout rate is 28%; 55% remain to graduate. About 20% of the graduates pursue advanced study; 3% enter medical school and 3% enter law school. Another 5% pursue careers in business and industry.

Services: Free career and psychological counseling, health care, tutoring, and remedial instruction are available. Placement services are also available, for a fee.

Programs of Study: The college confers the B.A., B.S., and B.S.W. degrees. Bachelor's degrees are offered in the following subjects: BUSINESS (accounting, business administration, business education, computer science, management), EDUCATION (early childhood, elementary, secondary), ENGLISH (English, journalism), FINE AND PERFORMING ARTS (art, art education, dance, music, music education, studio art, theater/dramatics), HEALTH SCIENCES (art therapy, dance therapy, medical technology, music therapy, nursing, physical therapy, speech therapy), LANGUAGES (French, German, Spanish), MATH AND SCIENCES (biology, mathematics), PHILOSOPHY (humanities, religion), PREPROFESSIONAL (dentistry, engineering, home economics, law, medicine, social work), SOCIAL SCIENCES (criminal justice, government/political science, history, psychology, social sciences, sociology). About 35% of the degrees conferred are in nursing.

Special: There is a study-abroad program, and students may create their own majors.

Honors: Honor and professional societies are open to eligible students.

Admissions: About 90% of those who applied were accepted for the 1981-82 freshman class. ACT scores of those who enrolled were as follows: 26% below 21, 23% between 21 and 23, 6% between 24 and 25, 7% between 26 and 28, and 7% above 28. Candidates for admission should have completed 15 Carnegie units and rank in the upper half of their graduating class. A minimum high school average of 2.0 is required. Recommendations and the student's interests, talents, and goals are also considered.

422 MINNESOTA

Procedure: Either the SAT or ACT must be taken; the PSAT is accepted if scores are at least 400 on each part. The college follows a rolling admissions plan. Freshmen are admitted for the fall, spring, and winter sessions. There are no application deadlines. A $15 application fee is required.

Special: There is an early admissions program.

Transfer: For fall 1981, 50 transfer students applied, 45 were accepted, and 42 enrolled. Students may not ordinarily transfer for the senior year, and D grades are not acceptable. A minimum GPA of 2.0 (2.5 is recommended) and SAT scores of at least 400 on each part or an ACT score of at least 16 are required. There is a 1-year residency requirement, and students must complete, at the college, 48 of the 192 quarter hours required for the bachelor's degree. A rolling admissions policy is used.

Visitors: Visits and tours can be arranged through the admissions office.

Financial Aid: Aid includes scholarships, grants, work contracts, and loans. The college participates in the BEOG, EOG, NDSL, CWS, and NSL programs. Fifty percent of the students work part-time on campus. Financial aid is awarded on the basis of academic achievement and need; applicants must file the FFS or FAF with CSS. About 75% of all students receive financial assistance; the average award to freshmen from all sources was $3100 in 1981–82.

Foreign Students: About 3% of the students are from foreign countries. An intensive English course, special counseling, and special organizations are available for these students.

Admissions: Minimum scores of 550 on the TOEFL, and 16 on the ACT or 400 on each part of the SAT are required.

Procedure: Foreign students are admitted for the fall, winter, and spring terms. There are no application deadlines. Students must present a health examination form signed by a physician, and must submit evidence of adequate funds for 1 year. Health insurance is not required, but is available through the college for a fee.

Admissions Contact: Sr. Katarina Schuth, Dean of Admissions.

COLLEGE OF ST. THOMAS   C–4
St. Paul, Minnesota 55105   (612) 647-5265

F/T, P/T:	Faculty: 265; IIA, av$
3470 M&W	Ph.D.'s: 45%
Grad: 1811M&W	S/F Ratio: 19 to 1
Year: 4-1-4, ss	Tuition: $3550
Appl: see profile	R and B: $1800
SAT or ACT: required	COMPETITIVE

The College of St. Thomas, founded in 1885, is an independent, coeducational, Roman Catholic liberal arts college. The college is a member of the Associated Colleges of the Twin Cities, which permits students to register for exchange courses at Augsburg College, Hamline University, and Macalester College. Its library contains 195,000 volumes and 1300 microfilm reels, and subscribes to 1100 periodicals.

Environment: The 45-acre campus contains 19 buildings, which include residence halls housing 900 students.

Student Life: Over 85% of the students come from Minnesota. About 30% live on campus.

Organizations: About 15% of the students belong to 1 of the 6 fraternities and 2 sororities. The student government sponsors social and cultural activities.

Sports: The college fields intercollegiate teams in 11 sports for men and 8 for women. About 24 intramural programs are open to men and women.

Handicapped: Special facilities for the handicapped include ramps, parking areas, elevators, and specially equipped rest rooms. Special class scheduling can be arranged. The campus is 95% accessible.

Graduates: The freshman dropout rate is 20%, and 50% remain to graduate. Of those, 50% continue their studies and 50% begin careers in business and industry.

Services: Free health care, placement aid, and career counseling are available. Other available services include tutoring or remedial instruction and psychological counseling.

Programs of Study: The college awards the B.A. degree. Master's degrees also are offered. Bachelor's degrees are offered in the following subjects: AREA (Asian–East Asian, Russian), BUSINESS (accounting, aerospace management, business administration, business education, computer science, finance, management, marketing), EDUCATION (elementary, health/physical, secondary), ENGLISH (English, journalism, speech), FINE AND PERFORMING ARTS (art, art education, film/photography, music, music education, radio/TV, theater/dramatics), LANGUAGES (French, German, Greek/Latin, Spanish), MATH AND SCIENCES (biology, chemistry, geology, mathematics, physics), PHILOSOPHY (humanities, philosophy, religion), PREPROFESSIONAL (aerospace studies, dentistry, engineering, home economics, law, library science, medicine, social work, veterinary), SOCIAL SCIENCES (economics, government/political science, history, international relations, psychology, public administration, social sciences, sociology).

Special: Students may study abroad and design their own majors. A combination degree program is available in engineering.

Honors: Four national honor societies are represented on campus.

Admissions: About 92% of those who applied were accepted for a recent freshman class. The SAT scores of those who enrolled were as follows: Verbal—31% between 500 and 600, 11% between 600 and 700, and 3% above 700; Math—37% between 500 and 600, 14% between 600 and 700, and 7% above 700. Of those who took the ACT, 25% scored between 20 and 23, 28% between 24 and 26, 19% between 27 and 28, and 6% above 28. The candidate should have completed 15 Carnegie units, graduated with a C average or better, and rank in the upper half of his or her high school class.

Procedure: The SAT, PSAT, or ACT is required and should be taken by December of the senior year. The priority-consideration deadline for applications is November 1. Freshmen are also admitted at midyear and in the summer. An interview is recommended. A $10 application fee should accompany all applications. Admissions are made on a rolling basis.

Special: A deferred admissions plan is available. AP and CLEP credit is accepted.

Transfer: For a recent year, 300 applications were received, 280 were accepted, and 220 students enrolled. A 2.0 GPA is required, and students must study at the college for at least 1 year to receive a degree. The application deadlines are August 1 (fall) and January 1 (spring).

Visiting: Tours can be arranged weekdays through the admissions office.

Financial Aid: About 70% of the students receive aid. Applicants should file the FFS or FAF. The deadline for aid applications is March 1.

Foreign Students: Special counseling is provided.

Admissions: Applicants must take the TOEFL.

Procedure: Application deadlines are the same as those for other students. Foreign students must subscribe to the college's health insurance program.

Admissions Contact: George E. Williams, Director of Admissions.

CONCORDIA COLLEGE/MOORHEAD   A–2
Moorhead, Minnesota 56560   (218) 299-3004

F/T: 1118M, 1432M	Faculty: 148; IIB, +$
P/T: 16M, 20W	Ph.D.'s: 55%
Grad: none	S/F Ratio: 16 to 1
Year: sems, ss	Tuition: $4805
Appl: July 1	R and B: $1645
1242 applied	1159 accepted 706 enrolled
SAT: 507V 541M	ACT: 22 COMPETITIVE+

Concordia College, founded in 1891, is a liberal arts institution affiliated with the American Lutheran Church. The library contains 253,000 volumes and 32,000 microtexts, and subscribes to 1360 periodicals.

Environment: The 120-acre suburban campus is located on the banks of the Red River in western Minnesota, in the twin cities of Moorhead and Fargo, North Dakota. New biology and home economics buildings were recently completed.

Student Life: Two-thirds of the students are from Minnesota, and the rest come from other states or 18 foreign countries. About 98% of entering freshmen come from public schools. Ninety-two percent of the students are Protestant (79% are Lutherans), and 6% are Catholic. People of all faiths are welcome. About 67% of the students live on campus. Four percent are minority-group members. Campus housing is single-sex, and there are visiting privileges. Students may keep cars on campus.

Organizations: There are no fraternities or sororities on campus, but 11% of the students belong to one of 6 men's or 5 women's societies.

Activities include student government; publications; music groups that include a world-famous choir; debating; drama; and clubs representing a variety of religions, academic departments, political viewpoints, and other special interests.

Sports: The college competes intercollegiately in 9 sports for men and 8 for women. There are 11 intramural sports for both men and women.

Handicapped: About 75% of the campus is accessible to physically handicapped students. Facilities include special parking, elevators, special class scheduling, and specially equipped restrooms. Special teaching aids are provided for visually or hearing impaired students.

Graduates: Twenty percent of the students drop out at the end of freshman year; 60% go on to graduate. Twenty percent of the graduates pursue advanced degrees: 2% enter medical school; another 2% enter dental school; and 3% enter law school.

Services: Free services for students include career and psychological counseling, remedial instruction, and health care. The college provides placement services and tutoring for a fee.

Programs of Study: The college awards B.A. and B.Mus. degrees. Bachelor's degrees are offered in the following subjects: AREA STUDIES (urban), BUSINESS (accounting, business administration, business education, computer science), EDUCATION (early childhood, elementary, health/physical, secondary), ENGLISH (English, literature, speech), FINE AND PERFORMING ARTS (art, art education, art history, music, music education, studio art, theater/dramatics), LANGUAGES (French, German, Greek/Latin, Russian, Spanish), MATH AND SCIENCES (biology, chemistry, mathematics, physics), PHILOSOPHY (classics, humanities, philosophy, religion), PREPROFESSIONAL (home economics, social work), SOCIAL SCIENCES (economics, government/political science, history, international relations, psychology, social sciences, sociology). Thirty-six percent of degrees are granted in the social sciences; 25% are in business; another 20% are in education; and 19% are in math and sciences.

Required: Each student is required to take 2 skills courses (in the areas of composition, argument, research, and reporting), 5 distribution courses from a list of options, 1 integration course, 2 religion courses, and one-half course in physical education.

Special: Students may register for junior year abroad, May semester abroad, Washington semester, co-op education programs, and paid internships in hospital administration. Degrees may be earned in three years.

Honors: Four national honor societies have chapters on campus.

Admissions: Ninety-three percent of applicants for admission to the 1981–82 freshman class were accepted. Of those who enrolled, the ACT scores were as follows: 35% scored below 21, 22% between 21 and 23, 16% between 24 and 25, 20% between 26 and 28, and 6% above 28. A general college preparatory curriculum is recommended. Admissions officers also consider, in diminishing order of importance, high school rank, test scores, and recommendations from school officials.

Procedure: Candidates must take the SAT or ACT and submit a $10 application fee. Prospective students may apply any time after their junior year. Application deadlines are July 1 (fall), December 1 (spring), and April 1 (summer). The college follows a rolling admissions policy.

Special: There is an early admissions plan under which applicants may be accepted during the first semester of their senior year of high school.

Transfer: For fall 1981, 274 transfer students applied, 183 were accepted, and 140 enrolled. Applicants must have a C average and be in good academic standing; 1 year must be spent in residence. Transfer students must complete, at the college, 7 of the 30.5 courses required for the bachelor's degree. Application deadlines are the same as for freshmen.

Visiting: There are group orientations at which prospective students can tour the campus and talk with admissions counselors and faculty members. Informal visits are also possible when classes are in session. Guides are provided and visitors can sit in on classes and stay overnight on campus. The admissions office handles arrangements.

Financial Aid: The college, a member of CSS, offers substantial assistance to freshmen, including scholarships, grants, loans, and CWS. Eighty percent of the students receive some type of financial aid; 60% work part-time on campus. The deadline for aid applications is April 1, and all applicants must submit the FFS or FAF.

Foreign Students: Two percent of the full-time students are from foreign countries. The college, which actively recruits these students, offers them special counseling and special organizations.

Admissions: Foreign students must achieve a score of 500 on the TOEFL. College entrance exams are not required.

Procedure: Application deadlines are April 1 (fall) and October 1 (spring). Foreign students must present a medical form completed by a physician as proof of health. They must also establish proof of funds adequate to cover 1 year of study. Health insurance, while not required, is available through the college.

Admissions Contact: James L. Hausmann, Vice President for Admissions.

MINNESOTA 423

CONCORDIA COLLEGE/ST. PAUL   C–4
St. Paul, Minnesota 55104   (612) 641-8231

F/T, P/T:	Faculty: 63; IIB, –$
700M&W	Ph.D.'s: 38%
Grad: none	S/F Ratio: 12 to 1
Year: qtrs, ss	Tuition: $3090
Appl: Aug. 15	R and B: $1590
298 applied	236 accepted	173 enrolled
ACT: required		COMPETITIVE

Concordia College, founded in 1893, is a church-related liberal arts and teachers' college affiliated with the Missouri Synod of the Lutheran Church. The library contains 80,000 volumes and 1100 microfilm items, and subscribes to 440 periodicals.

Environment: The 30-acre campus is located in the Midway area of the Twin Cities and consists of 17 buildings, including a campus center and 11 single-sex dormitories housing 450 students. Housing for married students also is available.

Student Life: About 60% of the students come from Minnesota, and 87% come from public schools. Two-thirds of the students live on campus. About 98% of the students are Protestant and 2% are Catholic. Daily attendance at chapel services is recommended. Drinking is forbidden on campus. All students must observe a sign-out procedure.

Organizations: The college sponsors several extracurricular activities, including a band, a choir, and a drama group. There are no fraternities or sororities.

Sports: The college competes on an intercollegiate level in 7 sports for men and 4 for women. Several intramural sports are available for men and women.

Handicapped: About 85% of the campus is accessible to the physically handicapped. Facilities include special parking, elevators, and special class scheduling. About 1% of the student body has visual impairments. Special tutors are available.

Graduates: The freshman dropout rate is 10%, and 60% remain to graduate.

Programs of Study: The college confers the B.A. degree. Bachelor's degrees are offered in the following subjects: BUSINESS (business administration), EDUCATION (Christian, early childhood, elementary, health/physical, special), ENGLISH (English), FINE AND PERFORMING ARTS (music), MATH AND SCIENCES (biology, ecology/environmental science, mathematics, natural sciences), PHILOSOPHY (religion), PREPROFESSIONAL (law, medicine, ministry, social work), SOCIAL SCIENCES (history, social sciences).

Special: Students may design their own majors and participate in a study-abroad program sponsored by another college.

Admissions: About 79% of those who applied were admitted to the 1981–82 freshman class. The ACT scores of those who enrolled were as follows: 40% below 21, 35% between 21 and 23, 7% between 24 and 25, 13% between 26 and 28, and 5% above 28. Forty-three percent of the freshmen ranked in the upper fifth of their high school class; 65% ranked in the upper two-fifths. Important factors include academic record, test scores, recommendations by school officials and personal qualities. The college gives special consideration to students entering its Metropolitan Teacher Education Program, designed for minority students from the Twin Cities area.

Procedure: The ACT is required and should be taken by July. Junior-year results are acceptable. The fall application deadline is August 15; deadlines for other terms are open. The college has a rolling admissions policy. A personal interview is recommended. There is a $10 application fee.

Special: The college offers early decision, early admissions, and deferred admissions plans. AP and CLEP credit is available.

Transfer: Recommendations and a C average are required. Forty-eight quarter hours must be taken in residence. Application deadlines are the same as those for freshmen.

424 MINNESOTA

Visiting: Orientations for prospective students are scheduled regularly. Informal guided tours and classroom visits can be arranged weekdays. For further information, contact the admissions office.

Financial Aid: About 95% of the students receive financial aid. Scholarships, loans, and work-study funds are available. The average aid package in 1981–82 totaled $3900. The FAF is required. The priority deadline for aid applications is April 1.

Foreign Students: About 4% of the students are from foreign countries. The college provides an intensive English course under its academic development program, and also offers special counseling and special organizations.

Admissions: Students must score at least 450 on the TOEFL or 70 on the University of Michigan Language Test. No academic exams are required.

Procedure: Application deadlines are open; students are admitted to all terms. Proof of good health and of adequate funds on a quarter-by-quarter basis is required. Students must carry health insurance, which is available through the college for a fee.

Admissions Contact: Myrtle Shira, Director of Admissions.

GUSTAVUS ADOLPHUS COLLEGE   C-4
St. Peter, Minnesota 56082   (507) 931-7676

F/T: 977M, 1289W	Faculty:	142; IIB, +$
P/T: 22M, 26W	Ph.D.'s:	78%
Grad: none	S/F Ratio:	15 to 1
Year: 4-1-4, ss	Tuition:	$5150
Appl: Apr. 1	R and B:	$2100
1150 applied	950 accepted	630 enrolled
SAT: 520V 580M	ACT: 25	VERY COMPETITIVE+

Gustavus Adolphus College is a liberal arts institution operated by the Lutheran Church in America. The library contains 189,000 volumes, subscribes to 1402 periodicals, and holds 33,000 microfilm items.

Environment: The college's 250-acre rural campus overlooks the Minnesota River Valley, about an hour's drive from Minneapolis. Among the prominent buildings on campus are Christ Chapel, the Schaeffer Fine Arts complex, and the Folke Bernadotte Memorial Library. There are 10 residence halls; 8 are coed.

Student Life: Although most of the students are from Minnesota, 45 states are represented in the student body. About 91% of entering freshmen come from public schools. Ninety-five percent of the students live in dormitories. Eighty-five percent of the students are Protestant and 13% are Catholic. The majority of students are members of the Lutheran Church, but there is no requirement to attend services. Three percent are minority-group members. Campus housing is both coed and single-sex. There are visiting privileges in single-sex dorms. Students may keep cars on campus.

Organizations: There are 8 local fraternities and 6 local sororities on campus; about 25% of the students belong. Extracurricular activities include a strong theater program and 20 musical organizations.

Sports: The college competes on an intercollegiate level in 12 sports for men and 11 for women. There are 14 intramural sports for men and 11 for women.

Handicapped: About 90% of the campus is accessible to the physically handicapped. Facilities for these students include wheelchair ramps, special parking, special telephones, elevators, specially equipped rest rooms, lowered drinking fountains, and special class scheduling.

Graduates: The freshman dropout rate is 8%; 67% remain to graduate. About 30% continue their studies in graduate or professional schools: 5% enter medical school; 2% enter dental school; and 6% enter law school. Approximately 35% pursue careers in business and industry.

Services: Students receive the following services free of charge: placement and career counseling, health care, tutoring, and psychological counseling.

Programs of Study: The college awards the B.A. degree. Bachelor's degrees are offered in the following subjects: AREA STUDIES (American, Latin American, Russian, Scandinavian), BUSINESS (accounting, business administration, business education, computer science), EDUCATION (early childhood, elementary, health/physical, secondary), ENGLISH (English), FINE AND PERFORMING ARTS (art, art education, music, music education, theater/dramatics), HEALTH SCIENCES (medical technology, nursing, physical therapy), LANGUAGES (French, German, Russian, Spanish, Swedish), MATH AND SCIENCES (biology, chemistry, earth science, geology, mathematics, physics), PHILOSOPHY (classics, philosophy, religion), PREPROFESSIONAL (dentistry, engineering, law, medicine, ministry, pharmacy, veterinary), SOCIAL SCIENCES (anthropology, economics, geography, government/political science, history, psychology, social sciences, sociology). About 22% of the degrees conferred are in math and sciences; 20% are in social sciences.

Special: Student-designed majors are allowed. Study abroad and a 3-2 engineering program with Washington University of St. Louis are available, as is an exchange program with Mankato State University.

Honors: There are 2 national honorary societies on campus.

Admissions: About 83% of those who applied were accepted for the 1981–82 freshman class. Of those who enrolled, the SAT scores were as follows: Verbal—45% below 500, 36% between 500 and 599, 16% between 600 and 700, and 3% above 700; Math—25% below 500, 41% between 500 and 599, 27% between 600 and 700, and 7% above 700. On the ACT, 12% scored below 21, 20% between 21 and 23, 23% between 24 and 25, 26% between 26 and 28, and 12% above 28. Candidates should rank in the upper third of their graduating class. High school preparation should include 4 units of English. Preference is given to students with averages of B or better. Other important factors are advanced placement or honor courses, personality, recommendations by high school officials, impressions made during interview, leadership, special talents, and extracurricular activities.

Procedure: Either the SAT or the ACT is required and should be taken by January of the senior year. The deadline for applications is 6 weeks prior to the beginning of any session. However, it is suggested that applications for the fall session be submitted by April 1 and applications for spring and summer by December 1. Freshmen are accepted for fall, midyear, and summer sessions. Early decision candidates receive notification after December 1. There is a $15 application fee.

Special: Early decision and early admissions plans are available. The deadline to apply for early admission is April 1.

Transfer: For fall 1981, 53 of 96 transfer applications were approved; 40 students were enrolled. An interview and a 2.4 GPA are required. Preference is given to community college graduates. There is a residency requirement of 1 year. Transfers must complete, at the college, 8 of the 36 courses required for the bachelor's degree. Application deadlines are the same as for freshmen.

Visiting: Classroom visits and informal guided tours are available. Visits are best scheduled during the period from September to March. Prospective students should contact the admissions office for further information.

Financial Aid: About 60% of the students receive financial aid; 45% work part-time on campus. A variety of scholarships and loans totaling $6 million are available. The FAF or FFS is required, and application for aid should be made by April 1 for fall or December 1 for winter or spring. The college is a member of CSS.

Foreign Students: Foreign students comprise about 2% of the full-time enrollment. The college, which actively recruits these students, offers them an intensive English course as well as special counseling and special organizations.

Admissions: Foreign students must take the TOEFL; the SAT or ACT is not required.

Procedure: Application deadlines are February 1 (fall) and October 1 (spring). Foreign students must furnish proof of health and must carry health insurance, which is available through the college for a fee. Proof of funds adequate to cover 1 year of study is also required.

Admissions Contact: Owen Sammelson, Director of Admissions.

HAMLINE UNIVERSITY   C-4
St. Paul, Minnesota 55104   (612) 641-2207

F/T: 643M, 582W	Faculty:	92; IIB, ++$
P/T: 33M, 40W	Ph.D.'s:	70%
Grad: 356M, 209W	S/F Ratio:	14 to 1
Year: 4-1-4, ss	Tuition:	$4950
Appl: open	R and B:	$1900
696 applied	621 accepted	324 enrolled
SAT: 500V 530M	ACT: 23	COMPETITIVE+

Hamline University, founded in 1854, is affiliated with the Methodist Church. The university consists of a college of liberal arts, a school of law, and a graduate program in liberal studies. Its library holds over 245,000 books and 2300 microfilm items, and subscribes to more than 80 periodicals.

Environment: The self-contained, 37-acre campus is located in the city of St. Paul. The university's 27 buildings include Old Main, built in 1884, which has been named to the National Register of Historic Places. Six residence halls house 700 students.

Student Life: Sixty-three percent of the students are from Minnesota. Fifty-three percent reside on campus. Fifty-two percent of the students are Protestant; 27% are Catholic; 1% are Jewish; 9% are of other faiths; and 11% are unaffiliated. Over 3% of the students are minority-group members. Campus housing is both coed and single-sex. There are visiting privileges in single-sex dorms. Students may keep cars on campus.

Organizations: Eighteen percent of the men belong to 1 of 2 national fraternities that have chapters on campus. There are no sororities. Extracurricular activities include music, drama, debating, publications, and religious and special-interest clubs. Cultural activities on campus include concerts, films, lectures, and theater.

Sports: Men can compete in 12 intercollegiate sports; women have a choice of 8 sports. There are 11 intramural sports for men and 10 for women.

Handicapped: Facilities provided for physically handicapped students include wheelchair ramps, special parking, elevators, specially equipped restrooms, and lowered telephones.

Graduates: Nineteen percent of the students drop out at the end of the freshman year; 52% remain to graduate, and 25% pursue advanced degrees; over 1% enter medical and dental school, and almost 4% enter law school. Thirty percent enter business and industry.

Services: The university provides free career and psychological counseling, health care, tutoring, and remedial instruction. Free placement services are available for undergraduates and graduates.

Programs of Study: The university awards the B.A. degree. Master's degrees are also awarded. Bachelor's degrees are offered in the following subjects: AREA STUDIES (American, Asian, Latin American, Russian, urban), BUSINESS (business administration), EDUCATION (elementary, secondary), ENGLISH (English), FINE AND PERFORMING ARTS (art, art education, art history, music, music education, studio art, theater/dramatics), HEALTH SCIENCES (medical technology), LANGUAGES (French, German, Spanish), MATH AND SCIENCES (biology, chemistry, ecology/environmental science, mathematics), PHILOSOPHY (philosophy, religion), PREPROFESSIONAL (dentistry, engineering, law, medicine, ministry), SOCIAL SCIENCES (anthropology, economics, government/political science, history, international relations, psychology, sociology).

Special: The university offers independent study. An intercampus curriculum in which students may take courses at St. Catherine's, Macalester, Augsburg, or St. Thomas and an open curriculum option under which students may plan their own majors or programs are also available. Foreign studies programs include the Student Project for Amity Among Nations (SPAN, a summer study plan), junior year abroad, a Brussels Semester, a London Semester, and a Hong Kong Semester. An Urban Studies Term is also offered.

Honors: Phi Beta Kappa and other honorary and professional societies have campus chapters. All departments offer senior honors programs for outstanding students.

Admissions: The university accepted 89% of those who applied for admission to the 1981-82 freshman class. The SAT scores of those who enrolled were as follows: Verbal—44% below 500, 32% between 500 and 599, 17% between 600 and 700, and 7% above 700; Math —33% below 500, 35% between 500 and 599, 27% between 600 and 700, and 5% above 700. On the ACT, 29% scored below 21, 24% between 21 and 23, 14% between 24 and 25, 24% between 26 and 28, and 9% above 28. Candidates should rank in the top half of their high school class and have completed 15 Carnegie units. Admissions officers also consider high school accreditation, recommendations by school officials, and the geographic distribution of Hamline's student body.

Procedure: Applicants must take the SAT or the ACT in December or January of their senior year. The application fee is $15. Freshmen may apply for fall and spring entry. The university considers applications on a rolling admissions basis.

Special: A deferred admissions plan is available. Students may earn credit through AP or CLEP tests.

Transfer: For fall 1981, 252 transfer students applied, 203 were accepted, and 132 enrolled. Applicants must have a GPA of at least 2.0 and plan to spend at least 1 year in residence. Transfers must complete, at the university, 9 of the 35 credits required for the bachelor's degree. Applicants are considered for fall and spring entry.

Visiting: Prospective students are welcome to visit the university during the week when classes are in session. The admissions office should be contacted to arrange guides, class visits, and a place to stay on campus.

Financial Aid: Seventy-one percent of the students receive financial aid; 30% work part-time on campus. The average award is $4500. The university has $710,000 available for scholarships for freshmen. Loans are provided by the federal government, local banks, and the university. The university is a member of the CSS and requires the FAF, FFS, or SFS from aid applicants. Aid application deadlines are August 1 (fall) and December 1 (spring).

Foreign Students: Foreign students comprise 4% of the full-time enrollment. The university offers these students special counseling and special organizations.

Admissions: Foreign students must achieve a score of 550 on the TOEFL. The SAT or ACT is not required.

Procedure: Application deadlines are April 1 (fall) and December 1 (spring). Foreign students must provide proof of funds adequate to cover the entire period of study. They must also carry health insurance, which is available through the university for a fee.

Admissions Contact: Daniel J. Murray, Director of Admissions.

MACALESTER COLLEGE C-4
St. Paul, Minnesota 55105 (612) 696-6357

F/T: 826M, 743W	Faculty: 125; IIB, + + $
P/T: 49M, 112W	Ph.D.'s: 84%
Grad: none	S/F Ratio: 14 to 1
Year: 4-1-4, ss	Tuition: $5480
Appl: Mar. 1	R and B: $1900
1075 applied	852 accepted	430 enrolled
SAT: 544V 563M	ACT: 25	VERY COMPETITIVE+

Macalester College is a liberal arts college affiliated with the United Presbyterian Church. Its library contains over 285,000 books and 7500 microfilm items, and subscribes to 1146 periodicals.

Environment: The 50-acre suburban campus is located halfway between downtown Minneapolis and St. Paul. Campus resources include two science halls considered among the best in the nation, a planetarium, a field house, and an outdoor track. The college owns a 280-acre natural history study center on the Mississippi River nearby.

Student Life: Macalester's student body is socially, geographically, religiously, and economically diverse. About 9% of the students are members of minority groups. About 80% of entering freshmen come from public schools. Seventy percent of the students live in dormitories —including special language housing for those interested in French, German, Russian, or Spanish—or in rented housing near campus. Campus housing is both coed and single-sex. There are visiting privileges in single-sex dorms. Students set dormitory regulations. Cars may be kept on campus.

Organizations: The college has no fraternities or sororities, but several honor societies, including Phi Beta Kappa, have chapters on campus. Activities include choir, drama, debate and forensics, symphonic orchestra and band, pipe band, and Highland dancers. There is an active campus ministry program. Students serve on policymaking committees of the faculty and board of trustees as well as in student government. Cultural facilities on campus include the Janet Wallace Fine Arts Center.

Sports: The college competes intercollegiately in 10 sports for men and 9 for women. Eleven intramural sports are open to both men and women.

Handicapped: About 20% of the campus is accessible to the physically handicapped. Facilities include special parking areas. Recently, the college provided tapes for its visually impaired students and the aid of work-study students to assist a wheelchair-bound student. A special counselor also is available.

Graduates: About 17% of the freshmen drop out at the end of their first year; more than 60% remain to graduate. Of these, about 33% enter graduate school immediately after graduation and another 50% do so within 10 years. About 4% of the graduates enter medical school; 1% enter dental school; and another 7% enter law school.

Services: Macalester offers students free health care, career and psychological counseling, tutoring, and remedial instruction. Free placement services for students include help in finding part-time and summer jobs and the Community Involvement Program, which places about 40% of the students in volunteer positions and internships in the Twin Cities.

Programs of Study: The college confers the B.A. degree in the following subjects: AREA STUDIES (East Asian, Russian, urban), EDUCATION (elementary, secondary), ENGLISH (English, journalism, speech), FINE AND PERFORMING ARTS (art, music, theater/dramatics), LANGUAGES (French, German, linguistics, Russian, Spanish), MATH AND SCIENCES (biology, chemistry, computer studies, ecology/environmental science, geology, mathematics, physics), PHILOSOPHY (classics, philosophy, religion), SOCIAL SCIENCES (an-

426 MINNESOTA

thropology, economics, geography, government/political science, history, international relations, law and society, psychology, social sciences, sociology). About half the students earn degrees in social sciences, 17% in math and sciences, 10% in English, and 9% in fine or performing arts.

Special: Freshmen take seminars focusing on single topics. During the January interim term each student selects a seminar, independent project, or field trip on which to concentrate.

All departments offer independent study. Interested students may design their own majors. The college offers a 5-year combined B.A.-B.S. engineering program in cooperation with Washington University. Other cooperative and exchange programs are offered in conjunction with institutions and organizations that include the Consortium for Urban Affairs and the Rush University College of Nursing.

About half the students study or travel overseas. Programs include language study in French, German, Japanese, Croatian, Russian, Norwegian, and Spanish; social science and humanities programs in Costa Rica, England, and Italy; and an exchange program with the University of Sterling in Scotland.

Honors: Virtually all departments offer honors sequences. Twelve honor societies have campus chapters.

Admissions: The college accepted 79% of those who applied to the 1981-82 freshman class. The SAT scores of those who enrolled were as follows: Verbal—33% below 500, 37% between 500 and 599, 23% between 600 and 700, and 6% above 700; Math—20% below 500, 41% between 500 and 599, 34% between 600 and 700, and 5% above 700. On the ACT, 1% scored below 21, 17% between 21 and 23, 24% between 24 and 25, 30% between 26 and 28, and 24% above 28. Other factors considered in determining admission include advanced placement or honor courses, extracurricular activities record, and leadership record.

Procedure: Applicants must take the ACT or SAT by January of the senior year. They must submit a $15 application fee and recommendations from 2 teachers and from their principal or counselor. For fall enrollment, those who apply by February 1 will be notified around March 1; those who apply by March 1 will be notified around April 1. Those interested in early decision must apply by December 15 and are notified around January 15.

Special: Early decision and early and deferred admissions plans are available. The application deadline for early admission is August 1. Students may earn credit through AP exams.

Transfer: For fall 1981, 169 transfer students applied, 122 were accepted, and 76 enrolled. Applicants must have at least a C average and submit a recommendation from the dean of students at the last college attended and a transcript of college work. Those with one year or less of college must submit high school transcripts and test scores. All students must study at Macalester at least 2 years to receive a degree, and must complete, at the college, 16 of the 31 courses required for the bachelor's degree. Application deadlines are June 1 (fall) and December 15 (spring).

Visiting: The college schedules group orientation sessions for prospective students. Also, individual visits are welcomed during the academic year; the college provides guides and can arrange for visitors to sit in on classes and stay overnight on campus. Those interested should contact the admissions office.

Financial Aid: Sixty percent of the students receive financial aid ranging from $100 a year to full cost. Seventy percent work part-time on campus. Aid packages usually include loans and jobs as well as scholarships. The average award to freshmen from all sources is 59% of college costs. A special program offers aid and academic support to economically disadvantaged minority students. Aid applicants must file the BEOG form and the FAF; Minnesota residents also must file the FFS and apply to the State Scholarship Program. Aid applications should be submitted by March 1. The college is a member of CSS.

Foreign Students: Almost 12% of the full-time students come from foreign countries. Macalester actively recruits these students and offers them an intensive English program in addition to special counseling and special organizations.

Admissions: Foreign students must achieve a score of 425 on the TOEFL. The SAT or ACT is not required.

Procedure: Application deadlines are March 15 (fall) and December 15 (spring). Foreign students must present proof of health and must carry health insurance, which is available through the college for a fee. Proof of funds adequate to cover 4 years of study is also required.

Admissions Contact: William M. Shain, Dean of Admissions.

MANKATO STATE UNIVERSITY C-4
Mankato, Minnesota 56001   (507) 389-1823

F/T: 4697M, 4925W	Faculty: 487; n/av
P/T: 453M, 747W	Ph.D.'s: 48%
Grad: 717M, 732W	S/F Ratio: 19 to 1
Year: qtrs, ss	Tuition: $750 ($1357)
Appl: open	R and B: $1313
3677 applied 3456 accepted 2123 enrolled	
ACT: 19	LESS COMPETITIVE

Mankato State University is a publicly controlled institution offering training in the liberal arts as well as in professional studies. The library contains over 600,000 volumes and 675,000 microfilm items, and subscribes to more than 2100 periodicals.

Environment: The university's 165-acre campus is set in a rural area, 85 miles from Minneapolis. The physical plant consists of classrooms, industrial arts facilities, a stadium, a field house, and a science building. About 3100 students are accommodated in the university's dormitories.

Student Life: About 97% of the students are residents of Minnesota; 99% of entering freshmen come from public schools. About 26% of the students live on campus. Four percent are minority-group members. Campus housing is coed. Students may keep cars on campus. The university provides day-care services to all students as well as to faculty and staff.

Organizations: There are 4 national fraternities and 2 national sororities on campus; about 5% of the men and 3% of the women belong. Many social and special interest groups, departmental clubs, and activities contribute to campus life.

Sports: The university competes on an intercollegiate level in 11 sports for men and 9 for women. Eleven intramural sports are open to men and 8 to women.

Handicapped: Special facilities for the physically handicapped include wheelchair ramps, special parking, elevators, specially equipped rest rooms, lowered drinking fountains, and lowered telephones. The campus is completely accessible to wheelchair students. A counselor is available for special assistance.

Graduates: The freshman dropout rate is 27%; 42% remain to graduate. About 15% of the students pursue graduate study after graduation; 55% pursue careers in business and industry.

Services: Students receive the following services free of charge: career counseling, tutoring, remedial instruction, and psychological counseling. In addition, free placement services and health care are available. Alumni may also take advantage of the placement services.

Programs of Study: The university offers B.A., B.F.A., B.G.S., and B.S., degrees. Associate, master's, and doctoral degrees are also conferred. Bachelor's degrees are offered in the following subjects: AREA STUDIES (American, minority, urban), BUSINESS (accounting, aviation management, business administration, business education, computer science, finance, industrial/technical studies, management, marketing, real estate/insurance), EDUCATION (adult, early childhood, elementary, health/physical, secondary, special), ENGLISH (English, journalism, literature, speech), FINE AND PERFORMING ARTS (art, art education, music, music education, studio art, theater/dramatics), HEALTH SCIENCES (environmental health, medical technology, nursing, occupational therapy, physical therapy, speech therapy), LANGUAGES (French, German, Spanish), MATH AND SCIENCES (astronomy, biology, chemistry, earth science, ecology/environmental science, mathematics, natural sciences, physical sciences, physics, statistics), PHILOSOPHY (philosophy), PREPROFESSIONAL (agriculture, dentistry, engineering, forestry, home economics, law, medicine, ministry, pharmacy, social work, veterinary), SOCIAL SCIENCES (anthropology, economics, geography, government/political science, history, international relations, psychology, social sciences, sociology). About 25% of degrees conferred are in business.

Special: The university offers opportunities for foreign travel as part of its regular curriculum. The B.G.S. degree is available.

Honors: There are 4 national honorary societies on campus. Many departments offer honors programs.

Admissions: About 94% of those who applied were accepted for the 1981-82 freshman class. Of those who enrolled, the ACT scores were as follows: 38% below 21, 41% between 21 and 23, 16% between 24 and 25, 3% between 26 and 28, and 1% above 28. Candidates must rank in the top 66% of their class and should be graduates of accredited high schools.

Procedure: New students may be admitted to any session. The SAT, ACT, or PSAT is required. There is a $10 application fee. Admissions are on a rolling basis. Application deadlines are open.

Transfer: For fall 1981, 1633 applications were received, 1376 were accepted, and 983 students actually enrolled. Transfers are accepted for all classes. D grades are acceptable. A 2.0 GPA is required. Students must study at the university for at least 1 year, and must complete in residence 45 of the 192 quarter hours required for the bachelor's degree. Transfer application deadlines are open.

Visiting: Informal guided tours and classroom visits can be arranged by the admissions office.

Financial Aid: About 53% of the students receive financial aid; 25% work part-time on campus. The average award to freshmen from all sources is $1590. Major financial assistance is from federal and state programs. The deadline for financial aid application is April 23.

Foreign Students: Four percent of the full-time students come from foreign countries. Special counseling and organizations as well as an intensive English course are available to these students.

Admissions: Foreign students must achieve a score of 500 on the TOEFL. College entrance exams are not required.

Procedure: Application deadlines are July 1 (fall), November 1 (winter), January 1 (spring), and April 1 (summer). Foreign students must present a doctor's certificate as proof of health. They must also provide proof of funds adequate to cover 1 year of study. Health insurance, although not required, is available through the university for a fee.

Admissions Contact: Jack Parkins, Director of Admissions.

MINNEAPOLIS COLLEGE OF ART AND DESIGN   C-4
Minneapolis, Minnesota 55404   (612) 870-3260

F/T: 212M, 277W	Faculty: 41; IIB, +$
P/T: 16M, 22W	Ph.D.'s: 2%
Grad: none	S/F Ratio: 9 to 1
Year: sems, ss	Tuition: $3700
Appl: July 31	R and B: $2000
381 applied 273 accepted	169 enrolled
SAT or ACT: not required	SPECIAL

The Minneapolis College of Art and Design, founded in 1886, is a coeducational, professional college of art. It is governed by the Minneapolis Society of Fine Arts, a nonprofit organization which is the parent body for both the college and the Minneapolis Institute of Arts. The library contains over 46,000 volumes and subscribes to more than 170 periodicals.

Environment: Located in Minneapolis, the college is convenient to downtown and suburban areas. Among the campus buildings is the Studio Arts Building which contains 3 studio technical centers: a lecture/critique core; an area for 2- and 3-dimensional construction; and a third area for large 3-dimensional work, photography, cinematography, video, and mural studios. Student apartment houses are directly across from the student core center.

Student Life: About 55% of the students come from Minnesota. Twenty-eight percent live on campus. Living accommodations are also available in the neighborhood. Six percent of the students are minority-group members. Campus housing is coed. Students may keep cars on campus.

Organizations: The college has no fraternities or sororities. Social life is varied. An active student council sponsors dances, lectures, an annual sale of student work, concerts, and films. A lecture series brings recognized authorities in various fields to the college each week. The college also provides opportunities for students to exhibit their work and to compete for scholarships and prizes.

Handicapped: Special facilities for handicapped students include wheelchair ramps and elevators.

Graduates: At the end of the freshman year, about 30% of the students drop out; 27% remain to graduate. Five percent of the students enter graduate or professional schools immediately after graduation.

Services: The following services are available to students free of charge: health care, psychological counseling, placement, career counseling, and remedial instruction. The part-time placement services may be used by graduates as well as undergraduates.

Programs of Study: The core of the institution is visual arts. The college offers a 4-year interdisciplinary studio/liberal arts program leading to the B.F.A. degree. Students take a year of visual studies. They choose between majors in fine arts or design. In design, they may select concentrations in environmental design, visual communications, or product design. Courses include architectural design, clothing design, drawing, film/video, furniture design, graphic design, illustration, interior design, painting, photography, printmaking, sculpture, and typography, in addition to a strong liberal arts core.

Special: The college offers visiting artist and visiting professor programs and a junior year abroad. As a member of the Union of Independent Colleges of Art, the college offers students an opportunity to participate in Student Mobility or Transfer programs.

Admissions: Seventy-two percent of those who applied were accepted for the 1981–82 freshman class. The college does not require specific credit unit distribution from high school, but strongly recommends a broad liberal arts program. Students should rank in the top half of their graduating class. Advanced placement or honors courses and evidence of special talents both weigh heavily in the admissions decision.

Procedure: Applications should be submitted by July 31. The ACT, SAT, or PSAT is requested for English placement or waiver. The application, with a $15 fee, must be sent before the applicant may receive an admissions packet, which includes instructions for portfolio, letters of reference, etc. New students may be admitted at midyear. Admissions are rolling.

Transfer: For the current academic year, of 191 students who applied, 135 were accepted and 97 chose to attend. A 2.0 GPA is required; D grades do not transfer. Students must spend the senior year in residence and must complete, at the college, 33 of the 135 credits necessary for the bachelor's degree. A rolling admissions policy for transfers is in effect.

Visiting: Orientation sessions for prospective students are available. Appointments must be made in advance. Guides are also available for informal visits to the school. Visitors may sit in on classes. The best time to visit is weekdays. Contact the admissions office for arrangements.

Financial Aid: Seventy-seven percent of the students receive financial aid; 50% work part-time on campus. Aid is available in a package that combines grants, EOG, NDEA, FWS, and CWS, and is based upon need and admission to the college. The average award to freshmen from all sources is $1914. Application must be made by March 1 and must be accompanied by either the FAF or the FFS. The college is a member of CSS.

Foreign Students: About 1% of the full-time students come from foreign countries. The college offers these students special counseling.

Admissions: Foreign students must achieve a score of 500 on the TOEFL. The ACT or SAT is not required, but students must submit a portfolio.

Procedure: Application deadlines are July 31 (fall), November 20 (spring), and June 14 (summer). To establish proof of health, foreign students must complete a health questionnaire. They must also carry health insurance, which is available through the college for a fee. Proof of funds adequate to cover 1 year of study is also required.

Admissions Contact: J. Thomas Reeve, Director of Admissions and Records.

MOORHEAD STATE UNIVERSITY   A-2
Moorhead, Minnesota 56560   (218) 236-2161

F/T: 2420M, 2849W	Faculty: 304; IIA, +$
P/T: 311M, 606W	Ph.D.'s: 55%
Grad: 145M, 337W	S/F Ratio: 19 to 1
Year: qtrs, ss	Tuition: $787 ($1435)
Appl: Aug. 15	R and B: $1311
1986 accepted	1340 enrolled
ACT: 21	COMPETITIVE

Moorhead State University, founded in 1887, is a publicly supported liberal arts and teacher training institution. The library contains over 218,000 volumes, and subscribes to more than 1756 periodicals.

Environment: The 104-acre wooded, suburban campus is located in the heart of the Red River Valley. The physical plant consists of 27 main buildings. Residence facilities include dormitories with single and double rooms, and suites.

Student Life: Most of the students come from Minnesota; 30% come from other states. About 72% of the students live on campus. Two percent are minority-group members. Campus housing is both coed and single-sex. There are visiting privileges in single-sex dorms. Students may keep cars on campus. Day-care services are provided to all students, faculty, and staff for a fee.

Organizations: There are 4 sororities and 4 fraternities on campus; about 3% of the men and 4% of the women belong. There are many extracurricular clubs including religious organizations for Catholics and Protestants.

Sports: The university competes on an intercollegiate level in 11 sports. Ten intramural sports are offered.

428 MINNESOTA

Handicapped: About 75% of the campus is accessible to physically handicapped students. Special facilities include wheelchair ramps, special parking, elevators, lowered drinking fountains, and lowered telephones. Two part-time counselors are also available.

Graduates: About 7% of the students pursue graduate study; 30% pursue careers in business and industry.

Services: Students receive the following services free of charge: career counseling, tutoring, remedial instruction, and psychological counseling. Placement and health care are also available. In addition, there are placement services for alumni.

Programs of Study: The university awards the B.A., B.F.A., B.S., B.S.N., and B.S.W. degrees. Associate and master's degrees are also conferred. Bachelor's degrees are offered in the following subjects: AREA STUDIES (American), BUSINESS (accounting, business administration, business education, computer science, finance, management, marketing, office administration), EDUCATION (early childhood, elementary, health/physical, industrial, secondary, special), ENGLISH (English, journalism, literature, speech), FINE AND PERFORMING ARTS (art, art education, art history, music, music education, radio/TV, studio art, theater/dramatics), HEALTH SCIENCES (medical technology, nursing, speech therapy), LANGUAGES (French, German, Spanish), MATH AND SCIENCES (biology, chemistry, earth science, mathematics, physics), PHILOSOPHY (humanities, philosophy), PREPROFESSIONAL (law, medicine, social work, veterinary), SOCIAL SCIENCES (anthropology, economics, geography, government/political science, history, psychology, sociology). About 34% of the degrees conferred are in education; 26% are in business.

Required: Courses in English, natural sciences, social sciences, humanities, and physical education are required of all students.

Special: Special programs include a fifth-year program in teacher education, the Washington Semester, individualized majors, EOMS for minority students, international internships, and Minority Group Studies. The Tri-College University Student Exchange Program makes it possible for Minnesota residents to take the first 3 years of certain majors at Moorhead before transferring to North Dakota State University to complete their degrees; some of the programs included are agriculture, architecture, engineering, geology, home economics, and pharmacy.

Honors: There are several honors programs.

Admissions: The ACT scores for the current freshman class are as follows: 24% below 21, 42% between 21 and 23, 13% between 24 and 25, 14% between 26 and 28, and 7% above 28. Applicants should rank in the upper half of their high school class, present a minimum ACT score of 20, or attain a comparable score on either the SAT or PSAT. Students who do not meet this standard may receive individual consideration if they can provide other evidence of college ability.

Procedure: The ACT, SAT, or PSAT should be taken by March of the senior year. It is suggested that application be made by May 1. August 15 is the deadline for the fall term; November 15 for the winter term; February 15 for the spring term; and June 1 for the summer sessions. Notification is made on a rolling basis. There is a $10 application fee.

Special: CLEP and AP credit is available.

Transfer: For fall 1981, 939 transfer students were accepted, and 658 enrolled. Transfers are accepted for all classes. A GPA of 2.0 is required. D grades transfer. The students must earn at least 45 quarter credits at the university of the 192 necessary for the bachelor's degree. The deadlines for transfer applicants are the same as for freshman applicants, except that May 15 is the deadline for summer entry.

Visiting: There are regularly scheduled orientations for prospective students. Informal guided tours and classroom visits can also be arranged 6 days a week. For further information prospective students should contact the admissions office.

Financial Aid: About 70% of the students receive financial aid; 25% work part-time on campus. The university provides scholarships, loans, and campus employment. The FFS is required; the priority deadline for fall aid applications is April 16. The regular deadlines are August 15 (fall), November 8 (winter), February 15 (spring), and June 1 (summer).

Foreign Students: Foreign students constitute about 2% of the full-time enrollment. There are special organizations available to these students.

Admissions: Foreign students must earn a score of 500 on the TOEFL. The SAT or ACT is not required.

Procedure: Application deadlines are the same as for transfer students. All foreign students must complete a medical history questionnaire. They must also present proof of funds sufficient to cover 4 years of study. Health insurance, while not required, is available to foreign students for a fee.

Admissions Contact: Floyd W. Brown, Director of Admissions.

NORTHWESTERN COLLEGE   C-4
Roseville, Minnesota 55113   (612) 636-4840

F/T: 372M, 414W	Faculty: 43; IIB, av$
P/T: 25M, 19W	Ph.D.'s: 26%
Grad: none	S/F Ratio: 19 to 1
Year: qtrs	Tuition: $3450
Appl: open	R and B: $1770
750 applied	600 accepted	432 enrolled
ACT: 20		COMPETITIVE

Northwestern College, founded in 1902, is a Christian college offering programs of study in the Bible, arts and sciences, and education. The library contains 60,000 volumes and 270 microfilm items, and subscribes to 400 periodicals.

Environment: The 95-acre campus is located in a suburb 10 miles from Minneapolis and St. Paul. Major buildings include a gymnasium, residence halls, and a student activity center. Construction of a fine arts center began in spring of 1980.

Student Life: Most students come from the Midwest. Campus activities are geared strongly toward religion, and attendance at regular chapel services is required. Campus housing is single-sex, and there are visiting privileges.

Organizations: There are no fraternities or sororities. Besides religious activities, students can participate in music groups, publications, and other clubs.

Sports: The college competes in 9 intercollegiate sports for men and 5 for women. Ten intramural sports are open to both men and women.

Graduates: About 40% of the graduates pursue advanced degrees. Forty-two percent enter business and industry.

Services: The college provides free health care for students. Free placement services, career and psychological counseling, and remedial instruction are also available.

Programs of Study: The college grants the bachelor's degree. Associate degrees are also awarded. Bachelor's degrees are offered in the following subjects: BUSINESS (accounting, business administration, business education, management), EDUCATION (elementary, secondary), PHILOSOPHY (religion), PREPROFESSIONAL (ministry). Specializations within the B.A. in Ministry include Christian education, church music, pre-seminary, communications, or recreation. Seventy-one percent of degrees conferred are in preprofessional subjects; 17% are in business.

Required: All students are required to take physical education.

Special: A combined B.A.-B.S. degree is possible in teacher education and business administration.

Admissions: Eighty percent of those who applied for admission to the 1981-82 freshman class were accepted. The ACT scores of a recent freshman class were: 24% between 20 and 23, 12% between 24 and 26, 6% between 27 and 28, and 2% above 28. Applicants should be high school graduates. Factors that enter into the admissions decision include advanced placement or honors courses, leadership record, personality, and school recommendations.

Procedure: Applicants must submit ACT scores, a $20 application fee, and recommendations from a pastor and a friend. Freshmen are admitted at the beginning of each quarter; application deadlines are open, but the beginning of August is preferred. The college follows a rolling admissions policy.

Special: Early decision and early admissions plans are available. Students may earn credit through AP and CLEP tests.

Transfer: For fall 1981, 99 transfer students enrolled. Applicants should apply at least 1 month before the quarter in which they would like to enroll. They must be in good standing at the last college attended, and must earn, in residence, 45 of the 188-234 credits necessary for the bachelor's degree.

Visiting: The college schedules group orientation sessions at which prospective students can observe classes, meet faculty members, and tour the campus. Those visiting informally when classes are in session will be provided with guides, and may sit in on classes, and stay overnight on campus. Arrangements should be made with the director of admissions.

Financial Aid: About 80% of the students receive financial aid; 16% work part-time on campus. Sources include scholarships, BEOG,

NDSL, short-term loans, CWS, SEOG, and campus employment. The average award to freshmen from all sources is 60% of college costs. The college is a member of CSS, and aid applicants must submit the FAF or FFS. There is no deadline for submitting financial aid applications, but receipt before April 23 is preferred.

Foreign Students: One percent of the full-time students come from foreign countries. Special counseling is available to these students.

Admissions: Foreign students must achieve a score of 450 on the TOEFL. If a lower score is obtained, intensive English study is required prior to admission. The ACT is also required.

Procedure: Applications should be received by the college 1 month prior to the beginning of each quarter. Foreign students must present proof of health. Proof of sufficient funds is also necessary. Foreign students must carry health insurance, which is available through the college for a fee.

Admissions Contact: Donald G. Lindahl, Director of Admissions.

ST. CLOUD STATE UNIVERSITY   C-3
St. Cloud, Minnesota 56301   (612) 255-2111

F/T: 4629M, 4754W	Faculty: 503; IIA, +$
P/T: 514M, 626W	Ph.D.'s: 60%
Grad: 557M, 940W	S/F Ratio: 21 to 1
Year: qtrs, ss	Tuition: $732 ($1449)
Appl: Aug. 15	R and B: $1265
3409 accepted	2246 enrolled
ACT: 20	COMPETITIVE

St. Cloud University, founded in 1869, is a coeducational, multi-purpose state institution. Its library contains 477,305 volumes and 167,151 reels of microfilm, and subscribes to 2024 periodicals.

Environment: The 82-acre campus is located in the city of St. Cloud. The university has 8 coed and single-sex residence halls.

Student Life: Ninety-eight percent of the students are from Minnesota. About 36% come from public schools. Twenty-five percent of the students live on campus. Fewer than 1% of the students are minority-group members. Campus housing is both single-sex and coed. There are visiting privileges in single-sex housing. Students may keep cars on campus. The university provides day-care services to all students, faculty, and staff for a fee.

Organizations: About 3% of the students belong to 6 fraternities and sororities. The student government and special interest groups provide social and cultural entertainment on campus. Nearby recreation areas include Minnesota Boundary Waters.

Sports: The university competes in 11 intercollegiate sports for men and 9 for women. There are 11 intramural sports for men and 11 for women.

Handicapped: Eighty percent of the campus is accessible to physically handicapped students. Special facilities include wheelchair ramps, parking areas, elevators, lowered drinking fountains and telephones, and specially equipped rest rooms. Special class scheduling is also available. Fewer than 1% of students have hearing or vision impairments. For them the university provides computer terminals, transcribers, and interpreters. Specialized counseling and service providers are available.

Graduates: About 38% of the freshmen drop out during the first year. Of those who graduate and pursue graduate study, 1% enter medical school, 2% enter dental school, and 1.2% enter law school. Fifty percent pursue careers in business and industry.

Services: The following services are available free to students: career counseling, psychological counseling, tutoring, and remedial instruction. Health care and placement services are also available on a fee basis.

Programs of Study: The university confers bachelor's degrees, including the B.A., B.E.S., B.F.A., B.M., and B.S. Associate and master's degrees are also granted. Bachelor's degrees are offered in the following subjects: AREA STUDIES (American, industrial, international, Latin American, urban), BUSINESS (accounting, business education, computer science, finance, management, marketing, office administration, real estate/insurance), EDUCATION (elementary, health/physical, industrial, reading, recreation, special, vocational/technical), ENGLISH (English, mass communications, speech), FINE AND PERFORMING ARTS (art, art history, arts administration, graphic design, music, studio art, theater/dramatics), HEALTH SCIENCES (medical technology, nuclear medical technology, physical therapy, speech science/pathology/audiology), LANGUAGES (French, German, Spanish), MATH AND SCIENCES (biology, biomedical science, chemistry, earth science, ecology/environmental science, general science, mathematics, physical sciences, physics), PHILOSOPHY (philosophy), PRE-PROFESSIONAL (criminal justice, engineering—industrial, engineering technology, photo-engineering technology, social work), SOCIAL SCIENCES (anthropology, economics, geography, government/political science, history, psychology, public administration, social sciences, social studies, sociology). About 32% of degrees conferred are in education, 30% are in business, and 14% are in social sciences.

Special: Study abroad, independent study, and internships are offered. The college allows student-designed majors.

Honors: There are 14 honor societies open to qualified students.

Admissions: Candidates should rank in the upper half of their class. The ACT scores of those who enrolled in the 1981–82 freshman class were as follows: 51% below 21, 31% between 21 and 23, 10% between 24 and 25, 7% between 26 and 28, and 1% above 28.

Procedure: The ACT, SAT, or PSAT is required. Application deadlines are August 15 (fall), November 15 (winter), March 1 (spring), and May 15 (summer). Generally, applications should be submitted at least 3 weeks prior to the beginning of the quarter of enrollment. The university uses a rolling admissions plan. There is a $10 application fee.

Special: Early decision and deferred admissions plans are available. AP and CLEP credit is granted.

Transfer: A 2.0 GPA is required; D grades transfer. At least 45 credits, of the 192 required for a bachelor's degree, must be taken in residence. Application deadlines are the same as those for freshmen.

Visiting: Informal tours of the campus with a guide can be arranged through the high school relations office. The best time for campus visits is weekdays from 9 A.M. to 1 P.M. only when classes are in session. Visitors may sit in on classes.

Financial Aid: In a recent year, 56% of all students received some form of aid. Scholarships, loans, and jobs are available through the university. The FAF, SFS, or FFS is required. Students are encouraged to apply for financial assistance by March 1.

Foreign Students: About 3% of full-time students come from foreign countries. The university offers these students an intensive English course, special counseling, and special organizations.

Admissions: Foreign students must take the TOEFL. No college entrance examination is required.

Procedure: Application deadlines are August 15 (fall), November 15 (winter), March 1 (spring), and May 15 (summer). Foreign students must present proof of health. They must also present proof of funds adequate for their entire period of study, and must pay a deposit equal to the cost of 1 year of study. Health insurance is not required, but is available through the university for a fee.

Admissions Contact: David Ellens, Admissions Counselor.

SAINT JOHN'S UNIVERSITY   B-3
Collegeville, Minnesota 56321   (612) 363-2196

F/T: 1807M	Faculty: 93; IIB, ++$
P/T: 46M, 17W	Ph.D.'s: 64%
Grad: 120M, 19W	S/F Ratio: 16 to 1
Year: 4-1-4	Tuition: $3945
Appl: June 1	R and B: $1825
1182 applied	789 accepted	509 enrolled
SAT: 510V 560M	ACT: 24	VERY COMPETITIVE

Saint John's University, established in 1857, is a Roman Catholic institution. The library contains over 310,000 volumes and 12,560 microfilm items, and subscribes to more than 1150 periodicals.

Environment: The campus is located on a 2400-acre tract of woodland and lakes, in a rural area 80 miles northwest of Minneapolis. Students enjoy both academic and social interaction with the College of Saint Benedict, a nearby women's college with an enrollment of 1850. On-campus apartments are available, in addition to dormitories.

Student Life: Over 75% of the students come from the Midwest; 25% are from other states and foreign countries. About 65% of entering freshmen come from public schools. Approximately 90% of the students reside on campus. Eighty-nine percent are Catholic and 9% are Protestant. About 7% are minority-group members. Campus housing is single-sex, and there are visiting privileges. Students may keep cars on campus.

Organizations: About 20% of the men belong to service fraternities.

Sports: The university competes on an intercollegiate level in 12 sports for men. There are 18 intramural sports for men and 3 for women.

Handicapped: Special facilities for the physically handicapped include wheelchair ramps, special parking, elevators, specially

430 MINNESOTA

equipped rest rooms, special class scheduling, and lowered telephones. About 75% of the campus is accessible to wheelchair students.

Graduates: The freshman dropout rate is 18%; 67% remain to graduate. About 50% of the graduates go on to further study: 9% enter medical school; 4% enter dental school; and 12% enter law school. Approximately 35% pursue careers in business and industry.

Services: The following free services are available to students: placement and career counseling, tutoring, remedial instruction, and psychological counseling. Health care is available for a fee. Placement services are offered to graduates as well as to undergraduates.

Programs of Study: The college awards B.A. and B.S. degrees. Master's degrees are also conferred. Bachelor's degrees are offered in the following subjects: AREA STUDIES (family, medieval), BUSINESS (accounting, business administration, management), EDUCATION (elementary, family life, home economics, religious), ENGLISH (English), FINE AND PERFORMING ARTS (art, art history, liturgical music, music, theater/dramatics), HEALTH SCIENCES (dietetics, medical technology, nursing, nutrition science, physical therapy), LANGUAGES (French, German, Greek/Latin, Spanish), MATH AND SCIENCES (biology, chemistry, mathematics, natural sciences, physics), PHILOSOPHY (classics, humanities, philosophy, theology), PREPROFESSIONAL (dentistry, divinity engineering, forestry, home economics, interior design, law, medicine, ministry, occupational food service, pharmacy, social work, veterinary), SOCIAL SCIENCES (economics, government/political science, history, psychology, social sciences, sociology). About 30% of the degrees conferred are in business; another 30% are in math and sciences.

Required: All students must register for 8 credits of freshman colloquia, 8 credits of natural science, 16 credits of humanities, 8 credits of social science, 4 credits of art, and 4 credits of analysis of values.

Special: Students are encouraged to spend the junior year abroad in university-arranged programs. Students may study in Austria, Spain, Germany, Italy, France, England, Greece, and Japan. Student-designed majors are allowed.

Honors: There are interdisciplinary honors programs.

Admissions: About 67% of those who applied were accepted for the 1981-82 freshman class. Of those who enrolled, the SAT scores were as follows: Verbal—44% below 500, Math—18% below 500, 46% between 500 and 599, 36% between 600 and 700 and 0% above 700. On the ACT, 13% scored below 21, 24% between 21 and 23, 25% between 24 and 25, 29% between 26 and 28, and 9% above 28. Candidates should rank in the upper 40% of their classes. They must also have at least a 2.5 GPA and present 15 units of high school work. Test scores, personality traits, and recommendations from the high school are also considered.

Procedure: Scores on the SAT, ACT, or PSAT will be accepted. The application deadlines are June 1 for fall and January 15 for spring. The application fee is $15. The university has a rolling admissions plan.

Special: Early and deferred admissions and early decision plans are offered. AP credit is available.

Transfer: For fall 1981, 165 transfer students applied, 98 were accepted, and 70 enrolled. A 2.5 GPA is required. D grades do not transfer. One year in-residence study is required. Transfers must also complete, at the university, 32 of the 120 credits necessary for the bachelor's degree. June 1 is the fall semester deadline; January 15 is the spring semester deadline.

Visiting: Informal guided tours, campus visits, and lodging can be arranged by the admissions office.

Financial Aid: About 60% to 65% of the students receive financial aid; 40% work part-time on campus. A variety of grants, loans, and scholarships are available. The average aid award is $3800. Applications for aid must be filed by April 23 for fall or January 15 for spring. The FAF or FFS is required by the university, which is a member of CSS.

Foreign Students: Three percent of the full-time students come from foreign countries. The university offers these students special counseling and special organizations.

Admissions: Foreign students must earn a score of 500 on the TOEFL. The SAT or ACT is also required.

Procedure: Application deadlines are February 1 (fall) and November 1 (spring). Foreign students must present proof of health and must carry health insurance, which is available through the university for a fee. Proof of funds adequate to cover study at the university is also required.

Admissions Contact: Roger C. Young, Director of Admissions.

SAINT MARY'S COLLEGE   D-5
Winona, Minnesota 55987   (507) 452-4430

F/T: 660M, 600W   Faculty: 88; IIB, av$
P/T: 50M, 50W   Ph.D.'s: 60%
Grad: 50M, 50W   S/F Ratio: 15 to 1
Year: sems   Tuition: $3790
Appl: June 1   R and B: $1760
850 applied   670 accepted   370 enrolled
ACT: 21   COMPETITIVE

Saint Mary's College, founded in 1912, is a Catholic liberal arts college conducted by the Brothers of the Christian Schools. The library contains over 150,000 volumes and subscribes to more than 575 periodicals.

Environment: The 350-acre suburban campus is set in rolling hills overlooking the Mississippi River, 110 miles from St. Paul. The physical plant includes the IBM Computer Center as well as the Mississippi River Hydrobiology Station.

Student Life: About 35% of the students come from Minnesota; 65% represent 20 other states and 6 foreign countries. Approximately 30% of entering freshmen come from public schools. Ninety percent of the students live on campus. Eighty percent are Catholic; 15% are Protestant. Three percent of the students are minority-group members. Campus housing is both coed and single-sex. There are visiting privileges in single-sex dorms. Students may keep cars on campus.

Organizations: There are 5 national fraternities; about 20% of the men belong. Student activities include a strong student government, a campus radio station, Theater St. Mary's, and departmental and special interest clubs.

Sports: The school competes on an intercollegiate level in 7 sports for men and 6 for women. There are 10 intramural sports for men and 9 for women.

Handicapped: Special facilities for the physically handicapped include wheelchair ramps, special parking, elevators, lowered drinking fountains, and lowered telephones. About 50% of the campus is accessible to handicapped students. Some students with visual impairments do attend.

Graduates: The freshman dropout rate is 15%; 75% remain to graduate. About 50% pursue graduate study after graduation: 5% enter medical school; 2% enter dental school; and 8% enter law school. Approximately 25% pursue careers in business and industry.

Services: Students receive the following services free of charge: placement and career counseling, health care, tutoring, remedial instruction, and psychological counseling. Placement services are available to graduates and undergraduates.

Programs of Study: The college confers the B.A. degree. Master's degrees are also awarded. Bachelor's degrees are offered in the following subjects: AREA STUDIES (American), BUSINESS (accounting, business administration, business education, computer science, finance, management, marketing), EDUCATION (early childhood, elementary, secondary, special), ENGLISH (English, journalism, literature), FINE AND PERFORMING ARTS (art, film/photography, music, music education, public relations, radio/TV, studio art, theater/dramatics), HEALTH SCIENCES (medical technology, nuclear medicine technology, physical therapy), LANGUAGES (French, German, Greek/Latin, Russian, Spanish), MATH AND SCIENCES (biology, chemistry, ecology/environmental science, mathematics, natural sciences, physics, statistics), PHILOSOPHY (classics, humanities, philosophy, religion), PREPROFESSIONAL (dentistry, engineering, law, medicine, ministry, veterinary), SOCIAL SCIENCES (economics, government/political science, history, psychology, sociology). About 25% of the degrees conferred are in business; 20% are in preprofessional studies; and another 20% are in math and sciences.

Required: Freshmen are required to complete 2 credits of physical education and 1 course in English composition.

Special: Student-designed majors are permitted. The college offers a course exchange program with the College of St. Theresa and Wonona State College. Cooperative degree programs in dentistry, law, medicine, and engineering are available as well as internship programs in accounting, governmental service, foreign study, and law enforcement.

Honors: The college has an interdisciplinary honors program.

Admissions: About 79% of those who applied were accepted for the 1981-82 freshman class. Of those who enrolled in a recent class, the ACT scores were as follows: 23% were between 20 and 23, 20% were between 24 and 26, 10% were between 27 and 28, and 3% were above 28. Candidates should rank in the upper 70% of their high school classes and present a minimum GPA of 2.2. Consideration is also given to leadership, extracurricular activities, special talents, impressions made during interview, recommendations by school officials, and advanced placement or honor courses.

Procedure: Either the SAT or ACT is required. The college uses a rolling admissions system. The application deadline is June 1, but it is recommended that applications be filed between September and January of the senior year. Freshmen may be admitted at midyear. The application fee is $15.

Special: CLEP and AP credit is available.

Transfer: For fall 1981, 100 transfer students applied, 80 were accepted, and 60 enrolled. Transfer students are admitted regularly each term. Application deadlines are the same as for freshmen. A 2.0 GPA is required. There is a residency requirement for 60 semester hours of the 122 required for the bachelor's degree.

Visiting: There are regularly scheduled orientations for prospective students. Informal tours and classroom visits can also be arranged by the director of admissions.

Financial Aid: About 55% of all students receive financial aid; 55% work part-time on campus. A variety of scholarships, grants, and loans are available. The college participates in the CSS and requires the FAF or FFS. The deadline for financial aid application is April 15 for fall or December 1 for winter.

Foreign Students: About 1% of the full-time students come from foreign countries. The college offers these students special counseling and special organizations.

Admissions: Foreign students must take the TOEFL; a minimum score is not required. College entrance exams also are not required.

Procedure: Application deadlines are June 1 (fall) and December 1 (winter). A physical examination and a health history are necessary as proof of health. Foreign students must carry health insurance, which is not available through the college. They must also present proof of funds adequate to cover 1 year of study.

Admissions Contact: Anthony M. Piscitiello, Director of Admissions Counseling.

ST. OLAF COLLEGE
Northfield, Minnesota 55057   C-4   (507) 663-3025

F/T: 1395M, 1640W	Faculty: 214; IIB, ++$
P/T: 22M, 40W	Ph.D.'s: 74%
Grad: none	S/F Ratio: 14 to 1
Year: 4-1-4, ss	Tuition: $4710
Appl: Feb. 15	R and B: $1714
1985 applied	1211 accepted 800 enrolled
SAT: 540V 590M	ACT: 26 **HIGHLY COMPETITIVE**

St. Olaf College is the largest liberal arts college associated with the American Lutheran Church. It was founded for the purpose of integrating young Norwegian men and women into American life and culture. The Department of Norwegian Studies and the Norwegian-American Historical Society reflect the continuation of this interest and the unique flavor of the college. An innovative approach to individualized education is offered by the St. Olaf Paracollege, founded in 1969. The Rolvaag Memorial Library contains over 325,000 volumes and 5500 microfilm items, and subscribes to more than 1100 periodicals.

Environment: The rural 350-acre campus is located 35 miles from Minneapolis.

Student Life: A little more than half the students are from Minnesota, but some 48 states and 26 foreign countries are represented in the student body. About 90% of entering freshmen come from public schools. Ninety-three percent of the students live on campus. Eighty-seven percent of the students are Protestant and 9% are Catholic. The majority of students are Lutheran, but attendance at daily services is voluntary. Two percent are minority-group members. Campus housing is both coed and single-sex. There are visiting privileges in single-sex dorms.

Organizations: Departmental and special interest clubs are available. On-campus organizations include 6 choirs, 2 bands, 3 orchestras, and 6 jazz ensembles. The St. Olaf Band and Choir were the first American collegiate musical organizations to appear before European audiences, more than 60 years ago.

Sports: The college competes on an intercollegiate level in 14 sports for men and 11 for women. Fifteen intramural sports are available to both men and women.

Handicapped: About 20% of the campus is accessible to the physically handicapped. Special facilities include wheelchair ramps, special parking, specially equipped rest rooms, and lowered drinking fountains and telephones.

Graduates: The freshman dropout rate is 2%; 75% remain to graduate. About 55% of the graduates eventually pursue graduate study. Five percent enter medical school, 1% enter dental school, and about 5% enter law school. Twenty percent pursue careers in business and industry.

Services: Students receive the following services free of charge: career counseling and placement, health care, tutoring, remedial instruction, and psychological counseling. Placement services are also available to alumni.

Programs of Study: The college confers the B.A., B.S., B.Mus., and B.S.N. degrees. Bachelor's degrees are offered in the following subjects: AREA STUDIES (Ancient and Medieval, American, Asian, Black/Afro-American, Hispanic, Russian, sports, urban, women's studies), BUSINESS (economics), EDUCATION (health/physical, secondary), ENGLISH (English, literature, speech), FINE AND PERFORMING ARTS (art, art education, art history, dance, fine arts, music, music education, theater/dramatics), HEALTH SCIENCES (health studies, nursing), LANGUAGES (French, German, Greek/Latin, Norwegian, Russian, Spanish), MATH AND SCIENCES (biology, chemistry, mathematics, physics, statistics), PHILOSOPHY (classics, philosophy, religion), PREPROFESSIONAL (architecture, dentistry, engineering, home economics, law, medicine, ministry, pharmacy, social work, veterinary), SOCIAL SCIENCES (anthropology, economics, government/political science, history, psychology, sociology). About 20% of the degrees conferred are in math and sciences, and 17% are in preprofessional studies.

Required: Students must fulfill the following requirements: 1 course in English; 3 in religion; 3 in foreign languages; 3 in history, literature, and philosophy; 2 in art, music, or speech; 2 in economics, political science, psychology, and sociology; and 2 in biology, chemistry, mathematics, and physics. Two semesters of physical education are also required.

Special: It is possible to earn a combined B.A.-B.S. degree in engineering. Student-designed majors are allowed. The college participates in the Urban Semester Teaching Program, the Newberry Library Humanities Seminar, the Argonne Semester Program in Atomic Studies in Chicago, the Wilderness Field Station Program, the American Indian Education Program, and the American Minorities Program. There is a Global Semester in cooperation with the Christian Ecumenical Center and an Interim Abroad academic program that offers foreign study in Europe, Japan, and Africa. A unique feature of St. Olaf's curriculum is the Great Conversation program—a creative approach to the study of the humanities—in which students and faculty examine the works of the great thinkers of Western civilization. The St. Olaf Paracollege offers an individualized alternative route to the B.A. degree. Utilizing the time-honored tutorial system, Paracollege students may design their own major in a field best suited to their intellectual interests and future plans.

Honors: There are 12 national honorary societies on campus and several departmental honors programs.

Admissions: About 61% of those who applied were accepted for the 1981–82 freshman class. Of those who enrolled, the SAT scores were as follows: Verbal—29% below 500, 45% between 500 and 599, 21% between 600 and 700, and 5% above 700; Math—17% below 500, 39% between 500 and 599, 34% between 600 and 700, and 10% above 700. The percentages for those submitting ACT scores were as follows: 5% scored below 21, 23% between 21 and 23, 22% between 24 and 25, 31% between 26 and 28, and 19% above 28. Applicants should rank in the upper 40% of their class, have at least a B average, be recommended by the high school, and present 15 Carnegie units of work. Other important factors in admission decisions include advanced placement or honor courses, evidence of special talent, leadership record, personality, and extracurricular activities. Some preference is given to children of alumni and to Lutherans.

Procedure: Either the SAT, PSAT, or ACT is required and should be taken by January of the senior year. The deadline for fall admission is February 15; for winter it is December 1. Notification takes place on a rolling basis. There is a $15 application fee.

Special: An early decision and early and deferred admissions plans are available. CLEP and AP credit is available.

Transfer: For fall 1981, 87 of 179 transfer applications were accepted; 59 students enrolled. A minimum GPA of 2.0 is necessary; D grades do not transfer. There is a 2-year residency requirement, during which transfers must complete 17 of the 35 courses required for the bachelor's degree. February 15 is the fall semester deadline; December 1, the spring deadline.

Financial Aid: Fifty-five percent of the students receive financial aid. The college offers scholarships ranging from $100 to $4000 from a fund of $2.5 million. Loans range from $100 to $2500. The average aid award to freshmen is $4000. About 50% of the students work part time. The deadline for financial aid application is February 15; the FAF or FFS is required. The college is a member of CSS.

Foreign Students: Foreign students comprise about 1% of the full-time enrollment. The college offers these students an intensive English course and special counseling and organizations.

Admissions: Foreign students must achieve a score of 500 on the TOEFL. The SAT or ACT is not required.

Procedure: February 1 is the application deadline for fall entry. Foreign students must take a complete physical examination to establish proof of health, and must carry health insurance, which is available through the college for a fee. Proof of funds adequate to cover 1 year of study is also required.

Admissions Contact: Bruce K. Moe, Director of Admissions.

SOUTHWEST STATE UNIVERSITY B-4
Marshall, Minnesota 56258   (507) 537-6286

F/T: 1687M&W	Faculty: n/av; IIB, ++$
P/T: 415M&W	Ph.D.'s: n/av
Grad: none	S/F Ratio: 18 to 1
Year: qtrs, ss	Tuition: $13.65 ($27.15) p/c
Appl: Aug. 27	R and B: $1500
941 applied	828 accepted 577 enrolled
SAT or ACT: required	LESS COMPETITIVE

Southwest State University, founded in 1963, is a liberal arts, technical, and professional college supported by the state of Minnesota. The library contains 135,000 volumes, subscribes to 1200 periodicals, and stores 12,000 microfilm items.

Environment: The rural 220-acre campus is located 150 miles from Minneapolis-St. Paul. Facilities include 7 residence halls, 8 academic buildings, 2 food service facilities, and 200 housing units for students who desire apartments.

Student Life: Seventy-five percent of the students come from Minnesota. About 55% reside on campus. Approximately 90% of entering freshmen come from public schools. About 2% of the students are minority-group members. Campus housing is both coed and single-sex; there are visiting privileges in single-sex dorms. Students may keep cars on campus.

Organizations: A variety of extracurricular activities are offered.

Sports: The university competes on an intercollegiate level in 6 sports for men and for women. There are 19 intramural sports for men and 15 for women.

Handicapped: Facilities for the handicapped include wheelchair ramps, special parking, elevators, specially equipped rest rooms, lowered drinking fountains, and lowered telephones. The campus is completely accessible to physically handicapped students.

Graduates: The freshman dropout rate is 19%. About 11% of the students pursue graduate study after graduation: 1% enter medical school; 1% enter dental school; and 1% enter law school. Sixty percent pursue careers in business and industry.

Services: Students receive the following services free of charge: placement, career and psychological counseling, health care, tutoring, and remedial instruction. Comprehensive placement services are also available to alumni during the first year following graduation.

Programs of Study: The university awards B.A., B.S., and B.E.T. degrees. Associate degrees are also conferred. Bachelor's degrees are offered in the following subjects: BUSINESS (accounting, agribusiness, business administration, business education, health care administration, hotel management, institutional management, management, marketing, restaurant management), EDUCATION (elementary, health/physical, secondary), ENGLISH (literature and language arts education, literature/creative writing, speech), FINE AND PERFORMING ARTS (art, art education, music, music education, radio/TV, speech/theater arts, speech/theater arts education, theater/dramatics), HEALTH SCIENCES (medical technology), MATH AND SCIENCES (biology, chemistry, earth science, mathematics, physics), PREPROFESSIONAL (dentistry, engineering—electronic, engineering—mechanical, law, medicine, ministry), SOCIAL SCIENCES (anthropology, history, psychology, sociology). About 30% of the degrees awarded are in business; 28% are in education.

Special: Student-designed majors are permitted. It is also possible to earn B.G.S. or combined B.A.-B.S. degrees.

Honors: There is one national honor society on campus.

Admissions: About 88% of those who applied for the 1981-82 freshman class were admitted. Of those who enrolled for a recent class, the ACT scores were as follows: 24% were between 20 and 23, 18% were between 24 and 26, 4% were between 27 and 28, and 4% were above 28. Applicants should rank in the upper half of their classes.

Procedure: The ACT, SAT, or PSAT/NMSQT is required. The deadline for fall admission is August 27; for winter, November 16; for spring, February 23; and for summer, May 10. There is a $10 application fee. Notification occurs on a rolling basis.

Special: An early decision is possible. Early admissions is also available. CLEP and AP credit is possible.

Transfer: For fall 1981, 241 transfer students were accepted. Transfers are considered for all classes. A 2.0 GPA is required. D grades do not transfer. All students must complete, at the university, 48 of the 192 quarter hours required for the bachelor's degree. Application deadlines are the same as for freshman applicants.

Visiting: There are regularly scheduled orientations for prospective students. Informal guided tours and classroom visits can also be arranged by the admissions office.

Financial Aid: About 75% of the students receive financial aid; 42% work part-time on campus. The average aid award to freshmen is $2200. The FAF or FFS is required; applications must be in by April 1. The university is a member of CSS.

Foreign Students: Foreign students constitute 2% of the full-time enrollment. The university offers these students special counseling and special organizations.

Admissions: A minimum score of 500 on the TOEFL is required for admission. The SAT or ACT is not necessary.

Procedure: Application deadlines are August 1 (fall), November 1 (winter), February 1 (spring), and May 1 (summer). Foreign students must provide proof of funds adequate to cover an entire year of study. They must also carry health insurance, which is available through the university for a fee.

Admissions Contact: Philip M. Coltart, Director of Admissions and Orientation.

UNIVERSITY OF MINNESOTA

The University of Minnesota, founded in 1851, is a state-supported institution with 5 campuses: Twin Cities (Minneapolis-St. Paul), Duluth, Morris, Crookston, and Waseca.

The Twin Cities, Duluth, and Morris campuses are full-time 4-year colleges. The Technical Colleges at Crookston and Waseca offer 2-year programs leading to the associate degree. Descriptions of the Duluth, Morris, and Twin Cities campuses follow.

UNIVERSITY OF MINNESOTA/DULUTH D-3
Duluth, Minnesota 55812   (218) 726-8282

F/T: 3411M, 2943W	Faculty: 413; IIA, +$
P/T: 274M, 404W	Ph.D.'s: 53%
Grad: 206M, 240W	S/F Ratio: 18 to 1
Year: qtrs, ss	Tuition: $1207 ($3010)
Appl: Aug. 15	R and B: $2050
3200 applied	3025 accepted 2008 enrolled
SAT: 441V 500M	ACT: 22 LESS COMPETITIVE

The University of Minnesota/Duluth, founded in 1947, is a rapidly growing center offering a liberal arts education. Though principally an undergraduate institution, it is expanding its graduate program. The library contains over 250,000 volumes and 54,000 microfilm items, and subscribes to more than 3532 periodicals.

Environment: The suburban campus, located approximately 150 miles north of Minneapolis, is divided into 2 parts: a 257-acre upper campus and a 10-acre lower campus. The university has a student center, a communications center, an art museum, a performing arts center, a planetarium, a School of Business, and a School of Medicine. There are dormitories accommodating 1100 students and apartments housing 1100.

Student Life: About 92% of the students are from Minnesota. Eight percent are minority-group members. Twenty-five percent live on campus. Campus housing is both coed and single-sex. There are visiting privileges in single-sex dorms. Students may keep cars on campus. The university provides day-care services to all students, faculty, and staff.

Organizations: There are 3 fraternities and 4 sororities on campus. Clubs and organizations sponsor a variety of cultural, social, and sports events. The campus has a student newspaper and radio station.

Sports: Intercollegiate competition is offered in 12 sports for men and 9 for women. Intramurals include 14 sports for men and 12 for women.

Handicapped: The entire campus is accessible to physically handicapped students. Special facilities include wheelchair ramps, special parking, elevators, specially equipped rest rooms, and lowered drinking fountains and telephones. There is 1 special counselor to assist handicapped students.

Graduates: Thirty-eight percent of the freshmen drop out by the end of the first year; 49% remain to graduate. Twenty percent of the students pursue graduate study after graduation.

Services: The following services are available to students free of charge: psychological counseling, career counseling, tutoring, and remedial instruction. Placement and health-care services are also available for a fee.

Programs of Study: The university offers the B.A., B.A.S., B.S., B.B.A., B.F.A., and B.Mus. degrees and Bachelors of Accounting, Social Development, Office Administration, Applied Science, and Applied Arts. Associate and master's degrees are also awarded. Bachelor's degrees are offered in the following subjects: AREA STUDIES (interdisciplinary, urban), BUSINESS (accounting, business administration, business education, computer science, finance, management, marketing), EDUCATION (early childhood, elementary, health/physical, industrial, secondary, special), ENGLISH (English, literature, speech), FINE AND PERFORMING ARTS (art, art education, art history, dance, music, music education, studio art, theater/dramatics), HEALTH SCIENCES, (speech therapy), LANGUAGES (French, German, Spanish), MATH AND SCIENCES (biolgoy, botany, chemistry, earth science, geology, mathematics, natural sciences, physical sciences, physics, statistics, zoology), PHILOSOPHY (classics, philosophy), PREPROFESSIONAL (agriculture, architecture, dentistry, engineering, forestry, home economics, law, medicine, ministry, pharmacy, social work, veterinary), SOCIAL SCIENCES (anthropology, economics, geography, government/political science, history, international relations, psychology, social sciences, sociology).

Special: Combined B.A.-B.S. degrees may be earned. Students are permitted to design their own majors.

Admissions: Ninety-five percent of those who applied for the 1981-82 freshman class were accepted. Of those who enrolled, the SAT scores were as follows: Verbal—74% below 500, 20% between 500 and 599, 6% between 600 and 700, and 0% above 700; Math—47% below 500, 32% between 500 and 599, 18% between 600 and 700, and 4% above 700. On the ACT, 47% scored below 21, 26% between 21 and 23, 12% between 24 and 25, 11% between 26 and 28, and 4% above 28. It is recommended that applicants have a strong preparatory background.

Procedure: The PSAT is preferred; the SAT or ACT is accepted. Application deadlines are August 15 (fall), November 15 (winter), and February 15 (spring). Admissions are made on a rolling basis. There is a $15 application fee.

Transfer: For fall 1981, 755 transfer students applied, 650 were accepted, and 490 enrolled. Transfers are accepted for all classes. A 2.0 GPA is required; D grades transfer. Transfer students must take 2 quarters in residence and complete, at the university, 30 of the 180 quarter credits necessary for the bachelor's degree. Application deadlines are the same as for freshmen.

Visiting: Campus tours and meetings with admissions counselors and faculty members are available to prospective students. Guides are also available for informal visits to the campus. Visitors may sit in on classes and may also stay at the school. The best time to visit is when classes are in session. The admissions office will make arrangements.

Financial Aid: Scholarships and loans are available. Currently about 71% of all students receive some form of financial aid; 22% work part-time on campus. The deadline for applications is March 1. The FFS is required; the university is a member of CSS.

Foreign Students: Over 2% of the full-time students come from foreign countries. The university offers these students an intensive English course, special counseling, and special organizations.

Admissions: Foreign students must achieve a score of 550 on the TOEFL. The ACT or SAT is also required.

Procedure: Application deadlines are July 15 (fall), November 15 (winter), and February 15 (spring). Foreign students must furnish a statement from a physician as proof of health and must carry health insurance, which is available through the university for a fee. Proof of funds adequate to cover 1 year of study is also necessary.

Admissions Contact: Gerald R. Allen, Director of Admissions and Registrar.

MINNESOTA 433

UNIVERSITY OF MINNESOTA/MORRIS B-3
Morris, Minnesota 56267 (612) 589-2116

F/T: 849M, 841W		Faculty:	108; IIB, + +$
P/T: none		Ph.D.'s:	68%
Grad: none		S/F Ratio:	17 to 1
Year: qtrs, ss		Tuition:	$1248 ($3075)
Appl: Sept. 15		R and B:	$1716
775 applied	739 accepted		494 enrolled
ACT: 22			COMPETITIVE

The University of Minnesota/Morris, established in 1959, offers a liberal arts and sciences curriculum. The library contains 105,000 volumes.

Environment: The self-contained campus is situated on 45 acres in a rural area about 150 miles northwest of Minneapolis. The nearly 30 buildings on campus include 5 residence halls and a student apartment complex.

Student Life: All but about 5% of the students are from Minnesota. About 80% live on campus or nearby. Ninety-eight percent come from public schools. About 5% of the students are minority-group members. Campus housing is both coed and single-sex; there are visiting privileges in single-sex dorms. Students may keep cars on campus.

Organizations: There are 2 fraternities and 1 sorority on campus. A cultural program brings lecturers, films, and art exhibits to the campus. Students are active in political groups, sports clubs, and special-interest organizations. Students can work on the yearbook, newspaper, and radio station.

Sports: Intercollegiate competition is offered in 8 sports for men and in 7 for women. There are 7 intramural sports each for men and women.

Handicapped: The entire campus is accessible to handicapped students. Facilities include wheelchair ramps, special parking, specially equipped rest rooms, and lowered drinking fountains and telephones. Special counselors are available to assist handicapped students. About 1% of the students have visual impairments.

Graduates: The freshman dropout rate is 4%; 45% remain to graduate. Twenty-five percent of the graduates pursue advanced study: 6% enter medical school, 2% enter dental school, and 15% enter law school. Another 35% pursue careers in business and industry.

Services: The following services are available to students free of charge: psychological counseling, career counseling, tutoring, and remedial instruction. Health care and placement services also are available.

Programs of Study: All undergraduate programs lead to the B.A. degree. Bachelor's degrees are offered in the following subjects: AREA STUDIES (Latin American), EDUCATION (elementary, health/physical, secondary), ENGLISH (English, literature, speech), FINE AND PERFORMING ARTS (art history, music, music education, studio art, theater/dramatics), LANGUAGES (French, German, Spanish), MATH AND SCIENCES (biology, chemistry, earth science, geology, mathematics, natural sciences, physical sciences, physics), PHILOSOPHY (humanities, philosophy), PREPROFESSIONAL (agriculture, architecture, computer science, dentistry, engineering, fisheries/wildlife, forestry, home economics, hospital and health care administration, journalism and mass communication, law, library science, medical technology, medicine, mortuary science, nursing, occupational therapy, optometry, osteopathic medicine, pharmacy, physical therapy, podiatric medicine, recreation and parks administration, veterinary), SOCIAL SCIENCES (anthropology, business economics, economics, geography, government–political science, history, psychology, social sciences, sociology).

Special: Students may design their own majors.

Admissions: Ninety-five percent of the applicants for the 1981-82 freshman class were accepted. The ACT scores of those who enrolled were as follows: 25% between 19 and 22, 35% between 23 and 25%, 35% between 26 and 28, and 4% above 28. Students should be high school graduates and should rank in the top half of their high school class. A strong academic background is recommended.

Procedure: The ACT or the PSAT is required. Applications are due September 15 for the fall quarter. New students also are admitted to other quarters. There is a $15 application fee. Admissions are granted on a rolling basis.

Special: The university has early decision, early admissions, and deferred admissions plans. AP and CLEP credit is accepted.

434 MINNESOTA

Transfer: Transfer students are accepted each term. A 2.0 GPA is required. Students must complete, at the university, 45 of the 180 quarter hours necessary to receive a bachelor's degree. The application deadline is the same as for freshmen.

Visiting: Campus tours and interviews with faculty members are offered. Guides are also available for informal visits. Visitors may sit in on classes and stay overnight on campus. The best time to visit is a weekday. The admissions office will make arrangements.

Financial Aid: Scholarships, grants, and loans are available to all needy students. The university also participates in CWS, and 69% of the students work part-time on campus. About 80% of all students receive aid; the average award to freshmen from all sources was $2537 in 1981–82. The FFS must be submitted by June 1 for fall, December 1 for winter, March 1 for spring, or May 1 for summer.

Foreign Students: Fewer than 1% of the students are from foreign countries. The university offers these students an intensive English course, special counseling, and special organizations.

Admissions: No college entrance exams are required. Students must achieve a minimum score of 525 on the TOEFL.

Procedure: The application deadline for foreign students is September 15. Proof of adequate funds for the first 2 years of study is required. Health insurance is also required, and is available through the university for a fee.

Admissions Contact: Ruth E. Olson, Admissions Counselor.

UNIVERSITY OF MINNESOTA/TWIN CITIES   C–4
Minneapolis, Minnesota 55455   (612) 373-3030

F/T: 15,077M, 12,574W	Faculty: 4655; I, +$
P/T: 2893M, 2674W	Ph.D.'s: n/av
Grad: 4525M, 3638W	S/F Ratio: n/av
Year: qtrs, ss	Tuition: $1265 ($3095)
Appl: July 15	R and B: $2175
10,887 applied	8799 accepted 5632 enrolled
SAT(mean): 495V 552M ACT: 21	COMPETITIVE+

The Twin Cities campus of the University of Minnesota is the site of the College of Liberal Arts; the Institute of Technology; the Law School; the College of Agriculture; the College of Forestry; the College of Home Economics; the Graduate School; the College of Education; the College of Biological Sciences; the College of Veterinary Medicine; the College of Pharmacy; the General College; the Library School; the University College; the School of Management; the School of Music; the School of Architecture; and the schools of Dentistry, Journalism, Medicine, Nursing, Public Health, and Social Work. The University College offers two innovative, student-designed programs—University Without Walls and the Inter-College Program—which provide flexible, individualized alternatives to traditionally structured degree majors. The library contains over 3,730,168 volumes and subscribes to more than 44,510 periodicals.

Environment: The campus occupies 230 acres in Minneapolis and 715 acres in St. Paul. Among its many buildings is Williamson Hall, an underground building completely heated and cooled by solar collection panels. The Law School building is used by the Minnesota Supreme Court for hearings. Campus dormitories accommodate 2000 men and 2000 women.

Student Life: About 95% of the students come from Minnesota; 3% come from other states. Almost 6% are minority-group members. A reciprocal agreement with Wisconsin, North Dakota, and South Dakota enables students from those states to attend the university at in-state costs. University housing is both coed and single-sex; there are visiting privileges in single-sex dorms. Students may keep cars on campus. Day-care services are provided to all students, faculty, and staff for a fee based on family income and number of children.

Organizations: There are over 500 registered student organizations which include political, social, and cultural groups as well as sports and student professional societies. There are 29 academic fraternities and 17 academic sororities, and 24 professional fraternities and 5 professional sororities on campus. Cultural programs on campus include theater, symphony, opera, and lectures. The cultural resources of Minneapolis and St. Paul are easily accessible to students.

Sports: The university competes intercollegiately in 12 sports for men and 11 for women. There are 17 intramural sports for men and 16 for women.

Handicapped: About 95% of the campus is accessible to physically handicapped students. Special facilities include wheelchair ramps, special parking, elevators, specially equipped rest rooms, and lowered drinking fountains and telephones. Special class scheduling is also available. Support services for handicapped students are available through several offices: Rehabilitation Services, the Department of Vocational Rehabilitation, 504 Handicapped Resource Coordinator, Student Counseling Bureau, and the Reading/Study-Skills Center. Special facilities for students with hearing or vision impairments include reader and taping services, special library facilities, elevators in braille, dial access to vital university information, and reading.

Graduates: At the end of the freshman year, 15% of the students drop out; 50% remain to graduate. Sixty percent of those students pursue graduate studies. Seventy-one percent enter careers in business or industry.

Services: The following services are available to students free of charge: health care, placement and career counseling (for graduates as well as undergraduates), and remedial instruction. Some psychological counseling and tutoring services require payment.

Programs of Study: The Twin Cities campus consists of 26 schools and colleges which offer degrees in more than 125 major fields. Degrees conferred include the B.A., B.Arch., B.Land.Arch., B.A.S., B.F.A., B.G.S., B.Mus., B.S., B.S.Bus., and Bachelor of Individualized Studies. Associate, master's and doctoral degrees are also awarded. Bachelor's degrees are offered in the following subjects: AREA STUDIES (African, American, American Indian, Black/Afro-American, Chicano, East Asian, Latin American, Near and Middle Eastern, Russian, South Asian, urban), BUSINESS (accounting, agricultural business administration, business administration, business education, computer science, finance, management, marketing, real estate/insurance, retail merchandising), EDUCATION (early childhood, elementary, foreign language, health/physical, industrial, secondary), ENGLISH (English, journalism, literature, speech), FINE AND PERFORMING ARTS (art, art education, art history, costume design, dance, music, music education, studio art, theater/dramatics), HEALTH SCIENCES (communication disorders, dance therapy, medical technology, mortuary science, nursing, occupational therapy, physical therapy, physiology, speech pathology, speech therapy), LANGUAGES (East Asian, French, German, Greek/Latin, Hebrew, Italian, Japanese, linguistics, Portuguese, Russian, Scandinavian, Slavic and East European, Spanish), MATH AND SCIENCES (astronomy, astrophysics, biochemistry, biology, biometry, botany, chemistry, earth science, ecology/environmental science, environmental design, geology, geophysics, mathematics, microbiology, physics, statistics), PHILOSOPHY (classics, humanities, philosophy, religion), PREPROFESSIONAL (agriculture—economics, agriculture—education, agriculture—journalism, agronomy, animal science, architecture, consumer food science, economics of public service, engineering—aeronautical, engineering—agricultural, engineering—chemical, engineering—civil, engineering—electrical, engineering—mechanical, engineering—metallurgical, engineering—mining, fisheries, food science and technology, forestry, general design, general home economics, home economics education, horticultural science, hospitality and food service management, housing, interior design, ministry, nutrition and dietetics, pharmacy, plant health technology, resource economics, social work, soil science, soil and water resource management, textiles and clothing, wildlife), SOCIAL SCIENCES (anthropology, child psychology, economics, family relationships, geography, government/political science, history, human services, international relations, psychology, social welfare/social work, sociology, speech communication, urban studies, women's studies).

Required: All undergraduate degree programs require that students distribute credits among 4 areas of knowledge: communication, language, and symbolic systems; physical and biological sciences; individual and society; and artistic expression. English composition is also required.

Special: In the field of engineering, the University offers a 4-year intern program whereby the student alternates 3 months of study and 3 months on the job after having completed 2 years of study. The university offers a summer travel program. A combined B.A.-B.S. degree may be earned in many subjects.

Two special programs are available within the University College. University Without Walls is an individualized degree program which offers participants access to the university's faculty, libraries, and other resources; permits them to select their own educational programs on campus or off; and allows credit for learning from a job or other life experiences. The Inter-College Program, a student-designed, credit-based alternative to conventional degree majors, encourages qualified students to implement a 190-credit intercollegiate or interdisciplinary program suited to their own objectives and plans, which results in either the B.A. or B.S. degree.

Honors: There are more than 40 honor societies with branches on campus. Many of the university's colleges and schools have separate honors programs as well.

Admissions: Over 80% of those who applied were accepted for the 1981-82 freshman class. Academic performance and test scores are basic to the admissions decision, but units, patterns, and curricula vary in importance according to the particular situation and the college of application. All students should have at least 9 academic units taken in the last 3 years of high school. Preference is given to Minnesota residents. The university considers advanced placement or honors courses, high school recommendations, and evidence of special talent in making admissions decisions.

Procedure: In-state applicants must submit the ACT, PSAT, or SAT scores. Either the SAT or the ACT is acceptable from out-of-state applicants. New students are admitted to most programs at all quarters. Application deadlines are July 15 (fall), November 15 (winter), and February 15 (spring). Applications may be considered after these dates if time allows. Notification is on a rolling basis. There is a $15 application fee.

Special: An early admissions plan is available. Non-high-school graduates who are over 19 years old may be admitted on the basis of tests and individual approval. High school graduates and prospective students with low test scores, or those who did not take entrance exams, may be admitted to the General College. CLEP and AP credit may be earned. Students are encouraged to submit applications as early as possible for fall admissions.

Transfer: Of the 7323 applications received for a recent school year, 5899 were accepted and 3136 students enrolled. Transfers are accepted for all classes. Requirements for transfer vary according to the admitting college. D grades transfer to some colleges. Preference is given to students transferring from other Minnesota colleges. Residency requirements vary according to the college attended or the degree earned. The deadlines for transfer applications are generally the same as those for freshmen applications, but some programs have earlier deadlines.

Visiting: The university conducts preview days for prospective students. Guides are also available for informal visits to the school. Visitors may sit in on classes with the instructor's permission. The best time to visit is weekdays from 8 A.M. to 3 P.M.. The university prefers 2 weeks' advance notice. The Prospective Student Services office will make arrangements.

Financial Aid: The federal government makes available about $3 million in the form of NDSL, BOG, BEOG, and CWS programs. In addition, the university grants funds of about $1 million through scholarships, loans, and grants. A student may earn up to $1500 per year. Currently about 66% of the students receive some form of aid; 50% work part-time on campus. The FFS-ACT Family Financial Statement is required. The deadline for aid application is March 1 for priority consideration.

Foreign Students: About 2% of the full-time students come from foreign countries. English courses and an intensive English program are available to these students. The university also offers them special counseling and special organizations.

Admissions: Either the TOEFL or the University of Michigan Language Test is required. Minimum acceptable scores on these tests are determined by the various colleges. The SAT or ACT is not required.

Procedure: Application deadlines are the same as for freshmen. Foreign students must provide proof of adequate funds. They must also carry health insurance, which is available through the university for a fee.

Admissions Contact: John R. Printz, Assistant Director of Admissions.

WINONA STATE UNIVERSITY D-5
Winona, Minnesota 55987 (507) 457-2065

F/T: 2000M, 2500W	Faculty: 210; IIA, av$
P/T: 200M, 200W	Ph.D.'s: 60%
Grad: 200M, 200W	S/F Ratio: 19 to 1
Year: qtrs, ss	Tuition: $880 ($1600)
Appl: see profile	R and B: $1450
1950 applied	1900 accepted 1135 enrolled
SAT: 440V 495M	ACT: 20 LESS COMPETITIVE

Winona State University is a publicly supported institution, established in 1858, offering training in the liberal arts, education, and preprofessional studies. Its library contains over 200,000 volumes and subscribes to more than 6000 periodicals.

Environment: The urban campus is situated in a beautiful region of the Mississippi Valley, 110 miles south of Minneapolis. The dormitories accommodate 1300 students. The university also sponsors off-campus apartments.

Student Life: About 70% of the students are from Minnesota; 75% come from public schools. Forty-two percent are Catholic, 37% are Protestant, and 1% are Jewish. Two percent of the students are minority-group members. Campus housing is both coed and single-sex. There are visiting privileges in single-sex dorms. Students may keep cars on campus. Forty percent of the students live off campus.

Organizations: There are 3 fraternities and 3 sororities on campus, but fewer than 2% of the students belong. There are other organizations that provide social and cultural opportunities for students.

Sports: The university competes in 8 intercollegiate sports for men and women. Intramural sports programs attract over 75% of the student body; 22 sports are open to men and 18 to women.

Handicapped: There are special facilities, housing, and a counselor available for the handicapped. Ninety percent of the campus is accessible to wheelchair students.

Graduates: The freshman dropout rate is 25%; 55% of the freshmen remain to graduate. About 10% of those who graduate enter graduate schools: 1% go to medical school, 1% go to dental school, and 1% go to law school. Another 25% pursue careers in business and industry.

Services: Free health care, tutoring, remedial instruction, psychological and career counseling, and job placement services are available to undergraduates.

Programs of Study: The university confers the B.A. and B.S. degrees. Associate, specialist, and master's degrees are also awarded. Bachelor's degrees are offered in the following subjects: AREA STUDIES (American), BUSINESS (accounting, business administration, business education, computer science, finance, management, marketing, personnel, public administration), EDUCATION (early childhood, elementary, health/physical, industrial, secondary, special), ENGLISH (English, journalism, speech), FINE AND PERFORMING ARTS (art, art education, film/photography, mass communication, music, music education, radio/TV, studio art, theater/dramatics), HEALTH SCIENCES (environmental health, medical technology, nursing, physical therapy, recreation and leisure studies, speech therapy, therapeutic recreation), LANGUAGES (French, German, Spanish), MATH AND SCIENCES (biology, botany, chemistry, earth science, ecology/environmental science, geology, mathematics, natural sciences, physical sciences, physics, statistics, zoology), PHILOSOPHY (philosophy), PREPROFESSIONAL (agriculture, architecture, dentistry, engineering, fisheries and wildlife, forestry, law, medicine, mortuary, optometry, pharmacy, podiatry, veterinary), SOCIAL SCIENCES (criminal justice, economics, geography, government/political science, history, paralegal, psychology, social sciences, social work, sociology). About 25% of degrees are conferred in business, 25% in education, and 25% in health science.

Special: The university sponsors overseas study programs. It is possible to earn a combined B.A.-B.S. degree and a B.G.S. degree. Students can design their own majors.

Honors: All departments have their own honors programs.

Admissions: Ninety-seven percent of those who applied were accepted for the 1981-82 freshman class. Of those who enrolled, the SAT scores were as follows: Verbal—58% below 500, 30% between 500 and 599, 10% between 600 and 700, and 2% above 700; Math—52% below 500, 30% between 500 and 599, 10% between 600 and 700, and 8% above 700. On the ACT, 40% scored below 21, 30% between 21 and 23, 20% between 24 and 25, 8% between 26 and 28, and 2% above 28. The candidates should have completed 15 Carnegie units, and rank in the top 66% of their graduating class. Students below these requirements may be admitted on a provisional basis. Freshmen are admitted in any session.

Procedure: The ACT, SAT, or PSAT is required. The admissions deadline is 1 week before the beginning of each quarter. The application fee is $10. There is a rolling admissions plan.

Special: Early decision and early and deferred admissions are available. AP and CLEP credit is offered.

Transfer: Of 635 applications received, 550 were accepted and 400 students enrolled for fall 1981. Good academic standing and a 2.0 GPA are required. Forty-eight quarter credits, of the 192 required for the bachelor's degree, must be earned in residence. The deadlines are the same as for freshman applications.

Visiting: Visits can be arranged weekdays through the office of admissions. Visitors can sit in on classes and stay overnight at the school.

Financial Aid: Cash awards based on merit are granted to high school seniors who rank in the top 20% of the graduating class and

436 MINNESOTA

have high admission-test scores. About 70% of the students receive some form of financial aid; 20% work part-time on campus. Scholarships averaging $1500 are available, and applications must be in by March 1. The FFS is preferred; the FAF is acceptable. The university is a member of CSS.

Foreign Students: Two percent of the full-time students are from foreign countries. The university offers these students an intensive English course as well as special counseling and special organizations.

Admissions: Foreign students must obtain a score of 500 on the TOEFL; the University of Michigan Language Test is also accepted. The SAT or ACT is not required.

Procedure: Applications should be received 6 months before the beginning of each quarter. Foreign students must complete a university health form and carry health insurance, which is available through the university for a fee. Proof of funds adequate to cover 1 year of study is also required.

MISSISSIPPI

ALCORN STATE UNIVERSITY   C-4
Lorman, Mississippi 39096   (601) 877-6147

F/T: 956M, 1135W	Faculty: 149; IIA, --$
P/T: 43M, 116W	Ph.D.'s: 50%
Grad: 39M, 98W	S/F Ratio: 14 to 1
Year: sems, ss	Tuition: $825 ($1751)
Appl: open	R and B: $686
2245 applied	1354 accepted	1013 enrolled
ACT: required		LESS COMPETITIVE

Alcorn State University, founded in 1830, offers undergraduate degree programs in agriculture, the arts and sciences, business, and education. The library contains 25,000 volumes.

Environment: The 720-acre campus is located in a rural area 36 miles south of Vicksburg and 40 miles north of Natchez. There are more than 15 major buildings, including dormitories for 890 men and 1175 women.

Student Life: About 95% of the students come from Mississippi; most are public school graduates. About 80% live on campus. The student body is predominantly black. Campus housing is single-sex, there are no visiting privileges. Students may keep cars on campus. Alcohol is not permitted on campus.

Organizations: Extracurricular activities include student government, clubs, performing groups, and social events. Ten percent of the women belong to sororities; 6% of the men to fraternities.

Sports: The university fields 6 intercollegiate teams for men and 6 for women. There are 7 intramural sports for men and 7 for women.

Handicapped: Most of the campus is accessible to handicapped students.

Graduates: The freshman dropout rate is 35%; 48% remain to graduate. About 10% of the graduates pursue advanced degrees.

Services: The university provides the following services free of charge: tutoring, remedial instruction, health care, career counseling, and placement.

Programs of Study: The B.A. and B.S. degrees are conferred. Associate and master's degrees are also awarded. Bachelor's degrees are offered in the following subjects: BUSINESS (accounting, business administration, business education, computer science, office administration), EDUCATION (early childhood, elementary, health/physical, industrial, secondary, special), ENGLISH (English, speech), FINE AND PERFORMING ARTS (music, music education), HEALTH SCIENCES (environmental health, medical technology, nursing, physical therapy), MATH AND SCIENCES (biology, chemistry, mathematics), PRE-PROFESSIONAL (agriculture, dentistry, home economics, law, medicine, pharmacy, social work, veterinary), SOCIAL SCIENCES (economics, government/political science, history, psychology, social sciences, sociology).

Required: There is a general education requirement.

Special: Dual-degree programs, cooperative education programs, and study abroad are offered.

Honors: There is an honors program. Qualified students may be elected to Alpha Kappa Mu.

Admissions: About 60% of those who applied were accepted for the 1981-82 freshman class. The ACT scores of those who enrolled were as follows: 96% below 21, 3% between 21 and 23, 1% between 24 and 25, 0% between 26 and 28, and 0% above 28. A high school diploma or GED is required. Students should have completed 15 Carnegie units. Admission is based on the applicant's academic record and ACT or SAT scores. State residents are given preference.

Procedure: The ACT is required. New students are admitted each semester. Application deadlines are open. There is no application fee.

Transfer: Transfers are accepted for the freshman and sophomore classes. A 2.0 GPA is needed; grades of C or above transfer. Sixty-seven semester hours must be completed in residence to earn a bachelor's degree, 133 credits are needed for the bachelor's degree.

Visiting: Campus tours with student guides can be arranged. Visitors may sit in on classes.

Financial Aid: About 90% of the students receive financial aid; 25% work part-time on campus. The university participates in federal programs such as NDSL, BEOG/SEOG, and CWS in addition to offering commercial loans and freshman scholarships. The university is a member of CSS, the FAF should be filed by April 15.

Foreign Students: The university offers foreign students an intensive English course.

Admissions: Foreign students must achieve an acceptable score on the university's own English proficiency test. They must also take the ACT.

Procedure: Application deadlines are open. Foreign students must present proof of health.

Admissions Contact: Alice Davis Gill, Registrar and Director of Admissions.

BELHAVEN COLLEGE   C-4
Jackson, Mississippi 39202   (601) 965-7400

F/T: 260M, 290W	Faculty: 39; IIB, --$
P/T: 220M, 251W	Ph.D.'s: 46%
Grad: none	S/F Ratio: 18 to 1
Year: sems, ss	Tuition: $2575
Appl: open	R and B: $1450
260 applied	192 accepted	141 enrolled
SAT: 520V 500M	ACT: 21	COMPETITIVE

Belhaven College is a small, coeducational, liberal arts college supported by the Presbyterian Church. The library houses 62,000 volumes, and subscribes to 400 periodicals.

Environment: The 45-acre campus, located in a suburban area, consists of colonial-style buildings and includes the recreational facilities of Belhaven Lake. Dormitories house 300 men and 300 women.

Student Life: About 68% of the students are Mississippi residents; 50% reside in dormitories. About 75% of entering freshmen come from public schools. Most students are members of the Presbyterian Church; all are required to attend chapel services once a week. About 4% of the students are minority-group members. Campus housing is single-sex; there are no visiting privileges. Students may keep cars on campus. Day-care services are available to all students for a fee.

Organizations: There are no fraternities or sororities. Extracurricular activities include an active student government. Religious organizations and counselors for all the major faiths are available.

Sports: The college fields 4 intercollegiate teams for men and 3 for women. There are 6 intramural sports for men and 6 for women.

Handicapped: About 60% of the campus is accessible to physically handicapped students, but facilities are extremely limited.

Graduates: The freshman dropout rate is 15%; 70% remain to graduate. Thirty-five percent of the graduates pursue graduate or professional study; 4% enter medical school, 5% law school, and 1% dental school. Forty percent pursue careers in business and industry.

Services: Students receive free placement services, health care, career counseling, psychological counseling, and remedial instruction. Tutoring is available on a fee basis.

Programs of Study: The college confers the B.B.A., B.A., B.S., and B.Mus. degrees. Bachelor's degrees are offered in the following subjects: BUSINESS (accounting, business administration, business education, finance, marketing, secretarial science), EDUCATION (early childhood, elementary, health/physical, secondary), ENGLISH (English, literature, speech), FINE AND PERFORMING ARTS (art, art education, music, music education), LANGUAGES (French, German, Greek/Latin, Spanish), MATH AND SCIENCES (biology, chemistry), PHILOSOPHY (Bible, Christian ministries, philosophy), PREPROFESSIONAL (dentistry, home economics, law, medicine, veterinary), SOCIAL SCIENCES (economics, history, psychology). Forty percent of the degrees are conferred in business, 20% in education, and 18% in math and science.

Required: All students must take 8 hours of religion.

Special: The college offers a B.G.S. degree. Student-designed majors are allowed. Interdepartmental courses are available in comparative literature. Courses in marine botany and invertebrate zoology are given at the Gulf Coast Research Laboratory.

Honors: Departmental honors programs are offered. There are 6 national honor societies with chapters on campus.

Admissions: Seventy-four percent of those who applied were accepted for the 1981–82 freshman class. The ACT scores of those who enrolled were as follows: 35% below 21, 25% between 21 and 23, 15% between 24 and 25, 15% between 26 and 28, and 10% above 28. Candidates must be graduates of an accredited high school, have 15 Carnegie units, have a C average or better, rank in the upper 50% of their graduating class, and score a minimum of 400 on each SAT section.

Procedure: The ACT or SAT is required. The application should be accompanied by a $10 fee. Application deadlines are open; a rolling admissions plan is in effect.

Special: AP and CLEP credit is available.

Transfer: For fall 1981, 250 transfer students applied, 180 were accepted, and 125 enrolled. A 2.0 GPA is required, a 2.5 GPA is recommended. Students must complete, at the college, 30 of the 124 hours required for a bachelor's degree. Grades of C and above transfer. Application deadlines are open.

Visiting: Orientations are held in February. Informal visits are best scheduled for Fridays; arrangements for guides can be made through the admissions office. Visitors may sit in on classes and stay overnight at the college.

Financial Aid: Fifty percent of the students receive financial aid; 30% work part-time on campus. Scholarships averaging about $650 for freshmen are available on the basis of need. Loans from federal government funds, the college, and private groups are available. The average award to freshmen from all sources is $1100. The college is a member of CSS. The deadline for scholarship applications is May 1. The FAF must be filed.

Foreign Students: Almost 4% of the full-time students are from foreign countries.

Admissions: Foreign students must achieve a minimum TOEFL score of 525; no college entrance exams are required.

Procedure: Application deadlines are open. Foreign students must complete the college's health form and present proof of funds adequate to cover 1 year of study.

Admissions Contact: R. Douglas Mickey, Director of Admissions.

BLUE MOUNTAIN COLLEGE D-1
Blue Mountain, Mississippi 38610 (601) 685-4161

F/T: 81M, 199W	Faculty: 28; IIB, n/av
P/T: 18M, 47W	Ph.D.'s: n/av
Grad: none	S/F Ratio: 15 to 1
Year: sems, ss	Tuition: $1850
Appl: open	R and B: $1410
SAT or ACT: recommended	LESS COMPETITIVE

Blue Mountain College is a liberal arts college for women, but local ministers are admitted as classroom participants. It is owned and operated by the Mississippi Baptist Convention. The library houses 44,914 volumes and 170 microfilm items, and subscribes to 229 periodicals.

Environment: The 44-acre campus, located in a rural area 70 miles from Memphis, Tennessee, is listed in the *National Register of Historical Places.* Among its facilities are a gymnasium, a fine arts building, tennis courts, a student union, an outdoor pool, and residence halls accommodating 250 women.

Student Life: Most students are from Mississippi; 13% are from other states. Seventy-nine percent of entering freshmen attended public schools. Most students are members of the Baptist Church. Chapel attendance is required 3 times a week. Dancing, smoking, and possession and/or use of alcohol are forbidden. Campus housing is single-sex, there are no visiting privileges. Students may keep cars on campus.

Organizations: There are no sororities. Students go to Memphis, Tennessee, for cultural programs.

Sports: The college fields 2 intercollegiate sports. There are 7 intramural sports.

Handicapped: Wheelchair ramps are provided for the physically handicapped; only 10% of the campus is accessible.

Graduates: The freshman dropout rate is about 5%; 45% remain to graduate. About 10% of the graduates pursue graduate and professional study; 2% enter law school, and 1% enter medical school. About 10% enter careers in business and industry.

Services: Students and graduates receive the following services free: confidential placement, resume preparation, and job listings. Health care is available on a fee basis.

Programs of Study: The college confers the B.A., B.S., B.S.Ed., and B.Mus. degrees. Bachelor's degrees are offered in the following subjects: BUSINESS (business education), EDUCATION (early childhood, elementary, health/physical, secondary, special), ENGLISH (English, speech), FINE AND PERFORMING ARTS (art, art education, music, music education), HEALTH SCIENCES (medical technology), LANGUAGES (French, Greek, Spanish), MATH AND SCIENCES (biology, chemistry, mathematics, natural sciences), PHILOSOPHY (religion), PREPROFESSIONAL (home economics, library science, ministry), SOCIAL SCIENCES (history, psychology, social sciences). Thirty-five percent of the degrees are conferred in education, 19% in social sciences, and 17% in philosophy.

Required: One year of physical education and 6 semesters of Bible are required.

Special: It is possible to earn combined B.A.-B.S. degrees in a 5-year curriculum. A pass/fail grading option is available.

Honors: The college has 2 national honor society chapters on campus —Phi Beta Lambda and the Student Education Association. Honors programs may be pursued in any major discipline. Juniors must have an overall GPA of 3.0 and 3.5 in their major, recommendation of the major professor, and approval by the honors committee.

Admissions: Eighty-seven percent of those who applied were accepted for a recent freshman class. Candidates must be graduates of an accredited high school. It is recommended that units be distributed as follows: 4 of English, 1 of social science, 2 of mathematics (1 should be algebra), 1 of science, and 4 electives. A C average or better is recommended.

Procedure: The SAT or ACT is recommended. There are no application deadlines. Freshmen are admitted to all sessions. The application fee is $10. A rolling admissions plan is used.

Special: CLEP credit is available.

Transfer: Most applications are approved; 53 students enrolled for a recent year. Transfers are accepted for all classes. A C average is preferred; D grades do transfer. Twenty-four semester hours must be taken in residence; 120 credits are required to earn the bachelor's degree. Application deadlines are open.

Visiting: Visitors may sit in on classes and stay overnight at the school. Arrangements can be made through the director of admissions.

Financial Aid: About 85% of the students receive some financial aid. Scholarships and aid totaling $200,000 are available; loan funds of $50,000 are available through NDSL and the Federally Insured Bank Loan; $50,000 more is dispensed through campus employment. The average amount of assistance granted to a freshman is $1700. The college is a member of CSS, the FAF must be filed. The application deadline is June 1.

Foreign Students: The college accepts foreign students.

Admissions Contact: Marcia Woodward, Director of Admissions.

DELTA STATE UNIVERSITY C-2
Cleveland, Mississippi 38733 (601) 843-4073

F/T: 935M, 1231W	Faculty: 192; IIA, –$
P/T: 207M, 345W	Ph.D.'s: 50%
Grad: 173M, 273W	S/F Ratio: 14 to 1
Year: sems, ss	Tuition: $770 ($1696)
Appl: see profile	R and B: $1206
689 applied	500 accepted	385 enrolled
ACT: 19		COMPETITIVE

Delta State University, founded in 1924, offers undergraduate degree programs in the arts and sciences, education, business, and nursing. The library has 226,295 volumes, and subscribes to 1611 periodicals.

438 MISSISSIPPI

Environment: The 274-acre campus, located in a rural setting, has 45 modern buildings, including 11 residence halls for 827 women and 680 men. There are also apartments for 48 married students.

Student Life: About 95% of the students come from Mississippi; 40% live on campus. Most are public school graduates. About 7% of the students are minority-group members. Campus housing is single-sex; there are visiting privileges. Students may keep cars on campus. Day-care services are available to all full-time students for a fee.

Organizations: On-campus activities include student government, clubs, publications, performing groups, dramatics, religious organizations, and social events. Ten percent of the students belong to 4 sororities and 4 fraternities.

Sports: The university fields 8 intercollegiate teams for men and 5 for women. There are 12 intramural sports for men and 12 for women.

Graduates: The freshman dropout rate is about 22%; about 45% remain to graduate. About 25% go on for further study after graduation; 1% enter medical school and 1% enter law school. Twenty percent enter careers in business and industry.

Services: The university provides free remedial instruction, health care, career counseling, placement, and psychological counseling. Tutoring is available for a fee.

Programs of Study: The B.A., B.S., B.S.Ed., B.B.A., B.F.A., B.G.S., B.M., B.M.Ed., B.S.C.J., B.S.N., and B.S.W. degrees are conferred. Master's and doctoral degrees are also awarded. Bachelor's degrees are offered in the following subjects: BUSINESS (accounting, business administration, business education, fashion merchandising, finance, management, management information systems, marketing, office administration, real estate/insurance), EDUCATION (early childhood, elementary, health/physical, secondary), ENGLISH (English, speech), FINE AND PERFORMING ARTS (art, art education, music, music education), HEALTH SCIENCES (nursing), LANGUAGES (Spanish), MATH AND SCIENCES (biology, chemistry, ecology/environmental science, mathematics, physics), PREPROFESSIONAL (dentistry, engineering, home economics, law, library science, medicine, pharmacy, social work, veterinary), SOCIAL SCIENCES (criminal justice, history, psychology, social sciences).

Required: There is a general education requirement for all students.

Special: Internships, exchange programs, and study abroad are offered.

Honors: An interdisciplinary honors program is available.

Admissions: About 73% of those who applied were accepted for the 1981-82 freshman class. The ACT scores of those who enrolled were as follows: 65% below 21, 15% between 21 and 23, 10% between 24 and 25, 4% between 26 and 28, and 1% above 28. A high school diploma or GED is required. Applicants should have completed 16 units of academic work. Out-of-state applicants need a 2.0 high school GPA. Recommendations are also considered important.

Procedure: An ACT composite score of 15 is required. New students are admitted each semester. Deadlines are open; applications should be submitted no later than 20 days before the beginning of the term. Notification is on a rolling basis. There is no application fee.

Special: There are early decision and early admissions plans. AP and CLEP credit is available.

Transfer: For fall 1981, 752 transfer students applied, 458 were accepted, and 302 enrolled. A 2.0 GPA is necessary; D grades are usually accepted. The last 30 semester hours must be completed at the university; the bachelor's degree requires completion of 133 credits. Application deadlines are the same as those for freshman applicants.

Visiting: Campus tours with student guides may be arranged. Visitors may sit in on classes.

Financial Aid: About 90% of the students receive aid; 40% work part-time on campus. The university participates in federal programs such as NDSL, BEOG/SEOG, and CWS in addition to offering commercial loans and freshman scholarships. Tuition may be paid in installments. The FAF should be filed; there is no application deadline.

Foreign Students: Fewer than 1% of the full-time students come from foreign countries.

Admissions: Foreign students must achieve a minimum TOEFL score of 525. They must also take the ACT or SAT.

Procedure: Application deadlines are May 1 (fall), October 1 (spring), and March 1 (summer). Foreign students must present proof of health as well as proof of funds adequate to cover their entire period of study.

Admissions Contact: Robert A. Bain, Director of Admissions.

JACKSON STATE UNIVERSITY C-4
Jackson, Mississippi 39217 (601) 968-2100

F/T: 3059M, 4027W Faculty: 423; IIA, av$
P/T: 432M, 928W Ph.D.'s: 52%
Grad: 329M, 621W S/F Ratio: 19 to 1
Year: sems, ss Tuition: $1664 ($2590)
Appl: Aug. 15 R and B: $1668
3200 applied 2400 accepted 1300 enrolled
ACT: 14 *LESS COMPETITIVE*

Jackson State University, established in 1877, offers undergraduate programs in the arts and sciences, business, education, and preprofessional areas. The library contains 45,000 volumes, and subscribes to more than 500 periodicals.

Environment: The 85-acre campus is located in Jackson, a city of 165,000 inhabitants. The 39 buildings include 6 residence halls that house 734 men and 1020 women. Facilities for commuting students also are available.

Student Life: About 92% of the students come from Mississippi, and most are public school graduates. About 20% live on campus in the single-sex dormitories. The student body is predominantly black. Alcohol is prohibited on campus.

Organizations: Activities include campus government, clubs, drama, publications, and social events. Four percent of the students are members of the 4 fraternities and 4 sororities on campus.

Sports: The university fields intercollegiate teams in 6 sports. Intramural sports also are available.

Handicapped: Most of the campus is accessible to handicapped students.

Graduates: The freshman dropout rate is 20%. About 30% of the graduates pursue advanced degrees.

Services: The university provides tutoring, remedial instruction, health care, career counseling, and placement services.

Programs of Study: The university confers the B.A. and B.S. degrees. Master's programs are also offered. Bachelor's degrees are awarded in the following subjects: BUSINESS (accounting, business administration, business education, computer science, finance, marketing), EDUCATION (early childhood, elementary, health/physical, industrial, recreation and leisure services, secondary, special), ENGLISH (English, literature, speech), FINE AND PERFORMING ARTS (art, art education, music, music education), HEALTH SCIENCES (medical records administration, medical technology), LANGUAGES (French, German, Spanish), MATH AND SCIENCES (biology, chemistry, mathematics, physics), PREPROFESSIONAL (dentistry, engineering, law, library science, medicine, pharmacy, social work, veterinary), SOCIAL SCIENCES (criminal justice, economics, geography, government/political science, history, psychology, social sciences, sociology).

Required: Students must fulfill general education requirements.

Special: Internships, study abroad, a cooperative education program, accelerated degrees, and exchange programs are offered.

Honors: An honors program is available. Three honor societies have chapters on campus.

Admissions: About 75% of those who applied were accepted for the 1981-82 freshman class. The ACT scores of those who enrolled were as follows: 75% below 21, 20% between 21 and 22, and 5% above 22. Applicants must have a high school diploma or GED. They must have completed 15 units of academic work with a 2.0 GPA. ACT scores, class rank (upper half preferred), recommendations, and leadership potential also are considered.

Procedure: The ACT is required. New students are admitted each semester. Application deadlines are August 15 (fall), December 15 (spring), and May 15 (summer). Notification is made on a rolling basis. There is no application fee.

Special: AP credit is granted.

Transfer: Applicants must have a 2.0 GPA. Thirty semester hours must be completed in residence.

Visiting: Campus tours with student guides can be arranged. Visitors may sit in on classes.

Financial Aid: About 85% of the students receive aid. The university participates in federal programs such as NDSL, BEOG/SEOG, and CWS, and also offers commercial loans and freshman scholarships. The average award to a 1981-82 freshman totaled $2356. The FAF or FFS should be filed by April 1.

Foreign Students: The 115 students from foreign countries make up about 2% of enrollment. Special counseling is provided for these students.

Admissions: Applicants must score 550 or better on the TOEFL. They also must take the ACT.

Procedure: Application deadlines are the same as those for American students. Students must present proof of good health. Health insurance is provided through the university at no charge.

Admissions Contact: Walter Crockett, Director of Admissions.

MILLSAPS COLLEGE C-4
Jackson, Mississippi 39210 (601) 354-5201

F/T: 465M, 418W	Faculty: 64; IIB, n/av
P/T: 78M, 113W	Ph.D.'s: 65%
Grad: 45M, 21W	S/F Ratio: 13 to 1
Year: sems, ss	Tuition: $3610
Appl: open	R and B: $1500
553 applied	449 accepted	227 enrolled
ACT: 24		**VERY COMPETITIVE**

Millsaps College, established in 1890, is a small, privately controlled, liberal arts college, affiliated with the Methodist Church. The library houses 140,000 volumes.

Environment: The campus is situated on 60 acres of rolling hills, in a city of 350,000. The surrounding environment is suburban. Dormitories, housing 100 to 175 students each, men's fraternity houses, and married student facilities accommodate most of the student body.

Student Life: Sixty-five percent of the students are Mississippi residents. About 85% attended public schools. Seventy-three percent reside on campus. Thirty-seven percent belong to the Methodist Church; chapel attendance is not required. Drinking is a violation of college policy. About 7% of the students are minority-group members. Campus housing is single-sex; there are visiting privileges. Students may keep cars on campus. Day-care services are available to all students, faculty, and staff for a fee.

Organizations: About 40% of the men and 40% of the women belong to 8 national fraternities and sororities. Student government sponsors numerous social and cultural activities. Religious counselors and organizations are provided for Catholic, Jewish, and Protestant students.

Sports: The college fields 5 intercollegiate teams for men and 2 for women. There are 5 intramural sports for men and 5 for women.

Handicapped: There are no special facilities for physically handicapped students.

Graduates: The freshman dropout rate is 27%; 60% remain to graduate. Forty-eight percent of the graduates pursue graduate study; 14% enter medical school.

Services: Students receive free placement and career counseling. A placement office provides job interviews for undergraduates and graduates. Health care, psychological counseling, and tutoring are available on a fee basis.

Programs of Study: The college confers the B.A., B.S., B.B.A., B.Mus. and the B.S.Ed. degrees. Master's programs are also available. Bachelor's degrees are offered in the following subjects: BUSINESS (accounting, business administration), EDUCATION (elementary, health/physical), ENGLISH (English), FINE AND PERFORMING ARTS (art, church music, music, music education, theater/dramatics), LANGUAGES (French, German, Spanish), MATH AND SCIENCES (biology, chemistry, geology, mathematics, physics), PHILOSOPHY (philosophy, religion), SOCIAL SCIENCES (economics, government/political science, history, psychology, sociology). Thirty-seven percent of the degrees are conferred in math and sciences, 24% in business, and 22% in social sciences.

Required: All students are required to take English composition and literature, behavioral science (1 year), mathematics, history (Western Civilization), religion, physical education (1 year), and natural sciences.

Special: Students may study abroad during the junior year. There is a Washington, D.C., semester. Cooperative programs in engineering are available at various universities.

Honors: There are 12 national honor societies represented on campus. Interdepartmental honors programs extending over 3 semesters are available. Honors I is a directed-study colloquium. Honors II and III are research-oriented. Candidates must prepare and defend a research paper.

Admissions: Eighty-one percent of those who applied were accepted for the 1981-82 freshman class. The ACT scores of those who enrolled were as follows: 16% below 21, 31% between 21 and 23, 16% between 24 and 25, 25% between 26 and 28, and 12% above 28. Candidates should have completed 16 Carnegie units and have a C average. The school also considers the following in order of importance: recommendations by school officials, advanced placement or honors courses, extracurricular activities record, leadership record, and evidence of special talents. Children of alumni have some preference.

Procedure: The SAT or ACT is required. Various tests are administered to entering freshmen for placement and counseling purposes. Application deadlines are open. Freshmen are admitted to all terms. A rolling admissions plan is used. The application fee is $20.

Special: There are early admissions and deferred admissions plans. AP credit is given.

Transfers: Transfers are accepted for all classes. A C average is required. A minimum of 30 hours must be taken in residence; the bachelor's degree requires 124 credits. D grades are acceptable. Application deadlines are the same as those for freshmen.

Visiting: Orientations are scheduled for prospective students. The overnight visit includes sleeping in a dorm, attending classes, lunch, and a seminar. Visits are best scheduled for Fridays. Arrangements can be made through the admissions office.

Financial Aid: Seventy-three percent of the students receive financial aid; 51% work part-time on campus. A fund of $30,000 provides 100 freshman scholarships ranging from $100 to $1200; the average is $600. Student loans average $586 for freshmen, and are available from federal and college funds. The average award to freshmen from all sources is $2500. The college is a member of the CSS. Applications are due by April 1. The FAF is required.

Foreign Students: Fewer than 1% of the full-time students come from foreign countries.

Admissions: Foreign students must achieve a minimum TOEFL score of 450; no college entrance exams are required.

Procedure: Application deadlines are June 1 (fall), October 1 (spring), and March 1 (summer). Foreign students must present proof of funds adequate to cover 1 year of study.

Admissions Contact: John H. Christmas, Director of Admissions.

MISSISSIPPI COLLEGE C-4
Clinton, Mississippi 39058 (601) 924-6082

F/T: 931M, 702W	Faculty: 120; n/av
P/T: 160M, 201W	Ph.D.'s: 50%
Grad: 313M, 301W	S/F Ratio: 19 to 1
Year: sems, ss	Tuition: $2338
Appl: open	R and B: $1400
425 applied	407 accepted	356 enrolled
ACT: 21		**LESS COMPETITIVE**

Mississippi College, founded in 1826, is affiliated with the Baptist Church and offers undergraduate training in the liberal arts and sciences as well as business, education, and health fields. The library has 185,000 volumes, 825 periodical subscriptions, and 1200 microfilm items.

Environment: The 40-acre small-town campus (population 14,000) is located 5 miles from Jackson. The 8 dormitories accommodate 492 men and 459 women. In addition, there are apartments for 40 married students and facilities for commuting students.

Student Life: About 90% of the students come from Mississippi; 50% reside on campus. Most of the students are Baptists; 5 semesters of chapel attendance (twice weekly) is required. Alcohol is not permitted on campus. About 6% of the students are minority-group members. Campus housing is single-sex; there are no visiting privileges. Students may keep cars on campus.

Organizations: The extracurricular program includes campus government, publications, performing groups, dramatics, social and cultural events, and religious and service organizations. There are no fraternities or sororities.

Sports: The college fields 7 intercollegiate teams for men and 6 for women. There are 6 intramural sports for men and 4 for women.

Graduates: The freshman dropout rate is 10%. About 45% remain to graduate. Fifty percent of the graduates go on for further study.

Services: The college provides tutoring, psychological counseling, health care, career counseling, and placement services to all students at no charge.

Programs of Study: The B.A., B.S., B.S.B.A., B.S.Ed., and B.S.N. degrees are conferred. Master's programs are also available. Bachelor's degrees are offered in the following subjects: BUSINESS (accounting, business administration, business education, computer science, management, marketing), EDUCATION (early childhood, elementary, health/physical), ENGLISH (English, speech), FINE AND PERFORMING ARTS (art, art education, music, music education), HEALTH SCIENCES (medical technology, nursing), LANGUAGES (French, German, Spanish), MATH AND SCIENCES (biology, chemistry, mathematics, physics), PHILOSOPHY (philosophy, religion), PRE-PROFESSIONAL (dentistry, home economics, law, medicine, social work), SOCIAL SCIENCES (economics, government/political science, history, psychology, social sciences, sociology).

Required: All students must complete a core curriculum.

Special: Study abroad, cooperative degree programs, internships, and dual degree programs are offered.

Honors: An honors program is offered in all departments.

Admissions: About 96% of the applicants for the 1981–82 freshman class were accepted. The ACT scores of those who enrolled were as follows: 46% below 21, 19% between 21 and 23, 9% between 24 and 25, 11% between 26 and 28, and 4% above 28. A high school diploma or GED and a satisfactory academic record are required. The minimum ACT score accepted is 15; the minimum SAT score is 700 (Math and Verbal combined).

Procedure: The ACT or SAT is required. New students are admitted each semester. Application deadlines are open; notification is on a rolling basis. There is a $15 application fee.

Special: There is an early admissions plan. CLEP credit is available.

Transfer: For fall 1981, 312 transfer students applied and 308 were accepted. A 2.0 GPA is recommended; D grades transfer if the overall average is 2.0. Thirty semester hours must be completed in residence; the bachelor's degree requires 130 semester hours. Application deadlines are open.

Visiting: Campus tours with student guides may be arranged. Visitors may sit in on classes.

Financial Aid: About 65% of the students receive financial aid. The college offers commercial and government loans, BEOG/SEOG grants, part-time work opportunities (including CWS), and freshman scholarships. The college is a member of CSS; the FAF should be filed by April 1.

Foreign Students: About 1% of the full-time students come from foreign countries.

Admissions: Foreign students must achieve a minimum TOEFL score of 550; they may take the SAT or ACT in lieu of the TOEFL.

Procedure: Application deadlines are 6 months prior to registration. Foreign students must present proof of funds adequate to cover 4 years of study.

Admissions Contact: Rory Lee, Director of Admissions.

MISSISSIPPI INDUSTRIAL COLLEGE D–1
Holly Springs, Mississippi 38635   (601) 252-4754

F/T: 186M, 174W	Faculty: n/av
P/T: 30M, 20W	Ph.D.'s: 5%
Grad: none	S/F Ratio: 11 to 1
Year: sems, ss	Tuition: $1800
Appl: open	R and B: $1420
SAT or ACT: required	NONCOMPETITIVE

Mississippi Industrial College, founded in 1905, is a private technically oriented institution offering programs in business and teacher education. It is affiliated with the Christian Methodist Episcopal Church.

Environment: The 105-acre urban campus has 14 buildings and is located 45 miles from Memphis, Tennessee. Campus facilities include a library, 4 dormitories, and athletic facilities.

Student Life: About 80% of the students come from Mississippi. Ninety percent reside on campus. Drinking is prohibited; students may have cars.

Organizations: There is 1 national fraternity to which 1% of the men belong, and a national sorority to which 1% of the women belong.

Sports: The college competes intercollegiately in 3 sports. There are 3 intramural sports for men and 3 for women.

Handicapped: The school indicates that the entire campus is accessible to handicapped students, but lists lowered telephones as the only special facility.

Graduates: Two percent of the graduates pursue graduate study; 1% enter careers in business and industry.

Services: Students receive the following services free: health care, career counseling, and tutoring, and remedial instruction.

Programs of Study: The college confers the B.A. and B.S. degrees. Associate degrees are also awarded. Bachelor's degrees are offered in the following subjects: BUSINESS (business administration, business education, industrial management), EDUCATION (elementary, secondary), ENGLISH (creative arts), MATH AND SCIENCES (biology, combined sciences, mathematics), SOCIAL SCIENCES (social sciences).

Admissions: Sixty-seven percent of those who applied were accepted for a recent freshman class. Candidates must have a high school diploma. The school also considers the following factors in order of importance: leadership record, personality, ability to finance college education, impression made during interview, and recommendations by school officials.

Procedure: The SAT or ACT is required. The college follows an open admissions policy. There are no application deadlines and freshmen are admitted at midyear.

Special: Early admissions are possible.

Transfer: Transfers are accepted to all classes. A C average is needed; D grades do not transfer. The last 30 credits must be taken in residence.

Visiting: Visits are best scheduled November through June. Visitors may sit in on classes. Arrangements can be made through the dean of student affairs.

Financial Aid: Ninety-eight percent of the students are receiving some form of financial aid. The application deadline is June. Tuition may be paid in installments. The FAF is required as early as possible.

Admissions Contact: Clarence W. Hunter, Associate Dean of Students.

MISSISSIPPI STATE UNIVERSITY E–3
Mississippi State, Mississippi 39762   (601) 325-2224

F/T: 5596M, 3664W	Faculty: 713; I, –$
P/T: 380M, 294W	Ph.D.'s: 72%
Grad: 1002M, 595W	S/F Ratio: 20 to 1
Year: sems, ss	Tuition: $1030 ($1956)
Appl: Aug. 3	R and B: $1700
2920 applied 2511 accepted	1601 enrolled
ACT (mean): 20	COMPETITIVE

Mississippi State University, founded in 1878, is a state-controlled institution and land-grant college with 9 undergraduate schools and colleges. The library houses 755,437 volumes and subscribes to 6550 periodicals and newspapers.

Environment: The 4000-acre campus includes farms, pastures, and woodlands used by the Experiment Station. The campus proper is 700 acres. The surrounding environment is rural. Seventeen residence halls accommodate 2657 men and 2425 women. Montgomery Hall is listed in the National Register of Historical Buildings. The university also sponsors fraternity houses, on-campus apartments, and married student housing.

Student Life: About 90% of the students come from Mississippi and 8% are from other states. Forty-three percent reside on campus. About 11% of the students are minority-group members. Campus housing is single-sex; there are no visiting privileges. Students may keep cars on campus. Day-care services are available to all students, faculty, and staff for a fee.

Organizations: Thirteen percent of the men and 21% of the women belong to the 18 fraternities and 12 sororities; members live in fraternity houses. Extracurricular activities include numerous religious clubs, student government, publications, lectures, and concerts.

Sports: The university fields 7 intercollegiate teams for men and 4 for women. There are 12 intramural sports for men and 10 for women.

Handicapped: Most of the campus is accessible to handicapped students. Special facilities are available in all buildings constructed after 1972 and include wheelchair ramps, parking areas, lowered drinking fountains and telephones, and specially equipped rest rooms. Special class scheduling is also possible. For students with visual impairments there is a visual aid room. An interpreter and amplification services are provided for students with hearing impairments. There are 2 special counselors.

Graduates: The freshman dropout rate is 25%. Ten percent of the graduates pursue graduate study; 1% enter medical school.

Services: Students receive free psychological counseling, placement, career counseling, health care, tutoring, and remedial instruction. Placement services are available for undergraduates and graduates.

Programs of Study: The university confers the B.A., B.B.A., B.Arch., B.L.A., B.Mus.Ed., B.P.A., B.S., and Bachelor of Surveying degrees. Master's and doctoral degrees are also awarded. Among the 102 majors leading to bachelor's degrees are the following: BUSINESS (accounting, business, business economics, business education, business statistics, finance, management, marketing, real estate/insurance, secretarial studies, transportation), EDUCATION (agricultural, educational psychology, elementary, secondary, health/physical, industrial, special, vocational/technical), ENGLISH (English, speech), FINE AND PERFORMING ARTS (art, art education, music, music education), HEALTH SCIENCES (medical technology), LANGUAGES (French, German, Spanish), MATH AND SCIENCES (biochemistry, botany, chemistry, entomology, geology, mathematics, microbiology, physics, plant pathology, zoology), PREPROFESSIONAL (agriculture, architecture, engineering—agricultural, engineering—biomedical, engineering—chemical, engineering—civil, engineering—electrical, engineering—industrial, engineering—mechanical, engineering—nuclear, engineering—petroleum), PHILOSOPHY (philosophy), SOCIAL SCIENCES (anthropology, economics, geography, government/political science, history, psychology, sociology). Twenty-three percent of the degrees are conferred in education and 20% in business.

Required: Freshman English is required of all students.

Special: A cooperative program enables students to spend alternate semesters in industry.

Honors: The university offers an honors program with courses in 19 departments.

Admissions: Eighty-six percent of those who applied were accepted for the 1981–82 freshman class. The ACT scores of those who enrolled were as follows: 57% below 21, 19% between 21 and 23, 11% between 24 and 25, 10% between 26 and 28, and 4% above 28. A high school GPA of at least 2.0 is required. There is a special admissions quota for students with ACT scores of less than 15. For regular admission, students must graduate from an approved secondary school with 15 Carnegie units. Nonresidents with combined SAT scores of 720 are accepted.

Procedure: The ACT is required. Application deadlines are August 3 (fall), December 21 (winter), and May 9 (summer). Freshmen are admitted to all terms. A rolling admissions plan is used. There is no application fee.

Special: AP and CLEP credit is available.

Transfer: For a recent school year, 1512 students applied for transfer, 1502 were accepted, and 1071 enrolled. A C average is required. D grades transfer. Thirty-two semester hours in junior-senior level courses must be taken in residence. Application deadlines are 20 days prior to the beginning of the semester.

Visiting: Seven orientation sessions are scheduled for June. Informal weekday visits are possible. Visitors may sit in on classes and stay overnight at the school. Arrangements can be made through the Director/School College Relations, Drawer NN.

Financial Aid: Fifty-five percent of the students receive financial aid; 20% of the students work part-time on campus. A fund of $90,000 provides scholarship aid for freshmen in amounts ranging from $200 to $1000. The average award to freshmen from all sources is $1160. Loans are available from the federal government, local banks, the university, and private sources. Depending on need, students may receive $200 to $1000 in loans, in addition to CWS. The university is a member of CSS; the FAF must be filed. Tuition may be paid in installments. The application deadline is April 1.

Foreign Students: There are 432 students who come from foreign countries. The university offers these students special organizations.

Admissions: Foreign students must achieve a minimum TOEFL score of between 475 and 525, depending on the discipline they wish to enter; in addition, they must also take the ACT.

Procedure: Application deadlines are August 3 (fall), December 21 (spring), and May 9 (summer). Foreign students must present proof of health as well as proof of funds adequate to cover 1 year of study. They must also carry health insurance, which is available through the university for a fee.

Admissions Contact: Jerry Inmon, Director of Admissions.

MISSISSIPPI UNIVERSITY FOR WOMEN E–2
Columbus, Mississippi 39701 (601) 328-5891

F/T: 1331W Faculty: 129; IIA, –$
P/T: 425W Ph.D.'s: 48%
Grad: 100W S/F Ratio: 11 to 1
Year: sems, ss Tuition: $800 ($1726)
Appl: open R and B: $1580
620 applied 595 accepted 552 enrolled
ACT: 20 **LESS COMPETITIVE**

Mississippi University for Women is the only state-supported institution of higher education for women in the United States. Degrees are offered in the schools of arts and sciences, education, nursing, and home economics. The library contains 304,000 volumes and 58,670 microfilm items, and subscribes to 3000 periodicals.

Environment: The 110-acre urban campus, situated in a town of 40,000, has buildings of historic and modern design. There are dormitories on campus.

Student Life: Sixty percent of the students live on campus. Eighteen percent are minority-group members. There are visiting privileges in the dormitories. Day-care services are available to all students. Students may keep cars on campus. Students govern themselves and are responsible for their own conduct.

Organizations: There are approximately 90 clubs and organizations on campus, including 14 local sororities to which 30% of the women belong.

Sports: The college competes intercollegiately in 4 sports. There are 9 intramural sports.

Handicapped: Wheelchair ramps, special parking, and elevators are provided for the physically handicapped.

Graduates: About 38% of the freshmen drop out; 45% remain to graduate. Twenty percent of the graduates pursue graduate study; 5%–10% enter medical school, and 5%–10% enter law school. Fifteen percent of the graduates enter business and industry.

Services: Students receive free health care, remedial instruction, psychological counseling, placement, and career counseling. Tutoring is available for a fee. Placement services are available for undergraduates and graduates.

Programs of Study: The university confers the B.A., B.S., B.S.N., B.Mus., B.F.A., and B.S.W. degrees. Associate and master's degrees are also awarded. Bachelor's degrees are offered in the following subjects: BUSINESS (accounting, business administration, business education, paralegal studies, secretarial science), EDUCATION (early childhood, elementary, health/physical, secondary), ENGLISH (English, journalism, speech), FINE AND PERFORMING ARTS (art, art education, art history, commercial art, dance, interior design, music, music education, music performance, radio/TV), HEALTH SCIENCES (medical technology, nursing, speech therapy), LANGUAGES (French, Spanish), MATH AND SCIENCES (biology, chemistry, mathematics, microbiology, physical sciences), PREPROFESSIONAL (foods and nutrition, home economics, library science, medical records administration, merchandising, social work), SOCIAL SCIENCES (government/political science, history, psychology, social sciences, sociology).

Required: All students must satisfy requirements in English, speech, laboratory science, world history, social studies, psychology, and physical education.

Special: It is possible to earn combined B.A.-B.S. degrees in a 5-year curriculum; 30 additional hours are required. Students are permitted to spend their junior year abroad, though not under college sponsorship. Students may design their own majors. Combination degree programs in social work and nursing are available. Independent study and seminar programs are available in Western Civilization.

Honors: Honor societies include Golden Key (organized by Phi Beta Kappa), Gamma Beta Phi, Phi Kappa Phi, Mortar Board, and 18 departmental societies.

Admissions: About 96% of those who applied were accepted for the 1981-82 freshman class. Candidates must graduate from an accredited high school and have at least 15 Carnegie units. Impressions made during an interview, extracurricular activities, advanced placement or honors courses, and leadership potential are also considered.

Procedure: The ACT is required (the SAT is required for out-of-state applicants). Application deadlines are open. Freshmen are admitted all semesters. The application should be accompanied by a $10 application fee and $25 room deposit (if applicant plans to dorm). A rolling admissions policy is in effect.

442 MISSISSIPPI

Special: CLEP and AP credit is available.

Transfer: For fall 1981, 193 students applied, 187 were accepted, and 175 enrolled. Good academic standing and a composite score of 725 on the SAT or 15 on the ACT are required; D grades do not transfer. For a bachelor's degree, 128 or more credits are required. Application deadlines are open.

Visiting: Regular orientations are scheduled for prospective students. Visits are best scheduled for weekdays. Visitors may sit in on classes and stay overnight at the university. Arrangements for a guide can be made through the admissions office.

Financial Aid: Fifty-five percent of the students receive financial aid. Twenty-four percent work part-time on campus. The university has a comprehensive program of student financial aid in the form of scholarships, loans, grants, and part-time employment. The FFS and the university aid application are required. The application deadline is June 1 (fall) or April 1 (summer).

Foreign Students: Fewer than 1% of the full-time students come from foreign countries. Special organizations are available for these students.

Admissions: Foreign students must achieve a TOEFL score of at least 525 and an ACT score of at least 20.

Procedure: Application deadlines are August 1 (fall), December 1 (spring), and May 1 (summer). Foreign students must complete a health form and must present proof of funds adequate to cover 1 year of study. Health insurance is required and is available through the university for a fee.

Admissions Contact: J.B. Alinder, Director of Admissions.

MISSISSIPPI VALLEY STATE UNIVERSITY C–2
Itta Bena, Mississippi 38941 (601) 254-9041

F/T: 1015M, 1218W Faculty: 147; IIA, – – $
P/T: 54M, 90W Ph.D.'s: 39%
Grad: 28M, 74W S/F Ratio: 14 to 1
Year: sems, ss Tuition: $800 ($1726)
Appl: open R and B: $1333
1536 applied 548 accepted 532 enrolled
ACT: 12 LESS COMPETITIVE

Mississippi Valley State University, founded in 1946, offers undergraduate degree programs in the arts and sciences, business, and education. The library has 90,000 volumes, 625 periodical subscriptions, and 1000 microfilm items.

Environment: The 450-acre rural campus is located in a small town of 1000, 12 miles from Greenwood. There are 35 buildings on campus, including 10 residence halls that accommodate 70% of the students.

Student Life: More than 90% of the students come from Mississippi. Most students are public school graduates. The student body is predominantly black. Alcohol is prohibited on campus. Campus housing is single-sex; there are no visiting privileges. Students may keep cars on campus. Day-care services are available for a fee.

Organizations: There are fraternities and sororities on campus. Extracurricular activities include student government, clubs, publications, social and cultural events, performing groups, and religious organizations.

Sports: The university fields intercollegiate teams in 6 sports. There are 9 intramural sports.

Handicapped: Most of the campus is accessible to handicapped students.

Graduates: The freshman dropout rate is about 17%, about 50% remain to graduate.

Services: The university provides free remedial instruction, tutoring, career counseling, and placement services. Health care is available on a fee basis.

Programs of Study: The B.A. and B.S. degrees are conferred. Associate and master's degrees are also awarded. Bachelor's degrees are offered in the following subjects: BUSINESS (accounting, business administration, business education, computer science, office administration), EDUCATION (elementary, health/physical, industrial, science, secondary), ENGLISH (English, speech), FINE AND PERFORMING ARTS (art, art education, music, music education), HEALTH SCIENCES (environmental health), MATH AND SCIENCES (biology, chemistry, mathematics, physics), SOCIAL SCIENCES (criminal justice, family and community services, gerontology, government/political science, history, social sciences, sociology).

Required: There is a general education requirement.

Special: A cooperative education program and study abroad are offered.

Honors: Alpha Kappa Mu has a chapter on campus.

Admissions: About 36% of those who applied were accepted for the 1981–82 freshman class. The ACT scores of those who enrolled were as follows: 98% under 21, 1% between 21 and 23, 0% between 24 and 25, 0% between 26 and 28, and less than 1% above 28. A high school diploma or GED is necessary as well as a 2.0 high school GPA. Candidates should present 16 units of academic work. Recommendations are also considered important.

Procedure: The ACT or SAT is required. New students are admitted each semester. Students should apply no later than 20 days prior to registration. Notification is on a rolling basis. There is no application fee.

Transfer: For fall 1981, 259 transfer students applied, 134 were accepted, and 117 enrolled. Transfers are accepted for all classes. A 2.0 GPA is needed; D grades are accepted. Thirty semester hours must be completed in residence; the bachelor's degree requires a minimum of 127 credits. Application deadlines are the same as those for freshmen.

Visiting: Campus tours with student guides can be arranged. Visitors may sit in on classes.

Financial Aid: About 98% of the students receive financial aid; 22% of the students work part-time on campus. The university participates in federal programs such as NDSL, BEOG/SEOG, and CWS in addition to offering commercial loans and freshman and athletic scholarships. Need is the main consideration in determining award of financial aid. The average award to freshmen from all sources is $2133. The university is a member of CSS. The FAF, SFS, or FFS should be filed by April 15.

Foreign Students: Fewer than 1% of the students come from foreign countries. The university offers these students an intensive English course, special counseling, and special organizations.

Admissions: Foreign students must achieve a minimum TOEFL score of 525; in addition, they must also take the ACT.

Procedure: Application deadlines are open; foreign students are admitted to all sessions. Foreign students must present the university's health form as well as proof of funds adequate to cover 4 years of study. They must also carry health insurance, which is available through the university for a fee.

Admissions Contact: Sara C. White, Director of Admissions and Recruitment.

RUST COLLEGE D–1
Holly Springs, Mississippi 38635 (601) 252-4661

F/T: 237M, 303W Faculty: 44; IIB, – – $
P/T: 26M, 127W Ph.D.'s: n/av
Grad: none S/F Ratio: 15 to 1
Year: 4-1-4, ss Tuition: $2242
Appl: open R and B: $1110
SAT or ACT: not required LESS COMPETITIVE

Rust College, founded in 1866, is a private college of liberal arts affiliated with the United Methodist Church. The library contains 60,000 volumes, and subscribes to 340 periodicals.

Environment: The 120-acre campus is located in a small town 35 miles from Memphis. The 23 buildings include dormitories that house 160 students, a combination gymnasium and 2500-seat auditorium, and a science hall that contains physics, chemistry, and biology laboratories.

Student Life: Ninety percent of the students are from the South, and 75% from Mississippi. The student body is predominantly black. Attendance at semi-weekly religious services is voluntary. Dormitories are single-sex.

Organizations: Three social fraternities and 2 sororities have chapters on campus. Extracurricular activities include religious organizations, a band, a choir, drama and dance groups, special-interest clubs, an international students' association, a student newspaper, and student government.

Sports: The college fields intercollegiate teams in 7 sports. Intramural sports also are offered.

Graduates: About a third of the freshmen drop out. Thirty percent of the graduates pursue further study.

Services: Students receive free health care, career counseling, and placement aid.

Programs of Study: The college awards the B.A. and B.S. degrees. Associate degrees also are available. Bachelor's degrees are offered in the following subjects: BUSINESS (business administration, business education), EDUCATION (general, health/physical), ENGLISH (English), FINE AND PERFORMING ARTS (music), HEALTH SCIENCES (nursing), MATH AND SCIENCES (biology, chemistry, mathematics, physics), PREPROFESSIONAL (social work), SOCIAL SCIENCES (economics, history, psychology, public service, sociology).

Required: All students must take courses in humanities, science and mathematics, social and behavioral sciences, and physical education.

Special: Non-major programs are offered in accounting, management, art, humanities, journalism, religion and philosophy, speech and drama, computer science, Afro-American studies, early childhood education, library science, military science, political science, public administration, and special education. Degrees in mass communication, engineering, and medical technology are offered in cooperative programs with other institutions. A general studies degree is available. Students may arrange to study abroad or to participate in independent study and undergraduate research.

Honors: A number of honor societies have chapters on campus.

Admissions: Twenty-five percent of those who applied were accepted for a recent freshman class. Candidates must have graduated from an accredited high school with an average of C or better in 15 Carnegie units. Students holding GED certificates also are eligible. Recommendations from the high school principal or counselor and 1 other person are required.

Procedure: The application fee is $10. Application deadlines are open. Admissions decisions are made on a rolling basis.

Special: Early decision and deferred admissions plans are available. CLEP and AP credit is accepted.

Transfer: Transfer students need not submit ACT or SAT scores if they have completed at least 15 semester hours of college work. D grades do not transfer. Students must study at the college for at least 1 year to receive a bachelor's degree.

Financial Aid: About 98% of the students receive aid. Academic scholarships of $100 to $1400 are awarded to students with a high school GPA of B or better. The college also offers denominational and special scholarships; grants-in-aid; EOG; federal, state, denominational, and college loans; and work-study jobs. The average aid award to freshmen is $3500. Tuition may be paid in installments. Students should contact the director of financial aid for information on applying.

Foreign Students: Foreign students at the college represent 10% of the student body. Special counseling and special organizations are provided.

Admissions: Applicants must score 500 or better on the TOEFL. No college entrance exams are required.

Procedure: Application deadlines are August 15 (fall), January 2 (spring), and April 30 (summer). Students must present a completed medical form as proof of good health and must show evidence of adequate funds for 1 year. Special fees are charged to foreign students.

Admissions Contact: Annie Lampley, Director of Admissions.

TOUGALOO COLLEGE C-4
Tougaloo, Mississippi 39174 (601) 956-4941

F/T: 274M, 446W	Faculty: 80; IIB, ––$
P/T: 4M, 87W	Ph.D.'s: 45%
Grad: none	S/F Ratio: 11 to 1
Year: sems	Tuition: $2450
Appl: open	R and B: $1320
800 applied	550 accepted	200 enrolled
SAT or ACT: recommended		COMPETITIVE

Tougaloo College, established in 1869, is a liberal arts college affiliated with the United Christian Missionary Society (Disciples of Christ) and the American Missionary Association. The library contains 85,120 volumes, subscribes to 425 periodicals, and has 3948 microfilm items on file.

Environment: The 500-acre suburban campus has 17 major buildings, including a dining hall and student union building. Dormitories house about 600 students.

Student Life: Ninety-one percent of the students are from Mississippi, and 95% come from public schools. The majority of the students are black. About 71% live on campus; dormitories are single-sex.

Organizations: Five national fraternities and 3 national sororities have chapters on campus. Student activities include debate, drama, and singing groups; news and literary organizations; student government; and departmental clubs.

Sports: The school participates in 3 intercollegiate sports. Intramural sports also are available.

Graduates: The freshman dropout rate is 10%. About 45% of the graduates enter graduate or professional schools; 25% enter medical school, 5% dental school, and 2% law school. Ten percent of the graduates pursue careers in business or industry.

Services: The following services are offered free to students: psychological counseling, tutoring, remedial instruction, health care, placement aid, and career counseling.

Programs of Study: The college confers the B.A. and B.S. degrees. Bachelor's degrees are offered in the following subjects: AREA STUDIES (Black/Afro-American), BUSINESS (accounting, business administration), EDUCATION (early childhood, elementary, health/physical, secondary), ENGLISH (English), FINE AND PERFORMING ARTS (art, music), MATH AND SCIENCES (biology, chemistry, computer science, mathematics, physics), PHILOSOPHY (humanities), SOCIAL SCIENCES (anthropology, economics, government/political science, history, psychology, sociology).

Special: Seminars and independent research, including a freshman social science seminar, are available in many departments. A Washington, D.C., semester, a Brookhaven Laboratories semester, and a Harvard-Yale-Columbia intensive summer program are offered. Tougaloo participates in a cooperative exchange program with Brown University. Preprofessional or cooperative programs are offered in medicine, nursing, dentistry, medical technology, and other health professions; journalism; engineering; laboratory technician; law; ministry; and social work. Students may design their own majors.

Honors: Alpha Kappa Mu has a chapter on campus.

Admissions: Sixty-nine percent of those who applied were accepted for the 1981-82 freshman class. Candidates must have completed 16 Carnegie units at an accredited high school with a 2.0 average and rank in the upper 50% of their graduating class. Other considerations are recommendations by school officials, friends, or college alumni; leadership potential; and evidence of significant contributions to school or community.

Procedure: The SAT or ACT is recommended and should be taken by March of the senior year. Application deadlines are open. Admissions are on a rolling basis. There is no application fee.

Special: An early admissions plan is offered. AP credit is given.

Transfer: Transfer students are accepted for all classes. D grades do not transfer. A minimum average of C and a statement of honorable dismissal from the last college are required. Students must earn at least 30 semester hours in residence of the 124 required for a bachelor's degree.

Visiting: Guides are available for informal visits. Visitors may sit in on classes. Overnight stays at the school can be arranged with the admissions office.

Financial Aid: About 95% of all students receive aid in the form of scholarships, loans, grants, and CWS. The average award to freshmen is $3250. The FAF or ACT analysis is required. The deadline to file aid applications is April 15.

Foreign Students: Students from foreign countries represent 2% of enrollment. The college offers these students special counseling and special organizations.

Admissions: Applicants must score 450 or better on the TOEFL. No academic exams are required.

Procedure: Foreign students are admitted in fall and spring; application deadlines are open. Students must submit a physician's statement as proof of good health and must show evidence of adequate funds for 1 year. Health insurance is included in the general fee.

Admissions Contact: Halbert F. Dockins, Director of Admissions and Academic Records.

UNIVERSITY OF MISSISSIPPI D-2
University, Mississippi 38677 (601) 232-7226

F/T: 3968M, 3456W	Faculty: n/av; I, ––$
P/T: 185M, 315W	Ph.D.'s: 70%
Grad: 555M, 563W	S/F Ratio: 17 to 1
Year: sems, ss	Tuition: $1085 ($2011)
Appl: open	R and B: $1832
2425 applied	2071 accepted	1919 enrolled
SAT: 490V 510M	ACT: 21	COMPETITIVE

444 MISSISSIPPI

University of Mississippi, established in 1848, is a state-supported institution, with programs in liberal arts, education, and various professions. The library houses 875,000 volumes and 210,000 microfilm items, and subscribes to 4600 periodicals.

Environment: The 1896-acre campus is located 75 miles from Memphis, Tennessee. The university has its own airport with scheduled commercial air transportation. Dormitories, fraternity and sorority houses, and married student apartments accommodate 5400 students. Day students have a cafeteria and student lounge. Resident Centers are located at Jackson and Tupelo, with a medical center in Jackson.

Student Life: Seventy-one percent of the students are residents of Mississippi, 24% are from other states, and 4% are from foreign countries. About 80% of entering freshmen come from public schools. About 70% of the students live on campus; all freshmen except commuters must live on campus. About 85% of the students are Protestant, 10% are Catholic, and 3% are Jewish. About 11% of the students are minority-group members. Campus housing is single-sex. Students may keep cars on campus.

Organizations: There are 21 national fraternities to which 40% of the men belong and 14 national sororities to which 44% of the women belong. Religious organizations and counselors are available to Catholic, Jewish, and Protestant students. Other organizations include special-interest groups, departmental clubs, publications, and student associations.

Sports: The university fields 6 intercollegiate sports. There are 13 intramural sports for men and women.

Handicapped: Special facilities for physically handicapped students include wheelchair ramps, special parking, elevators, and specially equipped rest rooms; 80% of the campus is accessible. Special class scheduling is possible. There is 1 special counselor and 1 assistant.

Graduates: The freshman dropout rate is 12%; 62% remain to graduate. About 40% of the graduates pursue graduate study; 8% enter law school, 4% medical school, and 1% dental school. Thirty percent enter careers in business and industry.

Services: Students receive the following services free: psychological counseling, placement, career counseling, tutoring, and remedial instruction. Health care is available on a fee basis. Placement services available to undergraduates and graduates include interview scheduling, resume storage, and counseling.

Programs of Study: The university confers the B.A., B.F.A., B.A.Ed., B.B.A., B.Mus., B.P.A., B.S., B.S.C., and B.S.J. degrees. Among the majors for which bachelor's degrees are conferred are the following: AREA STUDIES (American, Black/Afro-American, Southern, urban), BUSINESS (accounting, banking and finance, business (general), business education, computer science, economics, management, managerial finance, marketing, insurance), EDUCATION (early childhood, elementary, health/physical, home economics, secondary, special), ENGLISH (English, journalism, journalism and advertising, linguistics, literature, speech), FINE AND PERFORMING ARTS (art, art education, art history, ceramics, music, music education, music theory —composition, radio/TV, theater/dramatics), HEALTH SCIENCES (medical technology, nursing, occupational therapy, physical therapy, speech therapy), LANGUAGES (French, German, Greek/Latin, Spanish), MATH AND SCIENCES (astronomy and physics, biology, botany, chemistry, forensic, geology, mathematics, physics), PHILOSOPHY (classics, philosophy, religion), PREPROFESSIONAL (dentistry, engineering (general), engineering—chemical, engineering—civil, engineering—electrical, engineering—geological, engineering—mechanical, home economics, law, medicine, ministry, optometry, pharmacy, social work, veterinary), SOCIAL SCIENCES (anthropology, economics, government/political science, history, psychology, public administration, social sciences, sociology). Twenty-five percent of the degrees are conferred in business and 19% are in education.

Required: All students must take 12 hours of English.

Special: Although the university does not sponsor a junior-year abroad program, students do have the opportunity to earn credit from such experience.

Honors: The university has 8 national honor societies and 50 departmental societies.

Admissions: Eighty-five percent of those who applied were accepted for the 1981–82 freshman class. Candidates must ahve completed 7 semesters of secondary school work and have 15 high school units. The following factors are also considered: advanced placement or honors courses, evidence of special talents, leadership record, impressions made during an interview, recommendations by school officials, and extracurricular activities record.

Procedure: The SAT or ACT is required. The ACT should be taken by April of the senior year. The application deadline is 20 days prior to the registration date; applications may be submitted as early as a year before desired enrollment. Freshmen are also admitted in spring and summer. A rolling admissions plan is used. There is no application fee.

Special: There is an early admissions plan; students may apply anytime after completion of their senior year in high school and testing in the upper 30% in the nation. A deferred admissions plan is also available. CLEP general and subject exams are used; AP credit is also given.

Transfer: Transfers are accepted for all classes. A GPA of 2.0 in a previous term of full-time enrollment is required. Thirty semester hours in residence are also required to earn a bachelor's degree. D grades transfer. Application deadlines are the same as those for freshmen.

Visiting: Regularly scheduled orientations are held each summer. Informal visits are best scheduled for weekdays. Arrangements can be made through the admissions office. Visitors may stay overnight at the school.

Financial Aid: Fifty-one percent of the students receive financial aid. The university awards undergraduate scholarships ranging from $100 to $1500 yearly. Loans from the federal government range from $100 to $1800 per year; and $50 to $1000 loans are available from the university. Campus employment is available. Aid is awarded on the basis of scholarship and need; renewal requires maintenance of a specified grade average. Fees may be paid on a deferred payment plan. The university is a member of CSS; the deadlines for applications are March 1 for the FAF and April 1 for the university aid form.

Foreign Students: About 4% of the students come from foreign countries. The university offers these students an intensive English course, special counseling, and special organizations.

Admissions: Foreign students must achieve a minimum TOEFL score of 500; in addition, they must also take the SAT or ACT.

Procedure: Application deadlines are 45 days prior to registration for each semester. Foreign students must present proof of funds adequate to cover 1 year of study. They must also carry health insurance, which is available through the university for a fee. Foreign students must pay a $10 application fee.

Admissions Contact: Kenneth L. Wooten, Director of Admissions and Records.

UNIVERSITY OF SOUTHERN MISSISSIPPI D–5
Hattiesburg, Mississippi 39401 (601) 266-7111

F/T: 3668M, 4241W	Faculty: 520; I, – –$
P/T: 409M, 583W	Ph.D.'s: 64%
Grad: 676M, 841W	S/F Ratio: 15 to 1
Year: sems, ss	Tuition: $844 ($1694)
Appl: Aug. 6	R and B: $1290–1550
2551 applied 1944 accepted 1483 enrolled	
ACT: 19	LESS COMPETITIVE

University of Southern Mississippi, established in 1910, is a nonsectarian, state-supported institution. The library houses 1,165,000 volumes, subscribes to 4500 periodicals, and has 515,000 microtexts. The Computer Center contains a Xerox, Sigma 9 for faculty and student research and training.

Environment: The 840-acre, wooded campus contains 60 buildings and is located 85 miles from Jackson. The surrounding environment is urban. Regional campuses are located at Long Beach and Natchez; a resident center is at Gautier. Dormitories and fraternity houses accommodate more than 4000 students. Married-student apartments are also available.

Student Life: About 90% of the students are from Mississippi, 9% are from other states, and 1% are from foreign countries. Thirty-five percent reside on campus. Ninety-five percent of entering freshmen attended public schools. Drinking is prohibited on campus. About 14% of the students are minority-group members. Campus housing is single-sex; there are visiting privileges. Students may keep cars on campus.

Organizations: There are 10 national fraternities and 12 national sororities. Religious organizations and counselors are available to students of all the major faiths. Extracurricular activities include more than 100 organizations, student government, and numerous cultural and social events. The student union is the hub of many activities.

Sports: The university fields 8 intercollegiate teams for men and 4 for women. There are 20 intramural sports for men and 20 for women.

Handicapped: Special facilities for physically handicapped students include a special home and personal assistant for quadriplegics, wheelchair ramps, special parking, and elevators. About 80% of the campus is accessible. Special class scheduling is possible.

Graduates: The freshman dropout rate is 20%; 55% remain to graduate. Twenty percent of the graduates pursue graduate or professional study; 3% enter medical school, 4% law school, and 3% dental school. Fifty percent enter careers in business and industry.

Services: Students receive the following services free: placement, career counseling, health care, psychological counseling, tutoring, and remedial instruction. There is a nominal fee for medication.

Programs of Study: The university confers the B.A., B.F.A., B.Mus., B.Mus.Ed., B.S., B.S.B.A., and B.S.N. degrees. The university also offers 12 master's degrees and 4 doctoral degrees. Bachelor's degrees are offered in the following subjects: AREA STUDIES (American, Latin American), BUSINESS (accounting, business administration, business education, computer science, economics, finance, industrial management, management, marketing, personnel management, real estate/insurance), EDUCATION (elementary, health/physical, industrial, secondary, special), ENGLISH (advertising, communications, English, journalism, speech), FINE AND PERFORMING ARTS (art, art education, dance, film/photography, music, music education, radio/TV, theater/dramatics), HEALTH SCIENCES (dietetics, medical technology, nursing, social and rehabilitation services, speech therapy), LANGUAGES (French, German, Spanish), MATH AND SCIENCES (biology, chemistry, geology, mathematics, microbiology, physics, polymer science, statistics, technology), PHILOSOPHY (classics, philosophy), PREPROFESSIONAL (home economics, library science), SOCIAL SCIENCES (anthropology, criminal justice, economics, geography, government/political science, history, paralegal studies, psychology, social sciences, sociology). Thirty percent of the degrees are conferred in education and 16% in business.

Required: All students are required to take a general core curriculum.

Special: There are 400 combined study and work opportunities available to students.

Honors: The university has 5 general and 36 academic honor societies.

Admissions: Seventy-six percent of those who applied were accepted for the 1981-82 freshman class. The ACT scores of those who enrolled were as follows: 66% below 21, 17% between 21 and 23, 9% between 24 and 25, 6% between 26 and 28, and 2% above 28. Candidates must be high school graduates, have 12 units of academic subjects, a C average, and a score of at least 15 on the ACT.

Procedure: The ACT is required. The application deadlines are August 6 (fall), December 17 (spring), and May 10 (summer). Application, high school record, and test scores must be submitted 20 days prior to registration. A rolling admissions plan is used. There is no application fee.

Special: An early admissions plan is available. CLEP general and subject exams are accepted; AP credit is also given.

Transfers: For fall 1981, 2361 transfer students applied, 1711 were accepted, and 1248 enrolled. Transfers are accepted to all classes. A C average is required; D grades transfer. One year in residence is required. Students must complete, at the university, at least 32 of the 128 credits required for the bachelor's degree. The application deadlines are the same as those for freshmen.

Visiting: One- and 2-day orientation visits ending in pre-registration are scheduled July through August. Informal weekday visits can be arranged through the Department of High School and Junior College Relations. Visitors may stay overnight at the university.

Financial Aid: Sixty percent of the students receive financial aid; 13% of the students work part-time on campus. Scholarships are awarded to 125 students from a $400,000 fund. Federal government, state, local bank, and university loans are available in varying amounts depending on need. Employment can be arranged. The university is a member of CSS; the FFS application is required. The application deadline is March 15.

Foreign Students: About 2% of the students come from foreign countries. The university offers these students an intensive English program, special counseling, and special organizations.

Admissions: Foreign students must achieve a minimum TOEFL score of 525; in addition, they must also take the SAT or ACT.

Procedure: Application deadlines are May 1 (fall), October 1 (spring), and March 1 (summer). Foreign students must present proof of funds adequate to cover the duration of their programs.

Admissions Contact: Charles McNeil, Director of Admissions.

MISSISSIPPI 445

WILLIAM CAREY COLLEGE D-5
Hattiesburg, Mississippi 39401 (601) 582-5051

F/T, P/T:
1840M&W
Grad: 704M&W
Year: sems, ss
Appl: Aug. 15
471 applied
ACT: 17

Faculty: 144; n/av
Ph.D.'s: 60%
S/F Ratio: 19 to 1
Tuition: $67 p/c
R and B: $1690

432 accepted 394 enrolled
LESS COMPETITIVE

William Carey, founded in 1906, is a liberal arts college owned and operated by the Mississippi Baptist Convention. The libraries house 108,000 volumes and 370 microfilm items, and subscribe to 700 periodicals.

Environment: The 65-acre main campus is located in a small city 90 miles from Jackson and 100 miles from New Orleans. The administration building, 2 women's dormitories, the dining hall, the hospital, and the home economics building were constructed in 1925. Nine buildings have since been added. Single-sex dormitories accommodate 590 men and women, and there are facilities for 20 married couples. The Carey School of Nursing is located in New Orleans, and the Carey on the Coast campus is located in Gulfport.

Student Life: Fifty percent of the students are Mississippi residents, and about 90% come from public schools. About half the students live in the dormitories, which are single-sex. All unmarried students must live on campus unless living with relatives. Most students are members of the Baptist Church. Attendance at weekly religious services is required.

Organizations: There are no social fraternities or sororities. Extracurricular activities include a community concert series and theater productions.

Sports: The college fields intercollegiate teams in 3 sports. Intramural sports also are available.

Handicapped: About 80% of the campus is accessible to physically handicapped students. Wheelchair ramps are provided, and special class scheduling is possible.

Graduates: About 15% of the freshmen drop out, and 50% remain to graduate. Forty percent of the graduates pursue advanced degrees, while 10% begin careers in business and industry.

Services: Students receive free health care, placement aid, career counseling, tutoring, and remedial instruction.

Programs of Study: The college confers the B.A., B.F.A., B.S., B.Mus., and B.S.N. degrees. Master's degrees also are awarded. Bachelor's degrees are offered in the following subjects: BUSINESS (accounting, business administration), EDUCATION (elementary, health/physical, secondary, special), ENGLISH (communications, English, speech), FINE AND PERFORMING ARTS (art, church music, music, music education, music therapy, theater/dramatics), HEALTH SCIENCES (biological illustration, nursing), LANGUAGES (Spanish), MATH AND SCIENCES (biology, chemistry, mathematics), PHILOSOPHY (religion), PREPROFESSIONAL (home economics, ministry), SOCIAL SCIENCES (administration of justice, community services, economics, history, psychology, social sciences, sociology). About 10% of the students study for the Baptist ministry.

Required: Two semesters of physical education and 6 hours of Bible study are required.

Special: The college offers a B.G.S. degree and a 3-year bachelor's degree. There is a cooperative 3-2 program in forestry. A 6-year program in law leads to the B.A. from William Carey College and the LL.B. or J.D. from an accredited law school. There is also a 7-year cooperative program in medicine and a 3-1 program in medical technology. Two-year preprofessional programs are offered in engineering, medical technology, physical therapy, medical records administration, radiological technology, optometry, and pharmacy. Research and independent study are available in some departments. Study abroad can be arranged.

Honors: Several honor societies have chapters on campus.

Admissions: Ninety-two percent of those who applied were accepted for the 1981-82 freshman class. For an earlier class, the ACT scores were as follows: 15% between 20 and 23, 7% between 24 and 26, and 3% between 27 and 28. Candidates must be graduates of an accredited high school, have 16 Carnegie units, and present an average of 1.4 or better. Recommendations from high school officials and college alumni, extracurricular activities, advanced placement or honors courses, leadership potential, and ability to pay also are considered.

446 MISSISSIPPI

Procedure: The ACT is required. An interview is recommended. The application deadline for fall is August 15. Freshmen are admitted to all quarters. The application fee is $10. Admissions are on a rolling basis.

Special: Early admissions and early decision plans are available. CLEP and AP credit is given.

Transfer: Transfer students are accepted for all classes. Requirements include a GPA of at least 1.4 for freshmen, 1.7 for sophomores, and 2.0 for juniors. Some D grades transfer. Students must take at least 30 hours in residence of the 128 required for a bachelor's degree.

Visiting: Regularly scheduled orientations for prospective students include a campus tour, visits with faculty members, and financial aid information. Informal visits can be arranged through the director of admissions. Visitors may sit in on classes.

Financial Aid: About 87% of the students receive aid. Federal and private loans are available. Twenty-five academic scholarships and 25 "workships" are available to freshmen. All departments have work-study programs. The FAF or FFS should be filed by February 1.

Foreign Students: Students from foreign countries make up 4% of enrollment. The college offers these students an intensive English course, special counseling, and special organizations.

Admissions: Applicatns must score 500 or better on the TOEFL. No college entrance exams are required.

Procedure: Application deadlines are the same as those for American students. Foreign students must present proof of adequate funds for 1 year and carry health insurance, which is available through the college for a fee.

Admissions Contact: Antonio R. Pascale, Director of Admissions.

MISSOURI

AVILA COLLEGE   A-2
Kansas City, Missouri 64145   (816) 942-8400

F/T: 207M, 630W		Faculty:	74; IIB, av$
P/T: 221M, 469W		Ph.D.'s:	50%
Grad: 84M, 90W		S/F Ratio:	14 to 1
Year: sems, ss		Tuition:	$3526
Appl: open		R and B:	$1800
383 applied	337 accepted		185 enrolled
SAT: 400V 430M	ACT: 20		COMPETITIVE

Avila College, established in 1916 and affiliated with the Roman Catholic Church, offers undergraduate degree programs in business, education, health fields, and arts and sciences. Its library has 66,000 volumes and 224 microtexts, and subscribes to 417 periodicals.

Environment: The 48-acre suburban campus is located 7 miles from downtown Kansas City. Buildings include 2 residence halls, divided into men's floors and women's floors.

Student Life: About 80% of the students come from the Midwest. Sixty-four percent are graduates of public schools. About 88% live on campus. Fourteen percent of the students are minority-group members. About 43% are Catholic and 37% are Protestant. Campus housing is single-sex; there are visiting privileges. Students may keep cars on campus. Day-care services are available, for a fee, to all students.

Organizations: There are no sororities or fraternities. Extracurricular activities include theater, a lecture series, chorus, student government, publications, and clubs.

Sports: The college fields 3 intercollegiate teams for men and 3 for women. There are 8 intramural sports for men and 8 for women.

Handicapped: All of the campus is accessible to handicapped students. Special facilities include wheelchair ramps, parking areas, elevators, lowered drinking fountains and telephones, and specially equipped rest rooms.

Graduates: The freshman dropout rate is 14%; about 42% remain to graduate. About 38% of the graduates go on for further study (1% to medical school, 1% to law school); 47% enter careers in business and industry.

Services: Career counseling, placement service, health care, psychological counseling, and tutoring are offered without charge. Remedial instruction is available for a fee.

Programs of Study: The B.A., B.S., B.M., B.F.A., B.S.W., and B.S.N. degrees are offered. Associate and master's degrees are also awarded. Bachelor's degrees are available in the following subjects: BUSINESS (accounting, business administration, finance, international business, management, marketing, personnel), EDUCATION (early childhood, elementary, special), ENGLISH (English, speech), FINE AND PERFORMING ARTS (art, art education, communication, music, music education, studio art, theater/dramatics), HEALTH SCIENCES (medical records administration, medical technology, nursing, radiologic technology, respiratory therapy), LANGUAGES (French), MATH AND SCIENCES (biology, chemistry, mathematics, natural sciences), PHILOSOPHY (religion), PREPROFESSIONAL (dentistry, medicine, social work, veterinary), SOCIAL SCIENCES (economics, government/political science, history, psychology, sociology). About 30% of the degrees conferred are in business, and 26% in health sciences.

Required: There is a distribution requirement.

Special: Student-designed majors, internships, and study abroad are offered. A combined B.A.-B.S. degree can be earned in business/economics and art/education.

Admissions: About 88% of the 1981-82 applicants were accepted. The ACT scores of those who enrolled were as follows: 31% below 21, 26% between 21 and 23, 6% between 24 and 25, 6% between 26 and 28, and 9% above 28. Class rank should be in the top 50%; a high school GPA of 2.0 is required. Recommendations, the applicant's personality, and the extracurricular record are also considered important.

Procedure: The ACT or SAT is required. An interview is recommended. There are no application deadlines. Freshmen are admitted in the fall, spring, and summer terms. Notification is on a rolling basis. There is a $20 application fee.

Special: AP and CLEP credit is given.

Transfer: A GPA of 2.0 is required; D grades are accepted. Applicants must achieve a minimum composite score of 18 on the ACT or 900 on the SAT. All students must complete, at the college, 30 of the 129 credits required for a bachelor's degree. There are no application deadlines.

Visiting: Informal campus tours with student guides may be arranged through the coordinator of admissions. Visitors may sit in on classes and stay at the college. The best time to visit is during the day from 8 A.M. to 5 P.M.

Financial Aid: About 85% of the students receive assistance. About 18% work part-time on campus. Scholarships, grants (including BEOG), loans (including NDSL), and part-time campus employment (including CWS) are offered. Tuition may be paid in installments. The academic record and the applicant's need determine the award. The FAF or FFS should be filed as early as possible. The college is a member of CSS.

Foreign Students: One percent of the full-time students come from foreign countries. Special counseling and special organizations are available for these students.

Admissions: Foreign students must achieve a TOEFL score of at least 500. No college entrance exams are required.

Procedure: There are no application deadlines; foreign students are admitted in the fall, spring, and summer terms. They must present proof of funds adequate to cover 4 years of study and must carry health insurance, which is available through the college.

Admissions Contact: Gary R. Forney, Director of Admissions.

CARDINAL NEWMAN COLLEGE   D-2
St. Louis, Missouri 63121   (314) 261-2600
(Recognized Candidate for Accreditation)

F/T: 51M, 39W		Faculty:	18; IIB, - -$
P/T: 1M, 2W		Ph.D.'s:	83%
Grad: none		S/F Ratio:	5 to 1
Year: sems		Tuition:	$3980
Appl: Aug.25		R and B:	$1750
42 applied	38 accepted		26 enrolled
SAT: 440V 425M	ACT: 21		COMPETITIVE

Cardinal Newman College, founded in 1976, is a Roman-Catholic-affiliated institution offering undergraduate instruction in the liberal arts and business. Its library has 20,000 volumes and 39 microfilm items, and subscribes to 92 periodicals.

Environment: There are 12 buildings on the 20-acre urban campus, including 5 dormitories that can house 236 students.

Student Life: About 21% of the students come from Missouri. Seventy percent live on campus. The student body is predominantly (96%) Catholic. Three percent of the students are minority-group members. Campus housing is single-sex; there are no visiting privileges. Students may keep cars on campus.

Organizations: Extracurricular activities include a chorale, student government, and a legal society, in addition to on-campus social and cultural events. There are no fraternities or sororities.

Sports: There are 2 intercollegiate teams for men. There are 4 intramural sports for men and 3 for women.

Handicapped: There are no special facilities for handicapped students.

Graduates: The freshman dropout rate is 31%. About 42% of entering freshmen remain to graduate. Of those, 43% pursue advanced degrees (16% enter law school). About 53% enter business and industry.

Services: Career counseling, tutoring, and placement are offered free of charge. Health care is available for a fee.

Programs of Study: The B.A. and B.S. degrees are conferred. Bachelor's degrees are offered in the following subjects: BUSINESS (business administration), ENGLISH (English, journalism, literature), FINE AND PERFORMING ARTS (radio/TV), LANGUAGES (French, German, Greek/Latin, Spanish), MATH AND SCIENCES (biology), PHILOSOPHY (philosophy, religion), PREPROFESSIONAL (dentistry, law, medicine, pharmacy, veterinary), SOCIAL SCIENCES (government/political science, history). About 20% of the students major in media arts, and 17% in business.

Required: There is a core curriculum with integrative seminars weekly.

Honors: There are no honors programs, nor any honor societies.

Admissions: About 90% of the 1981–82 applicants were accepted. The SAT scores of those who enrolled were as follows: Verbal—67% below 500, 20% between 500 and 599, 13% between 600 and 700, and 0% above 700; Math—73% below 500, 27% between 500 and 599, and 0% above 599. On the ACT, 37% scored below 21, 31% between 21 and 23, 19% between 24 and 25, and 13% between 26 and 28. Applicants should rank in the top 60% of their high school class. A high school GPA of 2.0 is required. Also important are advanced placement or honors courses and recommendations.

Procedure: Either the ACT or the SAT is required. Deadlines are August 25 (fall) and January 10 (spring); notification is on a rolling basis. There is a $15 fee.

Special: AP and CLEP credit is offered.

Transfer: For fall 1981, 17 students applied, 15 were accepted, and 11 enrolled. An average of C and 2 letters of reference are required; D grades do not transfer. All students must complete, at the college, 45 of the 127 to 135 semester hours required for a bachelor's degree. Application deadlines are the same as those for freshmen.

Visiting: Informal campus tours with student guides can be arranged for weekdays from 9 A.M. to 5 P.M.. Visitors may attend classes and stay at the college. Arrangements should be made through the admissions office.

Financial Aid: About 78% of the students receive aid. Twenty-seven percent work part-time on campus. The FFS is required. Application deadlines are August 1 (fall) and December 1 (spring).

Foreign Students: Three percent of the students come from foreign countries. Special counseling is available for these students.

Admissions: Foreign students must take the TOEFL. No college entrance exams are required.

Procedure: Application deadlines are July 1 (fall) and November 1 (spring). Foreign students must present proof of funds adequate to cover 1 year of study and must have the college's health form completed by a physician. Health insurance is required and is available through the college for a fee.

Admissions Contact: John Herriage, Director of Admissions.

MISSOURI 447

CENTRAL METHODIST COLLEGE   C–2
Fayette, Missouri 65248   (816) 248-2452

F/T: 312M, 303W   Faculty: 65; IIB, –$
P/T: 25M, 31W   Ph.D.'s: 30%
Grad: none   S/F Ratio: 10 to 1
Year: sems, ss   Tuition: $3500
Appl: open   R and B: $1600
502 applied   462 accepted   303 enrolled
ACT: 18   **LESS COMPETITIVE**

Central Methodist College is a liberal arts institution affiliated with the Methodist Church. Its library contains 100,000 volumes and 3000 microtexts, and subscribes to 400 periodicals.

Environment: The 48-acre, small-town campus is located in a rural area 125 miles from Kansas City and 150 miles from St. Louis. College housing includes dormitories and apartments for married students.

Student Life: About 80% of the students come from Missouri. Sixty percent live on campus. There are religious requirements; students must attend 6 of 8 convocation programs per academic year. About 68% of the students are Protestant, and 10% are Catholic. Ten percent are minority-group members. Campus housing is single-sex; there are visiting privileges. Students may keep cars on campus.

Organizations: Five local fraternities and 4 local sororities attract 10% of the students. There is a full program of extracurricular activities.

Sports: The college fields 9 intercollegiate teams for men and 6 for women. There are 13 intramural sports for men and 10 for women.

Handicapped: There are no special facilities.

Graduates: About 60% of the students pursue graduate study. One percent enter law school, 1% dental school, and 1% medical school. Twenty-five percent pursue business careers.

Services: Career counseling, placement, psychological counseling, health care, tutoring, and remedial instruction are provided free of charge to students.

Programs of Study: The B.A., B.S., B.S.N., B.S.Ed., and B.Mus.Ed. degrees are offered. Associate degrees are also awarded. Bachelor's degrees are available in the following subjects: BUSINESS (accounting, business administration, business education), EDUCATION (adult, early childhood, elementary, health/physical, secondary), ENGLISH (English, literature, speech), FINE AND PERFORMING ARTS (art, art education, art history, music, music education), HEALTH SCIENCES (nursing), LANGUAGES (French, German, Spanish), MATH AND SCIENCES (biology, chemistry, geology, mathematics, natural sciences, physical sciences, physics, zoology), PHILOSOPHY (philosophy, religion), PREPROFESSIONAL (dentistry, engineering, law, ministry, social work, veterinary), SOCIAL SCIENCES (economics, geography, government/political science, history, psychology, social sciences, sociology). About 18% of the degrees conferred are in arts, 17% in business, and 14% in education.

Required: There is a general education requirement that includes course work in religion.

Special: Student-designed majors, study abroad, and combination degree programs are offered.

Honors: Eleven honor societies have chapters on campus. An honors program is available.

Admissions: About 92% of the applicants for the 1981–82 school year were accepted. The ACT scores of those who enrolled were as follows: 9% below 21, 60% between 21 and 23, 25% between 24 and 25, 11% between 26 and 28, and 5% above 28. Applicants should rank in the upper 25% of their class and have a GPA of at least 2.0. Advanced placement or honors courses, evidence of special talent, and leadership qualities are also considered important.

Procedure: The ACT is required. There are no application deadlines; freshmen are admitted in the fall, winter, and summer terms. Notification is on a rolling basis. There is a $10 application fee.

Special: CLEP is used. There is an early decision plan.

Transfer: For fall 1981, 70 students applied, 67 were accepted, and 67 enrolled. Applicants must have a GPA of at least 2.0. For the bachelor's degree, 120 credits are required. There are no application deadlines.

Visiting: There is an orientation program for new students. Informal campus tours with student guides may be arranged. Visitors may attend classes and stay at the school.

Financial Aid: About 72% of the students are receiving aid. About 46% work part-time on campus. The college offers merit and athletic scholarships and grants as well as ministerial and music grants. The

448 MISSOURI

college participates in CWS, BEOG, and NDSL. Tuition may be paid in installments. The FAF or FFS should be filed by August 15 (fall), January 15 (winter), or June 1 (summer).

Foreign Students: Two percent of the full-time students come from foreign countries. Special organizations are available for these students.

Admissions: Foreign students must achieve a TOEFL score of at least 550 and must take the ACT.

Procedure: Application deadlines are August 15 (fall) and January 15 (winter). Foreign students must present proof of funds adequate to cover 4 years of study and must present proof of health. Health insurance is required.

Admissions Contact: Tony Boes, Director of Admissions.

CENTRAL MISSOURI STATE UNIVERSITY   B-2
Warrensburg, Missouri 64093   (816) 429-4811

F/T: 4035M, 4129W	Faculty:	445; n/av
P/T: 249M, 215W	Ph.D.'s:	65%
Grad: 618M, 641W	S/F Ratio:	19 to 1
Year: qtrs, ss	Tuition:	$630
Appl: open	R and B:	$1650
3446 applied	3426 accepted	3233 enrolled
ACT: 18		LESS COMPETITIVE

Central Missouri State University, founded in 1871, offers undergraduate programs in agriculture, business, education, health fields, technology, and arts and sciences. Its library contains 325,000 volumes and subscribes to 2610 periodicals.

Environment: The 1000-acre campus (200 acres comprise the university farm) is located in a rural area. Warrensburg, a town of 13,000 people, is about 50 miles from Kansas City. There are 17 major buildings, including dormitories that house almost half the students. University housing also includes fraternity and sorority houses and married student housing.

Student Life: About 94% of the students come from Missouri. Forty-five percent live on campus. About 7% are minority-group members. Campus housing is both coed and single-sex; there are visiting privileges in the single-sex housing. Students may keep cars on campus.

Organizations: Fifteen percent of the men belong to one of 15 national fraternities; 10% of the women are members of one of 12 national sororities. There is a well-balanced extracurricular cultural and social program.

Sports: The university fields 8 intercollegiate teams for men and 8 for women. There are 13 intramural sports for men and 10 for women.

Handicapped: Special facilities for handicapped students include wheelchair ramps, parking areas, elevators, lowered drinking fountains, and specially equipped rest rooms. Special class scheduling is also available.

Graduates: Sixty percent of the entering freshmen remain to graduate. About 15% of the graduates go on for further education.

Services: Offered free to all students are psychological counseling, tutoring, remedial instruction, placement service, and career counseling. Health care sometimes requires payment.

Programs of Study: The B.A., B.S., B.S.B.A., B.M., B.S.Ed., B.S.Mus.Ed., and B.F.A. degrees are conferred. Associate, master's, and specialist degrees are also awarded. Bachelor's degrees are offered in the following subjects: BUSINESS (accounting, business administration, business education, computer science, finance, management, marketing), EDUCATION (adult, early childhood, elementary, health/physical, secondary, special), ENGLISH (English, journalism, literature, speech), FINE AND PERFORMING ARTS (art, art history, music, music education, radio/TV, studio art, theater/dramatics), HEALTH SCIENCES (medical technology, nursing, physical therapy, speech therapy), LANGUAGES (French, German, Spanish), MATH AND SCIENCES (biology, chemistry, earth science, geology, mathematics, physical sciences, physics), PREPROFESSIONAL (agriculture, dentistry, forestry, home economics, law, pharmacy, social work, veterinary), SOCIAL SCIENCES (economics, geography, government/political science, history, psychology, sociology).

Special: Study abroad is possible.

Honors: All departments participate in a university-wide honors program.

Admissions: About 99% of the applicants for 1981-82 were accepted. ACT scores of those who enrolled were as follows: 83% below 22, 14% between 23 and 26, and 3% above 26. Applicants should rank in the upper two-thirds of their class and have at least a 2.0 average.

Procedure: The ACT is required. Application deadlines are open; notification is on a rolling basis. New students are admitted each term. There is no application fee.

Special: There is an early admissions plan. CLEP and AP credit is offered.

Transfer: Over 600 transfer students enroll yearly. A 2.0 GPA is needed. D grades transfer. All students must reside at the university for at least 1 academic year and must complete, at the university, 30 of the 124 credits required for a bachelor's degree. There are no application deadlines.

Visiting: Week-day campus tours with student guides can be arranged. Although visitors may not attend classes, they may stay overnight at the university.

Financial Aid: About 65% of the students receive aid. Twenty-five percent work part-time on campus. There are freshman scholarships in addition to various loans, grants, and part-time campus employment. Programs such as NDSL and CWS are offered. The average freshman aid package is $700. The FFS is preferred and should be submitted no later than the day before the beginning of classes.

Foreign Students: Two percent of the full-time students come from foreign countries. Special counseling and special organizations are available for these students.

Admissions: Foreign students must achieve a TOEFL score of at least 500. No college entrance exams are required.

Procedure: Foreign students are admitted to all 4 terms. Applications must be submitted 3 months before the term begins if sent from outside the U.S., and 1 month before if sent from inside the U.S. Foreign students must present proof of health and proof of funds adequate to cover the intended period of study. They must also carry health insurance, which is available through the university for a fee.

Admissions Contact: A. Louie Sosebee, Dean of Admissions.

COLUMBIA COLLEGE   C-2
Columbia, Missouri 65216   (314) 875-7352

F/T: 302M, 365W	Faculty:	46; IIB, av$
P/T: 49M, 55W	Ph.D.'s:	39%
Grad: none	S/F Ratio:	14 to 1
Year: sems, ss	Tuition:	$3865
Appl: Aug.26	R and B:	$1950
349 applied	306 accepted	168 enrolled
ACT: recommended		LESS COMPETITIVE

Columbia College, founded in 1851, is an independent institution offering undergraduate curricula in the liberal arts and business. Its library has 57,000 volumes and 200 microfilm items, and subscribes to 422 periodicals.

Environment: The 25-acre campus is located in a suburban area midway between St. Louis and Kansas City, in a city of 70,000 people. There are 18 buildings, including 4 dormitories that house about half of the students.

Student Life: Twenty-seven states and 20 foreign countries are represented in the student body. About 50% of the students live on campus. Eighteen percent of the students are minority-group members. Campus housing is both coed and single-sex; there are visiting privileges in the single-sex housing. Students may keep cars on campus.

Organizations: There are no fraternities or sororities. Extracurricular activities include clubs, service groups, and social events.

Sports: The college fields 2 intercollegiate teams for men and 2 for women. There are 8 intramural sports for men and 8 for women.

Handicapped: There are facilities for handicapped students.

Graduates: The freshman dropout rate is 48%. About 25% of the students pursue advanced study after graduation: 1% enter medical school and 2% enter law school.

Services: Offered free are health care, psychological counseling, career counseling, tutoring, remedial instruction, and placement service.

Programs of Study: The B.A., B.S., B.F.A., B.A.I.S., and B.S.W. degrees are conferred. Associate degrees are also awarded. Bachelor's degrees are offered in the following subjects: BUSINESS (business administration), EDUCATION (elementary, secondary), ENGLISH (English), FINE AND PERFORMING ARTS (art, commercial art, music, music education), PREPROFESSIONAL (fashion), SOCIAL SCI-

ENCES (criminal justice administration, government/political science, history, psychology). There is also a major in individual studies.

Special: Student-designed majors, a general studies degree, and combined B.A.-B.S. degrees are offered.

Honors: There are 4 honor societies.

Admissions: About 88% of those who applied were accepted for the 1981-82 freshman class. Applicants should rank in the top 75% of their class and have a GPA of at least 1.8. A high school diploma (or GED) is required with 15 Carnegie units. Impressions made during the interview and advanced placement or honors courses are important factors.

Procedure: The ACT or SAT is recommended. Deadlines are August 26 (fall) and January 18 (winter). Notification is on a rolling basis; freshmen are admitted each semester. There is a $15 application fee.

Special: There are early decision, early admissions, and deferred admissions plans. CLEP credit is granted.

Transfer: For fall 1981, 147 students applied, 126 were accepted, and 99 enrolled. A GPA of at least 1.8 is recommended. Twelve credits worth of D grades transfer. All students must complete, at the college, 24 of the last 36 credits (120 credits are required for a bachelor's degree). Application deadlines are the same as those for freshman.

Visiting: There is an orientation program. Informal campus tours (Monday through Friday from 8 A.M. to 5 P.M., and Saturday by appointment only) with student guides can be arranged through the admissions office. Visitors may attend classes and stay overnight at the college.

Financial Aid: About 76% of the students receive aid. Ten percent work part-time on campus. The college administers freshman academic scholarships, federal loans (NDSL), and CWS in all departments. Tuition may be paid on the installment plan. The FAF or FFS is due by August (fall), January (winter), or June (summer).

Foreign Students: Nine percent of the full-time students come from foreign countries. Special counseling and special organizations are available for these students.

Admissions: Foreign students must achieve a minimum score of 500 on the TOEFL or 7 on the Comprehensive English Language Test. No college entrance exams are required.

Procedure: Application deadlines are July for fall entry and November for winter entry. Foreign students must complete the school health form and must present proof of funds adequate to cover 1 year of study. Health insurance is not required but is available through the college for a fee.

Admissions Contact: John J. Bart, Dean of Admissions.

CULVER-STOCKTON COLLEGE C-1
Canton, Missouri 63435 (314) 288-5221

F/T: 297M, 272W	Faculty: 35; IIB, av$
P/T: 20M, 54W	Ph.D.'s: 40%
Grad: none	S/F Ratio: 15 to 1
Year: 4-1-4, ss	Tuition: $3350
Appl: open	R and B: $1750
334 applied	333 accepted	172 enrolled
ACT: 17		LESS COMPETITIVE

Culver-Stockton College, established in 1853, is affiliated with the Christian Church (Disciples of Christ). It offers a liberal arts education. The library contains 104,000 books and 1000 microfilm items, and subscribes to 325 periodicals.

Environment: The 111-acre small-town campus has 16 buildings, including 4 dormitories housing 190 women and 200 men. There are also fraternity and sorority houses. The campus is located in a rural area 150 miles from St. Louis.

Student Life: About 46% of the students come from Missouri. Eighty-five percent reside on campus. The majority of the students (61%) are Protestant, but not all are members of the supporting church. Twenty percent are Catholic. Religious services are not compulsory. About 5% of the students are minority-group members. Campus housing is single-sex; there are visiting privileges. Students may keep cars on campus.

Organizations: Four fraternities attract 51% of the men and 3 sororities attract 52% of the women. The extracurricular program includes activities of religious, social, cultural, and political groups.

Sports: The college fields 5 intercollegiate teams for men and 4 for women. There are 8 intramural sports for men and 6 for women.

Handicapped: There are no special facilities.

Graduates: Sixteen percent of the freshmen drop out; 41% remain to graduate. Forty percent pursue graduate study. Five percent enter law school, 1% medical school, and 1% dental school. About 30% enter business and industry.

Services: Career counseling, tutoring, and remedial instruction are offered without charge. Health care and placement services are available for a fee.

Programs of Study: The B.A., B.S., B.F.A., and B.Mus. degrees are offered in the following subjects: BUSINESS (accounting, business administration, business administration/economics, business-agriculture, business education), EDUCATION (elementary, health/physical, secondary), ENGLISH (English, journalism, speech), FINE AND PERFORMING ARTS (art, art education, arts management, music, music education, theater/dramatics), MATH AND SCIENCES (biology, chemistry, mathematics), PHILOSOPHY (religion), PREPROFESSIONAL (agriculture, dentistry, engineering, law, library science, medicine, ministry, social work), SOCIAL SCIENCES (administration of justice, economics, government/political science, history, psychology, social sciences, sociology). About 30% of the degrees conferred are in business, 25% in social sciences, and 20% in education.

Required: Course work in religion is required.

Special: Student-designed majors, study abroad, a 3-2 engineering program, and work-study opportunities are offered.

Honors: There are 3 honor societies; honors work is offered in all fields.

Admissions: Almost 100% of the applicants for 1981-82 were accepted. The ACT scores of those who enrolled were as follows: 34% below 21, 26% between 21 and 23, 16% between 24 and 25, 18% between 26 and 28, and 5% above 28. Class rank should be in the upper 50%; minimum high school GPA required is 2.0. Advanced placement or honors courses are considered.

Procedure: The SAT or ACT should be taken by January of the senior year. Deadlines are open. New students are admitted to the fall, winter, and summer terms. Notification is on a rolling basis. There is no application fee.

Special: There are early decision, early admissions, and deferred admissions programs. AP and CLEP credit is given.

Transfer: For fall 1981, 84 students applied, 82 were accepted, and 64 enrolled. A 2.0 GPA and an ACT score of 14 are required. D grades do not transfer. All students must complete, at the college, 30 of the last 60 credits (124 credits are required for a bachelor's degree). There are no application deadlines.

Visiting: There is an orientation program for prospective applicants. Informal campus tours with student guides may be arranged. Visitors may attend classes and stay in the dormitories.

Financial Aid: About 64% of the students are receiving aid. About 33% work part-time on campus. Loans from the federal government, the state government, local banks, and the college itself are available, in addition to government grants and campus employment ($800 per year maximum). Aid is packaged. The average award to freshmen is $3950. The college is a member of CSS. The FAF or FFS should be filed by May 1 (fall entry) or December 18 (winter entry).

Foreign Students: Special counseling and special organizations are available for these students.

Admissions: Foreign students must achieve a TOEFL score of at least 500 and must take the ACT.

Procedure: Application deadlines are August 1 (fall), December 1 (winter), and May 1 (summer). Foreign students must present proof of adequate funds and must carry health insurance, which is available through the college.

Admissions Contact: Richard Valentine, Director of Admissions.

DRURY COLLEGE B-3
Springfield, Missouri 65802 (417) 862-0541

F/T: 557M, 641W	Faculty: 77; n/av
P/T: 518M, 818W	Ph.D.'s: n/av
Grad: 100M, 174W	S/F Ratio: 15 to 1
Year: 4-1-4, ss	Tuition: $3250
Appl: Aug. 15	R and B: $1630
462 applied	428 accepted	258 enrolled
SAT: 476V 502M	ACT: 20	COMPETITIVE

Established in 1873, Drury College is a liberal arts college affiliated with the United Church of Christ (Congregational) and the Christian

450 MISSOURI

Church (Disciples of Christ). Its library contains 100,000 volumes and 2100 microfilm items, and subscribes to 900 periodicals.

Environment: The 40-acre suburban campus is located 175 miles from Kansas City and 220 miles from St. Louis. There are 22 buildings, including 4 dormitories. There are also fraternity houses.

Student Life: About 70% of the students come from Missouri; 90% are public school graduates; 65% live on campus. Eighty percent of the students are Protestant, 8% are Catholic, and 1% are Jewish. Campus housing is single-sex; there are visiting privileges. Students may keep cars on campus.

Organizations: About half of the students belong to one of the 6 fraternities and 5 sororities with chapters on campus. Extracurricular activities include student publications, theater and music groups, clubs, and student government.

Sports: The college fields 5 intercollegiate teams for men and 2 for women. There are 6 intramural sports for men and 5 for women.

Handicapped: About 20% of the campus is accessible to physically handicapped students. Special facilities include wheelchair ramps, special parking areas, and elevators. Fewer than 2% of the students have visual or hearing impairments. Tutors, readers, and braille texts are available.

Graduates: Fifteen percent of the freshmen drop out; 65% remain to graduate. About 25% of the graduates pursue graduate study; 10% enter medical school, 8% enter dental school, and 10% enter law school. Thirty percent enter business and industry.

Services: Psychological counseling, health care, career counseling, and placement are offered without charge to students. Tutoring is available for a fee.

Programs of Study: The B.A., B.S., B.Mus., B.Mus.Ed., and B.S.N. degrees are conferred. Master's degrees are also awarded. Bachelor's degrees are offered in the following subjects: BUSINESS (accounting, business administration), EDUCATION (elementary, secondary, special), ENGLISH (English, journalism, literature, speech), FINE AND PERFORMING ARTS (art, art education, art history, film/photography, music, music education, radio/TV, studio art, theater/dramatics), HEALTH SCIENCES (medical technology, nursing), LANGUAGES (French, German, Spanish), MATH AND SCIENCES (biology, chemistry, ecology/environmental science, mathematics, physics), PHILOSOPHY (philosophy, religion), PREPROFESSIONAL (architecture, dentistry, engineering, law, medicine, pharmacy, veterinary), SOCIAL SCIENCES (anthropology, economics, government/political science, history, psychology, sociology). About 30% of the degrees conferred are in business and 15% in education.

Required: There is a general education requirement that includes foreign language and physical education.

Special: Student-designed majors, a 3-2 engineering program, a Washington semester, study abroad, internships, and independent study are offered.

Honors: Twelve honor societies have chapters on campus. Honors programs are available in all departments.

Admissions: About 93% of those who applied were accepted for the 1981-82 freshman class. The SAT scores of those who enrolled were as follows: Verbal—54% below 500, 25% between 500 and 599, 21% between 600 and 700, and 0% above 700; Math—49% below 500, 32% between 500 and 599, 10% between 600 and 700, and 3% above 700. On the ACT, 36% scored below 21, 17% between 21 and 23, 18% between 24 and 25, 18% between 26 and 28, and 11% above 28. Applicants should rank in the upper half of their class and have a GPA of at least 2.0. Advanced placement or honors courses, recommendations by school officials, and impressions made during the interview are also taken into consideration.

Procedure: The ACT or SAT is required. Deadlines are August 15 (fall), January 15 (spring), and May 15 (summer); notification is on a rolling basis. There is a $15 application fee.

Special: AP and CLEP are used. There are early decision, early admissions, and deferred admissions plans.

Transfer: For fall 1981, 91 students applied, 76 were accepted, and 55 enrolled. A 2.0 GPA is required. Grades earned in courses parallel to those offered at Drury transfer. All students must spend at least 1 year in residence and must complete, at the college, 30 of the 124 credits required for a bachelor's degree. Application deadlines are the same as those for freshmen.

Visiting: There is a formal orientation program for prospective applicants. Informal campus tours with student guides may be arranged. Visitors may sit in on classes and stay at the college.

Financial Aid: About 70% of the students receive aid. The college offers freshman scholarships, government and commercial loans (including NDSL), grants (such as BEOG and SEOG), and campus employment (CWS included). Need, achievement, and talent are the determining factors. The FAF or FFS is due by July 15.

Foreign Students: Two percent of the full-time students come from foreign countries. An intensive English course and special organizations are available for these students.

Admissions: Foreign students must take either the TOEFL, the University of Michigan Language Test, the Comprehensive English Language test, or the college's own test. On the TOEFL, a minimum score of 500 is required. Students must also take the SAT or ACT. On the SAT, a minimum score of 400 on each part is required; on the ACT, 15 composite.

Procedure: Application deadlines are the same as those for other students. Foreign students must complete the college's health form and must present proof of funds adequate to cover 1 year of study. They must also carry health insurance, which is available through the college for a fee.

Admissions Contact: Eltjen Flikkema, Dean of Admissions.

EVANGEL COLLEGE B-3
Springfield, Missouri 65802 (417) 865-2811

F/T: 754M, 1017W	Faculty: 60; n/av
P/T: 43M, 67W	Ph.D.'s: 50%
Grad: none	S/F Ratio: 20 to 1
Year: sems, ss	Tuition: $2222
Appl: Aug.15	R and B: $1740
634 applied	544 accepted 498 enrolled
ACT: 19	LESS COMPETITIVE

Evangel College, founded in 1955, is a liberal arts college affiliated with The Assemblies of God. Its library contains 88,000 volumes.

Environment: The 80-acre urban campus has 6 residence halls, accommodating more than 1400 students; there are apartments for married students.

Student Life: About 24% of the students come from Missouri. About 4% are minority-group members. Over 94% are Protestant. Seventy-nine percent live on campus. Campus housing is both coed and single-sex; there are no visiting privileges in the single-sex housing. Students may keep cars on campus. Daily chapel attendance is required, and smoking, alcohol, and gambling are prohibited.

Organizations: Religious activities are emphasized. There are no fraternities or sororities.

Sports: The college fields 4 intercollegiate teams for men and 3 for women. There are 4 intramural sports for men and 3 for women.

Graduates: The freshman dropout rate is 35%; about 53% remain to graduate. Fifteen percent of the graduates pursue advanced degrees; 1% enter law school.

Services: Health care, psychological and career counseling, placement, and tutoring are offered free of charge. Remedial instruction is available for a fee.

Programs of Study: The B.A., B.S., B.B.A., and B.M.Ed. degrees are conferred. Associate degrees are also awarded. Bachelor's degrees are offered in the following subjects: BUSINESS (accounting, business administration, business education, management, secretarial administration), EDUCATION (adult, elementary, health/physical, secondary, special), ENGLISH (English, journalism, speech), FINE AND PERFORMING ARTS (art, music education, theater/dramatics), HEALTH SCIENCES (medical technology, nursing), LANGUAGES (Spanish), MATH AND SCIENCES (biology, chemistry, mathematics), PHILOSOPHY (philosophy, religion), SOCIAL SCIENCES (government/political science, history, mental health, psychology, public administration, sociology).

Required: Sixteen hours of Bible studies are required.

Admissions: About 86% of the 1981-82 applicants were accepted. The ACT scores of those who enrolled were as follows: 67% below 21, 18% between 21 and 23, 8% between 24 and 25, 7 percent between 26 and 28, and 1% above 28. Applicants should rank in the upper 60% of their class and have a GPA of at least 2.0. Recommendations, personality, and leadership record are also considered.

Procedure: The ACT is required. Application deadlines are August 15 (fall), December 30 (spring), and May 1 (summer). There is a $25 application fee.

Special: AP and CLEP are used. There are early decision and deferred admissions plans.

Transfer: For fall 1981, 233 students applied, 199 were accepted, and 179 enrolled. A GPA of at least 2.0, a pastor's recommendation, and transfer clearance from the previous school are required. D grades do not transfer. All students must complete, at the college, 30 of the 124 credits required for a bachelor's degree. Application deadlines are the same as those for freshmen.

Visiting: Informal campus tours with student guides may be arranged; visitors may sit in on classes.

Financial Aid: About 84% of the students receive assistance. Sixteen percent work part-time on campus. Scholarships are available to freshmen. Federal and state loan and grant programs are offered in addition to loans from local banks. The FAF must be filed by June 1 (fall), October 1 (spring), or April 1 (summer). The college is a member of CSS.

Foreign Students: One percent of the full-time students come from foreign countries. Special counseling and special organizations are available for these students.

Admissions: Foreign students must achieve a TOEFL score of at least 500 and must take the ACT.

Procedure: The application deadline is March 1 for fall entry. Foreign students must present proof of health (a physician's statement) and proof of adequate funds. Health insurance is not required but is available through the college. There is a special $25 correspondence fee.

Admissions Contact: Eva Box, Director of Admissions.

FONTBONNE COLLEGE D-2
St. Louis, Missouri 63105 (314) 889-1400

F/T: 99M, 488W	Faculty: 61; n/av
P/T: 35M, 217W	Ph.D.'s: 30%
Grad: 5M, 38W	S/F Ratio: 10 to 1
Year: sems, ss	Tuition: $3660
Appl: Aug. 1	R and B: $1850–$2050
277 applied	241 accepted	140 enrolled
SAT: 402V 434M	ACT: 19	COMPETITIVE

Fontbonne College, established in 1917, is a liberal arts institution affiliated with the Sisters of St. Joseph of Carondelet. Its library has 85,600 volumes and subscribes to 510 periodicals.

Environment: The 13-acre suburban campus is about 5 miles from St. Louis. There are 8 buildings, including 2 dormitories that accommodate 200 men and women. There are also facilities for commuters.

Student Life: About 80% of the students come from Missouri. About 55% are from parochial schools. Only 25% live on campus. About 21% of the students are minority-group members. Campus housing is both coed and single-sex; there are visiting privileges in the single-sex housing. Students may keep cars on campus.

Organizations: The college sponsors religious and service groups, clubs, publications, student government, and social and cultural activities. There are no sororities or fraternities.

Sports: The college fields 2 intercollegiate teams for men and 4 for women. There are 5 intramural sports for men and 5 for women.

Handicapped: About 75% of the campus is accessible to handicapped students. Special facilities include wheelchair ramps, parking areas, elevators, lowered drinking fountains and telephones, and specially equipped rest rooms. Special class scheduling is also available.

Graduates: The freshman dropout rate is 30%; 50% remain to graduate. Thirty percent of the graduates go on for further study (1% to law school, 1% to medical school). About 30% enter careers in business or industry.

Services: Offered free of charge are psychological counseling, tutoring, remedial instruction, career counseling, and placement service. Health care is provided for a fee.

Programs of Study: The B.A., B.S., B.S.Med.Tech., B.Mus., and B.F.A. degrees are conferred. Associate and master's degrees are also awarded. Bachelor's degrees are offered in the following subjects: BUSINESS (accounting, computer programming, finance, human resources administration, management, marketing, retailing), EDUCATION (communication disorders, deaf, early childhood, elementary, secondary, special), ENGLISH (English), FINE AND PERFORMING ARTS (art, art education, broadcasting, music, music education, studio art, theater/dramatics), HEALTH SCIENCES (medical technology, speech therapy), MATH AND SCIENCES (biology, computer science, ecology/environmental science, mathematics, natural sciences), PRE-PROFESSIONAL (home economics, law, medicine, social work), SOCIAL SCIENCES (history, human services, social sciences). About 23% of the degrees are conferred in education, 29% in business, and 15% in fine/applied arts.

Special: A general studies degree, student-designed majors, and field work/internships including cooperative education are offered. There are 3-2 programs in business administration and engineering and social work with Washington University.

Honors: There are 2 honor societies.

Admissions: About 87% of the 1981–82 applicants were accepted. The ACT scores of those who enrolled were as follows: 13% below 12, 32% between 12 and 17, 40% between 18 and 23, and 15% above 23. Applicants should rank in the upper 60% of their class and have a B average. Recommendations, advanced placement or honors work, and leadership record are also considered important.

Procedure: Either the SAT or the ACT is required. August 1 is the deadline for fall; December 15, for spring; June 1, for summer. New students are admitted in the fall, spring, and summer terms. Notification is on a rolling basis. There is a $15 application fee.

Special: Early admissions and deferred admissions plans are offered. CLEP and AP credit is available.

Transfer: For fall 1981, 179 students applied, 160 were accepted, and 103 enrolled. Applicants must have a 2.0 GPA; those transferring with fewer than 30 credit hours must submit a high school transcript. All students must complete, at the college, 32 of the 128 semester hours required for a bachelor's degree. Applications are due at least 1 week prior to the beginning of any term.

Visiting: There is an orientation program for prospective applicants. Informal campus tours can be arranged for weekdays through the admissions office. Visitors may attend classes and stay at the school.

Financial Aid: About 63% of the students receive aid. Forty percent work part-time on campus. Freshman scholarships amounting to $43,000 are awarded each year. The average freshman award is $3000. Part-time jobs are available off campus. Academic promise and financial need are the bases for aid. The FAF is due by April 1 (fall) or December 15 (winter). The college is a member of CSS.

Foreign Students: Seven percent of the full-time students come from foreign countries. Special counseling and special organizations are available for these students.

Admissions: Foreign students must achieve a TOEFL score of at least 500. No college entrance exams are required.

Procedure: Application deadlines are August 1 (fall) and December 15 (winter). Foreign students must present proof of funds adequate to cover 1 year of study.

Admissions Contact: Charles E. Beech, Director of Admissions.

HARRIS-STOWE STATE COLLEGE D-2
St. Louis, Missouri 63103 (314) 533-3366

F/T, P/T:	Faculty: n/av; IIB, +$
1140 M&W	Ph.D.'s: 30%
Grad: none	S/F Ratio: 20 to 1
Year: sems, ss	Tuition: $450 ($854)
Appl: Aug. 1	R and B: n/app
350 applied	250 accepted	202 enrolled
SAT, ACT: not required		COMPETITIVE

Harris-Stowe State College, established in 1857 as Harris-Stowe College, recently joined the state's higher education system. It offers undergraduate training in elementary education. The library has 50,000 books and 30,000 microtexts, and subscribes to 330 periodicals.

Environment: The 8-acre urban campus has one main academic building and a student activity center. There are no residence halls.

Student Life: Nearly all of the students come from Missouri and are public school graduates.

Organizations: Clubs, on-campus social events, and performing groups are offered. The college sponsors 5 fraternities and 8 sororities.

Sports: The college fields intercollegiate teams in 4 sports, and a number of intramural sports are available to both sexes.

Handicapped: There are no special facilities for handicapped students.

Graduates: About 1% of the graduates seek advanced degrees.

Services: Placement services, health care, tutoring, and remedial instruction are offered free.

Programs of Study: The B.S. is offered in EDUCATION (elementary).

Required: General education requirements comprise about half the 4-year program. Students must maintain at least a 2.0 average to graduate.

452 MISSOURI

Special: In addition to elementary certification, the college offers extended certification in art education, health and physical education, librarianship, music education, special education, and junior-high-level subjects. Minors are offered in anthropology/sociology, art, biology, early childhood, counseling, history, English, journalism, speech, drama, library science, instructional media technology, mathematics, multicultural studies, music, psychology, physical education, social science, special education, and urban education. Independent study is available.

Honors: Four national honor societies have chapters on campus.

Admissions: About 71% of the applicants for the 1981-82 freshman class were accepted. Applicants should rank in the top half of their class and have at least a 2.0 GPA.

Procedure: Neither the SAT nor the ACT is required. Application deadlines are August 1 (fall) and January 1 (spring). Notification is on a rolling basis. There is no application fee.

Special: Early and deferred admissions plans are offered. CLEP credit is accepted.

Transfer: About 100 transfer students enroll each year. An average of C or better is preferred. D grades do not transfer. Students must earn at least 30 credits in residence.

Visiting: Campus tours may be arranged. Visitors may attend classes. Arrangements should be made through the director of admissions.

Financial Aid: About 80% of the students receive aid. The college administers funds from federal programs such as NDSL, BEOG, and CWS. The average award to a freshman in 1981-82 totaled about $800 from all sources. August 1 is the aid application deadline.

Foreign Students: Foreign students enrolled full-time represent about 1% of enrollment.

Admissions: Foreign applicants must take the TOEFL. No further academic exams are required.

Procedure: Application deadlines are the same as those for other students. Students must provide a physician's statement as proof of good health, and are required to submit evidence of adequate funds for 1 year. Health insurance is not required.

Admissions Contact: Valerie Beeson, Director of Admissions.

KANSAS CITY ART INSTITUTE A-2
Kansas City, Missouri 64111 (816) 561-4852

F/T: 245M, 231W Faculty: 48; IIB, +$
P/T: 18M, 24W Ph.D.'s: 8%
Grad: none S/F Ratio: 11 to 1
Year: sems, ss Tuition: $5100
Appl: open R and B: $1030
196 applied 88 accepted 64 enrolled
SAT or ACT: required SPECIAL

The Kansas City Art Institute, founded in 1885, is an independent professional college of art and design. The library contains 28,000 books and subscribes to 100 periodicals. The slide library has over 50,000 slides.

Environment: The 15-acre urban campus has 14 buildings including 1 dormitory. There are facilities for commuters.

Student Life: About 32% of the students come from Missouri. Sixty percent are public school graduates. About 79% live on campus. Ten percent of the students are minority-group members. Campus housing is both coed and single-sex; there are visiting privileges in the single-sex housing. Students may keep cars on campus.

Organizations: There are no fraternities or sororities on campus. Extracurricular activities include publications, cultural events, and a student gallery. Art shows, concerts, films, and lectures are offered.

Handicapped: About 50% of the campus is accessible to students with physical handicaps. Special facilities include wheelchair ramps and specially equipped rest rooms.

Graduates: The freshman dropout rate is 30%; 42% remain to graduate. About 50% of the graduates pursue graduate study. Forty-five percent enter careers in business and industry.

Services: Free psychological counseling, remedial instruction, career counseling, and placement services are provided to students. Health care and tutoring are available for a fee.

Programs of Study: The B.F.A. degree is offered in ceramics, design, fiber, painting, photography, printmaking, and sculpture.

Required: Two-thirds of the course work is studio work; the remainder is distributed over general education areas.

Special: Independent study programs, internships, and an exchange program are offered.

Admissions: About 45% of the 1981-82 applicants were accepted. Presentation of a portfolio of art work is required. Recommendations of high school officials should be submitted. A personal interview is suggested. Evidence of special talent is considered important.

Procedure: The ACT or SAT is required. New students are admitted each semester. Although there are no application deadlines, it is suggested that applications be submitted by February 1 (fall) or October 1 (spring). There is a $20 application fee.

Special: AP and CLEP credit is accepted.

Transfer: For fall 1981, 137 students applied, 71 were accepted, and 67 enrolled. A portfolio, a statement of purpose, and an interview are required. A 2.0 GPA, and an ACT score of 18 or SAT scores of 450 on each part, are recommended. D grades are not accepted. Four semesters of study must be completed in residence. All students must complete, at the institute, 48 of the 138 credits required for a bachelor's degree. There is a $20 application fee. Application deadlines are open.

Visiting: There is an orientation program for prospective applicants. Informal campus tours may be arranged.

Financial Aid: About 51% of the students are receiving assistance. Twenty percent work part-time on campus. The institute is a member of CSS and offers various loans and federal/state grant programs. The FAF and the student's and parents' IRS 1040 forms are required. The suggested aid application deadline is February 15.

Foreign Students: Two percent of the full-time students come from foreign countries.

Admissions: Foreign students must achieve a TOEFL score of at least 500. No college entrance exams are required.

Procedure: Application deadlines are February 1 (fall) and October 1 (spring). Foreign students must present proof of adequate funds and must have the institute's health form completed by a physician. They must also carry health insurance, which is available through the institute.

Admissions Contact: Director of Admissions.

LINCOLN UNIVERSITY C-2
Jefferson City, Missouri 65101 (314) 751-2325

F/T: 917M, 788W Faculty: 146; IIA, --$
P/T: 435M, 401W Ph.D.'s: 37%
Grad: 83M, 75W S/F Ratio: 19 to 1
Year: sems, ss Tuition: $500 ($900)
Appl: July 15 R and B: $1480
855 applied 806 accepted 505 enrolled
SAT: 269V 307M ACT: 20 NONCOMPETITIVE

Lincoln University, established in 1866 as Lincoln Institute, is a state-controlled institution offering undergraduate programs in the liberal arts and sciences, education, business, agriculture, and preprofessional areas. Its library has 132,097 books and 40,624 audiovisuals and subscribes to 1180 periodicals.

Environment: The urban main campus occupies 52 acres. Two farms comprising 522 acres are devoted to agricultural instruction. There are 55 buildings. The university maintains dormitories.

Student Life: The original purpose of the institution was to help educate blacks freed after the Civil War. The student body has remained largely (39%) black. Another 10% of the students are members of other minority groups. Twenty-three percent of the students live on campus. Campus housing is single-sex; there are visiting privileges. Students may keep cars on campus. Day-care services are available to all students, faculty, and staff for a fee.

Organizations: There are 4 local and 3 national fraternities (2% of the men are members), as well as 4 local and 3 national sororities (2% of the women are members). Social organizations and various clubs also are available on campus.

Sports: The university fields 8 intercollegiate teams for men and 5 for women. There are 3 intramural sports for men and 3 for women.

Handicapped: The campus is not readily accessible to physically handicapped students.

Services: Offered free to all students are psychological counseling, tutoring, remedial instruction, career counseling, and placement service. Health care is provided for a fee.

Programs of Study: The university confers the B.A., B.S., B.S.Ed., and B.Mus.Ed. degrees. Associate and master's degrees are also awarded. Bachelor's degrees may be earned in the following subjects: BUSINESS (accounting, business administration, business education, economics, marketing, public administration), EDUCATION (elementary, health/physical, special), ENGLISH (English, journalism, speech), FINE AND PERFORMING ARTS (art, mass communication, music education, theater/dramatics), HEALTH SCIENCES (communication disorders, medical technology), LANGUAGES (French), MATH AND SCIENCES (biology, chemistry, mathematics, physics), PHILOSOPHY (humanities, philosophy), PREPROFESSIONAL (agribusiness, agriculture, animal science, home economics, industrial arts education, natural resources management, plant and soil science), SOCIAL SCIENCES (criminal justice administration, economics, government/political science, history, psychology, social sciences, sociology). Most undergraduate degrees are awarded in business and the arts and sciences.

Special: The College of Applied Science and Technology offers 2-year terminal programs in several technological fields.

Admissions: About 94% of those who applied were accepted for the 1981-82 freshman class. There is an open enrollment policy for residents; out-of-state applicants need a C average. Advanced placement or honors courses and recommendations are considered important.

Procedure: The SAT or ACT and the SCAT are required. New students are admitted each term. Application deadlines are July 15 (fall), December 1 (spring), and May 1 (summer). There is a $12 application fee. Notification is on a rolling basis.

Special: There is a deferred admissions plan.

Transfer: For fall 1981, 430 students applied, 422 were accepted, and 257 enrolled. Good academic standing is necessary. D grades do not transfer. About 30 credits must be completed in residence. Application deadlines are the same as those for freshmen.

Visiting: There is an orientation program for new students. Informal campus tours with student guides can be arranged. Visitors may attend classes and stay overnight at the university; arrangements should be made through the admissions office.

Financial Aid: About 44% of the students receive aid. Twenty-six percent work part-time on campus. The university offers scholarships, federal/state grants, and government/commercial loans, and is a member of CSS. The FAF should be filed no later than April 30 for fall entry, April 1 for summer entry.

Foreign Students: Seven percent of the full-time students come from foreign countries. Special counseling and special organizations are available for these students.

Admissions: Foreign students must achieve a minimum score of 500 on the TOEFL or 80% on the University of Michigan Language Test. No college entrance exams are required.

Procedure: Application deadlines are the same as those for other students. Foreign students must complete a medical history form and must present proof of funds adequate to cover 1 academic year. Health insurance is required and is available through the university for a fee.

Admissions Contact: Charles E. Glasper, Director of Admissions.

THE LINDENWOOD COLLEGES D-2
St. Charles, Missouri 63301 (314) 723-7152

F/T: 307M, 461W	Faculty:	60; IIA, --$
P/T: 272M, 408W	Ph.D.'s:	30%
Grad: 188M, 280W	S/F Ratio:	12 to 1
Year: 4-1-4, ss	Tuition:	$4125
Appl: open	R and B:	$2700-3200
1096 applied	986 accepted	641 enrolled
SAT: 440V 450M	ACT: 18	LESS COMPETITIVE

The Lindenwood Colleges consist of Lindenwood College for Women, founded in 1827, Lindenwood College II (for men), Lindenwood College III (the evening school), and Lindenwood College for Individualized Education (LCIE). The colleges offer an innovative program in the liberal arts and sciences. Library resources include 77,000 volumes.

Environment: The 140-acre suburban campus is located 25 miles from St. Louis. The buildings on campus include 5 residence halls.

Student Life: About 83% of the students come from public schools. Twelve percent are minority-group members. About 35% live on campus. Campus housing is both coed and single-sex; there are visiting privileges in the single-sex housing. Students may keep cars on campus. Drinking is not permitted on campus.

Organizations: There are no fraternities or sororities. Extracurricular activities include student government, publications, a radio station, clubs, and regularly scheduled on-campus social and cultural events.

Sports: The colleges compete intercollegiately in 5 sports for men and 5 for women. There are 6 intramural sports for men and 6 for women.

Handicapped: About 80% of the campus is accessible to physically handicapped students. Special facilities include wheelchair ramps, parking areas, elevators, lowered drinking fountains and telephones, and specially equipped rest rooms. Special counselors are also available. Two percent of the students have visual impairments; 3% hearing impairments.

Graduates: The freshman dropout rate is 15%. Over 20% go on for further education.

Services: Career counseling, psychological counseling, tutoring, and remedial instruction are offered without charge to all students. Health care is provided for a fee.

Programs of Study: The B.A., B.S., B.S.N., and B.F.A. degrees are conferred. Associate and master's degrees are also awarded. Bachelor's degrees are offered in the following subjects: BUSINESS (business administration, business education), EDUCATION (early childhood, elementary, secondary, special), ENGLISH (English, mass communications), FINE AND PERFORMING ARTS (art, art education, music education, theater/dramatics), HEALTH SCIENCES (medical technology, nursing), LANGUAGES (French, Spanish), MATH AND SCIENCES (biology, chemistry, mathematics), PREPROFESSIONAL (dentistry, law, medicine, optometry, osteopathy, veterinary), SOCIAL SCIENCES (history, psychology, sociology).

Required: Two semesters of physical education are required.

Special: Student-designed majors, a general studies degree, study abroad, a Washington semester, and 3-2 programs (in engineering and in social work) with Washington University are offered. LCIE is designed to meet the needs of working adults; classes meet evenings and weekends.

Admissions: About 90% of the applicants for 1981-82 were accepted. The SAT scores of those who enrolled were as follows: Verbal —68% below 500, 26% between 500 and 599, 6% between 600 and 700, and 0% above 700; Math—66% below 500, 26% between 500 and 599, 8% between 600 and 700, and 0% above 700. Applicants should have a GPA of at least 2.0. Advanced placement or honor courses, recommendations, and special talents are considered important.

Procedure: The SAT or ACT is required. Application deadlines are open. New students are admitted each semester; notification is on a rolling basis. There is a $25 application fee.

Special: AP and CLEP credit is available. There are early decision, early admissions, and deferred admissions programs.

Transfer: About 70 students transfer yearly. A GPA of 2.0 is required. D grades do not transfer. All students must complete, at the college, 30 of the 120 credits required for a bachelor's degree. There are no application deadlines; transfer students are admitted in each term.

Visiting: There is an orientation program for prospective applicants. Informal campus tours on Monday through Saturday can be arranged through the admissions office. Visitors may sit in on classes and stay overnight at the colleges.

Financial Aid: About 86% of the students receive aid. Four percent work part-time on campus. The colleges offer various loans (NDSL included), government grants (BEOG), and part-time work opportunities (including CWS). There are also freshman scholarships. Aid packages average $2800 and are based primarily on need. The FAF is preferred bu the FFS is accepted; the deadline for filing is March 1 for fall entry. The college is a member of CSS.

Foreign Students: Thirteen percent of the full-time students come from foreign countries. An intensive English program and special counseling are available for these students.

Admissions: Foreign students must take the TOEFL or the University of Michigan Language Test. On the TOEFL, applicants must achieve a score of at least 500. No college entrance exams are required.

Procedure: Application deadlines are March 1 (fall), December 1 (winter), January 1 (spring), and April 1 (summer). Foreign students must have a physical exam and must present proof of funds adequate to cover 1 year of study. They must also carry health insurance, which is available through the colleges.

Admissions Contact: Sarah Fulton, Director of Admissions.

MARYVILLE COLLEGE
St. Louis, Missouri 63141
D-2
(314) 576-9300

F/T: 188M, 677W
P/T: 224M, 599W
Grad: 2M, 70W
Year: sems, ss
Appl: Sept. 1
433 applied 345 accepted 182 enrolled
ACT: 18 COMPETITIVE
Faculty: 59; n/av
Ph.D.'s: 65%
S/F Ratio: 14 to 1
Tuition: $3710
R and B: $1980

Maryville College, founded in 1872 by the Religious Order of the Sacred Heart but now governed by an independent board of trustees, offers undergraduate programs in the arts and sciences, business, education, and health fields. Its library has 90,000 volumes and subscribes to 550 periodicals.

Environment: The 300-acre suburban campus is located 20 miles from downtown St. Louis. Buildings include 2 dormitories, which are coed by floor. A gymnasium-multipurpose building and an ecumenical chapel were dedicated in 1980.

Student Life: About 94% of the students come from Missouri. Fifty-eight percent are from public schools. About 35% live on campus. Twelve percent are minority-group members. Campus housing is coed. Students may keep cars on campus. Day-care services are available for a fee to all students.

Organizations: There is a full extracurricular program of clubs and activities. On-campus cultural and social events are scheduled regularly. There is one service fraternity for men and women.

Sports: The college fields 6 intercollegiate teams for men and 7 for women. There are 3 intramural sports for men and 4 for women.

Handicapped: The classroom buildings are accessible to handicapped students, and modifications are in progress in the dormitories.

Services: Psychological counseling, career counseling, placement service, remedial instruction, and tutoring are provided without charge. Health care is provided for a fee.

Programs of Study: The B.A., B.S., B.S.N., and B.F.A. degrees are conferred. Associate and master's degrees are also awarded. Bachelor's degrees are offered in the following subjects: BUSINESS (health facilities management, information systems, legal administration, management), EDUCATION (early childhood, elementary, secondary, special), ENGLISH (communications, English, literature), FINE AND PERFORMING ARTS (art, art education, interior design, music, music education, therapeutic art), HEALTH SCIENCES (medical technology, music therapy, nursing, physical therapy, respiratory therapy), MATH AND SCIENCES (actuarial science, biology, chemistry, mathematics), PHILOSOPHY (humanities, philosophy, religion), PREPROFESSIONAL (dentistry, law, medicine), SOCIAL SCIENCES (government/political science, history, international understanding, psychology, sociology). About 48% of the students choose majors in health fields.

Required: There is a required core curriculum.

Special: Student-designed majors, independent study, and an internship in interior design are offered. A combined B.A.-B.S. degree can be earned (usually in a 5-year program). The Weekend College offers degrees in management, communications, and information systems and science. Students attend classes every other weekend and do much independent work. There are also cooperative education and intensive English programs.

Honors: There are 3 honor societies; honors work is offered in all academic areas during the junior and senior years.

Admissions: About 80% of the applicants for the 1981-82 school year were accepted. ACT scores of those who enrolled were as follows: 49% below 21, 26% between 21 and 23, 22% between 24 and 25, 3% between 26 and 28, and 0% above 28. A GPA of 2.0 is required; impressions made during the interview, recommendations, and advanced placement or honors courses are considered important.

Procedure: The ACT is required. September 1 is the fall deadline; December 15, the spring. Freshmen are admitted each semester. Notification is on a rolling basis. There is a $10 application fee.

Special: AP and CLEP credit is offered.

Transfer: For fall 1981, 611 students applied, 489 were accepted, and 337 enrolled. D grades are not accepted. A 2.0 GPA is required for most programs; an interview is required for some programs. All students must complete, at the college, the last 30 of the 128 credits required for a bachelor's degree. Applications are due September 1 (fall) or December 15 (spring).

Visiting: Open houses are scheduled 2 times a year. Informal campus tours can be arranged through the admissions office for Monday through Friday, from 9 A.M. to 3 P.M.. Visitors may attend classes and stay overnight at the college.

Financial Aid: About 75% of the students receive aid. Twelve percent work part-time on campus. The college offers grants, loans, and work opportunities (CWS included). The average aid package to freshmen is $3000. Need is the determining factor in granting assistance. Tuition may be paid in installments. The FAF is due by March 1; the college is a member of CSS.

Foreign Students: About 2% of the students come from foreign countries. An intensive English program, special counseling, and special organizations are available for these students.

Admissions: Foreign students must achieve a TOEFL score of at least 500 or a similar score on the University of Michigan Language Test. They must also take the college's placement exams in English composition and mathematics.

Procedure: Applications should be received 1 semester before entry. Foreign students are admitted in all terms. They must have a physician complete the college's health form and must present proof of funds adequate to cover 1 year of study. There is a special tuition fee for the intensive English program. Health insurance is required, but is not available through the college.

Admissions Contact: Michael J. Gillick, Director of Admissions.

MISSOURI BAPTIST COLLEGE
Creve Coeur, Missouri 63141
D-2
(314) 434-1115

F/T: 126M, 79W
P/T: 78M, 155W
Grad: none
Year: 4-4-1, ss
Appl: open
179 applied 150 accepted 120 enrolled
ACT: 18 LESS COMPETITIVE
Faculty: 16; IIB, av$
Ph.D.'s: 60%
S/F Ratio: 14 to 1
Tuition: $1800
R and B: $1750

Missouri Baptist College, established in 1963, is a liberal arts institution affiliated with the Missouri Baptist Convention. The library houses 30,000 volumes and holds subscriptions to 300 periodicals.

Environment: The college is located on an 81-acre suburban campus, 20 miles from downtown St. Louis. Campus facilities include a 2-story administration building housing classrooms and laboratories, a full-sized gymnasium, a multipurpose complex, and dormitories that house 50 men and 50 women.

Student Life: Ninety-eight percent of the students come from Missouri. Ninety-five percent of entering freshmen are from public schools. Fifteen percent live on campus. Six percent are minority-group members. About 88% of the students are Protestant and 10% are Catholic. Campus housing is single-sex; there are no visiting privileges. Students may keep cars on campus. Students must attend religious services 2 days a week, and drinking is prohibited on campus.

Organizations: Active groups are the Ministerial Alliance, Student Services Club, the student government, Perclesian Society, and Christian student ministries. There are no fraternities or sororities.

Sports: The college participates on an intercollegiate level in 3 sports for men. There are no intramural sports.

Graduates: The freshman dropout rate is 35%; 25% of the entering freshmen remain to graduate. Forty percent of those graduating enter careers in business and industry, and 40% pursue advanced degrees: 1% in medicine and 1% in law.

Services: Placement service, health care, and tutorial instruction are provided to students for a fee. Career counseling is provided free of charge.

Programs of Study: The college confers the B.A. and B.S. degrees, which are offered in the following subjects: BUSINESS (accounting, business administration, business education), EDUCATION (early childhood, elementary, health/physical, religious), ENGLISH (English), FINE AND PERFORMING ARTS (church music, music, music education), HEALTH SCIENCES (medical technology), LANGUAGES (Greek/Latin), MATH AND SCIENCES (biology, chemistry, mathematics, natural sciences), PHILOSOPHY (religion), PREPROFESSIONAL (ministry), SOCIAL SCIENCES (administration of justice, behavioral science, history, social sciences). The following majors are available by special arrangement: art, communication, driver education, economics, philosophy, physics, political science, psychology, sociology.

Required: There is a general education requirement, to which the freshman and sophomore years are largely devoted.

Special: Students in the honors program may create their own majors. Students may spend their junior year studying abroad.

Honors: An honors program is conducted by the college for qualified students.

Admissions: About 84% of those who applied were accepted for admission to the 1981–82 freshman class. The ACT scores of those who enrolled were as follows: 64% below 21, 20% between 21 and 23, 10% between 24 and 25, 5% between 26 and 28, and 1% above 28. Applicants should rank in the upper 50% of their high school class. An applicant must be a graduate of an accredited high school, or the equivalent. Recommendations and the interview are important.

Procedure: The ACT is required. There is no application deadline. A personal interview is preferred and may be taken with a college representative near the student's home. Freshmen are admitted in all terms. Notification is on a rolling basis. There is a $15 application fee.

Special: An early admissions plan is offered. CLEP credit is available.

Transfer: For fall 1981, 50 students applied, 40 were accepted, and 35 enrolled. Applicants for transfer must have a GPA of 2.0 in liberal arts courses. D grades do not transfer. Recommendations are required. All students must complete, at the college, 24 of the last 30 credits (128 credits are required for a bachelor's degree). There are no application deadlines.

Financial Aid: About 75% of all students receive aid. One third work part-time on campus. Scholarships, grants, loans, and a work-study program are available. The average scholarship is $300; the average loan, $400. The average total aid granted is $800. The college requires the FAF or FFS. There are no application deadlines.

Foreign Students: One percent of the full-time students come from foreign countries.

Admissions: Foreign students must achieve a TOEFL score of at least 500 and must take the ACT.

Procedure: Application deadlines are June (fall), October (spring), and February (summer). Foreign students must present proof of funds adequate to cover 1 year of study and must submit a physician's report as proof of good health. Health insurance is required and is available through the college for a fee.

Admissions Contact: Charles Bobbitt, Director of Admissions.

MISSOURI INSTITUTE OF TECHNOLOGY A-2
Kansas City, Missouri 64114   (816) 363-7030
(Recognized Candidate for Accreditation)

F/T: 1656M, 190W	Faculty: 37; n/av
P/T: 156M, 27W	Ph.D.'s: n/av
Grad: none	S/F Ratio: 20 to 1
Year: tri, ss	Tuition: $3025
Appl: October	R and B: n/app
SAT or ACT: required	LESS COMPETITIVE

Missouri Institute of Technology, an independent institution founded in 1931, is administered by the Bell & Howell Education Group. It offers undergraduate degrees in electronics engineering technology, computer science for business, and electronics technology.

Environment: The institute is located in Kansas City and has no housing facilities.

Student Life: Forty-four percent of the students come from Missouri. Twelve percent are members of minority groups. The housing office helps students find off-campus accommodations. Students may have cars on campus.

Organizations: The 11 extracurricular activities include professional organizations, a ham radio club, an audio club, a model rocketry club, a skydiving club, a computer club, and a photography club. There are no fraternities or sororities.

Sports: The institute does not participate in intercollegiate sports, but offers 2 intramural sports each for men and women.

Handicapped: All programs are accessible to handicapped students. Facilities include wheelchair ramps, special parking, elevators, specially equipped rest rooms, and lowered drinking fountains and telephones. Special class scheduling can be arranged, and the institute provides necessary tutoring and materials.

Graduates: More than 90% begin careers in business and industry.

Services: Placement aid, career counseling, and tutoring are provided free. Fees are charged for health-care services and remedial instruction.

Programs of Study: The institute awards the B.S.E.E. and the B.S. Comp. Sci. degrees. Associate degrees in electronics technology also are available. Bachelor's degrees are offered in: BUSINESS (computer science), PREPROFESSIONAL (engineering—electronics engineering technology).

Required: Students must follow a specified curriculum and maintain an average of 2.0 or better to graduate.

Honors: Tau Alpha Phi has a chapter on campus, and an honors program is offered in electronics engineering technology.

Admissions: Nineteen percent of the 1981–82 freshmen ranked in the upper fifth of their high school class, and 42% ranked in the upper two-fifths. Students must have a high school diploma or a GED. Besides high school record and test scores, admissions officers consider impressions made during a required personal interview and recommendations from high school officials.

Procedure: Students must take both the SAT or ACT and the Bell & Howell Education Group Entrance Exam. Applications must be submitted by October for fall admission, March for spring admission, or July for summer admission. The application fee is $25. Admissions decisions are made on a rolling basis.

Special: A deferred admissions plan is offered.

Transfer: Transfer students are accepted for all classes. A personal interview is required. D grades do not transfer. Students must earn, at the institute, at least 36 of the 160 credits required for a bachelor's degree, and must complete the last 2 trimesters of the program in residence. Application deadlines are the same as those for freshmen.

Visiting: Guides are provided for informal visits, which may be arranged for weekdays with the director of admissions.

Financial Aid: Eighty-five percent of the students receive aid through the school. Available aid includes scholarships (average $1500, maximum $4350), loans (average $2000, maximum $2500), and work contracts (average $3000, maximum $5000). The FAF is required; the institute is a member of the CSS.

Foreign Students: Four foreign students are enrolled at the institute.

Admissions: Foreign applicants must score at least 450 on the TOEFL or 106 on the ELS. They must take both the SAT and the Bell & Howell Education Group Entrance Exam.

Procedure: Application deadlines are the same as those for other freshmen. Students must provide a physician's certificate as proof of good health and must show evidence of adequate funds for 1 year. They are required to carry health insurance, which is available through the institute for a fee.

Admissions Contact: Joseph Buechner, Director of Admissions.

MISSOURI SOUTHERN STATE COLLEGE A-4
Joplin, Missouri 64801   (417) 624-8100

F/T: 1259M, 1346W	Faculty: 163; IIB, +$
P/T: 752M, 973W	Ph.D.'s: 46%
Grad: none	S/F Ratio: 16 to 1
Year: sems, ss	Tuition: $600 ($1200)
Appl: Sept.1	R and B: $1450
1283 applied	1283 accepted
ACT: 15	NONCOMPETITIVE

Missouri Southern State College, established in 1937, offers undergraduate programs in business, education, health fields, and the arts and sciences. Its library has 104,000 books and 82,000 microfilm items, and subscribes to 1055 periodicals.

Environment: The 350-acre suburban campus is located 3 miles from a city of 48,000. There are 30 buildings, including 7 residence halls.

Student Life: About 78% of the students come from Missouri. About 91% live on campus. Three percent are minority-group members. Student housing is single-sex; there are visiting privileges. Students may keep cars on campus.

Organizations: Clubs, religious groups, and social events are sponsored. About 4% of the students belong to fraternities (2 local, 2 national) and sororities (4 local, 4 national).

Sports: The college fields 8 intercollegiate teams for men and 7 for women. There are 7 intramural sports for men and 6 for women.

Handicapped: About 95% of the campus is accessible to handicapped students. Special facilities include wheelchair ramps, parking areas, and elevators. Special class scheduling is also available.

Graduates: The freshman dropout rate is 20%; 50% of the entering freshmen remain to graduate. Five percent of the students go on for further education; 2% each in medicine, dentistry, and law. Fifty percent enter careers in business and industry.

456 MISSOURI

Services: Psychological and career counseling and placement services are offered free of charge. There is sometimes a fee for tutoring and remedial instruction. Health care services require payment.

Programs of Study: The B.A., B.S., B.B.A., B.S. in Elem. Ed., B.S. in Sec. Ed., and B.T. degrees are conferred. Associate degrees are also awarded. Bachelor's degrees are offered in the following subjects: BUSINESS (accounting, business administration, business education, finance, management, marketing), EDUCATION (elementary, health/physical, secondary), ENGLISH (English, speech), FINE AND PERFORMING ARTS (art, art education, music, music education, theater/dramatics), HEALTH SCIENCES (environmental health, medical technology), LANGUAGES (Spanish), MATH AND SCIENCES (biology, chemistry, mathematics, physics), PREPROFESSIONAL (dentistry, law, medicine, pharmacy, veterinary), SOCIAL SCIENCES (economics, government/political science, psychology, sociology). About 33% of the degrees are conferred in business, and 33% in education.

Special: Student-designed majors and a general studies degree are offered, as well as a combined B.A.-B.S. degree.

Honors: Honors work is offered in 8 departments.

Admissions: All of the 1981–82 applicants were accepted. The ACT scores of those who enrolled were as follows: 73% below 21, 6% between 21 and 23, 12% between 24 and 25, 6% between 26 and 28, and 3% above 28. There is an "open door" admissions policy.

Procedure: The ACT is required; recommendations also are needed. Application deadlines are September 1 (fall), January 20 (spring), and June 7 (summer); notification is on a rolling basis. There is a $10 application fee.

Special: AP and CLEP are available. There are early decision, early admissions, and deferred admissions plans.

Transfer: For fall 1981, 500 students applied, 500 were accepted, and 368 enrolled. D grades transfer in the lower division only. All students must complete, at the college, 30 of the 124 credits required for a bachelor's degree. Application deadlines are the same as those for freshmen.

Visiting: Campus tours can be arranged. Visitors may attend classes and usually stay in the dormitories. Arrangements for visits on Monday through Friday, from 9 A.M. to 2 P.M., can be made through the admissions office.

Financial Aid: About 78% of the students receive aid. Ten percent work part-time on campus. The college offers federal/state grants, various loans, and part-time campus employment (including CWS). The average freshman aid package is $900. The FFS is due April 30 (fall), December 1 (spring), or May 1 (summer).

Foreign Students: Fewer than 1% of the full-time students come from foreign countries. Special counseling is available for these students.

Admissions: Foreign students must achieve a TOEFL score of at least 535 and an ACT score of at least 15.

Procedure: Application deadlines for foreign students are July 1 (fall), November 1 (spring), and April 1 (summer). Foreign students must present proof of funds adequate to cover 1 year of study and must carry health insurance, which is available through the college for a fee.

Admissions Contact: Richard D. Humphrey, Director of Admissions.

MISSOURI VALLEY COLLEGE B-2
Marshall, Missouri 65340 (816) 886-6924

F/T: 293M, 152W	Faculty: n/av; IIB, --$
P/T: 42M, 34W	Ph.D.'s: n/av
Grad: none	S/F Ratio: n/av
Year: sems, ss	Tuition: $3050
Appl: open	R and B: $1750
502 applied 321 accepted 211 enrolled	
SAT or ACT: required	COMPETITIVE

Missouri Valley College, founded in 1889, is a liberal arts institution affiliated with the United Presbyterian Church. Its library contains 100,000 books and subscribes to 500 periodicals.

Environment: The 40-acre campus is located in a rural area 65 miles from Kansas City. There are 14 buildings, which include dormitories for men and women.

Student Life: About 65% of the students come from Missouri. Seventy-five percent come from public schools and 70% reside on campus.

Organizations: On-campus activities include religious groups, clubs, student government, publications, dramatics, performing groups, service groups, and regularly scheduled social and cultural events. Two local and 3 national fraternities attract 80% of the men; 2 local and 2 national sororities attract 70% of the women.

Sports: The college offers both intercollegiate and intramural competition.

Handicapped: All of the campus is accessible to students with physical handicaps. One percent of the students have visual impairments; special equipment, special class scheduling, and tutoring services are available for these students.

Graduates: The freshman dropout rate is 15%; about 57% remain to graduate. Twenty-seven percent pursue further education and 42% enter careers in business or industry.

Services: Career counseling, placement, health care, tutoring, remedial instruction, and psychological counseling are offered to all students without charge.

Programs of Study: The B.A. and B.S. degrees are offered. Associate degrees are also awarded. Bachelor's degrees are offered in the following subjects: BUSINESS (accounting, business administration, computer science, management), EDUCATION (elementary, health/physical, secondary, special), ENGLISH (English), FINE AND PERFORMING ARTS (art, radio/TV, theater/dramatics), MATH AND SCIENCES (biology, chemistry, mathematics), PHILOSOPHY (humanities, philosophy, religion), SOCIAL SCIENCES (economics, government/political science, history, psychology, sociology). About 27% of the degrees conferred are in social sciences.

Required: There is a general education requirement that includes English, religion, and physical education.

Special: A general studies major is possible. Student-designed majors and study abroad are offered.

Admissions: About 64% of the 1981–82 applicants were accepted. The SAT scores of those who enrolled were as follows: Verbal—51% below 500, 48% between 500 and 599, 1% between 600 and 700, and 0% above 700; Math—52% below 500, 47% between 500 and 599, 1% between 600 and 700, and 0% above 700. On the ACT, 10% scored below 21, 33% between 21 and 23, 21% between 24 and 25, 2% between 26 and 28, and 0% above 28. Applicants should rank in the top half of their class and have a GPA of at least 2.0. Leadership record and advanced placement or honors courses are also considered important.

Procedure: The ACT or SAT is required by March of the senior year of high school. Application deadlines are open; notification is on a rolling basis. There is a $10 application fee.

Special: CLEP is used. There are early decision, early admissions, and deferred admissions plans.

Transfer: For fall 1981, 32 students applied, 28 were accepted, and 22 enrolled. A minimum GPA of 2.0 is required. D grades do not transfer. All students must complete, at the college, 30 of the 124 credits required for a bachelor's degree. Application deadlines are open.

Visiting: There is an orientation program for prospective applicants. Informal campus tours may be arranged. Visitors may attend classes and stay at the school.

Financial Aid: About 89% of the students are receiving assistance. Sixty-five percent work part-time on campus. The college offers scholarships, grants (federal and state), various loans (government and commercial), and campus employment. The average aid package is $2500; the maximum freshman award is $4305. Academic promise and need are the determining factors. The FAF or FFS should be filed; there is no deadline.

Foreign Students: Fewer than 1% of the full-time students come from foreign countries. An intensive English course, special counseling, and special organizations are available for these students.

Admissions: Foreign students must achieve minimum scores of 500 on the TOEFL and 500 on the verbal part of the SAT. They must also take the college's English proficiency exam.

Procedure: Application deadlines are May (fall), July (winter), September (spring), and January (summer). Foreign students must complete the college's health form and must present proof of funds adequate to cover 1 year of study. Health insurance is required and is available through the college for a fee.

Admissions Contact: Becky Mattei, Acting Director of Admissions.

MISSOURI WESTERN STATE COLLEGE   A-2
St. Joseph, Missouri 64507   (816) 271-4228

F/T: 1435M, 1456W	Faculty: n/av; IIB, +$
P/T: 578M, 802W	Ph.D.'s: 40%
Grad: none	S/F Ratio: 18 to 1
Year: sems, ss	Tuition: $680 ($1184)
Appl: Aug. 20	R and B: $1300
1800 applied	1750 accepted 1200 enrolled
ACT: required	NONCOMPETITIVE

Missouri Western State College, established in 1915, offers undergraduate programs in business, education, health fields, and the arts and sciences. Its library has 100,000 books and 15,000 microfilm items; it subscribes to 1420 periodicals.

Environment: The 750-acre suburban campus has 12 buildings, including 3 dormitories, each accommodating 184 students. There are also off-campus apartments.

Student Life: About 94% of the students come from Missouri. Ninety-five percent are graduates of public schools. Fifteen percent live on campus. Six percent are minority-group members. Campus housing is single-sex; there are visiting privileges. Students may keep cars on campus.

Organizations: Clubs, service groups, publications, performing groups, social events, and student government are available. Fifteen percent of the students belong to 5 national fraternities and 5 national sororities.

Sports: The college fields 5 intercollegiate teams for men and 4 for women. There are 9 intramural sports for men and 8 for women.

Handicapped: All of the campus is accessible to handicapped students. Special facilities include wheelchair ramps, parking areas, elevators, lowered drinking fountains and telephones, and specially equipped rest rooms. One percent of the students have visual impairments, and 1% have hearing impairments.

Graduates: The freshman dropout rate is 20%; about 55% remain to graduate; 12% go on to further study.

Services: Health care, psychological counseling, tutoring, remedial instruction, placement service, and career counseling are offered to students without charge.

Programs of Study: The B.A., B.S., B.S.B.A., B.S.Ed., B.S. Tech., and B.S.W. degrees are conferred. Associate degrees are also awarded. Bachelor's degrees are offered in the following subjects: BUSINESS (accounting, business administration, business education, computer science, management, marketing), EDUCATION (early childhood, elementary, health/physical, secondary, special), ENGLISH (English, speech), FINE AND PERFORMING ARTS (art, art education, music, music education, theater/dramatics), HEALTH SCIENCES (medical technology, nursing), MATH AND SCIENCES (biology, chemistry, mathematics), PREPROFESSIONAL (agriculture, social work), SOCIAL SCIENCES (economics, history, psychology, social sciences). Most of the students major in business or education.

Required: There is a distribution requirement. All freshmen must take 6 hours of English.

Special: Combined B.A.-B.S. degrees are available in several subjects. There is a 2-2 program for the B.S. Tech. degrees.

Admissions: About 97% of the 1981–82 applicants were accepted. There is an "open door" policy, but an applicant must have a high school diploma or have passed the GED.

Procedure: The ACT is required. August 20 is the fall application deadline; the deadline for spring is January 20, and for summer, June 3. There is a $5 application fee. Notification is on a rolling basis.

Special: There are early decision, early admissions, and deferred admissions plans. AP and CLEP credit is accepted.

Transfer: D grades transfer. All students must complete, at the college, 30 of the 124 credits required for a bachelor's degree. Application deadlines are the same as those for freshmen.

Visiting: Campus tours can be arranged. Visitors generally may not attend classes, but they may stay overnight in the residence halls. Arrangements for visits should be made through the College Relations Department.

Financial Aid: The college offers various loans, federal/state grants, and part-time campus employment (including CWS). About 60% of the students receive assistance. About 25% work part-time on campus. The FAF, FSF, or SFS is required by May 1.

Foreign Students: One percent of the full-time students come from foreign countries. Special counseling is available for these students.

Admissions: Foreign students must achieve a TOEFL score of at least 500 and must take the ACT.

Procedure: Application deadlines are July 10 (fall), December 5 (spring), and April 21 (summer). Foreign students must present proof of funds adequate to cover 1 year of study.

Admissions Contact: George Ashworth, Director of Admissions and Records.

NORTHEAST MISSOURI STATE UNIVERSITY   C-1
Kirksville, Missouri 63501   (816) 785-4116

F/T: 2423M, 3069W	Faculty: 250; IIA, av$
P/T: 206M, 279W	Ph.D.'s: 50%
Grad: 309M, 363W	S/F Ratio: 19 to 1
Year: sems, ss	Tuition: $480 ($960)
Appl: open	R and B: $1320
2500 applied	2200 accepted 1550 enrolled
ACT: 19	LESS COMPETITIVE

Northeast Missouri State University, founded in 1867, offers undergraduate programs in the arts and sciences, business, health fields, and education. Its library has 225,000 volumes and 400,000 microtexts, and subscribes to 1700 periodicals.

Environment: The 120-acre small-town campus is located in a rural area 160 miles from Kansas City and 180 miles from St. Louis. There are 30 major buildings. Apartments are available for 110 married students. Living facilities also include dormitories, fraternity houses, a sorority residence hall, and on-campus apartments.

Student Life: Over 73% of the students come from Missouri. Fifty-three percent live on campus. Nine percent are minority-group members. About 63% are Protestant, and 30% are Catholic. Campus housing is single-sex; there are visiting privileges. Students may keep cars on campus. Day-care services are available to all students for a fee.

Organizations: There is a traditional array of activities, social events, and on-campus groups. About 15% of the students belong to one of 14 national fraternities and 8 national sororities.

Sports: The university fields 12 intercollegiate teams for men and 11 for women. There are 21 intramural sports for men and 19 for women.

Handicapped: About 80% of the campus is accessible to students with physical handicaps.

Graduates: The freshman dropout rate is 5%; about 40% remain to graduate. Twenty-seven percent of the graduates go on for further study (3% to medical and dental schools and 1% to law school). Thirty percent enter careers in business and industry.

Services: Free to all students are career and psychological counseling, placement services, remedial instruction, and tutoring. Health care is provided for a fee.

Programs of Study: The B.A., B.S., B.S.Ed., B.F.A., B.S. Mus.Ed., B.S.N., and B.Mus. degrees are conferred. Master's and specialist degrees are also awarded. Bachelor's degrees are offered in the following subjects: AREA STUDIES (Latin American), BUSINESS (accounting, business administration, business education, computer science, finance, management, marketing, personnel management), EDUCATION (early childhood, elementary, health/physical, industrial, secondary, special), ENGLISH (English, mass communications, speech), FINE AND PERFORMING ARTS (art, art education, music, music education, radio/TV, studio art, theater/dramatics), HEALTH SCIENCES (environmental health, medical technology, nursing, speech therapy), LANGUAGES (French, German, Spanish), MATH AND SCIENCES (biology, botany, chemistry, earth science, ecology/environmental science, mathematics, natural sciences, physical sciences, physics, radiological surveillance, statistics, zoology), PHILOSOPHY (philosophy, religion), PREPROFESSIONAL (agriculture, dentistry, engineering, home economics, law, library science, medicine, pharmacy, social work, veterinary), SOCIAL SCIENCES (economics, geography, government/political science, history, psychology, sociology).

Honors: There are 13 honor societies on campus.

Admissions: About 88% of the applicants for the 1981–82 school year were accepted. Residents must be in the top 67% of their high school class and score at the 33rd percentile on the ACT, SAT, PSAT, or SCAT; nonresidents must rank in the top half of their class and score at the 40th percentile on those tests. Other factors considered in the admissions decision are recommendations, advanced placement or honors courses, and leadership record.

Procedure: The PSAT, SAT, or ACT is required. Missouri residents must take the SCAT. New students are admitted each semester; application deadlines are open. Notification is on a rolling basis. There is no application fee.

Special: AP and CLEP credit is available. There are early admissions, early decision, and deferred admissions plans.

Transfer: For fall 1981, 686 students applied, 565 were accepted, and 411 enrolled. A 2.0 GPA is required when transferring with 60 or more credits; D grades transfer. All students must complete, at the university, 30 of the 124 credits required for a bachelor's degree. Applications are due 2 weeks prior to each term.

Visiting: Campus tours with student guides can be arranged through the admissions office. Visitors may attend classes.

Financial Aid: About 81% of the students receive assistance. One-third work part-time on campus. The university offers various loans, grants, and employment opportunities (CWS is available in 62 departments). There are freshman scholarships from a $250,000 fund. The average aid package to a freshman is $1120. The FFS is required; deadlines for application are June 1 (fall), November 15 (spring), and April 15 (summer).

Foreign Students: Two percent of the full-time students come from foreign countries. An intensive English course, special counseling, and special organizations are available for these students.

Admissions: Foreign students must achieve a TOEFL score of at least 450. No college entrance exams are required.

Procedure: There are no application deadlines; foreign students are admitted in all terms. They must have a complete physical exam and must present proof of funds adequate to cover 4 years of study. Health insurance is required and is available through the university for a fee.

Admissions Contact: Regina Myers, Assistant Director of Admissions.

NORTHWEST MISSOURI STATE UNIVERSITY   A-1
Maryville, Missouri 64468   (816) 582-3011

F/T: 1950M, 2050W   Faculty: 225; IIA, av$
P/T: 200M, 100W   Ph.D.'s: 50%
Grad: 400M, 300W   S/F Ratio: 18 to 1
Year: sems, ss   Tuition: $550 ($930)
Appl: open   R and B: $1370
2300 applied   1944 accepted   1300 enrolled
ACT: 19   LESS COMPETITIVE

Northwest Missouri State University, established in 1905, offers undergraduate curricula in the arts and sciences, business, education, and health fields. Its library has 220,000 volumes and subscribes to 500 periodicals.

Environment: The small-town campus has 4 high-rise dormitories and 2 quads. There are also fraternity and sorority houses. The school is located in a rural area 90 miles from Kansas City.

Student Life: Most of the students come from Missouri and nearby states. About 90% are graduates of public schools. Forty-five percent of the students live on campus. About 75% are Protestant, 20% are Catholic, and 1% are Jewish. Five percent are minority-group members. Campus housing is both coed and single-sex; there are visiting privileges in the single-sex housing. Students may keep cars on campus.

Organizations: Ten percent of the students belong to one of 6 national fraternities and 5 national sororities. There is a full extracurricular program, including religious groups.

Sports: The university fields 8 intercollegiate teams for men and 7 for women. There are 9 intramural sports for men and 5 for women.

Handicapped: About 80% of the campus is accessible to handicapped students. Special facilities include wheelchair ramps, parking areas, elevators, lowered drinking fountains, and specially equipped rest rooms. Special class scheduling is also available.

Graduates: The freshman dropout rate is 40%; another 40% remain to graduate. About 10% of the graduates pursue further education; 25% enter careers in business and industry.

Services: Health care, psychological and career counseling, tutoring, and remedial instruction are available free of charge. Placement services are provided for a fee.

Programs of Study: The B.A., B.S., B.S.Ed., B.S.Med.Tech., B.S.N., and B.F.A. degrees are conferred. Master's degrees are also awarded. Bachelor's degrees are offered in the following subjects: BUSINESS (accounting, business administration, business education, computer science, finance, management, marketing), EDUCATION (early childhood, elementary, health/physical, industrial, secondary, special), ENGLISH (English, journalism, speech), FINE AND PERFORMING ARTS (art, art education, dance, music, music education, radio/TV, theater/dramatics), HEALTH SCIENCES (medical technology, nursing, speech therapy), LANGUAGES (French, German, Spanish), MATH AND SCIENCES (biology, botany, chemistry, earth science, ecology/environmental science, geology, mathematics, natural sciences, physical sciences, physics, statistics, zoology), PHILOSOPHY (humanities, philosophy), PREPROFESSIONAL (dentistry, engineering, forestry, home economics, law, medicine, pharmacy, veterinary), SOCIAL SCIENCES (economics, geography, government/political science, history, psychology, social sciences, sociology). About 45% of the degrees conferred are in education and 25% are in business.

Required: There is a general education requirement that varies with the degree program.

Special: There is a 2-2 engineering program with the University of Missouri. Study abroad is possible. There is an elementary school laboratory.

Honors: There are 5 honor societies on campus.

Admissions: About 85% of the applicants for the 1981–82 freshman class were accepted. The ACT scores of those who enrolled were as follows: 40% below 21, 30% between 21 and 23, 20% between 24 and 25, 8% between 26 and 28, and 2% above 28. Class rank should be in the top half. Recommendations and special talents are considered important.

Procedure: The ACT is required. Application deadlines are open. New students are admitted each semester. Notification is on a rolling basis. There is no application fee.

Special: CLEP credit is available.

Transfer: For fall 1981, 450 students applied, 450 were accepted, and 260 enrolled. A GPA of at least 2.0 is required. All grades transfer. Students must complete, at the university, 30 of the 120 credits required for a bachelor's degree. There are no application deadlines.

Visiting: Campus tours can be arranged through the admissions office. Visitors may attend classes and stay overnight at the university.

Financial Aid: About 65% of the students receive assistance. About 50% work part-time on campus. There are loans, grants, and employment opportunities. About 360 freshman scholarships are available, averaging $250. The average freshman aid package is $1000; the maximum, $2500. The FFS is due April 30 (fall), November 30 (winter), or May 1 (summer).

Foreign Students: Four percent of the students come from foreign countries. An intensive English course, special counseling, and special organizations are available for these students.

Admissions: Foreign students must achieve a TOEFL score of at least 500. No college entrance exams are required.

Procedure: Application deadlines are July 10 (fall), November 10 (spring), and April 7 (summer). Foreign students must have a physical exam and must present proof of funds adequate to cover 4 years of study. Health insurance is required and is available through the university for a fee.

Admissions Contact: James Goff, Director of Admissions.

PARK COLLEGE   A-2
Parkville, Missouri 64152   (816) 741-2000

F/T, P/T: Faculty: 50; n/av
500 M&W   Ph.D.'s: 60%
Grad: none   S/F Ratio: 14 to 1
Year: sems, ss   Tuition: $3290
Appl: open   R and B: $1700
380 applied   185 accepted   145 enrolled
SAT: 750 V&M   ACT: 16   LESS COMPETITIVE

Park College, founded in 1875, is affiliated with the Reorganized Church of Jesus Christ of the Latter-day Saints, and offers undergraduate programs in the arts and sciences, business, education, and nursing. Its library has 90,000 volumes and 800 microfilm items, and subscribes to 650 periodicals.

Environment: The 800-acre campus is located in a suburban area 10 miles from Kansas City. The 22 major buildings include dormitories that house about half the students.

Student Life: Most of the students come from Missouri and are members of the supporting church. Dormitories are single-sex. Unmarried students under 20 must live on campus unless living with parents.

Organizations: Extracurricular activities include clubs, service groups, student government, publications, and social and cultural events. There are no fraternities or sororities.

Sports: The college sponsors intercollegiate teams in 7 sports. Intramural competition is available for men and women in at least 8 sports.

Handicapped: About 10% of the campus is accessible to students with physical handicaps. Special facilities include wheelchair ramps, parking areas, and specially equipped rest rooms.

Graduates: About 25% of the graduates go on for further education, and about 15% enter careers in business or industry.

Services: Career counseling and placement services are offered free to students. Remedial instruction and personal counseling also are provided.

Programs of Study: The college confers the B.A. degree. Associate degrees also are awarded. Bachelor's degrees are offered in the following subjects: BUSINESS (accounting, business administration), EDUCATION (elementary/secondary), ENGLISH (communication arts, English, journalism), FINE AND PERFORMING ARTS (music, music education, radio/TV, theater/dramatics), HEALTH SCIENCES (prenursing), MATH AND SCIENCES (biology, chemistry, mathematics), SOCIAL SCIENCES (criminal justice administration, economics, government/political science, human services, psychology, social sciences, sociology).

Required: Students must complete 24 hours of general-education requirements, including courses in social sciences, natural sciences, and humanities.

Special: Students may design their own majors. A general studies degree is offered, as is an accelerated degree completion program for military personnel. Minors are offered in art, equine studies, history, philosophy, and religion.

Admissions: About 49% of the applicants for the 1981-82 freshman class were accepted. For an earlier class, the SAT scores were as follows: Verbal—5% between 500 and 599 and 1% above 600; Math—5% between 500 and 599 and 1% above 600. Of the 1981-82 freshmen who took the ACT, 65% scored below 21, 12% between 21 and 23, 10% between 24 and 25, 3% between 26 and 28, and 10% above 28. Applicants must rank in the top 60% of their high school class and have a GPA of 2.0 or better. Recommendations and special talents are also considered.

Procedure: The SAT or ACT is required. Application deadlines are open; new students are admitted each semester. Notification is made on a rolling basis. There is a $10 application fee.

Special: CLEP credit is accepted.

Transfer: Transfer applicants must be in good academic standing. D grades are not accepted. Students must complete at least 24 credits at the college of the 120 required for a bachelor's degree.

Visiting: Informal visits, including campus tours, may be arranged through the admissions office. Visitors may attend classes and stay overnight at the college.

Financial Aid: More than 80% of the students receive aid. The college offers scholarships, grants, loans, and campus jobs through federal programs such as BEOG, SEOG, NDSL, and CWS. Need and academic promise are the determining factors in awarding aid. The aid application should be submitted as soon as possible after January 1; priority consideration will be given to those submitted by April 30. The FAF is preferred, but the FFS also is accepted.

Foreign Students: Foreign students enrolled full-time at the college make up about 15% of the student body. The college offers these students an intensive English course, an intensive English program, special counseling, and special organizations.

Admissions: Foreign applicants must attain a score of 500 or better on the TOEFL. The University of Michigan Language Test can be taken instead. No academic exams are required.

Procedure: Application deadlines are open; new students are admitted to all terms. Students must submit a completed health form and show evidence of adequate funds for 1 year. Special fees are charged for counseling and additional services and for language instruction. Students are required to carry health insurance, which is available through the college.

Admissions Contact: Joseph V. Holst, Jr., Dean of Admissions.

ROCKHURST COLLEGE A-2
Kansas City, Missouri 64110 (816) 926-4100

F/T: 674M, 720W Faculty: 84; IIB, +$
P/T: 487M, 663W Ph.D.'s: 62%
Grad: 491M, 289W S/F Ratio: 16 to 1
Year: sems, ss Tuition: $3500
Appl: Aug. 1 R and B: $2100
1440 applied 1054 accepted 356 enrolled
ACT: 23 COMPETITIVE+

Rockhurst College, established in 1910, is affiliated with the Roman Catholic Church (Society of Jesus) and offers undergraduate programs in business, education, health fields, and arts and sciences. Its library has 108,000 volumes and 286 microtexts, and subscribes to 560 periodicals.

Environment: The 25-acre campus is located in a residential area of Kansas City. Buildings include 4 dormitories, 2 for men and 2 for women.

Student Life: Sixty-four percent of the students come from private schools. Half live on campus. About 72% are Catholic and 20% are Protestant. About 12% are members of minority groups. Campus housing is single-sex, with visiting privileges. Students may keep cars on campus.

Organizations: Four national fraternities attract 25% of the men; there are no sororities. Traditional extracurricular activities and groups are available.

Sports: The college fields 5 intercollegiate teams for men and 4 for women. There are 12 intramural sports for men and 10 for women.

Handicapped: About 75% of the campus is accessible to handicapped students. Special facilities include wheelchair ramps, parking areas, and elevators. Special class scheduling also is available.

Graduates: The freshman dropout rate is 24%, and 49% remain to graduate. Thirty-seven percent of the graduates go on for further study. About 3% enter medical school and 3% enter law school. About 59% pursue careers in business or industry.

Services: Offered without charge are health care, psychological and spiritual counseling, tutoring, remedial instruction, placement aid, and career counseling.

Programs of Study: The A.B., B.S., and B.S.B.A. degrees are conferred. Master's degrees are also awarded. Bachelor's degrees are offered in the following subjects: BUSINESS (accounting, business administration, business communications, finance—systems management, management, marketing, real estate/insurance), EDUCATION (elementary, secondary), ENGLISH (English, speech), HEALTH SCIENCES (medical technology, nursing, physical therapy, respiratory therapy), LANGUAGES (French, Spanish), MATH AND SCIENCES (biochemistry, biology, chemistry, computer science, mathematics, natural sciences, physics), PHILOSOPHY (humanities, philosophy, religion), PREPROFESSIONAL (dentistry, engineering, medicine, ministry, pharmacy, veterinary), SOCIAL SCIENCES (economics, government/political science, history, psychology, social sciences, sociology).

Required: Course work in theology and philosophy is required.

Special: Cooperative programs and study abroad are available. A combined B.A.-B.S. degree can be earned.

Honors: An honors program is offered. Honors courses are available in all major departments. Three honor societies have chapters on campus.

Admissions: About 73% of the applicants for the 1981-82 freshman class were accepted. The ACT scores of those who enrolled were as follows: 39% scored below 21, 24% between 21 and 23, 14% between 24 and 25, 14% between 26 and 28, and 6% above 28. Applicants should rank in the top 50% of their high school class and should have a high school average of at least 80%. Recommendations and advanced placement or honors courses also are considered.

Procedure: The ACT is required. Application deadlines are August 1 for fall, January 1 for spring, and June 1 for summer. Notification is made on a rolling basis. There is a $10 application fee.

Special: AP and CLEP credit is offered.

Transfer: For fall 1981, 444 transfer students applied, 255 were accepted, and 152 enrolled. A GPA of 2.0 is required; a 2.5 is recommended. An interview is also recommended. Grades of C or better transfer. Students must complete at least 30 credits in residence of the 128 required for a bachelor's degree. Application deadlines are the same as those for freshmen.

460 MISSOURI

Visiting: An orientation program is offered for prospective students. Informal campus tours can be scheduled for Monday, Wednesday, and Friday mornings, and for any weekday evening. Students may sit in on classes and stay in the dormitories. Arrangements should be made through the admissions office.

Financial Aid: About 70% of the students receive aid. Tuition may be paid in installments. Scholarships, grants, and part-time campus jobs (including CWS) are offered. Thirty percent of the students work part-time on campus. The average award to freshmen in 1981–82 was $3300. The FAF, FFS, or SFS is required; application deadlines are April 1 for fall and December 1 for winter.

Foreign Students: Fewer than 1% of the full-time students are from foreign countries.

Admissions: A TOEFL score of at least 550 is required. Applicants also must score at least 18 on the ACT or 800 on the SAT.

Procedure: Application deadlines are August 1 (fall), January 1 (spring), and June 1 (summer). Proof of adequate funds ($3000 before enrollment) is required. There is a special $10 application fee for foreign students. Health insurance, though not required, is available through the college for a fee.

Admissions Contact: Thomas J. Audley, Director of Admissions.

ST. LOUIS COLLEGE OF PHARMACY   D–2
St. Louis, Missouri 63110   (314) 367-8700

F/T: 331M, 316W	Faculty:	32; n/av
P/T: 10M, 7W	Ph.D.'s:	50%
Grad: none	S/F Ratio:	18 to 1
Year: sems, ss	Tuition:	$2358–3358
Appl: Aug. 1	R and B:	$1900
171 applied	137 accepted	98 enrolled
ACT: 23		VERY COMPETITIVE

St. Louis College of Pharmacy, founded in 1864, is an independent institution. Its library contains over 32,000 volumes and 5150 microfilm items, and subscribes to 400 periodicals.

Environment: The urban campus has 4 buildings, including a residence hall for first- and second-year students, and an apartment complex for married students and upperclassmen. The college also sponsors fraternity and sorority houses.

Student Life: About 48% of the students come from Missouri, and 90% come from public schools. Sixty percent live on campus. Seven percent of the students are minority-group members. Campus housing is coed. Students may keep cars on campus.

Organizations: About 35% of the men belong to one of the 4 fraternities on campus, and 40% of the women belong to one of the 2 sororities. Extracurricular activities include student government, publications, and performing groups.

Sports: The college sponsors intercollegiate teams in 3 sports for men. There are 3 intramural sports for men and 1 for women.

Handicapped: About 50% of the campus is accessible to physically handicapped students. Special facilities include wheelchair ramps, special parking areas, elevators, lowered drinking fountains, and specially equipped rest rooms.

Graduates: Fifteen percent of the freshmen drop out after the first year, and 58% remain to graduate. Ten percent of the graduates pursue advanced degrees, and 10% begin careers in business or industry.

Services: Career counseling, placement aid, remedial instruction, and psychological counseling are offered without charge. Fees are charged for health care and tutoring.

Programs of Study: The B.S. in Pharmacy is offered in a five-year program in pharmacy.

Special: Tuition is $2358 the first year, and $3358 for each of the next 4 years. The program may be completed in 4 years at an accelerated pace.

Honors: One honor society has a chapter on campus.

Admissions: About 80% of the 1981–82 applicants were accepted. The ACT scores of those who enrolled were as follows: 27% below 21, 32% between 21 and 23, 14% between 24 and 25, 18% between 26 and 28, and 9% above 28. Applicants should rank in the upper half of their high school class. Advanced placement or honors courses and extracurricular activities are also considered.

Procedure: The ACT is required. August 1 is the fall application deadline; December 1, the spring deadline; May 15, the summer deadline. Notification is made on a rolling basis. There is a $15 application fee.

Special: CLEP is used. Deferred admissions and early admissions plans are available.

Transfer: For fall 1981, 195 transfer students applied and 137 were accepted. A 2.0 GPA and an ACT score of 18 are required. (A GPA of 2.5 and an ACT of 23 are recommended.) Grades of C or better transfer. Students must spend at least 1 year in residence, earning at least 30 of the 158 credits required for a bachelor's degree. Application deadlines are the same as those for freshmen.

Visiting: An orientation program is held for new students. Informal campus tours may be arranged; visitors may sit in on classes.

Financial Aid: About 76% of the students receive aid. The college offers federal and state grants, various loans, CWS, and professional scholarships. Twenty-eight percent of students work part-time on campus. The average award to freshmen was $2200 in 1981–82. The FAF is required. Deadlines are May 1 for fall and May 31 for spring.

Foreign Students: One percent of the full-time students are from foreign countries. Special counseling and special organizations are available for these students.

Admissions: A score of 500 or better on the TOEFL is required. No college entrance exams are required.

Procedure: The application deadline is April 30 for the fall semester, the only one to which foreign students are admitted. Students must submit a documented health form and present proof of adequate funds for their entire period of study. Health insurance, though not required, is available through the college for a fee.

Admissions Contact: Taylor E. Lindhorst, Director of Admissions.

ST. LOUIS CONSERVATORY OF MUSIC   D–2
St. Louis, Missouri 63130   (314) 863-3033

F/T: 24M, 27W	Faculty:	n/av
P/T: 5M, 7W	Ph.D.'s:	n/av
Grad: 11M, 35W	S/F Ratio:	11 to 1
Year: sems	Tuition:	$4010
Appl: open	R and B:	n/app
SAT or ACT: required		SPECIAL

St. Louis Conservatory of Music, established in 1923, is a professional school of music under independent auspices. The conservatory's library holds 3500 volumes and more than 3000 music scores.

Environment: The 1-building campus is located in a suburban area minutes from downtown St. Louis. Facilities include 3 performance halls. There are no residence halls at the conservatory, but students may find dormitory accommodations at Fontbonne College, about a mile from the school.

Student Life: Over 50% of the students come from Missouri, and most are public school graduates.

Organizations: Campus activities are limited, but include music groups and student government.

Sports: The conservatory does not sponsor an athletic program.

Handicapped: The building is accessible to handicapped students.

Services: Health care, tutoring, and remedial instruction are offered.

Programs of Study: The conservatory awards the B.M. degree. Master's degrees in music also are offered. The bachelor's degree is awarded with majors in classical guitar, composition, all orchestral instruments, organ, piano, and voice.

Required: Core requirements include specific courses in performance, theory, music history, English, and humanities.

Special: There is a cooperative work-study program.

Admissions: About 50% of the applicants for the 1980–81 freshman class were accepted. A high school diploma and a satisfactory academic background are necessary. An audition is the primary criterion for admission.

Procedure: Either the SAT or ACT is required. New students are admitted each semester. Application deadlines are open. Notification is made on a rolling basis. There is a $25 application fee.

Special: AP and CLEP credit is available.

Transfer: Applicants must have at least a 2.0 GPA. D grades generally do not transfer. An audition is necessary. Students must complete the last 2 years in residence.

Visiting: Campus tours may be arranged.

Financial Aid: About 35% of the students receive financial aid. The conservatory participates in federal programs such as NDSL and

SAINT LOUIS UNIVERSITY D-2
St. Louis, Missouri 63103 (314) 658-2500

F/T: 2749M, 2079W	Faculty:	816; I, – – $
P/T: 714M, 1248W	Ph.D.'s:	75%
Grad: 2051M, 1555W	S/F Ratio:	12 to 1
Year: sems, ss	Tuition:	$4220
Appl: Aug. 1	R and B:	$2250
2732 applied	2377 accepted	1107 enrolled
SAT: 470V 512M	ACT: 23	COMPETITIVE+

St. Louis University, founded in 1818, is affiliated with the Jesuit Order of the Roman Catholic Church, and offers a wide variety of undergraduate- and graduate-degree programs. Its library has 1.2 million volumes and subscribes to 7270 periodicals; there is an extensive collection on microfilm of manuscripts in the Vatican Library.

Environment: The urban university has 3 campuses. The main campus contains most of the undergraduate facilities. The university sponsors on-campus apartments and married student housing, and there are 5 dormitories on campus. A new intramural and recreation complex opened in 1981.

Student Life: Sixty percent of the students come from parochial schools; 25% from public schools. Thirty-five percent live on campus. Fifty-five percent of the students are Catholic, 19% Protestant, and 5% Jewish. About 15% are minority-group members. University-sponsored housing is both single-sex and coed. There are visiting privileges in single-sex housing. Students may keep cars on campus.

Organizations: There is a full and traditional range of extracurricular activities. Religious groups are sponsored, and there are regularly scheduled on-campus social and cultural events. About 10% of the students belong to one of 7 national fraternities or 3 national sororities.

Sports: In addition to 6 intercollegiate sports for men and 6 for women, there are 15 intramural sports for men and 13 for women.

Handicapped: About 50% of the campus is accessible to physically handicapped students. Special facilities include parking areas, elevators, lowered drinking fountains and telephones, and specially equipped rest rooms. Special class scheduling is also available.

Graduates: Eighteen percent of freshmen drop out by the end of their first year. About 65% of those who enter remain to graduate. Fifty-five percent go on for further education.

Services: Career counseling, placement service, tutoring, remedial instruction, and psychological counseling are offered free of charge. Health care is available on a fee basis.

Programs of Study: The A.B., B.S., B.S.B.A., B.S. in C.D., B.S.Ch., B.S. in M.R.A., B.S.N., B.S. in M.T., B.S. in P.T., and B.S.S.W. degrees are granted. Associate, master's, and doctoral degrees are also conferred. Bachelor's degrees are offered in the following subjects: AREA STUDIES (American, Latin American, urban), BUSINESS (accounting, business administration, computer science, finance, management, marketing), EDUCATION (elementary), ENGLISH (English, speech), FINE AND PERFORMING ARTS (art, art history, music, music education, studio art, theater/dramatics), HEALTH SCIENCES (environmental health, medical technology, nursing, physical therapy, speech therapy), LANGUAGES (French, German, Greek/Latin, Russian, Spanish), MATH AND SCIENCES (biology, chemistry, earth science, geology, geophysics, mathematics, meteorology, physics, statistics), PHILOSOPHY (classics, humanities, philosophy, religion), PRE-PROFESSIONAL (dentistry, law, medicine, ministry, pharmacy, social work), SOCIAL SCIENCES (economics, government/political science, history, psychology, sociology, urban affairs). About 25% of the degrees are conferred in health sciences, and 22% in business.

Special: A student may design his or her own major. Combined B.A.-B.S. degrees can be earned in many areas.

Honors: Phi Beta Kappa and 14 other honor societies have chapters on campus. There is an honors program in the College of Arts and Sciences.

Admissions: About 87% of the applicants for the 1981–82 freshman class were accepted. SAT scores of those who enrolled were: Verbal—60% below 500, 29% between 500 and 599, 11% between 600 and 700, and fewer than 1% above 700; Math—45% below 500, 34% between 500 and 599, 18% between 600 and 700, and 3% above 700. On the ACT, 32% scored below 21, 24% between 21 and 23, 16% between 24 and 25, 22% between 26 and 28, and 6% above 28.

A GPA of 2.0 is needed. Honors work and advanced placement courses are also considered important factors.

Procedure: The SAT or ACT is required. Application deadlines are August 1 (fall), December 1 (spring), June 1 (summer). Freshmen are also admitted at midyear and in the summer. Notification is on a rolling basis. There is a $20 application fee.

Special: There is a deferred admissions plan. AP and CLEP credit is offered.

Transfer: For fall 1981, 1563 students applied, 1376 were accepted, and 890 enrolled. A GPA of 2.0 is necessary; D grades do not transfer. Thirty credits, of the 120 needed for a bachelor's degree, and 50% of the major requirements, must be completed in residence. Application deadlines are August 1 (fall), December 1 (spring), and June 1 (summer).

Visiting: Informal campus tours with student guides can be arranged through the admissions office. Visitors may attend classes and stay at the university.

Financial Aid: Seventy-five percent of the students receive assistance. Forty-five percent work part-time on campus. Average aid to freshmen from all sources is $4600. The university offers scholarships from a fund of $750,000. Additional aid is available in the form of loans and grants. The university is a member of CSS. The FAF is preferred; the FFS or SFS are accepted. Application deadlines are May 1 (fall), November 1 (spring), and April 1 (summer).

Foreign Students: About 6% of the full-time students come from foreign countries. The university offers these students an intensive English program, special counseling, and special organizations.

Admissions: Foreign students must achieve a passing score on the university's own language examination. They must also take the SAT or the ACT.

Procedure: Application deadlines are August 1 (fall), December 1 (spring), and June 1 (summer). Foreign students must present proof of funds adequate to cover 1 year of study.

Admissions Contact: Louis A. Menard, Dean of Admissions.

THE SCHOOL OF THE OZARKS B-4
Point Lookout, Missouri 65726 (417) 334-6411

F/T: 575M, 601W	Faculty:	78; IIB, av$
P/T: 68M, 99W	Ph.D.'s:	50%
Grad: none	S/F Ratio:	14 to 1
Year: tri, ss	Tuition:	see profile
Appl: Feb. 1	R and B:	see profile
800 applied	339 accepted	329 enrolled
ACT: 22		COMPETITIVE+

The School of the Ozarks, founded in 1906 as a high school and chartered in 1964 as a 4-year college, offers a liberal arts or business education. It is an independent institution. The library contains 82,500 volumes and 2500 microfilm items, and subscribes to over 500 periodicals. Instead of paying tuition, room, and board, students work a total of 960 hours a year in campus jobs.

Environment: The 1280-acre campus is located in a rural area 32 miles from Springfield. About 480 acres are rangeland devoted to cattle raising. Six dormitories accommodate 420 men and 465 women.

Student Life: About 75% of the students come from Missouri. Ninety-seven percent are graduates of public schools. About 80% live on campus. Eighty-five percent of the students are Protestant and 15% are Catholic. About 2% are minority-group members. Campus housing is single-sex; there are no visiting privileges. Students may keep cars on campus. Day-care services are available for a fee. All students are required to attend chapel services, and there is a midnight curfew from Monday through Friday.

Organizations: The school sponsors student government, publications, performing groups, clubs, religious and service organizations, and a radio station. Regularly scheduled cultural events take place. There are no sororities or fraternities.

Sports: Intercollegiate teams are fielded in 3 sports for men and 4 for women. There is intramural competition in 5 sports for men and 4 for women.

Handicapped: About 70% of the campus is accessible to handicapped students. Special facilities include wheelchair ramps, parking areas, elevators, and specially equipped rest rooms.

Graduates: Twenty percent of the freshmen drop out; 50% remain to graduate. Twenty percent of the graduates go on for further study (1% to medical school, 1% to law school). About 60% enter careers in business and industry.

462 MISSOURI

Services: Career counseling, placement service, health care, and psychological counseling are offered free to students.

Programs of Study: The B.A. and B.S. degrees are conferred. Bachelor's degrees are offered in the following subjects: BUSINESS (accounting, business administration, business education), EDUCATION (elementary, health/physical, industrial, secondary), ENGLISH (English, speech), FINE AND PERFORMING ARTS (art, art education, music, music education, theater/dramatics), LANGUAGES (French, German), MATH AND SCIENCES (biochemistry, biology, chemistry, mathematics), PHILOSOPHY (philosophy, religion), PREPROFESSIONAL (agriculture, home economics, law, medicine, veterinary), SOCIAL SCIENCES (government/political science, history, psychology, sociology).

Required: There is a 50-hour general education requirement.

Special: Resident students work 20 hours per week at a variety of campus jobs to pay costs. One 40-hour week per semester also is required. Independent study and cooperative programs in engineering (with the University of Missouri/Rolla) and medical technology (with Cox Medical Center) are offered.

Admissions: About 42% of the applicants for the 1981–82 school year were accepted. ACT scores of those who enrolled were as follows: 26% below 21, 50% between 21 and 23, 20% between 24 and 25, 3% between 26 and 28, and 1% above 28. Applicants should rank in the top 50% of their high school class and have a GPA of 2.0 or better. Financial need, recommendations, and extracurricular and leadership records are also considered.

Procedure: The ACT is required. There are rolling deadlines for all semesters; February 1 is the suggested application date for fall. Notification is made on a rolling basis. There is no application fee.

Special: Some CLEP credit is offered.

Transfer: For fall 1981, 50 transfer students applied, 43 were accepted, and 40 enrolled. A GPA of 2.0 is required. Students with fewer than 30 transfer hours should have an ACT score of at least 15. Grades of C or better transfer. Students must complete in residence at least 30 of the 124 credits necessary for a bachelor's degree.

Visiting: An orientation for prospective applicants is held each October. Informal campus tours can be arranged through Donald P. McMahon. Visitors may stay at the school and sit in on classes.

Financial Aid: The scholarship-work program eliminates tuition and room/board costs for all students in exchange for employment in one of 88 campus industries. The BEOG-SER application must be filed by June 1 for fall, November 1 for spring, or January 1 for summer.

Foreign Students: Three percent of the students are from foreign countries. Special counseling and special organizations are available.

Admissions: A minimum score of 550 on the TOEFL is required. No college entrance exam is needed.

Procedure: February 1 is the suggested application deadline for fall, spring, and summer terms. Students must submit a record of a physical and immunizations. Proof of adequate funds for 4 years is also required.

Admissions Contact: Donald P. McMahon, Director of Admissions and Career Development.

SOUTHEAST MISSOURI STATE UNIVERSITY
E-3

Cape Girardeau, Missouri 63701   (314) 651-2255

F/T: 3464M, 3992W   Faculty: 385; IIA, –$
P/T: 368M, 583W   Ph.D.'s: 50%
Grad: 268M, 452W   S/F Ratio: 25 to 1
Year: sems, ss   Tuition: $475 ($975)
Appl: Aug. 1   R and B: $1350
2975 applied   2676 accepted   2057 enrolled
ACT: 18   **LESS COMPETITIVE**

Southeast Missouri State University, established in 1873, offers undergraduate training in the arts and sciences, business, education, and health fields. Its library has 290,000 volumes and 200,000 microfilm items, and subscribes to 2200 periodicals.

Environment: The 200-acre campus is located in a rural community of 35,000 inhabitants about 120 miles from St. Louis. Residence halls accommodate 1600 women and 1400 men. The university also sponsors fraternity and sorority sections of dormitories.

Student Life: About 95% of the students come from Missouri. Eighty-six percent are graduates of public schools. About 35% live on campus. Fifty percent of the students are Protestant and 30% are Catholic. Five percent are minority-group members. Campus housing is single-sex, with visiting privileges. Students may keep cars on campus.

Organizations: There are 8 national fraternities, of which 10% of the men are members, and 5 national sororities, which attract 15% of the women. Traditional extracurricular and social activities are available.

Sports: There are 7 intercollegiate sports for men and 7 for women; 10 intramural programs are offered for men and 9 for women.

Handicapped: The campus is not readily accessible to physically handicapped students.

Graduates: Thirty-three percent of the freshmen drop out, and 45% remain to graduate. Eight percent go on for further education; 45% enter careers in business and industry.

Services: Career counseling, placement, psychological counseling, and tutoring are offered without charge. Fees are charged for remedial instruction and health care.

Programs of Study: The university confers the B.A., B.S., B.S.N., B.S.B.A., B.S.Ed., B.G.S., B.Mus., B.S. in Voc.HomeEcon., and B.S. in Interdisciplinary Studies degrees. Master's programs are also available. Bachelor's degrees are offered in the following subjects: AREA STUDIES (American, Latin American), BUSINESS (accounting, business education, computer science, finance, management, marketing), EDUCATION (early childhood, elementary, health/physical, secondary, special), ENGLISH (communications, English, speech), FINE AND PERFORMING ARTS (art, art education, mass communications, music, music education, theater/dramatics), HEALTH SCIENCES (medical technology, nursing, speech therapy), LANGUAGES (French, German, Spanish), MATH AND SCIENCES (biology, botany, chemistry, earth science, geology, mathematics, physics, zoology), PHILOSOPHY (classics, philosophy), PREPROFESSIONAL (agriculture, home economics, social work), SOCIAL SCIENCES (anthropology, economics, geography, government/political science, historic preservation, history, psychology, social sciences, sociology).

Special: A general-studies degree is offered. Students may design their own majors.

Honors: Eleven honor societies have chapters on campus.

Admissions: About 90% of the applicants for 1981–82 were accepted. The ACT scores of those who enrolled were as follows: 37% below 17, 42% between 17 and 22, 16% between 23 and 26, and 5% above 27. Applicants should rank in the top two-thirds of their high school class and have at least a C average.

Procedure: The ACT is required. Application deadlines are August 1 for fall, January 1 for spring, and June 1 for summer. Notification is made on a rolling basis. There is a $10 application fee.

Special: Early decision and early admissions plans are available. AP and CLEP credit is offered.

Transfer: For fall 1981, 917 transfer students applied, 789 were accepted, and 611 enrolled. A GPA of 2.0 is required. D grades transfer. At least 30 credits of the 124 required for a bachelor's degree must be completed at the university. There is a 1-year residency requirement. Application deadlines are the same as those for freshmen.

Visiting: Campus tours with student guides can be arranged. Visitors may attend classes and stay in the residence halls. Arrangements for visits can be made through the admissions office.

Financial Aid: About 50% of the students receive aid. The university offers government and commercial loans (including NDSL) and part-time campus work opportunities (including CWS). Twenty-two percent of students work part-time on campus. There are about 425 freshman scholarships, averaging $440. The maximum aid package for a freshman in 1981–82 was $3000; the average award was $2000. The FFS is required. For priority consideration, applications should be filed by June 1 for fall, November 1 for winter, or April 1 for summer.

Foreign Students: About 1% of the full-time students are from foreign countries. An intensive English course, special counseling, and special organizations are available for these students.

Admissions: A minimum score of 500 on the TOEFL is necessary. No college entrance exams are required.

Procedure: Application deadlines for foreign students are June 1 for fall, October 1 for spring, and March 1 for summer. Students must submit a completed health form and proof of adequate funds for 1 year. Health insurance is required, and is available through the university for a fee.

Admissions Contact: John A. Behrens, Director of Admissions.

SOUTHWEST BAPTIST UNIVERSITY B-3
(Formerly Southwest Baptist College)
Bolivar, Missouri 65613 (417) 326-5281

F/T: 626M, 761W		Faculty:	80; IIB, −$
P/T: 72M, 177W		Ph.D.'s:	38%
Grad: none		S/F Ratio:	17 to 1
Year: 4-1-4, ss		Tuition:	$2680
Appl: Sept. 10		R and B:	$1260
874 applied	683 accepted		601 enrolled
ACT: 18			COMPETITIVE

Southwest Baptist University, founded in 1878 and affiliated with the Baptist Church, offers undergraduate programs in the liberal arts and sciences, business, and education. Its library contains 80,000 books and subscribes to 130 periodicals.

Environment: The 123-acre campus is located in a rural area 28 miles from Springfield. The 39 buildings include 8 single-sex dormitories housing 1200 students.

Student Life: About 84% of the students come from Missouri. Ninety-eight percent come from public schools. Sixty-five percent live on campus. Most students are Baptists; attendance at chapel services is required. Campus housing is single-sex; there are no visiting privileges. Students may keep cars on campus.

Organizations: Campus activities include religious groups, clubs, social and cultural events, and student government. There are no fraternities or sororities.

Sports: The university fields 4 intercollegiate teams for men and 5 for women. There are 6 intramural sports for men and 5 for women.

Graduates: The freshman dropout rate is 40%, and about 40% remain to graduate. About 20% of the graduates pursue graduate study.

Services: Offered free are psychological counseling, placement aid, and career counseling. Health care and tutoring are available for a fee.

Programs of Study: The B.A., B.S., and B.Mus. degrees are conferred. Associate degrees are also awarded. Bachelor's degrees are offered in the following subjects: BUSINESS (accounting, business administration, business education), EDUCATION (elementary, health/physical, secondary, special), ENGLISH (English, speech), FINE AND PERFORMING ARTS (art, music, music education), MATH AND SCIENCES (biology, chemistry, mathematics), PHILOSOPHY (philosophy, religion), PREPROFESSIONAL (home economics), SOCIAL SCIENCES (government/political science, history, psychology, sociology).

Required: General-education requirements include courses in religion and physical education.

Special: The university offers a general-studies degree. Students may design their own majors. A 3-year bachelor's degree and study abroad are offered.

Admissions: About 78% of the 1980–81 applicants were accepted. Applicants must have a 2.0 high school GPA and rank in the top half of their class.

Procedure: The ACT or SAT is required. Application deadlines are September 10 (fall), January 6 (winter), February 10 (spring), and June 9 (summer). Notification is on a rolling basis. There is a $10 application fee.

Special: There are early decision and early admissions plans, as well as a deferred admissions plan. AP and CLEP credit is given.

Transfer: For fall 1981, 138 transfer students applied, 133 were accepted, and 124 enrolled. A GPA of 2.0 is required. Up to 6 hours of D grades are accepted. Thirty of the 124 credits required for the bachelor's degree must be earned in residence. Deadlines for applications are the same as those for freshmen.

Visiting: An orientation program is offered. Informal campus tours may be arranged. Visitors may attend classes and stay at the school.

Financial Aid: About 80% of the students receive aid; 40% work part-time on campus. The university administers funds for various loans, federal and state grants, and campus jobs. It participates in NDSL, BEOG, SEOG, and CWS. The average total award to freshmen from all sources covered 75% of costs in 1981–82. Missionaries and children of ministers receive a tuition reduction. The FAF or FFS and the aid application is due April 30.

Foreign Students: Special counseling is offered to foreign students.

Admissions: The TOEFL is required, as well as the SAT or ACT.

Procedure: Application deadlines are September 10 (fall), January 6 (winter), February 10 (spring), and June 9 (summer). Foreign students must present a record of a physical exam and show proof of adequate funds for 1 year. They must carry health insurance, which is available through the university for a fee.

Admissions Contact: Michael G. Thomas, Director of Admissions.

SOUTHWEST MISSOURI STATE UNIVERSITY B-3
Springfield, Missouri 65802 (417) 836-5517

F/T: 4992M, 5295W		Faculty:	511; IIA, av$
P/T: 1629M, 2275W		Ph.D.'s:	57%
Grad: 467M, 703W		S/F Ratio:	21 to 1
Year: sems, ss		Tuition:	$540 ($1080)
Appl: Aug. 1		R and B:	$1290
3799 applied	3456 accepted		2709 enrolled
ACT: 19			LESS COMPETITIVE

Southwest Missouri State University, founded in 1906, offers undergraduate preparation in the arts and sciences, business, health fields, and education. Its library contains 370,000 volumes and 364,000 microtexts, and subscribes to 4600 periodicals.

Environment: The 120-acre suburban campus is located in the Ozarks 180 miles from Kansas City and 220 miles from St. Louis. Campus housing is provided in residence halls and in fraternity and sorority houses. The university also sponsors off-campus apartments.

Student Life: About 95% of the students come from Missouri. Approximately 90% are graduates of public schools. About 20% live on campus. Two percent are minority-group members. Campus housing is single-sex; there are visiting privileges. Cars are permitted on campus.

Organizations: Eight percent of the students belong to the 12 national fraternities and 5 national sororities. The extracurricular and social programs are varied; cultural events are scheduled regularly.

Sports: There are 10 intercollegiate sports for men and 8 for women. Fifteen intramural sports are available for men and 15 for women.

Handicapped: About 95% of the campus is accessible to handicapped students. Special facilities include wheelchair ramps, parking areas, elevators, lowered drinking fountains, and specially equipped rest rooms. Special class scheduling is also available. Readers and interpreters are provided for visually impaired and hearing-impaired students.

Graduates: About 30% of the freshmen drop out by the end of the first year, and 30% remain to graduate. Ten percent of the graduates go on for further study, while 65% enter careers in business and industry.

Services: Career counseling, placement services, remedial instruction, and psychological counseling are offered free. Health care is available for a fee.

Programs of Study: The university confers the B.A., B.S., B.S.Ed., B.M., B.F.A., and B.S.N. degrees. Associate and master's degree programs are also available. Bachelor's degrees are offered in the following subjects: AREA STUDIES (Latin American, urban), BUSINESS (accounting, business education, computer science, finance, management, marketing), EDUCATION (early childhood, elementary, health/physical, industrial, secondary, special), ENGLISH (English, speech, writing), FINE AND PERFORMING ARTS (art, art education, art history, dance, film/photography, music, music education, radio/TV, studio art, theater/dramatics), HEALTH SCIENCES (medical technology, nursing, radiologic technology, respiratory therapy, speech therapy), LANGUAGES (French, German, Greek/Latin, Spanish), MATH AND SCIENCES (atmospheric science, biology, chemistry, earth science, environmental chemical technology, geology, mathematics, physics, technical physics), PHILOSOPHY (philosophy), PREPROFESSIONAL (agriculture, dentistry, engineering, home economics, law, medicine, pharmacy), SOCIAL SCIENCES (economics, geography, government/political science, history, psychology, social sciences, social work, sociology). About 25% of the students major in business, 20% in education, and 20% in math and sciences.

Required: There is a general-education requirement.

Special: A degree in general studies is offered. Students may design their own majors.

Honors: Twenty-six honor societies are represented on campus.

Admissions: About 91% of the 1981–82 applicants were accepted. The ACT scores of those who enrolled were as follows: 52% below 21, 15% between 21 and 23, 5% between 24 and 25, 6% between 26 and 28, and 2% above 28. Applicants should rank in the upper two-thirds of their high school class.

464 MISSOURI

Procedure: The ACT is required. Application deadlines are August 1 (fall), January 1 (spring), and May 25 (summer). Notification is made on a rolling basis. There is a $20 application fee.

Transfer: For fall 1981, 1143 transfer students applied, 916 were accepted, and 773 enrolled. A GPA of 2.0 is needed; D grades are accepted. The ACT is required if fewer than 20 credit hours have been earned. Thirty credits of the 124 required for a bachelor's degree must be completed in residence. Application deadlines are the same as those for freshmen.

Visiting: Campus tours with student guides may be arranged. Although visitors generally may not attend classes, they may stay in the dormitories when there is room. Arrangements for visits on Monday through Friday between 8 A.M. and 3 P.M. can be made through the admissions office.

Financial Aid: About 33% of the students receive assistance. A few scholarships are available, as are federal loans. Work-study programs are offered in all departments; 10% of the students work part-time on campus. The average award to freshmen from all sources totaled $1500 in 1981–82. The FAF or FFS is required (the FFS is preferred). Applications should be filed by March 31.

Foreign Students: Fewer than 1% of the full-time students are from foreign countries. Special counseling and special organizations are available for these students.

Admissions: A score of 500 or better on the TOEFL is necessary. No college entrance exams are required.

Procedure: The application deadline for foreign students is April 1. A complete physical-examination report is required before a student can enroll. Students also must present proof of adequate funds for their entire period of study. Health insurance is required, and is available through the university for a fee.

Admissions Contact: Edward F. Pierce, Director of Admissions and Records.

STEPHENS COLLEGE   C–2
Columbia, Missouri 65215   (314) 442-2211

F/T: 21M, 1241W   Faculty: 99; IV, –$
P/T: 72W   Ph.D.'s: 60%
Grad: none   S/F Ratio: 12 to 1
Year: modular, ss   Tuition: $4675
Appl: Aug. 15   R and B: $2100
868 applied   745 accepted   400 enrolled
SAT: 411V 419M   **LESS COMPETITIVE**

Stephens College, founded in 1833 is an independent college for women, offering undergraduate programs in the arts and sciences, business, education, and preprofessional fields. In addition to its traditional academic programs, Stephens has two innovative divisions: the Center for Conceptual Studies, an interdisciplinary program emphasizing holistic learning; and the Stephens House Plan, an experimental program in which freshmen live and study together. The college library has 125,000 volumes and over 200 microfilm items, and subscribes to 515 periodicals.

Environment: The 300-acre campus is located in a suburban area midway between St. Louis and Kansas City. There are 56 buildings, including 10 residence halls, each of which accommodates from 50 to 250 students.

Student Life: Most of the students are from out of state. Eighty percent are from public schools. Ninety-four percent live on campus. About 8% of the students are minority-group members. College housing is single-sex, with visiting privileges. Students may keep cars on campus.

Organizations: There are 4 local sororities, to which 15% of the women belong. There are also religious and service groups. The extracurricular program includes traditional activities and on-campus social and cultural events.

Sports: The college fields 6 intercollegiate teams for women. There are 2 intramural sports.

Handicapped: Special facilities for handicapped students include wheelchair ramps, parking areas, elevators, lowered drinking fountains, and specially equipped rest rooms. Special class scheduling is also available.

Graduates: The freshman dropout rate is 30%, and 47% of the freshmen remain to graduate. Twenty-five percent of the graduates seek advanced degrees; 1% enter medical school and 3% enter law school. Another 50% pursue careers in business and industry.

Services: Health care, psychological counseling, placement services, and career counseling are offered free to students. Some tutoring and all remedial instruction requires a fee.

Programs of Study: The college confers the B.A., B.F.A., and B.S. degrees. Associate degrees are also awarded. Bachelor's degrees are offered in the following subjects: BUSINESS (business administration, fashion merchandising), EDUCATION (child study, early childhood, elementary, human development), ENGLISH (creative writing, English, journalism, literature), FINE AND PERFORMING ARTS (art, dance, fashion design, film/photography, music, musical theater, radio/TV, studio art, theater/dramatics), LANGUAGES (foreign languages and business, French, Spanish), MATH AND SCIENCES (animal science, biology, chemistry, computer science, geology, mathematics), PHILOSOPHY (humanities, philosophy, religion), PREPROFESSIONAL (dentistry, engineering, law, medicine, ministry, veterinary), SOCIAL SCIENCES (government/political science, history, psychology, social sciences). A major in equestrian science also is available. About 28% of the degrees conferred are in the arts, and 25% in business.

Required: Freshman English, physical-education courses, and math competency are required. Liberal arts candidates, lower division, must also take 6 courses in 5 of 7 liberal arts areas. B.A. candidates, upper division, must take 1 course each in Intercultural Studies, Interdisciplinary Studies, and Senior Colloquium.

Special: A general-studies degree, study abroad, and exchange programs in theater are offered. Students may design their own majors. In addition, they may take any courses offered at the University of Missouri that are not given at Stephens. Each year, the Center for Conceptual Studies program enables a group of faculty and students to explore a single concept through a special series of courses. The House Plan liberal arts program is offered to incoming freshmen on the basis of interest and academic achievement; these students live in the only all-freshman hall on campus—a self-governing unit—and take courses that constitute a foundation for all liberal arts areas.

Honors: There are 11 honorary societies.

Admissions: About 86% of those who applied were accepted for the 1981–82 freshman class. The SAT scores of those who enrolled were as follows: Verbal—84% scored below 500, 12% between 500 and 599, 4% between 600 and 700, and 0% above 700; Math—78% scored below 500, 19% between 500 and 599, 3% between 600 and 700, and 0% above 700. Applicants must have a grade average of at least 2.0. Other factors considered include recommendations, advanced placement or honors courses, and extracurricular activities.

Procedure: The SAT or ACT is required. Application deadlines are August 15 (fall), January 1 (winter), and May 1 (summer). Notification is made on a rolling basis. There is a $25 application fee.

Special: There are early and deferred admissions plans. AP and CLEP credit is offered.

Transfer: For fall 1981, 120 students applied, 87 were accepted, and 56 enrolled. A GPA of 2.0 and a counselor's recommendation are needed to transfer; an interview is recommended. D grades are accepted. Three semesters must be completed in residence; 120 semester hours are necessary for a bachelor's degree. Deadliens for applications are the same as those for freshmen.

Visiting: An orientation program is offered. Informal campus tours with student guides also are provided. Visitors may attend classes and stay overnight at the college. Arrangements should be made through the admissions office.

Financial Aid: About 40% of the students receive aid. Fifty percent work part-time on campus. Average aid to freshmen in 1981–82 was $2700. There are academic scholarships, various loan programs, and government grants. Four-year honors scholarships of $1000 are available on the basis of academic achievement. The college is a member of CSS. The FAF or FFS is required; the deadlines for filing are March 15 (fall) and December 15 (winter).

Foreign Students: About 1% of the full-time students are from foreign countries. The college offers these students intensive English instruction through an exchange program with the University of Missouri/Columbia, special counseling, and special organizations.

Admissions: Foreign students must score at least 500 on the TOEFL. No college entrance exams are required.

Procedure: Application deadlines are August 1 (fall), January 1 (winter), and May 1 (summer session).

Admissions Contact: Martha G. Wade, Vice President and Dean of Admissions.

TARKIO COLLEGE
Tarkio, Missouri 64491   A-1
(816) 736-4131

F/T: 300M, 175W
P/T: 112 M&W
Grad: none
Year: 4-1-4
Appl: July 30
425 applied   300 accepted   226 enrolled
ACT: 16   LESS COMPETITIVE

Faculty: 31; n/av
Ph.D.'s: 17%
S/F Ratio: 12 to 1
Tuition: $3270
R and B: $1600

Tarkio College, established in 1883, is a liberal arts and sciences college affiliated with the Presbyterian Church. The library contains over 75,000 volumes and subscribes to 600 periodicals.

Environment: The 241-acre campus is located in a rural area 80 miles south of Omaha and 100 miles north of Kansas City. The 18 buildings on campus include single-sex residence halls that accommodate 400 men and 200 women. The college also sponsors on-campus apartments and married-student housing.

Student Life: About 40% of the students come from Missouri, and 90% live on campus. Alcohol is not permitted on campus. There are visiting privileges in dormitories. Students may keep cars on campus.

Organizations: Campus activities include clubs; campus government; publications; drama, social, and cultural events; and religious and service organizations. There are 6 fraternities and 3 sororities.

Sports: The college fields 8 intercollegiate teams for men and 7 for women. There are 8 intramural sports for men and 9 for women.

Handicapped: The college is working to make the campus accessible to handicapped students.

Graduates: The freshman dropout rate is about 25% and 50% of the students remain to graduate.

Services: The college provides free health care, remedial instruction, career counseling, and placement services. Tutoring is available for a fee.

Programs of Study: The college confers the B.A. and B.S. degrees. Associate degrees are also awarded. Bachelor's degrees are offered in the following subjects: BUSINESS (accounting, business administration, marketing), EDUCATION (elementary, health/physical, recreation, secondary, special), ENGLISH (creative writing, English, journalism, literature, speech), FINE AND PERFORMING ARTS (art, music, music education, performance production, theater/dramatics), HEALTH SCIENCES (nursing), MATH AND SCIENCES (biology, chemistry, computer science, mathematics), PHILOSOPHY (philosophy, religion), PREPROFESSIONAL (dentistry, engineering, law, medicine, pharmacy, social work, veterinary), SOCIAL SCIENCES (anthropology, economics, government/political science, history, psychology, sociology).

Required: All students must complete the core curriculum.

Special: Independent study and a summer-theater program are offered.

Honors: An honors program is available.

Admissions: About 70% of the applicants for the 1981-82 freshman class were accepted. Students should have completed 15 units of academic work and rank in the upper 60% of their graduating class. A high school GPA of at least 1.9 is required. Other factors considered are recommendations by school officials, personality, and impressions made during an interview.

Procedure: The ACT or SAT is required and may be taken at any time starting in May of the junior year. The application deadlines are July 30 for fall, October 1 for winter, and January for spring. Notification is made on a rolling basis. An interview is recommended. There is a $10 application fee.

Special: Early decision and early admissions plans are offered. AP and CLEP credit is accepted.

Transfer: For fall 1981, 72 transfer students applied, 54 were accepted, and 43 enrolled. Applicants should have earned a 2.0 GPA or better in a minimum of 15 credit hours. D grades are generally accepted. Twenty-four semester hours of the 124 required for a bachelor's degree must be completed in residence. An interview is recommended.

Visiting: Campus tours with student guides can be arranged. Visitors may sit in on classes.

Financial Aid: About 92% of the students receive financial aid; the average award to freshmen in 1981-82 was 80-90% of college costs. The college participates in federal programs such as NDSL, BEOG/SEOG, and CWS in addition to offering institutional funding, commercial loans, need and merit scholarships, and other part-time employment. Eighty percent of the students work part-time on campus. The college is a member of CSS. The FAF should be submitted as early as possible.

Foreign Students: Fewer than 1% of the full-time students are from foreign countries. The college offers an intensive English course.

Admissions: Applicants must take the TOEFL. No college entrance exams are required.

Procedure: Foreign students are admitted for the fall term only; applications should be submitted in May. Students must present proof of adequate funds for their entire period of study. Health insurance is required, and is available through the college for a fee.

Admissions Contact: Pam L. Jones, Admissions Office Manager.

UNIVERSITY OF MISSOURI

The University of Missouri system comprises 4 campuses with a combined faculty (full-time and part-time) of more than 3000 serving approximately 55,000 students. Its oldest campus, established at Columbia in 1839, is the system's largest, with a total enrollment of about 24,000 and 18 colleges and schools that offer more than 275 major programs through the doctoral level. The technologically oriented Rolla campus originally was established in the Ozarks in 1870 as the School of Mines and Metallurgy. Rolla now offers more than 75 major programs, including master's and doctoral programs in most areas. Serving the state's 2 most populated areas are the system's urban campuses at Kansas City and St. Louis. The former was founded in 1933 as the University of Kansas City and became part of the University of Missouri system in 1963. More than 140 major programs are available at the Kansas City campus and degrees are conferred through the doctoral level. Established in 1963, the St. Louis campus is the youngest of the 4 campuses. The campus first held classes as a 4-year institution in 1966 and now offers approximately 50 major programs leading to the bachelor's, first professional, master's, and doctoral degrees.

UNIVERSITY OF MISSOURI/COLUMBIA   C-2
Columbia, Missouri 65211   (314) 882-7651

F/T: 9060M, 8669W
P/T: 561M, 830W
Grad: 2502M, 2144W
Year: sems, ss
Appl: May 1
9072 applied   7183 accepted   4290 enrolled
SAT or ACT: required   COMPETITIVE

Faculty: n/av; I, av$
Ph.D.'s: n/av
S/F Ratio: 17 to 1
Tuition: $1020 ($3060)
R and B: $1525

The University of Missouri/Columbia, established in 1839, offers a variety of undergraduate and graduate programs. Its library houses 1.9 million volumes and 1.9 million microfilm items, and subscribes to 20,000 periodicals.

Environment: The 3600-acre campus is located in a rural area 35 miles north of Jefferson City. The 75 buildings include 22 dormitories that house 3472 women, 2903 men, and 360 married students. The university also sponsors fraternity and sorority houses. There are research facilities and an experimental field for soil and crop study.

Student Life: About 85% of the students come from Missouri. Ninety-five percent are graduates of public schools. About 45% live on campus. About 5% are minority-group members. Campus housing is both coed and single-sex; there are visiting privileges in the single-sex dorms. Students are permitted to keep cars on campus. Day-care services are provided. Drinking is not allowed on campus.

Organizations: The university sponsors numerous extracurricular activities and clubs, and social and cultural events are scheduled regularly. The 34 national fraternities with chapters on campus attract 20% of the men; the 18 national sororities attract 20% of the women.

Sports: The university fields teams in 10 intercollegiate sports for men and 10 for women. There are 14 intramural sports for men and 12 for women.

Handicapped: Special facilities for handicapped students include wheelchair ramps, parking areas, elevators, lowered drinking fountains and telephones, and specially equipped rest rooms. Special class scheduling is also available. The Center for Student Life provides an office for handicapped students, with special counselors.

Services: Free career counseling, placement services, tutoring, and psychological counseling are offered. Health care and remedial instruction are available for a fee.

Programs of Study: The university confers the following degrees: A.B., B.A., B.E.S., B.G.S., B.H.S., B.J., B.M., B.S.Ag., B.S.Ag.E.,

MISSOURI

B.S.Ch.E., B.S.C.I.E., B.S.E.E., B.S.Ed., B.S.F., B.S.F.W., B.S.H.E., B.S.I.E., and B.S.N. Master's and doctoral programs are also available. Bachelor's degrees are offered in: AREA STUDIES (Asian, Latin American, Russian), BUSINESS (accounting, business administration, computer science), EDUCATION (early childhood, elementary, health/physical, secondary, special), ENGLISH (English, journalism, speech), FINE AND PERFORMING ARTS (art, art education, music), HEALTH SCIENCES (medical technology, nursing, occupational therapy, physical therapy, speech therapy), LANGUAGES (French, German, Italian, Russian, Spanish), MATH AND SCIENCES (biochemistry, biology, chemistry, geology, mathematics, physical sciences, physics, statistics), PHILOSOPHY (classics, philosophy), PREPROFESSIONAL (agriculture, engineering—agricultural, engineering—chemical, engineering—computer, engineering—civil, engineering—electrical, engineering—industrial, engineering—mechanical, engineering—nuclear, forestry, home economics), SOCIAL SCIENCES (anthropology, economics, geography, government/political science, history, psychology, sociology).

Special: A general-studies degree, study abroad, and independent study are offered. Students may design their own majors. The College of Engineering has a 5-year work-study program.

Honors: Various departments offer honors work. Honor societies include Phi Beta Kappa.

Admissions: About 79% of the 1981–82 applicants were accepted. The SAT scores of those who enrolled were as follows: Verbal—80% below 599, 16% between 600 and 700, and 4% above 700; Math—85% below 599, 13% between 600 and 700, and 2% above 700.

Procedure: The ACT or SAT is required. Application deadlines are May 1 (fall), December 1 (spring), and March 1 (summer). Notification is made on a rolling basis. There is no application fee.

Special: AP and CLEP credit is available.

Transfer: For fall 1981, 2625 transfer students applied, 2296 were accepted, and 1516 enrolled. A 2.0 GPA is needed. The residency requirement varies with the individual program. Most programs require completion of 120 credits for a bachelor's degree. Application deadlines are May 1 (fall), July 1 (winter), and March 1 (summer).

Visiting: Campus tours with student guides may be arranged. Visitors may attend classes. Arrangements for campus visits, which should be scheduled between 8 A.M. and 12 noon and between 1 and 5 P.M. on Mondays through Fridays, can be made through the admissions office.

Financial Aid: About 50% of the students receive aid. Loans are available from the federal government, local banks, and the university. Opportunities for part-time campus jobs include CWS. About 1200 freshman scholarships are awarded. Aid is packaged. The university is a member of CSS. Aid applications are due April 1.

Foreign Students: The university offers these students an intensive English course and program, special counseling, and special organizations.

Admissions: Applicants must score at least 500 on the TOEFL, and must take the SAT or ACT.

Procedure: Application deadlines are May 1 for fall, July 1 for winter, and March 1 for summer. Students must present proof of adequate funds for 1 year. Health insurance is required, and is available through the university for a fee.

Admissions Contact: Gary L. Smith, Director of Admissions and Registrar.

UNIVERSITY OF MISSOURI/KANSAS CITY A–2

Kansas City, Missouri 64110 (816) 276-1125

F/T: 1970M, 2167W	Faculty: n/av; I, av$
P/T: 1028M, 1187W	Ph.D.'s: 60%
Grad: 2809M, 2610W	S/F Ratio: 12 to 1
Year: sems, ss	Tuition: $1102 ($3142)
Appl: see profile	R and B: $2100
1874 applied	1319 accepted	832 enrolled
SAT or ACT: required	VERY COMPETITIVE

The University of Missouri/Kansas City, established in 1929, offers undergraduate programs in the arts and sciences, business, education, health fields, and preprofessional areas. Its library has 616,000 volumes and 17,000 microfilm items, and subscribes to 7656 periodicals.

Environment: The 100-acre wooded campus is located in the cultural center of the city. Buildings include the Center for the Performing Arts and the Student Services Building. There is one dormitory accommodating 200 men and 100 women.

Student Life: About 80% of the students come from Missouri. Only 3% of the students live on campus. About 10% are minority-group members. University housing is coed. Students may keep cars on campus. Drinking on campus is prohibited. Day-care facilities are available.

Organizations: The 7 national fraternities attract 1% of the men; fewer than 1% of the women are members of 3 national sororities. A number of special-interest and departmental clubs are available. Regularly scheduled cultural and social events take place on campus.

Sports: The university fields 4 intercollegiate teams for men and 4 for women. There are 6 intramural sports for men and 6 for women.

Handicapped: About 50% of the campus is accessible to handicapped students. Special facilities include wheelchair ramps, parking areas, elevators, lowered drinking fountains, and specially equipped rest rooms. Special class scheduling is also available. There is special audiovisual equipment for hearing-impaired and visually impaired students. Four special counselors and 1 assistant are provided.

Graduates: The freshman dropout rate is 20%, and about 40% of the freshmen remain to graduate. Sixty percent of the graduates go on for further education; 20% enter careers in business and industry.

Services: Free psychological counseling, tutoring, remedial instruction, career counseling, and placement service are offered.

Programs of Study: The university confers the B.A., B.S., B.B.A., B.M., B.M.E., B.S.D.H., B.S.N., and B.S.Pharm. degrees. Master's and doctoral degrees are also awarded. Bachelor's degrees are offered in the following subjects: AREA STUDIES (American, Judaic, urban), BUSINESS (accounting, business administration, computer science, finance, management, marketing), EDUCATION (early childhood, elementary, health/physical, secondary), ENGLISH (English, journalism, literature), FINE AND PERFORMING ARTS (art, art education, art history, dance, music, music education, radio/TV, studio art, theater/dramatics), HEALTH SCIENCES (dental hygiene, medical technology, nursing, speech and hearing science), LANGUAGES (French, German, Spanish), MATH AND SCIENCES (biology, chemistry, computer science, earth science, geology, mathematics, physics), PHILOSOPHY (philosophy), PREPROFESSIONAL (agriculture, architecture, dentistry, engineering, forestry, home economics, law, library science, medicine, optometry, pharmacy, social work, veterinary), SOCIAL SCIENCES (economics, geography, government/political science, history, psychology, sociology).

Special: A 5-year combined B.A.-B.S. degree is offered; the same option is available in the accounting program. Honors admission to the pharmacy program is open to students directly from high school.

Honors: Honors work is offered in the College of Arts and Sciences. There are 15 honor societies.

Admissions: About 70% of those who applied were accepted for the 1981–82 freshman class. The ACT scores of those who enrolled were as follows: 34% scored below 21, 21% between 21 and 23, 15% between 24 and 25, 20% between 26 and 28, and 10% above 28. Admission is based on a combination of high school class rank and ACT or SAT score.

Procedure: The SAT, ACT, or PSAT/NMSQT is required; the ACT is required for applicants to the School of Medicine. Application deadlines are open, but preferred dates are July 1 (fall), December 1 (spring), and May 1 (summer). Notification is made on a rolling basis. There is no application fee.

Special: Early and deferred admissions plans and an early decision plan are available. AP and CLEP credit is offered.

Transfer: For fall 1981, 2600 students applied, 2100 were accepted, and 1800 enrolled. A 2.0 GPA and 12 completed credit hours are required. D grades do not transfer. Students must earn, at the college, at least 30 of the 120 credits necessary for a bachelor's degree. Application deadlines are open.

Visiting: Preferred times for campus tours are Monday through Friday from 10 A.M. to 2 P.M. Arrangements can be made through the School and College Relations Office (816-276-1115).

Financial Aid: About half the students receive assistance. Two percent work part-time on campus. The average freshman aid package was $2500 in 1981–82. Need and academic standing determine the award. The university, a member of CSS, awards scholarships and grants. There are also various loans available. The FFS is preferred (FAF accepted); the application deadline is March 15.

Foreign Students: About 1% of the full-time students come from foreign countries. The university offers these students special counseling and special organizations.

Admissions: Foreign students must score at least 500 on the TOEFL. The SAT or ACT is also required.

Procedure: Application deadlines are May 1 (fall), October 1 (spring), and March 1 (summer). Foreign students must present proof of adequate funds for 4 years of study. They also must carry health insurance, which is available through the university for a fee.

Admissions Contact: Leo J. Sweeney, Director of Admissions and Registrar.

UNIVERSITY OF MISSOURI/ROLLA   C-3
Rolla, Missouri 65401 (314) 341-4165

F/T: 5500M, 1500W	Faculty: 340; I, +$
P/T: 500M, 300W	Ph.D.'s: 85%
Grad: 800M, 100W	S/F Ratio: 14 to 1
Year: sems, ss	Tuition: $1015 ($2755)
Appl: July 1	R and B: $1914–2114
2550 applied	2100 accepted 1300 enrolled
SAT: 500V 600M	ACT: 25 VERY COMPETITIVE+

The University of Missouri/Rolla, established in 1870, offers undergraduate programs in the arts and sciences, technological areas, mining and metallurgy, and engineering. The library contains 300,000 volumes and 300,000 microtexts, and subscribes to 3000 periodicals.

Environment: The 258-acre rural campus is located in a town of 15,000 people in the Ozarks, about 90 miles from St. Louis. Six single-sex dormitories house about 33% of the students. On- and off-campus apartments, on-campus housing for married students, and fraternity and sorority houses also are provided.

Student Life: About 86% of the students come from Missouri. About 60% reside on campus. Thirteen percent of the students are minority-group members. Campus housing is both coed and single-sex; there are visiting privileges in the single-sex dorms. Students may keep cars on campus. Day-care services are available for a fee.

Organizations: About 27% of the men belong to the 1 local and 19 national fraternities on campus, and 18% of the women belong to the 1 local and 3 national sororities. Extracurricular activities include cultural events, clubs, and service organizations.

Sports: In addition to 11 intercollegiate teams for men and 3 for women, there are 9 intramural sports each for men and women.

Handicapped: The entire campus is accessible to handicapped students. Special facilities include wheelchair ramps, parking areas, elevators, lowered drinking fountains and telephones, and specially equipped rest rooms. Special class scheduling is also available. Four special counselors are provided for handicapped students.

Graduates: Ten percent of freshmen drop out by the end of the first year, and about 65% remain to graduate. Thirty percent of the graduates go on for further education.

Services: Career counseling, placement services, health care, and psychological counseling are offered without charge. Fees are charged for some remedial instruction and all tutoring.

Programs of Study: The university confers the B.A. and B.S. degrees. Master's and doctoral programs are also available. Bachelor's degrees are awarded in the following subjects: BUSINESS (computer science), ENGLISH (English), HEALTH SCIENCES (pre-nursing), MATH AND SCIENCES (biology, chemistry, geology, mathematics, physics, statistics), PHILOSOPHY (philosophy), PREPROFESSIONAL (engineering—aerospace, engineering—ceramic, engineering—chemical, engineering—civil, engineering—electrical, engineering—geological, engineering—mechanical, engineering—metallurgical, engineering—mining, engineering—nuclear, engineering—petroleum, engineering—engineering management, engineering—engineering mechanics), SOCIAL SCIENCES (economics, history, psychology).

Required: Individual programs of study have differing core requirements.

Special: Nursing and education programs are offered in conjunction with the University of Missouri/Columbia. A combined B.A.-B.S. degree can be earned in most areas.

Honors: All departments offer honors programs.

Admissions: About 82% of the 1981–82 applicants were admitted. The SAT scores of those who enrolled were as follows: Verbal—50% below 500, 30% between 500 and 599, 15% between 600 and 700, and 5% above 700; Math—22% below 500, 25% between 500 and 599, 39% between 600 and 700, and 14% above 700. Of those who took the ACT, 23% scored below 21, 14% between 21 and 23, 15% between 24 and 25, 26% between 26 and 28, and 22% above 28. Applicants should rank in the upper 50% of their high school class. Admission is based on a combination of high school class rank and ACT or SAT score.

Procedure: The ACT or SAT is required. Application deadlines are: fall, July 1; spring, December 1; summer, May 1. Notification is made on a rolling basis. The application fee is $20 for Missouri residents and $40 for nonresidents.

Special: AP and CLEP credit is offered.

Transfer: For fall 1981, 1000 transfer students applied, 800 were accepted, and 650 enrolled. A 2.0 GPA is required (a 3.0 GPA and an associate degree are recommended). All grades transfer. Students must complete in residence at least 30 of the 130 to 132 credits required for a bachelor's degree. Application deadlines are the same as those for freshmen.

Visiting: Campus tours with student guides can be arranged with the admissions office for Mondays through Fridays. Visitors may sit in on classes.

Financial Aid: About 30% of the students receive aid. The university offers traditional aid programs—loans, grants, scholarships, and part-time campus employment. About 5% of the students work part-time on campus. The average freshman aid package totaled $1200 in 1981–82. Freshmen should file the FFS by March 1; transfer students, by April 1.

Foreign Students: Seven percent of the full-time students are from foreign countries. An intensive English program, special counseling, and special organizations are available for these students.

Admissions: Applicants must score at least 550 on the TOEFL. Freshmen also must take the university's battery of placement tests.

Procedure: Application deadlines are June 1 for fall, October 1 for winter, and March 1 for summer. Proof of good health and adequate funds is required. Health insurance is required, and is available through the university for a fee.

Admissions Contact: Robert B. Lewis, Director of Admissions.

UNIVERSITY OF MISSOURI/ST. LOUIS   D-2
St. Louis, Missouri 63121 (314) 553-5451

F/T: 3144M, 2828W	Faculty: 315; I, –$
P/T: 2106M, 2107W	Ph.D.'s: 72%
Grad: 793M, 1070W	S/F Ratio: 26 to 1
Year: sems, ss	Tuition: $1090 ($3130)
Appl: July 1	R and B: n/app
2573 applied	1996 accepted 1292 enrolled
SAT: 426V 477M	ACT: 20 COMPETITIVE

The University of Missouri/St. Louis, established in 1963, offers undergraduate programs in the arts and sciences, business, education, and preprofessional areas. Its library has 347,000 volumes and 960,000 microfilm items, and subscribes to 2931 periodicals.

Environment: The 172-acre urban campus provides academic classrooms, laboratories, a life-sciences building, and a student activities center. There are no residence facilities.

Student Life: Nearly all students come from Missouri; most are from the St. Louis area. About 72% are graduates of public schools. About 13% are minority-group members. Day-care services are available for a fee.

Organizations: The university sponsors extracurricular activities, including 2 fraternities and 3 sororities, performing groups and departmental clubs. On-campus social and cultural events are scheduled regularly.

Sports: There are 7 intercollegiate sports for men and 6 for women. Six intramural sports are offered for men and 6 for women.

Handicapped: The entire campus is accessible to handicapped students. Special facilities include wheelchair ramps, parking areas, elevators, lowered drinking fountains and telephones, and specially equipped rest rooms. Auditory emergency signalers are provided for visually impaired students.

Graduates: The freshman dropout rate is 40%, and 30% remain to graduate.

Services: Offered free to students are career counseling, placement services, tutoring, health care, and psychological counseling. Remedial instruction is available for a fee.

Programs of Study: The university awards the B.A., B.S., B.G.S., B.M., and B.S.N. degrees. Master's and doctoral programs are also available. Bachelor's degrees are offered in the following subjects: BUSINESS (business administration), EDUCATION (early childhood, elementary, secondary, special), FINE AND PERFORMING ARTS (art history, music, music education), HEALTH SCIENCES (nursing), LANGUAGES (French, German, Spanish), MATH AND SCIENCES (applied mathematics, biology, chemistry, mathematics, physics), PHILOSOPHY (philosophy), PREPROFESSIONAL (dentistry, engineering, law, medicine, pharmacy, social work), SOCIAL SCIENCES (anthropology, economics, government/political science, history, psychology, sociology).

Required: Students must complete general-education requirements.

Special: A general-studies degree and a combined B.A.-B.S. degree are available. Students may design their own majors.

Honors: An honors program is offered for sophomores in the College of Arts and Sciences.

Admissions: About 78% of the 1981-82 applicants were accepted. The ACT scores of those who enrolled were as follows: 54% below 21, 22% between 22 and 23, 12% between 24 and 25, 10% between 26 and 28, and 2% above 28. Admission is based on a combination of high school class rank and SAT, ACT, or SCAT score.

Procedure: The SAT, ACT, or SCAT is required. Application deadlines are July 1 (fall), December 1 (spring), and May 1 (summer). Notification is made on a rolling basis. There is no application fee.

Special: AP and CLEP credit is available. Early admissions and early decision plans are offered.

Transfer: For fall 1981, 3445 transfer students applied, 2775 were accepted, and 1806 enrolled. A 2.0 GPA is needed; D grades usually do not transfer. Students must complete, at the university, 24 of the 120 credits required for a bachelor's degree. Application deadlines are the same as those for freshmen.

Visiting: Campus tours can be arranged through the student affairs office. Visitors may attend classes.

Financial Aid: About 33% of the students receive aid. The university offers loan programs, government grants, CWS and other part-time campus jobs, and scholarships. Ten percent of the students work part-time on campus. The average aid package for a freshman in 1981-82 was $1200; the maximum, $2800. The university is a member of CSS. The FAF is due March 30 (fall), December 1 (spring), or February 30 (summer).

Foreign Students: About 1% of the full-time students are from foreign countries. The university offers these students an intensive English course, special counseling, and special organizations.

Admissions: A minimum score of 500 on the TOEFL is required. Freshmen must take the SAT or ACT, if possible.

Procedure: Applications should be submitted 1 year in advance; foreign students are admitted to all terms. Students must present proof of adequate funds.

Admissions Contact: H. E. Mueller, Director of Admissions and Registrar.

WASHINGTON UNIVERSITY   D-2
St. Louis, Missouri 63130   (314) 889-6000

F/T: 2670M, 1891W	Faculty:	1366; I, +$
P/T: 1308M, 991W	Ph.D.'s:	98%
Grad: 3893 M&W	S/F Ratio:	14 to 1
Year: sems, ss	Tuition:	$6296
Appl: Feb. 15	R and B:	$2949
4851 applied	3968 accepted	1071 enrolled
SAT: 560V 610M	ACT: 27 HIGHLY COMPETITIVE+	

Washington University, established in 1853, is a private, independent institution offering undergraduate programs in the arts and sciences, business, architecture, fine arts, health fields, and engineering. Its library contains over 1.8 million books and 500,000 microfilm items, and subscribes to 15,200 periodicals.

Environment: The 176-acre, self-contained campus is located in a suburban area of St. Louis. The 90 major buildings include 14 dormitories housing 2100 men and women. The college also sponsors on- and off-campus apartments, fraternity houses, and married-student housing. Facilities are available for commuting students.

Student Life: About 20% of the students come from the metropolitan area. Seventy-five percent have had public school educations. Eighty percent live on campus. About 13% are minority-group members. Campus housing is both coed and single-sex; there are visiting privileges in the single-sex dorms. Juniors and seniors may keep cars on campus.

Organizations: The 10 fraternities attract 10% of the men; the 6 sororities attract 10% of the women. Extracurricular activities are extensive and varied. On-campus social and cultural events are scheduled regularly.

Sports: The university fields intercollegiate teams in 11 sports for men and 7 for women. Intramural competition is offered for men in 13 sports and for women in 10 sports.

Handicapped: About 55% of the campus is accessible to handicapped students. Special facilities include wheelchair ramps, parking areas, elevators, and specially equipped rest rooms. Special class scheduling is also available. Special personnel include a counselor, 2 assistants, and a coordinator for the handicapped.

Graduates: About 5% of the freshmen drop out, and 72% remain to graduate. Seventy percent of the graduates seek advanced degrees. Forty-five percent pursue careers in business and industry.

Services: Career counseling, placement, tutoring, remedial instruction, psychological counseling, and health care are offered without charge.

Programs of Study: The university confers the A.B., B.S., B.S.B.A., B.S.O.T., B.S.P.T., and B.F.A. degrees. Master's and doctoral programs are also available. Bachelor's degrees are offered in the following subjects: AREA STUDIES (Asian, Black/Afro-American, Jewish, Latin American, linguistic, Medieval and Renaissance, religious, urban, women's), BUSINESS (accounting, business administration, finance, management, marketing), EDUCATION (early childhood, elementary, secondary, special), ENGLISH (English, literature), FINE AND PERFORMING ARTS (art, art education, art history, dance, fashion design, graphics, music, music education, studio art, theater/dramatics), HEALTH SCIENCES (occupational therapy, physical therapy), LANGUAGES (Chinese, French, German, Greek/Latin, Hebrew, Japanese, Russian, Spanish), MATH AND SCIENCES (biology, chemistry, earth science, geology, mathematics, natural sciences, physical sciences, physics, statistics, zoology), PHILOSOPHY (classics, humanities, philosophy, religion), PREPROFESSIONAL (architecture, dentistry, engineering—chemical, engineering—civil, engineering—computer science, engineering—electrical, engineering—mechanical, engineering—physics, engineering—systems science and mathematics, engineering technology and human affairs, law, medicine, ministry, pharmacy, social work, veterinary), SOCIAL SCIENCES (economics, government/political science, history, international relations, psychology, social sciences, sociology).

Required: Distribution requirements include courses in English and mathematics.

Special: A general-studies major, student-designed majors, study abroad, independent study, and cooperative engineering programs are offered.

Honors: Several honor societies are represented on campus. Honors work is offered in nearly all areas.

Admissions: About 82% of the 1981-82 applicants were admitted. The SAT scores of those who enrolled were as follows: Verbal—22% below 500, 40% between 500 and 599, 29% between 600 and 700, and 9% above 700; Math—9% below 500, 31% between 500 and 599, 42% between 600 and 700, and 18% above 700. Of those who took the ACT, 9% scored below 21, 14% between 22 and 24, 32% between 25 and 27, 30% between 28 and 30, and 15% above 30. Besides academic record and test scores, admissions officers consider advanced placement or honors courses, recommendations, and extracurricular activities.

Procedure: The SAT or ACT is required; ATs are recommended. February 15 is the application deadline for fall; for spring it is November 1. Notification is made on a rolling basis. The application fee is $20.

Special: Early decision, early admissions, and deferred admissions plans are available. AP credit is granted.

Transfer: For fall 1981, 847 transfer students applied, 568 were accepted, and 244 enrolled. A 2.5 GPA and an interview are recommended. D grades do not transfer. Three semesters of study, and 30 of the 120 credits required for a bachelor's degree, must be completed in residence. Application deadlines are the same as those for freshmen.

Visiting: There is an orientation program. Informal campus tours may be arranged. Visitors may stay at the school and attend classes.

Financial Aid: About 54% of the students receive aid. Scholarships, grants, loans, and part-time jobs are available; 27% of students work part-time on campus. Need and academic merit determine the awards. The average award to freshmen in 1981-82 was $7032. The FAF should be filed with CSS no later than February 15 for fall or November 1 for spring.

Foreign Students: Twelve percent of the full-time students are from foreign countries. An intensive English course, special counseling, and special organizations are available for these students.

WEBSTER COLLEGE
Webster Groves, Missouri 63119   (314) 968-6985

F/T: 318M, 471W	Faculty:	70; IIA, –$
P/T: 336 M&W	Ph.D.'s:	52%
Grad: 3036 M&W	S/F Ratio:	13 to 1
Year: see profile, ss	Tuition:	$3675
Appl: open	R and B:	$1950
800 applied	400 accepted	150 enrolled
SAT: 510V 450M	ACT: 22	COMPETITIVE

Webster College, established in 1915, is a private, nonsectarian institution. The library contains 147,560 volumes and 4650 microfilm items, and subscribes to 887 periodicals.

Environment: The college is located in a suburban area of metropolitan St. Louis. One dormitory accommodates 200 students.

Student Life: About 81% of the students come from Missouri. Eighty-one percent come from public schools. Twenty-five percent live on campus. Thirty-one percent of the students are minority-group members. College housing is coed. Students may keep cars on campus.

Organizations: Activities include theater, films, recitals, guest lectures, and publications. The campus houses the Loretto-Hilton Center, which presents productions of the Loretto-Hilton Repertory Company, the Opera Theatre of St. Louis, and other cultural organizations. There are no fraternities or sororities.

Sports: There are no intercollegiate or intramural sports.

Handicapped: Facilities for physically handicapped students include an elevator and specially equipped rest rooms.

Graduates: The freshman dropout rate is 25%; 35% of the freshmen remain to graduate. Sixty percent of the graduates pursue further study.

Services: Students receive free placement aid, career counseling, psychological counseling, and remedial instruction. Health care and tutoring are available for a fee.

Programs of Study: The college confers the B.A., B.F.A., B.M., and B.Mus.Ed. degrees. Master's degrees also are awarded. Bachelor's degrees are offered in the following subjects: BUSINESS (computer science, management), EDUCATION (adult, early childhood, elementary, secondary, special), ENGLISH (English, journalism, literature), FINE AND PERFORMING ARTS (art, art education, art history, dance, film/photography, music, music education, studio art, theater/dramatics), HEALTH SCIENCES (nursing), LANGUAGES (French, German, Italian, Spanish), MATH AND SCIENCES (biology, mathematics, natural sciences, physical sciences), PHILOSOPHY (humanities, philosophy, religion), PREPROFESSIONAL (law, ministry, social work), SOCIAL SCIENCES (anthropology, government/political science, history, international relations, psychology, sociology).

Special: The school year is divided into a combination of 8-week terms and 16-week semesters. Students may design their own majors. Other programs include study abroad, off-campus semesters for credit, independent study, inter-institutional registration, and optional credit/no credit grading. A fully equipped professional theater offers students practical experience in drama.

Admissions: Fifty percent of those who applied were accepted for the 1981–82 freshman class. The SAT scores of those who enrolled were as follows: Verbal—50% scored below 500, 25% between 500 and 599, 15% between 600 and 700, and 10% above 700; Math—55% scored below 500, 25% between 500 and 599, 15% between 600 and 700, and 5% above 700. Candidates should have completed 16 units of work, rank in the upper 70% of their high school class, and have at least a C average. The reputation of the high school, advanced placement or honors courses, evidence of special talent, and leadership record also are considered.

Procedure: The SAT or ACT is required and should be taken by January of the senior year. Application deadlines are open. There is a rolling admissions plan. Students planning to major in theater or music must audition as part of the admissions procedure. Applications should be submitted with a $20 fee.

Special: Early and deferred admissions plans and an early decision plan are available. AP and CLEP credit is available.

Admissions: Applicants must score at least 500 on the TOEFL. The SAT or ACT is also required.

Procedure: Application deadlines are February 15 for fall and November 1 for spring. Foreign students are also admitted for the summer term. Students must present proof of adequate funds for 1 year. Health insurance is required, and is available through the university for a fee.

Admissions Contact: William H. Turner, Director of Admissions.

Transfer: For fall 1981, 400 students applied, 250 were accepted, and 180 enrolled. College transcripts (or high school transcripts when fewer than 60 credit hours have been completed) are required. Transfer students also need a GPA of at least 2.0. D grades do not transfer. Students must earn, at the college, at least 30 of the 128 credits necessary for a bachelor's degree. Deadlines for applications are open.

Visiting: Guides are available for informal visits; the director of admissions should be contacted for arrangements.

Financial Aid: Eighty percent of all students receive aid. Forty-five percent work part-time on campus. Average aid to 1981–82 freshmen was $4000. Sources of aid include EOG. The college is a member of CSS. Either the FAF or FFS must be submitted. Applications for aid should be received by April 1.

Foreign Students: Seven percent of the full-time students come from foreign countries. The college offers an intensive English course, an intensive English program, special counseling, and special organizations.

Admissions: No English proficiency or college entrance exams are required.

Procedure: Application deadlines are open. Foreign students must present a certificate of health and proof of adequate funds for 1 year.

Admissions Contact: Michael Newman, Director of Admissions.

WESTMINSTER COLLEGE
Fulton, Missouri 65251   (314) 642-3361

F/T: 581M, 133W	Faculty:	52; IIB, av$
P/T: 25M, 14W	Ph.D.'s:	60%
Grad: none	S/F Ratio:	14 to 1
Year: 5-4-1, ss	Tuition:	$4400
Appl: open	R and B:	$2200
493 applied	400 accepted	226 enrolled
SAT: 483V 528M	ACT: 24	COMPETITIVE+

Westminster College is a liberal arts institution founded in 1851 by the Presbyterian Church. It offers programs and facilities cooperatively with nearby William Woods College for women. The library has 140,000 volumes and 5000 microfilm items, and subscribes to 600 periodicals.

Environment: The 253-acre campus is located in a small town 100 miles west of St. Louis. Buildings include 7 residence halls. A freshman quadrangle houses all first-year students. The college also sponsors fraternity houses.

Student Life: About 51% of the students come from Missouri. Eighty percent are public school graduates. Almost all live on campus. Sixty-three percent of the students are Protestant, 35% are Catholic, and 1% are Jewish. Nineteen percent are minority-group members. Campus housing is single-sex, with visiting privileges. Students may keep cars on campus.

Organizations: About 65% of the men belong to one of the 7 national fraternities on campus. Extracurricular activities are provided.

Sports: The college fields 8 intercollegiate teams for men and 5 for women. There are 11 intramural sports for men and 7 for women.

Handicapped: About 75% of the campus is accessible to handicapped students. Special facilities include parking areas, elevators, and specially equipped rest rooms.

Graduates: Eight percent of the freshmen drop out by the end of the first year, and 60% remain to graduate. Of these, 45% seek advanced degrees (10% in medical school, 2% in dental school, and 12% in law school). Fifty percent begin careers in business or industry.

Services: Psychological counseling, career counseling, tutoring, and placement services are offered free.

Programs of Study: The college confers the B.A. and B.F.A. degrees. Bachelor's degrees are offered in the following subjects: BUSINESS (accounting, business administration, economics, finance, management), EDUCATION (elementary, health/physical, secondary), ENGLISH (English, literature, speech), FINE AND PERFORMING ARTS (art, art education, art history, dance, music, music education, theater/dramatics), LANGUAGES (French, German, Spanish), MATH AND SCIENCES (biology, chemistry, computer science, mathematics, physics), PHILOSOPHY (philosophy, religion), PREPROFESSIONAL (dentistry, engineering, law, medicine, veterinary), SOCIAL SCIENCES (anthropology, government/political science, history, psychology, sociology). Half the degrees conferred are in business, and one-quarter are in math and sciences.

Required: Distribution requirements include physical education.

Special: Independent study, Washington and United Nations semesters, study abroad, and combination-degree programs in engineering (a 3-2 program with Washington University) are offered. Students may design their own majors.

Honors: Nineteen honor societies are represented on campus.

Admissions: About 81% of the 1981-82 applicants were accepted. In an earlier class, 45% scored above 500 on the SAT verbal section and 52% scored above 500 on the math section. Of those who took the ACT, 25% scored between 20 and 23, 25% between 24 and 26, 15% between 27 and 28, 10% above 28. Applicants should have a high school GPA of at least 2.0. Advanced placement or honors courses, recommendations, and extracurricular activities also are considered.

Procedure: The ACT or SAT is required. There are no application deadlines; students are admitted to all terms. Notification is made on a rolling basis. There is a $20 application fee.

Special: Early and deferred admissions plans are offered. CLEP and AP credit is available.

Transfer: For fall 1981, all 26 transfer students who applied were accepted, and all enrolled. SAT or ACT scores are required; a 2.0 GPA and an interview are recommended. D grades do not transfer. Students must spend at least 2 years in residence and earn 122 credits for a bachelor's degree. Application deadlines are open.

Visiting: Campus tours can be arranged through the admissions office. Visitors may stay overnight at the school and attend classes. The best times for visits are 9 A.M. to noon on Saturdays and 8 A.M. to 5 P.M. on weekdays, from September to mid-December and from mid-January to May.

Financial Aid: About 86% of the students receive assistance. The college offers freshman scholarships, loans, grants, and part-time jobs. The average freshman aid package in 1981-82 was $3760. The FAF or FFS should be filed no later than April 1.

Foreign Students: The college actively recruits foreign students.

Admissions: Applicants must take the TOEFL as well as the SAT or ACT.

Procedure: Foreign students are admitted for the fall, winter, spring, and summer terms. Application deadlines are open.

Admissions Contact: Thomas N. King, Director of Admissions.

WILLIAM JEWELL COLLEGE B-2
Liberty, Missouri 64068 (816) 781-3806

F/T:	800M, 600W	Faculty:	91; IIB, av$
P/T:	none	Ph.D.'s:	70%
Grad:	none	S/F Ratio:	16 to 1
Year:	4-1-4, ss	Tuition:	$3580
Appl:	open	R and B:	$1820
1107 applied		408 accepted	376 enrolled
ACT: 22			VERY COMPETITIVE

William Jewell College, founded in 1849, is affiliated with the Baptist Church and offers undergraduate preparation in business, education, health fields, and arts and sciences. The library has 135,000 books and 4825 microfilm items, and subscribes to 900 periodicals.

Environment: The 500-acre campus is located in a suburban area 20 miles from Kansas City. The 12 buildings include 6 dormitories. The college also sponsors married-student housing.

Student Life: About 70% of the students come from Missouri, and 75% are graduates of public schools. Eighty percent live on campus. No drinking is permitted on campus. About 50% of the students are Baptist. About 5% are minority-group members. Campus housing is single-sex, with visiting privileges. Students may keep cars on campus.

Organizations: About 40% of the students belong to the 4 national fraternities and 4 national sororities with chapters on campus. Other activities include religious groups, performing groups, clubs, and publications.

Sports: The college fields 11 intercollegiate teams for men and 6 for women. There are 7 intramural sports for men and 7 for women.

Handicapped: The campus has no special facilities for handicapped students.

Graduates: The freshman dropout rate is 5%, and about 70% remain to graduate. About 85% of the graduates pursue further education.

Programs of Study: The B.A. and B.S. degrees are conferred. Bachelor's degrees are offered in the following subjects: BUSINESS (accounting, business administration, management), EDUCATION (elementary, health/physical, secondary), ENGLISH (English, public relations, speech), FINE AND PERFORMING ARTS (art, art education, communication, music, music education), HEALTH SCIENCES (medical technology, nursing), LANGUAGES (French, German, Greek/Latin, Japanese, Russian, Spanish), MATH AND SCIENCES (biology, chemistry, mathematics, physics), PHILOSOPHY (philosophy, religion), PREPROFESSIONAL (dentistry, engineering, forestry, law, medicine, ministry, social work), SOCIAL SCIENCES (economics, government/political science, history, international relations, psychology, public administration, sociology).

Required: Course work in religion is required.

Special: Study abroad and combination-degree programs in forestry (with Duke University) and engineering (with Columbia University) are offered. Students may design their own majors.

Honors: Twenty honor societies have chapters on campus.

Admissions: About 37% of the 1981-82 applicants were accepted. The ACT scores of those who enrolled were as follows: 23% below 21, 30% between 21 and 23, 16% between 24 and 25, 20% between 26 and 28, and 11% above 28. Applicants should rank in the top 50% of their high school class. Recommendations, extracurricular activities, and advanced placement or honors courses also are important factors.

Procedure: The ACT is required. New students may enter any semester; notification is made on a rolling basis. Application deadlines are open. There is a $10 application fee.

Special: Early decision, early admissions, and deferred admissions plans are offered. AP and CLEP credit is available.

Transfer: For fall 1981, 323 transfer students applied, 152 were accepted, and 124 enrolled. A 2.0 GPA is required (a 2.5 GPA and an interview are recommended). Grades of C or better transfer. Students must complete in residence at least 30 of the 124 credits required for the bachelor's degree.

Visiting: Informal campus tours with student guides can be arranged. Visitors may sit in on classes. Arrangements should be made through the admissions office.

Financial Aid: About 86% of the students receive aid; the average award to freshmen from all sources in 1981-82 was 64% of college costs. The college offers scholarships, loans, federal and state grants, and part-time campus jobs (including CWS). Forty-five percent of students work part-time on campus. The FAF or FFS is required. The application deadline for fall entry is open; for spring it is December 1, and for summer it is May 1.

Foreign Students: Fewer than 1% of the full-time students are from foreign countries. Special counseling and special organizations are available.

Admissions: Applicants must score at least 500 on the TOEFL and 21 on the ACT.

Procedure: Foreign students should apply by January for fall entry and by June for spring entry. Applications for the summer term are accepted on a rolling basis. Students must submit proof of adequate funds for 4 years. Health insurance is required, and is available thorugh the college for a fee.

Admissions Contact: Harley Wyatt, Jr., Director of Admissions.

WILLIAM WOODS COLLEGE C-2
Fulton, Missouri 65251 (314) 642-2251

F/T:	788W	Faculty:	59; IIB, −$
P/T:	303M, 52W	Ph.D.'s:	39%
Grad:	none	S/F Ratio:	13 to 1
Year:	5-4-1, ss	Tuition:	$4310
Appl:	open	R and B:	$1790
692 applied		605 accepted	261 enrolled
SAT: 490V 501M		ACT: 18	LESS COMPETITIVE

William Woods College, established in 1870, is an independent liberal arts college for women. It has a cooperative arrangement with nearby Westminster College for men. The William Woods library has 151,000 volumes and subscribes to 680 periodicals.

Environment: The 160-acre campus is located in a rural area 100 miles west of St. Louis and 150 miles east of Kansas City. The 38 major buildings include dormitories. The college also sponsors sorority houses.

Student Life: About 30% of the students come from Missouri. Eighty percent are graduates of public schools. Ninety percent of the students live on campus. About 6% of the students are minority-group members. There are visiting privileges in the dormitories.

Organizations: About 40% of the women belong to the 4 national sororities. Extracurricular activities include service organizations, clubs, student government, publications, performing groups, and regularly scheduled social and cultural events.

Sports: Women participate in 5 intercollegiate sports and 12 intramural sports.

Handicapped: The entire campus is accessible to handicapped students. Special facilities include wheelchair ramps and elevators.

Graduates: About 5% of the freshmen drop out, and 62% remain to graduate. About 10% of the graduates go on for further study; 1% enter medical school and 2% enter law school. Sixty percent begin careers in business or industry.

Programs of Study: The college confers the B.A., B.S., and B.F.A. degrees. Bachelor's degrees are offered in the following subjects: AREA STUDIES (American, arts and letters, humanistic, liberal), BUSINESS (accounting, business administration, business education, computer science, fashion merchandising, foods marketing and business administration, management, marketing, music and business administration, office management), EDUCATION (early childhood, elementary, health/physical, secondary, special), ENGLISH (English, English communications), FINE AND PERFORMING ARTS (art, art education, dance, music, music education, performing arts, radio/TV, studio art, theater/dramatics, theatrical design), HEALTH SCIENCES (medical technology), LANGUAGES (French, Spanish), MATH AND SCIENCES (biology, chemistry, earth science, mathematics, physics), PHILOSOPHY (humanities, philosophy, religion), PREPROFESSIONAL (engineering, home economics, law, library science, medicine, ministry, pharmacy, social work, veterinary), SOCIAL SCIENCES (economics, government/political science, history, psychology, social sciences, sociology). There is also a major in equestrian science. About 30% of the degrees are conferred in business.

Special: Cooperative degree programs are offered with other institutions in animal science, nursing, law, veterinary medicine, and engineering. Study abroad, independent study, and internships are available. Students may earn a combined B.A.-B.S. degree.

Honors: Several honor societies have chapters on campus.

Admissions: About 87% of the 1981-82 applicants were accepted. The SAT scores of those who enrolled were as follows: Verbal—76% below 500, 21% between 500 and 599, and 3% between 600 and 700; Math—71% below 500, 21% between 500 and 599, and 8% between 600 and 700. Of those who took the ACT, 50% scored below 21, 27% between 21 and 23, 7% between 24 and 25, 7% between 26 and 28, and 1% above 28. A high school GPA of 2.0 is required, and an interview is recommended. Also considered are recommendations, advanced placement or honors courses, and impressions made during an interview.

Procedure: The SAT or ACT is required. There are no application deadlines; new students are admitted each term. Notification is made on a rolling basis. There is a $25 application fee.

Special: Early decision, early admissions, and deferred admissions plans are available. AP and CLEP credit is accepted.

Transfer: For fall 1981, 32 transfer students applied, 29 were accepted, and 24 enrolled. A GPA of 2.0 is required. Grades of C or better transfer. Students must complete at least 1 year in residence, earning 30 of the 122 credits required for a bachelor's degree. There are no application deadlines.

Visiting: Informal campus tours with student guides can be arranged. Visitors may stay overnight at the school and attend classes. Arrangements for visits, preferably when classes are in session, can be made through the admissions office.

Financial Aid: About 31% of the students receive aid. The college offers a limited number of scholarships to freshmen. Also available are government and commercial loans, grants, and campus jobs. About 26% of the students work part-time on campus. Tuition may be paid in installments. Academic achievement determines recipients of scholarships; need determines recipients of grants. The college is a member of CSS; the FAF, FFS, or SFS should be submitted. Deadlines for filing are August 1 for fall and January 1 for winter.

Foreign Students: Fewer than 1% of the full-time students are from foreign countries. The college offers these students an intensive English course and special counseling.

Admissions: Applicants must score at least 500 on the TOEFL and take the SAT or the ACT.

Procedure: Application deadlines are August 1 for fall and December 15 for winter. Students must submit a completed college health form and proof of adequate funds for 4 years. Health insurance is required, and is available through the college for a fee.

Admissions Contact: Janet White, Acting Director of Admissions.

MONTANA

CARROLL COLLEGE C-2
Helena, Montana 59625 (406) 442-3450

F/T: 457M, 641W	Faculty:	73; IIB, av$
P/T: 98M, 162W	Ph.D.'s:	38%
Grad: none	S/F Ratio:	15 to 1
Year: sems, ss	Tuition:	$2588
Appl: Aug. 15	R and B:	$1756
518 applied	505 accepted	340 enrolled
SAT: 425V 448M	ACT: 21	COMPETITIVE

Carroll College, founded in 1909, is a small Roman Catholic institution devoted to the liberal arts and offering bachelor's degrees in business, education, health fields, and the arts and sciences. The library contains 90,000 volumes and subscribes to 500 periodicals.

Environment: The 64-acre campus is located in a suburban area 3 blocks from the city of Helena. Residence halls provide accommodations for 693 students.

Student Life: About 65% of the students are from Montana. Approximately 65% of the entering freshmen come from public schools. About 70% of the students live on campus. Seven percent are minority-group members. Sixty-five percent are Catholic. Campus housing is both coed and single-sex; there are visiting privileges in the single-sex housing. Students may keep cars on campus. Day-care services are available to all students.

Organizations: There are no fraternities or sororities. The college sponsors social events on campus, and the city offers entertainment opportunities.

Sports: The college fields 2 intercollegiate teams for men and 2 for women. There are 16 intramural sports for men and 15 for women.

Handicapped: There are no special facilities for physically handicapped students, and only half of the campus is accessible to them.

Graduates: About 10% of the freshmen drop out during their first year; 65% remain to graduate. Thirty-five percent of the graduates continue their education; 8% enter medical school, 3% enter dental school, and 7% enter law school. About 65% of the graduates pursue careers in industry and business.

Services: Free tutoring, remedial instruction, psychological counseling, health care, career counseling, and job placement services are offered to all students.

Programs of Study: The college offers the B.A. degree. Associate degrees are also awarded. Bachelor's degrees are offered in the following subjects: BUSINESS (accounting, business administration, finance), EDUCATION (elementary, health/physical, religious, secondary, special), ENGLISH (English, speech), FINE AND PERFORMING ARTS (theater/dramatics), HEALTH SCIENCES (dental hygiene, medical records administration, medical technology, nursing, speech therapy), LANGUAGES (French, Greek/Latin, Spanish), MATH AND SCIENCES (biology, mathematics), PHILOSOPHY (philosophy, theology), PREPROFESSIONAL (dentistry, engineering, law, medicine, ministry, optometry, pharmacy, social work, veterinary), SOCIAL SCIENCES (economics, government/political science, history, psychology, social sciences, sociology). About 28% of the degrees conferred are in health sciences and 18% in business.

Special: The college offers, in cooperation with several universities, a 3-2 program in math and engineering. Study abroad can also be arranged.

Honors: Two honor societies have chapters on campus.

Admissions: About 97% of those who applied were accepted for the 1981-82 freshman class. The SAT scores of those who enrolled were as follows: Verbal—74% scored below 500, 22% between 500 and 599, and 4% between 600 and 700; Math—69% scored below 500, 24% between 500 and 599, and 7% between 600 and 700. Of those who took the ACT, 38% scored below 20, 37% between 20 and 24, 23% between 25 and 29, and 2% above 30. Students should have a

472 MONTANA

C average or better. Advanced placement or honors courses and extracurricular activities are also considered.

Procedure: The SAT or ACT is required. The application deadlines are August 15 (fall) and December 31 (spring). Students are admitted each semester. Notification is on a rolling basis. A $20 application fee is required.

Special: Early decision, early admissions, and deferred admissions plans are available. AP and CLEP credit is given.

Transfer: For fall 1981, 123 applications were received, 122 applicants were accepted, and 82 enrolled. A GPA of 2.0 is recommended; D grades do not transfer. All students must complete, at the college, at least 30 of the 122 credits required for a bachelor's degree. Application deadlines are the same as those for freshmen.

Visiting: Regularly scheduled orientations for prospective students include a tour of the campus and meetings with faculty and the financial aid director. The office of admissions should be contacted to make arrangements for informal visits on Monday through Friday, from 8 A.M. to 5 P.M. Students may sit in on classes and stay overnight at the college.

Financial Aid: About 70% of all students receive aid. Sixty-five percent work part-time on campus. Scholarships and NDSL are available. The FAF or FFS should be filed by March 1 for priority consideration. The college is a member of CSS.

Foreign Students: Twenty-two students, or about 2% of the student body, come from foreign countries. Special counseling and special organizations are available for these students.

Admissions: Foreign students must achieve a TOEFL score of at least 500 and must take the SAT or ACT.

Procedure: Application deadlines are July 15 (fall) and November 31 (spring). Foreign students must present proof of health and of adequate funds for 1 calendar year. They also must carry health insurance, which is available through the college for a fee.

Admissions Contact: Allen Kohler, Director of Admissions.

COLLEGE OF GREAT FALLS C-2
Great Falls, Montana 59405 (406) 761-8210

F/T: 215M, 195W	Faculty: 35; IIB, −−$
P/T: 360M, 324W	Ph.D.'s: 33%
Grad: 6M, 20W	S/F Ratio: 12 to 1
Year: sems, ss	Tuition: $2990
Appl: Aug. 10	R and B: $1550
131 applied	131 accepted	90 enrolled
ACT: 18		NONCOMPETITIVE

The College of Great Falls, an independent Catholic institution conducted by the Sisters of Charity of Providence, offers 4-year programs in the liberal arts and sciences, business, teacher education, broadcast communications, and pre-professional areas. Its library contains 72,700 volumes and 12,612 microtexts, and subscribes to 376 periodicals.

Environment: The 71-acre suburban campus is located in Montana's second-largest city. College housing includes dormitories, off-campus apartments, and married-student housing.

Student Life: About 80% of the students are residents of Montana. Approximately 93% of the freshmen come from public schools. Most students commute, but 20% live on campus. About 40% of the students are Catholic. Campus housing is coed. Students may keep cars on campus.

Organizations: There are no national fraternities or sororities on campus. Clubs are available in many special-interest and recreational fields, as are college-sponsored concerts and debates.

Sports: The college fields 1 intercollegiate team for men and 1 for women. There are 8 intramural sports for men and 8 for women.

Handicapped: About 75% of the campus is accessible to handicapped students. Special parking and special class scheduling are provided.

Graduates: About 15% of the freshmen drop out by the end of their first year; 75% remain to graduate. Of these, 32% continue their education; 2% enter medical school, 1% enter dental school, and 1% enter law school. Another 20% of the graduates pursue careers in business and industry.

Services: Free tutoring, remedial instruction, career counseling, psychological counseling, health care, and job placement services are offered to all students.

Programs of Study: The college offers the B.A. and B.S. degrees. Associate and master's degrees are also awarded. Bachelor's degrees are offered in the following subjects: BUSINESS (accounting, business administration), EDUCATION (early childhood, elementary, health/physical, secondary), ENGLISH (English), FINE AND PERFORMING ARTS (radio/TV), HEALTH SCIENCES (medical technology), MATH AND SCIENCES (biology, chemistry, mathematics), PREPROFESSIONAL (dentistry, law, medicine, social work, veterinary), SOCIAL SCIENCES (government/political science, history, social sciences, sociology, sociology—criminal justice). About 30% of the degrees conferred are in education, and 25% in business.

Required: All students must take 2 courses in religious studies or philosophy.

Special: A general-studies degree can be earned.

Admissions: One hundred percent of those who applied were accepted for the 1981–82 freshman class. Preference is given to students who rank in the upper 50% of their graduating class.

Procedure: The SAT or ACT is required. Application deadlines are August 10 (fall), December 31 (spring), and June 1 (summer). Freshmen are admitted in the fall and spring. Notification is made on a rolling basis. There is a $20 application fee.

Transfer: For fall 1981, 109 students applied, 109 were accepted, and 85 enrolled. Students must wait one year before entering if they are not in good academic standing at the former institution. D grades do not transfer. All students must complete, at the college, 30 of the 128 credits required for a bachelor's degree. Application deadlines are the same as those for freshmen.

Visiting: Students can arrange visits to campus through the admissions office. Visitors may sit in on classes and stay at the school.

Financial Aid: About 60% of students receive financial assistance. Twenty percent work part-time on campus. The college awards about 30 freshman scholarships each year. In addition, loans are available through NDSL and United Student Aid Funds. The college takes part in CWS. Grants-in-aid and EOGs are also available. The college is a member of CSS. The FAF and the application for financial aid must be filed by April 1.

Foreign Students: Five percent of the full-time students come from foreign countries. Special counseling and special organizations are available for these students.

Admissions: Foreign students must achieve a TOEFL score of at least 500. No college entrance exams are required.

Procedure: Application deadlines are June 1 (fall) and November 1 (spring). Foreign students must present proof of adequate funds for the intended period of study. A special $100 annual fee covers intensive advising and tutoring. Health insurance is not required, but is available through the college for a fee.

Admissions Contact: Bruce N. Day, Director of Admissions.

EASTERN MONTANA COLLEGE D-3
Billings, Montana 59101 (406) 657-2158

F/T: 980M, 1585W	Faculty: 144; IIA, −$
P/T: 310M, 599W	Ph.D.'s: 85%
Grad: 19M, 83W	S/F Ratio: 18 to 1
Year: qtrs, ss	Tuition: $624 ($1758)
Appl: Sept. 15	R and B: $1995
1030 applied	1029 accepted	835 enrolled
SAT or ACT: required		NONCOMPETITIVE

Eastern Montana College, a state-supported institution founded in 1927 as a teacher-training school, offers programs in business, education, the liberal arts and sciences, and preprofessional fields. Its library contains 110,000 volumes and 140,000 microfilm items.

Environment: The campus is located in a suburban area of Billings, the largest city in Montana. The 14 major buildings include the Special Education Building, which houses the state handicapped center, and 3 high-rise dormitories. The college also maintains off-campus apartments.

Student Life: About 90% of the students are residents of Montana. About 75% live on campus. Four percent are minority-group members. Campus housing is both coed and single-sex. Day-care services are available to all students for a fee. Students may keep cars on campus.

Organizations: There is 1 national fraternity on campus, to which about 1% of the men belong. Special interest clubs and various political, religious, musical, and service organizations are available.

Sports: The college fields 6 intercollegiate teams for men and 6 for women. There are 13 intramural sports for men and 12 for women.

Handicapped: The entire campus is accessible to handicapped students. Facilities include lowered drinking fountains and telephones, elevators, wheelchair ramps, and special parking. About 1% of the students are visually impaired, and 1% hearing-impaired.

Graduates: Twenty-five percent of the full-time freshmen drop out by the end of their first year; 50% remain to graduate. About 20% of the graduates continue their education (1% in medical school, 1% in dental school, and 1% in law school). Another 25% pursue careers in industry and business.

Services: Free health care, psychological counseling, tutoring, remedial instruction, career counseling, and job placement services are available.

Programs of Study: The college confers the B.A., B.S., and B.S.Ed. degrees. Associate and master's degrees are also awarded. Bachelor's degrees are offered in the following subjects: BUSINESS (accounting, business administration, business education, finance, management, marketing), EDUCATION (early childhood, elementary, health/physical, secondary, special), ENGLISH (English, literature, speech), FINE AND PERFORMING ARTS (art, art education, music, music education, music therapy, theater/dramatics), LANGUAGES (French, German, Scandinavian studies, Spanish), MATH AND SCIENCES (biology, chemistry, geology, mathematics, physical sciences), PHILOSOPHY (philosophy), PREPROFESSIONAL (architecture, dentistry, engineering, home economics, law, library science, medicine, pharmacy, social work, veterinary), SOCIAL SCIENCES (economics, geography, government/political science, history, international relations, psychology, social sciences). About 45% of the degrees conferred are in education and 32% in business.

Required: All students must complete general-education requirements.

Special: A combined B.A.-B.S. degree is offered in business.

Honors: Six national honor societies have chapters on campus, and the school offers honors programs in mathematics, English, and foreign language.

Admissions: Almost 100% of those who applied were accepted for the 1981–82 freshman class. All candidates should have a high school diploma; nonresidents should rank in the upper 50% of their graduating class.

Procedure: The SAT or ACT is required. Application deadlines are September 15 for fall, December 15 for winter, March 15 for spring, and May 15 for summer. Freshmen are admitted each semester, and notification is on a rolling basis. There is a $20 application fee.

Special: An early admissions plan is available. CLEP credit is accepted.

Transfer: For fall 1981, 639 transfer students applied, and 479 enrolled. A GPA of 2.0 and an ACT score of at least 16 are required. D grades are transferable. A student must spend 12 months in residence and must complete, at the college, one full academic year's worth of credits out of the 192 required for a bachelor's degree.

Visiting: There is a regularly scheduled orientation 3 days before registration. Arrangements for informal visits (Monday through Friday, 9 A.M. to 3 P.M.) can be made through the admissions office. Visitors may stay overnight.

Financial Aid: About 65% of students receive financial assistance; 40% work part-time on campus. Freshman scholarships and federal loans are available. The FAF is required and must be filed by March 1. The college is a member of CSS.

Foreign Students: Fewer than 1% of the full-time students come from foreign countries. Special counseling and special organizations are available for these students.

Admissions: Foreign students must achieve a TOEFL score of at least 500 and an ACT score of at least 16.

Procedure: Application deadlines are September 1 (fall), December 1 (winter), March 1 (spring), and May 15 (summer). Foreign students must present proof of adequate funds for 1 year and submit evidence of good health. Health insurance, though not required, is available through the college for a fee.

Admissions Contact: Kathy Rumph, Admissions Representative.

MONTANA COLLEGE OF MINERAL SCIENCE AND TECHNOLOGY
B-3

Butte, Montana 59701   (406) 496-4178

F/T: 1200M&W	Faculty: n/av; IIA, +$
P/T: 350M&W	Ph.D.'s: 64%
Grad: 50M&W	S/F Ratio: 20 to 1
Year: early sems, ss	Tuition: $562 ($1930)
Appl: open	R and B: $1950
ACT: 21	361 enrolled COMPETITIVE

Montana College of Mineral Science and Technology, a state-supported institution, was established in 1895. It offers a variety of undergraduate degree programs in engineering, primarily in mining and mineralogy. The library includes 73,000 volumes and 24,000 microfilm items, and subscribes to 700 periodicals.

Environment: The 13-acre urban campus is located in the mining town of Butte, 60 miles from Helena. Coed residence halls accommodate over 200 students.

Student Life: About 83% of the students come from Montana, and 80% are public school graduates. About 25% reside on campus.

Organizations: Extracurricular activities include student government, clubs, and publications. There are 3 fraternities to which 5% of the men belong. There are no sororities.

Sports: The college fields intercollegiate teams in 6 sports. Seven intramural sports are offered.

Handicapped: About 50% of the campus is accessible to handicapped students. Special facilities include wheelchair ramps, parking areas, elevators, specially equipped rest rooms, and lowered drinking fountains. Special class scheduling is also available.

Graduates: About 12% of the graduates pursue advanced degrees, and 88% enter careers in business and industry.

Services: Career counseling and placement services are provided free. Tutoring or remedial instruction and health care require additional fees.

Programs of Study: The college awards the B.A. and B.S. degrees. Master's programs also are available. Bachelor's degrees are offered in the following subjects: BUSINESS (accounting, buisness administration, computer science, finance), HEALTH SCIENCES (occupational safety and health), MATH AND SCIENCES (chemistry, mathematics), PREPROFESSIONAL (engineering—engineering science, engineering—environmental, engineering—geological, engineering—geophysical, engineering—metallurgical, engineering—mineral, engineering—mineral processing, engineering—petroleum).

Required: Students must fulfill general-education requirements.

Special: Qualified upperclassmen may work in nearby mines, mills, or smelters to integrate engineering theory and practice. Students may combine a degree in society and technology with any other program on campus.

Admissions: About 92% of those who applied for a recent freshman class were accepted. SAT scores of those who enrolled were as follows: Verbal—18% between 500 and 599 and 6% between 600 and 700; Math—44% between 500 and 599, 15% between 600 and 700, and 3% above 700. ACT scores were as follows: 36% between 18 and 23, 33% between 24 and 30, 2% above 30. Out-of-state applicants should rank in the upper half of their high school class.

Procedure: The ACT or SAT is required. Application deadlines are open. New students are admitted in fall and at midyear. Notification is made on a rolling basis. There is a $20 application fee.

Special: Early admissions and early decision plans are offered. AP and CLEP credit is accepted.

Transfer: A 2.0 GPA is required. Some preference is given to students from other Montana University System Schools. Students must complete the senior year in residence.

Visiting: There is an orientation program for prospective applicants. Informal campus tours with student guides can be arranged. Visitors may sit in on classes and stay in the dormitories if rooms are available. The admissions office should be contacted for arrangements.

Financial Aid: About 64% of the students receive financial aid. Freshman scholarships, loans (bank and NDSL), grants (such as BEOG and SEOG), and part-time campus employment are offered. April 1 is the aid application deadline. The FAF should be filed.

Foreign Students: The 79 foreign students enrolled full-time make up about 5% of the student body. Special counseling and special

474 MONTANA

organizations are provided. An intensive English course is sometimes available.

Admissions: Applicants must score 500 or better on the TOEFL. If entering as freshmen, they also must take the SAT or ACT.

Procedure: Applications should be filed at least 3 months before the start of the semester in which the student seeks to enroll. The college requires proof of good health and evidence of adequate funds for 1 year. Health insurance, though not required, is available through the college at a fee.

Admissions Contact: Rich Meredith, Director of Admissions.

MONTANA STATE UNIVERSITY C–3
Bozeman, Montana 59717 (406) 994-2452

F/T: 5500M, 4000W	Faculty: n/av; I, – –$
P/T: 600M, 500W	Ph.D.'s: 70%
Grad: 400M, 300W	S/F Ratio: 20 to 1
Year: qtrs, ss	Tuition: $729 ($2168)
Appl: open	R and B: $2143
SAT or ACT: required	NONCOMPETITIVE

Montana State University, established in 1893, offers undergraduate degree programs in agriculture, arts and sciences, business, education, nursing, engineering, and preprofessional areas. The library contains over 500,000 volumes and 400,000 microfilm items, and subscribes to 10,000 periodicals.

Environment: The 1170-acre campus is located in a small city 90 miles north of Yellowstone National Park. The 40 major buildings include residence halls that accommodate 1196 women and 1608 men. Housing complexes for married students (646 families) and facilities for commuting students also are available.

Student Life: Most of the students come from Montana. About half live in the single-sex and coed dormitories. Most of the students come from public schools.

Organizations: Extracurricular activities include campus government, clubs, service and religious groups, publications, performing groups, and regularly scheduled on-campus social and cultural events. Five percent of the students belong to 1 of the 11 fraternities and 7 sororities.

Sports: The university fields intercollegiate teams in 7 sports for men and 5 for women. Coed riflery and rodeo teams also are available. At least 7 intramural sports are offered for both sexes.

Handicapped: About 85% of the campus is accessible to handicapped students. Special facilities include wheelchair ramps, elevators, parking areas, specially equipped rest rooms, and lowered drinking fountains and telephones. Three counselors are available to handicapped students.

Graduates: The freshman dropout rate is 20%. About 5% of the graduates pursue advanced degrees, and 60% enter careers in business and industry.

Services: Free career counseling, placement, health care, psychological counseling, and tutoring or remedial instruction are offered.

Programs of Study: The university confers the B.A., B.S., B.Arch., B.S.Ag., B.S.Bus., B.S.Comp.Sci, B.S.N., and B.S. in Engineering degrees. Master's and doctoral programs are also available. Bachelor's degrees are offered in the following subjects: AREA STUDIES (Native American), BUSINESS (accounting, agricultural business, business administration, business education, computer science, finance, management, marketing, office administration), EDUCATION (agricultural, elementary, health/physical, industrial, secondary), ENGLISH (English, literature, speech), FINE AND PERFORMING ARTS (art, art education, art history, music education, film/photography, radio/TV, theater/dramatics), HEALTH SCIENCES (environmental health, nursing), MATH AND SCIENCES (biology, botany, chemistry, earth science, entomology, geology, mathematics, meteorology, microbiology, natural sciences, physics, statistics, zoology), PHILOSOPHY (philosophy, religion), PREPROFESSIONAL (agriculture—animal science, agriculture—farm and ranch management, agriculture—mechanized agriculture, agriculture—plant protection, agriculture—plant and soil science, agriculture—range science, agriculture—land resources, agriculture—landscape horticulture, architecture, engineering—agricultural, engineering—chemical, engineering—civil, engineering—construction technology, engineering—electrical, engineering—electronic, engineering—engineering science, engineering—industrial and management, engineering—mechanical, forestry, home economics, law, library science, medicine, pharmacy), SOCIAL SCIENCES (anthropology, economics, geography, government/political science, history, psychology, public administration, sociology).

Required: Students must fulfill distribution requirements.

Special: Students may design their own majors. A 3-2 engineering program, independent study, study abroad, and exchange programs are offered.

Honors: Numerous honor societies have chapters on campus.

Admissions: About 86% of the applicants for a recent freshman class were accepted. Graduates of accredited Montana high schools are admitted upon the presentation of their certificates of graduation. Out-of-state applicants should rank in the upper half of their class and have completed 16 units of academic work.

Procedure: The SAT or ACT is required. New students are admitted each quarter; application deadlines are open. There is a $20 application fee. Early application for college housing is recommended.

Special: Early and deferred admissions plans are offered. AP and CLEP credit is given.

Transfer: A 2.0 GPA is necessary for out-of-state applicants. D grades transfer. There is a 1-year residency rule.

Visiting: There are regularly scheduled orientations for prospective students. Campus tours with student guides can be arranged. Visitors may sit in on classes and stay overnight at the school. The admissions office should be contacted for arrangements.

Financial Aid: About 75% of the students receive financial aid. The university participates in federal NDSL, BEOG/SEOG, and CWS programs and offers commercial loans, other kinds of campus employment, and freshman scholarships. Need is the determining factor. April 1 is the priority-consideration deadline for financial aid applications. The FAF is required.

Foreign Students: The university accepts foreign students.

Admissions: A score of 500 or better on the TOEFL is required.

Procedure: Application deadlines are open. Students must provide proof of adequate funds.

Admissions Contact: Mark A. Samaras, Assistant Director of Admissions.

NORTHERN MONTANA COLLEGE D–1
Havre, Montana 59501 (406) 265-7821

F/T: 758M, 526W	Faculty: 77; IIA, –$
P/T: 159M, 141W	Ph.D.'s: 34%
Grad: 68M, 70W	S/F Ratio: 14 to 1
Year: qtrs, ss	Tuition: $553 ($1561)
Appl: open	R and B: $1801
498 applied	495 accepted 474 enrolled
ACT: required	NONCOMPETITIVE

Northern Montana College, established in 1929, is a publicly supported unit of the Montana University System, offering teacher education, liberal arts, and technological programs. Its library contains 88,000 volumes and 145,000 microfilm items, and subscribes to 600 periodicals.

Environment: The 105-acre campus is located in the rural Northern High Plains region of the state, 110 miles north of Great Falls. The college maintains dormitories, on-campus apartments, and married student housing.

Student Life: Nearly all students are state residents, and 68% live on campus. About 90% of the freshmen come from public schools. One percent of the students are minority-group members. Campus housing is single-sex with visiting privileges. Students may keep cars on campus.

Organizations: There are no fraternities or sororities on campus. Religious, special-interest, and social organizations sponsor various events, usually at the student union.

Sports: The college fields 3 intercollegiate teams for men and 3 for women. There are 6 intramural sports for men and 6 for women.

Handicapped: Most of the campus is inaccessible to handicapped students. Specially equipped rest rooms and parking facilities are provided.

Graduates: About 8% of those who graduate continue their education; 40% of the graduates pursue careers in business and industry.

Services: Free tutoring, remedial instruction, career counseling, and job placement services are offered to students.

Programs of Study: The college confers the B.A., B.S., B.S.Ed., and B.T. degrees. Associate and master's degrees are also awarded. Bachelor's degrees are offered in the following subjects: BUSINESS (business administration, business education), EDUCATION (elementary, health/physical, industrial), ENGLISH (English), MATH AND

SCIENCES (mathematics), PREPROFESSIONAL (automotive mechanics, drafting, electronics, industrial arts), SOCIAL SCIENCES (history, social sciences).

Admissions: About 99% of those who applied were accepted for the 1981-82 freshman class. Candidates should be graduates of an accredited high school, have a GED, or be at least 21 years of age. Nonresidents must have graduated in the upper 50% of their high school class or have scored at least 16 on the ACT.

Procedure: The ACT is required, and can be taken on campus. There are no deadlines for applications, and freshmen are admitted to all terms. A $20 application fee is charged.

Transfer: For fall 1981, 185 students applied, 180 were accepted, and 155 enrolled. Good academic standing is required. D grades transfer. Students must reside at the college for at least 1 year and must complete, at the college, 45 of the 192 credits required for a bachelor's degree. There are no application deadlines; transfer students are admitted in all terms.

Visiting: Prospective students can visit the campus any time through arrangement with the admissions office. Tours of the campus and class observation are possible, and visitors may stay at the school.

Financial Aid: About 37% of students receive financial aid. Loans are available from the federal government, the college, and private sources. The aid application deadline is March 1.

Foreign Students: About 1% of the full-time students come from foreign countries. Special counseling is available.

Admissions: Foreign students must achieve a TOEFL score of at least 500. No college entrance exams are required.

Procedure: Foreign students are admitted in the fall, winter, and spring terms. The application is due on registration day. Foreign students must present proof of adequate funds and of good health.

Admissions Contact: Ralph A. Brigham, Director of Admissions.

ROCKY MOUNTAIN COLLEGE D-3
Billings, Montana 59102 (406) 245-6151

F/T: 203M, 168W Faculty: 30; IIB, —$
P/T: 16M, 7W Ph.D.'s: 47%
Grad: none S/F Ratio: 12 to 1
Year: 4-4-1, ss Tuition: $2905
Appl: Aug. 15 R and B: $1806
206 applied 194 accepted 140 enrolled
SAT: 495V 495M ACT:21 LESS COMPETITIVE

Rocky Mountain College, founded in 1878, is a liberal arts institution related to the United Methodist Church, the United Church of Christ, and the United Presbyterian Church in the United States of America. Its library contains 60,000 volumes and subscribes to 146 periodicals.

Environment: The 65-acre campus is located in the city of Billings (population over 100,000). The new Bair Center for the sciences opened in 1981. The dormitories on campus accommodate 375 students.

Student Life: About 64% of the students are residents of Montana. Approximately 96% of the freshmen come from public schools. About 70% of the students live on campus. Twenty-three percent of the students are Catholic and 65% are Protestant. Sixteen percent of the students are minority-group members. College housing is both single-sex and coed. There are visiting privileges in single-sex housing. Students may keep cars on campus.

Organizations: There are no fraternities or sororities. Special-interest and religious groups sponsor social and cultural events on campus.

Sports: The college competes in 2 intercollegiate sports for men and 2 for women. There are 13 intramural sports for men and 14 for women.

Handicapped: There are no special facilities for physically handicapped students. Fewer than 1% of the student body are visually impaired; tutoring is provided to help them.

Graduates: Forty percent of the freshmen drop out during their first year; 40% remain to graduate. Of these, 20% continue their education with graduate studies. Two percent enter medical school and 4% law school. Fifty-five percent pursue careers in business and industry.

Services: Free health care, psychological and career counseling, tutoring, remedial instruction, and job placement services are offered.

Programs of Study: The college confers the B.A. and B.S. degrees. Associate degrees are also granted. Bachelor's degrees are offered in the following subjects: BUSINESS (business administration), EDUCATION (elementary, physical, secondary), ENGLISH (English, English/ drama), FINE AND PERFORMING ARTS (art, music, music education), MATH AND SCIENCES (biology, chemistry, geology, mathematics, natural sciences), PHILOSOPHY (Christian thought, philosophy), PREPROFESSIONAL (dentistry, engineering, law, medicine, ministry, veterinary), SOCIAL SCIENCES (anthropology, history of ideas, history/political science, psychology, sociology).

Required: One course in Christian thought and various distribution requirements are part of the curriculum.

Special: Independent study, student-designed majors, junior-year-abroad programs, and a general studies degree are offered. Also available is the Cooperative Education Program, which provides an opportunity for students to work in an academically related occupation during the junior and senior years, receiving credit for the work.

Honors: Pi Kappa Delta and Alpha Psi Omega honor societies are represented on campus.

Admissions: About 94% of the students who applied were accepted for the 1981-82 freshman class. Their ACT scores were as follows: 50% below 21, 28% between 21 and 23; 7% between 24 and 25, 11% between 26 and 28, and 0% above 28. Candidates should have a 2.0 average or better. Recommendations, extracurricular activities, and leadership record are also considered.

Procedure: The ACT or SAT is required. Application deadlines are as follows: August 15 (fall), January 1 (winter), May 1 (summer). Freshmen are admitted each semester. There is a rolling admissions plan. The application fee is $15.

Special: Early admissions, early decision, and deferred admissions are possible. AP and CLEP credit is given.

Transfer: For fall 1981, 32 students applied, 30 were accepted, and 21 enrolled. A minimum GPA of 2.0 is required, and D grades do not transfer. There is a 1-year residency requirement, and students must complete, at the college, 30 of the 124 semester hours needed for a bachelor's degree. Application deadlines are August 15 (fall) and January 1 (spring).

Visiting: There is a regularly scheduled orientation for prospective students, who may tour the campus, visit classes, and talk with the faculty. Special arrangements can also be made through the admissions office for informal visits during regular class sessions. Visitors may stay at the school.

Financial Aid: About 80% of students receive financial assistance. Forty-four percent work part-time on campus. Freshman aid averages $2200. Grants and loans are also available from the federal government and the college. The college is a member of CSS. The FAF must be submitted. The deadlines for applying for aid are April 15 (fall) and January 1 (spring).

Foreign Students: About 5% of the full-time students come from foreign countries.

Admissions: Foreign students must score 500 on the TOEFL. No college entrance examination is required.

Procedure: Foreign students are admitted in the fall and the spring. They must present proof of funds adequate for at least 1 year of study, and must also carry health insurance.

Admissions Contact: Steve Olson, Director of Admissions.

UNIVERSITY OF MONTANA B-2
Missoula, Montana 59812 (406) 243-6266

F/T: 3739M, 3564W Faculty: 400; I, — —$
P/T: 397M, 480W Ph.D.'s: 82%
Grad: 557M, 500W S/F Ratio: 19 to 1
Year: qtrs, ss Tuition: $747 ($2115)
Appl: see profile R and B: $1900
1803 applied 1654 accepted 1230 enrolled
SAT or ACT: required NONCOMPETITIVE

The University of Montana, established in 1893, is a public institution offering undergraduate curricula in liberal arts and sciences, fine and applied arts, education, business, and several preprofessional areas. The library contains 550,000 volumes and 250,000 microfilm items, and subscribes to 1800 periodicals.

Environment: The university is composed of a 181-acre suburban main campus, an additional 519 mountainside acres, a 180-acre south campus, and additional experimental forestry and farmland acreage. University housing includes dormitories, on-campus apartments, off-campus apartments, fraternity and sorority houses, and married-student housing.

Student Life: About 75% of the students come from Montana. Most are public school graduates. About 75% live on campus. About 3% are

476 MONTANA

minority-group members. Campus housing is both coed and single-sex; there are visiting privileges in the single-sex housing. Students may keep cars on campus.

Organizations: The extracurricular program includes clubs, student government, dramatics, performing groups, publications, social and cultural events, and religious and service organizations. Five percent of the men and 11% of the women belong to fraternities and sororities.

Sports: The university fields 7 intercollegiate teams for men and 8 for women. There are 8 intramural sports for men and 8 for women.

Graduates: The freshman dropout rate is 30%; about 45% remain to graduate.

Services: Psychological counseling, remedial instruction, placement, and career counseling are offered free of charge. Health care and tutoring are available for a fee.

Programs of Study: The B.A., B.S., B.S.B.A., B.F.A., B.A.Ed., and B.M.E. degrees are conferred. Associate, master's, and doctoral degrees are also awarded. Bachelor's degrees are offered in the following subjects: BUSINESS (accounting, business administration, business education, computer science, finance, management), EDUCATION (early childhood, elementary, health/physical, home economics, secondary), ENGLISH (English, interpersonal communication, journalism), FINE AND PERFORMING ARTS (art, art education, art history, dance, music, music education, radio/TV, theater/dramatics), HEALTH SCIENCES (medical technology, physical therapy, speech therapy), LANGUAGES (French, German, Greek/Latin, Russian, Spanish), MATH AND SCIENCES (biology, botany, chemistry, geology, mathematics, microbiology, natural sciences, physical sciences, physics, resource conservation, wildlife biology, zoology), PHILOSOPHY (classics, humanities, philosophy, religion), PREPROFESSIONAL (agriculture, architecture, dentistry, engineering, forestry, law, library science, medicine, ministry, pharmacy, veterinary), SOCIAL SCIENCES (anthropology, economics, geography, government/political science, history, psychology, social sciences, sociology).

Required: Required courses depend on the individual major.

Special: A general-studies degree, study abroad, and an intensive humanities program are offered.

Honors: Various departments offer honors work. Numerous honor societies have chapters on campus.

Admissions: About 92% of those who applied for the 1981-82 freshman class were accepted. All Montana residents with high school or GED diplomas are accepted; out-of-state applicants must rank in the top half of their graduating class. Advanced placement or honors courses, recommendations, and leadership qualities are also considered. Each professional school requires a certain pattern of high school work.

Procedure: The ACT or SAT is required. New students are admitted each quarter. The application should be filed at least 1 month before the start of the term. Notification is on a rolling basis. There is a $20 application fee.

Special: There is an early admissions program. AP and CLEP credit is available.

Transfer: For fall 1981, 1350 students applied, 1205 were accepted, and 1071 enrolled. Transfers are accepted for all classes. A 2.0 GPA is needed. D grades are acceptable. Students must spend at least 12 months in residence and must complete, at the university, 45 of the 195 credits required for a bachelor's degree. Application deadlines are the same as those for freshmen.

Visiting: A tour of the campus with a student guide may be arranged. Visitors are allowed to sit in on classes.

Financial Aid: About 40% of the students receive financial aid. Forty percent work part-time on campus. The university participates in federal programs such as NDSL, BEOG/SEOG, and CWS in addition to offering loans and freshman scholarships. State assistance is also available. The average award to freshmen from all sources was $1100 in 1981-82. The university is a member of CSS. The FAF should be filed no later than April 1.

Foreign Students: Fewer than 2% of the full-time students come from foreign countries. Special counseling and special organizations are available for these students.

Admissions: Foreign students must achieve a TOEFL score of at least 500. No college entrance exams are required.

Procedure: Applications must be filed at least 30 days before the start of each term. Foreign students must present proof of good health (a self-report health form) and of adequate funds. They also must carry health insurance, which is available through the university for a fee.

Admissions Contact: Michael L. Akin, Director of Admissions.

WESTERN MONTANA COLLEGE B-3
Dillon, Montana 59725 (406) 683-7331

F/T: 330M, 291W Faculty: 43; IIA, –$
P/T: 51M, 78W Ph.D.'s: 47%
Grad: 6M, 1W S/F Ratio: 16 to 1
Year: sems, ss Tuition: $591 ($1599)
Appl: open R and B: $1924
230 applied 230 accepted 199 enrolled
ACT: 17 NONCOMPETITIVE

Western Montana College, a state-supported institution, offers 4-year undergraduate programs in natural heritage, human resource management, and education. Its library contains 80,000 volumes and 22,900 microfilm items, and subscribes to 320 periodicals.

Environment: The college is located in a rural area 65 miles from Butte. The college maintains dormitories and married-student housing.

Student Life: About 90% of the students are from Montana. Approximately 90% come from public schools. About 60% of the students live on campus. One percent of the students are minority-group members. Campus housing is both coed and single-sex; there are visiting privileges in the single-sex housing. Students may keep cars on campus.

Organizations: There are no fraternities or sororities. The college sponsors plays, lectures, and social affairs.

Sports: The college fields 5 intercollegiate teams for men and 4 for women. There are 8 intramural sports for men and 8 for women.

Handicapped: No special facilities are provided for physically handicapped students.

Graduates: About 20% of the freshmen drop out during their first year; 50% remain to graduate. Of those, about 13% enter business and industry.

Services: Free psychological counseling, career counseling, and job placement services are offered to students. Health care, tutoring, and remedial instruction are available for a fee.

Programs of Study: The college confers the B.S. in Elem. Ed., B.S. in Sec. Ed., B.A. in Natural Heritage, B.S. in Natural Heritage, and B.S. in Human Resource Management degrees. Associate and master's degrees are also awarded. Bachelor's degrees are offered in the following subjects: BUSINESS (business education, management), EDUCATION (elementary, health/physical, industrial, secondary), ENGLISH (English education), FINE AND PERFORMING ARTS (art education), MATH AND SCIENCES (biology education, mathematics education, physical sciences education), PREPROFESSIONAL (social work), SOCIAL SCIENCES (history and social science education).

Special: Students may earn a 3-year bachelor's degree. A combined B.A.-B.S. degree in education and natural heritage is offered.

Honors: Kappa Delta Pi has a chapter on campus.

Admissions: All applicants were accepted for the 1981-82 freshman class. The ACT scores of those who enrolled were as follows: 75% scored below 21, 21% between 21 and 25, and 4% above 25. Candidates should be graduates of an accredited high school.

Procedure: The college recommends the ACT, but will accept the SAT or ATP. Freshmen are admitted each semester. Notification is on a rolling basis. There is a $20 application fee.

Special: CLEP credit is offered.

Transfer: For fall 1981, 84 students applied, 84 were accepted, and 69 enrolled. Students must take the ACT or SAT and must have a GPA of at least 2.0. D grades transfer. Students must spend at least 2 semesters at the college and must complete, at the college, 30 of the 128 credits required for a bachelor's degree. There are no application deadlines.

Visiting: Special arrangements can be made through the admissions office for visits on Thursdays or Fridays. Visitors may sit in on classes and stay overnight at the school.

Financial Aid: About 65% of all students receive financial assistance. About 25% work part-time on campus. Approximately 100 freshman scholarships are awarded each year in amounts totaling $30,000. Pell grants and loans are available from the federal government, the college, and private sources. The average aid given to a freshman from all sources was about $1250 in 1981-82. This can be combined with part-time employment in some cases to pay a first-year student's full expenses. Either the FAF or FFS is required; the former is preferred. The college is a member of CSS. The deadline for aid application is April 1.

Foreign Students: No foreign students were enrolled at the college in 1981-82.

Admissions: Foreign students must achieve a TOEFL score of at least 500 and must take the ACT or SAT.

Procedure: Application deadlines are September 1 (fall), January 11 (spring), and June 15 (summer). Foreign students must present proof of adequate funds for 1 year. Health insurance is not required but is available through the college for a fee.

Admissions Contact: Bill Stenberg, Associate Director of Admissions.

NEBRASKA

BELLEVUE COLLEGE F-3
Bellevue, Nebraska 68005 (402) 291-8100

F/T: 458M, 317W	Faculty: 31; IIB, --$
P/T: 959M, 881W	Ph.D.'s: 39%
Grad: none	S/F Ratio: 25 to 1
Year: sems, tri, ss	Tuition: $1140
Appl: open	R and B: n/app
1101 applied	1101 accepted	1101 enrolled
ACT: 16		NONCOMPETITIVE

Bellevue College, founded in 1966, is a private, liberal arts, commuter college with day and evening classes. The library has 64,000 volumes and 5000 microfilm units, and subscribes to 300 periodicals.

Environment: The 7½-acre campus is located 1 mile from the center of suburban Bellevue (pop. 25,000). The 10 campus buildings include a science center, a physical-health center, and a new humanities center. There are no student residences.

Student Life: Ninety-five percent of the students are from Nebraska. Ninety percent come from public schools. About 17% of the students are minority-group members. Students may keep cars on campus.

Organizations: Students participate in school government and publications. There are no fraternities or sororities.

Sports: Two intercollegiate sports are available for men and 2 for women. There are 3 intramural programs each for men and women.

Handicapped: The entire campus is accessible to the physically handicapped. Facilities include parking, ramps, and lowered drinking fountains.

Graduates: About 12% of the students drop out by the end of the freshman year, and 40% remain to graduate. Twenty percent of the graduates seek advanced degrees, while 60% begin careers in business and industry.

Services: Services offered free to students include placement aid, psychological counseling, career counseling, and remedial instruction. Tutoring is available on a fee basis.

Programs of Study: The college confers the B.A. and B.F.A. degrees. Bachelor's degrees are offered in the following subjects: AREA STUDIES (urban), BUSINESS (business administration), EDUCATION (health/physical), ENGLISH (English), FINE AND PERFORMING ARTS (art, studio art), LANGUAGES (Spanish), MATH AND SCIENCES (mathematics), PHILOSOPHY (philosophy), SOCIAL SCIENCES (geography, government/political science, history, psychology, social sciences, sociology).

Required: All undergraduates must take 66 credit hours in the core curriculum. To graduate, a student must maintain an overall GPA of 2.0 and a GPA of 2.5 in the major.

Special: The college strives to offer individual attention and seeks to attract the nontraditional student. It operates on a traditional semester system for day classes, on the trimester system for evening classes. Students can earn the B.A. degree with a combination of day and night programs.

Honors: Alpha Chi and Alpha Kappa Psi have chapters on campus.

Admissions: All students who applied were accepted for the 1981–82 freshman class. On the ACT, 79% of those who enrolled scored below 21, 16% between 21 and 23, 3% between 24 and 25, 1% between 26 and 28, and 1% above 28. Applicants must be graduates of an accredited high school and rank in the upper two-thirds of their class. Other considerations include recommendations by school officials, personality, and impressions made during an interview.

Procedure: The ACT or SAT is required and may be taken at any time. Junior-year results are acceptable. Application deadlines are open. The college has a rolling admissions plan. A $10 fee must accompany the application.

Special: Early admissions and early decision plans are available. CLEP credit is accepted.

Transfer: For fall 1981, 652 students applied, were accepted, and enrolled. Applicants must rank in the upper two-thirds of their class. D grades do not transfer. Students must complete at least 30 hours in residence of the 127 required for a bachelor's degree. Application deadlines are open.

Visiting: Regularly scheduled orientations for prospective students include personal admissions counseling and advising sessions. Guides are provided for informal visits, and visitors may sit in on classes. The best time for campus visits is in the spring; the admissions office makes arrangements.

Financial Aid: About 63% of the students are receiving financial aid. About 3% work part-time on campus. Average aid to freshmen from all sources was $500 in 1981–82. Federal loan and work-study funds are available. Tuition may be paid on an installment plan. The college is a member of CSS. Need is the principal consideration in determining the award. The FAF is required. The application deadline is March 15 for all semesters.

Foreign Students: The 40 full-time students from foreign countries make up 5% of the enrollment. The college offers these students an intensive English course.

Admissions: Foreign students must score at least 470 on the TOEFL or at least 70 on the University of Michigan Language Test. No college entrance examination is required.

Procedure: Application deadlines are open; students are admitted to all terms. Foreign students must present proof of adequate funds for their entire period of study.

Admissions Contact: Pierre Flatowicz, Director of Admissions.

CHADRON STATE COLLEGE B-1
Chadron, Nebraska 69337 (308) 432-6263

F/T: 631M, 657W	Faculty: 89; IIA, av$
P/T: 242M, 449W	Ph.D.'s: 53%
Grad: 170M, 272W	S/F Ratio: 16 to 1
Year: sems, ss	Tuition: $724 ($1174)
Appl: see profile	R and B: $1500
490 applied	490 accepted	340 enrolled
ACT: 18		NONCOMPETITIVE

Chadron State College, established in 1911, is a state-administered liberal arts and teachers' college. The library contains 135,000 volumes and subscribes to 900 periodicals.

Environment: The campus occupies 213 acres in a rural setting at the edge of scenic Pine Ridge, 90 miles from Rapid City, South Dakota. Residence halls accommodate 1700 men and women, and there are 49 apartments for married students. Facilities for day students include a student lounge and a cafeteria.

Student Life: Eighty-two percent of the students come from Nebraska, and 95% come from public schools. About 41% live on campus. Two percent are minority-group members. Thirty-eight percent are Protestant, and 32% are Catholic. Campus housing is both coed and single-sex; there are visiting privileges in the single-sex housing. Students may keep cars on campus. Day-care services are available to all students.

Organizations: Five percent of the men and 5% of the women are members of fraternities or sororities. Numerous extracurricular activities are offered to students.

Sports: The college fields 7 intercollegiate teams for men and 6 for women. There are 8 intramural sports for men and 7 for women.

Graduates: Thirty percent of the freshmen drop out by the end of the first year, and 60% remain to graduate. Thirty percent of the graduates pursue further study.

Services: Career and psychological counseling, tutoring, and remedial instruction are offered free. Fees are charged for health care and placement services.

Programs of Study: The college confers the B.A. and B.S. degrees. Associate and master's degrees are also awarded. Bachelor's degrees are offered in the following subjects: BUSINESS (accounting, business administration, business education, computer science, management, marketing, real estate/insurance), EDUCATION (early childhood, elementary, health/physical, industrial, secondary, special), ENGLISH (English, speech), FINE AND PERFORMING ARTS (art, art education, music, music education, theater/dramatics), MATH AND SCIENCES (biology, chemistry, earth science, mathematics, natural sciences, physical sciences, physics), SOCIAL SCIENCES (criminal justice, economics, government/political science, history, psychology, social sciences, social work, sociology).

Special: The college offers a variety of summer workshops and also sponsors a number of European and American tours.

Admissions: All applicants were admitted to the 1981–82 freshman class. Applicants must have graduated from an accredited high school and have completed 15 units of high school work. The ACT score, the high school transcript, and the counselor's recommendation are all considered. Admission is open for Nebraska applicants; there are higher standards for nonresidents.

Procedure: The ACT is required. There are no application deadlines, but it is suggested that applications be submitted by August 15 for fall entry and December 15 for spring entry. Freshmen are also admitted to the summer term. Notification is made on a rolling basis. There is a $10 application fee.

Special: There is a deferred admissions plan. CLEP credit is used.

Transfer: Nearly all transfer applicants are accepted; about 100 enroll each year. Good academic standing is necessary. All students must complete, at the college, at least 30 of the 125 credits required for a bachelor's degree. Applications should be submitted by August 15 (fall) and December 15 (winter). Transfer students are also admitted in the summer.

Financial Aid: About 70% of the students receive aid. The average aid to freshmen in 1981–82 was $1250. CWS is available in all departments; 40% of the students work part-time. The BEOG must be filed. There are no application deadlines; awards are made on a first-come, first-served basis. The college is a member of CSS.

Foreign Students: The 29 full-time students from foreign countries make up 2% of enrollment. Special counseling and special organizations are available for these students.

Admissions: Foreign students must score at least 500 on the TOEFL. No college entrance exams are required.

Procedure: Application deadlines are July 15 (fall), December 15 (spring), and May 1 (summer). Foreign students must fill out a health form and present proof of adequate funds for 1 year. Health insurance is required and is available through the college.

Admissions Contact: Randy Bauer, Director of Admissions.

COLLEGE OF SAINT MARY F-2
Omaha, Nebraska 68124 (402) 393-8800

F/T: 16M, 408W		Faculty:	47; IIB, — —$
P/T: 125M, 348W		Ph.D.'s:	20%
Grad: none		S/F Ratio:	9 to 1
Year: sems, ss		Tuition:	$3606
Appl: open		R and B:	$1576
376 applied	340 accepted		232 enrolled
ACT: 18			LESS COMPETITIVE

The College of Saint Mary is a private, independent, 4-year liberal arts college for women conducted by the Sisters of Mercy. Men are accepted into the health-sciences programs. The library has 56,000 volumes.

Environment: The 43-acre campus is located in a suburban area of metropolitan Omaha. Facilities include an administration building with classrooms, an art gallery, 2 residence halls, a science hall, and a college center that contains the cafeteria, bookstore, lounges, recreation rooms, and snack bar.

Student Life: About 73% of students come from Nebraska. Seventy-four percent come from public schools. About 33% live on campus. Ten percent are minority-group members. About 59% are Catholic. Campus housing is single-sex, with visiting privileges. Students may keep cars on campus. Day-care services are available for a fee.

Organizations: Students participate in extracurricular clubs. Cultural activities on campus include exhibitions and performances of the arts by local and nationally known artists. There are no social sororities or fraternities.

Sports: The college fields 5 intercollegiate teams for women. There are 7 intramural sports for women.

Handicapped: The campus has no special facilities for the handicapped.

Graduates: About 12% of the freshmen drop out during the first year, and 51% remain to graduate.

Services: Students receive the following free services: placement, career counseling, health care, tutoring, and remedial instruction. Psychological counseling is provided on a fee basis.

Programs of Study: The college confers the B.A., B.S., and B.S. in Computer Information Management degrees. Associate degrees are also awarded. Bachelor's degrees are offered in the following subjects: BUSINESS (accounting, business administration, business education, computer science), EDUCATION (early childhood, elementary, recreation, secondary), ENGLISH (English, language arts), FINE AND PERFORMING ARTS (art, art education, music, music education), HEALTH SCIENCES (medical records administration, medical technology, respiratory therapy, therapeutic recreation), MATH AND SCIENCES (biology, chemistry), PHILOSOPHY (humanities), PREPROFESSIONAL (dentistry, law, medicine, pharmacy, social work), SOCIAL SCIENCES (history, social sciences). Seventy-eight percent of degrees conferred are in health sciences.

Required: Four-year students must complete general-education requirements.

Special: Some programs offer students a chance for on-the-job training.

Honors: Five national honor societies have chapters on campus. Five departments offer honors programs.

Admissions: Ninety percent of those who applied were accepted for the 1981–82 freshman class. The ACT scores of those who enrolled were as follows: 61% below 21, 17% between 21 and 23, 14% between 24 and 25, 6% between 26 and 28, and 3% above 28. Applicants should have a GPA of at least 2.0, rank in the upper half of their class, and have an ACT score of 17 or more. Other considerations include recommendations by high school officials, leadership record, advanced placement or honors courses, evidence of special talents, and impressions made during an interview.

Procedure: The ACT is required. There is a rolling admissions plan. Applications are accepted until the date of registration. The application fee is $15. Freshmen are admitted in the fall, at midyear, and in the summer.

Special: Early admissions and deferred admissions are available. CLEP and AP are used.

Transfer: For fall 1981, 126 students applied, 106 were accepted, and 88 enrolled. Applicants must meet basic freshman requirements. D grades do not transfer. All students must complete, at the college, at least 30 of the 128 credits required for a bachelor's degree. Application deadlines are open; students are admitted to all terms.

Visiting: Orientations for prospective students are usually held in November and March. Guided tours can be scheduled 5 days a week. Visitors may stay overnight at the school and sit in on classes. The admissions office arranges visits.

Financial Aid: About 80% of all students receive aid through scholarships, loans, jobs, and grants. About 40% work part-time on campus. All federal aid offered to college students is available. Either the FAF, FFS, or SFS is required; the FAF is preferred. The deadlines for aid applications are April 15 (fall), December 15 (spring), and May 15 (summer). The college is a member of CSS.

Foreign Students: The 7 full-time students from foreign countries make up less than 1% of enrollment.

Admissions: Foreign students must score at least 500 on the TOEFL. No college entrance exams are required.

Procedure: There are no application deadlines; foreign students are admitted to all terms. They must undergo a physical exam and present proof of adequate funds for 4 years.

Admissions Contact: Gary Johnson, Director of Admissions.

CONCORDIA TEACHERS COLLEGE E-3
Seward, Nebraska 68434 (402) 643-3651

F/T: 432M, 532W		Faculty:	n/av; IIA, — —$
P/T: 20M, 59W		Ph.D.'s:	45%
Grad: 10M, 13W		S/F Ratio:	16 to 1
Year: 4-1-4, ss		Tuition:	$2990
Appl: open		R and B:	$1570
389 applied	328 accepted		233 enrolled
ACT: 20			COMPETITIVE

Concordia Teachers College is affiliated with the Missouri Synod of the Lutheran Church. The library contains 120,000 volumes and 8000 microfilm items, and subscribes to 650 periodicals.

Environment: The 120-acre campus is located in a rural environment 25 miles from Lincoln. Living facilities include dormitories and married-student housing.

Student Life: About 75% of the students are from out of state. Ninety percent live on campus. Seventy percent come from public schools. All faculty members and most students are Lutheran; 1% of the students are Catholic. Six percent are minority-group members. Student regulations prohibit drinking on campus. Campus housing is single-sex; there are visiting privileges. Students may keep cars on campus.

Organizations: There are no Greek-letter societies on campus.

Sports: Concordia fields 9 intercollegiate teams for men and 7 for women. There are 7 intramural sports for men and 6 for women.

Handicapped: Sixty percent of the campus is accessible to the handicapped. There are ramps, special parking, lowered drinking fountains and phones, and specially equipped rest rooms.

Graduates: About 23% of the freshmen drop out, and 60% remain to graduate. Approximately 7% of the graduates pursue advanced degrees; 1% attend medical school. Five percent enter business and industry.

Services: The following services are available free to students: placement aid, career counseling, and tutoring. Health care and remedial instruction are provided on a fee basis.

Programs of Study: The college grants the B.A. and B.S.Ed. degrees. Master's degrees are also conferred. Bachelor's degrees are offered in the following subjects: BUSINESS (accounting, business administration, business education, management), EDUCATION (Christian, early childhood, elementary, secondary, special), ENGLISH (English, literature, speech), FINE AND PERFORMING ARTS (art education, music education, studio art), HEALTH SCIENCES (medical technology), MATH AND SCIENCES (biology, chemistry, mathematics), PHILOSOPHY (religion), PREPROFESSIONAL (dentistry, law, medicine, ministry, pharmacy, social work), SOCIAL SCIENCES (geography, history, social sciences, sociology). Eighty-five percent of the degrees conferred are in education.

Required: All students must complete general-education requirements, which include courses in religion.

Special: A fifth-year program is offered for classroom teachers, directors of Christian education, and youth workers. It is possible to earn a combined B.A.-B.S. degree in education and liberal arts.

Admissions: Approximately 84% of those who applied were accepted for the 1981–82 freshman class. Students must have an average of at least C, a good recommendation from the high school, and 15 Carnegie units. They must rank in the top half of their high school class. GPA, class rank, and ACT are considered. Other considerations include advanced placement or honors courses, and personality.

Procedure: Applicants are required to take the ACT. There is no application fee and the deadlines for applying are open; freshmen are admitted in the fall, spring, and summer terms. Admissions are on a rolling basis.

Special: There are early decision and early admissions plans. AP and CLEP are used.

Transfer: Recently, the college received 180 transfer applications, accepted 120, and enrolled 80 students. A 2.0 GPA is required and D grades will transfer. All students must complete, at the college, at least 30 of the 128 credits required for a bachelor's degree. Application deadlines are August 26 (fall), January 29 (spring), and June 5 (summer).

Visiting: Guides are provided for informal visits. Visitors may sit in on classes. Visits are permitted whenever classes are in session and there are facilities for overnight stays. Arrangements should be made through the admissions office.

Financial Aid: Ninety percent of all students receive aid. About 25% work part-time on campus. The average freshman award in 1981–82 was $2700. Scholarships and loans (federal and local) are available. The most financial assistance a freshman can expect from all sources, including college employment, is about $4500. Concordia is a member of the CSS and requires either the FAF, the FFS, or the SFS. Aid applications must be filed by April 15 (summer or fall entry) or December 1 (spring entry).

Foreign Students: The 26 full-time students from foreign countries make up 3% of enrollment. An intensive English course is available for these students.

Admissions: Foreign students must score at least 500 on the TOEFL. They also must take the ACT.

Procedure: Applications should be submitted by August for fall entry. Foreign students must present proof of good health and of adequate funds for 4 years. They must carry health insurance, which is available through the college for a fee.

Admissions Contact: E. F. Duensing, Director of Admissions.

CREIGHTON UNIVERSITY F-3
Omaha, Nebraska 68178 (402) 280-2703

F/T: 1825M, 1678W		Faculty:	n/av; IIA, av$
P/T: 117M, 168W		Ph.D.'s:	80%
Grad: 1114M, 412W		S/F Ratio:	14 to 1
Year: sems, ss		Tuition:	$3700
Appl: Aug. 1		R and B:	$1892
2288 applied	1972 accepted		1090 enrolled
ACT: 24			COMPETITIVE+

Creighton University, founded in 1878, is a private, coeducational Catholic institution conducted by the Society of Jesus. The university offers a liberal arts program and also includes professional and graduate divisions. The libraries have a combined total of 458,000 volumes.

Environment: The university's 85-acre urban campus is located in a residential area of Omaha. It has its own church; a communication and fine arts center; and medical, dental, and law centers. Living facilities include dormitories and on-campus apartments.

Student Life: More than half of the students come from outside Nebraska, representing all of the 50 states and many foreign countries. About 44% come from public schools. About 60% of the undergraduates live on campus. Ten percent are minority-group members. Seventy percent are Catholic and 10% are Protestant. Campus housing is both single-sex and coed; there are visiting privileges in the single-sex housing. Students may keep cars on campus.

Organizations: Approximately 25% of the men belong to the 6 fraternities on campus, and 17% of the women belong to the 6 sororities. Student organizations for each major school of study schedule many social and cultural activities.

Sports: The university fields 10 intercollegiate teams for men and 6 for women. There are 13 intramural sports for men and 13 for women.

Handicapped: Seventy-five percent of the campus is accessible to wheelchair-bound students. Special parking, ramps, and elevators are provided.

Graduates: About 15% of the freshmen drop out during the first year, and 54% remain to graduate. Approximately 35% of the graduates seek advanced degrees. Fifteen percent enter business and industry.

Services: The following services are available free to students: health care, tutoring, remedial instruction, psychological counseling, placement services, and career counseling.

Programs of Study: The university confers the B.A., B.S., B.F.A., B.S.Med.Tech., B.S.Rad.Tech., B.S.N., B.S. in Respiratory Therapy, B.S. in Social Work, and B.S.B.A. degrees. Associate, master's, and doctoral degrees are also awarded. Bachelor's degrees are offered in the following subjects: AREA STUDIES (American, Black/Afro-American), BUSINESS (accounting, business administration, computer science, economics, finance, management, marketing, organizational communications), EDUCATION (elementary, secondary, special), ENGLISH (creative writing, English, journalism, literature), FINE AND PERFORMING ARTS (art, art history, dance, film/photography, radio/TV, studio art, theater/dramatics), HEALTH SCIENCES (anesthesiology, medical technology, nursing, radiological technology, respiratory therapy), LANGUAGES (classical civilization, French, German, Greek/Latin, Spanish), MATH AND SCIENCES (biology, chemistry, mathematics, physics), PHILOSOPHY (classics, philosophy, theology), PREPROFESSIONAL (architecture, dentistry, law, medicine, pharmacy, social work), SOCIAL SCIENCES (economics, government/political science, history, psychology, sociology, speech). Thirty-three percent of degrees conferred are in health sciences, 24% are in math and sciences, and 11% are in business.

Required: All students in the College of Arts and Sciences must complete 60 hours within the General Education Component. These hours are divided among 4 areas: value consciousness, humanistic tradition, scientific inquiry, and modes of expression.

Special: Distinctive features are the Junior Year Abroad Program, the individual research projects open to outstanding freshmen in biology and chemistry, the Psychology Internship Program, and the Social Worker Internship Program. A 3-3 law program is also offered.

Honors: The university offers an interdepartmental honors program, and an English honors program. There are 13 undergraduate honor societies.

Admissions: Eighty-six percent of those who applied were accepted for the 1981–82 freshman class. The ACT scores of those who enrolled

480 NEBRASKA

were as follows: 18% below 21, 23% between 21 and 23, 20% between 24 and 25, 23% between 26 and 28, and 8% above 28. Applicants must have completed 15 academic units of high school work, should have a C average, and should rank in the upper 50% of the class. Other factors considered include recommendations, advanced placement or honors courses, and leadership potential. Non-high-school graduates may be admitted on a GED diploma.

Procedure: Either the SAT or the ACT is acceptable for admission; however, the ACT is required for placement. Freshmen are admitted to all sessions; application deadlines are August 1 (fall), January 1 (spring), and June 1 (summer). There is an application fee of $20. The university has a rolling admissions plan.

Special: CLEP and AP credit is available.

Transfer: For fall 1981, 351 students applied, 203 were accepted, and 81 enrolled. A GPA of 2.0 and good academic standing are required. D grades do not transfer. All students must complete, at the university, 64 of the 128 credits required for a bachelor's degree. Application deadlines are August 1 (fall), January 1 (spring), and June 1 (summer).

Visiting: Campus Days and summer orientation visits are held. Prospective students should contact the admissions office to make arrangements for scheduled or informal visits.

Financial Aid: About 70% of all students receive financial aid. Twenty percent work part-time on campus. The average freshman award was $3800 in 1981–82. University scholarships, BEOG, SEOG, CWS, NDSL, departmental scholarships, federal nursing scholarships, and nursing student loans are available. Awards depend upon need and the available funds. Short-term loans are available from university funds. Applications for financial aid should be filed by March 1. The university is a member of CSS. The FAF is required.

Foreign Students: The 120 full-time students from foreign countries make up 3% of enrollment. Intensive English courses, special counseling, and special organizations are available for these students.

Admissions: Foreign students must take the TOEFL. They also should take the ACT, if possible.

Procedure: Application deadlines are the same as those for other students. Foreign students must present proof of adequate funds for 1 year. Health insurance, though not required, is available through the university for a fee.

Admissions Contact: Howard J. Bachman, Director of Admissions.

DANA COLLEGE
Blair, Nebraska 68008 F-2
(402) 426-4101

F/T: 299M, 266W	Faculty:	37; IIB, av$
P/T: 8M, 22W	Ph.D.'s:	n/av
Grad: none	S/F Ratio:	15 to 1
Year: 4-1-4, ss	Tuition:	$3600
Appl: open	R and B:	$1505
686 applied	515 accepted	223 enrolled
ACT: 21		COMPETITIVE

Dana College, founded in 1884, is a private, liberal arts institution affiliated with the American Lutheran Church. Its library contains 113,000 volumes and 1500 reels of microfilm, and subscribes to more than 600 periodicals.

Environment: The 250-acre campus is located in a rural area just west of Blair, and 25 miles from Omaha. There are 16 major buildings on campus. Living facilities include dormitories and married-student housing.

Student Life: About 60% of the students are from out of state. Eighty percent are graduates of public schools. About 85% live on campus. About 83% are Protestant, most of them Lutheran. Fifteen percent are Catholic. Two percent are minority-group members. Campus housing is single-sex; there are visiting privileges. Students may keep cars on campus.

Organizations: Students may join fraternities and sororities. The student government sponsors social and cultural activities.

Sports: The college fields 8 intercollegiate teams for men and 8 for women. There are 6 intramural sports for men and 6 for women.

Graduates: About 30% of the freshmen drop out during the first year, and about 50% remain to graduate.

Services: Health care, placement and career counseling, psychological counseling, tutoring, and remedial instruction are provided free to students.

Programs of Study: The college confers the B.A. and B.S. degrees. Bachelor's degrees are offered in the following subjects: BUSINESS (accounting, business administration, computer science), EDUCATION (elementary, health/physical, secondary, special), ENGLISH (English, speech), FINE AND PERFORMING ARTS (art, art education, music, music education, radio/TV, studio art, theater/dramatics), HEALTH SCIENCES (environmental health, medical technology), LANGUAGES (Danish, French, German), MATH AND SCIENCES (biology, chemistry, earth science, general science, mathematics, physical sciences), PHILOSOPHY (humanities, religion), PREPROFESSIONAL (architecture, engineering, law, medicine, ministry, pharmacy, social work, veterinary), SOCIAL SCIENCES (economics, history, psychology, social sciences, sociology).

Required: All students must take courses in English composition, speech, social sciences, mathematics, natural sciences, humanities, religion, and physical education.

Special: Junior-year study abroad is offered.

Honors: Five honor societies are represented on campus.

Admissions: About 75% of those who applied were accepted for the 1981–82 freshman class. Candidates should rank in the upper 50% of their classes and have a 2.0 GPA. Advanced placement or honors courses, recommendations, and personality are also considered.

Procedure: Either ACT or SAT is required. There are no application deadlines; freshmen are admitted to all terms. A $10 fee should accompany all applications. Applicants are urged to undergo an interview. The college uses a rolling admissions plan.

Special: Early admissions and deferred admissions plans are offered. AP and CLEP credit is accepted.

Transfer: For fall 1981, 52 students applied, 40 were accepted, and 28 enrolled. A GPA of at least 2.0 is required. D grades do not transfer. All students must study at the college for at least 1 year, completing 30 of the 128 credits required for a bachelor's degree.

Visiting: Informal campus tours with guides can be arranged through the admissions office. Visitors may stay overnight at the school and sit in on classes.

Financial Aid: Eighty-four percent of the students receive aid. About 70% work part-time on campus. Scholarships, loans, and jobs are available. The FAF, BEOG, and SER forms are preferred, but the FFS also is accepted. The college is a member of CSS. There are no application deadlines.

Foreign Students: The 13 full-time students from foreign countries make up 2% of enrollment.

Admissions: Foreign students must score at least 500 on the TOEFL. No college entrance exams are required.

Procedure: There are no application deadlines; foreign students are admitted to all terms. They must present proof of adequate funds for 1 year.

Admissions Contact: Lee E. Johnson, Director of Admissions.

DOANE COLLEGE
Crete, Nebraska 68333 E-3
(402) 826-2161

F/T: 284M, 349W	Faculty:	n/av; IIB, –$
P/T: 21 M&W	Ph.D.'s:	51%
Grad: none	S/F Ratio:	14 to 1
Year: 4-1-4	Tuition:	$3750
Appl: Aug. 1	R and B:	$1450
463 applied	418 accepted	212 enrolled
ACT (mean): 21		COMPETITIVE

Doane College, founded in 1872, is a small, privately supported liberal arts college affiliated with the United Church of Christ. The Perkins library contains 128,417 volumes, 3,905 microfilm items, and 11,125 microfiche units, and subscribes to 420 periodicals.

Environment: The 300-acre, self-contained campus is located in a rural community 25 miles from Lincoln. The facilities include 20 buildings. Five dorms house about 600 students.

Student Life: Approximately 80% of the students come from Nebraska; 4 foreign countries and 22 states are represented. Ninety-seven percent of the entering freshmen come from public schools. Ninety percent of the students live in the dormitories. Campus housing is both coed and single-sex. Students may keep cars on campus.

Organizations: Religious organizations on campus include the Prayer and Praise Council, open to all students. Thirty-five percent of the students belong to the 9 local fraternities and sororities. Other organizations include art, drama, music, and various other special-interest clubs, as well as the staffs of the college newspaper, yearbook, and literary magazine. On-campus cultural events include a concert and lecture series.

NEBRASKA 481

Sports: The college fields intercollegiate teams in 14 men's and women's sports. Intramural sports are also offered.

Handicapped: There are no special facilities.

Graduates: The freshman dropout rate is 10%; 45% remain to graduate. Seventy-five percent pursue graduate study after graduation: 4% enter medical school and 3% enter law school. Thirty-eight percent pursue careers in business and industry.

Services: Students receive the following services free of charge: health care, placement, career counseling, and tutoring. Counseling for all freshmen is available through the GOALS (Goals Oriented toward Advising and Learning for Students) program. Through the Career Development Center any student who does not find placement may (at no cost) return to the college and "retool." Placement is high; 100% are placed in education. Doane is the site of the National Institute for Career Development. Its program, which features internships and intensive counseling, is nationally known.

Programs of Study: The college confers the B.A. degree in the following subjects: BUSINESS (accounting, business administration, business education, computer science, finance, management), EDUCATION (elementary, secondary), ENGLISH (English, speech), FINE AND PERFORMING ARTS (art), MATH AND SCIENCES (biology, chemistry, ecology/environmental science, mathematics, natural sciences), PHILOSOPHY (humanities, philosophy, religion), PREPROFESSIONAL (agriculture, architecture, dentistry, engineering, forestry, law, library science, medicine, ministry, pharmacy, social work, veterinary), SOCIAL SCIENCES (economics, government/political science, history, psychology, social sciences, sociology). Twenty-one percent of degrees conferred are in education and 18% are in business.

Required: A central core that includes fine arts, social science, humanities, and natural science, plus 2 terms of physical education, is required. In addition, all students must demonstrate proficiency in speech and writing.

Special: Student-designed majors are permitted. A 3-2 program in engineering is offered with Columbia University and Washington University, as well as a program in forestry with Duke University and Iowa State University. Off-campus semester programs are available in cooperation with American University in Washington, D.C., the University of Copenhagen in Denmark, and the Merrill Palmer Institute in Detroit.

Honors: There are 7 national honor societies on campus.

Admissions: Ninety percent of those who applied were accepted for the 1981–82 freshman class. The applicant should have completed 15 academic units and have a minimum GPA of C. In addition, the following factors are considered in order of importance: advanced placement or honors courses, recommendations, leadership record, and personality.

Procedure: The SAT or ACT is required and should be taken by May (preferably December or January) of the senior year. There is a $10 application fee.

Special: The college has early admissions and deferred admissions programs. There also is an early decision plan. AP and CLEP credit is available.

Transfer: About 80% of applications for transfer are approved, with about 20 students enrolling per year. An average of C is required. One year of resident study is also necessary; 132 credits are required for a bachelor's degree. August 1 (fall semester) and January 15 (spring semester) are the deadlines.

Visiting: Regularly scheduled orientation visits are available for prospective students. Contact the director of admissions to arrange for bus trips, guides, or overnight stays at the college.

Financial Aid: Ninety-two percent of all students receive financial aid. Scholarships based on need and on academic achievement are available, as well as scholarships for students with special skills in music, drama, art, or athletics. Long-term loans are awarded on the basis of need; funds are supplied by NDSL. The college participates in the PELL and SEOG programs and is VA-approved. There is no deadline for financial aid; however, early application is best. Either the FAF or the FFS is required.

Foreign Students: The Midwest Institute for International Studies, situated on the Doane campus, provides an extensive English language program for students from foreign countries. Through 8-week sessions offered 6 times each year, the institute prepares students to meet the English language requirements for admission to Doane and other American colleges and universities. Students live on campus and are considered to be part of the Doane community.

Admissions Contact: Steve Rasmussen, Director of Admissions.

HASTINGS COLLEGE D–3
Hastings, Nebraska 68901 (402) 463-2402

F/T: 343M, 428W	Faculty: 57; IIB, av$
P/T: 13M, 48W	Ph.D.'s: 54%
Grad: none	S/F Ratio: 14 to 1
Year: 4-1-4, ss	Tuition: $3430
Appl: Aug. 1	R and B: $2800
358 applied 356 accepted 236 enrolled
SAT: 440V 620M ACT: 19 COMPETITIVE

Hastings College is a 4-year liberal arts college affiliated with the United Presbyterian Church. The library contains 100,000 volumes and 12,000 microfilm items and subscribes to over 600 periodicals.

Environment: Located on an 80-acre campus in a rural area, the college's facilities include several nationally registered historic buildings, as well as a modern physical fitness center with indoor tennis courts and jogging track. Five dormitories house over 500 students.

Student Life: Approximately 80% of the students come from Nebraska. Five foreign nations and 19 states are represented. Sixty-five percent of the students live on campus. About 69% are Protestant, and 25% are Catholic. Campus housing is single-sex; there are visiting privileges. Students may keep cars on campus.

Organizations: The Religious Programs Committee is open to all students. There are 3 fraternities and 4 sororities to which 45% of the students belong.

Sports: The college fields 6 intercollegiate teams for men and 6 for women. There are 6 intramural sports for men and 6 for women.

Handicapped: Seventy-five percent of the campus is accessible to wheelchair students. Special parking and ramps are available.

Graduates: The freshman dropout rate is 19%; 58% remain to graduate. Thirty-five percent pursue graduate study after graduation: 5% enter medical school; 2% enter dental school; and 2% enter law school. Thirty-three percent pursue careers in business and industry.

Services: The following services are offered free of charge: placement and career counseling, psychological counseling, and health care. Tutoring is provided on a fee basis.

Programs of Study: The college confers the B.A. and B.M. degrees. Bachelor's degrees are offered in the following subjects: BUSINESS (business administration), EDUCATION (elementary, health/physical, secondary, special), ENGLISH (English, journalism, literature, speech), FINE AND PERFORMING ARTS (art, music, theater/dramatics), LANGUAGES (German, Spanish), MATH AND SCIENCES (biology, chemistry, mathematics, physics), PHILOSOPHY (philosophy, religion), PREPROFESSIONAL (dentistry, engineering, law, medicine, ministry, pharmacy, social work, veterinary), SOCIAL SCIENCES (economics, government/political science, history, psychology, sociology). Twenty-seven percent of degrees conferred are in business; 20% are in education; and 20% are in social sciences.

Required: A central core that includes fine arts, social science, humanities, and natural science, 2 terms of physical education, and a freshman life planning course, is required. The student is expected to develop a proficiency in speech and writing.

Special: A 3-2 program in engineering is offered with Columbia University, Washington University, and Georgia Tech. Off-campus semester programs are available in cooperation with American University in Washington, D.C., the University of Copenhagen in Denmark, and the Merrill Palmer Institute in Detroit. Student-designed majors are permitted.

Honors: One national honor society, Alpha Chi, is represented on campus.

Admissions: Ninety-nine percent of those who applied were accepted for the 1981–82 freshman class. The ACT scores of those who enrolled were as follows: 45% below 21, 24% between 21 and 23, 9% between 24 and 25, 13% between 26 and 28, and 5% above 28. Applicants should have completed 15 academic units in high school, have a 2.0 GPA, and rank in the upper 50% of their class. Recommendations are also considered important.

Procedure: The SAT or ACT is required and should be taken by May (preferably December or January) of the senior year. Application deadlines are August 1 (fall), December 1 (winter), January 1 (spring), and June 1 (summer). Notification is on a rolling basis. There is a $15 fee.

Special: There is an early decision plan. AP and CLEP credit is available.

Transfer: For fall 1981, 49 students applied, 49 were accepted, and 34 enrolled. D grades do not transfer; a C average is required. All

NEBRASKA

students must complete, at the college, 8 of the 35 units required for a bachelor's degree. Application deadlines are the same as those for freshmen.

Visiting: Prospective students are encouraged to visit at their own convenience. Contact the admissions office, Monday through Friday, to arrange for guides, for sitting in on classes, or for staying at the college.

Financial Aid: Eighty percent of all students receive financial aid. Thirty-eight percent work part-time on campus. The average freshman award is $4500. Scholarships based on need and on academic achievement are available, as well as scholarships for students with special skills in music, drama, art, athletics, or science. Long-term loans are awarded on the basis of need; funds are supplied by NDSL. The college participates in the EOG and CWS programs and is VA-approved. Either the FAF or the FFS is required. The college is a member of CSS. May 1 is the application deadline for fall entry.

Foreign Students: Fewer than 1% of the students come from foreign countries. Special counseling is available for these students.

Admissions: Foreign students must achieve a TOEFL score of at least 525. No college entrance exams are required.

Procedure: Application deadlines are the same as those for other students. Foreign students must present proof of health and of adequate funds. Health insurance is required.

Admissions Contact: Tracy Kramer, Admissions Counselor.

KEARNEY STATE COLLEGE D–3
Kearney, Nebraska, 68847 (308) 236-4216

F/T: 2174M, 2583W	Faculty: 245; IIA, – $
P/T: 408M, 680W	Ph.D.'s: 42%
Grad: 379M, 949W	S/F Ratio: 22 to 1
Year: sems, ss	Tuition: $630 ($1080)
Appl: Aug. 1	R and B: $1358
1386 enrolled	
SAT or ACT: recommended	NONCOMPETITIVE

This state-supported college, founded in 1903, trains teachers and also offers complete programs in the liberal arts at the bachelor's and master's degree levels. Its library contains 181,000 volumes and subscribes to 888 periodicals.

Environment: The college is located on a 235-acre campus, 140 miles from Lincoln. Living facilities include dormitories, married student apartments, off-campus housing, and fraternity and sorority houses.

Student Life: About 98% of students are from Nebraska. About 30% live in dormitories and 10% live in fraternity or sorority houses. Campus housing is both coed and single-sex.

Organizations: About 10% of men and women belong to 7 national fraternities and 4 national sororities. The college is nonsectarian but provides religious organizations for both Catholic and Protestant students. Extracurricular activities and 12 professional societies are open to students.

Sports: The college fields 8 intercollegiate teams for men and 7 for women. There are 15 intramural sports for men and 15 for women.

Handicapped: Facilities for the handicapped include wheelchair ramps, special parking, elevators, special class scheduling, and specially equipped rest rooms. Seventy percent of the campus is accessible to wheelchair students. A few books in braille, large-print books, and cassettes are available; other material can be ordered.

Graduates: At the end of the freshman year, about 35% of the class drop out, with 33% remaining to graduate. Sixty percent of those students go on to graduate studies: 1% go to medical school; 1% go to dental school; and 1% go to law school. Forty percent pursue careers in business and industry.

Services: Students receive the following services free of charge: career counseling, health care, tutoring, remedial instruction, and psychological counseling. Religious counseling is provided for both Catholic and Protestant students.

Programs of Study: The college confers the B.A., B.F.A., B.A.Ed., B.S., and B.S.Ed. degrees. There are also master's degree programs. Bachelor's degrees are offered in the following subjects: BUSINESS (business administration, business education, computer science, industrial management), EDUCATION (adult, early childhood, elementary, health/physical, industrial, special), ENGLISH (English, journalism, speech), FINE AND PERFORMING ARTS (art, art education, music, music education, theater/dramatics), HEALTH SCIENCES (medical technology, nursing, public health, speech therapy), LANGUAGES (French, German, Spanish), MATH AND SCIENCES (biology, chemistry, mathematics, physical sciences, physics, statistics), PREPROFESSIONAL (criminal justice, law enforcement), SOCIAL SCIENCES (economics, geography, government/political science, history, psychology, sociology). Secondary education degrees are awarded in the individual subject areas. Degrees are not conferred in preprofessional areas but studies in agriculture, architecture, dentistry, engineering, forestry, home economics, law, library science, medicine, pharmacy, social work, and veterinary medicine are offered. Thirty-five percent of degrees are conferred in education; 25% are in business; and 17% are in social sciences.

Required: A basic studies program totaling 45 semester hours must be completed by all students. It includes courses in science, mathematics, English-speech, social and political science, and humanities.

Special: Programs include credit and non-credit grading.

Honors: Nineteen national honor societies have chapters on campus. There are no departmental honors programs.

Admissions: Eligibility depends upon high school graduation with a total of 16 Carnegie units. The college seeks students who rank in the upper half of their graduating class and who come from accredited high schools. There is no selectivity for in-state high school graduates.

Procedure: Either the SAT or ACT is recommended. The deadline for application to the fall session is August 1; there is a rolling admission plan. New students are admitted for fall, midyear, and summer. There is a $10 application fee.

Special: The college has an early admissions plan, the application deadline for which is August 1. AP and CLEP are used.

Transfer: Good academic standing is required. Grades of D do not transfer. All students must complete, at the college, 32 of the 125 credits required for a bachelor's degree.

Visiting: There are regularly scheduled orientations that include a general information session, campus tours, registration for classes, and meetings with financial aid counselors. Guided informal visits can be arranged, preferably Monday through Friday from 10 A.M. to 1:30 P.M. Visitors can sit in on classes. Visits can be arranged through the admissions office.

Financial Aid: Eighty percent of all students receive financial aid. Students may also apply for loans from federal government sources, from the college, and from private funds. Either the FAF or the FFS is required. The deadline for financial aid application is March 15 for scholarships, or April 15 for other aid.

Foreign Students: An intensive English course, special counseling, and special organizations are available for these students.

Admissions: Foreign students must achieve a TOEFL score of at least 520. The SAT or ACT is recommended but not required.

Procedure: The application is due at least 6 months prior to the beginning of either semester. Foreign students must present proof of adequate funds and must carry health insurance, which is available through the college.

Admissions Contact: Wayne Samuelson, Director of Admissions.

MIDLAND LUTHERAN COLLEGE E–2
Fremont, Nebraska 68025 (402) 721-5480

F/T: 349M, 451W	Faculty: 56; IIB, – $
P/T: 24M, 27W	Ph.D.'s: 41%
Grad: none	S/F Ratio: 13 to 1
Year: 4-1-4, ss	Tuition: $3500
Appl: Sept. 1	R and B: $1630
592 applied 530 accepted 270 enrolled	
ACT: 21	COMPETITIVE

Midland Lutheran College is a 4-year, coeducational institution of the liberal arts and sciences affiliated with the Lutheran Church in America. The library houses 105,000 volumes and subscribes to 805 periodicals.

Environment: The compact, self-contained, 27-acre suburban campus, located 30 miles from Omaha, features among its structures a science complex, an art building, a physical education complex, an audiovisual center, and dormitories.

Student Life: Approximately 70% of the students are from Nebraska, but the college actively seeks to broaden its geographical base. Almost all the entering freshmen come from public schools. Seventy percent live on campus. Seven percent are minority-group members. Dormitories are single-sex; there are visiting privileges. Students may keep cars on campus. Religious services are held twice a week; attendance is voluntary.

Organizations: Approximately 40% of the women and 30% of the men are affiliated with 5 local sororities and 4 local fraternities.

Sports: The college fields 7 intercollegiate teams for men and 6 for women. There are 6 intramural sports for men and 5 for women.

Handicapped: About 90% of the campus is accessible to wheelchair-bound students. Special parking, wheelchair ramps, elevators, and specially equipped rest rooms are available.

Graduates: At the end of the freshman year, 25% of the class drop out, but 55% remain to graduate, and 16% of the graduates continue to work for higher degrees. Of graduates, 1% each enter law school, medical school, and dental school, while 28% pursue careers in business and industry.

Services: Students receive the following services free of charge: placement, health care, psychological counseling, career counseling, tutoring, and remedial instruction.

Programs of Study: The college awards the B.A. degree. Associate degrees are also awarded. Bachelor's degrees are offered in the following subjects: BUSINESS (accounting, business administration, business education, computer science, finance, management, marketing, real estate/insurance), EDUCATION (early childhood, elementary, health/physical, secondary, special), ENGLISH (English, journalism, speech), FINE AND PERFORMING ARTS (art, art education, music, music education, theater/dramatics), HEALTH SCIENCES (medical technology, nursing, respiratory therapy), LANGUAGES (French, German, Spanish), MATH AND SCIENCES (astronomy, biology, chemistry, earth science, mathematics, natural sciences, physical sciences), PHILOSOPHY (philosophy, religion), PREPROFESSIONAL (agriculture, architecture, dentistry, engineering, forestry, home economics, law, medicine, ministry, pharmacy, social work, veterinary), SOCIAL SCIENCES (anthropology, economics, history, psychology, social sciences, sociology). Twenty-eight percent of degrees conferred are in business, 26% are in education, and 25% are in health sciences.

Special: The B.G.S. degree is offered, and the college allows student-designed majors.

Honors: Two national honor societies, Blue Key and Cardinal Key, have chapters on campus.

Admissions: Ninety percent of those who applied were accepted for the 1981-82 freshman class. In evaluating candidates the 3 most important factors are class rank, ACT scores, and the high school evaluation. Students who rank in the upper half of their graduating classes and have the recommendation of their high schools are admitted in full standing; those with lower rank are considered after a review of their ACT scores and their personal educational objectives. The college indicates that in addition they consider impressions made during the interview and the applicant's personality.

Procedure: The ACT is required. The deadlines for regular admission are September 1 for fall, January 15 for spring, and June 1 for summer. Notification is on a rolling basis. The application fee is $10.

Special: Early admissions are available, with an application deadline of September 1. CLEP and AP are used.

Transfer: For fall 1981, 88 students applied, 76 were accepted, and 51 enrolled. Good academic standing is required. D grades do not transfer. One year must be completed in residence. All students must complete, at the college, 32 of the 128 credits required for a bachelor's degree. Application deadlines are the same as those for freshmen.

Visiting: Visitors can stay at the school and can sit in on classes. Regularly scheduled orientations for prospective students include a campus tour and visits with students and faculty. For information, the director of admissions should be contacted.

Financial Aid: About 90% of all students receive financial aid. About 45% work part-time on campus. The average freshman award is $3355. The college maintains an extensive program of assistance, in the form of grants, loans, CWS, and scholarships. Either the FAF or FFS is required. The deadline for financial aid application is April 1 (summer or fall entry) or January 1 (spring entry).

Foreign Students: One percent of the full-time students come from foreign countries.

Admissions: No English proficiency or college entrance exams are required.

Procedure: There are no application deadlines; foreign students are admitted in the fall, spring, and summer terms. They must present proof of funds adequate to cover 1 year of study. Health insurance is available through the college.

Admissions Contact: Roland R. Kahnk, Director of Admissions.

NEBRASKA 483

NEBRASKA WESLEYAN UNIVERSITY E-3
Lincoln, Nebraska 68504 (402) 466-2371

F/T: 492M, 537W Faculty: 90; IIB, av$
P/T: 50M, 128W Ph.D.'s: 76%
Grad: none S/F Ratio: 13 to 1
Year: sems, ss Tuition: $3750
Appl: Aug. 15 R and B: $1674
544 applied 530 accepted 341 enrolled
ACT: 23 COMPETITIVE+

Nebraska Wesleyan University, established in 1887, is a private liberal arts college related to the United Methodist Church. The library contains 160,000 volumes and 5000 microfilm items, and subscribes to 10,000 periodicals.

Environment: The 45-acre suburban campus, located 5 miles from the downtown center of Lincoln, includes 17 buildings and a football stadium. A new theater has just been completed. The Old Main Building has been declared a national historical monument. Living facilities include dormitories and fraternity and sorority houses.

Student Life: Eighty-one percent of the students come from Nebraska. Ninety percent are from public schools. Seventy-five percent of the students live on campus or in the 4 fraternity and 4 sorority houses immediately adjacent to the campus. The majority of the students are members of the Methodist, Lutheran, and Catholic faiths. There are numerous religious organizations on campus, and counselors are available for members of the major faiths. Campus housing is both coed and single-sex; there are visiting privileges in the single-sex housing. Students may keep cars on campus.

Organizations: Students participate in poetry recitals, drama productions, departmental clubs, musicals, and forensics.

Sports: The university competes on an intercollegiate level in 8 sports for men and 7 for women. There are 3 intramural sports for men and 2 for women.

Handicapped: About 50% of the campus is accessible to wheelchair-bound students. For these students, the following facilities are offered: wheelchair ramps, special parking, elevators, special class scheduling, specially equipped rest rooms, and lowered drinking fountains. Fewer than 1% of students have visual or hearing impairments. For these students there are some special facilities.

Graduates: The freshman dropout rate is 21%; 75% remain to graduate. Fifty percent of the graduates pursue advanced degrees; 10% enter medical school. About 35% of the graduates enter business and industry.

Services: Students receive the following services free of charge: health care, psychological counseling, remedial instruction, and career counseling. Tutoring and placement services are provided on a fee basis.

Programs of Study: The university awards the B.A., B.S., B.S.N., B.Mus., and B.L.A. degrees. Associate degrees are also conferred. Bachelor's degrees are offered in the following subjects: AREA STUDIES (American, Asian), BUSINESS (accounting, business administration, business education, computer science, finance, management, marketing), EDUCATION (elementary, health/physical, secondary, special), ENGLISH (English, literature, speech), FINE AND PERFORMING ARTS (art, art education, art history, music, music education, theater/dramatics), HEALTH SCIENCES (medical technology, nursing, physical therapy), LANGUAGES (French, German, Spanish), MATH AND SCIENCES (biochemistry, biology, botany, chemistry, mathematics, natural sciences, physical sciences, physics, statistics, zoology), PHILOSOPHY (philosophy, religion), PREPROFESSIONAL (dentistry, engineering, law, library science, medicine, ministry, pharmacy, social work, veterinary), SOCIAL SCIENCES (anthropology, economics, government/political science, history, international relations, psychology, social sciences, sociology).

Required: A basic curriculum of 37 hours is required of all students. This includes prescribed courses in freshman English, physical education, and speech, as well as course requirements in several broad fields.

Special: Work-study programs are offered. A limited pass/fail option is open to juniors and seniors. Off-campus study is available in Washington, D.C., in Latin America, at the United Nations, and at University Graz, Austria. There are 3-2 engineering programs with Georgia Tech, Columbia University, and Washington University.

Honors: The English department offers an honors program combining literature and composition. There is an accelerated program in chemistry.

Admissions: Ninety-seven percent of those who applied were accepted for the 1981-82 freshman class. Candidates should be gradu-

484 NEBRASKA

ates of accredited high schools and rank in the top 50% of their classes. They must have completed 15 academic units. The university indicates that in addition to these qualifications, the following factors are considered: evidence of special talents, advanced placement or honors courses, and extracurricular activities.

Procedure: The SAT or ACT is required and should be taken by March of the senior year. A personal interview, either on campus or with a field representative, is recommended. The application deadlines are August 15 (fall), January 2 (spring), and April 15 (summer). Notification is on a rolling basis. There is a $10 application fee.

Special: There are early admissions and deferred admissions plans. AP and CLEP (subject exams) is used.

Transfer: For fall 1981, 87 students applied, 82 were accepted, and 61 enrolled. A minimum composite score of 18 on the ACT or 800 on the SAT is required. A 2.0 GPA is recommended. One year of resident study is required. All students must complete, at the college, 30 of the 125 credits required for a bachelor's degree. Application deadlines are the same as those for freshmen.

Visiting: There are regularly scheduled orientations for prospective students, including a campus tour, faculty interview, and student meetings. Visitors can stay overnight at the school and sit in on classes. For information, contact the director of admissions.

Financial Aid: About 90% of all students receive financial aid. About 30% work part-time on campus. The average freshman award is $1800. The college is a member of CSS. The FAF is required. Application deadlines are June 1 (fall), November 15 (spring), and April 1 (summer).

Foreign Students: Three percent of the full-time students come from foreign countries. Special counseling and special organizations are available for these students.

Admissions: Foreign students must take the TOEFL or the University of Michigan Language Test. No college entrance exams are required.

Procedure: Application deadlines are July 1 (fall), November 1 (spring), and March 1 (summer). Foreign students must fill out a health form and must present proof of funds adequate to cover 1 year of study. Health insurance is required and is available through the university for a fee.

Admissions Contact: Ken Sieg, Director of Admissions.

PERU STATE COLLEGE
Peru, Nebraska 68421   F-3
(402) 872-3815

F/T: 294M, 293W
P/T: 83M, 177W
Grad: none
Year: sems, ss
Appl: Aug. 15
218 applied
ACT: 18

Faculty: 56; IIB, +$
Ph.D.'s: 52%
S/F Ratio: 14 to 1
Tuition: $740 ($1205)
R and B: $1624
190 accepted 170 enrolled
NONCOMPETITIVE

Peru State College is the oldest college in Nebraska, having been established in 1867, the same year in which Nebraska achieved statehood. The library houses 80,000 volumes and 425 microfilm items, and subscribes to over 526 periodicals.

Environment: Located in the city of Peru, 60 miles south of Omaha, the "Campus of a Thousand Oaks" overlooks the Missouri River and the neighboring states of Iowa and Missouri. A health and recreation complex features 4 basketball courts, an indoor track, tennis courts, and an Olympic-sized pool. There are fraternity houses, 4 dormitories for single students, and accommodations for married students. Off-campus housing is also available.

Student Life: About 80% of the students are from Nebraska; 70% of entering freshmen come from public schools. About 65% live on campus. Fifteen percent of the students are Catholic, 80% are Protestant, and 1% are Jewish. Eleven percent are minority-group members. Campus housing is both coed and single-sex. There are visiting privileges in single-sex dorms. Students may have cars on campus. Drinking is not allowed on campus.

Organizations: There are religious organizations for Catholic and Protestant students. The "Festival of a Thousand Oaks" features the Omaha Symphony on campus for five weeks in June and July.

Sports: Peru State College participates on an intercollegiate level in 7 sports for men and 6 for women. There are 12 intramural sports for men and 10 for women.

Handicapped: About 80% of the campus is accessible to wheelchair-bound students. Fewer than 1% of the students have visual impairments. For these students there are "talking books" and braille material.

Graduates: The freshman dropout rate is 35%; 50% remain to graduate. Ten percent pursue graduate study; 1% enter dental school, and 2% enter law school. Forty-eight percent pursue careers in business and industry.

Services: Students receive the following services free of charge: psychological counseling, career counseling, tutoring, and remedial instruction. Placement services and health care are also available for a fee.

Programs of Study: Peru State College confers the B.A., B.S., B.A.Ed., B.S.Ed., B.F.A. in Ed., and B.T. degrees. Associate degrees also are awarded. Bachelor's degrees are offered in the following subjects: BUSINESS (accounting, business administration, business education, computer science), EDUCATION (early childhood, elementary, health/physical, industrial, secondary, special), ENGLISH (English, journalism, literature, speech), FINE AND PERFORMING ARTS (art, art education, music, music education, theater/dramatics), HEALTH SCIENCES (medical technology), MATH AND SCIENCES (biology, chemistry, geology, mathematics, natural sciences, physics), PREPROFESSIONAL (agriculture, architecture, dentistry, engineering, forestry, home economics, law, medicine, mortuary, nursing, optometry, pharmacy, physical therapy, social work, veterinary, x-ray technology), SOCIAL SCIENCES (geography, history, psychology, social sciences, sociology). Twenty-eight percent of degrees conferred are in business; 18% are in education; and 10% are in math and sciences.

Required: All students must complete general education requirements.

Special: It is possible to earn combined B.A.-B.S. degrees. The college also allows student-designed majors.

Honors: There are 7 honor societies on campus, including Alpha Mu Omega and Alpha Chi.

Admissions: Eighty-seven percent of those who applied were accepted for the 1981–82 freshman class. The ACT scores of those who enrolled were as follows: 74% below 21, 11% between 21 and 23, 6% between 24 and 25, 6% between 26 and 28, and 1% above 28. Since the college is a public institution, there is no restriction on the admission of Nebraska high school graduates. In the case of out-of-state applicants, the college is interested in the high school record, ACT scores, a confidential summary, a rating by a high school counselor or principal, accreditation and reputation of high school, class rank, and the completion of 16 Carnegie units.

Procedure: The ACT is required and is used for placement purposes. The deadlines for regular admissions are August 15 (fall), December 15 (winter), and June 1 (summer). There is a rolling admissions policy. For early decision the notification date is within two weeks of application receipt. There is an application fee of $10.

Special: Early and deferred admissions are possible. CLEP subject exams are accepted.

Transfer: Approximately 90 applications were received for the current school year, 85 were accepted, and 62 transfers enrolled. Transfers are accepted for all classes; D grades are acceptable. Students must complete, at the college, 30 semester hours of the 126 required for the bachelor's degree. Transfer application deadlines are the same as for freshman applicants.

Visiting: Orientations for accepted students are held in July and August. Informal guided tours can be scheduled five days a week by contacting the director of admissions.

Financial Aid: About 70% of all students receive financial aid; 45% work part-time on campus. Scholarships, loans, and grants are available. The average scholarship granted to freshmen is $150; the average loan is $1000. College work-study is available in 7 departments. Either the FAF or the FFS is required. The deadlines for financial aid application are April 1 (fall), November 1 (winter), and May 1 (summer).

Foreign Students: One percent of the full-time students come from foreign countries. Special counseling is available to these students.

Admissions: Foreign students must achieve a score of at least 560 on the TOEFL. The SAT or ACT is not required.

Procedure: Application deadlines are July 1 (fall), December 1 (spring), and May 1 (summer). Proof of funds sufficient to cover 4 years of study is required.

Admissions Contact: Kenneth L. Steidle, Director of Admissions.

UNION COLLEGE
Lincoln, Nebraska 68516   E-3
(402) 488-2331

F/T, P/T:
453M, 489W
Grad: none
Year: sems, ss
Appl: Aug. 21
421 applied
ACT: required

Faculty: 60; n/av
Ph.D.'s: 29%
S/F Ratio: 15 to 1
Tuition: $4290
R and B: $1480–1550
367 accepted   257 enrolled
LESS COMPETITIVE

This coeducational liberal arts institution is owned and operated by the Seventh-Day Adventist Church. A balanced program of intellectual, moral, social, and physical education is offered; character development is stressed. The library houses over 103,455 volumes, more than 659 current periodicals, and 53 microfilm items.

Environment: The 26-acre campus is located in a suburban area 5 miles from downtown Lincoln. Dormitories accommodate over 600 students. Married student housing is also available. The health education center contains an Olympic-sized pool; basketball, racquetball, and tennis courts; and a gymnastics center.

Student Life: A majority of students come from outside the state; only 10% are Nebraska residents. Seventy-four percent of the students live on campus. Most are members of the Seventh-Day Adventist Church and all are required to attend chapel services. Sixteen percent of the students are minority-group members. Campus housing is single-sex, and there are no visiting privileges. Smoking and the use of alcoholic beverages are prohibited; a strict week-night curfew of 10:30 P.M. is observed by students. With the exception of first-semester freshmen, students may keep cars on campus.

Organizations: There are no sororities or fraternities, but various social and departmental groups invite student participation.

Sports: There are 9 intramural sports for men and 7 for women.

Handicapped: About 75% of the campus is accessible to wheelchair-bound students. Special parking, elevators, specially equipped rest rooms, and telephones are available.

Graduates: The freshman dropout rate is 30%; 35% remain to graduate. About 30% of the graduates continue to study for higher degrees; 1.5% enter medical school; 1.4% enter dental school; and 1.2% enter law school. Careers in business and industry are pursued by 40% of the graduates.

Services: Students receive free tutoring, remedial instruction, placement, and career and psychological counseling. Health care is available for a fee. Graduates are offered free placement and career counseling.

Programs of Study: All programs lead to the B.A., B.Mus., or B.S. degree. Associate degrees are also conferred. Bachelor's degrees are offered in the following subjects: BUSINESS (accounting, business administration, business education, computer science, management), EDUCATION (early childhood, elementary, health/physical, secondary), ENGLISH (English, journalism), FINE AND PERFORMING ARTS (music education, music performance), HEALTH SCIENCES (medical technology, nursing), MATH AND SCIENCES (biology, chemistry, mathematics, physics), PHILOSOPHY (religion), PREPROFESSIONAL (dentistry, home economics, law, medicine, ministry, social work, veterinary), SOCIAL SCIENCES (history, psychology, social sciences, sociology).

Required: All students must take a core curriculum of 48 semester hours, including 12 hours of religion.

Special: Students are offered opportunities to travel as part of the regular curriculum, but this does not constitute a formal study-abroad program.

Admissions: Eighty-seven percent of those who applied were accepted for the 1981–82 freshman class. The candidates must have completed 18 Carnegie high school units, have at least a C average, and bring a college-qualifying recommendation from the high school. In addition, the school considers the following factors in order of importance: advanced placement or honors courses, leadership record, and impressions made during the interview.

Procedure: The ACT is required. The deadlines for regular admission are August 21 (fall), January 5 (winter), and May 8 (summer). A rolling admissions plan is in effect. Applications should be submitted with a $10 fee.

Special: CLEP credit is available.

Transfer: For fall 1981, 173 applications were received; 132 were accepted; and 106 students enrolled. Transfers are accepted for all classes; D grades are acceptable. Thirty of the last 32 credits must be completed in residence; 128 credits are required for the bachelor's degree. Application deadlines are the same as for freshmen.

Visiting: Visits can be arranged through the admissions office.

Financial Aid: About 63% of all students receive aid through the college, a member of CSS, and 64% work part-time on campus. About 37% receive college money. Applicants must submit the PELL. The application deadlines are March 15 (fall) and September 1 (winter).

Foreign Students: The college actively recruits foreign students, who comprise 10% of the full-time enrollment.

Admissions: Foreign students must take the TOEFL; the SAT or ACT is not required.

Procedure: Information concerning application deadlines and other requirements is available from the college.

Admissions Contact: Leona Murray, Director of Admissions.

UNIVERSITY OF NEBRASKA

Two years after Nebraska became a state (February 15, 1869), the University of Nebraska was established. Classes began in 1871 with an enrollment of 20 students. By the turn of the century, the university had gained considerable stature among the leading educational institutions of the nation.

The university consists of 9 colleges, 5 schools, and a number of specialized divisions and agencies. There are 2 main campuses—the Lincoln City campus and the Lincoln East campus—plus a campus located in Omaha and a medical center, also in Omaha. Separate profiles follow for the Lincoln and Omaha campuses.

The medical center was absorbed into the University of Nebraska system in 1902. Included at the center are the College of Medicine and the College of Nursing. The 25-acre center consists of University Hospital and Clinics, Nebraska Psychiatric Institute, Eppley Institute for Research in Cancer and Allied Diseases, Children's Rehabilitation Institute, and the Hattie B. Munroe Pavilion. It is a center for programs of study in medicine, medical technology, nursing, physical therapy, and radiologic technology. Students are admitted as freshmen only to the A.S. program in nursing and radiologic technology. All other programs in the college require prior college work.

UNIVERSITY OF NEBRASKA AT OMAHA   F-3
Omaha, Nebraska 68182   (402) 554-2393

F/T: 3963M, 3297W
P/T: 3720M, 4512W
Grad: 804M, 1257W
Year: sems, ss
Appl: Aug. 1
2493 applied
SAT or ACT: required

Faculty: 400; IIA, av$
Ph.D.'s: 85%
S/F Ratio: 29 to 1
Tuition: $974 ($2489)
R and B: n/app
2493 accepted   2319 enrolled
NONCOMPETITIVE

The University of Nebraska at Omaha, founded in 1908 as the Municipal University of Omaha, became part of the University of Nebraska system in 1968. Now a public liberal arts university, it consists of the College of Arts and Sciences, the College of Business Administration, the College of Continuing Studies, the College of Education, the College of Engineering and Technology, the College of Public Affairs, the College of Home Economics, the College of Fine Art, and a graduate school. Its library contains over 400,000 volumes and 437,000 microforms, and subscribes to 6200 periodicals.

Environment: The 73-acre urban campus has 15 buildings and no dormitories. All students commute.

Student Life: About 94% of the students are from Nebraska, and 6% are from bordering states. Ninety-eight percent of the freshmen come from public schools. Nine percent of the students are minority-group members. Students may have cars on campus.

Organizations: There are 9 national fraternities and 4 national sororities to which 7% of the students belong. There are more than 100 extracurricular activities and groups, the most active of which are the student government, dramatics, and the Student Program Organization.

Sports: The university competes in 9 intercollegiate sports for men and 7 for women. Nine intramural sports are open to both men and women.

Handicapped: Eighty-five percent of the campus is accessible to physically handicapped students. Special facilities include wheelchair ramps, parking areas, elevators, lowered drinking fountains and telephones, and specially equipped rest rooms. There are no hearing or visually impaired students enrolled.

Graduates: About 60% of the freshmen drop out during the first year, and 10% remain to graduate.

Services: Free career and psychological counseling, job placement, tutoring, remedial instruction, and health care are available to all students.

Programs of Study: The university confers the B.A., B.S., B.F.A., B.M., B.S.Ed., B.S.B.A., B.S. in Criminal Justice, B.S.C.E., and B.S.Ind.Tech. degrees. Associate and master's degrees are also granted. Bachelor's degrees are offered in the following subjects: AREA STUDIES (Black/Afro-American, international studies, Latin American, urban), BUSINESS (accounting, business administration, business education, computer science, finance, management, marketing, real estate/insurance), EDUCATION (elementary, health/physical, secondary, special), ENGLISH (English, journalism, speech), FINE AND PERFORMING ARTS (art, art history, music, music education), LANGUAGES (French, German, Italian, Spanish), MATH AND SCIENCES (chemistry, earth science, geology, mathematics, physics), PHILOSOPHY (philosophy, religion), PREPROFESSIONAL (engineering, law, pharmacy), SOCIAL SCIENCES (economics, geography, government/political science, history, international relations, psychology, sociology). About 31% of the degrees conferred are in business, and 21% are in education.

Required: All students must participate in freshman orientation and take English Fundamentals.

Special: Study abroad, individualized majors, and independent study are offered to students.

Honors: Twenty-two national honor societies have chapters on campus, and the university has its own honors program.

Admissions: All those who applied were accepted for the 1981–82 freshman class. Candidates must be graduates of accredited high schools. Each curriculum has its own entrance criteria. The school operates under an open admissions policy.

Procedure: Either the SAT or ACT is required and should be taken by July 15. Application deadlines are August 1 (fall), December 1 (spring), and May 1 (summer). Notification is made on a rolling basis. Nebraska residents pay a $10 application fee, nonresidents pay $25.

Special: CLEP is used.

Transfer: For fall 1981, the 1212 transfer students who applied were accepted; 1150 enrolled. An average of C is required. D grades do not transfer. At least 30 semester hours of the 125 required for the bachelor's degree must be taken in residence. Transfers must also study for 6 months at the university. Application deadlines are the same as for freshmen.

Visiting: Informal tours of the campus can be arranged through the admissions office.

Financial Aid: About 25% of all students receive some form of financial aid. Ten percent work part-time on campus. There are 100 freshman scholarships and 200 athletic scholarships available to students. The university also administers $425,000 in federal loan funds and $100,000 in private loan funds. CWS funds are available in all departments. The university is a member of the CSS and the FAF is required. The deadline for financial applications is April 1.

Foreign Students: Currently 180 full-time foreign students are enrolled at the university. Both an English course and an intensive English program are available to these students. The university also provides special counseling and special organizations.

Admissions: Foreign students must earn a minimum score of 500 on the TOEFL. College entrance exams are also required.

Procedure: Application deadlines are July 1 (fall), November 1 (spring), and March 1 (summer). A physical examination is required to establish proof of health. Foreign students must also carry health insurance. Proof of funds adequate to cover 9 months of study is necessary.

Admissions Contact: Duncan M. Sargent, Director of Admissions.

UNIVERSITY OF NEBRASKA/LINCOLN   E-3
Lincoln, Nebraska 68588   (402) 472-3603

F/T: 9929M, 7231W
P/T: 1843M, 1584W
Grad: 2117M, 1597W
Year: sems, ss
Appl: Aug. 15
6562 applied   5944 accepted   4123 enrolled
ACT: 22   **NONCOMPETITIVE**

Faculty: 1071; I, −$
Ph.D.'s: 76%
S/F Ratio: 18 to 1
Tuition: $1025 ($2525)
R and B: $1825

Founded in 1869, this state-supported coed university is part of the University of Nebraska system. Love Memorial Library is administered to serve the entire university, and C. Y. Thompson Library serves the East Lincoln campus. The entire library system includes more than 1.4 million volumes, and subscribes to 19,800 periodicals.

Environment: The urban Lincoln campus consists of 545 acres and more than 5 million square feet of building space. The Sheldon Memorial Art Gallery, designed by Philip Johnson, is regarded as one of the finest small art galleries in the nation. There is also a large music complex.

Student Life: About 90% of the students are from Nebraska. Forty-four percent live on campus. All unmarried students who do not live with their parents are required to live in approved residences. About 3% of the students are minority-group members. University housing is both single-sex and coed. There are visiting privileges in single-sex housing. Students may keep cars on campus.

Organizations: There are 26 fraternities and 15 sororities on campus. The student government also sponsors social and cultural activities for students.

Sports: The university sponsors 15 intercollegiate sports for men and 12 for women. There are 11 intramural sports for men and 8 for women.

Handicapped: About one-third of the campus is accessible to handicapped students. Special facilities include wheelchair ramps, parking areas, elevators, lowered drinking fountains and telephones, and specially equipped rest rooms. Special class scheduling is also available. There are no hearing or visually impaired students enrolled.

Graduates: About 25% of the freshmen drop out during their first year; 52% remain to graduate. Of those, about 23% continue their studies and others pursue careers in business and industry.

Services: Free health care, psychological and career counseling are provided to all students. Job placement and tutoring are available both free and on a fee basis.

Programs of Study: The university confers the B.A., B.S., B.F.A., and B.Mus. degrees. Master's and doctoral degrees are also awarded. Bachelor's degrees are offered in the following subjects: AREA STUDIES (American, Latin American), BUSINESS (accounting, actuarial science, business administration, business education, computer science, finance, management, marketing), EDUCATION (early childhood, elementary, health/physical, industrial, secondary, special), ENGLISH (English, journalism, literature, speech), FINE AND PERFORMING ARTS (art, art education, art history, dance, film/photography, music, music education, radio/TV, studio art, theater/dramatics), HEALTH SCIENCES (environmental health, nursing, speech therapy), LANGUAGES (French, German, Greek/Latin, Spanish), MATH AND SCIENCES (astronomy, biology, chemistry, earth science, geology, mathematics, natural sciences, physics, statistics), PHILOSOPHY (classics, humanities, philosophy), PREPROFESSIONAL (agriculture, architecture, dentistry, engineering, forestry, home economics, law, library science, medicine, pharmacy, social work, veterinary), SOCIAL SCIENCES (anthropology, economics, geography, government/political science, history, international relations, psychology, social sciences, sociology).

Required: Required courses vary by college and by major.

Special: The university sponsors independent study, study abroad, and cooperative exchange programs.

Honors: Many national honor societies, including Phi Beta Kappa, are open to qualified students. There are also departmental honors programs.

Admissions: About 91% of those who applied were accepted for the 1981–82 freshman class. Of those who enrolled, the ACT scores were as follows: 38% below 21, 20% between 21 and 23, 15% between 24 and 25, 12% between 26 and 28, and 15% above 28. Nebraska residents are admitted if they are graduates of accredited high schools and have completed 13 units at a 3-year high school or 16 units at a 4-year high school. Nonresidents are admitted if they rank in the upper half of their graduating class and have completed the SAT or ACT. The university heavily considers class rank and test scores. Children of alumni are admitted on the same basis as Nebraska residents.

Procedure: The SAT or ACT should be taken by November of the senior year, and nonresidents should take the ATs in March. Application deadlines are August 15 (fall), January 1 (spring), and June 1 (summer). There is a rolling admissions plan. Applications must be accompanied by a $10 fee for Nebraska residents and a $25 fee for nonresidents.

Special: AP and CLEP credit is accepted.

Transfer: For fall 1981, 1700 students applied, and 1400 were accepted. A 2.0 GPA is generally required. Grades of 2.0 and higher will transfer. Students must earn 30 of the last 36 semester hours in residence; 127 semester hours are required for a bachelor's degree. Application deadlines are August 15 (fall), January 1 (spring), and June 1 (summer).

Visiting: Informal tours of the campus can be arranged through the admissions office. Visitors can stay overnight at the school.

Financial Aid: About 54% of all students receive some form of financial aid. Twenty-eight percent work part-time on campus. Several hundred freshman scholarships are available. Loans are also available. The university is a member of CSS. The FAF is required. Aid applications should be filed by February 1 (fall) or March 15 (spring and summer).

Foreign Students: About 4% of the full-time students come from foreign countries. The university offers these students an intensive English course, an intensive English program (summers only), special counseling, and special organizations.

Admissions: Foreign students must score at least 500 on the TOEFL or 80 on the University of Michigan Language Test. No college entrance examination is required.

Procedure: Application deadlines are June 1 (fall), November 1 (spring), and April 1 (summer). Foreign students must present proof of funds adequate to cover 4 years of study. They must also carry health insurance, which is available through the university for a fee.

Admissions Contact: Al Papik, Director of Admissions.

WAYNE STATE COLLEGE E-2
Wayne, Nebraska 68787 (402) 375-2200

F/T: 756M, 1005W Faculty: 86; IIA, –$
P/T: 176M, 296W Ph.D.'s: 52%
Grad: 79M, 87W S/F Ratio: 20 to 1
Year: sems, ss Tuition: $754 ($1204)
Appl: open R and B: $1560
689 applied 689 accepted 505 enrolled
SAT or ACT: required NONCOMPETITIVE

Wayne State College, established in 1910, is a state-supported college of teacher education and liberal arts which offers both undergraduate and master's degree programs. Its library contains about 140,000 volumes and 4850 reels of microfilm, and subscribes to more than 1250 current periodicals.

Environment: The 135-acre campus is located in a small town 45 miles from Sioux City, Iowa. The dormitories on campus accommodate about 1500 students. Married student housing is available.

Student Life: About 85% of the students are from Nebraska. More than 90% of the freshmen come from public schools. Approximately 60% of the students live on campus. Campus housing is both coed and single-sex. There are visiting privileges in single-sex dorms. Students may have cars on campus.

Organizations: There are 3 fraternities and 3 sororities represented on campus. The college sponsors social and cultural activities.

Sports: The college competes in 5 intercollegiate sports; its intramural program consists of 9 sports.

Graduates: Thirty-seven percent of the freshmen drop out by the end of the first year; 42% remain to graduate. About 10% of the graduates continue their education.

Services: Free career and psychological counseling as well as tutoring services are available to all students.

Programs of Study: The college confers the B.A., B.A.Ed., B.F.A. in Ed., B.S., and B.S.Ed. degrees. Master's programs are also available. Bachelor's degrees are offered in the following subjects: BUSINESS (accounting, business administration, business education, finance, management, marketing, real estate/insurance), EDUCATION (elementary, health/physical, industrial, secondary, special), ENGLISH (English, journalism, literature, speech), FINE AND PERFORMING ARTS (art, art education, music, music education, radio/TV, studio art, theater/dramatics), HEALTH SCIENCES (medical technology), LANGUAGES (French, German, Spanish), MATH AND SCIENCES (biology, chemistry, earth science, mathematics, natural sciences, physical sciences), PREPROFESSIONAL (agriculture, architecture, computer science, dentistry, environmental health, health education, home economics, medicine, nursing, oceanography, optometry, pharmacy, physical therapy, physician assistant, veterinary), SOCIAL SCIENCES (economics, government/political science, history, social sciences, sociology).

Special: The college offers a cooperative medical technology program. A 4-year degree in pre-law also is awarded.

Honors: There are 17 honor societies represented on campus.

Admissions: All those who applied were accepted for the 1981–82 freshman class. The ACT scores of those who enrolled were as follows: 63% below 21, 27% between 21 and 25, and 11% between 26 and 28. Candidates should have completed 16 Carnegie units. Out-of-state residents should also rank in the upper 50% of their class. State residents are given preference. Other factors entering into the admissions decision include recommendations by school officials, personality, and advanced placement or honors courses.

Procedure: Either the ACT or SAT is required from out-of-state residents. There are no application deadlines. Notification is on a rolling basis. There is a $10 fee.

Special: Early decision and early and deferred admissions are offered. AP and CLEP credit is given.

Transfer: For fall 1981, 185 transfer students applied, 178 were accepted, and 135 enrolled. Transfers are accepted into all classes. A minimum 2.0 GPA and good standing are required. C grades or better transfer. There is a 1-year residency requirement. Twenty-four of the last 30 credits must also be completed at the college. A total of 125 credits is required for the bachelor's degree. Application deadlines are open.

Financial Aid: Eighty percent of the students receive aid; 15% work part-time on campus. Scholarships, loans, and jobs are available to qualified students. Candidates for aid must file the AFAS. Application deadline for aid is May 15.

Foreign Students: Nine full-time foreign students are currently enrolled at the college. An intensive English course as well as special counseling and organizations are available to these students.

Admissions: Foreign students must attain a minimum score of 550 on the TOEFL. The ACT also is required.

Procedure: Application deadlines are the same as for freshmen. Foreign students must provide proof of funds adequate to cover 4 years of study. Health insurance, while not required, is available through the college for a fee.

Admissions Contact: Jim Hummel, Director of Admissions.

NEVADA

SIERRA NEVADA COLLEGE A-3
Incline Village, Nevada 89450 (702) 831-1314

F/T: 70M, 50W Faculty: 2; n/av
P/T: 40M, 59W Ph.D.'s: 20%
Grad: none S/F Ratio: 6 to 1
Year: qtrs, ss Tuition: $2000
Appl: open R and B: n/app
80 applied 75 accepted 68 enrolled
SAT or ACT: not required LESS COMPETITIVE

Sierra Nevada College, founded in 1969, is a private, nontraditional college offering undergraduate training in the liberal arts and sciences. The college, designed for students who prefer a more independent environment than can be found at the typical university, emphasizes small classes, personal attention to each student, informality, and relevance of educational programs. Students have a strong voice in college governance through weekly town meetings at which they join members of the faculty and administration in working out problems, discussing the future of the college, and interviewing applicants. The library contains more than 12,000 volumes and subscribes to 125 periodicals.

Environment: The 3-acre rural campus is located in a town of 4000 inhabitants about 35 miles from Reno. There is no on-campus housing.

Student Life: About 20% of the students come from Nevada. About 17% are members of minority groups.

Organizations: The student-run College Council helps support any activities approved by students, including a student newspaper, a ski team, environmental awareness campaigns, films, and parties. There are no fraternities or sororities.

Sports: Intramural competition in 4 sports is offered for men and women. The college does not participate in intercollegiate sports.

Handicapped: There are no special facilities for physically handicapped students.

Graduates: About 15% of the freshmen drop out, and 50% remain to graduate. About 30% of those who graduate seek advanced degrees; 2% enter medical school and 2% enter law school. About 30% pursue careers in business and industry; 20% begin careers in the environmental sciences.

Services: Placement aid, career counseling, and psychological counseling are offered free of charge.

Programs of Study: The B.A. and B.S. degrees are awarded. Associate degrees also are available. Bachelor's degrees are offered in creative arts, environmental science, alternative energy studies, and liberal arts.

Required: All undergraduates must complete course work in English, history, humanities, creative arts, science, and recreation.

Special: Students may design their own majors, earn a bachelor's degree in 3 years, and gain credit for independent study, internships, life experience, and volunteer work in the community.

Admissions: About 94% of the applicants for the 1981-82 freshman class were accepted. A GPA of 2.0 or better generally is required. All applicants should submit samples of creative work and a statement of their philosophy and goals, and have an interview.

Procedure: No standardized tests are required. There is a $20 application fee. Application deadlines are open; new students are admitted each quarter.

Special: Early decision and deferred admissions plans are offered.

Transfer: About 50 transfer students are admitted each year. Applicants should have a GPA of 2.0 or better and submit an autobiographical essay. D grades transfer. Students must spend at least 2 quarters in residence, completing at least 24 of the 180 credits required for a bachelor's degree.

Visiting: Informal campus tours can be arranged, and visitors may sit in on classes.

Financial Aid: About 30% of the students receive assistance; 30% work part-time on campus. The college offers work-study programs, BEOG, and federally insured loans (FISL, NDSL). The total amount of federal funds available is $90,000. Application deadlines are August 1 (fall), December 1 (winter), March 1 (spring), and May 1 (summer).

Foreign Students: Foreign students enrolled full-time make up about 13% of the student body.

Admissions: Foreign applicants must take the TOEFL or any other English proficiency exam. No academic tests are required.

Procedure: Application deadlines are September 1 (fall), January 1 (winter), or March 1 (spring). Students must present proof of adequate funds.

Admissiosn Contact: Nettie McClure, Director of Admissions and Records.

UNIVERSITY OF NEVADA

The University of Nevada was established in 1874 as a coeducational land-grant institution and comprises a central part of the University of Nevada system. Other members of the system include Northern Nevada Community College, the Desert Research Institute, Western Nevada Community College, and Clark County Community College.

The University of Nevada operates two campuses in Reno and in Las Vegas. The Reno campus is the older campus; the Las Vegas campus was founded in 1955 as an additional campus serving residents in the southern part of the state. Separate profiles on each campus follow.

UNIVERSITY OF NEVADA/LAS VEGAS   D-5
Las Vegas, Nevada 89123   (702) 739-3443

F/T: 2766M, 2271W   Faculty: 407; IIA, ++$
P/T: 1027M, 1373W   Ph.D.'s: 62%
Grad: 271M, 432W   S/F Ratio: 24 to 1
Year: sems, ss   Tuition: $900 ($2900)
Appl: see profile   R and B: $2100
2811 accepted   1116 enrolled
SAT or ACT: required   LESS COMPETITIVE

The University of Nevada at Las Vegas, founded in 1955, offers undergraduate instruction in the liberal arts and sciences, business, education, nursing, and engineering. The library contains 750,000 volumes and 355,000 microfilm items, and subscribes to over 5000 periodicals.

Environment: The 335-acre campus is located in a suburban area near downtown Las Vegas and has 21 buildings, including a coed dormitory that accommodates 260 students.

Student Life: About 75% of the students are from Nevada, and 3% live on campus. Students may keep cars on campus. Day-care services are available, for a fee, to all students, faculty, and staff.

Organizations: There are 7 national fraternities, to which 5% of the men belong; 2% of the women belong to the 2 national sororities. There are 38 extracurricular activities and groups on campus, including religious organizations for the 3 major faiths, a student theater program, a hotel association, a chorus, and a student activities board. Ten to 15 cultural events take place on campus each week.

Sports: The university fields intercollegiate teams in 9 sports for men and 5 for women. Twelve intramural sports are offered for men and 9 for women.

Handicapped: Approximately 95% of the campus is accessible to the physically handicapped. Facilities include wheelchair ramps, special parking, elevators, and lowered drinking fountains and telephones.

Graduates: About 26% of the freshmen drop out.

Services: Career counseling, health care, and most placement services are free. Fees are charged for some psychological counseling, tutoring, and remedial instruction.

Programs of Study: The B.A., B.S., and B.F.A. degrees are awarded. Associate, master's, and doctoral programs are also offered. Bachelor's degrees are offered in the following subjects: AREA STUDIES (Asian, comparative literature, film, Latin American, linguistics, social science, women's), BUSINESS (accounting, computer science, finance, management, marketing), EDUCATION (early childhood, elementary, health/physical, secondary, special), ENGLISH (English), FINE AND PERFORMING ARTS (art, music, theater/dramatics), HEALTH SCIENCES (nursing, radiologic technology), LANGUAGES (French, German, Spanish), MATH AND SCIENCES (biology, chemistry, computer science, earth science, geology, mathematics, physics), PHILOSOPHY (philosophy), SOCIAL SCIENCES (anthropology, criminal justice, economics, government/political science, history, psychology, public administration, social work, sociology).

Required: All undergraduates are required to take 6 credits of English, 3 of U.S. Constitution, and 3 of Nevada constitution.

Special: A combined B.A.-B.S. degree is offered in a 5-year program. The environmental science curriculum offers interdisciplinary courses. The College of Hotel Administration offers a 1-year internship program, and summer tours of European hotels and restaurants. Work-study programs are available in nursing, communication studies, hotel administration, social services, and radiologic technology.

Honors: Seven national honor societies have chapters on campus.

Admissions: Residents of Nevada should have at least a 2.0 GPA; out-of-state applicants must have at least a 2.3 GPA. All applicants must be graduates of accredited high schools.

Procedure: The SAT or ACT is required. Applications should be submitted at least 1 week before the first day of classes for the semester in which the student seeks to enroll. The university follows a rolling admissions policy. There is a $5 application fee.

Special: AP and CLEP credit is accepted. An early decision plan is offered. A deferred admissions plan is available for military personnel only.

Transfer: Over 1000 transfer students are accepted yearly. Applicants should have at least a 2.0 GPA; D grades transfer. At least 30 semester hours of the 124 to 128 required for a bachelor's degree must be taken in residence.

Visiting: The admissiosn office should be contacted to arrange campus visits.

Financial Aid: Approximately 14% of all students receive aid through the school. There are 722 academic scholarships, including 202 athletic scholarships, available. Federal, guaranteed, and private loan funds are available. Work-study is also offered, and 5% of the students work part-time on campus. Tuition may be paid on a deferment plan. Financial need and academic promise are the main factors in determining awards. The FAF or FFS is required; the deadline for priority consideration of aid applications is April 1. The university is a member of CSS.

Foreign Students: The 220 foreign students enrolled at the university make up about 3% of the student body. An intensive English course, special counseling, and special organizations are available.

Admissions: Students must score 500 or better on the TOEFL, or 70 or better on the University of Michigan Language Test. No academic exams are required.

Procedure: Application deadlines are May 1 (fall) and October 1 (spring). Students must present proof of good health (including a tuberculosis test) and evidence of adequate funds for 1 academic year. They must carry health insurance, which is available through the university for a fee.

Admissiosn Contact: Joe Ann Adler, Director of Admissions.

UNIVERSITY OF NEVADA/RENO   A-3
Reno, Nevada 89557   (702) 784-6865

F/T: 2903M, 2549W	Faculty: 330; I, av$
P/T: 973M, 1087W	Ph.D.'s: 75%
Grad: 895M, 835W	S/F Ratio: 20 to 1
Year: sems, ss	Tuition: $896 ($2896)
Appl: July 15	R and B: $3086
2081 accepted	1449 enrolled
SAT: 400V 600M ACT: 19	COMPETITIVE

The University of Nevada at Reno offers undergraduate curricula in the liberal arts and sciences, agriculture, engineering, business, the health sciences, home economics, nursing, and education. The library contains 680,272 volumes and 1.3 million microfilm items, and subscribes to 5100 periodicals.

Environment: The main campus, located on 200 acres of rolling hills north of Reno's business district, has both traditional, ivy-covered buildings and modernistic facilities. Students may live on campus in residence halls, fraternity and sorority houses, and married-student housing.

Student Life: Almost all students come from the mountain states or the west coast, and 97% of entering freshmen come from public schools. About 15% of the students live on campus. Ten percent are members of minority groups. Dorms are both single-sex and coed; there are visiting privileges in single-sex dorms. Students may keep cars on campus. Day care is available, for a fee, to all students, faculty, and staff.

Organizations: There are 7 national fraternities and 5 national sororities. Most of Reno's churches promote special religious activities for university students. Reno and its environs offer a variety of cultural and recreational activities.

Sports: The university fields intercollegiate teams in 10 sports for men and 7 for women. Nineteen intramural sports are offered for men and 15 for women.

Handicapped: Approximately 75% of the campus is accessible to the physically handicapped. Facilities include wheelchair ramps, special parking, elevators, specially equipped rest rooms, and lowered drinking fountains and telephones. Special class scheduling is also available.

Graduates: The freshman dropout rate is 12%, and 35% remain to graduate. Sixty percent of those who graduate pursue advanced degrees, including 1% each who enter medical, dental, or law school. Forty percent of the graduates begin careers in business and industry.

Services: Placement services, career counseling, psychological counseling, tutoring, remedial instruction, and health care are offered free of charge.

Programs of Study: The university confers 19 types of B.A. and B.S. degrees. Associate and master's degrees also are awarded. Bachelor's degrees are offered in the following subjects: BUSINESS (accounting, business administration, finance, management, marketing, real estate/insurance), EDUCATION (early childhood, elementary, health/physical, secondary, special), ENGLISH (journalism, speech), FINE AND PERFORMING ARTS (art, art education, music, music education, theater/dramatics), LANGUAGES (French, German, Spanish), MATH AND SCIENCES (astronomy, biochemistry, biology, botany, chemistry, earth science, geology, mathematics, physical sciences, physics, zoology), PREPROFESSIONAL (agriculture, dentistry, engineering, home economics, medicine, pharmacy, veterinary), SOCIAL SCIENCES (anthropology, geography, government/political science, history, psychology, social sciences, sociology).

Special: A junior year abroad and independent research are offered. Students may choose dual majors.

Honors: An honors program is open to qualified students.

Admissions: The ACT scores of those who enrolled in a recent class were as follows: 20% scored between 20 and 23, 19% between 24 and 26, 7% between 27 and 28, and 6% above 28. Nevada residents should have at least a 2.3 GPA, but are admitted on probation with a 2.0 average. Out-of-state applicants should have at least a 2.5 GPA.

Procedure: The ACT or SAT is required; the ACT is preferred. Application deadlines are July 15 (fall) and January 4 (spring). The university follows a rolling admissions policy. There is a $5 application fee.

Special: AP and CLEP credit is accepted. Early decision, early admissions, and deferred admissions plans are offered.

Transfer: For fall 1981, 2081 transfer students applied, all were accepted, and 1449 enrolled. A C average, at least 15 credit hours, and SAT or ACT scores are required. Students must complete, at the university, 32 of the 128 semester credits necessary for the bachelor's degree. There is a 6-month residency requirement. Application deadlines are the same as those for freshmen.

Visiting: Informal visits can be arranged for weekdays through the office of school relations. Guides are available, and visitors may sit in on classes.

Financial Aid: Approximately 60% of the students receive aid. A fund of $70,000 is available in scholarship aid; loans are available from several sources totaling about $3 million. About 10% of the students work part-time on campus. The average award to freshmen from all sources in 1981–82 was $2000. The deadlines for financial aid applications are April 1 (fall), October 1 (spring), and March 1 (summer). The FFS is required.

Foreign Students: Foreign students enrolled full-time make up about 3% of enrollment. Special counseling and organizations are available.

Admissions: Students must score 500 or better on the TOEFL. No academic exams are required.

Procedure: Application deadlines are June 1 (fall) and November 1 (spring). Students must submit a completed university medical form as proof of health and must show evidence of funds adequate for at least 1 academic year. Students also are required to carry health insurance, which is available through the university for a fee.

Admissions Contact: Jack H. Shirley, Director of Admissions and Registrar.

NEW HAMPSHIRE

COLBY-SAWYER COLLEGE   C-5
New London, New Hampshire 03257   (603) 526-2010

F/T: 650W	Faculty: 51; IIB, −$
P/T: 20W	Ph.D.'s: 70%
Grad: none	S/F Ratio: 13 to 1
Year: 4-1-4	Tuition: $5450
Appl: open	R and B: $2320
825 applied 625 accepted	275 enrolled
SAT: 450V 450M	COMPETITIVE

Colby-Sawyer College, founded in 1837 in the liberal Protestant tradition, offers associate and baccalaureate degree programs. The library contains 75,000 volumes and 20,000 microfilm items, and subscribes to 325 periodicals.

Environment: The 40-acre rural campus is 100 miles from Boston. The 23 buildings include 14 dormitories, a fine arts center, and a science center.

Student Life: About 25% of the students come from New Hampshire; 70% come from New England. Ninety-eight percent live on campus. Five percent of the students are minority-group members. College housing is single-sex. Students may keep cars on campus. Day-care services are available to all students, faculty, and staff.

Organizations: A variety of extracurricular activities is offered by the college, including music and drama groups, publications, and special-interest and service groups. The college is located near ski areas and Lake Sunapee.

Sports: Intercollegiate programs are offered in 8 sports. There are 9 intramural sports.

Handicapped: The needs of handicapped students are considered individually.

Graduates: Nineteen percent of the freshmen drop out by the end of their first year. Sixty percent remain to graduate. Fifteen percent of the students pursue advanced study after graduation. Twenty-five percent pursue careers in business or industry.

Services: Students receive the following services free of charge: psychological counseling, health care, tutoring, remedial instruction, placement, and career counseling.

Programs of Study: The college confers the B.A., B.S., and B.F.A. degrees. Associate degrees are also offered. Bachelor's degrees are offered in the following subjects: AREA STUDIES (American), BUSINESS (business administration), EDUCATION (early childhood), FINE AND PERFORMING ARTS (art, theater/dramatics), HEALTH SCIENCES (medical technology, nursing), MATH AND SCIENCES (biology).

Required: All freshmen must take courses in English, humanities, math and science, fine arts, and social sciences.

Special: Independent study, pass/fail options, study abroad, and student-designed internships and apprenticeships are offered.

Honors: Alpha Psi Omega and Phi Theta Kappa have chapters on campus.

Admissions: About 76% of those who applied were accepted for the 1981–82 freshman class. The SAT scores of those who enrolled were as follows: Verbal—75% below 500, 10% between 500 and 599, 1% between 600 and 700, and 0% above 700; Math—80% below 500, 9% between 500 and 599, 1% between 600 and 700, and 0% above 700. Equally important factors entering into an admissions decision are the applicant's high school transcript, SAT scores, advanced placement, recommendations, and impressions made during an interview.

Procedure: All candidates are required to take the SAT. Students planning to continue biology, chemistry, or a foreign language should take the AT in that area. These tests should be taken no later than January of the senior year. Application deadlines are open. A $25 application fee should be forwarded with each application.

Special: Early decision and early and deferred admissions plans are available. AP and CLEP credit is accepted.

Transfer: For fall 1981, 35 students applied, 25 were accepted, and 20 enrolled. A minimum 2.0 GPA from an accredited college is recommended. D grades do not transfer. Half of the 36 units needed for a bachelor's degree must be completed at Colby-Sawyer. Application deadlines are open.

Visiting: Two open houses that include an overnight visit, a theater performance, class visitation, and meals are held annually. Visits may be made on selected Saturdays by appointment only. The admissions office should be contacted to arrange visits.

Financial Aid: About 35% of all students receive aid from the following sources: scholarships, loans, and campus employment. Fifty percent of the students work part-time on campus. Average aid to freshmen from all sources is $3000. Scholarships are regularly given to from 60 to 80 freshmen. The college is a member of the CSS and requires the FAF. The preferred application deadline is February 15.

Foreign Students: Two percent of the full-time students come from foreign countries. The college offers these students special counseling and special organizations.

Admissions: Foreign students must score at least 500 on the TOEFL. No college entrance examination is required.

Procedure: Application deadlines are open. Foreign students must present the college's health form. They must also carry health insurance, which is available through the college.

Admissions Contact: Peter R. Dietrich, Dean of Admissions.

DANIEL WEBSTER COLLEGE   D–6
Nashua, New Hampshire 03063   (603) 883-3556

F/T: 349M, 81W	Faculty: 24; n/av
P/T: 8M, 3M	Ph.D.'s: 30%
Grad: none	S/F Ratio: 19 to 1
Year: sems	Tuition: $4650
Appl: July 1	R and B: $2300
831 applied	676 accepted	206 enrolled
SAT: 420V 470M	ACT: 23	COMPETITIVE+

Daniel Webster College, founded in 1965 as the New England Aeronautical Institute, is a private, nonsectarian college offering career training in aviation, business, computer systems, and engineering. The library contains 21,000 volumes and 20 microfilmed periodicals, and subscribes to 180 periodicals.

Environment: The 60-acre suburban campus is 45 miles from Boston. Although relatively new, the atmosphere is that of an old New England college. The college has 9 buildings, including the Flight Center, which contains a flight simulator, an aircraft construction laboratory, a flight observation tower, and a meterology center. The computer center has a Data General Eclipse C150 and a Data General MV 8000. There is also a gymnasium. Four dormitories house 300 students.

Student Life: Nearly 20% of the students are from New Hampshire. Twenty-four other states are also represented. Sixty percent of the students live on campus. Ten percent of the students are minority-group members. College housing is single-sex; there are visiting privileges. Students may keep cars on campus.

Organizations: There are no fraternities or sororities. The student senate, the student union, and the women's club are the largest and most active extracurricular groups on campus. Other campus events include dances, films, and lectures. The student government regulates dorm life, student discipline, student publications, and the chartering and financing of student activities.

Sports: The college competes intercollegiately in 5 sports for men and 4 for women. There are 6 intramural sports for men and 5 for women.

Handicapped: Approximately 42% of the campus is accessible to the physically handicapped. Special parking and special class scheduling are available.

Graduates: The freshman dropout rate is 15%; 60% remain to graduate. Five percent pursue advanced degrees after graduation. Ninety percent pursue careers in business and industry.

Services: Career counseling, placement services, psychological counseling, tutoring, and remedial instruction are offered to students free of charge. Health care is available on a fee basis.

Programs of Study: The college confers the B.S. degree. Associate degrees are also offered. Bachelor's degrees are granted in the following areas: BUSINESS (aviation management, computer science, flight training, management), PREPROFESSIONAL (air traffic control).

Required: All students must take courses in English, math, introduction to programming, introduction to processing, and psychology.

Special: Selected juniors and seniors may enroll in the Air Traffic Control Management program, affiliated with the Federal Aviation Administration. Participants alternate a semester of work with a semester of study and earn about $4000 per work semester. Admission to this program is highly competitive. Independent study programs are also available.

Admissions: About 81% of those who applied were accepted for the 1981–82 freshman class. The SAT scores of those who enrolled were as follows: Verbal—45% below 500, 42% between 500 and 599, 12% between 600 and 700, and 1% above 700; Math—40% below 500, 49% between 500 and 599, 10% between 600 and 700, and 1% above 700. Candidates must have graduated from an accredited high school (or received a high school equivalency certificate) and have completed 16 units. Students applying to the aviation or engineering division should have studied trigonometry and physics. All candidates must have at least a C average. In addition, the following factors are considered: recommendations, advanced placement or honors courses, extracurricular activities, impressions made during an interview, and personality.

Procedure: Students must apply to 1 of the 4 academic divisions: aviation, business, computer systems, or engineering. All applicants are required to take the SAT by June of their senior year. The college has a rolling admissions plan; freshmen are admitted to both terms. Application deadlines are July 1 (fall) and December 1 (winter). A personal interview is recommended but not required, except for candidates for the aviation consumer management sequence. There is no application fee.

Special: Under the early option plan, students apply by December 1 and are notified by January 15. Early admissions and deferred admissions plans are also available. AP and CLEP credit is accepted.

Transfer: For fall 1981, 70 students applied, 65 were accepted, and 32 enrolled. A 2.0 GPA and combined SAT scores of 900 or an ACT score of 22 are required. D grades do not transfer. Students must complete, at the college, 30 of the 120 credits needed for the bachelor's degree. There is a 1-year residency requirement. Transfer application deadlines are June 1 (fall) and December 1 (winter).

Visiting: There are no regularly scheduled orientations for prospective students. Guides are available for informal visits weekdays from 9 A.M. to 4 P.M. and Saturdays 9 A.M. to 1 P.M. Visitors may sit in on classes. The admissions office should be contacted to arrange visits.

Financial Aid: About 50% of all students receive some form of financial aid. Fifty percent work part-time on campus. The average financial aid package is $1200. The college is a member of the CSS. Tuition may be paid on an installment plan. The FAF and federal IRS form are required. The aid application deadline is April 1.

Foreign Students: Three percent of the full-time students come from foreign countries.

Admissions: Foreign students must score at least 500 on the TOEFL.

DARTMOUTH COLLEGE B-4
Hanover, New Hampshire 03755 (603) 646-1110

F/T: 2100M, 1400W
P/T: none
Grad: 878 M&W
Year: see profile
Appl: Jan. 1
8100 applied
SAT: 600V 600M
Faculty: 671; I, +$
Ph.D.'s: 90%
S/F Ratio: 12 to 1
Tuition: $7050
R and B: $3055
1770 accepted   1054 enrolled
MOST COMPETITIVE

Dartmouth College, a private institution chartered in 1769, is a member of the Ivy League. Primarily an undergraduate college of liberal arts, it has developed graduate programs in the arts and sciences and graduate schools in business administration, engineering, and medicine. The library contains more than 1.2 million volumes and 370,000 microfilm items, and subscribes to 14,000 periodicals.

Environment: The 175-acre campus is located in a small town 140 miles northwest of Boston. The more than 100 buildings, primarily of colonial architecture, include research laboratories, performing-arts facilities, and a well-equipped computer center. Students live in dormitories and in fraternity houses.

Student Life: About 6% of the students are New Hampshire residents. About 93% live on campus; freshmen are required to live on campus and upperclassmen are expected to do so. Both single-sex and coed dormitories are available. An honor code governs student conduct.

Organizations: About 40% of the men join 1 of the 22 fraternities on campus, and 13% of the women join 1 of the 2 sororities. Religious clubs and places of worship are available on campus for members of most major faiths. There are several governing bodies composed of students, faculty members, and administrators. The college sponsors a large number of social, cultural, and other extracurricular activities; students depend primarily on these for recreation.

Sports: The college fields more than 30 intercollegiate teams for men, women, or both in 19 sports. More than 20 intramural sports are available.

Graduates: About 10% of the freshmen drop out, and 80% remain to graduate. Forty percent of the graduates seek advanced degrees immediately upon graduation, including 10% who enter medical school and 10% who enter law school. About a quarter of the graduates begin careers in business and industry.

Services: Student services include health care and career and placement counseling.

Programs of Study: The college awards the B.A. degree. Master's and doctoral degrees also are available. Bachelor's degrees are offered in the following subjects: AREA STUDIES (Asian, Russian), ENGLISH (comparative literature, English, literature and creative writing), FINE AND PERFORMING ARTS (art, art history, music, theater/dramatics, visual studies), LANGUAGES (French, German, Greek/Latin, Italian, Romance languages, Russian, Spanish), MATH AND SCIENCES (biochemistry, biology, chemistry, computer science, earth science, mathematics, mathematics and social sciences, physics), PHILOSOPHY (classics, philosophy, religion), PREPROFESSIONAL (engineering—engineering sciences), SOCIAL SCIENCES (anthropology, archaeology, economics, geography, government/political science, history, policy studies, psychology, sociology). About 36% of degrees are conferred in social sciences, 15% in English, and 19% in physical and biological sciences.

Required: Students must take courses or demonstrate proficiency in English and in a foreign language. All students must take at least 3 physical education courses and 4 courses each in humanities, sciences, and social sciences. To graduate, students must be able to swim 50 yards.

Special: The college calendar, called the Dartmouth Plan, consists of 4 equal quarters each year and allows students to take vacation periods or off-campus study during any quarter.

Students may design their own majors or take modified majors that involve 2 or more fields. Non-major programs include Afro-American studies, native American studies, environmental studies, teacher preparation, studies in education, film studies, Romanian, health care studies, urban studies, and women's studies. A variety of interdisciplinary seminars is available. Students may propose and design seminars and, if the administration approves, a faculty member will be assigned to teach them.

Special programs include study abroad in such countries as England, Romania, Panama, Germany, and the Soviet Union; studies in Washington, D.C.; an exchange program with 13 U.S. and 2 foreign colleges; and hands-on training in computers for more than 80% of the students.

Honors: Each department provides a senior honors program. A number of national honor societies, including Phi Beta Kappa, have chapters on campus.

Admissions: About 22% of those who applied for admission to the 1981-82 freshman class were accepted. Students must be high school graduates and should have completed at least 16 Carnegie units. About 99% of the freshmen graduated in the top fifth of their high school class. Besides SAT scores and quality of high school work, admissions officers consider intellectual promise, character and motivation, and special talents. The college seeks a geographically diverse student body. Special consideration is given to children of alumni.

Procedure: Applicants must take the SAT by December of the senior year and any 3 ATs, including English Composition and Math I or II, by March. An interview is optional. New students are admitted only in fall. The application deadline is January 1, and students are notified by April 15. An early decision plan is available. The application fee is $20.

Special: Early decision, early admissions, and deferred admissions plans are available. The college grants credit through AP and CLEP exams.

Transfer: No transfer students are accepted.

Financial Aid: About 40% of the students receive aid. College scholarships; loans from the college, local banks, and federal government; and part-time jobs, including CWS, are available. The average award to 1981-82 freshmen was $7000. The application deadline for aid is February 1.

Foreign Students: Students from foreign countries make up about 2% of enrollment. The college offers these students special counseling and special organizations.

Admissions: Applicants must take the TOEFL, the SAT, and 3 ATs (including English Composition and Math I or II).

Procedure: The application deadline is January 1; new students are admitted only in fall. Students must submit a physician's statement as evidence of good health and present proof of adequate funds for 1 year. They must carry health insurance, which is available through the college for a fee.

Admissions Contact: Alfred Quirk, Director of Admissions.

FRANKLIN PIERCE COLLEGE C-6
Rindge, New Hampshire 03461 (603) 899-5111

F/T: 520M, 430W
P/T: 27M, 17W
Grad: none
Year: 4-1-4, ss
Appl: Aug. 15
4200 applied
SAT: 410V 426M
Faculty: 51; IIA, --$
Ph.D.'s: n/av
S/F Ratio: 16 to 1
Tuition: $4775
R and B: $2275
3000 accepted   460 enrolled
LESS COMPETITIVE

Franklin Pierce College, founded in 1962, is a private institution of higher learning. The library contains 45,000 volumes and 55,000 microfilm items, and subscribes to 355 periodicals.

Environment: The 750-acre campus, located in the southwestern part of New Hampshire in the rural town of Rindge, 65 miles from Boston, includes the Library Resource Center, a student union, a fieldhouse, and 6 dormitories that accommodate 350 women and 450 men. Other facilities include a cafeteria, coffeehouse, theater, dispensary, ski trails, ski jump, and waterfront.

Student Life: Only 12% of the students are from New Hampshire; 88% come from other states. Seventy-four percent of entering freshmen come from public schools. About 85% live on campus. Thirty-one percent of the students are Catholic, 27% Protestant, and 20% Jewish. About 10% of the students are minority-group members. College housing is both single-sex and coed. There are visiting privileges in single-sex housing. Students may keep cars on campus.

Organizations: There are no fraternities or sororities. There are about 30 student organizations and activities, which include special-interest clubs, publications, radio, chorus, and drama. The Manor is the hub of many student activities. The college sponsors a cultural program of guest speakers, musical programs, and dramatic productions. The Student Senate is concerned with student activities, welfare, and services. There is student-faculty participation in curriculum matters.

Procedure: The application deadlines are March 1 (fall) and September 1 (winter). Foreign students must submit the results of a physical examination. They must also present proof of funds adequate to cover 1 academic year. They must carry health insurance, which is available through the college for a fee.

Admissions Contact: David T. Leach, Director of Admissions.

492 NEW HAMPSHIRE

Sports: The college competes in 10 intercollegiate sports for men and 9 for women. There is an intramural program of 10 sports for men and 8 for women.

Handicapped: About 40% of the campus is accessible to wheelchair-bound students.

Graduates: The freshman dropout rate is 42%; 34% remain to graduate. Thirty-six percent of graduates pursue graduate study; 2% enter medical school, 3% dental school, and 6% law school. Thirty-two percent pursue careers in business and industry.

Services: There is free placement service, which includes assistance in resume writing. Other free services include health care, career counseling, psychological counseling, tutoring, and remedial instruction.

Programs of Study: The college confers the B.A. and B.S. degrees. Bachelor's degrees are offered in the following subjects: BUSINESS (accounting, business administration, computer science, finance, management, marketing), EDUCATION (elementary, secondary), ENGLISH (English, journalism, literature), FINE AND PERFORMING ARTS (art, art education, music, radio/TV, studio art, theater/dramatics), MATH AND SCIENCES (biology, ecology/environmental science), PREPROFESSIONAL (dentistry, law, medicine, social work, veterinary), SOCIAL SCIENCES (anthropology, economics, history, psychology, social sciences, sociology). Thirty-seven percent of degrees are conferred in business, 18% in math and sciences, and 14% in social sciences.

Required: Every student is required to take the core curriculum, which includes English composition, laboratory science, social science, humanities, and math.

Special: The archeology program includes a summer field session. Study abroad in Europe is available. Student-designed majors are also permitted.

Admissions: Approximately 71% of those who applied were accepted for the 1981-82 freshman class. The SAT scores of those who enrolled were as follows: Verbal—91% below 500, 7% between 500 and 599, 2% between 600 and 700, and 0% above 700; Math—83% below 500, 15% between 500 and 599, 2% between 600 and 700, and 0% above 700. Candidates must be high school graduates with at least a C average and 16 college preparatory units. Also important are the accreditation and reputation of the high school and the difficulty of the program chosen. The college prefers a total SAT score of at least 800. In addition, the following factors are considered, in order of importance: advanced placement or honors courses, recommendations, impressions made during an interview, and leadership record.

Procedure: Either the SAT or the ACT is required and should be taken no later than January of the senior year. The application, high school transcript and recommendations, and test scores should be filed during the senior year. Application deadlines are August 15 (fall), December 15 (intersession), and January 15 (spring). Notification is on a rolling basis. The college subscribes to the CRDA. There is no application fee.

Special: There are programs for deferred and early admissions. CLEP credit is accepted.

Transfer: For fall 1981, 347 students applied, 288 were accepted, and 31 enrolled. Students may not transfer for the senior year. One year in resident study is required. Students must complete, at the college, 9 of the 36 courses required for a bachelor's degree. Application deadlines are the same as those for freshman applicants.

Visiting: The college has an open house twice a year. Campus tours are also available. Prospective students should contact the admissions office for details and arrangements. Visitors can also arrange to stay at the college.

Financial Aid: Seventy percent of the students receive financial aid. Forty-five percent work part-time on campus. Average aid to freshmen from all sources is $4300. The college participates in the NDSL, BEOG, and CWS programs. New Hampshire residents may be awarded $400 per year. The college also awards scholarships to worthy students as supplements to the federal aid program. The college is a member of the CSS and requires the FPC-FAF. Application deadlines are open.

Foreign Students: About 2% of the full-time students come from foreign countries. The college offers these students special counseling.

Admissions: Foreign students must score at least 500 on the TOEFL.

Procedure: Application deadlines are open. Foreign students must present proof of funds adequate to cover 4 years of study. They must also carry health insurance, which is available through the college for a fee.

Admissions Contact: Thomas E. Desrosiers, Director of Admissions.

KEENE STATE COLLEGE
Keene, New Hampshire 03431

B-6
(603) 352-1909

F/T: 1125M, 1675W	Faculty: 130; n/av
P/T: 290M, 430W	Ph.D.'s: 65%
Grad: 80M, 120W	S/F Ratio: 18 to 1
Year: sems, ss	Tuition: $1312 ($3212)
Appl: June 1	R and B: $1935
2008 applied 1628 accepted	842 enrolled
SAT: required	COMPETITIVE

Keene State College, established in 1909, offers an educational program in the liberal arts and sciences, the fine and performing arts, industrial technology, management, teacher education, and preprofessional work. The college is a division of the University System of New Hampshire. The library contains 170,000 volumes and 45,000 microfilm items, and subscribes to 2000 periodicals. There is also an information retrieval system with more than 90 direct-dial video- and audio-terminal consoles located throughout the campus.

Environment: The 80-acre campus is located about 90 miles from Boston in the typically New England city of Keene in southwest New Hampshire. The facilities include 13 academic buildings, 20 auxiliary buildings, 3 dormitories, 2 residence halls, 9 garden-style, apartment-like units, 4 fraternity houses, 18 minidorms, and 46 units of family housing. Three major buildings have been officially designated national historical buildings.

Student Life: About 55% of the students come from New Hampshire. Ninety percent of entering freshmen come from public schools. Approximately 65% of the students live in college housing. Fewer than 2% of the students are minority-group members. College housing is both single-sex and coed. There are visiting privileges in single-sex housing. Students may keep cars on campus. Day-care services are available to all students, faculty, and staff for a fee.

Organizations: There are 4 fraternities, to which 20% of the men belong, and 2 sororities, to which 8% of the women belong. Protestant and Roman Catholic chaplains provide counseling and also serve as advisors to the respective religious organizations. The college presents a full and varied program of cocurricular activities. Students assume considerable responsibility for the control of student activities through the Board of Selectmen and the College Senate. A committee of students and faculty members arranges a balanced social program.

Sports: The intercollegiate athletic program includes 12 women's and 8 men's teams. There are 12 intramural sports for men and 11 for women.

Handicapped: Facilities for the physically handicapped include wheelchair ramps, special parking, elevators, specially equipped rest rooms, and lowered drinking fountains. Special class scheduling is also available. The services of the New Hampshire vocational rehabilitation program are available for visual and hearing-impaired students.

Graduates: Seventy percent of those who enter as freshmen remain to graduate. Sixty percent of the graduates pursue graduate study: about 1% enter medical school, 1% dental school, and 3% law school. Thirty-five percent pursue careers in business and industry.

Services: Career counseling, health care, tutoring, remedial instruction, psychological counseling, and placement services are offered to students free of charge. Placement services include preparation of credentials and scheduling of meetings with representatives of various career opportunities.

Programs of Study: The college confers the B.A., B.S., B.S.Ind. Tech., B.M., and B.S.Ed. degrees. Associate and master's programs are also offered. Bachelor's degrees are offered in the following subjects: AREA STUDIES (American), BUSINESS (management), EDUCATION (early childhood, elementary, health/physical, industrial, secondary, special, vocational), ENGLISH (English, public affairs/journalism), FINE AND PERFORMING ARTS (art, music, music education, music performance, theater/speech), LANGUAGES (French, German, Spanish), MATH AND SCIENCES (biochemistry, biology, chemistry—geology, chemistry—industrial, chemistry—physics, computer math, earth science, environmental science, mathematics, math physics); PREPROFESSIONAL (dietetics, drafting and design, general technology, home economics, industrial electronics, manufacturing technology, safety studies), SOCIAL SCIENCES (geography, political science, history, psychology, sociology). A 3-year R.N. diploma program is also offered. Forty percent of degrees are conferred in education, 12% in social sciences, and 10% in math and sciences.

Required: The requirements for degrees vary according to major, but all require a foundation in humanities, social science, mathematics, and science.

Special: The college offers an independent travel-study course and an interdisciplinary seminar in the humanities. The college also has consortium-sharing arrangements with 12 private and public colleges in New Hampshire through the New Hampshire College and University Council. A 3-year bachelor's degree is offered. Student-designed majors and a general studies degree are also available.

Honors: Four national honor societies have chapters on campus.

Admissions: Approximately 81% of those who applied were accepted for the 1981-82 freshman class. The SAT scores of those who enrolled were as follows: Verbal—64% below 500, 32% between 500 and 599, 3% between 600 and 700, and 1% above 700; Math—61% below 500, 32% between 500 and 599, 6% between 600 and 700, and 1% above 700. Students should be graduates of accredited high schools and have completed a college preparatory program. Non-high-school graduates must have a high school equivalency certificate. Students are expected to rank in the top half of their graduating class and have a C average or better. The college also considers the following factors, in order of importance: advanced placement or honors courses, recommendations, leadership record, evidence of special talents, and extracurricular activities. There is a 25% quota for out-of-state students, who must therefore meet higher admissions standards than New Hampshire residents.

Procedure: The SAT is required and should be taken no later than January of the senior year. Interviews are not required. Application should be made preferably by June 1 (fall) or January 1 (spring). There is a rolling admissions plan. New Hampshire residents should send a $10 fee with the application; nonresidents should send a $20 fee.

Special: There is a deferred admissions plan. AP and CLEP credit is accepted.

Transfer: For fall 1981, of the 457 applications received, 381 were accepted, and 251 students enrolled. A minimum GPA of 2.0 and recommendations are required. D grades do not transfer. Students must complete, at the college, at least the last 30 hours of the 120 to 126 needed for a bachelor's degree. Preference is given to students from New Hampshire. Application deadlines are July 1 (fall) and January 1 (spring).

Visiting: Visits to the campus are strongly recommended. In addition to regular campus tours on weekdays and Saturdays there is a special "Find Out Program" in which prospective students may spend a night on campus, visit classes, meet with faculty, and obtain information about financial aid and admissions. The admissions office should be contacted for details and arrangements.

Financial Aid: Seventy-three percent of the students receive financial aid. Twenty percent work part-time on campus. Average aid to freshmen from all sources is $1900. NDSL, BEOG, and CWS are available, as are state scholarship programs and Keene Endowment programs. The college is a member of CSS. Candidates for financial aid must file the FAF with the Keene State form. Applications for aid are due by March 1 (fall).

Foreign Students: Fewer than 1% of the full-time students come from foreign countries.

Admissions: Foreign students must score at least 500 on the TOEFL.

Procedure: The application deadlines are June 1 (fall) and January 1 (spring). Foreign students must present proof of funds adequate to cover 1 school year.

Admissions Contact: Donald N. Parker, Acting Director of Admissions.

NATHANIEL HAWTHORNE COLLEGE C-6
Antrim, New Hampshire 03440   (603) 588-6341

F/T: 270M, 100W	Faculty: 20; IIB, −$
P/T: none	Ph.D.'s: 17%
Grad: none	S/F Ratio: 12 to 1
Year: sems, ss	Tuition: $4600
Appl: open	R and B: $2100
675 applied	525 accepted 150 enrolled
SAT: 400V 430M	ACT: 17 LESS COMPETITIVE

Nathaniel Hawthorne College, founded in 1962, is a small, private, career-oriented college with specializations in aerospace education. The library contains 65,000 volumes and subscribes to 426 periodicals.

Environment: The 900-acre rural campus is 90 miles from Boston. Campus buildings include 9 dormitories that house 100 women and 270 men. A cafeteria and lounge are available to day students. The college maintains its own airport and aircraft.

Student Life: Ten percent of the students are from New Hampshire and 80% are from other states. Seventy percent come from public schools. Ninety-eight percent of the students live on campus. Eleven percent of the students are minority-group members. College housing is both single-sex and coed. There are visiting privileges in single-sex housing. Students may keep cars on campus.

Organizations: There are religious organizations on campus representing the 3 major faiths. There are 2 fraternities. Other student groups include special-interest clubs, an active student council, and campus publications.

Sports: The college competes intercollegiately in 5 sports for men and 3 for women. A program of intramural sports is also offered in 6 sports for men and 4 for women.

Graduates: The freshman dropout rate is 16%; 80% remain to graduate. Five percent pursue graduate study after graduation; 2% enter law school. Ninety percent pursue careers in business and industry.

Services: The following services are offered free of charge to all students: career counseling, placement, psychological counseling, tutoring, and remedial instruction. Health care is offered on a fee basis.

Programs of Study: The college awards the B.A. and B.S.B.A. degrees. Associate degrees are also offered. Bachelor's degrees are offered in the following subjects: BUSINESS (aviation management, business administration, computer science, recreation management), MATH AND SCIENCES (mathematics), PHILOSOPHY (humanities), SOCIAL SCIENCES (history, social sciences).

Special: It is possible to earn a combined B.A.-B.S. degree in aviation and business. Student-designed majors are permitted. The college's aircraft are used as part of the curriculum for field trips and vacation tours. Students also have the opportunity to spend their junior year abroad.

Admissions: About 78% of those who applied were accepted for the 1981-82 freshman class. Of those who enrolled, the SAT scores were as follows: Verbal—80% below 500, 14% between 500 and 599, 4% between 600 and 700, and 1% above 700; Math—80% below 500, 14% between 500 and 599, 4% between 600 and 700, and 1% above 700. Applicants should have completed 15 Carnegie units, have at least a C average, and be in the top half of their class. Other considerations in the admissions decision are: leadership record, recommendations, advanced placement, extracurricular record, and personality.

Procedure: The SAT or ACT is required. Students are admitted to either semester. The deadline for fall application is open. The college follows a rolling admissions policy. There is an application fee of $15.

Special: Early decision and deferred admissions plans are available. AP and CLEP credit is accepted.

Transfer: A 2.0 GPA is required. D grades do not transfer. Thirty hours must be earned in residence. Application deadlines are open.

Visiting: Guides are available for informal visits to the campus. Visitors may sit in on classes and stay overnight at the school. Scheduled open houses are also held by the college. The admissions office should be contacted to arrange visits.

Financial Aid: About 70% of all students receive some form of financial aid. Fifteen percent work part-time on campus. The college is a member of CSS. Applications for financial aid and the FAF must be filed by March 1 (fall).

Foreign Students: Ten percent of the full-time students come from foreign countries. The college offers these students an intensive English program, special counseling, and special organizations.

Admissions: Neither an English proficiency examination nor a college entrance examination is required.

Procedure: Application deadlines are open. Foreign students must present proof of health and of adequate funds. They must also carry health insurance, which is available through the college for a fee.

Admissions Contact: Ronald K. Cooper, Director of Admissions.

NEW ENGLAND COLLEGE C-5
Henniker, New Hampshire 03242   (603) 428-2223

F/T: 740M, 479W	Faculty: 86; IIB, +$
P/T: 6M, 4W	Ph.D.'s: 45%
Grad: none	S/F Ratio: 15 to 1
Year: 4-1-4	Tuition: $5280
Appl: Aug. 1	R and B: $2380
1240 applied	1116 accepted 393 enrolled
SAT: 400V 430M	LESS COMPETITIVE

New England College is an international institution with a curriculum designed to provide a liberal education that responds to career needs. The library contains 77,000 volumes and 3000 microfilm items, and subscribes to 500 periodicals.

494 NEW HAMPSHIRE

Environment: Situated on a rural 220-acre campus 16 miles from Concord, the college has over 20 buildings.

Student Life: Ten percent of the students are from New Hampshire, and 80% are from other states. Seventy percent of entering freshmen come from public schools. Sixty percent live on campus. College housing is both single-sex and coed. There are visiting privileges in single-sex housing. Students may keep cars on campus. Student regulations permit drinking only if the student is 18 years of age. Freshman women observe a curfew.

Organizations: There are religious organizations on campus representing the 3 major faiths. There are 3 fraternities, to which 10% of the men belong, and 1 sorority. Other student groups include special-interest clubs, an active student council, and campus publications. The college is near 7 major ski areas.

Sports: The college competes intercollegiately in 11 sports for men and 8 for women. There are 2 intramural sports for men and 2 for women.

Handicapped: There are no facilities for handicapped students.

Graduates: Twenty percent of graduates pursue graduate study; 50% pursue careers in business and industry.

Services: The following services are provided free of charge: career counseling, psychological counseling, placement, and health care.

Programs of Study: The college awards the B.A. and B.S. degrees. Master's degrees are also conferred. Bachelor's degrees are offered in the following subjects: AREA STUDIES (American), BUSINESS (accounting, finance, international administration, management, marketing, public administration), EDUCATION (elementary, health/physical, secondary), ENGLISH (English), FINE AND PERFORMING ARTS (theater/dramatics, visual arts), MATH AND SCIENCES (biology, ecology/environmental science, geology, mathematics, natural sciences), PHILOSOPHY (philosophy), PREPROFESSIONAL (engineering), SOCIAL SCIENCES (economics, government/political science, history, psychology, sociology). Forty percent of degrees are conferred in business and 20% are in education.

Special: The college operates a campus in Great Britain. It is possible to earn a combined B.A.-B.S. degree in any major that is combined with engineering. Student-designed majors are permitted, and a general studies degree is available.

Admissions: Ninety percent of those who applied were accepted for the 1981–82 freshman class. The SAT scores of those who enrolled were as follows: Verbal—88% below 500, 11% between 500 and 599, 1% between 600 and 700, and 0% above 700; Math—78% below 500, 16% between 500 and 599, 5% between 600 and 700, and fewer than 1% above 700. Admission is dependent on the applicant's academic preparation, personal qualifications, and potential for success at the college. The major criteria used are the applicant's 4-year academic record, class rank, SAT or ACT scores (or an interview in the case of students from other than American secondary schools). Other factors entering into the admissions decision are evidence of special talents and the applicant's extracurricular activities record.

Procedure: The SAT or ACT is required. Application deadlines are August 1 (fall) and January 1 (spring). The college has a rolling admissions plan. There is a $15 application fee.

Special: A deferred admissions plan is offered. AP and CLEP credit is accepted.

Transfer: For fall 1981, 160 students applied, 123 were accepted, and 70 enrolled. Both campuses of New England College welcome transfer applicants. The admissions criteria and procedures are the same as those for freshmen, except that transcripts from previous schools are required, as well as a Confidential Inquiry Form that is to be filled out by the dean of students at the last college attended. To receive a bachelor's degree, students must complete at least 32 credits at the college. There is a 1-year residency requirement. Application deadlines are the same as for freshman applicants.

Visiting: Prospective students may stay on campus. Guides are also available. The office of admissions should be contacted for details and arrangements.

Financial Aid: About 51% of all students receive some form of financial aid. Forty-eight percent work part-time on campus. Average aid to freshmen from all sources is $3500. The college is a member of CSS. Applications for financial aid and the FAF must be filed by April 15.

Foreign Students: Ten percent of the full-time students come from foreign countries. The college offers these students an intensive English course, special counseling, and special organizations.

Admissions: Foreign students must score at least 450 on the TOEFL. No college entrance examination is required.

Procedure: The application deadlines are August 1 (fall) and January 1 (spring). Foreign students must present proof of health. They must also present proof of funds adequate to cover 1 year of study.

Admissions Contact: Rick Stoerker, Dean of Admissions.

NEW HAMPSHIRE COLLEGE   D–6
Manchester, New Hampshire 03104   (603) 668-2211

F/T: 820M, 707W Faculty: 57; IIA, +$
P/T: 24M, 19W Ph.D.'s: 37%
Grad: 790M, 206W S/F Ratio: 27 to 1
Year: sems, ss Tuition: $4922
Appl: open R and B: $2872
2977 applied 2059 accepted 526 enrolled
SAT: required COMPETITIVE

New Hampshire College, founded in 1932, is a private, nonprofit, coeducational college offering a professional business curriculum. The college has 9 centers: Manchester, Salem, Portsmouth, Laconia, and Concord, New Hampshire; Brunswick and Winter Harbor, Maine; and Roosevelt Roads and San Juan, Puerto Rico. The library is a multimedia center that has 58,000 volumes, 33,000 microfilm items, and 3000 audio-visual materials; and subscribes to 800 periodicals.

Environment: The 160-acre suburban Manchester campus, located 3 miles from Manchester, has 20 modern buildings. Freshmen live in dormitories; upperclassmen live in apartments and townhouses. Fraternity and sorority houses also are available.

Student Life: About 30% of the students are residents of New Hampshire; 62% come from New England and the Middle Atlantic states. Nearly 80% of the students live in college housing. Thirty-eight percent of the students are Catholic, 40% Protestant, and 7% Jewish. Three percent of the students are minority-group members. College housing is both single-sex and coed. There are visiting privileges in single-sex housing. Students may keep cars on campus.

Organizations: There are 4 fraternities and 3 sororities on campus, to which 12% of the men and 10% of the women belong. There are 50 extracurricular activities groups. The student government organizes social and cultural events on campus.

Sports: The college competes in 6 intercollegiate sports for men and 4 for women. It offers 11 intramural programs for men and 10 for women.

Handicapped: About 90% of the campus is accessible to wheelchair-bound students. Lowered telephones and drinking fountains, specially equipped rest rooms, parking, and wheelchair ramps are offered to physically handicapped students. There are no hearing-impaired or visually handicapped students currently enrolled.

Graduates: About 12% of the graduates pursue advanced degrees; 90% pursue careers in business and industry.

Services: Free tutoring, remedial instruction, career and psychological counseling, and job placement services are available. The school also provides workshops on resume writing and interview techniques, and gives notification of job openings. Health care is available on a fee basis.

Programs of Study: The college grants the B.S. degree. Associate and master's degrees are also offered. The college grants bachelor's degrees in the following subjects: BUSINESS (accounting, business administration, business education, computer science, finance and economics, hotel/restaurant management, management, management advisory services, management information systems, marketing, office administration, retailing, techni-business).

Required: All 4-year students are required to take 9 credits of English, 6 credits each of math, economics, accounting, and management, and 3 credits of business data processing.

Special: Students in marketing, retailing, fashion merchandising, and hotel/restaurant management can spend a summer internship in a firm in Europe or Canada. Domestic internships are available in all of the 4-year majors and in some 2-year programs. Students who work in their area of expertise can earn up to 15 credits, be paid while on the job, and be given placement assistance in the geographic area of their choice. Students may also participate in study-abroad programs with a number of British schools.

Honors: Delta Mu Delta, Alpha Phi Omega, and Pi Omega Pi are represented on campus.

Admissions: About 69% of those who applied were accepted for the 1981–82 freshman class. On the SAT, 12% of those who enrolled in a recent freshman class scored above 500 Verbal and 27% above 500 Math. Candidates should be in the top 70% of their class and have a 2.5 GPA. GED diplomas are acceptable. The college strongly recommends an on-campus interview. Recommendations are also considered.

Procedure: The SAT is required. The deadline for admissions is open. The college follows a rolling admissions plan. There is no application fee.

Special: Early admissions and deferred admissions plans are offered. AP and CLEP credit is accepted.

Transfer: For fall 1981, 513 applications were received, 440 were accepted, and 150 students enrolled. A 2.2 GPA is necessary. D grades do not transfer. A minimum of 33 credits must be taken in residence to earn a bachelor's degree. Application deadlines are open.

Visiting: There are regularly scheduled orientations including a personal interview and a tour of the campus. Arrangements for campus visits can be made through the admissions office.

Financial Aid: About 78% of the students receive scholarship aid and financial loans, grants, and work-study assistance from a combination of federal and private sources. Forty-eight percent work part-time on campus. Average aid to freshmen from all sources is $5500. The college is a member of the CSS. The FAF and a college scholarship and assistance application form are required. The deadline for aid applications is March 15.

Foreign Students: One percent of the full-time students come from foreign countries. The college offers these students an intensive English program, special counseling, and special organizations.

Admissions: Foreign students must score at least 500 on the TOEFL. No college entrance examination is required.

Procedure: Application deadlines are open. Foreign students must submit a completed health form. They must also present proof of funds adequate to cover 1 year of study.

Admissions Contact: Michael DeBlasi, Director of Admissions.

NOTRE DAME COLLEGE D-6
Manchester, New Hampshire 03104 (603) 669-4298

F/T: 44M, 344W	Faculty: 37; IIB, --$
P/T: 28M, 159W	Ph.D.'s: 27%
Grad: 12M, 155W	S/F Ratio: 10 to 1
Year: sems, ss	Tuition: $2900
Appl: open	R and B: $1800
297 applied 250 accepted 136 enrolled	
SAT or ACT: not required	COMPETITIVE

Notre Dame College, founded in 1950, is a private liberal arts college primarily for women. The library contains 44,000 volumes and 3052 microfilm items, and subscribes to 278 periodicals.

Environment: The suburban campus, within reach of Manchester and Boston, has 15 buildings, including 8 women's dormitories with single, double, and triple rooms housing 150.

Student Life: About 35% of the women live in campus housing. Sixty-five percent of the students are Catholic, and 13% are Protestant. Fewer than 1% of the students are minority-group members. College housing is single-sex; there are visiting privileges. Students may keep cars on campus. Daily mass is available to all students.

Organizations: Special-interest clubs, organizations, and committees are offered.

Sports: There are 7 intramural sports for both men and women.

Handicapped: Approximately 80% of the campus is accessible to the physically handicapped. Facilities include wheelchair ramps, special parking, elevators, specially equipped rest rooms, electric door openers, and lowered drinking fountains and telephones. Special class scheduling is also available.

Graduates: Ten percent of the students who remain to graduate pursue graduate study.

Services: Students receive the following services free of charge: health care, psychological counseling, tutoring, remedial instruction, placement, and career counseling.

Programs of Study: The college confers the B.A. and B.S. degrees. Associate, master's, and doctoral programs are also offered. Bachelor's degrees are offered in the following subjects: BUSINESS (business education, secretarial science), EDUCATION (early childhood, elementary, secondary, special), ENGLISH (English), FINE AND PERFORMING ARTS (art, art education, commercial art, music, music education), HEALTH SCIENCES (cytotechnology, medical technology), LANGUAGES (French, Latin, Spanish), MATH AND SCIENCES (biology), PHILOSOPHY (religion), PREPROFESSIONAL (social work), SOCIAL SCIENCES (behavioral science, history, paralegal science). Thirty percent of degrees are conferred in education, 26% in fine and performing arts, and 16% in health sciences.

Special: The A.A. degree is offered in child study; legal, medical, and executive secretarial study; music performance; and pre-pharmacy.

Admissions: About 84% of those who applied were accepted for the 1981-82 freshman class. Requirements for admission are as follows: a high school diploma or the equivalent, the submission of the high school record, a rank in the top half of the class, and recommendations. Additional factors in an admissions decision are advanced placement and evidence of special talent. Portfolio reviews and music auditions are required of art and music applicants. Pre-pharmacy students must have an interview before acceptance.

Procedure: The SAT or ACT is optional. There is a rolling admissions program. A personal interview is strongly recommended. Applications should be submitted with a $15 fee.

Special: Deferred admissions and early decision plans are available.

Transfers: For fall 1981, 66 students applied, 50 were accepted, and 27 enrolled. Students must be in good standing at their previous college, with at least a 2.0 GPA. D grades transfer. Transfers are considered for all classes. Students must complete, at the college, 30 of the 122 credits needed for a bachelor's degree. There are no formal deadlines for applications.

Visiting: Fall and spring open houses are held by the college. Guides are also available for informal weekday visits to the campus. The admissions office should be contacted to arrange visits.

Financial Aid: About 60% of all students receive some form of financial aid. Fourteen percent work part-time on campus. Average aid to freshmen from all sources covers 95% of costs. Tuition may be paid on an installment plan. The college is a member of the CSS. The FAF is required of aid applicants along with the college's own form. The deadline for application is March 1 (fall).

Foreign Students: Fewer than 1% of the full-time students come from foreign countries.

Admissions: Foreign students must score at least 500 on the TOEFL. No college entrance examination is required.

Procedure: Application deadlines are open. Foreign students must present a health certificate. They must also present proof of funds adequate to cover 1 year of study. They must carry health insurance.

Admissions Contact: Barbara E. Schultze, Director of Admissions and Financial Aid.

PLYMOUTH STATE COLLEGE D-4
Plymouth, New Hampshire 03264 (603) 536-1550

F/T: 1500M, 1500W	Faculty: 170; n/av
P/T: 150M, 150W	Ph.D.'s: 75%
Grad: 50M, 50W	S/F Ratio: 21 to 1
Year: sems, ss	Tuition: $1325 ($3225)
Appl: June 1	R and B: $1850
2000 applied 1500 accepted 900 enrolled	
SAT or ACT: required	LESS COMPETITIVE

Plymouth State College, established in 1871 and governed by the University System of New Hampshire, is a coeducational public college emphasizing education curricula. Although historically a teacher-training institution, 70% of its students are now enrolled in the liberal arts and business administration divisions. The library contains 200,000 volumes and 230,000 microfilm items, and subscribes to 1200 periodicals.

Environment: The 66-acre suburban campus, located in the White Mountains and lakes region of New Hampshire 40 miles from Concord, plays a vital role in the life of the community. The campus consists of over 25 buildings, including an auditorium-gymnasium, 7 dormitories, student apartments, an infirmary, recreation fields, and a modern fieldhouse with an indoor pool, track, 3 gyms, and handball courts. Fraternity and sorority houses offer additional living facilities, and married student housing is also available. The college also owns a woodland park area for recreation and nature study and a cottage on a neighboring lake.

Student Life: Since preference is given to residents of New Hampshire, 70% of the students are from the state. Ninety-nine percent of entering freshmen come from public schools. Seventy percent of the students live on campus. Fewer than 1% of the students are minority-group members. College housing is both single-sex and coed. There are visiting privileges in single-sex housing. Students may keep cars on campus. Day-care services are available to all students, faculty, and staff for a fee. The college makes no requirements concerning religious

NEW HAMPSHIRE

attendance, but provides religious facilities for both Catholics and Protestants.

Organizations: There are 5 fraternities, to which 10% of the men belong, and 5 sororities, to which 10% of the women belong. There are also several religious clubs on campus. Five major ski areas are located within 25 miles.

Sports: The college competes intercollegiately in 12 sports for men and 7 for women. There are 9 intramural sports for men and 10 for women.

Handicapped: There are no special facilities for the physically handicapped.

Graduates: The freshman dropout rate is 25%; 75% remain to graduate. Ten percent of graduates go on to graduate study. Forty percent enter careers in business and industry.

Services: The following services are offered to students free of charge: career counseling, psychological counseling, placement, and health care. Tutoring and remedial instruction are available for a fee.

Programs of Study: The college confers the B.A., B.S., and B.F.A. degrees. Associate and master's programs are also offered. Bachelor's degrees are offered in the following subjects: BUSINESS (accounting, business administration, business education, management, marketing), EDUCATION (early childhood, elementary, health/physical, secondary), ENGLISH (English, journalism, literature), FINE AND PERFORMING ARTS (art, art education, music, music education, studio art), HEALTH SCIENCES (medical technology), LANGUAGES (French, Spanish), MATH AND SCIENCES (biology, chemistry, mathematics, physical sciences), PHILOSOPHY (philosophy), PREPROFESSIONAL (law, social work), SOCIAL SCIENCES (anthropology, geography, government/political science, history, psychology, social sciences, sociology).

Required: All students must complete courses in the standard liberal arts fields. Physical education is also required.

Special: The college considers noteworthy its International Understanding Program and the College Teachers Preparation Program in cooperation with the University of New Hampshire. Students may spend the junior year abroad, but the college does not include the program as part of the regular curriculum. Student-designed majors are permitted. It is possible to earn a general studies degree.

Honors: There are interdisciplinary honors seminars.

Admissions: Seventy-five percent of those who applied were accepted for the 1981–82 freshman class. The college requires graduation from an accredited high school, with 15 completed Carnegie units and a minimum C average. Students should rank in the top half of their graduating class. Factors considered most important by the college are the high school record, ACT or SAT scores, and recommendations. Also considered important are leadership potential, personality, and intellectual capacity. The college has a 25% quota on out-of-state students and therefore requires higher standards for their admissions.

Procedure: The SAT or ACT is required and should be taken in May of the junior year or in December of the senior year. Applications should be submitted as soon as possible in the year of desired enrollment; the deadlines are June 1 (fall) and January 1 (spring). The college follows a rolling admissions policy. The application fee is $10 for New Hampshire residents and $20 for nonresidents.

Special: There is an early admissions plan. AP and CLEP credit is accepted.

Transfer: For fall 1981, 300 students applied, 200 were accepted, and 150 enrolled. A 2.0 GPA is necessary. D grades do not transfer. Students must complete, at the college, 30 of the 122 credits needed for a bachelor's degree. Application deadlines are June 1 (fall) and January 1 (spring).

Visiting: Campus tours are available Monday through Friday at 11:00 A.M. and 2:00 P.M. Visitors can also make arrangements to stay at the college. The admissions office should be contacted for details.

Financial Aid: About 80% of all students receive financial aid in the form of scholarships, loans, grants and/or campus employment. Forty percent of the students work part-time on campus. Average aid to freshmen from all sources is $2412. Loans are available from the federal government, NDSL and EOG funds, and from a college fund. The college is a member of CSS. The FAF is required. Applications for scholarships and loans must be submitted by March 1 (fall) and January 1 (spring).

Foreign Students: Fewer than 1% of the full-time students come from foreign countries. The college offers these students special counseling and special organizations.

Admissions: Foreign students must take the TOEFL. No college entrance examination is required.

Procedure: The application deadlines are June 1 (fall) and January 1 (spring). Foreign students must present proof of funds adequate to cover 4 years of study.

Admissions Contact: C. W. Bailey, Director of Admissions.

RIVIER COLLEGE D–6
Nashua, New Hampshire 03060 (603) 888-1311

F/T: 670W Faculty: 40; IIA; n/av
P/T: 756 M&W Ph.D.'s: 25%
Grad: 683 M&W S/F Ratio: 17 to 1
Year: sems, ss Tuition: $3600
Appl: open R and B: $2400
516 applied 345 accepted 254 enrolled
SAT: 440V 450M **COMPETITIVE**

Rivier is a 4-year liberal arts college conducted by the Sisters of the Presentation of Mary. The library contains 86,000 volumes, and subscribes to 510 periodicals.

Environment: The 44-acre suburban campus is 50 minutes from Boston. The 19 buildings include 2 science buildings, the College Center, and 2 dormitories housing 300 students.

Student Life: Students come mostly from New England and the Middle Atlantic states. Seventy-five percent of students are graduates of public schools. About 45% live on campus. About 60% of the students are Catholic, and 40% are Protestant. Six percent of the students are minority-group members. College housing is single-sex; there are visiting privileges. Students may keep cars on campus. Use or possession of alcoholic beverages is permitted in students' rooms.

Organizations: There are no fraternities or sororities. Student groups include a student council and special-interest clubs. Ski tours, drama, films, concerts, and campus publications are available.

Sports: The college fields intercollegiate teams in 2 sports for women. There are 5 intramural sports for women.

Handicapped: About 85% of the campus is accessible by wheelchair. One percent of the students are visually impaired. Readers are available, and students may use tape recorders in class. Teachers are available to assist handicapped students. Special class scheduling is also possible.

Graduates: About 5% of the freshmen drop out by the end of the first year, and 80% remain to graduate. Twenty percent of the graduates pursue advanced degrees; 2% enter medical school, and 2% law school. Twenty percent enter careers in business and industry.

Services: Services available to students free of charge include health care, psychological and career counseling, placement, and remedial instruction. Tutoring is available on a fee basis.

Programs of Study: The B.A., B.F.A., and B.S. degrees are conferred. Associate and master's programs are also offered. Bachelor's degrees are offered in the following subjects: BUSINESS (accounting, business administration, business education, computer science, management, marketing), EDUCATION (early childhood, elementary, secondary, special), ENGLISH (English, English/business, English/computer science, English/design, English/education, English/political science, journalism, literature), FINE AND PERFORMING ARTS (art, art education, design, music, music education, pre-art therapy studio art), HEALTH SCIENCES (medical technology), MATH AND SCIENCES (biology, chemistry, mathematics), PREPROFESSIONAL (dentistry, law, medicine, social work), SOCIAL SCIENCES (psychology, sociology). Of the total degrees conferred, about 21% are in education, 23% in business, and 19% in health sciences.

Required: Courses in English literature, foreign language, science, mathematics, social sciences, philosophy, religious studies, and physical education are required of all students.

Special: A combination degree program in medical technology is offered.

Honors: Honor societies on campus include Delta Epsilon Sigma and Kappa Gamma Pi.

Admissions: About 67% of those who applied were accepted for the 1981–82 freshman class. The SAT scores of those who enrolled were as follows: Verbal—55% below 500, 30% between 500 and 599, 10% between 600 and 700, and 5% above 700; Math—52% below 500, 33% between 500 and 599, 10% between 600 and 700, and 5% above 700. Applicants should rank in the upper half of their graduating class and have a B average; exceptions may be made. Sixteen high school units are required. An interview and a campus visit are strongly recommended but not required. The following factors are also considered: advanced placement or honors courses, impressions made during an interview, leadership record, extracurricular activities record, and recommendations.

Procedure: The SAT is required for 4-year degree candidates only; it is usually taken in November or December. Application deadlines are open. The college follows a rolling admissions plan. There is a $15 application fee.

Special: The college has early decision and deferred admissions plans. AP and CLEP credit is accepted.

Transfer: For fall 1981, 52 students applied, 50 were accepted, and 50 enrolled. An average of at least C+ is required. D grades sometimes transfer. There is a residency requirement of 2 semesters and 30 credits out of the 120 needed for a bachelor's degree must be completed at the college. Application deadlines are open.

Financial Aid: About 62% of all students receive financial aid in the form of scholarships, grants-in-aid, and loans. Thirty-five percent work part-time on campus. Average aid awarded to freshmen from all sources covers about 67% of costs. Awards are based on academic record, promise of success, SAT scores, and financial need. The college is a member of CSS. The FAF, the college's financial aid form, academic credentials, and SAT scores must be received by the admissions office no later than February 15 (fall) or December 15 (spring).

Foreign Students: Fewer than 1% of the full-time students come from foreign countries.

Admissions: Foreign students must score within the 50th percentile on the TOEFL. No college entrance examination is required.

Procedure: Application deadlines are open. Foreign students must present proof of funds adequate to cover their entire period of study.

Admissions Contact: Sr. Florence Jasmin, Acting Director of Admissions.

ST. ANSELM COLLEGE D-6
Manchester, New Hampshire 03102 (603) 669-1030

F/T: 879M, 786W	Faculty: 107; IIB, av$
P/T: 127M, 109W	Ph.D.'s: 37%
Grad: none	S/F Ratio: 16 to 1
Year: sems, ss	Tuition: $4370
Appl: July 15	R and B: $2130
2292 applied	1383 accepted	539 enrolled
SAT: 456V 498M		COMPETITIVE

St. Anselm College is a private, Catholic, liberal arts college for men and women conducted by the Order of St. Benedict. The library contains 120,000 volumes and 50,000 microfilm items, and subscribes to 1200 periodicals.

Environment: The 300-acre campus is located in a beautiful suburban area. College property includes residence halls for men and women, a student union building, a gymnasium, and other academic and recreational facilities.

Student Life: About 28% of the students are from New Hampshire. Sixty-seven percent come from public schools; 67% live on campus. Eighty-nine percent of the students are Catholic, and 11% are Protestant. About 1% of the students are minority-group members. College housing is single-sex; there are visiting privileges. Students may keep cars on campus. Day-care services are available to all students free of charge.

Organizations: There are 2 local fraternities, to which 5% of the men belong. Five major ski slopes as well as other local facilities provide extracurricular activities.

Sports: The college participates on an intercollegiate level in 10 sports for men and 7 for women. There are 9 intramural sports for men and 11 for women.

Handicapped: There are no special facilities for the physically handicapped.

Graduates: Fifteen percent of the freshmen drop out by the end of their first year. About 67% remain to graduate. Fifty percent of those who remain pursue advanced study after graduation; about 1% enter medical school, 1% dental school, and 3% law school.

Services: Tutoring, placement, career counseling, psychological counseling, and health care are offered at no cost.

Programs of Study: The college confers the B.A. and B.S. degrees. Associate degrees are also offered. Bachelor's degrees are offered in the following subjects: AREA STUDIES (urban), BUSINESS (computer science, general business), EDUCATION (secondary), ENGLISH (English), HEALTH SCIENCES (nursing), LANGUAGES (French, Spanish), MATH AND SCIENCES (biology, chemistry, mathematics, natural sciences), PHILOSOPHY (classics, philosophy, religion), PREPROFESSIONAL (dentistry, engineering, law, medicine, social work, veterinary), SOCIAL SCIENCES (economics, geography, government/political science, history, psychology, sociology). Twenty percent of degrees are conferred in business, 20% in math and sciences, 16% in criminal justice, and 16% in health sciences.

Required: All students must take English composition, a lab science, the humanities program, courses in a foreign language, and philosophy. Catholic students must take 3 courses in theology.

Special: There is a 3-2 engineering program with Notre Dame University and the University of Lowell.

Honors: Delta Epsilon Sigma, Tau Kappa Alpha, and Phi Sigma Tau have chapters on campus.

Admissions: Sixty percent of those who applied were accepted for the 1981-82 freshman class. Candidates must have completed a strong college-preparatory program. Successful candidates generally rank in the top half of their class. Other considerations in the admissions decision include advanced placement, evidence of special talent, and recommendations.

Procedure: The SAT is required and should be taken by December of the senior year. The fall deadline is July 15. The application deadline for students planning to live on campus is April 15; the deadline for the nursing program is January 1. There is a rolling admissions plan. All applications must be accompanied by a $15 application fee.

Special: There are early decision and early and deferred admissions plans. AP and CLEP credit is accepted.

Transfer: About 57% of the applicants were accepted in a recent year. A 2.0 GPA and good academic standing are required. D grades do not transfer. Two years of study and 20 courses, of the 40 courses necessary for the bachelor's degree, must be completed in residence. Application deadlines are April 15 (fall) and December 15 (winter).

Visiting: Guides are available for informal visits to the campus. Visitors may sit in on classes and stay at the school. Arrangements should be made with the dean of students.

Financial Aid: About 62% of all students receive some form of financial aid. About 37% work part-time on campus. Average aid to freshmen from all sources is $2510. Scholarships, loan funds, and other forms of financial aid are available. The college is a member of CSS. The FAF must be filed along with the college's own form. The deadline is April 15.

Foreign Students: Fewer than 1% of the full-time students come from foreign countries.

Admissions: Foreign students must take the TOEFL. The SAT is recommended.

Procedure: Application deadlines are open. Foreign students are admitted in the fall, winter, and spring.

Admission Contact: Donald E. Healy, Director of Admissions.

UNIVERSITY OF NEW HAMPSHIRE E-5
Durham, New Hampshire 03824 (603) 862-1360

F/T: 4354M, 4986W	Faculty: 614; I, --$
P/T: 242M, 296W	Ph.D.'s: 80%
Grad: 482M, 465W	S/F Ratio: 17 to 1
Year: sems, ss	Tuition: $1728 ($4578)
Appl: Feb. 1	R and B: $1968
9037 applied	4523 accepted	2209 enrolled
SAT: 488V 541M		VERY COMPETITIVE

University of New Hampshire, established in 1886, is a state university and land-grant college. The library contains 732,368 volumes and 14,253 microfilm items, and subscribes to 5834 periodicals.

Environment: The university is located in a rural area. In addition to academic and recreational facilities, residential accommodations include fraternity and sorority housing, quads, high-rise dorms, mini-dorms, on-campus apartments, and married student housing.

Student Life: About 75% of the students are from New Hampshire. Forty-four percent of the students live on campus. Fewer than 2% of the students are minority-group members. University housing is both single-sex and coed. There are visiting privileges in single-sex housing. Freshmen and sophomores may not keep cars on campus.

Organizations: There are 10 fraternities, to which 20% of the men belong; 10% of the women belong to the 5 sororities. In addition to publications, drama, music, and theater groups, there are many special-interest clubs. Student social life centers largely around the residence hall units, fraternities and sororities.

498 NEW HAMPSHIRE

Sports: The university competes intercollegiately in 12 sports for men and 11 for women. There are 13 intramural sports for both men and women.

Handicapped: Facilities for the physically handicapped include special parking, elevators, and specially equipped rest rooms. Fewer than 1% of the students currently enrolled have visual or hearing impairments.

Graduates: The freshman dropout rate is 10%; about 55% remain to graduate. Fourteen percent pursue advanced study after graduation; 56% pursue careers in business and industry.

Services: The following services are offered free of charge: psychological and career counseling. Tutoring is available on a fee basis.

Programs of Study: The university confers the B.A., B.S., and B.F.A. degrees. Associate, master's, and doctoral programs are also offered. Bachelor's degrees are offered in the following subjects: AREA STUDIES (Russian), BUSINESS (business administration, computer science, hotel administration), EDUCATION (early childhood, elementary, health/physical, industrial, secondary), ENGLISH (English, literature, speech), FINE AND PERFORMING ARTS (art, art education, art history, music, music education, studio art, theater/dramatics), HEALTH SCIENCES (medical technology, nursing, occupational therapy, speech therapy), LANGUAGES (French, German, Greek/Latin, Russian, Spanish), MATH AND SCIENCES (biochemistry, biology, botany, chemistry, earth science, ecology/environmental science, geology, mathematics, oceanography, physical sciences, physics, zoology), PHILOSOPHY (classics, humanities, philosophy), PRE-PROFESSIONAL (agriculture, dentistry, engineering, forestry, home economics, medicine, social work, veterinary), SOCIAL SCIENCES (anthropology, economics, geography, government/political science, history, psychology, social sciences, sociology).

Required: Students must take a distribution of courses in English, science, social science, and the humanities.

Special: Students may spend the junior year abroad at the University of Marburg, Germany, or the University of Dijon, France. Disadvantaged students participate in a summer Bloomsburg College Upward Bound program before admission to the fall semester. A combined B.A.-B.S. degree in chemistry is offered in a 5-year program. Student-designed majors are permitted.

Admissions: Fifty percent of those who applied were accepted for the 1981-82 freshman class. Of those who enrolled in a recent freshman class, the SAT scores were as follows: Verbal—33% between 500 and 600, 7% between 600 and 700, and 1% above 700; Math—44% between 500 and 600, 22% between 600 and 700, and 1% above 700. Secondary school requirements vary according to the programs to which entrance is sought. Residents should rank in the top third of their class; nonresidents in the top 10% to 20%. A high school GPA of at least 3.0 is required. Special consideration is given to disadvantaged students and sons and daughters of alumni. In the admissions process, the most important considerations are SAT scores, class rank, overall record, and recommendations.

Procedure: Candidates are required to take the SAT in December or January of the senior year. New Hampshire residents must file their applications, accompanied by a $10 fee, by February 1; out-of-state candidates must file no later than February 15, with an application fee of $25.

Special: Early decision and deferred admissions plans are offered. AP and CLEP credit is accepted.

Transfer: For fall 1981, 1965 students applied, 1152 were accepted, and 717 enrolled. Students must have a 2.0 GPA. D grades do not transfer. Some preference is given to students transferring from other New Hampshire colleges. There is a 1-year residency requirement. Students must complete, at the university, 32 of the 128 credits needed for a bachelor's degree. Application deadlines are March 1 (fall) and November 1 (spring).

Visiting: Guides are available for informal visits to the campus. The best time for visits is on specific Saturday mornings during the fall, when group information sessions are scheduled.

Financial Aid: About 45% of all students receive some form of financial aid. Thirty-eight percent work part-time on campus. To retain a grant or scholarship in the sophomore year, the cumulative average must be 1.8. The university is a member of the CSS. Both the FAF and the university's financial aid application are required. The deadline for filing is February 15.

Foreign Students: About 1% of the full-time students come from foreign countries. The university offers these students an intensive English program, special counseling, and special organizations.

Admissions: Foreign students must score at least 550 on the TOEFL. They must also take the SAT.

Procedure: Foreign students must submit proof of funds adequate to cover 4 years of study. They must also carry health insurance, which is available through the university for a fee.

Admissions Contact: Stanwood C. Fish, Director of Admissions.

NEW JERSEY

BLOOMFIELD COLLEGE   E-2
Bloomfield, New Jersey 07003   (201) 748-9000

F/T: 394M, 680W	Faculty: 49; IIB, +$
P/T: 278M, 546W	Ph.D.'s: n/av
Grad: none	S/F Ratio: 11 to 1
Year: 4-1-4, ss	Tuition: $4080
Appl: Aug. 15	R and B: $2200
614 applied	525 accepted	181 enrolled
SAT: 370V 390M		LESS COMPETITIVE

Bloomfield College, founded in 1868, is affiliated with the Presbyterian Church. It offers undergraduate degree programs in the liberal arts and sciences, business, nursing, and education. The library has 90,000 volumes, and more than 2000 microfilm items, and subscribes to 1120 periodicals.

Environment: The 14-acre suburban campus is located 15 miles from New York City. There are 10 buildings on campus. Living facilities include dormitories and fraternity and sorority houses.

Student Life: About 89% of the students are from New Jersey, and 30% live on campus. There are no chapel attendance requirements. Campus housing is both coed and single-sex; there are visiting privileges in the single-sex housing. Students may keep cars on campus. Day-care services are provided free of charge to all students.

Organizations: Ten percent of the men and 10% of the women belong to 5 coed fraternities. Extracurricular activities include musical and performing groups, publications, student government, and special-interest clubs.

Sports: Intercollegiate competition is offered in 4 sports for men and 3 for women. There are 6 intramural sports for men and 5 for women.

Handicapped: Special facilities for handicapped students include parking areas and specially equipped rest rooms.

Graduates: The freshman dropout rate is 15%.

Services: Career counseling, placement (for students and graduates), remedial instruction, tutoring, health care, and psychological counseling are offered without charge to all students.

Programs of Study: The B.A. and B.S. degrees are awarded. Bachelor's degrees are offered in the following subjects: BUSINESS (accounting, business administration, finance, management, marketing), ENGLISH (English, journalism, literature), FINE AND PERFORMING ARTS (combined fine and performing arts), HEALTH SCIENCES (nursing), LANGUAGES (French, Spanish), MATH AND SCIENCES (biochemistry, biology, chemistry, physical sciences), PHILOSOPHY (philosophy, religion), PREPROFESSIONAL (chiropractic, dentistry, medicine, social work, veterinary), SOCIAL SCIENCES (economics, government/political science, history, psychology, social sciences, sociology).

Required: Freshmen must take an interdisciplinary studies program.

Special: Student-designed majors, independent study, the integrated core program, and the contract program are offered.

Honors: Four honor societies have chapters on campus.

Admissions: About 86% of those who applied were accepted for the 1981-82 freshman class. The SAT scores of those who enrolled were as follows: Verbal—80% below 500, 20% between 500 and 599, and 0% above 599; Math—80% below 500, 20% between 500 and 599, and 0% above 599. Applicants should be in the top 50% of their high school class, have a C average, and have completed 15 Carnegie units. Advanced placement or honors courses, extracurricular activities, and recommendations are also considered.

Procedure: The SAT or ACT should be taken by December of the senior year. There is a $20 application fee. Application deadlines are August 15 (fall), January 15 (spring), and May 1 (summer). Notification is on a rolling basis.

Special: There are early admissions, early decision, and deferred admissions plans. AP and CLEP credit is available.

Transfer: For fall 1981, 148 students applied, 130 were accepted, and 77 enrolled. A 2.0 GPA is required. D grades do not transfer. The final 8 courses must be taken in residence. All students must complete, at the college, 96 of the 128 credits required for a bachelor's degree.

Visiting: There is an orientation program for prospective students. Informal campus tours with student guides are possible. Visitors may sit in on classes but may not stay overnight at the school. Visits are best scheduled on weekdays and on Saturdays between 9 A.M. and noon.

Financial Aid: About 70% of the students receive financial aid. About 31% work part-time on campus. The average freshman award is $3093. The college offers freshman scholarships; federal, state, and bank loans; federal and state grants; and work-study. The FAF should be submitted; there are no application deadlines. The college is a member of CSS.

Foreign Students: Nine percent of the full-time students come from foreign countries. An intensive English program, special counseling, and special organizations are available for these students.

Admissions: Foreign students must achieve a TOEFL score of at least 550. No college entrance exams are required.

Procedure: Application deadlines are August 1 (fall) and January 10 (spring). Foreign students must present proof of funds adequate to cover 1 year of study.

Admissions Contact: Nancy M. Wolcott, Director of Admissions.

CALDWELL COLLEGE E-2
Caldwell, New Jersey 07006 (201) 228-4424

F/T: 455W		Faculty:	37; n/av
P/T: 311W		Ph.D.'s:	43%
Grad: none		S/F Ratio:	12 to 1
Year: sems, ss		Tuition:	$3250
Appl: open		R and B:	$2050
413 applied	344 accepted		158 enrolled
SAT: 431V 440M			LESS COMPETITIVE

Caldwell College, founded in 1939, is a liberal arts and sciences college for women affiliated with the Roman Catholic Church. Curricula in business, education, and health sciences are also offered. The library has 102,000 volumes and subscribes to 750 periodicals.

Environment: The 104-acre suburban campus is located in a town of 8000 inhabitants, about 20 miles from New York City. Dormitories house about 60% of the students.

Student Life: About 92% of the students come from New Jersey. Sixty percent live on campus. Thirteen percent are minority-group members. There are visiting privileges in the dormitories. Students may keep cars on campus. Day-care services are available to all students.

Organizations: There are 2 sororities; 10% of the women belong to one of them. Extracurricular activities include student government, publications, a dramatics group, musical groups, cultural and social events, special-interest clubs, and service organizations.

Sports: Intercollegiate competition is offered in 3 sports. There are 5 intramural sports.

Handicapped: About 75% of the campus is accessible to handicapped students. Facilities include parking areas, wheelchair ramps, elevators, and specially equipped rest rooms.

Graduates: The freshman dropout rate is 13%; about 57% remain to graduate. Ten percent of the graduates pursue advanced degrees: 1% enter medical school, and 1% enter law school. About 55% of the graduates enter business and industry.

Services: Placement, career counseling, tutoring, health care, and psychological counseling are offered free of charge to all students. Remedial instruction is provided on a fee basis.

Programs of Study: The B.A., B.S., and B.F.A. degrees are awarded. Bachelor's degrees are offered in the following subjects: BUSINESS (business administration), EDUCATION (early childhood, elementary, secondary), ENGLISH (English), FINE AND PERFORMING ARTS (art, art education, music, music education), HEALTH SCIENCES (medical technology), LANGUAGES (French, Spanish), MATH AND SCIENCES (biology, chemistry, mathematics), PHILOSOPHY (religion), SOCIAL SCIENCES (history, psychology, sociology).

Twenty-nine percent of degrees are awarded in social sciences, 21% in math and sciences.

Required: All students must take 9 semester hours of religion and 2 credits in physical education.

Special: Independent study, area studies, and internships are possible. There is a degree program for registered nurses.

Honors: Honors study is available for upperclassmen. Six honor societies have chapters on campus.

Admission: About 83% of the applicants for the 1981-82 freshman class were accepted. The SAT scores of those who enrolled were as follows: Verbal—80% below 500, 15% between 500 and 599, 5% between 600 and 700, and 0% above 700; Math—75% below 500, 20% between 500 and 599, 5% between 600 and 700, and 0% above 700. Applicants should have completed 16 units of academic work and should rank in the top 50% of the high school class. Also considered important are advanced placement or honors courses, recommendations, and extracurricular activities.

Procedure: The SAT or the ACT is required by January of the senior year. There is a $15 application fee. There are no application deadlines; freshmen are admitted in the fall, spring, and summer terms. An interview is recommended. Notification is on a rolling basis.

Special: There are early decision, early admissions, and deferred admissions plans. AP and CLEP credit is available.

Transfer: For fall 1981, 45 students applied, 33 were accepted, and 23 enrolled. A GPA of 2.0, a minimum composite score of 900 on the SAT, and a recommendation from a school official are required. All students must complete, at the college, 45 of the 120 credits required for a bachelor's degree. Fifty percent of the concentration must be completed in residence. There are no application deadlines; transfer students are admitted in all terms.

Visiting: There are regularly scheduled orientations for prospective students. Informal campus visits may be arranged; visitors may stay overnight at the school and sit in on classes. Visits are best scheduled on weekdays between 8:30 A.M. and 4:30 P.M. The admissions office should be contacted for information.

Financial Aid: About 68% of the students receive financial aid. About 37% work part-time on campus. The average freshman award is $2000. The college offers scholarships, grants (BEOG and SEOG), loans (government and commercial), and part-time employment (including work-study). Need is the determining factor. The college is a member of CSS and recommends that the FAF be filed by February 15.

Foreign Students: Six percent of the full-time students come from foreign countries. An intensive English program, special counseling, and special organizations are available for these students.

Admissions: Foreign students must achieve a TOEFL score of at least 500. No college entrance exams are required.

Procedure: There are no application deadlines; foreign students are admitted in the fall and spring terms. They must present proof of health and proof of adequate funds.

Admissions Contact: Sister Mary Joseph, Director of Admissions.

CENTENARY COLLEGE C-2
Hackettstown, New Jersey 07840 (201) 852-1400

F/T, P/T:	Faculty:	48; IIB, n/av
700W	Ph.D.'s:	15%
Grad: none	S/F Ratio:	14 to 1
Year: sems	Tuition:	$4000
Appl: open	R and B:	$3025
800 applied	640 accepted	330 enrolled
SAT or ACT: not required		LESS COMPETITIVE

Centenary College, founded in 1867, offers 2-year and 4-year career-oriented programs with a liberal arts base. The college is United Methodist in origin but ecumenical in its approach to student life. The library has 43,000 volumes and 9000 periodicals on microfilm.

Environment: The 42-acre suburban campus consists of 20 buildings, including 7 dormitories. New York City is 50 miles away. Facilities are available for commuter students.

Student Life: About 60% of the students come from New Jersey and 80% live on campus. There are visiting privileges in the dormitories. Students may keep cars on campus. Day-care services are available to all students.

Organizations: There are 4 sororities; 50% of the women belong to one of them. Extracurricular activities include clubs, student government, and publications.

Sports: Eight sports are offered on an intercollegiate level. Intramural competition is offered in 7 sports.

Handicapped: Plans are being made to make the campus accessible to handicapped students. Facilities include wheelchair ramps and parking areas.

Graduates: The freshman dropout rate is 30%; 70% remain to graduate.

Services: Placement, career counseling, tutoring, and remedial instruction are offered free of charge to all students.

Programs of Study: The B.A., B.S., and B.F.A. degrees are awarded. Associate degrees are also awarded. Bachelor's degrees are offered in the following subjects: BUSINESS (accounting, business administration, computer science, management), EDUCATION (early childhood, elementary, recreation management, special), FINE AND PERFORMING ARTS (art, dance, fashion design, interior design, radio/TV, studio art, theater/dramatics), PREPROFESSIONAL (equine studies, fashion merchandising/retailing).

Special: A general studies degree, student-designed majors, independent study, internships, and study abroad are offered.

Honors: There is a chapter of Phi Theta Kappa on campus.

Admissions: About 80% of those who applied for the 1981-82 freshman class were accepted. All applicants should present 16 units of academic work and a C average or better. Recommendations, impressions made during an interview, and leadership qualities are considered in addition to the applicant's academic record.

Procedure: Neither the SAT nor ACT is required. There is a $20 application fee. Deadlines are described as open; notification is on a rolling basis. Freshmen are admitted in the fall and spring. An interview is recommended.

Special: There are early decision, early admissions, and deferred admissions plans.

Transfer: Transfers are considered for the sophomore and junior years. Each applicant is considered individually; deadlines are open. The college requires 132 credits for a bachelor's degree.

Visiting: There is an orientation program for prospective students. Informal campus visits with guides can be arranged. Visitors may sit in on classes and stay overnight at the school. Visits are best scheduled on weekdays between 9 A.M. and 3 P.M. The admissions office should be contacted for arrangements.

Financial Aid: About 48% of the students receive financial aid. About 39% work part-time on campus. The college offers scholarships, grants, loans, and part-time employment. Need is the main factor in awarding aid. Tuition may be paid in installments. The FAF is required. The financial aid application should be submitted by April 1.

Foreign Students: One percent of the students come from foreign countries. Special counseling and special organizations are available for these students.

Admissions: Foreign students must take the TOEFL. No college entrance exams are required.

Procedure: There are no application deadlines; foreign students are admitted in the fall and spring terms. They must present proof of adequate funds.

Admissions Contact: Cynthia S. Rowan, Dean of Admissions.

COLLEGE OF SAINT ELIZABETH E-2
Convent Station, New Jersey 07961 (201) 539-1600

F/T: 2M, 517W	Faculty: 80; IIB, --$
P/T: 17M, 322W	Ph.D.'s: 49%
Grad: none	S/F Ratio: 11 to 1
Year: sems, ss	Tuition: $3600
Appl: Aug. 15	R and B: $2000
305 applied	262 accepted	142 enrolled
SAT: 410V 430M		LESS COMPETITIVE

The College of Saint Elizabeth is affiliated with the Roman Catholic Church. It offers undergraduate programs in the liberal arts and sciences, business administration, nursing, and education. The library has over 141,000 volumes and subscribes to more than 1000 periodicals.

Environment: The 400-acre suburban campus is located 40 miles from New York City. Facilities include residence halls, a science building, a chapel, a home economics management house, the Greek Theater, and the Shakespeare Garden. A student dining center has facilities for both residents and commuters.

Student Life: Most of the students come from New Jersey. Sixty-three percent come from public schools. About 65% live on campus. Eighty percent of the students are Catholic, 17% are Protestant, and 1% are Jewish. Twenty-four percent are minority-group members. Campus housing is single-sex, and there are visiting privileges. Students may keep cars on campus.

Organizations: There are no sororities on campus. Publications, clubs, a concert series, a lecture series, and student government are offered.

Sports: Intercollegiate teams are fielded in 6 sports. Intramural competition also is offered in 6 sports.

Handicapped: About 75% of the campus is accessible to handicapped students. Facilities include special parking and elevators. Special class scheduling is also available. The college provides 2 counselors for handicapped students.

Graduates: The freshman dropout rate is 18%; about 66% remain to graduate. Twenty-five percent of the graduates pursue advanced degrees. Of these students, 2% enter medical school, 1% dental school, and 2% law school. About 80% enter careers in business and industry.

Services: Placement (for students and graduates), career counseling, psychological counseling, tutoring, remedial instruction, and health care are offered free of charge to all students.

Programs of Study: The B.A., B.S., and B.S.N. degrees are awarded. Bachelor's degrees are offered in the following subjects: BUSINESS (accounting, computer science, management), EDUCATION (early childhood, elementary), ENGLISH (communications, English), FINE AND PERFORMING ARTS (art, music), HEALTH SCIENCES (nursing), LANGUAGES (French, Spanish), MATH AND SCIENCES (biology, chemistry, mathematics), PHILOSOPHY (philosophy), PREPROFESSIONAL (home economics, social work), SOCIAL SCIENCES (history, psychology, sociology). Twenty-five percent of degrees are conferred in education, 19% in preprofessional areas, 13% in business.

Required: All students must take a broad liberal arts program.

Special: There are combined B.A.-B.S. degree programs in biology and chemistry. Study abroad, cross-registration at nearby colleges, and an accelerated degree program are offered.

Honors: There are three honor societies on campus. An honors program is offered in all majors.

Admissions: About 86% of the applicants for the 1981-82 freshman class were accepted. SAT scores of enrolled students were as follows: Verbal—74% below 500, 22% between 500 and 599, 4% between 600 and 700, and 0% above 700; Math—74% below 500, 22% between 500 and 599, 3% between 600 and 700, and 1% above 700. Applicants should have a 2.5 GPA and rank in the top 50% of their high school class; 16 units of academic work should be completed. Also considered are advanced placement or honors courses, evidence of special talents, and recommendations.

Procedure: The SAT is required and should be taken by January of the senior year. There is a $15 application fee. The application deadlines are August 15 for fall admission and January 15 for spring; notification is on a rolling basis.

Special: There are early decision, early admissions, and deferred admissions plans. AP and CLEP credit is available.

Transfer: For fall 1981, 63 transfer students applied, 50 were accepted, and 46 enrolled. A 2.0 GPA is required. Transfer students are regularly accepted each semester. They must complete, at the college, 64 of the 128 credits required for the bachelor's degree. Application deadlines are the same as for freshmen.

Visiting: There are regularly scheduled orientations for prospective students. Informal campus visits with student guides may be arranged; visitors may attend classes. Visits are best scheduled on weekdays between 8:30 A.M. and 2:30 P.M. The admissions office should be contacted for arrangements.

Financial Aid: About 72% of the students receive financial aid. Thirty percent work part-time on campus. Thirty scholarships based on need are available to freshmen; awards range from $200 to $1800. A total of $50,000 in scholarship aid is available to freshmen. Grants and loans (federal and state) are also available. The college is a member of CSS. The FAF should be filed by February 15.

Foreign Students: Three percent of the full-time students come from foreign countries. The college, which actively recruits these students, offers them an intensive English course as well as special counseling and special organizations.

Admissions: A score of at least 500 must be achieved on the TOEFL. The SAT or ACT is not required.

Procedure: Application deadlines are the same as those for other freshmen. Proof of funds sufficient to cover 4 years of study is required.

Admissions Contact: Sister Maureen Sullivan, Director of Admissions.

DREW UNIVERSITY/COLLEGE OF LIBERAL ARTS D-2
Madison, New Jersey 07940 (201) 377-3000

F/T: 615M, 851W	Faculty: 100; IIA, +$
P/T: 27M, 83W	Ph.D.'s: 89%
Grad: 699M, 248W	S/F Ratio: 15 to 1
Year: 4-1-4, ss	Tuition: $5780
Appl: Mar. 1	R and B: $2100
1609 applied	1073 accepted 356 enrolled
SAT: 520V 540M	VERY COMPETITIVE

The College of Liberal Arts of Drew University is part of an educational complex that includes a theological school and a graduate school. The university library contains over 450,000 volumes and 68,000 microfilm items, and subscribes to more than 1700 periodicals.

Environment: The 186-acre suburban campus is about 30 miles from New York City. There are residence halls for men and women. On-campus apartments and married student housing are also available.

Student Life: About 50% of the students come from New Jersey; 70% come from public schools. Ninety percent live on campus. Twenty-eight percent of the students are Catholic, 25% are Protestant, and 11% are Jewish. There are religious organizations for students of the major faiths. About 9% of the students are minority-group members. Campus housing is both coed and single-sex. There are visiting privileges in single-sex dorms. Students may have cars on campus.

Organizations: There are no fraternities or sororities. Traditional extracurricular activities are available.

Sports: The university fields intercollegiate teams in 8 sports for men and 8 for women. There are 11 intramurals for men and 8 for women.

Handicapped: Most of the campus is accessible to the physically handicapped. Facilities include wheelchair ramps, special parking, elevators, specially equipped rest rooms, and lowered telephones; special class scheduling is also available.

Graduates: The freshman dropout rate is 12%; 68% remain to graduate. Approximately 70% of those who graduate pursue graduate study: 5% enter medical school, 2% enter dental school, and 12% enter law school; 30% pursue careers in business and industry.

Services: Placement services, career counseling, tutoring, and psychological counseling are offered free of charge. Health care is also available.

Programs of Study: The college confers the B.A. degree. Master's and doctoral programs are also offered. Bachelor's degrees are offered in the following subjects: AREA STUDIES (Russian), ENGLISH (literature), FINE AND PERFORMING ARTS (art history, music, music history, music theory, studio art), LANGUAGES (French, German, Greek/Latin, Russian, Spanish), MATH AND SCIENCES (biology, botany, chemistry, mathematics, physics, psychobiology, zoology), PHILOSOPHY (classics, philosophy, religion), PREPROFESSIONAL (business, dentistry, engineering, forestry, law, medicine, ministry, pharmacy, social work, veterinary), SOCIAL SCIENCES (anthropology, behavioral sciences, economics, government/political science, history, psychology, sociology). Sixty-one percent of degrees conferred are in social sciences and 14% are in math and sciences.

Required: Each student must complete 2 courses in 4 of 5 subject areas.

Special: Students may create their own majors. Students may study abroad in London (political science) or Brussels (economics); other opportunities include a Washington semester, a United Nations semester, an arts semester in New York, and a Miami semester in marine biology. A 3-2 forestry program is offered with Duke University; a 3-2 engineering program is offered with Washington University and Georgia Tech. A cooperative program in education with the College of Saint Elizabeth is also offered.

Honors: Four national honor societies have chapters on campus; honors work is available in most departments.

Admissions: About 67% of the applicants for the 1981-82 freshman class were accepted. The SAT scores of those who enrolled were as follows: Verbal—43% below 500, 40% between 500 and 599, 16% between 600 and 700, and 1% above 700; Math—36% below 500, 41% between 500 and 599, 21% between 600 and 700, and 2% above 700. Applicants should have completed 16 academic units.

Also important are advanced placement or honors courses, recommendations, leadership record, and impressions made during an interview.

Procedure: The SAT or ACT should be taken by January of the senior year. There is a $20 nonrefundable application fee. March 1 is the fall application deadline; December 1 is the deadline for spring. An interview is strongly recommended.

Special: AP and CLEP credit is accepted. There are early decision, early admissions, and deferred admissions plans.

Transfer: For fall 1981, 208 transfer students applied, 124 were accepted, and 68 enrolled. Satisfactory academic records are needed; D grades do not transfer. Transfers must complete, at the university, 48 of the 120 credits necessary for the bachelor's degree. June 1 is the fall semester application deadline; the deadline for spring is December 1.

Visiting: There are regularly scheduled orientation programs for prospective students. Informal campus visits with student guides may also be arranged; visitors may stay overnight at the school and sit in on classes. The admissions office should be contacted to arrange visits.

Financial Aid: About 42% of all students receive some form of financial aid. The school offers scholarships, grants, loans, and part-time employment. Thirty percent of the students work part-time on campus. The average grant to freshmen is $2177. The university is a member of CSS. The FAF or FFS should be filed by March 15.

Foreign Students: About 2% of the full-time students come from foreign countries. The university, which actively recruits these students, offers them an intensive English course and special organizations.

Admissions: Foreign students must achieve a minimum score of 550 on the TOEFL. College entrance exams are not required.

Procedure: Application deadlines are the same as those for other freshmen. Students must complete the university's health form to establish proof of health and must carry health insurance, which is available through the university for a fee. Proof of funds adequate to cover 1 year of study is required.

Admissions Contact: Beth Keane, Associate Director of Admissions.

FAIRLEIGH DICKINSON UNIVERSITY
Madison, New Jersey 07940	(201) 377-4700	D-2
Rutherford, New Jersey 07070	(201) 460-5000	E-2
Teaneck, New Jersey 07666	(201)692-2000	E-2

F/T: 2298M, 2285W	Faculty: 530; n/av
P/T: 3520M, 3055W	Ph.D.'s: 65%
Grad: 4128M, 2678W	S/F Ratio: 15 to 1
Year: sems, ss	Tuition: $4285
Appl: open	R and B: $2330
5679 applied	3422 accepted 1541 enrolled
SAT: required	COMPETITIVE

Fairleigh Dickinson University, founded in 1941, is a private multicampus institution offering undergraduate training in the liberal arts and sciences, business, education, engineering, and the health sciences. Total library resources include 550,000 volumes, 5800 reels of microfilm, and 3500 periodical subscriptions.

Environment: The 3 suburban campuses are situated in northern New Jersey at Madison, Rutherford, and Teaneck. Each campus has its own facilities. The dormitories accommodate a total of 3100 students. There is also a marine science laboratory in the U.S. Virgin Islands and a campus at Wroxton, England.

Student Life: About 80% of the full-time students come from New Jersey; 55% live on campus. Twelve percent of the students are minority-group members. University housing is both single-sex and coed. There are visiting privileges in single-sex housing. Students may keep cars on campus.

Organizations: Fraternities and sororities are available. The extracurricular program at each campus includes special-interest clubs, publications, performing groups, religious organizations, and student government.

Sports: The university fields intercollegiate teams in 11 sports for men and 11 for women. The intramural program includes 14 sports for men and 11 for women.

Services: Placement (for students and graduates), career counseling, tutoring, and remedial instruction are offered without charge.

Programs of Study: The B.A., B.S., B.S.E.E., B.S.I.E., and B.S.M.E. are conferred. There are also associate, master's, and doctoral programs. Bachelor's degrees are offered in the following subjects: AREA

502 NEW JERSEY

STUDIES (Russian, urban), BUSINESS (accounting, business education, computer science, finance, management, marketing), EDUCATION (elementary, health/physical, secondary), ENGLISH (communications, English, English education), FINE AND PERFORMING ARTS (fine arts, music education), HEALTH SCIENCES (dental hygiene, medical technology, nursing, radiologic technology), LANGUAGES (French, language education, Russian, Spanish), MATH AND SCIENCES (biochemistry, biology, chemistry, earth science, mathematics, mathematics education, physics, science education), PHILOSOPHY (humanities, philosophy), PREPROFESSIONAL (engineering, social work), SOCIAL SCIENCES (economics, government/political science, history, international studies, psychology, social studies education, sociology). About 32% of the degrees are conferred in arts and sciences, 43% in business.

Required: One semester of physical education is required of all students studying arts and sciences.

Special: Independent study, Upward Bound, study abroad, dual majors, internships, and scientific research programs are offered.

Honors: Nine honor societies have chapters on campus. Honors work is offered in all departments.

Admissions: About 60% of the 1981–82 freshman applicants were accepted. Candidates should have completed 16 Carnegie units. In addition to the high school academic record, the admissions committee considers SAT scores, recommendations, advanced placement or honors courses, and extracurricular activities.

Procedure: The SAT and the AT in English composition (for placement only) should be taken by January of the senior year. A student interested in majoring in science or engineering may take the Mathematics AT, Level I or II for placement only. Application deadlines are open. Notification is on a rolling basis. There is a $20 application fee.

Special: There are early decision, early admissions, and deferred admissions programs. AP and CLEP credit is available.

Transfer: For fall 1981, 2187 students applied, 1560 were accepted, and 973 enrolled. A 2.0 GPA is required. D grades do not transfer. The final 32 credits, of the 128 necessary for a bachelor's degree, must be taken in residence. Application deadlines are open.

Visiting: There is an orientation program for prospective students. Informal campus tours with student guides may be arranged. Open house programs are held twice a month on each campus, normally on Tuesday afternoons. Visitors may sit in on classes and stay overnight at the school. The admissions office of the particular campus in which the student is interested should be contacted for arrangements.

Financial Aid: About 73% of the students receive financial aid. Fifteen percent work part-time on campus. Average aid to freshmen from all sources is $3310. The university offers scholarships, grants (state and federal), loans (federal, state, bank, and short-term), and CWS. Tuition may be paid on the installment plan. Need and scholastic achievement are the determining factors in the award of aid. The university is a member of CSS. The FAF should be submitted by April 1 (fall) or November 15 (spring).

Foreign Students: Four percent of the full-time students come from foreign countries. The university offers these students special counseling and special organizations.

Admissions: Foreign students must score at least 500 on the TOEFL. No college entrance examination is required.

Procedure: Application deadlines are June 15 (fall) and November 15 (spring). Foreign students must present proof of funds adequate to cover their entire period of study. They must also carry health insurance, which is available through the university for a fee.

Admissions Contact: Howard Hamilton, Director of Admissions.

FELICIAN COLLEGE E–2
Lodi, New Jersey 07644 (201) 778-1190

F/T: 1M, 397W		Faculty:	51; IIB, – –$
P/T: 26M, 339W		Ph.D.'s:	26%
Grad: none		S/F Ratio:	10 to 1
Year: sems, ss		Tuition:	$2445
Appl: Aug. 15		R and B:	none
408 applied	264 accepted		199 enrolled
SAT: 350V 375M			LESS COMPETITIVE

Felician College, founded in 1923, is a Roman Catholic liberal arts college for women. It is conducted by the Felician Sisters. The evening and nursing programs are coeducational. The library contains almost 70,000 volumes.

Environment: The 27-acre urban campus is located about 15 miles from New York City. The campus is situated on the banks of the Saddle River. Facilities include modern science laboratories, art and music studios, and a 1500 seat theater. Felician College is a commuter school.

Student Life: Nearly all the students are from New Jersey or New York. Religion and spiritual development are considered of vital importance at Felician. Confession, chapel, and benediction services are held daily on campus. About 10% of the students are minority-group members. Students may keep cars on campus.

Organizations: There is 1 sorority at the college. Extracurricular activities include student government, Campus Ministry, and cultural, academic, and professional organizations and student publications.

Sports: There are 4 intramural sports.

Handicapped: Special facilities for handicapped students include wheelchair ramps, parking areas, elevators, specially equipped rest rooms, and lowered telephones.

Graduates: About 2% of the graduates pursue advanced study; about 1% enter medical school. About 98% enter careers in business and industry.

Services: The following services are provided to students free of charge: health care, career counseling, placement, and psychological counseling. Tutoring and remedial instruction are available on a fee basis.

Programs of Study: The college confers the B.S. and B.A. degrees. Associate degrees are also granted. The college offers the B.A. degree in the following subjects: AREA STUDIES (religious), EDUCATION (elementary, special), ENGLISH (English), FINE AND PERFORMING ARTS (art), HEALTH SCIENCES (nursing), MATH AND SCIENCES (biology, mathematics), PHILOSOPHY (philosophy), SOCIAL SCIENCES (history, psychology).

Required: All students must complete a core curriculum.

Special: Independent study, internships, study abroad, and community projects are available.

Admissions: About 65% of those who applied were accepted for the 1981–82 freshman class. The SAT scores of those who enrolled were as follows: Verbal—98% below 500, 1% between 500 and 599, 1% between 600 and 700, and 0% above 700; Math—94% below 500, 5% between 500 and 599, 1% between 600 and 700, and 0% above 700. Applicants must be high school graduates and must have completed at least 16 units of academic work. Advanced placement or honors courses, recommendations, leadership record, and impressions made during the interview are also taken into account.

Procedure: The SAT is required. An interview is required. Application deadlines are August 15 (fall) and December 1 (spring). Notification is on a rolling basis. There is a $25 application fee.

Special: The college has early decision, early admissions, and deferred admissions plans. CLEP and AP credit is available.

Transfer: For fall 1981, 67 transfer students enrolled. Transfer students are considered for all years. D grades do not transfer. Applicants must have at least a 2.0 GPA. Students must complete one-half of their total program in residence to receive a bachelor's degree. Application deadlines are the same as for freshman applicants.

Visiting: Guides are available for informal campus visits. Visitors may sit in on classes but may not stay overnight at the school. Visits are best scheduled on weekdays from 8:30 A.M. to 4:30 P.M. The admissions office should be contacted for arrangements.

Financial Aid: About 51% of the students receive financial aid. Six percent work part-time on campus. Average aid to freshmen from all sources covers 45% of costs. Federal and state aid programs including BEOG, SEOG, tuition aid grants, loans, scholarships, and CWS are available, as are scholarships administered by the college. The college is a member of CSS. The FAF is required. Applications should be submitted as soon as possible after January 1.

Foreign Students: About 2% of the full-time students come from foreign countries. The college offers these students an intensive English course.

Admissions: Foreign students must take the TOEFL and the New Jersey Skills Test; they must score 168–170 on the latter. No college entrance examination is required.

Procedure: Application deadlines are August 15 (fall) and December 1 (spring). Foreign students must present a certificate of health. They must also present proof of adequate funds.

Admissions Contact: Marie Ott Rossi, Director of Admissions.

GEORGIAN COURT COLLEGE
Lakewood, New Jersey 08701

E-4
(201) 367-4440

F/T: 14M, 644W
P/T: 57M, 278W
Grad: 97M, 309W
Year: sems, ss
Appl: Aug. 15
274 applied
SAT: 446V 443M

Faculty: 56; IIB, av$
Ph.D.'s: 32%
S/F Ratio: 12 to 1
Tuition: $2865
R and B: $1700

205 accepted

144 enrolled
COMPETITIVE

Georgian Court College, founded in 1908, is a liberal arts college for women. It is affiliated with the Roman Catholic Church. The library contains 67,000 volumes and 3000 microfilm items, and subscribes to 570 periodicals.

Environment: The 200-acre suburban campus has 17 buildings and is located 60 miles from both Philadelphia and New York City. Family-size dwellings and dormitories are available for residential students.

Student Life: About 75% of the students come from New Jersey, and 60% come from public schools. Thirty-six percent of the students live on campus. Campus housing is single-sex; there are no visiting privileges. Students may keep cars on campus.

Organizations: There are no sororities. Religious groups are available. Extracurricular activities include clubs, publications, dramatics, campus government, service organizations, and cultural groups.

Sports: There are 3 intercollegiate sports.

Handicapped: About 50% of the campus is accessible to students with physical handicaps.

Graduates: About 1% of the freshmen drop out by the end of their first year. Sixty percent remain to graduate; 25% of the graduates pursue graduate study. One percent enter medical school, fewer than 1% dental school, and 3% law school. Thirty-five percent enter careers in business and industry.

Services: Placement, career counseling, remedial instruction, and psychological and spiritual counseling are offered free of charge to all students. Health care and tutoring are available on a fee basis.

Programs of Study: The B.A. and B.S. are awarded. Master's programs are also offered. Bachelor's degrees are offered in the following subjects: BUSINESS (business administration), EDUCATION (elementary, secondary, special), ENGLISH (English), FINE AND PERFORMING ARTS (art education, art history, studio art), HEALTH SCIENCES (medical technology), LANGUAGES (French, German, Spanish), MATH AND SCIENCES (biochemistry, biology, chemistry, mathematics, physics), PHILOSOPHY (humanities), PREPROFESSIONAL (dentistry, law, medicine, ministry, social work), SOCIAL SCIENCES (history, psychology, sociology). Most degrees are awarded in education and the social sciences.

Special: Study abroad, off-campus studies, a general studies degree, and a premedical technology program are offered.

Honors: There are 9 honor societies open to qualified students.

Admissions: About 75% of the applicants for the 1981-82 freshman class were accepted. The SAT scores of those who enrolled were as follows: Verbal—44% below 500, 16% between 500 and 599, 3% between 600 and 700, and 2% above 700; Math—60% below 500, 15% between 500 and 599, 2% between 600 and 700, and 0% above 700. Applicants need a minimum C average and should rank in the top half of their class.

Procedure: The SAT should be taken by January of the senior year. An interview is strongly recommended. Application deadlines are August 15 (fall), December 15 (spring), June 1 (summer I), and June 15 (summer II). Notification is on a rolling basis. There is a $15 non-refundable application fee.

Special: There are early decision and early admissions plans. AP and CLEP credit is accepted.

Transfer: For fall 1981, 222 students applied, 220 were accepted, and 123 enrolled. Requirements are the same as those for freshmen. D grades transfer. Students must complete, at the college, 50 of the 132 credits necessary for a bachelor's degree. The deadlines are August 15 (fall), December 15 (spring), and June 15 (summer).

Visiting: There is no regularly scheduled orientation program for prospective students. Informal campus tours conducted by student guides may be arranged. Visitors may stay overnight at the school and sit in on classes. The admissions office should be contacted to arrange visits.

Financial Aid: About 60% of all students receive some form of financial aid. Twenty percent work part-time on campus. Average aid to freshmen from all sources is $2400. The college offers NDSL, CWS, and EOG. There is a special program for disadvantaged students. Scholarships and part-time employment are also offered. Tuition may be paid in installments. The college is a member of the CSS. The FAF should be submitted by March 1 (fall) or December 1 (spring).

Foreign Students: Two percent of the full-time students come from foreign countries. The college offers these students an intensive English course.

Admissions: Foreign students must take the TOEFL and the college's own English proficiency exam.

Procedure: Application deadlines are August 15 (fall), December 15 (spring), and June 15 (summer). Foreign students must present proof of health and proof of adequate funds. They must carry health insurance, which is available through the college for a fee.

Admissions Contact: John P. Burke, Director of Admissions.

GLASSBORO STATE COLLEGE
Glassboro, New Jersey 08028

C-4
(609) 445-5346

F/T: 2719M, 3306W
P/T: 1200M, 1200W
Grad: 742M, 691W
Year: sems, ss
Appl: Mar. 15
4300 applied
SAT: 430V 458M

Faculty: 460; IIA, ++$
Ph.D.'s: 60%
S/F Ratio: 18 to 1
Tuition: $1135($1995)
R and B: $1900

2300 accepted
ACT: 19

1330 enrolled
COMPETITIVE

Glassboro State College, founded in 1923, is a state-supported liberal arts institution, with a strong program in teacher education. The library has 380,000 volumes and 53,500 microform items, and subscribes to 160 periodicals.

Environment: The college is located on a 175-acre campus in a rural area 20 miles from Philadelphia. The campus consists of 23 buildings, including 7 dormitories for 850 students, and 3 apartment complexes.

Student Life: Almost all the students are from New Jersey. Eighty percent come from public schools. About 40% of the undergraduates live on campus. To be eligible for residence living, students must live outside a reasonable commuting distance. Dormitories are restricted to freshmen. Upperclassmen live in apartments on and off campus. Twenty percent of the students are minority-group members. College housing is both single-sex and coed. There are visiting privileges in single-sex housing. Students may not have cars on campus. Day-care services are available to all students.

Organizations: There are 7 fraternities to which 10% of the men belong; 6 sororities have 10% of the women as members. Glassboro students can participate in any of 60 student organizations, music and drama groups, a campus paper, and a variety of social and cultural affairs, including the Celebrity Concert Series. Atlantic City and Philadelphia offer additional recreational and cultural activities.

Sports: Students may participate in 13 intercollegiate sports for men and 11 for women. There are also 12 intramural sports for men and 11 for women.

Handicapped: About 75% of the campus is wheelchair accessible. Special facilities for the handicapped include wheelchair ramps, parking areas, elevators, lowered drinking fountains and telephones, and specially equipped rest rooms. Special class scheduling can be arranged. There are no visually or hearing-impaired students currently enrolled. A counselor is available for special assistance.

Graduates: The freshman dropout rate is 18%; 60% remain to graduate. Thirty-five percent of the graduates pursue graduate study: fewer than 1% enter medical school, fewer than 1% dental school, and 2% law school. About 35% of the graduates pursue careers in business and industry.

Services: The following services are available free to students: health care, placement, career counseling, tutoring, and psychological counseling. Remedial instruction is also available on a fee basis.

Programs of Study: The college confers the B.A. and B.S. degrees. It also offers master's programs. Bachelor's degrees are offered in the following subjects: BUSINESS (accounting, business administration, computer science, finance, management, management information systems, marketing, personnel management and labor relations, public administration, small business management), EDUCATION (early childhood, elementary, health/physical, industrial, secondary, special), ENGLISH (communications, English, journalism, speech), FINE AND PERFORMING ARTS (art, art education, dance, music, music education, radio/TV, studio art, theater/dramatics), LANGUAGES (French, Spanish), MATH AND SCIENCES (biology, chemistry, computer science, mathematics, physical sciences), PREPROFESSIONAL (dentistry, home economics, law, medicine), SOCIAL SCIENCES (economics, geography, government/political science, history, psychology, social sciences, sociology). Thirty-five percent of the degrees conferred are in education, 20% are in business, 15% are in communications, and 12% are in social sciences.

Required: All students must complete courses in general education, fundamental studies, derived studies, and competence-creative studies (including physical education).

Special: Special programs include semester abroad and independent study.

Honors: Chapters of 3 national honor societies are available for eligible students.

Admissions: Fifty-three percent of those who applied were accepted for the 1981–82 freshman class. The SAT scores of those who enrolled were as follows: Verbal—68% below 500, 28% between 500 and 599, 4% between 600 and 700, and 0% above 700; Math—63% below 500, 31% between 500 and 599, 5% between 600 and 700, and 1% above 700. On the ACT, 60% scored below 21, 31% between 21 and 23, 7% between 24 and 25, 2% between 26 and 28, and 0% above 28. Candidates for admission must have completed 16 units of study and should rank in the upper 60% of their graduating class. The following factors are also considered: special talents, advanced placement or honors courses, extracurricular activities, and recommendations by school officials. Five percent of the admitted freshmen may come from outside New Jersey.

Procedure: The SAT or ACT is required and should be taken in March or May of the junior year or December of the senior year. Application deadlines are March 15 (fall) and November 15 (spring). The rolling admissions plan is used. The CRDA is observed. An interview is recommended. There is a $10 application fee.

Special: There is a deferred admissions plan. AP and CLEP credit is available.

Transfer: For fall 1981, 1900 students applied, 1380 were accepted, and 890 enrolled. A minimum GPA of 2.0 is required. D grades do not transfer. Preference is given to graduates of New Jersey community colleges. The final 30 credit hours, of the 120–135 necessary for a bachelor's degree, must be earned in residence. June 1 (fall) and December 1 (spring) are the deadlines for applying.

Visiting: Fridays, from November through April, are scheduled as visiting days: a campus tour, slide show, and department open house are some of the features. Visitors may sit in on classes. Prospective students should contact the admissions office to make arrangements. Informal visits may also be made Monday through Friday when school is in session.

Financial Aid: Currently, 60% of the students receive financial aid. Twenty-nine percent work part-time on campus. The average award to freshmen from all sources is $1400. Freshman scholarships are available under the New Jersey state tuition program. Federal, state, and local bank loans are also available. Tuition may be paid in installments. Awards are based primarily on financial need; the academic record is considered only when the GPA falls into the probation category. The college is a member of CSS. The FAF is required. Applicants are notified by the end of June. Application for aid must be filed by April 30 (fall) or December 1 (spring).

Foreign Students: Fewer than 1% of the full-time students come from foreign countries. The college offers these students special counseling and special organizations.

Admissions: Foreign students must take the TOEFL or the University of Michigan Language Test. They must also take the SAT or ACT.

Procedure: The application deadline is March 15. Foreign students must provide proof of funds adequate to cover 4 years of study. They must also carry health insurance, which is available through the college for a fee.

Admissions Contact: John G. Davies, Director of Admissions.

JERSEY CITY STATE COLLEGE E-2
Jersey City, New Jersey 07305 (201) 547-3234

F/T: 2028M, 2229W Faculty: 294; IIA, ++$
P/T: 1018M, 1668W Ph.D.'s: 50%
Grad: 157M, 411W S/F Ratio: 16 to 1
Year: sems, ss Tuition: $34 ($61)p/c
Appl: May 15 R and B: $1400
2413 applied 1852 accepted 1213 enrolled
SAT: 395V 395M **LESS COMPETITIVE**

Jersey City State College, founded in 1929, is a public institution offering programs in the liberal arts and sciences, business, and education. The library has 216,000 volumes and 300,000 microfilm items, and subscribes to 1350 periodicals.

Environment: The 14-acre urban campus is located 2 miles from the downtown area. There are a dormitory for women students and college apartments for both men and women.

Student Life: Nearly all the students are from New Jersey. About 73% come from public schools. Two percent of the students live on campus. Forty-two percent are minority-group members. College housing is both single-sex and coed. Students may keep cars on campus. Day-care facilities are available to all students, faculty, and staff.

Organizations: There are 4 fraternities and 7 sororities on campus. Extracurricular activities include various clubs, programs of special interest, and social events. Across the Hudson River lies New York City, offering numerous cultural and recreational opportunities.

Sports: Eleven intercollegiate sports are offered for men and 7 for women. Both men and women participate on the intramural level in 10 sports.

Handicapped: About 80% of the campus is accessible to students with physical handicaps. Special facilities for the physically handicapped include wheelchair ramps, parking areas, elevators, lowered drinking fountains and telephones, and specially equipped rest rooms. Special class scheduling can be arranged.

Graduates: The freshman dropout rate is 5%. Sixty percent remain to graduate. After graduation, about 5% go on for advanced education: 1% enter medical school and 1% law school; 54% go into careers in industry and business.

Services: Career counseling, placement (undergraduates and alumni), tutoring, remedial instruction, health care, and psychological counseling are offered without charge.

Programs of Study: The B.A. and B.S. degrees are conferred. Master's degrees are also granted. Bachelor's degrees are offered in the following subjects: BUSINESS (accounting, business administration, computer science, finance, management, marketing, retail management), EDUCATION (early childhood, elementary, health/physical, secondary, special), ENGLISH (English), FINE AND PERFORMING ARTS (art, art education, art history, cinematography, film/photography, music, music education, radio/TV), HEALTH SCIENCES (nursing), LANGUAGES (Spanish), MATH AND SCIENCES (biology, chemistry, geoscience, mathematics), PHILOSOPHY (philosophy, religion), PREPROFESSIONAL (dentistry, law, medicine, veterinary), SOCIAL SCIENCES (anthropology, economics, geography, government/political science, history, psychology, sociology). About 28% of the degrees are offered in health sciences, 27% in education, and 18% in social sciences.

Special: There is a general studies degree. Study abroad is offered through college-sponsored summer tours.

Honors: Three national honor societies have chapters on campus. Honors work is offered in history, English, management, and biology-chemistry.

Admissions: About 77% of the applicants for the 1981–82 freshman class were accepted. The SAT scores of those who enrolled were as follows: Verbal—95% scored below 500, 4% between 500 and 599, 1% between 600 and 700, and 0% above 700; Math—95% scored below 500, 4% between 500 and 599, 1% between 600 and 700, and 0% above 700. Applicants should be in the top 65% of the high school class and have a C average. Also considered important are advanced placement or honors courses, special talents, recommendations by school officials, and extracurricular activities.

Procedure: The SAT or ACT is required. Application deadlines are May 15 (fall) and December 15 (spring). Notification is on a rolling basis. There is a $10 application fee.

Special: There are early decision, early admissions, and deferred admissions plans. AP and CLEP are used.

Transfer: For fall 1981, 1009 students applied, 837 were accepted, and 582 enrolled. A 2.0 GPA is required. D grades transfer only with an associate degree. Thirty-two credits, of the 128 required for a bachelor's degree, must be completed in residence. The deadlines are July 1 (fall) and December 15 (spring).

Visiting: On Wednesdays at 10 A.M. and 1:30 P.M. there is an orientation program for prospective applicants. For informal campus visits, student guides are usually provided. Visitors may attend classes. For further information, the admissions office should be contacted.

Financial Aid: Fifty-two percent of the students receive assistance. Fifteen percent work part-time on campus. Average aid to freshmen from all sources is $1010. Grants (federal and state), loans (governmental and commercial), and work-study are available. The college is a member of CSS. The FAF is required. The preferred due dates for aid application are May 1 (fall) and December 1 (spring).

NEW JERSEY 505

Foreign Students: Nine percent of the full-time students come from foreign countries. The college offers these students an intensive English course, special counseling, and special organizations.

Admissions: Foreign students must score at least 480 on the TOEFL. No college entrance examination is required.

Procedure: Application deadlines are April 15 (fall) and October 15 (spring). Foreign students must present proof of funds adequate for 4 years of study.

Admissions Contact: Samuel T. McGhee, Director of Admissions.

KEAN COLLEGE OF NEW JERSEY   E-2
Union, New Jersey 07083   (201) 527-2195

F/T: 2589M, 3534W	Faculty: 359; n/av
P/T: 1916M, 3254W	Ph.D.'s: 65%
Grad: 528M, 1637W	S/F Ratio: 17 to 1
Year: 4-1-4, ss	Tuition: $31 ($49) p/c
Appl: June 15	R and B: $1230
4493 applied	3569 accepted	1502 enrolled
SAT: 411V 423M		LESS COMPETITIVE

Kean College of New Jersey, founded in 1855, is a public institution offering undergraduate instruction in the liberal arts and sciences, business administration, and education. The library contains 300,000 volumes and 285,000 microfilm items, and subscribes to 1600 periodicals.

Environment: The 120-acre campus is located in a city of 55,000 inhabitants about 25 miles from New York City. Four dormitories accommodate 1000 men and women.

Student Life: Almost 99% of the students come from New Jersey. Eighty percent have had public school educations. About 9% reside on campus. Twenty-four percent are minority-group members. College housing is coed. Students may keep cars on campus. Day-care services are available to all students, faculty, and staff.

Organizations: There are 9 fraternities and 18 sororities on campus. Extracurricular activities include clubs, social and cultural events on campus, student government, publications, and dramatics.

Sports: The college fields intercollegiate teams in 9 sports for men and 8 for women. There are 9 intramural sports for men and 8 for women.

Handicapped: Over 85% of the campus is accessible to handicapped students. Facilities include wheelchair ramps, parking areas, elevators, and specially equipped rest rooms. Special class scheduling is also available. Three counselors are available to handicapped students.

Graduates: Twenty-nine percent of the freshmen drop out by the end of the first year. Twenty-four percent of the graduates go on for further education. A large number of graduates enter the teaching profession.

Services: Placement, career counseling, tutoring, remedial instruction, psychological counseling, and health care are offered without charge to all students.

Programs of Study: The college confers the B.A., B.S., and B.S.N. degrees. Master's degrees are also offered. The bachelor's degree is offered in the following subjects: BUSINESS (accounting, business administration, computer science, finance, management, marketing), EDUCATION (early childhood, elementary, health/physical, industrial, recreation, special), ENGLISH (English, literature, speech), FINE AND PERFORMING ARTS (art history, music, music education, studio art, theater/dramatics), HEALTH SCIENCES (medical records technology, medical technology, nursing, occupational therapy, physical therapy), LANGUAGES (French, Spanish), MATH AND SCIENCES (biology, chemistry, earth science, mathematics), PHILOSOPHY (philosophy, religion), PREPROFESSIONAL (library science, social work), SOCIAL SCIENCES (economics, government/political science, history, psychology, sociology). About 40% of the degrees are conferred in education.

Honors: Twelve honor societies have chapters on campus.

Admissions: About 79% of those who applied were accepted for the 1981-82 freshman class. The SAT scores of those who enrolled were as follows: Verbal—88% below 500, 11% between 500 and 599, fewer than 1% between 600 and 700, and 0% above 700; Math—83% below 500, 15% between 500 and 599, 2% between 600 and 700, and 0% above 700. Sixteen academic units are required. Out-of-state enrollment is limited to 5% of the student body.

Procedure: The SAT is required. The application deadlines are June 15 (fall) and December 15 (spring). Notification is on a rolling basis. There is a $10 application fee.

Special: There is an early decision plan. AP and CLEP credit is granted.

Transfer: For fall 1981, 2002 transfer applications were received, 771 were accepted, and 550 students enrolled. A C average is required. D grades do not transfer. Students must complete, at the college, 34 of the 124-132 credits necessary for a bachelor's degree. Application deadlines are July 15 (fall) and December 15 (spring).

Visiting: There is an orientation program for prospective students. Informal campus visits with student guides may be arranged. Visitors may sit in on classes and stay overnight at the school.

Financial Aid: Fifty percent of the students receive financial aid. Twenty percent work part-time on campus. Average aid to freshmen from all sources is $2133. The college offers scholarships, loans, and CWS. The college is a member of CSS. The FAF should be submitted by April 1 (fall) or December 1 (spring).

Foreign Students: About 5% of the full-time students come from foreign countries. The college offers these students an intensive English course, an intensive English program, special counseling, and special organizations.

Admissions: Foreign students must take the TOEFL or the University of Michigan Language Test. They must score at least 500 on the TOEFL. No college entrance examination is required.

Procedure: Application deadlines are June 15 (fall) and December 1 (spring). Foreign students must present proof of funds adequate to cover 1 year of study. Students must carry health insurance, which is available through the college for a fee.

Admissions Contact: Director of Admissions.

MONMOUTH COLLEGE   E-3
West Long Branch, New Jersey 07764   (201) 222-6600

F/T: 1000M, 1000W	Faculty: 208; IIA, +$
P/T: 450M, 450W	Ph.D.'s: 60%
Grad: 500M, 450W	S/F Ratio: 15 to 1
Year: sems, ss	Tuition: $4590
Appl: open	R and B: $2500
1636 applied	1018 accepted	545 enrolled
SAT: 442V 467M		COMPETITIVE

Monmouth College, established in 1933, is a private institution offering undergraduate programs in the liberal arts and sciences, business, and education. The library has 210,000 volumes and subscribes to over 1700 periodicals.

Environment: The 125-acre campus, located in a suburban area, occupies the former Guggenheim estate. Facilities include residence halls, a theater, science laboratories, and a student center. The college also sponsors fraternity houses.

Student Life: About 89% of the students come from New Jersey. Twenty-five percent live on campus. Campus housing is both coed and single-sex. Unmarried freshmen under 21 are required to live in campus housing unless living with relatives.

Organizations: Ten percent of the men belong to the 4 fraternities on campus, and 10% of the women belong to the 2 sororities. Extracurricular activities include clubs, student government, and publications.

Sports: The college sponsors intercollegiate teams in 10 sports for men and 8 for women. Seven intramural sports are offered for men and 5 for women.

Handicapped: About 90% of the campus is accessible to handicapped students. Facilities include special parking, elevators, wheelchair ramps, specially equipped rest rooms, and lowered drinking fountains and telephones. Special class scheduling is also available.

Graduates: About 20% of the freshmen drop out by the end of their first year, and 50% remain to graduate. Thirty percent of the graduates go on for further education.

Services: Placement, career counseling, psychological counseling, health care, tutoring, and remedial instruction are offered free to students. Placement services also are available to graduates.

Programs of Study: The college awards the B.A., B.F.A., B.S., and B.S.W. degrees. Associate and master's programs also are offered. Bachelor's degrees are conferred in the following subjects: BUSINESS (accounting, business administration, computer science, finance, management, marketing), EDUCATION (elementary, secondary), ENGLISH (English, media studies, speech), FINE AND PERFORMING ARTS (art, art education, music, music education, theater/dramatics), HEALTH SCIENCES (biology—health, medical technology), LANGUAGES (French, Spanish), MATH AND SCIENCES (biology, chemistry, ecology/environmental science, electron device physics, mathematics, physics), PHILOSOPHY (philosophy), PREPROFESSIONAL (engineering—electronic, social work), SOCIAL SCIENCES (anthropology, criminal justice, economics, government/political science, history, psychology, social sciences, sociology).

Required: Students must take 4 courses in English and meet distribution requirements.

Special: Preprofessional programs are offered in law, medicine, dentistry, veterinary science, optometry, and podiatry. The college offers a general-studies program, a peace studies program, interdisciplinary studies, and study abroad. Students may design their own majors.

Honors: Seventeen honor societies have chapters on campus. The college offers an honors program that includes seminars and an honors thesis.

Admissions: About 62% of the 1981-82 applicants were accepted. The SAT scores of those who enrolled were as follows: Verbal—60% below 500, 40% between 500 and 599, and 0% above 600; Math—50% below 500, 50% between 500 and 599, and 0% above 600. Applicants must have a high school GPA of at least 2.0, rank in the upper 50% of the high school class, and have completed 16 Carnegie units.

Procedure: The SAT is required and should be taken by January of the senior year. The application fee is $20. Application deadlines are open. Notification is made on a rolling basis.

Special: Early and deferred admissions plans are offered. AP and CLEP credit is available.

Transfer: Transfer applicants must be in good standing at their last school. D grades generally do not transfer. Students must earn at least 32 credits in residence for a bachelor's degree.

Visiting: An orientation program is held for prospective students. Informal visits with student guides may be arranged. Visitors may sit in on classes and stay overnight at the school. Visits are best scheduled in the fall. The admissions office should be contacted for arrangements.

Financial Aid: About 51% of the students receive aid. The college offers scholarships, federal and state grants, government and commercial loans, and CWS. The average award to 1981-82 freshmen totalled $3000. The FAF should be submitted by March 1 (fall) or November 1 (spring).

Foreign Students: Foreign students enrolled full-time make up about 7% of the student body. The college offers these students special counseling and special organizations.

Admissions: Foreign applicants generally must score 550 or better on the TOEFL. No college entrance exams are required.

Procedure: Application deadlines are August 1 (fall) and January 1 (spring). Students must submit a completed college medical form and show evidence of adequate funds for 1 year.

Admissions Contact: Robert N. Cristadoro, Director of Admissions.

MONTCLAIR STATE COLLEGE E-2
Upper Montclair, New Jersey 07043 (201) 893-4444

F/T: 3247M, 4803W
P/T: 1558M, 2507W
Grad: 1054M, 2200W
Year: sems, ss
Appl. Mar. 1
6400 applied
SAT: 450V 470M

Faculty: 475; IIA, +$
Ph.D.'s: 70%
S/F Ratio: 16 to 1
Tuition: $1029 ($2058)
R and B: $2500
3132 accepted 1679 enrolled
COMPETITIVE+

Montclair State College, established in 1908, offers undergraduate and graduate programs through the schools of fine and performing arts, humanities and social studies, mathematics and science, professional studies, and business administration. The library contains 315,182 volumes and 518,980 microfilm items, and subscribes to 25,500 periodicals.

Environment: The 200-acre suburban campus is located 14 miles from New York City. Facilities consist of 32 buildings, including dormitories and on-campus apartments.

Student Life: Most of the students come from New Jersey; 20% live on campus. About 80% come from public schools. Campus housing is both coed and single-sex; there are visiting privileges in the single-sex housing. Students may keep cars on campus.

Organizations: Student activities include 9 fraternities and 5 sororities, various social events, special-interest groups, and religious organizations.

Sports: The college fields 12 intercollegiate teams for men and 11 for women. There are 11 intramural sports for men and 11 for women.

Handicapped: About 80% of the campus is accessible to handicapped students. Facilities include wheelchair ramps, parking areas, elevators, specially equipped rest rooms, and lowered telephones. Special class scheduling is also available. There are 2 counselors available to handicapped students.

Graduates: The freshman dropout rate is 8%; 75% remain to graduate. Forty percent of the graduates pursue advanced degrees.

Services: Offered free of charge to all students are tutoring, remedial instruction, placement, health care, and career and psychological counseling.

Programs of Study: The college confers the B.A., B.S., B.F.A., and B.Mus. degrees. Master's programs are also offered. Bachelor's degrees are offered in the following subjects: BUSINESS (business administration, business education, computer science), EDUCATION (health/physical, industrial), ENGLISH (English), FINE AND PERFORMING ARTS (art, art education, art history, dance, music, music education, radio/TV, studio art, theater/dramatics), HEALTH SCIENCES (speech therapy), LANGUAGES (French, German, Greek/Latin, Italian, Spanish), MATH AND SCIENCES (biology, chemistry, earth science, mathematics, physical sciences, physics), PHILOSOPHY (philosophy), SOCIAL SCIENCES (anthropology, economics, geography, government/political science, history, psychology, sociology). Twenty-nine percent of degrees are conferred in education, 24% in business, and 13% in social sciences.

Required: Courses in English, natural science, mathematics, social science, humanities, and physical education are required of all students.

Special: Spanish and French majors may study abroad, and the college offers a spring semester at the University of Copenhagen.

Honors: There are honors programs available in biology, chemistry, mathematics, and psychology. Fifteen honor societies have chapters on campus.

Admissions: About 49% of those who applied were accepted for the 1981-82 freshman class. Candidates must have completed 16 Carnegie units. In addition, the following factors are considered in order of importance: advanced placement or honor courses, leadership, extracurricular activities, and evidence of special talent.

Procedure: The SAT is required by December of the senior year. Application deadlines are March 1 for fall entry and November 1 for spring entry. Notification is on a rolling basis. Students are encouraged to apply as early as possible in the senior year. There is a $10 application fee.

Special: There is a deferred admissions plan. AP and CLEP credit is available. The college has a special program for disadvantaged students.

Transfer: In 1981-82, 1816 students applied, 966 were accepted, and 758 enrolled. Transfers are considered for the sophomore, junior, and senior classes. Applicants must have a 2.0 GPA; D grades do not transfer. Preference is given to transfers from New Jersey community colleges. All students must complete, at the college, 30 of the 128 credits required for a bachelor's degree. Application deadlines are May 1 for fall and November 1 for spring.

Visiting: Tours and group meetings are available on a regular basis for prospective students. Guides are also available for informal visits. Visitors may not sit in on classes nor stay overnight at the school. The admissions office should be contacted for arrangements.

Financial Aid: About 65% of the students receive financial aid. Fifteen percent work part-time on campus. The average freshman award is $1132. The college is a member of CSS. Extremely needy freshmen can qualify for federally sponsored grants. Other financial aid for incoming students includes NDSL loans and student employment. The FAF is required. Application deadlines are March 15 (fall) and October 1 (spring).

Foreign Students: Two percent of the full-time students come from foreign countries. Special counseling and special organizations are available for these students.

Admissions: Foreign students must achieve a TOEFL score of at least 500. No college entrance exams are required.

Procedure: Application deadlines are April 1 (fall entry) and November 1 (spring entry). Foreign students must present proof of funds adequate to cover 1 year of study.

Admissions Contact: Alan Buechler, Director of Admissions.

NEW JERSEY INSTITUTE OF TECHNOLOGY
E-2
Newark, New Jersey 07102 (201) 645-5140

F/T: 2976M, 387W Faculty: 267; IIA, ++$
P/T: 1345M, 115W Ph.D.'s: 70%
Grad: 929M, 149W S/F Ratio: 14 to 1
Year: sems, ss Tuition: $1350 ($2460)
Appl: May 1 R: $2380
2128 applied 1128 accepted 557 enrolled
SAT: required COMPETITIVE

The New Jersey Institute of Technology, founded in 1919, is a state- and city-supported technological university. The library contains 125,000 volumes and 47,600 architectural slides, and subscribes to 1506 periodicals.

Environment: The 23-acre urban campus is located in downtown Newark, about 20 minutes from New York City. In addition to dormitories, there are facilities for commuter students.

Student Life: About 95% of the students come from New Jersey. Seventy-seven percent have had public school educations. Eight percent of the students live on campus. About 17% of the students are minority-group members. Campus housing is coed. Students may keep cars on campus.

Organizations: There are 13 national fraternities but no sororities. Extracurricular activities include special-interest clubs, religious groups, and student government.

Sports: The school competes intercollegiately in 16 sports for men and 15 for women. Men and women may compete on an intramural level in 6 sports.

Handicapped: Facilities for the physically handicapped include special parking and lowered drinking fountains and telephones.

Graduates: The freshman dropout rate is 20%; 60% remain to graduate. Twenty percent go on to graduate study; 3% enter medical school, 3% dental school, and 3% law school. Eighty-five percent of graduates pursue careers in business and industry.

Services: Career counseling, placement, tutoring, and health care are provided free of charge. Psychological counseling is also available on a fee basis.

Programs of Study: The institute confers the B.S. degree. Master's and doctoral programs are also offered. Bachelor's degrees are offered in the following subjects: BUSINESS (computer science, finance, management, marketing), PREPROFESSIONAL (architecture, engineering).

Required: Freshmen take a prescribed program in English, chemistry, mathematics, history, engineering graphics, physics, and physical education.

Special: Students may design their own majors. Independent study is possible. The B.S. is also offered in "Man and Technology."

Honors: Eight honor societies have chapters on campus.

Admissions: About 53% of the applicants for the 1981–82 freshman class were accepted. The SAT scores of those who enrolled were as follows: Verbal—68% below 500, 27% between 500 and 599, 4% between 600 and 700, and fewer than 1% above 700; Math—11% below 500, 59% between 500 and 599, 26% between 600 and 700, and 4% above 700. Applicants need a minimum B average with 16 academic units and a class rank in the top 40%. Advanced placement and honors courses are also considered.

Procedure: The SAT and the Mathematics I AT are required. Application deadlines are May 1 (fall) and December 1 (spring). Notification is on a rolling basis. There is a $20 application fee.

Special: AP and CLEP credit is accepted.

Transfer: For fall 1981, 1451 transfer students applied, 794 were accepted, and 698 enrolled. Each application is reviewed on an individual basis. A minimum GPA of 2.2 is required. D grades do not transfer. Thirty-three credits, of the 135 required for a bachelor's degree, must be completed in residence. The application deadlines are June 1 (fall) and November 1 (spring).

Visiting: There is an orientation program for prospective students. Informal campus visits with student guides may be arranged through the admissions office.

Financial Aid: Approximately 60% of all students receive some form of financial aid. Fewer than 1% work part-time on campus. Average aid to freshmen from all sources covers 50% of costs. Scholarships and loans are available to students showing need and scholastic ability.

Candidates may also be recommended by the institute for scholarships sponsored by various organizations or industries. Job opportunities are available, but not recommended until the student spends at least 1 year at the institute. The institute is a member of CSS. The FAF is required. Aid applications must be filed by March 15.

Foreign Students: Five percent of the full-time students come from foreign countries. The institute offers these students special counseling.

Admissions: No English proficiency examination is required. Foreign students must score at least 550 on the Math SAT and 550 on the Math Level I AT.

Procedure: Application deadlines are May 1 (fall) and December 1 (spring). Foreign students must provide proof of funds adequate to cover 4 years of study. They must also carry health insurance, which is available through the institute for a fee.

Admissions Contact: Neil D. Holtzman, Director of Admissions and Records.

PRINCETON UNIVERSITY
D-3
Princeton, New Jersey 08544 (609) 452-3060

F/T: 2821M, 1674W Faculty: 667; I, ++$
P/T: none Ph.D.'s: 100%
Grad: 1046M, 467W S/F Ratio: 7 to 1
Year: sems Tuition: $7250
Appl: Jan. 1 R and B: $2795
11,602 applied 2015 accepted 1140 enrolled
SAT (mean): 639V 680M MOST COMPETITIVE

Princeton University, established in 1746, is a private institution offering undergraduate degree programs in the liberal arts and sciences, engineering, and architecture. The university's library contains more than 3 million volumes and numerous microfilm items, and subscribes to 30,000 periodicals.

Environment: The 2600-acre suburban campus has 160 buildings, exclusive of residences. There are more than 30 dormitories. On-campus apartments and married student housing are also available. The campus is located 50 miles from New York City and 40 miles from Philadelphia.

Student Life: About 15% of the students come from New Jersey. Sixty percent are graduates of public schools. Nearly all 96% live on campus. Almost 18% of the students are minority-group members. Campus housing is both coed and single-sex. There are visiting privileges in single-sex dorms. Students may have cars on campus.

Organizations: There are no fraternities or sororities on campus. Religious organizations, clubs, service organizations, publications, performing groups, and other activities are offered. A variety of social and dining options are available, including 5 residential colleges, 3 non-residential societies, 13 eating clubs (open to upperclass students), and a kosher dining hall.

Sports: The university fields intercollegiate teams in 16 sports for men and 14 for women. Intramural competition is also offered in 15 sports for men and 10 for women.

Handicapped: About 60% of the campus is accessible to handicapped students. Special facilities include wheelchair ramps, parking areas, elevators, specially equipped rest rooms, and lowered telephones.

Graduates: The freshman dropout rate is 3%; about 90% of the students eventually graduate. About 37% of the graduates pursue advanced degrees: 8% enter medical school and 11% enter law school. About 43% pursue careers in business and industry.

Services: Placement for students and graduates, career counseling, health care, and psychological counseling are offered free of charge to all students. Tutoring is available on a fee basis.

Programs of Study: The A.B. and B.S. in E. degrees are awarded. Master's and doctoral programs are also available. Bachelor's degrees are offered in the following subjects: AREA STUDIES (African, American, Asian, Black/Afro-American, European, Latin American, Near Eastern, Russian, urban), BUSINESS (computer science), EDUCATION (secondary), ENGLISH (comparative literature, creative writing, English, linguistics, literature), FINE AND PERFORMING ARTS (art history, dance, music, studio art, theater/dramatics), LANGUAGES (Arabic, Chinese, French, German, Greek/Latin, Hebrew, Italian, Japanese, Portuguese, Russian, Spanish), MATH AND SCIENCES (astrophysics, biochemistry, biology, chemistry, geology, mathematics, physics, statistics), PHILOSOPHY (classics, philosophy, religion), PREPROFESSIONAL (architecture, engineering—aerospace and mechanical, engineering—chemical, engineering—civil, engineering—electrical and computer science, engineering—energy and environmental studies, engineering—physics, engineering—transportation),

SOCIAL SCIENCES (anthropology, economics, government/political science, history, international relations, psychology, sociology, statistics). Forty percent of the degrees are conferred in social sciences, 21% in preprofessional areas, and 17% in math and sciences.

Required: Core courses are required in 4 broad areas: natural sciences; social sciences; arts and letters; and history, philosophy, and religion. All A.B. students must achieve competence in a foreign language. Independent work and a senior thesis are required of all students.

Special: There is a teacher preparation program. Students may design their own majors. Study abroad, field study, urban work assignments, and student-initiated seminars are offered. There are University Scholar and Independent Concentrator programs. The Council of the Humanities is designed to strengthen the humanistic side of education not only in the conventional humanities but also in the humanistic aspects of the social and natural sciences.

Honors: Phi Beta Kappa and Sigma Xi have chapters on campus. Honors work is offered in all departments.

Admissions: About 17% of the applicants for the 1981–82 freshman class were accepted. The SAT scores of those who enrolled were as follows: Verbal—6% below 500, 22% between 500 and 599, 43% between 600 and 700, and 29% above 700; Math—2% below 500, 13% between 500 and 599, 34% between 600 and 700, and 50% above 700. Admission is based on a combination of factors. In addition to a strong high school record, the admissions committee considers the applicant's extracurricular activities and character. Candidates should present 16 units of academic work. A personal interview is strongly recommended.

Procedure: The SAT and 3 ATs should be taken by January of the senior year. There is a $35 application fee. The application deadline for the fall semester is January 1.

Special: There are early action and deferred admissions plans. AP and CLEP credit is available.

Transfer: In a recent year, 607 applications were received, 29 were accepted, and 27 students enrolled. An excellent college record, sound academic reasons for desiring to transfer, and recommendations are required. Applicants should have at least a 3.5 GPA. Grades of C or better transfer. Two years must be completed in residence. March 1 is the application deadline.

Visiting: There is a regularly scheduled orientation program for prospective students. Informal campus visits with guides can be arranged. Visitors may sit in on classes and stay overnight at the school. Visits are best scheduled between May 15 and December 15. The admissions office should be contacted for arrangements.

Financial Aid: About 44% of the students receive financial aid. Freshman scholarships, loans, grants, and part-time employment are offered. Sixty percent of the students work part-time on campus. The average award to freshmen is $4900. The university is a member of CSS. The FAF and an institutional application should be submitted by February 1.

Foreign Students: About 5% of the full-time students come from foreign countries. Princeton actively recruits these students and offers them special counseling and organizations.

Admissions: Foreign students must take the TOEFL. The SAT is also required, as are 3 ATs.

Procedure: The application deadline for fall entry is February 1. Although not required, health insurance is available through the university.

Admissions Contact: James W. Wickenden, Dean of Admission.

RAMAPO COLLEGE OF NEW JERSEY   D–2
Mahwah, New Jersey 07430   (201) 825-2800

F/T: 1383M, 1230W   Faculty: 147; IIB, ++$
P/T: 736M, 1181W   Ph.D.'s: 87%
Grad: none   S/F Ratio: 19 to 1
Year: sems, ss   Tuition: $35 ($55) p/c
Appl: Mar. 15   R and B: $2100
1958 applied   1152 accepted   587 enrolled
SAT: 430V 470M   COMPETITIVE

Ramapo College, a state-supported institution founded in 1969, offers undergraduate programs in the liberal arts and sciences and business administration. The library contains 120,000 volumes and 12,000 microfilm items, and subscribes to 500 periodicals.

Environment: The 350-acre campus is located in a small suburban town about 35 miles from New York City. There are 7 buildings on campus plus apartments that house 600 men and women.

Student Life: About 90% of the students come from New Jersey, and 97% come from public schools. Seventy percent live on campus. Thirteen percent of the students are minority-group members. Campus housing is coed. Students may keep cars on campus. Day-care services are available to all students, faculty, and staff.

Organizations: There are no fraternities or sororities. Extracurricular activities include clubs, student government, dramatics, and scheduled social and cultural events.

Sports: Ten intercollegiate sports are offered. The intramural program features 4 sports.

Handicapped: About 98% of the campus is accessible to students with physical handicaps. Special facilities include wheelchair ramps, elevators, special parking, specially equipped rest rooms, lowered drinking fountains and telephones, and housing. About 2% of the students have visual or hearing impairments; the library has material specifically for these students. The college assigns 1 counselor and 1 assistant to students with handicaps.

Graduates: Eighteen percent of the freshmen drop out by the end of their first year; 75% remain to graduate. Thirty percent pursue advanced study; 1% enter medical school, 1% dental school, and 3% law school. Twenty-five percent pursue careers in business and industry.

Services: Placement, career counseling, health care, psychological counseling, and remedial instruction are offered free of charge. Tutoring is offered on a fee basis.

Programs of Study: The B.A. and B.S. degrees are conferred. Bachelor's degrees are offered in the following subjects: AREA STUDIES (American, international, metropolitan), BUSINESS (business administration), ENGLISH (literature), FINE AND PERFORMING ARTS (communications arts, fine arts), MATH AND SCIENCES (biology, chemistry, ecology/environmental science, mathematics, mathematics/physics, physics), PHILOSOPHY (philosophy), PREPROFESSIONAL (dentistry, law, medicine, social work, veterinary), SOCIAL SCIENCES (anthropology, economics, government/political science, history, psychology, sociology). Approximately 35% of degrees conferred are in the sciences.

Required: All students must complete course work in the humanities, sciences, and social sciences.

Special: Student-designed majors, pass/fail options, a junior year abroad program, and intern programs in business, sociology, psychology, contemporary arts, and many other areas are offered. A 3-year bachelor's degree program is also available.

Admissions: About 59% of the applicants for the 1981–82 freshman class were accepted. The SAT scores of those who enrolled were as follows: Verbal—80% below 500, 16% between 500 and 599, 4% between 600 and 700, and 0% above 700; Math—66% below 500, 30% between 500 and 599, 4% between 600 and 700, and 0% above 700. The admissions quota for out-of-state students is 10%. In addition to having 16 Carnegie units, students must rank in the upper 40% of their class. Other factors in the admissions decision include recommendations, advanced placement or honors courses, and character. There is a special program for academically and financially disadvantaged students.

Procedure: The SAT or ACT should be taken by March of the senior year. Application deadlines are March 15 (fall) and December 15 (spring). Notification is on a rolling basis. An interview is recommended. There is a $10 application fee.

Special: There are early and deferred admissions plans. AP and CLEP credit is accepted.

Transfer: For fall 1981, 1046 students applied, 826 were accepted, and 481 enrolled. Good academic standing is required. D grades transfer only with an associate degree from a New Jersey 2-year college. Forty-five credits, of the 120 needed for a bachelor's degree, must be completed in residence. The deadlines are the same as those for incoming freshmen.

Visiting: There is a visiting program for prospective students. Visitors may sit in on classes. The admissions office should be contacted to arrange visits.

Financial Aid: About 50% of all students receive some form of financial aid. Fifteen percent work part-time on campus. Average aid to freshmen from all sources is $1100. The college offers grants (federal and state), loans (government and commercial), and CWS (in all departments). Tuition may be paid in installments by credit card. The college is a member of CSS. The FAF should be submitted by May 1 (fall) or December 15 (spring).

Foreign Students: Three percent of the full-time students come from foreign countries. The college offers these students an intensive English program, special counseling, and special organizations.

Admissions: Foreign students must take the TOEFL or the Comprehensive English Language Test. No college entrance examination is required.

Procedure: The application deadline is March 15 (fall). Foreign students must present proof of adequate funds, and must carry health insurance, which is available through the college for a fee.

Admissions Contact: Wayne C. Marshall, Director of Admissions.

RIDER COLLEGE D-3
Lawrenceville, New Jersey 08648 (609) 896-5041

F/T: 1654M, 1721W	Faculty: 209; IIA, +$
P/T: 610M, 635W	Ph.D.'s: 78%
Grad: 529M, 550W	S/F Ratio: 17 to 1
Year: 4-1-4, ss	Tuition: $4035
Appl: Aug. 30	R and B: $2400
2667 applied	1809 accepted	808 enrolled
SAT: 424V 472M		COMPETITIVE

Rider College, a private nonsectarian institution founded in 1865 as a business college, now offers curricula in 4 schools: Liberal Arts and Sciences, Business, Education, and Continuing Studies. Its library has a collection of 350,000 volumes and 19,000 microfilm items, and subscribes to 1807 periodicals.

Environment: The 333-acre suburban campus is located 3 miles from Trenton and 5 miles from Princeton. Eleven dormitories and 8 fraternity and sorority houses accommodate 2500 students.

Student Life: About 70% of the students come from New Jersey. Eighty-five percent have had public school educations. About 71% live on campus. Forty-seven percent of the students are Catholic, 20% Protestant, and 12% Jewish. Eleven percent are minority-group members. Campus housing is both single-sex and coed; there are visiting privileges in single-sex housing. Students may keep cars on campus.

Organizations: Twelve percent of the men belong to one of 4 national fraternities; 12% of the women are members of one of 4 national sororities. Religious organizations, clubs, student government, cultural groups, and a variety of social activities are offered. Nearby Princeton and Trenton afford many other opportunities for cultural and recreational activities.

Sports: Intercollegiate competition is offered in 9 sports for men and 6 for women. There are 6 sports available on an intramural level for men and 4 for women.

Handicapped: About 95% of the campus is accessible to students with physical handicaps. Special facilities include parking areas, wheelchair ramps, elevators, specially equipped rest rooms, and lowered telephones and drinking fountains. Class schedules can be individually arranged. The college provides a counseling staff to assist the handicapped student.

Graduates: Ten percent of the freshmen drop out by the end of their first year; 65% complete their degrees. Forty percent of the graduates continue their educations (1% in medical school and almost 2% in law school); 85% enter business and industry.

Services: The college offers free health care, psychological counseling, career counseling, and placement services. Tutoring and remedial help are offered on a fee basis.

Programs of Study: The college offers the B.A., B.S., and B.S.C. degrees. Associate and master's programs are also offered. Bachelor's degrees are offered in the following subjects: AREA STUDIES (American), BUSINESS (accounting, actuarial science, business administration, business education, computer science, finance, industrial relations, management, marketing), EDUCATION (early childhood, elementary, secondary), ENGLISH (English, journalism, literature, speech), FINE AND PERFORMING ARTS (fine arts), LANGUAGES (French, German, Russian, Spanish), MATH AND SCIENCES (biochemistry, biology, chemistry, geology, mathematics, physics, statistics), PHILOSOPHY (philosophy), PREPROFESSIONAL (dentistry, law, medicine, social work, veterinary), SOCIAL SCIENCES (economics, government/political science, history, psychology, sociology). About 55% of the degrees are awarded in business, 30% in the liberal arts and sciences, and 15% in education.

Required: A core curriculum must be completed.

Special: Student-designed majors, independent study, and study abroad are offered.

Honors: Twenty-one honor societies are represented on campus.

Admissions: About 68% of the 1981–82 freshman applicants were accepted. SAT scores of those who enrolled were as follows: Verbal—85% below 500, 13% between 500 and 599, 2% between 600 and 700, and 0% above 700; Math—71% below 500, 25% between 500 and 599, 3% between 600 and 700, and 1% above 700. Applicants should be in the top 50% of their class and have a 2.5 high school GPA. Other considerations include advanced placement or honors courses, impressions made during the interview, and extracurricular activities.

Procedure: The SAT or ACT is required. Application deadlines are August 30 (fall), January 15 (spring), and May 15 (summer). Notification is made within 1 month after the application file is complete. There is a $20 application fee.

Special: There are early decision and early admissions programs. AP and CLEP credit is granted.

Transfer: For fall 1981, 797 applications were received, 542 were accepted, and 260 transfer students enrolled. For business, a 2.75 GPA from a 2-year college or a 3.0 GPA from a 4-year college is required. For liberal arts and education, a 2.3 and a 2.5, respectively, are required. SAT scores must be submitted if fewer than 30 college credits have been earned. D grades do not transfer. Thirty credits must be completed in residence for liberal arts or education majors, 45 credits for business majors. A total of 126 credits is required for the bachelor's degree. The deadlines are the same as those for freshmen. A rolling admissions policy is used.

Visiting: The orientation program for prospective students includes discussions with faculty members and financial aid advisers. Informal campus tours with student guides may be arranged. Suggested visiting hours are weekdays from 9 A.M. to noon and from 1:30 P.M. to 4:30 P.M. Generally, visitors may not attend classes. For further information, the appointment secretary in the admissions office should be contacted.

Financial Aid: About 70% of the students are receiving aid administered by the college. Twenty percent work part-time on campus. Average aid to freshmen from all sources is $3800. Scholarships, grants (federal and state), loans (including NDSL), and work opportunities are available. Need and academic promise are determining factors. The college is a member of CSS. The FAF is required. Application deadlines are the same as those for freshman applicants.

Foreign Students: One percent of the full-time students come from foreign countries. The college offers these students special counseling and special organizations.

Admissions: Foreign students must score at least 500 on the TOEFL. No college entrance examination is required.

Procedure: Application deadlines are February (fall), October (spring), and April (summer). Foreign students must submit the college's health record form completed by a physician. They must also submit proof of funds adequate to cover 4 years of study.

Admissions Contact: Earl L. Davis, Director of Admissions.

RUTGERS UNIVERSITY

Rutgers was founded in 1766 as Queen's College and is one of the original colonial colleges. In 1864, it became New Jersey's land-grant college and has since become the state university with campuses in 3 locations and 13 undergraduate divisions, in addition to graduate and professional schools. It enrolls approximately 50,000 students.

In New Brunswick are located the undergraduate colleges: Douglass College (for women), Cook College, Livingston College, Rutgers College, Mason Gross School of the Arts, College of Engineering, College of Pharmacy, and one branch of University College. On the graduate level there are the Graduate School and the schools of Education, Library and Information Studies, Creative and Performing Arts, Applied and Professional Psychology, and Social Work. In Newark are the undergraduate College of Arts and Sciences, College of Nursing, and another branch of University College as well as the graduate-level Law School, School of Criminal Justice, Graduate School, and School of Management. In Camden are the undergraduate Camden College of Arts and Sciences, the third branch of University College, and another Law School. Separate profiles on each of the undergraduate colleges follow.

RUTGERS UNIVERSITY/CAMDEN C-4
COLLEGE OF ARTS AND SCIENCES
Camden, New Jersey 08102 (609) 757-6104

F/T: 1152M, 1095W	Faculty: 170; n/av
P/T: 264M, 441W	Ph.D.'s: 90%
Grad: none	S/F Ratio: 15 to 1
Year: sems, ss	Tuition: $1312 ($2422)
Appl: Mar. 15	R and B: none
1687 applied	1044 accepted	404 enrolled
SAT (mean): 450V 500M		COMPETITIVE

510 NEW JERSEY

Camden College of Arts and Sciences, founded in 1927, serves a commuting student body in the Camden and Philadelphia metropolitan area. Undergraduate programs are offered in the liberal arts and sciences, business, and education. Students may utilize any of the 18 libraries within the university system.

Environment: The 16-acre urban campus, 3 miles from Philadelphia, has 18 buildings. The college is part of an active industrial and cultural community where a wealth of educational and vocational opportunities exist. The college does not provide housing; many students live nearby in sorority and fraternity houses, cooperatives, or private apartments.

Student Life: About 97% of the students come from New Jersey. All students live off campus. Fourteen percent are minority-group members. The college offers day-care services, for a fee, to all students, faculty, and staff.

Organizations: There are 3 fraternities and 2 sororities. Extracurricular and co-curricular activities are generally held in the College Center, which includes a cafeteria, lounges, game room, meeting room, and a multipurpose room used for theater, lectures, films, and dances. Other activities include the student congress, campus newspaper, radio station, and over 30 academic and recreational organizations.

Sports: The college competes intercollegiately in 7 sports for men and 4 for women. There are 7 intramural sports for men and 8 for women.

Handicapped: Almost 100% of the campus is accessible to the physically handicapped. Facilities include wheelchair ramps, special parking, elevators, specially equipped rest rooms, and lowered drinking fountains and telephones; special class scheduling is also available. There is one student coordinator to assist handicapped students.

Graduates: Twenty-nine percent of the freshmen drop out by the end of the first year; 37% remain to graduate. Forty-three percent of those who graduate undertake further study immediately: 1% enter medical school, 1% dental school, and 4% law school. Seventy percent pursue careers in business and industry.

Services: Placement services, health care, psychological counseling, career counseling, and remedial instruction are offered to students free of charge. Tutoring is also available for a fee.

Programs of Study: The college confers the B.A. and B.S. degrees. Bachelor's degrees are offered in the following subjects: AREA STUDIES (Black/Afro-American, urban), BUSINESS (accounting, business administration), ENGLISH (English), FINE AND PERFORMING ARTS (art, music, theater/dramatics), HEALTH SCIENCES (medical technology, nursing), LANGUAGES (French, German, Spanish), MATH AND SCIENCES (biology, chemistry, general science, mathematics, physics), PHILOSOPHY (philosophy), PREPROFESSIONAL (dentistry, medicine, social work, veterinary), SOCIAL SCIENCES (economics, history, political science, psychology, sociology). Teacher certification is available in 13 majors. Thirty-seven percent of degrees are conferred in business/management, 8% in the health professions, 7% in the biological sciences, and 6% in psychology, letters, and fine/applied arts.

Required: All undergraduates are required to take 2 semesters of English composition, 1 of math, computer science, statistics, or logic, 1 of natural science, 2 of history, language and literature, and social science, and 1 of fine arts.

Special: Student-designed majors, a junior year abroad, and a combined B.A.-B.S. degree in engineering (requiring transfer to New Brunswick after 2 years) in a 5-year program are offered.

Honors: Eight honor societies have chapters on campus. Most merit award recipients participate in honors programs.

Admissions: Approximately 62% of those who applied were accepted for the 1981–82 freshman class. The mean SAT scores of those who enrolled were 450V, 500M. Candidates must be graduates of an accredited high school and have completed 16 Carnegie units. Candidates who do not have the required number or distribution of college preparatory units, or who have an equivalency diploma or a diploma from a non-accredited high school, may apply for admission by examination.

Procedure: The SAT is required (except for candidates out of high school 2 or more years, or with 12 or more college credits). Candidates for admission by examination must submit scores on 3 ATs in addition to the SAT. The deadlines for filing are March 15 (fall) and December 15 (spring). Applications are reviewed on a rolling basis. The college subscribes to the CRDA of May 1. The application fee is $15 for 1 college of Rutgers University, $20 for 2, and $25 for 3, applied to with a single application. The application fee may be deferred in cases of economic hardship.

Special: The college offers deferred admissions and early admissions plans. AP credit is accepted.

Transfer: Recently, 917 applications were received, 606 were accepted, and 365 transfer students enrolled. C grades or better transfer. Transfers must complete 30 of the last 42 credits at the college. A total of 128 credits must be completed for the bachelor's degree. Application deadlines are May 15 (fall) and December 15 (spring).

Visiting: There are regularly scheduled orientations for prospective students.

Financial Aid: University-wide, about 54% of the full-time students receive aid from funds totalling over $50 million. This may take the form of a scholarship, grant, loan, job, or combination thereof. Seventeen percent of the students work part-time on campus. All major federal and state programs are available. Merit awards have been established for students with outstanding academic/artistic ability. The average aid package is $2125, with a minimum of $100 to a maximum of $4600. Students must submit the FAF to CSS as soon as possible after January 1, but prior to March 1 for full consideration.

Foreign Students: Only 2 foreign students currently are enrolled at the college. An intensive English course and special counseling are available to foreign students.

Admissions: Students from non-English-speaking countries must take the TOEFL; those from English-speaking countries, the SAT. Candidates for admission by examination must also submit scores on 3 ATs.

Procedure: Application deadlines are March 15 (fall) and December 15 (spring). Proof of funds adequate to cover 4 years of study is required. Out-of-state tuition rates apply. Foreign students must carry health insurance, which is available through the college for a fee.

Admissions Contact: Deborah Brown, Director of Admissions.

RUTGERS UNIVERSITY/ COLLEGE OF ENGINEERING D-3
New Brunswick, New Jersey 08903   (201) 932-3770

F/T: 2155M, 457W   Faculty: 94; n/av
P/T: 47M, 6W   Ph.D.'s: 90%
Grad: none   S/F Ratio: 12 to 1
Year: sems, ss   Tuition: $1387 ($2497)
Appl: Feb. 1   R and B: $2000
3048 applied   1810 accepted   725 enrolled
SAT (mean): 479V 600M   **VERY COMPETITIVE**

Rutgers University College of Engineering, founded in 1864, is a coeducational professional college offering a sound technical and cultural education in addition to a thorough understanding of fundamental principles and engineering methods of reasoning and analysis. Engineering students may utilize any of the 18 libraries within the university system.

Environment: In proximity to the other New Brunswick divisions of the university, the College of Engineering is 35 miles south of New York City. The college provides modern facilities for instruction and research; engineering students affiliate with the New Brunswick liberal arts colleges for housing and other student services. A campus bus system provides regular, free service among the New Brunswick colleges, facilitating academic and social activities.

Student Life: Approximately 88% of the students come from New Jersey, and 54% live on campus in coed and single-sex dorms. Twelve percent are minority-group members. Day-care services are available through affiliated liberal arts colleges.

Organizations: Engineering students may participate in all of Rutgers' extracurricular activities and social and cultural events, including its 27 fraternities and 10 sororities.

Sports: Students may participate in 16 intercollegiate sports programs for men and 13 for women. Intramurals are available to both men and women through the college of affiliation.

Handicapped: Almost 100% of the Engineering Building is accessible to the physically handicapped. Facilities include wheelchair ramps, special parking, specially equipped rest rooms, and transportation; special class scheduling is also available. There is a student coordinator who assists handicapped students.

Graduates: Eleven percent of the freshmen drop out by the end of the first year; 70% remain to graduate. Thirty-one percent of those who remain pursue advanced degrees, and 69% enter careers in business and industry.

Services: Placement services, career counseling, health care, psychological counseling, tutoring, and remedial instruction are offered free of charge to engineering students through the university.

Programs of Study: The college confers the B.S. in Eng. degree in the following areas of specialization: PREPROFESSIONAL (engineering—agricultural, engineering—applied sciences, engineering—ceramics, engineering—chemical, engineering—civil, engineering—electrical, engineering—industrial, engineering—mechanical).

Required: All students must take an introduction to chemistry for engineers, calculus, analytical physics, and a college elective in the freshman year. All students follow the same program except for electives.

Special: The ceramic engineering program is one of the few such programs offered in the United States. A combined B.A.-B.S. degree is offered in a 5-year program in the liberal arts and engineering. In addition, a combined B.S. in Eng. and M.B.A. degree is offered in 5 years in cooperation with the Rutgers University Graduate School of Management.

Honors: Several honor societies have chapters on campus; honors programs are offered in all departments. The James J. Slade Scholars Honor Program offers independent study for qualified juniors and seniors. Most merit award recipients participate in honors programs.

Admissions: Approximately 59% of those who applied were accepted for the 1981–82 freshman class. The SAT scores of those who enrolled were as follows: Verbal—60% below 500, 32% between 500 and 599, 7% between 600 and 700, and 1% above 700; Math—11% below 500, 42% between 500 and 599, 40% between 600 and 700, and 7% above 700. Candidates should have 16 academic units from an accredited high school. Those who do not have the required number or distribution of college preparatory units, or who have an equivalency diploma or a diploma from a non-accredited high school, may apply for admission by examination. Other factors entering into the admissions decision are advanced placement or honors courses, extracurricular activities, recommendations, and character.

Procedure: The SAT is required (except for candidates out of high school 2 or more years or with 12 or more college credits). Candidates for admission by examination must submit scores from 3 ATs in addition to the SAT. The deadline for applications is February 1; the college follows a rolling admissions policy. Application fees are $15 for 1 college of the university, $20 for 2, and $25 for 3, applied to with a single application. The application fee may be deferred in cases of economic hardship.

Special: AP credit is accepted. There are early admissions and deferred admissions plans.

Transfer: For fall 1981, 665 applications were received, 210 were accepted, and 116 students enrolled. D grades do not transfer. Preference is given to graduates of New Jersey community colleges. The deadline for application is March 15 (fall). Thirty of the last 42 credits must be taken at Rutgers University (134–138 credits are required for the bachelor's degree).

Visiting: There are regularly scheduled orientations for prospective students. The office of undergraduate admissions should be contacted to arrange visits.

Financial Aid: University-wide, about 54% of the full-time students receive aid from funds totalling over $50 million. This may take the form of a scholarship, grant, loan, job, or combination thereof. Seventeen percent of the students work part-time on campus. All major federal and state programs are available. Merit awards have been established for students with outstanding academic/artistic ability. The average aid package is $2125, with a minimum of $100 to a maximum of $4600. Students must submit the FAF to CSS as soon as possible after January 1, but prior to March 1 for full consideration.

Foreign Students: About 4% of the full-time students come from foreign countries. An English course and an intensive English program are available to these students, as are special counseling and organizations.

Admissions: Foreign students must take the TOEFL. The SAT is also required. ATs are necessary only if the student is not a high school graduate, or if required entrance units are lacking.

Procedure: Application deadlines for fall entry are February 1 for students currently in the U.S., and March 15 for students residing overseas. Proof of funds adequate to cover 4 years of study is required. Out-of-state tuition rates apply. Foreign students must carry health insurance, which is available through the university and included in the student fee.

Admissions Contact: Natalie Aharonian, University Director of Undergraduate Admissions.

NEW JERSEY 511

RUTGERS UNIVERSITY/ COLLEGE OF NURSING
E-2

Newark, New Jersey 07102 (201) 648-5205

F/T: 26M, 422W		Faculty:	46; n/av
P/T: 7M, 111W		Ph.D.'s:	22%
Grad: none		S/F Ratio:	7 to 1
Year: sems, ss		Tuition:	$1287 ($2397)
Appl: Mar. 15		R:	$1010
451 applied	168 accepted		57 enrolled
SAT (mean): 450V 470M			COMPETITIVE+

Rutgers University College of Nursing, founded in 1956, is a professional school offering a Bachelor of Science curriculum in nursing. A four-year program, as well as a program for Registered Nurse students, is available. Students may utilize any of the 18 libraries within the university system.

Environment: The 23-acre urban campus, 10 miles from New York City, has well-equipped laboratories and classrooms. University-sponsored housing is available at the nearby YMWCA.

Student Life: Ninety-eight percent of the students are from New Jersey; 13% live in university-sponsored, coed housing. Twenty-three percent of the students are minority-group members. Students may keep cars on campus.

Organizations: The Newark campus has 4 national fraternities and 2 national sororities. Campus organizations related to academics, contemporary problems, the arts, and religion are available. The College of Nursing student senate represents the student body on important issues affecting college life.

Sports: Eight intercollegiate and 9 intramural sports for men and women are offered.

Handicapped: Almost the entire Newark campus is accessible to the physically handicapped. Facilities include wheelchair ramps, special parking, elevators, specially equipped rest rooms, and lowered drinking fountains and telephones; special class scheduling is also available. There is a student coordinator to assist handicapped students.

Graduates: Five percent of the freshmen drop out by the end of the first year; 70% remain to graduate. Twenty percent of those who remain go on to graduate study. Graduates hold staff and administrative positions in hospitals, public health agencies, and other health institutions.

Services: Placement services, health care, psychological counseling, tutoring, and remedial instruction are offered to students free of charge. Career counselors assist students with job search strategies, interviewing techniques, on-campus recruitment interviewing, graduate and professional school information, and part-time summer employment.

Programs of Study: The college confers the B.S. in nursing. The curriculum includes both liberal arts and professional education, and is designed to develop and foster intellectual curiosity, human understanding, and dedication to service. On completion of the degree, students are eligible to take nursing licensure examinations in New Jersey and all other states.

Required: An integral part of the nursing curriculum is clinical experience, which students obtain at hospitals and health agencies in northern New Jersey.

Honors: The Alpha Tau chapter of Sigma Tau, the national nursing honor society, is open to qualified students. Most merit award recipients participate in honors programs.

Admissions: Approximately 37% of those who applied were accepted for the 1981–82 freshman class. The mean SAT scores of those who enrolled were 450V, 470M. Candidates should have completed 16 academic units at an accredited high school. Those who do not have the required number or distribution of college preparatory units, or who have an equivalency diploma or a diploma from a non-accredited high school, may apply for admission by examination. Other factors entering into the admissions decision are advanced placement or honors courses, recommendations, and evidence of special talents.

Procedure: The SAT is required (except for candidates out of high school 2 or more years or with 12 or more college credits). Candidates for admission by examination must submit scores from 3 ATs in addition to the SAT. The college subscribes to the CRDA of May 1. The deadline for filing applications is March 15; applications are reviewed on a rolling basis. The application fee is $15 for 1 college of Rutgers University, $20 for 2, and $25 for 3, applied to with a single application. The application fee may be waived in cases of economic hardship.

512 NEW JERSEY

Special: CLEP and AP credit is accepted (AP grades of 4 and 5; CLEP 50% or better). There is an early admissions plan.

Transfer: For fall 1981, the college received 356 applications, accepted 182, and enrolled 104 students. Transfers are accepted for the sophomore year only. D grades do not transfer. Preference is given to graduates of state community colleges. There is a 3-year residency requirement. May 15 is the deadline for fall application.

Visiting: There are regularly scheduled orientations for prospective students.

Financial Aid: University-wide, about 54% of the full-time students receive aid from funds totalling over $50 million. This may take the form of a scholarship, grant, loan, job, or combination thereof. Seventeen percent of the students work part-time on campus. All major federal and state programs are available. Merit awards have been established for students with outstanding academic/artistic ability. The average aid package is $2125, with a minimum of $100 to a maximum of $4600. Students must submit the FAF to CSS as soon as possible after January 1, but prior to March 1 for full consideration.

Foreign Students: Fewer than 1% of the full-time students come from foreign countries. The college offers these students an intensive English course. Special counseling and special organizations are also available.

Admissions: Foreign students must achieve a minimum score of 550 on the TOEFL. The SAT is also required.

Procedure: Application deadlines are the same as for freshmen. Proof of funds adequate to cover 1 year of study is required. Out-of-state tuition rates apply. Foreign students must carry health insurance, which is available through the college and included in the student fee.

Admissions Contact: Cecile Stolbof, Dean of Admissions.

RUTGERS UNIVERSITY/ COLLEGE OF PHARMACY D-3
New Brunswick, New Jersey 08903 (201) 932-3770

F/T: 325M, 439W	Faculty: 28; n/av
P/T: 3M, 5W	Ph.D.'s: 90%
Grad: none	S/F Ratio: 14 to 1
Year: sems, ss	Tuition: $1387 ($2497)
Appl: Feb. 1	R and B: $2000
554 applied	407 accepted	230 enrolled
SAT (mean): 470V 530M	VERY COMPETITIVE

The College of Pharmacy, founded in 1892, is one of the 4 professional schools on the New Brunswick campus of Rutgers University. Its 5-year pharmacy curriculum combines science, humanities, and social sciences to provide theoretical and technical training to prepare students for careers in hospitals, government, business, industry, and community pharmacies. Students may utilize any of the 18 libraries within the university system.

Environment: In proximity to the other New Brunswick colleges of the university, the College of Pharmacy is located on the 200-acre New Brunswick campus, about 35 miles south of New York City, and is adjacent to the medical school and the library of science and medicine. Pharmacy students affiliate with Douglass, Livingston, or Rutgers Colleges for housing and other student services. A campus bus system provides regular, free service among the New Brunswick colleges, facilitating academic and social activities.

Student Life: Ninety-one percent of the students are from New Jersey and 53% live on campus. Thirteen percent are minority-group members. Day-care services are available through affiliated liberal arts colleges.

Organizations: Pharmacy students enjoy campus life through their college of affiliation. They also participate in a variety of professional and scientific programs. National fraternity and sorority chapters and a student chapter of the American Pharmaceutical Association sponsor many educational and social functions. Other activities include the yearbook, newspapers, musical organizations, and a variety of clubs.

Sports: Pharmacy students participate in 16 intercollegiate sports for men and 13 for women. Intramurals for both men and women are available through the college of affiliation.

Handicapped: Almost 100% of the Pharmacy Building is accessible to wheelchair students. For further details on facilities for the physically handicapped, see the entries for the New Brunswick liberal arts colleges.

Graduates: Nine percent of the freshmen drop out by the end of the first year. Seventy-five percent of those who enter remain to graduate; 2% pursue graduate study after graduation.

Services: Placement services, career counseling, health care, psychological counseling, tutoring, and remedial instruction are offered to students free of charge.

Programs of Study: The college confers the B.S. in pharmacy. It offers courses in pharmacy, pharmacy administration, pharmaceutical chemistry, pharmacognosy, and pharmacology. Students gain clinical experience working in one of several teaching hospitals.

Required: All students follow the same program except for electives.

Honors: The Rho Chi national honor society is open to qualified students. Most merit award recipients participate in honors programs.

Admissions: Approximately 73% of those who applied were accepted for the 1981-82 freshman class. The SAT scores of those who enrolled were as follows: Verbal—80% below 500, 19% between 500 and 599, 1% between 600 and 700, and 0% above 700; Math—67% below 500, 28% between 500 and 599, 4% between 600 and 700, and 1% above 700. Candidates should have completed 16 academic units at an accredited high school. The primary emphasis in the admissions decision is given to grades, class rank, the type of high school program followed, and SAT scores. Candidates who do not have the required number or distribution of college preparatory units, or who have an equivalency diploma or a diploma from a non-accredited high school, may apply for admission by examination.

Procedure: The SAT is required (except for candidates out of high school 2 or more years, or with 12 or more college credits). Candidates for admission by examination must submit scores from 3 ATs in addition to the SAT. The deadline for fall applications is February 1; applications are reviewed on a rolling basis. The college subscribes to the CRDA of May 1. The application fee is $15 for 1 college of Rutgers University, $20 for 2, and $25 for 3, applied to with a single application. The application fee may be deferred in cases of economic hardship.

Special: CLEP and AP credit is accepted. Deferred admissions and early admissions plans are available.

Transfer: For fall 1981, 268 transfer applications were received, 68 were accepted, and 40 students enrolled. Official transcripts of all high school and college work are required; D grades do not transfer. Preference is given to graduates of New Jersey community colleges. The last year of a 3-year full-time accredited pharmacy program must be taken at Rutgers; 169 credits are required for the bachelor's degree. The deadline for transfer applications is March 15 for fall; spring admission is not normally available.

Visiting: The admissions office should be contacted to arrange visits.

Financial Aid: University-wide, about 54% of the full-time students receive aid from funds totalling over $50 million. This may take the form of a scholarship, grant, loan, job, or combination thereof. Seventeen percent of the students work part-time on campus. All major federal and state programs are available. Merit awards have been established for students with outstanding academic/artistic ability. The average aid package is $2125, with a minimum of $100 to a maximum of $4600. Students must submit the FAF to CSS as soon as possible after January 1, but prior to March 1 for full consideration.

Foreign Students: Foreign students comprise less than 1% of the full-time enrollment. The college offers these students an intensive English course and an intensive English program. Special counseling and special organizations are also available.

Admissions: Foreign students must take the TOEFL. The SAT is also required.

Procedure: The application deadline for fall entry is February 1 for foreign students currently in the U.S. and March 15 for students from overseas. Proof of funds adequate to cover a full 5 years is required. Out-of-state tuition rates apply. Students must carry health insurance, which is available through the college and included in the student fee.

Admissions Contact: Natalie Aharonian, University Director of Undergraduate Admissions.

RUTGERS UNIVERSITY/ COOK COLLEGE D-3
New Brunswick, New Jersey 08903 (201) 932-3770

F/T: 1425M, 1253W	Faculty: 122; n/av
P/T: 73M, 65W	Ph.D.'s: 95%
Grad: none	S/F Ratio: 5 to 1
Year: sems, ss	Tuition: $1377 ($2487)
Appl: Feb. 1	R and B: $2000
6057 applied	2740 accepted	592 enrolled
SAT (mean): 500V 550M	VERY COMPETITIVE

Cook College, established in 1973, is a coeducational, residential college with a major emphasis in environmental and agricultural sciences. Many of the Cook programs draw to a large extent on the existing strengths of the former College of Agriculture and Environmental Science, and also introduce new fields of study emphasizing the relationship of man to his environment. Students may utilize any of the 18 libraries within the university system.

Environment: The suburban campus, adjacent to Douglass College of Rutgers University, is 35 miles from New York City. Housing includes dormitories, apartments, and a co-op for 40 students. A campus bus system provides regular, free service among the New Brunswick colleges, facilitating intercollegiate academic and social activities.

Student Life: Approximately 88% of the students come from New Jersey. Sixty-five percent live on campus. Fourteen percent are minority-group members. Campus housing is both coed and single-sex. There are visiting privileges in single-sex dorms. Juniors and seniors may keep cars on campus. Day-care services are available through affiliated liberal arts colleges.

Organizations: Students may join the 27 fraternities and 10 sororities of Rutgers College. Cook College has a student-life program designed to integrate the social, cultural, and educational opportunities in the college community. Campus activities include an annual spring program, the senior party, career seminars, the weekly newspaper, concerts, films, and special-interest clubs.

Sports: Cook students participate in Rutgers University's 16 men's and 13 women's intercollegiate teams. There are 7 intramural sports for both men and women.

Handicapped: Facilities, located on some parts of the campus, include wheelchair ramps, special parking, elevators, specially equipped rest rooms, lowered drinking fountains and telephones, and transportation. Special class scheduling is also available. There is a student coordinator to assist handicapped students.

Graduates: Ten percent of the freshmen drop out by the end of the first year. Seventy-eight percent of those who enter remain to graduate. Of those who remain, 31% pursue graduate study; 2% enter medical school and 1% enter law school. Seventy percent pursue careers in business and industry.

Services: Placement services, career counseling, health care, psychological counseling, tutoring, and remedial instruction are offered to students free of charge.

Programs of Study: The B.A. and B.S. degrees are awarded. Bachelor's degrees are offered in the following programs: BUSINESS (environmental and business economics), EDUCATION (health/physical, vocational/technical), HEALTH SCIENCES (public health), MATH AND SCIENCES (biology, chemistry, computer science, earth and atmospheric sciences, environmental planning and design, environmental studies, international environmental studies, natural resources management), PREPROFESSIONAL (agricultural engineering, agricultural science, animal science, food science, home economics, plant science), SOCIAL SCIENCES (geography, human ecology). A 5-year combined degree in agricultural engineering is offered in conjunction with the College of Engineering. Numerous interdisciplinary and/or preprofessional options are offered within the above degree programs. Forty-five percent of degrees conferred are in agriculture/natural resources, 22% are in the biological sciences, and 11% are in architecture and environmental design.

Required: All students must complete a distribution requirement of 36 credits in several areas including social and natural sciences and humanities.

Special: Student-designed majors and study abroad are offered. Cooperative education programs and a 5-year engineering program leading to 2 B.S. degrees are also available.

Honors: Eight honor and professional recognition societies have chapters on campus. All departments offer honors programs; the George H. Cook Scholars Honors Program offers independent study to seniors in the top 15% of their class. Most merit award recipients participate in honors programs.

Admissions: Approximately 45% of those who applied for the 1981-82 freshman class were accepted. The SAT scores of those who enrolled were as follows: Verbal—51% below 500, 36% between 500 and 599, 12% between 600 and 700, and 1% above 700; Math—27% below 500, 45% between 500 and 599, 26% between 600 and 700, and 2% above 700. Candidates should have completed 16 academic units at an accredited high school. Those who do not have the required number or distribution of college preparatory units, or who have an equivalency diploma or a diploma from a non-accredited high school, may apply for admission by examination. Other factors influencing the admissions decision are advanced placement or honors courses, extracurricular activities, and recommendations.

Procedure: The SAT is required (except for candidates out of high school 2 or more years, or with 12 or more college credits). Candidates for admission by examination must submit scores from 3 ATs in addition to the SAT. The deadline for fall application is February 1; the college follows a rolling admissions policy. Application fees are $15 for 1 college of the university, $20 for 2 and $25 for 3, applied to with a single application. The application fee may be deferred in cases of economic hardship.

Special: Early and deferred admissions plans are available. AP credit is accepted.

Transfer: For fall 1981, the college received 1667 transfer applications, accepted 474, and enrolled 175 students. The application deadline is March 15. D grades do not transfer. Preference is given to graduates of New Jersey community colleges. Thirty of the last 42 credits must be taken in residence. A minimum of 128 credits is necessary for the bachelor's degree.

Visiting: There are regularly scheduled orientations for prospective students. The undergraduate admissions office should be contacted to arrange visits.

Financial Aid: University-wide, about 54% of the full-time students receive aid from funds totalling over $50 million. This may take the form of a scholarship, grant, loan, job, or combination thereof. Seventeen percent of the students work part-time on campus. All major federal and state programs are available. Merit awards have been established for students with outstanding academic/artistic ability. The average aid package is $2125, with a minimum of $100 to a maximum of $4600. Students must submit the FAF to CSS as soon as possible after January 1, but prior to March 1 for full consideration.

Foreign Students: Fewer than 1% of the full-time students come from foreign countries. Cook offers these students an English course and an intensive English program. Special counseling and special organizations are also available.

Admissions: Students from non-English-speaking countries must take the TOEFL; those from English-speaking countries must submit the SAT instead.

Procedure: The application deadline for fall entry is February 1 for foreign students currently in the U.S. and March 15 for students from overseas. Proof of funds adequate to cover all 4 years of study is required. Out-of-state tuition rates apply. Foreign students must carry health insurance, which is available through the college and included in the student fee.

Admissions Contact: Natalie Aharonian, University Director of Undergraduate Admissions.

RUTGERS UNIVERSITY/ DOUGLASS COLLEGE   D-3
New Brunswick, New Jersey 08903   (201) 932-3770

F/T: 3492W   Faculty: 238; n/av
P/T: 182W   Ph.D.'s: 90%
Grad: none   S/F Ratio: 16 to 1
Year: sems, ss   Tuition: $1380 ($2490)
Appl: Feb. 1   R and B: $2000
4243 applied   3077 accepted   967 enrolled
SAT (mean): 470V 490M   COMPETITIVE

Douglass College, established in 1918 as the undergraduate women's division of Rutgers University, is a liberal arts college emphasizing the development of the talents of women for equal professional opportunity. The college offers teacher education, preprofessional, and professional curricula in addition to liberal arts programs. Students may utilize any of the 18 libraries within the university system.

Environment: The suburban campus, adjacent to Cook College of Rutgers University, is 35 miles south of New York City. Housing facilities include residence halls, apartments, and small houses. A campus bus system provides regular, free service among the New Brunswick colleges, facilitating academic and social activities.

Student Life: Approximately 94% of the students are from New Jersey; 62% live on campus. Fifteen percent are minority-group members. Campus housing is single-sex, and there are visiting privileges. Seniors may keep cars on campus. Day-care services are provided to all students for a fee.

Organizations: Students may join sororities through Rutgers College. A variety of organizations, clubs, and the student government association are available. There are lectures, concerts, and films related to the academic program.

Sports: Women may participate in the university's 13 intercollegiate and numerous intramural programs.

Handicapped: Facilities for the physically handicapped include wheelchair ramps, special parking, elevators, and specially equipped rest rooms; special class scheduling and transportation are also available. There is a student coordinator to assist handicapped students.

Graduates: Ten percent of the freshmen drop out by the end of the first year. Seventy-five percent of those who enter remain to graduate. Twenty-two percent of those who graduate pursue advanced degrees: about 1% enter medical and dental schools, and 1% enter law school.

Services: Placement services, career counseling, health care, psychological counseling, tutoring, and remedial instruction are offered to students free of charge.

Programs of Study: The B.A. and B.S. degrees are offered in the following subjects: AREA STUDIES (Africana, American, Hebraic, Latin American, Middle Eastern, Oriental, Puerto Rican, Soviet and East European), BUSINESS (computer science), EDUCATION (physical), ENGLISH (comparative literature, English, human communication, journalism, speech), FINE AND PERFORMING ARTS (art, art history, dance, music, theater/dramatics), HEALTH SCIENCES (medical technology), LANGUAGES (Chinese, French, German, Greek/Latin, Hebrew, Italian, Portuguese, Russian, Spanish), MATH AND SCIENCES (biochemistry, biology, biomathematics, botany, chemistry, ecology, geology, mathematics, microbiology, physics, physiology, statistics, zoology), PHILOSOPHY (classics, philosophy, religion), PREPROFESSIONAL (home economics), SOCIAL SCIENCES (anthropology, archeology, economics, geography, history, history and political science, labor studies, political science, psychology, sociology). Certificate programs are offered in 10 areas, including science management, teacher education, and women's studies. Twenty-three percent of degrees are conferred in social sciences, 12% in interdisciplinary studies, 10% in home economics, 9% in psychology, and 9% in fine/applied arts.

Required: All students must take English composition, a foreign language, and a core curriculum covering several academic disciplines.

Special: A junior year abroad program, language houses, student-designed majors, a 3-2 B.A./M.B.A. program in business administration, and a 5-year combined B.A./B.S. program in engineering are offered. The college participates in the Federal Summer Intern Program, which offers a salaried internship with a government agency in Washington, D.C. or New York City. Field work is also available in American studies, archeology, journalism, political science, science management, sociology, and personnel training in industry.

Honors: Fourteen honor societies have chapters on campus. Honors work is offered in all departments; the Douglass Scholars Program for selected students offers freshman seminars, sophomore tutorials, and independent research in the junior and senior years. Most merit award recipients participate in honors programs.

Admissions: Approximately 73% of those who applied were accepted for the 1981-82 freshman class. The SAT scores of those who enrolled were as follows: Verbal—66% below 500, 26% between 500 and 599, 6% between 600 and 700, and 2% above 700; Math—58% below 500, 35% between 500 and 599, 7% between 600 and 700, and 0% above 700. Candidates should have completed 16 academic units at an accredited high school. The main factors influencing the admissions decision are grades, class rank, the type of high school program followed, and SAT scores. Candidates who do not have the required number or distribution of college preparatory units, or who have an equivalency diploma or a diploma from a non-accredited high school, may apply for admission by examination.

Procedure: The SAT is required (except for candidates out of high school 2 or more years, or with 12 or more college credits). Candidates for admission by examination must also submit scores from 3 ATs. The deadline for fall applications is February 1; the college follows a rolling admissions policy and subscribes to the CRDA of May 1. The application fee is $15 for 1 college of Rutgers University, $20 for 2, and $25 for 3, applied to with a single application. The application fee may be deferred in cases of economic hardship.

Special: AP and CLEP credit is accepted. There are early admissions and deferred admissions plans.

Transfer: For fall 1981, the college received 1071 transfer applications, accepted 569, and enrolled 253 students. Transfers are accepted for the sophomore, junior, and senior years; D grades do not transfer. Official high school and college transcripts are required. Preference is given to graduates of New Jersey community colleges. Thirty of the last 42 credits must be earned in residence. A minimum of 120 credits is required for the bachelor's degree. The deadline for application is March 15 (fall). Deadlines for and availability of spring admission vary.

Visiting: There are regularly scheduled orientations for prospective students. The admissions office should be contacted to arrange visits.

Financial Aid: University-wide, about 54% of the full-time students receive aid from funds totalling over $50 million. This may take the form of a scholarship, grant, loan, job, or combination thereof. Seventeen percent of the students work part-time on campus. All major federal and state programs are available. Merit awards have been established for students with outstanding academic/artistic ability. The average aid package is $2125, with a minimum of $100 to a maximum of $4600. Students must submit the FAF to CSS as soon as possible after January 1, but prior to March 1 for full consideration.

Foreign Students: Twenty foreign students are currently enrolled at the college, which offers them an intensive English course and an intensive English program. Special counseling and special organizations are also available.

Admissions: Students from non-English-speaking countries must take the TOEFL. Those from English-speaking countries must submit the SAT instead.

Procedure: The application deadline for fall entry is February 1 for students currently residing in the United States and March 15 for students from overseas. Proof of funds adequate to cover 4 years of study is required. Out-of-state tuition rates apply. Foreign students must carry health insurance, which is available through the college and included in the student fee.

Admissions Contact: Natalie Aharonian, University Director of Admissions.

RUTGERS UNIVERSITY/ LIVINGSTON COLLEGE   D-3
New Brunswick, New Jersey 08903   (201) 932-3770

F/T: 1962M, 1275W	Faculty: 211; n/av
P/T: 137M, 120W	Ph.D.'s: 90%
Grad: none	S/F Ratio: 15 to 1
Year: sems, ss	Tuition: $1391 ($2501)
Appl: Feb. 1	R and B: $2000
4824 applied 3136 accepted	829 enrolled
SAT (mean): 440V 480M	COMPETITIVE

Livingston College, founded in 1969, is a coeducational, residential undergraduate college offering liberal arts, preprofessional, and professional programs. Students may utilize any of the 18 libraries within the university system.

Environment: The 200-acre campus is located 35 miles from New York City. There are 3 residential quadrangles, 2 high-rise residences, and apartment facilities. A campus bus system provides regular, free service among the New Brunswick colleges, facilitating academic and social activities.

Student Life: About 88% of the students are from New Jersey; 52% live on campus. Thirty percent are minority-group members. Campus housing is both coed and single-sex. There are visiting privileges in single-sex dorms. Students may keep cars on campus. Day-care services are available to all students for a fee.

Organizations: Students may join fraternities and sororities through Rutgers College. There are 33 clubs based at Livingston College plus an additional 13 university clubs and organizations recognized by Livingston.

Sports: The college competes intercollegiately in 16 sports for men and 13 for women. There are 14 intramural sports for men and 13 for women.

Handicapped: The entire Livingston campus is accessible to the physically handicapped. Facilities include wheelchair ramps, special parking, elevators, specially equipped rest rooms, and lowered drinking fountains and telephones. Special class scheduling and transportation are also provided. Modified living arrangements in the residence halls are available upon request.

Graduates: Twenty percent of the freshmen drop out at the end of the first year. Forty-eight percent of those who enter remain to graduate. Twenty-seven percent of students pursue graduate study after graduation: 1% enter medical school and 2% enter law school; 60% pursue careers in business and industry.

Services: Placement services, health care, psychological counseling, career counseling, tutoring, and remedial instruction are offered to students free of charge.

Programs of Study: The college confers the B.A. and B.S. degrees. Bachelor's degrees are offered in the following subjects: AREA STUDIES (Africana, American, Hebraic, Latin American, Middle Eastern, Oriental, Puerto Rican, Soviet and East European, urban), BUSINESS (accounting, computer science, management, marketing), EDUCATION (urban teacher education), ENGLISH (comparative literature,

English journalism/urban communications), FINE AND PERFORMING ARTS (art, art history, music, theater/dramatics), HEALTH SCIENCES (medical technology, physician's assistant, public health), LANGUAGES (Chinese, French, German, Greek/Latin, Hebrew, Italian, Portuguese, Russian, Spanish), MATH AND SCIENCES (biochemistry, biology, biomathematics, botany, chemistry, ecology, geology, mathematics, microbiology, physics, physiology, statistics, zoology), PHILOSOPHY (classics, philosophy, religion), PREPROFESSIONAL (social work), SOCIAL SCIENCES (anthropology, archeology, community development, economics, geography, history, history and political science, labor studies, political science, psychology, sociology). Thirty-four percent of degrees are conferred in the social sciences, 11% in psychology, 9% in communications, 8% in the biological sciences, and 7% in computer and information sciences.

Required: All students must complete a writing course. Through testing, all students are placed in an appropriate sequence of courses.

Special: A junior year abroad program, internships with structured learning contracts, a 5-year curriculum leading to a combined B.A.-B.S. degree in engineering, student-designed majors and certificate programs in 6 areas, are available.

Honors: Many departments offer honors programs; the Paul Robeson Scholar program of independent study is open to qualified students. Most merit award recipients participate in honors programs.

Admissions: Approximately 65% of those who applied were accepted for the 1981–82 freshman class. The SAT scores of those who enrolled were as follows: Verbal—77% below 500, 18% between 500 and 599, 4% between 600 and 700, and 1% above 700; Math—60% below 500, 31% between 500 and 599, 9% between 600 and 700, and 5% above 700. Candidates should have completed 16 academic units at an accredited high school. Those who do not have the required number or distribution of college preparatory units, or who have an equivalency diploma or a diploma from a non-accredited high school, may apply for admission by examination. Other factors entering into the admissions decision are advanced placement or honors courses, recommendations, and evidence of special talents.

Procedure: The SAT is required (except for candidates out of high school 2 or more years or with 12 or more college credits). Candidates for admission by examination must submit scores from 3 ATs in addition to the SAT. The deadline for filing applications is February 1; applications are reviewed on a rolling basis. The college subscribes to the CRDA of May 1. The application fee is $15 for 1 college of Rutgers University, $20 for 2, and $25 for 3, applied to with a single application. The application fee may be deferred in cases of economic hardship.

Special: CLEP and AP credit is accepted. There are early admissions and deferred admissions plans.

Transfer: For fall 1981, the college received 1885 applications, accepted 1023, and enrolled 402. Transfers are accepted for the sophomore, junior, and senior years. D grades do not transfer. Preference is given to graduates of New Jersey community colleges. The deadline for transfer applications is May 15 (fall). Deadlines for and availability of spring admission vary. Thirty of the last 42 credits must be taken at Rutgers University; 20 of the 30 credits must be taken at Livingston College. A minimum of 120 credits is required for the bachelor's degree.

Visiting: There are regularly scheduled orientations for prospective students.

Financial Aid: University-wide, about 54% of the full-time students receive aid from funds totalling over $50 million. This may take the form of a scholarship, grant, loan, job, or combination thereof. Seventeen percent of the students work part-time on campus. All major federal and state programs are available. Merit awards have been established for students with outstanding academic/artistic ability. The average aid package is $2125, with a minimum of $100 to a maximum of $4600. Students must submit the FAF to CSS as soon as possible after January 1, but prior to March 1 for full consideration.

Foreign Students: A little over 1% of the full-time students come from foreign countries. Livingston offers these students an English course and an intensive English program. Special counseling and special organizations are also available.

Admissions: Students from non-English-speaking countries must take the TOEFL; those from English-speaking countries must submit the SAT instead.

Procedure: The application deadline for fall entry is February 1. Proof of funds adequate to cover 4 years of study is required. Out-of-state tuition rates apply. Foreign students must carry health insurance, which is available through the college and included in the student fee.

Admissions Contact: Natalie Aharonian, University Director of Undergraduate Admissions.

RUTGERS UNIVERSITY/MASON GROSS SCHOOL OF THE ARTS   D–3

New Brunswick, New Jersey 08903   (201) 932-3770

F/T: 104M, 166W	Faculty: 79; n/av
P/T: 2M	Ph.D.'s: 100%
Grad: 58M, 73W	S/F Ratio: 12 to 1
Year: sems, ss	Tuition: $1387 ($2497)
Appl: Feb. 1	R and B: $2000
444 applied	131 accepted	85 enrolled
SAT (mean): 470V 480M		SPECIAL

The Mason Gross School of the Arts, founded in 1976, is a new unit of Rutgers University, offering B.F.A. and graduate programs to students of outstanding ability and talent who wish to pursue careers in the arts. Students may utilize any of the 18 libraries within the university system.

Environment: The school is located 35 miles south of New York City in a suburban area of central New Jersey. Facilities include several galleries and studios, a proscenium arch and cabaret theater, and a large, well-equipped, flexible space theater. A campus bus system provides regular, free service among the New Brunswick colleges, facilitating academic and social activities.

Student Life: Ninety-three percent of the students are from New Jersey. Nine percent are minority-group members. Mason Gross students affiliate with one of the New Brunswick liberal arts colleges of Rutgers University for housing and other student services.

Organizations: The fraternities, sororities, and other extracurricular groups and activities of Rutgers and Livingston Colleges are open to Mason Gross students. Students participate in approximately 45 theater productions each year.

Sports: Mason Gross students may participate in the sports programs offered by the New Brunswick liberal arts colleges.

Handicapped: See the entries for the New Brunswick liberal arts colleges.

Services: Free placement services, career counseling, health care, psychological counseling, tutoring, and remedial instruction are available through the New Brunswick liberal arts colleges.

Programs of Study: The school confers the B.F.A. degree. Master's degrees are also awarded. Bachelor's degrees are offered in dance, theater arts (acting, design, production), and visual arts (commercial design, drawing and painting, film and photography, sculpture, video).

Required: All students must take 36 credits in liberal arts distributed over disciplinary areas.

Special: A B.Mus. degree program is under development.

Admissions: Approximately 30% of those who applied were accepted for the 1981–82 freshman class. The SAT scores of those who enrolled were as follows: Verbal—67% below 500, 27% between 500 and 599, 4% between 600 and 700, and 2% above 700; Math—63% below 500, 30% between 500 and 599, 6% between 600 and 700, and 1% above 700. Candidates should have 16 academic units from an accredited high school. Other factors influencing the admissions decision are recommendations and evidence of special talents.

Procedure: An audition interview and/or portfolio are required for admission. The SAT is required; candidates for admission by examination must also submit scores from 3 ATs. The deadline for filing is February 1; applications are reviewed on a rolling basis. The school subscribes to the CRDA of May 1. The application fee is $15 for 1 college of Rutgers University, $20 for 2, and $25 for 3, applied to with a single application. The application fee may be deferred in cases of economic hardship.

Special: AP and CLEP credit is accepted. There are deferred admissions and early admissions plans.

Transfer: For fall 1981, the school received 100 transfer applications, accepted 40, and 27 students enrolled. Official high school and college transcripts are required; D grades do not transfer. Preference is given to community college graduates. Transfer students are accepted for the sophomore year only; there is a 3-year residency requirement. From 120 to 122 credits are required for the bachelor's degree. The deadline for fall applications is February 1. Spring admission is not normally available.

Visiting: There are regularly scheduled orientations for prospective students. The admissions office should be contacted to arrange visits.

Financial Aid: University-wide, about 54% of the full-time students receive aid from funds totalling over $50 million. This may take the form of a scholarship, grant, loan, job, or combination thereof. Seventeen percent of the students work part-time on campus. All major federal and state programs are available. Merit awards have been established for students with outstanding academic/artistic ability. The average aid package is $2125, with a minimum of $100 to a maximum of $4600. Students must submit the FAF to CSS as soon as possible after January 1, but prior to March 1 for full consideration.

Foreign Students: Fewer than 1% of the full-time students come from foreign countries. The school offers these students an English course and an intensive English program. Special counseling and special organizations are also available.

Admissions: Students from non-English-speaking countries must take the TOEFL. Those from English-speaking countries must submit the SAT instead.

Procedure: The application deadline for fall entry is February 1 for students currently residing in the U.S. and March 15 for students from overseas. Proof of funds adequate to cover 4 years of study is required. Out-of-state tuition rates apply. Foreign students must carry health insurance, which is available through the school and included in the student fee.

Admissions Contact: Natalie Aharonian, University Director of Undergraduate Admissions.

RUTGERS UNIVERSITY/NEWARK COLLEGE OF ARTS AND SCIENCES E-2
Newark, New Jersey 07102   (201) 648-5205

F/T: 1888M, 1423W	Faculty: 234; n/av
P/T: 274M, 210W	Ph.D.'s: 90%
Grad: none	S/F Ratio: 16 to 1
Year: sems, ss	Tuition: $1298 ($2408)
Appl: Mar. 15	R and B: n/app
3211 applied	1609 accepted	655 enrolled
SAT (mean): 450V 490M	VERY COMPETITIVE

The Newark College of Arts and Sciences, established in 1946, serves commuting students in the northern New Jersey area. Students may utilize any of the 18 libraries within the university system.

Environment: The modern 23-acre urban campus is located in the heart of the largest business community in New Jersey, 10 miles from New York City, and includes a dozen buildings. There is no on-campus housing.

Student Life: Ninety-eight percent of the students are from New Jersey; most commute. Twenty-nine percent are minority-group members.

Organizations: There are 4 fraternities and 2 sororities; 60 campus organizations related to academic interests, the arts, religion, and various professions are also available. The campus program board coordinates an extensive activity program. Other activities include musical performances, theater, a student newspaper, yearbook, literary magazine, and a radio station. The Paul Robeson Campus center, including an art gallery, a lounge, a dining hall, patio, meeting and game rooms, a pub, and a multi-purpose room, is the focal point of campus activities.

Sports: Eight intercollegiate and 10 intramural sports for men and women are offered.

Handicapped: Almost the entire campus is accessible to the physically handicapped. Facilities include wheelchair ramps, special parking, elevators, specially equipped rest rooms, and lowered drinking fountains and telephones; special class scheduling is also available. There is a student coordinator to assist handicapped students.

Graduates: Eighteen percent of the freshmen drop out by the end of the first year; 52% remain to graduate. About 37% of the seniors applied to graduate or professional schools. The admissions rate was: 37% medical school, 57% dental school, 41% business school, 51% law school, and 48% other professional.

Services: Placement services, career counseling, health care, psychological counseling, tutoring, and remedial instruction are offered to students free of charge.

Programs of Study: The B.A. and B.S. degrees are offered in the following subjects: AREA STUDIES (Afro-American and African, American, Hebraic, Puerto Rican, Slavic, urban), BUSINESS (accounting, business administration), ENGLISH (English, journalism), FINE AND PERFORMING ARTS (art, music, theater/dramatics), HEALTH SCIENCES (medical technology), LANGUAGES (French, German, Italian, Russian, Spanish), MATH AND SCIENCES (biological sciences education, botany, chemistry, earth sciences education, geology, mathematics, physics, zoology and physiology), PHILOSOPHY (classics, philosophy), PREPROFESSIONAL (engineering), SOCIAL SCIENCES (anthropology, criminal justice, economics, history, political science, psychology, sociology). Thirty-eight percent of degrees conferred are in business/management, 21% are in social sciences, and 13% are in biological sciences. State certification for secondary school is available with 15 majors.

Required: All students must take a core curriculum of 6 credits in English composition, 12 in humanities, 14 in natural sciences, and 12 in social sciences.

Special: A 5-year B.A./B.S. program in engineering, a B.A./M.B.A. program in business administration, a B.A./M.A. program in criminal justice, a B.A./M.P.A. program in public administration, a junior year abroad program, and student-designed majors are offered.

Honors: Eight national honor societies have chapters on campus. All departments have honors programs; independent study programs are open to outstanding juniors and seniors. Most merit award recipients participate in honors programs.

Admissions: Approximately 50% of those who applied were accepted for the 1981-82 freshman class. The mean SAT scores of those who enrolled were 450V, 490M. Candidates should have completed 16 academic units at an accredited high school. Other factors entering into the admissions decision are advanced placement or honors courses, recommendations, and evidence of special talents. Candidates who do not have the required number or distribution of college preparatory units, or who have an equivalency diploma or a diploma from a non-accredited high school, may apply for admission by examination.

Procedure: The SAT is required (except for candidates out of high school 2 or more years or with 12 or more college credits). Candidates for admission by examination must also take 3 ATs. The fall deadline is March 15; applications are reviewed on a rolling basis. The college subscribes to the CRDA of May 1. The application fee is $15 for 1 college of Rutgers University, $20 for 2, and $25 for 3, applied to with a single application; the application fee may be deferred in cases of economic hardship.

Special: AP and CLEP credit is accepted (AP grades of 4 and 5; CLEP, 50% or better). There is an early admissions plan.

Transfer: For fall 1981, recently 1205 transfer applications were received, 611 were accepted, and 373 students enrolled. Transfers are accepted for the sophomore, junior, and senior years. Official high school and college transcripts are required; D grades transfer only if the student has an A.A. from an accredited New Jersey community college. Preference is given to New Jersey community college graduates. Thirty percent to 50% of the major credits must be taken at the Newark College of Arts and Sciences; 124 credits are required for the bachelor's degree. Deadlines for application are May 15 (fall) and November 15 (spring, if space is available).

Visiting: There are regularly scheduled orientations for prospective students. The admissions office should be contacted to arrange visits.

Financial Aid: University-wide, about 54% of the full-time students receive aid from funds totalling over $50 million. This may take the form of a scholarship, grant, loan, job, or combination thereof. Seventeen percent of the students work part-time on campus. All major federal and state programs are available. Merit awards have been established for students with outstanding academic/artistic ability. The average aid package is $2125, with a minimum of $100 to a maximum of $4600. Students must submit the FAF to CSS as soon as possible after January 1, but prior to March 1 for full consideration.

Foreign Students: About 1% of the full-time students come from foreign countries. The college offers these students an intensive English course, special counseling, and special organizations.

Admissions: Students from non-English-speaking countries must achieve a minimum score of 550 on the TOEFL. Those from English-speaking countries must submit the SAT instead.

Procedure: Application deadlines are the same as those for other freshmen. Proof of funds adequate to cover 1 year of study is required. Out-of-state tuition rates apply. Foreign students must carry health insurance, which is available through the college and included in the student fee.

Admissions Contact: Cecile Stolbof, Dean of Admissions.

RUTGERS UNIVERSITY/ RUTGERS COLLEGE D-3
New Brunswick, New Jersey 08903   (201) 932-3770

F/T: 4442M, 3665W	Faculty: 492; n/av
P/T: 160M, 93W	Ph.D.'s: 90%
Grad: none	S/F Ratio: 17 to 1
Year: sems, ss	Tuition: $1387 ($2497)
Appl: Feb. 1	R and B: $2000
11,404 applied	6024 accepted	1934 enrolled
SAT (mean): 490V 540M	VERY COMPETITIVE

Rutgers College, the eighth oldest liberal arts college in the United States, was founded in 1766 as Queen's College. Originally a men's college, it became coeducational in 1972 and is the largest undergraduate residential college in New Jersey. Students may utilize any of the 18 libraries within the university system.

Environment: The 832-acre suburban campus, 35 miles south of New York City, contains 177 buildings. The college offers a variety of options in living styles, such as apartments, traditional residence halls with or without coed floors, and fraternity and sorority houses. A campus bus system provides regular, free service among the New Brunswick colleges, facilitating academic and social activities.

Student Life: Approximately 92% of the students come from New Jersey; 54% live on campus. Fifteen percent are minority-group members. Campus housing is both coed and single-sex. There are visiting privileges in single-sex dorms. Day-care services are available through affiliated liberal arts colleges. Students may keep cars on campus.

Organizations: There are 27 fraternities and 10 sororities, to which 20% of the students belong. Religious counselors and organizations for all the major faiths are sponsored by the university. Over 200 extracurricular activities are available; the most popular are Rutgers Community Action, the student government association, the daily student newspaper, and the radio station. The Octoberfest and the Cancer Marathon are 2 of the most popular on-campus events.

Sports: The college competes intercollegiately in 16 sports for men and 13 for women. There are 20 intramural sports for men and 13 for women.

Handicapped: Facilities for the physically handicapped include wheelchair ramps, special parking, elevators, specially equipped rest rooms, lowered drinking fountains, and transportation. Special class scheduling is also available. There is a coordinator for handicapped students.

Graduates: Eight percent of the freshmen drop out by the end of the first year; 77% remain to graduate. Of those who remain, 32% pursue graduate study; 3% enter medical school and 3% enter law school. Sixty percent pursue careers in business and industry.

Services: Health care, psychological counseling, tutoring, remedial instruction, career counseling, and placement services are offered to students free of charge.

Programs of Study: The B.A. and B.S. degrees are offered in the following subjects: AREA STUDIES (Africana, American, Hebraic, Latin American, Middle Eastern, Puerto Rican, Oriental, Soviet and East European), BUSINESS (business administration, computer science), ENGLISH (comparative literature, English, human communication), FINE AND PERFORMING ARTS (art, art history, music, theater/dramatics), HEALTH SCIENCES (human kinetics), LANGUAGES (Chinese, French, German, Greek/Latin, Hebrew, Italian, Middle Eastern, Oriental, Portuguese, Russian, Spanish), MATH AND SCIENCES (biochemistry, biology, biomathematics, botany, chemistry, ecology, geology, mathematics, microbiology, physics, physiology, statistics, zoology), PHILOSOPHY (classics, philosophy, religion), SOCIAL SCIENCES (anthropology, archeology, economics, geography, history and political science, labor studies, political science, psychology, sociology). Twenty-seven percent of degrees are conferred in the social sciences, 11% in the biological sciences, 8% in psychology, 13% in letters, and 14% in business and management.

Required: All students must take freshman English and select a major, a minor, and a "mini" from 3 different areas of the curriculum.

Special: Junior year abroad, national student exchange, student-designed majors, and a 5-year program leading to a B.A.-B.S. degree in engineering are offered. Certificate programs are available in 11 areas.

Honors: Phi Beta Kappa and several other honor societies have chapters on campus. Honors programs are available in all departments. The Henry Rutgers and Paul Robeson programs of independent study are available to qualified seniors. Most merit award recipients participate in honors programs.

Admissions: Approximately 53% of those who applied were accepted for the 1981–82 freshman class. The SAT scores of those who enrolled were as follows: Verbal—56% below 500, 35% between 500 and 599, 8% between 600 and 700, and 1% above 700; Math—32% below 500, 45% between 500 and 599, 20% between 600 and 700, and 3% above 700. Sixteen academic units from an accredited high school are required for admission. Candidates who do not have the required number or distribution of college preparatory units, or who have an equivalency diploma or a diploma from a non-accredited high school, may apply for admission by examination.

Procedure: The SAT is required (except for candidates out of high school 2 or more years, or with 12 or more college credits). Candidates for admission by examination must submit scores on 3 ATs in addition to the SAT. The deadline for fall applications is February 1; the college follows a rolling admissions policy. Application fees are $15 for 1 college of the university, $20 for 2, and $25 for 3, applied to with a single application. The application fee may be deferred in cases of economic hardship.

Special: CLEP and AP credit is accepted. There are early admissions and deferred admissions plans.

Transfer: For fall 1981, 2788 transfer applications were received, 933 were accepted, and 422 students enrolled. The application deadline is March 15 (fall). Deadlines for and availability of spring admission vary. D grades do not transfer. Preference is given to graduates of New Jersey community colleges. Thirty of the last 42 credits must be taken at the university. A minimum of 120 credits is required for the bachelor's degree.

Visiting: There are regularly scheduled orientations for prospective students. The undergraduate admissions office should be contacted to arrange visits.

Financial Aid: University-wide, about 54% of the full-time students receive aid from funds totalling over $50 million. This may take the form of a scholarship, grant, loan, job, or combination thereof. Seventeen percent of the students work part-time on campus. All major federal and state programs are available. Merit awards have been established for students with outstanding academic/artistic ability. The average aid package is $2125, with a minimum of $100 to a maximum of $4600. Students must submit the FAF to CSS as soon as possible after January 1, but prior to March 1 for full consideration.

Foreign Students: Fifty-seven foreign students are currently enrolled at Rutgers College, which offers these students an intensive English course and an intensive English program. Special counseling and special organizations are also available.

Admissions: Students from non-English-speaking countries must take the TOEFL. Those from English-speaking countries must submit the SAT instead.

Procedure: The application deadline for fall entry is February 1 for students currently residing in the United States and March 15 for students from overseas. Proof of funds adequate to cover 4 years of study is required. Out-of-state tuition rates apply. Foreign students must carry health insurance, which is available through the college and included in the student fee.

Admissions Contact: Natalie Aharonian, University Director of Undergraduate Admissions.

RUTGERS UNIVERSITY/UNIVERSITY COLLEGE—CAMDEN C-4
Camden, New Jersey 08100 (609) 757-6057

F/T: 61M, 63W	Faculty: 16; n/av
P/T: 510M, 442W	Ph.D.'s: n/av
Grad: none	S/F Ratio: 17 to 1
Year: sems, ss	Tuition: $38 ($76) p/c
Appl: July 30	R and B: n/app
610 applied 520 accepted	334 enrolled
SAT, ACT: not required	LESS COMPETITIVE

University College, founded in 1934, is an undergraduate evening college geared toward part-time adult students and is one of the few colleges for adults in the United States with its own full-time faculty. The college offers undergraduate programs in the liberal arts and sciences, social work, home economics, and business. Students may utilize any of the 18 libraries within the university system.

Environment: The 16-acre urban campus, 3 miles from Philadelphia, has 18 buildings. The college is part of an active industrial and cultural community where a wealth of educational and vocational opportunities exist.

Student Life: Ninety-eight percent of the students are from New Jersey. Twenty-four percent are minority-group members. About two-thirds are between 24 and 34 years of age; all students commute.

Organizations: Student government organizations represent student interests in matters affecting educational development and environment, and oversee college-wide events and publications. In addition to academic interest clubs, there is a wide variety of cultural and social activities.

Handicapped: Almost 100% of the campus is accessible to the physically handicapped. Facilities include wheelchair ramps, special parking, elevators, specially equipped rest rooms, and lowered drinking fountains and telephones; special class scheduling is also available. There is 1 student coordinator to assist handicapped students.

Graduates: Fifteen percent of those who graduate pursue graduate study; about 4% enter law school. Eighty percent of the graduates pursue careers in business and industry.

Services: Placement services, tutoring, remedial instruction, and career counseling are offered to students free of charge. Psychological counseling is available for a fee.

Programs of Study: The B.A. and B.S. degrees are conferred in the following subjects: AREA STUDIES (urban), BUSINESS (accounting, management), ENGLISH (English), MATH AND SCIENCES (chemistry, mathematics), PHILOSOPHY (philosophy), PREPROFESSIONAL (social work), SOCIAL SCIENCES (history, political science, psychology). Sixty-four percent of degrees are conferred in business, 17% in social sciences, and 8% in psychology.

Honors: Two national honor societies are open to qualified students; honors programs are also available.

Admissions: Approximately 85% of those who applied were accepted for the 1981–82 freshman class. The requirements for admission are flexible; more emphasis is placed on experience, motivation, and other personal qualities than on the usual indices of academic achievement. Candidates should have 16 academic units from an accredited high school.

Procedure: Students who do not have the required number and/or distribution of academic units, a high school diploma, or who have a diploma from a non-accredited high school may apply under an alternative arrangement. The deadline for applications is July 30; applications are reviewed on a rolling basis. The application fee is $10; students may also apply to other divisions of Rutgers University on a single application for an additional $5 per college choice. Neither the SAT nor ACT is required.

Special: CLEP and AP credit is accepted. The Educational Opportunity Fund permits financially and educationally disadvantaged students to enter.

Transfer: For fall 1981, the college received 450 transfer applications, accepted 400, and 315 students enrolled. Transfers are accepted for the sophomore, junior, and senior years; official transcripts of all secondary and college work are required. D grades transfer for graduates of county or community colleges. Thirty credits, of the 120 required for the bachelor's degree, must be taken in residence. The deadline for fall applications is July 30.

Visiting: The admissions office should be contacted to arrange visits.

Financial Aid: As most University College students are employed and self-supporting, only limited funds are available for financial aid. Some students may be reimbursed by their employers for tuition expenses. Students who wish to apply for financial aid should submit the FAF to the CSS as soon as possible after January 1, but prior to March 1 for full consideration.

Foreign Students: No foreign students are currently enrolled at the college. The college offers foreign students an intensive English course and special counseling.

Admissions Contact: Joanne Robinson, Admissions Officer.

RUTGERS UNIVERSITY/UNIVERSITY COLLEGE—NEWARK
E-Z

Newark, New Jersey 07100   (201) 648-5205

F/T: 160M, 218W   *Faculty:* 36; n/av
P/T: 694M, 925W   *Ph.D.'s:* 85%
Grad: none   *S/F Ratio:* 17 to 1
Year: sems, ss   *Tuition:* $38 ($76) p/c
Appl: Aug. 1   *R and B:* n/app
2122 enrolled
SAT or ACT: not required   **LESS COMPETITIVE**

University College, founded in 1934, is an undergraduate evening college geared toward part-time adult students and is one of the few colleges for adults in the United States with its own full-time faculty. The college offers undergraduate programs in the liberal arts and sciences, social work, and business.

Environment: The 23-acre, well-equipped, modern campus is located in the heart of the largest business community in New Jersey, 10 miles from New York City.

Student Life: Ninety-nine percent of the students are from New Jersey. Sixty-five percent are minority-group members. About two-thirds of the students are between 24 and 34 years of age. All students commute.

Organizations: Student government organizations represent student interests in matters affecting educational development and environment, and oversee college-wide events and publications. In addition to academic interest clubs, a wide variety of cultural and social activities is available.

Handicapped: Almost the entire campus is accessible to the physically handicapped. Facilities include wheelchair ramps, special parking, elevators, specially equipped rest rooms, and lowered drinking fountains and telephones; special class scheduling is also available. There is a student coordinator to assist handicapped students.

Graduates: Fifteen percent of those who graduate pursue graduate study; about 4% enter law school. Eighty percent of the graduates pursue careers in business and industry.

Services: Placement services, health care, tutoring, remedial instruction, career counseling, and psychological counseling are offered to students free of charge.

Programs of Study: The B.A. and B.S. degrees are conferred in the following subjects: AREA STUDIES (urban), BUSINESS (accounting, management, marketing), ENGLISH (English), LANGUAGES (Spanish), MATH AND SCIENCES (mathematics and computer science), PHILOSOPHY (philosophy), PREPROFESSIONAL (social welfare/social work), SOCIAL SCIENCES (criminal justice, economics, history, labor studies, political science, psychology, sociology). Sixty-one percent of degrees conferred are in business/management, 11% are in public affairs, 11% are in social sciences, and 9% are in psychology. Vocational education is also offered.

Special: A 3-2 combination B.A./M.B.A. program in business administration is offered; interdisciplinary, double, and student-designed majors are possible.

Honors: Two national honor societies are open to qualified students; honors programs are also available.

Admissions: Approximately 82% of those who applied were accepted for the 1981–82 freshman class. The requirements for admission are flexible; more emphasis is placed on experience, motivation, and other personal qualities than on the usual indices of academic achievement. Candidates should have 16 academic units from an accredited high school.

Procedure: Students who do not have the required number and/or distribution of academic units, or a high school diploma, or who have a diploma from a non-accredited high school may apply under an alternative arrangement. The deadline for applications is August 1; applications are reviewed on a rolling basis. The application fee is $10; students may also apply to other divisions of Rutgers University. Neither the SAT nor the ACT is required.

Special: CLEP and AP credit is accepted. The Educational Opportunity Fund permits financially and educationally disadvantaged students to enter.

Transfer: Transfers are accepted for the sophomore, junior, and senior years; official transcripts of all secondary and college work are required. D grades transfer for graduates of county or community colleges. Thirty credits must be completed at the college. The deadline for fall applications is August 1.

Visiting: The admissions office should be contacted to arrange visits.

Financial Aid: As most University College students are employed and self-supporting, only limited funds are available for financial aid. Some students may be reimbursed by their employers for tuition expenses. Students who wish to apply for financial aid should submit the FAF to CSS as soon as possible after January 1, but prior to March 1 for full consideration.

Foreign Students: No foreign students are currently enrolled at the college, although an intensive English course, special counseling, and special organizations are available to such students.

Admissions: Foreign students must achieve a minimum score of 550 on the TOEFL. Students from English-speaking countries should submit the SAT instead.

Procedure: Application deadlines are March 15 (fall) and December 1 (spring). Proof of funds adequate to cover 1 year of study is required. Out-of-state tuition rates apply. Foreign students must carry health insurance, which is available through the college.

Admissions Contact: Cecile Stolbof, Dean of Admissions.

RUTGERS UNIVERSITY/UNIVERSITY COLLEGE—NEW BRUNSWICK
D-3

New Brunswick, New Jersey 08903   (201) 932-7276

F/T: 219M, 186W	Faculty: 119; n/av
P/T: 1405M, 1618W	Ph.D.'s: n/av
Grad: none	S/F Ratio: 17 to 1
Year: sems, ss	Tuition: $38 ($76) p/c
Appl: July 30	R and B: n/app
2400 applied 1785 accepted	1079 enrolled
SAT: required	COMPETITIVE

Founded in 1934, University College—New Brunswick is one of the few undergraduate evening colleges in the nation that is served by its own adminstrative staff and faculty fellows whose predominant responsibility is to provide programs of study especially geared to adults and part-time students.

Environment: The college shares the facilities and faculties of the other undergraduate colleges on the urban New Brunswick campus.

Student Life: Ninety-eight percent of the students are from New Jersey. Thirteen percent are minority-group members. About two-thirds of the students are between 24 and 34 years of age. All students commute.

Organizations: Student government organizations represent student interests in matters affecting educational development and environment, and oversee college-wide events and publications. In addition to academic interest clubs, a wide variety of cultural and social activities is available through other divisions of Rutgers University.

Sports: Full-time students are permitted to play for Rutgers University teams.

Handicapped: Facilities for the physically handicapped include wheelchair ramps, special parking, elevators, specially equipped rest rooms, lowered drinking fountains, and transportation. Special class scheduling is also available. There is a coordinator for handicapped students.

Services: Placement services, psychological counseling, and career counseling are available to all students free of charge. Some free tutoring is also provided. Health care and remedial instruction are offered for a fee.

Programs of Study: The B.A. and B.S. degrees are conferred in the following subjects: AREA STUDIES (Africana, American, Hebraic, Latin American, Middle Eastern, Oriental, Puerto Rican, Soviet and East European), BUSINESS (accounting, computer science, management, marketing), ENGLISH (comparative literature, English), FINE AND PERFORMING ARTS (art history), LANGUAGES (Chinese, French, German, Greek/Latin, Italian, Middle Eastern, Oriental, Portuguese, Russian, Spanish), MATH AND SCIENCES (biochemistry, biology, biomathematics, botany, chemistry, ecology, geology, mathematics, microbiology, physics, physiology, statistics, zoology), PHILOSOPHY (classics, philosophy, religion), PREPROFESSIONAL (food science, home economics), SOCIAL SCIENCES (anthropology, archeology, criminal justice, economics, history, history and political science, labor studies, political science, psychology, sociology). Many of these majors require daytime attendance; some are offered only in the evening. Fifty-four percent of degrees conferred are in business and management, 11% are in social sciences, 8% are in psychology, and 6% are in letters and public affairs.

Special: A 3-2 combination B.A./M.B.A. program in business administration is offered; interdisciplinary, double, and student-designed majors are possible.

Honors: A national honor society is open to qualified students.

Admissions: Approximately 74% of those who applied were accepted for the 1981-82 freshman class. The requirements for admission are flexible; emphasis is placed on experience, motivation, and other personal qualities as well as the usual indices of academic achievement. Candidates should have 16 academic units from an accredited high school.

Procedure: Students who do not have the required number and/or distribution of academic units, or a high school diploma, or who have a diploma from a non-accredited high school may apply under an alternative arrangement. The deadline for applications is July 30; applications are reviewed on a rolling basis. The application fee is $10. Students may also apply to other divisions of Rutgers University. The SAT is required (except for candidates out of high school 2 or more years, or with 12 or more college credits).

Special: CLEP and AP credit is accepted. There is a deferred admissions plan. The Educational Opportunity Fund permits financially and educationally disadvantaged students to enter.

Transfer: For fall 1981, the college received 1936 transfer applications, accepted 1486, and 911 students enrolled. Transfers are accepted for the sophomore, junior, and senior years; official transcripts of all secondary and college work are required. Transfers must complete, at the college, 30 of the 120 credits required for the bachelor's degree. The deadline for fall applications is July 30.

Visiting: The admissions office should be contacted to arrange visits.

Financial Aid: As most University College students are employed and self-supporting, only limited funds are available for financial aid. Some students may be reimbursed by their employers for tuition expenses. Students who wish to apply for financial aid should submit the FAF to CSS as soon as possible after January 1, but prior to March 1 for full consideration.

Foreign Students: About 2% of the full-time students come from foreign countries. The college offers these students an intensive English course, an intensive English program, and special counseling and organizations.

Admissions: Students from non-English-speaking countries must achieve a minimum score of 500 on the TOEFL, or must submit the Comprehensive English Language Test. Those from English-speaking countries should take the SAT instead.

Procedure: Application deadlines are April 15 (fall) and November 1 (spring). Any required supporting documents must accompany the application. Proof of funds adequate to cover 1 year of study is required. Out-of-state tuition rates apply. Although not required, health insurance is available through the college for a fee.

Admissions Contact: William Callahan, Admissions Officer.

SAINT PETER'S COLLEGE
E-2

Jersey City, New Jersey 07306   (201) 333-4400

F/T: 1200M, 900W	Faculty: 124; IIB, +$
P/T: 50M, 150W	Ph.D.'s: 55%
Grad: 50M, 50W	S/F Ratio: 16 to 1
Year: sems, ss	Tuition: $3645
Appl: Mar. 1	R and B: none
1439 applied 1233 accepted	616 enrolled
SAT: 390V 410M	LESS COMPETITIVE

Saint Peter's College, a private Catholic institution founded in 1872, is built upon the traditional Jesuit base of a liberal education and offers programs in the liberal arts and sciences, education, and business. The library contains 200,880 volumes and subscribes to 1200 periodicals.

Environment: The 8-acre urban campus is located across the Hudson River from New York City and includes 14 buildings. There are no residence halls; private homes in the community provide boarding facilities for about 10% of the students.

Student Life: About 90% of the students come from New Jersey. Fifty percent have had public school educations. Eighty-five percent of the students are Roman Catholic, 5% are Protestant, and 5% are Jewish. Twenty-seven percent of the students are minority-group members. Students may keep cars on campus.

Organizations: One national and 3 local fraternities attract 5% of the men; about 5% of the women belong to 3 local sororities. Service organizations, religious groups, clubs, and student government are available to interested students.

Sports: The college competes intercollegiately in 14 sports for men and 11 for women. Intramural competition for men is offered in 11 sports and for women in 12.

Handicapped: Facilities for the physically handicapped include wheelchair ramps, special parking, elevators, specially equipped rest rooms, and lowered telephones. Special class scheduling is also available.

Graduates: The freshman dropout rate is 8%; 65% remain to graduate. Of those who pursue advanced study, 5% enter medical school, 5% dental school, and 5% law school. Sixty percent of the graduates pursue careers in business and industry.

Services: Placement services, career counseling, health care, remedial instruction, and psychological counseling are offered to students free of charge. Tutoring is available on a fee basis.

Programs of Study: The B.A. and B.S. degrees are awarded. Associate and master's programs are also offered. Bachelor's degrees are offered in the following subjects: BUSINESS (accounting, business administration, computer science, management, marketing), EDUCATION (elementary), ENGLISH (English), FINE AND PERFORMING ARTS (art), HEALTH SCIENCES (nursing), LANGUAGES (French, Spanish), MATH AND SCIENCES (biochemistry, biology, chemistry, mathematics, natural sciences, physics), PHILOSOPHY (philosophy, religion), PREPROFESSIONAL (dentistry, law, medicine, pharmacy, veterinary), SOCIAL SCIENCES (economics, government/political science, history, psychology, social sciences, sociology). Forty-one percent of degrees are conferred in business, 19% in math and sciences, and 12% in social sciences.

Required: The core curriculum consists of 22 courses, including courses in Catholic, Protestant, or Jewish theology. All students are also required to take courses in prose composition.

Special: Cooperative education programs, a junior year abroad, and student-designed majors are offered.

Honors: All departments offer honors programs.

Admissions: About 86% of the applicants for the 1981-82 freshman class were accepted. The SAT scores of those who enrolled were as follows: Verbal—89% below 500, 10% between 500 and 599, 1% between 600 and 700, and 0% above 700; Math—80% below 500, 16% between 500 and 599, 4% between 600 and 700, and 0% above 700. Applicants should rank within the top 60% of their class and have a 2.5 average. In addition to the applicant's academic record, the college considers the following factors: recommendations, advanced placement or honors courses, and the applicant's extracurricular record.

Procedure: The SAT should be taken by January of the senior year. Application deadlines are March 1 (fall) and December 15 (spring). Notification is on a rolling basis. There is a $15 application fee.

Special: There are early decision, early admissions, and deferred admissions plans. AP and CLEP credit is accepted.

Transfer: For fall 1981, 97 students applied, 69 were accepted, and 47 enrolled. A 2.0 GPA is required. D grades do not transfer. The college has a residency requirement of 1 year, plus a summer session. To receive a bachelor's degree, students must complete, at the college, 30 of the 129 credits necessary. Application deadlines are June 1 (fall) and January 1 (spring).

Visiting: There is an orientation program for prospective students. Informal campus visits with student guides may be arranged. Visitors may sit in on classes. The admissions office should be contacted to arrange visits.

Financial Aid: About 85% of all students receive some form of financial aid. Thirty percent work part-time on campus. The college offers scholarships, grants (federal and state), NDSL, and CWS. Disadvantaged students may receive sufficient aid to meet all college expenses. The college is a member of CSS. The FAF must be filed by March 1 (fall) or December 15 (spring).

Foreign Students: Three percent of the full-time students come from foreign countries. The college offers these students an intensive English course, an intensive English program, special counseling, and special organizations.

Admissions: Foreign students must score at least 500 on the TOEFL. No college entrance examination is required.

Procedure: Application deadlines are March 1 (fall) and December 15 (spring). Foreign students must submit a college health form before enrollment. They must also provide proof of funds adequate to cover 1 calendar year.

Admissions Contact: Robert J. Nilan, Dean of Admissions.

SETON HALL UNIVERSITY E-2
South Orange, New Jersey 07079 (201) 761-9331

F/T: 2756M, 2937W Faculty: 365; n/av
P/T: 494M, 529W Ph.D.'s: 65%
Grad: 1825M, 1675W S/F Ratio: 17 to 1
Year: sems, ss Tuition: $3880
Appl: Mar. 1 R and B: $2250
4229 applied 2960 accepted 1368 enrolled
SAT: 450V 480M COMPETITIVE

Seton Hall University, established in 1856, is a Roman Catholic institution offering undergraduate programs in the liberal arts and sciences, business, education, and the health sciences. Its library has 315,000 volumes and 10,000 microfilm items, and subscribes to 1700 periodicals.

Environment: The 56-acre suburban campus is 14 miles from New York City. Two residence halls accommodate 550 men and 550 women.

Student Life: About 90% of the students come from New Jersey; 22% live on campus. Sixty percent of the students are Catholic. Eighteen percent are minority-group members. Campus housing is coed. Students may keep cars on campus. Day-care services are available.

Organizations: There are 55 academic, social, political, and pre-professional clubs and organizations. Religious organizations are available, but participation in them is not required.

Sports: The school fields intercollegiate teams in 12 sports for men and 6 for women. There are 7 intramural sports for men and 5 for women.

Handicapped: Special facilities include ramps, elevators, and parking. Special class scheduling is possible.

Graduates: The freshman dropout rate is 17%; 75% remain to graduate. Forty-five percent pursue further education.

Services: Placement, career and psychological counseling, and health care are offered without charge to students.

Programs of Study: The university confers the B.A., B.S., and B.S.N. degrees. Master's and doctoral degrees are also granted. Bachelor's degrees are offered in the following subjects: AREA STUDIES (American, Asian, Black/Afro-American), BUSINESS (accounting, computer science, economics, finance, management, marketing), EDUCATION (early childhood, elementary, health/physical, secondary, special), ENGLISH (communications, English, journalism), FINE AND PERFORMING ARTS (art, art education, art history, music, radio/TV, theater/dramatics), HEALTH SCIENCES (medical technology, nuclear medicine technology, nursing), LANGUAGES (Chinese, French, German, Greek/Latin, Italian, Japanese, Russian, Spanish), MATH AND SCIENCES (biology, chemistry, mathematics, natural sciences, physics), PHILOSOPHY (philosophy, religion), PREPROFESSIONAL (dentistry, law, medicine, social work), SOCIAL SCIENCES (anthropology, criminal justice, economics, government/political science, history, psychology, social sciences, sociology). About 36% of the degrees are awarded in business, 22% in the social sciences, 10% in the health sciences, 8% in communications, 6% in education, 7% in mathematics and natural sciences, and 5% in humanities.

Required: Courses in English, philosophy, and speech are required. Catholic students must take courses in theology.

Special: A certificate is offered in Russian area studies. The university recently instituted a program through which high school seniors may enroll in college-level courses taught in their own schools. The university also offers a junior year in Mexico.

Honors: Seven honor societies have chapters on campus. There is an honors program in the College of Arts and Sciences.

Admissions: About 70% of the 1981-82 applicants for the freshman class were accepted. The SAT scores of those who enrolled were as follows: Verbal—79% below 500, 16% between 500 and 599, 2% between 600 and 700, and 1% above 700; Math—64% below 500, 27% between 500 and 599, 8% between 600 and 700, and 1% above 700. Students must have a C+ average and rank in the upper 40% of their class. In addition to scholastic record, the admissions committee considers important advanced placement or honors work, recommendations, and the applicant's leadership record.

Procedure: The SAT or ACT is required. New students are admitted to all semesters. The application deadlines are March 1 (fall) and December 1 (spring). Notification is on a rolling basis. There is a $25 application fee.

Special: There are early admissions and deferred admissions plans. AP and CLEP credit is accepted.

Transfer: For fall 1981, 971 students applied, 580 were accepted, and 321 enrolled. Students must have a 2.5 GPA. D grades are not acceptable. Students must complete, at the University, at least 30 credits of the 128-130 needed to receive a bachelor's degree. The application deadlines are March 1 (fall) and December 1 (spring).

Visiting: There is an admissions orientation program for prospective students. Informal campus visits with guides may be arranged. Visitors may attend classes and meet with professors.

Financial Aid: About 68% of the students receive aid. About 9% work part-time on campus. The university offers scholarships, government loans, and work-study. The university is a member of CSS. The FAF is required. Aid applications must be submitted by April 15.

Foreign Students: About 4% of the full-time students come from foreign countries. The university provides these students with an intensive English course, special counseling, and special organizations.

Admissions: Foreign students must score at least 500 on the TOEFL. No college entrance examination is required.

Procedure: Application deadlines are March 1 (fall) and November 1 (spring). Foreign students must submit a university health form. They must also provide proof of funds adequate to cover 1 year of study. They must carry health insurance, which is available through the university for a fee.

Admissions Contact: Lee W. Cooke, Director of Admissions.

STEVENS INSTITUTE OF TECHNOLOGY E-2
Hoboken, New Jersey 07030 (201) 420-5194

F/T: 1353M, 254W	Faculty: 140; I, ++$
P/T: none	Ph.D.'s: 92%
Grad: 1076M, 324W	S/F Ratio: 11 to 1
Year: sems, ss	Tuition: $5575
Appl: Mar. 1	R and B: $2810
1978 applied	1251 accepted 491 enrolled
SAT: 510V 620M	VERY COMPETITIVE+

Stevens Institute of Technology, founded in 1870, is a private institution offering degree programs in engineering, business, and the sciences. The library contains 90,000 volumes and 656 microfilm items, and subscribes to 944 periodicals.

Environment: The 54-acre urban campus at Castle Point overlooks the Hudson River and New York City. Residence halls accommodate 600 men and 80 married students; fraternity houses and on-and off-campus apartments are also available. The Davidson Laboratory, the world's largest nongovernmental hydrodynamics facility, is located on campus.

Student Life: About 50% of the students come from New Jersey and 75% come from public schools. Seventy-five percent live on campus. Sixteen percent of the students are minority-group members. Institute housing is single-sex; there are visiting privileges. All students except freshmen may keep cars on campus.

Organizations: About 33% of the men belong to 10 national fraternities and 10% of the women belong to 1 national sorority. Extracurricular activities include student government, special-interest clubs, cultural and service groups, and religious organizations. There are student branches of the American Society of Mechanical Engineers, the American Chemical Society, the American Institute of Aeronautics and Astronautics, and the American Society of Civil Engineers.

Sports: Thirteen intercollegiate teams are fielded for men and 5 for women. On the intramural level, men participate in 8 sports and women in 5.

Handicapped: Accessibility to the campus for individuals with physical handicaps is limited. Special parking and class scheduling are available.

Graduates: The freshman dropout rate is 15%; about 65% remain to graduate; 15% go on to graduate study. Fewer than 1% of the students go on to medical, dental, or law school. Eighty-five percent of the graduates pursue careers in business and industry.

Services: Career counseling, placement services, remedial instruction, psychological counseling, and health care are offered free of charge to all students. Tutoring is available on a fee basis.

Programs of Study: The B.E. and B.S. degrees are awarded. There are also master's and doctoral programs. Bachelor's degrees are offered in the following subjects: BUSINESS (computer science, management), MATH AND SCIENCES (biology, chemistry, mathematics, physics, statistics), PREPROFESSIONAL (engineering, law, medicine), SOCIAL SCIENCES (psychology). About 82% of degrees conferred are in engineering.

Required: All students must take courses in computer technology, mathematics, physics, chemistry, economics, humanities, and physical education.

Special: Pass/fail options are offered.

Honors: Five honor societies have chapters on campus. All engineering and science departments offer honors programs.

Admissions: About 63% of the applicants for the 1981–82 freshman class were accepted. The SAT scores of those who enrolled were as follows: Verbal—40% below 500, 43% between 500 and 599, 16% between 600 and 700, and 1% above 700; Math—2% below 500, 31% between 500 and 599, 50% between 600 and 700, and 15% above 700. Applicants need a B average and class rank in the top 25%. Recommendations, advanced placement or honors courses, and evidence of special talents are also considered.

Procedure: The SAT and 3 ATs (English Composition, Mathematics I or II, and Chemistry or Physics) should be taken by December of the senior year. The fall deadline is March 1. Notification is on a rolling basis. An interview is required. Freshmen are admitted to the fall term only. There is a $25 application fee.

Special: There are early decision, early admissions, and deferred admissions plans. AP and CLEP credit is accepted.

Transfer: For fall 1981, 200 transfer applications were received, 75 were accepted, and 33 students enrolled. Applications are considered on an individual basis. There is a 2-year residency requirement, and students must complete, at the institute, 76 of the 152 credits needed for a bachelor's degree. The deadlines for application are May 1 (fall) and November 1 (spring).

Visiting: There is no formal orientation program for prospective students. Informal campus visits with student guides can be arranged through the admissions office. Visitors may sit in on classes and stay overnight at the school.

Financial Aid: About 75% of all students receive some form of financial aid. Forty-five percent work part-time on campus. Average aid to freshmen from all sources is $5400. The institute offers scholarships, grants (federal and state), loans (governmental and commercial), and CWS. The institute is a member of the CSS. The FAF should be filed by February 1.

Foreign Students: About 5% of the full-time students come from foreign countries. The institute offers these students special counseling and special organizations.

Admissions: Foreign students must score at least 550 on the TOEFL or 5 to 6 on the American Language Institute of New York University Test. No college entrance examination is required.

Procedure: The application deadline is March 1. Foreign students must submit the results of a physical examination. They must also provide proof of funds adequate to cover 4 years of study. They must carry health insurance, which is available through the institute for a fee.

Admissions Contact: Robert H. Seavy, Director of Admissions.

STOCKTON STATE COLLEGE D-5
Pomona, New Jersey 08240 (609) 652-1776

F/T: 2666M, 2275W	Faculty: 173; IIB, +$
P/T: 501M, 531W	Ph.D.'s: 72%
Grad: none	S/F Ratio: 22 to 1
Year: sems, ss	Tuition: $915 ($1515)
Appl: June 1	R and B: $1100 ($2260)
2800 applied	1800 accepted 850 enrolled
SAT: 444V 479M	ACT: 21 COMPETITIVE

A member of the New Jersey State system, Stockton State College, founded in 1969, offers a liberal arts education. The library has 180,000 volumes of print and microfilm and 110,000 multimedia materials, and subscribes to 1900 periodicals.

Environment: Located on a 1600-acre, small-town campus in a rural setting 12 miles from Atlantic City, the college has 13 buildings, including a college center, a lecture hall, a gymnasium, a swimming pool, and a performing arts center. On-campus housing, consisting of garden-style apartments and a dormitory, is available. Other features include a 60-acre stream-fed lake, a 400-acre ecological preserve, a marine science field station, and a computer tie to the New Jersey State Computer Network.

Student Life: Only 5% of the students are from out of state. Forty percent live on campus. About 9% of the students are minority-group members. Campus housing is single-sex, and there are visiting privileges. Students may keep cars on campus. Day-care facilities are available to all students, faculty, and staff. Drinking is permitted on campus in accordance with state law.

Organizations: College-sponsored extracurricular activities and groups include a film club, International Student Organization, a sailing club, a women's union, an accounting society, the crew club, Hillel Foundation, and Unified Black Student Society. The college also sponsors films, plays, concerts, lectures, dance performances, exhibits, and a coffee house.

Sports: There are 6 intercollegiate sports for men and 8 for women. There are 15 intramural or club sports for men and 14 for women.

Handicapped: About 98% of the campus is accessible to physically handicapped students. Special facilities include wheelchair ramps, parking areas, elevators, lowered drinking fountains and telephones, and specially equipped rest rooms.

Services: The following services are available free to students: placement, tutoring, remedial instruction, health care, and career counseling.

Programs of Study: The B.A., B.S., B.S.N., B.S.W., and B.L.A. degrees are awarded. Bachelor's degrees are offered in the following subjects: BUSINESS (accounting, business administration, computer science, finance, management, marketing), EDUCATION (secondary), ENGLISH (English, journalism, literature), FINE AND PERFORMING ARTS (art, dance, film/photography, music, studio art, theater/dramatics), HEALTH SCIENCES (environmental health, nursing, speech therapy), LANGUAGES (French, German, Greek/Latin, Russian, Spanish), MATH AND SCIENCES (biology, botany, chemistry, earth science, ecology/environmental science, geology, mathematics, natural sciences, oceanography, physical sciences, physics), PHILOSOPHY (classics, humanities, philosophy, religion), PREPROFESSIONAL (dentistry, forestry, law, medicine, social work, veterinary), SOCIAL SCIENCES (anthropology, economics, government/political science, history, international relations, psychology, social sciences, sociology). Forty percent of the degrees conferred are in business studies.

Required: Bachelor of Arts candidates must earn a total of 64 credits in general studies; Bachelor of Science candidates must earn 48.

Special: Both independent and organized travel-abroad programs are possible. Interdisciplinary studies include studies in the arts (art, music, theater, media studies) and in teacher development. Students can choose from several instructional modes: traditional classroom lectures, small tutorials, independent studies, field trips, and internships. The liberal studies major allows students to design a degree program suited to career interests. There are remedial programs for students with deficiencies. It is possible to earn a combined B.A.-B.S. degree in 5 years. Student-designed majors are permitted.

Admissions: About 64% of those who applied were accepted for the 1981–82 freshman class. The SAT scores of those who enrolled were as follows: Verbal—80% below 500, 18% between 500 and 599, 2% between 600 and 700, and fewer than 1% above 700; Math—70% below 500, 25% between 500 and 599, 5% between 600 and 700, and fewer than 1% above 700. Graduation from high school is required. Candidates should rank in the top half of their graduating class. Nontraditional applicants (working adults, veterans, housewives, the financially and educationally disadvantaged, etc.) are urged to apply and will be carefully and individually evaluated. Other factors considered are advanced placement or honors courses, recommendations, leadership record, evidence of special talent, and impressions made during an interview.

Procedure: Either the SAT or ACT is required for applicants under 21 years of age. The latest acceptable test date is January; junior-year test results also are accepted. Admission deadlines are June 1 (fall) and December 1 (spring). The college uses a rolling admissions plan. The application must be submitted with a $10 fee.

Special: There is an early admissions plan. AP, CLEP, and PEP credit, as well as other forms of advanced placement credit, are accepted.

Transfer: For fall 1981, 1250 students applied, 950 were accepted, and 600 enrolled. Students must have at least a 2.0 GPA and must have earned 17 or more credits. Junior status is automatically granted to those transferring from a New Jersey community college with an associate degree. D grades do not transfer. Students must complete, at the college, 32 of the 128 credits required for a bachelor's degree. Application deadlines are June 1 (fall) and December 1 (spring).

Visiting: Regularly scheduled orientations for prospective students include sessions on admissions, housing, financial aid, and academic opportunities; guided campus tours; faculty open houses; interviews; transfer information sessions; and parents' "rap" sessions. The office of admissions should be contacted for details.

Financial Aid: Eighty-eight percent of students receive financial aid. The average aid awarded to freshmen from all sources covers 85% of costs. Aid is awarded in the forms of loans, grants, and campus employment. The college is a member of CSS. The FAF must be submitted. The application deadline is March 1 (fall).

Foreign Students: Two percent of the full-time students come from foreign countries. The college offers these students special counseling and special organizations.

Admissions: Foreign students must score at least 500 on the TOEFL. They must also take the SAT.

Procedure: The application deadline is March 15 (fall). Foreign students must provide proof of funds adequate to cover 4 years of study.

Admissions Contact: Nancy Iszard, Director of Admissions.

THOMAS A. EDISON STATE COLLEGE D–3
Trenton, New Jersey 08625 (609) 984-1170

F/T: none Faculty: n/av
P/T: 2300M, 2000W Ph.D.'s: n/av
Grad: none S/F Ratio: n/av
Year: none Tuition: see entry
Appl: open R and B: n/app
SAT or ACT: not required NONCOMPETITIVE

Thomas A. Edison State College, established in 1972, administers an external degree program that enables qualified students to earn or work toward a college degree without attending college in the usual way. There is no resident faculty, no campus, no classrooms, and no library. Administrative officers in Trenton evaluate college-level learning achieved through work or life experience, self-study, college courses taken previously, industry-sponsored education programs, military instruction, etc. The college accepts CLEP credit and administers its own examinations in the liberal arts and sciences, business, and radiologic technology under the Thomas Edison College Examination Program.

Graduates: About 40% of the graduates pursue advanced degrees. Eighty percent enter business careers.

Programs of Study: The B.A., B.S., and B.S.B.A. degrees are awarded. Associate degrees are also available. Bachelor's degrees are offered in the following subjects: BUSINESS (accounting, finance, human resources management, management, marketing, operations management), MATH AND SCIENCES (natural sciences, technical services), PHILOSOPHY (humanities), SOCIAL SCIENCES (human services, social sciences).

Special: Students may design their own majors.

Admissions: All applicants generally are accepted. Neither the SAT nor the ACT is required. Students may enroll at any time. AP and CLEP credit is accepted.

Visiting: Academic counselors hold regular meetings throughout the state. Prospective students may visit the college's headquarters in Trenton on weekdays from 9 A.M. to 4 P.M. The office of academic counseling should be contacted for information.

Financial Aid: Fewer than 1% of the students receive aid. The enrollment fee is $100 for state residents and $140 for out-of-state students. Other fees are variable.

Admissions Contact: Thomas P. McCarthy, Director of Admissions and Registrar.

TRENTON STATE COLLEGE D–3
Trenton, New Jersey 08625 (609) 771-2131

F/T: 2242M, 3433W Faculty: n/av
P/T: 1189M, 1641W Ph.D.'s: 61%
Grad: 512M, 1218W S/F Ratio: 19 to 1
Year: sems, ss Tuition: $780 ($1550)
Appl: Mar. 15 R and B: $2265
4802 applied 2100 accepted 1100 enrolled
SAT: 454V 496M COMPETITIVE+

Trenton State College, founded in 1855, is a public institution offering programs in the liberal arts and sciences, business, nursing, and education. It has a library collection of 355,000 volumes and subscribes to 1748 periodicals.

Environment: The 210-acre suburban campus is located 4 miles from Trenton and 9 miles from Princeton. The earlier colonial-style brick buildings are complemented by modern facilities, including a business building and a recreation center. Residence halls accommodate 2150 men and women.

Student Life: About 95% of the students are from New Jersey. Most are graduates of public schools. Thirty-three percent live on campus. About 12% of the students are minority-group members. College housing is both single-sex and coed. Students are not permitted to keep cars on campus. Day-care services are available to full-time students, faculty, and staff.

Organizations: There are 20 fraternities and sororities, to which 25% of the men and 25% of the women belong. Extracurricular activities include special-interest clubs, a modern dance group, student newspapers, and an FM radio station.

Sports: Nine intercollegiate sports for men and 10 for women are offered. On an intramural level, men and women compete in 14 sports.

Handicapped: Special facilities for the physically handicapped include wheelchair ramps, parking areas, elevators, and specially equipped rest rooms. The Office of Special Services provides 10 counselors and 2 assistants for students with physical handicaps.

Graduates: Sixteen percent drop out by the end of the first year; about 70% remain to graduate. Twelve percent go on for further education.

Services: Placement, career counseling, psychological counseling, remedial instruction, and tutoring are offered without charge. Health care is provided on a fee basis.

Programs of Study: The B.A. and B.S. are offered. There are also master's programs. Bachelor's degrees are offered in the following subjects: AREA STUDIES (urban), BUSINESS (accounting, administrative office management, business administration, business education, computer science, data processing, finance, management, marketing), EDUCATION (adult, early childhood, elementary, health/physical, industrial, secondary, special), ENGLISH (English, journalism, literature, speech), FINE AND PERFORMING ARTS (advertising design, art, art education, art history, art therapy, interior design, music, music education, radio/TV, studio art, theater/dramatics), HEALTH SCIENCES (nursing, physical therapy, speech therapy), MATH AND SCIENCES (biology, chemistry, earth science, ecology/environmental science, geology, mathematics, natural sciences, physical sciences, physics, statistics), PHILOSOPHY (philosophy, religion), PREPROFESSIONAL (dentistry, engineering, law, library science, medicine, social work, veterinary), SOCIAL SCIENCES (economics, geography, government/political science, history, psychology, social sciences, sociology).

Required: Students must take courses in English, western civilization, and speech.

Special: Study abroad, inner-city teaching opportunities, exchange programs, and independent study are offered, as well as a developmental program for students from disadvantaged backgrounds.

Honors: Eight national honor societies are represented on campus. Honors work is offered in 8 departments.

Admissions: About 44% of the 1981–82 freshman applicants were accepted. SAT scores of those who enrolled were as follows: Verbal—74% below 500, 24% between 500 and 599, 2% between 600 and 700, and 0% above 700; Math—52% below 500, 40% between 500 and 599, 8% between 600 and 700, and 0% above 700. Applicants must be graduates of accredited high schools and must have completed 16 Carnegie units. Advanced placement and honors work are considered important in addition to the applicant's academic record and SAT scores. Out-of-state freshman enrollment is limited to 5% of the total admitted.

Procedure: The SAT is required. Application deadlines are March 15 (fall) and November 15 (spring). Admission and notification are on a rolling basis. There is a $10 application fee.

Special: There are early decision, early admissions, and deferred admissions programs. AP and CLEP credit is granted.

Transfer: For fall 1981, 1873 students applied, 1281 were accepted, and 933 enrolled. A 2.0 GPA is required. Grades of D and above transfer. Students from New Jersey community colleges get preference. Thirty-two credits, of the 128 needed for a bachelor's degree, must be earned in residence. Application deadlines are May 20 (fall) and October 20 (spring).

Visiting: There are regularly scheduled orientations for prospective students; informal campus visits with student guides may also be arranged between the hours of 9 A.M. and 4:30 P.M. Visitors are allowed to attend classes. For further information, the admissions office should be contacted.

Financial Aid: About 58% of the students are getting aid. Twelve percent work part-time on campus. Garden State Scholarships, grants, and loans (government and commercial) are available to qualified students. Academic promise and need are the determining factors. The college is a member of CSS. The FAF and the SER-SEN are required. Application deadlines are March 15 (fall) and October 15 (spring).

Foreign Students: One percent of the full-time students come from foreign countries. The college offers these students special counseling and special organizations.

Admissions: Foreign students must score at least 500 on the TOEFL. No college entrance examination is required.

Procedure: Application deadlines are May 1 (fall) and November 1 (spring). Foreign students must present a certificate of health. They must also provide proof of funds adequate to cover 4 years of study.

Admissions Contact: Alfred W. Bridges, Director of Admissions.

UPSALA COLLEGE E-2
East Orange, New Jersey 07019 (201) 266-7191

F/T: 694M, 464W	Faculty:	79; IIA, –$
P/T: 154M, 396W	Ph.D.'s:	80%
Grad: 4M, 29W	S/F Ratio:	15 to 1
Year: 4-4-1, ss	Tuition:	$4312
Appl: open	R and B:	$2200
1530 applied	859 accepted	373 enrolled
SAT: 450V 460M		COMPETITIVE

Upsala College, founded in 1893, is a private liberal arts college affiliated with the Lutheran Church in America. The library contains 180,000 volumes and 10,622 microfilm items, and subscribes to 1100 periodicals.

Environment: The 48-acre suburban campus is located in a residential area of East Orange, 16 miles from New York City. There are 22 major buildings. The residence halls accommodate 880 students.

Student Life: About 90% of the students come from New Jersey. About 60% of the students live on campus. Thirty-five percent of the students are Catholic, 45% Protestant, and 12% Jewish. Thirty-one percent of the students are minority-group members. Campus housing is both single-sex and coed. There are visiting privileges in single-sex housing. Students may keep cars on campus. Day-care services are available to all students, faculty, and staff.

Organizations: About 25% of the students are affiliated with fraternities and sororities on campus. Extracurricular activities include service groups, student government, religious groups, special-interest clubs, musical groups, a drama group, a radio station, and publications.

Sports: There are 11 intercollegiate teams for men and 7 for women. Four intramural sports are offered for both men and women.

Graduates: About 7% of the students drop out by the end of the freshman year; 60% remain to graduate. Nearly 30% of the graduates pursue advanced degrees; 2% enter medical school, 1% dental school, and 4% law school.

Services: The following services are available to students free of charge: health care, psychological and career counseling, placement (for students and graduates), tutoring, and remedial instruction.

Programs of Study: The college confers the B.A., B.S., and B.S.W. degrees. Master's programs are also available. Bachelor's degrees are offered in the following subjects: AREA STUDIES (American, Ancient Near East, Black/Afro-American, Judaic, Scandinavian, urban), BUSINESS (accounting, business administration, computer science, human resources management, management, marketing, multinational corporate studies), EDUCATION (elementary, secondary), ENGLISH (English, literature), FINE AND PERFORMING ARTS (art, art history, music, studio art, theater/dramatics), HEALTH SCIENCES (cytotechnology), LANGUAGES (French, German, Italian, Spanish, Swedish), MATH AND SCIENCES (biochemistry, biology, chemistry, ecology/environmental science, geology, mathematics, physics), PHILOSOPHY (classics, philosophy, religion), PREPROFESSIONAL (architecture, dentistry, engineering, forestry, law, library science, medicine, ministry, social work, veterinary), SOCIAL SCIENCES (anthropology, economics, government/political science, history, international relations, psychology, public service, social sciences, sociology).

Special: The Ancient Near East area study program includes a summer in the Near East with work at an excavation site. Students who major in Scandinavian studies spend their junior year at the University of Stockholm. A junior year in Austria is also offered. The college has programs leading to state certification in primary and secondary education. There are 3-2 engineering programs with New Jersey Institute of Technology and Washington University, a 2-3 program in architecture with N.J.I.T., and a 3-2 program in forestry and environmental management with Duke University.

Honors: Six honor societies have chapters on campus. An honors program is available.

Admissions: About 56% of those who applied for the 1981–82 freshman class were accepted. Applicants must be graduates of accredited high schools, present 16 Carnegie units, and be recommended by high school officials. A high school GPA of at least 2.5 is required, and applicants should rank in the top 60% of their high school class. Advanced placement or honors courses, special talents, leadership record, and interview impressions are also considered important.

Procedure: The SAT is required and should be taken by January of the senior year. There are no application deadlines; freshmen are admitted for all terms. Notification is on a rolling basis. An interview is required. There is a $20 application fee.

Special: There are early decision, early admissions, and deferred admissions plans. AP and CLEP credit is available.

Transfer: For fall 1981, 170 students applied, 115 were accepted, and 68 enrolled. A GPA of 2.0 is required. D grades transfer in some cases. Students must complete, at the college, 32 of the 128 credits needed for a bachelor's degree. Application deadlines are August 15 (fall), January 15 (spring), and May 15 (summer).

Financial Aid: Seventy percent of the students receive financial aid. Twenty-two percent work part-time on campus. The average aid awarded to freshmen from all sources is $4900. Scholarships, grants, achievement awards, loans, and part-time employment (including CWS) are offered. Academic achievement, need, and character are the determining factors in awarding aid. The college is a member of the CSS. Applications for financial aid, the 1040 form, and the FAF should be filed by August 15 (fall), January 15 (spring), or May 15 (summer).

524 NEW JERSEY

Foreign Students: Three percent of the full-time students come from foreign countries. The college provides these students with special organizations.

Admissions: Foreign students must score at least 550 on the TOEFL. They may take the SAT instead.

Procedure: Application deadlines are August 15 (fall), January 15 (spring), and May 15 (summer). Foreign students must present proof of funds adequate to cover 1 year of study. They must also carry health insurance, which is available through the college for a fee.

Admissions Contact: Barry E. Abrams, Director of Enrollment Services.

WESTMINSTER CHOIR COLLEGE D-3
Princeton, New Jersey 08540 (609) 921-7144

F/T: 139M, 183W	Faculty: n/av; IIA, − −$
P/T: 3M, 24W	Ph.D.'s: 25%
Grad: 34M, 36W	S/F Ratio: 8 to 1
Year: sems, ss	Tuition: $4855
Appl: Aug. 1	R and B: $2265
210 applied 160 accepted 120 enrolled	
SAT: 440V 460M	SPECIAL

Westminster Choir College, established in 1926, is a private music college that provides undergraduate instruction for men and women who seek positions of music leadership in churches, schools, and communities. The library has 30,000 books and 380 microtexts, and subscribes to 90 periodicals.

Environment: The 22-acre suburban campus is located 50 miles from both New York City and Philadelphia. There are 13 buildings on campus, including 6 dormitories that house 370 students. There are also a student center and dining commons.

Student Life: About 33% of the students are from New Jersey. Sixty-eight percent come from public schools. Ninety-five percent reside on campus. Fourteen percent of the students are minority-group members. College housing is both single-sex and coed. There are visiting privileges in single-sex housing. Students may keep cars on campus.

Organizations: There are no sororities or fraternities. About 35% of the students hold weekend positions as organists, choir directors, and church singers. Extracurricular activities include drama, dance, and publications. Cultural and social events, such as a film series, a lecture series, operas, and recitals, take place regularly.

Sports: The college participates in no intercollegiate sports. There are 5 intramural athletics for men and women.

Handicapped: There are no special facilities for handicapped students.

Graduates: Ten percent of the freshmen drop out by the end of their first year; about 60% remain to graduate. Fifteen percent pursue advanced degrees.

Services: Offered free of charge to students are placement, career counseling, tutoring, and remedial instruction. Health care and psychological counseling are offered on a fee basis.

Programs of Study: The B.Mus. is awarded. There are also master's programs. Bachelor's degrees are offered in: EDUCATION (music), FINE AND PERFORMING ARTS (church music, music education, organ, piano, voice).

Required: All freshmen must take courses in English, choir, applied music, theory, music literature, and ear training. There are additional requirements for upperclass students.

Special: The 40-voice Westminster Choir performs yearly at the Festival of Two Worlds in Charleston, South Carolina, and Spoleto, Italy. A European organ study trip is scheduled for each January. Cross-registration is offered with Princeton University and Rider College.

Admissions: About 76% of the applicants for the 1981-82 freshman class were accepted. SAT scores of enrolled students were as follows: Verbal—57% below 500, 34% between 500 and 599, 9% between 600 and 700, and 0% above 700; Math—56% below 500, 39% between 500 and 599, 5% between 600 and 700, and 0% above 700. Applicants should present 16 Carnegie units, have a 2.0 high school GPA, and rank in the upper half of their class. Also considered important are evidence of special talents, recommendations, and extracurricular activities.

Procedure: The SAT or ACT is required and should be taken by January of the senior year. An audition and a basic musicianship test are required. Application deadlines are August 1 (fall) and December 1 (spring). An interview is strongly recommended. Notification is on a rolling basis. There is a $25 application fee.

Special: There are early decision, early admissions, and deferred admissions plans. AP credit is available.

Transfer: For fall 1981, 46 transfer applications were received, 37 were accepted, and 28 students enrolled. D grades do not transfer. Music courses transfer by exam only following matriculation. There is a 2-year residency requirement, and students must complete, at the college, 64 of the 124 credits needed for a bachelor's degree. Application deadlines are August 1 (fall) and December 1 (spring).

Visiting: There is an orientation program for prospective students. Informal campus visits with guides may be arranged. Visitors may stay overnight at the school and sit in on classes. The admissions office should be contacted for arrangements.

Financial Aid: In a recent year, about 57% of the students received financial aid. The average award to freshmen from all sources is $1500. The college offers scholarships, loans (federal, commercial, and college), work contracts, and grants. Need is the determining factor in the award of aid. The college is a member of CSS. The FAF should be submitted by April 15.

Foreign Students: Seven percent of the full-time students come from foreign countries. The college offers these students special organizations.

Admissions: Foreign students must score at least 500 on the TOEFL, and must pass the college's own music audition.

Procedure: Application deadlines are August 1 (fall) and December 1 (spring). Foreign students must present proof of funds adequate to cover 1 year of study. They must also carry health insurance, which is available through the college for a fee.

Admissions Contact: Steven Kreinberg, Director of Admissions.

WILLIAM PATERSON COLLEGE E-2
OF NEW JERSEY
Wayne, New Jersey 07470 (201) 595-2125

F/T: 4458M, 4544W	Faculty: 400; IIA, + +$
P/T: 1460M, 1001W	Ph.D.'s: n/av
Grad: 1169M, 1866W	S/F Ratio: 15 to 1
Year: sems, ss	Tuition: $1065 ($1665)
Appl: April 1	R and B: $2550
4963 applied 3224 accepted 1541 enrolled	
SAT: 823V&M	LESS COMPETITIVE

William Paterson College is a public institution offering programs in the liberal arts and sciences, business, education, and health sciences. Its library has 180,000 volumes and over 15,000 microfilm items, and subscribes to 3000 periodicals.

Environment: The 228-acre campus is located in a suburban area on a hilltop 3 miles from Paterson. High-rise dormitories house 530 men and women. All buildings on campus have been constructed since 1951.

Student Life: Most students come from New Jersey. The majority attended public schools. About 5% of the students live on campus. Dormitories are coed.

Organizations: Student activities include publications, student government, and special-interest clubs. There are sororities and fraternities on campus.

Sports: Intercollegiate competition is offered in 8 sports. Intramural sports also are offered.

Handicapped: About 90% of the campus is accessible to students with physical handicaps. Special parking areas are provided. Special class scheduling can be arranged. One counselor is available.

Graduates: The freshman dropout rate is 13%, and 70% remain to graduate. Of these, 30% go on for further education and 40% begin careers in business or industry.

Services: The following services are available on campus: placement and career counseling, health care, tutoring, remedial instruction, and psychological counseling.

Programs of Study: The college confers the B.A., B.S.N., B.S.M., B.Ed., and B.S. in Criminal Justice degrees. Master's degrees also are awarded. Bachelor's degrees are offered in the following subjects: AREA STUDIES (Black/Afro-American, urban), BUSINESS (accounting, business administration, computer science, management), EDUCATION (early childhood, elementary, health/physical, secondary, special), ENGLISH (English, journalism), FINE AND PERFORMING ARTS (art, art education, music, music education, radio/TV, studio art, theater/dramatics), HEALTH SCIENCES (nursing, speech therapy), LANGUAGES (French, Spanish), MATH AND SCIENCES (biology, chemistry, ecology/environmental science, mathematics), PHILOSO-

PHY (philosophy), PREPROFESSIONAL (dentistry, law, medicine, social work), SOCIAL SCIENCES (criminal justice, economics, geography, government/political science, history, psychology, sociology). Forty percent of the degrees conferred are in business, 15% are in education, and 15% are in social sciences.

Required: Students must complete 30 credits of liberal studies.

Special: Combined B.A.-B.S. degree programs and independent study programs are available.

Honors: Five honor societies have chapters on campus. Honors work is offered in 4 areas.

Admissions: About 65% of the applicants for the 1981-82 freshman class were accepted. The SAT scores of those who enrolled were as follows: Verbal—70% below 500, 17% between 500 and 599, 3% between 600 and 700, and 0% above 700; Math—71% below 500, 17% between 500 and 599, 2% between 600 and 700, and 0% above 700. Applicants should rank in the top 50% of their graduating class and have at least a C+ average in 16 Carnegie units. Advanced placement or honors courses, extracurricular activities, recommendations, and impressions made during an interview are also considered.

Procedure: The SAT or ACT is required and should be taken by December of the senior year. There is a $10 application fee. The application deadlines are April 1 (fall) and December 1 (spring). Notification is made on a rolling basis.

Special: Early decision, early admissions, and deferred admissions plans are offered. CLEP credit is accepted.

Transfer: About 800 transfer students are admitted yearly. A 2.0 GPA is required. D grades do not transfer. One year must be completed in residence.

Visiting: An orientation program is held for prospective applicants. Informal campus visits with student guides may be arranged. Visitors may attend classes. Arrangements can be made through the admissions office.

Financial Aid: About 35% of the students receive aid through the college. Grants (federal and state), loans (from NDSL, college, and bank funds), and work-study are available. The aid application and the FAF must be filed by April 1.

Foreign Students: About 1% of the full-time students come from foreign countries. The college offers these students special counseling and special organizations.

Admissions: Applicants must score 500 or better on the TOEFL. No college entrance exams are required.

Procedure: Application deadlines are April 1 (fall) and November 1 (spring). Students must submit a completed health report form and show evidence of adequate funds for 1 year. Foreign students must carry health insurance, which is available through the college for a fee.

Admissions Contact: Joseph NcNally, Director of Admissions.

NEW MEXICO

COLLEGE OF SANTA FE
Santa Fe, New Mexico 87501   C-2   (505) 473-6131

F/T: 309M, 430W   Faculty: 45; IIB, av$
P/T: 85M, 169W   Ph.D.'s: 65%
Grad: none   S/F Ratio: 18 to 1
Year: sems, ss   Tuition: $2900
Appl: open   R and B: $2060
500 applied   480 accepted   280 enrolled
ACT: required   **LESS COMPETITIVE**

Santa Fe, a Catholic college established in 1947, is a liberal arts institution founded by the Christian Brothers. The library contains 87,000 volumes and subscribes to 550 periodicals.

Environment: The 118-acre urban campus has 49 buildings, including dormitories for 610 men and 216 women. The self-contained campus is located near Santa Fe and 55 miles from Albuquerque.

Student Life: About 76% of the undergraduates are from New Mexico. Approximately 30% of the students live on campus. About 50% are minority-group members. About 70% are Catholic, 20% are Protestant, and 2% are Jewish. Attendance at religious services is not required. Campus housing is coed. Students may keep cars on campus.

Organizations: Two national fraternities have chapters on campus, and 10% of the men belong to one of them. There are 2 sororities. Campus organizations include professional, scientific, social, literary, drama, and art clubs. Other social outlets include dances, outings, cookouts, ski parties, summer opera, art galleries, and outdoor recreation.

Sports: The college fields 3 intercollegiate teams for men and 3 for women. There are 9 intramural sports for men and 6 for women.

Handicapped: The college offers no special facilities for the physically handicapped.

Graduates: About 30% of the freshmen drop out at the end of the year. Forty percent remain to graduate. Of the graduates, 20% pursue advanced degrees; 1% enter medical school and 5% go on to law school. Sixty percent of the graduates enter business and industry.

Services: The following services are available free of charge: tutoring, remedial instruction, psychological and career counseling, and placement.

Programs of Study: The college awards B.A., B.S., B.B.A., B.A.C., B.F.A., and B.C.S. degrees. Associate degrees are also awarded. Bachelor's degrees are offered in the following subjects: BUSINESS (business education, management, public administration), EDUCATION (bilingual, elementary, health/physical, recreation), ENGLISH (English, English education), FINE AND PERFORMING ARTS (art, art education, arts administration, design/theater technology, music/theater, studio art, theater/dramatics), HEALTH SCIENCES (medical technology), MATH AND SCIENCES (biology, chemistry, general science, mathematics), PHILOSOPHY (humanities, religion), PREPROFESSIONAL (dentistry, law, medicine), SOCIAL SCIENCES (government/political science, history, managerial psychology, psychology, social sciences, education, social work). Of degrees conferred, 25% are in social sciences, 24% in business, 16% in health sciences, and 12% in education.

Required: Students must satisfy course requirements in English, science, humanities, social sciences, philosophy, religion studies, and physical education.

Special: The college allows student-designed majors. Third-year students are permitted to study abroad; the college controls study arrangements. Certification in secondary education is available.

Admissions: Ninety-six percent of those who applied were accepted for the 1981-82 freshman class. ACT scores for those who enrolled were as follows: 60% below 21, 15% between 21 and 23, 10% between 24 and 25, 5% between 26 and 28, and 5% above 28. The accreditation and reputation of the high school; recommendations by high school officials, friends, and alumni; advanced placement or honors courses; and leadership potential are important factors in admission.

Procedure: Applicants must take the ACT. The college follows a rolling admissions policy. There are no application deadlines. Applications should be submitted with a $16 fee.

Special: There are early decision and early admissions plans. CLEP credit is granted.

Transfer: For fall 1981, 450 students applied, 390 were accepted, and 145 enrolled. D grades do not transfer. All students must complete, at the college, 30 of the 128 credits required for a bachelor's degree. There are no application deadlines.

Visiting: Guides are available for informal visits, which are best made when classes are in session. Visitors may sit in on classes and stay at the school. The office of admissions will make arrangements.

Financial Aid: About 65% of the students receive aid. The average award is $5500. More than $1 million in student aid is distributed each year. This aid includes scholarships, loans, and part-time employment. CWS programs are available in all departments; 30% of students work part-time on campus. The FAF must be filed by April 15 (fall), November 15 (spring), or March 15 (summer). The college is a member of CSS.

Foreign Students: One percent of the students come from foreign countries. An intensive English course and special counseling are available for these students.

Admissions: Foreign students must achieve a TOEFL score of at least 500. No college entrance exams are required.

Procedure: There are no application deadlines; foreign students are admitted in all terms. They must present proof of funds adequate to cover 1 year of study.

Admissions Contact: Mary Bacca, Director of Admissions.

COLLEGE OF THE SOUTHWEST   E-4
Hobbs, New Mexico 88240   (505) 392-6561

F/T: 27M, 58W
P/T: 38M, 85W
Grad: none
Year: sems, ss
Appl: open
ACT: required

Faculty: n/av; IV, av$
Ph.D.'s: 25%
S/F Ratio: 8 to 1
Tuition: $1070
R: $720
LESS COMPETITIVE

Founded in 1956 as a junior college, the College of the Southwest now offers liberal arts programs leading to the bachelor's degree. The library has 30,000 volumes and subscribes to 400 periodicals.

Environment: There are 9 buildings on the 162-acre campus, located 4 miles from the town of Hobbs. Lubbock, Texas, is 110 miles away; Albuquerque is 300 miles away. Single students are housed on campus in quadruplex apartment units.

Student Life: About 80% of the students come from New Mexico. About 5% of the students are minority-group members. Ninety-one percent are Protestant. All have public school backgrounds.

Organizations: There are 3 extracurricular groups on campus, and no fraternities or sororities. Recreation is also available in the nearby El Paso/Juarez, Mexico, area and the Sacramento Mountains.

Sports: The college does not participate in intercollegiate sports. At least 5 intramural sports are available for men and women.

Handicapped: The entire campus is accessible to the physically handicapped. Facilities include wheelchair ramps and specially equipped rest rooms.

Graduates: About 20% of the freshmen drop out by the end of the first year, and 20% remain to graduate.

Services: Psychological counseling and placement services are available.

Programs of Study: All programs lead to B.S. degrees. Bachelor's degrees are offered in the following subjects: BUSINESS (accounting, business administration, management), EDUCATION (early childhood, elementary, secondary, special), ENGLISH (English), MATH AND SCIENCES (biology), SOCIAL SCIENCES (history).

Special: The college offers the B.G.S. degree.

Admissiosn: Ninety percent of those who applied for a recent freshman class were accepted. The minimum grade average accepted from a high school student is 2.0. The college also considers the applicant's character, special talents, and leadership record.

Procedure: The ACT is required, but is used for counseling rather than for admissions purposes. There are no application deadlines. Admissions decisions are made on a rolling basis.

Special: An early decision plan and an early admissions plan are offered. AP and CLEP credit is accepted.

Transfer: D grades do not transfer. Students must earn at least 30 credits in residence to receive a bachelor's degree.

Visiting: Guides are available for informal visits. Visitors can sit in on class and stay overnight at the school. The admissions office will make arrangements.

Financial Aid: About 65% of the students receive aid. Pell grants, scholarships, GSLs, and work contracts are available. The college receives no federal funds. Tuition may be paid in installments. The deadline for financial aid applications is April 15.

Admissions Contact: Cynthia Cox, Director of Admissions.

EASTERN NEW MEXICO UNIVERSITY   E-3
Portales, New Mexico 88130   (505) 562-2178

F/T: 1260M, 1326W
P/T: 136M, 199W
Grad: 264M, 341W
Year: sems, ss
Appl: Aug. 1
1352 applied   1122 accepted   658 enrolled
SAT or ACT: required   LESS COMPETITIVE

Faculty: 140; IIA, +$
Ph.D.'s: 53%
S/F Ratio: 22 to 1
Tuition: $694 ($1809)
R and B: $1614

Eastern New Mexico University, established in 1934, is a state-supported institution. The university includes the colleges of Business, Education and Technology, Fine Arts, and Liberal Arts and Sciences. The library contains 368,000 volumes and subscribes to 1328 periodicals.

Environment: The university occupies more than 400 acres in a town of 12,000 people located in a rural area 120 miles from Amarillo and Lubbock, Texas. Most of the university's buildings have been constructed since 1950. Living facilities include 115 furnished apartments for married students, dormitories, on-campus apartments, and fraternity and sorority houses. The university recently constructed a solar-energy building.

Student Life: About 80% of the students come from New Mexico. Ninety percent come from public schools. About 34% live on campus. About 22% are minority-group members. Campus housing is both coed and single-sex; there are visiting privileges in the single-sex housing. Students may keep cars on campus. Drinking is forbidden on campus.

Organizations: There are 6 national fraternities and 3 national sororities; 16% of men and 11% of women belong. Religious facilities are available for Catholic and Protestant students.

Sports: The university fields 4 intercollegiate teams for men and 3 for women. There are 10 intramural sports for men and 10 for women.

Handicapped: Facilities for physically handicapped students include wheelchair ramps, special parking, elevators, and specially equipped rest rooms. Special class scheduling and location can be arranged.

Graduates: The freshman dropout rate is 35%; 30% remain to graduate. About 23% of the graduates go on to further study.

Services: Students receive the following services free of charge: health care, psychological and career counseling, tutoring, and remedial instruction. Free placement services for students and graduates include on-campus interviews and assistance in preparing resumes and writing letters.

Programs of Study: The university confers the B.A., B.S., B.F.A., B.U.S., B.S. in E., B.A.Ed., B.B.A., B.M., B.M.E., B.S.Bus.Ed., and B.S.Ind.Ed. degrees. Associate and master's degrees also are available. Bachelor's degrees are offered in the following subjects: AREA STUDIES (American, Latin American), BUSINESS (accounting, agricultural business and economics, business administration, business education, clerical, computer science, finance, legal secretary, management, management—personnel, management—production, marketing, medical secretary), EDUCATION (bilingual, counseling and guidance, early childhood, educational administration, elementary, health/physical, industrial, media, psychology, reading, recreation, secondary, special), ENGLISH (English, journalism, speech), FINE AND PERFORMING ARTS (art education, music, music education, radio/TV, theater/dramatics), HEALTH SCIENCES (audiology, environmental health, medical technology, speech therapy), LANGUAGES (Spanish), MATH AND SCIENCES (biology, chemistry, earth science, ecology/environmental science, geology, mathematics, physics, statistics, wildlife management), PHILOSOPHY (religion), PREPROFESSIONAL (agriculture, dentistry, engineering, forestry, law, medicine, pharmacy, social work, veterinary), SOCIAL SCIENCES (anthropology, government/political science, history, psychology, social sciences, sociology).

Special: Combined B.A.-B.S. degrees may be earned in 5 years. The university offers an ethnic studies minor. There is a summer program for incoming freshmen who need special assistance in preparing for college. Students may retake some courses failed.

Admissions: The university accepted 83% of the applicants for the 1981-82 freshmen class. Applicants should be graduates of an accredited high school and have completed at least 15 units of work. Students must have a 2.0 GPA or a minimum composite score of 900 on the SAT, 19 on the ACT, or 284 on the SCAT. Non-high-school graduates at least 18 years old may be admitted by examination. Special talents, extracurricular activities, and leadership record are considered important.

Procedure: There is a rolling admissions plan. A $10 application fee is required. The deadline for regular admission is August 1 (fall), December 31 (spring), and May 31 (summer). The ACT or SAT is required.

Special: There are early decision and early admissiosn plans. AP and CLEP credit is accepted.

Transfer: Most applications are approved; more than 400 students transfer yearly. A 2.0 GPA is necessary. D grades do not transfer. All students must complete, at the university, at least 32 of the 128 credits required for a bachelor's degree. Applications should be submitted 30 days before the beginning of a term.

Visiting: Guides are available for informal visits. Meals are provided, and visitors can stay overnight at the school when rooms are available. Visits may be scheduled for any time other than campus holidays. The admissions office handles arrangements.

Financial Aid: About 75% of the students receive aid. Fifty percent work part-time on campus. Approximately 150 freshman scholarships are offered each year. Federal, state, and college-administered loan funds provide additional aid. The average amount of aid for freshmen in 1981–82 was $2850. Applications for financial aid and the FAF must be filed by March 1 (summer or fall entry) or October 1 (spring entry). The university is a member of CSS.

Foreign Students: Three percent of the full-time students come from foreign countries. Special counseling and special organizations are available for these students.

Admissions: Foreign students must achieve a TOEFL score of at least 500 and must take the SAT or ACT.

Procedure: Application deadlines are July 15 (fall), November 15 (spring), and April 15 (summer). Foreign students must present evidence of good health and proof of adequate funds for 1 year. They also must carry health insurance, which is available through the university for a fee.

Admissions Contact: Larry N. Fuqua, Director of Admissions.

NEW MEXICO HIGHLANDS UNIVERSITY D-2
Las Vegas, New Mexico 87701 (505) 425-7511

F/T: 700M, 745W	Faculty:	120; IIA, –$
P/T: 101M, 220W	Ph.D.'s:	66%
Grad: 208M, 226W	S/F Ratio:	14 to 1
Year: sems, ss	Tuition:	$495 ($1609)
Appl: July 15	R and B:	$1460
552 applied	512 accepted	447 enrolled
ACT: required		LESS COMPETITIVE

New Mexico Highlands University, established in 1893, is a state-supported college that emphasizes teacher education. The library contains 220,000 volumes and subscribes to 12,000 periodicals. The library also serves as a repository of United States government documents.

Environment: The campus occupies 14 square blocks in a suburban area of Las Vegas. Living facilities include dormitories and apartments for married students.

Student Life: About 80% of the students are from New Mexico. About 25% live on campus. Sixty-five percent are minority-group members, primarily Hispanics. Sixty-eight percent are Catholic, and 22% are Protestant. Campus housing is single-sex, with visiting privileges. Students may keep cars on campus. The university had plans in 1981–82 to institute day-care services.

Organizations: Twenty percent of the students belong to sororities or fraternities. Extracurricular activities include the student senate, weekly newspaper, yearbook, choir, band, forensic club, religious societies, and departmental organizations. World-renowned skiing areas are a 2-hour drive from campus.

Sports: The university fields 6 intercollegiate teams for men and 2 for women. There are 8 intramural sports for men and 8 for women.

Handicapped: About 90% of the campus is accessible to handicapped students. Facilities include wheelchair ramps, special parking, elevators, and specially equipped rest rooms. About 1% of the students have impaired vision.

Graduates: Approximately 33% of the freshmen remain to graduate. About 60% pursue graduate study after graduation. About 20% pursue careers in business and industry.

Services: Students receive the following services free of charge: placement, career counseling, tutoring, remedial instruction, psychological counseling, and health care. The university has placement services for undergraduates and graduates.

Programs of Study: All programs lead to the B.A. degree. Associate and master's degrees are also awarded. Bachelor's degrees are offered in the following subjects: BUSINESS (accounting, business administration, business education), EDUCATION (elementary, health/physical, industrial), ENGLISH (English), FINE AND PERFORMING ARTS (art, music), HEALTH SCIENCES (environmental health, medical technology), LANGUAGES (Spanish), MATH AND SCIENCES (biology, chemistry, combined science, earth science, ecology/environmental science, mathematics), PHILOSOPHY (philosophy), PREPROFESSIONAL (dentistry, engineering, forestry, law, library science, medical technology, medicine, optometry, pharmacy, social work, veterinary), SOCIAL SCIENCES (government/political science, history, psychology, social sciences, sociology/anthropology).

Required: Two health and physical education courses are required.

Special: Programs include bilingual education and teaching English as a second language.

NEW MEXICO 527

Honors: The university has honors programs in foreign languages, social sciences, business education, psychology, and science. Eleven national honor societies have chapters on campus.

Admissions: Ninety-three percent of those who applied were accepted for the 1981–82 freshman class. Applicants must have at least a C average and must have completed 15 units of secondary school work.

Procedure: The ACT is required. Application deadlines are July 15 (fall), December 15 (spring), and May 1 (summer). Admissions decisions are made on a rolling basis.

Special: There is an early decision plan. CLEP and AP credit is accepted.

Transfer: An average of C is required of transfer students. D grades do not transfer. All students must complete, at the university, 32 of the 128 credits required for a bachelor's degree.

Visiting: Regularly scheduled orientations are provided for prospective students. Guides are provided for informal visits, and visitors may sit in on classes and stay overnight at the school. The dean of students or the admissions officer should be contacted to arrange visits.

Financial Aid: Scholarships and student loans are available. Applications for undergraduate financial aid must be in by March 1. About 85% of the students receive financial aid.

Foreign Students: Special counseling and special organizations are available for foreign students.

Admissions: Foreign students must achieve a TOEFL score of at least 520 to enter the business school or 480 to enter other programs. No college entrance exams are required.

Procedure: Application deadlines are the same as those for other freshmen. Foreign students must present proof of good health and of adequate funds.

Admissions Contact: E. Martinez, Director of Admissions.

NEW MEXICO INSTITUTE OF MINING AND TECHNOLOGY C-3
Socorro, New Mexico 87801 (505) 835-5424

F/T: 719M, 264W	Faculty:	85; I, –$
P/T: 78M, 81W	Ph.D.'s:	93%
Grad: 125M, 24W	S/F Ratio:	12 to 1
Year: sems, ss	Tuition:	$642 ($2154)
Appl: Aug. 15	R and B:	$2136
743 applied	551 accepted	241 enrolled
ACT: 24		VERY COMPETITIVE

New Mexico Institute of Mining and Technology, a state institution founded in 1889, trains men and women for careers in science and engineering. The institute is composed of the college, the New Mexico Bureau of Mines and Mineral Resources, the Research and Development Division, and the Petroleum Recovery Research Center. The library houses 80,000 volumes and subscribes to 1000 periodicals.

Environment: The 125-acre rural campus, located in a town of 7000 that is 75 miles from Albuquerque, includes a research laboratory for geological and atmospheric studies and the world-renowned Langmuir Laboratory for atmospheric research. Residence halls house 550 students, and there are 33 efficiency apartments for married students.

Student Life: Ninety-two percent of entering freshmen come from public schools. More than half the freshmen and most graduate students come from out of state. Forty-five percent live on campus. Twelve percent are minority-group members. Campus housing is both coed and single-sex; there are visiting privileges in the single-sex housing. Students may keep cars on campus. Day-care services are available, for a fee, to all students, faculty, and staff.

Organizations: There are no fraternities or sororities on campus. Various activities take place at the institute, including theater and films, concerts, and lectures. The campus is located in the scenic Rio Grande Valley, which offers recreational opportunities such as hiking and backpacking.

Sports: There are no intercollegiate sports. There are 16 intramural sports for men and 12 for women.

Handicapped: About 90% of the campus is accessible to wheelchair students. Facilities include wheelchair ramps, special parking, and specially equipped rest rooms.

Graduates: The freshman dropout rate is 18%; 52% of those who begin graduate. Thirteen percent of the graduates go on to further study: 2.75% enter medical school and 1% enter law school. Eighty percent pursue careers in business and industry.

NEW MEXICO

Services: Students receive free placement counseling and tutoring.

Programs of Study: The institute offers B.A., B.S., and B.G.S. degrees. Associate, master's and doctoral degrees are also awarded. Bachelor's degrees are offered in the following subjects: AREA STUDIES (general), BUSINESS (computer science), HEALTH SCIENCES (medical technology), MATH AND SCIENCES (basic sciences, biology, chemistry, geology, mathematics, physics), PREPROFESSIONAL (engineering—environmental, engineering—geological, engineering—materials, engineering—metallurgical, engineering—mining, engineering—petroleum), SOCIAL SCIENCES (history, psychology, social sciences). Forty-nine percent of all degrees are in math and the sciences, 10% are in social sciences, and 41% are in engineering.

Required: Courses in English, mathematics, science, social science, and fine arts are required.

Special: Outstanding students may participate in an undergraduate research program. The college has an exchange visitors program. There is a 6-week advanced field geology camp in unmapped areas. Combined B.A.-B.S. degrees are available. A general studies major is offered, and students may design their own majors.

Honors: The college has 2 honor societies on campus.

Admissions: Seventy-four percent of those who applied were accepted for the 1981–82 freshman class. ACT scores for those who enrolled were as follows: 23% below 21, 14% between 21 and 23, 15% between 24 and 25, 33% between 26 and 28, and 15% above 28. Applicants should have completed a minimum of 15 units of academic work and have at least a C average.

Procedure: The application fee is $10. The ACT is required. Applications should be submitted by August 15 (fall), December 15 (spring), or June 1 (summer). The institute follows a rolling admissions policy.

Special: The institute accepts AP credit.

Transfer: For the fall of 1981, 203 students applied, 123 were accepted, and 86 enrolled. A 2.0 GPA and an ACT score of 19 are required. Students must complete, at the institute, 30 of the 135 to 145 credits required for a bachelor's degree. Application deadlines are the same as those for freshmen.

Visiting: There are no scheduled orientations for prospective students. However, the institute will provide guides for informal visits. Visitors may sit in on classes and stay at the school. The admissions office should be contacted to arrange visits.

Financial Aid: About 63% of the students receive aid. Thirty-seven percent work part-time on campus. The average award to freshmen is $2280. Entering students may apply for aid in the form of scholarships, grants, part-time employment, student loans, and the institute's cooperative work-study program. The FAF or FFS and the institute's application form must be filed by March 1 for summer or fall entry and December 1 for spring entry. Merit scholarships of $1000 are also available.

Foreign Students: Five percent of the full-time students come from foreign countries.

Admissions: Foreign students must achieve a TOEFL score of at least 535. No college entrance exams are required.

Procedure: Application deadlines are June 1 (fall), October 15 (spring), and March 15 (summer). Foreign students must present proof of funds adequate to cover 4 years of study. Health insurance is required and is available through the institute for a fee.

Admissions Contact: Louise E. Chamberlin, Director of Admissions.

NEW MEXICO STATE UNIVERSITY   C-4
Las Cruces, New Mexico 88003   (505) 646-3121

F/T: 5132M, 3994W	Faculty: 986; I, —$
P/T: 623M, 956W	Ph.D.'s: 80%
Grad: 962M, 741W	S/F Ratio: 21 to 1
Year: sems, ss	Tuition: $744 ($2256)
Appl: Aug. 1	R and B: $1344–1544
ACT: required	LESS COMPETITIVE

New Mexico State University, established in 1888, is supported by the state of New Mexico. Its library contains 520,000 volumes and 200,000 microfilm items, and subscribes to 3690 periodicals.

Environment: The self-contained campus is located in a suburban area 40 miles north of El Paso, Texas, and includes 88 buildings on a 6250-acre site. The university also maintains a 289-acre irrigated experimental farm and orchard, a 61,760-acre cattle and experimental ranch, and a 2160-acre recreational area in the Organ Mountains. Living facilities include dormitories, fraternity and sorority houses, and married-student housing.

Student Life: Ninety percent of the students come from New Mexico. Ninety percent come from public schools. Most are from families of modest means. Forty percent live on campus. Twenty-nine percent are minority-group members, primarily Hispanic. Campus housing is single-sex, with visiting privileges. Students may keep cars on campus.

Organizations: Religious facilities are available for Catholic and Protestant students. Forty-five professional or special-interest clubs are open to qualified students. There are 11 national fraternities and 5 national sororities; about 7% of the men and 7% of the women belong.

Sports: The university fields 8 intercollegiate teams for men and 6 for women. There are 17 intramural sports for men and 15 for women.

Handicapped: About 90% of the campus is accessible to handicapped students. Facilities include wheelchair ramps, special parking, elevators, specially equipped rest rooms, specially equipped dormitory rooms, and lowered drinking fountains and telephones. Special class scheduling is available.

Graduates: About 25% of the freshmen drop out by the end of the first year, and 40% remain to graduate. Fifteen percent of the graduates pursue further study.

Services: The university offers the following services free of charge: placement, career counseling, tutoring, psychological counseling, and health care. Remedial instruction is provided for a fee. Placement services also are available for graduates.

Programs of Study: The university offers associate, bachelor's, master's, and doctoral degrees. Bachelor's degrees are offered in the following subjects: BUSINESS (accounting, business administration, business systems analysis, finance, management, marketing, real estate/insurance, trust and real property management), EDUCATION (bilingual, early childhood, elementary, health/physical, secondary, special), ENGLISH (English, journalism, literature, speech), FINE AND PERFORMING ARTS (art, art education, art history, film/photography, music, music education, radio/TV, theater/dramatics), HEALTH SCIENCES (audiology, community health, medical technology, nursing, physical therapy, speech therapy), LANGUAGES (French, German, Russian, Spanish), MATH AND SCIENCES (astronomy, biology, chemistry, computer science, earth science, ecology/environmental science, geology, mathematics, natural sciences, physical sciences, physics), PREPROFESSIONAL (dentistry, engineering—agricultural, engineering—chemical, engineering—civil, engineering—electrical/computer, engineering—geological, engineering—industrial, engineering—mechanical/solar, engineering technology, forestry, law, medicine, pharmacy, veterinary), SOCIAL SCIENCES (anthropology, economics, geography, government/political science, history, psychology, social sciences, sociology).

Special: It is possible to earn combined B.A.-B.S. degrees. The May interim semester offers courses not available during the regular school year that are graded on a satisfactory/unsatisfactory basis. Cooperative programs for engineering, mathematics, science, teacher education, and other majors allow students, after the first year, to help finance their education.

Honors: Twenty-five national honor societies have chapters on campus.

Admissions: Ninety percent of those who applied were accepted for the 1981–82 freshman class. The candidate must be a graduate of an accredited high school and have a C average or better or an ACT composite score of 19 or better. GED scores of applicants who are at least 18 years old may be accepted in lieu of a high school transcript.

Procedure: The ACT is required. The application deadlines for regular admission are August 1 for fall and January 1 for spring. Applications should be submitted with a $10 fee. Admissions decisions are made on a rolling basis.

Special: Early and deferred admissions plans are available. AP and CLEP credit is accepted.

Transfer: A GPA of 2.0 or better and an ACT score of at least 19 are required. D grades do not transfer. Students must complete, at the university, at least 30 of the 132 credits required for a bachelor's degree. Application deadlines are August 1 (fall), January 1 (spring), and May 15 (summer).

Visiting: There are 4 orientations for prospective students in June through August. Guides are always available for informal visits. Visitors may sit in on classes, tour the campus, and visit with faculty members. The best time for a visit is Monday through Friday. The admissions office will make arrangements.

Financial Aid: About 70% of students receive financial aid. Seventy percent work part-time on campus. The average freshman aid award was $1500 in 1981–82. Freshman scholarships as well as loans from federal and state governments, local banks, the university, and private sources are available. Aid applications must be filed by March 1 (summer or fall entry) or October 1 (spring entry). The university is a member of CSS and requires the FAF, FFS, or SFS (FAF preferred).

Admissions Contact: Bill J. Bruner, Director, Admissions and Records.

ST. JOHN'S COLLEGE
Santa Fe, New Mexico 87501   C-2
                               (505) 982-3691

F/T: 178M, 141W	Faculty: 43; n/av
P/T: 3M, 2W	Ph.D.'s: n/av
Grad: 14M, 17W	S/F Ratio: 9 to 1
Year: sems, ss	Tuition: $6000
Appl: open	R and B: $2400
148 applied	138 accepted	93 enrolled
SAT: 600V 590M		VERY COMPETITIVE

St. John's College, opened in 1964, is a private nonsectarian liberal arts college that is a sister campus of St. John's College at Annapolis, Maryland. Both campuses offer a 4-year all-required program in liberal arts. The library contains 50,000 volumes and subscribes to 200 periodicals.

Environment: The 330-acre suburban campus, located in the southeastern corner of the city, has 12 major buildings. The campus is on the side of a mountain and overlooks Santa Fe. Dormitories accommodate 146 men and 126 women.

Student Life: About 50% of the students come from the West and the Northwest. About 75% live on campus. One percent are minority-group members. Campus housing is both coed and single-sex; there are visiting privileges in the single-sex housing. Students may keep cars on campus.

Organizations: There are no fraternities or sororities, but professional and service organizations also serve as social groups. Extracurricular activities include theater and music groups, publications, poetry readings, concerts, and film series. Santa Fe also offers many cultural activities.

Sports: The college does not engage in intercollegiate sports. There are 10 intramural sports for men and 10 for women.

Handicapped: It is difficult for handicapped students to get around the campus. There are no special facilities for the handicapped.

Graduates: The freshman dropout rate is 25%; 50% remain to graduate. Half the graduates continue on to professional or graduate schools. Seven percent of the graduates enter medical school and 16% enter law school. About 23% pursue careers in business and industry.

Services: Students receive the following services free of charge: health care, placement aid, career and psychological counseling, tutoring, and remedial instruction. Placement services are available to graduates as well.

Programs of Study: The B.A. is conferred in liberal arts. Master's degrees are also awarded. Because all students follow a prescribed program, there are no majors and no electives.

Special: A unified curriculum, built around semi-weekly seminars on the great books of Western tradition, is required of all students. These seminars are supplemented by exercises in mathematics and translation, and by semi-weekly laboratories in the physical and biological sciences. The college also offers classes in painting, poetry, weaving, languages, dance, and karate.

Admissions: Ninety-three percent of those who applied were accepted for the 1981–82 freshman class. No minimum class rank or grade average is required of applicants. The most important factors considered are an applicant's essay, high school transcript, and letters of reference.

Procedure: The SAT or ACT is recommended but not required. Applications should be completed by early spring, but there is no deadline. The college does not require an application fee. Admissions decisions are made on a rolling basis.

Special: Early decision, early admissions, and deferred admissions plans are offered.

Transfer: About 30 students enter as transfers yearly. All must begin as freshmen, and therefore must meet the basic freshman requirements.

Visiting: St. John's schedules orientation sessions at which prospective students spend 3 days observing classes and being interviewed. The college provides room and board. Guides are provided for informal visits; visitors can sit in on classes and stay overnight at the school. The admissions office will make arrangements.

Financial Aid: Fifty-four percent of all students receive financial aid. About 25% work part-time on campus. Aid is awarded on the basis of need and renewed annually upon application. The FAF should be submitted by February 25. The college is a member of CSS.

Foreign Students: Fewer than 1% of the full-time students come from foreign countries.

Admissions: Foreign students must take the TOEFL exam. No college entrance exams are required.

Procedure: There are no application deadlines; foreign students are admitted in the fall and spring. They must undergo a physical exam and must present proof of adequate funds for 1 year. Health insurance is required and is available through the college.

Admissions Contact: Mary McCormick, Director of Admissions.

UNIVERSITY OF ALBUQUERQUE
Albuquerque, New Mexico 87140   C-2
                                  (505) 831-1111

F/T: 521M, 536W	Faculty: 155; n/av
P/T: 509M, 431W	Ph.D.'s: 64%
Grad: none	S/F Ratio: 22 to 1
Year: 4-1-4, ss	Tuition: $2300
Appl: Aug. 1	R and B: $1800
1172 applied	1172 accepted	447 enrolled
ACT: 15		LESS COMPETITIVE

The University of Albuquerque, founded in 1920, is a private, coeducational liberal arts college. The library contains 78,200 volumes and 25,754 microfilm items, and subscribes to 421 periodicals.

Environment: The 100-acre campus is located on the west bank of the Rio Grande overlooking the city of Albuquerque. Across the valley are the Sandia and Manzano Mountains. The main campus buildings are 2-story, mission-style structures. Since the university moved to this site in 1950, 10 buildings have been constructed, including two 2-story dormitories, one for men and one for women.

Student Life: About 15% of the students come from out of state. Ten percent of the students live on campus. The dormitories are single-sex.

Organizations: One national fraternity has a chapter on campus.

Sports: The university does not participate in intercollegiate sports. There are 15 intramural sports for men and 15 for women.

Handicapped: Sixty percent of the campus is accessible to physically handicapped students. Facilities include wheelchair ramps, special parking, special class scheduling, and specially equipped rest rooms.

Graduates: About 22% of the freshmen drop out at the end of the first year, and 45% remain to graduate. Twenty percent of the graduates pursue advanced degrees.

Services: Students receive the following services free of charge: placement, career counseling, health care, tutoring or remedial instruction, and psychological counseling. Placement services also are available for graduates.

Programs of Study: The college awards the B.A., B.S., B.S.Ed., B.S.B.A., B.F.A., and B.U.S. degrees. Associate degrees are also awarded. Bachelor's degrees are offered in the following subjects: AREA STUDIES (urban development), BUSINESS (accounting, business administration, computer science, real estate/insurance), EDUCATION (adult, elementary, health/physical, secondary, special), ENGLISH (English), FINE AND PERFORMING ARTS (art, theater/dramatics), HEALTH SCIENCES (nursing, radiographic technology, respiratory therapy), LANGUAGES (Spanish), MATH AND SCIENCES (biology, chemistry, mathematics, physical sciences), PHILOSOPHY (philosophy, religion), PREPROFESSIONAL (law, medicine, social work, veterinary), SOCIAL SCIENCES (criminology/corrections, economics, government/political science, psychology, sociology). Thirty-one percent of degrees conferred are in business, 17% in health sciences, and 10% in social sciences.

Special: Students may earn a combined B.A.-B.S. degree in 5 years. A general-studies degree is offered.

Honors: Honor students may join Delta Epsilon Sigma. The university also offers honors programs and seminars.

Admissions: All applicants were accepted for the 1981–82 freshman class. The ACT scores of those who enrolled were as follows: 12% between 20 and 23, 12% between 24 and 26, 10% between 27 and 28, and 7% above 28. Admissions decisions are based on the applicant's work in previous schools, recommendations, and ACT scores.

Procedure: Candidates must take the ACT or arrange for a special placement test on campus. Applications should be submitted by August 1 for fall, January 1 for spring, and June 1 for summer. There is

530 NEW MEXICO

an application fee of $15. The university follows a rolling admissions policy.

Special: AP and CLEP are used. Early and deferred admissions are possible; there are no application deadlines.

Transfer: D grades do not transfer. All students must complete, at the university, the last 30 of the 124 credits required for a bachelor's degree. August 1 is the fall semester application deadline; January 1 the spring deadline.

Visiting: Guides are available for informal visits. Visitors may sit in on classes and stay overnight at the school. The office of admissions will handle arrangements.

Financial Aid: Many scholarships and grants-in-aid are awarded to freshmen and upperclassmen in recognition of academic achievement and contribution to campus activities. The university also participates in several federally sponsored programs, including NDSL, SEOG, CWS, BEOG, GSL, Nursing Loan, and Nursing Scholarship. Aid awards, including campus jobs, are generally based on financial need. Sixty-eight percent of students receive aid. The FAF is required of all aid applicants. The application for aid should be filed by March 1.

Foreign Students: Special counseling and special organizations are available for these students.

Admissions: Foreign students must score at least 500 on the TOEFL or at least 75 on the University of Michigan English Language Test. No college entrance exams are required.

Procedure: Applications are due at least 1 month before registration for the fall, spring, or summer term. Foreign students must present proof of adequate funds.

Admissions Contact: Kip Allen, Director of Admissions.

UNIVERSITY OF NEW MEXICO C-2
Albuquerque, New Mexico 87131 (505) 277-2439

F/T: 6097M, 5853W	Faculty:	1038; I, av$
P/T: 2595M, 4101W	Ph.D.'s:	74%
Grad: 2099M, 2157W	S/F Ratio:	12 to 1
Year: sems, ss	Tuition:	$720 ($2232)
Appl: Aug. 1	R and B:	$1770
3686 applied	3197 accepted	2419 enrolled
ACT: 19		LESS COMPETITIVE

The University of New Mexico, established in 1889, is a state-supported institution that offers education in many liberal-arts, science, and professional fields. Its library contains 1,043,936 volumes and 71,300 reels of microfilm, and subscribes to 15,905 periodicals.

Environment: The 600-acre urban campus is located in the eastern section of the city. The 120 buildings exemplify the university's contemporary style, but show strong influence from the Spanish and Pueblo Indian cultures. Living facilities include dormitories, off-campus apartments, fraternity and sorority houses, and married-student housing.

Student Life: About 92% of the students come from New Mexico. About 8% live on campus. About 29% are minority-group members, primarily Hispanic. Campus housing is both coed and single-sex; there are visiting privileges in the single-sex housing. Day-care services are available for a fee. Cars are permitted. Drinking is not allowed on campus. Resident freshman women observe a curfew.

Organizations: There are 10 national fraternities and 7 national sororities on campus to which 26% of the students belong. A student government and special-interest clubs also provide social and cultural activities. The town offers off-campus entertainment.

Sports: The university fields 11 intercollegiate teams for men and 10 for women. There are 16 intramural sports for men and 16 for women.

Handicapped: About 90% of the campus is accessible to the physically handicapped. Special facilities are provided. A braille writer and dictionary, manual interpreters, and transcribers are available. There are also 3 special counselors.

Graduates: The freshman dropout rate is 33%; about 33% remain to graduate.

Services: Free health care, tutoring, remedial instruction, and career and psychological counseling are available to students.

Programs of Study: The university confers the B.A., B.B.A., B.F.A., B.S., B.S.Ed., B.S. in Eng., B.S.Med.Tech., B.S.N., and B.S.Pharm. degrees. Associate, master's, and doctoral degrees are also available. Bachelor's degrees are offered in the following subjects: AREA STUDIES (American, Latin American, Russian), BUSINESS (accounting, business administration, computer science, finance, management, marketing), EDUCATION (bilingual, elementary, English as a second language, English—philosophy, health/physical, industrial, recreation), ENGLISH (creative writing, English, journalism, literature, speech), FINE AND PERFORMING ARTS (art education, art history, dance, music, music education, music history, studio art, theater/dramatics), HEALTH SCIENCES (medical technology, nursing, physical therapy, speech therapy), LANGUAGES (French, German, linguistics, Portuguese, Spanish), MATH AND SCIENCES (astrophysics, biology, chemistry, earth science, geology, life science, physical sciences, physics), PHILOSOPHY (classics, philosophy), PREPROFESSIONAL (architecture, dietetics, engineering, home economics, library science, pharmacy), SOCIAL SCIENCES (anthropology, economics, economics—philosophy, geography, government/political science, history, psychology, social studies, sociology). About 20% of the degrees conferred are in preprofessional studies and 14% are in social sciences.

Required: Required courses vary according to the major.

Special: A cooperative program in engineering and combination degree programs for the M.B.A. are available. Students may also study abroad and earn a general-studies degree.

Honors: The university's General Honors Program is offered to juniors and seniors. Fifteen honor societies are represented on campus.

Admissions: About 87% of those who applied were accepted for the 1981-82 freshman class. The ACT scores of those who enrolled were as follows: 59% scored below 21, 19% between 21 and 23, 10% between 24 and 25, 9% between 26 and 28, and 3% above 28. The candidates should have completed 13 Carnegie units and have achieved at least a C average and good test scores. Other factors are considered in borderline cases.

Procedure: The ACT is required and should be taken in the fall of the senior year. The application and a $15 fee are due August 1 (fall), January 1 (spring), or June 1 (summer). Notification is made on a rolling basis.

Special: An early admissions plan is available. AP and CLEP credit is accepted.

Transfer: For fall 1981, 3565 students applied, 3057 were accepted, and 2240 enrolled. An average of C or better is required. D grades do not transfer. Students must complete, at the university, 30 of the 128 credits required for a bachelor's degree. Application deadlines are the same as those for freshmen.

Visiting: Visits can be arranged through the office of school relations.

Financial Aid: About 50% of all students receive aid. Seventeen percent work part-time on campus. The university awards 540 freshman scholarships, averaging $300. The average aid package awarded to a freshman was $525 in 1981-82. The college is a member of CSS, and the FAF is required. The deadline for financial aid applications is March 1.

Foreign Students: Three percent of the full-time students come from foreign countries. An intensive English program, special counseling, and special organizations are available for these students.

Admissions: Foreign students must achieve a TOEFL score of at least 540 and must take the ACT.

Procedure: Application deadlines are May 1 (fall), October 1 (spring), and April 1 (summer). Foreign students must present proof of adequate funds for 1 year. They must carry health insurance, which is available through the university for a fee.

Admissions Contact: Cynthia M. Stuart, Asst. Director of Admissions.

WESTERN NEW MEXICO UNIVERSITY B-4
Silver City, New Mexico 88061 (505) 538-6106

F/T: 427M, 431W	Faculty:	74; IIA, +$
P/T: 262M, 233W	Ph.D.'s:	51%
Grad: 97M, 124W	S/F Ratio:	12 to 1
Year: sems, ss	Tuition:	$510 ($1136)
Appl: August	R and B:	$1129
409 applied	389 accepted	341 enrolled
ACT: 15		LESS COMPETITIVE

Western New Mexico University, supported by the state, concentrates on teacher education, arts and sciences, and preprofessional training. The library contains 109,000 volumes and 195,000 microfilm items, and subscribes to 673 periodicals.

Environment: The 80-acre campus is located in a rural setting 150 miles from El Paso, Texas. The 25 main buildings include a $3.5 million physical education complex. Living facilities include dormitories and married student housing.

Student Life: About 75% of the students come from New Mexico. Twenty-four percent of the students live on campus. About 95% of entering freshmen come from public schools. About 47% of the students are minority-group members. Campus housing is single-sex; there are visiting privileges. Students may keep cars on campus.

Organizations: Religious counseling and organizations are provided for Protestant and Catholic students. A student government manages many phases of campus life. The Gila Cliff dwellings and the Gila National Forest are located nearby.

Sports: The university competes on an intercollegiate level in 7 sports for men and 5 for women. There are 3 intramural sports for men and 3 for women.

Handicapped: About 90% of the campus is accessible to the physically handicapped. Facilities include wheelchair ramps, special parking, elevators, specially equipped rest rooms, and a swimming pool ramp.

Graduates: An average of 35% of the students drop out at the end of the freshman year, 38% remain to graduate, and 45% of the graduates enter graduate or professional schools.

Services: The following services are available free of charge: career counseling, tutoring, and psychological counseling. Placement services and remedial instruction are provided for a fee.

Programs of Study: The university confers the B.A. and B.S. degrees. Associate and master's degrees are also awarded. Bachelor's degrees are offered in the following subjects: BUSINESS (accounting, business administration, business education, management, marketing), EDUCATION (early childhood, elementary, health/physical, secondary, special), ENGLISH (English), FINE AND PERFORMING ARTS (art, art education, music, music education, theater/dramatics), LANGUAGES (Spanish), MATH AND SCIENCES (biology, botany, chemistry, earth science, geology, mathematics, zoology), PRE PROFESSIONAL (architecture, dentistry, engineering, forestry, home economics, law, medicine, ministry, pharmacy, veterinary), SOCIAL SCIENCES (economics, history, psychology, sociology). About 30% of degrees conferred are in education and 27% are in business.

Special: The university offers a general studies degree and allows student-designed majors.

Admissions: About 95% of those who applied were accepted for the 1981–82 freshman class. Most students who have completed 15 Carnegie units at an accredited high school are accepted, although those who rank in the lowest quarter of their class are discouraged from applying. Candidates should have a grade average of C or better and show potential for leadership. Recommendations from high school officials, friends, and university alumni are welcome. The reputation of the applicant's high school also is considered.

Procedure: The ACT is required, and a personal interview is recommended. Applications should be submitted by August for fall entry, and by January for spring entry; the fee is $10. Notification is on a rolling basis.

Special: CLEP is used.

Transfer: For fall 1981, 62 students applied, 58 were accepted, and 48 enrolled. A 2.0 GPA is required. D grades do not transfer. One year (or two semesters) must be completed in residence; 132 credits are required for a bachelor's degree. Applications should be submitted by August for the fall semester, by January for the spring.

Visiting: Guides are available for informal visits, which are best scheduled in mid-fall and in spring. Visitors may stay at the school. The director of admissions will arrange visits.

Financial Aid: About 85% of all students receive financial aid. About 40% work part-time on campus. The FAF or FFS is required of aid applicants, and applications must be submitted by April 1. Aid is available through NDSL, CWS, BEOG, SEOG, the state, athletic grants, and scholarships. The average award to freshmen is $1500.

Foreign Students: One percent of the full-time students come from foreign countries. Special counseling is available for these students.

Admissions: Foreign students must achieve a TOEFL score of at least 550 and must take the ACT.

Procedure: Application deadlines are June for fall entry and November for spring entry. Foreign students must have a physical examination and must present proof of funds adequate to cover 1 year of study. Health insurance is required and is available through the university.

Admissions Contact: Daniel R. Chacon, Director of Admissions.

NEW YORK

ADELPHI UNIVERSITY D–5
Garden City, New York 11530 (516) 663-1104

F/T: 1470M, 3074W	Faculty: 383; I, av$
P/T: 654M, 1457W	Ph.D.'s: 61%
Grad: 1720M, 3461W	S/F Ratio: 15 to 1
Year: 4-1-4, ss	Tuition: $4660
Appl: open	R and B: $2600
3565 applied	2281 accepted	788 enrolled
SAT: 490V 474M		COMPETITIVE

Adelphi University, a private liberal arts institution, was founded in 1896. The library houses 377,941 volumes, 353,722 microform items and 27,481 listening and visual materials, and subscribes to 3292 periodicals.

Environment: The 75-acre suburban campus is located 25 miles from New York City. There are 17 buildings, including a 1.5 million dollar addition to the library and 5 dormitories.

Student Life: Most of the students are nearby residents. Fifteen percent come from out of state. About 20% of the students live on campus. Eighteen percent are minority-group members. University housing is both single-sex and coed. There are visiting privileges in single-sex housing. Upperclassmen may keep cars on campus.

Organizations: There are 4 fraternities and 5 sororities on campus. Ten percent of the men are fraternity members; 8% of the women belong to sororities. Clubs, special-interest groups, and a wide variety of extracurricular activities are available.

Sports: In addition to intercollegiate competition in 8 sports for men and 7 for women, there are 9 intramural sports for men and 9 for women.

Handicapped: Special facilities for physically handicapped students include wheelchair ramps, special parking, elevators, and special class scheduling.

Services: Free health care, psychological counseling, career counseling, placement services, tutoring, and remedial instruction are offered.

Programs of Study: The university awards the B.A., B.S., B.F.A., and B.B.A. degrees. Master's and doctoral degrees are also granted. The bachelor's degree is offered in the following subjects: AREA STUDIES (American, Latin American), BUSINESS (accounting, computer science, finance, management), EDUCATION (elementary), ENGLISH (English, speech), FINE AND PERFORMING ARTS (art, art education, communications, dance, music, theater/dramatics), HEALTH SCIENCES (medical technology, nursing, speech therapy), LANGUAGES (French, German, Spanish), MATH AND SCIENCES (biology, chemistry, earth science, mathematics, physics), PHILOSOPHY (philosophy, religion), PREPROFESSIONAL (engineering, law, medicine, social work), SOCIAL SCIENCES (anthropology, economics, political science, history, psychology, sociology).

Special: Junior year study abroad may be arranged. There is a 3-2 cooperative program in engineering.

Honors: There is an honors program in liberal studies.

Admissions: About 64% of the applicants were accepted for the 1981–82 freshman class. Of those who enrolled, the SAT scores were as follows: Verbal—68% scored below 500, 19% between 500 and 599, 5% between 600 and 700, and 1% above 700; Math—53% scored below 500, 31% between 500 and 599, 8% between 600 and 700, and 1% above 700. Candidates should graduate from approved high schools with 16 academic units and should receive good recommendations from their schools. Advanced placement or honors courses, extracurricular activities records, and leadership potential also are considered important.

Procedure: The SAT or ACT is required. The application deadline is open. Freshmen are admitted in the fall and spring. A rolling admissions plan is in operation. The application fee is $20.

Special: There are early and deferred admissions plans. AP and CLEP credit is offered.

Transfer: For fall 1981, 1791 students applied, 1113 were accepted, and 652 enrolled. A GPA of 2.5 is required. D grades do not transfer. Thirty credits must be earned in residence of the 120 needed for a bachelor's degree. Application deadlines are open.

532 NEW YORK

Visiting: Interviews with an admissions counselor and campus tours may be arranged by contacting the admissions office at (516) 663-1100.

Financial Aid: Seventy-five percent of students receive financial aid. Thirteen percent work part-time on campus. Scholarships, grants, loans, and campus employment (CWS) are available. In addition to financial aid awards based on need, there are also academic scholarships. Effective September 1982, freshmen who graduate in the top 10% of their high school class or who have a 3.0 academic average and 1100 combined score on the SAT are awarded one-third of their tuition a year for their 4 years at Adelphi as long as they maintain a 3.0 GPA. Transfer students with an associate degree and a 3.3 GPA or better receive one-third of their tuition per year for their 2 years at Adelphi. The university is a member of CSS. The FAF is required. Application deadlines are open.

Foreign Students: An intensive English course, an intensive English program in the summer, special counseling, and special organizations are available for foreign students.

Admissions: Foreign students must score 550 on the TOEFL. They may also take the SAT.

Procedure: Application deadlines are open; students are admitted to the fall and spring semesters. Foreign students must present proof of funds adequate to cover 4 years of study.

Admissions Contact: Susan D. Reardon, Director of Admissions.

ALBANY COLLEGE OF PHARMACY D-3
Albany, New York 12208 (518) 445-7221

F/T: 255M, 298W Faculty: 29; IIB, ++$
P/T: 1M, 4W Ph.D.'s: 62%
Grad: none S/F Ratio: 18 to 1
Year: sems Tuition: $2907
Appl: open R and B: n/app
230 applied 193 accepted 110 enrolled
SAT: 469V 551M COMPETITIVE

Albany College of Pharmacy, founded in 1881, is a division of Union University offering undergraduate training in pharmacy and medical technology. The library contains 6636 volumes and 100 microfilms, and subscribes to 100 periodicals.

Environment: The urban campus is located in 1 central building in downtown Albany. A new wing, which will provide more classroom and library space, is under construction. There is no on-campus housing.

Student Life: About 98% of the students come from New York. Three percent are minority-group members. All students live off campus. Students may keep cars on campus.

Organizations: There are 3 fraternities and 1 sorority; 46% of the men and 26% of the women belong to them. The college offers the traditional extracurricular activities as well. The Albany capital district and museums are nearby.

Sports: The college fields 4 intercollegiate teams for men and 4 for women. There are 6 intramural sports for men and 4 for women.

Handicapped: There are no special facilities at the college for the physically handicapped at this time, although construction is in progress.

Graduates: By the end of the freshman year, about 15% of the students withdraw; 68% remain to graduate. About 8% of the graduates go on to further study. Ninety-two percent pursue careers in business and industry.

Services: Placement services, tutoring, remedial instruction, and career and psychological counseling are provided to students free of charge. Health care is offered on a fee basis.

Programs of Study: The B.S.Med.Tech. and B.S.Pharm. degrees are conferred. Master's degrees are also awarded. Bachelor's degrees are offered in the following subjects: HEALTH SCIENCES (medical technology), PREPROFESSIONAL (pharmacy). About 95% of the students major in pharmacy.

Required: All students must complete a core curriculum.

Special: AP credit is offered.

Honors: The Rho Chi honor society has a chapter on campus.

Admissions: About 84% of those who applied were accepted for the 1981-82 freshman class. SAT scores of those who enrolled were as follows: Verbal—64% scored below 500, 28% between 500 and 599, 8% between 600 and 700, and 0% above 700; Math—20% scored below 500, 59% between 500 and 599, 18% between 600 and 700, and 3% above 700. Applicants must be high school graduates; they should have at least an 80 average, and rank in the top half of their graduating class. Sixteen Carnegie units are required. Other important factors are advanced placement or honors courses, school recommendations, and impressions made during an interview.

Procedure: The SAT is required. There are no application deadlines, but students are advised to apply as early as possible. A rolling admissions plan is used. Freshmen are admitted only in the fall. There is a $10 application fee.

Special: The college has an early decision plan with a December 1 notification date.

Transfer: For fall 1981, 92 students applied, 50 were accepted, and 33 enrolled. A GPA of 3.0 is recommended for transfer; D grades are not accepted. The application fee for transfers is $20. Three years must be spent in residence; 160 credits are required for a bachelor's degree. Application deadlines are open.

Visiting: No regular orientations are held for prospective students, but guides are available for informal visits to the college. Visitors may sit in on classes, but may not stay overnight at the school. Weekdays, when college is in session, are the best times to visit. The admissions office handles arrangements.

Financial Aid: About 86% of the students receive financial assistance. Eight percent work part-time on campus. The college is a member of CSS. Scholarships (none available to freshmen), federal loans, and state grants are offered. The FAF is required. The deadline for applications is March 1.

Foreign Students: Fewer than 1% of the full-time students come from foreign countries.

Admissions: Foreign students must take the TOEFL and the SAT.

Procedure: Foreign students are admitted in the fall semester. They must present proof of adequate funds.

Admissions Contact: Janis L. Fisher, Director of Admissions/Registrar.

ALFRED UNIVERSITY B-4
Alfred, New York 14802 (607) 871-2115

F/T: 984M, 895W Faculty: 136; IIA, av$
P/T: 39M, 164W Ph.D.'s: 68%
Grad: 123M, 118W S/F Ratio: 14 to 1
Year: sems, ss Tuition: $5650
Appl: Feb. 1 R and B: $2270
1775 applied 1250 accepted 480 enrolled
SAT: 500V 545M ACT: 24 VERY COMPETITIVE

Alfred University, founded in 1836, is a private liberal arts university offering undergraduate and graduate instruction in a broad range of programs. Undergraduate divisions include the College of Liberal Arts, the College of Nursing and Health Care, the School of Business and Administration, and the New York College of Ceramics, with divisions of engineering and art. The library contains 200,000 volumes and 11,500 microfilm items, and subscribes to 2500 periodicals.

Environment: The 232-acre rural campus, located in a small town 70 miles south of Rochester, has 53 buildings. Sixteen dormitories house 1200 students.

Student Life: Seventy percent of the students are from New York, 23% are from middle Atlantic and New England states, and 6% are from other states. About 85% reside on campus in dormitories or approved housing. About 81% of entering freshmen come from public schools. Upperclassmen are not required to live in the dorms. Two percent of the students are minority-group members. University housing is coed. Students may keep cars on campus.

Organizations: Twenty-two percent of the men belong to 5 fraternities and 10% of the women belong to 3 sororities. Numerous extracurricular activities and groups are sponsored by the university.

Sports: Men compete intercollegiately in 9 sports, women in 9. There are 17 intramural sports for men and 17 for women.

Handicapped: Special facilities for handicapped students include wheelchair ramps, parking areas, elevators, and specially equipped rest rooms. Special class scheduling is possible.

Graduates: The freshman dropout rate is 14%. Sixty-five percent remain to graduate. Forty percent of the graduates pursue advanced degrees; 2% enter medical school, 1% dental school, and 10% law school. Sixty percent enter careers in business and industry.

Services: Students receive the following services free of charge: psychological counseling, placement, career counseling, health care, and tutoring.

Programs of Study: The university confers the B.S., B.A., and B.F.A. degrees. Master's and doctoral degrees are also granted. Bachelor's degrees are offered in the following subjects: BUSINESS (accounting, business administration, business economics, business education, computer science, finance, management, marketing), EDUCATION (elementary, secondary, special), ENGLISH (English), FINE AND PERFORMING ARTS (art, art education, ceramics, design, film/photography, mixed media, printmaking, sculpture, studio art, theater/dramatics), HEALTH SCIENCES (nursing), LANGUAGES (French, German, Spanish), MATH AND SCIENCES (biology, chemistry, computer science, ecology/environmental science, general science, geology, mathematics, physics), PHILOSOPHY (humanities, philosophy), PREPROFESSIONAL (dentistry, engineering, forestry, law, library science, medicine, veterinary), SOCIAL SCIENCES (economics, gerontology, government/political science, history, psychology, sociology). About 50% of the degrees are conferred in the arts.

Required: All undergraduates are required to take physical education.

Special: The College of Ceramics, the only one of its kind, offers superior programs and facilities in ceramic engineering and science, art, and design. The tuition for this division differs from that of the other colleges. In-state students pay $1585 per year; out-of-state students pay $2285 per year. Interdisciplinary programs and flexibility permit students to study in a number of divisions. Students can design their own majors. A study-abroad program includes cooperatives with the Chapman College Afloat. A 3-2 engineering program with Columbia University, a Washington, D.C. Semester, a U.N. Semester, and a 4 + 1 M.B.A. program with Clarkson College are available. Combined B.A.-B.S. degrees and the B.G.S. degree are possible.

Honors: There are 10 honor societies on campus.

Admissions: Seventy percent of those who applied were accepted for the 1981–82 freshman class. Of those who enrolled, the SAT scores were as follows: Verbal—50% scored below 500, 36% between 500 and 599, 12% between 600 and 700, and 2% above 700; Math—25% scored below 500, 46% between 500 and 599, 25% between 600 and 700, and 4% above 700. Eighty-seven percent of the freshmen were in the top two-fifths of their high school class. Candidates should be graduates of accredited high schools (or have passed the GED exam), have completed 16 Carnegie units, and in most cases, have a GPA of 3.2. Other factors are recommendations, personal qualities, and advanced placement or honors courses. Some preference is given to children of alumni and applicants from geographic areas that are not well represented. There is special consideration given to students from culturally disadvantaged backgrounds.

Procedure: The ACT or SAT is required. The application deadline is February 1 (fall). New freshmen are also admitted at midyear. Late applications are taken on a space-available basis. Applicants must apply to the division in which they are interested. A personal interview is recommended. A modified rolling admissions plan is used, and the CRDA is observed. The application should be accompanied by a $20 fee.

Special: There are early decision and early admissions plans. AP and CLEP credit is given.

Transfer: For fall 1981, 350 students applied, 280 were accepted, and 175 enrolled. Transfers are accepted for all classes. A GPA of 2.0 and good standing at the former school is required. There is a residency requirement of 1 year. At least 30 semester hours must be completed at the university, out of the 124 needed for a bachelor's degree. The application deadlines are August 1 (fall) and December 1 (spring).

Visiting: There are scheduled orientations for prospective students. Informal visits are possible weekdays and Saturday mornings. The admissions office should be contacted for arrangements. Visitors may sit in on classes and stay overnight at the university.

Financial Aid: Sixty-two percent of the students receive financial aid. About 47% work part-time on campus. Average aid to freshmen from all sources is $4884. There are scholarships, NDEA loans, and NDSL. CWS funds are available in all departments. Financial aid packages are available. Tuition may be paid in installments. The university is a member of the CSS. The FAF is required. Need and academic potential are the main considerations in the awarding of financial aid. The application deadline for priority consideration is February 15.

Foreign Students: About 1% of the full-time students come from foreign countries. The university offers these students special counseling and special organizations.

Admissions: Foreign students must score 550 on the TOEFL. No college entrance examination is required.

Procedure: The application deadline is March 15 (fall). Foreign students must have the university's health form completed by a physician. They must also present proof of funds adequate to cover 4 years of study.

Admissions Contact: Paul P. Priggon, Director of Admissions.

ARNOLD AND MARIE SCHWARTZ COLLEGE OF PHARMACY AND HEALTH SCIENCES
D-5

Brooklyn, New York 11201   (212) 330-2710

F/T: 455M, 300W		Faculty:	35; n/av
P/T: none		Ph.D.'s:	n/av
Grad: 120M, 30W		S/F Ratio:	11 to 1
Year: sems, ss		Tuition:	$4710
Appl: open		R and B:	$2660
266 applied	196 accepted		102 enrolled
SAT: 470V 480M			COMPETITIVE

Arnold and Marie Schwartz College of Pharmacy and Health Sciences, formerly the Brooklyn College of Pharmacy, was chartered in 1886 and became affiliated with Long Island University in 1929. The Library Learning Center, which houses the pharmacy collection, contains 290,000 volumes and thousands of other materials.

Environment: The college is located in central Brooklyn in a modern pharmacy complex and classroom building specially designed for its curriculum. Residence facilities are provided in a 12-story dormitory. There is also a laboratory and library complex.

Student Life: Eighty percent of the students are from New York. About 80% of the students come from public schools. Forty percent are minority-group members. College housing is coed. Alcohol is prohibited on campus.

Organizations: Extracurricular activities include service clubs, an international students' club, publications, and student government. A large student branch of the American Pharmaceutical Association (SAPHA) is active on campus. One fraternity and 1 sorority have chapters on campus.

Sports: There are intercollegiate and intramural sports for both men and women.

Handicapped: The entire campus is accessible to handicapped students. Facilities include wheelchair ramps, parking areas, elevators, lowered drinking fountains, and specially equipped rest rooms. Special class scheduling is also available. Four counselors are available to handicapped students.

Graduates: The freshman dropout rate is 10%; 70% remain to graduate. Twenty-five percent of the graduates pursue advanced degrees; 1% enter medical school and 1% enter dental school. Forty percent pursue careers in business or industry.

Services: Psychological counseling, tutoring, remedial instruction, placement, and career counseling are offered free of charge to students. Health care is available on a fee basis.

Programs of Study: The college confers the B.S.Pharm. degree. Master's programs are also available. The bachelor's degree is conferred in the following subject: PREPROFESSIONAL (pharmacy).

Required: All students must follow a set sequence of courses, which provides a basic liberal arts background in the first 2 years and prepares students intensively in the third, fourth, and fifth year for the major field.

Admissions: Seventy-four percent of those who applied were accepted for the 1981–82 freshman class. The SAT scores of those who enrolled were as follows: Verbal—70% scored below 500, 20% between 500 and 599, 10% between 600 and 700, and 0% above 700; Math—70% scored below 500, 20% between 500 and 599, 10% between 600 and 700, and 0% above 700. Candidates should be graduates of accredited high schools, have completed 16 units, rank in the upper half of their graduating class, and have a 2.0 GPA or an average of 80 or above. Other considerations are evidence of special talent, recommendations, and advanced placement or honor courses.

Procedure: Either the SAT or ACT is required. The application deadline is open. Notification is on a rolling basis. There is a $15 application fee.

Special: AP credit is granted.

Transfer: For fall 1981, 220 students applied, 195 were accepted, and 125 enrolled. A 2.5 GPA is required. D grades do not transfer.

534 NEW YORK

There is a 2-year residency requirement. Sixty to 100 credits must be completed in residence, out of the 165 needed for a bachelor's degree. The application deadline is open.

Visiting: There are regularly scheduled orientations for prospective students. Guides are available for informal campus visits. Visitors may sit in on classes. Visits are best scheduled on weekdays. The admissions office should be contacted for arrangements.

Financial Aid: About 90% of the students have received financial aid in recent years. A wide range of financial aid is available, including scholarships and state and federal loans. The college is a member of CSS. The FAF is required. The application deadlines are May 15 (fall) and November 15 (spring).

Foreign Students: Six percent of the full-time students come from foreign countries. The college offers these students special counseling and special organizations.

Admissions: Foreign students must score 500 on the TOEFL. They must also take the college's own English proficiency examination. They must take the SAT or ACT and must have a combined score of 850 on the SAT.

Procedure: The application deadlines are May 1 (fall) and November 1 (spring). Foreign students must present proof of funds adequate for 24 credits. They must carry health insurance, which is available through the college for a fee.

Admissions Contact: F.A. Mantovani, Director of Admissions.

BARD COLLEGE   D-4
Annandale-on-Hudson, New York 12504   (914) 758-6822

F/T: 323M, 436W	Faculty: 55; IIB, ++$
P/T: 12M, 19W	Ph.D.'s: 60%
Grad: 15M, 15W	S/F Ratio: 10 to 1
Year: 4-1-4	Tuition: $7708
Appl: Mar. 15	R and B: $2555
802 applied	515 accepted	210 enrolled
SAT, ACT: not required		VERY COMPETITIVE

Bard College, founded in 1860, is a small, private college of liberal arts and sciences, which offers programs of individualized education designed to foster creative thought and the ability to effectively communicate that thought. There is much stress on independent work, and students play an active role in assessing and planning their intellectual growth throughout their undergraduate years. The library contains 146,000 volumes and 5195 microfilm items, and subscribes to 575 periodicals.

Environment: Nestled in a rural setting, the 1000-acre campus overlooks the Hudson River, 20 miles from Poughkeepsie and 100 miles north of New York City. A new art institute has just been completed. About 600 students are accommodated in college housing, which ranges in style from two Hudson River mansions to small, modern modular units.

Student Life: Bard students represent 37 states; their backgrounds are culturally and academically varied. Fewer than 50% of the students are from New York State. About 70% of entering freshmen come from public schools. Nineteen percent of the students live on campus. College housing is coed and single-sex; students in single-sex housing have visiting privileges. Students may keep cars on campus.

Organizations: There are no fraternities or sororities. Although the emphasis is on academic endeavor, there are many opportunities for participation in cultural, social, and cocurricular activities. Special academic interests are supported by various clubs, performing groups, and publications. The Bard Theater of Drama and Dance offers about 30 highly professional productions each year, to which admission is free.

Sports: The college fields 4 intercollegiate teams for men and 5 for women. There are 4 intramural sports for men and 4 for women.

Handicapped: There are some special facilities for the physically handicapped. Wheelchair ramps, special parking, and specially equipped rest rooms are available.

Graduates: The freshman dropout rate is 3%, and 55% of the freshmen remain to graduate. Fifty-five percent of the graduates go on to further education; 2% enter medical school, 1% enter dental school, and 5% enter law school. Another 40% pursue careers in business and industry.

Services: Students receive the following services free of charge: placement service, career counseling, health care, psychological counseling, tutoring, and remedial instruction.

Programs of Study: The academic work at Bard is organized under 4 divisions: Arts; Languages and Literature; Natural Sciences and Mathematics; and Social Studies. Students can become candidates for the B.A. degree in any of these divisions or concentrate in an individual discipline. The M.F.A. is also awarded. The bachelor's degree is awarded in the following subjects: AREA STUDIES (American, Asian, Black/Afro-American, community—regional/environmental, Latin American, Russian, urban), ENGLISH (creative writing, English, literature), FINE AND PERFORMING ARTS (art, art history, dance, film/photography, music, studio art, theater/dramatics), LANGUAGES (French, German, Greek/Latin, Hebrew, Spanish), MATH AND SCIENCES (biochemistry, biology, botany, chemistry, earth science, ecology/environmental science, mathematics, natural sciences, physical sciences, physics), PHILOSOPHY (classics, humanities, philosophy, religion), PREPROFESSIONAL (engineering, forestry, law, medicine), SOCIAL SCIENCES (anthropology, economics, government/political science, history, history of social ideas, psychology, social sciences, sociology, women's studies). Thirty-seven percent of degrees are conferred in fine and performing arts, 22% in social sciences, and 21% in languages and literature.

Required: All freshmen must take a 1-semester basic English course and a year-long Freshman Seminar. By the end of the sophomore year at least one 1-semester course in each of 3 divisions must be successfully completed; a second 1-semester course in each division is required for graduation.

Special: Each year of the 4-year curriculum is designed as a foundation for the next. Freshman Seminars create opportunities for exchanges with classmates, Sophomore Moderation enables students to evaluate their first 2 years and to plan for the next 2, and Major Conference during the junior year prepares the student for work on the Senior Project, an independent investigation in a subject chosen by the student. Underclassmen may experiment with a trial major before making a definite choice. Third-year students may participate in the Junior Year Abroad program, although this is not sponsored by the college. A student may spend the 4-week winter term in one of several ways: working off campus at a job usually related to the specialized field of study; embarking on an independent study project away from the college; taking a course at another college; or participating in the winter college, which offers a variety of courses. Bard is a member of the Associated Colleges of the Mid-Hudson Area, making cross-enrollments with member schools possible. A 3-2 engineering program is available in conjunction with Columbia University, and students may pursue a combined B.A.-M.S. degree in forestry and environmental studies with Duke University. Student-designed majors are permitted.

Honors: Five fellowship societies—1 for lower college students, 1 for languages and literature, 1 for the creative and performing arts, 1 for social studies, and 1 for science and math—have been established to recognize academic and artistic excellence.

Admissions: Sixty-four percent of those who applied were accepted for the 1981–82 freshman class. In selecting candidates for admission, Bard relies heavily on the secondary school record (advanced placement or honors courses, evidence of special talent, extracurricular activities) and essays which are submitted in conjunction with the application. Candidates must have completed at least 16 units of college preparatory work. Applicants should have had experience in independent study and research in the humanities or sciences, or in performance or creative work in the arts. A personal interview is strongly recommended.

Procedure: Neither the SAT nor the ACT is required. Application deadlines are March 15 for fall and January 1 for spring; freshmen are admitted both semesters. There is a $20 application fee.

Special: Early and deferred admissions plans are available, and there is an immediate decision plan whereby an applicant may complete the admissions process and be notified of the college's decision on the same day.

Transfer: For fall 1981, 154 students applied, 118 were accepted, and 65 enrolled. Students may not transfer into the senior class. A strong academic record with a minimum C+ grade average is required. Evidence of writing ability is also required, and evidence of other talents is helpful. An interview is recommended. D grades do not transfer. Students must complete 2 years in residence and complete at least 60 of the 124 credits necessary for a bachelor's degree.

Visiting: Prospective students may make an appointment to visit the campus. Such visits generally include an interview and an informal tour. Arrangements can be made through the admissions office.

Financial Aid: Approximately 54% of the students receive financial assistance, not including guaranteed student loans. Forty percent work part-time on campus. Average aid to freshmen is $4013. Financial aid is available from scholarships (including EOG) and loans (including NDSL). The college is a member of the CSS and requires the FAF. Applications for aid must be filed by March 15 for the fall semester or December 15 for spring.

Foreign Students: Five percent of the full-time students come from foreign countries. The college offers these students special counseling and special organizations.

Admissions: Foreign students must achieve a TOEFL score of at least 550. No college entrance exam must be taken.

Procedure: Application deadlines are March 15 (fall) and January 1 (spring). Foreign students must present a completed school health form and proof of funds adequate to cover the first year of study, with a projection for the full 4 years. They must also carry health insurance, which is available through the college for a fee.

Admissions Contact: Karen Wilcox, Director of Admissions.

BORICUA COLLEGE D–5
Broooklyn, New York 11211 (212) 782-2200
New York, New York 10032 (212) 865-9000

F/T: 350M, 654W	Faculty: 50; n/av
P/T: none	Ph.D.'s: 15%
Grad: none	S/F Ratio: 20 to 1
Year: tri	Tuition: $3500
Appl: see profile	R and B: n/app
436 applied	396 accepted	340 enrolled
SAT, ACT: not required		LESS COMPETITIVE

Boricua College, a private institution founded in 1973, offers 2- and 4-year degree programs for bilingual students. Designed to meet the educational needs of Puerto Ricans and other Spanish-speaking people in the United States, the college requires study in the areas of applied studies, cultural studies, and theoretical studies.

Environment: The college has Learning Centers in the urban settings of Manhattan and Brooklyn. There are no residence halls.

Student Life: All students are residents of New York State, and all are members of minority groups.

Organizations: Campus groups include a student council that sponsors social events, a student newspaper, drama and music ensembles, and a business club that schedules tours of Hispanic businesses.

Sports: Student-faculty sports nights are scheduled.

Handicapped: No special facilities are provided for handicapped students.

Services: The college provides career and psychological counseling, tutoring, and placement aid.

Programs of Study: The college confers the B.S. degree in: BUSINESS (business administration), EDUCATION (elementary), and PREPROFESSIONAL (human services). Associate degrees also are available in liberal arts.

Special: Nontraditional methods of teaching include individualized instruction, small learning groups, and independent study. In addition, students participate in internships throughout their 4 years of study. They are placed in jobs related to their career objectives.

Admissions: Ninety-one percent of those who applied were accepted for the 1981–82 freshman class. Applicants must be high school graduates or have earned a GED, and must demonstrate a working knowledge of English and Spanish to a faculty panel. Two letters of recommendation are required. Standardized test scores are also considered in the admissions decision.

Procedure: The college administers standardized tests, including the California Achievement Test, to prospective students. Applications should be submitted 6 weeks before the beginning of a semester. Notification is on a rolling basis. There is a $5 application fee.

Transfers: Applicants with A.A. degrees may transfer up to 60 credits; others may transfer up to 30 credits. Requirements are the same as those for freshmen, with minimum scores of 12.0 on the language exam and 7.0 on the math. D grades do not transfer. Students must earn, at the college, 64 of the 124 credits necessary for a bachelor's degree.

Financial Aid: Ninety-five percent of the students receive aid. Fifteen percent work part-time on campus. Grants and loans are also available. Most awards are need-based. The college is a member of CSS and requires the FAF. Applications must be submitted by March 31.

Admissions Contact: Senior Officer for Admissions.

CANISIUS COLLEGE A–3
Buffalo, New York 14208 (716) 883-7000

F/T: 1443M, 976W	Faculty: 162; IIA, +$
P/T: 138M, 268W	Ph.D.'s: 83%
Grad: 380M, 239W	S/F Ratio: 18 to 1
Year: sems, ss	Tuition: $4220
Appl: open	R and B: $2250
1810 applied	1185 accepted	603 enrolled
SAT: 477V 533M	ACT: 22	COMPETITIVE

Canisius College, founded in 1870 as a Roman Catholic college, is now a private, independent liberal arts institution in the Jesuit tradition. The library houses 221,895 volumes and 10,941 microfilm items, and subscribes to 1213 periodicals.

Environment: The 19-acre campus is located within the city limits of Buffalo. Among the buildings on the campus are a 6-floor dorm for 300 men and a similar structure for 300 women.

Student Life: About 90% of the students are residents of New York State. About 60% come from public schools. Twenty-five percent of the students live on campus. Eighty-two percent of the students are Catholic, 9% Protestant, and fewer than 1% Jewish; about 3% belong to other denominations; and 4% claim no religious affiliation. About 6% of the students are minority-group members. College housing is single-sex; there are visiting privileges. Students may keep cars on campus.

Organizations: One national fraternity and 1 national sorority are represented on campus. Clubs, special-interest groups, and social and cultural events are available.

Sports: There are 12 intercollegiate sports for men and 9 for women. There are 6 intramural sports for men and 5 for women.

Handicapped: Ninety percent of the campus is accessible to physically handicapped students. For their convenience there are lowered telephones and drinking fountains, special parking, specially equipped rest rooms, special class scheduling, wheelchair ramps, and elevators. There are 2 special counselors for these students.

Graduates: About 18% of the freshmen drop out by the end of their first year. Fifty-five percent remain to graduate, and 29% of these continue their studies in graduate or professional schools.

Services: Free health care, psychological counseling, tutoring, remedial instruction, placement service, and career counseling are available.

Programs of Study: Canisius confers the B.A. and B.S. degrees. Master's degrees are also offered. Bachelor's degrees are offered in the following subjects: AREA STUDIES (urban), BUSINESS (accounting, business education, computer science, finance, management, marketing), EDUCATION (health/physical, secondary), ENGLISH (English), FINE AND PERFORMING ARTS (art history), HEALTH SCIENCES (medical technology), LANGUAGES (French, German), MATH AND SCIENCES (biochemistry, biology, chemistry, mathematics, physics), PHILOSOPHY (philosophy, religion), PREPROFESSIONAL (dentistry, engineering, forestry, law, medicine, veterinary), SOCIAL SCIENCES (economics, government/political science, history, international relations, psychology, sociology).

Required: All students must take general education courses, including philosophy and religious studies.

Special: Internships are offered to qualified students in the School of Business and the School of Arts and Sciences. There is a cooperative program in fashion merchandising with the Fashion Institute of Technology.

Honors: Five national honor societies have chapters on campus. There is also an honors core curriculum.

Admissions: Sixty-five percent of the applicants for the 1981–82 freshman class were accepted. The SAT scores of those who enrolled were as follows: Verbal—58% scored below 500, 34% between 500 and 599, 8% between 600 and 700, and fewer than 1% above 700; Math—31% scored below 500, 47% between 500 and 599, 18% between 600 and 700, and 3% above 700. Candidates should rank in the upper 50% of their graduating class and should have completed 16 high school units. The minimum grade average is 80%. Advanced placement or honor courses, impressions made during the interview, and recommendations by school officials are also important.

Procedure: The SAT or ACT is required. There are no deadlines for application, and freshmen are admitted each semester. Admissions are made on a rolling basis. The application fee is $15.

Special: There are early admissions and deferred admissions plans. AP and CLEP credit is offered.

536 NEW YORK

Transfer: For fall 1981, 302 applications were received, 220 were accepted, and 156 students enrolled. A GPA of 2.25 is required. D grades do not transfer. Thirty hours must be taken in residence, out of the 120 needed for a bachelor's degree. Application deadlines are open.

Visiting: Regularly scheduled orientations take place in the fall with open house. Informal visits (Mondays through Fridays at 3 P.M.) may be arranged through the office of admissions. Visitors may stay overnight at the school. They will be provided with guides, and they may sit in on classes.

Financial Aid: Eighty percent of students receive financial aid. Twenty percent work part-time on campus. Average aid awarded to freshmen from all sources is $4280. The college is a member of CSS. The FAF is required. Financial aid applications must be submitted by March 1 (fall) or November 1 (spring).

Foreign Students: Fewer than 1% of the full-time students come from foreign countries.

Admissions: Foreign students must score 500 on the TOEFL. No college entrance examination is required.

Procedure: Application deadlines are open. Foreign students must present proof of health. They must also present proof of adequate funds.

Admissions Contact: Penelope H. Lips, Director of Admissions.

CITY UNIVERSITY OF NEW YORK

The City University of New York (CUNY), a public institution supported by both the city and the state, consists of 9 senior colleges, 7 community colleges, the University Graduate Center, and the affiliated Mount Sinai School of Medicine. The 9 senior colleges are Bernard M. Baruch College, Brooklyn College, City College, Hunter College, John Jay College of Criminal Justice, Herbert H. Lehman College, Queens College, College of Staten Island, and York College. The 7 community colleges are Borough of Manhattan Community College, Bronx Community College, Eugenio Maria de Hostos Community College, LaGuardia Community College, Kingsborough Community College, Medgar Evers College, and Queensborough Community College. Also included among CUNY colleges is the New York Technical College, with campuses in Manhattan and Brooklyn.

The Free Academy, now City College, which is the oldest college in the city university system, was established in 1847; in 1961 the 7 municipal colleges became the City University of New York through state legislation. The full-time undergraduate enrollment is approximately 103,472; the part-time enrollment is approximately 52,805. Master's degree programs are offered by the senior colleges and the Graduate Center; the university doctoral program offers the Ph.D. in 26 academic disciplines. To widen opportunity, the university has developed a program to help economically and educationally disadvantaged high school youth enter and stay in college through the College Discovery Program and SEEK (Search for Education, Elevation, and Knowledge).

Almost 200 programs are offered in 5 broad areas of study: community and social services; business; architecture, engineering, and related technologies; health sciences; and liberal arts and sciences. Preprofessional courses and academic majors from the diverse courses of study are available.

See the individual profiles for all information on the senior colleges of the university.

Standards: Under the open admissions plan adopted by the Board of Trustees in July, 1969, all New York State residents who receive a high school diploma are eligible for admission provided that they meet the health standards of the City University. A New York State Equivalency Diploma or the General Education Department Examination may be substituted for the high school diploma; a high school certificate is not acceptable. Students with an academic average of at least 80 or a rank in the upper 66% of their high school class are eligible for admission to the senior colleges; those with lower averages or class ranks are eligible for admission to the community colleges and the technical college. Students are given their choice of college in the order of their preference and seat availability.

CITY UNIVERSITY OF NEW YORK/   D-5
BERNARD M. BARUCH COLLEGE
New York, New York 10010   (212) 725-3158

F/T: 4195M, 4421W	Faculty: 500; IIA, ++$
P/T: 1927M, 2045W	Ph.D.'s: 76%
Grad: 1437M, 901W	S/F Ratio: 22 to 1
Year: sems, ss	Tuition: $976 ($1476)
Appl: open	R and B: n/app
SAT, ACT: not required	COMPETITIVE

Bernard M. Baruch College, which was originally a school of business attached to City College, became a separate unit of the City University of New York in 1968. It offers undergraduate programs in business, education, and liberal arts and sciences. The library contains 229,000 volumes and subscribes to 1500 periodicals.

Environment: The college is located in New York City. There are no dormitory facilities.

Student Life: Ninety-five percent of the students are from New York. All students live off campus.

Organizations: There are over 100 extracurricular activities and groups, the most active of which are Pride, Hillel, the Accounting Society, and the African Action Association. The major social events on campus are films, dances, receptions, concerts, art exhibitions, and small group discussions. Fraternities and sororities are on campus; 3% of the men and 2% of the women belong. Additional activities include choral groups, musical theater, student government, symphony orchestra, concert band, jazz band, and student newspaper.

Sports: Baruch College competes on an intercollegiate level in 8 sports for men and 5 for women. There are 5 intramural sports for men and 5 for women.

Graduates: The freshman dropout rate is 32%; 50% remain to graduate.

Services: Students receive the following services free of charge: career counseling, placement service, psychological counseling, tutoring, and remedial instruction. Health care is provided on a fee basis.

Programs of Study: The college confers B.A., B.B.A., and B.S. degrees. Master's degrees are also awarded. Bachelor's degrees are offered in the following subjects: BUSINESS (accounting, business education, computer science, economics, finance, industrial psychology, management, marketing, office administration and technology, public administration, real estate/insurance), EDUCATION (early childhood, elementary, secondary, special), ENGLISH (English, journalism, literature, speech), FINE AND PERFORMING ARTS (art, music, studio art, theater/dramatics), LANGUAGES (French, Hebrew, Spanish), MATH AND SCIENCES (biology, chemistry, mathematics, statistics), PHILOSOPHY (philosophy), PREPROFESSIONAL (law, medicine, pharmacy, social work, veterinary), SOCIAL SCIENCES (economics, government/political science, history, international relations, psychology, social sciences, sociology).

Special: The School of Liberal Arts and Sciences offers 3 other majors (art, natural science, and Romance languages) that require additional credits in the major field. A combined B.B.A.-M.B.A. can be earned in statistics, operations research, computer methodology, and other fields. The college participates in the CUNY study-abroad programs. Additional special academic programs include cooperative education, double majors, independent study, and internships.

Honors: Honors courses are available at the college. Six honor societies have chapters on campus.

Admissions: Although the City University of New York accepts all New York State residents who have a high school diploma and meet the university's health standards, applicants must have a high school average of 80 or rank in the upper two-thirds of their high school class to be eligible for admission to the senior colleges. Applicants with lower averages or class ranks are eligible for admission to the university's community colleges and technical college.

Procedure: Neither the SAT nor the ACT is required. There are no application deadlines; freshmen are admitted in the fall and spring terms. Notification is on a rolling basis. A $20 application fee is required.

Special: Early admission is possible; the application deadline is May 15. There is also a deferred admissions plan. AP and CLEP credit is given.

Transfer: Students transferring with fewer than 35 credits must have a GPA of at least 2.5; those with 35 or more credits must have a GPA of at least 2.0. All students must complete, at the college, 32 of the 128 credits required for a bachelor's degree. Application deadlines are May 1 (fall) and November 1 (spring). Transfer applications are handled through the CUNY Office of Admission Services.

Visiting: Students may visit Baruch, but must call ahead for arrangements; guided tours and interviews can be arranged through the admissions office.

Financial Aid: Seventy percent of all students receive aid through the school. The college offers grants based on the student's need. CWS funds are available in all departments. The college offers a financial aid package consisting of grants or stipend, loan, and/or work-study job for students other than freshmen; a combination of the 3 is generally given. The college is a member of CSS. The deadline for aid application is April 15.

NEW YORK 537

Foreign Students: Three percent of the full-time students come from foreign countries. Special counseling and special organizations are available for these students.

Admissions: Foreign students must achieve a TOEFL score of at least 500. No college entrance exams are required.

Procedure: Application deadlines are March 15 (fall entry) and November 1 (spring entry). Foreign students must complete a health form and must present proof of funds adequate to cover 1 year of study.

Admissions Contact: Patricia Hassett, Director of Admissions.

CITY UNIVERSITY OF NEW YORK/ BROOKLYN COLLEGE D-5

Brooklyn, New York 10031   (212) 690-6977

F/T: 5682M, 3359W		Faculty:	1500; IIA, ++$
P/T: 11,064M, 718W		Ph.D.'s:	over 50%
Grad: 1054M, 802W		S/F Ratio:	16 to 1
Year: sems, ss		Tuition:	$976 ($1476)
Appl: Jan. 15		R and B:	n/app
4000 applied	3000 accepted		1714 enrolled
SAT, ACT: not required			COMPETITIVE

Brooklyn College, established in 1930 by combining the Brooklyn campuses of City and Hunter Colleges, is a publicly supported college of liberal arts and a unit of the City University of New York. The main library contains 800,000 volumes and subscribes to 200 periodicals.

Environment: The 26-acre campus has 8 buildings, including the Walt Whitman Auditorium and the George Gershwin Theater. The library holds special collections on Henry James and Brooklyn history, as well as the Alice Morse Earle collection of first editions. There are no housing facilities.

Student Life: Almost all students are residents of New York City.

Organizations: There are 11 fraternities and 9 sororities, to which 18% of the men and 9% of the women belong. Over 250 organizations offer students social, academic, literary, religious, athletic, and recreational activities.

Sports: The college sponsors intercollegiate teams in 17 sports. Nine intramural sports also are available.

Handicapped: Services available to handicapped students include special parking privileges; wheelchair repair; book purchasing; proctoring of exams; reader services, orientation services, and recordings for the visually impaired; and note-taking for the hearing-impaired.

Graduates: Ten percent of the freshmen drop out by the end of their first year, and 90% remain to graduate. About 85% of the graduates pursue advanced degrees.

Services: Health services, psychological counseling, career counseling, and remedial instruction are provided free to students.

Programs of Study: The college confers the B.A. and B.S. degrees. Master's degrees also are awarded. Bachelor's degrees are offered in the following subjects: AREA STUDIES (African, American, Asian–East Asian, Judaic, Latin American, Middle Eastern, North African, Puerto Rican, Sub-Sahara African, urban, women's), BUSINESS (accounting), EDUCATION (bilingual, early childhood, elementary, health/physical, secondary, special), ENGLISH (English, comparative literature, speech), FINE AND PERFORMING ARTS (art, art history, dance, film/photography, music, radio/TV, theater/dramatics), HEALTH SCIENCES (health science, pre-nursing, speech therapy), LANGUAGES (Chinese, French, German, Greek/Latin, Hebrew, Italian, linguistics, Russian, Spanish), MATH AND SCIENCES (astronomy, astrophysics, biology, chemistry, computational mathematics, computer and information science, geology, mathematics, physics), PHILOSOPHY (classics, philosophy), PREPROFESSIONAL (consumer studies, home economics), SOCIAL SCIENCES (anthropology, archaeology, economics, government/political science, history, psychology, sociology). Nonmajor preprofessional programs are offered in dentistry, engineering, law, medicine, and library science.

Required: Students must fulfill distribution requirements.

Special: Four-year B.A.-M.A. programs are available in biology, chemistry, physics, and other fields. A 7-year B.A.-M.D. program involves 3 years at Brooklyn College and 4 years at Downstate Medical Center. Students may take joint programs, independent study, and interdisciplinary studies.

Honors: Numerous honor societies, including Phi Beta Kappa and Sigma Xi, have chapters on campus. Scholars Programs are offered for exceptional students, and various departments offer honors courses.

Admissions: Seventy-five percent of those who applied for the 1981–82 freshman class were accepted. Although the City University of New York accepts all New York State residents who have a high school diploma and meet the university's health standards, applicants must have a high school average of 80 or rank in the upper two-thirds of their high school class to be eligible for admission to the senior colleges. Applicants with lower averages or class ranks are eligible for admission to the university's community colleges and technical college. Brooklyn College recommends that applicants rank in the top third of their high school class.

Procedure: The SAT is recommended. Application deadlines are January 15 (fall) and October 15 (spring). Admissions are granted on a rolling basis. There is a $20 application fee.

Special: The college offers an early admissions plan. AP credit is accepted.

Transfer: Transfer students are accepted for the sophomore and junior classes. A minimum GPA of 2.0 is required. D grades do not transfer unless earned at other CUNY colleges. Students must earn 48 credits at the college of the 128 required for a bachelor's degree. Applications are handled through the CUNY Office of Admission Services.

Financial Aid: About 78% of the students receive aid. The college administers federal, state, and city grants and loans as well as work-study programs. Numerous scholarships are offered. Information on applying for aid is available from the college's Office of Financial Assistance.

Foreign Students: Students from foreign countries make up 8% of enrollment. The college offers these students an intensive English program and special counseling.

Admissions: Applicants must score 500 or better on the TOEFL. Students also must take the City University of New York's Skills Assessment Test.

Procedure: Students applying from outside the country are admitted to the fall semester only; students applying from within the United States also are admitted in spring. Application deadlines are the same as those for American students. Students must provide a physician's statement and must show evidence of adequate funds for 1 year.

Admissions Contact: Alan Sabal, Director of Admissions.

CITY UNIVERSITY OF NEW YORK/ CITY COLLEGE D-5

New York, New York 10031   (212) 690-6977

F/T: 5682M, 3559W		Faculty:	734; IIA, ++$
P/T: 1164M, 718W		Ph.D.'s:	85%
Grad: 1054M, 802W		S/F Ratio:	15 to 1
Year: sems, ss		Tuition:	$991 ($1491)
Appl: Jan. 15		R and B:	n/app
4000 applied	3050 accepted		1708 enrolled
SAT, ACT: not required			COMPETITIVE

Founded in 1847, City College is a publicly supported liberal arts institution and a unit of the City University of New York. The library contains 975,000 volumes and 440,000 microfilm items, and subscribes to 3300 periodicals.

Environment: The main campus covers 33 acres in uptown Manhattan. The 24 buildings include the Aaron Davis Hall, part of the Leonard Davis Center for the Performing Arts. There are no residence facilities.

Student Life: Most of the students are from New York. All students commute. Sixty-nine percent are minority-group members. Day-care services are available to all students.

Organizations: There are fraternities and sororities at the college, but only about 3% of the men and 3% of the women belong to them. There is student-faculty participation in administration matters, student government, publications, and the curriculum. The college is rich in extracurricular and on-campus cultural activities. Nevertheless, the cultural life of City College is synonymous with the cultural life of New York City.

Sports: There are intercollegiate teams in 10 sports for men and 7 for women. There are 8 intramural sports for men and 6 for women.

Handicapped: Handicapped students have special parking privileges, and special class scheduling also is available. There are counselors to assist handicapped students.

Graduates: About 10% of the freshmen drop out at the end of their first year, and 65% remain to graduate. About 70% of the graduates go on to further study.

Services: The following services are provided to students free of charge: psychological counseling, placement service, career counseling, tutoring, and remedial instruction.

538 NEW YORK

Programs of Study: The college offers the B.A., B.S., B.F.A., B.S.Ed., B.Eng., B.S.N., B.S.Arch., and B.Arch. degrees. Master's degrees are also awarded. Bachelor's degrees are offered in the following subjects: AREA STUDIES (American, Asian, Black/Afro-American, Jewish, Latin American, medieval and Renaissance, Puerto Rican, Russian), EDUCATION (adult, bilingual, early childhood, elementary, health/physical, industrial, occupational, secondary, special), ENGLISH (communications, English, journalism, literature, speech), FINE AND PERFORMING ARTS (art, art education, art history, dance, film/photography, music, music education, radio/TV, studio art, theater/dramatics), HEALTH SCIENCES (nursing, physician's assistant program, speech therapy), LANGUAGES (Chinese, French, German, Greek/Latin, Hebrew, Italian, Russian, Spanish), MATH AND SCIENCES (actuarial mathematics, biochemistry, biology, chemistry, earth science, geology, mathematics, meteorology, oceanography, physics, statistics), PHILOSOPHY (classics, philosophy), PREPROFESSIONAL (architecture, computer science, dentistry, engineering, law, medicine, pharmacy, technology), SOCIAL SCIENCES (anthropology, economics, geography, government/political science, history, international relations, psychology, sociology, women's studies).

Required: All liberal arts students are required to take 2 terms of physical education as well as introductory courses in humanities, science, and social science.

Special: There are accelerated bachelor's-master's programs in computer science, economics, engineering, English, mathematics, and Romance languages. A 7-year B.S.-M.D. biomedical program is offered. A 6-year B.A.-J.D. program is also available in urban legal studies. A B.F.A. degree is offered at the Leonard Davis Center for the Performing Arts. The university's Institute for Oceanography has its own sea-going research vessel. There are programs in urban design, urban landscape architecture, and urban and environmental engineering.

Honors: Under the Freshman Honors Program, selected freshmen may be permitted to complete the introductory courses in less time and devote more time to advanced work. Qualified upperclass students are encouraged to engage in independent research.

Admissions: About 76% of those who applied to the 1981–82 freshman class were accepted. Although the City University of New York accepts all New York State residents who have a high school diploma and meet the university's health standards, applicants must have a high school average of 80 or rank in the upper two-thirds of their high school class to be eligible for admission to the senior colleges. Applicants with lower averages or class ranks are eligible for admission to the university's community colleges and technical college.

Procedure: Neither the SAT nor the ACT is required. The preferred deadlines are January 15 (fall entry) and October 15 (winter entry). Admissions are granted on a rolling basis. There is a $20 application fee.

Special: The college has an early admissions program.

Transfer: For fall 1981, 2000 students applied, 1500 were accepted, and 1050 enrolled. Deadlines for transfer applicants are March 15 (fall) and November 1 (winter). D grades transfer. A 2.0 GPA is required. All students must complete, at the college, 60% of their major requirements and at least 32 of the 128 credits required for a bachelor's degree.

Visiting: Students may arrange their own tours of the college. Guides are available. Visitors may sit in on classes but may not stay on campus. The admissions office handles the arrangements.

Financial Aid: About 83% of the students receive aid. Fifteen percent work part-time on campus. The average freshman award is $2400. Federal and state grants and scholarships and BEOG, TAP, and NDSL funds are available. The City University aid form is required.

Foreign Students: Six percent of the full-time students come from foreign countries. An intensive English program and special organizations are available for these students.

Admissions: Foreign students must achieve a TOEFL score of at least 500. No college entrance exams are required.

Procedure: The application deadline is January 15 (fall entry). Foreign students are admitted in the winter term only if they are currently living in the U.S. They must fill out a health form and present proof of adequate funds.

Admissions Contact: Saul Friedman, Director of Admissions.

CITY UNIVERSITY OF NEW YORK/ COLLEGE OF STATEN ISLAND D-5
Staten Island, New York 10301 (212) 390-7557

F/T: 2600M, 2600W Faculty: 372; III, ++$
P/T: 2600M, 2600W Ph.D.'s: 56%
Grad: 270M, 270W S/F Ratio: 17 to 1
Year: sems, ss Tuition: $978 ($1478)
Appl: open R and B: n/app
3000 applied 3000 accepted 2100 enrolled
SAT, ACT: not required COMPETITIVE

The College of Staten Island, founded in 1976 by the merger of Richmond College and Staten Island Community College, offers liberal arts and technically oriented degree programs. The library contains 167,800 volumes and 232,850 microfilm items, and subscribes to 1550 periodicals.

Environment: The 36-acre campus is located in a suburban setting on Staten Island, a borough of New York City. There are no dormitory facilities.

Student Life: Nearly all the students are from New York State; most of them commute from homes on Staten Island. About 26% are minority-group members. Students may not keep cars on campus. Day-care services are available to all students on a fee basis.

Organizations: The college has no fraternities or sororities, but offers a traditional assortment of extracurricular activities. These include clubs, service organizations, and cultural groups.

Sports: The college fields 4 intercollegiate teams for men and 3 for women. There are 16 intramural sports for men and 15 for women.

Handicapped: One hundred percent of the campus is accessible to handicapped students. Special facilities include wheelchair ramps, special parking, elevators, specially equipped rest rooms, and lowered drinking fountains and telephones. Special class scheduling is also available. Fewer than 1% of the students have visual or hearing impairments. Readers are available for visually impaired students. One special counselor and 3 assistants work with handicapped students.

Graduates: The freshman dropout rate is 30%; 70% remain to graduate. Twenty-five percent of the graduates continue their education (1% in medicine, 1% in dentistry, and 1% in law). About 70% enter careers in business and industry.

Services: The following services are provided to students free of charge: psychological counseling, placement service, career counseling, tutoring, and remedial instruction.

Programs of Study: The college confers the B.A., B.S., B.S.E.S., and B.S.Med.Tech. degrees. Associate and master's degrees are also awarded. Bachelor's degrees are offered in the following subjects: AREA STUDIES (American, Black/Afro-American, women's studies), BUSINESS (business/economics, computer science), EDUCATION (education), ENGLISH (English), FINE AND PERFORMING ARTS (art, music, theater/dramatics), HEALTH SCIENCES (medical technology, nursing), LANGUAGES (French, Italian, Spanish), MATH AND SCIENCES (biochemistry, biology, chemistry, mathematics, physics), PHILOSOPHY (philosophy), PREPROFESSIONAL (engineering), SOCIAL SCIENCES (anthropology, economics, government/political science, history, international relations, psychology, sociology, women's studies). Fifty-nine percent of all degrees are conferred in the social sciences.

Required: All students must complete a core curriculum.

Special: Study abroad is possible through the international studies program.

Honors: Two national honor societies have chapters on campus. Special honors sections are available in most liberal arts departments.

Admissions: All those who applied to the 1981–82 freshman class were accepted. Although the City University of New York accepts all New York State residents who have a high school diploma and meet the university's health standards, applicants must have a high school average of 80 or rank in the upper two-thirds of their high school class to be eligible for admission to the senior colleges. Applicants with lower averages or class ranks are eligible for admission to the university's community colleges and technical college.

Procedure: Neither the SAT nor the ACT is required. Deadlines are open; freshmen are admitted in the fall, spring, and summer terms. Students are admitted on a rolling basis. There is a $20 application fee.

Transfer: For fall 1981, 620 students applied, 600 were accepted, and 430 enrolled. D grades do not transfer. A GPA of at least 2.0 is required. All students must complete, at the college, 30 of the 128 credits required for a bachelor's degree. Deadlines are open; transfer students are admitted in the fall, spring, and summer terms.

Visiting: The college has no regular orientation program for prospective students, and guides are not available for informal visits to the school.

Financial Aid: About 60% of the students receive some form of aid. Seven percent work part-time on campus. The college's aid application form is due May 15 (summer or fall entry) or December 23 (spring entry).

Foreign Students: Fewer than 1% of the full-time students come from foreign countries. Intensive English courses and programs, special counseling, and special organizations are available for these students.

Admissions: Foreign students must achieve a TOEFL score of at least 500. No college entrance exams are required.

Procedure: Application deadlines are August 1 (fall) and November 15 (spring). Foreign students must fill out a medical form and present proof of funds adequate to cover 4 years of study.

Admissions Contact: Ramon H. Hulsey, Director of Admissions.

CITY UNIVERSITY OF NEW YORK/ HERBERT H. LEHMAN COLLEGE
Bronx, New York 10468   D-5
(212) 960-8131

F/T: 1931M, 3379W   Faculty: 570; IIA, ++$
P/T: 1207M, 2116W   Ph.D.'s: 91%
Grad: 170M, 528W   S/F Ratio: 18 to 1
Year: sems, ss   Tuition: $976 ($1476)
Appl: Aug. 15   R and B: n/app
1625 applied   1208 accepted   910 enrolled
SAT, ACT: not required   COMPETITIVE

In 1968 the Bronx campus of Hunter College became a separate 4-year liberal arts college of the City University of New York and was named Herbert H. Lehman College. The library contains 350,000 volumes and 260,000 microfilm items, and subscribes to 1400 periodicals.

Environment: The 40-acre urban campus is located in a northern section of the Bronx, a borough of New York City, and is about 15 minutes from midtown Manhattan. There are no dormitories at the college.

Student Life: A majority of the students are from New York City; all but a few are from New York State. All students commute. About 74% of the students are minority-group members. Sixty-five percent are Catholic, 20% are Protestant, and 8% are Jewish. Students may keep cars on campus.

Organizations: There is 1 coeducational Greek letter society on campus, to which fewer than 1% of the men and women belong. The college offers publications, numerous academic departmental clubs, social organizations, and special-interest clubs, including the National Students' Club, the Musical Theater Society, political clubs, religious organizations for the major faiths, and foreign language clubs. The campus is within walking distance of the Bronx Zoo and the New York Botanical Garden.

Sports: There are intercollegiate teams in 8 sports for men and 8 sports for women. There are 9 intramural sports for men and 9 for women.

Handicapped: About 80% of the campus is accessible to handicapped students. Special facilities include wheelchair ramps, special parking, elevators, and specially equipped rest rooms. Fewer than 1% of the students have hearing or visual impairments.

Graduates: The freshman dropout rate is 28%; about 50% remain to graduate. About 50% of the graduates go on to further study; 2% enter medical school, 1% enter dental school, and 4% enter law school. Seventy percent of the students pursue careers in business and industry.

Services: The following services are available to students free of charge: psychological counseling, placement service, career counseling, tutoring, and remedial instruction.

Programs of Study: The college confers the B.A., B.F.A., and B.S. degrees. Master's and doctoral degrees are also awarded. Bachelor's degrees are offered in the following subjects: AREA STUDIES (American, Black/Afro-American, Puerto Rican), BUSINESS (accounting, business administration, business education, computer science, management), EDUCATION (health/physical), ENGLISH (English, speech), FINE AND PERFORMING ARTS (art, art education, art history, dance, music, music education, studio art, theater/dramatics), HEALTH SCIENCES (nursing, speech therapy), LANGUAGES (French, German, Greek/Latin, Hebrew, Italian, Portuguese, Russian, Spanish), MATH AND SCIENCES (biochemistry, biology, botany, chemistry, geology, mathematics, physics), PHILOSOPHY (classics, philosophy), PREPROFESSIONAL (social work), SOCIAL SCIENCES (anthropology, economics, geography, government/political science, history, psychology, sociology). Nonmajor preprofessional programs are available in dentistry, education, law, medicine, and veterinary.

Required: Students follow a core curriculum before specializing.

Special: The college offers a 4-year B.A.-M.A. combination degree program in mathematics. Students may design their own majors.

Honors: Most individual disciplines have their own honor societies with national affiliations. Phi Beta Kappa has a chapter on campus.

Admissions: About 74% of those who applied to the 1981–82 freshman class were accepted. Although the City University of New York accepts all New York State residents who have a high school diploma and meet the university's health standards, applicants must have a high school average of 80 or rank in the upper two-thirds of their high school class to be eligible for admission to the senior colleges. Applicants with lower averages or class ranks are eligible for admission to the university's community colleges and technical college.

Procedure: Applicants are not required to take the SAT or the ACT. The college prefers to receive applications by August 15 (fall entry) or December 15 (spring entry). Applications are processed on a rolling basis. There is a $20 application fee.

Special: The college has an early admissions plan. Applications should be sent in as early as possible; again, August 15 (fall) and December 15 (spring) are the deadlines. There is also a deferred admissions plan.

Transfer: For fall 1981, 1602 students applied, 950 were accepted, and 620 enrolled. D grades from other City University colleges transfer. All students must complete, at the college, at least half of their major requirements and at least 38 of the 128 credits required for a bachelor's degree. Deadlines are the same as those for freshmen. Transfer applications are processed through CUNY's centralized Office of Admission Services.

Visiting: The college schedules an "open house" for prospective students once each semester. Guides are also available for informal visits to the school. Visitors may sit in on classes with prior arrangement, but may not stay on campus. The number to call for visiting arrangements is (212) 960-8131.

Financial Aid: About 70% of the students receive some form of financial aid. About 25% work part-time on campus. Federal and state grants and scholarships and BEOG, TAP, and NDSL funds are available. The average freshman award is $1500. The City University aid form should be filed by June 30 (fall entry) or December 15 (spring entry).

Foreign Students: One percent of the full-time students come from foreign countries. Intensive English courses and programs, special counseling, and special organizations are available for these students.

Admissions: Foreign students must achieve a TOEFL score of at least 500. No college entrance exams are required.

Procedure: Application deadlines are the same as those for other students. Foreign students must present proof of funds adequate to cover 4 years of study.

Admissions Contact: Ann G. Quinley, Director of Admissions.

CITY UNIVERSITY OF NEW YORK/ HUNTER COLLEGE
New York, New York 10021   D-5
(212) 570-5149

F/T: 2120M, 6529W   Faculty: 612; IIA, ++$
P/T: 1468M, 4331W   Ph.D.'s: 95%
Grad: 743M, 2578W   S/F Ratio: 16 to 1
Year: sems, ss   Tuition: $950 ($1475)
Appl: Mar. 15   R and B: see profile
4446 applied   3247 accepted   1767 enrolled
SAT, ACT: not required   COMPETITIVE

Hunter College, a liberal arts institution founded in 1870, is one of the municipal colleges of New York City and receives support from both the city and the state. The library contains 495,036 volumes and 8962 microfilm items, and subscribes to 3274 periodicals.

Environment: The 3-acre urban campus is located on Park Avenue in Manhattan, close to several art museums and the central branch of the New York Public Library. The principal 16-story building contains a 2200-seat concert hall and a 700-seat theater in addition to classrooms, laboratories, and offices. Rooms are available on a limited basis at a cost of $950 per year for nursing and health science students.

540 NEW YORK

Student Life: Nearly 100% of the students come from the local area. All students commute except some in nursing and health science programs. About 40% of the students are minority-group members. The limited amount of dormitory housing is both coed and single-sex; there are visiting privileges in the single-sex dorms. Students may not keep cars on campus.

Organizations: Students enjoy a full college life with active participation in numerous student groups, social activities, and athletic events. There are religious organizations for students of all major faiths, and students are represented on the Hunter College Senate, the main policy-making body of the college. All the cultural and recreational advantages of Manhattan are available.

Sports: The college fields 8 intercollegiate teams for men and 7 for women. There are 4 intramural sports for men and 4 for women.

Handicapped: About 90% of the campus is accessible to handicapped students. Special facilities include wheelchair ramps, elevators, specially equipped rest rooms, and lowered telephones. The entire advising and counseling staff at the college is available to assist handicapped students, and there are 2 special counselors.

Graduates: The freshman dropout rate is 37%. About 54% of the entering freshmen remain to graduate, and 46% of the graduates go on to further study (6% in medicine, 1% in dentistry, and 9% in law). Sixty-seven percent pursue careers in business and industry.

Services: The following services are available to students free of charge: psychological counseling, placement service, career counseling, tutoring, and remedial instruction.

Programs of Study: The college confers the following undergraduate degrees: B.A., B.S., B.F.A., and B.Mus. Master's degrees are also awarded. Bachelor's degrees are offered in the following subjects: AREA STUDIES (American, Asian, Black/Afro-American, Puerto Rican, Russian, urban), BUSINESS (accounting, computer science), EDUCATION (adult, early childhood, elementary, health/physical, secondary, special), ENGLISH (English, literature), FINE AND PERFORMING ARTS (art, art education, art history, dance, film/photography, music, music education, studio art, theater/dramatics), HEALTH SCIENCES (environmental health, medical laboratory science, nursing, physical therapy, speech therapy), LANGUAGES (Chinese, French, German, Greek/Latin, Hebrew, Italian, Polish, Portuguese, Russian, Spanish, Swahili, Ukrainian), MATH AND SCIENCES (astronomy, biochemistry, biology, chemistry, ecology/environmental science, geology, mathematics, natural sciences, physical sciences, physics, statistics), PHILOSOPHY (classics, humanities, philosophy, religion), PREPROFESSIONAL (dentistry, home economics, law, medicine), SOCIAL SCIENCES (anthropology, economics, energy policy studies, geography, government/political science, history, international relations, psychology, social sciences, sociology). Twenty-eight percent of all degrees are conferred in social sciences, and 24% in health sciences.

Required: All students must take courses in freshman English and physical education, as well as a distribution of courses in 7 broad areas of study.

Special: Special programs are offered in cinema, comparative literature, comparative religions, East Asian studies, English language arts, and Inter-American affairs. Double majors and student-designed majors are permitted. There are B.A.-M.A. and B.A.-M.S. programs in sociology and social research.

Honors: Twenty-two national honor societies, including Phi Beta Kappa, have chapters on campus. In addition, any student who qualifies may participate in independent study projects that lead to departmental honors.

Admissions: About 73% of those who applied to the 1981–82 freshman class were accepted. Although the City University of New York accepts all New York State residents who have a high school diploma and meet the university's health standards, applicants must have a high school average of 80 or rank in the upper two-thirds of their high school class to be eligible for admission to the senior colleges. Applicants with lower averages or class ranks are eligible for admission to the university's community colleges and technical college.

Procedure: Neither the SAT nor the ACT is required. Applications are processed through the CUNY central processing center. Application deadlines are March 15 (fall) and October 15 (spring). Applicants are admitted on a rolling basis. There is a $20 application fee.

Special: The college has an early admissions plan with a May 15 application deadline. There is also an early decision plan. AP and CLEP credit is available.

Transfer: For fall 1981, 2191 applications were received, and 1337 students enrolled. D grades from other City University colleges transfer. Students transferring with fewer than 30 credits must have a 2.5 GPA; those with 30 or more, a 2.0. All students must complete, at the college, 30 of the 125–128 credits required for a bachelor's degree. Application deadlines are March 15 (fall) and November 1 (spring). Transfer applications are handled centrally by CUNY's Office of Admissions Services.

Visiting: A tour of the school, with an introduction to available programs, is available to prospective students. The Office of Admissions must be contacted for arrangements.

Financial Aid: Seventy-five percent of all students receive some form of financial aid. About 80% work part-time on campus. The average freshman award is $900. Federal and state grants and scholarships are available. The college is a member of CSS. The City University aid application form is required; May 13 is the deadline for fall entry.

Foreign Students: Three percent of the full-time students come from foreign countries. An intensive English course, special counseling, and special programs are available for these students.

Admissions: Foreign students must achieve a TOEFL score of at least 500. No college entrance exams are required.

Procedure: Application deadlines are January 15 (fall entry) and October 15 (spring entry). Foreign students must be examined by a physician and must present proof of adequate funds.

Admissions Contact: William DiBrienza, Director of Admissions.

CITY UNIVERSITY OF NEW YORK/ JOHN JAY COLLEGE OF CRIMINAL JUSTICE
D-5

New York, New York 10019   (212) 489-5080

F/T: 1920M, 1832W	Faculty: 257; IIA, + + $
P/T: 1035M, 599W	Ph.D.'s: 85%
Grad: 332M, 212W	S/F Ratio: 17 to 1
Year: sems, ss	Tuition: $964 ($1464)
Appl: open	R and B: n/app
1414 accepted	947 enrolled
SAT, ACT: not required	COMPETITIVE

John Jay College of Criminal Justice, a part of the City University of New York, is a college of liberal arts and sciences founded in 1964 to foster the professionalization of police and other law enforcement officers and to serve students interested in careers in criminal justice. The college is unique in that it schedules classes so that persons whose employment requires them to work a rotating shift can earn a degree while engaged in full-time employment. Each class is offered once in the daytime and once at night with the same instructor. The library contains 134,000 volumes and 12,000 microfilm items, and subscribes to 900 periodicals.

Environment: The college is located in Manhattan. There are no dormitory facilities.

Student Life: About 97% of the undergraduates are New Yorkers. All students commute. Seventy-five percent of the entering freshmen come from public schools; 12% from parochial schools. Fifty-three percent are minority-group members.

Organizations: There are no fraternities or sororities at the college, but numerous literary, dramatic, and other special-interest clubs are available. Lectures, plays, and other cultural events are presented frequently on campus. Lincoln Center and the Broadway theater district are readily accessible.

Sports: The college fields 7 intercollegiate teams for men and 7 for women. There are 6 intramural sports for men and 6 for women.

Handicapped: About 70–75% of the campus is accessible to handicapped students. Special facilities include wheelchair ramps, elevators, and lowered telephones. Fewer than 1% of the students have visual or hearing impairments.

Graduates: The freshman dropout rate is 20–25%; 40–45% of entering freshmen remain to graduate. About 40% of the graduates go on to further study, including 5–10% who enter law school. Five percent of the graduates pursue careers in business and industry. Most students seek employment in local, state, or federal government.

Services: The following services are provided to students free of charge: psychological counseling, placement service, career counseling, tutoring, and remedial instruction.

Programs of Study: The college offers the B.A. and B.S. degrees. Associate, master's, and doctoral degrees are also awarded. Bachelor's degrees are offered in the following subjects: MATH AND SCIENCES (fire science, forensic science), PREPROFESSIONAL (law, police science), SOCIAL SCIENCES (correction administration, criminal justice, deviant behavior and social control, forensic psychology, government and public administration).

Required: All undergraduates are required to take basic courses in humanities, science and mathematics, and the social sciences.

Special: A thematic studies program and 4-year B.A.-M.A. programs in public administration and criminal justice are offered. Study abroad is possible. A general studies degree is offered.

Honors: Two national honor societies have chapters on campus. Most departments have honors courses for seniors.

Admissions: Although the City University of New York accepts all New York State residents who have a high school diploma and meet the university's health standards, applicants must have a high school average of 80 or rank in the upper two-thirds of their high school class to be eligible for admission to the senior colleges. Applicants with lower averages or class ranks are eligible for admission to the university's community colleges and technical college.

Procedure: Neither the SAT nor the ACT is required. Deadlines are open; a rolling admissions plan is used. There is a $20 application fee.

Special: The college has an early admissions plan with an April 15 application deadline.

Transfer: For fall 1981, over 300 transfer students enrolled. A 2.0 GPA is required. D grades from other City University colleges transfer. All students must complete, at the college, at least half of their major and 32 of the 128 credits required for a bachelor's degree. Applications are processed centrally for all units of the City University of New York.

Visiting: The college has a regular open house program in which several departments are involved. Guides are also available for informal visits to the school. Visitors may sit in on classes but may not stay on campus. The best time to visit is during the spring semester. The Counseling Department should be contacted for arrangements.

Financial Aid: About 85% of all students receive some form of financial aid. About 20% work part-time on campus. The average freshman award is $1900. State and federal grants and scholarships are available. In addition, there are Police Department scholarships, and qualified students may participate in a work-study program. The CUNY aid application form is required; deadlines are open, but priority is given to aid applications received by June 15.

Foreign Students: Fewer than 1% of the full-time students come from foreign countries. An intensive English course, special counseling, and special organizations are available for these students.

Admissions: Foreign students must achieve a TOEFL score of at least 500. No college entrance exams are required.

Procedure: Application deadlines are open; foreign students are admitted in the fall and spring terms. They must complete a health form and present proof of funds adequate to cover 1 year of study.

Admissions Contact: Francis McHugh, Director of Admissions.

CITY UNIVERSITY OF NEW YORK/ MEDGAR EVERS COLLEGE D-5
Brooklyn, New York 11225   (212) 735-1947

F/T: 521M, 1101W	Faculty:	170; IIB, ++$
P/T: 207M, 864W	Ph.D.'s:	n/av
Grad: none	S/F Ratio:	23 to 1
Year: sems, ss	Tuition:	$976 ($1476)
Appl: open	R and B:	n/app
707 accepted		364 enrolled
SAT, ACT: not required		COMPETITIVE

Medgar Evers College was established in 1969 as part of the City University of New York, and today offers undergraduate preparation in accounting, business, education, public administration, nursing, and liberal arts and sciences. It has a strong mandate to serve the needs of the immediate community. Its library has 77,568 volumes and 18,000 microfilm items, and subscribes to 515 periodicals.

Environment: The urban campus is located in the Crown Heights section of central Brooklyn. There are no dormitories.

Student Life: About 98% of the students come from New York; nearly all are public school graduates. About 96% are minority-group members. All students commute.

Organizations: Special-interest clubs, performing groups, campus government, publications, social and cultural events, and service and religious organizations are sponsored. There are no fraternities or sororities.

NEW YORK   541

Sports: The college fields 4 intercollegiate teams for men and 3 for women. There are 3 intramural sports for men and 3 for women.

Handicapped: Most of the campus is accessible to physically handicapped individuals. There are ramps and elevators.

Graduates: The freshman dropout rate is about 25%.

Services: The following services are offered: tutoring, remedial instruction, health care, placement, and career counseling.

Programs of Study: The B.S. degree is conferred. Associate degrees are also awarded. Bachelor's degrees are offered in the following subjects: BUSINESS (accounting, business administration), EDUCATION (elementary), HEALTH SCIENCES (nursing), MATH AND SCIENCES (biology), PREPROFESSIONAL (engineering, medicine), SOCIAL SCIENCES (public administration).

Required: All students must take a core curriculum in the major field.

Special: Exchange programs with other CUNY units are available.

Honors: Honors work is possible.

Admissions: Although the City University of New York accepts all New York State residents who have a high school diploma and meet the university's health standards, applicants must have a high school average of 80 or rank in the upper two-thirds of their high school class to be eligible for admission to the senior colleges. Applicants with lower averages or class ranks are eligible for admission to the university's community colleges and technical college.

Procedure: The SAT or the ACT is not required. Deadlines are open; freshmen are admitted in the fall and spring. There is a $20 application fee.

Transfer: For fall 1981, over 140 transfer students enrolled. A GPA of 2.0 is needed. All students must complete, at the college, 32 of the 120–128 credits required for a bachelor's degree. Deadlines are open; transfer students are admitted in the fall, spring, and summer terms.

Financial Aid: About 87% of the students receive assistance. Eleven percent work part-time on campus. The college participates in federal and state aid programs and is a member of CSS. The CUNY financial aid application form is required. Deadlines are August 15 for fall entry and January 1 for spring entry.

Foreign Students: Three percent of the full-time students come from foreign countries. An intensive English course, special counseling, and special organizations are available for these students.

Admissions: Foreign students must achieve a TOEFL score of at least 500. No college entrance exams are required.

Procedure: Application deadlines are open. Foreign students are admitted in the fall; spring entry is possible for students already living in the U.S. Foreign students must present proof of funds adequate to cover 4 years of study.

Admissions Contact: Roberta Dannenfelser, Director of Admissions.

CITY UNIVERSITY OF NEW YORK/ QUEENS COLLEGE D-5
Flushing, New York 11367   (212) 520-7385

F/T: 4888M, 5905W	Faculty:	n/av; IIA, ++$
P/T: 1688M, 2886W	Ph.D.'s:	95%
Grad: 671M, 308W	S/F Ratio:	18 to 1
Year: sems, ss	Tuition:	$1050 ($1550)
Appl: see profile	R and B:	n/app
6066 accepted		3536 enrolled
SAT, ACT: not required		COMPETITIVE

Queens College is a large liberal arts commuter college, founded in 1939, operated by the city of New York, and supported by city and state funds. The library contains 450,000 volumes and 11,000 microfilm items, and subscribes to 4200 periodicals.

Environment: The 80-acre campus is located in an urban area of Long Island about 10 miles from Manhattan. Campus buildings include a science hall, a gymnasium, and a music and speech building. There are no residence facilities.

Student Life: Most of the students are residents of New York City. All students commute. About 18% are minority-group members. Students may keep cars on campus.

Organizations: Despite being a commuter college, Queens College offers a wide range of student activities, including theater, orchestra and choir, a student newspaper and literary magazine, student government, departmental clubs, political and religious organizations, and

542 NEW YORK

both local and national fraternal groups. The campus is located within an hour's drive of the beaches and recreational areas of Long Island.

Sports: Intercollegiate competitions are held in 8 sports. There are 4 intramural sports.

Graduates: The freshman dropout rate is 6%; 75% remain to graduate.

Services: The college offers placement services, career counseling, health care, and psychological counseling free of charge. Some tutoring services and all remedial instruction require payment.

Programs of Study: The college confers the B.A., B.F.A., B.S.P.E., and B. Mus. degrees. Master's degrees are also awarded. Bachelor's degrees are offered in the following subjects: AREA STUDIES (American, East Asian, Latin American), BUSINESS (accounting, computer science, economics), EDUCATION (early childhood, elementary, health/physical, secondary), ENGLISH (English, journalism, literature), FINE AND PERFORMING ARTS (art, art education, art history, dance, film/photography, music, music education, radio/TV, studio art, theater/dramatics), HEALTH SCIENCES (speech therapy), LANGUAGES (French, German, Greek/Latin, Hebrew, Italian, Portuguese, Russian, Spanish, Yiddish), MATH AND SCIENCES (biology, chemistry, earth science, ecology/environmental science, geology, mathematics, physics), PHILOSOPHY (philosophy), PREPROFESSIONAL (dentistry, engineering, home economics, law, medicine, pharmacy, social work, veterinary), SOCIAL SCIENCES (anthropology, economics, government/political science, history, psychology, sociology, urban studies).

Required: There are departmental requirements in the various major fields.

Special: Special programs include honors, independent study, seminars, interdisciplinary majors, summer foreign study, a junior or senior year abroad, and ACE (in which adult students meet degree requirements in basic work through seminars).

Admissions: Although the City University of New York accepts all New York State residents who have a high school diploma and meet the university's health standards, applicants must have a high school average of 80, or have a minimum composite score of 900 on the SAT or 20 on the ACT, or rank in the upper two-thirds of their high school class to be eligible for admission to the senior colleges. Applicants with lower averages or class ranks are eligible for admission to the university's community colleges and technical college.

Procedure: Applications are accepted until about 2 weeks before registration. Freshmen are admitted in the fall and spring terms. Notification is on a rolling basis. There is a $20 application fee.

Transfer: For fall 1981, 2090 students applied, 1627 were accepted, and 1125 enrolled. A 2.0 GPA is required. D grades do not transfer. All students must complete, at the college, 45 of the 128 credits required for a bachelor's degree. Deadlines are open; transfer students are admitted in the fall and spring terms. Transfer applications are processed centrally through CUNY's Office of Admissions Services.

Financial Aid: About 55% of the students receive some form of aid. State and federal grants and scholarships are available. The CUNY financial aid form is required.

Foreign Students: An intensive English course, an intensive English program, special counseling, and special organizations are available for foreign students.

Admissions: Foreign students must achieve a TOEFL score of at least 500 and must take the college's own English proficiency exam. No college entrance exams are required.

Procedure: Application deadlines are January 15 (fall entry) and October 15 (spring entry). Foreign students must complete a health form and must present proof of funds adequate to cover 4 years of study.

Admissions Contact: Richard Bory, Director of Preadmission Services.

CITY UNIVERSITY OF NEW YORK/ YORK COLLEGE
D-5

Jamaica, New York 11451   (212) 969-4215

F/T: 1024M, 1491W	Faculty: 162; IIB, ++$
P/T: 486M, 999W	Ph.D.'s: 72%
Grad: none	S/F Ratio: 16 to 1
Year: 4-1-4, ss	Tuition: $980 ($1480)
Appl: open	R and B: n/app
SAT, ACT: not required	**COMPETITIVE**

York College, founded in 1966, is a publicly supported liberal arts college and a unit of the City University of New York. The library contains 154,000 volumes and subscribes to 1013 periodicals.

Environment: The urban campus is located in Jamaica, Queens. A 50-acre site has been designated by the Board of Higher Education of New York as York's future permanent campus. There are no residential facilities.

Student Life: Ninety-nine percent of the students are from New York State; 94% are from New York City. About 60% are from Queens. Eighty percent of the entering freshmen come from public schools. All students commute. Students may keep cars on campus.

Organizations: Special-interest clubs; academic, social, and performing groups; student government; and publications are available. There are no fraternities or sororities.

Sports: The college fields 6 intercollegiate teams for men and 3 for women. There is 1 intramural sport for men and 1 for women.

Graduates: About 10% of the students drop out at the end of the freshman year.

Services: Placement services, career counseling, tutoring, remedial instruction, health care, and psychological counseling are offered free of charge.

Programs of Study: The college confers the B.A. and B.S. degrees. Bachelor's degrees are offered in the following subjects: AREA STUDIES (Black/Afro-American), BUSINESS (accounting, business administration, computer science, marketing), EDUCATION (elementary, health/physical), ENGLISH (English), FINE AND PERFORMING ARTS (art), HEALTH SCIENCES (environmental health, medical technology, occupational therapy), LANGUAGES (French, Italian, Spanish), MATH AND SCIENCES (biology, chemistry, geology, mathematics, physics), PHILOSOPHY (philosophy), PREPROFESSIONAL (social work), SOCIAL SCIENCES (anthropology, economics, government/political science, history, psychology, sociology). Preprofessional programs, although not majors, are available in architecture, dentistry, engineering, law, medicine, social work, and veterinary medicine.

Special: Cooperative education majors in business administration, gerontology, information systems management, and marketing are available.

Admissions: Although City University of New York accepts all New York State residents who have a high school diploma and meet the university's health standards, applicants must have a high school average of 80 or rank in the upper two-thirds of their high school class to be eligible for admission to the senior colleges. Applicants with lower averages or class ranks are eligible for admission to the university's community colleges and technical college.

Procedure: Neither the SAT nor the ACT is required. Deadlines are open; notification is on a rolling basis. Freshmen are admitted in the fall and spring terms. There is a $20 application fee.

Special: The college has an early admissions plan. AP credit is given.

Transfer: D grades from other CUNY colleges transfer. A minimum average of 2.0 is required. All students must complete, at the college, 30 of the 128 credits required for a bachelor's degree. Deadlines are open; transfer students are admitted in the fall and spring terms. Transfer applications are handled through the CUNY Office of Admission Services.

Visiting: The college holds regular orientation sessions for prospective students. Guides are also available for informal visits to the school. Visitors may sit in on classes but may not stay on campus. The admissions office handles the arrangements.

Financial Aid: About 50% of the students receive some form of financial aid. About 20% work part-time on campus. The average freshman award is $2000. Federal and state grants and scholarships are available. The CUNY financial aid form is required. The deadline for aid applications for the fall semester is May.

Foreign Students: Three percent of the full-time students come from foreign countries. An intensive English program, special counseling, and special organizations are available for these students.

Admissions: Foreign students must achieve a TOEFL score of at least 400. No college entrance exams are required.

Procedure: Applications are due in May; foreign students are admitted in the fall and spring terms. They must present proof of health and proof of funds adequate to cover 4 years of study.

Admissions Contact: Ronnie Levitt, Director of Admissions.

CLARKSON COLLEGE OF TECHNOLOGY
D-2

Potsdam, New York 13676   (315) 268-6479

F/T: 2800M, 770W   *Faculty: n/av; IIA, ++$*
P/T: 113M&W   *Ph.D.'s: 90%*
Grad: 272M, 71W   *S/F Ratio: 17 to 1*
Year: sems   *Tuition: $5500*
Appl: Feb. 15   *R and B: $2500*
3000 applied   2000 accepted   800 enrolled
SAT: 530V 640M   **HIGHLY COMPETITIVE**

Founded in 1896, Clarkson College is a private, nonsectarian, technological institution with 6 major organizational units: the School of Science, the School of Engineering, the School of Management, the Faculty of Liberal Studies, the Industrial Distribution Program, the Graduate School, and the Division of Research. The library contains over 130,000 volumes and subscribes to 1850 periodicals.

Environment: The 22 campus buildings and the grounds occupy 650 acres in this rural community. The residence halls accommodate 2800 students. Some sorority or fraternity housing is available.

Student Life: About 75% of the students are from New York. Eighty-five percent live on campus. Campus housing is both single-sex and coed. There are visiting privileges in single-sex housing. Freshmen may not keep cars on campus.

Organizations: There are 6 local and 7 national fraternities on campus, to which 25% of the men belong; there is 1 national sorority represented. Among the extracurricular activities available to Clarkson students are music and drama groups, special-interest and service organizations, and publications. Students have easy access to many cultural and recreational facilities in upper New York State, New England, and Canada.

Sports: The college participates on an intercollegiate level in 12 sports for men and 8 for women. There are 9 intramural sports for men and 7 for women.

Graduates: The freshman dropout rate is 10%; approximately 70% of enrolled freshmen graduate, and of those about 20% become candidates for graduate or professional degrees, while 70% pursue careers in business or industry.

Services: The college offers free tutoring, psychological and career counseling, and placement services. Health care is available on a fee basis.

Programs of Study: Undergraduate degrees offered are the B.S. and B.P.S. Clarkson also confers master's and doctoral degrees. Bachelor's degrees are offered in the following subjects: BUSINESS (accounting, economics, finance, management, marketing, psychology), ENGLISH (technical communications), HEALTH SCIENCES (industrial hygiene/environmental toxicology), MATH AND SCIENCES (biology, chemistry, computer science, mathematics, physics), PHILOSOPHY (humanities), SOCIAL SCIENCES (history, social sciences, sociology).

Required: Each student must complete a requirement either in ROTC or in physical education.

Special: Students have opportunities for interdisciplinary study, specialization within a given major, or study abroad. One of the college's distinctive educational programs is the Department of Industrial Distribution. This interarea program provides academic work in engineering, management, and arts and sciences.

Admissions: Sixty-seven percent of the students that applied for admission to the 1981–82 freshman class were admitted. The SAT scores of those who enrolled were as follows: Verbal—36% scored below 500, 48% between 500 and 599, 12% between 600 and 700, and 2% above 700; Math—1% scored below 500, 29% between 500 and 599, 56% between 600 and 700, and 14% above 700. Candidates must be graduates of an accredited high school, have completed 16 Carnegie units, and present a recommendation from the top school official.

Procedure: The SAT or ACT is required. The suggested deadline for application to the fall semester is February 15. Admissions are rolling after this date. There is a $25 application fee. A personal interview is recommended.

Special: Early decision, early admissions, and deferred admissions plans are offered. CLEP (subject) and AP exams are accepted.

Transfer: For fall 1981, 280 students enrolled. Transfers are accepted for the junior year. Generally, a 2.5 GPA is needed. D grades do not transfer. Students must study at the college at least 1 year; 120 credits are required to receive a bachelor's degree. Transfer application deadlines are May 1 (fall) and December 1 (spring).

NEW YORK   543

Visiting: When planning to visit, a student should write or telephone the admissions office, requesting an appointment. The admissions office is open September through May on weekdays from 9 A.M. to 4 P.M. and on Saturdays (by appointment) from 9 A.M. to noon.

Financial Aid: About 50% of all students receive some form of aid, including state awards and loans. Every effort is made to provide financial assistance for promising students who demonstrate genuine financial need. Financial aid can consist of scholarships, grants, loans, and employment, either singly or in combination. The college is a member of CSS. The FAF must be filed no later than February 15.

Foreign Students: Fewer than 5% of the full-time students come from foreign countries. The college offers these students special counseling and special organizations.

Admissions: Foreign students must take the TOEFL. No college entrance examination is required.

Procedure: The application deadline is February 15 (fall). Foreign students must present proof of adequate funds. They must also carry health insurance, which is available through the college.

Admissions Contact: Robert A. Croot, Director of Freshman Admissions.

COLGATE UNIVERSITY
C-3

Hamilton, New York 13346   (315) 824-1000

F/T: 1500M, 1100W   *Faculty: 200; IIA, ++$*
P/T: none   *Ph.D.'s: 87%*
Grad: 20M, 20W   *S/F Ratio: 13 to 1*
Year: 4-1-4   *Tuition: $6425*
Appl: Jan. 15   *R and B: $2425*
4920 applied   1980 accepted   694 enrolled
SAT: 581V 628M   ACT: 28 **HIGHLY COMPETITIVE+**

Colgate University, founded in 1819, is an independent liberal arts institution. Its curriculum is organized around the arts and emphasizes small classes, seminars, independent study, and individuality. The newly expanded library contains 356,000 volumes and subscribes to over 2000 periodicals.

Environment: The university is located in a rural town of 2500, 38 miles from Syracuse and 30 miles from Utica. The 1400-acre campus is situated among the rolling hills of the Chenango Valley. Noteworthy among campus facilities are a chemistry building and science library. Students are housed in four-class dorms, fraternities, sororities, special interest houses, and on-campus apartments.

Student Life: Seventy-five percent of the students come from the Northeast. Sixty-four percent attended public schools, 26% private schools, and 10% parochial schools. Eighty-two percent of the students live on campus. About 11% of the students are minority-group members. Campus housing is both single-sex and coed; there are visiting privileges in single-sex housing. Students may keep cars on campus.

Organizations: There are 10 fraternities to which 40% of the men belong. A small number of the women belong to 2 sororities. There is 1 coed fraternity. The annual Concert and Music Recital Series brings distinguished performers to the campus. A lecture series, poetry readings, weekend conferences, films, theater productions, art exhibits, and other events insure that the university's rural location does not mean cultural deprivation. There are numerous student publications, musical groups, special interest clubs, a radio and closed circuit TV station, religious organizations, and an active student government.

Sports: The university fields 24 intercollegiate teams for men and 22 for women. There are 27 intramural sports for men and 27 for women.

Handicapped: About 20% of the campus is accessible to handicapped students. Special facilities include wheelchair ramps and elevators.

Graduates: The academic dropout rate among freshmen is 4%; 86% remain to graduate. About 45% of the graduates pursue advanced degrees; 5% enter medical school, 1% enter dental school, and 15% enter law school. About 60% pursue careers in business and industry.

Services: The following services are provided to students free of charge: health care, psychological counseling, placement and career counseling (for students and graduates), tutoring, and remedial instruction.

Programs of Study: The university awards the B.A. degree. There are also several master's degree programs. Bachelor's degrees are offered in the following subjects: AREA STUDIES (American, Asian, Black/Afro-American, Russian), BUSINESS (computer science), ENGLISH (English), FINE AND PERFORMING ARTS (art, music), LANGUAGES (French, German, Greek/Latin, Russian, Spanish), MATH AND SCIENCES (astronomy, astro-geophysics, biochemistry, biology, chemistry, computer-mathematics, geology, marine science, mathematics, mathematics-economics, natural sciences, neuroscience, physics), PHILOSOPHY (classics, humanities, philosophy, religion), PRE-PROFESSIONAL (architecture, dentistry, engineering, law, medicine, ministry, veterinary), SOCIAL SCIENCES (anthropology, economics, geography, government/political science, history, international relations, peace and world order, psychology, social sciences, sociology). Forty-one percent of the degrees are conferred in social sciences and 28% in math and sciences.

Required: The university has a core curriculum with 5 required courses spread over 3 years. The core courses are specially integrated introductions to the humanities and sciences.

Special: During the January independent study period, students choose their own projects which are graded on a pass/fail basis. The university offers Washington, D.C. semesters and foreign study groups in many countries. Cooperative engineering programs (both bachelor's and master's) are offered with Columbia, Carnegie-Mellon, Cornell, R.I.T., and Dartmouth. Combined B.A.-B.S. degrees may be earned, and student-designed majors are permitted.

Honors: Seven honor societies have chapters on campus. All departments sponsor their own honors programs.

Admissions: About 40% of those who applied were accepted for the 1981-82 freshman class. SAT scores among freshmen were as follows: Verbal—15% scored below 500, 45% scored between 500 and 599, 36% between 600 and 700, and 4% above 700; Math—7% scored below 500, 27% between 500 and 599, 53% between 600 and 700, and 13% above 700.

Applicants should be graduates of accredited high schools, rank in the top 40% of their class, and have completed 16 units of high school work. Other important considerations include advanced placement or honor courses, standardized testing, recommendations, and evidence of special talents. Other qualifications being equal, special consideration is given to sons and daughters of Colgate alumni, and to those from geographical areas and ethnic groups in which the university desires greater representation.

Procedure: The SAT or ACT and 3 ATs (including English Composition) are required and should be taken by January of the senior year. Application deadlines are January 15 (fall) and November 1 (spring). Students are notified of fall admissions decisions in March and April. There is a $30 application fee.

Special: The university has an early decision plan; applicants are notified within a month after completion of their applications. There are also early and deferred admissions plans. AP and CLEP credit is given.

Transfer: For fall 1981, 342 transfer students applied, 145 were accepted, and 80 enrolled. A 3.0 GPA is recommended. The recommendation of the previous university's dean is required; students with associate degrees receive preference. C or better grades transfer. There is a 2-year residency requirement. Sixteen courses and 3 January terms must be completed at Colgate, out of a total of 35 courses required for the bachelor's degree. Application deadlines are March 1 (fall) and November 1 (spring).

Visiting: There is no regular orientation program for prospective students, but guides are available for informal weekday visits to the campus. Visitors may sit in on classes and may stay overnight at the school. The admissions office should be contacted for arrangements.

Financial Aid: Eighty-five percent of the students receive aid through the university. Fifty-six percent work part-time on campus. The average award to freshmen from all sources through the university is $6438. Scholarships, GSL and NDSL loans, and part-time work are the types of available aid. Tuition deferment plans are also available. The university is a member of CSS. The FAF and Colgate Financial Form are required. The deadlines for aid application are February 1 for fall and December 1 for spring.

Foreign Students: Two percent of the full-time students are from foreign countries. The university offers these students special counseling.

Admissions: The TOEFL and either the SAT or ACT are required; applicants must score a minimum of 550 on the TOEFL. Three ATs, English Composition and 2 others, are also required.

Procedure: Application deadlines are January 15 for fall and November 1 for spring. Foreign students must present proof of adequate funds for 4 years. They must also carry health insurance while in attendance at the university.

Admissions Contact: Thomas S. Anthony, Associate Dean of Admission.

COLLEGE FOR HUMAN SERVICES   D-5
New York, New York 10014   (212) 989-2002
(Recognized Candidate for Accreditation)

F/T: n/av   Faculty: n/av
P/T: n/av   Ph.D.'s: n/av
Grad: none   S/F Ratio: n/av
Year: tri, ss   Tuition: $3234
Appl: June 1   R and B: n/app
SAT, ACT: not required   LESS COMPETITIVE

Founded in 1964, the College for Human Services is an independent institution offering undergraduate professional education. The college offers a non-traditional program that consists of interdisciplinary, performance-based work/study. The purpose of this innovative educational design is to prepare graduates who can provide human services that result in greater self-sufficiency for the citizen involved.

Environment: The college is located in New York City. There are no college-sponsored living facilities for students.

Student Life: All of the students are New York residents. Ninety percent are minority-group members.

Organizations: The American Council for Human Service is the largest and most active college-sponsored organization.

Handicapped: Facilities for physically handicapped students include wheelchair ramps, elevators, and specially equipped rest rooms.

Graduates: Thirty-one percent of the freshmen drop out by the end of the first year. Ten percent of each graduating class enter careers in business and industry.

Services: The college offers placement services, psychological counseling, career counseling, tutoring, and remedial instruction to all students free of charge.

Programs of Study: All programs of study are in human services and lead to the Bachelor of Professional Studies in Human Service degree.

Required: The entire human service curriculum is required of all students.

Admissions: An eleventh-grade reading level is required of all freshman applicants. Other factors entering into the admissions decision include recommendations by school officials, personality, ability to finance college education, and evidence of special talents.

Procedure: The Stanford Task Test is required of all applicants. Application deadlines are June 1 (fall), October 1 (spring), and April 1 (summer). There is a rolling admissions plan. The application fee is $10.

Special: Early decision and early and deferred admissions plans are available.

Transfer: Students may transfer only into the freshman and sophomore classes. A minimum score of 450 on each part of the SAT is required. Transfers must submit an essay and recommendations. Transferable grades are determined through special assessment. Students must complete a total of 140 credits to receive a bachelor's degree. The application deadline for fall entry is July 1; for winter entry, November 1; and for summer entry, April 1.

Visiting: The college offers information sessions, tours, class visits, and field office orientation. The best times for visits are Monday and Tuesday from 9 A.M. to noon. Arrangements should be made through the admissions office.

Financial Aid: Ninety percent of the students receive aid through the college. Aid is available in the form of scholarships and loans; the average freshman scholarship totals $975, the average freshman loan, $2346. The FAF or FFS is required.

Admissions Contact: Madeline Marks, Director of Admissions.

COLLEGE OF INSURANCE   D-5
New York, New York 10038   (212) 962-4111

F/T: 212M, 82W   Faculty: 42; IIA, av$
P/T: 653M, 739W   Ph.D.'s: 48%
Grad: 84M, 17W   S/F Ratio: 15 to 1
Year: 3 4-month sems Tuition: $132 p/c
Appl: Aug. 1   R and B: $1900-3800
220 applied   108 accepted   92 enrolled
SAT: 530V 580M   VERY COMPETITIVE

The College of Insurance, founded in 1962, is a private, independent, professional school supported by insurance organizations—companies, service and professional organizations, brokerage firms, and agencies. The undergraduate, graduate, and special programs of the college are intended to fulfill the educational needs of the professional insurance practitioner. The college's Insurance and Frederic W. Ecker Liberal Arts libraries contain 70,390 volumes and 790 microfilm items, and subscribe to 350 periodicals.

Environment: Located in the heart of New York City's financial district, the college operates in space that has been leased in office buildings. Its classrooms, library, and administrative offices are convenient to public transportation. There are no student residences; students can reside at nearby colleges' dormitories.

Student Life: Approximately 60% of the students come from New York, and 90% of the students are from the Middle Atlantic area. Thirty percent live in other colleges' dorms. Housing is single-sex; there are visiting privileges. Students may keep cars on campus.

Organizations: There are no fraternities or sororities. Extracurricular activities include publications, drama, a Circle K organization, and various social and professional groups. The major social events on campus are dances and the awards program. New York City offers students innumerable cultural and social activities.

Sports: The college offers 1 intercollegiate team for men and 1 for women. Two intramural sports are available for men, none for women.

Handicapped: The entire campus is accessible to wheelchair students.

Graduates: At the end of the freshman year, about 10% of the students drop out; about 80% remain to graduate. Twenty percent of the graduates continue on to further study; 5% of these enter law school. Ninety-five percent of the graduates pursue careers in business and industry.

Services: Students receive the following services free of charge: placement, psychological and career counseling, and tutoring.

Programs of Study: The college confers the B.S. and B.B.A. degrees. Associate and master's degree programs are also offered. Bachelor's degrees are offered in the following subjects: BUSINESS (business administration, management, insurance), MATH AND SCIENCES (actuarial science, mathematics).

Required: All freshmen must take courses in freshman composition and literature, as well as a distribution of credits in 5 broad areas of study. All undergraduates must take 50–70% of their courses in the liberal arts; the remainder are equally divided between business administration and insurance subjects.

Special: Day division students in the B.S. and B.B.A. degrees participate in cooperative programs with insurance organizations. They must alternate 4-month periods of college study with 4-month periods of work, completing 128–132 credits in order to graduate.

Admissions: Forty-nine percent of those who applied were accepted for the 1981–82 class. Of those who enrolled, the SAT scores were as follows: Verbal—36% scored below 500, 44% between 500 and 599, 16% between 600 and 700, and 4% above 700; Math—27% scored below 500, 35% between 500 and 599, 28% between 600 and 700, and 10% above 700. All candidates must be graduates of accredited high schools, rank in the upper 50% of their graduating class, have a minimum GPA of 2.5, and have completed 16 Carnegie units. Also important are advanced placement or honors courses, impressions made during the interview, personality, and extracurricular activities record.

Procedure: The SAT or ACT is required. Applicants must also take the school's own College Qualification Test and Writing Sample. Students must have a personal interview either on campus or off campus (with a college representative near the student's hometown). Application deadlines are August 1 (fall) and December 1 (winter and spring). Freshmen are admitted each semester. Notification is on a rolling basis. The application fee is $20.

Special: There are early decision and early admissions plans. AP and CLEP credit is available.

Transfer: For fall 1981, 35 transfer students applied, 28 were accepted, and 27 enrolled. A 2.5 average is needed. D grades are accepted only as part of an associate degree. Applicants must have composite SAT scores of at least 950. Transfer students are not accepted for the senior class; all students are required to take at least 38 credits in residence. A total of 128 credits are required for the bachelor's degree. Applications are due by August 1 for fall and December 1 for winter and spring.

Visiting: There are no regularly scheduled orientations for prospective students. Guides are available for informal visits, and visitors may sit in on classes. Arrangements for visits can be made through Mrs. Paulette Fagone at the college.

Financial Aid: Approximately 95% of all students receive financial aid in the form of scholarships and loans. Twenty-five percent work part-time on campus. Freshmen receive from 95% to 100% of their demonstrated need. All freshmen are offered scholarships amounting to two-thirds of the cost of tuition through the cooperative programs with sponsoring insurance organizations, which pay two-thirds of the students' tuition and provide them with full-time employment during the work terms at salaries starting at $160 weekly. By the end of the 8 work terms, the student will have earned more than $18,000. In addition, if the student continues to work for his or her sponsor after graduation, the tuition paid by the student is reimbursed by the employer within 2 years. Tuition may be paid on the installment plan. The college is a member of the CSS, and requires the FAF from those applying for financial aid. There is no deadline for application for aid.

Foreign Students: The college actively recruits foreign students. Special counseling and organizations are available.

Admissions: The college requires that foreign applicants take the TOEFL; a minimum score of 500 is necessary for consideration. The SAT is also required.

Procedure: Application deadlines are June 15 for fall and November 15 for spring. Foreign students must present proof of funds adequate to cover at least 1 year of study. Health insurance is required; it is available through the college for a fee.

Admissions Contact: Russell F. Whiting, Director of Cooperative Education Admissions.

COLLEGE OF MOUNT SAINT VINCENT D–5
Riverdale, New York 10471   (212) 549-8000

F/T: 65M, 850W	Faculty:	64; IIB, –$
P/T: 25M, 305W	Ph.D.'s:	60%
Grad: none	S/F Ratio:	12 to 1
Year: sems, ss	Tuition:	$3880
Appl: open	R and B:	$2410
736 applied	489 accepted	210 enrolled
SAT: 475V 485M		COMPETITIVE

The College of Mount Saint Vincent, established in 1847, is a private, independent liberal arts college. The library houses 120,000 volumes, 10,000 microfilm items, and a special collection of Gaelic literature, and subscribes to 600 periodicals.

Environment: The 76-acre Riverdale campus borders the Hudson River in a suburban area just north of the George Washington Bridge, 30 minutes from midtown Manhattan. Campus facilities include Fonthill Castle, a New York State historical landmark, and 4 dormitories.

Student Life: Sixty percent of entering freshmen come from parochial schools; 40% from public. All students live on campus. Ninety-five percent of the students are Catholic. Campus housing is both single-sex and coed; there are visiting privileges in single-sex dorms. Students may keep cars on campus.

Organizations: There are no fraternities or sororities. Students are encouraged to participate in extracurricular activities and cultural events. A cooperative arrangement with Manhattan College, also in Riverdale, affords all students the use of both campuses.

Sports: The college fields 1 intercollegiate team for men and 5 for women. There are 3 intramural sports for men and 3 for women.

Handicapped: Special facilities available to physically handicapped students are wheelchair ramps, elevators, and specially equipped rest rooms; all buildings are accessible to them, but the campus terrain is very hilly. For visually impaired students there are readers. A designated coordinator and 1 special counselor are available for handicapped students.

Graduates: About 15% of the freshmen drop out by the end of the first year. Approximately 75% remain to graduate. Thirty-seven percent of the graduates pursue further study, 3% entering medical school and 4% entering law school. Thirty-five percent enter careers in business and industry.

Services: Students receive the following services free: psychological counseling, placement service, career counseling, tutoring, and health care.

Programs of Study: The college confers the B.A. and B.S. degrees in the following subjects: BUSINESS (computer science, general business), EDUCATION (elementary, health/physical, secondary), ENGLISH (English), FINE AND PERFORMING ARTS (art, art education, communication arts), HEALTH SCIENCES (nursing), LANGUAGES (French, German, Greek/Latin, Italian, Spanish), MATH AND SCIENCES (biochemistry, biology, chemistry, mathematics, physics), PHILOSOPHY (classics, philosophy, religion), PREPROFESSIONAL (dentistry, law, medicine, social work), SOCIAL SCIENCES (economics, government/political science, history, international business, psychology, social sciences, sociology). Thirty-three percent of the degrees are in nursing, 30% are in social sciences, and 10% are in education.

Required: All students must fulfill general education requirements.

Special: Three separate programs have been established for students wishing to major in liberal arts, a natural science, or liberal arts with preparation for teacher certification. Interdisciplinary and student-designed majors are possible, and a general studies degree is offered. The college has a Junior Year Abroad program. Biology majors may study at the Institute of Marine Biology in Nassau. Most majors have internship and field programs.

Honors: Eight honor societies have chapters on campus.

Admissions: Sixty-six percent of those who applied were accepted for the 1981–82 freshman class. The SAT scores for those who enrolled were as follows: Verbal—57% scored below 500, 35% between 500 and 599, 7% between 600 and 700, and 1% above 700; Math—48% scored below 500, 45% between 500 and 599, 6% between 600 and 700, and 1% above 700. Candidates should rank in the upper half of their class, have an 80% average or better, and demonstrate proficiency in a foreign language. Also of importance are recommendations by school officials, advanced placement or honors courses, and personality.

Procedure: The SAT is required. There is no application deadline; notification is on a rolling basis after December 15. Freshmen are admitted each semester. The application fee is $20.

Special: Early decision, early admissions, and deferred admissions plans are offered. The notification date for early decision is December 2. CLEP and AP credit is given.

Transfer: For fall 1981, 60 transfer applications were received, 38 were accepted, and 22 students enrolled. Transfers are considered for the freshman, sophomore, and junior years. Prospective transfers should have a minimum GPA of 2.5 and arrange for an interview. Evaluation is on an individual basis; D grades transfer with an associate degree. To receive a bachelor's degree, 45 credit hours, out of a total of 120 or 126, must be completed at the college. Application deadlines for transfer students are August 15 (fall) and December 15 (spring).

Visiting: Orientations for prospective students consist of a Sunday open house or weekday programs. November, February, and March are the best times to visit the campus. Visitors may sit in on classes and stay overnight at the school. Arrangements can be made through the admissions office.

Financial Aid: Eighty percent of the students receive financial aid. Each year full-tuition and partial scholarships are awarded to applicants on the basis of excellence of record, SAT scores, recommendation of the high school principal, and need. Service grants, NDSL, SEOG, BEOG, and CWS are available. The college is a member of the CSS. The FAF is required. The scholarship application deadlines are March 1 (fall) and December 1 (spring).

Foreign Students: One percent of the full-time students come from foreign countries. Special counseling is available for these students.

Admissions: Foreign applicants must take either the TOEFL or the SAT. A minimum score of 550 is required on the TOEFL.

Procedure: Application deadlines for foreign students are May 1 (fall) and August 1 (spring). The college requires proof of funds adequate to cover 1 year of study. Health insurance, available through the college for a fee, is also required.

Admissions Contact: William W. Hamilton, Director of Admissions.

COLLEGE OF NEW ROCHELLE D-5
New Rochelle, New York 10801   (914) 632-5300

F/T: 3M, 1157W	Faculty: n/av; IIA, –$
P/T: 92W	Ph.D.'s: 74%
Grad: none	S/F Ratio: 11 to 1
Year: sems, ss	Tuition: $4150
Appl: open	R and B: $2700
900 applied	610 accepted
SAT: 480V 495M	COMPETITIVE

The College of New Rochelle, chartered in 1904, is a private liberal arts college. The School of Arts and Sciences, a women's college since its founding, and the coeducational School of Nursing provide traditional undergraduate education. The library houses 160,000 volumes and 68,000 microfilm reels, and subscribes to over 687 periodicals.

Environment: The 30-acre campus is situated in the town of New Rochelle, 16 miles from New York City. Dormitories and small houses accommodate 645 students.

Student Life: Seventy-five percent of the students come from Mid-Atlantic states. Seventy percent reside in campus dormitories; students may live off campus. Fifty-two percent of entering freshmen come from public schools. Students may have cars on campus.

Organizations: There are no fraternities or sororities. Nearby New York City provides a wealth of educational and cultural opportunities.

Sports: The college competes intercollegiately in 5 sports and sponsors 5 intramural programs.

Handicapped: About 70% of the campus is accessible to handicapped students. Special facilities include wheelchair ramps, parking areas, elevators, specially equipped rest rooms, and lowered telephones. Special class scheduling is possible.

Graduates: The freshman dropout rate is about 11%; 80% remain to graduate. Twenty percent of the graduates pursue advanced degrees. About 40% enter careers in business and industry.

Services: Students receive the following services free of charge: psychological counseling, placement, career counseling, tutoring, and remedial instruction.

Programs of Study: The college confers the B.A., B.S., B.S.N., and B.F.A. degrees. Master's degrees are also awarded. Bachelor's degrees are offered in the following subjects: AREA STUDIES (American, women's), BUSINESS (general business), EDUCATION (elementary, special), ENGLISH (English), FINE AND PERFORMING ARTS (art, art education, art history, art therapy, communication arts, studio art), HEALTH SCIENCES (nursing), LANGUAGES (French, Greek/Latin, Italian, Spanish), MATH AND SCIENCES (biology, chemistry, mathematics, physics), PHILOSOPHY (classics, philosophy, religion), PRE-PROFESSIONAL (law, medicine, social work), SOCIAL SCIENCES (economics, government/political science, history, psychology, social sciences, sociology). Forty-five percent of the degrees are conferred in fine and performing arts.

Required: All students must take 18 hours in humanities, 12 hours in social sciences, and 6 hours in natural sciences and/or mathematics.

Special: Early childhood, elementary, secondary, and special education programs are available as a collaborative major leading to certification with the academic major. Interdisciplinary majors, student-designed majors, and study abroad are available. Students may earn a B.A. and M.S. in 4 years. Internships are available in most majors. Five-year programs in therapeutic education and psychology are offered. There is a cooperative program with Iona College.

Honors: Five honor societies have chapters on campus. There is a general interdisciplinary honors program.

Admissions: Sixty-two percent of those who applied were accepted for the 1981–82 freshman class. Of those who enrolled, the SAT scores were as follows: Verbal—35% between 500 and 599, 4% between 600 and 700, and 1% above 700; Math—25% scored between 500 and 599, 12% between 600 and 700, and 5% above 700. Candidates are selected on the basis of ability, preparation, and character; they should have completed 15 academic units and have a minimum average of 80%. Factors used in evaluating an applicant include GPA, class rank, advanced placement or honors courses, and recommendations.

Procedure: The SAT is required. A personal interview is recommended. Notification is on a rolling basis. The application fee is $15. There are no application deadlines; admissions and housing are offered on a first-come, first-served basis.

Special: Early decisions are possible. Early and deferred admissions plans are available. AP and CLEP credit is given.

Transfers: Transfers are accepted for the freshman, sophomore, and junior years; D grades are not acceptable. Fifty-two credits, of the 120 required for the bachelor's degree, must be completed in residence. Application deadlines are September 1 (fall) and January 15 (spring).

Visiting: Regular orientations are scheduled for prospective students. Visitors may sit in on classes and stay overnight at the college. The admissions office should be contacted for arrangements.

Financial Aid: Seventy-five percent of the students receive financial aid, which can take the form of scholarships, grants, low-interest loans, employment, or any combination thereof. Federal, state, and college aid programs are available. Freshmen and transfers are offered a number of scholarships ranging up to full tuition. Art scholarships and a Women's Leadership Scholarship are available. Awards are made on the basis of academic excellence, secondary school record, and personal qualifications. The college is a member of CSS. The FAF is required. The application deadline is March 1.

Foreign Students: The college welcomes foreign applicants and evaluates their transcripts in accordance with the educational procedures of the native country.

Admissions: Students whose native language is not English must submit results of the TOEFL.

Procedure: Application deadlines are open. Foreign students must submit a health report on a form provided by the college prior to the beginning of classes. They must also submit the Foreign Student Declaration and Certification of Finances.

Admissions Contact: Lynn McCaffrey, Director of Admissions.

COLLEGE OF SAINT ROSE D-5
Albany, New York 12203 (518) 454-5150

F/T: 238M, 963W	Faculty: 194; IIA, —$
P/T: 303M, 629W	Ph.D.'s: 41%
Grad: 205M, 559W	S/F Ratio: 12 to 1
Year: 5-1-5, ss	Tuition: $3440
Appl: open	R and B: $2000
512 applied 409 accepted 230 enrolled	
SAT or ACT: required	COMPETITIVE

The College of Saint Rose, founded in 1920, is a private liberal arts college. The library houses 125,000 volumes, 1738 microfilm reels, and 35,011 microfiche sheets, and subscribes to 800 periodicals.

Environment: The 22-acre campus is situated in the residential neighborhood of Pine Hills, just outside Albany. Dormitories accommodate 550 students.

Student Life: Almost all students are residents of New York State. Sixty percent come from public schools. Both single-sex and coed dormitories are available. Fewer than half the students live on campus.

Organizations: Students participate in many cultural and social activities, both on campus and with students from 14 other colleges in the area. There are no fraternities or sororities.

Sports: The college fields intercollegiate teams in 7 sports for men, women, or both. Intramural sports also are offered.

Handicapped: All major buildings, facilities, and services are accessible to the handicapped. Facilities include wheelchair ramps, special parking, elevators, specially equipped rest rooms, and lowered telephones and drinking fountains.

Graduates: About 70% of the freshmen remain to graduate. Forty percent of the graduates pursue advanced degrees; 2% enter law school. Thirty percent pursue careers in business and industry.

Services: Students receive the following free services: psychological counseling, health care, placement aid, career counseling, tutoring, and remedial instruction.

Programs of Study: The college confers the B.A. and B.S. degrees. Master's degrees also are awarded. Bachelor's degrees are offered in the following subjects: AREA STUDIES (American), BUSINESS (business administration), EDUCATION (communication disorders, elementary, special), ENGLISH (English), FINE AND PERFORMING ARTS (advertising design, art, art education, music, music education, studio art), HEALTH SCIENCES (medical technology), MATH AND SCIENCES (biology, biology/chemistry, chemistry, mathematics, mathematics/physical science), PHILOSOPHY (religion), SOCIAL SCIENCES (history, history/political science, international relations, social sciences, sociology, sociology/social work).

Required: All students must take writing and speech courses and earn 30 additional credits in 4 areas of liberal arts. Two physical education courses are also required.

Special: The college participates in junior-year-abroad and visiting-students programs, the Hudson-Mohawk Consortium, independent study, tutorial programs, and experienced adult programs. Students may design their own majors.

Honors: Three honor societies have chapters on campus.

Admissions: Eighty percent of those who applied were accepted for the 1981-82 freshman class. The SAT scores for an earlier freshman class were as follows: Verbal—26% between 500 and 599, 9% between 600 and 700, and less than 1% above 700; Math—38% between 500 and 599, 13% between 600 and 700, and less than 1% above 700. Candidates must be high school graduates or hold a GED diploma. They should rank in the upper half of their graduating class and have a B+ average. Recommendations by high school officials and advanced placement or honors courses also are considered. Students wishing to enter art or music programs should demonstrate special talents.

Procedure: The SAT or ACT is required. Application deadlines are open; March 15 is the recommended deadline for fall. There is a rolling admissions policy. The application fee is $15.

Special: Early decision, early admissions, and deferred admissions plans are available. AP and CLEP credit is given.

Transfers: For a recent year, 279 students applied, 232 were accepted, and 186 enrolled. A 2.0 GPA is necessary. D grades do not transfer. Students must earn at least 60 hours in residence of the 122 required for a bachelor's degree. Recommended application deadlines are April 1 (fall) and November 1 (spring).

Visiting: An admissions interview and campus visit are recommended for prospective students. Visitors may sit in on classes and stay overnight at the college. The admissions office should be contacted for arrangements.

Financial Aid: Eighty-five percent of the students receive aid. Several kinds of grants-in-aid are offered to freshmen. The college participates in NDSL, BEOG/SEOG, CWS, and state loan programs, and is a member of the CSS. Need is the main consideration in making awards. Application deadlines are March 1 (fall) and November 15 (spring).

Foreign Students: Two students from foreign countries were enrolled in 1981-82. Special counseling is provided.

Admissions: Applicants must score 520 or better on the TOEFL. No college entrance exams are required.

Procedure: Application deadlines are the same as those for American students. Foreign students must complete a college medical form and provide proof of adequate funds for 4 years. They also must arrange to carry health insurance.

Admissions Contact: Genevieve Ann Flaherty, Director of Admissions.

COLUMBIA UNIVERSITY

Columbia University, established in 1754 as King's College, has become one of the world's great centers of learning. Originally sponsored by the Episcopal Church, it is today privately supported and nonsectarian.

The urban campus is a 30-acre area on Morningside Heights, a section on the northwest side of Manhattan at the edge of the Hudson River. The campus, designed in grand American Renaissance style by McKim, Mead, and White in 1890 when Columbia moved from downtown New York, is generally regarded as one of the best laid-out urban campuses in America.

Undergraduate studies are offered by Columbia College (for men), Barnard (the affiliated women's college), the School of Engineering and Applied Science, the School of General Studies, and the College of Pharmaceutical Studies. The university has become widely known, however, for its graduate programs, which are offered by the School of Architecture, Graduate Faculties, School of Law, Graduate School of Business, School of International Affairs, Graduate School of Journalism, School of Fine Arts, School of Library Service, Teachers College, and School of Social Work. The university also operates the Columbia-Presbyterian Medical Center, which includes the College of Physicians and Surgeons and the School of Dental and Oral Surgery. All divisions except the Medical Center and the College of Pharmacy are located on the Morningside Campus.

Separate profiles on each of the undergraduate divisions follow.

COLUMBIA UNIVERSITY/ D-5
BARNARD COLLEGE
New York, New York 10027 (212) 280-2014

F/T: 2500W	Faculty: 139; IIB, ++$
P/T: none	Ph.D.'s: 98%
Grad: none	S/F Ratio: 13 to 1
Year: sems	Tuition: $7060
Appl: Jan. 15	R and B: $3280
2332 applied 1089 accepted 504 enrolled	
SAT: 620V 600M	HIGHLY COMPETITIVE

Barnard College, established in 1889, offers undergraduate programs in the liberal arts and sciences. Although part of Columbia University, Barnard maintains an independent status as a college for women. The library contains 150,000 volumes and subscribes to over 800 periodicals.

Environment: The urban campus occupies 4 acres of land adjacent to Columbia between 116th and 120th Streets in New York City. Living facilities include dormitories and on-campus and off-campus apartments.

NEW YORK

Student Life: A third of the students live within commuting distance of the college. Fifty-two percent come from public schools. About 45% live on campus. Campus housing is both coed and single-sex; there are visiting privileges in the single-sex housing. Students may not keep cars on campus.

Organizations: There are no sororities on campus. Extracurricular activities include publications, dramatics, performing groups, student government, special-interest clubs, and language clubs and centers.

Sports: The college fields intercollegiate teams in 9 sports. There are 6 intramural sports.

Handicapped: About 98% of the campus is accessible to handicapped students. Facilities include wheelchair ramps, elevators, lowered drinking fountains and telephones, specially equipped rest rooms, and tunnels connecting all campus buildings. Special class scheduling is also available. The office for disabled students provides counseling for handicapped students.

Graduates: The freshman dropout rate is 25%. About 80% of the freshmen remain to graduate. Of the graduates, 50% pursue advanced degrees; 8% enter medical or dental school and 8% enter law school. Thirty percent pursue careers in business or industry.

Services: Remedial instruction, placement, and career counseling are offered free of charge to students. Tutoring, health care, and psychological counseling are provided on a fee basis.

Programs of Study: The college confers the B.A. degree in the following subjects: AREA STUDIES (American, ancient, Asian, Latin American, medieval and Renaissance, Russian, urban, women's), ENGLISH (English), FINE AND PERFORMING ARTS (art history, dance, music, theater/dramatics), LANGUAGES (French, German, Greek/Latin, Italian, Russian, Spanish), MATH AND SCIENCES (biochemistry, biology, chemistry, computer science, ecology/environmental science, geology, mathematics, physics), PHILOSOPHY (philosophy, religion), PREPROFESSIONAL (architecture), SOCIAL SCIENCES (anthropology, economics, geography, government/political science, history, psychology, sociology). Twenty-five percent of the degrees are conferred in math and sciences, 24% in social sciences.

Special: Some undergraduate courses are held with Columbia College and a number of departments are conducted jointly with the university. Graduate courses are open to qualified students. A special program in education, offered in conjunction with the Teachers College, leads to certification. The Senior Scholar Program allows especially qualified students to undertake a single project with exemptions from all course and major requirements in their senior year. The Program of Health and Society introduces undergraduates to contemporary issues and problems in the field of health care. There is a combined degree program with the Seminary College of Jewish Studies.

Honors: There is a chapter of Phi Beta Kappa on campus.

Admissions: Forty-seven percent of those who applied were accepted for the 1981-82 freshman class. Of those who enrolled, the SAT scores were as follows: Verbal—5% below 500, 33% between 500 and 599, 50% between 600 and 700, and 13% above 700; Math—6% below 500, 42% between 500 and 599, 44% between 600 and 700, and 7% above 700. Candidates should present the following credentials: evidence of good character, which is obtained from confidential reports from the applicant's secondary school principal and teachers and, if possible, through a personal interview at the college; evidence of intellectual ability and achievement; and acceptable scores on the required SAT and ATs. Candidates must also offer a college preparatory program from an approved secondary school. A high school average of at least 3.5 is required. Advanced placement or honors courses, special talents, and the extracurricular activities record are also considered important.

Procedure: The SAT and 3 ATs (in English composition and 2 other subjects) should be taken no later than the fall of the senior year. The application deadline is January 15. Freshmen are admitted in the fall only. There is a $25 fee. Notification is in April.

Special: Early decision candidates must apply by November 15; notification is by mid-December. Deferred admissions and early admissions plans are offered. AP credit is available.

Transfer: For fall 1981, 442 students applied, 310 were accepted, and 199 enrolled. A strong academic record, recommendations, transcripts, and SAT scores are required. D grades do not transfer. All students must complete, at the college, 60 of the 120 credits required for a bachelor's degree. Deadlines are May 1 (fall entry) and November 1 (spring entry).

Visiting: Guides are available for informal visits to the campus. Visitors may sit in on classes and stay overnight at the school. Visits are best scheduled from May through January. The admissions office should be contacted for arrangements.

Financial Aid: About 40% of the students receive financial aid. About 25% work part-time on campus. In addition to grants and loan funds (including BEOG/SEOG and NDSL), opportunities for work-study (including CWS) are provided. The average aid to a freshman is $3150. Aid applications and the FAF should be filed by February 1; early decision candidates should file by November 1. The college is a member of CSS.

Foreign Students: Special counseling and special organizations are available for these students.

Admissions: Foreign students must achieve a TOEFL score of at least 550 and must take the SAT and 3 ATs (English Composition and 2 others).

Procedure: Application deadlines are January 15 (fall entry) and November 1 (spring entry). Foreign students must present proof of funds adequate to cover 1 year of study.

Admissions Contact: Yael Septee, Associate Director of Admissions.

COLUMBIA UNIVERSITY/ COLUMBIA COLLEGE
D-5

New York, New York 10027   (212) 280-2521

F/T: 2900M	Faculty: 500; I, ++$
P/T: none	Ph.D.'s: 100%
Grad: none	S/F Ratio: 6 to 1
Year: sems, ss	Tuition: $6772
Appl: Jan. 1	R and B: $3280
3410 applied	1491 accepted 746 enrolled
SAT: 620V 650M	MOST COMPETITIVE

Columbia College, founded in 1754, is the undergraduate liberal arts college of Columbia University. Formerly an all-male school, Columbia will begin admitting women for the 1983-84 freshman class. The library contains 4.9 million volumes and 1.7 million microfilm items, and subscribes to 57,000 periodicals.

Environment: Located in an urban setting, the college, which maintains some independence within the university, has its own sub-campus around South Field. In addition, the college shares in the enormous educational facilities of the whole university. There are 8 college residence halls that house from 250 to 600 students each. On- and off-campus apartments and fraternity houses are also available.

Student Life: About 42% of the students are from the tri-state New York metropolitan area. About 55% are graduates of public schools. More than 85% live in coed college residence halls, 8% in fraternity town houses, and 2% in apartments nearby. Twenty-one percent of the students are members of minority groups. Cars are not permitted on campus.

Organizations: Over 90% of the students traditionally participate in extracurricular activities such as publications, a drama group, service societies, performing groups, religious organizations, and the radio stations. There are 16 fraternities; 16% of the students belong to one of them.

Sports: The college fields 13 intercollegiate teams and offers intramural competition in 13 sports.

Handicapped: Facilities for handicapped students include wheelchair ramps and lowered drinking fountains and telephones.

Graduates: About 8% of the freshmen drop out by the end of their first year. About 80% graduate with their class. Of those who graduate, 90% pursue advanced degrees; 11% enter medical school, 2% dental school, and 21% law school.

Services: Psychological counseling, tutoring, placement, and career counseling are offered free of charge to students. Health care services are available for a fee.

Programs of Study: The college confers the B.A. degree. Bachelor's degrees are offered in the following subjects: AREA STUDIES (Asian, East Asian, Latin American, Middle Eastern, Russian, urban), ENGLISH (comparative literature, English, literature), FINE AND PERFORMING ARTS (art history, music), LANGUAGES (Chinese, French, German, Greek/Latin, Hebrew, Italian, Japanese, linguistics, Portuguese, Russian, Spanish), MATH AND SCIENCES (astronomy, biochemistry, biology, chemistry, computer science, earth science, geology, mathematics, physics, statistics), PHILOSOPHY (classics, philosophy, philosophy—economics, religion), PREPROFESSIONAL (architecture, dentistry, engineering, law, medicine), SOCIAL SCIENCES (ancient studies, anthropology, economics, geography, government/political science, history, international relations, Medieval-Renaissance studies, psychology, sociology).

Required: A core curriculum, emphasizing the achievements of Western civilization, must be completed by all students.

Special: Independent study is available to juniors and seniors in most departments. The study abroad program can include Columbia's own facility in Paris. A 5-year B.A.-B.S. degree program in liberal arts and engineering is offered in conjunction with Columbia's School of Engineering and Applied Science. Student-designed majors are permitted.

Honors: Phi Beta Kappa has a chapter on campus. Interdisciplinary seminars are offered for qualified students.

Admissions: Forty-four percent of those who applied were accepted for the 1981-82 freshman class. Of enrolled students, the SAT scores were as follows: Verbal—10% below 500, 31% between 500 and 599, 44% between 600 and 700, and 15% above 700; Math—5% below 500, 21% between 500 and 599, 50% between 600 and 700, and 24% above 700. Most students in the current freshman class ranked in the upper fifth of their high school class. The most important factors in the admissions decision are advanced placement or honor courses, extracurricular activities, recommendations by school officials, and special talents.

Procedure: The SAT and 3 ATs (including the AT in English composition) are required and should be taken in the senior year. On-campus interviews are available from June 1 to January 15. Applicants outside the New York metropolitan area may have an interview with an alumni representative. The application deadline is January 1; notification is made by April 15. There is a $30 application fee.

Special: Early decision, early admissions, and deferred admissions plans are available. The application deadline for early admission is January 1; the notification date for early decision is December 15. AP credit is offered.

Transfer: For fall 1981, 650 students applied, 70 were accepted, and 45 enrolled. A minimum GPA of 3.0 is recommended for transfer applicants. At least 15 credit hours must be completed. D grades do not transfer. There is a 2-year residency requirement. Students must complete, at the college, 64 of the 124 credits necessary for a bachelor's degree. Application deadlines are April 15 (fall) and November 1 (spring).

Visiting: Guides are available for informal campus visits. Visitors may sit in on classes and stay overnight at the school. The admissions office should be contacted for arrangements.

Financial Aid: About 55% of the students receive financial aid. The college awards scholarships, ranging from $100 to $5500, to about 55% of each entering class. CWS and other part-time employment is available, and 60% of the students work part-time on campus. In addition, $400,000 in loan funds is available for students. The average award to freshmen from all sources is $5200. Financial aid applications must be filed by February 15 for regular applicants and November 1 for early decision candidates. The FAF is required. The college is a member of CSS.

Foreign Students: About 6% of the students are from foreign countries. The college offers these students an intensive English course, an intensive English program, and special counseling and organizations.

Admissions: Foreign students must achieve an acceptable score on the college's own English proficiency exam. The SAT and 3 ATs, including English Composition, are also required.

Procedure: The application deadline for fall is January 1. Students must take a medical exam and are required to carry health insurance, which is available through the college for a fee.

Admissions Contact: James T. McMenamin, Director of Admissions.

COLUMBIA UNIVERSITY/ SCHOOL OF ENGINEERING AND APPLIED SCIENCE
D-5

New York, New York 10027 (212) 280-2931

F/T: 938M, 228W
P/T: none
Grad: 782M, 111W
Year: sems, ss
Appl: Jan. 20
1540 applied
SAT: 540V 670M

Faculty: 95; n/av
Ph.D.'s: 98%
S/F Ratio: 12 to 1
Tuition: $6842
R and B: $3280
643 accepted   253 enrolled
HIGHLY COMPETITIVE

The School of Engineering and Applied Science of Columbia University offers undergraduate degree programs in various fields of engineering and the sciences. The Ambrose Monell Engineering Library contains over 175,000 volumes and 850,000 technical reports, and subscribes to 1500 periodicals. In addition, students have access to over 5 million volumes in the university's other libraries.

Environment: The school forms part of the main university's urban campus at West 116th Street and Broadway. The Engineering Center, a 13-story laboratory and classroom building, is one of the most advanced teaching and research centers of its kind. The engineering and related science departments maintain extensive research facilities in many other buildings on campus as well as at off-campus sites. Living facilities include dormitories and fraternity houses.

Student Life: About 70% of the students come from public schools. About 85% live on campus. Thirty-four percent are minority-group members. Campus housing is coed. Students may not keep cars on campus.

Organizations: There are 15 fraternities on campus. The many cultural offerings of New York City are readily accessible to students.

Sports: The school fields 13 intercollegiate teams for men and 8 for women. There are 12 intramural sports for men and 9 for women.

Handicapped: About 70% of the campus is accessible to handicapped students. Facilities include wheelchair ramps, lowered drinking fountains and telephones, elevators, parking areas, and specially equipped rest rooms. Special class scheduling is also available. Two counselors are available to handicapped students.

Graduates: The freshman dropout rate is 5%; 67% of entering freshmen remain to graduate. Seventy percent of the graduates pursue advanced degrees; 5% enter medical school, 1% enter dental school, and 1% enter law school. Thirty percent enter business and industry.

Services: Psychological counseling, health care, remedial instruction, placement, and career counseling are offered free of charge to students. Tutoring is provided free of charge to freshmen and on a fee basis to other students.

Programs of Study: The school confers the B.S. in Eng. degree. Master's and doctoral degrees are also awarded. Bachelor's degrees are offered in the following subjects: MATH AND SCIENCES (chemistry, computer science, geophysics, mathematics, metallurgy and materials science, physics), PREPROFESSIONAL (engineering—bioengineering, engineering—chemical, engineering—civil, engineering—electrical, engineering—engineering mechanics, engineering—industrial, engineering—mechanical, engineering—mineral engineering and chemical metallurgy, engineering—mining, engineering—nuclear, operations research).

Special: The school also offers preparation in plasma physics, and solid state science and engineering. Students may study in Columbia College or any of 80 other liberal arts colleges throughout the country under the 5-year Combined Plan Program which leads to both the B.A. and B.S. degrees.

Admissions: Forty-two percent of those who applied were accepted for the 1981-82 freshman class. Of enrolled students, the SAT scores were as follows: Verbal—27% below 500, 43% between 500 and 599, 25% between 600 and 700, and 5% above 700; Math—1% below 500, 14% between 500 and 599, 47% between 600 and 700, and 38% above 700. Students should be graduates of accredited high schools, have at least a 3.0 high school GPA, and rank in the top 15% of their graduating class. Other factors considered are advanced placement or honors courses, recommendations, SAT scores, evidence of special talents, leadership record, and extracurricular activities.

Procedure: The SAT and 3 ATs (Math Level I or II, English Composition, and either Physics or Chemistry) are required and should be taken by December of the senior year. An interview on campus is required of all applicants who live within 50 miles of New York City. The application deadline is January 20. There is a $25 application fee.

Special: There are early decision, early admissions, and deferred admissions plans. The application deadline for early admissions is January 20; the notification date for early decision is December 15. AP credit is available.

Transfer: For fall 1981, 336 students applied, 160 were accepted, and 111 enrolled. D grades do not transfer. Students must have completed 1 year of calculus, 1 year of physics (with lab), 1 year of chemistry (with lab), and some liberal arts courses. All students must complete, at the school, 60 of the 128 or more credits required for a bachelor's degree. The application deadline for the fall semester is March 15.

Visiting: The school conducts regularly scheduled orientations for prospective students. Guides are available for informal campus visits. Visitors may sit in on classes and stay overnight at the school. The admissions office should be contacted for arrangements.

Financial Aid: About 75% of the students receive financial aid. About 30% work part-time on campus. The average freshman award is $3200. The school awards about 165 freshman scholarships ranging from $50 to $6000. In addition, there are state awards; federal, state, school, and private loans are also available. The financial aid

550 NEW YORK

application deadline is January 20. The FAF is required. The school is a member of CSS.

Foreign Students: Eight percent of the full-time students come from foreign countries. An intensive English course, an intensive English program, special counseling, and special organizations are available for these students.

Admissions: Foreign students must achieve a TOEFL score of at least 600 and must take the school's own English proficiency exam, the SAT, and 3 ATs (Math Level I or II, English Composition, and Physics or Chemistry).

Procedure: The application deadline for fall entry is January 20. Foreign students must present proof of funds adequate to cover 4 years of study and must carry health insurance, which is available through the school.

Admissions Contact: Thomas R. Phillips, Director of Admissions.

COLUMBIA UNIVERSITY/ SCHOOL OF GENERAL STUDIES   D-5
New York, New York 10027   (212) 280-2752

F/T: 630M, 313W		Faculty:	400; I, ++$
P/T: 440M, 500W		Ph.D.'s:	95%
Grad: none		S/F Ratio:	n/av
Year: sems, ss		Tuition:	$6090
Appl: July 15		R and B:	n/app
1465 applied	732 accepted		483 enrolled
ACT: 27			HIGHLY COMPETITIVE+

The Columbia University School of General Studies, which began granting degrees in 1947, is the university's coeducational liberal arts college for students who are 21 years of age and older or employed full time. The school has day and evening classes for full- and part-time students. The university library houses 4.9 million volumes and 1.3 million microfilm items, and subscribes to 59,400 periodicals.

Environment: The school shares the 30-acre campus of Columbia University. It has one building and uses 20 others of the university.

Student Life: Thirty-seven percent of the students are from New York. About 10% live on campus. University housing is both coed and single-sex. Students are of all ages and backgrounds. Most have transferred from other institutions.

Organizations: Interested students may participate in publications and radio. The school also sponsors art shows, science exhibits, and lectures.

Sports: Students may use Columbia athletic facilities and may be eligible for intercollegiate and intramural sports.

Handicapped: About 70% of the campus is accessible to handicapped students. Facilities include wheelchair ramps, specially equipped rest rooms, lowered drinking fountains and telephones, parking areas, and elevators. Special class scheduling is also available. A counselor is available to handicapped students.

Graduates: About 55% of the freshmen remain to graduate. Of those, 75% pursue advanced degrees. About 25% begin careers in business or industry.

Services: Psychological counseling, tutoring, remedial instruction, placement, and career counseling are offered free to students.

Programs of Study: The school offers the B.A. and B.S. degrees. Bachelor's degrees are offered in the following subjects: AREA STUDIES (ancient, Asian—East Asian, Latin American, urban), ENGLISH (comparative literature, English literature, linguistics, literature—writing), FINE AND PERFORMING ARTS (art history, music, film/photography, theater/dramatics, visual arts), LANGUAGES (French, German, Greek/Latin, Italian, Middle East languages and cultures, Polish, Russian, Spanish), MATH AND SCIENCES (applied mathematics, biology, chemistry, computer science, geology, mathematics, physics, statistics), PHILOSOPHY (philosophy, religion), SOCIAL SCIENCES (anthropology, economics, geography, government/political science, history, psychology, sociology). Twenty-five percent of the degrees are conferred in social sciences, and 19% in math and sciences.

Required: All students must complete general education requirements.

Special: Preprofessional programs are offered in architecture, dentistry, social work, and medicine. Combined degree programs are offered in international affairs, law, medicine, business, public affairs and administration, teaching, and engineering. Interdisciplinary major programs are conducted in Islamic studies, Jewish history, and other areas. Students may design their own majors.

Honors: Three honor societies, including Phi Beta Kappa, have chapters on campus. Almost all departments offer honors programs requiring an honors seminar and essay.

Admissions: About 50% of those who applied were accepted for the 1981-82 freshman class. All applicants must be 21 years of age or work full time, present evidence of superior academic ability, and be graduates of accredited high schools.

Procedure: The SAT or ACT generally is required. Application deadlines are July 15 (fall), December 1 (spring), and April 15 (summer). Notification is made on a rolling basis. There is a $20 application fee.

Special: A deferred admissions plan is offered. AP and CLEP credit is given.

Transfer: Applicants must be in good academic standing at their last school and meet the basic freshman criteria. Students must complete 60 semester hours in residence of the 124 required for a bachelor's degree.

Visiting: The school conducts regularly scheduled orientations for prospective students. Guides are available for informal campus visits. Visitors may sit in on classes and stay overnight at the school. The admissions office should be contacted for arrangements.

Financial Aid: About 15% of the students receive aid. Programs include scholarships, loans, and CWS. Students must use state loans before they are awarded money from Columbia or federal sources. Tuition may be paid on the installment plan. The deadline for aid applications is May 1. The FAF must be filed.

Foreign Students: About 10% to 15% of the students at the School of General Studies are from foreign countries. The university offers these students an intensive English course, an intensive English program, special counseling, and special organizations.

Admissions: Applicants must score at least 600 on the TOEFL. They also must take the SAT.

Procedure: Foreign students are admitted to all terms; applications must be filed 6 months before the start of the term in which the student seeks to enroll. Students must present proof of adequate funds for their entire period of study, and must carry health insurance, which is available through the university for a fee.

Admissions Contact: John Bamfield, Director of Admissions.

CONCORDIA COLLEGE   D-5
Bronxville, New York 10708   (914) 337-9300

F/T: 192M, 212W		Faculty:	40; IIB, -$
P/T: 18M, 24W		Ph.D.'s:	38%
Grad: none		S/F Ratio:	11 to 1
Year: sems		Tuition:	$3080
Appl: Aug. 28		R and B:	$2120
302 applied	232 accepted		164 enrolled
SAT: 410V 400M	ACT: 15		LESS COMPETITIVE

Concordia College is a private liberal arts college affiliated with the Lutheran Church, Missouri Synod. Founded in 1881, the college specializes in music, education, and social work. The library contains 65,000 volumes and subscribes to 500 periodicals.

Environment: The 32-acre campus is located in a suburban area 17 miles north of New York City. There are 17 buildings including a student union, modern labs, a physical education facility, and music halls. Athletic facilities include a field house, 5 outdoor tennis courts, 2 squash/racquetball courts, a weight room, and 3 athletic fields. Eight dormitories house 450 students.

Student Life: About two-thirds of the students are from New York. About 91% attended public schools. Eighty percent of the students live on campus. Seventy percent are Protestant, and 25% are Catholic; religious services are held daily, but are not compulsory. About 18% of the students are minority-group members. College housing is single-sex, and there are visiting privileges. Freshmen may not keep cars on campus.

Organizations: There are no fraternities or sororities, but professional and service organizations also serve as social groups. Extracurricular activities include musical groups, drama, publications, and off-campus cultural events.

Sports: The college fields 4 intercollegiate teams for men and 4 for women. There are 9 intramural sports for men and 8 for women.

Handicapped: The campus is accessible to physically handicapped students. Facilities include wheelchair ramps, specially equipped rest rooms, parking areas, lowered telephones, and an elevator in the library. Special class scheduling is also available. A counselor is available to handicapped students.

Services: Students receive the following services free of charge: placement, career counseling, health care, tutoring, remedial instruction, and psychological counseling.

Programs of Study: The college confers the B.A. and B.S. degrees. Associate degrees are also awarded. Bachelor's degrees are offered in the following subjects: BUSINESS (business education), EDUCATION (early childhood, educational services, elementary, secondary), ENGLISH (English), FINE AND PERFORMING ARTS (music, music education), MATH AND SCIENCES (biology, ecology/environmental science, mathematics), PHILOSOPHY (religion), PREPROFESSIONAL (ministry, social work), SOCIAL SCIENCES (behavioral science, history).

Required: A core curriculum is required of all students.

Special: Student-designed majors are permitted. A freshman seminar eases the transition from high school to college by developing the skills and discipline needed to succeed in college and in a career. Students may earn up to 15 credits studying for 1 semester in Germany, France, or England.

Honors: There is a chapter of Alpha Chi on campus.

Admissions: Seventy-seven percent of those who applied were accepted for the 1981-82 freshman class. The SAT scores of those enrolled were as follows: Verbal—81% scored below 500, 16% between 500 and 599, 3% between 600 and 700, and 0% above 700; Math—77% scored below 500, 21% between 500 and 599, 2% between 600 and 700, and 0% above 700. Applicants must graduate from an accredited high school with at least 16 high school units, a class rank in the upper half, and a 2.0 grade average. A personal interview is required. The school also considers advanced placement or honor courses, extracurricular activities, and evidence of special talents.

Procedure: Either SAT or ACT scores are required. Application deadlines are August 28 (fall) and January 17 (spring); freshmen are also admitted at midyear and in the summer. Notification is on a rolling basis. There is a $15 application fee.

Special: Early and deferred admissions plans are available. AP and CLEP credit is available.

Transfer: For fall 1981, 36 students applied, 34 were accepted, and 30 enrolled. Transfer students need a GPA of at least 1.875 and must have an interview at the school. D grades do not transfer. Students must earn, at the college, 30 of the 122 credits necessary for a bachelor's degree. Application deadlines are August 28 (fall) and January 17 (spring).

Visiting: Open-house visits are scheduled. Informal weekday visits, including guided tours and interviews, allow visitors to sit in on classes and stay overnight at the college. Arrangements should be made through the admissions office.

Financial Aid: Eighty-two percent of the students receive aid through the school. Sixty percent work part-time on campus. Average aid to freshmen is $3250; scholarships to freshmen average $300. Scholarships and loans are available, and tuition may be paid in installments. The college is a member of CSS. The FAF should be filed by April 15.

Foreign Students: One percent of the full-time students come from foreign countries. The college offers these students special counseling.

Admissions: Foreign students must achieve a TOEFL score of 500. No college entrance exam must be taken.

Procedure: Application deadlines are August 1 (fall) and January 1 (spring). Foreign students must present a completed health form issued by the college and proof of funds adequate to cover one year of study.

Admissions Contact: John Bahr, Director of Admissions.

THE COOPER UNION FOR THE ADVANCEMENT OF SCIENCE AND ART
D-5
New York, New York 10003   (212) 254-6300

F/T: 572M, 277W	Faculty: 58; IIA, ++$
P/T: 25M, 10W	Ph.D.'s: 40%
Grad: 31M, 3W	S/F Ratio: 15 to 1
Year: sems	Annual Fee: $300
Appl: see profile	R and B: n/app
1801 applied	318 accepted	206 enrolled
SAT(engineering): 600V 700M	MOST COMPETITIVE

The Cooper Union for the Advancement of Science and Art, founded in 1859, is a privately endowed institution providing free high-quality education in architecture, engineering, and fine arts. The library houses 84,000 volumes, subscribes to 280 periodicals, and has 40,000 slides on file.

Environment: The school occupies 3 buildings on Cooper Square in lower Manhattan. As a nonresidential institution, it provides no living quarters, but a cafeteria, lounges, and lockers are available.

Student Life: Most of the students are local residents. Seventy-three percent of the entering freshmen come from public schools. Sixteen percent of the students are minority-group members.

Organizations: About 15% of the men belong to fraternities. The extracurricular program includes social events, student clubs and publications, and student participation on faculty-student committees.

Sports: The college does not field any intercollegiate teams. There are 6 intramural sports for men and 6 for women.

Handicapped: The school estimates its buildings to be 50% accessible to handicapped students. Special facilities include wheelchair ramps, elevators, and specially equipped rest rooms. An interpreter is provided for hearing-impaired students.

Graduates: The freshman dropout rate is 12%; 75% remain to graduate. Sixty-five percent of the students go on to graduate studies; 80% enter careers in business and industry.

Services: Placement, tutoring, remedial instruction, and career and psychological counseling are offered at no charge to the student.

Programs of Study: The school confers the B.F.A., B.Arch., and B.En. degrees. Master's degrees are awarded in engineering. Bachelor's degrees are offered in the following subjects: architecture, design, engineering (chemical, civil, electrical, mechanical, or general), and fine arts. Sixty percent of the degrees recently conferred were in architecture and engineering, and 40% were in fine arts.

Special: Independent study is offered. A 5-year program leads to a combined B.En.-M.E. in engineering.

Honors: The honor society of Tau Beta Pi has a chapter on campus.

Admissions: Eighteen percent of those who applied were accepted for the 1981-82 freshman class. The SAT scores of those who enrolled in the engineering program were as follows: Verbal—8% scored below 500, 41% between 500 and 599, 40% between 600 and 700, and 11% above 700; Math—0% scored below 500, 2% between 500 and 599, 47% between 600 and 700, and 51% above 700. The school does not require a minimum grade average, but most engineering students have A averages. In evaluating a candidate for engineering, the high school average, SAT scores, and the score on designated ATs are the most important factors. Applicants for art or architecture are judged chiefly on evidence of artistic (design) talent. Other factors considered for all applicants are personality and the extracurricular activities record.

Procedure: Either the SAT or ACT is required. In addition, engineering applicants must take ATs in mathematics and either chemistry or physics, and art and architecture applicants must take the college's art test. The deadline for application is January 1 for art and architecture applicants, and February 1 for engineering applicants. Freshmen are admitted only in the fall. There is a $10 application fee.

Special: Early and deferred admissions plans are offered. AP and CLEP credit is available.

Transfer: For fall 1981, 973 students applied, 64 were accepted, and 57 enrolled. Requirements include a strong academic background and a curriculum similar to that of the school. Art and architecture students must present a portfolio. There is a 2-year residency requirement, during which students must complete at least half of the credits necessary for a bachelor's degree; requirements vary with the programs. Application deadlines are March 15 for art and architecture students, and June 1 for engineering students.

Visiting: Guides are available for informal visits to the campus on weekdays from 10 A.M. to 4 P.M. Arrangements should be made through the dean of admissions.

Financial Aid: All receive free tuition. Those requiring additional assistance may apply for federal, state, and union loans. Twenty-seven percent of the students receive aid. Five percent work part-time on campus. Average aid to freshmen is $1500. The college is a member of CSS and requires the FAF when aid is needed. The deadline for application is April 15.

Foreign Students: Two percent of the full-time students come from foreign countries.

Admissions: Foreign students must achieve a TOEFL score of 500. The SAT is also required. Engineering applicants must take ATs in mathematics and either chemistry or physics.

552 NEW YORK

Procedure: Application deadlines for fall entry are January 1 for fine arts and architecture students and February 1 for engineering students. Foreign students must present proof of funds adequate to cover 1 year of study.

Admissions Contact: Herbert Liebeskind, Dean of Admissions and Records.

CORNELL UNIVERSITY   C-3
Ithaca, New York 14853   (607) 256-3447

F/T: 6847M, 5420W	Faculty: n/av
P/T: 9M, 6W	Ph.D.'s: 90%
Grad: 3295M, 1739W	S/F Ratio: n/av
Year: sems, ss	Tuition: $2880-7000
Appl: Jan. 1	R and B: $2740
16,991 applied	5377 accepted	2860 enrolled
SAT: 590V 650M		MOST COMPETITIVE

Founded in 1865 as the land-grant university of New York and privately endowed by Ezra Cornell, Cornell University consists of 7 undergraduate divisions and several professional and graduate schools. Privately supported divisions offering undergraduate instruction are: the College of Arts and Sciences, the College of Architecture, Art, and Planning, the College of Engineering, and the School of Hotel Administration. Four divisions are state-supported units of the State University of New York: the College of Agriculture and Life Sciences, the College of Human Ecology, the College of Veterinary Medicine, and the School of Industrial and Labor Relations. Additional units include Cornell Medical College in New York City, the New York State Agricultural Experiment Station in Geneva, and the National Astronomy and Ionosphere Center in Puerto Rico. The various libraries contain over 4 million volumes and 2 million microfilm items, and subscribe to more than 51,000 periodicals.

Environment: The 740-acre Ithaca campus is situated on a hill overlooking Cayuga Lake in the rural Finger Lakes region of New York, about 60 miles from Syracuse. There are more than 400 university buildings, including several listed on the National Historic Register. Dormitories accommodate over 5500 students.

Student Life: Students come from all parts of the country, with 50% drawn from New York State. Thirty-six percent of the students live on campus. University housing is coed and single-sex; students in single-sex housing have visiting privileges. Students may keep cars on campus. Day-care facilities are available to full-time and part-time students, faculty, and staff for a fee.

Organizations: There are 48 fraternities and 12 sororities on campus; 36% of the men and 20% of the women belong to them. There are over 350 registered student organizations on campus. Year-round recreational facilities are only minutes away, supplementing campus facilities and social and cultural opportunities in Ithaca and Syracuse.

Sports: The university fields 21 intercollegiate teams for men and 18 for women. There are 23 intramural sports for men and 22 for women.

Handicapped: About 70% of the campus is accessible to handicapped students. Special facilities include wheelchair ramps, parking areas, elevators, specially equipped rest rooms, and lowered drinking fountains and telephones. Special class scheduling can be arranged. Reader services, braille and taped books, a teletype communication system, and a lending library for special equipment are all available to visually and hearing-impaired students. A special counselor and an assistant work with handicapped students.

Graduates: The freshman dropout rate is about 5%; about 80% of the freshmen remain to graduate.

Services: The following services are provided to students free of charge: psychological counseling, placement and career counseling (for graduates as well as undergraduates), health care, tutoring, and remedial instruction. Placement services include career centers, interview arrangements, files, and special libraries.

Programs of Study: Cornell confers the A.B., B.S., B.F.A., and B.Arch. degrees. Master's and doctoral degrees are also awarded. Bachelor's degrees are offered in the following subjects: AREA STUDIES (American, Asian, Black/Afro-American, European, Near Eastern, Russian), BUSINESS (hotel/restaurant management, labor/industrial relations), EDUCATION (agricultural, community service, general), ENGLISH (communication, comparative literature, creative writing, English, linguistics), FINE AND PERFORMING ARTS (art, art history, music, theater/dramatics), LANGUAGES (Chinese, French, German, Greek/Latin, Italian, Japanese, Russian, Spanish), MATH AND SCIENCES (applied math, astronomy, atmospheric sciences/meteorology, biochemistry, biology, biometrics/biostatistics, botany, chemistry, computer science, ecology/environmental science, entomology, genetics, geology, mathematics, microbiology, neurosciences, nutrition, physics, physiology, plant pathology, statistics), PHILOSOPHY (classics, philosophy), PREPROFESSIONAL (agriculture, architecture, engineering—agricultural, engineering—chemical, engineering—civil, engineering—electrical, engineering—general, engineering—industrial, engineering—materials, engineering—mechanical, engineering—physics, home economics), SOCIAL SCIENCES (anthropology, archaeology, economics, government/political science, history, international relations, psychology, social sciences, sociology). About 18% of the undergraduate degrees are conferred in engineering, 17% in agriculture and natural resources, and 11% in business.

Special: There are numerous cooperative programs with other colleges and universities. Student-designed majors and interdisciplinary studies may be arranged.

Honors: Many departments offer honors programs. About 25 national honor societies, including Phi Beta Kappa, have chapters on campus.

Admissions: About 32% of those who applied were accepted for the 1981-82 freshman class. The SAT scores of those who enrolled were as follows: Verbal—15% scored below 500, 35% between 500 and 599, 39% between 600 and 700, and 11% above 700; Math—4% scored below 500, 22% between 500 and 599, 45% between 600 and 700, and 29% above 700. Admissions requirements for any of the undergraduate divisions include a college-qualifying recommendation from the high school and the completion of 16 Carnegie units. A personal interview is required for the Schools of Hotel Administration and of Industrial and Labor Relations; for the College of Architecture, Art, and Planning; and for the veterinary divisions. The 3 major criteria affecting the admissions decision are the high school record, test scores, and extracurricular activities.

Procedure: The SAT or the ACT is required and should be taken by January of the senior year. ATs are required for several divisions. The application deadlines for most divisions are January 1 (fall) and November 1 (spring). Acceptance and notification procedures vary by school or college. There is a $30 application fee.

Special: The university has a deferred admissions plan and an early decision plan. AP credit may be earned.

Transfer: For fall 1981, 2940 students applied, 597 were accepted, and 480 enrolled. Transfers are accepted for all but the senior class. Preference is given to students applying from 2-year units of the State University of New York to the state-supported divisions at Cornell. D grades transfer in some divisions. Students must earn, at the university, at least 60 of the minimum 120 credits required for a bachelor's degree; numbers vary with the programs. Transfer application deadlines are March 15 (fall) and November 1 (spring).

Visiting: Cornell has a regular orientation program for prospective students which includes a campus visit and tour, and visits to classes, dorms, and dining facilities. Guides are also available for informal visits to the school. The best time to visit is before January or after April. The admissions office handles the arrangements.

Financial Aid: Seventy percent of the students receive aid. About 40% work part-time on campus. Financial aid is available to all students in the form of scholarships and loans and is awarded on the basis of need. Tuition may be paid in installments. Additional state aid programs are available to residents of New York. The college is a member of CSS and requires the FAF and parents' tax forms. The deadline for aid applications is January 1.

Foreign Students: There are more than 1340 foreign students from 96 different nations. The university offers these students an intensive English course, special counseling, and special organizations.

Admissions: Foreign students must achieve a TOEFL score of 560. The SAT is also required. ATs must be taken if required by the applicant's college.

Procedure: Application deadlines are the same as those for freshmen. Foreign students must present medical records and a chest X-ray after arrival. They must also present proof of funds adequate to cover the duration of study. Health insurance, available through the university for a fee, is also required.

Admissions Contact: Ann V. York, Director of Undergraduate Admissions.

DAEMEN COLLEGE   A-3
Amherst, New York 14226   (716) 839-3600

F/T: 344M, 854W	Faculty: 148; IIB, −$
P/T: n/av	Ph.D.'s: 80%
Grad: none	S/F Ratio: 13 to 1
Year: 4-1-4, ss	Tuition: $3825
Appl: open	R and B: $1950
1099 applied	882 accepted	365 enrolled
SAT: 448V 473M	ACT: 20	COMPETITIVE

Daemen College, founded in 1947 for the higher education of women, is now a private, coeducational liberal arts college. The library houses 100,000 volumes and subscribes to 462 periodicals.

Environment: The college campus, situated in a suburban area 10 miles from Buffalo, has 33 buildings, including an athletic facility. Living facilities sponsored by the college consist of dormitories and on-campus apartments.

Student Life: Eighty-nine percent of the students come from New York. Fifty percent of the students reside in campus housing administered by the student government. Campus housing is single-sex; there are visiting privileges. Students may keep cars on campus. The college provides day-care services.

Organizations: Four percent of the men belong to 1 fraternity, and 4% of the women to 1 sorority. There are numerous extracurricular activities.

Sports: The college competes intercollegiately in 2 sports for men and 3 sports for women. There are 4 intramural sports for men and 3 for women.

Handicapped: About 85% of the campus is accessible to handicapped students. Special facilities include wheelchair ramps, parking areas, elevators, specially equipped rest rooms, and lowered telephones.

Graduates: At the end of the freshman year, about 5% of the students drop out for academic reasons; 75% remain to graduate. Forty percent of the graduates pursue advanced degrees. About 68% enter careers in business and industry.

Services: Students receive the following services free of charge: psychological counseling, placement, career counseling, certain tutoring, and certain remedial instruction. Health care is available for a fee.

Programs of Study: The college confers the B.A., B.S., B.F.A., B.Mus., and B.S.W. degrees. Bachelor's degrees are offered in the following subjects: BUSINESS (accounting, business administration, business education, computer science, finance, management, marketing, transportation and travel management), EDUCATION (early childhood, elementary, secondary, special), ENGLISH (English), FINE AND PERFORMING ARTS (art, art education, graphic design, music, music education, theater/dramatics), HEALTH SCIENCES (medical technology, nursing, physical therapy), LANGUAGES (French, Spanish), MATH AND SCIENCES (biology, mathematics, natural sciences), PHILOSOPHY (humanities, philosophy), PREPROFESSIONAL (dentistry, law, medicine, social work, veterinary), SOCIAL SCIENCES (economics, government/political science, history, psychology, sociology). Thirty-two percent of the degrees are conferred in health sciences, 23% in social sciences, and 12% in business.

Required: All students must take courses in freshman English as well as a distribution of credits in 4 broad areas of study.

Special: A college-sponsored junior year abroad program is offered to students studying modern languages. English, history, art, and elementary education majors may also spend a year abroad. Combined B.A.-B.S. degrees and student-designed majors are permitted. The cooperative education program allows students to enhance their liberal arts education with valuable professional experience prior to graduation.

Honors: Nine honor societies have chapters on campus. Eight departments offer honors programs.

Admissions: Eighty percent of those who applied were accepted for the 1981-82 freshman class. For a recent freshman class, the SAT scores were as follows: Verbal—20% scored between 500 and 599, 5% between 600 and 700; Math—21% scored between 500 and 599, 5% between 600 and 700. On the ACT, 20% scored between 20 and 23, 18% between 24 and 26, and 2% between 27 and 28. Candidates should graduate from an accredited high school, have at least an 80% average, rank in the upper half of the graduating class, and have a college-qualifying recommendation from the secondary school. An SAT composite score of 800 to 900 is necessary to be considered for admission. Advanced placement or honor courses, personality and intangible qualities, and extracurricular activities record are also considered.

Procedure: The SAT or ACT is required and should be taken by March of the senior year. There are no application deadlines. Admissions are on a rolling basis. Freshmen are admitted for all semesters. The application fee is $15.

Special: An early admissions plan and a deferred admissions plan are available. AP and CLEP credit is given.

Transfer: For fall 1981, 399 transfer applications were received, 294 were accepted, and 151 students enrolled. Transfers are accepted for all classes. A 2.0 GPA is required; C and above grades are acceptable. Four semesters or 30 credit hours must be completed at the college; a total of 125 to 130 credit hours are required for the bachelor's degree. There are no application deadlines. Transfers are admitted to the fall, spring, and summer sessions on a rolling basis.

Visiting: There are regular orientation programs for prospective students. Informal visits are possible whenever classes are in session. Visitors may sit in on classes and stay overnight at the school. The admissions office should be contacted for arrangements.

Financial Aid: Eighty-nine percent of the students receive financial aid. Twelve percent work part-time on campus. The average aid to freshmen from all sources, including part-time employment, is $3150. Loans are available through a $130,000 NDSL fund, state government funds, and local banks. The college is a member of CSS; the FAF and the Daemen College Financial Aid Application are required. The application deadlines are February 15 (fall) and November 1 (spring).

Foreign Students: Fewer than 1% of the full-time students come from foreign countries.

Admissions: The college requires foreign applicants to take the TOEFL; a minimum score of 500 must be achieved for consideration. College entrance exams are not required.

Procedure: There are no application deadlines. Foreign students are admitted to the fall, spring, and summer sessions on a rolling basis. Proof of health, in the form of a physical examination, is required. Proof of funds adequate to cover the first year of study must be presented. Foreign students must carry health insurance, which is available through the college for a fee.

Admissions Contact: Peter W. Stevens, Vice President for Admissions.

DOMINICAN COLLEGE OF BLAUVELT D-5
Orangeburg, New York 10960 (914) 359-7800

F/T: 227M, 433W Faculty: 68; IIB, —$
P/T: 255M, 687W Ph.D.'s: 55%
Grad: none S/F Ratio: 17 to 1
Year: sems, ss Tuition: $2390
Appl: open R and B: n/app
305 applied 269 accepted 167 enrolled
SAT: 390V 415M **LESS COMPETITIVE**

Dominican College of Blauvelt is an independent liberal arts college, founded in 1952. The library contains 80,000 volumes and 7550 microfilm items, and subscribes to 700 periodicals.

Environment: The campus is located in a suburban area at the foothills of the Ramapo Mountains, 17 miles from New York City. There are no dorms, but listings for approved off-campus housing are available.

Student Life: Seventy-seven percent of the students are New York residents. No students live on campus. Seventy percent of the freshmen are public school graduates. About 8% of the students are minority-group members.

Organizations: There are no sororities or fraternities. Departmental and special interest clubs, a theater group, and publications, as well as concerts, films, and lectures, are available.

Sports: Three intercollegiate sports are offered for men and 3 for women. There are 4 intramural sports for men and 3 for women.

Handicapped: Eighty percent of the campus is accessible to physically handicapped students. Wheelchair ramps, special parking, elevators, specially equipped rest rooms, special class scheduling, and lowered telephone and drinking fountains are provided. Five percent of the students have visual impairments, and 5% have hearing impairments. In conjunction with the special education facilities in the college, tutors, readers, and special counselors are available.

Graduates: Twenty percent of the freshmen drop out. Sixty percent remain to graduate, and 45% go on to further study. Thirty-three percent enter careers in business and industry.

Services: Free career counseling, psychological counseling, placement service, and tutoring are provided. Remedial instruction is available on a fee basis.

Programs of Study: The college confers B.A., B.S., and B.S.N. degrees. Associate degree programs are also available. Bachelor's degrees are offered in the following subjects: AREA STUDIES (American), BUSINESS (accounting, business administration, computer science, economics, management), EDUCATION (elementary, special), ENGLISH (English), HEALTH SCIENCES (nursing), LANGUAGES (French, Spanish), MATH AND SCIENCES (mathematics, natural sciences), PREPROFESSIONAL (law, social work), SOCIAL SCIENCES (government/political science, history, psychology, social sciences, sociology). Twenty-eight percent of the degrees conferred are in nursing, and 9% in social sciences.

554 NEW YORK

Required: All students must complete a distributed liberal studies requirement.

Special: Students may participate in independent study and interdisciplinary courses. There is a Weekend College, offered on a trimester basis.

Honors: Honors colloquia are offered. There is a chapter of Alpha Chi at the school.

Admissions: For the 1981-82 class, 88% of those who applied were admitted. Of those who enrolled, the SAT scores were as follows: Verbal—58% scored below 500, 8% between 500 and 599, 6% between 600 and 700, and 0% above 700; Math—59% scored below 500, 15% between 500 and 599, 3% between 600 and 700, and 0% above 700. The composite score on the SAT should be at least 800-900. Applicants must rank in the upper three-fifths of their high school class and have a minimum average of 75. They must graduate from an accredited high school with 16 units completed. The extracurricular activities record, advanced placement or honor courses, and recommendations by high school officials are also important factors.

Procedure: The SAT is required. The suggested deadlines for applications are August 15 (fall) and January 1 (spring). Freshmen are admitted in the spring as well as in the fall. Notification is on a rolling basis. There is a $10 admission fee.

Special: Early admissions and early decision plans are available. CLEP and AP credit is offered. There is an open admissions policy for veterans.

Transfer: For fall 1981, 281 transfer applications were received, 236 were accepted, and 195 students enrolled. Transfers are accepted for freshman, sophomore, and junior classes. A minimum average of 2.0 and an interview are required; C or better grades transfer. Students must earn 30 credits in residence; a total of 120 credits are required for the bachelor's degree. Suggested application deadlines are the same as those for freshman applicants.

Visiting: In the fall and spring the school holds an open house, at which prospective students may speak with faculty and hear current students discuss academic programs, financial aid, and student activities. Campus tours are also given at this time. Informal visits may be scheduled for Mondays through Thursdays between 9 A.M. and 5 P.M. by contacting the admissions office. Visitors may sit in on classes.

Financial Aid: Sixty-five percent of students receive financial aid. Two percent work part-time on campus. The average award to freshmen is $500. The college is a member of CSS. The FAF must be filed by March 15.

Foreign Students: One percent of the student body come from foreign countries. The college offers these students an intensive English course.

Admissions: Foreign applicants must take the college's English proficiency exam. They are not required to take a college entrance exam.

Procedure: There are no application deadlines. Admissions are on a rolling basis for both the fall and spring semesters. A physician's statement must be presented. Proof of funds adequate to cover 1 year of study is required.

Admissions Contact: Dan Saraceno, Director of Admissions.

DOWLING COLLEGE E-5
Oakdale, New York 11769   (516) 589-1040

F/T: 750M, 750W   Faculty: 204; IIA, +$
P/T: 360M, 325W   Ph.D.'s: 74%
Grad: 129M, 137W   S/F Ratio: 18 to 1
Year: 4-1-4, ss   Tuition: $3900
Appl: open   R and B: $2100
950 applied   600 accepted   306 enrolled
SAT: 465V 468M   COMPETITIVE

Dowling College, founded in 1959, is a small, independent, coeducational liberal arts college. The library contains 88,000 volumes and subscribes to 762 periodicals.

Environment: The college is situated in a suburban area on the former Vanderbilt estate on Long Island, 50 miles from New York City. There are now 8 buildings, including the estate mansion and an apartment-type residence hall housing 200 students. Forty approved private homes, and 30 approved apartments also provide housing.

Student Life: Ninety-five percent of the undergraduates are from New York; 4% are from other states, and 1% are from foreign countries. Ten percent reside on campus, 89% reside at home, and 1% reside off campus. There are religious counselors and organizations on campus for all major faiths.

Organizations: There are no social fraternities or sororities, but professional and service organizations also serve as social groups. There are over 30 organizations including a student newspaper, Aero Club, and special interest clubs (music, art, drama). College-sponsored cultural events include art shows, concerts, debates, films, lectures, and plays.

Sports: The college competes on an intercollegiate level in 9 sports. There are 3 intramural sports for men and women.

Handicapped: About 80% of the campus is accessible to wheelchair-bound students. Wheelchair ramps, special parking, elevators, specially equipped rest rooms, lowered drinking fountains, and lowered telephones are available. Recorders and special tapes can be borrowed. Large print typewriters and braille typewriters are also available.

Graduates: The freshman dropout rate is 10% for academic reasons and 20% for other reasons; 50% remain to graduate. Fifty percent pursue advanced study after graduation. About 38% pursue careers in business and industry.

Services: Students receive the following services free of charge: placement, career counseling, tutoring, remedial instruction, and psychological counseling. Job listings are available through the placement office.

Programs of Study: The college confers the B.A. and B.S. degrees. Programs leading to master's degrees in education and business administration are also offered. Bachelor's degrees are offered in the following subjects: BUSINESS (accounting, management), EDUCATION (elementary, secondary, special), ENGLISH (English), FINE AND PERFORMING ARTS (art, music, music education), LANGUAGES (French, Spanish), MATH AND SCIENCES (biology, mathematics, natural sciences), SOCIAL SCIENCES (anthropology-sociology, history, social sciences). Forty percent of the degrees conferred are in business, 20% are in education, and 18% are in social sciences.

Required: A C average and 120 credits are required for graduation.

Special: A 3-year bachelor's degree is possible.

Honors: Kappa Delta Pi is represented at Dowling. Honors programs are available in education.

Admissions: Sixty-three percent of those who applied were accepted for a recent freshman class. The SAT scores of those who enrolled were as follows: Verbal—30% scored between 500 and 599, 9% between 600 and 700, and 1% above 700; Math—32% scored between 500 and 599, 13% between 600 and 700, and 2% above 700. Candidates for admission must be high school graduates and have completed at least 16 Carnegie units. They should rank in the upper half of their high school class. In evaluating a candidate, the 4 most important factors are advanced placement or honors courses, recommendations by school officials, impressions made during an interview, and extracurricular activities record.

Procedure: The SAT or ACT is required and should be taken before July of the senior year. Junior year results are acceptable. The candidate must also arrange for a personal interview. A rolling admissions plan is used. Freshmen are admitted in September and February. There is a $20 application fee.

Special: Early decision and deferred admissions plans are possible. AP and CLEP credit is given.

Transfer: Transfer students must have a C average; D grades do not transfer. There is a 1-year residency rule. A total of 120 credits are required for the bachelor's degree. Transfer application deadlines are July for the fall and December for the spring.

Visiting: Guided tours and interviews can be scheduled through the admissions office. Visitors may sit in on classes.

Financial Aid: Sixty-eight percent of all students receive some financial aid. Of those students receiving financial aid, 22% are receiving scholarship aid from a total amount of $41,900; 14% are receiving loan funds administered by the federal government from a total of $255,675; and 10% are receiving work contracts from the college. Work-study funds are available in all departments. Awards are based on demonstrated need. The average scholarship is $500 with a maximum of $1500; the average loan is $700 with a maximum of $1500; and the average work contract is $900 with a maximum of $1900. Tuition may be paid in installments. The FAF is required. The deadline to apply for financial aid is May 1.

Admissions Contact: William B. Galloway, Dean of Admissions.

D'YOUVILLE COLLEGE A-3
Buffalo, New York 14201 (716) 886-8100

F/T: 152M, 948W Faculty: 77; IIB, −$
P/T: 30M, 146W Ph.D.'s: 25%
Grad: none S/F Ratio: 13 to 1
Year: sems, ss Tuition: $3590
Appl: July 1 R and B: $1980
837 applied 653 accepted 226 enrolled
SAT: 391V 426M ACT: 17 LESS COMPETITIVE

Founded in 1908 by the Grey Nuns of the Sacred Heart, D'Youville College is a private, independent, liberal arts college. The library houses 110,400 volumes and 7850 microfilm items, and subscribes to 605 periodicals.

Environment: The campus is located in an urban area less than 1 mile from downtown Buffalo and 90 miles from Toronto, Canada. Facilities include a student center and a health-science building. The administration building, built in 1874, now houses reception rooms, administrative offices, the chapel, and the theater-auditorium. There are 2 dormitories.

Student Life: Students come from many states. Only 20% reside on campus. Seventy-five percent of the students are Catholic, 15% are Protestant, and 5% are Jewish. Nineteen percent are minority-group members. College housing is single-sex by floors, and there are visiting privileges. Students may keep cars on campus.

Organizations: There are no fraternities or sororities. Many social activities are held in cooperation with other private and public colleges and universities in the area. There are also many special-interest groups.

Sports: The college fields 1 intercollegiate team for men and 2 for women. There are 16 intramural sports for men and 16 for women.

Handicapped: Facilities for handicapped students are very limited. Further construction is planned.

Graduates: The freshman dropout rate is 20%, and 60% of the freshmen remain to graduate. Twelve percent of the graduates pursue advanced degrees; 1% enter medical school, 1% enter dental school, and 1% enter law school. Forty percent enter careers in business and industry.

Services: Students receive the following services free of charge: psychological counseling, health care, placement, career counseling, tutoring, and remedial instruction.

Programs of Study: The college confers the B.A., B.S., B.S.N., and B.S.G. degrees. Bachelor's degrees are offered in the following subjects: BUSINESS (accounting, business administration, business education, management, secretarial science), EDUCATION (bilingual, blind and visually handicapped, elementary, secondary, special), ENGLISH (English), HEALTH SCIENCES (medical technology, nursing), MATH AND SCIENCES (biology, chemistry, mathematics), PHILOSOPHY (philosophy), PREPROFESSIONAL (dentistry, law, medicine, social work, veterinary), SOCIAL SCIENCES (gerontology, government/political science, history, psychology, social sciences, sociology). Sixty-seven percent of the degrees are conferred in health sciences, 10% in education, and 10% in social sciences.

Required: Fifty-four credit hours are required in humanities, social science, and natural science courses.

Special: The college offers one of the largest 4-year nursing programs available at a private college in the U.S. Students may design their own majors in the general studies program. Independent study programs are offered in history, psychology, and the sciences. Combined B.A.-B.S. degrees may be earned.

Honors: There is 1 honor society on campus.

Admissions: Seventy-eight percent of those who applied were accepted for the 1981–82 freshman class. Of those who enrolled, the SAT scores were as follows: Verbal—73% below 500, 8% between 500 and 599, 1% between 600 and 700, and 0% above 700; Math—62% below 500, 17% between 500 and 599, 3% between 600 and 700, and 0% above 700. On the ACT, 100% scored below 21. Candidates must be graduates of an accredited high school, rank in the upper half of their class, and have a minimum grade average of 80. Admissions decisions are made on the basis of standardized test scores, advanced placement or honors courses, leadership record, and recommendations by school officials.

Procedure: The SAT or ACT is required and should be taken by January of the senior year. Applications should be received by July 1 for fall and December 1 for spring. Notification is on a rolling basis. The application fee is $15.

Special: An early admissions plan is available; the student must have a recommendation from the high school counselor. AP and CLEP credit is offered.

Transfer: For fall 1981, 254 students applied, 198 were accepted, and 113 enrolled. A 2.0 GPA and a combined score of 800 on the SAT or 18 on the ACT are required for liberal arts students; a 2.5 GPA and a combined score of 900 on the SAT or 20 on the ACT are required for nursing students. All applicants must present a minimum of 3 completed credit hours. D grades, pass/fail courses, clinicals, practicums, internships, field study, and independent study credits do not transfer. Students must spend the last 30 hours in residence and complete at least 30 of the 120 credits necessary for a bachelor's degree. Application deadlines are July 1 (fall) or December 1 (spring) for liberal arts students, and April 1 (fall) or November 1 (spring) for nursing students.

Visiting: Weekday visits are possible. Visitors may sit in on classes and stay overnight at the school. The admissions office should be contacted for arrangements.

Financial Aid: Eighty-six percent of the students receive financial aid. Ten percent work part-time on campus. Average aid to freshmen is $3750. Scholarships, grants-in-aid, and loans are available. The college is a member of CSS and requires the FAF. Application deadlines are April 1 (fall) and December 1 (spring).

Foreign Students: Fewer than one percent of the full-time students come from foreign countries. The college offers these students special counseling.

Admissions: Foreign students must achieve a TOEFL score of at least 500. No college entrance exam must be taken.

Procedure: Application deadlines are the same as those for other freshmen. Foreign students must present proof of funds adequate to cover 1 year of study. They must also carry health insurance, which is available through the college for a fee.

Admissions Contact: Carol J. Willson, Director of Admissions and Financial Aid.

EASTMAN SCHOOL OF MUSIC B-3
Rochester, New York 14604 (716) 275-3003

F/T: 208M, 200W Faculty: 89; n/av
P/T: 1M, 1W Ph.D.'s: 31%
Grad: 141M, 121W S/F Ratio: 4 to 1
Year: sems, ss Tuition: $6400
Appl: Feb. 20 R and B: $2369
760 applied 168 accepted 95 enrolled
SAT, ACT: not required SPECIAL

Eastman is a professional school of music within the University of Rochester. The school and the University of Rochester cooperatively offer the Bachelor of Arts degree with a music concentration. All the facilities of the University of Rochester are open to Eastman students. The school library contains 350,000 volumes and 4000 microfilm items, and subscribes to 475 periodicals.

Environment: Located in Rochester, Eastman's urban campus consists of the Eastman Theater, a classroom building, a music library, and a rehearsal building. Two dormitories accommodate over 300 students.

Student Life: Twenty-seven percent of the students are from New York State. Eighty-six percent of the students live on campus. Thirteen percent are minority-group members. Dormitories are both coed and single-sex; there are visiting privileges in single-sex dorms. Students may keep cars on campus.

Organizations: There are 2 fraternities and 1 sorority, to which 10% of the students belong. Major social events on campus include the First Fall Dance and the Christmas Sing. There are 12 extracurricular groups, including the Student Association and the Dorm Council.

Handicapped: There are no special facilities for handicapped students.

Graduates: Ten percent of the students drop out at the end of freshman year; 82% remain to graduate. About 48% of the graduates go on to graduate study, all of them in music.

Services: The following services are provided to students free of charge: psychological counseling, career counseling, tutoring, and remedial instruction. Health care and placement services are provided on a fee basis. Placement services for students and alumni include notices of employment, auditions, and resume development counseling.

Programs of Study: The school confers the B.A. and B.M. degrees. Master's and doctoral degrees are also awarded. Bachelor's degrees are offered in the following subjects: FINE AND PERFORMING ARTS (applied music, music, music composition, music education, music history, music performance, music theory).

Required: Courses in English, music theory, music literature, ensemble, and applied music are required.

Special: Combined 5-year B.A.-B.S. degrees may be earned in any subjects available at the University of Rochester.

Honors: There are 5 national honor societies with chapters on campus. In addition, the school's Graduate String Quartet is chosen from among top students.

Admissions: About 22% of those who applied were accepted for the 1981-82 freshman class. Applicants must be graduates of accredited high schools and should have completed 16 Carnegie units of work. Evidence of special talents, musical activities, advanced placement or honors courses, and recommendations from the high school are considered very important. Some preference is accorded to children of alumni.

Procedure: Neither the SAT nor the ACT is required. An interview (audition) is not required but is highly recommended and may be taken at a regularly scheduled Regional Audition Center. Application deadlines are February 20 (fall and summer) and December 1 (spring). Fall applicants are notified between March 15 and April 15. There is a $25 application fee.

Special: AP credit is granted.

Transfer: For fall 1981, 234 transfer applications were received, 69 were accepted, and 50 students enrolled. Transfers are accepted for all levels. Requirements include good academic standing at the previous institution, a music theory exam, and a successful audition. D grades do not transfer. Students rarely study at the school for less than 2 years; 120-140 credits are required for a bachelor's degree. Deadlines are the same as for freshmen.

Visiting: Scheduled audition days include orientation, audition, interview, campus tours, and informal student contact. No guides are available for informal visits to the school. Visitors may not sit in on classes and may not stay overnight on campus. The best days to visit are Monday, Wednesday, and Friday. The admissions office handles the arrangements.

Financial Aid: About 85% of the students receive aid. About 35% work part-time on campus. The average aid to a freshman is $3000. The college is a member of CSS and usually grants aid in combinations of scholarship, loan, and sometimes, work scholarship. A total of $184,000 is available for freshman scholarships. Work-study is available in all departments. Tuition may be paid in installments. The deadlines for aid applications are February 20 (summer and fall entry) and December 1 (winter entry), and the FAF is required. Musical merit and/or financial need are the primary considerations in awarding aid.

Foreign Students: Five percent of the full-time students come from foreign countries. An intensive English course, an intensive English program, special counseling, and special organizations are available for these students.

Admissions: Foreign students must take the TOEFL. No college entrance exams are required.

Procedure: Application deadlines are the same as those for other students. Foreign students must complete a school health form and must present proof of funds adequate to cover 1 year of study. Health insurance is required and is available through the school for a fee.

Admissions Contact: Charles Krusenstjerna, Director of Admissions.

EISENHOWER COLLEGE OF ROCHESTER INSTITUTE OF TECHNOLOGY C-3

Seneca Falls, New York 13148   (315) 568-7411

F/T: 331M, 235W	Faculty:	42; IIA, av$
P/T: 3M, 2W	Ph.D.'s:	74%
Grad: none	S/F Ratio:	13 to 1
Year: qtrs	Tuition:	$4491
Appl: open	R and B:	$2566
504 applied	421 accepted	245 enrolled
SAT: 480V 530M	ACT: 24	COMPETITIVE+

Eisenhower College, chartered in 1965 and opened in 1968, is an independent college and the liberal arts campus of the Rochester Institute of Technology. It is also the official national memorial to President Dwight D. Eisenhower. The college curriculum is entirely interdisciplinary and career-oriented. The library contains 97,000 volumes and 5750 microfilm items, and subscribes to over 800 periodicals.

Environment: The 272-acre campus is located in a rural setting 35 miles from Syracuse and 45 miles from Rochester and Ithaca, in the heart of the Finger Lakes region. College facilities include 14 buildings, a golf course, an athletic center, and a 143-year-old "Red Barn" housing a student pub. All residence halls are constructed on a "suite plan."

Student Life: Eighty-one percent of the students are from the Northeast. Eighty percent of entering freshmen come from public schools. Ninety-seven percent of the students reside on campus. College housing is coed and single-sex; students in single-sex housing have visiting privileges. Students may keep cars on campus.

Organizations: A wide variety of clubs, musical and dramatic groups, and student government and religious organizations are available. Off-campus recreational and cultural activities are provided by a state park, several nearby colleges, and the cities of Syracuse, Rochester, and Ithaca.

Sports: The college fields 6 intercollegiate teams for men and 8 for women. There are 14 intramural sports for men and 12 for women.

Handicapped: Ninety percent of the campus is accessible to the physically handicapped. Special facilities for these students include wheelchair ramps, parking areas, elevators, specially equipped rest rooms, and lowered drinking fountains.

Graduates: The freshman dropout rate is 29%, and 40% of the freshmen remain to graduate. Forty percent of the graduates pursue advanced study; 3% enter medical school, 3% enter dental school, and 7% enter law school. Another 30% enter careers in business and industry.

Services: Students receive the following services free: health care, psychological counseling, placement, career counseling, tutoring, and remedial instruction. Placement services available for undergraduates and alumni include a career library, professional orientation, testing services, and graduate school placement.

Programs of Study: The college confers the B.A. degree. Bachelor's degrees are offered in the following subjects: BUSINESS (managerial economics), ENGLISH (literature), FINE AND PERFORMING ARTS (art, interdisciplinary humanities, music, theater/dramatics), HEALTH SCIENCES (health care and community services), MATH AND SCIENCES (applied science, biology, chemistry, ecology/environmental science, interdisciplinary science), PHILOSOPHY (humanities, philosophy), PREPROFESSIONAL (dentistry, engineering, forestry, law, medicine, ministry, social work, veterinary), SOCIAL SCIENCES (community services, economics, gerontology, government/political science, history, international relations, psychology, public policy, social services management, sociology).

Required: All students are required to complete the World Studies core program designed to give a broad liberal arts background and an international orientation. Proficiency in writing and physical education should be demonstrated.

Special: The college has a strong international orientation, based in its nationally recognized core curriculum in World Studies. Qualified juniors may take a full program of study abroad. The environmental studies program utilizes a 37-foot laboratory-equipped houseboat.

Admissions: Eighty-four percent of those who applied were accepted for the 1981-82 freshman class. Of those who enrolled, the SAT scores were as follows: Verbal—58% scored below 500, 32% between 500 and 599, 9% between 600 and 700, and 1% above 700; Math—30% scored below 500, 45% between 500 and 599, 23% between 600 and 700, and 2% above 700. On the ACT, 14% scored below 21, 39% between 21 and 23, 14% between 24 and 25, 21% between 26 and 28, and 11% above 28. Eighty-four percent of the freshmen ranked in the top half of their high school graduating class, but no minimums are specified for class rank or GPA. Sixteen Carnegie units are required. Also considered important are advanced placement or honor courses, recommendations by school officials, impressions made during an interview, and leadership record.

Procedure: The SAT or ACT is required. Freshmen are admitted to the fall, winter, and spring terms; there are no application deadlines. Decisions regarding acceptance are made as soon as the application, supporting SAT or ACT scores, and appropriate transcripts are received; notification is on a rolling basis. The college subscribes to CRDA. The application fee is $25.

Special: Early and deferred admissions plans are available. The HEOP is offered to educationally and financially disadvantaged New York State students.

Transfer: For fall 1981, 45 students applied, 37 were accepted, and 26 enrolled. Transfers are considered for the freshman, sophomore, and junior classes. Good academic standing and a 2.25 GPA are needed; freshman transfers must also present standardized exam scores. An interview is recommended. With an associate degree, D grades transfer. Students must spend 2 years in residence and complete at least 90 of the minimum 180 quarter credit hours necessary for a bachelor's degree. No formal application deadline exists; students are admitted in the fall, winter, and spring.

Visiting: Orientation for prospective students includes a general introduction, guided tour, an interview, lunch, and a meeting with faculty. Visits are best scheduled mornings, Monday, Wednesday, and Friday. Visitors may sit in on classes and stay overnight at the college. Arrangements can be made through the admissions office.

Financial Aid: Seventy-two percent of the students receive financial assistance. Forty-seven percent work part-time on campus. Scholarships, grants, and loans are available. Eisenhower Scholarships, based on outstanding academic credentials, and merit awards, based on outstanding extracurricular participation, are awarded irrespective of financial need. The college is a member of CSS and requires the FAF. Application deadlines are open.

Foreign Students: Four percent of the full-time students come from foreign countries. The college offers these students an intensive English program, special counseling, and special organizations.

Admissions: Foreign students must achieve a TOEFL score of 550. Either the SAT or ACT is also required.

Procedure: Application deadlines are April 1 (fall), August 1 (winter), and November 1 (spring). Foreign students must present proof of a physical exam and proof of funds adequate to cover the anticipated period of study. They must also carry health insurance, which is available through the college for a fee.

Admissions Contact: Robert C. French, Coordinator of Admissions.

ELMIRA COLLEGE C–4
Elmira, New York 14901 (607) 734-3911

F/T: 433M, 576W	Faculty:	65; IIB, +$
P/T: 453M, 751W	Ph.D.'s:	68%
Grad: 64M, 202W	S/F Ratio:	17 to 1
Year: 4-4-1, ss	Tuition:	$4775
Appl: open	R and B:	$1975
1287 applied	952 accepted	389 enrolled
SAT: 450V 460M		COMPETITIVE

Elmira College, established in 1855 as a women's college, is now a coeducational, private, nonsectarian, liberal arts school. The Learning Center holds 130,000 volumes, 35,000 microfilm items, 160,000 government documents, and 1500 audio tapes, and subscribes to 700 periodicals.

Environment: The campus includes 28 major buildings on 38 acres in a suburban section of Elmira, as well as an additional 487 acres of land and an 18-hole golf course. Mark Twain's study is preserved on campus. Seven dormitories accommodate both men and women.

Student Life: Approximately 80% of the students live on campus in the dormitories. Sixty percent are from New York and surrounding states. About 65% of entering freshmen come from public schools. Campus housing is both single-sex and coed; there are visiting privileges in the single-sex facilities. Students may keep cars on campus.

Organizations: There are no fraternities or sororities. Extracurricular activities are traditional. Cultural opportunities are provided by such facilities as the Samuel Clemens Performing Arts Center, Elmira Symphony, Arnot Art Museum, and Elmira Little Theatre.

Sports: The men at Elmira participate in 6 sports at the intercollegiate level; the women, in 5. There are 7 intramural sports for men and 6 for women.

Handicapped: There are some special facilities for physically handicapped students: wheelchair ramps, parking areas, elevators (in the dorms), and specially equipped rest rooms. For further information, contact the dean of student services.

Graduates: At the end of the freshman year, 15% of the students drop out; 60% remain to graduate.

Services: Students receive the following services free of charge: placement, career counseling, psychological counseling, health care, tutoring, and remedial instruction.

Programs of Study: The college confers the B.A. and B.S. degrees. Associate and master's degrees are also awarded. Bachelor's degrees are offered in the following subjects: AREA STUDIES (American, international), BUSINESS (accounting, business administration, systems analysis), EDUCATION (early childhood, elementary, secondary), ENGLISH (English, literature), FINE AND PERFORMING ARTS (art, art education, art history, dance, music, studio art, theater/dramatics), HEALTH SCIENCES (medical technology, speech therapy), LANGUAGES (French, German, Greek/Latin, Italian, Spanish), MATH AND SCIENCES (biochemistry, biology, chemistry, ecology/environmental science, mathematics, physics), PHILOSOPHY (classics, philosophy, religion), PREPROFESSIONAL (dentistry, engineering, law, medicine, social work, veterinary), SOCIAL SCIENCES (anthropology, economics, government/political science, history, psychology, sociology).

Required: All students must take a core distribution.

Special: A combined B.A.-B.S. degree can be earned in engineering; this is a 3-2 program. The college sponsors a Junior Year Abroad program in the Far East and in Europe. Work-study experiences are offered in all fields. Students may design their own majors or take a general studies (no major) degree. In addition, an independent study program is available. The college maintains a Speech and Hearing Clinic for the benefit of students and the community. The college also offers the Washington Semester Program and the U.N. Semester sponsored by Drew University.

Honors: Five national honor societies have chapters on campus, including Phi Beta Kappa. The biology, history, and psychology departments offer honors programs.

Admissions: Seventy-four percent of those who applied were accepted for the 1981–82 freshman class. Candidates should rank in the upper half of their graduating class, have a B average or better, come from an accredited, well-reputed high school, have participated in extracurricular activities, and be recommended for college by the high school authorities. Impressions made during the interview, advanced placement or honor courses, and personality are also important. The college seeks a national geographic distribution in its student body.

Procedure: The SAT is recommended but not required. A personal interview is strongly recommended. New students are admitted in either the fall or spring semester. Suggested application deadlines are September 1 for fall, and January 2 for spring. Admissions and notification are on a rolling basis. There is a $20 application fee.

Special: The early admissions program is for mature students who are recommended by their guidance counselors. Early admissions candidates are required to have an interview. There are also early decision and deferred admissions plans. The notification date for early decision is December 1. AP and CLEP credit is granted. The freshman seminar program allows selected students who do not qualify for regular admission, but who show promise of being successful at Elmira, to attend a 3-week intensive study session during the summer.

Transfer: For fall 1981, 292 transfer students applied, 225 were accepted, and 135 enrolled. A GPA of 2.0 is required. C grades or better transfer. Thirty credits, out of a total of 120 credits required for the bachelor's degree, must be completed at Elmira. There are no application deadlines. Transfers are accepted for the fall and spring semesters on a rolling basis.

Visiting: Regularly scheduled orientations for prospective students include faculty presentations, student presentations, and interviews. Informal visits can be arranged for weekdays from 8:30 A.M. to 5 P.M. and Saturdays from 9 A.M. to noon. Guides are available, and visitors may stay overnight at the school and sit in on classes. Arrangements should be made through the admissions office.

Financial Aid: Approximately 75% of students receive financial aid. About 50% work part-time on campus. The average award to freshmen is $2885, not including Pell or TAP Grants. Aid is available in the form of scholarships, loans, and campus employment. The college is a member of CSS. The FAF is required and must be filed by August 1 (fall) and December 1 (spring).

Foreign Students: Foreign students represent 7% of the student body. The college offers an intensive English program, special counseling, and special organizations for these students.

Admissions: TOEFL is required; a minimum score of 500 must be achieved for consideration. College entrance exams are not required.

Procedure: Application deadlines for foreign students are June 1 for fall and October 1 for spring. Foreign students must present proof of health. They must also show proof of funds adequate to cover 1 year of study.

Admissions Contact: John W. Patience, Assistant Director of Admissions.

FASHION INSTITUTE OF TECHNOLOGY
(See State University of New York/Fashion Institute of Technology)

FORDHAM UNIVERSITY

Since its founding in 1846, Fordham University, an institution in the Jesuit tradition, has offered instruction in the liberal arts and selected

558 NEW YORK

professional areas, on both the undergraduate and graduate levels. Fordham's 3 undergraduate colleges are located on either the Manhattan (Lincoln Center) campus or the Bronx (Rose Hill) campus. Profiles of the undergraduate colleges follow.

FORDHAM UNIVERSITY/COLLEGE AT LINCOLN CENTER D-5
New York, New York 10023 (212) 841-5210

F/T: 642M, 842W	Faculty: 88; I, +$
P/T: 633M, 886W	Ph.D.'s: 87%
Grad: none	S/F Ratio: 17 to 1
Year: 4-1-4, ss	Tuition: $139 p/c
Appl: Feb. 15	R and B: $2700
844 applied	190 enrolled
SAT: 505V 500M	COMPETITIVE

The College at Lincoln Center was established in 1968 as a further manifestation of the university's long-standing commitment to the education of youth and adults. A coeducational institution, the college offers a strong liberal arts education to students of diverse religions, races, and backgrounds. It shares the university's library, which contains 1,309,264 volumes and 1 million microfilm items, and subscribes to 4872 periodicals.

Environment: The 8-acre Lincoln Center Campus is in mid-Manhattan, adjacent to Lincoln Center for the Performing Arts. It is housed in the modern, 14-story Leon Lowenstein Center. There are no residence halls at this campus; students may live at the Rose Hill Campus and commute by Fordham's shuttle bus service.

Student Life: About 79% of the students are from New York. Fifty-six percent of entering freshmen come from private schools; 40% come from public schools. Sixty-seven percent of the students are Catholic, 8% are Protestant, and 1% are Jewish. Thirty-four percent are minority-group members. Campus housing at the Rose Hill Campus is both coed and single-sex. There are visiting privileges in single-sex dorms.

Organizations: There are no social fraternities or sororities. A wide range of extracurricular and on-campus cultural activities is offered. New York City provides further cultural and recreational opportunities.

Sports: The college competes in 18 intercollegiate sports for men and 13 for women. There are 10 intramural sports for both men and women.

Handicapped: The campus is accessible to wheelchair-bound students. Special facilities for the physically handicapped include ramps, elevators, and specially equipped rest rooms.

Graduates: Some 8% of the freshmen drop out at the end of their first year; 72% remain to graduate. Seventy percent of the graduates pursue advanced study; 5% enter medical school, 2% enter dental school, and 15% enter law school. Thirty percent pursue careers in business or industry.

Services: Students receive the following services free of charge: placement, career counseling, health care, and psychological counseling. A career planning and placement center is located on the campus.

Programs of Study: The college confers the B.A. degree in the following subjects: AREA STUDIES (Black/Afro-American, Puerto Rican, urban), BUSINESS (business administration), EDUCATION (early childhood, elementary, secondary), ENGLISH (comparative literature, English, media studies), FINE AND PERFORMING ARTS (art history, studio art, theater/dramatics), LANGUAGES (French, Spanish), MATH AND SCIENCES (computer science, mathematics—computational, natural sciences), PHILOSOPHY (philosophy, religious studies), PREPROFESSIONAL (dentistry, engineering, law, medicine, social work), SOCIAL SCIENCES (anthropology, government/political science, history, psychology, social sciences, sociology).

Required: Each student must demonstrate proficiency in 4 areas: English, foreign languages, science, and math.

Special: Internships, interdisciplinary majors, and study abroad are offered. There is a 3-2 cooperative engineering program. Student-designed majors are allowed, with faculty approval.

Honors: Alpha Sigma Lambda has a chapter on campus. Honors programs are open to all majors, and honors seminars in the humanities are offered.

Admissions: Of the 844 students who applied, 190 were enrolled in the 1981-82 freshman class. The SAT scores of those who enrolled were as follows: Verbal—39% between 500 and 599, 13% between 600 and 700, and 1% above 700; Math—37% between 500 and 599, 12% between 600 and 700, and 1% above 700. Applicants should have completed 16 Carnegie units at an accredited high school and generally be in the top two-fifths of their class. The reputation of the high school is considered important. Advanced placement or honors courses, special talent, recommendations from school officials, leadership potential, and the extracurricular activities record are also taken into consideration.

Procedure: The SAT is required, and it is recommended that it be taken by January of the senior year. Application deadlines are February 15 (fall) and December 1 (spring). Notification is sent by April 1. There is a rolling admissions policy. An application fee of $20 is required.

Special: Early decision, early admissions, and deferred admissions plans are available. The notification date for early decision is December 15; the application deadline for early admission is February 15. AP and CLEP credit is granted.

Transfer: For fall 1981, 127 transfer students applied, 70 were accepted, and 56 enrolled. A 3.0 GPA is required; C grades or higher transfer. There is a 3-semester residency requirement at Lincoln Center. Students must complete, at the college, 48 of the 125 credits necessary for the bachelor's degree. Application deadlines are June 1 (fall) and December 1 (spring).

Visiting: Individual interviews and tours are scheduled most weekdays and certain Saturdays during the fall and spring. Visitors may sit in on classes. For information about visiting, the office of admissions should be contacted.

Financial Aid: About 50% of the students receive aid through the college; about 80% receive aid from both Fordham and outside sources. Forty percent of the students work part-time on campus. Tuition may be paid on the installment plan. Fordham is a member of CSS; aid applicants are asked to submit the FAF. The deadlines for aid application are February 15 (fall) and November 1 (spring).

Foreign Students: About 3% of the full-time students come from foreign countries. The college actively recruits these students and offers them special counseling and special organizations.

Admissions: Foreign students must achieve a minimum score of 525 on the TOEFL. The SAT or ACT is not required.

Procedure: Application deadlines are February 15 (fall) and September 1 (spring). As proof of health, students must present a medical report prepared by a physician. Proof of funds adequate to cover the length of stay in the U.S. is required.

Admissions Contact: Steve Lenhart, Associate Director of Admissions.

FORDHAM UNIVERSITY/COLLEGE OF BUSINESS ADMINISTRATION D-5
Bronx, New York 10458 (212) 579-2133

F/T: 842M, 447W	Faculty: 75; I, +$
P/T: none	Ph.D.'s: 80%
Grad: none	S/F Ratio: 17 to 1
Year: sems, ss	Tuition: $5010
Appl: Feb. 15	R and B: $2700
1175 applied	289 enrolled
SAT: 490V 540M	COMPETITIVE+

The College of Business Administration was established more than a half century ago in the financial district in lower Manhattan. Presently located on the Rose Hill Campus in the Bronx, it is an undergraduate school of business and maintains its independent status within the university. It shares in the university's library system, which contains 1,309,264 volumes and 1 million microfilm items, and subscribes to 4872 periodicals.

Environment: The college occupies a section of the picturesque Rose Hill Campus. Great care has been taken to preserve the neo-Gothic architectural style of the campus. In all, there are 40 buildings, including residence halls and apartment buildings that accommodate 1650 men and women.

Student Life: About 75% of the students are from the tri-state New York metropolitan area. Forty-two percent of the entering freshmen are from public schools, and 58% are from private schools. Forty percent of the students live on campus. Eighty-eight percent are Catholic, 5% Protestant, and 2% Jewish. Twelve percent are minority-group members. Campus housing is both coed and single-sex. There are visiting privileges in single-sex dorms. Students may keep cars on campus.

Organizations: The 125 university-wide organizations and activities are open to College of Business Administration students. In addition, the college itself supports and guides a number of student-managed societies and clubs in the areas of marketing, management, finance, and accounting. Other activities include student government and publications. New York City offers outstanding cultural and recreational opportunities.

Sports: The college competes intercollegiately in 18 sports for men and 12 for women. There are 10 intramural sports for men and women.

Handicapped: About 70% of the campus is accessible to wheelchair-bound students. Special facilities for the physically handicapped include ramps, elevators, parking areas, and specially equipped rest rooms. There are no students with visual or hearing impairments.

Graduates: About 8% of the freshmen drop out at the end of their first year; 72% remain to graduate, and 60% of the graduates become candidates for graduate or professional degrees. Forty percent pursue careers in business or industry.

Services: Students receive the following services free of charge: placement, career counseling, health care, and psychological counseling. Career planning and placement centers are also available.

Programs of Study: The college confers the B.S.B.A. degree in the following areas of concentration: BUSINESS (accounting—managerial and public, economics, finance, management, marketing, quantitative methods). Fifty percent of the degrees conferred are in accounting.

Required: Core, core area, and some advanced courses are required. About 50% of the total program is in the liberal arts.

Special: Internships, double majors, and study abroad are offered.

Honors: Three national honor societies (Beta Gamma Sigma, Alpha Kappa Psi, and Beta Alpha Psi) have chapters on campus.

Admissions: Of the 1175 students who applied, 289 were enrolled in the 1981–82 freshman class. The SAT scores of those who enrolled were as follows: Verbal—34% between 500 and 599, 8% between 600 and 700, and 1% above 700; Math—57% between 500 and 599, 18% between 600 and 700, and 2% above 700. Applicants should have completed 16 Carnegie units at an accredited high school and rank in the top two-fifths of their class. The reputation of the high school is considered important. Advanced placement or honors courses, special talent, recommendations by school officials, and leadership record are also taken into consideration.

Procedure: The SAT is required, and it is recommended that it be taken by January of the senior year. Application deadlines are February 15 (fall) and December 1 (spring). Notification is sent by April 1. There is a rolling admissions policy. An application fee of $20 is required.

Special: Early decision, early admissions, and deferred admissions plans are available. The notification date for early decision is December 15; the application deadline for early admission is February 15. AP and CLEP credit is granted.

Transfer: For fall 1981, 240 transfer students applied, 139 were accepted, and 96 enrolled. A 3.0 GPA is required; C grades or higher transfer. There is a 4-semester residency requirement. Students must complete, at the college, 64 of the 124 credits required for the bachelor's degree. Application deadlines are June 1 (fall) and December 1 (spring).

Visiting: Individual interviews and tours are scheduled most weekdays and certain Saturdays during the fall and spring. Group orientations are conducted on Sundays in October and November. Visitors may sit in on classes. For information about visiting, the admissions office should be contacted.

Financial Aid: About 50% of the students receive aid through the college; about 80% receive aid from both Fordham and outside sources. Thirty-five percent of the students work part-time on campus. Tuition may be paid on the installment plan. Fordham is a member of CSS and applicants for aid are asked to submit the FAF. The deadlines for aid applications are February 15 (fall) and November 1 (spring).

Foreign Students: About 2% of the full-time students come from foreign countries. The college offers these students special counseling and special organizations.

Admissions: Foreign students must achieve a minimum score of 525 on the TOEFL. The SAT or ACT is not required.

Procedure: Application deadlines are February 15 (fall) and September 1 (spring). Students must present a health report from a physician. Proof of funds adequate to cover the length of stay in the U.S. is required.

Admissions Contact: Richard T. Waldron, Director of Admissions.

NEW YORK 559

FORDHAM UNIVERSITY/ FORDHAM COLLEGE
Bronx, New York 10458

D–5

(212) 579-2133

F/T: 1641M, 1300W
P/T: none
Grad: none
Year: sems, ss
Appl: Feb. 15
2830 applied
SAT: 525V 540M

Faculty: 249; I, +$
Ph.D.'s: 87%
S/F Ratio: 12 to 1
Tuition: $5010
R and B: $2700
802 enrolled
VERY COMPETITIVE

Fordham College, founded in 1841, is the first liberal arts and science college established by the university. It is an independent college in the Jesuit tradition. The library contains 1,309,264 volumes and 1 million microfilm items, and subscribes to 4872 periodicals.

Environment: The college, which maintains its own identity within the university, is located on the picturesque, 86-acre Rose Hill Campus, adjacent to the New York Botanical Gardens and Bronx Zoological Park. There are 40 buildings; the predominant architectural style is neo-Gothic. The 10 residence halls accommodate 1650 students.

Student Life: About 75% of the students are from the tri-state New York metropolitan area. Sixty percent of entering freshmen come from private schools; 40% come from public schools. Forty percent of the students live on campus. Eighty-eight percent are Catholic, 5% are Protestant, and 2% are Jewish. Sixteen percent are minority-group members. Campus housing is both coed and single-sex. There are visiting privileges in single-sex dorms. Students may keep cars on campus.

Organizations: There are more than 125 extracurricular and on-campus cultural activities. About 80% of the students participate in such activities as publications, theater groups, service organizations, religious groups, the college radio station, academic clubs, political organizations, and community service societies. There are 7 service and 3 academic fraternities, in which 10% of the men participate. There are no fraternity houses. New York City offers outstanding cultural and recreational opportunities.

Sports: The college competes in 18 intercollegiate sports for men and 13 for women. There are 10 intramural sports for men and women.

Handicapped: About 70% of the campus is accessible to wheelchair-bound students. Special facilities for the physically handicapped include ramps, elevators, parking areas, and specially equipped rest rooms. There are no students with visual or hearing impairments.

Graduates: Some 8% of the freshmen drop out at the end of their first year; 72% remain to graduate. Seventy percent of the graduates pursue advanced study; 7% enter medical school, 1% enter dental school, and 10% enter law school. Twenty percent enter careers in business or industry.

Services: Students receive the following services free of charge: placement, career counseling, health care, and psychological counseling. Career planning and placement centers are located on the campus.

Programs of Study: The college confers the B.A. and B.S. degrees. Bachelor's degrees are offered in the following subjects: AREA STUDIES (American, Black/Afro-American, Latin American, Russian, urban, women's), ENGLISH (communications, English, journalism, literature), FINE AND PERFORMING ARTS (art history, film/photography, fine arts, radio/TV, theater/dramatics), LANGUAGES (French, German, Greek/Latin, Italian, Russian, Spanish), MATH AND SCIENCES (biology, chemistry, computer science, mathematics, physics), PHILOSOPHY (classics, medieval studies, philosophy, religion), PREPROFESSIONAL (architecture, dentistry, engineering, law, medicine), SOCIAL SCIENCES (anthropology, economics, government/political science, history, public administration, psychology, sociology). Twenty-nine percent of the degrees conferred are in social sciences and 15% are in preprofessional studies.

Required: Requirements include core, core area, and advanced courses.

Special: Internships, interdisciplinary majors, and study abroad are offered. There is a 3-2 cooperative engineering program. Student-designed majors are allowed, with faculty approval.

Honors: Three national honor societies, including Phi Beta Kappa, have chapters on campus. Honors programs are open to all majors; there are interdisciplinary honors programs with a guided research or seminar option.

Admissions: Of the 2830 students who applied, 802 were enrolled in the 1981–82 freshman class. The SAT scores of those who enrolled were as follows: Verbal—40% below 500, 40% between 500 and 599,

15% between 600 and 700, and 5% above 700; Math—32% below 500, 46% between 500 and 599, 19% between 600 and 700, and 3% above 700. Applicants should have completed 16 Carnegie units at an accredited high school and generally rank in the top two-fifths of their class. The reputation of the high school is considered important. Advanced placement or honors courses, special talents, recommendations by school officials, leadership potential, and the extracurricular activities record are also taken into consideration.

Procedure: The SAT is required, and it is recommended that it be taken by January of the senior year. Application deadlines are February 15 (fall) and December 1 (spring). Notification is sent by April 1. An application fee of $20 is required.

Special: Early decision, early admissions, and deferred admissions plans are available. The notification date for early decision is December 15; the application deadline for early admission is February 15. AP and CLEP credit is granted.

Transfer: For fall 1981, 415 transfer students applied, 238 were accepted, and 161 enrolled. A 3.0 GPA is required; C grades or higher transfer. There is a 4-semester residency requirement. Transfers must complete, at the college, 64 of the 124 credits necessary for the bachelor's degree. Application deadlines are June 1 (fall) and December 1 (spring).

Visiting: Individual interviews and tours are scheduled most weekdays and certain Saturdays during the fall and spring. Group orientations are conducted on Sundays in October and November. Visitors may sit in on classes. For information about visiting, the office of admissions should be contacted.

Financial Aid: About 50% of the students receive aid through the college; about 80% receive aid from both Fordham and outside sources. Thirty-five percent of the students work part-time on campus. Tuition may be paid on the installment plan. Fordham is a member of CSS and applicants for aid are asked to submit the FAF. The fall deadline for aid application is February 15; the spring deadline is November 1.

Foreign Students: About 3% of the full-time students come from foreign countries. The college offers these students special counseling and special organizations.

Admissions: Foreign students must achieve a minimum score of 525 on the TOEFL. The SAT or ACT is not required.

Procedure: Application deadlines are February 15 (fall) and September 1 (spring). As proof of health, students must present a medical report prepared by a physician. Proof of funds adequate to cover the length of stay in the U.S. is required.

Admissions Contact: Richard T. Waldron, Director of Admissions.

HAMILTON COLLEGE   C–3
Clinton, New York 13323   (315) 859-4421

F/T: 978M, 669W	Faculty: 132; IIB, ++$
P/T: 1W	Ph.D.'s: 80%
Grad: none	S/F Ratio: 12 to 1
Year: 4-1-4	Tuition: $7050
Appl: Feb. 1	R and B: $2250
2828 applied	1179 accepted 457 enrolled
SAT: 590V 620M	HIGHLY COMPETITIVE

Hamilton College, a small, independent liberal arts college, was founded in 1793 and named after Alexander Hamilton, who served on the first Board of Trustees. The library houses 365,000 volumes and 5000 microfilm reels. It subscribes to 2100 periodicals.

Environment: Located in a rural setting about 9 miles from Utica, the 350-acre wooded campus is divided into 2 sections. Hamilton's original 3 quadrangles of 26 buildings include the library, a science and chemistry building, and student center. The more modern Kirkland campus includes 7 dorms, a fine arts center, and a social science building. The chapel and the building which houses the admissions office are both registered landmarks. Students are housed in the original quads, more modern dorms, and townhouse-style dorms. Freshmen are housed in cluster groups of 30 to 40.

Student Life: Fifty percent of the students are from New York State. Thirty-eight percent come from private schools, the rest from public or parochial schools. Ninety-seven percent of the students live on campus. Five percent are minority-group members. Campus housing is coed. All except freshmen may keep cars on campus.

Organizations: Forty-five percent of the men belong to 1 of 9 fraternities on campus. There are no sororities. Hiking, camping, climbing, and cross-country skiing may be enjoyed in the 1500 acres of college-owned property or in the nearby Adirondacks. The Kirkland Art Center and the city of Utica offer cultural opportunities.

Sports: The college participates in a number of intercollegiate competitions: 20 for men, 17 for women. There are 15 intramural sports for men and 12 for women.

Handicapped: Thirty percent of the campus is accessible to the physically handicapped. Wheelchair ramps, elevators, and specially equipped rest rooms are provided.

Graduates: Seven percent of the freshmen drop out; 85% remain to graduate. Of those, about 40% go on to graduate schools: 6% enter medical school, 2% dental school, and 12% law school. About 40% begin careers in business and industry.

Services: Free health care, psychological counseling, career counseling, placement services, and tutoring are available. The Career Center offers employment counseling, hosts corporate and graduate school interviews, gives graduate study counseling, refers students to alumni resource people, and helps with internship and summer job placement.

Programs of Study: The College confers the B.A. degree in the following subjects: AREA STUDIES (American, Asian, foreign languages, Russian), ENGLISH (literature, writing), FINE AND PERFORMING ARTS (art history, dance, music, studio art, theater/dramatics), LANGUAGES (French, German, Greek/Latin, Spanish), MATH AND SCIENCES (biology, chemistry, geology, mathematics, physics), PHILOSOPHY (classics, philosophy, religion), SOCIAL SCIENCES (anthropology, economics, government/political science, history, psychobiology, psychology, public policy, sociology).

Required: Two semesters of physical education are required.

Special: The college offers independent study, student-designed majors, 3-2 cooperative programs in engineering with 4 other institutions, and a 3-3 cooperative program with Columbia School of Law. A junior year abroad program in France or Spain and a semester in Washington are offered.

Honors: There are 4 national honor societies with chapters on campus, including Phi Beta Kappa and Sigma Xi. Departmental honors may be earned in all concentrations by students who meet criteria which include an average of at least 88% and, usually, the writing of a thesis.

Admissions: The college accepted 42% of the applicants for the 1981–82 freshman class. The SAT scores of those who recently enrolled were as follows: Verbal—42% scored between 500 and 599, 39% between 600 and 700, and 6% above 700; Math—36% scored between 500 and 599, 46% between 600 and 700, and 11% above 700. Prospective students should graduate from an accredited high school and should have completed 16 Carnegie units. Admissions officers also give consideration to advanced placement or honor courses, recommendations by school officials, special talent, and extracurricular activities records.

Procedure: Requirements include a personal interview and the SAT or ACT. ATs are strongly recommended. Seniors should have taken the SAT by January. The deadline for fall application is February 1. A fee of $25 must accompany the application. Fall candidates are notified by April 15.

Special: Hamilton accepts students on an early decision basis; notification is on a rolling basis. There are also early admissions and deferred admissions plans; the deadline for early admissions is February 1. AP is offered.

Transfer: For fall 1981, 122 transfer applications were received, 26 were accepted, and 10 students were enrolled. Transfers are accepted for the sophomore and junior years. A 3.0 GPA and a significant activities record are recommended. There is a 2-year residency requirement. To earn the bachelor's degree, students must complete 35 courses. March 1 is the fall deadline; December 1, the spring.

Visiting: There are no regularly scheduled orientations for prospective students. Visitors may stay overnight at the school. They will be provided with guides and may sit in on classes. Plans can be made by contacting the admissions office receptionist.

Financial Aid: Forty-three percent of the students receive financial assistance. About 20% work part-time on campus. There is a total of $600,000 in scholarships available to freshmen and $200,000 in loans for all 4 classes. The average aid to freshmen is $7000. All candidates for aid should apply through the CSS. The FAF is required. February 15 is the deadline.

Foreign Students: Eight percent of the student body come from foreign countries. Special counseling and organizations are available.

Admissions: If the language of the candidate's secondary institution is not English, the applicant must take the TOEFL. The SAT or ACT is required and the ATs are strongly recommended.

Procedure: The application deadline for foreign freshman students is February 1 for fall entry. Foreign transfers may apply March 1 for fall

HARTWICK COLLEGE

Oneonta, New York 13820   D-3
(607) 432-4200

F/T: 583M, 841W		Faculty:	102; IIB, +$
P/T: 3M, 20W		Ph.D.'s:	62%
Grad: none		S/F Ratio:	14 to 1
Year: 4-1-4, ss		Tuition:	$5875
Appl: Mar. 1		R and B:	$2250
2219 applied	1626 accepted		441 enrolled
SAT: 482V 512M			COMPETITIVE

Hartwick College, founded in 1928, is a private liberal arts college. The library contains 166,955 volumes, subscribes to 1005 periodicals, and has 31,820 microfilm items on file.

Environment: There are 17 buildings on a 175-acre campus on Oyaron Hill, overlooking the city of Oneonta, 60 miles from Binghamton. The environment is rural. The college also maintains an 1100-acre ecological preserve, which is used for academic as well as recreational purposes. Seven dormitories with double rooms accommodate 1000 students.

Student Life: About 52% of the students come from New York. Ninety-nine percent live on campus. About 1 percent are minority-group members. Campus housing is both single-sex and coed; there are visiting privileges in the single-sex housing. Students may keep cars on campus.

Organizations: Twenty-six percent of the men belong to 2 local and 2 national fraternities; 14% of the women are members of 2 local and 1 national sorority. As many as 50 different clubs and organizations are open to students, and the college sponsors many functions, such as lectures, dances, open houses, and concerts. The Pine Lake Campus (8 miles from the main campus) provides facilities for hiking, swimming, boating, cross-country skiing, and skating.

Sports: Intercollegiate competition is offered in 10 sports for men and 9 for women. A program of intramural sports, 9 for men and 8 for women, is also available.

Handicapped: All of the academic facilities, as well as selected dormitories, are 100% accessible to handicapped students. Special class scheduling, special parking, elevators, and specially equipped rest rooms are available. Fewer than 2% of the student body have visual or hearing impairments. For these students, the library orders special records and other materials as needed.

Graduates: About 81% of the students return for their sophomore year, and 50% remain to graduate. Thirty percent pursue graduate study; 2% enter medical school, 2% enter dental school, and 4% enter law school. Seventy-five percent pursue careers in business or industry.

Services: Psychological counseling, tutoring, placement service, and career counseling are offered at no charge to the student. Health care is available for a fee.

Programs of Study: The college confers the B.A. and B.S. degrees. Programs leading to the bachelor's degree are offered in the following subjects: BUSINESS (management), EDUCATION (music, secondary), ENGLISH (English), FINE AND PERFORMING ARTS (art, theater/dramatics), HEALTH SCIENCES (medical technology, nursing), LANGUAGES (French, German, Spanish), MATH AND SCIENCES (biology, chemistry, geology, physics), PHILOSOPHY (philosophy, religion), SOCIAL SCIENCES (anthropology, economics, history, psychology, sociology). Of the degrees recently conferred, 39% were in social sciences, 19% were in health sciences, and 17% were in math and sciences.

Special: Students may develop their own independent study program subject to faculty approval and guidance. Directed study, independent study, and internship opportunities are available. The college offers a wide range of off-campus study programs abroad, in Washington, D.C., Philadelphia, and in the Bahamas. Dual-degree 3-2 programs are available in engineering in cooperation with Columbia University, Georgia Institute of Technology, and Clarkson College.

Honors: Ten national honor societies have chapters on campus.

Admissions: Seventy-three percent of those who applied were accepted for the 1981-82 freshman class. Of those who enrolled, the SAT scores were as follows: Verbal—62% scored below 500, 31% between 500 and 599, 6% between 600 and 700, and 1% above 700; Math—42% scored below 500, 47% between 500 and 599, 11% between 600 and 700, and 0% above 700. Important factors in the admission decision are recommendations by school officials, extracurricular activities, and evidence of special talent.

Procedure: The SAT or ACT is required. Applications, along with a $20 fee, must be submitted by March 1 (fall), December 1 (winter), and January 2 (spring). Freshmen are admitted each semester.

Special: There are early decision, early admissions, and deferred admissions plans. The notification date for early decision is February 1. The application deadline for early admissions is March 1. CLEP and AP credit is given.

Transfer: For fall 1981, 120 transfer applications were received, 70 were accepted, and 35 students were enrolled. A minimum average of 2.0, an A.A., or an A.S. degree is required for transfer. There is a 2-year residency requirement. Eighteen course units must be completed at Hartwick out of 36 course units required for the bachelor's degree. Transfer application deadlines are August 1 (fall), December 1 (winter), and January 15 (spring).

Visiting: Guides are available for informal visits to the college. Visitors may sit in on classes and stay overnight at the school. Visits should be arranged through the admissions office.

Financial Aid: About 50% of all students receive aid. About 33% work part-time on campus. The average award to freshmen from all sources is $4900. There are scholarships totaling $1,265,230, loans totaling $156,000 and employment grants totaling $450,000. The college is a member of CSS. The FAF, college application, and tax return are required; the deadline for aid application is April 1.

Foreign Students: Foreign students represent fewer than 1% of the student body.

Admissions: Hartwick requires foreign applicants to take the TOEFL. A college entrance exam is not necessary.

Procedure: Application deadlines for foreign students are March 1 (fall), December 1 (winter), and January 2 (spring). Proof of health in the form of a health certificate must be presented. Proof of funds adequate to cover 1 year of study is also required. Students must carry health insurance, which is available through the college.

Admissions Contact: John Muyskens, Jr., Dean of Admissions.

HOBART AND WILLIAM SMITH COLLEGES

Hobart and William Smith are coordinate institutions sharing facilities and faculty but maintaining separate campuses. Hobart enrolls only men; William Smith enrolls women. Separate profiles for each college follow.

HOBART AND WILLIAM SMITH COLLEGES/HOBART COLLEGE

C-3

Geneva, New York 14456   (315) 789-5500

F/T: 1100M		Faculty:	115; IIB, ++$
P/T: none		Ph.D.'s:	95%
Grad: none		S/F Ratio:	14 to 1
Year: tri		Tuition:	$6425
Appl: Feb. 15		R and B:	$2335
1593 applied	930 accepted		305 enrolled
SAT: 523V 581M	ACT: 26		VERY COMPETITIVE+

Hobart, a men's college founded in 1822, is the oldest private liberal arts college in western New York. The college is coordinate with William Smith College (see separate profile). The library houses 200,000 volumes and 23,000 microfilm items, and subscribes to 1250 periodicals.

Environment: Located halfway between Rochester and Syracuse in a rural residential area of Geneva overlooking Seneca Lake, the college shares the facilities of the 180-acre campus with William Smith College. The combined facilities include 13 classroom and administration buildings, 2 gymnasia, 2 dining halls, and 33 dormitories. Hobart College has 9 residence halls grouped around a quadrangle and along the lake front. Nine fraternity houses accommodate 201 students.

Student Life: Fifty percent of the students are from New York; 24% are from bordering states. Sixty percent of entering freshmen come from public schools. Eighty-eight percent reside on campus; about 15% leave the campus on weekends. Married students, nonfreshman fraternity members, some upperclassmen, and local students are not required to live in the dorms. Thirty percent of the students are Protestant, 27% are Catholic, and 22% are Jewish. Nine percent are minority-group members. College housing is coed and single-sex; students in single-sex housing have visiting privileges. Students may keep cars on campus.

Organizations: The 9 fraternities on campus play an important role in the social life of students; 40% of the men are members. There are over 35 college-sponsored extracurricular activities and groups. Fall, Winter, and Spring Weekends are the major campus social events. Cultural activities include nearby theaters and museums.

Sports: The college fields 13 intercollegiate teams. There are 24 intramural sports.

Handicapped: The entire campus is accessible to the physically handicapped. Elevators and student assistance are available for these students. Mechanical and human assistance is also provided for visually and hearing-impaired students. The dean's office and faculty advisers are available.

Graduates: The freshman dropout rate is 3%, and 82% of the freshmen remain to graduate. Sixty percent of the graduates pursue advanced study; 3% enter medical school and 4% enter law school. More than 35% enter careers in business and industry.

Services: Free placement and career counseling, psychological counseling, health care, tutoring, and remedial instruction are available to students. Placement services for undergraduates and alumni include counseling and reference materials.

Programs of Study: The college confers the B.A. and B.S. degrees. Bachelor's degrees are offered in the following subjects: AREA STUDIES (American, Asian, Black/Afro-American, urban, women's), ENGLISH (English), FINE AND PERFORMING ARTS (art, art history, studio art), LANGUAGES (French, German, Greek/Latin, Spanish), MATH AND SCIENCES (biology, chemistry, geology, mathematics, physics), PHILOSOPHY (classics, philosophy, religion), SOCIAL SCIENCES (anthropology, economics, government/political science, history, psychology, sociology). Recently, 45% of the degrees conferred were in social sciences, 27% in math and sciences, and 10% in English.

Required: Freshmen are required to take a program in General Education which comprises one third of the year. All undergraduates must write the Baccalaureate Essay before their senior year and attend the Baccalaureate Colloquium.

Special: Students may design their own major with faculty approval. Programs offered in addition to independent study and seminars include bidisciplinary majors and a binary program in engineering with either Columbia University or the University of Rochester. A program of provisional certification for either elementary or secondary school teaching is offered by the Education Department. Washington Semester, United Nations Semester, and a junior year study-abroad program are all available.

Honors: Honors programs are available to qualified students. Five honorary societies, including Phi Beta Kappa, have chapters on campus.

Admissions: Fifty-eight percent of those who applied were accepted for the 1981-82 freshman class. Of those who enrolled, the SAT scores were as follows: Verbal—40% scored below 500, 45% between 500 and 599, 13% between 600 and 700, and 2% above 700; Math—20% scored below 500, 55% between 500 and 599, 21% between 600 and 700, and 4% above 700. On the ACT, 0% scored below 21, 10% between 21 and 23, 60% between 24 and 25, 20% between 26 and 28, and 10% above 28. The college's selection methods are very individualistic. However, candidates should graduate from an accredited high school, offer 16 Carnegie units, rank in the upper three-fifths of their class, and have at least a 2.8 grade average. A personal interview is expected. Other factors considered are advanced placement or honor courses, recommendations by school officials, and the extracurricular activities record. Some preference is given to children of alumni and to those of geographic areas not well represented in the student body. The HEOP program is available to New York State residents from disadvantaged backgrounds.

Procedure: The SAT or ACT and the AT in English composition are required; the math AT is recommended for natural science majors. All tests should be taken by January of the senior year. The application deadline is February 15. Notification is sent by April 1. The college observes the CRDA. The application fee is $20.

Special: Early and deferred admissions plans and an early decision plan are available. AP and CLEP are accepted.

Transfers: For fall 1981, 78 students applied, 38 were accepted, and 28 enrolled. Transfer students need a GPA of at least 2.5, a combined SAT score of 1000 or an ACT score of 24, and completed credit hours from one year of study. An interview and recommendations are also required. Hobart's residency requirement is 2 years. The application deadlines are June 1 (fall), October 1 (winter), and January 1 (spring).

Visiting: Orientations for prospective students include an interview and tour of the campus. Informal visits are best planned for fall, winter, and spring. Visitors may sit in on classes and stay overnight at the college. Arrangements for a guide can be made through the admissions office.

Financial Aid: Forty percent of the students receive financial assistance. Twenty-five percent work part-time on campus. Average aid to freshmen is $6000. There are approximately 500 scholarships. Financial aid packages range in amounts from $250 to $6600 and must include loans and work contracts. The main considerations in determining the aid award are academic achievement and need. Tuition can be paid in installments through outside agencies. The college is a member of the CSS; the FAF is required. The aid application deadline is March 1.

Foreign Students: One percent of the full-time students come from foreign countries. The college offers these students an intensive English course and program as well as special counseling.

Admissions: Foreign students must take the TOEFL but are not required to take a college entrance exam.

Procedure: The application deadline for fall entry is February 15. Foreign students must take a standard physical exam. They must also carry health insurance, which is available through the college for a fee.

Admissions Contact: Leonard A. Wood, Jr., Director of Admissions.

HOBART AND WILLIAM SMITH COLLEGES/WILLIAM SMITH COLLEGE C-3

Geneva, New York 14456   (315) 789-5500

F/T: 750W   *Faculty:* 130; IIB, + + $
P/T: none   *Ph.D.'s:* 92%
Grad: none   *S/F Ratio:* 14 to 1
Year: tri   *Tuition:* $6450
Appl: Feb. 15   *R and B:* $2335
1100 applied   *650 accepted*   *213 enrolled*
SAT: 550V 550M   *ACT: 26*   *VERY COMPETITIVE+*

William Smith College, founded in 1908, is a private liberal arts college for women. The college is coordinate with Hobart College (see profile). The library has 200,000 volumes and 23,000 microfilm items, and subscribes to 1250 periodicals.

Environment: Located within an hour's drive from Rochester, Syracuse, and Ithaca, in a rural area on the northern shore of Seneca Lake, the college shares the facilities of the 180-acre campus with Hobart College. Each college has its own residential area, dean, admissions offices, and student government. The combined facilities of the colleges include 13 classrooms and administrative buildings, 2 gymnasia, 2 dining halls, and 33 dormitories. The college also sponsors off-campus apartments.

Student Life: Forty-five percent of the students are from New York; 22% are from bordering states. Eighty-five percent reside on campus; about 15% leave campus on weekends. Married students, some upperclassmen, and local students are not required to live in the dorms. Thirty-four percent of the students are Catholic, 23% are Protestant, and 23% are Jewish. Six percent are minority-group members. College housing is coed and single-sex; students in single-sex housing have visiting privileges. Students may keep cars on campus.

Organizations: There are no sororities. Together with Hobart College, the college sponsors over 35 different extracurricular activities and groups. The college's location in the midst of the Finger Lakes region, yet near 3 major cities, affords students a wide range of recreational, social, and cultural opportunities.

Sports: The college fields 8 intercollegiate teams. There are 7 intramural sports.

Handicapped: Fifty percent of the campus is accessible to the physically handicapped. Special facilities for these students include elevators, specially equipped rest rooms, and lowered drinking fountains and telephones. Special class scheduling can be arranged. There is special equipment for visually or hearing-impaired impaired students. Two special counselors are available.

Graduates: The freshman dropout rate is 5%, and 75% of the freshmen remain to graduate. Sixty-five percent of the graduates pursue graduate study; 3% enter medical school and 1% enter dental school. Thirty percent enter careers in business and industry.

Services: Students receive the following free services: health care, placement and career counseling, tutoring, remedial instruction, and psychological counseling. Placement services for undergraduates and alumnae include counseling and recruiting.

Programs of Study: The college confers the B.A. and B.S. degrees. Bachelor's degrees are offered in the following subjects: AREA STUDIES (American, Asian, Black/Afro-American, comparative literature, urban, women's), ENGLISH (English), FINE AND PERFORMING

ARTS (art history, dance, music, studio art), LANGUAGES (French, German, Greek/Latin, Russian, Spanish), MATH AND SCIENCES (biology, chemistry, geoscience, mathematics, physics), PHILOSOPHY (classics, philosophy, religion), SOCIAL SCIENCES (anthropology, economics, government/political science, history, psychology, sociology). Forty-five percent of the degrees conferred are in social sciences, 27% in math and sciences, and 10% in English.

Required: Freshmen are required to take a program in general education which comprises one-third of the year. All undergraduates are required to write the Baccalaureate Essay before the senior year and attend the Baccalaureate Colloquium.

Special: Qualified students may choose independent study and seminar options. The Washington Semester, the United Nations Semester, study abroad, and junior year study at the Institute of Architecture in New York City are available. Interdisciplinary and student-designed majors are possible. Binary programs in engineering and a 4+1 M.B.A. program are also offered. Courses leading to provisional certification for teaching in the elementary and secondary schools of New York State are offered by the Education Department.

Honors: All departments offer honors work. Five honor societies, including Phi Beta Kappa, have chapters on campus.

Admissions: Fifty-nine percent of those who applied were accepted for the 1981-82 freshman class. Of those who enrolled, the SAT scores were as follows: Verbal—20% scored below 500, 60% between 500 and 599, 18% between 600 and 700, and 2% above 700; Math—15% scored below 500, 63% between 500 and 599, 20% between 600 and 700, and 2% above 700. Sixty-five percent of those who were accepted were in the top fifth of their class. The college's selection methods are very individualistic; however, candidates should graduate from an accredited high school of good reputation, present 16 Carnegie units, and rank in the top two-fifths of their class. A personal interview is strongly recommended. Also considered are advanced placement or honor courses, recommendations by school officials, and evidence of special talents. Some preference is given to children of alumnae and to those from geographic areas not well represented in the student body. The HEOP program is available for New York State residents from disadvantaged backgrounds.

Procedure: The SAT or ACT and the AT in English composition are required; the math AT is suggested for natural science majors. These tests should be taken by January of the senior year. Freshmen are admitted in the fall; winter and spring admissions depend upon available space. Application deadlines are February 15 (fall), October 1 (winter), and January 1 (spring). Notification is sent by April 1. The application fee is $20.

Special: Early and deferred admissions plans and an early decision plan are available. AP and CLEP credit is granted.

Transfers: For fall 1981, 46 students applied, 21 were accepted, and 12 enrolled. A 3.0 GPA and recommendations by a professor and an academic dean are required; basic freshman requirements should be met. An interview is recommended. D grades do not transfer. The residency requirement is 2 years. The application deadlines are June 1 (fall), October 1 (winter), and January 1 (spring).

Visiting: Year-round interviews, preferably for students in their senior year of high school, are scheduled by appointment, except in March or on Saturdays from June through August. Visits are best scheduled for weekdays in the fall. Visitors may sit in on classes and stay overnight at the college. Arrangements can be made through the admissions office.

Financial Aid: Forty percent of the students receive financial assistance. Thirty-three percent work part-time on campus. Aid packages range in amounts from $250 to $7250 and include federal loans (NDSL and EOG) and work contracts. The main considerations in determining the aid award are academic achievement and need. Tuition can be paid in installments through outside agencies. The college is a member of the CSS; the FAF or FFS is required. The aid application deadline is February 15.

Foreign Students: Three percent of the full-time students come from foreign countries. The college offers these students special counseling and special organizations.

Admissions: Foreign students must achieve a TOEFL score of 500. No college entrance exam must be taken.

Procedure: Application deadlines are February 15 (fall), October 1 (winter), and January 1 (spring).

Admissions Contact: Mara O'Laughlin, Director of Admissions.

HOFSTRA UNIVERSITY D-5
Hempstead, New York 11550 (516) 560-3491

F/T: 3259M, 2727W Faculty: 375; I, av$
P/T: 680M, 684W Ph.D.'s: 80%
Grad: 1263M, 1620W S/F Ratio: 17 to 1
Year: 4-1-4, ss Tuition: $4350
Appl: Feb. 15 R and B: $2500
5000 applied 3500 accepted 1300 enrolled
SAT: 500V 520M ACT: 23 VERY COMPETITIVE

Hofstra University, founded in 1935, is a private liberal arts university. Its undergraduate divisions are the College of Liberal Arts and Sciences, the School of Business, the School of Education, University College, New College, and University Without Walls at New College. The library houses over 900,000 volumes, subscribes to 2300 periodicals, and has 374,500 microfilm items.

Environment: The 238-acre campus is located on Long Island in a suburban community 22 miles from New York City. Among the 48 buildings are high-rise residence towers that can accommodate 2300 students and new low-rise modular housing accommodating 500.

Student Life: The student body is drawn primarily from the northeast region of the United States but represents 35 states. Forty percent of the students are Catholic, 25% Protestant, and 35% Jewish. Six percent are minority-group members. University housing is both single-sex and coed; there are visiting privileges in single-sex housing. Students may keep cars on campus. Day-care services are available to all students, faculty, and staff.

Organizations: Student activities include about 50 special-interest clubs, publications, concerts, movies, and chapters of 8 fraternities and 6 sororities. Nearby Nassau Coliseum presents many major sports events and concerts.

Sports: The university participates on an intercollegiate level in 8 sports for men and 8 for women. The program of intramural sports includes 8 sports for men and 7 for women.

Handicapped: The campus is 100% accessible to wheelchair-bound students. Facilities and considerations include ramps, special class scheduling, designated handicapped parking, elevators, lowered drinking fountains and telephones, and specially equipped rest rooms. A staff of 2 is available to provide assistance and special counseling.

Graduates: Eleven percent of the freshmen drop out by the end of the first year. Sixty percent remain to graduate. Sixty percent of those who graduate enter graduate or professional schools; 5% enter medical school and 1% dental school. Forty percent pursue careers in business or industry.

Services: The following services are offered free of charge to students: psychological counseling, tutoring, remedial instruction, health care, placement, and career counseling.

Programs of Study: The university confers the B.A., B.S., B.E., B.S.Ed., and B.F.A. degrees. Master's and doctoral programs are also awarded. Bachelor's degrees are offered in the following subjects: AREA STUDIES (American, Asian), BUSINESS (accounting, business education, computer science, finance, international business, management, marketing), EDUCATION (early childhood, elementary, health/physical, music and art, secondary), ENGLISH (English, journalism, literature, speech), FINE AND PERFORMING ARTS (art, art education, art history, film/photography, music, music education, radio/TV, studio art, theater/dramatics), HEALTH SCIENCES (speech therapy), LANGUAGES (French, German, Greek/Latin, Hebrew, Italian, Russian, Spanish), MATH AND SCIENCES (biochemistry, biology, chemistry, computer science, ecology/environmental science, engineering science, geology, mathematics, physics), PHILOSOPHY (philosophy), SOCIAL SCIENCES (anthropology, economics, geography, government/political science, history, psychology, sociology). Of the degrees conferred, 33% are in business, 21% in social sciences, and 17% in fine and performing arts.

Required: All students must complete between 62 and 94 semester hours of liberal arts studies.

Special: New Opportunities at Hofstra (NOAH) is a special program for the economically and educationally deprived with high potential. A 3-2 program in forestry with Duke University, student-designed majors, and study abroad are available. New College, which provides liberal arts students with a small-college environment, offers the B.A. degree through interdisciplinary curricula in social sciences, natural sciences, humanities, and creative studies. Modes of learning include courses, seminars, independent study, and off-campus internships.

Honors: Phi Beta Kappa has a chapter on campus.

Admissions: Seventy percent of those who applied were accepted for the 1981-82 freshman class. Of those who enrolled, the SAT scores were as follows: Verbal—56% scored below 500, 35% between 500 and 599, 8% between 600 and 700, and 1% above 700; Math—32% scored below 500, 45% between 500 and 599, 20% between 600 and 700, and 2% above 700. Applicants should be graduates of accredited high schools, rank in the top 30% of their graduating class, and have acceptable SAT or ACT scores. Other important considerations are advanced placement or honors courses, leadership record, and evidence of special talent.

Procedure: The SAT or ACT is required and should be taken by December of the senior year. Those applying for mathematics, science, or engineering programs are urged to submit Math AT scores. The application deadlines are February 15 (fall) and January 15 (spring). The rolling admissions plan is used. There is a $25 application fee.

Special: Early decision, early admissions, and deferred admissions plans are offered. The early admissions application deadline is April 1. The notification date for early decision is December 15. CLEP and AP credit is accepted.

Transfer: For fall 1981, the university received 1674 transfer applications, accepted 1253 students, and enrolled 870. Transfers are accepted for all classes. Students from fully accredited schools must have a 2.0 GPA; those from partially accredited schools, a 2.5. Some D grades transfer. All students must complete their final 30 semester hours at the university as well as 15 in their department out of the 124 needed to receive a bachelor's degree. Application deadlines are March 15 (fall) and December 1 (spring).

Visiting: Gold Key student-conducted tours of the campus are available daily at 11 A.M. and 3 P.M.. Guides are available for informal visits. Visitors may sit in on classes. For information on overnight visits to the school or to make tour arrangements, contact the tour program at (516) 560-3433.

Financial Aid: About 60% of all students receive aid. Twenty-five percent work part-time on campus. The average freshman award is $1200. The university offers scholarships, grants-in-aid, and federal, state, bank, and university loans. The university is a member of CSS and requires the FAF. The deadlines for aid application are March 15 (fall) and November 15 (spring).

Foreign Students: Seven percent of the full-time students come from foreign countries. The university offers these students an intensive English program, special counseling, and special organizations.

Admissions: Foreign students must score 550 on the TOEFL. No college entrance examination is required.

Procedure: The application deadlines are March 1 (fall) and December 1 (spring). Foreign students must complete the infirmary medical statement. They must also present proof of funds adequate to cover 4 years of study. There is a special application fee of $50. Foreign students must carry health insurance, which is available through the university infirmary for a fee.

Admissions Contact: Joan E. Isaac, Director of Admissions.

HOUGHTON COLLEGE B-3
Houghton, New York 14744 (716) 567-2211

F/T: 500M, 690W	Faculty: 70; IIB, −$
P/T: 25M, 32W	Ph.D.'s: 50%
Grad: none	S/F Ratio: 14 to 1
Year: sems, ss	Tuition: $3920
Appl: Aug. 1	R and B: $1855
580 applied	504 accepted	304 enrolled
SAT: 505V 535M		COMPETITIVE+

Houghton College, established in 1883, is a small, liberal arts college under the auspices of the Wesleyan Church of America. The library contains 152,000 volumes and subscribes to 850 periodicals.

Environment: The central campus consists of 50 acres, plus 1200 additional acres, and is located in a rural area about 65 miles from Buffalo. There are 2 main classroom buildings, a science building, a student center, a gymnasium, a chapel-auditorium, a music building, and 8 dormitories which accommodate 500 women and 350 men. There are also off-campus apartments and married student housing.

Student Life: About 60% of the students come from New York State. Ninety-four percent of the entering freshmen come from public schools. About 65% of the students live on campus. Protestant students represent 95% of the enrollment. The majority of students are not members of the supporting church, but all are required to attend chapel services daily. About 4% are minority-group members. Campus housing is single-sex; there are visiting privileges. Students may keep cars on campus.

Organizations: There are no fraternities or sororities. There are 3 student publications, a radio station, 6 musical organizations, a branch of the Intervarsity Fellowship, and a strong student government. Places of worship are available on campus for Protestants.

Sports: Houghton fields 6 intercollegiate teams for men and 7 for women. There are 9 intramural sports for men and 10 for women.

Handicapped: Sixty-five percent of the campus is accessible to handicapped students. Special facilities include wheelchair ramps, special parking, elevators, and specially equipped rest rooms. Fewer than 1% of the students have visual impairments, fewer than 1% have hearing impairments. Readers, tutors, and audiovisual materials are available for these students. Special class scheduling is possible.

Graduates: At the end of the freshman year, 18% of the students drop out; 68% remain to graduate. About 70% of the graduates go on to graduate study; 8% enter medical school, 1% go on to dental school, and 4% enter law school. Thirty percent of the graduates pursue careers in business and industry.

Services: The following services are provided to students free of charge: health care, psychological counseling, placement, career counseling, tutoring, and remedial instruction.

Programs of Study: The college confers the B.A., B.S., and B.Mus. degrees. Associate degrees are also awarded. Bachelor's degrees are offered in the following subjects: BUSINESS (business administration), EDUCATION (Christian, elementary, health/physical, recreation, secondary), ENGLISH (communications, creative writing, English), FINE AND PERFORMING ARTS (art, music, music education), HEALTH SCIENCES (medical technology), LANGUAGES (French, German, Greek/Latin, Spanish), MATH AND SCIENCES (biology, chemistry, mathematics, physical sciences, physics), PHILOSOPHY (Bible, church ministries, classics, humanities, philosophy, religion), PRE-PROFESSIONAL (dentistry, engineering, forestry, law, medicine, ministry, veterinary), SOCIAL SCIENCES (history, psychology, social sciences, sociology). Fifteen percent of the degrees are conferred in each of the following: business, education, math and sciences, and preprofessional subjects.

Required: All students must take 32 to 64 hours in general education courses, including 7 in prescribed religion courses.

Special: Study abroad in the junior year is available through a college-sponsored program. The college has a particularly strong premedical program.

Honors: All departments have honors programs.

Admissions: About 87% of those who applied were accepted for the 1981–82 freshman class. The SAT scores of those who enrolled were as follows: Verbal—44% scored below 500, 40% between 500 and 599, 15% between 600 and 700, and 1% above 700; Math—33% scored below 500, 41% between 500 and 599, 20% between 600 and 700, and 6% above 700. Applicants should be graduates of accredited high schools, present a personal reference, be recommended by high school authorities, rank in the top half of their graduating class, have a B average or better, and have completed 16 Carnegie units of secondary school work. Verbal SAT scores must be above 450 for students to qualify. Other important considerations are advanced placement or honors courses, recommendations by school officials, personality, and leadership record.

Procedure: The SAT or ACT is required and should be taken in November or December of the senior year. A personal interview is recommended, but not required. The application deadlines are August 1 (fall) and December 1 (spring). Admissions are granted on a rolling basis. There is a $15 application fee.

Special: The college has an early decision plan with an October 31 notification date, an early admissions plan, and a deferred admissions plan. AP and CLEP credit is available.

Transfer: Most applicants are accepted and about 70 transfer each year. Transfers are accepted for all classes. A 2.0 GPA, minimum SAT scores of 450, and an interview are required. D grades do not transfer. Twenty-four hours must be earned in residence out of a total of 124 hours required for the bachelor's degree. Application deadlines are August 1 (fall), and December 1 (spring). Students are notified within 1 month after the application is submitted.

Visiting: There are no regular orientations for prospective students, but guides are available for informal visits to the college. Visitors may sit in on classes and may also stay overnight at the school. The best time to visit is during the fall. The admissions office handles arrangements.

Financial Aid: About 70% of the students receive financial aid. About 55% work part-time on campus. The average award to freshmen from all sources is $1650. Scholarships are given to freshmen in the form of a tuition discount. Loans are available from the federal and state governments, local banks, the college, and private sources. The maximum scholarship granted to freshmen is $3250. When loans are available to freshmen, they range from $200 to $3500; earnings from campus employment range from $200 to $1200. The FAF is required. The suggested deadline for financial aid applications is March 15 (fall); applications are processed on a rolling basis.

Foreign Students: Four percent of the full-time students come from foreign countries. The college offers special counseling and organizations for foreign students.

Admissions: Houghton requires foreign applicants to take the TOEFL; a minimum score of 500 is necessary for consideration. College entrance exams are not required.

Procedure: The admissions deadline for foreign applicants is March 1; they are admitted to the fall semester only. Proof of health must be presented. Proof of funds adequate to cover 1 year of study is also required.

Admissions Contact: Wayne A. MacBeth, Director of Admissions.

IONA COLLEGE   D-5
New Rochelle, New York 10801   (914) 636-2100

F/T: 2169M, 1435W	Faculty:	n/av; IIA, +$
P/T: 74M, 112W	Ph.D.'s:	65%
Grad: 698M, 491W	S/F Ratio:	23 to 1
Year: 4-1-4, ss	Tuition:	$3730
Appl: July 1	R and B:	$2350
2939 applied	2056 accepted	949 enrolled
SAT: 460V 500M	ACT: 20	COMPETITIVE

Iona College, established in 1940, is a liberal arts college founded by the Congregation of Christian Brothers. The library houses over 180,000 volumes and subscribes to 850 periodicals.

Environment: The 55-acre campus is located in the suburbs of New Rochelle, 14 miles from New York City. Noteworthy among the structures on campus is the Mulcahy Campus Center, which contains a 3000-seat gym and a 6-lane Olympic size pool. There are no dormitories on campus.

Student Life: The college draws 87% of its students from New York State. About 19% are resident students, who live in private homes in the community. Eighty-four percent of the students are Catholic, 4% are Protestant, and 1% are Jewish. Eleven percent are minority-group members. Students may keep cars on campus.

Organizations: There are 2 local fraternities and 1 local sorority. The student council supervises and promotes student activities. The traditional special-interest clubs and other groups are available.

Sports: The college fields 13 intercollegiate teams for men and 7 for women. There are 7 intramural sports for men and 6 for women.

Handicapped: Fifty percent of the campus is accessible to the physically handicapped. Wheelchair ramps, special parking, specially equipped rest rooms, elevators, lowered drinking fountains and telephones, and special class scheduling are provided.

Graduates: Eight percent of freshmen drop out. Thirty-five percent continue their studies in graduate or professional schools.

Services: Health care, psychological counseling, career counseling, tutoring, and remedial instruction are provided without charge, as is placement service for undergraduates and graduates.

Programs of Study: Iona confers the B.A., B.S., and B.B.A. degrees. Master's degrees are also awarded. Bachelor's degrees are offered in the following subjects: AREA STUDIES (urban), BUSINESS (accounting, business administration, business economics, computer science, decision science, finance, management, marketing), EDUCATION (elementary, secondary, special), ENGLISH (English, journalism, speech), FINE AND PERFORMING ARTS (art, film/photography, theater/dramatics), HEALTH SCIENCES (medical technology, speech therapy), LANGUAGES (French, Italian, Spanish), MATH AND SCIENCES (biochemistry, biology, chemistry, computer information science, ecology/environmental science, interdisciplinary science, mathematics, natural sciences, physics), PHILOSOPHY (philosophy, religion), PREPROFESSIONAL (dentistry, engineering, law, medicine, social work, veterinary), SOCIAL SCIENCES (economics, government/political science, history, international studies, psychology, social sciences, sociology).

Required: All students must take a core curriculum.

Special: A general studies degree can be earned. There is a 3-2 combination degree program in engineering with the University of Detroit. A junior year abroad program is offered. An internship program allows accounting majors to work for public accounting firms for 3 months during the senior year.

Honors: Ten national honor societies have chapters on campus.

Admissions: Seventy percent of those who applied were accepted for the 1981-82 freshman class. Candidates should be graduates of accredited high schools and have completed 16 academic units. A personal interview is recommended.

Procedure: The SAT or ACT is required. Applications should be filed by July (fall), January (spring), and June (summer). Notification is on a rolling basis. A fee of $15 must accompany the application.

Special: Early and deferred admissions plans and an early decision plan are available. AP credit is given.

Transfer: For fall 1981, 422 students applied, 341 were accepted, and 234 enrolled. A GPA of at least 2.0 and an interview are required. D grades do not transfer. Students who transfer from 2-year schools must earn, at the college, at least 60 of the credits necessary for a bachelor's degree; transfers from 4-year schools must earn at least 30. Application deadlines are the same as those for freshmen.

Visiting: There are regularly scheduled orientations for prospective students. No guides are provided for informal tours, but visitors may sit in on classes. The admissions office should be contacted for arrangements.

Financial Aid: Seventy-five percent of students receive financial aid. Campus employment, including CWS, is available. Aid in the form of scholarships, loans, and grants amounts to $900,000. The college is a member of CSS and requires the FAF. The filing deadline is April 15.

Foreign Students: Forty-one of the full-time students come from foreign countries. The college offers these students special counseling.

Admissions: Students must achieve a TOEFL score of 550. No college entrance exam must be taken.

Procedure: Application deadlines are March 30 (fall) and October 30 (spring), with summer entry also permitted. Foreign students must present proof of funds adequate to cover the duration of their studies. They must also carry health insurance, which is available free of charge through the college.

Admissions Contact: Brother Francis I. Offer, Director.

ITHACA COLLEGE   C-3
Ithaca, New York 14850   (607) 274-3124

F/T: 2070M, 2650W	Faculty:	293; IIB, ++$
P/T: 24M, 30W	Ph.D.'s:	49%
Grad: 64M, 109W	S/F Ratio:	15 to 1
Year: sems, ss	Tuition:	$5000
Appl: Mar. 1	R and B:	$2276
6884 applied	3851 accepted	1346 enrolled
SAT or ACT: required		COMPETITIVE

Ithaca College, founded in 1892, is a private liberal arts college with 6 schools: Humanities and Sciences, Communications, Music, Allied Health Professions, Health, Physical Education and Recreation, and Business. The library contains 265,670 volumes and 107,000 microform items, and subscribes to 1750 periodicals.

Environment: The 250-acre campus is located in a suburban setting overlooking Cayuga Lake. The 45 buildings include a physical education center, a laboratory science building, a music building, TV and radio stations, a fine arts center with 2 theaters, a student union, and an allied health/business center. There are 29 dormitories, including 2 14-story towers and 5 apartment-style dorms, which accommodate 80% of the students.

Student Life: About 50% of the students are from New York State, with virtually all states represented in the student population. Seventy-five percent of entering freshmen attended public schools. Approximately 80% of the students live on campus. Twenty-five percent are Catholic, 25% are Protestant, and 25% are Jewish. Four percent of the students are minority-group members. College housing is coed and single-sex; students in single-sex housing have visiting privileges. Students may keep cars on campus.

Organizations: About 4% each of the men and women are affiliated with 1 of 6 fraternities or 2 sororities. Four of these Greek-letter organizations are coed. Ithaca College has a variety of student organizations and clubs. The School of Music sponsors 24 performing groups. Cayuga Lake, 4 state parks, and a major ski area nearby offer abundant recreational activities.

Sports: Ithaca College fields 14 intercollegiate teams for men and 15 for women. There are 12 intramural sports for men and 9 for women.

Handicapped: About 20% of the campus is accessible to wheelchair students. Special facilities for the physically handicapped include wheelchair ramps, parking areas, elevators, lowered drinking fountains and telephones, and specially equipped restrooms. Special class scheduling can be arranged.

Graduates: By the end of the freshman year, 15% of the students drop out; 56% remain to graduate. Over 35% of the graduates pursue further studies immediately after graduation.

Services: Students receive the following services free of charge: placement, career counseling, health care, psychological counseling, tutoring, and remedial instruction.

Programs of Study: The college confers the B.A., B.S., B.F.A., and B.M. degrees. Master's degrees are also awarded. Bachelor's degrees are offered in the following subjects: BUSINESS (accounting, business administration, finance, management, personnel and industrial relations), EDUCATION (health/physical, recreation, secondary, speech and hearing for the handicapped), ENGLISH (English, speech), FINE AND PERFORMING ARTS (art, corporate/organizational media, film/photography, music, music education, radio/TV, studio art, theater/dramatics), HEALTH SCIENCES (administration of health services, medical record administration, physical therapy, speech pathology and audiology, speech therapy), LANGUAGES (French, German, Spanish), MATH AND SCIENCES (biology, chemistry, computer science—mathematics, physics—computing), PHILOSOPHY (philosophy), PREPROFESSIONAL (dentistry, law, medicine, veterinary), SOCIAL SCIENCES (anthropology, economics—management, government/political science, history, psychology—business, sociology). Twenty percent of the degrees conferred are in education, 18% in business, and 18% in social sciences.

Special: In the School of Humanities and Sciences, students may design their own course of study through the planned studies program. A 3-2 program with Cornell University allows chemistry or physics majors to receive their science degree from Ithaca and an engineering degree from Cornell.

Honors: Nine departments in the School of Humanities and Sciences have honors programs; there is also an honors program for physical education majors. Four national honor societies have chapters on campus.

Admissions: Fifty-six percent of those who applied were accepted for the 1981–82 freshman class. Of those who enrolled, the SAT scores were as follows: Verbal—the middle 50% had scores between 420 and 530; Math—the middle 50% had scores between 460 and 570. Eighty-five percent ranked in the top half of their graduating class. All candidates must be graduates of accredited high schools, and it is recommended that they have completed 15 Carnegie units.

Science and mathematics majors must have 4 years of mathematics; physical therapy majors must have 1 year of biology and 1 year of physics or chemistry; music and theater majors must audition; and art majors must submit a portfolio. Some non-high-school graduates may be admitted, provided they present satisfactory GED scores and a GED diploma. In general, the college considers class rank, SAT scores, academic courses, and an interview in its admission decision; advanced placement or honor courses, special talents, and recommendations by school officials are also taken into consideration.

Procedure: The SAT or ACT and the AT in English composition are required and should be taken by January of the senior year. Language majors should take a language AT. Application deadlines are March 1 (fall) and December 15 (spring). Notification is on a rolling basis, with applicants notified as soon as possible after all their credentials are complete. A $20 fee must accompany the application.

Special: Early and deferred admissions plans and an early decision plan are available. AP credit is offered.

Transfer: For fall 1981, 644 students applied, 311 were accepted, and 120 enrolled. Requirements vary with the different schools and divisions, but a minimum GPA of 2.0 is standard. D grades do not transfer. The last 30 credits must be completed in residence; the number of credits necessary for a bachelor's degree ranges from 120 to 138. Application deadlines are the same as those for freshmen.

Visiting: Tours of the campus and personal interviews are encouraged. For information about visiting the school, the director of admissions should be contacted.

Financial Aid: About 52% of all students receive financial aid administered by the college. Thirty percent work part-time on campus. Average aid to freshmen is $3500; the maximum award is full tuition. All such assistance is based on need. Scholarships are determined by academic promise and/or talent, where applicable. Student loans are available through the NDSL. The college is a member of the CSS, and the FAF is required of aid applicants. Deadlines for aid application are March 1 (fall) and December 1 (spring).

Foreign Students: One percent of the full-time students come from foreign countries. The college offers these students special counseling.

Admissions: Foreign students must achieve a TOEFL score of 550; English-speaking foreign students may take either the SAT or ACT instead.

Procedure: The application deadline for fall entry is March 1. Foreign students must present proof of funds adequate to cover 1 year of study. They must also carry health insurance, which is available through the college for a fee.

Admissions Contact: Peter A. Stace, Director of Admissions.

THE JEWISH THEOLOGICAL SEMINARY OF AMERICA D-5
New York, New York 10027   (212) 678-8828

F/T: 66M, 46W		Faculty:	57; n/av
P/T: 5M, 7W		Ph.D.'s:	60%
Grad: 253M, 98W		S/F Ratio:	2 to 1
Year: sems, ss		Tuition:	$3070
Appl: Feb. 1		R:	$1545
48 applied	42 accepted		23 enrolled
SAT: 575V 575M			COMPETITIVE+

Founded in 1886, The Jewish Theological Seminary of America is the academic and spiritual center of the Conservative movement in Judaism. With 5 schools at its New York campus (the Seminary College of Jewish Studies, the Graduate School-Institute for Advanced Studies in the Humanities, the Rabbinical School, the Cantors Institute, and the Seminary College of Jewish Music), a sixth in Los Angeles (the University of Judaism), and a seventh in Israel, the seminary has a student body exceeding 900, and a faculty of some 150 full- and part-time scholars.

Environment: The seminary's present buildings were erected in 1929–30 on a 1-acre campus on Broadway between 122nd and 123rd Streets. These buildings house classrooms and faculty studies, the Seminary College of Jewish Studies, the library, administrative offices, and the seminary synagogue; they also include 3 residence halls accommodating 100 men and 110 women. A new library building is now under construction.

Student Life: Thirty-five percent of the students are New York residents. Almost 100% are Jewish. Seminary housing is both coed and single-sex. There are visiting privileges in single-sex dorms. Married student housing is also available. Students may have cars on campus.

Organizations: The seminary sponsors numerous extracurricular activities and organizations, including student council, the Soviet Jewry committee, and a drama group. New York City provides additional cultural and recreational opportunities.

Services: The following services are provided to all students free of charge: placement, psychological counseling, and career counseling. Health care and some tutoring are available for a fee.

Programs of Study: The seminary confers the B.A. and Bachelor of Sacred Music degrees. Master's and doctoral degrees are also awarded. Bachelor's degrees are offered in the following subjects: EDUCATION (religious education), LANGUAGES (Hebrew), PHILOSOPHY (Bible, classics, humanities, philosophy, religion, Talmud and Rabbinics literature), SOCIAL SCIENCES (history).

Required: All students must complete 57 units of secular education.

Special: Study at the seminary combines traditional academic programs with opportunities for Jewish observance and study of Judaica. Student-designed majors and study abroad are offered.

Admissions: About 88% of those who applied were accepted for the 1981–82 freshman class. A high school diploma is required. A personal interview is recommended for regular applicants. Factors of importance to the admissions decision include personality, recommendations by school officials, extracurricular activities record, advanced placement or honors courses, and impressions made during an interview.

Procedure: The SAT is required. The application deadline for fall entry is February 1. Freshmen are admitted to both the fall and spring semesters. A rolling admissions policy is followed. An application fee of $20 is required.

Special: Early admissions and deferred admissions plans are available. AP credit is accepted.

Transfer: For fall 1981, 3 transfer students applied, 2 were accepted, and 1 enrolled. Transfers are accepted for the freshman and sophomore classes. There is a 2-year residency requirement. Transfers must earn, at the seminary, 96 of the 156 credits required for the bachelor's degree. Application deadlines are the same as those for freshmen.

Visiting: There are regularly scheduled orientations for prospective students. Visitors may sit in on classes and stay overnight at the school. Information regarding visit arrangements should be obtained from Rabbi Barry Starr, Director of Recruitment.

Financial Aid: Seventy-two percent of the students receive aid through the seminary; 3% work part-time on campus. Aid is available in the form of scholarships and loans. The average award to freshmen from all sources is $3500. The seminary is a member of CSS and requires that aid applicants submit the FAF in addition to the seminary application. The deadline for aid application is February 1.

Foreign Students: Almost 3% of the full-time students come from foreign countries.

Admissions: English proficiency exams and college entrance exams are not necessary.

Procedure: Application deadlines are the same as those for other freshmen. Foreign students must furnish proof of funds adequate to cover at least 1 calendar year of study. They must also carry health insurance, which is available through the seminary for a fee.

Admissions Contact: Paula Hyman, Dean.

THE JUILLIARD SCHOOL D-5
New York, New York 10023 (212) 799-5000

F/T: 304M, 341W Faculty: n/av
P/T: 1M, 1W Ph.D.'s: n/av
Grad: 194M, 119W S/F Ratio: 5 to 1
Year: sems Tuition: $4100
Appl: see profile R and B: $4800
174 accepted 160 enrolled
SAT or ACT: required SPECIAL

The Juilliard School, founded in 1905, is a private professional school of music, dance, and drama. The library contains 12,000 volumes, 38,000 musical scores, and 9000 recordings.

Environment: The school is located in a $30 million building in New York's Lincoln Center. There are no dormitory facilities; the figure given above for room and board is the school's estimate of the cost of housing in New York City.

Student Life: Twenty-five percent of the students are from New York. Twenty-two percent are minority-group members.

Organizations: The major social events are concerts and other professional productions, including operas, dance productions, and dramatic productions. The off-campus social life is, in effect, the social life of New York City.

Handicapped: The school estimates the building to be 100% accessible to physically handicapped students. Facilities include wheelchair ramps, elevators, specially equipped rest rooms, and wheelchair space in all theaters.

Graduates: Eighty-seven percent of the freshmen remain to graduate.

Programs of Study: The school confers the B.M. and B.F.A. degrees. Master's and doctoral degrees are also awarded. Bachelor's degrees are offered in dance, music, and theater/dramatics.

Required: Each division has a core of required courses.

Admissions: Admission is not based on high school grades, although 15 Carnegie units are needed. The entrance performance examination is the competitive basis for admission. In addition, there are placement tests in the literature and materials of music, ear training, and piano, and orchestra auditions for instrumentalists.

Procedure: The SAT or ACT is required. Freshmen are admitted only in the fall. Entrance examinations for music and dance applicants are conducted at the school 3 times a year. Applications should be submitted by January 15 for the March examination, April 15 for the May examination, and July 1 for the September examination. There is an $85 application and examination fee. For drama applicants, entrance auditions are held in February and March in New York and other major cities in the United States. For these students, there is a $30 application fee.

Transfer: For fall 1981, 69 transfer applicants were accepted and 64 enrolled. An entrance audition is required. Students must spend one year in residence and complete at least 30 of the minimum 133 credits necessary for a bachelor's degree. Application deadlines are the same as those for freshmen.

Financial Aid: Scholarships in varying amounts are awarded toward tuition charges, but there are no scholarships to cover living expenses. The school is a member of CSS and requires the FAF. The deadlines for aid application are January 15 for March examinations,

NEW YORK 567

April 15 for May examinations, and June 1 for September examinations.

Foreign Students: Twenty-one percent of the full-time students come from foreign countries. The school offers these students an English course and special counseling.

Admissions: Foreign students must achieve an acceptable score on the TOEFL. No college entrance exam must be taken.

Procedure: Application deadlines are the same as those for freshmen. Foreign students must present a school health form completed by a physician and proof of funds adequate to cover one year (9 months) of study.

Admissions Contact: Irene W. Anderson, Admissions Administrator.

KEUKA COLLEGE B-3
Keuka Park, New York 14478 (315) 536-4411

F/T: 2M, 490W Faculty: 49; IIB, −$
P/T: 2M, 30W Ph.D.'s: 43%
Grad: none S/F Ratio: 10 to 1
Year: qtrs, ss Tuition: $4960
Appl: open R and B: $1820
438 applied 380 accepted 131 enrolled
SAT: 450V 474M LESS COMPETITIVE

Keuka College, established in 1890, is an independent liberal arts college for women. The library houses 95,186 volumes and 5076 microfilm items, and subscribes to 558 periodicals.

Environment: The college is located on a 173-acre campus on the shore of Lake Keuka in the rural Finger Lakes region of New York, 50 miles from Rochester. Recent additions to the campus include a student activities center, a physical arts center, and a library. There are dormitory facilities on campus.

Student Life: Seventy-five percent of the students are from New York State. Fifty-five percent of entering freshmen come from public schools. About 95% of the students live on campus. Sixty-five percent are Protestant, 33% are Catholic, and 2% are Jewish. Eight percent are minority-group members. College housing is single-sex, and there are visiting privileges. Students may keep cars on campus.

Organizations: There are no national sororities. Campus extracurricular activities include a modern dance group, a drama club, a radio station, publications, a chorale group, and religious organizations.

Sports: The college fields 5 intercollegiate teams. There are 12 intramural sports.

Handicapped: There are no special facilities for handicapped students.

Graduates: The freshman dropout rate is 20%, and 51% of the freshmen remain to graduate. Twenty-one percent of those who graduate pursue further study.

Services: The following services are offered at no charge to the student: psychological counseling, health care, tutoring, remedial instruction, placement service, and career counseling.

Programs of Study: The college confers the B.A. or B.S. degree in the following subjects: BUSINESS (business administration), EDUCATION (elementary, special), ENGLISH (dramatic literature and theater arts, English), FINE AND PERFORMING ARTS (fine arts [art, dance, music]), HEALTH SCIENCES (medical technology, nursing), MATH AND SCIENCES (biochemistry, biology, mathematics), PHILOSOPHY (philosophy/religion), PREPROFESSIONAL (social work), SOCIAL SCIENCES (government/political science, history, psychology, public administration/management, sociology). Of the degrees conferred, 46% are in health sciences, 17% in social sciences, and 11% in education.

Required: Students must complete 4 units of supervised field experience in community service, cultural experience, and vocational experimentation. This work is generally done during a 5-week field period or during the summer.

Special: Opportunities for foreign study are offered under college sponsorship. Independent study and student-designed majors are permitted.

Honors: Sixteen national honor societies have chapters on campus.

Admissions: Eighty-seven percent of those who applied were accepted for the 1981–82 freshman class. Of those who enrolled, the SAT scores were as follows: Verbal—74% scored below 500, 22% between 500 and 599, 3% between 600 and 700, and 1% above 700; Math—63% scored below 500, 30% between 500 and 599, 7% be-

568 NEW YORK

tween 600 and 700, and 0% above 700. Factors of importance are advanced placement or honor courses, recommendations, and leadership record.

Procedure: The SAT or ACT is required. Deadlines for application are open. Freshmen are admitted to all semesters. Notification is on a rolling basis. There is a $15 application fee.

Special: Early and deferred admissions plans and an early decision plan are offered. AP and CLEP credit is available.

Transfer: For fall 1981, 101 students applied, 69 were accepted, and 36 enrolled. Students must spend 2 years at the college and complete 60 of the 120 semester credits necessary for a bachelor's degree. Application deadlines are open.

Visiting: Guides are available for informal visits to the campus. Visitors may sit in on classes and stay overnight at the college. Arrangements should be made through the admissions office.

Financial Aid: About 83% of all students receive aid. Fifty-five percent work part-time on campus. Average aid to freshmen is $2259. Scholarships, grants, and loans are available. The college is a member of CSS and requires the FAF. The deadline for aid application is August 1.

Foreign Students: Fewer than one percent of the full-time students come from foreign countries. The college offers these students special counseling.

Admissions: Foreign students must take the TOEFL, but are not required to take a college entrance exam.

Procedure: Application deadlines are open. Foreign students must present proof of health and proof of adequate funds. They must also carry health insurance, which is available through the college.

Admissions Contact: Bruce A. Westerdahl, Director of Admissions.

THE KING'S COLLEGE D–5
Briarcliff Manor, New York 10510 (914) 941-7200

F/T: 271M, 490W		Faculty:	46; IIB, – $
P/T: 10M, 16W		Ph.D.'s:	44%
Grad: none		S/F Ratio:	16 to 1
Year: sems, ss		Tuition:	$4050
Appl: open		R and B:	$1650
497 applied	446 accepted		241 enrolled
SAT: 430V 470M			LESS COMPETITIVE

The King's College, founded in 1938, is a private liberal arts college with religious emphasis. The library contains 77,735 volumes and 8624 microfilm reels, and subscribes to 550 periodicals.

Environment: The 80-acre campus overlooks the Hudson River Valley, in a suburban setting 40 miles from New York City. There are 8 buildings, including a science-classroom building. Five dormitories are available for resident students.

Student Life: Forty-six percent of the students are from New York. Eighty-five percent of entering freshmen come from public schools. Ninety percent of the students reside on campus. Ninety-six percent are Protestant and 3% are Catholic; attendance at daily chapel services is required. Twelve percent of the students are minority-group members. College housing is single-sex, and there are no visiting privileges. Students may keep cars on campus. Smoking, drinking, and dancing are not allowed.

Organizations: There are no fraternities or sororities. Special-interest groups include a band, chorus, orchestra, publications, and departmental clubs. The college sponsors many cultural events on campus.

Sports: The college fields 7 intercollegiate teams for men and 8 for women. Men's golf and volleyball clubs and a women's soccer club also compete with other colleges, but are not budgeted sports. There are 4 intramural sports for men.

Handicapped: The college estimates that the campus is 50% accessible to handicapped students. There are specially equipped rest rooms, special parking, elevators, and, if needed, special class scheduling.

Graduates: The freshman dropout rate is 24%, and 50% of the freshmen remain to graduate. Forty-five percent pursue careers in business or education.

Services: Tutoring, placement services, health care, and career counseling are offered at no charge. Psychological counseling is available for a fee.

Programs of Study: The college confers the B.A. and B.S. degrees. Associate degrees are also awarded. Bachelor's degrees are offered in the following subjects: BUSINESS (business administration), EDUCATION (elementary, health/physical), ENGLISH (English), FINE AND PERFORMING ARTS (music, music education), HEALTH SCIENCES (medical technology), LANGUAGES (French, Spanish), MATH AND SCIENCES (biology, chemistry, mathematics), PHILOSOPHY (philosophy, religion), PREPROFESSIONAL (law, medicine, ministry), SOCIAL SCIENCES (history, psychology, sociology). Of the degrees recently conferred, 23% were in education, 13% in math and sciences, and 22% in social sciences.

Required: There are core requirements for all students.

Special: Combination B.A.-B.S. degrees may be earned in any of the major fields of study offered. The college is an associate school of the Holy Land Institute, Jerusalem, Israel, and offers summer school, interim session, semester, or year abroad options there. Study abroad in France, Spain, England, and Germany is also available.

Admissions: Ninety percent of those who applied were accepted for the 1981–82 freshman class. Of those who enrolled, the SAT scores were as follows: Verbal—64% scored below 500, 20% between 500 and 599, 7% between 600 and 700, and 0% above 700; Math—56% scored below 500, 28% between 500 and 599, 7% between 600 and 700, and 0% above 700. Considerations in the admissions decision include test scores, advanced placement or honor courses, recommendations by school officials, and evidence of special talents.

Procedure: The SAT or ACT is required. Freshmen are admitted in the spring as well as in the fall. There are no application deadlines, and notification is on a rolling basis. There is a $10 application fee.

Special: An early admissions plan is offered. CLEP and AP credit is available.

Transfer: For fall 1981, 92 students applied, 88 were accepted, and 51 enrolled. A GPA of 2.0 and the basic freshman requirements must be met. D grades are not transferable. Students must complete, at the college, the last 30 credit hours of the 130 necessary for a bachelor's degree. Transfers are accepted for all classes. Application deadlines are open.

Visiting: The college conducts 2 "College for a Day" open houses each year. Guides are available for informal visits to the campus on Monday through Friday from 9 A.M. to 3 P.M.. Visitors may sit in on classes and stay overnight at the college. Arrangements should be made through the admissions office.

Financial Aid: About 75% of all students receive aid. Thirty-three percent work part-time on campus. The average freshman aid package is $3000, combining grants, loans, and campus employment. Approximately 110 scholarships with a total value of $51,000 are available to freshmen each year. The college is a member of CSS and requires the FAF. The deadline for filing aid applications is March 15.

Foreign Students: Fewer than one percent of the full-time students come from foreign countries.

Admissions: Foreign students are required to take the TOEFL and the SAT or ACT.

Procedure: Application deadlines are open. Foreign students must present a physician's report and proof of funds adequate to cover 4 years of study. They must also carry health insurance, which is available through the college as part of the general fee.

Admissions Contact: Roy McCandless, Director of Admissions.

LE MOYNE COLLEGE C–3
Syracuse, New York 13214 (315) 446-2882

F/T: 897M, 897W		Faculty:	110; IIB, +$
P/T: 98M, 130W		Ph.D.'s:	70%
Grad: none		S/F Ratio:	16 to 1
Year: sems, ss		Tuition:	$3930
Appl: see profile		R and B:	$2050
1268 applied	880 accepted		458 enrolled
SAT: 515V 560M	ACT: 25		VERY COMPETITIVE+

Le Moyne College, founded in 1946, is a coeducational private college under the sponsorship of the Society of Jesus. The library contains 151,000 volumes and 1400 microfilm items, and subscribes to 1300 periodicals.

Environment: The college is situated on a campus of 150 acres in a suburban area 2 miles from Syracuse. The buildings include 6 apartment-style residence halls.

Student Life: Eighty percent of the students come from New York State. About 60% of entering freshmen are graduates of public schools. Approximately 67% of the students live on campus. Eighty percent are Catholic, 14% are Protestant, and 2% are Jewish. Seven percent of the students are minority-group members. College housing is coed and single-sex; students in single-sex housing have visiting privileges. Students may keep cars on campus.

Organizations: There are no fraternities or sororities. Clubs, special-interest and performing groups, and social and cultural events are available.

Sports: Le Moyne fields 10 intercollegiate teams for men and 6 for women. There are 8 intramural sports for men and 7 for women.

Handicapped: The campus is 100% accessible to physically handicapped students. Special facilities include wheelchair ramps, elevators, and specially equipped rest rooms. Special housing arrangements are also available. A counselor and a group of readers provide special assistance.

Graduates: At the end of the freshman year 5% of the class generally drop out, but approximately 73% remain to graduate. About 47% of the graduates pursue advanced study; 4% enter medical school, 2% enter dental school, and 7% enter law school. Approximately 35% pursue careers in business and industry.

Services: Students receive the following services free of charge: placement, career counseling, psychological counseling, tutoring, and remedial instruction. Health care is available for a fee.

Programs of Study: The college offers the B.A. or B.S. degree in the following subjects: AREA STUDIES (urban), BUSINESS (accounting, business administration, business education, computer science, finance, industrial relations, management, marketing), EDUCATION (secondary), ENGLISH (English, English/communications, English/drama), LANGUAGES (French, Greek/Latin, Spanish), MATH AND SCIENCES (biology, chemistry, computer science, mathematics, multiple science, physics), PHILOSOPHY (philosophy, religion), PRE-PROFESSIONAL (dentistry, engineering, forestry, law, medicine, pharmacy, veterinary), SOCIAL SCIENCES (economics, government/political science, history, psychology, sociology). About 39% of the degrees conferred are in business, 22% in social sciences, and 17% in math and sciences.

Required: All students must complete a core curriculum.

Special: About 350–400 students are involved in Project Inner City, which encompasses a variety of individual projects and functions. The college offers a Junior Year Abroad program and also a 3-year bachelor's degree program. Students may engage in cross-registration with Syracuse University. An internship program in many departments and programs is also offered.

Honors: The college offers departmental and integral honors programs. There are 5 national honor societies on campus.

Admissions: About 69% of those who applied were accepted for the 1981–82 freshman class. Of those who enrolled, the SAT scores were as follows: Verbal—46% scored below 500, 46% between 500 and 599, 7% between 600 and 700, and 1% above 700; Math—23% scored below 500, 53% between 500 and 599, 21% between 600 and 700, and 3% above 700. The ACT scores were as follows: 8% scored below 21, 28% between 21 and 23, 24% between 24 and 25, 30% between 26 and 28, and 10% above 28. As a general rule, students should rank in the upper half of their graduating class and have an 80% average or better. Other important factors are advanced placement or honor courses, recommendations, special talents, and a leadership record.

Procedure: The SAT or ACT is required. The recommended application deadlines are March 1 (fall) and December 1 (spring). Notification is on a rolling basis. There is a $15 application fee.

Special: Early and deferred admissions plans and an early decision plan are available. AP and CLEP credit is accepted.

Transfer: For fall 1981, 388 students applied, 219 were accepted, and 145 enrolled. A minimum GPA of 2.5 is required; standardized test scores, an associate degree, and an interview are recommended. D grades receive transfer credit for no more than 2 courses and only as elective credits. Students must spend at least 1 year at the college and complete a minimum of 30 hours, including half of their major, toward the 120 credits necessary for a bachelor's degree. Recommended application deadlines are April 1 (fall) and December 1 (spring).

Visiting: Informal guided tours can be scheduled on weekdays from 8:30 A.M. to 4:30 P.M. and on Saturdays from 9 A.M. to noon in the fall or spring. Visitors may sit in on classes and stay overnight at the school. Arrangements should be made through the admissions office.

Financial Aid: About 65% of students receive financial aid. Twenty-six percent work part-time on campus. Average aid to freshmen from all sources is $2415. Each year the college offers 200 freshman scholarships totaling $160,000. Grants and loans are also available. The college is a member of CSS and requires the FAF. Application deadlines are March 1 (fall) and December 1 (spring).

Foreign Students: Fewer than one percent of the full-time students come from foreign countries. The college offers these students special counseling.

Admissions: Foreign students are required to take any one of the standard English proficiency exams or the college's own test. The SAT or ACT is recommended.

Procedure: The application deadline for fall entry is March 1. Foreign students must present proof of a recent medical examination by a physician and proof of funds adequate to cover 4 years of study.

Admissions Contact: Edward J. Gorman, Director of Admissions.

LONG ISLAND UNIVERSITY

Long Island University is a private independent institution composed of 4 main centers located on 3 campuses throughout Long Island. The oldest campus is the Brooklyn Center Campus in downtown Brooklyn, founded in 1926, on which is located the Richard L. Conolly College of Arts and Sciences and the School of Business and Public Administration, as well as the Arnold and Marie Schwartz College of Pharmacy and Health Sciences. The latter merged with Long Island University in 1929. Twenty-five miles from New York City is the C. W. Post Center in suburban Greenvale, Long Island. Founded in 1954, the undergraduate C. W. Post Center is situated on the 300-acre Marjorie Merriweather Post estate. The youngest of the 3 campuses is the 106-acre campus of Southampton Center, which was established in 1963.

Graduate programs are conducted by the Graduate Faculty of Arts and Sciences and the School of Business and Public Administration at the Brooklyn Center; the Arthur T. Roth Graduate School of Business Administration, the Graduate School of Education, the Carleton and Winthrop Palmer Graduate Library School, the School of the Arts, the School of Professional Accountancy, and the C. W. Post College of Arts and Sciences at the C. W. Post Center; the Education Faculty at Southampton Center, and the Arnold and Marie Schwartz College of Pharmacy and Health Sciences.

Profiles of the undergraduate colleges follow.

LONG ISLAND UNIVERSITY/ARNOLD AND MARIE SCHWARTZ COLLEGE OF PHARMACY AND HEALTH SCIENCES
(See Arnold and Marie Schwartz College of Pharmacy and Health Sciences)

LONG ISLAND UNIVERSITY/ BROOKLYN CENTER   D–5
Brooklyn, New York 11201   (212) 834-6100

F/T: 1499M, 1986W	Faculty:	n/av
P/T: 507M, 936W	Ph.D.'s:	90%
Grad: 1093M, 796W	S/F Ratio:	20 to 1
Year: sems, ss	Tuition:	$140p/c
Appl: June 1	R and B:	$1360–3490
1552 applied	733 accepted	683 enrolled
SAT: 450V 450M	ACT: 22	COMPETITIVE

The Brooklyn Center of Long Island University was founded in 1926 and is the oldest of the university's divisions. Undergraduate programs are conducted by the Richard L. Conolly College of Arts and Sciences and the School of Business Administration. The library contains more than 225,000 volumes and 54,800 microforms, and subscribes to 1900 periodicals.

Environment: The 22-acre downtown Brooklyn campus includes a 9-story humanities-social science center, 2 adjoining 11-story buildings, 2 smaller classroom buildings, a 16-story residence hall, and a library-learning center. The university also owns a large apartment development that provides additional housing.

Student Life: About 85% of the students are residents of New York City, and most of them commute to classes daily. About 20% of the students live on campus. University housing is coed. Students may keep cars on campus. Alcohol is not permitted in residence hall rooms.

Organizations: There are religious organizations for members of all major faiths. In addition to the usual college social activities, students take full advantage of the facilities that New York City makes available.

Sports: The university competes on an intercollegiate level in 9 sports for men and 7 for women.

Handicapped: The entire campus is accessible to handicapped students. Facilities include wheelchair ramps, parking areas, elevators, specially equipped rest rooms, and lowered drinking fountains and telephones. Special class scheduling is also available.

570 NEW YORK

Graduates: The average dropout rate for freshmen is 15%; 50% of the students remain to graduate. Forty-five percent pursue advanced study after graduation.

Services: Students receive the following services free of charge: placement, career counseling, health care, psychological counseling, and tutoring. Remedial instruction is available on a fee basis.

Programs of Study: The university confers the B.A. and B.S. degrees. Associate, master's and doctoral programs are also available. Bachelor's degrees are offered in the following subjects: BUSINESS (accounting, business administration, computer science, finance, management, marketing), EDUCATION (early childhood, elementary, health/physical, secondary, special), ENGLISH (English, journalism, literature, speech), FINE AND PERFORMING ARTS (art, art education, film/photography, music, music education, radio/TV, theater/dramatics), HEALTH SCIENCES (medical technology, nursing, physical therapy, physician assistant, respiratory therapy, speech therapy), LANGUAGES (French, Spanish), MATH AND SCIENCES (biology, chemistry, cytotechnology, mathematics, nuclear medicine technology), PHILOSOPHY (humanities, philosophy), PREPROFESSIONAL (dentistry, law, medicine, pharmacy, veterinary), SOCIAL SCIENCES (anthropology, economics, history, psychology, social sciences, sociology).

Special: The university offers a special education services program for disabled students. Various certificate programs are offered in criminal justice, American studies, ethnic studies, international studies, and social welfare. There is a 5-year B.S.-M.S. program in chemistry. It is possible to earn combined B.A.-B.S. degrees.

Honors: There are 15 honor societies on campus. Honor students may design their own majors.

Admissions: Forty-seven percent of those who applied were accepted for the 1981-82 freshman class. Applicants should have at least a C+ average, rank in the upper half of their graduating class, and have completed 16 Carnegie units. Admissions officers also consider the impressions made during the interview, extracurricular activities, recommendations, advanced placement or honor courses, personality, leadership potential, and evidence of special talent in making their decisions.

Procedure: Either the SAT or the ACT should be taken by January of the senior year. An interview is not required except in special cases. Application deadlines are June 1 (fall), December 1 (spring), and April 1 (summer). Notification is on a rolling basis. There is a $15 application fee.

Special: A deferred admissions plan is available. AP and CLEP credit is granted.

Transfer: For fall 1981, 1003 students applied, 600 were accepted, and 217 enrolled. SAT scores of 450 on both Verbal and Math tests are needed. A 2.0 GPA is required. D grades transfer only with an associate degree. There is a 1-year residency requirement. Thirty-two credits must be earned in residence, of the 128 to 132 needed for a bachelor's degree. Application deadlines are the same as those for freshman applicants.

Visiting: There are regularly scheduled orientations for prospective students. Guides are available for informal visits. Visitors may sit in on classes and stay overnight at the school. Visits are best scheduled on weekdays. The admissions office should be contacted for arrangements.

Financial Aid: About 80% of the students received financial aid in a recent year. Each year the university awards scholarships, grants, loans (including NDSL), and part-time employment. The university is a member of CSS. The FAF is required. The application deadlines for financial aid are May 15 (fall) and November 1 (spring).

Foreign Students: Seven percent of the full-time students come from foreign countries. The center offers these students an intensive English program, special counseling, and special organizations.

Admissions: Foreign students must score 500 on the TOEFL. They must also take the SAT and score 450 on both Verbal and Math tests, or take the university's own examination.

Procedure: The application deadlines are May 1 (fall), November 1 (spring), and March 1 (summer). Foreign students must present proof of funds adequate to cover 1 year of study. They must also carry health insurance, which is available through the university for a fee.

Admissions Contact: Ann A. Kaplan, Assistant to the Director of Admissions.

LONG ISLAND UNIVERSITY/ C. W. POST CENTER   D-5
Greenvale, New York 11548   (516) 299-2413

F/T: 2631M, 2755W	Faculty: 380; n/av
P/T: 770M, 1208W	Ph.D.'s: 68%
Grad: 1698M, 2455W	S/F Ratio: 14 to 1
Year: sems, ss	Tuition: $4590
Appl: open	R and B: $2628
3994 applied 3142 accepted	1346 enrolled
SAT: 432V 469M	COMPETITIVE

C. W. Post Center of Long Island University was established in 1954. The library houses 720,000 volumes and 242,000 microfilm items, and subscribes to 4400 periodicals.

Environment: The 360-acre, self-contained campus is set in a rural atmosphere and yet is only 25 miles from New York City. There are over 40 buildings, including the concert theater completed in 1981. Eight dorms provide residence for 1800 students.

Student Life: Over 40 states are represented at the school, although most students come from the Northeast. Seventy-five percent are public school graduates. Twenty-two percent of the students live in the dorms. Eighteen percent are minority-group members. Center housing is both single-sex and coed. There are visiting privileges in single-sex housing. Students may keep cars on campus.

Organizations: There are about 20 fraternities and sororities. Extracurricular activities include concerts, lectures, and sporting and social events. The proximity of New York City makes all of its cultural and recreational facilities easily accessible.

Sports: The intercollegiate athletic program includes 10 sports for men and 5 for women. There are 5 intramural sports for both men and women.

Handicapped: Eighty percent of the campus is accessible to handicapped students. Lowered telephones and drinking fountains as well as wheelchair ramps, elevators, parking areas, and specially equipped rest rooms are provided. Special counselors are available to assist the handicapped.

Graduates: Fifteen percent of the freshmen drop out by the end of their first year. Fifty percent remain to graduate. Forty-five percent of the graduates continue their studies. About 40% enter careers in business and industry.

Services: Free psychological counseling, tutoring, and remedial instruction are offered. Placement services for graduates and undergraduates, including career counseling, seminars, and on-campus recruiting, and health care are available on a fee basis.

Programs of Study: The university confers B.A., B.S., B.F.A. and B.P.S. degrees. Master's degrees are also offered. Bachelor's degrees are offered in the following subjects: AREA STUDIES (American, Latin American, Russian), BUSINESS (accounting, business administration, business education, computer science, finance, management, marketing), EDUCATION (elementary, health/physical, secondary, special), ENGLISH (English, journalism, speech), FINE AND PERFORMING ARTS (art, art education, art history, film/photography, music, music education, radio/TV, studio art, theater/dramatics), HEALTH SCIENCES (medical technology, nursing, speech therapy), LANGUAGES (French, German, Hebrew, Italian, Spanish), MATH AND SCIENCES (biology, chemistry, computational biology, computational mathematics, earth science, geology, mathematics, physics), PHILOSOPHY (philosophy), PREPROFESSIONAL (dentistry, law, medicine, pharmacy), SOCIAL SCIENCES (anthropology, economics, geography, government/political science, history, international relations, psychology, sociology). Thirty percent of the degrees conferred are in business, 20% in education, and 10% in English.

Required: All students are required to take English and a core curriculum of liberal arts courses.

Special: The college permits students to design their own majors. An accelerated B.A.-M.A. program is offered in various majors.

Honors: An honors program is available for outstanding students. Honor societies include Phi Eta, the preliminary group of a chapter of Phi Beta Kappa.

Admissions: Seventy-nine percent of those who applied for the 1981-82 freshman class were accepted. Of those who enrolled, the SAT scores were as follows: Verbal—77% scored below 500, 19% between 500 and 599, 2% between 600 and 700, and 2% above 700; Math—60% scored below 500, 30% between 500 and 599, 8% between 600 and 700, and 2% above 700. Sixteen Carnegie units are required. Students should rank in the upper 20% of their class, have a high-school grade average no lower than 75, and be recommended by the high school's principal or counselor. The school also considers the student's ability to finance his or her education, the parents' education, and the extracurricular activities record.

Procedure: The SAT or ACT is required and should be taken by December of the senior year. A personal interview is recommended. There is no application deadline; candidates are admitted and notified on a rolling basis. The application fee is $20.

Special: Early admissions and deferred admissions plans are available. AP and CLEP credit is granted.

Transfer: For fall 1981, 2315 students applied, 1903 were accepted, and 1225 enrolled. Transfer students are accepted for all classes. Students must have a combined SAT score of 900. A 2.0 GPA is required. D grades will transfer if the applicant holds an associate degree. A special program for students with associate degrees is designed to provide them with full transfer credit, counseling, and curriculum flexibility. Transfer students must complete, at the university, 32 of the 128 credits needed for a bachelor's degree. Deadlines for transfer application are open.

Visiting: There is an orientation in April for all accepted students. Campus visits may be arranged any time by contacting the admissions office. Guides are provided, and visitors may sit in on classes.

Financial Aid: Seventy-five percent of all students receive financial aid. Five percent work part-time on campus. The C. W. Post Center also offers 2 non-need scholarships: for students with an average of 85 or better and a combined SAT score of 900, and for students with an average of 90 or better and an 1100 combined SAT score. The center is a member of CSS. The FAF is required. Forms must be filed by March 31 (fall) and December 1 (spring).

Foreign Students: Two percent of the full-time students come from foreign countries. The center offers these students an intensive English course and special counseling.

Admissions: Foreign students must score 500 on the TOEFL. No college entrance examination is required.

Procedure: The application deadlines are June 15 (fall) and December 1 (spring). Foreign students must present proof of adequate funds. They must also carry health insurance, which is available through the center for a fee.

Admissions Contact: James Reilly, Director of Admissions.

LONG ISLAND UNIVERSITY/ SOUTHAMPTON COLLEGE
E-5

Southampton, New York 11968   (516) 283-4000

F/T: 658M, 604W	Faculty:	68; n/av
P/T: 28M, 52W	Ph.D.'s:	78%
Grad: 9M, 67W	S/F Ratio:	19 to 1
Year: 4-1-4, ss	Tuition:	$4740
Appl: Sept. 1	R and B:	$2770
786 applied	666 accepted	322 enrolled
SAT: 465V 487M		COMPETITIVE

Southampton College, founded in 1963, is the newest of the Long Island University campuses. The library houses 124,000 volumes and 10,000 microfilm items, and subscribes to 650 periodicals.

Environment: The 110-acre campus is located in rural eastern Suffolk County, Long Island, 90 miles from New York City. Campus facilities include a marine station with full laboratory facilities, vessels, and access to bays and the open ocean. Dormitories accommodate 700 students.

Student Life: Ninety-two percent of the students come from the Middle Atlantic states. About 70% of the students come from public schools. Fifty-two percent of the students are Catholic, 26% Protestant, and 12% Jewish; 10% belong to other denominations. Sixteen percent are minority-group members. College housing is both single-sex and coed. There are visiting privileges in single-sex housing. Students may keep cars on campus. There is a college-sponsored nursery school.

Organizations: There are no sororities or fraternities on campus. Extracurricular activities include publications, performing groups, and special-interest clubs. The area is noted for its swimming, surfing, and other ocean activities.

Sports: The college offers an intercollegiate athletics program in 7 sports for men and 5 for women. There are 3 intramural sports for men and 1 for women.

Handicapped: About 50% of the campus is accessible to handicapped students. There are no special facilities on campus.

NEW YORK   **571**

Graduates: Twenty-eight percent of the freshmen drop out by the end of their first year. Forty percent remain to graduate. About 35% of the graduates pursue advanced degrees; 5% enter law school, and 1% enter medical school. Forty percent enter careers in business and industry.

Services: Students receive the following services free of charge: psychological counseling, placement, career counseling, tutoring, and remedial instruction. Health care is available on a fee basis for doctor visits. The infirmary is free.

Programs of Study: The college confers the B.A., B.S., and B.F.A. degrees. Master's programs are also available. Bachelor's degrees are offered in the following subjects: BUSINESS (business administration), EDUCATION (elementary, secondary, special), ENGLISH (English, literature and writing), FINE AND PERFORMING ARTS (art, art education, studio art), MATH AND SCIENCES (biology, chemistry, ecology/environmental science, geology, oceanography), PREPROFESSIONAL (dentistry, law, medicine, veterinary), SOCIAL SCIENCES (government/political science, history, psychology, psychology/biology, social sciences, sociology). Forty-one percent of the degrees are conferred in math and sciences, 16% in social sciences, and 14% in fine and performing arts.

Required: Students must complete general education requirements in composition and writing, natural science, social science, humanities, and fine arts, plus winter session experiences.

Special: Cooperative programs with other Long Island University branches are offered in pharmacy and medical technology. A combination degree program is offered in pharmacy. Independent study, a 3-year bachelor's degree, off-campus internships, 3 summer sessions, a cooperative education program, and combined B.A.-B.S. degrees are offered.

Honors: There are 2 honor societies on campus.

Admissions: Eighty-five percent of those who applied were accepted for the 1981–82 freshman class. The SAT scores of those who enrolled were as follows: Verbal—53% scored below 500, 37% between 500 and 599, 8% between 600 and 700, and 2% above 700; Math—50% scored below 500, 31% between 500 and 599, 16% between 600 and 700, and 3% above 700. Candidates should have a minimum high school average of 80%, rank in the top 60% of their class, and earn combined SAT scores of 950 or higher. Advanced placement or honor courses, recommendations, and extracurricular activities are also considered.

Procedure: The SAT or ACT is required and should be taken by fall of the senior year. Application deadlines are September 1 (fall) and February 1 (spring). Notification is on a rolling basis. The application fee is $20.

Special: Early decision, early admissions, and deferred admissions plans are available. CLEP and AP credit is given.

Transfer: For fall 1981, 214 transfer applications were received, 176 were accepted, and 127 students enrolled. Transfers are accepted for all classes. A 2.0 GPA is required. D grades are acceptable only with an associate degree. College transcripts and recommendations are required. Students must complete 30 semester hours in residence, of the 128 needed to receive a bachelor's degree. Application deadlines are the same as those for freshmen.

Visiting: There are orientations for prospective students. Guides are available for informal campus visits. Visits are best scheduled on weekdays from 9 A.M. to 4 P.M. Visitors may sit in on classes and stay overnight at the school. The admissions office should be contacted for arrangements.

Financial Aid: Sixty-five percent of the students receive financial aid. Twenty percent work part-time on campus. The average aid awarded to freshmen from all sources is $3800. Scholarships, grants, CWS, and loans are available. Tuition may be paid in installments. The college is a member of CSS. The FAF should be submitted. Financial aid application deadlines are June 1 (fall) and December 1 (spring).

Foreign Students: One percent of the full-time students come from foreign countries. The college offers these students special counseling and special organizations.

Admissions: Foreign students must take the TOEFL, the University of Michigan Language Test, or the CELT. They must score 500 on the TOEFL. They must also take the SAT.

Procedure: Application deadlines are July 15 (fall) and January 1 (spring). Foreign students must submit a health form completed by a physician along with their tuition fee deposit. They must also present proof of funds adequate to cover 1 year of study. They must carry health insurance, which is available through the college for a fee.

Admissions Contact: Kevin Coveney, Director of Admissions.

572 NEW YORK

MANHATTAN COLLEGE D-5
Riverdale, New York 10471 (212) 920-0200

F/T: 2470M, 1034W Faculty: 239; IIA, +$
P/T: 352M, 257W Ph.D.'s: 70%
Grad: 617M, 297W S/F Ratio: 15 to 1
Year: sems, ss Tuition: $4200
Appl: Mar. 1 R and B: $3200
3446 applied 1991 accepted 829 enrolled
SAT: 490V 550M COMPETITIVE

Manhattan College, established in 1853, is a private college of liberal arts and professional schools sponsored by the Brothers of the Christian Schools of the Roman Catholic Church. The library contains 223,-206 volumes and subscribes to 2003 periodicals.

Environment: The 47-acre campus is located in the Riverdale section of the Bronx, an urban area 10 miles from mid-Manhattan. There are 5 dormitories housing 950 men and women. The college also sponsors on-campus apartments.

Student Life: About 85% of the students come from New York. Thirty-nine percent of entering freshmen are graduates of public schools. About 30% of the students live on campus. Ninety percent are Catholic, 3% are Jewish, and 2% are Protestant. Eight percent of the students are minority-group members. College housing is coed and single-sex; students in single-sex housing have visiting privileges. Students may keep cars on campus.

Organizations: Ten percent of men belong to 2 local and 7 national fraternities; 10% of women are members of 1 national sorority. There is a broad program of extracurricular activities.

Sports: The college fields 13 intercollegiate teams. There are 18 intramural sports.

Handicapped: The college estimates the campus to be 95% accessible to handicapped students. There are wheelchair ramps, specially equipped rest rooms, elevators, special parking, lowered drinking fountains and telephones, and special class scheduling.

Graduates: The freshman dropout rate is 10%; about 80% remain to graduate. Forty-six percent of the graduates pursue advanced study; 6% enter medical school, 1% enter dental school, and 4% enter law school. About 50% pursue careers in business and industry.

Services: Psychological counseling, health care, placement service, and career counseling are offered at no charge. Tutoring is available for a fee.

Programs of Study: The college confers the B.A., B.S., and B.E. degrees. Associate and master's degrees are also awarded. Bachelor's degrees are offered in the following subjects: AREA STUDIES (American, Russian, urban), BUSINESS (accounting, business administration, computer science, finance, management, marketing), EDUCATION (adult, early childhood, elementary, health/physical, secondary), ENGLISH (English, literature), FINE AND PERFORMING ARTS (art, art history, film/photography, radio/TV, studio art), LANGUAGES (French, German, Greek/Latin, Italian, Russian, Spanish), MATH AND SCIENCES (biochemistry, biology, chemistry, mathematics, natural sciences, physical sciences, physics), PHILOSOPHY (classics, humanities, philosophy, religion), PREPROFESSIONAL (dentistry, engineering—chemical, engineering—civil, engineering—electrical, engineering—mechanical, law, medicine, ministry, social work, veterinary), SOCIAL SCIENCES (economics, government/political science, history, psychology, social sciences, sociology). Of the degrees conferred in a recent year, 30% were in business, 20% were in preprofessional studies, and 15% were in math and sciences.

Special: The college has its own nuclear reactor and offers an exceptional nuclear science sequence for engineers and science students. Third-year students may participate in the Junior Year Abroad program. Manhattan College, Siena College, St. John Fisher College, Le Moyne College, and the College of Mount Saint Vincent offer a cooperative exchange program. Students may earn combined B.A.-B.S. degrees in the sciences. A general studies degree is also offered.

Honors: Eighteen national honor societies, including Phi Beta Kappa, have chapters on campus.

Admissions: Fifty-eight percent of those who applied were accepted for the 1981–82 freshman class. Of those who enrolled, the SAT scores were as follows: Verbal—50% scored below 500, 32% between 500 and 599, 11% between 600 and 700, and 2% above 700; Math—26% scored below 500, 30% between 500 and 599, 27% between 600 and 700, and 4% above 700. Applicants should rank in the upper half of their high school class and present a minimum grade average of about 83. Other important factors that may influence the admissions decision are advanced placement or honor courses, recommendations by school officials, and extracurricular activities record.

Procedure: The SAT or ACT is required. The application deadlines are March 1 (fall and summer) and December 1 (spring). Notification is on a rolling basis. There is a $20 application fee.

Special: A deferred admissions plan and an early decision plan are offered. AP and CLEP credit is available.

Transfer: For fall 1981, 650 students applied, 462 were accepted, and 311 enrolled. The requirements for transfer vary with the program, but a GPA of at least 2.4 is standard. An associate degree and an interview are recommended. Students must earn, at the college, at least 66 of the minimum 128 credits necessary for a bachelor's degree. Application deadlines are July 1 (fall) and December 1 (spring).

Visiting: There are regularly scheduled orientations. Informal visits permit visitors to sit in on classes and to stay at the college. Arrangements should be made through the admissions center.

Financial Aid: About 25% of all students receive aid. Five percent work part-time on campus. In addition to scholarships, loans are also available from the federal government, state government, the college, and private sources. The college is a member of CSS and requires the FAF. The deadline for aid application is February 1.

Foreign Students: Four percent of the full-time students come from foreign countries. The college offers these students special counseling and special organizations.

Admissions: Foreign students must achieve a TOEFL score of 500. The SAT or ACT is also required.

Procedure: Application deadlines are March 1 (fall), September 1 (winter), and March 1 (summer). Foreign students must present proof of funds adequate to cover 4 years of study. They must also carry health insurance, which is available through the college for a fee.

Admissions Contact: Brother William Batt, Director of Admissions.

MANHATTAN SCHOOL OF MUSIC D-5
New York, New York 10027 (212) 749-2802

F/T: 205M, 159W Faculty: 19; IV, ——$
P/T: 18M, 20W Ph.D.'s: n/av
Grad: 108M, 127W S/F Ratio: n/av
Year: sems Tuition: $4100
Appl: Aug. 1 R and B: n/app
231 applied 86 accepted 42 enrolled
SAT, ACT: not required SPECIAL

The Manhattan School of Music is a private institution established in 1917. Over the years, academic courses have been added to the instrumental program, and a broader curriculum made available to students. Nevertheless, the school's philosophy of education recognizes that music is the major interest of its students. The library contains 93,723 volumes and 26,838 sound recordings, and subscribes to 68 periodicals.

Environment: The school is located in an historic instructional complex designed for the training of the professional musician. It shares the Morningside Heights community with Columbia University, Barnard College, Riverside Church, and Riverside Park. The school provides no dormitory facilities.

Student Life: The school has trained students from all 50 states and from 70 foreign countries. Eighty-five percent of the entering freshmen come from public schools. About 11% of the students are minority-group members.

Organizations: There are no fraternities, sororities, or athletic programs. The school's location in New York affords students easy access to the city's concert halls, museums, theater, opera, and other activities.

Handicapped: There are no special facilities for handicapped students.

Graduates: Graduates of the school are accomplished soloists, members of leading opera companies, symphony orchestras, and chamber music groups, and recognized teachers in colleges and universities as well as in public and private schools. Eighty percent of the graduates go on to graduate study.

Services: The following services are available to students free of charge: psychological counseling, placement and career counseling (for graduates as well as undergraduates), tutoring, and remedial instruction. A limited amount of health care is free.

Programs of Study: The school confers the B.Mus. degree. Master's and doctoral degrees are also offered. The bachelor's degree is offered in the following fields: performance (bassoon, clarinet, composition and theory, double bass, flute, French horn, guitar, harp, oboe, organ, percussion, piano, saxophone, trombone, trumpet, tuba, viola, violin, violoncello, voice), composition, and theory. A diploma program offered requires the same music curriculum as the degree courses, but without certain academic requirements.

Admissions: About 37% of those who applied were accepted for the 1981-82 freshman class. Applicants must be graduates of accredited high schools. Candidates are given an aptitude test to evaluate ability in academic areas and must perform an audition. An examination in music theory is also necessary. Students who plan to major in piano, voice, or strings must perform their repertoire from memory; all auditions include sight-reading. Evidence of special talents is the most important criterion for admission.

Procedure: SAT scores should be submitted if available, but they are not required. Application deadlines are August 1 (fall) and November 15 (spring). Entrance examinations and auditions, required of all applicants, are administered by the school at designated intervals. There is an $85 application fee.

Special: CLEP credit is available.

Transfer: For fall 1981, 253 transfer students applied, 99 were accepted, and 64 enrolled. The criteria are basically the same as for entering freshmen. There is no time residency requirement; 122 credits are required to earn a bachelor's degree. Application deadlines are the same as for freshman applicants.

Visiting: The school has no regular orientation program for prospective students, but guides are available for informal visits. The admissions office handles arrangements.

Financial Aid: Scholarships are awarded from the school's scholarship fund, and a number of special endowed scholarships are also available. Grants of varying amounts are awarded in the form of tuition payments for 1 academic year, renewable upon application. Aid awards are based on the applicant's character, musical ability, financial need, and general scholastic achievement. The school has no loan funds of its own but participates in the NDSL program. About 69% of all students receive some form of financial aid; fewer than 1% of the students work part-time on campus. The school is a member of CSS; the FAF and an aid application must be submitted 4 weeks prior to the audition date.

Foreign Students: About 13% of the full-time students are from foreign countries. The college offers these students an intensive English course and special counseling.

Admissions: A minimum score of 500 on the TOEFL is required; no further exams are required.

Procedure: Application deadlines are the same as for freshman applicants. Students must present proof of funds adequate to cover 1 year of study.

Admissions Contact: Paul Wolfe, Director of Admissions.

MANHATTANVILLE COLLEGE D-5
Purchase, New York 10577 (914) 694-2200

F/T: 350M, 650W Faculty: 85; IIA, av$
P/T: 40M, 130W Ph.D.'s: 80%
Grad: 100M, 200W S/F Ratio: 11 to 1
Year: sems, ss Tuition: $5750
Appl: Mar. 1 R and B: $2950
1190 applied 705 accepted 319 enrolled
SAT: 532V 528M **VERY COMPETITIVE**

Manhattanville College, established in 1841, is an independent liberal arts college that was originally founded by the Religious of the Sacred Heart. The library contains 246,000 volumes and 3000 microfilm items, and subscribes to 1600 periodicals.

Environment: The 220-acre campus is located in a suburban area about 10 minutes from White Plains, New York, and 25 miles from New York City. Reid Hall, an historic landmark, is listed on the National Register. The dormitories accommodate 1100 students.

Student Life: About half the students are from New York State; 12% are from 42 foreign countries. Sixty-five percent of the entering freshmen attended public schools. Eighty-seven percent of the students live in the residence halls. About 70% of the students are Catholic. Eleven percent are minority-group members. Campus housing is both coed and single-sex; there are visiting privileges in single-sex dorms. Students may keep cars on campus.

Organizations: There are no fraternities or sororities at the college. Student life encompasses many activities, including music and drama groups, a film society, 2 newspapers, a literary magazine, and departmental clubs. The college sponsors many cultural and social events throughout the year. Students can take advantage of nearby New York City for cultural and social life. Catholic students have a place to worship on campus; students of other faiths, in the immediate community.

Sports: The college fields 12 intercollegiate teams and 11 intramural teams.

Handicapped: Ninety-five percent of the campus is accessible to handicapped students. Special facilities include wheelchair ramps, parking areas, elevators, and specially equipped rest rooms. Special class scheduling can be arranged.

Graduates: The freshman dropout rate is 4%; about 82% remain to graduate. Forty percent of the students pursue graduate study: 4% enter medical school, 6% law school, and 1% dental school. Forty-five percent of the graduates pursue careers in business and industry.

Services: The following services are available to students free of charge: health care, psychological counseling, placement and career counseling (for graduates as well as undergraduates), tutoring, and remedial instruction.

Programs of Study: The college confers the B.A., B.F.A., and B.Mus. degrees, as well as master's degrees. Bachelor's degrees are offered in the following subjects: AREA STUDIES (American, Asian, Russian), EDUCATION (elementary, secondary), ENGLISH (English), FINE AND PERFORMING ARTS (art, art education, art history, dance, music, film/photography, music, music education, studio art, theater/dramatics), LANGUAGES (French, German, Italian, Russian, Spanish), MATH AND SCIENCES (biochemistry, biology, chemistry, ecology/environmental science, mathematics, natural sciences, physics), PHILOSOPHY (philosophy, religion), PREPROFESSIONAL (dentistry, law, medicine, pharmacy, social work), SOCIAL SCIENCES (economics, government/political science, history, international relations, psychology, social sciences, sociology). Thirty-two percent of all undergraduate degrees are conferred in social sciences, 24% in the arts, and 18% in math and sciences.

Required: To satisfy degree requirements, each student presents a portfolio which encompasses all academic achievements in and out of the classroom.

Special: Students interested in studying abroad may take part in an archaeology and art summer program in Spain, spend a year at Oxford or other leading European universities, or study in Rome or Tokyo. There is also an exchange program with Mills College in California and a combined 6-year B.A.-J.D. program with New York Law School. Two 5-year programs with New York University lead to a B.A.-M.B.A. or B.A.-M.S. degree in computer science. Student-designed majors are permitted.

Honors: One national honor society has a chapter on campus. There are honors programs in 16 departments.

Admissions: About 59% of those who applied were accepted for the 1981-82 freshman class. The SAT scores of those who enrolled were as follows: Verbal—35% scored below 500, 48% between 500 and 599, 15% between 600 and 700, and 2% above 700; Math—34% scored below 500, 49% between 500 and 599, 16% between 600 and 700, and 1% above 700. Students must be high school graduates or hold a GED diploma. They must also rank in the upper three-fifths of their class. Selections are based primarily on the high school record, advanced placement or honor courses, and test scores.

Procedure: The SAT or ACT and 3 ATs are required. One of the ATs must be in English composition. These tests may be taken up to the end of January of the senior year. A personal interview is not required but is strongly recommended. The application deadline for fall is March 1. Freshmen are also admitted in the spring and summer. Admission and notification are on a rolling basis. There is a $20 application fee.

Special: The college has an early decision plan with a December 15 notification date, an early admissions plan with a March 1 application deadline, and a deferred admissions plan. CLEP credit is accepted.

Transfer: For fall 1981, 90 transfer students applied, 75 were accepted, and 40 enrolled. Four semesters must be taken in residence. A GPA of 2.5 is required; a GPA of 2.75 is recommended. Grades of C or better transfer. Application deadlines are the same as those for freshmen.

Visiting: The college holds 2 open houses in the fall, during which prospective students and their parents may tour the campus, attend classes, and meet with faculty and students. Guides are also available for informal visits to the school. Visitors may stay on campus. The best time to visit is Monday through Saturday in the fall or spring. The admissions office handles arrangements.

Financial Aid: About 85% of the students receive aid through the college; 20% work part-time on campus. The college is a member of the CSS and participates in EOG, NDSL, and CWS programs. Earnings from campus employment may bring a student about $750. Aid packages combine grants, loans, and employment. The average award to freshmen from all sources is $3600. Tuition may be paid in installments. The FAF is required, and the deadline for aid applications is April 1.

NEW YORK

Foreign Students: About 12% of the full-time students are from foreign countries. The college offers these students an intensive English course and program, special counseling, and organizations especially for foreign students.

Admissions: A minimum score of 550 on the TOEFL is required; no further exams are required.

Procedure: The application deadline for fall entry is March 1. Students must submit the college's health form, and must present proof of funds adequate to cover 1 year of study. Health insurance is required and is available through the college for a fee.

Admissions Contact: Marshall Raucci, Dean of Admissions.

MANNES COLLEGE OF MUSIC   D-5
New York, New York 10021   (212) 737-0700

F/T: 106M, 74W   Faculty: 30; IV, – – $
P/T: none   Ph.D.'s: 90%
Grad: 10M, 7W   S/F Ratio: 5 to 1
Year: sems   Tuition: $4050
Appl: July 15   R and B: n/app
SAT, ACT: not required   SPECIAL

The Mannes College of Music, founded in 1916 as a school of music and established as a college in 1953, is an independent, private music conservatory. The library contains approximately 30,000 volumes and 2600 records, and subscribes to 45 periodicals.

Environment: The college is situated in a 4-story colonial-style building on a residential street on the east side of Manhattan. There are no dormitory facilities. Students commonly share rented apartments in the vicinity of the college.

Student Life: Thirty-one percent of the students are from New York, 49% are from out of state, and 20% are from foreign countries. About 7% are minority-group members.

Organizations: The active student council makes valuable contributions to college programs. The college maintains an active schedule of performances. In addition, students have access to discount tickets and to the wide variety of activities in New York City.

Handicapped: There are no special facilities for the physically handicapped.

Graduates: Approximately 35% of the students pursue advanced study after graduation.

Services: Students receive career counseling and placement services free of charge. Remedial instruction and tutoring are offered as part of the curriculum. Health care is available for a fee.

Programs of Study: The college confers the B.S. and B.Mus. degrees. Master's degrees are also awarded. Bachelor's degrees are offered in music composition, performance, and theory. Candidates for the B.S. degree take a 5-year program; for the B.Mus. degree, a 4-year program. Mannes has a small academic faculty which is in charge of the special humanities curriculum. In addition, Marymount Manhattan and Hunter College provide Mannes with liberal arts electives and additional library and performance facilities.

Required: All students are required to take 4 years of the techniques of music and 2 years of music history. Performance majors must perform before a faculty jury each year and must participate in school performances on a regular basis.

Admissions: Twenty-eight percent of those who applied were accepted for the 1981–82 freshman class. Candidates are required to be high school graduates, show evidence of special talent, and make a good impression during personal interviews.

Procedure: The college administers an audition and its own placement examinations in theory, ear training and dictation, piano, and English. The entrance examinations for September admissions are held during March, May, and September. The examinations for January entrance are held the third week of January. An applicant may audition during any of these audition periods. A $50 application fee must accompany the application.

Special: Early admissions (application deadline, April 15, for the fall) early decision, and deferred admissions plans are available.

Transfer: For fall 1981, 28% of the transfer applicants were accepted. Transfers are accepted for all classes. Applicants must meet the audition requirements as well as basic freshman criteria. Academic credit will normally be accepted if it meets curriculum requirements and if the grade is satisfactory. Music credits are accepted only for music elective credit. There is a 2-year residency requirement. Application deadlines are the same as those for freshmen.

Visiting: Prospective applicants who are interested in visiting Mannes and sitting in on classes should contact the admissions office for further information.

Financial Aid: About 35% of all students are receiving financial aid; 29% are receiving scholarships; 17% of the students work part-time on campus. The college administers $115,000 in federal loan funds, and 33% of the students receive loans. Scholarships range from $200 to $5000, and loans from $300 to $2500. Students receive aid in the form of BEOG, SEOG, NDSL, CWS, GSL, and FISL, in addition to state and private scholarships. Talent and need are the main considerations in determining the award. The college is a member of CSS; the FAF must be filed. The aid application should be included with the regular application.

Foreign Students: About 20% of the full-time students are from foreign countries. The college actively recruits foreign students. These students are offered an intensive English course and special counseling.

Admissions: Students must take the college's own English proficiency exam and the college's own entrance exam; no further exams are required.

Procedure: Application deadlines are July 15 (fall) and December 15 (spring). Students must complete a Mannes Health Certificate or submit a letter from a physician to establish proof of health. They must also present proof of funds adequate to cover at least 1 year of study. Health insurance is available through the college for a fee.

Admissions Contact: Diane Newman, Admissions and Placement Officer.

MARIST COLLEGE   D-4
Poughkeepsie, New York 12601   (914) 471-3240

F/T: 950M, 950W   Faculty: 107; IIB, +$
P/T: 200M, 260W   Ph.D.'s: 81%
Grad: 150M, 150W   S/F Ratio: 18 to 1
Year: sems, ss   Tuition: $4030
Appl: open   R and B: $2530
2500 applied   1225 accepted   550 enrolled
SAT: 490V 510M   ACT: 23   COMPETITIVE+

Marist College, founded in 1946, is a private liberal arts college. The library houses over 88,000 volumes and subscribes to 1000 periodicals.

Environment: The campus is located in a suburban area on the banks of the Hudson River, 75 miles from New York City. The major buildings have all been completed since 1965. Dormitories accommodate 975 students. There are separate freshman dormitories. The college also sponsors on- and off-campus apartments and fraternity houses.

Student Life: Most of the students are from New York or surrounding states. Eighty-five percent reside in campus dormitories. Sixty percent of entering freshmen come from public schools. About 80% of the students are Catholic, 15% are Protestant, and 5% are Jewish. About 16% are minority-group members. Campus housing is coed. Students may keep cars on campus. Day-care facilities are available to all students, faculty, and staff.

Organizations: Five percent of the men belong to 1 fraternity. Lecture series, art exhibits, and 20 clubs provide a full activities calendar.

Sports: The college fields 10 intercollegiate teams for men and 6 for women. There are 14 intramural sports for men and 12 for women.

Handicapped: About 90% of the campus is accessible to handicapped students. Facilities include wheelchair ramps, parking areas, elevators, specially equipped rest rooms, and lowered drinking fountains and telephones. Tutors, readers, student aides, attendants, and note-takers are available. Four percent of the students are visually impaired; 7% have hearing impairments.

Graduates: The freshman dropout rate is 7%; 66% remain to graduate. About 49% of the graduates pursue advanced degrees; 2% enter medical school, 3% law school, and 1% dental school. About 71% enter careers in business or industry.

Services: Students receive the following services free of charge: psychological counseling, placement, career counseling, health care, tutoring, and remedial instruction.

Programs of Study: The college confers the B.A. and B.S. degrees. Master's degrees are also awarded. Bachelor's degrees are offered in the following subjects: AREA STUDIES (American), BUSINESS (accounting, business administration, computer science), EDUCATION (bilingual, elementary, secondary, special), ENGLISH (communication arts, English, professional writing), FINE AND PERFORMING ARTS (fashion design, studio art), HEALTH SCIENCES (medical technology), LANGUAGES (French, Russian, Spanish), MATH AND SCIENCES (biology, chemistry, computer mathematics, ecology/environmental science, mathematics), PREPROFESSIONAL (dentistry, law, ministry, paralegal studies, social work), SOCIAL SCIENCES (criminal justice, economics, government/political science, history, psychology, public administration, sociology). Forty-five percent of the degrees are conferred in business, 20% in math and sciences, and 18% in social sciences.

Required: Each student's required courses are determined by his or her major department.

Special: A 3-year bachelor's degree, student-designed majors, and study abroad are offered. The psychology major includes a 1-semester work-study program. Upperclassmen may enroll in a 1-semester program emphasizing learning-action projects undertaken in the mid-Hudson community. There are opportunities for internships in various majors. A 3-2 engineering program is offered with the University of Detroit. Students also may take courses at the other 7 member colleges of the Associated Colleges of the mid-Hudson area. Freshman seminar programs offer individualized attention in a small group setting.

Honors: Several honor societies are open to qualified students. There is a Science of Man honors program.

Admissions: Forty-nine percent of those who applied were accepted for the 1981–82 freshman class. The SAT scores of those who enrolled were as follows: Verbal—40% below 500, 45% between 500 and 599, 10% between 600 and 700, and 1% above 700; Math—38% below 500, 52% between 500 and 599, 0% between 600 and 700, and 0% above 700. Candidates must rank in the upper 60% of their high school class and have completed 15 Carnegie units. The accreditation, reputation, and recommendation of the high school are essential. SAT or ACT scores, advanced placement or honor courses, and leadership potential are also considered.

Procedure: The SAT or ACT is required. The SAT should be taken by January of the senior year. There are no application deadlines. Notification is made about 3 weeks after all materials are received. There is a $20 application fee.

Special: The application deadline is December 1 for early decision and early admissions. AP and CLEP credit is available.

Transfer: For fall 1981, 270 transfer students applied, 240 were accepted, and 209 enrolled. Transfers are accepted for all classes. A 2.0 GPA is required; a 2.5 GPA is recommended. Grades of C or better transfer. One year must be completed in residence, and students must earn, at the college, 30 of the 120 credits required for the bachelor's degree. Application deadlines are April 1 (fall) and December 1 (spring).

Visiting: Visitors may sit in on classes and stay overnight at the college. The admissions office should be contacted for arrangements.

Financial Aid: Eighty percent of the students receive financial aid; 45% work part-time on campus. Funded educational opportunities include laboratory teaching assistantships and technical positions, resident advisorships, and internships in educational administration. Qualified students are awarded grants-in-aid from a college fund; federal funds are also available. The average aid to freshmen is $1000. Tuition may be paid in installments. The college is a member of the CSS; the FAF must be submitted by March 1 for fall entry and December 1 for spring entry.

Foreign Students: About 2% of the full-time students are from foreign countries. The college offers these students special counseling and special organizations.

Admissions: A minimum score of 500 on the TOEFL is required; no further exams are necessary.

Procedure: Application deadlines are February 1 (fall) and November 1 (spring). Students must submit proof of vaccination, medical records, and a medical history. They must also present proof of funds adequate to cover 1 year of study. Health insurance is available through the college for a fee.

Admissions Contact: James Daly, Dean of Admissions.

MARYMOUNT COLLEGE D–5
Tarrytown, New York 10591 (914) 631-3200

F/T: 33M, 931W	Faculty: 66; IIB, +$
P/T: 35M, 258W	Ph.D.'s: 48%
Grad: none	S/F Ratio: 9 to 1
Year: sems, ss, weekend	Tuition: $4410
Appl: May 1	R and B: $2860
553 applied	433 accepted	209 enrolled
SAT: 407V 428M	LESS COMPETITIVE

Marymount College, an independent liberal arts college, was founded by the Religious of the Sacred Heart of Mary in 1919, but is today independent of formal ties with the Catholic Church. Marymount offers 2 formats of instruction: a traditional weekday program for women of all ages and an intensive weekend format for working men and women. The library houses 103,000 volumes and 5000 microfilm items, and subscribes to 550 periodicals.

Environment: The 60-acre campus is located in a suburban area overlooking the Hudson River, 25 miles north of New York City. The 11 buildings, 7 of which were constructed since 1950, include fully equipped science labs, art studios, a computer center, and a sports building. Four dormitories accommodate 700 women. Residence halls for students in the weekend program accommodate about 350 adult students.

Student Life: Students come from 21 states and 21 foreign countries. Fifty percent of the entering freshmen attended public schools. About 85% of the students live on campus. First-semester freshmen observe a curfew. About 14% of the students are minority-group members. Campus housing is single-sex; there are visiting privileges. Students may keep cars on campus.

Organizations: There are no sororities or fraternities. Student organizations include publications, special-interest clubs, and community service organizations. The college sponsors on-campus activities such as plays, films, and art exhibits. Students may travel to New York City to enjoy its many cultural and recreational attractions.

Sports: The college fields 6 intercollegiate teams for women. There are 5 intramural sports for women.

Handicapped: The entire campus is accessible to the physically handicapped. Wheelchair ramps, designated parking areas, and elevators are provided. Special counseling is available.

Graduates: About 15% of the freshmen drop out, and 78% remain to graduate. Thirty-three percent of the graduates continue their studies in graduate or professional schools; 2% enter law school. About 37% enter careers in business or industry.

Services: Free health care, psychological counseling, career counseling, tutoring, and remedial instruction are available. Free placement services for undergraduates and alumnae are also offered.

Programs of Study: The college confers the B.A. and B.S. degrees. Bachelor's degrees are offered in the following subjects: AREA STUDIES (American), BUSINESS (business administration), EDUCATION (elementary, secondary, special), ENGLISH (English), FINE AND PERFORMING ARTS (art, art history, theater/dramatics), HEALTH SCIENCES (medical technology), LANGUAGES (French, Spanish), MATH AND SCIENCES (biology, chemistry, mathematics), PHILOSOPHY (philosophy), PREPROFESSIONAL (foods and nutrition, home economics, law, medicine, social work), SOCIAL SCIENCES (art therapy, economics, governemnt/political science, history, international relations, psychology, sociology).

Required: General education and core curriculum requirements are flexible. Depending on the field of study, students are required to take 8 to 24 courses in the major. Weekday students need 128 credits to qualify for a degree; weekend students require 120.

Special: In addition to the weekend program, other special programs include an interdisciplinary major, junior year abroad and travel/study abroad, independent study, cross-cultural semesters, internships, a Community Leadership program, and student-designed majors.

Honors: Juniors and seniors with a cumulative index of 3.5 are eligible for membership in Delta Epsilon Sigma, a national honor society. There are freshman honors seminars.

Admissions: Seventy-eight percent of the applicants for the 1981–1982 freshman class were admitted. The SAT scores of those who enrolled were as follows: Verbal—85% below 500, 13% between 500 and 599, 2% between 600 and 700, and 0% above 700; Math—83% below 500, 14% between 500 and 599, 2% between 600 and 700, and 0% above 700. The school relies heavily on the student's secondary school record and letters of recommendation. Students should rank in the upper half of their graduating class. Sixteen academic high school units and a B average are required. Candidates should also show a good record of extracurricular activities and evidence of leadership. The college will consider a student who does not meet these requirements but shows academic potential and demonstrates financial need.

Procedure: The SAT or ACT is required. Applications should be submitted by May 1 for the fall term and by December 1 for the spring term. They should be accompanied by a fee of $20. Admission and notification are on a rolling basis. A personal interview is strongly recommended.

576 NEW YORK

Special: Early admissions, early decision, and deferred admissions plans are available. CLEP and AP credit is available.

Transfer: For fall 1981, 103 transfer students applied, 59 were accepted, and 26 enrolled. Transfers are accepted for all but the senior year and must complete, at the college, 48 of the 128 credits required to earn a bachelor's degree. Requirements include a cumulative index of 2.0, submission of college and high school transcripts, and 2 letters of recommendation. Grades of C or better transfer. Application deadlines are the same as those for freshmen. Transfer students are eligible for financial aid.

Visiting: Regularly scheduled orientations include campus tours, participation in classes, and discussions with faculty, students, and financial aid staff. The admissions office also arranges informal visits; suggested times are weekdays from 9 A.M. to 5 P.M. Prospective students may stay overnight at the school.

Financial Aid: Sixty-three percent of the students receive financial aid; 60% work part-time on campus. The average aid granted freshmen from all sources is $4690. The current freshman class has 209 students receiving a total of $105,830 in Marymount scholarships. Federal loans, grants, and work-study are available. Aid is awarded on the basis of need and is granted on a rolling basis. The college is a member of CSS, and it is recommended that the FAF be submitted by February 1. Notification of awards is made from January to June.

Foreign Students: About 7% of the full-time students are from foreign countries. The college offers these students an intensive English course, special counseling, and special organizations.

Admissions: A minimum score of 500 on the TOEFL is required; no further exams are necessary.

Procedure: The college follows a rolling admissions policy; students are admitted to the fall and spring semesters. Students must complete the college's health form and must present proof of funds adequate to cover 1 year of study. Health insurance is available through the college for a fee.

Admissions Contact: Micheileen J. Doran, Director of Admissions and Financial Aid.

MARYMOUNT MANHATTAN COLLEGE D-5
New York, New York 10021 (212) 472-3800

F/T: 69M, 808W	Faculty: 52; IIB, ++$
P/T: 123M, 1275W	Ph.D.'s: 58%
Grad: none	S/F Ratio: 17 to 1
Year: 4-1-4, ss	Tuition: $3590
Appl: open	R: $2590
520 applied	337 accepted	181 enrolled
SAT: 420V 400M		LESS COMPETITIVE

A private, independent, liberal arts college founded by the Religious of the Sacred Heart of Mary in 1947 as a branch of Marymount College in Tarrytown, New York, Marymount Manhattan College became a separate corporation in 1961. The library contains 66,865 volumes and 7020 audiovisual materials, and subscribes to 567 periodicals.

Environment: Marymount Manhattan's physical plant includes a 250-seat, professionally equipped theater, art studios, dance studios, a communication learning center, photography labs, and a swimming pool. Limited residence space is available in college-supervised apartments in a high-rise apartment building near the college. There are no campus dormitory facilities.

Student Life: Ninety-five percent of the students come from the middle Atlantic states. Fifty-one percent attended public schools. About 40% of the students are minority-group members.

Organizations: There are no social sororities at Marymount. There are, however, an active student government, a monthly newspaper, a dramatic workshop, and 17 clubs as well as other special-interest, departmental, and religious groups. The vast cultural and recreational resources of the New York metropolitan area are available to the students.

Sports: The college offers 2 intramural sports for women.

Handicapped: The entire campus is accessible to wheelchair-bound students, with the exception of the dining room. One percent of the students have visual impairments; 1% have hearing problems. There is a special counselor for handicapped students.

Graduates: The freshman dropout rate is 20%, about 75% of the entering freshmen remain to graduate. Twenty-five percent of graduates continue their studies in graduate or professional schools; about 3% enter medical school, about 3% law school.

Services: The following services are available to students free of charge: placement, career counseling, health care, and psychological counseling. Tutoring and remedial instruction are offered on a fee basis. Placement services for undergraduates include on-campus corporation recruitment.

Programs of Study: The college confers the B.A., B.S., and B.F.A. degrees. Bachelor's degrees are offered in the following subjects: BUSINESS (accounting, management), EDUCATION (early childhood, elementary, secondary, special, speech and hearing handicapped), ENGLISH (communication arts, literature, speech), FINE AND PERFORMING ARTS (acting, art, art history, dance, music, studio art, theater), HEALTH SCIENCES (speech pathology and audiology), LANGUAGES (French, Italian, Spanish), MATH AND SCIENCES (biology, chemistry, mathematics), PHILOSOPHY (philosophy, religion), PREPROFESSIONAL (law, medicine, social work), SOCIAL SCIENCES (economics, history, international studies, national studies, political science, psychology, sociology). Twenty-four percent of the degrees conferred are in social sciences, 18% in business, and 12% in fine and performing arts.

Required: Two semesters of Critical Thinking are required.

Special: Certificate programs in alcoholism counseling, business management, and gerontology are offered. The teacher education programs lead to New York State certification. There are study abroad and 3-year degree programs.

Honors: Two national honor societies have chapters on campus. Honors programs include the Women in Management program, which combines classroom learning with practical experience through internships and workshops.

Admissions: Sixty-five percent of those who applied were accepted for the 1981–82 freshman class. To receive serious consideration, students must rank in the top three-fifths of their class, have a minimum average of 80, and receive favorable recommendations from high school officials. Sixteen Carnegie units are required. The college will consider a student who does not meet the requirements but does show ability in other areas.

Procedure: The SAT is recommended but not required unless the applicant is applying for a scholarship. Regular admission is on a rolling basis; there is no deadline. Students are admitted to the fall, winter, spring, and summer terms. A $15 fee should accompany all applications.

Special: There is an early decision plan with a notification date of December 1. The college admits students on early admission after the junior year; the application deadline is November 15. A deferred admissions plan is also available. AP and CLEP credit is granted.

Transfer: For fall 1981, 224 transfer students applied, 177 were accepted, and 104 enrolled. An average of C is required; D grades transfer only with an associate degree. A GPA of 2.0 is required. Thirty credits must be taken in residence, of the 120 credits required for a bachelor's degree. The college uses a rolling admissions policy.

Visiting: Regularly scheduled orientations for prospective students include conversations with present students and administrators, tours, and class visits. Guides are available for informal visits. The college recommends visiting on weekdays from 9 A.M. to 7 P.M. The admissions office is also open Saturdays from 10 A.M. to 3 P.M. For information and an appointment, the admissions office should be contacted.

Financial Aid: Approximately 56% of the full-time students receive financial aid; 21% work part-time on campus. The college provides partial- and full-tuition scholarships, which are awarded on the basis of academic record, personal qualifications, and need. The average award to freshmen from all sources is $3550. If the student maintains an adequate academic record, scholarships are renewed. Also available are academic no-need scholarships based on competition. Students may secure loans through the New York State Higher Assistance Corporation as well as the NDSL program. The college also has Pell Grant, Tuition Assistance Program, and College Work-Study funds available. The college is a member of CSS; students are required to file the FAF. All applications should be filed by June 1 (fall), November 1 (winter and spring), and February 1 (summer).

Foreign Students: About 5% of the full-time students are from foreign countries. The college offers these students special counseling.

Admissions: A minimum score of 500 on the TOEFL is required. In addition, students must also take the college's own entrance exam.

Procedure: Foreign students are admitted to all terms; admissions are handled on a rolling basis. Students must submit a completed college health form and must present proof of funds adequate to cover 1 year of study.

Admissions Contact: Catherine O'Rourke, Director of Admissions.

MEDAILLE COLLEGE
Buffalo, New York 14214   (716) 884-3281

F/T: 313M, 398W
P/T: 30M, 50W
Grad: none
Year: sems, ss
Appl: Aug. 2
264 applied
SAT: 400V 415M

Faculty: 42; IIB, – – $
Ph.D.'s: 52%
S/F Ratio: 17 to 1
Tuition: $3060
R and B: n/app
208 accepted   178 enrolled
LESS COMPETITIVE

Medaille College, founded in 1937, is a private, independent college. The library contains 85,000 volumes and subscribes to 350 periodicals.

Environment: The 30-acre campus, located in an urban area, is within walking distance of Buffalo's Albright Knox Art Gallery overlooking Delaware Park. The campus consists of 3 buildings which include a demonstration school, a reading center, an educational resource center, and a recreational center. There are no dormitory facilities.

Student Life: Ninety-nine percent of the students come from New York State. All students commute. About 43% of the students are minority-group members. Students may keep cars on campus.

Organizations: There are no fraternities or sororities. Extracurricular activities include student government, newspaper, chorus, and drama club. The major social events on campus are dances and the Week of the Arts in spring.

Sports: The college fields 4 intercollegiate teams for men and 2 for women. There are 4 intramural sports for men and 3 for women.

Handicapped: About 30% of the campus is accessible to handicapped students. Special parking, elevators, and lowered drinking fountains are available.

Graduates: The freshman dropout rate is 20%; 65% remain to graduate. About 15% of the graduates go on for further study; 85% enter careers in business or industry.

Services: Students receive the following services free of charge: placement, career counseling, psychological counseling, tutoring, and remedial instruction.

Programs of Study: The college confers the B.A. and B.S. degrees. Associate degrees are also granted. Bachelor's degrees are offered in the following subjects: AREA STUDIES (urban), BUSINESS (advertising, business education, management, public relations, recreation and parks management), EDUCATION (adult, early childhood, elementary), ENGLISH (English, journalism, literature), FINE AND PERFORMING ARTS (arts management, radio/TV), PHILOSOPHY (humanities), PREPROFESSIONAL (social work), SOCIAL SCIENCES (government/political science, human services, social sciences).

Special: It is possible to earn combined B.A.-B.S. degrees in various subjects. Student-designed majors are permitted.

Honors: Delta Chi has a chapter on campus.

Admissions: Seventy-nine percent of those who applied were accepted for the 1981–82 freshman class. The SAT scores of those who enrolled were as follows: Verbal—80% below 500, 20% between 500 and 599, 0% between 600 and 700, and 0% above 700; Math—75% below 500, 23% between 500 and 599, 2% between 600 and 700, and 0% above 700. Requirements for admission are as follows: graduation from an accredited high school with an 80% average, rank in the top half of the class, and completion of 16 Carnegie units. The minimum composite SAT score acceptable is 800. The school also considers the following factors in order of importance: impressions made during an interview, personality, evidence of special talents, and recommendations by school officials.

Procedure: The SAT is required and should be taken by July following the senior year. The deadline for application to the fall semester is August 2. Freshmen are also admitted at midyear and for the summer; application deadlines are December 15 and May 31. The college has a rolling admissions plan and observes the CRDA. A personal interview is required. A $15 application fee must accompany the application.

Special: Early decision, early admissions, and deferred admissions plans are available. AP and CLEP credit is offered.

Transfer: For fall 1981, 111 transfer students applied, 78 were accepted, and 71 enrolled. A 2.0 GPA is required. Thirty hours of the 120 required for the bachelor's degree must be earned in residence. The application deadlines are the same as those for freshman applicants.

Visiting: Orientation is scheduled for prospective students. Informal campus visits may be made at any time. Visitors may sit in on classes. Guided tours and interviews can be arranged by the admissions office.

Financial Aid: Ninety-five percent of all students receive aid through the school; 2% work part-time on campus. The college offers limited scholarship aid and loan funds. Work contracts are available to freshmen. Tuition may be paid in installments. The college has no outside sources of funds other than student tuition money. All financial aid is based on individual need. The college is a member of CSS; the FAF is required. The deadline for financial aid application is April 1.

Foreign Students: About 1% of the full-time students are from foreign countries. The college offers these students an intensive English program and special counseling.

Admissions: A minimum score of 450 on the TOEFL is required; no further exams are necessary.

Procedure: There are no application deadlines. Students must present proof of funds adequate to cover 4 years of study.

Admissions Contact: Marilynn Propis, Director of Admissions.

MERCY COLLEGE
Dobbs Ferry, New York 10522   (914) 693-7600

F/T: 2362M, 3541W
P/T: 1422M, 2133W
Grad: none
Year: sems, ss
Appl: open
1908 applied
SAT: 410V 390M

Faculty: 200; IIB, +$
Ph.D.'s: 60%
S/F Ratio: 16 to 1
Tuition: $2550
R and B: n/app
1577 accepted   1266 enrolled
LESS COMPETITIVE

Mercy College, founded in 1950 under the auspices of the Sisters of Mercy, is now an independent, nonsectarian college offering undergraduate degree programs in liberal arts and sciences, education, business, and nursing. The library contains more than 280,000 volumes and subscribes to 1000 periodicals.

Environment: The 50-acre campus is located in a suburban area 10 miles north of New York City on the banks of the Hudson River in Westchester County. The college has a branch campus in Yorktown Heights and extension centers in Peekskill, White Plains, Yonkers, and the Bronx. Mercy is primarily a commuter campus; there are no residence halls.

Student Life: About 90% of the students are from New York. Sixty-five percent come from public schools. About 65% of the students are Catholic, 23% are Protestant, and 8% are Jewish. About 41% are minority-group members. Students may keep cars on campus.

Organizations: There are no fraternities or sororities on campus. Extracurricular activities include publications, departmental and special-interest clubs, performing and musical groups, and student government.

Sports: The college fields 6 intercollegiate teams for men and 5 for women. There is 1 intramural sport for men.

Handicapped: Classrooms, laboratories, rest rooms, the library, recreation rooms, and the dining hall are all easily accessible to handicapped students. Special parking is also available.

Graduates: At the end of the freshman year, 20% of the students drop out; 70% remain to graduate. About 30% of the graduates pursue advanced degrees; 5% enter medical school, 7% law school, and 5% dental school. About 45% enter careers in business or industry.

Services: Psychological counseling, placement, career counseling, health care, tutoring, and remedial instruction are available free of charge to all students.

Programs of Study: The college confers the B.A. and B.S. degrees. Associate degrees are also granted. Bachelor's degrees are offered in the following subjects: BUSINESS (accounting, business administration, finance, management, marketing), ENGLISH (English, journalism, speech), FINE AND PERFORMING ARTS (music), HEALTH SCIENCES (medical technology, nursing, speech therapy), LANGUAGES (French, Italian, Spanish), MATH AND SCIENCES (biology, mathematics, natural sciences), PREPROFESSIONAL (paralegal studies, pharmacy, social work, veterinary technology/management), SOCIAL SCIENCES (government/political science, history, psychology, sociology).

Required: All students are required to take courses in English, speech, and mathematics.

Special: A B.G.S. degree is offered. Study abroad, continuing education, independent study, and a 5-year coordinate program in phar-

578 NEW YORK

macy with Long Island University are available. An extension center in Miami, Florida, provides programs in bilingual studies.

Honors: There are 7 honor societies on campus.

Admissions: About 83% of the 1981-82 applicants were accepted. The SAT scores of those who enrolled were as follows: Verbal—80% below 500, 15% between 500 and 599, 3% between 600 and 700, and 2% above 700; Math—85% below 500, 8% between 500 and 599, 6% between 600 and 700, and 1% above 700. Applicants must be high school graduates and present at least 16 academic units. Important factors in the admissions decision include high school GPA, test scores, class rank, and impressions made during an interview.

Procedure: The SAT is required and should be taken by January of the senior year. There is a $15 application fee. There are no application deadlines. Notification is on a rolling basis.

Special: The college has an early decision plan. Early admissions and deferred admissions plans are also available. AP and CLEP credit is offered.

Transfer: For fall 1981, 1172 transfer students applied, 999 were accepted, and 935 enrolled. A 2.0 GPA is recommended. The last 30 semester hours, including 15 credits in the major, must be taken in residence; 120 credits are required to earn a bachelor's degree. There is a $20 application fee for transfer students. Grades of C or better transfer. There are no application deadlines.

Visiting: Prospective students are encouraged to visit the campus. Visitors may sit in on classes. The admissions office should be contacted for arrangements.

Financial Aid: About 70% of the students receive financial aid; 12% work part-time on campus. Aid is awarded primarily on the basis of need. A number of sources are available including scholarships, grants, campus employment, BEOG, SEOG, NDSL, and CWS. The college is a member of CSS; the FAF is required and should be filed by March 15.

Foreign Students: About 2% of the full-time students are from foreign countries. The college offers these students an intensive English program, special counseling, and special organizations.

Admissions: A minimum score of 500 on the TOEFL is required; no college entrance exams are necessary.

Procedure: There are no application deadlines. Students must present proof of funds adequate to cover 1 year of study.

Admissions Contact: Robert Sweeney, Director of Admissions.

MOLLOY COLLEGE   D-5
Rockville Centre, New York 11570   (516) 678-5000

F/T: 30M, 1131W	Faculty:	113; IIB, —$
P/T: 29M, 349W	Ph.D.'s:	37%
Grad: none	S/F Ratio:	10 to 1
Year: 4-1-4, ss	Tuition:	$3500
Appl: Aug. 15	R and B:	n/app
553 applied	430 accepted	271 enrolled
SAT: 447V 462M		**COMPETITIVE**

Molloy College, a private liberal arts college for women, is Catholic in origin, but is open to students of all denominations. Men are admitted to nursing, evening, and weekend programs. The library contains 80,000 volumes and 1100 microfilm items, and subscribes to 530 periodicals.

Environment: Situated on a 25-acre campus in a suburb of New York City, the college is readily accessible by car, bus, and train. There are 4 major buildings, including an arts center that houses art and music studios, theater facilities, and an auditorium.

Student Life: Ninety-five percent of the students are local residents; most commute from home, but a few live in private housing. About 65% are graduates of public schools. Attendance at religious services is not required.

Organizations: The college offers a variety of cultural, entertainment, and social activities, both on campus and taking advantage of the close proximity to New York City, in addition to coordinating events with such colleges as U.S. Merchant Marine Academy, Fairfield University, Adelphi, and Hofstra. Student government, clubs, and athletic activities are also available for interested students.

Sports: The college fields teams in 5 intercollegiate sports. There is 1 intramural sport.

Handicapped: The entire campus is accessible to handicapped students. Special facilities include wheelchair ramps, parking areas, elevators, lowered drinking fountains and telephones, and specially equipped rest rooms. Special class scheduling is also possible.

Graduates: The freshman dropout rate is 10%, but the majority remain to graduate. About 20% of the graduates pursue advanced degrees.

Services: Students receive the following services free of charge: placement, career counseling, health care, psychological counseling, and peer counseling for study skills.

Programs of Study: The college confers the B.A. and B.S. degrees. Associate degrees are also offered. Bachelor's degrees are offered in the following subjects: BUSINESS (management), EDUCATION (elementary, secondary), ENGLISH (English, speech), FINE AND PERFORMING ARTS (art, music), HEALTH SCIENCES (nursing), LANGUAGES (French, Spanish), MATH AND SCIENCES (biology, mathematics), PHILOSOPHY (philosophy, religion), PREPROFESSIONAL (social work), SOCIAL SCIENCES (government/political science, history, psychology, sociology).

Special: The music department offers a music therapy concentration. The business management major offers a cooperative work-study program in retailing and merchandising; minors are also offered in economics and computer science. Speech majors may take an optional concentration in dance and drama, or in speech pathology and audiology. Internships and independent study are available in most majors.

Honors: The 9 honor societies with chapters on campus include Epsilon Kappa, Sigma Theta Tau, the National Honor Society of Nursing, Delta Epsilon Sigma, the National Scholastic Honor Society, Alpha Mu Gamma, the National Foreign Language Honor Society, as well as the national societies in science, business, literature, math, and psychology.

Admissions: Seventy-eight percent of those who applied were accepted for the 1981-82 freshman class. The SAT scores of those who enrolled were as follows: Verbal—45% below 500, 22% between 500 and 599, 1% between 600 and 700, and 0% above 700; Math—38% below 500, 31% between 500 and 599, 6% between 600 and 700, and 0% above 700. Applicants should rank in the upper 60% of their graduating class, have a 3.0 high school GPA, and present acceptable SAT or ACT scores. An interview is strongly recommended. Advanced placement or honor courses, leadership record, extracurricular activities, and recommendations by school officials are also considered.

Procedure: The SAT or ACT is required. Applications for regular admissions should be received by August 15 (fall) and January 1 (spring). High school transcripts and SAT or ACT scores must also be forwarded for evaluation. The college uses a rolling admissions policy. The application fee is $15.00.

Special: Early admissions and deferred admissions plans are available; the application deadline for early admissions is April 1. AP and CLEP credit is accepted. Early decisions are possible on applications received by December 1.

Transfer: For fall 1981, 350 transfer students applied, 221 were accepted, and 151 enrolled. A 2.0 GPA is required of all liberal arts applicants. Grades of C or better are accepted for liberal arts students; grades of B or better for nursing students. The college accepts up to 73 credits from a 2-year college and 98 credits from a 4-year college. Thirty credits and at least half the credits in the major must be completed in residence. A total of 128 credits must be earned to receive a bachelor's degree. Application deadlines are the same as those for freshmen. There are special requirements for transferring into the nursing program. Nursing applicants are admitted only in the fall.

Visiting: Regularly scheduled orientations for prospective students include campus tours, department conferences, a financial aid presentation, and class visits. Informal weekday visits can be arranged; guides are available.

Financial Aid: About 82% of the students receive aid; 14% work part-time on campus. Scholarship funds total $270,000; the average aid to freshmen from all sources is $2389. The college is a member of CSS; financial aid applications and the FAF should be filed by February 15 (fall) and December 1 (spring).

Foreign Students: About 2% of the full-time students are from foreign countries. The college offers these students an intensive English course and special counseling.

Admissions: A minimum score of 500 on the TOEFL is required; no college entrance exams are necessary.

Procedure: Application deadlines are August 15 (fall) and January 1 (spring). A physical examination is required. Students must present proof of adequate funds. Health insurance is available through the college.

Admissions Contact: Francis A. Mullin, Director of Admissions and Freshman Financial Aid.

MOUNT SAINT MARY COLLEGE D–4
Newburgh, New York 12550 (914) 561-0800

F/T: 91M, 682W
P/T: 47M, 195W
Grad: none
Year: sems, ss
Appl: Aug. 15
423 applied
SAT: 390V 420M

Faculty: 50; IIB, –$
Ph.D.'s: n/av
S/F Ratio: 14 to 1
Tuition: $110 p/c
R and B: $1990

387 accepted 201 enrolled
LESS COMPETITIVE

Mount Saint Mary College, a private coeducational, liberal arts institution, was founded by the Dominican Sisters in 1954. The library houses 80,000 volumes, subscribes to 540 periodicals, and has 18,000 microfilm items on file.

Environment: The 63-acre campus is located in a suburban area 58 miles from New York City. Among its facilities are 2-story garden-apartment-style dormitories accommodating 575 students.

Student Life: Eighty percent of the students are from New York State. About 50% reside on campus. Sixty-nine percent of entering freshmen come from public schools. About 64% of the students are Catholic, 13% are Protestant, and 2% are Jewish. About 13% are minority-group members. Campus housing is single-sex; there are visiting privileges. Students may keep cars on campus.

Organizations: There are no fraternities or sororities, but students may participate in many special-interest groups. Community help and volunteer programs form a large part of campus life. The College Cultural Center brings many outstanding performers to the campus.

Sports: The college fields 2 intercollegiate teams for men and 4 for women. There are 4 intramural sports for men and 5 for women.

Handicapped: Special facilities for handicapped students include wheelchair ramps and elevators.

Graduates: The freshman dropout rate is 10%. Of the 65% that remain to graduate, 11% become candidates for graduate or professional degrees; 15% enter careers in business and industry.

Services: The following services are offered at no charge to the student: psychological counseling, tutoring, remedial instruction, placement service, and career counseling. Health care is available for a fee.

Programs of Study: The college confers the B.A., B.S., and B.S.N. degrees. Bachelor's degrees are offered in the following subjects: AREA STUDIES (social studies), BUSINESS (business administration, management), EDUCATION (elementary, secondary, special), ENGLISH (communication arts, English), FINE AND PERFORMING ARTS (radio/TV, theater/dramatics), HEALTH SCIENCES (medical technology, nursing), MATH AND SCIENCES (biology, chemistry, mathematics), PREPROFESSIONAL (dentistry, law, medicine), SOCIAL SCIENCES (government/political science, history, interdisciplinary studies, psychology, social sciences, sociology).

Required: All students must complete general education requirements.

Special: There is opportunity for independent study. Student-designed majors are permitted.

Honors: The national honor society of Beta Beta Beta has a chapter on campus.

Admissions: Ninety-one percent of those who applied were accepted for the 1981–1982 freshman class. The SAT scores of those who enrolled were as follows: Verbal—87% below 500, 13% between 500 and 599, 0% between 600 and 700, and 0% above 700; Math—80% below 500, 19% between 500 and 599, 1% between 600 and 700, and 0% above 700. A recommendation from the high school is required. Students should rank in the upper 60% of their graduating class. The college also considers advanced placement or honor courses, evidence of leadership potential, and the extracurricular activities record.

Procedure: The SAT or ACT is required. Application deadlines are August 15 (fall), December 15 (spring), and May 20 (summer). Notification is on a rolling basis. There is a $15 application fee.

Special: Early admissions and deferred admissions plans are offered. AP and CLEP credit is accepted.

Transfer: For fall 1981, 159 transfer students applied, 134 were accepted, and 73 enrolled. Transfers are accepted for all classes. Grades of C or better transfer. A GPA of 2.0 is required. Students must complete, at the college, 30 of the 120 credits required for the bachelor's degree. Application deadlines are the same as those for freshman applicants.

Visiting: A weekend orientation is conducted by the college for prospective students each year. Guides are available for informal visits to the campus, and visitors may sit in on classes and stay overnight at the school. Arrangements for visits (Monday through Friday from 8:30 A.M. to 4:00 P.M. and Saturday from 9:00 A.M. to noon) can be made through the admissions office.

Financial Aid: About 85% of the students receive aid. Aid is available in the form of scholarships, loans, and campus employment. The deadline for filing financial aid applications is March 15. The college is a member of CSS, and the FAF is required.

Foreign Students: About 1% of the full-time students are from foreign countries. Special organizations are available for these students.

Admissions: A minimum score of 500 on the TOEFL is required. Students must also take the SAT.

Procedure: The application deadline is March 15 for fall entry. Students must present proof of health. Proof of adequate funds is also required.

Admissions Contact: Anne Ayala-Earley, Admissions Counselor.

NAZARETH COLLEGE OF ROCHESTER B–3
Rochester, New York 14610 (716) 586-2525

F/T: 261M, 1127W
P/T: 130M, 383W
Grad: 150M, 850W
Year: sems, ss
Appl: open
1070 applied
SAT: 460V 480M

Faculty: 93; IIA, –$
Ph.D.'s: 55%
S/F Ratio: 12 to 1
Tuition: $3830
R and B: $2250

890 accepted 530 enrolled
ACT: 21 COMPETITIVE

Nazareth College of Rochester is an independent liberal arts college founded in 1924. The library houses 192,967 volumes and subscribes to 960 periodicals.

Environment: The 75-acre campus is located in a suburban setting 7 miles from Rochester. There are 14 buildings, including residence halls.

Student Life: About 85% of the students are from New York State, and 70% of the freshmen are graduates of public schools. Fifty-seven percent of the students live on campus. Seventy-five percent are Catholic, 21% are Protestant, and 1% belong to other denominations. Six percent of the students are minority-group members. College housing is both single-sex and coed. There are visiting privileges in single-sex housing. Students may keep cars on campus.

Organizations: There are no fraternities or sororities. Students may participate in school organizations and such activities as the chorus, clubs, and publications. The campus Arts Center presents student and professional performances.

Sports: In addition to intercollegiate sports competition in 7 sports for men and 7 for women, there are 3 intramural programs for both sexes.

Handicapped: Wheelchair ramps, special parking, and elevators are provided for physically handicapped students.

Graduates: About 3% of the freshmen drop out by the end of their first year. About 65% remain to graduate. Approximately 10% go on to graduate study; 1% enter law school. Forty-two percent pursue careers in business and industry.

Services: Health care, psychological counseling, career counseling, placement service, tutoring, and remedial instruction are provided without charge.

Programs of Study: The college confers the B.A. or B.S. degree. Master's degrees are also awarded. Bachelor's degrees are offered in the following subjects: AREA STUDIES (American), BUSINESS (accounting, business administration, business education, management), EDUCATION (elementary, secondary, special), ENGLISH (English), FINE AND PERFORMING ARTS (art, art education, art history, music, music education, music therapy, studio art, theater/dramatics), HEALTH SCIENCES (nursing, speech therapy), LANGUAGES (French, German, Italian, Spanish), MATH AND SCIENCES (biochemistry, biology, chemistry, mathematics), PHILOSOPHY (philosophy, religion), PREPROFESSIONAL (dentistry, law, medicine, social work), SOCIAL SCIENCES (government/political science, history, psychology, social sciences, sociology). Twenty-seven percent of degrees granted are in social sciences, 18% in education, and 13% in fine and performing arts.

Required: There are general education requirements.

Special: Other majors are available through the 14-college consortium of the Rochester Area Colleges. Internships, study abroad, and independent study are offered.

580 NEW YORK

Honors: There are campus chapters of national honor societies in the following areas: biology, modern foreign languages, music, social sciences and history, and psychology.

Admissions: Eighty-three percent of applicants were admitted to the 1981–82 freshman class. For those who enrolled, the SAT scores were as follows: Verbal—26% scored below 500, 30% between 500 and 599, 6% between 600 and 700, and 0% above 700. Math scores are not available. Candidates must be in the top half of their graduating class and have an average of 80. Advanced placement or honor courses, recommendations by school officials, and personality also are important in determining admissions.

Procedure: Either the SAT or ACT is required. Application deadlines are open. Freshmen are admitted to all semesters. Notification of acceptance is on a rolling basis. A fee of $20 must accompany the application.

Special: There are early and deferred admissions plans. AP and CLEP credit is given.

Transfer: For fall 1981, 320 students applied and 198 enrolled. Transfers with an associate degree are granted junior status, 60 hours of credit, and a waiver of core requirements. Students must have a 2.0 GPA. D grades do not transfer except with the associate degree. Students must complete, at the college, 30 of the 180 credits needed for a bachelor's degree. The application deadlines are July 30 (fall) and January 10 (spring).

Visiting: Informal visits may be scheduled for Monday through Friday from 9 A.M. to 3 P.M.. Guides are provided. Visitors may sit in on classes and stay overnight at the school. Arrangements can be made through the admissions office.

Financial Aid: Seventy-five percent of students receive financial aid. Competitive scholarships, campus employment (including CWS), and loans are available. The college is a member of CSS. The FAF is required. The application deadline is March 30 (fall). Awards are made on a rolling basis.

Foreign Students: Fewer than 1% of the full-time students come from foreign countries. The college offers these students special counseling.

Admissions: Foreign students must score 525 on the TOEFL. No college entrance examination is required.

Procedure: The application deadlines are July 1 (fall) and October 1 (spring). Foreign students must present a certificate of good health completed by a physician. They must also present proof of funds adequate to cover 1 year of study. They must carry health insurance, which is available through the college.

Admissions Contact: Paul Buntich, Director of Admissions.

NEW SCHOOL FOR SOCIAL RESEARCH/ SEMINAR COLLEGE
(See Seminar College)

NEW YORK INSTITUTE OF TECHNOLOGY   D-5

Old Westbury, New York 11568   (516) 686-7520
Commack, New York 11725   (516) 499-8800
New York, New York 10023   (212) 399-8351

F/T: 4738M, 1544W   Faculty: 187; n/av
P/T: 2231M, 1077W   Ph.D.'s: 61%
Grad: 861M, 456W   S/F Ratio: 31 to 1
Year: sems, ss   Tuition: $3241
Appl: open,   R and B: $1800
4418 applied   3869 accepted   1692 enrolled
SAT: 404V 451M   ACT: 20   COMPETITIVE

New York Institute of Technology, a career-oriented college founded in 1955, offers programs in business, education, arts and sciences, and preprofessional fields. The library houses 130,000 volumes and an extensive microfilm collection. It subscribes to over 1700 periodicals.

Environment: Three campuses are maintained: one spreading over 750 acres in suburban Old Westbury, Long Island, 20 miles from New York City; a metropolitan center in Manhattan; and the Commack College Center, also in suburban Long Island. The New York College of Osteopathic Medicine is also a part of the school. Housing is provided in off-campus apartments under college control.

Student Life: Ninety-three percent of students are from New York, and 3% are from bordering states. None of the students live on campus. Sixty-eight percent are Catholic, 12% Protestant, and 8% Jewish. Fourteen percent of the students are minority-group members. Students may keep cars on campus. Day-care services are available to all students at the Commack College Center only.

Organizations: There are over 25 extracurricular activities, including fraternities and sororities, publications, radio stations, social, academic, and religious organizations, special-interest groups, student government, student courts, and the Women's Association.

Sports: There are 9 intercollegiate sports for men, and 5 for women. Ten intramural programs for both men and women are also available.

Handicapped: Ninety-five percent of the campus is accessible to the physically handicapped. Special parking, specially equipped rest rooms, elevators, wheelchair ramps, lowered telephones, and special class scheduling are provided. One percent of the students are visually impaired, and 1% are hearing impaired. A special counselor with assistants is provided, and a staff with knowledge of sign language is available.

Graduates: Thirty-three percent of the freshmen remain to graduate. Thirty percent of graduates continue their studies: 1% enter medical school, 1% dental school, and 1% law school. Eighty-five percent pursue careers in business and industry.

Services: Free health care, psychological counseling, career counseling, tutoring, remedial instruction, and placement service are provided.

Programs of Study: The college confers the B.A., B.S., B.F.A., B.T., B.Arch., and B.P. degrees. Associate, master's, and doctoral degrees are also conferred. The bachelor's degree is offered in the following subjects: BUSINESS (accounting, applied economics, business administration, business education, hotel and restaurant administration), EDUCATION (chemistry, occupational, physics), FINE AND PERFORMING ARTS (art education, communication arts, design graphics, fine arts, interior design), HEALTH SCIENCES (medical technology), MATH AND SCIENCES (computer science, electrical engineering technology, electromechanical computer technology, life sciences, mechanical engineering technology, mechanical technology, physical sciences), PREPROFESSIONAL (architecture), SOCIAL SCIENCES (behavioral sciences, government/political science, technological management).

Required: All undergraduates are required to take 2 years of English, 1 semester of speech, 1 year of history, 1 semester of science, and 1 semester of psychology.

Special: A general studies degree is offered, and student-designed majors are permitted. The institute offers both regular semesters and 5 8-week cycles for evening programs.

Honors: All major departments offer honors programs.

Admissions: Eighty-eight percent of applicants for the 1981–82 freshman class were accepted. The SAT scores of those who enrolled were as follows: Verbal—84% scored below 500, 12% between 500 and 599, 3% between 600 and 700, and 1% above 700; Math—61% scored below 500, 32% between 500 and 599, 6% between 600 and 700, and 1% above 700. On the ACT, 15% scored below 21, 50% between 21 and 23, 27% between 24 and 25, 7% between 26 and 28, and 1% above 28. Grade average and class standing requirements are dependent on choice of major. The high-school record is of major importance. Students who score below 400 on the SAT must take preparatory work.

Procedure: The SAT or ACT is required. The application deadlines are open. There is a rolling admissions plan, and freshmen are admitted each semester. A fee of $15 must accompany the application.

Special: The college has early decision, early admissions, and deferred admissions plans. There are special admissions procedures for the combined Baccalaureate/Osteopathic Physician (7-year) program. AP and CLEP credit is offered.

Transfer: For fall 1981, 1934 students applied, 893 were accepted, and 602 enrolled. Good academic standing is necessary. One academic year or 24 credits must be completed in residence, of the 120–169 credits needed for a bachelor's degree. Application deadlines are open.

Visiting: There are regularly scheduled orientations for prospective students. Informal visits and tours with guides are arranged by the office of admissions on an individual basis as requested. Visitors are sometimes allowed to sit in on classes.

Financial Aid: Eighty-three percent of all students receive financial aid. Four percent work part-time on campus. Average aid to freshmen from all sources covers 70% of costs. Over 100 freshman scholarships are available. Federal and state loans and work-study programs are also offered. The college is a member of CSS. The FAF is required. There is no deadline for filing. Financial need is the principal consideration in awarding aid.

Foreign Students: Eleven percent of the full-time students come from foreign countries. The institute offers these students an intensive English course, special counseling, and special organizations.

NEW YORK UNIVERSITY
New York, New York 10003   D-5
(212) 598-3591

F/T: 5500M, 5500W
P/T: 1000M, 1000W
Grad: 7500M, 7500W
Year: sems, ss
Appl: Feb. 1
8300 applied
SAT: 545V 565M

Faculty: 1300; I, ++$
Ph.D.'s: 90%
S/F Ratio: 13 to 1
Tuition: $5820
R and B: $3000
4700 accepted   2160 enrolled
VERY COMPETITIVE

New York University, founded in 1831, is a private liberal arts university consisting of 7 undergraduate colleges, including the College of Arts and Sciences; School of Education, Health, and Nursing; School of Arts; School of Continuing Education; School of Social Work; and College of Business and Public Administration. The university's libraries contain over 2 million volumes and 1.16 million microfilm items, and subscribe to 13,635 periodicals.

Environment: The campus is located around Washington Square in Greenwich Village, New York City. In addition, its facilities occupy other locations. University property, including that at Sterling Forest, where there is a research center, totals 200 acres. There is a new 3-story indoor athletic facility. Three high-rise dormitories house 1800 undergraduate students. The university also sponsors fraternity houses and both on-campus and off-campus apartments.

Student Life: Students come from all states; the majority, however, are from the New York City metropolitan area. Sixty-five percent of entering freshmen come from public schools. About 18% of the students live on campus. Forty-two percent are Catholic, 30% are Jewish, and 17% are Protestant. About 25% of the students are minority-group members. University housing is coed.

Organizations: Ten percent of the men belong to 2 local and 6 national fraternities; 2% of the women are members of 2 local and 2 national sororities. There are numerous honor, scholastic, religious, and professional societies, as well as special-interest clubs, student newspapers, and musical and dramatic activities.

Sports: The university fields 8 intercollegiate teams for men and 5 for women. There are 9 intramural sports for men and 9 for women.

Handicapped: Approximately 95% of the campus is accessible to handicapped students. Special facilities include wheelchair ramps, elevators, lowered drinking fountains and telephones, and specially equipped rest rooms and dormitories. Special class scheduling is also available. Three percent of the student body have visual impairments; 3% have hearing impairments. For these students there are special audio and visual equipment and interpreters. There is a staff of 6 for special counseling and assistance to handicapped students.

Graduates: The freshman dropout rate is about 15%, and 65% of the freshmen remain to graduate. Seventy-five percent of the graduates pursue advanced study.

Services: Students receive the following services free of charge: career counseling, health care, psychological counseling, and remedial instruction. Placement services and tutoring are available for a fee.

Programs of Study: The university confers the B.A., B.S., and B.F.A. degrees. Associate, master's, and doctoral degrees are also awarded. Bachelor's degrees are offered in the following subjects: AREA STUDIES (Asian, Afro-American, Judaic, Latin American, Medieval/Renaissance, Russian, urban), BUSINESS (accounting, business administration, business education, computer science, finance, management, marketing), EDUCATION (early childhood, elementary, health/physical, industrial, secondary, special), ENGLISH (English, journalism, literature, speech), FINE AND PERFORMING ARTS (art, art education, art history, dance, film/photography, music, music education, radio/TV, studio art, theater/dramatics), HEALTH SCIENCES (environmental health, nursing, occupational therapy, physical therapy, speech therapy), LANGUAGES (French, German, Greek/Latin, Hebrew, Italian, Portuguese, Russian, Spanish), MATH AND SCIENCES (applied science, biochemistry, biology, chemistry, mathematics, natural sciences, physical sciences, physics, statistics, zoology), PHILOSOPHY (classics, humanities, philosophy, religion), PREPROFESSIONAL (dentistry, engineering, home economics, law, medicine, social work, veterinary), SOCIAL SCIENCES (anthropology, economics, geography, government/political science, history, international relations, psychology, social sciences, sociology).

Special: Independent study is available. Courses may be elected in other schools of the university. Junior Year Abroad programs are conducted in France and Spain, and a junior year in New York program is offered for students of other colleges. Student-designed majors are available.

Honors: Most departments offer honors programs for qualified students. Five national honor societies, including Phi Beta Kappa, have chapters on campus.

Admissions: Fifty-seven percent of those who applied were accepted for the 1981–82 freshman class. The SAT scores for a recent freshman class were as follows: Verbal—42% scored between 500 and 599, 20% between 600 and 700, and 4% above 700; Math—46% scored between 500 and 599, 28% between 600 and 700, and 4% above 700. While admissions requirements vary somewhat for the different colleges, in general a candidate should have a grade average of at least 80 and a combined score of 1100 or better on the SAT. Usually 16 Carnegie units are expected. Disadvantaged students with lower credentials have a stronger chance at admission than these figures suggest, however, and special academic support and financial aid programs are available. An interview or audition may be required at the discretion of the admissions office. Advanced placement or honor courses, high school recommendations, and evidence of special talent are also considered.

Procedure: The SAT or ACT is required. Freshmen are admitted to each semester. The deadlines for application are February 1 (fall), January 1 (spring), and May 1 (summer). Nonadmissible candidates are notified promptly. A $25 fee must accompany the application.

Special: Early and deferred admissions plans and an early decision plan are available. AP, CLEP, and PEP credit is given.

Transfer: For fall 1981, 4600 students applied, 2600 were accepted, and 1700 enrolled. A GPA of 2.5 is required for applicants from 4-year colleges, and 3.0 for applicants from 2-year colleges. D and C— grades do not transfer. Students must spend 2 semesters (fall and spring) in residence and complete at least 32 of the 128 credits necessary for a bachelor's degree. Application deadlines are July 1 (fall), January 1 (winter), and May 1 (summer).

Visiting: There are no regularly scheduled orientations for prospective students, but informal visits can be arranged for weekdays (9 A.M. to 5 P.M.) by calling (212) 598-3588. Guides are available, and visitors may sit in on classes.

Financial Aid: Approximately 67% of students receive financial aid administered by the university. Five percent work part-time on campus; there are good employment opportunities both in the city and at the university, as well as work-study programs in many departments. Average aid to freshmen is $2391. Scholarships, loans and grants are available. The university is a member of the CSS, and the FAF is required of aid applicants. Deadlines for aid application are February 15 (fall) and October 15 (spring).

Foreign Students: Seven percent of the full-time students come from 108 foreign countries. The university offers these students an intensive English course and program, special counseling, and special organizations.

Admissions: Foreign students must take an English proficiency exam but are not required to take a college entrance exam.

Procedure: Application deadlines are May 15 (fall), November 15 (spring), and April 1 (summer). Foreign students must present proof of a doctor's examination and proof of funds adequate to cover one year (9 months) of study. They must also carry health insurance, which is available through the university for a fee.

Admissions Contact: Harold R. Doughty, Director of Admissions.

NIAGARA UNIVERSITY
Niagara University, New York 14109   A-3
(716) 285-1212

F/T: 1300M, 1600W
P/T: 125M, 210W
Grad: 436M, 284W
Year: sems, ss
Appl: Aug. 1
2325 applied
SAT: 450V 450M

Faculty: 173; IIA, —$
Ph.D.'s: 42%
S/F Ratio: 16 to 1
Tuition: $3890
R and B: $2450
1951 accepted   771 enrolled
ACT: 20   COMPETITIVE

Niagara University, founded in 1856, is a Roman Catholic university operated by the Vincentian Fathers. The library contains 193,510 volumes and 24,500 microfilm items, and subscribes to 1454 periodicals.

Environment: The 160-acre suburban campus, located on a ridge overlooking the gorge of the Niagara River, is about 25 miles from Buffalo. There are 24 buildings, including an 8-story residence hall for men and women, a student center, and television and radio studios.

Student Life: Most students are from New York or surrounding states. Sixty-two percent of the entering freshmen come from public schools. Sixty percent of the students live on campus. Sixty-nine percent are Catholic, 15% Protestant, and 2% Jewish. University housing is single-sex; there are visiting privileges. Students may keep cars on campus.

Organizations: There are no fraternities or sororities at the university. Extracurricular activities and social events include theater performances, the University Singers, clubs, an art gallery, and special-interest organizations. The campus is 4 miles from Niagara Falls, 90 miles from Toronto, Canada.

Sports: There are 12 intercollegiate teams for men and 6 for women. There are also 5 intramural sports for men and 5 for women.

Handicapped: Special services for handicapped students include wheelchair ramps, parking areas, elevators, and specially equipped rest rooms. One special counselor works with handicapped students. There are no students with visual or hearing impairments.

Graduates: Nine percent of the freshmen drop out by the end of their first year. Sixty-five percent remain to graduate. Thirty-seven percent of the students go on to graduate school; 1% enter medical school, 1% dental school, and 2% law school. Forty-seven percent of the graduates pursue careers in business and industry.

Services: The following services are provided to students free of charge: health care, psychological counseling, placement and career counseling (for graduates as well as undergraduates), tutoring, and remedial instruction.

Programs of Study: The university confers the B.A., B.S., and B.B.A. degrees. It also offers associate and master's degrees. Bachelor's degrees are offered in the following subjects: BUSINESS (accounting, business administration, business education, finance, management, marketing, travel, transportation, and tourism), EDUCATION (secondary), ENGLISH (communications, English), FINE AND PERFORMING ARTS (theater/dramatics), HEALTH SCIENCES (nursing), LANGUAGES (French, Spanish), MATH AND SCIENCES (biochemistry, biology, chemistry, mathematics, natural sciences), PHILOSOPHY (philosophy, religion), PREPROFESSIONAL (dentistry, engineering, law, medicine), SOCIAL SCIENCES (criminal justice, government/political science, history, psychology, sociology, social work). Forty percent of all undergraduate degrees are conferred in business, 30% in health sciences, and 14% in social sciences.

Required: All students are required to earn 9 credits in religious studies.

Special: A study abroad program and a 3-year bachelor's degree are available. There is a preengineering program in conjunction with the University of Detroit.

Admissions: About 84% of those who applied were accepted for the 1981–82 freshman class. Among those who enrolled, the SAT scores were as follows: Verbal—82% scored below 500, 15% between 500 and 599, 2% between 600 and 700, and 1% above 700; Math—62% scored below 500, 30% between 500 and 599, 7% between 600 and 700, and 1% above 700. On the ACT, 46% scored below 21, 27% between 21 and 23, 15% between 24 and 25, 7% between 26 and 28, and 5% above 28. Applicants must be graduates of accredited high schools, should have completed at least 16 academic units of work, should have at least a 2.0 GPA, and should rank in the top half of their graduating class. In evaluating a candidate, the four most important factors are the high school record, test scores, class rank, and the recommendation of the high school.

Procedure: The SAT or ACT is required and should be taken by January of the senior year. Deadlines for applications are August 1 (fall) and December 15 (spring). Freshmen are also admitted in the summer. Admissions are granted on a rolling basis. There is a $15 application fee.

Special: The university has early decision, early admissions, and deferred admissions plans. AP and CLEP credit is available.

Transfer: For fall 1981, the university received 343 transfer applications, accepted 296, and enrolled 176 students. A 2.0 GPA is needed. D grades do not transfer. A combined SAT score of 850 and an ACT of 20 are required. The last 2 semesters must be completed in residence. From 120 to 126 credits are needed for a bachelor's degree. Application deadlines are August 1 (fall) and December 15 (spring).

Visiting: Interviews and campus tours are scheduled on a regular basis. Guides are also available for informal visits to the university. Visitors may sit in on classes but may not stay overnight at the school. Weekdays from 9:30 A.M. to 4 P.M. and Saturdays from 10 A.M. to 1 P.M. are the best times to visit. The office of admissions handles the arrangements.

Financial Aid: Eighty-nine percent of all students receive financial aid. Twenty-three percent work part-time on campus. Average aid to freshmen from all sources is $3600. Scholarships, nursing student loans, and NDSL are available. The university participates in the CWS program. The FAF is required. The deadline for aid applications is March 1.

Foreign Students: One percent of the full-time students come from foreign countries. The university offers these students special counseling and special organizations.

Admissions: Foreign students must score 500 on the TOEFL. No college entrance examination is required.

Procedure: The application deadlines are August 1 (fall) and December 15 (spring). Foreign students must submit the university's own health form. They must present proof of funds adequate to cover their entire period of study. They must also carry health insurance, which is available through the university for a fee.

Admissions Contact: George C. Pachter, Dean of Admissions.

NYACK COLLEGE D–5
Nyack, New York 10960 (914) 358-1710

F/T: 217M, 289W
P/T: 25M, 38W
Grad: 124M, 52W
Year: 4-1-4, ss
Appl: open
339 applied 188 accepted 137 enrolled
SAT: required ACT: 19 COMPETITIVE

Faculty: 35; IIA, n/av
Ph.D.'s: 31%
S/F Ratio: 14 to 1
Tuition: $3395
R and B: $1925

Nyack College, established in 1882, is a private liberal arts institution affiliated with the Christian and Missionary Alliance. It provides training for various vocations, including religious. The library contains 64,650 volumes and 563 microfilm items, and subscribes to 603 periodicals.

Environment: Located on a hillside overlooking the Hudson River 20 miles from New York City, the 66-acre suburban campus has 10 major buildings. About 506 students are housed in the 5 dormitories.

Student Life: About 49% of the students are from New York, and 50% come from bordering states. Approximately 80% of entering freshmen attended public schools. All but 15% reside on campus. Ninety-nine percent of students are Protestant. All students are required to attend daily chapel and must observe curfew and sign-out regulations. College housing is single-sex. There are no visiting privileges. Students may keep cars on campus.

Organizations: There are Protestant organizations on campus. Fifteen extracurricular activities are available to students. There are no fraternities or sororities.

Sports: Nyack College participates on an intercollegiate level in 6 sports for men and 5 for women. There are 4 intramural sports for men and 2 for women.

Handicapped: Special facilities for the physically handicapped will be available in new residence halls scheduled for completion in 1982.

Graduates: Recently, the freshman dropout rate has been 27%; 45% have remained to graduate. About 61% of the students pursued graduate study after graduation, with 1% entering law school.

Services: The following services are available free of charge to students: placement, career counseling, psychological counseling, and tutoring. Remedial instruction and health care are available on a fee basis.

Programs of Study: The college offers the B.A., B.S., and B.M. degrees. It also offers associate and master's degrees. Bachelor's degrees are offered in the following subjects: EDUCATION (elementary), ENGLISH (English), FINE AND PERFORMING ARTS (music, music education, sacred music), PHILOSOPHY (philosophy, religion), PREPROFESSIONAL (ministry, missions), SOCIAL SCIENCES (history, psychology, social sciences). About 41% of the degrees conferred are in preprofessional studies, 28% in social sciences, and 18% in English.

Required: All students are required to take courses in physical education, the Bible, history of Western Civilization, general psychology, introduction to the fine arts, English composition, and literature.

Special: Pass/no credit option is available for 1 elective per semester. Study abroad is offered.

Admissions: About 55% of those who applied were accepted for the 1981-82 freshman class. Of those who enrolled in a recent freshman class, the SAT scores were as follows: Verbal—22% scored between 500 and 599, and 6% between 600 and 700; Math—33% scored between 500 and 599, 16% between 600 and 700, and 2% above 700. Except in the case of disadvantaged students, the minimum acceptable SAT score is a composite of 850. The college's program for disadvantaged students includes pass/no credit options in all courses, unlimited time for completion of degree requirements, and special counseling. The college requires rank in the top two-fifths of the high school class. The minimum grade average is 2.0. The candidate must be a high school graduate and must present 16 Carnegie units. Other factors include impressions made during an interview, recommendations by school officials, and advanced placement or honor courses.

Procedure: The SAT or ACT is required and should be taken by July for fall admission. The college has a policy of rolling admission. Freshmen are admitted to all sessions. There is a $15 application fee. An interview is recommended.

Special: There is an early decision plan. AP and CLEP credit is available.

Transfer: For fall 1981, 54 transfer students enrolled. Students must have a composite SAT score of 850 and an ACT score of 19. A 2.0 GPA is required. D grades do not transfer. The last 30 credits must be earned in residence, out of the 130 needed for a bachelor's degree. Application deadlines are open.

Visiting: Regularly scheduled orientations are held for prospective students. Informal guided tours and classroom visits are also available. Visits are best scheduled Mondays, Thursdays, and Fridays. For further information pertaining to overnight accommodations and campus visits, prospective students should contact the office of admissions.

Financial Aid: About 52% of all students receive financial aid. The average aid awarded to freshmen from all sources is $600. Aid is available in the form of scholarships, NDSL, and work-study assignments. The FAF is required.

Foreign Students: Three percent of the full-time students come from foreign countries. The college offers these students special organizations.

Admissions: Foreign students must score 500 on the TOEFL. No college entrance examination is required.

Procedure: Application deadlines are open. Foreign students must present a medical form completed by a physician. They must also present proof of funds adequate for their entire period of study. They must carry health insurance, which is available through the college for a fee.

Admissions Contact: Dan Rinker, Director of Admissions and Financial Aid.

PACE UNIVERSITY/ COLLEGE OF WHITE PLAINS
White Plains, New York 10603   (914) 682-7070   D-5

F/T: 276M, 435W
P/T: 269M, 571W
Grad: 1081M, 871W
Year: 4-1-4, ss
Appl: Aug. 15
775 applied   390 accepted   175 enrolled
SAT: 480V 525M   COMPETITIVE
Faculty: 79; n/av
Ph.D.'s: n/av
S/F Ratio: 19 to 1
Tuition: $3848
R and B: $2700

The College of White Plains, founded in 1923, is a liberal arts college within Pace University. The library contains 94,500 volumes and 3650 microfilm reels, and subscribes to 810 periodicals.

Environment: The campus is situated in a suburban residential area of White Plains, 22 miles from New York City. Facilities include modern residence halls and dining facilities.

Student Life: Most of the students are from New York. About 15% of the students are minority-group members. College housing is coed. Students may keep cars on campus.

Organizations: Extracurricular activities include special-interest clubs, publications, performing groups, and service groups.

Sports: The college competes in 9 intercollegiate sports for men and 8 for women. There are 7 intramural sports for both men and women.

Handicapped: There are special facilities for handicapped students.

Graduates: Thirteen percent of the freshmen drop out by the end of their first year. About 27% remain to graduate.

Services: Students receive the following services free of charge: psychological counseling, placement, career counseling, tutoring, and remedial instruction. Health care is available on a fee basis.

Programs of Study: The college confers the B.A., B.S., B.B.A., and B.P.S. degrees. Associate programs are also available. Bachelor's degrees are offered in the following subjects: BUSINESS (accounting, business education, computer science, finance, international management, management, management information systems, marketing, retail management), EDUCATION (children's studies, early childhood, elementary), ENGLISH (English, journalism), FINE AND PERFORMING ARTS (performing arts), LANGUAGES (French, Spanish), MATH AND SCIENCES (mathematics), PREPROFESSIONAL (dentistry, law, medicine), SOCIAL SCIENCES (community development, history, human services, liberal studies). Forty-three percent of the degrees are conferred in social sciences, 37% in business, and 20% in English and journalism.

Special: Internships are available in most majors. A liberal studies program is offered.

Honors: An honors program is offered in all majors. Three honor societies have chapters on campus.

Admissions: Fifty percent of those who applied were accepted for the 1981-82 freshman class. Of those who enrolled, the SAT scores were as follows: Verbal—70% scored below 500, 25% between 500 and 599, 5% between 600 and 700, and 0% above 700; Math—54% scored below 500, 37% between 500 and 599, 8% between 600 and 700, and 1% above 700. Pace considers the student's high school average to be of primary importance. A minimum of 16 units from an accredited secondary school is required. Students should rank in the upper half of their class. A 3.0 GPA is recommended. Also considered are advanced placement or honor courses, recommendations, and extracurricular activities.

Procedure: The SAT or ACT is required. A personal interview is recommended. Application deadlines are August 15 (fall) and January 15 (winter and spring). A rolling admissions plan is followed. The application fee is $15.

Special: The college offers early decision, early admissions, and deferred admissions plans. AP and CLEP credit is granted.

Transfer: For fall 1981, 281 applications were received, 157 were accepted, and 100 students enrolled. A 2.5 GPA is necessary. D grades do not transfer. Fifty percent of the 128 credits needed for a bachelor's degree must be completed in residence. Application deadlines are August 15 (fall) and January 15 (spring).

Visiting: Orientations are scheduled regularly for prospective students. Guides are available for informal campus tours. Visitors may sit in on classes and stay overnight at the school. Visits are best scheduled on weekdays. The admissions office should be contacted for arrangements.

Financial Aid: Ninety-two percent of the students receive financial aid. Eleven percent work part-time on campus. Average aid to freshmen from all sources covers 23% of costs. University scholarships, grants-in-aid, PELL Grants, SEOG, NDSL, guaranteed loans, and campus employment (including CWS) are available. Tuition may be paid in installments. The college is a member of CSS. The FAF is required and should be filed by March 15.

Foreign Students: Two percent of the full-time students come from foreign countries. The college offers these students special organizations.

Admissions: Foreign students must score 500 on the TOEFL. No college entrance examination is required.

Procedure: Application deadlines are June 1 (fall) and November 1 (spring). Foreign students must present proof of adequate funds.

Admissions Contact: Mark Brooks, Director of Admissions.

PACE UNIVERSITY/ NEW YORK CAMPUS
New York, New York 10038   (212) 285-3323   D-5

F/T: 1969M, 2195W
P/T: 2549M, 3777W
Grad: 2177M, 1420W
Year: sems, ss
Appl: Aug. 15
3357 applied   2283 accepted   1108 enrolled
SAT: 480V 495M   COMPETITIVE
Faculty: 213; IIA, ++$
Ph.D.'s: n/av
S/F Ratio: 22 to 1
Tuition: $3848
R and B: $2700

Pace University, founded in 1906, is composed of the Dyson College of Arts and Sciences, the Lubin School of Business Administration, the School of Education, and the University College/Lubin Graduate

584 NEW YORK

School of Business. The library houses 293,000 volumes and 21,000 microfilm reels, and subscribes to 1290 periodicals.

Environment: The main campus, located in lower Manhattan, includes a residence tower for 380 students, a cafeteria, and a snack bar.

Student Life: About 70% of the undergraduates are from New York. Fifty-five percent of the students come from public schools. Seven percent of the students live in the dormitory; however, Pace is largely a commuter school. Forty percent of the students are minority-group members. Campus housing is coed. Day-care services are available to full-time students, faculty, and staff.

Organizations: There are 6 fraternities and 3 sororities. Extracurricular activities include special-interest clubs, debate team, ecology club, and publications.

Sports: Pace competes intercollegiately in 9 sports for men and 8 for women. There are 7 intramural sports for both men and women.

Handicapped: Special facilities are available for handicapped students.

Graduates: Eighteen percent of the freshmen drop out during their first year. Fifty-eight percent remain to graduate. About 33% of the graduates pursue advanced degrees.

Services: Students receive the following services free of charge: psychological counseling, placement and career counseling, tutoring, and remedial instruction. Health care is available on a fee basis.

Programs of Study: The university confers the B.A., B.S., B.B.A., and B.P.S. degrees. Associate, master's, and doctoral programs are also available. Bachelor's degrees are offered in the following subjects: BUSINESS (accounting, banking, business education, computer science, economics, finance, international management, labor management relations, management, management information systems, management science, marketing, real estate/insurance, retail management), EDUCATION (early childhood, elementary, office administration), ENGLISH (literature, speech, speech arts, speech communications, speech pathology, writing), FINE AND PERFORMING ARTS (history of drama, music education, theater/dramatics), HEALTH SCIENCES (medical technology, speech therapy), LANGUAGES (French, Spanish), MATH AND SCIENCES (biology, chemistry, computer science, mathematics, physical sciences), PREPROFESSIONAL (dentistry, law, medicine), SOCIAL SCIENCES (anthropology, economics, government/political science, history, human relations, industrial relations, psychology, social sciences, sociology). Sixty-eight percent of the degrees are conferred in business, 17% in social sciences.

Special: Pace offers a cooperative education program and an internship in public accounting. Students with superior grades can earn a combined B.B.A.-M.B.A. in public accounting in 4 or 5 years. Outstanding freshmen may plan their own programs in consultation with a faculty advisor.

Honors: Ten honor societies have chapters on campus.

Admissions: Sixty-eight percent of those who applied were accepted for the 1981–82 freshman class. Of those who enrolled, the SAT scores were as follows: Verbal—81% scored below 500, 16% between 500 and 599, 3% between 600 and 700, and 0% above 700; Math—64% scored below 500, 28% between 500 and 599, 7% between 600 and 700, and 1% above 700. Pace considers the student's high school average to be of primary importance. A minimum of 16 units from an accredited high school is required. Students should rank in the upper half of their class and have a 3.0 GPA. Also considered are advanced placement or honor courses, recommendations, and extracurricular activities.

Procedure: The SAT or ACT is required and should be taken by the fall of the senior year. Application deadlines are August 15 (fall), December 15 (spring), and May 15 (summer). Notification is on a rolling basis. The application fee is $15.

Special: Early admissions, early decision, and deferred admissions are available. CLEP and AP credit is given. Credit is also granted for AT scores of 600 or above.

Transfer: For fall 1981, 996 applications were received, 521 were accepted, and 289 students enrolled. Transfers are accepted for all classes. A 2.0 GPA must be maintained. D grades do not transfer. There is a 32-credit residency requirement; 128 credits must be completed for a bachelor's degree. The application deadlines are the same as those for freshmen.

Visiting: Orientations are scheduled regularly for prospective students. Guides are available for informal campus visits. Visitors may sit in on classes and stay overnight at the school. Visits are best scheduled on weekdays. The admissions office should be contacted for arrangements.

Financial Aid: About 91% of the students receive financial aid. The average aid awarded to freshmen from all sources is $3382. University scholarships, grants-in-aid, PELL Grants, SEOG, NDSL, guaranteed loans, and campus employment (including CWS) are available. Tuition may be paid in installments. The university is a member of CSS. The FAF is required and should be filed by March 15.

Foreign Students: Fewer than 1% of the full-time students come from foreign countries. The university offers these students an intensive English course, an intensive English program, special counseling, and special organizations.

Admissions: Foreign students must take the TOEFL or the university's own test. They must score 500 on the TOEFL. They must also take the SAT or ACT. ATs are recommended.

Procedure: Application deadlines are June 1 (fall) and November 1 (spring). Foreign students must present proof of funds adequate to cover 4 years of study. There is a special, one-time fee for English and speech tests.

Admissions Contact: Stuart L. Medow, Director of Admissions.

PACE UNIVERSITY/ PLEASANTVILLE/BRIARCLIFF D–5
Pleasantville, New York 10570   (914) 769-3788

F/T: 1158M, 1426W	Faculty: 160; n/av
P/T: 668M, 1126W	Ph.D.'s: n/av
Grad: 26M, 259W	S/F Ratio: 18 to 1
Year: 4-1-4, ss	Tuition: $3848
Appl: Aug. 15	R and B: $2700
2289 applied	1380 accepted	638 enrolled
SAT: 505V 500M		COMPETITIVE

Opened in 1963, Pace University in Pleasantville/Briarcliff maintains its individuality while drawing strength from the 75-year-old traditions of Pace University in New York. Undergraduate degree programs are offered in liberal arts and sciences, business, education, and nursing. The library contains 133,309 volumes and 8080 microfilm reels, and subscribes to 962 periodicals.

Environment: The 245-acre suburban Pleasantville/Briarcliff campus is located 35 miles north of New York City. Among the facilities are modern residence and dining halls and a student center.

Student Life: About 72% of the students come from public schools. Most students reside at home. University housing is coed. Students may keep cars on campus. Day-care services are available to full-time students, faculty, and staff for a fee.

Organizations: There are 1 fraternity and 1 sorority on campus. Student activities include performing groups, drama groups, and special-interest clubs.

Sports: An intercollegiate sports program is available in 11 sports for men and 9 for women. There are 8 intramural sports for both men and women.

Handicapped: Special facilities are available for handicapped students.

Graduates: Nineteen percent of the freshmen drop out during their first year. Forty-four percent remain to graduate.

Services: Students receive the following services free of charge: psychological counseling, placement and career counseling, tutoring, and remedial instruction. Health care is available on a fee basis.

Programs of Study: The college confers the B.A., B.S., B.B.A., and B.P.S. degrees. Associate and master's programs are also offered. Bachelor's degrees are offered in the following subjects: BUSINESS (accounting, business education, computer science, finance, international management, management, management information systems, marketing, retail management), EDUCATION (early childhood, elementary), ENGLISH (literature and communications), FINE AND PERFORMING ARTS (art, performing arts), HEALTH SCIENCES (nursing), LANGUAGES (French, Spanish), MATH AND SCIENCES (biology, chemistry, mathematics, physical sciences), PREPROFESSIONAL (dentistry, law, medicine, veterinary), SOCIAL SCIENCES (criminal justice, history, human relations, psychology, social sciences). Forty-seven percent of the degrees are conferred in business, 28% in health sciences.

Special: Student-designed majors are permitted. A restored farm on campus serves as an ecology center and provides facilities for interdisciplinary ecological studies and conservation programs.

Honors: There are 3 honor societies on campus.

Admissions: Sixty percent of those who applied were accepted for the 1981–82 freshman class. Of those who enrolled, the SAT scores were as follows: Verbal—72% scored below 500, 24% between 500 and 599, 4% between 600 and 700, and 0% above 700; Math—43% scored below 500, 42% between 500 and 599, 14% between 600 and 700, and 1% above 700. Pace considers the student's high school average to be of primary importance. A minimum of 16 units from an accredited secondary school is required. Students should rank in the upper half of their class and have a 3.0 high school GPA. Also considered are advanced placement or honor courses, recommendations, and extracurricular activities.

Procedure: The SAT or ACT is required. Application deadlines are August 15 (fall) and January 15 (spring). Notification is on a rolling basis. The application fee is $15.

Special: There are early decision, early admissions, and deferred admissions plans. AP and CLEP credit is granted, as is credit for AT scores of 600 or above.

Transfer: For fall 1981, 994 applications were received, 621 were accepted, and 359 students enrolled. An associate degree or good academic standing, and a 2.5 GPA are required. D grades do not transfer. Half of the 128 credits needed for a bachelor's degree must be completed in residence. Application deadlines are the same as those for freshman applicants.

Visiting: There are regularly scheduled orientations for prospective students. Guides are available for informal campus tours. Visits are best scheduled on weekdays. Visitors may sit in on classes and stay overnight at the school. The admissions office should be contacted for arrangements.

Financial Aid: About 81% of the students receive financial aid. Average aid awarded to freshmen from all sources is $3831. University scholarships, grants-in-aid, PELL Grants, SEOG, NDSL, guaranteed loans, campus employment (including CWS), and federal nursing scholarships and loans are available. Tuition may be paid in installments. The university is a member of CSS. The FAF must be filed by March 15.

Foreign Students: Fewer than 1% of the full-time students come from foreign countries. The university offers these students special counseling and special organizations.

Admissions: Foreign students must score 500 on the TOEFL. No college entrance examination is required.

Procedure: Application deadlines are June 1 (fall) and November 1 (spring). Foreign students must present proof of adequate funds.

Admissions Contact: Richard A. Avitabile, Director of Admissions.

PARSONS SCHOOL OF DESIGN   D-5
New York, New York 10011   (212) 741-8910

F/T: 650M, 850W   Faculty: n/av; IIB, —$
P/T: none   Ph.D.'s: n/av
Grad: 15M, 25W   S/F Ratio: n/av
Year: sems   Tuition: $5080
Appl: open   R and B: $2900
SAT: 510V 490M   ACT: 19   SPECIAL

Parsons School of Design is an independent, professional art school offering instruction in such disciplines as graphics, illustration, fine arts and crafts, environmental design, and fashion design. The library contains 33,000 volumes and 35,000 slides and plates, and subscribes to 130 periodicals.

Environment: The campus consists of 4 buildings and is located in the northern part of Greenwich Village, in Manhattan. There is 1 dormitory which accommodates 175 students.

Student Life: About 27% of the students come from New York State. Thirty-five percent of the students live in the dormitory. Twenty-seven percent of the students are minority-group members. School housing is coed. Students may keep cars on campus.

Organizations: There are no fraternities or sororities at the school. Extracurricular activities include a school newspaper, an exhibition committee, and a film and lecture series. Dances and parties are also popular. The cultural resources of New York City are within easy access to students.

Handicapped: One hundred percent of the campus is accessible to handicapped students. Special facilities include wheelchair ramps, elevators, specially equipped rest rooms, and lowered drinking fountains and telephones. There are no students with visual impairments. Fewer than 1% of the students have hearing impairments. Recording and note-taking services are available for these students.

Graduates: About 15% of the freshmen drop out by the end of their first year; 64% remain to graduate. About 15% of the students pursue graduate studies after leaving Parsons.

Services: Placement, career counseling services (for graduates as well as undergraduates), tutoring, and remedial instruction are provided without charge. Health care and psychological counseling are also available for a fee.

Programs of Study: The school confers the B.F.A. degree. Master's degrees are also granted. Bachelor's degrees are offered in the following subjects: FINE AND PERFORMING ARTS (art education, art history, crafts, environmental and interior design, fashion design, fashion illustration, film/photography, graphic design, illustration, product design, studio art).

Required: All students are required to take art history. The freshman year is a general art and design program taken by all students.

Special: The school offers a full-time program in Paris and a 3-year bachelor's degree program.

Admissions: About 38% of those who applied were accepted for the 1981-82 freshman class. The SAT scores of those who enrolled were as follows: Verbal—37% scored below 500, 46% between 500 and 599, 13% between 600 and 700, and 4% above 700; Math—52% scored below 500, 40% between 500 and 599, 7% between 600 and 700, and 1% above 700. No minimum class rank or grade average is required. Applicants must be graduates of accredited high schools and should have completed 16 Carnegie units of work, as much of it in art as possible. Evidence of special talents (portfolio), impressions made during an interview, leadership record, and character and personality are considered important.

Procedure: The SAT or ACT is required. A personal interview is required of applicants living within 200 miles of New York City. The deadline for applications is open. Admissions are granted on a rolling basis. The CRDA is observed. There is a $25 application fee.

Special: The school has an early admissions plan with a rolling deadline. Disadvantaged students from New York State may be admitted under the HEOP program.

Transfer: For fall 1981, 800 transfer applications were received, 350 were accepted, and 200 students were enrolled. Transfers are accepted in the freshman (second semester), sophomore, and junior classes. D grades do not transfer. Parsons has a residency requirement of 2 years. Sixty-seven credits must be completed at the school, out of the 134 needed for a bachelor's degree. Application deadlines are the same as those for freshmen.

Visiting: There are regularly scheduled orientations for prospective students. Student-guided tours are available by appointment. Visitors may sit in on classes but may not stay overnight at the school. The best time to visit is when classes are in session. The admissions office handles the arrangements.

Financial Aid: Seventy-eight percent of all students receive some form of financial aid from the school. Twenty-six percent work part-time on campus. About 100 scholarships are provided to freshmen yearly. Work-study is available in all departments. The school is a member of CSS. The FAF is required. Tuition may be payed in installments. The deadlines for aid applications are March 1 (fall) and December 1 (spring).

Foreign Students: The school offers foreign students special counseling.

Admissions: Foreign students must score 500 on the TOEFL. No college entrance examination is required.

Procedure: Application deadlines are open. Foreign students must present a physician's statement of health. They must also present proof of funds adequate to cover 1 year of study.

Admissions Contact: Thomas Heinegg, Director of Admissions.

POLYTECHNIC INSTITUTE   D-5
OF NEW YORK
Brooklyn, New York 11201   (212) 643-2150
Farmingdale, New York 11735   (516) 454-5101

F/T: 1836M, 251W   Faculty: 220; n/av
P/T: 582M, 72W   Ph.D.'s: 90%
Grad: 1837M, 250W   S/F Ratio: 10 to 1
Year: sems, ss   Tuition: $5510
Appl: open   R and B: $1150
1736 applied   1259 accepted   562 enrolled
SAT: 498V 620M   HIGHLY COMPETITIVE

Polytechnic Institute of New York, founded in 1854, is a nonsectarian, scientific-technological college under private control. In 1973, the institute merged with New York University's School of Engineering and Science. The library contains more than 265,000 volumes and 500,000 microfilm items, and subscribes to 2500 periodicals.

586 NEW YORK

Environment: The undergraduate campus occupies more than .3 acres in Brooklyn. A 25-acre suburban campus in Farmingdale, Long Island, offers a variety of undergraduate and graduate courses. An evening graduate program is available on the White Plains campus in Westchester. The Microwave Research Institute, the Polymer Research Institute, the Center for Urban Environmental Studies, and the Institute of Imaging Sciences are all headquartered at the Brooklyn campus. Limited housing is available near the Brooklyn campus. There is a residence hall at the Farmingdale campus.

Student Life: Most of the students come from the New York metropolitan area, although the institute seeks a wider distribution of its student body. About 2% of the students live in approved housing. Forty percent are minority-group members. Institute housing is coed. Students may keep cars on campus.

Organizations: There are 6 fraternities on campus, including 3 that offer housing facilities. There are no sororities. Extracurricular activities include special-interest clubs, religious groups, musical groups, publications, and student government.

Sports: The institute fields intercollegiate teams in 6 sports for men and 2 for women. There are 7 intramurals for men and 3 for women.

Handicapped: The small Brooklyn campus is generally accessible to handicapped students. The institute plans renovations to eliminate any existing barriers to handicapped students.

Graduates: Ten percent of the freshmen drop out by the end of their first year. About 65% of the students remain to graduate. Five percent pursue advanced study after graduation. Ninety-five percent enter careers in business and industry.

Services: Among the free services provided to students are career counseling, placement services, tutoring, and remedial instruction.

Programs of Study: The institute confers the B.S. degree. Master's and doctoral programs are also available. Bachelor's degrees are offered in the following subjects: BUSINESS (computer science, information management), ENGLISH (journalism), MATH AND SCIENCES (biology, chemistry, mathematics, physics), PHILOSOPHY (humanities), PREPROFESSIONAL (engineering—aerospace, engineering—chemical, engineering—civil, engineering—electrical, engineering—industrial, engineering—mechanical, engineering—metallurgical, engineering—nuclear), SOCIAL SCIENCES (social sciences).

Required: All students are required to take courses in composition and world history. Most students must take courses in mathematics, chemistry, physics, social sciences, physical education, and a foreign language in certain departments.

Special: An extensive system of computers for laboratory and independent studies permits course offerings in all aspects of computer science.

Honors: Thirteen honor societies have chapters on campus.

Admissions: About 73% of those who applied were accepted for the 1981–82 freshman class. The SAT scores of those who enrolled were as follows: Verbal—30% scored below 500, 57% between 500 and 599, 11% between 600 and 700, and 2% above 700; Math—2% scored below 500, 42% between 500 and 599, 45% between 600 and 700, and 11% above 700. Applicants must be graduates of accredited high schools with 18 units of academic work. Other factors considered are advanced placement or honor courses, special talents, and recommendations.

Procedure: The SAT or ACT is required, as are ATs in English composition, one laboratory science, and Math (Level I or II). The application deadline is open. Notification is on a rolling basis. There is a $20 application fee.

Special: The institute has early decision, early admissions, and deferred admissions plans. AP credit is available.

Transfer: For fall 1981, 557 students applied, 345 were accepted, and 225 enrolled. A 2.7 GPA is required. D grades do not transfer. Students must have a score of 550 on the Math SAT. Thirty-six semester hours in upperclass subjects must be taken in residence, of the 136 needed for a bachelor's degree. Application deadlines are open.

Financial Aid: About 80% of the students receive financial aid. Five percent work part-time on campus. Average aid awarded to freshmen from all sources is $2200. The institute offers scholarships and grants, loans, and part-time employment. The institute is a member of CSS. The FAF is required and must be filed by February 1 (fall) and October 1 (spring and summer).

Foreign Students: Twelve percent of the full-time students come from foreign countries. The institute offers these students special counseling and special organizations.

Admissions: Foreign students must score 500 on the TOEFL. They must also take the SAT or ACT. All except HEOP students must score 550 on each SAT.

Procedure: Application deadlines are May 1 (fall) and November 1 (spring). Foreign students must present proof of health. They must also carry health insurance. Proof of funds adequate to cover study at the institute is also required.

Admissions Contact: G. Peter Cooney, Associate Director of Admissions.

PRATT INSTITUTE D–5
Brooklyn, New York 11205 (212) 636-3669

F/T: 1843M, 1087W	Faculty: 131; IIA, +$
P/T: 263M, 138W	Ph.D.'s: n/av
Grad: 438M, 559W	S/F Ratio: 16 to 1
Year: 4-1-4, ss	Tuition: $5010
Appl: Apr. 1	R and B: $2700
1335 applied	661 accepted	301 enrolled
SAT: 454V 515M		COMPETITIVE

Pratt Institute, founded in 1887, is a private, nonsectarian institution offering training in specialized areas of business, science, and the fine arts. The institute has one of the largest professional art schools in the country. The library contains over 221,000 volumes and 16,000 microfilms, and subscribes to 1079 periodicals.

Environment: The 20-acre campus is located in a residential area of Brooklyn, 1 mile from Manhattan. Facilities include dormitories that accommodate 926 students. Apartments are available for married students.

Student Life: Fifty percent of the students come from New York State. About 84% of the entering freshmen are graduates of public schools. Thirty-three percent of the students live on campus. Thirty-seven percent are minority-group members. Institute housing is both single-sex and coed. There are visiting privileges in single-sex housing. Students may keep cars on campus.

Organizations: There are 1 fraternity and 1 sorority on campus; 1% of the men and 1% of the women belong to them. Campus activities include dances, lectures, sports events, movies, concerts, drama, modern dance presentations, and numerous special events. The institute benefits greatly from the cultural offerings of New York City.

Sports: Intercollegiate competition is offered in 6 sports for men and 4 for women. There are 8 intramural sports for men and 7 for women.

Handicapped: Special facilities on campus for handicapped students include wheelchair ramps, elevators, specially equipped rest rooms, and lowered telephones. Special class scheduling is available as well.

Graduates: About 9% of the students drop out by the end of the freshman year; 75% remain to graduate. Approximately 10% of the graduates go on to further study; 1% attend medical and dental school, and 2% law school. Sixty percent pursue careers in business and industry.

Services: The following services are available to students free of charge: health care, psychological counseling, placement service, career counseling, tutoring, and remedial instruction.

Programs of Study: The institute confers the B.S., B.Arch., B.F.A., B.Eng., B.I.D., and B.P.S. degrees. Associate and master's degrees can also be earned. Bachelor's degrees are offered in the following subjects: BUSINESS (computer science, management, marketing), EDUCATION (art), FINE AND PERFORMING ARTS (art, art education, film/photography, studio art), MATH AND SCIENCES (chemistry, ecology/environmental science, mathematics, natural sciences, physical sciences), PREPROFESSIONAL (architecture, dentistry, engineering, home economics, law, library science, medicine, pharmacy, veterinary). Fifty percent of the undergraduate degrees are conferred in the arts, and 42% in preprofessional areas.

Required: All students must take a core of courses in English, social science, and humanities.

Special: The institute is well known for its offerings in the fields of professional art, including communications design, industrial design, graphic arts, and interior design. The School of Architecture offers a 5-year program with an emphasis on design. Two-year degrees are offered in graphic design, illustration, and textile design. There are individualized programs in the upper divisions of the School of Art and Design. Cooperative work-study programs are available for all students. The institute offers a combined degree in architecture and planning. Student-designed majors are permitted, and a general studies degree is offered.

Honors: Four national honor societies have chapters on campus.

Admissions: About 50% of those who applied were accepted for the 1981–82 freshman class. SAT scores of those who enrolled were as follows: Verbal—76% scored below 500, 21% between 500 and 599, 3% between 600 and 700, and 0% above 700; Math—62% scored below 500, 34% between 500 and 599, 3% between 600 and 700, and 1% above 700. Candidates must be graduates of accredited high schools and have completed 16 units of work. The institute rarely considers for admission students whose class rank is below the top 50% and who do not score above 400 on the SAT. Other important factors include special talents, advanced placement or honors courses, recommendations, and impressions made during an interview.

Procedure: The SAT or ACT is required. Applicants to the School of Art and Design must complete the Home Exam as instructed by the institute. The deadlines for applications are April 1 (fall), December 1 (winter), January 1 (spring), and April 1 (summer). Freshmen are admitted each semester. Notification is on a rolling basis. There is a $30 application fee.

Special: The institute has an early decision plan, an early admissions plan, and a deferred admissions plan. CLEP and AP credit is offered.

Transfer: For fall 1981, 1079 applications were received, 675 were accepted, and 402 students enrolled. A GPA of 2.0 is required. D grades do not transfer. Transfers are considered for all but the senior class. A student must take, at the institute, a minimum of 48 credits of the 132 to 175 needed to receive a bachelor's degree. The application deadlines are July 1 (fall), December 1 (winter), January 1 (spring), and May 1 (summer).

Visiting: An orientation program held in the fall for prospective students includes meetings with admissions and financial aid officers, a tour, lunch, and classroom visits. Guides are also available for informal visits to the institute. Visitors may sit in on classes but may not stay overnight at the school. The best time to visit is between 10 A.M. and 2 P.M. on weekdays. The admissions office handles the arrangements.

Financial Aid: Eighty-five percent of students receive financial aid. Twenty percent work part-time on campus. Average aid to freshmen from all sources is $3670. The institute awards freshman scholarships yearly. Students may also apply for loans from federal and state government funds, from private sources, and from an institute fund. Tuition may be paid in installments. The institute is a member of CSS. The FAF is required. The deadlines for financial aid applications are April 1 (fall), December 1 (winter and spring), and May 1 (summer).

Foreign Students: Nine percent of the full-time students come from foreign countries. The institute offers these students special counseling and special organizations.

Admissions: Foreign students must score 500 on the TOEFL. They must also take the New York University-ALI Test. No college entrance examination is required.

Procedure: Application deadlines are April 1 (fall), November 1 (winter), December 1 (spring), and March 1 (summer). Foreign students must present proof of funds adequate for the academic year.

Admissions Contact: Daniel S. Kimball, Director of Admissions and Financial Aid.

RENSSELAER POLYTECHNIC INSTITUTE D-3
Troy, New York 12181 (518) 270-6216

F/T: 3503M, 831W
P/T: none
Grad: 1518M, 353W
Year: sems, ss
Appl: Jan. 1
6493 applied
SAT: 576V 688M

Faculty: 353; I, ++$
Ph.D.'s: 98%
S/F Ratio: 13 to 1
Tuition: $6500
R and B: $2300
2900 accepted 1200 enrolled
MOST COMPETITIVE

Founded in 1824 by Stephen Van Rensselaer, Rensselaer Polytechnic Institute is a privately endowed, nonsectarian institution. The oldest engineering and technical institution in the country and the first college to introduce the laboratory method of learning in the sciences, the institute offers programs in engineering science, architecture, management, humanities, and social sciences. The Folsom Library houses 265,000 volumes and over 300,000 technical research reports, periodicals, and serials.

Environment: The 260-acre suburban campus, located on a plateau overlooking the Hudson River, is 165 miles from Boston and New York. The 60 buildings include a linear accelerator, the Johnson Engineering Center, a science center, a communications center, the materials research building, the IBM 3033 computer center, and a field house that can seat 7000 for ice hockey and cultural events. Dormitories can accommodate 350 women and 2000 men. Fraternity and sorority residences and off-campus apartments provide additional living space.

Student Life: Forty-seven percent of the students come from New York State. Eighty percent of entering freshmen come from public schools. Eighty percent of the students live on campus. Unless freshmen live at home, they must live in institute housing. About 11% of the students are minority-group members. Institute housing is both single-sex and coed. There are visiting privileges in single-sex housing. Students may keep cars on campus.

Organizations: There are 24 fraternities, 3 coed fraternities, and 2 sororities. Extracurricular activities include musical groups, the RPI players, the FM radio station, and skiing. Religious organizations and activities are led by chaplains of the major faiths.

Sports: The institute competes intercollegiately in 17 sports for men and 12 for women. There are 15 intramural sports for men and 14 for women.

Handicapped: Facilities for handicapped students include wheelchair ramps, special parking, elevators, specially equipped rest rooms, lowered drinking fountains and telephones, a signer/interpreter, tapes, and readers. There is a counselor for handicapped students. Special class scheduling is possible.

Graduates: The freshman dropout rate is 8%. Seventy-nine percent remain to graduate. Sixty percent of the graduates pursue advanced degrees; 2% enter medical school. Forty percent enter careers in business and industry.

Services: Students receive the following services free of charge: psychological counseling, placement, career counseling, tutoring, and remedial instruction. Health care is covered by the annual health fee.

Programs of Study: The institute confers the B.S. and B.Arch. degrees. Master's and doctoral degrees are also awarded. Bachelor's degrees are offered in the following subjects: BUSINESS (communications, computer science, management), MATH AND SCIENCES (biology, chemistry, geology, interdisciplinary science, mathematics, physics), PHILOSOPHY (philosophy), PREPROFESSIONAL (architecture, dentistry, engineering, law, medicine, veterinary), SOCIAL SCIENCES (economics, psychology). Seventy percent of the degrees are conferred in preprofessional fields, and 24% in math and sciences.

Required: All except architecture students must take chemistry, physics, mathematics, humanities and social sciences (8 semesters), and physical education. Architecture students take a modified program. AP scores of 4 or 5 may satisfy requirements for 1 year of chemistry, physics, mathematics, foreign language, art and music, and humanities-social science.

Special: Rensselaer offers 6-year programs leading to the Biomedical B.S. and M.D. degrees in cooperation with Albany Medical School; the Management-Law B.S. and J.D. degrees in cooperation with Albany Law School; and a biodental program in conjunction with the University of Pennsylvania School of Dental Medicine. A special program offering remedial and tutorial services and a degree in 4 to 5 years is available for economically disadvantaged students. A 3-year bachelor's degree, combination degree programs, and 4- and 5-year accelerated master's programs are available.

Honors: There are chapters of Sigma Xi, Tau Beta Pi, and Eta Kappa Nu on campus. The math, chemistry, and physics departments offer advanced placement sections. Honors courses are available in humanities and physics.

Admissions: Forty-five percent of those who applied were accepted for the 1981–82 freshman class. Of those who enrolled, the SAT scores were as follows: Verbal—16% scored below 500, 40% between 500 and 599, 38% between 600 and 700, and 6% above 700; Math—2% scored below 500, 7% between 500 and 599, 43% between 600 and 700, and 48% above 700. Admission is based on several factors. The greatest stress is placed on the quality of work, rather than the particular subjects undertaken. Advanced placement or honor courses and recommendations by school officials are also considered.

Procedure: The SAT or ACT, and ATs in Mathematics, Level I or II, Physics or Chemistry, and English Composition are required of all students and should be taken before the senior year. Application deadlines are January 1 (fall) and November 1 (spring). Students are urged to apply prior to January 1 to assure full consideration. The application fee is $25 ($30 for applicants to accelerated programs).

Special: Early admissions, early decision, and deferred admissions plans are available.

Transfer: For fall 1981, 442 students applied, 173 were accepted, and 91 enrolled. Students from accredited 4-year colleges or universities, or 2-year community or junior colleges, who seek admission with advanced standing should have good academic standing, and must have an academic average of at least B. Advanced credit is granted

588 NEW YORK

for courses satisfactorily completed and comparable in content to Rensselaer courses. D grades do not transfer. Transfers are accepted for all classes. There is a 1-year residency requirement. Transfers must complete, at the institute, 30 hours of the 120 required for the bachelor's degree. Application deadlines are May 1 (fall) and November 1 (spring).

Visiting: Daily tours and scheduled interviews are available to prospective students. Visitors may sit in on classes and, if space is available, stay overnight at the institute.

Financial Aid: Sixty percent of the students receive financial aid in the form of scholarships, loans, and/or campus employment. Thirty-five percent of the students work part-time on campus. Freshman aid averages $6300. Many freshmen receive New York State Regents Scholarships or National Merit Scholarships. NDSL and institute loans are available. Aid is awarded on the basis of need and is reconsidered each year; students who qualify and maintain a good average continue to receive aid. The institute is a member of CSS. Early decision candidates should file the FAF by October 15, and all other applicants no later than January 31.

Foreign Students: About 3% of the full-time students come from foreign countries. The institute offers these students special counseling and special organizations.

Admissions: Foreign students must score 500 on the TOEFL. They must also take ATs in English Composition, Math Level I or II, and Physics or Chemistry.

Procedure: The application deadline is January 1 (fall). Foreign students must submit the institute's medical form. They must also submit proof of funds adequate to cover 4 years of study. They must carry health insurance, which is available through the institute.

Admissions Contact: Christopher M. Small, Dean of Admissions and Financial Aid.

ROBERTS WESLEYAN COLLEGE B-3
Rochester, New York 14624 (716) 594-9471

F/T: 183M, 392W
P/T: 9M, 29W
Grad: none
Year: sems, ss
Appl: open
241 applied 234 accepted 145 enrolled
SAT: 464V 505M ACT: 22 COMPETITIVE

Faculty: 53; IIB, – $
Ph.D.'s: 40%
S/F Ratio: 11 to 1
Tuition: $3686
R and B: $2000

Chili Seminary, founded more than a century ago as a small private school, eventually developed into Roberts Wesleyan College, a 4-year liberal arts college. The library houses 82,000 volumes and 5000 microfilm items, and subscribes to 514 periodicals.

Environment: The college is located in a suburban setting 8 miles southwest of Rochester and 12 miles from Lake Ontario.

Student Life: The majority of students are from the Middle Atlantic region. Ninety-eight percent of entering freshmen come from public schools. Eighty percent of all students live in dormitories. Four percent of the students are Catholic, 86% Protestant, and 10% claim no religious affiliation. About 8% of the students are minority-group members. College housing is single-sex; there are visiting privileges. Students may keep cars on campus. Tobacco, alcoholic beverages, dancing, and gambling are prohibited. Chapel is compulsory and is held twice a week.

Organizations: There are no fraternities or sororities. All students belong to the student association. Recreational and cultural activities include Rochester Philharmonic Orchestra, Memorial Art Gallery, the University of Rochester-Eastman Theater, and various state parks.

Sports: The college competes intercollegiately in 4 sports for men and 4 for women. There are 5 intramural sports for men and 4 for women.

Handicapped: There are no special facilities for handicapped students.

Graduates: Thirty percent of the freshmen drop out by the end of their first year. Fifty-two percent remain to graduate. About 20% of the graduates pursue advanced degrees; 2% enter law school.

Services: Students receive the following services free of charge: psychological counseling, placement, career counseling, and tutoring. Health care is available on a fee basis.

Programs of Study: The college confers the B.A. and B.S. degrees. Associate degrees are also available. Bachelor's degrees are offered in the following subjects: BUSINESS (business administration), EDUCATION (elementary, music, secondary), ENGLISH (English), FINE AND PERFORMING ARTS (art, music, music education), HEALTH SCIENCES (medical technology, nursing), MATH AND SCIENCES (biology, chemistry, mathematics, natural sciences, physics), PHILOSOPHY (humanities, religion), PREPROFESSIONAL (dentistry, engineering, law, library science, medicine, ministry, pharmacy, social work), SOCIAL SCIENCES (history, psychology, sociology). Thirty-two percent of the degrees are conferred in health sciences, 21% in social sciences, and 17% in fine and performing arts.

Required: The general education courses, given during the first 2 years, introduce 4 major fields of knowledge: the biological and physical sciences; history and social sciences; languages, literature, and the fine arts; and Bible and the philosophy of the Christian religion.

Special: Certification is available in art, music, elementary, and secondary education. There are 3-2 combination degree programs in pharmacy, engineering, and computer science, and a 3-1 program in medical technology.

Honors: There is a chapter of Alpha Kappa Sigma on campus.

Admissions: Ninety-seven percent of the applicants for the 1981–82 freshman class were accepted. Of those who enrolled, the SAT scores were as follows: Verbal—24% were between 500 and 599, 12% between 600 and 700, and fewer than 1% above 700; Math—29% were between 500 and 599, 14% between 600 and 700, and fewer than 1% above 700. On the ACT, 32% scored between 21 and 23, 21% between 24 and 27, and 16% 28 or above. Candidates must be graduates of an accredited high school, rank in the upper three-fifths of their graduating class, have at least a C average, and have completed 12 academic units. Also important are acceptable SAT or ACT scores, advanced placement or honor courses, recommendations, leadership record, and evidence of good physical and mental health.

Procedure: The SAT or ACT is required. The application deadlines are open. The college uses a rolling admissions plan. There is a $10 application fee.

Special: There are early decision, early admissions, and deferred admissions plans. AP and CLEP credit is offered.

Transfer: For fall 1981, 69 transfer students were accepted and 44 enrolled. Good academic standing is required. D grades are not acceptable. There is a 1-year residency requirement. Transfer students must complete 30 semester hours at the college, out of the 124 needed for a bachelor's degree. Application deadlines are open.

Visiting: Orientation for prospective students is usually scheduled for a summer weekend. Informal weekday visits can be arranged through the admissions office. Visitors may sit in on classes and stay overnight at the school.

Financial Aid: About 87% of the students receive financial aid. Thirty-seven percent work part-time on campus. In addition to financial need, the following are considered when assigning aid: scholarship record, personal character, and general cooperation in the affairs of college life. Promising students receive financial aid from the college insofar as its funds permit; loan funds and work opportunities are also available. Several states offer various types of financial assistance. The college is a member of CSS. The FAF is required. The application deadline is open.

Foreign Students: Four percent of the full-time students come from foreign countries. The college offers these students special counseling.

Admissions: Foreign students must score 550 on the TOEFL. No college entrance examination is required.

Procedure: Application deadlines are July (fall), September (spring), and April (summer). Foreign students must complete the college's health report form. They must also present proof of adequate funds. They must carry health insurance, which is available through the college for a fee.

Admissions Contact: Karl Somerville, Director of Admissions.

ROCHESTER INSTITUTE OF TECHNOLOGY B-3
Rochester, New York 14623 (716) 475-6631

F/T: 5265M, 2443W
P/T: 3784M, 2079W
Grad: 1094M, 477W
Year: qtrs, ss
Appl: open
4642 applied 2804 accepted 1351 enrolled
SAT: 473V 553M ACT: 23 VERY COMPETITIVE

Faculty: n/av; IIA, av$
Ph.D.'s: 35%
S/F Ratio: 18 to 1
Tuition: $4488
R and B: $2525

Rochester Institute of Technology was founded in 1829 as a private, nonsectarian institution offering a wide range of career-oriented programs of study. The multimedia library center contains 183,910 volumes and 114,222 microfilm items, and subscribes to 8579 periodicals.

Environment: The 1300-acre campus is located in the suburban community of Henrietta, 5 miles from Rochester. The 22 major buildings include a dormitory complex that accommodates 3500 men and women. Also located on the campus is the National Technical Institute for the Deaf, designated by Congress as the national center for postsecondary education for the hearing-impaired. Its current enrollment is 950 students.

Student Life: Approximately 60% of the student body comes from New York State; 42 other states are also represented. About 75% of the students reside on campus. About 8% are minority-group members. Institute housing is both single-sex and coed. There are visiting privileges in single-sex housing. Students may keep cars on campus. Day-care services are available to all students, faculty, and staff.

Organizations: There are 10 national fraternities, of which 10% of the men are members, and 4 national sororities, to which 4% of the women belong. There are numerous social, service, and performing groups, as well as special-interest organizations.

Sports: There are 11 intercollegiate sports for men and 7 for women. There are 5 intramural sports for both men and women.

Handicapped: Almost 100% of the campus is accessible to handicapped students. Special facilities include wheelchair ramps, parking areas, elevators, lowered drinking fountains and telephones, and specially equipped rest rooms. Special class scheduling is also available. Ten percent of the students have hearing impairments. The National Technical Institute for the Deaf offers complete services, both academic and residential, for these students. A full professional staff is available for counseling and assisting of handicapped students.

Graduates: By the end of the freshman year, 15% of the students drop out; 60% remain to graduate. Approximately 8% continue on to graduate or professional schools. Eighty-seven percent pursue careers in business and industry.

Services: Students receive the following services free of charge: placement, career counseling, psychological counseling, tutoring, and remedial instruction. Health care is available on a fee basis.

Programs of Study: The institute confers the B.S., B.F.A., B.S.W., and B.T. degrees. Associate and master's degrees are also available. The bachelor's degree is offered in the following subjects: BUSINESS (accounting, business administration, computer science), FINE AND PERFORMING ARTS (art, environmental design, film/photography, graphic design, medical illustration), HEALTH SCIENCES (biomedical computing, medical technology, nuclear medical technology), MATH AND SCIENCES (biochemistry, biology, chemistry, computational mathematics, mathematics, pharmacy, physics), PREPROFESSIONAL (dentistry, engineering, law, medicine, pharmacy, social work, veterinary). Thirty-eight percent of degrees are conferred in preprofessional studies, 28% in fine and performing arts, and 20% in business.

Required: There is a distribution requirement for all students.

Honors: Five national honor societies have chapters on campus. The following departments offer honors programs: business, engineering, fine and applied arts, science, and general studies.

Admissions: Sixty percent of those who applied were accepted for the 1981–82 freshman class. Of those who enrolled in a recent freshman class, the SAT scores were as follows: Verbal—26% scored between 500 and 599, 7% between 600 and 700, and 1% above 700; Math—37% scored between 500 and 599, 22% between 600 and 700, and 5% above 700. It is desirable for candidates to be graduates of accredited high schools, rank in the upper 50% of their class, and possess at least a C+ average. In addition, advanced placement or honor courses, impressions made during the interview, and the extracurricular activities record are considered. Admission interviews are encouraged but not required.

Procedure: The SAT or ACT is required. There are no application deadlines. The rolling admissions system is used. Students are usually admitted each semester. There is a $25 application fee.

Special: There are early and deferred admissions plans. CLEP and AP credit is given.

Transfer: For fall 1981, of 2605 applications received, 1929 were accepted, and 1261 students enrolled. Transfers are accepted for all classes, but students must reside a minimum of 1 year at the institute and complete 45 of the 180 hours needed to receive a bachelor's degree. Requirements for admission vary by program. The application deadlines are open.

Visiting: There are regularly scheduled orientations for prospective students. Guides are available for informal visits on weekdays from 9 A.M. to 4 P.M. Visitors may sit in on classes and stay overnight at the school. Campus visits can be arranged through the Department of Residence Halls.

Financial Aid: Approximately 58% of the students receive financial aid in the form of loans, grants, scholarships, or work-study. The average award to freshmen from all sources is $500. The institute is a member of the CSS. The FAF is required. The aid application must be received by March 1.

Foreign Students: Three percent of the full-time students come from 36 foreign countries. The institute offers these students an intensive English course, an intensive English program, special counseling, and special organizations.

Admissions: Foreign students must take the TOEFL or the University of Michigan Language Test. They must score 525 on the TOEFL. No college entrance examination is required.

Procedure: The application deadline is April 1 (fall). Foreign students must submit a completed health form. They must also present proof of funds adequate to cover 1 full year. They must carry health insurance, which is available through the college for a fee.

Admissions Contact: E. Louis Guard, Director of Admissions.

ROCHESTER INSTITUTE OF TECHNOLOGY/ EISENHOWER COLLEGE
(See Eisenhower College of Rochester Institute of Technology)

RUSSELL SAGE COLLEGE D-3
Troy, New York 12180 (518) 270-2217

F/T: 1389W	Faculty: 130; IIA, –$
P/T: 57W	Ph.D.'s: 52%
Grad: 78W	S/F Ratio: 12 to 1
Year: 4-1-4	Tuition: $4800
Appl: open	R and B: $2445
1077 applied	876 accepted	363 enrolled
SAT: 470V 510M		COMPETITIVE

Russell Sage College, established in 1916, is a moderately sized, private, nonsectarian liberal arts institution for women, offering professional and technical training in a variety of fields, including nursing, business, and education. The library houses 175,000 volumes and 5400 microfilm items, and subscribes to 1200 periodicals.

Environment: The 7½-acre urban campus is 10 miles from Albany in the educational center of Troy. Several of the buildings have historical significance. There are 5 dormitories accommodating 1250 women.

Student Life: Sixty-two percent of the students come from New York State. Eighty percent of the freshmen are graduates of public schools. About 70% of the students are residents. All students are required to live in college dormitories unless they commute from home. Seven percent of the students are minority-group members. College housing is single-sex; there are visiting privileges. Students may keep cars on campus. Day-care services are available to all students, faculty, and staff for a fee.

Organizations: There are no sororities. Students have a voice in student affairs through a strong student government, community council, and class council. They also have representatives on committees that formulate social regulations. Social activities are carried on in conjunction with nearby colleges.

Sports: The college competes on an intercollegiate level in 7 sports.

Handicapped: Only a limited part of the campus is accessible to handicapped students. Special facilities include parking areas and elevators. Special class scheduling and extra counseling are also available.

Graduates: Recently, about 8% of the freshman class dropped out by the end of the first year. Seventy-five percent of the students remained to graduate.

Services: Placement and career counseling are offered free of charge. Tutoring is on a fee basis.

Programs of Study: The college confers the B.A. and B.S. degrees. Associate and master's degrees are also granted. The bachelor's degree is offered in the following subjects: BUSINESS (accounting, computer science, management), EDUCATION (elementary, health/physical, secondary, special), ENGLISH (English), FINE AND PERFORMING ARTS (art, art history, dance, music, studio art, theater/dramatics), HEALTH SCIENCES (physical therapy), LANGUAGES (French, Spanish), MATH AND SCIENCES (biochemistry, biology, chemistry, mathematics), PHILOSOPHY (philosophy), PREPROFESSIONAL (dentistry, law, medicine, veterinary), SOCIAL SCIENCES (economics, government/political science, history, international relations, sociology). About 50% of all degrees conferred are in health sciences.

Required: All students must take a first semester English course plus 9 hours each of humanities, social sciences, and physical sciences.

Special: Independent study and student-designed majors are offered. Selected students may participate in the Drew University United Nations Semester. The college sponsors study abroad programs in Great Britain, Austria, France, Spain, and Colombia. A 3-2 combined B.A.-B.S. degree in mathematics/engineering is offered in conjunction with Rensselaer Polytechnic Institute. There are combination degree programs in physical therapy and laboratory technology. The college is part of the Hudson-Mohawk Consortium, and students may take courses at 14 other colleges in the area.

Honors: One national honor society has a chapter on campus. The college has honors programs in several areas for those with a GPA of 3.5 or better in their major field.

Admissions: Eighty-one percent of those who applied were accepted for the 1981–82 freshman class. Of those who enrolled in a recent freshman class, the SAT scores were as follows: Verbal—29% scored between 500 and 599, and 8% between 600 and 700; Math—35% scored between 500 and 599, and 11% between 600 and 700. All students must complete 16 Carnegie units. An acceptable score on the SAT is 450 on each part. Applicants must have at least a C average in high school work. Other considerations are advanced placement or honors courses, leadership potential, and extracurricular activities.

Procedure: The college requires the SAT or ACT. Candidates should arrange for a personal interview on campus. The fall application deadline is open. Notification is on a rolling basis. Freshmen are also admitted in the winter and the spring. There is a $20 application fee.

Special: Early admissions, early decision, and deferred admissions plans are available. AP and CLEP credit is available.

Transfer: For fall 1981, 275 applications were received; the college accepted 223, and enrolled 121 students. A combined SAT score of 850 and a 2.0 GPA are required. D grades are not transferable. A total of 120 credits is needed for a bachelor's degree. The application deadline is open.

Visiting: There are regularly scheduled orientations for prospective students, including a campus tour, personal interview, and departmental visit (if possible). Informal visits can be arranged for weekdays by the admissions house. Guided tours are available. Visitors may stay overnight at the school and sit in on classes.

Financial Aid: Approximately 65% of the students receive financial aid. About 50% of students work in jobs administered and/or funded by the college. About 170 freshman scholarships are awarded each year, and loans are available from the federal government, local banks, and the college. The FAF is required. The deadline for financial aid application is February.

Foreign Students: The college offers foreign students special counseling and special organizations.

Admissions: Foreign students must score 550 on the TOEFL. They must also take the SAT.

Procedure: Application deadlines are open. There is a rolling admissions procedure. Foreign students must submit the college's own health form completed by a physician. They must also present proof of funds adequate to cover 1 year of study.

Admissions Contact: Margaret B. Snyder, Acting Director of Admissions.

ST. BONAVENTURE UNIVERSITY A-3
St. Bonaventure, New York 14778   (716) 375-2400

F/T: 1162M, 1098W
P/T: 58M, 35W
Grad: 251M, 178W
Year: sems, ss
Appl: see profile
2030 applied
SAT: 481V 522M

Faculty: 152; IIA, —$
Ph.D.'s: 70%
S/F Ratio: 15 to 1
Tuition: $3845
R and B: $2150–2300
1382 accepted   622 enrolled
ACT: 24   COMPETITIVE+

St. Bonaventure University, established in 1856, is a Roman Catholic institution founded by the Franciscan Friars of the Holy Name Province. The library contains 250,000 volumes.

Environment: The university occupies 500 acres in the rural foothills of the Allegheny Mountains, 70 miles southeast of Buffalo. Residence halls on campus accommodate 809 women and 959 men; 2 two-story garden-style-apartment structures house 48 students each.

Student Life: The majority of the students are residents of New York; 22% come from other parts of the country. Fifty percent of entering freshmen are graduates of public schools. All resident students (about 85% of the student body) are required to live in campus dormitories. Most of the students are Catholic. University housing is single-sex; there are visiting privileges. Students may keep cars on campus.

Organizations: There are no social fraternities or sororities, but a number of other societies are open to undergraduates, including scholastic and professional organizations. The Garret Theater, on campus, offers many cultural events. Nearby recreational facilities include a skating rink, a ski area, and Allegheny State Park.

Sports: There are 13 intercollegiate sports for men and 10 for women. The university offers 20 intramural sports for men and 19 for women.

Handicapped: There are special facilities for the physically handicapped. These facilities include wheelchair ramps, elevators, lowered drinking fountains, and specially equipped rest rooms. For these students there is a counseling and career development center staffed by 4 professionals.

Graduates: Approximately 1% of the freshmen drop out by the end of the first year; 70% remain to graduate. Twenty-one percent of the graduates continue their studies. Seventy percent enter careers in business and industry.

Services: Students receive the following services free of charge: placement, career counseling, health care, psychological counseling, tutoring, and remedial instruction.

Programs of Study: The university confers the undergraduate degrees of B.A., B.S., and B.B.A.. It also offers master's degrees. Bachelor's degrees are offered in the following subjects: BUSINESS (accounting, finance, management, marketing), EDUCATION (elementary, secondary), ENGLISH (English, mass communications), HEALTH SCIENCES (medical technology), LANGUAGES (French, German, Spanish), MATH AND SCIENCES (biology, chemistry, computer science, mathematics, physics), PHILOSOPHY (philosophy, theology), PREPROFESSIONAL (dentistry, engineering, law, medicine, ministry, veterinary), SOCIAL SCIENCES (economics, history, psychology, social sciences, sociology). Forty percent of degrees conferred are in business, and 15% are in social sciences.

Required: All students must take 9 hours each of theology and philosophy. The GRE is also required.

Special: Students may, with faculty approval, design their own majors. A 2-3 B.S. in engineering is offered with the University of Detroit and with Manhattan College.

Honors: Honors programs are available depending on the individual student's choice and the goals and resources of the particular department.

Admissions: Sixty-eight percent of those who applied were accepted for the 1981–82 freshman class. Of those who enrolled, the SAT scores were as follows: Verbal—52% scored below 500, 32% between 500 and 599, 11% between 600 and 700, and 1% above 700; Math—28% scored below 500, 46% between 500 and 599, 20% between 600 and 700, and 2% above 700. Applicants must be high school graduates with 16 Carnegie units. Also important are recommendations by school officials, advanced placement or honors courses, and impressions made during the interview.

Procedure: The SAT or ACT is required. An interview is strongly recommended. The university maintains a rolling admissions policy, but takes applications until housing is filled, in early February. Freshmen are admitted each semester. Notification is on a rolling basis. A $20 fee must accompany the completed application.

Special: Early admissions and deferred admissions plans are available. AP and CLEP credit is available.

Transfer: For fall 1981, 235 students applied, 167 were accepted, and 81 enrolled. A minimum GPA of 2.0 is necessary. D grades transfer in nonmajor areas. The last 36 credits and half the major-area courses must be completed in residence. A total of 129 credits is needed for a bachelor's degree. Application deadlines are open.

Visiting: Regularly scheduled orientations for prospective students include an interview, a guided tour, and an optional overnight stay in a residence hall. Informal visits can be arranged for weekdays (9 A.M. to 2:30 P.M.) through the admissions office. Visitors may sit in on classes and stay overnight at the school.

Financial Aid: About 88% of students receive financial aid. Forty percent work part-time on campus. Average aid to freshmen from all sources is $1450. The university has a scholarship fund. Loans are available for freshmen from the federal government and local banks. The university is a member of CSS. St. Bonaventure's FAF and the FAF are required from all those applying for financial aid. Applications should be filed by March 1 (fall) and October 1 (spring).

Foreign Students: One percent of the full-time students come from foreign countries.

Admissions: Foreign students must take the TOEFL. College entrance exams are not required.

Procedure: Application deadlines are open. Foreign students must present the Datamation form as proof of health. They must also submit, on a yearly basis, proof of funds adequate to cover 4 years of study.

Admissions Contact: Donald Burkard, Director of Admissions.

ST. FRANCIS COLLEGE   D-5
Brooklyn Heights, New York 11201   (212) 522-2300

F/T: 1316M, 658W	Faculty: 190; IIB, ++$
P/T: 403M, 806W	Ph.D.'s: 36%
Grad: none	S/F Ratio: 17 to 1
Year: sems, ss	Tuition: $3000
Appl: Aug. 31	R and B: n/app
997 applied	887 accepted 475 enrolled
SAT: 410V 430M	LESS COMPETITIVE

St. Francis College, chartered in 1884, is a coeducational, nonresidential, independent liberal arts institution. The library houses 122,800 volumes and subscribes to more than 800 periodicals.

Environment: Located in Brooklyn Heights, the college's facilities include a science center, a student union building, a physical education building, and a main classroom building. There are no dormitories.

Student Life: About 97% of the students are state residents. All students commute.

Organizations: The college offers an extensive program of cocurricular and extracurricular activities. Religious activities are available to serve interested students. About 30% of the students are members of fraternities and sororities.

Sports: The college competes in 8 intercollegiate sports for men and 6 for women. There are 8 intramural sports for men and women.

Graduates: The freshman dropout rate is 8%, but 54% remain to graduate. About 70% of the graduates go on to graduate or professional schools.

Services: The college provides career counseling, health care, tutorial services, and a leadership training program; there are a campus guidance center and a reading clinic.

Programs of Study: The college confers the B.A., B.B.A., and B.S. degrees, as well as associate degrees. Bachelor's degrees are offered in the following subjects: BUSINESS (accounting, accounting and business practice, management), EDUCATION (elementary, physical, secondary), ENGLISH (communication arts, English), HEALTH SCIENCES (health care management, health science, health services administration, medical technology), LANGUAGES (French, Spanish), MATH AND SCIENCES (biology, chemistry, mathematics), PHILOSOPHY (philosophy, religious studies), PREPROFESSIONAL (dentistry, law, medicine, podiatry), SOCIAL SCIENCES (economics, history, political science, psychology, social studies, sociology).

Required: All bachelor's degree candidates must take courses in English, literature, fine arts, speech, mathematics or natural science, philosophy, history, and sociology.

Special: Junior year abroad, a 3-year bachelor's degree, and a general studies degree are possible. A 3-1 degree is offered in medical technology, and a 2-4 or 3-4 degree is offered in biomedical sciences (podiatry).

Admissions: Eighty-nine percent of those who applied were accepted for a recent freshman class. Applicants should hold a rank in the upper 50% of the graduating class and have a minimum B or C average, depending upon the school from which they are applying. The college requires recommendations from the high school and the completion of 16 Carnegie high school units. Leadership potential is another desirable quality.

Procedure: The college has a rolling admissions policy. Fall applications should be submitted by August 31; spring applications by January 15. Notification is usually made within a month after all credentials have been received. The SAT is recommended. There is a $20 application fee. A personal interview is encouraged.

Special: Early decision and deferred admissions plans are offered. CLEP subject and AP exams are accepted.

Transfer: Of 368 applications received for a recent school year, 323 were accepted and 123 students enrolled. Transfers are considered for all levels and must complete at least 30 credits at the college of the 126 required for the bachelor's degree. A 2.0 GPA is required; D grades sometimes transfer. Application deadlines are the same as for freshmen.

Financial Aid: Approximately $800,000 is awarded to freshmen in financial aid, in the form of scholarships or grants, student employment, and loans. The average award is $2400. Eighty-five percent of students who apply for financial aid receive some form of assistance. The FAF and supplement should be filed with the CSS by February 15, and application with the college should be made by February 15.

Foreign Students: A significant number of foreign students attend the college, which offers them special counseling and special organizations.

Admissions: Foreign students who seek admission must file an application, transcript of high school record, and proof of high school graduation. The submission of TOEFL scores well in advance of entrance is also recommended.

Procedure: Application deadlines are the same as for freshmen. A medical-accident insurance program is available to full-time day students through the college.

Admissions Contact: Br. George Larkin, O.S.F., Director of Admissions.

ST. JOHN FISHER COLLEGE   B-3
Rochester, New York 14450   (716) 586-4140

F/T: 838M, 837W	Faculty: 98; IIB, ++$
P/T: 1600M&W	Ph.D.'s: 70%
Grad: none	S/F Ratio: 17 to 1
Year: sems, ss	Tuition: $4276
Appl: open	R and B: $2363
1085 applied	833 accepted 399 enrolled
SAT: 490V 510M	ACT: 22 COMPETITIVE

St. John Fisher College, a private, independent liberal arts school, was founded in 1948. The library houses 125,000 volumes and 3000 microfilm items, and subscribes to 810 periodicals.

Environment: Situated on 125 suburban acres, the campus is a short distance from downtown Rochester. Among the facilities are 2 high-rise, suite-style dorms and 3 other modern residences that accommodate 700 men and women.

Student Life: Ninety-five percent of the students are from New York State. Fifty-three percent of the freshmen come from public schools. One-half of the students live on campus. About 3% of the students are minority-group members. College housing is single-sex; there are visiting privileges. Students may keep cars on campus.

Organizations: There are no sororities or fraternities, but clubs and other organizations representing many student interests have been chartered under the student association. There is also a student-run radio station, as well as various publications.

Sports: Students participate in 11 intercollegiate sports for men and 7 for women. There are 10 intramural sports for men and 9 for women.

Handicapped: Ninety percent of the campus is accessible to physically handicapped students. Wheelchair ramps, elevators, specially equipped rest rooms, and lowered drinking fountains are provided.

Graduates: The freshman dropout rate is about 8%. Seventy-five percent remain to graduate; and 20% pursue further study. About 65% of the graduates enter careers in business and industry.

Services: Free services available to students are career counseling, health care, placement service, psychological counseling, tutoring, and remedial instruction.

Programs of Study: The B.A., B.S., and B.B.A. degrees are offered. The bachelor's degree is granted in the following subjects: BUSINESS (accounting, business administration, computer science, management), EDUCATION (elementary, secondary), ENGLISH (English, journalism), HEALTH SCIENCES (nursing), LANGUAGES (French, German, Italian, Spanish), MATH AND SCIENCES (biology, chemistry, mathematics, physics), PHILOSOPHY (philosophy, religion), PREPROFESSIONAL (dentistry, engineering, health services, law, medicine, pharmacy, veterinary), SOCIAL SCIENCES (anthropology, economics, government/political science, history, psychology, sociology). Forty-eight percent of degrees conferred are in business, 19% in the social sciences, 17% in journalism/communications, and 11% in math and sciences.

Special: Students may design their own majors. A liberal studies major is offered. A junior year abroad is available under the Central College European Study Program. There is a 3-2 cooperative program in mathematics and computer science with the Rochester Institute of Technology, as well as a 2-3 program in engineering with the University of Detroit, Manhattan College, and Clarkson College.

Honors: Six national honor societies have chapters on the campus.

Admissions: Seventy-seven percent of those who applied for the 1981-82 freshman class were accepted. The SAT scores of those who enrolled were as follows: Verbal—60% scored below 500, 20% between 500 and 599, 4% between 600 and 700, and 1% above 700; Math—34% scored below 500, 41% between 500 and 599, 11% between 600 and 700, and 1% above 700. A candidate should have a high school average of 80% or above and a combined SAT score of 1000. Rank in the top half of the high school class is required. In judging prospective candidates, the college also considers advanced placement or honors courses, recommendations by school officials, impressions made during interviews, and personality.

Procedure: Either the SAT or ACT is required. There is no deadline for applications. The college has a rolling admissions plan. Freshmen are admitted each semester. The application fee is $20.

Special: There are early admissions and deferred admissions plans. AP and CLEP credit is offered.

Transfer: For fall 1981, 371 students applied, 303 were accepted, and 217 enrolled. Good academic standing (2.0 GPA) is required. D grades transfer only with an associate degree. The last 30 credits must be earned in residence, out of the 120 needed for a bachelor's degree. Application deadlines are open.

Visiting: Prospective students may attend regularly scheduled orientations. Informal visits may take place during the academic year when classes are in session. Arrangements can be made through the admissions office. Guides are provided for informal visits, which may include sitting in on classes and staying overnight at the school.

Financial Aid: Eighty percent of students receive financial aid. Thirty percent work part-time on campus. The average aid awarded to freshmen from all sources is $3006. Scholarships, grants, loans, and part-time employment, including CWS, are available. The college is a member of CSS. The FAF and the aid application should be filed by March 1.

Foreign Students: Fewer than 1% of the full-time students come from foreign countries. The college offers these students special counseling.

Admissions: Foreign students must score 500 on the TOEFL. No college entrance examination is required.

Procedure: The application deadlines are February 15 (fall) and November 15 (spring). Foreign students must submit the college's own health form completed by a physician. They must also present proof of adequate funds. They must carry health insurance, which is available through the college for a fee.

Admissions Contact: Jay S. Valentine, Dean of Admissions.

ST. JOHN'S UNIVERSITY D-5
Jamaica, New York 11439 (212) 990-6161
Staten Island, New York 10300 (212) 447-4343

F/T: 6231M, 4761W Faculty: 570; I, −$
P/T: 2637M, 2499W Ph.D.'s: n/av
Grad: 2979M, 2416W S/F Ratio: 20 to 1
Year: sems, ss Tuition: $3180
Appl: open R and B: n/app
7115 applied 4856 accepted 2671 enrolled
SAT: 450V 470M COMPETITIVE

St. John's University, founded in 1870 and affiliated with the Roman Catholic Church, offers programs in liberal arts and sciences, business, education, and preprofessional fields. The library houses 1,091,393 volumes and 131,496 microfilm items, and subscribes to 5023 periodicals.

Environment: The university, which occupies 112 acres in total, includes the main campus in Queens and a branch campus on Staten Island. An academic building on the Queens campus was recently completed. There are no student residences.

Student Life: Because the university is exclusively a commuting college, about 79% of the students are from the New York area. The university provides a registry of living accommodations for the other students. About 12% of the students are minority-group members. Students may keep cars on campus.

Organizations: There are 20 fraternities and 14 sororities on both campuses. Also available are clubs, special-interest and performing groups, and social and cultural events.

Sports: Students may participate in 14 intercollegiate sports for men and 10 for women. There are 12 intramural sports for men and 9 for women.

Handicapped: One hundred percent of the campus is accessible to handicapped students. The university provides special parking, wheelchair ramps, elevators, specially equipped rest rooms, lowered telephones, and cups for water fountain use. Special class scheduling and special laboratory facilities are also provided. For the small percentage of students who are visually impaired, readers and tapes are supplied, and raised numbers are to be installed on elevators and stairway landings. Appropriate seating is arranged for visually impaired and hearing impaired students. There is a special counselor for handicapped students.

Graduates: Sixteen percent of the freshmen drop out by the end of their first year. Recently, 25% of graduates pursued graduate study; 8% entered medical school, and 5% entered dental school. The great majority of students pursued careers in business and industry.

Services: Free health services, psychological counseling, tutoring, remedial instruction, career counseling, and placement service are provided.

Programs of Study: The university confers the B.A., B.S., B.F.A., B.S.Ed., B.S.Pharm., and B.S.Med.Tech. degrees. Associate, master's, and doctoral degrees are also granted. The bachelor's degree is offered in the following subjects: AREA STUDIES (American, Asian), BUSINESS (accounting, athletic administration, computer science, court management, economics, finance, funeral service administration, management, marketing, quantitative analysis, transportation), EDUCATION (elementary, human services, secondary, special, speech, speech and hearing handicapped), ENGLISH (English, journalism, literature, speech), FINE AND PERFORMING ARTS (art, film/photography), HEALTH SCIENCES (medical technology, pathologist's assistant, physician's assistant, speech pathology and audiology, urban health management), LANGUAGES (Chinese, French, German, Italian, Japanese, Spanish), MATH AND SCIENCES (biology, chemistry, mathematics, mathematical physics, physical sciences, physics), PHILOSOPHY (philosophy, religion), PREPROFESSIONAL (communications arts, correctional counseling, engineering, pharmacy), SOCIAL SCIENCES (anthropology, criminal justice, economics, environmental studies, government/political science, history, psychology, public administration, sociology). Thirty-five percent of degrees are awarded in business, and 27% in the social sciences.

Special: The university offers a special assessment program that enables students to receive academic credit for nontraditional learning. There are 3-2 programs in engineering and for physician's assistant. Independent study is available.

Honors: Fifteen honor societies have chapters on either or both campuses.

Admissions: Sixty-eight percent of those who applied were admitted to the 1981-82 freshman class. The mean high school GPA of accepted students is 84.8. An applicant must have 16 units from an accredited high school. Important in the admissions decision are advanced placement or honor courses, the extracurricular activities record, and the leadership record.

Procedure: The SAT is recommended. Application deadlines are open, but the following dates are recommended: March 1 (fall), November 1 (spring), May 1 (summer). Notification is on a rolling basis. Freshmen are admitted each semester. The application fee is $10.

Special: There is an early admissions plan; March 1 is the recommended date for application. AP and CLEP credit are given.

Transfer: For fall 1981, 1821 students applied, 1089 were accepted, and 688 enrolled. An average of 2.0 is required. D grades do not transfer. Students must complete at least 30 credits in residence to receive a bachelor's degree. Application deadlines are open.

Visiting: Bus tours and seminars are available for prospective students on a regularly scheduled basis. Informal visitors will be provided with guides and may sit in on classes between 9 A.M. and 5 P.M. Visits can be arranged by contacting the Office of University Information Services.

Financial Aid: About 80% of students receive assistance. About 6% work part-time on campus. Average aid to freshmen from all sources is $1775. About 300 scholarships based on a combination of high school academic achievement and need are available to freshmen. Federal and state loans are also available, and CWS is offered. The university is a member of CSS. The FAF is required. Aid applications are due by April 1.

Foreign Students: Seven percent of the full-time students come from foreign countries. The university offers these students an intensive English program, special counseling, and special organizations.

Admissions: Foreign students must take the TOEFL or the University of Michigan Language Test. They must score 500 on the TOEFL. They must also take the SAT or the ACT.

Procedure: The application deadlines are November (fall) and June (spring). Foreign students must present proof of funds adequate to cover each semester of study.

Admissions Contact: Henry F. Rossi, Dean of Admissions and Registrar, Queens Campus; Patricia A. Palermo, Dean of Admissions and Registrar, Staten Island Campus.

ST. JOSEPH'S COLLEGE D-5
Brooklyn, New York 11205 (212) 622-4696
Patchogue, New York 11772 (516) 289-3479

F/T: 198M, 1047W Faculty: 67; IIB, −$
P/T: 62M, 1004W Ph.D.'s: 25%
Grad: none S/F Ratio: 18 to 1
Year: 4-1-4, ss Tuition: $2760
Appl: Aug. 15 R and B: n/app
629 applied 478 accepted 249 enrolled
SAT: 445V 460M COMPETITIVE

St. Joseph's College, founded in 1916, is a small, private, liberal arts college. The library contains 110,000 volumes and 2360 microfilm items, and subscribes to about 500 periodicals.

Environment: The main campus is located in Brooklyn, 8 miles from New York City. In addition, the college has a branch campus in suburban Patchogue, Long Island. The Brooklyn campus comprises several buildings, including an outdoor theater and the Dillon Child Study Center, a laboratory preschool for 100 children from 3 to 5 years of age.

Student Life: St. Joseph's is basically a commuting college, and most of the students are residents of Brooklyn, Queens, and Long Island. Twenty-three percent of the freshmen come from public schools. Fifteen percent of the students are minority-group members. Students may keep cars on campus.

Organizations: Eight percent of the women belong to 1 local sorority. Special-interest clubs, drama groups, publications, and a modern dance program are available.

Sports: The college fields 1 intercollegiate team for men and 1 for women. There are 5 intramural sports for men and 5 for women.

Handicapped: There are no special facilities for physically handicapped students.

Graduates: The freshman dropout rate is 7%, and 70% of the freshmen remain to graduate. Thirty-three percent of the graduates continue their education; 4% enter medical school, 1% enter dental school, and 2% enter law school. About 60% pursue careers in business and industry.

Services: Students receive career counseling and psychological counseling free of charge.

Programs of Study: The college confers the B.A. or B.S. degree in the following subjects: AREA STUDIES (human relations), BUSINESS (business administration), EDUCATION (elementary, secondary, special), ENGLISH (English, speech), MATH AND SCIENCES (biology, chemistry, mathematics), PREPROFESSIONAL (law, medicine), SOCIAL SCIENCES (history, psychology, social sciences). Forty-six percent of degrees conferred are in education, 27% in social sciences, and 19% in math and sciences.

Required: Seminars are required for several majors. There is a distributional requirement for all students.

Special: A general studies degree is offered. Students may create their own programs from extensive options in humanities, social and behavioral sciences, natural sciences, and mathematics. Independent study and interdisciplinary courses are offered in some areas. During the interterm semester, students may attend a workshop at Oxford or London.

Honors: Three national honor societies have chapters on campus.

Admissions: Seventy-six percent of those who applied were accepted for the 1981–82 freshman class. Of those who enrolled, the SAT scores were as follows: Verbal—62% scored below 500, 26% between 500 and 599, 4% between 600 and 700, and 0% above 700; Math—56% scored below 500, 26% between 500 and 599, 6% between 600 and 700, and 0% above 700. Candidates for admission should be graduates of an accredited high school with 16 completed Carnegie units and a grade average of 80. In addition, the college considers important such factors as recommendations by school officials, leadership record, and advanced placement or honor courses.

Procedure: The SAT is required; the ACT is also accepted. The deadlines for application are August 15 (fall) and January 5 (spring). Notification is on a rolling basis. A $15 fee must accompany the application.

Special: Early and deferred admissions plans and an early decision plan are available. AP and CLEP credit is given.

Transfer: For fall 1981, 278 students applied, 234 were accepted, and 154 enrolled. Good academic standing with a minimum GPA of 2.0 is requested. Standardized exam scores are required if the applicant has completed less than 40 credits. An associate degree and an interview are recommended. D grades transfer only with an associate degree. Students must spend 3 semesters in residence and complete at least 48 of the 128 credits necessary for a bachelor's degree.

Visiting: Although there are no regularly scheduled orientations for prospective students, informal visits can be arranged for weekdays from 9 A.M. to 4 P.M.. Guides are available, and visitors may sit in on classes. Arrangements should be made through the assistant director of admissions.

Financial Aid: About 84% of all students receive financial aid. Fifteen percent work part-time on campus. Average aid to freshmen is $1500. The college offers full tuition scholarships each year on a competitive basis. Other aid is available in the form of scholarships, loans, and grants, and is based on need as well as ability. The college is a member of the CSS, and the FAF is required of aid applicants. Deadlines for aid application are February 25 (fall) and November 15 (spring) for freshmen, March 1 (fall) for transfers.

Foreign Students: One percent of the full-time students come from foreign countries.

Admissions: Foreign students must achieve a TOEFL score of 500. No college entrance exam must be taken.

Procedure: Application deadlines are August 15 (fall) and December 15 (spring). Foreign students must present a completed college health form and proof of funds adequate to cover one year of study.

Admissions Contact: Sherrie Van Arnam, Director of Admissions.

ST. LAWRENCE UNIVERSITY C-2
Canton, New York 13617 (315) 379-5261

F/T: 1193M, 1119W Faculty: 159; IIB, ++$
P/T: 3M, 3W Ph.D.'s: 70%
Grad: 71M, 73W S/F Ratio: 15 to 1
Year: 4-1-4, ss Tuition: $5845
Appl: Feb. 1 R and B: $2165
3000 applied 1600 accepted 635 enrolled
SAT: 550V 600M ACT: 28 VERY COMPETITIVE+

St. Lawrence University, founded in 1856, is a private liberal arts institution. The library contains 270,000 volumes and more than 1800 periodicals.

Environment: The 1500-acre rural campus is located 60 miles from Watertown, New York and 80 miles from Ottawa, Ontario. Other colleges, including Clarkson and SUNY at Potsdam, are nearby. Recent constructions include an addition to the library and computer facilities.

Student Life: About 60% of the students come from New York State, but 30 states are also represented. Seventy-five percent of the freshmen attended public schools. Ninety-nine percent of the students live on campus. About three percent are minority-group members. University housing is both single-sex and coed. There are visiting privileges in single-sex housing. Students may keep cars on campus.

Organizations: There are 7 fraternities and 6 sororities; 40% of the men and 33% of the women belong to them. There are many student organizations including religious groups for Catholic, Protestant, and Jewish students. The SLU Snowbowl is a popular winter event. There are some wilderness areas open to students.

Sports: There are intercollegiate teams in 15 sports for men and 11 sports for women. There are 17 intramurals for men and 10 for women.

Handicapped: About 75% of the campus is accessible to handicapped students. Special facilities include wheelchair ramps, special parking, elevators, and specially equipped rest rooms. Special class scheduling is possible.

Graduates: Two percent of the freshmen drop out by the end of their first year. Eighty-five percent remain to graduate. About 65% of the graduates go on to graduate study; 5% enter medical school, and 1% dental school. Thirty-six percent enter careers in business and industry.

Services: The following services are provided to students free of charge: placement, health care, psychological counseling, career counseling (for graduates as well as undergraduates), tutoring, and remedial instruction.

Programs of Study: The university confers the B.A. and B.S. degrees. Master's programs are also offered. Bachelor's degrees are offered in the following subjects: AREA STUDIES (Canadian), ENGLISH (literature, writing), FINE AND PERFORMING ARTS (art), LANGUAGES (French, German, Spanish), MATH AND SCIENCES (biology, chemistry, ecology/environmental science, geology, mathematics, physics), PHILOSOPHY (philosophy, religion), PREPROFESSIONAL (dentistry, engineering, law, medicine), SOCIAL SCIENCES (anthropology), economics, government/political science, history, psychology, sociology).

Required: One year of physical education is required.

Special: The university offers foreign study programs in Denmark, France, England, Kenya, Spain, Canada, and Austria. There is a 3-2 combination degree program in engineering and a 4-1 MBA program with Clarkson College. Student-designed majors are permitted.

Honors: There are 19 national honor societies with chapters on campus. All academic departments have their own honors programs as well.

Admissions: About 53% of those who applied were accepted for the 1981–82 freshman class. The SAT scores of those who enrolled were as follows: Verbal—84% scored below 600, 15% between 600 and 700, and 1% above 700; Math—62% scored below 600, 36% between 600 and 700, and 2% above 700. The secondary school record (average, courses, class rank, recommendations, and extracurricular activities) is considered the most important factor for admission. AP and honors courses are given special consideration.

Procedure: The SAT or ACT and the ATs in English Composition and 2 others are required. Tests should be taken in November, December, or January of the senior year. Applications should be filed by February 1 (fall) and December 1 (spring). Notification begins about March 15. There is a $20 application fee.

Special: The university has early decision, early admissions, and deferred admissions plans. AP and CLEP are used.

Transfer: For fall 1981, 155 students applied, 103 were accepted, and 58 enrolled. The university calls its transfer procedure "competitive." There is a 2-year residency requirement. Transfer students must complete 16 course credits at the university, out of the 32 needed for a bachelor's degree. March 1 is the deadline for fall applications, December 1 for spring.

Visiting: There are no regular orientations for prospective students, but guides are available for informal weekday visits. Visitors may sit in on classes and may also stay overnight at the school. The admissions office handles the arrangements.

Financial Aid: Thirty percent of the students receive scholarship aid. Thirty-five percent work part-time on campus. Average aid to freshmen from all sources is $3500. There are scholarship and loan funds, and most departments have work-study programs. The university is a member of CSS. The FAF is required, and the deadlines for aid applications are February 15 (freshmen) and March 1 (transfers) for fall and December 1 (spring).

Foreign Students: Two percent of the full-time students come from foreign countries.

Admissions: Foreign students must take the TOEFL, the SAT, or the ACT. They must also take ATs if the SAT is submitted.

Procedure: The application deadlines are February 1 (fall) and December 1 (spring). Foreign students must present proof of health. They must also submit proof of adequate funds. They must carry health insurance, which is available through the university.

Admissions Contact: Conrad J. Sharrow, Director of Admissions.

ST. THOMAS AQUINAS COLLEGE D-5
Sparkill, New York 10976 (914) 359-9500

F/T: 472M, 610W	Faculty: n/av; IIB, av$
P/T: 109M, 229W	Ph.D.'s: 70%
Grad: none	S/F Ratio: 15 to 1
Year: 4-1-4, ss	Tuition: $2600
Appl: open	R and B: $1800
517 applied	490 accepted	352 enrolled
SAT: 436V 449M		LESS COMPETITIVE

St. Thomas Aquinas College, founded under the auspices of the Sparkill Dominican Order in 1952, is a private liberal arts college. The library houses 104,000 volumes and subscribes to 75 periodicals.

Environment: The 24-acre campus, in a suburban area 13 miles from New York City, has 3 modern buildings, a residence hall, modern science laboratories, a dining hall, and student lounges.

Student Life: About 60% of the students are from New York. Sixty percent attended public schools. Ninety-six percent of the students live on campus. Fifty-five percent are Catholic, 25% Protestant, and 20% Jewish. About 16% of the students are minority-group members. College housing is single-sex; there are visiting privileges. Students may keep cars on campus.

Organizations: Extracurricular activities include special-interest groups and clubs and college-sponsored trips to plays and museums in New York City.

Sports: The college competes intercollegiately in 3 sports for men and 4 for women. There are 3 intramural sports for men and 4 for women.

Handicapped: About 80% of the campus is accessible to handicapped students. Special facilities include wheelchair ramps, special parking, and lowered drinking fountains. Special class scheduling is also available.

Graduates: The freshman dropout rate is 15%; 80% remain to graduate. Fifty percent of the graduates pursue advanced degrees; 3% enter law school. Forty-five percent pursue careers in business and industry.

Services: Free placement and career counseling are offered to students. Health care, tutoring, and remedial instruction are available on a fee basis.

Programs of Study: The college confers the B.A., B.S., and B.S. in Ed. degrees. Bachelor's degrees are offered in the following subjects: BUSINESS (accounting, business administration, finance, marketing, personnel management), EDUCATION (bilingual, early childhood, elementary, secondary, special), ENGLISH (English, journalism), FINE AND PERFORMING ARTS (art, art education, radio/TV), HEALTH SCIENCES (medical technology), LANGUAGES (French, Spanish), MATH AND SCIENCES (mathematics, natural sciences), PHILOSOPHY (philosophy, religion), PREPROFESSIONAL (dentistry, engineering, law, medicine), SOCIAL SCIENCES (criminal justice, gerontology, history, psychology, social sciences). Thirty-two percent of the degrees are conferred in business.

Required: Students must take either the GRE, URE, or UP tests for graduation.

Special: Teacher certification is available. There are special offerings in child care (leading to professional certification), gerontology, and learning disabilities. A dual degree in math and engineering is offered. A 5-year engineering program is available through George Washington University.

Honors: There is a chapter of Alpha Chi on campus.

Admissions: Ninety-five percent of those who applied were accepted for the 1981–82 freshman class. The SAT scores of those who enrolled were as follows: Verbal—80% scored below 500, 14% between 500 and 599, 6% between 600 and 700, and 0% above 700; Math—82% scored below 500, 16% between 500 and 599, 2% between 600 and 700, and 0% above 700. Candidates should have graduated from accredited high schools, have a good school recommendation, an average of 75% or better, and 15 Carnegie units. Advanced placement or honor courses are also considered.

Procedure: The SAT is required. A personal interview is recommended. Application deadlines are open. There is a rolling admissions policy. The application fee is $15.

Special: Early admissions and deferred admissions are available. AP and CLEP credit is given.

Transfer: For fall 1981, 321 applications were received, 317 were accepted, and 237 students enrolled. A 2.0 GPA is required. D grades do not transfer. Students must earn 30 credits at the college, out of the 120 needed for a bachelor's degree. Application deadlines are open.

Visiting: Informal weekday visits can be arranged by the admissions office. Visitors may sit in on classes.

Financial Aid: Seventy percent of the students receive financial aid. Eight percent work part-time on campus. Average aid to freshmen from all sources is $900. Loans are available from federal and state governments and local banks. The college is a member of the CSS. The FAF is required. The application deadline is March 1.

Foreign Students: Fewer than 1% of the full-time students come from foreign countries.

Admissions: Foreign students must take the TOEFL. No college entrance examination is required.

Procedure: Application deadlines are open. Foreign students must submit proof of funds adequate to cover 1 year of study. They must also carry health insurance, which is available through the college for a fee.

Admissions Contact: Andrea Kraeft, Director of Admissions.

SARAH LAWRENCE COLLEGE   D-5
Bronxville, New York 10708   (914) 793-4242

F/T: 190M, 670W	Faculty: 62; IV, ++$
P/T: 15M, 80W	Ph.D.'s: 62%
Grad: 10M, 100W	S/F Ratio: 9 to 1
Year: sems, ss	Tuition: $7260
Appl: Feb. 1	R and B: $3200
780 applied	500 accepted	225 enrolled
SAT or ACT: required		COMPETITIVE+

Sarah Lawrence College, a small, independent liberal arts college founded in 1928, has an individualized and nontraditional approach to education. Most courses are seminars of 15 students or less. Students are evaluated in written reports based on performance in class, biweekly tutorial conferences, written papers, and special projects. Letter grades are recorded on transcripts for graduate school and transfer purposes only. The college library contains over 155,000 volumes and 2750 microfilm items, and subscribes to 1000 periodicals.

Environment: The 30-acre campus is located in suburban Bronxville, 15 miles from New York City. There are 40 buildings, including 6 dormitories and 24 small residence houses with a capacity for 600 students.

Student Life: The geographic distribution of students is broad: 38% are from New York State and 52% are from other states. About 80% of the students reside on campus. Nineteen percent are minority-group members. College housing is both single-sex and coed. There are visiting privileges in single-sex housing. Students may keep cars on campus.

Organizations: There are no fraternities or sororities. A wide variety of cultural, social, and recreational activities is available.

Sports: The college offers intercollegiate competition in 4 sports for women and 1 for men. There are 4 intramural sports for both men and women.

Handicapped: Special facilities for handicapped students are very limited; there are wheelchair ramps. Fewer than 1% of the students have visual or hearing impairments.

Graduates: Ten percent of the freshmen drop out by the end of their first year. About 65% remain to graduate.

Services: The following services are available to students free of charge: placement service, career counseling, psychological counseling, and tutoring. Health care and tutoring are also available on a fee basis.

Programs of Study: The college confers the B.L.A. degree. Master's degrees are also granted. All programs are self-designed by the student, and no formal majors are declared. The bachelor's degree is offered in the following subjects: AREA STUDIES (American, Asian, women's), ENGLISH (English, creative writing, literature), FINE AND PERFORMING ARTS (art, art history, dance, film/photography, music, studio art, theater/dramatics), LANGUAGES (French, German, Greek/Latin, Italian, Russian, Spanish), MATH AND SCIENCES (biochemistry, biology, chemistry, ecology/environmental science, mathematics, natural sciences, physical sciences, physics), PHILOSOPHY (classics, humanities, philosophy, religion), PREPROFESSIONAL (architecture, dentistry, law, medicine), SOCIAL SCIENCES (anthropology, economics, government/political science, history, international relations, psychology, social sciences, sociology, women's studies).

Required: Undergraduates must take 2 lecture courses. There are no required courses for freshmen. However, each freshman is assigned one course, called freshman studies, on the basis of his or her expressed interests.

Special: The college's Horace Gregory Writing Program, with a faculty of well-known practicing authors, is one of the few undergraduate writing programs in the country. Study-abroad programs are available in Paris and Lacoste, France, as well as in London and Florence. Interdisciplinary and independent work is stressed. Students create their own programs. The creative arts are fully integrated with the liberal arts. Sarah Lawrence also has a cooperative program in architecture with the Institute of Architecture and Urban Studies in New York City. There are numerous combined study-work programs, including positions with art museums, theaters, hospitals, dance companies, publications, and orchestras, and in various social-action programs and government agencies.

Honors: There are no honors programs, but all departments offer advanced work opportunities.

Admissions: Sixty-four percent of those who applied were accepted for the 1981–82 freshman class. Of those who enrolled, the SAT scores were as follows: Verbal—14% scored below 500, 72% between 500 and 599, 10% between 600 and 700, 4% above 700; Math—20% scored below 500, 70% between 500 and 599, 7% between 600 and 700, and 3% above 700. The completion of 16 units of secondary school work or the equivalent is required for admission. Other important factors are advanced placement or honors courses, recommendations, and evidence of special talent.

Procedure: The SAT, 3 ATs, or the ACT is required of all freshmen and transfer applicants. The application deadline is February 1 (fall) and November 1 (spring). Freshmen are admitted to either semester. There is a $25 application fee.

Special: Candidates may apply for early admission after 3 exceptionally strong high school years. There are also early decision and deferred admissions plans. AP credit is available.

Transfer: For fall 1981, 135 students applied, 70 were accepted, and 55 enrolled. Requirements include strong academic and personal qualities. D grades do not transfer. A 2-year residency rule is in effect. Students must complete 60 credits at the college, out of the 120 needed for a bachelor's degree. The application deadlines are February 1 (financial aid), May 1 (fall), and November 1 (spring). Freshmen with one semester of college may be admitted in January. An interview is strongly recommended. No financial aid is awarded in January, however. Housing is extremely tight.

Visiting: There are regularly scheduled 1-day orientation programs for accepted students. Prospective students may visit the school on an informal basis any weekday from 9 A.M. to 5 P.M. and are encouraged to sit in on classes. Guided tours are available. Visitors may stay overnight at the school, hosted by students. Arrangements should be made through the admissions office.

Financial Aid: About 40% of students receive financial aid. Forty percent work part-time on campus. Average aid to freshmen from all sources is $4084. The college participates in NDSL, CWS, BEOG, and SEOG. Institutional funds are also available to students. All financial aid students are committed to a program of self-help, which includes a combination of loans and earnings. The college is a member of CSS. The SLC "D" form and the FAF are required. The deadline for application is February 1.

Foreign Students: Ten percent of the full-time students come from foreign countries. The college offers these students special organizations.

Admissions: Foreign students must score 500 on the TOEFL. No college entrance examination is required.

Procedure: The application deadlines are February 1 (fall) and November 1 (spring). Foreign students must present proof of funds adequate to cover a full academic year.

Admissions Contact: Sandra M. Moore, Associate Director of Admissions.

SCHOOL OF VISUAL ARTS   D-5
New York, New York 10010   (212) 679-7350

F/T: 1180M, 1109W	Faculty: 30; n/av
P/T: 1102M, 1753W	Ph.D.'s: 15%
Grad: none	S/F Ratio: 15 to 1
Year: 4-1-4, ss	Tuition: $4253
Appl: open	R and B: $2150
2331 applied	727 accepted	476 enrolled
SAT or ACT: not required		SPECIAL

The School of Visual Arts, founded in 1947, is a professional college of art that offers bachelor's degrees in fine and applied arts. The library contains 30,000 volumes, 60,500 slides, and 222,500 pictures, and subscribes to 135 periodicals.

Environment: The campus, located in midtown Manhattan, is made up of 5 buildings.

Student Life: About 71% of the students are residents of New York State. About 3% of the students live in school housing. About 12% of the students are minority-group members. School housing is both single-sex and coed.

Organizations: Extracurricular activities include student government; a newspaper and magazine; film, poster, and professional competitions; and drama.

Sports: The school sponsors intramural teams for both men and women in 3 sports.

Graduates: Sixteen percent of the freshmen drop out by the end of their first year. Sixty percent remain to graduate. Six percent of the graduates seek advanced degrees. Ninety-three percent pursue careers in business and industry.

Services: Free health care, placement and career counseling, tutoring, and remedial instruction are provided to students. Psychological counseling is available for a fee.

Programs of Study: The school offers the B.F.A. degree. The bachelor's degree is offered in the following areas: FINE AND PERFORMING ARTS (art, art education, art therapy, communication arts—journalism, film/photography, media arts—advertising, media arts—business, media arts—copywriting, media arts—design, media arts—illustration, radio/TV, studio art). The art-education program also leads to New York State teaching certification. About half the degrees are granted in media arts.

Special: Cooperative work-study and study-abroad programs are available. Summer abroad programs are offered in Dublin, Ireland and Tangier, Morocco.

Admissions: About 31% of those who applied were accepted for the 1981–82 freshman class. A high school diploma is required. The most important factors affecting the admissions decision are the applicant's portfolio, impressions made during the required interview, and recommendations by high school officials.

Procedure: Freshmen are admitted to all semesters. There are no application deadlines; a rolling admissions policy is used. The application fee is $15. The interview requirement may be waived if the applicant lives more than 100 miles from New York City.

Special: A deferred admissions plan is offered.

Transfer: For fall 1981, 1942 students applied, 495 were accepted, and 319 enrolled. Requirements are the same as those for freshman applicants. A 2.0 GPA is needed. D grades do not transfer. Students must complete at least 4 semesters in residence and earn 64 of the 128 credits needed for a bachelor's degree. Application deadlines are open.

Financial Aid: About 76% of the students receive aid. About 1% work part-time on campus. Average aid to freshmen from all sources covers 50% of costs. More than 30 freshman scholarships are available, as are federal and state loans. The school is a member of CSS. The FAF, the school's own form, and documents to substantiate income must be submitted by April 16 (fall) and November 15 (spring). Need is the primary consideration in awarding aid.

Foreign Students: Three percent of the full-time students come from foreign countries. The school offers these students an intensive English course and special counseling.

Admissions: Foreign students must score 500 on the TOEFL. No college entrance examination is required.

Procedure: Application deadlines are open. Foreign students must present proof of funds adequate to cover 4 years of study.

Admissions Contact: John Mulcahy, Director of Admissions.

SEMINAR COLLEGE D-3
New York, New York 10013 (212) 741-5665

F/T: 48M, 55W	Faculty: 23; I, ++$
P/T: 6M, 6W	Ph.D.'s: 30%
Grad: 1396M, 1516W	S/F Ratio: 5 to 1
Year: sems, ss	Tuition: $4600
Appl: open	R and B: $2900
112 applied	78 accepted 59 enrolled
SAT: 600V 580M	HIGHLY COMPETITIVE

Seminar College, an independent institution founded in 1976, is part of the undergraduate division of the New School for Social Research. The college developed from a one-year freshman program and an upper-division college that accepted only transfer students. It departs substantially from many of the principles that usually shape colleges today. Students read the original works of leading thinkers and confront intellectual issues and ideas through sustained writing and discussion. Students may study widely varied disciplines or closely related fields. The college uses the seminar method, and students work out individual programs with faculty advisers.

Environment: The college is located in the Greenwich Village area of Manhattan. Dormitories accommodate about 32 students; additional housing is available if necessary.

Student Life: About 55% of the freshmen come from New York State, and 68% are graduates of public schools. Eight percent are members of minority groups. Dormitories are coed.

Organizations: Students may participate in all the activities of the New School, which include an orchestra, acting and writing workshops, a student magazine, and a weekly newsletter. There are no fraternities or sororities.

Sports: The college has no athletics program.

Handicapped: All classrooms are accessible to handicapped students. Special facilities include elevators.

Graduates: About half the graduates seek advanced degrees.

Services: Career counseling is available free to students. Fees are charged for health care services.

Programs of Study: The college awards the B.A. degree. Master's and doctoral degrees are available through the New School. Students design their own major programs in conjunction with faculty members.

Required: Students must take 4 seminars in their freshman year; an intensive language course may substitute for 1 of the seminars. A GPA of 2.5 or better is required to graduate.

Admissions: Seventy percent of those who applied were accepted for the 1981–82 freshman class. The SAT scores of those who enrolled were as follows: Verbal—5% below 500, 53% between 500 and 599, 37% between 600 and 700, and 5% above 700; Math—6% below 500, 60% between 500 and 599, 30% between 600 and 700, and 4% above 700. Admissions requirements are flexible; graduation from high school is not required. Impressions made during the required personal interview, high school academic record, admission essay and recommendations from high school officials are very important. Advanced placement or honors courses, evidence of special talents, and leadership record also are considered.

Procedure: Applicants must take the SAT and arrange a personal interview. Freshmen are admitted in fall and spring. Application deadlines are open. The college follows a rolling admissions policy. The application fee is $25.

Special: Early and deferred admissions plans are offered. CLEP or AP credit is accepted.

Transfer: For fall 1981, 38 transfer students applied, 22 were accepted, and 16 enrolled. Transfers are accepted for all classes. Applicants must have a GPA of 2.5 or better and undergo an interview. The college recommends that they have SAT scores totaling at least 1150 and at least 15 credit hours. Grades of C or better generally transfer. Students must earn, at the college, at least 30 of the 120 credits required for a bachelor's degree.

Visiting: Guides are provided for informal visits, and students may sit in on classes and remain overnight at the school. Visits can be arranged with the admissions office, preferably for October, November, March, or April.

Financial Aid: About 48% of the students receive aid; 25% work part-time on campus. Scholarships averaging $1000, loans averaging $2500, and work contracts averaging $800 were available in 1981–82. The average award to freshmen from all sources totaled $3300. The college is a member of the CSS. The FAF and the aid application should be submitted by March 1 (fall) or September 1 (spring) for priority consideration.

Foreign Students: Three foreign students were enrolled in 1981–82. Special counseling and special organizations are provided for foreign students.

Admissions: Applicants must score 550 or better on the TOEFL. No college entrance exams are required.

Procedure: Application deadlines are June 1 (fall) and November 1 (spring). Students must present proof of adequate funds for 1 year. Health insurance, though not required, is available through the college for a fee.

Admissions Contact: Abigail Wender, Associate Director of Admissions.

SIENA COLLEGE D-3
Loudonville, New York 12211 (518) 783-2423

F/T: 1300M, 1200W	Faculty: 133; IIB, +$
P/T: 350M, 250W	Ph.D.'s: 56%
Grad: none	S/F Ratio: 18 to 1
Year: sems, ss	Tuition: $3780
Appl: Mar. 1	R and B: $2350
2200 applied	1335 accepted 595 enrolled
SAT: 498V 554M	VERY COMPETITIVE

Siena College, founded in 1937 by the Franciscan Fathers, is a private, Catholic, liberal arts college. The library contains over 175,000 volumes and 2780 reels of microfilm, and subscribes to 1100 periodicals.

Environment: The 120-acre campus is located in the suburban community of Loudonville, 2 miles from Albany. The 16 buildings include

4 dormitories housing 350 women and 550 men. The college also leases off-campus apartments for about 450 students.

Student Life: Eighty percent of the students are from New York State. Sixty-five percent of the entering freshmen come from public schools. Sixty-five percent of the students live on campus. Eighty percent are Catholic, and 15% are Protestant. Four percent are minority-group members. College housing is both single-sex and coed. There are visiting privileges in single-sex housing. Students may keep cars on campus.

Organizations: There are 2 service fraternities, to which 4% of the men belong. The many extracurricular activities include a radio station and publications. There are over 35 student organizations, including the Stage Three Theatre group, a jazz band, a debating group, and a choral group. Student organizations sponsor many social events throughout the academic year.

Sports: The college competes on an intercollegiate level in 12 sports for men and 8 for women. There are 6 intramural sports for men and 5 for women.

Handicapped: All of the campus is accessible to handicapped students. Special facilities include wheelchair ramps, parking areas, and elevators. Special counselors are also available.

Graduates: By the end of the freshman year, 9% of the students drop out, but 75% remain to graduate. Forty percent of the graduates go on to graduate or professional school; 2% enter medical school, 2% dental school, and 5% law school. Forty-five percent pursue careers in business or industry.

Services: The following services are available to students free of charge: placement, career counseling, health care, psychological counseling, tutoring, and remedial instruction.

Programs of Study: The college confers the B.A., B.S., or B.B.A. degree. Bachelor's degrees are offered in the following subjects: AREA STUDIES (American), BUSINESS (accounting, computer science, economics, finance, management, marketing), EDUCATION (secondary), ENGLISH (English), LANGUAGES (French, Greek/Latin, Spanish), MATH AND SCIENCES (biology, chemistry, mathematics, physics), PHILOSOPHY (philosophy, religion), SOCIAL SCIENCES (government/political science, history, international relations, psychology, sociology).

Required: All undergraduates are required to take 2 courses in religious studies and a core curriculum totaling 36 credit hours.

Special: The college offers the Hudson-Mohawk Association program, whereby students may take courses at any one of 12 other colleges in the area. A junior year abroad is available through several colleges in conjunction with this program. It is possible to earn combined B.A.-B.S. degrees in all majors. The college also offers a general studies degree.

Honors: Seven national honor societies have chapters on campus. Honors programs are offered in English and history.

Admissions: Sixty-one percent of those who applied were accepted for the 1981–82 freshman class. Of those who enrolled, the SAT scores were as follows: Verbal—51% scored below 500, 40% between 500 and 599, 9% between 600 and 700, and 1% above 700; Math—21% scored below 500, 53% between 500 and 599, 25% between 600 and 700, and 1% above 700. Applicants must be graduates of accredited high schools or have equivalency diplomas, have completed 16 Carnegie units, rank in the top 30% of their class, have a minimum grade average of 80, and score a minimum of 1000 on the SAT. Other important considerations are advanced placement or honor courses, leadership record, and recommendations by school officials.

Procedure: Either the SAT or ACT is required. The application deadlines are March 1 (fall) and December 1 (spring). Notification is on a rolling basis. A $15 fee must accompany the application.

Special: Early admissions, early decision, and deferred admissions plans are available. AP and CLEP credit is offered.

Transfer: For fall 1981, 505 students applied, 248 were accepted, and 183 enrolled. A GPA of 2.75 is required. D grades do not transfer. Thirty semester hours must be completed in residence, of the 120 needed for a bachelor's degree. Application deadlines are May 1 (fall) and December 1 (spring).

Visiting: Although there are no regularly scheduled orientations for prospective students, informal visits can be arranged through the admissions office for any day except Sunday. Visitors may stay overnight at the school and may sit in on classes. Guides are available.

Financial Aid: About 65% of students receive financial aid. Twenty-five percent work part-time on campus. Average aid to freshmen from all sources is $2600. The college offers college awards; federally sponsored EOG, NDSL, and CWS programs; state loans; and work

contracts. The college is a member of CSS. The FAF is required of all aid applicants. Need and academic record are the main considerations in determining the award of financial aid. The deadline for aid application is February 15.

Foreign Students: Fewer than 1% of the full-time students come from foreign countries.

Admissions: Foreign students must take the TOEFL, the SAT, or the ACT. They must score 500 on the TOEFL and achieve a combined score of 950 on the SAT.

Procedure: Application deadlines are March 1 (fall) and December 1 (spring). Foreign students must present proof of funds adequate to cover 1 year of study.

Admissions Contact: Harry W. Wood, Director of Admissions.

SKIDMORE COLLEGE D-3
Saratoga Springs, New York 12866　　(518) 584-5000

F/T: 562M, 1622W	Faculty: n/av; IIB, ++$
P/T: 5M, 18W	Ph.D.'s: 95%
Grad: none	S/F Ratio: 13 to 1
Year: 4-1-4, ss	Tuition: $6500
Appl: Feb. 1	R and B: $3010
2864 applied　　1844 accepted　　600 enrolled
SAT: 530V 540M	VERY COMPETITIVE+

Skidmore College, founded in 1911, is a privately controlled, independent liberal arts college. The library houses 264,122 volumes and 26,400 microfilm items, and subscribes to 1300 periodicals.

Environment: The 600-acre suburban campus is located on a wooded tract on the edge of Saratoga Springs, 30 miles north of Albany. The 41 buildings include dormitories and 15 clusters of townhouses. There are off-campus apartments as well.

Student Life: About 35% of the students are from New York State. About 75% live on campus. Ten percent are minority-group members. Campus housing is both coed and single-sex; there are visiting privileges in the single-sex housing. Students may keep cars on campus.

Organizations: There are no fraternities or sororities. Students enjoy a full schedule of cultural and intellectual activities—art exhibits, ballet, concerts, opera, theater, and lectures. Numerous recreational areas offer facilities for skiing, swimming, and riding. There are complete riding facilities on campus.

Sports: The college fields 9 intercollegiate teams for men and 14 for women. There are 9 intramural sports for men and 9 for women.

Handicapped: Nearly all of the campus is accessible to handicapped students. Special facilities include parking areas, elevators, lowered drinking fountains, and specially equipped rest rooms. Special class scheduling is also available. There are a few students with visual or hearing impairments, and the college tailors programs to their individual needs. Special counselors are available.

Graduates: The freshman dropout rate is 8%. Eighty-five percent remain to graduate, and 30% of the graduates continue on to graduate or professional school.

Services: Students receive the following services free of charge: placement and career counseling, health care, and psychological counseling. Tutoring services sometimes require payment.

Programs of Study: The college confers the degrees of B.A. and B.S. Bachelor's degrees are offered in the following subjects: AREA STUDIES (American), BUSINESS (accounting, business administration, management, marketing), EDUCATION (early childhood, elementary, health/physical, secondary), ENGLISH (English, literature), FINE AND PERFORMING ARTS (art, art education, art history, dance, music, music education, studio art, theater/dramatics), HEALTH SCIENCES (nursing), LANGUAGES (French, German, Greek/Latin, Spanish), MATH AND SCIENCES (biochemistry, biology, chemistry, geology, mathematics, physics), PHILOSOPHY (philosophy, religion), PREPROFESSIONAL (engineering, social work), SOCIAL SCIENCES (anthropology, economics, government/political science, history, psychology, sociology). In many liberal arts areas, students may qualify for certification for teaching in secondary schools. Fifty percent of degrees conferred are in liberal arts and sciences, 18% are in fine and performing arts, and 13% are in business.

Required: There are course distribution requirements in humanities, sciences, and social science areas.

Special: Juniors may study abroad under approved programs. During the winter term in January there are several projects involving travel and study abroad, as well as exchange programs with other colleges. Federal, state, and local internship programs in government are available. Cooperative plans include a 3-2 engineering program with Dartmouth and an M.B.A. program with Clarkson. The nursing program includes 2 years of residency in New York City, studying clinical nursing. Skidmore University Without Walls, a nontraditional, nonresidential program, offers students the opportunity to earn a B.A. or B.S. degree through a combination of course work, internships, independent studies, tutorials, and life experiences.

Honors: Four national honor societies have chapters on campus. All departments award honors, but there are no designated honors courses.

Admissions: Sixty-four percent of those who applied were accepted for the 1981–82 freshman class. Of those who enrolled in a recent class, the SAT scores were as follows: Verbal—45% scored between 500 and 599, 6% between 600 and 700, and 1% above 700; Math—53% scored between 500 and 599 and 11% between 600 and 700. Candidates should be graduates of accredited high schools, have good recommendations from the school and teachers, and have completed 16 Carnegie units. Also important are advanced placement or honor courses, leadership qualities, and evidence of special talent. A personal interview is not required, but is strongly recommended.

Procedure: The SAT is required. In addition, 3 ATs, in English composition and 2 other areas, are recommended. Application deadlines are February 1 (fall) and December 15 (spring). There is a $25 application fee.

Special: There are early decision, early admissions, and deferred admission plans. The application deadline for early admission is February 1. AP and CLEP credit is available.

Transfer: For fall 1981, 193 applications were received, 119 were accepted, and 40 students enrolled. A minimum GPA of 2.5 is required. D grades do not transfer. All students must complete, at the college, 18 of the 36 course units required for a bachelor's degree. The application deadline is April 1; transfer students are admitted in the fall and spring terms.

Visiting: Although there are no regularly scheduled orientations, informal visits can be arranged through the director of admissions. Visitors may stay overnight at the school and sit in on classes; guided tours are also available.

Financial Aid: Twenty-six percent of students receive aid. Twenty-six percent work part-time on campus. The average freshman award is $3000. Approximately $860,000 is available to freshmen. Tuition may be paid in installments, and loans and campus employment are available. Skidmore is a member of CSS. The FAF is required. The aid application deadline is February 1.

Foreign Students: Three percent of the full-time students come from foreign countries. Special counseling and special organizations are available for these students.

Admissions: Foreign students must achieve a TOEFL score of at least 550 and must take the SAT. It is recommended that they also take 3 ATs (English Composition and 2 others).

Procedure: Application deadlines are the same as those for other freshmen. Foreign students must present proof of funds adequate to cover 1 semester.

Admissions Contact: Louise Wise, Director of Admissions.

THE STATE UNIVERSITY OF NEW YORK

The State University of New York (SUNY) was established in 1948 to coordinate the state's public institutions of higher learning. Governed by a board of trustees appointed by the governor, SUNY is made up of all state-supported institutions of higher learning, except for the 2-year and 4-year colleges of the City University of New York. The SUNY system is the largest network of colleges and universities in the country and is the only system consciously designed to teach not only scholars and artists, but technicians and teachers. More than 380,000 students are currently enrolled in degree programs. The system includes the following 64 colleges, universities, and centers.

University Centers: State University of New York at Albany, State University of New York at Binghamton, State University of New York at Buffalo, and State University of New York at Stony Brook.

Colleges of Arts and Sciences: Empire State College, and the State University Colleges at Brockport, Buffalo, Cortland, Fredonia, Geneseo, New Paltz, Old Westbury, Oneonta, Oswego, Plattsburgh, Potsdam, and Purchase.

Centers for the Health Sciences: Downstate Medical Center, Upstate Medical Center, Buffalo, and Stony Brook.

Agricultural and Technical Colleges: The Agricultural and Technical Colleges at Alfred, Canton, Cobleskill, Delhi, Farmingdale, and Morrisville.

Specialized Colleges: College of Environmental Science and Forestry, College of Optometry, Maritime College, College of Technology at Utica/Rome, and Fashion Institute of Technology.

Statutory Colleges: College of Ceramics at Alfred University, and the Colleges of Agriculture and Life Sciences, Human Ecology, and Veterinary Medicine, and the School of Industrial and Labor Relations, all at Cornell University.

Community Colleges: Adirondack Community College, Broome Community College, Cayuga County Community College, Clinton Community College, Columbia-Greene Community College, Community College of the Finger Lakes, Corning Community College, Dutchess Community College, Erie Community College, Fulton-Montgomery Community College, Genesee Community College, Herkimer County Community College, Hudson Valley Community College, Jamestown Community College, Jefferson Community College, Mohawk Valley Community College, Monroe Community College, Nassau Community College, Niagara County Community College, North Country Community College, Onondaga Community College, Orange County Community College, Rockland Community College, Schenectady County Community College, Suffolk County Community College, Sullivan County Community College, Ulster County Community College, and Westchester Community College.

STATE UNIVERSITY OF NEW YORK AT ALBANY   D-3
Albany, New York 12222   (518) 457-8996

F/T: 4980M, 4990W   Faculty: 700; I, ++$
P/T: 200M, 220W   Ph.D.'s: 87%
Grad: 2700M, 2065W   S/F Ratio: 17 to 1
Year: sems, ss   Tuition: $1275 ($1975)
Appl: Apr. 1   R and B: $2020
12,355 applied   6440 accepted   2050 enrolled
SAT: 521V 580M   VERY COMPETITIVE

The State University of New York at Albany, founded in 1844, offers undergraduate and graduate programs in the liberal arts and sciences. It is made up of several colleges—Humanities and Fine Arts, Social and Behavioral Sciences, and Science and Mathematics—and schools—Business, Education, Social Welfare, and Public Affairs. Two libraries house a total of nearly 1 million volumes and more than 50,000 microfilm items, and subscribe to over 7000 periodicals.

Environment: The 382-acre suburban campus, located at the western edge of Albany, has 55 buildings, including 36 dormitories that accommodate 5500 students. The university operates 2 recreational campuses, one on the Mohawk River and the other in the Adirondacks.

Student Life: Ninety-eight percent of the students come from New York State. About 87% of the freshmen are graduates of public schools. Sixty-five percent of the students live on campus. Nine percent are minority-group members. Campus housing is both coed and single-sex. There are visiting privileges in single-sex dorms. Students may keep cars on campus. Day-care services are available to all students for a fee.

Organizations: About 2% of the students belong to the 5 fraternities and 3 sororities. There is a wide range of student-operated extracurricular activities, including student government and publications. Religious groups are available for Catholic, Protestant, and Jewish students.

Sports: The university fields intercollegiate teams in 12 sports for men and 10 for women. There are 11 intramural sports for men and 9 for women.

Handicapped: The entire campus is accessible to wheelchair-bound students. Facilities include ramps, elevators, special parking areas, specially equipped rest rooms, and lowered drinking fountains and telephones. Handicapped students also may register early. Approximately a third of the 150 handicapped students have impaired vision or hearing. Braille information on doors, special reading material, and an opticon are provided. Two special counselors are available.

Graduates: Thirteen percent of the freshmen drop out by the end of the first year; 61% remain to graduate. Thirty-eight percent of the graduates pursue advanced study; about 2% enter medical school, 1% enter dental school, and 6% enter law school. Twenty percent pursue careers in business or industry.

Services: The following services are offered free to students: psychological and career counseling, tutoring, and remedial instruction. Placement services are provided for students and alumni. Health care is available for a fee.

Programs of Study: The university confers the B.A. and B.S. degrees. Master's and doctoral degrees also are available. Bachelor's degrees are offered in the following subjects: AREA STUDIES (American, Asian, Black/Afro-American, Inter-American, Puerto Rican, Russian and East European), BUSINESS (accounting, business administration, business education), EDUCATION (secondary), ENGLISH (English, rhetoric and communication), FINE AND PERFORMING ARTS (music, studio art, theater/dramatics), HEALTH SCIENCES (medical technology), LANGUAGES (Chinese, French, German, Greek/Latin, Italian, Russian, Spanish), MATH AND SCIENCES (atmospheric science, biology, chemistry, computer science and applied mathematics, earth science, geology, mathematics, physics), PHILOSOPHY (classics, philosophy), PREPROFESSIONAL (social work), SOCIAL SCIENCES (anthropology, economics, geography, government/political science, history, psychology, public affairs, social studies, sociology). Thirty-four percent of the undergraduate degrees are conferred in social sciences, 23% in business, 15% in math and sciences, and 12% in English.

Special: Study-abroad programs are available. Students may design their own majors. Many departments offer opportunities for research and independent study. A pilot Liberal Education Advancement program is in effect.

Honors: Many departments provide honors programs. Phi Beta Kappa and 12 academic-area societies have chapters on campus.

Admissions: Fifty-two percent of those who applied were accepted for the 1981–82 freshman class. The SAT scores of those who enrolled were as follows: Verbal—36% below 500, 47% between 500 and 599, 15% between 600 and 700, and 2% above 700; Math—11% below 500, 50% between 500 and 599, 34% between 600 and 700, and 5% above 700.

Procedure: Applicants must take the SAT or ACT. Application deadlines are April 1 (fall) and December 1 (spring). Freshmen also are admitted in summer. Personal interviews may be required for some applicants. There is an application fee of $10. Admissions decisions are made on a rolling basis.

Special: Early and deferred admissions plans are available. AP and CLEP credit is accepted.

Transfer: For fall 1981, 4000 students applied, 1680 were accepted, and 950 enrolled. Applicants must present a GPA of at least 2.5 and meet basic freshman requirements. D grades do not transfer. Students must earn, at the university, the last 30 of the 120 credits required for the bachelor's degree. Application deadlines are May 15 (fall) and December 15 (spring).

Visiting: The university schedules orientation programs for prospective students. Guides also are available for informal visits. The best times for visits are the summer months and September, April, and May. Arrangements should be made with the admissions office.

Financial Aid: Financial aid programs include scholarships, grants, loans, and campus jobs. About 85% of the students receive aid; 20% work part-time on campus. The average award to freshmen is $2000. Applications should be filed 15 days after materials are received. The university is a member of CSS. The FAF is required.

Foreign Students: About 3% of the full-time students come from foreign countries. The university offers these students an intensive English course and an intensive English program. Special counseling and organizations are also available.

Admissions: Foreign students must achieve a minimum score of 550 on the TOEFL. The SAT or ACT is not required.

Procedure: The application deadline for fall entry is February 15. A physical examination is required to establish proof of health. Proof of funds adequate to cover the proposed period of study is required. Foreign students are strongly encouraged to carry health insurance, which is available through the university.

Admissions Contact: Rodney A. Hart, Director of Admissions and Records.

STATE UNIVERSITY OF NEW YORK AT BINGHAMTON C-4
Binghamton, New York 13901   (607) 798-2171

F/T: 3539M, 4235W	Faculty: 489; I, +$
P/T: 579M, 518W	Ph.D.'s: 86%
Grad: 1549M, 1172W	S/F Ratio: 20 to 1
Year: sems, ss	Tuition: $1175 ($1875)
Appl: Feb. 15	R and B: $2340–2540
12,362 applied	5523 accepted 1647 enrolled
SAT: 527V 579M	HIGHLY COMPETITIVE

The State University of New York at Binghamton was developed around Harpur College, established in 1946. Harpur College is still the liberal arts unit of the university. Schools of Nursing, Management, General Studies, and Professional Education also offer undergraduate programs. The library contains 1,001,230 volumes and 505,188 microfilm items, and subscribes to 13,718 periodicals.

Environment: The 606-acre suburban campus is located in the Susquehanna River Valley 5 miles from Binghamton. University housing is organized into 6 constituent colleges, 1 of which is located off campus.

Student Life: All but 4% of the students are residents of New York State. About half the students live on campus, and freshmen are required to do so. Campus housing is coed. Students may keep cars on campus. Day-care services are available to all students for a fee.

Organizations: There are no sororities or fraternities. Groups are available for students of all major faiths. Other social and special-interest groups also are available. Cultural activities in the Binghamton area include Roberson Center for the Arts and Sciences, Tri-Cities Opera, the Cider Mill Playhouse, and The Forum.

Sports: The university competes intercollegiately in 11 sports for men and 9 for women. There are 16 intramural sports for men and 15 for women.

Handicapped: Ninety percent of the campus is accessible to wheelchair-bound students. Facilities include wheelchair-accessible transportation, ramps, elevators, special parking areas, specially equipped rest rooms, and lowered drinking fountains and telephones. For students with visual or hearing impairments, the university provides print magnifiers, a variable-speed tape recorder, TTY, coordinate reader aid services, and sign language courses. Two special counselors are available, and special class scheduling can be arranged.

Graduates: Eleven percent of the freshmen drop out or transfer by the end of the first year; 66% remain to graduate. Two percent of the graduates enter dental school, 4% enter medical school, and 9% enter law school. About 35% enter business or industry.

Services: Students receive free career and psychological counseling, remedial instruction, and health care. Some of the tutoring available is free. Placement services may be used by students and alumni.

Programs of Study: The university confers B.A., B.S., and B.T. degrees. Master's and doctoral degrees are also awarded. Bachelor's degrees are offered in the following subjects: AREA STUDIES (Black/Afro-American, Latin American), BUSINESS (accounting, management science), ENGLISH (English, English and rhetoric), FINE AND PERFORMING ARTS (art history, film/photography, music, studio art, theater/dramatics), HEALTH SCIENCES (nursing), LANGUAGES (French, German, Greek/Latin, Hebrew, Italian, Spanish), MATH AND SCIENCES (biochemistry, biology, chemistry, ecology/environmental science, geology, geophysics, mathematics, mathematical physics, physics), PHILOSOPHY (philosophy), PREPROFESSIONAL (dentistry, engineering—electrical, engineering—electro-mechanical, engineering—industrial, engineering—mechanical, law, medicine, pharmacy, veterinary), SOCIAL SCIENCES (anthropology, American studies, applied social sciences, economics, geography, government/political science, history, psychology, social sciences, sociology). A third of the undergraduate degrees conferred are in math and sciences, 22% are in social sciences, and 14% are in business.

Special: Students may study abroad. A 3-2 combined B.A.-M.B.A. program is offered jointly by Harpur College and the School of Management. Five-year B.A.-B.S. degrees may be earned in liberal arts and management, accounting, or nursing, or in a 3-2 engineering program. Students may design their own majors.

Honors: Phi Beta Kappa has a chapter on campus. Most departments offer honors programs.

Admissions: Forty-five percent of those who applied were accepted for the 1981–82 freshman class. The SAT scores of those who enrolled were as follows: Verbal—34% below 500, 46% between 500 and 599, 18% between 600 and 700, and 2% above 700; Math—14% below 500, 45% between 500 and 599, 35% between 600 and 700, and 6% above 700. Harpur College requires applicants to present at least 15 Carnegie units. Besides high school record and test scores, admissions officers consider special talents, advanced placement or honors courses, extracurricular activities, recommendations by school officials, personality, and leadership record.

Procedure: Approximate application deadlines are February 15 (fall) and December 1 (spring). The SAT or ACT is required. Notification is made on a rolling basis beginning February 15. There is a $10 application fee.

Special: Early admissions and deferred admissions plans are available.

Transfer: For fall 1981, 3684 transfer students applied, 1829 were accepted, and 911 enrolled. Applicants should have an average of at least 2.5. C grades or better transfer. Students must complete the last

7½ courses in residence to graduate. Transfers must earn, at the university, 30 of the 120–128 credits necessary for the bachelor's degree. Students are admitted to the fall and spring semesters; application deadlines vary.

Visiting: Regularly scheduled orientations for prospective students include a campus tour and interviews with admissions counselors and current students. Visitors may sit in on classes, and may make arrangements with current students to stay overnight in their dormitory rooms. Visits should be scheduled for Wednesdays and Fridays at 1:30 P.M. and some Saturdays at 11 A.M.

Financial Aid: About 90% of the students receive aid through the university; 12% work part-time on campus. The average award to freshmen from all sources is $450. The university is a member of CSS. Applications and the FAF should be submitted by April 1 (fall), November 15 (spring), or March 15 (summer).

Foreign Students: About 3% of the full-time students come from foreign countries. The university offers these students an intensive English course, special counseling, and special organizations.

Admissions: Foreign students must achieve a minimum score of 550 on the TOEFL. The SAT or ACT is not required.

Procedure: Applications for admission must be received by April for fall entry and November for spring entry. All entering students must have a completed health form on file before enrollment. Proof of funds adequate to cover 1 calendar year of study is required; there are special insurance fees for foreign students. Health insurance is also required; it may be obtained through the university for a fee.

Admissions Contact: Geoffrey D. Gould, Assistant Vice President for Admissions and Financial Aid.

STATE UNIVERSITY OF NEW YORK AT BUFFALO   A-3
Buffalo, New York 14214   (716) 831-2111

F/T: 8682M, 5912W   Faculty: 1404; I, +$
P/T: 2260M, 2439W   Ph.D.'s: 95%
Grad: 4633M, 3464W   S/F Ratio: 10 to 1
Year: sems, ss   Tuition: $1237 ($1937)
Appl: Jan. 5   R and B: $1950
13,239 applied   10,095 accepted   3038 enrolled
SAT: 494V 567M   ACT: 24   VERY COMPETITIVE

The State University of New York at Buffalo, founded in 1846, became part of the SUNY system in September 1962. Undergraduate degrees are granted through a number of schools and faculties: Arts and Letters, Social Sciences, Natural Sciences and Mathematics, Engineering and Applied Science, Health Science, Pharmacy, Library and Information Science, Management, and Architecture and Environmental Design. The university also includes schools of Medicine, Dentistry, Law, and Social Work. The library contains more than 1.8 million volumes.

Environment: The university has 2 campuses. The 178-acre Main Street Campus, 5 miles from the center of Buffalo, eventually will house a health sciences center. The 1200-acre North Campus, still being constructed 12 miles away in suburban Amherst, will be the location of all other undergraduate and graduate education when it is completed in the mid to late 1980s. The university also rents a temporary Ridge Lea Campus near North Campus. Four large residence halls house 5000 students on the Main Street Campus and 3650 on the North Campus. Special interdisciplinary and theme-oriented residence centers are located in one of these halls.

Student Life: Almost all students are from the Mid-Atlantic states, and 6% are from foreign countries. Twenty-six percent live on campus. Eleven percent of the undergraduates are minority-group members. Campus housing is coed. Students may keep cars on campus.

Organizations: Nine fraternities and 4 sororities have chapters on campus. Counselors and groups are available for all major religious faiths. The Buffalo area provides a wealth of entertainment opportunities, including the Albright-Knox Art Gallery, Kleinhans Music Hall, the Chautauqua Institution, and the Shaw Festival in Ontario. Ski slopes, hiking and bicycle trails, camp grounds, and beaches are nearby.

Sports: The university competes on an intercollegiate level in 11 sports for men and 8 for women. There are 19 intramurals for both men and women.

Handicapped: About 90% of the campuses is accessible to wheelchair-bound students. All academic programs are accessible. Facilities include ramps, lowered drinking fountains and telephones, special parking areas, elevators, and specially equipped rest rooms. Thirty-two students have impaired vision and 6 have impaired hearing. An office of services for the handicapped can arrange special class scheduling and other academic support.

Graduates: About 18% of the freshmen drop out; 52% remain to graduate. Thirty-two percent of the graduates seek advanced degrees. Of those who apply, 55% enter medical or dental schools. About 53% of the graduates begin business careers.

Services: The following services are offered free to students: psychological and career counseling, health care, tutoring, and remedial instruction. Placement services are available to students and alumni.

Programs of Study: The university awards the B.A., B.S., B.F.A., and B.P.S. degrees. Master's and doctoral programs also are available. Bachelor's degrees are offered in the following subjects: AREA STUDIES (American, Black/Afro-American, urban), BUSINESS (accounting, computer science, management), EDUCATION (early childhood, health/physical, secondary), ENGLISH (English, literature), FINE AND PERFORMING ARTS (art, art education, art history, dance, film/photography, music, music education, studio art, theater/dramatics), HEALTH SCIENCES (medical technology, nursing, occupational therapy, physical therapy, speech therapy), LANGUAGES (French, German, Italian, Portuguese, Russian, Spanish), MATH AND SCIENCES (biochemistry, biology, chemistry, geology, mathematics, physics, statistics), PHILOSOPHY (classics, philosophy), PREPROFESSIONAL (architecture, dentistry, engineering—aerospace, engineering—chemical, engineering—civil, engineering—electrical, engineering—industrial, engineering—mechanical, law, medicine, pharmacy), SOCIAL SCIENCES (anthropology, economics, geography, government/political science, history, psychology, social sciences, sociology).

Special: Students may study abroad and design their own majors.

Honors: Eleven national honor societies, including Phi Beta Kappa, have chapters on campus. Honors programs are offered by the departments of anthropology, biochemistry, classics, economics, English, math, French, German, and sociology.

Admissions: Seventy-six percent of those who applied were accepted for the 1981–82 freshman class. The SAT scores of a recent class were as follows: Verbal—37% between 500 and 599 and 8% between 600 and 700; Math—46% between 500 and 599 and 30% between 600 and 700. Of those who took the ACT, 21% scored between 20 and 23, 29% between 24 and 26, 23% between 27 and 28, and 21% above 28. Applicants should have completed 16 Carnegie units.

Procedure: The SAT or ACT is required. Applications for fall admission should be submitted by January 5, but will be considered later if space is available. There is a $10 application fee. Freshmen also are admitted to the spring term. Admissions decisions are made on a rolling basis.

Special: The university has an early admissions plan. AP and CLEP credit is accepted.

Transfer: For fall 1981, 4359 transfer students applied, 3323 were accepted, and 1279 enrolled. A GPA of 2.0 or better is required. D grades transfer. Students must complete, at the university, 32 of the 128 credits required for the bachelor's degree. Application deadlines are March 15 (fall) and December 1 (spring).

Visiting: Group information and tour sessions for prospective students are scheduled regularly from October through mid-May. Guides are not provided for informal visits. Visitors may sit in on classes with the permission of the instructor. Campus visits may be arranged through the office of admissions and records.

Financial Aid: Financial aid programs include scholarships, grants, loans, and campus jobs. About 60% of the students receive aid; 12% work part-time on campus. The average award to freshmen is $1120. The university is a member of CSS. An institutional aid form and the FAF should be filed by January 31.

Foreign Students: About 6% of the full-time students come from foreign countries. The university offers these students an intensive English course and an intensive English program. Special counseling and special organizations are also available.

Admissions: Foreign students must achieve a minimum score of 500 on the TOEFL. The SAT or ACT is not required.

Procedure: The application deadline for fall entry is January 5. Foreign students are also admitted to the spring semester. Students must undergo a medical examination to establish proof of health and must carry health insurance, which is available through the university for a fee. Proof of funds adequate to cover 4 years of study at the university is required.

Admissions Contact: David C. Cook, Associate Director of Admissions.

STATE UNIVERSITY OF NEW YORK AT STONY BROOK
E-5

Stony Brook, New York 11794   (516) 246-5126
For health sciences: (516) 246-2109

F/T: 5259M, 4668W	Faculty: 1030; I, +$
P/T: 495M, 708W	Ph.D.'s: 95%
Grad: 2462M, 2131W	S/F Ratio: 15 to 1
Year: sems, ss	Tuition: $1155 ($1855)
Appl: open	R and B: $2340
11,598 applied 6476 accepted 1887 enrolled	
SAT: 480V 560M	**VERY COMPETITIVE**

The State University of New York at Stony Brook, established in 1957, awards undergraduate and graduate degrees through the College of Arts and Science, the College of Engineering and Applied Sciences, and the Harriman College of Urban and Policy Sciences. The Health Sciences comprise the schools of Medicine (including Basic Sciences), Dental Medicine, Nursing, Allied Health Professions, and Social Welfare. The library houses 1,275,000 volumes and 1,675,000 microfilm items, and subscribes to 17,425 periodicals.

Environment: The 1100-acre campus is located about 60 miles east of Manhattan in a suburban, wooded area on the north shore of Long Island, close to picturesque villages, harbors, and beaches. Residence halls and on-campus apartments house 7200 students. Nearby are Brookhaven National Laboratory and Cold Spring Harbor Laboratory, where collaborative research in several specialized fields is conducted by university faculty and graduate students.

Student Life: The majority of undergraduate students come from New York. About half the undergraduates and several hundred graduate students live on campus. Almost 14% of the students are minority-group members. Campus housing is coed. Students may keep cars on campus. Day-care services are available to all students for a fee.

Organizations: There are dozens of academic, athletic, social and cultural organizations on campus. Polity, the undergraduate student government, uses student fees to support more than 100 organizations, among them student newspapers, a radio station, and several club sports.

Sports: The university fields intercollegiate teams in 10 sports for men and 9 for women. Ten intramural sports for men and women also are available.

Handicapped: Facilities for wheelchair-bound students include ramps, special parking areas, elevators, specially equipped rest rooms, and lowered drinking fountains and telephones. There are also specially equipped living accommodations. The Office of the Disabled provides counseling and other assistance.

Graduates: About 18% of the freshmen drop out; 55% to 60% remain to graduate. Of those graduates who apply, 58% are accepted to medical schools, 76% to dental schools, and 85% to law schools.

Services: Free career and psychological counseling, tutoring, and remedial instruction are provided. Placement services are available to students and alumni.

Programs of Study: The university confers the B.A., B.S., and B.E. degrees. Master's, doctoral, and professional degrees also are available. Bachelor's degrees are offered in the following subjects: AREA STUDIES (Black/Afro-American), ENGLISH (comparative literature, English, linguistics), FINE AND PERFORMING ARTS (art history, music, studio art, theater/dramatics), HEALTH SCIENCES (cardiorespiratory science, medical technology, nursing, physical therapy, physician's assistant, social welfare), LANGUAGES (French, German, Italian, Russian, Spanish), MATH AND SCIENCES (biochemistry, biology, chemistry, computer science, earth science, engineering chemistry, mathematics, physics, statistics-applied mathematics), PHILOSOPHY (humanities, philosophy, religious studies), PREPROFESSIONAL (engineering—electrical, engineering—mechanical, engineering science), SOCIAL SCIENCES (anthropology, economics, government/political science, history, psychology, social sciences, sociology). Forty-six percent of the undergraduate degrees are conferred in social sciences, 22% in math and sciences, 10% in health sciences, 10% in preprofessional areas, 4% in English, 2% in languages, 1% in philosophy, and 5% in fine and performing arts.

Required: Students must demonstrate proficiency in English, math, and a foreign language. The university requires each student to take 12 credits in science and mathematics, 12 in social and behavioral science, and 12 in arts and humanities.

Special: Students may arrange to study in any of 30 countries, including England, Poland, Spain, Egypt, Israel, Mexico, Colombia, China, and Korea. Combined B.A.-B.S. degrees may be earned. Students may design their own majors. B.A. and B.S. candidates may earn teaching certificates in secondary levels.

NEW YORK   601

Honors: Phi Beta Kappa has a chapter on campus. Honors programs are offered by most major departments. The University Scholars Program awards scholarships to incoming freshmen with high academic credentials.

Admissions: About 56% of those who applied were accepted for the 1981–82 freshman class. The SAT scores of those who enrolled were as follows: Verbal—60% below 500, 30% between 500 and 599, 9% between 600 and 700, and 1% above 700; Math—31% below 500, 41% between 500 and 599, 24% between 600 and 700, and 4% above 700. Candidates should rank in the top 25% of their high school class and present an average of at least 85. Seventy percent of the freshmen are admitted by academic criteria and 30% for special talents in areas such as music, for leadership, for ethnic or cultural background, or for unusual academic strength in one area. Admissions officers also consider advanced placement or honors courses, extracurricular activities, and recommendations by school officials.

Procedure: The SAT or ACT is required. Applications are reviewed when received and candidates are notified on a rolling basis. Freshmen are admitted in summer. There is a $10 application fee.

Special: Early and deferred admissions plans are offered. CLEP and AP credit may be earned.

Transfer: For fall 1981, 3154 students applied, 1955 were accepted, and 1012 enrolled. D grades transfer; a 2.5 GPA is required. Students must complete at least 36 upper-division credits in residence and maintain a GPA of 2.0 or better to receive a bachelor's degree (which requires the completion of 120–128 credits).

Visiting: The university conducts orientations for prospective students on weekends. Tours also are available Wednesday and Friday at 3 P.M. from the Admissions Office when classes are in session.

Financial Aid: Financial aid programs include scholarships, grants, loans, and campus jobs. About 75% of the entering freshmen, 67% of entering transfers, and 54% of all undergraduate students receive aid. Applications for aid should be filed by February 19. The university is a member of CSS. The FAF is required.

Foreign Students: Almost 4% of the full-time undergraduate students come from foreign countries. The university offers these students an English course as well as an intensive English program held during the summer session. Special counseling and special organizations are also available.

Admissions: Foreign students must achieve a minimum score of 550 on the TOEFL. The SAT or ACT is not required.

Procedure: Fall application deadlines are July 1 for students residing abroad and July 15 for those in the U.S. Spring application deadlines are December 1 for applicants living abroad and December 15 for students in this country. A completed health form is required. Foreign students must also carry health insurance, which is available through the university for a fee. Proof of funds adequate to cover the full program of study is required.

Admissions Contact: Daniel M. Frisbie, Director of Admissions. For health sciences, contact the Office of Student Services.

STATE UNIVERSITY OF NEW YORK/ COLLEGE AT BROCKPORT
B-3

Brockport, New York 14420   (716) 395-2751

F/T: 2929M, 2928W	Faculty: n/av; IIA, +$
P/T: 430M, 577W	Ph.D.'s: 66%
Grad: 462M, 723W	S/F Ratio: 16 to 1
Year: sems, ss	Tuition: $1160 ($1860)
Appl: Jan. 15	R and B: $2170
7685 applied 4806 accepted 1088 enrolled	
SAT: 430V 478M	**COMPETITIVE**

The State University of New York/College at Brockport was founded in 1867. The library contains 400,000 volumes and 945,500 microfilm items, and subscribes to over 3500 periodicals.

Environment: The 590-acre campus is located in a village of 8000 people, about 16 miles from Rochester. The college also owns a 500-acre recreation area. There are 35 buildings on campus.

Student Life: The college draws 98% of its students from New York State and 1% from foreign countries. Ninety percent of the freshmen are graduates of public schools. Forty-five percent of the students live on campus. Nine percent are minority-group members. Campus housing is both coed and single-sex. There are visiting privileges in single-sex dorms. Students may keep cars on campus.

Organizations: One percent of the men belong to the 2 local fraternities. The college provides a typical program of activities, including student groups and social events. Cultural and recreational opportunities in the Rochester area include Letchworth State Park, Strasenberg Planetarium, and Eastman Theatre.

Sports: The college competes in 7 intercollegiate sports for men and 8 for women. There are 14 intramural sports for men and 11 for women.

Handicapped: The entire campus is accessible to wheelchair-bound students. Facilities include ramps, special parking areas, elevators, specially equipped rest rooms, and lowered drinking fountains and telephones. One special counselor is available.

Graduates: About 25% of the freshmen drop out; 45% remain to graduate. About a fourth of the graduates pursue advanced degrees. Another 35% begin careers in business and industry.

Services: Students receive free career and psychological counseling, health care, tutoring, and remedial instruction. Placement services are available for students.

Programs of Study: The college confers the B.A., B.S., B.P.S., and B.S.N. degrees. Master's degrees also are available. Bachelor's degrees are offered in the following subjects: AREA STUDIES (Black/Afro-American, global), BUSINESS (business administration), EDUCATION (health/physical), ENGLISH (English, speech), FINE AND PERFORMING ARTS (art, art history, dance, music, studio art, theater/dramatics), HEALTH SCIENCES (nursing), LANGUAGES (French, German, Spanish), MATH AND SCIENCES (biology, chemistry, earth science, geology, mathematics, meteorology, physics), PHILOSOPHY (philosophy), PREPROFESSIONAL (social work), SOCIAL SCIENCES (anthropology, economics, geography, government/political science, history, psychology, sociology). Teaching certificates may be earned in elementary education, elementary and early secondary education, health education, physical education, secondary education, speech education, and speech-and-hearing-handicapped education. Seventeen percent of the undergraduate degrees are conferred in social sciences, 14% in business, 12% in humanities, 17% in natural sciences, 8% in fine and performing arts, 11% in health sciences, and 21% in physical education and recreation.

Required: Students must complete general education requirements, which include a distribution of credits in 4 broad areas of study, during the first 2 years.

Special: An increasing number of independent-study and directed-study courses are available. Students may earn degrees in 3 years and design their own majors.

Admissions: Sixty-three percent of those who applied were accepted for the 1981–82 freshman class. The SAT scores of those who enrolled were as follows: Verbal—85% below 500, 13% between 500 and 599, 2% between 600 and 700, and 0% above 700; Math—65% below 500, 28% between 500 and 599, 6% between 600 and 700, and 1% above 700. Candidates must rank in the upper half of their class and have completed at least 14–16 academic units with an average of 80 or better.

Procedure: The SAT or ACT is required. New students are admitted in fall and spring. Applications for fall admission should be submitted by January 15. Notification is made on a rolling basis. There is a $10 application fee.

Special: Early and deferred admissions plans are available. CLEP and AP credit is accepted.

Transfer: For fall 1981, 2789 students applied, 2244 were accepted, and 821 enrolled. A GPA of 2.0 or better is required. D grades transfer only if the student has earned an associate degree. Transfer applicants are considered for all classes. Students must complete 24 of the last 30 credit hours at the college. A total of 120 credits is necessary for the bachelor's degree. The recommended application deadlines are March 15 (summer and fall) and December 15 (spring).

Visiting: Pre-admission orientation programs are scheduled in April. Informal campus visits and interviews can be arranged for weekdays, preferably in the early fall or late spring, through the admissions office. Guides are available, and visitors may sit in on classes.

Financial Aid: Financial aid programs include scholarships, grants, loans, and campus jobs. About 66% of the students receive aid; 11% work part-time on campus. The average award to freshmen is $3000. The college is a member of CSS. The FAF is preferred. Applications should be submitted by May 1.

Foreign Students: Foreign students constitute 1% of the full-time enrollment. The college offers these students an intensive English course, special counseling, and special organizations.

Admissions: Foreign students must achieve a minimum score of 550 on the TOEFL. The SAT or ACT is not required.

Procedure: Application deadlines are January 15 (fall) and December 15 (spring). A completed and certified medical form is necessary as proof of health. Proof of funds adequate to cover 1 year of study is required. Foreign students are strongly advised to carry health insurance, which is available through the college for a fee.

Admissions Contact: Marsha R. Gottovi, Director of Admissions.

STATE UNIVERSITY OF NEW YORK/ COLLEGE AT BUFFALO A–3
Buffalo, New York 14222 (716) 878-5511

F/T: 3787M, 4739W	Faculty: n/av; IIA, +$
P/T: 985M, 846W	Ph.D.'s: 64%
Grad: 391M, 1034W	S/F Ratio: 20 to 1
Year: sems, ss	Tuition: $1155 ($1605)
Appl: Aug. 1	R and B: $2200
6841 applied	4652 accepted	1827 enrolled
SAT: 428V 464M	ACT: 20	COMPETITIVE

The State University of New York/College at Buffalo, founded in 1871, is a liberal arts college. The library contains over 390,000 volumes and 225,000 microfilm items, and subscribes to more than 2200 periodicals.

Environment: The college is located in northwest Buffalo on a 110-acre campus. Ten dormitories house 1200 women and 600 men. Other buildings include a physical education and recreation center, a college union, and an infirmary. The college also operates the Great Lakes Laboratory for chemical and biological analysis of water and sediment.

Student Life: Almost all students come from New York State, and 25% live on campus. Twelve percent are minority-group members. College housing is both coed and single-sex. There are visiting privileges in single-sex dorms. Students may keep cars on campus. Daycare services are available to all students for a fee.

Organizations: Four percent of the men belong to the 5 fraternities and 2% of the women belong to the 3 sororities. More than 100 other student organizations also are available, including social clubs and religious organizations. Cultural and recreational opportunities in the city of Buffalo include Albright Knox Art Gallery and Delaware Park.

Sports: The college participates intercollegiately in 12 sports for men and 10 for women. There are 7 intramural sports for both men and women.

Handicapped: Ninety-five percent of the campus is accessible to wheelchair-bound students. Facilities include ramps, elevators, special parking areas, specially equipped rest rooms, and lowered drinking fountains. Fewer than 1% of the students have hearing or visual impairments. Special class scheduling can be arranged. No special counselors are available.

Graduates: Eight percent of the freshmen drop out; 55% remain to graduate. Since most graduates go directly into teaching, they begin graduate work to receive permanent teaching certification.

Services: Students receive free career and psychological counseling, health care, tutoring, and remedial instruction. Placement services for students and graduates include resume and job files and on-campus recruiting by businesses and schools.

Programs of Study: The college confers the B.A., B.F.A., B.S., B.S.Ed., and B.T. degrees. Master's degrees also are available. Bachelor's degrees are offered in the following subjects: AREA STUDIES (urban), BUSINESS (business administration, business education, computer science), EDUCATION (early childhood, elementary, industrial, secondary, special), ENGLISH (English, journalism, speech), FINE AND PERFORMING ARTS (art, art education, art history, music, studio art, theater/dramatics), HEALTH SCIENCES (speech therapy), LANGUAGES (French, German, Italian, Spanish), MATH AND SCIENCES (biology, chemistry, earth science, geology, mathematics, physics), PHILOSOPHY (philosophy), PREPROFESSIONAL (home economics, social work), SOCIAL SCIENCES (anthropology, economics, geography, government/political science, history, psychology, sociology).

Required: All students must take 60 hours of liberal arts courses.

Special: The college is a member of the International Student Exchange; juniors may study abroad in Siena, Italy; Australia; England; and Japan. An Individualized Degree Program emphasizes independent study. It is possible to earn 5-year combined B.A.-B.S. degrees.

Honors: A number of national honor societies are represented on campus, and the psychology department offers an honors program.

Admissions: Sixty-eight percent of those who applied were accepted for the 1981–82 freshman class. Applicants should be high school graduates or have earned an equivalency diploma. They should rank in the upper 50% of their high school class and present an average of 80 or better. Advanced placement or honors courses, recommendations by school officials, and the extracurricular activities record are also considered in the admissions decision.

Procedure: The SAT or ACT is required. Application deadlines are August 1 (fall) and January 1 (spring). Notification is made on a rolling basis. There is a $10 application fee.

Special: Early and deferred admissions plans are available. CLEP and AP credit is accepted.

Transfer: For fall 1981, 2816 transfer students applied, 1985 were accepted, and 1135 enrolled. Transfer students are considered for all classes. D grades transfer; a GPA of 2.0 is required. Students must earn, at the college, 32 credit hours of the 123 necessary for the bachelor's degree. Application deadlines are the same as those for freshmen.

Visiting: Applicants are encouraged to visit the campus, and orientations for prospective students are scheduled regularly. Guides also are available for informal visits, and visitors may sit in on classes. Visits should be arranged for weekday mornings with the admissions office.

Financial Aid: Financial aid programs include scholarships, grants, loans, and campus jobs. More than half the students receive aid; 35% work part-time on campus. Application deadlines are open. The college is a member of CSS. The FAF is required.

Foreign Students: Foreign students constitute almost 4% of the full-time enrollment. The college offers these students an intensive English course, special counseling, and special organizations.

Admissions: Foreign students must achieve a minimum score of 500 on the TOEFL. The SAT or ACT is not required.

Procedure: Application deadlines are June 1 (fall) and November 1 (spring). Proof of funds adequate to cover 4 years of study at the college is required. Out-of-state tuition rates apply. Foreign students must carry health insurance, which is available through the college for a fee.

Admissions Contact: Paul T. Collyer, Coordinator of Undergraduate Admissions.

STATE UNIVERSITY OF NEW YORK/ COLLEGE AT CORTLAND
C-5

Cortland, New York 13045   (607) 753-4711

F/T: 2126M, 3155W	Faculty:	362; IIA, av$
P/T: 89M, 32W	Ph.D.'s:	70%
Grad: 199M, 369W	S/F Ratio:	19 to 1
Year: sems, ss	Tuition:	$1162 ($1762)
Appl: Jan. 1	R and B:	$2006
6099 applied	4088 accepted	1277 enrolled
SAT: 428V 486M		COMPETITIVE

The State University of New York/College at Cortland, established in 1868, is an arts and sciences college with strong professional programs in education—elementary and secondary, health, physical, recreation, speech, and speech-hearing handicapped. The library houses over 225,000 volumes and subscribes to 1400 periodicals.

Environment: The 140-acre suburban campus is located about 30 miles from Syracuse in the Finger Lakes region. Thirteen residence halls accommodate 3300 students, and a 100-unit leased apartment complex houses another 368 students. Other facilities include a learning resources center, a fine arts center, a student union, and a physical education complex.

Student Life: Almost all students are from New York State. Ninety percent of the freshmen are graduates of public schools. Seventy percent of the students live on campus. About 5% are minority-group members. College housing is coed. Students may keep cars on campus.

Organizations: Religious organizations are provided for Catholic, Protestant, and Jewish students. Other student organizations include social and service groups. About 3% of the students belong to the 2 fraternities and 3 sororities. Area residents regularly attend drama festivals, concerts, and lectures sponsored by Cortland students. Several state parks and ski areas are nearby.

Sports: The college participates intercollegiately in 14 sports for men and 14 for women. There are 22 intramural sports for men and 21 for women.

Handicapped: Renovations are under way to make more of the campus accessible to wheelchair-bound students. Facilities include ramps, special parking areas, and elevators. Fewer than 1% of the students have visual impairments. A part-time counselor and assistant are available, and special class scheduling can be arranged.

Graduates: About 12% of the freshmen leave for academic reasons, and 60% remain to graduate. Twenty percent of the graduates pursue further study, including 2% who enter medical school, 2% who enter law school, and 1% who enter dental school.

Services: Students receive free career and psychological counseling, health care, and remedial instruction. Placement services are available to students and alumni. Tutoring is provided for a fee.

Programs of Study: The college confers the B.A., B.S., and B.S.Ed. degrees. Master's degrees also are available. Bachelor's degrees are offered in the following subjects: AREA STUDIES (Black/Afro-American), BUSINESS (computer science), EDUCATION (elementary, health/physical, secondary), ENGLISH (English, speech), FINE AND PERFORMING ARTS (art, art history, music, studio art, theater/dramatics), HEALTH SCIENCES (health education, health science, speech therapy), LANGUAGES (French, German, Spanish), MATH AND SCIENCES (biology, chemistry, earth science, geology, geophysics, mathematics, physics), PHILOSOPHY (philosophy), PREPROFESSIONAL (engineering, forestry, medicine), SOCIAL SCIENCES (anthropology, economics, geography, government/political science, history, international studies, psychology, sociology). Minors are available in Asian studies, journalism, management, philosophy in secondary education, psychology of exceptional children, Russian studies, and urban studies. Eighteen percent of the undergraduate degrees conferred are in social sciences, 10% are in math and sciences, and 6% are in health sciences.

Required: All students must take English composition.

Special: Programs include field experience for student teachers and political science majors, and independent study programs. Students may design their own majors or earn a general studies degree. Juniors may arrange to study in Switzerland, England, Ireland, Spain, or Germany. A Washington seminar also is available. Five-year combination degree programs are offered in engineering and forestry in conjunction with other institutions, and in other areas at the college itself.

Honors: Nine national honor societies have chapters on campus. The English, history, and psychology departments offer honors programs.

Admissions: Sixty-seven percent of those who applied were accepted for the 1981-82 freshman class. The SAT scores of those who enrolled were as follows: Verbal—84% below 500, 14% between 500 and 599, 1% between 600 and 700, and 0% above 700; Math—60% below 500, 33% between 500 and 599, 6% between 600 and 700, and 1% above 700. Applicants should have completed 17 high school units and generally must present an average of B— or better. Admissions officers also consider advanced placement or honors courses, although the high school grade average is the most important factor.

Procedure: Applicants must take the SAT or ACT. Application deadlines are flexible, but the recommended dates for filing are January 1 (fall) and December 15 (spring). A $10 application fee is charged.

Special: Early and deferred admissions plans are available. AP and CLEP credit is accepted.

Transfer: For fall 1981, 2024 transfer students applied, 1310 were accepted, and 591 enrolled. A GPA of 2.5 or better is recommended; D grades transfer. Students must earn, at the college, 45 semester hours of the 120-128 required for the bachelor's degree. Application deadlines are December 15 (fall) and June 1 (spring).

Visiting: Interviews may be scheduled with the admissions office. Guided tours and class visits also can be arranged. The admissions office will provide information.

Financial Aid: Financial aid programs include scholarships, grants, loans, and campus jobs. Seventy-three percent of the students receive aid; 38% work part-time on campus. The average award to freshmen is $798. The college is a member of CSS. Applications should be filed by May 1. The FAF is required.

Foreign Students: Fewer than 1% of the full-time students come from foreign countries. The college offers these students special counseling and special organizations.

Admissions: Foreign students must achieve a minimum score of 500 on the TOEFL. The SAT or ACT is not required.

Procedure: Applications must be received at least 6 months prior to enrollment. Foreign students are admitted to all semesters. Proof of health must be presented prior to arrival. Proof of funds adequate to cover 1 full year of study is required. Foreign students must carry health insurance, which is available through the college for a fee.

Admissions Contact: Thomas A. Syracuse, Director of Admissions.

STATE UNIVERSITY OF NEW YORK/ COLLEGE AT FREDONIA
A-4

Fredonia, New York 14063 (716) 673-3251

F/T, P/T:	Faculty:	258; IIA, +$
2400M, 2460W	Ph.D.'s:	78%
Grad: 120M, 232W	S/F Ratio:	18 to 1
Year: sems, ss	Tuition:	$1155 ($1855)
Appl: Aug. 1	R and B:	$2158
5876 applied	3379 accepted	1127 enrolled
SAT: 464V 511M	ACT: 23	COMPETITIVE+

The State University of New York/College at Fredonia, founded in 1826, offers degree programs in the liberal arts and sciences. The library houses 326,630 volumes and 630,500 microfilm items, and subscribes to 2094 periodicals.

Environment: The 232-acre rural campus is located in a village of 10,000 people, 45 miles southwest of Buffalo. The 29 major buildings include dormitories that accommodate 2600 students.

Student Life: More than 90% of the students come from New York State. Sixty percent live on campus. About 3% are minority-group members. Campus housing is both coed and single-sex. Students may keep cars on campus. The college provides day-care services to the community for a fee.

Organizations: About 3% of the men belong to the 2 fraternities, and 1% of women belong to a local sorority. Religious organizations are provided for students of the major faiths. The Student Association sponsors more than 200 activities each year, including lectures, concerts, exhibits, social activities and other special events. Student activities include music and drama, a campus newspaper and radio station, and special-interest clubs.

Sports: The college fields intercollegiate teams in 8 sports for men and 5 for women. There are 9 intramural sports for men and 7 for women.

Handicapped: About 25% of the campus is accessible to wheelchair-bound students. Special facilities include ramps, parking areas, elevators, and specially equipped rest rooms. Fewer than 1% of the students have visual or hearing impairments. Two special counselors and an assistant are available to handicapped students.

Graduates: Twenty-four percent of the freshmen drop out by the end of the first year; 46% remain to graduate. Of these, about 20% seek advanced degrees, including 1% who enter medical school, 1% who enter dental school, and 1% who enter law school.

Services: Students receive free health care, career and psychological counseling, tutoring, and remedial instruction. Placement services are provided for students and alumni.

Programs of Study: The college confers the B.A., B.S., B.F.A., B.M., B.S.Ed., B.A. Special Studies, and B.S. Special Studies degrees. Master's degrees also are available. Bachelor's degrees are offered in the following subjects: AREA STUDIES (American, special), BUSINESS (accounting, business administration, computer science), EDUCATION (early childhood, elementary, secondary, special, speech and hearing), ENGLISH (English), FINE AND PERFORMING ARTS (art, art history, music, music education, music theater, music therapy, performance, radio/TV, sound recording, studio art, theater/dramatics), HEALTH SCIENCES (medical technology, speech therapy), LANGUAGES (French, German, Spanish), MATH AND SCIENCES (biology, chemistry, geology, geophysics, mathematics), PHILOSOPHY (philosophy), PREPROFESSIONAL (dentistry, engineering, law, medicine, ministry), SOCIAL SCIENCES (anthropology, economics, government/political science, history, psychology, sociology). About 39% of the undergraduate degrees are awarded in liberal arts, 25% are in business, 16% are in fine and performing arts, and 15% are in education.

Special: Students may design their own majors or pursue a general studies degree. A cooperative program in special education is offered with D'Youville College, and a similar program in agriculture is offered with Cornell University. A dual-degree program in engineering is offered in conjunction with 11 other institutions. Juniors may study abroad. Bachelor's degrees may be earned in 3 years.

Honors: A number of honor societies are represented on campus.

Admissions: About 58% of those who applied were accepted for the 1981–82 freshman class. The SAT scores of those who enrolled broke down this way: Verbal—73% below 500, 22% between 500 and 599, 4% between 600 and 700, and 1% above 700; Math—49% below 500, 37% between 500 and 599, 13% between 600 and 700, and 1% above 700. Applicants must have graduated from an accredited high school or possess an equivalency certificate. They must rank in the top 60% of their high school class and present an average of 2.3 (C+) or better. Those who plan to study music must arrange an audition. Admissions officers also consider advanced placement or honors courses, recommendations by high school officials, evidence of special talent, extracurricular activities, impressions made during an interview, and leadership record.

Procedure: Applicants must take the SAT or ACT. Application deadlines are August 1 (fall) and January 1 (spring). Admissions decisions are made on a rolling basis. The application fee is $10.

Special: A deferred admissions plan is available. Students may earn credit through CLEP and AP exams.

Transfer: For a recent year, 1424 students applied, 847 were accepted, and 362 enrolled. Transfer students are accepted for all but the senior class, and must earn, at the college, 45 of the 120 credits required for the bachelor's degree. Applicants should have a GPA of 2.0 or better. D grades transfer. Application deadlines are the same as those for freshmen.

Visiting: Orientation programs for prospective students generally consist of a 1-hour information session and an hour-long tour of the campus. Guides are not provided for informal visits. Visitors may sit in on classes and arrange to stay overnight on campus. Visits are best scheduled with the admissions office for days in September, October, November, February, March, April, or May.

Financial Aid: Financial aid programs include scholarships, grants, loans, and campus jobs. About 68% of the students receive aid; 30% work part-time on campus. The average award to freshmen from all sources is $2827. The college is a member of CSS. The deadline for aid applications is open. The FAF is required.

Foreign Students: Foreign students constitute 1% of the full-time enrollment. Special counseling is available to these students.

Admissions: Foreign students must achieve a minimum score of 500 on the TOEFL. The SAT or ACT is not required.

Procedure: Application deadlines are May 1 (fall) and September 1 (spring). Proof of funds adequate to cover the first year of study is required. Out-of-state tuition rates apply. Although not required, health insurance is available through the college for a fee.

Admissions Contact: William S. Clark, Director of Admissions.

STATE UNIVERSITY OF NEW YORK/ COLLEGE AT GENESEO
B-3

Geneseo, New York 14454 (716) 245-5571

F/T: 1575M, 2787W	Faculty:	247; IIA, av$
P/T: 90M, 145W	Ph.D.'s:	74%
Grad: 57M, 133W	S/F Ratio:	18 to 1
Year: sems, ss	Tuition:	$1075 ($1775)
Appl: open	R and B:	$2000
6624 applied	3247 accepted	1182 enrolled
SAT: 512V 529M	ACT: 24	VERY COMPETITIVE

The State University of New York/College at Geneseo, established in 1867, offers degree programs in liberal arts and professional studies. The library contains 812,480 books, microtexts, and other documents, and subscribes to 2588 periodicals.

Environment: The 225-acre campus is located in a small town about 30 miles from Rochester. College dormitories accommodate 2104 women and 1091 men. Other facilities include a physical education complex, 3 theaters, 2 dance studios, an art gallery, a planetarium, a nuclear accelerator laboratory, 2 science complexes, and a student activities center.

Student Life: Almost all students are from New York, and 74% live on campus in coed and single-sex dorms. Three percent are minority-group members.

Organizations: About 12% of the men belong to the 6 fraternities, and 7% of the women belong to the 6 sororities. Religious counselors and organizations are provided for students of all major faiths. A full program of cultural, extracurricular, and social activities is available. The college is located 6 miles from Letchworth State Park, known as the "Grand Canyon of the East."

Sports: The college fields intercollegiate teams in 8 sports for men and 8 for women. There are 17 intramural sports for men and 16 for women.

Handicapped: About 70% of the campus is accessible to wheelchair-bound students. Facilities include ramps, special parking areas, elevators, specially equipped rest rooms, lowered drinking fountains, chairlifts, a swimming pool lift, portable lab tables, and fume hoods. For visually impaired students, the college provides readers, visual aid machines, cassettes, and talking calculators. Four special counselors are available.

Graduates: About 18% of the freshmen drop out, and 60% remain to graduate. Twenty-six percent of the graduates seek advanced degrees.

Services: The following services are offered free to students: psychological and career counseling, tutoring, and health care. Placement services are available to students and alumni.

Programs of Study: The college confers the B.A., B.S., and B.S.Ed. degrees. Master's programs also are available. Bachelor's degrees are offered in the following subjects: AREA STUDIES (American, Black/Afro-American), BUSINESS (accounting, business administration, management), EDUCATION (early childhood, elementary, secondary, special), ENGLISH (English, literature, speech), FINE AND PERFORMING ARTS (art history, music, radio/TV, studio art, theater/dramatics), HEALTH SCIENCES (medical technology, speech therapy), LANGUAGES (French, Spanish), MATH AND SCIENCES (biology, botany, chemistry, earth science, ecology/environmental science, geology, geophysics, mathematics, physics, zoology), PHILOSOPHY (philosophy), PREPROFESSIONAL (dentistry, engineering, forestry, law, library science, medicine, ministry, pharmacy, social work, veterinary), SOCIAL SCIENCES (anthropology, economics, geography, government/political science, history, psychology, sociology). Of the undergraduate degrees conferred, 27% are in social sciences, 15% are in education, and 17% are in math and sciences.

Required: Students must take 4 physical education courses and 34 hours of courses in a general-education curriculum.

Special: Combination degree programs include 3-2 programs in engineering with SUNY/Buffalo, Clarkson College, Columbia, Rochester Institute of Technology, SUNY/Stony Brook, Ohio State, Case Western Reserve, and Alfred University; a 3-2 M.B.A. with SUNY Buffalo; and a 2-2 forestry program with SUNY College of Environmental Science and Forestry. Most bachelor's degrees may be earned in 3 years.

Honors: Three national honor societies have chapters on campus.

Admissions: Forty-nine percent of those who applied were accepted for the 1981–82 freshman class. The SAT scores of those who enrolled broke down this way: Verbal—44% below 500, 42% between 500 and 599, 12% between 600 and 700, and 2% above 700; Math—21% below 500, 52% between 500 and 599, 17% between 600 and 700, and 10% above 700. On the ACT: 6% scored below 21, 32% between 21 and 23, 47% between 24 and 25, 10% between 26 and 28, and 5% above 28. Applicants must rank in the upper 40% of their graduating class and have an average of at least 80. Admissions officers also consider advanced placement or honors courses, leadership record, recommendations by high school officials, extracurricular activities, and special talents.

Procedure: The SAT or ACT is required. Application deadlines are open. Notification is made on a rolling basis, beginning in January for fall semester applicants. There is a $10 application fee.

Special: A deferred admissions plan is offered. AP and CLEP credit is accepted.

Transfer: For fall 1981, 1800 students applied, 802 were accepted, and 417 enrolled. A GPA of 2.0 or better is required. C grades transfer. Preference is given to transfers from SUNY community colleges. Students must earn in residence at least 32 of the 124 credits required for the bachelor's degree. Application deadlines are April 1 (fall) and October 1 (spring).

Visiting: Orientations for prospective students are scheduled regularly. Guides also are available for informal visits, and visitors may sit in on classes. The best times to visit are weekdays from 8 A.M. to 4:15 P.M. and Saturdays from 9 A.M. to 1 P.M. Arrangements should be made through the admissions office.

Financial Aid: Financial aid programs include scholarships, grants, loans, and campus jobs. About 85% of the students receive aid; 50% work part-time on campus. The college is a member of CSS; the FAF is required. Aid applications should be filed by February 1 (fall) or November 1 (spring).

Foreign Students: About 1% of the full-time students come from foreign countries.

Admissions: Foreign students must earn a minimum score of 600 on the TOEFL. The SAT or ACT is also required.

Procedure: Application deadlines are April 1 (fall) and October 1 (spring). Proof of funds adequate to cover 4 years of study is required. Foreign students must carry health insurance, which is available through the college for a fee.

Admissions Contact: William L. Caren, Dean of Admissions.

STATE UNIVERSITY OF NEW YORK/ COLLEGE AT NEW PALTZ   D-4
New Paltz, New York 12561   (914) 257-2414

F/T: 2064M, 2374W	Faculty: 314; IIA, +$
P/T: 478M, 749W	Ph.D.'s: 67%
Grad: 516M, 1023W	S/F Ratio: 18 to 1
Year: sems, ss	Tuition: $1213 ($1913)
Appl: July 1	R and B: $2200
5997 applied 3220 accepted 930 enrolled	
SAT: 450V 465M ACT: 20 COMPETITIVE	

The State University of New York/College at New Paltz, founded in 1828, is a liberal arts college. The library houses 350,000 volumes and subscribes to 1800 periodicals.

Environment: The 206-acre rural campus is located in a village of 4500 people, midway between Albany and metropolitan New York. Buildings include 11 dormitories that accommodate 2400 men and women, a college union, 2 science buildings, a gymnasium, a planetarium, and a fine-arts building. The college also owns a self-contained camping area 20 miles away for use by students.

Student Life: Ninety-one percent of the students come from New York State, and 37% are from the New York City area. About 52% live on campus. Forty-one percent of the students are Catholic, 13% are Protestant, and 17% are Jewish. Twenty-one percent are minority-group members. Campus housing is both coed and single-sex. There are visiting privileges in single-sex dorms. Students may keep cars on campus.

Organizations: Over 66 clubs and organizations offer students social, cultural, religious, academic, and political activities. Outdoor recreation areas nearby are available for climbing, hiking, skiing, and skating.

Sports: The college competes on an intercollegiate level in 9 sports for men and women. There are 13 intramural sports for men and 10 for women.

Handicapped: About 90% of the campus is accessible to wheelchair-bound students. Facilities include ramps, Braille elevators, special parking areas, and specially equipped rest rooms. A special counselor and 2 assistants are provided.

Graduates: About 15% of the freshmen drop out, and 60% remain to graduate. About 35% of the graduates continue their studies; 32% enter careers in business and industry.

Services: Students receive free placement, career and psychological counseling, tutoring, and remedial instruction. Health care is available for a fee. There is also a charge for some psychological counseling.

Programs of Study: The college confers the B.A., B.S., B.F.A., and B.S.N. degrees. Master's degrees also are available. Bachelor's degrees are offered in the following subjects: AREA STUDIES (Black/Afro-American), BUSINESS (business administration, computer science), EDUCATION (early childhood, secondary, speech and hearing handicapped), ENGLISH (English, journalism, speech), FINE AND PERFORMING ARTS (art education, art history, music, music therapy, studio art, theater/dramatics, visual arts), HEALTH SCIENCES (nursing), LANGUAGES (French, German, Spanish), MATH AND SCIENCES (biology, chemistry, geology, mathematics, physics), PHILOSOPHY (philosophy), PREPROFESSIONAL (dentistry, engineering, forestry, law, medicine, veterinary), SOCIAL SCIENCES (anthropology, economics, geography, government/political science, history, liberal studies, psychology, sociology).

Required: All students must take freshman English and a distribution of courses in several broad areas of study. Requirements may be satisfied by AP, CLEP, or New York State College Proficiency exams.

Special: Students may study abroad and design their own majors. A 3-2 engineering program is offered with SUNY/Buffalo and SUNY/Stony Brook, and a 3-2 geological engineering program with New Mexico Institute of Technology. There is also an approved transfer program with SUNY College of Environmental Science and Forestry. Combined B.A.-B.S. degrees may be earned in any combination of subjects.

Honors: A number of honor societies, including Delta Psi Omega, are represented on campus.

Admissions: Fifty-four percent of those who applied were accepted for the 1981–82 freshman class. The SAT scores of those who enrolled were as follows: Verbal—18% between 500 and 599, 6% between 600 and 700, and 1% above 700; Math—26% between 500 and 599, 8% between 600 and 700, and 1% above 700. Freshmen are admitted under 3 categories: competitive, discretionary, and Educational Opportunity Program. Freshmen admitted under the first 2 programs must

NEW YORK

have a high school average of 80 or better and rank in the upper 50% of their graduating class.

Procedure: Applicants must take the SAT or ACT. The application deadlines are July 1 (fall), December 1 (spring), and May 15 (summer). Interviews are required for EOP candidates and for some applicants under discretionary admissions. Notification is made on a rolling basis. There is a $10 application fee.

Special: AP and CLEP credit is accepted. Early and deferred admissions plans are available.

Transfer: For fall 1981, 2094 students applied, 1391 were accepted, and 660 enrolled. Most come from community colleges in New York State. A GPA of 2.0 or better is required. Transfers must complete, at the college, 45 of the 120 credits necessary for the bachelor's degree. Application deadlines are the same as for freshmen.

Visiting: Group information sessions for prospective students are conducted 3 times a week and on weekends. They include a campus tour and class visits. Visits should be arranged through the admissions office.

Financial Aid: Financial aid programs include scholarships, grants, loans, and campus jobs. About 68% of the students receive aid; 9% work part-time on campus. The college is a member of CSS. The FAF is required. Applications must be filed by March 1.

Foreign Students: About 4% of the full-time students come from foreign countries. The college offers these students an intensive English course as well as special counseling and special organizations.

Admissions: Foreign students must achieve a minimum score of 525 on the TOEFL. The SAT or ACT is not required.

Procedure: Application deadlines are April 1 (fall) and September 1 (spring). Foreign students must provide a physician's report and record of immunizations. Proof of funds adequate to cover 1 full year of study is required. Students must carry health insurance, which is available through the college for a fee.

Admissions Contact: Robert J. Seaman, Dean of Admissions.

STATE UNIVERSITY OF NEW YORK/ COLLEGE AT OLD WESTBURY   D-5
Old Westbury, New York 11568   (516) 876-3073

F/T: 1156M, 1359W   Faculty: 141; IIA, – –$
P/T: 344M, 586W   Ph.D.'s: 60%
Grad: none   S/F Ratio: 24 to 1
Year: sems, ss   Tuition: $1110 ($1810)
Appl: open   R and B: $2040
3176 applied   2418 accepted   1268 enrolled
SAT, ACT: not required   LESS COMPETITIVE

The State University of New York/College at Old Westbury, founded in 1966, is composed of the Division of Interdisciplinary Programs and the Division of Arts, Sciences, and Professional Studies. The library contains more than 115,000 volumes and 100,000 microtexts, and subscribes to 1500 periodicals.

Environment: The wooded, 600-acre campus is located in a suburban setting on Long Island, 22 miles from Manhattan. Dormitories accommodate 686 students.

Student Life: Approximately 75% of the students are Long Island residents, and 75% percent of the freshmen come from public schools. The students are, as a whole, older than those at other colleges, less affluent, and from varied racial, cultural, and ethnic backgrounds. About 50% are minority-group members. Campus housing is coed. Students may keep cars on campus. Day-care services are available to all students for a fee.

Organizations: There are a number of student activities and groups, largely student-initiated.

Sports: The college participates in 1 intercollegiate sport for men. There are 5 intramural sports for men and 4 for women.

Graduates: Almost 37% of the freshmen drop out, and 40% remain to graduate. About 50% of the graduates pursue advanced degrees; 1% enter medical school, nearly 1% enter dental school, and 3% enter law school. Forty percent pursue careers in business and industry.

Services: The following services are available to students free of charge: placement, health care, career and psychological counseling, and tutoring. An extensive remedial instruction program is provided.

Programs of Study: The college awards the B.A., B.S., and B.P.S. degrees. Bachelor's degrees are offered in the following subjects: AREA STUDIES (American, urban), BUSINESS (business administration, computer science), EDUCATION (early childhood, bilingual, elementary), FINE AND PERFORMING ARTS (art, music), HEALTH SCIENCES (community health), MATH AND SCIENCES (biology, chemistry, mathematics), PREPROFESSIONAL (dentistry, law, medicine, social work), SOCIAL SCIENCES (comparative history/ideas/culture, politics/economics/society). About 25% of the degrees are conferred in business, 16% in social sciences, 15% in education, and 13% in science.

Special: Students may arrange to spend a year abroad. Field projects may be arranged by students or offered by the school. Up to 32 credits may be granted for life experience. The college offers a general studies program.

Admissions: Seventy-six percent of those who applied were accepted for the 1981-82 freshman class. Admissions decisions are based on the student's motivation and readiness, rather than on test scores or class rank. Other factors influencing the decision are past employment, community and military service, and travel or other experiences.

Procedure: Application deadlines are open. Freshmen are admitted to all semesters. A rolling admissions plan is followed. There is a $10 application fee.

Special: A deferred admissions plan is available. CLEP credit is accepted.

Transfer: Transfer students are accepted for all classes. Some D grades transfer. A high school diploma is necessary. Students must earn, at the college, at least 48 of the 120 credits required for the bachelor's degree. Application deadlines are the same as those for freshmen.

Financial Aid: Financial aid programs include scholarships, grants, loans, and campus jobs. About 75% of the students receive aid; 40% work part-time on campus. The average award to freshmen from all sources is $2250. The college is a member of CSS. The FAF is required. The application deadline is April 1.

Foreign Students: About 3% of the full-time students come from foreign countries. The college offers these students an English course and an intensive English program. Special counseling and special organizations also are available.

Admissions: Foreign students must take an English proficiency exam given by the college. The SAT or ACT is not required.

Procedure: Foreign students are admitted to the fall and spring semesters. Application deadlines are open. Proof of funds adequate to cover 4 years of study is required. Health insurance, while not required, is available through the college for a fee.

Admissions Contact: Alan Chaves, Director of Admissions.

STATE UNIVERSITY OF NEW YORK/ COLLEGE AT ONEONTA   D-3
Oneonta, New York 13820   (607) 431-2524

F/T: 2331M, 3300W   Faculty: 350; IIA, +$
P/T: 92M, 132W   Ph.D.'s: 63%
Grad: 122M, 316W   S/F Ratio: 18 to 1
Year: sems, ss   Tuition: $1125 ($1825)
Appl: Apr. 1   R and B: $2165
6989 applied   4249 accepted   1225 enrolled
SAT: 471V 519M   ACT: 23   COMPETITIVE+

The State University of New York/College at Oneonta, founded in 1889, offers liberal arts and teacher education. The library houses over 350,000 books and 120,000 microtexts, and subscribes to 2800 periodicals.

Environment: The 204-acre campus is located in a rural town of 16,000 people, near Cooperstown and 75 miles from Albany. Dormitories, set up around quads, house 2160 women and 1300 men.

Student Life: Almost all students come from New York. About 65% live on campus. Campus housing is coed. Upperclassmen may keep cars on campus.

Organizations: About 6% of the students belong to the 4 fraternities and 5 sororities. Other campus activities include student government. The campus has its own ski area.

Sports: The college participates on an intercollegiate level in 8 sports for men and 7 for women. There are 20 intramural sports available to men and 18 to women.

Handicapped: About 60% of the campus is accessible to wheelchair-bound students. Facilities include ramps, elevators, special parking areas, and specially equipped rest rooms. Special class scheduling can be arranged. Fewer than 1% of the students have visual or hearing impairments.

Graduates: Eight to 10% of the freshmen drop out, and 70% remain to graduate. About half the graduates seek advanced degrees; of those who apply, 60% enter medical school, 65% enter dental school, and 40% enter law school. Another 20% of the graduates pursue careers in business or industry.

Services: Psychological and career counseling, tutoring, and remedial instruction are provided free. Health care is available on campus; fees are charged. Placement services are available to students and alumni.

Programs of Study: The college awards the B.A. and B.S. degrees. Master's degrees also are available. Bachelor's degrees are offered in the following subjects: AREA STUDIES (Black-Hispanic), BUSINESS (business economics), EDUCATION (elementary, secondary), ENGLISH (literature, speech), FINE AND PERFORMING ARTS (art history, music, studio art, theater/dramatics), HEALTH SCIENCES (school nurse teacher), LANGUAGES (French, German, Spanish), MATH AND SCIENCES (biology, chemistry, earth science, geology, mathematics, meteorology, physics, statistics, water resources), PHILOSOPHY (philosophy), PREPROFESSIONAL (dentistry, engineering, home economics, law, medicine, veterinary), SOCIAL SCIENCES (anthropology, economics, geography, government/political science, history, psychology, sociology). Of the undergraduate degrees conferred, 20% are in social sciences, 20% are in business, and 19% are in education.

Required: All students must complete a distribution of courses in the liberal arts and sciences.

Special: Study-abroad and independent study programs are available. The college offers a general studies degree. Two 3-2 cooperative programs are offered, one in engineering and one in accounting or business management.

Honors: Students may take any course for honors credit if they have a cumulative GPA of at least 3.0, a GPA for the last semester of at least 3.5, or permission of the instructor. Five national honor societies are represented on campus.

Admissions: Sixty-one percent of those who applied were accepted for the 1981–82 freshman class. Candidates must rank in the upper half of their graduating class, present a GPA of at least 2.0, and have completed 15 Carnegie units. Admissions officers also consider advanced placement or honors courses, recommendations by high school officials, impressions made during an interview, special talents, and leadership record.

Procedure: Applicants must take the SAT or ACT. Applications for fall admission should be submitted by January 1; final deadlines are April 1 (fall) and November 30 (spring). Notification is made on a rolling basis beginning January 1. There is a $10 application fee.

Special: Early and deferred admissions plans are offered. AP credit is accepted.

Transfer: For fall 1981, 2217 transfer students applied, 1140 were accepted, and 550 enrolled. A GPA of 2.0 is required. D grades transfer only if the student has earned an associate degree. Preference is given to graduates of state community colleges and agricultural/technical colleges. Students must complete, at the college, 45 of the 122 semester hours required for the bachelor's degree. State residents guaranteed transfer must apply by December 15 (fall) or October 15 (spring). Others must apply by July 1 (fall) or November 30 (spring).

Visiting: The college holds 2 spring orientation weekends for prospective students. Guides also are available for informal visits, and visitors may sit in on classes. Visits should be scheduled with the admissions office, preferably for October, November, March, or April.

Financial Aid: Financial aid programs include scholarships, grants, loans, and campus jobs. About 95% of the students receive aid; 34% work part-time on campus. The college is a member of CSS; the FAF is required. The application deadlines are April 15 (fall) and November 15 (spring).

Foreign Students: Foreign students constitute 1% of the full-time enrollment. The college offers these students special counseling and special organizations.

Admissions: Foreign students must achieve a minimum score of 500 on the TOEFL. The SAT or ACT is not required.

Procedure: Application deadlines are August 1 (fall) and September 30 (spring). Foreign students must complete a regulation physical examination form to establish proof of health. Proof of funds adequate to cover 1 academic year of study is required. Students must also carry health insurance, which is available through the college for a fee.

Admissions Contact: Margaret Serra-Lima, Admissions Counselor.

NEW YORK 607

STATE UNIVERSITY OF NEW YORK/ COLLEGE AT OSWEGO   C-3
Oswego, New York 13216   (315) 341-2250

F/T: 3347M, 3343W	Faculty:	371; IIA, +$
P/T: 139M, 191W	Ph.D.'s:	65%
Grad:174M, 347W	S/F Ratio:	20 to 1
Year: sems, ss	Tuition:	$1170 ($1870)
Appl: Jan. 15	R and B:	$2080
12,423 applied	6531 accepted	1557 enrolled
SAT: 480V 532M	ACT: 24	VERY COMPETITIVE

The State University of New York/College at Oswego, founded in 1861, is composed of the following divisions: Arts and Sciences, and Professional Studies. The library houses 457,542 volumes and 874,586 microfilm items, and subscribes to 3398 periodicals.

Environment: The 1000-acre rural campus is located on the shore of Lake Ontario, in a town of 19,000 people 35 miles from Syracuse. Twelve residence halls offer students a choice of suite, quad, or corridor arrangements; and such options as quiet, non-smoking, and special foreign-language floors. The 39 major buildings include the Tyler Fine Arts Building, which houses the Waterman Theatre, cited as one of the 50 best theatres built in the United States since 1960.

Student Life: About 63% of the students live on campus, and 2% live in off-campus fraternity or sorority houses. Students under 21 must have permission to live off campus. Forty percent of the students are Catholic and 15% are Jewish. Five percent are minority-group members. Campus housing is both coed and single-sex. There are visiting privileges in single-sex dorms. Students may keep cars on campus.

Organizations: About 7% of the students belong to the 7 fraternities and 4 sororities. The student-funded Program Policy Board schedules professional theatre, music and dance programs. Religious organizations are available for major faiths.

Sports: The college fields intercollegiate teams in 11 sports for men and 12 for women. There are 8 intramural sports for men and 18 for women.

Handicapped: About 85% of the campus is accessible to wheelchair-bound students. Facilities include elevators, ramps, specially equipped rest rooms, special parking areas, and lowered drinking fountains. Special class scheduling also is available. Fewer than 1% of the students have visual or hearing impairments. Limited tutorial assistance is provided for these students. Support services are available.

Graduates: About 20% of the freshmen drop out, and 50% remain to graduate. Ten percent of the graduates seek to further their education immediately upon graduation. Another 71% of the graduates are employed in business, industry, government, education, and human services.

Services: Psychological and career counseling, tutoring, remedial instruction, and health care are offered free to students. Placement services may be used by students and graduates.

Programs of Study: The college confers the B.A., B.F.A., and B.S. degrees. Master's degrees also are available. Bachelor's degrees are offered in the following subjects: AREA STUDIES (American, Russian), BUSINESS (accounting, business administration, computer science, management science), EDUCATION (early childhood, elementary, industrial, secondary), ENGLISH (communications, English), FINE AND PERFORMING ARTS (art, fine arts, music, theater/dramatics), LANGUAGES (French, German, linguistics, Russian, Spanish), MATH AND SCIENCES (biology, chemistry, geochemistry, geology, mathematics, meteorology, physics, zoology), PHILOSOPHY (philosophy, philosophy-psychology), PREPROFESSIONAL (engineering, forestry), SOCIAL SCIENCES (anthropology, economics, government/political science, history, psychology, public justice, sociology). Of the undergraduate degrees conferred, 22% are in education, 24% are in social sciences, and 25% are in business.

Required: Students must complete basic requirements in English composition, mathematics, and Western heritage; they must also complete 9 hours each in social and behavioral sciences, natural sciences, and humanities.

Special: Students may arrange to study abroad in the fall, spring, and summer at a wide range of locations available through the SUNY system. Minors are offered in such areas as: museum studies, art history, forensic science, marine science, European medieval studies, anthropology, biology, chemistry, geology, astronomy, music, history of philosophy, logic, political philosophy, social work/welfare, athletic coaching, health science, reading, women's studies, Afro-American studies, Native American studies, Russian and East European area studies, Asian studies, and Latin American studies.

Honors: Eleven national honor societies have chapters on campus. Honors programs are offered by the departments of chemistry, history, psychology, English, and math. The college also offers an honors program in liberal studies.

Admissions: Fifty-three percent of those who applied were accepted for the 1981-82 freshman class. The SAT scores of those who enrolled were as follows: Verbal—63% below 500, 31% between 500 and 599, 6% between 600 and 700, and fewer than 1% above 700; Math—33% below 500, 51% between 500 and 599, 15% between 600 and 700, and 1% above 700. On the ACT: 11% scored below 21, 32% between 21 and 23, 40% between 24 and 25, 11% between 26 and 28, and 6% above 28. Applicants must present an average of 80 or better and rank in the top 50% of their high school class. Admissions officers also consider advanced placement or honors courses, impressions made during an interview, and evidence of special talents.

Procedure: The SAT or ACT is required. Recommended application deadlines are January 15 (fall) and November 1 (spring). The application fee is $10. Applicants for fall admission are notified beginning January 1; applicants for spring admission, on a rolling basis.

Special: Early and deferred admissions plans are offered. Credit may be earned through AP and CLEP exams.

Transfer: For a recent year, 2498 students applied, 1830 were accepted, and 788 enrolled. A 2.0 or better GPA is required. D grades transfer. Transfers are accepted for all classes. There is a residency requirement of 1 year. Students must complete, at the college, 30 of the 122 hours necessary for the bachelor's degree. Application deadlines are the same as those for freshmen.

Visiting: Visits by prospective students and their parents are encouraged. The college holds an annual spring open house. Guides also are available for informal weekday visits, and students may sit in on classes and stay overnight in the residence halls. The admissions office handles arrangements.

Financial Aid: Financial aid programs include scholarships, grants, loans, and campus jobs. About 75% of the students receive aid. Applications must be filed by March 1 (fall) or November 15 (spring). The FFS or FAF is required.

Foreign Students: Fewer than 1% of the full-time students come from foreign countries. Special counseling and special organizations are available to these students.

Admissions: Foreign students must achieve a minimum score of 550 on the TOEFL. The SAT or ACT is not required.

Procedure: Application deadlines are March 1 (fall) and November 15 (spring). Foreign students must complete a university health form and carry health insurance, which is available through the college for a fee. Proof of funds adequate to cover 4 years of study is required.

Admissions Contact: Robert N. Stewart, Acting Director of Admissions.

STATE UNIVERSITY OF NEW YORK/ COLLEGE AT PLATTSBURGH
D-2

Plattsburgh, New York 12901   (518) 564-2040

F/T: 2268M, 3077W   Faculty: 301; IIA, av$
P/T: 252M, 232W   Ph.D.'s: 72%
Grad: 146M, 291W   S/F Ratio: 20 to 1
Year: sems, ss   Tuition: $1155 ($1855)
Appl: open   R and B: $2078-2164
6606 applied   3337 accepted   1127 enrolled
SAT: 447V 502M   COMPETITIVE

The State University of New York/College at Plattsburgh, founded in 1889, is a liberal arts college. The library contains over 260,000 volumes and more than 300,000 microfilm items, and subscribes to more than 1600 periodicals.

Environment: Highlights include a $7-million library and a fieldhouse that holds a 3000-seat ice arena and a 1000-seat track/basketball arena. The campus is located in a city of 23,000 people, 60 miles from Montreal and 45 miles from Lake Placid.

Student Life: About 95% of the students are residents of New York State. Ninety-five percent of the freshmen come from public schools. About half the students live on campus. Almost 4% are minority-group members. Dormitories are both coed and single-sex. There are visiting privileges in single-sex housing. Students may keep cars on campus.

Organizations: Twenty-five percent of the men belong to the 5 local fraternities, and 12% of the women belong to the 4 local sororities. Social, cultural, and special-interest groups are available, as are religious facilities for the major faiths.

Sports: The college competes intercollegiately in 7 sports for men and 7 for women. There are 16 intramural sports for men and 14 for women.

Handicapped: The college is working toward making the campus totally accessible to wheelchair-bound students. Facilities include ramps, special parking areas, elevators, and specially equipped rest rooms. A resource room and readers are available to the fewer than 1% of students who have visual impairments. A campus committee on the handicapped trains college staff members. Special class scheduling can be arranged.

Graduates: Sixteen percent of the freshmen drop out, and 45% remain to graduate. Thirteen percent of the graduates continue their studies. Another 10% begin careers in business and industry.

Services: Students receive free career and psychological counseling, health care, tutoring, and remedial instruction. Placement services are available to alumni as well as students.

Programs of Study: The college confers the B.A. and B.S. degrees. Certificates of advanced study and master's degrees are also awarded. Bachelor's degrees are offered in the following subjects: AREA STUDIES (Canadian, Latin American), BUSINESS (accounting, business administration, computer science, management, marketing), EDUCATION (early childhood, elementary, health, home economics, secondary, special), ENGLISH (English, speech), FINE AND PERFORMING ARTS (art, music, radio/TV, theater/dramatics), LANGUAGES (French, Spanish), MATH AND SCIENCES (biochemistry, biology, chemistry, ecology/environmental science, geology, mathematics, physics), PHILOSOPHY (philosophy), PREPROFESSIONAL (dentistry, engineering, home economics, law, medicine, pharmacy, social work), SOCIAL SCIENCES (anthropology, economics, geography, government/political science, history, psychology, sociology). Sixteen percent of the undergraduate degrees conferred are in social sciences, 20% are in education, and 24% are in business.

Special: Students may earn a general studies degree. A 3-2 engineering program is offered in conjunction with Clarkson College, Syracuse University, and SUNY at Stony Brook, and an *in vitro* cell biology program is offered in conjunction with the W. Alton Jones Cell Science Research Center in Lake Placid.

Honors: Four national honor societies have chapters on campus. The economics department offers an honors program.

Admissions: Fifty-one percent of those who applied were accepted for the 1981-82 freshman class. The SAT scores of those who enrolled were as follows: Verbal—21% between 500 and 599, and 4% above 599; Math—43% between 500 and 599, and 11% above 599. Most of those enrolled ranked in the top third of their high school class and presented an average of 84 or better. Candidates must have completed 15 Carnegie units. Besides high school record and test scores, admissions officers consider advanced placement or honors courses, leadership record, extracurricular activities, recommendations by high school officials, personality, impressions made during an interview, and special talents.

Procedure: Application deadlines are open. Applicants must take the SAT or ACT. The application fee is $10.

Special: An early admissions and a deferred admissions plan are available. AP and CLEP credit is accepted.

Transfer: For fall 1981, 2404 transfer students applied, 1377 were accepted, and 618 enrolled. Transfers are accepted for all but the senior class. A GPA of 2.0 or better is required. D grades transfer except in the major. Students must earn, at the college, 30 credits of the 122 required for the bachelor's degree. Application deadlines are open.

Visiting: An open house for prospective students is scheduled in April. Guides are available for informal weekday visits, and visitors may sit in on classes. Such visits should be arranged through the admissions office.

Financial Aid: Financial aid programs include scholarships, grants, loans, and campus jobs. About 70% of the students receive aid; 25% work part-time on campus. The average award to freshmen is $1000. The college is a member of CSS and the FAF is required. The application deadline is April 1.

Foreign Students: Almost 2% of the full-time students come from foreign countries. The college offers these students special counseling and special organizations.

Admissions: Foreign students must achieve a minimum score of 500 on the TOEFL. The SAT or ACT is not required.

Procedure: Foreign students are admitted to the fall and spring semesters; application deadlines are open. Completion of the college's health form is necessary to establish proof of health. Proof of funds adequate to cover 4 full years of study is required. Foreign students must also carry health insurance, which is available through the college for a fee.

Admissions Contact: David E. Truax, Director of Admissions.

STATE UNIVERSITY OF NEW YORK/ C-2
COLLEGE AT POTSDAM
Potsdam, New York 13676 (315) 267-2180

F/T: 2012M, 2336W	Faculty:	286; IIA, av$
P/T: 98M, 216W	Ph.D.'s:	53%
Grad: 143M, 408W	S/F Ratio:	19 to 1
Year: sems, ss	Tuition:	$1155 ($1855)
Appl: Mar. 1	R and B:	$2000
4091 applied	1683 accepted	999 enrolled
SAT: 475V 555M	ACT: 24	VERY COMPETITIVE

The State University of New York/College at Potsdam was established in 1866. The Crane Institute of Music, the first music school in the United States to prepare public school music teachers, became a major division of the college in 1926. The library contains 300,000 volumes and 200,000 microfilm items, and subscribes to over 2000 periodicals.

Environment: The 242-acre campus, located in a town of 10,000 people 100 miles from Montreal, houses 12 classroom buildings, a student union, and 9 dormitories that accommodate 2900 students.

Student Life: Almost all students come from New York State. Ninety-five percent of the freshmen are graduates of public schools. Seventy-five percent of the students live on campus. About 3% are minority-group members. Campus housing is both coed and single-sex. There are visiting privileges in single-sex dorms. Students may keep cars on campus.

Organizations: Student activities include drama, publications, special-interest groups, a concert and artist series, student government, and a social program planned with Clarkson College. The college's annual Spring Festival of the Arts is nationally known. Fifteen percent of the students belong to the 4 fraternities and 5 sororities.

Sports: The college fields intercollegiate teams in 8 sports for men and 7 for women. There are 8 intramural sports for men and 5 for women.

Handicapped: Approximately 95% of the campus is accessible to wheelchair-bound students. Special facilities include wheelchair ramps, elevators, and specially equipped rest rooms. Fewer than 1% of the students have visual or hearing impairments. A braille campus map and a special study center are available for the visually impaired. A special counselor is provided, and special class scheduling may be arranged.

Graduates: About 12% of the freshmen drop out, and 50% remain to graduate. Sixteen percent of the graduates seek advanced degrees. One percent enter medical school and 1% enter law school. Another 25% of the graduates pursue careers in business and industry.

Services: Students receive free career and psychological counseling, health care, tutoring, and remedial instruction. Placement services for undergraduates and graduates include counseling, a newsletter, a career library, a career development course, and job-search workshops.

Programs of Study: The college confers the B.A. and B.Mus. degrees, as well as master's degrees. Bachelor's degrees are offered in the following subjects: BUSINESS (computer science), EDUCATION (early childhood, elementary, secondary), ENGLISH (English), FINE AND PERFORMING ARTS (art education, art history, music, music education, studio art, theater/dramatics), LANGUAGES (French, Spanish), MATH AND SCIENCES (biology, chemistry, geology, mathematics, physics), PHILOSOPHY (philosophy, religion), SOCIAL SCIENCES (anthropology, economics, geography, government/political science, history, psychology, sociology).

Required: Students must take 4 semesters of physical education.

Special: The college offers a 4-year B.A.-M.A./M.S. degree in mathematics and a 3-2 degree in engineering. Students may earn New York State provisional certificates in early childhood, elementary, or secondary education. Other programs include a cooperative work-study program, a "school-within-a-school" interdisciplinary arts and science program for freshmen, a Focus program for exceptional students who have not decided on a career, cross-registration at other institutions in the Associated Colleges of the St. Lawrence Valley (Clarkson College, St. Lawrence University, and Canton Agricultural and Technical College), and student-designed majors.

Honors: Nine national honor societies have chapters on campus. An honors program in mathematics is available for freshmen.

Admissions: Forty-one percent of those who applied were accepted for the 1981–82 freshman class. The SAT scores of those who enrolled were as follows: Verbal—61% below 500, 31% between 500 and 599, 7% between 600 and 700, and 0% above 700; Math—22% below 500, 54% between 500 and 599, 22% between 600 and 700, and 3% above 700. Candidates should rank in the upper half of their graduating class, have completed 16 Carnegie units, and present an average of at least 80. Admissions officers also consider SAT or ACT scores, recommendations by high school officials, extracurricular activities, leadership record, personality, advanced placement or honors courses, special talents, and impressions made during an interview.

Procedure: The SAT or ACT is required. Applications should be submitted as early as possible after September 1 of the senior year. Suggested deadlines are March 1 (fall) and December 1 (spring). Music applicants must have an audition, and all applicants must arrange an interview on or off campus. The application fee is $10. Notification is made on a rolling basis beginning January 1 for the fall semester.

Special: Early and deferred admissions plans are available. AP and CLEP credit is awarded.

Transfer: For fall 1981, 998 students applied, 547 were accepted, and 284 enrolled. Students with less than 2 years of college must submit high school records. D grades transfer. Students must complete, at the college, 30 of the 120 credits required for the bachelor's degree. Suggested application deadlines are May 1 (fall) and December 15 (spring).

Visiting: Prospective freshmen may schedule the required personal interview on any weekday the college is in session. Guides are available, and visitors may stay overnight at the school and sit in on classes. The admissions office will make all arrangements.

Financial Aid: Financial aid programs include scholarships, grants, loans, and campus jobs. Three-fourths of the students receive aid; 30% work part-time on campus. The average award to freshmen from all sources is $2400. The college is a member of CSS; the FAF is required. The application deadline is March 1.

Foreign Students: About 1% of the full-time students come from foreign countries. The college offers these students an intensive English course, special counseling, and special organizations.

Admissions: Foreign students must achieve a minimum score of 500 on the TOEFL. The SAT or ACT is also required.

Procedure: Application deadlines are March 1 (fall) and October 1 (spring). Proof of funds adequate to cover the full period of study at the college is required. Although not obligatory, health insurance is available through the college for a fee.

Admissions Contact: Ross Pfeiffer, Director of Admissions.

STATE UNIVERSITY OF NEW YORK/ D-5
COLLEGE AT PURCHASE
Purchase, New York 12211 (914) 253-5068

F/T: 887M, 1225W	Faculty:	137; IIA, – –$
P/T: 34M, 69W	Ph.D.'s:	90%
Grad: none	S/F Ratio:	15 to 1
Year: sems, ss	Tuition:	$1285 ($1985)
Appl: see profile	R and B:	$1966
1600 applied	700 accepted	200 enrolled
SAT: 534V 529M		VERY COMPETITIVE

The State University of New York/College at Purchase was opened in 1971. Its divisions are the College of Letters and Sciences and the School of the Arts, which offers professional programs in dance, music, acting, theater design/technology, film, and visual arts. The library contains 165,000 volumes and 8400 microfilm items, and subscribes to 1100 periodicals.

Environment: The 500-acre campus, located on a rural estate 3 miles from White Plains and 25 miles from Midtown Manhattan, contains 18 buildings, including a Performing Arts Center, the Neuberger Museum, and residence halls that house 1600 students.

Student Life: Eighty-five percent of the students come from New York. Seventy percent live on campus. Seventy-one percent of the entering freshmen are graduates of public schools. Eighteen percent of the students are minority-group members. College housing is coed. Students may keep cars on campus. Day-care services are available to all students.

Organizations: Student activities include a film club, a newspaper, Hillel and Newman religious clubs, and student government. Cultural and social events are available, and the Performing Arts Center and Museum schedule extensive performance and exhibition programs. There are no fraternities or sororities.

610 NEW YORK

Sports: The college participates on an intercollegiate level in 5 sports for both men and women. There are 7 intramural sports for both men and women.

Handicapped: About 85% of the campus is accessible to wheelchair-bound students. Facilities include ramps, special parking areas, elevators, specially equipped rest rooms, and adapted dormitory facilities.

Graduates: About 20% of the freshmen drop out; and 45% eventually graduate. Fifty percent of the graduates go on to further study, including 6% who enter medical school and 9% who enter law school. Another 25% pursue careers in business or industry.

Services: Students receive free psychological and career counseling, health care, tutoring, remedial instruction, and placement services (available to graduates and students).

Programs of Study: The college confers the B.A. and B.F.A. degrees. Bachelor's degrees are offered in the following subjects: ENGLISH (English, literature), FINE AND PERFORMING ARTS (acting, dance, film/photography, music, theater design/technology, visual arts), LANGUAGES (French, Greek/Latin, Hebrew, Italian, Spanish), MATH AND SCIENCES (biochemistry, biology, chemistry, ecology/environmental science, mathematics, natural sciences, physical sciences), PHILOSOPHY (classics, humanities, philosophy), PRE-PROFESSIONAL (dentistry, law, medicine), SOCIAL SCIENCES (anthropology, economics, government/political science, history, psychology, social sciences, sociology). Of the degrees conferred, 30% are in fine and performing arts, 25% are in math and sciences, and 20% are in social sciences.

Required: Freshmen must participate in interdisciplinary courses, each dealing with a contemporary problem.

Special: The College of Letters and Sciences provides interdisciplinary study opportunities, the completion of a senior project/thesis, and the opportunity to shape an individualized program. Students may study abroad and design their own majors. Many opportunities exist for independent research, interdisciplinary study, and special projects. Instruction is given in seminars and small classes.

Honors: All liberal arts and science departments offer advanced research opportunities leading to a thesis or project.

Admissions: Forty-four percent of those who applied were accepted for the 1981–82 freshman class. The SAT scores of those who enrolled were as follows: Verbal—37% below 500, 44% between 500 and 599, 18% between 600 and 700, and 1% above 700; Math—43% below 500, 42% between 500 and 599, 12% between 600 and 700, and 3% above 700. Preference is given to those who present a background of strong preparation in a college-preparatory program. School of Arts candidates are admitted primarily on the basis of the required portfolio or audition.

Procedure: The SAT or ACT is required. Candidates should apply as early in the fall as possible. Applications received after mid-March will be considered if space is available. The College of Letters and Science admits students in the fall and spring; the School of the Arts in the fall only. There is a $10 application fee.

Special: Early and deferred admissions plans are available. AP and CLEP are used.

Transfer: For fall 1981, 600 students applied, 400 were accepted, and 200 enrolled. Transfer students are considered on the basis of background and preparation. A 2.75 GPA is required. D grades do not transfer. There is a 2-year residency requirement. Fifty-five credits must be completed, at the college, out of the 120 needed for a bachelor's degree. Application deadlines are the same as for freshman applicants.

Visiting: The office of admissions holds weekly orientations for prospective students.

Financial Aid: About 71% of the students receive aid. Thirty percent work part-time on campus. Average aid to freshmen from all sources is $2000. The college is a member of CSS. The FAF and the college's own form are required. The application deadlines are March 15 (fall) and June 1 (spring).

Foreign Students: Five percent of the full-time students come from foreign countries. The college offers these students an intensive English course, special counseling, and special organizations.

Admissions: Foreign students must score at least 550 on the TOEFL. No college entrance examination is required.

Procedure: Deadlines for application are May 1 (fall) and November 1 (spring). Foreign students must present proof of funds adequate to cover 4 years of study. They must also carry health insurance, which is available through the college for a fee.

Admissions Contact: Robert Maurovich, Director of Admissions.

STATE UNIVERSITY OF NEW YORK/ EMPIRE STATE COLLEGE D–3
Saratoga Springs, New York 12866   (518) 587-2100

F/T: 395M, 564W   Faculty: 207; IIB, +$
P/T: 1725M, 1150W   Ph.D.'s: n/av
Grad: none   S/F Ratio: n/av
Appl: open   Tuition: $1069 ($1769)
SAT, ACT: not required   NONCOMPETITIVE

Empire State College, a 4-year institution of liberal arts and sciences, was founded by SUNY in 1971 to help students meet their educational objectives through flexible, alternative modes of learning. Students may receive credit for earlier college study or for nonacademic experience, attend classes at other institutions, or attend programs sponsored by the college. The college has no campus, and has no libraries, laboratories, or other learning-related resources common to residential campuses. Instead, it operates through a network of more than 35 Learning Centers, where students meet with faculty "mentors" to discuss their work and plan individualized courses of study. These centers are located at Albany, Alfred, Auburn, Binghamton, Buffalo, Nanuet, New York City, Old Westbury, Plattsburgh, Rochester, Saratoga Springs, Syracuse, Utica, and other cities. Some centers offer special programs, such as the Center for Labor Studies in Manhattan, the Project for the Deaf, and a program for Hispanic students in New York City.

Each center is a regional clearinghouse for resources useful in planning the individualized study programs. Through them, students can arrange to use facilities of other SUNY and independent institutions, community and government agencies, businesses, labor unions, and other groups. Faculty members at each center help students plan their study programs, guide and evaluate their work, and ultimately recommend them for degrees. About 40% of the graduates pursue advanced degrees.

Programs of Study: The college recommends students for the B.A., B.S., and B.P.S. degrees. Associate degrees are also awarded. Bachelor's degree programs are divided into 10 general areas: business and economics, community/human services, cultural studies, educational studies, fine and performing arts, historical studies, human development, labor studies, math/sciences/technology, and social sciences. An interdisciplinary studies program also is possible.

Special: Each student develops a learning contract with a faculty mentor. The contract describes a series of activities both student and mentor agree are educationally valuable and fit the student's objectives. The contract specifies how long these activities will last and how they will be evaluated. The contracts are based on the individual degree program worked out by the student and the mentor, which also may include credit for earlier study or appropriate life learning. Students pursue full- or half-time academic work through the following activities: independent study of integrated readings; cooperative studies, in which several students who share similar interests create a group to coordinate activities; variable-length residences, which bring groups of students together to discuss general topics or specific issues; tutorials in which a faculty member helps a student pursue a specific area of knowledge; organized self-study programs, such as use of programmed learning materials; direct experiences such as travel, internships, paid employment, or volunteer activities; and formal courses offered by other colleges.

Admissions: Applicants must have completed high school or an equivalent experience. Admission also is dependent upon the college's ability to help the student meet his or her educational goals.

Procedure: New students are admitted monthly throughout the year. They must participate in an orientation workshop before beginning their studies. There is no application deadline or fee.

Visiting: Prospective students may attend information sessions at their local center. Appointments should be made through the center.

Financial Aid: About 56% of the students receive aid.

Admissions Contact: Robert Iannuzzo, Director of Admissions.

STATE UNIVERSITY OF NEW YORK/ FASHION INSTITUTE OF TECHNOLOGY D–5
New York, New York 10001   (212) 760-7675

F/T: 640M, 2971W   Faculty: 190; n/av
P/T: 1622M, 5516W   Ph.D.'s: n/av
Grad: none   S/F Ratio: 20 to 1
Year: 4-1-4, ss   Tuition: $1010 ($1910)
Appl: Mar. 15   R and B: $2350
5119 applied   2066 accepted   1731 enrolled
SAT or ACT: required   COMPETITIVE+

The Fashion Institute of Technology, founded in 1944, is a publicly controlled college that offers associate and bachelor's degrees in programs that prepare students for careers in the fashion industry. The library contains 125,000 volumes and 3400 audio materials, and subscribes to 600 periodicals.

Environment: The campus covers 1½ city blocks in the Garment District of Midtown Manhattan. The institute's 7 buildings include 2 dormitories that accommodate 750 students. The Design Center houses a collection of works by craftsmen and artists from around the world, a restoration laboratory, indexed collections of clothing and accessories, and more than a million fabric swatches. The Instructional Media Services Department has a complete TV studio.

Student Life: About 80% of the students come from New York. About 20% of the full-time students live on campus. Almost 17% are minority-group members. Campus housing is both coed and single-sex. There are visiting privileges in single-sex dorms.

Organizations: Student groups are organized and reorganized each year depending on interests. They include a newspaper, a senior yearbook, and student government. Various groups sponsor dances, concerts, trips, and flea markets. There are no fraternities or sororities. The cultural activities of New York City are readily accessible.

Sports: The institute participates in 4 intercollegiate sports for men and 3 for women.

Services: The institute provides free placement aid, health care, career and psychological counseling, tutoring, and remedial instruction.

Programs of Study: The institute awards the B.S. and B.F.A. degrees. Associate degrees also are available. Bachelor's degrees are offered in the following subjects: BUSINESS (marketing—fashion and related industries, production management—apparel, production management—textiles), PREPROFESSIONAL (advertising design, interior design, packaging design, product design—apparel and accessories, product design—textiles).

Required: Students must take a specified number of liberal arts courses, and participation in a cooperative work-study program is required in some majors.

Special: Study-abroad programs are available for certain majors at professional schools in England.

Admissions: All students first earn an A.A.S. degree, then, if they choose, go on to earn the B.F.A. or B.S. degree. Forty percent of those who applied were accepted in 1981-82. Candidates must possess a high school diploma or GED certificate and should have an average of 70 or better. An interview and portfolio are required of students who apply for an art or design program. Admissions officers also consider recommendations from high school officials, character, and leadership record.

Procedure: The SAT or, preferably, the ACT is required of applicants who have not completed at least 12 credits with an average of C or better at another accredited college or university. Applications for fall admission must be submitted by March 15. Some majors allow freshmen to enter at midyear, and the application deadline for those programs is November 15. There is a $10 application fee. An interview is recommended. Admissions decisions are made on a rolling basis.

Transfer: Applicants must have a GPA of 2.0 or better, and design majors must submit an acceptable portfolio. D grades do not transfer. Students must complete, at the institute, 30 of the 132-139 credits required for the bachelor's degree. Application deadlines are the same as those for freshmen.

Financial Aid: About 63% of the students receive aid. The institute is a member of CSS. The FAF is required. Application deadlines are March 1 (fall) and November 15 (spring).

Foreign Students: About 2% of the full-time students come from foreign countries. Student clubs are available to these students.

Admissions: Foreign students must achieve a minimum score of 500 on the TOEFL. Those students who are not college graduates must take college entrance exams available in their languages.

Procedure: The application deadline for fall entry is March 15. A medical examination is required. Proof of funds adequate to cover 1 year of study is necessary. Health insurance is available through the institute for a fee.

Admissions Contact: James Pidgeon, Admissions Director.

NEW YORK 611

STATE UNIVERSITY OF NEW YORK/ MARITIME COLLEGE
Bronx, New York 10465 (212) 892-3000 D-5

F/T: 860M, 68W   Faculty: 74; n/av
P/T: none   Ph.D.'s: 43%
Grad: 165M, 15W   S/F Ratio: 16 to 1
Year: sems, ss   Tuition: $1250
Appl: May 1   R and B: $2715
1360 applied   480 accepted   302 enrolled
SAT: 510V 580M   ACT: 25   VERY COMPETITIVE+

The State University of New York/Maritime College, founded in 1874, prepares young men and women to become licensed officers in the American Merchant Marine and to pursue professional careers ashore in the maritime industry and related fields. The college combines nautical and academic training. The library contains over 65,400 volumes and 12,300 microfilm items, and subscribes to 620 periodicals.

Environment: The 56-acre campus is located at Fort Schuyler on Throgs Neck, just outside New York City. The main college building is a former army fort completed in 1856. The 533-foot training ship *Empire State*, which cadets operate on required summer training cruises to foreign and domestic ports, is moored to the college pier.

Student Life: Eighty-five percent of the cadets come from New York State. Seventy percent of the freshmen are graduates of public schools. All cadets must live in coed college dormitories. Five percent of the cadets are minority-group members. Cars may be kept on campus.

Organizations: Religious counselors and organizations are available for Catholic, Protestant, and Jewish students.

Sports: The college fields intercollegiate teams in 18 sports for men and 11 for women. There are 15 intramural sports for men and 8 for women.

Handicapped: The college does not accept handicapped students. All students must be able to participate in all facets of the college program, including sea training. Physical standards set by the Coast Guard serve as a guide.

Graduates: About 10% of the freshmen drop out, and 75% to 85% remain to graduate. About half the graduates seek advanced degrees, including 10% who enter law school. Ninety percent of the graduates enter business and industry.

Services: Students receive free career and psychological counseling as well as tutoring. Free placement services are provided for students and alumni. There is a charge for health care.

Programs of Study: The college confers the B.S. and B.Eng. degrees. Master's degrees also are available. Bachelor's degrees are offered in the following subjects: BUSINESS (economics/management, marine transportation), ENGLISH (humanities), MATH AND SCIENCES (meteorology and oceanography), PREPROFESSIONAL (engineering—electrical, engineering—marine, engineering—naval architecture, engineering—nuclear science, engineering—ocean). Graduates also receive Coast Guard-issued licenses as third mates or third assistant engineers (steam and motor) for the American Merchant Marine. They are eligible for commissions as officers in the U.S. Naval Reserve or the Coast Guard. Half the undergraduate degrees conferred are in engineering, 35% are in business, and 15% are in math and sciences.

Required: All students must complete 3 summer cruises on the college training ship. Students also must meet distribution requirements.

Special: A modified program is available for veterans.

Admissions: Thirty-five percent of those who applied were accepted for the 1981-82 freshman class. The SAT scores of those who enrolled were as follows: Verbal—46% below 500, 47% between 500 and 599, 7% between 600 and 700, and 0% above 700; Math—3% below 500, 62% between 500 and 599, 33% between 600 and 700, and 2% above 700. Candidates must meet certain physical requirements and have completed at least 16 Carnegie units. Most successful applicants present 4 years of math and 4 of science. Besides test scores, class rank, and high school record, admissions officers also consider extracurricular activities, recommendations by high school officials, leadership, advanced placement or honors courses, and special talents.

Procedure: Candidates must take the SAT or ACT. The application deadline is May 1; new students are admitted only in the fall. Notification is made on a rolling basis beginning February 15. There is a $10 application fee.

Special: The college accepts economically and culturally disadvantaged students into a special Educational Opportunity Program. AP and CLEP credit is awarded. Early and deferred admissions plans are available.

612 NEW YORK

Transfer: A limited number of transfer students are accepted. Transfer applicants must meet freshman requirements. D grades do not transfer. Students must spend 3 years in residence to graduate, and must complete, at the college, 90 of the 160 credits required for the bachelor's degree. May 1 is the application deadline.

Visiting: Orientations for prospective students are scheduled regularly and include an interview and a cadet-guided tour. Visits may be made by appointment only from September to May. Guides are provided and visitors may sit in on classes. The admissions office will handle arrangements.

Financial Aid: Thirty-three percent of the students receive aid; 10% work part-time on campus. Each cadet who is a U.S. citizen and is physically qualified for a Merchant Marine officer's license and for a Midshipman status in the Navy Reserve is eligible for a $1200-a-year federal student incentive payment. All other forms of aid are based on need. The college is a member of CSS; the FAF is required. Aid applications should be submitted by April 15.

Foreign Students: Four percent of the full-time students come from foreign countries. The college, which actively recruits these students, offers them an intensive English course as well as special counseling and special organizations.

Admissions: Foreign students must take the TOEFL. The SAT or ACT is not required.

Procedure: The application deadline for fall entry is February 1. Proof of health must be presented. Foreign students must also carry health insurance, which is available through the college for a fee. Proof of funds adequate to cover 4 years of study is required. The tuition for foreign students is $1650.

Admissions Contact: R. Thomas Cerny, Director of Admissions.

STATE UNIVERSITY OF NEW YORK/ REGENTS EXTERNAL DEGREE PROGRAM
Albany, New York 12230   D-3   (518) 474-3703

The Regents External Degree Program, founded in 1971, makes it possible for students to earn a college degree without attending classes. Students may earn credit through college equivalency examinations (the Regents' own tests or the CLEP program), course credit from accredited colleges, appropriate military or corporate education programs, and special tests in cases where existing proficiency examinations are inappropriate or unavailable. The program offers no classroom instruction or correspondence courses, but instead allows students to bring together credits from various sources to meet flexible degree requirements.

Student Life: Students come from all parts of the United States, and many are stationed at military installations in the United States and abroad.

Programs of Study: The program awards eight degrees: the A.A., A.S., B.A., B.S., B.S.B.A., A.S.N., A.A.S.N., and B.S.N.

Special: B.A. or B.S. candidates may major in liberal studies or in most traditional academic areas. There is no time limit for completing degree requirements.

Admissions: There are no requirements for admission, and applicants need not be residents of New York State.

Expenses: Students are charged a $175 enrollment fee, a $75 to $100 records fee after the first year, and a $50 graduation fee. Examination fees range from $25 to $500.

STATE UNIVERSITY OF NEW YORK/ UPSTATE MEDICAL CENTER
Syracuse, New York 13210   C-3   (315) 473-4570

F/T: 53M, 178W	Faculty: 274; n/av
P/T: 6M, 14W	Ph.D.'s: 75% to 80%
Grad: 478M, 237W	S/F Ratio: n/av
Year: sems, ss	Tuition: $1130 ($1830)
Appl: open	R and B: $2364
303 applied	63 accepted 55 enrolled
SAT: 463V 470M	VERY COMPETITIVE

Upstate Medical Center has 3 component colleges: College of Medicine (graduate level only, leading to the M.D. degree); College of Graduate Studies (master's and graduate level only, leading to Ph.D. degrees); and College of Health Related Professions (offering associate and baccalaureate degrees as well as a certificate level program). The library contains over 130,000 volumes and subscribes to 2000 periodicals.

Environment: The 25-acre campus, located in the city of Syracuse, has 4 buildings, including 2 dormitories that house 338 students.

Student Life: About 95% of the students come from New York State. Thirty-five percent live on campus in coed dorms. Students may keep cars on campus. Day-care services are available to all students for a fee.

Organizations: The center sponsors a number of extracurricular activities.

Sports: There are 10 intramural sports for men and 8 for women.

Handicapped: About 90% of the campus is accessible to wheelchair-bound students. Facilities include ramps, special parking areas, elevators, specially equipped rest rooms, and lowered drinking fountains.

Graduates: Ten percent of the freshmen drop out; 90% remain to graduate. About 20% of the graduates go on to further study. Approximately 87% are employed in their fields.

Services: Career counseling, health care, and tutoring are offered free to students. Free placement services are also provided for both students and graduates.

Programs of Study: The center confers the B.S. degree. Associate, master's, and doctoral degrees also are available. Bachelor's degrees are offered in the following subjects: HEALTH SCIENCES (cytotechnology; medical technology, physical therapy, respiratory therapy). The center offers associate degrees in extracorporeal technology, radiation therapy, radiologic technology, and respiratory therapy. A certificate Nurse Practitioner Program is also available.

Admissions: Twenty-one percent of those who applied were accepted for the 1981–82 freshman class. Applications are processed by curriculum. Therefore, standardized test scores, high school averages, and class ranks for the entering class will vary from curriculum to curriculum and from year to year. In addition, each curriculum has specific course admissions requirements.

Procedure: The SAT or ACT is required; junior-year results are acceptable. There is a $10 application fee. Applicants must be invited for an interview. Notification is made on a rolling basis.

Special: An early admissions plan is offered. CLEP and AP credit is accepted.

Transfer: For fall 1981, 479 transfer students applied, 65 were accepted, and 51 enrolled. Requirements vary according to the major. D grades do not transfer. Students must complete, at the center, 24 of the 120 credit hours required for the bachelor's degree. Application deadlines are open.

Visiting: Applicants who are invited to the Medical Center for the required interview are given a tour of the campus. Tours are not regularly available.

Financial Aid: About 35% of the students receive aid; 23% work part-time on campus. The average award to freshmen is $1798. The center is a member of CSS; the FFS is required. The application deadline is May 1.

Foreign Students: Fewer than 1% of the full-time students come from foreign countries.

Admissions: The TOEFL is required of all foreign students. College entrance exams are not necessary.

Procedure: Foreign students are admitted to the fall semester only. The application deadline is open. Health forms must be completed after admission to establish proof of health. Proof of funds adequate to cover 2 years of study is required. Although not obligatory, health insurance is available through the center for a fee.

Admissions Contact: Lorraine Terracina, Assistant Dean of Admissions and Student Affairs.

STERN COLLEGE FOR WOMEN
(See Yeshiva University)

SYRACUSE UNIVERSITY
Syracuse, New York 13210   C-3   (315) 423-3611

F/T: 7351M, 6930W	Faculty: n/av; I, av$
P/T: 2195 M&W	Ph.D.'s: n/av
Grad: 21,023 M&W	S/F Ratio: 12 to 1
Year: sems, ss	Tuition: $5710
Appl: Feb. 1	R and B: $2718
13,511 applied	8907 accepted 3078 enrolled
SAT: 512V 535M	VERY COMPETITIVE

Syracuse University, founded in 1870, is a privately endowed, nonsectarian university. During the past century, it has developed from a small liberal arts college to a university of 16 degree-granting schools and colleges. The library contains 1.7 million volumes and 1.7 million microfilm items, and subscribes to 21,000 periodicals.

Environment: The main campus is located in the city of Syracuse and occupies about 900 acres; the urban campus of Utica College of Syracuse University is located in Utica, about 45 miles east of Syracuse. Facilities include a well-equipped laboratory for the sciences, a computer center, a nursery school, studios for art and music, and a new domed stadium. Living facilities include dormitories, on-campus and off-campus apartments, fraternity and sorority houses, and married student housing.

Student Life: About 45% of the students come from New York. About 90% live on campus. Twelve percent are minority-group members. Campus housing is both coed and single-sex; there are visiting privileges in the single-sex housing. Juniors and seniors may keep cars on campus. Day-care services are available to all students.

Organizations: There are 25 fraternities and 13 sororities; 12% of the students belong. Extracurricular activities include band and orchestra, cheerleading, journalism, publications, drama, and radio. Cultural events include shows, concerts, plays, debates, films, and lectures.

Sports: The university competes on an intercollegiate level in 10 sports for men and 9 for women. There are 9 intramural sports for men and 12 for women.

Handicapped: About 50% of the campus is accessible to handicapped students. Facilities include wheelchair ramps, parking areas, elevators, specially equipped rest rooms, and lowered telephones. Special class scheduling is possible. There is a coordinator of services for handicapped students.

Graduates: The freshman dropout rate is 9%; 69% remain to graduate. About 50% of the graduates pursue advanced degrees. Fifty percent enter business and industry.

Services: Students receive career and psychological counseling free of charge. Health care, tutoring, and placement services are provided on a fee basis.

Programs of Study: The university confers the B.A., B.S., B.Mus., B.F.A., and B.I.D. degrees. Master's and doctoral degrees are also offered. Bachelor's degrees are offered in the following subjects: AREA STUDIES (American, Asian, Black/Afro-American, Latin American, Russian, urban), BUSINESS (accounting, business administration, business education, computer science, finance, management, marketing, real estate/insurance), EDUCATION (early childhood, elementary, health/physical, secondary, special), ENGLISH (English, journalism, literature, speech), FINE AND PERFORMING ARTS (art, art education, art history, film/photography, music, music education, radio/TV, studio art, theater/dramatics), HEALTH SCIENCES (nursing), LANGUAGES (French, German, Greek/Latin, Italian, Russian, Spanish), MATH AND SCIENCES (biology, chemistry, geology, mathematics, physics), PHILOSOPHY (classics, philosophy, religion), PREPROFESSIONAL (architecture, dentistry, engineering, forestry, home economics, medicine, social work), SOCIAL SCIENCES (anthropology, economics, geography, government/political science, history, international relations, psychology, social sciences, sociology). Eighteen percent of degrees are conferred in fine and performing arts, 16% in business, 14% in social sciences, and 11% in communications.

Required: All students must meet the freshman English requirement and take a minimum of 15 hours in liberal arts courses.

Special: Combined B.A.-B.S. degrees, student-designed majors, and study abroad are available.

Honors: There is a well-established undergraduate honors program; 15 honor societies are represented on campus.

Admissions: Sixty-six percent of those who applied were accepted for the 1981-82 freshman class. The SAT scores of those who enrolled were as follows: Verbal—15% scored below 500, 50% between 500 and 599, 20% between 600 and 700, and 15% above 700; Math—10% scored below 500, 55% between 500 and 599, 25% between 600 and 700, and 10% above 700. The basic admissions requirement is graduation from an accredited high school with 16 units. No single criterion is used to evaluate students for admission, but the following factors are considered: scholastic achievement, the high school counselor's subjective evaluation, SAT or ACT results, the student's activities in and out of school, and the suggested essay on the application. Some preference is given to children of alumni. Other factors considered are advanced placement or honors courses, special talents, and recommendations.

Procedure: The deadline for application for the fall semester is February 1; for the spring semester, December 1. The admissions committee reviews applications from January 15 on; notification is on a rolling basis. There is a $30 application fee. The SAT or ACT is required and should be taken by December of the senior year. The university subscribes to the CRDA.

Special: Early decision is available; notification is made by January 15. Early admissions and deferred admissions are possible. The recommended deadline for early admissions is February 1. AP and CLEP credit is given.

Transfer: Over 1000 transfers enroll each year. In general, a 2.0 GPA is required; individual schools and colleges have specific criteria. D grades do not transfer. All students must complete, at the university, 30 of the 120 or more credits required for a bachelor's degree. Recommended application deadlines are June 1 (fall) and December 1 (spring).

Visiting: Regularly scheduled orientations include group interviews and tours of the campus. Informal weekday visits can also be made; the admissions office should be contacted for arrangements. Visitors may sit in on classes; overnight accommodations are available for a minimal fee.

Financial Aid: Seventy percent of all students receive some financial aid through scholarships, loans, grants, or work programs. The scholarship fund totals about $13 million. The university participates in the CWS program. Cooperative dormitories are available. A 12-month payment plan is possible. Financial aid from all sources ranges from $100 to $9500. The university is a member of the CSS. Applicants should submit the FAF before January 31.

Foreign Students: Ten percent of the full-time students come from foreign countries. An intensive English program, special counseling, and special organizations are available for these students.

Admissions: Foreign students must take the TOEFL and the SAT or ACT.

Procedure: Foreign students are admitted in the fall and spring terms. They must present proof of health and of funds adequate to cover their entire academic program. Health insurance is required and is available through the university for a fee.

Admissions Contact: William F. Bomhoff, Director of Admissions.

SYRACUSE UNIVERSITY/UTICA COLLEGE
(See Utica College of Syracuse University)

TOURO COLLEGE
New York, New York 10001   D-5
(212) 620-0090

F/T: 581M, 1093W   Faculty: 123; IIB, – – $
P/T: 99M, 168W   Ph.D.'s: 50%
Grad: 241M, 97W   S/F Ratio: 15 to 1
Year: sems, ss   Tuition: $3300
Appl: open   R and B: $2910
1405 applied   839 accepted   467 enrolled
SAT (mean): 520V 490M   COMPETITIVE

Touro College, founded in 1970, is a private liberal arts college. The library contains 130,000 volumes and subscribes to 650 periodicals.

Environment: The main campus is a 12-story building in the middle of Manhattan. Auxiliary centers are located throughout the metropolitan area. Two dormitories house 35 men and 100 women.

Student Life: Sixty-five percent of the students are from New York. Twenty percent live on campus. Dormitories are single-sex and there are no visiting privileges. Students may keep cars on campus.

Organizations: There are no fraternities or sororities, but professional and service organizations serve as social groups. Activities include student government and the school newspaper. A student-sponsored lecture series, student-faculty social events, a karate team, and a debating society are also available. Other activities vary from year to year.

Sports: Two intramural sports are offered for men and women.

Handicapped: The college has some facilities for handicapped students.

Graduates: About 20% of the freshmen drop out by the end of the first year. Eighty percent of the graduates seek advanced degrees, including 3% who enter medical school, 5% who enter dental school, and 15% who enter law school. About 50% pursue careers in business and industry.

Services: Students receive the following free services: placement aid, career counseling, tutoring, remedial instruction, and psychological counseling. Fees are charged for health care.

Programs of Study: The college's School of Liberal Arts and Sciences confers the B.A. and B.S. degrees. Associate and master's degrees also are awarded. Bachelor's degrees are offered in the following subjects: AREA STUDIES (Judaic), BUSINESS (accounting, business administration, computer science, finance, management), EDUCATION (elementary), ENGLISH (English, literature), HEALTH SCIENCES (medical records administration, physician's assistant), LANGUAGES (French, Hebrew), MATH AND SCIENCES (biology, chemistry, computer science, mathematics), PHILOSOPHY (humanities, philosophy), PREPROFESSIONAL (dentistry, law, medicine), SOCIAL SCIENCES (economics, government/political science, history, psychology, social sciences, sociology). Thirty percent of degrees are conferred in business, 15% in math and sciences, and 15% in health sciences.

Required: Students generally are required to take a core program in humanities and Judaic studies.

Special: Students may design their own majors or put together an interdisciplinary major.

Admissions: Sixty percent of those who applied were accepted for the 1981–82 freshman class. For an earlier class, the SAT scores were as follows: Verbal—45% between 500 and 599, 25% between 600 and 700, and 10% above 700; Math—40% between 500 and 599, 22% between 600 and 700, and 8% over 700. Applicants should be graduates of an accredited high school with at least a B average and 16 Carnegie units. The following factors are also considered: advanced placement or honors courses, recommendations, impressions made during an interview, extracurricular activities, personality, and leadership record.

Procedure: The SAT or ACT is recommended, and may be required for some students. Application deadlines are open, but priority is given to applications received by July 1 for the fall semester. Students also are admitted in spring and summer. Notification is on a rolling basis. A personal interview is generally required. A $20 fee must accompany the application.

Special: Early and deferred admissions plans are available.

Transfer: For fall 1981, 719 students applied, 572 were accepted, and 293 enrolled. Transfer applicants must be in good academic standing at their last school and have at least a 2.0 GPA. Transfer credits are usually given for liberal arts and science courses that have been completed with a grade of C or better. Students must complete at least 30 credits at the college of the 120 required for a bachelor's degree. Application deadlines are open.

Visiting: Orientation is held for prospective students. Informal visits can be scheduled with the admissions office during the academic year. Guided tours and interviews can be arranged, and visitors may sit in on classes and stay overnight on campus.

Financial Aid: About 85% of the students receive aid; 5% work part-time on campus. Sources of aid include NDSL, state scholarship programs, BEOG, G.I. benefits, and the Touro Scholarship Fund. The average award to 1981–82 freshmen totalled $3000. The college is a member of CSS; the FAF is required. Academic standing and need are the principal considerations in determining aid awards. Applications received by May 15 are given priority.

Foreign Students: The college offers these students an intensive English course, special counseling, and special organizations.

Admissions: Students must take the TOEFL or the college's own test of English proficiency, or otherwise demonstrate command of written and spoken English.

Procedure: Foreign students are admitted to all terms; application deadlines are open. Students must present proof of adequate funds for 1 year.

Admissions Contact: Norman Twersky, Director of Admissions.

UNION COLLEGE   D–3
Schenectady, New York 12308   (518) 370-6112

F/T: 1328M, 728W   Faculty: 150; IIA, +$
P/T: 384M, 87W   Ph.D.'s: 86%
Grad: 588M, 295W   S/F Ratio: 13 to 1
Year: tri, ss   Tuition: $6399
Appl: Feb. 1   R and B: $2300
3241 applied   1380 accepted   522 enrolled
SAT: 560V 620M   ACT: 29 HIGHLY COMPETITIVE+

Union College, founded in 1795, is an independent college of liberal arts and engineering. Originally a college for men, it has been coeducational since the fall of 1970. The library contains 400,000 volumes and 5000 microfilm items, and subscribes to 2369 periodicals.

Environment: The 100-acre urban campus lies 15 miles west of Albany and 170 miles north of New York City. There are 28 major buildings, including the Nott Memorial (the only 16-sided building in the Northern Hemisphere) and an $8-million science center. The 11 dormitories accommodate 800 men and 557 women. In addition, 16 fraternity houses accommodate 417 men, and 3 sororities accommodate 87 women.

Student Life: About 58% of the students come from New York. Approximately 74% of the entering freshmen attended public schools. Seventy-six percent of the students live in the residence halls. About 4% of the students are minority-group members. College housing is both single-sex and coed. There are visiting privileges in single-sex housing. Students may keep cars on campus.

Organizations: There are 16 national fraternities and 3 national sororities on campus. About 30% of the men and 8% of the women belong to these Greek-letter associations. Extracurricular activities on campus include music and theater groups, publications, Black Alliance, a film workshop, and other special-interest groups. The college sponsors art shows, recitals, films, lectures, and plays.

Sports: The college competes on an intercollegiate level in 14 sports for men and 9 for women. There are 16 intramural sports for men and 10 for women.

Handicapped: About 60% of the campus is accessible to the physically handicapped. Special facilities include elevators and designated parking areas.

Graduates: The freshman dropout rate is 4%; 80% remain to graduate. About 40% of the students pursue advanced study after graduation; of these, 10% enter medical school, 3% dental school, and 3% law school. About 55% of the graduates pursue careers in business and industry.

Services: Students receive the following services free of charge: placement, career counseling, health care, tutoring, remedial instruction, and psychological counseling.

Programs of Study: The college confers the B.A., B.S., and B.S. in E. degrees. It also offers master's and doctoral degrees. Bachelor's degrees are offered in the following subjects: AREA STUDIES (American, comparative Communist, Latin American), BUSINESS (computer science), ENGLISH (English, literature), FINE AND PERFORMING ARTS (art, music, theater/dramatics), LANGUAGES (Chinese, French, German, Greek/Latin, Hebrew, Italian, Russian, Spanish), MATH AND SCIENCES (biology, chemistry, mathematics, physics), PHILOSOPHY (classics, philosophy), PREPROFESSIONAL (dentistry, engineering, medicine), SOCIAL SCIENCES (economics, government/political science, history, psychology, sociology). About 13% of the degrees conferred are in interdisciplinary studies, 7% in the humanities, 25% in social sciences, 26% in sciences, and 29% in engineering.

Required: All students must take a distribution of liberal arts courses.

Special: There is cross-registration with 8 other area institutions. Interdepartmental majors, study abroad, and student-designed majors are offered. Internships are available in Washington, D.C., and in Albany. The college has a 6-year B.A.-J.D. program with Albany Law School and a 6-year B.S.-M.D. program with Albany Medical College. Other programs available combine bachelor's and master's degrees, and liberal arts and engineering degrees.

Honors: There are chapters of 5 national honor societies on campus, including Phi Beta Kappa and Sigma Xi.

Admissions: About 43% of those who applied were accepted for the 1981–82 freshman class. Of those who enrolled, the SAT scores were as follows: Verbal—19% scored below 500, 51% between 500 and 599, 26% between 600 and 700, and 4% above 700; Math—4% scored below 500, 34% between 500 and 599, 50% between 600 and 700, and 11% above 700. Eighty percent of the freshmen ranked in the top 20% of their high school class. Candidates must be graduates of an accredited high school and present 15 Carnegie units of work. Other important factors include extracurricular activities, recommendations by school officials, and advanced placement or honors courses.

Procedure: Either the ACT or SAT is required and must be taken by January of the senior year. Three ATs are required: English Composition, Math Level I or II, and 1 of the student's choice. Applications are due February 1 (fall) or January 1 for 6-year law and medical programs, and November 1 (winter). The college uses a block admissions notification plan. There is a $30 application fee for 4-year programs and a $35 application fee for 6-year programs. A personal interview is recommended.

Special: Early decision, early admissions, and deferred admissions plans are available. AP and CLEP credit is granted.

Transfer: For fall 1981, 255 students applied, 120 were accepted, and 74 students enrolled. Transfer applicants need a 3.0 GPA. D grades are not accepted for credit. Students must complete 9 courses in residence, out of the 36 needed for a bachelor's degree. Application must be made by April 1 (fall), November 1 (winter), and February 1 (spring).

Visiting: Regularly scheduled orientations for prospective students include personal interviews during the week (except February 1 to April 1) and group information sessions on selected Saturdays (October 1 to February 1). Informal guided tours, classroom visits, and overnight stays can be arranged during the week. The admissions office should be contacted for arrangements.

Financial Aid: About 46% of the students receive scholarship aid. Thirty-two percent work part-time on campus. Average aid to freshmen from all sources is $4700. The college is a member of CSS. The FAF is required. Financial aid is awarded on the basis of academic promise, character, leadership, need, and achievement in extracurricular activities. Application deadlines are February 1 (fall) and November 1 (winter).

Foreign Students: Fewer than 1% of the full-time students come from foreign countries. The college offers these students special counseling and special organizations.

Admissions: Foreign students must take the TOEFL and the SAT.

Procedure: The application deadline is February 1 (fall). Foreign students must submit the College Health Form completed by a physician. They must also present proof of funds adequate to cover 4 years of study.

Admissions Contact: Kenneth A. Nourse, Dean of Admissions and Financial Aid.

UNION UNIVERSITY/ALBANY COLLEGE OF PHARMACY
(See Albany College of Pharmacy)

UNITED STATES MERCHANT MARINE ACADEMY E-5
Kings Point, New York 11024 (516) 482-8200

F/T: 1020M, 84W Faculty: n/av; IIB, ++$
P/T: none Ph.D.'s: 37%
Grad: none S/F Ratio: 10 to 1
Year: qtrs Tuition: none
Appl: Mar. 1 R and B: none
2800 applied 943 accepted 352 enrolled
SAT: 525V 600M ACT: 27 HIGHLY COMPETITIVE+

The United States Merchant Marine Academy, founded in 1942, is one of the 5 service academies in the nation. It exists for the purpose of training officers for the Merchant Marine and leaders in the maritime industry. The academy was the first service institution to admit women. The library contains 89,000 volumes and subscribes to 1000 periodicals.

Environment: The 75-acre suburban campus is located on the former waterfront estate of Walter P. Chrysler. It is 20 miles from New York City on the north shore of Long Island. The American Merchant Marine Museum is located on the campus. A new science and engineering wing was recently added. Midshipmen live in 4-story dorms.

Student Life: Eighty percent of the students come from public schools. All students live at the academy and are under military discipline; midshipmen are permitted weekend liberty and leave. Nine percent of the students are minority-group members. About 55% are Catholic, 25% are Protestant, and 16% are Jewish. Campus housing is coed. Students may keep cars on campus.

Organizations: There are no fraternities or sororities at the academy. Religious facilities for students of all faiths are available.

Sports: The academy fields 16 intercollegiate teams for men and 11 for women. There are 7 intramural sports for men and 2 for women.

Handicapped: There are no special facilities for handicapped students.

Graduates: About 18% of the students drop out at the end of the first year; 72% remain to graduate. About 4% of the graduates pursue advanced degrees (3% enter law school). Ninety-two percent pursue careers in business and industry.

Services: The following services are available to students free of charge: health care, psychological counseling, tutoring, remedial instruction, placement, and career counseling.

Programs of Study: Midshipmen graduate with a B.S. degree, a license as ship's officer, and a commission in the U.S. Naval Reserve. Three professional curricula are offered: nautical science, marine engineering, and dual license. Nautical science instills professional competency in all the professional requirements of licensed mates on American ships, and provides unique laboratory and training facilities, including a stability tank and planetarium. Marine engineering provides all the professional competency requirements of licensed engineers on American ships. Laboratory and training facilities in this area include elements of a ship's power plant and nuclear training laboratories. The dual license curriculum provides professional competency in both nautical science and marine engineering. Elective courses are available which enable midshipmen to minor in specialized areas such as oceanography, management, naval architecture, and nuclear engineering.

One year is spent at sea. Midshipmen are assigned to American merchant vessels to acquire practical experience to match their classroom knowledge.

Required: All students must take courses in freshman English, as well as a distribution of credits in several broad areas of study.

Admissions: About 34% of those who applied were accepted for the 1981-82 freshman class. The SAT scores of those who enrolled were as follows: Verbal—36% scored below 500, 51% between 500 and 599, 12% between 600 and 700, and 2% above 700; Math—0% scored below 500, 49% between 500 and 599, 46% between 600 and 700, and 5% above 700.

Candidates must be nominated by their congressman or senator. Candidates from each state compete among themselves for the appointment allocated to their state. They can also compete for unfilled national quotas as alternates. Applicants must be between the ages of 17 and 25, United States citizens, and in excellent physical condition. Students should rank in the top 40% of their high school graduating class, should have a B average in math and science, and should have completed 15 units of academic work. Other important considerations are advanced placement or honor courses, recommendations, leadership record, and impressions made during the interview.

Procedure: The SAT or ACT is required and should be taken by February of the senior year. The application deadline is March 1. Notification is on a rolling basis. There is no application fee.

Transfer: The academy does not accept transfer students. Those students who enter after some college work must complete the full 4-year curriculum, but they can receive some credit for previous work. The academy requires 215-224 credits for a bachelor's degree. The application deadline is March 1.

Visiting: The academy has a regular interview and tour program for prospective students; no interviews are held between January 15 and May 1. Guides are available for informal visits. Visitors may sit in on classes and stay overnight at the school. The admissions office should be contacted for arrangements.

Financial Aid: Students make no conventional payments for tuition or room and board. During the year at sea they can earn $3500. Midshipmen make cash deposits in accordance with the following schedule: $450 at the beginning of the freshman year, $300 in both the sophomore and junior years, and $400 in the senior year. Essentially, these allowances and expenses equalize over the 4-year period of training. In effect, all midshipmen are on scholarship, but those requiring additional aid may apply for loans from local banks and private sources. The academy is a member of CSS.

Foreign Students: Fewer than 1% of the full-time students come from foreign countries. An intensive English course is available for these students.

Admissions: Foreign students must take either the TOEFL, the University of Michigan Language Test, the Comprehensive English Language Test, or the institute's own English proficiency exam. They must achieve SAT scores of at least 500 on the math section and 450 on the verbal section.

Procedure: The application deadline is March 1. Foreign students must present a statement from the health department certifying that they are free of communicable diseases.

Admissions Contact: Capt. Emmanuel L. Jenkins, Director of Admissions.

UNITED STATES MILITARY ACADEMY D-4
West Point, New York 10996 (914) 938-4041

F/T: 4013M, 426W Faculty: 632; n/av
P/T: none Ph.D.'s: 16%
Grad: none S/F Ratio: 7 to 1
Year: sems, ss Tuition: none
Appl: Jan. 15 R and B: none
11,047 applied 2148 accepted 1541 enrolled
SAT: 546V 623M ACT: 27 MOST COMPETITIVE

NEW YORK

The United States Military Academy was founded by Congress in 1802. The library contains 400,000 volumes and subscribes to 1600 current periodicals.

Environment: The campus is located in a rural area. Academic facilities include science laboratories, language labs, and a computer center that every cadet is trained to use. All students reside in a large dormitory complex.

Student Life: All students reside on campus. Thirteen percent are minority-group members. About 44% are Protestant, 41% are Catholic, and 1% are Jewish. Housing is coed. Seniors may keep cars on campus. New cadets enter the first week of July and receive military training until Academics begin in August; upperclassmen train for 2 months every summer.

Organizations: The Cadet Activities Directorate sponsors 87 extracurricular activities, all cadet-run and officer-advised. Eisenhower Hall is the forum for many visiting artists.

Sports: The academy fields 16 intercollegiate teams for men and 8 for women. There are 16 intramural sports for men and 12 for women. Either intercollegiate or intramural athletics are required of every student all 4 years.

Graduates: About 13% of entering freshmen drop out after 1 year; 65% remain to graduate. About 90% of those who stay on active duty for more than 10 years receive advanced degrees. Two percent of the graduates enter medical school.

Services: The following services are offered at no charge to cadets: psychological counseling, tutoring, remedial instruction, health care, placement, and career counseling.

Programs of Study: The graduate receives a B.S. degree (with no major) and a commission as a second lieutenant in the Regular Army. In addition to the required standard core curriculum, cadets are able to enroll in areas of elective concentration such as basic sciences (chemistry, mathematics, physics), applied sciences and engineering (aerospace, civil, computer science, electrical, engineering mechanics, nuclear, operations research, weapons systems), humanities (American studies, literature, Arabic, Chinese, French, German, Portuguese, Russian, Spanish), national security and public affairs (behavioral science, economics, geography, international affairs, military history, military studies, modern history, political science), and interdisciplinary fields in management and foreign area studies. Transcripts are annotated with the graduate's field of study.

Required: Core courses are required in chemistry, computer science, electrical engineering, general engineering, English, a foreign language, law, literature, mathematics, mechanics, military science, psychology, leadership, philosophy, physics, history, social sciences, and physical education.

Special: Advanced and honor courses are available to those who demonstrate exceptional ability. The academy also has a "Topics" series of elective courses which vary from semester to semester with demand and/or current relevancy.

Honors: There is a chapter of Phi Kappa Phi on campus. Each academic department offers an honors program which involves independent work.

Admissions: Only 19% of those who applied were accepted for the 1981–82 freshman class. Of those who enrolled, the SAT scores were as follows: Verbal—26% scored below 500, 48% between 500 and 599, 22% between 600 and 700, and 4% above 700; Math—1% scored below 500, 35% between 500 and 599, 50% between 600 and 700, and 14% above 700. On the ACT, 7% scored below 21, 17% between 21 and 23, 15% between 24 and 25, 24% between 26 and 28, and 37% above 28. To be considered for admission, a candidate must be nominated by a legal authority. Congressmen nominate 75% of the Corps; the remaining 25% receive military service-connected nominations.

Candidates must be United States citizens between the ages of 17 and 22 on July 1 of the year of admission, be unmarried, and have no legal obligation to support a child or children. Applications are evaluated on the basis of the following factors: academic qualification, medical examination, physical aptitude examination, and extracurricular activities.

Procedure: The ACT or SAT is required and should be taken no later than February of the year in which a candidate expects to enter. A physical aptitude exam and a medical exam are also required. There is no application fee. Candidates are urged to apply for a nomination as early as possible. A letter to the admissions office will open a file on the candidate. Notification is on a rolling basis.

Special: Equal Admission Opportunity Officers establish contact with prospective candidates, and encourage and offer help to minority-group members who apply. Currently, a 5-year active service obligation is incurred upon graduation from the academy. Under the Early Action Plan, those who notify the admissions office in writing by November 1 and complete their application file in November can be notified by December 15. Applicants under this plan need not have a nomination or the results from the medical examination to apply, but must have both prior to admission in July. CLEP and AP credit is available.

Transfer: For the current year, the academy enrolled 174 students with previous college experience. Transfer students must complete Cadet Basic Training, and then enter as first-semester freshmen (plebes). Requirements for admission and application deadlines are the same as for those with no prior college experience. At least 136.5 credits are required for a bachelor's degree.

Visiting: The academy conducts scheduled tours for prospective students. Visitors may sit in on classes. Overnight stays are possible. All arrangements should be made through the office of admissions.

Financial Aid: All students receive free room, board, and medical and dental care plus an annual salary of $5500.

Foreign Students: Fewer than 1% of the students come from foreign countries. Application procedures are the same as those for other students.

Admissions Contact: Col. Manley E. Rogers, Director of Admissions.

UNIVERSITY OF ROCHESTER   B–3
Rochester, New York 14627   (716) 275-3221

F/T: 2656M, 1847W   Faculty: 1056; I, av$
P/T: 245M, 317W   Ph.D.'s: 97%
Grad: 2226M, 1538W   S/F Ratio: 11 to 1
Year: sems + optional, ss   Tuition: $6169
Appl: Jan. 15   R and B: $2789
5694 applied   3757 accepted   1070 enrolled
SAT: 553V 617M   **HIGHLY COMPETITIVE**

The University of Rochester, a private, nonsectarian institution founded in 1850, includes the College of Arts and Science, the Graduate School of Education and Human Development, the College of Engineering and Applied Science, the Graduate School of Management, the University College, the School of Medicine and Dentistry, the School of Nursing, and the Eastman School of Music. The library houses 1,956,000 volumes and 1.6 million microfilm items. It subscribes to 12,500 periodicals.

Environment: University facilities include 132 buildings on 591 acres. All schools and colleges are on the suburban River Campus along the Genesee River in southwest Rochester except Medicine, Dentistry, and Nursing, which are located at the University Medical Center, and the Eastman School of Music, which is in downtown Rochester. Notable buildings include the Eastman Theater, the Memorial Art Gallery, the Nuclear Structure Research Laboratory, the Laboratory for Laser Energetics, Strong Memorial Hospital, Wilson Commons, and the Zornow Sports Center. Living facilities include dormitories, fraternity houses, on-campus and off-campus apartments, and married student housing.

Student Life: Fifty-six percent of the River Campus students come from New York State. Seventy-six percent of the freshmen attended public schools. About 85% of the students live on campus. Six percent are minority-group members. About 35% are Catholic, 23% are Protestant, and 24% are Jewish. Campus housing is both coed and single-sex; there are visiting privileges in the single-sex housing. Students may keep cars on campus.

Organizations: Sixteen percent of the men belong to 1 of 11 fraternities on campus; 6% of the women belong to 1 of 3 sororities. The many extracurricular activities include publications, drama, music, and academic and special-interest groups. The cultural and recreational facilities of Rochester are within easy reach.

Sports: The university fields 12 intercollegiate teams for men and 10 for women. There are 10 intramural sports for men and 9 for women.

Handicapped: Forty-one percent of the campus is accessible to the physically handicapped. Wheelchair ramps, parking areas, specially equipped rest rooms, elevators, and lowered drinking fountains and telephones are provided. Special class scheduling can be arranged. A counselor is provided to assist these students.

Graduates: The freshman dropout rate is 10%; 70% remain to graduate. Seventy-five percent of the graduates continue their studies, with 16% entering medical school, 2% dental school, and 15% law school. Thirty-two percent enter careers in business or industry.

Services: Free psychological counseling, career counseling, placement, and tutoring services are available. Health care is available for a fee.

Programs of Study: The University confers the B.A., B.S., and B.Mus. degrees. Master's and doctoral degrees are also awarded. Bachelor's degrees are offered in the following subjects: ENGLISH (English), FINE AND PERFORMING ARTS (art history, music, music composition, music education, music history, music theory, studio art), HEALTH SCIENCES (nursing), LANGUAGES (Chinese, comparative literature, French, German, foreign literature, linguistics, Russian, Spanish), MATH AND SCIENCES (biology, biology-geology, chemistry, general science, geology, geomechanics, mathematics, mathematics-statistics, microbiology, neuroscience, physics, physics-astronomy, statistics), PHILOSOPHY (philosophy, religion), PREPROFESSIONAL (engineering—chemical, engineering—electrical, engineering—mechanical, engineering and applied science, optics), SOCIAL SCIENCES (anthropology, economics, government/political science, history, psychology, sociology). Thirty-eight percent of the degrees conferred are in the social sciences, 23% in math and sciences, and 19% in preprofessional studies.

Required: River Campus undergraduates complete the first 2 years in the College of Arts and Science; the last 2 years are taken there or in one of the professional schools.

Special: It is possible to earn a combined B.S.-B.A. degree in an engineering discipline and an appropriate area. A 3-2 B.A.-M.S. program in public policy analysis, a 3-2 B.S.-M.S. program in biology-geology, a 3-2 B.A.- or B.S.-M.S. program in liberal arts and community health, a 3-2 B.A. or B.S. program and an M.S. program in human development, and a 3-2 program combining a bachelor's degree and an M.B.A. may be arranged. Interdepartmental studies, self-designed majors, and study abroad for a semester or a year are options offered. A general studies degree is available.

Honors: Every department has the degree with distinction option for students meeting the appropriate criteria. Seven honor societies, including Phi Beta Kappa, have chapters on campus.

Admissions: Sixty-six percent of the applicants to the 1981–82 freshman class were accepted. The SAT scores of those who enrolled were as follows: Verbal—23% scored below 500, 47% between 500 and 599, 26% between 600 and 700, and 4% above 700; Math—7% scored below 500, 29% between 500 and 599, 49% between 600 and 700, and 15% above 700. Quality rather than pattern of high school record is emphasized. Important factors in the admissions decision are advanced placement or honors courses, recommendations by school officials, extracurricular activities, personality, leadership record, and special talent.

Procedure: The SAT or ACT is required; ATs are also recommended. The SAT and ATs should be taken no later than February of the senior year. The deadline for regular fall admission is January 15. An application fee of $25 must accompany the form.

Special: The early decision deadline is November 15; the notification date is December 15. There are also early admissions and deferred admissions plans. AP credit is granted.

Transfer: For fall 1981, 347 students applied, 211 were accepted, and 130 enrolled. Transfer students are admitted for both the spring and fall semesters into the College of Arts and Sciences or the College of Engineering and Applied Science. D grades do not transfer. The university follows the rolling admissions plan. Two semesters in residence are required by the College of Arts and Science and the College of Engineering and Applied Science. All students must complete, at the university, at least 24 of the 128 credits required for a bachelor's degree. The School of Nursing accepts junior-level transfers.

Visiting: Regularly scheduled orientations for prospective students are Autumn Open House in the fall, Open Campus for admitted students in the spring, and summer orientation programs for enrolling students. Informal visits can be arranged throughout the year. Visitors are provided with guides and may sit in on classes and stay overnight at the school. Arrangements should be made through the admissions office receptionist.

Financial Aid: Fifty percent of the students receive financial aid from the University; 80%, from all sources. About 35% work part-time on campus. The average freshman award is $1900. HEOP is available. The university is a member of CSS. The financial aid package usually consists of a combination of scholarships, loans, and work scholarships. The FAF is required; aid application deadlines are January 31 (fall) and November 15 (spring).

Foreign Students: Seven percent of the full-time students come from foreign countries. An intensive English course, an intensive English program, special counseling, and special organizations are available for these students.

Admissions: The TOEFL is required only for foreign students applying to certain graduate programs. All foreign students must take the SAT or ACT.

Procedure: Application deadlines are January 15 (fall entry) and November 15 (spring entry). Foreign students must fill out the university's health form and must present proof of funds adequate to cover 4 years of study. Health insurance is required and is available through the university for a fee.

Admissions Contact: Timothy W. Scholl, Dean of Admissions and Student Aid.

UNIVERSITY OF ROCHESTER/ EASTMAN SCHOOL OF MUSIC
(See Eastman School of Music)

UTICA COLLEGE OF SYRACUSE UNIVERSITY
C-3

Utica, New York 13502   (315) 792-3006

F/T: 708M, 804W	Faculty: 91; IIB, +$
P/T: 190M, 197W	Ph.D.'s: 64%
Grad: none	S/F Ratio: 17 to 1
Year: sems, ss	Tuition: $4400
Appl: Feb. 1	R and B: $1700–2600
1134 applied	794 accepted	363 enrolled
SAT: 450V 490M	ACT: 23	COMPETITIVE+

A private liberal arts college, Utica College of Syracuse University, one of Syracuse University's 16 schools and colleges, is financially independent of the university. The library contains 123,134 volumes and 5383 microfilm items, and subscribes to 1220 periodicals.

Environment: Located in a city 50 miles from Syracuse, the 185-acre campus includes 2 residential halls, a student center, and a gymnasium.

Student Life: About 80% of the students come from New York State. Ninety percent of the students attended public schools. Forty-two percent of the students live on campus. About 13% are minority-group members. College housing is both single-sex and coed. There are visiting privileges in single-sex housing. Students may keep cars on campus.

Organizations: There are 6 national fraternities, 3 national sororities, and 3 local sororities. Other activities include publications, religious organizations, and numerous other special-interest groups.

Sports: The college participates in 10 intercollegiate sports for men and 5 for women. There are 8 intramural sports for men and 7 for women.

Handicapped: About 75% of the campus is accessible to wheelchair students. Special facilities for the physically handicapped include ramps, parking areas, and specially equipped rest rooms. There are no special counselors for handicapped students.

Graduates: Twenty-four percent of the freshmen drop out by the end of their first year. About 52% remain to graduate. Nine percent of the graduates go on to graduate or professional schools; 3% enter medical school, 2% law school, and 2% dental school. Thirty-nine percent enter careers in business and industry.

Services: Students receive the following services free of charge: placement, career counseling, health care, psychological counseling, tutoring, and remedial instruction.

Programs of Study: The college grants the B.A. and B.S. degrees. Associate degrees are also conferred. Bachelor's degrees are offered in the following subjects: BUSINESS (accounting, business administration, computer science, construction management, public relations), ENGLISH (English, journalism, speech), FINE AND PERFORMING ARTS (art, radio/TV, theater/dramatics), HEALTH SCIENCES (child life specialist, medical technology, occupational therapy), MATH AND SCIENCES (biology, chemistry, mathematics, physics, statistics), PHILOSOPHY (philosophy), PREPROFESSIONAL (dentistry, engineering, law, medicine, social work, veterinary), SOCIAL SCIENCES (economics, government/political science, history, international relations, psychology, social sciences, sociology). Forty percent of the degrees conferred are in business, 20% in health sciences, and 15% in social sciences.

Required: Students must exhibit competency in English composition.

Special: Independent study is available in some programs. There are 3-2 and 2-2 engineering programs in cooperation with the College of Engineering of Syracuse University and a geology program and a study-abroad program in cooperation with Syracuse University. An A.S. program in surgical technology is offered.

Honors: Honors study is available in some programs. Five national honor societies have chapters on campus.

618 NEW YORK

Admissions: Seventy percent of those who applied were accepted for the 1981-82 freshman class. The SAT scores of those who enrolled were as follows: Verbal—63% scored below 500, 25% between 500 and 599, 4% between 600 and 700, and 0% above 700; Math—50% scored below 500, 33% between 500 and 599, 8% between 600 and 700, and 2% above 700. Applicants should be in the top two-fifths of their high-school class and have a minimum average of B. The high school record is the most important factor in the admissions decision; it should include 16 Carnegie units. Candidates for the engineering program must have 3 to 4 years of mathematics. Aptitude test scores are important, as are special talents, extracurricular activities, leadership potential, and recommendations by school officials.

Procedure: The SAT or ACT is required. An interview is recommended. Applications should be submitted by February 1 (fall), December 1 (spring), and May 1 (summer). The college uses the rolling admissions plan. A $15 application fee must be included.

Special: Early decision, early admissions, and deferred admissions plans are available. CLEP subject exams are accepted. Students may also earn credit through AP exams.

Transfer: For fall 1981, 563 students applied, 444 were accepted, and 284 enrolled. Transfers are considered for all classes and must complete at least 30 hours at the college, of the 120 to 128 needed to receive a bachelor's degree. Application deadlines are the same as those for freshmen.

Visiting: Regularly scheduled orientations for prospective students include a campus tour, special activities, advising sessions, and course scheduling. Guides are available for informal visits. Visitors may stay overnight at the school and sit in on classes. Such visits can be arranged during the week from 10 A.M. to 4 P.M. by the admissions office.

Financial Aid: About 86% of all students receive aid. Eighty-two percent work part-time on campus. Average aid to freshmen from all sources is $1347. The college provides scholarship aid and administers NDSL, EOG, and CWS funds. The amount is based on need, and most aid is packaged. A Higher Education Opportunity Program is available for New York State residents. The FAF is required. A form from the college must also be filed. The application deadline is April 15.

Foreign Students: Fewer than 1% of the full-time students come from foreign countries. The college offers these students an intensive English course, special counseling, and special organizations.

Admissions: Foreign students must score 500 on the TOEFL. They must also take the SAT or the ACT, if English is the primary language.

Procedure: The application deadlines are February 1 (fall), December 1 (spring), and May 1 (summer). Foreign students must present proof of health. They must also present proof of funds adequate to cover their entire college budget. They must carry health insurance, which is available through the college for a fee.

Admissions Contact: Dominic Passalacqua, Director of Admissions.

VASSAR COLLEGE   D-4
Poughkeepsie, New York 12601   (914) 452-7000

F/T: 929M, 1290W	Faculty: 194; IIB, ++$
P/T: 40M, 74W	Ph.D.'s: 90%
Grad: 1M, 1W	S/F Ratio: 11 to 1
Year: sems	Tuition: $6560
Appl: Feb. 1	R and B: $2800
3698 applied	1598 accepted 583 enrolled
SAT: 600V 600M	**HIGHLY COMPETITIVE**

Vassar College, founded in 1861, is a nonsectarian, private liberal arts college. The library contains 545,000 volumes and 270,650 microforms, and subscribes to 3750 periodicals.

Environment: Vassar's 1000-acre campus, located 75 miles north of New York City, is noted for its beauty, with its diverse architecture, gardens, and 2 lakes. The college's surrounding environment is urban, suburban, and rural. Among the 10 dormitories are a steel and glass residence hall designed by Eero Saarinen and the Main Building (1865), patterned after the Tuilleries. There are also on-campus townhouse apartments and married student housing.

Student Life: Forty percent of the students are from New York State. About 65% of the entering freshmen attended public schools. Ninety-seven percent of the students live on campus. Eleven percent are minority-group members. Campus housing is both coed and single-sex; there are visiting privileges in the single-sex housing. Students may keep cars on campus.

Organizations: There are no sororities or fraternities on campus. Students participate in theater, concerts, recitals, special interest groups, 26 student organizations, 7 publications, and 10 sports clubs. A local opera house and a civic center offer cultural and social activities.

Sports: Vassar competes on an intercollegiate level in 8 sports for men and 9 for women. There are 11 intramural sports for men and 11 for women.

Handicapped: Special facilities for the physically handicapped include wheelchair ramps, parking areas, elevators, specially equipped rest rooms, and lowered drinking fountains and telephones. Class scheduling can be arranged to suit the needs of the handicapped person.

Graduates: The freshman dropout rate is 1%; 75% remain to graduate. About 50% of the students pursue graduate study after graduation.

Services: The following services are available free of charge to students: placement, career counseling, tutoring, remedial instruction, and psychological counseling. Health care is provided on a fee basis.

Programs of Study: The college confers the B.A. degree. Master's degrees are also awarded. Bachelor's degrees are offered in the following subjects: AREA STUDIES (American, Africana, Asian, Hispanic, Latin American, urban), BUSINESS (computer science), ENGLISH (English), FINE AND PERFORMING ARTS (art, music, theater/dramatics), LANGUAGES (French, German, Greek/Latin, Italian, Russian, Spanish), MATH AND SCIENCES (astronomy, biochemistry, biology, biopsychology, chemistry, ecology/environmental science, geology, mathematics, physics), PHILOSOPHY (classics, philosophy, religion), SOCIAL SCIENCES (anthropology, anthropology/sociology, economics, geography, geography/anthropology, government/political science, history, psychology, sociology). Of the degrees conferred, 46% are in social sciences, 16% in math and sciences, 12% in English, and 11% in the fine arts.

Required: All students must complete 34 units of study. Students are expected to spend 3 of their 4 years at Vassar.

Special: Off-campus study opportunities include junior year abroad, the Vassar-Wesleyan program in Spain, the Vassar-William and Mary program in Germany, a semester internship program in British primary schools, and a 12-college exchange program. Combined B.A.-M.A. degrees may be earned in 4 years through 3 departments: Chemistry, French, and Hispanic Studies. Other options include student-designed majors and multidisciplinary concentrations combining courses, seminars, and independent study or field work.

Honors: There are chapters of 8 national honor societies on campus, including Phi Beta Kappa.

Admissions: About 43% of those who applied were accepted for the 1981-82 freshman class. Of those who enrolled, the SAT scores were as follows: Verbal—7% scored below 500, 44% between 500 and 599, 42% between 600 and 700, and 7% above 700; Math—8% scored below 500, 42% between 500 and 599, 42% between 600 and 700, and 8% above 700. Although academic preparation is of great importance, the college's main criterion is the degree to which the candidate has taken advantage of the opportunities made available to him or her. Other important factors include advanced placement or honors courses, recommendations by school officials, leadership record, personality, extracurricular record, and impressions made during an interview.

Procedure: Candidates must take the SAT and any 3 ATs by January of the senior year. Applications should be submitted early in the senior year, and all credentials received no later than February 1 for the fall and December 1 for the spring. Notification is sent in April for regular fall candidates. There is a $20 application fee.

Special: Early admissions and deferred admissions plans are available. The notification date for early decision is 1 month after the credentials are complete.

Transfer: For fall 1981, 235 applications were received, 63 were accepted, and 26 students enrolled. An outstanding academic record is required (a B average or better). Applicants must take the SAT and 3 ATs. D grades do not transfer. All students must complete, at Vassar, 17 of the 34 units required for a bachelor's degree. Application deadlines are March 1 (fall), and December 1 (spring).

Visiting: Informal guided tours and classroom visits can be arranged through the admissions office throughout the year.

Financial Aid: About 68% of the students receive financial aid in the form of scholarships, loans, grants, and campus employment. About 53% work part-time on campus. The average freshman scholarship is

$4752; the average freshman loan, $2073. The college is a member of CSS. Awards are granted on the basis of need and academic qualification. The FAF is required. Deadline for financial aid application is February 1.

Foreign Students: Five percent of the full-time students come from foreign countries. Special counseling and special organizations are available for these students.

Admissions: Foreign students must take the TOEFL and the SAT.

Procedure: The application deadline is February 1. Foreign students must carry health insurance, which is available through the college for a fee.

Admissions Contact: Fred R. Brooks, Jr., Director of Admissions.

WAGNER COLLEGE
Staten Island, New York 10301

D-5
(212) 390-3011

F/T: 892M, 1021W
P/T: 88M, 138W
Grad: 168M, 232W
Year: sems, ss
Appl: May 30
1357 accepted
SAT: 450V 450M

Faculty: 85; IIA, +$
Ph.D.'s: 95%
S/F Ratio: 18 to 1
Tuition: $4262
R and B: $2576
578 enrolled
COMPETITIVE

Wagner College, established in 1883, is a liberal arts college recognized by the United Lutheran Church in America. The library contains over 250,000 volumes and 225,000 microfilm items, and subscribes to 950 periodicals.

Environment: The 86-acre suburban campus on Staten Island, 15 miles from Manhattan, is situated on a hill overlooking New York Harbor and the Atlantic Ocean. Within the campus boundaries are 20 buildings, including a solar energy facility and dormitory complexes with single, double, and suite facilities.

Student Life: About 50% of the students are from New York State. About 50% reside on campus. Half the entering freshmen come from public schools. Twelve percent are minority-group members. The majority of students are not members of the supporting church. About 55% are Catholic, 30% are Protestant, and 10% are Jewish. Campus housing is both coed and single-sex; there are visiting privileges in the single-sex housing. Students may keep cars on campus.

Organizations: Ten percent of men belong to 2 local and 4 national fraternities; 10% of women, to 3 local sororities and 1 national sorority. The college offers many extracurricular activities and organizations and encourages student participation.

Sports: The college fields 7 intercollegiate teams for men and 5 for women. There are 7 intramural sports for men and 6 for women.

Handicapped: About 35% of the campus is accessible to handicapped students. Special facilities include wheelchair ramps, parking areas, elevators, and specially equipped rest rooms. Special class scheduling is also available. One percent of the students have visual impairments. For these students there are readers and laboratory assistants.

Graduates: The freshman dropout rate is 10%; approximately 65% of the students remain to graduate. Eight percent of the graduates enter medical school, 5% enter dental school, and 10% enter law school. Twenty percent enter business and industry.

Services: Students receive the following services free of charge: placement service, career counseling, psychological counseling, health care, tutoring, and remedial instruction.

Programs of Study: The college confers the B.A., B.S., and B.S.Ed. degrees. Master's degrees are also awarded. Bachelor's degrees are offered in the following subjects: AREA STUDIES (American), BUSINESS (accounting, business administration, computer science, finance, management), EDUCATION (early childhood, elementary, secondary), ENGLISH (English, journalism, literature, speech), FINE AND PERFORMING ARTS (art, music, theater/dramatics), HEALTH SCIENCES (environmental health, medical technology, nursing), LANGUAGES (French, German, Greek/Latin, Italian, Spanish), MATH AND SCIENCES (biochemistry, biology, botany, chemistry, earth science, mathematics, natural sciences, physics, zoology), PHILOSOPHY (classics, humanities, philosophy, religion), PREPROFESSIONAL (dentistry, engineering, law, medicine, ministry, pharmacy), SOCIAL SCIENCES (anthropology, economics, government/political science, history, international relations, psychology, social sciences, sociology). Twenty-five percent of degrees conferred are in health sciences; 21% are in business; and 21% are in math and sciences.

Required: Each department sets its own requirements. Proficiency in English is required.

Special: A year abroad in Bregenz, Austria, is sponsored by the college and is open to all liberal arts majors. Both preprofessional and cooperative programs in engineering are available (both 2-2 and 3-2 plans). Students may design their own majors.

Honors: Twelve national honor societies have chapters on campus.

Admissions: Sixty-seven percent of those who applied were accepted for a recent freshman class. Candidates must present 16 complete Carnegie units of work and a minimum score of 450 on each part of the SAT. Applicants should rank in the upper half of their graduating class and have a B average or better. Also important are advanced placement or honors courses, recommendations, the extracurricular activities record, and leadership potential.

Procedure: The SAT or ACT is required. An interview is requested if it is possible. Application deadlines are May 30 (fall) and January 15 (spring). There is an application fee of $15.

Special: Early decision and early admissions plans are available. CLEP and AP credit is accepted.

Transfer: For fall 1981, 317 transfer applications were received, and 212 students enrolled. A GPA of 2.0 is required for transfer. The SAT or ACT is required. D grades do not transfer. All students must complete, at the college, 45 of the 128 credits required for a bachelor's degree. Application deadlines are June 30 (fall), and January 15 (spring).

Visiting: There are regularly scheduled orientations for prospective students. Guides are available for informal visits on weekdays. Visitors may stay overnight at the school and sit in on classes. Arrangements should be made through the admissions office.

Financial Aid: About 85% of students receive financial aid. About 25% work part-time on campus. The average freshman award is $500. Freshman scholarships are awarded each year on the basis of need and ability. Loans are also available from the federal and state governments, local banks, and the college. The deadline for financial aid application for the fall semester is April 1. The FAF is required.

Foreign Students: Twelve percent of the full-time students come from foreign countries. An intensive English program, special counseling, and special organizations are available for these students.

Admissions: Foreign students must take the TOEFL and the English Language Services test. No college entrance exams are required.

Procedure: Application deadlines are June 1 (fall) and December 1 (spring). Foreign students must present proof of health and proof of adequate funds. Health insurance is required and is available through the college.

Admissions Contact: James Keating, Director of Admissions.

WEBB INSTITUTE OF
NAVAL ARCHITECTURE
Glen Cove, New York 11542

D-5

(516) 671-2213

F/T: 77M, 5W
P/T: none
Grad: none
Year: sems
Appl: Feb. 15
79 applied
SAT: required

Faculty: 8; IIB, ++$
Ph.D.'s: 57%
S/F Ratio: 11 to 1
Tuition: none
R and B: $2580
27 accepted
26 enrolled
HIGHLY COMPETITIVE

The Webb Institute of Naval Architecture is a privately supported, nonsectarian, technological institution. The library contains over 32,000 volumes.

Environment: The 26-acre suburban campus, located 22 miles from New York City on Long Island's North Shore, has academic buildings, residence halls, and a ship model testing tank that is available for research, thesis work, and instruction.

Student Life: The student body is drawn equally from New York State and from other states. About 98% of the students live on campus. Eighty-four percent of the entering freshmen come from public schools. There are no minority-group members currently enrolled at the institute. Campus housing is single-sex; there are visiting privileges. Students may keep cars on campus.

Organizations: Student life is very much campus centered. Extracurricular campus activities include a humanities club, photography club, and yacht club. The close proximity of New York City provides students with a wide range of recreational and cultural facilities.

620 NEW YORK

Sports: The institute fields 3 intercollegiate teams. There are 2 intramural sports.

Handicapped: Special facilities for the physically handicapped are designated parking areas and elevators; wheelchair ramps are not needed. About 95% of the campus is accessible to these students. There are no hearing- or visually impaired students enrolled nor are there special counselors.

Graduates: The freshman dropout rate is 4%; 75% remain for the full program and graduate. About 98% of the graduates enter careers in business and industry.

Services: Health care and career and psychological counseling are provided free of charge to all students. Undergraduates and alumni receive free placement service including direct contact with potential employers.

Programs of Study: Graduates receive the B.S. degree. Degree programs are offered in naval architecture and marine engineering.

Required: The Webb program has 4 practical work periods, 1 for each academic year. During the freshman year, students work in a shipyard; in the sophomore year, students take a cruise and work as cadets in the engine room of the ship; during the junior and senior years, the work is of a more general nature in the shipbuilding profession. This is a prescribed curriculum.

Admissions: Thirty-four percent of those who applied were accepted for the 1981–82 freshman class. Of those who enrolled, the SAT scores were as follows: Verbal—0% scored below 500, 35% between 500 and 599, 57% between 600 and 700, and 8% above 700; Math—0% scored below 500, 0% between 500 and 599, 54% between 600 and 700, and 46% above 700. Candidates must be high school graduates, have 16 units of high school work, rank in the upper 20% of their class, and have at least a 3.4 average in mathematics and science and a satisfactory record in other subjects. Of importance are impressions made during the interview, recommendations, and advanced placement or honors courses.

Procedure: The SAT and 3 ATs (in English composition, math (level I or II), and physics or chemistry) are required and must be taken by January 31 of the senior year. The application deadline is February 15. The application fee is $25.

Transfers: For fall 1981, 3 transfer students enrolled. Transfers are not accepted for advanced standing and must enter as freshmen. All 143 of the credits required for a bachelor's degree must be completed at the institute.

Visiting: There are no scheduled orientations for prospective students, but visits can be arranged through the registrar. Weekdays during the school year are the best time to visit. Guides are available. Visitors are permitted to sit in on classes and stay overnight at the school.

Financial Aid: About 68% of the students receive financial aid. All students have complete scholarships covering tuition. There is no deadline for aid application. The institute is a member of CSS and requires the FAF.

Foreign Students: U.S. citizenship is required of all applicants.

Admissions Contact: W. G. Murray, Registrar.

WELLS COLLEGE C–3
Aurora, New York 13026 (315) 364-3264

F/T: 500W Faculty: 50; IIB, +$
P/T: 10W Ph.D.'s: 80%
Grad: none S/F Ratio: 9 to 1
Year: 4-1-4 Tuition: $6050
Appl: Mar. 1 R and B: $2200
400 applied 350 accepted 155 enrolled
SAT: 530V 530M ACT: 25 COMPETITIVE+

Wells College is a private nonsectarian women's college founded in 1868. The library contains 195,000 volumes and 2603 microfilm items, and subscribes to 642 periodicals.

Environment: The 360-acre wooded campus overlooks Cayuga Lake in the rural Finger Lakes region of New York, 50 miles from Syracuse and 26 miles from Ithaca. Among the 67 buildings are music and studio art buildings, an indoor athletic facility, and many older buildings dating from 1852. There are 7 dormitories interspersed throughout the campus.

Student Life: Forty percent of the students come from New York State. Eighty percent of the entering freshmen attended public schools. Ninety-nine percent of the students live on campus. Nine percent are minority-group members. Thirty-five percent are Protestant, 30% are Catholic, and 3% are Jewish. Campus housing is single-sex; there are visiting privileges. Students may keep cars on campus. Day-care services are available on a fee basis to part-time students.

Organizations: The college has no sororities. Extracurricular activities include student publications, music and vocal groups, a drama group, and many clubs. Five nearby colleges afford a variety of social and cultural interchanges.

Sports: The college fields 6 intercollegiate teams. There are 18 intramural sports.

Handicapped: About 75% of the campus is accessible to handicapped students. Special facilities include wheelchair ramps, parking areas, elevators, and specially equipped rest rooms. Class scheduling can be arranged. A very small percentage of the students have visual impairments, and a reader, tapes, and large print material are available for these students.

Graduates: The freshman dropout rate is 17%; 83% of entering freshmen remain to graduate. About 60% of the students go on to graduate school after finishing at Wells. Three percent enter medical school, 2% enter dental school, and 5% go on to law school.

Services: The following services are available to students free of charge: health care, psychological counseling, placement, career counseling (for graduates as well as undergraduates), tutoring, and remedial instruction.

Programs of Study: All programs lead to the B.A. degree. Bachelor's degrees are offered in the following subjects: AREA STUDIES (American, Italian, Russian), ENGLISH (English), FINE AND PERFORMING ARTS (art history, music, studio art, theater/dramatics), LANGUAGES (French, German, Greek/Latin, romance languages, Spanish), MATH AND SCIENCES (biology, biology/chemistry, biology/psychology, chemistry, mathematics, mathematics/physics), PHILOSOPHY (philosophy, philosophy/religion, religion), PRE-PROFESSIONAL (dentistry, engineering, law, medicine, veterinary), SOCIAL SCIENCES (economics, government/political science, history, psychology, sociology).

Special: Offerings include seminars, independent study, 3-year B.A. programs, winter term career internships, student-designed majors, and study-abroad opportunities in Germany, Great Britain, France, Israel, Italy, Spain, and the Soviet Union. A 3-2 degree is offered in business with the University of Rochester and in engineering with Columbia University, Washington University, and Texas A & M.

Honors: Phi Beta Kappa has a chapter on campus. All departments have their own honors programs.

Admissions: About 88% of those who applied were accepted for the 1981–82 freshman class. SAT scores of those who enrolled were as follows: Verbal—30% scored below 500, 29% between 500 and 599, 24% between 600 and 700, and 7% above 700; Math—31% scored below 500, 35% between 500 and 599, 18% between 600 and 700, and 3% above 700. The college considers each applicant individually; particularly important are the high school record, class rank, performance on the entrance exams, recommendations from the high school, advanced placement or honors courses, and extracurricular activities.

Procedure: The SAT or ACT is required. ATs are recommended. Students are also urged to arrange a personal interview. The deadline for applications is March 1 for fall admission or January 1 for spring admission. There is a $20 application fee. The college subscribes to the CRDA.

Special: The college has early decision, early admissions (with a March 1 deadline), and deferred admissions plans. AP credit is available.

Transfer: For fall 1981, 29 transfer applications were received, 25 were accepted, and 17 students enrolled. A C– average is required. D grades do not transfer. A 2-year residency is expected. All students must complete, at the college, 30 of the 60 credits required for a bachelor's degree. A rolling admissions policy is used, and financial aid is available. Application deadlines are the same as those for freshmen.

Visiting: The college interviews students on weekdays from 9 A.M. to 4 P.M. and Saturdays from 9 A.M. to noon from Labor Day until Commencement. Candidates may stay overnight in the dormitories with a student as hostess, tour the campus, attend classes, and visit with professors. Guides are also available for informal visits to the campus. The admissions office handles arrangements.

Financial Aid: Seventy-two percent of all students receive some form of financial aid. About 60% work part-time on campus. Scholarship aid available to freshmen totals $400,000. The college usually combines grants with loans and employment. The maximum aid to freshmen is $8000; the average is $5200. The college has no loan funds but will countersign loan requests under state programs. NDSL, SEOG, and CWS are available. The college is a member of CSS. The FAF is required. The deadline for aid applications is February 15 for regular applicants and December 31 for early decision.

Foreign Students: About 2% of the full-time students come from foreign countries. Special counseling and special organizations are available for these students.

Admissions: Foreign students must take the TOEFL or the SAT.

Procedure: Application deadlines are March 1 (fall) and January 1 (spring). Foreign students must present proof of adequate funds.

Admissions Contact: Joan C. Irving, Director of Admissions.

YESHIVA UNIVERSITY D-5
New York, New York 10033 (212) 960-5277

F/T: 688M, 456W	Faculty: 134; n/av
P/T: 96M, 64W	Ph.D.'s: 67%
Grad: 1424M, 1489W	S/F Ratio: 8 to 1
Year: sems	Tuition: $4600
Appl: open	R and B: $2380
806 applied	719 accepted 370 enrolled
SAT: (Yeshiva) 548V 593M	VERY COMPETITIVE+
(Stern) 517V 523M	

Yeshiva University, founded in 1886, is a multifaceted independent university under Jewish auspices. Liberal arts studies were initiated with the establishment of Yeshiva College (the undergraduate college for men) in 1928. Stern College for Women (the undergraduate college for women) was founded in 1954. Six undergraduate schools and 6 graduate and professional entities are located at 4 centers in Manhattan and the Bronx. The library houses 850,000 volumes, and 77,000 microfilm items, and subscribes to 4500 periodicals.

Environment: Yeshiva College is located at the main center in the Washington Heights section of Manhattan; Stern College for Women is located in midtown Manhattan. Dormitories with double, triple, and suite accommodations are available at both centers.

Student Life: Fifty-four percent of the men and 34% of the women come from New York State. Eighty-five percent of Yeshiva College students and 90% of Stern College students reside on campus. Dormitories are single-sex; there are visiting privileges. Students may keep cars on campus.

Organizations: There are no fraternities or sororities at Yeshiva, but a wide variety of student organizations and activities, including student government, publications, special-interest clubs, a radio station, and a dramatics society, are available to students. Students participate in institutional governance. New York City offers unparalleled cultural and recreational opportunities.

Sports: The university fields 5 intercollegiate teams for men and 1 for women. There are 7 intramural sports for men and 5 for women.

Handicapped: Ninety-five percent of the campus is accessible to wheelchair students. Special facilities for the physically handicapped include ramps and elevators. There are no special counselors for such students.

Graduates: The freshman dropout rate is 15% for Yeshiva College and 23% for Stern College. About 60% remain to graduate. More than 90% of Yeshiva College graduates and 65% of Stern College graduates go on to graduate or professional school. Twenty-two percent of Yeshiva College graduates and 3% of Stern College graduates enter medical school; 12% of Yeshiva College graduates and 8% of Stern College graduates enter law school; 8% of Yeshiva College graduates enter dental school.

Services: Students receive the following services free of charge: placement, health care, career counseling, psychological counseling, tutoring, and remedial instruction. Placement services for undergraduates are limited; graduate students, especially those in law and medicine, are given job placement assistance.

Programs of Study: The university confers the B.A. and B.S. degrees. Master's and doctoral degrees are also awarded. Bachelor's degrees are offered in the following subjects: BUSINESS (accounting, business administration, computer science, management), EDUCATION (elementary), ENGLISH (English, speech), FINE AND PERFORMING ARTS (music), HEALTH SCIENCES (nursing), LANGUAGES (French, Greek/Latin, Hebrew/Judaic studies), MATH AND SCIENCES (biology, chemistry, mathematics, physics), PHILOSOPHY (philosophy), PREPROFESSIONAL (dentistry, engineering, law, medicine), SOCIAL SCIENCES (economics, government/political science, history, psychology, sociology). Forty percent of the undergraduate degrees are conferred in the social sciences, 23% in the health sciences, and 11% in math and sciences.

Required: Under the Dual Program, students pursue a liberal arts curriculum together with courses in Hebrew language, literature, and culture. Courses in Jewish learning are geared to be students' level of preparation.

Special: The university has an optional pass/no credit system. It offers independent study, a junior year in Israel, and joint bachelor's-master's programs with its graduate schools. Stern College permits student-designed majors. For men there are 3-2 engineering programs in cooperation with Polytechnic Institute of New York and Columbia University and a 4-2 engineering program with Columbia. For women there is a nursing program in conjunction with Beth Israel Medical Center and a combined English communications program with Fashion Institute of Technology.

Honors: There are honors programs for all majors and minors. Nine national honor societies have chapters on campus.

Admissions: Eighty-nine percent of those who applied were accepted for the 1981–82 freshman class. The SAT scores of Yeshiva College freshmen were as follows: Verbal—25% scored below 500, 44% between 500 and 599, 26% between 600 and 700, and 5% above 700; Math—17% scored below 500, 30% between 500 and 599, 39% between 600 and 700, and 14% above 700. The SAT scores of freshmen at Stern College were as follows: Verbal—40% scored below 500, 39% between 500 and 599, 19% between 600 and 700, and 2% above 700; Math—39% scored below 500, 39% between 500 and 599, 20% between 600 and 700, and 2% above 700. Applicants must be graduates of academic high schools. An average of B or better is required, and preparation must comprise 16 Carnegie units. Other factors considered are impressions made during the interview, personality, recommendations by school officials, advanced placement or honors courses, and leadership potential.

Procedure: Candidates must take the SAT and the Hebrew AT by December of the senior year. This AT is not required of those who have not studied Hebrew for 2 years. There are no application deadlines; freshmen are admitted in the fall and spring terms. A personal interview is required. A $25 fee must accompany the application. The rolling admissions plan is used.

Special: Early admissions and deferred admissions plans are available. CLEP subject exams are accepted, and a student may earn credit through AP.

Transfer: For fall 1981, 88 students applied, 65 were accepted, and 42 enrolled. A student must be in good standing at his or her previous school and have a GPA of at least 2.6 to be eligible for transfer; D grades do not transfer. The SAT is required. All students must complete, at the university, 58 of the 128 credits required for a bachelor's degree. There are no application deadlines; transfer students are admitted in the fall and spring terms.

Visiting: Two open house programs—one at Yeshiva College and one at Stern College—are held each year, with presentations on academic programs and student life, as well as campus tours. Guided tours are available for informal visits; visitors may sit in on classes. For information about visiting the school, the admissions office should be contacted.

Financial Aid: About 75% of all students are receiving financial aid administered by the university. Scholarships, loans, and grants are awarded on the basis of individual need. The university also offers merit awards based on academic achievement. Work-study programs are available; 65% of Yeshiva College students and 50% of Stern College students earn part of their expenses through part-time employment. The aid application deadline is March 15 (fall) or January 1 (spring). The university is a member of CSS. The FAF is required.

Foreign Students: About 8% of the full-time students come from foreign countries. Special counseling and special organizations are available for these students.

Admissions: Foreign students must achieve a minimum score of 500 on the TOEFL or a minimum score of 500 on each part of the SAT. The Hebrew AT is required of applicants who have studied Hebrew for 2 or more years.

Procedure: The application deadline is April 15 (fall entry). Foreign students must complete a health form and must present proof of funds adequate to cover 1 year of study.

Admissions Contact: Paul S. Glasser, Director of admissions.

NORTH CAROLINA

APPALACHIAN STATE UNIVERSITY   B-2
Boone, North Carolina 28608   (704) 262-2120

F/T: 3904M, 4053W
P/T: 273M, 302W
Grad: 510M, 648W
Year: sems, ss
Appl: open
5420 applied
SAT: 427V 466M

Faculty: 525; IIA, +$
Ph.D.'s: 78%
S/F Ratio: 16 to 1
Tuition: $688 ($2475)
R and B: $1420
3808 accepted   1812 enrolled
COMPETITIVE

Appalachian State University, founded in 1899, is a liberal arts and teacher education institution administered by the state. The library contains 406,740 volumes and 308,000 microfilm items, and subscribes to 5030 periodicals.

Environment: The 255-acre rural campus, 100 miles from Charlotte and Winston-Salem, is located in the heart of the Blue Ridge of the Appalachian Mountains. There are 16 dormitories, 4 dining halls, and student apartments on campus.

Student Life: Ninety-two percent of the students are from North Carolina, and 79% come from public schools. Approximately half of the students live on campus; freshmen are required to live in dormitories. Eighty percent of the students are Protestant and 5% are Catholic. Six percent are members of minority groups. Campus housing is coed. Students may keep cars on campus. Day-care services are available for faculty and staff.

Organizations: There are 10 fraternities and sororities. The university offers a wide variety of extracurricular activities and cultural events; students participate in university administration and curriculum matters as well as in their own government and publications.

Sports: The university competes intercollegiately in 11 sports for women and 12 for men; an extensive intramural program includes 17 sports for women and 19 for men.

Handicapped: Approximately 50% of the campus is accessible to the physically handicapped. Facilities include wheelchair ramps, special parking, elevators, specially equipped rest rooms, and lowered drinking fountains and telephones. Special class scheduling is also available. Note takers and learning aides are available for students with visual or hearing impairments.

Graduates: Ten percent of freshmen drop out by the end of the first year. Forty-seven percent remain to graduate.

Services: Free placement services, career counseling, health care, psychological counseling, tutoring, and remedial instruction are offered to all students.

Programs of Study: The university confers the B.A., B.S., B.S.B.A., B.T., B.M., and B.S.C.J. degrees. Master's programs are also offered. Bachelor's degrees are offered in the following subjects: BUSINESS (accounting, banking, business education, computer science, economics, finance, management, marketing, real estate/insurance), EDUCATION (early childhood, elementary, health/physical, industrial, recreation, special), ENGLISH (English, speech), FINE AND PERFORMING ARTS (art, art education, music, music education, theater/dramatics), HEALTH SCIENCES (health care management, medical technology), LANGUAGES (French, Spanish) MATH AND SCIENCES (biology, chemistry, earth science, geology, mathematics, physics, statistics), PHILOSOPHY (philosophy, religion), PREPROFESSIONAL (home economics, library science), SOCIAL SCIENCES (anthropology, economics, geography, government/political science, history, psychology, social sciences, sociology). Forty-one percent of degrees are conferred in education, 20% in business, and 17% in social sciences.

Required: Courses in communications; humanities; mathematics; physical education; and social, natural, and behavioral sciences are required.

Special: A general studies (no major) degree, student-designed majors, and a combined B.A.-B.S. degree are offered.

Honors: Twelve national honor societies have chapters on campus. There is a general honors program, in addition to honors programs in economics, English, and history.

Admissions: Approximately 70% of those who applied were accepted for the 1981-82 freshman class. The SAT scores of those who enrolled were as follows: Verbal—82% below 500, 16% between 500 and 599, 2% between 600 and 700, and 0% above 700; Math—65% below 500, 30% between 500 and 599, 5% between 600 and 700, and 0% above 700. Applicants should have completed 16 Carnegie units at an accredited high school.

Procedure: The SAT or the ACT is required and should be taken in March of the junior year. Application deadlines are open; notification is on a rolling basis. There is a $15 application fee.

Special: CLEP credit in certain subject areas is accepted.

Transfer: For fall 1981, 1555 transfer students applied, 1144 were accepted, and 648 enrolled. Transfers are accepted for all classes. Students must have a 2.0 GPA and be in good standing at their former school. The time residency requirement is 2 semesters; the last 30 semester hours, of the 122 required for a bachelor's degree, must be taken at the university.

Visiting: There are regularly scheduled orientations for prospective students. Guides are also available for informal visits; visitors may sit in on classes. The admissions office should be contacted to arrange visits.

Financial Aid: Approximately 58% of all students receive some form of financial aid, and 18% of all students work part-time on campus. Loan funds are available from the federal and state governments. Tuition may be paid in installments. The college is a member of the CSS. The FAF or FFS is required. The deadline for financial aid applications is March 15 for fall or summer entry, November 1 for spring entry.

Foreign Students: Fewer than 1% of the students are from foreign countries. Special counseling is available to these students.

Admissions: A minimum score of 500 on the TOEFL is required; the SAT is also required.

Procedure: There is no fixed application deadline; however, receipt of applications by December 1 for the fall semester is preferred. Students must present as proof of health a medical form signed by a physician and must also present proof of adequate funds to cover the cost of 1 year of study. Health insurance is required, and is available through the college for a fee.

Admissions Contact: T. Joseph Watts, Director of Admissions.

ATLANTIC CHRISTIAN COLLEGE   E-2
Wilson, North Carolina 27893   (919) 237-3161

F/T: 510M, 868W
P/T: 74M, 112W
Grad: none
Year: early sems, ss
Appl: open
720 applied
SAT: 413V 454M

Faculty: 86; IIB, av$
Ph.D.'s: 42%
S/F Ratio: 16 to 1
Tuition: $2594
R and B: $1400
585 accepted   336 enrolled
LESS COMPETITIVE

Atlantic Christian College, established in 1902, offers undergraduate programs in liberal arts and sciences, business, and education. The college is affiliated with the Christian Church of the Disciples of Christ. The library has 105,000 books and 2556 microfilm items, and subscribes to 610 periodicals.

Environment: The 15-acre suburban campus has 21 major buildings. Single-sex dormitories accommodate 950 men and women. Additional housing accommodations are provided by fraternities.

Student Life: Most of the students are from North Carolina. About 90% of the freshmen come from public schools. Seventy percent of the students live on campus, including all freshmen, for whom this is a requirement. Eighty-three percent of the students are Protestant and 4% are Catholic. Minority-group members comprise 14% of the current enrollment. Dormitories are single-sex; visiting privileges are accorded. Students may keep cars on campus.

Organizations: Ten percent of the men belong to 4 national fraternities; 12% of the women, to 4 national sororities.

Sports: Intramural competition is available in 6 sports. There are 6 intercollegiate sports.

Handicapped: About 80% of the campus is accessible to physically handicapped students. Special facilities include wheelchair ramps, parking areas, elevators, lowered drinking fountains and telephones, and specially equipped rest rooms. Special class scheduling is also available.

Graduates: The freshman dropout rate is 12%. Forty-five percent of entering freshmen remain to graduate. About 25% of the students go on for further study after graduation (1% to medical school, 1% to dental school, and 1% to law school); 35% enter business and industry.

Services: Career counseling, tutoring, and psychological counseling are provided at no charge. Placement services, health care, and remedial instruction are available for a fee.

Programs of Study: The B.A., B.F.A., or B.S. degree is offered in the following subjects: BUSINESS (accounting, business administration, business education), EDUCATION (early childhood, elementary, health/physical, hearing impaired, secondary, special), ENGLISH (English), FINE AND PERFORMING ARTS (art, art education, music, music education, theater/dramatics), HEALTH SCIENCES (medical technology, nursing), MATH AND SCIENCES (biology, chemistry, mathematics), PHILOSOPHY (philosophy, religion), PREPROFESSIONAL (dentistry, law, medicine, ministry, social work, veterinary), SOCIAL SCIENCES (history, psychology, social sciences, sociology). About 28% of the degrees are conferred in education and 25% in business.

Required: Courses in English, religion, and physical education are required, in addition to a distribution requirement.

Honors: There are honors programs in 7 departments.

Admissions: About 81% of the 1981-82 applicants were accepted. The SAT scores of those who enrolled were as follows: Verbal—90% below 500, 5% between 500 and 599, 3% between 600 and 700, and 2% above 700; Math—84% below 500, 5% between 500 and 599, 9% between 600 and 700, and 2% above 700. Applicants must have completed at least 16 units at an accredited high school and have graduated in the top 60% of their class. Advanced placement or honors courses, special talents, leadership record, and recommendations are important.

Procedure: The SAT is required. The suggested application deadlines are July (fall), December (spring), and May (summer). Freshmen are admitted to all semesters. There is a $20 application fee.

Special: AP and CLEP credit is offered.

Transfer: For fall 1981, the college received 340 applications, accepted 288, and enrolled 195 students. A GPA of 2.0 is required. D grades are accepted if the GPA is above 2.0. Thirty of the 124 credits required for a bachelor's degree must be completed in residence. Suggested application deadlines are the same as those for entering freshmen.

Visiting: Informal campus tours can be arranged for weekdays. Visitors may attend classes and stay overnight in the dormitories. Arrangements should be made through the admissions office.

Financial Aid: About 75% of the students receive aid; 39% of all students work part-time on campus. The college offers scholarships and CWS in 13 departments. Tuition may be paid in installments. The college is a member of the CSS. The FAF or FFS should be submitted; deadlines for aid applications are April 15 for fall entry, November 15 for spring entry.

Foreign Students: There are 14 students from foreign countries currently attending the college. Special counseling is available.

Admissions: All foreign students are required to submit TOEFL scores. No college entrance exams are required.

Procedure: Application deadlines are April 15 for fall entry and November 15 for spring entry. Students must present proof of health in the form of a medical history and must provide proof of funds adequate to finance the first year of study. Health insurance is required and is available through the college for a fee.

Admissions Contact: James D. Daniell, Director of Admissions.

BARBER-SCOTIA COLLEGE C-3
Concord, North Carolina 28025 (704) 786-5171

F/T: 225M, 275W	Faculty: 19; n/av
P/T: 20M, 25W	Ph.D.'s: 31%
Grad: none	S/F Ratio: 17 to 1
Year: sems	Tuition: $2314
Appl: Aug. 1	R and B: $1679
SAT: 400V 400M	**LESS COMPETITIVE**

Founded in 1867, Barber-Scotia College is affiliated with the United Presbyterian Church and offers a liberal arts education. Its library has 65,000 books and 2500 microfilm items, and subscribes to 280 periodicals.

Environment: The 40-acre campus is located 20 miles from Charlotte. Two separate dormitories house men and women.

Student Life: About 85% of the students come from North Carolina; 98% attended public schools. The majority of students are not members of the supporting church.

Organizations: There are religious groups, clubs, performing groups, social and cultural events, and student government. About 25% of the men belong to 4 national fraternities, 35% of the women to 4 national sororities.

Sports: In addition to intercollegiate athletics, there is intramural competition in basketball, softball, tennis, and swimming.

Graduates: The freshman dropout rate is 13%; about 56% remain to graduate. About 30% of the graduates enter business careers; 5% of the graduates go on for further education: 1% to medical school and 2% to law school.

Services: Health care, psychological counseling, tutoring, remedial instruction, career counseling, and placement are offered free of charge. Placement services are available to graduates as well as currently enrolled students.

Programs of Study: The college awards the B.A. and B.S. degrees. Associate degrees are also awarded. Bachelor's degrees are offered in the following subjects: BUSINESS (accounting, business administration, business education, marketing), EDUCATION (early childhood, elementary, secondary), HEALTH SCIENCES (medical technology), MATH AND SCIENCES (biology, chemistry, mathematics), SOCIAL SCIENCES (government/political science, history, sociology). About 40% of the degrees are conferred in business and 30% in education.

Required: There is a general education requirement that includes courses in religion, English, physical education, and 13 others.

Special: It is possible to earn the B.G.S. degree.

Honors: There is one honor society, Alpha Kappa Mu.

Admissions: Applicants must be high school graduates. Recommendations, extracurricular activities, and the ability to finance a college education are important admissions factors.

Procedure: The SAT or ACT is required. August 1 is the fall application deadline; notification is on a rolling basis. There is a $10 fee.

Special: There is a deferred admissions plan.

Transfer: About 25 transfer students enroll yearly. A 2.0 GPA is necessary. All students must complete, at the college, 30 of the 125 credits required for a bachelor's degree.

Visiting: Campus tours with student guides can be arranged. Visitors may attend classes and stay overnight at the college.

Financial Aid: About 90% of the students are receiving aid. Students may earn $75 to $100 through campus employment. CWS and BEOG are offered. The FAF should be filed by April 15. Tuition can be paid in installments.

Foreign Students: Special counseling is available for students from foreign countries.

Admissions: Foreign students must present evidence of proficiency in English.

Procedure: Foreign students must present proof of funds adequate to cover 1 year of study and must submit a health report completed by a physician and a dental report completed by a dentist.

Admissions Contact: Brenda Gibbs, Director of Recruitment and Admissions.

BELMONT ABBEY COLLEGE C-3
Belmont, North Carolina 28012 (704) 825-3711

F/T: 474M, 337W	Faculty: 37; IIB, - - $
P/T: 29M&W	Ph.D.'s: 43%
Grad: none	S/F Ratio: 17 to 1
Year: sems	Tuition: $3170
Appl: Aug. 15	R and B: $1600
SAT or ACT: required	**LESS COMPETITIVE**

Belmont Abbey College, established in 1876, is a Roman-Catholic-affiliated institution offering undergraduate preparation in the liberal arts and sciences, business, education, and medical technology. The library has 80,000 volumes and 8000 microtexts, and subscribes to 485 periodicals.

Environment: The rural campus is located 12 miles from Charlotte. The Abbey Cathedral has been designated a national historic site. Single-sex residence halls accommodate 625 men and women.

Student Life: Thirty percent of the students come from North Carolina, and over 50% come from public schools. About 70% live on campus. Sixty-five percent of the students are Catholic; almost all others are of the Protestant faith. Minority-group members comprise 8% of the student body. There are visiting privileges in the single-sex

624 NORTH CAROLINA

dormitories. Students are permitted to keep cars on campus. Gambling is forbidden on campus.

Organizations: There are 4 fraternities, to which 18% of the men belong, and 4 sisterhood organizations affiliated with the fraternities. The college sponsors on-campus social and cultural events and extracurricular activities.

Sports: The college fields intercollegiate teams for men in 4 sports and for women in 3 sports. There are 5 intramural sports for men and 4 for women.

Handicapped: Special facilities for handicapped students include parking areas and specially equipped rest rooms.

Graduates: The freshman dropout rate is 25%; about 55% remain to graduate. Twenty percent of the graduates pursue advanced degrees.

Services: Career counseling, placement, health care, tutoring, remedial instruction, and psychological counseling are offered free of charge to all students.

Programs of Study: The B.A. and B.S. degrees are conferred. Bachelor's degrees are offered in the following subjects: BUSINESS (accounting, business administration, distribution management), EDUCATION (early childhood, elementary, religious, special), ENGLISH (English), FINE AND PERFORMING ARTS (art, art education), HEALTH SCIENCES (medical technology), MATH AND SCIENCES (biology, chemistry, ecology/environmental science), PHILOSOPHY (religion), PREPROFESSIONAL (dentistry, law, medicine, pharmacy, recreational studies), SOCIAL SCIENCES (economics, government/political science, history, psychology, sociology). About 42% of the degrees are conferred in business and 39% in social sciences.

Required: All students must take courses in English and literature, history, mathematics, philosophy, science, and theology.

Special: Internships in several areas, exchange programs, study abroad, and combined B.A.-B.S. degrees are offered.

Honors: Three honor societies have chapters on campus. An honors program is available in all departments.

Admissions: About 90% of those who applied were accepted for the 1981-82 freshman class. SAT scores of a recently enrolled freshman class were as follows: Verbal—86% below 500, 12% between 500 and 600, 2% between 600 and 700, and 0% above 700; Math—79% below 500, 17% between 500 and 600, 4% between 600 and 700, and 0% above 700. Students should present 15 Carnegie units of work and at least a 2.0 high school GPA. Other important factors include advanced placement or honors courses, recommendations, and impressions made during the interview.

Procedure: The SAT or ACT is required and should be taken by December of the senior year. August 15 is the fall deadline, January 1, the spring. An interview is recommended. Notification is on a rolling basis. There is a $15 application fee.

Special: There are early decision, early admissions, and deferred admissions plans. CLEP credit is available.

Transfer: Forty-four transfer students enrolled for fall 1981. A 2.0 GPA is needed; D grades are not accepted. One year of study must be completed in residence. Of the 130 credits required for a bachelor's degree, 30 must be completed at the college. Application deadlines are the same as for freshmen.

Visiting: There are regularly scheduled orientations for prospective students. Guides are available for informal campus tours. Visitors may sit in on classes and stay overnight at the school. Visits are best scheduled on weekdays. The admissions office should be contacted for arrangements.

Financial Aid: About 83% of the students receive financial aid. Twenty-five percent work part-time on campus. The college offers 20 freshman scholarships; the average award to freshmen is $2000. The college is a member of the CSS. NDSL, BEOG/SEOG, and CWS are also available. Tuition may be paid in installments. The FAF or FFS is required; April 1 is the aid application deadline.

Foreign Students: One percent of the students are from foreign countries. Special counseling is available.

Admissions: The TOEFL, minimum score 450, is required. The SAT or ACT is also required.

Procedure: Application deadlines are August 15 for the fall term and January 1 for the spring term. Students must present proof of health and must also present proof of adequate funds to cover the first year of study.

Admissions Contact: Robin R. Roberts, Director of Admissions.

BENNETT COLLEGE   D-2
Greensboro, North Carolina 27420   (919) 273-4431

F/T: 505W	Faculty: n/av; IIB, —$
P/T: 5W	Ph.D.'s: 55%
Grad: none	S/F Ratio: 12 to 1
Year: sems	Tuition: $2500
Appl: Aug. 10	R and B: $1300
255 applied	240 accepted	161 enrolled
SAT: 300V 310M		LESS COMPETITIVE

Bennett College, established in 1873, is a liberal arts and sciences college for women, affiliated with the United Methodist Church and the United Negro College Fund. The library contains 75,000 volumes and 300 microfilm items, and subscribes to 300 periodicals.

Environment: The campus is located in an urban area 1 mile from Greensboro's downtown section and 90 miles from Charlotte. There are 7 residence halls on campus.

Student Life: About 46% of the students come from North Carolina. About 90% live on campus. The majority (98%) of the students are black. Students may keep cars on campus. Day-care services are available to all students, faculty, and staff for a fee.

Organizations: There are 4 sororities on campus; 18% of the students are members. Extracurricular activities include student government, publications, special-interest clubs, and regularly scheduled on-campus social and cultural events.

Sports: The college fields 3 intercollegiate teams. There are 3 intramural sports.

Handicapped: The college has no facilities for handicapped students.

Graduates: About 58% of the freshmen remain to graduate. About 29% of the graduates pursue advanced degrees. About 33% enter careers in business and industry.

Services: Health care, psychological counseling, tutoring, remedial instruction, placement, and career counseling are provided free of charge to all students.

Programs of Study: The B.A., B.F.A., and B.S. degrees are conferred. Associate degrees are also awarded. Bachelor's degrees are offered in the following subjects: BUSINESS (accounting, business administration, computer science), EDUCATION (early childhood, elementary, health/physical, secondary, special), ENGLISH (English), FINE AND PERFORMING ARTS (art, art education, music education, theater/dramatics), HEALTH SCIENCES (medical technology, nursing), LANGUAGES (French), MATH AND SCIENCES (biology, chemistry, mathematics), PHILOSOPHY (interdisciplinary studies), PREPROFESSIONAL (dentistry, engineering, home economics, medicine, social work, veterinary), SOCIAL SCIENCES (history, psychology, social sciences, sociology). Thirty percent of the degrees are conferred in education and 16% in social sciences.

Required: All students must take courses in communication, humanities, mathematics, science, social science, philosophy, physical education, and religion.

Special: Student-designed majors, cooperative education, exchange programs, study abroad, and a combination degree in engineering are offered. Expanded course offerings are available by cross-registration through the Greensboro Regional Consortium.

Honors: There are 6 honor societies on campus.

Admissions: About 94% of the applicants for the 1981-82 freshman class were accepted. The SAT scores of those who enrolled were as follows: Verbal—75% below 500, 23% between 500 and 599, 2% between 600 and 700, and 0% above 700; Math—70% below 500, 25% between 500 and 599, 5% between 600 and 700, and 0% above 700. Candidates should have completed 16 units of high school work and have at least a C average. The applicant's high school record, class rank, SAT scores, and recommendations are all considered important in the admissions decision.

Procedure: The SAT or ACT is required; a personal interview is encouraged. The application deadline for fall is August 10; the spring deadline is January 15. A rolling admissions policy is used. There is a $10 application fee.

Special: There are early decision and early admissions plans. CLEP and AP credit is available.

Transfer: For fall 1981, 31 transfer students applied, 31 were accepted, and 18 enrolled. A 2.0 GPA is needed. One year must be completed in residence; 124 credits are required to earn the bachelor's degree. Grades of C or above transfer. Deadlines are the same as those for freshmen.

Visiting: Informal campus tours with student guides can be arranged. Visitors may sit in on classes and stay overnight at the school. The admissions office should be contacted for arrangements.

Financial Aid: About 94% of the students receive financial aid. The college offers funds from federal programs such as NDSL, BEOG/SEOG, and CWS. Scholarship assistance is also provided. The college is a member of CSS; the FAF should be filed by April 5.

Foreign Students: About 5% of the students come from foreign countries. There are special organizations for these students.

Admissions: Foreign students must take the SAT or ACT.

Procedure: Application deadlines are August 1 for fall and December 15 for spring. Foreign students must present a completed health certificate.

Admissions Contact: Phyllis V. Johnson, Director of Admissions.

CAMPBELL UNIVERSITY   D-3
Buies Creek, North Carolina 27506   (919) 893-4111

F/T: 1000M, 952W	Faculty: n/av
P/T: 500M, 300W	Ph.D.'s: 55%
Grad: 270M, 270W	S/F Ratio: 18 to 1
Year: sems, ss	Tuition: $3400 ($3450)
Appl: open	R and B: $1435
1575 applied 1400 accepted 863 enrolled	
SAT: 410V 420M	LESS COMPETITIVE

Campbell University, founded in 1887, is affiliated with the Baptist Church and offers undergraduate degree programs in liberal arts and sciences, business, education, and health fields. The library contains 170,000 volumes, and subscribes to 932 periodicals.

Environment: The 1000-acre rural campus has 30 buildings, including 6 residence halls for men and 7 for women. Married student housing is also available.

Student Life: About 70% of the students come from North Carolina, and 85% have had public school educations. About 75% live on campus. Ninety-five percent of the students are Protestant, 4% Catholic, and 1% Jewish. Minority-group members comprise 10% of the student body. Housing is single-sex; there are no visiting privileges. Students may keep cars on campus.

Organizations: Religious attendance is optional. There are no sororities or fraternities, but there are special-interest clubs, student government, and other extracurricular activities.

Sports: There are 8 intercollegiate sports for men and 4 for women. There are 11 intramural sports for men and 11 for women.

Graduates: The freshman dropout rate is 10%; about 65% of entering freshmen remain to graduate. Sixty percent of the graduates pursue advanced degrees.

Services: Offered free to all students are career counseling, placement, health care, tutoring, and remedial instruction. Health care and psychological counseling are available for a fee.

Programs of Study: The B.A., B.S., B.S.Bus., B.S.S., B.H.S., and B.Mus.Ed. degrees are conferred. Associate and master's programs are also available. Bachelor's degrees are offered in the following subjects: BUSINESS (accounting, business administration, business education, computer science, management, trust management), EDUCATION (early childhood, elementary, health/physical, secondary), ENGLISH (communications, English), FINE AND PERFORMING ARTS (music, music education), HEALTH SCIENCES (medical technology), LANGUAGES (French, Spanish), MATH AND SCIENCES (biology, chemistry, geology, mathematics, natural sciences, physical sciences), PHILOSOPHY (philosophy, religion), PREPROFESSIONAL (dentistry, home economics, law, medicine, ministry, pharmacy, social work), SOCIAL SCIENCES (economics, government/political science, history, psychology, social sciences, sociology). Forty percent of degrees are conferred in business.

Honors: Five honor societies have chapters on campus.

Admissions: Eighty-nine percent of those who applied were accepted for the 1981-82 freshman class. The SAT scores of those who enrolled were as follows: Verbal—65% below 500, 28% between 500 and 599, 5% between 600 and 700, and 2% above 700; Math—65% below 500, 28% between 500 and 599, 5% between 600 and 700, and 2% above 700. Applicants should have a 2.0 high school GPA and rank in the top half of their graduating class. Other criteria for admission include advanced placement or honors courses in high school, recommendations, and leadership record.

NORTH CAROLINA   625

Procedure: The SAT is required and should be taken by July following the senior year; the ACT may be substituted. Application deadlines are open. Notification is on a rolling basis. There is a $15 application fee.

Special: There is an early admissions plan. AP and CLEP credit is granted.

Transfer: For fall 1981, 401 students applied, 308 were accepted, and 250 enrolled. Transfer students are admitted to both semesters. A 2.0 GPA is required. Of the 128 semester hours required for a bachelor's degree, 32 must be completed in residence. Application deadlines are open.

Visiting: There is an orientation program for prospective students. Informal campus tours with guides are available. Visitors may attend classes and stay overnight at the school. The admissions office should be contacted for arrangements.

Financial Aid: About 85% of the students receive financial aid. Twenty-five percent work part-time on campus. The average award to freshmen is $650. The university offers scholarships, loans, grants, and work-study programs. The university is a member of the CSS. The FAF is required. The aid application should be filed by April 1 for fall entry, December 1 for spring entry.

Foreign Students: Three percent of the full-time students are from foreign countries. An intensive English course, a special English program, and counseling are offered.

Admissions: Applicants must take the TOEFL.

Procedure: Application deadlines are open; students may enroll at the beginning of any term. Students must submit a University Medical Form as proof of health. Proof of adequate funds to cover 1 academic year is also required. Health insurance is mandatory and is available through the university for a fee.

Admissions Contact: Winslow Carter, Director of Admissions.

CATAWBA COLLEGE   C-2
Salisbury, North Carolina 28144   (704) 637-4402

F/T, P/T:	Faculty: 70; IIB, av$
550M, 450W	Ph.D.'s: 55%
Grad: none	S/F Ratio: 15 to 1
Year: sems, ss	Tuition: $3356
Appl: open	R and B: $1500
822 applied 731 accepted 335 enrolled	
SAT: 410V 422M	LESS COMPETITIVE

Catawba College, established in 1851, is a private liberal arts college affiliated with the United Church of Christ. The library contains 168,000 volumes and 23,600 microfilm items, and subscribes to 1000 periodicals.

Environment: The 206-acre campus is located in a city of 25,000 people, 40 miles from Charlotte. Ten residence halls accommodate 410 women and 430 men.

Student Life: Approximately 47% of the students are from North Carolina, and 90% come from public schools. Seventy percent live on campus in single-sex dormitories.

Organizations: Student life centers around professional organizations, social and cultural activities, and student government. Chapel services, vespers, and convocation programs are held at various times during the school year. There are no fraternities or sororities.

Sports: The college fields intercollegiate teams in 11 sports. Intramural sports also are available.

Handicapped: There are no special facilities for the physically handicapped.

Graduates: About 10% of the freshmen drop out, and 60% remain to graduate. Twenty percent of the graduates pursue advanced degrees; 1% enter medical school, 1% dental school, and 5% law school. About 50% pursue careers in business and industry.

Services: Placement services, career counseling, health care, tutoring, and remedial instruction are offered free to students.

Programs of Study: The college confers the B.A. and B.S.W. degrees. Majors are offered in the following subjects: BUSINESS (accounting, business administration), EDUCATION (early childhood, elementary, health/physical, intermediate, recreation, secondary, special), ENGLISH (English, speech), FINE AND PERFORMING ARTS (music, music education, theater/dramatics), HEALTH SCIENCES (corrective therapy, medical technology, physician assistant), LANGUAGES (French, German, Spanish), MATH AND SCIENCES (biology, chemistry, computer science, ecology/environmental science, geology, mathematics), PHILOSOPHY (philosophy, religion), PRE-

626 NORTH CAROLINA

PROFESSIONAL (forestry, law, social work), SOCIAL SCIENCES (anthropology, economics, government/political science, history, psychology, sociology). About 25% of degrees are conferred in business and 20% in social sciences.

Required: Students must take at least 6 hours in English; mathematics, computer science, physics or a foreign language; social sciences; and the arts. They also must take 6 to 8 hours in natural science and 12 hours in humanities.

Special: A general studies degree, study abroad, and cooperative programs in adaptive physical education, engineering, forestry, medical technology, physician's assistant, and the exceptional child are offered. Students may design their own majors.

Honors: Four honor societies have chapters on campus.

Admissions: Approximately 89% of those who applied were accepted for the 1981-82 freshman class. Thirty percent of those who enrolled ranked in the top fifth of their high school class. For an earlier freshman class, the SAT scores were as follows: Verbal—10% between 500 and 600 and 1% between 600 and 700; Math—10% between 500 and 600 and 2% between 600 and 700. Candidates should have completed 16 Carnegie units at an accredited high school with a GPA of 2.0 or better. Other factors considered are advanced placement or honors courses, impressions made during an interview, recommendations, and extracurricular activities.

Procedure: The SAT is required and should be taken by December of the senior year. Application deadlines are open; the college follows a rolling admissions policy. There is a $15 application fee.

Special: AP and CLEP credit is accepted. There is an early decision plan.

Transfer: Approximately 60 transfer students enroll yearly. Transfers are accepted for all classes; requirements are the same as those for freshman applicants. Students must earn 30 credits in residence of the 120 required for a bachelor's degree.

Visiting: Regularly scheduled orientations are held for prospective students. Guides are also available for informal visits; visitors may sit in on classes and stay overnight at the school. The admissions office should be contacted to arrange visits.

Financial Aid: Approximately 62% of all students receive aid, which is available in the form of scholarships, loans, and part-time jobs. North Carolina residents with established need are eligible for state aid. The average award to freshmen is $1400. The FAF is required. The deadline for priority consideration of aid applications is February 15.

Foreign Students: Students from foreign countries represent less than 1% of enrollment. Special counseling is provided.

Admissions: Foreign students must score 500 or better on the TOEFL. No college entrance exams are required.

Procedure: Application deadlines are the same as those for American students. Foreign students must submit a medical form as proof of good health. They also must show evidence of adequate funds for 1 semester.

Admissions Contact: J. William Hall, Director of Admissions.

DAVIDSON COLLEGE C-3
Davidson, North Carolina 28036 (704) 892-2000

F/T: 919M, 484W Faculty: 98; IIB, ++$
P/T: 5M, 6W Ph.D.'s: 88%
Grad: none S/F Ratio: 14 to 1
Year: tri Tuition: $5220
Appl: Feb. 15 R and B: $1975
1699 applied 675 accepted 362 enrolled
SAT: 605V 620M **HIGHLY COMPETITIVE**

Davidson College is a private, coeducational, liberal arts college founded by the Presbyterian Church. The library contains 260,000 volumes and 12,000 microfilm items, and subscribes to 2000 periodicals.

Environment: The 450-acre rural campus, 18 miles from Charlotte, includes 9 dormitories accommodating 80% of the students. The college sponsors off-campus housing. Married student housing is also available.

Student Life: Approximately 30% of the students are from North Carolina, and 75% come from public schools. Eighty-seven percent of the students live on campus; all freshmen are required to do so. Approximately 85% of the students are Protestant and 7% are Catholic. Five percent are minority-group members. Both coed and single-sex housing is available; there are visiting privileges in single-sex housing. Students are permitted to keep cars on campus.

Organizations: There are 4 fraternities. Extracurricular activities include the student union; social clubs; art, music, and drama programs; lecture series; and service organizations.

Sports: The college competes intercollegiately in 12 sports for men and 7 sports for women. There are 5 intramural sports for men and 5 for women.

Handicapped: Approximately 20% of the campus is accessible to the physically handicapped. Facilities include wheelchair ramps, special parking, elevators, and specially equipped rest rooms. No students with visual or hearing impairments are currently enrolled.

Graduates: The freshman dropout rate is approximately 4%; 81% remain to graduate. About 70% of those who graduate pursue graduate study: 13% enter medical school, 0.6% dental school, and 12% law school; 15% pursue careers in business and industry.

Services: Placement services, career counseling, and psychological counseling are offered free of charge; health care and tutoring are also available for a fee.

Programs of Study: The B.A. or B.S. degree is offered in the following subjects: AREA STUDIES (American), BUSINESS (economics), EDUCATION (secondary), ENGLISH (English), FINE AND PERFORMING ARTS (art history, music, studio art, theater/dramatics/speech), LANGUAGES (French, German, Greek/Latin/classics, Spanish), MATH AND SCIENCES (biology, chemistry, mathematics, physics), PHILOSOPHY (classics, philosophy, religion), PREPROFESSIONAL (medicine), SOCIAL SCIENCES (anthropology, economics, government/political science, history, psychology, sociology). Forty-seven percent of degrees are conferred in social sciences; 33% in math and sciences; 16% in language, literature, and fine arts; 4% in philosophy and religion; and 4% in interdisciplinary programs.

Special: Student-designed majors, interdisciplinary study, study abroad programs, independent study, and a 3-2 combination degree program in engineering with Columbia University, North Carolina State University, Georgia Institute of Technology, or Washington University in St. Louis are offered.

Honors: Thirteen national honor societies have chapters on campus. Honors programs are offered in most departments.

Admissions: Approximately 40% of those who applied were accepted for the 1981-82 freshman class. The SAT scores of those who enrolled were as follows: Verbal—10% below 500, 41% between 500 and 599, 42% between 600 and 700, and 7% above 700; Math—4% below 500, 30% between 500 and 599, 53% between 600 and 700, and 13% above 700. The majority of those accepted rank in the top 20% of their class and have a GPA of 3.5 or better. Other factors entering into the admissions decision are advanced placement or honors courses, recommendations, evidence of special talents, and the candidate's extracurricular activities record. Applicants should have completed 16 Carnegie units.

Procedure: The SAT is required; 3 ATs are highly recommended. Tests should be taken by January of the senior year. A personal interview is highly recommended. The deadline for fall applications is February 15; there is a $25 application fee.

Special: There is an early decision plan. AP credit is accepted.

Transfer: For fall 1981, 87 transfer students applied and 5 were accepted and enrolled. Transfer applicants are considered for the beginning of any term; the likelihood of acceptance is greater for those who apply for a winter or spring term. A minimum GPA of 2.0 is required; a GPA of 3.0 is recommended. There is a 2-year residency requirement. Out of 36 courses required for a bachelor's degree, 18 must be taken at Davidson.

Visiting: There are no regularly scheduled orientations. Guides are available for informal visits; visitors may sit in on classes and stay overnight at the school. The admissions office should be contacted to arrange visits.

Financial Aid: Approximately 40% of all students receive some form of financial aid. Scholarships ranging from $270 to $5940 are available; loans of up to $1250, $2250 for employed students, are offered. The average award to freshmen from all sources is $4222. Work-study programs are offered by most departments; 20% of the students defray part of their expenses through part-time employment. The college is a member of CSS. The FAF is required. The deadline for aid applications is February 15.

Foreign Students: One percent of the students are from foreign countries. Special counseling is offered, and there are also organizations on campus especially for these students.

Admissions: The TOEFL, with a minimum score of 600, or the University of Michigan Language Test is required; the SAT is also required.

Procedure: Students are admitted at the beginning of the fall term only; the application deadline is March 1. Proof of health, consisting of a letter from a physician, and proof of adequate funds for 1 full year of study are required. Students must also carry health insurance, which is available through the college for a fee.

Admissions Contact: John V. Griffith, Director of Admissions.

DUKE UNIVERSITY   D-2
Durham, North Carolina 27706   (919) 684-3214

F/T: 3093M, 2670W
P/T: none
Grad: 2082M, 976W
Year: sems, ss
Appl: Jan. 15
10,088 applied   2868 accepted   1350 enrolled
SAT: 622V 663M   ACT: 30   MOST COMPETITIVE

Faculty: n/av; I, ++$
Ph.D.'s: n/av
S/F Ratio: 9 to 1
Tuition: $5745
R and B: $2690

Duke University, a private coeducational institution founded in 1838, includes the College of Law, the School of Engineering, the School of Nursing, and Trinity College of Arts and Sciences. The libraries contain more than 3 million volumes, 4 million manuscripts, and other materials, and subscribe to 14,500 periodicals.

Environment: The 8000-acre wooded West Campus is on the southwest fringe of Durham; the 110-acre East Campus is nearer the center of the city. Free buses connect the 2 campuses. Residence halls accommodate 4343 students; apartments are available for married students.

Student Life: Approximately 85% of the students are from out of state; all 50 states are represented in the student body. About 70% of entering freshmen come from public schools; 85% live in residence halls. About 10% of the students are minority-group members. University housing is both single-sex and coed. There are visiting privileges in single-sex housing. Students may keep cars on campus.

Organizations: There are 20 national fraternities, to which 38% of the men belong; 36% of the women belong to the 13 national sororities. Extracurricular activities include student government, a radio station, drama groups, a daily newspaper, quarterly magazines, and numerous musical groups.

Sports: The university competes intercollegiately in 19 sports for men and 16 for women. There are also 12 intramural sports for men and 7 for women.

Handicapped: Approximately 55% of the campus is accessible to the physically handicapped. Facilities include wheelchair ramps, special parking, elevators, specially equipped rest rooms, a wheelchair van, and lowered drinking fountains and telephones; special class scheduling is also available.

Graduates: About 3% of the freshmen drop out by the end of their first year. Eighty-five percent remain to graduate. About 60% of those who graduate pursue advanced study: 12% enter medical school, 2% dental school, and 18% law school.

Services: Placement services, career counseling, and psychological counseling, are offered to students free of charge. Health care is offered on a fee basis.

Programs of Study: The B.A., B.S., or B.S.E. degree is offered. Master's, and doctoral programs are also available. Bachelor's degrees are granted in the following subjects: AREA STUDIES (African, Asian, Black/Afro-American, Latin American, Mid East, Russian), BUSINESS (computer science), ENGLISH (literature), FINE AND PERFORMING ARTS (art history, music, studio art, theater/dramatics), LANGUAGES (French, German, Greek/Latin, Russian, Spanish), MATH AND SCIENCES (biology, botany, chemistry, engineering, geology, mathematics, physics, zoology), PHILOSOPHY (classics, philosophy, religion), PREPROFESSIONAL (architecture, dentistry, forestry, law, medicine), SOCIAL SCIENCES (anthropology, economics, government/political science, history, psychology, public policy, sociology).

Required: Every student chooses discussion groups and tutorial, preceptorial, and seminar courses to augment the regular course schedule.

Special: Student-designed majors, independent study, pass/fail options, study abroad, and cross-registration with the University of North Carolina are offered. Under a reciprocal agreement, students at Duke, the University of North Carolina, and North Carolina Central University share library facilities.

Honors: More than 20 national honor societies have chapters on campus. Honors programs are open to students displaying special ability.

Admissions: Approximately 28% of those who applied were accepted for the 1981–82 freshman class. The SAT scores of those who enrolled were as follows: Verbal—6% below 500, 28% between 500 and 599, 51% between 600 and 700, and 15% above 700; Math—3% below 500, 13% between 500 and 599, 48% between 600 and 700, and 36% above 700. Candidates should have completed 15 college preparatory units. Other factors entering into the admissions decision are advanced placement or honors courses, recommendations, evidence of special talents, and the applicant's extracurricular activities record. The candidate's personal statement should show competency in English.

Procedure: The SAT and 3 ATs (including the AT in English Composition) are required and should be taken by January of the senior year. Engineering applicants are required to take the Mathematics AT. The application deadlines for admission are January 15 (fall) and October 15 (spring). There is a $30 application fee.

Special: There are early decision and deferred admissions plans. AP credit is accepted.

Transfer: For fall 1981, 712 students applied, 85 were accepted, and 60 enrolled. Applicants must exhibit above-average academic qualifications. There is a 16-course residency requirement out of the 32 needed for a bachelor's degree. No on-campus housing is available for transfer students. Application deadlines are April 1 (fall) and October 15 (spring).

Visiting: There are regularly scheduled orientations for prospective students. Guides are also available for informal visits. Visitors may sit in on classes and stay overnight at the school. The admissions office should be contacted to arrange visits.

Financial Aid: Approximately 32% of all students receive some form of financial aid. Nineteen percent work part-time on campus. Scholarships, loans, grants, and part-time employment are available. Work-study opportunities are available in most departments. The university is a member of CSS. The federal tax return and the FAF are required. Aid application deadlines are January 15 (fall) and December 1 (early notification).

Foreign Students: The university offers foreign students special counseling.

Admissions: Foreign students must take the TOEFL. They must also take the SAT or ACT. They must take 3 ATs, including English Composition.

Procedure: The application deadlines are January 15 (fall) and October 15 (spring). Foreign students must present proof of health. They must also present proof of funds to cover airfare and 1 year of study. They must carry health insurance, which is available through the university for a fee.

Admissions Contact: Eugene Buckingham, Associate Director of Admissions.

EAST CAROLINA UNIVERSITY   E-2
Greenville, North Carolina 27834   (919) 757-6640

F/T: 4444M, 5756W
P/T: 411M, 516W
Grad: 827M, 1310W
Year: sems, ss
Appl: see profile
5849 applied   4837 accepted   2477 enrolled
SAT: 450V 450M   COMPETITIVE

Faculty: 763; IIA, +$
Ph.D.'s: 66%
S/F Ratio: 17 to 1
Tuition: $666 ($2454)
R and B: $1716

Founded in 1907, East Carolina University is a state-supported institution offering undergraduate programs in the arts and sciences, business, education, health fields, and applied technical fields. The library has over 600,000 books and 402,000 microfilm items, and subscribes to over 8000 periodicals.

Environment: The 411-acre campus is located in a suburban area 85 miles from Raleigh. Living facilities include dormitories, off-campus apartments, and fraternity and sorority houses. There are facilities for commuting students.

Student Life: About 88% of the students come from North Carolina; 75% live on or near the campus. About 53% of the students are Protestant and 13% are Catholic. About 12% of the students are minority-group members. Campus housing is both coed and single-sex, there are visiting privileges. Students may keep cars on campus.

Organizations: There is a traditional selection of extracurricular activities. About 12% of the students belong to 9 national sororities and 12 national fraternities. There are religious organizations for all major faiths.

Sports: The university fields 10 intercollegiate teams for men and 7 for women. There are 20 intramural sports for men and 16 for women.

Handicapped: About 80% of the campus is accessible to physically handicapped students. Special facilities include wheelchair ramps, parking areas, elevators, lowered drinking fountains and telephones, and specially equipped rest rooms. Special class scheduling is possible. Two counselors and 4 assistants are provided. There is a special outreach program for hearing impaired students, and special equipment for blind students.

Graduates: The freshman dropout rate is 25%; about 60% remain to graduate. Of these, 15% go on for further education; 1% enter medical school and 1% enter law school. About 25% enter careers in business and industry.

Services: Health care, psychological counseling, remedial instruction, career counseling, and placement are provided at no charge to full-time students. Tutoring is available; it may require payment.

Programs of Study: The B.A., B.S., B.Mus., B.S.N., B.S.B.A., B.F.A., and other degrees are conferred. Master's and doctoral programs are also offered. Bachelor's degrees are offered in the following subjects: AREA STUDIES (urban), BUSINESS (accounting, business administration, business education, computer science, finance, general business, management, marketing, real estate/insurance), EDUCATION (early childhood, elementary, health/physical, industrial, safety, secondary special), ENGLISH (English, writing), FINE AND PERFORMING ARTS (art, art education, art history, ceramics, church music, community arts management, dance, design, drawing, interior design, music, music education, music theory, music therapy, painting, printmaking, sculpture, studio art, theater/dramatics), HEALTH SCIENCES (environmental health, medical records science, medical technology, nursing, occupational therapy, physical therapy, speech therapy), LANGUAGES (French, German, Spanish), MATH AND SCIENCES (applied physics, biochemistry, biology, chemistry, coastal and marine studies, geology, mathematics, physics, science education), PHILOSOPHY (philosophy), PREPROFESSIONAL (dentistry, engineering, forestry, home economics, law, library science, medicine, pharmacy, veterinary), SOCIAL SCIENCES (anthropology, economics, geography, government/political science, history, psychology, sociology). About 25% of the degrees are conferred in education and 20% in business.

Required: There is a general education requirement that requires courses in English, sciences, math, social sciences, humanities and fine arts, and health and physical education.

Special: Study abroad is possible.

Honors: There are 90 honor societies and professional and service organizations as well as an interdisciplinary Great Books honors program.

Admissions: About 83% of the applicants for 1981–82 were accepted. The SAT scores of those who enrolled were as follows: Verbal—83% below 500, 15% between 500 and 599, 2% between 600 and 700, and fewer than 1% above 700; Math—71% below 500, 25% between 500 and 599, 4% between 600 and 700, and fewer than 1% above 700. Students should rank in the upper 75% of their graduating class. Advanced placement/honors courses, impressions made during an interview, and evidence of special talents are also considered important.

Procedure: The SAT or ACT is required. New students are admitted each semester. Applications must be received approximately 1 month before the beginning of each term; notification is on a rolling basis. There is a $15 application fee.

Special: There are early admissions and deferred admissions plans. CLEP and AP are used.

Transfer: For fall 1981, 1844 transfer students applied, 1334 were accepted, and 807 enrolled. A 2.0 GPA is required; D grades are accepted. Students must complete, at the university, 30 credits of the 120 to 134 credits required to earn a bachelor's degree. Application deadlines are the same as those for freshmen.

Visiting: There is an orientation program for new students. Campus tours with student guides can be arranged through the admissions office.

Financial Aid: About 46% of the students are receiving some aid. The average award to freshmen from all sources is $1500. Work-study programs are available in 26 departments; about 30% of the students work part-time on campus. The university is a member of CSS; the FAF or FFS should be filed by March 15.

Foreign Students: Fewer than 1% of the students come from foreign countries. The university offers these students special counseling and special organizations.

Admissions: Foreign students must achieve a minimum TOEFL score of 500; no college entrance exams are required.

Procedure: Application deadlines for fall, spring, and summer entry are 1 month prior to the beginning of the semester. Foreign students must present proof of health as well as proof of funds adequate to cover 1 year of study. They must also carry health insurance, which is available through the university for a fee.

Admissions Contact: Walter M. Bortz, III, Director of Admissions.

ELIZABETH CITY STATE UNIVERSITY F-2
Elizabeth City, North Carolina 27909   (919) 335-3305

F/T: 675M, 787W Faculty: 100; IIB, ++$
P/T: 61M, 85W Ph.D.'s: 46%
Grad: none S/F Ratio: 16 to 1
Year: sems, ss Tuition: $740 ($2322)
Appl: open R and B: $1580
1200 applied 1000 accepted 900 enrolled
SAT: 650 (composite) LESS COMPETITIVE

Elizabeth City State University, founded in 1891, is a 4-year college that is part of the University of North Carolina system. The library houses 80,000 volumes, and subscribes to 1000 periodicals.

Environment: The 160-acre campus is located in a town of 15,000 people, 55 miles from Norfolk, Virginia. The 16 campus buildings include 7 residence halls.

Student Life: About 87% of the students are from North Carolina. Sixty percent live on campus in the single-sex dorms. The student body is predominantly black.

Organizations: Extracurricular activities include religious organizations, student government, a newspaper, a yearbook, academic clubs, and music, drama, and dance groups. About 5% of the men belong to the 6 fraternities on campus, and 10% of the women belong to the 6 sororities.

Sports: The university fields intercollegiate teams in 6 sports. Intramural sports also are available.

Graduates: About half the freshmen eventually graduate, and 30% of the graduates seek advanced degrees.

Programs of Study: The university awards the B.A., B.S., and B.S.Ed. degrees. Bachelor's degrees are offered in the following subjects: BUSINESS (business administration, business education), EDUCATION (early childhood, intermediate, health/physical, industrial, reading, secondary), ENGLISH (English), FINE AND PERFORMING ARTS (art education, music, music education, theater/dramatics), MATH AND SCIENCES (biology, chemistry, ecology/environmental studies, geology, mathematics, physics), PREPROFESSIONAL (engineering—industrial engineering technology, law enforcement, police science technology, social work), SOCIAL SCIENCES (government/political science, history, social studies, sociology).

Required: Students must complete distribution requirements.

Special: Independent study, cooperative education, and an exchange program with Howard University are available. A summer program is offered for high school graduates who do not meet SAT-score requirements.

Honors: An honors program in language arts is available to qualified juniors and seniors.

Admissions: Eighty-three percent of those who applied were accepted for the 1981–82 freshman class. Applicants who are high school graduates should have completed 16 Carnegie units with a GPA of 2.0 or better. The university also accepts graduates of unaccredited high schools and mature applicants who are not high school graduates but pass an entrance examination.

Procedure: The SAT is required. Application deadlines are open; freshmen are admitted to both semesters. The application fee is $10. Notification is made on a rolling basis.

Special: Early and deferred admissions plans are available. CLEP and AP credit is accepted.

Transfer: Applicants must have an average of C or better. D grades do not transfer. Students must spend at least one year in residence to receive a bachelor's degree.

Financial Aid: Nearly 90% of the students receive aid. Scholarships and grants-in-aid are available. The university also administers loan funds and work programs. Students should submit the FAF and the aid application by April 15.

Foreign Students: About 15 students from foreign countries are enrolled. Special counseling and special organizations are available.

Admissions: Applicants must score 500 or better on the TOEFL. No college entrance exams are required.

ELON COLLEGE
Elon College, North Carolina 27244   **D–2**
(919) 584-2370

F/T: 1298M, 996W	Faculty: 113; IIB, av$
P/T: 173M, 286W	Ph.D.'s: 64%
Grad: none	S/F Ratio: 21 to 1
Year: 4-1-4, ss	Tuition: $2535
Appl: open	R and B: $1565
1611 applied	1300 accepted	716 enrolled
SAT: 393V 425M		LESS COMPETITIVE

Elon College, chartered in 1889 and affiliated with the United Church of Christ, offers undergraduate programs in the liberal arts and sciences, business, education, and health fields. Its library has 150,000 books and 1524 microfilm items, and subscribes to 645 periodicals.

Environment: The 95-acre campus is located in an urban area 17 miles from Greensboro. Dormitories house 1250 students. The college also sponsors fraternity and sorority houses.

Student Life: About 60% of the students come from North Carolina. Eighty percent are graduates of public schools. Sixty-five percent live on campus. About 68% of the students are Protestant, and 12% are Catholic. About 9% of the students are minority-group members. Campus housing is single-sex; there are visiting privileges. Students may keep cars on campus.

Organizations: There is a traditional extracurricular program, including social and cultural events regularly scheduled on campus. Twenty percent of the men belong to fraternities (2 local, 5 national), and 20% of the women to sororities (4 national).

Sports: The college fields 10 intercollegiate teams for men and 4 for women. There are 11 intramural sports for men and 7 for women.

Handicapped: Special facilities for handicapped students include wheelchair ramps, parking areas, and specially equipped rest rooms. Special class scheduling is also available.

Graduates: The freshman dropout rate is 10%; about 62% remain to graduate. Of these, 15% go on to graduate or professional school and about 35% enter business careers.

Services: Career counseling, placement service, and health care are offered free of charge to all students. Tutoring and remedial instruction are available for a fee.

Programs of Study: The B.A. or B.S. degree is conferred. Associate degrees are also awarded. Bachelor's degrees are offered in the following subjects: BUSINESS (accounting, business administration, business education), EDUCATION (early childhood, elementary, health/physical, secondary), ENGLISH (English, journalism), FINE AND PERFORMING ARTS (music, music education), HEALTH SCIENCES (medical technology), MATH AND SCIENCES (biology, chemistry, mathematics, physics), PHILOSOPHY (philosophy, religion), PRE-PROFESSIONAL (dentistry, medicine, ministry, social work, veterinary), SOCIAL SCIENCES (economics, government/political science, social sciences). About 45% of the degrees are conferred in social sciences, and 22% in business.

Required: Two courses in religion and 2 semesters of physical education are required.

Special: A 3-year bachelor's degree, student-designed majors, and study abroad are offered. A combined B.A.-B.S. degree can be earned in music and education.

Honors: There are 2 honor societies on campus. The honors program is interdisciplinary and college-wide.

Admissions: About 81% of the 1981–82 applicants were accepted. The SAT scores of those who enrolled were as follows: Verbal—88% below 500, 8% between 500 and 599, 1% between 600 and 700, and 1% above 700; Math—80% below 500, 7% between 500 and 599, 2% between 600 and 700, and 0% above 700. Admissions requirements are flexible and individualized. An interview is recommended. Important factors in the admissions decision are honors or advanced placement courses, recommendations, and impressions made during an interview.

Procedure: The SAT is required. Deadlines are open; new students are admitted each semester. Notification is on a rolling basis. There is a $10 application fee.

Special: AP and CLEP credit is given.

Transfer: For fall 1981, 305 transfer students applied, 238 were accepted, and 172 enrolled. An average of C is recommended; grades of C or above transfer. Thirty-two credits must be completed in residence; 126 credits are required to earn a bachelor's degree. Application deadlines are open.

Visiting: Campus tours with student guides can be arranged for weekdays from 8 A.M. to 5 P.M. and Saturdays from 9 A.M. to noon. Visitors may sit in on classes. Arrangements should be made through the admissions office.

Financial Aid: About 80% of the students receive aid; 35% of the students work part-time on campus. The college offers scholarships, loans, and part-time employment. About 250 freshman scholarships are awarded each year; scholarships or grants to freshmen range from $200 to $1600. Need and academic merit determine the award. Aid is generally packaged. The college is a member of CSS; the FAF or FFS should be filed. Deadlines are open.

Foreign Students: Fewer than 1% of the students come from foreign countries.

Admissions: Foreign students must achieve a minimum TOEFL score of 550; no college entrance exams are required.

Procedure: Application deadlines are April 1 (fall), August 1 (winter), September 1 (spring), and March 1 (summer). Foreign students must present proof of health as well as proof of funds adequate to cover 4 years of study. They must also carry health insurance, which is not available through the college.

Admissions Contact: Marydell R. Bright, Coordinator of Admissions and Financial Aid.

FAYETTEVILLE STATE UNIVERSITY
Fayetteville, North Carolina 28301   **D–3**
(919) 486-1371

F/T: 947M, 1103W	Faculty: 159; IIB, +$
P/T: 121M, 185W	Ph.D.'s: 51%
Grad: 27M, 102W	S/F Ratio: 13 to 1
Year: sems, ss	Tuition: $616 ($2198)
Appl: July 1	R and B: $1750
1033 applied	918 accepted	478 enrolled
SAT: required		LESS COMPETITIVE

Fayetteville State University is a state-controlled liberal arts college. The university was founded in 1867 as Howard School; in 1877 its name was changed to the State Colored Normal School. In 1939 it became the Fayetteville State Teachers College, and in 1963 it acquired its present name. The library contains 190,035 volumes and 5000 microfilm items, and subscribes to 800 periodicals.

Environment: The 156-acre campus, located in an urban area 60 miles from Raleigh, has 35 buildings, including residence halls accommodating 336 women and 142 men. A $5 million science building was recently completed.

Student Life: Fifty-six percent of the students are from the middle Atlantic region, 38% from the South, and 3% from New England. The majority of the students (80%) are black. Campus housing is both coed and single-sex; there are no visiting privileges. Students may keep cars on campus. Day-care services are available to all students, faculty, and staff.

Organizations: There are 4 local and 5 national fraternities, to which 3% of the men belong; 5% of the women belong to the 4 local and 5 national sororities. The university's community center accommodates student activities such as meetings, receptions, and exhibits. There are 15 social organizations on campus.

Sports: The university fields 5 intercollegiate teams for men and 1 team for women. There are 3 intramural sports for men and 3 for women.

Handicapped: Approximately 75% of the campus is accessible to the physically handicapped. Facilities include wheelchair ramps, special parking, elevators, specially equipped rest rooms, and lowered drinking fountains and telephones; special class scheduling is also available.

Graduates: The freshman dropout rate is 40%; 30% remain to graduate. Approximately 20% of those who graduate pursue graduate study.

Services: Placement services, career counseling, health care, psychological counseling, tutoring, and remedial instruction are offered to students free of charge.

Programs of Study: The B.A. or B.S. degree is conferred. Associate and master's degrees are also awarded. Bachelor's degrees are of-

630 NORTH CAROLINA

fered in the following subjects: AREA STUDIES (Black/Afro-American), BUSINESS (business administration, business education), EDUCATION (early childhood, elementary, health/physical, secondary), ENGLISH (English, literature, speech), FINE AND PERFORMING ARTS (music, music education), HEALTH SCIENCES (medical technology), MATH AND SCIENCES (biology, chemistry, mathematics), SOCIAL SCIENCES (economics, geography, government/political science, history, psychology, social sciences, sociology). About 37% of degrees are conferred in education, 32% in social sciences, and 23% in business.

Special: A 3-year bachelor's program is offered.

Honors: Twelve national honor societies have chapters on campus. There is a general studies honors program.

Admissions: Approximately 89% of those who applied were accepted for the 1981–1982 freshman class. Candidates should have a minimum 2.0 GPA with 16 Carnegie units. Graduates of 4-year nonstandard high schools may apply for admission by examination. Another factor entering into the admissions decision is recommendations by school officials.

Procedure: The SAT is required. The application deadline for fall admissions is July 1; freshmen are also admitted in the spring and summer terms. There is a $15 application fee. The university uses a rolling admissions policy.

Special: There is an early admissions plan. AP and CLEP credit is accepted.

Transfer: For fall 1981, 571 transfer students applied, 540 were accepted, and 352 enrolled. Transfers are accepted for all classes; grades of C or above transfer. A minimum 2.0 GPA is required. There is a 1-year residency requirement. For the bachelor's degree, 120 credits are required. Deadlines are the same as those for freshmen.

Visiting: There are regularly scheduled orientations for prospective students. Guides are also available for informal visits; visitors may sit in on classes and stay overnight at the school. The admissions office should be contacted to arrange visits.

Financial Aid: Approximately 81% of all students receive some form of financial aid. About 37% of the students work part-time on campus. The average award to freshmen from all sources is $1587. The university offers scholarships and loans. The college is a member of CSS; the FAF or FFS is required. The deadline for financial aid applications is May 1.

Foreign Students: Fewer than 1% of the students come from foreign countries.

Admissions: No English proficiency exam is required. Foreign students must take the SAT.

Procedure: Students must submit a physical exam form. They must also carry health insurance, which is available through the university for a fee.

Admissions Contact: Charles A. Darlington, Director of Admissions.

GARDNER-WEBB COLLEGE C–3
Boiling Springs, North Carolina 28017   (704) 434-2361

F/T: 742M, 771W
P/T: 8M, 20W
Grad: 27M, 58W
Year: sems, ss
Appl: Aug. 1
667 applied
SAT: 380V 409M
Faculty: n/av; IIB, n/av
Ph.D.'s: 70%
S/F Ratio: 17 to 1
Tuition: $2960
R and B: $1700
600 accepted 308 enrolled
ACT: 18 LESS COMPETITIVE

Gardner-Webb College, founded in 1928, is affiliated with the Baptist State Convention of North Carolina and offers undergraduate instruction in business, nursing, and the arts and sciences. Its library has 100,000 books, and subscribes to 750 periodicals.

Environment: The 137-acre campus is located in a rural area 50 miles from Charlotte. There are 34 buildings, including 9 dormitories that accommodate 561 men and 409 women. There is also housing for married students.

Student Life: About 95% of the students come from public schools. Most of the students are Baptist; convocation attendance is required. About 70% of the students live on campus. Eleven percent of the students are minority-group members. Campus housing is single-sex; there are no visiting privileges. Students may keep cars on campus.

Organizations: Religious groups, student government, clubs, publications, performing groups, and regularly scheduled cultural and social events are offered. There are no fraternities or sororities.

Sports: The college fields 6 intercollegiate teams for men and 4 for women. There are 7 intramural sports for men and 5 for women.

Handicapped: About 90% of the campus is accessible to wheelchair-bound students. Special facilities include wheelchair ramps, parking areas, lowered drinking fountains and telephones, and specially equipped rest rooms. Special class scheduling is possible.

Graduates: The freshman dropout rate is 25%; 60% remain to graduate. About 20% of the graduates go on for further education.

Services: Psychological counseling, career counseling, placement, health care, tutoring, and remedial instruction are available without charge.

Programs of Study: The B.A. or B.S. degree is conferred. Associate and master's degrees are also awarded. Bachelor's degrees are offered in the following subjects: BUSINESS (accounting, business administration, business education, computer science, finance, management), EDUCATION (early childhood, elementary, health/physical, secondary), ENGLISH (English), FINE AND PERFORMING ARTS (music, music education), HEALTH SCIENCES (medical technology, nursing), LANGUAGES (French, Greek/Latin, Hebrew, Spanish), MATH AND SCIENCES (biology, chemistry, mathematics), PHILOSOPHY (philosophy, religion), PREPROFESSIONAL (dentistry, engineering, law, medicine, ministry, veterinary), SOCIAL SCIENCES (government/political science, history, psychology, social sciences, sociology). About 24% of the degrees are conferred in religion.

Required: There is a general education requirement that includes courses in religion, English, and physical education.

Special: There are cooperative degree programs in engineering and medical technology.

Admissions: About 90% of the applicants for the 1981–82 school year were accepted. The SAT scores of those who enrolled were as follows: Verbal—88% below 500, 10% between 500 and 599, 1% between 600 and 700, and 1% above 700; Math—83% below 500, 15% between 500 and 599, 2% between 600 and 700, and 0% above 700. Class rank should be in the top 50%; high school GPA should be 2.0. Advanced placement or honors courses, recommendations, leadership record, and impressions made during an interview are also important.

Procedure: The SAT or the ACT is required. Application deadlines are August 1 (fall), December 1 (spring), and May 1 (summer). Notification is on a rolling basis. There is a $15 application fee.

Special: There are early decision, early admissions, and deferred admissions programs.

Transfer: For fall 1981, 389 transfer students applied, 365 were accepted, and 352 enrolled. A 2.0 GPA is required; grades of C or better transfer. Students must complete, at the college, 30 of the 128 credits required to earn a bachelor's degree. Application deadlines are the same as those for freshmen.

Visiting: There is an orientation program for prospective applicants. Informal campus tours with student guides can be arranged. Visitors may attend classes.

Financial Aid: About 65% of the students are receiving some aid; about 19% work part-time on campus. The college offers 10 freshman scholarships valued at $1500 each, academic departmental scholarships, endowed scholarships, various loan programs (including NDSL), and work-study opportunities. The average award to freshmen from all sources is $3500. The college is a member of CSS; the FFS and an income tax form must be submitted by April 1.

Foreign Students: The college accepts foreign students. The college offers these students special counseling and special organizations.

Admissions: Foreign students must achieve a minimum TOEFL score of 500; no college entrance exams are required.

Procedure: Application deadlines are May 1 (fall) and October 1 (spring). Foreign students must present proof of funds adequate to cover 1 year of study. They must also carry health insurance, which is available through the college for a fee.

Admissions Contact: Richard M. Holbrook, Director of Admissions.

GREENSBORO COLLEGE D–2
Greensboro, North Carolina 27420   (919) 272-7102

F/T: 192M, 387W
P/T: 18M, 37W
Grad: none
Year: sems, ss
Appl: open
558 applied
SAT or ACT: required
Faculty: 36; IIB, av$
Ph.D.'s: 60%
S/F Ratio: 16 to 1
Tuition: $3170
R and B: $1800
435 accepted 185 enrolled
LESS COMPETITIVE

Greensboro College is a small liberal arts institution affiliated with the Methodist Church, offering programs in the liberal arts and sciences, business, education, health sciences, and preprofessional areas. The library contains 75,000 volumes and 1397 microfilm items, subscribes to 412 periodicals, and has a reference computer tie-in.

Environment: The 30-acre campus, located in a suburban area, includes residence halls accommodating 350 women and 186 men.

Student Life: Seventy-five percent of the students are from the South; 80% live on campus. Student regulations prohibit drinking. About 22% of the students are minority-group members. Campus housing is single-sex; there are visiting privileges. With permission, students may keep cars on campus.

Organizations: There are no fraternities or sororities. Student life is closely knit; extracurricular activities include the Student Christian Fellowship, student government, and a variety of organizations. Worship facilities for most faiths are available in the community.

Sports: The college fields 5 intercollegiate teams for men and 4 for women. There are 8 intramural sports for men and 7 for women.

Handicapped: Facilities for the physically handicapped include wheelchair ramps, special parking, elevators, and specially equipped rest rooms (in some buildings).

Graduates: The freshman dropout rate is 22%; 47% remain to graduate. Approximately 18% of those who graduate pursue graduate study immediately after graduation: 6% enter medical school and 2% enter law school; 15% pursue careers in business and industry.

Services: Placement services, career counseling, health care, psychological counseling, tutoring, and remedial instruction are offered to students free of charge.

Programs of Study: The college confers the B.A., B.S., B.F.A., B.M., and B.Mus.Ed. degrees. Bachelor's degrees are offered in the following subjects: BUSINESS (accounting, business administration), EDUCATION (early childhood, elementary, health/physical, secondary, special), ENGLISH (English), FINE AND PERFORMING ARTS (art, art education, music, music education, theater/dramatics), HEALTH SCIENCES (medical technology, physician's assistant, radiology), LANGUAGES (French, Spanish), MATH AND SCIENCES (biology, chemistry, mathematics), PHILOSOPHY (philosophy, religion), PREPROFESSIONAL (dentistry, law, medicine, ministry, pharmacy, social work, veterinary), SOCIAL SCIENCES (sociology). Approximately 14% of degrees are conferred in fine and performing arts, 13% in business, and 12% in math and sciences.

Required: All students must take courses in English, history, religion, and mathematics.

Special: Student-designed majors are allowed. Combination degree programs are available in medical technology, physician's assistant, radiology, and registered nursing.

Honors: One national honor society has a chapter on campus.

Admissions: Approximately 78% of those who applied were accepted for the 1981-82 freshman class. Applicants should have completed 16 Carnegie units and have a minimum GPA of 2.0. Other factors entering into the admissions decision are the high school transcript, recommendations, extracurricular activities record, and impressions made during an interview. Mature persons who submit satisfactory GED scores may be admitted.

Procedure: The SAT or ACT is required. Deadlines are open; applications should be submitted as early as possible. Freshmen are admitted in the fall, spring, and summer terms. There is a $10 application fee. A personal interview is recommended. The college follows a rolling admissions policy.

Special: There are early decision, early admissions, and deferred admissions plans. AP and CLEP credit is accepted.

Transfer: For fall 1981, 196 transfer students applied, 123 were accepted, and 64 enrolled. Transfers are accepted for all classes; grades of C or better transfer. Thirty semester hours, of the 124 semester hours needed to earn a bachelor's degree, must be taken at the college. Application deadlines are open.

Visiting: There are regularly scheduled orientations for prospective students. Guides are also available for informal visits; visitors may sit in on classes and stay overnight at the school. The admissions office should be contacted to arrange visits.

Financial Aid: Approximately 72% of all students receive some form of financial aid. The average award to freshmen from all sources is $2500. Scholarships and loans are available. About 33% of the students work part-time on campus. Aid is granted through the results of the ACT. The college is a member of CSS; the FAF or FFS is required. Application deadlines are open, although the preferential date is May 1.

Foreign Students: About 1% of the students come from foreign countries.

Admissions: Foreign students must achieve a minimum TOEFL score of 550; no college entrance exams are required.

Procedure: Application deadlines are open. Foreign students must present the college's health form as well as proof of funds adequate to cover 1 year of study.

Admissions Contact: James M. Tucker, Jr., Director of Admissions.

GUILFORD COLLEGE D-2
Greensboro, North Carolina 27410 (919) 292-5511

F/T: 578M, 507W	Faculty: 85; IIB, +$
P/T: 10M, 5W	Ph.D.'s: 79%
Grad: none	S/F Ratio: 16 to 1
Year: sems, ss	Tuition: $3955
Appl: June 1	R and B: $1810
991 applied	609 accepted	309 enrolled
SAT: 510V 520M	ACT: 24	COMPETITIVE+

Guilford College, established in 1889, is affiliated with the Society of Friends (Quakers) and offers undergraduate instruction in the liberal arts and sciences. Its library has 175,000 books and 8700 microform items, and subscribes to 1000 periodicals. There are many special collections that pertain to Quaker history.

Environment: The 300-acre suburban campus includes dormitories and on-campus apartments. There are also facilities for married students, and French and German Language Houses.

Student Life: About 55% of the students come from the South. Seventy-five percent attended public schools; 87% live on campus. Fifteen percent of the students are Catholic, 70% Protestant, and 5% Jewish. Five percent of the students are minority-group members. College housing is both single-sex and coed. There are visiting privileges in single-sex housing. Students may keep cars on campus.

Organizations: There is a full extracurricular program; social and cultural events are regularly scheduled.

Sports: In addition to 7 intercollegiate athletics for men and 6 for women, there are 6 intramural sports for both men and women.

Handicapped: Special facilities for physically handicapped students include wheelchair ramps, parking areas, and elevators. Readers are provided for students who have visual impairments.

Graduates: Twelve percent of the students drop out by the end of their first year. Nearly 75% remain to graduate; 40% of these go on for additional degree work: 2% enter medical school, 2% dental school, and 3% law school. Thirty percent enter careers in business and industry.

Services: Health care, psychological counseling, tutoring, career counseling, and placement are offered free of charge.

Programs of Study: The college offers the B.A., B.S., and B.A.S. degrees. Associate degrees are also granted. Bachelor's degrees are offered in the following subjects: BUSINESS (accounting, management), EDUCATION (early childhood, elementary, health/physical, secondary, special), ENGLISH (English), FINE AND PERFORMING ARTS (art, art education, music, studio art, theater/dramatics), HEALTH SCIENCE (medical technology), LANGUAGES (French, German, Spanish), MATH AND SCIENCES (biology, chemistry, earth science, ecology/environmental science, geology, mathematics, physics), PHILOSOPHY (philosophy, religion), PREPROFESSIONAL (dentistry, engineering, forestry, law, medicine, ministry, pharmacy, social work, veterinary), SOCIAL SCIENCES (economics, government/political science, history, psychology, sociology). About 35% of the degrees are conferred in preprofessional areas and business; 28% are in social sciences.

Required: There are general course requirements for all students.

Special: Student-designed majors, independent study, exchange programs, study abroad, and 3-2 programs in forestry, engineering, and physician's assistantship are offered. It is possible to earn a bachelor's degree in 3 years.

Honors: Most departments offer honors work for those students who qualify with a 3.5 GPA.

Admissions: About 61% of the applicants for 1981-82 were accepted. The SAT scores of those who enrolled were: Verbal—31% below 500, 55% between 500 and 599, 12% between 600 and 700, and 2% above 700; Math—30% below 500, 55% between 500 and 599, 13% between 600 and 700, and 2% above 700. Class rank should be top 40%; a 3.0 high school GPA is needed. Special talents,

632 NORTH CAROLINA

honors/advanced placement courses, and leadership record are also considered important.

Procedure: New students are admitted all terms. The SAT or ACT should be taken by December of the senior year. The application deadlines are June 1 (fall), December 15 (spring), and May 20 (summer). Notification is on a rolling basis. There is a $15 application fee.

Special: There are early admissions, early decision, and deferred admissions programs. AP and CLEP are used.

Transfer: For fall 1981, 114 students applied, 80 were accepted, and 58 enrolled. A 2.0 GPA is necessary from a 4-year college and a 2.5 from a community college. D grades are not accepted. One year must be completed in residence. Thirty-two credits must be completed in residence, of the 128 needed for a bachelor's degree. Application deadlines are the same as those for freshman applicants.

Visiting: There is an orientation program for prospective students. Informal campus tours can also be arranged. Visitors may attend classes and stay overnight at the college.

Financial Aid: Eighty-four percent of the students are receiving assistance. Twenty-two percent work part-time on campus. Average aid to freshmen from all sources is $3200. Loans, grants, and work opportunities are offered. The college is a member of CSS. The FAF or FFS is required by April 15.

Foreign Students: Six percent of the full-time students come from foreign countries. The college offers these students an intensive English course, special counseling, and special organizations.

Admissions: Foreign students must score at least 500 on the TOEFL. No college entrance examination is required.

Procedure: The application deadlines are June 1 (fall), December 15 (spring), and May 20 (summer). Foreign students must complete the college's own health form. They must also present proof of funds adequate to cover 4 years of study. They must carry health insurance, which is available through the college for a fee.

Admissions Contact: John K. Bell, Associate Director of Admissions.

HIGH POINT COLLEGE D-2
High Point, North Carolina 27262 (919) 885-0414

F/T: 616M, 636W		Faculty:	60; IIB, −$
P/T: 51M, 82W		Ph.D.'s:	54%
Grad: none		S/F Ratio:	17 to 1
Year: sems, ss		Tuition:	$3330
Appl: open		R and B:	$1410
686 applied	588 accepted		221 enrolled
SAT: 420V 480M			COMPETITIVE

High Point College, established in 1924 and affiliated with the Methodist Church, offers programs in the liberal arts and sciences, education, and business. The library has 100,000 volumes and 1100 microfilm items, and subscribes to 600 periodicals.

Environment: The 75-acre campus is located in a suburban area 11 miles from Greensboro. Residence halls accommodate 814 students.

Student Life: About 60% of the students come from the South; 70% of the freshmen are graduates of public schools. About 75% of the students reside on campus. About 60% of the students are Protestant, 20% Catholic, and 1% Jewish. About 8% of the students are minority-group members. Campus housing is both coed and single-sex; there are visiting privileges. Students may keep cars on campus.

Organizations: Twenty-five percent of the men belong to 5 fraternities; 25% of the women, to 6 sororities. There are religious, service, and special-interest organizations. The extracurricular program also includes publications, performing groups, and student government.

Sports: The college fields 6 intercollegiate teams for men and 5 for women. There are 4 intramural sports for men and 3 for women.

Handicapped: There are no special facilities for handicapped students.

Graduates: The freshman dropout rate is 13%. About 70% remain to graduate. Thirty-three percent go on for further education; 2% enter medical school and 1% enter law school. About 20% enter careers in business and industry.

Services: Career counseling, placement service, psychological counseling, and remedial instruction are provided without charge. Health care and tutoring are available on a fee basis.

Programs of Study: The B.A. or B.S. degree is offered in the following subjects: BUSINESS (accounting, business administration, computer science, finance, management, marketing), EDUCATION (Christian, early childhood, elementary, health/physical, secondary, special), ENGLISH (English, journalism), FINE AND PERFORMING ARTS (art, art education, radio/TV), HEALTH SCIENCES (environmental health, medical technology), LANGUAGES (Spanish), MATH AND SCIENCES (biology, chemistry, ecology/environmental science, mathematics, oceanography), PHILOSOPHY (philosophy, religion), PREPROFESSIONAL (dentistry, law, medicine, ministry, pharmacy, veterinary), SOCIAL SCIENCES (government/political science, history, psychology, social sciences, sociology).

Required: Required courses include religion, philosophy, English, foreign language, and physical education.

Special: Student-designed majors, 3-2 programs in engineering, medical technology, and forestry, and study abroad are offered. There are cooperative programs with the Florida Institute of Technology in air commerce, business application of computers, applied math and computer science, environmental studies, oceanographic science, and photography.

Honors: There are 2 honor societies. All departments offer honors work.

Admissions: About 86% of the 1981–82 applicants were accepted. The SAT scores of those who enrolled were as follows: Verbal—82% below 500, 16% between 500 and 599, 2% between 600 and 700, and 0% above 700; Math—67% below 500, 26% between 500 and 599, 7% between 600 and 700, and 0% above 700. Class rank should be top 50%; a 2.5 high school GPA is required. Also important are advanced placement or honors courses.

Procedure: The SAT or ACT is required. Application deadlines are open; notification is on a rolling basis. Freshmen are admitted to all semesters. There is a $10 application fee.

Special: AP and CLEP credit is given.

Transfer: For fall 1981, 125 transfer students applied, 100 were accepted, and 80 enrolled. A GPA of 2.5 is recommended for transfer. Grades of C or better transfer. At least 32 credits of the 124 credits needed to earn a bachelor's degree must be completed in residence. Application deadlines are the same as those for freshmen.

Visiting: Informal campus tours with student guides can be arranged through the admissions office for weekdays (8:30 A.M. to 5 P.M.) or Saturday mornings. Visitors may attend classes and stay overnight at the college. There is an orientation program for new students.

Financial Aid: Sixty percent of the students receive financial aid; 15% of the students work part-time on campus. Scholarships, various loans, grants, and work opportunities (including CWS) are offered. The college is a member of CSS; the FAF or FFS is required. The deadline for aid application is May 1.

Foreign Students: About 1% of the students come from foreign countries.

Admissions: Foreign students must achieve a minimum TOEFL score of 500; in addition, they must also take the SAT.

Procedure: Application deadlines are open. Foreign students must present the college's medical form as well as proof of funds adequate to cover 4 years of study. They must also carry health insurance, which is available through the college for a fee.

Admissions Contact: Alfred S. Hassell, Director of Admissions.

JOHNSON C. SMITH UNIVERSITY C-3
Charlotte, North Carolina 28216 (704) 378-1010

F/T: 586M, 677W		Faculty:	92; IIB, −$
P/T: 21M, 26W		Ph.D.'s:	44%
Grad: none		S/F Ratio:	14 to 1
Year: sems, ss		Tuition:	$2482
Appl: Aug. 1		R and B:	$1418
1126 applied	739 accepted		393 enrolled
SAT: 310V 305M			LESS COMPETITIVE

Johnson C. Smith University, founded in 1867, is affiliated with the Presbyterian Church and offers undergraduate programs in the liberal arts and sciences, business, and education. The library contains 97,000 volumes and 5000 microfilm items, and subscribes to 795 periodicals.

Environment: The 85-acre urban campus includes 46 buildings. The dormitories accommodate 800 men and women. There are facilities for commuting students.

Student Life: About 45% of the students come from North Carolina and 55% live on campus. All come from minority backgrounds and nearly all have public school educations. About 85% of the students are Protestant and 5% are Catholic. Campus housing is single-sex; there are no visiting privileges. Students may keep cars on campus

NORTH CAROLINA 633

with the approval of the dean of students. Day-care services are available for all full-time students, faculty, and staff.

Organizations: Student activities include publications, student government, clubs, service organizations, religious groups, performing groups, and social events. Four fraternities and 4 sororities attract 15% of the students.

Sports: The university fields 8 intercollegiate teams for men and 5 for women. There are 6 intramural sports for men and 6 for women.

Handicapped: About 10% of the campus is accessible to handicapped students. Facilities include wheelchair ramps. Counselors are available to handicapped students.

Graduates: The freshman dropout rate is 20%; 60% remain to graduate. About 25% of the graduates go on for further education; 2% enter medical school, 4% law school, and 1% dental school. Seventy percent enter careers in industry or business.

Services: Career counseling, placement, health care, psychological counseling, tutoring, and remedial instruction are offered without charge to all students.

Programs of Study: The B.A., B.A. in Social Work, and B.S. degrees are offered. Bachelor's degrees are offered in the following subjects: AREA STUDIES (urban and community affairs), BUSINESS (accounting, business administration, computer science, finance and banking, marketing, music/business), EDUCATION (early childhood, elementary, health/physical, secondary), ENGLISH (English), FINE AND PERFORMING ARTS (communications, music, music education), MATH AND SCIENCES (biology, chemistry, mathematics, natural sciences, physics), PHILOSOPHY (philosophy), PREPROFESSIONAL (social work), SOCIAL SCIENCES (economics, government/political science, history, psychology, social sciences, sociology). About 24% of the degrees are conferred in business, 22% in education, and 20% in social sciences.

Required: All students must take courses in English, mathematics, physical education, and a distribution of credits from 4 broad areas.

Special: There is a church officers training program.

Honors: Several departments offer honors work. There are 5 honor societies on campus.

Admissions: About 66% of the applicants for the 1981–82 freshman class were accepted. Candidates should rank in the top half of their graduating class, have a minimum 2.0 high school GPA, and have completed 16 Carnegie units.

Procedure: The SAT is required. Application deadlines are August 1 (fall) and December 1 (spring). Notification is on a rolling basis. There is a $10 application fee.

Special: There are early decision, early admissions, and deferred admissions plans. AP and CLEP credit is available.

Transfer: For fall 1981, 91 transfer students applied and 49 were accepted. A 2.0 GPA is required; grades of C or above transfer. Students must complete, at the university, 30 credits of the 122 required to earn the bachelor's degree. Deadlines are the same as those for freshmen.

Visiting: There are orientation programs for prospective students. Informal campus tours with guides can be arranged; visitors may sit in on classes but may not stay overnight at the school. Visits are best scheduled during the spring semester. The admissions office should be contacted for arrangements.

Financial Aid: About 95% of the students receive financial aid; 45% work part-time on campus. The university offers loans, grants, and scholarships. The average award to freshmen from all sources is $2200. The university is a member of CSS; the FAF or FFS should be filed no later than April 15.

Foreign Students: About 2% of the students come from foreign countries. The university offers these students an intensive English course, special counseling, and special organizations.

Admissions: Foreign students must achieve a minimum TOEFL score of 500; no college entrance exams are required.

Procedure: Application deadlines are January 1 (fall) and August 1 (spring). Foreign students must present proof of health as well as proof of funds adequate to cover 1 year of study. They must also carry health insurance, which is available through the university for a fee.

Admissions Contact: Clyde H. Brown, Acting Director of Admissions.

LENOIR-RHYNE COLLEGE C–2
Hickory, North Carolina 28603 (704) 328-1741

F/T: 484M, 707W Faculty: 84; IIB, av$
P/T: 46M, 147W Ph.D.'s: 52%
Grad: 1M, 39W S/F Ratio: 14 to 1
Year: sems, ss Tuition: $3497
Appl: open R and B: $1610
790 applied 509 accepted 298 enrolled
SAT: 457V 477M COMPETITIVE

Lenoir-Rhyne College, founded in 1891 and affiliated with the Lutheran Church, offers undergraduate programs in the arts and sciences, business, education, and health fields. Its library has 109,400 books, and subscribes to 684 periodicals.

Environment: The 100-acre suburban campus is located in a town of 25,000 inhabitants about 50 miles from Charlotte. There are 26 buildings. Three men's and 4 women's residence halls accommodate over 900 students.

Student Life: About 70% of the students come from North Carolina. Eighty-eight percent of the freshmen are graduates of public schools; 70% of the students live on campus. Thirty percent of the students are Lutheran. About 7% of the students are minority-group members. Campus housing is single-sex; there are visiting privileges. Students may keep cars on campus.

Organizations: There is a full and varied extracurricular program, including regularly scheduled on-campus social and cultural events. Other activities include publications, debates, and student-produced radio and TV programs. About 25% of the men belong to 4 fraternities, and 25% of the women to 4 sororities.

Sports: The college fields 6 intercollegiate teams for men and 4 for women. There are 14 intramural sports for men and 13 for women.

Handicapped: About 90% of the campus is accessible to handicapped students. Special facilities include wheelchair ramps, parking areas, elevators, specially equipped rest rooms, and specially designed dorm rooms. Special class scheduling is also available. Tutors, note-takers, and 3 special counselors are provided to assist handicapped students.

Graduates: The freshman dropout rate is 18%; about 59% remain to graduate. Thirty percent go on for further education, and 45% enter careers in business and industry.

Services: Psychological counseling, health care, tutoring, remedial instruction, career counseling, and placement service are offered free.

Programs of Study: The B.A., B.S., B.S.N., and B.Mus.Ed. degrees are conferred. Master's degrees are also awarded. Bachelor's degrees are offered in the following subjects: BUSINESS (accounting, business administration), EDUCATION (Christian, early childhood, health/physical, intermediate, secondary, special hearing impaired), ENGLISH (English), FINE AND PERFORMING ARTS (music, music education, theater/dramatics), HEALTH SCIENCES (medical technology, nursing, physician's assistant), LANGUAGES (French, German, Spanish), MATH AND SCIENCES (biology, chemistry, computer science, ecology/environmental science, mathematics, physics), PHILOSOPHY (classics, philosophy, religion), PREPROFESSIONAL (dentistry, engineering, forestry, law, medicine, ministry, pharmacy, social work), SOCIAL SCIENCES (economics, government/political science, history, international relations, psychology, sociology). About 31% of the degrees are conferred in business and 15% in education.

Special: A general studies major, student-designed majors, and interdisciplinary programs are offered. Students may study abroad. A 3-2 engineering program is available with North Carolina State University, Georgia Institute of Technology, and Duke University. A 3-1(2) program in forestry is available with Duke University.

Honors: There are honors programs in 18 fields. Five honor societies have chapters on campus.

Admissions: About 75% of the 1981–82 applicants were accepted. The SAT scores of those who enrolled were as follows: Verbal—73% below 500, 20% between 500 and 599, 7% between 600 and 700, and 1% above 700; Math—59% below 500, 30% between 500 and 599, 10% between 600 and 700, and 1% above 700. Class rank should be in the upper 50%. Other important factors include honors or advanced placement courses, impressions made during an interview, leadership record, and recommendations.

Procedure: The SAT or ACT is required. New students are admitted to each semester; application deadlines are open. Notification is on a rolling basis. There is a $15 application fee.

Special: There are early decision, early admissions, and deferred admissions plans. CLEP and AP credit is given.

634 NORTH CAROLINA

Transfer: For fall 1981, 224 transfer students applied, 193 were accepted, and 132 enrolled. A GPA of 2.0 is necessary; D grades generally transfer. Students must complete, at the college, 32 credits of the 128 credits required to earn the bachelor's degree. Application deadlines are open.

Visiting: There are orientation programs for prospective applicants. Informal campus tours can be arranged through the admissions office for weekdays from 9 A.M. to 4 P.M. and Saturdays for 9 A.M. to noon. Visitors may attend classes and stay overnight at the school.

Financial Aid: About 60% of the students receive assistance; 13% of the students work part-time on campus. Scholarships, grants, various loans (commercial and governmental), and CWS in all departments are offered. The average award to freshmen from all sources is $2500. Tuition can be paid in installments. The college is a member of CSS; the FAF is required. Application deadlines are open.

Foreign Students: Fewer than 1% of the students are from foreign countries.

Admissions: Foreign students must achieve a minimum TOEFL score of 500; no college entrance exams are required.

Procedure: Application deadlines are open. Foreign students must submit the college's health form and present proof of funds adequate to cover 1 year of study. They must also carry health insurance, which is available through the college for a fee.

Admissions Contact: Richard P. Thompson, Dean of Admissions and Financial Aid.

LIVINGSTONE COLLEGE C–2
Salisbury, North Carolina 28144 (704) 633-7960

F/T: 413M, 267W Faculty: 65; IIB, – – $
P/T: 9M, 24W Ph.D.'s: 32%
Grad: none S/F Ratio: 18 to 1
Year: sems, ss Tuition: $2500
Appl: open R and B: $1596
543 applied 335 accepted 184 enrolled
SAT: 585 (composite) **LESS COMPETITIVE**

Livingstone College, founded in 1879, is affiliated with the African Methodist Episcopal Zion Church, and offers undergraduate programs in the arts and sciences, music, education, and business. Its library holds 70,000 books, and subscribes to 257 periodicals.

Environment: The college is located in a town of 26,000 inhabitants between Greensboro and Charlotte. The 23 buildings include dormitories for 600 students.

Student Life: About 58% of the students come from North Carolina. About 69% live on campus in the single-sex residence halls. The student body is predominantly black.

Organizations: There are 4 local and 4 national fraternities to which 20% of the men belong, and 3 local and 3 national sororities to which 30% of the women belong. Extracurricular activities include student government, music groups, drama, clubs, and religious organizations.

Sports: The college fields intercollegiate teams in 6 sports. Intramural competition also is offered.

Handicapped: There are no special facilities for physically handicapped students.

Graduates: About 20% of the graduates go on for further education (1% each to medical, dental, and law schools). About 25% pursue business careers.

Services: Students receive health care, tutoring, remedial instruction, placement aid, and career counseling. Placement services also are available to graduates.

Programs of Study: The college confers the B.A., B.S., and B.S.W. degrees. Master's degrees are also awarded through the School of Religion. Bachelor's degrees are offered in the following subjects: BUSINESS (accounting, business administration, business education, management, office management), EDUCATION (early childhood, elementary, health/physical, reading, secondary), ENGLISH (English), FINE AND PERFORMING ARTS (music, music education, music therapy), LANGUAGES (French), MATH AND SCIENCES (biology, chemistry, mathematics), PREPROFESSIONAL (engineering, social work), SOCIAL SCIENCES (government/political science, history, sociology). About 30% of the degrees are conferred in social sciences, 23% in education, and 20% in business.

Required: Students must complete a general-education requirement of 53 semester hours and a non-credit orientation course.

Special: A cooperative education program is open to sophomores, juniors, and seniors. The college offers a dual-degree program in engineering.

Honors: Two national honor societies have chapters on campus.

Admissions: About 62% of the 1981–82 applicants were accepted. The SAT scores of those who enrolled were as follows: Verbal—98% below 500 and 2% between 500 and 599; Math—100% below 500. A high school GPA of at least C+ is required. The ability to finance a college education, advanced placement or honors work, and recommendations are also considered.

Procedure: The SAT is required. Application deadlines are open; notification is made on a rolling basis. There is a $10 application fee.

Special: An early decision plan is offered.

Transfer: Transfers are considered for all classes. Applicants must be in good standing and have a 2.0 GPA and good recommendations from their former school. Applicants with fewer than 30 semester hours of college work must meet the regular freshman requirements. All students must complete at least 30 semester hours at the college of the 124 required for a bachelor's degree.

Visiting: Campus tours with student guides can be arranged. Visitors may sit in on classes and stay overnight in the dormitories.

Financial Aid: About 95% of the students receive aid. The college participates in federal and state programs such as NDSL, BEOG/SEOG, and CWS and also offers other loans and job opportunities. The average award to freshmen in 1981–82 was $3346. The FAF or FFS is required and should be filed by August 15.

Foreign Students: Students from foreign countries represent about 2% of enrollment. The college offers these students special counseling and special organizations.

Admissions: Applicants must score 500 or better on the TOEFL. They also must take the SAT.

Procedure: Application deadlines are open. Foreign students must present a physician's statement as proof of good health and show evidence of adequate funds for 1 year. Health insurance is required, and is available through the college for a fee.

Admissions Contact: Edward I. Clemmons, Registrar/Director of Admissions.

MARS HILL COLLEGE B–2
Mars Hill, North Carolina 28754 (704) 689-1201

F/T: 643M, 753W Faculty: 105; IIB, – $
P/T: 55M, 171W Ph.D.'s: 50%
Grad: none S/F Ratio: 13 to 1
Year: sems, ss Tuition: $3445
Appl: open R and B: $1488
836 applied 700 accepted 390 enrolled
SAT: 390V 430M **LESS COMPETITIVE**

Mars Hill College, founded in 1856, is a liberal arts college affiliated with the North Carolina Baptist Convention. The library contains 85,000 volumes, 10,545 bound volumes of periodicals, and 3470 microfilm items.

Environment: The 150-acre campus is located in a small town 18 miles from Asheville. The surrounding environment is rural. There are 30 buildings on campus; 11 dormitories accommodate 1200 students. There are also apartments and townhouses.

Student Life: Fifty-one percent of the students are from North Carolina; 62% live on campus. Ninety percent of entering freshmen come from public schools. Married students, those who are 21 years of age or older, and those living with close relatives are not required to live in the dormitories. About 88% of the students are Protestant, and 4% are Catholic. About 7% of the students are minority-group members. Campus housing is single-sex; there are limited visiting privileges. Students may keep cars on campus. Drinking on campus is prohibited. Freshmen must observe a curfew and a sign-out procedure for overnight absences.

Organizations: There are 3 local and 2 national fraternities and 1 national and 3 local sororities. Extracurricular activities include student government, band, theater, cultural and social events, publications, and service clubs. The college sponsors religious counselors and organizations for Protestant students.

Sports: The college fields 6 intercollegiate teams for men and 4 for women. There are 5 intramural sports for men and 5 for women.

Handicapped: Facilities for the physically handicapped include wheelchair ramps, special parking, elevators, and specially equipped rest rooms.

Services: Placement services, career counseling, health care, psychological counseling, tutoring, and remedial instruction are offered to students free of charge.

Programs of Study: The B.A., B.S., B.M., B.S.W., or Bachelor of Musical Theater Performance degree is offered in the following subjects: BUSINESS (accounting, business administration, business/mathematics, economics), EDUCATION (early childhood, elementary, health/physical, secondary), ENGLISH (English), FINE AND PERFORMING ARTS (art, art education, art history, church music, music, music education, music performance, theater/dramatics), HEALTH SCIENCES (allied health, medical technology, nursing), LANGUAGES (French, Spanish), MATH AND SCIENCES (biology, botany, chemistry, mathematics, zoology), PHILOSOPHY (religion), PREPROFESSIONAL (fashion merchandising, home economics, social work), SOCIAL SCIENCES (economics, government/political science, history, psychology, sociology).

Required: All students must demonstrate specified levels of competence in communications, personal development, cultural values, esthetics, sciences, and synoptics.

Special: Study abroad, student-designed majors, a 5-year combined B.A.-B.S. program, off-campus internships, independent study programs, and research projects are offered.

Honors: Five national honor societies have chapters on campus.

Admissions: Approximately 87% of those who applied were accepted for the 1981-82 freshman class. The SAT scores of those who enrolled were as follows: Verbal—99% below 500, 1% between 500 and 599, 0% between 600 and 700, and 0% above 700; Math—97% below 500, 3% between 500 and 599, 0% between 600 and 700, and 0% above 700. Candidates should be graduates of an accredited high school and have completed 16 Carnegie units with a minimum 1.5 GPA. Other factors entering into the admissions decision are recommendations by school officials, advanced placement or honor courses, and impressions made during an interview.

Procedure: The SAT or ACT is required and should be taken by May of the senior year; junior year results are acceptable. A personal interview is recommended but not required. Application deadlines are open; freshmen are admitted in the fall, spring, and summer terms. The college follows a rolling admissions policy. There is a $15 application fee.

Special: AP and CLEP credit is accepted.

Transfer: For fall 1981, 156 transfer students applied, 112 were accepted, and 103 enrolled. Transfers are accepted for all classes; grades of C or above transfer. A minimum 1.5 GPA and recommendations are required. Students must complete, at the college, 32 credits of the 128 credits required to earn the bachelor's degree. Application deadlines are open.

Visiting: There are regularly scheduled orientations for prospective students. Guides are also available for informal visits on weekdays; visitors may sit in on classes and stay overnight at the school. The admissions office should be contacted to arrange visits.

Financial Aid: Approximately 68% of all students receive some form of financial aid; about 22% of the students work part-time on campus. The average award to freshmen from all sources is $2900. Federal and private loan funds, work contracts, and CWS (in all departments) are available. Tuition may be paid in installments. The college is a member of the CSS and requires the FAF. Financial aid applications should be completed as soon as possible after January 1 for the following academic year.

Foreign Students: Fewer than 1% of the students come from foreign countries. Special counseling and special organizations are provided for these students.

Admissions: Foreign students must achieve a minimum TOEFL score of 450; in addition, students must also take the college's own entrance exam.

Procedure: Application deadlines are August 10 (fall) and January 5 (spring). Foreign students must present proof of health as well as proof of funds adequate to cover 1 year of study. They must also carry health insurance, which is available through the college for a fee.

Admissions Contact: W. Dennis Hill, Associate Dean of Admissions.

MEREDITH COLLEGE D-2
Raleigh, North Carolina 27611 (919) 833-6461

F/T: 1418W	Faculty: 76; IIB, —$
P/T: 177W	Ph.D.'s: 61%
Grad: none	S/F Ratio: 18 to 1
Year: sems, ss	Tuition: $2750
Appl: Feb. 15	R and B: $1250
767 applied	558 accepted 339 enrolled
SAT: 440V 470M	COMPETITIVE

Meredith College, founded in 1891, offers women undergraduate training in the liberal arts and sciences and business. The college is affiliated with the Baptist Church. The library contains 100,000 volumes, subscribes to 550 periodicals, and contains 50,000 microfilm and microfiche items.

Environment: The 225-acre campus, located in the city of Raleigh, has 21 buildings, including 7 dormitories. Two additional buildings are under construction. There are facilities for commuting students. The surrounding environment is suburban.

Student Life: About 85% of the students come from North Carolina. Eighty-seven percent come from public schools. About 89% of the students are Protestant, and 6% are Catholic. About 3% of the students are minority-group members. There are visiting privileges only in the first floor parlors of the dormitories. Juniors and seniors may keep cars on campus. Alcohol is not permitted on campus.

Organizations: There are no sororities. Extracurricular activities include clubs, student government, dramatics, musical groups, service organizations, religious groups, publications, and regularly scheduled social and cultural events.

Sports: The college fields intercollegiate teams in 5 sports. There are 6 intramural sports.

Handicapped: About 95% of the campus is accessible to physically handicapped students. Special facilities include wheelchair ramps, parking areas, elevators, and some specially equipped rest rooms. Special class scheduling is also available.

Graduates: Four percent of the freshmen drop out; 61% remain to graduate. Ten percent of the graduates pursue further study; 1% enter medical school, and 1% enter law school. Forty-nine percent enter careers in business and industry.

Services: Health care, career counseling, placement, and psychological counseling are provided free of charge to all students. Tutoring is available on a fee basis.

Programs of Study: The B.A., B.S., and B.M. degrees are conferred. Bachelor's degrees are offered in the following subjects: AREA STUDIES (American, non-Western), BUSINESS (business administration), ENGLISH (English), FINE AND PERFORMING ARTS (applied music, art, music, music education), LANGUAGES (French, Spanish), MATH AND SCIENCES (biology, chemistry, mathematics), PHILOSOPHY (religion), PREPROFESSIONAL (home economics), SOCIAL SCIENCES (economics, history, political studies, psychology, sociology). Certification in social work and teacher education (early childhood, intermediate, secondary, art, and music) is available. Except for music education, these fields of study must be taken in addition to a major field. Twenty-five percent of the degrees are conferred in social sciences, 21% in business, and 18% in home economics.

Required: Freshmen must take English composition. There are also general graduation requirements which must be fulfilled. Students typically concentrate on these requirements during the freshman and sophomore years.

Special: Student-designed majors; cooperative education; study abroad; a Capital City semester; a United Nations semester; a Washington, D.C., semester; and internships are offered. Joint-degree programs with North Carolina State University are available in some areas. Meredith is in a consortium with North Carolina State University, Peace College, St. Mary's College, St. Augustine's College, and Shaw University.

Honors: Seven honor societies have chapters on campus.

Admissions: About 73% of the 1981-82 applicants were accepted. The SAT scores of those who enrolled were as follows: Verbal—78% below 500, 19% between 500 and 599, 3% between 600 and 700, and 0% above 700; Math—60% below 500, 35% between 500 and 599, 5% between 600 and 700, and 0% above 700. Class rank of applicants should be in the upper 50%. Most students are in the top fourth of their classes. A 2.0 high school GPA is required; most students have a GPA of at least 2.5. Candidates should present 13 academic units of credit. Advanced placement or honors courses, recommendations, and evidence of special talents are considered in the admissions decision.

Procedure: The SAT or ACT is required and should be taken by December of the senior year. February 15 is the fall application deadline; December 1, the spring deadline. Notification is on a rolling basis. There is a $15 application fee.

Special: Early decision, early admissions, and deferred admissions plans are offered. AP credit is available.

Transfer: For fall 1981, 188 transfer students applied, 131 were accepted, and 92 enrolled. A 2.0 GPA is needed for transfer. The last 30 semester hours must be completed at Meredith in order to receive a degree from the college; 124 credits are required to earn the bachelor's degree. Application deadlines are the same as those for freshmen.

636 NORTH CAROLINA

Visiting: There is an orientation program for prospective students. Conferences and campus tours may be arranged on Open Days for high school seniors. Visitors may sit in on classes but generally may not stay overnight at the school. Visits are best scheduled on weekdays. The admissions office should be contacted for arrangements.

Financial Aid: About 26% of the students receive financial aid; about 11% of the students work part-time on campus. In a recent year the college offered scholarships and grants to 102 freshmen, from a fund of over $240,000. Various loans and part-time campus work opportunities (including CWS) are available. Aid is packaged and determined by the applicant's need. Average amount of need-based aid granted to freshmen from scholarships and grants is $2356; and from loans, $297. Tuition may be paid in installments. The college is a member of CSS; the FAF is required and should be filed by February 15. A Meredith financial aid form is also required.

Foreign Students: About 1% of the students come from foreign countries.

Admissions: Foreign students must take the TOEFL; if their principal language of instruction has been English, the college expects students to take the SAT.

Procedure: The recommended application deadline is February 15 for fall. Foreign students must complete the college's health form and present proof of funds adequate to cover each year of the student's projected enrollment. They must also carry health insurance, which is available through the college for a fee.

Admissions Contact: Mary Bland Josey, Director of Admissions.

METHODIST COLLEGE D-3
Fayetteville, North Carolina 28301 (919) 488-7110

F/T, P/T	Faculty:	57; IIB, — — $
759 M&W	Ph.D.'s:	52%
Grad: none	S/F Ratio:	17 to 1
Year: sems, ss	Tuition:	$2870
Appl: open	R and B:	$1780
418 applied	392 accepted	230 enrolled
SAT: 376V 415M		LESS COMPETITIVE

Methodist College, founded in 1956, is a church-related college of liberal arts and sciences. The library contains 66,000 volumes and 2452 microtexts, and subscribes to 426 periodicals.

Environment: The 600-acre wooded campus is located in a suburban area of a city of 60,000 inhabitants. Four dormitories accommodate 620 men and women. In all, there are 16 buildings on campus.

Student Life: About 86% of the students come from North Carolina. About 43% live on campus in the single-sex dorms. The majority of students are Methodist. Alcohol is not permitted on campus.

Organizations: Extracurricular activities include religious organizations, clubs, publications, service groups, student government, performing groups, and regularly scheduled social events. Three fraternities and 2 sororities have chapters on campus.

Sports: The college fields intercollegiate teams in 7 sports for men and 4 for women. Twelve intramural sports are available.

Handicapped: About 80% of the campus is accessible to handicapped students. Wheelchair ramps and special parking areas are provided. Special class scheduling can be arranged.

Services: Career counseling, placement aid, and health care are offered free to students. Fees are charged for psychological counseling, tutoring, and remedial instruction.

Programs of Study: The college confers the B.A., B.S., and B.Applied Sc. degrees. Bachelor's degrees are offered in the following subjects: BUSINESS (business administration), EDUCATION (early childhood, elementary, health/physical, secondary), ENGLISH (English), FINE AND PERFORMING ARTS (art, art education, music, music education), LANGUAGES (French, Spanish), MATH AND SCIENCES (biology, chemistry, mathematics, science), PHILOSOPHY (religion, religious education), PREPROFESSIONAL (social work), SOCIAL SCIENCES (government/political science, history, psychology, sociology). About 27% of the degrees are conferred in business, 13% in social sciences, and 12% in education.

Required: All students must complete course work in religion, philosophy, psychology, fine arts, foreign languages or cultures, history, mathematics, social sciences, natural sciences, and physical education.

Special: A 3-2 engineering program, a preprofessional program in the ministry, and a 3-year bachelor's degree are offered. Additional minors are offered in economics, German, philosophy, and theater.

Honors: Four honor societies have chapters on campus.

Admissions: About 94% of the applicants for the 1981–82 freshman class were accepted. The SAT scores of those who enrolled were as follows: Verbal—85% below 500, 8% between 500 and 599, and 0% above 600; Math—77% below 500, 15% between 500 and 599, 7% between 600 and 700, and 1% above 700. Candidates should rank in the top half of their high school class, have a 2.0 GPA, and have completed 16 units of work. Recommendations, advanced placement or honors courses, and extracurricular activities are also considered.

Procedure: Either the SAT or ACT is required. Students are admitted each semester; application deadlines are open. Notification is made on a rolling basis. There is a $15 application fee.

Special: Early and deferred admissions plans are offered. AP and CLEP credit is available.

Transfer: Transfers are accepted for all 4 years. A 2.0 GPA is recommended; D grades do not transfer. Students must earn at least 30 credits in residence of the 128 required for a bachelor's degree.

Visiting: An orientation program is held for prospective students. Campus tours with guides can be arranged with the admissions office. Visitors may sit in on classes and stay overnight at the school. Visits are best scheduled on weekdays.

Financial Aid: About 85% of the students receive aid. The college offers freshman scholarships, loans, grants, and campus jobs. The average award to a freshman in 1981–82 was $2000. Either the FFS or FAF is acceptable. Aid applications should be filed by May 1 for priority consideration.

Foreign Students: Students from foreign countries represent 6% of enrollment. The college offers these students an intensive English course, special counseling, and special organizations.

Admissions: Applicants must score 500 or better on the TOEFL. No college entrance exams are required.

Procedure: The application deadline for fall admission is July 1. Foreign students also are admitted in the spring. Students must submit a physician's statement as proof of good health and must show evidence of adequate funds for 1 year. Health insurance is required, and is available through the college for a fee.

Admissions Contact: Tommy Dent, Director of Admissions.

NORTH CAROLINA AGRICULTURAL D-2
AND TECHNICAL STATE UNIVERSITY
Greensboro, North Carolina 27411 (919) 379-7946

F/T: 2604M, 1859W	Faculty:	352; IIA, av$
P/T: 252M, 195W	Ph.D.'s:	56%
Grad: 269M, 271W	S/F Ratio:	16 to 1
Year: sems, ss	Tuition:	$799 ($2587)
Appl: June 1	R and B:	$1574
2549 applied	1860 accepted	1194 enrolled
SAT: 313V 354M		LESS COMPETITIVE

North Carolina Agricultural and Technical State University was founded in 1891 and granted university status in 1967. It is a state-supported liberal arts and professional-technical institution. The library contains over 433,000 volumes, and subscribes to over 1400 periodicals.

Environment: The 181-acre campus is located in a suburban environment near downtown Greensboro (pop. 156,000), 80 miles west of Raleigh. There are over 50 main buildings including 9 dormitories, which accommodate 1500 men and 1000 women. The university also owns a 600-acre experimental farm which is used for the agricultural program and for recreation.

Student Life: About 75% of the students are from North Carolina; 90% are from the South. A majority (86%) of the students are black; virtually all students are minority-group members. About 52% live on campus. Campus housing is single-sex; there are visiting privileges. Students may keep cars on campus. Day-care services are available to all students, faculty, and staff for a fee.

Organizations: Ten percent of the women belong to sororities; 5% of the men are members of fraternities. Extracurricular activities include dances, socials, athletic events, concerts, and movies. There are religious facilities on campus for Catholic and Protestant students.

Sports: The university fields 7 intercollegiate teams for men and 5 for women. There are 15 intramural sports for men and 14 for women.

Graduates: About 10% of the students drop out by the end of the freshman year; 55% remain to graduate. About 10% of the graduates pursue advanced degrees.

Services: Placement and career counseling are provided to all students free of charge. Health care and remedial instruction are available on a fee basis.

Programs of Study: The university confers the B.A. and B.S. degrees. Master's programs are also available. Bachelor's degrees are offered in the following subjects: BUSINESS (accounting, business administration, business education, computer science, economics, transportation), EDUCATION (early childhood, driver and safety, health/physical, industrial arts, industrial technology, recreation and leisure services, secondary), ENGLISH (English, speech), FINE AND PERFORMING ARTS (art, art education, music, music education, studio art, theater/dramatics), HEALTH SCIENCES (nursing), LANGUAGES (French), MATH AND SCIENCES (biology, chemistry, food sciences, mathematics, physics), PREPROFESSIONAL (agriculture, engineering—architectural, engineering—electrical, engineering—industrial, engineering—mechanical, engineering—mathematics, engineering—physics, home economics, social work), SOCIAL SCIENCES (government/political science, history, psychology, sociology).

Required: Students are required to take courses in health and physical education.

Special: Independent study, exchange programs, cooperative work-study, and study abroad are offered.

Honors: Ten honor societies have chapters on campus.

Admissions: About 73% of those who applied were accepted for the 1981–82 freshman class. All candidates must be high school graduates with 16 Carnegie units. Class rank (upper 60%), GPA (at least 2.0), recommendations, extracurricular activities, leadership potential, advanced placement or honor courses, and the reputation and accreditation of the candidate's high school are all considered in the admissions decision. Preference is given to state residents.

Procedure: Either the ACT or SAT is required. Application deadlines are June 1 (fall) and December 1 (spring). Notification is on a rolling basis. Freshmen are also admitted at midyear and in the summer. There is a $15 application fee.

Special: There is an early decision plan. AP and CLEP credit is available.

Transfer: Transfer students are accepted for all classes. A 2.0 GPA is required; grades of C or better transfer. Students must complete at least one-half of their major at the university; 124 credits are required to earn the bachelor's degree. Application deadlines are the same as those for freshmen.

Financial Aid: About 80% of the students receive financial aid; 3% work part-time on campus. Scholarships, grants, loans (from the federal and state governments, the university, and private funds), and campus employment (including CWS) are available. Applications for financial aid should be submitted by May 15. The FAF or FFS is required from all aid applicants.

Foreign Students: About 8% of the students come from foreign countries. The university offers these students special counseling and special organizations.

Admissions: Foreign students must achieve a minimum TOEFL score of 550; in addition, applicants for the nursing and engineering programs must take the SAT.

Procedure: Application deadlines are June 1 (fall) and December 1 (spring). Foreign students must present proof of health as well as proof of adequate funds. They must also carry health insurance, which is available through the university.

Admissions Contact: Clenton A. Blount, Jr., Director of Admissions.

NORTH CAROLINA CENTRAL UNIVERSITY   D-2
Durham, North Carolina 27707   (919) 683-6298

F/T: 1347M, 2082W   Faculty: 329; IIA, +$
P/T: 195M, 386W   Ph.D.'s: 46%
Grad: 373M, 534W   S/F Ratio: 16 to 1
Year: sems, ss   Tuition: $682 ($2470)
Appl: June 1   R and B: $1662
1551 applied   1321 accepted   989 enrolled
SAT: 650 (composite)   LESS COMPETITIVE

North Carolina Central University, established in 1909, is a state-supported university that offers a wide range of programs in liberal arts and in professional and technical fields. The library has more than 400,000 books and 26,400 microfilm items, and subscribes to 2500 periodicals.

Environment: The 109-acre campus, located in a city of 100,000 people, has 40 buildings, including 7 dormitories that house 1500 women and 1 dormitory that houses 660 men.

Student Life: About 90% of the students are from the South. The student body is predominantly black. Sixty-five percent of the students live on campus in the single-sex dormitories.

Organizations: Eight fraternities and 10 sororities have chapters on campus. Extracurricular activities include publications, special-interest and departmental clubs, music groups, religious organizations, and student government.

Sports: The university fields intercollegiate teams in 8 sports each for men and women. Intramural sports also are available.

Handicapped: The entire campus is accessible to physically handicapped students. Wheelchair ramps and special parking areas are provided.

Graduates: The freshman dropout rate is 12%.

Services: Career counseling and placement services are provided free. Health care and tutoring also are offered. Placement services are available to graduates.

Programs of Study: The university confers the B.A., B.S., B.S.N., B.B.A., B.S.H.E., and B.Mus. degrees. Master's degrees are also awarded. Bachelor's degrees are offered in the following subjects: AREA STUDIES (Black/Afro-American), BUSINESS (accounting, business administration, business education, finance), EDUCATION (early childhood, elementary, health/physical, intermediate, recreation, secondary), ENGLISH (English), FINE AND PERFORMING ARTS (art, music, theater/dramatics), HEALTH SCIENCES (nursing), LANGUAGES (French, German, Spanish), MATH AND SCIENCES (biology, chemistry, mathematics, physics), PHILOSOPHY (philosophy), PREPROFESSIONAL (home economics), SOCIAL SCIENCES (economics, geography, government/political science, history, psychology, sociology).

Required: All students must take freshman English as well as a distribution of courses in 7 areas of study.

Special: Students may earn 3-2 dual degrees in several fields in conjunction with the Georgia Institute of Technology.

Admissions: About 85% of the applicants for the 1981–82 freshman class were accepted. A GPA of at least C+ is required. Preference is given to state residents.

Procedure: Applicants must take the SAT or the ACT. Application deadlines are June 1 (fall) and October 1 (spring). Notification is made on a rolling basis. There is a $10 application fee.

Special: AP and CLEP credit is accepted.

Transfer: Over 200 transfer students are accepted each year. A 2.0 GPA is required. Grades below 2.0 do not transfer. Students must spend at least 1 year in residence, earning 30 of the 124 credits required for a bachelor's degree.

Visiting: Informal campus tours with student guides can be arranged. Visitors may attend classes and stay overnight in the dormitories. There is an orientation program in July for new students.

Financial Aid: About 88% of the students receive aid. The university offers scholarships, grants (BEOG/SEOG), campus employment (including CWS), and a variety of government and commercial loans (including NDSL). Need and academic merit are the determining factors. The FFS should be filed by May 1 (fall) or October 1 (spring).

Foreign Students: Students from foreign countries make up about 1% of the student body. The university offers these students special counseling and special organizations.

Admissions: Applicants must take the TOEFL and the SAT.

Procedure: Foreign students are admitted to all terms; the application deadline for fall is July 1. Students must submit a completed health form and present proof of adequate funds for 4 years. They are required to carry health insurance, which is available through the university.

Admissions Contact: Nancy Rowland, Director of Admissions.

NORTH CAROLINA SCHOOL OF THE ARTS   C-2
Winston-Salem, North Carolina 27117   (919) 784-7170

F/T: 272M, 216W   Faculty: 81; IV, +$
P/T: 10M, 7W   Ph.D.'s: 12%
Grad: none   S/F Ratio: 6 to 1
Year: tri, ss   Tuition: $981 ($2505)
Appl: see profile   R and B: $1855
486 applied   253 accepted   114 enrolled
SAT: 434V 452M   SPECIAL

638 NORTH CAROLINA

North Carolina School of the Arts, a state-related institution established in 1963, offers professional training in the fine, performing, and commercial arts. Its library holds 54,000 books, 2500 microfilm items, 22,000 music scores, and 23,000 recordings, and subscribes to 350 periodicals.

Environment: The 30-acre campus, located in an urban area, has 11 buildings, including 6 dormitories that accommodate 300 men and women.

Student Life: About 40% of the students come from North Carolina; 90% attended public schools. About 85% live on campus. About 13% of the students are minority-group members. Campus housing is coed. Students may keep cars on campus.

Organizations: There are no sororities or fraternities. Extracurricular activities are limited.

Sports: There is no organized athletic program, but there are facilities available for several sports.

Handicapped: About 10% of the campus is accessible to physically handicapped students. Special facilities include wheelchair ramps, parking areas, and elevators in the Workplace Building and the Administration Building.

Services: Psychological counseling, career counseling, placement, and remedial instruction are provided free of charge. Health care and tutoring are available on a fee basis.

Programs of Study: The B.F.A. or B.M. degree is offered in the following subjects: FINE AND PERFORMING ARTS (dance, music, theater/dramatics, theatrical design/technical production).

Required: All students must take 3 terms of freshman English.

Special: There are work-study options. Many design and production apprenticeships are possible.

Honors: There are no honors programs.

Admissions: About 52% of the 1981-82 applicants were accepted. A 2.0 high school GPA is recommended. Applicants must present evidence of special talents (portfolio or audition). Personality and recommendations are also considered important.

Procedure: The SAT or ACT is required. Applicants must attend scheduled auditions which usually end in late April or early May. New students are admitted each term if there are openings; the drama department does not enroll students at midyear. There are no application deadlines. There is a $15 application fee.

Special: There is an early admissions plan. CLEP is used.

Transfer: For fall 1981, 271 transfer students applied, 174 were accepted, and 103 enrolled. Special talents and good academic standing are required. Grades of C or better transfer. The number of credits required for the bachelor's degree varies with the major department. Application deadlines are the same as for freshmen.

Visiting: Informal campus tours with student guides can be arranged on weekdays.

Financial Aid: About 68% of the students receive some assistance. Freshman scholarships, various loans (government and commercial, including NDSL), grants (BEOG/SEOG), and part-time work opportunities (CWS included) are offered. The average award to freshmen from all sources is $1600. The school is a member of CSS; the FAF or FFS should be filed by March 15.

Foreign Students: About 2% of the students come from foreign countries.

Admissions: Foreign students must take the TOEFL; no college entrance exams are required.

Procedure: Application deadlines are the same as for all other students. Foreign students must present the school's official health examination report as well as proof of funds adequate to cover the entire length of their enrollment.

Admissions Contact: Dirk Dawson, Director of Admissions.

NORTH CAROLINA STATE UNIVERSITY D-2
Raleigh, North Carolina 27650   (919) 737-2434

F/T: 9694M, 4448W   Faculty: 1337; I, av$
P/T: 1590M, 1345W   Ph.D.'s: 71%
Grad: 2611M, 1866W   S/F Ratio: 14 to 1
Year: sems, ss   Tuition: $780 ($2604)
Appl: May 1   R and B: $2000
7935 applied   4938 accepted   2937 enrolled
SAT: 464V 536M   COMPETITIVE

North Carolina State University, founded in 1887, is a state-supported unit of the University of North Carolina. The major objective of the university's 8 degree-granting schools is to provide students with an opportunity to obtain the highest level of scientific and technical training as well as a broad general education. The library contains 920,000 volumes and 1 million microfilm items, and subscribes to 7000 periodicals.

Environment: The 600-acre campus, located in an urban area, has 120 major buildings. The engineering school possesses 2 nuclear reactors. A new school of veterinary medicine was completed in 1981. Dormitories accommodate 6021 students, apartments accommodate 331 married students, and fraternities and sororities house 1113. In addition to the university's holdings in the Raleigh area, the Agricultural Experiment Station operates test farms in 16 different parts of the state, and the School of Forestry has large holdings of experimental woodlands in each of the state's main geographical regions.

Student Life: Approximately 85% of the students are from North Carolina. About 26% live on campus. About 11% of the students are minority-group members. Campus housing is coed and single-sex; there are visiting privileges. Students may keep cars on campus.

Organizations: Fourteen percent of the men belong to the 22 national fraternities with chapters on campus; 14% of the women belong to the 5 national sororities. Extracurricular activities include concert and lecture series, glee club, band organizations, an extensive fine arts series, and religious facilities for the 3 major faiths.

Sports: The university fields 15 intercollegiate teams for men and 12 for women. There are 17 intramural sports for men and 16 for women.

Handicapped: Facilities for the physically handicapped include wheelchair ramps, special parking, elevators, and specially equipped rest rooms; special class scheduling is also available.

Graduates: The freshman dropout rate is 17%; 58% remain to graduate. About 28% of those who graduate pursue graduate study.

Services: Placement services, career counseling, health care, psychological counseling, and remedial instruction are offered free of charge; tutoring is available on a fee basis.

Programs of Study: The university confers the B.A. and B.S. degrees. Associate, master's, and doctoral programs are also offered. Bachelor's degrees are offered in the following subjects: AREA STUDIES (American, Asian, Latin American, Russian), BUSINESS (accounting, computer science, management), EDUCATION (agricultural, elementary, health, industrial, industrial arts, secondary, technical), ENGLISH (English, speech, writing-editing), LANGUAGES (French, Spanish), MATH AND SCIENCES (agricultural economics, agronomy, animal science, biochemistry, biology, botany, chemistry, conservation, crop science, food science, geology, horticultural pest management, mathematics, meteorology, physical sciences, physics, poultry science, recreation resource administration, soil science, statistics, wood science, zoology), PHILOSOPHY (philosophy), PREPROFESSIONAL (agriculture, architecture, dentistry, engineering—aerospace, engineering—chemical, engineering—civil, engineering—electrical, engineering—industrial, engineering—materials, engineering—mechanical, engineering—nuclear, engineering operations, forestry, furniture manufacturing and management, landscape architecture, medicine, product and visual design, social work, textile chemistry, textile management, textile science, veterinary), SOCIAL SCIENCES (economics, government/political science, history, psychology, sociology).

Required: All students must take courses in English, math, history, and physical education.

Special: Under an interinstitutional agreement with Meredith College, St. Augustine's College, and Shaw University, undergraduates may take any course at the individual college that is not taught at NCSU. Study-abroad opportunities in England and Spain are available.

Honors: Two national honor societies have chapters on campus. Honors programs featuring special advising, research, and courses are offered by each department.

Admissions: Approximately 62% of those who applied were accepted for the 1981-82 freshman class. The SAT scores of those who enrolled were as follows: Verbal—65% below 500, 28% between 500 and 599, 6% between 600 and 700, and 1% above 700; Math—31% below 500, 43% between 500 and 599, 23% between 600 and 700, and 3% above 700. The admissions decision is based on the student's high school record and test scores. Advanced placement or honors courses, recommendations, and evidence of special talent are also considered important.

Procedure: The SAT or ACT is required, and should be taken by December of the senior year. ATs are recommended, but are not used in admissions decisions. The application deadline for fall entry is May

1; for spring entry, November 1. Admissions are on a rolling basis. There is a $15 application fee.

Special: There is an early decision plan. AP and CLEP credit is accepted.

Transfer: For fall 1981, 2302 transfer students applied, 1307 were accepted, and 838 enrolled. A 2.0 GPA is required; some programs may require a higher GPA. Grades of C and above transfer. Twenty-four of the last 30 credits must be completed at the university. The bachelor's degree requires at least 124 credits. Deadlines are the same as those for freshmen.

Visiting: There are regularly scheduled orientations for prospective students. Guides are also available for informal visits; visitors may sit in on classes with the instructor's approval. The admissions office should be contacted to arrange visits.

Financial Aid: Approximately 30% of all students receive some form of financial aid, which is awarded on the basis of need, academic achievement and potential, character, and leadership ability. The university grants approximately 3000 financial awards each year. The average award to freshmen from all sources is $1780. CWS is available in 44 departments. The university is a member of CSS; the FAF is required. Financial aid applications should be filed by March 1.

Foreign Students: About 3% of the students come from foreign countries. The university offers these students an intensive English course, an intensive English program, special counseling, and special organizations.

Admissions: Foreign students must take the TOEFL; it is also recommended that they take ATs in math (Level I), chemistry, and/or biology and physics.

Procedure: The application deadline is March 1 for fall. Foreign students must present proof of health as well as proof of funds adequate to cover 4 years of study. Foreign students must also carry health insurance.

Admissions Contact: Anna P. Keller, Director of Admissions.

NORTH CAROLINA WESLEYAN COLLEGE   E-2
Rocky Mount, North Carolina 27801   (919) 442-7121

F/T: 349M, 277W	Faculty: 47; IIB, — $
P/T: 163M, 128W	Ph.D.'s: 55%
Grad: 70M, 56W	S/F Ratio: 13 to 1
Year: sems, ss	Tuition: $3300
Appl: Sept. 1	R and B: $1740
288 applied	278 accepted 130 enrolled
SAT: 400V 400M	**LESS COMPETITIVE**

North Carolina Wesleyan College is a private liberal arts college affiliated with the Methodist Church. The library contains 60,000 volumes and 35,000 microfilm items, and subscribes to 600 periodicals.

Environment: The 200-acre campus, located in a suburban area 60 miles east of Raleigh, includes dormitories housing 40% of the students.

Student Life: Seventy-five percent of the students are from North Carolina; 80% come from public schools. About 40% of the students live on campus. About 73% are Protestant, 8% are Catholic, and 1% are Jewish. About 21% are minority-group members. Campus housing is single-sex; there are visiting privileges. Students may keep cars on campus.

Organizations: There are 3 local fraternities, to which 10% of the men belong; 10% of the women belong to 2 local sororities. There are several religious and social clubs on campus, as well as a wide variety of extracurricular activities.

Sports: The college fields 5 intercollegiate teams for men and 3 for women. There are 7 intramural sports for men and 7 for women.

Handicapped: Approximately 90% of the campus is accessible to the physically handicapped. Facilities include wheelchair ramps and elevators.

Graduates: The freshman dropout rate is 25%; 35% remain to graduate. Thirty-five percent of those who graduate pursue graduate study: 1% enter medical school, 1% dental school, and 1% law school; 35% pursue careers in business and industry.

Services: Placement services, career counseling, psychological counseling, tutoring, and remedial instruction are offered to students free of charge. Health care is available on a fee basis.

NORTH CAROLINA 639

Programs of Study: The B.A. or B.S. degree is offered in the following subjects: BUSINESS (accounting, business administration, management), EDUCATION (early childhood, elementary, secondary), ENGLISH (English), FINE AND PERFORMING ARTS (music, music education, theater/dramatics), MATH AND SCIENCES (biology, chemistry, ecology/environmental science, mathematics), PHILOSOPHY (philosophy, religion), SOCIAL SCIENCES (economics, government/political science, history, psychology, sociology). About 35% of degrees are conferred in business, and 15% in education.

Required: Three semester hours of religion are required.

Special: Student-designed majors, a general studies degree, and study-abroad programs are possible. The 3-track program offers the choice of a conventional liberal arts program, half of the student's work in nontraditional courses, or student-designed programs.

Honors: Three national honor societies have chapters on campus.

Admissions: Approximately 97% of those who applied were accepted for the 1981–82 freshman class. The SAT scores of those who enrolled were as follows: Verbal—93% below 500, 6% between 500 and 599, 1% between 600 and 700, and 0% above 700; Math—87% below 500, 12% between 500 and 599, 1% between 600 and 700, and 0% above 700. Applicants should have completed 16 academic units at an accredited high school. Candidates usually rank in the top half of their class and have a minimum GPA of 2.0. Other factors entering into the admissions decision are advanced placement or honors courses, recommendations by school officials, and impressions made during an interview.

Procedure: The SAT or ACT is required. Application deadlines are September 1 (fall), January 1 (spring) and June 1 (summer); an earlier date is suggested for residential students. There is a $15 application fee. The college follows a rolling admissions policy.

Special: There are early admissions and deferred admissions plans. AP and CLEP credit is accepted.

Transfer: For fall 1981, 235 transfer students applied, 227 were accepted, and 169 enrolled. Transfers are considered for all classes. A minimum 2.0 GPA is required; a 2.5 GPA is recommended. Grades of C and above transfer. All students must complete, at the college, 24 of the 124 credits required for a bachelor's degree. Deadlines are the same as those for freshman applicants.

Visiting: There are regularly scheduled orientations for prospective students. Guides are also available for informal visits on weekday mornings; visitors may sit in on classes and stay overnight at the school. The admissions office should be contacted to arrange visits.

Financial Aid: Approximately 85% of all students receive some form of financial aid; 30% of the students work part-time on campus. Scholarships, loans, and part-time employment are available. The average award to freshmen from all sources is $2500. The college is a member of CSS; the FAF or FFS is required. The deadline for aid applications is May 1.

Foreign Students: About 1% of the students come from foreign countries.

Admissions: Foreign students must achieve a minimum TOEFL score of 500; in addition, they must also take the college's own entrance exam.

Procedure: Application deadlines are May 1 (fall) and November 1 (spring). Foreign students must present proof of health as well as proof of funds adequate to cover 1 year of study. There is a $10 processing fee.

Admissions Contact: R. Richard Davis, Director of Admissions.

PEMBROKE STATE UNIVERSITY   D-3
Pembroke, North Carolina 28372   (919) 521-4214

F/T: 756M, 902W	Faculty: 118; IIB, + + $
P/T: 116M, 225W	Ph.D.'s: 58%
Grad: 44M, 135W	S/F Ratio: 16 to 1
Year: sems, ss	Tuition: $548 ($2130)
Appl: June 30	R and B: $1210
709 applied	613 accepted 417 enrolled
SAT: 390V 419M	**LESS COMPETITIVE**

Pembroke State University is a publicly supported university of liberal arts and sciences providing liberal arts, teacher education, and professional programs. The library contains 170,000 volumes, and subscribes to 800 periodicals.

Environment: The 100-acre campus, located in a rural area 35 miles from Fayetteville, provides housing facilities for 400 women and 434 men. The gymnasium houses an Olympic-size swimming pool. There

640 NORTH CAROLINA

is also an educational center, a performing arts center, and a communicative arts building.

Student Life: Approximately 90% of the students are from North Carolina. About 75% come from public schools. Thirty-one percent of the students live on campus. About 37% are minority-group members. University housing is single-sex; there are visiting privileges. Students may keep cars on campus.

Organizations: There are 4 fraternities, to which 10% of the men belong; 10% of the women belong to the 3 sororities. There is an active student government, as well as many other organizations and activities, including dances, an arts series, a lyceum series, and numerous clubs.

Sports: The university competes in 8 intercollegiate sports for men and 3 for women. There are 6 intramural sports for men and 5 for women.

Handicapped: The entire campus is accessible to the physically handicapped. Facilities include wheelchair ramps, special parking, elevators, specially equipped rest rooms, and lowered drinking fountains.

Graduates: In a recent year, the freshman dropout rate was 28%; 30% remained to graduate. About 5% of those who graduated pursued graduate study; 93% pursued careers in business and industry.

Services: Placement services, career counseling, psychological counseling, tutoring, remedial instruction, and health care are offered to students free of charge.

Programs of Study: The B.A. or B.S. degree is offered. There are also master's programs. Bachelor's degrees are offered in the following subjects: AREA STUDIES (American Indian), BUSINESS (accounting, business administration, business education, management), EDUCATION (early childhood, elementary, health/physical, secondary), ENGLISH (English), FINE AND PERFORMING ARTS (art, art education, music, music education), HEALTH SCIENCES (medical technology), MATH AND SCIENCES (biochemistry, biology, chemistry, mathematics), PHILOSOPHY (philosophy), SOCIAL SCIENCES (economics, government/political science, history, psychology, sociology). About 38% of degrees are conferred in education and 35% in social sciences.

Required: All students must take courses in art or music; laboratory sciences; English; history; math; philosophy, psychology, or religion; health; and social science.

Special: A college opportunity program for disadvantaged students, combined B.A.-B.S. 5-year programs, and student-designed majors are offered.

Honors: Three national honor societies have chapters on campus.

Admissions: About 86% of those who applied were accepted for the 1981–82 freshman class. The SAT scores of those who enrolled were as follows: Verbal—95% below 500, 5% between 500 and 599, 0% between 600 and 700, and 0% above 700; Math—90% below 500, 9% between 500 and 599, 1% between 600 and 700, and 0% above 700. Candidates should rank in the top half of their class and have a minimum 2.0 GPA. Other factors influencing the admissions decision are advanced placement or honors courses, recommendations, the applicant's extracurricular activities record, and impressions made during an interview.

Procedure: The SAT or ACT is required. The deadlines for admission are June 30 (fall), December 1 (spring), and April 15 (summer). The university follows a rolling admissions policy. There is a $15 application fee.

Special: There are early decision and early admissions plans. CLEP credit is accepted.

Transfer: For fall 1981, 263 students applied, 218 were accepted, and 175 enrolled. A minimum 2.0 GPA is required. There is a 1-year residency requirement. Thirty credits must be completed in residence of the 120 needed for a bachelor's degree. The application deadline is June 30 (fall).

Visiting: There are regularly scheduled orientations for prospective students. Guides are also available for informal visits. Visitors may sit in on classes and stay overnight at the school. The admissions office should be contacted to arrange visits.

Financial Aid: Approximately 60% of all students receive financial aid, which is available in the form of scholarships and loans (including NDSL). Ten percent work part-time on campus. CWS is available in all departments. The university is a member of CSS. The FAF is required. Applications must be filed by April 15 (fall and summer) and November 15 (spring).

Foreign Students: One percent of the full-time students come from foreign countries. The university offers these students special counseling.

Admissions: Foreign students must take the TOEFL. They must also take the SAT or the ACT; they must have a composite score of 750 on the SAT.

Procedure: The application deadlines are June 30 (fall), December 15 (spring), and April 30 (summer). Foreign students must present proof of health and proof of funds adequate to cover 1 year of study.

Admissions Contact: Warren Baker, Director of Admissions.

PFEIFFER COLLEGE C–2
Misenheimer, North Carolina 28109 (704) 463-7343

F/T: 368M, 327W	Faculty: 46; IIB, –$
P/T: 59M, 46W	Ph.D.'s: n/av
Grad: 427M, 373W	S/F Ratio: 15 to 1
Year: sems, ss	Tuition: $3025
Appl: July 1	R and B: $1565
506 applied	447 accepted	188 enrolled
SAT: 392V 436M		LESS COMPETITIVE

Pfeiffer College, established in 1885, is a private coeducational liberal arts college affiliated with the United Methodist Church. The library contains 93,000 volumes and 7400 microform items, and subscribes to 460 periodicals.

Environment: The 365-acre campus, located in a rural area 40 miles northeast of Charlotte, includes a student center, a science building, and a gymnasium-swimming pool complex. Five dormitories accommodate 420 men and 380 women; apartments for married students are also available.

Student Life: Approximately 80% of the students are from the South. Ninety-five percent come from public schools. Seventy-one percent live on campus. Nine percent of the students are Catholic, 79% Protestant, and fewer than 1% Jewish. Twelve percent of the students are minority-group members. College housing is single-sex; there are visiting privileges. Students may keep cars on campus.

Organizations: There are no fraternities or sororities. There are 38 clubs and organizations on campus, including student government, special-interest groups, and religious organizations.

Sports: The college competes intercollegiately in 8 sports for men and 7 for women. There are 6 intramural sports for both men and women.

Handicapped: There are no special facilities for the physically handicapped.

Graduates: Twenty percent of the freshmen drop out by the end of their first year. Fifty percent remain to graduate. Twenty-five percent of those who graduate pursue advanced study; 1% enter medical school, 1% dental school, and 2% law school. Thirty percent pursue careers in business and industry.

Services: Placement services, career counseling, psychological counseling, tutoring, and remedial instruction are offered free of charge. Health care is available on a fee basis.

Programs of Study: The B.A. and B.S. degrees are conferred. Bachelor's degrees are offered in the following subjects: AREA STUDIES (American, British), BUSINESS (accounting, business administration, real estate/insurance), EDUCATION (early childhood, elementary, health/physical, secondary), ENGLISH (English), FINE AND PERFORMING ARTS (art administration, music, music education, theater/dramatics), HEALTH SCIENCES (allied health sciences, medical technology), MATH AND SCIENCES (biology, chemistry, mathematics, physical sciences, physics), PHILOSOPHY (religion), PREPROFESSIONAL (dentistry, engineering, medicine, social work), SOCIAL SCIENCES (economics, history, psychology, sociology).

Required: All students must take the GRE to fulfill graduation requirements.

Special: The college offers a dual degree nursing program with Case Western Reserve University, a 3-2 engineering program with Auburn University and Georgia Institute of Technology, and a 2-3 nursing program with Emory University.

Honors: All departments offer honors programs. The college has a liberal arts program that allows qualified students to engage in independent study projects and honors work in almost any course beyond the survey level. Evaluation of student progress is in terms of units rather than letter grades, which allows the student to accelerate his or her graduation.

Admissions: Approximately 88% of those who applied were accepted for the 1981–82 freshman class. The SAT scores of those who enrolled were as follows: Verbal—84% below 500, 7% between 500 and 599, 2% between 600 and 700, and 0% above 700; Math—68% below 500, 20% between 500 and 599, 4% between 600 and 700, and 0% above 700. Candidates should be high school graduates, rank in the top half of their class, have a minimum 2.0 GPA, and present 16 units of work. Veterans with 1 or more years of active service are considered on an individual basis; for such candidates a GED certificate will be accepted in lieu of a regular high school diploma.

Procedure: The SAT is required for all but transfer students. The application deadline is July 1 (fall). The college follows a rolling admissions policy. There is a $15 application fee.

Special: There are early and deferred admissions plans. AP and CLEP credit is accepted.

Transfer: For fall 1981, 121 transfer applications were received, 105 were accepted and 96 students enrolled. Transfers are accepted for all classes. An associate degree or a 2.0 GPA is required. D grades transfer. A minimum of 3 semesters must be completed in residence. Forty-five semester hours must be completed out of the 129 needed to receive a bachelor's degree. The application deadline is July 1 (fall).

Visiting: Guides are available for campus visits when classes are in session. Visitors may sit in on classes and stay overnight at the school. The student recruitment office should be contacted to arrange visits.

Financial Aid: Ninety-two percent of the students receive some form of financial aid. Scholarships, loans, and work-study are available. Forty-five percent work part-time on campus. Average aid to freshmen from all sources covers 75% of fees. About 60 competitive scholarships are available to entering students. A special scholarship series is offered for graduates of 2-year colleges. The college is a member of CSS. The FAF, FFS, or SFS can be submitted. The FFS is preferred. The deadline for financial aid applications is May 1 (fall); deadlines are open for winter, spring, or summer entry.

Foreign Students: One percent of the full-time students come from foreign countries. The college offers these students special counseling.

Admissions: Foreign students must score at least 550 on the TOEFL. They must also take the SAT.

Procedure: Application deadlines are open. Foreign students must present an affidavit of sufficient funds from their sponsor. They must also carry health insurance, which is available through the college for a fee.

Admissions Contact: Kenneth Sigler, Director of Admissions.

QUEENS COLLEGE   C-3
Charlotte, North Carolina 28274   (704) 332-7121

F/T: 413W	Faculty: 52; IIB, av$
P/T: 93M, 441W	Ph.D.'s: 54%
Grad: 85M, 36W	S/F Ratio: 8 to 1
Year: 4-1-4, ss	Tuition: $3750
Appl: open	R and B: $2110
444 applied	329 accepted	223 enrolled
SAT: 465V 445M		COMPETITIVE

Queens College is a small college affiliated with the Presbyterian Church. It offers undergraduate instruction for women primarily in the liberal arts and sciences. The library contains 100,000 books and more than 2600 microtexts, and subscribes to 600 periodicals.

Environment: The 35-acre campus is located in a suburban area. It has 28 buildings including 4 dormitories that house 500 women.

Student Life: About 55% of the students come from North Carolina. Sixty percent attended public schools; 60% live on campus. About 73% are Protestant, and 11% are Catholic. About 6% are members of minority groups. Campus housing is single-sex. Students may keep cars on campus.

Organizations: Extracurricular activities include clubs, religious groups, student government, and social events. Forty percent of the women belong to 4 national sororities.

Sports: Intercollegiate teams are fielded in 2 sports. There is 1 intramural sport.

Handicapped: Special facilities for physically handicapped students include wheelchair ramps, parking areas, and elevators. Special class scheduling is also available. One percent of the students have hearing impairments; 1% have visual impairments.

Graduates: The freshman dropout rate is about 5%; about 58% remain to graduate. About 20% of the graduates go on for further education. Fifteen percent enter business and industry.

Services: Career counseling, placement, health care, psychological counseling, and some remedial instruction are provided free of charge. Tutoring and some remedial instruction are available for a fee.

Programs of Study: The college awards the B.A., B.S., B.M., and B.G.S. degrees. Master's degree programs are also available. Bachelor's degrees are offered in the following subjects: AREA STUDIES (American, European, Latin American), BUSINESS (business, business/foreign language), EDUCATION (early childhood, elementary, religious), ENGLISH (English), FINE AND PERFORMING ARTS (art, music), HEALTH SCIENCES (medical technology, nuclear medical technology, nursing, radiological technology, speech therapy), LANGUAGES (French, Spanish), MATH AND SCIENCES (biochemistry, biology, computer science, mathematics), SOCIAL SCIENCES (history, political science, psychology, public administration). About 25% of the degrees are conferred in social sciences, and 19% in education.

Required: All students are required to take 1 or 2 courses in each of the following areas: English, foreign language or mathematics, humanities, sciences, social sciences, and fine arts. There also are required leadership training seminars for freshmen.

Special: Study abroad, exchange programs, and internships are offered. It is possible to earn the B.G.S. degree.

Honors: There are 2 honor societies at the college.

Admissions: Of those who applied for the 1981–82 class, 74% were accepted. The SAT scores of those who enrolled were as follows: Verbal—74% below 500, 11% between 500 and 599, 6% between 600 and 700, and 0% above 700; Math—65% below 500, 22% between 500 and 599, 4% between 600 and 700, and 0% above 700. A 2.0 high school GPA is required. Other factors include advanced placement/honors courses, special talents, and leadership record.

Procedure: The SAT or the ACT is required. All application deadlines are open; a rolling admissions policy is used. Freshmen may enter in the fall, spring, or summer. There is a $15 application fee.

Special: CLEP and AP credit is available.

Transfer: For fall 1981, 173 transfer students applied, 151 were accepted, and 110 enrolled. Transfers are accepted to all but the senior class. A 2.0 GPA is required; D grades do not transfer. Sixty credits (2 years) must be completed at the college, of a total 122 credits required for the bachelor's degree. Application deadlines are open; however, August is suggested for fall, January for spring, and May for summer.

Visiting: There is an orientation program for prospective applicants. Informal campus tours with student guides can be arranged. Visitors may stay overnight at the school and sit in on classes.

Financial Aid: About 52% of the students are receiving aid. About 20% work part-time on campus. The average award to freshmen from all sources available through the college is $3200. Scholarships, campus jobs (CWS included), loans (NDSL included), and grants (BEOG/SEOG), are offered. Scholarships range up to $4200, loans to $2500, and jobs to $1000. The college is a CSS member. The FAF is due March 1 for priority consideration in the fall and June 1 for the spring.

Foreign Students: Students from other countries represent about 2% of the enrollment. Special counseling and organizations are available.

Admissions: The TOEFL is required; a minimum score of 550 is necessary. College entrance exams are not required.

Procedure: Foreign candidates should apply by August (fall), January (spring), and May (summer). The college health form must be completed. Proof of adequate funds to cover 4 years must be presented.

Admissions Contact: Gene H. Burton, Director of Admissions.

SACRED HEART COLLEGE   C-3
Belmont, North Carolina 28012   (704) 825-8468

F/T: 88M, 268W	Faculty: n/av; IIB, − −$
P/T: 18M, 45W	Ph.D.'s: 40%
Grad: none	S/F Ratio: 10 to 1
Year: sems, ss	Tuition: $2310
Appl: Aug. 1	R and B: $1400
162 applied	135 accepted	107 enrolled
SAT: 365V 447M	ACT: 18	LESS COMPETITIVE

Founded in 1892, Sacred Heart College is affiliated with the Roman Catholic Church and offers a traditional liberal arts and sciences undergraduate education. The library contains 59,000 volumes and 3100 microfilm items, and subscribes to 245 periodicals.

Environment: The 100-acre campus is located in a small town 10 miles from Charlotte. There are 15 buildings, including 2 dormitories housing 450 students.

Student Life: About 50% of the students come from North Carolina; 60% come from public schools. About 40% live on campus. Over 40% of the students are Catholic; there are no chapel attendance requirements.

642 NORTH CAROLINA

Organizations: There is a full extracurricular program including student government, special-interest clubs, and social and cultural events.

Sports: Both intramural and intercollegiate athletics are offered.

Services: The college provides career counseling, placement, health care, psychological counseling, tutoring, and remedial instruction free of charge to all students.

Programs of Study: The B.A. and B.S. degrees are conferred. Bachelor's degrees are offered in the following subjects: BUSINESS (accounting, business administration, distribution management, management), EDUCATION (early childhood, elementary, special), ENGLISH (English), FINE AND PERFORMING ARTS (art, art education, studio art), HEALTH SCIENCES (medical technology), MATH AND SCIENCES (biology, chemistry, ecology/environmental science), PREPROFESSIONAL (dentistry, law, medicine, social work), SOCIAL SCIENCES (criminal justice, economics, government/political science, history, psychology, sociology).

Required: All students must take courses in communication skills, philosophy, theology, physical education, and health.

Special: A general studies degree, a combination degree program in medical technology, and a special education degree are offered.

Admissions: About 83% of those who applied for the 1981-82 freshman class were accepted. Candidates should have a 2.0 high school GPA and present 16 Carnegie units. A student's leadership record and personal qualities also enter into the admissions decision.

Procedure: Either the SAT or ACT is required. August 1 is the fall deadline; new students are also admitted at midyear. Notification is on a rolling basis. There is a $15 application fee. An interview is recommended.

Special: There is a deferred admissions plan. AP and CLEP credit is available.

Transfer: About 30 transfer students enroll annually. A 2.0 GPA is required. Transfers are accepted for all 4 years. One semester must be completed in residence. Applications must be submitted 1 month before registration.

Visiting: Campus tours with student guides can be arranged.

Financial Aid: About 60% of the students receive financial aid. The college offers scholarships for freshmen, loans (government and commercial), grants, and part-time campus work opportunities (including CWS). Aid is usually packaged. The FAF is preferred but the FFS is accepted. The deadline for applying for financial aid is March 15.

Admissions Contact: Director of Admissions.

ST. ANDREWS PRESBYTERIAN COLLEGE   D-3
Laurinburg, North Carolina 28352   (919) 276-3652

F/T: 354M, 351W	Faculty:	54; IIB, av$
P/T: 27M, 39W	Ph.D.'s:	77%
Grad: none	S/F Ratio:	15 to 1
Year: 4-1-4, ss	Tuition:	$3950
Appl: open	R and B:	$1950
452 applied	353 accepted	179 enrolled
SAT: 444V 470M		COMPETITIVE

St. Andrews Presbyterian College, established in 1958, is a coeducational liberal arts college owned by the Synod of North Carolina Presbyterian Church. The library contains 93,000 volumes and 7500 microfilm items, and subscribes to 500 periodicals.

Environment: The campus, located in a rural area along the northern and southern shores of a 70-acre lake, includes 820 acres of rolling farmland. Seven dormitories accommodate 580 students.

Student Life: Most of the students are from the South and the Middle Atlantic states, with 62% from North Carolina. Seventy-five percent live on campus. Unless the dormitories are full, students must live on campus except when they live within commuting distance. Eighty percent are Protestant, and 8% are Catholic. Thirteen percent are minority-group members. Campus housing is both single-sex and coed; there are visiting privileges. Students may keep cars on campus.

Organizations: There are no fraternities or sororities. Extracurricular activities include musical and dramatic groups, publications, a campus radio station, departmental clubs, and a concert and lecture series. The Student Christian Council coordinates religious activities on campus.

Sports: The college competes intercollegiately in 7 sports for men and 5 for women. There is also an extensive intramural program, which includes 8 teams for men and 7 for women.

Handicapped: The entire campus is accessible to the physically handicapped. Facilities include wheelchair ramps and special parking.

Graduates: The freshman dropout rate is 15%; about 60% remain to graduate. Fifty percent of those who graduate pursue graduate study: 6% enter medical school, 10% allied health graduate school, and 6% law school.

Services: Placement services, career counseling, health care, and psychological counseling are available free of charge. Tutoring is available for a fee.

Programs of Study: The B.A. or B.S. degree is offered in the following subjects: BUSINESS (business administration, business chemistry, computer science), EDUCATION (early childhood, elementary, health/physical, secondary, special), ENGLISH (English, English/writing, literature), FINE AND PERFORMING ARTS (art, music, theater/dramatics), HEALTH SCIENCES (allied health, medical technology), LANGUAGES (French, modern languages), MATH AND SCIENCES (biology, business chemistry, chemical physics, chemistry, mathematics, mathematics/computer science), PHILOSOPHY (philosophy, religion), PREPROFESSIONAL (dentistry, engineering, law, medicine, ministry, pharmacy, veterinary), SOCIAL SCIENCES (economics, government/political science, history, psychology).

Required: All students must complete a 3-year interdepartmental program in world cultures and 5 breadth courses (1 each in the arts, humanities, laboratory sciences, physical education, and social sciences).

Special: Student-designed majors, internships for career exploration, independent study, credit by examination, a 3-2 engineering program with Georgia Tech, regular Monday night programs in the arts, and study abroad are offered. A combination degree program is available in medical technology.

Admissions: Approximately 78% of those who applied were accepted for the 1981-82 freshman class. The SAT scores of those who enrolled were as follows: Verbal—75% below 500, 19% between 500 and 599, 5% between 600 and 700, 1% above 700; Math—61% below 500, 31% between 500 and 599, 8% between 600 and 700, and 0% above 700. Candidates should be graduates of an accredited high school, have a minimum 2.0 GPA, and rank in the upper 50% of their class. Other factors entering into the admissions decision are the candidate's extracurricular activities record, leadership record, and evidence of special talents. The college admits a limited number of special students who have been graduated from secondary schools but are not candidates for a degree.

Procedure: The SAT is required and should be taken between March of the junior year and January of the senior year. Application deadlines are open; the college follows a rolling admissions policy. There is a $15 application fee.

Special: There are early admissions and deferred admissions plans. AP and CLEP credit is accepted.

Transfer: For fall 1981, 163 transfer applications were received, 125 were accepted, and 80 students enrolled. Transfers are accepted for all classes. A minimum 2.0 GPA is required; D grades do not transfer. There is a 1-year residency requirement. Transfers must take at least 9 courses at the college, of a total 37 courses required for the bachelor's degree. There are no application deadlines.

Financial Aid: Approximately 78% of all students receive some form of financial aid. About 24% work part-time on campus. Aid sources include the Presbyterian Prospective Teacher Loan Program of North Carolina, the North Carolina Bankers' Student Loan Plan, the St. Andrews College Loan Fund, NDSL, EOG, and CWS. Awards are usually a combination of scholarship, loan, and grant. Tuition may be paid in installments. The college is a CSS member. The FAF or FFS is required. The deadline for aid applications is January 1.

Foreign Students: About 2% of the full-time students come from foreign countries.

Admissions: The TOEFL is required. College entrance exams are not necessary.

Procedure: There are no application deadlines. Admissions are on a rolling basis. Proof of adequate funds to cover 1 year must be presented.

Admissions Contact: Peggy Anderson, Director of Admissions.

SAINT AUGUSTINE'S COLLEGE   D-2
Raleigh, North Carolina 27611   (919) 828-4451

F/T: 1708M&W	Faculty: 74; IIB, – –$
P/T: 350M&W	Ph.D.'s: n/av
Grad: none	S/F Ratio: 24 to 1
Year: sems, ss	Tuition: $2550
Appl: open	R and B: $1350
1100 applied	1000 accepted	620 enrolled
SAT: 600 (composite)		LESS COMPETITIVE

Saint Augustine's College, founded in 1867 as a college for blacks, is an independent, 4-year liberal arts institution affiliated with the Episcopal Church. The library contains more than 113,000 volumes, and subscribes to 500 periodicals. Special collections focus on black history and culture.

Environment: The 96-acre urban campus is located in the city of Raleigh. Six residence halls house nearly 800 men and women. College-owned apartments also are available near campus.

Student Life: Most students come from North Carolina, South Carolina, and Virginia. The student body is predominantly black. Attendance at daily religious services is encouraged.

Organizations: Four fraternities and 4 sororities have chapters on campus. Extracurricular organizations include numerous special-interest and departmental clubs, student government, service organizations, publications, and religious clubs.

Sports: The college fields intercollegiate teams in 7 sports. Intramural activities also are available.

Graduates: More than 50% of those who enter remain to graduate. Thirty-five percent of the graduates seek advanced degrees.

Services: Students pay a fee for health services. Psychological, academic, and vocational counseling are available free. Placement services are provided to both undergraduates and alumni.

Programs of Study: The college confers the B.A. and B.S. degrees. Bachelor's degrees are offered in the following subjects: AREA STUDIES (urban), BUSINESS (accounting, business administration, business education, industrial hygiene and safety, industrial mathematics, management), EDUCATION (early childhood, health/physical, intermediate), ENGLISH (English), FINE AND PERFORMING ARTS (art, music), HEALTH SCIENCES (allied health), LANGUAGES (French), MATH AND SCIENCES (biology, chemistry, mathematics, physics), PRE-PROFESSIONAL (engineering, law, medicine), SOCIAL SCIENCES (criminal justice, economics, government/political science, history, psychology, social sciences, sociology). Most degrees are granted in education.

Required: Students are required to take a number of basic courses in such subjects as English composition and speech, physical education, natural science, humanities, mathematics, psychology, world civilization, reading, and the origin of beliefs and ethics.

Special: Students may study abroad. A cooperative program with Shaw University and North Carolina State University allows cross-registration.

Honors: Thirteen honor societies have chapters on campus. A college honors program offers students advanced study, independent study, and participation in honors courses and seminars.

Admissions: About 91% of those who applied for admission to the 1981–82 freshman class were accepted. Twenty-five percent ranked in the top fifth of their high school class. Applicants must be high school graduates and have completed 16 Carnegie units with a GPA of at least C+. Recommendations from the candidate's school and other references are also considered.

Procedure: The SAT is required. Application deadlines are open. There is a $10 application fee.

Transfer: Applicants must be in good standing at their previous college. D grades do not transfer. Students must spend at least 30 semester hours in residence of the 120 required for a bachelor's degree.

Financial Aid: About 90% of the students receive aid. Loans, campus jobs (including CWS), grants (including BEOG), and scholarships are available. The average award to a 1981–82 freshman totaled $4900. Applications for scholarships should be submitted by April 15. Loan applications are due 30 days before the start of the semester.

Foreign Students: Foreign students at the college represent 16% of enrollment. The college offers these students special counseling and special organizations.

Admissions: Applicants must take the TOEFL and the SAT.

NORTH CAROLINA 643

Procedure: Application deadlines are open. Foreign students must submit a physician's statement as proof of good health and must provide evidence of adequate funds for 1 year.

Admissions Contact: Igal E. Spraggins, Director of Admissions.

SALEM COLLEGE   C-2
Winston-Salem, North Carolina 27108   (919) 721-2622

F/T: 1M, 565W	Faculty: 57; IIB, av$
P/T: 3M, 96W	Ph.D.'s: 55%
Grad: none	S/F Ratio: 9 to 1
Year: 4-1-4	Tuition: $3565
Appl: open	R and B: $2610
399 applied	325 accepted	170 enrolled
SAT: 471V 485M		COMPETITIVE

Salem College, founded in 1772 by the Moravians, has had a long tradition as a liberal arts college for women. The library contains 106,000 volumes and 7000 microfilm items, and subscribes to 400 periodicals.

Environment: The 56-acre wooded campus is situated in an urban residential area—the heart of the Old Salem Restoration area. There are 21 buildings. Seven dormitories can accommodate 510 women. The fine arts center is one of the most outstanding in arrangement and equipment in the Southeast.

Student Life: Approximately 53% of the students are from North Carolina; 72% come from public schools. Eighty-eight percent of the students live on campus. About 3% are minority-group members. Campus housing is single-sex. Students may keep cars on campus.

Organizations: There are no fraternities or sororities. Extracurricular activities include fine arts, publications, forums, photography, science, service projects, films, cultural events, and symposiums.

Sports: The college competes intercollegiately in 3 sports for women. Intramural sports for women number 6.

Handicapped: Facilities for the physically handicapped include wheelchair ramps, special parking, and specially equipped rest rooms; special class scheduling is also available.

Graduates: About 15% of the freshmen drop out by the end of the first year; 49% remain to graduate. Approximately 30% of those who graduate pursue graduate study: 2% enter medical and dental school and 2% enter law school; 50% pursue careers in business and industry.

Services: Placement services, career counseling, health care, and psychological counseling are offered to students free of charge. Tutoring is available for a fee.

Programs of Study: The B.A., B.S., or B.M. degree is offered in the following subjects: AREA STUDIES (American), BUSINESS (arts management, economics/management), ENGLISH (English), FINE AND PERFORMING ARTS (art, art therapy, fine arts, music, music education), HEALTH SCIENCES (medical technology), LANGUAGES (French, German, Greek/Latin, Spanish), MATH AND SCIENCES (biology, chemistry, mathematics), PHILOSOPHY (classics, philosophy, religion), PREPROFESSIONAL (home economics), SOCIAL SCIENCES (economics, history, psychology, sociology). Thirty-nine percent of degrees are conferred in social sciences, 19% in fine and performing arts, and 10% in math and sciences.

Required: All students must complete a distribution requirement.

Special: Student-designed majors; off-campus internships; preprofessional advising in law, medicine, business, and graduate school; study abroad; teacher certification in early childhood, intermediate, secondary, learning disabilities, emotionally handicapped, art, and music; Washington semester; UN semester; American Dietetics Association accreditation; independent study; model UN program; communications program; and cross-registration with Wake Forest University are available.

Honors: Three national honor societies have chapters on campus. All departments offer honors programs.

Admissions: Eighty-one percent of those who applied for the 1981–82 freshman class were accepted. SAT scores for entering freshmen were as follows: Verbal—65% below 500, 27% between 500 and 599, 8% between 600 and 700, and 0% above 700; Math—59% below 500, 35% between 500 and 599, 5% between 600 and 700, 1% above 700. Admissions requirements are flexible, but it is recommended that applicants present 16 academic high school units. The college seeks diversity in its student body. Other factors entering into the admissions decision are advanced placement or honors courses, impressions made during an interview, and recommendations.

Procedure: The SAT or ACT is required and should be taken by January of the senior year. Departmental placement tests are given to

644 NORTH CAROLINA

entering freshmen in continuing subjects. A personal interview is recommended. Application deadlines are open; the college follows a rolling admissions policy. There is a $15 application fee.

Special: There are early admissions and deferred admissions plans. AP credit is accepted.

Transfer: For fall 1981, 21 transfer students applied, 15 were accepted, and 7 enrolled. Transfer students are accepted to all classes. A minimum 2.0 GPA is required for transfer. College entrance exam scores and 3 letters of recommendation must be submitted. There is a 1-year residency requirement and 6 courses must be taken at the college, of a total 32 courses required for the bachelor's degree. At least 1 January term must also be taken. Deadlines are open. Transfers may enter the fall, winter, or spring terms.

Visiting: There are regularly scheduled orientations for prospective students. Guides are also available for informal visits; visitors may sit in on classes and stay overnight at the school. The admissions office should be contacted to arrange visits.

Financial Aid: Approximately 60% of all students receive some form of financial aid. About 25% work part-time on campus. Scholarships, grants, loans (from federal and state governments and local banks), and campus employment are available. Recently 160 scholarships were awarded from funds totaling $315,000; the average scholarship is $2000, and the maximum, $5000. The average income from campus employment is $400; the maximum, $600. The average aid to a freshman from all sources combined is $3300; the maximum, $6000. Tuition may be paid in installments. The college is a member of CSS and requires the FAF or FFS. The priority deadline for fall aid applications is March 1. Applications for winter and spring are processed if funds are still available.

Foreign Students: Two percent of the students come from foreign countries. The college offers special counseling and organizations.

Admissions: The TOEFL is required; a minimum score of 580 is necessary. College entrance exams are not required.

Procedure: There are no deadlines for admissions applications. A rolling admissions procedure is used. Foreign students are admitted to the fall, winter, and spring terms. Proof of adequate funds to cover 1 academic year must be presented.

Admissions Contact: Jeannie Dorsey, Director of Admissions.

SHAW UNIVERSITY   D-2
Raleigh, North Carolina 27602   (919) 755-4800

F/T, P/T: 1500M&W	Faculty:	83; IIB, −$
Grad: none	Ph.D.'s:	50%
Year: sems, ss	S/F Ratio:	n/av
Appl: open	Tuition:	$3800
SAT or ACT: recommended	R and B:	$1500
		LESS COMPETITIVE

Shaw University, founded in 1865, is affiliated with the Baptist Church. It offers undergraduate programs in the arts and sciences as well as education and business. The library holds 80,000 volumes and over 15,000 microfilm items, and subscribes to 428 periodicals.

Environment: The 18-acre campus includes residence halls that accommodate 400 women and 400 men.

Student Life: About half the students are North Carolina residents. All students who are not residents of Raleigh must live in the single-sex dormitories. The student body is predominantly black.

Organizations: Extracurricular activities include fraternities and sororities, special-interest clubs, social and cultural events, publications, performing groups, religious organizations, and student government.

Sports: The university fields intercollegiate teams in 4 sports. Intramural sports are also offered.

Programs of Study: The university confers the B.A. and B.S. degrees. Bachelor's degrees are offered in the following subjects: BUSINESS (accounting, business administration, computer science, management), EDUCATION (child development, elementary, health/physical, secondary), ENGLISH (English, speech), FINE AND PERFORMING ARTS (music, radio/TV, theater/dramatics), HEALTH SCIENCES (speech therapy), MATH AND SCIENCES (biology, chemistry, mathematics), PREPROFESSIONAL (dentistry, engineering, medicine, ministry), SOCIAL SCIENCES (community development, evaluation research, international relations, planning and management, public administration and politics, sociology and criminal justice).

Required: All students must complete a core curriculum.

Special: The university participates in a cooperative program with 5 other North Carolina colleges. A combined B.A.-B.S. degree in engineering is available in conjunction with North Carolina State University.

Admissions: Most applicants are accepted. A high school diploma or GED and 15 units of academic work are required.

Procedure: The SAT or ACT is recommended. Application deadlines are open; new students are admitted each semester. Notification is made on a rolling basis.

Special: Early decision, early admissions, and deferred admissions plans are offered. CLEP credit is available.

Transfer: Most transfer students are accepted. A 2.0 GPA is necessary. D grades do not transfer. Students must complete at least 30 credits in residence for a bachelor's degree.

Visiting: Campus tours with student guides can be arranged.

Financial Aid: About 95% of the students receive financial aid. The university offers scholarships, grants (BEOG/SEOG), various government and commercial loan programs (including NDSL), and part-time campus jobs (including CWS). Tuition may be paid in installments. The FAF or FFS is required. The application deadline is May 15 for priority consideration.

Admissions Contact: Director of Admissions.

UNIVERSITY OF NORTH CAROLINA

University of North Carolina was chartered in 1789 and opened its doors to students at the Chapel Hill campus in 1795. By act of the General Assembly of 1931, the Chapel Hill campus, the North Carolina College for Women at Greensboro (founded 1891—now University of North Carolina at Greensboro), and the North Carolina College of Agriculture and Engineering at Raleigh (founded 1887—now North Carolina State University) were consolidated to form a multicampus institution designated the University of North Carolina. University of North Carolina at Charlotte was added in 1965, and in 1969 University of North Carolina at Wilmington and University of North Carolina at Asheville were added. In 1971, the General Assembly merged the remaining 10 state-supported senior institutions of higher education into the University of North Carolina: Appalachian State University, East Carolina University, Elizabeth City State University, Fayetteville State University, North Carolina Agricultural and Technical State University, North Carolina Central University, North Carolina School of the Arts, Pembroke State University, Western Carolina University, and Winston-Salem State University. There are 16 constituent institutions of the university.

The university is governed by a board of governors, and a president serves as the chief administrative and executive officer. Each constituent institution is headed by a chancellor, who is responsible to the president, and each has its own board of trustees.

All 16 constituent institutions are coeducational and grant the bachelor's degree. Graduate and professional degree programs are also offered by many of the campuses.

UNIVERSITY OF NORTH   B-2
CAROLINA AT ASHEVILLE
Asheville, North Carolina 28814   (704) 258-6480

F/T: 503M, 634W	Faculty:	87; IIB, + +$
P/T: 476M, 653W	Ph.D.'s:	78%
Grad: none	S/F Ratio:	16 to 1
Year: sems, ss	Tuition:	$586 ($2168)
Appl: see profile	R and B:	$1400
450 applied	338 accepted	230 enrolled
SAT or ACT: required		COMPETITIVE

University of North Carolina at Asheville is an undergraduate liberal arts campus of the University of North Carolina system. The library contains 110,000 volumes, 16,300 bound periodicals, 10,000 microfilm items, and 8000 microfiche items, and subscribes to 951 periodicals.

Environment: The 200-acre urban campus, located 1 mile from the center of Asheville (pop. 80,000), overlooks the gateway of the Great Smoky Mountains. A new student center is being built. There are 3 residence halls with both single and double accommodations, and a new residence hall is under construction.

Student Life: Ninety-two percent of the students are from North Carolina; 92% come from public schools. Ten percent live on campus. About 5% are minority-group members. Campus housing is both single-sex and coed; there are visiting privileges in the former. Students may keep cars on campus.

Organizations: There are 2 local fraternities, to which 6% of the men belong; 4% of the women belong to the 2 local sororities. Over 30 student organizations and societies affiliated with the university include social, professional, honor, academic, service, religious, literary, and special interest groups. The university sponsors lectures, jazz, folk, and rock concerts, dance and chamber music performances, and films. UNC-Asheville Theatre offers productions throughout the year, and the concert band and chorus perform regularly.

Sports: The university competes intercollegiately in 3 sports for men and 3 for women. Intramural sports are available for both men and women.

Handicapped: Approximately 60% of the campus is accessible to the physically handicapped. Facilities include wheelchair ramps, special parking, elevators, and specially equipped rest rooms; special class scheduling is also available.

Graduates: About 45% of the freshmen drop out; 30% remain to graduate. Approximately 15% of those who graduate pursue graduate study, with 2% entering medical school, 2% dental school, and 2% law school. Eighty percent pursue careers in business and industry.

Services: Placement services, career counseling, psychological counseling, tutoring, and remedial instruction are offered free of charge to all students. Health care is available for a fee.

Programs of Study: The B.A. or B.S. degree is awarded in the following subjects: BUSINESS (management), ENGLISH (communications, creative writing, journalism, literature), FINE AND PERFORMING ARTS (art, theater/dramatics), LANGUAGES (French, German, Spanish), MATH AND SCIENCES (biology, chemistry, computer science, mathematics, meteorology, physics), PHILOSOPHY (classics, philosophy), PREPROFESSIONAL (dentistry, engineering, forestry, law, medicine, pharmacy, veterinary), SOCIAL SCIENCES (economics, government/political science, history, psychology, social sciences, sociology). Fifty-two percent of degrees are conferred in social sciences, 22% in business, and 11% in math and sciences.

Required: Freshmen and sophomores must complete a general education program of 36 to 42 semester hours, including 16 hours in an integrated humanities sequence.

Special: The university offers teacher certification in art, early childhood, intermediate, reading, and secondary education; study-abroad programs; a joint program with North Carolina State University leading to the B.S. in engineering operations; and a cooperative nursing program with Western Carolina University. Combination degree programs are available in many fields; student-designed majors are also possible.

Honors: Several departments offer honors programs. The university also offers independent scholar and tutorial scholar honors programs.

Admissions: Approximately 75% of those who applied were accepted for the 1981–82 freshman class. The SAT scores of those who enrolled for a recent freshman class were as follows: Verbal—22% between 500 and 600; Math—29% between 500 and 600. Candidates should rank in the top half of their class and have a minimum GPA of 2.0. Other factors entering into the admissions decision are advanced placement or honors courses, leadership record, and recommendations.

Procedure: The SAT or ACT is required. The application deadlines are 2 weeks prior to registration for the fall, spring, or summer term. The university follows a rolling admissions policy. There is a $15 application fee.

Special: There is an early admission plan. AP and CLEP credit is accepted.

Transfer: Approximately 200 transfer students enroll yearly. Transfers are accepted for all classes. Minimum SAT scores of 400 verbal and 450 math and a minimum 2.0 GPA are required; all grades transfer. A minimum of 30 semester hours in residence and one-third of the requirements for the major are necessary to earn a bachelor's degree (120 semester hours). Deadlines are the same as those for freshman applicants. Transfers are admitted to the fall, spring, and summer terms.

Visiting: There are regularly scheduled orientations for prospective students. Guides are also available for informal visits on weekdays; visitors may sit in on classes. The admissions office should be contacted to arrange visits.

Financial Aid: Approximately 23% of all students receive financial aid in the form of scholarships, loans, or grants. Work-study is available in all departments. The FAF is required; the deadline for aid applications is March 1.

Foreign Students: About 1 percent of the students come from foreign countries. The university offers an intensive English course.

Admissions: The TOEFL is required; a minimum score of 500 is necessary. College entrance exams are not required.

Procedure: Applications are due 2 weeks prior to registration. Foreign students may enter in the fall, spring, or summer session. The university health form must be completed. Proof of adequate funds to cover 4 years must be presented. Health insurance must be carried while in attendance; it is available through the university for a fee.

Admissions Contact: Jean M. Luce, Associate Director of Admissions.

UNIVERSITY OF NORTH CAROLINA AT CHAPEL HILL D-2
Chapel Hill, North Carolina 27514 (919) 966-3621

F/T: 6096M, 7999W Faculty: 1887; I, ++$
P/T: 152M, 371W Ph.D.'s: 95%
Grad: 2453M, 2832W S/F Ratio: 14 to 1
Year: sems, ss Tuition: $675 ($2550)
Appl: Feb. 1 R and B: $2050
11,678 applied 5125 accepted 3201 enrolled
SAT: 506V 548M **VERY COMPETITIVE**

University of North Carolina at Chapel Hill, established in 1795, includes the following divisions: the College of Arts and Sciences, the schools of Business Administration, Dentistry, Education, Journalism, Law, Library Science, Medicine, Nursing, Pharmacy, Public Health, and Social Work, and the Institute of Government. The library contains 2.5 million volumes and 1 million microfilm items, and subscribes to 15,000 periodicals.

Environment: The 1200-acre campus, located 30 miles from Raleigh, is surrounded by an urban environment. There are residence facilities for 4430 men, 2248 women, and 400 families. Additional housing is provided by fraternity and sorority houses.

Student Life: Eighty-five percent of the students are from North Carolina; 86% come from public schools. Forty-five percent live on campus. Freshmen are required to live in residence halls. About 8% of the students are minority-group members. Campus housing is both single-sex and coed; there are visiting privileges in the single-sex dorms. Students may keep cars on campus.

Organizations: There are 30 fraternities, to which 20% of the men belong; 20% of the women belong to 15 sororities. Almost every aspect of student life is the concern of 1 or more offices of the Division of Student Life; numerous social and cultural activities are also available. There are religious organizations for Protestant, Catholic, Jewish, and Moslem students.

Sports: The university competes intercollegiately in 9 sports for men and 10 for women. Intramural sports for both men and women number 6.

Handicapped: Facilities for the physically handicapped include wheelchair ramps, special parking, and lowered drinking fountains; improvements are being made yearly.

Graduates: The freshman dropout rate is 5% to 10%; 70% remain to graduate. Forty-five percent of those who graduate pursue graduate study.

Services: Placement services, psychological counseling, health care, career counseling, tutoring, and remedial instruction are included in the regular tuition and fees.

Programs of Study: The university confers the B.A., B.M., B.S., and B.F.A. degrees. Master's and doctoral programs are also offered. Bachelor's degrees are offered in the following subjects: AREA STUDIES (African, American, Black/Afro-American, Latin American, urban), BUSINESS (accounting, business administration), EDUCATION (early childhood, health/physical, secondary), ENGLISH (English, journalism, literature, speech), FINE AND PERFORMING ARTS (art, art history, music, music education, radio/TV, studio art, theater/dramatics), HEALTH SCIENCES (dental hygiene, medical technology, nursing, physical therapy, public health, radiologic technology), LANGUAGES (French, German, Greek/Latin, Italian, linguistics, Portuguese, Russian, Spanish), MATH AND SCIENCES (astronomy/physics, biology, botany, chemistry, geology, mathematics, mathematical sciences, physics, zoology), PHILOSOPHY (classics, philosophy, religion), PREPROFESSIONAL (dentistry, pharmacy), SOCIAL SCIENCES (administration of criminal justice, anthropology, economics, geography, government/political science, history, industrial relations, international relations, psychology, public policy analysis, recreation administration, sociology). Fifty-three percent of degrees are conferred in liberal arts, 15% in business, and 13% in health sciences.

Required: All students must take courses in English, social sciences, natural sciences, foreign language or math, and humanities.

646 NORTH CAROLINA

Special: Student-designed majors, study-abroad opportunities, and political internship programs are offered. The facilities of the University Testing Service are available free of charge to all students to assist in selecting an appropriate major and ultimate vocation.

Honors: Phi Beta Kappa has a chapter on campus. Freshman and sophomore honors programs are available by invitation. Departmental honors programs are open to qualified upperclassmen.

Admissions: Approximately 44% of those who applied were accepted for the 1981-82 freshman class. SAT scores of entering freshmen were as follows: Verbal—45% below 500, 36% between 500 and 599, 16% between 600 and 700, 2% above 700; Math—26% below 500, 44% between 500 and 599, 25% between 600 and 700, 5% above 700. Applicants must be graduates of an accredited high school and present 16 academic units; recommendations are also required. Some individual variations may be allowed. The extracurricular activities record, evidence of special talents, and leadership record are also important factors in the admissions decision.

Procedure: The SAT is required and must be taken by December of the senior year; junior year results are acceptable. The deadline for fall admissions is February 1; for spring, November 1. The university follows a rolling admissions policy. There is a $15 application fee.

Special: AP credit is accepted.

Transfer: For fall 1981, 2832 transfer applications were received, 1188 were accepted, and 832 students enrolled. Transfers are accepted for the junior class only. A minimum GPA of 2.0 is required. C or above grades transfer. At least half of the major course requirements must be completed at the university. The bachelor's degree requires basically 120 credits plus 2 physical education courses. Application deadlines are February 1 (fall) and November 1 (spring).

Visiting: There are campus tours most weekdays at 2:00 P.M., followed by group information sessions at 3:00 P.M.. Guides are available for informal visits; visitors may sit in on classes. The office of undergraduate admissions should be contacted to arrange visits. Interviews are not part of the admissions process.

Financial Aid: Approximately 35% of all students receive some form of financial aid. About 37% work part-time on campus. Fellowships, scholarships, loans, and part-time employment are available. The average award to freshmen covers 58% of costs. The university is a CSS member. The FAF is required; the deadlines for aid applications are March 1 (fall and summer) and November 1 (spring).

Foreign Students: About 2% of the students are from foreign countries. The university offers special counseling and organizations.

Admissions: The TOEFL is required; a minimum score of 600 is necessary. College entrance exams are also required.

Procedure: February 1 and November 1 are the application deadlines for the fall and spring, respectively. The university health certificate must be completed. Proof of adequate funds to cover the length of the student's program must be presented. Health insurance is required; it can be arranged through the International Center.

Admissions Contact: Richard G. Cashwell, Director of Undergraduate Admissions.

UNIVERSITY OF NORTH CAROLINA AT CHARLOTTE   C-3
Charlotte, North Carolina 28223   (704) 597-2211

F/T: 3505M, 3039W
P/T: 991M, 888W
Grad: 465M, 686W
Year: sems, ss
Appl: July 1
3362 applied   2492 accepted   1336 enrolled
SAT: 430V 486M
Faculty: 447; IIA, +$
Ph.D.'s: 70%
S/F Ratio: 16 to 1
Tuition: $626 ($2414)
R and B: $1744-2160
COMPETITIVE

University of North Carolina at Charlotte is an urban-oriented university offering programs in the liberal arts and sciences, education, business, health sciences, and preprofessional areas. The library contains 313,792 volumes and 120,448 microfilm items, and subscribes to 4722 periodicals.

Environment: The 1000-acre campus is in an urban area 10 miles from downtown Charlotte. There are 33 buildings; high-rise and apartment-style dormitories accommodate 2954 students.

Student Life: Approximately 91% of the students are from North Carolina. About 31% live on campus. Twelve percent are minority-group members. Campus housing is both single-sex and coed; there are visiting privileges in the single-sex dorms. Students may keep cars on campus.

Organizations: There are 2 local and 11 national fraternities, and 1 local and 5 national sororities on campus. A social program is planned and conducted by students.

Sports: The university competes intercollegiately in 6 sports for men and 4 for women. Intramural sports for men number 16; for women, 14.

Handicapped: The entire campus is accessible to the physically handicapped. Facilities include wheelchair ramps, special parking, elevators, specially equipped rest rooms, lowered drinking fountains and telephones, and special auxiliary equipment. Housing facilities designed specifically for handicapped students in wheelchairs are available. Special registration is also available.

Graduates: The freshman dropout rate is 27%; 29% remain to graduate.

Services: Placement services, career counseling, health care, psychological counseling, and tutoring are offered to students free of charge.

Programs of Study: The university confers the B.A., B.Arch., B.C.A., B.S., B.S.N., B.S.E., and B.E.T. degrees. Master's programs are also offered. Bachelor's degrees are offered in the following subjects: AREA STUDIES (Black/Afro-American), BUSINESS (accounting, business administration, computer science), EDUCATION (early childhood, secondary), ENGLISH (English), FINE AND PERFORMING ARTS (art, art education, dance, music, theater/dramatics), HEALTH SCIENCES (medical technology, nursing), LANGUAGES (French, German, Spanish), MATH AND SCIENCES (biology, chemistry, earth science, mathematics, physics), PHILOSOPHY (philosophy, religion), PREPROFESSIONAL (architecture, criminal justice, engineering), SOCIAL SCIENCES (anthropology, economics, geography, government/political science, history, psychology, social sciences, sociology). Approximately 27% of degrees are conferred in business, 21% in social sciences, and 21% in preprofessional studies.

Required: English, mathematics or foreign language, laboratory science, humanities, and social science courses must be taken by all students.

Special: The university offers foreign exchange programs; student-designed majors; experiential learning programs including clinicals, cooperative education, internships, practica, and service-learning internships; and the venture program.

Honors: Three national honor societies have chapters on campus. Honors programs are offered in chemistry, history, nursing, math, and modern languages. A campus-wide honorary is also available for recognizing leadership in the university community.

Admissions: Approximately 74% of those who applied were accepted for the 1981-82 freshman class. The SAT scores of those who enrolled were as follows: Verbal—81% below 500, 17% between 500 and 599, 2% between 600 and 700, 0% above 700; Math—56% below 500, 35% between 500 and 599, 9% between 600 and 700, 1% above 700. Applicants should have completed 16 units at an accredited high school, have a C average, and rank in the upper half of their high school class.

Procedure: The SAT or ACT is required and should be taken by July of the senior year. The application deadlines are July 1 (fall), December 1 (spring), and May 1 (summer). The university follows a rolling admissions policy. There is a $15 application fee.

Special: There are early admissions and deferred admissions plans. AP and CLEP credit is available.

Transfer: For fall 1981, 2059 transfer students applied, 1816 were accepted, and 1206 enrolled. Transfer students are accepted for all classes. A minimum 2.0 GPA and a combined SAT score of 800 are required; D grades do not transfer. Thirty semester hours must be completed in residence, of a total 120 semester hours required for the bachelor's degree. Deadlines for application are July 1 (fall), December 1 (spring), and May 1 (summer).

Visiting: There are regularly scheduled orientations for prospective students. Guides are also available for informal visits; visitors may sit in on classes. The admissions office should be contacted to arrange visits.

Financial Aid: Approximately 30% of all students receive some form of financial aid. About 10% work part-time on campus. Applicants are considered for all available scholarships, grants, loans, and work assistance. Scholarships are awarded on the basis of academic promise; the amount is determined by need. The university is a member of CSS. The FAF and aid applications should be filed by April 15; notification of awards is on a rolling basis.

Foreign Students: About 3% of the students are from foreign countries. An intensive English program, special counseling, and organizations are available.

NORTH CAROLINA 647

Admissions: The TOEFL or University of Michigan Language Test is required; the minimum score on the TOEFL is 500, and on the Michigan, 80. College entrance exams are not required.

Procedure: Foreign applications should be complete at least 1 week before the following review dates for consideration: May 1 and July 1 (fall), November 15 (spring), and February 15 and May 1 (summer). A university medical form must be completed and returned to the University Health Center. Proof of adequate funds for the first year of study, as well as the means for meeting expenses for the remaining years of study, must be presented. Health insurance is required; it is available through the university for a fee.

Admissions Contact: Kathi M. Baucom, Director of Admissions.

UNIVERSITY OF NORTH CAROLINA AT GREENSBORO D-2
Greensboro, North Carolina 27412 (919) 379-5243

```
F/T:  1786M, 4348W          Faculty:   n/av; I, av$
P/T:  419M, 771W            Ph.D.'s:   66%
Grad: 1025M, 1852W          S/F Ratio: 15 to 1
Year: sems, ss              Tuition:   $724 ($2548)
Appl: Aug. 10               R and B:   $1610
3672 applied     2661 accepted     1294 enrolled
SAT: 462V 488M                     COMPETITIVE+
```

University of North Carolina at Greensboro, established in 1891, is a coeducational state-supported institution offering programs in the liberal arts and sciences, education, business, the health sciences, and preprofessional areas. The library contains 1.1 million volumes and 396,047 microfilm items, and subscribes to 6000 periodicals.

Environment: The 147-acre campus is surrounded by an urban environment. There are 74 buildings and a 9-hole golf course. Twenty-four dormitories accommodate 2961 women and 703 men.

Student Life: Since the university may admit only 15% of its students from outside the state, most students are residents of North Carolina. Ninety-five percent come from public schools. Thirty-six percent live on campus. Seventy-eight percent are Protestant, 11% are Catholic, and 1% are Jewish. Thirteen percent are minority-group members. Campus housing is single-sex; there are visiting privileges.

Organizations: There are fraternities and sororities. Extracurricular activities include a strong student government, departmental clubs, social and cultural events, and religious activities for members of all faiths.

Sports: The university competes intercollegiately in 4 sports for men and 4 for women. Intramural sports for men number 10; for women, 9.

Handicapped: Approximately 60% of the campus is accessible to the physically handicapped. Facilities include wheelchair ramps, special parking, elevators, and specially equipped rest rooms; special class scheduling is also available. Interpreters, portable cassette recorders, and braille material are provided for students with visual and hearing impairments.

Graduates: The freshman dropout rate is 20%; 62% remain to graduate.

Services: Placement services, career counseling, psychological counseling, tutoring, and remedial instruction are offered free of charge; health care is available for a fee.

Programs of Study: The university confers the B.A., B.M., B.S., B.S.N., B.S.H.E., B.S.P.E., B.S.Med.Tech., and B.F.A. degrees. Master's and doctoral programs are also offered. Bachelor's degrees are offered in the following subjects: AREA STUDIES (international, Latin American, linguistics, Russian, urban), BUSINESS (accounting, business administration, business education), EDUCATION (early childhood, elementary, health/physical, secondary, special/deaf), ENGLISH (English, speech), FINE AND PERFORMING ARTS (art education, art history, dance, dance education, music, music education, studio art, theater/dramatics), HEALTH SCIENCES (medical technology, nursing, speech therapy), LANGUAGES (French, German, Greek/Latin, Spanish), MATH AND SCIENCES (biology, chemistry, mathematics, physics), PHILOSOPHY (classics, philosophy, religion), PREPROFESSIONAL (dentistry, engineering, home economics, law, medicine, pharmacy, social work, veterinary), SOCIAL SCIENCES (anthropology, economics, geography, government/political science, history, psychology, sociology). Approximately 20% of degrees are conferred in education, 19% in social sciences, and 18% in business.

Required: English is required of all students; other requirements vary with major.

Special: Student-designed majors, a junior year abroad program, a 6-week summer institute abroad, an international studies program, cooperative education, internships, and work experiences in many academic majors are offered.

Honors: Ten national honor societies have chapters on campus. All departments in the College of Arts and Sciences offer honors programs. Freshman, sophomore and junior year special seminars are offered. Juniors may do honors independent work, and seniors may do a senior honors project.

Admissions: Approximately 72% of those who applied were accepted for the 1981-82 freshman class. The SAT scores of those who enrolled were as follows: Verbal—74% below 500, 21% between 500 and 599, 4% between 600 and 700, 1% above 700; Math—53% below 500, 40% between 500 and 599, 5% between 600 and 700, 1% above 700. Candidates should rank in the top half of their class and have a minimum 2.2 GPA with 15 Carnegie units from an accredited high school.

Procedure: The SAT or ACT is required and should be taken in May of the junior year for early decision or in the fall of the senior year. The application deadline for fall admission is August 10; for spring admission, December 10. The university follows a rolling admissions policy. There is a $15 application fee.

Special: The deadline for early admissions applications is November 1. AP and CLEP credit is accepted.

Transfer: For fall 1981, the university received 1489 transfer applications, accepted 1035, and enrolled 696 students. Transfers are accepted for all classes. A minimum C average is required. C grades and above transfer. Thirty hours must be completed in residence, of a total 122 credits required for the bachelor's degree. Deadlines for transfer application are the same as those for freshmen.

Visiting: There are regularly scheduled orientations for prospective students. Guides are also available for informal visits; visitors may sit in on classes.

Financial Aid: Approximately 50% of all students receive some form of financial aid. About 20% work part-time on campus. Scholarships, loans, grants, and work-study in all departments are available. Aid is usually granted in packets, and is based on need and academic potential. The average aid to freshmen from all sources available through the university is $760. The university is a member of CSS. The FAF is required; the deadlines for aid applications are March 1 (fall) and December 1 (spring).

Foreign Students: One percent of the full-time students come from foreign countries. The university offers special counseling.

Admissions: The TOEFL is required; a minimum score of 550 is necessary. College entrance exams are not required.

Procedure: Applications are due by August 10 for both semesters. Foreign students are admitted to the fall and spring semesters. A physical examination form must be completed. Proof of adequate funds to cover 1 semester must be presented.

Admissions Contact: Robert W. Hites, Director of Admissions.

UNIVERSITY OF NORTH CAROLINA AT WILMINGTON E-4
Wilmington, North Carolina 28406 (919) 791-4330

```
F/T:  2002M, 2058W          Faculty:   244; IIB, ++$
P/T:  352M, 538W            Ph.D.'s:   68%
Grad: 46M, 110W             S/F Ratio: 17 to 1
Year: sems, ss              Tuition:   $630 ($2212)
Appl: Aug. 1                R and B:   $1875
2761 applied     2061 accepted     1094 enrolled
SAT: 415V 458M                     LESS COMPETITIVE
```

University of North Carolina at Wilmington, founded in 1947, offers programs in the liberal arts and sciences, education, business, and preprofessional studies. The library contains 199,790 volumes and 272,909 microform items, and subscribes to 3130 periodicals.

Environment: The 620-acre campus, 4 miles east of Wilmington and 120 miles from Raleigh, is surrounded by an urban area. There are 14 fully air-conditioned buildings. Coed dormitories house 1000 students; 13 apartment-style units house 400 students.

Student Life: Approximately 98% of the students are from the South; 90% are from public schools. Twenty-seven percent live on campus. Eight percent are minority-group members. Campus housing is both single-sex and coed; there are visiting privileges in the former. Students may keep cars on campus.

648 NORTH CAROLINA

Organizations: There are 6 national fraternities, to which 5% of the men belong; 2% of the women belong to 3 national sororities. Extracurricular activities include an active student government, a newspaper, a university annual, and a literary magazine.

Sports: The university competes intercollegiately in 9 sports for men and 8 for women. Intramural sports for men number 12; for women, 10.

Handicapped: Approximately 90% of the campus is accessible to the physically handicapped. Facilities include wheelchair ramps, special parking, elevators, and specially equipped rest rooms; special class scheduling is also available. All of the dormitories are 100% accessible to the physically handicapped.

Graduates: Approximately 25% of those who enter as freshmen drop out; 46% remain to graduate. Twenty-three percent of those who graduate pursue graduate or professional degrees; 41% enter business and industry.

Services: Placement services, career counseling, health care, and psychological counseling are offered to students free of charge. Tutoring and remedial instruction are available for a fee.

Programs of Study: The university awards the B.A. and B.S. degrees. Associate and master's degrees are also available. Bachelor's degrees are offered in the following subjects: BUSINESS (accounting, business administration, business economics, computer science, management, marketing), EDUCATION (early childhood, elementary, health/physical, secondary, special), ENGLISH (English, speech), FINE AND PERFORMING ARTS (art, music, theater/dramatics), HEALTH SCIENCES (medical technology), LANGUAGES (French, Spanish), MATH AND SCIENCES (biology, chemistry, earth science, ecology/environmental science, geology, marine biology, mathematics, physics), PHILOSOPHY (philosophy, religion), SOCIAL SCIENCES (geography, government/political science, history, psychology, public affairs, social sciences, sociology). About 27% of degrees are conferred in math and sciences, 27% in social sciences, 17% in education, and 17% in business.

Required: All students must take courses in written composition, math, history, social science, humanities, natural science, modern language, and physical education.

Special: The university offers a Near Eastern archaeological seminar with the Institute for Mediterranean Studies, as well as independent study programs.

Honors: Two national honor societies have chapters on campus. Honors programs are open to qualified students.

Admissions: Approximately 75% of those who applied were accepted for the 1981-82 freshman class. The SAT scores of those who enrolled were as follows: Verbal—85% below 500, 13% between 500 and 599, 2% between 600 and 700, and 0% above 700; Math—71% below 500, 24% between 500 and 599, 5% between 600 and 700, and 0% above 700. Candidates must be graduates of an accredited high school, have a minimum 2.0 GPA, and have a minimum combined SAT score of 800.

Procedure: The SAT is required and should be taken in the fall of the senior year at the latest. The application deadline for fall admission is August 1; for spring admission, December 15. The university follows a rolling admissions policy. There is a $15 application fee.

Special: AP and CLEP credit is accepted.

Transfer: For fall 1981, 1086 transfer students applied, 727 were accepted, and 460 enrolled. Transfer students are accepted for all but the senior year. A minimum C average and a minimum combined SAT score of 800 are required. At least 32 credits must be taken at the university, of a total 124 required for the bachelor's degree. A rolling admissions policy is followed. Application deadlines are the same for transfers as they are for freshmen.

Visiting: The admissions office should be contacted to arrange campus visits.

Financial Aid: Approximately 41% of all students receive some form of financial aid. Fifteen percent work part-time on campus. Scholarships, work assistance loans, NDSL, and CWS are available. The university is a CSS member. Applicants for financial aid are required to submit the FAF, FFS, or BEOG. Applications are due April 1 (fall) and October 15 (spring). Those received by March 15 have priority.

Foreign Students: Fewer than 1% of the students come from foreign countries. Special counseling is available.

Admissions: The TOEFL or SAT is required; a minimum score of either 500 on the TOEFL or 800 (combined) on the SAT is necessary.

Procedure: August 1 is the application deadline for the fall; December 15, for the spring. The university's health report form must be completed by a physician. Proof of adequate funds to cover at least 1 year of study must be presented. Health insurance is required; it is available through the university for a fee.

Admissions Contact: Ralph H. Parker, Dean of Admissions.

WAKE FOREST UNIVERSITY C-2
Winston-Salem, North Carolina 27109   (919) 761-5201

F/T: 1862M, 1214W	Faculty: 218; IIA, ++$
P/T: 64M, 31W	Ph.D.'s: 85%
Grad: 1045M, 491W	S/F Ratio: 14 to 1
Year: sems, ss	Tuition: $4100
Appl: Jan. 15	R and B: $1710
3505 applied	1598 accepted 830 enrolled
SAT: 543V 585M	**HIGHLY COMPETITIVE**

Wake Forest University, chartered in 1834 and affiliated with the North Carolina Baptist State Convention, offers training in the liberal arts and sciences, business, education, and preprofessional fields. The library has 800,000 books and 225,000 microfilm items, and subscribes to 9800 periodicals.

Environment: The 350-acre campus, 4 miles from Winston-Salem, is surrounded by a suburban environment. There are 30 buildings. Ten residence halls accommodate 1017 women and 1510 men; there are also apartments for married students and fraternity houses.

Student Life: About 44% of the students come from North Carolina. Eighty-five percent are public school graduates. Eighty-five percent are campus residents. Seventy-five percent are Protestant, 15% are Catholic, 1% are Jewish. About 6% are minority-group members. Campus housing is both single-sex and coed; there are visiting privileges in the single-sex dorms. Students are permitted to keep cars on campus.

Organizations: Forty percent of the men belong to 10 national fraternities; 60% of the women, to 6 local societies. The student activity program includes clubs, government, publications, performing groups, dramatics, social and cultural events, and religious groups.

Sports: The university fields 9 intercollegiate teams for men and 7 for women. The intramural program includes 9 sports for men and 8 for women.

Handicapped: About 80% of the campus is accessible to physically handicapped individuals. Special facilities include wheelchair ramps, parking areas, elevators, lowered telephones, and specially equipped rest rooms and dorm rooms. Special class scheduling is also available. Fewer than 1% of the students have visual impairments. A special counselor is available for handicapped students.

Graduates: The freshman dropout rate is 3%; about 78% remain to graduate. Of these, 37% go on to advanced study (9% to law school, 5% to medical school, 1% to dental school), and 40% enter careers in business or industry.

Services: Career counseling, psychological counseling, and placement service are available without cost. Health care is available for a fee.

Programs of Study: The university awards the B.A. and B.S. degrees. Master's and doctoral degrees are also available. Bachelor's degrees are offered in the following subjects: AREA STUDIES (Asian), BUSINESS (accounting, business administration), EDUCATION (elementary, health/physical, intermediate, secondary), ENGLISH (English, speech), FINE AND PERFORMING ARTS (art, music, theater/dramatics), HEALTH SCIENCES (medical technology, physician's assistant), LANGUAGES (French, German, Greek/Latin, Spanish), MATH AND SCIENCES (biology, chemistry, mathematics, physics), PHILOSOPHY (humanities, philosophy, religion), PREPROFESSIONAL (dentistry, engineering, forestry, law, medicine, ministry), SOCIAL SCIENCES (anthropology, economics, government/political science, history, psychology, sociology). About 23% of the students major in math and sciences, and 19% in business.

Required: There is a broad distribution requirement for freshmen and sophomores.

Special: There are 3-2 programs in engineering with North Carolina State University and in forestry with Duke University. The university offers the junior year abroad program and residential learning centers in London and Venice. Wake Forest also arranges study in Dijon, France; Salamanca, Spain; Berlin, West Germany; and Bogotá, Colombia.

Honors: Honors work is offered in most areas, including an interdisciplinary program. Fifteen honor societies have chapters on campus.

Admissions: About 46% of the applicants for the 1981-82 freshman class were accepted. Their SAT scores were as follows: Verbal—28% below 500, 50% between 500 and 599, 19% between 600 and 700,

3% above 700; Math—14% below 500, 46% between 500 and 599, 35% between 600 and 700, 5% above 700. Applicants should have competitive rank in their high school class and in their grade average. Other important factors are honors or advanced placement work, recommendations, and the personality of the applicant.

Procedure: The SAT is required. Application deadlines are January 15 (fall), November 1 (spring), and May 1 (summer). There is a $20 application fee.

Special: There are early decision, early admissions, and deferred admissions plans. The notification date for early decision is early November. The application deadline for early admissions is January 1. CLEP and AP credit is given.

Transfer: For fall 1981, the university received 460 applications, accepted 184, and enrolled 113 students. Transfers are accepted for all but the senior class. A GPA of 2.0 is needed. D and better grades transfer. Four semesters must be completed in residence. Seventy-two credits must be completed at the university, of a total 144 credits required for the bachelor's degree. Application deadlines are the same as those for freshmen.

Visiting: There is an orientation program for prospective applicants. Informal campus tours with student guides can also be arranged, preferably during the spring or summer. Visitors may attend classes. Arrangements should be made through the admissions office.

Financial Aid: About 28% of the students receive assistance. Twenty-five percent work part-time on campus. The average award to freshmen is $1950. The university offers freshman scholarships, various loan programs, grants, and part-time campus work-study arrangements. Tuition may be paid on the installment plan. The university is a CSS member. The FAF should be filed by February 1 for priority consideration in the fall; December 15 is the deadline for the spring.

Foreign Students: One percent of the students are from foreign countries. The university offers special counseling and organizations.

Admissions: Both the TOEFL and the SAT are required.

Procedure: Application deadlines for foreign students are January 15 (fall) and November 1 (spring). A physician's form must be completed. Proof of adequate funds to cover 4 undergraduate years must be presented. Health insurance is required; it is available through the university for a fee.

Admissions Contact: W. G. Starling, Director of Admissions and Financial Aid.

WARREN WILSON COLLEGE B-2
Swannanoa, North Carolina 28778 (704) 298-3325

F/T: 265M, 269W Faculty: 55; IV, −−$
P/T: 7M, 13W Ph.D.'s: 50%
Grad: 19M, 10W S/F Ratio: 10 to 1
Year: see profile Tuition: $3950
Appl: Apr. 15 R and B: see profile
373 applied 245 accepted 174 enrolled
SAT: 490V 490M **COMPETITIVE**

Warren Wilson College, founded in 1894, is a small coeducational liberal arts institution associated with the United Presbyterian Church. The library contains 73,000 volumes and 4565 microfilm items, and subscribes to 500 periodicals.

Environment: The 1000-acre campus is located in a rural area, 9 miles from Asheville. There are 72 buildings, including 7 dormitories accommodating 484 students.

Student Life: Ninety percent of the students live on campus. Drinking is permitted in designated areas only. About 80% are Protestant, 8% are Catholic, and 3% are Jewish. Eight percent are minority-group members. Campus housing is single-sex; there are visiting privileges. Students may keep cars on campus. The college provides day-care services; all students, faculty, and staff are eligible.

Organizations: There are no fraternities or sororities. Student activities include choir, a dramatic association, publications, dances, and a variety of cultural events.

Sports: The college competes intercollegiately in 4 sports for men and 4 for women. Intramural sports for both men and women number 8.

Handicapped: Approximately 20% of the campus is accessible to the physically handicapped. Facilities include wheelchair ramps, special parking, specially equipped rest rooms, and lowered telephones; special class scheduling is also available.

Graduates: The freshman dropout rate is 18%; 65% remain to graduate. Of those who graduate, 35% pursue graduate study: 1% enter medical school, 1% dental school, and 5% law school; 10% pursue careers in business and industry.

Services: Placement services, career counseling, and psychological counseling are offered to students free of charge; health care and tutoring are available for a fee.

Programs of Study: The college confers the B.A. degree. Programs leading to the master's degree are also offered. Bachelor's degrees are offered in the following subjects: AREA STUDIES (American, intercultural), BUSINESS (business administration, management), EDUCATION (early childhood, elementary, secondary), ENGLISH (English, literature), FINE AND PERFORMING ARTS (music, music education, theater/dramatics), HEALTH SCIENCES (anesthesia), LANGUAGES (French, Spanish), MATH AND SCIENCES (biochemistry, biology, chemistry, ecology/environmental science, mathematics, natural sciences, physical sciences, physics), PREPROFESSIONAL (dentistry, forestry, law, medicine, ministry, social work, veterinary), SOCIAL SCIENCES (economics, government/political science, history, psychology, social sciences, sociology). Thirty-four percent of degrees are conferred in business and social sciences, 20% in math and sciences, 15% in education, and 15% in health sciences.

Required: All students must follow a core curriculum and complete a service project.

Special: The school year is divided into 2 semesters, each of which consists of 2 8-week terms. The student body maintains and operates every aspect of the college; each resident student works 15 hours per week on campus in exchange for room and board. A general studies (no major) degree, student-designed majors, study-abroad programs, and a 3-2 engineering program with Duke University and Tennessee Technological University are offered.

Honors: An honors program in English requiring an undergraduate thesis is open to qualified students.

Admissions: Approximately 66% of those who applied were accepted for the 1981–82 freshman class. The SAT scores of those who enrolled were as follows: Verbal—64% below 500, 30% between 500 and 599, 5% between 600 and 700, 1% above 700; Math—61% below 500, 31% between 500 and 599, 8% between 600 and 700, and 0% above 700. Candidates should rank in the top half of their class and have a minimum 2.0 GPA. Other factors entering into the admissions decision are impressions made during an interview, advanced placement or honors courses, extracurricular activities record, recommendations, and a personal essay.

Procedure: The SAT or ACT is required. Freshmen are admitted at the beginning of each semester. The application deadline for fall or summer admission is April 15; for spring admission, December 15. The college follows a rolling admissions policy. A personal interview is recommended but not required. There is a $10 application fee.

Special: There are early admissions and deferred admissions plans. AP and CLEP credit is accepted.

Transfer: For fall 1981, 85 transfer students applied, 72 were accepted, and 50 enrolled. Transfers are accepted for all classes. The requirements are basically the same as those for freshman applicants, except that no high school record is required if at least 2 years of college have been successfully completed. D grades do not transfer. The senior year must be completed at the college to receive a degree. Thirty-two credits must be completed at the college, of a total 128 credits required for the bachelor's degree. Application deadlines are April 15 (fall) and December 15 (spring).

Visiting: There are no regularly scheduled orientations for prospective students. Guides are available for informal visits Monday through Saturday; visitors may sit in on classes and stay overnight at the school. The admissions office should be contacted to arrange visits.

Financial Aid: Approximately 80% of all students receive some form of financial aid. All students work part-time on campus. All students participate in 15 hours per week of on-campus work, which defrays the total cost of room and board. A limited amount of loan funds are available from the federal and state governments and private sources. All departments have CWS programs. The average freshman scholarship is $1400; the average income from a work contract is $1600. Tuition may be paid in installments. Aid is determined by need and available resources. The college is a member of CSS. The FAF or FFS is required. The deadlines for financial aid applications are April 1 (fall) and November 15 (spring).

Foreign Students: Eleven percent of the students are from foreign countries. The college offers special counseling.

Admissions: The TOEFL is required; a minimum score of 500 is necessary. The SAT or ACT is not required.

Procedure: The application deadline for foreign students is April 15 for fall entry. The college health form must be completed. Proof of

650 NORTH CAROLINA

adequate funds to cover 4 years of study must be presented. Health insurance is required; it is available through the college for a fee.

Admissions Contact: Robert B. Glass, Director of Admissions.

WESTERN CAROLINA UNIVERSITY B-3
Cullowhee, North Carolina 28723 (704) 227-7317

F/T: 2514M, 2360W	Faculty: 325; IIA, +$
P/T: 242M, 315W	Ph.D.'s: 62%
Grad: 348M, 587W	S/F Ratio: 15 to 1
Year: sems, ss	Tuition: $673 ($2461)
Appl: Aug. 1	R and B: $1540
2776 applied	2337 accepted 1246 enrolled
SAT: 394V 422M	**LESS COMPETITIVE**

Founded in 1889, Western Carolina University is a state-supported institution offering undergraduate instruction in the arts and sciences, business, education, and health fields. Its library contains 375,000 books and nearly 627,000 microfilm/fiche items, and subscribes to 2355 periodicals.

Environment: The 400-acre campus is located in a rural area 52 miles west of Asheville in the scenic Appalachian Mountains. There are 10 residence halls that accommodate 1636 men and 1638 women.

Student Life: About 89% of the students come from North Carolina; 95% attended public schools; 51% live on campus. Eleven percent are members of various minority groups. Campus housing is single-sex; there are visiting privileges. Students may keep cars on campus.

Organizations: There are 9 fraternities and 6 sororities. Student organizations and activities include a weekly newspaper, a radio station, music and drama groups, and religious clubs.

Sports: The university fields 10 intercollegiate teams for men and 5 for women. There are 9 intramural sports for men and 8 for women.

Handicapped: The campus is entirely accessible to physically handicapped students. Special facilities include wheelchair ramps, parking areas, elevators, and specially equipped rest rooms. Special class scheduling is possible. A reading machine is supplied for students with visual impairments.

Graduates: Thirty-five percent of the freshmen drop out; 40% remain to graduate. About 20% of the graduates go on for further education. Sixty percent enter business and industry.

Services: Health care, psychological counseling, tutoring, remedial instruction, placement, and career counseling are provided free of charge.

Programs of Study: The university awards the B.A., B.S., B.S.Ed., B.S.B.A., B.F.A., B.S.N., B.S.M.T., B.S.M.R.A., and B.S.H.S. degrees. Master's programs are also available. Bachelor's degrees are offered in the following subjects: BUSINESS (accounting, business education, business law, finance, information systems, management, marketing, office administration), EDUCATION (early childhood, elementary, educational media, health/physical, industrial, reading, secondary, special), ENGLISH (English), FINE AND PERFORMING ARTS (art, art education, music, music education, theater/dramatics), HEALTH SCIENCES (emergency medical care, environmental health, medical record administration, medical technology, nursing), LANGUAGES (French, German, Spanish), MATH AND SCIENCES (biology, chemistry, computer science, earth science, geology, mathematics, physical sciences, physics), PREPROFESSIONAL (home economics, social work), SOCIAL SCIENCES (anthropology, economics, geography, government/political science, history, law enforcement/criminal justice, parks/recreation management, psychology, social sciences, sociology). About 20% of the degrees are conferred in education and 30% in business.

Required: The general education requirement includes physical education and English.

Special: Student-designed majors, study abroad, and overseas teaching are offered.

Honors: Various honor societies have chapters on campus.

Admissions: About 84% of the applicants for 1981–82 were accepted. The SAT scores of those who enrolled were as follows: Verbal—87% below 500, 11% between 500 and 599, 2% between 600 and 700, and 0% above 700; Math—81% below 500, 16% between 500 and 599, 3% between 600 and 700, and 0% above 700. Other factors that enter into the admissions decision include evidence of special talents and recommendations.

Procedure: The SAT is required. New students are admitted each semester and for summer sessions. Application deadlines are August 1 (fall), December 1 (spring), May 15 (summer I), and June 1 (summer II). Notification is on a rolling basis. There is a $15 application fee.

Special: There is an early admissions plan with a May 1 deadline. AP and CLEP are used.

Transfer: For fall 1981, 678 transfer students applied, 563 were accepted, and 361 enrolled. Transfer students are accepted for each class. A 2.0 GPA is needed; D grades are not accepted. Thirty credits must be completed in residence, of a total 128 credits required for the bachelor's degree. Application deadlines are the same as those for freshmen.

Visiting: There are scheduled orientations for prospective students. Informal campus tours can also be arranged. Visitors may attend classes and stay overnight in the dormitories.

Financial Aid: About 62% of the students are receiving assistance. Work-study programs are available, and 30% of the students work part-time. The fund for scholarships and grants totals nearly $5.5 million. Aid is awarded annually and must be renewed. The university is a member of CSS. The FAF is due April 1.

Foreign Students: One percent of the students are from foreign countries. The university offers special counseling and organizations.

Admissions: The TOEFL is required; a minimum score of 550 is necessary. College entrance exams are not required.

Procedure: The application deadlines for foreign students are August 1 (fall), December 1 (spring), and May 15 (summer). A medical examination form must be completed. Proof of adequate funds for the full 4 years must be presented.

Admissions Contact: Tyree H. Kiser, Jr., Director of Admissions.

WINGATE COLLEGE C-3
Wingate, North Carolina 28174 (704) 233-4061

F/T: 775M, 697W	Faculty: 75; IIB, −$
P/T: 21M, 61W	Ph.D.'s: 50%
Grad: none	S/F Ratio: 19 to 1
Year: sems, ss	Tuition: $2320
Appl: Sept. 1	R and B: $1320
791 applied	657 accepted 420 enrolled
SAT: 350V 412M	ACT: 17 **LESS COMPETITIVE**

Wingate College, affiliated with the Southern Baptist Church, offers undergraduate instruction in the liberal arts and sciences, business, and education. The library contains 76,000 volumes, and subscribes to 400 periodicals.

Environment: The 300-acre campus is located in a rural area 30 miles from Charlotte. There are 30 buildings, including 10 residence halls accommodating 1250 men and women.

Student Life: About 80% of the students come from North Carolina; 95% live on campus. There is no chapel attendance requirement. About 98% of the students are Protestant. Minority-group members represent about 7% of the student body. Campus housing is single-sex; there are no visiting privileges. Students may keep cars on campus. Alcohol is not permitted on campus.

Organizations: Activities include clubs, religious groups, student government, a debate society, and regularly scheduled social and cultural events. There are no fraternities or sororities.

Sports: The college fields intercollegiate teams in 5 sports for men and 4 for women. Intramurals number 8 for men and 6 for women.

Handicapped: All of the campus is accessible to handicapped students. Special facilities include wheelchair ramps, parking areas, elevators, and specially equipped rest rooms. Special class scheduling is also available.

Graduates: The freshman dropout rate is 25%. Fifty percent remain to graduate. About 5% of the graduates pursue advanced degrees. Fifty percent enter careers in business and industry.

Services: Psychological counseling, career counseling, placement, tutoring, and remedial instruction are offered free of charge to all students. Health care is available for a fee.

Programs of Study: The B.A., B.S., B.M., and B.Mus.Ed. degrees are conferred. Associate degree programs are also available. Bachelor's degrees are offered in the following subjects: AREA STUDIES (American), BUSINESS (business administration), EDUCATION (early childhood, elementary, social science), FINE AND PERFORMING ARTS (music, music education), MATH AND SCIENCES (biology, mathematics), PREPROFESSIONAL (engineering, law, medicine, social work, veterinary), SOCIAL SCIENCES (history, human services). Forty percent of the degrees are conferred in business and 24% in human services.

Required: All students must take courses in English, science, mathematics, history, religion, literature, physical education, fine arts, and social sciences.

Special: A 3-year bachelor's degree, study abroad, and "winternationals" are offered.

Honors: Honors work is offered in English and in history.

Admissions: About 83% of those who applied for the 1981-82 freshman class were accepted. SAT scores of entering freshmen were as follows: Verbal—80% below 500, 10% between 500 and 599, 10% between 600 and 700, and 0% above 700; Math—80% below 500, 10% between 500 and 599, 10% between 600 and 700, and 0% above 700. Candidates should rank in the top 75% of their class, have a 2.0 high school GPA, and present 16 Carnegie units. Advanced placement or honor courses, recommendations, and impressions made during an interview are also considered.

Procedure: Either the SAT or ACT is required. September 1 is the fall application deadline; January 17, the spring. Notification is on a rolling basis. There is a $15 application fee.

Special: There are early decision and deferred admissions plans; the notification date for early decision is December 31. AP and CLEP credit is available.

Transfer: For fall 1981, 110 transfer applications were received, 88 were accepted, and 75 students enrolled. Transfer students are accepted for all but the senior year. A 2.0 GPA is needed; C and above grades are accepted. Minimum SAT scores totalling 700 are recommended. At least 64 credits must be completed in residence, of a total 125 credits required for the bachelor's degree. Application deadlines are the same as those for freshmen. Transfers are admitted to the fall, spring, and summer sessions.

Visiting: There are orientation days throughout the year for prospective students. Informal campus tours with student guides can be arranged. Visitors may attend classes and stay overnight at the college. Visits are best scheduled on weekdays. The admissions office should be contacted for arrangements.

Financial Aid: About 65% of the students receive financial aid. About 15% work part-time on campus. The average award to freshmen from all sources available through the college is $800. The college offers 30 academic and 5 athletic scholarships for freshmen. Federal programs such as NDSL, BEOG/SEOG, and CWS (in 12 departments) are available. Tuition may be paid in installments. The college is a member of CSS. The FFS or FAF is required. The financial aid application deadlines are April 1 (fall) and December 1 (spring).

Foreign Students: One percent of the students come from foreign countries. The college offers special counseling and organizations.

Admissions: The TOEFL is required; a minimum score of 500 is necessary. College entrance exams are not required.

Procedure: Application deadlines for foreign students are August 15 (fall), December 15 (spring), and May 15 (summer). Proof of health must be shown. Proof of funds adequate to cover a full year of study must also be presented.

Admissions Contact: Dan M. Shive, Director of Student Recruitment and Financial Aid.

WINSTON-SALEM STATE UNIVERSITY C-2
Winston-Salem, North Carolina 27110 (919) 761-2070

F/T: 768M, 1139W Faculty: 128; IIB, +$
P/T: 162M, 225W Ph.D.'s: 39%
Grad: none S/F Ratio: 15 to 1
Year: sems, ss Tuition: $611 ($2193)
Appl: open R and B: $1669
1091 applied 845 accepted 515 enrolled
SAT: 320V 340M ACT: 12 **LESS COMPETITIVE**

Winston-Salem State University, established in 1892, is a coeducational, state-supported liberal arts institution offering programs in the liberal arts and sciences, education, business, and the health sciences. The library contains 153,800 volumes and 16,430 audiovisuals, and subscribes to 1150 periodicals.

Environment: The 64-acre campus is surrounded by an urban environment. The physical plant includes dormitories accommodating 256 men and 518 women. There is also a communications building housing a television studio, a radio station, and a 261-seat multi-media lecture hall.

Student Life: Approximately 95% of the students are from the South; 51% live on campus. The student body is predominantly black (85%). Campus housing is single-sex; there are no visiting privileges. Students may keep cars on campus.

Organizations: There are 4 national fraternities, to which 40% of the men belong; 40% of the women belong to the 5 national sororities. Extracurricular activities include student government, publications, Protestant and Catholic organizations, the NAACP, a drama guild, the Afro-American Society, music groups, and concert and lecture series.

Sports: The university competes intercollegiately in 7 sports for men and 4 for women. Intramural sports number 10 for men and 8 for women.

Handicapped: Facilities for the physically handicapped include wheelchair ramps, special parking, and elevators.

Graduates: The freshman dropout rate is 40%; 36% remain to graduate. Forty-two percent of those who graduate pursue graduate study: 1% enter medical school, 1% dental school, and 4% law school. Twenty percent pursue careers in business and industry.

Services: Placement services, some psychological counseling, career counseling, tutoring, and remedial instruction are offered to students free of charge. Health care and extensive psychological counseling are available for a fee.

Programs of Study: The B.A., B.S., B.S.Ed., B.S.N., or B.A.S. degrees are awarded. Bachelor's degrees are offered in the following subjects: BUSINESS (accounting, business administration, business education, computer science), EDUCATION (early childhood, elementary, health/physical, secondary, special), ENGLISH (English), FINE AND PERFORMING ARTS (art education, music, music education), HEALTH SCIENCES (medical technology, nursing), MATH AND SCIENCES (biology, chemistry, mathematics), PREPROFESSIONAL (social work), SOCIAL SCIENCES (government/political science, psychology, sociology). About 37% of degrees are conferred in education and 20% in business.

Required: All students must take courses in English, natural science, math, social science, physical education and health, and humanities.

Special: Student-designed majors and an enrichment center for students who wish to engage in self-directed study in addition to prescribed class work are offered.

Honors: Two national honor societies have chapters on campus. An honors program is open to qualified students.

Admissions: Approximately 77% of those who applied were accepted for the 1981-82 freshman class. On the SAT, entering freshmen scored as follows: Verbal—99% below 500, 1% between 500 and 599, 0% between 600 and 700, and 0% above 700; Math—98% below 500, 2% between 500 and 599, 0% between 600 and 700, and 0% above 700. Applicants must have completed 16 high school units with a grade average of C. Students are selected on the basis of their academic record, recommendations, SAT scores, and other information concerning health, abilities, and promise. Nonaccredited high school students and holders of equivalency certificates may be admitted with individual consideration. Standards for out-of-state applicants are slightly higher.

Procedure: The SAT or ACT is required. Application deadlines are open; the college follows a rolling admissions policy. Freshmen are admitted in the fall, spring, and summer. There is a $15 application fee.

Special: There is an early decision plan with a May 1 notification date. CLEP credit is accepted.

Transfer: For fall 1981, 234 transfer students applied; 147 were accepted, and 117 enrolled. Transfers are accepted to all but the senior class. State residents must have a minimum 2.0 GPA; out-of-state applicants must have a 2.5 GPA. All grades transfer. Thirty semester hours must be earned in residence, of a total 127 semester hours required for the bachelor's degree. Application deadlines are open. Transfers are admitted to the fall, spring, and summer sessions.

Visiting: There are no regularly scheduled orientations for prospective students. Guides are available for informal visits; visitors may sit in on classes. The recruitment office should be contacted to arrange visits.

Financial Aid: Approximately 80% of all students receive some form of financial aid, which is granted through scholarships, loans, grants (including EOG), and work (including CWS). About 75% of the students work part-time on campus. Need is the determining factor. The FAF or the FFS is required. The deadlines for aid applications are May 1 (fall) and December 1 (spring).

652 NORTH CAROLINA

Foreign Students: One percent of the students are from foreign countries. The university offers special counseling.

Admissions: The TOEFL is required; a minimum score of 500 is necessary. The SAT or the university's own entrance exam must also be taken. Applications should score at least 650 on the college entrance exam.

Procedure: There are no application deadlines. Admissions are on a rolling basis. Foreign students may enter the fall, spring, or summer sessions. A physical examination report must be completed. Proof of adequate funds to cover 1 year of study must be presented. Health insurance is required while in attendance; it is available through the university for a fee.

Admissions Contact: Emily H. Harper, Director of Admissions.

NORTH DAKOTA

DICKINSON STATE COLLEGE B–3
Dickinson, North Dakota 58601 (701) 227-2331

F/T: 407M, 555W
P/T: 36M, 95W
Grad: none
Year: qtrs, ss
Appl: open
400 applied
ACT: 18

Faculty: n/av; IIB, +$
Ph.D.'s: 22%
S/F Ratio: 15 to 1
Tuition: $708 ($1269)
R and B: $1041

383 accepted 337 enrolled
NONCOMPETITIVE

Dickinson State College offers education in the liberal arts and teacher training. Its library contains 65,000 volumes and 7179 microfilm items, and subscribes to over 630 periodicals.

Environment: The 67-acre campus is located 600 miles from Minneapolis. The dormitories accommodate more than 400 students, and apartments are available for married students.

Student Life: About 90% of the students are from North Dakota. Alcohol is prohibited on campus.

Organizations: There are 2 national fraternities and 2 national sororities, to which approximately 35% of the students belong.

Sports: The college has intercollegiate teams in 7 sports for men and 3 for women. There are also many intramural programs for men and women.

Handicapped: There are no special facilities for handicapped students.

Graduates: About 20% of the freshmen drop out after the first year. Approximately 40% remain to graduate; of those, 50% pursue advanced degrees.

Services: Free health care, tutoring, remedial instruction, career counseling, and placement services are offered to students.

Programs of Study: The college confers the B.A., B.S., and B.S.Ed. degrees. Associate degrees are also awarded. Bachelor's degrees are offered in the following subjects: BUSINESS (accounting, business administration, business education), EDUCATION (elementary, secondary), ENGLISH (English, speech), FINE AND PERFORMING ARTS (art, music), HEALTH SCIENCES (environmental health, nursing), MATH AND SCIENCES (biology, chemistry, earth science and geography, mathematics), SOCIAL SCIENCES (government/political science, social sciences). Most degrees are granted in education.

Special: Students may earn combined B.A.-B.S. degrees in all subjects. The college offers the Bachelor of College Studies (no major) degree.

Admissions: Ninety-six percent of those who applied were accepted for the 1981–82 freshman class. The college must by law admit all graduates of accredited high schools in North Dakota. Nonresident applicants must have completed 15 Carnegie units, score above 18 on the ACT, and rank in the top half of their graduating class.

Procedure: The ACT is required. The application, a $10 fee, a health certificate, transcripts, and test scores must be submitted. The college follows a rolling admissions plan. There is no application deadline.

Special: CLEP credit is accepted.

Transfer: For fall 1981, 150 transfers were accepted and 138 students enrolled. Transfers are accepted for all classes. A GPA of at least 2.0 is required; D grades may transfer. All students must complete, at the college, 90 of the 192–197 credits required for a bachelor's degree. Application deadlines are open.

Visiting: Orientations and tours of the campus are available for prospective students. Guides are available for informal visits. Visitors may sit in on classes. The admissions office should be contacted for arrangements.

Financial Aid: About 65% of the students receive financial aid. Scholarships and all federal aid programs are available. The FAF is required and should be filed by May 15.

Admissions Contact: Neil Ableidinger, Registrar and Director of Admissions.

JAMESTOWN COLLEGE E–3
Jamestown, North Dakota 58401 (701) 253-2557

F/T: 275M, 250W
P/T: 26M, 69W
Grad: none
Year: 4-1-4
Appl: open
460 applied
ACT: 21

Faculty: 37; IIB, +$
Ph.D.'s: 41%
S/F Ratio: 14 to 1
Tuition: $3900
R and B: $1575

449 accepted 165 enrolled
COMPETITIVE

Jamestown College, founded in 1883, is affiliated with the United Presbyterian Church. The library contains 60,000 volumes and 16,000 microfilm items, and subscribes to 350 periodicals.

Environment: The 107-acre campus is located in a rural area on a hill overlooking the city of Jamestown, 350 miles from Minneapolis. It has 13 major buildings, including 3 dormitories and 1 housing unit for married students.

Student Life: About 72% of the students are from North Dakota. Ten percent belong to the Presbyterian Church. Twenty-two percent are Catholic, and 63% are Protestant. Three percent of the students are minority-group members. Campus housing is coed. Freshmen must live on campus unless they are town residents or are living with a relative or guardian. Students may keep cars on campus.

Organizations: Student groups include the student government and various departmental, social, service, and religious organizations.

Sports: The college competes in 8 intercollegiate sports for men and 6 for women. Intramural programs are offered through the James Valley YMCA; there are no college-run intramural sports.

Handicapped: There are no special facilities for handicapped students, but 50% of the campus is accessible.

Graduates: Fifteen percent of entering freshmen drop out after their first year; 50% remain to graduate. Of these, 15% continue their studies, with 2% entering medical school, 2% entering dental school, and 2% entering law school. Another 30% pursue careers in business and industry.

Services: The following services are available free to students: health care, tutoring, remedial instruction, career counseling, and placement. Placement services may be used by alumni as well as students.

Programs of Study: The college confers the B.A. degree. Bachelor's degrees are offered in the following subjects: BUSINESS (business administration, computer science), EDUCATION (elementary, health/physical, secondary), ENGLISH (English), FINE AND PERFORMING ARTS (art, art/business, music, music education, theater/dramatics), HEALTH SCIENCES (medical technology, nursing), MATH AND SCIENCES (biology, chemistry, mathematics, physics), PHILOSOPHY (philosophy, religion), PREPROFESSIONAL (dentistry, engineering, law, medicine, ministry, optometry, pharmacy), SOCIAL SCIENCES (economics, government/political science, history, psychology). About 40% of the degrees are conferred in health sciences and 20% in business.

Required: There are certain liberal arts requirements. Course work is required in such major disciplines as English, philosophy, and the natural sciences. Physical education courses must also be taken.

Special: A 3-2 program in engineering and a junior-year-abroad program are available. An addiction counseling certification program is available in cooperation with the North Dakota State Hospital. The 4- or 5-year medical technology program is provided with the cooperation of 2 affiliated hospitals.

Honors: Alpha Chi has a chapter on campus. Departmental honors programs are available in art, English, math, biology, and chemistry.

Admissions: About 98% of those who applied were accepted for the 1981–82 freshman class. The ACT scores of those who enrolled were as follows: 47% below 21, 17% between 21 and 23, 15% between 24 and 25, 11% between 26 and 28, and 10% above 28. Candidates should have completed 15 Carnegie units and have a C average or higher. They should rank in the upper 50% of their graduating class. Advance placement or honors courses, recommendations, and personality are also considered important.

Procedure: Either the SAT or ACT should be taken during the senior year. There is no application deadline. All applications should be accompanied by a $15 fee. The college follows a rolling admissions plan.

Special: There are early admissions, early decision, and deferred admissions plans. CLEP credit is given.

Transfer: For fall 1981, 56 transfer students applied. Transfers are accepted for all classes. A minimum GPA of 2.0 is required. D grades do not transfer. Thirty-six of a minimum 140 semester credits required for a bachelor's degree must be taken in residence. The final semester prior to graduation must be taken at the college. There is a rolling admissions plan.

Visiting: Orientations are available to prospective students on weekdays. Guides are available for informal visits. Visitors may sit in on classes and stay overnight at the school. The admissions director should be contacted for arrangements.

Financial Aid: Eighty-five percent of all students receive some form of financial aid. The average award to freshmen from college sources is $3000. Thirty-four percent work part-time on campus. BEOG/SEOG, grants-in-aid, CWS, and state and federal loans are available. The college participates in the CSS; the FAF or FFS is required. There is no deadline for aid applications.

Foreign Students: Four percent of the full-time students come from foreign countries. The college offers these students an intensive English course and special counseling.

Admissions: Foreign students must achieve a minimum TOEFL score of 450 or an equally acceptable score on any other English proficiency exam. No college entrance examination is required.

Procedure: Admission is on a rolling basis. Foreign students must present proof of funds adequate to cover their length of study at the college. Proof of health must be presented in the form of a health certificate, signed by a qualified physician. Health insurance is available at cost through the college.

Admissions Contact: Clayton Ketterling, Director of Admissions.

MARY COLLEGE
Bismarck, North Dakota 58501   C-3
(701) 255-4681

F/T: 232M, 569W   Faculty: 89; n/av
P/T: 57M, 145W   Ph.D.'s: 17%
Grad: none   S/F Ratio: 17 to 1
Year: 4-4-1, ss   Tuition: $2690
Appl: Aug. 15   R and B: $1390
233 enrolled
ACT: 17   **COMPETITIVE**

Mary College, founded in 1955, is a Roman Catholic liberal arts college conducted by the Benedictine Sisters. Its library contains 56,000 volumes and 600 reels of microfilm, and subscribes to 7000 periodicals.

Environment: The 100-acre campus is located in a suburban area 7 miles from Bismarck. The buildings, designed by Marcel Breuer, a world-famous architect, include 5 dormitories. The college also sponsors on-campus apartments.

Student Life: About 85% of the students are from North Dakota. Forty-two percent of all students reside on campus. Sixty-one percent are Catholic, and 33% are Protestant; religious counseling is available for both denominations. Nine percent of the students are minority-group members. College housing is single-sex, and there are visiting privileges. Students may keep cars on campus.

Organizations: There are no fraternities or sororities on campus. Clubs on campus and local music and drama groups offer social and cultural entertainment.

Sports: The college fields 1 intercollegiate team for men and 3 for women. There are 7 intramural sports for men and 7 for women.

Handicapped: About 90% of the campus is accessible to the physically handicapped, and special facilities include wheelchair ramps, parking areas, elevators, and specially equipped rest rooms. A staff of 4 provides counseling and assistance.

NORTH DAKOTA 653

Graduates: The freshman dropout rate is 28%, and 32% of the freshmen remain to graduate. About 5% of the graduates continue their education, and 20% pursue careers in business and industry.

Services: Free health care, tutoring, placement, and career counseling are available to students.

Programs of Study: The college confers the B.A., B.S., and B.C.S. degrees. Associate degrees are also awarded. Bachelor's degrees are offered in the following subjects: BUSINESS (accounting, business administration), EDUCATION (early childhood, elementary, health/physical, secondary, special), ENGLISH (communications, English), FINE AND PERFORMING ARTS (music, music education), HEALTH SCIENCES (medical technology, nursing, radiological technology, respiratory therapy), MATH AND SCIENCES (natural sciences), PHILOSOPHY (Christian ministry), PREPROFESSIONAL (dentistry, engineering, law, medicine, pharmacy, social work, veterinary), SOCIAL SCIENCES (social sciences). About 29% of the degrees are conferred in health sciences, 23% in education, and 18% in social sciences.

Required: All students must take courses in the humanities, social science, mathematics, and philosophy-theology.

Special: Combined B.A.-B.S. degrees and general studies degrees are possible.

Admissions: ACT scores for the 1981–82 freshman class were as follows: 47% below 21, 21% between 21 and 23, 7% between 24 and 25, 3% between 26 and 28, and 1% above 28. Candidates must present 15 Carnegie units and have a minimum GPA of 2.0. An interview may be arranged. The ACT scores, recommendations, and advanced placement or honors courses are also important.

Procedure: The ACT or SAT is required. The deadline for applications is August 15 (fall), December 15 (spring), and May 15 (summer). Notification is on a rolling basis. There is a $15 application fee.

Special: Early and deferred admissions plans are available. AP and CLEP credit is granted.

Transfer: For fall 1981, 202 students enrolled. Transfers are accepted at all levels. Only students in good standing with a grade average of 2.0 or better are eligible; D grades transfer. Students must complete, at the college, at least 32 of the 128 semester hours necessary for a bachelor's degree. Application deadlines for the fall and spring terms are the same as those for freshmen.

Visiting: There are regularly scheduled orientations for prospective students. Guided tours of the campus are also available. Visitors may sit in on classes and stay overnight at the school. The director of admissions should be contacted for arrangements.

Financial Aid: About 75% of all students receive some form of financial aid. Twenty-five percent work part-time on campus. Federal loans are available in amounts from $200 to $1000; local bank loans, from $500 to $1500. Tuition may be paid in installments. The college is a member of CSS and requires the FFS. Application deadlines are June (fall and winter), November (spring), and March (summer).

Foreign Students: One percent of the full-time students come from foreign countries.

Admissions: Foreign students must achieve a minimum TOEFL score of 500. No college entrance exam must be taken.

Procedure: Foreign students must present proof of funds adequate to cover 1 year of study.

Admissions Contact: Leland D. Nagel, Director of Admissions.

MAYVILLE STATE COLLEGE
Mayville, North Dakota 58257   E-3
(701) 786-2301

F/T: 260M, 375W   Faculty: 43; IIB, +$
P/T: 11M, 50W   Ph.D.'s: 44%
Grad: none   S/F Ratio: 15 to 1
Year: qtrs, ss   Tuition: $702 ($1266)
Appl: Sept. 14   R and B: $1266
250 applied   246 accepted   184 enrolled
ACT: 18   **LESS COMPETITIVE**

Mayville State College, founded in 1890, is a small, coeducational, public college with preparation of teachers as its chief vocational concern. The library contains 75,000 volumes and 350 microfilm reels, and subscribes to 600 periodicals.

Environment: The 55-acre campus is set in a rural environment 58 miles from Fargo. Residence halls house 600 students, and on-campus apartments are available for 54 married students.

Student Life: About 73% of the students are from North Dakota; almost 95% of the entering freshmen come from public schools. Eighty-three percent of the students live on campus. About 4% are minority-

654 NORTH DAKOTA

group members. College housing is single-sex, and there are visiting privileges. Students may keep cars on campus. Day-care facilities are available for a fee to full-time and part-time students, faculty, and staff.

Organizations: There are no fraternities or sororities on campus. Student clubs and special-interest groups provide social and cultural activities. Popular outdoor sports are hunting, fishing, skiing, and skating.

Sports: The college fields 8 intercollegiate teams for men and 6 for women. There are 9 intramural sports for men and 9 for women.

Handicapped: Only 10% of the campus is accessible to physically handicapped students, and, except for designated parking areas, there are no special facilities. Two special counselors and 3 assistants are provided.

Graduates: The freshman dropout rate is 20%, and 65% of the freshmen remain to graduate. About 12% of the graduates continue their studies, while 45% enter business and industry.

Services: Free health care, career and psychological counseling, placement, tutoring, and remedial instruction are available.

Programs of Study: The college confers the B.A., B.S.Ed., B.S. General Studies, and B.S. Computer Studies degrees. Associate degrees are also offered. Bachelor's degrees are offered in the following subjects: BUSINESS (business administration, business education, computer science, management), EDUCATION (elementary, health/physical, secondary), ENGLISH (English), FINE AND PERFORMING ARTS (art, art education, music education), MATH AND SCIENCES (biology, chemistry, composite chemistry, composite science, general science, junior high science, mathematics, physical sciences), SOCIAL SCIENCES (social sciences, social sciences and geography). Nondegree preprofessional courses of study are also available. Most students major in elementary and secondary education.

Honors: Honors work is offered in business, social science, speech, and business. There are chapters of 4 professional societies on campus.

Admissions: Ninety-eight percent of those who applied for the 1981–82 freshman class were accepted. Candidates must be graduates of an accredited high school, should have completed 15 Carnegie units, and must have at least a 2.0 grade average. An interview is recommended. Advanced placement or honors courses are also considered.

Procedure: Students are strongly encouraged to take either the ACT or the SAT. Applications should be submitted by September 14 (fall), December 10 (winter), March 18 (spring), or June 9 (summer). Notification is on a rolling basis. There is a $10 fee.

Special: An early decision plan is available. CLEP credit is offered.

Transfer: For fall 1981, all of the 108 applicants were accepted and 88 enrolled. Transfers are accepted for all but the senior class. A minimum 2.0 GPA is required; standardized exam scores and an interview are recommended. D grades are acceptable. Students must spend at least 1 year in residence and complete, at the college, at least 45 of the 192 quarter hours necessary for a bachelor's degree.

Visiting: There are 2-day orientations in the summer for prospective students. Informal tours, class visits, and overnight stays during school sessions can be arranged in advance through the admissions office.

Financial Aid: About 75% of all students receive some form of financial aid. Forty-six percent work part-time on campus. Average aid to freshmen is $300. Scholarships, grants, and loans are available. The college is a member of CSS and requires the FFS. The application deadline for fall entry is April 15.

Foreign Students: Three percent of the full-time students come from foreign countries. The college offers these students special counseling.

Admissions: Foreign students must achieve a minimum TOEFL score of 525 or take the college's own English proficiency exam. No college entrance exam must be taken.

Procedure: Application deadlines are August 1 (fall), November 1 (winter), and May 1 (summer). Foreign students must present a completed medical form and proof of funds adequate to cover the entire period of study.

Admissions Contact: Ronald G. Brown, Director of Admissions.

MINOT STATE COLLEGE C–2
Minot, North Dakota 58701 (701) 857-3000

F/T: 898M, 1552W Faculty: 120; IIA, –$
P/T: 141M, 225W Ph.D.'s: 50%
Grad: 12M, 50W S/F Ratio: 20 to 1
Year: qtrs, ss Tuition: $792 ($1353)
Appl: open R and B: $1300
800 applied 800 accepted 800 enrolled
ACT: 19 NONCOMPETITIVE

Minot State College is a state-controlled institution offering programs in liberal arts, teacher education, and preprofessional and vocational areas. The library houses 100,000 volumes, and subscribes to 1400 periodicals.

Environment: The 103-acre campus is located in a city of 35,000 people, about 100 miles north of Bismarck. The dormitories house 710 students. Forty housing units are available for married students. Additional housing is provided by fraternities and sororities.

Student Life: About 95% of the students are from North Dakota. About 25% live in the residence halls, which are single-sex. Freshman and sophomore women must live in campus housing unless they live at home.

Organizations: There are 3 fraternities and 4 sororities on campus to which 25% of the men and 30% of the women belong. Campus activities include special-interest clubs and music and drama productions.

Sports: The college fields intercollegiate teams in 9 sports for men and 5 for women. Intramural programs also are available.

Handicapped: Special facilities for the physically handicapped include wheelchair ramps, parking areas, elevators, and specially equipped rest rooms and housing units. Special class scheduling can be arranged. A staff of 4 provides assistance and counseling.

Services: Free tutoring, remedial instruction, career and psychological counseling, and placement services are offered to students.

Programs of Study: The college confers the B.A., B.S., and B.S.W. degrees. Associate and master's degrees also are available. Bachelor's degrees are offered in the following subjects: BUSINESS (business administration, business education), EDUCATION (elementary, health/physical, recreation, secondary, special), ENGLISH (communication arts, English), FINE AND PERFORMING ARTS (art, music, music education, radio/TV), HEALTH SCIENCES (medical technology, nursing, speech therapy, X-ray technology), LANGUAGES (German), MATH AND SCIENCES (biology, chemistry, earth science, ecology/environmental science, mathematics, physical sciences, physics), PREPROFESSIONAL (dentistry, engineering, law, medicine, ministry, pharmacy, social work, veterinary), SOCIAL SCIENCES (criminal justice, economics, gerontology, history, psychology, social sciences, sociology).

Required: Students must take a number of general-education courses in humanities, communication, natural science, social and behavioral sciences, and leisure-time education.

Special: A general studies degree is available. The college offers distinctive educational programs (such as a radio program to teach vocal music to rural and grade schools) and independent research. A reading program for corrective and remedial purposes is also offered. Students may earn combined B.A.-B.S. degrees. Additional minors are offered in coaching, computer science, driver and safety education, French, geography, home economics, Indian studies, library science, and political science.

Admissions: All who applied for the 1981–82 freshman class were accepted. The ACT scores of those who enrolled were as follows: 31% between 21 and 25, and 27% above 26. Candidates must be graduates of accredited high schools and should present 17 Carnegie units. A minimum ACT score of 18 is required of out-of-state residents.

Procedure: The ACT is required. Application deadlines are open. A $10 application fee is required. The college uses a rolling admissions plan.

Special: CLEP credit is available.

Transfer: A 2.0 GPA is required. Students must earn, in residence, at least 45 of the 196 quarter credits required for a bachelor's degree.

Visiting: Prospective students can arrange visits to the campus on weekdays during the school year. Visits include campus tours and interviews with faculty members and with admissions and financial aid officers. Visitors may attend classes and stay overnight at the school. For further information, contact the admissions office.

Financial Aid: About 50% of the students receive aid. Scholarships, EOG, CWS, and student loans (including NDSL) are available. The average award to 1981–82 freshmen was $800. The FFS is required. Applications should be filed by March 1 for priority consideration.

Foreign Students: Students from foreign countries represent 2% of enrollment. The college offers these students an intensive English course and special counseling.

Admissions: Applicants must score at least 525 on the TOEFL. They also must take the ACT.

Procedure: Application deadlines are open. Students must present a physician's statement as proof of good health and must provide evidence of adequate funds. They also must arrange to carry health insurance.

Admissions Contact: Dawn Evenson, Director of Admissions.

NORTH DAKOTA STATE UNIVERSITY F-3
Fargo, North Dakota 58105 (701) 237-8643

F/T: 4466M, 2924W	Faculty: 510; I, — — $
P/T: 177M, 345W	Ph.D.'s: 62%
Grad: 560M, 270W	S/F Ratio: 15 to 1
Year: qtrs, ss	Tuition: $732 ($1500)
Appl: Aug. 1	R and B: $1550
2211 applied	1952 accepted 1604 enrolled
ACT: 21	LESS COMPETITIVE

North Dakota State University, established in 1890, is the traditional land-grant institution. It consists of 7 undergraduate colleges: Agriculture, Engineering and Architecture, Home Economics, Humanities and Social Sciences, Pharmacy, Science and Mathematics, and University Studies. The university also has a graduate school. The university library contains 335,493 volumes and 2200 reels of microfilm, and subscribes to 2789 periodicals.

Environment: The 100-acre campus is located in an urban setting, at the edge of the city of Fargo. The university owns another 2000 acres which are used in the courses of study. The 11 dormitories, which house 3200 students, include high-rise and 3-story buildings.

Student Life: Three-quarters of the students come from North Dakota; about 95% of entering freshmen attended public schools. Thirty-five percent of the students live on campus. Four percent are minority-group members. University housing is coed and single-sex; students in single-sex housing have visiting privileges. Students may keep cars on campus. Drinking on campus is prohibited. Day-care facilities are available free of charge to full-time and part-time students, faculty, and staff.

Organizations: There are 11 fraternities and 7 sororities on campus, to which 13% of the men and 11% of the women belong. Social and recreational activities are also arranged by the student government and other organizations. Some major events are Spring Blast, Homecoming, and a spring musical.

Sports: The college fields 11 intercollegiate teams. There are 7 intramural sports.

Handicapped: Ninety percent of the campus is accessible to the physically handicapped. Special facilities for these students include wheelchair ramps, parking areas, elevators, and specially equipped rest rooms. Special class scheduling and other services are offered by the Office of Special Student Services. A note-taking service and special library and computer terminal facilities are available for visually and hearing-impaired students.

Graduates: About 30% of the freshmen drop out after the first year; 55% remain to graduate.

Services: Free health care, tutoring, remedial instruction, career and psychological counseling, and job placement services are offered.

Programs of Study: Undergraduate programs lead to the B.A., B.S., B. University Studies, and B.F.A. in Drama degrees. Associate, master's, and doctoral programs are also available. Bachelor's degrees are offered in the following subjects: BUSINESS (business administration, computer science, construction management), EDUCATION (child development/family relations, health/physical, secondary), ENGLISH (English, speech), FINE AND PERFORMING ARTS (art, art education, art history, music, music education, theater/dramatics), HEALTH SCIENCES (food and nutrition, medical technology, speech therapy, veterinary science), LANGUAGES (French, German, Spanish), MATH AND SCIENCES (bacteriology, biochemistry, biology, botany, chemistry, earth science, entomology, geology, horticulture, mathematics, physics, statistics, zoology), PHILOSOPHY (humanities), PREPROFESSIONAL (agriculture, architecture, dentistry, engineering, home economics, law, medicine, pharmacy, veterinary), SOCIAL SCIENCES (economics, government/political science, history, leisure studies and community recreational services, psychology, social sciences, sociology). The most popular major is business.

Required: Freshman students are required to take a broad spectrum of general education courses, including English, speech, American history, science, mathematics, and psychology.

Special: Combined B.A.-B.S. degrees, student-designed majors, and a general studies degree are possible.

Honors: The university has a scholars program. There are a number of honor societies on campus.

Admissions: About 88% of those who applied for the 1981–82 freshman class were accepted. Applicants should have either a regular high school diploma or a GED certificate. Candidates should have completed 15 Carnegie units in an accredited high school and have a minimum grade average of 1.6.

Procedure: The SAT or ACT is required. Applications should be submitted by August 1 for fall entry. Notification is on a rolling basis. There is a $15 application fee.

Special: Early and deferred admissions plans are available. AP and CLEP credit is offered.

Transfer: For fall 1981, 1389 students applied, 1100 were accepted, and 1037 enrolled. Transfers are accepted for all but the freshman class. Students should have at least a 1.6 GPA for sophomore transfer, 1.75 for junior transfer, and 2.0 for senior transfer; standardized exam scores are also required. D grades do not transfer. Students must spend 1 year in residence and complete at least 45 of the 183 credits necessary for a bachelor's degree. The application deadline is the same as that for freshmen.

Visiting: Guided tours of the campus are available. Visitors are sometimes permitted to sit in on classes. The best times for visits are 10:30 A.M. and 1:30 P.M. on weekdays during the school year. The admissions office should be contacted for arrangements.

Financial Aid: About 30% of the students receive some form of campus aid. Twenty percent work part-time on campus. Federal and state loans are available. The FFS is required, and aid applications should be made by April 15.

Foreign Students: One percent of the full-time students come from foreign countries. The university offers these students an intensive English course and program, special counseling, and special organizations.

Admissions: Foreign students must achieve a minimum TOEFL score of 550. No college entrance exam must be taken.

Procedure: The application deadline for fall entry is June 1. Foreign students must present proof of funds adequate to cover the entire period of study. They must also carry health insurance, which is available through the university for a fee.

Admissions Contact: George Wallman, Director of Admissions.

UNIVERSITY OF NORTH DAKOTA E-2
Grand Forks, North Dakota 58201 (701) 777-2011

F/T, P/T:	Faculty: n/av; I, — — $
5450M, 5081W	Ph.D.'s: 54%
Grad: 1287M&W	S/F Ratio: 19 to 1
Year: sems, ss	Tuition: $766 ($1534)
Appl: July 1	R and B: $1550
3000 applied	2000 accepted 1800 enrolled
ACT: 21	NONCOMPETITIVE

University of North Dakota, established in 1883, is a state-supported institution offering undergraduate curricula in a wide variety of fields. The library contains over 500,000 volumes and periodical subscriptions.

Environment: The campus is located at the edge of Grand Forks, a city of 45,000 inhabitants. Living facilities include dormitories, on-campus apartments, married student housing, and fraternity and sorority houses.

Student Life: Most of the students come from North Dakota; 91% come from public schools. About 60% live on campus in single-sex and coed housing. Alcohol is prohibited on campus.

Organizations: There is a full program of extracurricular activities. About 21% of the women belong to 8 sororities; 25% of the men belong to 13 fraternities. On-campus social and cultural events are scheduled regularly.

Sports: The university fields intercollegiate teams in 11 sports for men and 11 for women. Intramural activities are offered in 21 sports.

Handicapped: The Student Opportunity Programs Office coordinates assistance and services for handicapped students.

Graduates: The freshman dropout rate is 20%; about 37% remain to graduate. Two-thirds of the men and one-third of the women go on to graduate study.

Services: The university offers the following services to all students: health care, tutoring, remedial instruction, placement, and career counseling.

Programs of Study: The B.A., B.S., B.S.B.A., B.S.P.A., B.M., B.F.A., and B.S.N. degrees are conferred. Master's and doctoral programs are

656 NORTH DAKOTA

also available. Bachelor's degrees are offered in the following subjects: AREA STUDIES (Indian), BUSINESS (accounting, aviation administration, banking and finance, business administration, business education, computer science, engineering management, management, marketing, office management, retail merchandising), EDUCATION (distributive, early childhood, elementary, health/physical, industrial, secondary, special), ENGLISH (communication, English, journalism, speech), FINE AND PERFORMING ARTS (art education, fine arts, music, music education, theater/dramatics, visual arts), HEALTH SCIENCES (medical technology, nursing, occupational therapy, physical therapy, speech therapy), LANGUAGES (French, German, Greek/Latin, Norwegian, Scandinavian languages, Spanish), MATH AND SCIENCES (biology, botany, chemistry, fishery and wildlife biology, geology, mathematics, physics, zoology), PHILOSOPHY (classics, philosophy, religious studies), PREPROFESSIONAL (bioengineering, engineering—chemical, engineering—civil, engineering—electrical, engineering—mechanical, home economics, law, library science, medicine, social work), SOCIAL SCIENCES (anthropology, criminal justice, economics, geography, government/political science, history, police administration, psychology, public administration, sociology).

Required: All students are required to take courses in English, the humanities, social science, and natural science.

Special: Study abroad and independent study are possible.

Honors: An honors program is available for superior students. There are numerous honor societies on campus, including a chapter of Phi Beta Kappa.

Admissions: About 67% of the applicants for the 1981–82 freshman class were accepted. The ACT scores of those who enrolled were as follows: 29% below 21, 37% between 21 and 25, and 21% above 26. All North Dakota residents who are high school graduates are eligible for admission. Nonresidents must rank in the upper half of their class.

Procedure: The ACT or SAT is required. July 1 is the application deadline for fall admission. New students are also admitted at midyear. Notification is on a rolling basis. There is a $15 application fee.

Special: There are early decision, early admissions, and deferred admissions plans. CLEP and AP credit is available.

Transfer: Transfers are considered for all classes. A GPA of at least 2.0 is required. All students must complete, at the university, 30 of the 125 credits required for a bachelor's degree.

Visiting: Campus tours with student guides can be arranged. Visitors may sit in on classes.

Financial Aid: The university offers freshman scholarships, various loans, grants, and campus work opportunities. CWS is offered. The FAF should be filed by March 15.

Foreign Students: About 1% of the full-time students come from foreign countries. Special counseling and special organizations are available for these students.

Admissions: Foreign students must achieve a TOEFL score of at least 525. No college entrance exams are required.

Procedure: The application deadline for fall entry is April 1. Foreign students must complete a health form and must present proof of funds adequate to cover 4 years of study. Health insurance is required.

Admissions Contact: Donna Bruce, Admissions Officer.

VALLEY CITY STATE COLLEGE   E-3
Valley City, North Dakota 58072   (701) 845-7412

F/T: 435M, 515W	Faculty: 51; IIB, +$
P/T: 89M, 169W	Ph.D.'s: 40%
Grad: none	S/F Ratio: 18 to 1
Year: qtrs, ss	Tuition: $707 ($1267)
Appl: open	R and B: $1428
290 applied	290 accepted 249 enrolled
ACT: 18	NONCOMPETITIVE

Valley City State, founded in 1889, is a state-supported college of liberal arts and education whose primary aim is to prepare teachers for the public elementary and secondary schools of North Dakota. The library contains 88,600 volumes and 2201 reels of microfilm, and subscribes to 381 periodicals.

Environment: The 94-acre campus is located in a rural setting 60 miles from Fargo. Its 32 buildings include a ceramics laboratory. Five residence halls (2 of which are rented to sorority and fraternity groups) house 382 students and 16 family units.

Student Life: About 93% of the students are from North Dakota. Forty percent of all students reside on campus. Three percent are minority-group members. College housing is single-sex, and there are visiting privileges. Students may keep cars on campus. Day-care facilities are available to full-time and part-time students, faculty, and staff.

Organizations: There are 4 fraternities and 4 sororities on campus, to which 40% of the men and 40% of the women belong. The student government and special-interest clubs also provide social and cultural activities.

Sports: The college fields 8 intercollegiate teams for men and 8 for women. There are 4 intramural sports for men and 2 for women.

Handicapped: About 60% of the campus is accessible to the physically handicapped. Facilities for these students include wheelchair ramps, elevators, lowered drinking fountains, and specially equipped rest rooms. Special class scheduling can be arranged. A counselor and an assistant are provided for handicapped students.

Graduates: The freshman dropout rate is 16%, and 40% of the freshmen remain to graduate. Of those, 5% continue their education; 1% enter medical school, and 1% enter law school. Another 40% pursue careers in business and industry.

Services: Free health care, tutoring, and career and psychological counseling are available to students. A job placement service, available for a fee to students and alumni, maintains a credentials file and lists job opportunities.

Programs of Study: The college confers the B.A., B.S., B.C.S., and B.S.Ed. degrees. Associate degrees are also awarded. Bachelor's degrees are offered in the following subjects: BUSINESS (business administration, business education), EDUCATION (elementary, health/physical, industrial), ENGLISH (English), FINE AND PERFORMING ARTS (art, art education, music, music education), LANGUAGES (Spanish), MATH AND SCIENCES (biology, chemistry, ecology/environmental science, mathematics), SOCIAL SCIENCES (history, human resources administration and management, social sciences). Most degrees are conferred in business.

Required: Freshmen must complete a general education requirement, including courses in English, speech, science, mathematics, psychology, and social science.

Special: A general studies degree is offered.

Honors: There are 5 honor societies represented on campus.

Admissions: ACT scores for the 1981–82 freshman class were as follows: 75% below 21, 16% between 21 and 23, 2% between 24 and 25, 1% between 26 and 28, and 0% above 28. All North Dakota high school graduates are admitted. Nonresidents must complete 15 Carnegie units, rank in the upper 50% of their graduating class, and be recommended by the high school. The ACT results are evaluated for placement purposes.

Procedure: The SAT or ACT is required. Application deadlines are open. Freshmen are admitted for all terms. Notification is on a rolling basis. A $10 application fee is required.

Special: CLEP credit is given.

Transfer: For fall 1981, 90 students applied, 89 were accepted, and 68 enrolled. A 2.0 GPA is required; D grades transfer. Students must spend 1 year in residence and complete at least 48 of the 198 quarter credits necessary for a bachelor's degree. Application deadlines are open.

Visiting: There are no regularly scheduled orientations for prospective students. Guides will be provided for informal tours; visitors may sit in on classes and stay overnight at the school. Arrangements can be made weekdays during the school year through the college relations office.

Financial Aid: Seventy percent of all students are receiving aid. Twenty percent work part-time on campus. Average aid to freshmen is $1800. About 240 scholarships totaling $40,000 are available to freshmen. Loans and grants are also available. The college is a member of the ACT and requires the FFS. Application deadlines are April 15 (fall), November 1 (winter), February 1 (spring), and June 1 (summer).

Foreign Students: One percent of the full-time students come from foreign countries.

Admissions: Foreign students must achieve a minimum TOEFL score of 500. No college entrance exam must be taken.

Procedure: Application deadlines are June 1 (fall), September 1 (winter), and December 1 (spring). Foreign students must present a completed school medical form as proof of a physical exam and proof of funds adequate to cover 4 years of study. They must also carry health insurance, which is available through the college for a fee.

Admissions Contact: Monte Johnson, Admissions Counselor.

OHIO

ANTIOCH COLLEGE
Yellow Springs, Ohio 45387

B-4
(513) 767-7047

F/T: 477M, 423W		Faculty:	75; n/av
P/T: 36M&W		Ph.D.'s:	73%
Grad: none		S/F Ratio:	9 to 1
Year: qtrs		Tuition:	$6320
Appl: Mar. 1		R and B:	$2180
402 applied	380 accepted		170 enrolled
SAT: 515V 513M	ACT: 24		COMPETITIVE+

Antioch College, founded in 1852, is an independent, nonsectarian, liberal arts institution at which students alternate full-time study on campus with full-time, related work experiences off campus. The library contains 250,000 volumes and 25,000 microfilm items, and subscribes to 1500 periodicals.

Environment: The 100-acre campus is located in a small rural town 19 miles from Dayton. The 40 buildings include a renovated science building, an art building, and a Greek amphitheater. Dormitories are available. Glen Helen, a 1000-acre nature preserve with an ecological study center, is adjacent to campus.

Student Life: The student body is geographically diverse. Ninety-five percent of the students live in dormitories while on campus. Only half the students are on campus at one time; the other half are engaged in the cooperative work-study program. Eighteen percent of the students are minority-group members. College housing is both single-sex and coed. There are visiting privileges in single-sex housing. Students may keep cars on campus.

Organizations: Extracurricular activities include student government, a 10,000-watt noncommercial FM radio station, theater and dance productions, special-interest clubs, a student fire department, and weekly dances, cabarets, and movies. There are no sororities or fraternities.

Sports: The college does not participate in intercollegiate sports. There are 19 intramural sports for men and 18 for women.

Handicapped: About half the campus is accessible to physically handicapped students. Special facilities include wheelchair ramps, parking areas, and elevators. No special counselors are available.

Graduates: About 70% of the entering freshmen eventually graduate. Of the graduates, almost half pursue advanced degrees immediately; another 15% do so within several years. Eight percent of the graduates enter medical school, 1% dental school, and 8% law school. At least 15% of the graduates pursue careers in business and industry.

Services: Health care, career and psychological counseling, tutoring, and remedial instruction are provided free to students. Placement services, which concentrate primarily on placing students in cooperative jobs, are available free to students and graduates.

Programs of Study: The college awards the B.A., B.S., and B.F.A. degrees. Bachelor's degrees are offered in the following subjects: AREA STUDIES (Asian, cross cultural, Latin American, urban, women's), BUSINESS (business administration, computer science), EDUCATION (early childhood, elementary, secondary), ENGLISH (communications, journalism, literature), FINE AND PERFORMING ARTS (art, art education, dance, film/photography, music, radio/TV, theater/dramatics), LANGUAGES (French, German, Japanese, Spanish), MATH AND SCIENCES (biochemistry, biology, botany, chemistry, earth science, ecology/environmental science, geology, mathematics, natural sciences, physical sciences, physics), PHILOSOPHY (humanities, philosophy, religion), PREPROFESSIONAL (architecture, dentistry, engineering, forestry, law, medicine, ministry, social work, veterinary), SOCIAL SCIENCES (anthropology, economics, geography, government/political science, history, international relations, psychology, social sciences, sociology). About 32% of degrees are conferred in social sciences and 21% in math and sciences.

Required: All students participate in the cooperative education program, alternating study on campus with full-time jobs the college arranges throughout the country. Students must take 6 required jobs for graduation. The Center of Cooperative Education has over 400 such positions available to the college.

Special: The college offers independent study, study abroad, and student-initiated courses. A 3-2 degree program in engineering is available in conjunction with other colleges. Students may design their own majors and take 5 years to earn a bachelor's degree. All courses are graded on a credit/no credit basis, and students are given written narrative evaluations by faculty members. (Students may request and receive an unofficial letter grade as an addendum on the evaluation.)

Honors: Because grading is noncompetitive, there are no honor societies or honors programs.

Admissions: About 95% of those who applied were accepted for the 1981-82 freshman class. The SAT scores of those who enrolled were as follows: Verbal—40% below 500, 40% between 500 and 599, 19% between 600 and 700, and 1% above 700; Math—50% below 500, 30% between 500 and 599, 17% between 600 and 700, and 3% above 700. Candidates must have completed 16 Carnegie units. The college recommends that they rank in the top half of their class and present an average of at least 2.5. The high school record is given more consideration than SAT scores. Other important factors include personality, impressions made during the interview, leadership record, recommendations by high school officials, advanced placement or honors courses, special talents, and extracurricular activities. Work experience and employers' recommendations are also important.

Procedure: The SAT or ACT is required and should be taken by January of the senior year. Applications should be filed by March 1 (fall), November 15 (winter), and March 1 (spring). Applications will be accepted until the class is filled. A rolling admissions plan is used. There is a $20 application fee. A personal interview on or off campus is required.

Special: Early decision and early and deferred admissions plans are available. AP and CLEP credit is accepted.

Transfer: For fall 1981, 90 students applied, 88 were accepted, and 87 enrolled. Students may not transfer for the senior year. An average of at least 2.0 is required. D grades do not transfer. Students must study at the college at least 2 years and complete 80 of the 120 credits needed to receive a bachelor's degree. Application deadlines are the same as those for freshmen.

Visiting: Prospective students may arrange campus visits for anytime the college is in session. Visitors may sit in on classes, tour the campus, meet students and faculty members, and stay overnight in the dorms. Arrangements should be made with the admissions office.

Financial Aid: About 60% of the students receive aid. Sixty percent work part-time on campus. Average aid to freshmen from all sources is $4282. Need is the only consideration in determining awards. Aid packages include outside aid such as BEOG, loans, CWS jobs, and Antioch tuition grants. The college is a member of CSS and requires aid applicants to submit the FAF. Aid applications are due March 1 (fall), November 15 (winter), and March 1 (spring). Candidates are notified of aid offers by mid-April, or within 2 weeks of the time their completed application is received. Students earn enough from cooperative jobs to pay their living expenses off campus and usually can save $500 or $600 for incidental expenses incurred during a term on campus.

Foreign Students: Four percent of the full-time students come from foreign countries. The college offers these students special counseling and special organizations.

Admissions: Foreign students must score at least 500 on the TOEFL. No college entrance examination is required.

Procedure: The application deadline is June 1 (fall). Foreign students must complete the standard physical examination form. They must also present proof of adequate funds. They must carry health insurance, which is available through the college.

Admissions Contact: Mary Jane Bachtell, Deputy Director of Admissions.

ASHLAND COLLEGE
Ashland, Ohio 44805

C-2
(419) 289-5079

F/T: 660M, 593W		Faculty:	105; IIB, av$
P/T: 33M, 66W		Ph.D's:	40%
Grad: 868M&W		S/F Ratio:	16 to 1
Year: sems, ss		Tuition:	$4706
Appl: open		R and B:	$2030
1009 applied	867 accepted		347 enrolled
SAT: 400V 440M	ACT: 19		LESS COMPETITIVE

Founded in 1878, Ashland College is a small liberal arts institution affiliated with the Brethren Church. The 9-story library contains 166,505 volumes and 99,915 microfilm items, and subscribes to 617 periodicals.

Environment: The college occupies a 70-acre site in a residential area of rural Ashland, 12 miles from Mansfield, Ohio. Among the buildings are fraternity row residences and dorms, a physical educa-

658 OHIO

tion center, and an arts building. Additional buildings are located off campus within easy walking distance. Sixteen acres of athletic fields are to the south of the main campus.

Student Life: About 80% of the students come from the Midwest; the balance come from the eastern states. Approximately 95% of the entering freshmen are graduates of public schools. Eighty-five percent of the students live on campus. Twenty-six percent are Catholic, 50% Protestant, and 1% Jewish. Chapel services are available to all students. Five percent of the students are minority-group members. College housing is single-sex; there are visiting privileges. Students may keep cars on campus.

Organizations: Twenty-five percent of the men belong to 6 national fraternities and 30% of the women belong to 5 national sororities. Student activities include band, choirs, drama, and a biweekly newspaper. A voice in school affairs is given through the Student Senate, Residence Hall Association, Student Judicial Boards, and the Campus Activity Board.

Sports: Intercollegiate competition for men is offered in 10 sports, and for women in 9. There are 15 intramural sports for men and 15 for women.

Handicapped: There are no special facilities for the physically handicapped.

Graduates: There is a freshman dropout rate of 28%; 53% remain to graduate. Fifteen percent of the graduates pursue advanced study; 2% enter medical school, 2% dental school, and 2% law school.

Services: Placement, career counseling, tutoring, remedial instruction, and psychological counseling are available free of charge. Health care is available on a fee basis.

Programs of Study: The college confers the B.A., B.M., B.S., B.S.B.A., B.S.C.J., B.S.Ed., B.S.W., and B.S. in Human Development degrees. Associate, master's, and doctoral degrees are also conferred. Bachelor's degrees are offered in the following subjects: AREA STUDIES (American), BUSINESS (accounting, business administration, business education, finance, health services management, hotel/restaurant management, management, marketing), EDUCATION (elementary, health/physical, secondary, special), ENGLISH (creative writing, English, journalism, speech), FINE AND PERFORMING ARTS (art, art education, music, music education, radio/TV, studio art, theater/dramatics), HEALTH SCIENCES (medical technology, speech therapy), MATH AND SCIENCES (biology, chemistry, earth science, energy resources management, geology, mathematics, physics), PHILOSOPHY (religion), PREPROFESSIONAL (dentistry, engineering, home economics, law, medicine, ministry, pharmacy, social work, veterinary), SOCIAL SCIENCES (economics, government/political science, history, international relations, psychology, social sciences, social work, sociology). Twenty-two percent of degrees are conferred in education, 45% in business, 10% in math and sciences, 13% in social sciences, and 11% in the fine and performing arts.

Special: There is no formal program for travel or study abroad, but the college will approve satisfactory arrangements sponsored by other institutions. The college participates in the Advanced Placement Program. Combination degree programs are offered in engineering, medical technology, nursing, social work, radio/TV, and art.

Honors: In addition to the Faculty Honors program, the following honor societies have chapters on campus: Phi Beta Theta, Phi Alpha Theta, Kappa Delta Pi, Kalon Logos, Omicron Delta Epsilon, Gamma Alpha Kappa, Beta Lambda, and Alpha Psi Omega.

Admissions: About 86% of those who applied were accepted for the 1981-82 freshman class. The SAT scores of those who enrolled were as follows: Verbal—85% below 500, 13% between 500 and 599, 1% between 600 and 700, and 0% above 700; Math—72% below 500, 22% between 500 and 599, 5% between 600 and 700, and 20% above 700. On the ACT, 60% scored below 21, 17% between 21 and 23, 8% between 24 and 25, 11% between 26 and 28, and 2% above 28. High school graduates must be in the top half of their class, with a 2.0 GPA. Also influencing the admissions decision are: recommendations by school officials, advanced placement or honors courses, impressions made during an interview, and personality.

Procedure: The SAT or ACT should be taken in May of the junior year or December of the senior year. Application deadlines are open. Admission is on a rolling basis. There is an application fee of $15.

Special: Early decision and deferred admissions plans are offered.

Transfer: For fall 1981, 280 applications were received, 175 were accepted, and 130 students enrolled. Transfers are accepted for all classes, with a minimum GPA of 2.0 required. D grades do not transfer. Students must study at the college for at least 64 hours of the 128 needed to qualify for a bachelor's degree. Application deadlines are August 1 (fall) and January 1 (winter).

Visiting: Visitors are invited to stay at the school and sit in on classes; guides will be assigned. Contact the admissions office.

Financial Aid: About 72% of all students receive financial aid. Twenty-five percent work part-time on campus. Average aid to freshmen from all sources is $3315. The college awards 320 freshman scholarships each year. Loans are available from the federal government and from local banks; some are guaranteed by the state or the United Student Aid Funds, Inc. Tuition may be paid in monthly installments through Education Funds, Inc. The college is a member of CSS. The FAF and the application should be filed by April 1 (fall) and November 1 (winter).

Foreign Students: Four percent of the full-time students come from foreign countries. The college offers these students an intensive English program, special counseling, and special organizations.

Admissions: Foreign students must score at least 500 on the TOEFL or 80 on the University of Michigan Language Test. No college entrance examination is required.

Procedure: The application deadlines are August 1 (fall) and January 1 (winter). Foreign students must complete the college's health form. They must also present proof of funds adequate to cover their entire period of study. They must carry health insurance, which is available through the college for a fee.

Admissions Contact: Carl A. Gerbasi, Executive Director of Admissions.

BALDWIN-WALLACE COLLEGE D-1
Berea, Ohio 44017 (216) 826-2222

F/T: 944M, 964W	Faculty:	134; IIB, ++$
P/T: 441M, 715W	Ph.D.'s:	60%
Grad: 546M, 205W	S/F Ratio:	15 to 1
Year: qtrs, ss	Tuition:	$4755
Appl: open	R and B:	$2340
1037 applied	830 accepted	454 enrolled
SAT: 450V 450M	ACT: 20	COMPETITIVE

Baldwin-Wallace, founded in 1845, is a private, liberal arts college affiliated with the United Methodist Church. The library houses 175,000 volumes and 102,865 microfilm items, and subscribes to 1000 periodicals.

Environment: The self-contained campus, located 14 miles from Cleveland, Ohio, with its 40 buildings on more than 50 acres of land, is woven into a suburban environment, and is a combination of old ivy-covered sandstone facilities and newer Georgian colonial buildings. An art and drama center, a stadium with artificial turf and track, and a large classroom building housing the departments of business, mathematics, and economics are recent additions. Residence halls of various architectural styles are interspersed throughout the campus. Fraternity and sorority facilities are incorporated into the residence halls.

Student Life: The college draws 75% of its students from Ohio. About 80% of the entering freshmen come from public schools. Seventy percent of the students live on campus. Sixty percent are Catholic, 30% Protestant, and 2% Jewish. There are no requirements for attendance at religious services. Eight percent of the students are minority-group members. College housing is both single-sex and coed. There are visiting privileges in single-sex housing. Students may keep cars on campus.

Organizations: There are 8 national fraternities, to which 37% of the men belong; 25% of the women belong to the 7 national sororities. There are many special-interest and religious groups.

Sports: The college competes intercollegiately in 9 sports for men and 6 for women. There are 15 intramural sports for men and 8 for women.

Handicapped: Facilities for the physically handicapped include wheelchair ramps, special parking, elevators, special class scheduling, specially equipped rest rooms, and lowered drinking fountains and telephones. There is 1 special counselor for handicapped students.

Graduates: Thirty percent of the freshmen drop out by the end of their first year. About 55% of those who enter remain to graduate. About 15% of the graduates go on to graduate study; 1% enter medical school, 1% dental school, and 2% law school. Fifty percent pursue careers in business and industry.

Services: The following services are offered free of charge to all students: placement, career counseling, health care, tutoring, remedial instruction, and psychological counseling. There are placement services for undergraduates that cover all aspects of the placement process from resume preparation to job interviews.

Programs of Study: The college confers the B.A., B.S., B.S.Ed., B.M., and B.Mus.Ed. degrees. Master's degrees are also awarded. Bachelor's degrees are offered in the following subjects: BUSINESS (accounting, business administration, finance, management, marketing), EDUCATION (elementary, health/physical, secondary, special), ENGLISH (English, speech), FINE AND PERFORMING ARTS (art, art education, art history, dance, music, music education, studio art, theater/dramatics), HEALTH SCIENCES (medical technology, speech therapy), LANGUAGES (French, German, Spanish), MATH AND SCIENCES (biology, chemistry, geology, mathematics, physics), PHILOSOPHY (philosophy, religion), PREPROFESSIONAL (dentistry, engineering, forestry, home economics, law, medicine, ministry, social work, veterinary), SOCIAL SCIENCES (economics, government/political science, history, international relations, psychology, social sciences, sociology). Forty percent of degrees are conferred in business, 21% in social sciences, and 16% in the fine and performing arts.

Special: A combined B.A.-B.S. degree can be earned in all major areas in the arts and sciences offered at the college; this is a 5-year curriculum. Student-designed majors are allowed with departmental approval. The college offers many opportunities for study and travel abroad each year: students may participate in programs in London, in Athens, and in many major cities throughout the world. Additional opportunities for international study exist in Austria and Germany; and the college sponsors its own 6-week study tour of western Europe. The college participates in the Washington semester at American University, and the Drew University semester on the United Nations. The college offers a 3-2 engineering program with Columbia University, Case Western Reserve, or Washington University, and several 2-2 programs in allied health. The field experience program provides varied off-campus educational experiences in business and industry, government and social agencies, and educational institutions. Independent studies can be arranged for in-depth study of academic topics outside the classroom setting. Newly established programs and services include an international studies major, a sport/dance/arts/management program, and a more comprehensive counseling program has been developed. Expanded computer capacity has made a computer science minor possible.

Honors: Sixteen national honor societies have chapters on campus. All departments offer honors courses to qualified juniors and seniors with permission of the dean of the college and appropriate department head.

Admissions: Eighty percent of those who applied for the 1981-82 freshman class were accepted. Of those who enrolled, the SAT scores were as follows: Verbal—74% below 500, 20% between 500 and 599, 5% between 600 and 700, and 1% above 700; Math—60% below 500, 28% between 500 and 599, 10% between 600 and 700, and 2% above 700. On the ACT, 54% scored below 21, 22% between 21 and 23, 13% between 24 and 25, 8% between 26 and 28, and 3% above 28. Candidates should rank in the top half of their class and present 16 completed high school units.

Procedure: Either the SAT or ACT is required. There is no cut-off date for admission. It is advisable, however, that students apply as early as possible in their senior year. There is a rolling admissions plan. A check for $15 should accompany the application.

Special: Early decision and deferred admissions plans are offered.

Transfer: For fall 1981, 316 students applied, 255 were accepted, and 189 enrolled. Transfers are accepted for all classes. A good academic standing with a minimum 2.0 GPA and good moral conduct are required for transfer. D grades do not transfer. Students must spend at least the last 48 quarter hours at the college, of the 186 needed to receive a bachelor's degree. Transfer application deadlines are the same as those for freshman applicants.

Visiting: Campus visiting programs include departmental interviews and a general introduction to the college, its academic programs, and facilities. There are guides for informal visits. Visitors may sit in on classes and stay at the school. Visits can take place throughout the academic year. The office of admissions should be contacted to make arrangements for a visit.

Financial Aid: Sixty-five percent of all students receive financial aid. Sixty-five percent work part-time on campus. Average aid to freshmen from all sources is $4600. Loans are available from federal government funds, the college, and private funds. The college attempts to provide financial assistance to all students who, without such aid, would not be able to further their education. The college is a member of the CSS and suggests that the FAF and financial aid application be filed by September 15 (fall), December 15 (winter), and March 15 (spring). The suggested application deadline for freshmen is April 15.

Foreign Students: Two percent of the full-time students come from foreign countries. The college offers these students an intensive English program, special counseling, and special organizations.

Admissions: Foreign students must score at least 500 on the TOEFL or 80 on the University of Michigan Language Test. No college entrance examination is required.

Procedure: Application deadlines are 3 months prior to the beginning of each quarter. Foreign students must present proof of funds adequate to cover 1 year of study. They must carry health insurance, which is available through the college.

Admissions Contact: John T. Amy, Director of Admissions and Registrar.

BLUFFTON COLLEGE B-2
Bluffton, Ohio 45817 (419) 358-8015

F/T: 288M, 309W	Faculty:	43; IIB, – $
P/T: 33M, 32W	Ph.D.'s:	50%
Grad: none	S/F Ratio:	13 to 1
Year: 1-3-3-2, ss	Tuition:	$3960
Appl: open	R and B:	$1660
676 applied	380 accepted	205 enrolled
ACT: 18		COMPETITIVE

Bluffton College, founded in 1899, is affiliated with the General Conference Mennonite Church. It is a small, private, liberal arts institution open to academic experimentation and innovation. The library contains 87,000 volumes and 6000 microfilm items, and subscribes to 650 periodicals.

Environment: The 65-acre campus is located in a rural area 16 miles from the town of Lima; small streams run through the heavily wooded grounds. Among the 22 buildings are a campus center with dining hall, snack shop, lounge, bookshop, and science center. There is also a 160-acre outdoor education center. Seven dormitories house 350 women and 258 men, along with 5 modular dormitories with 9 students residing on each of 3 floors.

Student Life: Eighty percent of the students are from Ohio. Eighty-five percent of the entering freshmen come from public schools. Although 80% of the students are Protestant, the majority are not members of the affiliated church. Attendance at chapel or religious services is not required. College housing is single-sex; there are visiting privileges. Students may keep cars on campus.

Organizations: There are no fraternities or sororities; there are several professional and service organizations. Students and faculty participate in administration and curriculum matters, student government, and publications. Students are represented on the board of trustees of the college.

Sports: The college competes intercollegiately in 8 sports for men and 4 for women. There are 7 intramural sports for both men and women.

Handicapped: About 25% of the campus is accessible to wheelchair-bound students. Facilities for handicapped students include wheelchair ramps, special rest rooms, and lowered drinking fountains. There are no students with visual impairments or hearing problems currently enrolled.

Graduates: The freshman dropout rate is 15%; 65% remain to graduate. About 25% go on to graduate study; 1% enter law school. Thirty percent pursue careers in business and industry.

Services: Students receive the following services free of charge: placement, career counseling, health care, and remedial instruction.

Programs of Study: Programs lead to the B.A. and B.S. degrees. Bachelor's degrees are offered in the following subjects: BUSINESS (accounting, business administration, business education, computer science), EDUCATION (adult, early childhood, elementary, health/physical, secondary, special), ENGLISH (English, journalism, literature, speech), FINE AND PERFORMING ARTS (art, art education, music, music education, theater/dramatics), HEALTH SCIENCES (medical technology, nursing), LANGUAGES (German, Spanish), MATH AND SCIENCES (biology, chemistry, mathematics), PHILOSOPHY (humanities, philosophy, religion), PREPROFESSIONAL (home economics, law, medicine, ministry, social work), SOCIAL SCIENCES (economics, history, psychology, social sciences, sociology). Twenty-eight percent of degrees are conferred in business, 11% in elementary education, and 9% in social sciences.

Required: There are no specific required courses for freshmen. Undergraduates are expected to take 2 courses in the following areas of human explorations at some time during their 4 years: Exploring the Natural Environment, Exploring the Cultural Environment, Exploring Creativity, Exploring Meaning and Faith, or Exploring World Peace. A satisfactory score on the URE is required for graduation.

Special: Through programs of the Council of Mennonite Colleges, students may spend a summer in intercultural study in Canada and Colombia, South America. Other special programs include Afro-

American intercultural studies; off-campus study-service programs; the September module and the April-May module, which provide opportunities for interdisciplinary study, study tours, and self-directed study; junior year abroad; semester abroad; and a comprehensive major. A combination program in engineering is available. Student-designed majors are permitted.

Honors: Pi Delta is the campus honor society. Qualified students may pursue independent study leading to departmental honors.

Admissions: Fifty-six percent of those who applied were accepted for the 1981–82 freshman class. Of those who enrolled the ACT scores were as follows: 72% below 21, 10% between 21 and 23, 6% between 24 and 25, 10% between 26 and 28, and 1% above 28. Candidates should be graduates of accredited high schools, have an average of at least C, and rank in the upper half of their class. A combined SAT of 1050 is recommended; an ACT composite score of at least 16 is recommended. The school also considers advanced placement or honors courses, recommendations by school officials, and leadership record.

Procedure: All candidates must take either the SAT or ACT in May of the junior year or December of the senior year. Application deadlines are open. Acceptance is on a rolling basis. An interview is strongly recommended. There is no application fee.

Special: An early admissions plan is available. The deadline for applications is June 1. CLEP and AP credit is accepted.

Transfer: For fall 1981, 50 students applied, 41 were accepted, and 33 enrolled. Transfers are accepted for all classes. Transfer students must study at the college for 1 year and must complete 11 of the 35 units needed to receive a bachelor's degree. The deadline for transfer applications is open.

Visiting: There are regularly scheduled orientations for prospective students. Visitors may sit in on classes and remain on campus overnight. Guided tours and interviews can be arranged through the admissions office.

Financial Aid: About 75% of all students receive financial aid. Twenty-two percent work part-time on campus. Scholarships are available to the top 15% of the freshmen. Scholarships range from $400 to $3960 per year. Packages are worked out to meet the needs of the students. Loans are available from the federal and state governments. Tuition may be paid on the installment plan. The FAF is required. The aid application deadline is open.

Foreign Students: About 4% of the full-time students come from foreign countries. The college offers these students special counseling and special organizations.

Admissions: Foreign students must score at least 500 on the TOEFL. No college entrance examination is required.

Procedure: Application deadlines are open. Foreign students must present proof of funds adequate to cover 4 years of study.

Admissions Contact: Glenn Snyder, Director of Admissions.

BOWLING GREEN STATE UNIVERSITY B-1
Bowling Green, Ohio 43403   (419) 372-2086

F/T: 6059M, 8187W	Faculty:	737; I, av$
P/T: 4080M, 452W	Ph.D.'s:	73%
Grad: 1046M, 928W	S/F Ratio:	19 to 1
Year: sems, ss	Tuition:	$1473 ($3228)
Appl: Feb. 1	R and B:	$1641
6760 applied	5720 accepted	3172 enrolled
SAT: 448V 485M	ACT: 21	COMPETITIVE

Bowling Green State University is located in northwest Ohio, and also operates the Firelands branch near Huron, Ohio. The library contains 635,485 volumes, over 1 million microfilm items, and 340,728 government documents, and subscribes to 6522 periodicals.

Environment: The 1200-acre campus, located in a rural area 23 miles south of Toledo, contains buildings with modern equipment and facilities for carrying on a broad, well-rounded program of education and extracurricular activity. The Student Recreation Center features a wide variety of indoor recreational activities. The Musical Arts Center offers a facility for music performance and education opportunities. Residences are grouped in fraternity/sorority rows and in quads. There are also 2 high-rise dorms. On or near the campus are an airport, a wildlife preserve, a golf course, and a chapel.

Student Life: Six percent of the students come from out of state. There are religious facilities available for students of all major faiths. Fifty percent of the students live on campus. Six percent are minority-group members. University housing is both single-sex and coed. There are visiting privileges in single-sex housing. Students may keep cars on campus. All automobiles must be registered with the university.

Organizations: There is 1 local fraternity and 23 national fraternities, to which 22% of the men belong. There are 15 national sororities and 1 local sorority, to which 15% of the women belong. The university offers over 200 student organizations, including the Student Body Organization, orchestra, band, choirs, newspaper, yearbook, debating, and dramatics. Religious clubs on campus include Newman, Jewish Congregation of Bowling Green, Christian Science, and Protestant sects.

Sports: The university offers 11 intercollegiate sports for men and 8 for women. There are 16 intramural sports for men and 11 for women.

Handicapped: Seventy-five percent of the campus is accessible to physically handicapped students. Facilities include wheelchair ramps, special parking, elevators, special class scheduling, specially equipped rest rooms, lowered drinking fountains and telephones, special housing, a tactile map of the campus, a counseling brochure in braille, and a volunteer braille group. Four percent of the students currently enrolled are visually impaired, 3% are hearing-impaired. There are visual smoke alarms for the hearing-impaired, and taped transcriptions for the visually impaired. There are no special counselors for the handicapped.

Graduates: There is a freshman dropout rate of 25%. Fifty-five percent remain to graduate.

Services: The following services are available free to all students: placement, career counseling, health care, tutoring, remedial instruction, and psychological counseling. Health care and tutoring are also offered on a fee basis. There are placement services for graduates but not for undergraduates. These provide counseling for students seeking jobs, with staff specializing in certain employment areas. Recruitment schedules are set up between prospective employers and students; student credentials are mailed on request.

Programs of Study: The university confers the B.A., B.S., B.F.A., B. Liberal Studies, B.M., B.A. in Communications, B.S.B.A., B.S.J., B.S.Ed., B.S.Tech., B.S.C.J., B.S.Med.Tech., B.S.N., B.S.W., and B.S. degrees in 11 other major areas. Associate, master's, and doctoral programs are also offered. Bachelor's degrees are offered in the following subjects: AREA STUDIES (American, Asian, Black/Afro-American, Latin American, Russian), BUSINESS (accounting, business administration, business education, computer science, finance, management, marketing, real estate/insurance), EDUCATION (early childhood, elementary, health/physical, industrial, secondary, special), ENGLISH (English, journalism, speech), FINE AND PERFORMING ARTS (art, art education, art history, film/photography, music, music education, radio/TV, studio art, theater/dramatics), HEALTH SCIENCES (art therapy, environmental health, medical technology, nursing, physical therapy, speech therapy), LANGUAGES (French, German, Greek/Latin, Russian, Spanish), MATH AND SCIENCES (biology, chemistry, earth science, ecology/environmental science, geology, mathematics, physics, statistics), PHILOSOPHY (philosophy), PREPROFESSIONAL (dentistry, engineering, home economics, law, library science, medicine, ministry, pharmacy, veterinary), SOCIAL SCIENCES (economics, geography, government/political science, history, international relations, psychology, social sciences, sociology). Thirty percent of degrees are conferred in education, 21% in business, and 2% in English.

Required: All students must fulfill an English and a physical education requirement.

Special: Combination degree programs are offered in dentistry, engineering, medicine, medical technology, and physical therapy. The university sponsors an academic year abroad in Austria, France, and Spain, and summer study programs in Austria and Spain. Student-designed majors are allowed.

Honors: Forty-seven national honor societies have chapters on campus. The honors program provides intellectually challenging experiences in general studies, small discussion groups, guest speakers, independent projects, travel/study seminars, recognition for outstanding performance, and opportunities for interaction with students of similar ability and motivation.

Admissions: Eighty-five percent of those who applied were accepted for the 1981–82 freshman class. Of those who enrolled, the SAT scores were as follows: Verbal—71% below 500, 24% between 500 and 599, 4% between 600 and 700, and fewer than 1% above 700; Math—53% below 500, 35% between 500 and 599, 10% between 600 and 700, and 1% above 700. On the ACT, 38% scored below 21, 29% between 21 and 23, 15% between 24 and 25, 13% between 26 and 28, and 4% above 28. Applicants must rank in the top 50% of their graduating class, have an average of at least C, and have completed at least 16 Carnegie units. Other important considerations include the recommendation of the applicant's high school, extracurricular activities, and advanced courses.

Procedure: Students should take the ACT or SAT in October of the senior year. The application deadline for the fall term is February 1. Spring and summer deadlines are open. There is a rolling admissions plan. There is a $25 application fee.

Special: CLEP and AP credit is accepted.

Transfer: For fall 1981, 870 applications were received, 631 were accepted, and 448 applicants enrolled. Transfers are accepted in all classes. To be eligible, the student must have 60 semester hours with a 2.0 average, or with less than 60 semester hours, a 2.5 average. D grades do not transfer. Students must complete the last 30 hours at the school, of the 122 hours needed to receive a bachelor's degree. Deadlines for transfer applications are February 1 (fall), December 10 (spring), and May 13 (summer).

Visiting: There are regularly scheduled orientations for prospective students, which include a brief talk with the admissions counselor, admissions material, discussion of questions, and a campus tour. There are guides for informal visits. The Director of Admissions should be contacted to arrange visits; the best times are 8 A.M. to 5 P.M. Monday through Friday and 9 A.M. to 12 noon Saturday.

Financial Aid: About 65% of all students receive financial aid. Thirty-five percent of the students earn part of their expenses with part-time work on campus. Scholarships, loans, and grants are available. Scholarships are awarded on the basis of scholastic achievement, participation in school activities, and evidence of good character. The average aid to freshmen is $1970. The university is a member of CSS. The FAF or FFS should be filed. The deadline for aid applications is April 1.

Foreign Students: About 2% of the full-time students come from foreign countries. The university offers these students an intensive English program and special counseling.

Admissions: Foreign students must take the TOEFL, the University of Michigan Language Test, or the university's own test. They must score at least 500 on the TOEFL. No college entrance examination is required.

Procedure: The application deadlines are July 1 (fall), November 1 (spring), and April 1 (summer). Foreign students must submit the results of a physical examination. They must also present proof of funds adequate to cover their entire period of study. They must carry health insurance, which is available through the university for a fee.

Admissions Contact: John W. Martin, Director of Admissions.

CAPITAL UNIVERSITY C–3
Columbus, Ohio 43209 (614) 236-6101

F/T: 638M, 834W	Faculty: 119; IIB, +$
P/T: 170M&W	Ph.D.'s: 65%
Grad: 927M&W	S/F Ratio: 15 to 1
Year: sems, ss	Tuition: $4720
Appl: Aug. 1	R and B: $2018
738 applied	432 accepted	388 enrolled
SAT: 450V 500M	ACT: 21	COMPETITIVE

Established in 1850, Capital University is a private educational institution of the American Lutheran Church. The undergraduate divisions comprise the College of Arts and Sciences, the School of Nursing, and the Conservatory of Music. The library contains more than 200,000 volumes, and subscribes to over 800 periodicals.

Environment: The 52-acre suburban campus has 27 buildings, including residence halls for more than 1300 men and women.

Student Life: About 87% of the students come from Ohio. Almost 90% of the entering freshmen attended public schools. About 65% of the students live on campus. The majority of students are Protestant. About 13% are minority-group members. University housing is single-sex; there are visiting privileges. Students may keep cars on campus only by special permission.

Organizations: About 25% of the students belong to 6 fraternities and 5 sororities. Extracurricular activities include student government, publications, clubs, religious and service groups, music and drama groups, and regularly scheduled cultural and social events on campus.

Sports: There are 8 intercollegiate sports for men, 5 for women. There are 3 intramural sports for men and 2 for women.

Graduates: Eighteen percent of the freshmen drop out by the end of their first year; 65% remain to graduate. Twenty percent go on for further education after graduation; 2% enter medical school, 1% dental school, and 6% law school. Thirty percent pursue careers in business and industry.

Services: Free career counseling, placement, psychological counseling, and remedial instruction are offered. Health care and tutoring are available on a fee basis.

Programs of Study: The university confers the B.A., B.G.S., B.S.N., B.F.A., B.M., and B.S.W. degrees. Master's degrees are also granted. Bachelor's degrees are offered in the following subjects: BUSINESS (accounting, business administration), EDUCATION (elementary, health/physical, secondary), ENGLISH (English, speech), FINE AND PERFORMING ARTS (art, art education, music, music education, theater/dramatics), HEALTH SCIENCES (medical technology, nursing), LANGUAGES (French, German, Spanish), MATH AND SCIENCES (biology, chemistry, mathematics), PHILOSOPHY (religion), PRE-PROFESSIONAL (dentistry, engineering, law, medicine, ministry, pharmacy, social work, veterinary), SOCIAL SCIENCES (economics, government/political science, history, psychology, sociology). Forty percent of the degrees are conferred in business.

Required: A core curriculum of 4 courses (in religion, English composition, ethnic relations, and humanities) is required of all students.

Special: A general studies degree is offered. Independent study, study abroad, individualized majors, exchange programs, and a B.A.-B.S. degree in engineering in conjunction with Washington University, St. Louis, Missouri, are also offered.

Honors: Honors programs are available in all departments. There are chapters of 9 national honor societies on campus.

Admissions: About 59% of the 1981–82 freshman applicants were accepted. Students must be graduates of an accredited high school or the equivalent. Class rank in the top 50% and a 2.0 GPA are required. Applicants to the Conservatory of Music are required to audition.

Procedure: The SAT or ACT should be taken by the end of the senior year. Two letters of recommendation must be submitted. Application deadlines are August 1 (fall), December 1 (winter), and April 15 (summer). Notification is on a rolling basis. There is a $15 application fee.

Special: There are deferred and early admissions plans. AP and CLEP credit is granted.

Transfer: For fall 1981, 125 students applied, 105 were accepted, and 96 enrolled. A 2.0 GPA is needed (2.75 for the School of Nursing). D grades transfer. Twenty-four of the final 122 to 136 hours needed for a bachelor's degree must be taken in residence. The application deadlines are the same as those for freshman applicants.

Visiting: Campus tours with student guides can be arranged. Visitors may attend classes and speak with faculty and admissions personnel. Arrangements should be made through the admissions office.

Financial Aid: About 70% of the students receive aid. Fifty-five percent work part-time on campus. Average aid to freshmen from all sources is $4200. Federal and commercial loans, nursing loans, freshman scholarships and grants (BEOG included), CWS and other campus employment opportunities are available. Tuition may be paid in installments. The university is a member of CSS. The FAF should be submitted by June 1.

Foreign Students: About 1% of the full-time students come from foreign countries.

Admissions: Foreign students must take the TOEFL or the University of Michigan Language Test. They must score at least 550 on the TOEFL. No college entrance examination is required.

Procedure: Application deadlines are July 1 (fall), November 15 (winter), and April 1 (summer). Foreign students must present proof of adequate funds. They must also carry health insurance, which is available through the university for a fee.

Admissions Contact: Diane Kohlmeyer, Director of Admissions.

CASE WESTERN RESERVE UNIVERSITY D–1
Cleveland, Ohio 44106 (216) 368-4450

F/T: 2109M, 807W	Faculty: 1335; I, +$
P/T: 139M, 172W	Ph.D.'s: 98%
Grad: 2946M, 2096W	S/F Ratio: 9 to 1
Year: sems, ss	Tuition: $5640
Appl: Mar. 15	R and B: $2680
2566 applied	2192 accepted	863 enrolled
SAT: 542V 618M	ACT: 27	VERY COMPETITIVE+

Case Western Reserve University is the educational center formed by the federation of Case Institute of Technology and Western Reserve University. It is a private, nonsectarian, semiurban university, consisting of 11 undergraduate, graduate, and professional schools and colleges. Of the 2 undergraduate colleges, Case Institute of Technology offers curricula in science and engineering; Western Reserve College, in the arts and sciences. The university's combined library facilities contain 1,392,317 volumes and 419,456 microfilm items, and subscribe to 13,691 periodicals.

Environment: The 115-acre campus is 4 miles from downtown Cleveland in parklike University Circle, a medical, cultural, and educational environment that encompasses University Hospital, the Cleveland Garden Center, the Cleveland Museum of Art, the Cleveland Music Settlement, the Institute of Music, and the Cleveland Orchestra. The Amasa Stone Chapel, in traditional Gothic style, is the site of numerous ceremonies and convocations. The campus also has a modern health science center, a law school complex, an engineering and computer building, 2 astronomical observatories, and a 272-acre biological field station. Undergraduate students are housed in 18 modern, low-rise residence halls; there are 2 fraternity quadrangles and a fraternity row.

Student Life: About 52% of the students come from Ohio. About 77% of the freshmen come from public schools. Unmarried students are required to live in residence halls until the age of 21; 85% of the students live on campus. Eight percent are minority-group members. University housing is both single-sex and coed. There are visiting privileges in single-sex housing. Students may keep cars on campus. Alcoholic beverage regulations conform with state laws.

Organizations: About 10% of the women belong to the 2 sororities, and 30% of the men belong to the 16 fraternities. Other organizations and activities include music, theater, publications, departmental clubs, and student government. Roman Catholic, Protestant, and Jewish religious centers provide religious and social activities. Extensive cultural and recreational facilities are within walking distance of the university.

Sports: Men participate in 12 intercollegiate sports and women in 5. There are 19 intramural sports for men and 17 for women.

Handicapped: Almost the entire campus is accessible to handicapped students. Special facilities include wheelchair ramps, special parking, elevators, specially equipped rest rooms, lowered telephones, light alarms for the hearing-impaired, a specially wired auditorium, and space for wheelchairs. Special class scheduling is also available. There are 2 special counselors for the handicapped.

Graduates: The freshman dropout rate is 10%. Sixty-seven percent remain to graduate. Thirty-nine percent go on to graduate or professional schools: 12% to medical school, 10% to dental school, and 6% to law school.

Services: Free placement, psychological and career counseling services, and remedial instruction are available to all students. Health care is available for a yearly fee.

Programs of Study: The university confers B.A., B.S., and B.F.A. degrees. Master's and doctoral programs are also offered. Bachelor's degrees are offered in the following subjects: AREA STUDIES (American, Asian), BUSINESS (accounting, computer science, management), ENGLISH (English), FINE AND PERFORMING ARTS (art education, art history, music, music education, theater/dramatics), HEALTH SCIENCES (medical technology, nursing, speech therapy), LANGUAGES (French, German, Greek/Latin, Russian), MATH AND SCIENCES (astronomy, biochemistry, biology, chemistry, earth science, geology, mathematics, natural sciences, physics, statistics), PHILOSOPHY (classics, humanities, philosophy, religion), PREPROFESSIONAL (architecture, dentistry, engineering—biomedical, engineering—chemical, engineering—civil, engineering—computer, engineering—electrical, engineering—mechanical and aerospace, engineering—systems and control, law, library science, medicine, social work, veterinary), SOCIAL SCIENCES (anthropology, economics, government/political science, history, psychology, sociology). About 26% of degrees are conferred in health sciences, 25% in engineering, and 12% in mathematics and science.

Required: One semester of freshman English is required as is 1 semester of computer skills. Case students must take 1 course in an analytical skill and 2 each in science, humanities, arts, history and cultures, and social and behavioral sciences. All students must take physical education.

Special: Special programs include a co-op program for students in engineering, mathematics, and science; junior year abroad; accelerated and independent study programs; advanced placement; individually designed programs; integrated graduate studies; senior year in absentia; Washington semester; and 3-2 B.S.-B.A. programs. A few highly qualified freshmen may enter a preprofessional scholars program for guaranteed admission to the university's schools of dentistry, law, nursing, and social work.

Honors: Virtually all departments offer honors programs. There are 15 honor societies on campus, including Phi Beta Kappa and Mortar Board.

Admissions: About 83% of those who applied were accepted for the 1981-82 freshman class. The SAT scores of those who enrolled were as follows: Verbal—28% below 500, 45% between 500 and 599, 22% between 600 and 700, and 5% above 700; Math—7% below 500, 31% between 500 and 599, 44% between 600 and 700, and 18% above 700. On the ACT, 5% scored below 21, 9% between 21 and 23, 13% between 24 and 25, 23% between 26 and 28, and 50% above 28. Students should be graduates of accredited high schools with a minimum GPA of 3.0. Special consideration is given to disadvantaged students. Both colleges require at least 16 units of full-credit high school work in solid academic subjects. The following factors are considered, in order of importance: recommendations by school officials, advanced placement or honors courses, impressions made during an interview, record in extracurricular activities, evidence of special talents, leadership record, and personality.

Procedure: Candidates for the freshman class should take either the SAT or the ACT no later than December of their senior year. Three ATs are also recommended, 1 in English composition and 2 others related to the student's area of study. New students are admitted to all terms. Application deadlines are March 15 (fall), December 15 (spring), and June 1 (summer). The university follows a rolling admissions policy. There is an application fee of $20, which may be waived for disadvantaged students who submit a request from their counselor.

Special: A deferred admissions plan is available. AP credit is accepted.

Transfer: For fall 1981, 364 students applied, and 101 enrolled. Transfers are considered for all classes. Students must study approximately 2 years at the university and complete 60% of the 120 semester hours needed to receive a bachelor's degree. Transfer requirements include high school and previous college transcripts. D grades do not transfer. Application deadlines are the same as those for freshmen.

Visiting: There are no regular orientations. Guides are available for informal visits. Visitors may sit in on classes and stay overnight at the school. Weekday mornings are best for visits; arrangements should be made with the undergraduate admissions office.

Financial Aid: About 64% of all students receive aid. Forty-five percent work part-time on campus. Average aid to freshmen from all sources is $5100. The university offers a comprehensive program of financial aid, including scholarships, grants-in-aid, employment, and loans. The university also awards to 68 entering freshmen with outstanding academic performance, 4-year, renewable scholarships ranging from half to full tuition. Financial need is not a prerequisite; all students with strong records are urged to apply to the dean's office for these scholarships. The university is a member of CSS. The FAF and a copy of the parents' most recent federal income tax return are required. The application deadline is April 15. Candidates for financial aid are notified about 3 weeks after notification of admission.

Foreign Students: Ten percent of the full-time students come from foreign countries. The university offers these students an intensive English program, special counseling, and special organizations.

Admissions: Foreign students must take the TOEFL or the university's own test. They must score at least 550 on the TOEFL. College entrance examinations are recommended.

Procedure: The application deadlines are July 15 (fall), December 1 (spring), and May 15 (summer). Foreign students must submit a physical examination form completed by a physician. They must also present proof of funds adequate to cover 1 year of study. Health insurance is required and is available through the university for a fee.

Admissions Contact: Lynn Farris, Assistant Director of Admissions.

CEDARVILLE COLLEGE   B-4
Cedarville, Ohio 45314   (513) 766-2211

F/T: 717M, 868W	Faculty:	68; IIB, av$
P/T: 36M, 36W	Ph.D.'s:	48%
Grad: none	S/F Ratio:	22 to 1
Year: qtrs, ss	Tuition:	$2958
Appl: Aug. 1	R and B:	$1935
784 applied	603 accepted	467 enrolled
SAT: 470V 470M	ACT: 21	COMPETITIVE

Cedarville College, founded in 1887, is a church-related liberal arts college affiliated with the General Association of Regular Baptists. The library contains 91,000 volumes and 7200 microfilm items, and subscribes to 750 periodicals.

Environment: The 105-acre campus is located in a small, rural town 10 miles from Springfield. It comprises almost 40 buildings including a science center, cafeteria, chapel, and a recreation center surrounding a 6-acre lake. Twelve dormitories house 1400 students; 1 more is under construction. Off-campus apartments are also available.

Student Life: Thirty-seven percent of the students are from Ohio, 40% from bordering states, and 1% from foreign countries. Eighty-two percent live on campus. All students are of the Protestant faith. There is daily compulsory chapel attendance. Three percent of the students are minority-group members. Campus housing is single-sex, and there are visiting privileges. Drinking on campus is forbidden. Only first quarter freshmen may not have cars on campus. All students must observe a curfew and a sign-out procedure.

Organizations: There are 24 extracurricular activities and groups. Each quarter, 5 to 10 cultural events take place on campus. The student government has representation in the areas of dorm regulations, student discipline, student publications, and student activities.

Sports: The college competes intercollegiately in 8 sports for men and 7 for women. There are 10 intramural sports for men, and 10 for women.

Handicapped: There are some facilities for the handicapped. Two counselors are available.

Graduates: Thirteen percent of freshmen drop out by the end of the first year; 47% remain to graduate. Twenty-five percent of those who remain pursue graduate study. Approximately 55% of the graduates enter business and industry.

Services: The college provides the following free services: placement, career counseling, psychological counseling, and health care. Tutoring services are available for a fee.

Programs of Study: The college confers the B.A., B.S.N., and B.Mus.Ed. degrees. Bachelor's degrees are offered in the following subjects: BUSINESS (accounting, business administration, business education), EDUCATION (elementary, health/physical, secondary, special), ENGLISH (English, speech), FINE AND PERFORMING ARTS (music, music education, radio/TV), HEALTH SCIENCES (medical technology, nursing), LANGUAGES (French, German, Greek, Hebrew, Spanish), MATH AND SCIENCES (biology, chemistry, mathematics), PHILOSOPHY (religion), PREPROFESSIONAL (agriculture, dentistry, engineering, law, medicine, ministry, pharmacy, social work, veterinary), SOCIAL SCIENCES (government/political science, history, psychology, social sciences, sociology).

Required: All undergraduates must take courses in the following areas: Bible education, communications, art and music in history, physical education, biological science, physical science, and social science.

Special: The college offers independent study and interdisciplinary studies. Students are permitted to participate in an established study-abroad program sponsored by another college.

Honors: There are no honor societies on campus.

Admissions: Seventy-seven percent of those who applied were accepted for the 1981-82 freshman class. Of those who enrolled the ACT scores were as follows: 48% below 21, 35% between 21 and 25, 12% between 26 and 28, and 2% above 28. Candidates must graduate from an accredited high school, have a GPA of at least 2.5, rank in the upper half of their graduating class, and have completed 15 Carnegie units.

Procedure: Either the SAT or the ACT is required; junior year results are acceptable. The college has a rolling admissions plan and observes the CRDA. Application deadlines are: August 1 (fall); February 15 (spring); May 15 (summer); November 15 (winter). A personal interview is recommended but not required. There is a $15 application fee.

Special: There is a deferred admissions plan. CLEP and AP credit is accepted.

Transfer: For fall 1981, 277 transfer students applied, 232 were accepted, and 164 enrolled. A GPA of 2.5 is required. Students must have minimum SAT verbal and math scores of 375 or a score of 16 on the ACT. D grades do not transfer. The student must complete 45 of the 192 quarter hours needed for a bachelor's degree in residence. The deadlines for transfer applicants are the same as those for freshman applicants.

Visiting: The best time for a visit is on Friday. There are no regularly scheduled visits; prospective students should contact the admissions office to make arrangements for guides or to stay at the campus.

Financial Aid: About 80% of all students receive financial aid. Thirty percent work part-time on campus. There are approximately 65 freshman scholarships and $127,000 in scholarship aid available to freshmen and upperclassmen. The college administers $2 million in federal loan funds and $1,540,000 in state and private loan funds. Work contracts are awarded to freshmen. Scholarships range from $500 to $1000, loans from $500 to $2500, and work contracts from $400 to $2000. The average award to freshmen from all sources is $2500. Tuition may be paid in installments. The college is a member of the CSS. The FAF is required from aid applicants. The deadline for applications is April 1.

Foreign Students: About 1% of the full-time students are from foreign countries. Special counseling is available for these students.

Admissions: Foreign students must achieve a minimum score of 500 on the TOEFL. They must also achieve a minimum score of 18 on the ACT or SAT scores of at least 410 on the verbal and 410 on the math.

Procedure: Application deadlines are the same as those for freshman applicants; foreign students are admitted throughout the academic year. Proof of funds adequate to cover 1 year of study must be presented. Foreign students must carry health insurance, which is available through the college for a fee.

Admissions Contact: David M. Ormsbee, Director of Admissions.

CENTRAL STATE UNIVERSITY B-4
Wilberforce, Ohio 45384 (513) 376-6011

F/T: 1223M, 1229W Faculty: 140; n/av
P/T: 80M, 164W Ph.D.'s: 50%
Grad: none S/F Ratio: 15 to 1
Year: qtrs, ss Tuition: $1173 ($2052)
Appl: open R and B: $2367
1734 applied 1635 accepted 847 enrolled
ACT: required NONCOMPETITIVE

Central State University, founded in 1887, offers undergraduate programs in the colleges of Arts and Sciences, Business Administration, and Education. Its library holds over 130,000 volumes and 250,000 microfilm items, and subscribes to 900 periodicals.

Environment: The 60-acre rural campus, located about 18 miles east of Dayton, was rebuilt in the years following a devastating 1974 tornado. Residence-hall complexes house approximately 1200 students. New buildings include the library, a performing arts center, a gymnasium, and a community health center.

Student Life: About 80% of the students come from Ohio. Eighty-five percent are black. About half live on campus in the single-sex dorms.

Organizations: About 25% of the students are members of fraternities and sororities. Extracurricular activities include special-interest and departmental groups, publications, dance, drama, music, and regularly scheduled social and cultural events.

Sports: The university fields intercollegiate teams in 14 sports. Intramural sports also are available.

Graduates: About 12% of the freshmen drop out, and 46% remain to graduate. Twenty percent of the graduates go on for further study.

Services: Career counseling and placement services are offered free. A health-care plan is available for a fee.

Programs of Study: The university confers the B.A., B.S., and B.S.Ed. degrees. Associate degrees also are awarded. Bachelor's degrees are offered in the following subjects: AREA STUDIES (African and Afro-American), BUSINESS (accounting, business administration, business education, data processing, finance, management, marketing, office administration), EDUCATION (elementary, health/physical, industrial, recreation, secondary, special), ENGLISH (English, journalism, literature, speech), FINE AND PERFORMING ARTS (art, dance, music, radio/TV, theater/dramatics), HEALTH SCIENCES (corrective and recreational therapy, medical technology), LANGUAGES (French, German, Spanish), MATH AND SCIENCES (biology, chemistry, computer science, earth science, geology, mathematics, physics), PHILOSOPHY (philosophy), PREPROFESSIONAL (dentistry, engineering, engineering—systems, industrial technology, law, medicine, ministry, social work), SOCIAL SCIENCES (anthropology, economics, geography, government/political science, history, psychology, public administration, sociology).

Required: Each student must take 57 quarter hours of core courses in English and speech, mathematics, humanities and fine arts, natural and social sciences, and health and physical education.

Special: Cooperative programs are offered to juniors and seniors. A special program provides academic assistance to entering freshmen from disadvantaged backgrounds. Combined B.A./B.S. and B.S.Ed. degrees are possible. Under a consortium arrangement, CSU students may register in courses offered by a member institution at no additional charge.

Honors: The university offers interdisciplinary and departmental honors programs. A Departmental Scholars Program offers seniors the opportunity to undertake specific research. One national honor society has a chapter on campus.

664 OHIO

Admissions: About 94% of the applicants for the 1981–82 freshman class were accepted. Central State has a policy of open admission for Ohio high school graduates or Ohio residents with a GED certificate. Admission of out-of-state students is limited to those who have a GPA of C+ or better and rank in the upper half of their high school class. Sixteen Carnegie units are required.

Procedure: The ACT is required for placement purposes only. New students are admitted to all quarters. Suggested application deadlines are June 15 (fall), October 15 (winter), February 15 (spring), and April 15 (summer). Applications are accepted as long as space is available. Notification is made on a rolling basis. There is a $15 application fee.

Special: AP and CLEP credit is granted.

Transfer: About 80 transfer students enroll yearly. Applicants must have at least a 2.0 GPA. D grades do not transfer. Students must earn at least 36 credits in residence of the 186 generally required for a bachelor's degree.

Financial Aid: About 80% of the students receive assistance. Loans (including NDSL), scholarships, grants (including BEOG), and campus jobs (including CWS) are available. The university aid form should be filed by April 15 for the fall term (June 15 for transfer students), October 15 for winter, February 15 for spring, and April 15 for summer. The FAF should be submitted by March 1. Need is the basis for aid awards.

Foreign Students: Students from foreign countries make up about 5% of enrollment. The university offers these students special counseling and special organizations.

Admissions: Applicants must score 500 or better on the TOEFL.

Procedure: Application deadlines are April 1 (fall), June 1 (winter), September 1 (spring), and January 1 (summer). Students must submit a physician's statement as proof of good health and provide evidence of adequate funds for 1 year. They also must carry health insurance, which is available through the university for a fee.

Admissions Contact: Edith Johnson, Director of Admissions.

CLEVELAND INSTITUTE OF ART   D-1
Cleveland, Ohio 44120   (216) 421-4322

F/T: 249M, 284W	Faculty: 53; III, n/av
P/T: 5M, 25W	Ph.D.'s: all M.F.A.'s
Grad: none	S/F Ratio: 10 to 1
Year: 4-1-4, ss	Tuition: $3575
Appl: Aug. 30	R and B: $2550
378 applied	220 accepted	116 enrolled
ACT: 18		SPECIAL

Cleveland Institute of Art, founded in 1882, is a private professional school of art. A comprehensive program of study is offered in the fine arts, design, the crafts, and teacher education. The library contains 30,000 volumes, 160 periodical subscriptions, and 40,000 slides.

Environment: The urban campus is located in the heart of Cleveland's University Circle, a complex of 35 educational and cultural institutions. Housing and dining facilities are available at Case Western Reserve University, which occupies a common campus with the institute.

Student Life: About 68% of the students are from Ohio. Twenty-five percent live on campus. Five percent of the students are minority-group members. Institute housing is single-sex; there are visiting privileges. Students may keep cars on campus.

Organizations: The institute shares many of its social, cultural, and extracurricular activities with Case Western Reserve. There is an active student government.

Sports: There is no athletic program.

Graduates: The freshman dropout rate is 10%. About 65% remain to graduate; 25% go on for further study.

Services: The institute offers free career counseling, placement services, psychological counseling, and tutoring to students. Health care is available on a fee basis.

Programs of Study: The B.F.A. is offered in the following subjects: FINE AND PERFORMING ARTS (art, art education, film/photography, studio art).

Required: All students must take the 2-year basic program.

Special: Study abroad is possible through a consortium of 9 professional schools of art.

Admissions: About 58% of those who applied were accepted for the 1981–82 freshman class. A high school diploma (or GED) and 16 Carnegie units are required. Evidence of special talents, the applicant's personal qualities, and recommendations are also considered.

Procedure: Neither the SAT nor the ACT is required. Application deadlines are August 30 (fall) and January 10 (spring). A rolling admissions policy is used. There is a $20 application fee.

Special: Early decision and early and deferred admissions plans are offered. AP and CLEP credit is available.

Transfer: About 65 transfer students enroll annually. Good academic standing (2.8 GPA) and evidence of special talents are required. D grades do not transfer. Students must complete a total of 178 credits to receive a bachelor's degree. Application deadlines are the same as those for freshman applicants.

Visiting: Campus tours may be arranged. Visitors may sit in on classes.

Financial Aid: About 71% of the students receive financial aid. The institute participates in CWS, NDSL, and BEOG/SEOG programs. It offers additional aid in the forms of other loans and limited part-time campus employment. Need is the determining factor. The institute is a member of CSS. The FAF should be filed no later than May 1.

Foreign Students: One percent of the full-time students come from foreign countries. The institute offers these students an intensive English course, special counseling, and special organizations.

Admissions: Foreign students must score at least 500 on the TOEFL. No college entrance examination is required.

Procedure: The deadlines for application are August 30 (fall) and January 1 (winter). Foreign students must submit proof of health and of adequate funds. They must also carry health insurance.

Admissions Contact: Ted Sherron, Director of Admissions.

CLEVELAND INSTITUTE OF MUSIC   D-1
Cleveland, Ohio 44106   (216) 791-5165

F/T: 72M, 70W	Faculty: 38; n/av
P/T: 1M, 3W	Ph.D.'s: 1%
Grad: 40M, 48W	S/F Ratio: 12 to 1
Year: sems, ss	Tuition: $5371
Appl: open	R and B: $2420
200 applied	66 accepted	36 enrolled
SAT: 510V 530M		SPECIAL

Cleveland Institute of Music, founded in 1920, is a conservatory affiliated with Case Western Reserve University. The music library contains 39,000 volumes and 8600 records, and subscribes to 150 periodicals.

Environment: The conservatory is located on the 400-acre university campus in urban Cleveland. Its 50 buildings include 2 concert halls, an electronic music studio, Dalcroze studio, an opera workshop, and 3 high-rise dormitories.

Student Life: Twenty percent of the students are from Ohio, and 20% are from bordering states. Ninety-five percent attended public schools. More than half live off campus. Fourteen percent of the students are minority-group members. Institute housing is coed. Students may keep cars on campus.

Organizations: Two fraternities have a membership of 2% of the men; 2% of the women belong to 2 sororities. Over 10 cultural events take place on campus each week. Off-campus cultural activities are also extremely important.

Sports: Athletics are available through Case Western Reserve University.

Handicapped: The campus is completely accessible to wheelchair-bound students. Facilities include wheelchair ramps, elevators, and lowered drinking fountains and telephones. One percent of the students currently enrolled are visually impaired. Special counseling is available through Case Western Reserve University.

Graduates: There is a freshman dropout rate of 10%; 40% remain to graduate. Ninety percent of graduates pursue advanced study.

Services: The following services are available free to students: placement, career counseling, psychological counseling, health care, tutoring, and remedial instruction. Tutoring is also available on a fee basis.

Programs of Study: The institute confers the B.Mus. and B.S.Mus.Ed. degrees. Master's and doctoral degrees also are awarded. Bachelor's degrees are offered in the following subjects: FINE AND PERFORMING ARTS (music, music education).

Required: A core curriculum of liberal arts, music history, theory, and literature is required. To graduate a student must earn 130 credits and have a GPA of at least 2.0. Evaluation is based on jury auditions, recitals, opera performance, exams, term papers, and research.

Special: A combined B.M.-B.S., degree is available through a 5-year program. Students benefit from special activities with the Cleveland Orchestra and a joint program with Case Western Reserve University.

Honors: There are 2 honor societies on campus: Pi Kappa Lambda and Mu Phi Epsilon.

Admissions: About 33% of those who applied were accepted for the 1981-82 freshman class. Of those who enrolled, the SAT scores were as follows: Verbal—10% below 500, 85% between 500 and 599, 4% between 600 and 700, and 1% above 700; Math—10% below 500, 85% between 500 and 599, 4% between 600 and 700, and 1% above 700. Applicants must be graduates of an accredited high school, with 16 Carnegie units. An audition and the required personal interview are especially important admission criteria. Other factors include evidence of special talent, extracurricular activities, recommendations, and advanced placement or honors courses.

Procedure: The institute requires the SAT. Freshmen are admitted at midyear and in the summer. There are no application deadlines. The $25 application fee is not refundable.

Special: Early decision and early admissions plans are available.

Transfer: In a recent year, 178 transfer applications were received, 95 were accepted, and 63 students enrolled. Freshmen, sophomores, juniors, and seniors may transfer. An audition and the college transcript are required. A 2.0 GPA is required. D grades do not transfer. A student must study at the institute for 1 year and complete 24 of the approximately 130 credits needed to receive a bachelor's degree. Application deadlines are the same as those for freshman applicants.

Visiting: There are no scheduled visits, but prospective students are welcome to come on informal visits. Contact the Housing Office at Case Western Reserve University to make arrangements.

Financial Aid: Sixty percent of the students receive financial aid. Fifty percent work part-time on campus. Average aid to freshmen from all sources is $2500. The institute administers scholarship aid, federal loans, and state loans. It is a CSS member and requires the FAF. The application deadlines are May 1 (fall) and December 1 (winter).

Foreign Students: Eleven percent of the full-time students come from foreign countries. The institute offers these students an intensive English course, special counseling, and special organizations.

Admissions: Foreign students must score at least 500 on the TOEFL. No college entrance examination is required.

Procedure: Application deadlines are open. Foreign students must submit a medical history report and proof of adequate funds. They must also carry health insurance, which is available through the institute for a fee.

Admissions Contact: Frank P. Caputo, Interim Dean.

CLEVELAND STATE UNIVERSITY D-1
Cleveland, Ohio 44114 (216) 687-3755

F/T: 4963M, 3902W Faculty: 525; IIA, ++$
P/T: 2161M, 1697W Ph.D.'s: 80%
Grad: 1501M, 1599W S/F Ratio: 22 to 1
Year: qtrs, ss Tuition: $1377 ($2754)
Appl: open R: $540
2691 applied 2673 accepted 1983 enrolled
SAT: 433V 469M ACT: 17 LESS COMPETITIVE

Cleveland State University, established in 1964, offers undergraduate programs in arts and sciences, business administration, education, engineering, urban affairs, and law. Optional cooperative education programs are also available. The library contains 461,793 volumes and 240,000 microfilm items, and subscribes to 6100 periodicals.

Environment: The campus, which is adjacent to downtown Cleveland, comprises about 38 acres and 23 buildings. There are limited dormitory accommodations as well as fraternity houses and off-campus apartments.

Student Life: The majority of the students come from the Cleveland area. About sixty-nine percent of the entering freshmen come from public schools. Ninety-nine percent of the students live off campus. Thirteen percent are minority-group members. University housing is both single-sex and coed. There are visiting privileges in single-sex dorms. Students may keep cars on campus. Day-care services are available for a fee to full-time and part-time students, faculty, and staff.

Organizations: About two percent of the men and 1% of the women join fraternities or sororities. Students may also participate in religious organizations, special-interest clubs, publications, musical groups, student government, and on-campus cultural and social events.

Sports: The university has 11 intercollegiate teams for men and 10 for women. Eleven intramural sports are offered for men and 9 for women.

Handicapped: About 99% of the campus is accessible to physically handicapped students. Facilities include wheelchair ramps, special parking, elevators, specially equipped rest rooms, and lowered drinking fountains and telephones. Special class scheduling is also available. One percent of the students currently enrolled have visual impairments. There is an equipment room with braille equipment and print magnification. There is 1 special counselor for handicapped students.

Graduates: About 40% of the men and 37% of the women entering as freshmen remain to graduate. About 10% of those who remain pursue full-time graduate or professional studies.

Services: Students receive the following services free of charge: placement, career counseling, health care, psychological counseling, tutoring, and remedial instruction.

Programs of Study: Four-year programs lead to the following degrees: B.A., B.S., B.S.N., B.S.Bus.Ed., B.S.C.I.S., B.S.T., B.S.Ed., B.B.A., B.Ch.E., B.E.E., B.M.E., and B.E.S. There are also master's and doctoral programs. Bachelor's degrees are offered in the following subjects: AREA STUDIES (American, Black/Afro-American, urban), BUSINESS (accounting, business administration, business education, computer science, finance, management, marketing, quantitative business analysis), EDUCATION (adult, early childhood, elementary, health/physical, industrial, secondary, special), ENGLISH (English, literature, speech), FINE AND PERFORMING ARTS (art, art education, music, music education, theater/dramatics), HEALTH SCIENCES (medical technology, nursing, occupational therapy, physical therapy, speech therapy), LANGUAGES (French, German, Italian, Spanish), MATH AND SCIENCES (biochemistry, biology, chemistry, geology, mathematics, physics), PHILOSOPHY (classics, philosophy, religion), PRE-PROFESSIONAL (dentistry, engineering, law, medicine, veterinary), SOCIAL SCIENCES (anthropology, economics, government/political science, history, psychology, social sciences, sociology). Thirty-five percent of degrees are conferred in arts and sciences, 20% in business administration, and 10% in engineering.

Required: All students must take courses in English composition, physical education, humanities, social sciences, science, and mathematics.

Special: It is possible to earn combined B.A.-B.S. degrees. There is a student development program for students not prepared for admission to a baccalaureate college. Cooperative education programs are also offered.

Honors: The university offers advanced placement and honors programs. There are 2 national honor societies on campus.

Admissions: Ninety-five percent of those who applied were accepted for the 1981-82 freshman class. Of those who enrolled, the SAT scores were as follows: Verbal—70% below 500, 25% between 500 and 599, 5% between 600 and 700, and 0% above 700; Math—52% below 500, 33% between 500 and 599, 15% between 600 and 700, and 0% above 700. The ACT scores were as follows: 49% below 21, 39% between 21 and 25, and 12% above 26. Freshmen should have satisfactory SAT or ACT scores for the program they intend to pursue. Ohio residents who have lower qualifications are admitted to the student development program. Subject matter requirements vary according to the program selected. Advanced placement or honors courses and recommendations are also considered.

Procedure: The SAT or ACT is required. Application deadlines are open; notification is on a rolling basis. Of the $25 application fee, $15 is refundable to those not granted admission. An interview is optional.

Transfer: For fall 1981, 2247 transfer applications were received, 2093 were accepted, and 1591 students enrolled. A minimum GPA of 2.0 is required, along with good academic standing. D grades do not transfer. Forty-five quarter credits of 192–200 needed for a bachelor's degree must be taken in residence. Application deadlines are open.

Visiting: There are regularly scheduled orientations for prospective students; guided tours can be scheduled during the quarter. For information, contact the community programs department.

Financial Aid: About 25% of all students receive financial aid, which is available in the form of university grants, activities awards, work-study, scholarships, federal aid funds, and loans. The average aid package for a student is $1470. The FAF is required; the aid application deadline is April 15.

Foreign Students: Two percent of the full-time students come from foreign countries. The university offers these students an intensive English program, special counseling, and special organizations.

Admissions: Foreign students must achieve a minimum score of 525 on TOEFL or 85 on the University of Michigan Language Test. The SAT or ACT is also required.

666 OHIO

Procedure: The application deadline for winter entry is December 4. Students are admitted throughout the year. Foreign students must present proof of funds adequate to cover 1 year of study.

Admissions Contact: Gregory T. Ross, Assistant Director of Admissions.

COLLEGE OF MOUNT SAINT JOSEPH ON THE OHIO A–5
Cincinnati, Ohio 45238 (513) 244-4531

F/T: 50M, 739W	Faculty: 91; IIB, –$
P/T: 129M, 811W	Ph.D.'s: 45%
Grad: 7M, 47W	S/F Ratio: 11 to 1
Year: sems, ss	Tuition: $103 p/c
Appl: July 15	R and B: $2100
430 applied	391 accepted	181 enrolled
SAT: 430V 450M	ACT: 19	COMPETITIVE

College of Mount St. Joseph on the Ohio, founded in 1920, is a Roman Catholic liberal arts college conducted by the Sisters of Charity. The library contains 105,000 volumes and 165 microfilm items, and subscribes to 525 periodicals.

Environment: The 250-acre campus is located in a suburban area 5 miles from Cincinnati proper. The 10 buildings include the administration building, the faculty residence, the chapel, the auditorium, the science building, and the gymnasium (which has a swimming pool). The residence halls accommodate 600 students.

Student Life: About 88% of the students are residents of Ohio. Approximately 46% of the students live on campus. Students must live on campus unless they commute from home. Half the freshmen come from private schools. Forty-nine percent of the students are Catholic and 49% are Protestant. Five percent are minority-group members. Campus housing is single-sex, and there are visiting privileges. Students may keep cars on campus. Day-care services are available free of charge to students, faculty, and staff.

Organizations: There are no fraternities or sororities on campus. The college sponsors lectures, concerts, and social activities.

Sports: The college has 4 intercollegiate teams for women. Two intramural sports are offered for women and 2 for men.

Handicapped: Special parking, elevators, and wheelchair ramps are offered for physically handicapped students. The entire campus is accessible to wheelchair-bound students. Fewer than 1% of the students have visual impairments.

Graduates: Twenty-one percent of the freshmen drop out by the end of their first year, and 66% remain to graduate. About 35% of the graduates pursue advanced degrees. About 2% enter medical school and 1% enter law school. Nineteen percent enter business and industry.

Services: Free career and psychological counseling, health care, job placement services, tutoring, and remedial instruction are offered.

Programs of Study: The college confers the B.A., B.F.A., and B.S.N. degrees. Associate degrees are also offered. Bachelor's degrees are offered in the following subjects: BUSINESS (accounting, business administration, marketing), EDUCATION (adult, early childhood, elementary, secondary, special), ENGLISH (English), FINE AND PERFORMING ARTS (art, art education, studio art), HEALTH SCIENCES (medical technology, nursing), MATH AND SCIENCES (biology/chemistry), PREPROFESSIONAL (dentistry, home economics, law, medicine, ministry, social work, veterinary), SOCIAL SCIENCES (history, sociology). A liberal studies program is also offered. About 37% of the degrees are conferred in the health sciences, and 16% in education.

Required: All students must complete at least 48 hours in liberal arts studies distributed in the following areas: religious studies/philosophy; humanities; history/social sciences; natural sciences/mathematics. In addition, students must satisfy the physical education requirement of 2 semester hours.

Special: Early field experience for credit is part of the curriculum of many majors. The programs in education are designed to lead toward multiple teacher certification in elementary, secondary, and special education.

Honors: Kappa Gamma Pi and Alpha Chi honor societies are represented on campus.

Admissions: Ninety-one percent of those who applied for the 1981–82 freshman class were accepted. The SAT scores of those who enrolled were as follows: Verbal—10% between 600 and 700, and 2% above 700; Math—13% between 600 and 700, and 3% above 700. On the ACT, 12% scored between 24 and 25, 14% between 26 and 28, and 6% above 28. Candidates should have completed 16 Carnegie units, rank in the upper 50% of their graduating class, have a high school GPA of 2.0 or more, and do well on the SAT or ACT. Impressions made during an interview, advanced placement or honors courses, extracurricular record, and recommendations are also taken into consideration.

Procedure: The SAT or ACT is required. Notification is on a rolling basis. The application deadline for fall is July 15. There is a $15 application fee.

Special: Early admissions, deferred admissions, and early decision plans are offered. AP and CLEP credit is accepted.

Transfer: Sixty-six applications were received for fall 1981; 58 students were accepted and 31 enrolled. Applicants should have a 2.0 minimum GPA. All students must complete, at the college, at least 32 of the 128 semester hours needed to earn a bachelor's degree. Transfers are considered for freshman, sophomore, and junior classes and admission is on a rolling basis with a July 15 deadline.

Visiting: Although there is no formal orientation session, special arrangements for visiting can be made through the admissions office. Tours of the campus, class observance, and overnight stays can be arranged.

Financial Aid: Scholarships and grants were received by about 56% of the entering freshmen for fall 1981. The average award to freshmen from sources available through the college was $1200. SEOG, NDSL, CWS, and campus jobs and nursing loans are also available. About 49% of all students receive some form of aid, and 47% work part-time on campus. The college is a member of CSS, and the FAF is required. The deadline for application is April 15.

Foreign Students: Fewer than 1% of the full-time students come from foreign countries.

Admissions: Foreign students must achieve a TOEFL score of at least 450. No college entrance examination is required.

Procedure: Application deadlines are March 15 (fall) and August 15 (winter). Foreign students must present a bank statement as proof of funds and a doctor's statement as proof of health. They must also carry health insurance, although it is not available through the college.

Admissions Contact: John Briggs, Director of Admissions.

COLLEGE OF STEUBENVILLE
(See University of Steubenville)

COLLEGE OF WOOSTER D–2
Wooster, Ohio 44691 (216) 264-1234

F/T: 909M, 817W	Faculty: n/av; IIB, ++$
P/T: 29M, 40W	Ph.D.'s: 83%
Grad: none	S/F Ratio: 12 to 1
Year: qtrs, ss	Tuition, R and B: $7930
Appl: May 1	
1317 applied	1168 accepted	519 enrolled
SAT: 509V 551M	ACT: 24	COMPETITIVE+

College of Wooster, a 4-year liberal arts college affiliated with the Presbyterian Church, was established in 1866. The library contains 258,000 books, 104,000 government documents, and 69,000 microfilm items, and subscribes to 1000 periodicals.

Environment: The 325-acre campus is situated in a rural setting 54 miles south of Cleveland. Students are housed in residence halls. Off-campus housing is also sponsored. There is a 9-hole golf course.

Student Life: About 50% of the students come from Ohio; the remainder represent 42 states and 48 foreign countries. All but 5% of the students live on campus. Freshmen must live on campus. Approximately 67% attended public high schools; 30% belong to the Presbyterian Church. Campus housing is both single-sex and coed, and there are visiting privileges. Students may keep cars on campus.

Organizations: Student life is regulated by the Student Government Association and a campus council composed of students, faculty, and administrators. Thirty percent of the men and 15% of the women are affiliated with the 6 local fraternities and 3 local sororities. Students take part in many extracurricular activities, including musical groups, publications, drama groups, and many social functions.

Sports: The college has 13 intercollegiate teams for men and 11 for women. Seven intramural sports are offered for men and 4 for women.

Handicapped: About 75% of the campus is accessible to the physically handicapped. Among the facilities available are wheelchair ramps, special parking, and elevators; special class scheduling is available on request.

Graduates: The freshman dropout rate is 12%; 66% remain to graduate. Fifty percent of those who remain pursue graduate study: 2% enter medical school, 1% enter dental school, and 3% enter law school. Thirty-five percent pursue careers in business and industry.

Services: Students receive placement services, career counseling, health care, tutoring, remedial instruction, and psychological counseling free of charge.

Programs of Study: The college offers the B.A., B.Mus., and B.Mus.Ed. degrees. Bachelor's degrees are offered in the following subjects: AREA STUDIES (African, Asian, Black/Afro-American, Latin American, Middle Eastern, modern Western European, Russian, urban), BUSINESS (business economics), EDUCATION (elementary, health/physical, secondary), ENGLISH (English, literature, speech), FINE AND PERFORMING ARTS (art, art history, music, music education, studio art, theater/dramatics), LANGUAGES (French, German, Greek/Latin, Spanish), MATH AND SCIENCES (biology, botany, chemical physics, chemistry, computer science, geology, mathematics, physics), PHILOSOPHY (classics, philosophy, religion), PREPROFESSIONAL (social work), SOCIAL SCIENCES (economics, government/political science, history, international relations, psychology, sociology). About thirty-four percent of degrees are conferred in social sciences, 27% in math and sciences, and 13% in English.

Special: The college offers extensive foreign study opportunities. The Department of Urban Studies offers students the opportunity to work and study in a variety of urban centers in this country; there are several other domestic special programs. Five-year cooperative programs with medical schools, a 6-year nursing program, and 3-2 engineering programs are offered, as well as teacher certification on the elementary and secondary levels.

Required: A freshman studies course, 3 courses in independent studies, 1 course in religion, and some work in foreign languages are required of all students.

Honors: Phi Beta Kappa and 11 other national honor societies have chapters on campus.

Admissions: Approximately 89% of those who applied were accepted for the 1981–82 freshman class. The SAT scores of those who enrolled were as follows: Verbal—38% below 500, 28% between 500 and 599, 15% between 600 and 700, and 2% above 700; Math—30% below 500, 31% between 500 and 599, 18% between 600 and 700, and 2% above 700. Candidates should have completed 15 academic units of secondary school work, have a GPA of at least 2.7, and rank in the top 40% of their class.

Procedure: The SAT or ACT is required and should be taken by January of the senior year. New students are admitted in the fall (application deadline May 1), winter (December 1), or spring (February 1). There is a $15 application fee.

Special: Early admissions and deferred admissions plans are available. AP credit is accepted.

Transfer: Seventy-eight applications for transfer were received for fall 1981; 55 students were accepted and 36 enrolled. A 2.5 minimum GPA is required, as is a combined SAT score of 900 or an ACT score of 18. D grades do not transfer. Two years (18 of 35 courses) must be taken in residence for a bachelor's degree. The application deadline is May 1.

Visiting: Guided tours are offered, visitors may sit in on classes, and, with 2 weeks' notice, may stay at the school.

Financial Aid: About 50% of all students receive aid. The college is a member of the CSS and awards $1.5 million in grants and $515,000 in loans annually. Average aid to a freshman is $5186. About 55% of the students earn part of their expenses. Tuition may be paid in installments through private plans. The FAF is required; notification is on a rolling basis. The application deadline is April 15.

Foreign Students: Ten percent of the full-time students come from foreign countries. The college offers these students special counseling services and special organizations.

Admissions: Foreign students must achieve a minimum score of 500 on the TOEFL, or 80 on the University of Michigan Language Test or the ALIGU exam. The SAT or ACT is also required.

Procedure: The application deadline for fall entry is May 1. Foreign students must present proof of funds adequate to cover 1 year of study. Proof of health must be presented; health insurance is available to foreign students through the college.

Admissions Contact: Samuel Barnett, Dean of Admissions.

OHIO 667

COLUMBUS COLLEGE OF ART AND DESIGN   C–3
Columbus, Ohio 43215   (614) 224-9101
(Recognized Candidate for Accreditation)

F/T: 349M, 372W	Faculty: 48; IIB, –$
P/T: 70M, 117W	Ph.D.'s: 1%
Grad: none	S/F Ratio: 15 to 1
Year: sems, ss	Tuition: $3574
Appl: see profile	R: $900
477 applied 319 accepted 261 enrolled	
SAT or ACT: required	SPECIAL

Columbus College of Art and Design, founded in 1879, is an independent institution providing undergraduate and professional instruction in the fine arts. The undergraduate divisions include advertising design, fine arts, illustration, industrial design, and retail advertising.

Environment: The 3-acre campus is located in the urban center of Columbus. Dormitories house 75 men and 75 women.

Student Life: About 80% of the students are residents of Ohio. About 9% are minority-group members. Sixteen percent of the students live on campus; freshmen must live on campus. Coed campus housing is available. Students may keep cars on campus.

Organizations: There are no fraternities or sororities on campus. Extracurricular activities include participation in student council and an intramural sports program.

Sports: There are no intercollegiate team sports. Two intramural sports are offered for men and 2 for women.

Handicapped: About 85% of the campus is accessible to physically handicapped students. Wheelchair ramps, elevators, special parking, specially equipped rest rooms, and lowered drinking fountains and telephones are available. Special class scheduling is also possible.

Graduates: Approximately 30% of the freshmen drop out by the end of their first year; 35% remain to graduate. About 15% of the students who remain pursue advanced study after graduation; 90% enter business and industry.

Services: Placement services, career and psychological counseling, and remedial instruction are offered free of charge. Tutoring is available on a fee basis.

Programs of Study: The college confers the B.F.A. degree in the following subjects: advertising design, illustration, industrial design, interior design, and studio art.

Required: Foundations Studies, 2 semester credits of art history, and physical education is required of all students. The graduation requirements include 145 semester credit hours, 60 credit hours in residency, and a minimum 2.0 GPA.

Admissions: About 67% of the students who applied were accepted for the 1981–82 freshman class. Applicants must have graduated from high school with a minimum GPA of 2.0. Other factors that enter into the admissions decision include, in order of importance, evidence of special talent(s), impressions made during an interview, recommendations from school officials, and personality.

Procedure: The SAT or ACT is required. Students are accepted up to two weeks into each semester, with notification on a rolling basis. The application fee is $25.

Transfer: Forty-nine transfer students were enrolled in fall 1981. Students must have a minimum GPA of 2.0; an interview and portfolio are recommended. D grades do not transfer. Students must complete, at the college, 60 of the 145 credits required for a bachelor's degree. Application deadlines are the same as those for freshmen.

Visiting: Visitors may sit in on classes and guides are available. Prospective students may visit Monday through Friday, 8:30 A.M. to 5:00 P.M. Contact Laurie Clements, Co-Director of Admissions, to arrange a visit.

Financial Aid: Fifty-six percent of the students are receiving financial aid. About 16% work part-time on campus. On the average, $1000 in scholarships are granted to students, $1000 in loans, and $900 in work contracts; the maximum awards are $3000 in scholarships, $1500 in loans, and $1600 in work contracts. The average award to freshmen from all sources available through the college is $3800. The college is a member of CSS; the FAF is required. The application deadlines are May 1 (fall), October 31 (winter), and March 15 (summer).

Foreign Students: Two percent of the full-time students are from foreign countries. An intensive English course and special counseling are available to these students.

668 OHIO

Admissions: Students must achieve a minimum score of 500 on the TOEFL or 80 on the University of Michigan Language Test. No college entrance exam is required.

Procedure: Students are accepted up to two weeks into each semester. Proof of health, a medical form, must be presented as well as proof of adequate funds to cover 4½ years of study. Health insurance is not required, but may be arranged through the college for a fee.

Admissions Contact: Patrick Marion or Laurie Clements, Co-Directors of Admissions.

THE DEFIANCE COLLEGE A-2
Defiance, Ohio 43512 (419) 784-4010

F/T: 303M, 324W	Faculty: 52; IIB, av$
P/T: 71M, 72W	Ph.D.'s: 40%
Grad: none	S/F Ratio: 15 to 1
Year: 4-4-1, ss	Tuition: $4090
Appl: open	R and B: $1870
718 applied	593 accepted	242 enrolled
ACT: 19		COMPETITIVE

The Defiance College, founded in 1850, is a small coeducational institution affiliated with the United Church of Christ, offering liberal arts and sciences, educational, and preprofessional programs. The library contains over 80,000 volumes.

Environment: The 150-acre campus is located in a rural setting 55 miles from Toledo. There are 8 dormitories accommodating 736 students. The 25 buildings on campus include a college community center, an art center and gallery, and a cafeteria and lounge for day students.

Student Life: About 85% of the students are residents of Ohio. Approximately 90% of the freshmen come from public schools. Housing facilities accommodate 72% of the students. Twenty-three percent of the students are Catholic, 44% Protestant, and fewer than 1% Jewish. Eleven percent are minority-group members. College housing is single-sex; there are visiting privileges. Students may keep cars on campus.

Organizations: There are 3 national fraternities, to which 33% of the men belong, and 3 sororities, to which 3% of the women belong. Special-interest groups sponsor social events, music, debates, dances, and other entertainment.

Sports: The college competes in 7 intercollegiate sports for men and 6 for women. There are 9 intramurals for men and 6 for women.

Services: Health care, tutoring, career counseling, and placement services are available to students.

Programs of Study: The college confers the B.A. and B.S. degrees. Associate degrees are also awarded. Bachelor's degrees are offered in the following subjects: BUSINESS (accounting, business administration, business education, computer science, finance, management, marketing), EDUCATION (elementary, health/physical, secondary, special), ENGLISH (English, journalism, literature, speech), FINE AND PERFORMING ARTS (art, art education, art history, music education, radio/TV, studio art, theater/dramatics), HEALTH SCIENCES (medical technology), LANGUAGES (French, German, Greek/Latin, Russian, Spanish), MATH AND SCIENCES (biochemistry, biology, botany, chemistry, earth science, ecology/environmental science, geology, mathematics, natural sciences, physical sciences, physics), PHILOSOPHY (humanities, philosophy, religion), PREPROFESSIONAL (dentistry, law, medicine, ministry, social work, veterinary), SOCIAL SCIENCES (criminal justice, economics, government/political science, history, psychology, social sciences, sociology). The most popular majors are business, physical education, and education.

Required: All undergraduates must fulfill general requirements in several broad disciplines or areas.

Special: During the winter term independent research on or off campus, group projects, or travel abroad replace the usual course work. Other special programs include junior year abroad; combined work-study in teaching and in specialized laboratory work; pass/fail options; student-designed majors; a student-planned and directed course in Afro-American history; and a 3-1 cooperative program in medical technology with Cleveland Metropolitan General Hospital. Teacher training programs lead to certification on the elementary and secondary levels, in physical education, and in special education.

Honors: There are 4 honor societies on campus.

Admissions: About 83% of those who applied were admitted to the 1981-82 freshman class. Candidates should have completed 14 Carnegie units, have an average of at least C, and rank in the upper 60% of their graduating class. SAT scores, impressions made during the interview, and the student's extracurricular record are also taken into consideration.

Procedure: The ACT is required and should be taken by December of the senior year. An interview is recommended. Application deadlines are open. There is a rolling admissions policy. A $15 fee is required.

Special: Early admissions and deferred admissions plans are available. AP and CLEP credit is accepted.

Transfer: Transfer students are accepted for all classes. A 2.0 GPA is required. D grades do not transfer. The final 8 academic units must be completed on campus.

Visiting: Tours can be arranged through the admissions office during the week. Students can sit in on classes and stay overnight at the college.

Financial Aid: Eighty percent of the students receive financial aid. Fifty percent work part-time on campus. About 150 freshman scholarships totaling $150,000 are offered each year. The college participates in the NDSL, CWS, and SEOG programs. Loans are available from federal and state government, local banks, and the college itself. Most aid is given in the form of a package consisting of work-study, grant, and loan. The maximum freshman scholarship is $2150; the maximum loan is $1500. A student can earn up to $550 from campus employment. Church vocation and valedictorian scholarships are available. Tuition may be paid in installments. The college is a member of the CSS. The FAF is required. Aid applications are handled on a rolling basis, but early applications have an advantage.

Foreign Students: Two percent of the full-time students come from foreign countries. The college offers these students special counseling and special organizations.

Admissions: Foreign students must take the TOEFL. No college entrance examination is required.

Procedure: Application deadlines are open.

Admissions Contact: Brian J. Lewis, Director of Admissions.

DENISON UNIVERSITY C-3
Granville, Ohio 43023 (614) 587-6276

F/T: 1054M, 1048W	Faculty: 161; IIB, ++$
P/T: 7M, 20W	Ph.D.'s: 75%
Grad: none	S/F Ratio: 13 to 1
Year: 4-1-4	Tuition: $5990
Appl: Feb. 1	R and B: $2065
2739 applied	1772 accepted	612 enrolled
SAT: 500V 540M	ACT: 24	COMPETITIVE+

Denison University, founded in 1831, is an independent 4-year college of liberal arts and sciences. The library contains 248,000 volumes and 4573 microfilm items, and subscribes to 1008 periodicals.

Environment: The campus of 1000 acres and more than 40 buildings is in a small New England-type village in rural central Ohio, 27 miles from Columbus. There is a biological reserve of 350 acres. Most students live in residence quads or fraternity houses.

Student Life: Seventy-four percent of students are from out of state. Sixty-six percent of the entering freshmen come from public schools. Ninety-one percent of the students live on campus. Five percent of the students are minority-group members. University housing is both single-sex and coed. There are visiting privileges in single-sex housing. All freshmen live in dormitories. Students may keep cars on campus. Weekly nonsectarian services are held on campus but are not compulsory.

Organizations: Fifty-seven percent of the men belong to 10 fraternities; 54% of the women are members of 5 sororities. Extracurricular activities include student government, a weekly newspaper, literary magazine, musical groups, student theater, Black Student Union, and departmental and special-interest clubs.

Sports: Intercollegiate competition for men is available in 13 sports, and for women in 11. There are 14 intramural sports for men and 12 for women.

Handicapped: Wheelchair ramps, parking, elevators, special rest rooms, and a lift chair make 40% of the campus available to wheelchair-bound students. There are no students with visual or hearing impairments currently enrolled; however, readers are available for the visually impaired.

Graduates: There is a freshman dropout rate of 14%; 70% remain to graduate. More than 50% of those who remain go on to graduate study; 4% enter medical school, 1% dental school, and 10% law school. Forty-three percent pursue careers in business and industry.

Services: The following services are available to students free of charge: health care, psychological counseling, career counseling, placement, and remedial instruction. Placement services include workshops, on-campus recruiting, summer jobs, internships, resume referrals, and individual job-hunt strategy. Tutoring is available on a fee basis.

Programs of Study: The university confers the B.A., B.S., B.Mus., and B.F.A. degrees. Bachelor's degrees are offered in the following subjects: AREA STUDIES (Black/Afro-American, French, Latin American, Russian, urban), BUSINESS (computer science), EDUCATION (health/physical), ENGLISH (English, literature, speech), FINE AND PERFORMING ARTS (art, art history, dance, film/photography, music, music education, studio art, theater/dramatics), LANGUAGES (French, German, Spanish), MATH AND SCIENCES (biology, chemistry, earth science, geology, mathematics, physics), PHILOSOPHY (classics, philosophy, religion), PREPROFESSIONAL (business, dentistry, engineering, forestry, medical technology, medicine, natural resources, veterinary), SOCIAL SCIENCES (economics, government/political science, history, psychology, sociology). Certification is available in secondary education. Forty-eight percent of degrees are conferred in social sciences, 16% in math and sciences, and 18% in English.

Required: The university has distribution requirements, but few are required to be taken in the freshman year.

Special: Programs include independent study, study abroad, a Washington Semester, and 3-2 programs in engineering, forestry, medical technology, and natural resources. Student-designed majors are permitted.

Honors: All departments offer students the opportunity to participate in honors projects. There are also 16 honor societies on campus.

Admissions: About 65% of those who applied were accepted for the 1981-82 freshman class. Of those who enrolled, the SAT scores were as follows: Verbal—50% below 500, 41% between 500 and 599, 8% between 600 and 700, and 1% above 700; Math—29% below 500, 51% between 500 and 599, 18% between 600 and 700, and 2% above 700. On the ACT, 20% scored below 21, 26% between 21 and 23, 18% between 24 and 25, 27% between 26 and 28, and 9% above 28. Applicants should have completed 15 Carnegie units. The university evaluates students on the following factors: advanced placement or honors courses, recommendations, leadership record, evidence of special talent, extracurricular activities, and personality.

Procedure: The SAT or ACT is required and should be taken by December of the senior year. The deadlines for application are February 1 (fall) and December 1 (spring). Applicants for fall are notified by April 15. The CRDA is observed. A personal interview is not required, but strongly recommended. There is a $20 application fee.

Special: There are early decision, and early and deferred admissions plans. AP and CLEP credit is accepted.

Transfer: For fall 1981, 86 applications were received, 32 were accepted, and 20 students enrolled. Generally, a B- or better average, high school and college transcripts (2.75 GPA), and recommendations from the dean and a faculty member of the last college attended are required. D grades do not transfer. There is a residency requirement of 2 years. Sixty semester hours must be completed, at the university, of the 127 needed to receive a bachelor's degree. May 1 is the fall semester deadline; December 1 for the spring semester.

Visiting: The university offers several regularly scheduled opportunities to visit the college, including campus tours, meetings with faculty members and coaches, socializers, and panel discussions. Contact the admissions office to make arrangements for formal or informal visits or stays; best times are late spring, summer, or fall.

Financial Aid: About 25% of all students receive financial aid. Fifty percent work part-time on campus. Average aid to freshmen from all sources is $5701. The university participates in the NDSL, GSL, SEOG, BEOG, OIG, and College Work-Study plans; it offers academic merit scholarships to superior students; and it sponsors National Merit Scholarships. The university is a member of CSS. The FAF should be filed. The application deadlines are February 15 (fall) and November 1 (spring).

Foreign Students: Two percent of the full-time students come from foreign countries. The university offers these students special counseling and special organizations.

Admissions: Foreign students must score at least 550 on the TOEFL. No college entrance examination is required.

Procedure: The application deadline is March 15 (fall). Foreign students must submit the IIE Form 101, certificate of health, signed by a physician. They must also submit proof of funds adequate for 4 years of study. They must carry health insurance, which is available through the university for a fee.

Admissions Contact: Richard F. Boyden, Director of Admissions.

OHIO 669

DYKE COLLEGE D-1
Cleveland, Ohio 44114 (216) 696-9000

F/T: 215M, 650W   Faculty: n/av; IIB, --$
P/T: 247M, 287W   Ph.D.'s: n/av
Grad: none   S/F Ratio: 19 to 1
Year: tri, ss   Tuition: $2575
Appl: open   R and B: n/app
691 applied   691 accepted   454 enrolled
SAT or ACT: required   NONCOMPETITIVE

Dyke College, founded in 1848, is an independent institution offering undergraduate programs in business. The library has 12,000 volumes, and subscribes to 120 periodicals.

Environment: The urban campus, located in downtown Cleveland, is for commuting students only. Duke also operates 2 suburban academic centers and on-site academic programs in greater Cleveland corporations.

Student Life: About 95% of the students come from Ohio; most have had public school educations. All students commute.

Organizations: On-campus activities include publications, clubs, fraternities and sororities, and professional societies.

Sports: The college fields 2 intercollegiate teams for men. There is 1 intramural sport for women.

Graduates: The freshman dropout rate is 45%. Five percent of the graduates go on for further study. About 90% of the graduates enter careers in business and industry.

Services: Placement, career counseling, and tutoring are offered free of charge to all students. Remedial instruction is available on a fee basis.

Programs of Study: The college confers the B.S. degree. Associate degrees are also awarded. Bachelor's degrees are offered in the following subjects: BUSINESS (accounting, business administration, finance, management, marketing, paralegal education, public administration, real estate/insurance, secretarial administration), HEALTH SCIENCES (health services management), SOCIAL SCIENCES (economics, social sciences).

Required: All students must complete a core curriculum.

Special: There is an external degree program for students who wish to earn bachelor's credit in ways other than through traditional classroom instruction. There is also a cooperative education program for accounting, management, marketing, paralegal, and secretarial science majors.

Admissions: All of those who applied were accepted for the 1981-82 freshman year. A high school diploma or GED is required. High school transcripts and ACT or SAT scores are considered in the admissions decision.

Procedure: The ACT or SAT is required. New students are admitted each term; deadlines are open. Notification is on a rolling basis. There is a $25 application fee.

Special: There is an early admissions plan.

Transfer: For fall 1981, 199 transfer students applied and all were accepted. Good academic standing is required; grades of C and above transfer. Thirty-three credits of advanced work must be completed in residence; 126 credits are required to earn the bachelor's degree. Application deadlines are open.

Visiting: Campus tours may be arranged by contacting the admissions office.

Financial Aid: About 75% of the students receive financial aid. The college offers federal programs such as NDSL, BEOG/SEOG, and CWS in addition to other loan programs. Scholarships are also available. The college is a member of CSS; the FAF is required (FFS accepted). It should be filed as early as possible, although the deadline is September 1.

Foreign Students: Fewer than 1% of the full-time students come from foreign countries. The college offers these students an intensive English course and special counseling.

Admissions: Foreign students must achieve a minimum TOEFL score of 475. They must also take the ACT and the college's own entrance exam.

Procedure: There are no application deadlines. Foreign students must present proof of funds adequate to cover their entire period of attendance.

Admissions Contact: Bruce T. Shields, Director of Admissions.

FINDLAY COLLEGE
Findlay, Ohio 45840

B-2
(419) 422-8313

F/T: 433M, 392W
P/T: 200M, 114W
Grad: none
Year: sems, ss
Appl: open
1052 applied
SAT or ACT: required

Faculty: 57; IIB, av$
Ph.D.'s: 30%
S/F Ratio: 15 to 1
Tuition: $4037
R and B: $1800
774 accepted   293 enrolled
COMPETITIVE

Findlay College was established in 1882 by the Churches of God in North America as a 4-year liberal arts college. The library contains 99,485 volumes and 14,991 microfilm items, and subscribes to 639 periodicals.

Environment: Located in the city of Findlay, which has a population of 40,000, the college is 38 miles from Toledo, in the farm area of northwestern Ohio. The main campus contains the administration and classroom building, science hall, fine arts center, student union, 2 gymnasiums and an Olympic-size swimming pool. A biology field station is located outside the city. Campus housing includes dormitories, fraternity houses, and sorority houses.

Student Life: Eighty percent of the students are from Ohio. All of the students live on campus, most of them in the dormitories, but a small percentage in fraternity or sorority houses. About 58% of the students are Protestant and 22% are Catholic. About 14% are minority-group members. Campus housing is single-sex; there are visiting privileges. Students may keep cars on campus.

Organizations: Four fraternities have a membership of 26% of the men; there are 3 sororities, to which 35% of the women belong. There are many recreational centers in the area.

Sports: The college fields 9 intercollegiate teams for men and 5 for women. There are 9 intramural sports for men and 3 for women.

Handicapped: Special parking and wheelchair ramps are provided for physically handicapped students, as well as special class scheduling.

Graduates: There is a freshman dropout rate of 30%; 40% remain to graduate. Eleven percent of those who remain pursue graduate study; 1% enter law school. Seventy-one percent of graduates pursue careers in business and industry.

Services: The college offers the following services free of charge to students: placement, career counseling, health care, tutoring, and remedial instruction.

Programs of Study: The college confers the B.A., and B.S. degrees. Associate degrees are also awarded. Bachelor's degrees are offered in the following subjects: BUSINESS (accounting, business administration, business education, computer science, finance, marketing), EDUCATION (elementary, health/physical, middle grade, secondary), ENGLISH (English, journalism, speech), FINE AND PERFORMING ARTS (art, art education, radio, theater/dramatics), HEALTH SCIENCES (medical technology), LANGUAGES (Spanish), MATH AND SCIENCES (biology, ecology/environmental science, mathematics), PHILOSOPHY (philosophy, religion), PREPROFESSIONAL (engineering, law, medicine, veterinary), SOCIAL SCIENCES (economics, government/political science, history, psychology, social sciences, sociology). Forty-six percent of degrees are conferred in business, 30% in education, 8% in math and sciences, and 8% in social sciences.

Special: Student-designed majors are permitted.

Honors: Honor and professional societies open to qualified students include Alpha Psi Omega, Phi Alpha Theta, Phi Mu Alpha, and Sigma Tau Delta.

Admissions: About 74% of those who applied were accepted for the 1981–82 freshman class. The ACT scores of those who enrolled were as follows: 67% below 21, 17% between 21 and 23, 5% between 24 and 25, 6% between 26 and 28, and 0% above 28. Applicants must be graduates of accredited high schools and should present 15 units of credit. A 2.0 grade average is required. Candidates should present SAT scores that indicate potential for academic success. Students must show evidence of intellectual and social maturity.

Procedure: The SAT or ACT is required. A personal interview is recommended. The application should be sent during the first semester of the senior year; a rolling admissions policy is followed. Students may be admitted to any session. There is no application fee.

Special: There is an early admissions plan. AP and CLEP credit is accepted.

Transfer: About 60 transfer students are accepted annually. A 2.0 GPA is recommended. Grades of C or better transfer. Nine courses must be taken in residence; 120 credits are required to earn the bachelor's degree. A rolling admissions policy is used.

Visiting: There are regularly scheduled tours of the campus; prospective students may visit classes, and speak with the professors. Contact the admissions office to make arrangements for visits or stays.

Financial Aid: In addition to NDSL, the college has available various other private and publicly supported loans and scholarships. About 64% of the students receive some form of financial aid; 37% work part-time on campus. To be eligible for a scholarship, loan, or job, a student must meet the admissions standards of the college and continue to make satisfactory progress in all academic work. The average award to freshmen from all sources is $2523. It is recommended that applications be filed by April 1. Findlay is a member of the CSS and requires the FAF.

Foreign Students: The college actively recruits foreign students and offers these students an intensive English program, special counseling, and special organizations.

Admissions: Foreign students must achieve a minimum TOEFL score of 500 or a score of at least 80 on the University of Michigan Language Test. No college entrance exams are required.

Procedure: There are no application deadlines. Foreign students must present proof of adequate funds.

Admissions Contact: J. Michael Turnbull, Director of Admissions.

FRANKLIN UNIVERSITY
Columbus, Ohio 43215

C-3
(614) 224-6413

F/T: 879M, 689W
P/T: 1482M, 1961W
Grad: none
Year: tri, ss
Appl: Sept. 1
2365 applied
SAT or ACT: recommended

Faculty: 47; IV, +$
Ph.D.'s: 38%
S/F Ratio: 28 to 1
Tuition: $1860
R and B: n/app
2300 accepted   1491 enrolled
NONCOMPETITIVE

Franklin University is an independent, coeducational business and technical university. Its divisions—the General College, College of Business and Public Administration, College of Science and Engineering Technology, and School of Baccalaureate Nursing—aim to prepare students for careers in business, government, engineering technologies, and nursing. The library contains 60,000 volumes, and subscribes to 1100 periodicals.

Environment: Essentially a commuter institution, the university is housed in 4 buildings on an 11-acre campus in downtown Columbus. While no dormitories are provided, suitable accommodations are available within walking distance of the campus. Parking facilities are also available to students at no additional cost.

Student Life: Ninety-eight percent of the students are Ohio residents; 1% are from bordering states, and 1% are from foreign countries. All students commute from either private homes or housing available in the campus vicinity. About 20% of the students are minority-group members. Students may keep cars on campus.

Organizations: Students are represented on curriculum, finance, and other university committees. There are curriculum-connected clubs and associations. The city of Columbus provides cultural activities.

Sports: The university fields 1 intercollegiate team for men. There are 2 intramural sports for men and 2 for women.

Handicapped: The entire campus is accessible to wheelchair-bound students. Facilities include wheelchair ramps, special parking and rest rooms, and lowered drinking fountains and telephones.

Graduates: Eight percent of the students pursue advanced study after graduation; 1% enter law school.

Services: Students receive the following services free of charge: placement, career counseling, tutoring, and psychological counseling. Placement counseling aids students with employment and provides career exploration seminars. Remedial instruction is available on a fee basis.

Programs of Study: The university confers the B.S.B.A., B.S.E.T., B.S.N., and B.P.A. degrees. Associate degrees are also awarded. Bachelor's degrees are offered in the following subjects: BUSINESS (accounting, business administration, computer science, finance, management, personnel and labor relations, real estate), HEALTH SCIENCES (nursing), PREPROFESSIONAL (engineering technology, engineering drawing technology), SOCIAL SCIENCES (government, public administration). Eighty-five percent of degrees are conferred in business and 15% in engineering technology and nursing.

Required: The bachelor's degree is conferred on those who have successfully completed a minimum of 120 semester hours, with a minimum GPA of 2.0. The A.S. is awarded to those who have successfully completed 60 semester hours of study. Although there is no time limit on receiving a degree, at least 30 semester hours must be taken in residence at Franklin.

Honors: Tau Alpha Pi, the national engineering technology honor society, has a chapter on campus.

Admissions: Ninety-seven percent of those who applied were accepted for the 1981–82 freshman class. Franklin maintains an open admissions policy. A high school diploma or GED is required. Three factors that enter into the admissions decision are advanced placement or honors courses, recommendations by school officials, and impressions made during an interview.

Procedure: The university suggests that candidates take the ACT or SAT. A personal interview is required. Applications must be submitted by September 1 for the fall trimester and January 1 for the spring trimester. Students are also admitted in the summer trimester; the application deadline is April 20. Notification is on a rolling basis. There is a $16 application fee.

Special: There are early admissions and deferred admissions plans. CLEP credit is accepted.

Transfer: For fall 1981, 715 transfer students applied, 550 were accepted, and 542 enrolled. The university's open door admission policy extends to transfer students as well. Transfer applications are accepted for the second trimester freshman, the sophomore, the junior, and the senior years. Transfer students must complete at least 30 semester hours at Franklin to receive their degree; 120 credits are required to earn the bachelor's degree. Deadlines for transfer applications are the same as those for entering freshmen.

Visiting: Two-hour orientations are scheduled prior to each trimester. Students can arrange to visit the campus and sit in on classes. Student guides provide tours of the campus; the best times for campus visits other than during orientation are weekdays.

Financial Aid: Twenty-one percent of all students receive some form of financial aid; 71% work part-time on campus. Approximately 112 scholarships are made available to freshmen annually. The average award to freshmen from all sources is $2200. Work-study programs are also available. Tuition may be paid in installments. The FFS or FAF is required. Financial aid applications should be filed by July 1.

Foreign Students: About 1% of the full-time students come from foreign countries. The university offers them an intensive English program, special counseling, and special organizations.

Admissions: Foreign students must achieve a minimum TOEFL score of 500 or a score of at least 85 on the University of Michigan Language Test. No college entrance exams are required.

Procedure: Application deadlines are August 1 (fall), December 1 (winter), March 1 (spring), and May 1 (summer). Foreign students must present proof of funds adequate to cover 4 years of study.

Admissions Contact: Stuart Tennant, Director of Admissions and Records.

HEIDELBERG COLLEGE C–2
Tiffin, Ohio 44883 (419) 448-2404

F/T: 384M, 307W	Faculty: n/av; IIB, av$
P/T: 35M, 51W	Ph.D.'s: 85%
Grad: none	S/F Ratio: 12 to 1
Year: sems, ss	Tuition: $4950
Appl: Aug. 1	R and B: $2000
643 applied	518 accepted	230 enrolled
SAT: 450V 470M	ACT: 22	COMPETITIVE

Heidelberg College, founded in 1850, is a private liberal arts institution affiliated with the United Church of Christ. The library contains 136,204 volumes, including the unique 5000-volume Besse Collection of published letters, which serves as valuable primary source material for scholarly research, as well as 6135 microfilm items, and subscriptions to 843 periodicals.

Environment: The 110-acre campus is located in a suburban area 50 miles southeast of Toledo. Residence halls accommodate 810 students.

Student Life: About 77% of the students come from Ohio. Chapel attendance is encouraged, but not required. About 5% of the students are minority-group members. Campus housing is coed and single-sex; there are visiting privileges in single-sex housing. Students may keep cars on campus.

OHIO 671

Organizations: There are 4 fraternities and 5 sororities to which 40% of the men and 40% of the women belong. The Campus Center Program Board sponsors social and cultural events; there are 70 organizations open to new members.

Sports: The college fields 7 intercollegiate teams for men and 5 for women. There are 3 intramural sports for men and 3 for women.

Graduates: There is a freshman dropout rate of 3%; 50% remain to graduate. Of those, 40% go on to graduate study: 8% enter medical school, 8% law school, and 3% dental school. Between 50% and 60% enter careers in business and industry.

Services: Free career counseling, job placement services, health care, and psychological counseling are available. Tutoring is available on a fee basis.

Programs of Study: The college confers the B.A., B.S., and B.Mus. degrees. Bachelor's degrees are offered in the following subjects: AREA STUDIES (American), BUSINESS (accounting, business administration, computer science, management), EDUCATION (elementary, health/physical, secondary, special), ENGLISH (English), FINE AND PERFORMING ARTS (art, music, music education, theater/dramatics), HEALTH SCIENCES (environmental health, medical technology), LANGUAGES (German, Spanish), MATH AND SCIENCES (biology, chemistry, mathematics, physics), PHILOSOPHY (humanities, philosophy, religion), PREPROFESSIONAL (agriculture, dentistry, engineering, forestry, law, medicine, ministry, pharmacy, veterinary), SOCIAL SCIENCES (economics, government/political science, history, psychology). About 18% of the degrees are conferred in math/sciences and 19% in fine and performing arts.

Required: All students must take 11 semester hours of sciences and mathematics, 9 hours of social sciences, and 20 of the humanities. Four semester hours of physical education are also required.

Special: The college offers cooperative degrees in many different subject areas. The Total Student Development Program attempts to integrate each student's social, cultural, and religious values with his or her academic program, activities, and career goals. The College Studies Program is offered primarily for freshmen. A pass/fail system of 1 course per term is optional for upperclassmen. Independent study and research semesters, junior year abroad, and the Washington Semester are offered to students.

Honors: There are 13 honor societies represented on campus; many departments also offer honors programs.

Admissions: About 81% of those who applied were accepted for the 1981–82 freshman class. The SAT scores of those who enrolled were as follows: Verbal—75% below 500, 23% between 500 and 599, 2% between 600 and 700, and 0% above 700; Math—75% below 500, 23% between 500 and 599, 2% between 600 and 700, and 0% above 700. The ACT scores of those who enrolled were as follows: 50% below 21, 30% between 21 and 23, 10% between 24 and 25, 5% between 26 and 28, and 5% above 28. Candidates should have completed a college preparatory program and have recommendations from their high school. Students should rank in the upper half of their graduating class and have a minimum high school GPA of 2.3.

Procedure: The SAT or ACT is required. An interview is recommended. Application deadlines are August 1 (fall), December 15 (spring), and May 15 (summer). There is a $15 application fee. The college uses a rolling admissions plan.

Special: Early decision, early admissions, and deferred admissions plans are available. AP and CLEP credit is accepted. The Non-Traditional Program gives older students the opportunity to work toward a degree without the necessity of on-campus residence.

Transfer: For fall 1981, 60 transfer students applied, 55 were accepted, and 12 enrolled. A minimum 2.3 GPA is required; grades of C or better transfer. At least 45 credits must be taken at the college to qualify for a degree; 120 credits are required to earn the bachelor's degree. Application deadlines are the same as those for freshmen.

Visiting: There is a regularly scheduled orientation including a campus tour and meetings with teachers and financial aid personnel. Special visits can be arranged through the admissions office while classes are in session.

Financial Aid: Funds amounting to $1.7 million are available for all types of aid. Grants-in-aid, SEOG, BEOG, EOG, NDSL, and CWS assistance, and Instructional Grants for Ohio residents, as well as scholarships, are awarded on the basis of financial need. Scholarship awards range between $500 and full tuition. Music scholarships, awarded on the basis of an audition, may be used to pursue a course of study in music. Some Trustees Scholarships are awarded without proof of need. The United Church of Christ also awards $800 tuition grants for members. Part-time employment is available; about 75% of the students work part-time on campus. About 75% of all students

672 OHIO

receive some form of financial assistance. The college is a member of CSS; the FAF is required. The deadline for application is June 1.

Foreign Students: About 1% of the full-time students come from foreign countries. The college offers these students an intensive English course, an intensive English program, and special counseling.

Admissions: Foreign students must achieve a minimum TOEFL score of 550; no college entrance exams are required.

Procedure: Application deadlines are August 1 (fall), December 15 (spring), and May 15 (summer). Foreign students must complete the college's health form and present proof of funds adequate to cover 4 years of study.

Admissions Contact: Steven W. Pochard, Dean of Admissions.

HIRAM COLLEGE E-1
Hiram, Ohio 44234 (216) 569-5169

F/T: 600M, 550W	Faculty: 80; IIB, +$
P/T: none	Ph.D.'s: 75%
Grad: none	S/F Ratio: 12 to 1
Year: 3-1-3-3, ss	Tuition: $5447
Appl: Aug. 1	R and B: $1730
705 applied	615 accepted	325 enrolled
ACT: 22		COMPETITIVE

Hiram College, founded in 1850, is a private, nonsectarian liberal arts college related to the Christian Church (Disciples of Christ). Historically the college has been known for its high academic standards and its tradition of innovation in education. The library contains 150,000 volumes and 16,000 microfilm items, and subscribes to 460 periodicals.

Environment: The 145-acre campus is located in a small village in the beautiful, rolling country of northeastern Ohio, within 35 miles of Cleveland, Akron, and Youngstown. There are 25 buildings including a social science-humanities building, a campus union, an art center, and a classroom-observation building at the 100-acre Biological Station. There are 11 dormitories and facilities for commuting students.

Student Life: Sixty-six percent of the students are from Ohio; 70% come from public schools. Ninety percent live on campus. Only 5% of the students are members of the affiliated church. About 59% of the students are Catholic, 35% are Protestant, and 4% are Jewish. About 9% are minority-group members. Campus housing is coed and single-sex; there are visiting privileges in single-sex dorms. Students may keep cars on campus.

Organizations: There are 3 local sororities and 3 local fraternities, to which 20% of the men and 20% of the women belong. There are also social, special-interest, and service clubs.

Sports: The college fields 12 intercollegiate teams for men and 10 for women. There are 5 intramural sports for men and 4 for women.

Graduates: The freshman dropout rate is 10%; 80% remain to graduate. Sixty percent of those who remain pursue graduate study. Thirty percent enter careers in business and industry.

Services: Students receive the following services free of charge: placement, career counseling, health care, and psychological counseling. Tutoring is also offered.

Programs of Study: All programs lead to the B.A. degree. Bachelor's degrees are offered in the following subjects: BUSINESS (computer science, management), EDUCATION (elementary, health/physical, secondary, special), ENGLISH (communications, English), FINE AND PERFORMING ARTS (art, art history, comparative arts, music, music education, studio art, theater/dramatics), HEALTH SCIENCES (medical technology), LANGUAGES (French, German, Spanish), MATH AND SCIENCES (biology, chemistry, mathematics, physics), PHILOSOPHY (classics, philosophy, religion), PREPROFESSIONAL (dentistry, engineering, forestry, law, medicine, ministry, veterinary), SOCIAL SCIENCES (economics, government/political science, history, psychology, social sciences, sociology).

Required: Freshmen are required to take the Freshman Institute and a freshman colloquium. Upperclassmen must take English composition, 2 selections from each of the divisions of fine arts, humanities, social sciences, and physical sciences, and an interdisciplinary experience.

Special: Student-designed majors are permitted. Special programs include enriched courses, independent study, small-group seminar activities, study abroad in Austria, England, France, Germany, Italy, Mexico, Spain, and Latin America, a combined degree program in engineering, the Washington and Drew Semesters, undergraduate research at the Biological Station, pass/fail options, and an Afro-American cultural center.

Honors: There are 7 honor societies on campus, including Phi Beta Kappa. All departments offer honors programs for outstanding students. There is also a general honors program.

Admissions: Eighty-seven percent of those who applied were accepted for the 1981–82 freshman class. The SAT scores of those who enrolled were as follows: Verbal—59% below 500, 30% between 500 and 599, 10% between 600 and 700, and 1% above 700; Math—48% below 500, 37% between 500 and 599, 14% between 600 and 700, and 1% above 700. The ACT scores were: 49% below 21, 20% between 21 and 23, 13% between 24 and 25, 13% between 26 and 28, and 5% above 28. Candidates should be graduates of an accredited high school, rank in the upper half of their graduating class, and have completed 16 Carnegie high school units. The college indicates that in addition to these qualifications it considers the following factors in order of importance: advanced placement or honors courses, recommendations by school officials, evidence of special talents, and leadership ability.

Procedure: Either the SAT or ACT is required. Freshmen are admitted to the fall term only; the application deadline is 30 days before registration, or August 1. A rolling admissions policy is observed. Candidates are notified 4 to 6 weeks after the application is complete. An interview is strongly recommended. There is a $15 application fee.

Special: Early admissions and deferred admissions plans are available. CLEP and AP credit is accepted.

Transfer: For fall 1981, 78 transfer students applied, 58 were accepted, and 32 enrolled. Transfer students are accepted for the freshman (2nd semester), sophomore, and junior years and must complete 90 hours of classwork at the college to receive a degree; 186 quarter hours are required for a bachelor's degree. They should be in good standing at the previous institution attended. A GPA of 2.25 is required. Grades of C or above transfer. Application deadlines are August 1 (fall), December 15 (winter), and March 15 (spring).

Visiting: Visits are scheduled on an individual basis on weekdays and Saturday mornings. Guided tours and interviews can be scheduled through the office of admissions. Visitors may sit in on classes and remain on campus overnight.

Financial Aid: About 70% of all students receive financial aid; 85% work part-time on campus. The college makes available 217 freshman grants each year, in amounts totaling $250,000. Loans can be secured from the federal government (total amount available $350,000), local banks, the college, and other sources. The college participates in NDSL, CWS, and EOG. Aid from all sources combined averages $3200. The college is a member of CSS. The FAF is required and should be submitted by August 1. The college has a rolling decision policy on aid applications.

Foreign Students: About 1% of the full-time students come from foreign countries.

Admissions: Foreign students must achieve a minimum TOEFL score of 450; no college entrance exams are required.

Procedure: Application deadlines are August 1 (fall), December 15 (winter), and March 15 (spring). Foreign students must present proof of funds adequate to cover 4 years of study.

Admissions Contact: John P. Pirozzi, Dean of Admissions.

JOHN CARROLL UNIVERSITY D-1
University Heights, Ohio 44118 (216) 491-4294

F/T: 1453M, 1669W	Faculty: 179; IIA, +$
P/T: 540M, 832W	Ph.D.'s: 83%
Grad: 412M, 337W	S/F Ratio: 15 to 1
Year: sems, ss	Tuition: $3700
Appl: open	R and B: $2000
1485 applied	1217 accepted	677 enrolled
SAT: 501V 536M	ACT: 23	COMPETITIVE+

Established in 1886, John Carroll University is a Roman Catholic (Jesuit) institution that consists of 3 schools: the School of Business, the College of Arts and Sciences, and the Graduate School. The library contains 340,000 volumes and 80,000 microfilm items, and subscribes to 1700 periodicals.

Environment: The 66-acre campus, located 12 miles east of Cleveland in suburban University Heights, consists of 22 Gothic-style buildings. Six dormitories accommodate 1500 students. The university also sponsors off-campus apartments.

Student Life: Sixty percent of students are from Ohio; about 70% of each freshman class are from parochial schools. About 45% commute; 55% live either on or off campus, in university-approved housing. About 70% of the students are Catholic, 20% are Protestant, and 10% are Jewish. Attendance at religious services is not required. About 4%

of the students are minority-group members. Campus housing is coed and single-sex; there are visiting privileges in single-sex dorms. Students may keep cars on campus.

Organizations: Forty percent of male students belong to 20 local fraternities; 30% of women students belong to 10 local sororities.

Sports: The university fields 14 intercollegiate teams for men and 7 for women. There are 13 intramural sports for men and 12 for women.

Handicapped: Eighty percent of the campus is accessible to physically handicapped students. Facilities include wheelchair ramps, special parking, elevators, and lowered telephones. Three special counselors assist the handicapped.

Graduates: There is a freshman dropout rate of about 3%; 65% remain to graduate. Sixty-three percent of those who remain pursue graduate studies: 4% enter medical school, 3% dental school, and 8% law school. Forty percent pursue careers in business and industry.

Services: Among the services provided free for students are placement and career counseling, psychological counseling, and tutoring. Health care and remedial instruction are available on a fee basis.

Programs of Study: The university confers the B.A. and B.S. degrees. Master's programs are also offered. Bachelor's degrees are offered in the following subjects: BUSINESS (accounting, business administration, computer science, finance, management, marketing), EDUCATION (elementary, health/physical, secondary, special), ENGLISH (English, journalism, speech), FINE AND PERFORMING ARTS (art history), LANGUAGES (French, German, Greek/Latin, Italian, Spanish), MATH AND SCIENCES (biology, chemistry, computer science, mathematics, physics), PHILOSOPHY (classics, humanities, philosophy, religion), PREPROFESSIONAL (architecture, dentistry, engineering, law, medicine, ministry, pharmacy, social work, veterinary), SOCIAL SCIENCES (economics, government/political science, history, international relations, psychology, sociology). Forty percent of degrees are conferred in business, 20% in health sciences, 10% in English, 10% in math and sciences, and 17% in preprofessional areas.

Required: All students are required to take religious studies for at least 2 semesters.

Special: Available to students is an interdepartmental major in humanities that leads to a B.A. or B.A. (Classics) degree; emphasis is on specialized and individually programmed study. Student-designed majors are also allowed. The university offers summer programs in Mexico and French-speaking Canada, and study abroad. Joint degree programs are offered in science and nursing with the Francis Payne Bolton School of Nursing. The university also offers a 2-3 engineering program with the University of Detroit, 3-2 engineering programs with Case Western Reserve University and Washington University, and a 2-2 engineering program with Case Western Reserve University.

Honors: The university has a nondepartmental honors program open to students by invitation only.

Admissions: Eighty-two percent of those who applied were accepted for the 1981–82 freshman class. The SAT scores of those who enrolled were as follows: Verbal—53% below 500, 35% between 500 and 599, 9% between 600 and 700, and 3% above 700; Math—26% below 500, 50% between 500 and 599, 20% between 600 and 700, and 4% above 700. The ACT scores were as follows: 14% below 21, 54% between 21 and 23, 14% between 24 and 25, 14% between 26 and 28, and 4% above 28. Applicants must be graduates of an accredited high school, rank in the upper half of their class, and have a GPA of at least 2.0. They must present 15 Carnegie units of work. The results of the SAT or ACT are very important in the admissions process. The university also lists the following factors in order of importance: impressions made during an interview, leadership record, extracurricular activities record, and advanced placement or honors courses. An interview is recommended.

Procedure: Applicants must take either the SAT or the ACT by July of the senior year. Applications should be filed after completion of the 7th semester; the deadline is open. Freshmen are also admitted for the spring term; the application deadline is open. The college has a rolling admissions plan. There is a $20 application fee.

Special: The college has an early admissions plan with an August 1 application deadline and a deferred admissions plan. AP credit is accepted.

Transfer: For fall 1981, 192 transfer students applied, 157 were accepted, and 105 enrolled. Good academic standing from the previous institution is required. A 2.0 GPA is required; a 2.5 GPA is recommended. Grades of C and above transfer. The last 32 hours must be taken in residence; 128 credits are required for the bachelor's degree. Application deadlines are open.

Visiting: Freshman orientation and registration are held in June or July. Informal campus visits can be arranged through the admissions office Monday through Friday. Visitors can stay at the school and sit in on classes.

Financial Aid: About 45% of all students receive financial aid; 15% work part-time on campus. Scholarships are available to 200 freshmen. The following loans are available: National Direct Student Loan (maximum $3000) and Ohio Guaranteed Student Loan (maximum $2500). Eighty percent of those students who applied for financial aid in fall 1981 received an award, composed of scholarships, loans, grants, and employment. The average award was $2900. The university is a member of the CSS and requires the FAF. The aid application deadline is March 1; notification is on a rolling basis.

Foreign Students: Eighteen foreign students are currently enrolled at the university, which offers them an intensive English course and special counseling.

Admissions: Foreign students must achieve a minimum TOEFL score of 500; they must also take the SAT or ACT.

Procedure: The application deadline is August 15 for fall entry. Foreign students must present proof of health as well as proof of funds adequate to cover 4 years of study.

Admissions Contact: John P. Sammon, Director of Admissions.

KENT STATE UNIVERSITY D–2
Kent, Ohio 44242 (216) 672-2444

F/T: 6313M, 6813W	Faculty: 668; I, –$
P/T: 1223M, 1421W	Ph.D.'s: n/av
Grad: 1674M, 2216W	S/F Ratio: 19 to 1
Year: sems, ss	Tuition: $1494 ($2694)
Appl: July 1	R and B: $1904
5745 applied	5634 accepted	3560 enrolled
ACT: 19	COMPETITIVE

Founded in 1910, Kent State University is a large, residential state-controlled university. There are 6 undergraduate colleges, a School of Physical Education, Recreation, and Dance, a School of Nursing, a School of Library Science, and a Graduate School. The library contains 1.5 million volumes and 500,000 microfilm items, and subscribes to 8000 periodicals.

Environment: The main campus encompasses 800 acres in a rural area 11 miles from Akron. The physical plant consists of 100 major buildings, including a library, 31 residence halls housing 4876 women and 3654 men, and various classroom facilities. The university also sponsors fraternity and sorority houses, and married student housing.

Student Life: About 83% of the students are from Ohio; 40% live on campus. About 40% of the freshmen are Catholic, 32% are Protestant, and 3% are Jewish. About 14% of the students are minority-group members. Campus housing is coed and single-sex; there are visiting privileges in single-sex dorms. Students may keep cars on campus.

Organizations: There are 13 national fraternities and 11 national sororities, to which 5% of the men and 4% of the women belong. Religious counselors and organizations are provided for students in the 3 major faiths. There are many student organizations and activities, including professional and governmental groups, a daily campus newspaper, theater, a debate team, and a radio station.

Sports: Kent State fields 12 intercollegiate teams for men and 10 for women. There are 23 intramural sports for men and 19 for women.

Handicapped: Almost 100% of the entire campus is accessible to physically handicapped students. Facilities include wheelchair ramps, special parking, elevators, specially equipped rest rooms, and lowered drinking fountains and telephones. Special class scheduling is also available. There is a staff of 2 for special counseling and assistance.

Graduates: The freshman dropout rate is 33%. About 40% of those who remain pursue graduate study.

Services: Students receive the following services free of charge: placement, career counseling, health care, remedial instruction, and psychological counseling. Tutoring is available on a fee basis.

Programs of Study: The university confers the B.A., B.Arch., B.B.A., B.F.A., B.Mus. and B.S. degrees. Master's and doctoral programs are also offered. Bachelor's degrees are offered in the following subjects: AREA STUDIES (American, Black/Afro-American, ethnic heritage, Latin American, Russian), BUSINESS (accounting, business administration, business education, computer science, economics, finance, human resource management, industrial management, management, marketing, real estate/insurance, transportation management), EDUCATION (community health, early childhood, elementary, health/physical, secondary, special, vocational), ENGLISH (advertising, English, journalism, literature, photojournalism, public relations, rhetoric and communication, speech), FINE AND PERFORMING ARTS (art, art education, art history, dance, fashion design, film/photography, interior design, music, music education, radio/TV, studio art, theater/dramatics), HEALTH SCIENCES (medical technology, nursing, recreational therapy, speech therapy), LANGUAGES (French, German, Greek/Latin, Russian, Spanish), MATH AND SCIENCES (biology, botany, chemistry, earth science, ecology/environmental science, geology, mathematics, physics, theoretical computer science, zoology), PHILOSOPHY (classics, general studies, philosophy), PREPROFESSIONAL (architecture, dentistry, forestry, home economics, law, medicine, social work, veterinary), SOCIAL SCIENCES (anthropology, economics, geography, government/political science, history, psychology, sociology). About 14% of degrees are conferred in business, 13% in education, 14% in preprofessional studies, and 8% in social sciences.

Special: It is possible to earn combined B.A.-B.S. degrees in many subjects. Student-designed majors are also permitted. A general studies degree is offered, which allows the student maximum freedom to design his or her own education and to develop his or her own areas of interest and concentration. Independent study is also available. Students may study abroad through formally organized programs with certain foreign institutions. Limited pass/fail options are available. A program in Afro-American studies has recently been introduced.

Honors: Over 25 national honor societies have chapters on campus. The Honors College works with all university programs.

Admissions: Ninety-eight percent of those who applied were accepted for the 1981–82 freshman class. The ACT scores of those who enrolled were as follows: 54% below 21, 23% between 21 and 23, 10% between 24 and 25, 9% between 26 and 28, and 4% above 28. Applicants from Ohio must have graduated from an accredited high school and completed 12 academic units. Out-of-state applicants must rank in the top half of their high school class, have completed 15 academic units, and be a graduate of an accredited high school.

Procedure: The ACT or SAT is required of all freshman applicants. The ACT or SAT should be taken in May of the junior year or August of the senior year. The application, a $25 fee, test scores, and scholastic transcripts should be submitted by July 1 (earlier for housing) (fall), December 15 (spring), and June 1 (summer). Notification is on a rolling basis. Students are admitted to all terms. An interview is recommended.

Special: There is an early admissions plan. CLEP and AP credit is accepted.

Transfer: For fall 1981, 1669 transfer students applied, 1601 were accepted, and 1024 enrolled. Transfers are considered for all classes. Students must have a 2.0 GPA. All students must complete at least 32 semester hours at the university to receive a degree; 128 semester hours are required to earn the bachelor's degree. Application deadlines are the same as those for freshman applicants.

Visiting: Orientation sessions are held for prospective students. College and Career Days are good opportunities for students to speak with faculty, take campus tours, and become familiar with the campus. Visitors may sit in on classes and remain on campus overnight. Informal guided tours can be arranged through the admissions office.

Financial Aid: About 55% of all students receive some form of financial aid; about 31% work part-time on campus. The university awards freshman scholarships. The average award to freshmen from all sources is $1875. Aid can also be obtained from federal and state governments. Application for aid is made to the Office of Student Financial Aids; the deadline is June 1. The FAF is required.

Foreign Students: About 4% of the full-time students come from foreign countries. The university offers these students special counseling and special organizations.

Admissions: Foreign students must achieve a minimum TOEFL score of 525; no college entrance exams are required.

Procedure: Application deadlines are July 1 (fall), December 15 (spring), and June 1 (summer). Foreign students must present proof of adequate funds. They must also carry health insurance, which is available through the university.

Admissions Contact: Bruce L. Riddle, Director of Admissions.

KENYON COLLEGE
Gambier, Ohio 43022   C-3
(614) 427-2244

F/T: 828M, 630W
P/T: 2M, 5W
Grad: none
Year: sems
Appl: Mar. 1
1702 applied
SAT: 571V 588M

Faculty: 110; IIB, ++$
Ph.D.'s: 94%
S/F Ratio: 13 to 1
Tuition: $6300
R and B: $2345
1061 accepted   415 enrolled
ACT: 27   HIGHLY COMPETITIVE+

Kenyon College is a private institution associated with the Protestant Episcopal Church. Formerly a liberal arts college for men, Kenyon was established in 1824 by Philander Chase, first Episcopal bishop in the Northwest Territory. The library contains 280,000 volumes and 1500 microfilm items, and subscribes to over 975 periodicals.

Environment: The 400-acre wooded campus is located in the rural village of Gambier (population 1000), 50 miles from Columbus. There are more than 45 buildings on campus, including a drama complex, a new sports-recreation complex, residence halls, and a dining-social commons.

Student Life: Thirty percent of the students come from Ohio and 68% from other states. Seventy-one percent of the entering freshmen come from public schools. Although the college is associated with the Episcopal Church, students of all faiths are enrolled, and counselors are available for Catholic, Protestant, and Jewish students. Attendance at religious services is voluntary. College housing is both single-sex and coed. There are visiting privileges in single-sex housing. Students may keep cars on campus.

Organizations: There are 3 local and 8 national fraternities, to which 36% of the men belong. There are no sororities on campus. Lectures, concerts, and other social and cultural opportunities enrich extracurricular activities. Students participate in student government, publications, and trustees' committees.

Sports: The college competes intercollegiately in 16 sports for men and 11 for women. There are 13 intramural sports for men and 12 for women.

Handicapped: The entire campus is accessible to wheelchair-bound students. Facilities include special parking and elevators. There are no students with visual or hearing impairments currently enrolled.

Graduates: The freshman dropout rate is 3%; 77% remain to graduate. Eighty percent of those who remain eventually pursue graduate study: 8% enter medical school, 1% dental school, and 12% law school. Fifty percent pursue careers in industry and business.

Services: Students receive the following services free of charge: placement and career counseling. Psychological counseling, health care, and tutoring are available on a fee basis.

Programs of Study: The college confers the B.A. degree. Bachelor's degrees are offered in the following subjects: ENGLISH (English, literature), FINE AND PERFORMING ARTS (art, art history, music, theater/dramatics), LANGUAGES (French, German, Greek/Latin, Spanish), MATH AND SCIENCES (biology, chemistry, mathematics, physics, zoology), PHILOSOPHY (classics, philosophy, religion), PREPROFESSIONAL (dentistry, engineering, law, medicine, pharmacy, veterinary), SOCIAL SCIENCES (anthropology, economics, government/political science, history, psychology, sociology). Twenty-eight percent of degrees are conferred in social sciences, 28% in math and sciences, 15% in fine and performing arts, and 16% in English.

Special: Students may spend a year abroad through Kenyon's program at the University of Exeter in Great Britain and through arrangements with the Great Lakes Colleges Association. A 5-year double-degree program may be arranged in engineering. Independent study, student-designed majors, and pass/fail options are offered.

Honors: The honor societies on campus include Phi Beta Kappa and Sigma Xi. There is an honors program in all departments, with seminars, tutorials, independent study, and outside examiners.

Admissions: Sixty-two percent of those who applied were accepted for the 1981–82 freshman class. Of those who enrolled, the SAT scores were as follows: Verbal—16% below 500, 59% between 500 and 599, 20% between 600 and 700, and 5% above 700; Math—10% below 500, 47% between 500 and 599, 34% between 600 and 700, and 9% above 700. On the ACT, the scores were as follows: 0% below 21, 1% between 21 and 23, 6% between 24 and 25, 48% between 26 and 28, and 45% above 28. Candidates must rank in the top half (preferably the top 25%) of their graduating class and have a B average. They must be graduates of accredited high schools and present 15 Carnegie units. The school indicates that in addition to these qualifications they consider the following factors: advanced placement or honors courses; recommendations by school officials, leadership record, extracurricular activities record, personality, and evidence of special talents.

Procedure: Either the SAT or ACT is required and should be taken in May of the junior year or November, December, or January of the senior year. The application deadline is March 1. The college participates in the CRDA program. An interview is recommended. The $20 application fee may be waived by written request.

Special: Early admissions, deferred admissions, and early decision plans are available.

Transfer: For fall 1981, 165 transfer applications were received, 37 were accepted, and 21 students enrolled. A GPA of at least 3.0 is required. D grades do not transfer. Students may not transfer for the senior year. There is a residency requirement of 2 years. Students must complete, at the college, 64 of the 128 semester hours needed for a bachelor's degree. May 1 is the fall semester deadline.

Visiting: Guided tours can be scheduled any time school is in session through the admissions office. Students may sit in on classes and remain on campus overnight.

Financial Aid: About 32% of all students receive some form of financial aid. Forty-eight percent work part-time on campus. Average aid to freshmen from all sources is $4700. About 135 scholarships are available to freshmen. Loans may be obtained from the federal and state governments, local banks, and the college itself. All aid offers are packages combining stipend, loan, and job. The college is a member of CSS. The FAF is required. The deadline for aid application is March 1 for regular admissions.

Foreign Students: Two percent of the full-time students come from foreign countries. The college offers these students special counseling and special organizations.

Admissions: Foreign students must score at least 500 on the TOEFL. They must also take the SAT or the ACT.

Procedure: The application deadline is March 1 (fall). Foreign students must complete the college's health form. They must also submit proof of funds adequate to cover 1 year of study. They must carry health insurance, which is available through the college for a fee.

Admissions Contact: John D. Kushan, Director of Admissions.

LAKE ERIE COLLEGE FOR WOMEN E-1
Painesville, Ohio 44077   (216) 352-3361

F/T: 350W	Faculty: 56; IIA, —$
P/T: 50W	Ph.D.'s: n/av
Grad: 85M, 115W	S/F Ratio: 13 to 1
Year: sems, ss	Tuition, R and B: $7450
Appl: open	
192 applied 160 accepted 86 enrolled	
SAT: 490V 490M ACT: 21 COMPETITIVE	

Lake Erie College, founded in 1856, is a private women's college that stresses student participation in the educational process. In addition to its traditional academic programs, the college offers Plan A; this "alternate plan" allows students to devise their own curriculum and modes of learning. The library contains 85,000 volumes and 4000 microfilm items, and subscribes to 325 periodicals.

Environment: The 60-acre suburban campus is located near Lake Erie, 29 miles from Cleveland. Residence halls can accommodate the entire student body. Nearby is the 400-acre, college-owned Morely Farm, home of the George Magoffin Humphrey Equestrian Center.

Student Life: About 65% of the students are residents of Ohio. Eighty percent of the freshmen come from public schools. Approximately 75% of the students live on campus. College housing is single-sex. Students may keep cars on campus. Day-care services are available to all students, faculty, and staff.

Organizations: There are no sororities on campus. Special-interest groups include madrigal singers, choir, dance club, and many others.

Sports: The college competes in 9 sports on the intercollegiate level.

Handicapped: The college is in process of complying with government regulations for facilities for the handicapped.

Graduates: Five percent of the freshmen drop out during their first year; 58% remain to graduate. Of those who remain, 30% go on to graduate study.

Services: Free career and psychological counseling, placement, and health care are available. Tutoring and remedial instruction are available on a fee basis.

Programs of Study: The college confers the B.A., B.S., B.S.Ed., and B.F.A. degrees. A master's program is also offered. Bachelor's degrees are offered in the following subjects: AREA STUDIES (American, European), BUSINESS (accounting, business administration, finance, international business, management, marketing, personnel management, small business management, taxation), EDUCATION (elementary, secondary), ENGLISH (English, literature), FINE AND PERFORMING ARTS (art, dance, music, studio art, theater/dramatics), LANGUAGES (French, German, Italian, Spanish), MATH AND SCIENCES (biology, chemistry, mathematics), PHILOSOPHY (humanities, philosophy, religion), PREPROFESSIONAL (physician assistant), SOCIAL SCIENCES (economics, government/political science, history, international relations, psychology, social sciences, sociology). The college also offers Equestrian Studies as one of its majors.

Special: Students can take the academic winter-term-abroad program, whereby they study at a European university and stay with a local family. A 3-1 physician's assistant program is available. Field studies, internships, and independent study are also offered. Students participating in Plan A may choose their own modes of learning, which might include person-to-person dialogs, internships, and outside readings.

Honors: The Alpha Lambda Delta and Mortar Board honor societies are represented on campus.

Admissions: About 83% of those who applied were accepted for the 1981–82 freshman class. The SAT scores of those who enrolled were as follows: Verbal—75% below 500, 25% between 500 and 599, 0% between 600 and 700, and 0% above 700; Math—75% below 500, 25% between 500 and 599, 0% between 600 and 700, and 0% above 700. On the ACT, 0% scored below 21, 75% between 21 and 23, 20% between 24 and 25, 5% between 26 and 28, and 0% above 28. Candidates should have completed 16 Carnegie units and have good test scores. Extracurricular activities and advanced placement or honors courses are also taken into consideration.

Procedure: The SAT or ACT is required, and should be taken by January of the senior year. A language placement test is given at the beginning of the freshman year. A personal interview is requested. Application deadlines are open. There is a $25 fee.

Special: Early decision and early and deferred admissions plans are offered. AP and CLEP credit is accepted.

Transfer: For fall 1981, 15 students applied, 10 were accepted, and 8 enrolled. Students should have a 2.5 GPA. D grades do not transfer. Thirty semester hours must be completed in residence, of the 120 needed to receive a bachelor's degree. The application deadlines are open.

Visiting: There is no formal orientation for students, but special arrangements can be made through the admissions office. Tours and class observations can be arranged, preferably on Fridays during the year.

Financial Aid: Sixty-three percent of the students receive financial aid. Sixty percent work part-time on campus. Average aid awarded to freshmen from all sources is $3800. The college is a member of the CSS. Tuition may be paid in installments. The FAF is required. There is no deadline for financial aid applications.

Foreign Students: Two percent of the full-time students come from foreign countries. The college offers these students an intensive English course and special counseling.

Admissions: Foreign students must score at least 500 on the TOEFL. No college entrance examination is required.

Procedure: Application deadlines are open. Foreign students must submit a certificate of good health. Proof of funds adequate to cover 1 year of study is also required. There is a special application fee of $50.

Admissions Contact: Frances J. Cook, Director of Admissions.

MALONE COLLEGE D-2
Canton, Ohio 44709   (216) 489-0800

F/T: 375M, 395W	Faculty: n/av; IIB, av$
P/T: none	Ph.D.'s: 60%
Grad: none	S/F Ratio: n/av
Year: sems, ss	Tuition: $3934
Appl: July 1	R and B: $1875
271 enrolled	
SAT or ACT: required COMPETITIVE	

Founded in 1892, Malone College is a small liberal arts institution affiliated with the Evangelical Friends Church. Present library facilities contain 85,000 volumes, and subscribe to 533 periodicals.

Environment: The present campus dates from 1957; its 63 acres are located in an urban area 3 miles from downtown Canton. The 16 buildings are contemporary in style. Six dormitories provide living quarters for 241 women and 215 men.

Student Life: Ninety-one percent of the students are from Ohio; 58% live on campus. The majority of students (74%) are Protestant, but less than 20% are members of the affiliated church. Attendance at chapel is required 3 days a week. Smoking and drinking are not permitted. There is a midnight curfew for women and freshman men; on weekends the curfew is extended to 2 A.M.. Campus housing is single-sex; there are visiting privileges. Students may keep cars on campus.

Organizations: There are no fraternities or sororities. There are Protestant religious counselors and organizations on campus.

676 OHIO

Sports: The college fields 8 intercollegiate teams for men and 5 for women. There are 3 intramural sports for men and 2 for women.

Handicapped: About 25% of the campus is accessible to wheelchair-bound students; specially equipped rest rooms are available.

Graduates: The freshman dropout rate is 15%; 65% remain to graduate.

Services: The college offers placement services, career counseling, and health care to students free of charge. Tutoring and remedial instruction are available on a fee basis.

Programs of Study: Degrees conferred are the B.A. and B.S.Ed. Associate degrees are also awarded. Bachelor's degrees are offered in the following subjects: BUSINESS (accounting, business administration, business education, computer science), EDUCATION (elementary, health/physical, secondary), ENGLISH (communications, English), FINE AND PERFORMING ARTS (art, art education, communications arts, music, music education), HEALTH SCIENCES (allied health, medical technology), MATH AND SCIENCES (biology, chemistry, mathematics), PHILOSOPHY (religion), PREPROFESSIONAL (engineering, law, medicine), SOCIAL SCIENCES (history, psychology, social work, sociology). The most popular major is elementary education.

Required: All undergraduates are required to take general education courses, 6 terms of physical education, and Bible study. Four courses required of students pursuing the B.A. degree are Computers for the Liberal Arts, Critical and Creative Thinking, the Nature of the Natural Sciences, and God, the World, and Man.

Special: Students have an opportunity to take a summer European tour for credits in history and literature. There is a junior year abroad program. A work-study program is being initiated.

Honors: Honor societies with chapters on campus are Pi Kappa Delta and Sigma Zeta.

Admissions: Most of those who applied were accepted for the 1981–82 freshman class. Candidates should have a 2.0 GPA. Sixteen Carnegie units are required.

Procedure: The ACT or SAT is required. Students are admitted to any term. Application deadlines are July 1 (fall), December 1 (winter), and May 1 (summer). There is a $20 application fee.

Special: The college gives placement tests in mathematics. There is an early admissions plan; the deadline is August 15. AP and CLEP credit is accepted.

Transfer: Recently the college received 99 applications for transfer; 99 were accepted, and 60 students enrolled. A 2.0 GPA is required. D grades and above transfer. Thirty semester hours, of the 124 required for the bachelor's degree, must be taken in residence. Deadlines are the same as those for freshmen.

Visiting: The best time to visit the campus is during the middle of terms. Contact the admissions office to make arrangements for guides, to sit in on classes, or to stay at the college.

Financial Aid: About 85% of all students receive some form of financial aid. Freshmen who have graduated in the top 10% of their class receive a scholarship; the average scholarship is $300. The total amount of aid available to freshmen is $25,000. The college belongs to the CSS; the FAF is required. The deadline for financial aid applications is April 15.

Foreign Students: About 4% of the full-time students are from foreign countries. The college offers them an intensive English program, special counseling, and special organizations.

Admissions: Foreign students must achieve a minimum TOEFL score of 525; no college entrance exams are required.

Procedure: Application deadlines are July 1 (fall) and December 1 (winter). Foreign students must present proof of health as well as proof of adequate funds. They must also carry health insurance, which is available through the college.

Admissions Contact: Lee Sommers, Director of Admissions.

MARIETTA COLLEGE
Marietta, Ohio 45750   E-4
(614) 373-4643

F/T: 841M, 445W	Faculty: 89; IIB, ++$
P/T: 32M, 19W	Ph.D.'s: 60%
Grad: none	S/F Ratio: 13 to 1
Year: sems, ss	Tuition: $5250
Appl: Aug. 1	R and B: $1900
1758 applied 1235 accepted	381 enrolled
SAT: 479V 537M ACT: 24	COMPETITIVE+

Established in 1835, Marietta College is a private, nonsectarian liberal arts college. The library contains 235,000 volumes and 4069 microfilm items, and subscribes to 2408 periodicals.

Environment: The 60-acre campus is located in a small city 114 miles from Columbus. The main campus is situated in a rural residential district.

Student Life: Students come from all parts of the country, with 40% from Ohio. Eighty percent of entering freshmen come from public schools. Ninety-two percent of students live on campus in dormitories and fraternity and sorority houses that accommodate 1300. About 1% of the students are minority-group members. College housing is both single-sex and coed. There are visiting privileges in single-sex housing. Students may keep cars on campus.

Organizations: About 35% of the students belong to 7 national fraternities and 5 national sororities.

Sports: The college competes intercollegiately in 8 sports for men and 7 for women. There are 14 intramural sports for men and 12 for women.

Handicapped: Ninety percent of the campus is accessible to physically handicapped students. Wheelchair ramps are provided. There are no students with visual or hearing impairments currently enrolled. There are no special counselors for the handicapped.

Graduates: The freshman dropout rate is 12%; 60% remain to graduate. Twenty-five percent go on to graduate study; 2% enter medical school, and 2% law school. Forty percent pursue careers in business and industry.

Services: Students receive the following services free of charge: psychological counseling, placement, career counseling, tutoring, remedial instruction, and health care.

Programs of Study: The B.A., B.S., B.F.A., and B.S. in Petroleum Engineering degrees are conferred. Bachelor's degrees are offered in the following subjects: AREA STUDIES (American, urban), BUSINESS (accounting, advertising, business administration, computer science, finance, industrial engineering, management, marketing, small business management), EDUCATION (early childhood, elementary, health/physical, secondary), ENGLISH (English, journalism, literature, speech), FINE AND PERFORMING ARTS (art, art education, art history, music, music education, radio/TV, studio art, theater/dramatics), HEALTH SCIENCES (athletic training, medical technology, nursing), LANGUAGES (French, German, Spanish), MATH AND SCIENCES (biochemistry, biology, chemistry, geology, mathematics, natural sciences, physics, statistics), PHILOSOPHY (philosophy, religion), PREPROFESSIONAL (dentistry, engineering—petroleum, forestry, law, medicine, pharmacy, social work, veterinary), SOCIAL SCIENCES (economics, government/political science, history, psychology, social sciences, sociology).

Required: Two semesters of physical education are required. Students must also take a course in English composition and public speaking. Two courses in literature, 2 in fine arts, 4 in the social sciences, 3 in the natural sciences, and 1 non-Western course are required. Three of these courses must be designated communications courses.

Special: The college confers combined B.A.-B.S. degrees in numerous subjects. A general studies degree is also offered. Juniors and seniors may take 1 course per semester on a pass/fail basis. There are 3-2 combination degree programs in engineering, natural resources, wildlife conservation, and forestry, and a 3-8 program in nursing. Students may spend a semester in Washington. Study abroad is possible for juniors. Interdisciplinary majors tailored to special interests and career plans are also available.

Honors: An honors program begins at the junior level. There are 15 honor and professional societies open to qualified students.

Admissions: Seventy percent of those who applied were accepted for the 1981–82 freshman class. The SAT scores of those who enrolled were as follows: Verbal—64% below 500, 30% between 500 and 599, 6% between 600 and 700, and 0% above 700; Math—32% below 500, 47% between 500 and 599, 20% between 600 and 700, and 1% above 700. On the ACT, 15% scored below 21, 35% between 21 and 23, 34% between 24 and 25, 11% between 26 and 28, and 5% above 28. High school records must be accompanied by a qualifying recommendation from the high school authorities. Other considerations are the recommendations of the school, friends, and alumni of the college, SAT or ACT scores, extracurricular activities, the reputation and accreditation of the applicant's high school, advanced placement or honors courses, leadership record, impressions made during an interview, and evidence of special talent. Children of former students are given preference.

Procedure: The SAT or ACT is required. The SAT must be taken between June of the junior year and February of the senior year. An interview is recommended. Application deadlines are August 1 (fall) and December 1 (spring). There is a rolling admissions plan. There is a $15 application fee.

Special: There are early and deferred admissions plans. AP and CLEP credit is accepted.

Transfer: For fall 1981, 157 applications were received, 90 were accepted, and 47 students enrolled. Three semesters must be taken in residence. Forty-five semester hours must also be completed out of the 127 to 136 needed for a bachelor's degree. The application deadlines are the same as those for freshman applicants.

Visiting: Guided informal tours can be arranged any time through the admissions office. Visitors can sit in on classes and stay at the school.

Financial Aid: Sixty-six percent of all students receive financial aid. Seventy-five percent work part-time on campus. Average aid to freshmen from all sources is $4000. The college is a member of CSS. The FAF must be filed. Application should be made by April 15 (fall) and December 15 (spring).

Foreign Students: About 1% of the full-time students come from foreign countries. The college offers these students special counseling and special organizations.

Admissions: Foreign students must score at least 550 on the TOEFL, 80 on the University of Michigan Language Test, or 550 on the Verbal SAT.

Procedure: The application deadlines are July 15 (fall) and November 15 (spring). Foreign students must submit the college's health form completed by a physician. They must also present proof of funds adequate to cover 4 years of study. Health insurance is required and is available through the college for a fee.

Admissions Contact: Daniel Jones, Director of Admissions.

MIAMI UNIVERSITY A-4
Oxford, Ohio 45056 (513) 529-2531

F/T: 6667M, 7830W	Faculty: 788; I, —$
P/T: 942M, 1238W	Ph.D.'s: 60%
Grad: 748M, 792W	S/F Ratio: 21 to 1
Year: sems, ss	Tuition: $1840 ($3740)
Appl: Mar. 1	R and B: $1910
7803 applied	5843 accepted 3370 enrolled
SAT: 494V 561M	ACT: 24 VERY COMPETITIVE

Miami University, founded in 1809, is a nonsectarian, state-supported institution. A variety of programs are offered in the liberal arts and in professional-vocational fields at both the undergraduate and graduate level. In addition to its traditional academic programs, Miami University has an innovative division, the School of Interdisciplinary Studies (Western College Program), which offers individualized majors and a residential learning program. The library contains 1 million volumes and 1.2 million microfilm items, and subscribes to 5000 periodicals.

Environment: The wooded, rolling campus is located in a rural area on 1400 acres, 35 miles from Cincinnati. Residence halls accommodate 4870 women and 2688 men. There are also fraternity houses and married student housing. Facilities for English and mathematics are available, along with a speech and hearing clinic. The entire Western College campus has been named a national historic landmark.

Student Life: Eighty percent of the students are residents of Ohio. About 86% of the entering freshmen come from public schools. Fifty-one percent of the students live in residence halls on campus; 8% live in off-campus fraternity houses. All freshmen are required to live in university housing unless they commute from home. Thirty-five percent of the students are Catholic, 48% are Protestant, and 4% are Jewish. Three percent are minority-group members. Campus housing is both single-sex and coed; there are visiting privileges in single-sex dorms.

Organizations: There are 24 national fraternities to which 26% of the men belong; 29% of the women belong to the 22 national sororities. Religious facilities are provided for students of all major faiths. Students hold membership in the University Senate, and are represented on many other university advisory committees.

Sports: The university has 20 intercollegiate teams for men and 18 for women. Eighteen intramural sports are offered for men and 20 for women.

Handicapped: Twenty-five percent of the campus is accessible to wheelchair-bound students. Facilities include wheelchair ramps, elevators, special parking, and specially equipped rest rooms. Special library facilities and a special counselor are also available.

Graduates: The freshman dropout rate is between 5% and 8%; between 60% and 65% remain to graduate. Thirty percent of those who remain pursue graduate study: 1% enter medical school, 4% law school, and about 1% dental school. Sixty percent pursue careers in business and industry.

Services: Students receive the following services free of charge: placement, career counseling, remedial instruction, and psychological counseling. Health care and tutoring services are available on a fee basis.

Programs of Study: The university confers the B.A., B.S., B.S.Ed., B.S.Bus., B.F.A., B.Mus., B.S. in Applied Science, B.S. in Paper Science and Engineering, B.S.N., B.S.H.E. and Consumer Sciences, B.A. in International Studies, B.Phil., and B.Environmental Design degrees. Associate, master's and doctoral programs are also offered. Bachelor's degrees are offered in the following subjects: AREA STUDIES (American, Black/Afro-American, international, urban), BUSINESS (accounting, business administration, business education, finance, food management, management, marketing, office administration, personnel management, systems analysis), EDUCATION (elementary, health/physical, industrial, secondary, special), ENGLISH (communication and theater, English, speech), FINE AND PERFORMING ARTS (art, art education, music, music education, radio/TV, theater/dramatics), HEALTH SCIENCES (medical technology, nursing, speech therapy), LANGUAGES (French, German, Greek/Latin, linguistics, Russian, Spanish), MATH AND SCIENCES (aeronautics, botany, chemistry, geology, mathematics, microbiology, mineralogy, paper science and engineering, physics, zoology), PHILOSOPHY (classics, philosophy, religion), PREPROFESSIONAL (architecture, engineering), SOCIAL SCIENCES (anthropology, consumer science, economics, geography, government/political science, history, international relations, psychology, sociology). Twenty-seven percent of degrees are conferred in business, 23% in education, 16% in social sciences, and 11% in math and sciences.

Required: All students are required to take freshman English and courses in the social sciences, natural sciences, and humanities. Two years of a language are required in the College of Arts and Science.

Special: The School of Interdisciplinary Studies is located on the campus of the former Western College and offers an interdisciplinary core curriculum integrating a completely residential pattern into an academic environment. Individualized majors are designed to meet students' needs and talents in this program. Students enrolled in the residential college live in the dormitories on the Western campus, accessible to the facilities of the main university. Students from all 6 divisions may arrange to spend a year abroad at the university's European Center in Luxembourg. Other special programs include independent study, combined programs with Duke University, and an engineering program with Massachusetts Institute of Technology, Case Western Reserve University, and Columbia University. Programs in medical technology are offered with several Ohio hospitals.

Honors: Eight honor societies, including Phi Beta Kappa, have chapters on campus. Honors programs are available to qualified students.

Admissions: Seventy-five percent of those who applied were accepted for the 1981–82 freshman class. Of those who enrolled, the SAT scores were as follows: Verbal—50% below 500, 40% between 500 and 599, 5% between 600 and 700, and 4% above 700; Math—18% below 500, 32% between 500 and 599, 30% between 600 and 700, and 20% above 700. On the ACT, 10% scored below 21, 27% between 21 and 23, 35% between 24 and 25, 23% between 26 and 28, and 5% above 28. Freshmen, on the average, ranked in the top 17% of their high school class. The candidate should have completed 17 Carnegie high school units and be a high school graduate.

Procedure: Either the ACT or the SAT is required, and should be taken by February of the senior year. Applications must be received prior to March 1, along with a $15 application fee. An interview is not required.

Special: There are special admissions programs for minority-group members and handicapped students.

Transfer: A limited number of transfer students are accepted regularly for most programs. Transfer students must present a GPA of at least 2.0 on previous college work. D grades do not transfer. Thirty-two semester hours must be taken in residence of the 128 needed for the bachelor's degree. The deadlines for transfer applications are August 1 for the first semester, December 10 for the second semester, and April 15 for the summer session. Students who wish to live in university housing should apply well in advance of these deadlines.

Visiting: There are regularly scheduled orientations for prospective students. Informal campus tours can be arranged through the admissions office. Visitors may sit in on classes.

Financial Aid: Twenty-nine percent of all students receive some form of financial aid. The average award to freshmen from all sources is $1675. Aid is available from funds administered by the university and from federal government funds. The university is a member of CCS. The FAF is required; the aid application deadline is March 1 for scholarships and loans.

678 OHIO

Foreign Students: Fewer than 1% of the students are from foreign countries. Special counseling and special organizations are offered for these students.

Admissions: Foreign students are required to take the TOEFL. No college entrance exam must be taken.

Procedure: Application deadlines are March 1 (fall), December 10 (spring), and April 15 (summer). Foreign students must present proof of adequate funds to cover 1 year of study. Health insurance must be carried and is available through the college for a fee.

Admissions Contact: Charles R. Schuler, Director of Admissions.

MOUNT UNION COLLEGE E-2
Alliance, Ohio 44601 (216) 821-5320

F/T: 574M, 472W	Faculty: 72; IIB, av$
P/T: 12M, 19W	Ph.D.'s: 70%
Grad: none	S/F Ratio: 13 to 1
Year: terms, ss	Tuition: $5040
Appl: May 1	R and B: $1710
691 applied	606 accepted	322 enrolled
SAT: 450V 525M	ACT: 21	COMPETITIVE

Mount Union College, founded in 1846, is a liberal arts college affiliated with the Methodist Church. The library contains 170,000 volumes, and subscribes to 950 periodicals.

Environment: The 72-acre campus is located in a pleasant residential section of Alliance, approximately 45 miles south of Cleveland and 75 miles west of Pittsburgh. Facilities include a theater and art studio, music complex, campus center, computer center, and an indoor track and tennis facility. Eight dormitories, as well as fraternities, house over 900 students.

Student Life: Seventy percent of students are from Ohio. About 94% of the entering freshmen come from public schools. Ninety percent of the students live on campus. Eighty percent are Protestant; 15% are Catholic. Eight percent are minority-group members. College housing is single-sex; there are visiting privileges. Students may keep cars on campus. Attendance at weekly chapel services is recommended.

Organizations: Thirty percent of the men belong to the 4 fraternities; 45% of women belong to the 4 sororities. There are religious clubs, a student senate, musical groups, publications, debating, and drama groups.

Sports: There is an intercollegiate program with 12 sports for men and 8 for women. There are 8 intramural sports for both men and women.

Handicapped: The campus is completely accessible to wheelchair-bound students. Wheelchair ramps, parking, elevators, and special rest rooms are available. There are no students with visual or hearing impairments currently enrolled.

Graduates: The freshman dropout rate is 10%; 55% remain to graduate. Thirty percent of graduates pursue advanced study, 6% enter medical school, 2% dental school, and 4% law school. Forty-five percent pursue careers in business and industry.

Services: The college offers the following services free of charge: health care, career and psychological counseling, placement, and tutoring.

Programs of Study: The college confers the B.A., B.S., B.Mus., and B.Mus.Ed. degrees. Bachelor's degrees are offered in the following subjects: AREA STUDIES (American), BUSINESS (accounting, business administration, computer science), EDUCATION (elementary, secondary), ENGLISH (English, speech), FINE AND PERFORMING ARTS (art, music, music education, theater/dramatics), HEALTH SCIENCES (medical technology, nursing), LANGUAGES (French, German, Greek/Latin, Italian, Spanish), MATH AND SCIENCES (astronomy, biology, chemistry, geology, mathematics, physics), PHILOSOPHY (philosophy, religion), PREPROFESSIONAL (dentistry, engineering, law, medicine, ministry, social work, veterinary), SOCIAL SCIENCES (anthropology, economics, government/political science, history, psychology, sociology). Thirty-five percent of degrees are conferred in business, 25% in preprofessional studies, 10% in the fine and performing arts, and 10% in social sciences.

Required: One course in college writing and 1 course in speech must be taken by all students. Three credits of physical education are also required.

Special: Special programs include pass/fail options, study abroad, 3-2 engineering programs with the University of Pennsylvania and Washington University, and United Nations semesters. Also available are a 4-1 program with the University of Pennsylvania and a Cooperative Urban Studies Center. Non-Western Studies is a comprehensive interdisciplinary major emphasizing the study of Asia and Africa. Student-designed majors and combined B.A.-B.S. degrees are also offered.

Honors: Honor and professional societies open to qualified students include Alpha Mu Gamma, Alpha Lambda Delta, Alpha Psi Omega, the American Chemical Society, Blue Key, Mu Phi Epsilon, Phi Sigma, and Pi Gamma Mu. Honors programs are also available.

Admissions: About 88% of those who applied were accepted for the 1981-82 freshman class. Of those who enrolled the SAT scores were as follows: Verbal—35% below 500, 45% between 500 and 599, 12% between 600 and 700, and 8% above 700; Math—35% below 500, 48% between 500 and 599, 10% between 600 and 700, and 7% above 700. On the ACT, 35% scored below 21, 40% between 21 and 23, 10% between 24 and 25, 10% between 26 and 28, and 5% above 28. Applicants should have completed 15 units of high school work, have an average of C or better, and rank in the upper half of their class. In addition, the college considers the following factors in order of importance: advanced placement or honors courses, leadership record, impressions made during a personal interview, and recommendations.

Procedure: Either the SAT or ACT is required and should be taken by December of the senior year. The application deadline for regular admissions is preferably May 1. Notification is on a rolling basis. The CRDA is observed. An interview is recommended unless distance is prohibitive. There is a $15 application fee.

Special: Early admissions and deferred admissions plans are available. There is no deadline for early admission. AP and CLEP credit is accepted.

Transfer: For fall 1981, 47 applications were received, 38 were accepted, and 21 transfer students enrolled. A GPA of at least 2.0 is required. D grades transfer. Fifteen courses must be taken in residence, out of the 36 needed for a bachelor's degree. Application deadlines are June 1 (fall), December 1 (winter), March 1 (spring), and May 1 (summer).

Visiting: Interviews and tours are available weekdays and Saturdays. Contact the admissions office to make arrangements for formal and informal visits or stays at the college.

Financial Aid: Seventy-five percent of the students receive financial aid. Sixty percent work part-time on campus. The average aid awarded to freshmen from all sources is $2000. The college is a member of CSS. The FAF should be submitted. The application deadlines are June 1 (fall), December 1 (winter), March 1 (spring), and May 1 (summer).

Foreign Students: Two percent of the full-time students come from foreign countries. The college offers these students special counseling and special organizations.

Admissions: Foreign students must score at least 500 on the TOEFL. No college entrance examination is required.

Procedure: The application deadlines are June 1 (fall), December 1 (winter), March 1 (spring), and May 1 (summer). Foreign students must submit proof of health. They must also provide proof of funds adequate to cover 4 years of study.

Admissions Contact: W. Edwin Seaver III, Director of Admissions.

MOUNT VERNON NAZARENE COLLEGE C-3
Mount Vernon, Ohio 43050 (614) 397-1244

F/T: 410M, 446W	Faculty: 64; IIB, −$
P/T: 69M, 52W	Ph.D.'s: 22%
Grad: none	S/F Ratio: 18 to 1
Year: 4-1-4, ss	Tuition: $2644
Appl: Aug. 15	R and B: $1634
431 applied	398 accepted	313 enrolled
ACT: 18		LESS COMPETITIVE

Mount Vernon Nazarene College, established in 1966, is a liberal arts institution affiliated with the Church of the Nazarene. The library contains 68,000 volumes and 5530 microtexts, and subscribes to 407 periodicals.

Environment: The 208-acre campus is located in a suburban area 40 miles from Columbus. The 20 campus buildings include dormitories and on-campus apartments that accommodate more than 700 men and women.

Student Life: About three-fourths of the students come from Ohio. Ninety percent are graduates of public schools. About 80% live on campus. Dormitories are single-sex. Most students are members of the Church of the Nazarene, but the college also welcomes those who share similar religious philosophies. Attendance at chapel services three times a week is expected. Drinking and smoking are prohibited on campus, and dancing and movie-going are discouraged.

Organizations: The student body is divided into 4 societies for social, service, and intramural activities. Cultural opportunities on campus include guest lecturers, music groups, and a drama club. Other campus organizations include student government and several religious groups, such as the Living Witnesses.

Sports: The college sponsors intercollegiate teams in 4 sports for men and 3 for women. At least 6 intramural sports are available.

Graduates: About 20% of the freshmen drop out, and 40% remain to graduate.

Programs of Study: The college grants the B.A. degree. Associate degrees also are offered. Bachelor's degrees are offered in the following subjects: BUSINESS (accounting, computer science, management, office administration), EDUCATION (Christian, elementary, health/physical, secondary), ENGLISH (English, speech), FINE AND PERFORMING ARTS (art, church music, music, music education), LANGUAGES (Spanish), MATH AND SCIENCES (biology, chemistry, mathematics), PHILOSOPHY (religion), PREPROFESSIONAL (church/Christian school administration, home economics, ministry), SOCIAL SCIENCES (history, psychology, sociology).

Required: Students must complete 42–44 hours of core courses and pass the GRE advanced test or UP field test to graduate.

Special: Students may arrange to study abroad. Degrees may be earned in fewer than 4 years. Preprofessional programs requiring transfer to another school include agriculture, engineering, medical technology, and nursing. Other preprofessional programs include law, medicine, and dentistry.

Admissions: About 92% of those who applied were accepted for the 1981–82 freshman class. The ACT scores of those who enrolled were as follows: 60% below 21, 12% between 21 and 23, 10% between 24 and 25, 12% between 26 and 28, and 6% above 28. Applicants should be graduates of an accredited high school, have completed 15 units of study, and rank in the top two-thirds of their class. Personality and character references also are considered.

Procedure: The ACT is required and should be taken in December of the senior year. The application deadline for fall is August 15. There is a $15 application fee. Admissions decisions are made on a rolling basis.

Special: Early and deferred admissions plans are available.

Transfer: For a recent year, the college received 112 applications, accepted 90, and enrolled 80 students. Applicants must submit transcripts of previous college work. D grades do not transfer. Students must earn at least 30 credits in residence of the 124 required for a bachelor's degree.

Financial Aid: Eighty percent of the students receive aid. Scholarships, grants, loans, and part-time jobs are available. Applicants must submit the FFS and the aid application by May 1.

Foreign Students: Four students from foreign countries were enrolled in 1981–82.

Admissions: Applicants must score at least 500 on the TOEFL. No other exams are required.

Procedure: The application deadline is June 1 for fall entry. Students must present proof of good health and evidence of adequate funds for 1 year. Health insurance is required, and may be obtained through the college for a fee.

Admissions Contact: Carolyn B. Learned, Director of Admissions.

MUSKINGUM COLLEGE D–3
New Concord, Ohio 43762 (614) 826-8137

F/T: 530M, 490W	Faculty:	72; IIB, av$
P/T: 20M, 40W	Ph.D.'s:	67%
Grad: none	S/F Ratio:	14 to 1
Year: sems, ss	Tuition:	$5010
Appl: Aug. 1	R and B:	$1880
745 applied	637 accepted	364 enrolled
ACT: 21		LESS COMPETITIVE

Muskingum College, a private liberal arts college founded in 1837, is affiliated with the United Presbyterian Church. The library contains 173,000 volumes, and subscribes to 850 periodicals.

Environment: Located on 215 acres in a small college town in a rural area within 15 miles of Zanesville, Ohio, and 70 miles from Columbus, the campus is made up of a series of hills and valleys with a lake between the educational quadrangle and the dormitories. Thirty-five acres and 7 buildings are part of the *National Registry of Historic Districts*. The college also owns a 57-acre environmental station with a mobile biology lab for ecology studies.

Student Life: About 70% of the students are Ohio residents, while about 80% of the entering freshmen come from public schools. All but 5% are campus residents living either in dormitories or in approved home or club houses. Twenty-five percent of the students are Catholic and 63% are Protestant. Four percent are minority-group members. College housing is single-sex; there are visiting privileges. Students may keep cars on campus.

Organizations: There are 4 social clubs for women, 3 for men, and 2 fraternities, to which 60% of the men and women belong. Other student activities include Student Forum, Community Council, Association of Women Students, publications, musical groups, a radio station, Forensic Club, Muskingum Players, and a television station.

Sports: The college competes intercollegiately in 10 sports for men and 9 for women. There are 12 intramural sports for men and 11 for women.

Handicapped: There are no special facilities for the physically handicapped.

Graduates: An average of 15% of the freshmen drop out each year; about 62% remain to graduate. An estimated 50% of the graduates become candidates for graduate or professional degrees; 4% enter medical school, 2% dental school, and 4% law school. Twenty percent enter elementary or secondary teaching. Sixty percent pursue careers in business and industry.

Services: Students receive free placement assistance, career counseling, tutoring, remedial instruction, psychological counseling, and health care.

Programs of Study: The college confers the B.A. and B.S. degrees. Bachelor's degrees are offered in the following subjects: AREA STUDIES (American, interdisciplinary), BUSINESS (accounting, business administration, computer science), EDUCATION (art, early childhood, elementary, health/physical, music, secondary, special), ENGLISH (English, speech), FINE AND PERFORMING ARTS (art, art education, music, music education, radio/TV, theater/dramatics), HEALTH SCIENCES (medical technology, nursing, physical therapy), LANGUAGES (French, German, Russian, Spanish), MATH AND SCIENCES (biology, chemistry, earth science, geology, mathematics), PHILOSOPHY (humanities, philosophy, religion), PREPROFESSIONAL (dentistry, engineering, law, medicine, ministry, social work, veterinary), SOCIAL SCIENCES (economics, government/political science, history, international relations, psychology, social sciences, sociology). Of the degrees conferred, 25% are in math and sciences, 25% in social sciences, and 21% in business.

Required: Students must complete a core curriculum of 1 semester each of philosophy of science, modern Christian thought, and composition, as well as 2 semesters of civilization courses. They must also fulfill a distribution requirement of 1 semester each of social science, alternative communications, and international perspective. Two semesters each of science and humanities, 1 to 3 hours of additional writing, and 3 hours of physical education are also required.

Special: The college offers combination degree programs: a 3-3 nursing program with Case Western Reserve and a 3-1 medical technology arrangement with a Cleveland-area hospital. Other programs include a Washington Semester, a U.N. Semester, the Merrill Palmer Institute Semester, and the Princeton Critical Languages Program.

Honors: All departments offer honors work in cooperation with the college's honors council. In addition, 17 honor societies have chapters on campus.

Admissions: About 86% of those who applied were accepted for the 1981–82 freshman class. The SAT scores of those who enrolled were: Verbal—70% below 500, 24% between 500 and 599, 4% between 600 and 700, and 2% above 700; Math—60% below 500, 27% between 500 and 599, 12% between 600 and 700, and 2% above 700. On the ACT, 55% scored below 21, 20% between 21 and 23, 13% between 24 and 25, 6% between 26 and 28, and 6% above 28. Candidates should rank in the top half of their class and present 15 completed Carnegie units. Students who meet the basic requirements are then evaluated on the basis of recommendations by school officials, extracurricular activities, advanced placement or honors courses, personality, impressions made during an interview, and special talents.

Procedure: The SAT or ACT is required and should be taken by January of the senior year. It is suggested that applications be filed by April 15 of the senior year. Deadlines are August 1 (fall), December 15 (spring), and May 15 (summer). The college follows a rolling admissions policy. An interview is recommended. There is a $15 application fee.

Special: Early and deferred admissions plans are available. AP and CLEP credit is accepted.

680 OHIO

Transfer: For fall 1981, 60 students applied, 50 were accepted, and 31 enrolled. A GPA of 2.0 and good academic standing are required. D grades do not transfer. Twenty-four semester hours must be taken in residence, out of the 124 needed for a bachelor's degree. Application deadlines are August 1 (fall) and December 15 (spring).

Visiting: Orientation programs for prospective students are scheduled on 8 dates in June. Visitors may sit in on classes and stay at the school.

Financial Aid: Sixty-five percent of all students receive financial aid. Fifty percent work part-time on campus. Average aid to freshmen from all sources is $3900. The college is a member of the CSS. Tuition may be paid in installments. Students must file the FAF. Application deadlines are May 15 (fall) and December 1 (winter).

Foreign Students: Two percent of the full-time students come from foreign countries. The college offers these students an intensive English course, special counseling, and special organizations.

Admissions: Foreign students must score at least 500 on the TOEFL. No college entrance examination is required.

Procedure: The application deadlines are July 1 (fall) and November 1 (winter). Foreign students must complete the college's health form. They must also submit proof of funds for the calendar year.

Admissions Contact: Jay R. Leiendecker, Director of Admissions.

NOTRE DAME COLLEGE OF OHIO   D-1
Cleveland, Ohio 44121   (216) 382-9806

F/T: 420W		Faculty:	36; IIB, – – $
P/T: 330W		Ph.D.'s:	40%
Grad: none		S/F Ratio:	11 to 1
Year: 4-1-4, ss		Tuition:	$2824
Appl: Aug. 15		R and B:	$1800
136 applied	114 accepted		78 enrolled
SAT: 420V 420M	ACT: 19	LESS COMPETITIVE	

Notre Dame College of Ohio is a small Roman Catholic college for women, founded in 1922 by the Sisters of Notre Dame. The library contains 82,000 volumes, and subscribes to 532 periodicals.

Environment: The 50-acre, self-contained campus is located in a suburban area 14 miles from downtown Cleveland. Facilities include the Liberal Arts building, the Connelly Student Center, and residence halls.

Student Life: Eighty-five percent of the students are Ohio residents. Forty-four percent come from parochial schools. Fifty percent of the women live on campus in the 2- and 3-story dorms. Eighty-seven percent of the students are Catholic, 7% Protestant, and 5% Jewish. Fourteen percent are minority-group members. College housing is single-sex; there are no visiting privileges. Students may keep cars on campus. Day-care services are available to all students.

Organizations: There are college publications, modern dance, choir, theater, departmental special-interest clubs, a lecture series, and a religious group.

Sports: The college fields 2 intercollegiate teams.

Handicapped: Fifty percent of the campus is accessible to physically handicapped students. Wheelchair ramps, special parking, elevators, specially equipped rest rooms, and lowered drinking fountains and telephones are available.

Graduates: Twenty percent drop out by the end of the freshman year, 60% graduate, and 27% of the graduates seek higher degrees in graduate or professional schools.

Services: The following services are available free to all students: placement, career counseling, health care, psychological counseling, and tutoring.

Programs of Study: The college confers the B.A. and B.S. degrees. Associate degrees are also offered. Bachelor's degrees are offered in the following subjects: BUSINESS (accounting, management), EDUCATION (elementary, health/physical, secondary, special), ENGLISH (English), FINE AND PERFORMING ARTS (art, art education, communication arts/theater), HEALTH SCIENCES (cytotechnology, dietetics, histotechnology, medical technology, nuclear medicine technology), LANGUAGES (French, German, Spanish), MATH AND SCIENCES (biology, chemistry, mathematics), PHILOSOPHY (catechetics), PRE-PROFESSIONAL (dentistry, engineering, medicine, pharmacy), SOCIAL SCIENCES (psychology, social sciences, sociology). Thirty-five percent of degrees are conferred in education, 22% in business, and 20% in math and sciences.

Special: Student travel is permitted in the junior year but is not offered as part of the college program. Undergraduate research is offered in biology, chemistry, and physics. A 3-2 binary program plan in engineering is offered in cooperation with Case Western Reserve University.

Honors: Kappa Gamma Pi has a chapter on campus.

Admissions: Eighty-four percent of those who applied were accepted for the 1981-82 freshman class. Of those who enrolled, the SAT scores were as follows: Verbal—80% below 500, 9% between 500 and 599, 11% between 600 and 700, and 0% above 700; Math—74% below 500, 20% between 500 and 599, 6% between 600 and 700, and 0% above 700. On the ACT, 41% scored below 21, 27% between 21 and 23, 8% between 24 and 25, 14% between 26 and 28, and 10% above 28. Recommendations by school officials are considered important in the admissions decision, as are high school performance as demonstrated through overall grade average, class rank, grade trends, and the level of courses completed.

Procedure: The SAT or ACT is required. Applications should be filed by August 15 (fall) and January 1 (winter). Notification is on a rolling basis. There is a $20 application fee.

Special: Deferred admission is possible. AP and CLEP credit is accepted.

Transfer: For fall 1981, 30 students applied, 26 were accepted, and 22 enrolled. A 2.0 GPA is required. D grades do not transfer. Thirty-two credit hours must be taken in residence, out of the 128 needed for a bachelor's degree. Application deadlines are the same as those for freshman applicants.

Visiting: There are guides for informal visits. Visitors may sit in on classes and stay at the school. The best times for visits are during regular semesters, weekdays. Sr. Dianne Piunno, S.N.D., should be contacted to arrange visits.

Financial Aid: Seventy-five percent of the students receive financial aid. Loans average $300 for freshmen and come from the federal government ($15,000), local banks, and the college. Aid from all sources, including part-time employment, can reach a maximum of $500 for a first-year student. The college is a member of CSS. The FAF or CFS is required. The aid application deadlines are March 1 (fall) and November 1 (winter). Notification is on a rolling basis.

Foreign Students: Two percent of the full-time students come from foreign countries. The college offers these students special counseling.

Admissions: Foreign students must score at least 500 on the TOEFL. No college entrance examination is required.

Procedure: The application deadlines are May 1 (fall) and October 1 (winter). Foreign students must submit proof of health and of adequate funds. They must carry health insurance.

Admissions Contact: Frank L. Stephenson, Director of Admissions.

OBERLIN COLLEGE   D-2
Oberlin, Ohio 44074   (216) 775-8411

F/T: 1245M, 1520W		Faculty:	n/av; IIB, + + $
P/T: 22M, 24W		Ph.D.'s:	73%
Grad: 4M, 6W		S/F Ratio:	14 to 1
Year: 4-1-4		Tuition:	$6780
Appl: Feb. 15		R and B:	$2570
3120 applied	1800 accepted		710 enrolled
SAT: 600V 602M	ACT: 27	HIGHLY COMPETITIVE+	

Oberlin College, founded in 1833, combines a distinguished private college of liberal arts and a conservatory of music. The library contains 800,000 volumes, and subscribes to 2500 periodicals.

Environment: The 440-acre campus is located in a rural area 35 miles from Cleveland. Facilities include a physical education center, a computer center, and the Conservatory of Music complex. The 28 dormitories, including cooperatives and language houses, house over 2200 students. Off-campus housing is available for upperclassmen.

Student Life: Twenty percent of the students come from Ohio. Seventy-four percent are graduates of public schools. Seventy percent live on campus. About 13% of the students are minority-group members. College housing is both single-sex and coed. There are visiting privileges in single-sex housing.

Organizations: There are no fraternities or sororities. Social life is informal; the campus atmosphere is democratic. Religious organizations are available for Catholic, Protestant, and Jewish students. The 90 student organizations, as well as other college facilities, offer opportunities for exceptional cultural enrichment. The Oberlin College Choir and Symphony Orchestra are among the best collegiate groups in the country.

Sports: There are 10 intercollegiate sports for men and 9 for women. There are 9 intramural sports for men and 7 for women.

Handicapped: Seventy-five percent of the campus is accessible to wheelchair-bound students. Facilities include wheelchair ramps, special parking, elevators, and specially equipped rest rooms. There are a few hearing- and visually impaired students currently enrolled.

Graduates: There is a freshman dropout rate of 8%; 70% remain to graduate. Of those who remain, 80% pursue graduate study; 9% enter medical school, and 7% law school. Ten percent enter careers in business and industry.

Services: The college offers the following services free of charge: career and psychological counseling, tutoring, remedial instruction, and placement services, including transcript and dossier distribution. Health care is available on a fee basis.

Programs of Study: Oberlin awards the B.A., B.M., and B.F.A. degrees. Bachelor's degrees are offered in the following subjects: AREA STUDIES (American, Asian, Black/Afro-American, Latin American, Russian, urban), EDUCATION (health/physical), ENGLISH (creative writing, English, literature), FINE AND PERFORMING ARTS (art, art history, dance, music, music education, studio art, theater/dramatics), LANGUAGES (Chinese, French, German, Greek/Latin, Russian, Spanish), MATH AND SCIENCES (biology, chemistry, ecology/environmental science, geology, mathematics, physics, psychobiology), PHILOSOPHY (classics, humanities, philosophy, religion), SOCIAL SCIENCES (anthropology, communications studies, economics, government/political science, history, psychology, sociology). Forty-one percent of degrees are conferred in social sciences, 26% in math and sciences, 15% in English, and 15% in the fine and performing arts.

Required: Student regulations prohibit ownership or operation of automobiles during the academic year except by permission of the deans.

Special: Student-designed majors are available. Students may arrange to spend their junior year abroad through the Great Lakes College Association. The college also offers 3 summer programs abroad, 3 semester programs abroad, and maintains 4 language houses on campus. The Experimental College offers 23 courses and emphasizes self-education and group discussion. Oberlin offers a 5-year program leading to the B.A. and B.Mus. and a 5-year program in engineering with Case Institute of Technology, Washington University, and the University of Pennsylvania, as well as exchange programs with Tougaloo College, Fisk University, Talladega College, and Gallaudet College for the Deaf.

Honors: An honors program and a senior scholar program are offered. Honor societies on campus include Phi Beta Kappa, Sigma Xi, Delta Sigma Rho, Tau Kappa Alpha, and Pi Kappa Lambda.

Admissions: Fifty-eight percent of those who applied were accepted for the 1981–82 freshman class. Of those who enrolled the SAT scores were as follows: Verbal—17% below 500, 38% between 500 and 599, 34% between 600 and 700, and 11% above 700; Math—14% below 500, 38% between 500 and 599, 37% between 600 and 700, and 11% above 700. Applicants should present 15 to 18 units of academic subjects. Successful applicants generally rank in the top 20% of their class and are highly recommended by their schools. Other factors considered are advanced placement or honors courses, personality, extracurricular activities, special talent, leadership, and impressions made during a personal interview. Children of alumni are given some preference. Application standards for the conservatory include an audition in the student's performing field.

Procedure: The SAT or ACT is required. The SAT should be taken by December of the senior year. ATs in foreign language are used for placement, and should be taken in May of the senior year. The deadlines for application to the college and conservatory are February 15 (fall) and December 1 (spring). The application fee is $25.

Special: The college offers early decision, deferred admissions, and early admissions plans. AP credit is accepted.

Transfer: For fall 1981, 332 applications were received, 153 were accepted, and 91 students enrolled. College transcripts, recommendations, good academic standing, and high school record are required. D grades do not transfer. There is a residency requirement of 4 semesters. Fifty-six of the 112 credits needed for a B.A. degree, and 62 of the 124 credits needed for a B.M. degree must be completed in residence. Application deadlines are March 15 (fall) and December 1 (spring).

Visiting: Campus visit days are scheduled each fall. Contact the admissions office to make arrangements for formal or informal visits or stays. The best time for visits is between September 5 and December 15.

Financial Aid: Forty-seven percent of the students receive financial aid. Fifty-one percent work part-time on campus. Average aid to freshmen from all sources is $4282. The college is a member of the CSS and participates in the CWS program. Oberlin's financial aid philosophy focuses on a self-help plan; students are expected to contribute toward their own support through summer earnings and prior savings. The FAF is required. The deadlines for application for financial aid are February 15 (fall) and December 1 (spring).

Foreign Students: Two percent of the full-time students come from foreign countries. The college offers these students special counseling and special organizations.

Admissions: Foreign students must score at least 550 on the TOEFL unless English is their first language; they must then take either the SAT or the ACT.

Procedure: The application deadline is January 15 (fall). Foreign students must submit proof of health and of funds adequate to cover 4 years of study. They must also carry health insurance, which is available through the college for a fee.

Admissions Contact: Carl W. Bewig, Director of Admissions.

OHIO DOMINICAN COLLEGE   C–3
Columbus, Ohio 43219   (614) 253-2741

F/T: 251M, 365W
P/T: 106M, 234W
Grad: none
Year: sems, ss
Appl: open
559 applied
ACT: 19

Faculty: 48; IIB, –$
Ph.D.'s: 38%
S/F Ratio: 13 to 1
Tuition: $3620
R and B: $2050

403 accepted   154 enrolled
COMPETITIVE

Ohio Dominican College, known until 1968 as the College of St. Mary of the Springs, is a private Roman Catholic coeducational college devoted to the liberal arts. The library contains 98,845 volumes and 5103 microfilm items, and subscribes to 596 periodicals.

Environment: The 43-acre campus is located in a suburban area at the east end of Columbus. Among the buildings are the gymnasium, auditorium, student lounge, music building, dining facility, fine arts building, science building, and residence halls.

Student Life: The majority of the students come from Ohio; 15% come from other states and countries. About 53% of the entering freshmen come from public schools. About 33% are campus residents. Fifty percent of the degree candidates are Catholic, 25% are Protestant, and 1% are Jewish. About 14% of the students are minority-group members. Campus housing is coed and single-sex; there are visiting privileges in single-sex dorms. Students may keep cars on campus.

Organizations: There are no fraternities or sororities, but other groups for social activity exist. All members of the college community belong to the Cooperative Government Association. There are special-interest groups, departmental clubs, and performing groups.

Sports: The college fields 2 intercollegiate teams for men and 2 for women. There are 10 intramural sports for men and 10 for women.

Handicapped: Ninety percent of the campus is accessible to wheelchair-bound students. Facilities for handicapped students include wheelchair ramps, elevators, special parking and rest rooms, and lowered drinking fountains. Special class scheduling is also available. Special counselors are available for assistance through the student services office.

Graduates: The freshman dropout rate is 36%; 44% remain to graduate. Thirty-four percent go on to graduate study; 2% enter law school. Thirty-seven percent pursue careers in business and industry.

Services: Students receive the following services free of charge: placement, career counseling, tutoring, remedial instruction, and psychological counseling. Health care is available on a fee basis. Job opportunities are posted on bulletin boards and various companies come to the campus for on-campus job recruitment.

Programs of Study: The college offers the B.A., B.S., and B.S.Ed. degrees. Associate degrees are also awarded. Bachelor's degrees are offered in the following subjects: BUSINESS (accounting, business administration, international business), EDUCATION (early childhood, elementary, secondary, special), ENGLISH (English, speech), FINE AND PERFORMING ARTS (art, art education, communications, theater/dramatics), LANGUAGES (Spanish), MATH AND SCIENCES (biology, chemistry, mathematics), PHILOSOPHY (philosophy, religion), PREPROFESSIONAL (dentistry, home economics, interior design and fashion merchandising, law, library science, medicine, pharmacy, social work, veterinary), SOCIAL SCIENCES (criminal justice, economics, government/political science, history, psychology, social sciences, social welfare, sociology). Twenty-nine percent of degrees are conferred in social sciences, 15% in business, 20% in education, and 6% in math and sciences.

682 OHIO

Special: Student-designed majors are permitted. Several summer study programs are also available. The college offers an honors program and study abroad. There is a combination degree program in engineering with the University of Detroit. The college offers a general studies degree.

Honors: The honors program is designed to provide unusual and challenging educational experiences for students and to encourage student initiative and involvement in learning. This program is open to students in all departments who maintain at least a 3.0 GPA.

Admissions: Seventy-two percent of those who applied were accepted for the 1981-82 freshman class. The ACT scores of those who enrolled were as follows: 59% below 21, 19% between 21 and 23, 17% between 24 and 25, 5% between 26 and 28, and 0% above 28. The candidate should have completed at least 15 Carnegie units, be a graduate of an accredited high school with an average of C or better, and must rank in the upper half of his or her class. The school indicates that in addition to these qualifications they consider the following factors in order of importance: advanced placement or honors courses, extracurricular activities record, and recommendations by school officials.

Procedure: The SAT or ACT is required. Application deadlines are open; there is no application fee. Students are admitted to all terms. The college uses a rolling admissions policy.

Special: There are early admissions and deferred admissions plans. CLEP and AP credit is accepted.

Transfer: For fall 1981, 159 transfer students applied, 152 were accepted, and 66 enrolled. A GPA of at least 2.0 is required. One year (32 semester hours) must be spent in resident study. Grades of C or better transfer. The bachelor's degree requires 124 semester hours. Deadlines are the same as those for freshmen.

Visiting: There is 1 open house each year, where faculty and administrators meet with parents and students, and tours and interviews are given. Informal visits may be made to the campus weekdays and Saturday mornings; guided tours can be taken. Visitors may sit in on classes and remain overnight on campus. Contact the admissions office to arrange such visits.

Financial Aid: About 33% of all students receive financial aid; 17% work part-time on campus. The average award to freshmen is $2680. Scholarships, grants, loans, and CWS are available. The requested deadline for scholarship applications is March 1; for other aid, March 15. The college is a member of CSS; the FAF is required of all aid applicants.

Foreign Students: About 21% of the full-time students come from foreign countries. The college offers them an intensive English course, an intensive English program, special counseling, and special organizations.

Admissions: Foreign students must take the University of Michigan Language Test; no college entrance exams are required.

Procedure: Application deadlines are August 15 (fall) and January 5 (winter). Foreign students must present proof of funds adequate to cover 1 year of study. They must also carry health insurance, which is available through the college for a fee.

Admissions Contact: James L. Sagona, Director of Admissions.

OHIO INSTITUTE OF TECHNOLOGY C-3
Columbus, Ohio 43209 (614) 228-1525
(Recognized Candidate for Accreditation)

F/T: 3316M, 398W Faculty: 52; n/av
P/T: 100M, 28W Ph.D.'s: n/av
Grad: none S/F Ratio: 14 to 1
Year: tri, ss Tuition: $3025
Appl: Oct. R and B: n/app
SAT or ACT: required LESS COMPETITIVE

Ohio Institute of Technology, an independent institution founded in 1952, is administered by the Bell & Howell Education Group. Its undergraduate divisions include electronics engineering technology, computer science for business, and electronics technology.

Environment: The campus is located in the city of Columbus. The institute has no housing facilities on campus, but sponsors off-campus apartments.

Student Life: About 42% of the students come from Ohio. About 16% are members of minority groups. The school's housing office helps students find off-campus accommodations. Students are permitted to have cars on campus.

Organizations: The 44 extracurricular activities available include professional organizations, a ski club, a jazz ensemble, and an adventurer's club. There are no fraternities or sororities.

Sports: The school does not participate in intercollegiate sports. Seven intramural sports are offered for men and 4 for women.

Handicapped: All programs are accessible to handicapped students. Facilities include wheelchair ramps, elevators, special parking, specially equipped rest rooms, and lowered drinking fountains and telephones. Special class scheduling can be arranged, and the school provides any needed tutoring or materials.

Graduates: Over 90% of each graduating class begin careers in business and industry.

Services: Placement aid, career counseling, and tutoring are provided free. Fees are charged for health-care services and remedial instruction.

Programs of Study: The school awards the B.S.E.E. and the B.S.Comp.Sci. degrees. Associate degrees in electronics technology also are available. Bachelor's degrees are offered in the following subjects: BUSINESS (computer science), PREPROFESSIONAL (electronics engineering technology).

Required: Students must follow a specified curriculum and maintain a GPA of 2.0 or better to graduate.

Honors: Tau Alpha Phi has a chapter on campus, and the electronics engineering technology department offers an honors program.

Admissions: Twenty-four percent of the 1981-82 freshmen ranked in the upper fifth of their class, and 47% ranked in the upper two-fifths. Applicants must be high school graduates or have earned a GED. An interview is required. In addition to grades and test scores, admissions officers consider impressions made during the interview and recommendations by high school officials.

Procedure: Applicants must take both the SAT or ACT and the Bell & Howell Education Group Entrance Exam. Applications should be submitted by October for fall admission, March for spring admission, and July for summer admission. The application fee is $25. Admissions decisions are made on a rolling basis.

Special: A deferred admissions plan is offered.

Transfer: Transfer students are accepted for all classes. Applicants must undergo a personal interview. Students must complete in residence at least 36 of the 160 credits required for a degree. Grades of C or better transfer. Application deadlines are the same as those for freshmen.

Visiting: Guides are available for informal visits, which may be arranged for weekdays with the director of admissions.

Financial Aid: Eighty-five percent of the students receive aid through the school; 1% work part-time on campus. Scholarships (average, $500; maximum, total cost of education) and loans (average, $2250; maximum, $2500) are available. Applicants must submit the FAF.

Foreign Students: Foreign students enrolled represent 1% of the student body.

Admissions: Applicants must score at least 450 on the TOEFL or 106 on the ELS. They also must take the SAT and the Bell & Howell Education Group Entrance Exam.

Procedure: Application deadlines are the same as those for other freshmen. Students must submit a physician's certificate as proof of good health and must show evidence of adequate funds for 1 year. They are required to carry health insurance, which is available through the institute for a fee.

Admissions Contact: Louis J. Collins, Director of Admissions.

OHIO NORTHERN UNIVERSITY B-2
Ada, Ohio 45810 (419) 634-9921

F/T: 1238M, 944W Faculty: 168; IIB, +$
P/T: 28M, 38W Ph.D.'s: 44%
Grad: 394M, 117W S/F Ratio: 15 to 1
Year: qtrs, ss Tuition: $4125
Appl: Aug. 15 R and B: $1755
1375 applied 1181 accepted 591 enrolled
SAT: 451V 514M ACT: 22 COMPETITIVE

Founded in 1871, Ohio Northern University is affiliated with the United Methodist Church. It consists of the colleges of Arts and Sciences, Business Administration, Engineering, Law, and Pharmacy and Allied Health Sciences. The university libraries house 320,099 volumes and subscribe to 1181 periodicals.

Environment: The 140-acre campus is located in rural Ada, 15 miles from Lima. All the 17 major academic buildings have been built or renovated within the last 15 years; the campus also has a lake. There are 5 dormitories, as well as fraternity houses.

Student Life: About 77% of the students come from Ohio. Ninety-three percent are from public schools. About 66% of the students live on campus: the residence halls house a total of 1396 students; the rest live in fraternity houses or approved private homes. Twenty-seven percent of the students are Catholic, 55% Protestant (25% Methodist), and 1% Jewish. There are weekly, voluntary, nonsectarian services. About 3% of the students are minority-group members. University housing is single-sex; there are visiting privileges. Students may keep cars on campus.

Organizations: Thirty-eight percent of the men belong to the 8 fraternities; 39% of the women belong to the 4 sororities. There are a number of extracurricular organizations and events.

Sports: The school competes intercollegiately in 11 sports for men and 7 for women. Intramurals include 13 sports for men and 9 for women.

Handicapped: About 90% of the campus is accessible to physically handicapped students. Facilities include special parking, wheelchair ramps, and specially equippped rest rooms.

Graduates: The freshman dropout rate is about 25%; 55% remain to graduate. Eight percent go on to further study after graduation; about 2% enter medical school, 1% dental school, and 9% law school. Students in the prelaw program are guaranteed admission to the Ohio Northern College of Law. Seventy-five percent of the students enter careers in business and industry.

Services: Students receive the following services free of charge: health care, psychological counseling, placement, and career counseling.

Programs of Study: The university confers the B.A., B.S., B.M., B.F.A., B.S.Med.Tech., B.S.C.E., B.S.E.E., B.S.M.E., B.S.Pharm., B.S.Ind.Tech., and B.S.B.A. degrees. Bachelor's degrees are offered in the following subjects: BUSINESS (accounting, computer science, finance, management, marketing), EDUCATION (early childhood, elementary, health/physical, industrial, secondary, student personnel administration), ENGLISH (English, literature, speech, writing), FINE AND PERFORMING ARTS (art—ceramics, art—graphic design, art—printmaking, art—sculpture, art education, music, music—performance, music—sacred, music education, theater/dramatics), HEALTH SCIENCES (medical technology, pharmacy), LANGUAGES (French, Spanish), MATH AND SCIENCES (biology, chemistry, mathematics, physics), PHILOSOPHY (philosophy, religion), PREPROFESSIONAL (dentistry, engineering—civil, engineering—electrical, engineering—mechanical, law, medicine, ministry, veterinary), SOCIAL SCIENCES (economics, gerontology, government/political science, history, political science—public personnel management, political science—urban affairs, psychology, public administration, social work, sociology).

Special: Students may receive credit by institutional examination in most courses and may elect 1 course per quarter on pass/fail in some colleges. Dual majors and dual degree programs are available. Independent study is also possible.

Admissions: About 86% of those who applied were accepted for the 1981–82 freshman class. The ACT scores of those who enrolled were as follows: 30% below 21, 31% between 21 and 23, 14% between 24 and 25, 18% between 26 and 28, and 7% above 28. Candidates should have completed 16 Carnegie units, have at least a 2.0 GPA, and rank in the top 50% of their class. Advanced placement or honors courses are also taken into consideration.

Procedure: Either the SAT or the ACT is required (the ACT is preferred). The deadline for the fall term is August 15; for the other terms it is 30 days before registration. There is a rolling admissions plan. The application fee is $20.

Special: Early decision and early admissions plans are available. AP and CLEP credit is accepted.

Transfer: For fall 1981, 202 students applied, 167 were admitted, and 91 enrolled. A GPA of at least 2.0 is recommended. D grades do not transfer. For the liberal arts program, 45 quarter hours must be taken in residence, out of the 182 credits needed for a bachelor's degree. Application deadlines are the same as those for regular admissions.

Visiting: Guided tours and interviews can be scheduled 6 days a week. Visitors may stay at the school and sit in on classes.

Financial Aid: About 60% of all students receive financial aid. Twenty-six percent work part-time on campus. The average freshman aid covers 55% of expenses. Church vocation and minister's children grants are available, as are loans to Methodist students from the church student loan fund. The university is a member of CSS. The FAF is required; the deadlines for financial aid applications are April 1 (fall), October 1 (winter), February 1 (spring), and May 1 (summer).

Foreign Students: About 2% of the full-time students come from foreign countries. The university offers these students special organizations.

Admissions: Foreign students must score at least 500 on the TOEFL. No college entrance examination is required.

Procedure: The application deadline is June 1 (fall). Foreign students must submit the results of a physical examination. They must also present proof of funds adequate to cover 1 year of study. They must carry health insurance, which is available through the university.

Admissions Contact: Ronald L. Knoble, Director of Admissions.

THE OHIO STATE UNIVERSITY

The Ohio State University is a multi-campus institution offering both undergraduate and graduate programs. The main campus is located in Columbus. There are 4 regional campuses located at Lima, Mansfield, Marion, Newark, and an Agricultural Technical Institute at Wooster (2-year programs only).

THE OHIO STATE UNIVERSITY C–3
Columbus, Ohio 43210 (614) 422-3980

F/T: 20,133M, 16,769W	Faculty: 2948; I, + + $
P/T: 1665M, 1745W	Ph.D.'s: 53%
Grad: 7068M, 5302W	S/F Ratio: 13 to 1
Year: qtrs, ss	Tuition: $1380 ($3510)
Appl: Mar. 1	R and B: $2271
13,486 applied	11,469 accepted 6677 enrolled
SAT: 456V 505M	ACT: 21 NONCOMPETITIVE

The Ohio State University, founded in 1870, includes 17 colleges, 9 schools, and a graduate school. The library contains 3.5 million volumes, houses 1.3 microfilm items, and subscribes to 23,303 periodicals.

Environment: The urban Columbus campus occupies more than 3250 acres of land and has more than 360 permanent buildings, including resident dormitories. There are 1190 acres for research and teaching in agriculture, a 500-acre airport, and two 18-hole golf courses.

Student Life: Students come from all 50 states. Twenty percent of the students live on campus. Eight percent are minority-group members. University housing is both single-sex and coed. There are visiting privileges in single-sex housing. Students may keep cars on campus. Day-care services are available to all students, faculty, and staff.

Organizations: There are 40 fraternities and 22 sororities with chapters on campus. A great variety of cultural, intellectual, recreational, and social activities is offered, including concerts, plays, visiting artists and special-interest clubs.

Sports: The university competes in 17 intercollegiate sports for men and 12 for women. There are 13 intramural sports for men and 12 for women.

Handicapped: The campus is 100% accessible to wheelchair-bound students. Facilities include wheelchair ramps, special parking, elevators, lowered drinking fountains and telephones, specially equipped rest rooms, and special class scheduling. Facilities for visually impaired and hearing-impaired students include reading programs, book recordings, transportation, and priority scheduling.

Graduates: Twenty-six percent of the freshmen drop out by the end of their first year. Forty-five percent remain to graduate.

Services: Students receive the following services free of charge: psychological counseling, tutoring, remedial instruction, placement, and career counseling. Health care is available on a fee basis.

Programs of Study: The university offers the B.S., B.A., B.F.A., and B.Mus. degrees. Master's and doctoral programs are also available. Among the 184 degree programs bachelor's degrees are offered in the following subjects: AREA STUDIES (Black/Afro-American, international, Islamic, Jewish, medieval and Renaissance, Russian, women's), BUSINESS (accounting, business administration, business education, computer science, finance, labor/industrial relations, management, marketing, real estate/insurance, restaurant management, transportation), EDUCATION (adult, early and middle childhood, elementary, health/physical, industrial, special), ENGLISH (communications, English, journalism, linguistics, speech), FINE AND PERFORMING ARTS (art, art education, art history, ceramic art, dance, drawing-painting-printmaking, film/photography, music, music education, music performance, music theater, music theory and composition, sculpture, theater/dramatics), HEALTH SCIENCES (environmental health, medical communications, medical dietetics, medical illustration, medical records administration, medical technology, nurse anesthesia, nursing, occupational therapy, physical therapy, radiologic technology, respiratory technology, speech and hearing science), LANGUAGES (Arabic, Chinese, French, German, Greek/Latin, Hebrew, Italian, Japanese, Russian, Slavic, Spanish), MATH AND SCIENCES (astronomy, biochemistry, biology, botany, chemistry, genetics, geology, mathematics, nutrition, physics, statistics, zoology), PHILOSOPHY (classics, humanities, philosophy), PREPROFESSIONAL (agriculture, architecture, aviation, dairy science, engineering, forestry, home economics, horticulture, pharmacy, social work, veterinary), SOCIAL SCIENCES (anthropology, criminology and criminal justice, economics, geography, government/political science, history, international relations, psychology, social sciences, sociology). Of the degrees conferred, 33% are in preprofessional studies, 16% in business, and 11% in education.

Special: It is possible to earn a combined B.A.-B.S. degree in arts and education. The university sponsors numerous studies in the international field and study tours abroad during the academic year. Other special programs include independent study, student-designed majors, and a rapidly expanding adult and continuing education program.

Honors: National honor societies with chapters on campus are Phi Beta Kappa, Phi Kappa Phi, and Mortarboard.

Admissions: Eighty-five percent of those who applied were accepted for the 1981–82 freshman class. The SAT scores of those who enrolled were as follows: Verbal—64% below 500, 27% between 500 and 599, 7% between 600 and 700, and 2% above 700; Math—46% below 500, 34% between 500 and 599, 15% between 600 and 700, and 5% above 700. On the ACT, 37% scored below 21, 19% between 21 and 23, 14% between 24 and 25, 16% between 26 and 28, and 14% above 28. Ohio residents who have never attended college may be accepted for admission as the enrollment ceiling permits. Nonresidents must be in the upper 50% of their grduating class and have a GPA of at least 2.5.

Procedure: Applicants for the freshman class are required to submit ACT or SAT scores to provide information for counseling and placement. The deadlines for admission are March 1 (fall and spring), December 1 (winter), and June 1 (summer). There is a rolling admissions plan. There is a $10 application fee.

Special: Early and deferred admissions plans are available. AP and CLEP credit is accepted.

Transfer: For fall 1981, 4874 students applied, 3519 were accepted, and 1862 enrolled. A GPA of at least 2.0 is required. D grades do not transfer. Two quarters and 45 of the 180 to 220 credits needed for a bachelor's degree must be completed at the university. Application deadlines are the same as those for freshman applicants.

Visiting: Regularly scheduled orientations are conducted by the university. Guides are available for informal visits to the campus.

Financial Aid: About 26% of all students receive aid. Ten percent work part-time on campus. Federal government funds and funds administered by the university provide student loans. The average freshman award from all sources is $600. The university is a member of CSS. The FAF is required. The aid application deadlines are March 1 (fall and spring), December 1 (winter), and June 1 (summer).

Foreign Students: Two percent of the full-time students come from foreign countries. The university offers these students special counseling and special organizations.

Admissions: Foreign students must score at least 500 on the TOEFL. No college entrance examination is required.

Procedure: The application deadlines are March 1 (fall and spring), December 1 (winter), and June 1 (summer). Foreign students must submit proof of health and proof of funds adequate to cover their entire period of study. They must carry health insurance, which is available through the university for a fee.

Admissions Contact: James J. Mager, Director of Admissions.

THE OHIO STATE UNIVERSITY AT LIMA B-2
Lima, Ohio 45804   (419) 228-2641

F/T: 360M, 457W	Faculty: 42; III, +$
P/T: 45M, 72W	Ph.D.'s: 76%
Grad: 2M, 23W	S/F Ratio: 18 to 1
Year: qtrs, ss	Tuition: $1335 ($3465)
Appl: Aug. 15	R and B: n/app
432 applied	424 accepted 351 enrolled
SAT: 424V 488M	ACT: 19 NONCOMPETITIVE

The Ohio State University's regional campus at Lima was established in 1960. The library contains 57,000 volumes, houses 2600 microfilm items, and subscribes to 538 periodicals.

Environment: The 565-acre wooded campus is located in a suburb 3 miles east of Lima. The physical plant is made up of 4 permanent structures and an outdoor classroom established for botanical research and nature study. The campus serves commuting students only.

Student Life: Almost all students come from Ohio. All students commute. Five percent of the students are minority-group members. Students may keep cars on campus.

Organizations: There are special-interest clubs, service groups, symposiums, concerts, publications, and student government.

Sports: The university offers 4 intercollegiate sports for men and 3 for women. There are 5 intramural sports for men and 3 for women.

Handicapped: The entire campus is accessible to wheelchair-bound students. Facilities include wheelchair ramps, special parking, elevators, lowered drinking fountains and telephones, and specially equipped rest rooms. Fewer than 1% of students currently enrolled have visual impairments. Tutors and readers are available for these students.

Services: Students receive the following services free of charge: tutoring, remedial instruction, placement, and career counseling.

Programs of Study: The Lima campus confers the B.S.Ed. degree. Associate degrees are also offered. The bachelor's degree is offered in the following subject: EDUCATION (elementary).

Special: Student-designed majors are permitted to a limited extent.

Honors: Honors courses are offered periodically on a departmental and interdisciplinary basis.

Admissions: About 98% of those who applied were accepted for the 1981–82 freshman class. Of those who enrolled, the ACT scores were as follows: 54% below 21, 17% between 21 and 23, 11% between 24 and 25, 9% between 26 and 28, and 9% above 28. All Ohio high school graduates are eligible. Out-of-state applicants are considered on an individual basis.

Procedure: SAT or ACT scores must be submitted for counseling and placement purposes. The application deadlines are August 15 (fall), December 1 (winter), March 1 (spring), and June 1 (summer). The university uses a rolling admissions plan. There is a $10 application fee.

Special: There is a deferred admissions plan. AP and CLEP credit is accepted.

Transfer: For fall 1981, 155 students applied, 136 were accepted, and 123 enrolled. An average of at least C is necessary. Preference is given to students from other OSU campuses. There is a residency requirement of 1 year. Students must complete, at the university, at least 45 of the 180 to 220 quarter hours needed for a bachelor's degree. Deadlines are the same as those for entering freshmen.

Visiting: Guides are available for informal visits to the campus. Regularly scheduled orientations are held for prospective students. For further information on these sessions, contact the Coordinator of Admissions.

Financial Aid: About 43% of all students receive financial aid, which is available in the form of CWS, NDSL, short-term and bank loans, university loans, EOG, scholarships, and instructional grants. Four percent of the students work part-time on campus. The average award to freshmen from all sources covers 30% of costs. The university is a member of CSS. The freshman deadline for filing of the FAF and the university's own financial aid form is March 15.

Foreign Students: No foreign students are currently enrolled.

Admissions: Foreign students must take the TOEFL or the University of Michigan Language Test. No college entrance examination is required.

Admissions Contact: James J. Mager, Director of Admissions.

THE OHIO STATE UNIVERSITY AT MANSFIELD C-2
Mansfield, Ohio 44906   (419) 755-4011

F/T: 383M, 389W	Faculty: 39; III, +$
P/T: 41M, 65W	Ph.D.'s: 75%
Grad: 7M, 50W	S/F Ratio: 20 to 1
Year: qtrs, ss	Tuition: $1335 ($3465)
Appl: Aug. 15	R and B: n/app
470 applied	462 accepted 368 enrolled
SAT: 482V 540M	ACT: 20 NONCOMPETITIVE

The Ohio State University at Mansfield is a public institution offering undergraduate programs in elementary education.

Environment: The campus is located in a suburban area 2 miles from Mansfield, a city of 110,000. The university has no student housing.

Student Life: About 99% of the students are from Ohio. Five percent are members of minority groups. Students may have cars on campus.

Organizations: The 50 extracurricular activities and organizations offered to students include a student ambassadors program, a traveling theater group, and a movie series.

Sports: The university fields intercollegiate teams in 2 sports for men. Seven intramural sports are available for both men and women.

Handicapped: The entire campus is accessible to physically handicapped students. Facilities include wheelchair ramps, elevators, special parking, specially equipped rest rooms, and lowered drinking fountains and telephones. One special counselor is available.

Services: Placement and career counseling, tutoring, and remedial instruction are available free to students.

Programs of Study: The univesity awards the B.S. in Elem. Ed. degree. Associate degrees also are conferred, and master's courses are offered on a nondegree basis. The bachelor's degree is offered in one subject: EDUCATION (elementary).

Special: A general studies degree (no major) is offered.

Honors: Three national honor societies have chapters on campus. Honors programs are available in all disciplines.

Admissions: About 98% of those who applied were accepted for the 1981-82 freshman class. The ACT scores of those who enrolled were as follows: 46% below 21, 22% between 21 and 23, 10% between 24 and 25, 9% between 26 and 28, and 13% above 28. Twenty-seven percent of the freshmen ranked in the upper fifth of their high school class, and 50% ranked in the upper two-fifths. Applicants must be high school graduates. The university follows an open-door admissions policy.

Procedure: The SAT or ACT is required. Application deadlines are August 15 (fall), December 1 (winter), March 1 (spring), and June 1 (summer). The application fee is $10.

Special: A deferred admissions plan is available.

Transfer: For fall 1981, 215 transfer students applied, 199 were accepted, and 168 enrolled. Students must spend at least 1 year in residence, earning 45 of the 180-220 credits required for a bachelor's degree. Grades of C or better transfer. Application deadlines are the same as those for freshmen.

Visiting: There are regularly scheduled orientations for prospective students. Informal visits may be scheduled with the admissions office. Guides are provided, and visitors may sit in on classes.

Financial Aid: Forty percent of the students receive aid through the university; 5% work part-time on campus. Scholarships (average $700, maximum $1200) and loans (average $500, maximum $1250) are available to freshmen; the average award from all sources in 1981-82 totaled $600. Students must submit the FAF and the aid application by March 15 (fall), December 1 (winter), March 1 (spring), or June 1 (summer).

Foreign Students: No foreign students are currently enrolled. An intensive English course, special organizations, and special counseling are available.

Admissions: Foreign applicants must take the TOEFL or the University of Michigan Language Test. The minimum acceptable score on the TOEFL is 500. No college entrance exams are required.

Procedure: Application deadlines are July 1 (fall), December 1 (winter), March 1 (spring), and June 1 (summer). Foreign students must present proof of good health and evidence of adequate funds for their entire period of enrollment. Health insurance is required, and is available through the university for a fee.

Admissions Contact: Karen Oberrath, Assistant Director of Admissions.

OHIO 685

THE OHIO STATE UNIVERSITY AT MARION   C-3
Marion, Ohio 43302   (614) 389-2361

F/T: 311M, 332W   Faculty: 24; III, + +$
P/T: 81M, 133W   Ph.D.'s: 75%
Grad: 4M, 23W   S/F Ratio: 26 to 1
Year: qtrs, ss   Tuition: $1335 ($3465)
Appl: Aug. 15   R and B: n/app
317 applied   316 accepted   285 enrolled
ACT: 19   NONCOMPETITIVE

The Ohio State University at Marion was founded in 1957. The library contains 28,500 volumes, subscribes to 285 periodicals, and houses 1700 microfilm items.

Environment: The 180-acre suburban campus is located east of the city. There are no dormitory facilities.

Student Life: Nearly all students come from Ohio. Five percent are minority-group members. Students may keep cars on campus. All students commute.

Organizations: Activities on campus are commuter-oriented, and include a standard selection of service groups, special-interest clubs, student government, publications, and social and cultural affairs.

Sports: The university competes on an intercollegiate level in 1 sport. There are 10 intramural sports.

Handicapped: The campus is 100% accessible to handicapped students. Special parking and elevators are provided. Assistance for visually impaired students is coordinated with the National Center on Educational Media.

Services: The following services are offered free of charge to all students: tutoring, remedial instruction, placement, and career counseling.

Programs of Study: The Marion campus confers the B.S.Ed. degree. Associate degrees are also awarded. The bachelor's degree is offered in the following subject: EDUCATION (elementary).

Special: Student-designed majors are permitted.

Honors: Twelve departments offer honors programs.

Admissions: Ninety-nine percent of those who applied were accepted for the 1981-82 freshman class. The ACT scores of those who enrolled were as follows: 58% below 21, 16% between 21 and 23, 8% between 24 and 25, 8% between 26 and 28, and 2% above 28. All graduates of accredited Ohio high schools are eligible; nonresident candidates must have a GPA of at least 2.5.

Procedure: The SAT or ACT is required and is used for guidance purposes. Deadlines are August 15 (fall), December 1 (winter), March 1 (spring), and June 1 (summer). There is a $10 application fee. Notification is on a rolling basis.

Special: AP and CLEP credit is accepted. Credit may also be granted for college-level U.S. Armed Forces Institute (DANTES) courses. There are early admissions and deferred admissions plans.

Transfer: For fall 1981, 136 students applied, 132 were accepted, and 126 enrolled. D grades do not transfer. All students must complete, at the university, 45 of the 180-220 credits required for a bachelor's degree. Application deadlines are the same as those for freshmen.

Visiting: A welcome evening program is conducted for parents and students. Guides are available for informal visits to the campus.

Financial Aid: About 30% of all students receive aid, offered in the form of scholarships, grants, and loans (federal, university, and bank). About 10% work part-time on campus. Aid applications are due by March 15 (fall), December 1 (winter), March 1 (spring), or June 1 (summer). The university is a member of CSS and requires the FAF.

Foreign Students: Fewer than 1% of the full-time students come from foreign countries.

Admissions: Foreign students must achieve a TOEFL score of at least 550. No college entrance exams are required.

Procedure: The application deadline for fall entry is June 15. Foreign students must present proof of funds adequate to cover 1 year of study and must complete a health form. The application fee for foreign students is $25.

Admissions Contact: Darlene S. Greenwood, Admissions Officer.

THE OHIO STATE UNIVERSITY AT NEWARK
Newark, Ohio 43055   (614) 386-3321   C-3

F/T: 400M, 412W
P/T: 77M, 91W
Grad: 19M, 61W
Year: qtrs, ss
Appl: Aug. 15
438 applied
ACT: 19

Faculty: * 27; III, +$
Ph.D.'s: 82%
S/F Ratio: 30 to 1
Tuition: $1335 ($3465)
R and B: n/app
425 accepted   346 enrolled
NONCOMPETITIVE

The Ohio State University at Newark was established in 1957. The library contains 40,000 volumes, and houses 5000 microfilm items, and subscribes to 407 periodicals.

Environment: The 150-acre suburban campus consists of 3 buildings with a capacity for 2000 students. The campus is shared with Central Ohio Technical College. There are no housing facilities.

Student Life: Ninety-six percent of the entering freshmen come from public schools. All students commute. Four percent of the students are minority-group members. Students may keep cars on campus. Day-care services are available to all students, faculty, and staff for a fee.

Organizations: Campus activities are commuter-oriented, and include publications, student government, and clubs.

Sports: Four intramural sports for men and 5 for women are offered. There are 12 intramural sports for men and 11 for women.

Handicapped: The campus is 100% accessible to wheelchair-bound students. Facilities for the handicapped include wheelchair ramps, lowered drinking fountains, and special parking.

Services: Tutoring, remedial instruction, placement, and career counseling are available free of charge to students. In addition to job listings, there are job seminars and workshops in career skills.

Programs of Study: The university offers the B.S.Ed. degree. Associate degrees are also offered. The bachelor's degree is offered in the following subject: EDUCATION (elementary).

Special: Student-designed majors are permitted.

Honors: The freshman honor societies of Alpha Lambda Delta and Phi Eta Sigma have chapters on campus. An honors interdisciplinary series is available.

Admissions: Ninety-seven percent of those who applied were accepted for the 1981-82 freshman class. The ACT scores of those who enrolled were as follows: 56% below 21, 12% between 21 and 23, 11% between 24 and 25, 11% between 26 and 28, and 10% above 28. Candidates must be graduates of an accredited high school.

Procedure: The ACT is required for placement only. The application deadlines are August 15 (fall), December 15 (winter), March 1 (spring), and June 1 (summer). The university follows a rolling admissions plan. There is a $10 application fee.

Special: There are early and deferred admissions plans. CLEP credit is accepted.

Transfer: For fall 1981, 155 students applied, 138 were accepted, and 121 enrolled. Good academic standing is necessary. A GPA of at least 2.0 in all courses is required. Students from other OSU campuses receive preference. There is a 12-month residency rule. Students must complete 45 of the 180 to 220 credits needed for a bachelor's degree. Application deadlines are March 1 (fall and spring), December 1 (winter), and June 1 (summer).

Visiting: Guides are available for informal visits to the campus. Visitors may sit in on classes.

Financial Aid: About 30% of all students receive aid. Forty-five academic scholarships are available to freshmen. In addition, grants, federal and state loans, CWS, and part-time employment are also offered. Ten percent of the students work part-time on campus. Average aid to freshmen from all sources is $600. The university is a member of CSS. Tuition may be paid in installments with a Visa charge card. The FAF is required. Application deadlines are March 15 (fall), December 1 (winter), March 1 (spring), and June 1 (summer).

Foreign Students: No foreign students are currently enrolled. The university offers foreign students special counseling and special organizations.

Admissions: Foreign students must score at least 500 on the TOEFL or 80 on the University of Michigan Language Test. No college entrance examination is required.

Procedure: The application deadlines are March 1 (fall), November 1 (winter), February 1 (spring), and May 1 (summer). Foreign students must submit proof of adequate funds.

Admissions Contact: David A. Breckenridge, Admissions Coordinator.

OHIO UNIVERSITY
Athens, Ohio 45701   (614) 594-5174   D-4

F/T: 5621M, 4912W
P/T: 1131M, 879W
Grad: 1184M, 763W
Year: qtrs, ss
Appl: June 15
5929 applied
SAT(mean): 435V 468M   ACT: 19

Faculty: 737; I, -$
Ph.D.'s: 73%
S/F Ratio: 14 to 1
Tuition: $1482 ($3183)
R and B: $2220
5330 accepted   2986 enrolled
COMPETITIVE

Ohio University, founded in 1804 in the former Northwest Territory, is a large state-assisted university consisting of 10 colleges: the University College, the Honors Tutorial College, and the colleges of Arts and Sciences, Business Administration, Communication, Education, Engineering and Technology, Fine Arts, Health and Human Services, and Osteopathic Medicine. The library contains 1,107,000 volumes and 680,000 microfilm items, and subscribes to 5700 periodicals.

Environment: Located on 641 acres in the rural town of Athens, 70 miles from Columbus, the campus has 100 major buildings, mainly of Colonial architecture. Cutler Hall, built in 1816, is a national historic landmark; the entire College Green was recently listed in the *National Register of Historic Places*. Residence halls accommodate 2800 women and 3800 men. Married student housing is available.

Student Life: Eighty percent of the students are from Ohio; 85% of entering freshmen come from public schools. About 16% of the students are minority-group members. About 58% of the students live on campus. Freshmen are required to live on campus unless they live nearby, are married, or are veterans. Campus housing is both single-sex and coed. There are visiting privileges in single-sex dorms. Students may keep cars on campus. Day-care services are available for a fee to full-time students, part-time students, faculty, and staff.

Organizations: There are 200 special-interest groups, 18 fraternities, 12 sororities, 1 main student governing board, and a dormitory government system. About 7% of the students are affiliated with Greek letter organizations. There are 17 religious organizations, including the Baptist Student Union, Christian Science, Hillel, Newman Club, Bible Fellowship, and Campus Crusade for Christ.

Sports: The university has 21 intercollegiate teams for men of which 10 are club sports and 11 varsity sports. There are 17 intercollegiate women's teams, 7 of which are club sports and 10 varsity sports. Thirteen intramural sports are offered for men and 11 for women.

Handicapped: About 35% of the campus is accessible to handicapped students. Wheelchair ramps, special parking, special class scheduling, specially equipped rest rooms, and lowered drinking fountains and telephones are available. For the hearing-impaired, there is a speech and hearing clinic; for the visually impaired, there are readers and large-type display terminals.

Graduates: By the end of the freshman year, about 30% of the students drop out; 54% remain to graduate. Thirty-five to 40% of those who remain pursue graduate study; 17% enter business or industry.

Services: Psychological counseling, career counseling, health care, and remedial instruction are offered free of charge. Placement services are available for a fee. Tutoring is also available at varying costs.

Programs of Study: The university confers the B.A., B.S., B.S.C., B.F.A., B.S.C.E., B.S.Ch.E., B.S.Ed., B.S.E.E., B.S.H.E., B.S.Ind.Tech., B.S.J., B.S.N., B.B.A., B.G.S., and B.S.I.E. degrees. Associate, master's, and doctoral programs are also offered. Bachelor's degrees are offered in the following subjects: AREA STUDIES (international), BUSINESS (accounting, business administration, business economics, business education, computer science, finance, health care management, management, marketing, production management, quantitative methods), EDUCATION (early childhood, elementary, health/physical, secondary, special), ENGLISH (English, journalism, speech), FINE AND PERFORMING ARTS (art, art education, art history, art therapy, dance, music, music education, music therapy, photography, radio/TV, studio art, theater/dramatics, visual communication), HEALTH SCIENCES (environmental health, medical technology, nursing, physical therapy, speech therapy), LANGUAGES (French, German, Latin, Russian, Spanish), MATH AND SCIENCES (botany, chemistry, forensic chemistry, geology, mathematics, microbiology, physics, zoology), PHILOSOPHY (philosophy), PREPROFESSIONAL (dentistry, engineering, home economics, law, medicine, pharmacy, social work, veterinary), SOCIAL SCIENCES (anthropology, economics, geography, government/political science, history, psychology, sociology). Seventeen percent of degrees are conferred in business, 16% in communication, 11% in health sciences, and 9% in education.

Required: Each college sets its own degree requirements, but all students must complete the university's general education requirements.

Special: The university offers study abroad programs in Spain, France, Austria, Italy, Mexico, and Canada. Other special programs include a 2-2 forestry program with North Carolina University, limited pass/fail options, a cooperative program in mental health technology with the Athens Mental Health Center, and a Center for Afro-American Studies.

Honors: Honors can be earned in any department; in certain departments, the Honors Tutorial College is a highly selective program offering one-to-one instruction. In addition to Phi Beta Kappa and Sigma Xi, there are 45 honor, professional, recognition, and departmental societies on campus.

Admissions: Approximately 90% of those who applied were accepted for the 1981-82 freshman class. The SAT scores of those who enrolled were as follows: Verbal—74% below 500, 20% between 500 and 599, 5% between 600 and 700, and 1% above 700; Math—63% below 500, 26% between 500 and 599, 10% between 600 and 700, and 1% above 700. On the ACT, 38% scored below 21, 18% between 21 and 23, 14% between 24 and 25, 18% between 26 and 28, and 11% above 28. There is open admission for Ohio residents. Besides standardized test scores, other factors taken into consideration are recommendations, special talents, advanced placement or honors courses, and extracurricular activities.

Procedure: The SAT or ACT is required (the ACT is preferred) and should be taken by March of the senior year. Deadlines for application are June 15 (fall), December 1 (winter), March 1 (spring), and May 1 (summer). Notification is on a rolling basis. Freshman are admitted at midyear and in the summer. An interview is not required, but is recommended. A $25 fee must accompany the application.

Special: Early admissions and deferred admissions plans are available. The application deadline for early admissions is June 15. AP and CLEP credit (for CLEP subject exams only) is accepted.

Transfer: For fall 1981, the university received 1172 transfer applications, accepted 874, and enrolled 542 students. A 2.0 GPA is required. A portfolio or an audition is required of Fine Arts applicants. D grades do not transfer. For students who complete fewer than 96 quarter hours at the university, the final year (three quarters) with 48 credit hours must be taken in residence; students who complete 96 or more quarter hours at the university only need to be in residence for the final quarter. The quarterly deadlines are August 1 (fall), December 1 (winter), March 1 (spring), and May 1 (summer).

Financial Aid: Sixty-eight percent of the students receive financial aid. About 30% work part-time on campus. The average award to freshmen from all sources totals $2000. The university is a member of CSS; the FAF is required. The application deadline for financial aid is April 1.

Foreign Students: About 10% of the full-time students are from foreign countries. An intensive English course, special counseling, and special organizations are available for these students.

Admissions: Foreign students must take the university's English proficiency exam. No college entrance exam is required.

Procedure: Application deadlines are May 1 (fall), September 1 (winter), December 1 (spring), and March 1 (summer). Proof of adequate funds for the calendar year must be presented. Foreign students must carry health insurance, which is available through the college for a fee.

Admissions Contact: James C. Walters, Director of Admissions.

OHIO WESLEYAN UNIVERSITY   C-3
Delaware, Ohio 43015   (614) 369-4431

F/T: 1155M, 1081W   Faculty: 137; IIB, ++$
P/T: 18M, 18W   Ph.D.'s: 74%
Grad: none   S/F Ratio: 14 to 1
Year: 3 10-wk terms, ss   Tuition: $5550
Appl: Mar. 1   R and B: $2110
2356 applied   1961 accepted   663 enrolled
SAT: 460V 493M   ACT: 22   COMPETITIVE

Ohio Wesleyan University, founded in 1842, is a private liberal arts institution affiliated with the Methodist Church. The library contains 400,000 volumes and 1140 microfilm items, and subscribes to 1200 periodicals.

Environment: The 200-acre campus is located in a town of 24,000, 20 miles from Columbus. A potpourri of architectural styles, the 70 buildings include a cafeteria and 3 dining halls, a physical education center, a science building, and a drama center; 2 buildings are listed in the *National Registry of Historic Buildings*. There are 7 dormitories; fraternity houses provide additional housing.

Student Life: Thirty percent of the students are from Ohio. Sixty-two percent come from public schools. Ninety percent live on campus. An estimated 20% of the students are members of the United Methodist Church; approximately 65% are Protestant. There are no compulsory religious services. Five percent of the students are minority-group members. University housing is both single-sex and coed. There are visiting privileges in single-sex housing. Students may keep cars on campus. Freshmen and sophomores must live in university housing. There are limited quiet hours and curfews.

Organizations: There are organizations on campus for Catholic, Jewish, and Protestant students. Fifty-four percent of the men belong to the 12 fraternities; 38% of the women are members of the 8 sororities. Students may choose from a wide range of special-interest, departmental and service clubs, music, drama, and publications groups, and on-campus cultural and social events. Students are actively involved in student government and participate with faculty members in all areas regarding student life, including administration and curriculum.

Sports: The university offers 15 intercollegiate sports for men and 11 for women. There are 11 intramural sports for both men and women.

Handicapped: Wheelchair ramps, special parking, elevators, and specially equipped rest rooms are available for physically handicapped students. Special class scheduling is also available. Fewer than 1% of the current student population are hearing-impaired.

Graduates: The freshman dropout rate is 20%; 60% remain to graduate. Eighty percent of those who graduate eventually pursue graduate study; about 3% enter medical school, and about 4% law school. About 65% pursue careers in business and industry.

Services: The university offers the following services free of charge: health care, psychological counseling, placement, career counseling, and tutoring.

Programs of Study: The university confers the B.A., B.Mus., B.S.N., and B.F.A. degrees. Bachelor's degrees are offered in the following subjects: AREA STUDIES (Black/Afro-American, family, urban), BUSINESS (accounting, management), EDUCATION (elementary, secondary), ENGLISH (English, journalism, literature, speech), FINE AND PERFORMING ARTS (art, art education, music, music education, theater/dramatics), HEALTH SCIENCES (art therapy, medical technology, music therapy, nursing, occupational therapy, physical therapy), LANGUAGES (French, German, Spanish), MATH AND SCIENCES (astronomy, botany, botany/bacteriology, chemistry, geology, mathematics, physics, zoology), PHILOSOPHY (humanities, philosophy, religion), PREPROFESSIONAL (dentistry, engineering, law, medicine, optometry, public administration, veterinary), SOCIAL SCIENCES (anthropology, economics, government/political science, history, human services, international business, international relations, psychology, sociology).

Required: There are 10 requirements to be selected from natural sciences, social sciences, humanities, and arts. One year of physical education is required.

Special: On a full-credit basis, self-instructional courses are available with native-speaking tutors in Arabic, Chinese, Greek, Hebrew, Hindi, Japanese, and Portuguese. Other special programs include limited pass/fail and credit/no entry options, and independent study. Achievement and university scholars, off-campus study from 1 term to a full year in Europe and in associated centers in Africa, the Middle East, India, Japan, and Latin America, and Washington and United Nations Semesters are also available. As part of Cross Cultural Studies, programs are available at 3 predominantly black southern universities. Courses on race and minorities, black history, black literature, and urbanization are offered. Teacher training programs lead to certification on the elementary and secondary levels. Students may design their own apprenticeship/work-study program, and also their own majors.

Honors: Virtually all departments offer honors programs. There are also 15 honor societies on campus, including Phi Beta Kappa.

Admissions: Eighty-three percent of those who applied were accepted for the 1981–82 freshman class. The SAT scores of those who enrolled were as follows: Verbal—71% below 500, 23% between 500 and 599, 5% between 600 and 700, and 1% above 700; Math—49% below 500, 40% between 500 and 599, 9% between 600 and 700, and 1% above 700. Candidates should be recommended by their schools and present 16 completed Carnegie units. Applicants should be in the upper half of their class and have a 2.0 average. The following factors are also considered important: advanced placement or honors courses, recommendations, impressions made during an interview, and extracurricular activities.

Procedure: The university requires the SAT or ACT and recommends a foreign language AT. The SAT or ACT may be taken in May of the junior year or December of the senior year. The preferred application deadlines are March 1 (fall), December 1 (winter), and February 1 (spring). An interview is strongly recommended but not required. There is an application fee of $20.

Special: Early decision and early and deferred admissions are possible. AP credit is accepted.

Transfer: For fall 1981, 139 students applied, 95 were accepted, and 55 enrolled. Transfers are considered for the freshman, sophomore, and junior classes. Applicants must have at least a 2.0 GPA; a 2.5 GPA is preferred. D grades do not transfer. All students must study at least 2 years at the university, and complete 18 credit units of the 37 needed to receive a bachelor's degree. Application deadlines are the same as those for freshman applicants.

Visiting: The university offers campus tours, including the "Slice of College Life" day-long program that shows all phases of campus life. Informal visits can also be arranged. Prospective students can sit in on classes or stay at the university. Contact the admissions office for details. The best times are Monday through Thursday, September through mid-November and January through May.

Financial Aid: Thirty percent of the students receive financial aid. Thirty percent work part-time on campus. Average aid to freshmen from all sources totals $5700. Most aid is available as packages consisting of grants, loans, and work-study. The university is a member of CSS. The FAF is required. The aid application deadline is February 15 (fall).

Foreign Students: About 4% of the full-time students come from foreign countries. The university offers these students an intensive English course, an intensive English program, special counseling, and sepcial organizations.

Admissions: Foreign students must score at least 500 on the TOEFL. No college entrance examination is required.

Procedure: The application deadlines are June 1 (fall), October 1 (winter), January 1 (spring), and March 1 (summer). Foreign students must present proof of adequate funds. They must also carry health insurance, which is available through the university.

Admissions Contact: Fred E. Weed, Dean of Admissions.

OTTERBEIN COLLEGE
Westerville, Ohio 43081

C-3

(614) 890-0004

F/T: 538M, 698W	Faculty: 90; IIB, av$
P/T: 137M, 319W	Ph.D.'s: 58%
Grad: none	S/F Ratio: 15 to 1
Year: qtrs, ss	Tuition: $4872
Appl: open	R and B: $1926
939 applied	686 accepted 342 enrolled
SAT or ACT: required	COMPETITIVE

Otterbein College, established in 1847 and affiliated with the United Methodist Church, sponsors a program of liberal arts education in the Christian tradition. The library contains 120,000 volumes and 8750 microfilm items, and subscribes to 850 periodicals.

Environment: The 70-acre campus is located in a suburban community adjoining Columbus. There are dining facilities for resident and nonresident students and a fine arts center. Nine dormitories accommodate about 800 students.

Student Life: Eighty percent of the students come from Ohio. Eighty-five percent are from public schools. Fifty-five percent live on campus. Only students who are local residents or who are 22 years of age may live off campus. Twenty-five percent of the students are Catholic, 50% Protestant, and 1% Jewish. Seven percent are minority-group members. College housing is single-sex; there are visiting privileges. Students may keep cars on campus.

Organizations: There are 6 fraternities, with a membership of 50% of the men, and 6 sororities, to which 50% of the women belong. Service and special-interest groups are active. Religious clubs on campus include the Council of Christian Associations and YM-YWCA. There is a strong campus government; excellent cooperation exists among faculty, administration, and students as members of college committees. There are 3 student-voting members on the Board of Trustees.

Sports: The college competes intercollegiately in 7 sports for men and 6 for women. There are 12 intramural sports for men and 8 for women.

Handicapped: Approximately 60% of the campus is accessible to wheelchair-bound students. Facilities include wheelchair ramps, special parking, elevators, specially equipped rest rooms, and lowered drinking fountains. Special class scheduling is also available. There are no visual or hearing-impaired students currently enrolled.

Graduates: The freshman dropout rate is 28%; 42% remain to graduate. About 15% of those who remain pursue graduate study; 4% enter medical school, 1% dental school, and 4% law school. Forty percent pursue careers in business and industry.

Services: The college offers free placement, career counseling, and tutoring. Placement services include a credential-resume service, and an on-campus employer interview program. Health care, psychological counseling, and remedial instruction are offered on a fee basis.

Programs of Study: The college confers the B.A., B.S., B.S.Ed., B.S.N., B.F.A., and B.Mus.Ed. degrees. Associate degrees are also offered. Bachelor's degrees are offered in the following subjects: BUSINESS (accounting, business administration, computer science), EDUCATION (elementary, health/physical, secondary), ENGLISH (English, journalism), FINE AND PERFORMING ARTS (art, art education, music, music education, theater/dramatics), HEALTH SCIENCES (medical technology, nursing), LANGUAGES (French, Spanish), MATH AND SCIENCES (biology, chemistry, mathematics, physics), PREPROFESSIONAL (dentistry, forestry, home economics, law, medicine, veterinary), SOCIAL SCIENCES (economics, government/political science, history, psychology, sociology). The college offers strong programs in premedicine and allied health areas, as well as radiologic technology and radiology management. Nineteen percent of degrees are conferred in education, 18% in health sciences, 15% in business, and 13% in social sciences.

Required: Directed toward the unifying theme of "human nature," the common courses allow the student to choose 10 of 18 offerings from various academic disciplines.

Special: The college offers a year abroad in France (Dijon) and Spain (Segovia), a term in Germany, Semester at Sea, the Washington Semester, and a term at McCurdy Schools, Vera Cruz, New Mexico. Also offered is an Individualized B.A. degree program. A 3-2 program in forestry and a 3-1 program in medical technology are offered. A cooperative education employment program offers the student up to 10 quarter hours of academic credit for 2 periods of paid employment.

Honors: Twelve national honor societies are open to qualified students.

Admissions: About 73% of those who applied were accepted for the 1981-82 freshman class. The SAT scores of those who enrolled were as follows: Verbal—60% below 500, 27% between 500 and 599, 10% between 600 and 700, and 3% above 700; Math—55% below 500, 30% between 500 and 599, 11% between 600 and 700, and 4% above 700. On the ACT, 48% scored below 21, 28% between 21 and 23, 14% between 24 and 25, 7% between 26 and 28, and 3% above 28. Applicants should score above 400 in each part of the SAT or 17 on the ACT. Candidates should be graduates of accredited high schools and rank in the upper half of their graduating class. Admissions officers also consider the following factors: advanced placement or honors courses, extracurricular activities, and evidence of special talent. Some preference is given to children of alumni.

Procedure: All candidates are required to take the SAT or the ACT in spring of the junior year or early in the senior year. New students may be admitted to any term. The college follows a rolling admissions policy. The application deadline is open. An interview is recommended. There is no application fee.

Special: There are early and deferred admissions plans. AP and CLEP credit is accepted.

Transfer: For fall 1981, 155 applications were received, 114 were accepted, and 69 students enrolled. Good academic standing is required. D grades do not transfer. The last 60 quarter hours must be taken at Otterbein, of the 180 needed for a bachelor's degree. The quarterly deadlines are the same as those for freshman applicants.

Visiting: There are no regularly scheduled visits; however, prospective students are welcome any time during the week for informal visits. Contact the admissions office for details and to make arrangements for sitting in on classes, guides, or to stay at the college.

Financial Aid: Sixty-five percent of all students receive financial aid. Sixty percent work part-time on campus. Average aid to freshmen from all sources is $3500. Loans are available from the federal government, local banks, and the college. Tuition may be paid in installments through one of several plans. The college is a member of the CSS. The FAF and the aid application should be filed. Application deadlines are open. Notification is on a rolling basis.

Foreign Students: About 3% of the full-time students come from foreign countries. The college offers these students an intensive English course, an intensive English program, special counseling, and special organizations.

Admissions: Foreign students must take the TOEFL or the University of Michigan Language Test. They must score at least 75 on the latter. No college entrance examination is required.

Procedure: The application deadlines are September 1 (fall), December 15 (winter), March 1 (spring), and June 1 (summer). Foreign students must present the results of a physical examination. They must also present proof of funds adequate to cover their entire period of study. They must carry health insurance, which is available through the college for a fee.

Admissions Contact: Morris F. Briggs, Dean of Admissions and Records.

RIO GRANDE COLLEGE   D-5
Rio Grande, Ohio 45674   (614) 245-5353

F/T: 526M, 747W   Faculty: 81; IIB, −$
P/T: none   Ph.D.'s: 48%
Grad: none   S/F Ratio: 15 to 1
Year: qtrs, ss   Tuition: $2700
Appl: open   R and B: $1920
500 applied   500 accepted   370 enrolled
ACT: 17   NONCOMPETITIVE

Rio Grande College is a private liberal arts college founded in 1876. It is under contract to operate a public 2-year community college. The library contains 70,000 volumes, subscribes to 550 periodicals, and has 8000 microfilm items.

Environment: The 170-acre campus is located in a rural area 12 miles from Gallipolis, Ohio. The 20 main buildings include a cafeteria, a physical-education building, and 6 dormitories that house 250 women and 300 men.

Student Life: Ninety-six percent of the students are from Ohio, and 75% live on campus in the single-sex dormitories.

Organizations: Campus activities include clubs, student government, and religious organizations for Catholics and Protestants. There are 4 fraternities, to which 28% of the men belong, and 4 sororities, to which 31% of the women belong.

Sports: The college participates on an intercollegiate level in 4 sports. Intramural sports also are offered.

Handicapped: About 40% of the campus is accessible to wheelchair-bound students. Newer buildings have wheelchair ramps, special parking areas, lowered drinking fountains, and specially equipped rest rooms. A staff of 3 assists handicapped students.

Graduates: Forty percent of the graduates pursue advanced degrees; 2% enter medical school, 1% dental school, and 2% law school. Thirty-five percent pursue careers in business or industry.

Services: The following services are offered free to students: diagnostic psychological counseling, health care, tutoring, remedial instruction, placement aid, and career counseling.

Programs of Study: The college awards the B.S. degree. Associate degrees also are available. Bachelor's degrees are offered in the following subjects: BUSINESS (accounting, business administration, business education, finance, management, marketing), EDUCATION (early childhood, elementary, health/physical, secondary, special), ENGLISH (English, speech), FINE AND PERFORMING ARTS (art, art education), HEALTH SCIENCES (medical technology, nursing), MATH AND SCIENCES (biology, chemistry, mathematics, natural sciences, physical sciences), PHILOSOPHY (humanities), PRE-PROFESSIONAL (dentistry, engineering, law, medicine, ministry, social work, veterinary), SOCIAL SCIENCES (economics, government/political science, history, social sciences, sociology). Sixty percent of the degrees are conferred in education, 35% in business, 2% in math and sciences, and 2% in the social sciences.

Special: The college offers remedial courses in English and mathematics. A general studies degree is offered. Students may design their own majors.

Admissions: All those who applied were accepted for the 1981–82 freshman class. Ten percent of those who enrolled ranked in the upper quarter of their graduating class, and 70% ranked in the upper half. Candidates should have a GPA of at least 1.7.

Procedure: Students must take the ACT as well as college placement examinations in English and math. There is a $15 application fee. Students are accepted for all terms.

Special: An early admissions plan is offered. AP and CLEP credit is accepted.

Transfer: Transfer students must be in good standing at their last school. At least 68 quarter hours must be taken in residence for a bachelor's degree.

Visiting: Regularly scheduled orientations include class visits, admissions and financial-aid interviews, and discussions with faculty members. Guides are available for informal visits. To arrange an overnight visit, contact the admissions office.

Financial Aid: About 65% of all students receive aid. Twenty-seven freshman scholarships are available. Loans may be secured from the federal and state governments, local banks, the college, and other sources. Campus jobs also are available. The average aid award to a freshman is $1800. The deadline for aid applications is April 15. The FAF is required.

Foreign Students: Students from foreign countries make up 5% of enrollment. The college offers these students an intensive English course and special counseling.

Admissions: Applicants must score at least 400 on the TOEFL. No college entrance exams are required.

Procedure: Application deadlines are open. Students must submit a completed medical form as proof of good health and must show evidence of adequate funds for 1 year. They also must carry health insurance, which is available through the college for a fee.

Admissions Contact: Lori Lowe, Director of Admissions.

UNIVERSITY OF AKRON   D-2
Akron, Ohio 44325   (216) 375-7100

F/T: 6873M, 6395W   Faculty: 731; I, −$
P/T: 4277M, 4622W   Ph.D.'s: 61%
Grad: 2418M, 2176W   S/F Ratio: 24 to 1
Year: sems, ss   Tuition: $1252 ($2722)
Appl: open   R and B: $1980
8244 applied   7664 accepted   4268 enrolled
SAT (mean): 438V 481M ACT: 18   LESS COMPETITIVE

University of Akron, founded in 1870, is a state-supported university, providing graduate and undergraduate instruction and research. The library contains 1,013,375 volumes and 687,926 microfilm items, and subscribes to 5013 periodicals.

Environment: The 140-acre campus is within walking distance from downtown Akron. There are 66 buildings, including the newly completed computer center. Thirteen dormitories in different styles can accommodate 2100 students. On- and off-campus apartments, fraternity houses, and sorority houses are also available.

Student Life: About 98% of the students are residents of Ohio. About 10% of the students live on campus; freshmen may live off campus. About 8% are minority-group members. Campus housing is single-sex, and there are visiting privileges. Students may keep cars on campus. Day-care facilities are available to full-time students, part-time students, faculty, and staff for a fee.

Organizations: There are 12 fraternities and 7 sororities on campus, to which 8% of the men and 5% of the women belong. Special-interest clubs, religious groups, and service clubs provide social and cultural entertainment. Art shows, concerts, debates, and films are sponsored by the various groups.

Sports: The university competes intercollegiately in 14 sports for men and 10 for women. There are 13 intramural sports for men and 9 for women.

Handicapped: The university has special facilities for physically handicapped students, but not in all buildings. About 85% of the campus is accessible to handicapped students. Fewer than 1% of the students currently enrolled have hearing or visual impairments.

Graduates: About 25% of the freshmen drop out during their first year; 75% remain to graduate. Ten percent of those who remain go on to graduate study.

Services: Free health care, tutoring, remedial instruction, career and psychological counseling, and job placement services are offered to all students. On-campus interviews and job listings are offered.

Programs of Study: The university confers the B.A., B.F.A., B.A. in Ed., B.S., B.S.M., B.Mus., B.S.Ed., and B.S.N. degrees among over 150 bachelor's degrees offered. Associate, master's, and doctoral programs are also available. Bachelor's degrees are offered in the following subjects: BUSINESS (accounting, business administration, business education, computer science, finance, management, marketing, real estate/insurance), EDUCATION (elementary, health/physical, secondary, special, technical), ENGLISH (English), FINE AND PERFORMING ARTS (art, art education, art history, dance, film/photography, music, music education, radio/TV, studio art, theater/dramatics),

690 OHIO

HEALTH SCIENCES (medical technology, nursing), LANGUAGES (French, German, Italian, Russian, Spanish), MATH AND SCIENCES (biology, chemistry, geology, mathematics, natural sciences, physics, statistics), PHILOSOPHY (classics, humanities, philosophy, religion), PREPROFESSIONAL (dentistry, law, medicine, veterinary), SOCIAL SCIENCES (economics, geography, government/political science, history, psychology, social sciences, sociology). Certificate programs are offered in computer science, life-span development, mid-careers, planning, public policy, and real estate. About 13% of the degrees are conferred in education and 15% in business.

Required: All students are required to take the general studies program.

Special: A 5-year cooperative program in engineering and combined B.A.-B.S. degrees are available.

Honors: There are 14 honor societies on campus. The university honors program is open to qualified students.

Admissions: About 93% of the students who applied were accepted for the 1981-82 freshman class. The SAT scores of those who enrolled were as follows: Verbal—70% below 500, 21% between 500 and 599, 6% between 600 and 700, and 0% above 700; Math—55% below 500, 30% between 500 and 599, 14% between 600 and 700, and 1% above 700. On the ACT, 32% scored below 21, 26% between 21 and 25, 10% between 26 and 29, and 1% above 30. Candidates should be high school graduates, and out-of-state students need a minimum GPA of 2.5. Only 20% of the freshman class can be from out of state. Other considerations, in order of importance, are advanced placement or honors courses, recommendations by school officials, and evidence of special talent.

Procedure: The SAT or ACT should be taken before January of the senior year. Applications should be submitted by January 1 in order to be considered for housing for the fall semester. There is a $25 fee; applications are accepted for all terms. Notification is on a rolling basis.

Special: AP and CLEP credit is accepted.

Transfer: For fall 1981, 1134 transfer students enrolled. A minimum GPA of 2.0 is required. D grades transfer. There is a 1-year residency requirement; 32 of 128 semester credits needed for a bachelor's degree must be completed at the university. Application deadlines are the same as those for freshmen.

Visiting: Tours of the campus are given Monday through Friday at 10:00 A.M. and 2:00 P.M. and on Saturdays at 9:30 A.M. and 10:30 A.M. Guides are available and prospective students can observe classes. Arrangements can be made through the admissions office.

Financial Aid: The university provides scholarships, grants, loans, and campus employment. There are 150 freshman scholarships available from a $50,000 fund. Loans can be secured from the federal and state governments, the university, and industrial, private or other sources. The university is a member of CSS and participates in the NDSL and BEOG federal programs. Average aid granted to freshmen from all sources combined is $1300. About 40% of all students receive financial assistance. Fifteen percent work part-time on campus. Applications for the presidential and honors scholarships should be filed by February 1; other university scholarship applications are due April 1. The FAF and University of Akron application are required.

Foreign Students: Five percent of the full-time students are from foreign countries. An intensive English program, special counseling, and special organizations are offered for these students.

Admissions: Foreign students must achieve a minimum score of 500 on the TOEFL or 150 on the University of Michigan Language Test. No college entrance exam is required.

Procedure: The application deadlines are June 15 (fall) and December 15 (winter). Foreign students must present proof of health consisting of references by a qualified physician. Proof of adequate funds to cover 1 academic year also must be presented. Foreign students must carry health insurance, which is available through the university for a fee.

Admissions Contact: John F. Stafford Jr., Assistant Director of Admissions.

UNIVERSITY OF CINCINNATI A-5
Cincinnati, Ohio 45226 (513) 475-3425

F/T: 10,105M, 8467W Faculty: n/av; I, +$
P/T: 6384M, 7442W Ph.D.'s: 75%
Grad: 2831M, 2514W S/F Ratio: 17 to 1
Year: qtrs, ss Tuition: $1479 ($3444)
Appl: open R and B: $2316
8204 applied 7009 accepted 5785 enrolled
SAT: 485V 495M ACT: 22 COMPETITIVE

University of Cincinnati, founded in 1819, is a state university consisting of 17 undergraduate and graduate divisions. The library contains 1.5 million volumes and 400,000 microfilm items, and subscribes to 8500 periodicals.

Environment: The campus is located in Clifton, a hilltop suburb 3 miles from downtown Cincinnati. The main campus has 65 buildings on 203 acres. The Medical Center, a 20-minute walk from the main campus, includes the College of Medicine, the General Hospital, the Kettering Laboratory, and the Holmes Hospital. There are 9 high-rise dorms, as well as fraternity and sorority houses.

Student Life: Approximately 52% of the students come from Cincinnati. About 40% of the students are residents: 20% live in residence halls, 2% in sorority houses, 6% in fraternity houses, and 12% in other university-approved facilities. University housing is both single-sex and coed. There are visiting privileges in single-sex housing. Day-care services are available to all full-time students. Smoking is allowed except in classes. Students may have cars, which must be registered.

Organizations: Approximately 645 women are affiliated with sororities and 750 men with fraternities. There are religious groups for students of all major faiths, and many other student groups as well. Cincinnati-area activities that appeal to students include the symphony, ballet, opera, zoo, Playhouse in the Park, and Kings Island.

Sports: The university competes intercollegiately in 11 sports. There are 21 intramural sports for men or women.

Handicapped: The entire campus is accessible to handicapped students. Facilities include special parking, wheelchair ramps, specially equipped rest rooms, and lowered telephones and drinking fountains.

Graduates: The freshman dropout rate is 15%; 60% remain to graduate. Of those who graduate, 25% go on to graduate study.

Services: Students receive the following services free of charge: psychological counseling, tutoring, remedial instruction, placement, and career counseling. Health care is available on a fee basis.

Programs of Study: The university confers the following degrees: B.A., B.S., B.M., and B.F.A. Associate, master's and doctoral programs are also offered. Bachelor's degrees are offered in the following subjects: AREA STUDIES (American, Black/Afro-American, Latin American, urban), BUSINESS (accounting, actuarial science, business administration, computer science, finance, management, marketing, quantitative analysis, real estate/insurance), EDUCATION (business, early childhood, elementary, health/physical, secondary, special), ENGLISH (English, journalism, literature, speech), FINE AND PERFORMING ARTS (art education, art history, dance, music, music education, radio/TV, studio art, theater/dramatics), HEALTH SCIENCES (medical technology, nursing), LANGUAGES (French, German, Greek/Latin, Hebrew, Russian, Spanish), MATH AND SCIENCES (biochemistry, biology, chemistry, earth science, geology, mathematics, natural sciences, physical sciences, physics, statistics), PHILOSOPHY (classics, humanities, philosophy), PREPROFESSIONAL (architecture, engineering, law, library science, medicine, pharmacy, social work), SOCIAL SCIENCES (anthropology, economics, geography, government/political science, history, international relations, psychology, social sciences, sociology).

Special: Cooperative plans, offering alternate work in academic subjects and industry, are available through the College of Business Administration (5 years), the College of Design, Architecture, and Art (6 years), the College of Engineering (5 years), and the Ohio College of Applied Science (2 years). The university also offers a unique 5-year cooperative program in city planning. Students in secondary education who pursue a 4-year program given jointly by the College of Arts and Sciences and the College of Education receive a degree from both colleges, as well as a state certificate for secondary teaching. Students in the College of Arts and Sciences may spend their junior year abroad, or 1 semester of the year at the American University in Washington, D.C.

Honors: An honors program is offered by the College of Arts and Sciences. Phi Beta Kappa and other honor societies are open to qualified students.

Admissions: Eighty-five percent of those who applied for the 1981-82 freshman class were accepted. The SAT scores of those who enrolled were as follows: Verbal—73% below 500, 15% between 500 and 599, 4% between 600 and 700, and 1% above 700; Math—55% below 500, 12% between 500 and 599, 15% between 600 and 700, and 2% above 700. On the ACT, 50% scored below 21, 12% between 21 and 23, 15% between 24 and 25, 11% between 26 and 28, and 2% above 28. Candidates should have completed 15 Carnegie units, have an average of at least C, and rank in the top half of their class. The university also considers recommendations by school officials, evidence of special talents, and advanced placement or honors courses.

Procedure: All applicants must take either the SAT or ACT. The SAT should be taken in May of the junior year or January or March of the senior year. Application deadlines are open. The university follows a rolling admissions plan. Applications should be submitted with a $25 fee.

Special: AP credit is accepted.

Transfer: For fall 1981, 2415 students applied, 1660 were accepted, and 1200 enrolled. A minimum GPA of 2.0 is required to apply from a 4-year college; 2.5 (or associate degree) from a 2-year college. Preference is given to students from other Ohio colleges. D grades do not transfer. There is a 1-year residency requirement. Transfer students must complete, at the university, 36 of the 190 to 200 credits needed for a bachelor's degree. Application deadlines are the same as those for freshman applicants.

Visiting: Guided tours can be arranged 6 days a week. Guides are also available for informal visits.

Financial Aid: About 52% of all students receive financial aid. University scholarships range from $100 to $2500 per year. EOG and CWS are also available. Tuition may be paid in installments through Tuition Plan, Inc. The university is a member of CSS. The FAF and the university's financial aid application are required. The deadline for both is June 1.

Foreign Students: Three percent of the full-time students come from foreign countries. The university offers these students an intensive English course and special counseling.

Admissions: Foreign students must score at least 520 on the TOEFL. No college entrance examination is required.

Procedure: The application deadlines are January 1 (fall and summer) and October 1 (winter). Foreign students must complete the university's health form. They must also submit proof of funds adequate to cover 1 year of study.

Admissions Contact: Robert W. Neel, Director of Admissions.

UNIVERSITY OF DAYTON B-4
Dayton, Ohio 45409 (513) 229-4411

F/T: 3520M, 2823W Faculty: 375; IIA, av$
P/T: 531M, 443W Ph.D.'s: 64%
Grad: 2072M, 1537W S/F Ratio: 18 to 1
Year: tri, ss Tuition: $3390
Appl: open R and B: $2010
4468 applied 3509 accepted 1760 enrolled
SAT: 467V 523M ACT: 22 COMPETITIVE

University of Dayton, founded in 1850, is a Roman Catholic university offering both liberal arts and technical training, as well as preparation for teaching, engineering, and business. The library contains over 800,000 volumes and 226,000 microfilm items, and subscribes to 6000 periodicals.

Environment: The university is located in a suburb on the southern edge of the city of Dayton on a 76-acre hilltop site. There are 35 buildings including a stadium, a physical activities center, 4 dormitories, a fine arts building, and music and theater halls.

Student Life: Approximately 50% of the students are from Ohio. Fifty percent of the students are residents. Fifty-six percent of entering freshmen come from public schools. About 73% of the students are Catholic, 18% percent are Protestant, and fewer than 1% are Jewish. About 7% are minority-group members. University housing is single-sex; there are visiting privileges. Students with permission may keep cars on campus.

Organizations: There are 15 local fraternities, to which 33% of the men belong, and 8 sororities, to which 33% of the women belong. Extracurricular activities include student government, the University Activities Committee, Central Women's Organization, a school newspaper, a literary magazine, various musical groups, University Players, and a debating team. There are religious organizations and places of worship on campus for Catholics, and nearby for other faiths.

Sports: The university competes intercollegiately in 10 sports for men and 6 for women. There are also 17 intramural sports for men and 13 for women.

Handicapped: Facilities for the physically handicapped include wheelchair ramps, special parking, elevators, and specially equipped rest rooms. A special counselor is available.

Graduates: The freshman dropout rate is 14%. Sixty percent remain to graduate. Eleven percent of those who remain pursue graduate study.

Services: Students receive the following services free of charge: placement, career counseling, tutoring, health care, and psychological counseling.

Programs of Study: The university confers the B.A. and B.S. degrees. Associate, master's, and doctoral degrees are also offered. Bachelor's degrees are offered in the following subjects: AREA STUDIES (American), BUSINESS (accounting, business administration, computer science, finance, management, marketing), EDUCATION (early childhood, elementary, health/physical, secondary, special), ENGLISH (English, journalism), FINE AND PERFORMING ARTS (art, art education, dance, film/photography, music, music education, radio/TV, theater/dramatics), HEALTH SCIENCES (medical technology), LANGUAGES (French, German, Spanish), MATH AND SCIENCES (biology, chemistry, geology, mathematics, physical sciences, physics), PHILOSOPHY (philosophy), PREPROFESSIONAL (dentistry, engineering, home economics, law, medicine, ministry, social work), SOCIAL SCIENCES (anthropology, economics, government/political science, history, international relations, psychology, social sciences, sociology).

Required: All students must take course work in English, communication skills, philosophy, and theology courses.

Special: Independent study programs are offered. There is a program in engineering with Wilberforce University. A General Studies degree (no major) is offered. Students may design their own majors. Recent curricular innovations include minicourses, interdisciplinary studies, internships, and self-directed learning. Cooperative programs are available in certain majors.

Honors: Honors programs are available to qualified students. Thirty selected freshmen participate each year.

Admissions: About 79% of those who applied were accepted for the 1981-82 freshman class. Of those who enrolled, the SAT scores were as follows: Verbal—64% below 500, 28% between 500 and 599, 7% between 600 and 700, and 1% above 700; Math—38% below 500, 37% between 500 and 599, 19% between 600 and 700, and 5% above 700. On the ACT, 28% scored below 21, 36% between 21 and 24, 30% between 25 and 29, and 6% above 30. Generally, candidates must be graduates of an accredited high school, rank in the top 60% of their graduating class, have an average of 80 or better, have good high school recommendations, and have completed 15 to 18 Carnegie units. The school indicates that in addition to these qualifications they consider the following factors: advanced placement or honors courses, extracurricular activities record, impressions made during an interview, personality, and leadership record.

Procedure: Either the SAT or ACT is acceptable and should be taken by April of the senior year, preferably in the junior year. Students may enter for the fall, spring, or summer terms. Application deadlines are open. Notification is on a rolling basis. An interview is recommended. A $15 application fee must accompany the student's credentials and application.

Special: Early decision and early admissions plans are avaialble. AP and CLEP credit is accepted.

Transfer: For fall 1981, the university received 631 transfer applications, accepted 410, and enrolled 284 students. An associate degree or good academic standing (2.0 GPA) is required. D grades do not transfer. There is a 30-hour residency requirement of the 120 hours needed for a bachelor's degree. Application deadlines are open.

Visiting: Orientations are held for prospective students. Guided tours and interviews can be scheduled any weekday 9 A.M. to 4 P.M. Daylong visits with a student guide can be arranged with the admissions office. Visitors may remain overnight on campus.

Financial Aid: About 78% of all students receive some form of financial aid. Thirty-five percent work part-time on campus. Average aid to freshmen from all sources is $3336. Loans are available from state and federal governments, the university, and private sources. The university is a member of the CSS. The FAF is required. The priority deadline for aid application is April 30. Notification is on a rolling basis.

Foreign Students: About 4% of the full-time students come from foreign countries. The university offers these students an intensive English course, special counseling, and special organizations.

Admissions: Foreign students must take the TOEFL or the Comprehensive English Language Test. No college entrance examination is required.

Procedure: The application deadlines are July 1 (fall), November 1 (winter), and April 1 (spring and summer). Foreign students must present proof of funds adequate to cover their entire period of study. They must pay a special application fee. They must also carry health insurance, which is available through the university for a fee.

Admissions Contact: Myron Achbach, Director of Admissions.

UNIVERSITY OF STEUBENVILLE E-3
(Formerly College of Steubenville)
Steubenville, Ohio 43952 (614) 283-3771

F/T: 297M, 366W	Faculty: 43; IIB, av$
P/T: 28M, 41W	Ph.D.'s: 33%
Grad: 67M, 23W	S/F Ratio: 15 to 1
Year: sems, ss	Tuition: $3690
Appl: see profile	R and B: $2178
437 applied	317 accepted	146 enrolled
SAT: 429V 455M	ACT: 20	COMPETITIVE

University of Steubenville, founded by the Franciscan Friars in 1946, is known internationally as a center for Christian renewal. High-quality education and a firm foundation for Christian living are stressed by the university. The library contains 135,000 volumes and 15,000 bound periodicals.

Environment: The 100-acre suburban campus is 700 feet above the Ohio River overlooking Steubenville and Weirton (West Virginia). It is 40 miles from Pittsburgh. The 11 college buildings include 4 dormitories, a chapel, and a College Center.

Student Life: About 35% of the students come from Ohio, and 58% are from public schools. Students come from 35 states and 5 foreign countries. Eight percent are minority-group members. About 67% of the students live on campus. Freshmen must live on campus. Campus housing is single-sex, and there are visiting privileges. There are also fraternities, sororities, and Christian faith "households." Students may keep cars on campus.

Organizations: Approximately 25% of the men belong to the 3 fraternities, and 35% of the women to the 3 sororities. The university offers a number of special-interest clubs and organizations. The Activities Board, a branch of student government, coordinates social and cultural activities.

Sports: The university has no intercollegiate teams. Eight intramural sports are offered for men and 7 for women.

Handicapped: Approximately 33% of the campus is accessible to physically handicapped students. Facilities include special parking, wheelchair ramps, and specially equipped rest rooms.

Graduates: The freshman dropout rate is 40%; 50% remain to graduate. Twenty-five percent of those who remain pursue graduate study, with 3% entering law school. About 40% pursue careers in business and industry.

Services: Students receive the following services free of charge: placement, health care, psychological counseling, tutoring, and career counseling. Placement services include job listings, job interviews, and resume writing.

Programs of Study: The university confers the B.A., B.S., and B.S.N. degrees. Associate and master's degree programs are also offered. Bachelor's degrees are offered in the following subjects: BUSINESS (accounting, business administration, finance, management), EDUCATION (elementary, secondary, special), ENGLISH (communications, drama, journalism, literature), HEALTH SCIENCES (medical technology, nursing), LANGUAGES (French), MATH AND SCIENCES (biology, chemistry, mathematics), PHILOSOPHY (humanities, philosophy, religion), PREPROFESSIONAL (engineering), SOCIAL SCIENCES (criminal justice, economics, government/political science, history, mental health, psychology, sociology). About twenty-nine percent of degrees are conferred in social sciences, 21% in business, 11% in math and sciences, and 11% in philosophy.

Special: The university offers a combination degree program in medical technology. A practicum is required in sociology, psychology, mental health, and education. Internships are available for many degree programs.

Honors: The university has 2 honor societies for qualified students.

Admissions: Approximately 73% of those who applied were accepted for the 1981–82 freshman class. The SAT scores of those who enrolled were as follows: Verbal—79% below 500, 17% between 500 and 599, 4% between 600 and 700, and 0% above 700; Math—60% below 500, 31% between 500 and 599, 9% between 600 and 700, and 0% above 700. On the ACT, 44% scored below 21, 36% between 21 and 23, 9% between 24 and 25, 7% between 26 and 28, and 4% above 28. Candidates should have completed 15 Carnegie units, have an average of at least C, have a minimum combined SAT score of 800 or a composite ACT score of 18, have a high school GPA of 2.0 or more, and rank in the top 60% of their graduating class. The college also considers the following factors, in order of importance: advanced placement or honors courses, recommendations, extracurricular activities, and special talents.

Procedure: The SAT or ACT is required. Admission decisions are made on a rolling basis. There is a $15 application fee.

Special: Early admission and early decision plans are available, with a January 15 deadline for the former. AP and CLEP credit is accepted.

Transfer: For fall 1981, 267 students applied, 202 were accepted, and 119 enrolled. Applicants should have a minimum GPA of 2.0, a minimum combined SAT score of 800, and a composite ACT score of at least 18. Grades of C or better transfer. Thirty of a minimum 124 semester hours must be taken in residence for a bachelor's degree. Transfers are considered for admission to fall, spring, and summer classes on a rolling basis.

Visiting: Scheduled visiting is recommended. Students should contact the admissions office to set up an appointment.

Financial Aid: Seventy percent of all students receive financial aid. Loans are available from the federal and state governments and local bank. Fifty-two percent of students work part-time on campus. The university is a member of CSS, and the FAF is required. Aid is distributed on a first-come, first-served basis; notification is on a rolling basis.

Foreign Students: Two percent of the full-time students come from foreign countries. The university offers these students participation in special organizations.

Admissions: Foreign students must achieve a TOEFL score of at least 400 to enter the university. A minimum combined SAT score of 800 or composite ACT score of at least 18 is also required.

Procedure: Admissions are on a rolling basis for fall and spring entry. Foreign students must present proof of funds adequate to cover 1 year of study. They must also present proof of health.

Admissions Contact: David Skiviat, Director of Admissions.

UNIVERSITY OF TOLEDO B-1
Toledo, Ohio 43606 (419) 537-2696

F/T: 6041M, 5056W	Faculty: 652; I, +$
P/T: 2963M, 3814W	Ph.D.'s: 64%
Grad: 1797M, 1446W	S/F Ratio: 17 to 1
Year: qtrs, ss	Tuition: $1260 ($2862)
Appl: Sept. 1	R and B: $2070
5551 applied	4973 accepted	3399 enrolled
SAT: 450V 450M	ACT: 19	COMPETITIVE

University of Toledo is a state-assisted institution, founded in 1872 in a democratic tradition of education. It offers 2-year technical college programs, baccalaureate degree programs, and graduate work. The library houses over 1 million volumes and 726,087 microfilm items, and subscribes to 4470 periodicals.

Environment: The university occupies 2 campuses that encompass 407 acres and are located in a residential section on the western edge of Toledo. Among the more prominent buildings are the Centennial Hall multi-purpose complex, the Center for the Performing Arts, and the Adult and Continuing Education Building.

Student Life: Approximately 58% of the students are residents of northwestern Ohio. Seventy-seven percent of entering freshmen come from public schools. About 8% of the students live on campus. University housing is both single-sex and coed. There are visiting privileges in single-sex housing. Students may keep cars on campus. Day-care services are available to all students, faculty, and staff.

Organizations: The university offers student governing bodies, professional and social societies, 21 national fraternities and sororities (to which 7% of the men and 5% of the women belong), and philosophic societies. There are religious organizations for the major faiths. The student body publishes a biweekly newspaper.

Sports: The university fields intercollegiate teams in 11 sports for men and in 7 for women. There are 10 intramural sports for men and 8 for women.

Handicapped: All of the campus is accessible to physically handicapped students. Wheelchair ramps, special parking, elevators, special rest rooms, lowered drinking fountains, and lowered telephones are available.

Graduates: The freshman dropout rate is 9%; 48% remain to graduate.

Services: The university offers placement services, career counseling, health care, tutoring, and psychological counseling to students free of charge. The placement program includes resume and interview seminars and part-time placement. Remedial instruction is available on a fee basis.

Programs of Study: The university confers the following degrees: B.A., B.S., B.B.A., B.Ed., B.S. in Eng., and B.S.Pharm. degrees. There are also associate, master's, and doctoral programs. Bachelor's degrees are offered in the following subjects: AREA STUDIES (American, Asian, Latin American, urban), BUSINESS (accounting, business administration, business education, computer science, finance, management, marketing, real estate/insurance), EDUCATION (early childhood, elementary, health/physical, physical therapy, recreation, secondary, special), ENGLISH (English, journalism, speech), FINE AND PERFORMING ARTS (art, art education, art history, dance, music, music education, radio/TV, theater/dramatics), HEALTH SCIENCES (medical technology, nursing, speech therapy), LANGUAGES (French, German, Greek/Latin, Spanish), MATH AND SCIENCES (biology, chemistry, earth science, geology, mathematics, physics), PHILOSOPHY (classics, humanities, philosophy), PRE-PROFESSIONAL (engineering, forestry, pharmacy, social work), SOCIAL SCIENCES (anthropology, economics, geography, government/political science, history, international relations, psychology, social sciences, sociology).

Required: Curriculum requirements vary among the various colleges of the university.

Special: The university offers seminars, independent study, and an experimental integrated curriculum open to students transferring to the University College after having completed 30 quarter hours.

Honors: A 4-year honors program includes exemption from required courses. Blue Key, Peppers, and 12 national honor societies have chapters on campus.

Admissions: Ninety percent of those who applied were accepted for the 1981–82 freshman class. Of those who enrolled in a recent freshman class, the ACT scores were as follows: 31% between 16 and 20, and 41% above 21. Candidates for admission to the colleges of Arts and Sciences, Business Administration, Education, and Pharmacy who are Ohio residents will receive immediate notice of acceptance if they have higher than a 2.0 GPA and SAT scores of more than 400 verbal and 400 mathematical, or an ACT composite score of 18. Out-of-state candidates should have slightly higher scores.

Procedure: The SAT or ACT is required; the ACT is preferred. The deadlines for application are September 1 (fall), December 1 (winter), March 1 (spring), and June 1 (summer). There is a rolling admissions policy. Applications should be submitted with a $20 fee.

Special: CLEP and AP credit is accepted.

Transfer: Recently, 1880 applications were received, and 1041 students enrolled. Transfers are accepted for all classes. Applicants must have a 2.0 GPA and good academic standing. D grades do not transfer. All students must complete, at the university, at least 45 of the 186 to 200 quarter hours needed to receive a bachelor's degree. Deadlines for transfer applications are September 1 (fall), December 1 (winter), March 1 (spring), and June 1 (summer).

Visiting: A visit and tour are strongly recommended. Regularly scheduled orientations, with guided tours, are arranged by the office of admissions.

Financial Aid: Thirty-three percent of all students receive financial aid in the form of scholarships, loans, or grants; 60% of the students work part-time. Average aid to freshmen is $1000. The university participates in the CSS and requires the FAF or FFS. There is CWS in all departments. The suggested aid application deadline is March 1.

Foreign Students: About 5% of the full-time students come from foreign countries. The university offers these students an intensive English course, an intensive English program, special counseling, and special organizations.

Admissions: Foreign students must score at least 80 on the University of Michigan Language Test. No college entrance examination is required. Placement tests must be taken in math, chemistry, and a verbal area.

Procedure: The application deadlines are September 1 (fall), December 1 (winter), March 1 (spring), and June 1 (summer). Foreign students must submit proof of funds adequate to cover 1 year of full-time study. They must pay out-of-state tuition fees. They must also carry health insurance, which is available through the university for a fee.

Admissions Contact: Richard J. Eastop, Director of Admissions.

OHIO 693

URBANA COLLEGE   B-3
Urbana, Ohio 43078   (513) 652-1301

F/T: 362M, 195W	Faculty: 27; n/av
P/T: 84M, 53W	Ph.D.'s: 50%
Grad: none	S/F Ratio: 14 to 1
Year: qtrs, ss	Tuition: $3007
Appl: open	R and B: $1890
167 applied   153 accepted   100 enrolled
ACT: 15	LESS COMPETITIVE

Founded in 1850, Urbana College is a church-related institution that offers curricula in the liberal arts and education. It is affiliated with the Swedenborgian Church. The library contains 57,000 volumes and 5000 microfilm items, and subscribes to 350 periodicals.

Environment: The 128-acre campus is in a rural environment 12 miles from Springfield in Urbana, a city of 13,000 people. Campus buildings include residence halls, a gymnasium, and a student lounge.

Student Life: Eighty-four percent of the students are from Ohio; 50% live on campus. Drinking is permitted on campus in compliance with Ohio state law. About 22% of the students are minority-group members. Campus housing is coed and single-sex; there are visiting privileges in single-sex dorms. Students may keep cars on campus.

Organizations: There are no fraternities or sororities. Extracurricular activities include the newspaper, choir, yearbook, theater productions, student government, film series, concert-lecture series, and dances.

Sports: The college fields 4 intercollegiate teams for men and 3 for women. There are 3 intramural sports for men and 3 for women.

Handicapped: About 50% of the campus is accessible to wheelchair-bound students. Facilities include wheelchair ramps, special parking, and specially equipped rest rooms.

Graduates: The freshman dropout rate is 20%; 60% remain to graduate. Fifteen percent of those who graduate pursue advanced study.

Services: Students receive the following services free of charge: placement, career counseling, health care, psychological counseling, tutoring, and remedial instruction.

Programs of Study: The college confers the B.A. and B.S. degrees. Associate degrees are also awarded. Bachelor's degrees are offered in the following subjects: BUSINESS (accounting, business administration, economics, management, marketing, personnel management, small business enterprise), EDUCATION (early childhood, elementary, health/physical, secondary, special), ENGLISH (English), MATH AND SCIENCES (biology, chemistry, mathematics, physics), PHILOSOPHY (humanities, philosophy, religion), SOCIAL SCIENCES (economics, social sciences). Fifty-four percent of the degrees are conferred in business, 20% are in education, and 14% are in student-designed majors.

Required: All students must take courses in the humanities, natural sciences, and social sciences.

Special: It is possible to earn combined B.A.-B.S. degrees in various subjects. Student-designed majors are permitted.

Admissions: Ninety-two percent of those who applied were accepted for the 1981–82 freshman class. The ACT scores of those who enrolled were as follows: 60% below 21, 35% between 21 and 23, 2% between 24 and 25, 2% between 26 and 28, and 1% above 28. Applicants must be recommended by high school authorities and have a minimum high school GPA of 2.0. They also should have completed 15 Carnegie units.

Procedure: The ACT or SAT is required. Application deadlines are open. A rolling admissions policy is used. There is a $10 application fee.

Special: Early admissions and deferred admissions plans are available. CLEP and AP credit is accepted.

Transfer: For fall 1981, 29 transfer students enrolled. A GPA of at least 2.0 is required. There is a residency requirement of 1 year. Students must complete, at the college, 45 of the 190 credits required for the bachelor's degree. Grades of C and above transfer. Application deadlines are open.

Visiting: Although there are no regularly scheduled orientations, prospective students may take guided tours of the campus on weekdays. Visitors may sit in on classes and remain overnight on campus. Visits can be arranged through the admissions office.

Financial Aid: About 70% of the students receive aid; 34% work part-time on campus. Loans may be obtained from federal and state funds, local banks, and the college. The FAF is required, and the application deadline is open.

694 OHIO

Foreign Students: About 3% of the full-time students come from foreign countries. The college offers these students an intensive English course, special counseling, and special organizations.

Admissions: Foreign students must achieve a minimum TOEFL score of 500; no college entrance exams are required.

Procedure: Application deadlines are August 15 (fall) and December 1 (winter). Foreign students must present proof of adequate funds. They must also carry health insurance, which is available through the college for a fee.

Admissions Contact: Vicky Dixon, Assistant Director of Admissions.

URSULINE COLLEGE   D-1
Pepper Pike, Ohio 44124   (216) 449-4200

F/T: 14M, 485W	Faculty:	48; IIB, – –$
P/T: 31M, 590W	Ph.D.'s:	27%
Grad: none	S/F Ratio:	14 to 1
Year: sems, ss	Tuition:	$2830
Appl: open	R and B:	$1700
212 applied	167 accepted	133 enrolled
SAT: 414V 420M	ACT: 17	LESS COMPETITIVE

Ursuline College, founded in 1871, is a private liberal arts college related to the Roman Catholic Church and conducted by the Ursuline Nuns of Cleveland. The library contains 70,000 volumes, and subscribes to 275 periodicals.

Environment: The 115-acre campus is in a suburban area 15 miles from Cleveland. There are 9 buildings, including an academic building, a science center, a student center, an art gallery, and 2 residence halls that can accommodate 200 women. The physical education center houses the student activity center, pool, and gym.

Student Life: Ninety-one percent of the students are from Ohio and 8% are from other states. About 45% of entering freshmen come from public schools. Thirty-eight percent of the students live on campus, 37% live in the dormitories, and 1% live in other college-approved housing. The majority of students (64%) are Catholic, but attendance at religious services is not required. Campus housing is single-sex; there are visiting privileges. Students may keep cars on campus.

Organizations: There are no fraternities or sororities; professional and service organizations serve as social groups. Extracurricular activities include chorus, drama, journalism, publications, service clubs, and a religious club (Christian Life Community). Cultural events include art shows, concerts, films, lectures, plays, and recitals.

Sports: There is no intercollegiate athletics program. There are 7 intramural sports.

Handicapped: The entire campus is accessible to wheelchair-bound students. Special facilities include wheelchair ramps and elevators.

Graduates: The freshman dropout rate is 14%; 70% remain to graduate. Eighteen percent of those who remain pursue graduate study.

Services: Students receive the following services free of charge: placement, career counseling, health care, and psychological counseling. Tutoring and remedial instruction are available on a fee basis.

Programs of Study: The college confers the B.A. and B.S.N. degrees. Associate and master's programs are also offered. Bachelor's degrees are offered in the following subjects: AREA STUDIES (American), BUSINESS (business administration, communication arts-public relations, fashion design, fashion merchandising), EDUCATION (adult, early childhood, elementary, secondary, special), ENGLISH (English), FINE AND PERFORMING ARTS (art, art education, graphic design, interior design, music, music education), HEALTH SCIENCES (dietetics, health services management, nursing), LANGUAGES (French, Spanish), MATH AND SCIENCES (biology, biology-chemistry, mathematics), PHILOSOPHY (humanities, philosophy), PRE-PROFESSIONAL (home economics), SOCIAL SCIENCES (behavioral sciences, history, psychology, social sciences, sociology). Thirty-one percent of degrees are conferred in health sciences, 26% in social sciences, and 22% in applied sciences.

Special: It is possible to earn combined B.A.-B.S. degrees in various subjects, including dietetics. Student-designed majors are permitted. The college offers admission to college after completion of the junior year in high school, independent study courses, pass/fail options, summer study abroad, advanced placement, and field work in sociology. The college also offers a 4-year, fully accredited baccalaureate program in nursing.

Honors: There are 3 honor societies on campus; honor programs are offered for qualified students.

Admissions: About 79% of those who applied were accepted for the 1981-82 freshman class. The SAT scores of those who enrolled were as follows: Verbal—79% below 500, 18% between 500 and 599, 3% between 600 and 700, and 0% above 700; Math—69% below 500, 27% between 500 and 599, 4% between 600 and 700, and 0% above 700. The ACT scores of those who enrolled were as follows: 40% below 21, 34% between 21 and 23, 24% between 24 and 25, 1% between 26 and 28, and 1% above 28. Applicants must be graduates of accredited high schools, have a high school GPA of 2.5 or better, and complete 15 Carnegie high school units. Other considerations are advanced placement or honors courses and recommendations by school officials.

Procedure: The SAT or ACT should be taken before March of the senior year. The application, a $15 fee, test scores, and high school record should be submitted to the college as soon as possible. The college follows a rolling admissions policy. Students are admitted to all terms.

Special: An early decision and an early admissions plan are available. AP and CLEP credit is accepted.

Transfer: For fall 1981, 61 transfer students applied, 43 were accepted, and 37 enrolled. Transfers are accepted for the freshman and sophomore classes; grades of C or above transfer. Students must be in good standing at their present college, have a GPA of at least 2.5, and complete at least 30 hours of the 128 required to earn a bachelor's degree, at Ursuline. Deadlines are the same as those for freshmen.

Visiting: Orientation for prospective students includes tours, interviews, class visits, and faculty and student presentations. Guided tours can be scheduled through the office of admissions on weekdays. Prospective students may remain overnight on campus.

Financial Aid: Sixty percent of all students receive financial aid; 30% work part-time on campus. The college provides scholarships, loans, grants, and campus employment. About 20 freshman scholarships are available. Loans are available through the federal and state governments, local banks, and the college. The average amount of aid from all sources is $2000; the maximum is $3700. The college is a member of CSS. The application deadline is open; the FAF must be filed.

Admissions Contact: Martin J. Carney, Assistant Director of Admissions.

WALSH COLLEGE   D-2
Canton, Ohio 44720   (216) 499-7090
 1(800) 362-9846 in Ohio

F/T: 237M, 482W	Faculty:	44; IIB, –$
P/T: 85M, 135W	Ph.D.'s:	55%
Grad: 16M, 65W	S/F Ratio:	18 to 1
Year: sems, ss	Tuition:	$3280
Appl: Aug. 26	R and B:	$1750
729 applied	644 accepted	265 enrolled
SAT: 438V 471M	ACT: 19	COMPETITIVE

Walsh College, founded in 1958, is a private liberal arts college operated by the Brothers of Christian Instruction. The library contains 75,000 volumes and 2700 microfilm items, and subscribes to 600 periodicals.

Environment: The 58-acre campus is in a suburban area 5 miles from Canton and 20 miles from Akron. There are 2 dormitories; 1 accommodates 200 men and the other accommodates 200 women.

Student Life: Eighty-five percent of the students are from Ohio. The majority are Catholic, but there are no compulsory church attendance requirements. Sixty percent of the entering freshmen come from public schools. Fifty percent of the students live on campus in the coed dorms. Cars are permitted with the permission of the dean of students.

Organizations: There are no fraternities or sororities. A wide variety of extracurricular activities and social and cultural events is available.

Sports: The college fields 7 intercollegiate teams for men and 3 for women. There are 8 intramural sports for men and 8 for women.

Handicapped: Fifty percent of the campus is accessible to the physically handicapped. Two percent of the students currently enrolled are visually impaired, 2% are hearing-impaired. There are no special facilities for the physically handicapped, and no special counselors.

Graduates: The freshman dropout rate is 20%; 80% remain to graduate. Fifteen percent of the students pursue graduate study after graduation; 3% percent enter medical school, 4% law school, 2% dental school. Forty percent pursue careers in business and industry.

Services: The following services are available free of charge: placement, career counseling, health care, tutoring, remedial instruction, and psychological counseling. Job placement services are available to undergraduates.

Programs of Study: The college confers the B.A. and B.S. degrees. Associate and master's programs are also offered. Bachelor's degrees are offered in the following subjects: AREA STUDIES (international studies), BUSINESS (accounting, business administration, computer science, finance, management, real estate/insurance), EDUCATION (early childhood, elementary, health/physical, secondary, special), ENGLISH (English, literature), HEALTH SCIENCES (medical technology, nursing), LANGUAGES (French, Spanish), MATH AND SCIENCES (biology, chemistry, integrated life science, mathematics, natural sciences), PHILOSOPHY (philosophy, religion), PREPROFESSIONAL (dentistry, forestry, law, medicine, pharmacy, veterinary), SOCIAL SCIENCES (economics, government/political science, history, international relations, psychology, social sciences, sociology). Thirty-five percent of degrees are conferred in business, 15% in education, and 4% in math and sciences.

Special: The college offers interdisciplinary seminars. Study abroad in Canada or Mexico is possible. The college also offers a 3-2 program in forestry in conjunction with the University of Michigan, leading to a B.A. from Walsh and a B.S. in forestry.

Honors: The English, history, and math departments offer honors programs.

Admissions: Eighty-eight percent of those who applied were accepted for the 1981–82 freshman class. The ACT scores of those who enrolled were as follows: 25% below 21, 38% between 21 and 23, 17% between 24 and 25, 17% between 26 and 28, and 3% above 28. Applicants should be graduates of an accredited high school, have a minimum GPA of 2.0, be recommended by their high school, rank in the top half of their class, and have completed 15 high school units. The following also enter into the admissions decision: the reputation of the candidate's high school, personality, extracurricular activities, leadership record, impressions made during a personal interview, and advanced placement or honors courses.

Procedure: The SAT or ACT is required. The application deadline for fall entry is August 26. A rolling admissions plan is used. There is a $15 application fee.

Special: Early and deferred admissions plans are available. The deadline for applying for early admission is 1 week prior to the start of the semester; an interview is recommended. CLEP credit is accepted.

Transfer: For fall 1981, 65 transfer students applied, 60 were accepted, and 60 enrolled. Transfers are accepted for all classes; grades of C and above transfer. Transfers must have a 2.0 minimum accumulated GPA; in secondary education, a 2.5 accumulated average at the end of the sophomore year is required. Students must complete, at the college, at least 32 of the 130 credits required to earn the bachelor's degree. Transfer deadlines are the same as those for freshman applicants.

Visiting: There are regularly scheduled orientations for prospective students. There are guides for informal visits; visitors may sit in on classes and stay at the school. Best times for campus visits are weekdays 8 A.M. to 5 P.M. The admissions office should be contacted to arrange a visit.

Financial Aid: The college awards many freshman scholarships each year in varying amounts. Financial assistance is available in the form of scholarships, grants-in-aid, and loans. About 85% of all students receive financial aid; about 53% work part-time on campus. The college is a member of CSS; the FAF is required. The application deadline is August 1.

Foreign Students: About 6% of the full-time students come from foreign countries. The college offers these students an intensive English course, special counseling, and special organizations.

Admissions: Foreign students must achieve a minimum TOEFL score of 500; no college entrance exams are required.

Procedure: Application deadlines are August 15 (fall) and January 4 (spring). Foreign students must present proof of funds adequate to cover 1 year of study. They must also carry health insurance, which is available through the college for a fee.

Admissions Contact: Fran Kehoe, Dean of Admissions.

WILBERFORCE UNIVERSITY
Wilberforce, Ohio 45384

B–4
(513) 376-2911

F/T: 492M, 542W
P/T: none
Grad: none
Year: tri, ss
Appl: June 1
1044 applied   630 accepted
ACT: required

Faculty: 47; IIB, – – $
Ph.D.'s: 30%
S/F Ratio: 16 to 1
Tuition: $2800
R and B: $1530
328 enrolled
COMPETITIVE

Wilberforce University, founded in 1856 and under the auspices of the African Methodist Episcopal Church since 1863, has continued for more than a century in dedicated service to black students. The library contains 55,000 volumes and subscribes to 350 periodicals.

Environment: The 152-acre campus, located in a rural area, contains 4 residence halls, a classroom-science building, a gymnasium, a learning center, a chapel, an administration building, a fine arts building, and an auditorium. The college also sponsors fraternity and sorority houses, on-campus apartments, and married student housing.

Student Life: Almost half of the students are from Middle Atlantic states. Although Wilberforce's religious tradition is historical and strong, there is no denominational program required of students or faculty. About 99% of the students are black. Almost all students live on campus. Campus housing is coed and single-sex; there are visiting privileges in single-sex housing. Students may keep cars on campus.

Organizations: There are 4 national and 2 local fraternities, to which 20% of the men belong. Twenty percent of the women belong to the 4 national and 4 local sororities. There are also many clubs, organizations, and religious facilities.

Sports: The university fields 1 intercollegiate team for men and 1 for women. There are 4 intramural sports for men and 4 for women.

Handicapped: There are no special facilities for the physically handicapped.

Graduates: The freshman dropout rate is 20%; 30% remain to graduate. Forty-five percent of the graduates pursue advanced study. Two percent enter medical school and 2% enter law school; 37% pursue careers in business and industry.

Services: Students receive the following services free of charge: placement, career counseling, tutoring, remedial instruction, and psychological counseling. Health care is available on a fee basis.

Programs of Study: The university confers the B.A. and B.S. degrees. Bachelor's degrees are offered in the following subjects: BUSINESS (accounting, business administration), ENGLISH (literature), FINE AND PERFORMING ARTS (art), HEALTH SCIENCES (health care administration, rehabilitation services), MATH AND SCIENCES (biology, chemistry, mathematics), PHILOSOPHY (liberal studies), PREPROFESSIONAL (engineering, law, medicine), SOCIAL SCIENCES (economics, government/political science, sociology).

Required: All students participate in a general studies program and take 4 credits of physical education.

Special: There is a cooperative education program, as well as dual degree programs in engineering, mathematics, and sciences.

Honors: The 3 honor societies on campus are Alpha Kappa Mu, Sigma Omega, and the Sons of Wilberforce. The university also has a special honors program that provides advanced and independent study for qualified students.

Admissions: Sixty percent of those who applied were accepted for the 1981–82 freshman class. Candidates should rank in the upper two-thirds of their graduating class and have a minimum of 12 units of acceptable credit. In addition to these qualifications the following factors are taken into consideration: advanced placement or honors courses, recommendations by school officials, and ability to finance college education.

Procedure: The ACT is required. Applications should be filed by June 1 (fall), November 15 (winter), and March 15 (spring-summer) trimester. There is a $10 application fee. Notification of admission is made on a rolling basis.

Special: An early decision plan is available. AP and CLEP credit is accepted.

Transfer: For fall 1981, 50 transfer students applied, 32 were accepted, and 32 enrolled. A minimum 2.0 GPA is required; grades of C or above transfer. There is a 1-year residency rule. The bachelor's degree requires 126 credits. Deadlines are the same as those for freshmen.

Visiting: Prospective students should contact the admissions office concerning on-campus visits.

Financial Aid: Ninety-five percent of all students receive some form of financial aid; 95% work part-time on campus. Financial aid includes BEOG, loans, and CWS, in addition to the university's own scholarships. As a general rule, students can expect to spend 1 trimester out of every 3 on a job, beginning in the sophomore year. The financial aid application deadline is July 31 for the fall term. The university is a member of CSS; the FAF is required. Notification of awards is made on a rolling basis.

696 OHIO

Foreign Students: Fewer than 1% of the full-time students come from foreign countries. The university offers these students special counseling and special organizations.

Admissions: Foreign students must achieve a minimum TOEFL score of 500. They must also take the ACT.

Procedure: Application deadlines are June 1 (fall), November 15 (winter), and March 15 (spring-summer). Foreign students must present proof of health as well as proof of adequate funds. They must also carry health insurance, which is available through the university.

Admissions Contact: Sheila L. Brown, Associate Director of Admissions.

WILMINGTON COLLEGE B-2
Wilmington, Ohio 45177 (513) 382-6661

F/T: 509M, 275W	Faculty: 47; IIB, −$
P/T: 20M, 19W	Ph.D.'s: 53%
Grad: none	S/F Ratio: 15 to 1
Year: qtrs, ss	Tuition: $3810
Appl: open	R and B: $1785
731 applied	514 accepted	290 enrolled
SAT: 402V 416M	ACT: 18	LESS COMPETITIVE

Wilmington College, founded in 1870, is a private liberal arts college sponsored by the Society of Friends (Quakers). The library contains 106,400 volumes and 2600 microfilm items, and subscribes to 614 periodicals.

Environment: The 86-acre campus and 1000 acres of farms are a 1-hour drive from Dayton, Cincinnati, and Columbus. There are six dormitories on campus. Three state parks are within a 20-mile radius.

Student Life: About 84% of the students come from Ohio, 11% from other states, and 5% from foreign countries. About 95% come from public schools. Sixty-three percent live on campus. Freshmen may live off campus. Religious affiliations vary widely, with Quakers representing about 11% of the students. Eighteen percent of the students are minority-group members. Campus housing is both single-sex and coed, and there are visiting privileges. Students may keep cars on campus.

Organizations: There are 4 local fraternities to which 12% of the men belong; eight percent of the women belong to the 3 local sororities. Religious organizations and counselors are available to students. There is active involvement in student government.

Sports: The college has 9 intercollegiate teams for men and 6 for women. Five intramural sports are offered for men and 4 for women.

Handicapped: Facilities for the physically handicapped include wheelchair ramps, special parking, elevators, and specially equipped rest rooms. Special class scheduling is also available. Fewer than 1% of the students have visual impairments; there are no students with hearing impairments.

Graduates: The freshman dropout rate is 20%; about 45% remain to graduate. Eighty-four percent pursue graduate study after graduation: 2% enter medical school, 1% dental school, and 2% law school. Forty percent pursue careers in business and industry.

Services: Students receive the following services free of charge: placement, career counseling, psychological counseling, tutoring, and remedial instruction. Health care is available for a fee.

Programs of Study: The college confers the B.A. and B.S. degrees. Wilmington also co-sponsors a master's program with Miami University. Bachelor's degrees are offered in the following subjects: BUSINESS (accounting, business administration, management, marketing), EDUCATION (early childhood, elementary, health/physical, industrial, secondary), FINE AND PERFORMING ARTS (art, art education, music, music education, theater/dramatics), HEALTH SCIENCES (medical technology), LANGUAGES (French, German, Spanish), MATH AND SCIENCES (biology, chemistry, mathematics), PHILOSOPHY (philosophy, religion), PREPROFESSIONAL (agriculture, dentistry, law, medicine, social work, veterinary), SOCIAL SCIENCES (economics, government/political science, history, human services, psychology, social sciences, sociology). Forty percent of the conferred degrees are in education, 20% in business, and 17% in social sciences.

Required: Undergraduates must take available courses only within the academic disciplines. Each student develops an individual program of study related to career and personal goals. This is done in consultation with a team of faculty and off-campus advisers. Each program is required to have breadth and depth.

Special: An Individualized Educational Planning (IEP) program, which makes it possible for students to make effective use of various resources, is available. An off-campus field team and/or field study are available, but not required. Overseas academic programs can be taken in Mexico, Italy, Switzerland, Austria, and other locations. A combination degree program is offered in medical technology. Student-designed majors are permitted. It is possible to earn combined B.A.-B.S. degrees.

Honors: Two honor societies have chapters on campus.

Admissions: Seventy percent of those who applied were accepted for the 1981–82 freshman class. The verbal SAT scores of those who enrolled were as follows: 86% below 500, 14% between 500 and 599, and 0% above 600. The ACT scores were as follows: 65% below 21, 19% between 21 and 23, 0% between 24 and 25, 16% between 26 and 28, and 0% above 28. The applicant should be a graduate of an accredited high school, have an average of at least C, have completed 16 Carnegie high school units, and be in the upper four-fifths of the graduating class. The school indicates that in addition to these qualifications it considers the following factors: advanced placement or honors courses, leadership record, extracurricular activities record, impressions made during an interview, personality, and recommendations.

Procedure: The college requires the SAT or ACT, which should be taken in November or December of the senior year. Applications are accepted any time after the junior year until June 1. Freshmen are admitted in the summer and at midyear. Admission is on a rolling basis. The deadline for early admissions applications is March 1. A personal interview is recommended.

Special: AP and CLEP credit is accepted.

Transfer: For fall 1981, 128 applications were received, 98 were accepted, and 61 students enrolled. Transfers are accepted for all classes. Students must be in good academic standing at their prior college, have a minimum 2.0 GPA, and have minimum scores of 500 on the SAT or 10 on the ACT. D grades do not transfer. At least 45 of 186 credit hours required for a bachelor's degree must be earned at the college. Transfer application deadlines are the same as those for freshman applicants.

Visiting: Guided tours and interviews can be scheduled on weekdays and Saturday mornings through the admissions office. Visitors may sit in on classes and remain overnight on campus.

Financial Aid: About 73% of all students receive some form of financial aid. The college awards freshman scholarships from a fund of $200,000; the average freshman scholarship is about $850. The maximum amount of aid a first-year student can usually expect to receive is $4500. Campus employment is sometimes awarded as part of the financial aid package; average yearly earnings are about $550. Tuition may be paid in installments. The college is a member of CSS. The FAF is required; the deadline for aid application is April.

Foreign Students: Five percent of the students are from foreign countries. Special counseling and special organizations are available to these students.

Admissions: Foreign students must take the TOEFL. No college entrance exam is required.

Procedure: Admissions are open and foreign students are admitted to all quarters. Proof of adequate funds must be presented. Foreign students must carry health insurance, which is available through the college for a fee.

Admissions Contact: Rhonda A. Inderhees, Director of Admissions.

WITTENBERG UNIVERSITY B-3
Springfield, Ohio 45501 (800) 543-5977

F/T: 1066M, 1199W	Faculty: 141; IIB, ++$
P/T: 13M, 28W	Ph.D.'s: 82%
Grad: none	S/F Ratio: 16 to 1
Year: terms, ss	Tuition: $6125
Appl: open	R and B: $2385
1926 applied	1660 accepted	625 enrolled
SAT: 492V 522M	ACT: 23	COMPETITIVE+

Wittenberg University is an institution of the Lutheran Church in America, founded in 1845. It stresses the liberal arts and is composed of 3 divisions: Wittenberg College, the School of Music, and the School of Community Education. The library contains 300,000 volumes and 40,000 microfilm items, and subscribes to 1427 periodicals.

Environment: Wittenberg's wooded campus is on a 71-acre tract located in a suburban area of Springfield, a city of 77,000 people, 24 miles from Dayton. Campus buildings include an art center and theater and a new library and field house.

Student Life: About 54% of the students come from Ohio. Eighty percent are from public schools. Ninety-five percent live on campus in the residence halls and in sorority and fraternity houses. Nineteen percent of the students are Catholic, 77% Protestant, and 2% Jewish. Seven percent are minority-group members. University housing is both single-sex and coed. There are visiting privileges in single-sex housing. Students may keep cars on campus. Chapel attendance is voluntary.

Organizations: There are 8 national fraternities, to which 45% of the men belong, and 9 national sororities, to which 47% of the women belong. Religious life on campus is coordinated by the Wittenberg Chapel Association.

Sports: The university competes on an intercollegiate level in 13 sports for men and 10 for women. There are 14 intramural sports for men and 11 for women.

Handicapped: Facilities for physically handicapped students include wheelchair ramps, special parking, and elevators.

Graduates: Eighteen percent of the freshmen drop out by the end of their first year. About 70% of those who enter remain to graduate. Thirty-two percent go on to graduate study; 4% enter medical school, 1% dental school, and 5% law school. Thirty-five percent pursue careers in business and industry.

Services: Students receive the following services free of charge: placement, career counseling, psychological counseling, tutoring, and remedial instruction. Health care is available on a fee basis.

Programs of Study: The university confers the B.A., B.F.A., B.Mus., and B.Mus. Ed. degrees. Bachelor's degrees are offered in the following subjects: AREA STUDIES (American, Asian, Russian, urban), BUSINESS (accounting, business administration, business education, computer science, finance, management, marketing), EDUCATION (elementary, health/physical, secondary, special), ENGLISH (English, literature, speech), FINE AND PERFORMING ARTS (art, art education, art history, music, music education, studio art, theater/dramatics), HEALTH SCIENCES (medical technology, nursing, radiation medicine), LANGUAGES (Chinese, French, German, Japanese, Russian, Spanish), MATH AND SCIENCES (biochemistry, biology, chemistry, earth science, geology, marine biology, mathematics, natural sciences, physical sciences, physics, statistics), PHILOSOPHY (humanities, philosophy, religion), PREPROFESSIONAL (dentistry, engineering, forestry, law, medicine, ministry, social work, veterinary), SOCIAL SCIENCES (economics, geography, government/political science, history, international relations, psychology, social sciences, sociology). Seventy-nine percent of the degrees are conferred in liberal arts, 12% in business, and 4% in education.

Required: Degree candidates must complete 12 institutional requirements, a major concentration, and such electives as may be needed to total 36 courses.

Special: Student-designed majors are permitted. A student may place out of any required or prerequisite course by examination. He or she may also, under certain conditions, acquire credit by examination. Each student may elect 1 course each term on a credit or no-credit basis. Study abroad and independent study are among the curriculum features. 3-2 programs are available in engineering, forestry, and nursing.

Honors: There are 23 honor societies on campus.

Admissions: Eighty-six percent of those who applied were accepted for the 1981–82 freshman class. The SAT scores of those who enrolled were as follows: Verbal—55% below 500, 35% between 500 and 599, 9% between 600 and 700, and 1% above 700; Math—37% below 500, 43% between 500 and 599, 17% between 600 and 700, and 3% above 700. The ACT scores were as follows: 30% below 21, 21% between 21 and 23, 19% between 24 and 25, 20% between 26 and 28, and 10% above 28. The university has a policy of selective admissions in which the applicant's school record, test scores, recommendations, and character are all taken into consideration. Each applicant is considered individually, and no single factor is given undue importance.

Procedure: All freshman applicants must take the SAT or ACT. ATs are recommended. Application deadlines are open. The university follows a rolling admissions plan. There is a $20 application fee.

Special: Early decision and deferred admissions plans are available. AP credit is accepted.

Transfer: For fall 1981, 120 students applied, 92 were accepted, and 61 enrolled. Transfers are accepted for all classes. A 2.0 GPA is required. D grades do not transfer. Students must study at the university for at least 1 year and complete 8 of the 36 courses needed to receive a bachelor's degree. Transfer application deadlines are August 15 (fall), December 15 (winter), and February 15 (spring).

Visiting: Orientations are scheduled for prospective students. Campus tours, departmental open houses, and admissions/financial aid information are available. Guided tours and interviews can be scheduled while classes are in session. Visitors may sit in on classes and remain overnight on campus.

Financial Aid: Forty percent of all students receive financial aid. Fifty percent work part-time on campus. Average aid to freshmen from all sources is $5200. The college participates in the CSS. NDEA loans are available. The FAF is required. The aid application deadlines are March 1 (fall), October 15 (winter), and February 1 (spring). Notification is on a rolling basis.

Foreign Students: About 2% of the full-time students come from foreign countries. The university offers these students an intensive English course, special counseling, and special organizations.

Admissions: Foreign students must take the TOEFL or the University of Michigan Language Test. They must score at least 500 on the TOEFL. No college entrance examination is required.

Procedure: The application deadlines are June 1 (fall), November 1 (winter), and January 15 (spring). Foreign students must submit the results of a physical examination. They must also submit proof of funds adequate to cover 1 year of study. They must carry health insurance, which is available through the university for a fee.

Admissions Contact: Kenneth G. Benne, Director of Admissions.

WRIGHT STATE UNIVERSITY   B-4
Dayton, Ohio 45435   (513) 873-2211

F/T: 3758M, 3464W   Faculty: 505; IIA, av$
P/T: 1768M, 1820W   Ph.D.'s: 80%
Grad: 1174M, 1899W   S/F Ratio: 14 to 1
Year: qtrs, ss   Tuition: $1278 ($2268)
Appl: Sept. 1   R and B: $556–644/qtr
2392 applied   2023 accepted   1567 enrolled
ACT: 19   LESS COMPETITIVE

Wright State University, founded in 1964, is a state-supported institution. In addition to the main campus at Dayton, there are the Western Ohio Branch Campus, and the Piqua Residence Credit Center. The university comprises the colleges of Liberal Arts, Business and Administration, Education, Science and Engineering, and the schools of Nursing, Medicine, and Professional Psychology. The library contains 345,000 volumes and 398,000 microfilm items, and subscribes to 6300 periodicals.

Environment: The 618-acre wooded suburban campus is about 9 miles from the center of Dayton. Its 20 buildings include a dormitory and university apartments adjacent to the campus, housing 600 students. Two new buildings, including an ambulatory care center, opened in fall 1981.

Student Life: Ninety-eight percent of the students are from Ohio and live off campus, mostly at home. About 9% of the students are minority-group members. Campus housing is coed. Students may keep cars on campus. Drinking on campus is restricted.

Organizations: Two percent of the men and 2% of the women belong to the 8 fraternities and 4 sororities. The university sponsors several extracurricular activities and groups, the most active of which are the orchestra, publications, plays, and the choir. Four to 6 cultural events are held each week on campus.

Sports: The university fields 7 intercollegiate teams for men and 6 for women. There are 17 intramural sports for men and 15 for women.

Handicapped: The university has extensive special facilities for handicapped students, including adapted athletics and transportation. Underground tunnels connect all buildings, making virtually the whole campus accessible by wheelchair. There are a tape center for the visually impaired, special support services for all handicapped, and 5 special counselors.

Graduates: There is a freshman dropout rate of 20%; 35% remain to graduate. Thirty-five percent of those who remain to graduate go on to graduate or professional schools: 2% enter medical school, 3% law school, and 2% dental school. Twenty-five percent pursue careers in business and industry.

Services: The university provides free placement services, health care, career and psychological counseling, tutoring, and remedial instruction. There is a co-op program for almost all majors except education and nursing. Career-planning and placement services are available for graduates.

Programs of Study: The university confers the following degrees: B.A., B.S., B.S.B.A., B.S.Ed., B.F.A., B.M., and B.S.N. Associate, master's, and doctoral degrees are also awarded. Bachelor's degrees are offered in the following subjects: AREA STUDIES (urban), BUSINESS (accounting, business administration, business economics, business education, computer science, finance, management, marketing, real estate/insurance), EDUCATION (early childhood, elementary, health/physical, secondary, special), ENGLISH (English, literature, speech) FINE AND PERFORMING ARTS (art, art education, art history, dance, film/photography, music, music education, theater/dramatics), HEALTH SCIENCES (environmental health, medical technology, nursing), LANGUAGES (French, German, Spanish), MATH AND SCIENCES (biochemistry, biology, chemistry, ecology/environmental science, geology, mathematics, natural sciences, physical sciences, physics, statistics), PHILOSOPHY (classics, humanities, philosophy, religion), PREPROFESSIONAL (dentistry, engineering, law, library science, medicine, social work, veterinary), SOCIAL SCIENCES (anthropology, economics, geography, government/political science, history, psychology, social sciences, sociology). Twenty-five percent of degrees are conferred in business, 20% in education, and 20% in science and engineering.

Required: All undergraduates must take 2 English courses, 3 science courses, and 9 courses in social sciences and the humanities. To graduate, a student must earn a minimum of 183 hours and maintain a 2.0 GPA.

Special: All freshmen are enrolled in the University Division for the first year. Students may spend their junior year abroad.

Honors: Eleven honor societies have chapters on campus. Honors programs are offered in classics, English, history, modern languages, political science, religion, anthropology, biological sciences, chemistry, computer science, geology, mathematics, physics, psychology, and nursing.

Admissions: Eighty-five percent of those who applied were accepted for the 1981-82 freshman class. The ACT scores of those who enrolled were as follows: 55% below 21, 31% between 21 and 25, and 14% between 26 and 30. Candidates are required to be graduates of high school and to have completed 16 Carnegie units. In a recent freshman class, 50% had been in the top half of their high school class, 5% in the top tenth.

Procedure: The ACT is required for admission, although it is used for advising purposes only. The deadlines for regular admission are: September 1 (fall); December 15 (winter); March 15 (spring); June 1 (summer). Admission is on a rolling basis. A $25 application fee is required.

Special: The university participates in CLEP and awards AP credit.

Transfer: For fall 1981, 1259 transfer students applied, 1007 were accepted, and 859 enrolled. Transfers are accepted for all classes. A 2.25 GPA is required from a regionally accredited college or university; grades of C or above are acceptable. Students must study at the university at least 45 quarter hours for a degree; 183 quarter units are required to earn the bachelor's degree. Application deadlines are the same as those for freshmen.

Visiting: Campus visits are encouraged for prospective students. Visits include a meeting with an admissions counselor, a visit with a faculty member, and a campus tour. There are guides for informal visits, and visitors may sit in on classes but may not stay on campus. The best times for visits are autumn and spring. Arrangements should be made through the Admissions Office.

Financial Aid: Approximately 34% of all students receive aid through the university. There are 448 scholarships totaling $284,000. The university administers $515,000 in federal loan funds, and $510,000 in Ohio Instructional Grants. About 10% of all students receive loans. Federal college work-study funds are available in 35 departments. Approximately 1172 students in a recent class qualified for work-study, and 1005 participated in the program. Scholarships range from $500 to $1800, loans from $500 to $2500, and work-study grants from $675 to $1200. Tuition may not be paid in installments. The university is a member of the CSS, and the FAF is required of aid applicants. The deadline for applications is March 1.

Foreign Students: Fewer than 1% of the full-time students come from foreign countries. The university offers these students special counseling and special organizations.

Admissions: Foreign students must achieve a minimum TOEFL score of 500; no college entrance exams are required.

Procedure: Application deadlines are July 15 (fall), November 1 (winter), February 15 (spring), and April 15 (summer). Foreign students must present proof of health as well as proof of funds adequate to cover 1 year of study. They must also carry health insurance, which is available through the university.

Admissions Contact: Kenneth Davenport, Director of Admissions.

XAVIER UNIVERSITY A-5
Cincinnati, Ohio 45207 (513) 745-3301

F/T: 1338M, 1218W	Faculty: 198; IIA, +$
P/T: 420M, 877W	Ph.D.'s: 70%
Grad: 1744M, 1299W	S/F Ratio: 16 to 1
Year: sems, ss	Tuition: $3700
Appl: open	R and B: $2100
1603 applied	1374 accepted	604 enrolled
SAT: 466V 492M	ACT: 22	COMPETITIVE

Xavier University, founded in 1831, is the fourth oldest Jesuit institution of higher education in the United States. It consists of the College of Arts and Sciences, the College of Business Administration, and the new Edgecliff College. The library contains 300,000 volumes and 20,000 microfilm items, and subscribes to 1200 periodicals.

Environment: The 85-acre, 2-campus university is located in a residential area 5 miles from downtown Cincinnati. Campus buildings include an athletic complex and a new business school. Dormitories and on-campus apartments are available.

Student Life: Seventy-five percent of the students come from Ohio; 20% are from public schools. About 45% live in 1 of the 6 dorms. Campus housing is coed. Freshmen who live outside a 35-mile radius are required to live on campus. About 65% of the students are Roman Catholic. About 12% are minority-group members. Cars are permitted on campus, but must be registered.

Organizations: There are no sororities; fraternal activity is minimal. In addition to extracurricular events on campus, students enjoy the numerous cultural and recreational opportunities available in the Cincinnati area.

Sports: The university competes intercollegiately in 8 sports for men and 6 for women. Three intramural sports are offered for men and 3 for women.

Handicapped: Facilities for handicapped students include special parking, wheelchair ramps, and lowered telephones and drinking fountains. Special class scheduling is also available.

Graduates: The freshman dropout rate is 7%; approximately 70% remain to graduate. About 80% of those who remain pursue graduate study.

Services: Students receive the following services free of charge: health care, psychological counseling, tutoring, career counseling, and job placement.

Programs of Study: The university offers the following degrees: B.S., B.A., B.F.A., and B.S.N. Associate and master's programs are also offered. Bachelor's degrees are offered in the following subjects: BUSINESS (accounting, business economics, finance, industrial relations, information systems, management, marketing), EDUCATION (early childhood, elementary, health/physical, secondary, special), ENGLISH (English), FINE AND PERFORMING ARTS (art, art education, art history, art therapy, music, music education, radio/TV, theater/dramatics), HEALTH SCIENCES (medical technology, nursing), LANGUAGES (French, Spanish), MATH AND SCIENCES (biology, chemistry, mathematics, natural sciences, physics), PHILOSOPHY (classics, philosophy, religion), PREPROFESSIONAL (dentistry, fashion merchandising, law, medicine, mortuary science, social work), SOCIAL SCIENCES (consumer science, criminal justice, economics, government/political science, history, international relations, psychology, social sciences, social work, sociology).

Special: Qualified students may study abroad in Austria, Colombia, France, or Italy.

Honors: The university offers an honors program: the Scholars Program involves intensive work in a core of liberal arts studies. Nine national honor societies have chapters on campus.

Admissions: Eighty-six percent of those who applied were accepted for the 1981-82 freshman class. The SAT scores of those who enrolled were as follows: Verbal—64% below 500, 23% between 500 and 599, 11% between 600 and 700, and 2% above 700; Math—50% below 500, 35% between 500 and 599, 14% between 600 and 700, and 1% above 700. On the ACT, 35% scored below 21, 25% between 21 and 23, 14% between 24 and 25, 16% between 26 and 28, and 7% above 28. Candidates should have completed 15 Carnegie units and have at least a C average. In addition to these qualifications, the school considers the following factors, in order of importance: advanced placement or honors courses, school recommendations, impression made during an interview, personality, and extracurricular activities.

Procedure: The SAT or ACT is required, and should be taken by April of the senior year. The application fee is $15. Notification is on a rolling basis.

Special: Early admissions is available. AP and CLEP credit is accepted.

Transfer: For fall 1981, 265 applications were made, 153 accepted, and 111 students enrolled. A minimum GPA of 2.0 from an accredited school is required; D grades do not transfer. The last 30 out of 120 semester hours needed for a bachelor's degree must be taken in residence. Application deadlines are open.

Visiting: Guided tours and interviews are scheduled on school days. Student visitors may stay at the school and sit in on classes.

Financial Aid: Sixty-four percent of all students receive financial aid. Twenty-seven percent work part-time on campus. Over 100 freshman scholarships are awarded each year; financial aid to undergraduates totals $4 million. The average award to freshmen from all sources is $2741. The university is a member of CSS. The FAF and the university's financial aid form are required. The deadlines for aid applications are April 1 (fall) and December 10 (spring), with notification on a rolling basis.

Foreign Students: About 3% of the full-time students are from foreign countries. An intensive English program, special counseling, and special organizations are available for these students.

Admissions: Foreign students must achieve a minimum score of 525 on the TOEFL or 85 on the University of Michigan Language Test. The SAT or ACT is recommended, but not required.

Procedure: Application deadlines are July 15 (fall), December 1 (spring), and May 1 (summer). Foreign students must present proof of health. Proof of adequate funds to cover the entire length of study must also be furnished. Foreign students must carry health insurance, which is available through the university for a fee.

Admissions Contact: Glen L. Glenn, Assistant Director of Admissions.

YOUNGSTOWN STATE UNIVERSITY C-2
Youngstown, Ohio 44555 (216) 742-3150

F/T: 5286M, 4613W	Faculty: 406; IIA, +$
P/T: 2214M, 2204W	Ph.D.'s: 60%
Grad: 632M, 715W	S/F Ratio: 21 to 1
Year: qtrs, ss	Tuition: $1065 ($1785)
Appl: Aug. 15	R and B: $1875
3618 applied	3453 accepted	2807 enrolled
SAT: 426V 482M	ACT: 17	LESS COMPETITIVE

Youngstown State University, founded in 1908, is a state-supported university of liberal arts, education, and professional training in business, engineering, and music. The library contains 385,859 volumes, 529,430 microfilm items, and 69,601 bound periodicals.

Environment: The 91-acre campus is located in downtown Youngstown and contains 26 buildings. Currently under construction is a sports complex consisting of a 16,000-seat stadium, softball fields, 10 lighted tennis courts, an all-weather running track, and space for other recreational activities. A dormitory houses 217 men and women. Fraternity houses and other university-authorized housing are available. A cafeteria, dining hall, student lounge, and locker facilities are available to day students.

Student Life: Ninety-two percent of the undergraduates are from Ohio, 6% from other states, and 2% from foreign countries. About 85% of the entering freshmen come from public schools. About 1 percent of the students live on campus; freshmen may live off campus. Eight percent of the students are minority-group members. Campus housing is coed. Students may keep cars on campus.

Organizations: About 3% of the men belong to 10 fraternities; 2% of the women belong to 4 sororities. Religious counselors and organizations are available for members of the Catholic, Protestant, Jewish, and Orthodox faiths. Student-faculty participation is encouraged in areas of administration, student publications, and curriculum matters. Extracurricular activities include music, art, drama, dance, science, service, debating, publications, and radio.

Sports: The university fields 9 intercollegiate teams for men and 7 for women. Sixteen intramural sports are offered for men and 13 for women.

Handicapped: Ninety percent of the campus is accessible to wheelchair-bound students; facilities include wheelchair ramps, special parking, elevators, specially equipped rest rooms, and lowered drinking fountains and telephones. Special class scheduling is also available. About 0.2% of the current student population are visually impaired, 0.2% are hearing-impaired. Recorded textbooks and other tapes are available, as well as a braille service and readers. There is a staff of 4 for special counseling and assistance.

Graduates: The freshman dropout rate is 28%; 35% remain to graduate. Thirty percent of the graduates become candidates for graduate or professional degrees.

Services: The following services are available free to students: health care, placement, career counseling, psychological counseling, and tutoring. Remedial instruction is available for a fee.

Programs of Study: Programs leading to the B.A., B.S., B.F.A., B.S.Ed., B.S.B.A., B.S.App.Sci., B.S.N., B.E., and B.Mus. are offered. Associate and master's degrees are also conferred. Bachelor's degrees are offered in the following subjects: AREA STUDIES (American, Black/ Afro-American), BUSINESS (accounting, business administration, business education, computer science, finance, management, marketing), EDUCATION (early childhood, elementary, health/physical, secondary, special), ENGLISH (English, speech), FINE AND PERFORMING ARTS (art, art education, art history, music, music education, studio art, theater/dramatics), HEALTH SCIENCES (medical technology, nursing), LANGUAGES (French, German, Italian, Latin, Russian, Spanish), MATH AND SCIENCES (biology, chemistry, earth science, geology, mathematics, physics), PHILOSOPHY (classics, humanities, philosophy, religion), PREPROFESSIONAL (engineering, home economics, social work), SOCIAL SCIENCES (anthropology, economics, geography, government/political science, history, psychology, social sciences, sociology). Twenty-two percent of degrees conferred are in business, 18% in education, and 11% in social sciences.

Required: All undergraduates must take courses in communications and literature, science, social science, and health and physical education.

Special: Combination degree programs are offered in medical technology (3-1) and forestry (3-2). Students have the opportunity to create their own major. It is also possible to earn combined B.A.-B.S. degrees.

Honors: There are 12 honor societies on campus.

Admissions: About 95% of those who applied were accepted for the 1981-82 freshman class. The SAT scores of those who enrolled are as follows: Verbal—77% below 500, 19% between 500 and 599, 4% between 600 and 700, and 0% above 700; Math—56% below 500, 29% between 500 and 599, 12% between 600 and 700, and 3% above 700. The ACT scores were as follows: 71% below 21, 15% between 21 and 23, 7% between 24 and 25, 6% between 26 and 28, and 1% above 28. Candidates must be high school graduates and have a 2.0 average; out-of-state applicants must be in the upper two-thirds of their class. Important considerations include the accreditation of the high school and results of entrance examinations. State residency is also important.

Procedure: The ACT or SAT is required. There is a rolling admissions plan. Deadlines for applications are August 15 (fall), March 15 (spring), May 15 (summer), and November 15 (winter). There is a $20 application fee.

Special: CLEP and AP credit is accepted.

Transfer: For fall 1981, 1004 students applied, 821 were accepted, and 654 enrolled. Transfers are accepted for all classes. A minimum 2.0 GPA is required for transfer. D grades do not transfer. Students must spend 1 year in residence. They must also complete, at the university, the last 45 of the 186 quarter hours required for the bachelor's degree. Transfer application deadlines are the same as those for freshman applicants.

Visiting: There are no formally scheduled visits; informal visitors can obtain guides to the campus. Contact the admissions office for details.

Financial Aid: About 750 scholarships totaling $450,000 are available to freshmen. Loans from federal and state governments, local banks, industrial and private sources, and the university are available. Because scholarships, loans, and grants are limited, the student's entire need cannot always be met from a single source; therefore packaged aid is offered. Average aid to freshmen from scholarships, loans, and campus employment is $600, $450, and $1500 respectively; the average award from all sources is $1000. About 40% of all students receive financial aid. Five percent work part-time on campus. The university is a member of CSS. The deadline for aid application is April 1.

Foreign Students: Two percent of all students are from foreign countries. The university offers these students an intensive English course, special counseling, and special organizations.

Admissions: Foreign students must achieve a minimum TOEFL score of 500. No college entrance exam is required.

Procedure: Application deadlines are April 1 (fall) and October 1 (spring). Foreign students must present the report from a medical exam. Proof of adequate funds for 4 years of study also must be presented. Foreign students are charged $67 per quarter in special fees. They must also carry health insurance, which is available through the university for a fee.

Admissions Contact: William Livosky, Director of Admissions.

OKLAHOMA

BARTLESVILLE WESLEYAN COLLEGE E-1
Bartlesville, Oklahoma 74003 (918) 333-6151

F/T: 186M, 219W
P/T: 138M, 278W
Grad: none
Year: sems, ss
Appl: open
311 enrolled
ACT: 19

Faculty: 37; IV, —$
Ph.D.'s: 27%
S/F Ratio: 20 to 1
Tuition: $2730
R and B: $1780

NONCOMPETITIVE

Bartlesville Wesleyan College, established in 1909, is a private, liberal arts college operated by the Wesleyan Church. The library contains 100,000 volumes and 48,000 microform items, and subscribes to 307 periodicals.

Environment: The college is situated on a 34-acre suburban campus 45 miles from Tulsa. Dormitory facilities are available for men and women. The Performance Center houses an auditorium and court athletic facilities.

Student Life: About 95% of the entering freshmen come from public schools. Forty-six percent of the students live on campus. Three percent of the students are Catholic, 90% Protestant, and 2% belong to other denominations; 5% claim no affiliation. Campus housing is single-sex; and there are visiting privileges. Students may keep cars on campus. All students observe a curfew.

Organizations: There are no fraternities or sororities on campus. Students may participate in a number of extracurricular activities offered by the college. Sources of entertainment are the choral society, little theater, civic ballet, and Bartlesville Symphony.

Sports: The college participates on an intercollegiate level in 4 sports for men and 1 for women. Intramural competition for men is offered in 9 sports and in 8 for women.

Handicapped: Wheelchair ramps and specially equipped rest rooms are provided for handicapped students.

Graduates: Fifteen percent of the students who graduate pursue further study; 40% pursue careers in business or industry.

Services: Psychological and career counseling, placement, tutoring, and remedial instruction are offered at no charge to the student.

Programs of Study: The college grants the B.A. and B.S. degrees. Associate degrees are also offered. Bachelor's degrees are offered in the following subjects: BUSINESS (accounting, business administration, business education, computer science), EDUCATION (elementary, health/physical, secondary), FINE AND PERFORMING ARTS (church music, music education, music performance), MATH AND SCIENCES (biology), PHILOSOPHY (religion), SOCIAL SCIENCES (behavioral science, government/political science, history). Of the degrees conferred, 25% are in education, and 18% are in social sciences.

Admissions: The college has an open admissions policy. The ACT scores of those accepted for the 1981–82 freshman class were as follows: 80% scored below 21, 15% between 21 and 23; 3% between 24 and 25; 1% between 26 and 28; 1% above 28. Students must be graduates of an accredited high school.

Procedure: The ACT is required. The application deadline is open. Admissions are made on a rolling basis. Freshmen are admitted to the fall and spring terms. There is no application fee.

Special: There is a deferred admissions plan. The college grants credit by examination.

Transfer: Transfer students must have been in good standing at the last school they attended. The college requires that the last 30 hours of credit be taken, in residence, of the 126 needed to obtain a bachelor's degree. Application deadlines are open.

Visiting: A Senior Day is conducted for prospective students from the western United States. Guides are available for informal visits to the campus. Visitors may sit in on classes and stay overnight at the college. Weekdays and Saturday mornings are the best time for visits. The Director of Public Affairs/Recruitment will make arrangements.

Financial Aid: About 55% of all students receive aid. Twenty percent work part-time on campus. Average aid to freshmen from all sources is $1500. Financial aid is available in the form of scholarships, federal assistance programs, and CWS. The FFS must be submitted. The aid application deadlines are May 1 (fall) and November 1 (spring).

Admissions Contact: Wendell O. Rovenstine, Director of Public Relations and Admissions.

BETHANY NAZARENE COLLEGE D-3
Bethany, Oklahoma 73008 (405) 789-6400

F/T: 472M, 606W
P/T: 90M, 109W
Grad: 44M, 42W
Year: sems, ss
Appl: Aug. 15
362 applied   355 accepted   288 enrolled
ACT: 19

Faculty: 68; IIA, —$
Ph.D.'s: 41%
S/F Ratio: 16 to 1
Tuition: $2294
R and B: $1660

LESS COMPETITIVE

Bethany Nazarene College, founded in 1899, is a Christian institution of higher education affiliated with the Church of the Nazarene. It offers training in liberal arts, business, health fields, and education. The library contains 96,318 volumes and 42,109 microfilm items, and subscribes to 648 periodicals.

Environment: The 40-acre suburban campus is located in the center of Bethany, about 10 miles from downtown Oklahoma City. Facilities include 5 dormitories that accommodate 480 women and 464 men. Additional housing is provided for about 75 students in private homes. There is a cafeteria and lounge for day students.

Student Life: About 40% of the students are from Oklahoma. Ninety-five percent of the students come from public schools. Sixty-five percent live on campus. Ninety-four percent of the students are members of the supporting church and all are required to attend religious services 3 times a week. Fewer than 1% of the students are Catholic, fewer than 1% are Jewish; 1% belong to other denominations; and 4% claim no affiliation. Nine percent are minority-group members. College housing is single-sex, and there are no visiting privileges. Students may keep cars on campus. Drinking and smoking are not allowed on campus.

Organizations: There are no fraternities or sororities on campus. Activities and social events center around 6 societies; students choose the one to which they wish to belong. Religious clubs and organizations meet regularly and conduct services in surrounding churches. There is a student government, a student newspaper, and a yearbook.

Sports: There are intercollegiate teams in 6 sports for men and 3 for women. There are 10 intramural sports for men and 9 for women.

Handicapped: About 50% of the campus is accessible to handicapped students. Special facilities include wheelchair ramps and elevators. Three counselors are available to handicapped students.

Graduates: About 20% of the freshmen drop out by the end of the first year; 45% remain to graduate. About 45% of the graduates pursue advanced degrees; 10% enter medical school, 2% dental school, and 3% law school. Thirty-five percent pursue careers in business or industry.

Services: The following services are provided to students free of charge: psychological counseling, placement, and career counseling. Health care, tutoring, and remedial instruction are available on a fee basis.

Programs of Study: The college confers the B.A., B.S., and B.Mus.Ed. degrees. Master's programs are also available. Bachelor's degrees are offered in the following subjects: BUSINESS (accounting, business administration, business education, computer science, management, marketing), EDUCATION (early childhood, elementary, health/physical, secondary), ENGLISH (English, journalism, speech), FINE AND PERFORMING ARTS (art, music, music education), HEALTH SCIENCES (medical technology, nursing), LANGUAGES (French, German, Greek/Latin, Spanish), MATH AND SCIENCES (biology, botany, chemistry, mathematics, physics, zoology), PHILOSOPHY (philosophy, religion), PREPROFESSIONAL (home economics, ministry), SOCIAL SCIENCES (economics, government/political science, history, psychology, social sciences, sociology).

Special: Study abroad, sponsored by the college and other institutions, is available. Student-designed majors are permitted.

Admissions: About 98% of those who applied for the 1981–82 freshman class were accepted. ACT scores of enrolled students were as follows: 60% scored below 21, 20% scored between 21 and 23, 11% between 24 and 25, 8% between 26 and 28, and 1% above 28. Applicants must be high school graduates and must have at least a 2.0 GPA. High school recommendations, personality, and advanced placement or honor courses are also considered in the admissions decision.

Procedure: The ACT is required. Application deadlines are August 15 (fall), December 15 (spring), and May 15 (summer). Test scores, a transcript, and the results of a physical examination must be submitted. There is a $35 application fee.

Special: CLEP and AP credit is accepted.

Transfer: For fall 1981, 134 students applied, and 132 were accepted. The only requirement is that the student may not be on suspension from another college. To receive a degree a transfer student must have 30 hours of resident credit of the 124 needed for a bachelor's degree. Deadlines are the same as those for freshman applicants.

Visiting: The college schedules regular orientation programs for prospective students in November, April, June, July, and August. Guides are also available for informal visits. Visitors may sit in on classes and stay overnight at the college in some cases. The dean of student affairs should be contacted for arrangements.

Financial Aid: About 70% of the students receive financial aid. Fifteen percent work part-time on campus. The average aid to freshmen from all sources is $975. Scholarships, loans, and grants are available. There are work-study programs in all departments. Tuition may be paid in installments. The FAF, FFS, or SFS may be filed. The deadlines for aid applications are June 1 (fall), November 1 (spring), and March 1 (summer).

Foreign Students: About 2% of the full-time students come from foreign countries.

Admissions: Foreign students must score 500 on the TOEFL. No college entrance examination is required.

Procedure: Application deadlines are August 1 (fall), December 1 (winter), and May 1 (summer). Foreign students must have a physician fill out the college's own health form. They must also present proof of funds adequate to cover their entire course of study. There is a special application fee. Foreign students must carry health insurance, which is available through the college for a fee.

Admissions Contact: Vernon A. Snowbarger, Director of Admissions and Registrar.

CAMERON UNIVERSITY D-4
Lawton, Oklahoma 73505 (405) 248-2200

F/T: 1392M, 1511W	Faculty: 184; IIB, ++$
P/T: 1148M, 987W	Ph.D.'s: 39%
Grad: none	S/F Ratio: 24 to 1
Year: sems, ss	Tuition: $14($35) p/c
Appl: open	R and B: $1540
1027 applied	993 accepted 825 enrolled
ACT: required	LESS COMPETITIVE

Cameron University, founded in 1908, is a state-supported institution offering liberal arts, technological, and teacher education programs. The library contains 140,000 volumes and subscribes to 1435 periodicals.

Environment: The 25-acre urban campus consists of 25 buildings, more than half of which have been constructed since 1970. A fine arts complex contains separate buildings for art, music, and speech, and a 500-seat auditorium for the performing arts. Two dormitories house 1100 students.

Student Life: All but 5% of the students are from Oklahoma; 10% live on campus. Twenty-two percent of the students are minority-group members. Campus housing is single-sex; there are visiting privileges. Students may keep cars on campus.

Organizations: There are 2 national and 2 local fraternities, to which fewer than 1% of the men belong; fewer than 1% of the women belong to the 2 national sororities. There are 40 extracurricular groups and activities.

Sports: The university competes intercollegiately in 5 sports for men and 3 for women. There are 4 intramural sports for men and 4 for women.

Handicapped: Approximately 60% of the campus is accessible to the physically handicapped. Facilities include wheelchair ramps, special parking, specially equipped rest rooms, and lowered drinking fountains and telephones. Special class scheduling is also available. There are no visually or hearing impaired students currently enrolled.

Graduates: The freshman dropout rate is 45%; 45% remain to graduate. Fourteen percent of those who graduate pursue graduate study.

Services: Career counseling, placement services, and remedial instruction are offered free of charge. Health care is available on a fee basis.

Programs of Study: The college grants the B.A. or B.S. degree. Associate degrees are also offered. The bachelor's degree is offered in the following subjects: BUSINESS (accounting, business administration), EDUCATION (elementary, health/physical, secondary), ENGLISH (English, speech), FINE AND PERFORMING ARTS (art, music), HEALTH SCIENCES (medical technology, nursing), MATH AND SCIENCES (biology, chemistry, mathematics, natural sciences, physics), PREPROFESSIONAL (agriculture, dentistry, engineering, home economics, law, medicine, pharmacy, veterinary), SOCIAL SCIENCES (government/political science, history, sociology). Of the degrees conferred, 14% are in social sciences.

Required: All students must complete a 50-hour core curriculum.

Special: The university offers freshman remedial programs in mathematics, English, and physical science.

Honors: Phi Kappa Phi has a chapter on campus. Honors programs are offered in English and social sciences.

Admissions: Approximately 97% of those who applied were accepted for the 1981-82 freshman class. The ACT scores of those who enrolled in a recent year were as follows: 11% scored between 20 and 23, 7% between 24 and 26, 3% between 27 and 28, and 2% above 28. Candidates should have 18 Carnegie units, be graduates of an accredited high school, and have a minimum 2.0 GPA. Oklahoma residents must rank in the top 75% of their class; nonresidents must rank in the top half of their class and score in the top half on the ACT. The minimum acceptable ACT score for residents is 13; for nonresidents, 16.

Procedure: The ACT is required and should be taken no later than the last spring date. Application deadlines are open. The university follows a rolling admissions policy. There is no application fee.

Special: AP and CLEP credit is accepted.

Transfer: For fall 1981, the university received 653 transfer applications, accepted 639, and 498 students enrolled. A minimum 2.0 GPA is required. An ACT score of 16 is needed. D grades transfer. There is a 1-year residency requirement; 30 of the last 45 credits must be completed, in residence, of the 128 needed for a bachelor's degree. Deadlines are open.

Visiting: Six days are set aside for freshman orientation and enrollment each year.

Financial Aid: Thirty-five percent of all students receive some form of financial aid. Eleven percent work part-time on campus. The college offers 28 academic and 20 athletic scholarships to freshmen. Federal and state loan funds administered by the college are also available. CWS is offered in all departments. The college requires the FAF, FFS, or SFS. The deadlines for aid applications are May 15 (fall) and October 15 (spring).

Foreign Students: Fewer than 1% of the full-time students come from foreign countries.

Admissions: Foreign students must score 500 on the TOEFL. No college entrance examination is required.

Procedure: Application deadlines are April 15 (fall), September 15 (spring), and March 15 (summer). Foreign students must present proof of funds adequate to cover their first and last semesters. They must also pay a special tuition fee.

Admissions Contact: Raymond Chapman, Director of Admissions and Records.

CENTRAL STATE UNIVERSITY E-5
Edmond, Oklahoma 73034 (405) 341-2980

F/T: 2613M, 3202W	Faculty: 336; IIA, +$
P/T: 1285M, 1704W	Ph.D.'s: n/av
Grad: 1345M, 1855W	S/F Ratio: n/av
Year: sems, ss	Tuition: $450 ($900)
Appl: Aug. 23	R and B: $1550
4928 applied	4682 accepted 3252 enrolled
ACT: 17	LESS COMPETITIVE

Central State University was established in 1890, and today offers undergraduate curricula in the arts and sciences, business, education, and music. Its library has 552,000 books and 271,000 microfilm items, and subscribes to 4300 periodicals.

Environment: The 200-acre campus, located in a suburban setting, has 38 major buildings, including residence halls for 592 men and 716 women, apartments for 158 married students, and facilities for commuters.

Student Life: About 95% of the students come from Oklahoma; the majority are public school graduates. Ten percent of the students live on campus. About 19% of the students are minority-group members. University housing is single-sex; and there are visiting privileges. Students may keep cars on campus. Day-care services are available to all students.

Organizations: There is a full and traditional extracurricular program. Five percent of the men and 7% of the women belong to fraternities and sororities. On-campus social and cultural events are regularly scheduled.

Sports: There are 9 intercollegiate sports for men and 6 for women. There are 9 intramural sports for both men and women.

Graduates: The freshman dropout rate is 40%. Recently, 25% have remained to graduate; 50% of those went on for further study.

Services: The university provides health care, career and psychological counseling, and placement services for all students.

Programs of Study: The university offers the B.A., B.S., B.B.A., B.A. Ed., B.S.Ed., B.Mus., and B.Mus.Ed. degrees. Master's degrees are also granted. Bachelor's degrees are offered in the following subjects: BUSINESS (accounting, business administration, business education, finance, management, marketing), EDUCATION (early childhood, elementary, health/physical, industrial, secondary, special), ENGLISH (English, journalism), FINE AND PERFORMING ARTS (art, art education, music, music education), HEALTH SCIENCES (medical technology, nursing), MATH AND SCIENCES (biology, chemistry, mathematics, physics), SOCIAL SCIENCES (economics, geography, history, psychology, sociology). Most of the degrees are conferred in education and business.

Required: There is a basic education requirement.

Special: Study abroad, independent study, and exchange programs are offered.

Honors: Students may pursue honors work in several academic areas.

Admissions: About 95% of the applicants were accepted for the 1981-82 freshman class. A high school diploma or GED is usually required. Generally, class rank should be in top 66%, and high school average should be C.

Procedure: ACT scores must be submitted. New students are admitted each semester. Application deadlines are August 23 (fall), January 8 (spring), and June 2 (summer). Notification is on a rolling basis. There is no application fee.

Special: AP and CLEP are used.

Transfer: Recently, over 1740 transfer students have enrolled each year. A 2.0 GPA is needed. One year (30 credits) must be completed, in residence, of the 124 needed for a bachelor's degree. Application deadlines are the same as those for freshman applicants.

Visiting: Campus tours with student guides can be arranged. Visitors are allowed to sit in on classes.

Financial Aid: About 25% of the students are receiving assistance. Twelve percent work part-time on campus. Average aid to freshman from all sources is $1310. The university participates in federal programs such as NDSL, BEOG/SEOG, and CWS in addition to offering commercial (bank) and short-term university loans, state assistance, and several freshman scholarships. The FAF or FFS should be filed. The aid application is due by March 1.

Foreign Students: Seven percent of the full-time students come from foreign countries. The university offers these students an intensive English course, special counseling, and special organizations.

Admissions: Foreign students must score 500 on the TOEFL.

Procedure: Application deadlines are July 1 (fall), November 1 (spring), and April 1 (summer). Foreign students must present proof of funds. There are state-required enrollment fees for the fall, spring, and summer. Foreign students must carry health insurance, which is available through the university for a fee.

Admissions Contact: Jack Beeson, Director of Admissions.

EAST CENTRAL OKLAHOMA STATE UNIVERSITY
E-4

Ada, Oklahoma 74820   (405) 332-8000

F/T: 1176M, 1572W	Faculty: 183; IIA, av$
P/T: 193M, 347W	Ph.D.'s: 45%
Grad: 208M, 445W	S/F Ratio: 15 to 1
Year: sems, ss	Tuition: $1300 ($1600)
Appl: Aug. 20	R and B: $1403
829 applied	825 accepted	679 enrolled
ACT: 16		LESS COMPETITIVE

East Central Oklahoma State University, founded in 1909, is a publicly controlled, coeducational institution devoted to the liberal arts and the training of teachers. The library contains 130,657 volumes and 190,000 microfilm items, and subscribes to 1000 periodicals.

Environment: The 130-acre urban campus is located in the city of Ada, 88 miles from Oklahoma City. Living facilities include dormitories, on-campus apartments, and married student housing.

Student Life: Ninety-seven percent of the students are residents of Oklahoma. About 90% live on campus. Twelve percent are minority-group members. Campus housing is both coed and single-sex; there are visiting privileges in the single-sex housing. Students may keep cars on campus.

Organizations: There are 3 national sororities to which 7% of the women belong and 3 national fraternities to which 6% of the men belong. Religious facilities are available for Catholic and Protestant students.

Sports: The university fields 6 intercollegiate teams for men and 1 team for women. There are 7 intramural sports for men and 3 for women.

Handicapped: The campus is 100% accessible to physically handicapped students. Special facilities include wheelchair ramps, parking areas, elevators, lowered drinking fountains and telephones, and specially equipped rest rooms. Special class scheduling is also available. Visually impaired and hearing impaired students each comprise 1% of the student body. There is special tutoring provided and interpreters are available for certain classes.

Graduates: The freshman dropout rate is about 10%; 45% remain to graduate. Thirty percent of those who graduate pursue further study; 3% enter medical school, and 2% enter law school. About 65% enter business and industry.

Services: Tutoring, remedial instruction, and career counseling are offered at no charge to the student. Health care and placement services are provided on a fee basis.

Programs of Study: The university offers the B.A., B.S., B.A.Ed., B.S.Ed., and B.Mus.Ed. degrees. Master's degrees are also available. Bachelor's degrees are offered in the following subjects: BUSINESS (accounting, business administration, business education), EDUCATION (elementary, health/physical, industrial, special), ENGLISH (English, journalism, speech), FINE AND PERFORMING ARTS (art, art education, music, music education), HEALTH SCIENCES (environmental health, medical technology, nursing), MATH AND SCIENCES (biology, chemistry, ecology/environmental science, mathematics, physics), PREPROFESSIONAL (home economics, social work), SOCIAL SCIENCES (geography, government/political science, history, psychology, sociology). Of the degrees conferred 14% were in business, 13% were in social sciences, and 8% were in area studies.

Special: There are several specialized programs in teacher education. A degree minor in military science is available.

Honors: Two national honor societies have chapters on campus.

Admissions: Ninety-nine percent of those who applied were accepted for the 1981-82 freshman class. The ACT scores of those who enrolled were as follows: 82% scored below 21, 11% between 21 and 23, 5% between 24 and 25, 2% between 26 and 28, and 0% above 28. Requirements for Oklahoma residents are a score of 14 or higher on the ACT, a rank in the upper two-thirds of the graduating class, and an average of 2.2 or better. Nonresidents must rank in the upper 50% on tests or in the graduating class, or score 18 or more on the ACT. Oklahoma residents over 19 years of age who are not high school graduates may be admitted on a provisional basis with a satisfactory score on the ACT.

Procedure: The ACT is required. Application deadlines are August 20 (fall), January 15 (spring), and June 1 (summer). Admission is on a rolling basis. There is no application fee.

Special: The university admits a limited number of students under early decision and early admissions plans. CLEP credit is accepted.

Transfer: Approximately 500 applications were received for the 1981-82 school year, approximately 495 students were accepted, and 477 enrolled. Transfers are accepted for all classes. D grades are acceptable. The student must be in good standing at the college last attended. All students must complete, at the university, 30 of the 124 credits required for a bachelor's degree. Application deadlines are the same as those for freshmen.

Visiting: Guides are available for informal visits to the campus. Visitors may not sit in on classes or stay overnight at the school. The best time to visit is mid-semester. Arrangements can be made through the personnel office.

Financial Aid: About 68% of all students receive aid. About 24% work part-time on campus. The average freshman award is $1200. Scholarships, loans, and work-study are available. The FFS must be filed. Aid application deadlines are August 1 (fall) November 1 (spring), and March 1 (summer).

Foreign Students: Fewer than 1% of the full-time students come from foreign countries.

Admissions: Foreign students must achieve minimum scores of 500 on the TOEFL and 18 on the ACT.

Procedure: Application deadlines are the same as those for other students. Foreign students must present proof of adequate funds.

Admissions Contact: Merle Boatwright, Registrar.

FLAMING RAINBOW UNIVERSITY F-3
Stilwell, Oklahoma 74960 (918) 696-3644
(Recognized Candidate for Accreditation)

F/T: 46M, 232W	Faculty: 8; n/av
P/T: none	Ph.D.'s: 7%
Grad: none	S/F Ratio: 35 to 1
Year: 4-1-4	Tuition: $1920
Appl: Sept. 15	R and B: n/app
113 applied	113 accepted	113 enrolled
SAT, ACT: not required	NONCOMPETITIVE

Flaming Rainbow University is a 4-year, undergraduate institution with campuses in Tahlequah, Stilwell, and Oaks. The university's mission is to provide innovative higher education programs to the non-traditional student population in Eastern Oklahoma. The main academic thrust is to assist these students, primarily Native Americans, in obtaining the knowledge and ability to assume participation and leadership in the social, economic, and political systems of their communities.

Student Life: All students live off campus. Seventy-seven percent are minority-group members (76% are Native Americans).

Graduates: Thirty-seven percent of the freshmen drop out by the end of the first year. Fifteen percent of the full-time students pursue advanced study after graduation; 48% enter careers in business and industry.

Services: The following services are provided free of charge to all students: placement, career counseling, tutoring, and remedial instruction.

Programs of Study: The university confers the B.A. degree in the following areas of concentration: AREA STUDIES (American), BUSINESS (accounting, business administration, management, marketing, real estate/insurance), ENGLISH (journalism), FINE AND PERFORMING ARTS (art, art history, film/photography, radio/TV, studio art), MATH AND SCIENCES (biology, ecology/environmental science, natural sciences, physical sciences), PHILOSOPHY (humanities, religion), PREPROFESSIONAL (forestry, social work), SOCIAL SCIENCES (economics, government/political science, psychology, social sciences, sociology).

Required: Students must complete 42 units of credit in general education and a major area of concentration. This academic unit system was developed to meet the needs of measuring academic accomplishment—1 unit equals 3 semester credit hours; 42 units equal the 126 credit hours required for graduation at traditional institutions.

Special: The B.A. degree is defined in terms of its educational mission and commitment. The academic process—from lower division exploratory and interdisciplinary studies to upper division work in the major area of concentration—is directed toward helping each student achieve the objectives of the 5 degree requirements: personal learning skills, breadth of knowledge, depth of knowledge, social consciousness, and wholeness.

Admissions: All of those who applied were accepted for the 1981–82 freshman class. Anyone 18 years of age or possessing a high school diploma or GED may apply. Applicants are not rejected because of past school records. All applicants are given individual attention by the Admissions Committee.

Procedure: College entrance exams are not required. Application deadlines are September 15 (fall) and February 15 (spring). Applicants should submit a completed admissions form, a financial aid general information form and required applications for specific aid, transcripts, GED certificates, and any other proof of previous learning experiences. An interview with an academic counselor is also required. There is no application fee.

Transfer: For fall 1981, 6 transfer students applied and all were accepted. Transfers are accepted for all classes. Students who transfer from other institutions with 3 or more years of credit must spend 1 year in residence at the university. Application deadlines are the same as those for freshmen.

Financial Aid: Seventy-nine percent of the students receive aid through the university; 36% work part-time on campus. The university offers financial aid in cooperation with federal and state agencies, including CWS, FISL, BEOG, SEOG, Bureau of Indian Affairs scholarships, and state tuition aid grants. Aid applications and the FAF should be submitted by September 15 for fall entry or March 15 for spring entry.

Foreign Students: No foreign students are currently enrolled at the university.

Admissions Contact: Wanda Smith, Registrar.

LANGSTON UNIVERSITY D-3
Langston, Oklahoma 73050 (405) 466-2231

F/T: 826M, 515W	Faculty: 46; IIB, +$
P/T: 67M, 104W	Ph.D.'s: 54%
Grad: none	S/F Ratio: 19 to 1
Year: sems, ss	Tuition: $435 ($750)
Appl: see profile	R and B: $1550
427 enrolled	
ACT: required	LESS COMPETITIVE

Langston is a state-controlled university and land-grant college offering liberal arts, teacher education, and vocational instruction. It was founded as the Colored Agricultural and Normal University, a college for black students, in 1897. The present name was adopted in 1941. The library contains 147,000 volumes and 3771 microfilm items, and subscribes to 346 periodicals.

Environment: The 40-acre campus is located in a rural area about 45 miles from Oklahoma City. The university's farm has 110 acres, with 260 acres of pasture. Major buildings include the Learning and Resources Center, language and reading laboratories, residence halls which accommodate 302 men and 302 women, and institutional apartments for 72 married students. The library contains a special Black Heritage Collection.

Student Life: About 66% of the students are from Oklahoma; 98% come from public schools. Eighty-five percent are minority-group members. About 42% of the students live on campus. Alcohol is prohibited on campus. Campus housing is both coed and single-sex; there are visiting privileges in the single-sex housing. Students may keep cars on campus.

Organizations: There are 4 fraternities and 4 sororities on campus; 25% of the men and 30% of the women belong to one of them. The university has numerous special interest clubs, publications, theater and musical groups, student government, and religious groups.

Sports: The university fields intercollegiate teams in 4 sports for men and 2 for women. There are 6 intramural sports for men and 5 for women.

Handicapped: About 70% of the campus is accessible to handicapped students. Special facilities include wheelchair ramps, parking areas, elevators, and specially equipped rest rooms. Special class scheduling is also available. Five counselors are available to handicapped students.

Graduates: About 65% of entering freshmen remain to graduate. Five percent of the graduates pursue advanced degrees. Sixty-five percent pursue careers in business and industry.

Services: The following services are available to students free of charge: health care, psychological counseling, placement, career counseling, and tutoring.

Programs of Study: The university confers the B.S., B.S.Ed., and B.S.N. degrees. Bachelor's degrees are offered in the following subjects: AREA STUDIES (urban), BUSINESS (accounting, business administration, business education, computer science, management), EDUCATION (early childhood), ENGLISH (English), FINE AND PERFORMING ARTS (art, art education, music, music education, radio/TV, theater/dramatics), HEALTH SCIENCES (medical technology, nursing, physical therapy), MATH AND SCIENCES (biology, chemistry, mathematics), SOCIAL SCIENCES (economics, history, psychology, social sciences, sociology, urban studies). Twenty percent of the degrees are conferred in social sciences, 20% in business, and 15% in education.

Required: Two years of physical education are required.

Special: A freshman development program offers guidance and counseling to students both within small classes and on an individual basis.

704 OKLAHOMA

Honors: Seven honor societies have chapters on campus. Honors programs are available in several departments.

Admissions: Recently, 52% of those who applied were accepted. All applicants must be graduates of accredited high schools and present 15 Carnegie units. Oklahoma residents must have either a 2.0 GPA, a rank in the upper 75% of their class, or a composite ACT score in the upper 75% of their class. Standards are higher for out-of-state applicants. Oklahoma applicants who do not meet the minimum requirements but are high school graduates and have taken the ACT may be admitted on probation during the summer session.

Procedure: The ACT is required and must be taken by July following the senior year. An interview at the university must be arranged by July 15. Applications should be submitted by July 15, but students may be admitted until 2 weeks after the start of the fall and spring terms, and 1 week after the start of the summer term. Notification is on a rolling basis. There is a $12 application fee.

Special: CLEP and AP credit may be earned.

Transfer: Transfer applicants are accepted for all classes. They must have an honorable dismissal from their previous college and a 2.0 GPA. D grades do not transfer. All students must complete, at the university, 30 of the 124 credits required for a bachelor's degree. Application deadlines are September 15 (fall) and December 15 (spring).

Visiting: There is an orientation program for prospective students. Guides are available for informal campus visits. Visitors may sit in on classes and stay overnight at the school. Visits are best scheduled on weekdays. The high school and college relations office should be contacted for arrangements.

Financial Aid: About 60% of the students receive financial aid. Thirty percent work part-time on campus. Funds are available under the following programs: NDSL ($29,530), EOG ($511,263), and CWS ($276,731). Work-study programs are available in all departments. Tuition may be paid in installments. It is suggested that the application be filed by May 1. The FAF is required.

Foreign Students: Seventeen percent of the full-time students come from foreign countries. Special counseling and special organizations are available for these students.

Admissions: Foreign students must achieve a TOEFL score of at least 500. No college entrance exams are required.

Procedure: Application deadlines are September 15 (fall) and December 15 (spring or summer). Foreign students must present proof of funds adequate to cover 2 semesters of study.

Admissions Contact: John Smith, Director of Admissions.

NORTHEASTERN OKLAHOMA STATE UNIVERSITY   F-3
Tahlequah, Oklahoma 74464   (918) 456-5511

F/T: 1819M, 1971W	Faculty: 226; IIA, av$
P/T: 393M, 425W	Ph.D.'s: 64%
Grad: 673M, 730W	S/F Ratio: 22 to 1
Year: sems, ss	Tuition: $475 ($1150)
Appl: Aug. 1	R and B: $1875
ACT: 16	LESS COMPETITIVE

Northeastern Oklahoma State University was founded in 1846 when the Cherokee National Council passed an act providing for the establishment of the National Male Seminary and the National Female Seminary. It is now a state-supported comprehensive coed university. The library contains 185,000 volumes and 85,000 microfilm items, and subscribes to 1500 periodicals.

Environment: The 176-acre self-contained campus is located in a rural area 70 miles from Tulsa and 35 miles from Muskogee. Seminary Hall, built in 1878, still remains on campus from the Cherokee seminary days. Living facilities include dormitories, fraternity houses, and married student housing.

Student Life: Over 95% of the students are from Oklahoma, and most others are from the West. Twenty-four percent are minority-group members. Sixty-eight percent are Protestant, 30% are Catholic, and 1% are Jewish. Campus housing is single-sex; there are visiting privileges. Students may keep cars on campus.

Organizations: There are 4 fraternities and 3 sororities on campus; 10% of the men and 10% of the women belong. Departmental clubs and activities, the university band, the choir, and the debate team are among the important extracurricular activities. Canoeing, water skiing, and fishing at nearby recreation areas are all popular with students.

Sports: Intercollegiate teams are sponsored in 8 sports. There are 12 intramural sports.

Handicapped: Ninety-eight percent of the campus is accessible to handicapped students. Special facilities include wheelchair ramps, special parking, elevators, and special class scheduling. There are no students with visual or hearing impairments.

Graduates: The freshman dropout rate is 30%. About 10% of the graduates enter graduate or professional school; 1% enter medical school, 1% enter dental school, and 1% enter law school. Twenty-five percent pursue careers in business or industry.

Services: The following services are provided to students without charge: psychological counseling, placement and career counseling (for graduates as well as undergraduates), tutoring, and remedial instruction. Health care is available for a fee.

Programs of Study: The university confers the B.A., B.A.Ed., B.S., B.S.Ed., B.S.N., and B.S. in Visual Science degrees. Master's degrees also are available. Bachelor's degrees are offered in the following subjects: AREA STUDIES (Black/Afro-American), BUSINESS (accounting, business administration, business education, computer science, finance, management, marketing, real estate/insurance, touristry management), EDUCATION (adult, early childhood, elementary, health/physical, industrial, secondary, special), ENGLISH (English, journalism, speech), FINE AND PERFORMING ARTS (art, art education, music, music education, studio art, theater/dramatics), HEALTH SCIENCES (medical technology, nursing, speech therapy), LANGUAGES (Cherokee, French, German, Spanish), MATH AND SCIENCES (biology, botany, chemistry, geology, mathematics, physics, physics—engineering, zoology), PREPROFESSIONAL (dentistry, engineering, law, library science, medicine, pharmacy, social work, veterinary), SOCIAL SCIENCES (criminology, economics, geography, government/political science, history, psychology, social sciences, sociology). Thirty-five percent of all undergraduate degrees are conferred in education, 30% in business.

Required: During the first 2 years students must take prescribed courses in English, the arts, humanities, social studies, natural sciences, and health and physical education.

Special: Combined B.A.-B.S. degrees may be earned in any 2 subjects.

Admissions: Recently, about 98% of those who applied were accepted. In-state applicants should be graduates of accredited high schools, should rank in the top three-fourths of their graduating class, and should have at least a 2.0 GPA. Out-of-state candidates must be in the top half of their class. Applicants not meeting these basic criteria may be admitted on probation. Advanced placement or honors courses, leadership qualities, and special talents are considered important.

Procedure: The ACT is required. Applications must be filed by August 1 (fall), December 15 (spring), and May 1 (summer). There is no application fee. Admissions are granted on a rolling basis.

Special: The university has an early decision plan (with notification as soon as the application is received) and an early admissions plan. CLEP credit is available.

Transfer: Transfers are accepted for the sophomore, junior, and senior classes. Students must be in good standing at their former school. A GPA of at least 2.0 and an ACT score of at least 14 are required. D grades transfer. All students must complete, at the university, 30 of the 124 credits required for a bachelor's degree. Application deadlines are the same as those for freshmen.

Visiting: The university holds 5 summer freshman orientation sessions which include a tour, advising, and registration. Guides are also available for informal visits to the school. Visitors may sit in on classes and may also stay overnight on campus. The best time to visit is Monday through Friday when classes are in session. The University Relations Office handles arrangements.

Financial Aid: About 75% of the students receive some form of financial aid. About 15% work part-time on campus. Scholarships are available, and loans may be obtained from several sources, including a fund established by members of the faculty and friends of the university. The FAF is required. The deadline for aid applications is April 1.

Foreign Students: One percent of the full-time students come from foreign countries. Special counseling and special organizations are available for these students.

Admissions: Foreign students must achieve a TOEFL score of at least 500. No college entrance exams are required.

Procedure: Application deadlines are July 1 (fall), November 15 (spring), and April 1 (summer). Foreign students must present proof of health and adequate funds and must carry health insurance, which is available through the university for a fee.

OKLAHOMA 705

Admissions Contact: James A. Watkins, Director of Admissions and Registrar.

NORTHWESTERN OKLAHOMA STATE UNIVERSITY C-1
Alva, Oklahoma 73717 (405) 327-1700

F/T: 667M, 674W	Faculty: 72; IIA, av$
P/T: 163M, 355W	Ph.D.'s: 40%
Grad: 142M, 303W	S/F Ratio: 19 to 1
Year: sems, ss	Tuition: $420–450 ($1061–1162)
Appl: open	R and B: $1272
738 applied	738 accepted 547 enrolled
ACT: 19	NONCOMPETITIVE

Northwestern Oklahoma State University, established in 1897, is a state-controlled university of liberal arts and teacher education. The library contains 211,455 volumes and 202,669 microfilm items, and subscribes to 1128 periodicals.

Environment: The 140-acre campus is located in a suburban area 150 miles northwest of Oklahoma City. Residence halls accommodate 1450 men and women. Recreational facilities include 6 tennis courts, and all-weather track, and 2 softball diamonds.

Student Life: Oklahoma residents make up 79% of the student body; the rest of the students come from 25 states and 19 foreign countries. Ninety-eight percent are graduates of public schools. About 25% live on campus. Dormitories are coed.

Organizations: Five percent of the men belong to the 1 fraternity on campus, and 5% of the women belong to the 1 sorority. Extracurricular activities include the student senate and special-interest groups for agriculture, dramatics, home economics, international relations, music, and religion.

Sports: The university fields intercollegiate teams in several sports. Intramural sports also are offered.

Handicapped: Approximately 45% of the campus is accessible to the physically handicapped. Facilities include wheelchair ramps, special parking, and elevators.

Graduates: Eighteen percent of the graduates pursue graduate study.

Services: Placement services, career counseling, health care, psychological counseling, tutoring, and remedial instruction are offered free to students.

Programs of Study: The university confers the B.A., B.S., B.A.Ed., B.S.Ed., and master's degrees. Bachelor's degrees are offered in the following subjects: BUSINESS (accounting, agribusiness, business administration, business education, secretarial administration), EDUCATION (elementary, health/physical, industrial, secondary), ENGLISH (English, speech), FINE AND PERFORMING ARTS (art, art education, music, music education, theater/dramatics), LANGUAGES (Spanish), MATH AND SCIENCES (biology, botany, chemistry, mathematics, natural sciences, physics, zoology), PREPROFESSIONAL (agriculture, home economics, library science, social work, veterinary), SOCIAL SCIENCES (economics, government/political science, history, law enforcement, psychology, sociology).

Required: Education majors must take 50 semester hours of general-education courses; others must take 35 hours.

Special: Interdepartmental programs are offered in agriculture, ecology, conservation, law enforcement, and social welfare. The university offers independent study, "short courses," and summer workshops.

Honors: Six national honor societies have chapters on campus.

Admissions: All of those who applied were accepted for the 1981-82 freshman class. For an earlier class, the ACT scores were as follows: 18% between 20 and 23, 10% between 24 and 26, 4% between 27 and 28, and 2% above 28. Applicants must be graduates of accredited high schools, have a C average or better, rank in the upper 75% of their class, and submit recommendations from high school officials. Standards may be higher for out-of-state applicants. Oklahoma residents 18 years of age or older who are not high school graduates may be admitted on a provisional basis depending on ACT or GED scores.

Procedure: The ACT is required; out-of-state applicants may submit SAT scores. Application deadlines are open. There is no application fee.

Special: CLEP credit is accepted.

Transfer: Over 240 transfer students are accepted annually. A GPA of at least 1.4 is required of Oklahoma residents; out-of-state applicants must present at least a 2.0. There is a 1-year residency requirement.

Visiting: Guides are available for informal visits. Visitors may sit in on classes and stay overnight at the school. The admissions counselor should be contacted for arrangements.

Financial Aid: About 70% of all students receive aid. Scholarships, loans, and CWS are available. The FFS is required. The suggested deadline for aid applications is November 1.

Foreign Students: About 56 foreign students are enrolled at the university. An intensive English course, special counseling, and special organizations are provided.

Admissions: Foreign applicants must score at least 500 on the TOEFL. No college entrance exams are required.

Procedure: Students are admitted to the fall, spring, and summer terms. Applications should be filed at least 6 weeks before the start of the fall term and 2 to 5 weeks before the start of the spring term. Students must submit a completed university health form and present proof of adequate funds for 1 year.

Admissions Contact: Bettielou Lane, Admissions Counselor.

OKLAHOMA BAPTIST UNIVERSITY E-3
Shawnee, Oklahoma 74801 (405) 275-2850

F/T: 583M, 704W	Faculty: 100; IIB, –$
P/T: 64M, 76W	Ph.D.'s: 43%
Grad: none	S/F Ratio: 13 to 1
Year: 4-1-4, ss	Tuition: $2335 ($2435)
Appl: Aug. 1	R and B: $1500
452 applied	434 accepted 402 enrolled
SAT: 438V 474M	ACT: 20 COMPETITIVE

Oklahoma Baptist University is a liberal arts institution affiliated with the Baptist Church. The library contains 165,000 volumes and 22,000 microfilm items, and subscribes to 650 periodicals.

Environment: The 122-acre campus is located in a suburban area about 25 miles from Oklahoma City. The 27 buildings, largely of Georgian design, are situated on a hill overlooking miles of rolling countryside. Dormitories accommodate about 1000 men and women.

Student Life: About 65% of the students come from Oklahoma. Ninety-five percent graduate from public schools. Seventy percent live on campus. Ninety-eight percent are Protestant and 1% are Catholic. The majority of the students are members of the Baptist Church and attendance at chapel or assembly is required once a week. Nine percent of the students are minority-group members. Campus housing is single-sex; there are no visiting privileges. Students may keep cars on campus. Drinking on campus is prohibited.

Organizations: There are 16 fraternities and 18 sororities on campus, to which 25% of the men and 30% of the women belong. Other organizations provide students with the opportunity to participate in scholarship, athletics, and social, political, and religious affairs.

Sports: The university fields intercollegiate teams in 5 sports for men and 3 for women. There is 1 intramural sport for men.

Handicapped: About 90% of the campus is accessible to physically handicapped students. Facilities include wheelchair ramps, special parking, elevators, specially equipped rest rooms, and lowered telephones. About 2% of the students are visually impaired; 1% have hearing impairments.

Graduates: The freshman dropout rate is 12%; 45% remain to graduate. About 45% of the graduates go on to graduate or professional study: 1% in medicine, 1% in dentistry, and 1% in law. Thirty-five percent pursue careers in business and industry.

Services: The following services are provided to students free of charge: health care, psychological counseling, career counseling, tutoring, and remedial instruction. Some placement services require payment.

Programs of Study: The university confers the following degrees: B.A., B.S., B.B.A. B.F.A. B.Humanities, B.Mus., and B.Mus.Ed. Associate degrees are also awarded. Bachelor's degrees are offered in the following subjects: AREA STUDIES (American), BUSINESS (accounting, business administration, business education, computer science, finance, health care administration, management, marketing), EDUCATION (early childhood, elementary, health/physical, secondary), ENGLISH (English, journalism, speech), FINE AND PERFORMING ARTS (art, art education, music, music education, theater/dramatics), HEALTH SCIENCES (medical technology, nursing), LANGUAGES (French, German, Spanish), MATH AND SCIENCES (biology, chemistry, mathematics, physical sciences, physics), PHILOSOPHY (philosophy, religion), PREPROFESSIONAL (dentistry, engineering, law, medicine, ministry), SOCIAL SCIENCES (economics, government/political science, history, international relations, psychology, social

706 OKLAHOMA

sciences, sociology). Twenty percent of all undergraduate degrees are conferred in the arts, 20% in business, and 15% in area studies and education.

Required: All students must complete a core of 17 unified studies courses.

Special: There is a junior-year exchange program with Sainon Gakuin University in Japan. The university offers a European Study Tour each summer, taught by resident faculty, which enables the student to earn 8 semester hours in art, music, history, government, education, or other areas. The group spends 4 weeks at a European educational institution and also tours several countries. Dual 3-2 degrees are available in medical technology, engineering, and pharmacy. The university offers a B.G.S. degree. Student-designed majors are permitted.

Honors: Three honor societies have chapters on campus, and 14 departments offer honors programs.

Admissions: About 96% of those who applied were accepted for the 1981-82 freshman class. The ACT scores of those who enrolled were as follows: 43% scored below 21, 28% between 21 and 23, 11% between 24 and 25, 12% between 26 and 28, and 6% above 28. Applicants must be graduates of accredited high schools, rank in the upper 50% of their class, and have a C average or better.

Procedure: Either the ACT or the SAT is required and should be taken by December of the senior year. Application deadlines are August 1 (fall), January 1 (spring), May 1 (summer), and December 1 (for the January interim session). Admissions are granted on a rolling basis. There is a $25 application fee.

Special: There is a deferred admissions plan. CLEP and AP credit may be earned.

Transfer: For fall 1981, 181 students applied, 164 were accepted, and 146 enrolled. Transfers are considered for all classes. Applicants must have a C average, have an ACT score of at least 13, and be in good standing at their former school. D grades do not transfer. All students must complete, at the university, 40 of the 133 credits required for a bachelor's degree. Application deadlines are the same as for freshman applicants.

Visiting: The university holds fall and spring preview days to introduce the school to prospective students. Guides are also available for informal visits to the campus. Visitors may sit in on classes and stay overnight at the school. Weekdays are the best times to visit. The director of admissions handles arrangements.

Financial Aid: Ninety percent of the students receive some form of financial aid. Twenty-five percent work part-time on campus. The average amount given to students is $1600 per year. Scholarships, grants, loans, and work-study programs are available. The FFS is required. The application deadlines are April 15 (fall), October 15 (January interim and spring), and March 15 (summer).

Foreign Students: Two percent of the full-time students come from foreign countries. Special counseling and special organizations are available for these students.

Admissions: Foreign students must achieve a TOEFL score of at least 500. No college entrance exams are required.

Procedure: Application deadlines are the same as those for other students. Foreign students must present proof of health and proof of adequate funds. Health insurance is required, but is not available through the university.

Admissions Contact: John Fluke, Director of Admissions.

OKLAHOMA CHRISTIAN COLLEGE   D-3
Oklahoma City, Oklahoma 73111   (405) 478-1661

F/T: 675M, 813W	Faculty: 61; IIB, +$
P/T: 71M, 54W	Ph.D.'s: 51%
Grad: none	S/F Ratio: 25 to 1
Year: tri, ss	Tuition: $2010
Appl: Sept. 2	R and B: $1500
685 applied	685 accepted 488 enrolled
ACT: required	NONCOMPETITIVE

Oklahoma Christian College, founded in 1950, is a private liberal arts college affiliated with the Church of Christ. The library contains 100,000 volumes and 3000 microfilm items, and subscribes to 465 periodicals.

Environment: The 200-acre suburban campus consists of 25 buildings, including a new fine arts center and apartment complex. Living facilities include dormitories, on-campus apartments, and married student housing.

Student Life: About 45% of the students are from Oklahoma. Eighty-eight percent live on campus. About 96% are Protestant. Nine percent are minority-group members. Campus housing is single-sex; there are no visiting privileges. Students may keep cars on campus. Daily attendance at chapel is required. Alcohol is not permitted on campus.

Organizations: There are no fraternities or sororities on campus. The college sponsors many extracurricular activities, including student government. Religious counselors and organizations are available on campus.

Sports: There are intercollegiate teams in 6 sports for men and 3 for women. There are 9 intramural sports for men and 7 for women.

Handicapped: About 90% of the campus is accessible to handicapped students. Special facilities include wheelchair ramps, parking areas, and specially equipped rest rooms. Special class scheduling is also available.

Graduates: The freshman dropout rate is 32%; 25% remain to graduate. About 30% of the graduates pursue advanced degrees, 4% enter medical school and 2% enter law school. About 25% of the graduates pursue careers in business and industry.

Services: The following services are available to students free of charge: health care, psychological counseling, placement, career counseling, and remedial instruction. Some tutoring services require payment.

Programs of Study: The college confers the B.A., B.S., B.Mus.Ed., and B.S.Ed. degrees. Bachelor's degrees are offered in the following subjects: AREA STUDIES (American), BUSINESS (accounting, business administration, business education, computer science, management, marketing), EDUCATION (early childhood, elementary, health/physical, secondary, special), ENGLISH (English, journalism, literature, speech), FINE AND PERFORMING ARTS (art, art education, music, music education, radio/TV, studio art, theater/dramatics), HEALTH SCIENCES (medical technology, nursing, speech therapy), MATH AND SCIENCES (biochemistry, biology, chemistry, mathematics), PHILOSOPHY (religion), PREPROFESSIONAL (home economics, law, library science, ministry, social work), SOCIAL SCIENCES (history, human behavior, psychology, sociology). Twenty-five percent of degrees are conferred in education, 17% in business, and 17% in math and sciences.

Required: All students must take a core curriculum that includes humanities, communication, social science, physical education, science, and Bible.

Special: Students may study abroad. There is cross-registration with Central State University.

Honors: There is a chapter of Alpha Chi on campus.

Admissions: All of those who applied were accepted for the 1981-82 freshman class. Candidates must either be high school graduates or 19 years old to be admitted. Admissions are open.

Procedure: The ACT is required. The application deadline for fall admission is September 2; notification is on a rolling basis. There is a $10 application fee.

Special: AP and CLEP credit is available.

Transfer: For fall 1981, 220 students applied, 220 were accepted, and 152 enrolled. Good academic standing is required of transfer students. D grades transfer. All students must complete, at the college, 30 of the 126 credits required for a bachelor's degree. The application deadline for fall entry is September 2.

Visiting: There are regularly scheduled orientations for prospective students. Guides are available for informal campus visits. Visitors may sit in on classes and stay overnight at the school. The admissions office should be contacted for arrangements.

Financial Aid: About 80% of all students receive financial aid. The college offers several freshman scholarships. The deadline for aid applications is April 15; the FFS must be filed.

Foreign Students: Special counseling and special organizations are available for these students.

Admissions: Foreign students must achieve a TOEFL score of at least 500 and must take the ELS. No college entrance exams are required.

Procedure: There are no application deadlines; foreign students are admitted in all terms. Foreign students must present proof of health and proof of funds adequate to cover 1 year of study. Health insurance is available through the college.

Admissions Contact: Bob D. Smith, Dean of Admissions and Registrar.

OKLAHOMA CITY UNIVERSITY D-3
Oklahoma City, Oklahoma 73111 (405) 521-5050

F/T: 471M, 491W	Faculty: 200; IIA, −$
P/T: 260M, 260W	Ph.D.'s: 68%
Grad: 1020M, 337W	S/F Ratio: 17 to 1
Year: sems, ss	Tuition: $2140
Appl: open	R and B: n/av
998 applied	912 accepted 727 enrolled
ACT: 22	COMPETITIVE

Oklahoma City University was established in 1904 and is affiliated with the Methodist Church. It offers undergraduate programs in the liberal arts and sciences, business, education, and preprofessional areas. The library contains 150,000 volumes and 900 microtexts, and subscribes to more than 1000 periodicals.

Environment: The 60-acre campus, located in the center of Oklahoma City, has 24 buildings, including 5 residence halls that accommodate about 350 men and 250 women. There are also facilities for commuting students.

Student Life: About 70% of the students come from Oklahoma. About 85% are graduates of public schools. Sixty percent live on campus. Most students are Protestant. Dormitories are single-sex.

Organizations: Campus activities include student government, clubs, religious and service organizations, publications, drama and other performing groups, and social and cultural events. About 12% of the men belong to the 4 fraternities on campus, and 14% of the women belong to the 4 sororities.

Sports: The university fields intercollegiate teams in 6 sports for men and 4 for women. Intramural sports for men and women also are available.

Handicapped: The entire campus is accessible to handicapped students.

Graduates: The freshman dropout rate is 15%, and about 65% remain to graduate. About 45% of the graduates go on for further study.

Services: The university provides health care, tutoring, remedial instruction, career counseling, and placement services.

Programs of Study: The university confers the B.A., B.S., B.S. in Bus., B.Mus., and B.Perf.Arts degrees. Associate and master's programs are also available. Bachelor's degrees are offered in the following subjects: BUSINESS (accounting, aviation management, business administration, computer science, finance, management, marketing, technical management), EDUCATION (early childhood, elementary, health/physical, secondary), ENGLISH (English, mass communications), FINE AND PERFORMING ARTS (art, dance, film/photography, Indian art, music, music education, theater/dramatics), LANGUAGES (French, German, Spanish), MATH AND SCIENCES (biology, chemistry, mathematics, physics), PHILOSOPHY (humanities, philosophy), SOCIAL SCIENCES (corrections, economics, government/political science, history, law enforcement, psychology, sociology).

Required: Students must take courses in English, religion, physical education, and other basic academic areas.

Special: Independent study, study abroad, exchange programs, a Washington semester, a 3-year bachelor's degree, and an external degree program are offered.

Honors: Thirteen honor societies have chapters on campus.

Admissions: Almost all (91%) of the applicants for the 1981–82 freshman class were accepted. Applicants should be high school graduates, have at least a 2.0 GPA, and rank in the top 30% of their class. Recommendations are also necessary.

Procedure: Either the SAT or the ACT is required. Application deadlines are open. Notification is made on a rolling basis. A personal interview is recommended. The application fee is $20.

Special: Early and deferred admissions plans are offered. AP and CLEP credit is available.

Transfer: Transfer students are considered for all classes. A 2.0 GPA is needed. Thirty semester hours must be completed in residence.

Visiting: Campus tours with student guides may be arranged. Visitors may sit in on classes.

Financial Aid: The university participates in federal (NDSL, CWS, BEOG/SEOG) and state aid programs. It also offers commercial loans and freshman scholarships. Need and academic merit are the determining factors for awards. The FAF should be filed by March 1.

Foreign Students: Full-time students from foreign countries represent about 10% of enrollment.

Admissions: Foreign applicants generally must score 500–550 on the TOEFL. No college entrance exams are required.

Procedure: Students are admitted in fall, spring, and summer. Applications should be filed at least 1 month before the start of the term in which the student seeks to enroll. Students must present proof of adequate funds for 1 year.

Admissions Contact: Kenneth Doake, Director of Undergraduate Admissions.

OKLAHOMA PANHANDLE STATE UNIVERSITY B-2
Goodwell, Oklahoma 73939 (405) 349-2611

F/T: 575M, 340W	Faculty: 64; IIB, +$
P/T: 75M, 210W	Ph.D.'s: 30%
Grad: none	S/F Ratio: 17 to 1
Year: sems, ss	Tuition: $411 ($994)
Appl: open	R and B: $1370
340 applied	320 accepted 285 enrolled
ACT: 17	NON COMPETITIVE

Oklahoma Panhandle State University, founded in 1909, is a state-supported institution offering undergraduate study in agribusiness, agriculture, business, home economics, industrial arts, literature, music, and science. The library contains 75,500 volumes and subscribes to 500 periodicals.

Environment: The 120-acre campus is located in a rural area about 100 miles from Amarillo, Texas. Facilities include an on-campus, 9-hole golf course. Living facilities consist of dormitories and married student housing.

Student Life: Two-thirds of the students are from Oklahoma; 20% come from Texas, Kansas, Colorado, and New Mexico. Ninety-seven percent of entering freshmen come from public schools. About 60% of all students reside on campus. Twelve percent are minority-group members. Ninety-five percent are Protestant, 2% are Catholic, and 1% are Jewish. Campus housing is single-sex; there are visiting privileges. Students may keep cars on campus.

Organizations: There are no fraternities or sororities on campus, but students have the opportunity to participate in many other activities.

Sports: The university fields 5 intercollegiate teams. There are 8 intramural sports.

Handicapped: About 70% of the campus is accessible to physically handicapped students, with further alterations in progress. Fewer than 1% of the students are visually impaired; there are no hearing impaired students.

Graduates: The freshman dropout rate is 25%; 40% remain to graduate. Fifteen percent of the students who graduate pursue further study; 1% enter medical school, 1% enter dental school, and 1% enter law school. Sixty-five percent pursue careers in business or industry.

Services: The following services are offered at no charge to students: remedial instruction, placement and career counseling. Health care and psychological counseling are provided on a fee basis.

Programs of Study: The university confers the B.A. and B.S. degrees. Bachelor's degrees are offered in the following subjects: BUSINESS (accounting, agribusiness, business administration, business education, computer science), EDUCATION (elementary, health/physical, secondary), ENGLISH (English, speech), FINE AND PERFORMING ARTS (music, music education), HEALTH SCIENCES (medical technology), MATH AND SCIENCES (biology, chemistry, mathematics, natural sciences), PREPROFESSIONAL (agriculture, home economics, library science), SOCIAL SCIENCES (government/political science, history, psychology, social sciences).

Special: A cooperative medical technology program is offered.

Honors: The national honor society Alpha Psi Omega has a chapter on campus.

Admissions: Ninety-four percent of those who applied were accepted for the 1981–82 freshman class. All candidates must be high school graduates and have completed 16 units of secondary school study. Out-of-state residents must be in the upper 50% of their class. Other important considerations in the admissions decision are: recommendations by school officials, leadership record, and evidence of special talent.

Procedure: The SAT or ACT is required. There are no application deadlines; freshmen are admitted in the fall, spring, and summer terms. The university has a rolling admissions plan. There is no application fee.

OKLAHOMA

Special: CLEP credit is accepted.

Transfer: For fall 1981, 80 students applied, 75 were accepted, and 70 enrolled. Transfers are considered for all classes. Applicants must be in good standing at their previous school. D grades transfer. All students must complete, at the university, 24 of the 124 credits required for a bachelor's degree. Application deadlines are August 15 (fall), December 15 (spring), and May 1 (summer).

Visiting: The university holds pre-enrollment clinics for interested students. Guides may be requested for informal visits to the campus. Visitors may sit in on classes and arrange to stay overnight at the school. Weekday mornings are the best times for visiting. The director of admissions will make arrangements.

Financial Aid: About 30% of all students receive aid. Forty percent work part-time on campus. The university awards many freshman scholarships each year. The university is a member of CSS; the FAF, FFS, or SFS is required. Application deadlines are December 18 (fall) and May 10 (summer).

Foreign Students: Two percent of the full-time students come from foreign countries. Special organizations are available for these students.

Admissions: Foreign students must achieve a TOEFL score of at least 500. No college entrance exams are required.

Procedure: Application deadlines are June 1 (fall), November 1 (spring), and March 1 (summer). Foreign students must have a physical exam and must present proof of funds adequate to cover 1 year of study.

Admissions Contact: Jack V. Begley, Director of Admissions.

OKLAHOMA STATE UNIVERSITY E-2
Stillwater, Oklahoma 74078 (405) 624-6857

F/T: 10,606M, 7599W	Faculty:	995; I, − $
P/T: 578M, 554W	Ph.D.'s:	82%
Grad: 1960M, 1412W	S/F Ratio:	18 to 1
Year: sems, ss	Tuition:	$625 ($1675)
Appl: Aug. 20	R and B:	$1642
4594 applied	4518 accepted	3607 enrolled
ACT: 20		COMPETITIVE

Oklahoma State University was established in 1890 and offers undergraduate degree programs in liberal arts and sciences, business, education, agriculture, engineering, home economics, and applied science/technology areas. The library contains nearly 2 million items.

Environment: The main campus is located on more than 480 acres in a suburban/rural setting. The university farmland totals 2352 acres and adjoins the campus. There are also 2 branch campuses and 17 experimental agricultural stations throughout the state. Living facilities include dormitories, on-campus apartments, married student housing, and sorority and fraternity houses.

Student Life: About 85% of the students come from Oklahoma; the majority are public school graduates. Half of the students live on campus. Seven percent are minority-group members. Campus housing is single-sex; there are visiting privileges. Students may keep cars on campus.

Organizations: There is a full and varied extracurricular program. The university sponsors all traditional groups and schedules on-campus cultural and social events regularly. About 20% of the men and women are members of 39 nationally affiliated fraternities and sororities.

Sports: Intercollegiate teams are organized in 8 sports for men and 7 for women. There are 20 intramural sports for men and 16 for women.

Graduates: The freshman dropout rate is 28%; 50% remain to graduate.

Services: The university provides health care, psychological counseling, tutoring, career counseling, and placement services for all students.

Programs of Study: The university offers the B.A., B.S., B.F.A., B.S. Art Ed., and B.Mus. degrees. Associate, master's, and doctoral degrees are also awarded. Bachelor's degrees are offered in the following subjects: BUSINESS (accounting, business administration, business education, computer science, finance, management, marketing, real estate/insurance), EDUCATION (adult, distributive education, early childhood, elementary, health/physical, industrial, secondary, special, technical), ENGLISH (English, journalism, literature, speech), FINE AND PERFORMING ARTS (art, art education, film/photography, music, music education, radio/TV, theater/dramatics), HEALTH SCIENCES (medical technology, speech therapy), LANGUAGES (French, German, Spanish), MATH AND SCIENCES (aerospace, biochemistry, biology, botany, chemistry, earth science, ecology/environmental science, geology, mathematics, military science, natural sciences, physical sciences, physics, physiology, statistics, zoology), PHILOSOPHY (humanities, philosophy, religion), PREPROFESSIONAL (agriculture, architecture, dentistry, engineering, forestry, home economics, law, medicine, social work, veterinary), SOCIAL SCIENCES (anthropology, economics, geography, government/political science, history, psychology, social sciences, sociology).

Required: There is a general education requirement for all degrees including courses in English and American history/government.

Special: Study abroad, independent study, dual degree programs, exchange programs, internships, and a 3-year bachelor's degree are offered. It is possible to earn the B.G.S. degree.

Honors: Several honorary societies have chapters on campus. Honors work is possible in all departments.

Admissions: About 98% of the most recent freshman applicants were accepted. The ACT scores of those who enrolled were as follows: 55% scored below 21, 20% between 21 and 23, 11% between 24 and 25, 11% between 26 and 28, and 3% above 28. A high school diploma (or GED) and class rank in the top 50% are required in addition to a satisfactory score on the ACT. Nonresidents also need a 2.0 high school GPA.

Procedure: The ACT is required of Oklahoma residents; nonresidents must take either the ACT or the SAT. Application deadlines are August 20 (fall), January 8 (spring), and June 4 (summer). Notification is on a rolling basis. There is a $10 application fee for out-of-state applicants.

Special: CLEP and AP are used. There are early decision, early admissions, and deferred admissions plans.

Transfer: For fall 1981, 2358 students applied, 2272 were accepted, and 2032 enrolled. A 2.0 GPA is necessary; D grades to transfer. All students must complete, at the university, 24 of the 120–144 credits required for a bachelor's degree. Application deadlines are the same as those for freshmen.

Visiting: Campus tours with student guides can be arranged. Visitors may attend classes.

Financial Aid: About 25% of the students are receiving assistance. Ten percent work part-time on campus. The average freshman award is $1200. The university participates in federal (NDSL, BEOG/SEOG, CWS) and state aid programs in addition to offering commercial (bank) loans and a limited number of freshman scholarships. The FFS is required. Application deadlines are March 1 (fall), November 1 (spring), and January 1 (summer).

Foreign Students: Eight percent of the full-time students come from foreign countries. Special counseling and special organizations are available for these students.

Admissions: Foreign students must achieve a TOEFL score of at least 500. No college entrance exams are required.

Procedure: Application deadlines are June 15 (fall), November 1 (spring), and April 1 (summer). Foreign students must submit a medical history report and must present proof of funds adequate to cover 4 years of study. There is a special $15 fee for foreign students, which covers special processing and reporting.

Admissions Contact: Raymond Girod, Director of Admissions and Registrar.

ORAL ROBERTS UNIVERSITY E-2
Tulsa, Oklahoma 74171 (918) 495-6518

F/T: 1468M, 1578W	Faculty:	292; n/av
P/T: 267M, 196W	Ph.D.'s:	67%
Grad: 547M, 128W	S/F Ratio:	11 to 1
Year: sems, ss	Tuition:	$3360
Appl: open	R and B:	$1962
2359 applied	1929 accepted	1335 enrolled
SAT: 463V 490M		COMPETITIVE

Oral Roberts University, founded in 1963, is a private liberal arts institution, committed to the Christian faith. The library contains 500,000 volumes and 165,000 microfilm items, and subscribes to 4000 periodicals.

Environment: The 520-acre suburban campus is located 8 miles from downtown Tulsa. There are 20 major buildings; the City of Faith Medical and Research Center has partially opened; the hospital and clinic are accepting patients, and the research center will open in 1982. Living facilities include dormitories and off-campus apartments for graduate students.

Student Life: About 18% of the students are from Oklahoma. About 82% live on campus. Twelve percent are minority-group members.

Ninety-nine percent are Protestant. Campus housing is single-sex; there are visiting privileges. Students may keep cars on campus. Students must attend religious services twice a week. There are religious counselors for Catholic and Protestant students. Drinking and smoking are prohibited on and off campus.

Organizations: There are no fraternities or sororities on campus. Activities include religious groups, special interest clubs, student government, and social and cultural events. The Christian Service Council coordinates volunteer opportunities for students.

Sports: The university fields teams in 5 intercollegiate sports for men and 4 sports for women. There are 12 intramural sports for men and 11 for women.

Handicapped: About 90% of the campus is accessible to handicapped students. Facilities include wheelchair ramps, parking areas, elevators, specially equipped rest rooms, lowered drinking fountains and telephones, and individual classroom modifications. Special class scheduling is also available.

Graduates: The freshman dropout rate is 20%. About 40% of the graduates pursue advanced degrees: 5% in medicine, 1% in dentistry, and 3% in law.

Services: Students receive the following services free of charge: placement, health care, psychological and career counseling, and tutoring.

Programs of Study: The B.A., B.M., B.Mus.Ed., and B.S. degrees are conferred. Master's and doctoral degrees are also awarded. Bachelor's degrees are offered in the following subjects: BUSINESS (accounting, business administration, business education, computer science, management, marketing), EDUCATION (aerobics, elementary, health/physical, religious, secondary, special), ENGLISH (communication arts, interpersonal communication, literature), FINE AND PERFORMING ARTS (art, art education, music, music—composition, music—performance, music—sacred, music education, radio/TV, studio art, theater/dramatics), HEALTH SCIENCES (medical technology, nursing), LANGUAGES (French, German, Spanish), MATH AND SCIENCES (biochemistry, biology, chemistry, mathematics), PHILOSOPHY (Biblical literature), PREPROFESSIONAL (dentistry, law, medicine, ministry, social work), SOCIAL SCIENCES (history, liberal arts, psychology, sociology). Most degrees are conferred in theology and music.

Required: All students are required to take courses in the humanities, social sciences, natural and biological sciences, physical education, the Bible, and theology.

Special: Combined B.A.-B.S. degrees, student-designed majors, study abroad, independent study, and a program in humanities are offered.

Honors: There are 6 honor societies on campus.

Admissions: Eighty-two percent of those who applied for the 1981–82 freshman class were accepted. Applicants should be high school graduates, rank in the upper half of the class, and present satisfactory SAT or ACT scores. Other factors considered are impressions made during the interview, evidence of special talent, and advanced placement or honor courses.

Procedure: The SAT or ACT is required and should be taken by the fall of the senior year. Placement tests are given by the university. Students are accepted for the fall, spring, and summer terms. There is a rolling admissions plan. Though there is no application deadline, students should apply by October 1. The application fee is $15.

Special: There are early decision and early admissions plans. CLEP and AP credit is given.

Transfer: For fall 1981, 233 students enrolled. A minister's recommendation is required. D grades do not transfer. Students must complete, at the university, 30 of the 128 credits required for a bachelor's degree. There is no deadline for transfer applications, but July 1 is suggested for fall admission.

Visiting: Orientations for prospective students are scheduled during Thanksgiving and Easter vacations. Attendance is by application only; the only cost to the student is transportation to the campus. Other campus visits are best scheduled on weekdays from 8:30 A.M. to 4 P.M. Visitors may sit in on classes. Overnight accommodations are available for prospective students by invitation. The admissions office should be contacted for arrangements.

Financial Aid: About 72% of the students receive financial aid. Nineteen percent work part-time on campus. The university provides academic scholarships. Government, bank, and university loans are available, as is part-time employment. Most financial aid is in package form. The university is a member of CSS and requires the FAF and the university's own financial aid form. The deadlines for financial aid applications are April 1 (fall) and November 1 (spring).

Foreign Students: Five percent of the full-time students come from foreign countries. Special counseling and special organizations are available for these students.

Admissions: Foreign students must take either the TOEFL or the SAT. On the TOEFL, a minimum score of 500 is required.

Procedure: There are no application deadlines; foreign students are admitted in all terms. They must present proof of funds adequate to cover 1 year of study and must carry health insurance, which is available through the university for a fee.

Admissions Contact: Tim Cameron, Admissions Director.

PHILLIPS UNIVERSITY   D–2
Enid, Oklahoma 73701   (405) 237-4433

F/T: 500M, 400W   Faculty: 73; IIA, – – $
P/T: 200M, 200W   Ph.D.'s: 75%
Grad: 50M, 30W   S/F Ratio: 11 to 1
Year: sems, ss   Tuition: $2846
Appl: open   R and B: $1760
348 applied   294 accepted   168 enrolled
ACT: 20   COMPETITIVE

Phillips University is a private liberal arts institution affiliated with the Disciples of Christ. The library contains 220,000 volumes and subscribes to 1020 periodicals.

Environment: The 140-acre campus is located in a suburban area about 60 miles from Oklahoma City. The 4000-seat Mabee Center is an athletic facility used for varsity basketball and intramural sports. Two dormitories on campus accommodate 245 women and 254 men. There are also three 20-unit apartment buildings for married students.

Student Life: About 50% of the students are from Oklahoma; 90% come from public schools. Forty-eight percent of the students live on campus. Ten percent of the students are Catholic; 40% are Protestant. Thirteen percent are minority-group members. University housing is single-sex; there are visiting privileges. Alcohol is not permitted on campus.

Organizations: There are 6 fraternities and 6 sororities on campus; 15% of the men and 15% of the women belong to them. Extracurricular activities include musical groups, publications, special-interest clubs, and religious groups.

Sports: There are 3 intercollegiate teams for men and 2 for women. There are 8 intramurals for men and 7 for women.

Handicapped: About 70% of the campus is accessible to handicapped students. Special facilities include wheelchair ramps, parking areas, elevators, and lowered drinking fountains and telephones. Special class scheduling is also available. Two counselors are available to handicapped students.

Graduates: About 5% of the freshmen drop out by the end of the first year; 52% remain to graduate. Forty-seven percent of the graduates pursue advanced degrees; 2% enter medical school, 1% dental school, and 1% law school. Thirty percent pursue careers in business and industry.

Services: The following services are provided to students free of charge: health care, placement, psychological counseling, and career counseling.

Programs of Study: The university confers the B.A., B.S., and B.Mus.Ed. degrees. Associate and master's programs are also offered. Bachelor's degrees are offered in the following subjects: AREA STUDIES (American, urban), BUSINESS (accounting, business administration, business education, computer science, finance, management, marketing, real estate/insurance), EDUCATION (adult, early childhood, elementary, health/physical, industrial, secondary, special), ENGLISH (English, journalism, literature, speech), FINE AND PERFORMING ARTS (art, art education, art history, music, music education, radio/TV, studio art, theater/dramatics), HEALTH SCIENCES (medical technology, nursing, occupational therapy, physical therapy, speech therapy), LANGUAGES (French, German, Greek/Latin, Hebrew), MATH AND SCIENCES (biochemistry, biology, botany, chemistry, earth science, geology, mathematics, natural sciences, physical sciences, physics, statistics, zoology), PHILOSOPHY (humanities, philosophy, religion), PREPROFESSIONAL (dentistry, engineering, law, library science, medicine, ministry, pharmacy, social work, veterinary), SOCIAL SCIENCES (anthropology, economics, geography, government/political science, history, international relations, psychology, social sciences, sociology), Fifteen percent of degrees are awarded in education, 15% in health sciences, and 15% in preprofessional subjects.

Required: Each student must satisfy 12 goals that provide balance between a broad liberal arts education and responsible career preparation.

710 OKLAHOMA

Special: Students may participate in the junior-year-abroad program. Courses in geology, art, and biology are offered at the University Summer Campus in the Colorado mountains. Through Hebrew Union College, students may earn credit by participating in an archaeological dig in Israel, or spend a semester in Sweden. A 3-2 engineering program is offered in conjunction with Washington University in St. Louis. The B.G.S. degree is offered. Students may design their own majors.

Honors: Honors courses are offered in many areas. There are several honor societies on campus.

Admissions: About 84% of those who applied were accepted for the 1981–82 freshman class. Applicants should have completed 15 Carnegie units, have at least a 2.0 GPA, and be recommended by their high school. Leadership record, extracurricular activities, special talents, and personality are also considered in the admissions decision.

Procedure: The ACT or SAT is required. The university arranges for either a campus interview or an off-campus interview with a Phillips representative, and this is generally important in the admissions process. Candidates should apply early in their senior year. The deadline is open. Notification is on a rolling basis. There is a $10 application fee.

Special: AP and CLEP credit is granted.

Transfer: For fall 1981, 129 students applied, 118 were accepted, and 88 enrolled. A 2.0 GPA is recommended. Students must complete, in residence, all 124 of the credits needed for a bachelor's degree. Deadlines are the same as for freshmen.

Visiting: There are regularly scheduled orientations for prospective students. Guides are available for informal visits. Visitors may sit in on classes and stay overnight at the school. Visits are best scheduled between 8 A.M. and 3 P.M. on weekdays. The admissions department should be contacted for arrangements.

Financial Aid: About 65% of the students receive financial aid. Sixty percent work part-time on campus. Average aid to freshmen from all sources covers 10% of costs. Freshman scholarships, NDSL, BEOG/SEOG, CWS, and other loans, and part-time employment are available. Installment financing is also available. Aid is usually awarded in packages tailored to the applicant's financial need. Aid is awarded on the basis of the student's GPA, test scores, character, and aptitude. The university is a member of CSS. The FAF is required. The deadline for aid applications is March 1.

Foreign Students: Three percent of the full-time students come from foreign countries. The university offers these students an intensive English course, an intensive English program, special counseling, and special organizations.

Admissions: No English-language or college entrance examination is required.

Procedure: Application deadlines are open; students are admitted to all terms. Health insurance is required.

Admissions Contact: Rick Ziegler, Director of Admissions.

SOUTHEASTERN OKLAHOMA STATE UNIVERSITY D–3
Durant, Oklahoma 74701 (405) 924-0121

F/T: 1513M, 1137W	Faculty: 154; IIA, –$
P/T: 430M, 716W	Ph.D.'s: 47%
Grad: 208M, 328W	S/F Ratio: 26 to 1
Year: sems, ss	Tuition: $460 ($1138)
Appl: Aug. 15	R and B: $1740
1080 applied	1058 accepted 980 enrolled
ACT: 21	LESS COMPETITIVE

Southeastern Oklahoma State University, established in 1909, is a college of liberal arts and teacher education. The library contains 135,000 volumes, and 4000 microfilm items, and subscribes to 921 periodicals.

Environment: The 100-acre campus is located near rural Lake Texoma. The residence halls accommodate 420 men and 330 women; institutional apartments accommodate married students. The campus also includes a power technology building and an industrial technology building.

Student Life: Seventy-five percent of the students are from the north central United States, and 23% are from the South. Ninety-eight percent of the entering freshmen come from public schools. Twenty-five percent of the students live on campus. Fifty-three percent are minority-group members. University housing is both single-sex and coed. There are visiting privileges in single-sex housing. Students may keep cars on campus.

Organizations: There are 4 fraternities and 3 sororities, to which 10% of the students belong.

Sports: The university competes intercollegiately in 8 sports for men and 7 for women. There are 8 intramural sports for men and 6 for women.

Handicapped: Approximately 30% of the campus is accessible to the physically handicapped. Facilities include wheelchair ramps, special parking, elevators, and specially equipped rest rooms. Special class scheduling is also available. There are no students with visual or hearing impairments currently enrolled.

Graduates: The freshman dropout rate is 35%. Fifty-five percent go on to graduate. Of those who graduate, 35% pursue graduate study, 1% enter medical school, 1% enter dental school, and 1% enter law school; 30% pursue careers in business and industry.

Services: Placement services, career counseling, tutoring, and remedial instruction are offered free of charge. Health care is available for a fee.

Programs of Study: The university offers the B.A., B.S., B.A.Ed., and B.S.Ed. degrees. Master's programs are also available. Bachelor's degrees are offered in the following subjects: AREA STUDIES (American, Latin American), BUSINESS (accounting, business administration, business education, computer science, finance, management, marketing), EDUCATION (bilingual, early childhood, elementary, health/physical, industrial, science, secondary, special), ENGLISH (English, speech), FINE AND PERFORMING ARTS (art, art education, music, music education, theater/dramatics), HEALTH SCIENCES (medical technology, speech therapy), LANGUAGES (French, Spanish), MATH AND SCIENCES (biochemistry, biology, chemistry, ecology/environmental science, mathematics, physics, recombinant DNA technology), PREPROFESSIONAL (home economics, social work), SOCIAL SCIENCES (criminal justice, economics, geography, government/political science, history, psychology, social sciences, sociology). Forty-five percent of degrees conferred are in education, 25% in business, and 7% in math and sciences.

Special: A combined B.A.-B.S. degree may be earned in a variety of subjects.

Honors: There are 5 national honor societies with chapters on campus. There is a university-wide honors program with preference given to Native Americans.

Admissions: Ninety-eight percent of those who applied were accepted for the 1981–82 freshman class. Of those who enrolled in a recent year, the ACT scores were as follows: 12% scored between 20 and 23, 8% between 24 and 26, 5% between 27 and 28, and 1% above 28. All applicants must be high school graduates. Oklahoma residents must have at least a C average, or rank in the top 75% of their graduating class. Out-of-state applicants must rank in the top half of their class or have an ACT score of at least 16.

Procedure: The ACT is required. Application deadlines are August 15 (fall), January 15 (spring), and June 1 (summer). Notification is on a rolling basis. There is no application fee.

Special: The university has early admissions and deferred admissions plans. CLEP exams are accepted for advanced placement.

Transfer: For fall 1981, 418 students applied, 402 were accepted, and 380 enrolled. Transfers are accepted for all classes and should have at least a 2.0 GPA. All grades transfer. In-state students must score 12 on the ACT, out-of-state, 16. To receivce a degree, students must study a minimum of 30 hours, at the university, out of the 124 needed for a bachelor's degree. Application deadlines are the same as those for freshmen.

Visiting: Guides are available for informal visits to the campus. Visitors may stay overnight at the school. The office of high school relations should be contacted to arrange visits.

Financial Aid: About 48% of all students receive some form of financial aid. Nineteen percent work part-time on campus. Average aid to freshmen from all sources covers 36% of costs. Loans, scholarships, and part-time jobs are available. The FFS is required. The deadlines for aid applications are May 1 (fall), December 1 (spring), and April 1 (summer).

Foreign Students: Ten percent of the full-time students come from foreign countries. The university offers these students an intensive English course, an intensive English program, special counseling, and special organizations.

Admissions: Foreign students must score 500 on the TOEFL. No college entrance examination is required.

Procedure: Application deadlines are June 15 (fall), November 15 (spring), and April 1 (summer). Foreign students must present proof of

SOUTHWESTERN OKLAHOMA STATE UNIVERSITY D-3
Weatherford, Oklahoma 73096   (405) 772-6611

F/T: 1646M, 1856W	Faculty: 200; IIA, +$
P/T: 304M, 392W	Ph.D.'s: 55%
Grad: 267M, 467W	S/F Ratio: 18 to 1
Year: sems, ss	Tuition: $650 ($1600)
Appl: open	R and B: $1200
1625 applied	1620 accepted 1585 enrolled
ACT: 18	LESS COMPETITIVE

Southwestern Oklahoma State University, founded in 1903, offers undergraduate degree programs in the liberal arts and sciences, business, education, health fields, and preprofessional areas. The library has 186,089 volumes and 265,000 microfilm items, and subscribes to 1405 periodicals.

Environment: The 73-acre campus is located in a small rural town 75 miles from Oklahoma City. Residence halls accommodate about 710 men and 830 women. There are apartments for married students and cafeteria facilities for commuters.

Student Life: About 95% of the students come from Oklahoma; most are public school graduates. About 50% reside on campus. Twenty percent of the students are Catholic, 18% Protestant, and 1% Jewish; 1% claim no religious affiliation. Twenty percent of the students are minority-group members. University housing is both single-sex and coed. There are visiting privileges in single-sex housing. Students may keep cars on campus. Alcohol is not permitted on campus.

Organizations: The extracurricular program includes campus government, clubs, service and religious organizations, performing groups, dramatics, and publications. About 5% of the students belong to fraternities and sororities. There are regularly scheduled on-campus social and cultural events.

Sports: The university fields intercollegiate teams in 7 sports for men and 5 for women. The intramural program includes 8 sports for both men and women.

Handicapped: Most of the campus is accessible to handicapped students.

Graduates: The freshman dropout rate is 13%. Recently, about 65% remained to graduate. Of the graduates, nearly 20% went on for further study.

Services: The university provides free tutoring, placement, and career counseling. Health care and remedial instruction are available on a fee basis.

Programs of Study: The B.A., B.S., B.A.Ed., B.S.Ed., and B.S.Pharm. degrees are conferred. There are also master's programs. Bachelor's degrees are offered in the following subjects: BUSINESS (accounting, business administration, business education, computer science, finance, management, marketing), EDUCATION (elementary, health/physical, secondary, special), ENGLISH (English, journalism, literature, speech), FINE AND PERFORMING ARTS (art, art education, music, music education, theater/dramatics), HEALTH SCIENCES (medical technology, nursing), LANGUAGES (Spanish), MATH AND SCIENCES (biology, chemistry, mathematics, natural sciences, physics, zoology), PREPROFESSIONAL (home economics, library science, pharmacy, social work), SOCIAL SCIENCES (economics, geography, history, psychology, social sciences, sociology).

Required: All students must complete the general education requirement.

Honors: Various honor societies have chapters on campus.

Admissions: About 99% of those who applied were accepted for the 1981–82 freshman class. The ACT scores of those who enrolled were as follows: 20% scored below 21, 50% between 21 and 23, 5% between 24 and 25, 5% between 26 and 28, and 20% above 28. A high school diploma or GED is required. Out-of-state applicants should rank in the top half of their high school class. An interview is recommended.

Procedure: The ACT is required. New students are admitted each semester. Application deadlines are open. Notification is on a rolling basis. There is no application fee.

Special: There is an early admissions plan. AP and CLEP credit is available.

Transfer: For fall 1981, 200 students applied, 195 were admitted, and 180 enrolled. A 2.0 GPA, an ACT score of 14, and good academic standing are necessary. State residents are given preference. Students must complete all 124 credits needed to obtain a bachelor's degree. Application deadlines are the same as those for freshman applicants.

Visiting: Campus tours with student guides can be arranged. Visitors may sit in on classes.

Financial Aid: About 30% of the students receive financial aid. Ten percent work part-time on campus. The university participates in federal (NDSL, CWS, BEOG/SEOG) and state assistance programs in addition to offering commercial loans and a limited number of freshman scholarships. Installment financing is available. Need and academic achievement are the determining factors. The college is a member of CSS. The FFS is required. Application deadlines are open.

Foreign Students: About 3% of the full-time students come from foreign countries. The university offers these students special organizations.

Admissions: Foreign students must score 500 on the TOEFL. They must also take the ACT.

Procedure: Application deadlines are June 1 (fall), October 1 (spring), and March 1 (summer). Foreign students must present proof of funds adequate to cover 4 years of study. They must pay out-of-state tuition fees.

Admissions Contact: Bob Klaassen, Director of Admissions.

UNIVERSITY OF OKLAHOMA D-3
Norman, Oklahoma 73019   (405) 325-2251

F/T: 8352M, 5922W	Faculty: 753; I, −$
P/T: 1296M, 1096W	Ph.D.'s: 75%
Grad: 2092M, 1794W	S/F Ratio: 21 to 1
Year: sems, ss	Tuition: $575 ($1565)
Appl: June 1	R and B: $1532
4712 applied	4458 accepted 3136 enrolled
ACT: 21	COMPETITIVE

The University of Oklahoma, founded in 1890, is part of the state educational system and presently includes 15 colleges. The library contains 1.8 million volumes and 850,000 microfilm items, and subscribes to 20,149 periodicals.

Environment: The 1029-acre, suburban main campus is in Norman, 20 miles from Oklahoma City. The university now owns an additional 2077 acres. Dormitory facilities are extensive. Instruction in the health sciences is given in Oklahoma City; instruction in biology is offered during summer sessions at the biological station at Lake Texoma. All other departments of instruction and administrative offices are in Norman.

Student Life: Approximately 80% of the students are from Oklahoma. Nine percent of the students are minority-group members. University housing is coed. Students may keep cars on campus.

Organizations: There are 24 fraternities and 15 sororities, to which 18% of the men and 20% of the women belong. Almost every department has a club that students of similar occupational or professional interests may join.

Sports: The university competes intercollegiately in 11 sports for men and 11 for women. There are 8 intramural sports for men and 4 for women.

Handicapped: Approximately 75% of the campus is accessible to the physically handicapped. Facilities include wheelchair ramps, special parking, elevators, specially equipped rest rooms, and lowered drinking fountains and telephones. Special class scheduling, individual counseling, and an attendant referral service are also available. Notetakers and special facilities are available for hearing and visually impaired students.

Graduates: The freshman dropout rate is 36%; 33% remained to graduate in recent years.

Services: Placement services, career counseling, psychological counseling, tutoring, and remedial instruction are offered free of charge. Health care is also available on a fee basis.

Programs of Study: The university confers the B.A., B.S., B.B.A., B.Arch., B.A., B.F.A., B.M., and B.Mus.Ed. degrees. Master's and doctoral degrees are also offered. Bachelor's degrees are offered in the following subjects: AREA STUDIES (American, Asian, Latin American, Russian, urban), BUSINESS (accounting, business administration, business education, computer science, finance, management, marketing, real estate/insurance), EDUCATION (early childhood, elementary, health/physical, secondary, special), ENGLISH (English, journalism, speech), FINE AND PERFORMING ARTS (art, art education, art history, dance, film/photography, music, music education, radio/TV, theater/dramatics), HEALTH SCIENCES (medical technology, nurs-

712 OKLAHOMA

ing, occupational therapy, physical therapy, speech therapy), LANGUAGES (French, German, Russian, Spanish), MATH AND SCIENCES (astronomy, botany, chemistry, geology, mathematics, physics, zoology), PHILOSOPHY (philosophy, religion), PREPROFESSIONAL (architecture, engineering, home economics, pharmacy, social work), SOCIAL SCIENCES (anthropology, economics, geography, government/political science, history, psychology, sociology).

Required: All undergraduates must complete 2 courses in English composition and 2 in American history and government; these courses are usually taken during the freshman year.

Special: Student-designed majors, combined programs in dentistry and medicine, and a 5-year combined degree program in arts and sciences and engineering are offered. The Oklahoma Center for Continuing Education offers educational and cultural services to individuals, organizations, and communities of Oklahoma, other states, and foreign countries.

Honors: Approximately 75 national honor societies have chapters on campus. Honors programs are offered in arts and sciences, business, engineering, and fine arts.

Admissions: Approximately 95% of those who applied were accepted for the 1981–82 freshman class. The ACT scores of those who enrolled were as follows: 46% scored below 21, 20% between 21 and 23, 12% between 24 and 25, 15% between 26 and 28, and 7% above 28. Any Oklahoma resident who is a graduate of an accredited high school, has taken the ACT, and meets at least 1 of the following requirements is eligible for admission: (1) a minimum 3.0 high school GPA; (2) rank in the top half of the graduating class; (3) a composite standard ACT score placing the candidate in the top half of high school seniors, based on twelfth-grade national norms. Students not eligible for normal admission may be admitted provisionally for the summer session.

Procedure: The ACT is required of Oklahoma residents; nonresidents may substitute the SAT. The deadlines for applications are June 1 (fall), October 15 (spring), and April 1 (summer). The university follows a rolling admissions policy. There is a $10 application fee for nonresidents.

Special: The university participates in the CLEP program (subject exams only).

Transfer: For fall 1981, 2440 students applied, 2270 transfer applicants were accepted, and the university enrolled 1589. Transfers are accepted for all classes. A GPA of 2.0 is required. D grades are accepted. Students must complete 45 of their last 60 credits in residence; 124 credits are required for a bachelor's degree.

Visiting: Guides are available for informal visits to the campus. There are also regularly scheduled campus tours. Visitors may sit in on classes. To arrange an appointment for a visit or an overnight stay, the office of high school relations should be contacted.

Financial Aid: Twenty-three percent of the freshmen and about 21% of all other students receive some form of financial aid. Twenty percent work part-time on campus. Average aid awarded to freshmen from all sources is $1150. Many scholarships, fellowships, and assistantships are open to undergraduate and graduate students. Loans and part-time employment are also available. The university is a member of CSS. The FAF is required. There is no formal deadline for aid applications.

Foreign Students: Seven percent of the full-time students come from foreign countries. The university offers these students special counseling and special organizations.

Admissions: Foreign students must score 550 on the TOEFL. No college entrance examination is required.

Procedure: Application deadlines are June 1 (fall), October 15 (spring), and April 1 (summer). Foreign students must present proof of funds adequate to cover 1 calendar year. They must also pay a special fee of $15 a semester to process their immigration papers and for special services. They must carry health insurance, which is available through the university without charge.

Admissions Contact: Barbara E. Cousins, Director of Admissions.

UNIVERSITY OF SCIENCE AND ARTS OF OKLAHOMA D-4
Chickasha, Oklahoma 73018   (405) 224-3140

F/T: 262M, 432W	Faculty: 54; IIB, +$
P/T: 183M, 475W	Ph.D.'s: 65%
Grad: none	S/F Ratio: 14 to 1
Year: tri, ss	Tuition: $480 ($1150)
Appl: open	R and B: $1400
279 applied	251 accepted 209 enrolled
ACT: 19	LESS COMPETITIVE

The University of Science and Arts of Oklahoma, established in 1908, is a state-supported university offering undergraduate programs in liberal arts and sciences, business, education, and health fields. The library contains 85,000 volumes and subscribes to 1200 periodicals.

Environment: The 75-acre campus is located in a rural setting, 50 miles from Oklahoma City. Facilities include the student union, 6 dormitories accommodating 300 men and 300 women, and a student lounge and dining hall for commuting students.

Student Life: About 90% of the students come from Oklahoma. Thirty percent of the students live on campus. Thirteen percent are minority-group members. University housing is single-sex; there are visiting privileges. Students may keep cars on campus. Alcohol is not permitted on campus.

Organizations: There are 3 sororities and 3 fraternities on campus; 2% of the men and 2% of the women belong to them. Student activities include religious organizations, student government, publications, musical groups, and special-interest clubs.

Sports: Intercollegiate teams are fielded in 3 sports for men and 2 for women. There are 10 intramural sports for men and 9 for women.

Handicapped: The university is working to make the campus accessible to handicapped students.

Graduates: The freshman dropout rate is 25%; 25% remain to graduate. Twenty percent of the graduates pursue advanced degrees; 1% enter medical school, 1% dental school, and 3% law school. Ninety percent eventually enter careers in business and industry.

Services: Students receive the following services free of charge: career and psychological counseling, health care, and placement services. Tutoring and remedial instruction are on a fee basis.

Programs of Study: The university confers the B.A. and B.S. degrees. Bachelor's degrees are offered in the following subjects: AREA STUDIES (Indian), BUSINESS (accounting, business administration, business education, computer science, management), EDUCATION (early childhood, elementary, secondary, special), ENGLISH (English, literature, speech), FINE AND PERFORMING ARTS (art, art education, music, music education, theater/dramatics), HEALTH SCIENCES (medical technology, nursing, speech therapy), LANGUAGES (French, Spanish), MATH AND SCIENCES (biology, chemistry, mathematics, natural sciences, physics), PREPROFESSIONAL (home economics), SOCIAL SCIENCES (economics, government/political science, history, psychology, sociology). Twenty-seven percent of degrees are conferred in business, 23% in education, and 14% in social sciences.

Special: Independent study is offered during the first 5 weeks of the third trimester. A 3-year bachelor's degree is available.

Honors: Seven honor societies have chapters on campus.

Admissions: Ninety percent of those who applied were accepted for the 1981–82 freshman class. The ACT scores of those who enrolled were as follows: 70% scored below 21, 17% between 21 and 23, 6% between 24 and 25, 5% between 26 and 28, and 2% above 28. Candidates must be graduates of accredited high schools. Out-of-state candidates must rank in the upper half of the graduating class or have a 2.0 high school GPA.

Procedure: The ACT is required. Application deadlines are open; however, the following deadlines are suggested: August 1 (fall), December 1 (spring), and April 1 (summer). Notification is on a rolling basis. There is no application fee.

Special: AP and CLEP credit is available.

Transfer: For fall 1981, 87 students applied, 87 were accepted, and 61 enrolled. Transfer students are accepted for all classes. A GPA of 2.0 is required; an ACT score of 17 is also required. Students must study at the university for at least 30 semester hours of the 124 needed to receive a bachelor's degree. Transfer application deadlines are the same as for freshmen.

Visiting: Guided tours are available. The admissions office should be contacted for arrangements.

Financial Aid: About 48% of the students receive financial aid. Thirty-five percent work part-time on campus. Average aid awarded to freshmen from all sources covers 70% of college costs. Freshman scholarships are awarded each year. Loans are available from the federal government and from the university. Part-time campus employment is also offered. Tuition may not be paid in installments. The FFS is required. Financial aid application deadlines are July 1 (fall), November 1 (spring), and March 1 (summer).

Foreign Students: Four percent of the full-time students come from foreign countries. The university provides these students with special counseling and special organizations.

Admissions: Foreign students must score 500 on the TOEFL and 17 on the ACT.

Procedure: The deadlines for application are August 1 (fall), December 1 (spring), and April 1 (summer). Foreign students must present proof of funds adequate to cover 1 academic year. They must pay out-of-state tuition fees. They must also carry health insurance, which is available through the university for a fee.

Admissions Contact: Jack D. Hudson, Registrar and Director of Admissions.

UNIVERSITY OF TULSA E-2
Tulsa, Oklahoma 74104 (918) 592-6000

F/T: 1782M, 1573W	Faculty: 311; I, — — $
P/T: 564M, 651W	Ph.D.'s: 70%
Grad: 1071M, 741W	S/F Ratio: 16 to 1
Year: 4-4-1, ss	Tuition: $2770
Appl: open	R and B: $1515
1534 applied 1318 accepted 763 enrolled	
SAT: 471V 520M ACT: 23 COMPETITIVE	

The University of Tulsa was founded in 1894 and is affiliated with the United Presbyterian Church. The Kendall campus houses 5 colleges: Arts and Sciences, Business Administration, Education, Nursing, and Law. The North Campus contains the College of Engineering and Physical Sciences. The library contains 1 million volumes and 134,000 microfilm items, and subscribes to 4650 periodicals.

Environment: The 2 campuses cover 120 acres in an urban setting and house a total of 50 buildings, including dormitory facilities, a drilling research laboratory, and the Westby Student Center.

Student Life: Fifty-five percent of the students are from Oklahoma. Forty percent of the students live on campus. Nineteen percent of the students are Catholic, 58% Protestant, and 1% Jewish; 13% belong to other denominations; and 8% claim no religious affiliation. Fifteen percent of the students are minority-group members. University housing is single-sex; there are visiting privileges. Students may keep cars on campus.

Organizations: There are 6 fraternities, to which 20% of the men belong; 25% of the women belong to the 8 sororities. Thirty professional societies have chapters on campus.

Sports: The university competes intercollegiately in 7 sports for men and 7 for women. There are 17 intramural sports for men and 17 for women.

Handicapped: Approximately 90% of the campus is accessible to the physically handicapped. Facilities include wheelchair ramps, special parking, specially equipped rest rooms, and lowered drinking fountains and telephones.

Services: Career counseling, placement services, health care, and psychological counseling are offered free of charge. Tutoring is also available on a fee basis.

Programs of Study: The university confers the B.A., B.S., B.F.A., B.Mus., B.Mus.Ed., and B.S.N. degrees. Master's and doctoral programs are also offered. Bachelor's degrees are offered in the following subjects: AREA STUDIES (urban), BUSINESS (accounting, computer science, finance, management, marketing, real estate/insurance), EDUCATION (adult, deaf, early childhood, elementary, health/physical, industrial, secondary, special, speech pathology/audiology), ENGLISH (English, literature), FINE AND PERFORMING ARTS (art, art education, art history, music, music education, radio/TV, studio art, theater/dramatics), HEALTH SCIENCES (medical technology, nursing, physical therapy, speech therapy), LANGUAGES (French, Spanish), MATH AND SCIENCES (biology, botany, chemistry, geology, mathematics, natural sciences, physical sciences, physics, zoology), PHILOSOPHY (humanities, philosophy, religion), PREPROFESSIONAL (dentistry, engineering, law, medicine, pharmacy, social work, veterinary), SOCIAL SCIENCES (anthropology, economics, government/political science, history, psychology, sociology). Twenty-two percent of degrees conferred are in business, 12% in education, and 10% in health sciences.

Special: Students may arrange to spend their third year abroad with individual approval of the program to be completed.

Honors: There are 18 national honor societies with chapters on campus.

Admissions: Eighty-six percent of those who applied were accepted for the 1981–82 freshman class. Of those who enrolled, the SAT scores were as follows: Verbal—61% scored below 500, 24% between 500 and 599, 13% between 600 and 700, and 2% above 700; Math—39% scored below 500, 35% between 500 and 599, 20% between 600 and 700, and 6% above 700. The ACT scores of those who enrolled were as follows: 19% scored below 21, 35% between 21 and 23, 20% between 24 and 25, 18% between 26 and 28, and 8% above 28. Applicants should be graduates of accredited high schools, have at least a C average, and rank in the top half of their class. Recommendations by school officials may also influence an admissions decision.

Procedure: The SAT or ACT is required. There are no formal application deadlines. Notification is on a rolling basis. There is a $10 application fee.

Special: Early admissions are available. CLEP and AP credit is accepted.

Transfer: For fall 1981, 1115 students applied, 721 were accepted, and 524 enrolled. Transfers are accepted for all classes. D grades do not transfer. A 2.0 GPA is required. Students must study at the university, at least 30 of the 124–128 hours needed to receive a bachelor's degree. Application deadlines are open.

Visiting: Guides are available for informal visits to the campus. Visitors may sit in on classes and stay overnight at the school. The admissions office should be contacted to arrange visits.

Financial Aid: About 75% of all students receive some form of financial aid. Twenty-five percent work part-time on campus. Average aid awarded to freshmen from all sources is $1000. The university is a member of CSS. The FAF or FFS should be filed. The deadline for financial aid application is March 1. Notification of awards is made May 1.

Foreign Students: Eight percent of the full-time students come from foreign countries. The university offers these students an intensive English course, an intensive English program, special counseling, and special organizations.

Admissions: Foreign students must score 500 on the TOEFL. No college entrance examination is required.

Procedure: Application deadlines are July 1 (fall), November 1 (spring), and March 1 (summer). Foreign students must present proof of funds adqaute to cover 1 calendar year. They must pay a special fee for additional services.

Admissions Contact: Clark W. Fowler, Admissions Counselor.

OREGON

CONCORDIA COLLEGE B-1
Portland, Oregon 97211 (503) 288-9371

F/T: 108M, 146W	Faculty: n/av; III, — — $
P/T: 15M, 4W	Ph.D.'s: n/av
Grad: none	S/F Ratio: 8 to 1
Year: tri, ss	Tuition: $3200
Appl: Sept. 1	R and B: $1970
218 applied 208 accepted 110 enrolled	
ACT: required LESS COMPETITIVE	

Concordia College is owned and maintained by the Lutheran Church-Missouri Synod. Concordia was founded in 1905 and became a 4-year college in 1977. The library has over 33,000 volumes.

Environment: The 10-acre campus is located on a slope overlooking the Columbia River in the city of Portland. The surrounding environment is suburban. The college is minutes away from downtown Portland. Dormitories accommodate most students.

Student Life: Religious activities and convictions are considered the compelling motive for behavior and discipline at the college. Worship services are offered twice each day. About 40% of the students come from Oregon. About 95% of the students are Protestant. About 11% of the students are minority-group members. Eighty-five percent live on campus. Campus housing is coed and single-sex; there are visiting privileges. Students may keep cars on campus.

Organizations: There are no fraternities or sororities on campus. The most popular extracurricular activities include student government, choir, the Concordia Players, concert band and other ensembles, Chi Rho (a Christian service organization), a monthly arts and lectures series, and college social events such as holiday banquets, and beach and skating parties.

Sports: The college fields 4 intercollegiate teams for men and 4 for women. There are 7 intramural sports for men and 7 for women.

Services: Students receive the following services free of charge: placement, career counseling, health care, psychological counseling, tutoring, and remedial instruction.

Programs of Study: The college confers the B.A. degree. Associate degrees are also awarded. Bachelor's degrees are offered in the following subjects: BUSINESS (accounting, business administration), EDUCATION (Christian, elementary, secondary), PREPROFESSIONAL (dentistry, medicine, ministry, social work, veterinary), SOCIAL SCIENCES (social sciences).

Special: Cooperative programs with local universities allow students to take courses in their major areas of study not offered at Concordia. The Independent Learning Center and the Educational Media Center offer students access to many different learning methods and educational tools.

Required: Students must fulfill the general education requirements by completing course work in the sciences, math, physical education, the humanities, fine arts, English, and religion (15 credit hours).

Honors: Students who attain a 3.5 GPA are recognized annually at an Honors Convocation.

Admissions: About 95% of those who applied were accepted for the 1981-82 freshman class. Admissions standards include a 2.25 GPA, or a score of 400 on the verbal section of the SAT, or a composite score of 18 on the ACT. All candidates must be recommended by either their pastor, former teacher, or a friend.

Procedure: The SAT, ACT, or Washington Pre-College Test (WPCT) is required, and should be taken in the junior year or early in the senior year. Test scores, transcript, letters of recommendation, and a $25 application fee must be submitted to the college by September 1 (fall), December 1 (winter), March 1 (spring), or June 1 (summer). Notification is usually within 2 weeks after receipt of the application materials.

Special: CLEP credit may be earned.

Transfer: For fall 1981, 57 transfer students applied, 56 were accepted, and 25 enrolled. A 2.0 GPA in previous college work is required. Students must earn, at the college, at least 45 of the 180 credits necessary for a bachelor's degree. D grades transfer. Deadlines are the same as those for freshmen.

Visiting: An orientation for new students is held just prior to the beginning of each term. Informal visits by prospective students are also possible. The admissions office handles the arrangements.

Financial Aid: A "package" of financial aid sources including scholarships and grants, loans, and part-time employment, is generally worked out for students. The average award to freshmen from all sources is $4000. Aid is awarded on the basis of need, and over 88% of all students receive some form of financial assistance. About 85% of the students work part-time on campus. The college is a member of CSS; the FAF is required and the deadline for aid applications is March 1 (fall or spring), December 1 (winter), or June 1 (summer).

Foreign Students: About 3% of the students come from foreign countries.

Admissions: Foreign students must achieve a minimum TOEFL score of 500; in addition, they must also take the SAT or ACT.

Procedure: Application deadlines are September 1 (fall), December 1 (winter), March 1 (spring), and June 1 (summer). Foreign students must present proof of funds adequate to cover 1 year of study.

Admissions Contact: Bill Cullen, Dean of Admissions.

EASTERN OREGON STATE COLLEGE   D-2
La Grande, Oregon 97850   (503) 963-2171

F/T: 662M, 669W	Faculty:	120; IIA, av$
P/T: 88M, 212W	Ph.D.'s:	49%
Grad: 136M, 254W	S/F Ratio:	9 to 1
Year: terms, ss	Tuition:	$1200
Appl: open	R and B:	$2015
516 applied	513 accepted	319 enrolled
SAT: 399V 432M		LESS COMPETITIVE

Eastern Oregon State College, founded in 1929, is a state-supported liberal arts, business, and teacher education college. The library contains 89,000 volumes and 27,400 microfilms, and subscribes to 1200 periodicals.

Environment: The 120-acre campus is located 260 miles from Portland in the Grande Ronde Valley, a rural area surrounded by the Blue and Wallowa Mountains. There are 11 buildings including 3 dormitories with accommodations for 230 women and 240 men. Housing is also available for married students.

Student Life: About 85% of the students come from Oregon. About 21% live on campus. Drinking is prohibited on campus, except in private rooms by students 21 and older. Nine percent of the students are members of various minority groups. Campus housing is both single-sex and coed; there are visiting privileges in some of the dorms. Students may keep cars on campus.

Organizations: No fraternities or sororities exist at the college, but there is a wide variety of activities, including a radio station, newspaper, literary magazine, active student government, music groups, summer stock theater, and educational, social, and cultural clubs. There are no religious groups on campus, but local churches have active organizations. Outdoor recreational facilities off-campus are popular with students.

Sports: There are intercollegiate teams for men in 6 sports and for women in 6. Intramural sports for both sexes number 3.

Handicapped: The campus is 100% accessible to handicapped students. Special facilities include wheelchair ramps, special parking, elevators, specially equipped rest rooms, and lowered telephones. Special class scheduling is also available. There are 3 counselors to assist handicapped students.

Graduates: An average of 38% of the freshmen drop out at the end of the year, and 30% remain to graduate. Nine percent of the students enter graduate or professional study after graduation.

Services: The following services are provided to students free of charge: psychological counseling, career counseling, tutoring, and health care. Placement services and remedial instruction are available for a fee.

Programs of Study: The college confers the B.A. and B.S. degrees. Associate and master's degree programs are also offered. Bachelor's degrees are offered in the following subjects: BUSINESS (agriculture/business, business/economics), EDUCATION (elementary, secondary), ENGLISH (English), FINE AND PERFORMING ARTS (art, music), MATH AND SCIENCES (biology, chemistry, mathematics, physics), PREPROFESSIONAL (engineering), SOCIAL SCIENCES (anthropology/sociology, community services, fire administration, history, psychology). Preprofessional programs, although not majors, are offered in computer science, dentistry, fisheries, forestry, geology, home economics, journalism, medicine, law, oceanography, pharmacy, veterinary medicine, and wildlife. Fifty percent of all degrees are conferred in education, 19% in social sciences, and 15% in business.

Special: The nursing program is offered in cooperation with the University of Oregon Medical School. There are courses in secretarial science, early childhood education, and community service leading to the A.S. degree. The college has an Indian Education Institute and a program in bilingual education (Spanish-English). Students may design their own majors. A 3-year degree is possible, and a general studies degree is offered. A combination degree (3-2) program is offered in physics/engineering.

Honors: Four national honor societies have chapters on campus.

Admissions: About 99% of those who applied were accepted for the 1981-82 freshman class. SAT scores for a recent freshman class were as follows: Verbal—16% between 500 and 599, 5% between 600 and 700, and 1% above 700; Math—20% between 500 and 599, 6% between 600 and 700, and 1% above 700. All Oregon residents who have graduated from an accredited high school and have completed 15 Carnegie units of work are accepted provided they have a GPA of at least 2.5 or a minimum combined score of 890 on the SAT. Out-of-state residents must have a GPA of at least 2.75. Other factors that enter into the admissions decision are advanced placement or honors courses and recommendations by school officials.

Procedure: The SAT is required. There are no application deadlines. Freshmen are admitted to each term, beginning in the fall, winter, spring, and summer. The college uses a rolling admissions policy. There is a $25 application fee.

Special: The university has early decision, early admissions, and deferred admissions plans. Early decision candidates are notified upon receipt of required materials. CLEP and AP credit may be earned.

Transfer: For a recent class, the college received 295 transfer applications, accepted 292, and enrolled 225 students. Transfers are accepted for all classes. A minimum GPA of 2.0 to 2.75 and combined SAT scores of 890 are necessary. A, B, C, and D grades transfer. Students must study at the college for at least 3 terms to receive a degree. Thirty-five credits, of a total 186 required for the bachelor's degree, must be completed at Eastern Oregon State College. There are no deadlines. Students may enter the fall, winter, spring, or summer terms.

Visiting: An orientation program, including campus tour, visit with admissions, financial aid officers, and faculty, class visits, two cafeteria meals, and an overnight stay in the dorms, is available for prospective

OREGON 715

students. Guides are also provided for informal visits to the college. Visitors may sit in on classes and also stay overnight on campus. The best time to visit is weekdays while school is in session. The admissions office will handle arrangements.

Financial Aid: About 56% of all students receive some form of financial aid. About 20% work part-time on campus. The college awards over 100 freshman scholarships each year. Aid is also offered from federal funds, a college-administered fund, and local banks. The college is a CSS member. The FAF is required. The deadline for aid applications is open.

Foreign Students: About 3% of the students come from foreign countries. An intensive English course and special counseling are available.

Admissions: The TOEFL is required; a minimum score of 500 is necessary. College entrance exams are not necessary.

Procedure: Application deadlines for foreign students are June 15 (fall), August 15 (winter), December 15 (spring), and March 15 (summer). Proof of adequate funds to cover all obligations while attending college must be presented. Health insurance is required; it is available through the college for a fee.

Admissions Contact: Terral Schut, Director of Admissions.

GEORGE FOX COLLEGE   B-2
Newberg, Oregon 97132   (503) 538-8383

F/T: 283M, 412W	Faculty: 44; IIB, av$
P/T: 15M, 33W	Ph.D.'s: 58%
Grad: none	S/F Ratio: 17 to 1
Year: qtrs	Tuition: $4165
Appl: Sept. 1	R and B: $1840
380 applied	313 accepted	216 enrolled
SAT: 440V 450M		COMPETITIVE

George Fox College, an evangelical Christian college organized in 1891, is operated by the Northwest Yearly Meeting of Friends Church (Quaker). The library contains 66,000 volumes and 1200 microfilm items, and subscribes to 575 periodicals.

Environment: The 90-acre campus is located in a town of 10,000 people, 23 miles from Portland. The area that surrounds the campus is suburban. Campus buildings include a gymnasium, a classroom and laboratory complex, an educational center, and 5 residence halls that accommodate 430 students. Living facilities sponsored by the college also include on-campus apartments and married student housing.

Student Life: Seventy percent of the students are residents of Oregon. About 90% of the freshmen come from public schools. Forty percent of the students live on campus. About 3% are minority-group members. Attendance at twice-weekly chapel services is required, and students may not drink, smoke, gamble, or dance. Campus housing is both single-sex and coed. Students may keep cars on campus.

Organizations: Student activities include music, drama, religious, and service groups; student government; a newspaper; and a radio station.

Sports: The college fields varsity teams in 4 sports for men and 5 for women. Intramural sports number 5 for both men and women.

Handicapped: About 60% of the campus is accessible to wheelchair-bound students. Facilities include ramps, special parking areas, elevators, and special class scheduling. No special counselors are available.

Graduates: About 35% of the freshmen remain to graduate. Of the graduates, 10% seek advanced degrees.

Services: The following services are offered free to students: placement, career counseling, remedial instruction, and health care. Tutoring services are available for a fee.

Programs of Study: The college confers the B.A. and B.S. degrees. Bachelor's degrees are offered in the following subjects: BUSINESS (business administration), EDUCATION (elementary, health/physical, secondary, religion), ENGLISH (communication arts, language arts, literature, writing/literature), FINE AND PERFORMING ARTS (music, music education, music/religion), MATH AND SCIENCES (biology, chemistry, mathematics, science/business), PHILOSOPHY (religion), PREPROFESSIONAL (home economics, home economics/business, ministry, social work), SOCIAL SCIENCES (economics/business, history, psychology, sociology). Of the degrees conferred, 31% are in social sciences, 16% in education, and 13% in philosophy.

Required: Students must take courses in art or music, physical education, Bible, literature, social studies, science, and foreign language or music theory or mathematics.

Special: The college offers preprofessional programs in banking, counseling, law, management, medicine, ministry, and science research. A 1-week fall mini-term centers around subjects of special interest that are not normally part of the curriculum. Students may arrange to study abroad through other institutions. A general studies degree is offered, and students may design their own majors.

Honors: All departments offer intensified study programs. No national honor societies are represented on campus.

Admissions: Eighty-two percent of those who applied were accepted for the 1981–82 freshman class. The SAT scores of a recent freshman class were as follows: Verbal—71% below 500, 24% between 500 and 599, 4% between 600 and 700, 1% above 700; Math—61% below 500, 26% between 500 and 599, 12% between 600 and 700, 1% above 700. Admissions decisions are based on high school grades and on recommendations by high school officials or the applicant's friends. SAT or ACT scores and the applicant's motivation and goals also are considered.

Procedure: The SAT, ACT, or Washington Pre-College Test is required. Application deadlines are September 1 (fall), December 1 (winter), and March 1 (spring). There is a $15 application fee. Admissions decisions are made on a rolling basis.

Special: An early admissions plan is available; application should be made the September before the senior year in high school. CLEP and AP credit is granted.

Transfer: For fall 1981, 95 transfers applied, 74 were accepted, and 48 enrolled. Transfers are accepted for all classes. Applicants should have a GPA of 2.0 or better and must submit recommendations. D grades do not transfer. Students must study at least 45 hours (2 terms in the senior year) at the college to receive a degree. The bachelor's degree requires a total of 189 quarter hours. Application deadlines are the same as those for freshmen. Transfers may enter any term.

Visiting: Guides are available for informal visits by prospective students. Visitors may sit in on classes and stay overnight in the residence halls. Visits should be scheduled with the director of admissions, preferably for weekdays between 10 A.M. and 2 P.M.

Financial Aid: About 77% of the students receive aid. About half work part-time on campus. The average award to freshmen covers about 64% of costs. Honors-on-Entrance Scholarships are available to freshmen who graduated in the upper 10% of their high school class and meet other requirements. Federal loans, BEOG, and CWS also are available. The college is a member of CSS. The FAF, FFS, or SFS is required. The deadline for aid application is March 1.

Foreign Students: Fewer than 1% of the student body are from foreign countries. There are special organizations on campus for foreign students.

Admissions: The TOEFL is required; a minimum score of 500 is necessary. College entrance exams are not necessary.

Procedure: Application deadlines for foreign students are September 1 (fall), December 1 (winter), and March 1 (spring). Proof of health, consisting of the DASH of Datamation, must be presented. Proof of adequate funds to cover 4 years must also be shown. Health insurance is required; it is available through the college for a fee.

Admissions Contact: James E. Settle, Director of Admissions.

LEWIS AND CLARK COLLEGE   B-1
Portland, Oregon 97219   (503) 244-6161

F/T: 775M, 916W	Faculty: 117; IIA, ++$
P/T: 26M, 38W	Ph.D.'s: 76%
Grad: 646M, 642W	S/F Ratio: 17 to 1
Year: qtrs, ss	Tuition: $5653
Appl: Mar. 1	R and B: $2264
1495 applied	1098 accepted	495 enrolled
SAT: 510V 530M		COMPETITIVE+

Lewis and Clark College, a 4-year college affiliated historically with the United Presbyterian Church, offers programs in the liberal arts and sciences, business, and education. The library contains 340,914 volumes.

Environment: The college is located on Palatine Hill overlooking the Willamette River about 6 miles from downtown Portland. The environment surrounding the college is suburban. The 130-acre campus was at one time a country estate. Its 55 buildings include a new science building containing a seismograph and an observatory, and dormitories accommodating 1150 men and women.

Student Life: About 35% of the students come from Oregon. About 75% are graduates of public schools. Sixty percent of the students live on campus. About 34% are Protestant, 9% Catholic, and 2% Jewish. About 24% are minority-group members. Campus housing is both single-sex and coed; there are visiting privileges. All students except freshmen may keep cars on campus.

716 OREGON

Organizations: There are 2 national fraternities on campus, to which 5% of the men belong; there are no sororities. Numerous extracurricular organizations and activities are available to students.

Sports: There are intercollegiate teams in 10 sports for men and 9 for women. Intramural sports for both men and women number 7.

Handicapped: Special facilities on campus for handicapped students include wheelchair ramps, special parking, elevators, specially equipped rest rooms, and lowered drinking fountains and telephones.

Graduates: At the end of the freshman year, about 25% of the students drop out; about 60% remain to graduate. Over 50% of the graduates go on to further study; 7% enter medical school, 2% dental school, and 3% law school. Thirty-eight percent of the graduates pursue careers in business or industry.

Services: Students receive the following services free of charge: placement, career counseling, health care, psychological counseling, and tutoring.

Programs of Study: The college confers the B.A., B.S., and B.Mus. degrees. Master's degree programs are also offered. Bachelor's degrees are offered in the following subjects: BUSINESS (business administration), EDUCATION (elementary, health/physical, secondary), ENGLISH (English/foreign literature, literature), FINE AND PERFORMING ARTS (art, music, music education, theater/dramatics), LANGUAGES (French, German, foreign languages/literatures, Spanish), MATH AND SCIENCES (biology, chemistry, mathematics, natural sciences, physics), PHILOSOPHY (philosophy, religion), PREPROFESSIONAL (dentistry, engineering, medicine), SOCIAL SCIENCES (communications, economics, history, international affairs, political science, psychology, sociology).

Special: There is the Overseas Study Program, in which 40% of a recent graduating class participated in 6 to 8 trips during the year. The college offers intensive language study in foreign countries, including a full-year program in Munich. Many students also participate in off-campus study programs in Washington, D.C., and New York City, scientific field study, internships, and independent study. A program for training teachers of the deaf is offered in cooperation with Washington State School for the Deaf in Vancouver, Washington. The college offers a general studies degree. Combined B.A.-B.S. degrees may be earned in all subjects. Twenty percent of all undergraduates have double or self-designed majors.

Admissions: About 73% of those who applied were accepted for the 1981-82 freshman class. SAT scores for a recent freshman class were as follows: Verbal—38% between 500 and 599, 15% between 600 and 700, and 5% above 700; Math—35% between 500 and 599, 20% between 600 and 700, and 7% above 700. Sixty percent of the students admitted as freshmen rank in the upper 20% of their graduating class. The admissions officers give more consideration to the student's academic achievement and the recommendations of high school counselors and teachers than to the results of standardized testing. Also important are advanced placement or honors courses, the student's school and community involvement, and his or her creativity, curiosity, and motivation.

Procedure: The SAT or ACT is required. The deadline for regular application is March 1 (fall). Fall notification is made by April 1. There is a $25 application fee.

Special: The college has an early decision plan with a December 15 application deadline and rolling notification. There is a deferred admissions plan as well. AP credit may be earned.

Transfers: For fall 1981, 187 transfer students applied, 110 were accepted, and approximately 75 enrolled. Transfers are accepted for all classes. C and above grades transfer. There is no fixed grade requirement; previous academic achievement and indicated aptitude and motivation are considered. A minimum GPA of 2.5 is recommended. To receive a degree, students must study for at least 3 terms at the college. At least 9 credits, out of 37 credits required for the bachelor's degree, must be taken at the college. Application deadlines are May 1 (fall), December 1 (winter), March 1 (spring), and June 1 (summer).

Visiting: Prospective students may visit at any time during the year. However, to insure greatest access to opportunities, the best time to visit is when classes are in session. At these times, the admissions office can arrange class visits, overnights, tours of campus, and department meetings or interviews.

Financial Aid: About 42% of the students receive financial aid in the form of grants, scholarships, loans, and work opportunities. About 35% work part-time on campus. The average award to freshmen from all sources is $4400. Aid packages vary in size, depending on the student's financial needs. Loans are available from the federal government, local banks, the college, and private funds. Tuition may be paid in installments. Aid is awarded on the basis of academic record, test scores, and personal qualities and development, as well as on financial need. The college is a member of the CSS and requires the FAF, which should be filed by February 15.

Foreign Students: Foreign students represent 6% of the student body. An intensive English program, special counseling, and organizations are available.

Admissions: The TOEFL or University of Michigan Language Test is required; a minimum score of 525 is required on the TOEFL. The SAT or ACT is also required.

Procedure: Application deadlines for foreign applicants are May 1 (fall), December 1 (winter), March 1 (spring), and June 1 (summer). Proof of adequate funds to cover a full year must be presented each year. Health insurance is required; it is part of the regular tuition/fees.

Admissions Contact: Robert H. Loeb III, Dean of Admissions.

LINFIELD COLLEGE B-2
McMinnville, Oregon 97128 (503) 472-4121

F/T: 578M, 618W	Faculty: 82; IIA, —$
P/T: 25M, 31W	Ph.D.'s: 75%
Grad: 16M, 20W	S/F Ratio: 14 to 1
Year: 4-1-4, ss	Tuition: $4500
Appl: Aug. 15	R and B: $1920
1035 applied	792 accepted	407 enrolled
SAT: 463V 502M	ACT: 23	COMPETITIVE+

Linfield College, established in 1849, is one of the oldest private liberal arts colleges in the West. It is affiliated with the American Baptist Church. The library contains 100,000 volumes, and subscribes to 811 periodicals.

Environment: The 90-acre campus is located 38 miles southwest of Portland, in a community of 14,000 people. The environment surrounding the campus is rural. There are 30 buildings on campus, including Pioneer Hall, a national historic landmark. Fourteen dormitories, 9 single-sex and 5 coed, are grouped into 2 resident quads. Other college-sponsored living facilities include on- and off-campus apartments, fraternity houses, and married student housing.

Student Life: Forty-four percent of the students are from outside Oregon; 14 foreign countries are represented. About 74% of the students live on campus. Ninety percent of the freshmen attended public schools. Forty-nine percent are Protestant, 20% are Catholic, and 1% are Jewish. About 12% are members of various minority groups. Campus housing is both single-sex and coed; there are visiting privileges. Students may keep cars on campus.

Organizations: There are 3 fraternities and 4 sororities to which 25% of the men and 35% of the women belong. There are language clubs, engineering societies, future-teacher organizations, student government, and art, science, music, and drama activities. Outdoor activities, such as camping, backpacking, and skiing in the Oregon Cascades, are also very popular among the students.

Sports: The college fields 10 intercollegiate teams for men and 8 for women. Intramurals for men number 18; for women, 17.

Handicapped: About 80% of the campus is accessible to handicapped students. Special facilities include wheelchair ramps, special parking, specially equipped rest rooms, and lowered drinking fountains and telephones.

Graduates: About one-third of the freshmen drop out at the end of their first year; about half remain to graduate. Thirty percent of the students pursue graduate study after graduation; about 3% enter medical school, 1% dental school, and 2% law school. Thirty percent of each graduating class enter business and industry.

Services: The following services are provided to students free of charge: psychological counseling, placement, career counseling, tutoring, and remedial instruction. Health care is available for a fee.

Programs of Study: The college confers the B.A. and B.S. degrees. There are also programs leading to the master's degree. Bachelor's degrees are offered in the following subjects: BUSINESS (accounting, business administration, systems analysis), EDUCATION (early childhood, elementary, health/physical, secondary), ENGLISH (English, creative writing, journalism, literature, speech), FINE AND PERFORMING ARTS (art, art education, art history, music, music education, radio/TV, studio art, theater/dramatics), HEALTH SCIENCES (medical technology, nursing), LANGUAGES (French, German, Greek/Latin, Japanese, Spanish), MATH AND SCIENCES (biochemistry, biology, chemistry, ecology/environmental science, general science, mathematics, natural sciences, physics, systems analysis), PHILOSOPHY (philosophy, religion), PREPROFESSIONAL (dentistry, engineering, home economics, law, medicine, ministry, pharmacy, veterinary), SOCIAL SCIENCES (anthropology, economics, government/political science, history, psychology, sociology). Twenty-five percent of all undergraduate degrees are conferred in business, and 20% in social sciences.

Required: Students are required to take 1 course in each of 6 general areas, including the humanities, social science, natural science, arts and letters, philosophy, and communicative arts. Competence in foreign language or 1 semester of computer programming and 1 semester of statistics will satisfy the language requirement. All language majors must spend their junior year in a country where the language is spoken.

Special: An overseas study program is designed to place junior-year students in already existing programs of study. An international program is also available to freshmen and sophomores. The college offers a 3-year bachelor's degree, a 3-2 combined engineering degree, a B.G.S. degree, and student-designed majors. An off-campus degree program provides a comprehensive program of courses, independent study, prior learning assessment, and student services to adults who want a bachelor's degree in liberal studies, at times and locations convenient to them.

Honors: There are 8 honor societies with chapters on campus. The college has an honors program for entering freshmen as well.

Admissions: About 77% of those who applied were accepted for the 1981–82 freshman class. Students are considered on the basis of their GPA in all academic courses completed in the last 3 years of high school; a 2.5 is required but a faculty review committee will consider those whose grades fall between 2.0 and 2.5. Eligibility is also based on test scores and a counselor's recommendation.

Procedure: The SAT, ACT, or Washington Pre-College Test (WPCT) is required. Applications are processed on a rolling basis. Application deadlines are August 15 (fall), December 15 (winter), January 15 (spring), and May 15 (summer). Freshmen are admitted all terms. There is a $20 application fee.

Special: The college has an early decision plan, with a December 15 notification date; an early admissions plan, with no deadline; and a deferred admissions plan. AP and CLEP exams are used for placement and/or credit.

Transfer: Of 125 transfer applications received for fall 1981, 96 were accepted, and 61 students enrolled. Transfers are accepted for all years. D grades do not transfer. A 2.0 GPA is required. Students must study at the college for at least 30 semester hours, of a total 125 semester hours required for the bachelor's degree. Application deadlines are the same as those for freshmen. Transfers are notified within 1 month.

Visiting: The college sponsors area coffee hours and a campus open house in April for prospective students. Guides are also available for informal, weekday visits to the campus. Visitors may sit in on classes and may also stay overnight at the college. The admissions office handles arrangements.

Financial Aid: Seventy-five percent of all students receive some aid. About 48% work part-time on campus. Scholarships range from $200 to $1400 per year depending on need and academic achievement. Grants-in-aid may range from $200 to $800. The average financial assistance package for freshmen is $2600, which includes scholarships, grants, and work. The deadlines for aid applications are April 1 (fall) and November 30 (winter).

Foreign Students: Students from foreign countries represent 4% of the enrollment. An intensive English program, special counseling, and organizations especially for foreign students are available.

Admissions: The TOEFL or the college's own language test must be taken by foreign applicants; a minimum score of 500 is necessary on the TOEFL. College entrance exams are not necessary.

Procedure: Application deadlines for foreign students are July 1 (fall), October 1 (winter), December 1 (spring), and March 1 (summer). Proof of adequate funds to cover 2 academic semesters must be presented. Health insurance is required; it is available through the college for a fee.

Admissions Contact: Thomas Meicho, Dean of Admissions.

MARYLHURST COLLEGE FOR LIFELONG LEARNING B–1
(Formerly Marylhurst Education Center)
Marylhurst, Oregon 97036   (503) 636-8141

F/T: 58M, 98W
P/T: 125M, 363W
Grad: 42M, 164W
Year: qtrs, ss
Appl: open
13 applied   13 accepted   13 enrolled
SAT, ACT: not required   NONCOMPETITIVE

Faculty: 25; n/av
Ph.D.'s: 25%
S/F Ratio: 12 to 1
Tuition: $2520
R and B: n/app

Marylhurst College for Lifelong Learning, founded in 1893, is an independent, coeducational liberal arts college that emphasizes lifelong education for adults. The library contains 105,000 volumes, and subscribes to 200 periodicals.

Environment: The 75-acre campus is located in a suburban area on Lake Oswego about 10 miles from Portland. Marylhurst also has off-campus centers in the Portland metropolitan area. There are no residential facilities.

Student Life: Students range in age from 18 to 80; the average age is 37 years. Most are working adults who transfer with about 2 years of previous college education. All live off campus. About 6% are minority-group members.

Organizations: There are no fraternities, sororities, or traditional collegiate extracurricular organizations.

Sports: Marylhurst does not offer any intercollegiate or intramural sports.

Handicapped: Wheelchair ramps and elevators are provided for handicapped persons.

Graduates: About 5% of the freshmen drop out by the end of the first year; 75% remain to graduate. About 25% pursue advanced study after graduation; 1% enter medical school, 1% dental school, and 5% law school. Thirty percent of the students pursue careers in business and industry after graduation.

Services: Psychological counseling, placement, and career counseling are provided to students free of charge. Tutoring is available for a fee.

Programs of Study: The center confers the B.A., B.S., and B.M. degrees. Bachelor's degrees are offered in the following subjects: BUSINESS (management), ENGLISH (communication), FINE AND PERFORMING ARTS (art, crafts, music), MATH AND SCIENCES (mathematics, natural sciences), PHILOSOPHY (humanities), PRE-PROFESSIONAL (pastoral ministry), SOCIAL SCIENCES (interdisciplinary, social sciences). Thirty percent of all degrees are conferred in business.

Required: Students are required to take the LIFE residential seminar. The center also has liberal arts distribution requirements.

Special: The Life Planning Center assists adults in transition in integrating their interests and goals with their career and educational needs. Information and counseling are provided. Life Planning Studies offer courses and workshops to assist adults with career choices and changes, self-identity, self-evaluation, and life enrichment. The Prior Learning Experience Program is based on the premise that knowledge and skills are achieved in many ways and in a variety of places. Up to 90 quarter hours of credit for college-level life experiences may be earned through this program. Courses are offered mainly in the evenings and on weekends for the working adult.

Admissions: Marylhurst has an open admissions policy. All of those who applied for the current freshman class were accepted. A high school diploma or the equivalent is required.

Procedure: Completion of the admissions form and payment of a $50 application fee are required. The form must be accompanied by official transcripts from all colleges attended previously and for armed forces courses, if applicable. Admissions are made on a rolling basis, and there are no deadlines. Freshmen may enter in the fall, winter, spring, or summer quarter.

Financial Aid: Grants, loans, and work-study employment are available. The college is a CSS member. The FAF must accompany the aid application. Applications must be submitted by May 1 (fall), November 1 (winter), February 1 (spring), and April 1 (summer).

Foreign Students: One percent of the students come from foreign countries. The college offers special counseling.

Admissions: The TOEFL or the college's own test is required; a minimum score of 550 is necessary. The college's own entrance exam must be taken; the results should show proficiency in writing English.

Procedure: There are no application deadlines. Foreign applicants may apply for entrance to the fall, winter, spring, or summer quarter. Proof of adequate funds to cover the period required to complete the degree must be shown.

Admissions Contact: Nancy Rich, Dean of Student Services.

MUSEUM ART SCHOOL
(See Pacific Northwest College of Art)

OREGON COLLEGE OF EDUCATION
(See Western Oregon State College)

OREGON INSTITUTE OF TECHNOLOGY B-4
Klamath Falls, Oregon 97601　　　　　　(503) 882-6321

F/T: 1569M, 574W	Faculty: 145; IIB, ++$
P/T: 726M&W	Ph.D.'s: 11%
Grad: none	S/F Ratio: 14 to 1
Year: qtrs, ss	Tuition: $1456 ($4132)
Appl: Aug. 15	R and B: $1995–2195
1324 applied　1145 accepted　726 enrolled	
SAT: 404V 443M　ACT: 21　COMPETITIVE	

Oregon Institute of Technology, founded in 1947, is the polytechnic college of the Oregon State System of Higher Education. The library contains 52,501 volumes, and subscribes to 1248 periodicals.

Environment: The 158-acre campus is located in a suburban area just outside the town of Klamath Falls (pop. 17,000). The 10 buildings include a new $2.6 million learning resources center. One coed dormitory accommodates 558 students. There is a cafeteria to serve commuter students.

Student Life: About 87% of the students are from Oregon; 7% are from bordering states. About 98% of the entering freshmen come from public schools. Twenty-one percent of the students live on campus. Drinking is permitted on campus in the over-21 floor of the dorm, and there is no curfew. About 6% are minority-group members. Campus housing is coed. Students may keep cars on campus.

Organizations: There are 4 fraternities and 2 sororities on campus. Other extracurricular organizations include special interest clubs and service groups. There are religious groups on campus for Protestant and Catholic students. The institute sponsors regular social and cultural events.

Sports: Intercollegiate teams are sponsored in 8 sports for men and 6 for women. Intramural sports for men number 13; for women, 12.

Handicapped: One hundred percent of the campus is accessible to handicapped students. Special facilities include wheelchair ramps, special parking, specially equipped rest rooms, lowered drinking fountains, and elevators.

Programs of Study: The B.S. degree is awarded. Programs leading to the associate degree are also available. Bachelor's degrees are offered in the following areas: BUSINESS (computer science, management), HEALTH SCIENCES (dental hygiene, medical technology, nursing, radiologic technology), PREPROFESSIONAL (diesel technology, engineering technology—civil, engineering technology—computer systems, engineering technology—electronics, engineering technology—mechanical, manufacturing technology). Forty-six percent of all degrees are conferred in engineering technology, and 22% in health sciences.

Required: English composition and physical education are required.

Special: Cooperative work-study programs are available for several majors. There is a reverse curriculum program in which students take major courses the first 2 years and liberal arts, management, and advanced technology in their upperclass work.

Admissions: Eighty-six percent of those who applied were accepted for the 1981–82 freshman class. SAT scores for freshmen were as follows: Verbal—82% below 500, 14% between 500 and 599, 3% between 600 and 700, 1% above 700; Math—57% below 500, 27% between 500 and 599, 14% between 600 and 700, 2% above 700. A high school diploma and a GPA of 2.25 are required.

Procedure: The SAT or ACT is required. The application deadlines are August 15 (fall), December 4 (winter), February 29 (spring), and open (summer). The institute uses a rolling admissions policy. There is a $25 application fee.

Special: The institute has an early decision plan. AP and CLEP credit is offered.

Transfer: For fall 1981, the institute accepted 304 transfer students. Transfers are accepted for the freshman and sophomore classes. A GPA of at least 2.25 is needed; D grades do not transfer. There is usually a 2-year residency rule. Out of a total 198 quarter credits required for the bachelor's degree, 45 must be taken at the institute. The application deadlines are the same as those for freshmen.

Visiting: An open house, with a tour of the institute, is held in May for prospective students. Guides are also available for informal visits to the school. Visitors may sit in on classes but may not stay overnight on campus. The best times to visit are during the open house and on weekdays. The assistant director of admissions is in charge of arrangements.

Financial Aid: About 15% of the students receive some form of aid. About 20% work part-time on campus. The average award to freshmen from all sources is $1500. Financial aid is awarded on the basis of need and includes scholarships, BEOG, state grants and loans, NSDL, and CWS in all departments. The institute is a member of the CSS and requires the FAF. The deadline for aid applications is March 1. Tuition may be paid in installments.

Foreign Students: Two percent of the student body are from foreign countries. Special counseling and organizations are available on campus.

Admissions: The TOEFL is required; a minimum score of 540 is necessary. College entrance exams are not required.

Procedure: The deadline for foreign applicants is August 1 (fall). Students must fill out a health questionnaire and receive shots, if necessary. Proof of adequate funds to cover the full period of enrollment must be presented.

Admissions Contact: Al Roberson, Director of Admissions.

OREGON STATE UNIVERSITY B-2
Corvallis, Oregon 97331　　　　　　(503) 754-4411

F/T: 8120M, 5895W	Faculty: 1075; I, –$
P/T: 377M, 308W	Ph.D.'s: 87%
Grad: 1806M, 954W	S/F Ratio: 17 to 1
Year: qtrs, ss	Tuition: $1077 ($3753)
Appl: see profile	R and B: $1920
4757 applied　4366 accepted　3105 enrolled	
SAT or ACT: required　COMPETITIVE	

Oregon State University, established in 1868, is the oldest member of the Oregon State System of Higher Education. Nearly all of the university's 12 schools have undergraduate divisions. The library contains 910,214 volumes, and subscribes to 17,559 periodicals.

Environment: The university is located in a city of 40,000 people about 80 miles from Portland, in the central Willamette Valley between the Cascade Mountains and the Coast Range. The environment surrounding the campus is suburban. The 397-acre main campus includes a recreation park and an outdoor laboratory. Beyond it are nearly 15,000 acres of university forest and agricultural land. University-sponsored living facilities include dormitories, on- and off-campus apartments, fraternity and sorority houses, and married student housing.

Student Life: About 85% of the students are from Oregon; the remainder are drawn from all parts of the United States and from a number of foreign countries. Drinking is prohibited on campus. Forty percent live on campus. Six percent are minority-group members. Campus housing is both single-sex and coed; there are visiting privileges. Students may keep cars on campus. The university provides day-care services on a first come, first served basis.

Organizations: There are 27 fraternities and 14 sororities, to which 10% of the men and 7% of the women belong. Students may participate in a full range of extracurricular activities, including numerous special interest groups. A number of student-staffed governing organizations regulate student activities and conduct. Many local churches, serving most major Catholic and Protestant denominations, maintain houses adjacent to the campus and encourage student participation in their religious and social affairs.

Sports: Intercollegiate teams are sponsored in 8 sports for men and 11 for women. There are 14 intramural sports for men and 9 for women.

Handicapped: Special facilities for handicapped students on campus include wheelchair ramps, special parking, elevators, specially equipped rest rooms, and lowered drinking fountains and telephones. Special class counseling is also available. There are 3 special counselors on campus to assist handicapped students. Special tutors are provided for students with hearing or visual impairments.

Graduates: At the end of the freshman year, about 33% of the students drop out; 13% remain to graduate.

Services: The following services are available to students free of charge: placement service, career counseling, tutoring, remedial instruction, and psychological counseling. Health care is available for a fee.

Programs of Study: The university awards the B.A., B.S., B.F.A., and B.Agri. Programs leading to the master's and doctoral degrees are also available. Bachelor's degrees are offered in the following subjects: AREA STUDIES (American), BUSINESS (business administration, business education, computer science), EDUCATION (agriculture, business, elementary, health/physical, industrial, science, vocational), ENGLISH (communications, journalism), FINE AND PERFORMING ARTS (art, art education, music), HEALTH SCIENCES (health, health care administration), LANGUAGES (French, German, Spanish), MATH AND SCIENCES (biochemistry, biophysics, biology, botany, chemistry, geology, geophysics, mathematics, natural sciences, physical sciences, zoology), PHILOSOPHY (philosophy, religion), PRE-PROFESSIONAL (agriculture, engineering, pharmacy), SOCIAL SCIENCES (anthropology, geography, government/political science, history, psychology, sociology). Twenty-two percent of the undergraduate degrees are conferred in business, 14% in science, and 18% in engineering.

Required: All students must take 3 hours of English composition and 3 terms of physical education.

Special: Study abroad is possible. Combined B.A.-B.S. degrees may be earned in some subjects.

Admissions: Ninety-two percent of those who applied were accepted for the 1981-82 class. The SAT scores for the entering freshmen were as follows: Verbal (men)—62% below 500, 29% between 500 and 599, 8% between 600 and 700, and 1% above 700; Verbal (women)—70% below 500, 23% between 500 and 599, 6% between 600 and 700, and 1% above 700; Math (men)—31% below 500, 38% between 500 and 599, 25% between 600 and 700, and 6% above 700; Math (women)—56% below 500, 33% between 500 and 599, 10% between 600 and 700, and 1% above 700. Oregon residents who apply must be graduates of standard high schools and have a minimum GPA of 2.75. An applicant with a GPA of 2.25-2.74 may be admitted on predicted success based on a combination of GPA and test scores.

Procedure: Either the ACT or SAT is required. Freshmen are admitted to all quarters. Applications should be submitted 30 days before the opening of the term. There is a $25 application fee. A rolling admissions plan is used.

Special: The university has an early decision plan; applicants are notified after October 15. CLEP and AP credit may be earned.

Transfer: For fall 1981, 2670 transfer applicants applied, 2221 were accepted, and 1670 enrolled. Transfers are accepted for all classes. Applicants from Oregon must have a minimum GPA of 2.0; nonresidents, a GPA of at least 2.5. All passing grades for college-level courses are accepted. To receive a degree, the student must study for at least 45 quarter hours at the university. The bachelor's degree requires a total of 192 to 204 credits. Transfers should apply at least 30 days prior to the opening of the term. They are admitted to all terms.

Visiting: The university holds a regular orientation program for prospective students, which includes a tour of the grounds and buildings and presentation of the various schools. Guides are also available for informal visits to the campus. Visitors may sit in on classes and may also stay overnight at the school if advance arrangements are made. Weekdays from 8 A.M. to 5 P.M. are the best times to visit. Franz Haun in the New Student Services Office is in charge of arrangements.

Financial Aid: About 65% of all students receive some form of financial aid. About 60% work part-time on campus. The average aid to freshmen is $2300. Federal and private loans are available; scholarships, grants, and work assistance are also awarded on the basis of academic performance and financial need. Financial need is the prime consideration. The university is a CSS member. The FAF must be filed with the CSS by February 1. The priority date for aid applications to the university is March 1.

Foreign Students: Five percent of the students come from foreign countries. The university offers an intensive English program, special counseling, and organizations especially for foreign students.

Admissions: The TOEFL is required; a minimum score of 500 is necessary. College entrance exams are not required.

Procedure: Foreign candidates should apply by May 15 (fall), September 15 (winter), and December 15 (spring). A physical examination is necessary, and an OSO form must be completed. Proof of funds adequate to cover the first year of study must be presented. Health insurance is required; it is available through the university for a fee.

Admissions Contact: Wallace E. Gibbs, Registrar and Director of Admissions.

PACIFIC NORTHWEST COLLEGE OF ART
Portland, Oregon 97205   B-1

(503) 226-4391

F/T: 59M, 112W   Faculty: 16; IV, —$
P/T: 6M, 14W   Ph.D.'s: 0%
Grad: none   S/F Ratio: 7 to 1
Year: sems, ss   Tuition: $3400
Appl: June 15   R and B: n/app
80 applied   55 accepted   55 enrolled
SAT, ACT: not required   SPECIAL

Founded in 1909, the Pacific Northwest College of Art is a private, coeducational school for professional training in the visual arts. The school and the Portland Art Museum, which share the same building, are both directed and maintained by the Portland Art Association. The library contains 8300 volumes, subscribes to over 50 periodicals, and houses more than 40,000 slides.

Environment: The college is located in downtown Portland and with the Portland Art Museum is the state's largest metropolitan art center. The environment surrounding the college is urban. Students enjoy the benefits of a small art school environment. There are no student residence facilities.

Student Life: About 75% of the students come from Oregon; the remainder are from other states and foreign countries. All students live off campus. About 7% are members of minority groups.

Organizations: Many of the student activities are organized by the students themselves. School facilities are available for the viewing of films, slide presentations, lectures, and entertainment. Artists are frequently invited to the school for workshops and informal discussions of their work. Popular social events are the Halloween Party and a spring picnic. Students have immediate access to events at the museum and the Film Study Center.

Sports: There is no organized athletic program.

Programs of Study: The college grants the B.F.A. degree with concentrations in the following areas: FINE AND PERFORMING ARTS (ceramics, drawing, graphic design, illustration, mixed media, painting, photography, printmaking, sculpture, studio art), PHILOSOPHY (humanities).

Required: In the first year, students are required to take a program consisting of visual elements, life drawing, humanities, 3-dimensional design, art history, and electives.

Special: The school cooperates with Reed college in a 5-year program leading to a combined B.A.-B.F.A. degree.

Admissions: About 69% of those who applied were accepted for the 1981-82 freshman class. Applicants must have completed high school or the equivalent. Admissions decisions are made on the basis of the high school or college record, 3 letters of recommendation, the portfolio, and a letter stating the candidate's personal interests and background.

Procedure: Neither the SAT nor the ACT is required. The PNCA Home Exam, primarily a drawing test, is required. Applications, accompanied by other admissions materials, should be sent to the school between January 1 and March 31; the $40 fee must be sent between April 1 and June 15. New students are not admitted to the spring semester. Admissions are on a rolling basis.

Special: There are early decision and deferred admissions plans.

Transfer: For fall 1981, 7 students applied, and 7 enrolled. The school usually accepts credits from liberal arts institutions as part of the humanities requirement. A, B, and C grades are accepted. Studio credits, unless earned in a professional B.F.A. program, are judged more critically. Transfers from colleges in the National Association of Schools of Art Accredited Colleges are given preference. Two years of study at the college are required. Out of a total of 148 credits, 74 must be taken at Pacific Northwest. Application deadlines for transfers are June 15 (fall) and December 15 (spring).

Financial Aid: About 71% of the students receive aid through the college. About 42% work part-time on campus. The average aid to freshmen from all sources available through the college is $2500. Numerous forms of financial aid are available to qualified students including BEOG, SEOG, CWS, Oregon state scholarships, school scholarships, and student loans. Aid is usually based only on continued need, satisfactory progress, and completion of at least 13.5 credits per semester. Students must mail the FAF to the CSS by April 1. Notification is made by May 10. Students must reapply for aid each year.

Foreign Students: Students from foreign countries represent 3% of the enrollment. The college offers an intensive English course.

Admissions: The TOEFL is required. Foreign applicants must also take the college's own entrance exam and receive a passing grade for acceptance.

Procedure: Foreign candidates must apply by June 15 for fall entry.

Admissions Contact: Bonnie Laing-Malcolmson, Admissions and Student Affairs Officer.

PACIFIC UNIVERSITY
Forest Grove, Oregon 97116   (503) 357-6151   B-1

F/T: 457M, 361W	Faculty: 77; IIA, −$
P/T: 7M, 11W	Ph.D.'s: 75%
Grad: 141M, 58W	S/F Ratio: 11 to 1
Year: 7-7-3, ss	Tuition: $5000
Appl: open	R and B: $2150
573 applied	439 accepted	190 enrolled
SAT: 430V 470M		COMPETITIVE

Pacific University, established in 1849 by the United Church of Christ, offers programs in the liberal arts and sciences. It also has professional schools of optometry and physical therapy, which together enroll about 340 students. The library contains 122,000 volumes and 855 microfilms, and subscribes to 855 periodicals.

Environment: The 55-acre campus is located in a rural area about 25 miles from Portland. The 16 major buildings include Old College Hall, the oldest continuously used educational building in the West, 3 dormitories accommodating 357 women and 338 men, and a 100-apartment complex for adult and married students.

Student Life: About 35% of the students come from Oregon; about 3% are from foreign countries. Eighty-five percent of the entering freshmen are graduates of public schools. Forty-four percent of the students live on campus. About 14% are minority-group members. Campus housing is both single-sex and coed; there are visiting privileges in the single-sex dorms. Students may keep cars on campus.

Organizations: There are 1 fraternity and 2 sororities on campus, to which 5% of the men and 5% of the women belong. Extracurricular activities include music and theater groups, publications, and service and special interest groups. The university also sponsors concerts, plays, films, lectures, and major social events such as Homecoming, Hawaiian Luau, Black Culture Week, and the Wassail Party. Religious counselors and organizations are available for Catholic and Protestant students.

Sports: There are intercollegiate teams for men in 10 sports, and for women in 8. There are 6 intramural sports for men and 4 for women.

Handicapped: Special facilities for handicapped students include wheelchair ramps, elevators, special parking, specially equipped rest rooms, and lowered drinking fountains. Special class scheduling is also available.

Graduates: At the end of the freshman year, 16% of the students transfer or drop out; 26% remain to graduate. About 30% of the graduates go on to further study.

Services: The following services are available to students free of charge: psychological counseling, placement service, career counseling, and tutoring. Health care is available for a fee.

Programs of Study: The university confers the B.A., B.S., B.M., and B.M.E. degrees. Master's and doctoral degrees are also offered. Bachelor's degrees are offered in the following subjects: BUSINESS (business/economics), EDUCATION (elementary, health/physical, recreation, secondary), ENGLISH (communications, English, speech), FINE AND PERFORMING ARTS (art, music, music education, studio art, theater/dramatics), HEALTH SCIENCES (communication disorders, physical therapy, therapeutic recreation), LANGUAGES (French, German, Spanish), MATH AND SCIENCES (biology, chemistry, ecology/environmental science, mathematics, physics, science, visual science), PHILOSOPHY (humanities, philosophy, religion), PRE-PROFESSIONAL (electronic science, engineering, social work), SOCIAL SCIENCES (government/political science, history, psychology, sociology). Forty-two percent of the undergraduate degrees are conferred in health sciences, and 22% in social sciences.

Required: All students must demonstrate proficiency in speech and English composition, and must take courses in science, social science, humanities, speech, and physical education.

Special: The university operates a biological field station in southeast Oregon, where students stay while doing research in environmental biology in the Malheur Wildlife Refuge. Programs in psychology and sociology emphasize field work and independent study. Students may spend their junior year abroad. A 3-2 program is available in engineering.

Honors: Several honor societies have chapters on campus. In addition, the university has an honors program for juniors and seniors and a freshman honors seminar.

Admissions: About 77% of those who applied were accepted for the 1981-82 freshman class. Applicants must be graduates of accredited high schools. Advanced placement or honors courses, recommendations by school officials, leadership record, and extracurricular activities are also considered important.

Procedure: The SAT, ACT, or Washington Pre-College Test is required. Application deadlines are open. Freshmen are admitted to each semester. A rolling admissions plan is used. There is a $20 application fee.

Special: The university has an early admissions plan, with no set deadline, and a deferred admissions plan. CLEP and AP credit may be earned.

Transfer: For fall 1981, the university received 121 applications, 84 were accepted, and 78 students enrolled. Transfers are admitted to all classes. The university requires a minimum GPA of 2.0 at the previous college; D grades do not transfer. The student must take at least 30 semester hours at the university, out of a total of 124 semester hours required to receive the bachelor's degree. Transfer application deadlines are open. Transfers may enter each semester. Notification is given within 2 weeks.

Visiting: Guides are available for informal visits to the university. Visitors may sit in on classes and may also stay overnight at the school. The best time to visit is when classes are in session. The admissions office handles arrangements.

Financial Aid: About 70% of the students receive financial aid. Sixty-eight percent work part-time on campus. The average award to freshmen covers 65% of costs. About 150 scholarships are available to freshmen. Loans may be obtained from a variety of sources, and campus employment also is available. Attempts are made to fill the total financial need of students by combining grant, loan, and work funds. Tuition may be paid in installments. The university is a member of the CSS and requires the FAF. The deadline for applications is July 1 (fall), December 1 (winter), January 1 (spring), and May 1 (summer).

Foreign Students: About 3% of the students come from foreign countries. The university offers special counseling and organizations for foreign students.

Admissions: The TOEFL is required; a minimum score of 500 is necessary. College entrance exams are not required.

Procedure: Foreign candidates should apply by July 1 for fall entry. They are admitted to the winter or spring semesters also, but there are no deadlines for these terms. A health form must be completed. Proof of adequate funds to cover 12 months must be presented. Health insurance must be carried; it is available through the university for a fee.

Admissions Contact: Marie B. Williams, Director of Admissions.

PORTLAND STATE UNIVERSITY
Portland, Oregon 97207   (503) 229-3511   B-1

F/T: 3380M, 2904W	Faculty: 477; IIA, +$
P/T: 2269M, 2532W	Ph.D.'s: 70%
Grad: 1970M, 2416W	S/F Ratio: 13 to 1
Year: qtrs, ss	Tuition: $1068 ($3762)
Appl: Aug. 1	R and B: n/app
1614 applied	1393 accepted	862 enrolled
SAT: 851 (composite)	ACT: 18	COMPETITIVE

Portland State University began in 1946 as an extension center and in 1955 became a 4-year degree-granting institution. It is a liberal arts university under state control. Eight schools and colleges and 1 division confer undergraduate and professional degrees. The library contains 621,352 volumes, and subscribes to 11,783 periodicals.

Environment: The campus occupies 46 acres in downtown Portland. The environment surrounding the campus is urban. University facilities include 2 historic buildings: Lincoln Hall, built in 1911, and the Social Work building, a converted pioneer home built in 1897. The university does not sponsor dormitory facilities; however, Portland Student Services, a nonprofit housing corporation, operates housing near or on campus which is available to students.

Student Life: About 90% of the students are from Oregon. All students commute to school. Eight percent are minority-group members. Students may keep cars on campus. The university provides day-care services for all students, faculty, and staff for a fee.

Organizations: There are 3 fraternities and 3 sororities on campus. Other extracurricular activities include music and theater groups, athletic clubs, forensics, a newspaper and other publications, an outdoor program, and student government. The university sponsors 10 different religious clubs. In addition, a unique campus building houses 8 Christian faiths. Places of worship are available within walking distance for Catholic, Jewish, and Protestant students.

Sports: There are intercollegiate teams for men in 6 sports, for women in 6 sports. Intramural teams number 19 for men and 13 for women.

Handicapped: About 92% of the campus is accessible to handicapped students. Special facilities include wheelchair ramps, special parking, elevators, specially equipped rest rooms, lowered drinking fountains and telephones, paraplegic showers, and a swimming pool lift. One special counselor is available to assist handicapped students. Fewer than 1% of the students have hearing impairments; fewer than 1% are visually impaired. The university has interpreters, referral and pick-up/drop-off services, and a resource library for these students.

Services: The following services are provided to students free of charge: health care, psychological counseling, placement and career counseling, and tutoring. A fee is charged for remedial instruction, psychological testing, placement file service, and additional health insurance.

Programs of Study: The university confers the B.A. and B.S. degrees. Master's and doctoral degrees are also awarded. Bachelor's degrees are offered in the following subjects: BUSINESS (accounting, business administration, computer science, finance, management, marketing), EDUCATION (elementary, health/physical), ENGLISH (English, speech), FINE AND PERFORMING ARTS (art, art history, arts/letters, music, theater/dramatics), LANGUAGES (foreign languages, French, German, Russian, Spanish), MATH AND SCIENCES (biology, chemistry, earth science, mathematics, physics, science), PHILOSOPHY (philosophy), PREPROFESSIONAL (engineering, social work), SOCIAL SCIENCES (administration of justice, anthropology, economics, geography, government/political science, history, psychology, social sciences, sociology). About 27% of all undergraduate degrees are conferred in the social sciences, 29% in business, and 6% in education.

Required: All students must take English composition, physical education, and health, as well as various major and distribution requirements.

Special: Certificate programs in 12 areas, including dance, Black studies, urban studies, women's studies, international business, public health studies, and teaching English as a second language, supplement courses taken in regular major fields. The university's international program offers area studies both at the university and abroad. Area concentrations are offered in Central Europe, the Middle East, and Latin America. Summer study/travel programs are offered in Japan, Ireland, Yugoslavia, Tunisia, Israel, London and the west of England, Brazil and Spain. The university also sponsors a German summer school program in which students live together for 7 weeks speaking only German, and intensive language programs in French, Spanish, and Italian, which take place on Mount Hood.

Honors: There are 3 honor societies with chapters on campus. There is also a school-wide honors system, the university scholars program.

Admissions: About 86% of those who applied were accepted for the 1981–82 freshman class. On the SAT, those who enrolled achieved the following composite scores: 81% below 1000, 16% between 1000 and 1199, 3% between 1200 and 1399. On the ACT, freshmen scored as follows: 50% below 20, 22% between 20 and 23, 14% between 24 and 25, 7% between 26 and 28, 7% above 28. Oregon residents must have at least a 2.5 high school GPA; out-of-state residents must have a 2.75. Applicants with lower averages may be admitted on the basis of superior scores on the SAT (at least 890 combined scores), or the ACT (a composite score of at least 20). Applicants may also be admitted by achieving a 2.0 GPA in 12 hours of course work taken during a college summer session.

Procedure: The SAT or ACT is required. Test results and application must be submitted by August 1 for fall admissions. Other deadlines are December 1 (winter), March 1 (spring), and June 15 (summer). New students are admitted all terms. A rolling admissions plan is used and notification is made as soon as all records are received. There is a $25 application fee.

Special: Oregon high school students who have a cumulative 2.5 GPA or an SAT score of 890, and who are recommended by their high school principals, may apply for early admissions at the conclusion of their sixth semester. There is also a deferred admissions plan. AP and CLEP credit is given.

Transfer: About 4000 transfer students are admitted each year. For fall 1981, 2909 applied, 2342 were accepted, and 1579 enrolled. Transfers are accepted for all classes. Oregon residents receive preference. A 2.25 GPA is required. The university requires that 45 credits of the final 60 or 165 of the total credits presented be taken at PSU; the bachelor's degree requires 186 credits. Deadlines are the same for transfers as for freshmen.

Visiting: A regular orientation program is available for prospective students. Guides are also available for informal, weekday visits to the school. Visitors may sit in on classes. Accommodations can be arranged through the university.

Financial Aid: About 49% of all students receive some form of financial aid. About 14% work part-time on campus. Scholarships, loans, and CWS are available from federal, state, and university funds. Scholarships are awarded on the basis of financial need, academic standing, character, and promise. The university is a member of CSS. The FAF is required and should be filed by February 1.

Foreign Students: Students from foreign countries comprise 10% of the student body. The university offers an intensive English course, special counseling, and organizations especially for foreign students.

Admissions: The TOEFL is required; a minimum score of 525 is necessary. College entrance exams are not necessary.

Procedure: Foreign candidates should apply by August 1 (fall), November 1 (winter), February 1 (spring), or April 15 (summer). Proof of funds adequate to cover 1 year must be presented.

Admissions Contact: Eileen Rose, Director of Admissions.

REED COLLEGE
Portland, Oregon 97202

B-1
(503) 777-7511

F/T: 622M, 474W	Faculty: 74; IIA, + +$
P/T: 5M, 5W	Ph.D.'s: 87%
Grad: 1M, 2W	S/F Ratio: 12 to 1
Year: 4-1-4	Tuition: $6400
Appl: Feb. 15	R and B: $2350
899 applied	689 accepted 260 enrolled
SAT: 621V 631M	HIGHLY COMPETITIVE+

Reed College, founded in 1911, is an independent, coeducational institution for the liberal arts and sciences. The college's traditional curriculum includes a broad scope of reading and writing, small conference-style classes, and a faculty committed primarily to teaching. There is an emphasis on research in the sciences and all students undertake a thesis in their senior year. The library contains 274,184 volumes, 80,000 government publications, and 16,100 microfilm items, and subscribes to 1221 periodicals.

Environment: The 98-acre campus is located in a wooded, residential area about 5 miles from downtown Portland. The science facilities, available to all undergraduates, are extensive, including a sophisticated computer center open on a 24-hour basis. A multi-use College Center and new research facilities in psychology were completed recently. Dormitory facilities are available to all freshmen; the most common arrangement is a divided double or single room.

Student Life: Approximately 25% of the students come from the Pacific Northwest, 25% from the Northeast, and 20% from California. About 7% are minority-group members. About half the students live in dormitories; freshmen may live off campus. Campus housing is both single-sex and coed. There are visiting privileges in single-sex dorms. Students may keep cars on campus.

Organizations: There are no fraternities or sororities at the college, although students are involved in many informal clubs and activities. The participation of both students and faculty in determining college policy is encouraged. The college owns a ski lodge on Mt. Hood, only 50 miles from the campus, and mountain climbing in the nearby Cascades attracts many students. The cultural offerings of Portland are within easy access.

Sports: The college has 6 intercollegiate teams for men and 5 for women. Ten intramural sports are offered for men and 10 for women.

Handicapped: About 50% of the campus is accessible to handicapped students; special facilities include wheelchair ramps and special parking. Special class scheduling is also available.

Graduates: About 18% of entering freshmen drop out by the end of the first year; 56% remain to graduate. Sixty percent of the graduates go on to further study; 5% enter medical school and 8% law school. About 25% of the graduates enter business and industry.

Services: The following services are available free of charge: health care, psychological counseling, placement service, career counseling, and remedial instruction. Tutoring is also available at varying costs.

Programs of Study: Undergraduate programs lead to B.A. degree. Bachelor's degrees are offered in the following subjects: AREA STUDIES (American, international, medieval), ENGLISH (English, literature), FINE AND PERFORMING ARTS (art, dance/theater, music, theater/dramatics), LANGUAGES (French, German, Greek/Latin, Russian), MATH AND SCIENCES (biology, chemistry, mathematics, physics), PHILOSOPHY (classics, philosophy, religion), SOCIAL SCIENCES (anthropology, economics, government/political science, history, international relations, psychology, sociology). Twenty-five percent of all undergraduate degrees are conferred in social sciences, 21% in math and sciences, and 15% in health sciences.

Required: The only academic course specifically required is the interdisciplinary humanities course. Students must satisfy distribution requirements by selecting courses in each of 4 areas of study. One and a half years of physical education are also required. Each senior must complete a thesis and pass an oral examination in order to graduate.

Special: Study abroad permits juniors to travel and study in a wide variety of areas. Student exchange programs exist with universities in England and Germany. A combination (3-2) degree program is offered in engineering with California Institute of Technology, Columbia University, and Rensselaer Polytechnic Institute; in forestry with Duke University; in computer science with the University of Washington; and with the Pacific Northwest College of Art. Students may design their own majors. A number of interdisciplinary programs are available. The Young Scholars program is available for gifted high school students, and the Eliot Scholars program is for adults returning to undergraduate studies.

Honors: Phi Beta Kappa has a chapter on campus.

Admissions: About 77% of those who applied were accepted for the 1981–82 freshman class. The SAT scores for entering freshmen were as follows: Verbal—7% below 500, 33% between 500 and 599, 40% between 600 and 700, and 20% above 700; Math—4% below 500, 26% between 500 and 599, 52% between 600 and 700, and 18% above 700. Advanced placement or honors courses, high school recommendations, extracurricular activities record, and special talents are considered important.

Procedure: The SAT or ACT is required (the SAT is preferred). Achievement tests are recommended but not required. Application deadlines are February 15 (fall) and November 1 (spring). Notification is on a rolling basis. There is a $20 application fee.

Special: The college has an early decision plan with a November 1 deadline and an early December notification date. Early admissions and deferred admissions plans are also available. AP credit is offered for scores of 4 and 5 on the AP test.

Transfer: Of 163 applications received for fall 1981, 101 were accepted, and 53 students eventually enrolled. Transfers are accepted for the freshman, sophomore, and junior years. D grades are not acceptable. A transfer student must study a minimum of 2 years at the college to receive a degree; at least 12 out of 30 credits required for a bachelor's degree must be completed at the college. Deadlines are April 1 (with some flexibility) for fall and November 1 for spring.

Visiting: Prospective students who visit the college receive a tour of the campus, are interviewed by an admissions officer, are encouraged to sit in on classes, and are invited to stay overnight. The best time to visit is when classes are in session, from September 1 through December 12 and from January 21 through April 25. Mrs. June Call in the office of admissions is in charge of arrangements.

Financial Aid: About 44% of the students receive some form of financial aid. A fund is used for freshman scholarships, and a self-help element of loan or employment is offered as part of all aid awards. The average freshman scholarship is $4100. Part-time jobs are available on campus and in the community; 60% of the students work part-time on campus. Work-study is available in all departments. The college is a member of CSS. Applications for financial aid must be submitted by March 1. The FAF and Reed Aid Application are required.

Foreign Students: About 6% of the full-time students are from foreign countries. Special counseling and special organizations are offered for these students.

Admissions: Foreign students must take the TOEFL. The SAT is also required.

Procedure: The application deadlines are February 15 (fall) and November 1 (spring). Foreign students must present proof of funds adequate to cover 1 year of study. Health insurance is available through the college and is covered in the tuition costs.

Admissions Contact: Robin Cody, Dean of Admissions.

SOUTHERN OREGON STATE COLLEGE B-4
Ashland, Oregon 97520 (503) 482-6411

F/T: 1681M, 1622W   Faculty: 200; IIA, av$
P/T: 421M, 433W   Ph.D.'s: 65%
Grad: 174M, 253W   S/F Ratio: 20 to 1
Year: qtrs, ss   Tuition: $1132 ($3448)
Appl: open   R and B: $2000
1210 applied   1024 accepted   756 enrolled
SAT: 410V 420M   ACT: 19   LESS COMPETITIVE

Southern Oregon State College, established in 1926, is a state-supported liberal arts, business, and teacher education institution. The library contains 200,000 volumes and 250,000 microfilm items, and subscribes to 2100 periodicals.

Environment: The 175-acre campus is located in a town of approximately 15,000 people, 280 miles south of Portland. The environment surrounding the campus is rural. There is a new theater arts building. Dormitories are small, and many are special interest residences, such as the math-science dorm, business hall, and foreign language dorm.

Student Life: Most of the students come from the West; about 90% come from Oregon. Unmarried freshmen under 21 must live in residence halls unless commuting from home. Drinking is prohibited on campus. About 30% live on campus. Six percent are minority-group members. Campus housing is both single-sex and coed; there are visiting privileges in the single-sex dorms. Students may keep cars on campus.

Organizations: There are no fraternities or sororities on campus. The college and its strong student government sponsor numerous cultural, social, and athletic events. The campus is within easy driving distance of the Oregon coast, Crater Lake, and the ski resort on Mt. Ashland. Outdoor activities are popular with students. Ashland hosts the Oregon Shakespeare Festival every year.

Sports: There are intercollegiate teams in 11 sports for men and 5 for women. Intramural athletics for men number 7; for women, 6.

Handicapped: About 50% of the campus is accessible to handicapped students. Special facilities include elevators, special parking, and specially equipped rest rooms. Special class scheduling is also available. About 1% of the students have visual impairments; 1% are hearing impaired.

Graduates: The freshman dropout rate is about 45%. About 30% of the freshmen remain to graduate. Approximately 30% of the graduates go on to further study; 1% enter medical school, 1% dental school, and 1% law school. Fifty percent enter careers in business and industry.

Services: The following services are available to students free of charge: health care, psychological counseling, placement service, and career counseling.

Programs of Study: The university confers B.A., B.S., and B.F.A. degrees. Associate and master's degree programs are also available. Bachelor's degrees are offered in the following subjects: BUSINESS (accounting, business administration, management, marketing), EDUCATION (early childhood, elementary, health/physical, secondary), ENGLISH (English), FINE AND PERFORMING ARTS (art, art education, music, music education, radio/TV, theater/dramatics), HEALTH SCIENCES (nursing), LANGUAGES (French, German, Russian, Spanish), MATH AND SCIENCES (biology, chemistry, mathematics, natural sciences, physical sciences, physics), PREPROFESSIONAL (agriculture, dentistry, engineering, forestry, law, medicine, pharmacy, physical therapy, social work, veterinary), SOCIAL SCIENCES (criminology, economics, geography, government/political science, history, psychology, social sciences, sociology).

Required: All students must take a distribution of credits in general education courses.

Special: Cooperative degree programs are offered in the areas of applied optics, dental education, dental hygiene, medical technology, medicine, nursing, physical therapy, prelaw, preoptometry, and presocial work. The college has 2 overseas study groups. Combined B.A.-B.S. degrees may be earned in many subjects, and a general studies degree is offered.

Admissions: About 85% of those who applied were accepted for the 1981–82 freshman class. The SAT scores of a recent freshman class were as follows: Verbal—16% between 500 and 599, 4% between 600 and 700, and 1% above 700; Math—22% between 500 and 599, 6% between 600 and 700, and 1% above 700. On the ACT, 19% scored between 20 and 23, 15% between 24 and 26, 6% between 27 and 28, and 1% above 28. Applicants must be graduates of accredited high schools with at least a 2.5 average or a composite score of at least 890 on the SAT or 20 on the ACT. Advanced placement or honor courses, evidence of special talent, and extracurricular activities record are also considered important.

Procedure: Either the SAT or ACT is required. Application deadlines are open. Freshmen are admitted to all quarters. Admissions are granted on a rolling basis. There is a $25 application fee.

Special: The college has early decision, early admissions, and deferred admissions plans. CLEP and AP credit is available.

Transfer: For fall 1981, 727 transfer students applied, 640 were accepted, and 581 enrolled. Transfers are accepted for all classes. Applicants must show a minimum GPA of 2.0, honorable dismissal from the previous college, and at least 12 quarter hours of transferable credit. D grades are acceptable. One year and a minimum of 45 quarter hours must be taken in residence. A total of 186 quarter hours are required for the bachelor's degree. There are no application deadlines. Transfers are admitted to all terms.

Visiting: The college schedules regular orientation sessions for prospective students. Guides are also available for informal visits. Student visitors may sit in on classes and may stay overnight at the school, space permitting. The best time to visit is when classes are in session. The office of admissions handles arrangements.

Financial Aid: About 60% of the students receive financial aid from the following sources: scholarships, loans, and campus employment. About 10% work part-time on campus. There are work-study programs in many departments. Tuition may be paid in installments. The college is a CSS member. The FAF must be filed. Applications should be made prior to March 1 to receive maximum consideration.

Foreign Students: Two percent of the student body are from foreign countries. The college offers an intensive English program, special counseling, and organizations especially for foreign students.

Admissions: The TOEFL is required; a minimum score of 500 is necessary. College entrance exams are not required.

Procedure: There are no deadlines for applying. Foreign students are admitted to the fall, winter, spring, or summer quarter. Proof of adequate funds to cover each year must be shown. Health insurance is required; it is available through the college for a fee.

Admissions Contact: Allen H. Blaszak, Director of Admissions.

UNIVERSITY OF OREGON B-2
Eugene, Oregon 97403 (503) 686-3201

F/T: 5670M, 5394W	Faculty: n/av; I, –$
P/T: 692M, 778W	Ph.D.'s: 90%
Grad: 2362M, 2020W	S/F Ratio: 19 to 1
Year: qtrs, ss	Tuition: $969 ($3282)
Appl: Aug. 15	R and B: $2000
4500 applied 4200 accepted	3100 enrolled
SAT: 440V 460M	COMPETITIVE

University of Oregon, founded in 1872, is a state-supported institution offering undergraduate programs in the College of Arts and Sciences, the College of Business Administration, the College of Education, the College of Health, Physical Education, and Recreation, the Honors College, the School of Architecture and Allied Arts, the School of Community Service and Public Affairs, the School of Journalism, and the School of Music. The library contains 1.8 million volumes and 200,000 microfilm items, and subscribes to 20,000 periodicals.

Environment: The 250-acre main campus is located in a city of about 110,000 people, 106 miles south of Portland, and is bordered on the north by the Willamette River. Over 30 major buildings include Deady Hall and Villard Hall, which are both national historic landmarks. There are dormitories with single and double rooms. Lounges are provided for commuting students.

Student Life: About 73% of the students come from Oregon; 90% are from the West. About 95% of entering freshmen are graduates of public schools. Twenty-five percent of the students live in coed and single-sex dormitories, and 6% in fraternity and sorority houses.

Organizations: There are 14 national fraternities and 12 national sororities at the university, to which 4% of the men and 4% of the women belong. Students pursue many different extracurricular activities, and the relative isolation of the campus from any major cultural center causes students to rely on university activities. Social activities are sponsored both by student groups and by the university. Religious groups are available for Catholic, Protestant, and Jewish students. Recreational areas, including the Cascade Mountains and the Pacific Ocean, are within easy reach of Eugene.

Sports: There are intercollegiate teams in 8 sports for men and 8 for women. There are over 18 intramural sports.

Handicapped: About 60% of the campus is accessible to handicapped students. Special facilities include wheelchair ramps, special parking, elevators, specially equipped rest rooms, and lowered drinking fountains and telephones. Special class scheduling is also available.

Graduates: Approximately 30% of the entering freshmen remain to graduate. About 40% of the graduates go on to further study; 10% go to medical school, and 10% enter law school.

Services: Placement services and career counseling are available to students free of charge.

Programs of Study: The university confers the following undergraduate degrees: B.A., B.S., B.Arch., B.Int.Arch., B.F.A., B.B.A., B.Ed., B.Mus., B.Phys.Ed., and B.Land.Arch. Master's and doctoral degrees are also awarded. Bachelor's degrees are offered in the following subjects: AREA STUDIES (Asian, Latin American, Russian), BUSINESS (accounting, business administration, computer science, finance, management, marketing, real estate/insurance), EDUCA-TION (elementary), ENGLISH (English, journalism, literature, speech), FINE AND PERFORMING ARTS (art, art education, art history, dance, film/photography, music, music education, radio/TV, studio art, theater/dramatics), HEALTH SCIENCES (medical technology), LANGUAGES (Chinese, French, German, Greek/Latin, Italian, Japanese, Russian, Spanish), MATH AND SCIENCES (biochemistry, biology, chemistry, geology, mathematics, physics), PHILOSOPHY (classics, philosophy, religion), PREPROFESSIONAL (architecture, interior architecture, landscape architecture, social work), SOCIAL SCIENCES (anthropology, economics, geography, government/political science, history, psychology, sociology). Preprofessional programs, although not majors, are offered in dentistry, law, medicine, ministry, pharmacy, and veterinary.

Required: Required courses vary with the school or college.

Special: There are study-abroad programs for students in business administration, music, and romance languages, as well as a direct exchange program for juniors with a school in The Netherlands. Other students make their own contacts and arrangements for foreign study, but the university cooperates in every way it can and discusses acceptance of work to be taken abroad. Student-designed majors are permitted.

Honors: Fifteen honor societies, including Phi Beta Kappa, have chapters on campus. In addition, all departments in the College of Arts and Sciences offer honors programs. The Honors College provides full opportunity for superior students to develop their potential in liberal education and specialized training. Students take part of their work in regular university courses and part in Honors College courses. Independent work is encouraged.

Admissions: About 93% of those who applied were accepted for the 1981–82 freshman class. All applicants must be graduates of accredited high schools. Oregon residents must have, at the minimum, either a GPA of 2.75 or a total score of 890 on the SAT; out-of-state residents must have either a 2.75 GPA, or a 2.25 GPA and a satisfactory score on the SAT. Although class rank is not stipulated, successful applicants usually are in the upper 50% of their high school classes. The reputation of the high school and advanced placement or honors courses are considered important.

Procedure: The SAT or ACT is required. The deadlines for applications are August 15 (fall), December 15 (winter), March 15 (spring), and May 15 (summer). Freshmen are admitted to each quarter. Notification is on a rolling basis. There is a $25 application fee.

Special: The university has a deferred admissions plan. AP and CLEP credit is available.

Transfer: Transfers are considered for all classes. A GPA of at least 2.0 is required; D grades are acceptable. All students must complete, at the university, 45 of the 186–220 credits required for a bachelor's degree.

Visiting: An orientation program for prospective students includes preview, tour, academic advising, and registration. Guides are also available for informal visits to the school. Visitors may sit in on classes but may not stay overnight on campus. Weekdays from 8 A.M. to 5 P.M. are the best times to visit. The admissions office handles arrangements.

Financial Aid: About 45% of students receive financial aid. Aid is available from the following sources: scholarships (including EOG), loans (including NDSL), and campus employment (including CWS). Over 1000 scholarships are available to students. Aid is awarded on the basis of financial need; however, academic achievement is also considered. The university is a member of the CSS and requires the FAF and student budget report from aid applicants. The deadline for applications is March 1.

Foreign Students: About 9% of the full-time students come from foreign countries. Special counseling and special organizations are available for these students.

Admissions: Foreign students must take the TOEFL.

Procedure: Application deadlines are May 1 (fall), October 15 (winter), January 15 (spring), and April 1 (summer).

Admissions Contact: James K. Buch, Director of Admissions.

UNIVERSITY OF PORTLAND B-1
Portland, Oregon 97203 (503) 283-7147

F/T: 878M, 838W	Faculty: 110; IIA, –$
P/T: 352M, 103W	Ph.D.'s: 60%
Grad: 335M, 197W	S/F Ratio: 17 to 1
Year: sems, ss	Tuition: $3950
Appl: open	R and B: $2050
1037 applied 852 accepted	412 enrolled
SAT: 430V 470M	COMPETITIVE

724 OREGON

University of Portland, founded in 1901, is affiliated with the Catholic Church. The university consists of 5 undergraduate colleges and a graduate school. The library contains 175,000 volumes and 100,000 microfilm items, and subscribes to 1250 periodicals.

Environment: The 90-acre campus is situated in an urban residential district of North Portland, overlooking the Willamette River. It consists of 20 buildings including West Hall, built in 1891, which has been designated a national historical monument. Five dormitories accommodate about half the students. A cafeteria, dining hall, and lounge are available for commuting students.

Student Life: Less than 50% of the students come from Oregon; about 50% come from private schools. Although the university is Catholic-related, 60% of the students are non-Catholic. About 8% of the students are minority-group members. Half of the students live on campus; freshmen may live off campus. Campus housing is single-sex, and there are visiting privileges. Students may keep cars on campus.

Organizations: The university has social, professional, and honor fraternities and sororities. Numerous special-interest groups provide extracurricular activities for students. The cultural offerings of Portland are easily accessible.

Sports: The university competes intercollegiately in 7 sports for men and 6 for women. Seven intramural sports are offered for men and 7 for women.

Handicapped: There are no special facilities for handicapped students at the university.

Graduates: About 26% of the freshmen drop out by the end of the first year; 45% remain to graduate. About 40% of the graduates pursue advanced degrees.

Services: The following services are available to students free of charge: health care, psychological counseling, placement, and career counseling.

Programs of Study: The university confers the B.A., B.S., B.S.N., B.S.E., and B.B.A. degrees. Master's programs are also available. Bachelor's degrees are offered in the following subjects: BUSINESS (accounting, computer applications management, communications management, management, marketing), EDUCATION (elementary, secondary, special), ENGLISH (English, journalism/communications, speech/communications), FINE AND PERFORMING ARTS (fine arts, music, music education, theater/dramatics), HEALTH SCIENCES (medical technology, nursing), LANGUAGES (modern languages), MATH AND SCIENCES (biology, chemistry, mathematics, physics, science communication), PHILOSOPHY (philosophy, theology), PREPROFESSIONAL (dentistry, engineering—civil, engineering—computer, engineering—electrical, engineering—general, engineering—industrial, law, medicine), SOCIAL SCIENCES (administration of justice, government/political science, history, psychology, social services, society and justice, sociology).

Required: All students must take courses in fine arts, communications, mathematics, physical or biological sciences, social science or history, philosophy, and theology.

Special: Teacher training programs lead to certification at the elementary, secondary, and special education levels. Seminars, interdisciplinary majors, study abroad, independent study, and combined B.A.-B.S. degrees are offered.

Honors: The university provides special programs for honor and college scholars. There are honor societies on campus.

Admissions: Eighty-two percent of those who applied were accepted for the 1981–82 freshman class. Students must have graduated from an accredited high school and must have achieved success in an academic program. They should have a minimum GPA of 2.0. Advanced placement or honor courses and recommendations from high school officials also enter into the admissions decision.

Procedure: Either the SAT or ACT is required and should be taken by March of the senior year. A rolling admissions plan is used; there is no application deadline. Applicants must submit a $25 application fee.

Special: The university has early decision, early admissions, and deferred admissions plans. CLEP and AP credit may be earned.

Transfer: In fall 1981, 723 transfer students applied, 570 were accepted, and 188 enrolled. Transfers are accepted for all classes; D grades are not acceptable. Generally, a 2.0 minimum GPA is required for previous college work. Students must complete, at the university, 30 of the 120 credits required for a bachelor's degree. Application deadlines are open.

Visiting: The university has a regular orientation program for prospective students. Guides are available for informal campus visits. Visitors may sit in on classes and stay overnight at the school. Visits are best scheduled on weekdays. The admissions office should be contacted for arrangements.

Financial Aid: About 70% of the students receive financial aid. Twenty-four percent work part-time on campus. Loans are available from the federal government, local banks, and the university. The average award to freshmen from all sources is $1700. The university is a member of CSS. The FAF is required; applications for financial aid should be filed by March 15. Notification is on a rolling basis. Tuition must be paid in full before classes begin.

Foreign Students: About 20% of the full-time students come from foreign countries. An intensive English course, special counseling, and special organizations are offered for these students.

Admissions: Foreign students must achieve a minimum score of 500 on the TOEFL. No college entrance exams are required.

Procedure: Application deadlines are open; students are admitted to all terms. Foreign students must present proof of health. Proof of adequate funds to cover 1 year of study must also be presented. Health insurance must be carried and is available through the college for a fee.

Admissions Contact: Daniel B. Reilly, Director of Admissions.

WARNER PACIFIC COLLEGE B-1
Portland, Oregon 97215   (503) 775-4366

F/T, P/T: 229M, 176W	Faculty: 44; IIA, ——$
Grad: 5M, 4W	Ph.D.'s: 40%
Year: qtrs, ss	S/F Ratio: 9 to 1
Appl: Sept. 17	Tuition: $75 p/c
310 applied 185 accepted	R and B: $2340
SAT: 800 (composite) ACT: 23	99 enrolled LESS COMPETITIVE

Warner Pacific College, founded in 1937, is a liberal arts college affiliated with the Church of God. The library contains over 50,000 volumes.

Environment: The 28-acre campus, located in the heart of Portland, is adjacent to Mount Tabor Park, which provides recreational facilities for students. The campus has 16 major buildings, including dormitories that house about 140 men and 150 women. Sixteen apartments are available for married students. A cafeteria serves both resident and commuting students.

Student Life: About 80% of the students are from the West, and 40% are from Oregon. Most are members of the supporting church. All students are required to attend twice-a-week chapel services and other religious events. About 70% of the students live on campus; all unmarried students not living at home must do so. Dormitories are single-sex. Drinking and smoking are not permitted. Students may have cars on campus.

Organizations: The college sponsors numerous clubs and activities, including student ministries and religious-involvement groups. There are no fraternities or sororities. The cultural offerings of downtown Portland are easily accessible.

Sports: The college fields intercollegiate teams in 4 sports for men and 4 for women. Intramural sports also are available.

Handicapped: About 90% of the campus is accessible to handicapped students. Special facilities include parking areas and specially equipped rest rooms. Counselors are available.

Graduates: About 10% of the graduates pursue advanced degrees.

Services: The following services are provided free to students: psychological counseling, placement aid, career counseling, tutoring, and remedial instruction. Fees are charged for health care.

Programs of Study: The college confers the B.A. and B.S. degrees. Associate and master's degree programs are also available. Bachelor's degrees are offered in the following subjects: AREA STUDIES (American), BUSINESS (business administration), EDUCATION (early childhood, elementary, health/physical, recreation, secondary), ENGLISH (English, journalism), FINE AND PERFORMING ARTS (church music, music, music education), MATH AND SCIENCES (biology, general science, mathematics, physical sciences), PHILOSOPHY (humanities, philosophy, religion), PREPROFESSIONAL (ministry, social work), SOCIAL SCIENCES (history, psychology, social sciences, sociology).

Required: All students must take courses in English, religion, fine arts, and science. They also must participate in the Aerobics Physical Fitness Program.

Special: Interdepartmental majors are offered in several areas. A general studies degree is offered. Students may design their own majors.

Admissions: About 60% of those who applied were accepted for the 1981–82 freshman class. Applicants must be graduates of accredited high schools and have a GPA of at least 2.0. Recommendations, extracurricular activities, and advanced placement or honors courses also are considered.

Procedure: The SAT or ACT is required and should be taken by the July following the senior year. A personal interview is recommended. The application deadline for fall admission is September 17, although applications for all terms should be submitted at least 1 month before registration for priority consideration. Notification is made on a rolling basis. There is a $15 application fee.

Special: The college offers early decision and deferred admissions plans. CLEP and AP credit is available.

Transfer: Transfers are accepted for all classes. The applicant must have a 2.0 GPA. D grades do not transfer. Students must earn at least 45 quarter credits at the college of the 186 required for a bachelor's degree.

Visiting: A regular orientation program is held for prospective students. Guides are available for informal visits. Visitors may sit in on classes and stay overnight at the school. The admissions office should be contacted for arrangements.

Financial Aid: About 85% of the students receive aid. Scholarships (including BEOG/SEOG), loans (including NDSL), and campus jobs (including CWS) are available. Aid is awarded on the basis of need, academic record, personal qualifications, and extracurricular activities. The college is a member of the CSS and requires the FAF from aid applicants. Applications should be submitted as early as possible.

Foreign Students: Students from foreign countries make up about 5% of enrollment. The college offers these students an intensive English course, an intensive English program, special counseling, and special organizations.

Admissions: Applicants must score 500 or better on the TOEFL. They also must take the SAT or the ACT.

Procedure: Application deadlines are the same as those for American students. Foreign students must submit a completed medical form as proof of good health and present evidence of adequate funds for their full period of study. Health insurance is required, and is available through the college for a fee.

Admissions Contact: Roberta Petersen, Admissions Office Manager.

WESTERN OREGON STATE COLLEGE B–2
(Formerly Oregon College of Education)
Monmouth, Oregon 97361   (503) 838-1220

F/T: 878M, 1445W	Faculty:	n/av; IIA, +$
P/T: 120M, 263W	Ph.D.'s:	n/av
Grad: 127M, 294W	S/F Ratio:	20 to 1
Year: qtrs, ss	Tuition:	$1088 ($3404)
Appl: open	R and B:	$1998
667 applied		572 enrolled
SAT: 350V 450M	ACT: 15	LESS COMPETITIVE

Western Oregon State College, founded in 1856, is a liberal arts college under state control. The library contains 198,834 volumes and subscribes to 1620 periodicals. Its holdings include a valuable Oregon history collection.

Environment: The campus occupies 122 acres in an urban setting 15 miles from Salem. There are 4 dormitories with single and double rooms and suites accommodating 750 students.

Student Life: Most students come from the West Coast. About 96% of the students are from Oregon. About 25% of the students live on campus. Five percent of the students are minority-group members. Campus housing is single-sex and coed; there are visiting privileges in single-sex dorms. Students may keep cars on campus. Day-care services are available to all students for a fee.

Organizations: There are no fraternities or sororities at the college, but there are numerous extracurricular activities and religious organizations.

Sports: The college fields 9 intercollegiate teams for men and 9 for women. There is also an intramural sports program for men and women.

Handicapped: About 90% of the campus is accessible to handicapped students. Special facilities include wheelchair ramps, special parking, elevators, specially equipped rest rooms, and lowered drinking fountains and telephones. There are 2 counselors to serve handicapped students. About 2% of the students are hearing impaired. The Regional Resource Center for the Deaf helps serve these students. In addition 9 interpreters are available. Special class scheduling is possible.

Graduates: The freshman dropout rate is 10%; 75% remain to graduate 4 years later. Twenty-five percent of the graduates pursue advanced study.

Services: The following services are available to students free of charge: health care, psychological counseling, placement and career counseling (for graduates as well as undergraduates), and tutoring. Remedial instruction is available on a fee basis.

Programs of Study: The college confers the B.S. and B.A. degrees. Associate and master's degrees are also awarded. Bachelor's degrees are offered in the following subjects: EDUCATION (elementary, secondary), ENGLISH (humanities), FINE AND PERFORMING ARTS (art), LANGUAGES (French, German, Spanish), MATH AND SCIENCES (biology, mathematics, natural sciences), SOCIAL SCIENCES (corrections, economics, geography, history, law enforcement, psychology, social sciences).

Special: Study abroad is available. Students may design their own majors. There is an interdisciplinary studies major combining English, French, German, Spanish, philosophy and religion, and speech and journalism.

Honors: Phi Kappa Phi has a chapter on campus. A general honors program in the humanities and social sciences is also available.

Admissions: About 97% of those who applied were accepted for a recent freshman class. The SAT scores of those who enrolled were as follows: Verbal—98% below 500, 2% between 500 and 599, and 0% above 600; Math—99% below 500, 1% between 500 and 599, and 0% above 600. The ACT scores of those who enrolled were as follows: 97% below 21, 3% between 21 and 23, and 0% above 24. The minimum requirements for applicants are graduation from an accredited high school and a 2.25 GPA (2.5 for out-of-state applicants) in all high school subjects.

Procedure: The SAT or ACT is required. Application deadlines are open. New students are admitted to all quarters. Admissions are on a rolling basis. There is a $25 application fee.

Special: CLEP and AP credit may be granted.

Transfer: For fall 1981, 457 transfer students enrolled. Transfers are accepted for all classes. D grades are acceptable. A minimum GPA of 2.5 is required. Students must study at the college for at least 45 credit hours to receive a degree. The bachelor's degree requires 192 credits. Application deadlines are open.

Visiting: The college holds a regular orientation program for prospective students. Guides are also available for informal, weekday visits to the school. Visitors may sit in on classes. The admissions office handles arrangements.

Financial Aid: Over $2 million is available in financial aid from federal, state, college, and private sources. Aid is offered in the form of scholarships, grants, loans, and part-time work. About 60% of all students receive some form of financial aid; about 15% work part-time on campus. The FAF must be filed and the application for aid should be submitted by March 1 to receive priority consideration. The college is a member of CSS.

Foreign Students: About 3% of the full-time students come from foreign countries. The college offers these students special counseling.

Admissions: Foreign students must achieve a minimum score of 500 on the TOEFL or 85 on the University of Michigan Language Test; no college entrance exams are required.

Procedure: Application deadlines are open. Foreign students must present proof of health and proof of funds adequate to cover 4 years of study. They must also carry health insurance, which is available through the college for a fee.

Admissions Contact: Barbara Gianneschi, Director of Admissions.

WILLAMETTE UNIVERSITY B–2
Salem, Oregon 97301   (503) 370-6303

F/T: 668M, 638W	Faculty:	91; IIA, +$
P/T: 9M, 15W	Ph.D.'s:	70%
Grad: 399M, 187W	S/F Ratio:	14 to 1
Year: sems	Tuition:	$4930
Appl: Mar. 1	R and B:	$2150
876 applied	735 accepted	334 enrolled
SAT: 480V 510M	ACT: 24	COMPETITIVE+

Willamette University, founded in 1842, is a private liberal arts school affiliated with the United Methodist Church. The university has 3 colleges: Liberal Arts, Management, and Law. The library contains 131,004 volumes, and subscribes to 1125 periodicals.

OREGON

Environment: The 57-acre, landscaped campus is in an urban area adjacent to the state capitol and within walking distance of downtown Salem. It is 45 miles from Portland. There are 34 buildings on campus including 3 single-sex dormitories, 6 coed dormitories, 6 fraternities, and 3 sororities.

Student Life: Fifty-four percent of the students are from Oregon; 80% attended public schools. Seventy percent live on campus. Although 60% of the students are Protestant, the majority of them are not members of the affiliated church. Attendance at chapel services is not required. Eight percent of the students are members of minority groups. Campus housing is both single-sex and coed; there are visiting privileges. Students may keep cars on campus.

Organizations: There are 6 fraternities and 3 sororities on campus; 35% of the men and 25% of the women belong. Student organizations and activities include special-interest clubs, a weekly newspaper, service clubs, and music activities. Art shows, concerts, debates, films, lectures, operas, plays, and social activities are scheduled regularly. Student government is active. There are religious organizations for Catholic, Jewish, and Protestant students.

Sports: There are intercollegiate teams in 13 sports for men and 12 for women. There are 10 intramural teams for men and 7 for women.

Handicapped: About 60% of the campus is accessible to handicapped students. Special facilities include wheelchair ramps, special parking, elevators, and specially equipped rest rooms. About 1% of the students are visually impaired; 1% are hearing impaired.

Graduates: At the end of the freshman year 20% of the students drop out; 55% remain to graduate. About 50% of the graduates pursue graduate study.

Services: The following services are available to students free of charge: health care, psychological counseling, career counseling, and tutoring.

Programs of Study: The university confers the B.A., B.S., B.Mus., B.Mus.Ed., and B. of Theater degrees. Other programs lead to master's and doctoral degrees. Bachelor's degrees are offered in the following subjects: AREA STUDIES (American, British, French, German, Hispanic, Russian), EDUCATION (health/physical, secondary), ENGLISH (English, speech), FINE AND PERFORMING ARTS (art, music, music education, theater/dramatics), LANGUAGES (French, German, Spanish), MATH AND SCIENCES (Biology, chemistry, ecology/environmental science, mathematics, natural sciences, physics), PHILOSOPHY (humanities, philosophy, religion), PREPROFESSIONAL (architecture, dentistry, engineering, forestry, law, medicine, ministry, pharmacy, veterinary), SOCIAL SCIENCES (economics, government/political science, history, international relations, psychology, social sciences, sociology). Sixty percent of all undergraduate degrees are conferred in social sciences.

Special: The university offers study abroad, a pass/fail system, and an internship program that permits students to work in many levels of the Oregon state government. Three-two degree programs are offered in forestry with Duke University, in engineering with Stanford and Columbia universities, and in management with Williamette's own Atkinson Graduate School of Management. Students may design their own majors.

Honors: Fourteen honor societies have chapters on campus.

Admissions: About 84% of those who applied were accepted for the 1981-82 freshman class. SAT scores of those who enrolled were as follows: Verbal—50% below 500, 39% between 500 and 599, 9% between 600 and 700, 2% above 700; Math—39% below 500, 37% between 500 and 599, 20% between 600 and 700, and 4% above 700. On the ACT, 22% scored below 20, 27% between 20 and 23, 23% between 24 and 25, 24% between 26 and 28, 4% above 28. Applicants must be graduates of accredited high schools, rank in the top half of their class, have a GPA of approximately 2.5, and have completed 15 Carnegie units. Other important considerations are advanced placement or honors courses, extracurricular activities, special talents, and recommendations by high school officials.

Procedure: The SAT or ACT is required. Application deadlines are March 1 (fall) and November 1 (spring). New students are admitted both terms. There is a $20 application fee.

Special: The university has an early decision plan with a January 15 notification date, an early admissions plan with a March 1 (junior year in high school) deadline, and a deferred admissions plan. AP and CLEP may be used.

Transfer: Of 225 applications received for fall 1981, 180 transfer students were accepted, and 117 enrolled. Transfers are accepted for the freshman and sophomore years; D grades do not transfer. The applicant must have at least a 2.0 GPA in previous college work and must submit all previous college and high school transcripts along with the application. Transfers must take at least 60 semester hours at the university, out of a total of 124 required for the bachelor's degree. Application deadlines are March 1 (fall) and November 1 (spring).

Visiting: The university does not have an orientation program for prospective students, but guides are available for informal visits to the campus. Visitors may sit in on classes and may also stay overnight at the school. Visitors are encouraged to contact the admissions office in advance to schedule an appointment.

Financial Aid: About 62% of the students receive aid through the university. Forty-five percent work part-time on campus. The average award to freshmen from all sources available through the university is $3590. The university provides scholarships, grants, loans, and employment. About 180 grants and scholarships are available to freshmen. Loans may be secured from the federal and state governments, local banks, the university, and industrial, private or other sources. The university employs the package approach in awarding aid. The university is a member of CSS. The FAF must be filed. The application deadline is March 1. Notification is made by April 10.

Foreign Students: About 5% of the student body are from foreign countries. The university offers special counseling and special organizations for foreign students.

Admissions: Foreign applicants must take the TOEFL and achieve a minimum score of 500. College entrance exams are not required.

Procedure: The deadlines for applying are March 1 (fall) and November 1 (spring). Students must fill out the university's own health history form. Proof of adequate funds to cover the academic year must also be presented. Health insurance is required; the university offers insurance for a fee.

Admissions Contact: Franklin D. Meyer, Director of Admissions.

PENNSYLVANIA

ALBRIGHT COLLEGE
Reading, Pennsylvania 19603　　　　　　　　　E-3
(215) 921-2381

F/T: 660M, 760W
P/T: 375M, 310W
Grad: none
Year: 4-1-5, ss
Appl: Mar. 15
1396 applied
SAT: 520V 570M

Faculty: 90; IIB, ++$
Ph.D.'s: 65%
S/F Ratio: 16 to 1
Tuition: $4865
R and B: $1880
860 accepted　　　375 enrolled
ACT: 25　VERY COMPETITIVE+

Established in 1856 and affiliated with the United Methodist Church, Albright is a liberal arts college. The library contains 136,000 volumes and 5345 microfilm items, and subscribes to 725 periodicals.

Environment: The 80-acre campus is located in a residential section of Reading, a city of 80,000 residets, which is 60 miles from Philadelphia. Seven women's and 5 men's residences and 1 coed dormitory are arranged in a complex. Four fraternity houses, 2 sorority houses, and on-campus apartments provide additional housing. A social-science center and a life-sports center are under construction. Facilities for day students include a cafeteria, a dining hall, a lounge, and lockers.

Student Life: About 50% of the students come from Pennsylvania and 48% from other states. About 84% are graduates of public schools. Eighty percent live on campus. Fifty-one percent are Protestant, 35% are Catholic, and 9% are Jewish. College housing is both single-sex and coed. There are visiting privileges in single-sex housing. Places of worship are available on campus for Protestants and Catholics, and in the immediate community for Jews. Resident freshmen may not keep cars on campus.

Organizations: Twenty-four percent of the men belong to 3 local and 2 national fraternities; 20% of the women belong to 4 local sororities and 2 national sororities. Campus organizations include the student council and departmental groups. Cultural opportunities include visits by music and theater companies, concerts, opera, and art galleries.

Sports: The college competes in 9 intercollegiate sports for men and 7 for women. There are 4 intramural sports for men and 6 for women.

Handicapped: Ninety percent of the campus is accessible to handicapped students. Special facilities include wheelchair ramps, parking areas, elevators, lowered drinking fountains, and specially equipped rest rooms. Special class scheduling is also available. Individual arrangements are made for students with visual or hearing impairments.

Graduates: About 5% of the freshmen drop out by the end of their first year. Seventy-five percent remain to graduate. Of those, about 40% go on to further study, including 10% to medical school, 4% to dental school, and 2% to law school. Fifty percent pursue careers in business and industry.

Services: Students receive the following free services: placement and, career counseling, health care, psychological counseling, and tutoring.

Programs of Study: The college confers A.B. and B.S. degrees. Bachelor's degrees are offered in the following subjects: AREA STUDIES (American), BUSINESS (accounting, business administration, business/psychology, computer science), ENGLISH (English), FINE AND PERFORMING ARTS (art), HEALTH SCIENCES (medical technology, nursing), LANGUAGES (French, German, Spanish), MATH AND SCIENCES (biochemistry, biology, chemistry, mathematics, physics, psychobiology), PHILOSOPHY (philosophy, religion), PREPROFESSIONAL (dentistry, forestry, home economics, law, medicine, ministry, social work, veterinary), SOCIAL SCIENCES (economics, government/political science, history, international relations, psychology, sociology). Field-work experience is required of students in the home economics, social welfare, and psychology programs, as well as those in the nonmajor communications arts program. Twenty-five percent of degrees conferred are in preprofessional studies, 19% in social sciences, 25% in math and sciences, 12% in humanities, and 19% in business.

Required: All students must take freshman English as well as a distribution of credits in traditional areas of study.

Special: Students may participate in the Washington Semester program. Study abroad is encouraged. A 3-2 combination-degree program in forestry is offered in cooperation with Duke University; 3-2 programs in engineering are offered with Bucknell University, Pennsylvania State University, and the University of Pennsylvania; and a 4-1 program in engineering is offered with the University of Pennsylvania. Students may create their own majors.

Honors: Nine national honor societies have chapters on campus.

Admissions: About 62% of those who applied were accepted for the 1981-82 freshman class. For those who enrolled, the SAT scores were as follows: Verbal—36% below 500, 52% between 500 and 599, 11% between 600 and 700, and 1% above 700; Math—17% below 500, 53% between 500 and 599, 27% between 600 and 700, and 3% above 700. All applicants must have completed 15 Carnegie units of work, be high school graduates, rank in the upper 40% of their class, have a GPA of at least 3.0, and be recommended by their high school. The college seeks a national geographic representation in its student body, and children of alumni are given preference. Advanced placement or honors courses, extracurricular activities, impressions made during an interview, recommendations, and special talents are also taken into consideration.

Procedure: Applicants must take the SAT or ACT. For placement purposes, ATs are required in English composition, in math for those planning to enter a B.S. program, and in the appropriate language for those planning to study a language. Application deadlines are March 15 (fall), and December 15 (winter and spring). New students are admitted on a rolling basis. There is an application fee of $15.

Special: Early admissions, deferred admissions, and early decision plans are available. The college accepts CLEP and some AP exams for credit.

Transfer: For fall 1981, 84 students were accepted and 62 enrolled. A 2.0 average, good standing at the previous institution, and an interview are required. D grades are not accepted. At least 60 credits must be taken at the college of the 122 required for a bachelor's degree. Application deadlines are August 1 (fall) and December 15 (winter and spring).

Visiting: There are regularly scheduled orientations for prospective students. Guides are available for informal visits on weekdays and Saturday mornings throughout the school year. Visitors may stay overnight at the school and sit in on classes. Campus visits can be arranged through the admissions office.

Financial Aid: Eighty-two percent of the students receive aid. About 50% work part-time on campus. The average award to freshmen from all sources was $4000 in 1981-82. Scholarships, loans, grants, and campus jobs are available. Students may receive federal and state grants. Financial aid is awarded on the basis of need, but merit awards are based solely on the individual's academic and leadership potential. The college is a member of the CSS. Applicants must submit the FAF and the aid application by April 1.

Foreign Students: One percent of the full-time students come from foreign countries. The college offers these students special counseling and special organizations.

Admissions: Foreign students must score 500 on the TOEFL. No college entrance examination is required.

Procedure: Application deadlines are April 15 (fall) and December 15 (winter and spring). Foreign students must submit a physician's report and proof of adequate funds for their entire period of study. They must carry health insurance, which is included in the college's comprehensive fee.

Admissions Contact: Dale H. Reinhart, Director of Admissions.

ALLEGHENY COLLEGE B-1
Meadville, Pennsylvania 16335   (814) 724-4351

F/T: 963M, 925W	Faculty: 130; IIB, +$
P/T: 1M, 10W	Ph.D.'s: 75%
Grad: 5M, 11W	S/F Ratio: 15 to 1
Year: see entry, ss	Tuition: $4950
Appl: Mar. 1	R and B: $1850
2097 applied	1611 accepted	618 enrolled
SAT: 535V 564M		VERY COMPETITIVE

Allegheny College, an independent liberal arts college affiliated with the Methodist Church, was founded in 1815. The library contains 300,000 volumes and 24,293 microfilm items, and subscribes to 1143 periodicals.

Environment: The campus extends over 150 acres, 65 of which are used for 30 buildings and the remainder for athletic and recreational purposes. It is located in Meadville, a small city with a population of 18,000 that is 35 miles from Erie and 90 miles north of Pittsburgh. The college sponsors dormitories, off-campus apartments, and fraternity houses.

Student Life: Fifty-four percent of the students are from Pennsylvania. Eighty-two percent come from public schools. Eighty-three percent live in college housing. Thirty-five percent are Catholic, 41% Protestant, and 3% Jewish. Eight percent are minority-group members. Campus housing is both single-sex and coed. There are visiting privileges in single-sex housing. Freshmen, students receiving financial aid, and those on academic probation may not have cars on campus.

Organizations: Forty percent of the men belong to 8 national fraternities, and 35% of the women belong to 4 national sororities. The college offers a variety of cultural and recreational opportunities.

Sports: The college participates in 15 intercollegiate sports for men and 9 for women. There are 16 intramural sports for men and 16 for women.

Handicapped: Thirty percent of the campus is accessible to handicapped students. Facilities include specially equipped rest rooms and dormitory rooms, and lowered drinking fountains and telephones.

Graduates: About 8% of freshmen drop out by the end of the first year, and 75% remain to graduate. About 70% of the graduates continue their studies. Seven percent enter medical school, 3% enter dental school, and 6% enter law school. Twenty-four percent pursue careers in business and industry.

Services: Students receive the following free services: placement aid, career counseling, psychological counseling, tutoring, and remedial instruction.

Programs of Study: The college confers the B.A. and B.S. degrees. Master's degrees are also granted. Bachelor's degrees are offered in the following subjects: BUSINESS (computer science), EDUCATION (elementary, secondary), ENGLISH (English, literature, speech), FINE AND PERFORMING ARTS (art, art history, radio/TV, studio art, theater/dramatics), HEALTH SCIENCES (medical technology), LANGUAGES (French, German, Greek/Latin, Russian, Spanish), MATH AND SCIENCES (biology, chemistry, ecology/environmental science, geology, mathematics, physics), PHILOSOPHY (classics, philosophy, religion), PREPROFESSIONAL (dentistry, engineering, forestry, law, medicine, ministry, pharmacy, veterinary), SOCIAL SCIENCES (anthropology, economics, government/political science, history, international relations, psychology, sociology). Eighteen percent of the degrees are conferred in business.

Required: Students must complete distribution requirements.

Special: Allegheny uses a 3-term, 3-course calendar. Work in a field of concentration or specialized area may be initiated in the freshman year. A Washington semester, a junior year abroad, an exchange program with Fisk University, and a 3-year bachelor's degree are offered. Cooperative 5-year B.S.-M.S. programs in forestry (with Duke University and the University of Michigan) are available. The 5-year teacher-education program in elementary and secondary education, which includes a 1-year internship, culminates in the M.A.Ed. degree. Independent study and interdepartmental programs are offered. Joint and double majors and internships can be arranged. Students may design their own majors.

Honors: Several national honor societies, including Phi Beta Kappa, have chapters on campus.

Admissions: Seventy-seven percent of those who applied were accepted for the 1981–82 freshman class. For those who enrolled, the SAT scores were as follows: Verbal—33% below 500, 46% between 500 and 599, 17% between 600 and 700, and 3% above 700; Math—22% below 500, 42% between 500 and 599, 29% between 600 and 700, and 6% above 700. Each applicant is evaluated on the basis of achievement in school, standardized test results, the counselor's recommendation, and various nonintellectual factors. No preestablished standards are in effect, although students generally should rank in the top half of their high school class. Advanced placement or honors courses and impressions made during the interview also are taken into consideration.

Procedure: Either the SAT or the ACT is required. Three ATs (in English composition and 2 other areas) are recommended. Application deadlines are March 1 (fall), November 1 (winter), February 1 (spring), and May 1 (summer). The application fee is $20.

Special: The college offers early admissions, deferred admissions, and early decision plans. CLEP general and subject exams are accepted. Credit also can be earned through AP.

Transfer: For fall 1981, 92 students applied, 79 were accepted, and 48 enrolled. Transfer students are accepted for the freshman, sophomore, and junior years. College grades, secondary school records, and test scores are considered. D grades are not acceptable. Students must complete a minimum of 2 academic years or 18 term courses at Allegheny of the 36 term courses (120 credits) needed to receive a bachelor's degree. Application deadlines are May 1 (fall), November 1 (winter), February 1 (spring), and May 1 (summer).

Visiting: Day-long orientations provide contact with faculty members, administrators, and students. Guides are available for informal visits. Visitors may stay overnight at the school and sit in on classes. Visits can be arranged for weekdays and Saturday mornings through the admissions office.

Financial Aid: Fifty-eight percent of all students receive financial aid. Thirty-three percent work part-time on campus. Average aid to freshmen from all sources was $4000 in 1981–82. College assistance includes grants-in-aid, loans, and campus jobs. Costs may be paid in installments. The college is a member of CSS. The FAF is required. The deadlines for filing aid applications are March 1 (fall), November 1 (winter), February 1 (spring), and May 1 (summer).

Foreign Students: Two percent of the full-time students come from foreign countries. The college offers these students special counseling and special organizations.

Admissions: Foreign students must score at least 600 on the TOEFL. No college entrance examination is required.

Procedure: Application deadlines are March 1 (fall), November 1 (winter), February 1 (spring), and May 1 (summer). Foreign students must complete a college physical-examination form and must present proof of adequate funds for 1 year. They also must carry health insurance, which is available through the college for a fee.

Admissions Contact: Richard A. Stewart, Dean of Admissions.

ALLENTOWN COLLEGE OF ST. FRANCIS DE SALES   E–3
Center Valley, Pennsylvania 18034   (215) 282-4443

F/T: 343M, 366W   Faculty: 43; IIB, –$
P/T: 22M, 50W   Ph.D.'s: 54%
Grad: none   S/F Ratio: 16 to 1
Year: sems, ss   Tuition: $3700
Appl: open   R and B: $2180
640 applied   506 accepted   246 enrolled
SAT: 460V 490M   COMPETITIVE

Allentown College, a private liberal arts college affiliated with the Roman Catholic Church, was founded in 1965 and is conducted by the Oblate Fathers of St. Francis de Sales. The library contains 95,000 volumes and 600 microfilm items, and subscribes to 600 periodicals.

Environment: The 300-acre campus is located in a rural setting 7 miles from Allentown and Bethlehem. Seven dormitories accommodate 496 students.

Student Life: About 70% of the students are from Pennsylvania. Approximately 40% are graduates of public schools. Sixty-five percent live on campus. Eighty-four percent are Catholic, 7% are Protestant, and fewer than 1% are Jewish. About 4% of the students are minority-group members. Campus housing is single-sex, with visiting privileges. Students may keep cars on campus. Day-care services are available to all students, faculty, and staff for a fee.

Organizations: Special-interest clubs and other extracurricular activities are available. Students may visit the Allentown Art Museum and attend concerts given by the Allentown Symphonic Orchestra.

Sports: The college fields intercollegiate teams in 5 sports for men and 5 for women. There are 4 intramural sports for men and 3 for women.

Handicapped: Eighty percent of the campus is accessible to handicapped students. Wheelchair ramps, special parking, and elevators are provided.

Graduates: Twenty-nine percent of the freshmen drop out by the end of the first year, and 55% remain to graduate. Ten percent of the graduates continue their studies. About 1% enter medical school, 1% enter dental school, and 2% enter law school. About 19% pursue careers in business and industry.

Services: Health care, psychological counseling, career counseling, and placement aid are provided free. Fees are charged for some tutoring and remedial instruction.

Programs of Study: The college confers the B.A., B.S., and B.S.N. degrees. Bachelor's degrees are offered in the following subjects: BUSINESS (accounting, computer science, management), ENGLISH (English), FINE AND PERFORMING ARTS (dance, theater/dramatics), HEALTH SCIENCES (nursing), LANGUAGES (foreign languages), MATH AND SCIENCES (biology, chemistry, computer science, mathematics), PHILOSOPHY (liberal studies, religion), SOCIAL SCIENCES (criminal justice, government/political science, psychology). Twenty-six percent of degrees are conferred in the health sciences, 23% in social sciences, and 16% in business.

Required: Two courses in theology, two in philosophy, and two in physical education are required.

Special: Students may earn combined B.A.-B.S. degrees in biology, chemistry, and mathematics. The college is a member of the Lehigh Valley Association of Independent Colleges and permits cross-registration with all member institutions. Study abroad in the junior year is offered. Certification in secondary education is available.

Honors: Two national honor societies have chapters on campus.

Admissions: Seventy-nine percent of the applications for the 1981–82 freshman class were accepted. The SAT scores of those who enrolled were as follows: Verbal—77% scored below 500, 20% between 500 and 599, 3% between 600 and 700, and 0% above 700; Math—68% scored below 500, 25% between 500 and 599, 6% between 600 and 700, and 1% above 700. Applicants should have completed 16 Carnegie units, have a C average or better, and rank in the upper 60% of their graduating class.

Procedure: The SAT is required. There are no application deadlines, and notification is made on a rolling basis. Freshmen are admitted to all semesters. The application fee is $10.

Special: Early admissions and deferred admissions plans are offered. CLEP and AP credit is available.

Transfer: For a recent semester, 55 applications were received and 52 were accepted, and 27 students enrolled. Applicants must be in good standing at their former school with at least a 2.0 GPA. D grades do not transfer. Students must spend 2 years in residence, earning at least 60 of the 120 credits required for a bachelor's degree. There is no application deadline.

Visiting: A prospective student can contact the admissions office to arrange a visit, which normally includes a campus tour and an interview with an admissions counselor and a faculty member. Guides will be provided. Visitors may sit in on classes, and prospective students may stay overnight on campus. Weekdays from 9 A.M. to 4 P.M. are the best times to visit.

Financial Aid: Eighty-three percent of the students receive aid. Thirty percent work part-time on campus. The average award to freshmen from all sources in 1981–82 covered 60% of costs. Federal and state loans and campus employment are available. Tuition may be paid in installments. The college is a member of CSS. The FAF is required, and the Pennsylvania State Grant Application must be filed by state residents. There is no application deadline.

Foreign Students: Fewer than 1% of the full-time students come from foreign countries.

Admissions: Foreign students must take the TOEFL. No college entrance examination is required.

ALLIANCE COLLEGE B–1
Cambridge Springs, Pennsylvania 16403　　(814) 398-4611

F/T: 129M, 40W	Faculty:	17; IIB, — $
P/T: 40M, 7W	Ph.D.'s:	40%
Grad: none	S/F Ratio:	15 to 1
Year: sems, ss	Tuition:	$2910
Appl: open	R and B:	$1900
220 applied	192 accepted	113 enrolled
SAT: 410V 420M	ACT: 18	LESS COMPETITIVE

Alliance College, an independent college of liberal and applied arts, was founded in 1912 by the Polish National Alliance, a fraternal organization of Americans of Polish descent. The library contains 90,000 volumes and 10,000 microfilm items, and subscribes to 100 periodicals.

Environment: The campus covers 200 acres in a rural area 24 miles from Erie. The 3 dormitories accommodate 200 women and 410 men. The college also sponsors fraternity houses.

Student Life: Eighty percent of the students come from Pennsylvania, New Jersey, and New York. About 95% live on campus. Sixty percent are Catholic, and 35% are Protestant. Three percent are minority-group members. Campus housing is both single-sex and coed. There are visiting privileges in single-sex housing. Students may keep cars on campus.

Organizations: There are 3 fraternities and 1 sorority; 30% of the men and 15% of the women belong. Students may participate in student government, publications, and special-interest groups, and may attend various social and cultural events.

Sports: The college competes on an intercollegiate level in 3 sports for men. There are 8 intramural sports for men and 7 for women.

Handicapped: About 80% of the campus is accessible to wheelchair-bound students. No special facilities are available.

Graduates: About 20% of the freshmen drop out by the end of their first year, and 60% remain to graduate. Fifteen percent of the graduates pursue advanced degrees; 2% enter medical school, 1% enter dental school, and 2% enter law school. Forty-five percent pursue careers in business and industry.

Services: Students receive free placement aid, career counseling, health care, tutoring, and remedial instruction. Placement services for undergraduates and alumni include a job bank and resource files.

Programs of Study: The college confers the B.A. and B.S. degrees. Associate degrees also are granted. Bachelor's degrees are offered in the following subjects: AREA STUDIES (Slavic), BUSINESS (accounting, international business, management), ENGLISH (English), LANGUAGES (Polish, Russian), MATH AND SCIENCES (biology, chemistry, mathematics), PREPROFESSIONAL (dentistry, law, library science, medicine, social work, veterinary), SOCIAL SCIENCES (psychology, social sciences, sociology). Forty-five percent of the degrees conferred are in business, 20% in math and sciences, and 20% in social sciences.

Required: All students must take courses in English, fine arts, a foreign language, natural science, religion or philosophy, social science, physical education, and (for all but 3 majors) mathematics.

Special: Students may design their own majors.

Honors: Four honor societies have chapters on campus.

Admissions: Eighty-seven percent of those who applied were accepted for the 1981–82 freshman class. Applicants should have completed 16 units of secondary school work, rank in the top 60% of their class, and have at least a 2.0 GPA. The recommendations of the high school, high school record, and ACT or SAT scores are the main criteria used in the admissions process.

Procedure: Applicants should take the ACT or SAT by March of the senior year. Freshmen are admitted to both semesters. Students can apply at the end of their junior year in high school. Notification is made on a rolling basis. There is a $15 application fee. An interview is encouraged.

Special: Early admissions, deferred admissions, and early decision plans are offered. CLEP and AP credit is accepted. Veterans may earn credit for USAF and service school courses.

Transfer: Of 18 applications received for the fall of 1981, 14 were accepted, and 10 students enrolled. Transfers are accepted for the freshman, sophomore, and junior years. A 2.0 average is required. D grades are not acceptable. Transfer students must earn a minimum of 30 credits at Alliance of the 128 needed to receive a bachelor's degree. Applications should be submitted at least 2 weeks before the beginning of the term.

Visiting: Orientation programs for prospective students include campus tours, meetings with faculty members, lunch, financial-aid seminars, and special programs. Informal visits can be arranged through the admissions office. Guided tours, interviews, class visits, and overnight stays can be scheduled during the fall and spring.

Financial Aid: About 70% of all students receive aid through the school. Forty percent work part-time on campus. The average award to freshmen from all sources in 1981–82 covered 60% of costs. The college offers scholarships, NDSL, BEOG, SEOG, CWS, and United Student Aid Funds loans. Students in good academic standing with demonstrated financial need are considered for aid. The college is a member of CSS. The SFS is required. The deadline for aid applications is March 1.

Foreign Students: Fewer than 1% of the full-time students come from foreign countries. The college offers these students special counseling.

Admissions: Foreign students must score at least 500 on the TOEFL or attain an equivalent score on the college's own language test. No academic exams are required.

Procedure: Application deadlines are August 15 (fall) and December 15 (spring). Foreign students must present a completed health form. They also must present proof of adequate funds for at least 1 year. Foreign students are required to carry health insurance, which is available through the college for a fee.

Admissions Contact: Robert A. Stephens, Dean of Admissions and Records.

ALVERNIA COLLEGE E–3
Reading, Pennsylvania 19601　　(215) 777-5411

F/T: 133M, 150W	Faculty:	33; IIB, —$
P/T: 116M, 455W	Ph.D.'s:	24%
Grad: none	S/F Ratio:	11 to 1
Year: sems, ss	Tuition:	$2150
Appl: May 1	R and B:	$1700
300 applied	240 accepted	124 enrolled
SAT: 450V 500M		COMPETITIVE

Alvernia College, a small Roman Catholic liberal arts college, was established in 1958. The library houses 65,000 volumes and 15,400 microfilm items, and subscribes to 1500 periodicals.

Environment: The 85-acre campus is located in a rural setting 3 miles from Reading, Pennsylvania. The campus consists of 8 major buildings. Residence facilities are provided.

Student Life: Seventy percent of the students come from Pennsylvania, and most of the rest are from the Middle Atlantic states. Seventy-five percent are public-school graduates. About 40% live on campus. Sixty percent are Catholic and 25% are Protestant. Ten percent are minority-group members. Campus housing is coed. Students may keep cars on campus.

Organizations: Alvernia has no fraternities or sororities. There is an active student government. Recreational areas adjacent to the campus include Angelica Park.

Sports: The college fields 4 intercollegiate teams for men and 2 for women. There are 2 intramural sports for both men and women.

Graduates: Ten percent of the freshmen drop out by the end of their first year. Eighty percent remain to graduate. Thirty-five percent of the graduates continue their studies, including 2% who enter medical school, 2% who enter dental school, and 5% who enter law school. Thirty-five percent of the graduates pursue careers in business and industry.

Services: Health care, psychological counseling, tutoring, remedial instruction, career counseling, and placement aid are available free to students.

Programs of Study: The college confers the B.A. and B.S. degrees. Associate degrees are also granted. Bachelor's degrees are offered in the following subjects: BUSINESS (accounting, business administration, finance), EDUCATION (elementary, secondary), ENGLISH, (English, journalism), FINE AND PERFORMING ARTS (music), HEALTH SCIENCES (medical technology, nursing), LANGUAGES (French, German, Spanish), MATH AND SCIENCES (biochemistry, biology, chemistry, mathematics), PHILOSOPHY (religion), PREPROFESSIONAL (dentistry, law, medicine, social work, veterinary), SOCIAL SCIENCES (psychology, social sciences, sociology). Forty percent of

730 PENNSYLVANIA

the degrees are awarded in the social sciences, 25% in business, and 10% in the health sciences.

Required: Students must take English composition and a liberal arts core consisting of philosophy/theology, science/mathematics, a foreign language, fine arts, social sciences, and physical education.

Special: Students may earn combined B.A.-B.S. degrees in biology, psychology, and chemistry. A general-studies degree is offered.

Admissions: Eighty percent of the applicants for the 1981-82 freshman class were accepted. The SAT scores of those who enrolled were as follows: Verbal—82% scored below 500, 12% between 500 and 599, 5% between 600 and 700, and 0% above 700; Math—71% scored below 500, 22% between 500 and 599, 12% between 600 and 700, and 0% above 700. Of those who took the ACT, 65% scored below 21, 20% between 21 and 23, 15% between 24 and 25, and 0% above 26. Requirements include 16 high school units, a grade average of 2.0 or above, and a rank in the upper four-fifths of the graduating class. The college also considers advanced placement or honors courses, recommendations by school officials, impressions made during an interview, and extracurricular activities.

Procedure: The SAT or the ACT is required. The application deadlines are May 1 (fall) and January 1 (spring). Notification is made on a rolling basis. The application fee is $10.

Special: Early and deferred admissions are possible. CLEP exams are accepted.

Transfer: For fall 1981, 75 students applied, 55 were accepted, and 40 enrolled. A GPA of 2.0 is necessary. D grades do not transfer. Students must earn at least 30 credits at Alvernia of the 120 needed to receive a bachelor's degree. Application deadlines are the same as those for freshman applicants.

Visiting: Informal visits may be made any time classes are in session. Visitors may stay overnight at the school. They will be provided with guides and may sit in on classes. Arrangements can be made through the director of admissions.

Financial Aid: Sixty percent of the students receive financial aid. Thirty-five percent work part-time on campus. The average aid to freshmen from all sources covered 90% of costs in 1981-82. Aid is offered in the form of scholarships, loans, or grants. The college is a member of CSS. The FAF or state grant application should be filed. Application deadlines are April 1 (fall), December 15 (spring), and April 1 (summer).

Foreign Students: About 3% of the full-time students come from foreign countries. The college provides these students with an intensive English course.

Admissions: Foreign students must take the TOEFL. No college entrance examination is required.

Procedure: Application deadlines are May 1 (fall and summer) and December 1 (spring). Foreign students must present proof of adequate funds for 4 years.

Admissions Contact: Joel R. Wincowski, Director of Admissions and Financial Aid.

BEAVER COLLEGE
Glenside, Pennsylvania 19038   F-3
                                      (215) 572-0132

F/T: 146M, 575W   Faculty: 63; IIB, +$
P/T: 168M, 439W   Ph.D.'s: 54%
Grad: 114M, 681W   S/F Ratio: 12 to 1
Year: 4-1-4, ss   Tuition: $4970
Appl: Aug. 1   R and B: $2250
859 applied   557 accepted   207 enrolled
SAT or ACT: required   COMPETITIVE

Beaver College, founded in 1853, is a nonsectarian, privately endowed, liberal arts college affiliated with the United Presbyterian Church. The library houses 121,720 volumes and 5475 microfilm items, and subscribes to 550 periodicals.

Environment: The college is located in a suburb 10 miles from Philadelphia on a 55-acre campus. The 16 buildings include a computer center and 5 dormitories. Grey Towers Castle, inspired by a medieval English castle, is registered as an historical landmark.

Student Life: About 64% of the students are residents of Pennsylvania. Sixty-four percent live on campus. Twenty-six percent are Catholic, 31% Protestant, and 11% Jewish. Nineteen percent are minority-group members. Campus housing is both single-sex and coed; there are visiting privileges in single-sex housing. Students may keep cars on campus. Day-care services are available to all students, faculty, and staff for a fee.

Organizations: There are no fraternities or sororities, but other student organizations provide social opportunities. These include religious organizations, departmental clubs, special-interest groups, and workshops.

Sports: The intercollegiate athletic program consists of 8 sports for men and 10 for women. There are 8 intramural sports for men and 7 for women.

Handicapped: About 50% of the campus is accessible to handicapped students. Designated parking areas and special class scheduling are available.

Graduates: The freshman dropout rate is 10%. Of the 55% of freshmen who remain to graduate, 55% continue their education. Five percent enter medical school, 2% enter dental school, and 2% enter law school. Forty-five percent of the graduates pursue careers in business or industry.

Services: Health care, psychological counseling, tutoring, placement aid, and career counseling are offered free.

Programs of Study: The college confers the B.A., B.S., and B.F.A. degrees. Associate and master's degrees are also offered. Bachelor's degrees are awarded in the following subjects: BUSINESS (accounting, business administration, computer science), EDUCATION (early childhood, elementary, secondary, special), ENGLISH (English, literature), FINE AND PERFORMING ARTS (art, art education, art history, art/science, film/photography, studio art, theater/dramatics), HEALTH SCIENCES (medical technology, physical therapy), MATH AND SCIENCES (biology, chemistry, interdisciplinary science, mathematics, psychobiology), PHILOSOPHY (humanities, philosophy, religion), PREPROFESSIONAL (dentistry, engineering, law, library science, medicine, ministry, nursing, pharmacy, social work, veterinary), SOCIAL SCIENCES (government/political science, history, psychology, sociology). Thirty-two percent of degrees are conferred in fine and performing arts, 19% in social sciences, 25% in math and sciences and 15% in business.

Required: Distribution requirements include 2 semesters of English composition, a laboratory science and physical education.

Special: Selected upperclass students are permitted to enroll in 1 course per semester at the University of Pennsylvania. There is a cooperative nursing program with the University of Pennsylvania, as well as 3-2 engineering programs with Columbia University, Washington University, and Widener University that lead to a combined B.A.-B.S. degree. Independent study, interdisciplinary programs, and undergraduate research programs are available. Students may design their own majors. A junior year abroad, semesters in London and Vienna, a Harrisburg Urban Semester, a Philadelphia semester, and a Washington semester are offered. Internships are available in social work, corrections, and psychology.

Honors: Six national honor societies have chapters on campus. All departments offer honors programs consisting of colloquia and independent studies.

Admissions: Sixty-five percent of those who applied were accepted for the 1981-82 freshman class. Students should have completed at least 16 academic courses, rank in the top 50% of their class, and have a good recommendation from the high school. Also important are advanced placement or honors courses, evidence of special talent, leadership record, and personality.

Procedure: The SAT or ACT is required. Application deadlines are August 1 (fall) and December 15 (spring). There is a rolling admissions plan. The application fee is $15.

Special: Early decision, early admissions, and deferred admissions plans are offered. CLEP and AP credit is accepted.

Transfer: For fall 1981, 147 students applied, 83 were accepted, and 43 enrolled. Applicants must be in good standing at an accredited college and have at least a 2.5 GPA. One D grade per year is transferable provided that it is not in the major area. Students must complete at least 12 course units at the college of the 32 required for a bachelor's degree. Application deadlines are August 1 (fall) and December 15 (spring).

Visiting: The college schedules orientations for prospective students. Guides also are available for informal visits, and visitors may sit in on classes and stay overnight at the school. Visits can be arranged for any time except December 15 through February 1 with the office of admissions.

Financial Aid: Forty-eight percent of all students receive aid. Twenty percent work part-time on campus. The average award to freshmen from all sources in 1981-82 was $1888. The college awards a number of freshman scholarships. Grants, loans, and work-study also are available. The FAF is required. Aid applications should be submitted by February 1 for priority consideration.

Foreign Students: Five percent of the full-time students come from foreign countries. The college offers these students an intensive English program, special counseling, and special organizations.

Admissions: Foreign students must score at least 500 on the TOEFL. No college entrance examination is required.

Procedure: Application deadlines are May 1 (fall) and October 1 (spring). Foreign students must present a completed college health form and proof of adequate funds for their entire course of study. They also must carry health insurance.

Admissions Contact: T. Edwards Townsley, Dean of Admissions.

BLOOMSBURG STATE COLLEGE E-2
Bloomsburg, Pennsylvania 17815 (717) 389-3316

F/T: 1927M, 2953W	Faculty:	302; IIA, ++$
P/T: 275M, 541W	Ph.D.'s:	50%
Grad: 202M, 379W	S/F Ratio:	19 to 1
Year: sems, ss	Tuition:	$1352 ($2282)
Appl: open	R and B:	$1314
4520 applied	2203 accepted	1079 enrolled
SAT: 470V 510M		COMPETITIVE+

Bloomsburg State College is a state-controlled institution founded in 1839. The library contains 295,500 volumes and 1,020,000 microfilm items, and subscribes to 850 periodicals.

Environment: The 173-acre campus is located in a rural town of 12,000 people, 40 miles from Wilkes-Barre and 80 from Harrisburg. The oldest of the 30 buildings on campus, Carver Hall, is a local landmark. There are 7 dormitories on campus.

Student Life: About 94% of the students come from Pennsylvania. Forty-eight percent are Catholic, 38% are Protestant, and 1% are Jewish. Nearly 4% are minority-group members. Seventy-three percent of the students live on campus. Campus housing is both coed and single-sex; there are visiting privileges in single-sex dorms. Drinking is prohibited for students under 21. Freshmen may not have cars on campus. Day-care services are available.

Organizations: About 15% of the students belong to 1 of the 9 fraternities and 8 sororities. The college has a recreational center and offers a number of extracurricular activities, including religious organizations. The Pocono Mountain ski area is nearby.

Sports: The college fields intercollegiate teams in 11 sports for men and 10 for women, and offers 8 intramural sports for men and 7 for women.

Handicapped: About half the campus is accessible to wheelchair-bound students. Facilities include ramps, special parking areas, elevators, special class scheduling, specially equipped rest rooms, and lowered drinking fountains and telephones.

Graduates: Sixteen percent of the freshmen drop out, and 66% remain to graduate. Twenty-five percent of the graduates pursue further study; 1% enter medical school, 1% enter dental school, and 1% enter law school. Another 40% of the graduates begin careers in business and industry.

Services: Students receive free career and psychological counseling, placement services, health care, tutoring, and remedial instruction. Placement services also are available to graduates.

Programs of Study: The college awards the B.A., B.S., B.S.B.A., B.S.Ed., B.S.N., and B.S.O.A. degrees. Associate and master's degrees also are available. Bachelor's degrees are offered in the following subjects: AREA STUDIES (American), BUSINESS (accounting, business administration, business education, computer science, finance, management, marketing, office administration), EDUCATION (early childhood, elementary, secondary, special), ENGLISH (English, speech), FINE AND PERFORMING ARTS (art, art history, mass communications, music, studio art), HEALTH SCIENCES (dental hygiene, medical technology, nursing, radiologic technology, speech therapy), LANGUAGES (French, Spanish), MATH AND SCIENCES (biology, chemistry, earth science, geology, mathematics, natural sciences, physical sciences, physics), PHILOSOPHY (philosophy), SOCIAL SCIENCES (anthropology, economics, geography, government/political science, history, psychology, sociology). About 34% of the undergraduate degrees are conferred in professional studies, 34% in business, and 32% in arts and sciences.

Required: Students must take physical education and fulfill general-education requirements.

Special: The college has a 3-2 cooperative program in engineering with Pennsylvania State University.

Honors: Nineteen honor societies are represented on campus.

Admissions: About 49% of the applicants were accepted for the 1981–82 freshman class. The SAT scores of those who enrolled were as follows: Verbal—79% below 500, 19% between 500 and 599, 2% between 600 and 700, and 0% above 700; Math—52% below 500, 42% between 500 and 599, 6% between 600 and 700, and 0% above 700. Pennsylvania residents must have completed 16 academic units, score at least 400 on each portion of the SAT, rank in the upper 50% of their graduating class, and present at least a C+ average. Out-of-state applicants must have at least a B average and a total score of 1000 on the SAT, and must rank in the upper two-fifths of their class. Admissions officers also consider recommendations by high school officials, extracurricular activities, and advanced placement or honors courses.

Procedure: The SAT is required. Application deadlines are open, and new students are admitted to both semesters. The college follows a rolling admissions plan. The application fee is $10.

Special: Early admissions and deferred admissions plans are available. CLEP and AP credit is given.

Transfer: For fall 1981, 701 students applied, 371 were accepted, and 206 enrolled. Transfer students are accepted for all classes. Applicants must have an average of 2.0 or better and a minimum of 30 credit hours. D grades transfer. Students must study at least 1 year on campus, earning 32 of the 128 credits necessary to receive a bachelor's degree.

Visiting: Orientations for prospective students are held regularly. Informal visits should be scheduled with the admissions office for Mondays, Thursdays, and Fridays between 9 A.M. and 3 P.M. Visitors may sit in on classes.

Financial Aid: Ninety-five percent of the students receive aid. Loans are available from the college and from federal and state governments. Thirty-two percent of the students work part-time on campus. The aid application deadline is March 15. The college is a member of CSS.

Foreign Students: Foreign students at Bloomsburg represent less than 1% of the full-time enrollment. Special counseling and organizations are available for these students.

Admissions: Foreign students must take the TOEFL. No college entrance exams are required.

Procedure: Application deadlines are January 1 (fall), July 1 (spring), and November 1 (summer). Students must present proof of adequate funds for 1 year. They are required to carry health insurance, which is available through the college for a fee.

Admissions Contact: Thomas L. Cooper, Dean of Admissions.

BRYN MAWR COLLEGE F-3
Bryn Mawr, Pennsylvania 19010 (215) 645-5152

F/T: 1104W	Faculty:	n/av; I, –$
P/T: 8W	Ph.D.'s:	89%
Grad: 129M, 472W	S/F Ratio:	9 to 1
Year: sems	Tuition:	$7050
Appl: Feb. 1	R and B:	$3050
1200 applied	607 accepted	280 enrolled
SAT: 660V 630M		MOST COMPETITIVE

Bryn Mawr College, founded in 1855 by members of the Society of Friends, is an independent, nonsectarian liberal arts college. It provides instruction on graduate and undergraduate levels. The library contains 500,000 volumes and subscribes to 2500 periodicals.

Environment: The 112-acre campus is located in a suburban area 11 miles west of Philadelphia. The federal government has declared the college an historic district. There are 10 residence halls and a group of language houses for upperclassmen who speak French, German, or Spanish. Students from Bryn Mawr and from Haverford, a mile away, live in coed dorms at both schools under a cooperative plan.

Student Life: Students come from all areas of the country. Ninety-four percent live on campus. About 9% are minority-group members. Housing is both single-sex and coed, with visiting privileges in single-sex housing. Students may keep cars on campus. Day-care services are available.

Organizations: Activities include the Interfaith Association, a weekly newspaper, music groups, student theater, political and service groups, films, music, and lecture series. There are no sororities or fraternities. Philadelphia offers additional cultural and recreational opportunities.

Sports: The college competes in 8 intercollegiate sports for women. There are 6 intramural sports for men and 9 for women.

Handicapped: About 75% of the campus is accessible to wheelchair-bound students. Special facilities include ramps, parking areas, and elevators. Special class scheduling can be arranged. Readers and a scanner are provided for visually impaired students.

Graduates: Fewer than 4% of the freshmen drop out by the end of their first year, and 82% remain to graduate. About 70% of the graduates pursue further study, including about 13% who enter medical school and 15% who enter law school. Ten percent of the graduates pursue careers in business and industry.

Services: Students receive free placement aid, career counseling, health care, and psychological counseling. Tutoring is available on a fee basis.

Programs of Study: The B.A. degree is offered. Master's and doctoral degrees also are conferred. Bachelor's degrees are available in the following subjects: AREA STUDIES (Hispanic, Hispanic-American, Russian, urban), ENGLISH (English), FINE AND PERFORMING ARTS (art, art history, music), LANGUAGES (French, German, Greek/Latin, Italian, Russian, Spanish), MATH AND SCIENCES (astronomy, biology, chemistry, geology, mathematics, physics), PHILOSOPHY (philosophy, religion), SOCIAL SCIENCES (anthropology, classical and Near-Eastern archaeology, economics, government/political science, growth and structure of cities, history, psychology, sociology).

Required: All students must complete 1 course in English composition, humanities, literature, natural sciences, and social sciences. Proficiency in 2 languages or in 1 language and mathematics must be shown. A comprehensive exam in the major is required.

Special: Students may spend the junior year abroad or attend summer institutes in France or Spain between the junior and senior years. Through a cooperative plan, students may take courses for credit at Haverford, Swarthmore, or the University of Pennsylvania. A 3-2 program can lead to a B.A. from Bryn Mawr and a B.S. in engineering from California Institute of Technology. The education department offers no major but maintains a nursery school as a laboratory for child study. Independent study, a premedical program, and interdepartmental courses are offered.

Honors: All departments offer honors programs. Part of the senior year may be spent on an honors project, working independently with faculty supervision.

Admissions: About 51% of the students who applied for the 1981–82 freshman class were accepted. Of those who enrolled, the SAT scores were as follows: Verbal—0% below 500, 19% between 500 and 599, 50% between 600 and 700, and 26% above 700; Math—0% below 500, 36% between 500 and 599, 48% between 600 and 700, and 12% above 700. Applicants should have completed 16 academic units, rank high in the graduating class, and achieve good scores on the SAT and the ATs. Other factors considered are advanced placement or honors courses, recommendations by school officials, and special talents.

Procedure: The SAT and 3 ATs (in English composition, a foreign language, and another area) should be taken by January of the senior year. An interview is recommended. The application deadlines are February 1 (fall) and November 1 (winter). Notification is made by late April. The CRDA is observed. The $20 application fee may be waived in cases of financial need.

Special: Early decision, early admissions, and deferred admissions plans are available. AP credit is given.

Transfer: For fall 1981, the college received 68 transfer applications, accepted 35, and enrolled 26 students. Transfers are considered for the sophomore and junior classes. Requirements include a B average and an interview. D grades do not transfer. Students must spend at least 2 years in residence, earning 64 of the 128 semester hours required for a bachelor's degree. Application deadlines are March 15 (fall), and November 1 (winter).

Visiting: Orientations are scheduled regularly. Guides are available for informal visits weekdays during the fall. Arrangements should be made with the Director of Admissions. Visitors may sit in on classes and stay overnight at the school.

Financial Aid: Forty-two percent of all students receive financial aid. Fifty-five percent work part-time on campus. The average award to freshmen from all sources in 1981–82 was $4400. Scholarships, loans, and campus jobs are provided by the school. Aid is awarded on the basis of need and academic record. The college is a member of CSS. The FAF and the college's own aid form are required. Application for aid must be made by January 15.

Foreign Students: Seven percent of the full-time students come from foreign countries. The college offers these students special counseling and special organizations.

Admissions: Foreign students must score at least 600 on the TOEFL. They also must take the SAT.

Procedure: Application deadlines are February 1 (fall) and November 1 (winter). Foreign students must present a physician's report. They must carry health insurance, which is available through the college for a fee.

Admissions Contact: Elizabeth G. Vermey, Director of Admissions.

BUCKNELL UNIVERSITY   D–2
Lewisburg, Pennsylvania 17837   (717) 524-1101

F/T: 1670M, 1471W   Faculty: 241; IIA, ++$
P/T: 19M, 26W   Ph.D.'s: 84%
Grad: 110M, 103W   S/F Ratio: 15 to 1
Year: 4-1-4, ss   Tuition: $6467
Appl. Jan. 1   R and B: $1850
6284 applied   2277 accepted   804 enrolled
SAT: 554V 616M   HIGHLY COMPETITIVE

Bucknell University, founded in 1846, is a private university offering programs in liberal arts and sciences, business, education, and pre-professional areas. The library contains 450,000 volumes.

Environment: The 300-acre campus is located in a rural area 60 miles from Harrisburg. The 60 buildings include a student center and 11 coed and single-sex dormitories accommodating 2100 students. The university also sponsors on-campus apartments and fraternity houses.

Student Life: Thirty-eight percent of the students are from Pennsylvania. Eighty-two percent come from public schools. About 86% live on campus. Thirty-one percent of the students are Catholic, 45% Protestant, and 6% Jewish. Eleven percent are minority-group members. University housing is both single-sex and coed. There are visiting privileges in single-sex housing. First-semester freshmen and aid recipients may not have cars on campus.

Organizations: There are 12 fraternities, to which 48% of the men belong; and 10 sororities, of which 40% of the women are members. Extracurricular groups include special-interest, religious, and service organizations. The university sponsors cultural events such as art shows, concerts, debates, films, lectures, plays, recitals, and science exhibits.

Sports: The university fields intercollegiate teams in 20 sports for men and 15 for women. There are 14 intramural sports for men and 12 for women.

Handicapped: About 60% of the campus is accessible to handicapped students. Facilities include wheelchair ramps, designated parking areas, elevators, specially equipped rest rooms, and lowered drinking fountains. One percent of the students have visual impairments. Two special counselors are available.

Graduates: The freshman dropout rate is 5%. Eighty-one percent of the freshmen remain to graduate. Forty percent of the graduates go on to further study. Six percent enter medical school, 3% enter dental school, and 6% enter law school. Fifty-five percent pursue careers in business or industry.

Services: Psychological counseling, health care, placement aid, and career counseling are offered free.

Programs of Study: The university confers the B.A., B.S., B.S.B.A., and B.S. in E. degrees. Master's degrees are also offered. Bachelor's degrees are awarded in the following subjects: BUSINESS (accounting, business administration, computer science, management), EDUCATION (early childhood, elementary, secondary), ENGLISH (English, literature), FINE AND PERFORMING ARTS (art, art history, music, music education, studio art, theater/dramatics), LANGUAGES (French, German, Japanese, Russian, Spanish), MATH AND SCIENCES (biochemistry, biology, chemistry, geology, mathematics, physics), PHILOSOPHY (classics, philosophy, religion), SOCIAL SCIENCES (economics, geography, government/political science, international relations, psychology, sociology).

Required: Required courses vary with the major. Students in certain majors are required to take the URE.

Special: The university offers interdepartmental majors, a voluntary noncredit January program of independent study, a 5-year combined B.A.-B.S. degree in engineering and arts, and a 4-year combined B.S.-M.S. program in biology, chemistry, mathematics, or mechanical engineering. Students may spend the sophomore or junior year abroad and design their own majors.

Honors: Sixteen national honor societies, including Phi Beta Kappa, have chapters on campus.

Admissions: Thirty-six percent of those who applied were accepted for the 1981–82 freshman class. The SAT scores of those who enrolled were as follows: Verbal—18% scored below 500, 52% between 500 and 599, 25% between 600 and 700, and 5% above 700; Math—5% scored below 500, 30% between 500 and 599, 49% between 600 and 700, and 16% above 700. Candidates should be graduates of an accredited high school and have completed 15 Carnegie units. Other factors considered are advanced placement or honors courses, recommendations by school officials, evidence of special talent, and extracurricular activities.

Procedure: The SAT and 3 ATs are required. ATs should include English composition, a foreign language for candidates in the arts and sciences, and mathematics for those in mathematics/science or engineering programs. The deadline for application is January 1. Freshmen are admitted only in the fall. Notification is given by April 1. A $20 fee must accompany the application.

Special: Early decision, early admissions, and deferred admissions plans are offered.

Transfers: For fall 1981, 220 students applied, 70 were accepted, and 37 enrolled. Transfers are considered for the sophomore and junior classes only. Applicants must have a GPA of at least 2.5. D grades are not acceptable. Students must study a minimum of 3 semesters at the university, earning 48 of the 128 credits required for a bachelor's degree. Application deadlines are March 1 (fall) and December 1 (spring).

Visiting: Guides are available for informal visits.

Financial Aid: Twenty-eight percent of the students receive aid. Thirty-five percent work part-time on campus. Average aid to freshmen from all sources was $5000 in 1981-82. Aid is available in the form of scholarships, loans, and campus jobs. Tuition may be paid in installments. The university is a member of the CSS and requires the FAF. The deadline for aid application is February 1.

Foreign Students: About 7% of the full-time students come from foreign countries. The university offers these students special counseling and special organizations.

Admissions: Foreign students must score at least 550 on the TOEFL. No college entrance examination is required.

Procedure: The application deadline is April 1 for fall admission. Foreign students must present the record of a physical examination. They must carry health insurance, which is available through the university for a fee.

Admissions Contact: Richard C. Skelton, Director of Admissions.

CABRINI COLLEGE F-4
Radnor, Pennsylvania 19087 (215) 687-2100

F/T: 120M, 460W	Faculty:	33; n/av
P/T: 25M, 115W	Ph.D.'s:	37%
Grad: none	S/F Ratio:	18 to 1
Year: sems, ss	Tuition:	$3740
Appl: open	R and B:	$2350
395 applied	323 accepted	176 enrolled
SAT: 450V 450M		COMPETITIVE

Cabrini College, established in 1957, is a private, liberal arts institution affiliated with the Roman Catholic Church and operated by the Missionary Sisters of the Sacred Heart. The library contains 66,500 volumes and 2700 microfilm items, and subscribes to 345 periodicals.

Environment: The 110-acre, wooded campus is located in a suburban town on the Main Line, 18 miles from Philadelphia. The original buildings are Elizabethan-style structures dating back to the turn of the century. Buildings include 7 residence halls, a chapel, a science hall, a children's school, and a new campus center.

Student Life: About 68% of the students come from Pennsylvania, and 39% are graduates of public schools. Sixty-five percent live on campus. Eighty-two percent are Catholic, 10% are Protestant, and 1% are Jewish. Ten percent are minority-group members. Campus housing is single-sex, with visiting privileges. Students may keep cars on campus. Freshmen living in residence halls must observe curfews.

Organizations: Student activities include publications, theater, departmental clubs, film festivals, a social-action program, a lecture series, and a glee club. There are no fraternities or sororities. Additional cultural and recreational facilities are available in Philadelphia.

Sports: The college fields 4 intercollegiate teams for men and 6 for women. There are 3 intramural sports for both men and women.

Handicapped: No special facilities are provided for handicapped students.

Graduates: Fifteen percent of the freshmen drop out by the end of their first year, and 60% eventually graduate. Thirty-five percent of the graduates seek advanced degrees.

Services: Free placement assistance, health care, psychological and career counseling, tutoring, and remedial instruction are provided.

Programs of Study: The college awards the B.A., B.S., and B.S.Ed. degrees. Bachelor's degrees are offered in the following subjects: AREA STUDIES (American), BUSINESS (business administration), EDUCATION (early childhood, elementary, secondary, special), ENGLISH (communications, English), FINE AND PERFORMING ARTS (arts administration, studio art), HEALTH SCIENCES (medical technology, pre-nursing), LANGUAGES (French, Spanish), MATH AND SCIENCES (biology, chemistry, mathematics), PHILOSOPHY (philosophy, religion), PREPROFESSIONAL (dentistry, law, medicine, pharmacy, social work, veterinary), SOCIAL SCIENCES (history, psychology, social sciences). About 32% of the degrees conferred are in education, 20% are in business, 12% are in social sciences, 19% are in math and sciences, and 17% are in communications/humanities.

Required: Students must take a specified number of hours in English, fine arts, history, mathematics, philosophy, psychology, science, foreign language, religion, and physical education.

Special: Combined B.A.-B.S. degrees may be earned. Students may design their own majors. A study-abroad program is offered. A freshman honors program, field work, and internships are also available.

Honors: Five honor societies are represented on campus.

Admissions: Eighty-two percent of those who applied for admission to the 1981-82 freshman class were accepted. Candidates should have completed 16 high school units, rank in the upper half of their graduating class, and present a grade average of 80 or better. Admissions officers also consider recommendations by high school officials, extracurricular activities, and special talents.

Procedure: The SAT or ACT is required and should be taken early in the senior year. Application deadlines are open. The college follows a rolling admissions plan. Freshmen are admitted to the fall and spring terms. The application fee is $20.

Special: Early and deferred admissions plans are available. CLEP and AP credit is given.

Transfer: For fall 1981, 99 students applied, 84 were accepted, and 61 enrolled. Transfer students are accepted in all classes. Applicants must have an average of 2.0 or better at their previous college. D grades do not transfer. Students must earn at least 60 credits on campus of the 130 needed for a bachelor's degree. Application deadlines are the same as those for freshman applicants.

Visiting: Regularly scheduled orientations for prospective students include information sessions, lunch with students and faculty members, and classroom visits. Guides are available for informal visits. Visitors may sit in on classes and arrange to stay overnight in the residence halls. Appointments should be made with the admissions office.

Financial Aid: Eighty-five percent of the students receive aid. Thirty percent work part-time on campus. Average aid to freshmen from all sources in 1981-82 was $3000. Scholarships, loans, grants, and part-time jobs are awarded on the basis of financial need and academic achievement. The college is a member of CSS. The FAF is required. The State Grant Application is also required of Pennsylvania residents. Aid applications should be submitted by April 1.

Foreign Students: No foreign students were enrolled in 1981-82.

Admissions: Applicants must score at least 500 on the TOEFL. They also must score at least 450 on each section of the SAT, or attain acceptable scores on the ACT.

Procedure: The application deadline is February 1. Foreign students must submit a completed health form. They must also present proof of adequate funds for each year of study.

Admissions Contact: Estelle Travis Oristaglio, Director of Admissions.

CALIFORNIA STATE COLLEGE B-3
California, Pennsylvania 15419 (412) 938-4404

F/T: 1600M, 1500W	Faculty:	370; IIA, ++$
P/T: 375M, 350W	Ph.D.'s:	47%
Grad: 300M, 330W	S/F Ratio:	16 to 1
Year: sems, ss	Tuition:	$1350 ($2190)
Appl: Aug. 1	R and B:	$1550
2518 applied	1994 accepted	1318 enrolled
SAT: required		COMPETITIVE

California State College, established in 1852, is a public institution that offers degree programs in the liberal arts, in teacher training, and in technical fields. The library contains 250,000 volumes, subscribes to 2100 periodicals, and houses 250,000 microfilm items.

734 PENNSYLVANIA

Environment: The college occupies 75 acres in a suburban area 35 miles south of Pittsburgh. It also owns an 88-acre farm. Campus buildings include 2 high-rise dormitories that accommodate 2300 students. The college also sponsors fraternity and sorority houses.

Student Life: Almost all students are residents of Pennsylvania. About 90% come from public schools. About 50% live on campus. Dormitories are single-sex.

Organizations: There are 10 fraternities and 11 sororities to which 15% of the men and 20% of the women belong. Professional societies are also open to students.

Sports: The college competes on an intercollegiate level in 7 sports. At least 4 intramural sports are offered for men and women.

Handicapped: About 60% of the campus is accessible to wheelchair-bound students. Special parking, wheelchair ramps, elevators, and special rest rooms are available. Special class scheduling can be arranged.

Graduates: About 30% of the freshmen drop out, and 55% remain to graduate. Fifteen percent of the graduates pursue graduate study; 2% enter medical school, 1% dental school, and 2% law school. About 20% pursue careers in business and industry.

Services: Students receive the following free services: placement aid, career counseling, health care, tutoring, remedial instruction, and psychological counseling.

Programs of Study: The college confers the B.A., B.S., and B.S.Ed. degrees. Associate and master's programs are also offered. Bachelor's degrees are offered in the following subjects: AREA STUDIES (American, urban), BUSINESS (accounting, business administration, computer science), EDUCATION (adult, early childhood, elementary, industrial, secondary, special), ENGLISH (creative writing, English, journalism, professional writing, speech), FINE AND PERFORMING ARTS (art, film/photography, printing and graphic communications, radio/TV, theater/dramatics), HEALTH SCIENCES (medical technology, speech therapy), LANGUAGES (French, German, Spanish), MATH AND SCIENCES (biology, chemistry, earth science, ecology/environmental science, geology, mathematics, mathematics and computer science, natural sciences, physical sciences, physics), PHILOSOPHY (humanities, philosophy), PREPROFESSIONAL (chiropractic, energy technology, industrial technology, law, manufacturing technology, mortuary science, optometry, osteopathy, pharmacy, podiatry, recreation and parks, social work, veterinary), SOCIAL SCIENCES (anthropology, economics, geography, gerontology, government/political science, history, international studies, psychology, social sciences, sociology).

Special: Combined B.A.-B.S. degrees may be earned in various subjects. A 5-year B.A.-B.S. curriculum is offered and a general-studies degree is possible. Students may design their own majors. Sophomores may study abroad in college-sponsored programs in France, Spain, and Mexico.

Admissions: About 79% of those who applied were accepted for the 1981–82 freshman class. For an earlier class, the SAT scores were as follows: Verbal—10% between 500 and 600, 2% between 600 and 700, and 1% above 700; Math—12% between 500 and 600, 5% between 600 and 700, and 1% above 700. Candidates must have at least a C average in 15 Carnegie units and rank in the upper 60% of their high school class. The college also considers the following factors: recommendations by school officials, extracurricular activities, advanced placement or honors courses, evidence of special talents, leadership record, personality, and impressions made during an interview.

Procedure: Candidates must take the SAT in May of the junior year or November, December, or January of the senior year. Application deadlines are August 1 (fall) and December 1 (spring). Notification is sent as soon as all credentials are complete. The application fee is $10.

Special: The college has early decision, early admissions, and deferred admissions plans. CLEP and AP credit is accepted.

Transfer: Transfers are considered for all classes. A minimum C average is required. D grades do not transfer. Students must study at least 1 year at the college to receive a bachelor's degree.

Visiting: An orientation program is held for prospective students in the summer. Informal visits can also be arranged through the admissions office. Guides are provided, and visitors may sit in on classes and stay overnight at the college.

Financial Aid: About 73% of all students receive aid. Loans are available from the federal government and the college. The FAF must be filed with the CSS. The aid application deadline is April 1.

Foreign Students: Foreign students enrolled full-time make up 6% of the student body. The college offers an intensive English course, an intensive English program, special counseling, and special organizations.

Admissions: Applicants must take the TOEFL (attaining a score of at least 450) or the college's own English proficiency test. The college recommends that applicants also take the SAT.

Procedure: Students should submit applications at least 6 months before the start of the term in which they wish to enroll. They must present a physician's statement and proof of adequate funds for 1 year. They also must carry health insurance, which is available through the college.

Admissions Contact: Norman Hasbrouck, Dean of Admissions.

CARLOW COLLEGE B-3
Pittsburgh, Pennsylvania 15213 (412) 578-6059

F/T: 29M, 698W	Faculty: 52; IIB, −$
P/T: 14M, 272W	Ph.D.'s: 56%
Grad: none	S/F Ratio: 14 to 1
Year: sems, ss	Tuition: $4294
Appl: open	R and B: $2297
611 applied	480 accepted	192 enrolled
SAT: 420V 440M		LESS COMPETITIVE

Carlow College, established in 1929 as Mount Mercy College, is an independent women's liberal arts college operated by the Sisters of Mercy. The library contains 107,572 volumes and 10,168 microfilm items, and subscribes to 427 periodicals.

Environment: The 13-acre urban campus is located in the Oakland district and has 12 buildings, including dormitories that house 600 women.

Student Life: All but 15% of the students are residents of Pennsylvania. About 38% live on campus. Nearly 13% are minority-group members. About 54% are Catholic, 20% are Protestant, and 1% are Jewish. Campus housing is single-sex, and there are visiting privileges. Day-care services are available for a fee.

Organizations: There are no sororities. Student activities include publications, drama and music groups, and other organizations. Students also attend events in Pittsburgh and at nearby colleges.

Sports: The college offers 2 intercollegiate and 6 intramural sports for women.

Handicapped: Special facilities include parking areas, elevators, and tutoring services. Special class scheduling can be arranged.

Graduates: About 20% of the freshmen drop out, and 50% remain to graduate. Twelve percent of the graduates pursue further study; 1% enter medical school, 1% enter dental school, and 2% enter law school. Another 1% pursue careers in business and industry.

Services: Students receive free placement services, career counseling, health care, tutoring, remedial instruction, and psychological counseling.

Programs of Study: The college confers the B.A., B.S., and B.S.N. degrees. Bachelor's degrees are offered in the following subjects: BUSINESS (management), EDUCATION (early childhood, elementary, secondary, special), ENGLISH (literature), FINE AND PERFORMING ARTS (art, art education, music, music education, theater/dramatics), HEALTH SCIENCES (medical technology, nursing, speech therapy), MATH AND SCIENCES (biology, mathematics), PREPROFESSIONAL (dentistry, law, medicine, social work, veterinary), SOCIAL SCIENCES (anthropology, government/political science, history, psychology, social sciences, sociology). Twenty-four percent of the degrees conferred are in social sciences, 47% are in health sciences, and 9% are in business.

Required: Students must demonstrate competence in English composition, speech, reading, and math. All students are required to take courses in history; literature; biology, chemistry, or physics; math or logic; anthropology, psychology, or sociology; theology; and art, music, or drama. Two interdisciplinary courses are also required.

Special: Junior year abroad, independent study, and cross-registration (by upperclassmen only) at any of the 9 other member colleges and universities of the Pittsburgh Council are available. Off-campus field work for credit is an option offered in a number of departments.

Honors: Three honor societies have chapters on campus.

Admissions: Seventy-nine percent of those who applied were accepted for the 1981–82 freshman class. The SAT scores of those who enrolled were as follows: Verbal—87% below 500, 11% between 500 and 599, 2% between 600 and 700, and 0% above 700; Math—82% below 500, 17% between 500 and 599, 1% between 600 and 700, and 0% above 700. Applicants must be high school graduates, rank in the top 50% of their class, have at least a B− average, be recommended by high school authorities, and have completed 16 Carnegie units. Additional factors considered include recommendations by school officials, advanced placement or honors courses, and evidence of special talents.

Procedure: The SAT or ACT should be taken by December of the senior year. A personal interview is recommended. There are no deadlines for application. Students may be admitted in the fall or the spring. A rolling admissions policy is used. There is no application fee.

Special: Early decision, deferred admissions, and early admissions plans are offered. AP and CLEP credit is given.

Transfer: For fall 1981, 72 students applied, 34 were accepted, and 22 enrolled. A 2.0 GPA is required; a 2.2 is recommended. D grades do not transfer. All students must complete, at the college, at least 32 of the 128 credits required for a bachelor's degree. Transfer application deadlines are open.

Visiting: Regularly scheduled orientations are held for prospective students. Guided tours, interviews, class visits, and overnight stays can be scheduled for weekdays through the admissions office.

Financial Aid: About 84% of all students receive aid through the school; 52% work part-time on campus. The college is a member of CSS. Scholarships, loans, and student jobs are available. The Pennsylvania State Grant and Federal Student Aid applications are required. Applications may be filed at any time.

Foreign Students: The college actively recruits foreign students; 1 such student was enrolled in 1981-82. Special counseling and an intensive English program are available.

Admissions: Students must score at least 70% on the University of Michigan Language Test. No college entrance exams are required.

Procedure: The application deadlines are July 1 (fall) and November 1 (spring). Students must present proof of adequate funds for 4 years of study, and must submit a health form completed by a physician. Health insurance is required and is available through the college for a fee.

Admissions Contact: John P. Hine, Jr., Director of Admissions and Financial Aid.

CARNEGIE-MELLON UNIVERSITY B-3
Pittsburgh, Pennsylvania 15213   (412) 578-2082

F/T: 2690M, 1301W   Faculty: 440; I, +$
P/T: 67M, 40W   Ph.D.'s: 85%
Grad: 1226M, 363W   S/F Ratio: 9 to 1
Year: sems, ss   Tuition: $5450
Appl: Mar. 1   R and B: $2720
4957 applied   2978 accepted   1190 enrolled
SAT: 580V 600M   HIGHLY COMPETITIVE

Carnegie-Mellon University is an independent, nonsectarian liberal arts and professional institution. The university consists of the Carnegie Institute of Technology, the Mellon College of Science, the College of Humanities and Social Sciences, the College of Fine Arts, the Graduate School of Industrial Administration (which includes undergraduate programs in administration and management science), and the School of Urban and Public Affairs. The library contains 604,128 volumes, subscribes to 2687 periodicals, and has 121,822 microfilm items on file.

Environment: The 90-acre urban campus is situated 4 miles from downtown Pittsburgh. The 32 buildings on campus include 10 dormitories. Fraternity and sorority houses and on- and off-campus apartments are also available.

Student Life: About 47% of the students come from Pennsylvania. Eighty percent live on campus. About 65% come from public schools. About 12% are minority-group members. Campus housing is both coed and single-sex; there are visiting privileges in single-sex dorms. Students may keep cars on campus. Day-care services are available for a fee.

Organizations: Twenty percent of the men belong to the 12 fraternities on campus, and 11% of the women belong to the 5 sororities. The university provides a variety of student organizations, clubs, activities, publications, and lectures. It sponsors 15 major drama productions yearly. There are religious organizations for all major faiths.

Sports: The athletic program features intercollegiate competition in 13 sports for men and 11 for women, and offers 16 intramural sports each for men and women.

Handicapped: Ninety-five percent of the campus is accessible to handicapped students. Facilities include wheelchair ramps, lowered drinking fountains and telephones, handicapped parking areas, elevators, and specially equipped rest rooms. Special class scheduling is also available. One percent of the students have visual impairments. Applications from handicapped students are encouraged; accommodations are made to meet their individual situations.

Graduates: About 7% of the freshmen drop out, and 75% remain to graduate. Of those who graduate, 40% go on to further study; 5% enter medical school, 3% enter dental school, and 10% enter law school. About 60% begin careers in business or industry.

Services: The following services are offered free to students: psychological counseling, tutoring, health care, placement aid, and career counseling.

Programs of Study: The university confers the B.A., B.S., B.F.A., and B.Arch. degrees. Associate, master's, and doctoral degrees also are awarded. Bachelor's degrees are offered in the following subjects: AREA STUDIES (European, urban), BUSINESS (accounting, business administration, computer science, finance, management, marketing), EDUCATION (early childhood), ENGLISH (creative writing, English, journalism, literature, professional writing, technical writing/editing), FINE AND PERFORMING ARTS (design, music, studio art, theater/dramatics), LANGUAGES (French, German, Italian, Spanish), MATH AND SCIENCES (biochemistry, biology, chemistry, ecology/environmental science, mathematics, natural sciences, physical sciences, physics, statistics), PHILOSOPHY (humanities, philosophy), PRE-PROFESSIONAL (architecture, dentistry, engineering and nuclear science, engineering and public policy, engineering—biomedical, engineering—chemical, engineering—civil, engineering—electrical, engineering—mechanical, law, medicine, metallurgy and materials science, veterinary), SOCIAL SCIENCES (economics, government/political science, history, information systems, political economy, psychology, public policy/management, social sciences, sociology). About 33% of the degrees conferred are in preprofessional studies, 31% in fine and performing arts, and 14% in math and sciences.

Special: Students may spend a semester in Washington, or their junior year abroad. They may design their own majors. Five-year programs in the liberal arts and sciences lead to combined B.A.-B.S. degrees.

Admissions: Sixty percent of those who applied were accepted for the 1981-82 freshman class. The standards and requirements of the 5 colleges vary. In general, candidates for the Carnegie Institute of Technology, the Mellon College of Science, the College of Humanities and Social Sciences, and the administration and management science programs must have a strong B average, have good school recommendations, rank in the upper third of their graduating class, have scores of at least 500-550 on the Verbal SAT and 550-600 on the Math, and have completed 16 Carnegie units. For the College of Fine Arts, a portfolio is required in the art and design departments, and an audition in the music and drama departments. In addition, high school performance and standardized test results are reviewed.

Procedure: All 5 colleges require the SAT and the AT in English composition. In addition, the Carnegie Institute of Technology and the Mellon College of Science require ATs in chemistry or physics and in mathematics (level I or II); the College of Humanities and Social Sciences and the administration and management science programs require the mathematics AT (level I or II) and 1 additional AT of the candidate's choice; and the College of Fine Arts requires 2 additional ATs of the candidate's choice (architecture candidates are required to have ATs in mathematics and in chemistry or physics). The application deadline is March 1, and freshmen are admitted only in the fall. There is a $25 application fee.

Special: Early decision, early admissions, and deferred admissions plans are offered. Students may earn credit through AP exams.

Transfer: For fall 1981, the university received 687 transfer applications, accepted 269, and enrolled 185 students. Transfer candidates must have demonstrated satisfactory performance at their former school and have an appropriate background for the intended major. A 3.0 GPA is recommended. D grades do not transfer. The fall application deadline for the College of Fine Arts is March 1; for all other students the deadline is May 1. There are no spring admissions to the College of Fine Arts except for the departments of music and design. Students desiring spring entry must apply by December. Students must study at the university for at least 1 year, completing at least 30 of the approximately 90 credits necessary for a bachelor's degree.

Visiting: The university conducts regularly scheduled orientations for prospective students. Guides are available for informal visits when classes are in session. Visitors may sit in on all classes except drama. Overnight stays at the school are possible on "Sleeping Bag Weekends." The admissions office arranges visits.

Financial Aid: About 66% of all students receive aid. The university is a member of the CSS. The average award to freshmen in 1981-82 was $5950. Approximately 450 freshmen receive scholarships each year. Loans are available from the federal and state governments, local banks, and the university. The FAF is required. The aid application deadlines for regular admission are March 1 (fall) and December 1 (spring).

736 PENNSYLVANIA

Foreign Students: The 50 foreign students at the university represent 1% of the full-time enrollment. Special organizations are available for these students.

Admissions: Students must score at least 600 on the TOEFL. They also should take the SAT and 3 ATs, if possible.

Procedure: The application deadline for fall, the only semester to which students are admitted, is March 1. Students must present proof of adequate funds for 1 year. They are required to carry health insurance, which is available through the university for a fee.

Admissions Contact: William F. Elliott, Vice President for Enrollment.

CEDAR CREST COLLEGE E-3
Allentown, Pennsylvania 18104 (215) 437-4471

F/T: 800W	Faculty: 58; IIB, +$
P/T: 325W	Ph.D.'s: n/av
Grad: none	S/F Ratio: 13 to 1
Year: sems, ss	Tuition: $4500
Appl: open	R and B: $2100
609 applied	448 accepted	190 enrolled
SAT: 433V 447M		COMPETITIVE

Cedar Crest College, founded in 1867, is a small, liberal arts women's college affiliated with the United Church of Christ. The library contains 106,217 volumes and 10,862 microforms, and subscribes to 748 periodicals.

Environment: The 100-acre suburban campus is located in the city of Allentown, 50 miles from Philadelphia. The 12 campus buildings include a science center, 4 dormitories accommodating 684 women, several classroom buildings, a small art gallery, language laboratories, and art and music studios.

Student Life: Forty-five percent of the students are from Pennsylvania. About 85% attended public schools. Almost 90% live on campus. About 5% of the students are minority-group members. There are visiting privileges in the dorms, and students may keep cars on campus. Day-care services are available. Cedar Crest is nonsectarian and welcomes students of all religious preferences.

Organizations: There are no social sororities. There are many campus-centered activities, including excellent concert, lecture, and film series. Because Lehigh Valley is a collegiate center, with over 12,000 college students attending 6 private colleges, the social life is not limited exclusively to weekends.

Sports: The college competes on an intercollegiate level in 6 sports. Two intramural sports are offered.

Handicapped: Special arrangements, including class schedules, are made on an individual basis for handicapped students. Wheelchair ramps, designated parking areas, and specially equipped rest rooms in the new buildings are available.

Graduates: The freshman dropout rate is 5%; 60% remain to graduate. Twenty percent of the graduates pursue graduate study.

Services: Students receive free placement aid, career counseling, health care, tutoring, remedial instruction, and psychological counseling.

Programs of Study: The college confers the B.A. and B.S. degrees. Bachelor's degrees are offered in the following subjects: BUSINESS (accounting, business administration, management), EDUCATION (dance/physical, elementary, secondary), ENGLISH (communications studies, English), FINE AND PERFORMING ARTS (art, music, studio art, theater/dramatics), HEALTH SCIENCES (medical technology, nuclear medicine technology, nursing), LANGUAGES (French, German, Spanish), MATH AND SCIENCES (biology, chemistry, mathematics), PHILOSOPHY (classics, humanities, philosophy), PREPROFESSIONAL (dentistry, engineering, law, medicine, social work, veterinary), SOCIAL SCIENCES (government/political science, history, psychology, social sciences, sociology).

Required: Each student must take 3 semester courses in each of the 4 divisions: fine arts, humanities, social sciences, and mathematical/natural science. Psychology majors are required to sit for the URE.

Special: Students may design their own majors. It is possible to earn a general-studies degree or combined B.A.-B.S. degrees in various subjects. The college offers independent-study programs, study abroad for a semester or a year, and a variety of internships. A full program of cross-registration is offered in cooperation with other Lehigh Valley colleges (Lehigh University, Lafayette College, Moravian College, Muhlenberg College, Allentown College of St. Francis de Sales). Certification is offered in elementary and secondary education.

Honors: Seven national honor societies have chapters on campus.

Admissions: Seventy-four percent of those who applied were accepted for the 1981-82 freshman class. SAT scores of those who enrolled were as follows: Verbal—81% below 500, 17% between 500 and 599, 1% between 600 and 700, and 1% above 700; Math—73% below 500, 25% between 500 and 599, 1% between 600 and 700, and 1% above 700. Candidates must be well-recommended by an accredited high school, should rank in the upper 40% of the graduating class, should have earned a 2.5 GPA, and should have completed 15 Carnegie units. Additional factors considered are impressions made during an interview, advanced placement or honors courses, and special talents. Daughters of alumnae are given some preference.

Procedure: A personal interview is recommended but not required, except for applicants to nursing and nuclear medicine technology. All applicants must submit SAT scores. Applications should be filed as early as possible during the fall of the senior year. The college uses the rolling admissions procedure and participates in the CRDA. There is a $20 application fee. Freshmen are admitted to both semesters.

Special: Early admissions and deferred admissions plans are available. CLEP and AP credit is accepted.

Transfer: For fall 1981, 68 students applied, 46 were accepted, and 31 enrolled. Transfers are considered for all classes except senior year. Students must be in good academic standing at the previous college and should have a GPA of at least 2.5 and SAT scores of at least 900. An interview is recommended. D grades will transfer if the GPA is 2.5 or higher. Students must earn a minimum of 30 credits at the college of the 120 required for a bachelor's degree.

Visiting: Orientations are scheduled on Columbus Day, Veteran's Day, and Foreign Language Day. Informal guided tours and interviews can be arranged through the admissions office on weekdays from 9 A.M. to 3:30 P.M. and Saturdays from 9 A.M. to 11 A.M.. Visitors may sit in on classes; overnight accommodations are available.

Financial Aid: Sixty percent of all students receive aid through the school. Freshman scholarships, as well as loans from the federal government, local banks, the college, and private funds are available. Tuition may be paid on the installment plan. The college is a member of the CSS and requires the FAF with aid applications. Deadlines for aid applications are February 1 for fall and December 1 for spring.

Foreign Students: The 4 students from foreign countries make up less than 1% of enrollment. Special counseling and special organizations are available.

Admissions: Students must take the TOEFL. No college entrance exams are required.

Procedure: Application deadlines are April 15 (fall) and November 15 (spring). Students must submit a physician's report as well as proof of adequate funds. Health insurance is available through the college at no fee.

Admissions Contact: Dana Lim Lacis, Director of Admissions.

CHATHAM COLLEGE B-3
Pittsburgh, Pennsylvania 15232 (412) 441-8200

F/T: 518W	Faculty: 57; IIB, +$
P/T: 157W	Ph.D.'s: 89%
Grad: none	S/F Ratio: 9 to 1
Year: 4-1-4, ss	Tuition: $5055
Appl: open	R and B: $2475
332 applied	252 accepted	117 enrolled
SAT: 410V 420M		COMPETITIVE

Chatham College, established in 1869, is a private, nonsectarian liberal arts institution for women. The library contains more than 110,000 volumes and 19,000 microfilm items, and subscribes to 460 periodicals.

Environment: The 55-acre campus is located on a wooded hilltop in a residential section of Pittsburgh. The college has a variety of residence halls, many of which once were private homes of prominent citizens. Academic buildings, concentrated around a quadrangle, include science laboratories and a music center. Other buildings include a 275-seat theater, a student center, and a physical-education center.

Student Life: About 60% of the students come from Pennsylvania; the rest are from 24 states and several foreign countries. About 17% are minority-group members. About 70% live on campus. There are visiting privileges in the dormitories. Students may keep cars on campus. Day-care services are available.

Organizations: Extracurricular activities include student government, publications, and academic and special-interest clubs. The college sponsors visits by theater and music groups, artists, and prominent professionals. Religious counselors and organizations are provided for students of the major faiths. The college has no sororities.

Sports: The college fields intercollegiate teams in 5 sports. There are 2 intramural sports.

Graduates: About 21% of the freshmen drop out, and 55%–60% remain to graduate. Sixty percent of the graduates go on to further study. One percent enter medical school, 1% enter dental school, and 7% to 9% enter law school. Another 50% pursue careers in business and industry.

Services: Fees are charged for health care and infirmary treatment. Free psychological counseling, career counseling, and tutoring are available.

Programs of Study: The college awards the B.A. and B.S. degrees. Bachelor's degrees are offered in the following subjects: AREA STUDIES (Black/Afro-American, women's), BUSINESS (business administration, management), EDUCATION (early childhood, elementary, secondary), ENGLISH (English, communication), FINE AND PERFORMING ARTS (art, music, theater/dramatics), LANGUAGES (French, German, Spanish), MATH AND SCIENCES (biology, chemistry, mathematics), PHILOSOPHY (philosophy, religion), SOCIAL SCIENCES (anthropology, economics, government/political science, history, psychology, sociology).

Required: Students must complete a freshman seminar, a course in expository writing, 2 special in-depth courses offered during the 4-week January Interim, and an individually designed independent-study project for the senior year.

Special: Students may design their own majors or pursue a general-studies degree. Through an exchange program, students may take courses at no extra charge at 9 other area institutions. Study-abroad programs may be arranged through other universities, and Chatham sponsors several such programs during the Interim. The college offers special freshmen seminars and faculty symposiums on topics of interest. All departmental areas offer independent-study programs and internships. Students interested in teaching careers can take courses that will enable them to earn elementary and secondary certification.

Honors: Phi Beta Kappa and Mortar Board are represented on campus.

Admissions: About 76% of those who applied were accepted for the 1981–82 freshman class. Applicants should be high school graduates and should rank in the top half of their class. Admissions officers consider each candidate's academic record, recommendations, and other information furnished by the high school. The college seeks a culturally, geographically, and economically diverse student body with a wide range of interests.

Procedure: No standardized tests are required. A campus interview is recommended. There are no application deadlines. Admissions decisions are made on a rolling basis beginning in January. There is a $15 application fee.

Special: The college offers early admissions and deferred admissions plans. AP credit may be earned.

Transfer: For fall 1981, 34 students applied, 24 were accepted, and 18 enrolled. A GPA of at least 2.0 is required. High school and college transcripts must be submitted, and an interview is recommended. D grades do not transfer. Students must complete, at the college, at least 13 of the 34 course credits necessary for the bachelor's degree.

Visiting: Prospective students are encouraged to visit the campus for a personal interview, a student-guided tour, conversations with faculty members and current students, observation of classes, and a night in the residence halls. Live-in programs of overnight visits are scheduled regularly throughout the school year. Arrangements should be made with the admissions office.

Financial Aid: Merit scholarships are awarded to entering freshmen on the basis of academic achievement and contributions to school and community. Scholarships also are available to students who demonstrate outstanding ability in vocal music. Other aid awards are based on financial need. Aid packages may include a grant, a part-time job, and a loan. Fifteen percent of the students work part-time on campus. About 48% of the students receive aid ranging from $100 to $6000 a year; the average award to 1981–82 freshmen was $3090. Aid candidates must submit the FAF. Application deadlines are March 15 (fall) and January 15 (spring). The college is a member of the CSS.

Foreign Students: The 6 students from foreign countries represent about 1% of enrollment. Special counseling is available for these students.

Admissions: Students must take either the TOEFL (attaining a score of at least 500) or the SAT.

Procedure: Application deadlines are June 15 (fall) and September 15 (spring). Proof of good health and of adequate funds for 1 year are required. Students must carry health insurance, which is available through the college for a fee.

Admissions Contact: Kathy F. Williams, Director of Admissions.

CHESTNUT HILL COLLEGE F-3
Philadelphia, Pennsylvania 19118 (215) 248-7000

F/T: 660W	Faculty: 100; n/av
P/T: 20M, 200W	Ph.D.'s: n/av
Grad: none	S/F Ratio: 12 to 1
Year: sems, ss	Tuition: $2850
Appl: May 1	R and B: $2000
SAT: 900 (composite)	COMPETITIVE

Chestnut Hill College, a private liberal arts institution for women founded in 1924, is operated by the Sisters of St. Joseph of the Roman Catholic Church. The library contains more than 90,000 volumes and subscribes to more than 825 periodicals.

Environment: The 45-acre campus is located in Chestnut Hill, a residential section of Philadelphia. Buildings include residence halls, the Gruber Theater, science laboratories, art and music studios, a planetarium, and an observatory.

Student Life: More than 60% of the students are from Pennsylvania. About half live on campus.

Organizations: The student government is primarily responsible for social, cultural, and athletic activities at the college. A range of extracurricular activities and organizations is available. There are no sororities.

Sports: The college fields intercollegiate teams in 7 sports. Intramural sports also are available.

Graduates: About 10% of the freshmen drop out, and 70% remain to graduate.

Services: Basic health services, placement aid, career counseling, and tutoring are provided free to students.

Programs of Study: The college awards the B.A. and B.S. degrees. Bachelor's degrees are offered in the following subjects: AREA STUDIES (American), EDUCATION (early childhood, elementary), ENGLISH (English), FINE AND PERFORMING ARTS (art, music, music education), LANGUAGES (French, German, Greek/Latin, Spanish), MATH AND SCIENCES (biochemistry, biology, chemistry, mathematics), PHILOSOPHY (classics, philosophy), SOCIAL SCIENCES (economics, government/political science, history, psychology, sociology). Non-major preprofessional programs are offered in medicine, law, and allied health fields.

Required: Students must take 11 hours of natural sciences, 9 of social sciences, 21 of humanities, 6 of religion, 6 of advanced foreign language, and 3 of English composition.

Special: The college offers a Women in Management Program for students of all majors. Students may design their own majors or combine two existing ones. Medical technology programs are offered in conjunction with Thomas Jefferson University. A cooperative nursing program is offered with Chestnut Hill Hospital and Methodist Hospital Schools of Nursing. A cooperative program in podiatry is offered with the Pennsylvania College of Podiatric Medicine, and a dual-degree program in engineering is offered with George Washington University. Cooperative programs in special education, accounting, finance, marketing, personnel and labor relations, and quantitative analysis are offered with La Salle College. Students may enroll in courses or major programs offered by La Salle at no extra charge. Students may study abroad or in other areas of the country during the summer or the month-long interim between semesters, and the college also offers semester-long or year-long programs in Paris. Many departments offer internship or cooperative education programs, sometimes for credit.

Honors: Freshmen and sophomores may participate in an interdisciplinary honors program. Sophomores may be invited to participate in honors programs in their majors for their junior and senior years. Delta Epsilon Sigma and Kappa Gamma Pi have chapters on campus.

Admissions: Applicants must be high school graduates and have completed 16 Carnegie units. They should rank in the top 40% of their class. High school grades, class rank, test scores, and recommendations by high school officials are the primary factors considered.

Procedure: The SAT is required. Applications for fall admission should be submitted by May 1. Decisions are made on a rolling basis. There is a $15 application fee.

Special: An early admissions plan is available. AP and CLEP credit is accepted.

738 PENNSYLVANIA

Transfer: Applicants must submit transcripts of all college and high school work and a recommendation from their current school. Students must earn, in residence, at least 60 of the 120 credits required for a bachelor's degree.

Financial Aid: Scholarships, grants, federal and private loans, SEOG, and campus jobs are available. Full-tuition Presidential Scholarships are awarded on the basis of ability; other aid is awarded on the basis of need. Candidates must submit the FAF and the aid application by January 15. About half the students receive aid.

Foreign Students: Twenty-two foreign students are enrolled at the college.

Admissions Contact: Sister Roberta Archibald, Director of Admissions.

CHEYNEY STATE COLLEGE   F-4
Cheyney, Pennsylvania 19319   (215) 758-2275

F/T: 1337M, 1369W	Faculty: 193; IIB, + + $
P/T: 163M, 98W	Ph.D.'s: 39%
Grad: 130M, 120W	S/F Ratio: 12 to 1
Year: sems, ss	Tuition: $1380 ($2320)
Appl: June 1	R and B: $1550
1600 applied	900 accepted
SAT: 850 (composite)	COMPETITIVE

Cheyney State College, a state-supported institution founded in 1837 as a college for blacks, provides programs in the liberal arts and sciences, in education, and in technical and applied sciences. The library contains 160,000 volumes and 8600 microfilm items, and subscribes to 1637 periodicals.

Environment: The college occupies a 276-acre site in a rural area 24 miles from Philadelphia. Buildings include a health center and 4 residence halls that house 1300 students.

Student Life: Eighty-three percent of the students are state residents. About 92% are black. About half live in residence halls, which are single-sex.

Organizations: There are 4 fraternities and 4 sororities, to which 1% of the men and 3% of the women belong. Political and professional organizations are available.

Sports: The college competes on an intercollegiate level in 6 sports for men and 5 for women. Six intramural sports also are available.

Handicapped: About 5% of the campus is accessible to wheelchair-bound students. The newer buildings have wheelchair ramps and specially equipped rest rooms.

Graduates: About 10% of the freshmen drop out, and 60% to 70% remain to graduate. About 20% of the graduates pursue further study; 3% enter medical school, 1% dental school, and 10% law school. Forty percent pursue careers in business and industry.

Services: Students receive the following free services: placement aid, career counseling, health care, tutoring, remedial instruction, and psychological counseling.

Programs of Study: The college confers the B.A., B.S., and B.S.Ed. degrees. Master's programs are also offered. Bachelor's degrees are offered in the following subjects: AREA STUDIES (Black/Afro-American, urban), BUSINESS (accounting, business administration, computer science, hotel/restaurant/institutional management, management, marketing), EDUCATION (early childhood, elementary, industrial, secondary, special), ENGLISH (English), FINE AND PERFORMING ARTS (art, music), HEALTH SCIENCES (dietetics), LANGUAGES (French, Spanish), MATH AND SCIENCES (biology, chemistry, earth science, ecology/environmental science, general science, marine biology, mathematics), PREPROFESSIONAL (clothing and textiles, home economics, industrial technology, social work), SOCIAL SCIENCES (anthropology, criminal justice, economics, geography, government/political science, history, psychology, recreation, social sciences, sociology).

Required: Students must take courses in English, world literature, humanities, social sciences, health and physical education, physical sciences, and life sciences. A Common Program of 60 semester hours includes these core courses. Students also must attend the college lecture series.

Special: Combined B.A.-B.S. degrees may be earned in mathematics, computer and information sciences, biology, and chemistry. A five-year curriculum is offered.

Honors: Eight national honor societies have chapters on campus.

Admissions: Fifty-six percent of those who applied were accepted for the 1981–82 freshman class. Students must have at least a C average, present recommendations from their high school, and submit SAT or ACT scores. State residents are given preference.

Procedure: Applicants must take the SAT or the ACT. The SAT should be taken in July, December, January, or March of the senior year. ATs in English composition and math are used for placement. Application deadlines are June 1 (fall) and November 1 (spring). There is a $10 application fee.

Special: Early decision, early admissions, and deferred admissions plans are offered. CLEP and AP credit is accepted.

Transfer: In a recent year, 358 transfer students applied, 232 were accepted, and 109 enrolled. Applicants are considered for all levels and should have at least a 2.0 GPA. An interview is required. D grades do not transfer. Preference is given to state residents. To receive a bachelor's degree, students must study at least 1 year at the college and earn 128 credits. Application deadlines are the same as those for freshmen.

Visiting: Two orientation sessions, each lasting 4 days, are held during the summer. They include parents' sessions, residence hall orientation, campus tours, placement exams, seminars, and pre-registration. Guided tours and interviews also may be scheduled during the fall and spring semesters and summer sessions through the admissions office. Visitors may sit in on classes, and overnight accommodations are available.

Financial Aid: About 85% of all students receive aid. Scholarships, grants, part-time jobs, cooperative education (work-study programs), and other funds are awarded on the basis of need. The FAF and college aid form are required. Aid applications should be filed by May 1 (fall) or November 1 (spring).

Foreign Students: Students from foreign countries make up about 4% of enrollment. The college offers these students special organizations and special counseling.

Admissions: Applicants from non-English-speaking countries must take the TOEFL. A score of at least 550 is required. Applicants also must take the SAT or ACT.

Procedure: Application deadlines are the same as those for other students. Foreign students must present the record of a medical examination and submit evidence of adequate funds. They also must carry health insurance, which is available through the college for a fee.

Admissions Contact: Christopher M. Rouhlac, Jr., Director of Admissions.

CLARION STATE COLLEGE   B-2
Clarion, Pennsylvania 16214   (814) 226-2306

F/T: 2300M, 2800W	Faculty: 280; IIA, + + $
P/T: 100M, 200W	Ph.D.'s: 70%
Grad: 155M, 175W	S/F Ratio: 18 to 1
Year: sems, ss	Tuition: $1350 ($2100)
Appl: May 1	R and B: $1250
3700 applied	2500 accepted	1740 enrolled
SAT: 449V 500M		COMPETITIVE

Founded in 1867 and publicly supported, Clarion State College offers programs in education, business, the liberal arts and sciences, and preprofessional fields. The library contains 400,000 volumes and subscribes to 300 periodicals.

Environment: The 84-acre campus is located in a rural town of 6000 people, 85 miles from Pittsburgh. The college's 23 buildings include 9 coed and single-sex dormitories accommodating 1100 men and 1400 women. The college also sponsors on- and off-campus apartments. For commuting students, there are lounges, lockers, and a snack bar.

Student Life: Eighty-three percent of the students are from Pennsylvania, and 80% come from public schools. About 75% live on campus. Fifty percent are Protestant, 35% are Catholic, and 2% are Jewish. About 9% are minority-group members. Campus housing is both coed and single-sex; there are visiting privileges in the single-sex dorms. Students may keep cars on campus.

Organizations: Fifteen percent of the men belong to the 2 local and 8 national fraternities on campus, and 15% of the women belong to the 9 national sororities. The student senate sponsors social, athletic, and cultural events.

Sports: The college competes in 12 intercollegiate sports for men and 11 for women. There are 7 intramural sports for men and 5 for women.

Handicapped: Facilities for the physically handicapped include special parking and elevators. Special counselors also are available.

Graduates: The freshman dropout rate is about 31%, and 64% of the freshmen remain to graduate. Of these, 55% seek advanced degrees.

Services: Students receive the following free services: health care, placement aid, career counseling, psychological counseling, tutoring, and remedial instruction.

Programs of Study: The college confers the B.A., B.S., and B.F.A. degrees. Associate and master's degrees also are awarded. Bachelor's degrees are offered in the following subjects: BUSINESS (accounting, business administration, computer science, finance, industrial and labor relations, management, marketing, real estate/insurance), EDUCATION (early childhood, elementary, secondary, special), ENGLISH (English, journalism, speech), FINE AND PERFORMING ARTS (art, film/photography, music, music education, radio/TV, studio art, theater/dramatics), HEALTH SCIENCES (medical technology, nursing, speech therapy), LANGUAGES (French, German, Russian, Spanish), MATH AND SCIENCES (astronomy, biochemistry, biology, chemistry, earth science, ecology/environmental science, geology, mathematics, natural sciences, physical sciences, physics, statistics), PHILOSOPHY (humanities, philosophy), PREPROFESSIONAL (dentistry, engineering, law, library science, medicine, ministry, pharmacy, social work, veterinary), SOCIAL SCIENCES (anthropology, economics, geography, government/political science, history, psychology, social sciences, sociology).

Required: Courses in English composition, humanities, natural sciences, mathematics, social sciences, and health and physical education are required of all students.

Special: Foreign-language students may spend the junior year abroad, and the college sponsors special summer study programs in Spain and South America. Prospective teachers may earn certification in athletic coaching, driver-safety education, and environmental education.

Admissions: Sixty-eight percent of those who applied were accepted for the 1981–82 freshman class. SAT scores of those who enrolled were as follows: Verbal—52% below 500, 42% between 500 and 599, 5% between 600 and 700, and 1% above 700; Math—48% below 500, 44% between 500 and 599, 7% between 600 and 700, and 1% above 700. Applicants should be graduates of accredited high schools, have a GPA of 2.0 or better, and rank in the upper half of their graduating class. They should be recommended for college by their high schools and show good records of extracurricular or athletic activities and leadership. Advanced placement or honors courses are highly regarded.

Procedure: All candidates must take the SAT or the ACT; potential liberal arts and foreign-language majors must also take a foreign-language AT. May 1 is the application deadline for fall; freshmen are also admitted for spring and summer semesters. Admission is on a rolling basis. There is an application fee of $10.

Special: Early decision, early admissions, and deferred admissions plans are available. CLEP general and subject exams are accepted; AP credit is also given.

Transfer: For fall 1981, 300 students applied, 225 were accepted, and 180 enrolled. Transfers are accepted for all classes except the senior class. D grades do not transfer. Applicants must have at least a 2.0 GPA, and be in good standing at their previous school. Students must complete at least 30 credits in residence of the 126 required for a bachelor's degree. The fall application deadline is the same as that for freshmen; transfer students are also admitted for the spring semester.

Visiting: There are regularly scheduled orientations for prospective students. Guides are available for informal visits, and visitors may sit in on classes by prearrangement with faculty members. During the summer session, visitors may stay overnight at the school. The college considers summer the best time of year for visiting the campus. Information can be obtained from the admissions office.

Financial Aid: Seventy percent of the students receive aid. Federal and state loans and campus jobs are available; half of the students work part-time on campus. The financial package available to a freshman averaged $1300 in 1981–82. Aid awards are based on financial need. The FAF should be filed before March 1 of the senior year. Pennsylvania residents also should file the state grant application. June is the deadline for aid applications. The college is a member of the CSS.

Foreign Students: The 102 students from foreign countries make up 3% of enrollment.

Admissions: Students must score at least 500 on the TOEFL.

Procedure: Foreign students are admitted for the fall, spring, and summer semesters. Proof of good health and of adequate funds is required. Students also must carry health insurance.

Admissions Contact: John S. Shropshire, Director of Admissions.

PENNSYLVANIA 739

COLLEGE MISERICORDIA B–2
Dallas, Pennsylvania 18612 (717) 675-2181

F/T: 140M, 715W Faculty: 61; IIB, –$
P/T: 44M, 245W Ph.D.'s: 18%
Grad: 6M, 51W S/F Ratio: 12 to 1
Year: sems, ss Tuition: $3265
Appl: open R and B: $1925
678 applied 565 accepted 338 enrolled
SAT: 425V 410M LESS COMPETITIVE

College Misericordia, founded in 1924, is a Roman Catholic liberal arts college conducted by the Sisters of Mercy of the Union. The library holds 93,800 volumes and microfilm items.

Environment: The 100-acre suburban campus is located in a small town of 15,000, 9 miles from Wilkes-Barre. The campus consists of 18 buildings, including 4 dormitories that accommodate 440 men and women.

Student Life: Seventy percent of the students are from Pennsylvania and 29% are from bordering states. Fifty-one percent attended public schools. Fifty-three percent live on campus. About 70% of the students are Catholic, 18% are Protestant, and 1% are Jewish. About 3% are minority-group members. Campus housing is single-sex, with visiting privileges. Students may keep cars on campus. Day-care services are available for a fee.

Organizations: There are no social fraternities or sororities, but professional and service organizations serve as social groups. The college sponsors 28 extracurricular activities, the most active of which are the Nursing Club, the Misericordia Athletic Association, the Misericordia Players, the Council on Exceptional Children, and the Education Council. A nearby state park and the Pocono Mountains, 45 minutes away by car, offer a wide range of recreational opportunities.

Sports: The college competes on an intercollegiate level in 6 sports for women and 3 for men. There are 5 intramural sports each for men and women.

Handicapped: About 85% of the campus is accessible to wheelchair-bound students. Designated parking areas, elevators, special class scheduling, specially equipped rest rooms, and lowered telephones are available. A special counselor assists handicapped students. Individual counseling and study aids are provided for students with visual or hearing impairments.

Graduates: The freshman dropout rate is 6%; 68% of the freshmen remain to graduate. About 41% of the graduates pursue graduate study; 1% enter medical school and 1% enter law school. Twenty-five percent pursue careers in business and industry.

Services: Students receive free placement aid, career counseling, health care, tutoring, remedial instruction, and psychological counseling.

Programs of Study: The college grants the B.A., B.S., B.Mus., B.S.N., and B.S.W. degrees. Associate and master's degrees are also available. Bachelor's degrees are offered in the following subjects: AREA STUDIES (general, liberal), BUSINESS (business administration, computer science, fashion merchandising), EDUCATION (early childhood, elementary, secondary, special), ENGLISH (English), FINE AND PERFORMING ARTS (art, art education, music, music education, music therapy, studio art), HEALTH SCIENCES (food and nutrition, medical technology, nursing, occupational therapy, radiologic technology), MATH AND SCIENCES (biology, mathematics), PREPROFESSIONAL (art therapy, dentistry, law, medicine, optometry, social work), SOCIAL SCIENCES (government/political science, history, psychology, sociology).

Required: All undergraduates must take courses in English composition and literature, history, philosophy, behavioral and natural sciences or mathematics, art or music appreciation, speech, and physical education. Catholic students must take theology.

Special: Students may earn combined B.A.-B.S. degrees in various subjects or a general-studies degree, or design their own majors. They may spend the junior year abroad on their own or participate in an established study-abroad program sponsored by another college. The School of Music is affiliated with Trinity College of Music in London.

Honors: Two honor societies have chapters on campus.

Admissions: Eighty-three percent of those who applied were accepted for the 1981–82 freshman class. The SAT scores of those who enrolled were as follows: Verbal—95% below 500, 4% between 500 and 599, 1% between 600 and 700, and 0% above 700; Math—94% below 500, 4% between 500 and 599, 2% between 600 and 700, and 0% above 700. Students should rank in the top 50% of their high

740 PENNSYLVANIA

school class and have an average of at least 85. Nursing students are required to have taken courses in biology and chemistry. Other factors affecting the admissions decision include extracurricular activities, recommendations by school officials, leadership record, and personality. Preference is given to children of alumni.

Procedure: Applicants must take the SAT or ACT. Junior-year results are acceptable. Music applicants must undergo an audition. A personal interview is recommended. There are no application deadlines; the college uses a rolling admissions plan. Notification is given 3 weeks after application, transcript, and test scores are received. Freshmen are admitted in the fall, spring, and summer. A $15 application fee is required.

Special: Early decision and early admissions plans are available. AP and CLEP are used.

Transfer: For fall 1981, 139 transfer students applied, 109 were accepted, and 77 enrolled. Transfers are accepted for all classes. A minimum GPA of 2.0 is required, and applicants should have a combined SAT score of at least 950. Students must complete at least 32 credits in residence of the 126 necessary for a bachelor's degree. D grades do not transfer. There are no application deadlines.

Visiting: Informal visits can be made on weekdays between 8:30 A.M. and 3 P.M. Guided tours and interviews can be scheduled through the admissions office. Visitors may sit in on classes; overnight accommodations are available.

Financial Aid: Eighty percent of all students receive aid. There are 45 freshman scholarships. About 55% of the students receive loans. About 20% of the freshmen have work contracts, including CWS. The average award to 1981-82 freshmen from all sources was $3455. Financial need is the main consideration in determining awards. The FAF is required; the college is a member of the CSS. Pennsylvania residents also must file the state grant application. Applications should be filed by April 1 for fall and November 1 for spring.

Foreign Students: The 9 students from foreign countries make up 1% of enrollment.

Admissions: No English-proficiency or college-entrance exams are required.

Procedure: Foreign students are admitted in the fall, spring, and summer. There are no application deadlines. A physical exam is required, and students must present proof of adequate funds for each academic year. Health insurance is required, and is available through the college for a fee.

Admissions Contact: David M. Payne, Dean of Admissions.

COMBS COLLEGE OF MUSIC F-3
Philadelphia, Pennsylvania 19119 (215) 951-2250

F/T: 41M, 36W	Faculty:	12; n/av
P/T: 7M, 8W	Ph.D.'s:	57%
Grad: 10M, 6W	S/F Ratio:	3 to 1
Year: sems, ss	Tuition:	$3490
Appl: open	R and B:	$1850
60 applied	20 accepted	20 enrolled
SAT: 540V 560M		SPECIAL

Combs College of Music, founded in 1885, is a privately supported college of music. The library contains 9500 volumes and 1002 microfilm items, and subscribes to 124 periodicals.

Environment: The 5-acre campus is located in a suburban area and consists of 4 large, old mansions. One residence hall houses 14 students. Dining facilities are not available. There is an apartment complex nearby.

Student Life: Seventy-five percent of the undergraduates are from Pennsylvania. Forty-three percent are minority-group members. Eighty percent live off campus. Campus housing is coed, and students may keep cars on campus.

Organizations: Fifteen percent of the men belong to a national fraternity; there are no sororities. The college does not sponsor extracurricular activities, but 1 or 2 cultural events take place on campus each week. Philadelphia offers additional cultural and recreational activities.

Handicapped: The campus is not accessible to handicapped students.

Graduates: The freshman dropout rate is 3%; about 80% of the freshmen remain to graduate. Twenty percent of the graduates pursue graduate study; 20% enter business and industry.

Services: Students receive free placement services, career counseling, and tutoring. Remedial instruction is available on a fee basis.

Programs of Study: Undergraduate programs lead to the B.Mus. degree. Master's and doctoral programs are also offered. Bachelor's degrees are offered in: FINE AND PERFORMING ARTS (applied music, music education, music therapy). Fifty percent of the degrees conferred are in applied music, 25% in music education, and 25% in music therapy.

Required: Students must study a major musical instrument and earn 130 credits for graduation.

Special: The college is purposely small to permit individual attention. A general-studies degree is available.

Admissions: Thirty-three percent of those who applied were accepted for the 1981-82 freshman class. The primary considerations in the admissions process are an audition and a theory placement examination. Candidates should rank in the top 50% of their high school class, should have at least a C average in 16 Carnegie units, and must be graduates of an accredited high school. The school also considers impressions made during an interview, advanced placement or honors courses, extracurricular activities, and recommendations by high school officials.

Procedure: The SAT is required, but scores are used for counseling purposes only. An interview and audition are required of all students. Applications are processed on a rolling basis. There is a $20 application fee. The CRDA is observed.

Special: AP and CLEP credit is granted.

Transfer: For fall 1981, 26 students applied, 11 were accepted, and all enrolled. Applicants must have at least a 2.0 GPA and pass an audition; an interview is required. D grades do not transfer. A student must remain at the college for 1 year, completing at least 36 of the 130 credits required, to receive a bachelor's degree. Deadlines for applications are open. Transfer students are accepted for all levels except senior year.

Visiting: Regularly scheduled orientations, including workshops and auditions, are held for prospective students. Informal visits can be made at any time; visitors may sit in on classes and stay overnight. Arrangements can be made through the admissions office.

Financial Aid: Forty-nine percent of all students are receiving scholarships, federal and state loans, or work contracts. Three percent work part-time on campus. Four academic scholarships are available to freshmen. The average award to freshmen from all sources was $450 in 1981-82. Tuition may be paid on the installment plan. The school is a member of CSS; the FAF is required. The deadline for aid applications is April 30.

Foreign Students: Four students are from foreign countries. The college offers an intensive English course.

Admissions: Both the TOEFL and the college's own entrance exam are required.

Procedure: Foreign students are admitted for all semesters; there are no application deadlines. Students must present proof of adequate funds for the school year.

Admissions Contact: Morton Berger, Director of Admissions.

DELAWARE VALLEY COLLEGE F-3
(Formerly Delaware Valley College of Science and Agriculture)
Doylestown, Pennsylvania 18901 (215) 345-1500

F/T: 919M, 442W	Faculty:	79; IIB, +$
P/T: 21M, 12W	Ph.D.'s:	49%
Grad: none	S/F Ratio:	18 to 1
Year: sems, ss	Tuition:	$3890
Appl: open	R and B:	$1805
898 applied	694 accepted	422 enrolled
SAT: 418V 466M		COMPETITIVE

Delaware Valley College, a private, nonsectarian institution founded in 1896, offers a scientific education in specialized fields of agriculture, sciences, and business administration. The library contains 50,119 volumes and 1425 microfilm items, and subscribes to 611 periodicals.

Environment: The college is located in rural Bucks County, Pennsylvania, 30 miles from Philadelphia. The 35-acre campus includes a science building, an agriculture building, dairy beef and swine barns, greenhouses, and 11 dormitories that accommodate 923 men and women. The college also maintains 725 acres of farmland, including pastureland, orchards, and field crops.

Student Life: About 69% of the students come from Pennsylvania, and about 66% live on campus. Campus housing is single-sex; there are visiting privileges. About 78% of the freshmen come from public schools. Nearly 3% of the students are minority-group members. Alcoholic beverages are prohibited, and freshmen may not have cars on campus.

Organizations: There are no social fraternities or sororities. Denominational services, activities, and organizations are forbidden on campus, but there are places of worship for most religious faiths in the vicinity. Extracurricular activities include special-interest clubs, and dairy, livestock, and soil-judging contests.

Sports: Men compete in 8 intercollegiate sports and women in 7. There are 5 intramural sports for men and 4 for women.

Handicapped: Most of the campus is accessible to handicapped students. Special facilities include wheelchair ramps, parking areas, elevators, lowered drinking fountains, and specially equipped rest rooms. Special class scheduling is also available.

Graduates: About 15% of the freshmen drop out by the end of the first year, and 65% remain to graduate. From 10% to 15% of the graduates go on to further study. Seventy percent pursue careers in business and industry.

Services: Students receive the following free services: placement aid, career counseling, health care, tutoring, and remedial instruction. Psychological counseling is available on a fee basis.

Programs of Study: The college offers the B.S. degree in the following subjects: BUSINESS (business administration), MATH AND SCIENCES (biology, chemistry), PREPROFESSIONAL (agronomy, animal husbandry, dairy husbandry, food industry, horticulture, ornamental horticulture). Seventy-three percent of the degrees conferred are in agriculture, 19% are in business, and 8% are in sciences.

Required: All freshmen majoring in agriculture, biology, or chemistry must take biology, chemistry, English, mathematics, and physical education. Freshman business-administration majors take a course in natural science. In addition, all undergraduates must complete a distribution of courses in liberal arts, basic sciences, and professional subjects.

Special: The college offers a specialized methods and techniques program that enables students to learn laboratory techniques and gain experience in the practical aspects of their majors. Students must find summer employment of 24 weeks or campus employment related to their majors.

Admissions: Seventy-seven percent of those who applied were accepted for the 1981–82 freshman class. The SAT scores for a recent freshman class were as follows: Verbal—13% between 500 and 599 and 3% between 600 and 700; Math—33% were between 500 and 599 and 6% between 600 and 700. Candidates must be graduates of approved secondary schools, rank in the upper half of their class, have at least a C average in required courses, be recommended by their school, and have completed 15 units of high school work. Candidates are selected for admission on the basis of their high school academic work, rank in class, SAT or ACT scores, letters of recommendation, and personal interview; advanced placement or honors courses are also taken into consideration.

Procedure: The SAT or ACT is required. Applications are considered on a rolling basis. There is a $15 application fee.

Transfer: For fall 1981, 165 students applied, 128 were accepted, and 92 enrolled. Transfers are considered for all classes. Requirements are the same as those for freshmen. D grades are not acceptable. To receive a bachelor's degree, students must earn half of the credit requirements for their major at the college.

Visiting: Guides are available for informal visits, and visitors may sit in on classes. Campus visits can be arranged when school is in session through the director of admissions.

Financial Aid: Sixty-six percent of the students receive financial aid. The college participates with the federal government in the SEOG, NDSL, and CWS programs. About 17% of the students work part-time on campus. A few scholarships are available from the college and individual donors. Loans are also available from the state government, local banks, and private sources. Awards are based on need and academic qualification; the average award to 1981–82 freshmen from all sources was $2700. Tuition may be paid in installments. The college is a member of the CSS. The Pennsylvania State Grant–Federal Student Aid Application must be filed by March 1. Students must also file the FAF.

Foreign Students: The 6 students from foreign countries make up less than 1% of enrollment. Special counseling is available.

Admissions: Students must take the TOEFL. They also must take either the SAT or the ACT.

Procedure: Foreign students are admitted in the fall and spring. There are no application deadlines. Proof of good health (in the form of a statement on the application) is required. Students must also submit proof of adequate funds for 4 years. Health insurance is required, and is available through the college for a fee.

Admissions Contact: H. William Craver, Director of Admissions.

DICKINSON COLLEGE D-3
Carlisle, Pennsylvania 17013   (717) 245-1231

F/T: 811M, 931W   Faculty: 113; IIB, ++$
P/T: 18M, 29W   Ph.D.'s: 90%
Grad: none   S/F Ratio: 12 to 1
Year: sems, ss   Tuition: $5915
Appl: Mar. 1   R and B: $2150
3068 applied   1695 accepted   575 enrolled
SAT: 539V 571M   HIGHLY COMPETITIVE

Dickinson College, founded in 1773, is a private liberal arts institution that also offers teacher-training programs and preprofessional preparation. The library houses 328,303 volumes, subscribes to 1204 periodicals, and contains 5961 microfilm items.

Environment: The 55-acre tree-lined suburban campus includes a planetarium, a physical education center, and dormitories that house 1475 students. The college also sponsors fraternity houses and on-campus apartments.

Student Life: More than 90% of the students come from the Middle Atlantic and New England states. About 77% have graduated from public schools. All freshmen must live in dormitories, and upperclassmen must live in dormitories or fraternity houses unless they commute from home or receive special permission to live off campus. Fifty percent of the students are Protestant, 34% are Catholic, and 15% are Jewish. About 4% are minority-group members. Campus housing is both coed and single-sex; there are visiting privileges in the single-sex dormitories. Freshmen may not keep cars on campus.

Organizations: Sixty percent of the students belong to the 10 fraternities and 4 sororities on campus. Extracurricular activities include special-interest clubs, student government, publications, music and drama groups, concerts, lecture series, and a campus radio station.

Sports: The college fields intercollegiate teams in 11 sports for men and 9 for women. There are 15 intramural sports for men and 13 for women.

Handicapped: Approximately 45% of the campus is accessible to the physically handicapped. Facilities include wheelchair ramps, special parking, elevators, and specially equipped rest rooms.

Graduates: The freshman dropout rate is 4%; 80% of the freshmen remain to graduate. Forty-five percent of the graduates go on to further study; 3% enter medical school, 1% enter dental school, and 20% enter law school. About 25% pursue careers in business and industry.

Services: Placement services, career counseling, health care, psychological counseling, tutoring, and remedial instruction are offered free.

Programs of Study: The college confers the B.A. and B.S. degrees. Bachelor's degrees are offered in the following subjects: AREA STUDIES (American, Judaic, Russian), ENGLISH (English), FINE AND PERFORMING ARTS (art, music, theater/dramatics), LANGUAGES (French, German, Greek/Latin, Spanish), MATH AND SCIENCES (biology, chemistry, computer science, geology, mathematics, physics), PHILOSOPHY (philosophy, religion), SOCIAL SCIENCES (anthropology, economics, government/political science, history, international relations, psychology, sociology). Of the degrees conferred, 55% are in social sciences, 18% in math and sciences, and 6% in education certification.

Required: All students must complete a core curriculum that includes foreign language, comparative civilizations, and physical education.

Special: The college operates a Center for International Studies in Bologna, Italy; participates in the Institute for European Studies; offers study-abroad programs in 5 countries; and sponsors semesters in Appalachia, Harrisburg (urban), and Washington. Students may design their own majors. Tutorial majors are also available. Preprofessional preparation is offered in dentistry, law, medicine, ministry, social work, and veterinary science.

Honors: Fourteen national honor societies have chapters on campus. All departments offer honors programs.

Admissions: Fifty-five percent of those who applied were accepted for the 1981–82 freshman class. The SAT scores of those who enrolled were as follows: Verbal—27% below 500, 51% between 500 and 599, 19% between 600 and 700, and 3% above 700; Math—13% below 500, 52% between 500 and 599, 30% between 600 and 700, and 5% above 700. Besides academic record and test scores, the college considers advanced placement or honors courses, recommendations by school officials, personality, and leadership record.

742 PENNSYLVANIA

Procedure: The SAT or ACT is required and should be taken no later than January of the senior year. Application deadlines are March 1 (fall) and December 1 (spring). There is a $20 application fee.

Special: Early decision, early admissions, and deferred admissions plans are offered. Students may earn credit through AP exams.

Transfer: For fall 1981, the college received 181 applications, accepted 39, and enrolled 27 students. A personal interview is required, and applicants must submit college and high school transcripts. D grades do not transfer. To receive a bachelor's degree, students must study at least 4 semesters at the college, completing 17 of the 34 courses required. Application deadlines are June 1 (fall) and December 1 (spring).

Visiting: Guides are available for informal visits. Visitors may sit in on classes and stay overnight at the college. The admissions office should be contacted to arrange visits.

Financial Aid: About 76% of all students receive aid. Scholarships, loans, and jobs are offered to freshmen and upperclassmen; programs include NDSL, SEOG, and CWS. Forty percent of the students work part-time on campus. The average award to freshmen from all sources in 1981–82 was $4947. The FAF or FFS is required. Pennsylvania residents must also file the state grant application. The deadlines for filing aid applications are February 15 for fall and November 15 for spring. The college is a member of CSS.

Foreign Students: The 17 students from foreign countries represent 1% of enrollment. Special counseling and special organizations are available for these students.

Admissions: Students must take the TOEFL. SATs are strongly recommended.

Procedure: The application deadline is March 1 for fall entry. Students are required to carry health insurance, which is available through the college for a fee.

Admissions Contact: J. Larry Mench, Director of Admissions.

DREXEL UNIVERSITY F–3
Philadelphia, Pennsylvania 19104 (215) 895-2400

F/T: 5064M, 2156W	Faculty:	303; IIA, + + $
P/T: 2643M, 835W	Ph.D.'s:	85%
Grad: 1906M, 914W	S/F Ratio:	20 to 1
Year: qtrs	Tuition:	$4011
Appl: Apr. 1	R and B:	$2950
4858 applied	3361 accepted	1750 enrolled
SAT: 500V 580M	ACT: 25	VERY COMPETITIVE

Drexel University, founded in 1891, has the following undergraduate divisions: the College of Business and Administration, the College of Engineering, the College of Humanities and Social Science, the Nesbitt College of Design/Nutrition/Human Behavior/Home Economics, and the College of Science. The library contains 400,000 volumes and subscribes to 8000 periodicals.

Environment: The campus, occupying 27 acres near the heart of metropolitan Philadelphia, has more than 37 buildings, including 5 residence halls and 12 fraternity houses that accommodate 1650 students.

Student Life: About 50% of entering freshmen come from public schools. Twelve percent of the students are minority-group members. Forty-five percent of the students live in campus housing. Dormitories are coed. Students are permitted to keep cars on campus.

Organizations: There are 10 local and 2 national fraternities, to which 20% of the men belong, and 4 national sororities, to which 25% of the women belong. Students may participate in extracurricular activities including campus publications, religious organizations, service clubs, music groups, student government, and drama.

Sports: The university offers intercollegiate competition in 14 sports for men and 10 for women. Eleven intramural sports are offered for men and 7 for women.

Handicapped: About 85% of the campus is accessible to handicapped students. Special facilities include wheelchair ramps and elevators.

Graduates: Approximately 20% of the graduates enter graduate or professional schools, and 80% pursue careers in business or industry.

Services: The following services are offered free to students: psychological counseling, tutoring, remedial instruction, placement aid, and career counseling.

Programs of Study: The university confers the B.S. degree, as well as master's and doctoral degrees. Bachelor's degrees are offered in the following subjects: BUSINESS (accounting, administrative systems management, commerce and engineering, computer science, consumer food services, economics, finance, manpower management, marketing management, retail management), EDUCATION (early childhood, home economics), FINE AND PERFORMING ARTS (design and merchandising, fashion design, interior design), HEALTH SCIENCES (consumer food services, dietetics, food science, food service system management, nutrition), MATH AND SCIENCES (biochemistry, biology, biophysical chemistry, chemistry, computer science, ecology/environmental science, inorganic chemistry, mathematics, physics and atmosphere science, unified science), PRE-PROFESSIONAL (engineering—chemical, engineering—civil, engineering—electrical and computer, engineering—general, engineering—materials, engineering—mechanical), SOCIAL SCIENCES (anthropology, government/political science, history, human behavior and development, humanities/communication, human systems management, psychology, sociology).

Special: Five-year cooperative programs are offered in engineering. Under those plans, students spend alternating terms in paid employment with more than 1114 companies and other institutions in 1248 locations. Combined bachelor's-master's degree programs are available.

Honors: Nineteen national honor societies have chapters on campus.

Admission: Seventy percent of those who applied were accepted for the 1981–82 freshman class. Candidates must have completed an accredited academic course of study with a minimum grade average of C and a rank in the upper two-fifths of the class, have the recommendation of their high school principals, and show ability to perform at the college level. All the colleges require at least 1 year of a laboratory science and 3 years of mathematics. The colleges of Engineering and Science require 2 years of laboratory science and 4 years of mathematics through trigonometry, with more advanced math, chemistry, and physics recommended. Other considerations are advanced placement or honors courses and extracurricular activities.

Procedure: The SAT is required. Engineering and science students also must take 3 ATs (in English composition, mathematics, and either chemistry or physics). The deadline for fall application is April 1. A limited number of freshmen are admitted to the winter quarter. Notification is made on a rolling basis. There is a $10 application fee.

Special: Early decision and early admissions plans are available. CLEP and AP credit is accepted.

Transfer: For fall 1981, the university received 738 transfer applications, accepted 470, and enrolled 266 students. Applicants must have a 2.5 GPA (2.75 for engineering students) and have been enrolled in a program comparable to the one they plan to enter. D grades do not transfer. All students must spend their final year at Drexel to qualify for a bachelor's degree. Application deadlines are August 1 (fall), February 1 (spring), May 1 (summer), and November 1 (winter).

Visiting: Campus tours are available at scheduled times during the week. Appointments must be made with the office of admissions.

Financial Aid: About 60% of all students receive aid in the form of scholarships, grants, loans, and work-study. The FAF is required. Applications for undergraduate scholarships close March 1.

Foreign Students: The 216 students from foreign countries make up 4% of enrollment. Special counseling and special organizations are available.

Admissions: Students must score at least 500 on the TOEFL. They also must take the SAT or the ACT. Engineering students are required to take ATs in mathematics, English composition, and either physics or chemistry.

Procedure: The application deadline is April 1 for fall admission. Proof of good health and adequate funds is required. Health insurance, though not required, is available through the university for a fee.

Admissions Contact: John R. McCullough, Dean of Admissions and Financial Aid.

DUQUESNE UNIVERSITY B–3
Pittsburgh, Pennsylvania 15282 (412) 434-6207

F/T: 1899M, 2215W	Faculty:	287; IIA, + $
P/T: 202M, 260W	Ph.D.'s:	42%
Grad: 630M, 705W	S/F Ratio:	15 to 1
Year: sems, ss	Tuition:	$4175
Appl: July 1	R and B:	$2013
2391 applied	1995 accepted	937 enrolled
SAT or ACT: required		COMPETITIVE

Duquesne University, founded in 1878, is a private institution affiliated with the Roman Catholic Church and conducted by the Holy Ghost

Fathers. It has 6 undergraduate divisions: the College of Liberal Arts and Sciences and the schools of Business Administration, Pharmacy, Education, Music, and Nursing. The library contains 402,000 volumes and 31,952 microfilm items, and subscribes to 3600 periodicals.

Environment: The hilltop campus is located on 38 acres in downtown Pittsburgh. The university's 20 buildings include a campus center, a communication center, a science center, a modern music building, and 4 dormitories that house 1392 women and 1157 men.

Student Life: Eighty-one percent of the students are from Pennsylvania. Seventy-one percent come from public schools. About 55% live in dormitories. Sixty percent of the students are Catholic, 17% are Protestant, and 2% are Jewish. Ten percent are minority-group members. Campus housing is both coed and single-sex; there are visiting privileges in the single-sex dormitories. Students may keep cars on campus.

Organizations: There are 7 fraternities and 6 sororities; about 10% of the students belong. Student organizations include special-interest clubs, publications, music ensembles, a radio station, a chorus, a closed-circuit TV studio, service clubs, and religious groups for the 3 major faiths. Cultural events are sponsored on campus, and major social events include special dances, Greek Week, Spring Weekend, and Fall Carnival. Pittsburgh's recreational and cultural facilities are within easy access.

Sports: Duquesne competes in 10 intercollegiate sports for men and 6 for women. There are 5 intramural sports for men and 3 for women.

Handicapped: About 85% of the campus is accessible to wheelchair-bound students. Special class scheduling, wheelchair ramps, and elevators are available. The university provides a special counselor for the handicapped and a reader service for visually impaired students.

Graduates: The freshman dropout rate is 10%; 68% of the freshmen remain to graduate. Fifty-three percent of the graduates pursue advanced degrees. About 35% begin careers in business and industry.

Services: Students receive free health care, placement aid, career counseling, tutoring, remedial instruction, and psychological counseling.

Programs of Study: The university confers the B.S., B.S.Pharm., B.S.Med.Tech., B.S. in Radiological Health, B.S.Ed., B.S.Mus., B.S.Music Therapy, B.S.Mus.Ed., B.S.N., and B.A. degrees. Master's and doctoral programs are also available. Bachelor's degrees are offered in the following subjects: BUSINESS (accounting, business administration, economics, finance, international business, law administration, management, marketing), EDUCATION (early childhood, elementary, secondary), ENGLISH (English, journalism, literature, speech), FINE AND PERFORMING ARTS (music, music education, music therapy, radio/TV, theater/dramatics), HEALTH SCIENCES (medical media communication, medical technology, nursing, radiological health, speech pathology and audiology), LANGUAGES (French, German, Spanish), MATH AND SCIENCES (biochemistry, biology, chemistry, computer science, mathematics, physics), PHILOSOPHY (classics, philosophy, religion), PREPROFESSIONAL (dentistry, engineering, law, medicine, pharmacy, social work, veterinary), SOCIAL SCIENCES (classical civilizations, criminal justice, economics, gerontology, government/political science, history, psychology, sociology). Thirty-four percent of the degrees conferred are in health sciences, 25% in business, and 14% in social sciences.

Required: English composition is generally required of freshmen. All undergraduates must complete the core curriculum of the school in which they are enrolled.

Special: Students may earn 5-year combined B.A.-B.S. degrees in liberal arts and engineering. A cross-registration program permits students to register for 1 course per semester at Carnegie-Mellon University, the University of Pittsburgh, or 5 other institutions. A 3-2 program in engineering is offered in cooperation with Case Western Reserve University. Also offered are a Black Studies program, junior year abroad, work-study programs, a 3-year bachelor's degree, and pass/fail grading.

Honors: Eleven national honor societies have chapters on campus. Honors programs are available for qualified students.

Admissions: Eighty-three percent of those who applied were accepted for the 1981–82 freshman class. The SAT scores of those who enrolled were as follows: Verbal—70% below 500, 25% between 500 and 599, 5% between 600 and 700, and less than 1% above 700; Math—56% below 500, 32% between 500 and 599, 11% between 600 and 700, and 1% above 700. Applicants must be graduates of accredited high schools, rank in the upper three-fifths of their class, have a GPA of at least 2.5, and complete 16 high school units. Additional factors considered are advanced placement or honors courses, impressions made during an interview, recommendations by school officials, and extracurricular activities.

Procedure: The SAT or the ACT is required. The application, a $20 fee, test scores, and high school record should be submitted by July 1 for the fall semester and December 15 for the spring. Admission and notification are on a rolling basis.

Special: Early and deferred admissions plans are available. CLEP and AP credit is granted.

Transfer: Of 515 transfer applications received for fall 1981, 376 were accepted, and 264 students enrolled. Transfers are considered for all except senior years. Requirements include an interview and a GPA of at least 2.0 from an accredited institution or at least 3.0 from a nonaccredited institution. Students should have a minimum of 12 credit hours earned. D grades will transfer with an associate degree in arts and sciences or in education. To receive a bachelor's degree, the student must earn at least 30 credits in residence of the 120 required.

Visiting: A campus visit for prospective students includes an interview with an admissions counselor and a tour. Informal visits can be arranged on weekdays from 8:30 A.M. to 4:30 P.M. through the office of residence life or admissions. Visitors may sit in on classes and stay overnight.

Financial Aid: Seventy-five percent of all students receive aid. The university provides scholarships, loans, grants, and student jobs. Nine percent of the students work part-time on campus. Aid is awarded on the basis of financial need and academic record. Applications must be filed by May 1 for fall or December 1 for spring. The FAF is required; the university is a member of CSS.

Foreign Students: The 87 students from foreign countries make up 2% of enrollment. The university offers these students an intensive English course, special counseling, and special organizations.

Admissions: Students must score at least 500 on the TOEFL. The SAT or ACT is also required.

Procedure: Application deadlines are July 1 for fall and November 1 for spring. Students must undergo a physical examination and present proof of adequate funds for 1 year. Health insurance is also required, and is available through the university for a fee.

Admissions Contact: Dr. Frederick H. Lorensen, Director of Admissions.

EASTERN COLLEGE F-3
St. Davids, Pennsylvania 19087 (215) 688-3300

F/T: 250M, 400W Faculty: 37; IIB, +$
P/T: 50M, 100W Ph.D.'s: 42%
Grad: n/av S/F Ratio: 13 to 1
Year: sems, ss Tuition: $4290
Appl: Aug. 15 R and B: $1700
443 applied 360 accepted 230 enrolled
SAT: 440V 440M COMPETITIVE

Eastern College is a private liberal arts college founded by the American Baptist Churches. The library contains 65,000 volumes and subscribes to 276 periodicals.

Environment: The 92-acre campus is located in a suburban area 16 miles outside of Philadelphia. Four dormitories house 266 women and 138 men. On-campus apartments are also available.

Student Life: About 70% of the students come from Pennsylvania and 29% are from other states. About 67% live in college housing. Housing is both coed and single-sex; there are visiting privileges in single-sex dorms. Ninety-one percent of the entering freshmen attended public schools. Twenty-seven percent of the students are minority-group members. Most students are not members of the affiliated church. Chapel attendance is expected, but not required. Daycare services are available to all students.

Organizations: Extracurricular activities include student government, publications, drama and choral groups, concert band, and service fraternities and sororities.

Sports: The college competes on an intercollegiate level in 6 sports for men and 6 for women. There are 6 intramural sports for men and 5 for women.

Graduates: About 20% of the freshmen drop out, and 50% remain to graduate. Thirty percent of the graduates pursue further study; 1% enter medical school and 1% enter law school. About 13% pursue careers in business and industry.

Services: Students receive the following free services: career and psychological counseling, health services, placement aid, tutoring, and remedial instruction. Placement services also are available for graduates.

Programs of Study: The college confers the B.A., B.S., and B.S.W. degrees. Master's degrees are also awarded. Bachelor's degrees are offered in the following subjects: AREA STUDIES (American), BUSINESS (accounting, business administration, computer science), EDUCATION (elementary, health/physical, secondary, special), ENGLISH (English, journalism, literature), HEALTH SCIENCES (medical technology), LANGUAGES (French, Spanish), MATH AND SCIENCES (biology, chemistry, mathematics), PHILOSOPHY (philosophy, religion), PREPROFESSIONAL (social work), SOCIAL SCIENCES (economics, history, psychology, sociology, youth ministries). A nursing major was planned for fall 1983. Sixty-three percent of degrees conferred are in arts and sciences, 15% are in education, and 15% are in business.

Required: All students must satisfy a general distribution requirement.

Special: The American Studies Seminar, study-abroad, work-training, and cross-registration programs are available. Combination-degree programs are available in medical technology and nursing. Students may create their own majors.

Honors: An honors research program is offered at the Argonne National Laboratory.

Admissions: Eighty-one percent of those who applied were accepted for the 1981-82 freshman class. The SAT scores of those who enrolled were as follows: Verbal—56% below 500, 18% between 500 and 599, 2% between 600 and 700, 1% above 700, and 23% unreported; Math—47% below 500, 20% between 500 and 599, 8% between 600 and 700, 1% above 700, and 24% unreported. Candidates should have completed at least 15 Carnegie units at an accredited high school and be recommended by school officials. Also important are SAT scores, advanced placement or honors courses, and extracurricular activities.

Procedure: The SAT or ACT is required. The SAT should be taken in November of the senior year. Scores of 450 or more on each part are preferred. Candidates should apply no later than August 15 for fall admission and December 15 for spring. Notification is made on a rolling basis. The application fee is $10.

Special: Early decision, deferred admissions, and early admissions plans are offered. CLEP and AP subject exams are accepted.

Transfer: For fall 1981, 125 applications were received, 115 were accepted, and 100 students enrolled. Transfers are accepted for all classes. D grades are not acceptable. A minimum average of 2.0 is required. Students must complete, at the college, at least 32 of the 127 credit hours necessary to receive a bachelor's degree. Application deadlines are the same as those for freshmen.

Visiting: Guided tours and interviews can be arranged through the admissions office.

Financial Aid: Eighty percent of the students receive aid; 70% work part-time on campus. Scholarships are apportioned among all classes on the basis of need and merit. The aid application deadline is May 15. Tuition may be paid in installments. The college is a member of the CSS, and the FAF is required.

Foreign Students: The 30 students from foreign countries make up 4% of enrollment. The college offers these students an intensive English course, special counseling, and special organizations.

Admissions: Students must take the TOEFL or the college's own English-proficiency exam. No college entrance exams are required.

Procedure: Application deadlines are August 15 (fall) and December 15 (spring). Students must submit a completed college health form, and must present proof of adequate funds for the first year of study.

Admissions Contact: William A. Zulker, Dean of Admissions.

EAST STROUDSBURG STATE COLLEGE F-2
East Stroudsburg, Pennsylvania 18301   (717) 424-3542

F/T: 1505M, 1769W   Faculty: n/av; IIA, ++$
P/T: 124M, 188W   Ph.D.'s: n/av
Grad: 130M, 170W   S/F Ratio: n/av
Year: sems, ss   Tuition: $1358 ($2298)
Appl: open   R and B: $1476
2881 applied   1742 accepted   828 enrolled
SAT: 430V 460M   COMPETITIVE

East Stroudsburg State College, a state institution established in 1893, offers over 50 undergraduate programs through the schools of Arts and Sciences, Professional Studies, and Health Sciences and Physical Education. The library houses 300,032 volumes, subscribes to 2810 periodicals, and has 641,655 microfilm items on file.

Environment: The 210-acre campus is located in a rural area on a hilltop overlooking the town of East Stroudsburg, 45 miles from Allentown. The 34 college buildings include 8 dormitories that house 1185 women and 750 men, a library, a fine-arts center, and a biological-sciences center.

Student Life: Seventy-five percent of the students are from Pennsylvania. Approximately 60% live in the dormitories. Campus housing is both coed and single-sex; there are visiting privileges in single-sex dorms. No alcoholic beverages are allowed on campus. Freshmen and sophomores may not have cars on campus. Day-care services are available.

Organizations: Seven fraternities and 6 sororities have chapters on campus. The Pocono Mountain ski resorts are easily accessible.

Sports: The college fields intercollegiate teams in 13 sports for men and 11 for women. Twelve intramural sports are offered for men and 11 for women.

Handicapped: About 65% of the campus is accessible to handicapped students. Facilities include wheelchair ramps, lowered drinking fountains and telephones, elevators, designated parking, and specially equipped rest rooms. Special class scheduling is also available.

Graduates: About 20% of the graduates go on to further study, and 25% pursue careers in business and industry.

Services: The following services are offered free to students: psychological counseling, tutoring, remedial instruction, health care, placement aid, and career counseling.

Programs of Study: The college confers the B.S. and B.A. degrees. Associate and master's degrees are also awarded. Bachelor's degrees are offered in the following subjects: BUSINESS (computer science, hotel/resort management, recreation/leisure services management), EDUCATION (early childhood, elementary, health/physical, secondary, special), ENGLISH (communication, English, speech), FINE AND PERFORMING ARTS (art, media/communication and technology, music, theater/dramatics), HEALTH SCIENCES (medical technology, nursing, speech therapy), LANGUAGES (French, German, Spanish), MATH AND SCIENCES (biochemistry, biology, chemistry, earth science, ecology/environmental science, mathematics, natural sciences, physical sciences, physics), PHILOSOPHY (philosophy), PREPROFESSIONAL (pharmacy), SOCIAL SCIENCES (economics, geography, government/political science, history, psychology, sociology).

Special: Students may spend their junior year abroad and design their own majors. Cooperative degree programs are offered in clinical chemistry with Hahnemann Medical College, in engineering with Pennsylvania State University, in pharmacy with Temple University, and in podiatric medicine with the Pennsylvania College of Podiatric Medicine. Combined B.A.-B.S. degrees can be earned in a variety of subjects.

Honors: Eleven national honor societies have chapters on campus.

Admissions: Sixty percent of those who applied were accepted for the 1981-82 freshman class. For an earlier class, the SAT scores were as follows: Verbal—13% between 500 and 599, 1% between 600 and 700, and 1% above 700; Math—29% between 500 and 599, and 6% between 600 and 700. Applicants should be graduates of accredited high schools, have completed 12 academic units of work, and be recommended for college by the high school authorities. Other factors considered include advanced placement or honors courses, recommendations by school officials, evidence of special talent, and impressions made during an interview.

Procedure: The SAT or ACT is required. The college uses the rolling admissions plan, but suggests February 1 as the application deadline for fall and November 15 as the deadline for spring. There is a $10 application fee.

Special: CLEP and AP credit is granted.

Transfer: Of 620 students who applied during a recent school year, 496 were accepted and 272 enrolled. Transfers are accepted for all classes. Applicants must present a GPA of 2.0 or better. D grades transfer if outside the student's major. Students must complete, at the college, at least 32 of the 128 credits required for a bachelor's degree.

Visiting: The college conducts regularly scheduled orientations for prospective students. Visitors may sit in on classes with the permission of the instructor. The best times for campus visits, which should be arranged through the office of admissions, are Tuesday mornings and Thursday afternoons.

Financial Aid: About 80% of the students receive aid; 27% work part-time on campus. No scholarships are awarded. Grants and loans are available through federal and state sources. The BEOG/state grant composite application is required and is provided by the college, a member of the CSS. The deadline for aid application is March 1.

Foreign Students: The 25 students from foreign countries make up less than 1% of enrollment. Special counseling and special organizations are available.

Admissions: Students must score at least 500 on the TOEFL. No college entrance exams are required.

Procedure: Application deadlines are March 1 (fall) and November 1 (spring). Students must present proof of adequate funds for 1 year. They are required to carry health insurance, which is available through the college for a fee.

Admissions Contact: Alan T. Chesterton, Director of Admissions.

EDINBORO STATE COLLEGE   B–1
Edinboro, Pennsylvania 16444   (814) 732-2761

F/T: 1951M, 2467W	Faculty: 353; IIA, ++$
P/T: 367M, 417W	Ph.D.'s: 55%
Grad: 182M, 464W	S/F Ratio: 16 to 1
Year: sems, ss	Tuition: $1398 ($2338)
Appl: open	R and B: $1460
2509 applied	2251 accepted 1258 enrolled
SAT: 416V 429M	LESS COMPETITIVE

Edinboro State College, founded in 1857, is a state-run college offering programs in the arts and sciences, business, education, and health fields. The library houses 340,000 volumes, subscribes to 2200 periodicals, and has 500,000 microfilm items on file.

Environment: The 600-acre campus is located at the southern edge of the rural lake-resort community of Edinboro, 20 miles from Erie. Facilities include a college union, a fieldhouse with health suite and swimming pool, and residence halls housing 2000 students.

Student Life: About ninety percent of the students come from Pennsylvania. Campus housing is both coed and single-sex; there are visiting privileges in single-sex dorms. About 48% of the students are campus residents; another 48% live in other college-approved housing. Six percent of the students are minority-group members. Drinking is forbidden on campus. Resident freshmen may not have cars on campus. Day-care services are available for a fee.

Organizations: Student organizations include music groups, professional groups, special-interest clubs, and religious organizations for the 3 major faiths. There are 10 sororities, to which 15% of the women belong, and 10 fraternities, to which 10% of the men belong. Extracurricular activities include a radio station, publications, and drama. Facilities for skiing, horseback riding, mountaineering, and water sports are easily accessible from the campus.

Sports: The athletic program includes 12 intercollegiate sports for men and 8 for women. Seven intramural sports are available for men and 6 for women.

Handicapped: The college is accessible to handicapped students. Facilities include wheelchair ramps, elevators, lowered drinking fountains and telephones, designated parking areas, specially equipped rest rooms, transportation, meal aids, and academic aids. Special class scheduling is also available. For students with visual or hearing impairments, the college offers recording equipment, library aids, table and hand-held magnifiers, interpreters, and personal care. A counselor is on hand to provide special assistance.

Graduates: The freshman dropout rate is 32%; 42% remain to graduate. Of those, 15% go on to further study. Fifty-five percent pursue careers in business or industry.

Services: Psychological counseling, tutoring, remedial instruction, placement services, and career counseling are offered free to students.

Programs of Study: The college awards the B.A., B.S., B.S.Ed., B.F.A., and B.S.Art Ed. degrees. Associate and master's degrees also are conferred. Bachelor's degrees are offered in the following subjects: AREA STUDIES (Black/Afro-American, Russian, urban), BUSINESS (accounting, business administration, computer science, secretarial science), EDUCATION (early childhood, elementary, health/physical, secondary, special), ENGLISH (English, journalism, literature, speech), FINE AND PERFORMING ARTS (art, art education, art history, film/photography, music, music education, studio art, theater/dramatics), HEALTH SCIENCES (anesthesia, dental hygiene, medical technology, nursing, nutrition, speech therapy), LANGUAGES (French, German, Russian, Spanish), MATH AND SCIENCES (biology, chemistry, earth science, ecology/environmental science, geology, mathematics, natural sciences, physical sciences, physics), PHILOSOPHY (humanities, philosophy), PREPROFESSIONAL (dentistry, engineering, law, library science, medicine, osteopathy, pharmacy, social work, veterinary), SOCIAL SCIENCES (anthropology, criminal justice, economics, geography, government/political science, history, human services, psychology, social sciences, sociology). Of the degrees conferred, 30% are in education, 6% are in social sciences, and 8% are in fine and performing arts.

Required: Students must take 60 hours of general-education courses in the humanities, natural sciences and mathematics, and social and behavioral sciences.

Special: Students are encouraged to participate in field experiences (Marine Science Consortium on Chesapeake Bay, teacher training in Mexico, travel in Europe) and internships. A 3-2 program in engineering with Case Western Reserve, Pennsylvania State University, or the University of Pittsburgh leads to a combined B.A.-B.S. degree. Interinstitutional cooperation also exists on such programs as nutrition, anesthesia, medical technology, and pharmacy. Students may design their own majors.

Honors: Eight national honor societies have chapters on campus. An interdepartmental honors program and an all-college honors program are offered.

Admissions: Ninety percent of those who applied were accepted for the 1981–82 freshman class. Applicants must be graduates of an approved high school or equivalent institution. Preference is given to residents of Pennsylvania. Other considerations are advanced placement or honors courses, recommendations by school officials, and evidence of special talents.

Procedure: The SAT or ACT is required. There are no application deadlines, but the college recommends that students apply no later than 1 month before the fall or spring term. Freshmen also are admitted in summer. Notification is made on a rolling basis. There is a $10 application fee.

Special: Early decision, early admissions, and deferred admissions plans are offered. Students may earn credit through CLEP and CEEB advanced-placement exams.

Transfer: For fall 1981, the college received 544 applications, accepted 472, and enrolled 345 transfer students. A GPA of 2.0 is recommended. D grades do not transfer. Students must study at least 1 year at the college, completing the last 32 of the 128 credits required for a bachelor's degree. Preference is given to state residents. The nursing program does not admit transfers. Application deadlines are open.

Visiting: The college conducts regularly scheduled orientations for prospective students. Guides are available for informal visits. Visitors may sit in on classes and stay overnight at the school. Arrangements for visits should be made through the admissions office.

Financial Aid: About 75% of the students receive aid. Several freshman scholarships are awarded each year. Students receive nearly $8 million in aid from federal, state, and institutional programs. The average award to freshmen from all sources in 1981–82 was $2000. The FAF is recommended. Deadlines for aid applications are March 15 (fall), July 15 (winter and spring), and January 15 (summer).

Foreign Students: The 47 students from foreign countries make up less than 1% of enrollment. The college offers these students an intensive English course, special counseling, and special organizations.

Admissions: The University of Michigan Language Test is required. No college entrance exams are necessary.

Procedure: Foreign students are admitted to all terms. Applications should be filed several months in advance. Students must present proof of adequate funds for 1 year, and must submit a completed college medical-history form. Health insurance is required, and is available through the college for a fee.

Admissions Contact: Harold Umbarger, Dean of Admissions.

ELIZABETHTOWN COLLEGE   D–3
Elizabethtown, Pennsylvania 17022   (717) 367-1151

F/T: 539M, 848W	Faculty: n/av; IIB, ++$
P/T: none	Ph.D.'s: 47%
Grad: none	S/F Ratio: 14 to 1
Year: sems, ss	Tuition: $4365
Appl: see profile	R and B: $2135
1300 applied	1204 accepted 474 enrolled
SAT: 445V 480M	LESS COMPETITIVE

Elizabethtown College, founded in 1899, is a small, private liberal arts college affiliated with the Church of the Brethren. The library houses 150,000 volumes and 5902 microfilms, and subscribes to 665 periodicals.

Environment: The 110-acre campus is located in a rural area 20 miles from Lancaster. Campus facilities include 15 major buildings, a student center, and 5 single-sex dormitories accommodating about 1200 men and women. The college also sponsors off-campus cooperative houses.

746 PENNSYLVANIA

Student Life: About 70% of the students are from Pennsylvania. About 85% reside in campus dormitories. About 5% are minority-group members. Campus housing is both single-sex and coed; there are visiting privileges in single-sex housing. Students may keep cars on campus.

Organizations: There are no fraternities or sororities. Student organizations include special-interest clubs, religious groups, publications, a radio station, musical groups, forensics, and political and service clubs. Off-campus cultural and recreational facilities include Hershey Cultural Center (10 miles away) and nearby skiing and horseback riding facilities.

Sports: The college fields 7 intercollegiate teams for men and 7 for women. There are 13 intramural sports for men and women.

Handicapped: Special parking areas are available for physically handicapped students. Special educational materials can be provided for visually or hearing impaired students. There are no special counselors.

Graduates: The freshman dropout rate is about 15%. Sixty percent remain to graduate. Twenty-five percent of the graduates pursue advanced study. Forty percent enter careers in business and industry.

Services: Students receive free health care, tutoring, remedial instruction, career and psychological counseling, and placement services. Certain remedial instruction may require a fee.

Programs of Study: The college confers the B.A. and B.S. degrees. Associate degree programs are also available. Bachelor's degrees are offered in the following subjects: BUSINESS (accounting, business administration, business education, computer science, management, marketing), EDUCATION (early childhood, elementary, secondary), ENGLISH (English), FINE AND PERFORMING ARTS (music, music education), HEALTH SCIENCES (medical technology, music therapy, occupational therapy), LANGUAGES (French, German, Spanish), MATH AND SCIENCES (biology, chemistry, mathematics, physics), PHILOSOPHY (religion/philosophy), PREPROFESSIONAL (dentistry, engineering, forestry, law, medicine, ministry, pharmacy, social work, veterinary), SOCIAL SCIENCES (economics, government/political science, history, psychology, social sciences, sociology). Twenty-five percent of the degrees conferred are in business, 20% are in health sciences, and 13% are in social sciences.

Required: All students are required to take courses in English and literature, fine arts, history, mathematics or logic, natural science, physical education, religion and philosophy, and social science. B.A. candidates are also required to take a modern language.

Special: Cooperative programs are offered in engineering with Pennsylvania State University, in forestry with Duke University, and in nursing with Georgetown University. Junior year abroad programs and a program of study at the University of Ghana in West Africa are available.

Honors: Six honor societies have chapters on campus.

Admissions: Ninety-three percent of those who applied were accepted for the 1981–82 freshman class. The SAT scores of those who enrolled were as follows: Verbal—70% below 500, 21% between 500 and 599, 5% between 600 and 700, and 0% above 700; Math—63% below 500, 30% between 500 and 599, 6% between 600 and 700, and 1% above 700. Candidates should be graduates of an accredited high school, have an average of 2.3 or better, rank in the upper 50% of the graduating class, and complete 15 units of high school work. Other considerations are advanced placement or honors courses, impressions made during an interview, and recommendations by school officials.

Procedure: The SAT is required and should be taken before January of the senior year. It is recommended that the application, test scores, high school record, and a $15 fee be submitted before March 1 of the senior year (before December 1 for occupational therapy applicants). Admission and notification are on a rolling basis.

Special: Early admissions and deferred admissions are available. CLEP subject exams are accepted; AP credit is granted.

Transfer: For fall 1981, about 60 transfer students enrolled. To be considered for admission, transfer students must have a GPA of 2.0 or better. Contingent on the registrar's approval, credit for grades of C or P or better will transfer. Elizabethtown has a residency requirement of 30 semester hours; a total of 128 credits must be completed for the bachelor's degree. Transfer application deadlines are August 1 (fall), January 1 (spring), and June 1 (summer).

Visiting: Orientation for prospective students includes testing for placement, parent activities, student scheduling, and social activities for students. Informal visits are best planned for Monday through Friday, 9:30 A.M. to 2:30 P.M. Arrangements for a guided tour and class visits can be made through the admissions office.

Financial Aid: More than 60% of the students receive college-administered financial aid. Fifty percent of the students work part-time on campus. The college provides scholarships, loans, grants, and campus-employment. Loans are available from the federal government, local banks, and various private funds. Aid is awarded on the basis of financial need and academic record; academic scholarships are based on the scholastic record only. The college is a CSS member. The FAF must be filed (except for academic scholarship application), and, when appropriate, the Pell Grant Form. Application deadlines are March 1 for academic scholarships and April 1 for other aid.

Foreign Students: One percent of the students are from foreign countries. Special counseling is available.

Admissions: Foreign applicants must take the TOEFL or SAT. The minimum TOEFL score should be in the high 400s.

Procedure: Foreign students should apply by April for the fall semester and by February for the spring semester. They must present proof of health in the form of a physical examination. Health insurance is available through the college.

Admissions Contact: Sandra Zerby, Acting Director of Admissions.

FRANKLIN AND MARSHALL COLLEGE   E-3
Lancaster, Pennsylvania 17604   (717) 291-3951

F/T: 1129M, 928W	Faculty: 134; IIB, ++$
P/T: 29M, 21W	Ph.D.'s: 92%
Grad: none	S/F Ratio: 15 to 1
Year: sems, ss	Tuition: $5650
Appl: Feb. 10	R and B: $2050
3701 applied	1701 accepted 570 enrolled
SAT (mean): 561V 584M	HIGHLY COMPETITIVE

Franklin and Marshall College, founded in 1787, is an independent, coeducational, liberal arts college, which retains an historical relationship with the United Church of Christ. The library contains over 188,000 volumes and over 68,000 microfilm items, and subscribes to more than 1700 periodicals.

Environment: The campus is located in a suburban area about 1 mile from downtown Lancaster, a city of 60,000, and 60 miles from Philadelphia. The main campus covers 52 acres. Coed facilities, arranged in a quad and having single-sex floors or wings, accommodate 1250 students; a cafeteria, lounge, and lockers are available for commuting students. Playing fields near the college cover 54 acres.

Student Life: Approximately 32% of the students come from Pennsylvania. About 67% of the entering freshmen are graduates of public schools. Approximately 80% of the students live on campus, either in dormitories or in fraternity houses. Forty-one percent of the students are Protestant, 31% are Catholic, and 21% are Jewish. Eight percent are minority-group members. Campus housing is coed. Students may keep cars on campus.

Organizations: Thirty-five percent of the men belong to 10 national fraternities; 5% of the women, to 2 national sororities. There are religious counselors and organizations for Catholic, Protestant, and Jewish students. There are over 70 campus extracurricular activities and organizations, including publications, radio, and active musical and dramatic groups, as well as an artists-in-concert series and 2 film series. Numerous theatrical and musical organizations in Lancaster also attract many students.

Sports: The college fields 13 intercollegiate teams for men and 12 for women. There are 12 intramural sports for men and 11 for women. In addition, students may participate in club sports.

Handicapped: Franklin and Marshall College admits students without regard to physical handicap. Its facilities and programs are fully available as required for all students. Special facilities include wheelchair ramps, parking areas, elevators, and specially equipped rest rooms. Special class scheduling is also available. Fewer than 1% of students have visual or hearing impairments; for these students there are taped classes and special readers. Tutoring and counseling are available.

Graduates: Three percent of the freshman class drop out for academic reasons at the end of the first year. Seventy-four percent of entering freshmen remain to graduate. Thirty-two percent of the graduates pursue further study immediately upon graduation; 10% enter law school, 6% enter medical school, and 4% enter dental school. Forty-six percent of the graduates pursue careers in business and industry.

Services: Students receive the following services free of charge: placement service, career counseling, health care, psychological counseling, tutoring, and remedial instruction.

Programs of Study: All programs lead to the B.A. degree, which is offered in the following subjects: AREA STUDIES (American, Russian), BUSINESS (accounting, management), ENGLISH (English), FINE AND

PERFORMING ARTS (art history, studio art, theater/dramatics), LANGUAGES (French, German, Greek/Latin, Russian, Spanish), MATH AND SCIENCES (biology, chemistry, geology, mathematics, physics, psychology), PHILOSOPHY (classics, philosophy, religion), SOCIAL SCIENCES (anthropology, economics, government/political science, history, sociology). Although not majors, preprofessional programs in law and healing arts (medicine, dentistry, and veterinary) involve 40–50% of the students. Thirty-two percent of degrees are conferred in math and sciences, 31% in social sciences, 18% in business, 15% in humanities, and 3% in fine arts and drama.

Required: The curriculum, though structural, is highly flexible and offers the student unlimited options. No specific courses are required, but all students must take courses in the following areas: scientific inquiry, social analysis (2 courses in each); arts, foreign cultures, historical studies, literature, systems of knowledge and belief (1 course in each). Some freshmen may be asked to take a writing course.

Special: Certification in secondary education is available. Through cooperative arrangements, students may pursue studies in the following areas: a government semester at American University; oceanography in cooperation with Columbia University and The Johns Hopkins University; a 3-2 engineering program with R.P.I., Case Western Reserve, Columbia, Georgia Tech, University of Pennsylvania, and Washington University (St. Louis); a 3-2 program in forestry and environmental studies with Duke University; a one-year program in New York City with the Institute for Architecture and Urban Studies; West African and Black studies at Lincoln University; and an urban semester in Harrisburg, PA. There is active participation in study abroad programs.

Honors: Eight national honor societies, including Phi Beta Kappa, have chapters on campus. The economics and physics departments offer honors programs, which entail 2–3 semesters of independent research with a final thesis or presentation.

Admissions: Forty-six percent of those who applied for the 1981–82 class were accepted. Of those who enrolled, the SAT scores were as follows: Verbal—15% below 500, 56% between 500 and 599, 26% between 600 and 700, and 3% above 700; Math—12% below 500, 47% between 500 and 599, 35% between 600 and 700, and 6% above 700. The college requires that all students be graduates of accredited high schools and have completed 16 units of secondary school work. Applicants should not rank lower than the third quintile (75% of those accepted are in the top 20%), and records must be accompanied by a qualifying recommendation. SAT scores should be above 500, although all scores are considered in the admissions process. The college also considers such factors as advanced placement or honors courses, recommendations by school officials, extracurricular activities, and evidence of special talents.

Procedure: All students are required to take the SAT (preferred) or the ACT and the English Composition AT. A personal interview is recommended but not required, except for early admission and early decision candidates. Students should apply by February 10 for fall admission, December 1 for spring, or June 8 for summer. Students are notified on or about April 1 for fall semester admission. There is a $25 application fee.

Special: Early admissions, deferred admissions, and early decision plans are available. Early decision applications are accepted between November 15 and February 1. Candidates are notified within 1 month of the receipt of the completed application. CLEP subject exams and AP exams are accepted.

Transfer: For fall 1981, 82 transfer students applied, 35 were accepted, and 19 enrolled. Transfers are considered for the freshman (second semester), sophomore, and junior years; an applicant must have a 3.0 average or better for the freshman year from an accredited college. An interview, 3 faculty references, and an essay on reasons for transfer are also required. Students must complete 16 courses at the college out of a total of 32 courses required for the bachelor's degree. Transfer application deadlines are May 1 for the fall term, December 1 for the spring term, and June 8 for the summer sessions.

Visiting: Regularly scheduled orientations for prospective students include personal or group interviews, a slide show presentation, and a campus tour. Guides are available for campus tours on weekdays from September to January and from April to August. Visitors may stay overnight at the school and sit in on classes. Visits can be arranged by contacting the host/hostess coordinator at the college.

Financial Aid: Twenty-two percent of the students receive aid through the college; approximately 65% receive aid from all sources. Twenty-five percent work part-time on campus. The average aid award to freshmen from all sources available through the college is $4600. The college is a member of the CSS and awards aid from a scholarship fund of $685,000 and a loan fund of $200,000, plus $1.3 million from outside sources. The FAF is required, and application for aid should be made by March 1 for winter and by January 1 for spring.

Foreign Students: One percent of the students are from foreign countries. Special counseling and organizations are available to foreign students.

Admissions: The TOEFL, SAT, and English Composition AT are required. Applicants must achieve a minimum score of 570 on the TOEFL.

Procedure: Application deadlines for foreign students are February 10 for fall, December 1 for spring, and June 8 for summer. A college health form must be completed. While health insurance is not required, it is available for a fee through the college.

Admissions Contact: Ronald D. Potier, Director of Admissions.

GANNON UNIVERSITY B-1
Erie, Pennsylvania 16541   (814) 871-7240

F/T: 1550M, 1350W	Faculty: 127; IIA, –$
P/T: 350M, 295W	Ph.D.'s: 48%
Grad: 400M, 250W	S/F Ratio: 22 to 1
Year: sems, ss	Tuition: $2970
Appl: open	R and B: $1600
1873 applied	1592 accepted	810 enrolled
SAT: 480V 530M	ACT: 19	COMPETITIVE

Gannon University, which is under the direction of the Roman Catholic diocese of Erie, offers programs in the liberal arts and sciences, business, education, and health and preprofessional fields. The library houses 187,000 volumes and 500 microfilm items, and subscribes to 1150 periodicals.

Environment: The 13-acre campus, located in downtown Erie, has 17 buildings. In addition to dormitory facilities that house 500 men and 250 women, a townhouse and apartment complex accommodates 250 upperclass students.

Student Life: Seventy-two percent of the students are from Pennsylvania. Forty-five percent of entering freshmen come from public schools. About 52% of the students reside on campus. Sixty percent are Catholic, 32% are Protestant, and 2% are Jewish. Eleven percent are minority-group members. Campus housing is both single-sex and coed; there are visiting privileges in single-sex housing. Students may keep cars on campus.

Organizations: Nine percent of the men belong to 12 fraternities; 6% of the women, to 5 sororities. The facilities of Presque Isle State Park include 7 miles of beaches and woods on Lake Erie.

Sports: The university fields 7 intercollegiate teams for men and 5 for women. There are 10 intramural sports for men and 9 for women.

Handicapped: Eighty-five percent of the campus is accessible to the handicapped student. Special facilities include specially equipped rest rooms, wheelchair ramps, and elevators. Special class scheduling is also available. One percent of the students are visually impaired; 1%, hearing impaired. Two special counselors are available for handicapped students.

Graduates: The freshman dropout rate is 18%. Sixty percent of the students remain to graduate. Of each graduating class, 10% pursue graduate study: 5% enter medical school; 2%, dental school; 2%, law school. Twenty-five percent pursue careers in business or industry.

Services: The following services are offered at no charge to the student: psychological counseling, tutoring, remedial instruction, health care, placement service, and career counseling.

Programs of Study: The university confers the B.A., B.S., B.E.E., B.M.E., and B.S.I.M. degrees. Associate (2-year) and master's degrees are also conferred. Bachelor's degrees are offered in the following subjects: BUSINESS (accounting, business education, computer science, finance, management, marketing), EDUCATION (early childhood, elementary, secondary, special), ENGLISH (English, journalism), FINE AND PERFORMING ARTS (art, art education, radio/TV, theater/dramatics), HEALTH SCIENCES (medical technology, nursing), LANGUAGES (French, German, Spanish), MATH AND SCIENCES (biology, chemistry, earth science, mathematics, physics), PHILOSOPHY (humanities, philosophy), PREPROFESSIONAL (dentistry, engineering, law, medicine, ministry, pharmacy, social work, veterinary), SOCIAL SCIENCES (anthropology, economics, history, psychology, social sciences, sociology). Of the degrees recently conferred, 30% were in preprofessional studies; 25%, in business; 10%, in health sciences.

Special: Students may spend their third year abroad. A general studies degree is offered. Student-designed majors are permitted.

Honors: Four national honor societies have chapters on campus.

Admissions: Eighty-five percent of those who applied were accepted for the 1981–82 freshman class. Of those who enrolled, the

748 PENNSYLVANIA

SAT scores were as follows: Verbal—71% below 500, 20% between 500 and 599, 7% between 600 and 700, and 2% above 700; Math—67% below 500, 22% between 500 and 599, 8% between 600 and 700, and 3% above 700. Students must have completed 16 Carnegie units with a GPA of 2.4. Other factors that enter into the admissions decision are advanced placement or honors courses, recommendations by school officials, impressions made during the interview, and the extracurricular activities record.

Procedure: The SAT or the ACT is required. There are no deadlines for admission; the university uses a rolling admissions plan. Freshmen are admitted to each semester. There is a $15 application fee.

Special: Early decision, early admissions, and deferred admissions plans are offered. CLEP general and subject exams are accepted; students may also earn AP credit.

Transfer: For fall 1981, 254 transfer students applied. An applicant must have a GPA of 2.0 and be in good standing at the former school. A, B, and C grades transfer. All students must complete at least 30 credits at the university out of a total of 128 credits required for the bachelor's degree. Applications are processed on a rolling basis.

Visiting: Guides are available for informal visits to the campus on weekdays from 9 A.M. to 3 P.M. Visitors may sit in on classes and stay overnight at the school. Arrangements should be made through the admissions office.

Financial Aid: About 87% of all students receive aid in the form of scholarships and federal, state, and industrial loans. About 30% of the students work part-time on campus. Tuition may be paid in installments. The university is a member of the CSS. The PHEEA/Pell Grant Form is required and must be filed by March 1.

Foreign Students: Two percent of the students are from foreign countries. The university offers an intensive English course and special counseling for foreign students.

Admissions: Foreign applicants must take the TOEFL and achieve a minimum score of 500. College entrance exams are not required.

Procedure: Foreign students may apply for admission at any time for entry to the fall, spring, or summer sessions. Acceptance notification is on a rolling basis. Proof of funds adequate to cover 1 year of study must be shown. Health insurance is required; it is available through the university for a fee.

Admissions Contact: Gary D. Froehlich, Assistant Director of Admissions.

GENEVA COLLEGE A–3
Beaver Falls, Pennsylvania 15010 (412) 843-2400

F/T: 651M, 511W	Faculty:	58; IIB, ++$
P/T: 158M, 91W	Ph.D.'s:	51%
Grad: none	S/F Ratio:	17 to 1
Year: sems, ss	Tuition:	$4200
Appl: July 31	R and B:	$2130
823 applied	666 accepted	310 enrolled
SAT: 450V 500M		COMPETITIVE

Geneva College, founded in 1848, is a liberal arts college controlled by the Synod of the Reformed Presbyterian Church of North America. The library contains 120,000 volumes and 66,000 microfilm items, and subscribes to 600 periodicals.

Environment: The campus occupies 60 acres on a hill overlooking the Beaver River in a suburban area 30 miles from Pittsburgh. Among the buildings are a science-engineering complex, a student center, and 5 dormitories and some supplementary housing facilities with total accommodations for 400 women and 400 men.

Student Life: About 65% of the students are residents of Pennsylvania. Ninety percent of the entering freshmen come from public schools. About 75% of the students live on campus. All students must attend chapel services one day a week; the majority of students are not members of the Reformed Presbyterian Church. About 85% are Protestant; 15% are Catholic. Six percent are minority-group members. Campus housing is single-sex. Students may keep cars on campus. Profanity, the use of alcohol and tobacco, gambling, and social dancing are prohibited.

Organizations: There are no social fraternities or sororities, but service organizations also serve as social groups. Pittsburgh provides cultural events as well as recreational activities.

Sports: Geneva College competes on an intercollegiate level in 7 sports for men and 4 for women. There are 6 intramural sports for men and 4 for women.

Graduates: The freshman dropout rate is 8%; 60% remain to graduate. Twenty percent pursue advanced study after graduation; 1% enter medical school and 1% enter law school.

Services: Students receive free placement services, career counseling, tutoring, remedial instruction, health care, and psychological counseling.

Programs of Study: Geneva confers the B.A., B.S., B.S.B.A., B.S.E., B.S.Ed., B.S.C.E., B.S.Ch.E., B.S.E.E., B.S.I.E., and B.S.M.E. degrees. The associate degree is also awarded. Bachelor's degrees are offered in the following subjects: BUSINESS (accounting, business administration, business education, computer science, information systems), EDUCATION (Christian school teaching, elementary, secondary), ENGLISH (English, journalism, speech/communications), FINE AND PERFORMING ARTS (applied music, music, music education), HEALTH SCIENCES (life support technology, medical technology), LANGUAGES (German), MATH AND SCIENCES (biology, chemistry, general science, mathematics, physics), PHILOSOPHY (Biblical studies, philosophy), PREPROFESSIONAL (engineering—chemical, engineering—civil, engineering—electrical, engineering—industrial, engineering—mechanical, law, (medicine, ministry, social work), SOCIAL SCIENCES (counseling, economics, government/political science, history, psychology, sociology). Forty percent of the degrees conferred are in math and sciences, 23% are in business, and 12% are in social sciences.

Required: Two semesters of physical education are required in addition to courses in liberal arts and sciences, including Bible Study.

Special: Special programs include an optional Experimester from May to June, study abroad, and student-designed majors. Independent study is available in some departments.

Honors: Two honor societies are open to students.

Admissions: About 81% of those who applied were accepted for the 1981–82 freshman class. The SAT scores of those who enrolled were as follows: Verbal—66% below 500, 26% between 500 and 599, 8% between 600 and 700, and 0% above 700; Math—50% below 500, 36% between 500 and 599, 14% between 600 and 700, and 0% above 700. Applicants must be graduates of accredited high schools, have a C average, and rank in the upper three-fifths of their high school graduating class. They must present 16 Carnegie units and the results of either the SAT or ACT. Other factors considered, in order of importance, are extracurricular activities record, evidence of special talents, advanced placement or honors courses, and impressions made during the interview.

Procedure: The SAT or ACT should be taken in the early part of the senior year. The deadlines for application are July 31 (fall), December 15 (spring), and May 10 (summer). The application fee is $10. The college uses a rolling admissions plan. A personal interview, either on or off campus, is strongly recommended.

Special: Early admissions and deferred admissions plans are available. CLEP subject exams are accepted; students may also earn credit through AP exams.

Transfer: The college received 211 transfer applications for fall 1981, accepted 172, and enrolled 95 students. Transfers are considered for all years except the senior year and must have at least a 2.0 GPA and good standing at the previous institution. D grades transfer if the GPA is over 2.0. Students must earn at least 30 credits at the college, with 6 in the major area, to earn the bachelor's degree. There is a residency requirement of one full year. Transfer deadlines are the same as for freshmen.

Visiting: During regularly scheduled orientations, prospective students can meet the faculty and student leaders, engage in social and sport activities, and take placement exams. Informal visits may be made to the campus during the week; arrangements can be made by the admissions office. Visitors may sit in on classes; overnight accommodations are available.

Financial Aid: Ninety percent of all students receive aid through the school. Sixty percent work part-time on campus. The average award to freshmen from all sources available through the college is $3500. Scholarships, loans, and grants are available. Tuition may be paid on the installment plan. The college is a member of the CSS. The FAF and the Geneva Assistance Form are required, and application for aid should be made by March 15.

Foreign Students: Two percent of the students come from foreign countries. There are special organizations for foreign students.

Admissions: Foreign applicants are required to take the TOEFL and to achieve a minimum score of 500. The SAT, ACT, and ATs are not required.

Procedure: Application deadlines for foreign students are June 1 (fall), October 1 (spring), and March 1 (summer). Proof of adequate funds

GETTYSBURG COLLEGE   D-4
Gettysburg, Pennsylvania 17325   (717) 334-3131

F/T: 975M, 975W	Faculty: 141; IIB, ++$
P/T: none	Ph.D.'s: 82%
Grad: none	S/F Ratio: 14 to 1
Year: 4-1-4	Tuition: $5300
Appl: Feb. 15	R and B: $1900
2502 applied	1529 accepted 580 enrolled
SAT: 521V 555M	VERY COMPETITIVE

Gettysburg College, founded in 1832, is a private liberal arts institution affiliated with the Lutheran Church in America. The library houses 247,000 volumes and 32,650 microfilm items, and subscribes to 1130 periodicals.

Environment: The 200-acre campus is located in a suburban area next to the Civil War battlefield, 30 miles from Harrisburg and 80 miles from Washington, D.C. The 48 buildings include a student union, an observatory, a planetarium, a life sciences building, library/learning center, and a new fine arts center. Other facilities include a physical education center, fieldhouses, and a stadium. Ten dormitories house 1250 students; other students live in 3 common-interest houses. Fraternity houses are also available.

Student Life: Thirty percent of the students come from Pennsylvania. Eighty percent of the freshmen are graduates of public schools. Eighty-five percent of the students live on or close to campus. A third of the men live in fraternity houses. Fifty-five percent are Protestant; 31% are Catholic, and 2% are Jewish. Two percent are members of minority groups. College housing is both single-sex and coed; there are visiting privileges in the single-sex dormitories. Students receiving financial aid may not have cars. An honor system governs student conduct.

Organizations: Half the women belong to 1 of the 7 sororities, and 70% of the men belong to 1 of the 11 fraternities. Other activities include music, drama, lectures, publications, a radio station, and student government. The college provides numerous worship opportunities each week and schedules a full program of religious activities.

Sports: The college fields intercollegiate teams in 14 sports for men and 13 for women. There are 13 intramural sports for men and 8 for women.

Handicapped: No special facilities for physically handicapped students are provided. The school schedules programs or classes chosen by handicapped students in accessible buildings.

Graduates: About 10% of the freshmen drop out, and 73% remain to graduate. About 20% of the graduates seek advanced degrees; of those who graduate, 3% are admitted to medical and dental schools and 4% to law schools. Fifty to seventy-five percent of the graduates pursue careers in business and industry.

Services: Students receive free health care, psychological and career counseling, tutoring, and placement services.

Programs of Study: The college awards the B.A. and B.S.Mus.Ed. degrees. Bachelor's degrees are offered in the following subjects: BUSINESS (business administration), EDUCATION (elementary, health/physical, secondary), ENGLISH (English), FINE AND PERFORMING ARTS (art, music, music education, theater/dramatics), LANGUAGES (French, German, Greek/Latin, Spanish), MATH AND SCIENCES (biology, chemistry, mathematics, physics), PHILOSOPHY (classics, philosophy, religion), PREPROFESSIONAL (dentistry, engineering, forestry, law, medicine, ministry, veterinary), SOCIAL SCIENCES (anthropology, economics, government/political science, history, psychology, sociology). Of the degrees conferred, 25% are in business, 20% are in social sciences, and 15% are in math and sciences.

Required: Students must take courses in a foreign language, religion, history and philosophy, literature, the arts, a laboratory science, and the social sciences; and proficiency in written English must be demonstrated.

Special: Students may design their own majors. A Junior-Year-Abroad program, 5-year cooperative programs in forestry and engineering, Washington and United Nations semesters, and the Harrisburg Urban Semester are offered. Up to 50 students at a time hold paid internships with the Mental Health Council. The January term provides an opportunity for independent study on and off campus. Also available are courses in black studies and exchange programs with other Central Pennsylvania colleges. Students may take programs in Indian, Japanese, and Asian studies at other colleges.

Honors: Twenty-two national honor societies, including Phi Beta Kappa, have chapters on campus. A senior scholars program is offered.

Admissions: About 61% of the applicants for the 1981-82 freshman class were accepted. The SAT scores of those who enrolled were as follows: Verbal—38% below 500, 52% between 500 and 599, 9% between 600 and 700, and 1% above 700; Math—19% below 500, 57% between 500 and 599, 23% between 600 and 700, and 1% above 700. Most applicants rank in the upper two-fifths of their class and present an average of B or better. Applicants must be graduates of approved high schools. Admissions officers consider advanced placement or honors courses, recommendations by school officials, evidence of special talents, personality, and leadership record.

Procedure: Applicants should take the SAT, preferably no later than January of the senior year. The ACT also may be acceptable. Application deadline is February 15 (fall). The application fee is $20.

Special: Early and deferred admissions plans are available. The application deadline for early decision is December 1. AP credit is given.

Transfer: For fall 1981, 80 students applied, 38 were accepted, and 22 enrolled. Transfer students are accepted in all classes. An average of B or better is required. A, B, and C grades transfer. There is a minimum residency requirement of 1 year, and 9 of the 35 credits required for the bachelor's degree must be completed at Gettysburg. The application deadline is the same as that for freshmen.

Visiting: Orientations for prospective students are held regularly, and interviews can be arranged throughout the year with the admissions office. Guides are available for informal visits when the school is in session. Visitors may sit in on classes and arrange to stay overnight in the dormitories.

Financial Aid: Thirty percent of the students receive financial aid through the college. Twenty-seven percent work part-time on campus or in town. The average aid to freshmen from all sources available through the college is $4089. The award is usually a combination of grant and loan. The college is a member of the CSS. Aid candidates must submit the FAF and the aid application by February 15.

Foreign Students: Ten foreign students are enrolled at Gettysburg.

Admissions: Foreign applicants must take the TOEFL and the SAT. No minimum scores are required.

Procedure: The application deadline is February 15 (fall). Proof of health must be presented.

Admissions Contact: Delwin K. Gustafson, Director of Admissions.

GROVE CITY COLLEGE   B-2
Grove City, Pennsylvania 16127   (412) 458-6600

F/T: 1156M, 1074W	Faculty: 94
P/T: 15M, 11W	Ph.D.'s: 40%
Grad: none	S/F Ratio: 20 to 1
Year: sems	Tuition: $2370
Appl: open	R and B: $1580
1692 applied	926 accepted 611 enrolled
SAT: 492V 553M	ACT: 24 VERY COMPETITIVE

Grove City College is a liberal arts college related to the United Presbyterian Church. The library contains 142,750 volumes and 2150 microfilm items, and subscribes to 510 periodicals.

Environment: The 150-acre campus is located in a rural community of 8500, 65 miles from Pittsburgh. Facilities include 11 dormitories accommodating 1810 students, an engineering building, a health center, a chapel, and science, recreation, music, administration, and liberal arts buildings. A new fieldhouse and stadium were recently dedicated.

Student Life: Seventy-five percent of the students are from Pennsylvania. Ninety percent are from public schools. About 86% are campus residents. About 60% of the students are Protestant; 36% are members of the Presbyterian church. Another 25% are Catholic. One percent are minority-group members. Campus housing is single-sex; there are visiting privileges. Students may keep cars on campus. Drinking is prohibited on campus. Students are required to attend convocation once a week.

Organizations: There are 11 fraternities and 9 sororities, to which 41% of the men and 45% of the women belong. Extracurricular activities include music, theater, publications, and radio. Christian outreach groups are offered.

Sports: The college fields 9 intercollegiate teams for men and 5 for women. There are 8 intramural sports for men and 4 for women.

750 PENNSYLVANIA

Handicapped: The campus is not readily accessible to physically handicapped students. There are no students currently enrolled with visual or hearing impairments.

Graduates: The freshmen dropout rate is 4%; 75% remain to graduate. Twenty-five percent pursue advanced study after graduation; 1% enter medical school, 1% enter dental school, and 2% enter law school. Thirty percent pursue careers in business and industry.

Services: Students receive health care and career counseling services free of charge. Tutoring and placement services are available for a fee.

Programs of Study: The college confers the B.A., B.S., and B.Mus. degrees. Bachelor's degrees are offered in the following subjects: BUSINESS (accounting, business administration, business education), EDUCATION (elementary, secondary), ENGLISH (communication arts), FINE AND PERFORMING ARTS (music education), LANGUAGES (French, German, Spanish), MATH AND SCIENCES (biology, chemistry, mathematics), PHILOSOPHY (philosophy, religion), PREPROFESSIONAL (dentistry, engineering, medicine, ministry, social work), SOCIAL SCIENCES (economics, government/political science, history, psychology, sociology). Thirty-three percent of degrees are conferred in business, 22% in engineering, and 18% in social sciences.

Required: All students are required to complete the 18 semester hours, including 4 interdisciplinary courses, designed to introduce the student to fundamental concepts in the humanities, the sciences, and the social sciences.

Special: Third-year students may arrange to study abroad if they desire, but must do so independently since the college does not sponsor such a program. Students may also plan an interdisciplinary major with the help of their faculty adviser. Student-designed majors are permitted; a general studies degree is offered.

Honors: The college has a well-established undergraduate honors program in all departments. Nine national honor societies have chapters on campus.

Admissions: Fifty-five percent of those who applied were accepted for the 1981–82 freshman class. The SAT scores of those who enrolled were as follows: Verbal—51% below 500, 41% between 500 and 599, 7% between 600 and 700, and 1% above 700; Math—23% below 500, 48% between 500 and 599, 26% between 600 and 700, and 3% above 700. ACT scores were as follows: 16% below 21, 20% between 21 and 23, 22% between 24 and 25, 33% between 26 and 28, and 9% above 28. Requirements include graduation from an accredited high school. Applicants must have completed 15 Carnegie units of high school work. The college indicates that in addition to these qualifications it considers the following factors, in order of importance: advanced placement or honors courses, recommendations by school officials, extracurricular activities, evidence of special talents, and impressions made during an interview.

Procedure: All candidates are required to take the SAT or ACT in the spring of the junior year (for early decision) or in the fall of the senior year. A personal interview is not required but is recommended. Applications are processed on a rolling basis beginning about October 1. The application fee is $15. Freshmen are also admitted at midyear.

Special: Early decision is available; the notification date is November 15. Deferred admissions are possible. CLEP and AP credit is accepted.

Transfer: For fall 1981, 171 transfer students applied, 35 were accepted, and 26 enrolled. Transfers are admitted to all classes. Transfer applicants must present a 2.0 GPA and have good academic and social standing at the previous college. A, B, and C grades transfer. There is a minimum residency requirement of 1 year. To receive a degree, students must complete at least 32 hours at the college; the college requires a total of 128 credits for the B.A. and 136 credits for the B.S. in engineering. Transfer application deadlines are July 31 for the fall term and January 1 for the spring term.

Visiting: Orientation is scheduled for prospective students. Guided tours and interviews can be scheduled through the admissions office. Visitors may sit in on classes.

Financial Aid: Forty-five percent of all students receive some form of financial aid. Twenty-five percent work part-time on campus. The average award to freshmen is $460. The college is a member of the CSS and has scholarship funds. Loan funds are provided by the state government, local banks, the college, and private sources. The FAF is required; application for aid should be made by March 15.

Foreign Students: Fewer than 1% of the students come from foreign countries.

Admission: Foreign applicants are required to take the TOEFL. The ACT, SAT, and ATs are not required.

Procedure: Application deadlines for the fall and spring semesters are open; notification is on a rolling basis. Proof of health must be presented. Proof of adequate funds to cover 1 year of study must be shown.

Admissions Contact: John H. Moser, Director of Admissions.

GWYNEDD-MERCY COLLEGE   F–4
Gwynedd Valley, Pennsylvania 19437   (215) 641-5510

F/T: 105M, 785W	Faculty: 105; IIB, – – $
P/T: 145M, 1088W	Ph.D.'s: 40%
Grad: none	S/F Ratio: 11 to 1
Year: sems, ss	Tuition: $3000
Appl: open	R and B: $2100
1300 applied	513 accepted	322 enrolled
SAT: 470V 490M	ACT: 21	COMPETITIVE+

Gwynedd-Mercy College, established in 1948, is a small independent coeducational college of arts and sciences sponsored by the Sisters of Mercy. The library contains 60,000 volumes, subscribes to 445 periodicals, and has 116 hardware and 13,989 software microfilm items.

Environment: The 315-acre campus is situated in a suburban area 20 miles from Philadelphia. Dormitories and on-campus apartments accommodate 190 women and 9 men.

Student Life: Seventy percent of the students come from Pennsylvania. About 50% of the entering freshmen come from public schools. About 28% of the students live on campus. Seventy percent are Catholic, 20% are Protestant, and 2% are Jewish. Seven percent are minority-group members. Campus housing is single-sex; there are visiting privileges. Students may keep cars on campus. Drinking on campus is prohibited.

Organizations: A strong student government sponsors many extracurricular activities; a faculty moderator is assigned to each club.

Sports: The college fields 2 intercollegiate teams for men and 4 for women. There are 2 intramural sports for men and 2 for women.

Handicapped: The campus is 90% accessible to wheelchair-bound students. Facilities include wheelchair ramps, elevators, lowered drinking fountains and telephones, and specially equipped rest rooms. Special class scheduling is also available.

Graduates: About 4% of the freshmen drop out. Ninety-three percent of those who enter remain to graduate. Of those who graduate, 52% pursue advanced study: 1% enter medical school, 1% enter dental school, and 2% enter law school. Forty-three percent enter business and industry.

Services: Psychological counseling, remedial instruction, placement, and career counseling are offered free of charge. Health care is available for a fee.

Programs of Study: The college confers the B.A. and B.S. degrees. The associate degree is also awarded. Bachelor's degrees are awarded in the following subjects: BUSINESS (accounting, business administration, business education, computer science), EDUCATION (elementary, special), ENGLISH (English), HEALTH SCIENCES (medical technology, nursing), LANGUAGES (French), MATH AND SCIENCES (biology, mathematics), PREPROFESSIONAL (dentistry, law, medicine, veterinary), SOCIAL SCIENCES (psychology, sociology). Forty percent of degrees conferred are in business, 40% are in health sciences, and 8% are in preprofessional studies.

Special: Students in the A.S. programs in nursing, secretarial science, and medical secretarial may continue to earn bachelor's degrees in their respective fields. Registered nurses from diploma schools may apply for the B.S. in Nursing. Five-year combined degree programs are offered. Other special programs include junior year abroad, interdisciplinary courses, and independent study.

Honors: Four national honor societies have chapters on campus.

Admissions: Thirty-nine percent of those who applied were accepted for the 1981–82 freshman class. Of those who enrolled, the SAT scores were as follows: Verbal—60% below 500, 39% between 500 and 599, 1% between 600 and 700, and 0% above 700; Math—58% below 500, 40% between 500 and 599, 2% between 600 and 700, and less than 1% above 700. Applicants must be graduates of an accredited high school with 16 Carnegie units and should rank in the top 50% of their class with an average of 80 or better. Other factors that enter into the admissions decision are advanced placement or honors courses, recommendations by school officials, evidence of special talents, and personality.

Procedure: The SAT or ACT and 3 ATs (in English composition, math, and one in area of choice) are required and should be taken no later than January of the senior year. Application deadlines are open; the college uses a rolling admissions procedure. There is a $20 application fee.

Special: There are early decision, early admissions, and deferred admissions plans. The application deadline for early admission is August 1; the notification date for early decision is December 1. CLEP and AP credit is accepted.

Transfer: For fall 1981, 306 transfer students applied, 198 were accepted, and 164 enrolled. A recommendation from the school counselor is required. A, B, and C grades transfer. A minimum GPA of 2.0 is required. Students must earn 60 credits at the college of the 125 to 130 credits required for the bachelor's degree. Application deadlines for transfer students are August 1 for fall, December 1 for spring, and April 1 for summer.

Visiting: The college conducts open houses for prospective students. Guides are available for informal visits to the campus. The admissions office should be contacted to arrange visits.

Financial Aid: About 48% of all students receive aid through the college. Six percent work part-time on campus. The average award to freshmen is about $2500. Federal and state government loans, scholastic grants, and grants-in-aid are available. The college is a member of the CSS. The FAF, state, and federal forms are required. The deadlines for aid application are March 1 for fall, October 15 for spring, and March 1 for summer.

Foreign Students: Seven percent of the students come from foreign countries. The college offers an intense English course and special counseling for foreign students.

Admissions: Foreign applicants are required to take the TOEFL and to achieve a minimum score of 500. College entrance exams are not required.

Procedure: Application deadlines for foreign students are August 1 for fall, December 1 for spring, and April 1 for summer. Proof of adequate funds to cover from 2 to 4 years of study must be presented. Foreign students are required to carry health insurance; it is available through the college for a fee.

Admissions Contact: Sister Helen Cahill, R.S.M., Director of Admissions.

HAVERFORD COLLEGE E-4
Haverford, Pennsylvania 19041 (215) 896-1350

F/T: 700M, 300W
P/T: none
Grad: none
Year: sems
Appl: Jan. 31
1322 applied
SAT: required

Faculty: 67; IIB, ++$
Ph.D.'s: n/av
S/F Ratio: 12 to 1
Tuition: $7230
R and B: $2510
550 accepted 260 enrolled
MOST COMPETITIVE

Haverford College, an undergraduate college of arts and sciences founded in 1833, was the first college established by the Society of Friends (Quakers). Women were admitted as freshmen for the first time in 1980. The library houses 421,000 volumes and subscribes to 1200 periodicals.

Environment: The 230-acre campus, located in a suburban area 10 miles from Philadelphia, has been designated an Arboretum. Facilities include science laboratories, classrooms, a library, a computer center, a dining center, and 14 dormitories.

Student Life: Sixty-five percent of the students come from the Middle Atlantic area, including 20% from Pennsylvania. About 70% come from public schools. Ninety-five percent live on campus. About 10% are minority-group members. Campus housing is single-sex and coed. Students may keep cars on campus. There is no requirement to attend the weekly Quaker Meeting.

Organizations: Student activities, almost all conducted jointly with Bryn Mawr, include a newspaper, radio station, dramatic society, instrumental and vocal groups, and numerous volunteer social service programs. There are no fraternities or sororities. Student government includes the administration of an effective honor code.

Sports: The college fields 10 intercollegiate teams for men and 5 for women. There are 5 intramural sports, all of which are coed.

Handicapped: Sixty percent of the campus is accessible to the physically handicapped. Wheelchair ramps, special parking and rest rooms, elevators, lowered telephones, and special class scheduling are provided.

Graduates: Fewer than 2% of the freshmen drop out; about 90% remain to graduate. Of the graduates, 45% go on immediately to graduate or professional schools: 15% enter medical school, 10% enter law school, and 1% enter dental school. Forty percent pursue careers in business or industry.

Services: Free health care, psychological counseling, tutoring, remedial instruction, career counseling, and placement services are provided.

Programs of Study: The college confers the B.A. or B.S. degrees in the following subjects: ENGLISH (English), FINE AND PERFORMING ARTS (art, art history, music), LANGUAGES (French, German, Greek/Latin, Italian, Russian, Spanish), MATH AND SCIENCES (astronomy, biology, chemistry, geology, mathematics, physics), PHILOSOPHY (classics, philosophy, religion), SOCIAL SCIENCES (anthropology, economics, government/political science, history, psychology, sociology).

Required: All freshmen must take a writing seminar. A year of foreign language and 1 course in each of 7 dimensional areas are also required.

Special: An extensive cooperative program with nearby Bryn Mawr College permits students to take courses, major, or live at either college. There are more than 3000 cross-registrations yearly. Students may also take courses at Swarthmore or the University of Pennsylvania. The Academic Flexibility Program includes independent study, project courses, student-designed majors, a 4-year combined B.A.-M.A. program, and a 3-year bachelor's degree program. Ten endowed funds bring more than 100 guest faculty and artists to the campus each year. The Gest Center for Cross Cultural Study of Religion offers seminars and lectures.

Honors: Students may work for honors in every department. There is a chapter of Phi Beta Kappa on campus.

Admissions: Forty-two percent of those who applied for the 1981–82 freshman class were accepted. Of those who enrolled, SAT scores were as follows: Verbal—66% between 600 and 800; Math—75% between 600 and 800. Some preference is given to children of alumni and Quakers, who account for 10–15% of the student body. Minority students are encouraged to apply. Other factors weighed equally by admissions officers are advanced placement or honors courses, extracurricular activities record, recommendations by school officials, personality, leadership record, impressions made during an interview, and evidence of special talents.

Procedure: The SAT and 3 ATs (including English composition) are required; all should be taken by January of the senior year. The application deadline is January 31, with notification in early April. The application fee is $25. An interview is recommended.

Special: The early decision deadlines are November 15 (fall) and January 5 (spring); fall early decision applicants are notified by December 15. The early admissions application deadline is January 31. There are also deferred admissions.

Transfer: For fall 1981, 119 transfer students applied, 19 were accepted, and 13 enrolled. Transfer students are accepted for the sophomore and junior classes only; at least 2 years must be completed at the college. A, B, and C grades transfer. Sixteen courses must be completed at Haverford out of a total of 32 courses required for the bachelor's degree. The application deadline is March 31 (fall); decisions are announced by June 15.

Visiting: The time between April 1 and February 1 is best for visiting the college. Guides are available; visitors may sit in on classes.

Financial Aid: About 40% of all students receive financial aid from scholarships, loans, and campus employment. Forty percent work part-time on campus. The school is a member of CSS and requires the FAF. Applications for aid must be made by January 31.

Foreign Students: Three percent of the student body are foreign nationals. The college actively recruits foreign students and sponsors special organizations for them.

Admissions: Foreign applicants must take either the TOEFL or the SAT.

Procedure: The application deadline for foreign students is January 31 (fall). Proof of health consisting of a completed medical form must be presented. Proof of funds adequate to cover 1 year of study must be shown.

Admissions Contact: William W. Ambler, Director of Admissions.

HOLY FAMILY COLLEGE F-3
Philadelphia, Pennsylvania 19114 (215) 637-7700

F/T: 59M, 467W
P/T: 161M, 719W
Grad: none
Year: sems, ss
Appl: open
329 applied
SAT: 450V 451M

Faculty: 45; IIB, n/av
Ph.D.'s: 35%
S/F Ratio: 10 to 1
Tuition: $2650
R and B: none
163 accepted 122 enrolled
COMPETITIVE

752 PENNSYLVANIA

Holy Family College, founded in 1954, is a nonresidential liberal arts college conducted by the Sisters of the Holy Family of Nazareth. The library houses 90,740 volumes, subscribes to 390 periodicals, and has 1446 microtext volumes on file.

Environment: The college's 46-acre campus is located in a suburban section of Philadelphia. Facilities include a nursing education building, a writing skills center, and a nursery school and kindergarten. There are no residence halls on campus.

Student Life: Almost all of the students come from the Middle Atlantic area. About 85% of the students are from private or church-related high schools. None of the students live on campus. About 85% of the students are Catholic, 10% are Protestant, and 3% are Jewish. About 7% are minority-group members.

Organizations: There are no fraternities or sororities. Extracurricular activities on campus include the student government association, publications, athletic programs, a glee club, and various special-interest groups.

Sports: The college fields 1 intercollegiate team for men and 1 for women. There is 1 intramural sport for men and 1 for women.

Handicapped: Special facilities for handicapped students include wheelchair ramps, designated parking, and specially equipped rest rooms and lowered drinking fountains and telephones in 50% of the academic buildings and the library. Special class scheduling is also available. There is one special counselor for handicapped students.

Graduates: Nine percent of the freshmen drop out. Eighty percent remain to graduate. Of these, 10% go on to graduate or professional schools; 1% enter medical school, and 1% enter law school. About 18% pursue careers in business or industry.

Services: The following services are offered at no charge to the student: psychological counseling, tutoring, remedial instruction, health care, placement service, and career counseling.

Programs of Study: The college confers the B.A., B.S., and B.S.N. degrees. Bachelor's degrees are offered in the following subjects: BUSINESS (accounting, international business, management, marketing), EDUCATION (elementary), ENGLISH (English, literature), FINE AND PERFORMING ARTS (art, art education), HEALTH SCIENCES (medical technology, nursing), LANGUAGES (French, Spanish), MATH AND SCIENCES (biochemistry, biology, chemistry, mathematics), PHILOSOPHY (humanities), PREPROFESSIONAL (social work), SOCIAL SCIENCES (child care, criminal justice, economics, fire science administration, history, psychobiology, psychology, psychology for business, social sciences, sociology).

Required: For certain majors, the GRE is required for graduation.

Special: There are special programs in most preprofessional fields.

Honors: Eight national honor societies have chapters on campus.

Admissions: Fifty percent of those who applied were accepted for the 1981–82 freshmen class. Of those who enrolled, the SAT scores were as follows: Verbal—75% below 500, 25% above 500; Math—78% below 500, 22% above 500. All applicants must be graduates of accredited high schools and have completed 16 high school units with a minimum average grade of B. Other important considerations in the admissions decision are evidence of special talent, advanced placement or honors courses, and recommendations by school officials.

Procedure: The SAT is required. There are no application deadlines, and the college follows the rolling admissions policy. Freshmen are admitted to all semesters. There is a $15 application fee.

Special: There is an early admissions plan; applicants should apply by May 15. CLEP and AP credit is granted.

Transfer: For fall 1981, 101 transfer students applied, 26 were accepted, and 22 enrolled. Applicants must have a minimum GPA of 2.5 and character references. D grades do not transfer. The college requires residency of at least 1 year. Transfer students must complete 30 credit hours at the college of a total of 120 credits required for the bachelor's degree. There are no application deadlines.

Visiting: Regularly scheduled orientations are conducted by the college for prospective students. Guides are available for informal visits to the campus, and visitors may sit in on classes. Arrangements should be made through the director of admissions.

Financial Aid: About 80% of all students receive aid from the following sources: scholarships (including EOG), loans (including NDSL), and campus employment (including CWS). Forty percent work part-time on campus. The average award to freshmen from all sources is $1800. Financial aid is awarded on the basis of academic standing and financial need. The college is a member of the CSS and requires the FAF from all those applying for aid. There is no application deadline.

Foreign Students: One foreign student is enrolled at Holy Family. Special counseling is available.

Admissions: The college requires foreign students to take the TOEFL and to score a minimum of 530. College entrance exams are not required.

Procedure: There is no application deadline. Foreign students are admitted to the fall, spring, or summer sessions. Students must present proof of health consisting of a college health form completed by a physician. They must also show proof of funds adequate to cover 4 years of study.

Admissions Contact: Angela Godshall, Director of Admissions and Financial Aid.

IMMACULATA COLLEGE   E-4
Immaculata, Pennsylvania 19345   (215) 296-9067

F/T: 2M, 557W	Faculty: n/av
P/T: 164M, 846W	Ph.D.'s: 32%
Grad: 3M, 33W	S/F Ratio: 18 to 1
Year: sems, ss	Tuition: $2800
Appl: June 1	R and B: $1850
294 applied	248 accepted	166 enrolled
SAT: 460V 490M	ACT: 21	COMPETITIVE

Immaculata College, conducted by the Sisters, Servants of the Immaculate Heart of Mary, was chartered in 1920. The college offers programs in the arts and sciences, business, education, and preprofessional areas of study. The library contains 125,000 volumes and subscribes to 587 periodicals.

Environment: The 400-acre campus, located in a suburban area 20 miles from Philadelphia, overlooks the beautiful Chester Valley. Facilities include an electronic language laboratory. Residence halls (including a freshman dormitory) accommodate 500 women.

Student Life: The present college community includes students from 18 states and 9 foreign countries. About 75% of the students live on campus. About 70% are Catholic, about 30% are Protestant, and less than 1% are Jewish. About 17% are minority-group members. Campus housing is single-sex. The college permits students to keep cars on campus. The college provides day-care services for part-time students.

Organizations: There are no Greek letter organizations on campus. Student activities include a student council, a newspaper and a magazine, musical groups, a speech club, and Cue and Curtain Players. Also on campus are other special-interest, departmental, and religious groups.

Sports: The college fields 5 intercollegiate teams for women and none for men. There are 14 intramural sports for women and none for men.

Handicapped: The campus is 90% accessible to wheelchair-bound students. Facilities and considerations include specially equipped rest rooms, ramps, designated handicapped parking, elevators, and special class scheduling. The college also offers braille edition textbooks and tapes and cassettes for visually impaired students, and hearing aids for hearing-impaired students.

Services: The following services are offered at no charge to the student: psychological counseling, tutoring, remedial instruction, some aspects of health care, placement services, and career counseling.

Programs of Study: The college awards the A.B., B.S., and B.Mus. degrees. Associate degrees are also awarded. Bachelor's degrees are offered in the following subjects: BUSINESS (accounting, business administration, computer science, management, marketing), EDUCATION (early childhood, elementary, secondary), ENGLISH (English, literature), FINE AND PERFORMING ARTS (music, music education), LANGUAGES (French, German, Greek/Latin, Spanish), MATH AND SCIENCES (biochemistry, biology, chemistry, mathematics, physics), PREPROFESSIONAL (dentistry, engineering, home economics, law, medicine, social work, veterinary), SOCIAL SCIENCES (economics, government/political science, history, psychology, sociology).

Required: All students must take physical education. Theology is mandatory for Catholic students. The URE is required in the senior year.

Special: Independent study and interdisciplinary courses are offered.

Honors: Outstanding students are invited to participate in honors sections in English, history, philosophy, or theology.

Admissions: Eighty-four percent of those who applied were accepted for the 1981–82 freshman class. Of those who enrolled, SAT scores were as follows: Verbal—62% below 500, 35% between 500 and 599, 2% between 600 and 700, and 1% above 700; Math—50% below 500, 46% between 500 and 599, 3% between 600 and 700, and 1% above 700. Applicants must be high school graduates with 16 units of academic work completed, should rank in the upper 50% of the class, have a minimum GPA of 2.0, and must present the principal's recommendation. Other important considerations are impressions made during an interview, evidence of special talent, and advanced placement or honors courses.

Procedure: The SAT or ACT is required. June 1 is the deadline for application to the fall session. December 1 is the deadline for the spring session. Freshmen are normally admitted only in the fall. There is a $20 application fee. Admission and notification are on a rolling basis. An interview is recommended.

Special: An early admissions plan is offered; the application deadline is June 1. Deferred admissions are possible. AP and CLEP credit is offered.

Transfer: For fall 1981, 30 transfers applied, 24 were accepted, and 18 enrolled. Transfers should have a minimum GPA of 2.0 and minimum SAT scores of 400. A, B, and C grades transfer. Thirty of the 126 credits required for the bachelor's degree must be taken at Immaculata. Prospective transfers should apply by June 1 for the fall or December 1 for the spring.

Visiting: There are no regularly scheduled orientations. Guides are available for informal visits to the campus. Prospective students may sit in on classes and may arrange an overnight stay at the campus by contacting the director of admissions.

Financial Aid: About 72% of all students receive aid. About 45% work part-time on campus. The average aid award to freshmen is $1500. Immaculata College academic grants are awarded annually to properly qualified students. Federal and state loans and campus employment are available. Applications for academic grants close February 1; a personal interview is required of these applicants. The college is a member of the CSS. The FAF and the PHCAA are required. Application deadlines are March 1 for fall and December 1 for spring.

Foreign Students: Five percent of the students come from foreign countries. The college offers an intensive English program, special counseling, and special organizations.

Admissions: The college requires that foreign applicants take the TOEFL and score a minimum of 550. College entrance exams are not required.

Procedure: Application deadlines for foreign students are July 1 for fall entry and January 1 for spring entry. Proof of health and adequate funds must be presented. Health insurance is required; it is available through the college for a fee.

Admissions Contact: Sr. Maria Claudia, Director of Admissions.

INDIANA UNIVERSITY OF PENNSYLVANIA
B-3

Indiana, Pennsylvania 15705   (412) 357-2230

F/T: 4449M, 6143W
P/T: 369M, 453W
Grad: 411M, 530W
Year: sems, ss
Appl: Dec. 31
6703 applied
SAT: 484V 527M

Faculty: 625; I, +$
Ph.D.'s: 50%
S/F Ratio: 17 to 1
Tuition: $1473 ($2523)
R and B: $1520
3082 accepted   1667 enrolled
VERY COMPETITIVE

Indiana University of Pennsylvania, founded in 1875, is part of the Pennsylvania State College and University System. The undergraduate university is composed of 7 schools: Social Sciences and Humanities, Natural Sciences and Mathematics, Business, Fine Arts, Education, Health Services, and Home Economics. The library contains over 450,000 volumes and 840,000 microform units, and subscribes to more than 3000 periodicals.

Environment: The 106-acre campus is located in a rural town in the foothills of the Alleghenies 60 miles from Pittsburgh. Many of the campus' 79 buildings form a quadrangle around the Oak Grove at the center of the campus. The 13 residence halls are grouped into 4 quads. The University Lodge, located a few miles from the town and surrounded by 280 acres of woods, offers opportunities for nature study, hiking, and skiing. The university also operates branch campuses at Punxsutawney and Kittanning, both 28 miles from the main campus.

Student Life: Almost all students are from Pennsylvania. About 60% live on campus. About 6% are minority-group members. Campus housing is both coed and single-sex. There are visiting privileges in single-sex dorms. Students may have cars on campus. The university provides day-care services to all students.

Organizations: About 1200 students belong to the 15 fraternities and 13 sororities. Other activities include student government, an activities board, concert committee, a lecture series, student publications, university radio and TV stations, and more than 100 other departmental, special-interest, drama, music, and religious organizations.

Sports: The university sponsors intercollegiate teams in 13 sports for men and 9 for women. There are 6 coed intramurals.

Graduates: About 21% of the freshmen drop out, and 74% remain to graduate. About 8% of the graduates go on for further study.

Services: Most routine health services are provided to students free. Psychological counseling, career counseling, remedial instruction, tutoring, and placement services also are available without charge.

Programs of Study: The university confers the B.A., B.S., B.S.Ed., and B.F.A. degrees. Associate, master's, and doctoral degrees also are available. Bachelor's degrees are offered in the following subjects: BUSINESS (business administration, business education, distributive education), EDUCATION (elementary, health/physical, rehabilitation, secondary, special), ENGLISH (English, journalism, speech), FINE AND PERFORMING ARTS (art, art education, art history, music, music education, studio art, theater/dramatics), HEALTH SCIENCES (audiology, dental hygiene, environmental health, medical technology, nursing, public school nursing, respiratory therapy, speech therapy), LANGUAGES (French, German, Russian, Spanish), MATH AND SCIENCES (applied mathematics, biology, chemistry, computer science, geology, geoscience, mathematics, natural sciences, physics), PHILOSOPHY (philosophy), PREPROFESSIONAL (home economics, law, ministry), SOCIAL SCIENCES (anthropology, criminology, economics, geography, government/political science, history, international relations, psychology, public service, regional planning, sociology).

Required: Students must take courses in English, art, music, mathematics, and physical education.

Special: Students may study abroad. The computer center offers instruction and facilities to students from several departments.

Honors: Nineteen honor societies have chapters on campus.

Admissions: About 46% of those who applied were accepted for the 1981–82 freshmen class. The SAT scores of those who enrolled were as follows: Verbal—66% below 500, 29% between 500 and 599, 8% between 600 and 700, and 0.43% above 700; Math—40% below 500, 48% between 500 and 599, 12% between 600 and 700, and 0% above 700. Applicants should be graduates of an accredited high school or hold a GED. The admissions committee considers the candidate's academic record, test scores, recommendations by high school officials, extracurricular activities and other pertinent information.

Procedure: The SAT or ACT is required. Applications should be submitted by December 31, but are accepted until the class is filled. There is a $10 application fee. Prospective art and music majors must arrange an audition or submit a portfolio.

Special: The university offers an early decision plan. AP credit is accepted.

Transfer: For fall 1981, 1054 transfer students applied, 820 were accepted, and 482 enrolled. A 2.0 GPA is required. Applicants should apply by February 1 for fall, and by September 15 for spring, although applications may be considered after those dates. The last 30 credits of the 124 necessary for the bachelor's degree must be earned in residence.

Visiting: An orientation program is held for incoming students at the start of each semester.

Financial Aid: Loans, jobs, grants, and scholarships are available. Ten percent of the students receive aid; 33% work part-time on campus. The FAF is required. The deadline for aid applications is March 15.

Foreign Students: About 1% of the full-time students come from foreign countries. The university offers these students special counseling and special organizations.

Admissions: Foreign students must achieve a minimum score of 500 on the TOEFL. The SAT is also required.

Procedure: Application deadlines are the same as for other freshmen. The examination required for a visa will suffice as proof of health. Foreign students must carry health insurance, which is available through the university for a fee. Proof of adequate funds is also required.

Admissions Contact: Fred Dakak, Dean of Admissions.

JUNIATA COLLEGE C-3
Huntingdon, Pennsylvania 16652 (814) 643-4310

F/T: 694M, 604W
P/T: 4M, 5W
Grad: none
Year: 3 terms, ss
Appl: Apr. 1
1341 applied
SAT: 500V 540M
Faculty: 74; IIB, ++$
Ph.D.'s: 61%
S/F Ratio: 18 to 1
Tuition: $4740
R and B: $2055
1059 accepted 394 enrolled
COMPETITIVE+

Juniata College, established in 1876, is a private, independent college of liberal arts founded by the members of the Church of the Brethren. The library contains 177,392 volumes and 41,221 microform volume equivalents, and subscribes to 698 periodicals.

Environment: The rural campus comprises 100 acres, 90 miles from Harrisburg and 32 miles from Altoona. There are some 32 buildings, including academic buildings, a science center, a student center, and a humanities center. A new sports complex is under construction. Dormitories accommodate 1174 students.

Student Life: The college draws 75% of its students from Pennsylvania. About 91% of the entering freshmen come from public schools. About 92% of the students live in residence halls on the campus. Thirty percent are Catholic, 64% Protestant, and 1% Jewish. About 4% are minority-group members. Campus housing is both coed and single-sex. There are visiting privileges in single-sex dorms. Students may keep cars on campus.

Organizations: There are no social sororities or fraternities on campus. Student activities include a newspaper and a radio station. There are special-interest groups, religious groups, a choir, a band, and an orchestra. The college sponsors an artist series and an extensive film series.

Sports: The college competes in 9 intercollegiate sports for men and 6 for women. There are 12 intramural sports for men and 8 for women.

Handicapped: Fifty percent of the campus is accessible to handicapped students. Special facilities include wheelchair ramps, elevators, and specially equipped rest rooms.

Graduates: At the end of the freshman year about 15% of the students drop out. Sixty-five percent remain to graduate, and 40% of the graduates go directly on to further study. Five percent enter medical school; 2% law school; and 2% dental school. Forty percent of the alumni hold graduate degrees. Thirty-five percent of the graduates pursue careers in business and industry.

Services: Students receive the following services free of charge: placement services, career counseling, health care, psychological counseling, and remedial instruction. Tutoring is available for a fee.

Programs of Study: The college confers the B.A. and B.S. degrees. Bachelor's degrees are offered in the following subjects: BUSINESS (accounting, business administration, computer science, management), EDUCATION (early childhood, elementary, secondary), ENGLISH (English), FINE AND PERFORMING ARTS (art, music), HEALTH SCIENCES (medical technology, nursing, occupational therapy, physical therapy), LANGUAGES (French, German, Russian, Spanish), MATH AND SCIENCES (biochemistry, biology, chemistry, ecology/environmental science, geology, mathematics, natural sciences, physics), PHILOSOPHY (humanities, philosophy, religion), PREPROFESSIONAL (dentistry, engineering, forestry, law, medicine, ministry, social work, veterinary), SOCIAL SCIENCES (economics, government/political science, history, international relations, peace and conflict studies, psychology, social sciences, sociology). Twenty-five percent of degrees conferred are in math and sciences; 25% are in business; and 22% are in social sciences.

Special: The college offers Washington, United Nations, and urban semesters. Internships are available in several fields. French, Spanish, and German majors are encouraged to spend their junior year abroad in the Brethren Colleges Abroad Program. Foreign study exchange programs are available in Germany, France, and Japan. The college offers a 3-2 combined B.A.-B.S. program in engineering in cooperation with Columbia University, Washington University, Georgia Institute of Technology, and Penn State University. There are cooperative programs in forestry with Duke University, and in medical technology with several hospitals. Cooperative programs in nursing and allied health fields are available in conjunction with Thomas Jefferson University. Students also have the opportunity to create their own majors or to take a general studies (no major) degree.

Honors: Four national honor societies have chapters on campus.

Admissions: Seventy-nine percent of those who applied were accepted for the 1981-82 freshman class. Of those who enrolled, the SAT scores were as follows: Verbal—50% below 500, 39% between 500 and 599, 10% between 600 and 700, and 1% above 700; Math—28% below 500, 50% between 500 and 599, 20% between 600 and 700, and 2% above 700. Applicants must be high school graduates and must have completed 16 academic units at an approved secondary school. Other considerations are results of the SAT (or ACT in special cases), advanced placement or honors courses, impressions made during interview, the leadership record, and evidence of special talents.

Procedure: The SAT is required. Application deadlines are as follows: April 1 (fall), September 1 (winter), and December 1 (spring). Freshmen are admitted to all semesters, except the summer term. Notification on a rolling basis begins shortly after receipt of all necessary credentials. There is a $20 application fee.

Special: Deferred admissions and early decision plans are available. AP credit is possible.

Transfer: For fall 1981, 66 transfer students applied, 41 were accepted, and 24 enrolled. Associate degrees are preferred. Applicants must have acceptable high school, test, and college records. A GPA of 2.0 is necessary. The last 3 terms must be taken at the college. Transfers must complete in residence 9 of the 36 units required for the bachelor's degree. Application deadlines are the same as for freshmen. An interview is required.

Visiting: There are regularly scheduled fall and spring open houses and summer orientations for prospective students. Guides are available for informal visits; students may stay overnight at the school and sit in on classes. Visits can be arranged for times when classes are in session through the admissions office.

Financial Aid: Approximately 85% of the students receive financial assistance. The college provides scholarships and grants. Approximately half of the students earn some of their expenses in on- or off-campus part-time work. Aid is awarded on the basis of financial need. Application must be made by March 1; the FAF must also be filed. The college is a member of CSS. Notification is made by May 1.

Foreign Students: About 1% of the full-time students come from foreign countries. Special counseling is available for these students.

Admissions: The TOEFL is required. The SAT or ACT is not necessary.

Procedure: Application deadlines are the same as for freshmen. Foreign students are admitted to all terms. Proof of funds adequate to cover the academic year and summer term is required. A hospitalization insurance policy is available through the college, though this is not required.

Admissions Contact: Gayle W. Kreider, Director of Admissions.

KING'S COLLEGE E-2
Wilkes-Barre, Pennsylvania 18711 (717) 826-5858

F/T: 976M, 803W
P/T: 272M, 292W
Grad: none
Year: sems, ss
Appl: open
1197 applied
SAT: 440V 470M
Faculty: 100; IIB, +$
Ph.D.'s: 55%
S/F Ratio: 17 to 1
Tuition: $3660
R and B: $1980
1075 accepted 526 enrolled
LESS COMPETITIVE

Founded in 1946 under the direction of the Holy Cross Fathers from the University of Notre Dame, King's College is a coeducational Roman Catholic liberal arts institution that offers programs in science, business, social science, and humanities. The library contains 154,000 volumes and 507,000 microfilm items, and subscribes to over 1120 periodicals.

Environment: The main campus covers 12 acres in the city of Wilkes-Barre, 140 miles from New York City and 120 miles from Philadelphia. Facilities include 3 dormitories that accommodate about 675 students. A separate cafeteria and dining hall serve resident and nonresident students.

Student Life: About 59% of the undergraduates are from public schools; 60% reside in the dormitories. Eighty-eight percent of the students are Catholic, 8% are Protestant, and 1% are Jewish. There are places of worship available on campus for Catholics and in the immediate community for Protestant and Jewish students. Four percent of the students are minority-group members. Campus housing is single-sex, and there are visiting privileges. Students may keep cars on campus.

Organizations: There are no fraternities or sororities on campus; professional and service organizations also serve as social groups. Extracurricular activities include departmental clubs, professional associations, service groups, publications, area clubs, music groups, theater, and forensic groups. The college is located 40 to 60 minutes from Pocono ski resorts.

Sports: King's College competes on an intercollegiate level in 10 sports for men and 7 sports for women. There are 4 intramural sports for men and 2 for women.

Handicapped: Ninety-nine percent of the campus is accessible to wheelchair-bound students. Special parking, wheelchair ramps, elevators, specially equipped rest rooms, and lowered telephones are available. Arrangements can be made for live-in aides; the college provides electric wheelchairs for all non-ambulatory students. There are no students currently enrolled with hearing impairments; fewer than 1% have visual impairments. Students with visual impairments can use braille textbooks, tape cassettes of all lectures, oral examinations, and tutors when needed. There are 2 counselors to assist handicapped students.

Graduates: The freshman dropout rate is about 10%; 60% remain to graduate. About 14% pursue graduate study after graduation. Fifty-nine percent of graduates enter careers in business and industry.

Services: Students receive the following services free of charge: placement, career counseling, health care, tutoring, remedial instruction, and psychological counseling.

Programs of Study: The college confers the B.A. and B.S. degrees. Associate degrees are also awarded. Bachelor's degrees are offered in the following subjects: BUSINESS (accounting, business administration, computer science, marketing), EDUCATION (early childhood, elementary, secondary, special), ENGLISH (communications, English), FINE AND PERFORMING ARTS (radio/TV, theater/dramatics), HEALTH SCIENCES (health services administration, medical technology, physician's assistant), LANGUAGES (French, German, Spanish), MATH AND SCIENCES (biology, chemistry, computer science, mathematics, natural sciences, physics), PHILOSOPHY (philosophy, theology), PREPROFESSIONAL (dentistry, engineering, law, medicine, pharmacy, social work, veterinary), SOCIAL SCIENCES (criminal justice, economics, gerontology, government/political science, history, psychology, social work, sociology). Forty-four percent of degrees conferred are in social sciences, 34% are in business, and 13% are in math and sciences.

Required: All students must take 6 hours of theology. The core curriculum eliminates all other course requirements except those required by a specific major sequence.

Special: Student-designed majors are permitted; a general studies (no major) degree is offered. Secondary education programs are offered to liberal arts and science students only. Elementary education and special education programs are available to freshmen only through a cooperative program with College Misericordia. Study abroad for juniors, sponsored by other institutions, is possible.

Honors: Honors programs are available through the Center for Independent Learning. Three honor societies have chapters on campus.

Admissions: Ninety percent of those who applied were accepted for the 1981–82 freshman class. The SAT scores of those who enrolled were as follows: Verbal—72% below 500, 13% between 500 and 599, 2% between 600 and 700, and 0.1% above 700; Math—61% below 500, 23% between 500 and 599, 4% between 600 and 700, and 0.3% above 700. Entering students are expected to have completed 15 academic units and have a minimum C average. The college indicates that in addition to these qualifications it considers the following factors: advanced placement or honors courses, recommendations by school officials, and impressions made during an interview.

Procedure: Either the SAT or ACT is required. Campus visits and interviews are not required, but are recommended and encouraged. Applications for each term are accepted until such time as residence and classroom facilities are filled. There is no application deadline; freshmen are admitted to all terms. The college employs a rolling admission plan whereby a student is notified of the decision by the college within 6 weeks from the date of his application. There is a $15 application fee.

Special: Early decision is possible; notification is made by September 15. Early admission is available; the deadline for application is June 1 of the junior year. Deferred admission is also possible. CLEP and AP credit is accepted.

Transfer: For fall 1981, the college received 241 applications, accepted 236, and enrolled 152 students. Transfers are accepted for all classes except the senior year and are admitted to all sessions. They should have a 2.0 minimum average for liberal arts and business programs, a 2.5 for science. Holders of associate degrees may transfer with junior-year status. D grades transfer if the student has an associate degree. Students must earn, at the college, 60 of the 120 credits required for the bachelor's degree. Transfer application deadlines are August 15 (fall), December 15 (spring), and May 15 (summer).

Visiting: There is an orientation at which time students may arrange for interviews and tours of the campus. Informal visits can be arranged through the admissions office; visitors may sit in on classes.

Financial Aid: About 72% of all students receive some form of financial aid. Ten percent work part-time on campus. The average award to freshmen from all sources is $2900. The college is a member of CSS; the FAF or BEOG/PHEAA must be on file for students to be considered for financial assistance. April 1 is the deadline for fall and summer aid applications; the spring deadline is September 1.

Foreign Students: Two percent of the full-time students come from foreign countries. An English course, an intensive English program, and special counseling are available to these students.

Admissions: Either the University of Michigan Language Test or the Comprehensive English Language Test is required. College entrance exams are not necessary.

Procedure: Application deadlines are July 1 (fall), November 1 (spring), and April 1 (summer). Foreign students must complete the college's medical history form to establish proof of health. Proof of funds adequate to cover 1 year of study is required. Health insurance, while not required, is available through the college for a fee.

Admissions Contact: George J. Machinchick, Director of Admissions.

KUTZTOWN STATE COLLEGE   E-3
Kutztown, Pennsylvania 19350   (215) 683-4060

F/T: 2269M, 3230W   Faculty: n/av; IIA, ++$
P/T: none   Ph.D.'s: n/av
Grad: 210M, 301W   S/F Ratio: 18 to 1
Year: sems, ss   Tuition: $1372 ($2312)
Appl: Sept. 1   R and B: $1480
4000 applied   2972 accepted   1705 enrolled
SAT: 450V 460M   ACT: 16   COMPETITIVE

Kutztown State College, a publicly supported institution founded in 1866, offers programs in the liberal arts and sciences. The library contains over 230,000 volumes and microtexts, and subscribes to 1800 current periodicals.

Environment: The campus, located in a rural community of 3500, about 18 miles from Allentown and Reading, covers 210 acres. The buildings include a fine arts studio, an elementary laboratory school, an electronics classroom building, a planetarium, a special education building, and dormitories accommodating 2000 men and women.

Student Life: Eighty-five percent of the students come from Pennsylvania, and about half of them are campus residents living in the dormitories; the remainder commute. Almost 12% are minority-group members. Campus housing is both coed and single-sex. There are visiting privileges in single-sex dorms. Drinking is forbidden. Resident freshmen and sophomores may not have cars on campus.

Organizations: Fifteen percent of the students belong to social fraternities and sororities.

Sports: The college offers 10 intercollegiate sports for men and 9 for women. There are 11 intramurals for men and 10 for women.

Handicapped: Ninety-five percent of the campus is accessible to handicapped students. Special facilities include wheelchair ramps, parking areas, elevators, lowered drinking fountains and telephones, and specially equipped rest rooms. Special class scheduling is also available. Fewer than 1% of the students have hearing or visual impairments; special tutoring and housing are available.

Graduates: About 17% of the freshmen fail to return after the first year; 65% of the students graduate. More than 45% of the full-time students pursue advanced study after graduation; 9% enter medical school and 10% law school. Forty-five percent enter business and industry.

Services: Students receive the following services free of charge: placement service, career counseling, psychological counseling, and tutoring. Health care and remedial instruction are available for a fee.

Programs of Study: The college confers B.A., B.F.A., B.S.Ed., and B.S. degrees, as well as master's degrees. Bachelor's degrees are offered in the following subjects: AREA STUDIES (American, Russian), BUSINESS (accounting, business/administration, computer science, economics, finance, management, marketing), EDUCATION (adult, early childhood, elementary, health/physical, secondary, special), ENGLISH (English, literature, speech), FINE AND PERFORMING ARTS (art, art education, dance, music, radio/TV, studio art, theater/dramatics), HEALTH SCIENCES (environmental health, medical technology, nursing, speech therapy), LANGUAGES (French, German, Russian, Spanish), MATH AND SCIENCES (biology, chemistry, earth science, ecology/environmental science, geology, mathematics, natural sciences, oceanography, physics), PHILOSOPHY (philosophy), PREPROFESSIONAL (engineering, forestry, law, library science, social work), SOCIAL SCIENCES (anthropology, criminal justice, geography, government/political science, history, psychology, social sciences, sociology).

Special: There are opportunities for foreign travel in certain curricula, although the college does not sponsor a program of study abroad. A professional semester is offered in the junior year for education majors. There is an accelerated degree program. It is possible to earn a combined B.A.-B.S. degree (5-year program) or a general studies degree. The college has a 3-2 cooperative program in engineering with Penn State. Student-designed majors are permitted.

Honors: Honor students may become eligible for membership in Kappa Delta Pi.

Admissions: Seventy-four percent of those who applied were accepted for the 1981–82 freshman class. The SAT scores of those who enrolled were as follows: Verbal—50% below 500, 35% between 500 and 599, 10% between 600 and 700, and 5% above 700; Math—42% below 500, 45% between 500 and 599, 10% between 600 and 700, and 3% above 700. The college requires graduation from an accredited high school with 16 completed Carnegie units. There is no cutoff by class rank or grade average. The college also considers seriously the recommendations of high school officials, and advanced placement or honors courses.

Procedure: The SAT or ACT is required. Applications should be submitted by September 1 for the fall term, and by January 15 for the spring term. There is a $10 application fee.

Special: Early and deferred admissions plans are available. AP and CLEP credit is offered.

Transfer: For fall 1981, 801 transfer students applied, 658 were accepted, and 413 enrolled. Transfers must complete, at the college, 30 of the 128 credits required for the bachelor's degree. Application deadlines are the same as those for freshmen.

Visiting: Special visiting days are held in the fall. Visitors may sit in on classes, and may stay overnight at the college by arrangement with a student friend.

Financial Aid: Eighty-five percent of the students receive financial aid; 65% work part-time on campus. Aid is available to freshmen in the form of scholarships and loans from the federal government or the college on the basis of need; CWS also is offered. Tuition may be paid on the installment plan. Those applying for financial aid should submit the FAF to the CSS before March 15 of the senior year; this is also the deadline for fall financial aid application. The spring deadline is November 1.

Foreign Students: Foreign students comprise 1% of the full-time enrollment. The college offers these students an intensive English course as well as special counseling and organizations.

Admissions: Foreign students must achieve a minimum score of 500 on the TOEFL. The SAT or ACT is also required.

Procedure: Application deadlines are June 1 (fall) and November 1 (spring). Foreign students must complete the college's health form and carry health insurance, which is available through the college for a fee. Proof of funds sufficient to cover 1 year of study is also required.

Admissions Contact: George E. McKinley, Director of Admissions.

LAFAYETTE COLLEGE F–3
Easton, Pennsylvania 18042 (215) 250-5100

F/T: 1155M, 861W	Faculty:	159; IIB, ++$
P/T: 283M, 117W	Ph.D.'s:	82%
Grad: none	S/F Ratio:	13 to 1
Year: sems, ss	Tuition:	$6000
Appl: Mar. 1	R and B:	$2275
4677 applied	1431 accepted	500 enrolled
SAT: 560V 620M		HIGHLY COMPETITIVE

Lafayette College, a private, coeducational college established in 1826, offers programs in the arts and sciences. The library contains 350,000 volumes, subscribes to 1600 periodicals, and has 7500 microfilm items on file.

Environment: Lafayette is located on a 100-acre campus in a suburban area overlooking the city of Easton, 60 miles from Philadelphia. The campus includes over 50 buildings, ranging from contemporary Kunkel Biology Hall to stately, 19th-century Pardee Hall.

Student Life: The majority of freshmen come from the Middle Atlantic States; 79% are graduates of public high schools. About 94% of the students live on campus. Thirty-eight percent are Catholic, 34% Protestant, and 12% Jewish. About 4% are minority-group members. Campus housing is both coed and single-sex. There are visiting privileges in single-sex dorms. Resident freshmen may not have cars.

Organizations: There are 17 fraternities, to which 74% of the men belong, and 5 sororities, of which 46% of the women are members. A comprehensive program of more than 70 extracurricular activities provides for the social, professional, cultural, and personal needs of the students. Nearby are the Pennsylvania Dutch country and the Pocono Mountains.

Sports: The college fields 13 intercollegiate teams for men and 11 for women. There are 25 intramural sports for men and 22 for women.

Handicapped: The campus is 60% accessible to the handicapped student. Facilities include wheelchair ramps, designated parking, elevators, and specially equipped rest rooms. One percent of the students have visual impairments, and 1% are hearing impaired. A special counselor is on hand to provide advice and assistance.

Graduates: Two percent of the freshmen drop out; 90% remain to graduate. Forty percent of the students who graduate go on to further study: 3% enter medical school; 1% dental school; and 6% law school. Sixty-one percent pursue careers in business or industry.

Services: The following services are offered at no charge to the student: psychological counseling, tutoring, remedial instruction, health care, placement service, and career counseling.

Programs of Study: The following degrees are granted: B.A., B.S., B.S.Ch., B.S.Ch.E., B.S.E.E., B.S.M.E., and B.S.Met.E. Bachelor's degrees are offered in the following subjects: AREA STUDIES (American), ENGLISH (English), FINE AND PERFORMING ARTS (art history, music, studio art), LANGUAGES (French, German, Greek/Latin, Russian, Spanish), MATH AND SCIENCES (biology, chemistry, geology, mathematics, physics), PHILOSOPHY (classics, philosophy, religion), PREPROFESSIONAL (architecture, engineering, law, medicine, ministry, veterinary), SOCIAL SCIENCES (anthropology, economics/business, government/political science, history, international relations, psychology, sociology). It is possible to earn certification in elementary and secondary education. Programs, although not majors, are available in medicine, law, and business administration. Of the degrees recently conferred, 37% were in math and sciences and 25% were in social sciences.

Special: Among the special programs offered are interdepartmental majors in history and literature, American civilization, and international affairs. A 5-year B.A.-B.S. program with different combinations available is also offered, as well as independent study. Student-designed majors are permitted. In addition to formal majors, students may take "course clusters" in a wide variety of specialized fields. Study-abroad programs sponsored by other institutions, as well as Lafayette-sponsored programs, are offered.

Honors: Seven national honor societies, including Phi Beta Kappa, have chapters on campus. Almost all departments offer honors programs.

Admissions: Thirty-one percent of those who applied were accepted for the 1981–82 freshman class. Of those who enrolled, the SAT scores were as follows: Verbal—19% below 500, 51% between 500 and 599, 28% between 600 and 700, and 2% above 700; Math—5% below 500, 33% between 500 and 599, 49% between 600 and 700, and 13% above 700. Freshmen should rank in the top 20% of their class. The candidate is expected to have satisfactorily completed 16 academic units in a college preparatory program. In addition to academic achievement and academic potential as shown by test results, the following factors are important: advanced placement or honors courses, the extracurricular record, recommendations, personality, the leadership record, and evidence of special talents.

Procedure: The SAT or ACT and 3 ATs, including the AT in English composition, are required. B.S. applicants should also take mathematics and chemistry or physics. The fall application deadline is March 1; the deadline for spring is December 15. There is a $25 application fee.

Special: Early decision, early admissions, and deferred admissions plans are offered. The application deadline for early admission is March 1; the notification date for early decision is within a month of receipt of the application. AP credit is available.

Transfer: For fall 1981, the college received 258 applications, accepted 31, and enrolled 20 students. The majority of those offered admission have achieved an above-average record at the previous institution attended. D grades do not transfer. There is a 2-year residency requirement. Students must complete, at the college, at least half of the 120–130 credits required for the bachelor's degree. Transfer application deadlines are July 1 for the fall term and December 15 for the spring term.

Visiting: The college conducts regularly scheduled orientations for prospective students. Guides are available for informal visits to the campus. Visitors may sit in on classes and stay overnight at the school. Arrangements should be made through the office of admission.

Financial Aid: About 30% of the students receive aid; 30% work part-time on campus. Financial awards such as grants, loans, work opportunities, and combinations thereof are made to freshmen. These awards range from $200 to $9225, the average being $5115. The FAF should be filed with CSS by February 1.

Foreign Students: Two percent of the full-time students come from foreign countries. The college, which actively recruits these students, offers them special counseling and special organizations.

Admissions: Foreign students must achieve a minimum score of 550 on the TOEFL. The SAT is also required.

Procedure: The application deadline is March 1 for fall entry. Students must complete a certificate-of-health form. They must also provide proof of funds adequate to cover 4 years of study. Health insurance, although not required, is available through the college for a fee.

Admissions Contact: Richard W. Haines, Director of Admissions.

LA ROCHE COLLEGE B-3
Pittsburgh, Pennsylvania 15237   (412) 367-9300

F/T: 278M, 403W		Faculty:	32; IIB, --$
P/T: 199M, 562W		Ph.D.'s:	47%
Grad: 39M, 67W		S/F Ratio:	21 to 1
Year: sems, ss		Tuition:	$2750
Appl: open		R and B:	$2050
351 applied	285 accepted		149 enrolled
SAT, ACT: not required			COMPETITIVE

La Roche College, founded in 1963, is a small, coeducational liberal arts college. The library contains 65,000 volumes and subscribes to 500 periodicals.

Environment: The 160-acre campus is located in a suburban area 12 miles from Pittsburgh. Its facilities include 5 classroom buildings and a cafeteria. The art building is equipped with laboratories and studios for the graphic arts and houses a printing plant. The Science Center provides expanded laboratory and classroom space, faculty offices, snack bar, bookstore, and Student Activities Office. Three residence halls accommodate 242 students.

Student Life: About 85% of the undergraduates are from Pennsylvania. Sixteen percent live in dormitories. Fifty-two percent of the students are Catholic, 24% are Protestant, and 1% are Jewish. About 13% are minority-group members. College housing is coed. Students may keep cars on campus.

Organizations: There is 1 national fraternity on campus. Professional and service organizations also serve as social groups. Student activities include student government, student newspaper, yearbook, drama, and choral groups.

Sports: The college fields 1 intercollegiate team for men. There are 7 intramural sports for men and 6 for women.

Handicapped: Seventy-five percent of the campus is accessible to physically handicapped students. Special facilities include special parking, wheelchair ramps, elevators, specially equipped rest rooms, lowered drinking fountains, and lowered telephones.

Graduates: The freshman dropout rate is 20%. Thirty percent of those who graduate pursue advanced study; 2% enter law school. Seventy percent enter careers in business and industry.

Services: Students receive the following services free of charge: career counseling, tutoring, remedial instruction, psychological counseling, and placement. A hospital located next to the college provides health care for a fee.

Programs of Study: All programs lead to the B.A., B.S., and B.S.N. degrees. Master's degrees are also awarded. Bachelor's degrees are offered in the following subjects: BUSINESS (accounting, bilingual administration, business administration, management), ENGLISH (English, literature, writing), FINE AND PERFORMING ARTS (communications, graphic arts, graphic design, interior design), HEALTH SCIENCES (medical technology, nursing, nursing anesthesia, radiography), LANGUAGES (bilingual administration, French, German, Spanish), MATH AND SCIENCES (biology, chemistry, mathematics, medical technology chemistry, natural sciences), PHILOSOPHY (religion), PREPROFESSIONAL (dentistry, law, medicine, veterinary), SOCIAL SCIENCES (history, psychology, social sciences, sociology). Twenty-one percent of degrees conferred are in business, 15% are in health sciences, and 15% are in social sciences.

Special: Special academic programs include internships, practicum, directed research, independent study, study abroad, and cross-registration with 9 other area institutions.

Honors: An honors program is open to qualifying seniors who are allowed to pursue independent projects.

Admissions: Eighty-one percent of those who applied were accepted for the 1981-82 freshman class. Applicants should be graduates of accredited high schools, have completed 14-16 academic units, rank in the upper 70% of their graduating class, have a C average, and have a good school recommendation. Other factors considered in the decision include personality, extracurricular activities record, and advanced placement or honors courses.

Procedure: Either the SAT or ACT is strongly recommended. Application deadlines are open. Freshmen are admitted in the fall and at midyear. Notification is on a rolling basis. There is a $15 application fee.

Special: Early and deferred admissions plans are available. CLEP and AP credit is given.

Transfer: For fall 1981, 154 students applied for full-time enrollment, 132 were accepted, and 98 enrolled. Transfers are considered for all classes. Candidates must be in good standing at the previous institution attended, with a GPA of at least 2.0. D grades are not accepted. Students must earn, at the college, at least 30 of the 120 credits necessary for a bachelor's degree. Application deadlines are open.

Visiting: Orientation is held for prospective students. Informal visits, including guided tours and interviews, can be arranged through the admissions office; visitors may sit in on classes.

Financial Aid: Eighty-five percent of all students receive some financial aid. Twenty percent work part-time on campus. Average aid to freshmen is $3304. Scholarships, grants, and loans are available. The college is a member of CSS. The State Grant Federal Student Aid Form is required. June 30 is the deadline to apply for financial aid.

Foreign Students: Fewer than one percent of the full-time students come from foreign countries. The college offers these students special counseling and special organizations.

Admissions: Foreign students must take the TOEFL but are not required to take a college entrance exam.

Procedure: Application deadlines are open. Foreign students must present a completed health form issued by the college and proof of funds adequate to cover 1 year of study. Students are also required to carry health insurance, which is available through the college for a fee.

Admissions Contact: Valerie C. Donohue, Director of Admissions.

LA SALLE COLLEGE F-3
Philadelphia, Pennsylvania 19141   (215) 951-1500

F/T: 2212M, 1746W		Faculty:	200; IIB, ++$
P/T: 2406M&W		Ph.D.'s:	70%
Grad: 1119M&W		S/F Ratio:	15 to 1
Year: sems, ss		Tuition:	$3865
Appl: Aug.1		R and B:	$2500
2924 applied	2000 accepted		900 enrolled
SAT: 490V 540M			COMPETITIVE+

La Salle College is a liberal arts institution under the auspices of the Brothers of the Christian Schools of the Roman Catholic Church. The library houses 250,000 volumes and 6378 microfilm items, and subscribes to over 1100 periodicals.

Environment: The 60-acre campus is 6 miles from the center of Philadelphia, on the eastern edge of historic Germantown. Nine residence halls accommodate 1000 men and women.

Student Life: About 70% of the students come from Pennsylvania. About 20% of entering freshmen attended public schools. Approximately 30% reside on campus. Eighty percent of the students are Catholic, 10% are Protestant, and 10% are Jewish. Eleven percent are minority-group members. Religious counselors include a chaplain for Jewish students. Chapel services are available but not required. Campus housing is both coed and single-sex. There are visiting privileges in single-sex dorms. Students may keep cars on campus. Day-care services are available to all students.

Organizations: There are 9 fraternities and 3 sororities. The student union is the center of social activities; there are also 45 extracurricular and co-curricular organizations. Off-campus recreational facilities include Fairmont Park, the world's largest city park.

Sports: There are 13 intercollegiate sports for men and 10 for women. There are 13 intramural sports for both men and women.

Handicapped: Wheelchair ramps, special parking, elevators, and specially equipped rest rooms are available for physically handicapped students.

Graduates: The freshman dropout rate is 7%; 65% remain to graduate. Forty-five percent of the graduates pursue graduate study.

758 PENNSYLVANIA

Services: Students receive free placement, health care, career and psychological counseling, tutoring, and remedial instruction.

Programs of Study: The college confers the B.A. and B.S. degrees. Associate and master's degrees are also awarded. Bachelor's degrees are offered in the following subjects: AREA STUDIES (Russian, urban), BUSINESS (accounting, business administration, business education, computer science, finance, industrial relations, management, marketing, real estate/insurance), EDUCATION (elementary, secondary, special), ENGLISH (English, journalism, literature, writing), FINE AND PERFORMING ARTS (art history, music, music education, radio/TV), LANGUAGES (French, German, Greek/Latin, Italian, Portuguese, Russian, Spanish), MATH AND SCIENCES (biology, botany, chemistry, earth science, geology, mathematics, natural sciences, physical sciences, physics, statistics, zoology), PHILOSOPHY (classics, humanities, philosophy, religion), PREPROFESSIONAL (dentistry, law, medicine, ministry, pharmacy, social work, veterinary), SOCIAL SCIENCES (economics, government/political science, history, international relations, psychology, social sciences, sociology).

Required: All students are required to take courses outside the major area. The curriculum permits students to select almost half of all courses required to graduate.

Special: The college participates in the advanced placement program. A 1-year program of studies in Switzerland or Spain and a cooperative education program, alternating work and study, are available.

Honors: Selected students are invited to participate in the honors program.

Admissions: Sixty-eight percent of those who applied were accepted for the 1981–82 freshman class. Of those who enrolled in a recent class, the SAT scores were as follows: Verbal—35% between 500 and 599, 15% between 600 and 700, and 5% above 700; Math—43% between 500 and 599, 20% between 600 and 700, and 2% above 700. Candidates must have completed at least 16 units of high school work, rank in the top 50% of their class, and have at least an 80% average. The admissions committee decision is based on the high school record, SAT scores, recommendations from high school authorities, evidence of motivation and readiness for college, and impressions made during an interview.

Procedure: The SAT or ACT is required and should be taken before February of the senior year. It is recommended that students take ATs in English composition, mathematics, and a foreign language (if the language will be continued). Those planning to live on campus should take tests no later than January of the senior year. Application deadlines are August 1 (fall) and December 15 (spring). The rolling admissions system is used. The application fee is $15.

Special: The early admissions application deadline is December 1 of the high school junior year. A deferred admissions plan is also available. CLEP general exams (except English composition) and subject exams are accepted; AP credit is given.

Transfer: For fall 1981, 458 applications were received, 340 were accepted, and 225 students enrolled. Transfers are considered for all levels. The minimum acceptable GPA is 2.25 from an accredited college or 2.75 GPA from an institution applying for accreditation; D grades do not transfer. La Salle has a 1-year residency rule. Students must complete, at the college, 50 of the 120 credits required for the bachelor's degree. Application deadlines are the same as those for freshmen.

Visiting: There is no regularly scheduled orientation for prospective students. Visits are best planned for Monday through Friday. Arrangements for a guide can be made with the admissions office. Visitors may sit in on classes and stay overnight at the school.

Financial Aid: Seventy-five percent of the students receive financial aid. Forty percent work part-time on campus. Qualified students are awarded competitive and appointive academic scholarships; all other aid is awarded on the basis of need. Federal funds through BEOG, NDSL, and CWS programs and several state loan plans are available. The college Bank Loan Plan makes it possible to spread payment over a 5-year period. The PHEAA/Composite Form is required; the college is a member of CSS. The aid application deadline is February 15.

Foreign Students: Fifty foreign students are currently enrolled at the college, which offers these students an intensive English course as well as special counseling and special organizations.

Admissions: Foreign students must achieve a score of at least 500 on the TOEFL. The SAT or ACT is also required.

Procedure: Application deadlines are August 1 (fall) and December 15 (spring). Students must present a physician's record of physical examination as proof of health. Proof of funds adequate to cover the entire period of study is also required.

Admissions Contact: Br. Lewis Mullin, F.S.C., Director of Admissions.

LEBANON VALLEY COLLEGE   E–3
Annville, Pennsylvania 17003   (717) 867-4411

F/T: 421M, 408W	Faculty:	76; IIB, +$
P/T: 35M, 58W	Ph.D.'s:	80%
Grad: none	S/F Ratio:	11 to 1
Year: sems, ss	Tuition:	$4790
Appl: May 1	R and B:	$2185
900 applied	625 accepted	275 enrolled
SAT: 460V 510M		COMPETITIVE

Lebanon Valley College, a small, private liberal arts college founded in 1866 and related to the United Methodist Church, emphasizes a rigorous academic program and individual attention to each student. Its library contains over 111,000 volumes and 11,000 microfilm items, and subscribes to more than 600 periodicals.

Environment: The campus is situated on 80 acres in a small town 6 miles from Hershey. The 35 buildings include residences, grouped in a quad, for 850 men and women, and a new music building. A $5 million science center is scheduled for completion in 1982.

Student Life: All but 30% of the students come from Pennsylvania, and 81% live on campus in the residence halls. About 85% of the freshmen come from public schools. Twenty-five percent of the students are Catholic, 70% are Protestant, and 2% are Jewish. About 3% are minority-group members. Campus housing is single-sex, and there are visiting privileges. Students may keep cars on campus. Drinking is not permitted on campus or at college functions.

Organizations: Thirty-five percent of the men belong to 3 local fraternities; 35% of the women, to 2 local sororities. There are many opportunities for students to pursue their special interests. The surrounding Pennsylvania Dutch country and nearby Hershey are popular attractions for students.

Sports: The college participates in 10 intercollegiate sports for men and 8 for women. There are 12 intramural sports available to men and 11 to women.

Graduates: About 10% of the students drop out at the end of the freshman year, and 70% remain to receive their degrees. About 60% of the graduates go on to further study; 30% pursue careers in business and industry.

Services: Students receive the following services free of charge: placement services, career counseling, health care, tutoring, and remedial instruction. Psychological counseling is available for a fee.

Programs of Study: The college confers 4 bachelor's degrees: B.A., B.S., B.S.Ch., and B.S.Med.Tech. Bachelor's degrees are offered in the following subjects: BUSINESS (accounting, business administration, computer science), EDUCATION (elementary, secondary), ENGLISH (English), FINE AND PERFORMING ARTS (music, music education), HEALTH SCIENCES (medical technology, nursing), LANGUAGES (French, German, Greek/Latin, Spanish), MATH AND SCIENCES (actuarial science, biochemistry, biology, chemistry, mathematics, operations research, physics), PHILOSOPHY (philosophy, religion), PREPROFESSIONAL (dentistry, engineering, forestry, law, medicine, ministry, pharmacy, social work, veterinary), SOCIAL SCIENCES (economics, government/political science, history, psychology, social sciences, sociology). Thirty-five percent of degrees conferred are in math and sciences; 22% are in fine and performing arts; and 25% are in business.

Required: All students are required to take courses in English composition, humanities, natural sciences, physical education, and social sciences.

Special: The college offers independent study programs in all departments. A cooperative marine biology program has recently been instituted. Study abroad, arranged by the college or other institutions, permits sophomores and juniors to travel to several foreign countries. It is possible to earn combined B.A.-B.S. degrees; student-designed majors are allowed. The college offers a cooperative program with Thomas Jefferson University in Philadelphia. This 2+2 program allows students to pursue majors in nursing, medical technology, cytotechnology, radiological technology, dental hygiene, physical therapy, and occupational therapy.

Honors: Honors programs are available in all departments of the college. Five national honor societies have chapters on campus.

Admissions: Sixty-nine percent of those who applied were accepted for the 1981–82 freshman class. For those who enrolled, the SAT scores were as follows: Verbal—62% below 500, 16% between 500 and 599, 7% between 600 and 700, and 1% above 700; Math—42%

below 500, 32% between 500 and 599, 11% between 600 and 700, and 3% above 700. Graduation from an accredited high school with a total of 16 Carnegie units is required. Records must be accompanied by a recommendation from the high school authorities. Preference is given to sons and daughters of graduates, to those with the highest SAT scores, to those who can present advanced placement or honors courses, and to those who show evidence of special talents.

Procedure: The SAT or ACT is required. A personal interview with a member of the admissions staff is necessary. The system of rolling admissions is used, and the college accepts students for both the February and September semesters. The deadline for fall admission is May 1; for spring admission, January 1. There is a $15 application fee.

Special: Early admissions, deferred admissions, and early decision plans are available. The application deadline for early admission is November 15. Advanced placement or credit or both may be given to students who score 3 or higher on the APs.

Transfer: Of 100 applications received for the current school year, 70 were accepted and 60 students enrolled. Transfers are considered for all levels. Requirements include a personal interview, high school and college transcripts, and a minimum GPA of 2.0; D grades are not accepted. To receive a bachelor's degree, students must earn 30 of the required 122 credits at the college. Deadlines are the same as for freshmen. Associate degree holders are usually granted junior status.

Visiting: Regularly scheduled orientations include course scheduling and meetings with advisors and prospective roommates. Guides are available for informal visits; visitors may stay overnight at the school and sit in on classes. Visits during the fall (September 10 to December 15) and spring (January 15 to May 15) semesters can be arranged through the dean of admissions.

Financial Aid: Eighty percent of the students receive financial assistance; 30% work part-time on campus. The college awards approximately 145 freshman scholarships each year. NDSL funds averaging $700 are granted to about 35% of the students; loans are also available from funds administered by the college and from various private sources. The maximum aid a student can expect in the freshman year is $3900 from scholarships, $2500 from loans, and $500 from campus jobs. The average amount of aid awarded is $4300 yearly. Aid is awarded on the basis of need and academic performance. The college is a member of CSS; the FAF is required, and the deadline for financial aid application is March 1.

Foreign Students: Fewer than 1% of the full-time students come from foreign countries. The college offers these students an intensive English course as well as special counseling and special organizations.

Admissions: Foreign students must achieve a score of at least 500 on the TOEFL. The SAT or ACT is not required.

Procedure: Application deadlines are the same as for freshmen. Students must take a physical examination to establish proof of health. Proof of funds sufficient to cover 12 months of study is required.

Admissions Contact: Gregory G. Stanson, Dean of Admissions.

LEHIGH UNIVERSITY   F-3
Bethlehem, Pennsylvania 18015   (215) 861-3100

F/T: 3143M, 1180W	Faculty: 399; I, +$
P/T: none	Ph.D.'s: 85%
Grad: 1289M, 756W	S/F Ratio: 15 to 1
Year: sems, ss	Tuition: $6140
Appl: Mar. 1	R and B: $2400
6796 applied	2961 accepted	1073 enrolled
SAT: 560V 640M	**HIGHLY COMPETITIVE**

Now coeducational, Lehigh University was founded in 1865 as a private, nonsectarian, residential university for men. There are 3 undergraduate colleges (Arts and Sciences, Business and Economics, and Engineering and Physical Sciences), a graduate school, and a research institute. The library contains 750,000 volumes, subscribes to 8000 periodicals, and has 480,000 microfilm items, 10,000 audiovisual units, and 80,000 government documents on file.

Environment: The university is located on a 700-acre wooded campus overlooking the Lehigh Valley in southeastern Pennsylvania, 60 miles from Philadelphia. Among the university's 64 buildings are historic Packer Chapel and the new 6000-seat Arts and Convocation Center. Eighteen dormitories, including a new 6-story apartment building, house 2255 students. Accommodations are also available in 32 fraternity houses and 3 sorority houses.

Student Life: Sixty percent of the students are from outside Pennsylvania. Forty-five percent are Catholic, 37% are Protestant, and 13% are Jewish. Three percent of the students are minority-group members. About 91% live on campus. Fraternity and sorority houses accommodate 41% of the students; 50% live in campus apartments and dormitories. Freshmen live in dormitories. Campus housing is both coed and single-sex. There are visiting privileges in single-sex dorms. Students may keep cars on campus. The university provides day-care services to children of students and faculty for a fee.

Organizations: Extracurricular activities include broadcasting, debating, drama, journalism, music, photography, and science. In addition to the more than 100 clubs, there are many campus cultural and social events, including concerts, lectures, athletic events, house parties, and exchanges with such nearby colleges as Moravian, Muhlenberg, Cedar Crest, and Lafayette. There are 32 fraternities, to which 33% of the men belong, and 3 sororities, to which 11% of the women belong.

Sports: The university participates on an intercollegiate level in 18 sports for men and 13 for women. There are 18 intramural sports for men and 19 for women.

Handicapped: The university estimates the campus to be 100% accessible to the wheelchair-bound student. Special class scheduling is available. There are 2 students with either visual or hearing impairments currently enrolled.

Graduates: The freshman dropout rate is 2%; 81% remain to graduate. Forty-four percent of the liberal arts graduates enter graduate or professional schools: 8% enter medical school, 2% dental school, and 13% law school. Ten percent of the business and engineering graduates go on for further education; 79% pursue careers in business or industry.

Services: Free services available on campus to all students include placement, career counseling, health care, tutoring, remedial instruction, and psychological counseling. Among the placement services offered to both students and alumni are on-campus interviews with representatives from business and industry. Almost 916 interviewers conducted interviews with the Class of 1981 on campus.

Programs of Study: Lehigh confers the B.A. and B.S. degrees, as well as master's and doctoral degrees. Bachelor's degrees are offered in the following subjects: AREA STUDIES (American, Italian, Jewish, Latin American, Russian, urban), BUSINESS (accounting, computer science, economics, finance, management, marketing), ENGLISH (English, journalism, literature), FINE AND PERFORMING ARTS (art, art history, music, theater/dramatics), LANGUAGES (French, German, Greek/Latin, Russian, Spanish), MATH AND SCIENCES (biochemistry, biology, chemistry, ecology/environmental science, geology, mathematics, natural sciences, physical sciences, physics, statistics, zoology), PHILOSOPHY (classics, humanities, philosophy, religion), PREPROFESSIONAL (architecture, dentistry, engineering—chemical, engineering—civil, engineering—computer, engineering—electrical, engineering—fundamental sciences, engineering—industrial, engineering—materials, engineering—mechanical, engineering—metallurgy, engineering—physics, law, medicine, ministry, pharmacy, social work), SOCIAL SCIENCES (economics, government/political science, history, international relations, psychology, social sciences, sociology). Most degrees are conferred in engineering and business.

Required: All undergraduates must take at least 1 year of English. All liberal arts undergraduates must take 1 year of study of a foreign language or culture.

Special: Curricular offerings include junior year abroad programs and programs in urban affairs and environmental and water pollution control. Also available are a 5-year B.A.-B.S. degree in liberal arts and engineering, a 5-year B.S. in engineering and M.B.A., and a 6-year medical program with the Medical College of Pennsylvania. Student-designed majors are permitted in the liberal arts.

Honors: There are 16 national honor societies, including Phi Beta Kappa and Tau Beta Pi, which was founded at Lehigh. All departments offer honors programs.

Admissions: Forty-four percent of those who applied were accepted for the 1981–82 freshman class. Of those who enrolled, the SAT scores were as follows: Verbal—17% below 500, 56% between 500 and 599, 25% between 600 and 700, and 2% above 700; Math—2% scored below 500, 22% between 500 and 599, 56% between 600 and 700, and 20% above 700. Seventy-two percent of the applicants ranked in the top fifth of their high school class. Applicants must present a minimum of 16 Carnegie units. There are no established minimums for high school class rank and GPA. The freshman class is selected on the basis of quality of secondary school records, aptitude for college study, proficiency in preparatory subjects, SAT scores, and personal qualifications. Other factors considered are advanced placement or honors courses, the extracurricular activities record, and special talent.

Procedure: The SAT, the English composition AT, and 2 additional Tests of the College Board must be taken by January of the senior year. All candidates for science and engineering are urged to take the math AT (level I or II) and the chemistry or physics AT. The deadline for application is March 1 for the fall term; a few freshmen are admitted in the spring. There is a $25 application fee. The CRDA is observed.

760 PENNSYLVANIA

Special: The university offers early admission after the junior year and early decision in the senior year (apply no later than November 1). The early decision notification date is December 15. AP credit is offered.

Transfer: For fall 1981, 370 transfer students applied, 240 were accepted, and 106 enrolled. Transfers are accepted for the freshman (second semester), sophomore, and junior years. Requirements include good standing at the previous institution attended, a B average, and the same preparatory courses required of freshmen. D grades do not transfer. The residency requirement is 1 year. Transfers must complete, at the university, 30 of the 120–140 credits necessary for the bachelor's degree. Transfer application deadlines are March 1 (fall) and October 1 (spring).

Visiting: Guides are available for informal afternoon visits to the campus when classes are in session. Visitors may sit in on classes or stay overnight at the school. For arrangements, prospective students should contact other students at Lehigh.

Financial Aid: About 20% of all students receive aid. Financial aid available to freshmen in the form of 214 scholarships totals $590,914. In addition, loans may be granted from federal and state government, local bank, and university-administered funds. Part-time work is available through CWS and institutional employment, and 10% of the students work part-time on campus. The university tries to package most awards. Amounts of aid granted to freshmen are as follows: scholarships average $2760, maximum $4700; loans or campus employment average $600, maximum $2000; all sources combined average $2700, maximum $8600. Financial need, the academic record, and leadership potential are the criteria for aid awards. Tuition may be paid in installments. The FAF should be filed with CSS before March 1.

Foreign Students: About 1% of the full-time students come from foreign countries. The university, which actively recruits these students, offers them an intensive English course as well as special counseling and special organizations.

Admissions: An English proficiency exam is not necessary. The SAT, however, is required, as are 3 ATs (English and 2 additional tests).

Procedure: The application deadline for fall entry is March 1. Foreign students must present proof of funds adequate to cover 4 years of study. They must also carry health insurance, which is available through the university for a fee.

Admissions Contact: S. H. Missimer, Director of Admission.

LINCOLN UNIVERSITY E-4
Lincoln University, Pennsylvania 19352   (215) 932-8300

F/T: 535M, 479W   Faculty: 70; IIA, +$
P/T: 18M, 22W   Ph.D.'s: 52%
Grad: 73M, 91W   S/F Ratio: 15 to 1
Year: tri, ss   Tuition: $1450 ($2150)
Appl: open   R and B: $2000
1448 applied   1013 accepted   556 enrolled
SAT: 375V 375M   LESS COMPETITIVE

Lincoln University is a state-related liberal arts institution. The library contains 160,000 volumes and 22,020 microfilm items, and subscribes to over 588 periodicals.

Environment: The 442-acre campus is located in a rural area 45 miles southwest of Philadelphia. Facilities include 12 dormitories, a life-science building, and a fine arts building.

Student Life: The university draws 33% of its students from Pennsylvania. About 80% of the students reside on campus. The student body is predominantly black. Campus housing is single-sex, and there are visiting privileges. Students may keep cars on campus.

Organizations: There are 5 fraternities and 5 sororities. Extracurricular activities include student government, special-interest clubs, movies, Varsity Club, and the newspaper. Recitals, concerts, and forums are conducted periodically, and various student dances are held by clubs and organizations.

Sports: Lincoln competes on an intercollegiate level in 8 sports for men and 6 for women. There are 13 intramural sports available to men and 10 to women.

Handicapped: There are no special facilities for the physically handicapped. No students with visual or hearing impairments are currently enrolled.

Graduates: The freshman dropout rate is 20%; 80% remain to graduate. Forty-six percent pursue graduate study after graduation, with 3% entering dental school. Forty percent pursue careers in business and industry.

Programs of Study: Undergraduate programs lead to the B.A. and B.S. degrees; master's programs are also available. Bachelor's degrees are offered in the following subjects: BUSINESS (accounting, business administration, computer science, economics), EDUCATION (secondary), ENGLISH (English), LANGUAGES (Chinese, French, German, Russian, Spanish), MATH AND SCIENCES (biology, chemistry, mathematics, physics), PHILOSOPHY (classics, philosophy, religion), PREPROFESSIONAL (architecture, dentistry, engineering, law, medicine, ministry, pharmacy, social work, veterinary), SOCIAL SCIENCES (anthropology, economics, history, international relations, psychology, social welfare, sociology).

Required: The UGRE is required during the senior year.

Special: Student-designed majors and study abroad are possible. Programs include a Black Studies Institute; a cooperative engineering program with Pennsylvania State University, Drexel Institute of Technology, and Lafayette College; exchange programs with Colgate University (students) and Princeton University (faculty); and a cooperative program in international service with American University.

Honors: Departmental honor societies include Alpha Kappa Alpha (philosophy), Beta Kappa Chi Scientific Society, Phi Kappa Epsilon (scholarship), and Mu Phi Alpha (music).

Admissions: Seventy percent of those who applied were accepted for the 1981–82 freshman class. The candidate should be a graduate of an accredited high school, rank in the upper 75% of the graduating class, have a C average or better, and have completed 15 Carnegie units. The school indicates that the minimum acceptable SAT score is 750; the minimum ACT, 16. Other factors considered are advanced placement or honors courses, recommendations by school officials, personality, extracurricular activities record, and leadership record. Some preference is given to residents of Pennsylvania.

Procedure: All candidates are required to take either the SAT or the ACT. Records should be accompanied by college-qualifying recommendations from the high school authorities. A personal interview is recommended. The university uses the system of rolling admissions. Application deadlines are open. There is a $10 application fee.

Special: An early admissions plan is offered. Early decision is available; the notification date is December 1. AP and CLEP credit is granted.

Transfer: For fall 1981, 300 applications were received, 150 were accepted, and 39 applicants were enrolled. An average of C is required; D grades do not transfer. There is a 1-year residency rule. Transfers must complete, at the university, 16 of the 128 credits required for the bachelor's degree. A rolling admissions plan is used.

Visiting: Guided tours, class visits, overnight stays, and interviews can be scheduled through the admissions office. The recommended time for visiting is Thursday evening through Saturday morning.

Financial Aid: About 87% of all students receive aid through the university. Sixty-one percent work part-time on campus. Aid awards are based on need. Students receive assistance in the form of packages which include scholarships, federal grants and NDSL, loans, and CWS. Tuition may be paid on the installment plan. The university is a member of CSS, and the FAF is required. The application deadline is June 15.

Foreign Students: Almost 7% of the full-time students come from foreign countries. An English course, an intensive English program, special counseling, and special organizations are available to these students.

Admissions: Foreign students must achieve a minimum score of 550 on the TOEFL. The SAT or ACT is not required.

Procedure: There are no application deadlines; a rolling admissions plan is used. A health form must be completed. Tuition for foreign students is $1930; fees amount to $220. Although not required, health insurance is available through the university for a fee.

Admissions Contact: Darrell C. Davis, Director of Admissions.

LOCK HAVEN STATE COLLEGE D-2
Lock Haven, Pennsylvania 17745   (800) 233-8978

F/T: 1100M, 1312W   Faculty: 166; IIB, ++$
P/T: 57M, 62W   Ph.D.'s: 46%
Grad: none   S/F Ratio: 16 to 1
Year: sems, ss   Tuition: $1372 ($2312)
Appl: June 1   R and B: $1500
1985 applied   1237 accepted   612 enrolled
SAT: 420V 460M   COMPETITIVE

Lock Haven State College is a coeducational multi-purpose institution owned by the Commonwealth of Pennsylvania and chartered in 1870. The library contains over 280,000 volumes and 213,955 microfilm items, and subscribes to more than 1234 periodicals.

Environment: The compact 135-acre rural campus is located in a town of 12,000. Residence halls accommodate 605 men and 1019 women. Off campus is the Sieg Conference Center, a 44-acre college-owned woodland with fresh-water streams.

Student Life: Eighty-one percent of the students come from Pennsylvania. About 85% of entering freshmen come from public schools. Sixty-five percent live in dormitories or fraternity houses, or other college-approved housing. Thirty-seven percent are Catholic, 44% are Protestant, and 1% are Jewish. About 4% are minority-group members. Campus housing is both coed and single-sex. There are visiting privileges in single-sex dorms. Students may keep cars on campus.

Organizations: There are 6 fraternities and 4 sororities, to which 17% of the men and 10% of the women belong. Organizations exist for Catholic and Protestant students. Cultural events take place at the John Sloan Fine Arts Center and Parsons Union Building.

Sports: Lock Haven competes on an intercollegiate level in 9 sports for men and 9 for women. There are 3 intramural sports for men and 2 for women.

Handicapped: About 50% of the campus is accessible to wheelchair students. Special rest rooms, wheelchair ramps, and elevators are available. Fewer than 1% of the students currently enrolled have visual or hearing impairments.

Graduates: The freshman dropout rate is 25%; 65% remain to graduate. About 15% of the graduates go on to full-time graduate or professional schools immediately after graduation; fewer than 5% enter medical, dental, or law school. About 25% pursue careers in business and industry.

Services: Students receive the following services free of charge: placement, career counseling, health care, tutoring, remedial instruction, and psychological counseling.

Programs of Study: The college confers the B.A., B.S., or B.S.Ed. degree in the following subjects: AREA STUDIES (Latin American), BUSINESS (computer science, management), EDUCATION (early childhood, elementary, health/physical, secondary, special), ENGLISH (English, journalism, speech), FINE AND PERFORMING ARTS (art, music, theater/dramatics), HEALTH SCIENCES (medical technology, physical therapy), LANGUAGES (French, German, Spanish), MATH AND SCIENCES (biology, chemistry, earth science, mathematics, natural sciences, physics), PHILOSOPHY (philosophy), PRE-PROFESSIONAL (dentistry, engineering, law, medicine, pharmacy, veterinary), SOCIAL SCIENCES (geography, government/political science, history, international relations, psychology, social sciences, social work, sociology). Certification programs are offered in athletic coaching and athletic training. Forty percent of degrees are conferred in education, 25% in social sciences, and 35% in math and sciences.

Required: All students must take 3 hours of physical education.

Special: Student-designed majors are permitted; a general studies (no major) degree is offered. Five-year curriculum programs are also available. Study abroad, sponsored by the college or other institutions, is available to juniors; students have traveled through such programs to England, France, Spain, Germany, Austria, Poland, and Ecuador.

Honors: The college offers (by examination) honors courses with credit to superior students. There are 2 honor societies: Kappa Delta Pi (national honor society) and Phi Kappa Phi (education).

Admissions: Sixty-two percent of those who applied were accepted for the 1981-82 freshman class. The SAT scores of those who enrolled were as follows: Verbal—88% below 500, 11% between 500 and 599, 1% between 600 and 700, and 0% above 700; Math—70% below 500, 25% between 500 and 599, 4.5% between 600 and 700, and 0.5% above 700. Applicants must be graduates of accredited 4-year high schools. The school indicates that in addition to these qualifications they consider the following factors, in order of importance: advanced placement or honors courses, recommendations by school officials, impressions made during an interview, leadership record, and extracurricular activities record.

Procedure: The SAT is required. Freshmen are admitted in September and January. Application deadlines are June 1 (fall) and December 1 (spring). The application fee is $10. The college observes a rolling admissions procedure.

Special: Early admission is possible; the application deadline is June 1 of the junior year. Deferred admission is available. Students may earn credit through AP exams.

Transfer: For fall 1981, 262 applications were received, 172 were accepted, and 115 students enrolled. Transfers are considered for all but the senior year and must present a minimum of 24 credits and a 2.0 GPA. D grades do not transfer unless an associate degree is held. Students must study at least 1 year at the college, and complete 32 of the 128 credits necessary for the bachelor's degree. Transfer application deadlines are August 1 (fall) and December 15 (spring).

Visiting: Orientation is held for prospective students, and includes a campus tour. Informal visits may be arranged through the admissions office; visitors may sit in on classes.

Financial Aid: About 85% of all students receive some form of financial aid. Thirty percent work part-time on campus. A comprehensive program of school financial aid includes scholarships, federal opportunity grants, NDSL, BEOG, work-study, and regular part-time student employment. The average award to freshmen is $2300. April 15 is the deadline for financial aid applications; the FAF is required. The college is a member of CSS.

Foreign Students: Two percent of the full-time students come from foreign countries. The college, which actively recruits these students, offers them special counseling.

Admissions: Foreign students must achieve a minimum score of 500 on the TOEFL. The ACT or SAT is not required.

Procedure: Foreign students are admitted in fall and spring. Proof of adequate funds is required.

Admissions Contact: Joseph Coldren, Director of Admissions.

LYCOMING COLLEGE D-2
Williamsport, Pennsylvania 17701 (717) 326-1951

F/T: 630M, 501W Faculty: 74; IIB, av$
P/T: 41M, 32W Ph.D.'s: 70%
Grad: none S/F Ratio: 15 to 1
Year: 4-4-1, ss Tuition: $4280
Appl. Apr. 1 R and B: $1990
1057 applied 810 accepted 318 enrolled
SAT: 440V 480M COMPETITIVE

Lycoming College is a small liberal arts and sciences institution related to the Methodist Church. The library contains over 130,000 volumes and 11,000 microfilm items, and subscribes to more than 875 periodicals.

Environment: On the 36-acre rural campus are 19 modern buildings. The academic center houses the library, a theater, a planetarium, a computer, and laboratories. There are 8 residence halls with a capacity for 450 women and 650 men.

Student Life: Sixty percent of the students come from Pennsylvania. About 75% live on campus in dormitories and fraternity houses. Thirty-three percent are Catholic, 41% are Protestant, and almost 1% are Jewish. Religious services are scheduled for various times of the year, but chapel attendance is not required. About 1% of the students are minority-group members. Campus housing is both coed and single-sex. There are visiting privileges in single-sex dorms. Students may keep cars on campus.

Organizations: Lycoming has 6 fraternities and 3 sororities; 30% of the men and 10% of the women belong. There are religious organizations for the major faiths. Other student activities include publications, dramatic and musical productions, special-interest clubs, an international semester, and a great-artists' series. Skiing, canoeing, backpacking, and hiking are popular recreational activities.

Sports: Lycoming competes on an intercollegiate level in 7 sports for men and 4 for women. There are 3 coed intramurals.

Handicapped: About 20% of the campus is accessible to wheelchair-bound students. There are no students enrolled with visual or hearing impairments. Facilities are limited: some wheelchair ramps, special parking, and elevators.

Graduates: The freshman dropout rate is 8%; 60% remain to graduate. Twenty-five percent pursue graduate study after graduation: 5% enter medical school, 5% law school, and 5% dental school. Twenty-five percent pursue careers in business and industry.

Services: Students receive free placement services, career counseling, health care, tutoring, remedial instruction, and psychological counseling. Religious counseling for students of the major faiths is also available.

Programs of Study: The college offers the B.A. degree in the following subjects: AREA STUDIES (American), BUSINESS (accounting, business administration, computer science), EDUCATION (elementary, secondary), ENGLISH (communications, English), FINE AND PERFORMING ARTS (art, music, theater/dramatics), HEALTH SCIENCES (medical technology), LANGUAGES (French, German, Spanish), MATH AND SCIENCES (astronomy, biology, chemistry, mathematics, physics), PHILOSOPHY (philosophy, religion), PRE-PROFESSIONAL (dentistry, engineering, forestry, law, medicine, veterinary), SOCIAL SCIENCES (anthropology, criminal justice, economics, government/political science, history, international relations, psychology, sociology). Twenty percent of the degrees conferred are

762 PENNSYLVANIA

in social sciences, 20% are in math and sciences, and 16% are in business.

Required: Liberal arts distribution courses are required.

Special: Programs in engineering with Pennsylvania State University and Bucknell University (3-2) and in forestry with Duke University (3-2) are offered. A B.F.A. in sculpture is offered as a cooperative program (3-1) with Johnson Atelier, Princeton, New Jersey. Other special programs include junior year abroad, an accelerated degree program, a self-designed major, and Washington, United Nations, and London Semesters.

Honors: All departments offer honors programs and internships. The Lycoming Scholar Program has been developed for students with high academic promise; it permits an increased amount of interdisciplinary study. There are 9 honor societies on campus.

Admissions: Seventy-seven percent of those who applied were accepted for the 1981–82 freshman class. The SAT scores of those who enrolled were as follows: Verbal—80% below 500, 15% between 500 and 599, 4% between 600 and 700, and 1% above 700; Math—55% below 500, 35% between 500 and 599, 8% between 600 and 700, and 2% above 700. The candidate should have completed 16 Carnegie units, be a graduate of an accredited secondary school, rank in the upper two-fifths of the class (for public school students), and be recommended by school officials. Private school students, from smaller classes, are evaluated on an individual basis. Additional factors considered, in order of importance, are the secondary school record, advanced placement or honors courses, personality, extracurricular activities, and leadership potential.

Procedure: Either the SAT or the ACT is required. There is a non-refundable application fee of $15. The college subscribes to the CRDA. Freshmen are admitted on a rolling schedule. The preferred deadlines for application are April 1 (fall), December 1 (spring), and May 1 (summer).

Special: Early admissions, early decision, and deferred admissions plans are available. CLEP general and subject exams are accepted; AP credit is also given.

Transfer: For fall 1981, 95 applications were received, 75 were accepted, and 52 applicants enrolled. Transfers are considered for all levels and must have a minimum 2.0 GPA. D grades are accepted. Students must complete, at the college, 32 of the 128 credit hours required for the bachelor's degree. Transfer application deadlines are August 1 (fall) and December 1 (spring).

Visiting: There are no regularly scheduled orientations for prospective students. Visitors are encouraged to write or call for an appointment. Guided tours, class visits, and interviews can be arranged through the admissions office. Visitors may remain overnight on campus (Sunday night through Thursday night).

Financial Aid: Forty-five percent of all students receive aid through the school, 33% work part-time on campus. Recently, 175 freshman scholarships averaging $900 were awarded. Financial aid is available through federal, state, and local banks loans and campus employment. Tuition may be paid on the installment plan. The college is a member of the CSS. The FAF is required, and the aid application should be filed by April 1.

Foreign Students: Lycoming accepts foreign students.

Admissions: The TOEFL is required. Students must score in the 50th percentile. College entrance exams are not necessary. Each applicant is evaluated individually.

Procedure: Application deadlines are April 1 (fall), December 1 (spring), and May 1 (summer).

Admissions Contact: Office of Admissions.

MANSFIELD STATE COLLEGE D-1
Mansfield, Pennsylvania 16933 (717) 662-4243

F/T: 1066M, 1084W	Faculty:	193; IIA, ++$
P/T: 113M, 191W	Ph.D.'s:	50%
Grad: 54M, 167W	S/F Ratio:	14 to 1
Year: sems, ss	Tuition:	$1366 ($2306)
Appl: Mar 1	R and B:	$1626
1882 applied	1638 accepted	671 enrolled
SAT: 487V 520M		COMPETITIVE

Mansfield State College, founded in 1857, is a publicly supported institution offering programs in education, liberal arts, and preprofessional fields. The library contains over 180,000 volumes and 470,000 microfilm items, and subscribes to more than 2340 periodicals.

Environment: The campus is located in a rural setting. Five dormitories provide housing for 2000 students; a cafeteria, student lounge, dining hall, and lockers are available to commuting students.

Student Life: Ninety-three percent of the students come from Pennsylvania and about 90% are graduates of public schools. About 80% live on campus. Six percent of the students are minority-group members. College housing is both coed and single-sex. There are visiting privileges in single-sex dorms. Students may keep cars on campus. Alcoholic beverages are prohibited on campus. Day-care services are available to all students.

Organizations: Twenty percent of the men belong to 4 national fraternities, and 20% of the women belong to 4 national sororities. About 100 cocurricular activities, including student government, politics, debate, art, music, science, dramatics, religion, education, and community services, are available. College assemblies and evening performances feature concerts, guest speakers, and similar programs.

Sports: The college participates in 16 intercollegiate sports; 8 for men and 8 for women. There are 11 intramural sports for men and 9 for women.

Handicapped: Five percent of the campus is accessible to handicapped students. Special facilities include wheelchair ramps, parking areas, elevators, and specially-equipped rest rooms.

Graduates: Thirty percent of the freshmen drop out by the end of the first year; 55% remain to graduate. Forty percent of the graduates pursue study in graduate or professional schools.

Services: Students receive the following services free of charge: placement services, career counseling, health care, psychological counseling, tutoring, and remedial instruction.

Programs of Study: The college confers the degrees of B.A., B.M., B.S., and B.S.Ed., as well as master's and associate (2-year) degrees. Bachelor's degrees are offered in the following subjects: BUSINESS (accounting, business administration, computer science), EDUCATION (adult, early childhood, elementary, secondary, special), ENGLISH (English, literature, speech), FINE AND PERFORMING ARTS (art, art education, art history, music, music education, radio/TV, studio art, theater/dramatics), HEALTH SCIENCES (medical technology), LANGUAGES (Spanish), MATH AND SCIENCES (biology, chemistry, earth science, mathematics, physical sciences, physics), PHILOSOPHY (philosophy), PREPROFESSIONAL (engineering, home economics, law, medicine, social work), SOCIAL SCIENCES (anthropology, economics, geography, government/political science, history, psychology, social sciences, sociology).

Special: Students may arrange to spend their junior year abroad. Public school nursing certification is offered. Also available are the Washington semester, a general studies (no major) degree, a self-designed major, and the upper-lower division concept, in which a student need not declare a major until the beginning of the junior year. Combined B.A.-B.S.Ed. degrees can be earned in biology, earth science, engineering, and other areas.

Honors: Thirteen national honor societies have chapters on campus. All departments of the college participate in a campus-wide honors program.

Admissions: Eighty-seven percent of those who applied were accepted for the 1981–82 freshman class. For those who enrolled in a recent class, the SAT scores were as follows: Verbal—2% were between 500 and 599, and 2% between 600 and 700; Math—2% were between 500 and 599. A candidate must graduate from an accredited high school and have completed 15 Carnegie units. Applicants should rank in the top 60% of the high school class and have a grade average of at least 2.5. Of primary importance in the admissions decision are test scores and recommendations from the student's high school. Also considered are advanced placement or honors courses, impressions made during the interview, and evidence of special talent.

Procedure: The SAT or ACT is required. The application deadline for fall admission is March 1. Freshmen are admitted in the fall, spring, and summer. Applicants are notified on a rolling basis. There is a $10 application fee.

Special: Early admissions and early decision plans are available. CLEP general exams are accepted; students may also earn AP credit.

Transfer: For fall 1981, the college enrolled 154 transfer students. Transfers are accepted for all but the senior year and must complete, at the college, 30 of the 128 credits required for the bachelor's degree. There is also a 1-year residency requirement. A GPA of 2.0 is required, as well as honorable dismissal from the previous institution. D grades are accepted. Transfer application deadlines are the same as for freshmen.

Visiting: Regularly scheduled visitation days include presentations by the offices of admissions, placement, financial aid, and student affairs;

tours; and meetings with the faculty. Guides are available for informal visits by appointment; visitors may stay overnight at the school and sit in on classes. Arrangements should be made through the admissions office.

Financial Aid: Seventy-five percent of the students receive aid in the form of scholarships, state and federal employment, federal grants, and NDSL, state higher-education, and college loans. Fifteen percent work part-time on campus. Tuition may be paid in installments. Deadlines for financial aid are August 15 for the fall term and January 1 for the spring term; the FAF and PHEAA must be filed. The college is a member of CSS.

Foreign Students: Foreign students comprise less than 1% of the full-time enrollment. The college actively recruits these students and offers them an intensive English program as well as special counseling and special organizations.

Admissions: A score of 500 must be achieved on the TOEFL. The SAT or ACT is also required.

Procedure: Application deadlines are June 1 (fall), December 1 (spring), and March 1 (summer). Students must take a physical exam to establish proof of health. Proof of funds adequate to cover at least 1 year is required. Although not required, health insurance is available through the college for a fee.

Admissions Contact: John J. Abplanalp, Director of Admissions.

MARYWOOD COLLEGE E–2
Scranton, Pennsylvania 18509 (717) 348-6234

F/T: 188M, 1490W   Faculty: 160; IIA, –$
P/T: 27M, 149W   Ph.D.'s: 80%
Grad: 327M, 714W   S/F Ratio: 16 to 1
Year: sems, ss   Tuition: $2590
Appl: Mar. 1   R and B: $1850
837 applied   700 accepted   425 enrolled
SAT: 440V 450M   ACT: 22   LESS COMPETITIVE

Marywood College, founded in 1915, is conducted by the Sisters, Servants of the Immaculate Heart of Mary, and offers a liberal arts education on the graduate and undergraduate levels. The Learning Resource Center houses a library that contains over 157,000 volumes and 3419 microfilms, and subscribes to 1500 periodicals.

Environment: The 180-acre campus is located in a suburban area 110 miles from Philadelphia and 120 miles from New York City. Among the 20 major buildings are 3 dormitories and 3 townhouses accommodating over 600 women. A new physical education building is under construction.

Student Life: About 81% of the students are from Pennsylvania. Approximately 40% live on campus. About 62% of entering freshmen come from public schools. The majority of students are Catholic. Religious service attendance is not compulsory. Eight percent of the students are minority-group members. College housing is single-sex, and there are no visiting privileges. A liberal and flexible curfew is observed. Students may keep cars on campus.

Organizations: There are no sororities or fraternities. Extracurricular activities include departmental clubs, drama and music groups, and publications; social and cultural events including formal dances, concerts, mixers, plays, and guest artists and lecturers. Nearby, the Pocono Mountains provide skiing and other recreational facilities.

Sports: The college competes intercollegiately in 8 sports for women. There are 16 intramural sports for women, none for men.

Handicapped: Wheelchair ramps, elevators, and lowered telephones and drinking fountains are available for the physically handicapped; 100% of the campus is accessible to these students. Fewer than 1% of the students have visual impairments, and 1% are hearing impaired. Services are provided by the tutoring center.

Graduates: Five percent of the freshmen drop out by the end of the first year; 66% remain to graduate. Of those, 30% pursue graduate study.

Services: Students receive free psychological counseling, health care, placement services, career counseling, tutoring, and remedial instruction. The Psycho-Educational Clinic provides diagnostic and remedial services. Pastoral counseling is also available for Catholic students.

Programs of Study: The college confers the B.A., B.Mus., B.S., B.S.N., B.S.W., and master's degrees. Bachelor's degrees are offered in the following subjects: BUSINESS (accounting, business administration, business education, computer science, management, marketing), EDUCATION (adult, early childhood, elementary, health/physical, secondary, special), ENGLISH (English, journalism, literature), FINE AND PERFORMING ARTS (art, art education, art history, music, music education, radio/TV, studio art, theater/dramatics), HEALTH SCIENCES (medical technology, nursing, speech therapy), LANGUAGES (French, German, Italian, Spanish), MATH AND SCIENCES (biology, chemistry, mathematics, physics), PREPROFESSIONAL (engineering, law, library science, medicine, ministry, pharmacy, social work, veterinary), SOCIAL SCIENCES (government/political science, international relations, psychology, social sciences, sociology).

Required: A candidate for the B.S. must complete courses in the liberal arts, including the humanities, foreign language and literature, social science, and natural sciences.

Special: Students may study abroad for a year, a semester, or a summer. Also available are joint majors, a 3-year bachelor's degree, a combined 5-year B.A.-B.S. degree, opportunity courses (in which students and faculty initiate courses), student-designed majors, a 5-year master's program, and independent study.

Honors: Ten honor societies have chapters on campus. Honors research provides advanced students with the opportunity for research, culminating in a long essay.

Admissions: Eighty-four percent of those who applied were accepted for the 1981–82 freshman class. Candidates should graduate from an accredited school and should complete 16 academic units. Candidates should rank in the top two-fifths of their class and have a GPA of at least 2.5. The standards and reputation of the high school are also considered. Other important factors include test scores, advanced placement or honors courses, recommendations from high school officials, leadership potential, and the extracurricular activities record.

Procedure: The SAT or ACT is required and should be taken no later than February of the senior year. The application, high school record, test scores, and a $20 nonrefundable fee should be submitted by March 1 (fall) and December 1 (spring). Notification on a rolling basis starts 1 month after receipt of all credentials. Freshmen are also admitted in the summer.

Special: The application deadline for early decision is November 1; notification is by December 1. The early admissions application deadline is March 1. A deferred admissions plan is also offered. CLEP and AP credit is granted.

Transfer: For fall 1981, 200 applications were received, 180 were accepted, and 150 students enrolled. Transfers are not considered for the senior year. A 2.5 GPA is required; D grades are not acceptable. Transfers must complete in residence 60 of the 124 credits required for the bachelor's degree. Application deadlines are the same as for freshmen.

Visiting: There are regularly scheduled orientations for prospective students. Visits are best scheduled in the fall or spring; arrangements for a guided tour, class visits, and overnight stays can be made through the admissions office.

Financial Aid: Eighty percent of the students receive financial aid; 75% work part-time on campus. The college, a member of CSS, grants several freshman scholarships; in addition, students receive grants and scholarships from other public and private sources. Federal and state government loans are available to qualified students. Earnings from campus employment average about $500. A number of talent scholarships are granted to students in music, art, and drama. Aid awards are based on need and academic promise. The FAF must be filed. The aid application deadline is February 1.

Foreign Students: Forty-five foreign students are currently enrolled at the college. An English course, an intensive English program, special counseling, and special organizations are available to these students.

Admissions: Foreign students must achieve a minimum score of 500 on the TOEFL. The SAT or ACT is also required.

Procedure: The application deadline for fall entry is March 1. Students must furnish proof of health and carry health insurance, which is available through the college. Proof of adequate funds for study at the college is also required.

Admissions Contact: Sr. M. Gabriel Kane, Director of Admissions.

MERCYHURST COLLEGE B–1
Erie, Pennsylvania 16546 (814) 825-4000

F/T: 428M, 667W   Faculty: 75; IIB, av$
P/T: 131M, 215W   Ph.D.'s: 50%
Grad: 21M, 16W   S/F Ratio: 15 to 1
Year: 4-3-3, ss   Tuition: $3777
Appl: open   R and B: $1775
800 applied   680 accepted   357 enrolled
SAT: 450V 450M   ACT: 20   LESS COMPETITIVE

764 PENNSYLVANIA

Founded in 1926 by the Sisters of Mercy, Mercyhurst is a distinctive liberal arts college with a Catholic heritage. It is a fully accredited, 4-year institution with programs in the arts and sciences, professional preparation, and technology. The library contains over 75,000 volumes and subscribes to more than 600 periodicals.

Environment: The 75-acre campus is in the suburban Glenwood Hills section of Erie, centrally located between Pittsburgh (125 miles away), Buffalo, and Cleveland. Buildings include a campus center (athletic facility) that seats 2000 people. Three dormitories, 8 townhouses, and 3 apartment houses accommodate 750 students.

Student Life: About 70% of the students come from Pennsylvania; the rest come from 14 other states and 8 foreign countries. Sixty-five percent live on campus. Sixty percent of the students are Catholic, 38% are Protestant, and 1% are Jewish. Eight percent are minority-group members. Campus housing is single-sex, and there are visiting privileges. Students may have cars on campus. The college provides day-care services to all students for a fee.

Organizations: There are no fraternities or sororities. Nearby recreational facilities include the Erie County Fieldhouse and the Erie Playhouse. There are over 30 clubs and organizations available to students, including student government and 2 publications. The Campus Ministry provides spiritual and community services to the student population.

Sports: There are 8 intercollegiate sports for men and 7 for women. Intramurals consists of 8 sports for men and 8 for women.

Handicapped: Eighty-five percent of the campus is accessible to the physically handicapped. Specially equipped rest rooms and elevators are provided. There is one special counselor for handicapped students.

Graduates: At the end of the freshman year 23% of the students drop out; 60% remain to graduate. Fifteen percent of the graduates continue their studies in the areas of business, law, and medicine.

Services: Health care, tutoring, remedial instruction, career counseling, and placement services are provided without charge.

Programs of Study: The college offers the B.A., B.M., or B.S. degree. Associate and master's degrees are also awarded. Bachelor's degrees are offered in the following subjects: BUSINESS (accounting, business administration, business education, computer science, hotel and restaurant management, management), EDUCATION (early childhood, elementary, secondary, special), ENGLISH (English, journalism), FINE AND PERFORMING ARTS (art, art education, art therapy, dance, music, music education, radio/TV, studio art), HEALTH SCIENCES (foods and nutrition/dietetics, medical technology, nursing), MATH AND SCIENCES (biology, chemistry, earth science, ecology/environmental science, geology, mathematics, petroleum geology), PHILOSOPHY (lay ministry, religious education), PREPROFESSIONAL (dentistry, fashion merchandising, home economics, interior design, law, medicine, pharmacy, social work), SOCIAL SCIENCES (government/political science, history, psychology, public administration, social sciences, sociology). Forty percent of degrees are conferred in business, 20% in education, and 18% in the social sciences.

Special: Student-designed majors are allowed, and a general studies degree is offered. The college offers independent study, a 3-year bachelor's degree program, a seminar in business enterprises, and studio art courses for liberal arts students. Paid internships are offered in 23 of the 35 major programs with no restrictions on location.

Honors: There are 7 honor societies for qualified students.

Admissions: Eighty-five percent of the applicants to the 1981-82 freshman class were accepted. The SAT scores of those who enrolled were as follows: Verbal—74% below 500, 20% between 500 and 599, 5% between 600 and 700, and 1% above 700; Math—74% below 500, 20% between 500 and 599, 5% between 600 and 700, and 1% above 700. On the ACT, 74% sscored below 21, 15% between 21 and 23, 7% between 24 and 25, 3% between 26 and 28, and 1% above 28. An applicant should have completed 16 Carnegie units with a grade average of at least C+. Other factors considered are advanced placement or honors courses, recommendations by school officials, impressions made during an interview, and the extracurricular activities record.

Procedure: The SAT or the ACT is required. There is no application deadline. Admissions are made on a rolling basis. Freshmen are admitted to all terms. The application fee is $20.

Special: There are early admissions, early decision, and deferred admissions plans. CLEP and AP credit is given.

Transfer: For fall 1981, 180 transfer students applied, 150 were accepted, and 80 enrolled. Transfer students must have GPA of 2.0 and a recommendation from the dean of students. D grades do not transfer. Students must complete, at the college, 45 of the 120 credit hours required for the bachelor's degree. There is no application deadline.

Visiting: There are regularly scheduled orientations for prospective students. Informal visits can be arranged through the admissions office. Tours will be provided; visitors may sit in on classes and stay overnight at the school. The beginning of each term is the most favorable time for visitors.

Financial Aid: Eighty-five percent of the students receive financial aid. Fifty percent work part-time on campus. The average award to freshmen is $2000. Sources of funds include PHEAA grants and loans, athletic grants from the college, federal grants and loans, and work-study. Applications for aid should be submitted by March 15. The FAF and PHEAA must be filed. The college is a member of CSS.

Foreign Students: About 1% of the full-time students come from foreign countries. The college offers these students special counseling and special organizations.

Admissions: A score of 550 must be achieved on the TOEFL. The SAT or ACT is not required.

Procedure: Application deadlines are July 15 (fall), November 15 (winter), January 15 (spring), and April 15 (summer). Proof of funds adequate to cover 4 years of study is required. Students must carry health insurance, which is available through the college for a fee.

Admissions Contact: Thomas A. Billingsley, Director of Admissions.

MESSIAH COLLEGE D-3
Grantham, Pennsylvania 17027 (717) 766-2511

F/T: 535M, 836W	Faculty: 60; IIB, +$
P/T: 31M, 63W	Ph.D.'s: 63%
Grad: none	S/F Ratio: 18 to 1
Year: 4-1-4, ss	Tuition: $3690
Appl: July 1	R and B: $1900
835 applied	678 accepted 441 enrolled
SAT: 502V 530M	ACT: 23 COMPETITIVE+

Messiah College, founded in 1909, is a Christian liberal arts institution. The library houses over 110,000 volumes and 500,000 microfilm items, and subscribes to more than 180 periodicals.

Environment: The 175-acre suburban campus, located 10 miles from Harrisburg, has a branch campus in Philadelphia. Among the 21 buildings are a science building, a fine arts building, and 7 dormitories with double rooms accommodating 600 women and 500 men.

Student Life: Sixty-eight percent of the students come from Philadelphia. About 93% reside on campus. Ninety-eight percent of the students are Protestant; chapel attendance is required twice a week. Six percent of the students are minority-group members. Campus housing is single-sex, and there are visiting privileges. Smoking and alcoholic beverages are prohibited on campus. Freshmen may not have cars on campus.

Organizations: There are no sororities or fraternities. Extracurricular activities include a variety of special-interest clubs, publications, Christian service organizations, music and drama groups, and a music-lecture series. Popular outdoor recreational activities include hiking, skiing, canoeing, fishing, and ice skating.

Sports: The college competes on an intercollegiate level in 6 sports for men and 5 for women. There are 5 intramural sports for men and 6 for women.

Handicapped: Wheelchair ramps, special parking, elevators, specially equipped rest rooms, and lowered telephones and drinking fountains are available for the physically handicapped; 80% of the campus is accessible to these students. One percent of the students are visually impaired.

Graduates: The freshman dropout rate is 22%; 57% remain to graduate. Thirty percent of the graduates pursue graduate study, with 1% entering medical school and 1% entering law school. Twenty-three percent begin careers in business and industry.

Services: Students receive free psychological counseling, health care, placement services, and career counseling.

Programs of Study: The college confers the B.A. and B.S. degrees. Bachelor's degrees are offered in the following subjects: BUSINESS (accounting, business administration, computer science), EDUCATION (Christian education, early childhood, elementary, health/physical, secondary), ENGLISH (English, journalism, speech), FINE AND PERFORMING ARTS (art, film/photography, music, music education, radio/TV, theater/dramatics), HEALTH SCIENCES (dietetics, medical technology, nursing), LANGUAGES (French, German, Spanish), MATH AND SCIENCES (biology, chemistry, mathematics, natural sciences, physics), PHILOSOPHY (philosophy, religion), PREPROFESSIONAL (dentistry, engineering, home economics, law, library science, medicine, ministry, pharmacy, social work, veterinary), SOCIAL

SCIENCES (government/political science, history, psychology, sociology). Thirty percent of the degrees are conferred in business, 20% in education, and 15% in math and sciences.

Required: All students must take interdisciplinary courses in the liberal arts area, Biblical literature, and physical education.

Special: A cooperative arrangement with Temple University gives students access to most of the major programs available there. Independent study, junior year abroad, and student-designed major programs are possible.

Admissions: Eighty-one percent of those who applied were accepted for the 1981–82 freshman class. Of those who enrolled, the SAT scores were as follows: Verbal—61% below 500, 31% between 500 and 599, 7% between 600 and 700, and 1% above 700; Math—46% below 500, 35% between 500 and 599, 18% between 600 and 700, and 1% above 700. Candidates should graduate from an accredited high school, should rank in the upper half of their graduating class, and should have completed 16 Carnegie units. Recommendations from the school and friends are required. The minimum composite SAT score expected is 850; the minimum composite ACT score is 19. Also considered are advanced placement or honors courses, special talents, and leadership record.

Procedure: The SAT or ACT is required and should be taken by March of the senior year. A personal interview is important but not required. Application deadlines are July 1 (fall), December 1 (spring), and May 1 (summer). Admission is on a rolling basis. The application fee is $15.

Special: Early decision and deferred admissions plans are available. CLEP general and subject exams are accepted.

Transfer: For fall 1981, 160 applications were received, 121 were accepted, and 79 students enrolled. Transfers are considered for all classes. A 2.5 GPA is required; D grades do not transfer. Students must complete, at the college, 30 of the 123 credits required for the bachelor's degree. Application deadlines are the same as for freshmen.

Visiting: The orientation program includes a tour of the campus, an admission and financial aid session, a meal, and a meeting with the curriculum counselor. Informal visits are best planned for late in the morning before lunch. Visit arrangements, including a guided tour, can be made through the admissions office. Visitors may sit in on classes and stay overnight at the school.

Financial Aid: Seventy percent of the students receive financial aid. Thirty-one percent work part-time on campus. Loans and grants are available from the federal and state governments, the college, and private sources. The college also provides academic scholarships and employment opportunities. The average award to freshmen is $1150. The college is a member of CSS and requires the FAF. The application deadline is April 1. Tuition may be paid in installments.

Foreign Students: Two percent of the full-time students come from foreign countries. The college offers these students special counseling and special organizations.

Admissions: Students must obtain a minimum score of 550 on the TOEFL. The SAT or ACT is also required. A composite score of 850 on the SAT is necessary.

Procedure: Application deadlines are April 1 (fall) and September 1 (spring). Proof of funds adequate to cover 4 years of study is required. Health insurance, while not required, is available through the college for a fee.

Admissions Contact: Ron E. Long, Director of Admissions.

MILLERSVILLE STATE COLLEGE E-4
Millersville, Pennsylvania 17551 (717) 872-3371

F/T: 2090M, 2504W	Faculty:	308; IIA, ++$
P/T: 443M, 726W	Ph.D.'s:	56%
Grad: 218M, 483W	S/F Ratio:	15 to 1
Year: sems, ss	Tuition:	$1398 ($2338)
Appl: open	R and B:	$1502
3945 applied	2996 accepted	1661 enrolled
SAT: 459V 502M		COMPETITIVE

Millersville State College was founded as the Millersville Normal School in 1855. The library contains over 360,000 volumes and 48,450 microfilm items, and subscribes to more than 3145 periodicals.

Environment: The suburban campus is located 3 miles from Lancaster, and is 60 miles from Philadelphia. Eleven dormitories, 3 of them coed, accommodate 2650 students; private dormitories are available off campus for upperclassmen. A few male students live in private homes.

Student Life: All but 5% of the students are from Pennsylvania, and 86% are public school graduates. About 42% of the students commute; 58% live on campus. Almost 9% of the students are minority-group members. College housing is both coed and single-sex. There are visiting privileges in single-sex dorms. Upperclassmen may have cars on campus.

Organizations: There are 10 fraternities and 10 sororities to which 18% of the men and 20% of the women belong. Activities center around some 40 clubs, religious organizations, civic groups, and professional societies.

Sports: The college competes in 11 intercollegiate sports for men and 7 for women. There are 10 intramural sports for men and 8 for women.

Handicapped: About 20% of the campus is accessible to wheelchair students. Ramps, special parking, and special class scheduling are provided for these students.

Graduates: Eighteen percent of the freshmen drop out by the end of the first year; about 64% remain to graduate. Some 24% of the graduates pursue graduate studies; 1% enter medical school. Fifteen percent pursue careers in business and industry.

Services: Students receive the following services free of charge: placement, health care, psychological counseling, career counseling, tutoring, and remedial instruction. There are placement services for both students and graduates.

Programs of Study: The college confers the B.A., B.S., and B.S.Ed. degrees. Associate and master's degrees are also given. Bachelor's degrees are offered in the following subjects: BUSINESS (business administration, computer science), EDUCATION (early childhood, elementary, secondary, special), ENGLISH (English), FINE AND PERFORMING ARTS (art, art education, music, music education), HEALTH SCIENCES (medical technology), LANGUAGES (French, German, Greek/Latin, Russian, Spanish), MATH AND SCIENCES (biochemistry, biology, chemistry, earth science, ecology/environmental science, mathematics, physics), PHILOSOPHY (philosophy), PRE-PROFESSIONAL (dentistry, engineering, law, medicine, social work), SOCIAL SCIENCES (anthropology, economics, geography, government/political science, history, psychology, social sciences, sociology). About 40% of the undergraduate degrees conferred are in education, 24% are in math and sciences, and 15% are in social sciences.

Required: All students must take 60 hours of general education and 4 or 5 hours of physical education.

Special: A study-abroad program is available to juniors. There is a 3-2 engineering program with Pennsylvania State University and the University of Pennsylvania.

Honors: A departmental honors program allows superior students intensive study within their major.

Admissions: About 76% of the students who applied for the 1981–82 freshman class were accepted. Of those who enrolled, the SAT scores were as follows: Verbal—70% below 500, 25% between 500 and 599, 4% between 600 and 700, and 0.1% above 700; Math—47% below 500, 44% between 500 and 599, 8% between 600 and 700, and 1% above 700. Admission is based on the secondary school record, class rank, and SAT scores. Other factors considered by the school in order of importance are: advanced placement or honors courses, evidence of special talent, and the extracurricular activities record. Pennsylvania residents are given preference.

Procedure: The SAT or ACT is required. There is a rolling admissions program with no application deadline. The application fee is $10.

Special: There is an early admissions plan with an application deadline of the end of the junior year. CLEP and AP credit is given.

Transfer: For fall 1981, 521 applications were received, 435 were accepted, and 296 students enrolled. Transfers are considered for the sophomore and junior classes. Applicants must have a minimum 2.0 average for 1 year; D grades transfer only for Pennsylvania community college graduates. Preference is given to state residents. Transfers must complete, at the college, 30 of the 120–128 credits necessary for the bachelor's degree. Deadlines are the same as for freshmen.

Visiting: Orientations are held regularly. Guides are available for informal visits while school is in session; visitors may sit in on classes. Arrangements should be made with the admissions office.

Financial Aid: About 80% of all students receive some financial aid. Thirty percent work part-time on campus. Limited scholarships are available for freshmen. The average award to freshmen is $1100. Loans are available. Aid applications must be submitted by May 1. The college is a member of CSS.

Foreign Students: Foreign students comprise about 1% of the full-time enrollment. Special counseling and special organizations are available to these students.

PENNSYLVANIA

Admissions: Students must achieve a minimum score of 500 on the TOEFL. College entrance exams are not required.

Procedure: Application deadlines are April 1 (fall), October 1 (spring), and March 1 (summer). Students must furnish a physician's statement as proof of health and carry health insurance, which is available through the college for a fee. Proof of funds sufficient to cover 1 year of study is required.

Admissions Contact: Blair E. Treasure, Director of Admissions.

MOORE COLLEGE OF ART F-3
Philadelphia, Pennsylvania 19103 (215) 568-4515

F/T: 450W		Faculty:	51; IIB, –$
P/T: 100W		Ph.D.'s:	6%
Grad: none		S/F Ratio:	9 to 1
Year: sems, ss		Tuition:	$4400
Appl: open		R and B:	$2150
220 applied	138 accepted		86 enrolled
SAT: 450V 350M	ACT: 17		SPECIAL

Founded in 1844, Moore is the only college of art exclusively for women in the United States. It is privately endowed and nonsectarian, and seeks to prepare young women for careers in the fine and applied arts. The library contains over 31,000 volumes, a 190,000-item picture collection, and 40,000 slides, and subscribes to more than 245 periodicals.

Environment: The campus is located in the center of Philadelphia and consists of 8 major buildings. Residence halls accommodate 60% of the student body. The freshman dormitory is located next to the main classroom building; upperclass students are transported by college bus to apartment-type dorms several blocks away.

Student Life: Approximately 50% of the students come from Pennsylvania; 75% are graduates of public schools. Three percent are minority-group members. There are visiting privileges in the dorms. Cars are permitted, but parking is a problem.

Organizations: There are no sororities. Extracurricular activities include a concert and lecture series, an art gallery program, and a film series. Social life is augmented by mixers with nearby colleges. Student government is in the hands of the student government association, the residence council, and the judiciary committee. Popular off-campus attractions include the Philadelphia Museum of Art, the Rodin Museum, and the Academy of Natural Sciences.

Handicapped: The entire campus is accessible to wheelchair-bound students; there are elevators for their use.

Graduates: No more than 11% of the students drop out at the end of the freshman year; 85% remain to graduate. Two percent of graduates pursue further education after graduation; 1% enter medical school.

Services: Students receive the following services free of charge: placement service, career counseling, psychological counseling, tutoring, and remedial instruction. Health care is available for a fee.

Programs of Study: The college offers the B.F.A. degree in 11 fields: advertising, ceramics, fashion illustration and design, illustration, interior design, jewelry, painting, photography, printmaking, sculpture, and textiles. Sixty percent of degrees conferred are in applied arts; 40% are in fine arts.

Required: All freshmen must take courses in drawing, figure drawing, design, lettering, general studies, and the history of world art. Upperclass students must complete courses in humanities, science, social science, art history, and related arts.

Special: The college offers a cooperative education program during the senior year. It is possible to earn combined B.F.A.-B.S. degrees in fine or applied arts/art education; student-designed majors are available. Study abroad is possible.

Admissions: Sixty-three percent of those who applied were accepted for the 1981–82 freshman class. The college preferes scores of 400 or better on the verbal SAT (recently 17% scored between 500 and 600), but allows some flexibility. Students must graduate from an accredited high school or the equivalent with a minimum class rank in the upper 40% and a grade average of at least 2.0. As many art courses as possible should be included in the high school program. Important factors are evidence of special talents, advanced placement or honors courses, and recommendations by school officials.

Procedure: The SAT or ACT is required. In addition, a portfolio must be submitted. A personal interview, though not required, should be arranged when possible. There is no application deadline; notification is made on a rolling basis approximately 30 days after all credentials have been received. New students are admitted in the spring as well as in the fall. There is a $20 application fee.

Special: Early admissions, deferred admissions, and early decision plans are available; there is a rolling application deadline for early admission.

Transfer: For fall 1981, 81 transfer students applied, 51 were accepted, and 34 enrolled. Applicants must present a portfolio and evidence of good academic standing at the previous school attended. Transfers must earn, at the college, 48 of the 124–126 credits required for the bachelor's degree. There is no application deadline; notification is on a rolling basis.

Visiting: There are no regularly scheduled orientations for prospective students. Informal visits during the fall and spring semesters can be arranged by the admissions office; visitors may stay overnight at the school and sit in on classes.

Financial Aid: Approximately 65% of the students receive financial aid; 16% work part-time on campus. Financial aid is available to freshmen in the form of scholarships and federal loans. Tuition may be paid in installments. The deadline for financial aid applications is April 1. The college is a member of CSS. The FAF must be filed.

Foreign Students: Moore actively recruits foreign students and offers them an intensive English course.

Admissions: Students must achieve a minimum score of 500 on the TOEFL. The SAT or ACT is not required.

Procedure: Foreign students are admitted to the fall and spring semesters; notification is on a rolling basis. Proof of funds adequate to cover the first year of study is required.

Admissions Contact: Linda K. Harper, Director of Admissions.

MORAVIAN COLLEGE F-3
Bethlehem, Pennsylvania 18017 (215) 861-1320

F/T: 657M, 622W		Faculty:	87; IIB, +$
P/T: 18M, 28W		Ph.D.'s:	64%
Grad: none		S/F Ratio:	17 to 1
Year: 4-1-4, ss		Tuition:	$5060
Appl: Mar. 15		R and B:	$1980
1048 applied	735 accepted		310 enrolled
SAT or ACT: required			COMPETITIVE

The nation's sixth oldest educational institution, Moravian College, a private, coeducational liberal arts school, began with a women's program in 1742. Men were admitted in 1746, and a full collegiate curriculum started in 1807. The library houses over 161,866 volumes and 7601 microfilm items, and subscribes to 1186 periodicals.

Environment: Located in Bethlehem, a city of 75,000, the college is 60 miles from Philadelphia. Its Church Street campus is on the National Register of Historic Buildings; its oldest building dates from 1748. The residence halls and fraternity and sorority houses accommodate 431 men and 459 women. On- and off-campus apartments are also available.

Student Life: About 85% of the entering freshmen come from public schools; 20% of the students live on campus. Forty percent are Catholic, 55% are Protestant, and 5% are Jewish. About 1% of the students are minority-group members. College housing is single-sex, and there are visiting privileges. Students may have cars on campus.

Organizations: The school's music traditions bring symphony orchestras and major soloists to the area. The student choir, band, orchestra, and special ensemble groups offer many performance opportunities. Some 25% of the students belong to 3 fraternities and 3 sororities. Activities also include a newspaper, literary magazine, radio station, film society, and a variety of special-interest, cultural, and recreational groups.

Sports: The college competes in 8 intercollegiate sports for men and 8 for women. There are 12 intramural sports for men and 11 for women.

Handicapped: Educational programs and many facilities are available to the handicapped student.

Graduates: Sixty-nine percent of entering freshmen remain to graduate. About 15% of the students pursue graduate study after graduation: 3% enter medical school, 3% dental school, and 3% law school. About 76% find careers in business and industry.

Services: The following services are offered free to students: placement, career counseling, health care, psychological counseling, and tutoring. Placement services for students and graduates include information files, resume preparation, videotaped and evaluated practice interviews, alumni contacts, recruiting, information files, and interest/ability assessment.

Programs of Study: All programs lead to the B.A. or B.S. degree. Bachelor's degrees are offered in the following subjects: BUSINESS (accounting, computer science, management), EDUCATION (elementary, secondary), ENGLISH (English, journalism, literature), FINE AND PERFORMING ARTS (art, art history, music, music education), HEALTH SCIENCES (medical technology), LANGUAGES (French, German, Greek/Latin, Russian, Spanish), MATH AND SCIENCES (biology, chemistry, earth science, geology, mathematics, physics), PHILOSOPHY (classics, philosophy, religion), PREPROFESSIONAL (dentistry, engineering, forestry, law, medicine, ministry, social work, veterinary), SOCIAL SCIENCES (economics, government/political science, history, psychology, sociology). Of the degrees conferred, 20% are in social sciences, 19% are in business, and 16% each are in math/sciences and preprofessional areas.

Required: The following courses are required of all students: English, foreign language, math-logic-computer science, physical education, fine arts, religion-philosophy, history, behavioral science, natural science, and participation in 2 January terms. Course requirements can be fulfilled through AP or other tests.

Special: Student-designed majors are possible. Study abroad is available to juniors. Cooperative programs exist in engineering with the University of Pennsylvania and Lafayette College, and in forestry with Duke University. Interdisciplinary programs and cross-registration with other colleges are allowed. Internship and field study is offered to all students. The January term offers diverse studies, both off- and on-campus. Washington, D.C. and Harrisburg urban semesters are available.

Honors: All departments offer honors programs featuring independent study. The programs include research, thesis preparation, and oral examinations. There are 5 national honor societies on campus.

Admissions: About 70% of the students who applied for the 1981-82 freshman class were accepted. Of those who enrolled, the SAT scores were as follows: Verbal—63% below 500, 32% between 500 and 599, 5% between 600 and 700, and 0% above 700; Math—35% below 500, 48% between 500 and 599, 16% between 600 and 700, and 1% above 700. The school considers the high school record the most important criterion for admission; an average of B is the general standard. Test scores, especially the SAT verbal scores, are given consideration. The applicant should have completed 16 units of work and should rank in the top 40% of the class. An interview is recommended. Other factors considered by the school in order of importance are: advanced placement or honors courses, evidence of special talent, and personality.

Procedure: The SAT or ACT is required. ATs in mathematics, language, and English are used for placement purposes. The SAT should be taken by January of the senior year. The deadlines for admission are March 15 (fall), December 31 (spring), and May 15 (summer). There is a rolling admissions plan. Applications should be submitted with a $25 fee.

Special: The notification date for early decision is December 1; application should be made by November 1. The application deadline for the early admissions plan is March 15 of the junior year; there also is a deferred admissions plan. CLEP and AP credit is given.

Transfer: For fall 1981, 198 applications were received, 120 were accepted, and 85 students enrolled. Transfers are considered for all classes. A minimum 2.5 average in liberal arts is required. D grades do not transfer. There is a residency requirement of 1 year, and transfers must complete, at the college, 32 of the 128 credits required for the bachelor's degree. Application deadlines are March 15 (fall), December 15 (spring), and May 15 (summer).

Visiting: A freshman registration and orientation is held in May. Guides are available for informal weekday visits during the regular semester; arrangements can be made with the admissions office. Visitors may sit in on classes.

Financial Aid: Some 53% of all students receive aid. Thirty-two percent work part-time on campus. Approximately 138 freshman scholarships are available from a fund of $126,000; the average award is $1234. Loans are available from NDSL and State Guarantee funds of $310,300. The deadline for aid application is March 1; the FAF is required. The college is a member of CSS.

Foreign Students: Foreign students comprise about 1% of the full-time enrollment. The college actively recruits these students and offers them special organizations.

Admissions: A minimum score of 550 must be obtained on the TOEFL. The SAT is also required.

Procedure: Application deadlines are March 15 (fall) and December 15 (spring). Proof of funds adequate to cover 4 years of study is required. Foreign students must also present proof of health and carry health insurance, which is available through the college.

Admissions Contact: John T. McKeown, Director of Admissions.

PENNSYLVANIA 767

MUHLENBERG COLLEGE E-3
Allentown, Pennsylvania 18104 (215) 433-3191

F/T: 826M, 707W	Faculty: 122; IIB, + + $
P/T: 28M, 32W	Ph.D.'s: 80%
Grad: none	S/F Ratio: 13 to 1
Year: sems, ss	Tuition: $5150
Appl: Feb. 15	R and B: $1750
1825 applied	1105 accepted 397 enrolled
SAT: 540V 586M	VERY COMPETITIVE

Founded in 1848, Muhlenberg is a small liberal arts college affiliated with the Lutheran Church in America. The library contains 180,000 volumes and 15,000 microfilm items, and subscribes to over 800 periodicals.

Environment: The 75-acre campus is located in a residential section of Allentown, 60 miles from Philadelphia and 90 miles from New York. Residential facilities include 6 residence halls, accommodating 512 men and 521 women, 5 small community houses, a new on-campus village of self-contained, 1-story apartment units, and 5 fraternity houses. The Center for the Arts includes a 950-seat theater, a formal gallery, art studios, recital halls, and recording studios.

Student Life: About 39% of the undergraduates come from Pennsylvania. Seventy-five percent attended public schools. About 90% live on campus. Thirteen percent of the students are Catholic, 42% are Protestant, and 22% are Jewish. About 4% are minority-group members. Campus housing is both coed and single-sex. There are visiting privileges in single-sex dorms. Students may have cars on campus.

Organizations: There are 5 fraternities on campus and no sororities; 45% of the men belong. In addition to unusual offerings in drama and art, the college and various student groups sponsor a wide variety of social, cultural, and political programs. There are interdenominational student organizations on campus. For other recreational and cultural facilities, the Pocono Mountains, Philadelphia, and New York City are within easy driving range.

Sports: Muhlenberg competes on an intercollegiate level in 10 sports for men and 6 for women. There are 11 intramural sports for men; 10 for women.

Handicapped: About 70% of the campus is accessible to wheelchair-bound students. Designated parking, wheelchair ramps, elevators, and specially equipped rest rooms are available. There are no students enrolled with visual impairments or hearing problems; any special facilities or counseling for such students is provided on an individual basis. Special class scheduling can be arranged.

Graduates: The freshman dropout rate is 9%; 76% remain to graduate. Sixty percent pursue graduate study after graduation: 15% enter medical school, 2% dental school, and 8% law school. Fifteen percent pursue careers in industry and business.

Services: Students receive free placement services, career counseling, health care, tutoring, and psychological counseling. Placement services for undergraduates and alumni include job counseling, job listings, and campus visits by graduate schools and employers.

Programs of Study: Muhlenberg confers the A.B. and B.S. degrees. Bachelor's degrees are offered in the following subjects: AREA STUDIES (American, Russian), BUSINESS (accounting, business administration), ENGLISH (English), FINE AND PERFORMING ARTS (art, art history, music, theater/dramatics), LANGUAGES (French, German, Greek/Latin, Hebrew, Russian, Spanish), MATH AND SCIENCES (biology, chemistry, ecology/environmental science, mathematics, natural sciences, physics), PHILOSOPHY (classics, humanities, philosophy), PREPROFESSIONAL (dentistry, law, medicine, ministry, social work, veterinary), SOCIAL SCIENCES (economics, government/political science, history, psychology, social sciences, social work, sociology). Thirty-nine percent of the degrees are conferred in math and sciences, 31% in social sciences, and 16% in business.

Required: All students are required to take 1 semester of freshman English, 4 courses in the humanities, 4 courses in the math/science areas, 5 courses in the social sciences, 2 courses in religion, a foreign language through the intermediate level, and 4 semesters of physical education.

Special: Student-designed majors are permitted. Also available are programs leading to certification in elementary and secondary education and a cooperative (3-2) program in engineering with Columbia University, the University of Pennsylvania, and Washington University. Study abroad, sponsored by the college or other institutions, is primarily a self-designed program for juniors.

Honors: An honors program includes seminars, guided independent study, and individual research. There are 11 honor societies at Muhlenberg, including Phi Beta Kappa.

Admissions: Sixty-one percent of those who applied were accepted for the 1981–82 freshman class. The SAT scores of those who enrolled were as follows: Verbal—34% below 500, 49% between 500 and 599, 13% between 600 and 700, and 2% above 700; Math—8% below 500, 47% between 500 and 599, 39% between 600 and 700, and 4% above 700. An applicant must graduate from an accredited high school, rank in the top 50%, have a 2.5 GPA or better, and have completed 16 Carnegie units. Generally, scores on each part of the SAT should be above 500. Other important factors are advanced placement or honors courses, recommendations by school officials, extracurricular activities, special talents, and leadership ability.

Procedure: Candidates are required to take the SAT and 3 ATs (including the AT in English composition). The SAT should be taken in November or December of the senior year and the ATs in December or January of that year. Application deadlines are February 15 (fall) and the first day of classes (summer). There is a $20 application fee.

Special: Early decision is possible; notification is between December 15 and January 15. The application deadline for early admissions is February 15; an interview is required. A deferred admissions plan is also available. CLEP subject exams are accepted; credit may be earned through AP exams.

Transfer: Of 113 applicants for the current school year, 51 were accepted and 34 enrolled. Transfers are accepted for the sophomore and junior years and must have a minimum 2.5 GPA (preferably 3.0) from an accredited institution. D grades are not accepted. Students must complete, at the college, at least 60 of the 120 credit hours (2 years) required for the bachelor's degree. The application deadline for the fall semester is June 1; for the winter semester, November 15.

Visiting: Regularly scheduled orientations are held. Guided tours and interviews can be scheduled. Students may sit in on classes and stay overnight upon special request. The admissions office handles all arrangements.

Financial Aid: About 67% of all students receive aid through the school. Seventeen percent work part-time on campus. The college awards aid from a fund of more than $2 million. Loans may be obtained from the federal government, local banks, and private funds. The average award to freshmen is $2780. The deadline for aid applications is February 1; the FAF must be filed. The college is a member of CSS.

Foreign Students: About 1% of the full-time students come from foreign countries. The college offers these students special counseling and special organizations.

Admissions: Foreign students must achieve a minimum score of 550 on the TOEFL. The SAT or ACT is not required.

Procedure: The application deadline for fall entry is February 15. Foreign students must complete the college's health form and carry health insurance, which is available through the college for a fee. It is recommended that additional health insurance be obtained to supplement the college insurance plan. Proof of funds adequate to cover a full year of study is required.

Admissions Contact: George Gibbs, Dean of Admissions and Freshmen.

NEUMANN COLLEGE E-4
(Formerly Our Lady of Angels College)
Aston, Pennsylvania 19014 (215) 459-0905

F/T: 31M, 331W	Faculty:	34; IIB, n/av
P/T: 57M, 367W	Ph.D.'s:	27%
Grad: none	S/F Ratio:	13 to 1
Year: sems, ss	Tuition:	$3025
Appl: Aug. 15	R and B:	none
271 applied	186 accepted	124 enrolled
SAT: 440V 465M		COMPETITIVE

Neumann College, founded in 1965, is a Roman Catholic nonresidential liberal arts college. The library houses over 63,195 volumes, subscribes to 600 periodicals, and has 13,500 microfilm items.

Environment: The 14-acre suburban campus is located 20 miles from Philadelphia and 9 miles from Wilmington. Campus buildings include an outside sports complex and the Tau Center for meetings and other student-oriented activities. There are no dormitory facilities.

Student Life: Seventy-four percent of the students come from Pennsylvania; the rest, from New Jersey and Delaware. About 48% of the freshmen are graduates of public schools. Five percent of the students are minority-group members. The college provides day-care services to all students for a fee.

Organizations: There are no fraternities or sororities. The college sponsors an ongoing program of guest speakers, lectures, colloquia, workshops, and discussions. Other activities include dance, gymnastics, and yoga.

Sports: The college participates on an intercollegiate level in 4 sports for women. In addition, 7 intramural sports are offered for both men and women.

Handicapped: The campus is 100% accessible to the handicapped student. Special facilities include wheelchair ramps, designated parking, elevators, and specially equipped rest rooms.

Graduates: The freshman dropout rate is 20%, about 70% of the students remain to graduate. Of those who graduate, 50% go on to further study; 5% pursue careers in business or industry.

Services: The following services are offered at no charge to the student: psychological counseling, health care, placement service, and career counseling. Tutoring and remedial instruction are available for a fee.

Programs of Study: The college confers the B.A. and B.S. degrees. Bachelor's degrees are offered in the following subjects: BUSINESS (business administration), EDUCATION (early childhood, elementary), ENGLISH (communications, English), HEALTH SCIENCES (medical technology, nursing), MATH AND SCIENCES (biology), PHILOSOPHY (religion), PREPROFESSIONAL (law), SOCIAL SCIENCES (social sciences). Of the degrees recently conferred, 43% were in health sciences; 37%, in student-designed majors; 12%, in social sciences.

Special: All majors offer internship programs. Juniors may participate in study abroad sponsored by other institutions. Independent study is available. Combined B.A.-B.S. degrees in all subjects and general studies degrees are offered. Students may design their own majors.

Honors: The national honor society Sigma Theta Tau has a chapter on campus.

Admissions: Sixty-nine percent of those who applied were accepted for the 1981–82 freshman class. Of those who enrolled, the SAT scores were as follows: Verbal—77% below 500, 20% between 500 and 599, 3% between 600 and 700, and 0% above 700; Math—70% below 500, 28% between 500 and 599, 3% between 600 and 700, and 0% above 700. Requirements for admission include graduation from high school with a rank in the upper two fifths of the class, and completion of 16 Carnegie units with a GPA of at least 2.5. Other factors that enter into the admissions decision are advanced placement or honors courses, recommendations by school officials, and extracurricular activities record.

Procedure: The SAT or the ACT is required. Application deadlines are August 15 (fall) and December 15 (spring). Freshmen are admitted to all semesters. Notification is on a rolling basis. There is a $15 application fee.

Special: There are early decision, early admissions, and deferred admissions plans. CLEP and AP credit is given.

Transfer: For fall 1981, the college received 67 transfer applications, accepted 34, and enrolled 23 students. Applicants must have a GPA of 3.0. D grades do not transfer. All students must complete, at the college, the last 30 credits of the approximately 124 necessary for the bachelor's degree. Nursing majors must apply for admission by May 1.

Visiting: The college conducts regularly scheduled orientations, including a campus tour and picnic, for prospective students. Guides are available for informal visits to the campus on Monday through Thursday while school is in session. Visitors may sit in on classes. Arrangements should be made through the admissions office.

Financial Aid: About 72% of all students receive financial aid. Nine percent work part-time on campus. Work contracts are awarded to freshmen. Academic scholarships are available. The FAF and the college's scholarship form are required. The deadline for aid application is June 1. The college is a member of CSS.

Foreign Students: No foreign students are currently enrolled at the college.

Admissions: Foreign applicants must take the TOEFL. College entrance exams are not required.

Procedure: Application deadlines are open; notification is on a rolling basis. Foreign students must complete the standard college health form and must carry health insurance, which is not available through the college.

Admissions Contact: Patricia Tamborello, Director of Admissions.

NEW SCHOOL OF MUSIC F-3
Philadelphia, Pennsylvania 19103　　(215) 732-3966

F/T: 38M, 45W	Faculty: 5; n/av
P/T: none	Ph.D.'s: 20%
Grad: none	S/F Ratio: 17 to 1
Year: sems, ss	Tuition: $3435
Appl: Feb. 1	R and B: $2350
45 applied　　30 accepted　　25 enrolled	
SAT or ACT: not required	SPECIAL

The New School of Music is a private professional institution offering preparation for performing careers in instrumental ensemble and symphony orchestra music. All faculty members are performing musicians —principally, members of the Curtis String Quartet and Philadelphia Orchestra. The library contains over 9000 volumes.

Environment: The school is housed in a single building in a residential area of downtown Philadelphia and has no dormitory facilities; the figure above indicates the school's estimate of cost of housing off campus in Philadelphia. Students reside in nearby apartments and institutional residences.

Student Life: No students live on campus. Eleven percent of the students are minority-group members.

Organizations: There are no Greek letter or other student organizations. The sophisticated musical environment of Philadelphia surrounds the school.

Graduates: Four percent of the freshmen drop out by the end of the first year; 80% remain to graduate. Ten percent of the graduates pursue further study after graduation. Alumni are members of over 100 professional symphony orchestras in America and the world.

Services: Remedial instruction, career counseling, and psychological counseling are available to students. No placement or health care services are offered.

Programs of Study: All programs lead to the B.Mus. degree; the performance majors offered are in symphony orchestra instruments or piano.

Admissions: Sixty-seven percent of those who applied were accepted for the 1981–82 freshman class. Candidates must be high school graduates. No minimum GPA is specified.

Procedure: An audition (either in person or on tape) is required. Application deadlines are February 1 for the fall semester and October 1 for the spring. The application fee is $25.

Special: An early admissions plan is offered; the application deadline is February 1.

Transfer: For fall 1981, 15 transfer students applied, 10 were accepted, and 5 enrolled. Transfer applicants are admitted for every year. Previous courses must be approved by the school, and an in-person or on-tape audition is required. Students must complete, at the college, 44 of the 124 credits required for the bachelor's degree. There is a 2-year residency requirement.

Visiting: The school conducts regularly scheduled orientations for prospective students, including interviews with the dean and instrumental instructors and a visit to an orchestra rehearsal. Guides are available for informal visits to the campus. Visitors may sit in on classes. Weekdays are recommended for visiting.

Financial Aid: About 65% of all students receive aid, which is provided in a variety of ways. Twenty-five percent work part-time on campus. The deadline for aid application is February 1. The FAF must be filed. The school is a member of CSS.

Foreign Students: Foreign students compromise 6% of the full-time enrollment. Special counseling is offered to these students.

Admissions: The TOEFL is required. College entrance exams are not necessary.

Procedure: Application deadlines are February 1 (fall) and October 1 (spring). Foreign students must present a health certificate signed by a physician. Proof of funds adequate to cover 4 years of study is required.

Admissions Contact: James Leitch, Registrar.

OUR LADY OF ANGELS COLLEGE
(See Neumann College)

PENNSYLVANIA STATE UNIVERSITY

Pennsylvania State University, the land-grant institution of the Commonwealth of Pennsylvania, was established in 1855. In addition to the main campus at University Park, full-time instruction is also available at 19 branch campuses. Total university library resources include 2.3 million volumes, 25,800 periodical subscriptions, and 1.7 million microfilm items.

Seventeen of the branch campuses offer the first 2 years of baccalaureate work; all except Allentown also offer 2-year associate degree programs. They are located in Allentown, Altoona, Beaver, Berks, Delaware County, DuBois, Fayette, Hazleton, McKeesport, Mont Alto, New Kensington, Ogontz, Schuylkill, Scranton, Shenango Valley, Wilkes-Barre, and York. Behrend College in Erie offers 4-year programs and Capital Campus in Middletown offers the third and fourth years of baccalaureate programs and graduate study. Part-time graduate study is available at the Radnor Graduate Center.

The branch campuses are within commuting distance of about 95% of the state's population. Several of the Commonwealth Campuses have limited residence facilities for students who cannot commute. Admission requirements, courses, and credits in the baccalaureate degree program are the same throughout the university system. Students may transfer from the lower division campuses to the University Park Campus, Capitol Campus, Behrend College, or another university to complete their degree work. Separate profiles on the University Park Campus and Behrend College follow.

PENNSYLVANIA STATE UNIVERSITY/ B-1
BEHREND COLLEGE
Erie, Pennsylvania 16563　　(814) 898-1511

F/T: 957M, 509W	Faculty: 97; n/av
P/T: 216M, 107W	Ph.D.'s: 60%
Grad: 10M	S/F Ratio: 15 to 1
Year: terms, ss	Tuition: $1677 ($3711)
Appl: open	R and B: $2037
2117 applied　　1925 accepted　　648 enrolled	
SAT: 445V 505M	LESS COMPETITIVE

Pennsylvania State University/Behrend College, a state-supported institution, was founded in 1948. It is the only campus in the Commonwealth of Pennsylvania to receive college status within the university. The library contains more than 92,000 volumes and subscribes to 500 periodicals.

Environment: The 420-acre suburban campus is located 10 miles from downtown Erie. Residence halls accommodate 600 students.

Student Life: More than 95% of the students are from Pennsylvania. Four percent are minority-group members. About 50% live on campus. Campus housing is single-sex, and there are visiting privileges. Students may have cars on campus. Alcohol is not permitted on campus.

Organizations: Extracurricular activities include special-interest groups, publications, student government, and musical and dramatic groups.

Sports: The college fields intercollegiate teams in 4 sports for men and 4 for women. There are 7 intramural sports for men and 6 for women.

Handicapped: The college is working to make the campus accessible to handicapped students.

Graduates: Thirty-five percent of the freshmen drop out by the end of the first year; 65% remain to graduate. Ten percent pursue advanced study after graduation.

Programs of Study: The college confers the B.A. and B.S. degrees. Associate and master's programs are also available. Bachelor's degrees are offered in the following subjects: BUSINESS (accounting, business administration, business economics, general business, management, marketing), ENGLISH (communications, literature), MATH AND SCIENCES (biology, mathematics, physical sciences), SOCIAL SCIENCES (economics, government/political science, history).

Required: All students must complete a core curriculum.

Special: Study abroad and student-designed majors are available.

Honors: There is an honors program.

Admissions: Ninety-one percent of those who applied were accepted for the 1981–82 freshman class. Students are admitted on the basis of the high school GPA and SAT scores. Preference is given to state residents.

Procedure: The SAT or ACT is required. Although there are no deadlines, students should apply by November for fall admission. Notification is on a rolling basis. There is a $20 application fee.

770 PENNSYLVANIA

Transfers: A 2.0 GPA is required. D grades do not transfer. There are no application deadlines; notification is on a rolling basis.

Financial Aid: About 65% of all students receive financial aid. Scholarships, grants (including BEOG/SEOG and state grants), loans (including NDSL), and part-time employment (including CWS) are available. The FAF and PHEAA/BEOG are required. The college is a member of CSS. Financial aid applications must be filed by February 15.

Foreign Students: The university accepts applications from foreign students and offers them special counseling and special organizations.

Admissions: The TOEFL is required; college entrance exams are not necessary.

Procedure: Foreign students are admitted to all terms. Proof of health is necessary. Proof of funds sufficient to cover study at the university is also required.

Admissions Contact: Benjamin A. Lane, Director of Admissions.

PENNSYLVANIA STATE UNIVERSITY/ UNIVERSITY PARK CAMPUS   C-3
University Park, Pennsylvania 16802   (814) 865-5471

F/T: 28,101M, 18,719W	Faculty: 3026; I, +$
P/T: 4508M, 4479W	Ph.D.'s: 65%
Grad: 4748M, 3245W	S/F Ratio: 22 to 1
Year: terms, ss	Tuition: $1848 ($3711)
Appl: open	R and B: $2037
27,942 applied 21,888 accepted 10,820 enrolled	
SAT: 509V 564M	VERY COMPETITIVE

The University Park Campus offers undergraduate degree programs in the liberal arts and sciences; agriculture; arts and architecture; business administration; earth and mineral sciences; education; engineering; health, physical education, and recreation; and human development. The library contains 2.5 million volumes and 2.2 million microfilm items, and subscribes to 24,475 periodicals.

Environment: The University Park Campus is located in the geographic center of the state on a 5005-acre tract. The rural campus is 90 miles from Harrisburg. There are 291 major buildings.

Student Life: Most of the students come from Pennsylvania and are graduates of public schools. About 4% are minority-group members. About 40% reside on campus; the remainder live in off-campus apartments, fraternity houses, or at home. Campus housing is single-sex, and there are visiting privileges. Upperclassmen may have cars on campus. Alcohol is not permitted on campus. Day-care services are open to the public. Space is limited; there is a fee.

Organizations: The extracurricular program includes student government, publications, musical and dramatic groups, and religious organizations. There are 50 fraternities and 19 sororities. Regularly scheduled social and cultural events take place on campus.

Sports: The university fields intercollegiate teams in 17 sports for men and 15 for women. Intramural competition is offered for men and women in 16 sports.

Handicapped: About 60% of the campus is accessible to handicapped students. Special facilities include wheelchair ramps, elevators, parking areas, and specially equipped rest rooms. A coordinator for the handicapped supervises supportive services.

Graduates: The freshman dropout rate for academic reasons is 2%; about 62% of the baccalaureate degree freshmen remain to graduate.

Services: The university provides free health care, psychological counseling, tutoring, remedial instruction, career counseling, and placement for all students.

Programs of Study: The university confers the B.A., B.S., B.Arch., B.Arch.Eng., B.F.A., B.L.A., B.M., and B.Tech. degrees. Associate, master's, and doctoral programs are also offered. Bachelor's degrees are offered in the following subjects: AREA STUDIES (American, East Asian, Latin American), BUSINESS (accounting, business administration, business logistics, computer science, finance, management, marketing, operations management, quantitative business analysis, real estate/insurance), EDUCATION (elementary, health/physical, industrial, rehabilitation, secondary, special), ENGLISH (English, journalism, literature, speech), FINE AND PERFORMING ARTS (art, art education, art history, film/photography, music, music education, theater/dramatics), HEALTH SCIENCES (health planning and administration, medical technology, nursing, nutrition, speech therapy), LANGUAGES (French, German, Italian, Russian, Russian technical translation, Spanish), MATH AND SCIENCES (astronomy, biochemistry, biology, chemistry, earth science, ecology/environmental science, geosciences, mathematics, microbiology, molecular and cell biology, natural sciences, physical sciences, physics), PHILOSOPHY (classics, humanities, philosophy, religious studies), PREPROFESSIONAL (architecture, engineering, forestry, home economics, landscape architecture, law, medicine, social work, veterinary), SOCIAL SCIENCES (administration of justice, anthropology, economics, geography, government/political science, history, individual and family studies, international relations, psychology, recreation and parks, social sciences, sociology).

Required: All students must take 46 credits in arts, communications, health sciences and physical education, humanities, natural sciences, and quantification.

Special: Study abroad, student-designed majors, liberal arts seminars, and combined B.A.-B.S. degrees in liberal arts/earth and mineral sciences or liberal arts/engineering are offered.

Honors: There are numerous honor societies, including a chapter of Phi Beta Kappa. Most departments offer honors programs.

Admissions: About 78% of the applicants for the 1981-82 freshman class were accepted. SAT scores of enrolled students were as follows: Verbal—62% below 500, 30% between 500 and 599, 7% between 600 and 700, and 1% above 700; Math—36% below 500, 41% between 500 and 599, 20% between 600 and 700, and 3% above 700. Admission is based on a combination of high school GPA and SAT scores. Applicants must be graduates of an accredited high school and have completed 15 Carnegie units. Each academic division has its own specific requirements.

Procedure: The SAT is required and should be taken during the junior year; applicants presenting junior year scores are given first preference. New students are admitted to each term. Applications should be on file by November 30, although there are no set deadlines. A rolling admissions policy is used. There is a $20 application fee.

Special: AP and CLEP credit is available.

Transfer: For fall 1981, 3909 transfer students applied, 2472 were accepted, and 1569 enrolled. Students who have completed 60 semester hours of work at an accredited institution are considered for transfer. A 2.0 GPA is needed; D grades are not accepted. Preference is given to state residents. The application deadline is the same as for freshman admission.

Visiting: General orientations for prospective students are held each weekday at 10 A.M. and 1 P.M.. Informal campus tours with student guides can be arranged. Visitors may sit in on classes but may not stay overnight at the school. The admissions office should be contacted for arrangements.

Financial Aid: About 79% of the students receive financial aid. Assistance is available in the form of scholarships, BEOG/SEOG, NDSL funds, and campus employment (including CWS). Need and academic merit are the determining factors. The average award to freshmen is $2515. The FAF is required and should be filed no later than February 15; the university is a member of CSS.

Foreign Students: Almost 2% of the full-time students come from foreign countries. Special counseling and special organizations are available to these students.

Admissions: Foreign students must achieve a minimum score of 550 on the TOEFL. College entrance exams are not required.

Procedure: Foreign students are admitted to all terms. Applications should be on file by November 30. Proof of funds adequate to cover study at the university is necessary and varies according to the program selected.

Admissions Contact: Donald G. Dickason, Dean of Admissions.

PHILADELPHIA COLLEGE OF ART   F-3
Philadelphia, Pennsylvania 19102   (215) 893-3174

F/T: 446M, 608W	Faculty: 60; IIA, +$
P/T: 48M, 127W	Ph.D.'s: n/av
Grad: n/av	S/F Ratio: 11 to 1
Year: sems, ss	Tuition: $5110
Appl: Feb. 1	R and B: $2100
1161 applied 810 accepted 400 enrolled	
SAT: 450V 400M	SPECIAL

Philadelphia College of Art, established in 1876 as part of the Philadelphia Museum of Art, is a private, nonsectarian, professional school of art. The library contains 43,000 volumes, 25,000 prints, and 75,000 slides, and subscribes to 270 periodicals.

Environment: Located in downtown Philadelphia, the college's facilities include a 13-story apartment-style residence hall and a sculpture garden.

Student Life: About 40% of the undergraduates are from Pennsylvania. Twenty percent are campus residents. College housing is coed.

Organizations: Campus activities include student government, campus publications, concerts, lectures, and social events. There are no fraternities or sororities.

Sports: There is no sports program.

Handicapped: Facilities for the physically handicapped include elevators.

Graduates: About 15% of the graduates become candidates for higher degrees.

Services: Students receive the following free services: placement aid, career counseling, tutoring, remedial instruction, and psychological counseling. Placement services include referrals, on-campus interviews, internships, and career counseling. Health care is available for a fee.

Programs of Study: The college confers the B.F.A. and B.S. degrees. Master's degrees are also awarded. Bachelor's degrees are offered in crafts, environmental design, graphic design, illustration, industrial design, painting and drawing, photography and film, printmaking, and sculpture.

Required: All students must take a freshman foundation studio program consisting of 18 credits, as well as a distribution of credits in the studio major and electives and in the liberal arts.

Special: Students may design their own majors. Special programs are offered in art education and art therapy. As a member of the East Coast Consortium of Art Schools, the college participates in the Student Exchange Program.

Admissions: Seventy percent of those who applied were accepted for the 1981–82 freshman class. The SAT scores of an earlier class were as follows: Verbal—21% scored between 500 and 599, 1% between 600 and 700, and 1% above 700; Math—21% scored between 500 and 599, 5% between 600 and 700, and 5% above 700. Applicants should have completed a college-preparatory program. They must rank in the upper half of their class and have at least a C average. The school also considers evidence of special talents, advanced placement or honors courses, impressions made during an interview, and personality.

Procedure: The SAT is required. The application consists of the candidate's academic record, SAT scores, portfolio of art work, and at least 1 of the following: an interview, an autobiography, additional written or visual material, and references. Application deadlines are February 1 (fall) and November 15 (spring). Notification is on a rolling basis. There is a $20 application fee.

Special: Early and deferred admissions plans are available. CLEP and AP credit is accepted.

Transfer: In a recent year, 200 transfer students applied, 88 were accepted, and 51 enrolled. Transfers are considered for the sophomore, junior, and senior years. A portfolio of artwork is the main criterion; transcripts of previous college work are also required. An interview is recommended. Grades of 2.5 and above transfer. There is a 1-year residency requirement toward the 132 credits necessary for a bachelor's degree. Transfer application deadlines are April 15 (fall) and November 15 (spring).

Visiting: An open house held each spring includes tours, career panels, financial-aid seminars, and special exhibits. Guided tours can be scheduled during the week. Visitors may sit in on classes. Arrangements should be made through the admissions office.

Financial Aid: Seventy-five percent of all students receive aid. Twenty percent work part-time on campus; only upperclassmen may take campus jobs. Average aid to freshmen covered 100% of costs in 1981–82. Financial aid is awarded on the basis of need and usually takes the form of a package consisting of a scholarship, NDSL, and EOG. The college is a member of CSS and requires the FAF. Applications should be submitted by March 15.

Foreign Students: The 7 students from foreign countries make up 1% of enrollment. The college offers these students an intensive English course.

Admissions: Foreign students must take the TOEFL or the college's own English-proficiency exam. No college entrance exams are required.

Procedure: Application deadlines are February 1 (fall) and October 15 (spring). Foreign students must present proof of adequate funds. Health insurance, though not required, is available through the school.

Admissions Contact: Caroline Kelsey, Director of Admissions.

PENNSYLVANIA 771

PHILADELPHIA COLLEGE OF PHARMACY AND SCIENCE
Philadelphia, Pennsylvania 19104   (215) 596-8810

F-3

F/T: 530M, 504W   Faculty: 73; IIA, +$
P/T: 9M, 22W   Ph.D.'s: 74%
Grad: 31M, 12W   S/F Ratio: 12 to 1
Year: sems   Tuition: $4000
Appl: open   R and B: $2100
540 applied   389 accepted   202 enrolled
SAT: 500V 540M   **VERY COMPETITIVE**

The Philadelphia College of Pharmacy and Science, a privately controlled professional college founded in 1821, offers programs in pharmacy and health-related sciences. The library houses 70,000 volumes and subscribes to 762 periodicals.

Environment: Located in urban surroundings, the 10-acre campus has 11 buildings, including 2 dormitories that accommodate 295 students.

Student Life: About 65% of the students are residents of Pennsylvania. Seventy-seven percent live on campus. Four percent are minority-group members. College housing is coed. Students may keep cars on campus.

Organizations: Twenty-two percent of the men belong to the 6 fraternities on campus, and 25% of the women belong to the 1 sorority. Organizations for the major religious faiths are provided. The cultural and recreational facilities of Philadelphia are readily accessible.

Sports: The college fields 6 intercollegiate teams for men and 4 for women. There are 12 intramural sports for men and 6 for women.

Handicapped: The entire campus is accessible to handicapped students. Facilities include wheelchair ramps and elevators.

Graduates: Fifty-one percent of the freshmen remain to graduate.

Services: Psychological counseling, health care, and career counseling are offered free to students.

Programs of Study: The college confers the B.S. degree. Master's and doctoral degrees are also awarded. Bachelor's degrees are offered in the following subjects: HEALTH SCIENCES (medical technology, physical therapy), MATH AND SCIENCES (biology, chemistry, toxicology), PREPROFESSIONAL (pharmacy). Eighty-two percent of degrees are conferred in health sciences (including pharmacy) and 18% in math and sciences.

Required: All students must take freshman English, as well as a distribution of credits in 6 broad areas.

Honors: Three national honor societies have chapters on campus.

Admissions: Seventy-two percent of those who applied were accepted for the 1981–82 freshman class. The SAT scores of those who enrolled were as follows: Verbal—57% scored below 500, 33% between 500 and 599, 9% between 600 and 700, and 1% above 700; Math—19% scored below 500, 57% between 500 and 599, 21% between 600 and 700, and 3% above 700. Candidates should have graduated from an accredited high school, have completed 16 Carnegie units, and rank in the upper 40% of their high school class. Also considered are extracurricular activities, recommendations by school officials, advanced placement or honors courses, and personality. Admission to the physical therapy program is by invitation, and an interview is required.

Procedure: The SAT is required. Students are admitted to the fall term only. Application deadlines are open. Notification is on a rolling basis. There is a $15 application fee.

Special: CLEP credit is granted.

Transfer: For fall 1981, 271 students applied, 115 were accepted, and 43 enrolled. Transfer students are accepted for freshmen, sophomore, and junior classes. A GPA of 2.5 is required; an interview is recommended. D grades do not transfer. There are no residency requirements, and the number of credits required for a bachelor's degree varies.

Visiting: There is an orientation program in the spring for all accepted students and their families. Guides are available for informal visits, and visitors may sit in on classes. Visits may be arranged for weekdays through the registrar's office.

Financial Aid: About 65% of the students receive aid. Ten percent work part-time on campus. Average aid to freshmen was $1200 in 1981–82. Scholarships and loans are available, and tuition may be paid in installments. The college is a member of the CSS and requires the Pennsylvania State grant application. Applications for aid should be submitted by March 15.

Foreign Students: The 18 students from foreign countries make up 2% of enrollment. The college offers these students an intensive English course, special counseling, and special organizations.

Admissions: Foreign students must score at least 550 on the TOEFL. They also must take the SAT, and may be asked to take ATs.

Procedure: Foreign students are admitted only in the fall. The application deadline is June 16. Students must present a health certificate and proof of adequate funds for 4 years of study.

Admissions Contact: Richard C. Kent, Registrar.

PHILADELPHIA COLLEGE OF TEXTILES AND SCIENCE   F-3
Philadelphia, Pennsylvania 19144   (215) 951-2800

F/T: 758M, 893W		Faculty:	86; IIB, ++$
P/T: 40M, 54W		Ph.D.'s:	n/av
Grad: 117M, 22W		S/F Ratio:	16 to 1
Year: sems, ss		Tuition:	$4020
Appl: n/av		R and B:	$2350
1459 applied	760 accepted		510 enrolled
SAT: 486V 490M	ACT: 20		COMPETITIVE

The Philadelphia College of Textiles and Science, founded in 1884, is an independent, primarily career-oriented 4-year college offering preprofessional programs in business, sciences, fashion, apparel, and textiles. The library houses 63,000 volumes and 4200 microfilm items, and subscribes to 1200 periodicals.

Environment: The college is located on an 85-acre, tree-lined campus in a suburban residential area. Students live in a dormitory and townhouses.

Student Life: About 48% of the students come from Pennsylvania. Sixty-two percent live in college housing. Housing is single-sex, and there are visiting privileges. Students may keep cars on campus.

Organizations: Ten percent of the men belong to the 3 fraternities on campus; 10% of the women belong to the 1 sorority. Another 10% of the students belong to 2 professional fraternities. A wide variety of extracurricular activities is available, including a weekly student newspaper and a number of special-interest clubs.

Sports: The college fields 9 intercollegiate teams. There are 6 intramural sports.

Handicapped: Facilities for handicapped students include wheelchair ramps and special parking.

Graduates: The freshman dropout rate is 1%, and 88% remain to graduate. Twenty-five percent of the graduates go on to further study; 2% enter medical school and 2% enter law school.

Services: The following services are offered free to students: psychological counseling, tutoring, remedial instruction, health care, placement aid, and career counseling.

Programs of Study: The college conferes the B.S. degree. Master's degrees are also awarded. Bachelor's degrees are offered in the following subjects: BUSINESS (accounting, apparel management, business administration, computer management, computer science, fashion merchandising, finance, management, marketing, retail management, textile management and marketing), FINE AND PERFORMING ARTS (textile design), MATH AND SCIENCES (chemistry, life science, textile chemistry), PREPROFESSIONAL (dentistry, medicine, textile engineering).

Required: All students must take courses in English, history, sociology, psychology, political science, and mathematics.

Admissions: Fifty-two percent of those who applied were accepted for the 1981–82 freshman class. A basic admissions requirement is graduation from secondary school. The following credentials are evaluated on an individual basis: the student's high school academic record, recommendations from teachers, SAT scores, extracurricular activities, and class rank. Other considerations include AP or honors courses and evidence of special talents.

Procedure: The SAT or ACT is required. The completed application, high school record and recommendation, and SAT or ACT scores should be submitted. Freshmen are admitted to each semester. Admissions are on a rolling basis. There is a $20 application fee.

Special: Early and deferred admissions plans and an early decision plan are offered. CLEP and AP credit is given.

Transfer: For fall 1981, 14% of those who applied for transfer were accepted. Transfer applicants should meet the requirements outlined for regular admission and also present a transcript of their previous college record. An interview is recommended. Students must earn, at the college, at least 60 credits toward a bachelor's degree.

Visiting: Guides are available for informal visits to the campus; visitors may sit in on classes. Arrangements for visits, preferably on weekdays from 9 A.M. to 5 P.M., can be made through the director of admissions.

Financial Aid: Seventy-six percent of the students receive aid. Sixty-four percent work part-time on campus. Scholarships, loans, and campus jobs are available, as are funds from corporations, state agencies, and the federal government. The FAF is required. Applications for aid should be submitted by May 1.

Foreign Students: About 200 students come from foreign countries. The college offers these students an intensive English course, special counseling, and special organizations.

Admissions: No English-proficiency or college-entrance exams are required.

Procedure: Application deadlines are the same as those for other freshmen. Foreign students must present proof of good health and of adequate funds.

Admissions Contact: Mott Linn, Director of Admissions.

PHILADELPHIA COLLEGE OF THE PERFORMING ARTS   F-3
Philadelphia, Pennsylvania 19102   (215) 875-2228

F/T: 135M, 157W		Faculty:	20; n/av
P/T: 26M, 28W		Ph.D.'s:	12%
Grad: 13M, 8W		S/F Ratio:	14 to 1
Year: sems, ss		Tuition:	$4560
Appl: May 1		R and B:	$2350
256 applied	166 accepted		119 enrolled
SAT: 455V 445M			SPECIAL

Philadelphia College of the Performing Arts, founded in 1870, is a private, independent college of music and dance. The library contains over 18,000 volumes and 13,000 records, and subscribes to 39 periodicals.

Environment: The college is located in downtown Philadelphia. Facilities include dance studios and a new dormitory.

Student Life: Most students come from Pennsylvania. About 70% come from public schools. Forty percent live on campus. Twenty-two percent are minority-group members. College housing is coed. Students may keep cars on campus.

Organizations: Student activities include concerts, master classes, recitals, lectures, study tours, productions, and student government. There are no fraternities or sororities. Nearby cultural facilities include the Academy of Music, major theaters, and Independence Hall and other historical landmarks.

Handicapped: The entire campus is accessible to the handicapped. Facilities include wheelchair ramps, elevators, specially equipped rest rooms, and lowered drinking fountains, telephones, and light switches.

Graduates: The freshman dropout rate is 15%, and 60% of the freshmen remain to graduate. Eight percent of those who graduate go on to further study.

Programs of Study: The college confers the B.Mus., B.Mus.Ed., and B.F.A. degrees. Master's degrees are also awarded. Bachelor's degrees are offered in FINE AND PERFORMING ARTS (dance, dance education, music, music education). Within these broad fields, a wide variety of majors is offered.

Required: All students must take a general distribution of humanities courses.

Special: The college offers extensive performance opportunities in large and chamber ensembles, as well as solo appearances. Many students study privately with members of the Philadelphia Orchestra. A large number of elective courses is offered in such areas as electronic music, jazz, and opera.

Admissions: Sixty-five percent of those who applied were accepted for the 1981–82 freshman class. The SAT scores of those who enrolled were as follows: Verbal—85% scored below 500, 10% between 500 and 599, 4% between 600 and 700, and 1% above 700; Math—85% scored below 500, 10% between 500 and 599, 4% between 600 and 700, and 1% above 700. Applicants must be graduates of an accredited high school and audition at the college. Admissions requirements are flexible. Evidence of special talent, impressions made during the audition, and recommendations are helpful.

Procedure: The SAT or ACT is required in addition to the audition. The deadlines for application are May 1 for fall and December 1 for spring. Notification is made immediately after testing. There is a $25 application fee.

Special: Early and deferred admissions plans and an early decision plan are offered.

Transfer: Good academic standing, the SAT or ACT, and an audition are necessary. D grades do not transfer. There is a 2-year residency requirement toward the 136 credits generally necessary for a bachelor's degree. Application deadlines are the same as those for freshmen.

Visiting: Guides are available for informal visits, and visitors may sit in on classes. Arrangements can be made through the director of admissions.

Financial Aid: About 72% of the students receive aid. Ten percent work part-time on campus. The college provides scholarships and loans from federal and state sources. Private scholarships are also awarded based on talent. The college is a member of CSS and requires the FAF. The deadline for aid applications is April 1.

Foreign Students: The 23 students from foreign countries make up 6% of enrollment.

Admissions: Foreign students must score at least 450 on the TOEFL or present other verification of English proficiency. No college entrance exams are required.

Procedure: Application deadlines are the same as those for other students.

Admissions Contact: Edward T. Brake, Director of Admissions.

POINT PARK COLLEGE B–3
Pittsburgh, Pennsylvania 15222   (412) 391-4100

F/T: 651M, 530W		Faculty:	72; IIB, av$
P/T: 797M, 596W		Ph.D.'s:	45%
Grad: 9M, 12W		S/F Ratio:	16 to 1
Year: sems, ss		Tuition:	$3955
Appl: open		R and B:	$2000
983 applied	809 accepted		328 enrolled
SAT: 434V 434M	ACT: 18		LESS COMPETITIVE

Point Park College, an independent institution of liberal arts and sciences, was founded in 1960. The library contains 104,034 volumes and 23,990 microfilm items, and subscribes to 1310 periodicals.

Environment: The campus consists of 3 high-rise buildings and the Pittsburgh Playhouse in downtown Pittsburgh. A communications center provides journalism students with practical experience in editing, typesetting, and printing. The buildings also contain laboratories, radio and TV studios, an art gallery, a student union, and recreational facilities. The playhouse has facilities for drama and music. Two high-rise dormitories house 725 students.

Student Life: About 83% of the students come from the Middle Atlantic states; others come from one of 19 states. About 35% live in the residence halls. Twenty-one percent are minority-group members. College housing is both coed and single-sex; students in single-sex housing have visiting privileges. Students may keep cars on campus. Day care services are available for a fee.

Organizations: Extracurricular activities include publications, student government, fraternities, and departmental and service organizations. The city provides additional cultural and recreational opportunities.

Sports: The college fields 2 intercollegiate teams for men and 2 for women. There are 7 intramural sports for men and 5 for women.

Handicapped: Nearly all of the campus is accessible to wheelchair-bound students. Facilities include ramps, elevators, and lowered telephones. Special class scheduling can be arranged. For students with impaired vision or hearing, the college provides readers and tape-recording facilities. A special counselor and an assistant are available.

Graduates: About 31% of the freshmen drop out during their first year, and 44% remain to graduate. About 12% of the graduates seek advanced degrees. Fifty-one percent of the graduates pursue careers in business and industry.

Services: Students receive free placement aid, career and psychological counseling, health care, tutoring, and remedial instruction. Placement services also are available for graduates.

Programs of Study: The college awards the B.A., B.F.A., and B.S. degrees. Associate and master's degrees are also awarded. Bachelor's degrees are offered in the following subjects: BUSINESS (accounting, computer science, management), EDUCATION (early childhood, elementary), ENGLISH (English, journalism), FINE AND PERFORMING ARTS (dance, film/photography, radio/TV, theater/dramatics, visual arts and design), HEALTH SCIENCES (health services, medical technology), LANGUAGES (French, Spanish), MATH AND SCIENCES (biology, chemistry, mathematics), PHILOSOPHY (philosophy), PRE-PROFESSIONAL (dentistry, engineering—civil engineering technology, engineering—electrical engineering technology, engineering—mechanical engineering technology, law, medicine, mortuary science), SOCIAL SCIENCES (government/political science, history, psychology, public administration, social sciences). Of the degrees conferred, 30% are in business, 24% in natural sciences and technology, and 20% in journalism and communications.

Special: Combined B.A.-B.S. degrees may be earned in programs that generally take 5 years. Students may design their own majors. The college offers interdepartmental programs, cross-registration with other colleges, and a work-study program. It is associated with the Pittsburgh Playhouse.

Honors: A number of honor societies are represented on campus.

Admissions: About 82% of those who applied for admission to the 1981–82 freshman class were accepted. The SAT scores of those who enrolled were as follows: Verbal—75% scored below 500, 20% between 500 and 599, 2% between 600 and 700, and 0% above 700; Math—69% scored below 500, 22% between 500 and 599, 4% between 600 and 700, and 1% above 700. Of those who took the ACT, 64% scored below 21, 22% between 21 and 23, 3% between 24 and 25, 3% between 26 and 28, and 4% above 28. Candidates must be high school graduates or hold a GED certificate. They must rank in the upper half of their graduating class. Admissions officers also consider advanced placement or honors courses, recommendations by school officials, impressions made during an interview, and extracurricular activities. Veterans are given special admissions consideration.

Procedure: Applicants must take the SAT or ACT. Application deadlines are open; candidates desiring fall admission are advised to apply by early spring. Students are admitted to all terms. The college follows a rolling admissions policy and adheres to the CRDA. The application fee is $15.

Special: Early and deferred admissions plans are offered. CLEP and AP credit is granted.

Transfer: For fall 1981, 260 students applied, 189 were accepted, and 115 enrolled. Transfer students must present an average of 2.0 or better, a transfer information form, and a history of financial aid; an interview is recommended. D grades transfer if the student holds an associate degree. Students must earn at least 30 credits in residence to qualify for a bachelor's degree.

Visiting: Guides are provided for informal visits by prospective students. Visitors may sit in on classes. Recommended times for visits are weekdays from 9 A.M. to 5 P.M. Arrangements should be made with the admissions office.

Financial Aid: Seventy-eight percent of the students receive aid. Thirty-two percent work part-time during the school year, earning an average of $900. Average aid to freshmen in 1981–82 was $3750. Scholarships, EOG, and NDSL are available. Pennsylvania residents may receive state grants or low-interest guaranteed loans. The college is a member of CSS and requires aid candidates to submit the FAF; Pennsylvania residents must submit the state grant application. The aid application deadline is May 1.

Foreign Students: The 208 students from foreign countries make up 18% of enrollment. The college offers these students an intensive English program, special counseling, and special organizations.

Admissions: Students must take the TOEFL for diagnostic purposes only. No college entrance exams are required.

Procedure: Application deadlines are August 1 (fall), November 25 (spring), and April 1 (summer). Foreign students must present proof of adequate funds for 4 years of study. Health insurance, though not required, is available through the college for a fee.

Admissions Contact: Richard K. Watson, Dean of Enrollment Planning.

ROBERT MORRIS COLLEGE B–3
Coraopolis, Pennsylvania 15108   (412) 264-9300

F/T: 1362M, 1552W		Faculty:	122; n/av
P/T: 832M, 1353W		Ph.D.'s:	32%
Grad: 338M, 85W		S/F Ratio:	24 to 1
Year: sems, ss		Tuition:	$2580
Appl: open		R and B:	$1700
1086 applied	858 accepted		678 enrolled
SAT: required			COMPETITIVE

Robert Morris College, founded in 1921, is a private college of business education that also offers a 2-year liberal arts transfer program. The library contains 93,005 volumes and 6000 microfilm items, and subscribes to 950 periodicals.

Environment: The 230-acre main campus, located in a small town in a suburban area 17 miles from Pittsburgh, was once a private estate. The campus has 21 buildings, including a theater and 9 dormitories that house 1072 students. The college's Pittsburgh Center, located in downtown Pittsburgh, consists of an 8-story building; there are no dormitories. Both campuses are under the same management and offer identical programs.

Student Life: Eighty percent of the students are from Pennsylvania. Thirty-five percent live on the main campus. Freshmen live in single-sex dorms, upperclassmen in suites; there are visiting privileges. Students may keep cars on campus.

Organizations: There are 2 local and 4 national fraternities, to which 25% of the men belong, and 2 local and 6 national sororities, to which 30% of the women belong. Spring Weekend and the Snow Ball are major campus events. Several cultural and social events take place on campus each week.

Sports: The college fields 7 intercollegiate teams. There are 4 intramural sports.

Handicapped: Twenty-five percent of the main campus and 100% of the Pittsburgh Center campus are accessible to the physically handicapped. Special parking areas, elevators, special class scheduling, and specially equipped rest rooms are available.

Graduates: The freshman dropout rate is 15%, and 81% of the freshmen remain to graduate. Twenty-five percent of the graduates pursue advanced degrees. Virtually all eventually enter careers in business and industry.

Services: Students receive free psychological counseling, health care, placement aid, career counseling, tutoring, and remedial instruction. Placement services also are available to alumni.

Programs of Study: The college confers associate, bachelor's, and master's degrees. The B.S.B.A. is offered in the following subjects: BUSINESS (accounting, business administration, business education, business information systems, computer science, economics, industrial communications, management, marketing, office administration, real estate/insurance, sports management, transportation).

Required: All undergraduates must complete a core curriculum that includes physical education.

Special: Students may cross-register for courses at 9 other schools in the area. Internship programs are available in selected areas of the business-administration programs.

Honors: Eight national honor societies have chapters on campus.

Admissions: Seventy-nine percent of those who applied for the 1981–82 freshman class were accepted. The SAT scores of those who enrolled were as follows: Verbal—10% scored between 500 and 599, and 1% between 600 and 700; Math—13% scored between 500 and 599, and 1% between 600 and 700. Of those who took the ACT, 30% scored between 21 and 23, 10% between 24 and 25, and 1% between 26 and 28. Candidates should be graduates of an accredited high school, rank in the upper 10% of their class, and have at least a 2.0 GPA. An interview is recommended.

Procedure: The SAT or ACT is required for placement purposes only. Freshmen must apply to the academic division they seek to enter: Business Administration, Secretarial Administration, or Liberal Arts. Students are admitted to all terms. Application deadlines are open. Notification is on a rolling basis. The application should be accompanied by a $20 fee.

Special: An early admissions plan is available. CLEP and AP credit is granted.

Transfer: For fall 1981, 406 students applied, 335 were accepted, and 307 enrolled. Transfers are considered for all classes and should have at least a 2.0 GPA; an interview is recommended. D grades transfer with an associate degree. Students must spend at least 1 year in residence, completing 30 of the 120 credits necessary for a bachelor's degree. Application deadlines are open.

Visiting: Orientation involves a day on campus meeting the faculty, visiting classes, touring the campus, dining, and attending social functions. Informal visits are best planned on weekdays from 9 A.M. to 5 P.M.; visitors may sit in on classes. Arrangements for a guide can be made through the admissions office.

Financial Aid: Seventy-four percent of the students receive aid. Work contracts, including CWS, are awarded to freshmen. The number of freshman scholarships varies. Athletic scholarships are available to men and women in intercollegiate sports. Federal and state loans are also available. Need is the main consideration in determining awards. The college is a member of the CSS. The FAF and the college's own form are required. The aid application deadline is May 15.

Foreign Students: The 28 students from foreign countries represent 1% of enrollment. The college offers these students an intensive English course and special counseling.

Admissions: Foreign students must score at least 500 on the TOEFL. No college entrance exams are required.

Procedure: Foreign students must apply during the semester before the one in which they seek to enroll. They must present a completed physical-examination record and proof of adequate funds for 1 year. They also must carry health insurance, which is available through the college for a fee.

Admissions Contact: Helen Mullen, Dean of Admissions.

ROSEMONT COLLEGE   F–4
Rosemont, Pennsylvania 19010   (215) 525-6420

F/T: 495W	Faculty:	38; IIB, ++$
P/T: 208W	Ph.D.'s:	60%
Grad: none	S/F Ratio:	12 to 1
Year: sems, ss	Tuition:	$4300
Appl: open	R and B:	$2665
405 applied	291 accepted	168 enrolled
SAT: 450V 450M		COMPETITIVE

Rosemont College, founded by a Roman Catholic order, the Religious of the Society of the Holy Child Jesus, in 1921, is a small, private liberal arts college. The library contains 135,600 volumes and 18,650 microfilm items, and subscribes to 610 periodicals.

Environment: The 56-acre campus is located in a suburb about 11 miles west of Philadelphia. Four dormitories, including 1 primarily for seniors, accommodate more than 410 students.

Student Life: Fewer than 40% of the students come from Pennsylvania. Eighty-five percent live on campus. About 47% attended public schools. Most are Catholic. About 5% are minority-group members. There are visiting privileges in college housing. Students may keep cars on campus. Day-care services are available.

Organizations: Campus activities include lectures, concerts, movies, dances, and plays. There are no sororities. Off campus, Philadelphia provides numerous cultural activities.

Sports: The college competes on an intercollegiate level in 6 sports. Four club sports are offered cooperatively with Villanova University.

Handicapped: There are no special facilities for physically handicapped students.

Graduates: About 4% of the freshmen drop out during their first year, and 75% remain to graduate. Twenty-five percent of the graduates pursue advanced degrees; 1% enter medical school, 1% enter dental school, and 2% enter law school. About 50% pursue careers in business and industry.

Services: Students receive free career counseling, health care, tutoring, and remedial instruction. Psychological counseling is available on a fee basis.

Programs of Study: The college awards the B.A., B.S., and B.F.A. degrees. Bachelor's degrees are offered in the following subjects: AREA STUDIES (American, Italian), BUSINESS (accounting, business administration), ENGLISH (English), FINE AND PERFORMING ARTS (art history, studio art, theater/dramatics), LANGUAGES (French, German, Italian, Spanish), MATH AND SCIENCES (biology, chemistry, mathematics), PHILOSOPHY (humanities, philosophy, religion), SOCIAL SCIENCES (economics, government/political science, history, psychology, social sciences, sociology). Candidates for teacher education complete a liberal arts major and an education certification program. Certification is given in art, elementary, secondary, and special education. Twenty-four percent of the degrees conferred are in social sciences, 11% in fine and performing arts, 9% in English, and 8% in natural sciences.

Required: Students must complete a core curriculum that includes courses in rhetoric, religious studies, literature, a foreign language, philosophy, history, natural science and math, social science, and 2 semesters of physical education.

Special: Students may design their own majors. The college offers a cooperative education program, summer study in Siena, Italy, and shared courses with Villanova University. The college also offers an exchange program with several commercial art schools and a business concentration.

Honors: Delta Epsilon, the national honor society of Catholic colleges and universities, has a chapter on campus. Honors programs are available in studio art.

Admissions: Seventy-two percent of those who applied were accepted for the 1981–82 freshman class. The SAT scores of those who enrolled were as follows: Verbal—70% scored below 500, 25% between 500 and 599, 5% between 600 and 700, and 0% above 700; Math—69% scored below 500, 25% between 500 and 599, 5% between 600 and 700, and 1% above 700. The school recommends that students rank in the top half of their high-school class and have a 2.0 average. Candidates are primarily selected on the basis of academic record, class rank, recommendations, and SAT scores. Additional factors considered include advanced placement or honors courses, recommendations, leadership record, and extracurricular activities.

Procedure: The SAT is required and must be taken by January of the senior year. Applications should be filed as early as possible. The rolling admissions plan is used. Freshmen are admitted at midyear as well as in the fall. All candidates are notified 4 weeks after receipt of credentials. The $15 application fee is waived for applicants upon request.

Special: Early admissions and deferred admissions plans are available. AP and CLEP are used.

Transfer: For fall 1981, 39 students applied, 26 were admitted, and 15 enrolled. An average of 2.0 is necessary. D grades do not transfer. Students must study at the college for at least 2 years, completing 20 of the 39 units needed for a bachelor's degree. Application deadlines are open.

Visiting: Campus visit days are held for prospective students. Programs include tours of the campus, lunch, discussion sessions, class visits, and interviews. Appointments can be arranged through the admissions office while college is in session. Visitors may sit in on classes. Overnight accommodations are available.

Financial Aid: Over 60% of the students receive aid through the school. Twenty percent work part-time on campus. The average aid awarded to freshmen from all sources in 1981–82 was $2300. Aid is awarded on the basis of need. Students receiving aid are required to contribute a limited amount of service in the library, laboratories, or offices. The college is a member of CSS. The FAF should be filed. Applications should be submitted by April 15 (fall) and by December 15 (winter).

Foreign Students: The 8 students from foreign countries make up nearly 2% of enrollment. The college offers these students an individualized English program.

Admissions: Foreign students must score at least 500 on the TOEFL. No college entrance examination is required.

Procedure: The recommended application deadlines are April 1 (fall) and November 15 (winter). Foreign students must submit the college's health form. They also must carry health insurance, which is available through the college for a fee.

Admissions Contact: Jane A. Maloney, Director of Admissions.

SAINT FRANCIS COLLEGE   C–3
Loretto, Pennsylvania 15940   (814) 472-7000

F/T: 594M, 531W	Faculty:	65; n/av
P/T: 23M, 18W	Ph.D.'s:	52%
Grad: 163M, 69W	S/F Ratio:	15 to 1
Year: sems, ss	Tuition:	$110 p/c +$290
Appl: open	R and B:	$2000
840 applied	457 accepted	343 enrolled
SAT: 450V 475M	ACT: 21	COMPETITIVE

Saint Francis is a Roman Catholic liberal arts college. The library houses 160,000 volumes and 5500 microfilm items, and subscribes to 694 periodicals.

Environment: Located in a rural area on the western slopes of the Allegheny mountains, the 600-acre campus is surrounded by lakes. It is 20 miles from Altoona and 25 miles from Johnstown. The campus has 21 modern buildings, including an art museum and 8 dormitories. The college also sponsors on-campus apartments, married-student housing, 4 fraternity houses, and 1 sorority house.

Student Life: Fifty-seven percent of the students are from Pennsylvania. Thirty-five percent attended public schools. Eighty percent live on campus. Ninety percent are Catholic, 4% are Protestant, and 2% are Jewish. Three percent of the students are minority-group members. College housing is single-sex, with visiting privileges. First-semester freshmen may not have cars on campus.

Organizations: There are 4 national fraternities, to which 10% of the men belong, and 2 national sororities, to which 4% of the women belong. Activities include a special cultural program of professional artists, campus socials, coffeehouse programs, special-interest groups, religious groups, service and departmental clubs, and student government. Major ski resorts are nearby.

Sports: The college fields 7 intercollegiate teams for men and 5 for women. There are 8 intramural sports for men and 8 for women.

Handicapped: More than half the campus is accessible to the physically handicapped. There are special facilities for these students, including elevators in some buildings. A special support staff is also available.

Graduates: The freshman dropout rate is 18%. About 79% of the freshmen remain to graduate. Seven percent of the graduates pursue advanced study; 1% enter medical school and 4% enter law school. Another 80% enter careers in business and industry.

Services: Health care, placement services, and career counseling are available free to students. Placement services include counseling and interviews with recruiters. Some tutoring and all remedial instruction requires a fee. Referrals are given for psychological counseling.

Programs of Study: The college confers the B.A., B.S., and B.S.N. degrees. Associate and master's degrees are also awarded. Bachelor's degrees are offered in the following subjects: AREA STUDIES (American), BUSINESS (accounting, business administration, computer science, management), EDUCATION (elementary, library science, secondary), ENGLISH (broadcasting, English, journalism), FINE AND PERFORMING ARTS (art, art education, radio/TV, theater/dramatics), HEALTH SCIENCES (medical technology, nursing, physician assistant), LANGUAGES (French, Spanish), MATH AND SCIENCES (biology, chemistry, ecology/environmental science, mathematics, oceanography), PHILOSOPHY (philosophy, religion), PREPROFESSIONAL (dentistry, engineering, law, medicine, social work), SOCIAL SCIENCES (anthropology, criminal justice, economics, government/political science, history, psychology, social sciences, sociology). Thirty-two percent of the degrees conferred are in business, 16% in health sciences, and 16% in social sciences.

Required: All students must take 17 general-education courses, including 2 in philosophy and 2 in religious studies.

Special: Students may earn combined B.A.-B.S. degrees. A library-science certification program is available. Juniors may participate in the junior-year-abroad program sponsored by New York University. There is a cooperative 3-2 program in engineering with Pennsylvania State University. Students may design their own majors.

Honors: Most departments offer independent-study honors programs. Six honor societies have chapters on campus.

Admissions: Fifty-four percent of those who applied were accepted for the 1981–82 freshman class. The SAT scores of those who enrolled were as follows: Verbal—79% scored below 500, 16% between 500 and 599, 4% between 600 and 700, and 1% above 700, Math—50% scored below 500, 22% between 500 and 599, 7% between 600 and 700, and 1% above 700. On the ACT, 10% scored below 21, 8% between 21 and 23, and 2% between 24 and 25. Candidates should be graduates of an accredited high school and have 16 Carnegie units, a class rank in the top two-fifths, a grade average of at least 2.5, and an SAT score above 400 on each part. An interview is encouraged. Sons and daughters of alumni receive preference. Also considered are advanced placement or honors courses, recommendations by school officials, leadership record, and extracurricular activities.

Procedure: The SAT or ACT is required and should be taken by January of the senior year. Freshmen are admitted to all semesters. The application should be submitted early in the senior year, but deadlines are open. Notification is made on a rolling basis. There is a $15 application fee.

Special: Early and deferred admissions plans are available. CLEP and AP credit is granted.

Transfer: For fall 1981, 167 students applied, 105 were accepted, and 79 enrolled. Transfers are considered for all classes. A minimum GPA of 2.5 and 25 completed credit hours are required; an interview is recommended. D grades transfer with an associate degree. State residents receive preference. Students must spend at least 1 year in residence, completing 32 of the 128 credits necessary for a bachelor's degrees. Application deadlines are open.

Visiting: A scheduled orientation includes a faculty reception, a tour, and entertainment. Informal visits are encouraged, and visitors may sit in on classes and stay overnight at the school. Visits are best scheduled for the middle of the week. Arrangements for a guide can be made with the director of admissions.

Financial Aid: Eighty-five percent of the students receive aid. About 35% work part-time on campus. Average aid to freshmen covered 77% of costs in 1981–82. Freshman scholarships are awarded according to need. SEOG work-study programs, and loans from both the federal government (including NDSL) and the college are also availa-

776 PENNSYLVANIA

ble. Tuition can be paid in installments. The college is a CSS member. Either the FAF or the FFS is required. The application deadline is May 1, but it is advisable to apply as soon after January 1 as possible.

Foreign Students: The 4 students from foreign countries represent less than 1% of enrollment. The college offers these students special counseling.

Admissions: Foreign students must take the TOEFL. No college entrance exams are required.

Procedure: Application deadlines are open. Foreign students must present proof of adequate funds. Health insurance, though not required, is available through the college.

Admissions Contact: Edward E. Kale, Jr., Director of Admissions.

SAINT JOSEPH'S UNIVERSITY F-3
Philadelphia, Pennsylvania 19131 (215) 879-7400

F/T: 1274M, 1056W	Faculty: 173; IIB, ++$
P/T: 51M, 38W	Ph.D.'s: 80%
Grad: 1172M&W	S/F Ratio: 15 to 1
Year: sems, ss	Tuition: $3700
Appl: Mar. 1	R and B: $2450
2056 applied	1364 accepted 655 enrolled
SAT: 520V 528M	VERY COMPETITIVE

Founded in 1851, St. Joseph's is a private liberal arts university affiliated with the Roman Catholic Church and administered by the Jesuits. The library contains 190,412 volumes and 260,000 microforms, and subscribes to 1415 periodicals. It also contains special theological collections.

Environment: The 47-acre campus is located in a suburban residential area at the western edge of Philadelphia. A new athletic facility, a new residence center, and an addition to the library all have been completed within the past few years. Two high-rise dorms and residential houses are scattered throughout the campus and accommodate 950 students.

Student Life: About 44% of the students live on campus. About 23% come from public schools. Ninety-two percent are Catholic. Eight percent are minority-group members. University housing is coed and single-sex; students in single-sex housing have visiting privileges. Students may keep cars on campus.

Organizations: Three national fraternities and 3 local sororities are represented on campus. There are more than 60 clubs and special-interest groups. Cultural attractions in the area include the Barnes Foundation, the Museum of Art, the Franklin Institute, and the Academy of Natural Sciences.

Sports: The college fields 7 intercollegiate teams for men and 7 for women. There are 2 intramural sports for men. Students have formed clubs in 5 other sports.

Graduates: Ten percent of the freshmen drop out by the end of the first year, and 67% remain to graduate. About 40% of the graduates seek advanced degrees; 10% enter medical school, 2% enter dental school, and 3% enter law school. About 35% pursue careers in business or industry.

Services: Health care, psychological counseling, tutoring, remedial instruction, placement aid, and career counseling are available free to students.

Programs of Study: The university confers the A.B. and B.S. degrees. Master's degrees are also awarded. Bachelor's degrees are offered in the following subjects: BUSINESS (accounting, business administration, finance, food marketing, industrial relations, information systems, management, marketing), ENGLISH (English), LANGUAGES (French, German, Spanish), MATH AND SCIENCES (biology, chemistry, computer science, mathematics, natural sciences, physics), PHILOSOPHY (philosophy, religion), PREPROFESSIONAL (dentistry, law, medicine), SOCIAL SCIENCES (economics, government/political science, history, international relations, psychology, social sciences, sociology). Fifty percent of degrees are conferred in business, 20% in math and sciences, and 20% in social sciences.

Required: Students must take courses in English, foreign or classical languages, history, mathematics, science, philosophy, social sciences, and theology.

Special: The university offers cooperative programs in electronics and physics (work-training employment during alternate terms begins in the junior year) and in chemistry. Internships in Washington and exchange programs with other Jesuit universities are available. Students may study abroad in the junior year. The university also offers summer programs in Latin American countries and a semester in Mexico City.

Honors: Ten national honor societies have chapters on campus. Honors programs are available in most of the major fields and include seminars, colloquia, tutorials, independent study, independent laboratory projects, and directed research.

Admissions: Sixty-six percent of those who applied were accepted for the 1981–82 freshman class. The SAT scores for a recent class were as follows: Verbal—45% between 500 and 599, 16% between 600 and 700, and 2% above 700; Math—46% between 500 and 599, 24% between 600 and 700, and 4% above 700. Applicants should rank in the upper two-fifths of their class and have at least a B average. The high school transcript and SAT scores are of primary importance in the admissions decision. Also considered are advanced placement or honor courses, extracurricular activities, recommendations of school officials, and impressions made during an interview.

Procedure: The SAT is required. Freshmen are admitted only in the fall, for which the application deadline is March 1. There is a $20 application fee.

Special: Early and deferred admissions plans and an early decision plan are available. AP exams are accepted.

Transfer: For fall 1981, 349 students applied, 199 were accepted, and 114 enrolled. Applicants must have at least a 2.5 average; a combined score of 1050 on the SAT is recommended. D grades do not transfer. Students must spend 2 years in residence, completing at least half of the 40 courses required for a bachelor's degree. Applications must be submitted by June 30 for the fall semester and by December 1 for the spring semester.

Visiting: Guided tours of the campus are available. Visitors may sit in on classes and stay overnight at the school. Admissions personnel are available Monday through Friday from 9:30 A.M. to 4:30 P.M. From October to March, interviews can be arranged on Saturday mornings from 9:30 A.M. to 12 P.M. Arrangements should be made through the admissions office.

Financial Aid: Eighty-three percent of the students receive aid. Fourteen percent work part-time on campus. Average aid to freshmen in 1981–82 was $2860. Approximately 50 scholarships are awarded to freshmen on the basis of outstanding academic ability and financial need. EOG and loans from the federal government and local banks are available. The college is a member of CSS and requires the FAF. Applications should be submitted by March 1.

Foreign Students: Eight percent of the full-time students come from foreign countries. The university offers these students an intensive English program, special counseling, and special organizations.

Admissions: Foreign students must score at least 500 on the TOEFL. No college entrance exams are required.

Procedure: Application deadlines are March 1 (fall) and November 1 (spring). Foreign students must present proof of adequate funds. They also must carry health insurance, which is available through the university for a fee.

Admissions Contact: Director of Admissions.

SAINT VINCENT COLLEGE B-3
Latrobe, Pennsylvania 15650 (412) 539-9761

F/T: 772M	Faculty: 51; IIB, av$
P/T: 211M	Ph.D.'s: 44%
Grad: none	S/F Ratio: 12 to 1
Year: sems, ss	Tuition: $3813
Appl: Aug. 15	R and B: $1800
446 applied	373 accepted 222 enrolled
SAT or ACT: required	COMPETITIVE

St. Vincent College, established in 1846, is a Roman Catholic liberal arts institution for men. The library houses 215,527 volumes and 90,921 microfilm items, and subscribes to 760 periodicals.

Environment: The 80-acre campus is located in the Laurel Highlands, a rural area 38 miles from Pittsburgh. The 22 campus buildings include a community center and 3 dormitories that house 608 men.

Student Life: Over 60% of the students come from public schools. About 79% live in the dormitories. Three percent are minority-group members. There are visiting privileges in college housing. Students may keep cars on campus.

Organizations: Extracurricular activities include lectures, dances, concerts, and social events in coordination with Seton Hill College for women. There are no fraternities.

Sports: The college fields 7 intercollegiate teams. There are 9 intramural sports.

Handicapped: About 40% of the campus is accessible to handicapped students. Special facilities include wheelchair ramps, lowered telephones, elevators, and designated parking areas. Special class scheduling is also available.

Graduates: The freshman dropout rate is 8%, and 70% of the freshmen remain to graduate. Of those who graduate, 26% pursue further study; 7% enter medical school, 4% enter dental school, and 5% enter law school. Seventy percent pursue careers in business and industry.

Services: The following services are offered free to students: psychological counseling, health care, tutoring, remedial instruction, placement aid, and career counseling.

Programs of Study: The college confers the B.A. and B.S. degrees. Bachelor's degrees are offered in the following subjects: BUSINESS (accounting, business administration, computer science, finance, industrial relations, management), ENGLISH (English, journalism, literature), FINE AND PERFORMING ARTS (art, art education, art history, art theraphy, graphic design, music, music education, theater/dramatics), HEALTH SCIENCES (medical technology), LANGUAGES (French, Spanish), MATH AND SCIENCES (biology, chemistry, mathematics, physics), PHILOSOPHY (philosophy, religion), PREPROFESSIONAL (dentistry, engineering, home economics, law, medicine, ministry, optometry, pharmacy, podiatry, social work, veterinary), SOCIAL SCIENCES (economics, government/political science, history, psychology, sociology). Twenty-eight percent of degrees are conferred in business, 23% in social sciences, and 20% in math and sciences.

Required: Students must complete a core curriculum.

Special: The college participates in an academic exchange program with Seton Hill College. Juniors may study abroad for a year in England, France, Spain, or Taiwan. Students may design their own majors. Cooperative work-study programs are available.

Admissions: Eighty-four percent of those who applied were accepted for the 1981–82 freshman class. Thirty percent of those who enrolled ranked in the top fifth of their high school class. Applicants must be graduates of accredited high schools, have completed 15 Carnegie units, rank in the upper half of their class, and have a minimum grade average of C+. Other considerations include advanced placement or honors courses, recommendations by school officials, and leadership record.

Procedure: The SAT or ACT is required. Application deadlines are August 15 for fall and January 1 for spring. Notification is made on a rolling basis. There is a $15 application fee.

Special: A deferred admissions plan is available. CLEP and AP credit is granted.

Transfer: For fall 1981, 66 students applied, 57 were accepted, and 45 enrolled. A GPA of 2.0 is required; an interview is recommended. D grades transfer if the applicant has an associate degree. Students must spend at least 2 semesters in residence, earning 34 of the 124 credits necessary for a bachelor's degree. Transfer application deadlines are the same as those for freshmen.

Visiting: The college conducts regularly scheduled orientations for prospective students. Guides are available for informal visits to the campus when classes are in session. Visitors may sit in on classes and may stay overnight at the school. Arrangements should be made through the admissions office.

Financial Aid: About 86% of all students receive aid. Forty percent work part-time on campus. Freshmen aid awards in 1981–82 averaged $2500; the maximum a freshman could expect from all sources combined, including campus employment, was $5800. Scholarships, grants, and loans are available, and tuition may be paid in installments. The college is a member of CSS. The Pennsylvania state grant application must be submitted. Application deadlines are May 1 (fall) and December 1 (spring).

Foreign Students: The 24 students from foreign countries represent 3% of enrollment. The college offers these students an intensive English course, special counseling, and special organizations.

Admissions: Foreign students must score at least 500 on the TOEFL. No college entrance exams are required.

Procedure: Application deadlines are August 15 (fall) and January 1 (spring). Foreign students must present proof of adequate funds for the duration of their studies. They also must carry health insurance, which is available through the college for a fee.

Admissions Contact: Rev. Earl J. Henry, Director of Admissions.

PENNSYLVANIA 777

SETON HILL COLLEGE B-4
Greensburg, Pennsylvania 15601 (412) 834-2200

F/T: 727W	Faculty:	51; IIB, av$
P/T: 27M, 219W	Ph.D.'s:	43%
Grad: none	S/F Ratio:	13 to 1
Year: sems, ss	Tuition:	$3670 ($3745)
Appl: open	R and B:	$2000
386 applied	295 accepted	180 enrolled
SAT: 457V 466M		COMPETITIVE

Seton Hill, founded as an academy in 1883, is a Roman Catholic liberal arts college for women. The library contains 69,000 volumes and 1300 microfilm items, and subscribes to 434 periodicals.

Environment: The 205-acre campus is located in a suburban area 30 miles east of Pittsburgh. Its 21 buildings include a classroom/laboratory building for home economics, theater labs, a music wing, and computer facilities. There are 2 residence halls for freshmen and 4 for upperclassmen, accommodating 570 students.

Student Life: Eighty percent of the students come from Pennsylvania. Over 80% attended public schools. Eighty-four percent live in the dormitories. Seven percent are minority-group members. College housing is single-sex. Students may keep cars on campus.

Organizations: Students participate in special-interest clubs and organizations. There are no sororities. Off-campus recreational facilities and activities include nearby ski and winter sports resorts, parks and recreation areas, whitewater rafting, and golf courses.

Sports: The college fields 5 intercollegiate teams. There are 8 intramural sports.

Handicapped: Ninety percent of the campus is accessible to the physically handicapped. Wheelchair ramps, parking areas, elevators, specially equipped rest rooms, specially equipped housing, and lowered drinking fountains and telephones are available. Tutorial assistants and readers are provided for students with visual or hearing impairments.

Graduates: About 15% of the freshmen drop out, and 83% remain to graduate. Forty percent of the graduates pursue advanced degrees; 2% enter medical school, 1% enter dental school, and 1% enter law school. Another 25% begin careers in business and industry.

Services: Students receive free psychological and career counseling, placement aid, tutoring, and remedial instruction. Health care is available for a fee. Placement services also are available to alumni.

Programs of Study: The college confers the B.A., B.F.A., B.Mus., B.S., B.S.H.E., B.S.Med.Tech., and B.S. in Nurse Anesthesia degrees. Bachelor's degrees are offered in the following subjects: AREA STUDIES (American), BUSINESS (accounting, business administration, computer science and mathematics, finance, management), EDUCATION (early childhood, elementary, secondary), ENGLISH (communications, English, journalism, speech), FINE AND PERFORMING ARTS (art, art education, art therapy, film/photography, music, music education, studio art, theater/dramatics), HEALTH SCIENCES (medical technology, nurse anesthesia, pre-nursing), LANGUAGES (French, Spanish), MATH AND SCIENCES (biochemistry, biology, chemistry, computer science and mathematics, physics), PHILOSOPHY (philosophy, religion), PREPROFESSIONAL (dentistry, engineering, home economics, law, medicine, social work, veterinary), SOCIAL SCIENCES (economics, government/political science, history, psychology, social sciences, sociology). Twenty-six percent of the degrees conferred are in preprofessional fields, 23% in math and sciences, and 20% in the fine and performing arts.

Required: All students must complete 2 courses in religious studies, 2 courses in philosophy (including 1 in ethics), 1 English composition course, 2 English literature courses, and 1 course in language on an intermediate level. Seniors must pass a comprehensive exam in their major.

Special: Students have the option of 3 curriculum plans: a departmental major, an interdisciplinary major, and a self-designed curriculum. Combined 5-year B.A.-B.S. degrees are available in biology/medical technology and engineering. A 3-2 program in engineering with Georgia Tech, Notre Dame, and Penn State and a 2-2 program in nursing with Catholic University are offered. An academic exchange program is available with Saint Vincent College for men. Through the Coordinated Undergraduate Program (CUP) in Dietetics, a student is eligible to take the exam to become a registered dietitian. The Quality Undergraduate Education freshmen seminar is designed to foster critical thinking, effective communication, creativity, and growth in implications of personal freedom. Another innovative Program is the Opportunity summer session, designed to help students deficient in basic English or math skills adjust to college work.

778 PENNSYLVANIA

Honors: An honors program is open to students with a high academic average. Three honor societies have chapters on campus.

Admissions: Seventy-six percent of those who applied were accepted for the 1981–82 freshman class. Of those who enrolled, the SAT scores were as follows: Verbal—67% scored below 500, 10% between 500 and 599, 5% between 600 and 700, and 1% above 700; Math—78% scored below 500, 11% between 500 and 599, 5% between 600 and 700, and 0% above 700. Candidates must have a high school diploma or a GED, have completed 15 Carnegie units, rank in the upper 40% of their class, and have at least a 2.5 grade average. Advanced placement or honors courses, evidence of special talents, and personality are also considered.

Procedure: The SAT or ACT is required and should be taken by March of the senior year. Application deadlines are open; freshmen are admitted in fall and spring. Notification is made on a rolling basis. There is a $10 application fee.

Special: Early and deferred admissions plans and an early decision plan are available. CLEP and AP credit is accepted.

Transfer: For fall 1981, 136 students applied, 101 were accepted, and 78 enrolled. Transfers are accepted for all classes. A minimum 2.0 grade average and 12 completed credit hours are required; the SAT or ACT and an interview are recommended. D grades transfer if the applicant has a 2.0 average. Students must earn, at the college, 64 of the 128 credits necessary for a bachelor's degree. Application deadlines are open.

Visiting: Orientation for prospective students includes a personal interview, a campus tour, an interview with the financial aid officer, and a meeting with faculty members and students. Guided informal tours, which allow for class visits and overnight stays, are best scheduled when classes are in session during the academic year or summers. Arrangements can be made through the director of admissions.

Financial Aid: Eighty-five percent of the students receive aid. Nine percent work part-time on campus. The college provides freshman scholarships and grants. Federal and state loans and other aid programs are available. The college is a member of CSS and requires the FAF or college aid form. The aid application deadline is July 1.

Foreign Students: The 16 students from foreign countries make up 2% of enrollment. The college offers these students an intensive English course, special counseling, and special organizations.

Admissions: Foreign students must score at least 500 on the TOEFL. No college entrance exams are required.

Procedure: Application deadlines are open. Foreign students must present a completed health form and proof of adequate funds for 1 year. They also must carry health insurance, which is available through the college for a fee.

Admissions Contact: Jean Boggs, S.C., Director of Admissions.

SHIPPENSBURG STATE COLLEGE C–4
Shippensburg, Pennsylvania 17257 (717) 532-1233

F/T: 2048M, 2406W
P/T: 112M, 101W
Grad: 501M, 538W
Year: sems, ss
Appl: open
3087 applied 1258 accepted
SAT: 450V 510M

Faculty: 265; IIA, ++$
Ph.D.'s: 72%
S/F Ratio: 21 to 1
Tuition: $1414 ($2354)
R and B: $1470
1113 enrolled
COMPETITIVE+

Shippensburg State College is a public 4-year college offering programs in the schools of Arts and Humanities, Behavioral and Social Sciences, Business, Education and Professional Studies, and Mathematics and Natural Sciences. The library contains 352,920 volumes and 924,083 microfilm items, and subscribes to 1550 periodicals.

Environment: The 200-acre campus is located in a rural area 40 miles southwest of Harrisburg. The 35 buildings include a health center, student apartments, and 9 residence halls.

Student Life: The majority of students come from Pennsylvania. Forty-nine percent live on campus. Eight percent are minority-group members. College housing is both coed and single-sex; students in single-sex housing have visiting privileges. Students may keep cars on campus.

Organizations: About 17% of the men belong to the 9 national fraternities on campus, and 15% of the women belong to the 4 national and 5 local sororities. Student activities include student government.

Sports: The college fields 12 intercollegiate teams for men and 10 for women. There are 6 intramural sports for men and 6 for women.

Handicapped: Most of the campus is accessible to wheelchair-bound students. Special facilities include ramps, parking areas, specially equipped rest rooms, and lowered drinking fountains and telephones. Special class scheduling can be arranged.

Graduates: The freshman dropout rate is 15%, and 57% remain to graduate.

Services: The following services are free to students: placement aid, health care, psychological counseling, career counseling, tutoring, and remedial instruction. Placement services also are available to graduates.

Programs of Study: The college confers the B.A., B.S., B.S.B.A., and B.S.Ed. degrees. Master's degrees also are awarded. Bachelor's degrees are offered in the following subjects: BUSINESS (accounting, data processing, finance, labor relations, management, marketing, office administration, real estate/insurance, secretarial, transportation), EDUCATION (elementary), ENGLISH (English, journalism, speech), FINE AND PERFORMING ARTS (art, radio/TV, theater/dramatics), HEALTH SCIENCES (medical technology), LANGUAGES (French, German, Spanish), MATH AND SCIENCES (biology, chemistry, computer and information sciences, earth science, engineering, geo-environmental studies, mathematics, physics), PHILOSOPHY (humanities), PREPROFESSIONAL (engineering), SOCIAL SCIENCES (administration of justice, economics, geography, government/political science, history, psychology, public administration, social sciences, social welfare, sociology, urban studies). Forty-four percent of the degrees conferred are in arts and sciences, 31% in business, and 25% in education.

Required: General-education requirements include courses in the humanities, social sciences, and natural sciences.

Special: Students may participate in an extensive internship program, in independent study, and in cooperative programs such as preengineering and medical technology. Study-abroad programs in Europe are available.

Honors: Thirteen national honor societies have chapters on campus.

Admissions: Forty-one percent of those who applied were accepted for the 1981–82 freshman class. The SAT scores of those who enrolled were as follows: Verbal—76% scored below 500, 22% between 500 and 599, 2% between 600 and 700, and 0% above 700; Math—40% scored below 500, 48% between 500 and 599, 12% between 600 and 700, and 0% above 700. Applicants should be graduates of an accredited high school. Consideration is also given to test scores, advanced placement or honors courses, leadership record, and recommendations by school officials.

Procedure: The SAT is required; transfers from junior colleges must present ACT scores. Application deadlines are open. Notification is on a rolling basis. The application should be submitted with a $15 fee.

Special: There is a deferred admissions plan. CLEP and AP credit is accepted.

Transfer: For fall 1981, 514 students applied, 309 were accepted, and 214 enrolled. Transfers are accepted at all levels. A 2.0 average and 15 completed credit hours are required. D grades do not transfer. Students must spend 1 year in residence, completing at least 30 of the 120 credits necessary for a bachelor's degree. There are no application deadlines.

Visiting: Orientations are held regularly and include group interviews with the admissions, financial-aid, and student-life staffs; meetings with faculty; and tours. Visits should be arranged with the dean of admissions.

Financial Aid: About 85% of all students receive aid. Three percent work part-time on campus. Average aid to freshmen in 1981–82 was $700. Most aid comes from the Pennsylvania Higher Education Assistance Agency grant or loan program. NDSL and BEOG funds are available, as are a limited number of merit scholarships. The college is a member of CSS and requires the Pennsylvania state grant application. The deadlines for aid applications are April 1 for fall and summer entry and November 1 for spring entry.

Foreign Students: The 21 students from foreign countries make up less than 1% of enrollment. The college offers these students special counseling.

Admissions: Foreign students must score at least 500 on the TOEFL. The SAT is also required.

Procedure: Application deadlines are June 1 (fall) and October 1 (spring). Foreign students must present the record of a physical examination and proof of adequate funds for 1 year. They also must carry health insurance, which is available through the college for a fee.

Admissions Contact: Albert Drachbar, Dean of Admissions.

SLIPPERY ROCK STATE COLLEGE B-2
Slippery Rock, Pennsylvania 16057 (412) 794-7203

F/T: 2283M, 2417W	Faculty:	303; IIA, ++$
P/T: 104M, 160W	Ph.D.'s:	58%
Grad: 139M, 285W	S/F Ratio:	16 to 1
Year: sems, ss	Tuition:	$1250 ($2190)
Appl: Aug. 15	R and B:	$1398
3262 applied	2668 accepted	1314 enrolled
SAT: 385V 425M	ACT: 18	LESS COMPETITIVE

Slippery Rock State College offers programs in liberal arts and teacher education. It was founded in 1889 and is controlled by the Commonwealth of Pennsylvania. The library contains 423,248 volumes and subscribes to 1618 periodicals.

Environment: The 600-acre campus is located in a rural area 50 miles north of Pittsburgh. Among the 35 buildings are the college union and 11 dormitories capable of housing 1910 women and 1360 men.

Student Life: About 90% of the students are from Pennsylvania, and 90% come from public schools. Sixty-five percent live on campus. Four percent of the students are minority-group members. College housing is coed and single-sex; students in single-sex housing have visiting privileges. Students may keep cars on campus. Day care services are available for a fee.

Organizations: There are 8 fraternities and 8 sororities; 10% of the men and 8% of the women belong. Student activities include student government, the newspaper, yearbook, radio, drama, choral groups, concert band, and theater.

Sports: The college fields 13 intercollegiate teams for men and 13 for women. There are 7 intramural sports for men and 7 for women.

Handicapped: Sixty percent of the campus is accessible to wheelchair-bound students. Special parking, wheelchair ramps, elevators, especially equipped rest rooms, student aides, and lowered drinking fountains are available. Readers and tape recorders are available for students with visual impairments. Special class scheduling can be arranged.

Graduates: The freshman dropout rate is 26%, and 45% of the freshmen remain to graduate. About 9% of the graduates seek advanced degrees, and 60% begin careers in business and industry.

Services: Students receive the following free services: placement aid, career counseling, tutoring, remedial instruction, and psychological counseling. Health care is available for a fee. Placement services also are available to alumni.

Programs of Study: The college offers the B.A., B.F.A., B.M., B.S., B.S.B.A., B.S.Ed., and B.S.N. degrees. Master's degrees are also awarded. Bachelor's degrees are offered in the following subjects: BUSINESS (accounting, business administration, computer science, finance, management, marketing), EDUCATION (elementary, environmental, health/physical, library science, recreation, secondary, special), ENGLISH (communication, English), FINE AND PERFORMING ARTS (art, music, music therapy), HEALTH SCIENCES (medical technology, nursing), LANGUAGES (French, German, Spanish), MATH AND SCIENCES (biology, chemistry, earth science, ecology/environmental science, geology, mathematics, physics), PHILOSOPHY (philosophy), SOCIAL SCIENCES (anthropology, economics, environmental studies, geography, government/political science, history, psychology, public administration, rural and urban studies, social work, sociology).

Required: Freshmen must take English composition, public speaking, physical education, and basic mathematics.

Special: Overseas-study programs include a semester in Spain, summer sessions in Salzburg and Nairobi, and an academic year in Basel. Interdisciplinary studies include environmental science, marine science, and administrative science. A 3-2 engineering program is offered in cooperation with Pennsylvania State University.

Honors: Honors programs are offered in many departments. There are 15 honor societies.

Admissions: Eighty-two percent of those who applied were accepted for the 1981–82 freshman class. The SAT scores of those who enrolled were as follows: Verbal—88% scored below 500, 11% between 500 and 599, 1% between 600 and 700, and 0% above 700; Math—88% scored below 500, 11% between 500 and 599, 1% between 600 and 700, and 0% above 700. Requirements for admission are flexible. Students should have a minimum 2.0 grade average, satisfactory character, and good SAT scores. The school also considers such factors as advanced placement or honors courses, impressions made during an interview, and recommendations by school officials.

Procedure: The SAT or ACT is required and should be taken in December or January of the senior year. Freshmen are admitted to both semesters and the summer session. Application deadlines are August 15 (fall) and January 1 (winter). A rolling admissions plan is used; applicants are notified 4 weeks after all information has been received. There is a $10 application fee.

Special: Early and deferred admissions plans are available. Students may earn credit through AP exams.

Transfer: For fall 1981, 644 students applied, 526 were accepted, and 351 enrolled. Transfers are considered for all years. Applicants should have a minimum of 12 completed credit hours with an overall GPA of 2.0. They must present official transcripts from every college attended. An interview is also recommended. D grades are acceptable in many cases. Students must complete, at the college, at least 30 of the 128 or more credits necessary for a bachelor's degree. Application deadlines are the same as those for freshmen.

Visiting: An orientation is held for prospective students. Informal visits with guided tours are also available. Visitors may sit in on classes; overnight accommodations are available. Visits and interviews can be arranged through the admissions office.

Financial Aid: Eighty percent of all students receive aid through the school. Forty percent work part-time on campus. Average aid to freshmen covered 80% of costs in 1981–82. Scholarships for freshmen are limited; loans are available. Students must submit Pennsylvania State Grant and Federal Student Aid forms by May 1 for fall and spring entry.

Foreign Students: The 52 students from foreign countries make up less than 1% of enrollment. The college offers these students an intensive English course, special counseling, and special organizations.

Admissions: Foreign students must score at least 550 on the TOEFL. No college entrance exams are required.

Procedure: The application deadline is February 15 for the fall semester, the only one to which foreign students are admitted. Students must present a health record and proof of adequate funds for 1 year. They also must carry health insurance, which is available through the college for a fee.

Admissions Contact: Eliott Baker, Director of Admissions.

SPRING GARDEN COLLEGE F-3
Chestnut Hill, Pennsylvania 19118 (215) 242-3700

F/T: 657M, 140W	Faculty:	68; IIB, +$
P/T: 430M, 118W	Ph.D.'s:	34%
Grad: none	S/F Ratio:	16 to 1
Year: 4-1-4, ss	Tuition:	$3550
Appl: Sept. 1	R and B:	$2000
555 applied	345 accepted	245 enrolled
SAT: 387V 452M		COMPETITIVE

Spring Garden College, founded in 1851, is a private professional and technical college. The library contains 13,000 volumes and subscribes to 400 periodicals.

Environment: The 7-acre campus is located in a suburban area 12 miles from the center of Philadelphia. There are no dormitories, but about 250 students live in approved off-campus housing.

Student Life: About 70% of the students are from Pennsylvania, and 40% attended public schools. About 92% live at home. Eight percent are minority-group members. Students may keep cars on campus.

Organizations: There are 3 fraternities, to which 10% of the men belong. Dances, lectures, and concerts are held regularly. Activities include a literary magazine, yearbook, the International Student Club, and special-interest groups.

Sports: The college fields 3 intercollegiate teams for men and 1 for women. There are 7 intramural sports for men and 6 for women.

Handicapped: About 60% of the campus is accessible to wheelchair-bound students. Special facilities include ramps and parking areas.

Graduates: The freshman dropout rate is 20%. Approximately 10% of the graduates seek advanced degrees, while 90% pursue careers in business and industry.

Services: The following services are available free to students: placement aid, career counseling, psychological counseling, health care, tutoring, and remedial instruction. According to the college, 87% of graduates find jobs through the campus placement service.

Programs of Study: The B.A., B.Arch., B.S., and B.S.Tech. degrees are offered. Associate degrees also are awarded. Bachelor's degrees are offered in the following subjects: BUSINESS (accounting, adminis-

780 PENNSYLVANIA

tration for registered nurses, business administration, computer science, management), FINE AND PERFORMING ARTS (interior design), HEALTH SCIENCES (biochemical technology, medical technology), MATH AND SCIENCES (biochemistry, chemistry, life sciences for registered nurses), PREPROFESSIONAL (architecture, engineering technology).

Special: There is a work-stdy program. Students with a bachelor's degree in any field can pursue a second degree in computer systems.

Admissions: Sixty-two percent of those who applied were accepted for the 1981–82 freshman class. The SAT scores of those who enrolled were as follows: Verbal—58% scored below 500, 42% between 500 and 599, 0% between 600 and 700, and 0% above 700, Math—39% scored below 500, 58% between 500 and 599, 3% between 600 and 700, and 0% above 700. Candidates should have completed 16 Carnegie units and rank in the upper 50% of their high school class. Other factors considered by the college are impressions made during an interview, evidence of special talent in architecture or interior design, and recommendations by school officials.

Procedure: The SAT is required. The deadlines for admission are September 1 for the fall semester and January 15 for spring. Notification is on a rolling basis. A $20 application fee is required.

Special: Early admissions and early decision plans are available. CLEP and AP credit is given.

Transfer: For fall 1981, 288 students applied, 201 were accepted, and 141 enrolled. Transfers are accepted for all levels. A minimum 2.0 GPA and standardized exam scores are required. Students must earn, at the college, at least 30 of the average 130 credits necessary for a bachelor's degree. Application deadlines are the same as those for freshmen.

Visiting: Guides for informal visits are available weekdays from 9 A.M. to 3 P.M.. Visitors may sit in on classes. Arrangements should be made with the office of admissions.

Financial Aid: About 60% of all students receive aid. Twenty-two percent work part-time on campus. Average aid to freshmen covered 35% of costs in 1981–82. NDSL and BEOG are available to qualified students. The college is a member of the CSS. The FAF is required; applications are due by May 1 (fall) or December 1 (spring).

Foreign Students: The 64 students from foreign countries make up 3% of enrollment. The college offers these students special organizations.

Admissions: Foreign students must score at least 450 on the TOEFL. No college entrance exams are required.

Procedure: Application deadlines are August 15 (fall) and December 15 (spring). Foreign students must present proof of adequate funds for 1 year. Health insurance, though not required, is available through the college for a fee.

Admissions Contact: Peter J. Bonasto, Director of Admissions.

SUSQUEHANNA UNIVERSITY D–3
Selinsgrove, Pennsylvania 17870   (717) 374-0101

F/T: 769M, 710W	Faculty: 98; IIB, + +$
P/T: 6M, 12W	Ph.D.'s: 50%
Grad: none	S/F Ratio: 15 to 1
Year: tri, ss	Tuition: $4745
Appl: Mar. 15	R and B: $1977
1516 applied	1048 accepted 409 enrolled
SAT: 470V 520M	COMPETITIVE

Susquehanna University, founded in 1858 and related to the Lutheran Church in America, offers programs in business, the liberal arts and sciences, music, and preprofessional fields. The library contains 120,000 volumes and 20,937 microfilm items, and subscribes to 1115 periodicals.

Environment: The 185-acre campus is located in a small town in a rural area 50 miles from Harrisburg. Buildings include a complex of modular houses for resident students and an extensive physical-education center. Selinsgrove Hall, the main administration building, and Seibert Hall, a dormitory for women, have recently been declared historical monuments. Residence facilities include 7 dormitories and 5 fraternity houses.

Student Life: Forty-five percent of the students come from Pennsylvania. About 90% are public-school graduates. Eighty-one percent live on campus. Fifty-three percent are Protestant, 27% are Catholic, and 10% are Jewish. Two percent are minority-group members. University housing is both coed and single-sex; students in single-sex housing have visiting privileges. Students may keep cars on campus.

Organizations: Twenty-nine percent of the men are members of the 5 national fraternities on campus, and 27% of the women belong to the 4 sororities. The university sponsors social and extracurricular activities. Nearby recreational facilities include the Raymond B. Winter State Park.

Sports: The university fields 10 intercollegiate teams for men and 6 for women. There are 6 intramural sports for men and 4 for women.

Handicapped: Thirty percent of the campus is accessible to the physically handicapped. Wheelchair ramps, special parking, specially equipped rest rooms, elevators, and special class scheduling are provided. Outside personnel are hired to assist visually impaired and hearing-impaired students when needed.

Graduates: About 12% of the freshmen drop out, and 75% remain to graduate. Of those who graduate, 30% seek advanced degrees; 2% enter medical school and 3% enter law school. Sixty percent pursue careers in business or industry.

Services: Health care, psychological counseling, career counseling, tutoring, and placement services are available free to students.

Programs of Study: The university confers the B.A., B.S.Bus., and B.M. degrees. Associate degrees are also awarded. Bachelor's degrees are offered in the following subjects: BUSINESS (accounting, business administration, computer science, finance, management, marketing), EDUCATION (elementary, secondary), ENGLISH (English), FINE AND PERFORMING ARTS (music, music education, radio/TV, theater/dramatics), LANGUAGES (French, German, Greek/Latin, Spanish), MATH AND SCIENCES (biology, chemistry, geology, mathematics, physics), PHILOSOPHY (philosophy, religion), SOCIAL SCIENCES (economics, government/political science, history, psychology, sociology). Non-major preprofessional programs are available in dentistry, engineering, forestry, law, medicine, ministry, social work, and veterinary science. Forty percent of degrees are conferred in business, 18% in social sciences, 15% in math and sciences, and 17% in fine and performing arts.

Required: All students must take courses in writing, science or mathematics, physical education, humanities, social sciences, and fine arts.

Special: Combined B.A.-B.S. degrees may be earned in engineering in conjunction with the University of Pennsylvania. Interdepartmental majors are offered in several areas, and students may design their own majors. Internships are available in 13 departments. Students may spend their junior year abroad, or a summer at Oxford University. Other programs include a U.N. semester at Drew University, a Washington semester at American University, an Appalachian semester at Union College, and urban semesters in Baltimore or Harrisburg.

Honors: Honors programs are offered by the departments of chemistry, English, geological and environmental sciences, history, modern languages, political science, and religion and philosophy. Ten national honor societies have chapters on campus.

Admissions: Sixty-nine percent of the applicants for the 1981–82 freshman class were accepted. The SAT scores of those who enrolled were as follows: Verbal—69% scored below 500, 29% between 500 and 599, 3% between 600 and 700, and 0% above 700; Math—41% scored below 500, 43% between 500 and 599, 15% between 600 and 700, and 1% above 700. Applicants should rank in the upper three-fifths of their high school class and have a minimum grade average of 2.5. Other considerations include advanced placement or honors courses, impressions made during an interview, recommendations by school officials, extracurricular activities, and leadership record.

Procedure: The SAT or the ACT is required. Two ATs, including English Composition, are recommended for placement purposes. The application deadlines are March 15 (fall), November 4 (winter), and February 10 (spring). Notification is made on a rolling basis. There is an application fee of $20.

Special: The university offers early admissions, deferred admissions, and early decision plans. CLEP and AP credit is accepted.

Transfer: For fall 1981, 111 students applied, 76 were accepted, and 46 enrolled. Transfer students need a GPA of at least 2.0 and an interview; Bachelor of Music candidates must audition. D grades do not transfer. Students must study at the university for at least 2 years, completing at least 18 of the 35 credits necessary for a bachelor's degree. Application deadlines are May 1 (fall), November 4 (winter), and February 10 (spring).

Visiting: Regularly scheduled orientations for prospective students include financial-aid discussions, campus tours, meetings with departmental representatives, and admissions talks. For informal tours, visitors are provided with guides and may sit in on classes and stay overnight at the school. Visits may be made from 9 A.M. to 3 P.M. when school is in session. All visiting plans should be made through the admissions office secretary.

Financial Aid: Seventy-two percent of all students receive aid. Thirty-nine percent work part-time on campus. Average aid to freshmen was $3707 in 1981–82. Scholarships, loans, BEOG, NDSL, work-study, and grants-in-aid are available. The FAF is required. The aid application deadline is February 15.

Foreign Students: The 8 students from foreign countries make up less than 1% of enrollment. The university offers these students special organizations.

Admissions: Foreign students must score at least 550 on the TOEFL. The university recommends that applicants also take the SAT or the ACT.

Procedure: Application deadlines are March 15 (fall), November 4 (winter), and February 10 (spring). Foreign students must present a university health form completed by a physician. They also must provide proof of adequate funds for the first year of study. Health insurance is included in the standard student fee.

Admissions Contact: Paul W. Beardslee, Director of Admissions.

SWARTHMORE COLLEGE   F–4
Swarthmore, Pennsylvania 19081   (215) 447-7300

F/T: 730M, 590W	Faculty: 145; IIB, ++$
P/T: 11M, 16W	Ph.D.'s: 90%
Grad: none	S/F Ratio: 9 to 1
Year: sems	Tuition: $6730
Appl: Feb. 1	R and B: $2650
2000 applied	737 accepted	318 enrolled
SAT: 640V 670M		MOST COMPETITIVE

Swarthmore College, a privately endowed nonsectarian college, was founded by the Society of Friends in 1864. The libraries have 573,000 volumes and 210,000 microfilm items, and subscribe to 2450 periodicals.

Environment: The 300-acre campus is located in a suburban area 11 miles from Philadelphia. Campus facilities include the Tarble Athletic Pavilion, Ware Swimming Pool, Mertz Dormitory, and Papazian Hall. Dormitories accommodate 1210 students.

Student Life: More than 80% of the students come from outside Pennsylvania. About 72% are public-school graduates. Ninety percent live in the dormitories. Nineteen percent are minority-group members. College housing is both coed and single-sex; students in single-sex housing have visiting privileges.

Organizations: Ten percent of the men are members of the 1 national and 2 local fraternities on campus. There is a Student Council, and students are represented on the major college committees. Religious associations for Jewish, Catholic, and Protestant students operate at the school; services in the Quaker tradition also are held.

Sports: The college fields 13 intercollegiate teams for men and 13 for women. There are 13 intramural sports for men and 12 for women.

Handicapped: Seventy-five percent of the campus is accessible to the physically handicapped. Wheelchair ramps, elevators, special parking and rest rooms, and special class scheduling are provided. There is a special counselor to assist handicapped students.

Graduates: The freshman dropout rate is 3%, and 85% of the freshmen remain to graduate. About 70% of graduates pursue advanced degrees; 15% enter medical school, 1% enter dental school, and 15% enter law school. Twenty percent pursue careers in business and industry.

Services: Free psychological counseling, remedial instruction, career counseling, placement services, and health care are offered. Some tutoring requires a fee.

Programs of Study: The college confers the B.A. and B.S. degrees. Bachelor's degrees are offered in the following subjects: AREA (Asian, medieval), ENGLISH (English, literature), FINE AND PERFORMING ARTS (art, music, theater/dramatics), LANGUAGES (French, German, Russian, Spanish), MATH AND SCIENCES (astronomy, biology, chemistry, mathematics, physics), PHILOSOPHY (classics, philosophy, religion), PREPROFESSIONAL (engineering), SOCIAL SCIENCES (anthropology, economics, government/political science, history, international relations, psychology, sociology). Twenty-five percent of degrees conferred are in math and sciences, 25% in social sciences, and 15% in engineering.

Required: Students must take courses in 4 general areas of study.

Special: A 5-year program leads to a combined B.A.-B.S. degree in engineering and liberal arts. Students may design their own majors. All freshman courses in the first semester are graded on a pass/fail basis. There is a cross-registration program with nearby colleges, including Bryn Mawr, Haverford, and the University of Pennsylvania. Juniors and sophomores may study abroad in a wide variety of places, including 2 Swarthmore centers in France and Spain.

Honors: All departments offer honors programs. The seminar method is used during the last 2 years; students are evaluated by outside examiners. Phi Beta Kappa and Sigma Xi have chapters on campus.

Admissions: Thirty-seven percent of those who applied were accepted for the 1981–82 freshman class. The SAT scores of those who enrolled were as follows: Verbal—9% scored below 500, 22% between 500 and 599, 45% between 600 and 700, and 24% above 700; Math—6% scored below 500, 16% between 500 and 599, 43% between 600 and 700, and 35% above 700. Twenty-seven freshmen were National Merit Scholars. Students must show evidence of ability to maintain the high standards of the college. An interview is recommended. Admissions officers consider the applicant's high school record, college-board scores, extracurricular activities, advanced placement or honors courses, and recommendations by school officials.

Procedures: The SAT and 3 ATs, including English Composition, are required and should be taken by January of the senior year. The application deadline for fall, the only semester to which freshmen are admitted, is February 1. There is a $25 application fee.

Special: Deferred admissions and early decision plans are available. AP credit is accepted.

Transfer: For fall 1981, 200 students applied, 15 were accepted, and 10 enrolled. Transfers are accepted for the sophomore and junior years and should have an excellent record at their previous college. A minimum GPA of 3.0, 8 completed courses, and an interview are recommended. D grades do not transfer. Students must study at the college for 2 years, completing at least 16 of the 32 courses necessary for a bachelor's degree. Transfer application deadlines are April 15 (fall) and November 15 (winter).

Financial Aid: Approximately 46% of all students receive aid. Sixty percent work part-time on campus. Average aid to freshmen in 1981–82 was $3700. About 250 freshman scholarships are offered each year. Loans are also available. The college is a member of CSS. Financial aid is given on the basis of need as determined by the FAF, which must be submitted by February 1.

Foreign Students: The 90 students from foreign countries make up 7% of enrollment. The college offers these students special counseling and special organizations.

Admissions: Foreign students must score at least 600 on the TOEFL. The SAT is also required.

Procedure: The application deadline is February 1 for fall entry. Foreign students must present proof of adequate funds for 1 year. They must also carry health insurance, which is available through the college.

Admissions Contact: Robert A. Barr, Jr., Dean of Admissions.

TEMPLE UNIVERSITY   F–3
Philadelphia, Pennsylvania 19122   (215) 787-7200

F/T: 7270M, 7037W	Faculty: 1781; I, +$
P/T: 3873M, 3352W	Ph.D.'s: 90%
Grad: 4153M, 4202W	S/F Ratio: 8 to 1
Year: sems, ss	Tuition: $2382 ($4440)
Appl: June 15	R and B: $2425
8267 applied	5088 accepted	2423 enrolled
SAT: 481V 512M		COMPETITIVE

Temple University, founded in 1884, is one of the largest universities in the country. There are 6 campuses under common administrative control. The undergraduate divisions include 5 schools (Business Administration, Communications and Theater, Dental Hygiene, Social Administration, and Tyler School of Art), 6 colleges (Allied Health Professions, Education, Engineering Technology, Health/Physical Education/Recreation and Dance, Liberal Arts, and Music), and the department of criminal justice. The library contains over 1.1 million volumes and 536,000 microfilm items, and subscribes to 11,780 periodicals.

Environment: The main campus is located near the center of the Delaware Valley. Dormitory space there is available for 1200 students. The 187-acre Ambler Campus accommodates 5500 commuter and resident students. The Tyler School of Art is located in Elkins Park, Pennsylvania. The Health Sciences Campus, located about 1 mile north of the Main Campus, houses the schools of Medicine, Dentistry, Pharmacy, and Dental Hygiene, and the College of Allied Health Professions. Dormitory space is also available on all campuses.

Student Life: About 83% of the students come from Pennsylvania. Sixty percent come from public schools. About 18% live on campus or in approved off-campus housing. Forty-three percent are Catholic,

19% are Protestant, and 14% are Jewish. About 21% are minority-group members. Campus housing is both coed and single-sex; there are visiting privileges in single-sex dorms. Students may keep cars on campus. Day-care services are provided for a fee.

Organizations: There are 8 fraternities and 7 sororities. The university sponsors more than 52 special-interest and social groups. Activities include a student-run radio station, a campus newspaper, theater productions, and student/faculty music and dance recitals.

Sports: The university competes on an intercollegiate level in 13 sports for men and 13 for women. Eleven intramural sports are open to both men and women.

Handicapped: About 75% of the campus is accessible to wheelchair-bound students. Special parking, wheelchair ramps, elevators, special rest rooms, and motorized carts are available. Reader services are available for students with visual impairments, and interpreters for those with hearing impairments.

Services: Students receive the following free services: placement aid, career counseling, remedial instruction, health care, and psychological counseling. Tutoring is available for a fee.

Programs of Study: The university confers the B.A., B.S., B.B.A., B.S.Ed., B.Mus., B.M.Ed., B.S.W., and B.F.A. degrees. Associate, master's, and doctoral programs are also offered. Bachelor's degrees are offered in the following subjects: AREA STUDIES (American, Asian, Black/Afro-American, Puerto Rican, urban, women's), BUSINESS (accounting, actuarial science, business administration, business education, business law, computer science, finance, industrial relations, management, marketing, real estate/insurance), EDUCATION (early childhood, elementary, health/physical, industrial, secondary), ENGLISH (English, journalism, speech), FINE AND PERFORMING ARTS (art, art education, art history, dance, film/photography, music, music education, radio/TV, studio art, theater/dramatics), HEALTH SCIENCES (health records administration, medical technology, nursing, occupational therapy, physical therapy, speech therapy), LANGUAGES (Chinese, French, German, Greek/Latin, Hebrew, Italian, Portuguese, Russian, Spanish), MATH AND SCIENCES (biochemistry, biology, chemistry, geology, mathematics, physics, statistics), PHILOSOPHY (classics, philosophy, religion), PREPROFESSIONAL (architecture, dentistry, engineering—civil/construction, engineering—electrical, engineering—mechanical, engineering—biomedical engineering technology, engineering—civil/construction engineering technology, engineering—electrical engineering technology, engineering—environmental engineering technology, engineering—mechanical engineering technology, law, medicine, pharmacy, social work, veterinary), SOCIAL SCIENCES (anthropology, child care, criminal justice, economics, geography, government/political science, history, psychology, recreation and leisure studies, social work, sociology). Twenty-two percent of degrees conferred are in business, 21% in education, and 17% in social sciences.

Special: Students may design their own majors. Qualified students majoring in any subject may spend a year at Temple's campus in Rome, Italy. Theater students may study at Temple's program in London, and students interested in Irish culture and history may study in the university's program in Dublin. Exchange programs are available with the University of Puerto Rico, the University of Hamburg, the Nijenrode School of Business, and Nankai University in the People's Republic of China. Summer programs at a variety of locations are also offered. Cooperative programs are offered in most colleges to help prepare students for specific occupations. A 3-year bachelor's degree can be earned in some fields.

Honors: Honors programs are available to students in the College of Liberal Arts. Other departments offer honors work for juniors and seniors. Twelve national honor societies have chapters on campus.

Admissions: Sixty-two percent of those who enrolled were accepted for the 1981-82 freshman class. The SAT scores of those enrolled were as follows: Verbal—59% scored below 500, 31% between 500 and 599, 8% between 600 and 700, and 1% above 700; Math—42% scored below 500, 45% between 500 and 599, 12% between 600 and 700, and 2% above 700. Candidates must be high school graduates, rank in the top 60% of their class, and have completed 16 high school units. The school also considers advanced placement or honors courses, extracurricular activities record, leadership record, recommendations by school officials, and evidence of special talents.

Procedure: The SAT or ACT is required and should be taken between March of the junior year and April of the senior year. Application deadlines are June 15 (fall) and November 15 (spring). Candidates are notified on a rolling basis. There is a $15 application fee.

Special: Early admissions and deferred admissions plans are available. CLEP and AP credit is accepted.

Transfer: For fall 1981, 4654 transfer students applied, 3135 were accepted, and 2035 enrolled. Transfers are considered for all classes and should have an A.S. degree or a minimum 2.0 GPA. D grades do not transfer. Students must complete, at the university, at least 30 semester hours of the 128 necessary for the bachelor's degree. Transfer application deadlines are the same as those for freshmen.

Visiting: Interviews are scheduled during the week and on Saturdays during the academic semesters. Informal visits can be arranged through the undergraduate admissions office.

Financial Aid: About 60% of all students receive aid in the form of scholarships (including Pell Grants), loans (including NDSL), and campus employment (including CWS). Six percent of the students work part-time on campus. The average award to freshmen in 1981-82 was $2163. Loans are provided by the federal government, local banks, the university, and private funds. Financial aid is awarded on the basis of need; renewal is contingent upon continued need and academic record. The university is a member of CSS and requires the FAF or FFS. Applications for aid must be submitted by May 1.

Foreign Students: About 10 students come from foreign countries. The university offers these students an intensive English program as well as special counseling and special organizations.

Admissions: Foreign students must score at least 500 on the TOEFL. The SAT or ACT is also required.

Procedure: Application deadlines are April 15 (fall) and November 1 (spring). Students must submit a completed university health form and show proof of adequate funds for the duration of their studies at the university. Foreign students must carry health insurance, which is available through the university for a fee.

Admissions Contact: R. Kenneth Haldeman, Director of Admissions.

THIEL COLLEGE   A-2
Greenville, Pennsylvania 16125   (412) 588-7700

F/T: 468M, 453W   Faculty: 63; IIB, av$
P/T: 12M, 27W   Ph.D.'s: 52%
Grad: none   S/F Ratio: 14 to 1
Year: 4-1-4, ss   Tuition: $4318
Appl: open   R and B: $2076
935 applied   752 accepted   322 enrolled
SAT: 445V 440M   ACT: 18   COMPETITIVE

Thiel College, founded in 1866, is a liberal arts college affiliated with the Lutheran Church. The library contains 110,000 volumes and 13,000 microfilm items, and subscribes to 774 periodicals.

Environment: The 135-acre campus is situated in a rural area near the northwestern Pennsylvania town of Greenville in the Allegheny foothills, 70 miles from Pittsburgh. Facilities include a language laboratory, a 2000-seat auditorium, a fraternity row of 5 houses, and a quad with 4 dormitories.

Student Life: More than 20% of the students are from out of state. About 90% attended public schools. Eighty-six percent live on campus. Three percent are minirity-group members. About 20% of the students are Lutheran, 31% are Catholic, and 1% are Protestant. Campus housing is single-sex; there are visiting privileges. Students may keep cars on campus.

Organizations: There are 1 local and 3 national fraternities to which 50% of the men belong; 5 national sororities attract 50% of the women. Off-campus recreational activities include 3 nearby parks.

Sports: The college fields 8 intercollegiate teams for men and 7 for women. There are 4 intramural sports for men and 3 for women.

Handicapped: About 85% of the campus is accessible to handicapped students. Wheelchair ramps, parking areas, elevators, and specially equipped rest rooms are available. The Learning Skills Center, readers, tutors, and special equipment are offered for visually impaired students. The college has a special counselor for the handicapped.

Graduates: The freshman dropout rate is 22%; 65% of the freshmen remain to graduate. Eighteen percent of the graduates pursue advanced degrees. Twenty percent begin careers in business and industry.

Services: Students receive free health care, career counseling, placement aid, tutoring, and remedial instruction.

Programs of Study: The college confers the B.A. and B.S. degrees. Associate degrees are also awarded. Bachelor's degrees are offered in the following subjects: BUSINESS (accounting, business administration, computer science), EDUCATION (elementary, environmental, secondary), ENGLISH (English), FINE AND PERFORMING ARTS (art), HEALTH SCIENCES (medical technology, nursing, speech therapy), LANGUAGES (French, Spanish), MATH AND SCIENCES (biology, chemistry, ecology/environmental science, geology, mathematics, physics), PHILOSOPHY (philosophy, religion), PREPROFESSIONAL (dentistry, engineering, forestry, law, medicine, ministry, pharmacy, veterinary), SOCIAL SCIENCES (economics, government/political science, history, psychology, sociology). Thirty-eight percent of the degrees conferred are in business, 24% in social sciences, and 21% in math and sciences.

Required: All students must complete a general distribution of courses in English, the humanities, social sciences, science, and physical education.

Special: The college offers combination-degree programs in medical technology, nursing (with Case Western Reserve), and engineering (with Case Western Reserve). Teacher certification is offered for elementary, secondary, and environmental education. The Washington Semester, United Nations Semester, and junior-year-abroad programs are available.

Honors: Twelve national honor societies have chapters on campus. Honors programs are available in all areas.

Admissions: Eighty percent of those who applied were accepted for the 1981–82 freshman class. The SAT scores of those who enrolled were as follows: Verbal—68% scored below 500, 16% between 500 and 599, 4% between 600 and 700, and 0% above 700; Math—54% scored below 500, 27% between 500 and 599, 7% between 600 and 700, and 0% above 700. Of those who took the ACT, 53% scored below 20, 37% between 21 and 23, 0% between 24 and 25, 11% between 26 and 28, and 0% above 28. Candidates should present 16 units of high school credit, rank in the upper 80% of their class, and have at least a 2.5 average. Advanced placement or honors courses and recommendations also are considered.

Procedure: The SAT or ACT is required. An interview is recommended. There are no application deadlines; freshmen are admitted to all terms. Admission is on a rolling basis. The application fee is $15.

Special: An early admissions plan is available. AP and CLEP credit is granted.

Transfer: For fall 1981, 62 students applied, 46 were accepted, and 26 enrolled. D grades do not transfer. A 2.0 GPA is required. Application deadlines are August 15 (fall) and May 15 (summer). Students must complete, at the college, at least 30 of the 128 credits required for a bachelor's degree.

Visiting: Orientations for prospective students include campus tours, lunch, class visits, meetings with professors, admissions interviews, and financial-aid seminars. Informal visits are best scheduled Monday through Friday from 8:30 A.M. to 4:00 P.M. and Saturdays from 9 A.M. to noon. Guides are provided. Visitors may sit in on classes and stay overnight at the school. Arrangements should be made through the admissions office.

Financial Aid: Sixty-four percent of the students receive aid. Forty-six percent work part-time on campus. The college awards a combination of scholarships, loans, and campus employment to qualified students. The average aid to freshmen covered 32% of costs in 1981–82. Several departments have CWS. The college is a member of CSS. The FAF is required. The application deadline is May 1.

Foreign Students: One percent of the students come from foreign countries. An intensive English course and special counseling are available for these students.

Admissions: Foreign students must score at least 500 on the TOEFL. No college entrance exams are required.

Procedure: Application deadlines are May 1 (fall), October 1 (spring), and February 1 (summer). Foreign students must submit a completed health form and present proof of adequate funds for their entire period of study. They also must carry health insurance, which is available through the college for a fee.

Admissions Contact: John R. Hauser, Director of Admissions and Financial Aid.

UNIVERSITY OF PENNSYLVANIA F–3
Philadelphia, Pennsylvania 19104 (215) 243-7509

F/T: 5300M, 3400W	Faculty: 1800; I, ++$
P/T: 306M, 261W	Ph.D.'s: 86%
Grad: 5488M, 1806W	S/F Ratio: 7 to 1
Year: sems, ss	Tuition: $6900
Appl: Jan. 1	R and B: $3350
11,367 applied	4470 accepted 2149 enrolled
SAT: 620V 680M	MOST COMPETITIVE

Founded in 1740 as a private, nonsectarian school, the University of Pennsylvania was the first institution of higher learning to offer subjects such as applied mathematics, modern languages, economics, public law, the sciences, and medicine, and thus is considered the nation's first true university. A member of the Ivy League, Penn makes all the facilities of its 4 undergraduate and 13 graduate divisions accessible to all students. The undergraduate divisions are the College (arts and sciences), the Wharton School of Business, the School of Engineering and Applied Science, and the School of Nursing. The main library—the largest completely open-stack library of any American university—contains 2.9 million volumes and 46,000 microfilm items, and subscribes to over 13,000 periodicals.

Environment: Separated from the center of Philadelphia by the Schuylkill River, the 247-acre campus has more than 150 buildings, including an ice pavilion, the Annenberg Center for Communications and Performing Arts, a hospital, and the University Museum. Student residences include dormitories, college houses that provide living-learning experiences, on- and off-campus apartments, married-student quarters, and fraternity and sorority houses.

Student Life: About 25% of the students come from Pennsylvania. Ninety percent live on campus. Nearly 70% are graduates of public schools. Twenty-two percent are minority-group members. Campus housing is coed. Students may have cars on campus. The university provides day-care services.

Organizations: More than 225 extracurricular activities are available on campus, including student government, publications, performing-arts groups, and an FM radio station. Religious counselors and organizations are available for students of all major faiths. The university schedules on-campus cultural and social events. Twenty-eight fraternities and 3 sororities have chapters on campus.

Sports: The university fields intercollegiate teams in 17 sports for men and 15 for women. Nineteen intramural sports are available for men and 18 for women.

Graduates: About 3% of the freshmen drop out by the end of their first year, and 85% remain to graduate. About 70% of the graduates pursue advanced degrees; 12% enter medical school and 1% enter dental school.

Services: Free placement services, career and psychological counseling, tutoring, and remedial instruction are available to students. Fees are charged for some health-care services.

Programs of Study: The university confers the B.A., B.S., B.S. in E., B.S.N., and B.Applied Sci. in Eng. degrees. Master's and doctoral programs are also available. Bachelor's degrees are offered in the following subjects: AREA STUDIES (American, Asian, Black/Afro-American, East Asian, Latin American, Russian, Southeast Asian, urban), BUSINESS (accounting, actuarial science, business administration, computer science, finance, management, marketing, real estate/insurance), EDUCATION (elementary), ENGLISH (English, linguistics, literature), FINE AND PERFORMING ARTS (art history, fine arts, music, theater/dramatics), HEALTH SCIENCES (environmental science, nursing), LANGUAGES (Chinese, French, German, Greek/Latin, Hebrew, Italian, Japanese, Portuguese, Russian, Spanish), MATH AND SCIENCES (astronomy, biochemistry, biology, botany, chemistry, earth science, ecology/environmental science, geology, mathematics, natural sciences, physics, statistics, zoology), PHILOSOPHY (classics, philosophy, religion), PREPROFESSIONAL (architecture, engineering—bioengineering, engineering—chemical, engineering—civil and urban, engineering—computer science, engineering—electrical, engineering—materials, engineering—mechanical, engineering—systems), SOCIAL SCIENCES (anthropology, economics, government/political science, history, international relations, psychology, sociology). Non-major preprofessional programs are available in dentistry, law, medicine, ministry, social work, and veterinary medicine. About 25% of the undergraduate degrees are conferred in business and 22% in social sciences.

Required: Liberal arts students must complete 3 related courses in humanities, in social sciences, and in natural sciences. They also must demonstrate proficiency in a foreign language. Nursing, engineering, and business students must complete a number of liberal arts courses.

Special: Qualified students may take courses in all undergraduate and many graduate programs. They also may design their own majors or pursue 2 majors simultaneously. An example of such a dual program is management/technology, which leads to degrees from both the Wharton School and the Engineering School. The University Scholars Program combines graduate and undergraduate study. The Freshman Seminar Program offers at least 1 class per semester with 17 students or fewer. There are many opportunities for study abroad.

Honors: Twenty-four honor societies, including Phi Beta Kappa, have chapters on campus. The university offers a general honors program.

Admissions: About 39% of the applicants for the 1981–82 freshman class were accepted. Candidates must have graduated from accredited high schools and have completed a well-rounded curriculum, including math, science, English, history, and foreign language. Requirements are flexible, but 90% of the 1981–82 freshmen ranked in the top 10% of their high school class. Admissions officers also consider advanced placement or honors courses. The university seeks a socially, culturally, and economically diverse student body.

Procedure: Applicants must take the SAT and 3 ATs, including English Composition. Wharton and Engineering School candidates also must take the AT in mathematics, and any students interested in science-related fields are advised to take a science AT. These tests should be taken by December of the senior year. An interview is recommended. Freshmen are admitted only in the fall, and applications must be submitted by January 1. The application fee is $30. Notifications are mailed in mid-April.

Special: Early decision, early admissions, and deferred admissions plans are available. AP credit is given.

Transfer: For fall 1981, 1589 transfer students applied, 559 were accepted, and 384 enrolled. Applicants must possess excellent academic credentials and must have completed 8 transferable courses. Students must complete at least 2 years in residence, earning 16–20 of the 32–40 course units necessary for the bachelor's degree. Application deadlines are April 1 (fall) and October 15 (spring).

Visiting: Campus tours for prospective students are given daily during the school year. Information sessions are held daily at 1 P.M. Visitors may sit in on classes and stay overnight at the school. The admissions office should be contacted for arrangements.

Financial Aid: About 53% of the students receive financial aid. Loans are available from federal and state governments, local banks, private sources, and the university. The university also provides scholarships, and CWS is available. The average award from all sources totaled $7072 in 1981–82. Tuition may be paid in installments. The university is a member of the CSS and requires aid candidates to submit the FAF. Aid applications should be filed by February 15.

Foreign Students: About 1500 students from foreign countries are enrolled at Penn, most as graduate students. The university actively recruits foreign students and offers them an intensive English course, an intensive English program, special counseling, and special organizations.

Admissions: Foreign students must score at least 550 on the TOEFL. The SAT and 3 ATs also are required.

Procedure: The application deadline is Jan. 1 for fall admission. Proof of adequate funds for 12 months of study is required. Students must carry health insurance, which is available through the university for a fee.

Admissions Contact: Willis J. Stetson, Jr., Director of Admissions.

UNIVERSITY OF PITTSBURGH

The University of Pittsburgh was established in 1787. It is a private and state-related institution, one-third of whose trustees are appointed by the Commonwealth of Pennsylvania. In addition to the main campus in Pittsburgh, there are independent regional campuses in Bradford, Greensburg, and Johnstown. Separate profiles on all 4 campuses follow.

UNIVERSITY OF PITTSBURGH B–3
Pittsburgh, Pennsylvania 15260 (412) 624-5761

F/T: 6109M, 5870W	Faculty: 2104; I, +$
P/T: 2663M, 4334W	Ph.D.'s: 58%
Grad: 4732M, 5498W	S/F Ratio: 6 to 1
Year: tri, ss	Tuition: $2060 ($4030)
Appl: open	R and B: $2250
6385 applied	4776 accepted 2600 enrolled
SAT: 480V 530M	VERY COMPETITIVE

The University of Pittsburgh's main campus offers undergraduate instruction in the liberal arts and sciences, business, education, health fields, engineering, and preprofessional and professional areas. The library contains 3.5 million volumes.

Environment: The 125-acre urban campus is located about 3 miles from downtown Pittsburgh. The 52 buildings on campus include residence halls that accommodate about 4200 students. There are facilities for commuters.

Student Life: About 91% of the students come from Pennsylvania. Most are public-school graduates. About 15% live on campus. Twelve percent are minority-group members. Campus housing is both coed and single-sex; there are visiting privileges in the single-sex dorms. Students may keep cars on campus. Day-care services are available.

Organizations: Extracurricular activities include student government, special-interest clubs, religious and service organizations, publications, and music and drama groups. Ten percent of the students belong to the 24 fraternities and 16 sororities.

Sports: The university fields intercollegiate teams in 12 sports for men and 9 for women. There are 12 intramural sports for men and 11 for women.

Handicapped: About 80% of the campus is accessible to handicapped students. Special facilities include wheelchair ramps, elevators, parking areas, specially equipped rest rooms, lowered drinking fountains and telephones, and transportation service. Special class scheduling is also available. Counselors are available.

Graduates: About 33% of the graduates pursue advanced degrees.

Services: The university provides psychological counseling, tutoring, remedial instruction, career counseling, and placement services free to students. Health care is available on a fee basis.

Programs of Study: The university confers the B.A. and B.S. degrees. Associate, master's, and doctoral degrees are also awarded. Bachelor's degrees are offered in the following subjects: AREA STUDIES (Black/Afro-American, urban), BUSINESS (accounting, business administration, computer science), EDUCATION (early childhood, elementary, health/physical, industrial/vocational, language communications, secondary), ENGLISH (English, literature, media communications, speech, writing), FINE AND PERFORMING ARTS (art, music, studio art), HEALTH SCIENCES (anesthesiology, child development and child care, health records administration, interdisciplinary health professions, medical technology, nursing, nutrition, physical therapy), LANGUAGES (Chinese, French, German, Italian, linguistics, Polish language/literature/culture, Russian, Spanish), MATH AND SCIENCES (behavioral science, behavioral neuroscience, biochemistry, biology, biophysics, chemistry, geology, mathematics, microbiology, natural sciences, physics, statistics), PHILOSOPHY (classics, humanities, philosophy), PREPROFESSIONAL (architectural studies, engineering, legal studies, pharmacy, social work), SOCIAL SCIENCES (administration of justice, anthropology, economics, geography, government/political science, history, history and philosophy of science, politics and philosophy, psychology, public administration, social sciences, sociology).

Required: Students must complete 9 hours each in humanities, natural sciences, and social sciences.

Special: Study abroad, independent study, a general-studies degree, and double majors for either a B.A. or B.S. degree are offered. Students may design their own majors.

Honors: Phi Beta Kappa and other honor societies have chapters on campus. Honors work is offered on a university-wide basis.

Admissions: About 75% of the applicants for the 1981–82 freshman class were accepted. About 56% of those who enrolled ranked in the top fifth of their high school class, 85% in the top two-fifths. For an earlier freshman class, the SAT scores were as follows: Verbal—47% between 500 and 599, 8% between 600 and 700, 2% above 700; Math—39% between 500 and 599, 20% between 600 and 700, 3% above 700. Candidates should have completed 15 Carnegie units and should have a GPA of at least 2.5. Other considerations are selection of courses and SAT or ACT scores.

Procedure: The SAT or ACT is required and should be taken by January of the senior year. There are no application deadlines; notification is made on a rolling basis. Freshmen are admitted in all 4 terms. There is a $15 application fee.

Special: Early admissions and deferred admissions plans are available. AP credit is given.

Transfer: For fall 1981, 2043 applications were received, 1181 were accepted, and 833 students enrolled. Transfers are accepted for all classes; D grades do not transfer. A 2.5 GPA is needed. All students must complete, at the university, 30 of the 120 credits required for a bachelor's degree, including half the courses in their major. Application deadlines are open.

Visiting: Orientations are regularly scheduled for prospective students. Guides are available for informal visits. Visitors may sit in on classes; between April and August, they may stay overnight on campus. Visits are best scheduled on weekdays between 9 A.M. and 4 P.M. and on Saturdays between 9 A.M. and noon. The admissions office should be contacted for arrangements.

Financial Aid: About 66% of the students receive aid. About 62% work part-time on campus. Scholarships, loans, and part-time jobs are available. The average award to freshmen in 1981–82 totaled $2400. The university is a member of CSS. The FAF should be filed by March 1.

Foreign Students: The 1186 students from foreign countries make up 7% of enrollment. An intensive English program, an intensive English course, special counseling, and special organizations are available for these students.

Admissions: Foreign students must score at least 500 on the TOEFL or 80 on the University of Michigan Language Test. No college entrance exams are required.

Procedure: Application deadlines are July 15 (fall), November 15 (winter), and March 15 (spring or summer). Students must present a physician's statement certified by a U.S. consulate. They also must show evidence of adequate funds for 1 year. Health insurance is required and is available through the university for a fee.

Admissions Contact: Joseph A. Merante, Director of Admissions.

UNIVERSITY OF PITTSBURGH AT BRADFORD   C-2

Bradford, Pennsylvania 16701   (814) 362-3801

F/T: 425M, 375W
P/T: 175M, 125W
Grad: none
Year: tri, ss
Appl: July 1
651 applied
SAT: 450V 550M

Faculty: 50; III, av$
Ph.D.'s: 85%
S/F Ratio: 17 to 1
Tuition: $2020 ($3940)
R and B: $2310
546 accepted   335 enrolled
ACT: 23   COMPETITIVE

The University of Pittsburgh at Bradford, established in 1963, offers undergraduate programs in the arts and sciences and in business. The library contains 50,000 volumes and 1800 microfilm items, and subscribes to 430 periodicals.

Environment: The 125-acre campus is located in a suburban area 85 miles from Buffalo, New York. There are 4 major buildings. On-campus apartments accommodate 450 men and women. There are also facilities for commuters. A new library/administration complex is under construction.

Student Life: About 90% of the students come from Pennsylvania. Most are public-school graduates. Forty-five percent live on campus. Ten percent are minority-group members. Campus housing is single-sex, with visiting privileges. Students may keep cars on campus.

Organizations: Extracurricular activities include special-interest clubs, publications, and student government. There are no fraternities or sororities.

Sports: The university fields intercollegiate teams in 3 sports for men and 3 for women. There are 10 intramural sports for men and 10 for women.

Handicapped: The entire campus is accessible to handicapped students. Special facilities include wheelchair ramps, elevators, specially equipped rest rooms, and lowered drinking fountains and telephones.

Graduates: The freshman dropout rate is 10%; about 75% remain to graduate. Twenty-five percent of the graduates pursue advanced degrees.

Services: The university provides health care, placement aid, career counseling, tutoring, and remedial instruction free to students. Psychological counseling is provided for a fee.

Programs of Study: The Bradford campus confers the B.A. and B.S. degrees. Associate degrees are also awarded. Bachelor's degrees are offered in the following subjects: BUSINESS (business administration, public administration), ENGLISH (English writing, literature, public relations), MATH AND SCIENCES (ecology/environmental science, environmental biology, mathematics/computer science, physical sciences), SOCIAL SCIENCES (human relations, social sciences).

Required: Students must take 3 courses each in humanities, in social sciences, and in natural sciences.

Special: Independent study, a general-studies degree, and a 3-year bachelor's degree are offered. Students may design their own majors.

Admissions: About 84% of those who applied for the 1981–82 freshman class were accepted. The SAT scores of those who enrolled were as follows: Verbal—55% scored below 500, 40% between 500 and 599, 4% between 600 and 700, and 1% above 700; Math—45% scored below 500, 45% between 500 and 599, 9% between 600 and 700, and 1% above 700. Applicants should have completed 15 units of academic work, rank in the upper 60% of their class, and have a GPA of at least 2.5. Advanced placement or honors courses, recommendations, and extracurricular activities also are considered.

Procedure: Either the SAT or the ACT is required. Application deadlines are July 1 (fall), December 1 (winter), April 15 (spring), and June 15 (summer). Notification is made on a rolling basis. There is a $15 application fee.

Special: Early decision, early admissions, and deferred admissions plans are offered. AP and CLEP credit is available.

Transfer: For fall 1981, 40 students applied, 35 were accepted, and 30 enrolled. Transfer students are accepted for all classes. A 2.5 GPA and at least 15 earned credits are required. D grades do not transfer. Students must complete, at the university, at least 30 of the 120 credits required for a bachelor's degree. Application deadlines are the same as those for freshmen.

Visiting: There are regularly scheduled orientations for prospective students. Guides are available for informal visits. Visitors may sit in on classes. Visits are best scheduled on weekdays. The admissions office should be contacted for arrangements.

Financial Aid: About 65% of the students receive aid. Ten percent work part-time on campus. The university is a member of CSS. Scholarships, grants, loans, and part-time jobs are available. The FAF or FFS should be filed by March 15 (fall), November 15 (winter), April 15 (spring), or June 15 (summer).

Foreign Students: The 3 students from foreign countries make up less than 1% of enrollment. Special counseling is available for these students.

Admissions: Foreign students must score at least 550 on the TOEFL. No college entrance exams are required.

Procedure: Application deadlines are April 1 (summer or fall entry), October 1 (winter entry), and February 1 (spring entry). Foreign students must present proof of adequate funds for 1 year. They also must carry health insurance, which is available through the university for a fee.

Admissions Contact: Stephen E. Eidson, Admissions and Aid Counselor.

UNIVERSITY OF PITTSBURGH AT GREENSBURG   B-3

Greensburg, Pennsylvania 15601   (412) 837-7040

F/T: 395M, 255W
P/T: 305M, 305W
Grad: none
Year: tri, ss
Appl: open
400 applied
SAT: 420V 480M

Faculty: 35; III, +$
Ph.D.'s: 80%
S/F Ratio: 19 to 1
Tuition: $2000 ($3570)
R and B: n/app
360 accepted   245 enrolled
COMPETITIVE

The University of Pittsburgh at Greensburg, established in 1963, offers undergraduate degrees in the arts and sciences and in business. The library has 54,000 volumes and subscribes to 135 periodicals.

Environment: The 160-acre campus is located in a suburban area 30 miles east of Pittsburgh. No student housing is provided.

Student Life: About 99% of the students come from Pennsylvania. Most are public-school graduates. One percent are minority-group members.

Organizations: Extracurricular activities include student government, the student newspaper, and special-interest clubs. There are no fraternities or sororities.

Sports: The university sponsors no intercollegiate sports. There is intramural football for men.

Handicapped: About 80% of the campus is accessible to handicapped students. Special facilities include wheelchair ramps, parking areas, and elevators. A special counselor is available.

Graduates: The freshman dropout rate is about 20%; 70% remain to graduate. About 25% of the graduates pursue advanced degrees.

Services: Career and psychological counseling are provided free to students.

Programs of Study: The campus confers the B.A. and B.S. degrees. Bachelor's degrees are offered in the following subjects: BUSINESS (accounting, business administration), ENGLISH (journalism, literature, writing), PHILOSOPHY (humanities), SOCIAL SCIENCES (government/political science, psychology, social sciences). In addition, students may complete the first 2 years of work in arts and sciences, engineering, education, social work, or health-related professions on the Greensburg campus. Students in arts and sciences and in engineering relocate automatically to the Pittsburgh campus to finish their degree programs. Those in one of the professional programs must apply for admission to the appropriate school at the Pittsburgh campus.

Required: Students must take courses in communications, humanities, social sciences, and natural sciences.

786 PENNSYLVANIA

Special: A general-studies degree, independent study, and a 3-year bachelor's degree are offered. Students may design their own majors.

Admissions: About 90% of the applicants for the 1981–82 freshman class were accepted. Candidates should have a 2.0 high school GPA, rank in the upper 60% of their class, and present 15 units of academic work. The admissions committee also considers advanced placement or honors courses, recommendations, and impressions made during an interview.

Procedure: The SAT or ACT is required. There are no application deadlines; freshmen are admitted to all 4 terms. Notification is made on a rolling basis. There is a $15 application fee.

Special: Early and deferred admissions plans are offered. AP and CLEP credit is available.

Transfer: For fall 1981, 60 students applied, 50 were accepted, and 40 enrolled. D grades do not transfer. A 2.0 GPA and a minimum composite SAT score of 700 are required. All students must complete, at the university, at least 30 of the 120 credits required for a bachelor's degree.

Visiting: Guides are available for informal visits. Visitors may sit in on classes. The admissions office should be contacted for arrangements.

Financial Aid: About 78% of the full-time students receive aid. Four percent work part-time on campus. Scholarships, grants (including BEOG/SEOG), loans (including NDSL), and part-time jobs (including CWS) are available. The FAF should be filed by June 1 (fall), November 1 (winter), or April 1 (spring). The university is a member of CSS.

Foreign Students: Fewer than 1% of the students come from foreign countries.

Admissions: Foreign students must score at least 500 on the TOEFL. They may take the university's own English-proficiency test instead. No college entrance exams are required.

Procedure: Application deadlines are June 1 (fall), October 1 (winter), March 1 (spring), and April 1 (summer). Foreign students must submit a completed health form and present proof of adequate funds for 3 terms.

Admissions Contact: Larry J. Whatule, Director of Admissions and Financial Aid.

UNIVERSITY OF PITTSBURGH AT JOHNSTOWN C–3
Johnstown, Pennsylvania 15904 (814) 266-9661

F/T: 1296M, 1104W Faculty: 130; IIB, +$
P/T: 380M, 320W Ph.D.'s: 80%
Grad: none S/F Ratio: 20 to 1
Year: tri, ss Tuition: $2040 ($4010)
Appl: see profile R and B: $1930
1703 applied 1256 accepted 820 enrolled
SAT: 510V 565M ACT: 23 VERY COMPETITIVE

The University of Pittsburgh at Johnstown, established in 1927, offers undergraduate programs in the arts and sciences, business, education, and engineering technology. The library contains over 80,000 volumes.

Environment: The 635-acre campus is located in a suburban area 70 miles east of Pittsburgh. The university has 26 buildings, including 5 single-sex residence halls, 7 small-group lodges, and 46 townhouse apartment units. Fraternity and sorority houses also are provided, as are facilities for commuting students.

Student Life: About 93% of the students come from Pennsylvania. Most are public-school graduates. About 60% live on campus. Eight percent are minority-group members. Campus housing is single-sex, with visiting privileges. Students may keep cars on campus.

Organizations: Extracurricular activities include student government, service and religious groups, publications, and performing groups. There are 4 fraternities to which 21% of the men belong, and 4 sororities to which 18% of the women belong.

Sports: The university fields intercollegiate teams in 7 sports for men and 3 for women. There are 11 intramural sports for men and 8 for women.

Handicapped: About 90% of the campus is accessible to handicapped students. Special facilities include wheelchair ramps, parking areas, elevators, specially equipped rest rooms, and lowered drinking fountains. Special class scheduling is also available.

Graduates: The freshman dropout rate is 10%, and about 70% remain to graduate. About 45% of the graduates pursue advanced degrees; 3% enter medical school, 4% enter dental school, and 4% enter law school. About 45% of the graduates begin careers in business and industry.

Services: Placement aid, career counseling, psychological counseling, tutoring, and remedial instruction are offered free to students. Health care is available on a fee basis.

Programs of Study: The university confers the B.A. and B.S. degrees. Bachelor's degrees are offered in the following subjects: AREA STUDIES (American), BUSINESS (accounting, business administration, computer science, finance, management), EDUCATION (elementary, secondary), ENGLISH (creative writing, English, journalism, literature, speech), FINE AND PERFORMING ARTS (theater/dramatics), HEALTH SCIENCES (medical technology), MATH AND SCIENCES (biology, chemistry, ecology/environmental science, geology, mathematics, natural sciences, statistics), PHILOSOPHY (humanities), PREPROFESSIONAL (architecture, dentistry, engineering—civil engineering technology, engineering—electrical engineering technology, engineering—mechanical engineering technology, forestry, law, library science, medicine, ministry, pharmacy, social work, veterinary), SOCIAL SCIENCES (economics, geography, government/political science, history, psychology, social sciences, sociology). Students are guaranteed relocation to the university's main campus in Pittsburgh for completion of degree programs not offered at Johnstown. About 33% of the degrees are conferred in preprofessional areas, 22% in social sciences, and 19% in math and sciences.

Required: Students must complete 9 hours each in humanities, natural sciences, and social sciences.

Special: A general-studies degree, independent study, internships, and combined B.A.-B.S. degrees are offered. Students may design their own majors.

Honors: A President's Scholars Program is offered in all departments.

Admissions: About 74% of the applicants for the 1981–82 freshman class were accepted. SAT scores of those who enrolled were as follows: Verbal—50% scored below 500, 35% between 500 and 599, 13% between 600 and 700, and 2% above 700; Math—36% scored below 500, 46% between 500 and 599, 13% between 600 and 700, and 5% above 700. Candidates should have completed 15 units of academic work. Rank in class is important. Other considerations include advanced placement or honors courses, evidence of special talents, recommendations, and impressions made during an interview.

Procedure: The SAT or ACT is required and should be taken by January of the senior year. Although application deadlines are open, students should apply by March 15 (fall), December 15 (winter), April 1 (spring), or June 1 (summer) for priority consideration. Notification is made on a rolling basis. There is a $15 application fee.

Special: Early decision, early admissions, and deferred admissions plans are available. AP credit is granted.

Transfer: For fall 1981, 120 students applied, 55 were accepted, and 40 enrolled. A 2.5 GPA is required. D grades do not transfer. Students must complete, at the university, at least 30 of the 120 credits required for a bachelor's degree.

Visiting: Guides are available for informal campus visits. Visitors may sit in on classes and stay overnight at the school. Visits are best scheduled on weekdays between 9 A.M. and 3 P.M. The admissions office should be contacted for arrangements.

Financial Aid: About 70% of the students receive aid. Ten percent work part-time on campus. Scholarships, grants, loans, and CWS are available. The FAF should be filed by March 1 (fall) or May 1 (spring). The university is a member of CSS.

Foreign Students: The university accepts foreign students.

Admissions: Foreign students must score at least 550 on the TOEFL. The university recommends that they also take the SAT.

Procedure: Application deadlines are March 15 (fall) and December 1 (winter). Foreign students must present proof of adequate funds for at least 1 year of study. They must carry health insurance, which is available through the university for a fee.

Admissions Contact: Thomas J. Wonders, Director of Admissions and Financial Aid.

UNIVERSITY OF SCRANTON E–2
Scranton, Pennsylvania 18510 (717) 961-7540

F/T: 1700M, 1300W Faculty: 157; IIA, av$
P/T: 400M, 350W Ph.D.'s: 70%
Grad: 425M, 350W S/F Ratio: 20 to 1
Year: 4-1-4, ss Tuition: $3300
Appl: July 1 R and B: $1700
2766 applied 1668 accepted 871 enrolled
SAT: 477V 520M COMPETITIVE

The University of Scranton, founded in 1888, is operated by the Jesuit Fathers of the Roman Catholic Church. It includes the undergraduate College of Arts and Sciences, the School of Management, the Graduate School, and the Evening College. The library houses 200,000 volumes and 20,000 microfilm items, and subscribes to 1225 periodicals.

Environment: The 37-acre urban campus is located in Scranton, 25 minutes from the Pocono Mountains and 125 miles from Philadelphia and New York City. The campus includes a student center, a science building, a physical education facility, and a swimming pool. Twenty residence halls, arranged in quads, accommodate 1200 students. On-campus apartments are also available. Recent additions include an outdoor recreational facility and the University Commons.

Student Life: Most students come from Pennsylvania, New Jersey, and New York; 20 other states and 10 foreign countries are also represented. Fifty-five percent of the students attended public schools. Sixty percent live on campus. Six percent are members of minority groups. About 85% are Catholic, 11% are Protestant, and 2% are Jewish. Campus housing is single-sex, with visiting privileges. Students may have cars on campus.

Organizations: Extracurricular activities include debating, drama, publications, a glee club, service organizations, and 30 other clubs. A lecture and cultural series is offered. There are no fraternities or sororities. Elk Mountain, Pocono ski resorts, and 7 colleges within a 15-mile radius provide off-campus activities.

Sports: The university fields intercollegiate teams in 9 sports for men and 6 sports for women. Fifteen intramural sports also are available.

Handicapped: The entire campus is accessible to handicapped students. Wheelchair ramps, parking areas, elevators, specially equipped rest rooms, and lowered drinking fountains and telephones are available. Special class scheduling can be arranged. One percent of the students are visually impaired, and 1% have hearing impairments. Services available to these students include human resource labs and lounges, and the facilities of the Pennsylvania Association for the Blind (1 block from the campus). There are 2 special counselors and 1 assistant.

Graduates: About 9% of the freshmen drop out by the end of their first year, and 75% remain to graduate. Thirty-six percent of the graduates pursue advanced degrees; 7% enter medical school, 2% enter dental school, and 7% enter law school. About 65% begin careers in business and industry.

Services: Students receive free psychological counseling, placement aid, career counseling, tutoring, and remedial instruction.

Programs of Study: The university confers the A.B., B.S., and B.S.N. degrees. Associate and master's degrees also are awarded. Bachelor's degrees are offered in the following subjects: BUSINESS (accounting, chemistry/business, computer science, electronics/business, finance, management, marketing), EDUCATION (secondary), ENGLISH (English, journalism), FINE AND PERFORMING ARTS (radio/TV), HEALTH SCIENCES (medical technology, nursing, physical therapy), LANGUAGES (French, German, Greek/Latin, Spanish), MATH AND SCIENCES (biochemistry, biology, biophysics, chemistry, electronics engineering, food science, mathematics, physics), PHILOSOPHY (classics, philosophy, religion), PREPROFESSIONAL (dentistry, engineering, law, medicine, pharmacy, social work, veterinary), SOCIAL SCIENCES (criminal justice, economics, family studies, gerontology, government/political science, history, international relations, psychology, public administration). Thirty-one percent of the degrees are conferred in business, 25% in social sciences, and 13% in math and sciences.

Required: Students must take courses in each of the following general-education areas: natural science and quantitative studies, social and behavioral science, communications, humanities, and philosophy and religious studies.

Special: A 2-3 program leading to the B.S. in engineering is given in conjunction with the University of Detroit or with Widener College. Internships, study abroad, a semester at another U.S. Jesuit university, a 3-year A.B. program, and cross-registration with nearby Marywood College are available. Students may design their own majors. A special freshman academic development program is available for applicants not meeting all the admissions requirements. The university has graduated 28 Fulbright scholars in the past 10 years.

Honors: Sixteen honor societies have chapters on campus. The open-ended honors program offers interdisciplinary seminars and tutorials. The special Jesuit Liberal Arts Program follows a more traditional core-curriculum approach.

Admissions: Sixty percent of those who applied were accepted for the 1981–82 freshman class. The SAT scores of those who enrolled were as follows: Verbal—60% below 500, 34% between 500 and 599, 6% between 600 and 700, and 1% above 700; Math—35% below 500, 49% between 500 and 599, 15% between 600 and 700, and 1% above 700. Admission is based primarily on the high school record (including recommendations from school authorities) and SAT or ACT scores. Applicants must rank in the top 60% of their high school class and have completed 16 Carnegie units. Also considered are impressions made during an interview, advanced placement or honors courses, leadership record, and extracurricular activities. Disadvantaged students and veterans receive special consideration; out-of-state and foreign students are encouraged to apply.

Procedure: The SAT or ACT is required and should be taken between March of the junior year and April of the senior year. An interview is recommended. Application deadlines are July 1 (fall), December 15 (spring), and June 1 (summer). Admission is on a rolling basis. There is a $20 application fee.

Special: Early decision, early admissions, and deferred admissions plans are offered. CLEP and AP credit is accepted.

Transfer: For fall 1981, 220 students applied, 140 were accepted, and 92 enrolled. Transfers are accepted for the freshman (second semester), sophomore, and junior years. Applicants must have a GPA of 2.5 or better in at least 15 credits. D grades are not acceptable. Students must earn, in residence, at least 52 of the 129–152 credits required for a bachelor's degree. Application deadlines are the same as those for freshmen.

Visiting: Visits are best planned when classes are in session. Guides are available. The admissions office is open weekdays and Saturday by appointment. Visitors may sit in on classes. They also may stay overnight at the school if they make arrangements with a student currently attending the university.

Financial Aid: Seventy-five percent of the students receive aid; 15% work part-time on campus. Scholarships are awarded on the basis of scholastic excellence and financial need. Presidential scholarships are available for outstanding high school seniors; debating and athletic scholarships are also offered. The maximum scholarship award is about $4000. State and federal grants and loans and part-time jobs are available to freshmen; the average award to freshmen in 1981–82 totaled $900. Those wishing to pay tuition in installments should consult local banks. The university is a member of CSS and requires the FAF and the federal income tax form. Aid application deadlines are July 1 (fall), December 15 (spring), and June 1 (summer).

Foreign Students: Foreign students make up 2% of the student body. The university offers these students special counseling and special organizations.

Admissions: Applicants must score 500 or better on the TOEFL. No academic exams are required.

Procedure: Application deadlines are March 1 (fall), September 15 (spring), and February 1 (summer). Students must present proof of adequate funds for 4 years.

Admissions Contact: Rev. Bernard R. McIlhenny, S.J., Dean of Admissions.

URSINUS COLLEGE E–3
Collegeville, Pennsylvania 19426   (215) 489-4111

F/T: 586M, 521W	Faculty: 82; IIB, av$
P/T: 15M, 27W	Ph.D.'s: 64%
Grad: none	S/F Ratio: 12 to 1
Year: sems, ss	Tuition: $4650
Appl: open	R and B: $2000
1341 applied	639 accepted	309 enrolled
SAT: 540V 590M	VERY COMPETITIVE+

Established in 1869, Ursinus is a small, privately endowed liberal arts college affiliated with the United Church of Christ. The library contains 174,400 volumes and 125,000 microfilm items, and subscribes to 700 periodicals.

Environment: The 140-acre campus is located in a suburban area 28 miles from Philadelphia. Residence halls accommodate about 1000 students.

Student Life: Sixty-three percent of the undergraduates are from Pennsylvania. About 92% live on campus. About 85% come from public schools. Nine percent are minority-group members. About 44% are Protestant, 36% are Catholic, and 4% are Jewish. Campus housing is single-sex. Students may keep cars on campus.

Organizations: Forty percent of the men belong to the 8 local fraternities on campus, and 35% of the women belong to the 5 local sororities. There are numerous extracurricular activities. For additional activities, students travel to Philadelphia.

788 PENNSYLVANIA

Sports: The intercollegiate athletic program includes 14 sports for men and 11 for women. There are 7 intramural sports for men and 7 for women.

Handicapped: About 90% of the campus is accessible to handicapped students. Designated parking areas, wheelchair ramps, elevators, special class scheduling, and specially equipped rest rooms are available.

Graduates: The freshman dropout rate is 15%; 62% remain to graduate. Of those, 65% pursue graduate study; 10% enter medical school, 2% enter dental school, and 9% enter law school. Forty percent pursue careers in business and industry.

Services: Students receive the following free services: placement aid, career counseling, tutoring, and health care.

Programs of Study: The college confers the B.A., B.S., and B.B.A. degrees. Associate degrees are also awarded. Bachelor's degrees are offered in the following subjects: AREA STUDIES (American), BUSINESS (accounting, business administration, computer science, economics, management), EDUCATION (health/physical, secondary), ENGLISH (English), LANGUAGES (French, German, Greek/Latin, Spanish), MATH AND SCIENCES (biology, chemistry, mathematics, natural sciences, physics), PHILOSOPHY (classics, humanities, philosophy, religion), PREPROFESSIONAL (dentistry, engineering, law, medicine, ministry, veterinary), SOCIAL SCIENCES (economics, government/political science, history, international relations, psychology, social sciences). Thirty-six percent of the degrees conferred are in social sciences, 30% in math and sciences, and 21% in business and economics.

Required: Freshmen must take physical education.

Special: Students may design their own majors. A 3-2 program in engineering is offered with the University of Pennsylvania, the University of Southern California, and Georgia Institute of Technology. Also available are a junior-year-abroad program, senior seminars, and a 3-year bachelor's degree.

Honors: Six honor societies have chapters on campus. Ursinus has an independent-study honors program.

Admissions: Forty-eight percent of those who applied were accepted for the 1981–82 freshman class. The SAT scores of those who enrolled were as follows: Verbal—35% scored below 500, 49% between 500 and 599, 14% between 600 and 700, and 2% above 700; Math—18% scored below 500, 43% between 500 and 599, 34% between 600 and 700, and 5% above 700. Applicants must be graduates of an accredited high school, having completed a college-preparatory program. GEDs may be accepted. Besides academic factors, the college considers advanced placement or honors courses, extracurricular activities, and special talents.

Procedure: The SAT is required and should be taken by January of the senior year. Applicants who live reasonably near the college should visit the campus for a personal interview. Applications should be filed as early as possible; deadlines are open, but admissions are usually closed 2 weeks before classes start. Freshmen are admitted to all terms. The rolling admissions procedure is followed. There is a $20 application fee.

Special: Early decision, early admissions, and deferred admissions plans are available. CLEP and AP credit is considered.

Transfer: For fall 1981, 121 students applied, 58 were accepted, and 46 enrolled. Transfers are considered for all but the senior year. Applicants should have a clear record and a 2.5 GPA. D grades are not acceptable. All students must complete, at the college, at least 60 of the 122 credits required for a bachelor's degree. Applications should be filed at least 2 weeks before the start of the term.

Visiting: Informal guided tours and interviews can be arranged 6 days a week through the admissions office. Visitors may sit in on classes with prior arrangement.

Financial Aid: Eighty-three percent of all students receive aid through the school. Forty-two percent work part-time on campus. The college is a member of CSS. Freshman scholarships and campus jobs are available. The FAF is required; Pennsylvania residents must file the state grant application. The application deadline for financial aid is March 1.

Foreign Students: The 22 students from foreign countries make up 2% of enrollment. Special counseling and special organizations are available for these students.

Admissions: Foreign students must score at least 550 on the TOEFL. They also must take the SAT.

Procedure: Application deadlines are June 1 (fall), September 1 (spring), and March 1 (summer). Students must fill out a health form and must present proof of adequate funds for 4 years of study.

Admissions Contact: Kenneth L. Schaefer, Dean of Admissions.

VILLA MARIA COLLEGE B-1
Erie, Pennsylvania 16505 (814) 838-1966

F/T: 6M, 560W Faculty: 62; IIB, −$
P/T: 6M, 154W Ph.D.'s: 15%
Grad: none S/F Ratio: 12 to 1
Year: sems, ss Tuition: $3520
Appl: open R and B: $1900
367 applied 315 accepted 144 enrolled
SAT: 400V 450M ACT: 19 LESS COMPETITIVE

Villa Maria College, founded in 1925, is a Roman Catholic liberal arts college conducted by the Sisters of St. Joseph. The library contains 43,100 volumes and subscribes to 310 periodicals.

Environment: The 45-acre campus is located in a suburban area of a small city of 250,000 people, halfway between Cleveland and Buffalo. The campus consists of 8 buildings, including 2 dormitories, a gymnasium with a swimming pool, tennis courts, and a lecture hall.

Student Life: About 93% of the students come from Pennsylvania. About 76% attended public schools. Fifty-nine percent live on campus. Dormitories are single-sex, with visiting privileges. Students may keep cars on campus. Day-care services are available to full-time students.

Organizations: Extracurricular activities include religious groups. Cultural events include plays, concerts, films, and lectures.

Sports: The college competes on an intercollegiate level in 4 sports for women. There are 6 intramural sports for women.

Graduates: The freshman dropout rate is 25%; 65% remain to graduate. Twelve percent of the graduates pursue further study. Five percent enter business and industry.

Services: Students receive the following free services: health care, career counseling, placement aid, and tutoring.

Programs of Study: The college confers the B.A., B.S., and B.S.N. degrees. Associate degrees are also awarded. Bachelor's degrees are offered in the following subjects: BUSINESS (accounting, management, marketing), EDUCATION (early childhood, elementary, secondary, special), ENGLISH (English), HEALTH SCIENCES (dietetics, medical technology, nursing), LANGUAGES (Spanish), MATH AND SCIENCES (biology, chemistry, mathematics), PREPROFESSIONAL (home economics, law, pharmacy, social work), SOCIAL SCIENCES (psychology, sociology, therapeutic recreation). Forty-seven percent of degrees conferred are in health professions, 23% are in education, and 11% are in home economics.

Required: All undergraduates must take a freshman-studies program, physical education, and 17 general-education courses.

Special: Academic programs include participation in American University's Washington, D.C., Semester, intercollegiate exchange programs, and study abroad. Internships are available in every academic discipline.

Admissions: Eighty-six percent of those who applied were accepted for the 1981–82 freshman class. The SAT scores of those who enrolled were as follows: Verbal—68% scored below 500, 19% between 500 and 599, 1% between 600 and 700, and 1% above 700; Math—81% scored below 500, 14% between 500 and 599, 4% between 600 and 700, and 1% above 700. Of those who took the ACT, 68% scored below 21, 13% between 21 and 23, 11% between 24 and 25, 8% between 26 and 28, and 1% above 28. Applicants must be graduates of an accredited high school with 16 Carnegie units and a GPA of at least 2.0. Prospective nursing majors must meet special requirements.

Procedure: The SAT or ACT is required. Junior-year results are acceptable but not final. Admissions decisions are made on a rolling basis. Application deadlines are open; new students are admitted in the fall, spring, and summer terms. A personal interview is recommended. Arrangements can be made for an interview with a college representative in or near the student's hometown. A $15 fee must accompany the application.

Special: CLEP and AP credit is accepted.

Transfer: For fall 1981, 24 students applied, 21 were accepted, and 20 enrolled. Transfers are considered for the freshman, sophomore, and junior classes. Applicants must submit high school transcripts and SAT or ACT scores, and must have a C average. On the SAT, a minimum composite score of 800 is required. D grades do not transfer. Students must complete, at the college, at least 62 of the 126 credits required for a bachelor's degree. There are no application deadlines.

Visiting: Guided tours and interviews can be scheduled through the admissions office.

Financial Aid: About 69% of all students receive aid through the school. About 25% work part-time on campus. The average award to freshmen in 1981-82 was $3264. Scholarships, grants, and loans are packaged to meet individual needs. Federal work-study and BEOG funds are available. Students participate in the Guaranteed Student Loan program. The college is a member of CSS; the FAF is required of all aid applicants. The deadline for aid applications is February 15.

Foreign Students: No students from foreign countries were enrolled in 1981-82.

Admissions: Foreign students must take the TOEFL and the SAT or ACT. A minimum composite score of 800 on the SAT is required. Students also must submit recommendations from school officials.

Procedure: Application deadlines are open; foreign students are admitted to all terms. They must present proof of adequate funds for 1 year and must carry health insurance.

Admissions Contact: Director of Admissions.

VILLANOVA UNIVERSITY F-4
Villanova, Pennsylvania 19085 (215) 645-4000

F/T: 3449M, 2592W Faculty: 452; IIA, +$
P/T: 921M, 956W Ph.D.'s: 70%
Grad: 1480M, 1172W S/F Ratio: 15 to 1
Year: sems, ss Tuition: $4550
Appl: Feb. 15 R and B: $2700
7303 applied 3619 accepted 1456 enrolled
SAT: 500V 560M **VERY COMPETITIVE**

Villanova University, founded in 1842, is a Roman Catholic institution sponsored by the Augustinian Fathers. The university has the following undergraduate divisions: the College of Arts and Sciences, the College of Commerce and Finance, the College of Engineering, the College of Nursing, and the University College. The library contains 454,000 volumes and 43,500 microfilm items, and subscribes to 2676 periodicals.

Environment: The 240-acre suburban campus is located near a small town of 2500 people, 12 miles west of Philadelphia. The 43 buildings include 14 dormitories. The Connelly Center offers programs, services, and activities for students, faculty, and alumni.

Student Life: Forty-three percent of the students are from Pennsylvania. Fifty percent live on campus. Almost half come from public schools. Resident freshmen and sophomores may not have cars on campus. Six percent of the students are minority-group members. Ninety-two percent are Catholic, 5% are Protestant, and 1% are Jewish. Campus housing is single-sex, with visiting privileges.

Organizations: Twenty percent of the men belong to the 5 national and 4 local fraternities; 20% of the women belong to the 3 local sororities. The university sponsors religious counselors and organizations for Catholic and Jewish students, as well as 113 extracurricular activities. Each week, 2 to 5 cultural events take place on campus.

Sports: The university fields teams in 13 intercollegiate sports for men and 13 for women. There are 3 intramural sports for men and 3 for women.

Graduates: The freshman dropout rate is 10%. About 40% of the graduates pursue advanced degrees: 2% enter medical school and 4% enter law school. About 73% enter business and industry.

Services: Students receive placement services free of charge. Some health care services require payment.

Programs of Study: The university confers the B.A., B.S., B.F.A., B.Ch.E., B.C.E., B.E.E., and B.M.E. degrees. Associate, master's, and doctoral degrees are also awarded. Bachelor's degrees are offered in the following subjects: BUSINESS (accounting, business administration, economics), EDUCATION (elementary, secondary, special), ENGLISH (English), FINE AND PERFORMING ARTS (art, theater/dramatics), HEALTH SCIENCES (nursing), LANGUAGES (French, German, Greek/Latin, Italian, Russian, Spanish), MATH AND SCIENCES (astronomy, biology, chemistry, mathematics, physics), PHILOSOPHY (philosophy), PREPROFESSIONAL (engineering—chemical, engineering—civil, engineering—electrical, engineering—mechanical), SOCIAL SCIENCES (criminal justice, economics, geography, government/political science, history, psychology, sociology). Thirty-one percent of the degrees conferred are in business, 22% in social sciences, and 15% in preprofessional studies.

Required: A core curriculum in the College of Arts and Sciences is required. Students must maintain a GPA of least 2.0 to graduate.

Special: The university has special programs in astronomy and criminal justice. Students may spend their junior year abroad on their own or participate in an established study-abroad program sponsored by another college. Students may choose a general-studies degree or design their own majors.

Honors: Eighteen national honor societies have chapters on campus. Honors programs are avaiable in arts and sciences.

Admissions: Fifty percent of those who applied were accepted for the 1981-82 freshman class. The SAT scores of those who enrolled were as follows: Verbal—47% scored below 500, 42% between 500 and 599, 9% between 600 and 700, and 0% above 700, Math—19% scored below 500, 50% between 500 and 599, 28% between 600 and 700, and 3% above 700. Applicants must be graduates of an accredited high school with a B average and a rank in the upper two-fifths of their class. They must have completed 16 Carnegie units. Other factors considered are recommendations by school officials, advanced placement or honors courses, and extracurricular activities.

Procedure: Applicants must take either the SAT or the ACT. Applicants to the College of Arts and Sciences must take a language AT. An applicant must apply to the particular academic division in which he or she is interested. The application deadline for fall is February 15; for spring, October 15. There are rolling admissions for commuting students. A visit to the campus is recommended. There is an application fee of $25.

Special: Early admissions and early decision plans are offered. Credit may be earned through AP exams.

Transfer: For fall 1981, 184 students applied, 156 were accepted, and 88 enrolled. Transfers are considered for the sophomore, junior, and senior years. Applicants should have a GPA of 2.5, a minimum score of 500 on each part of the SAT, and good standing at their last school. D grades are not acceptable. All students must complete, at the university, at least 30 of the 122 credits required for a bachelor's degree. Application deadlines are the same as those for freshmen. The College of Commerce and Finance does not accept transfer applications.

Visiting: The admissions office arranges campus tours for weekdays from 10 A.M. to 2 P.M. Visitors may sit in on classes.

Financial Aid: Seventy percent of the students receive aid. Sixteen percent work part-time on campus. There are 347 freshman grants and 34 athletic scholarships; the total amount of grant aid available to freshmen is $175,000. The university administers $1.56 million in federal loan funds and $3.5 million in state loan funds; 40% of the students receive loans. Aid packages are a combination of grants and loans. Grants and loans range in amount from $200 to $2500. The average freshman award in 1981-82 was $3500. The university is a member of CSS. Either the FAF or FFS is acceptable. Financial need is the principal consideration in determining awards. The application deadline is March 15.

Foreign Students: The 131 students from foreign countries make up 2% of enrollment.

Admissions: Foreign students must score at least 500 on the TOEFL.

Procedure: Students are admitted to all terms. Application deadlines are open. Students must present proof of adequate funds and must carry health insurance, which is available through the university.

Admissions Contact: Rev. Harry J. Erdlen, Dean of Admissions.

WASHINGTON AND JEFFERSON COLLEGE A-3
Washington, Pennsylvania 15301 (412) 222-4400

F/T: 654M, 404W Faculty: 90; IIB, +$
P/T: none Ph.D.'s: 70%
Grad: none S/F Ratio: 10 to 1
Year: 4-1-4, ss Tuition: $5310
Appl: Mar. 1 R and B: $1990
750 applied 600 accepted 300 enrolled
SAT: 1070 (composite) ACT: 23 **VERY COMPETITIVE**

Washington and Jefferson College, founded in 1781, is one of America's oldest institutions of higher learning. The library contains 175,000 volumes and 5400 microfilm items, and subscribes to 739 periodicals.

Environment: The campus is situated on 40 acres in a suburban area 25 miles from Pittsburgh. Among its 32 buildings are 5 dormitories that house 654 men and 404 women. There are also fraternity houses.

Student Life: About 70% of the students are from Pennsylvania. Seventy percent come from public schools. About 95% live on cam-

790 PENNSYLVANIA

pus, half in the dormitories and half in the 11 fraternity houses. Campus housing is single-sex, with visiting privileges. Students may keep cars on campus.

Organizations: Fifty-five percent of the men belong to the 11 national fraternities; 2 national sororities also are represented on campus. There is a wide variety of special-interest groups and departmental clubs. Popular cultural and recreational areas off campus include Heinz Hall and Three Rivers Stadium in Pittsburgh, and the nearby Seven Springs resort.

Sports: The college fields 11 intercollegiate teams for men and 9 for women. There are 10 intramural sports for men and 9 for women.

Graduates: About 4%–11% of the freshmen drop out during their first year, and 83% remain to graduate. About 60% of the graduates seek advanced degrees; 10% enter law school. Thirty percent pursue careers in business and industry.

Services: Career counseling, health care, tutoring, personal counseling, and placement aid are available free to students.

Programs of Study: The college offers the B.A. degree. The 4-1-4 curriculum structures the courses under the divisions of humanities, social sciences, and science and mathematics. Bachelor's degrees are offered in the following subjects: BUSINESS (accounting, business administration), EDUCATION (secondary), ENGLISH (English), FINE AND PERFORMING ARTS (art), HEALTH SCIENCES (medical technology), LANGUAGES (French, German, Spanish), MATH AND SCIENCES (biology, chemistry, mathematics, physics), PHILOSOPHY (philosophy), PREPROFESSIONAL (dentistry, engineering, law, medicine, ministry, veterinary), SOCIAL SCIENCES (economics, government/political science, history, psychology, sociology). Twenty-eight percent of degrees conferred are in business, 16% are in biology, and 13% are in chemistry.

Required: Students must take a course in freshman English and 2 courses in physical education or ROTC. They also must complete a core curriculum of 14 courses.

Special: There are 3-2 cooperative programs in engineering and 3-4 cooperative programs in optometry and in podiatry. Students may spend a semester in Washington or their third year abroad. The January interim may be used for travel/study. A work-study program is available. Students may design their own majors.

Honors: Twenty national honor societies, including Phi Beta Kappa, have chapters on campus.

Admissions: Eighty percent of those who applied were accepted for the 1981–82 freshman class. Applicants must have completed 15 Carnegie high school units and rank in the upper 40% of their class. Also considered are advanced placement or honors courses, leadership qualities, and recommendations by school officials.

Procedure: Students must take either the SAT and 3 ATs (including English Composition), or the ACT. The application deadlines are March 1 (fall), December 15 (winter), January 15 (spring), and March 1 (summer). Notification is made on a rolling basis. There is a $15 application fee.

Special: Early admissions, early decision, and deferred admissions plans are available. Students may earn credit through AP exams.

Transfer: For fall 1981, 70 students applied, 45 were accepted, and 40 enrolled. Transfers are considered for the freshman and sophomore classes. Applicants must submit SAT or ACT scores and their high school transcript. D grades do not transfer. All students must study at least 4 terms and 2 intersessions at the college to receive a degree. Thirty-six courses are required for a bachelor's degree. Application deadlines are the same as those for freshmen.

Visiting: Campus visits should be scheduled for September through November or February through April. Guides are available. Visitors may stay overnight at the school and sit in on classes. Visits can be arranged for any day except Sunday through the admissions office.

Financial Aid: Fifty-three percent of the students receive aid. Aid packages (scholarships, loans, campus jobs) are granted in accordance with need as assessed by the FAF in academic competition with all other aid applicants. The average freshman award in 1981–82 was $1550. Tuition may be paid in installments through private plans. The college is a member of the CSS. The aid application deadline is March 15 for regular admission. The FAF is required.

Foreign Students: The 20 students from foreign countries make up 2% of enrollment.

Admissions: Foreign students must score at least 500 on the TOEFL. No college entrance exams are required.

Procedure: Application deadlines are the same as those for other freshmen. Students must complete a health form and must present proof of adequate funds for 1 year. They also must carry health insurance.

Admissions Contact: Thomas P. O'Connor, Director of Admissions.

WAYNESBURG COLLEGE B-4
Waynesburg, Pennsylvania 15370 (412) 627-6233

F/T: 370M, 304W
P/T: 20M, 37W
Grad: none
Year: sems, ss
Appl: open
627 applied 608 accepted 258 enrolled
SAT or ACT: required

Faculty: 54; IIB, av$
Ph.D.'s: 61%
S/F Ratio: 14 to 1
Tuition: $4350
R and B: $1950

LESS COMPETITIVE

Waynesburg College, founded in 1849, is a small, privately controlled liberal arts college related to the United Presbyterian Church. The library contains 115,000 volumes and 2500 microfilm items, and subscribes to 750 periodicals.

Environment: The college's 16 buildings are located on a 30-acre tract in a rural area 45 miles south of Pittsburgh. Notable buildings include a seismology station and a museum of mineralogical, petrological, and archaeological material. The campus also contains 6 dormitories. Fraternity houses provide additional accommodations.

Student Life: About 75% of the students are from Pennsylvania. Ninety percent attended public schools. Twenty percent live on campus. About 50% are Protestant, 30% are Catholic, and 1% are Jewish. Eight percent are minority-group members. Campus housing is single-sex, with visiting privileges. Students may keep cars on campus.

Organizations: There are 3 fraternities and 3 sororities; 35% of the men and 25% of the women belong. Extracurricular activities include special-interest clubs and religious organizations. Nearby ski resorts provide additional recreation.

Sports: Waynesburg competes on an intercollegiate level in 7 sports for men and 3 for women. There are 4 intramural sports for men and 3 for women.

Handicapped: Facilities for handicapped students include wheelchair ramps and special parking areas.

Graduates: The freshman dropout rate is 30%; 55% remain to graduate. Two percent of the graduates enter medical school, 1% enter dental school, and 5% enter law school.

Services: Students receive free placement aid, career counseling, health care, tutoring, remedial instruction, and psychological counseling.

Programs of Study: The B.A., B.S., and B.S.B.A. degrees are conferred. Associate degrees are also awarded. Bachelor's degrees are offered in the following subjects: BUSINESS (accounting, business administration, computer science, finance, management, marketing, small business management), EDUCATION (elementary, secondary), ENGLISH (communications arts, English), FINE AND PERFORMING ARTS (art, art education), HEALTH SCIENCES (medical technology), LANGUAGES (modern languages, Spanish), MATH AND SCIENCES (biology, chemistry, earth science, geology, mathematics), SOCIAL SCIENCES (economics, government/political science, history, psychology, public service administration, social sciences, sociology). Fifty percent of the degrees conferred are in business, 15% in math and sciences, and 12% in English.

Required: All students must take courses in the fine arts, humanities, and social and natural sciences.

Special: A 3-year bachelor's degree, combined B.A.-B.S. degrees, and summer study tours in Mexico and France are offered. Internships are available for senior accounting majors and public-administration students. An intensive summer course in Rocky Mountain field geology is offered by the Rocky Mountain Geology Station in Colorado.

Honors: Honors programs are offered by the departments of fine arts, English, history, political science, and sociology. Ten national honor societies have chapters on campus.

Admissions: Ninety-seven percent of those who applied were accepted for the 1981–82 freshman class. The SAT scores of those who enrolled were as follows: Verbal—85% scored below 500, 13% between 500 and 599, 2% between 600 and 700, and 0% above 700; Math—69% scored below 500, 21% between 500 and 599, 9% between 600 and 700, and 1% above 700. Candidates must be graduates of an accredited high school with 16 units of work. The school also considers the following factors: advanced placement or honors courses, recommendations by school officials, and impressions made during an interview.

Procedure: The SAT or ACT is required and should be taken in April of the junior year or by December of the senior year. Applications should be submitted as early as possible. There are no deadlines. Students are notified within 2 weeks after their application is received. There is a $15 application fee.

Special: Early decision and early admissions plans are available. AP exams and CLEP general exams are accepted.

Transfer: For fall 1981, 38 students applied, 38 were accepted, and 38 enrolled. Transfers are considered for all years. D grades are not acceptable. All students must complete, at the college, at least 24 of the 124 credits required for a bachelor's degree. There are no application deadlines.

Visiting: The college schedules an orientation in the spring. Informal visits also can be arranged through the admissions office. Visitors may sit in on classes, and overnight accommodations are available. Guided tours and interviews can be scheduled weekdays between 9 A.M. and 4 P.M.

Financial Aid: Ninety percent of all students receive aid through the school. About 33% work part-time on campus. The average award to freshmen in 1981–82 was $3200. The college is a member of the CSS. Aid comes in the form of college scholarships and loans from local banks, federal and state government, and private sources. Tuition may be paid on the installment plan. The deadline for aid applications is May 1; the FAF also must be filed.

Foreign Students: The 12 students from foreign countries make up about 1% of enrollment. Special counseling is available for these students.

Admissions: Foreign students must score at least 500 on the TOEFL. No college entrance exams are required.

Procedure: Application deadlines are open; students are admitted to all terms. They must present proof of adequate funds for 1 year and must carry health insurance, which is available through the college for a fee.

Admissions Contact: Ronald L. Shunk, Director of Admissions and Financial Aid.

WEST CHESTER STATE COLLEGE   F–4
West Chester, Pennsylvania 19380   (215) 436-3411

F/T: 2586M, 3969W	Faculty: 457; IIA, ++$
P/T: 993M, 1623W	Ph.D.'s: 40%
Grad: 482M, 773W	S/F Ratio: 18 to 1
Year: sems, ss	Tuition: $1374 ($2314)
Appl: Aug. 1	R and B: $1590
4704 applied	2893 accepted	1779 enrolled
SAT: 468V 512M		COMPETITIVE

West Chester State College, established in 1812, is a nonsectarian, publicly controlled college offering programs in business, education, the liberal arts and sciences, and preprofessional fields. The library contains 350,000 volumes and 300,000 microfilm items, and subscribes to 2500 periodicals.

Environment: The 551-acre suburban campus is located 27 miles west of Philadelphia in a historic area near the Valley Forge Campgrounds and the Brandywine Battlefield. Facilities include dormitories that house 3100 men and women.

Student Life: All but 18% of the students are residents of Pennsylvania. About 85% live on campus. Twelve percent are minority-group members. About 50% are Catholic, 44% are Protestant, and 5% are Jewish. Dormitories are both coed and single-sex; there are visiting privileges in the single-sex dorms. Students may keep cars on campus. Day-care services are available.

Organizations: Twenty percent of the men belong to the 7 national and 2 local fraternities on campus; 15% of the women belong to the 7 national sororities. Religious organizations are available for students of all faiths. The college sponsors cultural activities, including music, and recreational services. Other activities are within driving distance of the campus.

Sports: The college fields 13 intercollegiate teams for men and 13 for women. There are 7 intramural sports for men and 4 for women.

Handicapped: Eighty percent of the campus is accessible to handicapped students. Special facilities include wheelchair ramps, parking areas, and elevators (in most buildings). Special class scheduling is also available.

Graduates: No more than 20% of the freshmen drop out by the end of their first year, and 60% remain to graduate. About 65% of the graduates seek advanced degrees.

Services: Students receive the following free services: placement aid, career counseling, psychological counseling, tutoring, and remedial instruction. Health care is provided on a fee basis.

Programs of Study: The college confers the B.A., B.S., B.S.N., and B.S.Ed. degrees. Associate and master's degrees are also awarded. Bachelor's degrees are offered in the following subjects: AREA STUDIES (American), BUSINESS (business administration, computer science), EDUCATION (early childhood, elementary, health/physical, secondary, special), ENGLISH (literature), FINE AND PERFORMING ARTS (art, music, music education, theater/dramatics), HEALTH SCIENCES (environmental health, nursing, public health, speech therapy), LANGUAGES (French, German, Greek/Latin, Russian, Spanish), MATH AND SCIENCES (biochemistry, biology, chemistry, clinical chemistry, earth science, forensic chemistry, mathematics, physical sciences, physics), PHILOSOPHY (philosophy), PREPROFESSIONAL (dentistry, engineering, law, medicine, veterinary), SOCIAL SCIENCES (anthropology, economics, geography, government/political science, history, psychology, social work, sociology).

Special: The college offers a combined B.A.-B.S. degree in liberal studies. A junior-year-abroad program is offered for prospective teachers of French at the University of Montpelier near Marseilles, France. There is a 3-2 program in engineering. Students may design their own majors in physical education.

Honors: Seventeen national honor societies have chapters on campus. An interdisciplinary honors program is offered.

Admissions: Sixty-two percent of those who applied were accepted for the 1981–82 freshman class. Applicants must be graduates of an accredited high school and rank in the upper 60% of their class. Also considered are advanced placement or honors courses, evidence of special talent, and recommendations. Out-of-state students must rank in the top 50% of their class and submit combined SAT scores above 950 or an ACT score above 21.

Procedure: The SAT or ACT is required. Application deadlines are August 1 for admission to the fall semester and December 1 for the spring semester. Applicants are notified on a rolling basis. There is a $15 application fee.

Special: Early admissions and deferred admissions plans are offered. CLEP and AP credit is accepted.

Transfer: The college accepted 1004 of 1519 applications for fall 1981, and 702 students enrolled. Transfers are accepted for all classes. A GPA of at least 2.0 is required. D grades in the major field do not transfer. Students must study at the college for at least 1 year, earning 30 of the 128 credits required for a bachelor's degree. Application deadlines are the same as those for freshman applicants.

Visiting: Open-house programs are scheduled throughout the year for prospective students. Guides are available for informal visits, which can be arranged for Monday through Friday, from 8 A.M. to 4:30 P.M., through the admissions office.

Financial Aid: Fifty-five percent of the students receive aid. Eight percent work part-time on campus. The average award to freshmen in 1981–82 was $1200. Scholarships usually are awarded to about 50 freshmen. Loans are available from the federal and state governments, the college, and private sources. Tuition may be paid in installments. The deadline for aid applications is May 1; the FAF must be filed. The college is a member of CSS. Candidates are notified on a rolling basis.

Foreign Students: The 52 students from foreign countries make up less than 1% of enrollment. An intensive English course, special counseling, and special organizations are available for these students.

Admissions: Foreign students must score at least 550 on the TOEFL. No college entrance exams are required.

Procedure: The application deadline is July 1 for fall entry. Foreign students must submit a physician's report and proof of adequate funds for 1 year. They also must carry health insurance, which is available through the college.

Admissions Contact: William E. Kipp, Director of Admissions.

WESTMINSTER COLLEGE   A–2
New Wilmington, Pennsylvania 16142   (412) 946-8761

F/T: 680M, 755W	Faculty: 118; IIA, av$
P/T: 45M, 118W	Ph.D.'s: 72%
Grad: 57M, 65W	S/F Ratio: 14 to 1
Year: 4-1-4, ss	Tuition: $4376
Appl: open	R and B: $1824
939 applied	805 accepted	361 enrolled
SAT: 459V 502M	ACT: 23	COMPETITIVE+

792 PENNSYLVANIA

Founded in 1852, Westminster is a coeducational liberal arts college related to the United Presbyterian Church. The library contains 202,000 volumes and 3000 microfilm items, and subscribes to 1112 periodicals.

Environment: The 300-acre campus, located in a rural area 60 miles from Pittsburgh and 17 miles from Youngstown, Ohio, includes 16 major buildings, athletic fields, and a lake. Eight dormitories accommodate over 630 women and 570 men; 5 fraternity houses also are provided.

Student Life: Two-thirds of the students come from Pennsylvania. Virtually all come from public schools. About 90% live on campus, including 7% in fraternity houses. Two percent are minority-group members. About 70% are Protestant, and 25% are Catholic. Campus housing is single-sex; there are visiting privileges. Students may keep cars on campus. Alcoholic beverages are prohibited on campus.

Organizations: Fifty percent of the men belong to the 5 national fraternities; 48% of the women, to the 5 national sororities. There is a wide variety of extracurricular activities. Speakers, political leaders, scientists, and music and theater groups often visit the campus.

Sports: The college fields 9 intercollegiate teams for men and 7 for women. There are 6 intramural sports for men and 11 for women.

Handicapped: There are no special facilities for the physically handicapped; accommodations are made on the basis of individual needs.

Graduates: About 15% of the freshmen drop out by the end of the first year, and 68% remain to graduate. Thirty percent of the graduates become candidates for higher degrees; 4% enter medical school, 4% enter dental school, and 3% enter law school. Fifty percent pursue careers in business and industry.

Services: Students receive the following free services: placement aid, career counseling, health care, and psychological counseling. Tutoring and remedial instruction are provided on a fee basis.

Programs of Study: The college confers the B.A., B.S., and B.Mus. degrees. Master's degrees are also awarded. Bachelor's degrees are offered in the following subjects: BUSINESS (accounting, business administration, industrial relations, international economics and business, international politics, management, management science), EDUCATION (elementary, secondary), ENGLISH (English), FINE AND PERFORMING ARTS (art, art education, music, music education, radio/TV, speech, theater/dramatics, theater/dramatics—literature), HEALTH SCIENCES (health science), LANGUAGES (classics, French, German, Greek/Latin, Spanish), MATH AND SCIENCES (biology, chemistry, computer science, ecology/environmental science, mathematics, physics), PHILOSOPHY (philosophy, religion), PREPROFESSIONAL (dentistry, engineering, law, medicine, ministry, veterinary), SOCIAL SCIENCES (economics, government/political science, history, intercultural studies, psychology, sociology and Spanish). Twenty-three percent of degrees conferred are in social sciences, 18% are in math and sciences, and 16% are in fine and performing arts.

Required: Freshmen must take a course in writing, and all undergraduates must take physical education.

Special: Students may arrange to take the junior year abroad. Available are several interdisciplinary programs, an urban-study center, and cooperative programs developed by the East Central College Consortium, a group of 7 colleges of which Westminster is a member.

Honors: Honors are available in all departments. Honors and independent study programs are offered for outstanding upperclassmen. A special elective humanities program is available in both the freshman and sophomore years. About 23 national honor societies have chapters on campus.

Admissions: Eighty-six percent of those who applied were accepted for the 1981-82 freshman class. The SAT scores of those who enrolled were as follows: Verbal—72% scored below 500, 23% between 500 and 599, 5% between 600 and 700, and 0% above 700; Math—56% scored below 500, 33% between 500 and 599, 9% between 600 and 700, and 2% above 700. An applicant should be a graduate of an accredited high school and have completed 15 Carnegie units.

Procedure: The SAT or the ACT is required. Applicants who wish to satisfy language and freshman writing requirements by examination should take ATs in English and a foreign language. There are no application deadlines; freshmen are admitted in all 4 terms. Candidates are notified on a rolling basis. There is a $15 application fee.

Special: Early admissions, deferred admissions, and early decision plans are available. AP credit is offered.

Transfer: For fall 1981, 84 applications were received, 73 were accepted, and 49 students enrolled. Transfers are accepted for all classes. The requirements are the same as those for freshmen, plus a 2.0 average and good standing at the previous college. D grades do not transfer. All students must complete, at the college, 12 of the 35 courses required for a bachelor's degree. The deadlines for transfer applications are August 1 (fall), December 1 (winter), January 1 (spring), and May 1 (summer).

Visiting: Informal visits can be made when classes are in session. Guides are available, and visitors may stay overnight at the school and sit in on classes. Arrangements should be made through the admissions office.

Financial Aid: Sixty-five percent of the students receive aid. Thirty percent work part-time on campus. When possible, the college prefers to package aid awards. The average freshman award in 1981-82 was $2000. Tuition may be paid in installments. Applications for aid should be filed by April 1 (summer and fall), September 1 (winter), and October 1 (spring). The college is a member of CSS; the FAF is required. Candidates are notified on a rolling basis.

Foreign Students: The 8 students from foreign countries make up less than 1% of enrollment. Special counseling is available for these students.

Admissions: Foreign students must score at least 475 on the TOEFL. No college entrance exams are required.

Procedure: Application deadlines are June 1 (fall), September 1 (winter and spring), and February 1 (summer). Foreign students must present proof of adequate funds for 1 year. They also must carry health insurance, which is available through the college.

Admissions Contact: Edwin G. Tobin, Director of Admissions.

WIDENER COLLEGE F-4
Chester, Pennsylvania 19013 (215) 499-4000

F/T: 1191M, 905W Faculty: 291; n/av
P/T: 23M, 48W Ph.D.'s: n/av
Grad: 626M&W S/F Ratio: 13 to 1
Year: tri, ss Tuition: $4635
Appl: open R and B: $2160
2134 applied 1175 accepted 547 enrolled
SAT: 500V 500M COMPETITIVE

Widener College is a private institution founded in 1821. In 1976, the school became affiliated with Brandywine College in Delaware. The library contains more than 160,000 volumes and 3600 microfilm items, and subscribes to over 1400 periodicals.

Environment: The college is located in a community of 57,000 people, 15 miles from Philadelphia. The 87-acre campus contains 31 buildings, including a 400-seat auditorium, extensive health-education facilities, dormitories, and fraternity and sorority houses.

Student Life: Seventy percent of the students are Pennsylvania residents. More than half live on campus. Dormitories are both single-sex and coed. Single-sex dorms have visiting privileges.

Organizations: Activities include student government; publications; a campus radio station; music and drama groups; religious clubs for the major faiths; and special-interest, academic, and service organizations. Thirty percent of the men belong to the 7 fraternities on campus, and 20% of the women belong to the 2 sororities.

Sports: The school sponsors intercollegiate teams in 14 sports for men and 6 for women. Ten intramural sports are offered.

Graduates: About 23% of the freshmen drop out, and 70% remain to graduate. About 25% of the graduates seek advanced degrees.

Services: Counseling and health-care services are provided. Placement assistance is available for students and graduates.

Programs of Study: The university confers the B.A., B.S., B.S.B.A., B.S. in Eng., B.S.N., and B.S.W. degrees. Associate and master's degrees also are available. Bachelor's degrees are offered in the following subjects: BUSINESS (accounting, management), ENGLISH (English), HEALTH SCIENCES (nursing, radiologic technology, respiratory therapy), LANGUAGES (French, German, Spanish), MATH AND SCIENCES (biology, chemistry, computer science, mathematics, physical sciences, physics, science administration), PHILOSOPHY (humanities), PREPROFESSIONAL (engineering—chemical, engineering—civil, engineering—electrical, engineering—engineering mechanics, engineering—general, engineering—mechanical, medicine, social work), SOCIAL SCIENCES (behavioral science, community psychology, economics, government/political science, history, psychology, sociology). Students may earn teaching certification in early childhood education or a secondary subject field.

Special: Project Prepare helps educationally and economically disadvantaged students get ready for college through a summer tutorial and counseling program. The engineering internship program allows students to spend 2 periods working in industry and still graduate with a B.S. in 4 years. A similar cooperative education program is available for business majors. A general-studies degree is available, and students may design their own majors.

Admissions: About 55% of those who applied were accepted for the 1981–82 freshman class. Applicants should have completed a college-preparatory program in an accredited high school and rank in the top half of their class. Other considerations include extracurricular activities, AP and honors courses, and recommendations by high school officials. A GED certificate is acceptable.

Procedure: Applicants should take the SAT or the ACT. An interview is recommended. The university follows a rolling admissions policy. Freshmen are admitted to all terms. Application deadlines are open, but it is recommended that candidates for fall admission apply by December 31. There is a $15 application fee.

Special: Early decision, early admissions, and deferred admissions plans are offered. CLEP credit may be earned.

Transfer: A GPA of 2.0 or better is required. Applicants must be in good standing at their last school. Decisions on whether D grades transfer are made on an individual basis. Students must spend at least 3 terms in residence to graduate.

Financial Aid: About 73% of the students receive aid. The university awards more than 260 freshman scholarships each year, some on the basis of academic ability alone. Loans are available from the federal government, local banks, and the college. The FAF is required. Applications should be filed by March 1.

Foreign Students: About 5% of the students are from foreign countries. The college offers these students an intensive English program, special counseling, and special organizations.

Admissions: Applicants must score 500 or better on the TOEFL. No college entrance exams are required.

Procedure: Application deadlines are open; students are admitted in fall and spring. Foreign students must present proof of adequate funds for 1 year.

Admissions Contact: Vincent F. Lindsley, Dean of Admissions.

WILKES COLLEGE E–2
Wilkes-Barre, Pennsylvania 18766 (717) 824-4651

F/T: 1079M, 1011W	Faculty: 159; IIA, –$
P/T: 830M&W	Ph.D.'s: n/av
Grad: 279M&W	S/F Ratio: 13 to 1
Year: sems, ss	Tuition: $4250
Appl: open	R and B: $2100
1518 applied	1398 accepted	625 enrolled
SAT: 430V 480M		COMPETITIVE

Wilkes College, established in 1933, is a privately controlled liberal arts college. The library contains 125,000 volumes and subscribes to 1125 periodicals.

Environment: Located in an urban community of 60,000, the 50-acre campus occupies 3 city blocks and contains 58 buildings. Facilities include an art gallery, a music building, a gymnasium, the guidance center, the student union, and residence halls.

Student Life: About 75% of the students are from Pennsylvania. Half live on campus. Dormitories are single-sex; there are visiting privileges. Students may keep cars on campus. Day-care services are available.

Organizations: Student activities include a radio station, newspaper, theater, symphonic band, chorus, and pep band. There are no sororities or fraternities.

Sports: The college competes on an intercollegiate level in 10 sports for men and 9 for women. There are 3 intramural sports for men and 1 for women.

Handicapped: The campus is partially accessible to wheelchair-bound students. Facilities include special parking, wheelchair ramps, specially equipped rest rooms, and lowered telephones.

Graduates: The freshman dropout rate is 11%; 87% remain to graduate. Forty percent pursue graduate study after graduation: 6% enter medical school, 2% enter dental school, and 3% enter law school. Thirty-five percent pursue careers in business and industry.

Services: Students receive the following free services: placement, career counseling, tutoring, remedial instruction, and psychological counseling. Some health-care services require payment.

Programs of Study: The college offers the B.A. and B.S. degrees. Master's degrees are also awarded. Bachelor's degrees are offered in the following subjects: BUSINESS (accounting, business administration, computer science), EDUCATION (elementary, secondary), ENGLISH (communications, English), FINE AND PERFORMING ARTS (art, art education, music, music education, theater/dramatics), HEALTH SCIENCES (medical technology, nursing), LANGUAGES (French, German, Spanish), MATH AND SCIENCES (biology, chemistry, earth science, ecology/environmental science, mathematics, physics), PHILOSOPHY (philosophy), PRE-PROFESSIONAL (dentistry, engineering—electrical, engineering—materials, optometry, pharmacy, podiatry), SOCIAL SCIENCES (economics, government/political science, history, international studies, psychology, sociology).

Required: All students must complete general-education requirements and 2 years of physical education.

Special: Junior year abroad is possible, usually for language majors. A 3-year bachelor's degree is offered. Students may create their own majors. A B.G.S. degree is offered.

Honors: Three honor societies have chapters on campus. An honors program is available in English by invitation of the department.

Admissions: Ninety-two percent of those who applied were accepted for the 1981–82 freshman class. About 75% of those who enrolled ranked in the upper fifth of their high school class. For an earlier freshman class, the SAT scores were as follows: Verbal—16% between 500 and 599, 4% between 600 and 700, and 1% above 700; Math—25% between 500 and 599, 7% between 600 and 700, and 1% above 700. Candidates must rank in the upper 40% of their graduating class and have completed 15 Carnegie units.

Procedure: The SAT is required and should be taken by December or January of the senior year. Application deadlines are open; freshmen are admitted in the fall, spring, and summer terms. There is a $15 application fee. Acceptance notifications are on a rolling basis. The college participates in the CRDA.

Special: Early decision and early admissions plans are available. CLEP and AP credit is given.

Transfer: For fall 1981, 305 students applied, 281 were accepted, and 159 enrolled. Transfers are accepted for all classes. D grades do not transfer. All students must complete, at the college, 60 of the 120–131 credits required for a bachelor's degree. Transfer application deadlines are open.

Visiting: Orientation is held for prospective students in March. Informal visits, guided tours, and interviews can be arranged through the admissions office. Visitors may sit in on classes and remain overnight on campus.

Financial Aid: Eighty-six percent of all students receive aid through the school. Eleven percent work part-time on campus. Financial assistance is offered in the form of scholarships, grants-in-aid, loans, and college employment. The college is a member of the CSS. The FAF is required. There are no application deadlines.

Foreign Students: The 30 students from foreign countries make up 2% of enrollment. An intensive English course, special counseling, and special organizations are available for these students.

Admissions: Foreign students must take the TOEFL, the University of Michigan Language Test, or the ALIGU test. On the TOEFL, a score of at least 500 is required. Students also should take the SAT, if possible.

Procedure: Application deadlines are July 15 (fall), November 15 (spring), and May 1 (summer). Foreign students must present proof of adequate funds for 9 months and must carry health insurance, which is available through the college for a fee.

Admissions Contact: Gerald K. Wuori, Dean of Admissions.

WILSON COLLEGE D–4
Chambersburg, Pennsylvania 17201 (717) 264-4141

F/T: 210W	Faculty: 35; IIB, av$
P/T: 1M, 23W	Ph.D.'s: 69%
Grad: none	S/F Ratio: 6 to 1
Year: 4-1-4	Tuition: $5420
Appl: open	R and B: $2280
257 applied	207 accepted	100 enrolled
SAT: 461V 449M	ACT: 22	COMPETITIVE

Wilson College, founded in 1869, is a small liberal arts college affiliated with the United Presbyterian Church. The library includes 150,000 volumes and 7102 microfilm items, and subscribes to 620 periodicals.

Environment: The 300-acre suburban campus is located in a residential section of Chambersburg, midway between Pittsburgh and Philadelphia. The 39 buildings include dormitories that house 600 students.

794 PENNSYLVANIA

Student Life: About 78% of the students come from Pennsylvania. Eighty-five percent attended public schools. Ninety-nine percent live on campus. Five percent are minority-group members. There are visiting privileges in the dormitories. The college welcomes students of all faiths.

Organizations: There are no fraternities or sororities. Extracurricular activities include singing groups; publications; language, academic, and athletic clubs; student government; and the Afro-American Society.

Sports: Nine intercollegiate sports for women are offered. There are 4 intramural sports for women.

Handicapped: The campus is working to meet government standards concerning facilities for the handicapped. Wheelchair ramps are available.

Graduates: The freshman dropout rate is 9%; 60% remain to graduate. Forty percent of the graduates pursue further study.

Services: Students receive free placement services, career counseling, tutoring, remedial instruction, and psychological counseling. Health care is available on a fee basis. Job-listing files also are available to alumni.

Programs of Study: The college confers the B.A. and B.S. degrees. Associate degrees are also awarded. Bachelor's degrees are offered in the following subjects: AREA STUDIES (American, Western heritage), BUSINESS (business administration), EDUCATION (early childhood, elementary, secondary), ENGLISH (English, journalism, literature), FINE AND PERFORMING ARTS (art, dance, music, radio/TV, studio art) HEALTH SCIENCES (medical technology), LANGUAGES (French, German, Greek/Latin, Spanish), MATH AND SCIENCES (biology, chemistry, mathematics, physics), PHILOSOPHY (classics, philosophy, religion), PREPROFESSIONAL (dentistry, engineering, law, medicine, ministry, social work, veterinary), SOCIAL SCIENCES (behavioral studies, economics, government/political science, history, international relations, psychology, social sciences, sociology). Twenty-two percent of degrees are conferred in the social sciences, 19% in math and sciences, and 8% in fine and performing arts.

Required: All students must complete a distribution requirement of at least 7 courses.

Special: It is possible to earn a 5-year combined B.A.-B.S. degree in engineering and management. A 4-year degree program is offered with Thomas Jefferson University in the allied-health fields of cytotechnology, dental hygiene, medical technology, nursing, occupational therapy, physical therapy, and radiology. Independent study and junior year abroad are offered. There is a cooperative major in equestrian studies. Students may design their own majors.

Honors: Honors programs are available.

Admissions: Eighty-one percent of those who applied were accepted for the 1981-82 freshman class. The SAT scores of those who enrolled were as follows: Verbal—27% scored between 500 and 599, 6% between 600 and 700, and 2% above 700; Math—24% scored between 500 and 599, 8% between 600 and 700, and 0% above 700. Candidates should be recommended by an accredited high school, should rank in the upper half of the graduating class, should have a GPA of at least 2.0, and should have completed a college-preparatory program. The school also considers the following factors: advanced placement or honors courses, extracurricular activities, and personality.

Procedure: The SAT or the ACT is required, and a personal interview is recommended. Placement examinations in foreign languages are given during orientation. Admission is on a rolling basis, and there are no specified deadlines. Freshmen are admitted in the fall and spring terms. There is a $15 application fee. Students can expect a decision within 4 to 6 weeks. The CRDA is observed.

Special: There are early admissions and deferred admissions plans. Students may earn credit with AP and CLEP exams.

Transfer: Transfers are accepted for the freshman (second semester), sophomore, and junior classes. D grades do not transfer. Applicants should have a GPA of at least 2.0. Students must complete, at the college, at least 14 of the 36 courses required for a bachelor's degree. Application deadlines are July 1 (fall) and January 1 (spring).

Visiting: On College Days, prospective students may visit classes and meet with faculty, current students, and admissions and financial-aid directors. For informal visits, a guided tour, class visits, and an overnight stay can be arranged through the admissions office.

Financial Aid: Sixty-nine percent of all students receive aid through the school. Forty-two percent work part-time on campus. The college is a member of the CSS. Tuition may be paid on the installment plan. Loans are available from the federal and state governments and the college. Aid applications should be filed as soon as possible. The FAF and the state grant application are required.

Foreign Students: The 25 students from foreign countries make up 9% of enrollment. Special organizations are available for these students.

Admissions: Foreign students must score at least 600 on the TOEFL. They also should take the SAT if possible.

Procedure: There are no application deadlines; foreign students are admitted in the fall and spring terms. They must undergo a physical examination and present proof of adequate funds for the duration of their stay.

Admissions Contact: Director of Admissions.

YORK COLLEGE OF PENNSYLVANIA D-4
York, Pennsylvania 17405 (717) 846-7788

F/T: 930M, 1309W Faculty: 103; IIA, −$
P/T: 843M, 1072W Ph.D.'s: 50%
Grad: 105M, 18W S/F Ratio: 20 to 1
Year: sems, ss Tuition: $2598
Appl: open R and B: $1708
2026 applied 1671 accepted 729 enrolled
SAT: 406V 436M LESS COMPETITIVE

York College of Pennsylvania, founded in 1941, is a private liberal arts college. The library contains over 100,000 volumes and 35,000 microfilm items, and subscribes to more than 1100 periodicals.

Environment: The 57-acre suburban campus is located on the southern edge of the city, 45 miles from Baltimore and 25 miles from Harrisburg. The 9 buildings on campus include 6 dormitories housing 686 students. The college also owns an on-campus apartment complex that houses 200 students.

Student Life: Eighty percent of the students are from Pennsylvania. Seventy-five percent come from public schools, 20% from parochial. Sixty percent live on campus. Six percent are minority-group members. About 60% are Protestant, 35% are Catholic, and 3% are Jewish. Campus housing is single-sex; there are visiting privileges. Students may keep cars on campus.

Organizations: There are 4 fraternities and 4 sororities; 5% of the men and 5% of the women belong. The college sponsors over 30 extracurricular activities, the most active of which are the drama group, the choir, the varsity club, the veterans' club, and the student senate. Other activities include a movie series, a concert series, and student dances.

Sports: The college competes on an intercollegiate level in 10 sports for men and 7 sports for women. There are 11 intramural sports for men and 8 for women.

Handicapped: About 50% of the campus is accessible to wheelchair-bound students. Special facilities include wheelchair ramps, parking areas, lowered drinking fountains, and specially equipped rest rooms. Facilities available to visually impaired students include a large-screen reading machine and sound tapes. A counselor assists handicapped students.

Graduates: The freshman dropout rate is 38%; 48% remain to graduate. Fifteen percent of the graduates pursue graduate study. Sixty percent pursue careers in business and industry.

Services: Students receive free placement services, career counseling, health care, tutoring, remedial instruction, and psychological counseling.

Programs of Study: The college grants the B.A. and B.S. degrees. Master's degrees are also awarded. Bachelor's degrees are offered in the following subjects: BUSINESS (accounting, business education, computer science, management, marketing), EDUCATION (elementary, secondary), ENGLISH (English, speech), FINE AND PERFORMING ARTS (art, music), HEALTH SCIENCES (medical technology, nursing), MATH AND SCIENCES (biology), PHILOSOPHY (humanities), SOCIAL SCIENCES (criminal justice, government/political science, history, international relations, psychology, sociology). Forty-six percent of the degrees conferred are in business, 33% are in social sciences, and 6% are in math and sciences.

Required: All undergraduates must take physical education and the core curriculum, which consists of English, mathematics, a lab science, humanities, social studies, and foreign culture.

Special: The college offers programs in medical records administration and police science and corrections.

Honors: Honors programs are offered in all departments. Four honor societies have chapters on campus.

Admissions: Eighty-two percent of those who applied were accepted for the 1981-82 freshman class. The SAT scores of those who enrolled were as follows: Verbal—88% scored below 500, 11% between 500 and 599, 1% between 600 and 700, and 0% above 700; Math—79% scored below 500, 19% between 500 and 599, 2% between 600 and 700, and 0% above 700. Candidates must be graduates of an accredited high school and rank in the upper three-fifths of their class. Recommended minimum test scores are 800 on the SAT and 18 on the ACT. Fifteen Carnegie units are required. Additional factors considered, in order of importance, are advanced placement or honors courses, recommendations by school officials, and impressions made during an interview.

Procedure: The SAT or ACT is required and should be taken by January. Junior-year results are acceptable. Application deadlines are open. Freshmen are admitted in fall and spring. There is a rolling admissions plan. A personal interview is recommended. A $15 application fee must accompany the application.

Special: Early admissions and deferred admissions plans are available. CLEP and AP credit is granted.

Transfer: For fall 1981, 395 applications were received, 315 were accepted, and 135 students enrolled. D grades are acceptable with an associate degree. All students must complete, at the college, 30 of the 124 credits required for a bachelor's degree. Application deadlines are open.

Visiting: Orientation for prospective students includes campus tours, introduction to school officials and student leaders, academic advising, and pre-scheduling. Informal visits can be arranged weekdays through the admissions office; visitors may sit in on classes and stay overnight if accommodations are available.

Financial Aid: Seventy percent of all students receive aid through the school. Ten percent work part-time on campus. The college awards several freshman scholarships; the total amount of scholarship aid available to freshmen is $20,000. The average freshman award in 1981-82 was $1500. The college has $1 million in federal and state loan funds. Work contracts are available. The college is a member of the CSS and requires the FAF. Need and scholarship are the main considerations determining awards. Aid application deadlines are May 1 (fall) and January 1 (spring).

Foreign Students: The 18 students from foreign countries make up less than 1% of enrollment. Special counseling is available for these students.

Admissions: Foreign students must score at least 500 on the TOEFL. No college entrance exams are required.

Procedure: There are no application deadlines; foreign students are admitted in the fall and spring terms. They must fill out the college's health form and must present proof of adequate funds for 1 year.

Admissions Contact: Nancy Clingan, Director of Admissions.

PUERTO RICO

ANTILLIAN COLLEGE A-1
Mayaguez, Puerto Rico 00709 (809) 832-9595

F/T: 260M, 395W Faculty: 45; n/av
P/T: 34M, 64W Ph.D.'s: 29%
Grad: none S/F Ratio: 16 to 1
Year: sems, ss Tuition: $1882
Appl: Aug. 15 R and B: $1660
260 applied 252 accepted 188 enrolled
SAT, ACT not required LESS COMPETITIVE

Antillian College, founded in 1957, is affiliated with the Seventh-day Adventist Church. The library contains 40,000 volumes and subscribes to 379 periodicals.

Environment: The 284-acre suburban campus is located on hills overlooking the city and the Atlantic Ocean. Two residence halls house 328 students. The college also sponsors married student housing.

Student Life: Most students come from Puerto Rico; others come from the mainland or one of 21 foreign countries. About 89% of the students are Protestant and 7% are Catholic. Campus housing is single-sex; there are no visiting privileges. Students may keep cars on campus. About 41% of the students live on campus.

Organizations: Social and special-interest clubs are available.

Sports: There is no intercollegiate athletics program. There are 6 intramural sports for men and 6 for women.

Graduates: The freshman dropout rate is 7%; about 35% remain to graduate.

Services: The college provides free placement services, career counseling, and health care. Remedial instruction is available on a fee basis.

Programs of Study: The college awards the B.A. and B.S. degrees. Associate degrees also are available. Bachelor's degrees are offered in the following subjects: BUSINESS (business administration, business education, secretarial science), EDUCATION (elementary, secondary), FINE AND PERFORMING ARTS (music), HEALTH SCIENCES (nursing), LANGUAGES (Spanish), MATH AND SCIENCES (biology, chemistry), PHILOSOPHY (religion, theology), PREPROFESSIONAL (dentistry, medicine), SOCIAL SCIENCES (history). Minors are offered in business administration, biology, secretarial science, accounting, secondary education, Spanish, history, English, Biblical languages, mathematics, music, psychology, chemistry, religion, and pastoral theology. Associate degrees are offered in secretarial science, nursing, and religion.

Required: Students must complete a 2-part general-education program. The basic skills sequence requires courses in Spanish, English, mathematics, vocational studies, and health and physical education. The second section includes courses in history, literature, fine arts, science, human relations, and religion.

Admissions: Applicants must be high school graduates and present a GPA of 2.0 or better. Students with lower qualifications may be admitted on probation.

Procedure: CEEB exams and the college's own entrance exam are required. There is a $15 application fee. Admissions decisions are made on a rolling basis.

Special: Early decision, early admissions, and deferred admissions plans are available.

Transfer: For fall 1981, 41 transfer students applied, 41 were accepted, and 35 enrolled. Applicants must have a GPA of 2.0 or better and be in good standing at their previous school. Students must complete, at the college, 30 of the 128 credits required to earn the bachelor's degree. Grades of C or above transfer. Application deadlines are the same as those for freshmen.

Financial Aid: Deadlines for financial aid applications are May 30 (fall and summer) and October 30 (winter). College and church scholarships, federal loans, and jobs are available. About 86% of the students receive financial aid; 38% work part-time on campus.

Foreign Students: About 14% of the students come from foreign countries. The college offers these students special counseling.

Admissions: Foreign students must take the University of Michigan Language Test or the college's own test; in addition, they must take the CEEB exam, on which a minimum score of 1200 is required.

Procedure: Application deadlines are August 5 for fall, December 31 for winter, and May 10 for summer. Foreign students must present the college's medical report as well as proof of funds adequate to cover their entire period of study. Foreign students must also carry health insurance, which is available through the college.

Admissions Contact: Guivi Rodriguez, Assistant Director of Admissions and Records.

BAYAMON CENTRAL UNIVERSITY C-1
Bayamon, Puerto Rico 00619 (809) 786-3030

F/T: 1100M, 1200W Faculty: 100; n/av
P/T: 100M, 140W Ph.D.'s: n/av
Grad: none S/F Ratio: n/av
Year: sems, ss Tuition: $1500
Appl: Aug. 10 R and B: n/app
SAT: required LESS COMPETITIVE

Bayamon Central University, founded in 1961, is an independent Catholic liberal-arts institution. The library contains more than 20,000 volumes and subscribes to 250 periodicals.

Environment: The campus is located in the heart of Bayamon, on land that once was part of a Dominican seminary. There are no residence halls. Most students commute from home.

Student Life: Almost all students are from Puerto Rico. Drinking is restricted on campus.

Organizations: Religious counseling is available for Catholic and Protestant students, and mass is held daily at a Catholic church adjoining campus. The university sponsors social and cultural events, including

796 PUERTO RICO

music recitals, poetry readings, films, and art exhibits. Other activities include student government, publications, departmental and special-interest clubs, and fraternities and sororities. The clubs and classes sponsor social activities and outings.

Sports: The intercollegiate athletic program, which the university is expanding, includes 2 sports for men and women. There is also an intramural sports program.

Services: The university provides free placement services, health care, career and psychological counseling, tutoring, and remedial instruction.

Programs of Study: The university awards the B.A., B.S., B.A.Ed., and B.B.A. degrees. Associate degrees also are available. Bachelor's degrees are offered in the following subjects: BUSINESS (accounting, business administration, management, marketing), EDUCATION (early childhood, elementary, health/physical, secondary, special), LANGUAGES (English, Spanish), MATH AND SCIENCES (biology, chemistry, general science, mathematics), PHILOSOPHY (philosophy, religion), PREPROFESSIONAL (social work), SOCIAL SCIENCES (government/political science, history, psychology, sociology). About 35% of the degrees are conferred in education and 35% in business.

Required: All students must take 55 credits distributed among specific required courses in theology, philosophy, Spanish, English, humanities, social sciences, mathematics, science, methodology, and physical education. Further general-education requirements are enforced in each degree area. Students must maintain an average of 2.0 or better to graduate. Class attendance is required.

Admissions: Candidates must be graduates of accredited high schools, have a GPA of 2.0 or better, speak Spanish, and have a good knowledge of English. Other important factors are recommendations by high school officials, and special talents.

Procedure: The SAT is required. Admissions decisions are made on a rolling basis. Application deadlines are August 10 (fall) and January 5 (spring). There is a $20 application fee.

Special: An early admissions plan is offered. AP credit is granted.

Transfer: Students must submit transcripts of previous college work and, if they have earned fewer than 24 credits, high school transcripts. A 2.0 GPA is required. Students generally must earn 30 credits at Bayamon to graduate. Application deadlines are the same as those for freshmen. Grades of C and above transfer.

Financial Aid: About 94% of the students receive aid. Loans are available from the federal government, and scholarships and grants are available from federal and territorial governments. CWS funds are offered in all departments. Aid applicants must submit a parent's financial statement. The deadline for aid applications is March 15.

Foreign Students: Fewer than 1% of the full-time students are from foreign countries.

Admissions: Foreign students must take the SAT; no English proficiency exam is required.

Procedure: Application deadlines are August 10 (fall), January 5 (spring), and May 28 (summer). Students must present proof of health.

Admissions Contact: Inez Gascot, Dean of Admissions.

CARIBBEAN UNIVERSITY COLLEGE C–1
Bayamon, Puerto Rico 00619 (809) 780-0070

F/T, P/T:
1850 M&W
Grad: none
Year: sems, ss
Appl: July 24
SAT, ACT: not required

Faculty: n/av
Ph.D.'s: n/av
S/F Ratio: n/av
Tuition: $1410
NONCOMPETITIVE

The Caribbean University College, founded in 1969, is an independent liberal arts institution offering associate and bachelor's degrees. The college has extension centers at Vega-Baja and Carolina.

Environment: The 16-acre campus is located in an urban area. The college has no on-campus housing facilities.

Student Life: More than 90% of the students are from Puerto Rico. All students live off campus.

Sports: The college is in the process of developing an athletics program. Currently, 1 intramural sport is offered.

Handicapped: The campus is completely accessible to physically handicapped students. Wheelchair ramps and special parking are available. Special counseling is provided.

Services: Free placement services, health counseling, career counseling, tutoring, and remedial instruction are available.

Programs of Study: The college confers the B.A., B.A. in Ed., B.B.A., and B. Secretarial Science degrees. Associate degrees are also awarded. Bachelor's degrees are offered in the following subjects: BUSINESS (accounting, business administration), EDUCATION (elementary, secondary), PREPROFESSIONAL (law, medicine, secretarial science).

Required: Students must complete a core curriculum (consisting of courses in English, Spanish, humanities, social sciences, biology, science, math, and history) and maintain a GPA of 2.0 or better to graduate.

Admissions: The college has an open-door admissions policy for high school graduates. Admissions considerations include the applicant's academic record and test scores. An interview is required.

Procedure: CEEB exams are required. Application deadlines are July 24 (fall), November 20 (spring), and March 27 (summer). Notification is on a rolling basis. There is a $15 application fee.

Transfer: Transfers are accepted for all classes. Thirty credit hours must be completed at the college for a bachelor's degree. Application deadlines are the same as those for freshmen.

Financial Aid: Ninety-seven percent of the students receive aid through the college. Application deadlines are June 29 (fall), October 26 (spring), and March 1 (summer).

Admissions Contact: Director of Admissions.

CATHOLIC UNIVERSITY OF PUERTO RICO C–2
Ponce, Puerto Rico 00731 (809) 844-4150

F/T: 2964M, 5579W
P/T: n/av
Grad: n/av
Year: sems, ss
Appl: July 15
4160 applied   3676 accepted   2311 enrolled
SAT: 475V 475M

Faculty: 294; n/av
Ph.D.'s: 13%
S/F Ratio: 20 to 1
Tuition: $1750
R and B: $1200
LESS COMPETITIVE

Catholic University, founded in 1948, is a 4-year bilingual institution affiliated with the Catholic Church. The library contains more than 100,000 volumes and 1600 microfilm items, and subscribes to 600 periodicals.

Environment: The 92-acre campus is located on the southern part of the island, in a metropolitan area 9 miles from San Juan. The 23 buildings include 7 dormitories that house 200 men and 300 women.

Student Life: Almost all students are residents of Puerto Rico. About 10% live in the single-sex dormitories. About 80% leave campus on weekends.

Organizations: Eight percent of the women belong to the 7 sororities, and 15% of the men belong to the 16 fraternities. Other student activities include student government, publications, a radio station, drama and choral groups, a band, and religious, political, and service groups.

Sports: The university participates on an intercollegiate level in 9 sports. Intramural sports are offered as well.

Graduates: About 20% of the freshmen drop out. Of the 70% who remain to graduate, 10% seek graduate or professional degrees.

Services: The university provides counseling and health care. Placement services are available to graduates and undergraduates.

Programs of Study: The university awards the B.S., B.A., B.B.A., B.Ed, and B.S.N. degrees. Graduate degrees also are available. Bachelor's degrees are offered in the following subjects: BUSINESS (accounting, business administration, business education, finance, management, marketing, secretarial science), EDUCATION (early childhood, elementary, health/physical, secondary, special), FINE AND PERFORMING ARTS (art, art education), HEALTH SCIENCES (medical technology, nursing), LANGUAGES (English, French, Spanish), MATH AND SCIENCES (biology, chemistry, mathematics, natural sciences, physics), PHILOSOPHY (philosophy, religion), PREPROFESSIONAL (home economics, law, social work), SOCIAL SCIENCES (psychology). About 20% of the undergraduate degrees are awarded in business, 20% in education, 13% in social sciences, and 10% in health sciences.

Required: Students must take courses in English, Spanish, social science, history, theology, philosophy, and science or mathematics.

Special: Independent study and undergraduate research programs are available.

Honors: The university offers an honors program.

Admissions: The university prefers applicants with a GPA of 2.0 or better. Grades and SAT scores largely determine the admissions decision. Applicants should be high school graduates and have completed 16 Carnegie units.

Procedure: The SAT and 3 ATs (in Mathematics, Spanish, and English as a second language) are required. The application deadline for fall is July 15. There is a $10 application fee. Notification is made on a rolling basis beginning in February.

Special: AP and CLEP credit is granted.

Transfer: About 200 transfer students are accepted each year. Applicants must have a GPA of 2.0. Students must spend 3 years in residence to graduate.

Financial Aid: The university grants honors, athletic, and band scholarships to freshmen. Loans are available from the federal government, local banks, and private sources. The deadline for financial aid applications is April 30. The FFS is required. About 92% of the students receive aid, which is awarded primarily on the basis of need. Residents receive priority.

Admissions Contact: Carmen Willims, Assistant Director of Admissions.

CHRISTIAN UNIVERSITY COLLEGE OF THE AMERICAS   D-1
San Juan, Puerto Rico 00936

Christian University College of the Americas is a private, church-related institution that offers associate and bachelor's degrees. The college has an enrollment of 135 full-time students and 85 part-time students.

COLEGIO UNIVERSITARIO METROPOLITANO
Rio Piedras, Puerto Rico 00928   (809) 767-9730

Colegio Universitario Metropolitano is a private, coeducational institution with a total of 4000 undergraduates. The school operates on the semester system; there is a summer session for undergraduates. The deadline for fall application is December. Tuition is $45 per credit; there are no dormitories on campus. The majority of the students are from Puerto Rico.

CONSERVATORY OF MUSIC OF PUERTO RICO   D-1
Hato Rey, Puerto Rico 00918   (809) 751-0160

F/T: 190M&W	Faculty: 22; n/av
P/T: 80M&W	Ph.D.'s: n/av
Grad: none	S/F Ratio: 6 to 1
Year: sems	Tuition: $210
Appl: Apr. 15	R and B: n/app
135 applied	70 enrolled
SAT: required	SPECIAL

The Conservatory of Music is a specialized college supported by the Commonwealth of Puerto Rico.

Environment: The urban campus is located midway between San Juan and Rio Piedras. There are 3 buildings on campus.

Student Life: About 98% of the students are Puerto Rican residents. There are no dormitories on campus; all students commute.

Services: Tutoring and placement services are offered free to students. Health care and remedial instruction are available on a fee basis.

Programs of Study: The school offers 4- and 5-year programs leading to the bachelor's degree in: FINE AND PERFORMING ARTS (music performance). Associate degrees also are available.

Admissions: About 50% of those who applied were accepted for the 1981–82 freshman class. Applicants must be high school graduates with an average of 2.0 or better and must take exams in theory and instruments.

Procedure: The SAT is required. The application deadline is April 15. An interview and an audition are required. There is no application fee.

Financial Aid: About 55% of the students receive aid. Scholarships, loans, and college work-study are available. Application deadlines are open. The conservatory is a member of CSS.

Admissions Contact: Zulma Palos de Santini, Registrar.

PUERTO RICO   797

INTER-AMERICAN UNIVERSITY OF PUERTO RICO/ARECIBO REGIONAL COLLEGE   B-1
Arecibo, Puerto Rico 00612   (809) 878-5475

F/T, P/T: 3000M&W	Faculty: n/av
	Ph.D.'s: n/av
Grad: none	S/F Ratio: n/av
Year: sems, ss	Tuition: $45 p/c
Appl: July 1	R and B: n/app
SAT: required	LESS COMPETITIVE

Inter-American University of Puerto Rico/Arecibo Regional College is an independent, coeducational institution that offers undergraduate instruction. Most students are from Puerto Rico. About 95% of the students receive financial aid. The university offers B.A. and B.S. degrees as well as associate degrees. Bachelor's degrees are offered in: BUSINESS (business administration), MATH AND SCIENCES (biology), PREPROFESSIONAL (social work).

INTER-AMERICAN UNIVERSITY OF PUERTO RICO/METROPOLITAN CAMPUS
Hato Rey, Puerto Rico 00657   (809) 751-8000

F/T: 3677M, 5292W	Faculty: 239; n/av
P/T: 1574M, 2086W	Ph.D.'s: 31%
Grad: 404M, 420W	S/F Ratio: 35 to 1
Year: sems, ss	Tuition: $45 p/c
Appl: May 1	R and B: n/app
3034 applied 2535 accepted	1935 enrolled
SAT: 478V 479M	COMPETITIVE

The Inter-American University of Puerto Rico/Metropolitan Campus, a private, bilingual institution, was established in 1966. The library houses 85,400 volumes and 8150 microfilm items, and subscribes to 1900 periodicals.

Environment: The campus is located in the city of San Juan. Facilities include laboratories and a cafeteria. There are no residence halls.

Student Life: Students may keep cars on campus.

Organizations: Extracurricular activities include clubs, intramural sports, publications, and student government. One national fraternity has a chapter on campus.

Sports: The university fields 9 intercollegiate teams for men and 6 for women. There are 9 intramural sports for men and 6 for women.

Handicapped: About 80% of the campus is accessible to wheelchair-bound students. Facilities include elevators and special parking areas.

Graduates: The freshman dropout rate is 15%; about 50% remain to graduate. Ten percent pursue advanced study after graduation. Five percent of the graduates enter medical school, 5% enter law school, 3% enter dental school. Thirty-five percent begin careers in business and industry.

Services: The university provides free psychological counseling, placement, career counseling, and tutoring. Health care and remedial instruction are available on a fee basis.

Programs of Study: The university awards the B.A. and B.S. degrees. Associate, master's, and doctoral degrees also are available. Bachelor's degrees are offered in the following subjects: BUSINESS (accounting, banking, business administration, computer science, economics, finance, insurance, management, public administration, secretarial sciences), EDUCATION (early childhood, elementary, health/physical, secondary, special), FINE AND PERFORMING ARTS (art, art education, music), HEALTH SCIENCES (medical technology, nursing), LANGUAGES (English, English as a second language, Spanish), MATH AND SCIENCES (biology, chemistry, mathematics, natural sciences), PREPROFESSIONAL (mental health, social work), SOCIAL SCIENCES (anthropology, economics, government/political science, history, psychology, sociology). Of the undergraduate degrees conferred, 29% are in business, 28% are in social sciences, 28% are in education, and 13% are in math and sciences.

Special: Combined B.A.-B.S. degrees may be earned.

Honors: Two national honor societies have chapters on campus.

Admission: Eighty-four percent of those who applied were accepted for the 1981–82 freshman class. The SAT scores of those who enrolled were as follows: Verbal—65% below 500, 15% between 500 and 599, 10% between 600 and 700, and 10% above 700; Math—60% below 500, 15% between 500 and 599, 15% between 600 and 700, and 10% above 700. Applicants must be high school graduates. Besides academic record and SAT scores, admissions officers consider ability

PUERTO RICO

to finance a college education, extracurricular activities, special talents, and advanced placement or honors courses.

Procedure: The SAT is required. Applications for admission are due May 1 for fall, November 15 for spring, and April 15 for summer. The application fee is $15.

Special: Deferred and early admissions plans are offered. AP and CLEP credit is accepted.

Transfer: For fall 1981, 742 transfer students applied, 688 were accepted, and 525 enrolled. A GPA of 2.0 or better is required. Students must complete 24 of the last 60 hours in residence to graduate. The bachelor's degree requires the completion of 120 credits.

Visiting: The university schedules orientations for prospective students during the academic year. Guides also are available for informal visits to campus.

Financial Aid: About 90% of the students receive aid; 50% work part-time on campus. Scholarships, NDSL, BEOG, CWS, grants, short-term loans, and part-time jobs are available. Tuition may be paid in installments. Aid applications are due March 15 (fall) or May 1 (spring). The university is a member of CSS.

Foreign Students: The university actively recruits foreign students and offers these students intensive English courses and programs, special counseling, and special organizations.

Admissions: Foreign students are not required to take an English proficiency exam; however, they must take the SAT.

Procedure: Foreign students are admitted in the fall, spring, and summer. They must present proof of health. They must also carry health insurance, which is available through the university for a fee.

Admissions Contact: Neftaly Tosado, Director of Admissions.

INTER-AMERICAN UNIVERSITY OF PUERTO RICO/SAN GERMAN B-2
San German, Puerto Rico 00753 (809) 892-1095

F/T: 7700M, 14,800W
P/T: 2600M, 4600W
Grad: n/av
Year: sems, ss
Appl: June 1
SAT, ACT: not required

Faculty: 159; n/av
Ph.D.'s: 21%
S/F Ratio: 80 to 1
Tuition: $45 p/c
R and B: $1500

LESS COMPETITIVE

Inter-American University, established in 1912, is affiliated with the United Presbyterian Church. The university has a second major campus at Hato Rey as well as 7 regional colleges that grant 2-year degrees. The library contains more than 70,000 volumes and subscribes to 400 periodicals.

Environment: The 300-acre campus in the town of San German, 15 miles from Mayaguez, has 4 dormitories that house 5% of the students, 6 classroom buildings, an administrative center, and a chapel.

Student Life: Almost all students are residents of Puerto Rico. Drinking is prohibited on campus. Campus housing is single-sex; there are no visiting privileges.

Organizations: Campus groups include fraternities, sororities, and 20 other student organizations sponsored by the student government. Students organize many social events. Protestant and Catholic religious counselors are available.

Sports: The university participates on an intercollegiate level in more than 10 sports and offers several intramural sports.

Graduates: About 30% of the freshmen drop out, and 60% remain to graduate. About half the graduates seek advanced degrees.

Programs of Study: The university awards the B.A., B.S., and B.B.A. degrees. Master's degrees also are available. Bachelor's degrees are offered in the following subjects: AREA STUDIES (Latin American), BUSINESS (accounting, business administration, secretarial science), EDUCATION (early childhood, elementary, health/physical, secondary), FINE AND PERFORMING ARTS (art, music), HEALTH SCIENCES (medical technology, nursing), LANGUAGES (French, German, Greek/Latin, Italian, Russian, Spanish), MATH AND SCIENCES (biology, chemistry, mathematics, physics), PHILOSOPHY (philosophy, religion), PREPROFESSIONAL (home economics, social work), SOCIAL SCIENCES (economics, geography, government/political science, history, psychology, sociology). Almost half the undergraduate degrees conferred are in education, 20% are in business, and 10% are in social science.

Required: Students must take courses in English; Spanish; mathematics; religion; philosophy; social sciences; history; biology, chemistry, physics, geology, or geography; and music or art.

Admissions: Applicants must be graduates of accredited high schools and present an average of 2.0 or better in 12 or more academic units. A personal interview may be required. Other important factors include extracurricular activities, advanced placement or honors courses, recommendations from high school officials, and leadership record. Non-high-school graduates may be admitted on the basis of GED tests.

Procedure: The CEEB exam is required. The application deadlines are June 1 (fall), September 1 (winter), December 1 (spring), and March 1 (summer). Admissions decisions are made on a rolling basis. There is a $15 application fee.

Special: An early admissions plan is available. AP and CLEP credit is granted.

Transfer: Most transfer applications are approved. A GPA of 2.0 or better is necessary. Students must complete 24 of the last 60 hours in residence to graduate.

Financial Aid: The university provides 500 to 600 freshman scholarships each year. Honors scholarships are available for students with a GPA of 3.75 or above. Federal and university loans as well as CWS jobs also are provided. The aid application deadline is April 15. About 75% of the students receive aid.

INTERNATIONAL INSTITUTE OF THE AMERICAS OF WORLD UNIVERSITY
San Juan, Puerto Rico 00917 D-1
(809) 765-4646
Ponce, Puerto Rico 00731 C-2
Bayamon, Puerto Rico 00619 C-1

F/T: 1790M, 1974W
P/T: 250M, 268W
Grad: 178M, 76W
Year: qtrs, ss
Appl: open
1597 applied 1597 accepted 1476 enrolled
SAT, ACT: not required

Faculty: 236; n/av
Ph.D.'s: 20%
S/F Ratio: 18 to 1
Tuition: $1963
R and B: n/app

NONCOMPETITIVE

The International Institute of the Americas of World University, an independent institution founded in 1965, has centers in San Juan, Ponce, and Bayamon. Each campus includes 6 schools: Behavioral Sciences, Business Administration, Human Resource Development and Administration, Languages, Science and Technology, and World Affairs. University library facilities house more than 85,000 volumes and subscribe to 450 periodicals.

Environment: Each center is located within city limits and is housed in one modern, air-conditioned building. There are no residence halls. Science and language laboratories, audio-visual centers and social halls are provided.

Student Life: Ninety-six percent of the students are from Puerto Rico. Most are Spanish-speaking. Students may keep cars on campus.

Handicapped: Campuses are entirely accessible to wheelchair-bound students. Facilities include elevators.

Graduates: Thirty-six percent of the graduates become candidates for advanced degrees.

Services: Career counseling, placement, tutoring, and remedial instruction are offered free to students. Health care is available on a fee basis.

Programs of Study: The university offers the B.A., B.S., B.B.A., and B.Applied Arts. Associate and master's degrees also are available. Bachelor's degrees are offered in the following subjects: AREA STUDIES (world affairs), BUSINESS (accounting, business administration, computer science, finance, health care management, industrial relations, management, marketing), EDUCATION (bilingual, elementary), HEALTH SCIENCES (dental technology, radiology), LANGUAGES (English, French, Spanish), MATH AND SCIENCES (biology, chemistry, mathematics), PREPROFESSIONAL (social work), SOCIAL SCIENCES (criminal justice, psychology, vocational rehabilitation). Forty-nine percent of the bachelor's degrees are awarded in business, 17% in human resource development and administration, 16% in behavioral sciences, and 15% in science and technology.

Requirements: Students must maintain a GPA of 2.0 and pass 2 oral and written comprehensive exams to graduate. Core curricula often require courses in human relations, leadership, world cultures, social change, Spanish, and English.

Special: Students may participate in study/travel programs during the summer quarter. The university also offers cultural exchange programs.

Admissions: All those who applied were accepted for the 1981-82 freshman class. Applicants must be graduates of accredited high schools and should present a minimum GPA of 2.0; students with a lower average may be admitted on probation.

Procedure: Applications are due 2 weeks before the start of each quarter. New students are admitted to all quarters. There is a $15 application fee. Admissions decisions are made on a rolling basis.

Transfer: Transfer students are accepted for all classes. A 2.0 GPA is required. Application deadlines are the same as those for freshmen.

Visiting: The university schedules orientations for prospective students. Guides are available, and visitors may sit in on classes. Arrangements should be made through the admissions office.

Financial Aid: About 85% of the students receive aid. Loans are available from federal and local governments, the university, and other sources. Work-study opportunities are also available. The deadline for aid applications is June 30.

Foreign Students: About 1% of the full-time students are from foreign countries. The university offers these students special counseling.

Admissions: Foreign students are not required to take an English proficiency exam or any other entrance exams.

Procedure: Application deadlines are open. Foreign students must present a medical certificate.

Admissions Contact: Luis Aquiles, Director of Admissions.

POLYTECHNIC UNIVERSITY OF PUERTO RICO D-1
San Juan, Puerto Rico 00918 (809) 754-8000

Polytechnic University of Puerto Rico is a private, coeducational institution that offers bachelor's degrees. The university operates on the quarter system, and application deadlines are open. Tuition and fees are $465 per quarter; there is no housing on campus. About 85% of the students come from Puerto Rico, and the remainder are from foreign countries. About 60% of the students receive financial aid; the average award to freshmen from all sources is $350 per quarter. The university offers bachelor's degrees in: PREPROFESSIONAL (engineering—civil, engineering—industrial, land surveying, mapping).

TURABO UNIVERSITY D-1
Caguas, Puerto Rico 00625 (809) 744-8791

F/T, P/T: 5700 M&W
Grad: 55M, 20W
Year: sems, ss
Appl: open
2194 applied 2044 accepted 1718 enrolled
SAT, ACT: not required
Faculty: 80; n/av
Ph.D.'s: n/av
S/F Ratio: 21 to 1
Tuition: $1035
R and B: n/app
LESS COMPETITIVE

Turabo University is a private, nonsectarian liberal-arts institution that began offering 4-year degrees in 1972. It is organized into 7 institutes: English and Communications, Education, Business Administration, Spanish, Humanities and History, Social Sciences, and Natural Sciences and Technology.

Environment: The 116-acre urban campus is located on a former estate in an industrial section 30 minutes from Rio Piedras. Buildings include the Learning Resources Center and a gymnasium. There are no dormitories on campus.

Student Life: Students may keep cars on campus.

Organizations: Student groups include an orchestra, the Association of Christian Youth, the Bahai Association, and clubs for students interested in natural sciences, physical education, business, and psychology. There also is a student council.

Sports: The college fields 3 intercollegiate teams. There are 3 intramural sports.

Services: Health care and career counseling are provided at no charge to students.

Programs of Study: The college awards the B.A., B.S., and B.B.A. degrees. Associate and master's degrees also are awarded. Bachelor's degrees are offered in the following subjects: BUSINESS (accounting, business administration, computer science, management), EDUCATION (adult, early childhood, elementary, health/physical, secondary, special), LANGUAGES (English, Spanish), MATH AND SCIENCES (natural sciences), PHILOSOPHY (humanities), SOCIAL SCIENCES (criminology, economics, government/political science, history, psychology, social sciences, sociology).

Required: Students must maintain an average of 2.0 or better to graduate.

Admission: Applicants must be high school graduates and submit high school records. A 2.0 GPA is required.

Procedure: The CEEB exam is required. There is a $15 application fee. A personal interview is required. The university should be contacted for information on application deadlines.

Transfer: For fall 1981, 325 transfer students applied and 248 enrolled. Applicants must be in good standing at the last institution and present a GPA of at least 2.0 in at least 24 credits. Students must earn, at the university, 30 hours, including 9 in the major field, of the 139 hours required to receive a bachelor's degree. Grades of C and above transfer.

Financial Aid: Scholarships, loans, and work-study jobs are available. Honors scholarships are awarded to students with GPAs of 3.8 or better, and athletic scholarships also are available. BEOG, SEOG, and legislative grants are offered. Aid applications should be submitted by April 20.

Admissions Contact: Gladys Betancourt, Director of Admissions.

UNIVERSITY OF PUERTO RICO

The University of Puerto Rico, established in 1903, is a publicly supported institution that offers undergraduate, graduate, and professional programs in a variety of fields. The main campus, a 4-year school, is located at Rio Piedras. Other 4-year campuses are located at Bayamon, Cayey, Humacao, Mayaguez, and San Juan. Two-year regional colleges are at Arecibo, Carolina, Ponce, Ramay, and Utuado.

UNIVERSITY OF PUERTO RICO/ C-1
BAYAMON TECHNOLOGICAL UNIVERSITY COLLEGE
Bayamon, Puerto Rico 00619 (809) 786-2885

The University of Puerto Rico/Bayamon Technological University College is a public, coeducational institution that offers undergraduate instruction. There are 4000 men and women currently attending the school. The application deadline for fall admission is November 30. Tuition is $15 per credit; the school does not offer residential facilities. The school operates on a semester system with a summer session. Almost all the students are from Puerto Rico.

The university confers bachelor's degrees in: BUSINESS (business administration, computer science, secretarial science), PREPROFESSIONAL (electronics technology). All students must take courses in English, Spanish, mathematics, social sciences, and humanities.

UNIVERSITY OF PUERTO RICO/ C-2
CAYEY UNIVERSITY COLLEGE
Cayey, Puerto Rico 00633 (809) 738-2161

F/T: 950M, 1500W
P/T: 115M, 150W
Grad: none
Year: sems, ss
Appl: Nov. 30
SAT: required
Faculty: n/av
Ph.D.'s: 35
S/F Ratio: 23 to 1
Tuition: $175
R and B: n/app
COMPETITIVE

The University of Puerto Rico/Cayey University College, founded in 1967, is a state-supported 4-year college. The library houses more than 20,000 volumes.

Environment: The campus is located in a small city about 30 miles from San Juan.

Student Life: Almost all students are residents of Puerto Rico.

Organizations: Activities include student government, drama and choral groups, and religious, political and academic clubs.

Sports: The university fields intercollegiate teams in 10 sports for men and 7 for women. There are 8 intramural sports for men and women.

Services: The university provides health care and career counseling for students at no charge. Placement services are provided for students and alumni.

Programs of Study: The university awards the B.A., B.S., and B.B.A. degrees. Bachelor's degrees are offered in the following subjects: BUSINESS (business administration), EDUCATION (elementary, secondary), LANGUAGES (English, Spanish), MATH AND SCIENCES (biology, chemistry, mathematics), PHILOSOPHY (humanities), SO-

800 PUERTO RICO

CIAL SCIENCES (psychology, social sciences). About 25% of the degrees are awarded in education and 19% in business.

Admissions: Students must be high school graduates.

Procedure: The CEEB test is required. The application deadline is November 30. There is no application fee.

Special: AP credit is granted.

Financial Aid: About 90% of the students receive aid. Scholarships, loans, and work-study are available.

Admissions Contact: Fernando Torres, Director of Admissions.

UNIVERSITY OF PUERTO RICO/ HUMACAO D-2
Humacao, Puerto Rico 00601 (809) 852-2525

The University of Puerto Rico/Humacao is a public, coeducational institution with a total of 3200 undergraduates. Approximately 97% of the students are from Puerto Rico; 3% come from foreign countries. Tuition is $15 per credit; there are no residential facilities on campus.

The university confers the B.A. or B.S. degree in: BUSINESS (business administration, human resources, management), EDUCATION (elementary), HEALTH SCIENCES (nursing, speech therapy), LANGUAGES (English), MATH AND SCIENCES (applied physics and electronics, chemistry, marine biology), PREPROFESSIONAL (social welfare). All students must take 12 semester hours each in Spanish and English.

The school considers the high school average and SAT scores in determining admissions. About 80% of the students are receiving financial aid through the school. The application deadline for fall admission is November 30, and the application deadline for financial aid is June 30.

UNIVERSITY OF PUERTO RICO/ MAYAGUEZ A-1
Mayaguez, Puerto Rico 00708 (809) 832-4040

F/T: 4751M, 3152W	Faculty:	558; n/av
P/T: 780M, 556W	Ph.D.'s:	38%
Grad: 193M, 104W	S/F Ratio:	15 to 1
Year: sems, ss	Tuition:	$495 ($2045)
Appl: Nov. 30	R and B:	n/app
5275 applied	3079 accepted	2546 enrolled
SAT or ACT: required		COMPETITIVE

The Mayaguez campus of the University of Puerto Rico was founded in 1911. Its undergraduate divisions are the Faculty of Arts and Sciences, the College of Agriculture, the College of Business Administration, and the College of Engineering. The library houses more than 600,000 volumes.

Environment: The campus, located in the city of Mayaguez, has no dormitories. The university sponsors off-campus apartments.

Student Life: Almost all students are residents of Puerto Rico. Most students commute. Students may keep cars on campus.

Organizations: Extracurricular activities include student government, lectures, concerts, and films.

Sports: The university fields intercollegiate teams in 7 sports for men and 6 for women. There are 6 intramural sports for men and 5 for women.

Graduates: About 10% of the freshmen eventually graduate.

Programs of Study: The university awards the B.A., B.S.Ag., B.S.E.E., B.S.I.E., B.S.Civil Eng., and B.S. Chemical Eng. degrees. Associate, master's, and doctoral degrees also are available. Bachelor's degrees are offered in the following subjects: BUSINESS (accounting, business administration, finance, marketing, office management), EDUCATION (physical), ENGLISH (English, literature), FINE AND PERFORMING ARTS (art theory, plastic arts), HEALTH SCIENCES (nursing), LANGUAGES (English, French, Spanish), MATH AND SCIENCES (biology, chemistry, geology, mathematics, physical sciences, physics), PHILOSOPHY (humanities, philosophy), PREPROFESSIONAL(agriculture—agricultural economics, agriculture—agricultural education, agriculture—agricultural extension, agriculture—agricultural sciences, agriculture—animal sciences, agriculture—horticulture, agriculture—soil and crop sciences, engineering—chemical, engineering—civil, engineering—computer, engineering—electrical, engineering—industrial; engineering—mechanical, engineering—surveying, medicine),SOCIAL SCIENCES (economics, government/political science, history, psychology, social sciences, sociology).

Required: Students must take specified courses in humanities, Spanish, English, physical sciences, biology, social sciences, mathematics, and physical education.

Special: The university offers study-abroad and student exchange programs.

Admissions: Students must have a high school GPA of 2.0.

Procedure: Either the SAT or the ACT is required. The application fee is $15.

Transfer: Transfer students are accepted for the sophomore and junior classes. A GPA of 2.0 is required. Grades of C and above transfer.

Financial Aid: About 83% of the students receive aid; 14% work part-time on campus. The deadline for financial aid application is March 15.

Foreign Students: About 2% of the students come from foreign countries.

Admissions: Foreign students are not required to take an English proficiency exam; however, they must take the SAT or the ACT.

Procedure: The application deadline is November 30 for fall. Foreign students must present proof of adequate funds. They must also carry health insurance. Special fees apply to foreign students.

Admissions Contact: Pedro Montalvo, Director of Admissions.

UNIVERSITY OF PUERTO RICO/ RIO PIEDRAS
Rio Piedras, Puerto Rico 00931 (809) 765-6385

F/T: 6000M, 10,300W	Faculty:	1400
P/T: 3000M, 4300W	Ph.D.'s:	n/av
Grad: 3000M&W	S/F Ratio:	n/av
Year: sems, ss	Tuition:	$200
Appl: Nov. 30	R and B:	$2320
12,000 applied	3600 accepted	3000 enrolled
SAT: required		COMPETITIVE+

The University of Puerto Rico at Rio Piedras is a publicly supported institution founded in 1900. Divisions include the colleges of Humanities, Natural Sciences, Education, Social Sciences, General Studies, Business Administration, Engineering, and Pharmacy, and the School of Architecture. The library houses more than 2.1 million volumes and 17,700 microfilm items, and subscribes to 35,700 periodicals.

Environment: The 281-acre campus is located in the San Juan metropolitan area. The 115 buildings include several museums and theaters, a planetarium, and residence halls that house 437 men and 384 women.

Student Life: About 99% of the students are from Puerto Rico. About 68% of the freshmen come from public schools. Three percent of the students live on campus. Drinking on campus is prohibited, and freshmen and sophomores may not have cars.

Organizations: Activities include 2 fraternities to which 1% of the men belong, student government, music and theater groups, radio and TV stations, publications, lecture series, concerts, and special-interest groups. Religious organizations and counselors are available to Catholic and Protestant students.

Sports: The university fields intercollegiate teams in 8 sports for men and 7 for women. There is a wide variety of intramural sports for men and women.

Handicapped: About 14% of the campus is accessible to wheelchair-bound students. Facilities include ramps, special parking areas, elevators, specially equipped rest rooms, and lowered drinking fountains and telephones. Facilities for visually impaired students include readers, braille and tape library resources, and physical, occupational, and speech therapy. Four counselors and aides are available.

Services: The following services are offered free to students: psychological and career counseling and health care. Placement services are available to students and alumni.

Programs of Study: The university awards the B.A., B.S., B.B.A., B.Secretarial Science, and B. in Environmental Design degrees. Associate, master's, and doctoral degrees also are available. Bachelor's degrees are offered in the following subjects: AREA STUDIES (Latin American), BUSINESS (accounting, business administration, business education, computer science, finance, human resources administration, management, marketing, production management, statistics), EDUCATION (early childhood, elementary, health/physical, secondary, special), FINE AND PERFORMING ARTS (art, art education, art history, music, music education, public communication, theater/dramatics), LANGUAGES (English, French, Spanish), MATH AND SCIENCES (biology, chemistry, ecology/environmental sciences, mathematics, physics), PHILOSOPHY (humanities, philosophy), PRE-PROFESSIONAL (communications, environmental design, home economics, secretarial science), SOCIAL SCIENCES (anthropology, economics, geography, government/political science, history, labor relations, psychology, social sciences, social welfare, sociology). Of the undergraduate degrees conferred, 27% are in business, 25% in education, and 22% in social sciences.

Required: Students must take stipulated courses in humanities, Spanish, English, physical sciences, biology, social sciences, and mathematics.

Special: A general studies degree is offered. A student exchange program with accredited U.S. universities enables mainland students who speak Spanish to attend the University of Puerto Rico for their junior year. The university also sponsors a junior-year-abroad program and offers organized trips to the United States.

Honors: One national honor society has a chapter on campus. The university offers an honors program designed for independent work.

Admissions: Thirty percent of those who applied were accepted for the 1981–82 freshman class. High school GPA and test scores are the most important factors in admissions decisions.

Procedure: Application deadlines are November 30 (fall), September 15 (spring) and February 15 (summer). The SAT or PAA is required. Students must also take 3 ATs (in English, Spanish, and mathematics).

Transfer: For a recent year, 1104 students applied, 321 were accepted, and 224 enrolled. Applicants with 48 to 60 hours must have a GPA of 2.5. Those with more than 60 semester hours should have a GPA of 2.0. There is a 28-credit-hour residency requirement. Grades of C and above transfer. Application deadlines are the same as those for freshmen.

Visiting: Guides are available for informal visits to the campus. Arrangements should be made with the admissions office.

Financial Aid: About 72% of the students receive aid. Scholarships, loans, and college work-study are available.

Admissions Contact: Ana Haydee G. de Hernandez, Acting Director of Admissions.

UNIVERSITY OF THE SACRED HEART
Santurce, Puerto Rico 00914   (809) 727-7800

F/T: 1700M, 2900W
P/T: 700M, 1200W
Grad: n/av
Year: sems, ss
Appl: open
SAT: required

Faculty: n/av
Ph.D.'s: n/av
S/F Ratio: 22 to 1
Tuition: $45 p/c
Room: $900

COMPETITIVE

The University of the Sacred Heart is a private liberal arts institution founded by the sisters of the Society of the Sacred Heart and affiliated with the Roman Catholic Church. The library contains 55,000 volumes and 1000 microfilm items, and subscribes to 456 periodicals.

Environment: The 30-acre campus, located in the city of San Juan, consists of an administration/academic building, a residence hall for 145 students, and a lecture hall.

Student Life: All but 2% of the students come from Puerto Rico. Drinking and smoking are restricted, and curfews are enforced.

Organizations: Ten percent of the women belong to sororities. Thirteen other extracurricular activities also are available.

Sports: The university fields 6 intercollegiate teams. Eight intramural sports are offered.

Graduates: The freshman dropout rate is about 20%. Half the students remain to graduate, and 10% enter graduate or professional schools.

Programs of Study: The university confers the B.A., B.B.A., B.S., and B.Secretarial Science degrees. Associate and master's degrees also are available. Bachelor's degrees are offered in the following subjects: AREA STUDIES (world), BUSINESS (accounting, business administration, computer and information science, finance, labor relations, management, marketing, personnel, insurance, secretarial studies), EDUCATION (general, elementary, secondary, special), ENGLISH (English, communications, literature), FINE AND PERFORMING ARTS (art), HEALTH SCIENCES (dental technology, medical technology, nursing), LANGUAGES (Chinese, English, French, German, Spanish), MATH AND SCIENCES (biology, chemistry, mathematics, physics, statistics), PHILOSOPHY (philosophy), PRE-PROFESSIONAL (engineering—aeronautical, engineering—architectural, engineering—biomedical, engineering—civil, engineering—general, engineering—industrial, engineering—mechanical, home economics, social work), SOCIAL SCIENCES (criminal justice, economics, government/political science, history, psychology, social sciences, sociology).

Required: Students must take 16 credits of theology, 12 each of philosophy and humanities, 9 each of English and Spanish, and 6 each of mathematics and science.

Special: Students may spend their junior year abroad and participate in summer study trips abroad. Classes generally are conducted in the language of the professor.

Honors: Kappa Gamma Pi has a chapter on campus.

Admissions: Students must be graduates of accredited high schools and have completed 16 Carnegie units.

Procedure: The SAT, 3 ATs (in English composition, Spanish, and mathematics), and university-administered tests are required. An interview also is mandatory. There is no application deadline. There is a $15 application fee. A rolling admissions policy is followed.

Special: An early admissions plan is available. CLEP and AP credit is accepted.

Transfer: Grades of C and above transfer. Transfers are accepted for all classes except the senior class. Students must earn 60 credits in residence to graduate.

Financial Aid: About 80% of the students receive aid; 12% of the students work part-time on campus. Aid is available in the form of commonwealth- and university-administered scholarships and grants, Cuban Refugee Loans, NDSL, EOG, and CWS. There is no aid application deadline.

Foreign Students: The university accepts foreign students.

Admissions: Foreign students must take the SAT and 3 ATs (English, Spanish, and mathematics).

Procedure: Application deadlines are open.

Admissions Contact: Angie Rodriguez, Dean of Admissions.

RHODE ISLAND

BARRINGTON COLLEGE   D-3
Barrington, Rhode Island 02806   (401) 246-1200

F/T: 182M, 273W
P/T: 50M&W
Grad: none
Year: 4-1-4
Appl: open
SAT: 428V 445M

Faculty: n/av; IIB, – – $
Ph.D.'s: 60%
S/F Ratio: 15 to 1
Tuition: $4425
R and B: $2250

LESS COMPETITIVE

Barrington College, founded in 1900, is a private nonsectarian liberal arts institution in the evangelical Protestant tradition. Its library contains 61,000 volumes and subscribes to 280 periodicals.

Environment: The 110-acre campus is located in a suburban area 7 miles from Providence. The 10 major buildings on campus include dormitories that house about 400 students.

Student Life: About 30% of the students are from Rhode Island; 89% of the freshmen come from public schools. About 70% reside on campus. Students participate in a biweekly convocation and a 2-hour College Service Corps experience. The college prohibits smoking, alcohol, gambling, and illegal drugs on campus. Dormitories are single-sex. Students may keep cars on campus.

Organizations: There are no sororities or fraternities on campus. A majority of the students are involved in some form of student government. There are prayer groups and creative workshop opportunities.

Sports: The college competes in 4 intercollegiate sports for men and 4 for women. There are 7 intramural sports for men and 7 for women.

Handicapped: Facilities include wheelchair ramps and special parking. Special class scheduling is possible.

Graduates: About 25% of the freshmen drop out during the first year; 50% remain to graduate and 35% of those continue their education.

Programs of Study: The college confers the B.A., B.S., and B.Mus. degrees. Associate degrees are also awarded. Bachelor's degrees are offered in the following subjects: AREA STUDIES (American), BUSI-

802 RHODE ISLAND

NESS (accounting, business administration, business education, computer science, finance, management), EDUCATION (elementary, health/physical, secondary, special), FINE AND PERFORMING ARTS (art, art education, music, music education, studio art), LANGUAGES (Greek/Latin), MATH AND SCIENCES (astronomy, biology, chemistry, geology, mathematics, natural sciences, physics), PHILOSOPHY (humanities, philosophy, religion), PREPROFESSIONAL (engineering, ministry, social work), SOCIAL SCIENCES (economics, government/political science, history, psychology, social sciences, sociology).

Required: All students must take interdisciplinary courses during the January "winterim" term.

Special: Study abroad and student-designed majors are available.

Honors: Departmental honors courses are offered. Honor students may be elected to an honor society.

Admissions: Candidates should have completed 16 Carnegie units, rank in the top 40% of their class, and have a C average or better. Recommendations and extracurricular activities are also considered.

Procedure: The SAT or ACT is required, and an interview is strongly recommended. Applications should be accompanied by a $15 fee; there are no application deadlines. Notification is on a rolling basis.

Special: Early admission and early decision are possible. The early decision deadline is October 15 of the senior year. AP and CLEP credit is given.

Transfer: A minimum 2.0 GPA is required, and D grades do not transfer. All students must complete, at the college, 32 of the 132 credits required for a bachelor's degree.

Financial Aid: About 60% of all students receive some form of financial assistance. Loans, scholarships, and grants are available to qualified students. More than $500,000 is awarded annually. The college is a member of the CSS and requires the FAF as well as the college's own application form. Applications filed by February 1 receive priority, but there is no deadline.

Foreign Students: Special organizations are available for these students.

Admissions: Foreign students must achieve a TOEFL score of at least 500 and must take the SAT or ACT.

Procedure: There are no application deadlines. Health insurance is required and is available through the college.

Admissions Contact: Don Anderson, Director of Admissions.

BROWN UNIVERSITY C-2
Providence, Rhode Island 02912 (401) 863-2703

F/T: 2870M, 2430W   Faculty: 560; I, ++$
P/T: none   Ph.D.'s: 95%
Grad: 700M, 480W   S/F Ratio: 10 to 1
Year: sems   Tuition: $7140
Appl: Jan. 1   R and B: $2500
11,854 applied   2433 accepted   1302 enrolled
SAT: 630V 640M   MOST COMPETITIVE

Founded in 1764 by Baptists and now a privately endowed, nonsectarian institution, Brown University is among the smallest of the Ivy League colleges. Pembroke College, established in 1891 as the university's undergraduate college for women, merged with the undergraduate college for men in 1971. The library contains 2.5 million volumes and subscribes to 12,500 periodicals.

Environment: Brown's campus of more than 100 acres dominates the top of College Hill on the East Side residential section of Providence. The campus has 150 buildings, including a newly renovated theater and dance studio. Residence facilities, which range from quadrangle-type dormitories to special-interest language-study houses, accommodate 3750 students. Brown also owns a 475-acre former estate in Bristol, Rhode Island, that contains recreational facilities and the Haffenreffer Museum, which houses the world's largest private collection of Indian artifacts.

Student Life: Nearly one-third of the students are from New England. Most students come from middle- and upper-middle-class backgrounds. About 70% of the students come from public schools. More than 76% of the men and women live on campus. Most others live within walking distance.

Organizations: There are 9 fraternities on campus, 8 national and 1 local, to which 15% of the men belong. There is 1 sorority to which 1% of the women belong. Extracurricular activities include student government, publications, a 50,000-watt AM-FM radio station, dramatics, music groups, special-interest clubs, and service organizations. Social events include lectures, concerts, faculty hours, athletic contests, dances, parties, and movies. There are several undergraduate religious organizations, including the ecumenical University Christian Movement and the Hillel Foundation.

Sports: Brown fields intercollegiate teams in 13 sports for men and 14 for women. The water polo, crew, and soccer teams are nationally ranked. A number of intramural sports also are available for men and women.

Handicapped: The entire campus is accessible to handicapped students. Facilities include wheelchair ramps, special parking, and elevators. Counseling and other assistance is provided. The university has tape recorders for use by students with visual impairments.

Graduates: Three percent of the students drop out by the end of the freshman year; between 80% and 85% remain to graduate. About 55% of the graduates pursue advanced degrees; 12% enter medical school and 12% enter law school. More than 25% pursue careers in business and industry.

Services: The following services are provided free to students: health care; psychological, placement, and career counseling; tutoring; and remedial instruction. Job placement services may be used by graduates as well as undergraduates.

Programs of Study: The university confers the B.A. and B.S. degrees. Master's and doctoral degrees also are awarded. Bachelor's degrees are offered in the following subjects: AREA STUDIES (American, Asian, Black/Afro-American, Latin American, Russian, urban), BUSINESS (computer science, organizational behavior), EDUCATION (early childhood, elementary, secondary), ENGLISH (comparative literature, creative writing, English, literature, literature and society), FINE AND PERFORMING ARTS (art history, film, music, semiotics, studio art, theater/dramatics), HEALTH SCIENCES (biomedical engineering, environmental health), LANGUAGES (Chinese, Czech, French, German, Greek/Latin, Hebrew, Italian, Japanese, Portuguese, Russian, Spanish), MATH AND SCIENCES (biochemistry, biology, chemistry, ecology/environmental science, geology, mathematics, natural sciences, oceanography, physical sciences, physics, statistics), PHILOSOPHY (classics, humanities, philosophy, religion), PREPROFESSIONAL (engineering), SOCIAL SCIENCES (anthropology, economics, history, international relations, law and society, political science, psychology, sociology). Education students must complete a second academic major. Other languages may be studied by arrangement. A nonmajor pre-medical program is recommended for all students planning to apply to medical school.

Required: All students must take 32 courses and pass 28 of them.

Special: Special features include seminars, foreign study, teacher training, a cooperative arrangement with Rhode Island School of Design, and government internships. Combined B.A.-B.S. degrees may be earned in several subjects. Students may design their own majors.

Honors: Phi Beta Kappa has a chapter on campus. Almost all departments offer honors programs, most of which include departmental seminars and a senior thesis.

Admissions: Twenty-one percent of those who applied were accepted for the 1981-82 freshman class. Admissions decisions are based on high school record, class rank, school recommendation, teacher references, personal essay, and entrance examination scores. Special consideration is given to honors or advanced placement courses, special talents, extracurricular activities, and personality. Brown actively seeks qualified minority students.

Procedure: The SAT and any 3 ATs, or the ACT, are required and should be taken by January of the senior year. Applications for the fall semester should be submitted by January 1; notification is made about April 15. The university must receive the application, a $30 fee (waived in cases of financial hardship), test scores, and references from the high school and 2 teachers. Candidates for science degrees should supply an additional reference from a mathematics or science teacher.

Special: The university has an early action (decision) plan, an early admissions plan, and a deferred admissions plan. Students may earn credit through AP exams.

Transfer: A limited number of highly qualified transfer applicants are accepted. For a recent year, 750 applications were received and 50 accepted, and 45 students enrolled. There is a two-year residency requirement. April 1 is the application deadline.

Visiting: Group information sessions for prospective students are held on weekdays at 10 A.M. and 2 P.M. all year long, and Saturdays at 10 A.M. and 11 A.M. from October to mid-December. Guides are available for informal visits. Visitors may sit in on classes and stay overnight at the school. The best time to visit is when school is in session, from late September to early May. The admissions office will make arrangements.

RHODE ISLAND 803

Financial Aid: About 35% of the students receive aid from the university. The average aid package awarded to a freshman in 1981-82 totaled $6300. In a recent year, more than 400 scholarships were awarded to freshmen. About half the students work part-time during the school year. Loans are also available. Tuition may be paid in installments. Financial aid is awarded solely on the basis of need. All factors relevant to the award, including academic performance, are re-examined each year. The university is a member of the CSS and requires the FAF. Applications should be submitted by January 15. Notification is made about April 15.

Foreign Students: About 5% of the students are from foreign countries. Special counseling and special organizations are available for these students.

Admissions: It is recommended that foreign applicants take the TOEFL, and they must score over 600 to qualify for admission. They also must take the SAT and 3 ATs.

Procedure: The application deadline is January 1 for fall admission. Students must submit proof of good health. Health insurance is available through the university.

Admissions Contact: James H. Rogers, Director of Admission.

BRYANT COLLEGE   C-2
Smithfield, Rhode Island 02917   (401) 231-1200

F/T: 1684M, 1334W   Faculty: 98; IIA, ++$
P/T: 831M, 1040W   Ph.D.'s: 49%
Grad: 1026M, 372W   S/F Ratio: 30 to 1
Year: sems, ss   Tuition: $3375
Appl: open   R and B: $2495
4400 applied   1689 accepted   870 enrolled
SAT: 470V 540M   VERY COMPETITIVE

Bryant College is one of the oldest institutions of professional business study in the country. Established in 1863, Bryant is a private, coeducational college that provides 4-year programs of study which lead to bachelor's and master's degrees. Courses of study represent affirmations of commitment to education for business and public service. The college's programs in professional studies are balanced by a broad and varied curriculum in the liberal arts. The library contains 92,000 volumes and 7000 microfilm items, and subscribes to 1000 periodicals.

Environment: In 1971, Bryant moved to its present 295-acre suburban location, 12 miles from Providence and 43 miles from Boston. The hub of this modern campus is the glass-domed, multi-purpose Unistructure and the adjacent student center. These buildings contain classrooms, a computer center and labs, a library, dining rooms, an indoor swimming pool, student lounges, faculty and administrative offices, and an auditorium. There is a variety of student residences, including a new 300-student dormitory, 52 townhouse-style apartments, and a "dormitory village" with suites accommodating 1200 students.

Student Life: About 25% of the students are from Rhode Island. Eighty percent of the freshmen come from public schools. Eighty-nine percent of the students live on campus. One percent are minority-group members. Campus housing is both coed and single-sex. There are visiting privileges in single-sex dorms. Students may keep cars on campus.

Organizations: There are eight fraternities, 6 local and 2 national, and 6 local sororities on campus. About 32% of the students belong to 1 of them. Religious counselors and organizations are available for Catholics, Protestants, and Jews. Other activities include student government, publications, an FM radio station, drama, special-interest clubs, service organizations, and athletic events.

Sports: The college fields intercollegiate teams in 9 sports for both men and women. There are 8 intramural sports for men and 7 for women.

Handicapped: About 90% of the campus is accessible to handicapped students. Facilities include wheelchair ramps, special parking, elevators, special class scheduling, specially equipped rest rooms, and lowered drinking fountains and telephones. There is 1 counselor and 1 assistant for handicapped students. Fewer than 1% of the students have visual or hearing impairments.

Graduates: About 7% drop out at the end of the freshman year, while 75% remain to graduate. About 20% of the students pursue graduate studies after graduation; 3% go on to law school. Ninety-seven percent of the graduates pursue careers in business and industry.

Services: The following services are available to students free of charge: health care; psychological, placement, and career counseling; tutoring; and remedial instruction. Placement services are available for graduates as well as undergraduates.

Programs of Study: The college confers the B.S. degree. Master's degrees are also awarded. Bachelor's degrees are offered in the following subjects: BUSINESS (accounting, applied actuarial mathematics, business administration, business communications, computer science, economics, finance, hotel management, institutional management, management, marketing, systems management), PREPROFESSIONAL (criminal justice). Eighty-six percent of all undergraduate degrees are awarded in business.

Required: All students are normally required to complete the core program by the end of the sophomore year. This program consists of 6 semester hours of accounting, 6 of economics, 6 of English composition, 6 of mathematics, 3 of management, 3 of marketing, and 3 of computer information systems.

Special: Internships are offered in each area of professional study. A number of opportunities to study abroad during the junior year are available.

Honors: Two national honor societies have chapters on campus.

Admissions: Thirty-eight percent of those who applied were accepted for the 1981-82 freshman class. The SAT scores of those freshmen were as follows: Verbal—65% below 500, 32% between 500 and 599, 2% between 600 and 700, and 1% above 700; Math—25% below 500, 55% between 500 and 599, 18% between 600 and 700; and 2% above 700. Candidates should be graduates of a college-preparatory program of an approved secondary school. They must have completed 16 Carnegie units. Applicants should rank in the top half of their graduating class and have at least a B average. Other important factors are recommendations from school officials, advanced placement or honors courses, leadership, and extracurricular activities.

Procedure: Applicants should take the SAT or ACT in November, December, or January of their senior year. All credentials should be submitted as early as possible in the senior year, although the deadline for applications is open. The application fee is $20. There is a rolling admissions plan.

Special: The college has an early decision plan with a December 20 notification date, and early and deferred admissions plans. Deadline for early decision applications is November 15. CLEP and AP credit is accepted.

Transfer: For fall 1981, 683 transfer students applied, 363 were accepted, and 190 enrolled. Transfers are accepted for the 2nd semester of the freshman class, and for the sophomore and junior classes. A minimum GPA of 2.0 is required. D grades usually do not transfer. The student must complete, at the college, 30 credit hours of the 120 required for the bachelor's degree. Transfer admissions are accepted on a rolling basis.

Visiting: There are no regular orientation programs for prospective students, but guides are available for informal visits. Visitors may sit in on classes but may not stay overnight on campus. The best time to visit is when classes are in session. The admissions office will make arrangements.

Financial Aid: Sixty-five percent of the students receive aid; 10% work part-time on campus. Financial assistance consists of scholarship grants, NDSL, and part-time work opportunities. Aid awards are based on financial need. The average award is $2500. The deadline for financial aid applications is February 15; the FAF is required.

Foreign Students: Sixty-four full-time foreign students are currently enrolled at the college, which actively recruits applicants from other countries. Special counseling and special organizations are available to these students.

Admissions: Foreign students must achieve a minimum score of 500 on the TOEFL. The SAT or ACT is also required.

Procedure: Applications for admission are accepted on a rolling basis. A physical examination is required to establish proof of health. Foreign students must carry health insurance, which is available through the college for a fee. Proof of funds adequate to cover 1 year of study is necessary.

Admissions Contact: Roy A. Nelson, Dean of Admissions.

PROVIDENCE COLLEGE   C-2
Providence, Rhode Island 02918   (401) 865-2141

F/T: 1775M, 1850W   Faculty: 220; IIA, +$
P/T: 6M, 11W   Ph.D.'s: 45%
Grad: 515M, 221W   S/F Ratio: n/av
Year: sems, ss   Tuition: $4732
Appl: Feb. 15   R and B: $2900
3511 applied   2206 accepted   954 enrolled
SAT: 510V 530M   ACT: 24   VERY COMPETITIVE

804 RHODE ISLAND

Providence College, established in 1917, is a liberal arts and sciences institution operated by the Dominican Fathers of the Roman Catholic Church. The library contains 241,000 volumes and subscribes to 1846 periodicals. About one-fifth of the faculty members are Dominican Fathers.

Environment: The 125-acre, self-contained campus is 5 miles from downtown Providence. There are 26 buildings on campus including the library, which won an architectural award; a large fieldhouse; and an ice arena. Living facilities include dormitories and off-campus apartments.

Student Life: About one-third of the students come from Rhode Island. Most (95%) are Catholic; 3% are Protestant and 2% are Jewish. Nearly 6% are members of minority groups. Sixty-two percent of the students come from public schools, and 60% live on campus. Campus housing is single-sex; there are visiting privileges. Students may keep cars on campus.

Organizations: There are no fraternities or sororities. Extracurricular activities include a weekly newspaper and other publications, and departmental, service, and special-interest organizations. Cultural events in Providence are easily accessible.

Sports: The college sponsors intercollegiate teams in 10 sports for men and 10 for women, and offers 13 intramural sports each for men and women.

Handicapped: About 80% of the campus is accessible to handicapped students. Facilities include wheelchair ramps, special parking, elevators, and specially equipped rest rooms. Fewer than 1% of the students have visual or hearing impairments. There are no special counselors for handicapped students.

Graduates: Eleven percent of freshmen drop out in the first year; 72% remain to graduate. Twenty-five percent of the graduates pursue advanced study.

Services: The following services are available free to students: health care, placement and career counseling, tutoring, and remedial instruction. Placement services may be used by graduates as well.

Programs of Study: All undergraduate programs lead to the B.A. or B.S. degree. Master's and doctoral degrees also are conferred. Bachelor's degrees are offered in the following subjects: AREA STUDIES (American, Latin American), BUSINESS (accounting, computer science, finance, management, marketing), EDUCATION (secondary, special), FINE AND PERFORMING ARTS (art history, music, studio art, theater/dramatics), HEALTH SCIENCES (health services administration), LANGUAGES (French, German, Italian, Portuguese, Russian, Spanish), MATH AND SCIENCES (biology, chemistry, clinical chemistry, mathematics, physics), PHILOSOPHY (philosophy, religion), PRE-PROFESSIONAL (dentistry, engineering, medicine, social work), SOCIAL SCIENCES (anthropology, economics, government/political science, history, psychology, social studies, sociology). About 30% of all undergraduate degrees are conferred in business, 23% in social sciences, and 11% in math and sciences.

Required: All students must take 20 semester hours of Development of Western Civilization, 6 hours of social science, 6 hours of natural science, 6 hours of philosophy, 6 hours of religious studies, and 3 hours of English composition.

Special: Students may study abroad during the junior year. The B.G.S. degree is offered, and student-designed majors are permitted. A 3-2 cooperative engineering program is offered with Columbia, Notre Dame, and Washington Universities.

Honors: Two national honor societies have chapters on campus. The Liberal Arts Honors Program permits superior students to pursue their studies in greater depth.

Admissions: Sixty-three percent of those who applied were accepted for the 1981-82 freshman class. SAT scores for freshmen were as follows: Verbal—46% below 500, 47% between 500 and 599, 6% between 600 and 700, and 1% above 700; Math—32% below 500, 53% between 500 and 599, 14% between 600 and 700, and 1% over 700. The college requires graduation from an accredited high school, completion of 15 Carnegie units, and a positive recommendation from the high school. Applicants should have a 2.5 average and rank in the top 50% of their class. Other factors considered important are advanced placement or honors courses, leadership, extracurricular activities, and interview impressions.

Procedure: The SAT or ACT is required. The SAT should be taken in November or December of the senior year. Application deadlines are February 15 (fall) and November 15 (spring). Admissions decisions are made in March. There is a $25 application fee.

Special: The college offers an early decision plan (with a January 31 notification date), an early admissions plan (with a February 15 deadline), and a deferred admissions plan. AP and CLEP credit is accepted.

Transfer: For fall 1981, 344 students applied, 219 were accepted, and 135 enrolled. Transfers are accepted for freshman, sophomore, and junior classes. A minimum GPA of 3.0 is required, and an interview is recommended. D grades are not acceptable. Students must complete, at the college, at least 56 of the 104 credits necessary to receive a bachelor's degree; there is a 2-year residency requirement. Transfer application deadlines are March 15 (fall) and November 15 (spring).

Visiting: Regular orientation sessions for prospective students are held Monday, Wednesday, and Friday at 10:30 A.M. and 2:30 P.M. Guides are also available for informal visits. Visitors may sit in on classes and stay overnight at the school. Visits should be scheduled September through November or January through March. Students must register in advance for the orientations. The admissions office will make arrangements.

Financial Aid: The college is a member of the CSS and provides eligible freshmen with scholarships, loans, and part-time employment. About 50% of all students receive aid; the average award to freshmen from all sources is $5000. Scholarships are awarded and renewed depending on academic record and need. Loans are awarded on the basis of need only. Applications for scholarship and loans must be submitted by February 15. The FAF also must be filed. Scholarship decisions are made on a rolling basis.

Foreign Students: One percent of the full-time students are from foreign countries.

Admissions: A minimum score of 600 on the TOEFL is required. Students must also take the SAT or the ACT.

Procedure: The application deadline for fall is February 15. Students must submit proof of health in the form of a personal statement, and are required to carry health insurance. Proof of funds adequate to cover 1 academic year is also required.

Admissions Contact: Michael G. Backes, Director of Admissions.

RHODE ISLAND COLLEGE C-2
Providence, Rhode Island 02908 (401) 456-8234

F/T: 1417M, 3007W
P/T: 1093M, 1957W
Grad: 515M, 1188W
Year: sems, ss
Appl: May 1
2260 applied
SAT: 410V 435M

Faculty: 369; IIA, +$
Ph.D.'s: 67%
S/F Ratio: 17 to 1
Tuition: $854 ($2838)
R and B: $2200
1700 accepted 1054 enrolled
COMPETITIVE

Rhode Island College is a state-supported liberal arts and education college established in 1854. The library has over 240,000 volumes and subscribes to more than 2100 periodicals.

Environment: The 125-acre, self-contained campus is 3 miles from downtown Providence. There are 24 buildings on campus, including 4 dormitories accommodating 480 women and 140 men.

Student Life: The college is intended to serve residents of the state, and 90% of the student body comes from Rhode Island. About 75% of the students are from public schools. Fifteen percent live on campus; most students commute. Nine percent of the students are minority-group members. Campus housing is both coed and single-sex. There are visiting privileges in single-sex dorms. Students may keep cars on campus. Day-care services are provided to all students, faculty, and staff for a fee.

Organizations: There are fraternities and sororities on campus to which 5% of the men and 5% of the women belong. Extracurricular activities include theater and music groups, publications, recitals, films, poetry readings, a student parliament, religious and special-interest clubs, and student-faculty committees. Places of worship are available on campus for Catholics and nearby for other major faiths.

Sports: The college offers intercollegiate competition in 7 sports for men and 8 for women. There are 9 coed intramural sports.

Handicapped: About 90% of the campus is accessible to handicapped students. Facilities include wheelchair ramps, special parking, elevators, special class scheduling, and lowered drinking fountains and telephones. Two counselors and 1 assistant staff an office to assist handicapped students. Telecommunication systems are available for hearing-impaired students.

Graduates: About 15% of the students drop out by the end of the freshman year; 50% remain to graduate. Of the graduates, 90% go on to full-time graduate study; 1% enter medical school, 1% enter dental school, and 1% enter law school.

Services: The following services are provided to students free of charge: health care; psychological, placement, and career counseling;

tutoring; and remedial instruction. The placement office helps both students and alumni.

Programs of Study: The college confers the B.A., B.S., B.S.W., B.G.S., and Bachelor of Music in Performance degrees. It also awards master's degrees. Bachelor's degrees are offered in the following subjects: AREA STUDIES (Black/Afro-American, classical, general, Latin American, Medieval and Renaissance, urban, women's), BUSINESS (computer science, industrial arts education, industrial technology, management), EDUCATION (early childhood, elementary, health/physical, industrial, secondary, special), ENGLISH (communications, English), FINE AND PERFORMING ARTS (art, art education, art history, film studies, music, music education, studio art, theater/dramatics), HEALTH SCIENCES (medical technology, nursing, radiologic technology), LANGUAGES (French, Spanish), MATH AND SCIENCES (biology, chemistry, general science, mathematics, physical sciences), PHILOSOPHY (philosophy), PREPROFESSIONAL (dentistry, law, medicine, optometry, social work, veterinary), SOCIAL SCIENCES (anthropology, anthropology/public archeology, economics, geography, government/political science, history, psychology, social sciences, sociology). Twenty-eight percent of all undergraduate degrees are conferred in education, 14% in health sciences, and 15% in social sciences.

Required: All students are required to complete a general education program that includes course work in 7 areas: other cultures, natural science/mathematics, fine/performing arts, history, English, social/behavioral sciences, and contemporary values.

Special: The special education program is one of the few in the nation backed by federal grants. The college has a laboratory school for education majors. It is possible to earn combined B.A.-B.S. degrees. A general studies degree is offered and student-designed majors are permitted.

Honors: One honor society has a chapter on campus.

Admissions: Seventy-five percent of those who applied were accepted for the 1981-82 freshman class. Among freshmen, SAT scores were as follows: Verbal—83% below 500, 14% between 500 and 599, 2% between 600 and 700, and 1% above 700; Math—75% below 500, 21% between 500 and 599, 3% between 600 and 700, and 1% above 700. Applicants should have a minimum high school grade average of 2.0. Other factors considered are advanced placement or honors courses, interview, extracurricular activities, and special talents.

Procedure: The SAT is required and should be taken by December of the senior year. Applications for the fall term should be submitted by May 1 and those for the spring term by December 1. Admissions are made on a rolling basis from September to July. There is a $15 application fee.

Special: The college has an early decision plan with a December 25 notification date. There is an early admissions plan with a May 1 deadline. There is no formal admission for the summer session, but students may begin their study in the summer if they are accepted and enrolled for the fall. CLEP and AP may be available.

Transfer: For fall 1981, 916 transfer students were accepted, and 779 enrolled. Transfers are accepted for all classes. Transfers from junior colleges must have an A.A. and a 2.5 GPA; from a senior college or university a 2.0 GPA is required. D grades do not transfer. The student must study at least 1 year at the college and must complete in residence 30 of the 120 credits required for the bachelor's degree. The application deadline for the fall semester is June 1; for the spring semester, December 1.

Visiting: Personal interviews and campus tours are available for prospective students. Visitors may sit in on classes and stay at the school. The best times for campus visits are Monday through Friday when classes are in session. The admissions office will make arrangements.

Financial Aid: About 49% of the students receive financial aid; 62% work part-time on campus. The average aid to freshmen from college-administered scholarships and loans is $2000. Work-study programs also are available. The college is a member of CSS. Financial aid is awarded primarily on the basis of need. It is renewed on a basis of continued need and satisfactory academic performance. The FAF, BEOG, and the college's own form must be filed by February 28.

Foreign Students: One percent of the full-time students come from foreign countries. Special counseling is available to these students.

Admissions: Foreign students must obtain a minimum score of 500 on the TOEFL. The SAT also is required.

Procedure: Application deadlines are March 1 (fall) and December 1 (spring). Proof of funds sufficient to cover 1 year of study is required. Foreign students must carry health insurance, which is available through the college for a fee.

Admissions Contact: James M. Colman, Director of Admissions.

RHODE ISLAND SCHOOL OF DESIGN C-2
Providence, Rhode Island 02903 (401) 331-3511

F/T: 742M, 854W		Faculty:	84; IIA,—$
P/T: none		Ph.D.'s:	n/app
Grad: 52M, 56W		S/F Ratio:	18 to 1
Year: 4-1-4		Tuition:	$5960
Appl. Jan. 21		R and B:	$2510
1500 applied	500 accepted		310 enrolled
SAT: 500V 510M			SPECIAL

Rhode Island School of Design, founded in 1877, is a privately endowed 4-year college that prepares students to enter the professional art world. The school is made up of the divisions of Fine Arts, Architecture, Illustration and Photographic Studies, Design, and Graduate Studies. The library contains over 56,000 volumes and 87,000 slides, and subscribes to 232 periodicals.

Environment: The campus occupies 3 blocks on Providence's East Side. A separate residence center houses students in single and double rooms. There are 23 main buildings, some built as early as the 1700s, others as late as the 1960s. The school also maintains a 33-acre seaside tract 12 miles from Providence that is used for outdoor activities and research in landscape architecture. The Museum of Art is open to the public and available for research and study.

Student Life: The school, which enjoys an international reputation, draws students from all parts of the United States and 50 foreign countries. About 10% of the students are minority-group members. Nearly 80% of the entering freshmen come from public schools. Ninety-six percent of the freshmen and 30% of the upperclass students live on campus. Authorized off-campus apartments are also available. Campus housing is coed.

Organizations: There are no fraternities or sororities at the school, and no honor or professional societies. Extracurricular activities include dances, publications, art shows, concerts, films, lectures, plays, and professional demonstrations. Religious facilities for all major faiths are available; religious clubs on campus include Newman and Hillel.

Sports: There are 4 intramural sports for men and women. There are no intercollegiate activities.

Handicapped: About a fourth of the campus is accessible to handicapped students. Special facilities include wheelchair ramps and elevators. There are no special counselors for handicapped students. There are no students with visual or hearing impairments.

Graduates: Between 5% and 12% drop out by the end of the freshman year, and approximately 65% remain to graduate. Twenty percent of the students pursue graduate studies after graduation.

Services: The following services are provided to students free of charge: health care, psychological and career counseling, placement, and remedial instruction in English. The Career Planning Office, which assists students in selecting goals, preparing portfolios, writing resumes, and obtaining interviews, is open to graduates as well as undergraduates.

Programs of Study: The school confers the B.F.A., B.Arch., B.Land. Arch., B.Int.Arch., and B.ID. degrees. Master's degrees also are awarded. Bachelor's degrees are offered in the following major fields of concentration: apparel design, ceramics, film/photography, film/video, glass design, graphic design, illustration, industrial design, interior architecture, jewelry/metals, landscape architecture, painting, print-making, sculpture, textile design, wood-furniture design. The programs leading to degrees in architecture take 5 years. All others take 4 years. Sixty-five percent of all degrees are conferred in the arts, 35% in preprofessional subjects.

Required: All freshmen are required to take art history, English, life drawing, 2-dimensional design, 3-dimensional design, and a studio elective. An additional 24 credits in liberal arts and departmental sequences are required in the sophomore, junior, and senior years.

Special: Students selected for a European Honors program study for a year in the school's studios in Rome. Students who spend their fourth year abroad make their own living arrangements, but the study arrangements are controlled by the school. An agreement with neighboring Brown University allows students of each school to elect courses at the other. During the 6-week winter session between semesters, courses are suspended and students work outside their major fields.

Admissions: About 33% of those who applied were accepted for the 1981-82 freshman class. The SAT scores of those who enrolled were as follows: Verbal—53% below 500, 34% between 500 and 599, 12% between 600 and 700, and 1% above 700; Math—47% below 500, 36% between 500 and 599, 14% between 600 and 700, and 2% above 700. About 70% of the students were in the top quarter of their

RHODE ISLAND

high school class. Candidates must submit 3 drawings and a portfolio and must have graduated from an accredited high school. Acceptance is based on the quality of the drawings and the portfolio; academic performance takes secondary importance.

Procedure: The SAT or ACT is required. Candidates are usually accepted for the fall term only. The application deadline is January 21. Notification of acceptance is sent no later than April 10. There is a $20 application fee.

Special: An early admissions plan is offered; the application deadline is December 15. A deferred admissions plan is also available.

Transfer: Of 830 applications received in 1980–81, 280 were accepted, and 210 applicants enrolled. Transfers are accepted only for the sophomore class. D grades do not transfer. A transfer student must study at the school 2 years to receive a bachelor's degree, for which 120 credits are required. The deadlines for applications are January 31 (fall), November 4 (winter), and March 31 (spring).

Visiting: Orientation sessions are held for prospective students every Monday, Wednesday, and Friday from October through January, and every Wednesday and Friday from February through September. The admissions office handles arrangements. Guides are not available for informal visitors, who may not sit in on classes or stay overnight on campus.

Financial Aid: An average of 150 freshman students receive financial assistance each year. Aid is awarded in packages that include institutional scholarships and federal loan, grant, and work awards. The awards average about $3000 with a maximum of $5500. Aid awarded in the first year usually is continued as long as the student is enrolled if circumstances do not change. Approximately 68% of all students receive financial aid. The FAF is required, and financial aid applications should be submitted by February 28. The school is a member of CSS.

Foreign Students: The full-time foreign student enrollment currently numbers 150. The school offers foreign students special counseling and special organizations.

Admissions: Foreign students must take the TOEFL. The SAT also is required.

Procedure: Application deadlines are December 15 (fall), November 4 (winter), and March 31 (spring). Foreign students must present proof of health and carry health insurance. Proof of adequate funds is also required.

Admissions Contact: Edward Newhall, Director of Admissions.

ROGER WILLIAMS COLLEGE D-3
Bristol, Rhode Island 20871 (401) 255-2151

F/T: 1400M, 1000W	Faculty: 100; IV, +$
P/T: 1000M, 500W	Ph.D.'s: 30%
Grad: none	S/F Ratio: 24 to 1
Year: 4-1-4, ss	Tuition: $4030
Appl: open	R and B: $2538
3000 applied	1700 accepted	800 enrolled
SAT, ACT: not required		COMPETITIVE

Roger Williams College, founded in 1919, is a private liberal arts and professional college. The library houses 80,000 volumes and subscribes to 850 periodicals.

Environment: The suburban campus is situated on 83 acres overlooking Mt. Hope Bay. It is located in Bristol, about 15 miles from Providence. The Division of Continuing Education also maintains facilities in Providence and North Kingston. The campus consists of about 10 buildings, including 3 dormitories housing 800 students. A new apartment complex 1½ miles from campus accommodates 325 upperclassmen. Sailing facilities, beaches, and historic Newport are nearby.

Student Life: About half the students are from New England, including 10% from Rhode Island. Eighty-five percent of the entering freshmen come from public schools. About 50% of the students live on campus, and 20% commute. Fifty percent of the students are Catholic, 30% are Protestant, and 15% are Jewish. About 5% are minority-group members. Campus housing is both coed and single-sex. There are visiting privileges in single-sex dorms. Students may keep cars on campus.

Organizations: There are no fraternities or sororities at the college. Extracurricular activities include drama, the college newspaper, a student assistance service, and student government. Social events on campus include student-sponsored concerts and plays. Student delegates sit and vote on faculty and administration committees dealing with student regulations, discipline, policymaking, and curriculum. Religious counseling is available from ministers, priests, and rabbis in the community.

Sports: The college participates intercollegiately in 8 sports for men and 7 for women. There are 8 intramural sports for men and 7 for women.

Handicapped: Ninety percent of the campus is accessible to handicapped students. Facilities include wheelchair ramps, special parking, elevators, special class scheduling, specially equipped rest rooms, and lowered telephones. There is 1 special counselor for handicapped students.

Graduates: About 25% of the students drop out by the end of the freshman year; 68% remain to graduate. About 20% of the students pursue graduate study; 1% enter medical school, 1% enter dental school, and 1% enter law school. Seventy percent enter business and industry.

Services: The college provides free psychological counseling, placement, career counseling, and remedial instruction. Health care and tutoring are available for a fee.

Programs of Study: All programs lead to the B.A., B.F.A., or B.S. degree. Bachelor's degrees are offered in the following subjects: AREA STUDIES (American, urban), BUSINESS (accounting, business administration, computer science, finance, management, marketing), EDUCATION (elementary), ENGLISH (English, career writing, creative writing), FINE AND PERFORMING ARTS (art, studio art, theater/dramatics), MATH AND SCIENCES (biochemistry, biology, chemistry, ecology/environmental science, natural sciences, oceanography, zoology), PHILOSOPHY (philosophy), PREPROFESSIONAL (architecture, engineering, forestry, law, social work), SOCIAL SCIENCES (government/political science, history, social sciences, sociology).

Required: All undergraduates must take expository writing and 1 course from each of 4 divisions.

Special: The college has humanities seminars that introduce students to the topic-and-discussion approach to college work. Cooperative education is available in several programs, including business and engineering. Education students will be certified to teach in the elementary schools of Rhode Island and its reciprocal states. One semester of the junior year may be spent abroad. The B.G.S. degree is available. Student-designed majors are permitted.

Admissions: Fifty-seven percent of those who applied were accepted for the 1981–82 freshman class. The SAT scores of those who enrolled were as follows: Verbal—20% below 500, 70% between 500 and 599, 10% between 600 and 700, and 1% above 700; Math—40% below 500, 50% between 500 and 599, 5% between 600 and 700, and 0% above 700. A high school diploma is required for admission. Recommendations by school officials, advanced placement or honors courses, evidence of special talents, and personality also are considered important.

Procedure: Freshmen are admitted in the summer, spring, and fall. The college has a rolling admissions plan. A personal interview is recommended, but not required. There is a $20 application fee.

Special: The college has early decision, early admissions, and deferred admissions plans. CLEP and AP credit is available.

Transfer: For fall 1981, 400 transfer students applied, 300 were accepted, and 200 enrolled. Transfer students are accepted in each class. D grades transfer if the GPA is at least 2.0 and the D is not in the student's major. Students must spend 1 year in residence and must complete, at the college, 30 of the 120 credits required for the bachelor's degree. Transfer applications are accepted on a rolling basis.

Visiting: Orientation sessions are offered to prospective students. Guides also are available for informal visits. Visitors may sit in on classes but may not stay overnight at the school. The best time to visit is during the school day. The admissions office will make arrangements.

Financial Aid: Sixty-two percent of all students receive aid; 10% work part-time on campus. The college administers $180,000 in federal loan funds, and 15% of the students receive loans. Work-study programs are available to freshmen, and 20% of the students participate. Aid packages include grants, loans, and part-time jobs. Scholarships and loans each range from $450 to $1000. The college is a member of the CSS. The FAF, FFS, or SFS is required of all aid applicants. Need is the main consideration in determining awards. Aid applications are accepted on a rolling basis. Students will be considered as long as funds are available.

Foreign Students: Seven percent of the full-time students come from foreign countries. The college, which actively recruits these students, offers them an intensive English course as well as special counseling and organizations.

Admissions: Foreign students must take an English proficiency examination given by the college. The SAT or ACT is not required.

Procedure: Applications are accepted on a rolling basis. Foreign students must complete a health form and carry health insurance, which is available through the college. Proof of funds adequate to cover 1 year of study is required.

Admissions Contact: Robert P. Nemec, Dean of Admissions and Financial Aid.

SALVE REGINA—THE NEWPORT COLLEGE D-4
Newport, Rhode Island 02840 (401) 847-6650

F/T: 186M, 1042W	Faculty: 81; IIA, --$
P/T: 103M, 417W	Ph.D.'s: 32%
Grad: 76M, 136W	S/F Ratio: 20 to 1
Year: sems, ss	Tuition: $4000
Appl: open	R and B: $2300
953 applied 890 accepted 424 enrolled	
SAT: 400V 420M	LESS COMPETITIVE

Salve Regina—The Newport College, founded in 1947, is a private college of arts and sciences affiliated with the Roman Catholic Church. It is conducted by the Religious Sisters of Mercy of the Union. Its library contains more than 70,000 volumes and 4300 microfilm items, and subscribes to 625 periodicals.

Environment: Located in an urban area 40 miles from Providence on a 50-acre campus, the college overlooks the Atlantic Ocean. The administration building is the former Goelet mansion, Ochre Court. It was built in the late 19th century and is a reproduction of a baroque French chateau. The residence halls accommodate 800 students. The college also sponsors off-campus apartments.

Student Life: About 80% of the students are from New England. Thirty-four percent live on campus. Over 95% are Catholic. Two percent of the students are minority-group members. College housing is single-sex, and there are visiting privileges. Students may keep cars on campus.

Organizations: There are no fraternities or sororities on campus. The college sponsors 25 student clubs and 3 student government organizations.

Sports: The college fields 5 intercollegiate teams for men and 5 for women. There are 5 intramural sports for men and 6 for women.

Handicapped: Twenty percent of the campus is accessible to physically handicapped students. Special facilities include wheelchair ramps, parking areas, elevators, and specially equipped rest rooms. Special class scheduling is also available.

Graduates: Ten percent of the entering freshmen drop out after their first year; 80% remain to graduate.

Services: Free health care, career and psychological counseling, job placement, tutoring, and remedial instruction are offered to all students.

Programs of Study: The college confers the B.A., B.S., and B.A.S. degrees. Associate and master's degrees are also awarded. Bachelor's degrees are offered in the following subjects: AREA STUDIES (American), BUSINESS (accounting, computer science, management), EDUCATION (elementary, secondary, special), ENGLISH (English, literature), FINE AND PERFORMING ARTS (art, art education, theater/dramatics), HEALTH SCIENCES (medical technology, nursing), LANGUAGES (French, Spanish), MATH AND SCIENCES (biology, chemistry, mathematics), PHILOSOPHY (philosophy, religion), PREPROFESSIONAL (social work), SOCIAL SCIENCES (economics, government/political science, history, psychology, sociology). About 47% of all degrees conferred are in health sciences, and 26% are in social sciences.

Special: Independent study and study abroad are possible. The nursing curriculum provides an integrated program that prepares the student for the practice of professional nursing in first-level positions and provides a foundation for further study. A number of hospitals and community health centers in the Rhode Island and the southeastern Massachusetts areas are used. Students in medical technology spend their senior year in a clinical setting at numerous hospitals.

Honors: There are 3 honor society chapters on campus.

Admissions: About 93% of those who applied for the 1981–82 freshman class were accepted. The SAT scores of those who enrolled were as follows: Verbal—85% below 500, 14% between 500 and 599, 1% between 600 and 700, and 0% above 700; Math—78% below 500, 18% between 500 and 599, 3% between 600 and 700, and 0% above 700. Candidates should have completed 16 high school units. They must rank in the upper half of their graduating class, have a grade average of at least 2.0, and present a statement from the principal or guidance counselor regarding character, personality, and scholarship. An interview is recommended. Other factors considered are advanced placement or honors courses and the extracurricular activities record.

Procedure: Either the SAT or ACT is required. Applications should be submitted by the early fall of the senior year. Notification is on a rolling basis. There is a $20 application fee.

Special: Early and deferred admissions plans and an early decision plan are offered. AP and CLEP credit is given.

Transfer: For fall 1981, 185 students applied, 137 were accepted, and 94 enrolled. A 2.0 GPA is required, and standardized exam scores are recommended. D grades do not transfer. Students must spend 30 semester hours in residence and earn at least 30 of the 120 credits necessary for a bachelor's degree. Application deadlines are open.

Visiting: Informal tours of the campus can be arranged through the admissions office. Visitors can sit in on classes.

Financial Aid: About 64% of all students receive financial aid. Work assistance is available. Scholarships, grants, and loans are awarded annually on the basis of academic performance and financial need. Funds include NDSL, SEOG, CWS, BEOG, and NSL. The college is a member of CSS and requires the FAF. Application for aid should be made by February 15.

Foreign Students: One percent of the full-time students come from foreign countries.

Admissions: Foreign students must take the TOEFL but are not required to take a college entrance exam.

Procedure: Application deadlines are open. Foreign students must present proof of funds adequate to cover 1 year of study.

Admissions Contact: Christopher M. Kiernan, Dean of Admissions.

UNIVERSITY OF RHODE ISLAND C-4
Kingston, Rhode Island 02881 (401) 792-2164

F/T: 4430M, 4394W	Faculty: 702; I, +$
P/T: 434M, 705W	Ph.D.'s: 72%
Grad: 1618M, 1448W	S/F Ratio: 13 to 1
Year: sems, ss	Tuition: $1368 ($3892)
Appl: Mar. 1	R and B: $2618
7433 applied 5277 accepted 2333 enrolled	
SAT: 442V 501M	COMPETITIVE

The University of Rhode Island is a state-supported institution offering undergraduate programs in 7 colleges: Arts and Sciences, Business Administration, Engineering, Human Sciences and Services, Nursing, Pharmacy, and Resource Development. The library contains 650,000 volumes.

Environment: The university occupies a 1200-acre central campus in Kingston, close to the Atlantic Ocean and 30 miles from Providence. The school has two other campuses, the 165-acre Bay campus and the 2300-acre Jones campus. Dormitories accommodate 2009 women and 1850 men.

Student Life: Seventy percent of the students are from Rhode Island. Slightly less than half the students live on campus. About 85% of entering freshmen come from public schools. Three percent of the students are minority-group members. Campus housing is both coed and single-sex. There are visiting privileges in single-sex dorms. Students may keep cars on campus. Day-care services are provided to all students, faculty, and staff for a fee.

Organizations: There are 14 fraternities and 8 sororities on campus; 13% of the men and 14% of the women belong to 1 of them. Other student organizations include music groups, a campus newspaper, a literary magazine, a radio station, and student government. Religious organizations exist on campus for all major faiths. The Atlantic Ocean is nearby, and historic Newport is just across Narragansett Bay.

Sports: The university competes intercollegiately in 9 sports for men and 10 for women. There are 18 intramural sports for men and 15 for women.

Handicapped: About 25% of the campus is accessible to handicapped students. Facilities include wheelchair ramps, special parking, elevators, special class scheduling, specially equipped rest rooms, and lowered drinking fountains and telephones. There is 1 special counselor for the handicapped.

Graduates: About 7% of the freshmen drop out after the first year, and 65% percent remain to graduate. About 15% of the students pursue graduate studies.

RHODE ISLAND

Services: The university offers free placement and career and psychological counseling. Health care, tutoring, and remedial instruction also are available for a fee. Graduates as well as undergraduates may use placement services.

Programs of Study: Undergraduate studies lead to the B.A., B.S., B.F.A., and B.Mus. degrees. The university also awards associate, master's and doctoral degrees. Bachelor's degrees are offered in the following subjects: AREA STUDIES (Latin American, urban, women's), BUSINESS (accounting, business administration, business education, computer science, finance, management, management science, marketing, production and operations management, real estate/insurance), EDUCATION (early childhood, elementary, health/physical, home economics, secondary), ENGLISH (comparative literature, English, journalism, linguistics, speech), FINE AND PERFORMING ARTS (art, music, theater/dramatics), HEALTH SCIENCES (dental hygiene, food science and nutrition, medical technology, nursing, pharmacy, respiratory therapy), LANGUAGES (French, German, Italian, Russian, Spanish), MATH AND SCIENCES (biology, botany, chemistry, geography, geology, mathematics, marine affairs, microbiology, natural sciences, physics, zoology), PHILOSOPHY (classics, philosophy), PRE-PROFESSIONAL (agriculture, animal science and technology, aquaculture and fishery technology, engineering, pharmacy, plant science and technology), SOCIAL SCIENCES (anthropology, consumer affairs, economics, geography, government/political science, history, psychology, sociology). Black studies, consumer affairs, gerontology, textile marketing, and women's studies are also offered as "areas of interest." Thirty-seven percent of all undergraduate degrees are conferred in liberal arts, 15% are in business, and 14% are in agriculture.

Special: Juniors may study abroad.

Honors: Several honor societies have chapters on campus. The Honors Colloquium, a series of lectures, is open to students ranking in the upper tenth of each academic concentration. A freshman honors program is available.

Admissions: Seventy-one percent of those who applied were accepted for the 1981–82 freshman class. SAT scores for those freshmen were as follows: Verbal—72% below 500, 22% between 500 and 599, 4% between 600 and 700, and 1% above 700; Math—45% below 500, 39% between 500 and 599, 14% between 600 and 700, and 1% above 700. Requirements vary according to whether the candidate is a state resident and what curriculum he or she intends to follow. Generally, the candidate should rank in the top 40% of his or her graduating class and have at least a B average. Students must have completed 16 Carnegie units at an accredited high school and be recommended for college by high school authorities. Advanced placement or honors courses and special talents also are considered important.

Procedure: All candidates must take the SAT or ACT, preferably by January of the senior year. The DHAT is required for dental hygiene applicants. The deadlines for applications are March 1 (fall) and December 1 (spring). There is a $15 application fee. Admissions decisions are made on a rolling basis.

Special: The university has an early admissions plan with the same March 1 deadline. An early decision plan is available; the notification date is December 15. CLEP and AP credit is available.

Transfer: Of 1573 applications received for fall 1981, 888 were accepted, and 560 students enrolled. Transfers are accepted for all classes. A 2.5 GPA is required; A student must take half his or her major requirement (15 hours) at the university. A minimum of 24 credit hours must have been completed at the university by the end of the senior year. There is a 1-year residency requirement. Application deadlines are the same as for freshmen.

Visiting: Group orientations for prospective students are held Mondays and Fridays. Guides are also provided for informal visits to the university. Visitors may sit in on classes and stay on campus. The best time to visit is Monday through Saturday. The community relations office should be contacted for arrangements.

Financial Aid: The university awards financial aid to about 45% of each entering class. Awards include grants, loans, and part-time employment. Individual awards depend on financial need and aid sources available. Entering freshmen must submit applications for financial aid by March 1. The FAF must be filed by February 1. Freshman aid decisions are made around April 15.

Foreign Students: The university accepts applicants from foreign countries and offers these students special counseling and special organizations.

Admissions: Foreign students must take either the TOEFL or the University of Michigan Language Test. A minimum score of 550 on the TOEFL must be obtained. The SAT is also required.

Procedure: Application deadlines are March 1 (fall) and October 15 (spring). Foreign students must take a complete physical examination to establish proof of health and must carry health insurance, which is available through the university for a fee. Proof of funds sufficient to cover the total undergraduate program is also required.

Admissions Contact: Catherine Serdakowski, Assistant Director of Admissions.

SOUTH CAROLINA

BAPTIST COLLEGE AT CHARLESTON D-4
Charleston, South Carolina 29411 (803) 797-4326

F/T: 2300M&W
P/T: 700M&W
Grad: none
Year: sems, ss
Appl: open
382 applied
SAT: 750 (composite)

Faculty: 78; IIB, - - $
Ph.D.'s: 47%
S/F Ratio: 24 to 1
Tuition: $2972 ($3456)
R and B: $2192
359 accepted 359 enrolled
LESS COMPETITIVE

Baptist College at Charleston, established in 1965, is affiliated with the South Carolina Baptist Convention. It offers undergraduate programs in the liberal arts and sciences, business, and education. The library contains 70,000 volumes, and subscribes to 750 periodicals.

Environment: The 500-acre campus is located in a suburban area 15 miles from downtown Charleston. There are over 10 major buildings, including 4 residence halls that house 350 men and 350 women. Facilities for commuting students also are available.

Student Life: About 90% of the students come from South Carolina. Forty-five percent live on campus in the single-sex dorms; full-time single students under 25 must do so unless they are veterans or living with relatives. Most students are Baptist; chapel attendance is required.

Organizations: Campus activities include student government, music and drama groups, publications, clubs, religious and service organizations, and social and cultural events. There are no fraternities or sororities.

Sports: Intercollegiate teams are organized in 7 sports for men and 3 for women. Intramural competition also is offered.

Graduates: Ten percent of the freshmen drop out, and 75% remain to graduate.

Services: The college provides tutoring, remedial instruction, health care, and career counseling.

Programs of Study: The college offers the B.A., B.S., and B. Applied Sc. degrees. Associate degrees also are available. Bachelor's degrees are offered in the following subjects: BUSINESS (business administration, business education), EDUCATION (early childhood, elementary, guidance and counseling, health/physical, secondary), ENGLISH (English, speech), FINE AND PERFORMING ARTS (art, music, theater/dramatics), HEALTH SCIENCES (music therapy), LANGUAGES (French, German, Spanish), MATH AND SCIENCES (biology, chemistry, mathematics, physics), PHILOSOPHY (religion), SOCIAL SCIENCES (criminal justice, economics, government/political science, history, psychology, sociology).

Required: There is a required core curriculum.

Special: Independent study, study abroad, and exchange programs are offered. Additional minors are available in computer science, library science, and philosophy. Nonmajor preprofessional programs are offered in dentistry, engineering, law, medicine, and ministry.

Honors: Several departments offer honors work.

Admissions: About 95% of the applicants for the 1981–82 freshman class were accepted. A high school diploma or GED is required.

Procedure: Applicants must take the SAT or ACT. Application deadlines are open. New students are admitted each semester. Notification is made on a rolling basis. There is a $20 application fee. An interview is recommended.

Special: The college offers early and deferred admissions programs. AP and CLEP credit is available.

Transfer: Over 200 transfer students are accepted annually. Applicants must have a C average. Students must earn at least 18 credits in residence of the 125 required for a bachelor's degree.

SOUTH CAROLINA 809

Visiting: Prospective students may arrange visits through the admissions office.

Financial Aid: About 98% of the students receive aid. The college participates in NDSL, BEOG/SEOG, and CWS. Bank loans and freshman scholarships also are available. The FFS should be submitted by May 1.

Foreign Students: Students from foreign countries make up about 5% of enrollment. The college offers these students an intensive English course, special counseling, and special organizations.

Admissions: Applicants must score at least 500 on the TOEFL. They also must take the SAT or ACT.

Procedure: Foreign students are admitted to all terms, and must file applications at least 30 days before registration. Students must provide a physician's statement as proof of good health and must show evidence of adequate funds for 1 year. Health insurance is required, and is available through the college for a fee.

Admissions Contact: Barbara C. Mead, Director of Admissions.

BENEDICT COLLEGE C–3
Columbia, South Carolina 29284   (803) 256-4220

F/T: 458M, 823W	Faculty: 106; IIB, – –$
P/T: 11M, 18W	Ph.D.'s: 36%
Grad: none	S/F Ratio: 16 to 1
Year: sems, ss	Tuition: $2684
Appl: open	R and B: $1600
900 applied	800 accepted 454 enrolled
SAT or ACT: required	LESS COMPETITIVE

Benedict College, founded in 1870 and affiliated with the Baptist Church, offers undergraduate degrees in the liberal arts and sciences, business, and education. The library contains 139,220 volumes and 1159 microfilm items, and subscribes to 581 periodicals.

Environment: The 20-acre campus is located in downtown Columbia, a city of 130,000. Buildings include a 12-story dormitory.

Student Life: Virtually all the students are from the South. About 99% are graduates of public schools. All students from more than 50 miles from Columbia are required to live on campus in the single-sex dorms. Benedict was founded as a college for blacks and continues to attract a primarily black student body.

Organizations: Four fraternities and 4 sororities have chapters on campus. The college sponsors clubs and other organizations. Additional recreational and cultural facilities are available in Columbia.

Sports: Intercollegiate and intramural sports are available.

Graduates: Twelve percent of the graduates pursue advanced degrees; 3% enter medical school, 1% dental school, and 5% law school. Thirty percent begin careers in business and industry.

Services: Students receive free placement aid and career counseling.

Programs of Study: The college awards the B.A. and B.S. degrees. Bachelor's degrees are offered in the following subjects: BUSINESS (accounting, business administration, business education, finance, management, marketing, office administration), EDUCATION (elementary, health/physical, recreation), ENGLISH (English, journalism), FINE AND PERFORMING ARTS (art education, music), MATH AND SCIENCES (biology, chemistry, mathematics, physics), PHILOSOPHY (religion), SOCIAL SCIENCES (economics, government/political science, history, sociology). Nonmajor preprofessional programs are available in dentistry, engineering, law, medicine, and social work.

Required: Entering freshmen take an intensified program in communications and mathematics, designed to correct deficiencies and strengthen skills in these areas.

Honors: Four honor societies have chapters on campus. The division of social science offers honors courses.

Admissions: Eighty-nine percent of those who applied were accepted for 1981–82 freshman class. Applicants should be high school graduates with at least 18 academic units. The GED also is accepted.

Procedure: The SAT or ACT is required. There are no application deadlines. Admission is on a rolling basis. There is a $10 application fee.

Special: An early admissions plan is available. AP and CLEP credit is granted.

Transfer: Transfer students must be in good standing at their last school. The final 30 hours must be taken in residence.

Visiting: Prospective students are encouraged to arrange visits to campus through the admissions office. Guided tours can be scheduled at any time except exam weeks. Visitors may sit in on classes and, if space is available, stay overnight on campus.

Financial Aid: About 97% of the students receive aid. A limited number of scholarships is available, and the college participates in federal programs such as CWS, NDSL, and EOG. The average aid award to freshmen in 1981–82 was $3700. The deadline for aid applications is March 15. The FAF is required.

Foreign Students: Students from foreign countries make up 3% of enrollment. The college offers these students special counseling.

Admissions: No English proficiency exams are required. Students must take the California Achievement Test.

Procedure: Application deadlines are open; foreign students are admitted to all terms. They must submit a physician's statement as proof of good health and provide a $1500 deposit as evidence of adequate funds. Health insurance, though not required, is available through the college for a fee.

Admissions Contact: Director of Admissions.

CENTRAL WESLEYAN COLLEGE A–2
Central, South Carolina 29630   (803) 639-2453

F/T: 178M, 198W	Faculty: 22; IIB, – –$
P/T: 15M, 40W	Ph.D.'s: 50%
Grad: none	S/F Ratio: 16 to 1
Year: sems, ss	Tuition: $3200
Appl: Aug. 15	R and B: $1750
SAT or ACT: required	LESS COMPETITIVE

Central Wesleyan College, established in 1906, is a church-controlled liberal arts institution affiliated with the Wesleyan Church. The library contains 50,000 volumes and subscribes to 370 periodicals.

Environment: The college's 190-acre campus is located in a rural area 25 miles from Greenville. The 10 buildings include dormitories with a capacity of 184 women and 102 men. A cafeteria, student lounge, and locker facilities are available to day students.

Student Life: About 55% of the students come from South Carolina. Approximately 50% reside on campus. The majority are members of the Wesleyan Church; 75% are Protestant and 2% Catholic. The college requires that students attend daily chapel services. Drinking and smoking are prohibited on campus, and all students must observe a curfew. Twelve percent of the students are minority-group members. College housing is single-sex; there are no visiting privileges. Students may keep cars on campus.

Organizations: There are no social fraternities or sororities. The college sponsors extracurricular groups, such as music and drama groups and science groups, as well as publications, films, lectures, concerts, and recitals. There is student-faculty particpation in student government and student publications.

Sports: There are 4 intercollegiate sports for men and 2 for women. There are 6 intramural sports for both men and women.

Handicapped: Ninety-five percent of the campus is accessible to handicapped students. Facilities include wheelchair ramps, special parking, elevators, and specially equipped rest rooms. Special class scheduling is also available.

Graduates: The freshman dropout rate is 15%.

Services: Students receive the following services free of charge: career counseling, psychological counseling, and placement. Health care, tutoring, and remedial instruction are available on a fee basis.

Programs of Study: The college confers the B.A. degree. Bachelor's degrees are offered in the following subjects: BUSINESS (accounting, business administration, business education, computer science), EDUCATION (early childhood, elementary, health/physical, secondary, special), ENGLISH (English, English education), FINE AND PERFORMING ARTS (music, music education), HEALTH SCIENCES (medical technology, nursing), MATH AND SCIENCES (biology, chemistry, mathematics), PHILOSOPHY (religion), PREPROFESSIONAL (dentistry, law, medicine, ministry, pharmacy, social work, veterinary), SOCIAL SCIENCES (history, psychology).

Required: All students must take a core curriculum.

Special: There are cooperative programs with Clemson University in mathematics, medical technology, and nursing. Combined study-work experience programs are offered in psychology and social work. The special education major has a concentration in mental retardation.

Honors: There are independent study programs for superior students.

Admissions: Applicants must have 16 Carnegie units, a GPA of 2.0, a rank in the upper 50% of their high school class, and recommendations from the high school. Also important in the admissions decision are the accreditation of the high school, extracurricular activities, and the impressions made during a personal interview either on or off campus.

Procedure: Either the SAT or ACT is required. The deadlines for application are August 15 (fall), January 10 (spring), and May 15 (summer). Notification is on a rolling basis. There is a $50 admission fee required from accepted students.

Special: CLEP and AP subject exams are accepted.

Transfer: Transfer students are accepted regularly for all classes. A GPA of 2.0 is required. D grades are acceptable if not in the major. A student must complete, at the college, 32 semester hours of the 128 needed to receive a bachelor's degree. The deadlines for applications are the same as those for freshman applicants.

Visiting: Orientation is scheduled for prospective students. Visits with a student guide can be arranged through the admissions office. Visitors may sit in on classes.

Financial Aid: Eighty-eight percent of the students receive financial aid. Twenty-two percent work part-time on campus. Average aid to freshmen from all sources is $2000. Financial assistance is offered to students who need it. The college is a member of CSS. The FAF and FFS are required. There is no deadline for financial aid applications, but preference is given to applicants filing before June 1.

Foreign Students: The college accepts qualified foreign applicants.

Admissions: Foreign students must take the TOEFL and the college's own language test. They must achieve a combined score of 750 on the SAT or 20 on the ACT. They must also take the college's own entrance examination.

Procedure: Application deadlines are August 15 (fall), January 10 (spring), and May 15 (summer). Foreign students must present proof of health. They must also provide proof of funds adequate for each year of study. They must carry health insurance, which is available through the college.

Admissions Contact: Lillian A. Robbins, Director of Admissions.

THE CITADEL   D-4
Charleston, South Carolina 29409   (803) 792-5230

F/T: 2023M   Faculty: 135; IIA, ++$
P/T: none   Ph.D.'s: 73%
Grad: none   S/F Ratio: 13 to 1
Year: sems, ss   Tuition: *
Appl: June 1   R and B: *
1826 applied   1172 accepted   685 enrolled
SAT: 456V 500M   ACT: 23   COMPETITIVE+

The Citadel is a liberal arts, military college supported by the state of South Carolina. Its library has over 167,000 volumes and 106,000 microfilm reels, and subscribes to 1375 periodicals.

Environment: The 100-acre riverside campus is located in a suburban area of Charleston, near the ocean. Its facilities, compactly grouped around a large parade ground, include academic buildings, barracks, administrative buildings, a chapel, a student activities building, and recreational and athletic facilities.

Student Life: Fifty percent of the students come from South Carolina. About 74% attended public schools. All undergraduates are uniformed cadets who must live on campus. All freshmen take part in the training program known as the "Knob system." Twenty-five percent of the students are Catholic, 72% Protestant, and 1% Jewish. Six percent are minority-group members. Housing is single-sex; there are no visiting privileges. Students may keep cars on campus.

Organizations: The extracurricular program includes a wide variety of clubs, performing groups, publications, student government, religious and service groups, and regularly scheduled on-campus social and cultural events. There are no fraternities.

Sports: Eighteen intercollegiate sports are offered. Nineteen intramural sports are available.

Graduates: Twenty-seven percent of the freshmen drop out; 63% remain to graduate. About 30% go on for further study; 3% enter medical school, 1% dental school, and 7% law school. Fifty percent initially enter active military service. Twenty percent become career officers.

Services: Career counseling, placement services, health care, psychological counseling, remedial instruction, and tutoring are provided free of charge.

Programs of Study: The Citadel offers the B.A., B.S., B.S.B.A., B.S.C.E., and B.S.E.E. degrees. Bachelor's degrees are offered in the following subjects: BUSINESS (business administration), EDUCATION (elementary, secondary), ENGLISH (English), LANGUAGES (modern languages), MATH AND SCIENCES (biology, chemistry, computer science, mathematics, physics), PREPROFESSIONAL (dentistry, engineering—civil, engineering—electrical), SOCIAL SCIENCES (government/political science, history, psychology).

Required: All students must take ROTC as well as a distribution requirement that includes English composition and literature, mathematics, science, and U.S. history.

Special: Independent study is possible.

Honors: Superior students may pursue honors work.

Admissions: About 64% of the applicants for the 1981–82 freshman class were accepted. Candidates must be between 16 and 21 years of age, must be unmarried, and must meet certain physical standards. A diploma from an accredited high school, 15 Carnegie units, a recommendation from the school principal, and a good extracurricular record are required. Evidence of leadership qualities and SAT scores are also important. Residents of South Carolina are given some preference, but the college seeks others who have a B average or higher.

Procedure: The SAT or ACT is required; ATs—English Composition and Mathematics I or II—are recommended. The tests should be taken by December of the senior year. Applications for admission should be submitted early in the senior year; June 1 (fall) is the deadline. An interview is recommended. There is a $15 application fee.

Special: AP and CLEP are used.

Transfer: For fall 1981, 55 students applied, 46 were accepted, and 38 enrolled. Transfer applicants must have a combined SAT score of 800 or an ACT score of 17, be in good academic standing, and meet basic freshman criteria. At least two years and 50% of course requirements must be completed in residence; a minimum of 122 hours is needed for a bachelor's degree. The application deadline is June 1 (fall).

Visiting: Weekend visits by prospective cadets are encouraged. They should make arrangements for the particular weekend in advance with the admissions office. Visitors stay in barracks and eat in the dining room. A reception, campus tour, orientation, faculty interviews, and athletic events or a visit to historic Charleston are part of the program. Prospective visitors are requested to notify the admissions office at least 2 weeks before the visit.

Financial Aid: About 65% of the students receive aid. Thirty-one percent work part-time on campus. Average aid to freshmen from all sources is $1200. Academic scholarships based on merit can range to cover from part to all expenses. Grants (BEOG/SEOG) and loans (governmental and commercial) to freshmen are based on need (primarily) and academic record. CWS is also available. Tuition may be paid in installments. The college is a member of CSS. The FAF should be filed by February 15.

Foreign Students: Two percent of the full-time students come from foreign countries.

Admissions: Foreign students must score at least 450 on the TOEFL. They must have a combined score of 800 on the SAT. They may also take the ACT.

Procedure: The application deadline is June 1 (fall). Foreign students must present the results of medical and physical examinations. They must present proof of funds adequate to cover 1 year of study. They must also carry health insurance, which is available through the college for a fee.

Admissions Contact: Captain Wallace West, Assistant Director of Admissions.

CLAFLIN COLLEGE   C-3
Orangeburg, South Carolina 29115   (803) 536-5635

F/T: 205M, 433W   Faculty: n/av; IIB, --$
P/T: 6M, 6W   Ph.D.'s: 36%
Grad: none   S/F Ratio: 16 to 1
Year: sems, ss   Tuition: $4100
Appl: Sept. 9   R and B: $1634
407 applied   304 accepted   203 enrolled
SAT: 500V 500M   ACT: 13   LESS COMPETITIVE

*For the freshman year, tuition, student fees, room, board, and fees for uniforms, books, laundry, dry cleaning, haircuts, and athletic events come to $3990 for South Carolina residents and $5190 for others. Expenses are somewhat lower in subsequent years.

Claflin College, established in 1869, is a private liberal arts and teacher education college affiliated with the United Methodist Church. The college is organized into 4 divisions: Education, Humanities, Natural Science and Mathematics, and Social Sciences. The library contains more than 55,000 volumes and 4000 microfilm items, and subscribes to 519 periodicals.

Environment: The 25-acre urban campus is located in a town of approximately 15,000 people in the center of South Carolina. There are 18 buildings on campus, including dormitories that accommodate 240 men and 350 women.

Student Life: About 90% of the students come from South Carolina. Fewer than 1% of the students are Catholic, and 84% are Protestant. A strong emphasis is placed on chapel and church attendance. Almost 100% of the students are minority-group members. College housing is single-sex; there are no visiting privileges. Students may keep cars on campus.

Organizations: There are 4 sororities and 4 fraternities at the college. Other student organizations include student government, social and service groups, a drama guild, music and dance groups, religious organizations, and publications.

Sports: There are intercollegiate teams in 3 sports for men and 4 for women.

Graduates: By the end of the freshman year, 48% of the students drop out. Twenty percent pursue advanced study after graduation; 1% enter medical school, 1% dental school, and 1% law school. Ten percent pursue careers in business and industry.

Services: The following services are provided to students free of charge: health care, placement, career counseling, tutoring, and remedial instruction.

Programs of Study: The college confers the B.A., B.S., and B.S.B.A. degrees. Bachelor's degrees are offered in the following subjects: BUSINESS (business administration), EDUCATION (elementary, health/physical, secondary), ENGLISH (English), FINE AND PERFORMING ARTS (art, art education, music education), MATH AND SCIENCES (biology, chemistry, mathematics), PHILOSOPHY (religion and philosophy), PREPROFESSIONAL (dentistry, law, medicine, ministry), SOCIAL SCIENCES (social sciences).

Required: Students must complete a core curriculum, including courses in English, health, mathematics, physical education, religion, science, and social sciences.

Special: The college has a special program for freshmen with deficiencies in English, mathematics, or reading.

Honors: There are chapters of 2 national honor societies on campus.

Admissions: About 75% of those who applied were accepted for the 1981–82 freshman class. Students should have a high school diploma or the equivalent and should present 16 completed Carnegie units. Admissions decisions are based on the following criteria: secondary school record, test scores, recommendations of the high school, personal qualities, health record, and educational objectives.

Procedure: The SAT or ACT is required, as is a recommendation from the secondary school. The deadlines for application are September 9 (fall) and January 12 (spring). There is a $10 application fee.

Special: Early decision and early admissions plans are available. AP and CLEP credit is granted.

Transfer: For fall 1981, 17 students applied, 17 were admitted, and 17 enrolled. Transfer applicants must be in good standing with their previous college. They must have a 2.0 GPA and SAT scores of 500 or ACT scores of 9. D grades do not transfer. Transfer students must complete 2 semesters in residence to receive a bachelor's degree. Application deadlines are the same as those for freshmen.

Visiting: Prospective students may arrange to visit the college and have a personal interview with the director of admissions. Appointments for visits should be made in advance with the admissions office.

Financial Aid: Ninety-six percent of the students receive financial aid. Thirty-five percent work part-time on campus. Scholarships, loans, grants, and employment are all available. The college is a member of CSS. The FAF and FFS should be filed by June 1 (fall) and December 1 (spring).

Foreign Students: Fewer than 1% of the full-time students come from foreign countries.

Admissions: Foreign students must take the TOEFL. They must also take the SAT or ACT. They must score at least 500 on the SAT.

Procedure: Application deadlines are March 1 (fall), July 30 (spring), and December 1 (summer). Foreign students must complete the college's own medical examination form. They must also present proof of funds adequate to cover 1 year of study.

Admissions Contact: George F. Lee, Admissions Officer.

CLEMSON UNIVERSITY A–2
Clemson, South Carolina 29631 (803) 656-2287

F/T: 5626M, 3802W Faculty: 975; I, av$
P/T: 295M, 147W Ph.D.'s: 67%
Grad: 871M, 550W S/F Ratio: 16 to 1
Year: sems, ss Tuition: $1350 ($2788)
Appl: open R and B: $1570
6309 applied 3947 accepted 2284 enrolled
SAT: 470V 537M COMPETITIVE

Clemson University is a state-supported institution that provides programs in liberal arts and applied scientific education. The library contains 801,023 volumes, subscribes to 13,390 periodicals, and has 14,500 microfilm items.

Environment: The university is located in a rural area 30 miles from Greenville and has a campus of 600 acres plus 26,000 acres in experimental farm and forest lands. There are dormitories for about 6600 students and apartments for married students. The college also sponsors on-campus apartments, fraternity houses, and sorority houses.

Student Life: About 80% of the undergraduates are from South Carolina and 19% come from other states. Sixty-five percent of the students live on campus. About 5% are minority-group members. Campus housing is single-sex; there are visiting privileges. Students may keep cars on campus.

Organizations: There are 14 fraternities and 7 sororities, to which 6% of the men and 8% of the women belong. There are also religious organizations and counselors for members of the Catholic, Protestant, and Jewish faiths. Students may also participate in the student government.

Sports: The university fields 15 intercollegiate teams for men and 10 for women. There are 7 intramural sports for men and 7 for women.

Handicapped: Special facilities for the physically handicapped include wheelchair ramps, special parking, elevators, special class scheduling, and specially equipped rest rooms.

Graduates: The freshman dropout rate is 17%; between 50% and 60% remain to graduate.

Services: Students receive the following services free of charge: placement, career counseling, and psychological counseling. Health care is also available for a fee.

Programs of Study: The university confers the B.A., B.S., B.Arch., and B.T.T. degrees. Master's and doctoral programs are also offered. Bachelor's degrees are offered in the following subjects: BUSINESS (accounting, business administration, computer science, finance, management), EDUCATION (early childhood, elementary, industrial, secondary), ENGLISH (English), HEALTH SCIENCES (medical technology, nursing), LANGUAGES (French, German, Spanish), MATH AND SCIENCES (biochemistry, chemistry, geology, mathematics, physics, zoology), PREPROFESSIONAL (agriculture—economics, agriculture —engineering, agriculture—mechanization and business, animal industries, architecture, building science, community and rural development, design, economic biology, engineering—ceramic, engineering —chemical, engineering—civil, engineering—computer, engineering —electrical, engineering—mechanical, engineering analysis, engineering technology, food science, forest management, law, medicine, plant sciences, recreation and park administration, textile chemistry, textile science, textile technology), SOCIAL SCIENCES (economics, government/political science, history, psychology, sociology). The most popular major courses are in engineering and business management.

Special: It is possible to earn combined B.A.-B.S. degrees in various subjects.

Honors: Thirty national honor societies have chapters on campus. There is a university-wide honors program for qualified students.

Admissions: Sixty-three percent of those who applied were accepted for the 1981–82 freshman class. The SAT scores of those who enrolled were as follows: Verbal—62% below 500, 32% between 500 and 599, 5% between 600 and 700, and 1% above 700; Math—30% below 500, 46% between 500 and 599, 21% between 600 and 700, and 3% above 700.

Procedure: The SAT and ATs should be taken preferably in the spring of the junior year. The AT in mathematics is required for placement purposes in most curricula. Applicants wishing to continue in a modern foreign language should take the appropriate language AT; this may

812 SOUTH CAROLINA

qualify them for advanced placement. There is no application deadline. New students are admitted in any term, and applications are accepted as soon as the student can present College Board reports and a high school transcript complete through 6 semesters. There is a rolling admissions policy. The application fee is $15.

Special: There are early decision and early admissions plans. CLEP and AP credit is accepted.

Transfer: For fall 1981, 1609 transfer students applied, 751 were accepted, and 505 enrolled. Applicants should have a minimum 2.5 GPA. All students must complete 1 year's work at the university. Grades of C or better transfer. There are no application deadlines, but early application is encouraged.

Visiting: Guided tours can be scheduled with the admissions office. The best times for campus visits are Mondays and Fridays.

Financial Aid: About 33% of all students receive some form of financial aid. The university participates in the CSS. Aid is available from scholarships, BEOG, NDSL, and Guaranteed Student Loans on the basis of academic record and need. The FAF is required. Applications for scholarship aid should be filed by February 15; applications for loans should be filed by April 1.

Foreign Students: One percent of the full-time students are from foreign countries. The university offers these students special counseling and special organizations.

Admissions: A minimum score of 550 on the TOEFL is required; students must also take the SAT.

Procedure: Application deadlines are six weeks prior to the start of each semester. Foreign students are admitted to all terms. They must complete the university's medical form and present proof of funds adequate to cover 1 year of study. They must also carry health insurance, which is available through the university for a fee.

Admissions Contact: W. Richard Mattox, Director of Admissions.

COKER COLLEGE D-2
Hartsville, South Carolina 29550 (803) 332-1381

F/T: 97M, 120W	Faculty: 38; IIB, −$
P/T: 23M, 29W	Ph.D.'s: 55%
Grad: none	S/F Ratio: 6 to 1
Year: sems, ss	Tuition: $3580
Appl: see profile	R and B: $1840
183 applied	104 accepted	65 enrolled
SAT: 382V 394M		LESS COMPETITIVE

Coker College, a small, independent, coeducational institution, offers programs in business, education, and the liberal arts and sciences. The library contains 61,000 volumes and more than 4000 microfilms, and subscribes to 276 periodicals.

Environment: The 25-acre urban campus, located in a town of 25,000 people, includes dormitories with single and double rooms. In addition to the main campus, 25 acres have been developed into a natural botanical garden and recreation park.

Student Life: Currently, about 80% of the students come from South Carolina, although 10 states are represented. About 84% of the entering freshmen are graduates of public schools. About 61% of the students live on campus. About 23% are minority-group members. Campus housing is both coed and single-sex. There are visiting privileges in single-sex dorms. Students may keep cars on campus.

Organizations: There are no social fraternities or sororities. Extracurricular groups and activities include religious organizations, music and drama groups, clubs, publications, student government, and concert and lecture series. A college-owned boathouse on Prestwood Lake provides sailing and other recreational opportunities.

Sports: The college fields 2 intercollegiate teams for men and 3 for women. There are 6 intramural sports for men and 4 for women.

Handicapped: No facilities are available for physically handicapped students; there are no students with visual or hearing impairments.

Graduates: Ten percent of the freshmen drop out by the end of their first year; approximately 40% remain to graduate. Twenty-five percent of the graduates pursue further study.

Services: Students receive the following services free of charge: placement, career counseling, tutoring, remedial instruction, psychological counseling, and health care.

Programs of Study: All programs lead to the B.A. or B.S. degrees. Bachelor's degrees are offered in the following subjects: BUSINESS (accounting, business administration, business education, management, marketing), EDUCATION (early childhood, elementary, health/physical, secondary, special), ENGLISH (communications, English), FINE AND PERFORMING ARTS (art, art education, art history, film/photography, modern dance, music, music education, studio art, theater/dramatics), HEALTH SCIENCES (medical technology), MATH AND SCIENCES (biology, chemistry), PHILOSOPHY (religion), SOCIAL SCIENCES (government/political science, history, psychology, social sciences, sociology). Preprofessional studies, although not major programs, are available in dentistry, law, and medicine. Thirty-five percent of the degrees conferred are in business; 19% are in social sciences; 18% are in fine and performing arts; and 11% are in education.

Required: All students are required to take a distribution of courses in the arts, social sciences, natural sciences, literature, and the humanities.

Special: There are special-topic courses in all disciplines. Study abroad is sponsored, and scholarships are available for these programs. It is possible to earn combined B.A.-B.S. degrees in various subjects. Student-designed majors are permitted.

Admissions: Fifty-seven percent of those who applied were accepted for the 1981–1982 freshman class. The SAT scores of those who enrolled were as follows: Verbal—80% below 500 and 20% between 500 and 599; Math—80% below 500 and 20% between 500 and 599. All applicants should have at least a 2.0 average. In addition to these qualifications, the following factors are considered important: impressions made during an interview, recommendations by school officials, and the leadership record.

Procedure: The SAT or ACT is required. An interview is recommended, but not required. The deadline for regular admission is 30 days prior to registration, and notification is made on a rolling basis. Freshmen are admitted to all semesters. There is a $15 application fee.

Special: Early decision and early admissions plans are available. CLEP and AP credit is given.

Transfer: For fall 1981, the college received 69 transfer applications, accepted 40, and enrolled 27 students. Transfers are accepted for all but the senior year. Transfer students must have a GPA of at least 2.0 and a combined SAT score of 750 if they have completed fewer than 30 semester hours at the previous school. Grades of C or better transfer. The student must complete at least 30 semester hours, of the 120 required for graduation, in residence at Coker. Students should apply at least 30 days prior to the beginning of all semesters.

Visiting: Orientation is scheduled for prospective students. Informal guided tours can be scheduled during the week; visitors may sit in on classes and remain overnight on campus. Arrangements for visits should be made through the director of admissions.

Financial Aid: About 69% of the students receive aid from the following sources: scholarships, grants, loans, and campus employment. Thirty-seven percent of the students work part-time on campus. Academic scholarships range from small awards to $12,000 for 4 years of study. The average award to freshmen from all sources available through the college is $3920. Financial aid is awarded and renewed on the basis of academic record and financial need. The college is a member of the CSS and requires the FAF. Applications for aid should be submitted by June 1 (fall), December 1 (spring), and April 1 (summer).

Foreign Students: The college offers foreign students an intensive English course.

Admissions: A minimum score of 500 on the TOEFL is required. Students must also take the SAT.

Procedure: Application deadlines are 90 days prior to the beginning of each semester. Students must present proof of funds adequate to cover 1 academic year of study. Health insurance is not required, but is available through the college for a fee.

Admissions Contact: Mike Stephens, Admissions Counselor.

COLLEGE OF CHARLESTON D-4
Charleston, South Carolina 29401 (803) 792-5670

F/T: 1386M, 2177W	Faculty: 209; IIA, av$
P/T: 426M, 830W	Ph.D.'s: 85%
Grad: 38M, 167W	S/F Ratio: 20 to 1
Year: sems, ss	Tuition: $950 ($1850)
Appl: Aug. 1	R and B: $1770
1970 applied	1514 accepted	1017 enrolled
SAT: 468V 486M		COMPETITIVE

College of Charleston, founded in 1770, is a state-supported liberal arts college. The library contains 215,000 volumes and nearly 200,000 microfilm items, and subscribes to 2000 periodicals.

Environment: The 12-acre campus, located in an urban area, contains 80 buildings including 6 dormitories and numerous houses accommodating 1077 women and 462 men. The college also sponsors fraternity and sorority houses, and on-campus apartments.

Student Life: About 90% of the students are from South Carolina; 10% are from out of state or from foreign countries. About 75% come from public schools; 40% live on campus. About 7% of the students are minority-group members. Campus housing is single-sex; there are visiting privileges. Students may keep cars on campus. Day-care services are available to all students.

Organizations: There are 7 fraternities and 7 sororities to which 15–20% of the men and women belong. Religious organizations are provided for all interested students. Cultural events include the Charleston Museum, Charleston Symphony Orchestra, Gibbs Art Gallery, and Dock Street Theater.

Sports: The college fields 7 intercollegiate teams for men and 6 for women. There are 12 intramural sports for men and 12 for women.

Handicapped: About 80% of the campus is accessible to wheelchair-bound students. Facilities include wheelchair ramps, special parking, elevators, special class scheduling, specially equipped rest rooms, and lowered drinking fountains. There are several students with visual and hearing impairments currently enrolled.

Graduates: The freshman dropout rate is 12%.

Services: Students receive the following services free of charge: placement, career counseling, health care, tutoring, remedial instruction, and psychological counseling.

Programs of Study: The college confers the B.A. and B.S. degrees. Master's programs are also offered. Bachelor's degrees are offered in the following subjects: AREA STUDIES (urban), BUSINESS (business administration, computer science), EDUCATION (elementary, secondary, special), ENGLISH (English), FINE AND PERFORMING ARTS (fine arts), LANGUAGES (French, German, Greek/Latin, Italian, Spanish), MATH AND SCIENCES (biochemistry, biology, biometry, chemistry, geology, marine biology, mathematics, physics), PHILOSOPHY (philosophy), PREPROFESSIONAL (dentistry, engineering, law, medicine, pharmacy, veterinary), SOCIAL SCIENCES (economics, government/political science, history, psychology, sociology). Twenty-eight percent of degrees conferred are in business, 20% in math and sciences, and 18% in education.

Required: All students must take freshman English and a distribution of credits in 4 broad areas of study.

Special: The college offers independent study programs. Credits for the junior year abroad are accepted if a student selects a well-established program at a recognized university. A Sea Semester program is offered by the Sea Education Association in Woods Hole, Massachusetts. Cooperative education and internships in Washington, D.C. are also offered. A very broad Continuing Education Program has been established.

Honors: Five national honor societies have chapters on campus. There is a departmental honors program, as well as an honors program for entering freshmen.

Admissions: Seventy-seven percent of those who applied were accepted for the 1981–82 freshman class. The SAT scores of those who enrolled were as follows: Verbal—61% below 500, 25% between 500 and 599, 5% between 600 and 700, and fewer than 1% above 700; Math—52% below 500, 30% between 500 and 599, 8% between 600 and 700, and 1% above 700. Candidates who have completed 18 units of high school work and whose work in class and SAT scores are sufficiently high will receive consideration for admission.

Procedure: The SAT is required and should be taken in May of the junior year and in November or December of the senior year. A personal interview is not required. Application deadlines are August 1 (fall) and December 1 (spring). Applications for students desiring dormitory space should be made by February (fall). Freshmen may also be admitted in the summer. The application fee is $20. Admissions are on a rolling basis.

Special: Deferred admission is available. CLEP and AP credit is accepted.

Transfer: For fall 1981, 831 transfer students applied, 692 were accepted, and 538 enrolled. Transfers are accepted for all classes. Students must have 9 transferable semester hours for each semester they have been in college. Grades of C or better transfer. A 2.0 GPA is recommended. At least 1 year (30 semester hours) of study at the college is required to receive a degree. For the bachelor's degree, 122 credits are required. The deadlines for transfer applications are the same as those for freshman applicants.

Visiting: Although orientation is not scheduled for prospective students, informal visits can be made to the campus. Guided tours and interviews can be scheduled during the week; visits can be arranged through the admissions office. Prospective students may sit in on classes.

Financial Aid: Forty percent of all students receive some form of financial aid. Twelve percent work part-time on campus. The college has a scholarship fund of $180,000 for 300 students. Loans are available from the federal government, local banks, and the college. Scholarships range from an average of $200 to a maximum of $1500; loans range from $200 to a maximum of $2500; campus employment is available. The average award to freshmen from all sources available through the college is $1075. The college is a member of the CSS and requires the FAF. Applications for aid should be submitted by April 1.

Foreign Students: Two percent of the full-time students are from foreign countries. The college offers these students special counseling and special organizations.

Admissions: A minimum score of 500 on the TOEFL is required. Students must also take the SAT.

Procedure: Application deadlines are April 1 (fall) and September 1 (spring). Students must present proof of funds adequate to cover 1 year of study. Health insurance is required and is available through the college for a fee.

Admissions Contact: Frederick W. Daniels, Dean of Admissions.

COLUMBIA COLLEGE   C–3
Columbia, South Carolina 29203   (803) 786-3871

F/T: 920W	Faculty: 74; IIB, av$
P/T: 125W	Ph.D.'s: 60%
Grad: 25W	S/F Ratio: 14 to 1
Year: early sem, ss	Tuition: $3300
Appl: open	R and B: $1900
536 applied	454 accepted	266 enrolled
SAT: 410V 430M		LESS COMPETITIVE

Columbia College is a career-oriented liberal arts college for women. The library contains 145,000 volumes and 6000 microfilm items, and subscribes to 800 periodicals.

Environment: The 32-acre urban campus is located in Eau Claire on the north side of Columbia. There are 25 buildings including a student center and 6 dormitories housing 725 women.

Student Life: About 90% of the students are residents of South Carolina; 70% of the women live in the dormitories. About 30% of the students are members of the United Methodist Church. About 17% are minority-group members. Students may keep cars on campus.

Organizations: There are no sororities. Lectures, plays and concerts are brought to Columbia and are made available to the students. The Social Recreation Association, elected by the student government, in cooperation with the Dean of Student Life, plans the social life of the college community. Students serve on various committees.

Sports: The college fields 3 intercollegiate teams. Intramural sports are not offered.

Handicapped: About 80% of the campus is accessible to wheelchair-bound students. Wheelchair ramps, special parking, elevators, and specially equipped rest rooms are available.

Graduates: The freshman dropout rate is 24%; 52% remain to graduate. Thirty percent pursue advanced study after graduation.

Services: Students receive the following services free of charge: placement, career counseling, health care, and remedial instruction. Tutoring and psychological counseling are available for a fee.

Programs of Study: The college confers the B.A. or B.Mus. degree. Master's degrees are also awarded. Bachelor's degrees are offered in the following subjects: BUSINESS (accounting, business administration), EDUCATION (early childhood, elementary, special), ENGLISH (English, literature, speech, writing), FINE AND PERFORMING ARTS (art, dance, music, music education, theater/dramatics), HEALTH SCIENCES (medical technology, speech therapy), LANGUAGES (French, German, Spanish), MATH AND SCIENCES (biology, chemistry, mathematics, natural sciences), PHILOSOPHY (religion), PREPROFESSIONAL (social work), SOCIAL SCIENCES (history, public affairs, psychology, sociology).

Required: All students are required to take courses in art or music, English, a foreign language, mathematics and natural science, social science, religion, speech, and physical education.

Special: Student-designed majors are permitted. Advanced placement credit is given in some courses. Also, certain course requirements can be met by satisfactory scores on a departmental examination. Internship programs are also offered.

SOUTH CAROLINA

Admissions: Eighty-five percent of those who applied were accepted for the 1981–82 freshman class. Combined SAT scores of 720 are usually necessary, but in some cases lower scores are acceptable. In addition, applicants must have at least a C average and present qualifying recommendations from their high schools. Preparation must consist of 18 Carnegie units and graduation from an accredited high school.

Procedure: The SAT or ACT is required and should be taken in the junior or senior year. Applications for the fall semester should be submitted as early as possible; there is no formal deadline. Qualified applicants are notified of acceptance on a rolling admissions basis. Freshmen may also be admitted at midyear and in the summer. There is a $15 application fee.

Special: AP credit is accepted.

Transfer: For fall 1981, 90 applications were received, 70 were accepted, and 48 students enrolled. Transfers are considered for all classes. Students must complete, at the college, 30 of the 127 credits required to earn a bachelor's degree. Applicants must meet regular entrance requirements and be in good standing at their previous institution. All credits earned transfer if the GPA is at least 2.0. There are no application deadlines.

Visiting: Orientation is scheduled for prospective students; informal visits may be made on weekdays. Guided tours and interviews can be scheduled through the admissions office; visitors may sit in on classes and remain on campus overnight.

Financial Aid: Seventy percent of all students receive some form of financial aid. Aid is awarded on the basis of financial need and academic performance. The college is a member of the CSS; aid to freshmen averages $2900. Work-study programs are available in all departments. Applicants should file the FAF with the CSS by April 1.

Foreign Students: The college offers organizations especially for foreign students.

Admissions: A minimum score of 550 on the TOEFL is required. Students must also take the SAT.

Procedure: Application deadlines are April 1 (fall) and October 1 (winter). Students must submit results of a physician's examination. Proof of funds adequate to cover 1 academic year of study is also required. There is a $500 refundable travel deposit fee. Health insurance is available to foreign students through the college.

Admissions Contact: Joe Mitchell, Dean of Admissions.

CONVERSE COLLEGE B-1
Spartanburg, South Carolina 29301 (803) 585-6421

F/T: 731W	Faculty:	72; IIA, — $
P/T: 32W	Ph.D.'s:	75%
Grad: 37M, 252W	S/F Ratio:	11 to 1
Year: 4-2-4, ss	Tuition:	$4110
Appl: open	R and B:	$2250
603 applied	530 accepted	247 enrolled
SAT (mean): 466V 473M		COMPETITIVE

Converse College, a private nondenominational liberal arts college for women, has a professional school of music. The library contains over 110,000 volumes, and subscribes to 550 periodicals.

Environment: The 70-acre urban campus, about 70 miles south of Charlotte, North Carolina, includes 27 buildings, with dormitories housing 700 women.

Student Life: Approximately 90% of the students are from the South; 63% of the entering freshmen come from public schools. About 94% of the women live in dormitories. About 92% of the students are Protestant, and 7% are Catholic; attendance at religious services is voluntary. About 4% of the students are minority-group members. Students may keep cars on campus.

Organizations: There are no sororities. The Student Christian Association, and the Athletic Association are open to all students. Extracurricular activities include leadership groups, publications, orchestra, band, chorus, riding, modern dance, clubs focusing on various fields of study, and campus-wide social groups.

Sports: The college fields 2 intercollegiate teams and offers 2 intramural sports.

Handicapped: Facilities for the physically handicapped include wheelchair ramps, special parking, and elevators.

Graduates: The freshman dropout rate is 15%; about 50% remain to graduate. Of those who graduate, about 25% pursue advanced study immediately.

Services: Placement services, career counseling, and health care are offered free of charge. Tutoring and psychological counseling are available for a fee.

Programs of Study: The college confers the B.A., B.F.A., and B.Mus. degrees. Master's programs are also offered. Bachelor's degrees are offered in the following subjects: BUSINESS (accounting), EDUCATION (early childhood, elementary, special), ENGLISH (English), FINE AND PERFORMING ARTS (art, art history, interior design, music, music education, studio art, theater/dramatics), HEALTH SCIENCES (medical technology), LANGUAGES (French, modern languages, Spanish), MATH AND SCIENCES (biology, chemistry, comprehensive science, mathematics, physics), PHILOSOPHY (humanities, philosophy, religion), SOCIAL SCIENCES (economics, government/political science, history, psychology, sociology).

Required: All students must fulfill the requirements of the general education program with courses in the natural sciences and mathematics, social sciences, humanities, fine arts, and physical education.

Special: Students may arrange to spend their third year abroad with credit or a fall term in London. A certified program of teaching the deaf is offered.

Honors: Three national honor societies have chapters on campus.

Admissions: Approximately 88% of the students who applied were accepted to the 1981–82 freshman class. The SAT scores of those who enrolled were as follows: Verbal—63% below 500, 28% between 500 and 599, 9% between 600 and 700, and 0% above 700; Math—62% below 500, 30% between 500 and 599, 8% between 600 and 700, and 0% above 700. Candidates should have at least a C average, rank in the top half of their high school class, and have completed 16 high school units. Other factors entering into the admissions decision are advanced placement or honors courses, recommendations from school officials, leadership record, and extracurricular activities record.

Procedure: The SAT or ACT is required and should be taken between March of the junior year and March of the senior year. Application deadlines are open. The college follows a rolling admissions plan. There is a $20 application fee.

Special: AP and CLEP credit is accepted.

Transfer: For fall 1981, 54 transfer students applied, 45 were accepted, and 28 enrolled. An average of C is required. Grades of C or better transfer. Students must complete, at the college, 42 of the 120 semester hours required to earn a bachelor's degree. Application deadlines are open.

Visiting: Regularly scheduled orientation sessions for prospective students are held in which an overview of the college is presented by administrators. The sessions also include talks with department chairmen, student panels, and lunch. Guided tours may be arranged Monday through Friday between 8:30 A.M. and 4:30 P.M. Visitors may sit in on classes and prospective students may stay at the school while visiting. The admissions office should be contacted to arrange visits.

Financial Aid: About 57% of all students receive financial aid from sources that include scholarships, grants, loans, and campus employment. Financial aid is awarded and renewed on the basis of academic record and financial need. The college is a member of the CSS and requires the FAF from all those applying for aid except for merit awards. Applications for aid should be submitted preferably by February 15.

Foreign Students: No foreign students are currently enrolled at Converse.

Admissions Contact: Margaret A. Printz, Director of Admissions.

ERSKINE COLLEGE B-2
Due West, South Carolina 29639 (803) 379-8838

F/T: 309M, 313W	Faculty:	47; IIA, — — $
P/T: 10M, 15W	Ph.D.'s:	63%
Grad: 72M, 9W	S/F Ratio:	15 to 1
Year: 4-1-4, ss	Tuition:	$3750
Appl: Aug. 1	R and B:	$1650
434 applied	358 accepted	151 enrolled
SAT or ACT: required		COMPETITIVE

Erskine College, sponsored by the Associate Reformed Presbyterian Church, was founded in 1839 as South Carolina's first 4-year sectarian college. In addition to its undergraduate program, it operates a 3-year theological seminary. The library houses 110,000 volumes and 2700 microfilm items, and subscribes to 800 periodicals.

Environment: The 75-acre campus is located in a rural area 40 miles from Greenville. Philomathean Hall, the oldest building on campus, dates back to 1859. The 6 residences housing 284 women and 283 men offer a choice of single or double rooms or suites. Off-campus housing is available for married students.

Student Life: Approximately 75% of the students are from South Carolina; 93% live in dormitories. About 92% of the students are Protestant and 7% are Catholic. About 6% are minority-group members. Campus housing is single-sex; there are visiting privileges. Students may keep cars on campus.

Organizations: There are 3 local fraternities and 3 local sororities, to which 40% of the men and 30% of the women belong. Extracurricular activities include student government, dances, a fine arts series, and numerous clubs and organizations.

Sports: The college fields 5 intercollegiate teams for men and 4 for women. There are 6 intramural sports for men and 5 for women.

Handicapped: Approximately 90% of the campus is accessible to the physically handicapped. Facilities include wheelchair ramps and elevators.

Graduates: The freshman dropout rate is 20%; 60% remain to graduate. Approximately 30% of those who graduate pursue advanced study.

Services: Placement services, career counseling, psychological counseling, and tutoring are offered free of charge. Health care is available for a fee.

Programs of Study: The college confers the B.A. and B.S. degrees. Bachelor's degrees are offered in the following subjects: BUSINESS (business administration), EDUCATION (Christian, early childhood, elementary, health/physical, secondary), ENGLISH (English), FINE AND PERFORMING ARTS (music, music education), HEALTH SCIENCES (medical technology), LANGUAGES (French, German, Spanish), MATH AND SCIENCES (biology, chemistry, mathematics, natural sciences, physics), PHILOSOPHY (Bible), SOCIAL SCIENCES (behavioral science, history, psychology, social sciences, Southern studies).

Required: All students must take Bible, English, science, mathematics, social science, physical education, and 1 course in fine arts or philosophy.

Special: Student-designed majors are allowed. There is a summer study-travel program, and foreign study is permitted during January. The January interim is open to innovative courses designed by students and faculty. Other programs include nursing with Clemson University, early childhood education with Spartanburg Junior College, engineering with the Georgia Institute of Technology and Clemson, and programs leading to certification in special education and early childhood education.

Honors: The Erskine Scholars Program, designed to encourage academic excellence, allows students to design their own programs. The Garnet Circle, an academic honor society, is open to qualified students. Five national honor societies have chapters on campus.

Admissions: Of those who applied for the 1981-82 freshman class, 82% were accepted. Candidates should have completed 16 academic units, rank in the top half of their graduating class, and have a minimum 2.0 GPA. Other factors entering into the admissions decision are advanced placement or honors courses, extracurricular activities record, personality, and evidence of special talents.

Procedure: All candidates must take either the SAT or the ACT. New students are admitted to all terms. Applications should be submitted by August 1 for fall; there is a rolling admissions plan. Acceptance can begin 1 year in advance for superior students, 6 months ahead for others. The $15 application fee may be waived for financial reasons.

Special: CLEP and AP credit is accepted.

Transfer: For fall 1981, 70 transfer students applied, 60 were accepted, and 55 enrolled. Transfers are accepted for all classes. Requirements include a transcript of previous work and eligibility to return to previous school or an associate degree. Grades of C or above transfer. All students must complete 1 year at the college to be eligible for a bachelor's degree, which requires 120 hours. Deadlines are the same as those for freshman applicants.

Visiting: Orientation sessions include a campus tour, meeting with faculty, a financial aid workshop, and social activities. Guides are available on weekdays for informal tours; arrangements can be made with the admissions office. Visitors may sit in on classes and stay overnight at the school.

Financial Aid: About 80% of all students receive some form of financial aid. About 25% work part-time on campus. Approximately 100 scholarships are awarded to freshmen each year. In addition, South Carolina students are eligible for tuition equalization grants of up to $2000. Government and college loans are also available. The average amount of scholarship aid awarded to freshmen is $700; the average amount of each loan is $700. The college is a member of CSS and requires the FAF. The deadline for financial aid application is 1 month prior to the start of the term.

Foreign Students: Almost 3% of the students are from foreign countries.

Admissions: Foreign students must take the TOEFL. The SAT or ACT is not required.

Procedure: Application deadlines are August 1 (fall), December 1 (winter), January 1 (spring), and May 1 (summer). Students must submit a doctor's certificate and must present proof of funds to cover 1 year. Health insurance is available through the college for a fee.

Admissions Contact: Robin Livingston, Admissions Counselor.

FRANCIS MARION COLLEGE D-2
Florence, South Carolina 29501 (803) 669-4121

F/T:	930M, 960W	Faculty:	103; IIB, + + $
P/T:	205M, 346W	Ph.D.'s:	67%
Grad:	45M, 242W	S/F Ratio:	18 to 1
Year:	sems, ss	Tuition:	$680 ($1320)
Appl:	open	R and B:	$1900
1218 applied		1062 accepted	649 enrolled
SAT or ACT: required			COMPETITIVE

Founded in 1970, Francis Marion College is a state-controlled liberal arts institution offering selected professional programs in business, education, and engineering technology. The library contains 228,810 volumes and 58,000 microfilm items, and subscribes to 1412 periodicals.

Environment: Located in a rural area 7 miles from Florence, the 309-acre campus has 9 buildings including the Smith College Center and private on-campus apartment complexes. Limited college housing is also available.

Student Life: All but 1% of the students are from South Carolina. About 86% of the entering freshmen come from public schools. About 10% of the students live on campus. About 11% are minority-group members. Campus housing is coed. Students may keep cars on campus.

Organizations: There are 7 national fraternities and 5 national sororities to which 12% of the men and 6% of the women belong. Extracurricular activities include religious organizations, special-interest groups, dances, concerts, and films. The student government has voting delegates on college committees concerned with discipline, curriculum, student regulations, and entertainment.

Sports: The university fields 6 intercollegiate teams for men and 4 for women. There are 17 intramural sports for men and 16 for women.

Handicapped: The entire campus is accessible to wheelchair-bound students. Wheelchair ramps, special parking, elevators, special rest rooms, lowered drinking fountains, and lowered telephones are available. Readers are available for students with visual impairments.

Graduates: The freshman dropout rate is 40%. Thirty-five percent remain to graduate. Ten percent pursue advanced study after graduation. Twenty percent enter careers in business and industry.

Services: Students receive the following services free of charge: placement, career counseling, and remedial instruction.

Programs of Study: The college confers the B.A., B.S., and B.G.S. degrees. Associate and master's programs are also offered. Bachelor's degrees are offered in the following subjects: BUSINESS (administrative technology, business administration, computer science), EDUCATION (elementary), ENGLISH (English), FINE AND PERFORMING ARTS (art), HEALTH SCIENCES (medical technology), LANGUAGES (French, Spanish), MATH AND SCIENCES (biology, chemistry, geology, health physics, mathematics), PREPROFESSIONAL (engineering technologies, forestry), SOCIAL SCIENCES (anthropology, economics, geography, government/political science, history, psychology, sociology). Twenty-four percent of degrees conferred are in education, 19% in business, and 11% in sociology.

Required: Each student is required to complete 12 hours in basic communications, 9 in social sciences, 15 in the humanities, and 12 in the sciences. Twelve hours are required in foreign language for the B.A. degree.

Special: A general studies (no major) degree is offered. Study abroad is possible. Cooperative programs in civil engineering technology, electronic engineering technology, administrative technology, anthropology, art, computer science, geography, geology, engineering, and forestry management are available.

816 SOUTH CAROLINA

Honors: There are 6 national honor societies on campus. Honors courses are offered in some disciplines.

Admissions: Eighty-seven percent of those who applied were accepted for the 1981–82 freshman class. The college requires a high school diploma or the equivalent, SAT or ACT scores or standing in the top half of the high school graduating class, and recommendations from the candidate's high school.

Procedure: The SAT or ACT is required; July is generally the latest test date acceptable for fall admission. Junior year results may also be submitted. Application deadlines are open. Freshmen are admitted to all terms. Students are notified of the admissions decision immediately upon completion of the application form. The college follows a rolling admissions procedure. There is a $10 application fee.

Special: Early admission is possible. CLEP subject exams are accepted.

Transfer: For fall 1981, 365 transfer students applied, 327 were accepted, and 158 enrolled. Transfers are accepted for all classes. To be eligible for transfer, students must be academically eligible to return to the school they last attended. All students must complete, at the college, 30 of the 120 hours required to earn a bachelor's degree. The deadlines for transfer applications are the same as those for freshman applicants.

Visiting: Orientation for prospective students includes a half day for pre-registration and advising and a full day for orientation of campus, rules, and requirements. Guided tours can be scheduled through the director of admissions. Visitors may sit in on classes.

Financial Aid: Forty-five percent of all students receive some form of financial aid. Ten percent work part-time on campus. Some freshman scholarships are available, including athletic scholarships. Thirty-six departments offer CWS. Work contracts are awarded to 5% of the students, including freshmen. The college is a member of CSS; the FAF or FFS is required. The deadline for aid applications is April 1.

Foreign Students: About 2% of the full-time students are from foreign countries.

Admissions: A minimum score of 500 on the TOEFL is required. No college entrance exams are necessary.

Procedure: Application deadlines are the same as those for freshmen. Students must present proof of adequate funds to undertake study at the college.

Admissions Contact: Marvin W. Lynch, Director of Admissions.

FURMAN UNIVERSITY B-1
Greenville, South Carolina 29613 (803) 294-2034

F/T: 1186M, 1056W	Faculty:	150; IIA, av$
P/T: 136M, 254W	Ph.D.'s:	87%
Grad: 251M, 234W	S/F Ratio:	14 to 1
Year: 3-2-3, ss	Tuition:	$3800
Appl: Feb. 1	R and B:	$2400
1891 applied	1041 accepted	597 enrolled
SAT: 548V 559M		**VERY COMPETITIVE**

Furman University, founded in 1826, is a coeducational liberal arts university affiliated with the South Carolina Baptist Convention. The library contains 275,000 volumes, and subscribes to 1700 periodicals.

Environment: The 750-acre campus is located in a suburban area 5 miles from the city of Greenville. Facilities include a 30-acre lake, all-weather tennis courts, and residence halls with a capacity for 649 women and 791 men. The university also sponsors on-campus apartments.

Student Life: Forty percent of the students are residents of South Carolina. Thirty-four percent are members of the Baptist Church; 80% are Protestant, 15% Catholic, and 1% Jewish. About 72% of the students live in the residence halls. Seven percent are minority-group members. Campus housing is single-sex. There are visiting privileges. Students may keep cars on campus.

Organizations: There are 5 fraternities to which 12% of the men belong. There are also 3 sororities. Social clubs, departmental clubs, and honor organizations are among the extracurricular activities available on campus.

Sports: The university fields 12 intercollegiate sports for men and 8 for women. There are 11 intramural sports for men and 11 for women.

Handicapped: Ninety-five percent of the campus is accessible to wheelchair-bound students. Facilities include wheelchair ramps, special parking, elevators, and specially equipped rest rooms; special class scheduling is also available. Two counselors are available for special counseling and assistance.

Graduates: The freshman dropout rate is 9%; 68% remain to graduate. Fifty-eight percent pursue graduate study: 4% enter medical school, 20% law school, and 2% dental school. Thirty-five percent pursue careers in business and industry.

Services: Students receive the following services free of charge: placement, career counseling, health care, and psychological counseling. Tutoring is available for a fee.

Programs of Study: The university confers the B.A., B.S., B.Mus., and B.G.S. degrees. Master's degrees also are awarded. Bachelor's degrees are offered in the following subjects: AREA STUDIES (urban), BUSINESS (business administration, computer science, finance, management, marketing), EDUCATION (early childhood, elementary, health/physical, secondary, special), ENGLISH (English), FINE AND PERFORMING ARTS (art, art education, art history, church music, music, music education, studio art, theater/dramatics), HEALTH SCIENCES (medical technology, physical therapy), LANGUAGES (French, German, Greek/Latin, Spanish), MATH AND SCIENCES (biology, chemistry, geology, mathematics, physics), PHILOSOPHY (classics, philosophy, religion), PREPROFESSIONAL (dentistry, engineering, forestry, law, medicine, ministry, pharmacy, social work, veterinary), SOCIAL SCIENCES (economics, government/political science, history, psychology, sociology). About 20% of degrees conferred are in business, 15% in social sciences, and a great majority in preprofessional studies.

Required: Courses in English, history, social sciences, natural sciences, fine arts, religion, foreign language, mathematics, and physical education are required. One term of independent study is required for most majors.

Special: It is possible to earn combined B.A.-B.S. degrees in mathematics, business administration, chemistry, and biology. Student-designed majors are permitted. Various foreign study programs are available, including the junior year abroad, as well as a term in England, France, Spain, Austria, and Japan. There is also a 2-month Holy Land archeological study tour during the winter term each year. Combination degree programs are offered in engineering with Georgia Tech, Clemson, and Auburn, and in forestry with Duke University. The university offers a 3-year bachelor's degree.

Honors: Phi Beta Kappa and several other national honor societies have chapters on campus.

Admissions: Fifty-five percent of those who applied were accepted for the 1981–82 freshman class. The SAT scores of those who enrolled were as follows: Verbal—18% below 500, 49% between 500 and 599, 22% between 600 and 700, and 11% above 700; Math—21% below 500, 41% between 500 and 600, 23% between 600 and 700, and 15% above 700. Applicants should score at least 500 on both the verbal and mathematical sections of the SAT, rank in the top fifth of their graduating class, and present a good recommendation from an accredited high school. The following factors also enter into the admissions decision: advanced placement or honors courses, extracurricular activities record, evidence of special talents, and recommendations by school officials.

Procedure: All applicants are required to take the SAT. The university recommends at least 2 testings by January of the senior year. The application deadlines are as follows: February 1 (fall), February 15 (spring), June 10 (summer), and December 15 (winter). The application fee is $20. An interview is strongly recommended.

Special: An early decision plan is available; notification is by December 15. Early admission is also possible; the application deadline is February 1. AP credit is accepted.

Transfer: For fall 1981, 226 transfer students applied, 192 were accepted, and 115 enrolled. Transfers are accepted for all but the senior class. A 3.0 average on all work is required. Grades of C or better transfer. All students must study at least 1 year at the university to receive a degree. They must also complete, at the university, 30 of the 126 credits required for a bachelor's degree. Deadlines for transfer applications are the same as those for freshman applicants.

Visiting: Guided tours can be scheduled in the fall and spring through the admissions office. Visitors may sit in on classes and remain overnight on campus.

Financial Aid: Fifty-nine percent of all students receive some form of financial aid. Twenty-five percent work part-time on campus. Aid may be obtained in the form of scholarships, loans, or campus employment. The average award to freshmen from all sources available through the university is $2800. Installment financing is available if arrangements are made in advance with outside corporations providing such services. The FAF should be filed with the CSS by the second week of January; applications for aid should be sent to the university by February 1.

Foreign Students: One percent of the full-time students are from foreign countries. The university offers these students special counseling and special organizations.

Admissions: A minimum score of 550 is required on the TOEFL. The SAT or ACT is not required.

Procedure: Application deadlines are February 1 (fall), December 15 (winter), February 15 (spring), and June 10 (summer). Students must submit a completed university health form and present proof of funds to cover 1 year of study. They must also carry health insurance.

Admissions Contact: Charles E. Brock, Director of Admissions.

LANDER COLLEGE B-2
Greenwood, South Carolina 29646   (803) 229-8307

F/T: 554M, 904W	Faculty: 92; IIB, ++$
P/T: 153M, 214W	Ph.D.'s: 58%
Grad: none	S/F Ratio: 12 to 1
Year: sems, ss	Tuition: $1050 ($1650)
Appl: Aug. 1	R and B: $1550
690 applied	608 accepted	417 enrolled
SAT or ACT: required		LESS COMPETITIVE

Lander College is a publicly controlled, coeducational college of liberal arts. It was established as the Williamston Female College in 1872; in 1904, it moved to Greenwood, and the name was changed to its present one in honor of its founder, Dr. Samuel Lander. The library contains 115,907 volumes and 12,653 microfilm items, and subscribes to 958 periodicals.

Environment: The 75-acre campus is located in an urban area 50 miles from Greenville. A new learning/classroom building is scheduled for completion in 1982. A modern residence hall accommodates 700 students.

Student Life: Most of the students are from South Carolina; 42% live on campus. Campus housing is single-sex, with visiting privileges. Students may keep cars on campus.

Organizations: There are 5 fraternities and 4 sororities. Extracurricular activities include student government, publications, theater, and choir. There are also Protestant and Catholic organizations.

Sports: The college fields 3 intercollegiate teams for men and 3 for women. There are 13 intramural sports for men and 12 for women.

Handicapped: Eighty percent of the campus is accessible to wheelchair-bound students. Wheelchair ramps, special parking, elevators, specially equipped rest rooms, lowered drinking fountains, and lowered telephones are available. Special class scheduling can also be arranged.

Graduates: The freshman dropout rate is 27%. Fourteen percent of the students pursue advanced study after graduation; 1% enter law school. About 32% pursue careers in business and industry.

Services: Students receive the following services free of charge: placement, career counseling, remedial instruction, tutoring, and psychological counseling. Health care is available for a fee.

Programs of Study: The college confers the B.A. and B.S. degrees. An associate degree is available in nursing. Bachelor's degrees are offered in the following subjects: BUSINESS (accounting, business administration, business education, computer science, economics, management), EDUCATION (early childhood, elementary, health/physical, home economics, recreation), ENGLISH (English), FINE AND PERFORMING ARTS (art, art education, music education, theater/dramatics), HEALTH SCIENCES (medical technology, nursing), LANGUAGES (French), MATH AND SCIENCES (biology, chemistry, computer science, mathematics), PHILOSOPHY (interdisciplinary science), PREPROFESSIONAL (dentistry, engineering, home economics, law, medicine, pharmacy, veterinary), SOCIAL SCIENCES (government/political science, history, psychology, sociology). Thirty-four percent of degrees conferred are in business, 19% in education, and 15% in social sciences.

Required: Courses required of all students are literature, composition, history, science, speech, and physical education.

Honors: Six national honor societies have chapters on campus.

Admissions: Eighty-eight percent of those who applied were accepted for the 1981-82 freshman class. Applicants must be graduates of accredited high schools with 18 units of work, have maintained a C average, rank in the upper half of their high school class, and show evidence of social responsibility, personality adjustment, and general fitness.

Procedure: Either the SAT or ACT is required and should be taken by December of the senior year; applications should be submitted by August 1 (fall) and December 1 (spring). A $15 fee must accompany the application.

Special: There are early decision, early admissions, and deferred admissions plans. CLEP and AP credit is accepted.

Transfer: For fall 1981, 366 transfer students applied, 330 were accepted, and 233 enrolled. Applicants with fewer than 30 semester hours must meet basic freshman criteria. Junior college transfers must earn, in residence, 60 of the 124 semester hours needed for a bachelor's degree. Senior college transfers must earn 30 of the last 36 semester hours in residence. Application deadlines are the same as those for freshmen.

Visiting: Summer orientations are required for freshmen. Prospective students can also make informal visits; guided tours can be scheduled through the admissions office. Visitors may sit in on classes.

Financial Aid: About 54% of the students receive some form of financial aid. About 23% work part-time on campus. A limited number of honor, departmental, and alumni scholarships are awarded annually. NDSL loans and Basic Grants are available, as well as loans from civic clubs, patriotic organizations, and the alumni association. CWS is offered in all departments. The average award to freshmen from all sources is $200. Need is the prime consideration, but promise and academic performance are also considered. The college is a member of CSS; the FAF should be submitted. Applications for aid should be filed by April 15 (fall and summer) and November 15 (spring).

Foreign Students: About 1% of the full-time students are from foreign countries. Special counseling and organizations are available to these students.

Admissions: A minimum TOEFL score of 550 is required. College entrance exams are not necessary.

Procedure: Application deadlines are 6 months prior to the start of any semester. Foreign students are admitted to all terms. Students must present proof of adequate funds to cover 1 year of study. Health insurance is not required but is available to foreign students through the college for a fee.

Admissions Contact: Jacquelyn DeVore Roark, Director of Admissions.

LIMESTONE COLLEGE B-1
Gaffney, South Carolina 29340   (803) 489-7151

F/T: 200M, 200W	Faculty: n/av; IIB, av$
P/T: 5M, 10W	Ph.D.'s: 50%
Grad: none	S/F Ratio: 13 to 1
Year: sems, ss	Tuition: $3470
Appl: open	R and B: $1830
313 applied	257 accepted	163 enrolled
SAT: 388V 417M		LESS COMPETITIVE

Limestone College, established in 1845, is an independent liberal arts and sciences college. The library houses 65,000 volumes, and subscribes to 450 periodicals.

Environment: The 111-acre campus is located in a suburban area 50 miles from Charlotte, North Carolina. There are 15 major buildings, including 2 residence halls for 300 women and 150 men. There are also apartments for 10 married students and facilities for commuters.

Student Life: About 75% of the students come from South Carolina; 95% are graduates of public schools. About 65% of the students reside on campus. Campus housing is single-sex. Students may keep cars on campus.

Organizations: Student government, clubs, publications, performing groups (musical and dramatic), religious and service organizations, and regularly scheduled on-campus social and cultural events are sponsored by the college. There are fraternities and sororities.

Sports: The college fields 3 intercollegiate sports for men and 3 for women. There are 8 intramural sports for men and 8 for women.

Graduates: Ten percent of the freshmen drop out, 35% remain to graduate, and 3% of the graduates continue their education.

Services: The college provides the following services free of charge: placement, career counseling, health care, tutoring, remedial instruction, and psychological counseling.

Programs of Study: The B.A. or B.S. degree is offered in the following subjects: BUSINESS (accounting, business administration, finance, management), EDUCATION (early childhood, elementary, health/physical, secondary), ENGLISH (English), FINE AND PERFORMING ARTS (art, art education, music, music education, studio art, theater/dramatics), LANGUAGES (French, German, Spanish), MATH AND SCIENCES (biology, chemistry, mathematics), PHILOSOPHY

SOUTH CAROLINA

(humanities, philosophy, religion), PREPROFESSIONAL (dentistry, law, medicine, ministry, pharmacy, pre-medical technology, social work, veterinary), SOCIAL SCIENCES (government/political science, history, psychology, sociology).

Required: There are no required courses at this time.

Special: Student-designed majors, a general studies major, study abroad, combination degrees in preprofessional programs, and a 3-year bachelor's degree are offered.

Honors: Several departments offer honors work.

Admissions: About 82% of the 1981–82 freshman applicants were accepted. A high school diploma or GED plus rank in the top 50% and a 2.0 high school GPA are necessary. Other factors include extracurricular activities record, advanced placement or honors courses, and recommendations by school officials.

Procedure: The SAT or ACT should be taken by December of the senior year. New students are admitted each semester. Deadlines are open. Notification is on a rolling basis. There is a $15 application fee.

Special: There are early decision, early admissions, and deferred admissions programs. AP and CLEP credit is available.

Transfer: For fall 1981, 80 transfer students applied and 53 enrolled. A C average is recommended; D grades are sometimes accepted. Thirty credits, of the 120 required to earn a bachelor's degree, must be taken in residence. There are no application deadlines.

Financial Aid: Over 75% of the students are receiving aid. The college participates in federal CWS, BEOG/SEOG, and NDSL programs in addition to offering commercial (bank) loans and a limited number of freshman scholarships. Academic performance and need are the determining factors. The college is a member of CSS; the FAF should be filed by March 31.

Foreign Students: Fewer than 1% of the full-time students are from foreign countries.

Admissions: A minimum score of 500 on the TOEFL is required. Students must also take the SAT.

Procedure: There are no application deadlines. Students must submit the college's health form. Proof of funds adequate to cover 4 years of study is required. Health insurance is available through the college.

Admissions Contact: Anslie J. Waters, Director of Admissions.

MORRIS COLLEGE D–3
Sumter, South Carolina 29150 (803) 775-9371

F/T: 229M, 404W	Faculty:	47; IIB, – – $
P/T: 14M, 11W	Ph.D.'s:	46%
Grad: none	S/F Ratio:	15 to 1
Year: sems, ss	Tuition:	$2261
Appl: open	R and B:	$1502
425 applied	400 accepted	188 enrolled
SAT or ACT: not required		NONCOMPETITIVE

Morris College, a small, coeducational, liberal arts college affiliated with the Baptist Church, was founded in 1908. The library houses 98,245 volumes and 36,496 microform items, and subscribes to 601 periodicals.

Environment: The campus is situated 20 miles east of Columbia in an urban area. The campus includes a fine arts center, a learning resource center, and 4 student residences. There is also approved local housing.

Student Life: The majority of students come from South Carolina; the student body is predominantly black. Chapel services are held twice a week; attendance is voluntary. Campus housing is single-sex, there are visiting privileges. Students may keep cars on campus.

Organizations: There are 3 national fraternities and 1 local fraternity on campus, and 2 local and 3 national sororities, to which 7% of the men and 12% of the women belong. Extracurricular activities include a literary group, science and social studies clubs, the choir, choral society, and publications.

Sports: The college fields 3 intercollegiate teams for men and 3 for women. There is 1 intramural sport for men.

Handicapped: There are limited provisions for the physically handicapped.

Graduates: The freshman dropout rate is 5%; about 54% remain to graduate. About 16% of the graduates pursue advanced studies; 1% enter medical school, and 36% go on to careers in business and industry.

Services: Students receive the following services free of charge: placement, career counseling, tutoring, remedial instruction, and psychological counseling. Health care and insurance are available for a fee.

Programs of Study: The college confers the B.A., B.F.A., B.S., and B.S. in Elem.Ed. degrees. Bachelor's degrees are offered in the following subjects: BUSINESS (business administration), EDUCATION (elementary, secondary), ENGLISH (English, liberal studies, liberal/technical studies), FINE AND PERFORMING ARTS (media arts, music), MATH AND SCIENCES (biology, mathematics, math/physics), SOCIAL SCIENCES (history, political science, social sciences). Of the degrees conferred, 29% are in social sciences, 24% in business, and 23% in education.

Special: A general studies degree and a general studies/technical degree are offered. The college participates in the Upward Bound-Special Services program, which provides tutoring and counseling for freshmen from disadvantaged backgrounds. A summer program, Helping Hand, is offered for disadvantaged high school students.

Honors: The honors program in social sciences promotes advanced study for promising students. There is 1 national honor society on campus.

Admissions: Of those who applied for the 1981–82 freshman class, 94% were accepted. Candidates should have completed 18 credits of work. The college prefers that applicants rank in the top two-thirds of their class, but the admissions policy is open-door.

Procedure: The SAT or ACT is not required. There is no formal application deadline, but applicants are encouraged to file as early as possible. Applications should be submitted with a $10 fee. There is a rolling admissions plan.

Special: There are early decision, early admissions, and deferred admissions plans.

Transfer: For fall 1981, 57 transfer students applied, 50 were accepted, and 45 enrolled. Good academic standing (a 2.0 GPA) is required. Grades of C or better transfer. Students must complete, at the college, 30 of the 124 semester hours required to earn a bachelor's degree. Application deadlines are open.

Visiting: Guides are available for informal visits between 1 and 5 P.M. Visitors may sit in on classes and stay overnight at the school. The dean of students should be contacted to arrange visits.

Financial Aid: Ninety-five percent of all students receive some form of financial aid. About 63% work part-time on campus. Sources of aid include scholarships, EOG, NDSL, CWS, BEOG, SEOG, and South Carolina tuition grants. The college is a member of CSS; the FAF is required. There are no application deadlines.

Foreign Students: There are no foreign students currently enrolled at the college.

Admissions: Foreign students must demonstrate ability in written English. College entrance exams are not required.

Procedure: Application deadlines are open; students are admitted to all terms. Completion of a health certificate by a physician is required. Proof of funds adequate to cover the entire period of attendance is also necessary. Foreign students must carry health insurance, which is availble through the college for a fee.

Admissions Contact: Queen W. Spann, Admissions and Records Officer.

NEWBERRY COLLEGE B–2
Newberry, South Carolina 29108 (803) 276-6974

F/T: 422M, 298W	Faculty:	65; IIB, – $
P/T: 5M, 12W	Ph.D.'s:	66%
Grad: none	S/F Ratio:	15 to 1
Year: sems, ss	Tuition:	$3665
Appl: Aug. 1	R and B:	$1685
617 applied	495 accepted	289 enrolled
SAT: 430V 450M	ACT: 20	COMPETITIVE

Newberry College, established in 1856, is a privately controlled, liberal arts college affiliated with the Lutheran Church in America. The library houses 95,000 volumes and 5000 microfilm items, and subscribes to 600 periodicals.

Environment: The 55-acre campus is located in a rural area 40 miles northwest of Columbia. Residence halls accommodate 550 men and 230 women. The college also sponsors fraternity and sorority houses.

Student Life: About 95% of the students come from the South; the remainder come from 24 other states. Approximately 80% of the students live on campus. Students are required to live on campus unless they commute from home. Ninety percent of the students are Protestant and 7% are Catholic; attendance at religious services is voluntary. Ten percent of the students are minority-group members. Campus housing is single-sex; there are visiting privileges. Students may keep cars on campus.

Organizations: About 30% of the men are members of the 4 local and 4 national fraternities; 15% of the women belong to the 3 national and 3 local sororities.

Sports: The college fields 5 intercollegiate teams for men and 4 for women. There are 5 intramural sports for men and 5 for women.

Handicapped: Ninety-eight percent of the campus is accessible to wheelchair-bound students. Facilities include wheelchair ramps, special parking, elevators, and specially equipped rest rooms. Special class scheduling is also available.

Graduates: The freshman dropout rate is 12%; 56% remain to graduate. About 40% of the graduates go on to graduate study: 6% enter medical school, 3% dental school, and 3% law school; 40% pursue careers in business and industry.

Services: Students receive the following services free of charge: placement, career counseling, health care, tutoring, remedial instruction, and psychological counseling.

Programs of Study: The college confers the B.A., B.S., B.M., B.Mus.Ed., and B.S. Tech. degrees. Bachelor's degrees are offered in the following subjects: AREA STUDIES (urban), BUSINESS (accounting, business administration, computer science), EDUCATION (early childhood, elementary, secondary), ENGLISH (English), FINE AND PERFORMING ARTS (art, music, music education, theater/dramatics), LANGUAGES (French, German, Greek/Latin, Spanish), MATH AND SCIENCES (biology, chemistry, mathematics), PHILOSOPHY (philosophy, religion), SOCIAL SCIENCES (economics, government/political science, history, international relations, psychology, sociology). Of the degrees conferred, 24% are in business, 19% in social sciences, and 12% in education.

Required: All students are required to take English, foreign language, history, mathematics, science, religion, and physical education courses.

Special: The 3-2 cooperative programs available include an arrangement with Duke University in forestry and with Georgia Tech and Clemson University in engineering. For South Carolina residents there is a 2-3 medical program with the Medical University of South Carolina.

Admissions: Of those who applied for the 1981–82 freshman class, 80% were accepted. The SAT scores of those who enrolled were as follows: Verbal—87% below 500, 10% between 500 and 599, 2% between 600 and 700, and 1% above 700; Math—87% below 500, 10% between 500 and 599, 2% between 600 and 700, and 1% above 700. Candidates should have completed 18 units of work, rank in the top 75% of their class, and have a minimum average of C. Other factors entering into the admissions decision are recommendations by school officials, impressions made during an interview, and leadership record.

Procedure: The SAT or ACT is required. Application deadlines are August 1 (fall), December 1 (spring), and May 1 (summer). Applicants are notified on a rolling basis. There is a $15 application fee.

Special: There are early admissions and deferred admissions plans. CLEP credit is accepted.

Transfer: For fall 1981, 113 transfer students applied, 90 were accepted, and 54 enrolled. Transfers are accepted for all classes. The applicant must be eligible to return to the previous school. A 2.0 GPA is recommended. Grades of C or better transfer. Students must complete, at the college, 30 of the 126 credits needed to earn a bachelor's degree. Application deadlines are the same as those for freshmen.

Visiting: Orientations are held twice a year. Guides are available for informal visits on weekdays from 9 A.M. to 4 P.M. Arrangements can be made through the admissions office. Visitors may sit in on classes and stay overnight at the school, if advance notice is given.

Financial Aid: About 84% of all students recieve some form of financial aid; 25% work part-time on campus. The average financial aid package is approximately $3400. Work-study is available in all departments. The college is a member of the CSS; the FAF is required. The deadline for financial aid applications is May 1.

Foreign Students: The college accepts foreign students.

Admissions: A minimum score of 500 on the TOEFL is required; no college entrance exams are required.

Procedure: There are no application deadlines.

Admissions Contact: H. Ray Sharpe, Dean of Admissions.

SOUTH CAROLINA 819

PRESBYTERIAN COLLEGE B–2
Clinton, South Carolina 29325 (803) 833-2820

F/T: 524M, 424W	Faculty: 65; IIB, +$
P/T: none	Ph.D.'s: 75%
Grad: none	S/F Ratio: 14 to 1
Year: sems, ss	Tuition: $3705
Appl: open	R and B: $1835
900 applied	650 accepted	261 enrolled
SAT: 450V 490M		COMPETITIVE

Presbyterian College is a 4-year institution controlled and supported by Presbyterians of the Synod of the Southeast (Georgia and South Carolina). The library contains 115,000 volumes, and subscribes to 650 periodicals.

Environment: The 175-acre campus, located in a suburban area 35 miles from Greenville, features 2 avenues with most of the Georgian colonial style buildings facing a central plaza. Four men's and 3 women's dormitories have a variety of room arrangements. The college also sponsors fraternity houses and married student housing.

Student Life: About 52% of the students are from South Carolina. About 90% live on campus. Ninety-one percent are Protestant (37% Presbyterian) and 3% are Catholic. About 4% of the students are minority-group members. Campus housing is single-sex; there are no visiting privileges. Students may keep cars on campus.

Organizations: The small enrollment allows each student to take part in some phase of campus activities, which include student government, publications, and other organizations. Half the men belong to 6 national fraternities.

Sports: The college fields 7 intercollegiate teams for men and 4 for women. There are 5 intramural sports for men and 5 for women.

Handicapped: Facilities for the physically handicapped include wheelchair ramps, special parking, elevators, and specially equipped rest rooms. About 60% of the campus is accessible to handicapped students.

Graduates: The freshman dropout rate is 20%; 58% remain to graduate. About 45% pursue advanced study after graduation: 7% enter medical school, 5% dental school, and 5% law school; 25% pursue careers in business and industry.

Services: The following services are available to all students free of charge: placement, career counseling, health care, psychological counseling, and remedial instruction. Tutoring is available for a fee.

Programs of Study: The college confers the B.A. or B.S. degree in the following subjects: BUSINESS (business administration, management), EDUCATION (elementary, secondary, special), ENGLISH (English), FINE AND PERFORMING ARTS (art, music, music education, theater/dramatics), LANGUAGES (French, German, Spanish), MATH AND SCIENCES (biology, chemistry, mathematics, physics), PHILOSOPHY (religion), PREPROFESSIONAL (dentistry, engineering, forestry, law, medicine, ministry, pharmacy, social work, veterinary), SOCIAL SCIENCES (economics, government/political science, history, psychology, sociology). Of the degrees conferred, 25% are in business, 20% each in preprofessional and social sciences, and 10% each in education and math/sciences.

Required: The following courses are required for all students: English, a foreign language, mathematics, science, religion, history, and 1 social science.

Special: It is possible to earn a bachelor's degree in 3 years. The college offers 3-2 programs in engineering in conjunction with Clemson, Vanderbilt, and Auburn Universities and a dual-degree program in forestry in conjunction with Duke University.

Admissions: Approximately 72% of those who applied were accepted for the 1981–82 freshman class. The SAT scores of those who enrolled were as follows: Verbal—73% below 500, 20% between 500 and 599, 6% between 600 and 700, and 1% above 700; Math—56% below 500, 32% between 500 and 599, 9% between 600 and 700, and 3% above 700. Candidates should have completed 15 Carnegie units and have maintained a GPA of at least 2.25. Students should rank in the top half of their class and achieve scores of 400 on each part of the SAT to receive serious consideration. Other qualifications noted by the school in order of importance are: advanced placement or honors courses, recommendations by school officials, leadership record, and extracurricular activities record. Sons and daughters of alumni are given preference.

Procedure: Applicants are required to take the SAT or ACT, preferably in August, December, or January of the senior year. It is suggested that the application be filed before April 1, although there are no deadlines. Notification is on a rolling basis. The application fee is $15. Freshmen are admitted to all terms.

820 SOUTH CAROLINA

Special: There is an early admissions plan. The deadline for applying is March 15.

Transfer: For fall 1981, 65 transfer students applied, 50 were accepted, and 30 enrolled. An average of C is necessary for transfer students. Grades of C or better transfer. There is a residency requirement of 1 year. Students must complete the last 24 hours of credit at the college; 122 credits are required to earn a bachelor's degree. There are no application deadlines.

Visiting: A senior visitation day is scheduled in the fall in which academic departments and campus activities are presented to prospective students. There are also guides for informal visits to the college. Visitors may sit in on classes and stay overnight. The best time for visits are weekdays in the early fall and spring. The director of admissions should be contacted to arrange visits.

Financial Aid: About 65% of all students receive some form of financial aid. About 25% work part-time on campus. The college has a variety of aid programs, including Founder's Scholarships and church vocational grants. Loan funds and part-time employment are also available. Some awards are based on need alone, while others are based on grades, leadership, and vocational plans. The deadline for applying for the Founder's scholarship is December 1; for other forms of aid applicants should submit the FAF by March 15. The college is a member of CSS.

Foreign Students: Fewer than 1% of the full-time students are from foreign countries. The school offers these students special counseling.

Admissions: Foreign students must take the TOEFL. The SAT is also required.

Procedure: Application deadlines are June 15 (fall), October 15 (winter), and March 15 (summer). Students must complete the college's medical form. They must also present proof of funds adequate to cover 1 year of study plus transportation.

Admissions Contact: William K. Jackson, Director of Admissions.

SOUTH CAROLINA STATE COLLEGE   C-3
Orangeburg, South Carolina 29117   (803) 536-7185

F/T: 1434M, 1759W	Faculty: 247; IIA, —$
P/T: 151M, 212W	Ph.D.'s: 43%
Grad: 114M, 373W	S/F Ratio: 16 to 1
Year: sems, ss	Tuition: $750 ($1500)
Appl: July 31	R and B: $1516
1831 applied	1026 accepted	918 enrolled
SAT: 305V 336M	ACT: 16	LESS COMPETITIVE

South Carolina State College, established in 1895, comprises 5 schools: Arts and Sciences, Education, Home Economics, Industrial Education and Engineering Technology, and Graduate Studies. Its library has nearly 220,000 volumes and 192,000 microfilm items, and subscribes to 929 periodicals.

Environment: The 147-acre small-town campus is located in a rural area 40 miles east of Columbia and has more than 60 buildings, including 13 residence halls that accommodate 1177 women and 850 men. The college also has 32 apartments for married students.

Student Life: About 94% of the students come from South Carolina. The majority are public school graduates. Three-quarters of the students reside on campus. About 96% are minority-group members. Campus housing is single-sex; there are no visiting privileges. Students may keep cars on campus.

Organizations: Twelve percent of the men belong to 1 of 7 fraternities; 10% of the women join 1 of the 6 sororities. The extracurricular program is traditional. Performing groups include band, choir, dramatics, chorus, dance, jazz, and orchestra. On campus are a theater and museum/planetarium.

Sports: The college fields 9 intercollegiate teams for men and 4 for women. There are 3 intramural sports for men and 2 for women.

Handicapped: About 60% of the campus is accessible to handicapped students. Wheelchair ramps, elevators, designated parking areas, and lowered drinking fountains and telephones are provided. No students with visual or hearing impairments are currently enrolled.

Graduates: Twenty-two percent of the freshmen drop out; 32% remain to graduate. About 32% of the graduates enter business and industry.

Services: Free career counseling, placement services, health care, psychological counseling, tutoring, and remedial instruction are offered.

Programs of Study: The B.A. and B.S. degrees are conferred. Master's degrees are also available. Bachelor's degrees are offered in the following subjects: BUSINESS (accounting, business administration, business education, computer science, economics, marketing, office management and administration), EDUCATION (counselor, early childhood, elementary, health/physical, industrial, secondary, special), ENGLISH (English), FINE AND PERFORMING ARTS (art education, music education, theater/dramatics), HEALTH SCIENCES (food and nutrition, nursing, speech pathology and audiology), LANGUAGES (French, Spanish), MATH AND SCIENCES (biology, chemistry, mathematics, physics), PREPROFESSIONAL (agriculture, dentistry, engineering technology—civil, engineering technology—electrical, engineering technology—mechanical, home economics, library science, medicine, optometry, pharmacy, social welfare, veterinary), SOCIAL SCIENCES (criminal justice, government/political science, history, psychology, social studies, sociology). Most of the degrees are conferred in education and business.

Required: The distribution requirement includes course work in English, mathematics, science, and physical education.

Special: Cooperative education programs are offered. The college has a program that enables educationally disadvantaged students who do not meet regular admission requirements to attend.

Honors: There are 3 honor societies on campus.

Admissions: About 56% of the 1981–82 freshman applicants were accepted. Candidates must have a diploma from an accredited high school (or GED), should have a GPA of at least 2.0, and should rank in the top half of the graduating class. The college also considers test scores, recommendations from school officials, and advanced placement or honors courses.

Procedure: The SAT or ACT is required. July 31 is the fall deadline; November 30, the spring. There is a $10 application fee ($15 for out-of-state applicants).

Special: AP and CLEP credit is granted.

Transfer: Transfers are accepted for all classes. A GPA of at least 1.9 and a composite SAT score of at least 650 are required. All students must complete, at the college, 30 of the total hours required for a bachelor's degree. Application deadlines are July 30 (fall), November 30 (spring), and June 8 (summer).

Visiting: There is an orientation program for prospective students. Student guides give tours of the campus. Visitors may sit in on classes. To arrange a visit, the director of admissions should be contacted.

Financial Aid: About 85% of the students are receiving assistance. Twelve percent work part-time on campus. The college participates in federal and state aid programs such as NDSL, BEOG/SEOG, and CWS in addition to offering commercial (bank) loans and freshman scholarships. Aid is packaged. Need is the determining factor for most aid. The college's aid application should be filed by June 1. The FAF is also required. The college is a member of CSS.

Foreign Students: Two percent of the full-time students come from foreign countries. Special counseling and special organizations are available for these students.

Admissions: Foreign students must achieve a TOEFL score of at least 500 and an SAT composite score of at least 750.

Procedure: The application deadline is July 31 for fall entry. Foreign students must present proof of funds adequate to cover 4 years of study.

Admissions Contact: Dorothy L. Brown, Director of Admissions and Records.

UNIVERSITY OF SOUTH CAROLINA

University of South Carolina, a state-supported system of higher education, was established in 1801. In addition to the main campus in Columbia, it consists of three 4-year campuses at Aiken, Conway (Coastal Carolina College), and Spartanburg, and five 2-year campuses at Allendale, Beaufort, Lancaster, Sumter, and Union. Individual profiles on the 4-year campuses follow.

UNIVERSITY OF SOUTH CAROLINA   C-3
Columbia, South Carolina 29208   (803) 777-7700

F/T: 7586M, 6934W	Faculty: n/av; I, av$
P/T: 1720M, 2005W	Ph.D.'s: 76%
Grad: 3456M, 4133W	S/F Ratio: n/av
Year: sems, ss	Tuition: $1180 ($2460)
Appl: Aug. 1	R and B: $1590
5201 applied	3693 accepted	2110 enrolled
SAT (mean): 463V 491M	ACT: 23	COMPETITIVE+

University of South Carolina offers undergraduate degree programs in the arts and sciences, business, education, health fields, engineering, and pharmacy. The library contains 1.9 million volumes and 1.8 million microfilm items, and subscribes to 16,800 periodicals.

Environment: Situated in a downtown area of the state capital, the 230-acre campus includes about 150 buildings. Renovation and restoration of the historic Horseshoe (old campus) buildings is near completion. Recent additions to the campus include the life and physical science centers and the social sciences center. Residence facilities accommodate 7600 students. The university also sponsors on-campus apartments and married student housing.

Student Life: About 82% of the students are from South Carolina; 42% of the undergraduates live on campus. About 15% of the students are minority-group members. Campus housing is both single-sex and coed; there are visiting privileges in single-sex dorms. Students may keep cars on campus. Day-care services are available to all students, faculty, and staff for a fee.

Organizations: There are 20 fraternities and 14 sororities, to which 11% of the men and 8% of the women belong. Extracurricular activities include religious groups, forensic and literary clubs, publications, and dramatic and musical groups.

Sports: The university fields 9 intercollegiate teams for men and 6 for women. There are 11 intramural sports for men and 8 for women.

Handicapped: Special facilities for physically handicapped students include wheelchair ramps, special parking, elevators, specially equipped rest rooms, and lowered drinking fountains and telephones. Counseling services and special class scheduling are also available. There are special facilities for visually impaired students.

Graduates: The freshman dropout rate is 25%; 49% remain to graduate.

Services: Students receive the following services free of charge: placement, psychological and career counseling, tutoring, and remedial instruction. Health care is included in full-time student fees.

Programs of Study: The following undergraduate degrees are offered: B.A., B.S., B.F.A., B.M., B.Mus.Ed., and B. of Media Arts. Associate, master's, and doctoral programs are also offered. Bachelor's degrees are offered in the following subjects: AREA STUDIES (Black/Afro-American, Latin American), BUSINESS (accounting, business economics, business education, computer science, finance, insurance, management, management science, marketing, office administration), EDUCATION (distributive, early childhood, elementary, health/physical, secondary), ENGLISH (English, journalism), FINE AND PERFORMING ARTS (art education, art history, media arts, music, music education, radio/TV, studio art, theater/dramatics), HEALTH SCIENCES (medical technology, nursing), LANGUAGES (French, German, Greek/Latin, Italian, Spanish), MATH AND SCIENCES (biology, chemistry, geology, marine science, mathematics, physics), PHILOSOPHY (classics, philosophy, religion), PREPROFESSIONAL (engineering—chemical, engineering—civil, engineering—electrical, engineering—mechanical, pharmacy), SOCIAL SCIENCES (anthropology, criminal justice, economics, geography, government/political science, history, interdisciplinary studies, international relations, psychology, sociology). Preprofessional training is offered in dentistry, law, and medicine. Twenty-five percent of the degrees are conferred in business, 11% in education, and 9% in social sciences.

Special: It is possible to earn combined B.A.-B.S. degrees in the humanities, social sciences, math, and science. A general studies degree is offered. Student-designed majors are permitted.

Honors: South Carolina College, the honors college of the university, offers honors programs in all majors. Eighteen honor societies have chapters on campus.

Admissions: Seventy-one percent of those who applied for the 1981-82 freshman class were accepted. The SAT scores of those who enrolled were as follows: Verbal—67% below 500, 26% between 500 and 599, 6% between 600 and 700, and 1% above 700; Math—52% below 500, 36% between 500 and 599, 11% between 600 and 700, and 1% above 700. On the ACT, 23% scored below 21, 29% between 21 and 23, 23% between 24 and 25, 20% between 26 and 28, and 5% above 28. Admission is based on a predicted GPA obtained by considering high school rank and test scores. Candidates must rank in the top 75% of their graduating class. In addition, the school considers the following factors, in order of importance: advanced placement or honor courses and evidence of special talents.

Procedure: The SAT or ACT is required and should be taken by May of the senior year. Applications should be submitted by August 1 (fall), December 1 (spring), and 2 weeks before each summer session. Dormitory space may be reserved by February. Notification is on a rolling basis. Freshmen are also admitted at midyear and in the summer. There is a $25 application fee.

Special: CLEP and AP credit is accepted.

Transfer: For fall 1981, 1988 transfer students applied, 1260 were accepted, and 862 enrolled. Transfers are accepted for all classes. A GPA of 2.0 is required for transfers from 4-year institutions; a GPA of 2.5 is required of transfers from 2-year institutions. Some colleges of the university may have higher requirements. SAT or ACT scores and a high school transcript are needed if the transfer applicant has fewer than 30 semester hours of college credit. Grades of C or better transfer. Thirty semester hours must be completed in residence; 120 semester hours are required to earn a bachelor's degree. Application deadlines are the same as those for freshmen. Notification is on a rolling basis.

Visiting: One-day orientation sessions, including registration, are scheduled throughout the summer for accepted applicants. Guides are available for informal visits. Visitors may sit in on classes. Visits are best scheduled on weekdays between 9 A.M. and 3 P.M.. The admissions office should be contacted for arrangements.

Financial Aid: About 35% of all students receive some form of financial aid; 8% work part-time on campus. Scholarship funds total $250,000 annually. An estimated $2 million is available through institutional loan funds. The average freshman award is $1400. Most institutional funds are awarded on the basis of demonstrated financial need. The university is a member of CSS; either the FAF or FFS should be submitted. The priority deadline for financial aid applications is February 15.

Foreign Students: About 3% of the full-time students are from foreign countries. The university offers these students an intensive English program, special counseling, and special organizations.

Admissions: A minimum score of 500 on the TOEFL is required. Students must also take the SAT.

Procedure: Application deadlines are June 1 (fall) and December 1 (spring). Students must present proof of funds adequate to cover 1 year of study. There is a $25 visa-processing fee. Health insurance is required and is available through the university for a fee.

Admissions Contact: Elizabeth T. Wills, Associate Director of Admissions.

UNIVERSITY OF SOUTH CAROLINA AT AIKEN B-3
Aiken, South Carolina 29801   (803) 648-6851

F/T, P/T:	Faculty: 135; IIB, +$
720M, 1080W	Ph.D.'s: 58%
Grad: 300M&W	S/F Ratio: 13 to 1
Year: sems, ss	Tuition: $900 ($1890)
Appl: Aug. 1	R and B: n/app
475 applied	425 accepted	375 enrolled
SAT: 445V 490M	ACT: 18	LESS COMPETITIVE

University of South Carolina at Aiken, established in 1961, offers programs in the liberal arts and sciences, business, and education. The library contains 56,805 volumes and 7700 microfilm and microfiche items, and subscribes to 904 periodicals.

Environment: The 144-acre campus is located in a small town 15 miles from Augusta, Georgia. The university has 6 main buildings. There are no residence halls.

Student Life: About 85% of the students come from South Carolina. Most are public-school graduates. All students commute.

Organizations: Extracurricular activities include student government, regularly scheduled social and cultural events, special-interest clubs, publications, closed-circuit TV, religious and service organizations, and 1 fraternity and 1 sorority.

Sports: The university fields intercollegiate teams in 3 sports for men and 2 for women. Intramural sports also are available.

Handicapped: About 75% of the campus is accessible to handicapped students. Special facilities include wheelchair ramps, parking areas, elevators, lowered drinking fountains and telephones, and specially equipped rest rooms.

Graduates: About 18% of the freshmen drop out, and 79% remain to graduate. About 30% of the graduates pursue advanced degrees, while 18% enter careers in business and industry.

Services: Tutoring, remedial instruction, psychological and career counseling, and placement services are provided free to students. Fees are charged for health care.

Programs of Study: The university confers the B.A., B.S., B.I.S., and B.F.A. degrees. Associate and master's programs are also offered. Bachelor's degrees are granted in the following subjects: BUSINESS (accounting, business economics, business education, finance, management, marketing, office administration), EDUCATION (early child-

822 SOUTH CAROLINA

hood, elementary, health/physical, secondary), ENGLISH (English), FINE AND PERFORMING ARTS (studio art), MATH AND SCIENCES (biology, chemistry, mathematics/computer science, natural sciences), SOCIAL SCIENCES (economics, government/political science, history, psychology, social studies).

Required: All students must take courses in English, mathematics, science, and history.

Special: The B.I.S. degree program permits students to design their own majors. Internships and a general-studies degree are offered. The university offers up to 3 years of work in the following majors: art, foreign languages, journalism, media arts, music, theater/speech, chemistry, computer science, engineering, geology, physics, prepharmacy, allied health sciences, anthropology, geography, philosophy, and international studies. Students wishing to complete a degree in these fields must transfer.

Honors: One honor society has a chapter on campus.

Admissions: About 89% of those who applied for the 1981–82 freshman class were accepted. Twenty-two percent of those who enrolled ranked in the top fifth of their high school class. A high school diploma or GED is required. Academic record, class rank, SAT or ACT scores, and recommendations are considered. Students must have SAT scores of 350 Verbal and 350 Math or an ACT composite score of 17 for regular admission. Applicants with combined SAT scores of 600 or lower may be admitted provisionally.

Procedure: The SAT or ACT is required. New students are admitted each semester. Application deadlines are August 1 (fall), December 1 (spring), and May 1 (summer). Notification is made on a rolling basis. An interview is recommended. There is a $15 application fee.

Special: Early and deferred admissions plans are available. AP and CLEP credit is granted.

Transfer: Transfer applicants must be in good standing at their last college and have a 2.0 GPA. D grades do not transfer. Students must earn at least 30 credits in residence of the 120 generally required for a bachelor's degree. Application deadlines are the same as those for freshmen.

Visiting: Campus tours with student guides can be arranged with the admissions office. Visitors may sit in on classes. Visits are best scheduled for weekdays.

Financial Aid: About 65% of the students receive aid. Awards are based on financial need, academic achievement, and future promise. The university participates in federal NDSL, CWS, and BEOG/SEOG programs. Freshman academic scholarships, state aid, and commercial loans also are offered. The deadline for priority consideration of aid applications is April 1. Both the university aid form and the FAF must be filed.

Foreign Students: Students from foreign countries make up less than 1% of enrollment. The university offers these students special counseling and special organizations.

Admissions: Applicants must score at least 500 on the TOEFL. They also must take the SAT.

Procedure: Application deadlines are open; foreign students are admitted to all terms. They must present proof of adequate funds for 1 year.

Admissions Contact: Robert Moldenhauer, Director of Admissions.

UNIVERSITY OF SOUTH CAROLINA AT SPARTANBURG B–1

Spartanburg, South Carolina 29303   (803) 578-1800

F/T: 625M, 980W
P/T: 391M, 611W
Grad: none
Year: sems, ss
Appl: Aug. 1
SAT: 380V 410M

Faculty: 95; IIB, av$
Ph.D.'s: 75%
S/F Ratio: 17 to 1
Tuition: $825 ($1840)
R and B: n/app

NONCOMPETITIVE

University of South Carolina at Spartanburg, established in 1967, offers undergraduate degree programs in the liberal arts and sciences, business, education, and nursing. The library contains more than 100,000 volumes.

Environment: There are 6 major buildings on the campus, which is located in a suburban area 60 miles from Charlotte, North Carolina. There are no residence halls.

Student Life: About 95% of the students come from South Carolina. The majority are public school graduates. All students commute. About 15% of the students are minority-group members. Day-care services are provided for all students, faculty, and staff.

Organizations: On-campus activities include student government, clubs, publications, religious and service groups, performing groups, and regularly scheduled social and cultural events. There is 1 fraternity and 1 sorority.

Sports: The university fields 5 intercollegiate teams for men and 3 for women. There are 5 intramural sports for men and 4 for women.

Handicapped: Special facilities for handicapped students include wheelchair ramps, elevators, specially equipped rest rooms, designated parking areas, and lowered drinking fountains. One counselor is available to handicapped students.

Graduates: Twenty percent of freshmen drop out by the end of the first year; 45% remain to graduate. Twenty-five percent of the graduates pursue advanced study; 1% enter medical school, 1% dental school, and 5% law school. Thirty-five percent enter careers in business and industry.

Services: Free career counseling, placement, tutoring, remedial instruction, and psychological counseling are provided. Health-care services are provided for a fee.

Programs of Study: The university confers the B.A. and B.S. degrees, as well as associate degrees. Bachelor's degrees are offered in the following subjects: BUSINESS (accounting, business administration, computer science, management), EDUCATION (early childhood, elementary, health/physical, secondary), ENGLISH (English), HEALTH SCIENCES (nursing), MATH AND SCIENCES (biology), SOCIAL SCIENCES (criminal justice, economics, government/political science, history, psychology, sociology). Most degrees are granted in business, nursing, education, and humanities.

Required: The general education requirement includes courses in English and American government.

Special: An interdisciplinary studies degree, student-designed majors, and cooperative education programs are offered.

Honors: There are chapters of 2 honor societies on campus.

Admissions: The SAT scores of those who enrolled in the 1981–82 freshman class were as follows: Verbal—88% below 500, 8% between 500 and 599, 4% between 600 and 700, and 0% above 700; Math —84% below 500, 10% between 500 and 599, 5% between 600 and 700, and 1% above 700. A diploma from an accredited high school or a GED diploma is required. The campus has an open admissions policy.

Procedure: The SAT or ACT is required. New students are admitted each semester. Application deadlines are August 1 (fall), December 15 (spring), and June 1 (summer). Notification is on a rolling basis. There is a $15 application fee.

Special: Early decision and early admissions plans are availble. AP and CLEP credit is granted.

Transfer: For fall 1981, 452 transfer students applied, 363 were accepted, and 325 enrolled. A 2.0 GPA is necessary. Grades of C or better transfer. One academic year (30 semester hours) must be completed in residence; 120 credits are required to earn a bachelor's degree in most areas. Deadlines are the same as those for freshman applicants.

Visiting: There are regularly scheduled orientations for prospective students. Campus tours with student guides can be arranged. Visitors may sit in on classes. The admissions office should be contacted for arrangements.

Financial Aid: About 60% of the students receive financial aid through the university; 45% work part-time on campus. Federal programs, such as NDSL and BEOG/SEOG, commercial loans, state funds, campus employment (including CWS), and 10 freshman scholarships are available. There are also 25 athletic scholarships. Federal loan funds total $50,000. The average scholarship is $500, the maximum $850; the average loan is $1000, the maximum $1500; the average work contract is $1000, the maximum $2500. The university is a member of CSS; the FFS or FAF is required and should be submitted by April 1.

Foreign Students: About 2% of the full-time students are from foreign countries. The university offers these students special organizations.

Admissions: A minimum score of 550 on the TOEFL is required; the University of Michigan Language Test is also acceptable. Students must also take the SAT or the ACT.

Procedure: Application deadlines are June 1 (fall), October 1 (spring), and March 1 (summer). Students must present proof of funds adequate to cover 1 year of study. Health insurance is available through the university for a fee.

Admissions Contact: Kevin C. Smith, Director of Admissions.

UNIVERSITY OF SOUTH CAROLINA/ COASTAL CAROLINA COLLEGE
E-3

Conway, South Carolina 29526   (803) 347-3161

F/T: 846M, 869W   Faculty: 109; IIB, +$
P/T: 351M, 313W   Ph.D.'s: 56%
Grad: none   S/F Ratio: 19 to 1
Year: sems, ss   Tuition: $850 ($1840)
Appl: Aug. 15   R and B: $1950
956 applied   909 accepted   784 enrolled
SAT: 400V 410M   *LESS COMPETITIVE*

University of South Carolina/Coastal Carolina College offers undergraduate degrees in the liberal arts and sciences, education, and business. The library contains 80,000 volumes and 11,000 microfilm items, and subscribes to 875 periodicals.

Environment: The 185-acre campus is located in a small town 9 miles from Myrtle Beach. The 7 major buildings include a gymnasium, a fine arts building, and a student union. The college also has a 17,500-acre research facility used for marine biology. There are no residence halls (the figure above indicates the school's estimate of the cost of living off campus).

Student Life: About 91% of the students come from South Carolina. Seventy percent live at home; all students live off campus. About 10% of the students are minority-group members. Students may keep cars on campus.

Organizations: Extracurricular activities include student government, special-interest and service clubs, religious organizations for Protestant students, and music and drama groups. The college schedules one or 2 social or cultural events each week, including concerts, dances, the Spring Arts Festival and International Day. Ten percent of the men belong to the 3 fraternities, and 2% of the women belong to 1 sorority.

Sports: The college fields 5 intercollegiate teams for men and 4 for women. There are 2 intramural sports for men and 2 for women.

Handicapped: Special facilities for handicapped students include wheelchair ramps, special parking, elevators, specially equipped rest rooms, and lowered drinking fountains and telephones. Special class scheduling also is available.

Graduates: Fifty-two percent of the freshmen drop out, and 12% remain to graduate. Forty percent of the graduates pursue advanced degrees and 21% begin business careers.

Services: The following services are offered free of charge to students: placement, career counseling, tutoring, remedial instruction, and psychological counseling. Health care is available for a fee.

Programs of Study: The college confers the B.A., B.S., and B.I.S. degrees. Associate degrees also are available. Bachelor's degrees are offered in the following subjects: BUSINESS (accounting, business administration, finance, management, marketing, real estate/insurance), EDUCATION (early childhood, elementary, health/physical, secondary), ENGLISH (English), FINE AND PERFORMING ARTS (art education, music education), MATH AND SCIENCES (biology, mathematics, oceanography), PHILOSOPHY (philosophy), PREPROFESSIONAL (allied health services, dentistry, engineering, law, medicine, pharmacy), SOCIAL SCIENCES (government/political science, history, psychology). Twenty percent of the degrees are conferred in business and 18% in education.

Required: All students must take English and complete general education requirements in their major. They must maintain a GPA of 2.0 or better to graduate.

Special: Students may design their own majors or pursue a general studies degree through the Interdisciplinary Studies Program. Study abroad is possible.

Honors: Two honor societies are represented on campus.

Admissions: About 95% of those who applied for the 1981-82 freshman class were accepted. The SAT scores of those who enrolled were as follows: Verbal—91% below 500, 7% between 500 and 599, 2% between 600 and 700, and 0% above 700; Math—89% below 500, 8% between 500 and 599, 3% between 600 and 700, and 0% above 700. Applicants must present a high school diploma or GED and rank in the top 60% of their graduating class. Admissions officers also consider recommendations by high school officials, impressions made during an interview, and evidence of special talents.

Procedure: The SAT or ACT is required. An interview is recommended. New students are admitted each semester; the application deadlines are August 15 (fall) and December 1 (spring). Notification is on a rolling basis. There is a $15 application fee.

Special: There is a deferred admissions plan. AP and CLEP credit is accepted.

Transfer: For fall 1981, 285 transfer students applied, 280 were accepted, and 275 enrolled. A 2.0 GPA is necessary. Grades of C or better transfer. Students must complete, at the college, 30 of the 120 credits required to earn a bachelor's degree. Application deadlines are August 15 (fall) and December 1 (spring). There is no deadline for summer entry.

Visiting: Guides are provided for informal visits by prospective students, and visitors may sit in on classes. Visits should be arranged, preferably for the fall or spring, with the admissions office.

Financial Aid: About 60% of the students receive financial aid. About 10% work part-time on campus. Eighteen percent of the students receive scholarships; 25 academic and 35 athletic scholarships are available. Federal loan funds total $58,000; state loan funds total $7500. CWS jobs also are available. For freshmen, the average loan is $150 and the maximum $300, the average scholarship is $355 and the maximum $500, the average work contract is $1000 and the maximum $2000. Aid candidates should file the FAF or, preferably, the FFS. The college is a member of CSS. The aid application deadline is March 1.

Foreign Students: Fewer than 1% of the full-time students are from foreign countries. The university offers these students special counseling and special organizations.

Admissions: A minimum score of 500 on the TOEFL is required. Students must also take the SAT and achieve scores of at least 400 (Verbal) and 410 (Math).

Procedure: Application deadlines are June 1 (fall) and October 1 (spring). Students must present proof of funds adequate to cover 1 year. Health insurance is required and is available through the college.

Admissions Contact: Marsh H. Myers, Jr., Director of Admissions and Registration.

VOORHEES COLLEGE
C-4

Denmark, South Carolina 29042   (803) 793-3351

F/T: 207M, 396W   Faculty: 57; IIB, −−$
P/T: 7M, 15W   Ph.D.'s: 35%
Grad: none   S/F Ratio: 14 to 1
Year: sems, ss   Tuition: $2329
Appl: open   R and B: $1583-1862
691 applied   432 accepted   230 enrolled
SAT or ACT: required   *NONCOMPETITIVE*

Voorhees College is a coeducational liberal arts institution related to the Protestant Episcopal Church. It was founded in 1897 as a junior college for blacks and became a 4-year institution in 1962. The library contains 90,000 volumes and 20,000 microfilm items, and subscribes to 500 periodicals.

Environment: The 350-acre campus is located in the southern part of the state, about a mile from the center of Denmark (population 3500) and about 50 miles from Columbia. Among the more than 25 campus buildings are 5 dormitories accommodating 250 men and 380 women.

Student Life: About four-fifths of the students are from the South, and most of the remainder are from Middle Atlantic states. More than 90% of the students live on campus in single-sex dorms. Most of the students are black and many are members of the supporting church.

Organizations: There are 5 fraternities to which 34% of the men belong, and 5 sororities, to which 30% of the women belong. A variety of activities is available, including publications and special-interest clubs.

Sports: The college competes intercollegiately in 4 sports. Intramural sports are also offered.

Handicapped: There are no special facilities for the physically handicapped. There are no students currently enrolled with visual or hearing impairments.

Graduates: The freshman dropout rate is 10%. Three percent pursue graduate study after graduation; 19% pursue careers in business and industry.

Services: Students receive the following services free of charge: placement, career counseling, tutoring, remedial instruction, and psychological counseling.

Programs of Study: The college confers the B.A., and B.S. degrees. Associate degrees are also awarded. Bachelor's degrees are offered in the following subjects: BUSINESS (business administration, business education, office administration), EDUCATION (elementary), EN-

824 SOUTH CAROLINA

GLISH (English), MATH AND SCIENCES (biology, mathematics), PHILOSOPHY (humanities), SOCIAL SCIENCES (history, political science, sociology). Thirty percent of all degrees are conferred in business, 29% in social sciences, and 23% in education.

Honors: Two national honor societies have chapters on campus.

Admissions: Sixty-three percent of those who applied were accepted for the 1981–82 freshman class. Candidates must be high school graduates or GED recipients and have completed 18 units. Applicants should also be in the middle third of their graduating class and have a minimum 2.0 average. The following factors also enter into the admissions decision: impressions made during an interview, ability to finance college education, recommendations from school officials, and advanced placement or honors courses.

Procedure: The SAT or ACT is required; ATs in areas of the student's interests are recommended. All credentials, together with a $10 application fee, must be submitted before the beginning of classes. An open admissions policy is followed.

Special: AP credit is accepted.

Transfer: Transfer students are accepted each term. A minimum 2.0 GPA is necessary; D grades do not transfer. There is a 1-year residency requirement. Transfers must complete, at the college, 30 of the 122 semester hours of credit required for the bachelor's degree.

Visiting: Orientation is held immediately preceding the registration period. Informal campus visits can be arranged with the admissions office. Visitors may sit in on classes and remain overnight on campus.

Financial Aid: Ninety-eight percent of all students receive some form of financial aid. Sources include scholarships, NDSL, SEOG, and CWS. The FAF is required. Aid applications should be received by March 1.

Foreign Students: Voorhees admits foreign applications who are deemed best qualified to profit from its educational programs.

Admissions: Foreign students must achieve a minimum score of 500 on the TOEFL. The SAT is required. An official transcript and 2 letters of recommendation are also necessary.

Procedure: Application deadlines are open. A current health certificate must be presented. A completed "Declaration and Certificate of Finances" form signed by the student's sponsor is also required. Foreign students are expected to have funds adequate to cover college expenses, periods during which college is not in session, and return travel.

Admissions Contact: Iris D. Bomar, Director, Admissions and Records.

WINTHROP COLLEGE   C–1
Rock Hill, South Carolina 29733   (803) 323-2191

F/T: 1064M, 2552W   Faculty: 253; IIA, +$
P/T: 177M, 286W   Ph.D.'s: 49%
Grad: 227M, 654W   S/F Ratio: 14 to 1
Year: sems, ss   Tuition: $1012 ($1800)
Appl: open   R and B: $1372
1804 applied   1445 accepted   909 enrolled
SAT or ACT: required   LESS COMPETITIVE

Winthrop College is a state-controlled college of liberal arts. The library contains 289,306 volumes and 537,719 microfilm items, and subscribes to 3064 periodicals.

Environment: The 85-acre campus is located in a suburban area 20 miles from Charlotte, North Carolina, and 70 miles from Columbia. It has 34 buildings, the oldest of which, Tillman Building, is listed in the *National Register of Historic Places*. A multipurpose field house is presently under construction. The 9 dormitories accommodate 2664 students. The college also sponsors on-campus apartments and married student housing.

Student Life: About 84% of the students are from South Carolina. About 58% of the students live on campus. About 17% are minority-group members. College-sponsored housing is both coed and single-sex; there are visiting privileges in single-sex dorms. Students may keep cars on campus.

Organizations: There are 7 sororities and 6 fraternities on campus. The college features recreational facilities—including a golf course, soccer and baseball fields, lake for fishing, and lodge for parties—on a 400-acre former farm.

Sports: The college fields 4 intercollegiate teams for men and 4 for women. There are 15 intramural sports for men and 14 for women.

Handicapped: The campus is completely accessible to handicapped students. Special facilities include wheelchair ramps, parking areas, and elevators. Special class scheduling and counselors are also available.

Services: Students receive the following services free of charge: placement, career and psychological counseling, and health care. Tutoring is available for a fee.

Programs of Study: The college confers the B.A., B.Mus., B.Mus.Ed., B.S., B.S.W., and B.V.A. degrees. Master's and specialist degrees are also awarded. Bachelor's degrees are offered in the following subjects: BUSINESS (business administration, business education), EDUCATION (distributive, early childhood, elementary, health/physical, special), ENGLISH (communications, English, speech), FINE AND PERFORMING ARTS (art, music, music education, visual art), HEALTH SCIENCES (medical technology), LANGUAGES (French, Spanish), MATH AND SCIENCES (biology, chemistry, mathematics), PHILOSOPHY (philosophy/religion), PREPROFESSIONAL (consumer technology, dietetics, family and child development, fashion merchandising, food and nutrition, home economics, interior design, social work), SOCIAL SCIENCES (economics, government and public service, history, political science, psychology, sociology). About 40% of the degrees are conferred in education, 22% in business, 10% in home economics, and 7% in social sciences.

Required: All students must take courses in basic communications, foreign languages or mathematics, humanities, sciences, and social sciences.

Honors: Seventeen honor societies have chapters on campus. General and departmental honors programs are offered.

Admissions: About 80% of those who applied for the 1981–82 freshman class were accepted. The major factors determining admission are results of entrance examinations, class rank, and recommendations by school officials. Outstanding high school students who have completed the 11th grade with senior-level English may apply for admission by examination.

Procedure: The SAT or ACT is required; the SAT is preferred. Application deadlines are open; notification is on a rolling basis. There is a $15 application fee.

Special: CLEP, AP, and AT credit is available.

Transfer: For fall 1981, 508 transfer students applied and 368 were accepted. A 2.0 GPA is required. Grades of C or better transfer. Students must complete 30 semester hours in residence to receive a degree; a minimum of 122 credits is required for the bachelor's degree. Application deadlines are open.

Visiting: There are regularly scheduled orientations for prospective students. Guides are available for informal campus tours. Visitors may sit in on classes. Visits are best scheduled on weekdays. The admissions office should be contacted for arrangements.

Financial Aid: About 49% of the students receive financial aid from the college; 26% work part-time on campus. The average scholarship for freshmen is $900; average BEOG award is $976; average NDSL is $800; average CWS earnings are $700. The college is a member of the CSS and requires the FAF from financial aid applicants. The deadline for financial aid applications is February 1.

Foreign Students: One percent of the full-time students are from foreign countries. The college offers these students special counseling and special organizations.

Admissions: A minimum score of 530 on the TOEFL is necessary; no college entrance exams are required.

Procedure: Application deadlines are August 1 (fall) and December 1 (spring). Students must submit the college's health form signed by a physician and must present proof of funds adequate to cover 1 year of study. Health insurance is available through the college; there is no fee for full-time students.

Admissions Contact: James R. McCammon, Director of Admissions.

WOFFORD COLLEGE   B–1
Spartanburg, South Carolina 29301   (803) 585-4821

F/T: 725M, 250W   Faculty: 63; IIB, +$
P/T: 21M, 16W   Ph.D.'s: 86%
Grad: none   S/F Ratio: 16 to 1
Year: 4-1-4, ss   Tuition: $4005
Appl: open   R and B: $2040
824 applied   577 accepted   233 enrolled
SAT(mean): 486V 521M   COMPETITIVE

Wofford College is a private liberal arts college associated with the Methodist Church. The library contains 159,448 volumes and 15,041 microfilm items, and subscribes to 18,088 periodicals.

Environment: The 90-acre campus, located in an urban area, is 70 miles from Charlotte. A student life center and gymnasium are recent additions to the modern campus. About 782 students are housed in the 5 dormitories.

Student Life: About 73% of the students come from South Carolina; 73% of entering freshmen come from public schools. About 77% of the students live on campus. Seventy-six percent are Protestant; 7% are Catholic. About 72% are not members of the supporting church. Nine percent of the students are minority-group members. Campus housing is both single-sex and coed. There are visiting privileges in single-sex dorms. Students may keep cars on campus.

Organizations: Approximately 35% of the men belong to the 7 national fraternities; 17% of the women belong to 2 national sororities. Extracurricular activities include a debate group, publications, an active student union, religious organizations, and a glee club.

Sports: The college fields 8 intercollegiate teams for men and 4 for women. There are 6 intramural sports for men and 6 for women.

Handicapped: About 80% of the campus is accessible to wheelchair-bound students. Wheelchair ramps, special parking, and elevators are provided; special class scheduling is also available.

Graduates: The freshman dropout rate is 22%; 85% remain to graduate. About 45% of the graduates pursue advanced study: 8% enter medical school, 5% law school, and 2% dental school; 15% pursue careers in business and industry.

Services: The following services are offered free of charge to students: placement, career counseling, health care, tutoring, and psychological counseling.

Programs of Study: The college confers the B.A. or B.S. degree in the following subjects: BUSINESS (accounting), ENGLISH (English, literature), LANGUAGES (French, German, Spanish), MATH AND SCIENCES (biology, chemistry, mathematics, physics), PHILOSOPHY (humanities, philosophy, religion), PREPROFESSIONAL (business and management, dentistry, education, engineering, law, medicine, ministry, pharmacy, veterinary), SOCIAL SCIENCES (economics, government/political science, history, psychology, sociology). Of the degrees conferred, 50% are in social sciences and 20% in math and sciences.

Required: All students must take English composition and literature, a foreign language or literature, history, natural science, philosophy, religion, fine arts, and physical education.

Special: It is possible to earn a combined B.A.-B.S. degree in any major. Student-designed majors are permitted. Third year students may participate in the junior year abroad program. A combined medical program is offered with South Carolina Medical College.

Honors: All departments offer honors programs. Eight national honor societies have chapters on campus.

Admissions: Of those who applied for the 1981–82 freshman class, 70% were accepted. The SAT scores of those who enrolled were as follows: Verbal—59% below 500, 28% between 500 and 599, 11% between 600 and 700, and 2% above 700; Math—40% below 500, 42% between 500 and 599, 16% between 600 and 700, and 2% above 700. Candidates should have completed 16 units, have a minimum grade average of B, and rank in the top 50% of their class. Other factors considered by the college are: advanced placement or honors courses, leadership record, extracurricular activities record, recommendations by school officials, and impressions made during an interview. The admissions office welcomes interviews with applicants from nontraditional situations.

Procedure: The SAT or ACT is required, and must be taken between March of the junior year and January of the senior year. The English Composition AT and 1 other AT must be taken before enrollment for placement purposes. Deadlines are open. There is a rolling admission plan. Freshmen may also be admitted at midyear and in the summer. The application fee is $15.

Special: Deferred admission is possible. The college subscribes to the CRDA. CLEP, AP, and CPT credit is accepted.

Transfer: For fall 1981, 98 transfer students applied, 65 were accepted, and 41 enrolled. Transfers are considered for all classes except the senior year. Applicants must have an average of C, satisfactory scores on the SAT or ACT, and be in good standing at the previous school. Grades of C or better transfer. Students must complete the final 30 hours at the college to graduate. Acceptance is on a rolling admissions basis with no formal deadlines.

Visiting: Orientation sessions for prospective students are held in July and August. Guides for informal visits are available weekdays and Saturday mornings. Arrangements for visits should be made with the admissions office. Visitors may sit in on classes and stay overnight at the school.

Financial Aid: Approximately 32% of the students receive some form of financial aid. About 20% work part-time on campus. Scholarships for freshmen total $73,000; loan funds total $45,000. The average aid granted to freshmen is $1300. The college is a member of the CSS and requires the FAF. Applications for aid should be submitted by March 1.

Foreign Students: Fewer than 1% of the full-time students are from foreign countries. Special counseling is available for these students.

Admissions: A minimum score of 550 on the TOEFL is necessary; no college entrance exams are required.

Procedure: The college uses a rolling admissions policy for foreign students. Students must complete the college's medical questionnaire and must present proof of adequate funds as outlined in the college's financial questionnaire. Health insurance is available through the college for a fee.

Admissions Contact: Charles H. Gray, Director of Admissions.

SOUTH DAKOTA

AUGUSTANA COLLEGE   F-3
Sioux Falls, South Dakota 57197   (605) 336-5516

F/T: 605M, 1061W
P/T: 150M, 223W
Grad: 11M, 38W
Year: 4-1-4, ss
Appl: open
953 applied   742 accepted   471 enrolled
SAT: 498V 538M   ACT: 23   COMPETITIVE +
Faculty: 123; IIA, –$
Ph.D.'s: 58%
S/F Ratio: 15 to 1
Tuition: $4680
R and B: $1700

Augustana College, founded in 1860, is affiliated with the American Lutheran Church. It is a private liberal arts college. Its library contains 125,000 volumes and subscribes to 1000 periodicals. Special collections include the Dakota Historical Collection, the Stavig Theological Collection, and the Norwegian Collection.

Environment: The 100-acre campus is located in the city of Sioux Falls. Six residence halls accommodate 1382 students.

Student Life: About 55% of the students are from out of state. Seventy-five percent live on campus. Eleven percent are Catholic, 59% belong to the Lutheran Church, 28% to other Protestant denominations; and 2% claim no affiliation. Six percent of the students are minority-group members. College housing is both single-sex and coed. There are visiting privileges in single-sex housing. Students may keep cars on campus. Day-care services are available to all students, faculty, and staff for a fee.

Organizations: There are 3 fraternities and 3 sororities. Forty percent of men and 35% of women belong. The student association also sponsors social and cultural activities.

Sports: The college competes in 9 intercollegiate sports for men and 7 for women; and offers 8 intramural programs for men, 7 for women.

Handicapped: About 50% of the campus is accessible to the physically handicapped. Special facilities include wheelchair ramps, parking areas, and elevators.

Graduates: Twenty-five percent of the freshmen drop out during their first year; 58% remain to graduate. Of those, 34% continue their education; 5% enter medical schools, 3% dental schools, and 6% law schools. Another 14% pursue careers in business and industry.

Services: Free placement, career counseling, psychological counseling, health care, tutoring, and remedial instruction are offered.

Programs of Study: The college confers the B.A. degree. It also offers master's programs. Bachelor's degrees are offered in the following subjects: BUSINESS (accounting, business administration, computer science, economic aviation administration, health and hospital administration), EDUCATION (early childhood, elementary, health/physical, secondary, special), ENGLISH (English, journalism, literature, speech), FINE AND PERFORMING ARTS (art, art education, music, music education, theater/dramatics), HEALTH SCIENCES (medical technology, nursing), LANGUAGES (French, German, Spanish), MATH AND SCIENCES (biochemistry, biology, chemistry, ecology/environmental science, mathematics, physics), PHILOSO-

826 SOUTH DAKOTA

PHY (philosophy, religion), PREPROFESSIONAL (architecture, dentistry, engineering, law, medicine, ministry, pharmacy, social work, veterinary), SOCIAL SCIENCES (economics, geography, government/political science, history, international relations, psychology, social sciences, sociology). About 25% of the degrees granted are in education, and 17% are in health sciences.

Required: Courses in English, religion, philosophy, literature, speech, history, physical education, laboratory science, and social sciences are required.

Special: The college offers study abroad, combination degrees in engineering, and a B.G.S. degree.

Honors: There are 6 honor societies represented on campus.

Admissions: About 78% of those who applied were accepted for the 1981–82 freshman class. The ACT scores of those who enrolled in a recent freshman class were as follows: 26% scored between 20 and 23, 14% between 24 and 26, 13% between 27 and 28, and 16% above 28. Candidates should have completed 16 Carnegie units and have at least a C average. Recommendations and interview impressions are also strongly considered.

Procedure: The ACT or SAT should be taken by April of the senior year. Application deadlines are open. Freshmen are admitted all terms. Notification is on a rolling basis. There is a $15 application fee.

Special: Deferred admissions are available. AP and CLEP credit is given.

Transfer: For fall 1981, 129 students applied, 115 were accepted, and 69 enrolled. The requirements are the same as for freshmen. D grades transfer. Transfers must complete, at the college, 30 semester hours of the 130 needed for a bachelor's degree. Applications should be filed by September 1 (fall), February 1 (spring), and June 1 (summer).

Visiting: Weekday tours of the campus can be arranged through the office of admissions. Visitors may sit in on classes and stay overnight at the school.

Financial Aid: About 80% of the students receive financial aid. Forty-five percent work part-time on campus. Average aid to freshmen from all sources is $4300. NDSL and other loans are available; CWS is also offered. The college is a member of CSS. The FAF or FFS should be filed. Application deadlines are open.

Foreign Students: One percent of the full-time students come from foreign countries. The college offers these students an intensive English course and special organizations.

Admissions: Foreign students must score 550 on the TOEFL. No college entrance examination is required.

Procedure: The application deadline is July 1 (fall). Foreign students must present doctor's certification of good health. They must also present proof of funds adequate to cover 1 year of study. They must carry health insurance, which is available through the college for a fee.

Admissions Contact: Dean A. Schueler, Director of Admissions.

BLACK HILLS STATE COLLEGE A-2
Spearfish, South Dakota 57783   (605) 642-6343

F/T: 866M, 1091W Faculty: n/av; IIA, –$
P/T: 89M, 127W Ph.D.'s: 46%
Grad: n/av   S/F Ratio: 21 to 1
Year: sems, ss Tuition: $984 ($1787)
Appl: open   R and B: $1337
784 applied 693 accepted 582 enrolled
ACT: 21   LESS COMPETITIVE

Black Hills State College, founded in 1883, is a state-supported college of education and liberal arts. The college trains its students in teacher education, business, liberal arts, and preprofessional areas. Its library contains 150,000 volumes and 25,000 microfilm items, and subscribes to 695 periodicals. It has computer access to 7.5 million volumes.

Environment: The 123-acre campus is located in a rural setting 50 miles from Rapid City, in the Black Hills of South Dakota. Among the 10 buildings are 5 dormitories that house 654 students.

Student Life: About 90% of the students are from South Dakota; 30% live on campus. Eight percent of the students are minority-group members. College housing is both single-sex and coed. There are visiting privileges in single-sex housing. Students may keep cars on campus.

Organizations: There are 2 national fraternities and 2 national sororities on campus to which 10% of the students belong. The college sponsors 78 extracurricular activities and groups. The student senate, the ski club, the science club, the rodeo club, and the outdoor club are the most active.

Sports: The college competes in 8 intercollegiate sports for men and 6 for women. Intramural programs include 13 sports for men and 11 for women.

Handicapped: About 70% of the campus is accessible to physically handicapped students. Special facilities include wheelchair ramps, parking areas, elevators, and lowered telephones. Special class scheduling is possible.

Graduates: About 16% of the freshmen drop out during the first year; 80% remain to graduate. About 30% of graduates continue their studies: 2% enter medical school, 2% dental school, and 2% law school. Another 35% pursue careers in business and industry.

Services: Free tutoring, remedial instruction, psychological counseling, and career counseling are offered to all students. Free health care and placement services are also available.

Programs of Study: The college confers the B.A., B.S., and B.S.Ed. degrees. Associate and master's programs are also offered. Bachelor's degrees are offered in the following subjects: AREA STUDIES (American), BUSINESS (accounting, business administration, business education, computer science, management, travel industries management), EDUCATION (adult, early childhood, elementary, health/physical, industrial, secondary, special), ENGLISH (English, journalism, literature, speech), FINE AND PERFORMING ARTS (art, art education, music, music education, film/photography, radio/TV, theater/dramatics), HEALTH SCIENCES (physical therapy), LANGUAGES (Spanish), MATH AND SCIENCES (biology, chemistry, earth science, mathematics, physical sciences, physics), PREPROFESSIONAL (agriculture, architecture, chiropractic, dental hygiene, dentistry, engineering, forestry, law, medical technology, medicine, mortuary science, occupational therapy, optometry, pharmacy, veterinary, wildlife management), SOCIAL SCIENCES (criminal justice, economics, government/political science, history, psychology, social sciences, sociology).

Required: All students must take the basic curriculum courses and 4 hours of physical education.

Special: The college has Indian Education programs, teacher corps programs, and student teacher internships.

Honors: There are 11 honor societies represented on campus. All divisions have honors programs.

Admissions: About 88% of those who applied for the 1981–82 freshman class were accepted. The ACT scores of those who enrolled were as follows: 53% scored below 21, 22% between 21 and 23, 13% between 24 and 25, 7% between 26 and 28, and 5% above 28. Candidates should have completed 15 Carnegie units and rank in the upper two-thirds of their graduating class. There are higher requirements for out-of-state students.

Procedure: The SAT or ACT is required and should be taken by July. The deadlines for applications are open. Freshmen are admitted at all sessions. Admissions are on a rolling basis. There is a $15 application fee.

Special: Early decision, and early and deferred admissions plans are available. CLEP credit is given.

Transfer: For fall 1981, 349 students applied, 284 were accepted, and 257 enrolled. A 2.0 GPA with 65 semester hours is required; a lower GPA is allowed with fewer credits. D grades transfer. Transfers are accepted for all classes, but at least 32 hours must be spent at the college, out of the 128 needed to earn a bachelor's degree. Application deadlines are the same as for freshmen.

Visiting: Tours of the campus while school is in session can be arranged through the admissions office. Visitors can sit in on classes and stay overnight at the school.

Financial Aid: About 80% of the students receive some form of financial assistance. Seventeen percent work part-time on campus. Average aid to freshmen from all sources is $1800. The college is a member of CSS. The FFS is required. The deadlines for application are May 1 (fall), December 1 (spring), and April 1 (summer).

Foreign Students: Two percent of the full-time students come from foreign countries. The college offers these students a full tutoring program in English and other subjects, special counseling, and special organizations.

Admissions: Foreign students must score 490 on the TOEFL, and 55 on the University of Michigan Language Test. No college entrance examination is required.

Procedure: Application deadlines are two months prior to registration. Foreign students must complete the college's own medical history form. They must also present proof of funds adequate to cover 1 academic year.

Admissions Contact: Gene Bauer, Director of Admissions.

DAKOTA STATE COLLEGE
Madison, South Dakota 57042

E–3
(605) 256-3551

F/T: 426M, 533W
P/T: 55M, 93W
Grad: none
Year: sems, ss
Appl: open
394 applied   383 accepted   318 enrolled
ACT: 18   LESS COMPETITIVE

Faculty: 53; IIB, av$
Ph.D.'s: 27%
S/F Ratio: 14 to 1
Tuition: $949 ($1742)
R and B: $1390

Founded in 1881, the college is devoted to the training of public school teachers. It also offers programs in business administration and numerous two-year career programs. There is also an extension school. The library contains 77,428 volumes and 3750 microfilm items, and subscribes to 644 periodicals.

Environment: The 25-acre campus is in a rural setting 50 miles from Sioux Falls. Dormitories accommodate about 650 students in single and double rooms.

Student Life: Nearly all of the students come from South Dakota; 6% are from other states. About 50% of the students live on campus. About 3% of the students are minority-group members. College housing is both single-sex and coed. There are visiting privileges in single-sex housing. Students may keep cars on campus.

Organizations: There are no fraternities or sororities, but an active student board is concerned with social life on campus.

Sports: The college competes on the intercollegiate level in 7 sports for men and 7 for women. There are 3 intramural sports for both men and women.

Handicapped: Fifty percent of the campus is accessible to handicapped students, and facilities for them include elevators and specially equipped rest rooms.

Graduates: By the end of the freshman year approximately 20% of the students drop out, while 67% remain to graduate. About 6% of the graduates pursue graduate study; 1% go to law school. Thirty-two percent enter careers in business and industry.

Services: Placement and health care are offered to students on a fee basis.

Programs of Study: All programs lead to the B.S. and B.S.Ed. degrees. Associate degrees are also granted. Bachelor's degrees are offered in the following subjects: BUSINESS (business administration, business education), EDUCATION (elementary, health/physical, secondary), ENGLISH (English, speech), FINE AND PERFORMING ARTS (art education, music, music education, theater/dramatics), HEALTH SCIENCES (medical records administration), MATH AND SCIENCES (biology, chemistry, mathematics, physical sciences), SOCIAL SCIENCES (history, social sciences). Forty-five percent of all degrees are in business; 29% are in education; and 17% are in social sciences.

Special: Two-year programs are offered in secretarial work, health claims technology, respiratory therapy, accounting, data processing, medical records technology, small business management, and travel specialist.

Honors: Honor societies on campus include Delta Nu Delta and Kappa Sigma Iota.

Admissions: About 97% of the students who applied for admission to the college were accepted for the 1981–82 school year. Applicants must be in the upper two-thirds of their graduating class; requirements for out-of-state students are higher.

Procedure: Students are required to take the ACT. There are no application deadlines. There is a rolling admissions plan. Freshmen are admitted all sessions. The application fee is $15.

Special: CLEP and general subject exams are accepted.

Transfer: For fall 1981, 157 applications were received, 147 were accepted, and 123 students enrolled. Transfers are accepted for all classes. Students must be in good standing and eligible to return to their previous college. They must have a GPA of 2.0 and an ACT score of 18. D grades transfer. Students must complete at least 32 hours, at the college, out of the 128 needed to receive a bachelor's degree. Transfer application deadlines are open.

Visiting: Regularly scheduled orientations are presented for prospective students. Informal visits can be arranged on weekdays through the admissions office. Visitors can sit in on classes and stay overnight at the school.

SOUTH DAKOTA   827

Financial Aid: About 72% of all students receive financial aid. Twenty-two percent work part-time on campus. Average aid to freshmen from all sources is $2500. A fund is available for freshman scholarships each year, and part-time work is possible. The college is a member of CSS. The FFS is required. Application deadlines are open.

Foreign Students: Fewer than 1% of the full-time students come from foreign countries. The college offers these students an intensive English course, special counseling, and special organizations.

Admissions: Foreign students must score 500 on the TOEFL. They can also take the University of Michigan Language Test. They must take the college's own entrance examination.

Procedure: The application deadlines are May (fall), October (spring), and March (summer). Foreign students must present proof of funds adequate to cover 1 year of study.

Admissions Contact: Kathy Schneider, Director of Admissions.

DAKOTA WESLEYAN UNIVERSITY
Mitchell, South Dakota 57301

E–3
(605) 996-5510

F/T: 206M, 298W
P/T: 35M, 25W
Grad: none
Year: 4-1-4, ss
Appl: open
434 applied   335 accepted   202 enrolled
ACT: 19   COMPETITIVE

Faculty: 37; IIB, av$
Ph.D.'s: 40%
S/F Ratio: 12 to 1
Tuition: $3165
R and B: $1700

Dakota Wesleyan University is a privately endowed liberal arts institution affiliated with the United Methodist Church. Its library contains 85,000 volumes, and subscribes to 300 periodicals.

Environment: The 40-acre campus is located in the city of Mitchell, 71 miles from Sioux Falls. The residence halls accommodate 500 students.

Student Life: About 75% of the students are from South Dakota; 95% of the entering freshmen come from public schools. About 90% of the students live on campus. Women's curfew hours are set by each residence hall. Fifty-five percent of the students are Catholic, 35% Protestant, and 15% belong to other denominations. Twelve percent are minority-group members. University housing is both single-sex and coed. There are visiting privileges in single-sex housing. Students may keep cars on campus. Day-care services are available to full-time students, faculty, and staff.

Organizations: There are no fraternities or sororities on campus. Social groups and the student government sponsor various activities.

Sports: The college competes in 8 intercollegiate sports for men and 7 for women. It offers 10 intramural programs for both men and women.

Handicapped: About 50% of the campus is accessible to handicapped students. There are some special facilities available.

Graduates: Seven percent of the freshmen drop out during their first year; 46% remain to graduate. Of those, 10% continue their education; 5% enter medical school and 4% law school. Thirty-five percent pursue careers in business and industry.

Services: Free tutoring, remedial instruction, career and psychological counseling, job placement, and health care are available to all students. Health care, psychological counseling, and remedial instruction are also available on a fee basis.

Programs of Study: The university confers the B.A. and B.M.E. degrees. Associate degrees are also offered. Bachelor's degrees are offered in the following subjects: AREA STUDIES (American), BUSINESS (accounting, business administration, business education, computer science), EDUCATION (early childhood, elementary, health/physical, secondary), ENGLISH (English, journalism, literature, speech), FINE AND PERFORMING ARTS (art, art education, music, music education, radio/TV, theater/dramatics), HEALTH SCIENCES (medical technology), LANGUAGES (German, Spanish), MATH AND SCIENCES (biology, chemistry, mathematics, natural sciences, physics), PHILOSOPHY (philosophy, religion), PREPROFESSIONAL (engineering, law, medicine, ministry, social work), SOCIAL SCIENCES (economics, government/political science, history, international relations, psychology, sociology). About 33% of the degrees are conferred in the social sciences and 16% in education.

Required: Students must take 11½ units of General Education.

Special: Independent study, pass/fail grading, and student-designed majors are available. A 3-1 program in law, and a 3-2 program in engineering can be arranged with other schools.

828 SOUTH DAKOTA

Honors: There are 5 national honor societies represented on campus.

Admissions: About 77% of those who applied were accepted for the 1981-82 freshman class. The SAT scores of those who enrolled were as follows: Verbal—27% scored below 500, 46% between 500 and 599, 22% between 600 and 700, and 5% above 700; Math—30% scored below 500, 59% between 500 and 599, 4% between 600 and 700, and 7% above 700. On the ACT, 43% scored below 21, 27% between 21 and 23, 15% between 24 and 25, 11% between 26 and 28, and 4% above 28. Candidates should have completed high school and rank in the upper half of their graduating class.

Procedure: The ACT is required. The application deadlines are open. Admissions are on a rolling basis. Freshmen are admitted all sessions. A $10 fee is required.

Special: CLEP and AP exams are offered credit.

Transfer: For fall 1981, 5 students applied, 5 were accepted, and 2 enrolled. A 2.0 GPA is required. Transfers must complete, at the university, 4 units of the 34 needed for a bachelor's degree. There are no deadlines for applications.

Visiting: Tours of the campus can be arranged through the admissions office. Visitors can sit in on classes and stay overnight at the school.

Financial Aid: About 80% of all students receive some form of aid. Thirty-six percent work part-time on campus. Average aid to freshmen from all sources is $1950. Scholarships, loans, and work-study programs are available to qualified students. The college is a member of CSS. The FFS is required. The suggested filing dates for applications are March 1 (fall), December 1 (winter), January 1 (spring), and May 1 (summer).

Foreign Students: Three percent of the full-time students come from foreign countries. The university offers these students an intensive English course, special counseling, and special organizations.

Admissions: Foreign students must score 550 on the TOEFL. They must take the university's own college entrance examination. They must also take the General Education Examination in reading, writing, and mathematics.

Procedure: Application deadlines are September 1 (fall), December 15 (winter), and January 15 (spring). Foreign students must present a documented statement of health. They must also present proof of funds adequate to cover 1 year of study.

Admissions Contact: Lee Hoellwarth, Director of Admissions.

HURON COLLEGE   E-2
Huron, South Dakota 57350   (605) 352-8721

F/T: 183M, 167W	Faculty: 39; IIB, — — $
P/T: 16M, 42W	Ph.D.'s: 26%
Grad: none	S/F Ratio: 11 to 1
Year: 4-1-4, ss	Tuition: $3155
Appl: open	R and B: $1839
216 applied	170 accepted 110 enrolled
ACT: 14	LESS COMPETITIVE

Huron College, established in 1883, is a private liberal arts college affiliated with the United Presbyterian Church. Its library contains 58,000 volumes and 200 microfilm items, and subscribes to 300 periodicals.

Environment: The 15-acre campus is located in Huron, a town of about 15,000 people 120 miles northeast of Sioux Falls. The college's 9 buildings include 3 residence halls housing 413 students.

Student Life: About 75% of the students are from South Dakota. Two-thirds come from public schools. About 53% live on campus. Most are Protestant. Dormitories are single-sex.

Organizations: There are 3 fraternities and 3 sororities; 25% of the men and 20% of the women belong. The student government sponsors social and cultural activities.

Sports: The college fields intercollegiate teams in 6 sports for men and at least 3 for women. Intramural sports also are available.

Handicapped: Forty percent of the campus is accessible to physically handicapped students. Special facilities include wheelchair ramps, parking areas, elevators, and lowered drinking fountains and telephones.

Graduates: About 25% of the freshmen drop out during their first year, and 55% remain to graduate. Of those, 40% continue their studies.

Services: Tutoring, remedial instruction, psychological counseling, career counseling, placement aid, and health care are available free to students.

Programs of Study: The college confers the B.A., B.Mus., and B.S. degrees. Associate degrees also are available. Bachelor's degrees are offered in the following subjects: AREA STUDIES (American), BUSINESS (accounting, agribusiness, business administration), EDUCATION (elementary, health/physical, secondary, special), ENGLISH (literature, speech, writing), FINE AND PERFORMING ARTS (art, communications, music, theater/dramatics), LANGUAGES (German, Spanish), MATH AND SCIENCES (biology, mathematics), PHILOSOPHY (philosophy, religion), PREPROFESSIONAL (dentistry, law, medicine, ministry, veterinary), SOCIAL SCIENCES (criminal justice, economics, gerontology, government/political science, history, psychology, sociology).

Required: Students must complete a general-education program that requires courses in science, humanities, social sciences, and physical education.

Special: Independent study, internships, and study abroad are available. Paraprofessional work-study programs in public schools are offered. Students may design their own majors.

Honors: Departmental honors programs are offered.

Admissions: About 79% of those who applied were accepted for the 1981-82 freshman class. Candidates should have completed 15 Carnegie units and rank in the upper half of their high school class.

Procedure: The SAT or ACT is required and should be taken by February of the senior year. Application deadlines are open. Freshmen are admitted to all sessions. There is a $10 application fee.

Special: Early decision and deferred admissions plans are available. CLEP credit is given.

Transfer: A 2.0 GPA is required. Students must earn in residence at least 6 of the 34 credits required for a bachelor's degree.

Visiting: Weekday tours of the campus can be arranged through the admissions office. Visitors may sit in on classes and stay overnight at the school.

Financial Aid: Scholarships, loans, and work-study programs are available. About 90% of all students receive aid. The FFS is required; the suggested filing date is April 1.

Foreign Students: Three foreign students were enrolled at the college in 1981-82.

Admissions: Foreign applicants must take the TOEFL.

Procedure: Students are admitted to all terms; application deadlines are open. Students must submit a physician's statement and proof of adequate funds for 4 years. Health insurance also is required.

Admissions Contact: Douglas E. Almond, Director of Admissions.

MOUNT MARTY COLLEGE   E-4
Yankton, South Dakota 57078   (605) 668-1524

F/T: 98M, 339W	Faculty: n/av; IIB, — — $
P/T: 36M, 80W	Ph.D.'s: 35%
Grad: none	S/F Ratio: 10 to 1
Year: 4-1-4, ss	Tuition: $3200
Appl: Aug. 15	R and B: $1580
190 applied	180 accepted 140 enrolled
ACT: 21	COMPETITIVE

Mount Marty College, founded in 1936, is a Roman Catholic liberal arts college conducted by the Benedictine Sisters of the Sacred Heart Convent. Its library contains 71,000 volumes and 344 microfilm items, and subscribes to 800 periodicals.

Environment: The 20-acre campus is in a rural setting 60 miles from Sioux City, Iowa. The college's 10 buildings include 4 residence halls for 426 students.

Student Life: About 46% of the students are from South Dakota; 75% come from public schools. About 70% of the students live on campus. Approximately 65% are Catholic, 30% Protestant; and 5% belong to other denominations. About 3% of the students are minority-group members. College housing is single-sex; there are visiting privileges. Students may keep cars on campus. Day-care services are available to full-time students, faculty, and staff for a fee.

Organizations: There are no fraternities or sororities on campus. The college sponsors other extracurricular activities and a variety of social and cultural events.

Sports: The college competes on the intercollegiate level in 1 sport for men and 3 for women.

Handicapped: About 90% of the campus is accessible to the handicapped. There are some special facilities for physically handicapped students, including ramps, elevators, and parking areas.

Graduates: About 20% of the freshmen drop out during their first year; 65% remain to graduate. Of those, 15% continue their education; fewer than 1% enter medical school. Five percent enter careers in business and industry.

Services: The college offers placement, psychological and career counseling, tutoring, and remedial instruction free of charge. Health care is available on a fee basis.

Programs of Study: The college confers the B.A. and B.S. degrees. Bachelor's degrees are offered in the following subjects: BUSINESS (accounting, business administration), EDUCATION (elementary, health/physical, secondary), ENGLISH (English, journalism), FINE AND PERFORMING ARTS (music, music education), HEALTH SCIENCES (anesthesia, dietetics, medical technology, nursing), MATH AND SCIENCES (mathematics, physics), PHILOSOPHY (philosophy), PREPROFESSIONAL (dentistry, engineering, law, medicine, social work, veterinary), SOCIAL SCIENCES (social sciences).

Required: All undergraduates must take 4 hour courses of science and/or math, 2 of humanities, 2 of social science, and 2 in religious studies or philosophy.

Special: A 3-2 dual degree program in engineering is offered. It is possible to earn a combined B.A.-B.S. degree in selected majors. Student-designed majors are possible. Students may participate in study-abroad programs.

Honors: There are numerous honor societies.

Admissions: About 95% of the students who applied for the 1981–82 freshman class were accepted. The ACT scores of those who enrolled were as follows: 35% scored below 21, 20% between 21 and 23, 20% between 24 and 25, 20% between 26 and 28, and 5% above 28. Candidates should have a C average and rank in the top 50% of the graduating class. Interview impressions and recommendations are also considered.

Procedure: The ACT or SAT is required. Applications should be filed by August 15 (fall), January 15 (winter), January 25 (spring), and May 25 (summer). There is a $10 application fee.

Special: The college offers early decision and deferred admissions plans. AP and CLEP credit is available.

Transfer: For fall 1981, 100 students applied, 65 were accepted, and 40 enrolled. A GPA of 2.0 is required. Grades lower than C transfer if the GPA at the former institution and the number of semester hours taken are sufficient. There is a residency requirement of 2 semesters. Students must complete, at the college, 36 credits of the 120 needed for a bachelor's degree. The application deadline is the same as for freshmen.

Visiting: Tours of the campus can be arranged through the admissions office during the week. Visitors can sit in on classes and stay overnight at the college.

Financial Aid: About 76% of the students receive financial aid. Average aid to freshmen from all sources is $2700. Loans and campus employment are available in addition to scholarships. The college is a member of CSS. The FFS, FAF, or SFS should be filed. The application deadlines are March 1 (fall), December 15 (winter), December 30 (spring), and May 15 (summer).

Foreign Students: Five percent of the full-time students come from foreign countries. The college offers these students special counseling.

Admissions: Foreign students must score 500 on the TOEFL. They must also take the college's own entrance examination.

Procedure: Application deadlines are August 15 (fall), January 15 (winter), January 25 (spring), and May 25 (summer). Foreign students must present proof of funds adequate to cover 1 year of study.

Admissions Contact: Tom Streveler, Director of Admissions.

NATIONAL COLLEGE   B-3
Rapid City, South Dakota 57701   (605) 394-4820
(Recognized Candidate for Accreditation)

F/T: 383M, 679W	Faculty: 50; IV, –$
P/T: 79M, 32W	Ph.D.'s: 11%
Grad: none	S/F Ratio: 18 to 1
Year: qtrs, ss	Tuition: $3450
Appl: open	R and B: $2333
1198 applied	1190 accepted 565 enrolled
ACT: 16	LESS COMPETITIVE

National College, founded in 1941, is an independent institution offering undergraduate programs in business and business technology.

Environment: The main campus is located in a suburban area of Rapid City. Living facilities sponsored by the college include off-campus apartments, fraternity and sorority houses, and dormitories accommodating 80 men and 220 women.

Student Life: Fifty percent of the students are residents of South Dakota. Almost all entering freshmen come from public schools. Thirty percent of the students live on campus. Ten percent are minority-group members. Campus housing is coed. Students may keep cars on campus.

Organizations: There are 2 fraternities on campus to which 7% of the men belong, and 2 sororities of which 6% of the women are members. The college sponsors about 25 extra-curricular activities and organizations, including student government, a ski club, and the Vets Club.

Sports: Intercollegiate competition is offered in 2 sports for men and 3 for women. There are 8 intramural sports for men and 7 for women.

Handicapped: About 95% of the campus is accessible to physically handicapped students. Special facilities include wheelchair ramps, elevators, special parking, specially equipped rest rooms, and lowered drinking fountains and telephones. Special class scheduling is possible.

Graduates: Forty percent of the freshmen drop out by the end of the first year; 50% remain to graduate. Fifteen percent of the students pursue advanced study after graduation; 85% enter careers in business and industry.

Services: The following services are offered free of charge to all students: placement, career and psychological counseling, health care, tutoring, and remedial instruction.

Programs of Study: The college confers the B.S. degree. Associate degrees are also awarded. Bachelor's degrees are offered in the following subjects: BUSINESS (accounting, business administration, computer science, management, marketing, travel and tourism management), HEALTH SCIENCES (medical services administration). All undergraduate degrees conferred are in business or business technology.

Required: All students must take a course in orientation (college survival). A business core is common in almost all curricula, including technological specialty courses.

Special: A B.G.S. degree is offered.

Admissions: Ninety-nine percent of those who applied were accepted for the 1981–82 freshman class. The ACT scores of those who enrolled were as follows: 68% below 23, 11% between 24 and 29, and 1% above 30. A high school diploma is required for admission. Standardized test scores are used for placement purposes.

Procedure: The ACT is required. There are no application deadlines; students are admitted to all 4 quarters. There is a $25 application fee.

Special: CLEP credit is accepted.

Transfer: For fall 1981, 98 transfer students enrolled. Transfers are admitted to all classes. There is a residency requirement of 1 year. Transfer students must complete, at the college, 48 of the 192 credits required for the bachelor's degree. Application deadlines are open.

Visiting: The college offers orientation sessions for new students at the beginning of each quarter. Informal guided tours also are available. Visitors may sit in on classes and stay at the college. The office of admissions handles all arrangements.

Financial Aid: Seventy-five percent of the students receive aid through the college; 26% work part-time on campus. Aid is available in the form of scholarships, loans, and work contracts. The average award to freshmen from all sources is $4800. The FFS is required. There are no deadlines for financial aid application.

Foreign Students: Fewer than 1% of the full-time students come from foreign countries. The college offers these students an intensive English course as well as special counseling.

Admissions: Foreign students must achieve a minimum score of 490 on the TOEFL. The ACT is also required.

Procedure: Applications for admission must be submitted by the first day of the quarter for all terms. Proof of funds adequate to cover the entire course of study at the college is required. Although not required, health insurance is available through the college for a fee.

Admissions Contact: Earle Sutton, Director of Admissions.

SOUTH DAKOTA

NORTHERN STATE COLLEGE D-1
Aberdeen, South Dakota 57401   (605) 622-2544

F/T: 908M, 1181W	Faculty: n/av; IIA, – – $
P/T: 174M, 312W	Ph.D.'s: 47%
Grad: 45M, 86W	S/F Ratio: 20 to 1
Year: sems, ss	Tuition: $906 ($1710)
Appl: Aug. 1	R and B: $1317
855 applied	826 accepted	691 enrolled
ACT: 18		LESS COMPETITIVE

Northern State College, founded in 1901, is one of 4 state colleges in South Dakota. It offers liberal arts, teacher education, business, and preprofessional majors. Its library contains 180,000 volumes and 30,000 microfilm items, and subscribes to 700 periodicals.

Environment: The 50-acre campus is located in the city of Aberdeen. The 6 dormitories accommodate 966 students.

Student Life: Most of the students are from South Dakota; 85% come from public schools. About 37% of the students live on campus. Forty-three percent of the students are Catholic, 55% Protestant, and fewer than 1% Jewish; about 2% claim no religious affiliation. About 2% of the students are minority-group members. College housing is both single-sex and coed. There are visiting privileges in single-sex housing. Students may keep cars on campus. Day-care services are available to all students, faculty, and staff for a fee.

Organizations: There are no fraternities or sororities on campus. Various social, professional, and religious groups provide extracurricular activities.

Sports: The college competes in 9 intercollegiate sports and offers 11 sports on the intramural level.

Handicapped: About 60% of the campus is accessible to physically handicapped students. Special facilities include wheelchair ramps, parking areas, elevators, lowered drinking fountains and telephones, and specially equipped rest rooms. Special class scheduling is also possible.

Graduates: About 31% of the freshmen drop out during their first year; 51% remain to graduate. Of those, 25% continue their studies; 2% enter medical school, 1% dental school, and 8% law school. Thirty percent pursue careers in business and industry.

Services: Free psychological and career counseling and tutoring are offered to all students. Health care, placement, and remedial instruction are available on a fee basis.

Programs of Study: The college confers the B.A., B.S., B.M.E. and B.S.Ed. degrees. It offers associate and master's degrees as well. Bachelor's degrees are offered in the following subjects: BUSINESS (accounting, business administration, business education, finance, management, marketing), EDUCATION (elementary, health/physical, industrial, secondary, special), ENGLISH (English), FINE AND PERFORMING ARTS (art, art education, music, music education, theater/dramatics), HEALTH SCIENCES (medical technology, speech therapy), MATH AND SCIENCES (biology, chemistry, ecology/environmental science, mathematics), SOCIAL SCIENCES (economics, government/political science, history, psychology, social sciences, sociology).

Admissions: About 97% of those who applied were accepted for the 1981-82 freshman class. The ACT scores of those who enrolled were as follows: 64% scored below 21, 17% between 21 and 23, 7% between 24 and 25, 4% between 26 and 28, and 1% above 28. Candidates should be high school graduates and rank in the upper two-thirds of their graduating class, or in the upper half for out-of-state applicants. Recommendations and test scores are also considered.

Procedure: The ACT is required. Application deadlines are August 1 (fall), and December 1 (spring). Freshmen are admitted all sessions. Admissions are on a rolling basis. There is a $15 application fee.

Special: Early decision, early admissions, and deferred admissions plans are available. AP and CLEP credit is given.

Transfer: For fall 1981, 215 students applied, 200 were accepted, and 161 enrolled. A 2.0 GPA is required; D grades are accepted. At least 2 semesters must be taken in residence, of the full course (128 credits) needed to earn a bachelor's degree. Application deadlines are the same as for freshman applicants.

Visiting: Weekday tours of the campus can be arranged by contacting the admissions office. Visitors can sit in on classes and stay overnight at the school.

Financial Aid: Seventy-five percent of the students receive financial aid. Forty percent work part-time on campus. Average aid to freshmen from all sources is $1000. Scholarships, loans, and work-study grants are available. The FFS must be filed, and the recommended deadline is April 1.

Foreign Students: Fewer than 1% of the full-time students come from foreign countries. The college offers these students special organizations.

Admissions: Foreign students must score 500 on the TOEFL. They must also take the ACT.

Procedure: Application deadlines are June 1 (fall) and November 1 (winter). Foreign students must present proof of health. They must also present proof of funds adequate to cover costs. They must carry health insurance, which is available through the college for a fee.

Admissions Contact: Richard W. Van Beek, Director of Admissions.

SIOUX FALLS COLLEGE F-3
Sioux Falls, South Dakota 57101   (605) 331-6604

F/T: 246M, 363W	Faculty: 42; IIB, – $
P/T: 89M, 204W	Ph.D.'s: 48%
Grad: 1M, 8W	S/F Ratio: 12 to 1
Year: 4-1-4, ss	Tuition: $3240
Appl: open	R and B: $1690
299 applied	251 accepted	178 enrolled
ACT: required		COMPETITIVE

Sioux Falls College is a private liberal arts college affiliated with the American Baptist Convention. The library contains more than 75,000 volumes and subscribes to 450 periodicals.

Environment: The campus occupies 12 acres in suburban Sioux Falls. The 13 major buildings include a science center, a student union, a fine arts center, a gymnasium, and a music conservatory. There are 2 dormitories for men, 2 for women, and a separate residence hall for married students.

Student Life: Almost half of the students are from South Dakota. Fifty-three percent of the students live on campus. Ten percent of the students are Catholic, 71% are Protestant; and about 5% belong to other denominations; 14% claim no religious affiliation. About four percent of the students are minority-group members. College housing is single-sex; there are visiting privileges. Students may keep cars on campus. Day-care services are available to all students, faculty, and staff. Drinking is not permitted on campus.

Organizations: The college has no fraternities or sororities, but most students are involved in other types of social groups and activities.

Sports: The college sponsors 7 intercollegiate teams for men and 7 for women. There are 3 intramural sports for men and 2 for women.

Graduates: Eighteen percent of freshmen drop out by the end of their first year; 62% remain to graduate. About 25% of the graduates pursue graduate study.

Services: The following services are offered free of charge: placement, health care, psychological and career counseling, tutoring, and remedial instruction.

Programs of Study: All programs lead to the B.A. or B.S. degree. Associate and master's degrees are also offered. Bachelor's degrees are offered in the following subjects: BUSINESS (accounting, business administration), EDUCATION (elementary, health/physical), ENGLISH (English, speech), FINE AND PERFORMING ARTS (art, art education, music, music education, radio/TV), HEALTH SCIENCES (medical technology, nursing), MATH AND SCIENCES (biology, chemistry, mathematics), PHILOSOPHY (religion), PREPROFESSIONAL (law, social work), SOCIAL SCIENCES (criminal justice, history, psychology, social sciences, sociology).

Required: All students must take 1 religion course and physical education.

Special: Third-year students may study abroad. The B.G.S. degree is available. Student-designed majors are permitted.

Admissions: Eighty-four percent of those who applied were accepted for the 1981-82 freshman class. Applicants must have completed 15 Carnegie units and be recommended by their high school. The college seeks students who rank in the upper half of their graduating class, have at least a C average, and score at least 19 (composite) on the ACT. An applicant's ability to finance his or her education is also considered.

Procedure: The ACT is required and should be taken by November or December of the senior year. Application deadlines are open, and notifications are made on a rolling basis. There is a $10 application fee.

Special: CLEP credit is accepted.

Transfer: For fall 1981, 118 students applied, 96 were accepted, and 67 enrolled. A GPA of 2.0 is required. An ACT score of 19 is also needed. D grades do not transfer. Students must complete 32 credits, in residence, of the 128 needed for a bachelor's degree. Application deadlines are open.

Financial Aid: Ninety percent of the students receive financial aid. Thirty-five percent work part-time on campus. Average aid awarded to freshmen from all sources is $3000. Loans are available from the federal government, the college, and private sources. The FAF must be submitted. Application deadlines are open.

Foreign Students: One percent of the full-time students come from foreign countries. The college offers these students special counseling.

Admissions: Foreign students must score 500 on the TOEFL. No college entrance examination is required.

Procedure: Application deadlines are June 1 (fall), October 1 (winter), November 1 (spring), and March 1 (summer). Foreign students must present proof of health. They must also present proof of funds adequate to cover study at the college. They must carry health insurance, which is available through the college for a fee.

Admissions Contact: Garry Schwerin, Associate Director of Admissions.

SOUTH DAKOTA SCHOOL OF MINES AND TECHNOLOGY   B–3
Rapid City, South Dakota 57701   (605) 394-2414

F/T: 1563M, 442W	Faculty: 108; IIA, +$
P/T: 207M, 311W	Ph.D.'s: 55%
Grad: 182M, 21W	S/F Ratio: 20 to 1
Year: sems, ss	Tuition: $1022 ($2027)
Appl: Aug. 15	R and B: $1400
583 enrolled	
ACT: 23	COMPETITIVE+

The South Dakota School of Mines and Technology is a publicly supported institution devoted to sophisticated education and training of engineers and scientists. Its library contains 176,000 volumes and 99,434 microfilm items, and subscribes to 1075 periodicals.

Environment: The 120-acre campus is located in the east section of the city. Its 12 buildings include residence halls for 565 students.

Student Life: About 81% of the students are from South Dakota. Twenty-five percent of the students live on campus. About 3% are minority-group members. Campus housing is single-sex; there are visiting privileges. Students may keep cars on campus.

Organizations: There are 4 fraternities on campus, to which 10% of the students belong. Societies, clubs, and other groups provide social and cultural entertainment.

Sports: The school competes in 7 intercollegiate sports and offers intramural programs for men and women in 5 sports.

Handicapped: About 24% of the campus is accessible to physically handicapped students. Special facilities include wheelchair ramps, parking areas, elevators, lowered drinking fountains, and specially equipped rest rooms.

Graduates: About 30% of the freshmen drop out during their first year; 55% remain to graduate. Twenty percent of graduates continue their education; 1% enter medical school and 1% enter law school. About 78% of the students pursue careers in business and industry.

Services: Health care, remedial instruction, and job placement are available to students for a fee. Career counseling is free to students and alumni.

Programs of Study: The college confers the B.S. degree. It also offers master's and doctoral degrees. Bachelor's degrees are offered in the following subjects: MATH AND SCIENCES (chemistry, computer science, geology, mathematics, physics), PREPROFESSIONAL (engineering—chemical, engineering—civil, engineering—electrical, engineering—geological, engineering—mechanical, engineering—metallurgical, engineering—mining).

Special: The Army Corps of Engineers ROTC program is available.

Honors: There are 5 national honor societies represented on campus.

Admissions: About 98% of those who applied were accepted for a recent freshman class. The ACT scores of those who enrolled were as follows: 27% scored between 20 and 23, 28% between 24 and 26, 14% between 27 and 28, and 9% above 28. Candidates should have completed 15 Carnegie units. Residents must rank in the upper 66%, nonresidents in the upper half, of their graduating class.

Procedure: The ACT and placement tests are required. Application deadlines are August 15 for fall and December 15 for spring. Notification is on a rolling basis. A $15 application fee is required.

Special: AP and CLEP credit is offered.

Transfer: For fall 1981, 152 students enrolled. Course work at a prior institution that has a similar curriculum is required. A GPA of 2.0 and an ACT score of 20 are necessary. D grades do not transfer. There is a one-year residency requirement. Transfers must also complete, in residence, 30 of the 136 credits required for the bachelor's degree. Application deadlines are the same as those for freshmen.

Visiting: Tours of the campus can be arranged through the admissions office while school is in session. Visitors may sit in on classes.

Financial Aid: About 65% of all students receive some form of financial aid. Twenty percent work part-time on campus. Average aid to freshmen from all sources is $2000. The FFS is required, as well as the ACT Student Data Form. The deadline for application is May 1 (fall and winter).

Foreign Students: Eleven percent of the full-time students come from foreign countries. The school offers these students special organizations.

Admissions: Foreign students must score 530 on the TOEFL. No college entrance examination is required.

Procedure: Application deadlines are June 15 (fall) and November 15 (winter). Foreign students must present proof of funds adequate to cover 1 year of study. They must also carry health insurance, which is available through the school for a fee.

Admissions Contact: J. A. Mack, Associate Director of Admissions.

SOUTH DAKOTA STATE UNIVERSITY   F–3
Brookings, South Dakota 57007   (605) 688-4121

F/T: 3406M, 2823W	Faculty: 381; IIA, –$
P/T: 176M, 226W	Ph.D.'s: 56%
Grad: 318M, 218W	S/F Ratio: 22 to 1
Year: sems, ss	Tuition: $971 ($1915)
Appl: Aug. 1	R and B: $1352
ACT: 21	COMPETITIVE

South Dakota State University, established in 1881, is a state-supported institution. The library contains 300,000 volumes and 89,600 microfilm items, and subscribes to 3500 periodicals.

Environment: The 200-acre campus is located in a rural setting 60 miles from Sioux Falls. Its 40 buildings include dormitories housing 2985 students with 88 family housing units.

Student Life: About 90% of the students are from South Dakota. Fifty percent of the students live on campus. University housing is both single-sex and coed. There are visiting privileges in single-sex housing. Students may keep cars on campus. Day-care services are available to all students, faculty, and staff for a fee. No drinking is allowed on campus.

Organizations: There are 5 fraternities and 3 sororities as well as professional and religious groups. The student government also sponsors social and cultural events.

Sports: The university competes in 12 intercollegiate sports for men and 11 for women. There are 8 intramural sports for men and 9 for women.

Graduates: About 20% of the freshmen drop out during their first year; 30% remain to graduate and 10% of those continue their education.

Services: Health care, tutoring, and job placement services are available on a fee basis. Psychological counseling and career counseling services, including resume workshops, interviews, and a career information library, are available free of charge.

Programs of Study: The university confers the B.A., B.S., and B.M.Ed. degrees. Associate, master's and doctoral programs are also offered. Bachelor's degrees are offered in the following subjects: AREA STUDIES (Latin American), BUSINESS (economics), EDUCATION (agricultural, music, secondary), ENGLISH (English, journalism, speech), FINE AND PERFORMING ARTS (art), HEALTH SCIENCES (medical technology, nursing, physical therapy), LANGUAGES (French, German, Spanish), MATH AND SCIENCES (biology, botany, chemistry, mathematics, physics, zoology), PREPROFESSIONAL (dentistry, engineering, forestry, home economics, law, medicine, ministry, pharmacy, veterinary), SOCIAL SCIENCES (economics, geography, government/political science, history, psychology, sociology). About 15% of the degrees conferred are in the sciences and 5% are in business.

Required: Freshman English, physical education, and speech are required of all students.

Special: Overseas study is possible.

832 SOUTH DAKOTA

Honors: There are numerous honor societies represented on campus. An honors program is available in English.

Admissions: About 96% of those who applied for a recent freshman class were accepted. The ACT scores of those who enrolled were as follows: 75% scored between 20 and 23, 55% between 24 and 26, 25% between 27 and 28, and 10% above 28. Candidates should have completed 15 Carnegie units and rank in the upper 75% of their graduating class. Recommendations and extracurricular activities are also considered.

Procedure: The ACT is required. The application deadlines are August 1 (fall), December 1 (spring), and May 15 (summer). There is a $15 application fee.

Special: Early admissions are possible. AP and CLEP credit is offered.

Transfer: For fall 1981, about 100 transfer students applied for admission. A 2.25 GPA is required. D grades do not transfer. There is a one-year residency requirement. Sixty-four credits must be completed at the university, if transferring from a junior college, and 32, if from another college or university, of the 128 to 136 needed for a bachelor's degree. Application deadlines are June 1 (fall), November 1 (spring), and March 15 (summer).

Visiting: Tours of the campus can be arranged through the admissions office. Visitors can sit in on classes and stay overnight at the university.

Financial Aid: Eighty-six percent of the students receive financial aid. Twenty-one percent work part-time on campus. Average aid awarded to freshmen from all sources is $2600. Scholarships, loans, and CWS are all available. The university is a member of CSS. The FFS or FAF is required. The application deadline for financial aid is open.

Foreign Students: About 3% of the full-time students come from foreign countries. The university offers these students special counseling and special organizations.

Admissions: Foreign students must score 500 on the TOEFL, and 85 on the University of Michigan Language Test. No college entrance examination is required.

Procedure: Application deadlines are June 1 (fall), November 1 (spring), and March 15 (summer). Foreign students must present the results of a physical examination. They must also present proof of funds adequate to cover their first year of study. There is a special fee for services, payable one time only. Foreign students must also carry health insurance, which is available through the university for a fee.

Admissions Contact: Vincent O. Heer, Director of Admissions.

UNIVERSITY OF SOUTH DAKOTA F-4
Vermillion, South Dakota 57069 (605) 677-5434

F/T: 2200M, 2200W	Faculty: 476; I, --$
P/T: n/av	Ph.D.'s: 59%
Grad: 800M, 450W	S/F Ratio: 19 to 1
Year: sems, ss	Tuition: $783 ($1720)
Appl: see entry	R and B: $1400
1640 applied	1339 accepted	1141 enrolled
ACT: 21		COMPETITIVE

The University of South Dakota, founded in 1862, is a state-controlled university. Its library contains 425,000 volumes and 225,348 microfilm items, and subscribes to 2346 periodicals.

Environment: The 133-acre campus, located in a rural area 35 miles from Sioux City, Iowa, consists of 40 buildings, including a radio and television station and the largest museum in the state. A recent addition, the Dakota Dome, is an indoor football and multi-purpose athletic facility. The university provides residence halls, married-student housing, and fraternity and sorority houses.

Student Life: About 80% of the students are from South Dakota, and 85% live on campus. University housing is both single-sex and coed.

Organizations: There are 9 fraternities and 5 sororities on campus to which 11% of men and 9% of women belong. Extracurricular activities include music and drama groups, publications, student government, religious groups, and special-interest clubs.

Sports: The university competes in 10 intercollegiate sports for men, women, or both. More than 20 intramural or club sports are available.

Handicapped: There are limited facilities for the physically handicapped students.

Graduates: About 50% of the freshmen remain to graduate, and 25% of graduates pursue careers in business and industry.

Services: Free counseling and placement services are offered. Health care and tutoring are also available.

Programs of Study: The university confers the B.A., B.S., B.S.Ed., B.S.Med., B.S.Med. Tech., and B.F.A. degrees. Associate, master's, and doctoral degrees are also offered. Bachelor's degrees are offered in the following subjects: BUSINESS (accounting, business administration, business education, chemistry—business, computer science management), EDUCATION (elementary, health/physical, secondary, special), ENGLISH (communication, English, journalism, mass communication, speech), FINE AND PERFORMING ARTS (art, art education, music, music education, film/photography, radio/TV, theater/dramatics), HEALTH SCIENCES (alcohol and drug abuse studies, health services administration, medical technology, pre-occupational therapy, pre-physical therapy, speech therapy), LANGUAGES (French, German, Greek/Latin, Spanish), MATH AND SCIENCES (biology, chemistry, chemistry—business, earth science, mathematics, physics), PHILOSOPHY (classics, humanities, philosophy), PREPROFESSIONAL (dentistry, engineering, law, library science, medicine, optometry, osteopathy, social work, veterinary), SOCIAL SCIENCES (anthropology, criminal justice, economics, government/political science, history, human services, psychology, sociology). About 24% of all degrees conferred are in business and 15% are in the social sciences.

Special: The university has an Institute of Indian Studies. Students may design their own majors.

Honors: Nine honor societies are represented on campus.

Admissions: About 82% of those who applied were accepted for the 1981–82 freshman class. The ACT scores of those who enrolled were as follows: 40% below 21, 30% between 21 and 23, 13% between 24 and 25, 14% between 26 and 28, and 4% above 28. Candidates should have completed 16 Carnegie units, rank in the upper two-thirds of their graduating class, and have good ACT scores.

Procedure: The ACT is required. Applications are accepted up to 2 weeks before registration. Freshmen are accepted all sessions. There is a $15 application fee. Admission is on a rolling basis.

Special: Early and deferred admissions and early decision plans are offered. AP and CLEP credit is given.

Transfer: Students must have a 2.0 GPA and be in good standing at their last school. D grades transfer. Students must earn at least 30 semester hours in residence of the 128 required for a bachelor's degree. Application deadlines are the same as those for freshmen.

Visiting: Weekday tours of the campus can be arranged through the admissions office. Visitors may sit in on classes and stay overnight at the school.

Financial Aid: About 85% of the students receive aid. Scholarships and loans are available. The average award to freshmen in 1981–82 totalled $1314. The FAF or FFS is required. Aid applications should be submitted by March 1 for priority consideration.

Foreign Students: Foreign students enrolled full-time make up about 1% of the student body. The university provides these students with special counseling.

Admissions: Applicants must score at least 550 on the TOEFL. They also must take the ACT.

Procedure: Foreign students are admitted only in the fall, and must file applications by May 1. Students must submit a medical history and show proof of adequate funds for 4 years of study.

Admissions Contact: Gary Gullickson, Director of Admissions.

UNIVERSITY OF SOUTH DAKOTA AT SPRINGFIELD E-4
Springfield, South Dakota 57062 (605) 369-2289

F/T: 503M, 204W	Faculty: 50; IIB, av$
P/T: 40M, 17W	Ph.D.'s: 9%
Grad: none	S/F Ratio: 14 to 1
Year: sems, ss	Tuition: $927 ($1731)
Appl: Sept. 8	R and B: $1320
302 applied	302 accepted	246 enrolled
ACT: required		NONCOMPETITIVE

The University of South Dakota at Springfield, founded in 1881, is a state-supported technical university that offers a complete junior college program and 4-year programs in technology. It is a branch of the University of South Dakota at Vermillion. Its library contains 70,000 volumes and subscribes to 700 periodicals.

Environment: The 57-acre campus is located in a rural setting 100 miles from Sioux Falls. There are 22 buildings, including 3 dormitories housing 550 students.

Student Life: About 90% of the students are from South Dakota; 60% live on campus. Five percent of the students are minority-group members. University housing is both single-sex and coed. There are visiting privileges in single-sex housing. Students may keep cars on campus.

Organizations: The student government and special-interest clubs sponsor numerous social and cultural events.

Sports: The college competes in 7 intercollegiate sports for men and 4 sports for women. There are 12 intramural programs open to men and 11 to women.

Handicapped: About 70% of the campus is accessible to physically handicapped students. Special facilities include ramps and parking areas.

Graduates: About 20% of the freshmen drop out during their first year; 65% remain to graduate. Of those, 5% continue with graduate education. Eighty percent go on to careers in business and industry.

Services: Free remedial instruction, job placement, and career counseling are offered to all students. Health care and tutoring are on a fee basis.

Programs of Study: The university confers the B.A., B.S., B.S.Ed., B.S.Ed. Industrial Arts, and B.S.T. degrees. Associate degrees are also offered. Bachelor's degrees are offered in the following areas: EDUCATION (industrial, technical, vocational), PREPROFESSIONAL (engineering—construction technology, engineering—electronics technology, engineering—mechanical technology).

Required: All undergraduates must take courses in humanities, physical education and recreation, physical and natural science, and behavioral science.

Special: There is a freshman pretechnology program. Cooperative work experience is available in the 4-year vocational education program. It is possible to earn a combined B.A.-B.S. degree.

Admissions: The university has an open admissions policy. Candidates should have completed 15 Carnegie units.

Procedure: The ACT is required. Freshmen are admitted to all semesters. A rolling admissions policy is used. There is a $15 application fee.

Special: CLEP is accepted.

Transfer: For fall 1981, 138 students applied, 138 were admitted, and 103 enrolled. A 2.0 GPA is required. Students must complete 30 semester hours in residence and must complete 64 of the 128 semester hours needed for a bachelor's degree. Application deadlines are the same as those for freshman applicants.

Visiting: Tours of the campus can be arranged through the admissions office.

Financial Aid: About 80% of all students receive some form of aid. Forty-three percent work part-time on campus. Average aid awarded to freshmen from all sources cover 90% of costs. Scholarships, loans, and grants are awarded to all qualified students. The university is a member of CSS. The FAF or FFS is required. The application deadlines are April 30 (fall), November 30 (spring), and March 31 (summer).

Foreign Students: Four percent of the full-time students come from foreign countries. The university offers these students an intensive English course and special counseling.

Admissions: Foreign students must score 500 on the TOEFL. No college entrance examination is required.

Procedure: Application deadlines are April 20 (fall), September 12 (spring), and February 6 (summer). Foreign students must present proof of funds adequate to cover 1 year of study. They must also pay a special admissions fee of $50, $2200 in tuition, and $1800 for room and board, among other fees.

Admissions Contact: Tim Witte, Director of Admissions.

YANKTON COLLEGE E-4
Yankton, South Dakota 57078 (605) 665-3661

F/T: 148M, 95W	Faculty: 25; IIB, — —$
P/T: 5M, 5W	Ph.D.'s: 36%
Grad: none	S/F Ratio: 10 to 1
Year: 4-1-4, ss	Tuition: $3580
Appl: Aug. 15	R and B: $1690
SAT or ACT: required	*LESS COMPETITIVE*

Yankton College, founded in 1881, is a privately endowed institution affiliated with the United Church of Christ (Congregational). The library contains 60,000 volumes and 300 microfilm items, and subscribes to 600 periodicals.

Environment: The 55-acre campus is located in a rural area 65 miles from Sioux City, Iowa. The Conservatory of Music has recently been named to the National Registry for Historical Sites. Three dormitories accommodate 500 students, and apartment complexes are available for married students.

Student Life: About half the students are from South Dakota; 85% of the students come from public schools. Seventy-six percent live on campus. Thirty-four percent of the students are Catholic and 58% Protestant; 4% belong to other denominations; and 4% claim no religious affiliation. Twenty-four percent of the students are minority-group members. College housing is single-sex; there are visiting privileges. Students may keep cars on campus.

Organizations: There are no fraternities or sororities on campus. The student government and special-interest clubs sponsor social and cultural events on campus.

Sports: The college participates in 7 sports for men and 6 for women on the intercollegiate level, and offers 3 intramural programs for both men and women.

Handicapped: There are no special facilities for physically handicapped students.

Graduates: Thirty-five percent of the freshmen drop out by the end of their first year. About 39% of the freshmen remain to graduate, and 40% continue their education. Of those, 2% enter medical school, 1% dental school, and 7% law school. Twenty percent enter careers in business and industry.

Services: Free health care, tutoring, career counseling, and job placement are available to all students. Remedial instruction is available on a fee basis.

Programs of Study: The college confers the B.A., B.Mus., and B.S.Med.Tech. degrees. Associate degrees are also offered. Bachelor's degrees are offered in the following subjects: BUSINESS (accounting, management), EDUCATION (elementary, health/physical, secondary), ENGLISH (English, literature, speech), FINE AND PERFORMING ARTS (art, art education, music, music education, theater/dramatics), HEALTH SCIENCES (medical technology), MATH AND SCIENCES (biology, chemistry), PREPROFESSIONAL (dentistry, law, medicine, ministry, veterinary), SOCIAL SCIENCES (criminal justice, government/political science, history, human services, psychology, sociology). About 40% of the degrees conferred are in education.

Required: All students are required to take English, communications, fine arts, literature, history, science, logic or mathematics, physical education, and electives from natural science, social science, fine arts, and humanities.

Special: Student-designed majors are available.

Honors: Departmental honors programs are offered.

Admissions: About 96% of those who applied for the 1981–82 freshman class were accepted. Candidates should have completed 15 Carnegie units, have a C average, and rank in the upper 60% of the graduating class. Advanced placement and honor courses, leadership record, and special talents are also considered.

Procedure: The SAT or ACT is required. A personal interview is recommended. Application deadlines are August 15 (fall) and January 5 (spring). Admissions are on a rolling basis. Freshmen are admitted in all sessions. The application fee is $10.

Special: AP and CLEP credit is given.

Transfer: Transfer students are accepted for all classes. A 1.5 GPA is required. D grades transfer. The last 30 hours must be taken at the college to earn a bachelor's degree. Application deadlines are the same as those for freshmen.

Visiting: Tours of the campus can be arranged through the admissions office. Visitors can sit in on classes and stay overnight at the college.

Financial Aid: About 95% of all students receive some form of financial assistance. The maximum amount awarded in a scholarship or a loan is $1200. There are work-study programs in all departments. The college is a member of CSS. The FAF is required. The deadlines for financial aid application are August 15 (fall) and January 5 (spring).

Foreign Students: Fewer than 1% of the full-time students come from foreign countries.

Admissions: Foreign students must take the TOEFL. They must also take the ACT or the SAT. They must score 14 on the ACT, or achieve a combined score of 600 on the SAT.

Procedure: The application deadlines are July 15 (fall) and December 5 (spring). Foreign students must present proof of funds adequate to cover at least 12 months of study. They must also carry health insurance.

Admissions Contact: Mary R. Johnson, Acting Director of Admissions.

TENNESSEE

AUSTIN PEAY STATE UNIVERSITY C-2
Clarksville, Tennessee 37040 (615) 648-7121

F/T: 1700M, 1725W	Faculty: n/av; IIA, −$
P/T: 850M, 650W	Ph.D.'s: 70%
Grad: 230M, 450W	S/F Ratio: 20 to 1
Year: qtrs, ss	Tuition: $654 ($2184)
Appl: Sept. 1	R and B: $1610
ACT: 16	NONCOMPETITIVE

Austin Peay is a state-supported institution offering bachelor's degrees in the liberal arts. The library houses 199,220 volumes, holds subscriptions to 1466 periodicals, and has 12,869 microfilm items.

Environment: The 150-acre campus is located about 47 miles from Nashville and contains 42 buildings, including residence halls for 620 women and 539 men.

Student Life: About 83% of the students are Tennessee residents. Twenty percent live on campus.

Organizations: There are 7 fraternities and 5 sororities on campus; 12% of the men and 10% of the women belong. The university maintains religious facilities through the Baptist Student Union, Church of Christ Student Center, and the Wesley Foundation.

Sports: The university participates on an intercollegiate level in 7 sports.

Handicapped: Approximately 95% of the campus is accessible to wheelchair-bound students. Facilities and considerations include ramps, designated handicapped parking, elevators, lowered drinking fountains, and special class scheduling. A special counselor and an assistant are available.

Graduates: The freshman dropout rate is 20%, with 60% remaining to graduate. Twenty percent of those who graduate pursue further study; 2% enter medical school, 1% dental school, and 3% law school.

Services: Health care, psychological counseling, placement services, and career counseling are offered at no charge to the student.

Programs of Study: The university confers bachelor's and master's degrees. Bachelor's degrees are offered in the following subjects: BUSINESS (accounting, business administration, business education, computer science, finance, management, marketing), EDUCATION (early childhood, elementary, health/physical, secondary, special), ENGLISH (English), FINE AND PERFORMING ARTS (art, music), HEALTH SCIENCES (medical technology, nursing, physical therapy), LANGUAGES (French), MATH AND SCIENCES (biology, earth science, geology, mathematics, physics), PHILOSOPHY (philosophy), PREPROFESSIONAL (agriculture), SOCIAL SCIENCES (economics, geography, government/political science, history, psychology, sociology). Of the degrees conferred, 40% are in business, 33% in education, and 6% in health sciences.

Special: Although there is no undergraduate major in secondary education, students may prepare to teach, and there are graduate programs in education.

Honors: An interdepartmental honors program is offered.

Admissions: Eighty percent of those who applied were accepted for the 1980–81 freshman class. Under the open admissions policy, all graduates of accredited Tennessee high schools are eligible for admission. Out-of-state students must have a composite ACT score of at least 16 or a GPA of at least 2.25.

Procedure: The ACT is required for guidance purposes. Application deadlines are September 1 (fall), December 1 (winter), March 1 (spring), and May 10 (summer). There is a rolling admissions program. The application fee is $5.

Special: An early admissions plan is offered; the application deadline is September 1. AP and CLEP credit is available.

Transfer: Applicants must have a 2.0 GPA and may transfer credits earned with a grade of D. Application deadlines are the same as those for freshmen.

Visiting: The university conducts regularly scheduled orientations for prospective students. Guides are available for informal visits to the campus. To arrange classroom visits and an overnight stay at the school, the Office of University School Relations should be contacted.

Financial Aid: About 66% of all students receive aid. During a recent year, 2574 students received aid totaling $2,633,279 from sources related to the university. The FFS is required, as well as an institutional application. The priority application deadline is March 1.

Admissions Contact: Glenn S. Gentry, Dean of Admissions and Records.

BELMONT COLLEGE C-3
Nashville, Tennessee 37203 (615) 383-7001

F/T: 691M, 692W	Faculty: 89; IIB, av$
P/T: 143M, 267W	Ph.D.'s: 46%
Grad: none	S/F Ratio: 17 to 1
Year: sems, ss	Tuition: $2315
Appl: July 15	R and B: $1670
802 applied	784 accepted	721 enrolled
ACT: 19	LESS COMPETITIVE

Founded in 1951, Belmont is a private coeducational college of liberal arts related to the Baptist Convention. The library contains 87,000 volumes and subscribes to 400 periodicals.

Environment: The 35-acre campus, located on the antebellum Acklen estate, is surrounded by an urban environment. The old Acklen residence, "Belmont," is at the nucleus of the college, with later additions surrounding it in a quadrangle. About 555 students are housed in the residence halls.

Student Life: Students not living with their parents must live in dormitories; 31% of the students live on campus. Gambling and drinking are prohibited. Chapel attendance is expected twice a week. About 91% of the students are Protestant, and 9% are Catholic. About 6% of the students are minority-group members. Campus housing is single-sex; there are visiting privileges. Students may keep cars on campus.

Organizations: There are 2 local fraternities, to which 40% of the men belong, and 2 local sororities, to which 40% of the women belong. There are also departmental, religious, and special-interest clubs. Other extracurricular activities include the student government association, a student newspaper and other publications, musical groups, debate club, and the Student Players.

Sports: The college fields 4 intercollegiate teams for men and 3 for women. There are 6 intramural sports for men and 5 for women.

Graduates: Seventy-five percent of the freshmen remain to graduate. Forty-five percent of the graduates pursue graduate study: 3% enter medical school and 3% law school; 50% pursue careers in business and industry.

Services: The following free services are available: career counseling, health care, and job placement services.

Programs of Study: The college confers the B.A., B.B.A., B.M., and B.S. degrees. Associate degrees are also awarded. Bachelor's degrees are offered in the following subjects: BUSINESS (accounting, business administration, business education, finance, hospitality business, information systems management, management, marketing, music business), EDUCATION (early childhood, elementary, health/physical, secondary, special), ENGLISH (English, journalism, speech), FINE AND PERFORMING ARTS (church music, commercial music, music, music education, music performance, piano pedagogy, radio/TV, theater/dramatics, theory and composition), HEALTH SCIENCES (medical technology, nursing), LANGUAGES (foreign language), MATH AND SCIENCES (actuarial science, biology, chemistry, mathematics, physics), PHILOSOPHY (philosophy, religion), PREPROFESSIONAL (dentistry, engineering, law, library science, medicine, ministry, pharmacy, social work, veterinary), SOCIAL SCIENCES (criminal justice, economics, government/political science, history, international relations, psychology, sociology).

Required: The college requires each student to take 2 semesters of religion and 4 physical education courses during the freshman and sophomore years. Candidates for graduation must score satisfactorily on the UP Area Tests, UP Field Tests, and URE.

Special: The college has cooperative arrangements with the University of Tennessee, offering the B.S. degree in pre-law (3–3) and pre-engineering (3–2).

Admissions: Ninety-eight percent of those who applied for the 1981–82 freshman class were accepted. The ACT scores of those who enrolled were as follows: 59% below 21, 16% between 21 and 23, 9% between 24 and 25, 7% between 26 and 28, and 5% above 28. The most important criteria used by the college in evaluating applications for admission are the transcript of grades, ACT or SAT scores, character reference, and the medical form. Leadership qualities, advanced placement or honors courses, and evidence of special talent are also considered important. Applicants must be high school graduates. A minimum C average is recommended. Students should rank in the upper half of their graduating class.

Procedure: The deadline for applications for fall admission is July 15; for spring, November 15; for summer session, June 1. The ACT or SAT is required and should be taken by April of the senior year. Applications should be submitted with a $15 fee for commuters, and a $25 fee for resident students. Notification is made on a rolling basis.

Special: There are early decision and early admissions plans. AP and CLEP credit is accepted.

Transfer: For fall 1981, 368 transfer students applied, 346 were accepted, and 310 enrolled. Applicants must be eligible to return to their former schools. A minimum 2.0 GPA is required; a 2.5 GPA is recommended. D grades are granted transfer credit. All students must complete, at the college, at least 24 semester hours of the 128 credits required to earn a bachelor's degree. Deadlines are the same as those for entering freshmen.

Visiting: There are no regularly scheduled orientations for prospective students. Guides are available for informal visits on weekday mornings; visitors may sit in on classes and stay overnight at the school. The admissions office should be contacted to arrange visits.

Financial Aid: Athletic scholarships of about $1500 each are awarded. Student loans are administered by the Tennessee Baptist Foundation. The college also participates in the ACT Financial Aid Services, EOG, and CWS. About 75% of all students receive financial aid; 10% of the students work part-time on campus. Applicants for financial aid must submit the FFS or FAF; the college is a member of CSS. The aid application deadline is March 15.

Foreign Students: About 7% of the students are from foreign countries. The college offers these students an intensive English course, special counseling, and special organizations.

Admissions: Foreign students must achieve a minimum TOEFL score of 450; no further exams are required.

Procedure: Application deadlines are July 15 (fall), November 15 (spring), and June 1 (summer). Foreign students must present proof of health by completing the college's medical form, and they must present proof of funds adequate to cover 4 years of study. Special fees include a $1000 deposit and a $50 application fee. Health insurance is available through the college for a fee.

Admissions Contact: Martha Kelley, Assistant Registrar.

BETHEL COLLEGE   B–3
McKenzie, Tennessee 38201   (901) 352-5321

F/T: 183M, 180W	Faculty:	n/av; IIB, – – $
P/T: 24M, 37W	Ph.D.'s:	50%
Grad: none	S/F Ratio:	15 to 1
Year: qtrs, ss	Tuition:	$1980
Appl: Aug. 31	R and B:	$1500
319 applied	179 accepted	119 enrolled
ACT: 17		COMPETITIVE

Established in 1842, Bethel is a coeducational, privately controlled college of liberal arts related to the Cumberland Presbyterian Church. The library contains 67,000 volumes, holds subscriptions to 360 periodicals, and has 675 microfilm items.

Environment: The 155-acre campus is located in a rural area 120 miles northeast of Memphis. Residence halls accommodate 150 women and 180 men.

Student Life: Seventy-two percent of the students come from Tennessee; 50% live on campus. About 97% of the students are Protestant. About 15% of the students are minority-group members. Campus housing is single-sex; there are visiting privileges. Students may keep cars on campus.

Organizations: There are 4 local fraternities, to which 15% of the men belong, and 4 local sororities, to which 15% of the women belong.

Sports: The college fields 4 intercollegiate teams for men and 3 for women. There are 9 intramural sports for men and 9 for women.

Handicapped: Approximately 75% of the campus is accessible to the physically handicapped. Facilities include special parking, specially equipped rest rooms, and lowered drinking fountains and telephones; special class scheduling is also available.

Graduates: The freshman dropout rate is 25%; 25% remain to graduate. Ten percent of those who graduate pursue advanced study.

Services: Placement services, career counseling, psychological counseling, tutoring, and remedial instruction are offered free of charge; health care is available for a fee.

Programs of Study: The college confers the B.A. or B.S. degree in the following subjects: BUSINESS (accounting, business administration, business education, general business), EDUCATION (elementary, health/physical, secondary, special), ENGLISH (English), FINE AND PERFORMING ARTS (music, music education), MATH AND SCIENCES (applied math, biology, natural sciences), PHILOSOPHY (lay ministries, religion), PREPROFESSIONAL (dentistry, law, medicine, ministry), SOCIAL SCIENCES (social sciences). Thirty-four percent of degrees conferred are in business, 17% in education, and 13% in social sciences.

Required: All students must complete 192 quarter hours with an average of at least C, basic course requirements, and major and minor requirements; 60 hours must be on the junior and senior level.

Special: Some of the educational programs offered are evening classes for adults and in-service training for teachers. Student-designed majors are permitted.

Honors: There are 3 national honor societies with chapters on campus.

Admissions: Fifty-six percent of those who applied were accepted for the 1981–82 freshman class. The ACT scores of those who enrolled were as follows: 57% below 21, 15% between 21 and 23, 9% between 24 and 25, 5% between 26 and 28, and 0% above 28. Candidates must have graduated from an accredited high school with a minimum C average, rank in the top half of their class, and have an ACT score of 16 or a combined SAT score of 800. Impressions made during an interview, evidence of special talent, and personality are also considered important. Admission may be based on GED tests or other high school equivalency tests in special cases.

Procedure: The ACT or SAT is required. Applications should be submitted no later than August 31 (fall), January 3 (winter), March 15 (spring), and June 13 (summer). The college follows a rolling admissions plan. There is a $10 application fee.

Special: There is an early decision plan, with a notification date of April 1, and an early admissions plan, with an application deadline of May 30. There is also a deferred admissions plan. CLEP credit is accepted.

Transfer: For fall 1981, 32 transfer students applied, 28 were accepted, and 21 enrolled. A minimum 2.0 GPA is required for transfer. D grades are transferable. Students must complete, at the college, at least 45 credits of the 192 required to earn the bachelor's degree. Application deadlines are the same as those for regular admission.

Visiting: The college conducts regularly scheduled orientations for prospective students. Guides are also available for informal visits to the campus. The office of admissions should be contacted to arrange visits.

Financial Aid: About 80% of all students receive some form of aid; 25% of the students work part-time on campus. There is no deadline for financial aid applications. The FFS is the preferred form, although the FAF may be submitted.

Foreign Students: Fewer than 1% of the students are from foreign countries. The college offers these students special counseling and special organizations.

Admissions: Foreign students must achieve a minimum score of 450 on the TOEFL; they must also take the college's own placement exams.

Procedure: Foreign students must present proof of health and of adequate funds.

Admissions Contact: Delores Mann, Director of Admissions.

BRYAN COLLEGE   D–3
Dayton, Tennessee 37321   (615) 775-2041

F/T: 258M, 309W	Faculty:	37; IIB, – $
P/T: 61M&W	Ph.D.'s:	40%
Grad: none	S/F Ratio:	16 to 1
Year: sems, ss	Tuition:	$2550
Appl: July 31	R and B:	$2200
507 applied	434 accepted	235 enrolled
ACT: 19		COMPETITIVE

Bryan College, founded in 1930, is a private liberal arts institution. The library houses 70,000 volumes, holds subscriptions to 410 periodicals, and has 2000 microfilm items.

Environment: The 100-acre campus is located on a hilltop overlooking Chickamauga Lake and the town of Dayton, approximately 40 miles from Chattanooga. The environment surrounding the campus is rural. College buildings include a fine arts building, a chapel, and 3 dormitories.

Student Life: Only 12% of the students come from Tennessee. The college is interdenominational; attendance at the 3 weekly chapel *services is required.* About 95% of the students reside in the dormitories. There are curfew regulations. Drinking and smoking are prohibited. About 3% of the students are minority-group members. Campus housing is single-sex; there are no visiting privileges. Students may keep cars on campus.

Organizations: There are no sororities or fraternities on campus. Activities include publications, drama club, band, choir, Practical Christian Involvement, the Student Union, and numerous cultural and social activities sponsored by the college.

Sports: The college fields 5 intercollegiate teams for men and 5 for women. There are 6 intramural sports for men and 5 for women.

Handicapped: Forty percent of the campus is accessible to handicapped students. Wheelchair ramps are provided. There are no special counselors.

Graduates: The freshman dropout rate is 30%; 35% remain to graduate. Of the graduates, 45% go on to further study, with 2% entering law school. Ten percent pursue careers in business or industry.

Services: Tutoring, health care, placement services, and career counseling are offered at no charge to the student.

Programs of Study: The college confers the B.A. and B.S. degrees. Bachelor's degrees are offered in the following subjects: BUSINESS (accounting, business administration, business education), EDUCATION (elementary), ENGLISH (English), MATH AND SCIENCES (biology, chemistry, mathematics, natural sciences), PHILOSOPHY (Bible), PREPROFESSIONAL (Christian education), SOCIAL SCIENCES (history, psychology). Of the degrees conferred, 31% were in education, 16% in social sciences, and 13% in business.

Required: All freshmen are required to take courses in grammar and composition, general psychology, fundamentals of speech, history of Western civilization, physical education, Bible, and laboratory science or language.

Special: Student-designed majors are permitted. Students have the opportunity to study abroad through the Institute of Holy Land Studies and the study abroad program of the Christian Colleges.

Admissions: Eighty-six percent of those who applied were accepted for the 1981–82 freshman class. Candidates should have completed 15 Carnegie units of high school work with at least a 2.5 GPA. Factors affecting acceptance are high school grades, character references, and ACT or SAT scores.

Procedure: The ACT or SAT is required. Application deadlines are July 31 (fall) and November 15 (spring). Applications are reviewed on a rolling basis. There is no application fee.

Special: An early admissions plan is offered. The application deadline for early admission is May 1. Credit is given for CLEP subject exams and AP exams.

Transfer: For fall 1981, 55 transfer students enrolled. Transfers are accepted for all classes. A 2.5 GPA and character references are required for admission. D grades are transferable if they constitute less than 12 hours and are not in the major field. Students must complete, at the college, 30 credits of the 124 credits required to earn the bachelor's degree. The application deadlines are the same as those for freshmen.

Visiting: The college conducts spring and fall orientations for prospective students. Guides are available for informal visits to the campus. Visitors may sit in on classes and stay overnight at the school. The dean of admissions and records makes arrangements for such visits. Recommended times for visiting are October, November, February, and March.

Financial Aid: About 70% of all students receive aid; about 55% of all students work part-time on campus. Loan funds administered by the college and federal loan funds available total $20,000 and $150,000 respectively. About 20 freshman scholarships are awarded annually. The average amount of aid given to freshmen from all sources is $2200; the maximum is $4800. Package aid is based on need. The college is a member of the CSS; the FAF or FFS is required. The suggested filing date for aid applications is May 1.

Foreign Students: About 3% of the students are from foreign countries. The college offers these students special counseling and special organizations.

Admissions: Foreign students must achieve a TOEFL score of at least 500; they must also take the California Achievement Test. No college entrance exams are required.

Procedure: Application deadlines are July 31 (fall) and November 15 (spring). Foreign students must present proof of health and of adequate funds. They must also carry health insurance, which is available through the college for a fee.

Admissions Contact: Virginia Seguine, Director of Admissions.

CARSON-NEWMAN COLLEGE E-3
Jefferson City, Tennessee 37760   (615) 475-9061

F/T: 810M, 852W   Faculty: 83; IIB, av$
P/T: 32M, 27W   Ph.D.'s: 49%
Grad: none   S/F Ratio: 16 to 1
Year: 4-1-4, ss   Tuition: $2800 ($2900)
Appl: open   R and B: $1700
675 applied   675 accepted
ACT: 19   NONCOMPETITIVE

Founded in 1851, Carson-Newman College is a private liberal arts institution affiliated with the Tennessee Baptist Convention. The library houses 135,000 volumes, holds subscriptions to 1000 periodicals, and has 6500 microfilm items.

Environment: The 130-acre campus, located in a rural area about 25 miles from Knoxville, has 25 buildings, including 5 dormitories. The college also sponsors on-campus apartments, off-campus apartments, and married student housing.

Student Life: About 50% of the students are from Tennessee. Eighty-five percent live on campus. About 80% of the entering freshmen attended public schools. Eighty percent are Protestant, and 2% are Catholic. The majority of students are members of the Baptist Church. Attendance at weekly chapel service is required. About 15% of the students are minority-group members. Campus housing is single-sex; there are no visiting privileges. Students may keep cars on campus.

Organizations: Ten percent of the men belong to 1 of 2 local fraternities, 15% of the women to 1 of 2 local sororities. Over 70 other campus organizations, including religious groups for Baptist students, provide a variety of activities. Recreational opportunities abound in nearby Tennessee Valley Authority lakes and the Great Smoky Mountains National Park.

Sports: The college fields 10 intercollegiate teams for men and 3 for women. There are 4 intramural sports for men and 4 for women.

Handicapped: The college estimates the campus to be 50% accessible to the handicapped student. There are specially equipped rest rooms on campus. Special class scheduling may be arranged. There are no special counselors.

Graduates: The freshman dropout rate is 35%; 45% remain to graduate. Of the graduates, 35% go on to further study: 2% enter medical school, 1% dental school, and 2% law school. About 40% enter careers in business and industry.

Services: The following services are offered at no charge to the student: psychological counseling, tutoring, remedial instruction, health care, placement services, and career counseling.

Programs of Study: The college offers the B.A., B.M., and B.S. degrees. Bachelor's degrees are offered in the following subjects: BUSINESS (accounting, business administration, business economics, business education, computer science, management, public administration), EDUCATION (early childhood, elementary, secondary, special), ENGLISH (English, speech), FINE AND PERFORMING ARTS (art, film/photography, music, music education, piano pedagogy, studio art, theater/dramatics), HEALTH SCIENCES (medical records administration, medical technology, nursing, physical therapy), LANGUAGES (French, German, Spanish), MATH AND SCIENCES (biology, chemistry, mathematics, physics), PHILOSOPHY (philosophy, religion), PREPROFESSIONAL (dentistry, engineering, forestry, home economics, law, medicine, ministry, pharmacy, veterinary), SOCIAL SCIENCES (economics, government/political science, history, psychology, social sciences, sociology). Students may also major in church recreation, human services, and recreation. Of the degrees conferred, 22% are in education, 12% in business, and 13% in the fine and performing arts.

Required: All students must take 6 semester hours of religion.

Special: Students may receive permission to spend their junior year abroad, but this is not a college-sponsored program. Combined 5-year B.A.-B.S. degrees are offered in many areas of study. Student-designed majors are permitted. A general studies degree is offered.

Honors: There are 12 national honor societies with chapters on campus. Honors programs are offered by the Departments of Religion, Philosophy, English, and Science.

Admissions: All of those who applied were accepted for the 1981–82 freshman class. The ACT scores of those who enrolled were as follows: 59% below 21, 15% between 21 and 23, 14% between 24 and 25, 7% between 26 and 28, and 5% above 28. Eligibility depends upon graduation from an accredited high school with 16 completed Carnegie units of work, a rank in the upper half of the class, and a 2.0 GPA. Other factors influencing the admissions decision are recommendations by school officials, leadership record, and personality.

Procedure: The ACT is required. Applications should be submitted, along with a $15 fee, preferably by August 15 for the fall term. Freshmen are admitted to all terms, including the summer. Applications are considered on a rolling basis.

Special: An early admissions plan is offered; the application deadline is May 1. There is also a deferred admissions plan. CLEP subject exams and AP exams are accepted for credit.

Transfer: For fall 1981, 190 transfer students applied, 163 were accepted, and 132 enrolled. A 2.0 GPA from an accredited institution is required. D grades can be transferred. Students must complete, at the college, 32 credits of the 128 credits required to earn a bachelor's degree. Application deadlines are the same as those for freshmen.

Visiting: Regularly scheduled orientations, including campus tours, faculty-student discussions, financial aid workshops, and an athletic event, are conducted by the college for prospective students. Guides are available for informal visits to the campus. To arrange class visits and an overnight stay at the school, the director of admissions should be contacted. The recommended time for such visits is weekdays during the fall and spring.

Financial Aid: About 75% of all students receive aid; about 25% of the students work part-time on campus. There are 2 comprehensive financial aid programs, which include loans, grants, and work-study. A number of freshman scholarships are available. The average aid to freshmen is $1300. The FAF must be filed; the college is a member of the CSS. The deadline for aid application is May 15. Tuition may be paid in installments.

Foreign Students: About 2% of the students are from foreign countries. The college offers these students special counseling and special organizations.

Admissions: Foreign students must achieve a minimum TOEFL score of 500; in addition, they must take the ACT.

Procedure: Application deadlines are June 1 (fall), December 1 (spring), and May 1 (summer). Foreign students must present proof of health, as well as proof of adequate funds. An advance tuition deposit of $1000 is held by the college. Foreign students must carry health insurance, which is available through the college for a fee.

Admissions Contact: Jack Shannon, Director of Admissions.

CHRISTIAN BROTHERS COLLEGE   A-4
Memphis, Tennessee 38104   (901) 278-0100

F/T: 750M, 516W	Faculty:	72; IIB, av$
P/T: 85M, 132W	Ph.D.'s:	70%
Grad: none	S/F Ratio:	16 to 1
Year: sems, ss	Tuition:	$3050
Appl: March 15	R and B:	$1012
881 applied	827 accepted	341 enrolled
ACT: 24		COMPETITIVE+

Christian Brothers College, founded in 1871 and reopened as a 4-year college in 1954, is a private coeducational institution run by the Christian Brothers. The library houses 79,577 volumes and 2600 microfilm items, and subscribes to 495 periodicals.

Environment: The 57-acre campus is located in an urban area and contains 18 buildings, including 2 dormitories.

Student Life: Tennessee residents account for 53% of the students, while 46% come from other states. About 29% of the students live on campus. Fifty-six percent of the students are Protestant; 33% Catholic. Religious services are held daily; attendance is voluntary. About 19% of the students are minority-group members. Campus housing is single-sex; there are visiting privileges. Students may keep cars on campus.

Organizations: There are 3 fraternities, to which 25% of the men belong, and 1 sorority, to which 2% of the women belong. Extracurricular activities include professional clubs, choral club, plays, discussion groups, a college newspaper and yearbook, field trips, dances, and lectures.

Sports: The college fields 3 intercollegiate teams for men and 3 for women. There are 9 intramural sports for men and 8 for women.

Handicapped: Approximately 75% of the campus is accessible to the physically handicapped. Facilities include wheelchair ramps and special parking.

Graduates: The freshman dropout rate is 35%; 45% remain to graduate. About 15% of the graduates pursue graduate study; 2% enter medical school, 1% dental school, and 2% law school.

Services: Placement services, career counseling, health care, and psychological counseling are offered free of charge. Tutoring is available for a fee.

Programs of Study: The college confers the B.A. and B.S. degrees. Associate degrees are also available. Certification in elementary, secondary, and K-12 education is also offered. Bachelor's degrees are offered in the following subjects: BUSINESS (accounting, finance/economics, general business, management, marketing), ENGLISH (english), HEALTH SCIENCES (medical technology), MATH AND SCIENCES (biology, chemistry, engineering physics, mathematics, natural sciences, physics), PHILOSOPHY (humanities), PREPROFESSIONAL (engineering—chemical, engineering—civil, engineering—electrical, engineering—mechanical), SOCIAL SCIENCES (history, human development and learning). Forty percent of degrees conferred are in engineering, 18% in math and sciences, and 7% in social sciences.

Special: It is possible to earn combined B.A.-B.S. degrees in math-engineering and engineering-biology.

Honors: One national honor society has a chapter on campus.

Admissions: Approximately 94% of those who applied were accepted for the 1981-82 freshman class. The ACT scores of those who enrolled were as follows: 13% below 21, 34% between 21 and 23, 16% between 24 and 25, 17% between 26 and 28, and 20% above 28. Candidates should be graduates of an accredited high school, have a minimum 2.0 GPA, rank in the top two-thirds of their class, and present recommendations from their high school. Applicants over the age of 21 who are not high school graduates may be admitted on the basis of the GED.

Procedure: The ACT is required. New students are admitted to all terms. The application deadline for the fall term is March 15; the college follows a rolling admissions policy. There is a $25 application fee.

Special: AP and CLEP subject exam credit is accepted.

Transfer: For fall 1981, 189 transfer students applied. Transfers are accepted for all classes. Grades of C or above transfer. High school and college transcripts and a minimum 2.2 GPA are required. Students must complete 35 of the last 70 credits at the college; 138 credits are required to earn the bachelor's degree. Application deadlines are the same as those for freshmen.

Visiting: There are no regularly scheduled orientations for prospective students. Guides are available for informal weekday visits to the campus; visitors may sit in on classes. The admissions office should be contacted to arrange visits.

Financial Aid: About 83% of all students receive some form of financial aid; 40% of the students work part-time on campus. There are no formal deadlines for financial aid applications. There are work-study programs in all departments. The college is a member of the CSS; the FAF or the FFS must be submitted.

Foreign Students: About 4% of the students are from foreign countries. The college offers these students special counseling and special organizations.

Admissions: Foreign students must achieve a minimum TOEFL score of 500; no further exams are required.

Procedure: The application deadline is March 15 for fall. Foreign students must present proof of adequate funds.

Admissions Contact: Dayna Street, Director of Day Admissions.

COVENANT COLLEGE   D-4
Lookout Mountain, Tennessee 37350   (404) 820-1560

F/T: 244M, 253W	Faculty:	33; n/av
P/T: 20M, 12W	Ph.D.'s:	63%
Grad: none	S/F Ratio:	16 to 1
Year: sems, ss	Tuition:	$3890
Appl: see profile	R and B:	$2080
261 applied	219 accepted	159 enrolled
SAT: 476V 489M	ACT: 19	COMPETITIVE

Founded in 1955, Covenant College is a Christian liberal arts college affiliated with the Reformed Presbyterian Church, Evangelical Synod, and the Presbyterian Church in America. The library contains over 50,000 books and 30,000 microfilm items, and subscribes to 1535 periodicals.

Environment: The 60-acre campus is located in a rural area atop Lookout Mountain, in the northwest corner of Georgia, overlooking the city of Chattanooga, Tennessee. There are 7 major buildings, including 2 dormitories for 190 men and 215 women.

TENNESSEE

Student Life: Most of the students come from the South. Eighty percent live on campus. Ninety-eight percent are Protestant. Most of the students are members of the supporting church; daily chapel attendance is required. All freshmen, sophomores, and juniors, unless 21 years of age or older, must live in the residence halls unless excused by the dean of students. Alcoholic beverages, tobacco, and social dancing are not permitted. About 5% of the students are minority-group members. Campus housing is single-sex; there are visiting privileges. Students may keep cars on campus.

Organizations: Clubs, religious and service organizations, campus government, performing groups, and publications are sponsored. There are regularly scheduled social and cultural events. There are no fraternities or sororities.

Sports: The college fields 4 intercollegiate teams for men and 3 for women. There are 4 intramural sports for men and 5 for women.

Graduates: The freshman dropout rate is about 37%; about 23% remain to graduate. Of the graduates, 20% go on for further study; 1% enter medical school and 1% law school. About 14% enter careers in business and industry.

Services: Placement services, career counseling, psychological counseling, and tutoring are available free of charge. Health care is available for a fee.

Programs of Study: The college confers the B.A. and B.M. degrees. Associate degrees are also awarded. Bachelor's degrees are offered in the following subjects: BUSINESS (accounting, business administration, computer science), EDUCATION (early childhood, elementary, health/physical, recreation, secondary), ENGLISH (English), FINE AND PERFORMING ARTS (music, music education), HEALTH SCIENCES (medical technology, nursing), MATH AND SCIENCES (biology, chemistry), PHILOSOPHY (philosophy, religion), SOCIAL SCIENCES (economics, history, psychology, sociology).

Required: There is a core curriculum.

Special: Three-two, dual-degree engineering, physics, and applied mathematics degrees are offered in conjunction with Georgia Institute of Technology. Study abroad, interdisciplinary studies, and independent study are also offered. Every student engages in 1 to 3 hours of practical work on campus each week.

Honors: Graduation with honors is possible.

Admissions: About 84% of the students who applied for the 1981–82 freshman class were accepted. A high school diploma from an approved secondary school (or a GED diploma) is required as well as a C average, a minimum combined SAT score of 800, secondary school recommendations, and 15 Carnegie units. A credible profession of faith in Christianity is also required.

Procedure: The SAT is required and should be taken by January of the senior year. New students are admitted both semesters. The application deadline is 2 weeks before the start of the semester. Admission and notification are on a rolling basis. There is a $15 application fee.

Special: There is a deferred admissions plan. AP and CLEP credit is granted.

Transfer: For fall 1981, 110 transfer students applied, 95 were accepted, and 45 enrolled. Transfer students are accepted for all classes. A C average is requested; Grades of C or better are accepted. Students must complete, at the college, 30 credits of the 126 credits required to earn a bachelor's degree. Application deadlines are the same as those for freshmen.

Visiting: Regularly scheduled orientations are held for new students. The program includes campus tours, lectures, placement tests, counseling, and social gatherings.

Financial Aid: About 80% of the students are getting aid; 56% of the students work part-time on campus. The college offers federal aid programs such as NDSL, BEOG/SEOG, and CWS, in addition to athletic, music, and academic scholarships and local bank loans. The college is a member of CSS; its own aid application and the FAF are required. Georgia residents receive a $675 state tuition grant.

Foreign Students: About 8% of the students come from foreign countries.

Admissions: Foreign students must achieve a minimum TOEFL score of 500. In addition, students must take the SAT or ACT.

Procedure: Application deadlines are August 15 (fall) and December 5 (spring). Health insurance is available through the college for a fee.

Admissions Contact: Arline Cadwell, Director of Admissions Counseling.

DAVID LIPSCOMB COLLEGE   C–3
Nashville, Tennessee 37203   (615) 385-3855

F/T: 1060M, 1184W   Faculty: 101; IIB, −$
P/T: 73M, 58W   Ph.D.'s: 60%
Grad: none   S/F Ratio: 20 to 1
Year: qtrs, ss   Tuition: $2343
Appl: see profile   R and B: $1680
846 applied   665 accepted   602 enrolled
ACT: 20   COMPETITIVE

David Lipscomb College, founded in 1891, is a liberal arts college related to the Church of Christ. The library contains over 140,000 volumes, holds subscriptions to 850 periodicals, and has 4200 microfilm items.

Environment: The 56-acre campus, with its colonial style buildings, is situated in a suburban area of Nashville. There are dormitory facilities for 1400 students.

Student Life: Over fifty percent of the students are from Tennessee. About 80% of the freshmen come from public schools; 60% live in dormitories. Ninety-eight percent are Protestant; the majority of the students are members of the Church of Christ, as are all faculty members. Daily attendance at both chapel service and Bible class is required of all students. Drinking is prohibited. About 5% of the students are minority-group members. Campus housing is single-sex; there are no visiting privileges. Students may keep cars on campus.

Organizations: There are 10 men's and 11 women's social clubs on campus.

Sports: The college fields 6 intercollegiate teams for men and 2 for women. There are 7 intramural sports for men and 6 for women.

Graduates: The freshman dropout rate is 26%; 51% remain to graduate.

Services: Career counseling, placement, health care, and psychological counseling are offered free of charge. Tutoring and remedial instruction are available for a fee.

Programs of Study: The college confers the B.A. or B.S. degree in the following subjects: AREA STUDIES (American, urban), BUSINESS (accounting, business education, management, office administration), EDUCATION (early childhood, elementary, health/physical, secondary), ENGLISH (English, literature, speech), FINE AND PERFORMING ARTS (art, art education, music, music education), HEALTH SCIENCES (medical technology), LANGUAGES (Biblical languages, French, German, Spanish), MATH AND SCIENCES (biochemistry, biology, chemistry, mathematics, physics), PHILOSOPHY (religion), PREPROFESSIONAL (dentistry, engineering, law, medicine, ministry, pharmacy, social work, veterinary), SOCIAL SCIENCES (economics, government/political science, history, psychology, sociology).

Admissions: Approximately 79% of those who applied were accepted for the 1981–1982 freshman class. The ACT scores of those who enrolled were as follows: 49% below 21, 18% between 21 and 23, 20% between 24 and 25, 7% between 26 and 28, and 6% above 28. Eligibility is based on rank in the top 75% of the senior high school class, a C average or better, and completion of 15 Carnegie units. Applicants should be graduates of accredited high schools and present strong recommendations.

Procedure: The ACT is required. There is no formal deadline, but application should be made by August 15. Freshman are admitted in all 4 quarters. There is a $25 application fee. The college uses a rolling admissions plan.

Special: An early admissions plan is offered. AP and CLEP credit is accepted.

Transfer: For fall 1981, 235 transfer students applied, 191 were accepted, and 143 enrolled. Transfer students are admitted each term. A 2.0 GPA is needed. Students must complete, at the college, 36 of the 198 credits required to earn a bachelor's degree. Deadlines are the same as those for freshman applicants.

Visiting: Regularly scheduled orientations are conducted by the college. Guides are also available for informal visits to the campus. Overnight visits to the college may be made if space permits. The admissions office should be contacted to arrange visits.

Financial Aid: About 70% of all students receive some form of financial aid; about 30% of the students work part-time on campus. Scholarship funds total over $400,000; loan funds total $215,000. The college participates in SEOG, Pell Grant, and NDSL programs. The FAF or the FFS are required. The financial aid application deadline for the fall quarter is June 1.

Foreign Students: Fewer than 1% of the students come from foreign countries.

Admissions: Foreign students must achieve a score of 500 on the TOEFL; no further exams are required.

Procedure: There are no application deadlines. Foreign students must present the college's student health form, and they must present proof of adequate funds each year. Health insurance is available through the college for a fee.

Admissions Contact: Steven M. Davidson, Director of Admissions.

EAST TENNESSEE STATE UNIVERSITY   F-2
Johnson City, Tennessee 37614   (615) 929-4213

F/T: 2881M, 3530W	Faculty: n/av; IIA, av$
P/T: 625M, 888W	Ph.D.'s: 59%
Grad: 637M, 911W	S/F Ratio: 23 to 1
Year: sems, ss	Tuition: $714 ($2244)
Appl: open	R and B: $1600
2910 applied	2738 accepted 1728 enrolled
ACT: 18	LESS COMPETITIVE

East Tennessee State University, established in 1911, is a state-supported institution. Its undergraduate divisions include 5 schools: Arts and Sciences, Business and Economics, Education, Health, and Nursing. The library houses 559,090 volumes, holds subscriptions to 4050 periodicals, and has 337,939 microfilm items.

Environment: Located in the foothills of the Appalachian Mountains, the campus consists of 92 buildings on 438 acres. The surrounding area is urban. There are 14 dormitories and 2 efficiency apartments housing 2800 men and women, apartments for married students, 7 sorority houses, and 10 fraternity houses.

Student Life: About 88% of the students come from Tennessee. Seventy percent reside on campus. Campus housing is single-sex; there are visiting privileges. Students may keep cars on campus.

Organizations: Student activities include student government, drama and choral groups, and a weekly newspaper. There are 11 fraternities and 7 sororities with chapters on campus; 20% of the men and 15% of the women belong.

Sports: The university fields 12 intercollegiate teams. There are 11 intramural sports.

Handicapped: The university estimates the campus to be 90% accessible to the wheelchair-bound student. Facilities and considerations include ramps, designated handicapped parking, special class scheduling, lowered drinking fountains and telephones, and specially equipped rest rooms (in dorms only). One special counselor is available to assist handicapped students.

Services: Health care, placement services, and career counseling are offered at no charge to the student.

Programs of Study: The B.A., B.S. in Environmental Health, B.F.A., B.S.Med.Tech., B.S.Mus.Ed., B.S.N., and B.S.W. degrees are conferred. Associate, master's, and doctoral degrees are also awarded. Bachelor's degrees are offered in the following subjects: AREA STUDIES (American), BUSINESS (accounting, business administration, business education, computer science, finance, management, marketing, real estate/insurance), EDUCATION (early childhood, elementary, health/physical, industrial, secondary, special), ENGLISH (English, journalism, speech), FINE AND PERFORMING ARTS (art, art education, music education, radio/TV, theater/dramatics), HEALTH SCIENCES (environmental health, medical technology, nursing, physical therapy, speech therapy), LANGUAGES (French, German, Spanish), MATH AND SCIENCES (biology, chemistry, geology, mathematics, physics), PHILOSOPHY (humanities, philosophy), PREPROFESSIONAL (dentistry, engineering, home economics, medicine, pharmacy, veterinary), SOCIAL SCIENCES (economics, geography, government/political science, history, psychology, social sciences, sociology). Of the degrees conferred, 22% are in education, 17% in business, and 6% in math and sciences.

Special: Combined study is offered in corrective therapy and manual arts therapy.

Honors: There are 8 national honor societies with chapters on campus.

Admissions: Ninety-four percent of those who applied were accepted for the 1981-82 freshman class. The ACT scores of those who enrolled were as follows: 65% below 21, 22% between 21 and 23, 7% between 24 and 25, 5% between 26 and 28, and 1% above 28. Candidates must have a diploma from an accredited high school, have at least a 2.3 GPA, and submit satisfactory ACT or SAT test scores. Non-high-school graduates may be accepted with a GED diploma.

Procedure: The ACT or SAT is required and should be taken in the fall of the senior year. There is no deadline for applications; applications are considered on a rolling basis. Freshmen are admitted to all terms. There is a $5 application fee.

Special: An early admissions plan is offered. Credit is given for the CLEP general exam and AP exams.

Transfer: Recently, 1024 applications were received, 945 were accepted, and 647 transfer students enrolled. Transfers are accepted for all classes. A 2.0 GPA is required in addition to a clear social report from the last college attended. D grades are transferable. Students must complete, at the university, 34 quarter credits of the 128 quarter credits required to earn the bachelor's degree. There are no application deadlines.

Visiting: There are no regularly scheduled orientations for prospective students. Guides are available for informal visits to the campus. Visitors may sit in on classes. The university recommends weekdays during the fall, from 8 A.M. to 4:30 P.M., as the best time to visit.

Financial Aid: About 40% of all students receive aid; 12% of the students work part-time on campus. The average award to freshmen from all sources is $1200. The FAF is required. The university is a member of CSS. The filing deadline for aid is April 15. There are work-study programs in all departments.

Foreign Students: About 2% of the students are from foreign countries. The university offers these students special counseling and special organizations.

Admissions: Foreign students must achieve a minimum TOEFL score of 500; no further exams are required.

Procedure: Application deadlines are June 1 (fall), September 1 (spring), and March 1 (summer). Foreign students must present a medical report; they must also present proof of funds adequate to cover their entire period of study. Foreign students must carry health insurance, which is available through the university for a fee.

Admissions Contact: James W. Loyd, Dean of Admissions and Records.

FISK UNIVERSITY   C-3
Nashville, Tennessee 37203   (615) 329-8585

F/T: 263M, 571W	Faculty: 67; IIA, --$
P/T: 4M, 6W	Ph.D.'s: 60%
Grad: 18M, 24W	S/F Ratio: 13 to 1
Year: sems	Tuition: $4900
Appl: June 15	R and B: $2085
1012 applied	711 accepted 217 enrolled
SAT or ACT: recommended	COMPETITIVE

Fisk University, a privately controlled, nonsectarian college of liberal arts, is affiliated with the American Missionary Association. It was established in 1866 as a college for blacks. Fisk has always accepted students regardless of race. The library contains 186,174 volumes and 4270 microfilm items, and subscribes to 595 periodicals.

Environment: The 40-acre campus is located in an urban area and includes residence halls that accommodate 1030 men and women.

Student Life: About 12% of the students are from Tennessee. Fisk became known as one of the best Negro colleges, and the student body is still predominately (95%) black. Campus housing is single-sex; there are visiting privileges. Students may keep cars on campus.

Organizations: About 25% of the men belong to 5 fraternities; 15% of the women are affiliated with 4 sororities. Extracurricular activities include dramatic and musical groups, publications, radio station, concerts, lectures, and departmental clubs.

Sports: The university fields 6 intercollegiate teams for men and 5 for women. There are 8 intramural sports for men and 8 for women.

Handicapped: About 80% of the campus is accessible to handicapped students; there are no special facilities.

Graduates: Twenty percent of the freshmen drop out at the end of their first year; 60% remain to graduate. About 50% of the graduates pursue advanced degrees and 40-45% enter careers in business and industry.

Services: Psychological counseling, placement, career counseling, tutoring, and remedial instruction are offered free of charge to students. Health care is available for a fee.

Programs of Study: The university confers the B.A., B.S., and B.M. degrees. Master's degrees are also offered. Bachelor's degrees are offered in the following subjects: BUSINESS (management), ENGLISH (English), FINE AND PERFORMING ARTS (art, education, dramatics and speech, music, music education), HEALTH SCIENCES (health care administration and planning), LANGUAGES (French, Spanish), MATH AND SCIENCES (biology, chemistry, mathematics, physics),

PHILOSOPHY (religious and philosophical studies), PREPROFESSIONAL (dentistry, engineering, law, medicine, ministry), SOCIAL SCIENCES (economics, history, political science, psychology, sociology). Of the degrees conferred, 61% are in social sciences, 26% in math and sciences, and 13% in humanities and fine arts.

Required: All students must complete a 36-credit core curriculum in communications, creative arts, humanistic experience and thought, natural sciences and mathematics, social sciences, and the world and its peoples; and a 1-semester freshman orientation course.

Special: Student-designed majors, exchange programs, and cross-registration are available. Five-year, dual-degree programs in science and engineering (leading to B.A.-B.E. degrees) or management (leading to B.S.-M.B.A. degrees) are offered in conjunction with Vanderbilt University.

Honors: Five honor societies, including Phi Beta Kappa, have chapters on campus. There is a university-wide honors program.

Admissions: Seventy percent of those who applied were accepted for the 1981-82 freshman class. Applicants must present 15 acceptable units of high school studies and must rank in the upper half of their class. Other factors considered include advanced placement or honors courses, leadership record, evidence of special talents, and aptitude test scores.

Procedure: The SAT or ACT is strongly recommended. Applications should be submitted by June 15 for the fall semester, November 1 for spring. Decisions are made on a rolling basis. There is a $10 application fee.

Special: There is an early admissions plan with an application deadline of June 15. AP credit is granted.

Transfer: For fall 1981, 132 transfer students applied, 46 were accepted, and 18 enrolled. A 2.0 GPA is required. Grades of C or better transfer. Students must complete, at the university, 30 of the 120 credits required for the bachelor's degree. Application deadlines are the same as those for freshmen.

Visiting: Guides are available for informal campus visits. Visitors may sit in on classes and stay overnight at the school. Visits are best scheduled between September 15 and December 1, and between January 15 and April 15. The admissions office should be contacted for arrangements.

Financial Aid: About 72% of all students receive financial aid; 42% of the students work part-time on campus. Fisk participates in the CSS and is a member of the United Negro College Fund. Need-based financial aid packages range from $2060 to $7225 a year; the average package is $4800. Tuition may be paid in installments; CWS is available. The FAF and a university application are required. The deadline for financial aid applications is April 1.

Foreign Students: About 4% of the students come from foreign countries. The university offers these students an intensive English course and special counseling.

Admissions: Foreign students must take the TOEFL; no further exams are required.

Procedure: Application deadlines are June 15 (fall) and November 1 (spring). Foreign students must present proof of health in the form of a physician's statement; they must also present proof of adequate funds. Foreign students must carry health insurance, which is available through the university for a fee.

Admissions Contact: Aline Rivers, Director of Admissions.

FREED-HARDEMAN COLLEGE   B-3
Henderson, Tennessee 38340   (901) 989-4611

F/T: 576M, 705W
P/T: 32M, 48W
Grad: none
Year: sems, ss
Appl: open
718 applied
ACT: 18

Faculty: 68; IV, —$
Ph.D.'s: 38%
S/F Ratio: 20 to 1
Tuition: $2450
R and B: $1615
623 accepted
539 enrolled
LESS COMPETITIVE

Freed-Hardeman College, founded in 1869, is affiliated with the Churches of Christ and offers liberal arts programs. The library contains 90,000 volumes and 3698 microfilm items, and subscribes to 584 periodicals.

Environment: The 85-acre campus, located in a rural area 17 miles from Jackson, has 25 buildings. Nine dormitories house 1218 students. Married student housing is also available. A cafeteria, an auditorium, athletic facilities, and a student center are also located on campus.

Student Life: About 39% of the students are from Tennessee. Over 85% reside on campus. Most students belong to the affiliated church; virtually all students are Protestant. Daily chapel attendance is compulsory. Drinking is forbidden on campus. About 5% of the students are minority-group members. Campus housing is single-sex; there are no visiting privileges. Students may keep cars on campus.

Organizations: There are over 30 extracurricular groups on campus, but there are no fraternities or sororities.

Sports: The college fields 6 intercollegiate teams for men and 2 for women. There are 9 intramural sports for men and 8 for women.

Handicapped: About 90% of the campus is accessible to handicapped students. Facilities include wheelchair ramps, parking areas, and specially equipped rest rooms. A counselor is available to handicapped students.

Graduates: The freshman dropout rate is 20%; 35% remain to graduate. About 71% of the graduates pursue advanced degrees; 2% enter medical school, 2% dental school, and 3% law school. Twenty-nine percent pursue careers in business or industry.

Services: Psychological counseling, remedial instruction, placement, career counseling, and health care are offered free of charge to students. Tutoring is available for a fee.

Programs of Study: The college confers the B.A. and B.S. degrees. Associate degrees are also awarded. Bachelor's degrees are offered in the following subjects: BUSINESS (accounting, business administration, business education, computer science, finance, management, marketing), EDUCATION (early childhood, elementary, health/physical, secondary), ENGLISH (speech), FINE AND PERFORMING ARTS (art, music, radio/TV, theater/dramatics), MATH AND SCIENCES (biology, chemistry, mathematics), PHILOSOPHY (religion), PREPROFESSIONAL (home economics, law, medicine, ministry, social work), SOCIAL SCIENCES (history, psychology). Of the degrees conferred, 24% are in education, 20% in philosophy, and 19% in business.

Required: All full-time students must study Bible each semester. A distribution of core courses is also necessary for graduation.

Special: With guidance, students may create their own majors. Double majors and second degrees are offered. Study abroad is possible; cooperative education programs are available in some areas.

Honors: Two honor societies have chapters on campus. All departments offer honors programs.

Admissions: Eighty-seven percent of those who applied were accepted for the 1981-1982 freshman class. The ACT scores of those who enrolled were as follows: 60% below 21, 22% between 21 and 23, 8% between 24 and 25, 6% between 26 and 28, and 4% above 28. Candidates must be graduates of accredited high schools and have either a 2.0 high school GPA or an ACT score of 14. Other factors considered in the admissions decision are recommendations, personality, and evidence of special talents.

Procedure: The ACT is required; junior year results are acceptable. There are no application deadlines; freshmen are admitted in the fall, spring, and summer terms. Notification is on a rolling basis. An interview is recommended for all prospective students. There is a $15 application fee.

Special: AP and CLEP credit is available.

Transfer: For fall 1981, 73 transfer students applied, 53 were accepted, and 48 enrolled. Requirements are the same as for freshman students. D grades transfer. A 2.0 GPA is recommended. Students must complete, at the college, 30 of the 132 credits required to earn a bachelor's degree. Application deadlines are September 1 (fall), January 2 (spring), and June 1 (summer).

Visiting: The college conducts 2 orientations each year for prospective students. Guides are available for informal campus visits. Visitors may sit in on classes and stay overnight at the school. The admissions office should be contacted for arrangements.

Financial Aid: About 80% of all students receive financial aid; 44% of the students work part-time on campus. Scholarships, federal loans, and CWS in all departments are available. The average aid to a freshman from all sources combined is $2527. The application deadline for priority consideration is May 15. The FFS must be submitted.

Foreign Students: About 2% of the students come from foreign countries. The college offers these students special counseling and special organizations.

Admissions: An English proficiency exam is not required; however, students must take the ACT.

Procedure: Application deadlines are September 1 (fall), January 2 (spring), and June 1 (summer). Foreign students must present the college's health form; they must also present proof of funds adequate to cover 4 years of study. Health insurance is available through the college for a fee.

Admissions Contact: Billy R. Smith, Director of Admissions.

KING COLLEGE   F-2
Bristol, Tennessee 37620   (615) 968-1187

F/T: 159M, 130W	Faculty: 26; IIB, —$
P/T: 15M, 27W	Ph.D.'s: 80%
Grad: none	S/F Ratio: 9 to 1
Year: 4-1-4, ss	Tuition: $3440
Appl: open	R and B: $2060
232 applied	167 accepted	99 enrolled
SAT: 449V 512M		COMPETITIVE

King College, established in 1867, is a small liberal arts Christian college affiliated with the Presbyterian Church. The library has 80,000 volumes and 2855 microfilm items, and subscribes to 500 periodicals. Through SOLINET, a computerized bibliographical service, library users have access to over 7 million titles.

Environment: Located in the foothills of the Appalachian Mountains, the 135-acre wooded campus is in a suburban area near the Tennessee-Virginia border. There are residence hall facilities for 160 women and 160 men.

Student Life: About 72% of the students are from Tennessee and Virginia. About 84% attended public school. Eighty-three percent live on campus. Ninety-five percent of the students are Protestant, and 2% are Catholic. Thirty-two percent of the students are Presbyterian. Attendance is required at 75% of the weekly chapel services and convocations. About 9% of the students are minority-group members. Campus housing is single-sex; there are visiting privileges. Students may keep cars on campus.

Organizations: There is a traditional extracurricular activities program, including choir, publications, drama groups, and clubs. Popular social and cultural events are the Autumn Banquet, Dogwood Festival, lectures, and concerts. There are no fraternities or sororities. Within a short drive of the campus are outstanding recreational facilities for sports of all seasons.

Sports: The college fields 6 intercollegiate teams for men and 4 for women. There are 9 intramural sports for men and 7 for women.

Graduates: The freshman dropout rate is about 25%; 45% remain to graduate. Twenty percent of the graduates go on for further study. About 30% enter careers in business and industry.

Services: The college provides free career and psychological counseling, placement services, health care, and tutoring.

Programs of Study: The B.A., B.S., and B.S.Ed. degrees are awarded. Bachelor's degrees are offered in the following subjects: BUSINESS (business administration), EDUCATION (elementary), ENGLISH (English), HEALTH SCIENCES (medical technology), LANGUAGES (French, Greek/Latin), MATH AND SCIENCES (applied math and science, biology, chemistry, mathematics, physics), PREPROFESSIONAL (dentistry, engineering, law, medicine, ministry, pharmacy, social work, veterinary), SOCIAL SCIENCES (government/political science, history, psychology).

Required: To meet general education core requirements, all students must take courses in English, Bible and religion, history, foreign language, and physical education.

Special: Independent study, summer study abroad, off-campus externships during the January term, and teacher certification are offered. There are 3-2 cooperative programs in engineering with the University of Tennessee, University of Maryland, and Georgia Institute of Technology. Under a cooperative arrangement, King College students may take courses at Virginia Intermont College.

Honors: Graduation with honors and with honors in independent study are possible.

Admissions: About 72% of the 1981-82 freshman applicants were accepted. SAT scores of those who enrolled were as follows: Verbal—65% below 500, 27% between 500 and 599, 8% between 600 and 700, and 0% above 700; Math—46% below 500, 47% between 500 and 599, 7% between 600 and 700, and 0% above 700. Candidates should be graduates of accredited high schools, complete 16 Carnegie units, rank in the top half of the high school class, demonstrate a desire for a Christian education, be recommended by secondary school officials, and have a minimum score of 19 on the ACT or of 900 combined math and verbal on the SAT.

Procedure: The SAT or ACT is required. Freshmen are admitted to both semesters and, under certain circumstances, to the summer session. Admission and notification are on a rolling basis. Deadlines are open. There is a $15 application fee.

Special: There is an early admissions plan. CLEP credit is granted.

Transfer: For fall 1981, 69 transfer students applied, 58 were accepted, and 35 enrolled. Transfers are accepted for all classes. A 2.0 GPA is required; D grades are accepted. One academic year should be taken in residence. Students must complete, at the college, 50 of the 130 credits required to earn a bachelor's degree. Transfer application deadlines are open.

Visiting: All new students participate in an orientation program. Informal campus tours with student guides and interviews with faculty and staff members can be arranged. Suggested visiting times are 8 A.M. to noon and 1 P.M. to 5 P.M. on weekdays. The admissions office is open on Saturdays upon request.

Financial Aid: About 84% of the students are receiving aid; 70% of the students work part-time on campus. The college offers 18 freshman merit scholarships, ranging from $1250 to $2500 and 10 transfer scholarships for the same amounts. Grants (BEOG/SEOG), government and commercial loans, and CWS are offered. Children of Presbyterian ministers and missionaries qualify for tuition discounts. The college is a member of CSS; either the FAF or FFS is required. There is no deadline for aid applications; priority is given to those filed by May 31.

Foreign Students: About 8% of the students come from foreign countries. The college offers these students an intensive English course and special organizations.

Admissions: Foreign students must achieve a minimum TOEFL score of 550; they must also take either the SAT or ACT. The minimum acceptable score on the SAT is 900 (combined); on the ACT, the minimum acceptable composite score is 19.

Procedure: Application deadlines are August 1 (fall), January 15 (spring), and June 1 (summer). Foreign students must have a physical examination and present proof of funds adequate to cover 4 years of study. They must also carry health insurance, which is available through the college for a fee.

Admissions Contact: Thomas N. Daniel, Director of Admissions.

KNOXVILLE COLLEGE   E-3
Knoxville, Tennessee 37921   (615) 524-6512

F/T: 388M, 253W	Faculty: 34; n/av
P/T: 17M, 41W	Ph.D.'s: 42%
Grad: none	S/F Ratio: 18 to 1
Year: qtrs, ss	Tuition: $4200
Appl: July 15	R and B: $1632
137 applied		127 enrolled
SAT or ACT: required		LESS COMPETITIVE

Knoxville College, established in 1875, offers undergraduate instruction in the liberal arts and professional areas. It is affiliated with the United Presbyterian Church. The library contains 65,000 volumes and more than 1100 microfilm items, and subscribes to 450 periodicals.

Environment: The 39-acre campus is located in the city of Knoxville. The 22 buildings include the Colston Center for the Performing Arts and 6 dormitories.

Student Life: One-quarter of the students are from Tennessee. About 95% come from public schools. The student body is predominately black. Most students are not members of the supporting church. More than 80% of the students live on campus in the single-sex dorms.

Organizations: About 20% of the students belong to 1 of the 10 sororities and fraternities. Campus activities include student government, the student newspaper, drama and choral groups, departmental and religious clubs, and the school band.

Sports: The college fields intercollegiate teams in 4 sports for men and 3 for women. Four intramural sports also are offered.

Graduates: Almost half the freshmen remain to graduate. Nearly one-quarter of the graduates pursue advanced degrees.

Services: The college provides counseling, remedial instruction, placement services, and tutoring.

Programs of Study: The college confers the B.A., B.S., B.S.Ed., and B.S.Mus.Ed. degrees. Associate degrees are also offered. Bachelor's degrees are available in the following subjects: BUSINESS (business education, food and lodging administration, general business, secretarial science), EDUCATION (early childhood, elementary, health/physical, recreation, secondary), ENGLISH (English, literature), FINE AND PERFORMING ARTS (art, art education, music, music education), LANGUAGES (French, Spanish), MATH AND SCIENCES (biology, chemistry, general sciences, mathematics), PHILOSOPHY (philosophy, religion), PREPROFESSIONAL (engineering), SOCIAL

842 TENNESSEE

SCIENCES (economics, government/political science, history, psychology, social studies, sociology).

Required: Students must complete a basic studies program made up of 3 interdisciplinary courses—Humanities and Art, Social Science, and Natural Science—and 3 seminars.

Special: The college offers 3-2 engineering programs in cooperation with Lafayette College and the University of Tennessee that lead to degrees in administrative, chemical, electrical, and mechanical engineering. Dual majors, internships, cooperative education plans, and 3-2 programs in liberal arts and a career area are also available. No major preprofessional programs are offered in law, medicine, and health professions.

Honors: The college has an honors program.

Admissions: Almost all applicants for the 1981-82 freshman class were accepted. Applicants should be graduates of an accredited high school with a GPA of at least 1.7 in 15 Carnegie units and a class rank in the top 50%. GED diplomas also are accepted. Culturally disadvantaged students may be admitted under a special program. Applicants to the music program must audition.

Procedure: Students must take the SAT or ACT for placement purposes. Application deadlines are July 15 (fall) and March 15 (spring). A rolling admissions plan is used. The $10 application fee may be waived for applicants with financial need.

Transfer: Transfer applicants should have a GPA of 2.5. D grades do not transfer. Transfers are accepted for all classes. Students must complete at least 36 credits in residence of the 186 required for a bachelor's degree.

Financial Aid: About 90% of the students receive aid. Scholarships, performance awards, BEOG, NDSL, CWS, and special awards are available. The FAF must be filed by March 15.

Foreign Students: Students from foreign countries make up 8% of enrollment. The college offers these students special counseling.

Admissions: Applicants must score at least 475 on the TOEFL. No college entrance exams are required.

Procedure: Application deadlines are the same as those for American students. Foreign students must present a physician's statement as proof of good health and show evidence of adequate funds for 1 year. Special fees may be charged. Health insurance is required, and is available through the college for a fee.

Admissions Contact: Director of Admissions.

LAMBUTH COLLEGE B-3
Jackson, Tennessee 38301 (901) 427-6743

F/T: 211M, 379W	Faculty:	n/av; IIB, —$
P/T: 59M, 89W	Ph.D.'s:	50%
Grad: none	S/F Ratio:	12 to 1
Year: sems, ss	Tuition:	$2685
Appl: Sept. 1	R and B:	$1470
315 applied	275 accepted	150 enrolled
SAT: 450V 400M	ACT: 19	COMPETITIVE

Lambuth College is a United Methodist liberal arts college controlled by the Memphis Conference and open to students of any faith. The library houses 105,000 volumes, holds subscriptions to 500 periodicals, and has 1000 microfilm items.

Environment: The 50-acre campus is located in an urban area 85 miles from Memphis and has a physical plant that includes 4 dormitory facilities.

Student Life: Eighty-five percent of the students come from Tennessee. About 50% live in dormitories. The majority of students are Protestant. Students are encouraged to attend church services and to participate in Christian work. About 20% of the students are minority-group members. Campus housing is single-sex. Students may keep cars on campus.

Organizations: There are 3 fraternities and 4 sororities with chapters on campus; 50% of the men and women belong. Religious clubs on campus include Church Vocations Association and the Campus Congregation.

Sports: The college fields 3 intercollegiate teams for men and 3 for women. There are 3 intramural sports for men and 2 for women.

Handicapped: The college estimates that 10% of the campus is accessible to wheelchair-bound students. Ramps and elevators are provided.

Graduates: The freshman dropout rate is 10%; 60% remain to graduate. Of those who graduate, 25% enter graduate or professional schools; 1% enter medical school, 1% dental school, and 2% law school.

Services: Psychological counseling, tutoring, remedial instruction, placement services, career counseling, and health care are offered at no charge to the student.

Programs of Study: The college confers the B.A., B.S., B.M., and B.B.A. degrees. Bachelor's degrees are offered in the following subjects: BUSINESS (accounting, business education, computer science, industrial management, management, marketing), EDUCATION (elementary, secondary, special), ENGLISH (English), FINE AND PERFORMING ARTS (art, music, music education, theater/dramatics), HEALTH SCIENCES (medical technology, physical therapy), LANGUAGES (German, Italian, Spanish), MATH AND SCIENCES (biology, chemistry, mathematics, physical sciences), PHILOSOPHY (philosophy, religion), PREPROFESSIONAL (architecture, dentistry, engineering, law, medicine, ministry, pharmacy, social work, veterinary), SOCIAL SCIENCES (economics, government/political science, history, psychology, sociology). Of the undergraduate degrees conferred, 27% are in business, 17% in humanities, and 16% in education.

Required: Two hours of physical education are required. UP area tests are required for graduation.

Special: A review program is offered for entering students with inadequate verbal and reading achievement levels. Student-designed majors and a general studies degree are permitted.

Honors: There are 5 national honor societies with chapters on campus. A campus-wide honors program is conducted by the college.

Admissions: Eighty-seven percent of those who applied were accepted for the 1981-82 freshman class. The ACT scores of those who enrolled were as follows: 50% below 21, 16% between 21 and 23, 15% between 24 and 25, 14% between 26 and 28, and 5% above 28. The applicant must have completed 16 Carnegie units at an accredited high school, have at least a 2.0 GPA, and rank in the top half of the graduating class. Other factors of importance are recommendations, extracurricular activities, advanced placement or honors courses, and impressions made during an interview.

Procedure: The ACT or SAT is required. The college uses rolling admissions. Application deadlines are September 1 (fall), January 1 (spring), and June 1 (summer). The application fee is $10. An interview is recommended.

Special: An early admissions plan is offered. CLEP and AP credit is granted.

Transfer: For fall 1981, 199 transfer students applied, and 124 enrolled. Transfers are considered for all classes. Applicants must be in good standing at their previous school. A 2.0 GPA is required. Grades of C or above transfer. Students must complete, at the college, 32 of the 128 credits required to earn a bachelor's degree. Application deadlines are the same as those for freshmen.

Visiting: The best times for visiting are Monday through Friday from 8:30 A.M. to 4:30 P.M.. Other arrangements (weekends and evenings) can be made with the admissions office. Student guides are available for informal visits to the campus.

Financial Aid: About 75% of all students receive aid; 15% of the students work part-time on campus. The college tries to help financially needy freshmen with scholarships and state grants and with federal and private loan funds, including NDSL. The average award to freshmen from all sources is $2600. The FFS is required. The priority deadline for filing the aid application is April 15, although some aid is still available after that date. Tuition may be paid in installments.

Foreign Students: About 1% of the students come from foreign countries. The college offers these students special organizations.

Admissions: Foreign students must achieve a minimum TOEFL score of 450; they must also achieve a score of at least 15 on the ACT.

Procedure: The application deadline for fall is September 1. Foreign students must present proof of health as well as proof of funds adequate to cover 1 year of study.

Admissions Contact: David Ogden, Director of Admissions.

LANE COLLEGE B-3
Jackson, Tennessee 38301 (901) 424-4600

F/T: 639M&W	Faculty:	42; IIB, ——$
P/T: 9M, 9W	Ph.D.'s:	19%
Grad: none	S/F Ratio:	18 to 1
Year: sems, ss	Tuition:	$2064
Appl: see profile	R and B:	$1400
418 applied	375 accepted	194 enrolled
ACT: 10		LESS COMPETITIVE

Lane College, founded in 1882 as a college for blacks, is a liberal arts institution affiliated with the Christian Methodist Episcopal Church. The library contains 80,000 volumes, and subscribes to 450 periodicals.

Environment: The 15-acre campus is located in northeast Jackson, 79 miles from Memphis. The campus has 14 main buildings, including 4 dormitories that house more than 600 students.

Student Life: About 60% of the students come from Tennessee. More than 50% live on campus in the single-sex dorms. The students are predominately black and Protestant. Students are encouraged to participate in weekly chapel services and other religious activities. All single, full-time freshmen and sophomores who do not live at home are required to live on campus.

Organizations: Five fraternities and 4 sororities have chapters on campus. The college sponsors numerous extracurricular activities, including a marching band, college and gospel choirs, departmental and professional clubs, religious organizations, and student publications.

Sports: The college fields intercollegiate teams in 4 sports for men and 1 for women. Intramural sports also are available.

Graduates: About 8% of the freshmen drop out by the end of their first year, and 80% remain to graduate. Of those, 5% seek advanced degrees.

Services: Psychological counseling, placement services, and career counseling are provided free to students. A yearly fee is charged for health services.

Programs of Study: The college confers the B.A. and B.S. degrees. Bachelor's degrees are offered in the following subjects: BUSINESS (computer science, general business), EDUCATION (elementary, health/physical), ENGLISH (communications, English), FINE AND PERFORMING ARTS (music), MATH AND SCIENCES (biology, chemistry, mathematics), PHILOSOPHY (religion), SOCIAL SCIENCES (history, sociology).

Required: Students must complete a core program of 49 semester hours that includes courses in communications, mathematics, physical education, religion, and other subjects.

Special: Remedial programs are available in mathematics, English, and reading. The college also has a writing laboratory. Students may design their own majors. Cooperative programs are available in computer programming with Jackson State University and in physics with Howard University.

Honors: Two national honor societies have chapters on campus.

Admissions: About 90% of those who applied were accepted for the 1981–82 freshman class. Of those who enrolled, 94% scored below 21 on the ACT and 6% between 21 and 23. Applicants must be graduates of an accredited high school or the equivalent and should have completed at least 15 units of academic work.

Procedure: Applicants must take the SAT or, preferably, the ACT. These tests are used for counseling and placement purposes only. Applications should be filed at least 30 days before registration. They are processed on a rolling basis.

Special: AP and CLEP credit is granted.

Transfer: Transfer applicants must be in good standing at their last college. D grades transfer only for students with associate degrees. Students must study on campus for at least 1 year, earning 32 of the 128 credits required for graduation.

Visiting: Prospective students may visit and stay overnight on campus. Arrangements should be made with the office of the director of residential life.

Financial Aid: About 95% of the students receive aid. NDSL, GSLP, CWS, SEOG, and BEOG are all available, along with local grants, loans, and scholarships. Average awards to freshmen range from $900 to $1200. The college is a member of CSS and requires the FFS or FAF. The aid application deadlines are May 1 (fall) and November 1 (spring).

Foreign Students: Students from foreign countries make up less than 1% of enrollment. The college offers these students an intensive English course, an intensive English program, and special counseling.

Admissions: Applicants must take the TOEFL and the SAT or ACT.

Procedure: Application deadlines are the same as those for American students. Foreign students must provide a physician's statement as evidence of good health and show proof of adequate funds for 1 year. There is a special $10 registration fee. Students are required to carry health insurance, which is available through the college for a fee.

Admissions Contact: E. Ruth Maddox, Director of Admissions.

LEE COLLEGE D-4
Cleveland, Tennessee 37311 (615) 472-2111

F/T: 644M, 658W	Faculty: n/av; IIB, –$
P/T: 117M, 53W	Ph.D.'s: 75%
Grad: none	S/F Ratio: 20 to 1
Year: 4-1-4, ss	Tuition: $1980
Appl: open	R and B: $1480
ACT: required	**LESS COMPETITIVE**

Lee College, founded in 1918, is a liberal arts and teachers college affiliated with the Church of God. The library contains 83,427 volumes, and subscribes to 700 periodicals.

Environment: The 23-acre campus is located in a town of 30,000 people, 30 miles from Chattanooga. The 21 buildings include a science building, a gymnasium, and 7 single-sex dormitories which accommodate 750 students.

Student Life: Thirty-five percent of the students are from Tennessee. About 75% live on campus. There is compulsory chapel attendance 3 times a week. Drinking and smoking are forbidden on campus.

Organizations: The college sponsors religious counselors and organizations for its students. Many extracurricular activities are available. There are no fraternities or sororities.

Sports: The college fields intercollegiate teams in 5 sports. Intramural sports for men and women include basketball and tennis.

Handicapped: There are no special facilities for handicapped students.

Graduates: Thirty percent of the graduates pursue advanced degrees; 2% enter medical school and 1% dental school. Thirty-five percent pursue careers in business and industry.

Services: The following services are offered free of charge to students: psychological counseling, health care, tutoring, remedial instruction, placement, and career counseling.

Programs of Study: The college confers the B.A. and B.S. degrees. Bachelor's degrees are offered in the following subjects: BUSINESS (accounting, business administration, management), EDUCATION (elementary, health/physical, secondary, special), ENGLISH (English, speech), FINE AND PERFORMING ARTS (music, music education), HEALTH SCIENCES (medical technology), LANGUAGES (French, Spanish), MATH AND SCIENCES (biology, chemistry, mathematics, natural sciences), PHILOSOPHY (religion), PREPROFESSIONAL (medicine, social work), SOCIAL SCIENCES (geography, psychology, sociology). Of the degrees conferred, 30% are in education, 25% in business, 15% in preprofessional areas, and 15% in math and sciences.

Required: All students must complete the core curriculum plus Bible-related courses.

Special: Holy Land tours are offered during the January term. Combined B.A.-B.S. degrees are available.

Honors: The English department offers an honors program.

Admissions: Candidates must be graduates of accredited high schools, have a C average, and have completed 15 Carnegie units. The minimum ACT score accepted is 17. Other factors considered in the admissions decision are the applicant's personal qualities, recommendations by school officials, and advanced placement or honor courses.

Procedure: The ACT is required and should be taken by July following the senior year. Freshmen are admitted in the fall, summer, and spring. Application deadlines are open. Notification is on a rolling basis. There is a $20 application fee.

Special: The application deadline for early admissions is August. AP and CLEP credit is available.

Transfer: A 2.0 GPA is required. All students must complete, at the college, 30 of the 130 credits required for a bachelor's degree.

Visiting: Guides are available for informal campus visits. Visitors may sit in on classes. Overnight stays may be arranged with the permission of the Dean of Students. The admissions office should be contacted for arrangements.

Financial Aid: About 80% of all students receive financial aid. Scholarships, BEOG/SEOG, NDSL, and CWS are available. Tuition may be paid in installments. The FAF is required. Need is the main consideration in the award of aid. The deadline for aid application is April 1.

Foreign Students: Special counseling is available for students from foreign countries.

844 TENNESSEE

Admissions: Foreign students must take the TOEFL.

Procedure: There are no application deadlines. Foreign students must present proof of adequate funds.

Admissions Contact: Stanley Butler, Dean of Admissions and Records.

LeMOYNE-OWEN COLLEGE   A-4
Memphis, Tennessee 38126   (901) 774-9090

F/T: 342M, 681W	Faculty: 52; IIB, --$
P/T: 15M, 27W	Ph.D.'s: 46%
Grad: none	S/F Ratio: 20 to 1
Year: tri, ss	Tuition: $2500
Appl: July 15	R and B: n/app
350 applied	315 accepted 298 enrolled
ACT: required	LESS COMPETITIVE

LeMoyne-Owen is a privately controlled college of liberal arts and cooperative education affiliated with the United Church of Christ. LeMoyne College was established as a junior college for blacks in 1870, and merged with Owens College in 1968. The library contains 83,030 volumes and 125 microforms, and subscribes to 220 periodicals.

Environment: The 15-acre campus is located in an urban environment in south Memphis. Facilities include a student center, science hall, and gymnasium. There are no dormitory facilities.

Student Life: Almost all the students are from the South. All students live off campus. About 98% of the students are black. Although LeMoyne-Owen is a church-related institution, it makes no religious demands on students. About 89% of the students are Protestant, and 10% are Catholic.

Organizations: There are 4 sororities and 4 fraternities on campus; 45% of the women and 35% of the men belong. In addition, students participate in clubs, special-interest groups, and organizations.

Sports: The college fields 5 intercollegiate teams for men and 5 for women. There are 2 intramural sports for men and 2 for women.

Graduates: The freshman dropout rate is 20%; 35% remain to graduate. Twenty percent pursue graduate study after graduation; 1% enter medical school, 1% law school, and 1% dental school. About 20% enter careers in business and industry.

Services: The college assists the student in finding off-campus housing. The following services are available at no charge to the student: placement, career counseling, health care, tutoring, and remedial instruction.

Programs of Study: B.A., B.S., and B.B.A. degrees are conferred. Bachelor's degrees are offered in the following subjects: BUSINESS (accounting, business administration, business education), EDUCATION (elementary, health/physical, secondary), ENGLISH (English, literature), FINE AND PERFORMING ARTS (art, music), MATH AND SCIENCES (chemistry, mathematics, natural sciences, physical sciences, physics), PHILOSOPHY (humanities, religion), PREPROFESSIONAL (engineering, law, medicine, ministry, social work), SOCIAL SCIENCES (economics, history, social sciences, sociology). Thirty-seven percent of the degrees conferred are in education, 24% in business, and 18% in social sciences.

Required: All students must take a core curriculum including course offerings in the humanities, the social sciences, and the natural sciences.

Special: Cooperative education is a part of the graduation requirements. During the Coop Work Trimester, the student is employed as a trainee in a field of career interest by a business, an industrial firm, or a government, public, or private institution. An on-the-job internship is an integral part of the degree program. Other special programs include independent study, Washington Semester, and exchange programs with the University of Iowa, Grinnell College, and Stephens College. There is a 3-2 engineering program with Tuskegee Institute.

Honors: An honors program is available at the college.

Admissions: About 90% of those who applied were accepted for the 1981-82 freshman class. The ACT scores of those who enrolled were as follows: 40% below 21, 30% between 21 and 23, 20% between 24 and 25, 10% between 26 and 28, and 0% above 28. Applicants must be graduates of accredited high schools. The major emphasis is on entrance examinations; no cut-off scores are specified. Sixteen high school units are required. Students should rank in the upper 65% of their graduating class and have a 2.0 high school GPA. Advanced placement or honors courses, special talent, and impressions made during an interview are also considered important.

Procedure: All applicants must take the ACT by April of the senior year. Application deadlines are July 15 (fall), December 15 (spring), and April 15 (summer). Applicants are notified on a rolling basis. A $25 application fee is required. Freshmen are admitted to both semesters. The CRDA is observed.

Special: Early decision and early admissions plans are available.

Transfer: For fall 1981, 100 transfer students applied, 85 were accepted, and 65 enrolled. A 2.0 GPA is required. Students must complete, at the college, 30 of the 124 credits required for the bachelor's degree. Deadlines are the same as those for freshman applicants.

Financial Aid: About 97% of the students receive aid, which is determined by need. About 60% of the students work part-time on campus. NDSL, BEOG, and SEOG programs are available. A student must maintain a C average to be eligible for loans and CWS; scholarship students must maintain a B average. The FFS is required. Aid applications should be filed by July 15.

Foreign Students: About 2% of the students come from foreign countries. The college offers these students an intensive English course, an intensive English program, and special counseling.

Admissions: Foreign students must take the Comprehensive English Language Test and the ACT.

Procedure: Application deadlines are May 15 (fall), October 15 (spring), and February 15 (summer). Foreign students must present proof of health and must also present proof of funds adequate to cover at least 2 trimesters. They must also carry health insurance, which is available through the college.

Admissions Contact: Carolyn Bishop, Director of Admissions.

LINCOLN MEMORIAL UNIVERSITY   E-2
Harrogate, Tennessee 37752   (615) 869-3611

F/T: 382M, 522W	Faculty: 43; IIB, --$
P/T: 107M, 267W	Ph.D.'s: 40%
Grad: none	S/F Ratio: 21 to 1
Year: qtrs, ss	Tuition: $2260
Appl: open	R and B: $1656
1100 applied	1100 accepted 425 enrolled
ACT: 17	NONCOMPETITIVE

Lincoln Memorial University, established in 1897, is a private nonsectarian coeducational college of arts and sciences. The library contains 60,000 volumes, and subscribes to 800 periodicals.

Environment: The large campus is located in a rural area adjacent to the Cumberland Gap National Historical Park. There are dormitory facilities available for 300 men and 220 women. Housing facilities for married students are also available. The university also sponsors fraternity houses.

Student Life: Ninety percent of the entering freshmen come from public schools; 40% live on campus. About 13% of the students are minority-group members. Campus housing is both coed and single-sex; there are visiting privileges. Students may keep cars on campus. Day-care services are available to full-time students, faculty, and staff for a fee.

Organizations: Three national service organizations, 7 social organizations, and numerous departmental and specialized clubs are open to interested students. Religious facilities are available for Catholic and Protestant students.

Sports: The university fields 5 intercollegiate teams for men and 3 for women. There are 5 intramural sports for men and 3 for women.

Handicapped: Approximately 95% of the campus is accessible to the physically handicapped. Facilities include special parking and elevators; special class scheduling is also available.

Graduates: The freshman dropout rate is 25%; 45% remain to graduate. Fifteen percent of the graduates pursue advanced study; 1% enter medical school, 2% law school, and 1% dental school. About 81% pursue careers in business and industry.

Services: Placement services, career counseling, tutoring, remedial instruction, and psychological counseling are offered free of charge.

Programs of Study: The university confers the B.A. and B.S. degrees. Associate degrees are also awarded. Bachelor's degrees are offered in the following subjects: BUSINESS (accounting, business administration, business education, marketing), EDUCATION (early childhood, elementary, health/physical, secondary, special), ENGLISH (English), FINE AND PERFORMING ARTS (art, art education, music, music education), HEALTH SCIENCES (medical technology, nursing), MATH AND SCIENCES (applied sciences, biology, chemistry, mathematics), PREPROFESSIONAL (dentistry, engineering, forestry, law, medicine, pharmacy, social work), SOCIAL SCIENCES (economics, history, psychology, social sciences). Thirty-eight percent of degrees conferred are in business, 37% in education, and 10% in math and sciences.

Special: The university has a center for research on Lincoln and the Civil War. It is possible to earn a combined B.A.-B.S. degree. Student-designed majors are permitted.

Honors: There are 5 national honor societies with chapters on campus.

Admissions: All of those who applied were accepted for the 1981-82 freshman class. Candidates must be graduates of accredited high schools and have completed 15 units of study. The minimum high school GPA required is 1.5. Candidates without a high school diploma may be admitted on the basis of the GED.

Procedure: The SAT or ACT is required. There are no application deadlines. Freshmen are admitted in all 4 terms. A rolling admissions policy is used. There is a $10 application fee. An interview is recommended.

Special: An early admissions plan is offered. CLEP and AP credit is accepted.

Transfer: For fall 1981, 160 transfer students applied, 160 were accepted, and 132 enrolled. A 2.0 average is recommended. Students must complete, at the university, at least 45 quarter hours of the 192 quarter hours required to earn a bachelor's degree. There are no application deadlines.

Visiting: There are regularly scheduled orientations for prospective students. Guides are also available for informal weekday visits; visitors may sit in on classes and stay overnight at the school. The admissions office should be contacted to arrange visits.

Financial Aid: About 70% of all students receive some form of financial aid; 40% of the students work part-time on campus. Assistance programs include the NDSL, CWS, and the EOG. The average award to freshmen from all sources is $2500. Applications are processed on a rolling basis. The FFS or FAF is required. There is no application deadline.

Foreign Students: About 3% of the students come from foreign countries. The university offers these students special counseling and special organizations.

Admissions: Foreign students must achieve a minimum TOEFL score of 450; no further exams are required.

Procedure: There are no application deadlines. Foreign students must present proof of funds adequate to cover 1 year of study.

Admissions Contact: Conrad Daniels, Director of Admissions.

MARYVILLE COLLEGE   E-3
Maryville, Tennessee 37801   (615) 982-6412

F/T: 307M, 282W	Faculty:	48; IIB, --$
P/T: 11M, 6W	Ph.D.'s:	75%
Grad: none	S/F Ratio:	12 to 1
Year: see profile	Tuition:	$3520
Appl: Sept. 14	R and B:	$1810
491 applied	384 accepted	189 enrolled
SAT: 450V 490M	ACT: 21	COMPETITIVE

Maryville College, established in 1819, is a private liberal arts college affiliated with the United Presbyterian Church. Its library has 110,000 books, and subscribes to 619 periodicals.

Environment: The 375-acre suburban campus is located near the entrance to the Great Smoky Mountains National Park, about 15 miles from Knoxville. There are 20 buildings, including 6 residence halls.

Student Life: About 35% of the students come from Tennessee. Sixty percent are public school graduates. Eighty percent of the students reside on campus. Ten percent are minority-group members. About 61% are Protestant, and 19% are Catholic. Campus housing is both coed and single-sex; there are visiting privileges in the single-sex housing. Students may keep cars on campus. Chapel attendance is not required.

Organizations: The extracurricular program includes religious groups, student government, clubs, service organizations, publications, music and theater groups, and regularly scheduled on-campus social and cultural events. There are no fraternities or sororities.

Sports: The college fields 6 intercollegiate teams for men and 5 for women. There are 6 intramural sports for men and 6 for women.

Handicapped: Wheelchair ramps and special telephones for the hearing-impaired are provided. There are 2 counselors assigned to physically handicapped students. Fewer than 1% of the students have hearing impairments; there are no visually impaired students presently enrolled. Interpreters are provided for students with hearing impairments.

Graduates: Five percent of the freshmen drop out; 50% remain to graduate. About 30% of the graduates go on for further study (4% to medical school, 4% to law school, and 4% to dental school); 65% enter business and industry.

Services: The college provides free health care, psychological counseling, remedial instruction, career counseling, and placement services. Tutoring is available on a fee basis.

Programs of Study: The college confers the B.A. and B.M. degrees. Bachelor's degrees are offered in the following subjects: BUSINESS (business administration, management), EDUCATION (early childhood, elementary, gifted children, health/physical, secondary), ENGLISH (English), FINE AND PERFORMING ARTS (art, art education, music, music education), HEALTH SCIENCES (medical technology, physical therapy), MATH AND SCIENCES (biology, chemistry, mathematics), PHILOSOPHY (philosophy, religion), PREPROFESSIONAL (dentistry, engineering, law, medicine, pharmacy, veterinary), SOCIAL SCIENCES (economics, government/political science, history, psychology). About 21% of the degrees are conferred in business, 16% in math and sciences, and 11% in preprofessional fields.

Required: All students must complete a core curriculum, which includes courses in the humanities and fine arts, the natural sciences, and the social sciences.

Special: A 3-1 medical technology program, independent study, junior year abroad, a 3-year bachelor's degree, individualized majors, internships, and a combination degree program in liberal arts and engineering are offered.

Honors: There are chapters of 15 honor and professional societies on campus. A general honors program, with independent study and research, is offered to qualified students.

Admissions: About 78% of the 1981-82 applicants were accepted. The SAT scores of those who enrolled were as follows: Verbal—71% below 500, 21% between 500 and 599, 7% between 600 and 700, and 1% above 700; Math—58% below 500, 32% between 500 and 599, 10% between 600 and 700, and 0% above 700. On the ACT, 47% scored below 21, 39% between 21 and 23, 10% between 24 and 28, and 4% above 28. Candidates should be graduates of an accredited high school or the equivalent and should have completed 15 Carnegie units. Class rank should be in the top 50%; a 2.0 high school GPA is required. Also considered are the SAT or ACT scores, impressions made during an interview, personality, and the extracurricular activities record.

Procedure: The SAT or ACT should be taken by December of the senior year. Deadlines are September 14 (fall), January 4 (winter), March 23 (spring), and the first day of classes (summer). There are three 10-week terms, a 3-week interim term, and 2 summer sessions. New students are admitted in any 10-week term. Admission and notification are on a rolling basis. There is a $10 application fee.

Special: There are early admissions and deferred admissions programs. CLEP and AP are used.

Transfer: Transfers are accepted for all classes. A 2.0 GPA is needed; D grades usually do not transfer. All students must complete, at the college, 6 of the 40 courses required for a bachelor's degree. Application deadlines are the same as those for freshmen.

Visiting: There is an orientation program for prospective students. Campus tours with student guides can be arranged. Visitors may attend classes and stay in the dormitories. For further information, the admissions office should be contacted.

Financial Aid: About 70% of the students are receiving aid. Ten percent work part-time on campus. The average award to freshmen is $3370. The college offers academic scholarships ($200 to $2500 yearly), grants (including BEOG/SEOG), loans (government and commercial), and part-time campus employment. The FAF should be filed as early as possible. Application deadlines are September 1 (fall), January 4 (winter), and March 15 (spring). The college is a member of CSS. Tuition may be paid in installments.

Foreign Students: Three percent of the full-time students come from foreign countries. An intensive English course, special counseling, and special organizations are available for these students.

Admissions: Foreign students must achieve a TOEFL score of at least 500. No college entrance exams are required.

Procedure: Application deadlines are September 1 (fall), January 4 (winter), March 15 (spring), and June 5 (summer). Foreign students must present a physician's report and must present proof of funds adequate to cover 1 year of study. Health insurance is required and is available through the college for a fee.

846 TENNESSEE

Admissions Contact: Norma Edmondson, Assistant Director of Admissions.

MEMPHIS ACADEMY OF ARTS A-4
Memphis, Tennessee 38112 (901) 726-4085

F/T: 87M, 100W	Faculty:	14; IIB, av$
P/T: 5M, 20W	Ph.D.'s:	n/av
Grad: none	S/F Ratio:	12 to 1
Year: sems, ss	Tuition:	$2500
Appl: Aug. 1	R and B:	n/app
113 applied	78 accepted	55 enrolled
ACT: 15		SPECIAL

Established in 1936, the Memphis Academy of Arts is an independent professional college of art offering undergraduate work only. Its library has 17,000 books and 22,000 slides, and subscribes to 110 periodicals.

Environment: The academy is located in 320-acre Overton Park in midtown Memphis. There are no dormitory facilities. A workshop/sculpture studio adjoins the main building.

Student Life: About one-half of the students come from Memphis and its environs. The majority are public school graduates. All students commute. About 21% of the students are minority-group members. Students may keep cars on campus.

Organizations: The student council, special-interest groups, and college-sponsored cultural events (art shows, films, lectures, and field trips) are offered. There are no fraternities or sororities. The many cultural and recreational facilities of Memphis are available to students.

Graduates: The freshman dropout rate is 12%; 70% remain to graduate. About 20% go on for further study.

Services: A special committee of the student council operates a housing bureau to help new students find appropriate quarters. Placement, career counseling, tutoring, and remedial instruction are offered free of charge. Health care and psychological counseling are available for a fee.

Programs of Study: The academy confers the B.F.A. degree. Certificate programs are also available. Bachelor's degrees are offered in the following subjects: FINE AND PERFORMING ARTS (advertising/illustration, art, clay, fiber, film/photography, metals, painting, printmaking, sculpture, studio art).

Required: The first year's curriculum is prescribed and includes course work in English, art history, and studio arts.

Special: Students may plan their own majors. Exchange programs with 4 other member institutions of the Greater Memphis Consortium are also offered.

Admissions: About 69% of the applicants for the 1981-82 freshman class were accepted. The ACT scores of those who enrolled were as follows: 60% below 21, 20% between 21 and 23, 10% between 24 and 25, 10% between 26 and 28, and 0% above 28. A diploma from an accredited high school or a GED diploma is required. Students should rank in the upper half of their graduating class and have at least a 2.0 GPA. All applicants must present a portfolio of at least 10 and not more than 20 works. Other factors influencing the admissions decision are evidence of special talent and recommendations by school officials.

Procedure: The SAT or ACT is required. The application deadlines are August 1 (fall), December 1 (spring), and June 1 (summer). Notification is sent within 30 days. There is a $10 application fee.

Special: There is a deferred admissions plan. AP and CLEP credit is available.

Transfer: For fall 1981, 49 transfer students applied, 45 were accepted, and 34 enrolled. Transfer students are accepted for all classes. Good academic standing is required: students must also submit a portfolio. Grades of C or above transfer. One year must be completed in residence; 132 credits are required to earn a bachelor's degree. Application deadlines are the same as those for freshmen.

Visiting: Prospective students are encouraged to visit the academy. A tour of the campus with a student guide must be arranged through the director of admissions.

Financial Aid: About 45% of the students are getting aid; 34% of the students work part-time on campus. The academy offers 5 to 10 freshman scholarships each year, federal and state grants, various commercial (bank) and governmental loans, and work-study (CWS). Aid is usually awarded in the form of a package. In some cases tuition may be paid in installments. The academy is a member of CSS; the FAF or FFS should be filed by August 1 for fall admission.

Foreign Students: About 1% of the students come from foreign countries.

Admissions: Foreign students must take the TOEFL; no further exams are required.

Procedure: Application deadlines are April 1 (fall) and December 1 (spring). Foreign students must present proof of funds adequate to cover 1 year of study.

Admissions Contact: Carol DeForest, Director of Admissions.

MEMPHIS STATE UNIVERSITY A-4
Memphis, Tennessee 38152 (901) 454-2101

F/T: 5315M, 5316W	Faculty:	749; I, --$
P/T: 1911M, 2628W	Ph.D.'s:	70%
Grad: 1806M, 2538W	S/F Ratio:	21 to 1
Year: sems, ss	Tuition:	$732 ($2660)
Appl: Aug. 1	R:	$860
3367 applied	2894 accepted	2124 enrolled
ACT: 20		LESS COMPETITIVE

Memphis State University, established in 1912, is a state-controlled institution. In addition to its traditional academic program, Memphis State has an innovative division, University College, which awards degrees on the basis of individualized programs of study. The university library contains 700,000 volumes and 1.4 million microfilm items, and subscribes to 4700 periodicals.

Environment: Located in an urban area, the 120-acre campus houses 54 major buildings, including residence halls that accommodate 2116 men and women. There are also apartments for 120 married students and fraternity houses. There is no University Meal Plan available, but cafeterias are located on campus.

Student Life: Ninety-three percent of the students are from Tennessee. Twelve percent live on campus. Nineteen percent of the students are minority-group members. University housing is single-sex, and there are visiting privileges. Students may keep cars on campus.

Organizations: There are 14 national fraternities and 8 national sororities on campus, to which 8% of the men and 5% of the women belong. Concerts, lectures, plays, and other social and cultural activities are sponsored by the students and the university. Students also participate in 29 professional and departmental clubs.

Sports: The university fields 10 intercollegiate teams for men and 9 for women. There are 12 intramural sports for men and 10 for women.

Handicapped: The university estimates the campus to be 89% accessible to wheelchair-bound students. Facilities include ramps, elevators, designated parking areas, specially equipped rest rooms, lowered drinking fountains and telephones, and a specially equipped bus. A reader machine is available for the visually impaired. A staff of 4 counselors is on hand to provide assistance.

Graduates: The freshman dropout rate is 14%, and 29% of the freshmen remain to graduate.

Services: The following services are offered at no charge to the student: psychological counseling, tutoring, remedial instruction, health care, placement services, and career counseling.

Programs of Study: The university confers the B.A., B.S., B.B.A., B.F.A., B.M., B.S.C.E., B.S.E.E., B.S.M.E., B.S.T., B.S.E.T., B.S.H.E., B.S.M.T., B.S.G., B.S.N., and B.S.Ed. degrees; its University College division offers the B.L.S. and B.P.S. degrees. Master's and doctoral degrees are also awarded. Bachelor's degrees are offered in the following subjects: AREA STUDIES (Latin American, urban), BUSINESS (accounting, business administration, business education, finance, international business, management, marketing, office administration, real estate/insurance), EDUCATION (early childhood, elementary, health/physical, recreation/park administration, secondary, special, vocational home economics), ENGLISH (English, journalism, speech), FINE AND PERFORMING ARTS (art, art history, commercial music, music, theater/dramatics), HEALTH SCIENCES (medical technology, nursing, occupational therapy), LANGUAGES (French, German, Greek/Latin, Italian, Russian, Spanish), MATH AND SCIENCES (biology, chemistry, geology, mathematics, physical sciences, physics), PHILOSOPHY (philosophy), PREPROFESSIONAL (dentistry, medicine, veterinary), SOCIAL SCIENCES (anthropology, criminal justice, economics, geography, government/political science, history, international relations, psychology, social work, sociology). Of the degrees conferred, 26% are in business, 18% in preprofessional studies, and 18% in education.

Special: Junior year study abroad, a general studies degree, and student-designed majors are permitted. Combined B.A.-B.S. degrees may be earned in any of the majors offered if all requirements are met.

Programs of study in University College are based upon individual learning contracts.

Honors: A variety of honors programs is offered by the university. There are 16 national honor societies and 10 professional honor societies with chapters on campus.

Admissions: Eighty-six percent of those who applied were accepted for the 1981-82 freshman class. Of those who enrolled, the ACT scores were as follows: 64% below 21, 19% between 21 and 23, 9% between 24 and 25, 6% between 26 and 28, and 2% above 28. Applicants must be graduates of accredited high schools and have at least a 2.0 grade average. Out-of-state applicants must rank in the upper 50% of their graduating classes. The minimum acceptable ACT score is 16. The university also considers evidence of special talents and the ability to finance a college education.

Procedure: The ACT and the SCAT are required. Applications are due August 1 (fall), December 1 (spring), or May 1 (summer). Notification is on a rolling basis. There is a $5 application fee.

Special: An early decision plan is available. AP credit is given.

Transfer: For fall 1981, 3011 students applied, 2333 were accepted, and 1236 enrolled. Transfers are accepted for all classes. A minimum ACT score of 18 and 3 completed credit hours are required. All grades transfer. Students must complete, at the university, 33 of the final 66 credits toward the 132 credits necessary for a bachelor's degree. Transfer application deadlines are the same as those for freshmen.

Visiting: The university conducts regularly scheduled orientations for prospective students. Guides are available for informal visits to the campus. Visitors may sit in on classes if the instructor permits or may stay overnight at the campus. The school recommends weekdays, from 8 A.M. to 4:30 P.M., as the best time for visits. The student relations office (901) 454-2169 handles arrangements.

Financial Aid: About 30% of all students receive aid. Ten percent work part-time on campus. Average aid to freshmen is $900. Scholarships, loans, and grants are available. The FAF, FFS, or SFS is required. The deadline for filing aid applications is April 1.

Foreign Students: Two percent of the full-time students come from foreign countries. The university offers these students special counseling and special organizations.

Admissions: Foreign students must achieve a TOEFL score of at least 500 or take an equivalent English proficiency exam. They must also achieve a combined SAT score of 800 or an ACT score of 18.

Procedure: Application deadlines are May 1 (fall), September 15 (spring), and February 1 (summer). Foreign students must present certification of good health by a licensed physician, proof of adequate funds, and a special out-of-state fee of $1130. They must also carry health insurance, which is available through the university for a fee.

Admissions Contact: David R. Wallace, Associate Dean.

MIDDLE TENNESSEE STATE UNIVERSITY
C-3

Murfreesboro, Tennessee 37132   (615) 898-2111

F/T: 3965M, 4100W   Faculty: 408; I, --$
P/T: 709M, 717W   Ph.D.'s: 63%
Grad: 631M, 809W   S/F Ratio: 20 to 1
Year: sems, ss   Tuition: $707 ($2237)
Appl: open   R and B: $1306
3148 applied   2945 accepted   1862 enrolled
ACT: 17   LESS COMPETITIVE

Middle Tennessee State University, founded in 1911, is a publicly supported institution offering training in general education, professional fields, teacher education, arts and science, and business and industry. The library contains 403,795 volumes, has 572,254 microfilm items, and holds subscriptions to 2883 periodicals.

Environment: The $55-million physical plant is located on a 600-acre campus in the heart of Tennessee. The environment surrounding the campus is rural. Facilities include 23 dormitories accommodating 3312 students; there are also 192 apartments for married students.

Student Life: About 95% of the students come from the South; 29% live on campus. Drinking is not permitted on state property. About 70% of the students are Protestant, and 8% are Catholic. About 12% of the students are minority-group members. Campus housing is single-sex; there are visiting privileges. Students may keep cars on campus. Day-care services are available to all students, faculty, and staff for a fee.

Organizations: There are 14 national fraternities, to which 12% of the men belong; 8% of the women belong to the 6 national sororities. There is a wide variety of extracurricular activities, including an active student government.

Sports: The university fields 7 intercollegiate teams for men and 4 for women. There are 15 intramural sports for men and 14 for women.

Handicapped: Approximately 70% of the campus is accessible to the physically handicapped. Facilities include wheelchair ramps, special parking, elevators, specially equipped rest rooms, and lowered drinking fountains and telephones; special class scheduling is also available. A vocational rehabilitation counselor comes to the campus once a week.

Graduates: The freshman dropout rate is 20%; 40% remain to graduate. About 10% of the men and 5% of the women who graduate pursue graduate study.

Services: Placement services, career counseling, health care, and psychological counseling are offered free of charge. Tutoring and remedial instruction are available for a fee.

Programs of Study: The university confers the B.A., B.S., B.U.S., B.F.A., B.B.A., B.M., and B.S.S.W. degrees. Associate, master's, and doctoral programs are also offered. Bachelor's degrees are offered in the following subjects: BUSINESS (accounting, business administration, business education, computer science, distributive education, finance, information systems, management, marketing, office management, university studies), EDUCATION (early childhood, elementary, health/physical, industrial, special), ENGLISH (English, journalism, speech), FINE AND PERFORMING ARTS (art, art education, mass communications, music, recording industry management, theater/dramatics), HEALTH SCIENCES (medical technology, nursing, speech therapy), LANGUAGES (French, German, Spanish), MATH AND SCIENCES (biology, chemistry, earth science, mathematics, physics, science), PHILOSOPHY (philosophy), PREPROFESSIONAL (aerospace, agriculture, architecture, dentistry, engineering, forestry, home economics, law, medicine, pharmacy, social work, veterinary), SOCIAL SCIENCES (economics, geography, government/political science, history, international relations, psychology, social sciences, sociology).

Special: A Bachelor of University Studies degree designed for mature adult students is offered.

Honors: There are 15 national honor societies with chapters on campus. Nineteen university departments offer honors programs.

Admissions: Ninety-four percent of those who applied were accepted for the 1981-82 freshman class. The ACT scores of those who enrolled were as follows: 72% below 21, 15% between 21 and 23, 8% between 24 and 25, 5% between 26 and 28, and 2% above 28. Candidates must be graduates of approved high schools and have a minimum score of 16 on the ACT or a C average in all subjects.

Procedure: The ACT is required for Tennessee residents; out-of-state applicants may substitute the SAT. There is no formal application deadline; freshmen are admitted in the fall, spring, and summer terms. Admissions are on a rolling basis. There is a $5 application fee.

Special: An early admissions plan is offered. CLEP and AP credit is accepted.

Transfer: For fall 1981, 1467 transfer students applied, 1144 were accepted, and 873 enrolled. Transfers are accepted for all classes. D grades transfer. Students must complete, at the university, 30 credits of the 132 credits required to earn a bachelor's degree. A 1.5 GPA is required. There are no formal application deadlines.

Visiting: There are regularly scheduled orientations for prospective students. Guides are also available for informal visits; visitors may sit in on classes. The admissions office should be contacted to arrange visits.

Financial Aid: About 60% of all students receive some form of aid. Financial aid ranges from $50 through total cost. The average aid to freshmen is between $1100 and $1400. There are work-study programs in all departments. The university is a member of CSS; the FFS is required. The deadline for financial aid applications is May 15.

Foreign Students: About 2% of the students come from foreign countries. The university offers these students special counseling and special organizations.

Admissions: Foreign students must achieve a minimum TOEFL score of 450 or a minimum score of 75 on the University of Michigan Language Test; no further exams are required.

Procedure: Application deadlines are August 1 (fall), December 1 (spring), and June 1 (summer). Foreign students must present proof of health, and they must present proof of funds adequate to cover 1 year of study. Health insurance is strongly recommended and is available through the university for a fee.

Admissions Contact: W. Wes Williams, Director of Admissions.

848 TENNESSEE

MILLIGAN COLLEGE F-2
Milligan College, Tennessee 37682   (615) 929-0116

F/T: 306M, 368W	Faculty: 38; n/av
P/T: 55M, 43W	Ph.D.'s: 60%
Grad: 361M, 411W	S/F Ratio: 14 to 1
Year: sems, ss	Tuition: $2824
Appl: Aug. 1	R and B: $1992
342 applied	298 accepted	172 enrolled
SAT or ACT: required	LESS COMPETITIVE

Founded in 1881, Milligan College is a private liberal arts college affiliated with the Christian Church. The library houses 110,000 volumes and microfilm items, and holds subscriptions to 440 periodicals.

Environment: Located 3 miles from Johnson City, the 135-acre campus has a physical plant that includes dormitories and housing for married students.

Student Life: About 25% of the students are from Tennessee. Seventy-three percent of the students are campus residents. Ninety-eight percent are Protestant, and 1% are Catholic; the majority of students are members of the Christian Church. All students are required to attend religious services twice a week. About 4% of the students are minority-group members. Campus housing is single-sex; there are no visiting privileges. Students may keep cars on campus.

Organizations: There are no fraternities or sororities. Student activities include participation in student government, parties, weekly movies, and sponsoring of outside concerts, lectures, and other events. Nearby attractions are a theater, a civic center, ski resorts, and lakes.

Sports: The college fields 7 intercollegiate teams for men and 7 for women. There are 2 intramural sports for men and 1 for women.

Handicapped: Special facilities for the physically handicapped include designated parking areas, elevators, specially equipped rest rooms, and lowered drinking fountains. Fifty percent of the campus is accessible to these students. There are no special counselors.

Graduates: The freshman dropout rate is 23%; 48% remain to graduate. Of the latter, 20% pursue further study. Twenty-five percent pursue careers in business or industry.

Services: The following services are offered at no charge to the student: psychological counseling, tutoring, remedial instruction, health care, placement services, and career counseling.

Programs of Study: The college confers the A.B. and B.S. degrees. Associate degrees are also awarded. Bachelor's degrees are offered in the following subjects: BUSINESS (accounting, business administration), EDUCATION (early childhood, elementary, health/physical, secondary, special), ENGLISH (English), FINE AND PERFORMING ARTS (music, music education), MATH AND SCIENCES (biology, chemistry, mathematics), PHILOSOPHY (humanities, religion), PRE-PROFESSIONAL (dentistry, engineering, home economics, law, medicine, ministry, pharmacy, social work, veterinary), SOCIAL SCIENCES (economics, history, psychology, social sciences, sociology).

Required: All students must take more than 50 hours of general education requirements, including 9 hours of Bible study and 2 hours of physical education.

Special: Cooperative programs are available with East Tennessee State University. Summer study tours to Europe are offered.

Honors: The philosophy honor society, Phi Sigma Tau, has a chapter on campus.

Admissions: About 87% of those who applied were accepted for the 1981-82 freshman class. The SAT scores of those who enrolled were as follows: Verbal—78% below 500, 19% between 500 and 599, 3% between 600 and 700, and 0% above 700; Math—63% below 500, 31% between 500 and 599, 3% between 600 and 700, and 3% above 700. The ACT scores of those who enrolled were as follows: 58% below 21, 21% between 21 and 23, 7% between 24 and 25, 8% between 26 and 28, and 6% above 28. Candidates should have completed 16 academic units of high school work. Recommendations by school officials are important considerations in the admissions decision.

Procedure: The ACT or SAT is required. Application deadlines are August 1 (fall), December 1 (spring), and May 1 (summer). There is a $10 application fee. Admissions are considered on a rolling basis.

Special: There are early decision, early admissions, and deferred admissions plans. CLEP and AP credit is granted.

Transfer: For fall 1981, 81 transfer students applied, 71 were accepted, and 49 enrolled. A 2.0 GPA is required. Students must complete, at the college, 30 of the 128 credits required to earn a bachelor's degree. Application deadlines are the same as those for freshman applicants.

Visiting: The college conducts regularly scheduled orientations for the prospective student. Guides are available for informal visits to the campus. Visitors may sit in on classes and stay at the school. To arrange a visit, the office of student enlistment should be contacted.

Financial Aid: About 52% of all students receive aid. Scholarships, loans, and campus employment are available. The FAF is required. The deadline for aid application is April 1.

Foreign Students: About 1% of the students come from foreign countries. The college offers these students special organizations.

Admissions: Foreign students must achieve a minimum TOEFL score of 550; in addition, they must take the SAT or ACT.

Procedure: Application deadlines are August 1 (fall), December 1 (spring), and May 1 (summer). Foreign students must present proof of health as well as proof of funds adequate to cover 1 year of study. They must also carry health insurance, which is available through the college for a fee.

Admissions Contact: Paul Bader, Director of Enlistment.

SOUTHERN MISSIONARY COLLEGE D-4
Collegedale, Tennessee 37315   (615) 396-4008

F/T: 656M, 782W	Faculty: 112; IIB, – – $
P/T: 159M, 248W	Ph.D.'s: 33%
Grad: none	S/F Ratio: 14 to 1
Year: sems, ss	Tuition: $3780
Appl: open	R and B: $1900
731 applied	721 accepted	540 enrolled
ACT: 18	LESS COMPETITIVE

Founded in 1892, Southern Missionary College is a private coeducational liberal arts college affiliated with the Seventh-day Adventist Church. The library contains 110,000 volumes and holds subscriptions to 1120 periodicals.

Environment: The 900-acre campus is located in a rural area about 18 miles from Chattanooga. There are residence halls, on-campus apartments, and married student housing.

Student Life: Most of the students are from the southeastern states. Many students are members of the supporting church. A large percentage of the student body live in dormitories or other college-approved housing. Drinking and smoking are prohibited. Students living in residence halls are required to attend weekly chapel services. An 11 P.M. curfew is observed. About 12% of the students are minority-group members. Campus housing is single-sex; there are no visiting privileges. Students may keep cars on campus. Day-care services are available for all students, faculty, and staff.

Organizations: There are no sororities or fraternities, but students can belong to various professional clubs.

Sports: There is no intercollegiate sports program. There are 13 intramural sports for men and 13 for women.

Handicapped: The college estimates the campus to be 25% accessible to wheelchair-bound students. Special facilities include wheelchair ramps, designated handicapped parking, and elevators.

Graduates: The freshman dropout rate is 42%; 25-30% remain to receive their degrees. Of those who graduate, 35% pursue further study. Ten percent pursue careers in business and industry.

Services: The following services are offered free of charge: psychological counseling, health care, placement, and career counseling. Tutoring and remedial instruction are also available.

Programs of Study: The college confers the B.S., B.A., and B. Med. Tech. degrees. Associate degrees are also offered. Bachelor's degrees are offered in the following subjects: BUSINESS (accounting, business administration, business education, computer science, management), EDUCATION (elementary, secondary), ENGLISH (English, journalism, speech), FINE AND PERFORMING ARTS (art, radio/TV), HEALTH SCIENCES (medical technology, nursing), LANGUAGES (French, German), MATH AND SCIENCES (biology, chemistry, mathematics, physics), PHILOSOPHY (religion), PREPROFESSIONAL (ministry), SOCIAL SCIENCES (history, international relations, psychology, sociology). Thirty percent of degrees conferred are in health sciences, 20% in math and sciences, and 15% in education.

Honors: An honors program is offered by the English department.

Admissions: Almost 99% of those who applied were accepted for the 1981-82 freshman class. The ACT scores of those who enrolled were as follows: 24% between 21 and 23, 14% between 24 and 25, 2% between 26 and 28, and 1% above 28. Applicants must be graduates of accredited high schools or academies, have completed 16 units of work, and have a C average or better. Students from nonaccredited high schools are admitted on the basis of examinations; mature students are admitted on the basis of the GED.

Procedure: The ACT is required. There are no deadlines for application. Freshmen are admitted in the fall, winter, and summer terms. There is a $15 application fee. The college follows a rolling admissions plan.

Special: CLEP credit is accepted.

Transfer: For fall 1981, 252 transfer students applied, and 249 were accepted. A minimum average of 2.0 is required for transfer. D grades are acceptable. Students must complete, at the college, 30 of the 124–128 credits required to earn a bachelor's degree. Application deadlines are August 1 (fall) and December 1 (winter).

Visiting: Overnight visits to the college are permitted on a limited basis. The admissions office should be contacted to arrange visits.

Financial Aid: About 65% of all students receive some form of financial aid. Eighty-five percent work part-time on campus. There are work-study programs in 7 departments. Applications for aid must be filed by August 1. The FAF is required.

Foreign Students: The college accepts foreign students but does not actively recruit them. The college offers these students an intensive English course and special counseling.

Admissions: Foreign students must achieve a minimum score of 90 on the University of Michigan Language Test; they must also take the ACT.

Procedure: Application deadlines are August 1 (fall) and December 1 (winter). Foreign students must present proof of health as well as proof of funds adequate to cover 1 year of study.

Admissions Contact: Ronald Barrow, Director of Admissions.

SOUTHWESTERN AT MEMPHIS A-4
Memphis, Tennessee 38112 (901) 274-1800

F/T: 528M, 527W	Faculty:	86; IIB, ++$
P/T: 8M, 17W	Ph.D.'s:	80%
Grad: none	S/F Ratio:	11 to 1
Year: 4-4-2, ss	Tuition:	$4500
Appl: Feb. 15	R and B:	$2280
787 applied	663 accepted	282 enrolled
SAT: 544V 584M	ACT: 26	VERY COMPETITIVE+

Founded in 1848, Southwestern at Memphis is a college of liberal arts affiliated with the Presbyterian Church. The library contains 173,000 volumes and 1100 microfilm items, and subscribes to 950 periodicals.

Environment: The college is situated on a 100-acre tract of land in the center of Memphis. Its buildings are of collegiate Gothic style. There are men's and women's residence halls.

Student Life: Fewer than 50% of the students come from Tennessee. About 95% live on campus. Twelve percent are Catholic, 68% are Protestant; 30% are members of the Presbyterian Church. About 60% of the entering freshmen come from public schools. Alcohol is permitted in residence halls. About 3% are minority-group members. Campus housing is single-sex; there are visiting privileges. Students may keep cars on campus.

Organizations: Six fraternities and 4 sororities have chapters on campus; 45% of the men and 40% of the women belong to one of them. A full extracurricular activities program is offered.

Sports: The college fields intercollegiate teams in 8 sports for men and 3 for women. There are 15 intramural teams for men and 14 for women.

Handicapped: About 90% of the campus is accessible to handicapped students. Facilities include wheelchair ramps, elevators, and parking areas. Three counselors are available to handicapped students.

Graduates: The freshman dropout rate is 2%; 75% of the students remain to graduate; about 60% of the graduates pursue advanced degrees.

Services: Psychological counseling, health care, placement, and career counseling are offered free of charge to students. Tutoring and remedial instruction are available on a fee basis.

Programs of Study: The college confers the B.A., B.S., and B.Mus. degrees. Bachelor's degrees are offered in the following subjects: AREA STUDIES (American, urban), BUSINESS (accounting, business administration, economics, finance, management, marketing), EDUCATION (elementary, secondary), ENGLISH (English), FINE AND PERFORMING ARTS (art, art education, art history, communications, music, music education, studio art), HEALTH SCIENCES (nursing, physical therapy), LANGUAGES (French, German, Greek/Latin, Spanish), MATH AND SCIENCES (biology, chemistry, mathematics, physics), PHILOSOPHY (classics, philosophy, religion), PREPROFESSIONAL (architecture, dentistry, engineering, law, medicine, ministry, pharmacy, social work), SOCIAL SCIENCES (economics, history, international relations, psychology, sociology).

Required: The required core curriculum includes courses in humanities, natural sciences, social sciences, and arts and communication.

Special: Student-designed majors, study abroad, directed inquiry seminars, tutorial programs, and a 3–2 combination degree in engineering are offered.

Honors: Eight honor societies, including Phi Beta Kappa, have chapters on campus. Honors programs are available.

Admissions: Eighty-four percent of those who applied were accepted for the 1981–82 freshman class. The SAT scores of those who enrolled were as follows: Verbal—26% below 500, 47% between 500 and 599, 21% between 600 and 700, and 5% above 700; Math—15% below 500, 41% between 500 and 599, 30% between 600 and 700, and 13% above 700. Applicants must be graduates of accredited high schools and have completed 16 units of work. Those who rank in the upper half of their class and have a 3.0 high school GPA are most likely to be accepted.

Procedure: The ACT or SAT is required and should be taken by January of the senior year. Application deadlines are February 15 (fall) and December 1 (winter). Students who intend to live on campus should apply by February 1. There is a $15 application fee. Notification is on a rolling basis beginning March 15.

Special: There are early decision, early admissions, and deferred admissions plans. The notification date for early decision is December 1; the application deadline for early admissions is November 15. AP credit is given.

Transfer: For fall 1981, 107 transfer students applied, 84 were accepted, and 54 enrolled. A 2.0 GPA is required. Students must complete, at the college, 60 of the 124 credits required to earn a bachelor's degree. Grades of C or above transfer. Application deadlines are the same as those for freshman applicants.

Visiting: Guides are available for informal campus visits. Visitors may sit in on classes and stay overnight at the school. Visits are best scheduled on Thursday, Friday, or Saturday. The admissions office should be contacted for arrangements.

Financial Aid: About 60% of all students receive financial aid; 29% of the students work part-time on campus. The college offers scholarships from a fund of $800,000; other aid may be obtained through federal loan funds, BEOG/SEOG, CWS, and guaranteed loans. The average award to freshmen from all sources available through the college is $3662. Tuition may be paid in installments. The college is a member of the CSS. The FAF is required; aid applications must be submitted by February 15.

Foreign Students: About 2% of the students come from foreign countries. The college offers these students an intensive English course and special counseling.

Admissions: Foreign students must achieve a minimum TOEFL score of 500; no further exams are required.

Procedure: Application deadlines are February 15 (fall) and December 1 (winter). Foreign students must present proof of funds adequate to cover 4 years of study. They must also carry health insurance, which is not available through the college.

Admissions Contact: Mary Jo Miller, Director of Admissions.

TENNESSEE STATE UNIVERSITY C-3
Nashville, Tennessee 37221 (615) 320-3420

F/T: 2328M, 2430W	Faculty:	500; IIA, av$
P/T: 1151M, 1497W	Ph.D.'s:	n/av
Grad: 500M, 532W	S/F Ratio:	15 to 1
Year: sems, ss	Tuition:	$792 ($2550)
Appl: open	R and B:	$1790
2000 applied	1500 accepted	997 enrolled
ACT: 14		LESS COMPETITIVE

Tennessee State University, established in 1912, includes the schools of Agriculture and Home Economics, Engineering, Arts and Sciences, and Education, the divisions of Business and Field Services, the Department of Air Sciences, and the Graduate School. The library contains more than 120,000 volumes, and subscribes to about 2000 periodicals.

850 TENNESSEE

Environment: The university's campus, farmlands, and pastures occupy 450 acres. The central campus, located in an urban setting, has more than 30 buildings. Students may live in 6 residence halls or a limited number of university-approved homes in the city.

Student Life: About three-fourths of the students are from Tennessee; 90% are from the South. The student body is predominately black. About 30% of the students live in the dormitories, which are single-sex.

Organizations: Four fraternities and 4 sororities have chapters on campus. The university sponsors many cultural, social, and recreational activities. Extracurricular activities include student government, publications, music and drama groups, and religious organizations.

Sports: The university fields intercollegiate teams in 8 sports for men and 2 for women. Intramural sports also are available.

Handicapped: The university is working to make the campus accessible to handicapped students.

Graduates: About 40% of the freshmen drop out. About 10% of the graduates pursue advanced degrees.

Services: Health care, psychological counseling, placement aid, and career counseling are available to students.

Programs of Study: The university confers the B.A., B.S., and B.S.E. degrees. Associate and master's degrees also are available. Bachelor's degrees are offered in the following subjects: BUSINESS (business administration, business education, office administration), EDUCATION (early childhood, elementary, health/physical, recreation, secondary), ENGLISH (English, speech), FINE AND PERFORMING ARTS (art, music, theater/dramatics), HEALTH SCIENCES (dental hygiene, health care administration, medical records, medical technology, nursing, speech therapy), LANGUAGES (French, Spanish), MATH AND SCIENCES (biology, chemistry, mathematics, physics), PREPROFESSIONAL (aeronautics, agriculture—animal science, agriculture—plant science, agriculture—rural development, engineering, engineering—architectural, engineering—civil, engineering—electrical, engineering—mechanical, home economics, industrial technology, social work, transportation technology), SOCIAL SCIENCES (criminal justice, geography, government/political science, history, psychology, sociology).

Required: All students are required to take physical education and complete general education requirements.

Special: A communications clinic offers training in speech, writing, and other communications skills. Cooperative education and cross-registration programs are available. Additional minors include special education and Afro-American studies.

Honors: Honors programs are available.

Admissions: Seventy-five percent of those who applied were accepted for the 1981–82 freshman class. Applicants must have a high school diploma or a passing grade on the GED. Preference is given to Tennessee residents. Out-of-state applicants must have a GPA of at least 2.35.

Procedure: The ACT or SAT is required. Credentials should be submitted in the final semester of the senior year. Applications should be filed at least 45 days before the start of a semester. Notification is made on a rolling basis. The application fee is $5.

Special: An early admissions plan is available.

Transfer: Transfer students are accepted for all classes. D grades transfer. A 2.0 GPA is required of nonresidents who are not transferring from Tennessee colleges. Transfer students must spend at least 1 year in residence, earning 30 of the 132 credits required for a bachelor's degree.

Financial Aid: About 95% of the students receive aid. Scholarships, federal loans, and campus jobs are available. Either the FAF or the FFS must be filed by May 1.

Foreign Students: Students from foreign countries make up 5% of enrollment. The university offers these students special counseling and special organizations.

Admissions: Applicants must score 500 or better on the TOEFL. No college entrance exams are required.

Procedure: Overseas students must apply at least 1 year in advance of the time they seek to enroll. They must provide a physician's statement as proof of good health and show evidence of adequate funds for 4 years. Special fees are charged; in 1981–82 the amount was $25 per semester.

Admissions Contact: J. Grey Hall, Dean of Admissions and Records.

TENNESSEE TECHNOLOGICAL UNIVERSITY D–3
Cookeville, Tennessee 38501   (615) 528-3888

F/T: 3735M, 2562W   Faculty: 376; IIA, +$
P/T: 222M, 349W   Ph.D.'s: 60%
Grad: 301M, 354W   S/F Ratio: 19 to 1
Year: qtrs, ss   Tuition: $705 ($2235)
Appl: see profile   R and B: $1479
2224 enrolled
ACT: 20   **COMPETITIVE**

Established as Tennessee Polytechnic Institute in 1915, Tennessee Technological University is a coeducational, multi-purpose institution under state control. The undergraduate divisions include 6 colleges: Arts and Sciences, Agriculture and Home Economics, Business, Education, Engineering, and Nursing. The library contains 346,831 volumes, holds subscriptions to 1994 periodicals, and has 489,495 microfilm items.

Environment: The 235-acre campus, with a 300-acre farm adjoining, is located in a rural area 80 miles east of Nashville. There are 73 buildings, including a university center, an engineering-science complex, a computer center, a new fine arts building, and residence halls that accommodate 1786 men, 1487 women, and 304 married students (in apartment units). The university also sponsors fraternity houses.

Student Life: Ninety percent of the students are from Tennessee; 50% live in dormitories or fraternity or sorority houses. About 55% of the students are Protestant and 7% are Catholic. About 6% of the students are minority-group members. Campus housing is single-sex; there are visiting privileges. Students may keep cars on campus.

Organizations: There are 13 fraternities, to which 20–25% of the men belong; 10% of the women belong to the 6 sororities. Extracurricular activities include departmental and nondepartmental clubs.

Sports: The university fields 9 intercollegiate teams for men and 4 for women. There are 10 intramural sports for men and 8 for women.

Handicapped: The campus has an exterior accessibility of 60% and an interior accessibility of 50% for the physically handicapped. Facilities include wheelchair ramps, special parking, elevators (in some buildings), and specially equipped rest rooms; special class scheduling can also be arranged. Special tutors, assistance, and testing facilities are available for students with visual or hearing impairments.

Graduates: The freshman dropout rate is 25%; 45% remain to graduate. Twenty-five percent of the graduates pursue graduate study.

Services: Placement services, career counseling, health care, psychological counseling, tutoring, and remedial instruction are offered free of charge.

Programs of Study: The university confers the B.A., B.S., and B.F.A. degrees. Associate, master's, and doctoral programs are also offered. Bachelor's degrees are offered in the following subjects: BUSINESS (accounting, business administration, computer science, finance, management, marketing), EDUCATION (early childhood, elementary, health/physical, secondary, special), ENGLISH (English, journalism, speech), FINE AND PERFORMING ARTS (art education, music, music education, music therapy), HEALTH SCIENCES (nursing), LANGUAGES (French, German, Spanish), MATH AND SCIENCES (biology, chemistry, geology, mathematics, physics), PREPROFESSIONAL (dentistry, engineering, forestry, law, medicine, pharmacy, pre-medical technology, pre-physical therapy, veterinary), SOCIAL SCIENCES (economics, government/political science, history, psychology, sociology). The majority of degrees conferred are in engineering; 21% are in education, and 12% in business.

Special: A cooperative work-study plan permits students to alternate yearly between study at the university and employment with industry, business, a school system, or a government agency. Additional programs include Tech Aqua (biological research station), and Tech Farm.

Honors: Thirteen departments participate in the university's honors program.

Admissions: More than 95% of those who applied were accepted for a recent freshman class. The ACT scores of those who enrolled were as follows: 47% below 21, 23% between 21 and 23, 13% between 24 and 25, 13% between 26 and 28, and 5% above 28. Applicants must be graduates of approved or accredited high schools and have a minimum high school average of 2.35 and/or an ACT composite of 17. Engineering applicants must have an ACT composite and math score of at least 18 in addition to the 2.35 average. The minimum GED score is 50.

Procedure: Applications should be submitted no later than 2 weeks prior to the start of each quarter. The ACT is required. There is a $5 application fee. Admissions are on a rolling basis.

Special: The application deadline for early admission is 2 weeks prior to the start of each quarter. AP and CLEP credit is accepted.

Transfer: For fall 1981, 463 transfer students enrolled. Transfers are accepted for the freshman, sophomore, junior, and senior classes; D grades transfer. A 2.35 GPA and an ACT composite score of 17 are required for transfer. Students must complete, at the university, at least 45 quarter hours to receive a bachelor's degree; 198 quarter hours are required to earn the bachelor's degree. Application deadlines are the same as those for freshmen.

Visiting: The university conducts regularly scheduled orientations for prospective students. Visitors may sit in on classes and stay overnight at the school when space is available. The admissions office should be contacted to arrange visits.

Financial Aid: About 70% of all students receive some form of financial aid; 35% of the students work part-time on campus. A variety of scholarships, loans, and work opportunities are available. Applications for aid must be submitted by April 15. The FFS is required.

Foreign Students: About 4% of the students come from foreign countries. The university offers these students an intensive English program, special counseling, and special organizations.

Admissions: Foreign students must take the TOEFL, the University of Michigan Language Test, or the university's own test of English proficiency. No further exams are required.

Procedure: Application deadlines are August 1 (fall), November 15 (winter), February 1 (spring), and May 1 (summer). Foreign students must present the university's health form, and present proof of funds adequate to cover 1 year of study. Foreign students pay $7228 per year (4 quarters). They must carry health insurance, which is available through the university for a fee.

Admissions Contact: James C. Perry, Director of Admissions.

TENNESSEE WESLEYAN COLLEGE D-4
Athens, Tennessee 37303 (615) 745-5872

F/T, P/T: 504M&W
Grad: none
Year: qtrs, ss
Appl: open
200 applied
ACT: 19

Faculty: 31; IIB, — $
Ph.D.'s: 55%
S/F Ratio: 18 to 1
Tuition: $2800
R and B: $2000
175 accepted 125 enrolled
COMPETITIVE

Tennessee Wesleyan College, founded in 1857, is a liberal arts college operated by the United Methodist Church. The library contains more than 70,000 volumes and subscribes to 350 periodicals.

Environment: The campus and grounds occupy 24 acres in a town of 15,000 in the foothills of the Great Smoky Mountains, 58 miles southwest of Knoxville. The 14 campus buildings include dormitories housing about 250 men and 300 women.

Student Life: About 80% of the students come from Tennessee. Half are members of the United Methodist Church. Eighty-seven percent are graduates of public schools. Half live on campus in the single-sex dorms. Alcohol is not permitted on campus.

Organizations: Four sororities and 3 fraternities have chapters on campus. Extracurricular activities include music and drama groups, religious organizations, special-interest clubs, student government, and publications.

Sports: The college fields intercollegiate teams in 5 sports. Intramural sports also are available.

Handicapped: The college is working to make the campus accessible to handicapped students.

Graduates: About 15% of the graduates pursue advanced degrees.

Services: The college provides health care, psychological counseling, placement aid, and career counseling free to students.

Programs of Study: The college confers the B.A., B.S., B. Applied Sc., and B.Mus.Ed. degrees. Bachelor's degrees are offered in the following subjects: BUSINESS (accounting, business education, management), EDUCATION (elementary, health/physical, recreation, secondary, special), ENGLISH (communications, English, speech), FINE AND PERFORMING ARTS (music, music education, theater/dramatics), HEALTH SCIENCES (medical technology), MATH AND SCIENCES (biology, chemistry, mathematics, mathematics and physical sciences), PHILOSOPHY (philosophy, religion), PREPROFES-SIONAL (aviation, church vocations, ministry), SOCIAL SCIENCES (behavioral sciences, criminal justice, history, human services, psychology, public administration, social sciences).

Required: Students must take courses in English composition, mathematics, physical education, religion, history, social sciences, and natural and physical sciences.

Special: The college offers 3-2 engineering programs with Auburn University, the University of Southern California, and the University of Tennessee; a 3-2 program in forestry with Duke University; and a working relationship with the School of Nursing at Emory University. A 3-year bachelor's degree is available.

Honors: Three honor societies have chapters on campus. An honors program is offered.

Admissions: Eighty-eight percent of those who applied were accepted for the 1981–82 freshman class. Candidates must be high school graduates with at least a C average.

Procedure: Applicants must take the SAT or ACT. Application deadlines are open. Admissions are granted on a rolling basis; notification is made 2 weeks after the application is complete. There is a $25 application fee.

Special: AP and CLEP credit is accepted.

Transfer: A 2.0 GPA is generally required. Transfers who hold an A.A. or A.S. degree are granted junior standing and are considered to have completed core requirements. If the associate degree does not include religion and philosophy, the student must meet this requirement. Students must complete at least 45 quarter hours in residence of the 192 required for a bachelor's degree.

Visiting: Prospective students are encouraged to visit the campus and have a personal interview. The admissions office should be contacted for arrangements.

Financial Aid: About 70% of the students receive aid. Scholarships, grants (including BEOG/SEOG), loans (including NDSL), and part-time jobs (including CWS) are available. The average award to freshmen is $1500. The FFS or FAF is required; students are urged to apply as early as possible.

Foreign Students: Students from foreign countries make up 3% of enrollment.

Admissions: Applicants must score at least 500 on the TOEFL. No college entrance exams are required.

Procedure: Application deadlines are open. Students must submit a completed health form and provide proof of adequate funds for 1 year.

Admissions Contact: Damon B. Mitchell, Director of Admissions.

TREVECCA NAZARENE COLLEGE C-3
Nashville, Tennessee 37203 (615) 248-1320

F/T: 445M, 427W
P/T: 27M, 62W
Grad: none
Year: qtrs, ss
Appl: open
533 applied
ACT: 17

Faculty: 63; IIB, — $
Ph.D.'s: 40%
S/F Ratio: 14 to 1
Tuition: $2607
R and B: $1728
531 accepted 341 enrolled
LESS COMPETITIVE

Founded in 1901, Trevecca Nazarene is a small private liberal arts and teachers college under the control of the Church of the Nazarene. The library contains 75,000 volumes, holds subscriptions to 450 periodicals, and has 73,535 microfilm items.

Environment: An urban environment surrounds the campus. There are 20 buildings on the 75-acre campus, including 6 residence halls, a science building, and a physical education center. The college also sponsors on-campus apartments, off-campus apartments, and married student housing.

Student Life: Eighty-nine percent of the students come from out of state; 65% live on campus. Ninety-nine percent are Protestant, and 1% are Catholic. The majority of the students are members of the affiliated church; attendance at chapel services is required 3 days a week. Drinking and smoking are prohibited; freshmen and sophomores observe a curfew. About 5% of the students are minority-group members. Campus housing is single-sex; there are no visiting privileges. Students may keep cars on campus.

Organizations: There are Protestant organizations on campus. Extracurricular activities include special-interest and service groups and a variety of social and cultural events. Students are members of all major councils and committees.

852 TENNESSEE

Sports: The college fields 4 intercollegiate teams for men and 2 for women. There are 6 intramural sports for men and 3 for women.

Handicapped: Approximately 10% of the campus is accessible to the physically handicapped. Some buildings have wheelchair ramps and specially equipped rest rooms.

Graduates: The freshman dropout rate is 22%; 30% remain to graduate. Approximately 30% of the graduates pursue graduate study; 2% enter medical school, 2% law school, and 1% dental school. About 25% enter careers in business and industry.

Services: Placement services, career counseling, tutoring, and remedial instruction are offered free of charge. Health care and psychological counseling are available for a fee.

Programs of Study: The college confers the B.A. and B.S. degrees. Associate degrees are also awarded. Bachelor's degrees are offered in the following subjects: BUSINESS (accounting, business administration, business education, executive secretary), EDUCATION (early childhood, elementary, health/physical, special), ENGLISH (broadcasting and broadcasting journalism, communication and human relations, English education, speech), FINE AND PERFORMING ARTS (church music, creative and performing arts, music, music education), HEALTH SCIENCES (medical technology, physician assistant), MATH AND SCIENCES (biology, chemistry, general science, mathematics), PHILOSOPHY (religion, youth ministry, youth and music ministry), PREPROFESSIONAL (dentistry, engineering, law, medicine, ministry, pharmacy), SOCIAL SCIENCES (communications and human relations, cross-cultural communication). Thirty percent of degrees conferred are in business, 13% in humanities, and 11% in social sciences.

Special: Under its Academic Enrichment Program the college admits freshmen who have less than 15 on the ACT and gives them special tutorial help. An Afro-American literature seminar is offered.

Admissions: Ninety-nine percent of those who applied were accepted for the 1981–82 freshman class. The ACT scores of those who enrolled were as follows: 66% below 21, 20% between 21 and 23, 8% between 24 and 25, 5% between 26 and 28, and 1% above 28. Candidates must be high school graduates.

Procedure: The ACT is required. Application deadlines are open. Freshmen are admitted in all 4 terms. There is a rolling admissions plan. There is a $15 application fee.

Special: The college offers an early admissions plan; applications should be submitted by the summer after the junior year. CLEP credit is accepted.

Transfer: For fall 1981, 114 transfer students applied, 99 were accepted, and 37 enrolled. Applicants must have a C average or better. D grades transfer. At least 36 quarter hours of the final year must be taken in residence; 192 quarter hours are required to earn a bachelor's degree. There are no application deadlines.

Visiting: The college conducts regularly scheduled orientations for prospective students. Guides are also available for informal visits to the campus. Visitors may sit in on classes and stay at the school. The admissions office should be contacted to arrange visits.

Financial Aid: About 80% of all students receive some form of financial aid; 70% of the students work part-time on campus. The total amount of aid available is $2 million. There are 40 freshman scholarships available; loans are also available from the federal and state governments, local banks, and the college. The FFS or FAF is required. April 15 is the deadline for aid applications.

Foreign Students: About 2% of the students come from foreign countries. The college offers these students an intensive English course and special counseling.

Admissions: Foreign students must achieve a minimum TOEFL score of 450; no further exams are required.

Procedure: There are no application deadlines. Foreign students must present proof of health as well as proof of funds adequate to cover 1 year of study. They must also carry health insurance, which is available through the college for a fee.

Admissions Contact: Howard T. Wall, Director of Admissions.

TUSCULUM COLLEGE F–3
Greeneville, Tennessee 37743   (615) 639-2931

F/T: 140M, 146W	Faculty: 31; IIB, ––$
P/T: 5M, 7W	Ph.D.'s: 30%
Grad: none	S/F Ratio: 13 to 1
Year: sems, ss	Tuition: $3100
Appl: open	R and B: $2030
269 applied	224 accepted 84 enrolled
SAT: 402V 438M	ACT: 17 LESS COMPETITIVE

Tusculum College, founded in 1794, is a small, private, liberal arts institution affiliated with the Presbyterian Church. The library contains 67,000 volumes and 6310 microfilm items, and subscribes to 400 periodicals.

Environment: The college occupies 140 acres in a rural area of the Great Smoky Mountains. There are dormitory facilities to accommodate 550 men and women.

Student Life: The college draws 49% of its students from outside Tennessee. Sixty-two percent of the students live on campus. The majority of the students are not Presbyterian. About 13% of the students are minority-group members. Campus housing is single-sex; there are visiting privileges. Students may keep cars on campus.

Organizations: Extracurricular activities include films, concerts, convocations, formal and informal dances, and student clubs.

Sports: The college fields 5 intercollegiate teams for men and 5 for women. There are 7 intramural sports for men and 7 for women.

Graduates: The freshman dropout rate is 10%; 40% remain to graduate. Twenty-five percent of the graduates pursue graduate study: 5% enter medical school, 3% law school, and 2% dental school; 25% pursue careers in business and industry.

Services: Placement services, career counseling, psychological counseling, tutoring, and remedial instruction are available free of charge.

Programs of Study: The college confers the B.A. and B.S. degrees with majors in the following subjects: BUSINESS (business administration), EDUCATION (elementary, health/physical, secondary, special), ENGLISH (literature), FINE AND PERFORMING ARTS (art, music), HEALTH SCIENCES (medical technology), MATH AND SCIENCES (biology), PREPROFESSIONAL (social work), SOCIAL SCIENCES (psychology). Thirty-two percent of degrees conferred are in education, 15% in social sciences, and 19% in business.

Special: Student-designed majors are permitted. The college offers a developmental skills program aimed at helping students overcome deficiencies in English, mathematics, and reading.

Admissions: Eighty-three percent of those who applied were accepted for the 1981–82 freshman class. The SAT scores of those who enrolled were as follows: Verbal—80% below 500, 16% between 500 and 599, 4% between 600 and 700, and 0% above 700; Math—73% below 500, 26% between 500 and 599, 1% between 600 and 700, and 0% above 700. The ACT scores of those who enrolled were as follows: 62% below 21, 26% between 21 and 23, 8% between 24 and 25, 4% between 26 and 28, and fewer than 1% above 28. Candidates must be graduates of accredited high schools, rank in the top half of their graduating class, and have completed 16 Carnegie units. The minimum high school GPA required is 2.0.

Procedure: The SAT or ACT is required. There is no formal application deadline, but students are urged to apply early in the senior year. Freshmen are admitted in the fall and spring terms. Notification is on a rolling basis. There is a $10 application fee.

Special: Early admissions and deferred admissions plans are offered. CLEP credit is accepted.

Transfer: For fall 1981, 77 transfer students applied, 70 were accepted, and 43 enrolled. Transfers are accepted during the first 3 years. A 2.0 GPA and the eligibility to return to the prior school are required. Students must complete, at the college, 30 of the 128 credits required to earn a bachelor's degree. There are no application deadlines.

Visiting: Guides are available for informal visits to the campus. Visitors may sit in on classes and stay at the school. The admissions office should be contacted to arrange visits.

Financial Aid: About 82% of all students receive some form of financial aid; 40% of the students work part-time on campus. The college uses the CSS. Honors scholarships and other scholarships are available to freshmen, as are loans from the federal government, BEOG, EOG, CWS, and on- and off-campus employment. The FAF is required. There is no aid application deadline.

Foreign Students: Almost 2% of the students come from foreign countries.

Admissions: Foreign students must achieve a minimum TOEFL score of 500; they must also take the ACT.

Procedure: There are no application deadlines. Foreign students must present a health certificate completed by a physician, and they must present proof of funds adequate to cover 4 years of study. Health insurance is available through the college for a fee.

Admissions Contact: Estel C. Hurley, Dean of Admissions.

UNION UNIVERSITY   B-3
Jackson, Tennessee 38301   (901) 668-1818

F/T: 444M, 659W	Faculty: 64; IIB, av$
P/T: 79M, 200W	Ph.D.'s: 53%
Grad: none	S/F Ratio: 17 to 1
Year: 4-1-4, ss	Tuition: $2050
Appl: Aug. 31	R and B: $1350
467 applied	419 accepted	349 enrolled
ACT: 19		COMPETITIVE

Union University, founded in 1825, is a private liberal arts college owned and operated by the Tennessee Baptist Convention. The library contains 72,909 volumes and 1596 microfilm items, and subscribes to 575 periodicals.

Environment: The 153-acre suburban campus is located 75 miles from Memphis. Buildings include an academic multi-center complex and separate men's and women's apartment housing complexes. Married student housing is also available.

Student Life: About 78% of the students are from Tennessee. Ninety-six percent are Protestant. About 5% are minority-group members. Sixty-seven percent of the students live on campus; freshmen may live off campus. Campus housing is single-sex, and there are no visiting privileges. Students may keep cars on campus. Attendance at 21 of the 34 chapel services each term is required. All students observe curfew regulations.

Organizations: There are 3 national fraternities and 2 national sororities on campus; 18% of the men and 19% of the women belong. Extracurricular activities include band, chorus, glee club, student publications, and a drama group. The university also sponsors off-campus art shows, concerts, lectures, operas, and plays.

Sports: Four intercollegiate sports are offered for men and 2 for women. Eight intramural sports are available for men and 7 for women.

Handicapped: The university estimates the campus to be 100% accessible to wheelchair-bound students. Facilities include ramps, designated handicapped parking, specially equipped rest rooms, and lowered telephones. Fewer than 1% of the students are visually impaired; there are no students with hearing impairments.

Graduates: The freshman dropout rate is 33%; 56% remain to graduate. Forty percent of those who remain pursue further study: 1% enter medical school, 1% dental school, and 2% law school.

Services: Health care, tutoring, remedial instruction, placement services, psychological counseling, and career counseling are offered free of charge to the student.

Programs of Study: The B.S., B.A., B.S.N., and B.Mus. degrees are offered. Associate degree programs are also available. Bachelor's degrees are offered in the following subjects: BUSINESS (accounting, business administration, business education, computer science, finance, management, marketing), EDUCATION (elementary, health/physical, secondary, special), ENGLISH (English, journalism), FINE AND PERFORMING ARTS (art, art education, art history, music, music education, radio/TV, theater/dramatics), HEALTH SCIENCES (medical technology, nursing), LANGUAGES (French, German, Greek, Hebrew, Spanish), MATH AND SCIENCES (biochemistry, biology, botany, chemistry, mathematics, natural sciences, physical sciences, physics), PHILOSOPHY (humanities, philosophy, religion—Greek, religion—philosophy), PREPROFESSIONAL (dentistry, law, library science, medicine, ministry, pharmacy, social work, veterinary), SOCIAL SCIENCES (economics, government/political science, history, psychology, social sciences, sociology). Of the degrees conferred, 28% are in health sciences, 17% in business, and 15% in education.

Required: All students must complete courses in English, history, religion, fine arts, physical education, and social sciences. All candidates for graduation must take the UP Area Tests.

Special: The nursing program allows students to work as nurse assistants at the local hospital.

Honors: Six national honor societies have chapters on campus. An interdisciplinary honors program spanning all majors is offered.

Admissions: Ninety percent of those who applied were accepted for the 1981-82 freshman class. Of those who enrolled, the ACT scores were as follows: 56% below 21, 28% between 21 and 23, 15% between 24 and 28, and fewer than 1% above 28. The candidate must have completed 16 units of work at an accredited high school, with at least a C average. The result of the entrance examination is a most important factor in judging a candidate; a minimum ACT score of 15 is required. Advanced placement or honors courses, evidence of special talents, personality, and ability to finance a college education also enter into the admissions decision.

Procedure: The SAT or ACT is required. Students should apply by August 31 for fall; the deadline for winter, spring, and summer is the last day of registration. A rolling admissions plan is in effect. The application fee is $10.

Special: An early admissions plan is offered, with an application deadline of August 25. AP and CLEP credit is granted.

Transfer: For fall 1981, 377 students applied and 201 enrolled. Applicants must be eligible to return to their previous school. A minimum GPA of 2.0 and a score of at least 15 on the ACT is required. D grades do not transfer. At least 32 of 128 semester hours required for a bachelor's degree must be completed in residence. Application deadlines are the same as those for freshmen.

Visiting: There are regularly scheduled orientations for prospective students. Guides are available for informal visits. Visitors may sit in on classes or stay overnight at the school. For arrangements, the director of student enlistment should be contacted.

Financial Aid: About 70% of all students receive aid. Twenty percent work part-time on campus. The university provides academic scholarships for freshmen. Loans and grants are available from federal, state, banking, and private sources, and from the university. The average award to freshman from all sources is $1600. The FFS is required. The deadline for aid application is June 1. Tuition may be paid on the installment plan.

Foreign Students: Fewer than 1% of full-time students are from foreign countries.

Admissions: Foreign students must achieve a minimum score of 500 on the TOEFL. The ACT is also required.

Procedure: The application deadlines are the same as those for other freshmen. Foreign students must present a certified health card from a physician as proof of health. Proof of adequate funds for 1 year's tuition and fees must also be presented. Health insurance must be carried and is available through the university for a fee.

Admissions Contact: Joe S. Layman, Director of Student Enlistment.

UNIVERSITY OF TENNESSEE

University of Tennessee, founded in 1794, serves as a federal land-grant college and the state university for the citizens of Tennessee. The largest campus is located in Knoxville; other primary campuses offering undergraduate instruction are located at Chattanooga, Martin, and Memphis (upper division only). Graduate degree programs are offered at the Space Institute at Tullahoma, the School of Biomedical Sciences at Oak Ridge, and at all primary campuses and off-campus centers.

UNIVERSITY OF TENNESSEE AT   D-4
CHATTANOOGA
Chattanooga, Tennessee 37402   (615) 755-4157

F/T: 2235M, 2234W	Faculty: 265; IIA, av$
P/T: 676M, 883W	Ph.D.'s: 74%
Grad: 689M, 763W	S/F Ratio: 18 to 1
Year: sems, ss	Tuition: $620 ($1840)
Appl: see profile	R and B: $1800
1710 applied	1592 accepted	1076 enrolled
ACT: 18		LESS COMPETITIVE

Founded in 1886 as a private nonsectarian institution, University of Tennessee at Chattanooga became part of the University of Tennessee in 1969. The library houses 272,177 volumes and 380,820 microfilm items, and subscribes to 2980 periodicals.

Environment: The campus, comprising over 60 acres and 30 buildings, is located in the center of the city of Chattanooga, which has a population of 169,000. A $6.2 million Fine Arts Center opened during 1980, and a $15 million Sports Arena/Physical Education building will be completed in 1982. Residence halls, accommodating 786 men and women, include both the traditional dormitory style, and village apartments with kitchens, housing 4 students per unit. A new 200-bed apartment housing unit was scheduled to open in fall 1982.

Student Life: Approximately 85% of the students are from Tennessee; 10% live on campus, either in residence halls or in fraternity houses. About 13% of the students are minority-group members. Campus housing is both coed and single-sex; there are visiting privileges. Students may keep cars on campus. Day-care services are available to all students, faculty, and staff for a fee.

Organizations: Ten percent of the men belong to the 7 national fraternities; 12% of the women belong to the 6 national sororities. Extracurricular activities include student government, special-interest groups, departmental clubs, and professional societies. There are religious organizations or counselors for students of all major faiths.

Sports: The university fields 11 intercollegiate teams for men and 4 for women. There are 16 intramural sports for men and 12 for women.

Handicapped: Approximately 75% of the campus is accessible to the physically handicapped. Facilities include wheelchair ramps, special parking, elevators, and lowered drinking fountains and telephones; special class scheduling is also available.

Graduates: The freshman dropout rate is 12%; 50% remain to graduate. Twelve percent of the graduates go on to graduate study: 5% enter medical school, 1% dental school, and 5% law school; 30% pursue careers in business and industry.

Services: Placement services, career counseling, psychological counseling, health care, tutoring, and remedial instruction are available free of charge.

Programs of Study: The university confers the B.A., B.S., B.F.A., B.Mus. B.S.N., and B.S.E. degrees. Master's programs are also offered. Bachelor's degrees are offered in the following subjects: AREA STUDIES (American, urban), BUSINESS (accounting, business administration, computer science, finance, management, marketing, office administration), EDUCATION (early childhood, elementary, health/physical, secondary, special), ENGLISH (English, communications), FINE AND PERFORMING ARTS (art, art education, music, music education, theater/drama), HEALTH SCIENCES (medical technology, nursing), LANGUAGES (French, Greek/Latin, Spanish), MATH AND SCIENCES (astronomy, biology, chemistry, ecology/environmental science, geology, mathematics, physics), PHILOSOPHY (philosophy, religion), PREPROFESSIONAL (engineering, engineering management, home economics, social work), SOCIAL SCIENCES (anthropology, economics, geography, government/political science, history, psychology, sociology). Twenty-five percent of the degrees are conferred in business, 20% in education, and 11% in social sciences.

Special: Interdepartmental majors are offered in classical civilization, combined sciences, and humanities.

Honors: Twenty-three national honor societies have chapters on campus. There is a university scholars program, as well as an honors program in which all departments participate.

Admissions: Approximately 93% of those who applied were accepted for the 1981-82 freshman class. The most important factors in evaluating applicants are the GPA for grades 9 through 12 and the composite ACT score. Candidates must have an average of 2.0 or better, or have a composite score of 18 on the ACT, or 850 on the SAT, have completed 16 Carnegie units, and be graduates of accredited high schools. Some exceptions are made by the Dean of Admissions and Records.

Procedure: The ACT or SAT is required. The application deadlines are 30 days prior to the beginning of the semester, the university follows a rolling admissions policy. There is a $10 application fee.

Special: There is an early decision plan. AP and CLEP credit is accepted.

Transfer: For fall 1981, 887 transfer students applied, 845 were accepted, and 623 enrolled. Transfers are accepted for all classes; D grades transfer. A 2.0 GPA is required. The deadline for transfer applications is 4 weeks prior to the first day of class. Sixty hours must be completed in residence to earn a degree if the student is transferring from a 2-year college; 30 hours are required if the student is transferring from a 4-year college. The bachelor's degree requires the completion of 128 credits.

Visiting: There are regularly scheduled orientations for prospective students. Guides are also available for informal visits; visitors may sit in on classes and stay overnight at the school. The admissions office should be contacted to arrange visits.

Financial Aid: Approximately 60% of all students receive some form of financial aid; 4% of the students work part-time on campus. Scholarships, loans, and grants-in-aid are available; CWS is offered in many departments. Tuition may be paid in installments. The FAF or FFS is required. The aid application deadline is March 1.

Foreign Students: About 1% of the students come from foreign countries. The university offers these students an intensive English course and special organizations.

Admissions: Foreign students must achieve a minimum TOEFL score of 500; no further exams are required.

Procedure: Application deadlines are August 1 (fall) and December 1 (spring). Foreign students must present proof of health and proof of adequate funds. Health insurance is available through the university for a fee.

Admissions Contact: Michael White, Director of Admissions.

UNIVERSITY OF TENNESSEE AT MARTIN

B-2

Martin, Tennessee 38238   (901) 587-7026

F/T: 2100M, 2000W   Faculty: n/av; IIA, av$
P/T: 425M, 465W   Ph.D.'s: 52%
Grad: 110M, 210W   S/F Ratio: 20 to 1
Year: qtrs, ss   Tuition: $660 ($1800)
Appl: Sept. 1   R and B: $1600
ACT: 17   **LESS COMPETITIVE**

University of Tennessee at Martin, founded in 1927, is part of the state's higher education system. It has 6 schools: Liberal Arts, Business, Education, Engineering, Home Economics, and Agriculture. The library contains over 200,000 volumes and 13,000 microfilm items, and subscribes to 1600 periodicals.

Environment: The 200-acre campus is located in a small town 125 miles from Memphis. An adjoining 700 acres is used for agricultural research by the university. There are 28 major buildings, including 6 dormitories, accommodating 2629 men and women, and 320 apartments for married students and faculty. There is also fraternity housing for 115 men.

Student Life: About 95% of the students come from Tennessee. The majority (85%) are public school graduates. Sixty-five percent live on campus. Campus housing is both coed and single-sex. Students may keep cars on campus. Day-care services are available to all students, faculty, and staff.

Organizations: Sixteen percent of the men and 13% of the women join 1 of 18 Greek letter organizations. Over 90 extracurricular groups are sponsored, including special-interest clubs, publications, dramatics, musical groups, service groups, religious organizations, and student government. Popular campus events include Homecoming, Winter Wonderland Dance, and regularly scheduled cultural events. The campus is within easy driving distance of a number of the state's most famous recreation areas.

Sports: The university fields 5 intercollegiate teams for men and 4 for women. There are 6 intramural sports for men and 6 for women.

Graduates: The freshman dropout rate is about 30%; 50% remain to graduate. More than 10% go on for further study.

Services: The university provides health care, psychological counseling, remedial instruction, tutoring, career counseling, and placement services at no charge to the student.

Program of Study: The university campus at Martin confers the B.A., B.S., B.S.Ed., and B.M. degrees, as well as associate and master's degrees. Bachelor's degrees are offered in the following subjects: BUSINESS (accounting, business administration, business education, business/foreign studies, computer science, economics, management, health services, marketing, office administration), EDUCATION (early childhood, elementary, health/physical, home economics, secondary, special), ENGLISH (English), FINE AND PERFORMING ARTS (art education, communications, music, music education), HEALTH SCIENCES (cytotechnology, dental hygiene, food systems management, medical records administration, medical technology, nursing, physical therapy, radiologic technology), LANGUAGES (French, Spanish), MATH AND SCIENCES (biology, chemistry, earth science, geology, mathematics), PREPROFESSIONAL (agriculture, architecture, dentistry, (engineering—aerospace, engineering—biomedical, engineering—chemical, engineering—civil, engineering—electrical, engineering—industrial, engineering—mechanical, engineering—metallurgical, engineering—nuclear, engineering physics, engineering science, engineering technology—civil, engineering technology—electrical, engineering technology—mechanical), home economics, law, medicine, optometry, pharmacy, social work, veterinary), SOCIAL SCIENCES (criminal justice, government/political science, history, psychology, sociology).

Required: All students must complete course work in English as well as in physical education and/or military science.

Special: Study abroad, individualized programs, 5-year cooperative degree programs, interdisciplinary programs, and independent study are offered.

Honors: There is an honors program. Seventeen honor and professional societies are represented on campus.

Admissions: About 94% of a recent freshman class were accepted. A high school diploma (or the equivalent) is necessary, with 16 Carnegie units completed. The minimum ACT score accepted is 17; a 2.2 high school average is also required.

Procedure: The ACT is required and should be taken by June of the senior year. New students are admitted each quarter. Application deadlines are September 1 (fall), March 1 (spring), January 1 (winter), and June 1 (summer). Notification is on a rolling basis. There is a $10 application fee.

Special: There is an early admissions plan. AP and CLEP credit is granted.

Transfer: Of 450 applications recently received, 400 were accepted and 361 transfer students enrolled. Transfers are accepted for all classes. A 2.2 GPA is necessary; D grades are usually accepted. The last 45 credits must be completed in residence, 96 quarter hours must be completed to earn a bachelor's degree. Application deadlines are the same as those for freshmen.

Financial Aid: About 68% of the students are receiving aid. The university participates in federal programs such as NDSL, BEOG/SEOG, and CWS (all departments) in addition to offering commercial (bank) loans and scholarships (about 600 academic and 130 athletic). Aid is generally packaged: need and academic achievement are the determining factors. Scholarships range from $300 to $750, loans from $600 to $1000, and work contracts from $600 to $1000. The FFS should be filed by March 1.

Foreign Students: About 200 students come from foreign countries. The university offers these students an intensive English program and special counseling.

Admissions: Foreign students must achieve a minimum TOEFL score of 450; no further exams are required.

Procedure: Application deadlines are September 1 (fall), January 1 (winter), March 1 (spring), and June 1 (summer). Foreign students must present proof of health as well as proof of funds adequate to cover 1 year of study. They must also carry health insurance, which is available through the university for a fee.

Admissions Contact: Paul Kelley, Associate Dean of Admissions.

UNIVERSITY OF TENNESSEE/ KNOXVILLE E-3
Knoxville, Tennessee 37996 (615) 974-2184

F/T, P/T: Faculty: 1250; I, — $
12,624M, 10,583W Ph.D.'s: 80%
Grad: 3494M, 3120W S/F Ratio: 17 to 1
Year: qtrs, ss Tuition: $741 ($2271)
Appl: Aug. 1 R and B: $1803
5423 applied 4670 accepted 3917 enrolled
ACT: 21 COMPETITIVE

The original campus of the University of Tennessee, founded in 1794, and its central administrative offices are located in Knoxville. The university is organized into 19 colleges and schools; 2 branches of the University of Tennessee Center for the Health Sciences are located here. The library contains about 1.4 million volumes, and subscribes to 25,000 periodicals.

Environment: The Knoxville campus is located about a mile from the downtown area, on the banks of the Tennessee River. The main campus (which includes 98 buildings) and the agriculture campus together occupy 1000 acres. Residence halls and apartments for married students accommodate more than 7000 students. The university also sponsors fraternity houses and off-campus apartments.

Student Life: About 80% of the students come from Tennessee, and 85% of the entering freshmen come from public schools. About 36% of the students live in the residence halls. There are restrictions on the drinking of alcoholic beverages. About 62% of the students are Protestant, 12% are Catholic, and 1% are Jewish. About 8% of the students are minority-group members. Campus housing is coed and single-sex, there are visiting privileges. Students may keep cars on campus.

Organizations: There are 26 fraternities and 20 sororities on campus. Extracurricular activities include musical, dramatic and other cultural organizations, special-interest clubs, publications, student government, a campus radio station, religious activities, social programs, and recreational and avocational activities. More than 200 different extracurricular organizations and activities are maintained.

Sports: The university fields 10 intercollegiate teams for men and 6 for women. There are 22 intramural sports for men and 22 for women.

Handicapped: The university is coordinating efforts to eliminate physical barriers with priority given to access and facilities for academic buildings. Special services for handicapped students include assistance during registration (manual interpretation for the deaf), parking areas, elevators, and tickets for special events. The Hearing and Speech Center offers complete diagnostic and therapeutic services to all students with hearing and/or speech impairments.

Graduates: The freshman dropout rate is 35%; about 39% remain to graduate. Sixty percent of the graduates pursue advanced degrees.

Services: The following services are provided to students free of charge: psychological counseling, placement, and career counseling. Health care and tutoring are available for a fee.

Programs of Study: The university offers the B.A., B.Arch., B.S.Ed., B.F.A., B.Mus., and B.S.N. and 21 other degrees. More than 120 majors are available in the fields of agriculture , architecture , business administration , communications , education , health, physical education, and recreation , engineering , home economics , liberal arts , and nursing .

Special: Study-abroad programs are offered in Spain, France, Austria, and Mexico. The university offers cooperative work-study programs in engineering and business. A combination degree program is available in medicine.

Honors: Special honors courses are available to qualified students.

Admissions: About 86% of those who applied were accepted for the 1981-82 freshman class. The ACT scores of those who enrolled were as follows: 47% below 21, 22% between 21 and 23, 13% between 24 and 25, 13% between 26 and 28, and 5% above 28. The minimum high school GPA required is 2.0 for in-state students and 2.25 for out-of-state students.

Procedure: The ACT is required. There is a $10 application fee. The application deadlines are August 1 for fall and 3 weeks prior to the start of the quarter for winter, spring, and summer. Preference is given to students from Tennessee. There is a rolling admissions plan.

Transfer: For fall 1981, 1963 transfer students applied, 1372 were accepted, and 1105 enrolled. A 2.0 average and good standing at the student's previous college are required. A 2.5 average is recommended. D grades may transfer. All students must complete the last 45 quarter hours at the university. Between 180 and 220 quarter hours are required for the bachelor's degree. Preference is given to students transferring from colleges within the state. Deadlines are the same as those for entering freshmen.

Financial Aid: About 50% of the students receive aid through the university; 20% of the students work part-time on campus. Scholarships, grants, CWS and other part-time work programs, and loans are all available. The average award to freshmen from all sources available through the university is $2100. The university is a member of CSS. The FAF or FFS is required; applications for financial aid must be submitted by March 1 for incoming freshmen and by April 1 for upperclass transfer students.

Foreign Students: About 4% of the students are from foreign countries. The university offers these students an intensive English course and an intensive English program, special counseling, and special organizations.

Admissions: Foreign students must achieve a minimum TOEFL score of 525; an English placement exam is required of non-native English speakers.

Procedure: Application deadlines are August 1 (fall), December 1 (winter), February 20 (spring), and May 15 (summer). Foreign students must present proof of funds adequate to cover at least 1 year of study. They must also carry health insurance, which is available through the university for a fee.

Admissions Contact: Charles Edington, Director of Admissions.

THE UNIVERSITY OF THE SOUTH D-4
Sewanee, Tennessee 37375 (615) 598-5931

F/T: 600M, 400W Faculty: 101; IIB, ++$
P/T: 5M, 30W Ph.D.'s: 80%
Grad: 70M, 10W S/F Ratio: 10 to 1
Year: sems, ss Tuition: $5680
Appl: Mar. 10 R and B: $1590
844 applied 535 accepted 281 enrolled
SAT: 550V 600M VERY COMPETITIVE+

The university is owned and operated by the Protestant Episcopal Church and consists of the College of Arts and Sciences and the School of Theology (graduate). The library houses 435,000 volumes, holds subscriptions to 1850 periodicals, and has 24,700 microfilm items.

Environment: Located 50 miles from Chattanooga in a rural area, at an elevation of 2000 feet, the 10,000-acre wooded campus has Tudor-Gothic style buildings that include 13 dormitories to accommodate 700 men and 270 women, and apartments for 8 married couples.

Student Life: Only 21% of the students come from Tennessee. About 98% reside on campus. Fifty-seven percent of entering freshmen attended public schools. Eighty-five percent are Protestant, and 9% are Catholic. Approximately half the students are members of the Protestant Episcopal Church. About 2% of the students are members of minority groups. Campus housing is both coed and single-sex; there are visiting privileges. Students may keep cars on campus.

Organizations: Extracurricular activities include band, chorus, drama productions, publications, an FM radio station, concerts, films, lectures, and art shows. About 50% of the students belong to the Ski and Outing Club. There are 11 national fraternities and 4 local sororities with chapters on campus; 65% of the men and 45% of the women belong.

Sports: The university fields 12 intercollegiate teams for men and 10 for women. There are 9 intramural sports for men and 6 for women.

Graduates: Fewer than 1% drop out at the end of the freshman year; 70% remain to graduate. Seventy percent of the graduates pursue further study.

Services: The following services are offered at no charge to the student: psychological counseling, tutoring, placement services, and career counseling. Health care is available on a fee basis.

Programs of Study: B.A. and B.S. degrees are offered through the College of Arts and Sciences. The School of Theology confers master's and doctoral degrees. Bachelor's degrees are offered in the following subjects: AREA STUDIES (American, Asian, medieval, Russian), EDUCATION (secondary), ENGLISH (comparative literature, English, literature), FINE AND PERFORMING ARTS (art, art history, music, studio art, theater/dramatics), LANGUAGES (French, German, Greek/Latin, Italian, Russian, Spanish), MATH AND SCIENCES (biology, chemistry, computer science, mathematics, natural sciences, physics), PHILOSOPHY (classics, philosophy, religion), PREPROFESSIONAL (dentistry, forestry, medicine, ministry, pharmacy, veterinary), SOCIAL SCIENCES (economics, government/political science, history, psychology). Thirty percent of the degrees conferred are in the sciences.

Required: Baccalaureate degree candidates must take courses in English literature, foreign language, experimental science, mathematics, history, economics, political science, philosophy, religion, physical education, and in either fine arts, music, or drama.

Special: Independent study and study abroad are offered. A combined degree may be earned in liberal arts and engineering in cooperation with Columbia University, Georgia Institute of Technology, and Rensselaer Polytechnic Institute.

Honors: There are 4 national honor societies, including Phi Beta Kappa, with chapters on campus. Honors programs are conducted by all departments offering a major field of study.

Admissions: Sixty-three percent of those who applied were accepted for the 1981–82 freshman class. Of those who enrolled, the range of the middle 50% of SAT verbal scores was between 500 and 600; the middle 50% on math scores ranged between 550 and 650. Applicants must be high school graduates with 15 completed Carnegie units (which include 3 years of college preparatory math and at least 2 years of a foreign language). The most important factors affecting acceptance are the high school average, recommendations by teachers, friends, and alumni of the university, reputation and accreditation of the high school, extracurricular activities, and the results of the SAT.

Procedure: The SAT should be taken by December of the senior year. Application should be made by March 10 (fall) and December 1 (spring). Freshmen are allowed to attend in the summer. However, summer attendance does not constitute admission for the following academic year. The application fee is $15. There is a rolling admissions plan. The CRDA is observed.

Special: The application deadline for early admission is March 10; December 10 is the notification date for early decision. A deferred admissions plan is also offered. AP credit is granted.

Transfer: For fall 1981, 56 transfer students applied, 29 were accepted, and 19 enrolled. Transfer students are accepted for all but the senior year. A 3.0 GPA is recommended for transfer, and four semesters must be spent at the university in order to graduate. The bachelor's degree requires 123 credits. Grades of C or better transfer. Application deadlines are the same as those for freshmen.

Visiting: There are no scheduled visitations for prospective students. Guides are always available for informal visits to the campus. Prospective students may sit in on classes and stay overnight at the school. The office of admissions handles such arrangements.

Financial Aid: About 40% of all students receive aid; 32% of the students work part-time on campus. Aid is granted in a combination of at least 2 of the 3 types available: scholarships, loans (federal and university), and jobs, although freshmen are not encouraged to hold jobs. The maximum aid granted to a freshman is $8000. The average award to freshmen from all sources is $2407. The university is a member of CSS and requires the FAF or FFS. The deadline for aid application is March 10. Tuition may be paid on the installment plan.

Foreign Students: About 1% of the students come from foreign countries. The university offers these students special counseling.

Admissions: Foreign students must achieve a minimum TOEFL score of 550; in addition, they must take the SAT.

Procedure: Application deadlines are March 10 (fall) and December 15 (spring). Foreign students must present the university's health form, and they must also present proof of funds adequate to cover 4 years of study. They must also carry health insurance, which is not available through the university.

Admissions Contact: Albert S. Gooch, Jr., Director of Admissions.

VANDERBILT UNIVERSITY C–3
Nashville, Tennessee 37212 (615) 322-2561

F/T, P/T: 2686M, 2787W
Grad: 2062M, 1376W
Year: sems, ss
Appl: Feb. 15
5319 applied 3438 accepted 1405 enrolled
SAT: 550V 600M ACT: 26 HIGHLY COMPETITIVE

Faculty: n/av; I, av$
Ph.D.'s: 95%
S/F Ratio: 9 to 1
Tuition: $5560
R and B: $2540

Vanderbilt University is a private, nonsectarian university founded in 1873. In 1979 it merged with George Peabody College for Teachers. It has 4 undergraduate schools: Arts and Science, Engineering, Nursing, and George Peabody College for Teachers. The library contains 1.5 million volumes, and subscribes to 5000 periodicals.

Environment: Located 2 miles from downtown Nashville, the 320-acre campus contains a hospital and medical school building and 31 dormitories. The university also sponsors fraternity and sorority houses, on-campus apartments, and married student housing.

Student Life: Twenty percent of the students come from Tennessee. About 57% of the entering freshmen attended public schools. Five percent of the students are minority-group members. About 84% live on campus; freshmen may not live off campus. Campus housing is both single-sex and coed, and there are visiting privileges. Students may keep cars on campus.

Organizations: There are 15 national fraternities and 11 national sororities to which 45% of the students belong. Other activities include special-interest groups, student publications, service groups, a jazz ensemble, a drama club, concerts, plays, films, and lectures. The many recreational and cultural facilities of Nashville are easily accessible.

Sports: The university offers 8 intercollegiate sports for men and 6 for women. Sixteen intramural sports are available for men and 9 for women.

Handicapped: Facilities for handicapped students include elevators and designated parking areas. Handicapped students are advised on an individual basis; special class scheduling can be arranged. Facilities are provided as required.

Graduates: The freshman dropout rate is 5%; 72% remain to graduate. Of the graduates, 50% go on to graduate or professional schools: 10% enter medical school, 1% dental school, and 17% law school. Fifty percent enter business and industry.

Services: The following services are offered free of charge to the student: psychological counseling, tutoring, remedial instruction, health care, placement services, and career counseling.

Programs of Study: The university confers the B.A., B.S., B.Eng., and B.S.N. degrees. Master's and doctoral degree programs are also offered. Bachelor's degrees are offered in the following subjects: AREA STUDIES (Asian, Black/Afro-American, Chinese, environmental, Latin American, Medieval, Russian, urban, women's), EDUCATION (early childhood, elementary, health/physical, special), ENGLISH (English), FINE AND PERFORMING ARTS (fine arts, theater/dramatics), HEALTH SCIENCES (nursing), LANGUAGES (French, German, Greek/Latin, Portuguese, Russian, Spanish), MATH AND SCIENCES (astronomy, biology, biology—molecular, chemistry, geology, mathematics, physics), PHILOSOPHY (classics, philosophy, religion).PREPROFESSIONAL (engineering—biomedical, engineering—chemical, engineering—civil and environmental, engineering—computer science, engineering—electrical, engineering—environmental and water resources, engineering—mechanical and materials, engineering science),SOCIAL SCIENCES (anthropology, economics, government/political science, history, psychology, sociology). Of the degrees conferred, 31% are in social sciences and 17% are in preprofessional studies.

Special: Among the study abroad programs offered are the Experiment in International Living, the university-sponsored junior year abroad programs, and an annual summer program of British studies at Oxford. Student-designed majors are permitted.

Honors: Five national honor societies, including Phi Beta Kappa, have chapters on campus. Honors programs are offered in many major fields for selected candidates, beginning with the junior year.

Admissions: Sixty-five percent of those who applied were accepted for the freshman class. The SAT scores of those who enrolled were as follows: Verbal—24% below 500, 50% between 500 and 599, 24% between 600 and 700, and 2% above 700; Math—12% below 500, 43% between 500 and 599, 38% between 600 and 700, and 7% above 700. On the ACT, 5% scored below 21, 10% between 21 and 23, 19% between 24 and 25, 39% between 26 and 28, and 27% above 28. Candidates should generally be in the upper third of their graduating class and have at least a B+ average. Fifteen Carnegie units are required. Also considered in the admissions decision are the entrance examinations results, the accreditation of the high school, recommendations by school officials, extracurricular record, and advanced placement or honors courses.

Procedure: The SAT or ACT and 3 ATs (in English composition, mathematics, and a subject of the student's choice) are required. These should be taken by December of the senior year. The application deadline for the fall term is February 15; notification is sent by April 15. Freshmen are also admitted in the summer with an application deadline of June 1. There is a $15 application fee.

Special: The deadline for early decision applications is November 1; the notification date is December 1. Admission is available for qualified high school juniors. A deferred admissions plan is also available. AP credit is offered.

Transfer: For fall 1981, 353 students applied, 252 were accepted, and 84 enrolled. Applicants must meet basic freshman requirements. A minimum of 24 semester hours must have been earned. D grades do not transfer. There is a residency requirement of 4 full semesters; 60 of 120 semester hours required for a bachelor's degree must be completed at the university. Application deadlines are February 15 (fall and summer) and November 15 (spring).

Visiting: The university conducts regularly scheduled orientations for prospective students, including campus tours with student guides and interviews with admissions personnel. Visitors are permitted to sit in on classes. The recommended times for visiting are weekdays from 8:30 A.M. to 4:30 P.M. when school is in session.

Financial Aid: About a third of all students receive aid. About 30% work part-time on campus. Almost all aid packages involve combinations of scholarship, grant, and self-help (loan and job). A limited number of honor scholarships are offered on a competitive basis; financial need is not a criterion for selection. The university is a member of CSS. The FAF is required. The deadlines for aid application are February 15 (fall), November 1 (spring), and June 1 (summer).

Foreign Students: About 1% of the undergraduate students are from foreign countries. The university offers an intensive English course, an intensive English program, special counseling, and special organizations for these students.

Admissions: Foreign students must achieve a minimum score of 550 on the TOEFL. The SAT or ACT is required. Three ATs—English Composition, Mathematics, and one of the student's choice—are also required.

Procedure: The application deadlines are February 1 (fall), November 1 (spring—for transfer students only), and June 1 (summer). Foreign students must present a health form completed by a physician as proof of health. Proof of adequate funds for 1 year of study must also be presented. Foreign students must carry health insurance, which is available through the college for a fee.

Admissions Contact: Kathlynn C. Ciompi, Director of Undergraduate Admissions.

TEXAS

ABILENE CHRISTIAN UNIVERSITY C-2
Abilene, Texas 79699   (915) 677-1911

F/T: 1713M, 1774W	Faculty: 174; IIA, av$
P/T: 173M, 186W	Ph.D.'s: 60%
Grad: 305M, 154W	S/F Ratio: 22 to 1
Year: sems, ss	Tuition: $2624
Appl: open	R and B: $1640
1100 applied	1050 accepted 963 enrolled
ACT: 20	LESS COMPETITIVE

Abilene Christian University is a private liberal arts institution affiliated with the Church of Christ but open to members of any faith. The library contains 251,457 volumes and 297,536 microfilm items, and subscribes to 1495 periodicals.

Environment: The campus is located in a suburban area, 180 miles from Dallas. It consists of 29 buildings on 102 acres. There is a 700-acre farm operated by the Agriculture Department. The dormitories accommodate 1160 men and 1365 women.

Student Life: Sixty-nine percent of the students come from Texas. Ninety-five percent of the freshmen are graduates of public schools. About 53% of the students live on campus; freshmen may not live off campus. Most students are of the Protestant faith. About 6% are minority-group members. Students attend religious services daily and observe a curfew. Smoking is not permitted on campus. Campus housing is single-sex, and there are no visiting privileges. Students may keep cars on campus.

Organizations: There are no fraternities or sororities on campus. Campus activities include theater productions and song festivals.

Sports: The university competes in 6 intercollegiate sports for men and 5 for women. Four intramural sports are offered for men and 3 for women.

Handicapped: All of the campus is accessible to handicapped students. Special facilities include wheelchair ramps and elevators.

Graduates: About 7% of the freshmen drop out by the end of the first year; 50% remain to graduate. About 30% of the graduates go on to further study: 5% enter medical school, 2% dental school, and 3% law school. Forty percent pursue careers in business and industry.

Services: Students receive the following services free of charge: placement service, psychological counseling, career counseling, health care, tutoring, and remedial instruction.

Programs of Study: The B.A., B.B.A., B.F.A., B.S., B.S.Ed., B.S.H.E., B.Mus.Ed., and B.S.N. degrees are awarded. Associate and master's degree programs are also offered. Bachelor's degrees are offered in the following subjects: BUSINESS (accounting, business administration, business education, computer science, finance, management, marketing, office management), EDUCATION (early childhood, elementary, health/physical, industrial, secondary), ENGLISH (English, speech), FINE AND PERFORMING ARTS (art, art education, music, music education, radio/TV, theater/dramatics), HEALTH SCIENCES (medical technology, nursing, speech therapy), LANGUAGES (French, German, Spanish), MATH AND SCIENCES (biology, chemistry, engineering physics, geology, mathematics, physics), PHILOSOPHY (religion), PREPROFESSIONAL (agriculture, home economics, ministry, social work), SOCIAL SCIENCES (government/political science, history, psychology). Thirty percent of the undergraduate degrees are conferred in education, 20% in business, and 8% in math and sciences.

Required: All students must take English, the Bible, and physical education. Some requirements may be satisfied by acceptable scores on AP and CLEP exams. Up to 30 semester hours of credit can be earned by these exams.

Special: Student-designed majors are permitted. There is a 6-week summer seminar in missions for practicing or prospective missionaries.

Admissions: Of those who applied for the 1981–82 freshman class, 95% were accepted. Of those who enrolled, the ACT scores were as follows: 59% below 21, 17% between 21 and 23, 10% between 24 and 25, 11% between 26 and 28, and 3% above 28. The candidate should have completed 15 Carnegie units, rank in the upper 75% of the class, and have a minimum grade average of C. Other factors considered include, in order of importance, advanced placement or honors courses, recommendations by school officials, leadership record, and extracurricular activities.

Procedure: The ACT is required. The university prefers to receive applications by June 1. Notification is on a rolling basis. There is a $10 application fee.

Special: A deferred admissions plan is available. AP and CLEP credit is given.

Transfer: For fall 1981, 250 transfer students applied, 225 were accepted, and 200 enrolled. Transfers are accepted for all classes; D grades transfer. An average of 2.0 is required. A student must complete 24 of 128 semester hours required for a bachelor's degree at the

858 TEXAS

university; there is a time residency requirement of 1 year. The application deadlines are March 1 (fall) and November 15 (spring).

Visiting: High school days are held in spring and fall for prospective students. The director of admissions should be contacted to arrange guides for informal visits. Visitors may sit in on classes and stay overnight at the school.

Financial Aid: Seventy-five percent of the students receive financial aid. About 16% work part-time on campus. Government and university loans are available. The average dollar award to freshmen from all sources is $2000. The deadline for application is April 15 (fall) or November 15 (spring). The university is a member of the CSS and requires the FFS.

Foreign Students: About 3% of the full-time students are from foreign countries. An intensive English course, special counseling, and special organizations are offered for these students.

Admissions: Foreign students must achieve a minimum score of 500 on the TOEFL and a minimum composite score of 15 on the ACT.

Procedure: The application deadlines are March 15 (fall) and September 1 (spring). A medical exam form filled out by a certified physician must be presented as proof of health. Proof of adequate funds for 1 year of study also must be presented. Health insurance, while not required, is available through the college for a fee.

Admissions Contact: Clint Howeth, Director of Admissions.

AMBER UNIVERSITY D-2
(Formerly Abilene Christian University at Dallas)
Garland, Texas 75041 (214) 279-6511
(Recognized Candidate for Accreditation)

F/T, P/T:	Faculty: 15; n/av
500M&W	Ph.D.'s: 75%
Grad: n/av	S/F Ratio: 10 to 1
Year: sems, ss	Tuition: $1810
Appl: open	R and B: n/app
SAT or ACT: not required	NONCOMPETITIVE

Amber University, founded in 1971, is an independent institution offering undergraduate instruction in business administration and management, communications, and psychology, as well as graduate studies. The average age of the students is 35, and the majority are evening students; courses are offered once a week and on weekends.

Environment: The 5-acre campus is located in a suburban area 8 miles from Dallas. There is no student housing available on campus.

Student Life: Twenty-five percent of the students are minority-group members. Students may keep cars on campus.

Organizations: There are no fraternities or sororities.

Sports: The university does not offer a sports program.

Handicapped: The entire campus is accessible to the physically handicapped. Facilities for these students include wheelchair ramps, elevators, special parking, and specially equipped rest rooms. A counselor is available to handicapped students.

Services: Students receive the following services free of charge: placement, career counseling, and psychological counseling.

Programs of Study: The university confers the B.S. and B.B.A. degrees. Master's degrees are also awarded. Bachelor's degrees are offered in the following subjects: BUSINESS (career development, management), SOCIAL SCIENCES (human relations). Sixty percent of the degrees conferred are in business and 40% are in social sciences.

Required: Students must complete general education requirements and take courses in religion. A 2.0 GPA is required for graduation.

Special: Student-designed majors are allowed.

Admissions: The university follows an open admissions policy.

Procedure: Entrance exams are not required. Application deadlines are open. There is a $10 application fee.

Transfer: Applicants are accepted for all years. A GPA of at least 2.0 is required. D grades do not transfer. Students must complete, at the university, at least 30 of the 126 semester hours necessary for a bachelor's degree. Application deadlines are open.

Visiting: There are no regularly scheduled orientations for prospective students.

Financial Aid: None of the students receive financial aid from the university.

Foreign Students: About 4% of the full-time students come from foreign countries. The university offers these students special counseling.

Admissions: Undergraduate foreign students are required to have completed a minimum of 30 semester hours at an accredited American college. Students do not need to take either an English proficiency exam or a college entrance exam.

Procedure: Application deadlines are July 25 (fall), December 15 (spring), and May 1 (summer). Foreign students must present proof of funds adequate to cover the duration of study.

Admissions Contact: Lee Paul, Director of University Services.

ANGELO STATE UNIVERSITY C-3
San Angelo, Texas 76909 (915) 942-2041

F/T: 2020M, 2018W	Faculty: 192; IIA, av$
P/T: 542M, 720W	Ph.D.'s: 75%
Grad: 151M, 141W	S/F Ratio: 25 to 1
Year: sems, ss	Tuition: $412 ($1492)
Appl: Aug. 16	R and B: $1984
1802 applied	1259 enrolled
ACT: 18	LESS COMPETITIVE

Angelo State University, founded in 1928, is a state-supported liberal arts institution. The library contains 501,208 volumes and 12,893 microfilm reels, and subscribes to 2000 periodicals.

Environment: The 268-acre campus is located in an urban area 200 miles from Austin. Its 41 buildings include 6 dormitories housing 1400 students. The university also sponsors on-campus apartments and married student housing.

Student Life: Ninety-four percent of the students are from Texas. About 25% live on campus. Drinking on campus is not permitted. About 15% of the students are minority-group members. Campus housing is single-sex; there are visiting privileges. Students may keep cars on campus.

Organizations: Four percent of the men belong to 4 national fraternities and 1% of the women to 2 national sororities. About 60 extracurricular activities and groups are available to undergraduates. Each week 5-10 cultural events take place on campus.

Sports: The university fields 6 intercollegiate teams for men and 5 for women. There are 6 intramural sports for men and 6 for women.

Handicapped: Special facilities for handicapped students include wheelchair ramps, lowered drinking fountains and telephones, elevators, designated parking, and specially equipped rest rooms. Special class scheduling is also available. Special library facilities are available for handicapped students.

Services: Psychological counseling, placement service, career counseling, health care, tutoring, and remedial instruction are offered at no charge to the student.

Programs of Study: The university confers the B.A., B.B.A., B.S., B.Mus.Ed., and B.S.N. degrees, as well as the Associate in Nursing (R.N.) and master's degrees. Bachelor's degrees are offered in the following subjects: BUSINESS (accounting, business administration, computer science, distributive education, economics, finance, management, marketing, secretarial science), EDUCATION (elementary, health/physical), ENGLISH (English, journalism, speech), FINE AND PERFORMING ARTS (art, music education, theater/dramatics), HEALTH SCIENCES (medical technology, nursing), LANGUAGES (French, German, Spanish), MATH AND SCIENCES (biology, chemistry, mathematics, physics), PREPROFESSIONAL (animal science, dentistry, medicine), SOCIAL SCIENCES (government/political science, history, psychology, sociology). Of the degrees conferred, 28% are in business and 9% are in education.

Required: All students must take courses in English, history, government, and physical education.

Special: The university offers the following special programs: a journalism internship program in collaboration with the Harte-Hanks newspaper chain; a distributive education degree program with a teacher certification option; and a summer European studies program. There are 2-year and 4-year programs in nursing.

Honors: Nineteen national honor societies have chapters on campus.

Admissions: About 80% of those who applied were accepted for the 1981-82 freshman class. The ACT scores of those who enrolled were as follows: 67% below 21, 15% between 21 and 23, 8% between 24 and 25, 7% between 26 and 28, and 3% above 28. Candidates must be high school graduates and have a score of at least 15 on the ACT or a combined SAT score of 700 or graduate in the top 50% of their class.

Procedure: The ACT or SAT is required. Application deadlines are August 16 for fall and January 3 for spring. There is no application fee.

Special: Early decision and early admissions plans are offered.

Transfer: For fall 1981, 736 transfer students applied and 487 enrolled. Transfers are accepted for all classes. D grades transfer. The GPA required of transfer students is determined according to a sliding scale based on hours attempted; 2.0 is recommended. To receive a degree, 30 semester hours, 24 of which are advanced, must be taken at the university. The bachelor's degree requires the completion of 130 credits. Application deadlines are the same as those for freshmen.

Visiting: The university conducts regularly scheduled orientations for prospective students. Guides are available for informal visits to the campus anytime except holidays and weekends. Visitors may sit in on classes and stay overnight at the school (spring only). Arrangements can be made through the Office of Student Life.

Financial Aid: About 38% of the students receive aid; 8% work part-time on campus. The university administers $120,000 in federal loan funds (excluding federally insured loans), and $5,000 in state loan funds. CWS funds are available in all departments. Scholarships range in amount from $120 to $1600, loans from $100 to $2500, and work contracts from $723 to $2000. The university is a member of CSS; either the FAF or FFS is required. The recommended deadlines for filing aid applications are April 15 (fall), October 15 (spring), and March 15 (summer).

Foreign Students: Fewer than 1% of the students are from foreign countries. The university offers these students special organizations.

Admissions: Foreign students must achieve a minimum TOEFL score of 500; no further exams are required.

Procedure: Application deadlines are July 1 for fall, November 1 for spring, and April 1 for summer. Foreign students must present proof of health as well as proof of funds adequate to cover 1 year of study.

Admissions Contact: Steven G. Gamble, Director of Admissions.

AUSTIN COLLEGE
Sherman, Texas 75090   D-2   (214) 892-9101

F/T: 623M, 495W	Faculty: 93; IIA, av$
P/T: 9M, 10W	Ph.D.'s: 82%
Grad: 9M, 9W	S/F Ratio: 12 to 1
Year: 4-1-4, ss	Tuition: $3600
Appl: Aug. 1	R and B: $1800
629 applied	520 accepted	306 enrolled
SAT: 500V 520M		COMPETITIVE

Austin College, established in 1849, is a liberal arts college affiliated with the Presbyterian Church in the United States. The library houses 180,000 volumes and 78,000 microfilm items, and subscribes to 712 periodicals.

Environment: The 65-acre suburban campus, located in a city of 35,000, is 65 miles north of Dallas and close to Lake Taxoma. The facilities comprise 28 buildings, 15 of which have been built since 1947. The Wortham Visitors Center is noteworthy. Dormitories accommodate 393 women and 500 men. The college also sponsors on- and off-campus apartments.

Student Life: Eighty percent of the students live on campus. Chapel attendance is not required. Many denominations are represented in the student body; 71% of the students are Protestant, 16% are Catholic, and 2% are Jewish. About 14% are minority-group members. Campus housing is both single-sex and coed; there are visiting privileges in the single-sex dorms. Students may keep cars on campus. The college provides day-care services for a fee; all students, faculty, and staff members are eligible.

Organizations: Approximately half of the students are affiliated with the social, nonresidential fraternities and sororities.

Sports: The college competes on an intercollegiate level in 10 sports for men and 8 for women. There are 4 intramural sports for men and 5 for women.

Handicapped: Facilities for the physically handicapped include wheelchair ramps and special parking.

Graduates: The freshman dropout rate is 12%; 60% remain to graduate. Fifty-five percent of the graduates pursue advanced degrees; 12% enter medical school, 4% dental school, and 10% law school. Fifteen percent pursue careers in business and industry.

Services: Placement services, health care, and psychological counseling are offered free of charge. Career counseling, tutoring, and remedial instruction are available for a fee.

Programs of Study: The college confers the B.A. degree. Master's programs are also offered. Bachelor's degrees are offered in the following subjects: AREA STUDIES (American, Asian), BUSINESS (business administration, computer science), EDUCATION (elementary, health/physical, secondary), ENGLISH (English, speech), FINE AND PERFORMING ARTS (art, music, theater/dramatics), LANGUAGES (French, German, Greek/Latin, Spanish), MATH AND SCIENCES (biology, chemistry, mathematics, physics), PHILOSOPHY (classics, philosophy, religion), PREPROFESSIONAL (dentistry, engineering, law, medicine, ministry), SOCIAL SCIENCES (economics, government/political science, history, psychology, sociology). Twenty-five percent of degrees are conferred in social sciences, 20% in business, and 15% in math and sciences.

Required: Usually students take 6 core courses and 6 exploratory courses (in broad areas other than their concentration).

Special: Cooperative programs in engineering are offered with the University of Texas, Texas A&M, Southern Methodist University, Washington University, and Polytechnic Institute of New York. Science and mathematics students can do additional research study or gain work experience at the Graduate Research Center of the Southwest. Students wishing to study abroad during their junior year may receive permission to do so independently. There is a Washington Semester. Other programs include a communication inquiry group for first-year students, an individual development program (in which mentors individualize a student's total education), a flexible degree plan, flexible grading system, and student-designed majors. The AT and AP examinations and CLEP are used to determine advanced standing and placement.

Honors: Nine national honor societies have chapters on campus. All departments have honors programs.

Admissions: Approximately 83% of those who applied were accepted for the 1981–82 freshman class. The SAT scores of those who enrolled were as follows: Verbal—49% below 500, 37% between 500 and 599, 13% between 600 and 700, and 1% above 700; Math—46% below 500, 38% between 500 and 599, 15% between 600 and 700, and 1% above 700. Candidates must be graduates of an accredited high school, rank in the top half of their class, have an average of C or C+; be recommended by their high schools; present adequate SAT scores; and have completed 15 units of high school work. Also considered are advanced placement or honors courses, impressions made during an interview, and the applicant's extracurricular activities record. Freshmen are also admitted to the spring and summer terms.

Procedure: The SAT or ACT is required and should be taken in December or January of the senior year. It is strongly recommended that freshman and transfer candidates visit the campus. The one application deadline is August 1 (fall); all others are open. The college employs a rolling admissions plan. There is an application fee of $20.

Special: An early decision plan exists, with notification on a rolling basis. Early admissions and deferred admissions plans are also available. Credit is accepted for CLEP subject exams and AP exams.

Transfer: For fall 1981, 119 transfer students applied, 88 were accepted, and 62 enrolled. Transfers are accepted for all but the senior class; D grades do not transfer. Transfer requirements include 2 teacher recommendations, high school and college transcripts, a 2.5 GPA, good standing at the previous school, and the SAT if fewer than 24 hours have been completed. There is an 8-course residency rule. A total of 34 courses is required for the bachelor's degree. Application deadlines are the same as those for freshman applicants.

Visits: Orientation for prospective students includes an open house with the president of the college, classes, tours, lunch with faculty, and a visit with student leaders. Visits are best scheduled for Monday through Friday, 8 A.M. to 5 P.M. Arrangements for a guide can be made with the admissions office. Visitors may stay at the school only for visitation or by special arrangement; they may sit in on classes.

Financial Aid: Eighty percent of all students receive some form of financial aid. Forty-six percent work part-time on campus. The average award to freshmen from all sources through the college is $2873. Tuition, fees, and room and board are paid in two equal payments. Student aid is available in the form of grants, loans, and employment. Total aid is based on financial need as determined by the FAF and Austin College Financial Aid Application, which are required from those applying for aid. The college is a CSS member. There is no formal application deadline; notification is on a rolling basis.

Foreign Students: About 2% of the students come from foreign countries. An intensive English program and special counseling are available.

Admissions: The TOEFL is required; a minimum score of 550 to 600 is necessary for admission. College entrance exams are not required.

Procedure: Application deadlines are the same for foreign students as for other freshman applicants. The college's health form must be com-

860 TEXAS

pleted. Proof of adequate funds to cover 4 years of study must be presented. Health insurance is required; it is available through the college for a fee.

Admissions Contact: Howard Starr, Vice President for College Relations.

BAYLOR UNIVERSITY D-3
Waco, Texas 76706 (817) 755-3435

F/T: 4015M, 4714W	Faculty: 500; I, –$
P/T: 219M, 240W	Ph.D.'s: 75%
Grad: 775M, 449W	S/F Ratio: 21 to 1
Year: sems, ss	Tuition: $2844
Appl: Apr. 1	R and B: $1995
SAT: 485V 521M	ACT: 23 VERY COMPETITIVE

Baylor University, established in 1845, is affiliated with the Baptist Church. The main campus, located in Waco, houses the College of Arts and Sciences and the schools of Business, Education, Law, Music, and Nursing. Dental and medical centers are located in Dallas. The library houses 869,000 volumes and 44,000 microfilm items, and subscribes to 5000 periodicals.

Environment: The 350-acre campus is located in a suburban area 100 miles from Dallas-Fort Worth. The 45 buildings include a fine-arts building with 2 theaters and 10 dormitories for 3900 men and women. Housing for married students also is available.

Student Life: About 77% of the students come from Texas; the rest come from all other states and several foreign countries. Forty percent live on campus. University forum attendance is required, and drinking is forbidden. About 88% of the students are Protestant, and 8% are Catholic. Minority-group members comprise 6% of the enrollment. Campus housing is single-sex; there are visiting privileges. Students may keep cars on campus.

Organizations: Activities include student government, publications, radio and television, music and drama, religious groups for Catholic and Protestant students, and political and special-interest clubs. About 24% of the men belong to the 14 fraternities and 18% of the women to the 8 sororities.

Sports: The university fields intercollegiate teams in 15 sports for men and 14 for women. There are 13 intramural sports for both men and women.

Handicapped: About 95% of the campus is accessible to physically handicapped students. Facilities include wheelchair ramps, specially equipped rest rooms, elevators, special parking areas, and lowered drinking fountains. No special counselors are available.

Graduates: About 17% of the freshmen drop out, and 70% remain to graduate. Sixty percent of the graduates go on for further education, including 3% who enter medical school, 1% who go to dental school, and 1% who enter law school.

Services: Free career and psychological counseling, placement, and tutoring services are available. Health care is available for a fee.

Programs of Study: The university awards the B.A., B.S., B.F.A., B.Mus., B.M.Ed., B.B.A., B.S.Ed., and B.H.E. degrees. Master's and doctoral degrees also are available. Bachelor's degrees are offered in the following subjects: AREA STUDIES (American, Latin American, urban), BUSINESS (accounting, business administration, business education, business journalism, business law, computer science, entrepreneurship, finance, international business, management, marketing, office administration, quantitative business analysis, real estate/insurance), EDUCATION (bilingual, elementary, health/physical, library science, reading, recreation, secondary, special), ENGLISH (English, journalism, literature, speech), FINE AND PERFORMING ARTS (art, art education, art history, music, music education, radio/TV, studio art, theater/dramatics), HEALTH SCIENCES (art therapy, medical technology, nursing, physical therapy, speech therapy), LANGUAGES (French, German, Greek/Latin, Hebrew, Italian, Japanese, Portuguese, Russian, Spanish), MATH AND SCIENCES (biochemistry, biology, chemistry, earth science, ecology/environmental science, geology, mathematics, natural sciences, physics), PHILOSOPHY (classics, humanities, philosophy, religion), PREPROFESSIONAL (dentistry, engineering, forestry, law, medicine, pharmacy), SOCIAL SCIENCES (anthropology, economics, government/political science, history, international relations, psychology, social sciences, sociology). About 32% of the undergraduate degrees are conferred in business and 25% in education.

Required: Courses in religion and physical education, plus traditional liberal arts distribution requirements, are required.

Special: Study abroad, internships, exchange programs, concentrated summer study, and combination degree programs in medical technology and physical therapy are offered.

Honors: An honors program is available. Seven national honor societies, including Phi Beta Kappa, have chapters on campus.

Admissions: About 64% of the applicants for the 1980–81 freshman class were accepted. The SAT scores of a recent freshman class were: Verbal—57% below 500, 32% between 500 and 599, 9% between 600 and 700, and 2% above 700; Math—37% below 500, 41% between 500 and 599, 19% between 600 and 700, and 3% above 700. Of those who took the ACT, 20% scored below 21, 24% between 21 and 23, 15% between 24 and 25, 22% between 26 and 28, and 11% above 28. Applicants must be high school graduates with at least 16 Carnegie units and rank in the upper half of their class.

Procedure: The SAT or ACT is required. An interview is recommended. New students are admitted each semester; application deadlines are April 1 (fall), November 1 (spring), and May 1 (summer). Notification is made on a rolling basis. There is a $30 application fee.

Special: Early decision and early and deferred admissions plans are available. AP and CLEP credit is accepted. Students may also earn credits by ATP, ACT, and Baylor examination scores.

Transfer: For fall 1981, 842 transfer students applied, 517 were accepted, and 368 enrolled. Transfers are accepted for all but the senior class. Applicants must have a GPA of 2.5 or better after 30 hours. D grades do not transfer. Students must complete 60 semester hours in residence, out of a total of 124 semester hours required for the bachelor's degree. Application deadlines are the same for transfers as they are for freshman applicants.

Visiting: Prospective students may arrange visits for weekdays (except holidays) with the admissions office. Guides are available, and visitors may sit in on classes and stay overnight in the dormitories.

Financial Aid: About 65% of the students receive aid. About 35% work part-time on campus. Freshman scholarships are available, and students may apply for federal, university, or private loans. The university is a member of CSS. Applicants must submit the FAF. Application deadlines are open, but those received by March 1 (fall) or November 1 (spring) are given priority consideration.

Foreign Students: One percent of the students are from foreign countries. The university offers these students special counseling and organizations.

Admissions: The TOEFL is required; a minimum score of 540 is necessary for admission. The SAT or ACT is also required.

Procedure: Admissions application deadlines are April 1 (fall), November 1 (spring), and May 1 (summer). The university's health form must be completed by the student's doctor. Proof of adequate funds to cover 2 semesters must be presented. Health insurance is required.

Admissions Contact: Bobby D. Schrade, Director of School Relations and Freshman Admissions.

BISHOP COLLEGE D-2
Dallas, Texas 75241 (214) 376-4311

F/T: 659M, 343W	Faculty: 52; IIB, av$
P/T: 74M&W	Ph.D.'s: 60%
Grad: none	S/F Ratio: 18 to 1
Year: sems, ss	Tuition: $82 p/c
Appl: Apr. 1	R and B: $1990
SAT: 1030 (composite)	COMPETITIVE

Bishop College, founded in 1881, is a private liberal arts college affiliated with the Baptist Church. The library contains more than 75,000 volumes, and subscribes to 660 periodicals.

Environment: The 389-acre campus is located in a suburban area of Dallas, 12 miles from downtown. The 20 major campus buildings include a chapel, a student center, a science building, and 5 dormitories that house about 800 men and women.

Student Life: About half the students come from Texas, and another quarter from other Southern states. About two-thirds of the students live on campus in the single-sex dorms. The student body is predominantly black. Drinking is prohibited on campus. Attendance at chapel is required.

Organizations: About 40% of the students belong to fraternities and sororities. Other extracurricular activities include special-interest clubs, drama and music groups, publications, and student government.

Sports: The college fields intercollegiate teams in 8 sports for men and 5 for women. Intramural sports also are available.

Graduates: About 30% of the freshmen drop out, and 15% remain to graduate. Ten percent of the graduates go on to further study.

Services: The following services are available free to students: health care, placement aid, and psychological and career counseling. Placement services also are available for graduates.

Programs of Study: The college confers the B.A. and B.S. degrees. Bachelor's degrees are offered in the following subjects: AREA STUDIES (Black/Afro-American, urban), BUSINESS (accounting, business administration, computer science, finance, management, marketing, secretarial studies/office management), EDUCATION (early childhood, elementary, health/physical, recreation), ENGLISH (English, speech), FINE AND PERFORMING ARTS (music, sacred music, theater/dramatics), HEALTH SCIENCES (gerontology, nursing), LANGUAGES (French, German, Spanish), MATH AND SCIENCES (biology, chemistry, geology, mathematics, physics), PHILOSOPHY (humanities, philosophy, religion), PREPROFESSIONAL (dentistry, law, medicine, veterinary), SOCIAL SCIENCES (corrections, economics, government/political science, history, law enforcement, psychology, sociology).

Required: Students must take courses in religion, physical education, and the liberal arts.

Special: Students may arrange to study abroad. The college participates in a 13-institution consortium. Independent study opportunities are available.

Honors: Two honor societies have chapters on campus.

Admissions: Applicants must be graduates of accredited high schools and should have completed 15 Carnegie units. They should rank in the top 50% of their class. The college also considers advanced placement or honors courses, recommendations by high school officials, and impressions made during an interview.

Procedure: The ACT or SAT is required and should be taken in December of the senior year. An interview is recommended. Application deadlines are April 1 (fall) and November 1 (spring). Decisions are made on a rolling basis. There is a $10 application fee.

Special: AP and CLEP credit is accepted.

Transfer: Most transfer applicants are accepted. A GPA of 2.0 or better is required. Students must complete 30 hours in residence to graduate.

Financial Aid: About 65% of the students receive aid. Scholarships are available, as are loans from state and federal governments and local banks. CWS jobs also are provided. The FAF is required.

Foreign Students: Students from foreign countries make up about 10% of enrollment. The college offers these students special counseling and special organizations.

Admissions: Applicants must score 550 or better on the TOEFL. They also must take the SAT or ACT.

Procedure: Foreign students are admitted to all terms. Students must present proof of good health and show evidence of adequate funds for 4 years. They are required to carry health insurance, which is available through the college for a fee.

Admissions Contact: H. D. Thomas, Director of Admissions.

DALLAS BAPTIST COLLEGE D-2
Dallas, Texas 75211 (214) 331-8311

F/T: 396M, 207W Faculty: n/av
P/T: 280M, 222W Ph.D.'s: 43%
Grad: 9M, 7W   S/F Ratio: 19 to 1
Year: 4-1-4, ss Tuition: $2025
Appl: open   R and B: $1820
191 enrolled
ACT: 15   LESS COMPETITIVE

Dallas Baptist College, founded in 1965, is a liberal arts college affiliated with the Southern Baptist Church. The library houses 135,552 printed volumes, 43,000 government documents, and 195,600 microfilm items, and subscribes to 126 periodicals.

Environment: The 200-acre campus, located in a suburban area 13 miles from downtown Dallas, consists of 10 buildings. Dormitories house 450 students.

Student Life: About 80% of the students come from Texas; 15% are from out-of-state; and 5% are from foreign countries. About 25% live on campus, and 10% reside in off-campus housing. Weekly chapel attendance is compulsory for 4 semesters. About 30% of the students are minority-group members. Campus housing is single-sex; there are visiting privileges. Students may keep cars on campus.

Organizations: There are 3 local fraternities and 1 national sorority, to which 10% of the men and 5% of the women belong. A variety of activities are offered, and cultural events are scheduled several times weekly. Major social events include Focus Week, Commitment Week, and the cultural arts festival.

Sports: The college fields 2 intercollegiate teams for men and 1 for women. There are 5 intramural sports for men and 2 for women.

Handicapped: There are no special facilities for the physically handicapped.

Graduates: The freshman dropout rate is 10%; 55% remain to graduate.

Services: There are free placement services for graduates and alumni.

Programs of Study: The college confers the B.A., B.S., B.B.A., B.M., and B. of Career Arts degrees. Bachelor's degrees are offered in the following subjects: BUSINESS (accounting, business administration, career arts, corporate security management, finance, management, marketing), EDUCATION (elementary, health/physical, religious, secondary), ENGLISH (English, journalism, speech), FINE AND PERFORMING ARTS (art, music, music education, radio/TV, theater/dramatics), HEALTH SCIENCES (nursing), LANGUAGES (Spanish), MATH AND SCIENCES (biology, chemistry, mathematics, physics), PHILOSOPHY (religion), PREPROFESSIONAL (criminal justice, law, ministry), SOCIAL SCIENCES (government/political science, history, psychology, sociology).

Required: The following courses are required for all students: English, history, science, religion, mathematics, political science, and physical education.

Special: A general studies degree is offered. Student-designed majors, double majors, independent study, and internships are also permitted. There is a study-abroad program available during the summer sessions.

Honors: There are 5 honor society chapters on campus.

Admissions: All of the students who applied for a recent freshman class were accepted. Candidates should have graduated from an accredited high school with a minimum average of C, rank in the top 75% of their class, and score a minimum of 15 on the ACT.

Procedure: The ACT or SAT is required. Application deadlines are open; there is a rolling admissions plan. Applications should be submitted with a $25 fee.

Special: There is an early decision plan. CLEP credit is accepted.

Transfer: Transfers are accepted for all classes. D grades are accepted. The student must be eligible to return to his or her prior school. A 2.0 GPA is required, and students should have a minimum SAT score of 650 or an ACT score of at least 15. A minimum of 30 hours must be completed in residence to qualify for a degree; the bachelor's degree requires 126 credits. Application deadlines are the same as those for freshmen.

Visiting: Guides are available for tours weekdays from 8 A.M. to 5 P.M.; arrangements should be made with the admissions office. Visitors may sit in on classes.

Financial Aid: About 68% of all students receive financial assistance; 3% of the students work part-time on campus. NDSL funds are available. Work contracts are awarded to freshmen. Tuition may be paid in installments. The college is a member of the CSS; the FAF is required. There is no deadline for aid applications, but priority is given to applications received by May 1.

Foreign Students: About 5% of the students come from foreign countries. The college offers these students special organizations.

Admissions: Foreign students must achieve a minimum TOEFL score of 500; they must also take the SAT or ACT.

Procedure: Application deadlines are open; foreign students may enroll for any semester. Foreign students must present proof of health as well as proof of funds adequate to cover 1 year of study. They must also carry health insurance, which is available through the college for a fee.

Admissions Contact: Ray Bratcher, Director of Admissions.

DE VRY INSTITUTE OF TECHNOLOGY D-2
Irving, Texas 75062 (214) 258-6330
(Recognized Candidate for Accreditation)

F/T: 1357M, 176W   Faculty: 28; n/av
P/T: 62M, 10W   Ph.D.'s: 10%
Grad: none   S/F Ratio: 19 to 1
Year: tri, ss   Tuition: $4110-4500
Appl: open   R and B: n/app
1555 applied   789 accepted   729 enrolled
SAT or ACT: required   VERY COMPETITIVE

862 TEXAS

De Vry Institute of Technology, an independent institution administered by the Bell & Howell Education Group, was founded in 1969. It has undergraduate divisions in computer science for business, electronics engineering technology, and electronics technology.

Environment: The institute is located in a suburban area 14 miles from Dallas. It has no housing facilities.

Student Life: Sixty-five percent of the students come from Texas, and 35% are members of minority groups. The institute's housing office helps students find off-campus housing.

Organizations: No special organizations are available.

Sports: The institute does not offer intramural or intercollegiate sports.

Handicapped: The entire campus is accessible to handicapped students. Wheelchair ramps, special parking, elevators, and specially equipped rest rooms are available.

Graduates: Virtually all the graduates begin careers in business and industry.

Services: Placement aid, career counseling, psychological counseling, and tutoring are available free of charge.

Programs of Study: The institute awards the B.S.Comp.Sci. and the B.S.E.E. degrees. Associate degrees in electronics technology also are available. Bachelor's degrees are offered in: BUSINESS (computer science), PREPROFESSIONAL (engineering—electronics engineering technology).

Required: Students must maintain a GPA of 2.0 or better to graduate. Class attendance is compulsory.

Admissions: Fifty-one percent of those who applied for the 1981–82 freshman class were accepted. Of those who enrolled, none scored below 480 on the verbal portion of the SAT or below 23 on the ACT. Applicants must be high school graduates. A personal interview is required.

Procedure: Students must take both the SAT or ACT and the institute's entrance/placement exam. Application deadlines are open; new students are accepted to any trimester. The application fee is $25 plus a $50 tuition deposit.

Special: The institute offers an early admissions plan.

Transfer: For fall 1981, all 9 transfer students who applied were accepted and enrolled.

Visiting: Orientations for prospective students are scheduled regularly. Guides are provided for informal visits, which may be scheduled with the director of admissions.

Financial Aid: About 95% of the students receive aid through the school. Available aid includes scholarships (average $11,000) and loans (average $2500, maximum $6000). Part-time campus jobs also are available. The FAF is required. Aid application deadlines are open.

Foreign Students: Foreign students represent about 3% of the student body.

Admissions: Applicants must score 450 or better on the TOEFL or show evidence that they have completed English courses. They also must take both the SAT or ACT and the institute's entrance exam.

Procedure: Application deadlines are open. Students must present a physician's certificate as proof of good health and must show evidence of adequate funds for 1 year. Students must carry health insurance, which is available through the institute for a fee.

Admissions Contact: Vijay Shah, Director of Admissions.

EAST TEXAS BAPTIST COLLEGE E-2
Marshall, Texas 75670 (214) 935-7963

F/T: 398M, 391W	Faculty: 45; n/av
P/T: 68M, 59W	Ph.D.'s: 72%
Grad: none	S/F Ratio: 19 to 1
Year: sems, ss	Tuition: $1950
Appl: Aug. 1	R and B: $1748
467 applied	465 accepted 378 enrolled
ACT: 18	LESS COMPETITIVE

East Texas Baptist College, founded in 1912, is a liberal arts college affiliated with the Southern Baptist Convention. The library contains 90,421 volumes and 4700 microfilm items, and subscribes to 576 periodicals.

Environment: The 160-acre campus near the suburban town of Marshall, 35 miles from Shreveport, Louisiana, and 150 miles from Dallas, has 12 buildings, including a $1.5 million library. Five dormitories accommodate approximately 650 men and women, plus 90 married students. Day students have their own cafeteria and lounge.

Student Life: Eighty-five percent of the students are Texans, and 13% are from out of state. Ninety-eight percent of the freshmen are graduates of public schools. About 35% of the students live on campus. Ninety-five percent are Protestant, and 1% are Catholic; attendance at religious services twice weekly is compulsory. Eleven percent of the students are minority-group members. College housing is single-sex, and there are no visiting privileges. Study hours and curfew are variable. Students may keep cars on campus. Alcoholic beverages are prohibited.

Organizations: There are no fraternities or sororities; however, students may participate in a wide range of extracurricular activities, including theatrical and musical presentations, publications, concerts, films, and lectures. There are several major social events on campus during the school year, and a coffeehouse is available. Recreational facilities in the surrounding area include Lake O' Pines.

Sports: The college fields 4 intercollegiate teams for men and 2 for women. There are 4 intramural sports for men and 3 for women.

Handicapped: No special facilities are offered.

Graduates: The freshman dropout rate is 45%, and 28% of the freshmen remain to graduate. Of the graduates, 20% pursue advanced degrees; 1% enter medical school, and 1% enter law school. About 10% pursue careers in business and industry.

Services: Students receive the following services free of charge: health care, career counseling, placement, and tutoring. Remedial instruction is available for a fee.

Programs of Study: The B.A., B.S., and B. Applied Science degrees are awarded. Associate degrees are also conferred. Bachelor's degrees are offered in the following subjects: BUSINESS (business administration, business education), EDUCATION (elementary, health/physical, secondary), ENGLISH (English, speech), FINE AND PERFORMING ARTS (music education, piano, sacred music, voice), HEALTH SCIENCES (medical technology, nursing), LANGUAGES (Spanish), MATH AND SCIENCES (biology, chemistry, mathematics), PHILOSOPHY (religion), PREPROFESSIONAL (law, medicine), SOCIAL SCIENCES (history, sociology). Most degrees are granted in education.

Required: Freshman programs must include English, mathematics, natural science, social sciences, and physical activity. Seniors are required to take the URE.

Special: There is an all-level program for teachers of health and physical education. It is possible to earn a combined B.A.-B.S. degree.

Honors: There are approved honors programs within departments. Four honor societies are open to students.

Admissions: Almost all those who applied were accepted for the 1981–82 freshman class. Of those who enrolled, the ACT scores were as follows: 50% below 21, 20% between 21 and 23, 15% between 24 and 25, 15% between 26 and 28, and 0% above 28. A candidate must have completed 16 high school units, rank in the upper 50% of the class, and have at least a C average. Nongraduates over 21 and veterans over 18 may be admitted on the basis of GED tests. The following factors are also important in the admissions decision: evidence of special talent, advanced placement or honors courses, and recommendations by school officials.

Procedure: The ACT is required. Application deadlines for regular admission are August 1 (fall), December 1 (spring), and May 1 (summer). Applications should be submitted with a $15 fee.

Special: An early admissions plan is available. CLEP and AP credit is accepted.

Transfer: For fall 1981, all of the 88 applicants were accepted, and 52 enrolled. Transfers are considered for all classes. A minimum GPA of 2.0 and an ACT score of 15 are required; an interview is recommended. D grades transfer in all except major, minor, and English courses. Students must complete, at the college, at least 30 semester hours toward the 128 necessary for a bachelor's degree. Application deadlines are the same as those for freshmen.

Visiting: Regularly scheduled orientations for prospective students include campus tours and scholarship tryouts. Informal weekday visits allow visitors to sit in on classes and stay overnight at the school. The director of admissions should be contacted for arrangements.

Financial Aid: About 80% of the students receive aid through the school. Fifteen percent work part-time on campus. Scholarships and loans are available, and tuition may be paid in installments. The FFS is required. Application deadlines are June 15 (fall), November 15 (spring), and March 15 (summer).

Foreign Students: Two percent of the full-time students come from foreign countries. The college offers these students special counseling and special organizations.

Admissions: Foreign students must take the TOEFL. They must also achieve an ACT score of 15.

Procedure: Application deadlines are August 1 (fall), December 1 (spring), and May 1 (summer). Foreign students must present proof of a physical exam by a physician, proof of adequate funds, and an initial deposit of $1500. They must also carry health insurance, which is available through the college for a fee.

Admissions Contact: Paul L. Saylors, Director of Admissions.

EAST TEXAS STATE UNIVERSITY   E-2
Commerce, Texas 75428   (214) 886-5081

F/T: 2650M, 2115W	Faculty: 363; I, — — $
P/T: 750M, 600W	Ph.D.'s: 70%
Grad: 1680M, 1610W	S/F Ratio: 20 to 1
Year: sems, ss	Tuition: $450 ($1530)
Appl: open	R and B: $1940
SAT or ACT: required	LESS COMPETITIVE

East Texas State University, a multi-campus state-supported institution founded in 1889, offers undergraduate and graduate programs in the liberal and fine arts, business, education, sciences, and technology. The main library contains nearly 600,000 volumes, and subscribes to 3000 periodicals.

Environment: The 140-acre main campus is located in a community of 10,000 persons 65 miles from Dallas. There are 80 buildings, including dormitories for 2700 men and women. Three housing projects accommodate 350 married couples. The university also has an upper-division branch—serving juniors, seniors, and graduate students—in Texarkana and the Metroplex Center in Dallas, which offers graduate programs.

Student Life: About 96% of the students come from Texas. The majority are public school graduates. Thirty percent live on campus. Both single-sex and coed housing is available.

Organizations: Among the more than 100 extracurricular activities are special-interest clubs, religious and service groups, publications, music, and drama. A number of sororities and fraternities have chapters on campus. Campus social and cultural events include concerts, movies, and museum and ski trips.

Sports: Intercollegiate competition is offered in 5 sports for men and 5 for women. An intramural program also is available.

Graduates: About 25% of the freshmen drop out, and 60% remain to graduate. About 35% of the graduates go on for further study.

Services: The university provides free health care, personal and career counseling, placement services, tutoring, and remedial instruction. Placement services also are available to graduates.

Programs of Study: The university confers the B.A., B.S., B.S.W., B.F.A., B.Mus., B.Mus.Ed., B.B.A., and B.A. or B.S. in Criminal Justice. Master's and doctoral degrees also are available. Bachelor's degrees are offered in the following subjects: AREA STUDIES (Latin American), BUSINESS (accounting, agribusiness, business administration, business education, finance, general business, management, marketing, personnel and human resources management, production and operations management, office administration), EDUCATION (agricultural, counseling and guidance, elementary, health/physical, industrial, secondary, special), ENGLISH (English, journalism, speech), FINE AND PERFORMING ARTS (advertising art, art, art education, film/photography, music, music education, radio/TV, theater/dramatics), HEALTH SCIENCES (health care administration, speech therapy), LANGUAGES (French, German, Spanish), MATH AND SCIENCES (biology, botany, chemistry, computer science, earth science, geology, geophysics, mathematics, physics, zoology), PREPROFESSIONAL (agriculture, agriculture—animal science, agriculture—plant and soil science, fashion, food and nutrition, home economics, interior design, printing, social work, technology), SOCIAL SCIENCES (anthropology, economics, geography, law enforcement, government/political science, history, psychology, social sciences, sociology).

Required: Students must fulfill general education requirements, which include 4 semester hours of physical education.

Special: Independent study, double majors, cooperative education, and exchange programs are possible. An ethnic studies minor is available. Preprofessional programs are offered in law, ministry, health professions, wildlife, and engineering. Students may design their own majors. A general studies degree is available.

Honors: Eligible students may participate in the honors programs.

TEXAS 863

Admissions: About 70% of the applicants for a recent freshman class were accepted. A high school diploma or GED is required. The university prefers that students score 18 or higher on the ACT, or at least 800 when both sections of the SAT are combined.

Procedure: Either the ACT or the SAT is required. New students are admitted each semester. Application deadlines are open. Notification is made on a rolling basis. There is no application fee.

Special: Early decision and early admissions plans are offered. CLEP and AP credit is accepted.

Transfer: A 2.0 GPA is necessary. D grades are usually accepted. Students must complete at least 10 courses (including 8 advanced courses) in residence for a bachelor's degree. Applications should be submitted at least 60 days before the start of the semester.

Visiting: Parents and prospective students are invited to attend Early Enrollment Conference programs. Informal campus tours with student guides can be arranged. Visitors may sit in on classes.

Financial Aid: About 33% of the students receive aid. The university participates in federal and state grant and loan programs such as NDSL and BEOG/SEOG. A limited number of freshman scholarships, commercial (bank) loans, and campus jobs, including CWS, also are offered. The average freshman aid package is $2000. Most aid awards are based on financial need. The FFS is required. All applications must be made by June 1 to ensure availability of funds.

Foreign Students: About 2% of the students come from foreign countries. An intensive English course and special counseling are available.

Admissions: Applicants must score at least 500 on the TOEFL.

Procedure: Students should apply at least 3 months before the start of the semester in which they wish to enroll. Health insurance is required, and is available through the university.

Admissions Contact: Director of Admissions.

HARDIN-SIMMONS UNIVERSITY   C-2
Abilene, Texas 79698   (915) 677-7281

F/T: 632M, 689W	Faculty: 94; IIA, — — $
P/T: 241M, 240W	Ph.D.'s: 73%
Grad: 154M, 93W	S/F Ratio: 19 to 1
Year: sems, ss	Tuition: $2460
Appl: see profile	R and B: $1700
447 applied 390 accepted	345 enrolled
ACT: 18	LESS COMPETITIVE

Hardin-Simmons University is a privately controlled institution affiliated with the Baptist General Convention of Texas. Its library houses 300,000 volumes and 15,204 microfilm items, and subscribes to 725 periodicals.

Environment: The 40-acre campus is located in an urban area 150 miles west of Fort Worth. Residence halls accommodate 400 men and 528 women; there are housing facilities for 42 married students.

Student Life: About 85% of the students come from Texas, and 95% are graduates of public schools. About 88% of the students are Protestant (68% are Southern Baptists) and 4% are Catholic. Resident students must attend chapel-assembly during half their college experience; students are urged to attend their own churches. All unmarried students who do not live at home must live in dormitories. Drinking is prohibited. About 7% of the students are minority-group members. Campus housing is single-sex; there are no visiting privileges. Students may keep cars on campus.

Organizations: There are campus social clubs for men and women and there are numerous special-interest clubs, a biweekly newspaper and other publications, theater and music groups, and religious activities.

Sports: The university fields 8 intercollegiate teams for men and 6 for women. There are 3 intramural sports for men and 3 for women.

Handicapped: About 90% of the campus is accessible to wheelchair-bound students. Facilities include wheelchair ramps, special parking, elevators, specially equipped rest rooms, and handrails. A special counselor is available for assisting handicapped students. Special class scheduling can be arranged.

Services: Students receive the following services free of charge: placement, limited health care, psychological counseling, career counseling, and tutoring in some departments.

Programs of Study: The university confers the B.A., B.S., B.B.A., B.F.A., B.Mus., and B.S.N. degrees. Master's degrees are also awarded. Bachelor's degrees are offered in the following subjects: BUSINESS (accounting, business administration, business education, computer science, finance, management, marketing), EDUCATION (elementary, health/physical, reading, secondary, special), ENGLISH (English, mass communications, speech), FINE AND PERFORMING ARTS (art, art education, music, music education, studio art, theater/dramatics), HEALTH SCIENCES (medical technology, nursing, speech therapy), LANGUAGES (French, German, Spanish), MATH AND SCIENCES (biology, chemistry, earth science, geology, mathematics, physical sciences, physics), PHILOSOPHY (Bible, religion, religious education), PREPROFESSIONAL (agriculture, dentistry, engineering, law, medicine, ministry, pharmacy, social work, veterinary), SOCIAL SCIENCES (government/political science, history, psychology, social sciences, sociology). Half of the degrees conferred are in education.

Required: All students must take 6 semester hours in Bible and 4 semester hours in either ROTC or physical education.

Special: Cooperative programs with Abilene Christian University are offered in agriculture, geology, law enforcement, military science, and speech pathology and audiology.

Honors: Seventeen national honor societies have chapters on campus.

Admissions: Of the students who applied for the 1981–82 freshman class, 87% were accepted. The SAT scores of those who enrolled were as follows: Verbal—82% below 500, 14% between 500 and 599, 4% between 600 and 700, and 0% above 700; Math—74% below 500, 21% between 500 and 599, 5% between 600 and 700, and 1% above 700. On the ACT, 65% scored below 21, 20% between 21 and 23, 8% between 24 and 25, 6% between 26 and 28, and 1% above 28. Candidates should have completed 16 units of high school work. Other factors considered by the school are the high school transcript, the counselor's reference, and ACT or SAT scores. Applicants who do not have a diploma from an accredited high school may be admitted on the basis of the GED. Admission to the School of Music requires an audition and a written examination.

Procedure: The ACT or SAT is required. To facilitate processing, applications should be submitted at least 30 days prior to the start of the semester. Applying as early as possible is recommended. The official deadline is registration day. Notification is made on a rolling basis. Freshmen are admitted to every semester. There is a $25 application fee.

Special: Notification for early decision is December 15. Early and deferred admissions are possible. CLEP and AP credit is accepted.

Transfer: For fall 1981, 236 transfer students applied, 205 were accepted, and 173 enrolled. Transfers are considered for all classes. The requirements are the same as for freshmen. Grades of C and above transfer. All students must complete 30 credit hours on campus to qualify for a degree; the bachelor's degree requires the completion of 124 credit hours. Transfer students are encouraged to apply at least 30 days prior to the start of the semester.

Visiting: There are June or July 3-day orientation sessions and an orientation in late August. Guides are available for informal tours on weekdays; arrangements should be made with the office of admissions. Visitors may sit in on classes and stay overnight at the school if space permits.

Financial Aid: About 80% of all students receive some form of financial aid; about 30% of the students work part-time on campus. The university participates in NDSL, guaranteed student loans, BEOG, SEOG, TEG, and federal nursing scholarships and loans programs. Aid application should be made by April 15, but commitments are made as long as funds are available. The university is a member of CSS. The FFS or FAF must be filed.

Foreign Students: Fewer than 1% of the students come from foreign countries.

Admissions: Foreign students must achieve a minimum TOEFL score of 550; they must also take the SAT or ACT.

Procedure: Application deadlines are the same as those for other freshmen. Foreign students must present proof of health as well as proof of funds adequate to cover their entire period of study. They must also carry health insurance, which is available through the university for a fee.

Admissions Contact: David Smith, Director of Admissions.

HOUSTON BAPTIST UNIVERSITY E-3
Houston, Texas 77074 (713) 774-7661

F/T: 768M, 936W Faculty: 103; IIB, +$
P/T: 291M, 375W Ph.D.'s: 65%
Grad: 131M, 176W S/F Ratio: 18 to 1
Year: qtrs, ss Tuition: $95 p/c
Appl: open R and B: $1725
594 applied 520 accepted 394 enrolled
SAT: 420V 460M ACT: 20 COMPETITIVE

Houston Baptist University, founded in 1960, is a liberal arts college controlled by the Southern Baptist Convention. The library houses more than 96,830 volumes and 2000 microfilm items, and subscribes to 572 periodicals.

Environment: The 100-acre campus, located in an urban section of Houston, includes 2 dormitories that house 128 students each, an apartment complex, a gymnasium, and an academic quadrangle. There are also theology, teaching, and science buildings.

Student Life: Eighty percent of the students come from a 25-mile radius of Houston. Convocation once a week is required. Drinking is prohibited at the university. Fifteen percent of the students live on campus. Unmarried students must live on campus, in approved off-campus housing, or with relatives. Forty-six percent of the students are Protestant, 14% are Catholic, and 4% are Jewish. Twenty percent are minority-group members. Campus housing is single-sex; there are visiting privileges. Students may keep cars on campus.

Organizations: Extracurricular activities include art, band, debating, student government, drama, glee club, student publications, films, plays, and concerts. A nationally known lecturer is invited to campus each week. About 15% of the students belong to fraternities or sororities.

Sports: The university fields intercollegiate teams in 6 sports for men and 2 for women. There are 8 intramural sports for men and 6 for women.

Graduates: About 20% of the freshmen drop out. Of the 66% who remain to graduate, 15% go on to further education.

Programs of Study: The university awards the B.A., B.S., B.S.N., B.Mus., and B.Mus.Ed. degrees. Master's degrees also are available. Bachelor's degrees are offered in the following subjects: BUSINESS (accounting, computer science, economics, finance, management, marketing), EDUCATION (early childhood, elementary, secondary), ENGLISH (English), FINE AND PERFORMING ARTS (art, art education, music, music education), HEALTH SCIENCES (medical technology, nursing), LANGUAGES (French, German, Spanish), MATH AND SCIENCES (biology, chemistry, mathematics, physics), PHILOSOPHY (religion), PREPROFESSIONAL (dentistry, law, medicine), SOCIAL SCIENCES (government/political science, history, psychology, sociology).

Required: Students must take 3 courses in religion, 6 hours of an interdisciplinary course, and 8 hours of a senior seminar. They also must maintain an average of 2.0 or better to graduate.

Special: English majors may study at Stratford-on-Avon for 4 weeks during April. Credit also is given to students participating in study-abroad programs, generally lasting 3 weeks, in Christianity, English, and the sophomore interdisciplinary course.

Admissions: Eighty-eight percent of those who applied were accepted for the 1981–82 freshman class. On the SAT, entering freshmen scored as follows: Verbal—60% below 500, 33% between 500 and 599, 7% between 600 and 700, and 0% above 700; Math—44% below 500, 31% between 500 and 599, 21% between 600 and 700, and 4% above 700. On the ACT, freshmen scored as follows: 35% below 21, 20% between 21 and 23, 28% between 24 and 25, 16% between 26 and 28, and 1% above 28. Applicants must be high school graduates. Acceptable composite test scores are 800 on the SAT and 18 on the ACT if taken in the first half of the senior year, 850 and 19 if taken during the third quarter, and 900 and 20 if taken in the final quarter. Other important considerations are high school grades, extracurricular activities, impressions made during an interview, and relationship to alumni.

Procedure: The SAT or ACT is required and should be taken by January of the senior year. The application deadlines are open. Freshmen are accepted to all quarters. There is a $15 application fee. Admissions decisions are made on a rolling basis.

Special: The university employs early admissions and deferred admissions plans. AP and CLEP credit is accepted.

Transfer: Transfers are accepted for all classes. D grades do not transfer. Applicants must be in good standing at their last school and have a GPA of 2.0 or better. Students must take at least 32 semester hours at the university, out of the 130 required for the bachelor's degree. There are no application deadlines. Transfers are admitted to all quarters.

Financial Aid: About 60% of the students receive aid. About 15% work part-time on campus. The average award to freshmen from all sources available through the university is $900. Full-tuition scholarships for students who maintain a GPA of 3.5 or better and partial scholarships for nursing students who keep a GPA of 2.5 or better are awarded on the basis of academic standing alone. Other scholarships are available to Baptist ministers and music majors. Grants-in-aid are awarded to students whose grades are not outstanding but who have special abilities in music, debate, drama, or other areas. Other aid sources include federal loans, BEOG, state grants, CWS jobs, and off-campus employment. The university is a member of the CSS, and aid applicants must submit the FAF. The deadline for aid application is May 1.

Foreign Students: Four percent of the full-time students come from foreign countries. An intensive English course and special organizations for foreign students are available.

Admissions: The TOEFL is required; a minimum score of 500 is necessary for acceptance. College entrance exams are not necessary.

Procedure: There are no application deadlines. Foreign students may enter any quarter. The university health form must be completed by the student's physician. Proof of adequate funds for the first year must be presented.

Admissions Contact: Brenda Davis, Director of Admissions.

HOWARD PAYNE UNIVERSITY C-3
Brownwood, Texas 76801 (915) 646-2502

F/T: 464M, 472W	Faculty: 89; IIB, — $
P/T: 104M, 132W	Ph.D.'s: 47%
Grad: none	S/F Ratio: 14 to 1
Year: sems, ss	Tuition: $60 p/c
Appl: Aug. 15	R and B: $1650
500 applied	450 accepted 300 enrolled
ACT: 16	LESS COMPETITIVE

Howard Payne University, established in 1890, is a private college of liberal arts affiliated with the Baptist Church. The library houses 130,000 volumes, and subscribes to 783 periodicals.

Environment: The 40-acre campus, divided into 2 sections, is located in a town of 18,000 persons, 165 miles from Dallas and 125 miles from Fort Worth. The 25-acre main campus has air-conditioned dormitories and a religious center. The older section contains the main building, the auditorium, and a gymnasium. Married-student housing is available.

Student Life: Ninety percent of the students are from Texas. About half live on campus in the single-sex dorms. Most students are members of the Baptist Church, and all are required to attend chapel 3 times a week. Drinking is prohibited; smoking is discouraged. Unmarried undergraduates are required to live on campus as long as space is available.

Organizations: Eight fraternities and 9 sororities have chapters on campus; 29% of the men and 40% of the women belong. Campus activities include student government, departmental and religious groups, and publications.

Sports: The university fields intercollegiate teams in 3 sports for men and 2 for women. Intramural sports also are available.

Handicapped: There are no special facilities for the physically handicapped.

Graduates: About 15% of the freshmen drop out, and 40% remain to graduate. Thirty percent of the graduates pursue advanced degrees; 2% enter medical school, 2% enter dental school, and 5% enter law school. About 30% begin careers in business and industry.

Services: Placement services, health care, and psychological counseling are offered free.

Programs of Study: The university confers the B.A., B.B.A., B.A.Ed., B.S.Ed., B.Mus., and B.Mus.Ed. degrees. Bachelor's degrees are offered in the following subjects: BUSINESS (accounting, finance, marketing, office administration and secretarial science), EDUCATION (elementary, health/physical, religious, secondary), ENGLISH (English, journalism, speech), FINE AND PERFORMING ARTS (art education, music, music education, studio art, theater/dramatics), HEALTH SCIENCES (medical technology, speech therapy), LANGUAGES (French, German, Spanish), MATH AND SCIENCES (biology, chemistry, mathematics, physics), PHILOSOPHY (philosophy, religion), PRE-PROFESSIONAL (ministry), SOCIAL SCIENCES (economics, government/political science, history, psychology, sociology).

Required: All students must take a distribution of courses in English, humanities, religion, mathematics, science, and social sciences. Two years of physical education are required.

Special: A behavioral science program is available. The college confers combined B.A.-B.S. degrees. A general studies degree is offered.

Honors: Five honor societies have chapters on campus. The university offers a general honors program and special programs in social sciences and theology.

Admissions: Ninety percent of those who applied were accepted for the 1981–82 freshman class. The ACT scores of those who enrolled were: 50% below 21, 10% between 21 and 23, 10% between 24 and 25, 5% between 26 and 28, and 2% above 28. Candidates must rank in the top 75% of their graduating class, and have an average of 70 (C) or better. Students with a class rank in the bottom quarter will be admitted only with a personal interview. Completion of 15 Carnegie units is recommended. The GED also is accepted.

Procedure: All candidates must take the ACT by April of the senior year, preferably in November. Application deadlines are August 15 (fall), January 15 (spring), and June 1 (summer). Notification is made about June 1. The application fee is $15.

Special: CLEP subject exams are accepted.

Transfer: In a recent year, 118 transfer students applied, 117 were accepted, and 102 enrolled. Transfers are considered for all classes; they must be in good standing at their previous school. Up to 6 hours of D grades transfer. Students must earn at least 30 semester hours in residence of the 128 or more required for a bachelor's degree.

Visiting: Orientations are scheduled for prospective students, who also may visit at their own convenience. Guides can be arranged, and visitors may sit in on classes and stay overnight at the school.

Financial Aid: About 75% of the students receive aid. Tuition may be paid in installments. Scholarships and loans are available to freshmen. The application deadlines are June 1 (fall), November 15 (spring), and April 15 (summer) for priority consideration.

Foreign Students: Eight students from foreign countries were enrolled in 1981–82.

Admissions: Applicants must score 450 or better on the TOEFL. No college entrance exams are required.

Procedure: Foreign students are admitted to all semesters. They must submit a physician's statement as proof of good health and show evidence of adequate funds for at least 1 year. Health insurance is included in their activity fee.

Admissions Contact: W. Bennett Ragsdale, Director of Admissions and Registrar.

HUSTON-TILLOTSON COLLEGE D-3
Austin, Texas 78702 (512) 476-7421

F/T: 479M, 315W	Faculty: 36; IIB, — $
P/T: 22M, 20W	Ph.D.'s: 40%
Grad: none	S/F Ratio: 16 to 1
Year: sems, ss	Tuition: $2430
Appl: open	R and B: $1826
226 applied	224 accepted 212 enrolled
SAT or ACT: required	NONCOMPETITIVE

Huston-Tillotson College was formed in 1952 by the merger of Tillotson College (founded in 1875) and Samuel Huston College (founded in 1876). This private liberal arts institution is supported by the United Methodist Church and the United Church of Christ. The library contains more than 64,000 volumes, and subscribes to 399 periodicals.

Environment: The 23-acre campus is located in the eastern section of Austin, an urban setting about a mile from downtown. There are 13 campus buildings, including 2 dormitories, which house more than 600 students.

Student Life: Seventy percent of the students come from Texas. About 55% live on campus; all freshmen, unless excused by the dean of student affairs, are required to live on campus. The majority of students are Protestant, and attendance at weekly chapel services is recommended. About 69% of the students are minority-group members. College housing is single-sex, and there are visiting privileges. Students may keep cars on campus.

Organizations: There are 4 fraternities and 4 sororities on campus. The Cultural and Special Events Committee sponsors lectures, musical programs, panel discussions, and symposiums. Other activities include student government, social clubs, academic and professional groups, and publications.

Sports: The college fields 4 intercollegiate teams for men and 3 for women. There are 5 intramural sports for men and 5 for women.

Graduates: Seventeen percent of the graduates pursue advanced study.

Services: The college provides free placement services, career counseling, health services, tutoring, and remedial instruction.

Programs of Study: The college confers the B.A. and B.S. degrees. Bachelor's degrees are offered in the following subjects: BUSINESS

866　TEXAS

(accounting, business administration, business education, hotel and restaurant management, industrial relations and personnel management, marketing), EDUCATION (elementary, health/physical, secondary), ENGLISH (English), FINE AND PERFORMING ARTS (music), HEALTH SCIENCES (medical technology, prenursing), MATH AND SCIENCES (biology, chemistry, mathematics), PREPROFESSIONAL (dentistry, law, medicine), SOCIAL SCIENCES (economics, government/political science, history, sociology).

Required: During the freshman and sophomore years, students must fulfill general education requirements in English, mathematics, social science, science, physical education, humanities, foreign languages, philosophy, and health.

Special: Cooperative academic arrangements have been developed with 4 other colleges and universities in the Austin area.

Honors: Three national honor societies have chapters on campus.

Admissions: Almost all of those who applied were accepted for the 1981-82 freshman class. Applicants must be graduates of an accredited high school or have a satisfactory score on the GED test. Fifteen units of high school work are required. The admissions decision is based on academic records, SAT or ACT scores, and other evidence of potential for academic success. An interview is recommended.

Procedure: The ACT or SAT is required but is used for placement purposes only. Freshmen are admitted to fall, spring, and summer sessions; application deadlines are open. Notification is on a rolling basis. There is a $10 application fee.

Transfer: For fall 1981, 101 students applied, 75 were accepted, and 67 enrolled. Transfers are accepted for all classes. In all transfer cases, satisfactory academic achievement, good character, and honorable separation from the previous college are required. Students must complete, at the college, the last 24 semester hours toward the 120 necessary for a bachelor's degree. Application deadlines are open.

Visiting: A freshman orientation session is held before the start of each semester. Prospective students are encouraged to arrange visits to the college and interviews with the director of admissions.

Financial Aid: Sixty-seven percent of the students receive financial aid. Sixteen percent work part-time on campus. Average aid to freshmen covers 55% of costs. Numerous scholarships are available to qualified students from the sponsoring churches, the United Negro College Fund, and other sources. Pell, SEOG, NDSL, and other grant and loan programs are offered. Financial assistance is based primarily on financial need and academic performance. A deferred payment plan is available. Tuition discounts are offered to children of ministers of the sponsoring churches. The FAF or FFS is required and must be submitted with the college's own aid application by March 1.

Foreign Students: Twenty-four percent of the full-time students come from foreign countries. The college offers these students an intensive English course, special counseling, and special organizations.

Admissions: Foreign students must achieve a minimum TOEFL score of 350. They must also take the college's own entrance exam.

Procedure: Application deadlines are open. Foreign students must present a health record and proof of immunizations, as well as proof of funds adequate to cover the duration of study. They must also carry health insurance, which is available through the college and included in the basic fees.

Admissions Contact: Margaret McCracken, Vice President for Student Affairs.

INCARNATE WORD COLLEGE　　　D-4
San Antonio, Texas 78209　　　(512) 828-1261

F/T: 204M, 770W　　　Faculty: 73; IIA, --$
P/T: 64M, 244W　　　Ph.D.'s: 78%
Grad: 51M, 220W　　　S/F Ratio: 13 to 1
Year: sems, ss　　　Tuition: $3036
Appl: Aug. 15　　　R and B: $1664
524 applied　　　440 accepted　　　238 enrolled
SAT: 401V 408M　　　ACT: 17　　　LESS COMPETITIVE

Incarnate Word College, founded in 1881, is a Catholic college of liberal arts and professional studies conducted by the Sisters of Charity of the Incarnate Word. The library contains 119,533 volumes and 12,168 microfilm items, and subscribes to 611 periodicals.

Environment: Located in a suburban area 5 minutes from downtown San Antonio, the self-contained campus consists of 18 buildings including 4 residence halls for men and women. Some 13 prehistoric and historic sites and 100 acres of the campus are contained in the *National Register of Historic Places.* A $2.6 million teaching theater was dedicated in 1980.

Student Life: The majority of students are from Texas; about 85% of the freshmen come from public schools. About 22% of the students live on campus. Although this is a Catholic college, approximately half of the students are non-Catholic. About 44% of the students are minority-group members. Campus housing is coed and single-sex; there are visiting privileges in single-sex dorms. Students may keep cars on campus. Day-care services are available to all students, faculty, and staff for a fee.

Organizations: There are 3 fraternities and 2 sororities on campus. An active social and cultural life is maintained by departmental and college-wide organizations. Extracurricular activities include student government, touring groups, lectures, concerts, films, dances, a coffee house, and a cafe theater.

Sports: The college fields 2 intercollegiate teams for men and 4 for women. There are 7 intramural sports.

Handicapped: The campus is completely accessible to wheelchair-bound students. Special facilities include wheelchair ramps, special parking, and elevators.

Graduates: The freshman dropout rate is 20%; 68% remain to graduate. About 50% of the students go on to graduate school; 4% enter medical school, 2% enter dental school, and 2% enter law school. About 28% pursue careers in business and industry.

Services: Students receive the following services free of charge: placement, psychological counseling, career counseling, tutoring, and remedial instruction. Health care is available on a fee basis.

Programs of Study: The college confers the B.A., B.B.A., B.M., B.S., and B.S.N. degrees. Master's programs are also offered. Bachelor's degrees are offered in the following subjects: AREA STUDIES (American), BUSINESS (accounting, business administration, finance, management, marketing), EDUCATION (adult, early childhood, elementary, health/physical, secondary, special), ENGLISH (communication arts, English, speech), FINE AND PERFORMING ARTS (art, music, music education, studio art, theater/dramatics), HEALTH SCIENCES (medical records administration, medical technology, nuclear medical science, nursing), LANGUAGES (Spanish), MATH AND SCIENCES (biology, chemistry, mathematics), PHILOSOPHY (philosophy, religion), PREPROFESSIONAL (dentistry, dietetics, fashion design, fashion merchandising, home economics, interior design, law, medicine, veterinary), SOCIAL SCIENCES (anthropology, child care work, economics, government/political science, history, human relations, psychology, sociology). Forty-five percent of degrees conferred are in health sciences, 15% in social sciences, and 14% in education.

Required: All degree programs require 51 credits from a core curriculum chosen from 6 areas of study. All students must take 2 semesters of physical education.

Special: A 3-year bachelor's program is offered. There is a study-abroad program. The academic year consists of 2 traditional semesters followed by a short term prior to summer sessions. Students can earn 3 credits in the short term.

Honors: Two national honor societies have chapters on campus.

Admissions: About 84% of those who applied for the 1981-82 freshman class were accepted. The SAT scores of those who enrolled were as follows: Verbal—91% below 500, 8% between 500 and 599, 1% between 600 and 700, and 0% above 700; Math—90% below 500, 8% between 500 and 599, 2% between 600 and 700, and 0% above 700. The ACT scores were as follows: 79% below 21, 18% between 21 and 23, 2% between 24 and 25, 1% between 26 and 28, and 0% above 28. Candidates should have completed 16 units of high school work, have at least an average of C, and rank in the top 60% of their class. Other factors, considered in order of importance, are impressions made during an interview, advanced placement or honors courses, and evidence of special talents. Students ranked in the lower quartile may be admitted if there are indications that high school deficiencies may be overcome in college.

Procedure: The SAT or ACT is required. The fall application deadline is August 15. A rolling admissions plan is used. Applications should be submitted with a $15 fee.

Special: The notification date for early decision is December 15. A deferred admissions plan is also available. CLEP and AP credit is accepted. College credit courses are available for high school seniors.

Transfer: For fall 1981, 329 transfer students applied, 293 were accepted, and 189 enrolled. Applicants must have a 2.0 average and may not be on scholastic probation; D grades transfer when there are B grades to balance them. Students must take 36 semester hours on campus to qualify for a degree; the bachelor's degree requires 128 semester hours. Application deadlines are the same as those for freshmen.

Visiting: Two-day orientation sessions are held for freshmen. There are separate sessions for transfer students. Guides are also available for informal tours weekdays; the admissions office should be contacted for arrangements. Visitors may stay at the school and sit in on classes.

Financial Aid: About 85% of all students receive some form of financial aid; 33% work part-time on campus. There are 115 types of scholarships available, 22 of them administered by the college. There are 6 government grant and 4 loan programs available. The average award to freshmen from all sources is $3500. The FFS is required. The deadline for aid applications is March 1 for priority consideration.

Foreign Students: About 5% of the full-time students come from foreign countries. The college offers these students an intensive English course, special counseling, and special organizations.

Admissions: Foreign students must achieve a minimum TOEFL score of 500; no college entrance exams are required.

Procedure: Application deadlines are August 1 for fall, December 1 for spring, and May 1 for summer. Foreign students must present proof of funds adequate to cover 1 year of study. They must also carry health insurance.

Admissions Contact: Judith Watson, Director of Enrollment Development.

JARVIS CHRISTIAN COLLEGE E-2
Hawkins, Texas 75765   (214) 769-2174

F/T: 214M, 217W   *Faculty: 65; IIB, −$*
P/T: 7M, 18W   *Ph.D.'s: 45%*
Grad: none   *S/F Ratio: 16 to 1*
Year: sems   *Tuition: $4112*
Appl: see profile   *R and B: $1585*
217 applied   *212 accepted*
ACT: 10   **NONCOMPETITIVE**

Jarvis Christian College, founded in 1912, is a liberal arts institution affiliated with the Disciples of Christ Church. The library contains more than 45,000 volumes, and subscribes to more than 500 periodicals.

Environment: The 243-acre campus is located in a rural area about 100 miles east of Dallas. The more than 50 campus buildings include dormitories that house about 400 students. Married-student housing also is available.

Student Life: About 80% of the students come from Texas, and 10% of the rest come from other Southern states. The student body is predominately black. More than 95% of the freshmen are graduates of public schools. Dormitories are single-sex. Drinking is prohibited on campus.

Organizations: About 30% of the students belong to the 8 sororities and fraternities with chapters on campus. Extracurricular activities include student government, performing-arts groups, and departmental, professional, and social clubs. Religious organizations include the United Church of Christ Christian Fellowship, YMCA, YWCA, Bible School, and College Church.

Sports: The college fields intercollegiate teams in 3 sports. Intramural sports also are available.

Graduates: About 45% of the freshmen drop out, and 45% remain to graduate. About 10% of the graduates go on to further study.

Services: A health center is located on campus.

Programs of Study: The college confers the B.A., B.S., B.B.A., and B.S.Ed. degrees. Associate degrees also are available. Bachelor's degrees are offered in the following subjects: BUSINESS (accounting, business administration, business education, office management), EDUCATION (elementary, secondary), ENGLISH (English), MATH AND SCIENCES (biology, chemistry, ecology/environmental science, mathematics, physics), PHILOSOPHY (religion), SOCIAL SCIENCES (economics, government/political science, history, social sciences, sociology).

Required: Students must complete a core curriculum that includes 6 credit hours in religion. To graduate, they must pass GRE Aptitude and Advanced tests. A Sophomore Comprehensive Exam also is required.

Special: The college participates in a curriculum consortium with 8 other institutions of higher learning nearby. Additional minors include art, drama, earth science, music, physical education, psychology, and speech. Students may design their own majors. Other special programs include a semester at Brookhaven National Laboratory, cooperative education, summer premedical programs, and a Black Executive Exchange Program.

Honors: Four honor societies have chapters on campus. The college offers an honors program that includes seminars and research papers.

Admissions: Almost all who applied were accepted for the 1981–82 freshman class. Candidates must be graduates of accredited high schools. The college follows an open admissions policy.

Procedure: The ACT or the SAT is required. Applicants are admitted on a rolling basis. Applications are due at least 30 days before registration. Students are admitted to all terms. There is a $5 application fee.

Transfer: Transfer students are accepted for the freshman, sophomore, and junior classes. Applicants must be in good standing at their last school. D grades do not transfer. Students must complete at least 30 semester hours in residence of the 124 required for a bachelor's degree.

Financial Aid: About 95% of the students receive aid, usually in a package that combines scholarships, loans, and part-time jobs. The average package awarded to a freshman in 1981–82 totaled $2300. Aid is awarded on the basis of academic record and financial need. Applicants must submit the FAF or the FFS. The college will provide information on application deadlines.

Foreign Students: Three students from foreign countries were enrolled in 1981–82. The college actively recruits foreign students.

Admissions: Applicants must take the TOEFL and either the SAT or ACT.

Procedure: Students must apply at least 1 semester before the start of the term. They must present a completed medical form as proof of good health and must show evidence of adequate funds for 1 year. Health insurance is required, and is available through the college for a fee.

Admissions Contact: Director of Admissions.

LAMAR UNIVERSITY E-3
Beaumont, Texas 77710   (713) 838-7619

F/T: 4139M, 4292W   *Faculty: 436; IIA, −$*
P/T: 2365M, 2456W   *Ph.D.'s: n/av*
Grad: 160M, 350W   *S/F Ratio: 19 to 1*
Year: sems, ss   *Tuition: $555 ($1845)*
Appl: Aug. 15   *R and B: $1746*
4000 applied   *2706 enrolled*
SAT or ACT: required   **NONCOMPETITIVE**

Lamar University, a state-supported institution established in 1923, offers programs in liberal arts and sciences and in technical fields. Its library contains 415,000 volumes and 210,000 microfilm items, and subscribes to 3158 periodicals.

Environment: The 200-acre campus is located in a city of 120,000 people, 85 miles from Houston. The 48 buildings include 8 residence halls that house 887 men and 683 women. Seventy units for married students also are provided. Major buildings include health sciences and speech and hearing therapy centers and the Brown Center, a mansion built in the antebellum tradition and surrounded by landscaped grounds. The university also sponsors fraternity and sorority houses.

Student Life: About 93% of the students come from Texas and 4% from foreign countries. Fifteen percent live on campus. Drinking is allowed in certain areas of the campus. About 30% of the students are minority-group members. Campus housing is coed and single-sex; there are visiting privileges in single-sex dorms. Students may keep cars on campus. Day-care services are available to all students, faculty, and staff.

Organizations: About 4% of the men belong to the 14 fraternities and 2% of the women to the 9 sororities. Extracurricular activities include student government, publications, radio and television, drama, choral and orchestral groups, and religious, professional, and special-interest groups.

Sports: The university fields 8 intercollegiate teams for men and 7 for women. There are 4 intramural sports for men and 2 for women.

Handicapped: The entire campus is accessible to wheelchair-bound students. Ramps and special parking areas are provided, and special class scheduling may be arranged. Special counselors also are available.

Graduates: About 15% of the freshmen drop out, and 50% remain to graduate. About 10% of the graduates seek advanced degrees. Eighty-five percent enter careers in business and industry.

Services: Free career and psychological counseling are provided. Placement services are available to students and graduates.

Programs of Study: The university confers the B.A., B.S., B.B.A., B.M., B.S.W., B.F.A., and B.G.S. degrees. Associate, master's, and doctoral degrees also are available. Bachelor's degrees are offered in the following subjects: BUSINESS (accounting, business administration, computer science, finance, management, marketing, office administration), EDUCATION (elementary, health/physical, home economics, secondary, special), ENGLISH (English, speech), FINE AND PERFORMING ARTS (art, dance, music, music education, studio art, theater/dramatics), HEALTH SCIENCES (medical technology, nursing, occupational therapy, speech therapy), LANGUAGES (French, Spanish), MATH AND SCIENCES (biology, chemistry, ecology/environmental science, energy resource management, geology, mathematics, oceanography, physics), PREPROFESSIONAL (engineering—chemical, engineering—civil, engineering—electrical, engineering—industrial, engineering—mechanical, law, medicine, social work), SOCIAL SCIENCES (criminal justice, economics, government/political science, history, psychology, sociology). Twenty-eight percent of the undergraduate degrees are conferred in education, 20% in business, 16% in engineering, and 12% in fine and performing arts.

Required: Students must take 6 hours in government, 6 in American history, 6 in English composition, and 3 in literature; 4 courses in mathematics, laboratory science or a foreign language; and 4 semesters of physical education. They must also maintain a GPA of 2.0 or better to graduate.

Special: Students may earn a general studies degree. Internship and study-abroad programs also are available. A cooperative education program is offered for engineering majors.

Honors: Honors seminars are run for students in all majors by the College of Liberal Arts.

Admissions: The university follows an open admissions policy. The SAT scores of those who enrolled in the 1981–82 freshman class were as follows: Verbal—87% below 500, 11% between 500 and 599, 2% between 600 and 700, and 0% above 700; Math—74% below 500, 20% between 500 and 599, 5% between 600 and 700, and 1% above 700. Applicants should be graduates of accredited high schools and have completed 16 Carnegie units.

Procedure: The SAT or ACT is required and should be taken by April of the senior year. Application deadlines are August 15 (fall), December 15 (spring), and May 30 (summer sessions). There is no application fee.

Special: AP and CLEP credit is granted.

Transfer: Transfers are accepted for all classes. An average of C or better is required. D grades transfer. Students must complete 30 credits in residence to graduate; the bachelor's degree requires 132 credits. Application deadlines are the same as those for freshmen.

Visiting: Guides are provided for informal visits by prospective students. The students may stay overnight in the dormitories. Arrangements should be made with the director of recruitment.

Financial Aid: About 41% of the students receive aid; 4% work part-time on campus. The university offers 100 freshman scholarships. Loans are available from the university and local banks. The university is a member of CSS; the FAF should be filed by April 1.

Foreign Students: About 4% of the full-time students come from foreign countries. The university actively recruits foreign students and offers them an intensive English course and program, and special organizations.

Admissions: Foreign students must achieve a minimum TOEFL score of 500. They must also take the SAT or ACT.

Procedure: Application deadlines are June 15 for fall, November 1 for spring, and March 15 for summer. Foreign students must present proof of health as well as proof of adequate funds. There is a $20 orientation fee. Foreign students must also carry health insurance, which is available through the university for a fee.

Admissions Contact: Elmer Rode, Dean of Admissions and Registrar.

LE TOURNEAU COLLEGE   E–2
Longview, Texas 75607   (214) 753-0231

F/T: 902M, 114W	Faculty:	57; IIB, –$
P/T: 10M, 12W	Ph.D.'s:	39%
Grad: none	S/F Ratio:	18 to 1
Year: sems, ss	Tuition:	$3178
Appl: July 1	R and B:	$1800
710 applied	423 accepted	322 enrolled
SAT or ACT: required		COMPETITIVE

Le Tourneau College, founded in 1946, is a private liberal arts and technical college. The library contains 92,000 volumes, and subscribes to 539 periodicals.

Environment: The 162-acre campus, located in an urban area of 60,000, is located 120 miles from Dallas, and has 48 buildings including temporary barrack-style as well as permanent brick structures. Thirteen dormitories house 700 students. Apartment housing for 36 married students also is available.

Student Life: Approximately 21% of the students come from Texas and bordering states; the rest, from other states and abroad. Ninety-six percent of the students belong to the Protestant faith, and daily chapel attendance is compulsory. All women and freshmen must observe a curfew, and all students follow sign-out procedures. Alcoholic beverages on campus are prohibited. Ninety-six percent of the students live on campus; other students must live at home with their families or in authorized apartments. Campus housing is single-sex; there are no visiting privileges. Students may keep cars on campus.

Organizations: There are no fraternities or sororities. The college sponsors 12 extracurricular activities, the most active of which are the American Welding Society, the Mechanical Engineering Society, and the Missionary Fellowship. Each week there are cultural events scheduled on campus, and only about 2% of the students leave the campus on weekends. Community theater, symphony, and nearby lakes provide additional cultural and recreational opportunities.

Sports: The college fields 5 intercollegiate teams for men and 3 for women. There are 11 intramural sports for men and 8 for women.

Handicapped: There are no special facilities or services for handicapped students.

Graduates: About 40% of the students drop out by the end of the freshman year. Fifty percent remain to graduate; of those, 5% go on to further study.

Services: Students receive the following services free of charge: health care, psychological counseling, career counseling, and placement service.

Programs of Study: The college confers the B.A. and B.S. degrees, as well as associate degrees. Bachelor's degrees are offered in the following subjects: BUSINESS (accounting, business administration, industrial management, public administration, recreation and camp administration), EDUCATION (health/physical, secondary), ENGLISH (English), HEALTH SCIENCES (medical technology), MATH AND SCIENCES (biology, chemistry, computer science and engineering, mathematics), PREPROFESSIONAL (dentistry, engineering, law, medicine, ministry, veterinary), SOCIAL SCIENCES (government/political science, history). There are also major programs in engineering technology, aviation technology, and in missions. The most popular major is engineering.

Required: All undergraduates are required to take Old and New Testament literature, English composition, physical education, natural science, and mathematics.

Special: The Department of Overseas Education sponsors extensive student tours abroad, for college credit.

Honors: Gold Key Society has a chapter on campus.

Admissions: Sixty percent of those who applied were accepted for the 1981–82 freshman class. A candidate should have completed 16 Carnegie high school units, have at least a C average, and rank in the upper 50% of the class. Engineering students are strongly advised to have 4 Carnegie units of mathematics (exclusive of general math), including one course in trigonometry and one or more units of mechanical drawing. The minimum acceptable ACT score is 18.

Procedure: The ACT or SAT is required. Admissions are on a rolling basis, and personal interviews are not required. The deadlines for application are July 1 (fall), December 1 (spring), and April 1 (summer). Freshmen are admitted in the spring as well as the fall. There is a $20 application fee.

Special: There is a deferred admissions plan. CLEP and AP credit is accepted.

Transfer: For fall 1981, 125 transfer students enrolled at the school. A GPA of 2.0 is required; grades of C and above transfer. At least 30 semester hours must be spent in residence to qualify for a degree. The bachelor's degree requires 123 credits. Deadlines are the same as those for entering freshmen.

Visiting: There are regularly scheduled orientations for prospective students. Weekdays from 8 A.M. to 5 P.M. are recommended for informal visits. Guides are available, and visitors may sit in on classes and stay at the school. Arrangements can be made through the director of admissions.

Financial Aid: About 63% of the students receive aid through the school. In addition to scholarships, federal loans are available, as well as federal work-study in all departments; 37% of the students receive work contracts. The FAF must be filed. The application deadline is April 1.

Foreign Students: About 4% of the full-time students come from foreign countries.

Admissions: Foreign students must achieve a minimum TOEFL score of 500. They must also take the SAT or ACT.

Procedure: Application deadlines are July 1 for fall and December 1 for spring. Foreign students must present proof of health as well as proof of funds adequate to cover 1 year of study.

Admissions Contact: Linda H. Fitzhugh, Director of Admissions.

LUBBOCK CHRISTIAN COLLEGE   B-2
Lubbock, Texas 79407   (806) 792-3221

F/T: 575M, 519W	Faculty: 40; IIB, – –$
P/T: 70M, 73W	Ph.D.'s: 60%
Grad: none	S/F Ratio: 25 to 1
Year: sems, ss	Tuition: $2880
Appl: Sept. 1	R and B: $1200
ACT: 18	NONCOMPETITIVE

Lubbock Christian College, founded in 1956, is a liberal arts institution affiliated with the Church of Christ. The library houses 60,000 volumes, and subscribes to 400 periodicals.

Environment: The 120-acre urban campus is located in a city of 155,000 in northern Texas. The 14 buildings on campus include 2 dormitories and 3 sets of apartments housing a total of 572 men and women.

Student Life: Two-thirds of the students come from Texas. Sixty percent of the student body lives on campus. About 11% of the students are minority-group members. Seventy percent are members of the affiliated church, and daily chapel attendance is compulsory. Alcoholic beverages on campus are prohibited. Women students observe a curfew and sign-out procedure. There are no visiting privileges in the dormitories.

Organizations: Sixty percent of the men and women belong to the 10 social clubs that exist on campus. Extracurricular groups include service organizations and various clubs. There are social and cultural events on campus. Lubbock, also the home of Texas Tech with an additional 24,000 college students, affords further recreational opportunities.

Sports: The college fields 7 intercollegiate teams. There are 9 intramural sports.

Handicapped: About 50% of the campus is accessible to handicapped students; wheelchair ramps are provided.

Graduates: The freshman dropout rate is 20%; 35% remain to graduate. Of the graduates, 25% go on to further study: 3% enter medical school, 3% enter law school, and 3% enter dental school. Twenty percent pursue careers in business and industry.

Services: Students receive the following services free of charge: health care, psychological counseling, career counseling, tutoring, and remedial instruction.

Programs of Study: The B.A. and B.S. degrees are conferred. Associate degrees also are awarded. Bachelor's degrees are offered in the following subjects: AREA STUDIES (American), BUSINESS (accounting, business administration), EDUCATION (elementary, health/physical, secondary), ENGLISH (English, literature, speech), FINE AND PERFORMING ARTS (art, art education, music, music education), LANGUAGES (French, German, Greek/Latin, Hebrew, Spanish), MATH AND SCIENCES (biology, chemistry, mathematics), PHILOSOPHY (religion), PREPROFESSIONAL (agriculture, dentistry, engineering, forestry, law, library science, medicine, ministry, pharmacy, social work, veterinary), SOCIAL SCIENCES (government/political science, history, psychology, social sciences, sociology). Twenty-seven percent of the degrees conferred are in education, 22% in business, and 19% in preprofessional studies.

Required: All students must take courses in English, the Bible, history, mathematics, and laboratory science.

Special: There is a cooperative program with Texas Tech University. A general studies degree is offered.

Honors: There is a chapter of Alpha Chi on campus.

Admissions: All of those who applied were accepted for the 1981–82 freshman class. A diploma from an accredited high school is required. The applicant's character is given strong consideration. Children of alumni receive preference.

Procedure: The ACT is required. Freshmen are admitted each semester. There is a $10 application fee. Application deadlines are September 1 (fall) and January 5 (spring).

Special: AP and CLEP credit is accepted.

Transfer: For fall 1981, 109 transfer students applied, all were accepted, and 105 enrolled. A GPA of 1.8 and character references are requested. D grades transfer. Thirty semester hours must be spent on campus to qualify for a degree; the bachelor's degree requires 132 hours. Application deadlines are the same as those for freshmen.

Visiting: A 2- to 3-day orientation session is scheduled each fall. Informal visits, with guides, on weekdays and special Guest Days can be arranged by writing to John King in the admissions office. Visitors may sit in on classes and stay overnight at the school.

Financial Aid: About 80% of the students receive aid through the college, on the basis of need. About 33% work part-time on campus. Financial aid is available in the form of scholarships, federal and state loans, and CWS in all departments. The college is a member of CSS; the FFS must be filed by July 6.

Foreign Students: About 4% of the full-time students come from foreign countries. The college offers these students an intensive English course, an intensive English program, and special counseling.

Admissions: Foreign students must take the TOEFL; no college entrance exams are required.

Procedure: Application deadlines are September 1 for fall and January 5 for spring. Foreign students must present proof of health as well as proof of adequate funds. They must also carry health insurance, which is available through the college for a fee.

Admissions Contact: John King, Director of Admissions.

McMURRY COLLEGE   C-2
Abilene, Texas 79697   (915) 692-4130

F/T: 475M, 443W	Faculty: 59; IIB, –$
P/T: 364M, 266W	Ph.D.'s: 68%
Grad: none	S/F Ratio: 15 to 1
Year: 4-4-1, ss	Tuition: $2445
Appl: Aug. 15	R and B: $1625
535 applied	349 accepted 311 enrolled
ACT: 18	COMPETITIVE

McMurry College, founded in 1920, is a liberal arts institution affiliated with the Methodist Church. The library houses 149,000 volumes and 2000 microfilm items, and subscribes to 457 periodicals. A carefully selected collection of books is of special value to students in the field of education.

Environment: The 51-acre campus, located in a suburban area, has residence halls accommodating 324 men and 331 women; a central cafeteria serves all the dorms. The college also sponsors married student housing.

Student Life: Most students are from Texas. Forty-five percent of the students live on campus; students not within commuting distance are required to live in dorms. About 83% of the students are Protestant, and 12% are Catholic. About 14% are minority-group members. Campus housing is single-sex; there are no visiting privileges. Students may keep cars on campus. Alcoholic beverages on campus are prohibited.

Organizations: There are 7 fraternities and 5 sororities, as well as special-interest, service, and religious groups. Other activities include Fall Homecoming.

Sports: The college fields 5 intercollegiate teams for men and 5 for women. There are 8 intramural sports for men and 8 for women.

Handicapped: Wheelchair ramps and elevators are available for physically handicapped students; 85% of the campus is accessible to them.

Graduates: Fifty-seven percent of entering freshmen remain to graduate. Twenty-two percent of the graduates pursue advanced study: 2% enter medical school, 1% enter dental school, and 1% enter law school. Thirty-eight percent pursue careers in business and industry.

Services: Free placement, career counseling, health care, tutoring, and remedial instruction are provided. Psychological counseling is available on a fee basis.

Programs of Study: The college confers the B.A., B.S., B.B.A., B.S.N., B.M., B.Mus.Ed., and B.F.A. degrees. Associate degrees are also awarded. Bachelor's degrees are offered in the following subjects: BUSINESS (accounting, business administration, business education, finance, management, marketing), EDUCATION (bilingual, elementary, health/physical, reading, secondary, special), ENGLISH (English, speech, writing), FINE AND PERFORMING ARTS (art, music, music education, theater/dramatics), HEALTH SCIENCES (medical technology, nursing), LANGUAGES (French, German, Spanish), MATH AND SCIENCES (biology, chemistry, geology, mathematics, natural sciences, physics), PHILOSOPHY (philosophy, religion), PREPROFESSIONAL (dentistry, engineering, law, medicine, ministry, pharmacy, veterinary), SOCIAL SCIENCES (applied sociology, criminal justice, economics, government/political science, history, mental health and social services, psychology, social sciences, sociology). Thirty-one percent of degrees conferred are in business, 31% in education, and 8% in English.

Required: Four semesters of physical education are required for the freshman and sophomore years.

Special: Individual study and travel are available. A combination degree program is offered in medical technology.

Honors: Eleven national honor societies have chapters on campus.

Admissions: Sixty-five percent of those who applied were accepted for the 1981–82 freshman class. The ACT scores of those who enrolled were as follows: 69% below 21, 12% between 21 and 23, 11% between 24 and 25, 7% between 26 and 28, and 1% above 28. Candidates must be graduates of accredited high schools, rank in the top 75% of their graduating class, and have completed 16 units of high school work. A student may be admitted if his ACT composite score ranks him in the 25th percentile or higher; variations are handled individually. Also considered are extracurricular activities record, advanced placement or honors courses, and leadership record.

Procedure: The ACT or SAT is required and should be taken in November of the senior year. The application deadline is August 15 for the fall. A personal interview may be requested of the applicant. Admissions are on a rolling basis. There is an application fee of $15.

Special: There are early admissions and deferred admissions plans. AP and CLEP credit is accepted.

Transfer: Transfer students are admitted each session; a 2.0 GPA is required; grades of C or above transfer. There is a 30-hour residency rule; the bachelor's degree requires 120 credits. Application deadlines are the same as those for freshmen.

Visiting: Prospective students attend 3-day "Student Weekends." Visits can be scheduled any time through the office of admissions; visitors may sit in on classes and stay overnight at the school.

Financial Aid: Eighty-five percent of the students receive financial aid; 35% work part-time on campus. Scholarships range from $100 to $1500 per year. If the proper average is maintained, the scholarship is good for 4 years. SEOG, BEOG, and SSIG grants are available to those showing need. About 20% of the students earn 25% or more of their expenses. The average award to freshmen from all sources is $1800. The college is a CSS member. The FAF or FFS must be filed; the FFS is preferred. The Tuition Plan, Inc. is also available. The aid application deadline is March 15.

Foreign Students: About 1% of the full-time students come from foreign countries. The college offers these students special counseling and special organizations.

Admissions: Foreign students must achieve a minimum TOEFL score of 500. They must also take the SAT or ACT.

Procedure: Application deadlines are January 1 (fall and summer) and August 1 (spring). Foreign students must present proof of funds adequate to cover their entire period of study.

Admissions Contact: O. Douglas Wofford, Director of Admissions.

MIDWESTERN STATE UNIVERSITY D-2
Wichita Falls, Texas 76308 (817) 692-6611

F/T: 1177M, 1229W
P/T: 648M, 891W
Grad: 247M, 263W
Year: sems, ss
Appl: Aug. 15
1010 applied
SAT: 400V 450M
Faculty: 144; IIA, av$
Ph.D.'s: 54%
S/F Ratio: 20 to 1
Tuition: $475 ($1561)
R and B: $1440
1010 accepted 882 enrolled
ACT: 18 NONCOMPETITIVE

Midwestern State University, founded in 1922, is a state-supported institution offering degrees in the liberal arts and sciences, business, education, and professional areas. The library holds 350,000 volumes and nearly 20,000 microfilm items, and subscribes to over 1100 periodicals.

Environment: There are 27 major buildings on the 165-acre campus, located in a large city 150 miles northwest of Dallas. Two residence halls accommodate 450 students. The university also sponsors fraternity and sorority houses.

Student Life: About 98% of the students come from Texas. Ten percent live on campus; all unmarried freshmen and sophomores generally must do so if they do not live at home. About 7% of the students are minority-group members. Campus housing is coed and single-sex; there are visiting privileges in single-sex dorms. Students may keep cars on campus.

Organizations: Campus activities include regularly scheduled social and cultural events, student government, clubs, publications, music and drama groups, and service and departmental clubs. About 5% of the students belong to the 5 national sororities and 6 fraternities.

Sports: The university fields 4 intercollegiate teams for men and 3 for women. There are 17 intramural sports for men and 13 for women.

Graduates: About 20% of the freshmen drop out, and 50% remain to graduate. Fifteen percent of the graduates go on for further study.

Services: Health care, counseling, and placement services for graduates and students are provided free of charge. Tutoring and remedial instruction are available on a fee basis.

Programs of Study: The university awards the B.A., B.B.A., B.M., B.Mus.Ed., B.F.A., B.A.A.S., B.S., and B.S.Ed. degrees. Associate and master's degrees also are available. Bachelor's degrees are offered in the following subjects: BUSINESS (accounting, business administration, computer science, finance, management, marketing, secretarial science), EDUCATION (elementary, health/physical, secondary, special), ENGLISH (English, journalism, speech), FINE AND PERFORMING ARTS (art, music, music education, theater/dramatics), HEALTH SCIENCES (dental hygiene, medical technology, radiologic technology, speech therapy), LANGUAGES (Spanish), MATH AND SCIENCES (biology, chemistry, geology, geophysics, mathematics, physics), PHILOSOPHY (humanities), PREPROFESSIONAL (architecture, dentistry, engineering, law, medicine, pharmacy, social work, veterinary), SOCIAL SCIENCES (criminal justice, economics, government/political science, history, psychology, social sciences, sociology). Twenty-seven percent of the undergraduate degrees are conferred in education, 25% in business, and 13% in social science.

Required: Students must take courses in English, U.S. and Texas government, history, physical education, mathematics, computer science, fine arts, social sciences, and natural sciences.

Special: A general studies major, independent study, and an accelerated bachelor's degree program are offered. Preprofessional programs are available in dentistry, engineering, law, medicine, nursing, optometry, osteopathy, pharmacy, and veterinary medicine.

Honors: The honors program offers scholarships and special courses to selected students. Fifteen national honor societies have chapters on campus.

Admissions: All of the applicants were accepted for the 1981–82 freshman class. The SAT scores of those who enrolled were as follows: Verbal—80% below 500, 15% between 500 and 599, 4% between 600 and 700, and 1% above 700; Math—70% below 500, 22% between 500 and 599, 7% between 600 and 700, and 1% above 700. The ACT scores were as follows: 65% below 21, 15% between 21 and 23, 10% between 24 and 25, 6% between 26 and 28, and 4% above 28. Applicants should be graduates of accredited high schools or pass special university examinations. The university follows an open admissions policy.

Procedure: The SAT or ACT is required and should be taken by January of the senior year. Application deadlines are August 15 (fall), January 6 (spring), and May 26 (summer). Notification is made on a rolling basis. There is no application fee.

Special: AP and CLEP credit is accepted. An early decision plan is available.

Transfer: For fall 1981, 507 transfer students applied, 507 were accepted, and 440 enrolled. D grades generally transfer. Students must earn 24 credits in residence to graduate; the bachelor's degree requires 124 credits. Application deadlines are the same as those for freshmen.

Financial Aid: About 24% of the students receive aid; 40% work part-time on campus. The number of scholarships varies from year to year. Students may apply for loans from the federal government, the university, or private sources. Preference is given to students who establish need by filing the FAF or FFS. The university is a member of CSS. The application deadline is July 1.

Foreign Students: Fewer than 1% of the full-time students come from foreign countries. The university offers these students special counseling and special organizations.

Admissions: Foreign students must achieve a minimum TOEFL score of 500; no college entrance exams are required.

Procedure: Application deadlines are August 15 (fall), January 6 (spring), and May 26 (summer). Foreign students must present proof of health as well as proof of funds adequate to cover their entire period of study. There is a $25 application fee and a $500 deposit is required. Out-of-state fees apply.

Admissions Contact: Donita Shaddock, Director of Admissions.

NORTH TEXAS STATE UNIVERSITY D-2
Denton, Texas 75063 (817) 788-2681

F/T: 4821M, 5227W	Faculty: 690; I, – – $
P/T: 1224M, 1107W	Ph.D's: 75%
Grad: 2427M, 2681W	S/F Ratio: 17 to 1
Year: sems, ss	Tuition: $438 ($1518)
Appl: Aug. 1	R and B: $2000
3858 applied	2875 accepted	1771 enrolled
SAT: 416V 444M	ACT: 23	COMPETITIVE+

North Texas State University, established in 1890, is a coeducational, state-controlled institution offering liberal arts and teacher education. The library houses 1.2 million volumes and 280,257 microfilm items, and subscribes to 4882 periodicals. Special collections include a music library of 76,328 volumes and 21,453 recordings.

Environment: The university buildings and grounds are located on 380 acres in a suburban area 35 miles northwest of Dallas. In addition to dormitories, the university sponsors married student housing.

Student Life: Ninety percent of the students are from Texas. The majority of entering freshmen come from public schools. Twenty percent live on campus. Undergraduates who have completed fewer than 30 hours of university work, with some exceptions, are required to live in dorms. Seventeen percent of the students are minority-group members. University housing is coed and single-sex; students in single-sex housing have visiting privileges. Students may keep cars on campus. Day-care facilities are available for a fee to full-time and part-time students, faculty, and staff.

Organizations: Six hundred men belong to the 15 fraternities; 500 women belong to the 9 sororities. Activities include student publications, student government, musical or theatrical organizations, and Jewish, Catholic, and Protestant religious organizations.

Sports: The university fields 9 intercollegiate teams for men and 5 for women. There are 15 intramural sports for men and 13 for women.

Handicapped: Sixty percent of the campus is accessible to the physically handicapped. Facilities for these students include wheelchair ramps, special parking, elevators, specially equipped rest rooms, and lowered telephones and drinking fountains. Special class scheduling is also available. For visually and hearing-impaired students, there are interpreters and special library equipment that includes braille books and tapes. Counseling is provided for the handicapped.

Services: Students receive the following services free: psychological counseling, career counseling, and placement.

Programs of Study: The college confers the B.A., B.S., B.B.A., B.F.A., and B.M. degrees. Master's and doctoral degrees are also awarded. Bachelor's degrees are offered in the following subjects: BUSINESS (accounting, business administration, business education, computer science, finance, management, marketing, real estate/insurance), EDUCATION (early childhood, elementary, health/physical, industrial, recreation, secondary, special), ENGLISH (English, journalism, speech), FINE AND PERFORMING ARTS (art, dance, film/photography, music, music education, radio/TV, studio art, theater/dramatics), HEALTH SCIENCES (medical technology, speech therapy), LANGUAGES (French, German, Greek/Latin, Spanish), MATH AND SCIENCES (biochemistry, biology, chemistry, mathematics, physics), PHILOSOPHY (philosophy), PREPROFESSIONAL (home economics, library science, social work), SOCIAL SCIENCES (anthropology, geography, government/political science, history, psychology, social sciences, social work, sociology). Twenty-eight percent of degrees conferred are in business, 24% in education, and 11% in fine and performing arts.

Required: All students in the arts and sciences curriculum are required to take English composition, literature, American history, federal and state constitutions, laboratory science, physical education, and a foreign language.

Honors: Five national honor societies have chapters on campus.

Admissions: Seventy-five percent of those who applied were accepted for the 1981–82 freshman class. Of those who enrolled for a recent freshman class, the SAT scores were: Verbal—16% between 500 and 599, 3% between 600 and 700, and 1% above 700; Math—23% between 500 and 599, 7% between 600 and 700, and 1% above 700. Applicants must be high school graduates with 16 units of study. The SAT and ACT scores and rank in the high school class are important considerations; minimum acceptable scores for the SAT and ACT vary with the applicant's rank in class. An interview is recommended for applicants with a particular problem.

Procedure: The SAT or ACT is required and should be taken by March of the senior year. Application deadlines are August 1 (fall), January 2 (spring), May 25 (first summer session), and July 2 (second summer session). Notification is on a rolling basis. There is no application fee.

Special: Early admissions for qualified students and early decision plans are available. AP and CLEP credit is accepted.

Transfer: For fall 1981, 3375 students applied, 2458 were accepted, and 1862 enrolled. Applicants must have at least a 2.0 GPA and be eligible to return to their former school; standardized exam scores are also required if the student has completed less than 30 semester hours. D grades are transferable. All students must complete 24 of the last 30 semester hours in residence. Application deadlines are the same as those for freshmen.

Visiting: There is a regularly scheduled orientation for prospective students. Guides are available for informal visits, during which visitors may sit in on classes and stay overnight at the school with advance notification. Visits can be scheduled weekdays at 10 A.M. and from 2 to 4 P.M.. Arrangements should be made through the admissions office.

Financial Aid: Twenty-five percent of the students receive financial aid. Thirty-five percent work part-time on campus. Approximately 1000 undergraduate scholarships are awarded; several student loan programs are available to students enrolled on at least a half-time basis. Financial aid is awarded on the basis of need, as well as academic performance for some scholarships. The university is a member of CSS and requires the FAF. Application deadlines are June 1 (fall), October 1 (spring), and April 1 (summer).

Foreign Students: Eight percent of the full-time students come from foreign countries. The university offers these students an intensive English course and program, special counseling, and special organizations.

Admissions: Foreign students must achieve a minimum TOEFL score of 500. They are also given a screening test, but are not required to take a standardized college entrance exam.

Procedure: Applications must be submitted 3 months in advance for fall, winter, and spring entry; 2 months in advance for summer entry. Foreign students must present proof of health, proof of funds adequate to cover 1 year of study, and a special evaluation fee of $25. They must also carry health insurance, which is available through the university.

Admissions Contact: Dan C. Palermo, Director of Admissions and School Relations.

OUR LADY OF THE LAKE UNIVERSITY D-4
OF SAN ANTONIO
San Antonio, Texas 78285 (512) 434-6711

F/T: 198M, 494W	Faculty: 72; IIA, – – $
P/T: 172M, 393W	Ph.D.'s: 50%
Grad: 137M, 301W	S/F Ratio: 10 to 1
Year: sems, ss	Tuition: $2900
Appl: open	R and B: $2400
620 applied	350 accepted	145 enrolled
SAT: 420V 440M	ACT: 18	COMPETITIVE

Our Lady of the Lake University, founded in 1911, is a private liberal arts institution affiliated with the Roman Catholic Church and offering undergraduate programs in business, education, the arts and sciences, and preprofessional fields. The library holds 226,000 volumes and 5000 microfilm items, and subscribes to 500 periodicals.

Environment: The 115-acre campus is located in an urban area 4 miles from downtown San Antonio. Three residence halls accommodate 300 women and 80 men.

Student Life: About 85% of the students are from Texas. Seventy-four percent are Catholic and 20% are Protestant. Sixty-six percent are minority-group members. University housing is single-sex, and there are visiting privileges. Students may keep cars on campus.

Organizations: There are no fraternities or sororities on campus. Campus organizations include a forensic society and other special-interest clubs; there is a university newspaper. The city offers cultural and recreational opportunities such as a symphony orchestra, a ballet company, opera, and numerous parks.

Sports: The university fields 1 intercollegiate team for men and 1 for women. There are 3 intramural sports for men and 2 for women.

Handicapped: About 70% of the campus is accessible to handicapped students. Special facilities include wheelchair ramps, parking, elevators, and specially equipped rest rooms. Special class scheduling is also available. Tutors and readers are available for the visually impaired. A staff of 3 exists for special counseling.

872 TEXAS

Graduates: The freshman dropout rate is 25%, and 45% of the freshmen remain to graduate. About 25% of the graduates go on to further study; 5% enter medical school, 5% enter dental school, and 5% enter law school. Another 25% pursue careers in business and industry.

Services: Students receive the following services free of charge: placement, health care, psychological counseling, career counseling, and tutoring. Remedial instruction is available for a fee.

Programs of Study: Undergraduate degrees offered are the B.A., B.S., B. Applied Studies, B.B.A., and B.S.W. Master's degrees also are conferred. Bachelor's degrees are offered in the following subjects: BUSINESS (accounting, business education, computer science, fashion merchandising, management, marketing, public administration), EDUCATION (bilingual, elementary, secondary, special), ENGLISH (English), FINE AND PERFORMING ARTS (art, media communication arts, speech and drama), HEALTH SCIENCES (speech therapy), LANGUAGES (Spanish), MATH AND SCIENCES (biology, chemistry, mathematics), PHILOSOPHY (philosophy, religion), PREPROFESSIONAL (law, medical technology, medicine, social work), SOCIAL SCIENCES (psychology, social sciences, sociology). Of the undergraduate degrees conferred, 30% are in business, and 20% each in education and social sciences.

Special: Study abroad is available during the spring interterm. The "Curriculum of Alternatives" offers an individualized degree plan, open registration throughout the year, college credit through exams, and assessment of life and work experience. The university belongs to a four-member consortium, the United Colleges of San Antonio, and students have the opportunity to take courses at the other 3 colleges.

Admissions: Fifty-six percent of the students who applied for the 1981–82 freshman class were accepted. Of those who enrolled, the SAT scores were as follows: Verbal—85% below 500, 10% between 500 and 599, 5% between 600 and 700, and 0% above 700; Math—76% below 500, 18% between 500 and 599, 6% between 600 and 700, and 0% above 700. The candidate should have completed 16 units of high school work, have a grade average of 2.25, and have a combined SAT score of 700 or a composite ACT score of 15. Provisional admission is allowed with an SAT of 600 or an ACT of 13. Admission depends only on GPA and test results.

Procedure: The SAT or ACT is required. Application deadlines are open; freshmen are admitted to all semesters. Notification is on a rolling basis. The application fee is $15.

Special: CLEP and AP credit is given.

Transfer: For fall 1981, 180 students applied, 150 were accepted, and 100 enrolled. A minimum GPA of 2.25 and SAT scores are required. D grades do not transfer. The student must complete, at the university, 30 semester hours of the 128 necessary for a bachelor's degree. Application deadlines are open.

Visiting: There are no regularly scheduled orientations. Guides are available for informal tours during school sessions. Visitors may sit in on classes and stay overnight at the school. Arrangements may be made with the admissions office.

Financial Aid: Eighty-five percent of the students receive financial aid. Forty-five percent work part-time on campus. Scholarships, loans, and grants are offered. Scholarships are awarded on the basis of academic achievement as indicated by SAT or ACT scores and GPA. Other financial aid is based on need. The university is a member of CSS and requires the FAF. Application deadlines are open.

Foreign Students: Six percent of the full-time students come from foreign countries. The university offers these students an intensive English course, special counseling, and special organizations.

Admissions: Foreign students must achieve a minimum TOEFL score of 500.

Procedure: Application deadlines are open for all sessions. Foreign students must present proof of health and proof of adequate funds. They must also carry health insurance, which is available through the university for a fee.

Admissions Contact: Loretta A. Schlegel, Director of Admissions.

PAN AMERICAN UNIVERSITY D–5
Edinburg, Texas 78539 (512) 381-2206

F/T: 2592M, 2897W
P/T: 1094M, 1768W
Grad: 554M, 698W
Year: sems, ss
Appl: Aug. 4
ACT: 12

Faculty: n/av; IIA, av$
Ph.D.'s: 65%
S/F Ratio: 22 to 1
Tuition: $270 ($1350)
R and B: $1350–1390
NONCOMPETITIVE

Pan American University, founded in 1927, is a state-supported institution offering programs in the liberal arts and sciences, business, and education. The library contains 187,000 volumes and 105,895 microfilm items, and subscribes to 2788 periodicals.

Environment: The 200-acre campus is set in an area composed of 20 small towns whose entire population is about 300,000. It is 230 miles from San Antonio. The 23 buildings include 2 dormitories accommodating 200 women and 200 men.

Student Life: Ninety-seven percent of the students come from Texas. Six percent reside on campus. There is religious counseling for Protestant and Catholic students.

Organizations: There are 10 national fraternities, of which 5% of the men are members, and 5 sororities, to which 5% of the women belong. On-campus activities and organizations include publications, special-interest groups, music groups, and service clubs. Cultural and social opportunities are offered through art shows, concerts, debates, films, lectures, plays, readings, recitals, science exhibits, and dances.

Sports: The university competes in 5 intercollegiate sports for men and 4 for women; 7 intramural sports are offered.

Handicapped: Facilities for handicapped students include wheelchair ramps, parking, elevators, specially equipped rest rooms, and lowered drinking fountains and telephones.

Graduates: The freshman dropout rate is 30%; 15% remain to graduate. About 1% of the graduates enter medical school; 1%, dental school; 1%, law school. Another 35% pursue careers in business and industry.

Services: The following services are provided to students free of charge: placement service, health care, psychological counseling, career counseling, tutoring, and remedial instruction.

Programs of Study: Undergraduate programs lead to the B.A., B.F.A., B.C.J., B.S., and B.B.A. degrees. Master's degrees also are awarded. Bachelor's degrees are offered in the following subjects: AREA STUDIES (Mexican-American heritage), BUSINESS (accounting, business administration, computer science, finance, management, marketing, office administration), EDUCATION (elementary, health/physical, secondary), ENGLISH (English, journalism, speech), FINE AND PERFORMING ARTS (art, art education, music, music education, theater/dramatics), HEALTH SCIENCES (medical technology, speech therapy), LANGUAGES (Spanish), MATH AND SCIENCES (biology, chemistry, mathematics, physics), PREPROFESSIONAL (social work), SOCIAL SCIENCES (economics, government/political science, history, psychology, sociology).

Required: All students are required to take 48 hours of general liberal education.

Honors: An honors colloquium program is offered for the superior student.

Admissions: All of the students who applied for the 1981–82 freshman class were accepted. The candidate should be a graduate of an accredited high school and have completed 16 Carnegie units.

Procedure: The ACT is required. The application deadlines for regular admission are August 4 (fall), December 3 (spring), and April 18 (summer). There is a rolling admissions plan. Freshmen are admitted each semester. There is no application fee.

Special: CLEP credit is given.

Transfer: Recently, 750 applications were received; all were accepted, and 628 students were enrolled. D grades transfer. All students must complete, at the university, 30 of the 124 credits required for a bachelor's degree. Deadlines are the same as those for entering freshmen.

Visiting: Regularly scheduled orientations include campus tours, counseling, and course selection. The best time for informal campus visits is spring. Visitors may sit in on classes. Arrangements for visits can be made with Gilbert Dominguez.

Financial Aid: About 78% of the students receive financial aid. Scholarships and employment are available, as well as government, bank, and university loans. The deadline for application is July 1.

Foreign Students: An intensive English course, special counseling, and special organizations are available for students from foreign countries.

Admissions: Foreign students must achieve a TOEFL score of at least 500. No college entrance exams are required.

Procedure: Foreign students must present proof of adequate funds.

Admissions Contact: David Zuniga, Registrar and Director of Admissions.

PAUL QUINN COLLEGE D-3
Waco, Texas 76704   (817) 753-6565

F/T: 238M, 237W	Faculty: 32; IIB, – – $
P/T: 12M, 15W	Ph.D.'s: 34%
Grad: none	S/F Ratio: 16 to 1
Year: sems, ss	Tuition: $2200
Appl: June 1	R and B: $2150
380 applied	380 accepted	185 enrolled
ACT: 12		NONCOMPETITIVE

Paul Quinn College, founded in 1872, is a liberal arts college affiliated with the African Methodist Episcopal Church. The library houses 81,000 volumes and 35,000 microfilm items, and subscribes to 462 periodicals.

Environment: The 22-acre suburban campus is located in the heart of East Waco. The 14 buildings include 3 dormitories.

Student Life: Seventy-two percent of the students come from Texas, and 26% from bordering states. All come from public schools. Virtually all students are minority-group members. Ninety-two percent are Protestant, and 3% are Catholic. Campus housing is single-sex; there are visiting privileges. Students not living at home must live in the dorms; about 80% of the students live on campus. Drinking on campus is forbidden. Students may keep cars on campus.

Organizations: About 20% of the men belong to 4 fraternities; 30% of the women, to 4 sororities. The most popular campus activities are the choir, the band, and the ministerial club. Honors Day and Founder's Day are major social events.

Sports: The college fields 4 intercollegiate teams for men and 4 for women. There are 5 intramural sports for men and 4 for women.

Handicapped: There are no visually impaired or hearing impaired students on campus. No special facilities are provided for handicapped students.

Graduates: The freshman dropout rate is 14%; 42% of the students remain to graduate. About 14% of the graduates go on to further study; 30% pursue careers in business and industry.

Services: Students receive the following services free of charge: placement service, career counseling, tutoring, and remedial instruction. Health care is provided for a fee.

Programs of Study: The college awards the B.A., B.S., B.S.Ed., and B. Applied Sc. degrees. Bachelor's degrees are offered in the following subjects: BUSINESS (accounting, business administration), EDUCATION (elementary, health/physical, secondary), ENGLISH (English), HEALTH SCIENCES (medical technology), MATH AND SCIENCES (biology, mathematics), PHILOSOPHY (religion), PREPROFESSIONAL (social work), SOCIAL SCIENCES (history, sociology). About 45% of the degrees are conferred in business, 35% in education, and 10% in preprofessional areas.

Required: All students are required to take health, physical education, and a core curriculum. There is a required internship in all programs.

Admissions: All of the students who applied for the 1981–82 freshman class were accepted. The candidate should be a high school graduate with 15 Carnegie units. The college has an open door policy on admissions.

Procedure: The SAT or ACT is required. Application deadlines are June 1 (fall), November 11 (spring), and March 1 (summer). There is a rolling admissions plan. Applications should be submitted with a $6 fee. A personal interview is recommended.

Special: CLEP credit is given.

Transfers: For fall 1981, 84 applications were received, all were accepted, and 58 students enrolled. Transfer students are admitted each term. D grades do not transfer. All students must complete, at the college, 30 of the final 36 credits; 128 credits are required for a bachelor's degree. Application deadlines are the same as those for freshmen.

Visiting: Regularly scheduled orientation sessions include campus tours and testing. The Dean of Student Life will arrange guides for informal visits. Visitors may sit in on classes and stay overnight at the school.

Financial Aid: About 81% of the students receive financial aid through the college. Scholarships, loans, and work contracts are available. CWS funds are available in all departments. Tuition may be paid on the installment plan. The college is a CSS member and requires the FAF. Application deadlines are June 1 (fall), November 1 (spring), and March 1 (summer).

Foreign Students: Fewer than 1% of the full-time students come from foreign countries. An intensive English course and special counseling are available for these students.

Admissions: Foreign students must achieve a TOEFL score of at least 550 and must take the SAT or ACT.

Procedure: Application deadlines are the same as those for other students. Foreign students must complete a medical form and present proof of funds adequate to cover 4 years of study. Health insurance is required and is available through the college for a fee.

Admissions Contact: Sarah J. Seldon, Director of Admissions and Financial Aid.

PRAIRIE VIEW A&M UNIVERSITY E-3
Prairie View, Texas 77445   (713) 857-4723

F/T, P/T, Grad: 2500M, 2500W	Faculty: 279; IIA, – – $
	Ph.D.'s: 42%
	S/F Ratio: 19 to 1
Year: sems, ss	Tuition, R and B:
Appl: Aug. 1	$1200 ($1800)
3000 applied	2000 accepted	1700 enrolled
SAT: 700 (composite)	ACT: 13	LESS COMPETITIVE

Prairie View A&M University, a state-supported institution established in 1878 as a college for blacks, is part of the Texas A&M University System. The university is composed of 9 academic divisions: the colleges of Agriculture, Arts and Sciences, Business, Education, Engineering, Home Economics, Industrial Education and Technology, and Nursing, and the Graduate School. The library contains 245,000 books and 103,000 microfilm items, and subscribes to 2200 periodicals.

Environment: The 1440-acre campus is located in a small town 46 miles northwest of Houston. The dormitories house more than 3500 men and women.

Student Life: Almost all of the students are from Texas. Most are black. Ninety-five percent come from public schools. Most students live on campus in the single-sex dormitories.

Organizations: Four sororities and 4 fraternities have chapters on campus. Social clubs, academic and special-interest organizations, religious groups, and cultural events are available.

Sports: The university fields intercollegiate teams in 6 sports for men and 3 for women. Intramural sports also are available.

Graduates: About 33% of the freshmen drop out by the end of their freshman year, and 33% remain to graduate.

Services: Students pay a small health fee each semester. Psychological and career counseling, placement services, tutoring, and remedial instruction are provided free. Placement services also are provided for alumni.

Programs of Study: The university awards these undergraduate degrees: B.A., B.S., B.S.Ag., B.S.Ed., B.Mus., B.B.A., B.S.N., B.S.Arch., B.S.H.E., B.S.C.E., B.S.E.E., B.S.I.E., B.S.Ch.E., and B.S.M.E. Master's degrees also are conferred. Bachelor's degrees are offered in the following subjects: BUSINESS (accounting, business education, finance, management, marketing, office administration), EDUCATION (agricultural, elementary, health/physical, industrial, recreation, secondary), ENGLISH (communications, English, speech), FINE AND PERFORMING ARTS (advertising art, art education, music, music education, radio/TV, theater/dramatics), HEALTH SCIENCES (medical technology, nursing), LANGUAGES (French, German, Spanish), MATH AND SCIENCES (biology, chemistry, computer science, mathematics, physics, statistics), PREPROFESSIONAL (agriculture—animal science, agriculture—economics, agriculture—engineering, agriculture—plant science, agriculture—soil science, architecture, dentistry, dietetics, engineering—civil, engineering—electrical, engineering—industrial, engineering—mechanical, home economics, industrial arts, library science, medicine, social work), SOCIAL SCIENCES (economics, geography, political science, history, law enforcement, psychology, sociology).

Required: All students are required to take courses in English, humanities, mathematics, science, social science, health, and physical education. Male students must take a 2-year ROTC course.

Special: Cooperative education programs, independent study, and internships are available.

Honors: Twenty-four honor societies have chapters on campus.

Admissions: About two-thirds of those who applied were accepted for the 1981–82 freshman class. The SAT scores of those who enrolled were as follows: Verbal—90% below 500 and 10% between 500 and 599; Math—90% below 500 and 10% between 500 and 599. Of those

874 TEXAS

who took the ACT, 90% scored below 21 and 10% between 21 and 24. Applicants must rank in the top half of their high school class and have a GPA of at least 2.0 in 15 Carnegie units. Preference is given to state residents.

Procedure: The ACT or SAT is required. Students are admitted to all terms; applications must be filed at least 30 days before the start of a semester.

Special: AP and CLEP credit is granted.

Transfer: Transfer students must be in good standing at their last school. D grades do not transfer. There is a 1-year residency requirement.

Financial Aid: About 90% of the students receive aid. The university offers part-time jobs, loans (all types), scholarships, and grants. Aid awards generally are based on need. The FAF is required. The deadline for some aid programs is as early as February 1.

Foreign Students: Foreign students enrolled at the university make up 4% of the student body. Special counseling and special organizations are provided.

Admissions: Applicants must take the TOEFL and the SAT or ACT.

Procedure: Application deadlines are the same as those for American students. Foreign students must present a physician's report of their health and show evidence of adequate funds for 1 year. Health insurance is required, and is available through the university for a fee.

Admissions Contact: George H. Stafford, Director of Admissions.

RICE UNIVERSITY E-3
Houston, Texas 77001 (713) 527-4036

F/T: 1549M, 899W Faculty: 400; I, ++$
P/T: none Ph.D.'s: 90%
Grad: 606M, 315W S/F Ratio: 9 to 1
Year: sems Tuition: $3400
Appl: Feb. 1 R and B: $2900
2826 applied 1025 accepted 580 enrolled
SAT: 621V 671M **MOST COMPETITIVE**

Rice University, a private, nonsectarian institution founded in 1891, offers science, technological, and liberal arts programs. The library contains 1 million volumes and 250,000 microfilm items, and subscribes to more than 5000 periodicals.

Environment: The 300-acre campus is located in a suburban area 4 miles from downtown Houston. The more than 45 buildings are predominately Mediterranean in style. Facilities include dormitories that house 1380 men and 600 women.

Student Life: About 54% of the students come from Texas, and 85% of the freshmen are graduates of public schools. Eighty-five percent of the students live on campus. Nine percent are minority-group members. University housing is coed and single-sex; students in single-sex housing have visiting privileges. Students may keep cars on campus.

Organizations: Each student belongs to 1 of the 8 residential colleges around which social, athletic, and cultural programs are based. Each college has its own student government, as well as faculty members who live in or are associated with it. Other activities include choral groups, dance, drama, film, radio, a student newspaper, and ethnic, religious, academic, and special-interest clubs. A chapel lecture series features visiting theologians.

Sports: Rice University fields 12 intercollegiate teams for men and 11 for women. There are 12 intramural sports for men and 12 for women.

Graduates: About 7% of the freshmen drop out, and 85% remain to graduate. About 65% of the graduates seek advanced degrees; 15% enter medical school, 3% enter dental school, and 10% enter law school.

Services: Career and psychological counseling, placement services, and tutoring are offered to students free of charge. Health care is available for a fee.

Programs of Study: The university confers the B.A., B.Arch., B.F.A., B.Mus., and B.S. degrees. Master's and doctoral degrees also are available. Bachelor's degrees are offered in the following subjects: BUSINESS (business administration, computer science, management), EDUCATION (health/physical), ENGLISH (English, literature), FINE AND PERFORMING ARTS (art, art history, music, studio art), LANGUAGES (French, German, Greek/Latin, Spanish), MATH AND SCIENCES (biochemistry, biology, chemistry, earth science, geology, mathematics, physics), PHILOSOPHY (classics, philosophy, religion), PREPROFESSIONAL (architecture, engineering—aerospace, engineering—chemical, engineering—civil, engineering—electrical, engineering—environmental, engineering—mechanical), SOCIAL SCIENCES (anthropology, economics, government/political science, history, psychology, sociology). A third of the undergraduate degrees conferred are in engineering, 18% in social sciences, and 8% in business.

Required: All students must pass examinations in composition and expression and take 2 semesters of health and physical education.

Special: A student may design his or her own major. A cooperative program in African studies is offered jointly by Rice, the University of Houston, and Texas Southern University. An exchange program with Cambridge University and Swarthmore College is available. Juniors may arrange, on their own, to spend a year abroad.

Honors: An honors program is available. Eight honor societies, including Phi Beta Kappa, are represented on campus.

Admissions: Thirty-six percent of those who applied were accepted for the 1981-82 freshman class. The SAT scores of those who enrolled were as follows: Verbal—8% below 500, 25% between 500 and 599, 49% between 600 and 700, and 18% above 700; Math—4% below 500, 10% between 500 and 599, 43% between 600 and 700, and 43% above 700. Applicants should have completed 16 Carnegie units. Admissions officers consider class rank and SAT scores, advanced placement or honors courses, recommendations by high school officials, and personality. Students should arrange for an interview on campus or with a university representative in their hometown. Rice seeks a culturally and geographically diverse student body, and foreign students as well as those from disadvantaged backgrounds are encouraged to apply.

Procedure: The SAT and 3 ATs (including English composition) must be taken, preferably in December or January of the senior year. Prospective math, science, or engineering majors must take ATs in English composition, mathematics, and chemistry or physics. Chemistry CLEP exams also are accepted. The application deadline is February 1. Notification is made by November 15 for early decision and by April 10 for regular admission. The CRDA is observed. There is no application fee.

Special: Early and deferred admissions plans and an early decision plan are available. AP and CLEP credit is accepted.

Transfer: For fall 1981, 596 students applied, 127 were accepted, and 85 enrolled. Applicants must present satisfactory SAT scores and college record transcripts, and arrange for an interview; a minimum 3.5 GPA and 30 completed credit hours are recommended. D grades do not transfer. Students must spend 2 years in residence on a full-time basis and complete at least 20 of the 40 courses necessary for a bachelor's degree. Application deadlines are April 1 (fall) and November 1 (winter).

Financial Aid: About 80% of the students receive aid. Twelve percent work part-time on campus. Average aid to freshmen is $3445. Federal and university loans and tuition grants are available. Rice is a member of CSS, and aid applicants must submit the FAF. Aid applications are due February 1 (fall) and November 1 (winter).

Foreign Students: Two percent of the full-time students come from foreign countries. The university offers these students special counseling.

Admissions: Foreign students whose first language is not English must take the TOEFL; a minimum score of 550 is required. All foreign students must take the SAT and, if freshman applicants, 3 ATs (including English composition).

Procedure: Application deadlines are February 1 (fall) and, for transfers only, November 1 (winter). Foreign students must present proof of adequate funds each year.

Admissions Contact: Richard Stabell, Assistant to the President for Admissions and Records.

ST. EDWARD'S UNIVERSITY D-3
Austin, Texas 78704 (512) 444-2621

F/T: 750M, 562W Faculty: 90; IIB, av$
P/T: 180M, 162W Ph.D.'s: 70%
Grad: 225M, 101W S/F Ratio: 22 to 1
Year: 4-1-4, ss Tuition: $2840
Appl: Aug. 15 R and B: $2160
670 applied 600 accepted 380 enrolled
SAT: 410V 430M ACT: 16 **LESS COMPETITIVE**

St. Edward's University, established in 1885, is a college privately controlled by a corporate board of trustees, and dedicated to the basic Judaic-Christian spirit. It is staffed by lay men and women, the Brothers of Holy Cross, and the Sisters of the Immaculate Heart of Mary, and offers programs in arts and sciences, business, and bilingual elementary and secondary teacher preparation. The library houses 100,000 volumes and numerous microfilm items, and subscribes to 9000 periodicals.

Environment: The 180-acre campus is in an urban area 2 miles from downtown Austin. Facilities include a nationally historic main building, a dining hall, and residence halls accommodating 300 men and 300 women.

Student Life: About 70% of the students come from Texas. Eighty percent of entering freshmen come from public schools. Twenty percent of the students live on campus; freshmen out of high school less than a year and not married must live in dorms. Fifty percent of the students are Catholic, 40% are Protestant, and 1% are Jewish; places of worship are available on campus for Catholics, and nearby for Protestants and Jews. Thirty-three percent of the students are minority-group members. University housing is single-sex, and there are visiting privileges. Students may keep cars on campus.

Organizations: There are no fraternities or sororities. Students enjoy a diversified extracurricular and academic life, including the Student Activities Council, numerous special-interest groups, geographical and academic groups, a newspaper and other publications, theater and music groups, lecture series, films, and art exhibits.

Sports: The university fields 4 intercollegiate teams for men and 3 for women. There are 6 intramural sports for men and 5 for women.

Handicapped: Fifty percent of the campus is accessible to the physically handicapped. Wheelchair ramps, special parking, and special class scheduling are available to these students. There is 1 special counselor.

Graduates: Forty percent of the freshmen remain to graduate. Of the graduates who pursue advanced study, 2% enter medical school, 1% enter dental school, and 2% enter law school. Fifty percent pursue careers in business and industry.

Services: Students receive the following services free of charge: placement, career and psychological counseling, health care, tutoring, and remedial instruction.

Programs of Study: The university confers the B.A., B.S., B.B.A., and B.L.S. degrees. Master's degrees are also awarded. Bachelor's degrees are offered in the following subjects: BUSINESS (accounting, business administration, business education, computer science, finance, health care administration, management, marketing), EDUCATION (elementary, secondary), ENGLISH (English), FINE AND PERFORMING ARTS (art, art education, film/photography, theater/dramatics), HEALTH SCIENCES (medical technology), MATH AND SCIENCES (biology, chemistry, ecology/environmental science), PHILOSOPHY (religious education), PREPROFESSIONAL (engineering, law, medicine, social work, veterinary), SOCIAL SCIENCES (economics, gerontology, history, psychology, sociology). Teacher certification is offered in elementary and secondary education. Twenty-five percent of degrees conferred are in business, 25% in social sciences, and 20% in education.

Special: There is an opportunity to spend a semester studying in Rome.

Admissions: Ninety percent of those who applied were accepted for the 1981-82 freshman class. Of those who enrolled, the SAT scores were: Verbal—80% below 500, 15% between 500 and 599, 5% between 600 and 700, and 0% above 700; Math—80% below 500, 15% between 500 and 599, 5% between 600 and 700, and 0% above 700. On the ACT, 75% scored below 21, 10% between 21 and 23, 10% between 24 and 25, 3% between 26 and 28, and 2% above 28. Applicants must rank in the top two-thirds of their graduating class. Other factors considered in the admissions decision are recommendations by school officials, impressions made during an interview, personality, and leadership record.

Procedure: The SAT or ACT is required. Application deadlines are August 15 (fall), January 15 (spring), and May 15 (summer). Notification is on a rolling basis. The application fee is $20.

Special: AP and CLEP credit is accepted.

Transfer: For fall 1981, 400 students applied, 350 were accepted, and 275 enrolled. A 2.0 average is required. D grades do not transfer. Students must complete, at the university, at least 30 of the 120 credits necessary for a bachelor's degree. Application deadlines are the same as those for freshmen.

Visiting: Orientation for prospective students includes campus tours and class visitation. Informal tours allow visitors to sit in on classes and stay overnight at the school. These visits are best scheduled Monday through Friday between 8 A.M. and 5 P.M. Arrangements for a guide can be made with the director of admissions.

Financial Aid: Sixty percent of the students receive some form of financial aid. Thirty percent work part-time on campus. Average aid to freshmen is $4700. Scholarships available through the St. Edward's Scholarship Foundation are awarded on the basis of academic record; scholarships are open to freshmen in varying amounts. Federal and state loans and grants (including BEOG) are also available. The university is a member of CSS and requires the FAF, FFS, or SFS. Application deadlines for financial aid are March 1 (fall) and November 1 (spring); applications received later will be considered if funds are still available.

Foreign Students: Sixteen percent of the full-time students come from foreign countries. The university offers these students an intensive English course, special counseling, and special organizations.

Admissions: Foreign students must achieve a minimum TOEFL score of 450. No college entrance exam must be taken.

Procedure: Application deadlines are August 15 (fall), January 15 (spring), and May 15 (summer). Foreign students must present proof of adequate funds.

Admissions Contact: John Lucas, Director of Admissions.

ST. MARY'S UNIVERSITY
San Antonio, Texas 78240   (512) 436-3011   D-4

F/T: 905M, 880W   Faculty: 116; IIA, av$
P/T: 173M, 114W   Ph.D.'s: 55%
Grad: 706M, 428W   S/F Ratio: 21 to 1
Year: sems, ss   Tuition: $2974
Appl: Aug. 15   R and B: $1910
981 applied   789 accepted   468 enrolled
SAT: 469V 491M   ACT: 21   COMPETITIVE

Established in 1852, St. Mary's University is a Roman Catholic institution. The library houses 160,000 volumes, 50,000 microfilm items, and 148,000 government documents, and subscribes to 1000 periodicals.

Environment: The 135-acre campus is in a suburban area 5 miles north of downtown San Antonio. Buildings include a math/engineering complex, a life sciences building, a law school complex, and a newly constructed business school complex. In addition to dormitories, the university sponsors fraternity houses.

Student Life: Seventy-five percent of the students are from Texas. Sixty percent of entering freshmen come from public schools. About 40% of the students live on campus. Seventy-five percent are Catholic, and 19% are Protestant; there are religious counselors and organizations for all denominations. Fifty percent of the students are minority-group members. University housing is single-sex, and there are visiting privileges. Students may keep cars on campus. Drinking is permitted at school functions open to the entire student body.

Organizations: There are 9 fraternities, to which 30% of the men belong, and 5 sororities, to which 25% of the women belong.

Sports: The university fields 5 intercollegiate teams for men and 4 for women. There are 9 intramural sports for men and 8 for women.

Handicapped: Ninety-five percent of the campus is accessible to the physically handicapped. Wheelchair ramps, special parking, elevators, special class scheduling, and specially equipped rest rooms are available.

Graduates: The freshman dropout rate is 10%, and 75% of the entering freshmen remain to graduate. Sixty percent of the graduates pursue advanced study; 12% enter medical school, 3% enter dental school, and 14% enter law school. Thirty-five percent pursue careers in business and industry.

Services: Students receive the following services free: psychological counseling, career counseling, placement, and tutoring.

Programs of Study: The university confers the B.A., B.S., and B.B.A. degrees. Master's degrees are also offered. Bachelor's degrees are offered in the following subjects: AREA STUDIES (Latin American, urban), BUSINESS (accounting, business education, computer science, economics, finance, management, marketing, real estate/insurance), EDUCATION (elementary, secondary), ENGLISH (communication arts, English), FINE AND PERFORMING ARTS (music), HEALTH SCIENCES (medical technology), LANGUAGES (French, German, Spanish), MATH AND SCIENCES (biology, chemistry, earth science, geology, mathematics, physics), PHILOSOPHY (philosophy), PREPROFESSIONAL (dentistry, law, medicine, ministry), SOCIAL SCIENCES (economics, government/political science, history, international relations, psychology, sociology). Preprofessional programs are incorporated within other majors. Forty-two percent of degrees conferred are in social sciences, 31% in business, 22% in math and sciences, and 5% in education.

Required: All students are required to take 6 hours of theology and 9 hours of philosophy. Students in the School of Arts and Sciences must also take 2 semesters of physical education.

Honors: Six national honor societies have chapters on campus.

Admissions: Eighty percent of those who applied were accepted for the 1981–82 freshman class. Of those who enrolled, the SAT scores were: Verbal—67% below 500, 23% between 500 and 599, 8% between 600 and 700, and 2% above 700; Math—52% below 500, 40% between 500 and 599, 6% between 600 and 700, and 2% above 700. On the ACT, 18% scored below 19, 54% between 19 and 23, 25% between 24 and 29, and 3% above 29. Candidates must be graduates of an accredited high school and rank in the top half of their graduating class. Students planning to enter the fields of engineering, physics, chemistry, or geology are expected to present 4 units of mathematics (including trigonometry or analysis) and 2 units of a laboratory science (1 in either physics or chemistry). ACT or SAT scores, high school record, and rank in class are the 3 most important factors in evaluating a candidate. Also considered are the recommendations of the applicant's high school and any alumni he or she may know, advanced placement or honors courses, evidence of leadership potential, and the reputation of the high school. It is recommended that applicants arrange for an interview on or off campus with a representative of the school.

Procedure: The ACT or SAT is required and should be taken in October, December, or February of the senior year. Application deadlines are August 15 (fall), December 31 (spring), and May 15 (summer). Notification is on a rolling basis. The application fee is $15.

Special: Deferred admissions are available. CLEP and AP credit is accepted.

Transfer: For fall 1981, 385 students applied, 259 were accepted, and 167 enrolled. Transfers are considered for all but the senior class. A 2.0 GPA and good standing at the former school are required; an interview is recommended. D grades do not transfer. Students must complete, at the university, at least 30 of the 128 semester credit hours necessary for a bachelor's degree. Application deadlines are the same as those for freshmen.

Visiting: A late August orientation is required of all entering freshmen. In-town students can visit throughout the year; campus visitation weekends are scheduled for out-of-towners. Visitors may sit in on classes and stay overnight at the school. Visits are best scheduled weekdays or Saturday mornings until 1 P.M. Arrangements for a guide can be made through the admissions office.

Financial Aid: Seventy-three percent of all students receive financial aid. Twenty-two percent work part-time on campus. Average aid to freshmen is $3500. Scholarships range from $500 per year to full tuition. More than 60 freshmen received scholarships recently. Loans are available from St. Mary's fund, local banks, private sources, and the federal government. The university is a CSS member. The FAF and the university's own aid application are required. The priority deadline for aid applications is March 1.

Foreign Students: Three percent of the full-time students come from foreign countries. The university offers these students special counseling and special organizations.

Admissions: Foreign students must achieve a minimum TOEFL score of 500. No college entrance exam must be taken.

Procedure: Application deadlines are June 25 (fall), November 15 (spring), and March 25 (summer). Foreign students must present a university health form completed by a licensed physician, proof of funds adequate to cover 1 year of study, and an application processing fee of $15. They must also carry health insurance, which is available through the university for a fee.

Admissions Contact: Fernando Yarrito, Director of Admissions.

SAM HOUSTON STATE UNIVERSITY E–3
Huntsville, Texas 77341   (713) 294-1056

F/T: 3832M, 4033W
P/T: 604M, 439W
Grad: 513M, 869W
Year: sems, ss
Appl: open
3264 applied 2611 accepted 1963 enrolled
ACT: 17
Faculty: 400; IIA, +$
Ph.D.'s: n/av
S/F Ratio: 22 to 1
Tuition: $420 ($1500)
R and B: $1800

LESS COMPETITIVE

Sam Houston State University, established in 1879 to prepare teachers for the public schools of Texas, is a publicly supported institution. Preprofessional preparation and liberal arts education are also offered. The library houses 472,127 volumes and 246,863 microfilm items, and subscribes to 3525 periodicals.

Environment: The 60-acre campus, located in a rural environment, is 60 miles from Houston. The university also has an agricultural farm of 1000 acres. Five cafeterias and 5 dining halls are available to residents and nonresidents. Dormitories accommodate 1510 men, 2253 women, and 191 married students. The university also sponsors fraternity and sorority houses.

Student Life: Ninety-five percent of the students are from Texas. Ninety-eight percent of entering freshmen come from public schools. Approximately 40% live in dormitories, fraternity or sorority houses, or approved private homes. About 12% of the students are minority-group members. Campus housing is single-sex; there are visiting privileges. Students may keep cars on campus.

Organizations: There are 6 national fraternities and 6 national sororities. The director of student activities coordinates organizational activities and directs the Student Center. The student senate governs the student body; the officers and representatives are directly responsible to the dean of students.

Sports: The college fields 8 intercollegiate teams for men and 7 for women. There are 9 intramural sports for men and 8 for women.

Handicapped: There are no special facilities for physically handicapped students.

Graduates: Twenty percent of the graduates pursue graduate study: 2% enter medical school, 1% enter dental school, and 1% enter law school. Twenty-one percent pursue careers in business and industry.

Services: Students receive free placement, career and psychological counseling, and tutoring. A placement service sets up interviews with prospective employers.

Programs of Study: The university confers the B.A., B.S., B.A.A.S., B.A.T., B.B.A., B.F.A., B.Mus., and B.Mus. Ed. degrees. Master's and doctoral programs are also offered. Bachelor's degrees are offered in the following subjects: BUSINESS (accounting, business administration, business education, computer science, finance, management, marketing), EDUCATION (early childhood, elementary, health/physical, industrial, special), ENGLISH (English, journalism, speech), FINE AND PERFORMING ARTS (art, art education, dance, film/photography, music, music education, radio/TV, studio art, theater/dramatics), HEALTH SCIENCES (medical technology), LANGUAGES (French, Spanish), MATH AND SCIENCES (biology, chemistry, earth science, mathematics, physics), PHILOSOPHY (humanities), PREPROFESSIONAL (agriculture, home economics, library science, social work), SOCIAL SCIENCES (economics, geography, government/political science, history, psychology). Forty-six percent of degrees conferred are in social sciences, 27% in business, and 23% in education.

Special: The undergraduate program in American Ethnic Studies provides an analysis of the contributions of the Latin, German, Jewish, Oriental, Indian, and black subcultures to the development of American civilization.

Admissions: About 80% of the applicants for the 1981–82 freshman class were accepted. Candidates must be graduates of an accredited high school and have completed 15 Carnegie units. State residents are given preference, as are those with advanced placement or honors courses, rank in the top half of their graduating class, and an average of B or better. Also considered are recommendations of secondary school authorities and school reputation. Non-high-school graduates over 21 having a GED diploma may be admitted on the basis of individual approval.

Procedure: SAT or ACT scores must be presented. There is no formal application deadline. Admissions are on a rolling basis.

Special: CLEP and AP credit is accepted.

Transfer: For fall 1981, 1923 transfer students applied, 1538 were accepted, and 1188 enrolled. D grades are acceptable. A 2.0 GPA is required. There is a 1-year residency rule. Students must complete, at the university, 30 of the 128 credits required for the bachelor's degree. Application deadlines are open.

Visiting: There is a regularly scheduled orientation for prospective students. Informal visits can also be scheduled; arrangements for a guide can be made with George L. Morton. Visitors may sit in on classes and stay overnight at the university.

Financial Aid: About 25% of the students receive aid. Student aid is available in the form of scholarships, federal and university loans, and campus employment. The FAF is required.

Foreign Students: About 3% of the full-time students come from foreign countries.

Admissions: Foreign students must achieve a minimum TOEFL score of 550; no college entrance exams are required.

Procedure: Application deadlines are July 1 for fall, November 1 for spring, and April 1 for summer. Foreign students must present proof of health as well as proof of funds adequate to cover 1 year of study.

Admissions Contact: H. A. Bass, Director of Admissions.

SOUTHERN METHODIST UNIVERSITY D-2
Dallas, Texas 75275 (214) 692-2058

F/T: 2754M, 2750W	Faculty: 479; I, av$
P/T: 331M, 282W	Ph.D.'s: 70%
Grad: 2120M, 1035W	S/F Ratio: 15 to 1
Year: sems, ss	Tuition: $4910
Appl: Apr. 1	R and B: $2753
3160 applied	2550 accepted 1377 enrolled
SAT: 500V 550M	ACT: 25 COMPETITIVE+

Southern Methodist University, founded in 1911, is a private, nonsectarian institution affiliated with the Methodist Church. The library contains nearly 1 million volumes and 155,257 microfilm items, and subscribes to 152,350 periodicals.

Environment: The 164-acre campus, located in a suburban setting 5 miles from downtown Dallas, has 80 buildings. Nineteen residence halls house 1512 women and 1332 men. Auxiliary housing exists for 140 married students.

Student Life: Forty-five percent of the students are from Texas. Seventy-three percent of the freshmen come from public schools. Sixty percent of the students live on campus. Fifty percent are Protestant, 30% are Catholic, and 3% are Jewish; there are religious counselors for members of all major faiths. About 8% of the students are minority-group members. University housing is coed and single-sex; students in single-sex housing have visiting privileges. Students may keep cars on campus. Day-care facilities are available for a fee to full-time and part-time students, faculty, and staff.

Organizations: Forty-five percent of the men and 45% of the women belong to 15 national fraternities and 12 sororities. In addition to a wide range of on-campus extracurricular activities, students have access to all the cultural (theater, symphony hall, art museum) and recreational opportunities of downtown Dallas.

Sports: The university fields 8 intercollegiate teams for men and 5 for women. There are 15 intramural sports for men and 14 for women.

Handicapped: About 95% of the campus is accessible to handicapped students. Special facilities include wheelchair ramps, parking areas, elevators, lowered drinking fountains and telephones, and specially equipped rest rooms. Special class scheduling is also available. A staff of 5 assists handicapped students.

Graduates: The freshman dropout rate is 12%, and 65% of the freshmen remain to graduate. Of these, 63% go on to further study. Fifty percent pursue careers in business and industry.

Services: Students receive the following services free of charge: health care, psychological counseling, career counseling, placement service, and remedial instruction. Tutoring is available for a fee.

Programs of Study: The university confers the B.A., B.S., B.A.S., B.B.A., B.F.A., B.M., and B.S. in Eng. degrees. Master's and doctoral degrees are also awarded. Bachelor's degrees are offered in the following subjects: AREA STUDIES (Black/Afro-American, Latin American), BUSINESS (accounting, business administration, computer science, finance, management, marketing, real estate/insurance), ENGLISH (English, journalism), FINE AND PERFORMING ARTS (art, art education, art history, dance, film/photography, music, music education, radio/TV, studio art, theater/dramatics), LANGUAGES (French, German, Italian, Russian, Spanish), MATH AND SCIENCES (biology, chemistry, geology, mathematics, physics, statistics), PHILOSOPHY (philosophy, religion), PREPROFESSIONAL (dentistry, engineering—civil, engineering—computer, engineering—electrical, engineering—mechanical, engineering management, law, medicine, ministry, social work), SOCIAL SCIENCES (anthropology, economics, government/political science, history, psychology, social sciences, sociology). Teacher certification is offered in elementary, health/physical, and secondary education. Thirty-six percent of degrees conferred are in business, 19% in social sciences, and 16% in fine and performing arts.

Special: Interdisciplinary courses are available, and a combined B.A.-B.S. degree is offered in humanities and sciences. Student-designed majors are permitted, and study abroad options are available in many parts of the world. A work-study program enables engineering students to gain valuable field experience with selected Dallas industries.

Honors: The university has a well-established honors program in many departments. There are 7 national honor societies on campus, including Phi Beta Kappa.

Admissions: Eighty-one percent of those who applied were accepted for the 1981–82 freshman class. Of those who enrolled, the SAT scores were as follows: Verbal—54% below 500, 37% between 500 and 599, 8% between 600 and 700, and 1% above 700; Math—35% below 500, 42% between 500 and 599, 19% between 600 and 700, and 4% above 700. The candidate should have completed 13 Carnegie high school units. Factors important in the admissions decision are advanced placement or honors courses, the leadership record, recommendations by school officials, and the extracurricular activities record.

Procedure: The SAT or ACT is required. Application deadlines are April 1 (fall), December 1 (spring), and May 1 (summer). Notification is on a rolling basis. There is a $20 application fee.

Special: A deferred admissions plan is available.

Transfer: For fall 1981, 995 students applied, 940 were accepted, and 535 enrolled. The GPA required for entrance is determined by the applicant's major but should be no lower than 2.0; an interview is recommended. D grades do not transfer. Students must complete, at the university, at least 60 of the 122 hours necessary for a bachelor's degree. Application deadlines are July 1 (fall) and December 1 (spring).

Visiting: There are regularly scheduled orientation programs for prospective students during spring, summer, and preregistration. Guides are available for informal visits, and visitors may sit in on classes and stay overnight at the school. Midweek is the best time for these visits. Arrangements can be made through the admissions office.

Financial Aid: About 40% of the students receive aid through the school. Twenty percent work part-time on campus and earn between $800 and $1500. Average aid to freshmen is $2000, with the average freshman scholarship, $1500, and the average loan, $1000. The university is a member of CSS. The FAF must be filed by scholarship applicants. Application deadlines are March 1 (fall and summer) and October 1 (spring).

Foreign Students: Five percent of the full-time students come from foreign countries. The university offers these students special counseling and special organizations.

Admissions: Foreign students must achieve a minimum TOEFL score of 550. They must also take either the SAT or the ACT.

Procedure: Application deadlines are April 1 (fall and summer) and December 1 (spring). Foreign students must present proof of health and proof of funds adequate to cover 1 year of study. They must also carry health insurance.

Admissions Contact: Scott F. Healy, Director of Admissions.

SOUTHWESTERN ADVENTIST COLLEGE D-2
Keene, Texas 76059 (817) 645-3921

F/T: 302M, 342W	Faculty: 46; IIB, n/av
P/T: 49M, 51W	Ph.D.'s: 42%
Grad: none	S/F Ratio: 14 to 1
Year: sems, ss	Tuition: $4140
Appl: open	R and B: $2074
469 applied	335 accepted 228 enrolled
ACT: 14	LESS COMPETITIVE

Southwestern Adventist College, established in 1893, is affiliated with the Seventh-day Adventist Church. It offers undergraduate programs in the liberal arts and sciences, business, education, and nursing. The library contains 65,000 volumes and 13,000 microfilm items, and subscribes to 500 periodicals.

Environment: The 140-acre small-town campus is located in a rural setting 25 miles south of Fort Worth. Residence halls accommodate about 200 men and 200 women. There are apartments for 22 married students.

Student Life: About 50% of the students come from Texas. Nearly all (99%) are members of the supporting church. Fifty-three percent live on campus. About 29% of the students are minority-group members. Campus housing is single-sex; there are no visiting privileges. Students may keep cars on campus. Weekly chapel attendance is required. The use of alcohol and tobacco is prohibited.

Organizations: Religious and service groups, student government, clubs, publications, musical groups, and social and cultural events are offered. There are no fraternities or sororities.

Sports: There are no intercollegiate teams. There are 4 intramural sports.

Graduates: The freshman dropout rate is 30%; 30% remain to graduate. About 19% of the graduates pursue advanced degrees; 7% enter medical school.

Services: The college provides health care, tutoring, remedial instruction, placement, and career counseling at no charge to the student.

878 TEXAS

Programs of Study: The B.A., B.B.A., B.M., and B.S. degrees are conferred. Associate degrees are also offered. Bachelor's degrees are offered in the following subjects: BUSINESS (accounting, business administration, management, office administration), EDUCATION (elementary, health/physical, industrial, secondary), ENGLISH (communications, English), FINE AND PERFORMING ARTS (music, music education), HEALTH SCIENCES (dietetics, health care administration, medical technology, nursing), LANGUAGES (French, German, Greek/Latin, Spanish), MATH AND SCIENCES (biology, chemistry, industrial technology, mathematics), PHILOSOPHY (religion), PREPROFESSIONAL (home economics), SOCIAL SCIENCES (history, social sciences). About 19% of the degrees are conferred in business and 20% in education.

Required: Course work in religion, physical education, English, fine arts, mathematics, laboratory sciences, and social sciences is required.

Special: Internships, independent study, student-designed majors, and study abroad are offered.

Honors: There is an honors program.

Admissions: About 71% of the applicants were accepted for the 1981–82 freshman class. The ACT scores of those who enrolled were as follows: 70% below 21, 16% between 21 and 23, 6% between 24 and 25, 5% between 26 and 28, and 3% above 28. Students should be graduates of accredited high schools, have a 2.0 high school GPA, and present 16 units of work.

Procedure: The ACT is required. New students are admitted each semester. Application deadlines are open. An interview is recommended. Notification is on a rolling basis. There is no application fee.

Special: There are early admissions and deferred admissions programs. AP and CLEP credit is available.

Transfer: For fall 1981, 188 transfer students applied, 133 were accepted, and 78 enrolled. A 2.0 GPA is needed. Thirty semester hours must be completed in residence; the bachelor's degree requires 128 semester hours. Application deadlines are open.

Visiting: Campus tours with student guides are available. Visitors may sit in on classes. The admissions office should be contacted for arrangements.

Financial Aid: About 95% of the students receive financial aid; 90% work part-time on campus. The college offers scholarships, governmental (NDSL) and commercial loans, grants (BEOG/SEOG), and part-time campus employment (including CWS). The average award to freshmen from all sources is $3700. Tuition may be paid in installments. The college is a member of CSS; the FAF is required. Priority is given to aid applications received by July 15.

Foreign Students: About 9% of the full-time students come from foreign countries. The college offers these students an intensive English program, special counseling, and special organizations.

Admissions: Foreign students must take the college's own test of English proficiency. They must also take the ACT.

Procedure: Application deadlines are open. Foreign students must complete the college's medical form and present proof of adequate funds. They must also carry health insurance, which is available through the college for a fee.

Admissions Contact: Dallas Kindopp, Director of Admissions and Registrar.

SOUTHWESTERN UNIVERSITY D–3
Georgetown, Texas 78626   (512) 863-1460

F/T: 418M, 497W   Faculty: 57; IIB, +$
P/T: 40M, 45W   Ph.D.'s: 90%
Grad: none   S/F Ratio: 15 to 1
Year: sems, ss   Tuition: $3500
Appl: Aug. 1   R and B: $2511
487 applied   355 accepted   250 enrolled
SAT: 494V 515M ACT: 23   COMPETITIVE+

Founded in 1840, Southwestern University offers an undergraduate education in the liberal and fine arts under the auspices of the Methodist Church. The library houses 125,000 volumes, and subscribes to 550 periodicals.

Environment: The 500-acre campus, located in a rural area 28 miles north of Austin, has 34 buildings and a golf course. Seven dormitories accommodate 354 women and 300 men; 100 men live in the 4 fraternity houses.

Student Life: Ninety-two percent of the students come from Texas, and 6% come from out of state. Seventy-five percent of the students live on campus. Seventy-nine percent are Protestant, 10% are Catholic, and 1% are Jewish; chapel services are held once a week, with attendance voluntary. Catholic and Protestant counselors are available. Seven percent of the students are minority-group members. University housing is single-sex. Students may keep cars on campus. Drinking is prohibited.

Organizations: Thirty-five percent of the men and 45% of the women belong to the 4 fraternities and 5 sororities. Extracurricular activities include an active union program and an artist series.

Sports: The university fields 3 intercollegiate teams for men and 3 for women. There are 8 intramural sports for men and 6 for women.

Handicapped: Ninety percent of the campus is accessible to the physically handicapped. Wheelchair ramps, special parking, elevators, specially equipped rest rooms, and lowered drinking fountains are available for these students.

Graduates: The freshman dropout rate is 20%, and 50% of the freshmen remain to graduate. Fifty percent of the graduates pursue advanced study; 2% enter medical school, 1% enter dental school, and 2% enter law school. Twenty percent pursue careers in business and industry.

Services: Placement, career counseling, psychological counseling, and health care are available free of charge.

Programs of Study: The university confers the B.A., B.S., B.B.A., B.F.A., B.S.Ed., B.S. in Soc. Sci., and B. Applied Sc. degrees. Bachelor's degrees are offered in the following subjects: AREA STUDIES (American), BUSINESS (accounting, business administration, computer science, finance, management, marketing), EDUCATION (early childhood, elementary, health/physical, secondary, special), ENGLISH (English, speech), FINE AND PERFORMING ARTS (art, art education, art history, music, music education, studio art, theater/dramatics), HEALTH SCIENCES (medical technology, nursing, physical therapy), LANGUAGES (French, German, Greek/Latin, Spanish), MATH AND SCIENCES (biology, chemistry, mathematics, physics), PHILOSOPHY (philosophy, religion), PREPROFESSIONAL (dentistry, engineering, law, medicine, ministry, pharmacy, social work, veterinary), SOCIAL SCIENCES (economics, government/political science, history, international relations, psychology, sociology).

Required: Thirty-seven semester hours of liberal arts training in the common core program are required of all freshmen; the program, covering English, science, fine arts, religion, social studies, and history, must be completed before a degree is received.

Special: Independent study opportunities are available. Students are permitted to spend their junior year abroad. Internships are offered in a variety of subjects; in this program students work in their major field away from campus and receive semester hour credit. Some pass/fail courses are allowed in the senior year. Three-year bachelor's programs in allied health sciences, engineering, or medical technology are available. Combined degrees are available in several subjects; this is usually a 5-year curriculum.

Honors: Seven honor societies have chapters on campus.

Admissions: Seventy-three percent of those who applied were accepted for the 1981–82 freshman class. Candidates must have completed 16 Carnegie units at an accredited high school and rank in the top half of their graduating class. Other factors considered in the admissions decision are advanced placement or honors courses, recommendations by school officials, leadership record, and evidence of special talent.

Procedure: The SAT or ACT is required and should be taken by January of the senior year. Application deadlines are August 1 (fall), December 1 (winter), and April 1 (summer). Notification is on a rolling basis. There is an application fee of $10.

Special: There is an early admissions plan. AP and CLEP credit is accepted.

Transfer: For fall 1981, 139 students applied, 120 were accepted, and 89 enrolled. A 2.0 GPA is expected; ACT or SAT scores are also considered. D grades transfer only in elective courses. Students must spend 2 semesters in residence and complete at least 30 of the 124 credits necessary for a bachelor's degree. Application deadlines are the same as those for freshmen.

Visiting: Orientation for prospective students is held prior to fall registration. Guides are available for informal visits, during which visitors may sit in on classes and stay overnight at the school. Visits can be scheduled Monday through Friday. Arrangements can be made through the office of admissions.

Financial Aid: Sixty-two percent of all students receive some form of financial aid. Twenty percent work part-time on campus; work is required if the student receives aid on the basis of financial need as determined by the CSS. Average aid to freshmen covers 62% of costs; recently, 130 freshmen received an average of $1200 each. Federal, state, and university loans are available. The university is a CSS member and requires the FAF. Application deadlines are May 1 (fall), November 1 (spring), and April 1 (summer).

Foreign Students: Two percent of the full-time students come from foreign countries.

Admissions: Foreign students must achieve a minimum TOEFL score of 550. They must also take either the SAT or the ACT.

Procedure: Application deadlines are January 1 (fall), September 1 (spring), and December 1 (summer). Foreign students must present proof of a medical exam by a licensed physician and an immunization record. They must also furnish proof of funds adequate to cover 4 years of study and are required to carry health insurance.

Admissions Contact: William D. Swift, Vice President for Admissions and Student Development.

SOUTHWEST TEXAS STATE UNIVERSITY D-4
San Marcos, Texas 78666   (512) 245-2364

F/T: 5683M, 6216W	Faculty: 485; IIA, –$
P/T: 1190M, 1113W	Ph.D.'s: 60%
Grad: 526M, 549W	S/F Ratio: 23 to 1
Year: sems, ss	Tuition: $426 ($1506)
Appl: July 19	R and B: $1755
6362 applied	3276 accepted	2873 enrolled
ACT: 18		COMPETITIVE

Southwest Texas State University, founded in 1899, is a publicly controlled institution offering programs in business, education, the liberal arts and sciences, and preprofessional fields. The library contains 528,000 volumes and 504,690 microfilm items, and subscribes to 4800 periodicals.

Environment: The 155-acre campus is located in a suburban setting within the city limits of San Marcos, 30 miles from Austin. The university also maintains a 450-acre farm. The buildings include a sports coliseum and physical education facilities; a new football stadium will be constructed shortly. There are 21 dormitories accommodating 3101 women, 1715 men, and 125 married students.

Student Life: All but 5% of the student body are residents of Texas. Ninety-eight percent of the freshmen come from public schools. Thirty-four percent of the students live on campus. Twenty percent are Protestant, and 10% are Catholic; religious facilities are available for these students. Fourteen percent are minority-group members. University housing is coed and single-sex; students in single-sex housing have visiting privileges. Students may keep cars on campus.

Organizations: Six percent of the men belong to 12 national fraternities; 7% of the women, to 1 local and 7 national sororities. Swimming and sunbathing facilities are available to students in Sewell Park, a university-owned park located in the center of campus. Off-campus attractions include Aquarena Springs and Wonder World.

Sports: The university fields 6 intercollegiate teams for men and 6 for women. A full intramural program for both men and women is also available.

Handicapped: The campus is 50% accessible to the handicapped student. Facilities include wheelchair ramps, specially equipped rest rooms, designated parking, lowered drinking fountains, and elevators. Special class scheduling is also available. There is a special counselor to assist handicapped students.

Graduates: The freshman dropout rate is 44%.

Services: The following services are offered at no charge to the student: psychological counseling, health care, remedial instruction, placement service, and career counseling. Tutoring is available for a fee.

Programs of Study: The degrees of B.A., B.Mus.Ed., B.B.A., B.S.H.E., B.S.Ind.Arts, B.S.Voc.Agr., and B.S.Ed. are conferred. Associate and master's degrees are also awarded. Bachelor's degrees are offered in the following subjects: BUSINESS (business administration, computer science), EDUCATION (elementary, guidance studies, health/physical, industrial arts, recreational administration), ENGLISH (English, journalism, speech), FINE AND PERFORMING ARTS (art, music, studio art, theater/dramatics), HEALTH SCIENCES (health professions, medical technology, speech pathology and audiology), LANGUAGES (French, German, Spanish), MATH AND SCIENCES (biology, chemistry, computer science, mathematics, physics), PHILOSOPHY (philosophy), PREPROFESSIONAL (agriculture, criminal justice, home economics, social work), SOCIAL SCIENCES (economics, geography, government/political science, history, international relations, physical and applied geography, psychology, social sciences, sociology). Of the degrees conferred, 31% are in preprofessional studies, 25% in business, and 17% in education.

Honors: A general honors program is offered. Entrance to the program is by invitation only, and an honors thesis is required. Sixteen national honor societies have chapters on campus.

Admissions: Fifty-two percent of those who applied were accepted for the 1981–82 freshman class. Of those who enrolled for a recent freshman class, the ACT scores were as follows: 24% between 21 and 23, 13% between 24 and 26, 5% between 27 and 28, and 1% above 28. Applicants must be graduates of accredited high schools, have completed 15 Carnegie units, and have a minimum ACT score of 15. The minimum required high school grade average varies according to the applicant's ACT score.

Procedure: The ACT or SAT is required. Formal application must be made at least 6 weeks before the registration date; suggested deadlines are July 19 (fall), December 10 (spring), April 22 (first summer session), and June 17 (second summer session). Freshmen are admitted each semester. Notification is on a rolling basis. There is no application fee.

Special: Early and deferred admissions plans are offered. CLEP credit is granted.

Transfer: For fall 1981, 3763 students applied, 2082 were accepted, and 1849 enrolled. A GPA of 2.0, 12 completed credit hours, and eligibility to return to the previous school are required. An interview is also required for specific programs. All grades transfer. Students must complete, at the university, the last 30 of the 128 semester hours necessary for a bachelor's degree. Suggested application deadlines are the same as those for freshmen.

Visiting: Guides are available for informal weekday visits to the campus from 8 A.M. to noon and from 1 P.M. to 5 P.M. Visitors may sit in on classes and stay overnight at the school. Arrangements can be made through the Office of Admissions and School Relations.

Financial Aid: Thirty-one percent of the students receive aid. Nine percent work part-time on campus. Scholarships and loans are available; loans range from $1200 to $2500 per year. The university is a member of the CSS and requires the FFS. Aid application deadlines are May 1 (fall), October 15 (spring), and March 15 (summer).

Foreign Students: One percent of the full-time students come from foreign countries. The university offers these students some special counseling and special organizations.

Admissions: Foreign students must achieve a minimum TOEFL score of 550. Applicants who are graduates of American high schools, which they attended 2 or more years, must also take the ACT or SAT.

Procedure: Application deadlines are June 15 (fall), November 1 (spring), and April 1 (summer). Foreign students must present certification of immunization and proof of funds adequate to cover at least the first year of study and preferably all 4 years. A $3400 deposit, which covers the first year's basic expenses, is required prior to acceptance.

Admissions Contact: Debra Evans, Director of Admissions.

STEPHEN F. AUSTIN STATE UNIVERSITY E-3
Nacogdoches, Texas 75962   (713) 569-2504

F/T: 4300M, 4900W	Faculty: 438; IIA, av$
P/T: 400M, 300W	Ph.D.'s: 70%
Grad: 500M, 600W	S/F Ratio: 24 to 1
Year: sems, ss	Tuition: $420 ($1620)
Appl: open	R and B: $2000
3400 applied	3000 accepted	2400 enrolled
SAT: 450V 450M	ACT: 20	COMPETITIVE

Stephen F. Austin University, founded in 1923, is a liberal arts institution under state control. The library contains 625,000 volumes.

Environment: Located in a rural setting, the self-contained campus contains several buildings, including those for forestry, music, home economics, computer science, and science, and an auditorium-fine arts building. In addition to dormitories, the college sponsors married student housing.

Student Life: Ninety-six percent of the students come from Texas. Ninety-five percent of the freshmen are graduates of public schools. Fifty-five percent of the students live on campus. Five percent are minority-group members. University housing is single-sex, and there are visiting privileges. Students may keep cars on campus.

Organizations: There are 12 national fraternities and 6 national sororities on campus; 8% of the men are fraternity members, and 5% of the women belong to sororities.

880 TEXAS

Sports: The university fields 12 intercollegiate teams for men and 10 for women. There are 14 intramural sports for men and 14 for women.

Handicapped: Some special facilities are offered for handicapped students.

Graduates: The freshman dropout rate is 35%; 45% remain to graduate. Twenty percent of the graduates pursue further study; 2% enter medical school, 2% enter dental school, and 2% enter law school. Thirty percent enter careers in business and industry.

Services: Students receive the following services free of charge: placement service, health care, psychological counseling, and career counseling. Tutoring and some remedial instruction require a fee.

Programs of Study: The undergraduate degrees offered are the B.A., B.B.A., B.F.A., B.M., B.S., B.S.Comp.Sci., B.S.Ed., B.S.Agr., B.S.H.E., B.S.N., and B.S.Soc.Work degrees. Master's and doctoral degrees also are conferred. Bachelor's degrees are offered in the following subjects: BUSINESS (business administration, computer science), EDUCATION (general education, health/physical), ENGLISH (communications, English, speech), FINE AND PERFORMING ARTS (art, music, theater/dramatics), HEALTH SCIENCES (medical technology), LANGUAGES (foreign languages), MATH AND SCIENCES (biology, chemistry, mathematics, physics), PHILOSOPHY (religion—Bible), PREPROFESSIONAL (agriculture, engineering, forestry, home economics), SOCIAL SCIENCES (criminal justice, economics, geography, government/political science, history, psychology/philosophy, sociology).

Required: Requirements vary with the particular program in which the student is enrolled.

Special: The university offers a B.A.A.S. degree, a 2+2 program designed for students with A.A. degrees in vocational areas and for mature students who have expertise in specialized areas and want a bachelor's degree. A 3-year bachelor's degree program is also offered. The programs in medical technology and in pre-engineering lead to combination degrees.

Honors: There are 24 honor societies on campus.

Admissions: Eighty-eight percent of those who applied for the 1981–82 freshman class were accepted. Of those who enrolled for a recent freshman class, the ACT scores were as follows: 60% between 21 and 23, 20% between 24 and 26, 6% between 27 and 28, and 3% above 28. Applicants must be graduates of accredited high schools and should have acceptable ACT or SAT scores. The university mainly accepts applicants who rank in the upper half of their class.

Procedure: The ACT or SAT is required. In addition, various tests are given for placement and guidance. The application deadlines are open, but applicants are encouraged to apply at least 30 days before the start of the semester. Freshmen are admitted in the fall, midyear, and summer. There is no application fee.

Special: A deferred admissions plan is available for the summer session.

Transfer: Recently, 3100 applications were received, 2500 were accepted, and 1900 students enrolled. The candidate must have a 2.0 average and be in good standing at the previous institution. A minimum of 42 hours must be taken on campus to qualify for a bachelor's degree.

Financial Aid: About 15% of the students receive financial aid. Campus employment offers students the opportunity to earn 25% or more of their expenses. Scholarships are available, as well as loans from government, private, bank, and university funds.

Foreign Students: Fewer than 1% of the full-time students come from foreign countries.

Admissions: Foreign students must achieve a minimum TOEFL score of 550. They must also take either the SAT or ACT.

Procedure: Application deadlines are open for all sessions. Foreign students must present proof of health and proof of funds in the form of a $3800 deposit fee.

Admissions Contact: Clyde Iglinsky, Director of Admissions.

SUL ROSS STATE UNIVERSITY
Alpine, Texas 79830   B–3   (915) 837-8052

F/T: 691M, 527W   Faculty: 79; IIA, –$
P/T: 140M, 177W   Ph.D.'s: 62%
Grad: 244M, 269W   S/F Ratio: 16 to 1
Year: sems, ss   Tuition: $292 ($1444)
Appl: open   R and B: $1800
508 applied   368 accepted   331 enrolled
SAT: 370V 400M   ACT: 14   LESS COMPETITIVE

Sul Ross State University, founded in 1917, is a state-controlled liberal arts institution with 7 major divisions: Science, Teacher Education, Liberal Arts, Range Animal Science, Fine Arts, Business Administration, and Adult and Continuing Education. The library houses 203,638 volumes, 19,150 microfilm items, and 4936 audiovisual items, and subscribes to 1375 periodicals.

Environment: The campus is situated on a 700-acre tract in a rural area 165 miles from Odessa. Seven dormitories house 500 students; there are 109 apartments for married students. The university also sponsors fraternity houses.

Student Life: About 89% of the students are from Texas, 5% are from other states, and 3% are from foreign countries. Forty-six percent reside on campus; freshmen and sophomores are required to do so. About 36% of the students are minority-group members. Campus housing is single-sex; there are visiting privileges. Students may keep cars on campus.

Organizations: There is 1 national fraternity on campus, but no sororities. There are several special-interest groups. Extracurricular activities include publications, dances, and cultural events. Among the off-campus attractions are Big Bend National Park, Fort Davis, and McDonald Observatory.

Sports: The university fields 5 intercollegiate teams for men and 5 for women. There are 12 intramural sports for men and women.

Handicapped: Ninety percent of the campus is accessible to handicapped students. Special facilities include wheelchair ramps, parking, elevators, and specially equipped rest rooms. Special class scheduling is also available.

Services: The following services are provided to all students free of charge: placement, career counseling, limited health care, tutoring, and remedial instruction.

Programs of Study: The B.A., B.B.A., B.M., B.F.A., and B.S. degrees are conferred. Master's degrees are also awarded. Bachelor's degrees are offered in the following subjects: BUSINESS (business administration, business education), EDUCATION (elementary, industrial, physical), ENGLISH (English, speech), FINE AND PERFORMING ARTS (art, art education, music, music education, theater/dramatics), LANGUAGES (Spanish), MATH AND SCIENCES (biology, chemistry, earth science, geology, mathematics), PREPROFESSIONAL (range animal science), SOCIAL SCIENCES (criminal justice, government/political science, history, social sciences). Thirty-four percent of the undergraduate degrees are conferred in education, 32% in math and sciences, and 16% in social sciences.

Special: There are 1-year certificate programs in vocational nursing and business administration, and 2-year certificate programs in animal health technology, meat inspection technology, and horse science.

Honors: There are 7 national honor societies on campus.

Admissions: About 72% of the students who applied for the 1981–82 freshman class were accepted. The SAT scores of those who enrolled were as follows: Verbal—95% below 500, 2% between 500 and 599, 2% between 600 and 700, and 0% above 700; Math—89% below 500, 6% between 500 and 599, 5% between 600 and 700, and 0% above 700. The ACT scores were as follows: 87% below 21, 8% between 21 and 23, 4% between 24 and 25, 1% between 26 and 28, and 0% above 28. The candidate should be a graduate of an accredited high school or hold a GED certificate and have a minimum grade average of 70.

Procedure: The SAT or ACT is required. Freshmen are admitted to all sessions. There are no deadlines for application. A rolling admissions plan is followed. There is no application fee.

Special: AP and CLEP credit is given.

Transfer: For fall 1981, 210 transfer students applied, 154 were accepted, and 129 enrolled. An average of 2.0 is recommended. The student must take 30 credit hours on campus to qualify for a degree; the bachelor's degree requires 130 credits. Application deadlines are open.

Visiting: Regularly scheduled orientation sessions include academic advisement and information on registration and campus facilities. Guides are available for informal tours weekdays from 8 A.M. to 5 P.M.; arrangements should be made with the Student Life Office. Visitors may sit in on classes and stay overnight at the school.

Financial Aid: About 60% of the students receive financial aid; 57% work part-time on campus. Departmental and academic scholarships are available. State loans totaling more than $15,000 are administered by the university, in addition to NDSL loans of $181,500. All departments offer CWS. The average award to freshmen from all sources is between $800 and $850. The deadlines for financial aid application are June 1 (fall) and November 1 (spring). The university is a member of CSS; the FFS is required.

Foreign Students: Almost 3% of the full-time students come from foreign countries. The university offers these students an intensive English program, special counseling, and special organizations.

Admissions: Foreign students must achieve a minimum TOEFL score of 500; no college entrance exams are required.

Procedure: Application deadlines are 30 days prior to registration for each semester. Foreign students must present a completed medical report form as well as proof of funds adequate to cover their entire period of study. They must also pay a $150 deposit, which is applied to the housing deposit and tuition and fees after enrollment.

Admissions Contact: Dorothy M. Leavitt, Registrar.

TARLETON STATE UNIVERSITY D-2
Stephenville, Texas 76401 (817) 968-9000

F/T: 1447M, 1219W	Faculty: 132; IIA, –$
P/T: 120M, 130W	Ph.D.'s: 35%
Grad: 700M&W	S/F Ratio: 25 to 1
Year: sems, ss	Tuition: $460 ($1080)
Appl: Aug. 13	R and B: $1648
1100 applied 1000 accepted	840 enrolled
SAT: 800 (composite)	LESS COMPETITIVE

Tarleton State University, established in 1899, is part of the Texas A & M University System. The university offers undergraduate degrees in the arts and sciences as well as technical fields. The library contains more than 150,000 volumes.

Environment: The 125-acre campus is located in west Texas, in a town of 12,000 persons 65 miles southwest of Fort Worth. The 38 major campus buildings include residence halls housing 600 men and 400 women.

Student Life: About 95% of the students come from Texas. Most are public school graduates. Seventy percent live on campus in the single-sex dorms.

Organizations: Extracurricular activities include student government, departmental clubs, service and religious groups, publications, performing arts groups, and regularly scheduled social and cultural events.

Sports: The university fields intercollegiate teams in 4 sports for men and 4 for women. Intramural sports also are available.

Handicapped: The university is working to make the campus accessible to handicapped students.

Graduates: About 45% of the freshmen drop out, and 20% remain to graduate. More than 10% of the graduates pursue advanced degrees.

Services: The university provides health care, psychological counseling, tutoring, remedial instruction, career counseling, and placement aid.

Programs of Study: The university confers the B.A., B.S., B.B.A., B.S.W., and B. Applied A.S. degrees. Associate and master's programs are also offered. Bachelor's degrees are offered in the following subjects: BUSINESS (accounting, agribusiness, business education, finance, management, marketing, office administration), EDUCATION (agricultural, elementary, health/physical, industrial, secondary), ENGLISH (English, speech), FINE AND PERFORMING ARTS (music education), HEALTH SCIENCES (medical technology), LANGUAGES (Spanish), MATH AND SCIENCES (biology, chemistry, mathematics, physics), PREPROFESSIONAL (agriculture, agriculture—agricultural economics, agriculture—animal production, agriculture—animal science, agriculture—floriculture and landscape design, agriculture—horse production and management, agriculture—mechanized agriculture, agriculture—plant and soil science, home economics, industrial arts, social work), SOCIAL SCIENCES (criminal justice, economics, government/political science, history, sociology).

Required: All students must complete distribution requirements including courses in physical education.

Special: Independent study, a 3-year bachelor's degree, study abroad, and exchange programs are offered. A general studies degree is available.

Honors: Three honor societies have chapters on campus.

Admissions: About 91% of the applicants for the 1981-82 freshman class were accepted. The SAT scores of those who enrolled were as follows: Verbal—87% below 500, 10% between 500 and 599, 1% between 600 and 700, and 2% above 700; Math—80% below 500, 16% between 500 and 599, 3% between 600 and 700, and 1% above 700. Candidates must have a high school diploma and have completed 15 Carnegie units. Texas residents generally should have combined SAT scores of 700 or an ACT composite of 16.

TEXAS 881

Procedure: Either the SAT or ACT is required. New students are admitted both to semesters; August 13 is the application deadline for fall admission. Notification is made on a rolling basis. There is no application fee.

Special: Early decision, early admissions, and deferred admissions plans are available. AP and CLEP credit is accepted.

Transfer: Transfer applicants must have a 2.0 GPA. Students must earn at least 30 semester hours in residence of the 120 or more required for a bachelor's degree.

Visiting: Campus tours with student guides can be arranged. Visitors may sit in on classes.

Financial Aid: About 42% of the students receive aid. The university participates in federal and state programs such as NDSL, CWS, and BEOG/SEOG. Scholarships are awarded on the basis of academic merit. The FAF should be filed by June 15.

Foreign Students: Students from foreign countries make up 9% of enrollment. The university offers these students special organizations.

Admissions: Applicants must score 550 or better on the TOEFL. They also must take the SAT or ACT.

Procedure: Application deadlines are July 23 (fall), December 9 (spring), and May 5 (summer). Foreign students must submit a medical statement of good health and must show evidence of adequate funds for 4 years. They also must be prepared to deposit $3000 toward expenses.

Admissions Contact: Conley Jenkins, Director of Admissions.

TEXAS A&I UNIVERSITY D-5
Kingsville, Texas 78363 (512) 595-2811

F/T, P/T, Grad:	Faculty: n/av; IIA, av$
5194M&W	Ph.D.'s: 67%
	S/F Ratio: 18 to 1
Year: sems, ss	Tuition: $300 ($1200)
Appl: Aug. 19	R and B: $1400
1800 applied	
SAT or ACT: required	LESS COMPETITIVE

Originally established as a teacher training institution in 1925, Texas A&I University is a publicly controlled institution composed of 6 colleges: Agriculture, Arts and Sciences, Business Administration, Engineering, Teacher Education, and Graduate Studies. Other campuses are at Laredo and Corpus Christi. The library houses 400,635 volumes and 162,153 microfilm items, and subscribes to 2142 periodicals.

Environment: The 255-acre main campus, located in an urban area 40 miles from Corpus Christi, has 32 buildings, the major ones of Spanish architecture. A 534-acre experimental farm adjoins the campus; a 237-acre Citrus and Vegetable Training Center is located in the lower Rio Grande Valley. Twelve dormitories accommodate 2582 students; institutional apartments are available for married students.

Student Life: Approximately 90% of the students are from Texas. About 95% of entering freshmen come from public schools. About 50% of the students live on campus; all students except those with more than 60 semester hours, married students, and those under 21 living at home are required to live on campus. University housing is coed and single-sex; visiting hours in single-sex dorms are determined by the residents. Students may keep cars on campus.

Organizations: The numerous and varied extracurricular activities and groups include 8 fraternities, 6 sororities, and religious organizations for Catholic and Protestant students. Students have voting delegates on all university committees.

Sports: The university fields 8 intercollegiate teams for men and 6 for women. There are 18 intramural sports for men and 17 for women.

Handicapped: The entire campus is accessible to the physically handicapped. Facilities include wheelchair ramps, special parking, elevators, and lowered drinking fountains and telephones. Readers and tapes are provided for students with visual impairments.

Graduates: Of the graduates who pursue advanced study, 5% enter medical school, 5% enter dental school, and 5% enter law school. Twenty percent pursue careers in business and industry.

Services: Placement services, career counseling, psychological counseling, tutoring, and remedial instruction are offered free of charge. Health care is available for a fee.

Programs of Study: The university confers the B.A., B.S., and B.B.A. degrees. Master's and doctoral degrees are also offered. Bachelor's degrees are offered in the following subjects: BUSINESS (accounting, business administration, business education, computer science, fi-

882 TEXAS

nance, management, marketing, real estate/insurance), EDUCATION (adult, early childhood, elementary, health/physical, secondary, special), ENGLISH (English, journalism, literature, speech), FINE AND PERFORMING ARTS (art, art education, art history, dance, music, music education, radio/TV, theater/dramatics), HEALTH SCIENCES (environmental health, medical technology, speech therapy), MATH AND SCIENCES (astronomy, biochemistry, biology, botany, chemistry, earth science, geology, mathematics, natural sciences, physical sciences, physics, zoology), PREPROFESSIONAL (agriculture, engineering, home economics, social work, veterinary), SOCIAL SCIENCES (anthropology, geography, government/political science, history, psychology, social sciences, sociology).

Required: There are course requirements in English, government, history, physical education, and science.

Special: A bilingual program providing instruction in English and Spanish qualifies a student to secure employment in Mexico and Latin America; students may spend a junior year abroad, on their own or through a program with another institution. Work-study is offered in conjunction with the National Aeronautics and Space Administration; after the freshman year a student can alternate a semester in school and a semester at NASA, with 2 summer terms counting as a semester. Combined B.A.-B.S. programs are offered in various subjects in the College of Arts and Sciences; this is a 5-year program.

Honors: Two national honor societies have chapters on campus.

Admissions: About 80% of the applicants for a recent freshman class were accepted. The ACT scores of the freshmen who enrolled were: 9% between 21 and 23, 4% between 24 and 26, and 2% between 27 and 28. The university requires graduation from an accredited high school and completion of 16 Carnegie units. Standardized exam scores are also considered in the admissions decision.

Procedure: The ACT is required; SAT scores can be converted. August is the latest test date acceptable for fall; junior year results are acceptable. Application deadlines are August 19 (fall), January 7 (winter), and May 26 (summer). Notification is about 2 weeks after receipt of all credentials. There is no application fee.

Special: Early admissions and early decision plans are available. Credit is accepted for CLEP subject exams and AP exams.

Transfer: For fall 1981, 408 students applied. A minimum SAT score of 680 or ACT score of 15 is required; a GPA of at least 2.5 is recommended. D grades are accepted for credit. In-state students must spend 1 year in residence; all transfers must complete, at the university, the last 30 of the 128–135 hours necessary for a bachelor's degree. Application deadlines are the same as those for freshmen.

Visiting: Orientation is scheduled for a day immediately before registration. Guides are available for informal visits, during which visitors may sit in on classes and stay overnight at the school. Visits are best scheduled from the middle to the end of the semester. Arrangements can be made with the dean of student life.

Financial Aid: Ten percent of the students receive financial aid. Some freshmen are awarded work contracts. Twenty-six academic and 16 athletic scholarships are available to freshmen. Federal (NDSL) and state loans are administered by the university. Application deadlines are June 1 (fall), October 15 (spring), and February 1 (summer).

Foreign Students: Ten percent of the full-time students come from foreign countries. The university offers these students special counseling and special organizations.

Admissions: Foreign students must achieve a minimum TOEFL score of 550. No college entrance exam must be taken.

Procedure: Application deadlines are September 1 (fall) and April 1 (spring). Foreign students must present an I-94 form as proof of health and proof of funds adequate to cover 1 year of study.

Admissions Contact: Frederick G. Harvey, Coordinator of Admissions.

TEXAS A&M UNIVERSITY D-3
College Station, Texas 77843 (713) 845-1031

F/T: 16,939M, 10,277W
P/T: 1252M, 838W
Grad: 3518M, 1766W
Year: sems, ss
Appl: July 31
11,398 applied 9648 accepted
SAT: 486V 517M

Faculty: n/av; I, av$
Ph.D.'s: 78%
S/F Ratio: 25 to 1
Tuition: $520 ($1600)
R and B: $2086–2302
6063 enrolled
COMPETITIVE

Texas A&M University, founded in 1876, is a publicly controlled agricultural and technological college, consisting of the colleges of Agriculture, Architecture, Business Administration, Education, Engineering, Science, Geosciences, Veterinary Medicine, Medicine, and Liberal Arts, and a Graduate College. One of 4 university members of the Texas A&M University System of 11 universities and agencies, it offers a wide range of studies and research. The library contains 1.3 million volumes and subscribes to 16,000 periodicals. The Corps of Cadets, to which about 2100 students belong, affords the opportunity to experience military life and obtain commissions in all branches of the Service.

Environment: The 5200-acre campus, in rural surroundings of a town of 100,000, is 90 miles from Houston. Forty dormitories, arranged in commons and quadrangles, house 10,000 men and women. About 24,000 students live in private homes and apartments. There are 708 university-operated apartments for married students. Three dining halls and several cafeterias provide facilities for both day and resident students.

Student Life: About 85% of the students come from Texas, and 9% come from other states. Thirty-three percent live on campus. Attendance at religious services is voluntary. Six percent of the students are minority-group members. University housing is single-sex, and there are visiting privileges. Students may keep cars on campus but must register them with the university. Alcoholic beverages on campus are prohibited. Undergraduate students who join the Cadet Corps are organized along military lines, observe military practice, and wear the prescribed uniform. Freshman and sophomore cadets observe a 7:30 curfew, except for Saturdays; bedtime is at taps.

Organizations: There are no fraternities or sororities officially recognized by the university, but extracurricular activities are numerous. There is a cultural activities center on campus, and many other cultural and recreational opportunities in the surrounding area.

Sports: The university fields 10 intercollegiate teams for men and 10 for women. The Extramural Sports Clubs, consisting of 25 clubs and 45 teams, give students the opportunity to compete in intercollegiate activities that cannot be offered through the Athletic Department. There is also an extensive intramural program.

Handicapped: Approximately 97% of the campus is accessible to the physically handicapped. Facilities include wheelchair ramps, curb cuts, special parking, a shuttle bus (van with a lift) system, elevators, specially equipped rest rooms and residence hall rooms, and lowered drinking fountains and telephones. There are 2 special counselors to assist handicapped students.

Graduates: The freshman dropout rate is 20%, and 69% remain to graduate. Of these, 35% pursue advanced study. Engineering students account for approximately 32% of the total enrollment.

Services: Students receive the following services free of charge: psychological counseling, tutoring, and career and placement counseling from a highly successful placement center serving both graduates and undergraduates. Some health care requires a fee.

Programs of Study: The university confers the B.A., B.S., B.B.A., and B.E.D. degrees. Master's and doctoral degrees are also awarded. Bachelor's degrees are offered in the following subjects: BUSINESS (accounting, computer science, finance, management, marketing), EDUCATION (agricultural, elementary, health/physical, industrial, secondary, technical), ENGLISH (English, journalism), FINE AND PERFORMING ARTS (theater/dramatics), LANGUAGES (foreign languages), MATH AND SCIENCES (applied mathematical sciences, biochemistry, biology, botany, chemistry, geology, geophysics, mathematics, meteorology, microbiology, physics, zoology), PHILOSOPHY (philosophy), PREPROFESSIONAL (agriculture, architecture, engineering, environmental design, geosciences, science), SOCIAL SCIENCES (anthropology, economics, geography, government/political science, history, psychology, sociology). Fifty-seven percent of degrees conferred are in preprofessional areas, 19% in business, 7% in education, and 8% in liberal arts.

Required: Biology, chemistry, English, history, mathematics, and 2 years of physical education are required of all students.

Special: Professional degrees are offered in medicine and veterinary medicine.

Honors: The university offers a university honors program with courses in many departments. There are 34 national honor societies on campus.

Admissions: Eighty-five percent of those who applied were accepted for the 1981–82 freshman class. Of those who enrolled, the SAT scores were as follows: Verbal—60% below 500, 30% between 500 and 599, 9% between 600 and 700, and 1% above 700; Math—33% below 500, 42% between 500 and 599, 22% between 600 and 700, and 3% above 700. Candidates should have completed 16 Carnegie units and rank in the top 75% of their graduating class. Other factors considered in the admissions decision are advanced placement or honors courses, impressions made during an interview, extracurricular activities record, and leadership record. The school attempts to achieve national geographic distribution of the student body, although Texas residents are given preference. Out-of-state applicants must rank in the top quarter of their class and score 1000 on the SAT.

Procedure: The SAT is required and should be taken by January of the senior year. The deadline for fall admissions is July 31; applications for spring and summer entry should be submitted as soon as possible. Notification is on a rolling basis. There is no application fee.

Special: Early admissions and early decision plans are available. CLEP and AP credit is accepted.

Transfer: For fall 1981, 8060 students applied, 7701 were accepted, and 2973 enrolled. Transfer students must be in good standing at their previous school. Those entering with 45 or less completed credit hours must have a 3.0 GPA; with 46 to 60, a 2.5; and with 61 or more, a 2.0. D grades transfer. Students must complete, at the university, 30 of the last 36 credits—including 12 hours of upper division work in their major—toward the 128 credit hours necessary for a bachelor's degree. Application deadlines are the same as those for freshmen.

Visiting: There are regularly scheduled orientations for prospective students. Guides are also available for informal campus visits; visits should be arranged through the information center.

Financial Aid: About 33% of all students receive some form of financial aid. Twenty-five percent work part-time on campus. Average aid to freshmen is $1584. Two hundred and fifty scholarships are awarded annually to freshmen. The university is a member of CSS and requires the FAF. Application deadlines are April 1 (fall), September 15 (spring), and January 15 (summer).

Foreign Students: Five percent of the full-time students come from foreign countries. The university offers these students an intensive English course and program, special counseling, and special organizations.

Admissions: Foreign students must achieve a minimum TOEFL score of 550 or take either the University of Michigan Language Test or the university's own English proficiency exam. Freshmen applicants who have been attending an American high school must achieve a combined SAT score of 800 and rank in the top 10% of their class.

Procedure: Application deadlines are June 15 (fall), November 1 (spring), and March 15 (summer). Foreign students must present a completed university health form with proof of immunizations and proof of funds adequate to cover 1 year of study. Special fees include $50 for evaluation of credentials and $45 for English assessment.

Admissions Contact: Billy G. Lay, Director of Admissions.

TEXAS A&M UNIVERSITY AT GALVESTON   E-4
Galveston, Texas 77553   (713) 845-1031

F/T: 392M, 112W   Faculty: 53; IIB, av$
P/T: 43M, 33W   Ph.D.'s: 78%
Grad: none   S/F Ratio: 13 to 1
Year: sems, ss   Tuition: $379 ($1359)
Appl: open   R and B: $2491
SAT: required   LESS COMPETITIVE

Texas A&M University at Galveston is a publicly controlled undergraduate institution that offers programs in marine sciences.

Environment: The urban campus includes 2 dormitories that house 241 students. The campus also includes a swimming pool and tennis courts.

Student Life: About 88% of the students live on campus. Drinking is forbidden. Campus housing is both coed and single-sex; there are visiting privileges in the single-sex housing. Students may keep cars on campus.

Organizations: The 10 extracurricular activity clubs include social service groups and dorm organizations. There are no sororities, fraternities, or religious organizations. The university generally sponsors 1 or 2 events, such as films or dances, each week.

Sports: The university fields 1 intercollegiate team for men. There are 8 intramural sports for men and 7 for women.

Graduates: About 12% of the freshmen drop out, and almost all the rest remain to graduate.

Services: Psychological and career counseling, health care, and placement assistance are offered free to students. Tutoring is provided for a fee.

Programs of Study: The university awards the B.S. degree. Bachelor's degrees are offered in the following subjects: BUSINESS (maritime administration), MATH AND SCIENCES (marine biology, marine fisheries, marine sciences), PREPROFESSIONAL (engineering—marine, engineering—maritime systems, marine transportation).

Required: Students must maintain an average of 2.0 in all courses and in the major field to graduate.

Honors: All departments offer honors programs.

Admissions: Applicants must be graduates of accredited high schools.

Procedure: The SAT and ATs in English and mathematics are required. Admissions decisions are made on a rolling basis. There is no application fee. Deadlines are open; freshmen are admitted in the fall, spring, and summer terms.

Special: Early decision and early admissions plans are offered. AP and CLEP credit may be earned.

Transfer: Applicants must present a GPA of 2.0 or better from their previous school. D grades generally transfer. All students must complete, at the university, 30 of the 128 credits required for a bachelor's degree.

Visiting: The university schedules orientations for prospective students. Guides also are available for informal weekday visits.

Financial Aid: Fifty percent of the students receive aid through the university. Twenty percent work part-time on campus. University-administered state and federal loan funds are available. CWS jobs also are available in all departments. The university is a member of CSS; the FAF and the IRS 1040 or 1040A are required. Applications should be submitted by April 1.

Foreign Students: One percent of the full-time students come from foreign countries.

Admissions: For information on admissions criteria, foreign students should contact the admissions office.

Procedure: Application deadlines are June 15 (fall), November 1 (spring), and March 15 (summer).

Admissions Contact: Registrar's Office.

TEXAS CHRISTIAN UNIVERSITY   D-2
Fort Worth, Texas 76129   (817) 921-7490

F/T: 1848M, 2572W   Faculty: 366; I, — —$
P/T: 586M, 628W   Ph.D.'s: 80%
Grad: 485M, 439W   S/F Ratio: 16 to 1
Year: sems, ss   Tuition: $3300
Appl: June 1   R and B: $1374–1710
2225 applied   1879 accepted   1089 enrolled
SAT: 493V 460M   ACT: 21   COMPETITIVE

Texas Christian University, founded in 1873, is a private university affiliated with the Disciples of Christ but open to students of all faiths. The library, which contains over 1 million volumes and subscribes to 9000 periodicals, is being doubled in size.

Environment: The 243-acre campus, located in a suburban area 4 miles from downtown Fort Worth, includes a golf course and a 5-court indoor tennis center. There is a new visual arts and communications building. Sixteen residence halls house approximately 4000 students. The university also sponsors fraternity and sorority houses.

Student Life: About 56% of the students are from Texas. Sixty-six percent of the students live in dormitories. Twenty percent of the students are Catholic. Eight percent are minority-group members. University housing is single-sex, and there are visiting privileges. Alcoholic beverages are permitted only in dorm rooms. Students may keep cars on campus.

Organizations: Thirty percent of the men and 38% of the women belong to 10 national fraternities and 12 national sororities. Extracurricular activities are numerous, and there are religious organizations for most of the faiths represented on campus. Art museums, opera, ballet, and the Fort Worth Symphony attract many students to cultural events off campus.

Sports: The university fields 11 intercollegiate sports for men and 8 for women. There are 12 intramural sports for men and 11 for women.

Handicapped: Facilities for disabled students include special parking, special rest rooms, elevators, and wheelchair ramps.

Graduates: Fifty-five percent of the freshmen remain to graduate. Of the graduates, 25% pursue advanced study; 2% enter medical school.

Services: Students receive the following services free of charge: placement service, psychological counseling, career counseling, and tutoring. Health care is available for a fee.

884 TEXAS

Programs of Study: The university confers the B.A., B.F.A., B.M., B.M.Ed., B.B.A., B.S., and B.S.N. degrees. Master's and doctoral degrees are also awarded. Bachelor's degrees are offered in the following subjects: AREA STUDIES (Latin American, urban), BUSINESS (accounting, business administration, computer science, finance, management, marketing, real estate/insurance), EDUCATION (bilingual, elementary, health/physical, secondary, special), ENGLISH (advertising/public relations, broadcast journalism, English, journalism, speech), FINE AND PERFORMING ARTS (art, art education, art history, ballet, church music, commercial art, dance, film/photography, history/literature of music, human relations, music, music education, music performance, music theory/composition, musical theater, radio/TV/film, speech education, studio art, theater/dramatics, theater education), HEALTH SCIENCES (medical technology, nursing, speech pathology/deaf education), LANGUAGES (French, German, Spanish), MATH AND SCIENCES (astronomy, biochemistry, biology, chemistry, ecology/environmental science, geology, mathematics, neuroscience, physics), PHILOSOPHY (classics, philosophy, religion), PREPROFESSIONAL (child development, fashion/clothing/textiles, home economics, home economics education, interior design, nutrition and dietetics), SOCIAL SCIENCES (archival studies, comparative studies, criminal justice, economics, government/political science, history, international relations, psychology, social work, sociology).

Required: One semester of religion and 2 semesters of physical education are required.

Special: It is possible to earn combined B.A.-B.S. degrees in comparative studies, environmental science, and premedicine. Student-designed majors are allowed, and a general studies degree is available. Cooperative degree programs are offered with the School of Fine Arts, as well as a cooperative 4-year program in medical technology with Harris Hospital, and a cooperative 9-month work-study ranch training program with various ranches in the Southwest. Language study in Europe and Mexico is available.

Honors: The university has a 4-year honors program, as well as honors sections, upperclass research and tutorials, and interdepartmental colloquia. The national honor societies Phi Beta Kappa and Sigma Xi are represented on campus.

Admissions: Eighty-four percent of those who applied were accepted for the 1981–82 freshman class. Of those who enrolled, the SAT scores were as follows: Verbal—66% below 500, 25% between 500 and 599, 8% between 600 and 700, and 1% above 700; Math—52% below 500, 32% between 500 and 599, 13% between 600 and 700, and 3% above 700. Candidates should have completed 13 Carnegie high school units and have a class rank in the upper 50%. A personal interview is recommended. Also important in the admissions decision are advanced placement or honors courses, recommendations by school officials, and the extracurricular activities record.

Procedure: The SAT or ACT is required. The university prefers to receive applications by June 1 (fall), December 1 (spring), and May 1 (summer). Notification is on a rolling basis. Applications should be submitted with a $15 fee.

Transfer: For fall 1981, 904 students applied, 741 were accepted, and 554 enrolled. A minimum GPA of 2.0 is required; D grades transfer. Students must complete, at the university, 30 of the 124 credits necessary for a bachelor's degree. Application deadlines are August 1 (fall), December 1 (spring), and May 1 (summer).

Visiting: There is a Friday on Campus program for prospective students every fall and spring. Informal weekday visits can be scheduled, except during Thanksgiving and Christmas holidays. Guides are available, and visitors may sit in on classes. Prospective students, but not parents, may stay overnight at the school. Arrangements should be made through the admissions office.

Financial Aid: Over 60% of the students receive aid through the school. Twenty-five percent work part-time on campus. The university provides freshman scholarships each year. Loans and EOG grants also are available. The university is a member of CSS and requires the FAF. Application deadlines are June 1 (fall), December 1 (spring), and April 1 (summer).

Foreign Students: Six percent of the full-time students come from foreign countries. The university offers these students special counseling and special organizations.

Admissions: Foreign students must achieve a minimum TOEFL score of 450 or take the university's own English proficiency exam. No college entrance exam must be taken.

Procedure: Application deadlines are July 15 (fall) and December 4 (spring). Foreign students must present proof of funds adequate to cover 4 years of study. They must also carry health insurance, which is available through the university for a fee.

Admissions Contact: Edward G. Boehm, Jr., Dean of Admissions.

TEXAS COLLEGE E–2
Tyler, Texas 75701 (214) 593-8311

F/T: 252M, 265W	Faculty: 56; IIB, ––$
P/T: 85M, 27W	Ph.D.'s: 40%
Grad: none	S/F Ratio: 16 to 1
Year: sems, ss	Tuition: $3700
Appl: Aug. 15	R and B: $1800
300 applied	270 accepted	240 enrolled
SAT: required		LESS COMPETITIVE

Texas College, founded in 1894, is a liberal arts institution affiliated with the Colored Methodist Episcopal Church. The library contains more than 70,000 volumes, and subscribes to more than 500 periodicals.

Environment: The 66-acre campus is located in a city of 66,000 people, about 100 miles from Dallas. The 16 campus buildings include 5 dormitories that house more than 400 students. Other students live in a 120-unit apartment complex and in several single-family homes.

Student Life: About 70% of the students come from Texas. More than half live on campus in the single-sex dorms. The student body is predominately black. Drinking is forbidden on campus. Vespers and special chapel programs are held.

Organizations: Most of the students belong to a fraternity or sorority. Extracurricular activities include student government, publications, music and drama, and academic clubs. The major campus social events are the Homecoming Ball and football game, and the coronation of Miss Texas College.

Sports: The college sponsors intercollegiate teams in 2 sports for men and 2 for women. Intramural sports also are available.

Graduates: About 15% of the freshmen drop out, and 66% remain to graduate. Eleven percent of the graduates seek advanced degrees.

Services: The college provides free placement services, career and psychological counseling, tutoring, and remedial instruction.

Programs of Study: The college confers the B.A. and B.S. degrees. Bachelor's degrees are offered in the following subjects: BUSINESS (business administration, business education, office administration), EDUCATION (elementary, health/physical, secondary, vocational), ENGLISH (English), FINE AND PERFORMING ARTS (music, music education), HEALTH SCIENCES (medical technology), MATH AND SCIENCES (biology, mathematics), PREPROFESSIONAL (home economics), SOCIAL SCIENCES (history, psychology, social sciences, social services, sociology).

Required: All students must take courses in religion, English, foreign language, history, political science, physical education, a lab science, and mathematics. Freshmen must complete a speech and reading-development program.

Special: Students may spend their junior year abroad and design their own majors.

Admissions: About 90% of those who applied were accepted for the 1981–82 freshman class. Applicants must be graduates of accredited high schools, rank in the top 75% of their class, and have completed 16 Carnegie units with a C average or better. A GED also is acceptable.

Procedure: The SAT is required for guidance purposes only. The application deadline for fall entry is August 15. Students also are admitted to other terms; applications must be filed at least 2 weeks before registration. There is a $10 application fee. Students are admitted on a rolling basis. An interview is recommended.

Special: The college offers an early admissions plan.

Transfer: Applicants should have an average of C or better. Students must complete at least 30 semester hours in residence of the 124 required for a bachelor's degree.

Financial Aid: About 95% of the students receive aid. Need and athletic scholarships, state and federal loans, work contracts, and CWS jobs are available. Tuition may be paid in installments. Need is the primary consideration in determining awards. The FAF is required, and aid applications must be submitted 2 weeks before the beginning of the semester.

Foreign Students: Students from foreign countries make up 18% of enrollment. The college offers these students special counseling.

Admissions: Applicants must score 500 or better on the TOEFL. They also must take the SAT.

Procedure: Application deadlines are the same as those for American students. Foreign students must submit a completed medical form and show evidence of adequate funds for 1 year. Health insurance is required and is available through the college for a fee.

Admissions Contact: Mac T. Turner, Director of Admissions.

TEXAS LUTHERAN COLLEGE D-4
Seguin, Texas 78155 (512) 379-4161

F/T: 480M, 505W	*Faculty:* 59; IIB, av$
P/T: 208M, 140W	*Ph.D.'s:* 62%
Grad: none	*S/F Ratio:* 15 to 1
Year: 4-1-4	*Tuition:* $2550
Appl: Aug. 1	*R and B:* $1525
559 applied	435 accepted	292 enrolled
SAT: 480V 440M	*ACT:* 21	COMPETITIVE

Texas Lutheran College, founded in 1891, is a liberal arts college owned and operated by the American Lutheran Church. The library contains 87,000 volumes.

Environment: Located in a suburban area 34 miles from San Antonio, the 101-acre campus has 17 major buildings. The 9 dormitories accommodate 362 women and 340 men. There are on-campus apartments for upperclassmen.

Student Life: About 79% of the students are from Texas. About 90% live in dormitories. Seventy-seven percent of the students are Protestant, 15% are Catholic, and 3% are Jewish. Sixteen percent are minority-group members. College housing is coed and single-sex; students in single-sex housing have visiting privileges. Students may keep cars on campus. Alcohol is prohibited on campus.

Organizations: There are 5 fraternities and 4 sororities, to which 18% of the men and 19% of the women belong.

Sports: The college fields 5 intercollegiate teams for men and 4 for women. There are 3 intramural sports for men and 2 for women.

Handicapped: Special facilities for wheelchair-bound students include ramps and elevators.

Graduates: The freshman dropout rate is 30%, and 40% remain to graduate. About 20% of the graduates go on to graduate school; 3% enter medical school, 2% enter dental school, and 2% enter law school. Sixty percent pursue careers in business and industry.

Services: Students receive the following services free of charge: health care, psychological counseling, career counseling, tutoring, and remedial instruction. Placement services are available for a fee.

Programs of Study: The college confers the B.A., B.S., and B.Mus.Ed. degrees with majors in the following subjects: BUSINESS (accounting, business administration, business education, finance, management, marketing), EDUCATION (elementary, health/physical, secondary), ENGLISH (English), FINE AND PERFORMING ARTS (art education, communication arts, music, music education, visual arts), HEALTH SCIENCES (physical therapy), LANGUAGES (German, Spanish), MATH AND SCIENCES (biology, chemistry, mathematics), PHILOSOPHY (philosophy, religion), PREPROFESSIONAL (dentistry, engineering, law, medicine, ministry, pharmacy, social work, veterinary), SOCIAL SCIENCES (economics, government/political science, history, psychology, sociology). Thirty percent of the degrees conferred are in education, 18% in social sciences, and 17% in business.

Required: All students must take theology courses and 29 hours of general courses fulfilling the distribution requirement, including 12 hours of humanities for sophomores.

Special: A select number of qualified students may design their own curricula. There is a 2-year engineering program. There is a junior year abroad program (a cooperative exchange with the University of Bonn in Germany) and travel tours during the January interim. The interim exchange program is conducted with 10 colleges around the country. Pass/fail options are available in all interim courses.

Honors: There is a campus-wide scholars program.

Admissions: About 78% of the students who applied for the 1981–82 freshman class were accepted. Of those who enrolled for a recent freshman class, the SAT scores were as follows: Verbal—11% between 500 and 599, and 1% between 600 and 700; Math—17% between 500 and 599, 6% between 600 and 700, and 1% above 700. Candidates should have completed 16 Carnegie units, including 13 in academic areas, rank in the top 40% of their class, and have a minimum SAT total score of 750 or an ACT composite of 15. Recommendations from school officials are also considered in the admissions decision.

Procedure: The PSAT should be taken in March of the junior year. The SAT or ACT is required and should be taken by the beginning of the senior year. Application deadlines are August 1 (fall), January 1 (spring), and May 1 (summer). Notification is on a rolling basis. There is a $10 application fee.

Special: Early admissions and early decision plans are available. AP and CLEP credit is accepted.

Transfer: For fall 1981, 134 students applied, 99 were accepted, and 80 enrolled. A 2.0 average is required for transfer; standardized exam scores and an interview are also required. D grades transfer. Students must complete, at the college, 30 semester hours toward a bachelor's degree. Application deadlines are the same as those for freshmen.

Visiting: Prospective students are invited to orientation weekends in the spring. Guides are available for tours on class days from 9 to 11 A.M. and from 2 to 4 P.M. Visitors may sit in on classes and stay overnight at the school. Arrangements should be made with the admissions office.

Financial Aid: About 80% of all students receive financial aid. Thirty-one percent work part-time on campus. Average aid to freshmen covers 58% of costs. Scholarships and loans are available. The college is a member of the CSS and requires the FAF. Aid applications must be submitted by March.

Foreign Students: Fewer than 1% of the full-time students come from foreign countries. The college offers these students special counseling.

Admissions: Foreign students must achieve a minimum TOEFL score of 500. No college entrance exam must be taken.

Procedure: Application deadlines are March 1 (fall), August 1 (spring), and December 1 (summer). Foreign students must present proof of health and proof of adequate funds. They must also carry health insurance, which is available through the college for a fee.

Admissions Contact: Robert A. Miller, Director of Admissions.

TEXAS SOUTHERN UNIVERSITY E-3
Houston, Texas 77004 (713) 527-7011

F/T: 3400M, 3000W	*Faculty:* 498; I, --$
P/T: 900M, 700W	*Ph.D.'s:* 50%
Grad: 800M, 600W	*S/F Ratio:* 14 to 1
Year: sems, ss	*Tuition:* $532 ($1828)
Appl: Aug. 14	*R and B:* $2000
SAT or ACT: required	NONCOMPETITIVE

Texas Southern University, founded in 1947, is a state-supported institution offering programs in business, education, the liberal arts and sciences, and preprofessional fields. The library contains 265,000 volumes and 131,000 microfilm items, and subscribes to 2093 periodicals.

Environment: The 59-acre campus is located 5 miles from downtown Houston, between Rice University and the University of Houston. It has 7 dormitories housing 424 women and 446 men as well as accommodations for 54 married couples. Day students have a cafeteria, dining hall, lounge, and lockers.

Student Life: About 90% of the students are from Texas. Eleven percent live on campus in single-sex dorms. The student body is predominately black. Drinking is prohibited, and smoking is not allowed in classrooms.

Organizations: Four percent of the men and 4% of the women belong to 7 fraternities and 7 sororities with chapters on campus. Religious organizations and counselors are available for Catholic and Protestant students.

Sports: The university competes on an intercollegiate level in 7 sports. Intramural sports also are offered.

Handicapped: About 80% of the campus is accessible to handicapped students. Special facilities include wheelchair ramps, elevators, and lowered drinking fountains.

Graduates: About 40% of the freshmen drop out, and 25% remain to graduate. Eight percent of the graduates go on to further study; 1% enter medical school and 2% enter law school. Ten percent pursue careers in business and industry.

Services: Students receive the following free services: psychological counseling, career counseling, placement aid, tutoring, and remedial instruction.

Programs of Study: The university confers the B.A., B.B.A., B.F.A., B.M., B.Mus.Ed., B.S., B.S.Elem.Ed., B.S.H.E., B.S.Bus., B.S.Med.Tech., B.S.Tech., and B.S.Pharm. degrees. Master's and doctoral degrees also are awarded. Bachelor's degrees are offered in the following subjects: AREA STUDIES (Black/Afro-American), BUSINESS (accounting, business administration, business education, computer science, housing management, office administration), EDUCATION (early

886 TEXAS

childhood, elementary, health/physical, industrial, secondary), ENGLISH (communications, English, journalism), FINE AND PERFORMING ARTS (art, art education, music, music education, film/photography, theater/dramatics), HEALTH SCIENCES (dietetics, medical records administration, medical technology, physical therapy, respiratory therapy), LANGUAGES (French, German, Spanish), MATH AND SCIENCES (biology, chemistry, mathematics, physics), PREPROFESSIONAL (home economics, industrial arts, law, pharmacy, social work, technology), SOCIAL SCIENCES (administration of justice, economics, government/political science, history, psychology, public affairs, public services, sociology).

Required: All students must take a distribution of academic courses.

Special: Work-study programs are provided in several areas.

Honors: An honors program is available.

Admissions: The university has an open enrollment policy; all who applied were accepted for a recent freshman class. A candidate should have completed 15 Carnegie high school units with an average of at least C+. Non-high-school graduates may sometimes be admitted on the basis of GED test scores. For out-of-state applicants, a letter of recommendation from the high school is required.

Procedure: The SAT or ACT is required. A rolling admissions policy is used. The deadlines for application are August 14 (fall) and December 24 (spring). There is no application fee.

Transfer: An average of C is necessary for transfer. Students must spend at least 1 year in residence to qualify for a bachelor's degree.

Visiting: Guides are available for informal visits. Overnight accommodations can be arranged with the office of recruitment.

Financial Aid: About 80% of the students receive aid through the school. Freshman scholarships, grants, state and federal loans, and campus jobs are available. Either the FAF or FFS must be filed. Aid application deadlines are April 1 (fall) and November 1 (spring).

Admissions Contact: Director of Admissions.

TEXAS TECH UNIVERSITY B-2
Lubbock, Texas 79409 (806) 742-3661

F/T: 9529M, 7402W Faculty: 982; I, --$
P/T: 1240M, 1117W Ph.D.'s: 79%
Grad: 1651M, 1356W S/F Ratio: 17 to 1
Year: sems, ss Tuition: $460 ($1540)
Appl: Aug. 15 R and B: $1800
SAT or ACT: required LESS COMPETITIVE

Texas Tech University, established in 1923, is a state-controlled institution offering undergraduate degree programs in a variety of applied, technical, and vocational areas. The library contains 1.5 million volumes and 421,000 microfilm items, and subscribes to 6600 periodicals.

Environment: The 1839-acre campus is located in an urban area 320 miles west of Dallas. Residence halls accommodate 3466 men and 4312 women.

Student Life: About 95% of the students come from Texas; the majority are public school graduates. Nine percent of the students are minority-group members. University housing is coed and single-sex; students in single-sex housing have visiting privileges. Students may keep cars on campus.

Organizations: Eight percent of the men belong to 20 fraternities; 7% of the women belong to 15 sororities. Extracurricular activities include publications, student government, religious organizations, and music and drama groups.

Sports: The university fields 16 intercollegiate teams for men and 12 for women. There are 10 intramural sports for men and 7 for women.

Handicapped: Facilities for handicapped students include wheelchair ramps and parking areas. Two counselors are available to handicapped students.

Graduates: The freshman dropout rate is 25%; about 40% remain to graduate. Thirty-five percent of the graduates pursue advanced degrees.

Services: Career counseling, placement, and health care are provided free of charge to all students. Some tutoring, some psychological counseling, and all health care require a fee.

Programs of Study: The university confers the B.A., B.B.A., B.F.A., B.Mus., B.Mus.Ed., B.Arch., B.S., B.S.Ed., B.S.Med.Tech., B.S. in Eng., B.S. in Eng. Physics, B.S. in Textile Technology and Management, B.S. in P.Ed., B.S. in Mech. Agr., and B.S.H.E. degrees. Master's and doctoral degrees are also offered. Bachelor's degrees are offered in the following subjects: AREA STUDIES (Latin American), BUSINESS (accounting, business administration, computer science, finance, management, marketing), EDUCATION (adult, early childhood, elementary, health/physical, secondary, special), ENGLISH (English, journalism, speech), FINE AND PERFORMING ARTS (art, art education, art history, dance, music, music education, studio art, theater/dramatics), HEALTH SCIENCES (medical technology, nursing, occupational therapy, physical therapy), LANGUAGES (French, German, Greek/Latin, Spanish), MATH AND SCIENCES (biology, botany, chemistry, geology, mathematics, physics, zoology), PHILOSOPHY (philosophy), PREPROFESSIONAL (agriculture, architecture, dentistry, engineering, home economics, law, medicine, pharmacy, social work, veterinary), SOCIAL SCIENCES (anthropology, economics, geography, government/political science, history, international relations, psychology, sociology). About 22% of the degrees are conferred in business and 17% in math and sciences.

Required: Required courses include English, American history, political science, mathematics, science, and physical education.

Special: Student-designed majors, a B.G.S. degree, independent study, study abroad, internships, and exchange programs are offered.

Honors: Honors work is possible in many departments. There are several honor societies on campus.

Admissions: Ninety-five percent of those who applied were accepted for the 1981-82 freshman class. The SAT scores of those who enrolled were as follows: Verbal—77% below 500, 18% between 500 and 599, 4% between 600 and 700, and 1% above 700; Math—60% below 500, 27% between 500 and 599, 12% between 600 and 700, and 1% above 700. On the ACT, 58% scored below 21, 19% between 21 and 23, 13% between 24 and 25, 6% between 26 and 28, and 4% above 28. Candidates should be graduates of accredited high schools and rank in the upper 75% of the graduating class. Out-of-state applicants should rank in the upper 50%. Standardized exam scores also enter into the admissions decision.

Procedure: Either the SAT or ACT is required and should be taken by March of the senior year. Application deadlines are August 15 (fall), December 15 (spring), and May 15 (summer). Notification is on a rolling basis. There is no application fee.

Special: AP and CLEP credit is available.

Transfer: For fall 1981, 2467 students applied, 1889 were accepted, and 1449 enrolled. A 2.0 GPA is needed; standardized exam scores are required if less than 15 hours are transferred. D grades are not acceptable. Thirty semester hours must be completed in residence. Application deadlines are the same as those for freshmen.

Visiting: Campus tours with student guides can be arranged. Visitors may sit in on classes and stay overnight at the school. Visits are best scheduled on weekdays. The office of new student relations should be contacted for arrangements.

Financial Aid: About 25% of the students receive financial aid. Nine percent work part-time on campus. Average aid to freshmen is $1200. The university participates in state and federal assistance programs such as NDSL, CWS, and BEOG/SEOG, in addition to offering commercial loans, short-term university loans, and both academic merit and need-based scholarships. Preference is given to state residents. The university is a member of CSS. The FFS is preferred, although the FAF is accepted. Deadlines for financial aid applications are June 1 (fall), October 1 (spring), and March 1 (summer).

Foreign Students: The university offers foreign students an intensive English program, special counseling, and special organizations.

Admissions: Foreign students must achieve a minimum TOEFL score of 550. They must also take either the SAT (scoring at least 1000) or the ACT.

Procedure: Application deadlines are April 30 (fall) and October 1 (spring). Foreign students must present a completed university health form and proof of funds adequate to cover a 12-month period, except for students who go home for the summer.

Admissions Contact: Dale Grusing, Director of Undergraduate Admissions.

TEXAS WESLEYAN COLLEGE D-2
Fort Worth, Texas 76105 (817) 534-0251

F/T: 750M, 850W Faculty: 114; IIB, av$
P/T: 175M&W Ph.D.'s: 54%
Grad: 57M, 123W S/F Ratio: 12 to 1
Year: sems, ss Tuition: $2900
Appl: see profile R and B: $2500
620 applied 510 accepted 320 enrolled
SAT: 885 (composite) ACT: 20 COMPETITIVE

Texas Wesleyan College, established in 1891 and affiliated with the United Methodist Church, includes 4 undergraduate schools: the School of Business, the School of Education, the School of Fine Arts, and the School of Science and Humanities. The library contains 126,030 volumes and 20,000 microfilm items, and subscribes to 840 periodicals.

Environment: The 50-acre hilltop campus, overlooking Fort Worth and the surrounding area, has 23 buildings. Three residence halls house approximately 300 men and women.

Student Life: All but 10% of the students come from Texas. About 10% live on campus. Both single-sex and coed dorms are available.

Organizations: Eleven percent of the men and 9% of the women belong to the 3 national fraternities and 3 sororities with chapters on campus. There are 2 national service fraternities as well. In addition to campus activities, organizations, and publications, students have access to cultural and recreational opportunities in Fort Worth.

Sports: The college competes on an intercollegiate level in 4 sports for men and 4 for women. Intramural sports also are available.

Handicapped: About 75% of the campus is accessible to handicapped students. Special facilities include wheelchair ramps, parking areas, and elevators. Special class scheduling is also available.

Graduates: Thirty percent of graduates go on to further study. Thirty-five percent begin careers in business and industry.

Services: Students receive the following services free: health care, psychological counseling, career counseling, and placement aid.

Programs of Study: The university confers the B.A., B.S., B.B.A., and B.M. degrees. Master's degrees also are awarded. Bachelor's degrees are offered in the following subjects: BUSINESS (accounting, business administration, business education, business/psychology, international business, management, marketing, office administration), EDUCATION (Christian, early childhood, elementary, health/physical, secondary), ENGLISH (English, mass communications, speech), FINE AND PERFORMING ARTS (art, art education, music, music education, theater/dramatics), HEALTH SCIENCES (medical technology), LANGUAGES (French, German, Spanish), MATH AND SCIENCES (biology, chemistry, ecology/environmental science, geology, mathematics, natural sciences, physics), PHILOSOPHY (humanities, philosophy, religion), SOCIAL SCIENCES (criminal justice, economics, government/political science, history, psychology, social sciences, sociology).

Special: Nonmajor preprofessional programs are offered in medicine, dentistry, law, ministry, and church administration.

Required: Students must take a core of courses in English, laboratory science, history, physical education, political science, mathematics, social sciences, fine arts, and humanities.

Honors: Six national honor societies have chapters on campus.

Admissions: Eighty-two percent of those who applied were accepted for the 1981-82 freshman class. Of those who enrolled, the SAT scores were as follows: Verbal—38% below 500, 31% between 500 and 599, 21% between 600 and 700, and 1% above 700; Math—50% below 500, 25% between 500 and 599, 20% between 600 and 700, and 5% above 700. Of those who took the ACT, 62% scored below 21, 20% between 21 and 23, 5% between 24 and 25, 4% between 26 and 28, and 8% above 28. Applicants should have completed 16 Carnegie units and should rank in the upper 50% of their high school class.

Procedure: Either the SAT or ACT is required. Admission is on a rolling basis. Freshmen are admitted each semester; applications must be filed at least 30 days before registration. The application fee is $10.

Special: A deferred admissions plan is available. CLEP and AP credit is accepted.

Transfer: Applicants must have a minimum GPA of 1.65-2.0, depending on the number of credit hours earned. Students must earn at least 30 semester hours at the college of the 124 required for a bachelor's degree.

Visiting: Orientation weekends are held in the fall and spring. Informal visits can be arranged for Monday through Thursday with the admissions office. Guides are available, and visitors may sit in on classes and stay overnight at the school.

Financial Aid: About 74% of the students receive aid in the form of scholarships, grants, loans, and campus jobs. Merit scholarships are awarded to freshmen. The average aid award to a 1981-82 freshman totaled $1720. The Wesleyan Fellow Program offers full tuition, fees, and books to high school class valedictorians and full tuition to salutatorians. Applications should be submitted by April 15 for priority consideration.

Foreign Students: Students from foreign countries make up about 3% of enrollment. The college offers these students an intensive English course, an intensive English program, special counseling, and special organizations.

Admissions: Applicants must take the TOEFL or the college's own test of English proficiency. The minimum acceptable score on the TOEFL is 550. No college entrance exams are required.

Procedure: Foreign students are admitted to all terms. They must apply at least 45 days before registration. A completed health form and proof of adequate funds for 1 year are required. Students must carry health insurance, which is available through the college for a fee.

Admissions Contact: Larry Smith, Director of Admissions.

TEXAS WOMAN'S UNIVERSITY   D-2
Denton, Texas 76204   (817) 566-1451

F/T: 110M, 2966W
P/T: 26M, 836W
Grad: 443M, 3117W
Year: sems, ss
Appl: open
1100 applied
SAT or ACT: required

Faculty: n/av; I, --$
Ph.D.'s: n/av
S/F Ratio: 18 to 1
Tuition: $226 ($1418)
R and B: $1966-2370

900 accepted   750 enrolled
LESS COMPETITIVE

Texas Woman's University, a state-controlled institution established in 1901, offers degree programs in the liberal arts and sciences, business, education, health fields, and the professions. The library holds 816,000 volumes and 181,000 microfilm items, and subscribes to more than 2700 periodicals.

Environment: The 270-acre suburban campus is located in a city of 50,000 people, about 35 miles from Dallas-Forth Worth. The residence halls accommodate 2800 students. Research facilities include radiation-chemistry equipment, nutrition laboratories, and an electron microscope. Art, music, radio, and television studios; therapy laboratories; and a nursery school and child-care center also are available.

Student Life: About 85% of the students come from Texas, and 98% are public-school graduates. Forty percent live on campus. About 19% of the students are minority-group members. Campus housing is single-sex; there are visiting privileges. Students may keep cars on campus. Day-care services are available to all students, faculty, and staff.

Organizations: The extracurricular program includes student government, publications, music and drama groups, special-interest clubs, and religious and service organizations. The university sponsors various cultural events, and additional cultural and recreational activities are available in Denton and in Dallas-Fort Worth. About 35% of the women belong to sororities; there are no fraternities.

Sports: The university fields 8 intercollegiate teams for women. There are 8 intramural sports for women.

Handicapped: About 95% of the campus is accessible to physically handicapped students. Facilities include wheelchair ramps, elevators, specially equipped rest rooms, special parking areas, lowered drinking fountains and telephones, and audiovisual materials. Student assistants, sign-language courses, and audiovisual materials are available to visually or hearing impaired students. Special counselors are provided.

Graduates: About 10% of the freshmen drop out, and 35% remain to graduate. Thirty-five percent of the graduates go on for further study (including 1% to medical school, 1% to dental school, and 2% to law school). Another 15% of the graduates begin business careers.

Services: Free psychological, career, and placement counseling; tutoring; and remedial instruction are provided. Health care is available on a fee basis.

Programs of Study: The university awards the B.A., B.S., B.F.A., and B.S.W. degrees. Master's and doctoral degrees also are available. Bachelor's degrees are offered in the following subjects: BUSINESS (accounting, business administration, business education, management, marketing), EDUCATION (early childhood, elementary, health/physical, secondary, special), ENGLISH (English, journalism, speech), FINE AND PERFORMING ARTS (art, art education, film/photography, dance, music, music education, radio/TV, studio art, theater/dramatics), HEALTH SCIENCES (medical technology, nursing, occupational therapy, physical therapy, speech therapy), LANGUAGES (French, Spanish), MATH AND SCIENCES (biology, chemistry, mathematics, physics), PREPROFESSIONAL (library science, social work), SOCIAL SCIENCES (economics, government/political science, history, psychology, sociology). About 44% of the undergraduate degrees are conferred in health sciences, 15% in fine and performing arts, 14% in math and sciences, and 10% in education.

888 TEXAS

Required: All students must fulfill general-education requirements.

Special: Independent study, study abroad, combination B.A.-B.S. degree programs, and exchange programs are offered.

Honors: Students may enroll in honors sections of courses, in regular courses on an honors basis, and in an honors lecture series.

Admissions: About 82% of the applicants were accepted for the 1981-82 freshman class. Applicants must be graduates of accredited high schools with 16 Carnegie units and a GPA of C or better. High school grades and SAT or ACT scores are of primary importance in the admissions decisions.

Procedure: The SAT or ACT is required. New students are admitted each semester; application deadlines are open. A rolling admissions plan is used. There is no application fee.

Special: Early decision and early admissions programs are available. AP and CLEP credit is accepted.

Transfer: For fall 1981, 1474 transfer students applied, 1200 were accepted, and 1000 enrolled. Applicants should have a C average. D grades generally do not transfer. Students must complete 36 semester hours at the university to graduate; 124 semester hours are required for the bachelor's degree. Application deadlines are open.

Visiting: Guides are provided for informal weekday visits by prospective students. Visitors may attend classes and stay overnight in the dormitories. Arrangements should be made with the admissions office.

Financial Aid: About 45% of the students receive aid. Student loans, part-time jobs, and about 1000 scholarships are available. The FAF must be submitted by June 1.

Foreign Students: About 5% of the full-time students come from foreign countries. The university offers these students special organizations.

Admissions: Foreign students must take the TOEFL or the university's own test of English proficiency. They must also take the SAT or ACT.

Procedure: Application deadlines are open. Foreign students must present proof of health as well as proof of funds adequate to cover 1 semester of study.

Admissions Contact: J. E. Tompkins Jr., Director of Admissions and Registrar.

TRINITY UNIVERSITY D-4
San Antonio, Texas 78284 (512) 736-7207

F/T: 1097M, 1220W	Faculty: 204; IIA, +$
P/T: 138M, 128W	Ph.D.'s: 80%
Grad: 360M, 326W	S/F Ratio: 12 to 1
Year: sems, ss	Tuition: $4021
Appl: July 30	R and B: $2200
1413 applied	1010 accepted 529 enrolled
SAT: 520V 580M	ACT: 26 VERY COMPETITIVE+

Trinity University, founded in 1869, is a private, independent institution. A large new central library holds 485,000 volumes and 205,000 microfilm items, and subscribes to more than 600 periodicals.

Environment: The 107-acre urban campus has 44 buildings, including a communications center, an administrative studies center, and an education building. Coates University Center includes game rooms, TV and music rooms, ballroom, forum, and a coffee house. Fourteen residence halls accommodate over 1400 men and women in a variety of styles, from high-rise to breezeway-connected quads. Additional housing is available in several small apartment complexes adjacent to the campus.

Student Life: Sixty-six percent of the students are from Texas; 65% of entering freshmen come from public schools. Sixty percent of the students live on campus. About 14% are minority-group members. Twenty-five percent are Catholic, 20% are Protestant, and 3% are Jewish. Religious services are held twice weekly but attendance is not compulsory. Campus housing is both coed and single-sex; there are visiting privileges in single-sex dorms. Students may keep cars on campus.

Organizations: Fifteen percent of the men and 20% of the women belong to the 5 local fraternities and 5 sororities. On-campus facilities and extracurricular activities include a bowling alley, a film series, and symphony concerts.

Sports: The university competes on an intercollegiate level in 7 sports for men and 6 for women. There are 15 intramural sports for men and 13 for women.

Handicapped: About 60% of the campus is accessible to wheelchair-bound students. Facilities include wheelchair ramps, special parking, and lowered telephones; special class scheduling can be arranged. For students with visual impairments, or the 4% with hearing impairments, the school provides special assistance when necessary.

Graduates: The freshman dropout rate is 12%; 52% remain to graduate. Of these, 42% go on to graduate study; 3% enter law school, and 4% enter medical school. About 34% pursue careers in business and industry.

Services: Students receive the following services free of charge: psychological counseling, career counseling, placement, health care, tutoring, and remedial instruction.

Programs of Study: The university confers the B.A., B.Mus., and B.S. degrees. Master's degrees are also awarded. Bachelor's degrees are offered in the following subjects: AREA STUDIES (American, Asian, border, inter-American, Latin American), BUSINESS (business administration, computer science), EDUCATION (early childhood, elementary, health/physical, hearing-impaired, secondary, special), ENGLISH (English, journalism, speech), FINE AND PERFORMING ARTS (art, art history, music, music education, radio/TV, studio art, theater/dramatics), LANGUAGES (classical languages, French, German, Spanish), MATH AND SCIENCES (biology, biophysics, chemistry, ecology/environmental science, geology, mathematics, physics), PHILOSOPHY (philosophy, religion), PREPROFESSIONAL (dentistry, engineering, law, medical technology, medicine, ministry, pharmacy, physical therapy, veterinary), SOCIAL SCIENCES (economics, government/political science, history, international relations, psychology, sociology). Twenty-four percent of degrees conferred are in business, 14% in fine and performing arts, 13% in preprofessional studies, and 12% in education.

Required: Freshmen choose from a list of liberal studies in 4 basic groups in the general curriculum.

Special: Combination degree programs are offered in medical technology, physical therapy, and premed. There are interdisciplinary programs in American, Latin American, European, Asian, and border studies, as well as in biophysics. Advanced placement is possible based on high school grades and entrance exam scores. An optional pass/fail system may be used in some courses. Student-designed majors are allowed under carefully monitored conditions. The drama program utilizes the special facilities of the Ruth Taylor Theater on Trinity Hill and the Dallas Theater Center. Study abroad options are also available, although not as part of the regular curriculum.

Honors: Trinity University has an extensive honors program in 8 departments, involving independent study and junior/senior theses. There are 12 national honor societies on campus, including Phi Beta Kappa.

Admissions: Seventy-one percent of those who applied were accepted for the 1981-82 freshman class. Of those who enrolled, the SAT scores were as follows: Verbal—40% below 500, 42% between 500 and 599, 15% between 600 and 700, and 3% above 700; Math—19% below 500, 44% between 500 and 599, 30% between 600 and 700, and 6% above 700. Candidates should have completed a total of 16 high school units. A GPA of at least 3.0 and a high school class rank in the upper 50% are preferred. Engineering and business school applicants must have 2 extra units in math and science. A personal interview is recommended, but not required. Advanced placement or honors courses, recommendations, and evidence of special talent are also considered important.

Procedure: The SAT is required, but the ACT is accepted if the SAT is not available; it should be taken in December, January, or April of the senior year. Deadlines for regular admission are: July 30 (fall), December 1 (spring), and May 1 (summer). Early application for fall admission is urged, as residence spaces are usually filled by mid-June. Freshmen are admitted to all semesters. There is a $15 application fee.

Special: Early decision, early admissions, and deferred admissions plans are available. CLEP and AP credit is accepted.

Transfer: For fall 1981, 354 applications were received, 236 were accepted, and 158 students enrolled. A 2.5 GPA is required: D grades do not transfer. All students must complete, at the university, 30 of the 124 hours required for a bachelor's degree. Application deadlines are the same as those for freshmen.

Visiting: The recommended times for campus visits are October through November or February through March. Guides are available and visitors may sit in on classes. Arrangements can be made by contacting the admissions office.

Financial Aid: Approximately 50% of all students receive some form of financial aid. Twenty-six percent work part-time on campus. Loan funds are available from the federal government, local banks, and private sources, as well as from the university. Merit-based scholarships are also available. The average award to freshmen is $3010. Tuition may be paid in installments. The university is a member of the

CSS and requires the FAF. The deadlines for aid applications are July 30 (May 1 is preferred) for fall entry, December 1 for spring entry, and May 1 for summer entry.

Foreign Students: Four percent of the full-time students come from foreign countries. Special counseling and special organizations are available for these students.

Admissions: Foreign students must achieve a TOEFL score of at least 550. No college entrance exams are required.

Procedure: Application deadlines are May 1 (fall), October 1 (spring), and April 1 (summer). It is recommended that application for fall admission be made by March 1 in order to ensure on-campus residence. Foreign students must present proof of funds adequate to cover 1 year of study. Health insurance is required and is available through the university for a fee.

Admissions Contact: Alberta Meyer, Director of Admissions.

UNIVERSITY OF DALLAS   D-2
Irving, Texas 75061   (214) 579-5266

F/T: 561M, 515W	Faculty: 97; I, --$
P/T: 27M, 51W	Ph.D.'s: 85%
Grad: 1223M, 438W	S/F Ratio: 15 to 1
Year: sems, ss	Tuition: $3272
Appl: Aug. 15	R and B: $2050
862 applied	666 accepted	324 enrolled
SAT: 585V 590M	ACT: 26 HIGHLY COMPETITIVE

University of Dallas, established in 1955, is a small Catholic liberal arts institution, open to all faiths. The library contains 218,800 volumes and 910,015 microfilm items, and subscribes to 1148 periodicals.

Environment: The 1000-acre campus, located in a suburban area 12 miles from Dallas, has 34 air-conditioned buildings, including a student center with an art gallery. Residence halls house 610 men and women. New furnished apartments house an additional 118 students.

Student Life: Seventy-five percent of the students live on campus. Seventy percent are Catholic, 17% are Protestant, and 1% are Jewish. Ten percent of the students are minority-group members. University housing is single-sex, and there are visiting privileges. Students may keep cars on campus.

Organizations: There are no fraternities or sororities. Extracurricular activities include special dinners, dances, plays, publications, and tutorial programs with the underprivileged. There are music and theater groups and special-interest clubs. In addition, students have access to all the cultural (ballet, opera, theater) and recreational opportunities of Dallas.

Sports: The university fields 5 intercollegiate teams for men and 3 for women. There are 7 intramural sports for men and 7 for women.

Handicapped: About 77% of the campus is accessible to handicapped students. Special facilities include wheelchair ramps, designated parking, and elevators.

Graduates: The freshman dropout rate is 18%, and 60% remain to graduate. Seventy percent of the graduates pursue advanced study; 7% enter medical school, and 7% enter law school. Eighteen percent pursue careers in business and industry.

Services: Students receive the following services free of charge: health care (nurse), psychological counseling, and career counseling. Tutoring is available for a fee.

Programs of Study: The university confers the B.S. degree in biochemistry and the B.A. degree in all other areas. Master's and doctoral degrees are also awarded. Bachelor's degrees are offered in the following subjects: EDUCATION (elementary, secondary), ENGLISH (English, literature), FINE AND PERFORMING ARTS (art, art education, art history, studio art, theater/dramatics), LANGUAGES (classics, French, German, Greek/Latin, Spanish), MATH AND SCIENCES (biochemistry, biology, chemistry, mathematics, physics), PHILOSOPHY (classics, philosophy, religion), PREPROFESSIONAL (architecture, dentistry, engineering, law, medicine, ministry, veterinary), SOCIAL SCIENCES (economics, government/political science, history, psychology). The most popular fields of concentration are, in the order listed, biology, economics, psychology, government/political science, and English.

Required: All students must complete a core curriculum.

Special: A semester in Rome is available for sophomores; about 75% of all sophomores participate in this program. Courses appropriate to the locale are selected from the core curriculum to form the central offerings at the Rome campus. Third-year abroad options are also available.

Honors: There is a chapter of Kappa Delta Pi on campus.

Admissions: Seventy-seven percent of those who applied were accepted for the 1981–82 freshman class. Of those who enrolled, the SAT scores were as follows: Verbal—26% below 500, 37% between 500 and 599, 31% between 600 and 700, and 6% above 700; Math—22% below 500, 36% between 500 and 599, 33% between 600 and 700, and 9% above 700. On the ACT, 9% scored below 21, 19% between 21 and 23, 18% between 24 and 25, 28% between 26 and 28, and 26% above 28. A candidate should have completed 16 college prep units, rank in the upper third of the class, and have a minimum grade average of 80. Also important are recommendations by school officials, the extracurricular activities record, the leadership record, and evidence of special talent.

Procedure: Either the SAT or ACT is required. Deadlines for application are August 15 (fall), January 4 (spring), and May 15 (summer). Notification is on a rolling basis. A $15 application fee is charged.

Special: Early and deferred admissions plans and an early decision plan are available. AP credit is accepted.

Transfer: For fall 1981, 150 students applied, 125 were accepted, and 78 enrolled. A GPA of 2.5 and a recommendation are required; an interview is recommended. Students must spend 1 year in residence and complete at least 60 of the 126 credits necessary for a bachelor's degree. Application deadlines are August 15 (fall), January 15 (spring), and May 15 (summer).

Visiting: Guides are available for informal visits. Visitors may sit in on classes and stay at the school. Mondays, Wednesdays, and Fridays are recommended for these visits. Arrangements can be made with Mrs. Margie Cruse in the admissions office.

Financial Aid: About 72% of all students receive aid through the school. Twenty-five percent work part-time on campus. Average aid to freshmen is $3716. The university administers annual scholarship exams, awarding 53 4-year, full-tuition scholarships. Grants and federal and state loans are also available. The university is a member of CSS and requires either the FAF or the FFS. The deadlines for financial aid application are April 1 for fall and November 1 for spring.

Foreign Students: Five percent of the full-time students come from foreign countries. The university offers these students special counseling and special organizations.

Admissions: Foreign students must achieve a minimum TOEFL score of 550. No college entrance exam must be taken.

Procedure: The application deadline for fall entry is June 15. Foreign students must present proof of health and proof of funds adequate to cover 1 year of study. They must also carry health insurance, which is available through the university.

Admissions Contact: Daniel J. Davis, Director of Admissions.

UNIVERSITY OF HOUSTON/   E-3
CENTRAL CAMPUS
Houston, Texas 77004   (713) 749-2949

F/T: 15,178M&W	Faculty: 2260; I, +$
P/T: 13,117M&W	Ph.D.'s: 70%
Grad: 5441M&W	S/F Ratio: 11 to 1
Year: sems, ss	Tuition: $400 ($1260)
Appl: July 15	R and B: $2140–2460
7500 applied	3500 accepted	1750 enrolled
SAT: 446V 500M		COMPETITIVE+

University of Houston/Central Campus, established in 1927 as a community junior college, became a 4-year institution in 1934. Since 1963, this 4-year campus university system has been supported by the state of Texas. Degrees are offered through the colleges of Architecture, Business Administration, Education, Engineering, Hotel and Restaurant Management, Humanities and Fine Arts, Law, Natural Sciences and Mathematics, Optometry, Pharmacy, Social Sciences, and Technology, and the Graduate School of Social Work. The libraries contain 1,240,000 volumes, subscribe to 13,329 periodicals, and hold over 900,000 microfilm items.

Environment: The 384-acre campus located 3 miles from the business district, includes an educational television station. Dormitories house 1110 women and 1100 men.

Student Life: Almost 90% of the students are from Texas. About 8% live on campus in single-sex dorms.

Organizations: Fifteen national fraternities and 10 national sororities have chapters on campus, and 4% of the men and 4% of the women belong. Extracurricular activities include departmental clubs, religious organizations, political groups, publications, band, symphony, chorale, and student government.

890 TEXAS

Sports: The university fields intercollegiate teams in 9 sports. Intramural sports also are available.

Handicapped: The entire campus is accessible to the physically handicapped. Facilities include wheelchair ramps, special parking, elevators, specially equipped rest rooms, and lowered drinking fountains and telephones. Special class scheduling, assistance in the bookstore, and special programming are also provided. A tape library and a specially equipped reading area are provided for students with visual impairments. A coordinator of handicapped student services and 2 counselors are available.

Graduates: About 36% of the freshmen drop out, and 25% remain to graduate. Approximately 35% of the graduates pursue advanced degrees; 5% enter medical school, 5% enter dental school, and 5% enter law school. Forty percent begin careers in business and industry.

Services: Placement services, career counseling, health care, psychological counseling, tutoring, and remedial instruction are offered free.

Programs of Study: The university confers the B.A., B.S., B.F.A., B.S.Ch.E., B.S.C.E., B.S.E.E., B.S.I.E., B.S.M.E., B.S.Tech., B.S.Pharm., B.S.Ed., B.M., B.B.A., B.Arch., and B.Acc. Master's and doctoral programs are also offered. Bachelor's degrees are awarded in the following subjects: AREA STUDIES (German, Russian, urban), BUSINESS (accounting, business administration, business education, computer science, economics, finance, hotel and restaurant management, management, marketing, organizational behavior and management, production-logistics management, quantitative management science), EDUCATION (elementary, health/physical, industrial, secondary), ENGLISH (English, journalism, speech), FINE AND PERFORMING ARTS (art, art education, music, music education, radio/TV, theater/dramatics), HEALTH SCIENCES (medical technology, nutrition, speech therapy), LANGUAGES (French, German, Spanish), MATH AND SCIENCES (biology, biophysical sciences, chemistry, computer science, geology, mathematics, physics), PHILOSOPHY (classics, philosophy), PREPROFESSIONAL (architecture, consumer sciences and merchandising, construction technology, drafting technology, electrical technology, electronics technology, engineering—chemical, engineering—civil, engineering—electrical, engineering—industrial, engineering—mechanical, home economics, industrial technology, law, manufacturing technology, mechanical environmental systems technology, optometry, pharmacy), SOCIAL SCIENCES (anthropology, economics, geography, government/political science, history, psychology, public administration, sociology).

Required: Two semester hours of physical education are required.

Special: Preprofessional and teacher certification programs in several fields are available. There are programs leading to certificates in Afro-American studies and in Mexican-American studies. The Houston Inter-University African Studies Program also offers opportunities for study to those interested in Africa.

Honors: Numerous national honor societies have chapters on campus. All departments offer honors programs.

Admissions: About 47% of those who applied were accepted for the 1981-82 freshman class. The SAT scores of those who enrolled were as follows: Verbal—71% below 500, 11% between 500 and 599, and 18% above 600; Math—17% below 500, 55% between 500 and 599, and 27% above 600. Candidates must be graduates of an accredited high school, ranking in the top 75% of their class, with 16 Carnegie units of work and at least a C average.

Procedure: The SAT or ACT is required and should be taken by January of the senior year. Applications deadlines are July 15 (fall), December 5 (spring), May 1 (first summer session), and June 12 (second summer session). There is no application fee for U.S. residents.

Special: An early admissions plan is offered. CLEP credit is accepted.

Transfer: Over 3600 transfer students are admitted each year. Applicants must be eligible to return to their last college. D grades are transferable if offset by an A or B grade in another course. Students must earn at least 30 credits in residence of the 122 or more required for a bachelor's degree. Application deadlines are the same as those for entering freshmen.

Visiting: The university holds orientations for prospective students. Guides also are available for informal visits to the campus. Visitors may sit in on classes.

Financial Aid: About 35% of all students receive aid. Four major sources of funding are available for students: grants, loans, college work-study, and scholarships. The FFS is required. The priority application deadline for all programs is April 1.

Foreign Students: Students from foreign countries make up 10% of enrollment. The university offers these students an intensive English course, an intensive English program, special counseling, and special organizations.

Admissions: Applicants must score 550 or better on the TOEFL. No college entrance exams are required.

Procedure: The application deadline for fall entry is June 1; foreign students also are admitted in spring. They must provide a physician's statement as proof of good health and must show evidence of adequate funds for 4 years. There is a special $50 application fee for foreign students. They are required to carry health insurance, which is available through the university for a fee.

Admissions Contact: Lee Elliott Brown, Director of Admissions.

UNIVERSITY OF HOUSTON/ DOWNTOWN CAMPUS E-3
Houston, Texas 77002 (713) 749-2001

F/T: 1221M, 1041W Faculty: 123; IIB, av$
P/T: 1774M, 1730W Ph.D's: n/av
Grad: none S/F Ratio: n/av
Year: sems, ss Tuition: $400 ($1260)
Appl: open R and B: $1305-1950
1492 enrolled
SAT or ACT: not required NONCOMPETITIVE

University of Houston/Downtown Campus, a state-controlled institution founded in 1974, offers undergraduate degrees in the arts and sciences, business, and technology.

Environment: The 8-acre campus is located in the city of Houston. University dormitories accommodate 400 students.

Student Life: About 92% of the students come from Texas; 98% are graduates of public schools. About 60% of the students are minority-group members. Campus housing is single-sex; there are visiting privileges. Students may keep cars on campus.

Organizations: There is 1 national sorority on campus, but no fraternities. Students may participate in a variety of organizations. Popular groups include the Black Student Union, Christian Student Union, International Student Organization, and the Latin American Student Organization.

Sports: There is no intercollegiate athletics program. There are 7 intramural sports for men and 7 for women.

Handicapped: The entire campus is accessible to physically handicapped students. Special facilities include wheelchair ramps, elevators, special parking, specially equipped rest rooms, and lowered drinking fountains and telephones. Special class scheduling is also available. There is 1 special counselor for handicapped students.

Services: Students receive the following services free of charge: placement, career counseling, psychological counseling, health care, and remedial instruction. Tutoring is available on a fee basis.

Programs of Study: The university offers bachelor's degrees in the following subjects: BUSINESS (business and commerce, business services), PREPROFESSIONAL (criminal justice, engineering technology, petroleum land management). About 65% of the degrees conferred are in business.

Required: Students must complete 120 credit hours with a minimum GPA of 2.0. The last 36 hours must be taken in residence.

Special: The university offers a general studies degree.

Admissions: Graduation from high school is not required.

Procedure: Neither the SAT nor ACT is required. There is no application deadline. There is no application fee.

Special: CLEP credit is accepted.

Transfer: For fall 1981, 2192 transfer students applied, 2189 were accepted, and 1094 enrolled. A minimum GPA of 1.5 is required. Transfer students are accepted for all classes. Students must complete, at the university, 36 of the 120 credits required to earn the bachelor's degree. There are no application deadlines.

Visiting: There are no regularly scheduled orientations for prospective students. Guides are available for informal visits; visitors may not stay overnight at the school.

Financial Aid: About 21% of the students receive aid through the university; 2% work part-time on campus. Scholarships averaging $225 (maximum, $400) and work contracts averaging $2000 (maximum, $2600) are available. The average award to freshmen from all sources is $1800. The FFS must be submitted; there is no application deadline.

Foreign Students: About 8% of the full-time students come from foreign countries. The university offers these students an intensive English program, special counseling, and special organizations.

Admissions: Foreign students must achieve a minimum TOEFL score of 550. They must also take the university's own entrance exams in English, mathematics, and reading.

Procedure: Application deadlines are open; foreign students are admitted in the fall, spring, and summer. Foreign students must present proof of funds adequate to cover their entire period of study. There is an application fee of $25. Foreign students must carry health insurance, which is available through the university for a fee.

Admissions Contact: Beth Lasswell, Director of Admissions.

UNIVERSITY OF MARY HARDIN-BAYLOR   D-3
Belton, Texas 76513   (817) 939-5811

F/T: 263M, 485W	Faculty: 63; IIB, −−$
P/T: 102M, 182W	Ph.D.'s: 46%
Grad: none	S/F Ratio: 16 to 1
Year: sems, ss	Tuition: $2060
Appl: July 15	R and B: $1590
197 applied	192 accepted	181 enrolled
SAT: 410V 460M	ACT: 18	LESS COMPETITIVE

University of Mary Hardin-Baylor, chartered in 1845, is affiliated with the Baptist General Convention of Texas. It offers undergraduate degrees in the arts and sciences, business, education, and nursing. The library has 104,000 volumes and nearly 20,000 microfilm items, and subscribes to 1100 periodicals.

Environment: The 100-acre campus is located in a small town 60 miles from Austin. The surrounding environment is rural. The 19 buildings include 4 residence halls that house 120 men and 180 women, a health center, a gymnasium, and a student union.

Student Life: About 65% of the students come from Texas. About 40% live on campus. Chapel attendance is required. About 53% of the students are Protestant and 15% are Catholic. About 20% are minority-group members. Campus housing is single-sex. Students may keep cars on campus. Day-care services are available to all students, faculty, and staff for a fee.

Organizations: Extracurricular activities include departmental clubs, a literary society, and the Baptist Student Union. There are no fraternities or sororities.

Sports: The university fields intercollegiate teams in 4 sports for men and 3 for women. There are 4 intramural sports for men and 3 for women.

Handicapped: About 75% of the campus is accessible to wheelchair-bound students. Ramps, elevators, special parking areas, and special class scheduling are provided. One counselor is available.

Graduates: About 15% of the freshmen drop out, and 45% remain to graduate. Fifteen percent of the graduates seek advanced degrees; 1% enter medical school and 1% enter law school.

Services: Free health care, psychological and career counseling, and placement services are available for students and graduates. Tutoring and remedial instruction are available for a fee.

Programs of Study: The university awards the B.A., B.B.A., B.F.A., B.G.S., B.S., B.S.Ed., B.S.N., and B.Mus. degrees. Bachelor's degrees are offered in the following subjects: BUSINESS (accounting, finance, management, secretarial science), EDUCATION (early childhood, elementary, health/physical, secondary, special), ENGLISH (English, speech), FINE AND PERFORMING ARTS (art, art education, music, music education), HEALTH SCIENCES (medical technology, nursing), LANGUAGES (Spanish), MATH AND SCIENCES (biology, chemistry, mathematics), PHILOSOPHY (religion), PREPROFESSIONAL (dentistry, home economics, law, medicine, ministry, social work), SOCIAL SCIENCES (economics, government/political science, history, psychology, social sciences, sociology).

Required: Students must take courses in religion and physical education.

Special: Independent study, study abroad, and exchange programs are offered. Students may earn a general studies degree.

Honors: An honors program, consisting of special seminars and independent research, is available to juniors and seniors with a GPA of 3.5 or better.

Admissions: About 97% of the applicants for the 1981-82 freshman class were accepted. The ACT scores of those who enrolled were as follows: 50% below 21, 36% between 21 and 23, 8% between 24 and 25, 5% between 26 and 28, and 1% above 28. Applicants must score 15 or higher on the ACT, have graduated from high school with 15 Carnegie units, have a C average, and rank in the top half of their graduating class. The university also considers recommendations by school officials, advanced placement or honors courses, and impressions made during an interview.

Procedure: The ACT is required. New students are admitted to both semesters; applications are due July 15 for fall, December 15 for spring, and May 1 for summer. There is a $25 application fee. The university uses a rolling admissions plan.

Special: Early admissions and early decision plans are available. AP and CLEP credit is accepted.

Transfer: For fall 1981, 271 transfer students applied and 251 were accepted. Applicants must have a GPA of 2.0 or better and be in good standing at their last school. D grades generally do not transfer. Students must complete 30 credits in residence to graduate. The bachelor's degree requires between 124 and 132 credits. Application deadlines are the same as those for freshmen.

Visiting: Orientations for prospective students are scheduled regularly. Guides also are available for informal visits. Visitors may sit in on classes and stay in the dormitories. Arrangements should be made with the director of admissions.

Financial Aid: About 65% of the students receive aid; 16% work part-time on campus. The university participates in federal programs such as NDSL, BEOG/SEOG, and CWS. Loans also are available from banks, the university, and the state. State tuition grants are available to Texas residents. Freshman scholarships are awarded on the basis of financial need or academic ability. Tuition may be paid in installments. The FFS is required. Aid applications are due April 1.

Foreign Students: The university actively recruits foreign students and offers these students an intensive English program, special counseling, and special organizations.

Admissions: Foreign students must achieve a minimum TOEFL score of 400; no college entrance exams are required.

Procedure: Application deadlines are May 1 for fall and October 1 for spring. Foreign students must present proof of health as well as proof of funds adequate to cover 1 semester of study. They must also carry health insurance, which is available through the university.

Admissions Contact: Carla Price, Director of Financial Aid and Admissions.

UNIVERSITY OF ST. THOMAS   E-3
Houston, Texas 77006   (713) 522-7911

F/T: 333M, 622W	Faculty: 96; IIA, −−$
P/T: 195M, 387W	Ph.D.'s: 65%
Grad: 230M, 172W	S/F Ratio: 16 to 1
Year: sems, ss	Tuition: $2650
Appl: Aug. 15	R and B: $1690
525 applied	470 accepted	325 enrolled
SAT: 425V 425M	ACT: 15	LESS COMPETITIVE

University of St. Thomas, established in 1947, is a private coeducational college of liberal arts related to the Roman Catholic Church. The library houses 85,000 volumes, and subscribes to 620 periodicals.

Environment: The undergraduate campus buildings and grounds occupy 12 city blocks in a residential area of Houston. The School of Theology is 10 minutes from the St. Thomas campus. Boarding students reside in the one dorm accommodating 100 men and 100 women. Campus buildings include the Cullen Music Building, Crooker Student Center, School for Young Children, and the Cameron School of Business building. A new athletic center is under construction.

Student Life: Ninety percent of the students are from the Houston area; 7% are from foreign countries. About 5% of the men and 10% of the women live on campus. Attendance at Mass is voluntary. About 65% of the students are Catholic, 15% are Protestant, and 5% are Jewish. About 24% are minority-group members. Campus housing is single-sex; there are visiting privileges. Students may keep cars on campus.

Organizations: There is 1 sorority, to which 5% of the women belong; there are no fraternities. Clubs include accounting, philosophy, nursing, music, and others.

Sports: The college fields 1 intercollegiate team for men and 1 for women. There are 4 intramural sports for men and 1 for women.

Handicapped: Wheelchair ramps, special parking, elevators, and specially equipped rest rooms are available for physically handicapped students; 50% of the campus is accessible.

Graduates: The freshman dropout rate is 23%; 25% remain to graduate. About 10% of the graduates pursue advanced study: 5% enter law school, 1% enter medical school, and 5% enter dental school. Twenty percent pursue careers in business and industry.

Services: Students receive psychological counseling, career counseling, placement, and remedial instruction free of charge. Tutoring is available on a fee basis.

Programs of Study: The college confers the B.A., B.B.A., B.M., and B.S.N. degrees. Master's and doctoral degrees are also awarded. Bachelor's degrees are offered in the following subjects: BUSINESS (accounting, business administration), EDUCATION (early childhood, elementary, secondary), ENGLISH (communications, English), FINE AND PERFORMING ARTS (art, music, theater/dramatics), HEALTH SCIENCES (medical technology, nursing), LANGUAGES (French, German, Spanish), MATH AND SCIENCES (biology, chemistry, mathematics), PHILOSOPHY (philosophy), PREPROFESSIONAL (dentistry, engineering, law, medicine, ministry), SOCIAL SCIENCES (economics, government/political science, history, international studies, psychology, sociology). Thirty percent of the degrees conferred are in business and 20% in education.

Honors: Eight national honor societies have chapters on campus.

Admissions: Ninety percent of those who applied were accepted for the 1981-82 freshman class. The SAT scores of those who enrolled were as follows: Verbal—55% below 500, 35% between 500 and 599, 8% between 600 and 700, and 2% above 700; Math—55% below 500, 35% between 500 and 599, 8% between 600 and 700, and 2% above 700. The ACT scores were as follows: 65% below 21, 16% between 21 and 23, 7% between 24 and 25, 7% between 26 and 28, and 5% above 28. Candidates must be graduates of an approved secondary school with 16 units of work; have a minimum average of C, and rank in the top 75% of their graduating class. Preference is given to those graduating in the top half of their class, except where high school standards are exceptionally high. Also considered are advanced placement or honors courses, impressions made during an interview, evidence of special talents, and the candidate's extracurricular activities record.

Procedure: The SAT or ACT is required. An interview is strongly recommended. The university follows a rolling admissions policy. The application fee is $15; the deadline is August 15.

Special: Early admissions, early decision, and deferred admissions plans are available.

Transfer: For fall 1981, 685 transfer students enrolled. An average of C is necessary: D grades transfer with an overall GPA of 2.0. There is a 1-year residency rule. Students must complete, at the university, 30 of the 120 semester hours required for the bachelor's degree. Application deadlines are the same as those for freshmen.

Visiting: There are no regularly scheduled orientations. Visits are best scheduled Monday through Friday. Arrangements for a guide can be made through the office of admissions. Visitors may sit in on classes and stay overnight at the school.

Financial Aid: Fifty percent of all students receive some form of financial aid; 47% work part-time on campus. The university subscribes to all state and federal fund loan and grant programs. The university is a member of CSS; the FAF is required of all applicants. The application deadline for scholarships is open.

Foreign Students: About 7% of the full-time students come from foreign countries. The university offers these students special organizations.

Admissions: Foreign students must achieve a minimum TOEFL score of 550; no college entrance exams are required.

Procedure: Application deadlines are July 15 for fall and December 1 for spring. Foreign students must present the results of a physical examination as well as proof of funds adequate to cover 1 year of study. A $40 international student fee is charged each semester, and a $500 deposit is required. Foreign students must also carry health insurance, which is available through the university.

Admissions Contact: George A. Knaggs, Dean of Admissions.

UNIVERSITY OF TEXAS

University of Texas was founded at Austin in 1883, with a medical branch opening at Galveston in 1891. Today, it has grown to a statewide system of 14 major components at Arlington, Austin, Dallas, El Paso, Galveston, Houston, Odessa, San Antonio, and Tyler. Seven component institutions are general academic institutions and 4 are health science centers with 4 medical schools, 2 dental schools, 7 nursing schools, 4 schools of allied health science, 4 graduate schools of biomedical science, 2 speech and hearing institutes, 1 school of public health, a comprehensive cancer research and treatment center, and over 2000 hospital beds. The university operates a marine biomedical institute and a marine science institute with ocean-going vessels as well as an environmental science park. Austin's famed McDonald Observatory in West Texas is renowned worldwide. Austin is also the location of the LBJ Presidential Library and Archives, the nation's first presidential collection to be housed on a university campus.

The combined system enrollment of over 110,000 students is taught by over 9,000 faculty and supported by over 32,000 staff personnel in over 800 classroom and service buildings. The university's endowment funds, among the largest for U.S. schools and colleges, are generated largely from surface and sub-surface income from 2.1 million acres of land in 19 west Texas counties.

Separate profiles of the universities at Arlington, Austin, El Paso, and San Antonio, which offer bachelor's degrees, follow.

UNIVERSITY OF TEXAS AT ARLINGTON D-2
Arlington, Texas 76017   (817) 273-3401

F/T: 6958M, 4891W   Faculty: 677; IIA, +$
P/T: 3631M, 2762W   Ph.D.'s: 53%
Grad: 1638M, 1073W   S/F Ratio: 24 to 1
Year: sems, ss   Tuition: $464 ($1524)
Appl: Aug. 15   R and B: $2650
3750 applied   2650 accepted   2014 enrolled
SAT: 435V 475M   COMPETITIVE

University of Texas at Arlington, established in 1895, consists of the College of Business Administration, the College of Engineering, the College of Liberal Arts, the College of Science, the School of Architecture and Environmental Design, the School of Nursing, and the Graduate School. The library contains 750,000 volumes and 30,000 microfilm items, and subscribes to 3000 periodicals.

Environment: The 201-acre campus is located in a suburban area midway between Dallas and Fort Worth. There are over 40 buildings. A new School of Nursing building will be completed in 1982. Student dorms and apartments accommodate 1580 students. Privately owned housing is available adjacent to the campus.

Student Life: Ninety-five percent of the undergraduates are from Texas, and 95% of entering freshmen are public school graduates. Seven percent of the students live on campus. There are religious groups of all faiths. About 14% of the students are minority-group members. Campus housing is coed and single-sex; there are visiting privileges in single-sex dorms. Students may keep cars on campus.

Organizations: Seven percent of the men belong to the 15 national fraternities; 6% of the women are members of the 9 national sororities. There are various professional and social organizations on campus.

Sports: The university fields 10 intercollegiate teams for men and 8 for women. There are 12 intramural sports for men and 9 for women.

Handicapped: Ninety percent of the campus is accessible to physically handicapped students. Wheelchair ramps, elevators, special parking and rest rooms, lowered drinking fountains and telephones, and special class scheduling are provided. There is a handicapped students services office.

Graduates: The freshman dropout rate is 33%; 30% remain to graduate. Thirty percent of graduates pursue careers in business or industry; 25% go on to graduate study.

Services: Free placement services, remedial instruction, and career counseling are offered. Health care, psychological counseling, and tutoring are available on a fee basis.

Programs of Study: The university offers bachelor's, master's, and doctoral degrees. Bachelor's degrees are offered in the following subjects: BUSINESS (accounting, business administration), ENGLISH (English, journalism, speech), FINE AND PERFORMING ARTS (art, art education, music, music education, radio/TV, theater/dramatics), HEALTH SCIENCES (medical technology, nursing), LANGUAGES (French, German, Russian, Spanish), MATH AND SCIENCES (biochemistry, biology, chemistry, geology, mathematics, physics), PHILOSOPHY (philosophy), PREPROFESSIONAL (architecture, engineering, social work), SOCIAL SCIENCES (economics, government/political science, history, psychology, sociology). Thirty percent of degrees conferred are in business, 16% in preprofessional areas, 15% in math and sciences, and 11% in health sciences.

Honors: Twenty-eight national honor societies have chapters on campus. The College of Liberal Arts offers an honors program for high academic achievers.

Admissions: Seventy-one percent of the applicants for the 1981-82 freshman class were accepted. The SAT scores of those who enrolled were as follows: Verbal—74% below 500, 20% between 500 and 599, 5% between 600 and 700, and 1% above 700; Math—60% below 500, 29% between 500 and 599, 9% between 600 and 700, and 2% above 700. Completion of 15 Carnegie units is required. A balance is struck between SAT or ACT scores and class rank which requires increasingly higher SAT or ACT scores as the applicant's rank diminishes. Class rank, total SAT or ACT score, and the secondary school curriculum are the major factors in determining admissions.

Procedure: The SAT or ACT is required and should be taken by fall of the senior year. Application deadlines are August 15 (fall), December 18 (spring), and June 1 (summer). Notification is on a rolling basis. There is no application fee.

Special: AP and CLEP credit is accepted.

Transfer: For fall 1981, 5650 transfer students applied, 4300 were accepted, and 3579 enrolled. Transfers are accepted for all classes. A 2.0 GPA is required. D grades are acceptable. Students must study at the university for 30 semester hours to receive a degree; the bachelor's degree requires between 124 and 140 semester hours. Application deadlines are the same as those for freshmen.

Visiting: Campus visits may be made on Monday through Friday in the afternoon. Guides are provided, and visitors may sit in on classes. Arrangements may be made by contacting the admissions office.

Financial Aid: About 67% of the students receive some form of financial aid. Part-time work is available; 20% of students earn part of their expenses. The average award to freshmen from all sources is $800. The university is a member of CSS; the FAF is required. Application must be made by June 1.

Foreign Students: About 10% of the full-time students come from foreign countries. The university offers these students an intensive English course and program, special counseling, and special organizations.

Admissions: Foreign students are not required to take an English proficiency test; however, they must take the SAT and achieve a combined score of 700 (800 for engineering).

Procedure: Application deadlines are June 1 for fall, November 1 for spring, and March 15 for summer. Foreign students must present proof of health as well as proof of funds adequate to cover 1 year of study. They must also carry health insurance.

Admissions Contact: Glenn Read, Director of Admission Services.

UNIVERSITY OF TEXAS AT AUSTIN   D-3
Austin, Texas 78712   (512) 471-1711

F/T, P/T: Faculty: n/av; I, av$
 20,301M, 17,810W   Ph.D.'s: n/av
Grad: 5968M, 4066W   S/F Ratio: 23 to 1
Year: sems, ss   Tuition: $420 ($1506)
Appl: June 1   R and B: $2980
14,108 applied   10,048 accepted   6136 enrolled
SAT or ACT: required   VERY COMPETITIVE

University of Texas at Austin, established in 1883, consists of 8 colleges, the Graduate School, the Law School, the School of Architecture, the School of Nursing, the Graduate School of Library Science, and the Lyndon B. Johnson School of Public Affairs. The library is the largest and most comprehensive in the Southwest and the tenth largest academic library in the United States. It houses more than 4 million volumes and 665,000 microfilm items, and subscribes to over 40,000 periodicals.

Environment: The 440-acre main campus is situated in a residential area of Austin adjoining the State Capitol Complex. The Lyndon B. Johnson Library is the first presidential library on a university campus; the Computation Center holds one of the largest educational computer systems in the country; the world's fourth largest telescope is an additional feature. The 17 dormitories accommodate 3500 women and 1980 men. Other housing includes apartments for married students, a mobile home park, and a fraternity row. A shuttle bus service is provided for students who live off campus. Parking is limited.

Student Life: The university has one of the largest enrollments in the country and draws students from all 50 states and 90 foreign countries. Seventy percent of the students are residents of Texas; 14% are campus residents. About 12% of the students are minority-group members. Campus housing is coed and single-sex; there are visiting privileges in single-sex dorms. Students may keep cars on campus.

Organizations: There are 33 national fraternities and 21 national sororities on campus. Extracurricular activities include the Students' Association, Student Assembly, a daily newspaper, a magazine, the yearbook, and numerous musical, dramatic, debate, service, religious, and special-interest groups.

Sports: The university fields 9 intercollegiate teams for men and 8 for women. There are 20 intramural sports for men and 18 for women.

Handicapped: Ninety percent of the campus is accessible to the physically handicapped. Facilities include wheelchair ramps, elevators, special parking and rest rooms, and lowered telephones and drinking fountains. There are 4 special counselors and 4 assistants to aid handicapped students.

Graduates: About 20% of the freshmen drop out at the end of the first year. Forty percent remain to graduate. Over 500 graduates enter medical school every year. The university is represented in every medical school in the United States and in many located in foreign countries. Graduates are enrolled at the 3 dental schools in Texas and many others as well. The top-ranked law schools also accept numerous U.T. graduates. Other graduates enter all areas of business and industry.

Services: There is a Career Choice Center which offers free career counseling and placement services to both undergraduates and graduates. Free psychological counseling is also available. Tutoring and health care services are available on a fee basis.

Programs of Study: Undergraduate degrees conferred by the university are the B.A., B.S., B.A.B., B.F.A., B.J., and B. Mus. Master's and doctoral programs are also available. Bachelor's degrees are offered in the following subjects: AREA STUDIES (American, Asian, Latin American), BUSINESS (accounting, business administration, business education, finance, international business, management, marketing, petroleum land management, real estate/insurance), EDUCATION (early childhood, elementary, health/physical, secondary, special), ENGLISH (English, journalism, speech), FINE AND PERFORMING ARTS (art education, art history, dance music), HEALTH SCIENCES (medical technology, nursing, speech therapy), LANGUAGES (French, German, Greek/Latin, Hebrew, Italian, Portuguese, Russian, Spanish), MATH AND SCIENCES (astronomy, biochemistry, biology, botany, chemistry, geology, mathematics, natural sciences, physics, zoology), PHILOSOPHY (classics, humanities, philosophy), PRE-PROFESSIONAL (agriculture, architecture, dentistry, engineering, forestry, home economics, law, library science, medicine, ministry, pharmacy, social work, veterinary), SOCIAL SCIENCES (anthropology, economics, geography, government/political science, history, psychology, sociology). The most popular majors are business, engineering, and math and sciences.

Required: Freshmen working toward a B.A. degree are required to take English, science, and a foreign language or mathematics. All undergraduates must take 6 hours in United States history and 6 in national and state government.

Special: The university offers a general studies (no major) degree and allows student-designed majors. Study abroad in the junior year is possible. There is a cooperative work-study program in engineering. A 3-year bachelor's degree program is available.

Honors: A Junior Fellows Program and departmental honors programs are offered by every college and school. Plan II (Honors Program) is an alternate route to the B.A. degree for approximately 200 new students each year. The University has one of the oldest and largest honors programs in the country. There is a chapter of Phi Beta Kappa on campus.

Admissions: Seventy-one percent of the applicants were accepted for the 1981-82 freshman class. The minimum SAT score for Texas residents is 1100 if the student ranks in the lower three quarters of his class; any SAT score is accepted from Texas residents who rank in the top quarter of their class. For out-of-state students, the minimum SAT score is 1100. Nonresident students must also rank in the top quarter of their graduating class. Well-qualified applicants from out of state are encouraged to apply.

Procedure: The SAT or ACT is required and should be taken as early as possible in the senior year. The deadline for application to the fall session is June 1; for the spring, November 1. Admission is on a rolling basis. There is no application fee for residents of the United States.

Special: AP and CLEP exams may be taken for credit.

Transfer: For fall 1981, 9382 transfer students applied, 5832 were accepted, and 3774 enrolled. A 3.0 GPA is required of students who have completed up to 53 credits; students who have completed more than 53 credits must have a 2.5 GPA. Grades of C and above transfer. SAT scores, high school rank, and GPA are considered. At least 24 of the last 30 hours must be taken at the university. The bachelor's degree requires at least 120 hours. Application deadlines are the same as those for freshmen.

Visiting: There are regularly scheduled "U. T. Days," one in mid-fall and one in mid-spring. Informal visitors must make arrangements through the admissions office at least a week in advance. With permission, visitors may sit in on classes.

Financial Aid: Forty percent of all students receive some form of financial aid; 40% work part-time on campus. Package aid is offered in all cases where required to provide the financial resources needed in order to attend the university. The average award to freshmen from all sources is $1000. The university is a member of CSS; the FFS is required. The deadlines for financial aid applications are March 1 for the fall term and October 1 for the spring term.

Foreign Students: About 5% of the full-time students come from foreign countries. The university offers these students an intensive English course and program, special counseling, and special organizations.

Admissions: Foreign students must achieve a minimum TOEFL score of 550. They must also take the SAT or ACT.

Procedure: Application deadlines are May 1 for fall and summer, and November 1 for spring. Foreign students must complete the student health form; they must also present proof of adequate funds. There is a $25 application fee for foreign students.

Admissions Contact: Shirley Binder, Director of Admissions and Records.

UNIVERSITY OF TEXAS AT EL PASO A-3
El Paso, Texas 79968 (915) 747-5550

F/T: 4703M, 4484W	Faculty: 430; IIA, av$
P/T: 2247M, 2179W	Ph.D.'s: 75%
Grad: 921M, 884W	S/F Ratio: n/av
Year: sems, ss	Tuition: $396 ($1476)
Appl: open	R and B: $1920
SAT or ACT: required	LESS COMPETITIVE

University of Texas at El Paso, established in 1913 as the Texas State School of Mines, is a liberal arts and technical institution under public control. The university comprises 6 colleges (Business Administration, Education, Engineering, Liberal Arts, Science, and Nursing) and the Graduate School. The library contains 618,489 volumes and 636,828 microform texts, and subscribes to 3380 periodicals.

Environment: The 333-acre campus is located in the city of El Paso in a rugged mountain setting just across the Rio Grande from Mexico. The distinguishing characteristic of the campus is the Bhutanese architectural style. There are 2 high-rise dormitories, which accommodate more than 700 students. The married student complex consists of 60 apartments.

Student Life: Most of the students come from Texas, but 48 states and 65 foreign countries are also represented. The university has the largest enrollment of Mexican citizens of any college or university in the United States. Most students commute. About 46% of the students are minority-group members. Campus housing is coed. Students may keep cars on campus.

Organizations: There are 14 Greek letter organizations and more than 100 registered student organizations. On-campus events include a film series, art exhibits, plays, and lectures. Special-interest clubs, publications, religious and service organizations, and music and drama groups provide extracurricular activities.

Sports: The university fields 7 intercollegiate teams for men and 6 for women. There are 24 intramural sports for men and 22 for women.

Handicapped: The university is committed to provide equal educational opportunities to handicapped students and has initiated an effort to make the physical facilities as accessible as possible.

Services: The following services are provided to students free of charge: health care, psychological counseling, placement and career counseling (for graduates as well as undergraduates), tutoring, and remedial instruction.

Programs of Study: There are bachelor's, master's, and doctoral programs. The university confers the following undergraduate degrees: B.A., B.S., B.B.A., B.S.Ed., B.S.N., B.S.Med.Tech., B.Mus., B.F.A., B.S.W., and B.S. in Computer Science. Bachelor's degrees are offered in the following subjects: AREA STUDIES (Chicano, Latin American), BUSINESS (accounting, administrative services, business administration, commercial banking, computer science, finance, management, marketing, real estate), EDUCATION (deaf and/or severely hard of hearing, elementary, health/physical, secondary), ENGLISH (English, creative writing, journalism, literature, linguistics, speech), FINE AND PERFORMING ARTS (art—ceramics, art—metals, art—painting, art—printmaking, art—sculpture, broadcasting, drama, music education, music performance, music theory and composition), HEALTH SCIENCES (allied health, medical technology, nursing, speech, hearing, language disorders), LANGUAGES (French, German, Spanish), MATH AND SCIENCES (biology, botany, chemistry, geology, geophysics, mathematics, physics, zoology), PHILOSOPHY (philosophy), PREPROFESSIONAL (engineering—civil, engineering—electrical, engineering—industrial, engineering—mechanical, engineering—metallurgical, social work), SOCIAL SCIENCES (anthropology, criminal justice, economics, government/political science, history, psychology, sociology).

Required: All students must complete general foundation requirements.

Special: Cooperative education, internships, and a 5-year combined B.S.-M.S. degree in chemistry are offered.

Honors: There are chapters of 18 honor societies on campus. An honors program is offered.

Admissions: About 93% of those who applied were accepted for a recent freshman class. Applicants must be graduates of an accredited high school or score at least 45 on the GED test. Students graduating in the upper half of their class must score a minimum of 700 on the SAT or 15 on the ACT to be admitted in good standing. Students graduating in the lower half must score 800 (SAT) or 18 (ACT).

Procedure: The SAT or ACT is required and should be taken by March of the senior year. There is no formal deadline for application. Freshmen may be admitted to any session. Admissions are granted on a rolling basis. There is no application fee.

Special: The university has early admissions, early decision, and deferred admissions plans. AP and CLEP credit is granted.

Transfer: For fall 1981, 890 transfer students enrolled. Transfer applicants who have completed 30 semester hours at their previous college with at least a C average and who are in good standing are eligible for admission. Students who have not completed 30 hours must submit ACT or SAT scores. Students must complete 30 credits at the university to receive a degree; the bachelor's degree requires at least 120 credits. Application deadlines are open.

Visiting: Orientation sessions are held for new students at the start of the fall and spring semesters.

Financial Aid: About 60% of the students receive aid; almost 7% work part-time on campus. Scholarships, grants, loans, and work-study opportunities are available. Scholarships are based on academic merit; all other forms of aid are based on a combination of academic merit and financial need. The average award to freshmen from all sources is $2000. The university is a member of CSS; the FFS or FAF is required. Priority is given to applications received by April 1.

Foreign Students: About 8% of the full-time students come from foreign countries. The university offers these students an intensive English course and program, special counseling, and special organizations.

Admissions: Foreign students must achieve a minimum TOEFL score of 500; no college entrance exams are required.

Procedure: Application deadlines are 60 days prior to the start of each semester. Foreign students must present proof of health as well as proof of funds adequate to cover 4 years of study.

Admissions Contact: William P. Nelsen, Registrar and Director of Admissions.

UNIVERSITY OF TEXAS AT SAN ANTONIO D-4
San Antonio, Texas 78285 (512) 691-4535

F/T, P/T: 4309M, 4622W	Faculty: 354; IIA, —$
Grad: 704M, 927W	Ph.D.'s: n/av
Year: sems, ss	S/F Ratio: 24 to 1
Appl: Aug. 1	Tuition: $150 ($1230)
3154 applied	R and B: n/app
2321 accepted	1548 enrolled
SAT or ACT: required	LESS COMPETITIVE

University of Texas at San Antonio, established in 1969, offers 4-year programs in business, fine and applied arts, music, humanities and social sciences, math and science, and multidisciplinary studies. The library contains 328,476 volumes and 110,294 microfilm items, and subscribes to 2126 periodicals.

Environment: The 600-acre campus, 5 miles from San Antonio, includes 5 colleges and the John Peace Library, plus complete physical education facilities.

Student Life: The university is a commuter institution, with 84% of the students coming from public schools. About 25% of the students are minority-group members. Students may keep cars on campus.

Organizations: There are 4 national fraternities and 4 national sororities represented on campus. Students may join traditional clubs and service groups, and there are university-sponsored social events.

Sports: The university fields 4 intercollegiate teams for men and 4 for women. There are 3 intramural sports for men and 3 for women.

Handicapped: The entire campus is accessible to the physically handicapped. Wheelchair ramps, lowered drinking fountains, special parking, and specially equipped rest rooms are provided. There are 2 special counselors; individualized help is given when needed.

Graduates: Fifteen percent of the graduates continue their studies in graduate or professional schools.

Services: Free health care, psychological counseling, tutoring, and remedial instruction are available. The Office of Career Planning and Placement provides free placement and career counseling services to graduates and undergraduates.

Programs of Study: The university confers the B.A., B.S., B.B.A., B.M., B.M.E., and B.F.A. degrees. Master's programs are also offered. Bachelor's degrees are offered in the following subjects: AREA STUDIES (American), BUSINESS (accounting, business administration, economics, finance, management, marketing), EDUCATION (early childhood, health/physical), ENGLISH (English), FINE AND PERFORMING ARTS (art, music, music education), HEALTH SCIENCES (medical technology, occupational therapy, physical therapy), LANGUAGES (French, German, Russian, Spanish), MATH AND SCIENCES (biology, chemistry, computer science, ecology/environmental science, geology, mathematics, physics), PHILOSOPHY (humanities), PREPROFESSIONAL (architecture), SOCIAL SCIENCES (anthropology, criminal justice, economics, geography, government/political science, history, psychology, sociology). Twenty-five percent of degrees conferred are in business, 20% in education, 19% in mathematics and sciences, and 18% in social sciences.

Admissions: About 74% of the applicants for the 1981–82 freshman class were accepted. Applicants must be high school graduates with 13 recommended academic units, and must rank in the top 25% of their high school class. A minimum C average is required.

Procedure: The SAT or ACT is required. Application deadlines are August 1 (fall), December 1 (spring), and May 1 (summer). There is no application fee. The university follows a rolling admissions plan.

Special: AP and CLEP credit is accepted.

Transfer: For fall 1981, 3888 transfer students enrolled. A minimum C average and good academic standing are required for transfer. Students must complete, at the university, 30 of the 120 credits required to earn the bachelor's degree. D grades transfer. Application deadlines are the same as those for freshmen.

Visiting: There are regularly scheduled orientations for prospective students. There are also guides for informal visits. Arrangements can be made through the office of news and information.

Financial Aid: Ten percent of all students receive some form of financial aid, which is administered in the form of CWS, FISL, BEOG, LEEP, and state-funded programs. About 5% of the students work part-time on campus. The average award to freshmen from all sources ranges from $200 to $858. The university is a member of CSS; the FAF must be filed. For deadlines, contact the office of financial aid.

Foreign Students: Fewer than 1% of the full-time students come from foreign countries. The university offers these students special counseling and special organizations.

Admissions: Foreign students must achieve a minimum TOEFL score of 550. They must also take the SAT or ACT.

Procedure: Application deadlines are August 1 for fall, December 1 for spring, and May 1 for summer. Foreign students must present proof of health as well as proof of funds adequate to cover 1 year of study. They must also carry health insurance, which is available through the university for a fee.

Admissions Contact: John H. Brown, Director of Admissions and Registrar.

WAYLAND BAPTIST UNIVERSITY   B-2
(Formerly Wayland Baptist College)
Plainview, Texas 79072   (806) 296-5521

F/T: 349M, 329W   Faculty: 73; n/av
P/T: 520M, 196W   Ph.D.'s: 33%
Grad: none   S/F Ratio: 16 to 1
Year: 4-1-4, ss   Tuition: $68 p/c
Appl: Aug. 1   R and B: $1988
167 applied   165 accepted   140 enrolled
ACT: 19   LESS COMPETITIVE

Wayland Baptist University, founded in 1908 and affiliated with the Baptist General Convention of Texas, offers undergraduate training in liberal arts and sciences, business, and education. Its library holds 87,000 volumes and subscribes to 675 periodicals.

Environment: The 40-acre campus is located in a city of 23,000 people, about 45 miles north of Lubbock. The 13 major buildings include 9 residence halls that house 292 women and 242 men. Married student housing also is available.

Student Life: About 75% of the students come from Texas, and an equal percentage live on campus. Unmarried students not living with their immediate families must live in the residence halls, which are single-sex. Weekly chapel attendance is required, and drinking is forbidden on campus.

Organizations: Extracurricular activities include special-interest, service, and religious groups, publications, student government, music and drama, and social and cultural events. There are no fraternities or sororities.

Sports: The university fields intercollegiate teams in 4 sports for men and 2 for women. Intramural sports also are available.

Graduates: About 25% of the freshmen drop out, and 35% remain to graduate. Thirty-five percent of the graduates go on for further study.

Services: Career counseling, placement aid, health care, tutoring, and remedial instruction are provided.

Programs of Study: The university awards the B.A., B.S., B.M., and B.S.O.E. degrees. Bachelor's degrees are offered in the following subjects: AREA STUDIES (American), BUSINESS (business administration), EDUCATION (elementary, health/physical, occupational, religious, vocational), ENGLISH (communication, English, speech), FINE AND PERFORMING ARTS (church music, music, music education), LANGUAGES (Spanish), MATH AND SCIENCES (biology, chemistry, composite science, earth science, mathematics, physical sciences), PHILOSOPHY (religion), SOCIAL SCIENCES (criminal justice, government/political science, history, psychology, public administration, sociology).

Required: Students must take 2 courses in religion. Non-veterans must take 4 hours of physical education. A GPA of 2.0 or better is required for graduation.

Special: Independent study and study-abroad programs are offered. Additional minors are available in art, data processing, German, journalism, and philosophy.

Honors: Four honor societies are represented on campus. An honors program is available for juniors and seniors.

Admissions: Almost all of the applicants for the 1981–82 freshman class were accepted. Applicants must be high school graduates, have completed 15 Carnegie units, and rank in the top 70% of their class.

Procedure: The ACT is required. The application deadline for fall is August 1; students also are admitted in spring. Notification is made on a rolling basis. There is a $15 application fee.

Special: Early and deferred admissions programs are available. AP credit is accepted.

Transfer: Applicants must have a C average. D grades do not transfer. Students must complete at least 30 credits in residence of the 124 required for a bachelor's degree.

Financial Aid: About 80% of the students receive aid. The university offers academic, athletic, religious, and music scholarships; loans from the federal government, local banks, and private sources; and part-time jobs. The average award to 1981–82 freshmen was $1000. Aid candidates must submit the FAF. Scholarship applications must be received by August 1, loan applications by 3 weeks before registration.

Foreign Students: Students from foreign countries make up fewer than 1% of the student body. The university offers these students special counseling and an intensive English course.

Admissions: Applicants must take the TOEFL. No college entrance exams are required.

Procedure: The application deadline for fall admission is June 1; foreign students also are admitted to other terms. They must provide a medical certificate as proof of good health and show evidence of adequate funds for 1 year. They are required to carry health insurance, which is available through the university for a fee.

Admissions Contact: Audrey H. Boles, Registrar.

WEST TEXAS STATE UNIVERSITY   B-1
Canyon, Texas 79016   (806) 656-3331

F/T: 5458M&W   Faculty: 217; IIA, – $
P/T: 1023M&W   Ph.D.'s: 50%
Grad: 1235M&W   S/F Ratio: 19 to 1
Year: sems, ss   Tuition: $500 ($1480)
Appl: open   R and B: $1730
1561 applied   1083 enrolled
SAT: 650 (composite)   ACT: 12   LESS COMPETITIVE

896 TEXAS

West Texas State University, established in 1909, is a state-controlled institution made up of the colleges of Education and Arts and Sciences; the schools of Business, Fine Arts, Agriculture, and Nursing; and the Graduate School. The library contains more than 750,000 volumes and 400,000 microfilm items, and subscribes to 2580 periodicals.

Environment: The 120-acre campus is located in a community of 11,000 people, 17 miles south of Amarillo. Facilities include fine-arts, research, and science centers; a stadium; a chapel; and the Panhandle-Plains Historical Museum. Twelve dormitories accommodate about 2400 students. The university also owns a 186-acre farm and a 240-acre ranch.

Student Life: More than 95% of the students come from Texas. About 30% live on campus; unmarried freshmen and sophomores must do so. Dormitories are single-sex.

Organizations: Nine percent of the women belong to the 4 sororities with chapters on campus, and 7% of the men belong to the 6 fraternities. Other campus activities include student government, music, drama, publications, radio and television, debate, and special-interest, religious, and departmental groups.

Sports: West Texas State College competes on an intercollegiate level in 7 sports for men and 6 for women. Sixteen intramural sports are available.

Graduates: About 25% of the freshmen drop out, and 30% remain to graduate. About 25% of the graduates seek advanced degrees.

Services: Students receive free counseling and health care. Placement services are available for both students and graduates.

Programs of Study: The university confers the undergraduate degrees of B.A., B.A.A.S., B.B.A., B.F.A., B.Mus., B.B.E., B.Mus.Ed., B.S., B.S.Med.Tech., and B.S.N. Master's degrees also are available. Bachelor's degrees are offered in the following subjects: BUSINESS (accounting, administrative services, agricultural business administration, business education, computer science, finance, industrial distribution, industrial technology, management, marketing), EDUCATION (elementary, health/physical, industrial, recreation, secondary), ENGLISH (English, journalism, speech), FINE AND PERFORMING ARTS (art, art education, communications graphics, music, music education, radio/TV, theater/dramatics), HEALTH SCIENCES (medical technology, music therapy, nursing, speech and hearing, therapy), LANGUAGES (French, German, Spanish), MATH AND SCIENCES (biology, biomedicine, chemistry, geology, mathematics, physics), PREPROFESSIONAL (agriculture, agriculture—animal science, agriculture—plant science, building construction, dentistry, engineering, law, medicine, social work, wildlife science), SOCIAL SCIENCES (criminal justice administration, economics, geography, government/political science, history, psychology, public administration, social sciences, sociology).

Required: All students must take a distribution of courses in English, communications, fine arts and humanities, natural science, social sciences, and physical education.

Special: Combination bachelor's and professional degrees are available in dentistry, engineering, law, veterinary medicine, and medicine. Independent study is offered.

Honors: Four national honor societies are represented on campus. A university-wide honors program is offered.

Admissions: Almost all who applied were accepted for a recent freshman class. Applicants should be graduates of accredited high schools, preferably having completed 16 units. Non-high-school graduates 18 or older with GED certificates also are eligible. The most important factors in the admissions decision are high school record and ACT or SAT scores.

Procedure: Applicants must take the ACT or SAT. Application deadlines are open. There is no application fee.

Special: An early admissions plan is available. AP and CLEP credit is accepted.

Transfer: Applicants must be in good standing at their last school. D grades may transfer if the student has earned Bs for the same number of credits. Students must earn at least 30 credits in residence of the 124 required for a bachelor's degree.

Financial Aid: Over 25% of the students receive aid. Freshman scholarships are granted each year, and students also may apply for federal, state, or private loans. Campus jobs, including CWS, also are available. Financial aid is awarded on the basis of financial need, academic record, character, and promise. The average award to a 1981–82 freshman was $1800. Aid candidates must submit the FAF or FFS, and applications should be filed 6 weeks before registration for priority consideration.

Foreign Students: Students from foreign countries make up 3% of enrollment. The university offers these students special counseling and special organizations.

Admissions: Applicants must score at least 525 on the TOEFL. They also must take the SAT or ACT.

Procedure: Application deadlines are open. Students must present a completed medical form as proof of good health and must show evidence of adequate funds for the full period they plan to study at the university. They also must arrange for health insurance.

Admissions Contact: Donald Cates, Dean of Admissions and Registrar.

WILEY COLLEGE E-2
Marshall, Texas 75670 (214) 938-8341

F/T: 295M, 308W Faculty: 34; IIB, — —$
P/T: 18M, 17W Ph.D.'s: 26%
Grad: none S/F Ratio: 18 to 1
Year: sems, ss Tuition: $2195
Appl: Aug. 10 R and B: $1754
800 applied 800 accepted 285 enrolled
SAT or ACT: not required NONCOMPETITIVE

Wiley College, founded in 1873 as a college for blacks, offers programs in the liberal arts, the sciences, and teacher training. It is affiliated with the United Methodist Church. The library contains about 80,000 volumes.

Environment: The 58-acre campus is located in a community of about 25,000 people, 35 miles from Shreveport, Louisiana. Major buildings on campus include a science facility, the library, a student union, and 2 dormitories.

Student Life: About 80% of the students come from Texas or neighboring states. Most of the students are black. Three-fourths live on campus in the single-sex dorms. A weekly chapel hour is held.

Organizations: Eight fraternities and 8 sororities have chapters on campus. The college sponsors music groups, departmental clubs, religious organizations, publications, cultural events, and other extracurricular activities.

Sports: The college participates in intercollegiate competition and also offers an intramural program.

Services: The following services are provided free to students: health services, personal counseling, placement and career counseling, tutoring, and remedial instruction. Placement services also are provided for graduates.

Programs of Study: The college awards the B.A., B.S., and B.B.A. degrees. Associate degrees also are offered. Bachelor's degrees are conferred in the following subjects: BUSINESS (business education, general business, hotel and restaurant management, management, nursing home administration, office administration), EDUCATION (elementary, health/physical, secondary, special), ENGLISH (English), FINE AND PERFORMING ARTS (art education, music, music education), MATH AND SCIENCES (biology, chemistry, mathematics), PHILOSOPHY (philosophy, religion), SOCIAL SCIENCES (history, sociology).

Required: Students must take basic courses in English, history, religion, mathematics, science, humanities, political science, psychology or sociology, education, and physical education.

Special: The college has a concurrent registration program with East Texas Baptist College.

Honors: Four honor societies have chapters on campus.

Admissions: All who applied were accepted for the 1981–82 freshman class. Wiley maintains an open admissions policy. Freshman applicants must be high school graduates or have GED test scores of at least 40.

Procedure: The ACT or SAT is used for counseling purposes only. A letter of recommendation from a high school counselor or teacher is required. Application deadlines are August 10 (fall), December 10 (spring), and April 10 (summer). There is a $10 application fee.

Special: The college has an early admissions plan.

Transfer: Transfer applicants must be in good standing at their last college. D grades do not transfer. Students must complete at least 30 hours in residence of the 124 required for a bachelor's degree.

Financial Aid: About 98% of the students receive aid. Wiley participates in NDSL, CWS, and other programs. Loans, grants, and scholarships are offered by the United Methodist Church. Part-time campus jobs are available. Aid is awarded according to need and academic achievement. Applications for aid should be submitted at least 2 months before enrollment. A deferred payment plan is available. Dependents of ministers of the supporting church and of faculty and staff are eligible for a 40% reduction of tuition.

Foreign Students: Students from foreign countries represent 4% of enrollment. Special counseling and special organizations are provided.

Admissions: Applicants must score at least 400 on the TOEFL. Other tests may be required.

Procedure: Application deadlines are the same as those for American students. Foreign students must submit a completed medical form and provide proof of adequate funds for 4 years.

Admissions Contact: Susie Robinson, Director of Admissions.

UTAH

BRIGHAM YOUNG UNIVERSITY C-2
Provo, Utah 84602 (801) 378-2537

F/T: 12,874M, 11,692W	Faculty: n/av
P/T: 302M, 3434W	Ph.D.'s: 63%
Grad: 1943M, 839W	S/F Ratio: 19 to 1
Year: tri, ss	Tuition: $1100 (Latter-Day Saints)
	$1650 (others)
Appl: Apr. 30	R and B: $1740
6198 applied	4742 accepted	3904 enrolled
ACT: 23		COMPETITIVE

Brigham Young University, established in 1876, is a private institution operated by the Church of Jesus Christ of the Latter-Day Saints. The library holds 1.5 million volumes and 720,000 microfilm items, and subscribes to 17,000 periodicals.

Environment: The 536-acre campus, located 45 miles south of Salt Lake City in the heart of the Rocky Mountains, overlooks Provo and the Utah Valley. Forty-one residence halls house 3355 women and 2061 men. There are 812 units, including 150 trailers, for married couples. Apartment-type buildings for women also are available.

Student Life: About 32% of the students come from Utah. About a third live on campus. Dormitories are single-sex. Students are governed by an honor code that requires them to maintain high standards of morality. Abstinence from tobacco, alcohol, tea, and coffee is mandatory. There is a campus dress code.

Organizations: Among the distinctive features of student social life are geographical organizations representing all sections of the United States and many foreign countries, and 139 church groups (wards) that provide religious and social programs and opportunities for leadership. There are no fraternities or sororities. Off-campus recreational facilities include theaters and a ski resort.

Sports: The university competes on an intercollegiate level in 11 sports for men and 8 for women. Intramural sports also are offered.

Handicapped: The entire campus is accessible to handicapped students. Special facilities include wheelchair ramps, designated parking areas, elevators, and specially equipped rest rooms. Seven percent of the students are visually impaired; special reading rooms and elevator buttons are provided. Nine staff members offer other assistance to handicapped students.

Graduates: Twenty percent of the graduates pursue further study.

Services: Psychological counseling, placement aid, and career counseling are offered free.

Programs of Study: The university confers the B.A., B.S., B.Mus., and B.F.A. degrees. Associate, master's, and doctoral degrees also are awarded. Bachelor's degrees are offered in the following subjects: AREA STUDIES (American, Asian, European, Latin American, Mexican, Near-Eastern, Spanish-speaking American), BUSINESS (accounting, agricultural, business education, computer science, management, travel/tourism), EDUCATION (early childhood, elementary, health/physical, industrial, recreation, secondary, special), ENGLISH (communications, English, journalism, literature), FINE AND PERFORMING ARTS (art, art education, dance, design and graphics technology, environmental design, music, music education, film/photography, radio/TV, theater/dramatics), HEALTH SCIENCES (food science, health science, medical dietetics, medical technology, nursing, nutrition, pre-physical therapy, speech therapy), LANGUAGES (Chinese, French, German, Greek/Latin, Italian, Japanese, linguistics, Portuguese, Russian, Spanish), MATH AND SCIENCES (botany, chemistry, ecology/environmental science, geology, mathematics, microbiology, physics, statistics, zoology), PHILOSOPHY (classics, humanities, philosophy), PREPROFESSIONAL (agriculture—agronomy, agriculture—animal science, building construction, clothing and textiles, electronics technology, engineering—chemical, engineering—civil, engineering—mechanical, home economics, horticulture, interior environment, law, manufacturing technology, range science, social work, veterinary), SOCIAL SCIENCES (anthropology, economics, geography, government/political science, history, international relations, justice administration, psychology, public policy, sociology, youth leadership).

Required: Each student is required to take a 2-hour course in religion every semester. Students also must fulfill general education requirements.

Special: An entire college of 6 departments is devoted to major and minor programs on family life. Students may obtain credit for travel under the travel-study program and may create their own majors. An independent studies degree is available.

Honors: Four national honor societies have chapters on campus. The university offers a general honors program.

Admissions: About 77% of those who applied were accepted for the 1981–82 freshman class. The ACT scores of those who enrolled were as follows: 31% below 21, 38% between 21 and 25, and 31% above 25. Admission is based on "expected GPA," a combination of the high school GPA and the ACT score; there is unconditional acceptance at 2.4. Also important is a confidential interview with the applicant's bishop or ecclesiastical leader. A student who has not graduated but has completed 16 Carnegie units may receive special consideration. Persons 19 or over may take the highest level GED.

Procedure: The ACT is required. Application deadlines are April 30 (fall), November 1 (winter), March 1 (spring), and April 30 (summer). Freshmen are admitted each semester. There is a $15 application fee.

Special: An early admissions plan is available.

Transfer: In a recent year, 3549 students applied, 2591 were accepted, and 2382 enrolled. A GPA of at least 2.5 is required. Transfers are accepted for all classes. Students must study at the university for at least 30 credit hours of the 128 or more required for a bachelor's degree. The fall application deadline is July 1.

Visiting: Guides are available for informal visits to the campus on weekdays from 11 A.M. to 2 P.M. Visitors may sit in on classes and to stay overnight at the school. Visits can be arranged through Campus Tours (801) 378-1211.

Financial Aid: About 26% of the students receive aid in the form of institutional loans, scholarships, and grants (exclusive of government loans, grants, etc.). Campus jobs also are available. The FFS is required. The deadlines for aid applications are April 30 for freshmen and July 1 for transfer students.

Foreign Students: Five percent of the full-time students come from foreign countries. The university offers these students an intensive English course, special counseling, and special organizations.

Admissions: Students must score 500 or better on the TOEFL. They also must take the SAT or the ACT.

Procedure: Application deadlines for fall admission are May 30 for incoming freshmen and June 15 for transfer students. The deadline for winter entry is October 15; for spring entry, February 1; and for summer entry, April 15. Foreign students must submit a completed medical form as proof of good health and must show evidence of funds adequate to cover the entire period of study.

Admissions Contact: Jeffrey M. Tanner, Director of Admissions.

SOUTHERN UTAH STATE COLLEGE B-4
Cedar City, Utah 84720 (801) 586-7740

F/T, P/T:	Faculty: 96; IIB, +$
1036M, 1070W	Ph.D.'s: 55%
Grad: n/av	S/F Ratio: 14 to 1
Year: qtrs, ss	Tuition: $684 ($1722)
Appl: Sept. 1	R and B: $585–1545
171 applied	171 accepted	171 enrolled
SAT, ACT: not required		NONCOMPETITIVE

Southern Utah State College, established in 1897, is a state institution offering programs in the arts and sciences, education, business, and technology. The library contains 125,500 volumes and subscribes to 800 periodicals.

Environment: The college's 105-acre main campus is located in a small rural community about 260 miles south of Salt Lake City. There are 27 buildings, including coed dormitories and apartments that ac-

898 UTAH

commodate 502 men and women and 48 married families. The college also operates a 3700-acre ranch and a 1000-acre farm.

Student Life: Eighty percent of the undergraduates are from Utah. About 21% of the students live on campus. About 5% of the students are minority-group members. Campus housing is single-sex; there are visiting privileges. Students may keep cars on campus.

Organizations: There are 4 fraternities and 3 sororities; about 7% of the men and 16% of the women belong. Extracurricular activities include student government, publications, departmental and recreational clubs, cultural and service organizations, choral groups, theater, and jazz band.

Sports: The college fields 8 intercollegiate teams for men and 3 for women. There are 6 intramural sports for men and 5 for women.

Graduates: The freshman dropout rate is about 46%; 50% remain to graduate. Twelve percent pursue graduate study after graduation.

Services: Students receive the following services free of charge: personal and career counseling, placement service, and remedial instruction. Health care, tutoring, and psychological counseling are available for a fee.

Programs of Study: All programs lead to the B.A. or B.S. degree. Bachelor's degrees are offered in the following subjects: BUSINESS (accounting, business administration, computer science, marketing), EDUCATION (elementary, health/physical, industrial, reading, secondary), ENGLISH (communications, English), FINE AND PERFORMING ARTS (art, art education, music, music education, theater/dramatics), LANGUAGES (German, Spanish), MATH AND SCIENCES (biology, botany, chemistry, earth science, mathematics, physical sciences, physics, zoology), PREPROFESSIONAL (agriculture, dentistry, engineering, forestry, home economics/family life, law, medicine, pharmacy, veterinary), SOCIAL SCIENCES (anthropology, economics, government/political science, history, psychology, sociology). Thirty-three percent of the degrees conferred are in education, 18% in business and management, and 11% in biological sciences.

Required: All students must complete 53 credit hours of general education requirements, including courses in physical education, language arts, applied sciences, behavioral and social sciences, humanities, life sciences, and physical sciences.

Special: The college offers an Upward Bound program for economically deprived students. Independent study and cooperative education programs are possible. Certificates are awarded to students completing vocational (nondegree) programs.

Admissions: One hundred percent of those who applied were accepted for the 1981-82 freshman class. All applicants who have graduated from an accredited high school or who have passed the GED test are eligible for admission. The minimum high school grade average required is 2.0.

Procedure: All freshman applicants are encouraged to take the ACT. The application deadlines are September 1 (fall), December 1 (winter), March 1 (spring), and June 1 (summer). Admission is on a rolling basis. The application fee is $10.

Special: Early admissions and early decision programs are offered. AP and CLEP credit is available.

Transfer: For fall 1981, 313 transfer students applied. All were accepted and all enrolled. The college will accept a maximum of 112 credit hours earned at an accredited junior college. Students with less than 45 quarter hours of college credit must submit an ACT Student Profile. All passing grades are accepted for credit. Transcripts of all previous college work are required. All students must complete, at the college, at least 50% of the major; 183 credits are required for the bachelor's degree. Application deadlines are the same as for freshmen.

Financial Aid: About 55% of all students receive aid through the college; 22% work part-time on campus. Financial need is the basis for most awards (except scholarships). Available programs include BEOG, SEOG, NDSL, and CWS. In addition, the college offers regular part-time employment and loan and scholarship programs. The average award to freshmen is $650. The FAF is required; the aid application deadline is May 1. Notification of awards is sent by April 1.

Foreign Students: About 1% of the students come from foreign countries. The college offers these students an intensive English course, special counseling, and special organizations.

Admissions: Foreign students must achieve a minimum TOEFL score of 500; no further exams are required.

Procedure: Application deadlines are September 1 for fall, December 1 for winter, March 1 for spring, and June 1 for summer. Foreign students must present proof of health and proof of funds adequate to cover 1 year of study. They must also carry health insurance, which is available through the college for a fee.

Admissions Contact: Ward Robb, Director of Admissions.

UNIVERSITY OF UTAH   C-2
Salt Lake City, Utah 84112   (801) 581-7281

F/T: 8943M, 4770W
P/T: 2717M, 2360W
Grad: 2028M, 1344W
Year: qtrs, ss
Appl: Aug. 1
4739 applied
ACT: 20

Faculty: 1370; I, +$
Ph.D.'s: 89%
S/F Ratio: 17 to 1
Tuition: $1930 ($5120)
R and B: $2700
3901 accepted   2872 enrolled
COMPETITIVE

Founded in 1850, the University of Utah is a tax-assisted institution that serves as the major research center of the region. The library contains 1.9 million volumes and 1.3 million microfilm items, and subscribes to 17,250 periodicals.

Environment: The 1500-acre suburban campus, located along the western edge of the Wasatch Mountains, houses 214 permanent buildings; a $70-million addition to the College of Medicine has recently been completed. Living facilities include dormitories, on-campus apartments, married student housing, and sorority and fraternity houses.

Student Life: The students attending the university represent every county in Utah and every state in the union. About 95% come from public schools. Ten percent live in university housing. Six percent of the students are minority-group members. University housing is both single-sex and coed. There are visiting privileges in some single-sex housing. Students may keep cars on campus.

Organizations: Eight sororities and 11 fraternities have chapters on campus; 7% of the women and 7% of the men are members. A full schedule of cultural programs is presented each year, including musical and dramatic productions, films, concerts, and performances by the university opera and ballet companies. Six major ski resorts are located less than 45 minutes from campus, and the adjacent mountain country also provides outdoor diversion.

Sports: The university participates in 10 sports on an intercollegiate level for men and 10 for women. The extensive intramural program includes 15 sports for both men and women.

Handicapped: The campus is 90% accessible to the handicapped student. Special facilities include wheelchair ramps, elevators, specially equipped rest rooms, lowered drinking fountains and telephones, and designated parking. Special class scheduling is also available. The Counseling Office for the Handicapped has a staff of 3 to provide special assistance.

Graduates: Twenty percent of the freshmen drop out by the end of their first year. About half of the freshmen remain to graduate. Recently, more than 20% of the graduates pursued further study. About 56% pursued careers in business and industry.

Services: Health care, tutoring, remedial instruction, psychological counseling, placement service, and career counseling are all offered for a fee to students.

Programs of Study: The university confers the B.F.A., B.S., B.A., B.Mus., and Bachelor of University Studies degrees. Master's and doctoral degrees are also granted. Bachelor's degrees are offered in the following subjects: AREA STUDIES (family and consumer, leisure, Middle East, urban), BUSINESS (accounting, computer science, economics, management, marketing), EDUCATION (early childhood, elementary, health/physical, industrial, secondary, special), ENGLISH (English, speech), FINE AND PERFORMING ARTS (art, art history, dance, music, speech/theater, theater/dramatics), HEALTH SCIENCES (nursing, physical therapy, speech therapy), LANGUAGES (French, German, Greek/Latin), MATH AND SCIENCES (biology, chemistry, geology, geophysics, materials science, mathematics, meteorology, physics), PHILOSOPHY (philosophy), PREPROFESSIONAL (engineering—chemical, engineering—electrical, engineering—fuels, engineering—mechanical, engineering—metallurgical, engineering—mining), SOCIAL SCIENCES (anthropology, economics, government/political science, psychology, social sciences, sociology). Of the degrees conferred, 24% are in social sciences, 18% in preprofessional studies, and 17% in business.

Required: All students must complete liberal education requirements.

Special: The university offers a unique program in liberal education known as the Utah Plan. A self-designed Bachelor of University Studies degree is offered. Study abroad programs are available.

Honors: Sixteen honor societies, including Phi Beta Kappa, have chapters on campus. Honors programs are available in all departments.

Admissions: About 82% of those who applied were accepted for the 1981-82 freshman class. Of those who enrolled, the ACT scores were as follows: 47% below 21, 24% between 21 and 23, 12% between 24 and 25, 12% between 26 and 28, and 5% above 28. Applicants are required to be graduates of accredited high schools with a GPA of 2.5 or a sufficiently high ACT score to predict reasonable success.

Procedure: The ACT is required of in-state students. The SAT is accepted from out-of-state students only. Deadlines are August 1 (fall), December 1 (winter), February 25 (spring), and May 25 (summer). Notification is on a rolling basis. There is a $25 application fee. An additional $15 is charged for late applications.

Special: There is an early admissions plan. AP and CLEP credit is granted.

Transfer: For fall 1981, 2428 students applied, and 2138 were accepted. A GPA of 2.0 is required. Thirty of the final 45 quarter hours must be completed in residence of the 183 needed for a bachelor's degree. Application deadlines are the same as those for freshman applicants.

Visiting: Guides are available for informal weekday visits to the campus. Visitors may sit in on classes and stay at the school if space permits. Arrangements for visits can be made through the Office of High School Services.

Financial Aid: About 53% of the students receive aid. Three percent work part-time on campus. The average aid to freshmen from all sources is $1138. Work-study programs are available in 25 departments. The university is a member of CSS. The FAF is required. The aid application deadline for the fall is February 1 (merit) and April 1 (need).

Foreign Students: Four percent of the full-time students come from foreign countries. The university offers these students special counseling and special organizations.

Admissions: Foreign students must achieve a score of at least 500 on the TOEFL. No college entrance examination is required.

Procedure: The application deadline is April 1 (fall). Foreign students must submit a physician's statement certifying good health. Foreign students must also provide proof of funds adequate to cover 9 months, or of $6021. They must also pay a special processing fee of $25.

Admissions Contact: Robert E. Finley, Director of Admissions.

UTAH STATE UNIVERSITY
Logan, Utah 84322 C-1
(801) 750-1106

F/T: 2819M, 2170W
P/T: 2123M, 1630W
Grad: 1026M, 522W
Year: qtrs, ss
Appl: Sept. 1
2983 applied   2852 accepted   2119 enrolled
ACT: required   LESS COMPETITIVE

Faculty: 447; I, −$
Ph.D.'s: 60%
S/F Ratio: 20 to 1
Tuition: $786 ($2103)
R and B: $1800

Established in 1888, Utah State University, which is under public control, has been designated as a world center for arid land ecology. Undergraduate divisions include 8 colleges: Agriculture; Business; Education; Engineering; Family Life; Humanities, Arts, and Social Sciences; Natural Resources; and Science. The library contains 525,-265 volumes, 130,519 bound serials, and 527,728 microfilm items, and subscribes to 6500 periodicals.

Environment: The 332-acre campus, located in a suburban area 80 miles north of Salt Lake City, houses Old Main, an historical monument. Dormitories are available for 976 men and 976 women, and there are institutional apartments for 505 married student families. In addition, there are 153 spaces in the university's Trailor Courts. The college also sponsors fraternity and sorority houses.

Student Life: The student body comes largely from Utah and other western states, although all states and some 90 foreign countries are represented. Most students live either in dormitories or in apartments near the campus. Drinking is prohibited on campus. About 3% of the students are minority-group members. Campus housing is single-sex; there are visiting privileges. Students may keep cars on campus. Daycare services are available to all students, faculty, and staff.

Organizations: There are 6 fraternities and 3 sororities on campus; membership is negligible. Extracurricular activities available to students include concerts, plays, theater, dances, and local skiing.

Sports: The university fields 9 intercollegiate teams for men and 7 for women. There are 13 intramural sports for men and 10 for women.

Handicapped: The campus is 90% accessible to the handicapped student. Special facilities include wheelchair ramps, designated parking, elevators, specially equipped rest rooms, and lowered drinking fountains and telephones. Special class scheduling can also be arranged. Special facilities available to visually impaired students are tape recorders and braille computers. Special assistance is available for hearing impaired students through the Hearing and Speech Impairment Department.

Graduates: The freshman dropout rate is 55%; 20% remain to graduate. Twenty-two percent of the students go on to further study after graduation. Seventy percent pursue careers in business or industry.

Services: Students are offered the following services free of charge: health care, psychological counseling, placement service, career counseling, and remedial instruction.

Programs of Study: The university confers the B.A., B.S., B.F.A., and B.L.A. degrees. Master's and doctoral degrees are also awarded. Bachelor's degrees are offered in the following subjects: AREA STUDIES (American), BUSINESS (accounting, agricultural economics, agribusiness, business administration, business education, finance, management, marketing, personnel and industrial relations), EDUCATION (early childhood, elementary, health/physical, industrial, secondary, special), ENGLISH (English, journalism, speech), FINE AND PERFORMING ARTS (art, dance, music, theater/dramatics), LANGUAGES (French, German, Spanish), MATH AND SCIENCES (biology, chemistry, geology, mathematics, physics, statistics), PHILOSOPHY (philosophy), PREPROFESSIONAL (animal science, architecture, clothing and textiles, dairy science, dentistry, engineering—agriculture and irrigation, engineering—civil and environmental, engineering—electrical, engineering—mechanical, forestry, home economics, international agriculture, landscape architecture/environmental planning, law, medicine, plant science/soil science, range science, social work, veterinary, watershed science, wildlife science), SOCIAL SCIENCES (economics, family/human development, general family life, geography, government/political science, history, outdoor recreation, psychology, sociology).

Required: All students must take 6 units in basic communication, and distribution units in 4 broad areas.

Special: Experimental curricula are offered; these include curricula as a function of the learning-living environment and with respect to general education requirements. Another innovation is the SILEX (Student-Initiated Learning Experience) Program. A major in liberal arts is offered. Student-designed majors are permitted.

Honors: A general honors program is offered in which most departments participate.

Admissions: About 96% of those who applied were accepted for the 1981-82 freshman class. The ACT scores of those who enrolled were as follows: 59% below 21, 16% between 21 and 23, 15% between 24 and 25, 6% between 26 and 28, and 4% above 28. Applicants must be graduates of approved schools or the equivalent.

Procedure: The ACT is required. (The SAT will be accepted if the combined score exceeds 900.) Application deadlines are September 1 (fall), December 1 (winter), March 1 (spring), and June 1 (summer). Notification is on a rolling basis. Freshmen are admitted each quarter. There is an application fee of $15.

Special: Early decision and early admissions plans are available. The application deadline for early admission is September 1. CLEP and AP credit is granted.

Transfer: For a recent year 437 transfer students were accepted for all classes. A minimum 2.2 GPA is required. Students are required to complete, at the university, at least 45 of the 186 quarter credits required to earn a bachelor's degree. Deadlines for application are the same as those for freshmen.

Visiting: Guides are available for informal visits to the campus. Visitors may sit in on classes and stay at the school. Arrangements for visits, preferably at 10:30 A.M., can be made through School Services.

Financial Aid: About 33% of the students receive aid; about 20% of the students work part-time on campus. Federal loans and scholarships are available. Work-study programs are offered in practically all departments. The university is a member of the CSS and requires the FAF. The deadline for aid applications is March 1.

Foreign Students: About 10% of the students are from foreign countries. The university offers these students an intensive English course, special counseling, and special organizations.

Admissions: Foreign students must achieve a satisfactory TOEFL score; no further exams are required.

Procedure: Application deadlines are September 1 for fall, December 1 for winter, March 1 for spring, and June 1 for summer. Foreign students must present proof of funds adequate to cover 1 year of study.

900 UTAH

They must also carry health insurance, which is available through the university for a fee.

Admissions Contact: Lynn J. Poulsen, Assistant Director for Admission and Registration Services.

WEBER STATE COLLEGE C–1
Ogden, Utah 84408 (801) 626-6046

F/T: 4204M, 3748W *Faculty:* 425; IIB, ++$
P/T: 1473M, 715W *Ph.D.'s:* 80%
Grad: 34M, 56W *S/F Ratio:* 20 to 1
Year: qtrs, ss *Tuition:* $705 ($1785)
Appl: Sept. 1 *R and B:* $1950
2265 applied 2137 accepted 1823 enrolled
ACT: 17 **LESS COMPETITIVE**

Weber State College, a state-controlled institution founded in 1889, offers programs in liberal arts and sciences, business, education, and preprofessional fields. The library contains over 250,000 volumes, subscribes to 2160 periodicals, and has 100,000 microfilm items.

Environment: The college's 375-acre campus is located in a suburban area 35 miles from Salt Lake City. The residence halls house 700 undergraduates.

Student Life: All but 40% of the students come from the metropolitan area nearby, and many more are Utah residents. Ninety percent of the entering freshmen come from public schools. Ten percent of the students live on campus. Counselors are available for members of all faiths. A curfew is observed in the residence halls. About 7% of the students are minority-group members. Campus housing is single-sex; there are visiting privileges. Students may keep cars on campus.

Organizations: Two percent of the men belong to 3 national fraternities; 2% of the women, to 3 local sororities. An active student government sponsors lectures, concerts, debates, and social activities. Professional clubs also supplement the varieties of educational experience that the college affords.

Sports: The college fields 7 intercollegiate teams for men and 7 for women. There are 13 intramural sports for men and 10 for women.

Handicapped: The campus is 100% accessible to the handicapped student. Special facilities include wheelchair ramps, elevators, designated parking, specially equipped rest rooms, and lowered drinking fountains. Special class scheduling is also available.

Graduates: The freshman dropout rate is 45%; 35% remain to graduate. Of those who graduate, 20% pursue further study.

Services: Tutoring, remedial instruction, psychological counseling, placement service, career counseling, and health care are offered at no charge to the student.

Programs of Study: The college confers the B.A. and B.S. degrees. Associate and master's degrees are also awarded. Bachelor's degrees are offered in the following subjects: BUSINESS (accounting, business education, computer science, finance, management, marketing, office administration), EDUCATION (early childhood, elementary, family relations, health/physical, secondary), ENGLISH (English, journalism, speech), FINE AND PERFORMING ARTS (art, broadcasting, music, theater/dramatics), HEALTH SCIENCES (allied health sciences, medical technology), LANGUAGES (French, German, Spanish), MATH AND SCIENCES (botany, chemistry, geology, mathematics, microbiology, physics, zoology), PREPROFESSIONAL (engineering, social work), SOCIAL SCIENCES (economics, geography, government/political science, history, police science, psychology, sociology).

Required: All students must take courses in English, health education, physical education, humanities, life sciences, physical sciences, and social sciences.

Special: A general studies degree program is available. One quarter may be spent studying in Mexico.

Honors: Phi Kappa Phi has a chapter on campus.

Admissions: Ninety-four percent of those who applied were accepted for the 1981–82 freshman class. Candidates must be graduates of accredited high schools. The ACT is used mainly for placement purposes.

Procedure: The ACT is strongly preferred; the SAT is accepted. Application deadlines are September 1 (fall), December 1 (winter), March 1 (spring), and June 1 (summer). Freshmen are admitted each semester. Notification is on a rolling basis. There is a $15 application fee.

Special: Early decision, early admissions, and deferred admissions plans are offered. AP and CLEP credit is available.

Transfer: For fall 1981, 1071 transfer students applied and 935 were accepted. Applicants must be in good standing, be eligible to return to their previous colleges, and have a GPA of 2.0. D grades may be transferred. Students must complete, at the college, at least 45 of the 183 credits required for the bachelor's degree. Deadlines are the same as those for freshmen.

Visiting: There are regularly scheduled orientations for prospective students. Guides are available for informal visits to the campus during regular quarters. Visitors are permitted to sit in on classes and stay at the school. Arrangements can be made with the Director of High School and College Relations.

Financial Aid: Approximately 38% of the students receive aid; 18% work part-time on campus. Financial aid is available in the form of scholarships, loans, and grants. Work-study programs are available in all departments. The average award to freshmen from all sources is $850. The college requires students to file the Pell Grant financial statement. Deadline for scholarship applications is February; for other financial aid, August 15.

Foreign Students: About 4% of the students come from foreign countries. The college offers these students special counseling and special organizations.

Admissions: Foreign students must achieve a TOEFL score of 550 or a score of 85 on the University of Michigan Language Test; no further exams are required.

Procedure: Application deadlines are 60 days before the start of each quarter. Foreign students must present proof of funds adequate to cover 1 year of study. Health insurance is available through the college for a fee.

Admissions Contact: L. Winslow Hurst, Director of Admissions.

WESTMINSTER COLLEGE C–2
Salt Lake City, Utah 84105 (801) 484-7651

F/T: 253M, 289W *Faculty:* 59; IIB, –$
P/T: 253M, 364W *Ph.D.'s:* 60%
Grad: 19M, 25W *S/F Ratio:* 17 to 1
Year: 4-1-4, ss *Tuition:* $3290
Appl: Sept. 1 *R and B:* $2097
246 applied 186 accepted 109 enrolled
ACT: 19 **COMPETITIVE**

Westminster College, founded in 1875, is a nonsectarian liberal arts college affiliated with the United Presbyterian Church, the United Methodist Church, and the United Church of Christ. The library contains 60,000 volumes, subscribes to 400 periodicals, and has 1550 microfilm items.

Environment: The 27-acre campus is located in a residential, urban area 2 miles from Salt Lake City. The 14 buildings include 2 dormitories housing 120 women and 125 men.

Student Life: Approximately 70% of the students come from Utah. Twenty percent reside in dormitories. Eighty percent of the freshmen come from public schools. Although the college has a trichurch affiliation, the student body is made up of all religious faiths. Campus housing is single-sex; there are visiting privileges. Students may keep cars on campus.

Organizations: There are no fraternities or sororities. The college sponsors on-campus art shows, films, lectures, plays, recitals, and other cultural and social events. Major ski areas are 30 minutes from the campus.

Sports: There are no intercollegiate sports. There are 9 intramural sports for men and 9 for women.

Handicapped: The campus is 20% accessible to the handicapped student. Special facilities are wheelchair ramps, designated parking, and elevators.

Graduates: The freshman dropout rate is 20%; 40% remain to graduate. Of the graduates, 10% pursue further study. Fifty-nine percent pursue careers in business or industry.

Services: The following services are offered at no charge to students: psychological counseling, remedial instruction, health care, and career counseling. Placement and tutoring are available for a fee.

Programs of Study: The college confers the B.A. and B.S. degrees. Master's degrees are also awarded. Bachelor's degrees are offered in the following subjects: BUSINESS (accounting, computer science, finance, management, marketing), EDUCATION (early childhood, elementary, secondary), ENGLISH (English), FINE AND PERFORMING ARTS (art, theater/dramatics), HEALTH SCIENCES (medical technology, nursing), LANGUAGES (French, Spanish), MATH AND SCIENCES (biology, chemistry, mathematics, natural sciences, physical sciences, physics), PHILOSOPHY (philosophy, religion), PRE-PROFESSIONAL (dentistry, law, medicine, veterinary), SOCIAL SCIENCES (government/political science, history, psychology, sociology). Of the degrees conferred, 23% are in health sciences; 22%, in social sciences; 16%, in business.

Required: All students must take courses in one or more of the following areas: English, history, religion, natural science or math, philosophy, social science, fine arts, and (for the B.A.) a foreign language.

Special: The college offers a general studies degree. Student-designed majors are permitted.

Honors: An honors seminar is available to students with a GPA of 3.5. The humanities department (philosophy and religion) offers honors programs.

Admissions: Seventy-six percent of those who applied were accepted for the 1981-82 freshman class. Candidates should have a C average, and come from an accredited high school with recommendations from the high school authorities. Other factors in the admissions decision, in order of importance, are leadership record, advanced placement or honor courses, and extracurricular activities record.

Procedure: Either the SAT or ACT should be taken. Application deadlines are September 1 for the fall, and December 1 for the spring. Notification is on a rolling basis. Freshmen are admitted each semester. There is a $20 application fee.

Special: Early decision and early admissions plans are offered. The application deadline for early admission is 1 month before the registration date. CLEP and AP credit is granted to qualified students.

Transfer: For fall 1981, 221 transfer students applied, 181 were accepted, and 128 enrolled. Transfers are considered for all classes. Students must complete, at the college, 30 credits of the 124 required for the bachelor's degree. Applicants should have at least a C average; grades of C or higher transfer. Application deadlines are 30 days prior to the start of the semester.

Visiting: A campus open house is held each spring. Guides are available for informal visits to the campus, preferably in the middle of a semester. Visitors may sit in on classes and stay at the school. Arrangements can be made with the dean of admissions.

Financial Aid: About 55% of the students receive aid; 20% of the students work part-time on campus. A comprehensive federal and college financial program is available, including tuition grants for the disadvantaged. The average award to a freshman is $3500. Tuition may be paid in installments. The college is a member of CSS and requires either the FAF, FFS, or SFS. The aid application should be received by the college by February 1.

Foreign Students: About 5% of the full-time students are from foreign countries. The college offers these students an intensive English program, special counseling, and special organizations.

Admissions: Foreign students must achieve a TOEFL score of 500 or a score of 82 on the University of Michigan Language Test; no further exams are required.

Procedure: Application deadlines are August 1 for fall and December 1 for spring. Foreign students must present proof of funds adequate to cover 1 year of study. Health insurance is available through the college for a fee.

Admissions Contact: Craig Green, Dean of Admissions.

VERMONT

BENNINGTON COLLEGE A-6
Bennington, Vermont 05201   (802) 442-6349

F/T: 189M, 439W
P/T: 4M
Grad: 4M, 3W
Year: see profile
Appl: Mar. 1
472 applied   374 accepted   208 enrolled
SAT, ACT: not required   VERY COMPETITIVE

Faculty: 58; n/av
Ph.D.'s: 25%
S/F Ratio: 9 to 1
Tuition: $8260
R and B: $2300

Bennington College, founded in 1925, is an experimental liberal arts institution limited to approximately 600 students. The Edward Clark Crossett Library houses over 90,000 volumes and subscribes to more than 500 periodicals.

Environment: The 550-acre, self-contained campus is located in a rural area of Vermont 40 miles from Albany, New York. The campus is arranged in the style of a New England village, with student houses set around a green, and the library and other campus buildings nearby. The 32 buildings include 15 student houses, a science building, and a recently constructed Visual and Performing Arts Center.

Student Life: About 95% of the students come from out of state; 85% live in college-owned housing. Four percent are minority-group members. Students in each of the coeducational houses determine their own social regulations. A few of the houses are located just off campus. Fifteen percent of the students find private housing off campus. Students may keep cars on campus.

Organizations: Bennington College has no religious organizations and no sororities or fraternities. Extracurricular activities include concerts, dance and drama performances, art and photography exhibits, films, workshops, and lectures. All members of the student body, the faculty, the administration, and the staff are members of the Bennington College Community, which has an elected government that deals with all aspects of the community and campus life.

Sports: There is no organized sports program.

Graduates: About 15% of the freshmen drop out by the end of the first year; 60% remain to graduate. About 40% of the graduates pursue graduate study; 10% enter medical school and 10% enter law school. About 12% pursue careers in business and industry.

Programs of Study: The college confers the B.A. degree. Master's degrees also are awarded. Bachelor's degrees are offered in the following subjects: AREA STUDIES (American, Latin American), EDUCATION (early childhood), ENGLISH (English, literature), FINE AND PERFORMING ARTS (art, dance, music, studio art, theater/dramatics), HEALTH SCIENCES (environmental health), LANGUAGES (French, German, Spanish), MATH AND SCIENCES (biochemistry, biology, botany, chemistry, earth science, ecology/environmental science, mathematics, natural sciences, physical sciences, physics, statistics), PHILOSOPHY (humanities, philosophy), PREPROFESSIONAL (architecture), SOCIAL SCIENCES (anthropology, economics, government/political science, history, international relations, psychology, social sciences). The academic areas are divided into broadly conceived divisions that include Black music, dance, drama, literature and languages, music, natural science and mathematics, social science, and visual arts.

Special: Bennington's educational philosophy and curriculum are based on the progressive ideology of Dewey. Each student follows an individually tailored program. Many students construct inter-divisional majors. The college emphasizes independent study. Descriptive critical evaluations, which focus on the individual development within a discipline, are used instead of letter grades. The college calendar is broken into two 14-week terms and a 9-week nonresident term. The latter is designed to provide students with practical job experience. Employment and student reports are evaluated and become part of the permanent academic record.

Admissions: About 79% of the applicants for the 1981-82 freshman class were accepted. The evaluation of applicants is based on all of the following, which are studied in relation to one another: the ability the candidate possesses, the way in which that ability has been used, the scholastic standards that have been met, and the scope of the secondary school program. The school record is viewed in the context of the Personal Statement and the observations of parents, counselors, teachers, and interviewers. Standardized tests are recommended, but not required.

Procedure: Each applicant should submit the Biographical and Personal Statements along with a $25 application fee. The student's parents should submit the Family Statement, and the Secondary School report should be sent directly to the college. One recommendation should also be submitted by someone who knows the applicant, preferably a high school teacher. Each applicant must have an interview, either on or off campus. Application deadlines are March 1 for the fall and February 1 for the spring. The college follows a rolling admissions plan after January 15.

Special: There are early decision and early and deferred admissions plans.

Transfer: About 25% of all students are transfers. For fall 1981, 84 transfers applied, 67 were accepted, and 45 enrolled. An interview is required of transfer students. No less than 2 years may be spent at the

902 VERMONT

college to qualify for a bachelor's degree. Application deadlines are May 1 (fall) and February 1 (spring).

Financial Aid: Fifty percent of all students receive financial aid; 70% work part-time on campus. All aid recipients are responsible for raising $3000 from on-campus work and/or loan sources during the year. The college is a member of CSS. The college aid application and the FAF are required. The aid application deadline is February 1.

Foreign Students: Ten percent of the full-time students come from foreign countries. The college offers these students an intensive English course and special counseling.

Admissions: The TOEFL is required. College entrance exams are not necessary.

Procedure: Application deadlines are March 1 (fall) and February 1 (spring). Foreign students must furnish proof of funds adequate to cover 1 year of study. Health insurance, while not required, is available through the college for a fee.

Admissions Contact: John Nissen, Director of Admissions.

BURLINGTON COLLEGE A-2
Burlington, Vermont 05401 (802) 862-9616
(Recognized Candidate for Accreditation)

F/T: 29M, 40W Faculty: 55(p/t); n/av
P/T: 18M, 66W Ph.D.'s: 26%
Grad: none S/F Ratio: 3 to 1
Year: sems, ss Tuition: $3181
Appl: open R and B: n/app
31 enrolled
SAT or ACT: not required LESS COMPETITIVE

Burlington College, founded in 1972, is an independent liberal arts college that offers an alternative education. Students design their own programs of study; contract-based learning enables them to choose the method of evaluation.

Environment: The half-acre campus, located in the city of Burlington, does not include any living facilities.

Student Life: About 85% of the students come from Vermont. Four percent are minority-group members. All students live off campus.

Organizations: There are no fraternities or sororities. Students sit on the 7 college committees.

Sports: There are no intercollegiate or intramural sports.

Handicapped: The campus is totally accessible to handicapped students. Wheelchair ramps, special class scheduling, and specially equipped rest rooms are provided. There are no students with visual or hearing impairments now enrolled at the college.

Graduates: The freshman dropout rate is 15%; 50% remain to graduate. Twenty percent of the graduates pursue advanced degrees; 1% enter law school, and 10% enter careers in business and industry.

Services: Career counseling, tutoring, remedial instruction, and psychological counseling are provided free of charge.

Programs of Study: The college confers the B.A. degree. Associate degrees are also awarded. Almost all programs are interdisciplinary. A major in transpersonal psychology is offered.

Required: All students must take a course in communications and must complete a final project.

Special: Students design their own majors. A general studies degree is offered.

Admissions: Applicants must be high school graduates. The student's ability to benefit from the college, impressions made during the interview, and personality are important factors in the admissions decision.

Procedure: No entrance exams are required. There are no application deadlines; students are admitted in the fall, spring, and summer terms. An interview is required. The application fee is $25. Notification is on a rolling basis.

Special: AP and CLEP credit is accepted.

Transfer: For fall 1981, 22 transfer students enrolled. D grades do not transfer. All students must complete, at the college, 30 of the 120 credits required for a bachelor's degree. There are no application deadlines; transfer students are admitted in the fall, spring, and summer semesters.

Visiting: Guides are available for informal visits; visitors may sit in on classes. Early in the semester is the best time for visiting. John Owen should be contacted about arrangements.

Financial Aid: Ninety percent of the students receive aid through the college. Fifty percent work part-time on campus. The FAF, FFS, or SFS should be submitted by September 30 (fall), January 30 (spring), or June 30 (summer).

Foreign Students: No foreign students are currently enrolled at the college, but they are accepted.

Admissions: No English proficiency exams or college entrance exams are required.

Procedure: There are no application deadlines; foreign students are admitted in the fall, spring, and summer terms. They must present proof of funds adequate to cover 1 year of study.

Admissions Contact: John Owen, Admissions Director.

CASTLETON STATE COLLEGE B-4
Castleton, Vermont 05735 (802) 468-5611

F/T: 549M, 667W Faculty: 98; IIA, – – $
P/T: 196M, 389W Ph.D.'s: 45%
Grad: 95M, 132W S/F Ratio: 14 to 1
Year: sems Tuition: $1412 ($3212)
Appl: Aug. 21 R and B: $2400
1300 applied 1140 accepted 544 enrolled
SAT: 410V 430M NONCOMPETITIVE

Castleton State College, founded in 1787, is the oldest institution of higher learning in Vermont. It is a state-supported liberal arts and sciences college. Its library contains 75,000 volumes and 17,000 microfilm items, and subscribes to over 400 periodicals.

Environment: The 130-acre self-contained campus is located in Castleton, a community of 2800 12 miles from Rutland. Sixteen modern buildings include a campus center and an academic center. Four 4-story suite-type dormitories house 448 students; 1 traditional corridor-type dorm accommodates 130.

Student Life: Almost all students come from the Northeast; 60% are from Vermont. Six percent are minority-group members. Fifty percent of the students live in dormitories; 50% live off campus or commute from home. All students who do not live with parents or guardians are required to live in a college dormitory. Campus housing is both coed and single-sex. There are visiting privileges in single-sex dorms. Freshman women who live on campus must observe a curfew. Students may keep cars on campus. The college offers day-care services to all students, faculty, and staff for a fee.

Organizations: Every student is automatically a member of the Student Association and of the Athletic Association. There are various clubs and service organizations on campus. Eight percent of the men belong to 1 of 2 local fraternities; 3 percent of the women belong to the 1 national sorority. Other popular cultural and recreational activities include concerts, plays, and musicals. Skiing is available at nearby slopes.

Sports: The college competes intercollegiately in 7 sports for men and 8 for women. There are 8 intramural sports for men and 7 for women.

Handicapped: Castleton has no special facilities for the physically handicapped other than parking. About 75% of the campus is accessible to these students.

Graduates: About 15% of the freshmen drop out for academic reasons, and 65% go on to graduate. Of the graduates, 40% continue their studies: 2% enter medical school, 1% dental school, and 2% law school. Sixty percent pursue careers in business and industry.

Services: Students receive the following services free of charge: placement, career counseling, tutoring, remedial instruction, health care, and psychological counseling. The placement service for undergraduates provides job listings, a newsletter, portfolio distribution, referrals, and interview and resume preparation.

Programs of Study: The college confers the B.A. and B.S. degrees. Associate and master's degrees are also awarded. Bachelor's degrees are offered in the following subjects: BUSINESS (accounting, business education, management, marketing, small business management), EDUCATION (athletic training and exercise technology, early childhood, elementary, health/physical, secondary, special), ENGLISH (English, journalism, literature, mass media, speech), FINE AND PERFORMING ARTS (art, art education, art history, crafts, graphic arts, music, music education, radio/TV, theater/dramatics), HEALTH SCIENCES (nursing), LANGUAGES (French, Spanish), MATH AND SCIENCES (biology, mathematics, natural sciences), PREPROFESSIONAL (dentistry, law, medicine, social work, veterinary), SOCIAL SCIENCES (economics, geography, government/political science, history, psychology, social sciences, sociology). Twenty-three percent of degrees conferred are in education, 21% are in social sciences, 19% are in health sciences, and 19% are in business.

Required: All students in the teacher education program must take three-quarters of their credits in the area of general education and one-quarter in professional courses. Students must also observe public school classes and student-teach for 15 weeks.

Special: The college offers a general studies degree and allows student-designed majors. The nursing program, carried out in cooperation with Rutland Hospital, is completed in 2 academic years with a summer session after the first year. Study abroad is available.

Honors: Various honor societies have chapters on campus.

Admissions: Eighty-eight percent of the freshmen who applied were accepted for the 1981–82 class. Candidates for the freshman class should be secondary school graduates with satisfactory class standing. Out-of-state applicants should rank in the upper half of their high school class. Castleton offers open admission to all Vermont high school graduates up to the enrollment limit established by the Vermont State Colleges Board of Trustees. Admission to the nursing program is selective. The college considers the following factors: recommendations by school officials, impressions made during an interview, advanced placement or honors courses, leadership record, and evidence of special talent.

Procedure: The SAT or ACT is required. Application deadlines are August 21 (fall) and January 5 (spring). State residents are admitted on a rolling basis. A $25 fee must accompany applications.

Special: Deferred admissions requests are handled individually.

Transfer: For fall 1981, 147 transfer students enrolled at the college. All students must take, in residence, at least 30 of the 122 semester credits required for the bachelor's degree. A 2.0 GPA is necessary; D grades do not transfer. Application deadlines are the same as for freshmen.

Visiting: There are regularly scheduled orientations for prospective students. Guides are available for informal visits, during which visitors may sit in on classes. Visitors may stay overnight at the school. The best time for visits is when the college is in session; advance arrangements must be made with the admissions office.

Financial Aid: About 75% of all students receive financial aid; 30% work part-time on campus. The college, a member of CSS, awards scholarships and grants from a total fund of $717,500, which includes Vermont Incentive Grants, awarded by the Vermont Student Assistance Corporation. Available loan funds total $481,997 (with NDSL). Approximately 400 students earn $1000 each year through part-time work on and off campus. The FFS should be submitted by March 1.

Foreign Students: Fewer than 1% of the full-time students come from foreign countries. The college offers these students an intensive English course and special counseling.

Admissions: Foreign students must achieve a minimum score of 500 on the TOEFL. The SAT or ACT is not required.

Procedure: Application deadlines are January 1 (fall) and November 1 (spring). Foreign students must provide proof of funds adequate to cover 1 year of study. They must also carry health insurance, which is available through the college for a fee.

Admissions Contact: Gary Fallis, Director of Admissions.

COLLEGE OF ST. JOSEPH THE PROVIDER   B-4
Rutland, Vermont 05701   (802) 775-0806

F/T: 31M, 123W	Faculty: 9; IV, n/av
P/T: 38M, 98W	Ph.D.'s: 33%
Grad: 6M, 36W	S/F Ratio: 17 to 1
Year: sems, ss	Tuition: $3380
Appl: open	R and B: $2039
139 applied	126 accepted 56 enrolled
SAT or ACT: recommended	LESS COMPETITIVE

College of St. Joseph the Provider, founded in 1954, is an independent liberal arts and teachers' college affiliated with the Roman Catholic Sisters of St. Joseph. The library contains over 20,000 volumes and 141 microfilm items, and subscribes to more than 96 periodicals.

Environment: The 99-acre, self-contained campus is located 1 mile outside Rutland and about 160 miles from Boston. There are 5 buildings, including 2 dormitories and a central administration and classroom building that were built in the 1960s. The student center is located in the carriage house of an old estate.

Student Life: About three-fourths of the students come from Vermont. Two percent are minority-group members. Sixty-seven percent live on campus in dormitories. Campus housing is both coed and single-sex. There are visiting privileges in single-sex dorms. Students may keep cars on campus. The college provides day-care services to all students for a fee.

Organizations: The college has no fraternities or sororities. Extracurricular activities include drama, student publications, student government, and films, lectures, and plays. Two major ski areas are within 15 miles.

Sports: Three intercollegiate sports are offered for women; 1 for men. There are 3 intramural sports for men and women.

Handicapped: About 95% of the campus is accessible to handicapped students. Special facilities include wheelchair ramps, special parking, specially equipped rest rooms, and lowered drinking fountains. At present, there are no visually or hearing impaired students on campus.

Graduates: About 36% of the entering freshmen drop out at the end of the first year; 46% remain to graduate. Two percent of the graduates enter law school.

Services: The following services are provided to students free of charge: placement, psychological and career counseling, and remedial instruction.

Programs of Study: The college confers the B.A. and B.S. degrees. Associate and master's degrees are also awarded. Bachelor's degrees are offered in the following subjects: BUSINESS (accounting, business administration), EDUCATION (early childhood, elementary, special), ENGLISH (English), PREPROFESSIONAL (law), SOCIAL SCIENCES (human services, social sciences). About three-fourths of the undergraduate degrees are conferred in education.

Required: All students must complete a core requirement, which includes English, social sciences, mathematics, foreign language or linquistics, fine arts, and philosophy.

Admissions: Ninety-one percent of those who applied were accepted for the 1981–82 freshman class. Applicants should be graduates of an accredited high school. A minimum average of 2.0 is required. Other factors considered important by the college are impressions made during an interview, recommendations by school officials, and personality.

Procedure: The SAT or ACT is recommended and should be taken in December of the senior year. An interview is also recommended. The deadline for applications is open; the college has a rolling admissions policy. There is a $15 application fee.

Special: The college has a deferred admissions plan. A Life Experience Program allows credit to be granted in lieu of basic academic courses.

Transfer: For fall 1981, 32 transfer students applied, 29 were accepted, and 20 enrolled. Thirty credits, of the 127 required for the bachelor's degree, must be taken in residence. A 2.0 GPA is necessary. D grades do not transfer. Transfer students are accepted for all college years. There are no deadlines.

Visiting: The college has a regular orientation program for prospective students. Guides are also available for informal visits to the school. Visitors may sit in on classes and may also stay overnight at the school. The best time to visit is when classes are in session. The admissions office should be contacted for arrangements.

Financial Aid: About 89% of all students receive some form of aid; 39% work part-time on campus. The college, a member of CSS, participates in all federally funded financial programs. It also awards its own scholarships, some of which are available to freshmen. The average award to freshmen is $1716. The college requires the FAF or FFS from aid applicants. The deadline for applications for the fall semester is March 1. Tuition may be paid in installments.

Foreign Students: About 1% of the full-time students come from foreign countries.

Admissions: Foreign students must take an English proficiency examination. The SAT or ACT is not required.

Procedure: Foreign students are admitted to the fall and spring semesters. Proof of funds sufficient to cover 1 year of study is required.

Admissions Contact: Amy M. Barna, Dean of Admissions.

GODDARD COLLEGE   C-2
Plainfield, Vermont 05667   (802) 454-8311

F/T: 50M, 55W	Faculty: 7; IV, — $
P/T: 1M, 2W	Ph.D.'s: 60%
Grad: 6M, 5W	S/F Ratio: 12 to 1
Year: terms, ss	Tuition: $3600–7900
Appl: open	R and B: $2000
SAT: recommended	NONCOMPETITIVE

904 VERMONT

Goddard College, founded in 1938, is a private liberal arts college that stresses progressive, individualized education largely based on John Dewey's "Learning by Doing" theory. Its library contains 70,000 volumes and more than 3500 microfilm items, and subscribes to 510 periodicals.

Environment: The 200-acre campus is located in the rural foothills of the Green Mountains, 10 miles from Montpelier.

Student Life: Over 90% of the students are from out of state. Fifty percent of all students live on campus. Eleven percent are minority-group members. College housing is coed and single-sex; students in single-sex housing have visiting privileges. Students may keep cars on campus.

Organizations: There are no fraternities or sororities on campus. The student government sponsors social and cultural events.

Sports: The college does not field any intercollegiate teams. There are 8 intramural sports for men and 8 for women.

Graduates: The freshman dropout rate is 3%, and 80% of the freshmen remain to graduate. Fifty-five percent of the graduates continue their studies on a higher level.

Services: Students receive the following services free of charge: career counseling, psychological counseling, tutoring, remedial instruction, and limited placement counseling.

Programs of Study: The college confers the B.A. degree. Master's degrees are also awarded. Bachelor's degrees are offered in the following subjects: AREA STUDIES (American, Asian, Black/Afro-American, Middle Eastern, urban), EDUCATION (adult, early childhood, elementary, secondary), ENGLISH (English, journalism, literature, speech), FINE AND PERFORMING ARTS (art, art education, dance, music, radio/TV, studio art, theater/dramatics), HEALTH SCIENCES (environmental health), MATH AND SCIENCES (biology, botany, earth science, ecology/environmental science, mathematics, natural sciences, physics), PHILOSOPHY (classics, humanities, philosophy), PREPROFESSIONAL (agriculture, law, library science, medicine, social work), SOCIAL SCIENCES (anthropology, economics, government/political science, history, international relations, psychology, social sciences, sociology).

Required: To earn each 30 credits a student must complete 2 high-residency terms or 3 low-residency terms. The former consists of full-time, on-campus study; the latter, independent study with faculty supervision. All students must attend a nine-day meeting at the beginning of each term. While on campus, students must work 8 hours a week to help maintain and operate the college.

Special: There are no prescribed courses. Students progress in their thinking skills by engaging in real problem-solving while supported by their peers and the faculty. Studies are student-designed and some are pursued independently. No grades are given; students and teachers write evaluations. Specially designed workshops and seminars are integrated into the curriculum.

Admissions: A deliberately small student body enhances the community aspect of the college's educational philosophy. Factors that enter into the admissions decision include standardized test scores, the applicant's personality and leadership record, and evidence of special talent.

Procedure: The SAT is preferred and an interview is required. The personal statement form is an important part of the application. Application deadlines are open. Notification is on a rolling basis. A $20 fee is required.

Special: Early and deferred admissions plans and an early decision plan are available. AP and CLEP credit is given.

Transfer: For fall 1981, 52 students applied, 50 were accepted, and 33 enrolled. An interview is required, during which the student must show evidence of maturity and an interest in progressive education; standardized exam scores are also recommended. D grades do not transfer. Transfer students must spend at least one year at the college toward completion of the 120 semester hours necessary for a bachelor's degree. Application deadlines are open.

Visiting: Students are required to visit the campus and tours can be arranged through the admissions office.

Financial Aid: About 54% of all students receive some form of financial aid. Thirty percent work part-time on campus. Average aid to freshmen is $2500. College grants are awarded according to need. The college is a member of the CSS and requires the FAF. Deadlines for application are March 1 for freshmen and May 1 for transfer students.

Foreign Students: The personal environment here well supports foreign students.

Admissions: No English proficiency exam or college entrance exam must be taken.

Procedure: Application deadlines are open. Foreign students must present proof of health and proof of adequate funds.

Admissions Contact: Cynthia Drown, Admissions Coordinator.

GREEN MOUNTAIN COLLEGE A-4
Poultney, Vermont 05764 (802) 287-9313

F/T: 110M, 300W Faculty: 28; IIB, −$
P/T: 3M, 12W Ph.D.'s: 21%
Grad: none S/F Ratio: 14 to 1
Year: sems Tuition: $4680
Appl: open R and B: $2900
452 applied 421 accepted 161 enrolled
SAT: 426V 425M LESS COMPETITIVE

Green Mountain College is a private, nonsectarian liberal arts college offering undergraduate programs in business, health, recreation, and education. Founded in 1834 as a junior college, Green Mountain started offering B.S. degrees in 1974. Its library contains over 63,000 volumes and 28,000 microfilm items, and subscribes to more than 150 periodicals.

Environment: The 155-acre campus and its 25 buildings are located in a rural setting 22 miles from Rutland.

Student Life: Only 10% of the students are from Vermont; 82% of all students come from public schools. Ninety-eight percent of the students live on campus. Five percent are minority-group members. Campus housing is both coed and single-sex. The student government and each dormitory determine visiting hours. Students may keep cars on campus.

Organizations: There are no fraternities or sororities on campus. Social clubs and the student government sponsor social and cultural activities.

Sports: The college competes in 9 intercollegiate sports for both men and women. There are 5 intramural programs open to men and women.

Handicapped: There are no facilities for physically handicapped students.

Graduates: Eighteen percent of the freshmen drop out during their first year; 75% remain to graduate. Five percent of the students pursue advanced study after graduation. Fifty-two percent enter business and industry.

Services: Free tutoring and psychological counseling are available to all students. Free career counseling and job placement services are offered for students and alumni. Health care is available for a fee.

Programs of Study: The college confers the B.S. degree. Associate degrees are also awarded. Bachelor's degrees are offered in the following subjects: BUSINESS (accounting, business administration, retail management), EDUCATION (elementary, special), HEALTH SCIENCES (recreation, therapeutic recreation). About 25% of the degrees conferred are in education, and 20% are in business.

Required: One year of freshman English and 5 liberal arts courses in humanities, fine arts, social science, mathematics, or natural science are required.

Special: Most courses offer off-campus internships.

Honors: Phi Theta Kappa and Delta Psi Omega honor societies have chapters on campus.

Admissions: About 93% of those who applied for the 1981–82 freshman class were accepted. The SAT scores of those who enrolled were as follows: Verbal—80% below 500, 18% between 500 and 599, 2% between 600 and 700, and 0% above 700; Math—78% below 500, 18% between 500 and 599, 4% between 600 and 700, and 0% above 700. Candidates should have completed 16 Carnegie units and have a C average. Recommendations, character and personality, and impressions made during an interview all enter into the admissions decision.

Procedure: Either the SAT or the ACT must be taken by June of the senior year. Application deadlines are open. Freshmen are admitted both terms. There is no application fee. Admissions are on a rolling basis.

Special: Early admissions are allowed: the deadline is July 1. AP and CLEP credit is given.

Transfer: For fall 1981, 16 transfer students applied, 14 were accepted, and 9 enrolled. Students must have a C average; D grades do not transfer. There is a one-year residency requirement. Transfers must complete, at the college, 30 of the 120 credits necessary for the bachelor's degree. Applications should be submitted by August 15 for fall or December 15 for the spring semester.

Visiting: Tours of the campus can be arranged weekdays through the admissions office.

Financial Aid: Scholarships, loans, and work contracts are awarded to qualified students. About 73% of all students receive some form of financial assistance; 35% work part-time on campus. The college is a member of the CSS and requires the FAF or FFS. The application deadline is April 1.

Foreign Students: Nearly 2% of the full-time students come from foreign countries.

Admissions: The TOEFL is required. The SAT or ACT is not necessary.

Procedure: Application deadlines are August 15 (fall) and December 15 (spring). Foreign students must present proof of health and proof of adequate funds. Health insurance is not required, but is available through the college for a fee.

Admissions Contact: Douglas W. Durkee, Dean of Admissions.

JOHNSON STATE COLLEGE   C-2
Johnson, Vermont 05656   (802) 635-2356

F/T: 450M, 450W		Faculty:	47; IIA, — $
P/T: 42M, 71W		Ph.D.'s:	65%
Grad: 23M, 52W		S/F Ratio:	16 to 1
Year: sems, ss		Tuition:	$1438 ($3238)
Appl: open		R and B:	$2396
604 applied	528 accepted		239 enrolled
SAT, ACT: not required			LESS COMPETITIVE

Johnson State College, founded in 1828, is a publicly controlled liberal arts and teachers' college. The library contains over 83,453 volumes and 20,000 microfilm items, and subscribes to 450 periodicals.

Environment: The 500-acre campus is located in a rural setting on a hilltop overlooking the village of Johnson, in the heart of ski country. Living facilities include dormitories, on-campus apartments, and married student housing. The nearest large cities, Burlington and Montpelier, are both located 45 miles away.

Student Life: Approximately 75% of the students come from Vermont; 50% reside on campus. Fewer than 1% are minority-group members. Campus housing is coed. Students may keep cars on campus. Day-care services are available to all students.

Organizations: There are no social fraternities or sororities, but there are religious organizations for Catholic, Protestant, and Jewish students, and an ecumenical council, as well as a variety of student clubs and activities. On-campus events include concerts, plays, films, dances, the Winter Carnival, and Spring Weekend. Several major ski areas are within easy driving distance.

Sports: The college fields 5 intercollegiate teams for men and 5 for women. There are 8 intramural sports for men and 8 for women.

Handicapped: Johnson State College provides some wheelchair ramps, elevators, specially equipped rest rooms, and lowered drinking fountains for the handicapped. About 20% of the campus is accessible to wheelchair-bound students. Fewer than 1% of the students are visually or hearing impaired.

Graduates: About 40% of the freshmen drop out at the end of the first year; 20% remain to graduate and 6% of those pursue graduate study. About 35% seek careers in business and industry.

Services: Placement, career counseling, tutoring, remedial instruction, and psychological counseling are available on campus free of charge. Health care is available for a fee. Placement services for all students and alumni include resume writing, credential files, notification of job openings, career advising, and job skills development.

Programs of Study: The B.A., B.F.A., and B.S. degrees are offered. Associate and master's degrees are also awarded. Bachelor's degrees are offered in the following subjects: BUSINESS (business management/economics, recreation facilities management), EDUCATION (early childhood, elementary, health/physical, secondary, special), ENGLISH (creative writing), FINE AND PERFORMING ARTS (art, art education, dance, music, music education, studio art, theater/dramatics), HEALTH SCIENCES (pre-allied medical professions), MATH AND SCIENCES (ecology/environmental science), SOCIAL SCIENCES (anthropology/sociology, government/political science, human services certification, psychology). Thirty percent of the degrees conferred are in education, 12% are in business, and 11% are in math and sciences.

Required: All students must take 2 courses in each of the following: English, mathematics, science, social/behavioral sciences, humanities, arts.

Special: The college offers the opportunity to do fieldwork or an internship, and has exceptional student support services.

Admissions: Eighty-seven percent of those who applied were accepted for the 1981–82 freshman class. The SAT scores of those who enrolled were as follows: Verbal—80% below 500, 15% between 500 and 599, 5% between 600 and 700, and 0% above 700; Math—75% below 500, 20% between 500 and 599, 5% between 600 and 700, and 0% above 700. Applicants should be graduates of accredited high schools and have completed 15 Carnegie high school credits. They should rank in the upper 80% of their class and have a GPA of at least 1.0. Advanced placement or honors courses, recommendations, and extracurricular activities are also considered.

Procedure: Neither the SAT nor the ACT is required, but either is strongly recommended. There are no application deadlines; freshmen are admitted in the fall, spring, and summer terms. Notification is on a rolling basis. The application fee is $25.

Special: There is a deferred admissions plan. AP and CLEP credit is given.

Transfer: For fall 1981, 90 students applied, 85 were accepted, and 65 enrolled. A 2.0 GPA is usually required. All students must complete, at the college, 30 of the 120 credits required for a bachelor's degree. Application deadlines are August 1 (fall), January 15 (spring), and June 1 (summer).

Visiting: Regularly scheduled orientations for prospective students include interviews and campus tours. Guides are also available for informal visits. Visitors can sit in on classes but cannot stay overnight at the school. The best times for campus visits are Monday through Friday from 8 A.M. to 4 P.M. The admissions office should be contacted for further information.

Financial Aid: Sixty-five percent of all students receive financial aid. Forty percent work part-time on campus. The average freshman award is $3904. Loans are available from the federal and state governments, from local banks, and from funds administered by the college. A combination of grant, scholarship, loan, and work is offered to meet financial need. Tuition may be paid on the installment plan. The college requires the FAF or FFS. Aid applications should be filed by March 1 (fall) or November 1 (spring).

Foreign Students: One percent of the full-time students come from foreign countries. An intensive English course is available for these students.

Admissions: Foreign students must achieve a TOEFL score of at least 500. No college entrance exams are required.

Procedure: Application deadlines are July 1 (fall), December 15 (winter interim and spring), and March 1 (summer). Foreign students must have the college's health form completed by a physician and must present proof of funds adequate to cover 1 year of study. Health insurance is required and is available through the college for a fee.

Admissions Contact: James McWilliam, Director of Admissions.

LYNDON STATE COLLEGE   D-2
Lyndonville, Vermont 05851   (802) 626-9371

F/T: 544M, 426W		Faculty:	40; IIB, — $
P/T: 31M, 77W		Ph.D.'s:	25%
Grad: 14M, 25W		S/F Ratio:	17 to 1
Year: sems		Tuition:	$1465 ($3265)
Appl: open		R and B:	$2396
534 applied	478 accepted		258 enrolled
SAT or ACT: required			LESS COMPETITIVE

Lyndon State College, established in 1911 as a state teachers' college, became a liberal arts institution in 1962. The library houses over 57,000 volumes and 3300 microfilm items, and subscribes to more than 346 periodicals.

Environment: The 175-acre campus is in a rural setting in the heart of ski country. Its buildings include a dining hall, a student center, an activities building, a theater, a gymnasium, and a music department. Seven dormitories accommodate 221 women and 221 men.

Student Life: About 70% of the students are from Vermont, and about 55% of the students live on the campus in coed and single-sex dormitories. Eighty-five percent of entering freshmen come from public schools. Two percent of the students are minority-group members. Students may keep cars on campus.

Organizations: Lyndon has 2 national fraternities and 1 national sorority. A variety of extracurricular activities are offered.

906 VERMONT

Sports: Lyndon competes on an intercollegiate level in 8 sports. There are 5 intramural sports.

Handicapped: Special facilities for the handicapped include wheelchair ramps, elevators, and specially equipped rest rooms. Seventy-five percent of the campus is accessible to these students. There are no visually handicapped or hearing-impaired students at Lyndon.

Graduates: About 30% of the students drop out at the end of their freshman year, and 70% remain to graduate; 10% of the graduates go on for further degrees.

Services: The following services are included in the general fee: placement and career counseling; tutoring; remedial instruction; health care; and psychological counseling. There are placement services for alumni and undergraduate students.

Programs of Study: The college confers the B.A. and B.S. degrees and also awards associate and master's degrees. Bachelor's degrees are offered in the following subjects: BUSINESS (business administration, computer science, management), EDUCATION (early childhood, elementary, health/physical, secondary, special), ENGLISH (English, literature), FINE AND PERFORMING ARTS (radio/TV, theater/dramatics), MATH AND SCIENCES (biology, ecology/environmental science, natural sciences, physical sciences), SOCIAL SCIENCES (social sciences). Twenty-five percent of the degrees conferred are in education.

Required: All students must take a distribution of general education courses.

Special: A general studies degree is offered.

Admissions: Ninety percent of those who applied were accepted for the 1981-82 freshman class. Of those, the SAT scores were as follows: Verbal—85% below 500, 10% between 500 and 599, 5% between 600 and 700, and 0% above 700; Math—85% below 500, 10% between 500 and 599, 5% between 600 and 700, and 0% above 700. The candidate should have completed 15 Carnegie units. Other factors considered by the admissions committee are the accreditation and reputation of the high school, extracurricular activities, honors and advanced placement courses, leadership potential, and impressions made during a personal interview.

Procedure: The ACT or SAT is required and should be taken in the junior year or by January of the senior year. Applications are accepted for both fall and spring semesters. Application deadlines are open; notification is on a rolling basis. There is a $25 application fee.

Transfer: For fall 1981, 168 applications were received, 151 were accepted and 96 students enrolled. Transfers are accepted for all classes; D grades are not acceptable. Transfer application deadlines are open. Students must complete, at the college, the last 30 credit hours of the 122 required for the bachelor's degree.

Visiting: There are regularly scheduled orientations for students, which take place during preregistration. Guides are provided by the college for informal visits. Visitors are permitted to sit in on classes, but may not stay overnight at the college. The admissions office should be contacted to arrange such visits.

Financial Aid: About 80% of all students receive financial aid. Forty percent work part-time on campus. The deadlines for aid application are April 1 (fall) and September 1 (spring). Assistance is given in the form of grants, low-interest loans, campus work opportunities, or a combination of one or more of these programs. The college is a member of CSS. The FAF or FFS is required of all applicants for financial aid.

Foreign Students: Foreign students comprise less than 1% of the full-time enrollment.

Procedure: A rolling admissions policy is followed for foreign students, who are admitted to both fall and spring semesters.

Admissions Contact: Russell S. Powden, Jr., Director of Admissions.

MARLBORO COLLEGE
Marlboro, Vermont 05344   B-6
                                       (802) 257-4333

F/T: 110M, 115W   Faculty: 31; IV, —$
P/T: n/av   Ph.D.'s: 60%
Grad: none   S/F Ratio: 8 to 1
Year: 4-1-4   Tuition: $5880
Appl: open   R and B: $2600
225 applied   150 accepted   85 enrolled
SAT: 533V 519M   VERY COMPETITIVE

Marlboro College, founded in 1947, is a private liberal arts college. Its library contains 45,000 volumes and subscribes to over 700 periodicals.

Environment: The 350-acre campus is located in a rural setting in the Green Mountains, 100 miles from Boston. There are 13 dormitories on campus.

Student Life: Only 15% of the students are from Vermont; 74% of the students are from public schools. Approximately 73% live on campus. Fourteen percent of the students are minority-group members. Campus housing is both coed and single-sex. There are visiting privileges in single-sex dorms. Students may keep cars on campus. The college provides day-care services to all students for a fee.

Organizations: There are no sororities or fraternities on campus. Student organizations provide social and cultural events.

Sports: Although the college does not participate in intercollegiate competition, there are 8 intramural sports.

Handicapped: Work has been done to make the campus barrier-free for the physically handicapped, and special class scheduling is possible. About 3% of the students have hearing impairments, and 2% have visual impairments. There are counselors to help these students.

Graduates: About 20% of the freshmen drop out after their first year; 40% remain to graduate. Of those, 35% continue their education; 2% enter medical school, and 1% enter law school.

Services: Free health care, tutoring, remedial instruction, career counseling, and job placement services are offered to students. Psychological counseling is available for a fee.

Programs of Study: The college confers the B.A. and B.S. degrees. Bachelor's degrees are offered in the following subjects: AREA STUDIES (American), ENGLISH (English, literature), FINE AND PERFORMING ARTS (art, art history, music, theater/dramatics), LANGUAGES (French, German, Greek/Latin, Italian, Japanese, Portuguese, Russian, Spanish), MATH AND SCIENCES (astronomy, biochemistry, biology, botany, chemistry, ecology/environmental science, geology, mathematics, natural sciences, physical sciences, physics, zoology), PHILOSOPHY (classics, humanities, philosophy, religion), PREPROFESSIONAL (law, medicine), SOCIAL SCIENCES (anthropology, economics, government/political science, history, international relations, psychology, social sciences, sociology).

Required: Students must pass English requirements.

Special: Students are able to design their own majors.

Admissions: About 67% of the students who applied for the 1981-82 freshman class were accepted. The SAT scores of those who enrolled were as follows: Verbal—50% scored between 500 and 599; Math—50% scored between 500 and 599. Candidates should have completed 15 Carnegie units, should have a 2.5 GPA, and should rank in the upper 50% of their graduating class. Advanced placement or honors courses, recommendations by school officials, and personality also enter into the admissions decision.

Procedure: The SAT is required and should be taken by January of the senior year. An English Composition AT is recommended. There are no application deadlines. The application fee is $20. There is a rolling admissions policy.

Special: Early and deferred admissions are available. AP and CLEP credit is given.

Transfer: Thirty-two transfer students enrolled in fall 1981. Transfers are accepted in all classes. Recommendations, a writing sample, an autobiography, and high school transcripts are required. The SAT or ACT is recommended. There is a rolling admissions policy.

Visiting: Tours of the campus can be arranged through the office of admissions. Visitors can sit in on classes and stay overnight at the school.

Financial Aid: About 45% of all students receive financial aid. Forty percent work part-time on campus. Scholarships, grants, and loans are available. The average award to freshmen is $3734. The college is a member of CSS, and the FAF or FFS is required by March 1.

Foreign Students: Foreign students comprise less than 3% of the full-time enrollment.

Admissions: A score of at least 550 must be achieved on the TOEFL. The SAT or ACT is not required.

Procedure: Foreign students are admitted to the fall, winter and spring terms. A rolling admissions policy is followed. Proof of funds adequate to cover 4 years of study is required. Foreign students must carry health insurance, which is available through the college for a fee.

Admissions Contact: Nancy W. Leach, Director of Admissions.

MIDDLEBURY COLLEGE   A-3
Middlebury, Vermont 05753   (802) 388-3711

F/T: 1031M, 911W	Faculty:	146; IIB, ++$
P/T: 3M, 7W	Ph.D.'s:	74%
Grad: 2M	S/F Ratio:	13 to 1
Year: 4-1-4, ss	Tuition:	*
Appl: Jan. 15	R and B:	*
3460 applied	1101 accepted	499 enrolled
SAT: 590V 620M		HIGHLY COMPETITIVE

Middlebury College, founded in 1800, is a small, private, coeducational institution which concentrates on the humanities, languages, and social and natural sciences. Its library contains 440,256 volumes and 27,185 microfilm items, and subscribes to 1694 periodicals.

Environment: The 500-acre main campus is located on a hill adjacent to the town of Middlebury, in the Champlain Valley 35 miles south of Burlington. The college operates a Bread Loaf Mountain campus nearby in the Green Mountains.

Student Life: Students come from 38 states. Fifty-seven percent come from public schools. Six percent are minority-group members. About 98% of all students live in dormitories and freshmen live in freshman dorms. Campus housing is both coed and single-sex. There are visiting privileges in single-sex dorms. Students may have cars on campus.

Organizations: There are 6 fraternities to which 10% of the students belong. The student government and 45 student interest groups sponsor social and cultural activities on campus.

Sports: The college competes in 11 intercollegiate sports for men and 13 for women. There are 14 intramural sports for men and 13 for women.

Handicapped: Wheelchair ramps and special parking are provided for physically handicapped students.

Graduates: Only 3% of the freshmen drop out after their first year; 70% remain to graduate. Of those, 32% continue their education immediately after graduation; 1% enter medical school, and 5% to 8% enter law school.

Services: Free tutoring, psychological counseling, and career counseling are offered to students. Basic health care, student employment advising, and financial aid counseling are also available. Placement services available to students and alumni include internship listings, job placement, seminars, and advanced training.

Programs of Study: The college confers the B.A. degree. Master's and doctoral degrees are also awarded. Bachelor's degrees are offered in the following subjects: AREA STUDIES (American, classical, East Asian, environmental, literary, Northern), ENGLISH (English, literature), FINE AND PERFORMING ARTS (art, art history, music, theater/dramatics), LANGUAGES (Chinese, French, German, Italian, Russian, Spanish), MATH AND SCIENCES (biochemistry, biology, chemistry, environmental studies, geology, mathematics, physics), PHILOSOPHY (classics, philosophy, religion), SOCIAL SCIENCES (anthropology/sociology, economics, geography, history, Northern studies, political science, psychology).

Special: Independent scholar; junior year in a Middlebury School in Paris, Florence, Mainz, Madrid, or Moscow; teacher education; Washington Semester; a semester at the Institute for Architecture and Urban Studies in New York City; and exchange programs are offered. Undergraduates may take courses for credit during the summer at any of the 8 Middlebury College Languages Schools or at the Bread Loaf School of English in Vermont or Oxford, England. There are preprofessional programs in law, medicine, dentistry, veterinary medicine, business/management, and engineering. Cooperative programs with other institutions allow combined degrees such as B.A.-B.S. (engineering), B.A.-M.B.A., B.A.-J.D., B.A.-M.D., and B.A.-D.D.S./D.M.D.

Honors: Phi Beta Kappa and departmental honors are available to qualified students.

Admissions: About 32% of those who applied for the 1981-82 freshman class were accepted. The SAT scores of those who enrolled were as follows: Verbal—9% below 500, 40% between 500 and 599, 43% between 600 and 700, and 8% above 700; Math—5% below 500, 27% between 500 and 599, 53% between 600 and 700, and 15% above 700. Candidates should have completed 15 Carnegie units and have a high GPA. Personal characteristics and recommendations are also strongly considered.

Procedure: The SAT and 3 ATs are required, 1 of which should be English. The SAT should be taken by January of the senior year. The application deadline is January 15. There is a $30 application fee.

*Students pay a comprehensive fee of $9360.

Special: Early decision and deferred admissions plans are offered. AP credit is available.

Transfer: For fall 1981, 99 students applied, 14 were accepted, and 6 enrolled. There is a 2-year residency requirement. D grades do not transfer. Students must complete, at the college, 18 of the 36 courses required for the bachelor's degree. Applications are due March 1.

Visiting: Tours of the campus can be arranged through the admissions office.

Financial Aid: Sixty-four percent of the students receive financial aid in the form of grants or loans from federal, state, or college sources. Thirty-one percent receive aid directly from the college; 65% work part-time on campus. The college, a member of CSS, offers CWS. The FAF is required and applications are due by February 1.

Foreign Students: Almost 3% of the full-time students come from foreign countries. Special organizations are available to these students.

Admissions: The TOEFL is required. The SAT or ACT is not necessary.

Procedure: The application deadline is the same as that for freshmen. Foreign students must present a satisfactory health certificate and must carry health insurance, which is available through the college for a fee.

Admissions Contact: Fred F. Neuberger, Director of Admissions.

NORWICH UNIVERSITY   C-3
Northfield, Vermont 05663   (802) 485-5011

F/T: 1264M, 165W	Faculty:	111; IIB, +$
P/T: 11M, 13W	Ph.D.'s:	60%
Grad: 12M, 3W	S/F Ratio:	14 to 1
Year: sems, ss	Tuition:	*
Appl: open	R and B:	*
1409 applied	1333 accepted	575 enrolled
SAT, ACT: not required		COMPETITIVE

Norwich University, founded as a military college in 1819, continues to educate students within a military environment. Since its merger with Vermont College in 1972, it offers a coordinated education program with that college. Army and Air Force ROTC programs and a Marine PLC program are available. The Norwich University library contains 150,000 volumes and 6000 reels of microfilm, and subscribes to over 700 periodicals.

Environment: The campus is located 12 miles from Montpelier in a small town. The dorms are grouped around a central area called the Upper Parade Ground.

Student Life: About 90% of the students come from out of state. About 75% of the freshmen come from public schools. Ninety-nine percent of the students live on campus. Six percent are minority-group members. Campus housing is single-sex, and there are visiting privileges. Upperclassmen may keep cars on campus. The university is nonsectarian but encourages attendance at weekly religious services. Military rules and regulations are followed.

Organizations: All students are members of, and participate in, the Corps of Cadets, a self-governing organization that has as its purpose the development of leadership abilities in students. There are no fraternities or sororities. Both formal and informal social activities are conducted by class organizations. Each class has its own club. The university operates a student center/rathskeller on campus. Extracurricular activities include orchestra and band, debating, drama clubs, campus radio, and publications.

Sports: The school has a full intercollegiate sports program consisting of 15 sports for men and 10 for women. There are 18 intramural sports for men and 12 for women.

Handicapped: No special facilities are available for handicapped students.

Graduates: Thirty-three percent of the freshmen drop out by the end of the first year; 58% remain to graduate. About 33% of the graduates continue their education and 40% pursue careers in business and industry. Of the graduates, 5% enter dental school.

Services: Free health care, tutoring, remedial instruction, career and psychological counseling, and job placement are available to students.

Programs of Study: The university confers the B.A. and B.S. degrees. Master's degrees are also awarded. Bachelor's degrees are offered in the following subjects: BUSINESS (accounting, business administration, business education, computer science), EDUCATION (elementary, health/physical, secondary), ENGLISH (communications,

*A comprehensive fee of $7650 includes tuition, room, board, acivity fee, infirmary fee, and uniform fee.

908 VERMONT

English), LANGUAGES (French, German, Spanish), MATH AND SCIENCES (biology, chemistry, computer science, mathematics, physics), PHILOSOPHY (humanities, philosophy, religion), PREPROFESSIONAL (engineering—civil, engineering—electrical, engineering—environmental technology, engineering—mechanical), SOCIAL SCIENCES (economics, government/political science, history, international relations, military studies, psychology).

Required: ROTC training is required of all men and women at the Northfield campus. Students are not required to enter military service upon graduation. Freshmen are required to take English, physical education, and mathematics. All undergraduates are required to complete 2 semesters of physical education, 1 year of English, and 1 semester of American history.

Special: There is a 3-1 combined degree program in medical technology, and junior-year study abroad.

Honors: There are 4 honor societies represented on campus.

Admissions: About 95% of those who applied were accepted for the 1981–82 freshman class. Candidates should have completed 16 Carnegie units, should have a C+ average, and should rank in the upper half of their graduating class. Secondary school record, recommendations by school officials, and advanced placement or honors courses figure heavily in the admissions decision.

Procedure: Neither the SAT nor the ACT is required. It is recommended that all applicants have a personal interview. The application deadlines are open. An application fee of $20 must be submitted. The university uses a rolling admissions plan.

Special: Early decision and deferred admissions plans are available. CLEP credit is available.

Transfer: For fall 1981, 75 transfer students applied and were accepted, and 31 enrolled. To receive a bachelor's degree, students must complete half their credits (60) at the university and must study 2 years in residence. A GPA of 2.0 is required. C grades or better transfer. Application deadlines are the same as those for freshmen.

Visiting: It is recommended that students visit the campus. Guided tours can be arranged weekdays through the admissions office. Visitors may sit in on classes and stay overnight at the school.

Financial Aid: About 60% of all students receive financial assistance. Forty-five percent work part-time on campus. Norwich participates in all the federal programs and has its own scholarship fund. In addition, the U.S. Army and the U.S. Air Force provide 4-, 3-, 2-, and 1-year ROTC scholarships to qualified students. The university participates in CSS and in the ACT Financial Aid Services. It requires that its own aid application be filed by March 1.

Foreign Students: About 2% of the full-time students come from foreign countries. The university offers these students an intensive English course.

Admissions: Foreign students must achieve a minimum score of 500 on the TOEFL. A college entrance exam is required.

Procedure: Application deadlines are March 1 (fall) and October 1 (spring). Foreign students must complete a university physical examination form and carry health insurance, which is available through the university for a fee. Proof of funds adequate to cover 1 year of study is required, as is a uniform fee of $1050.

Admissions Contact: William S. Neal, Dean of Admissions.

SAINT MICHAEL'S COLLEGE A-2
Winooski, Vermont 05404 (802) 655-2017

F/T: 877M, 761W	Faculty:	105; IIA, −$
P/T: 54M, 8W	Ph.D.'s:	60%
Grad: 256 M&W	S/F Ratio:	16 to 1
Year: sems, ss	Tuition:	$4680
Appl: open	R and B:	$2170
1883 applied	1004 accepted	411 enrolled
SAT: 490V 521M		COMPETITIVE

Saint Michael's College, established in 1904, is located in an educational center that also contains a 2-year college, a women's college, and a larger university. A 3-level circular library houses over 100,000 volumes and subscribes to more than 992 periodicals.

Environment: The college is in a suburban setting near the town of Winooski, only 98 miles from Montreal. There are 25 buildings on the 400-acre campus.

Student Life: About 85% of the students are from out-of-state, and 76% reside on campus. Three percent are minority-group members. Chapel attendance is not required. Campus housing is single-sex and there are visiting privileges. Students may have cars on campus. Dormitory regulations are in effect.

Organizations: There are no fraternities or sororities on campus; the college sponsors music and theater groups, publications, and various special-interest groups, as well as cultural activities.

Sports: The college competes on the intercollegiate level in 11 sports for men and 9 for women. There are 8 intramural programs for both men and women.

Handicapped: There are some facilities for physically handicapped students, and 30% of the campus is accessible to them. Wheelchair ramps, elevators, and specially equipped rest rooms are available; special class scheduling is possible.

Graduates: Only 8% of the freshmen drop out during their first year; 70% remain to graduate. Of those, 60% continue their education; 2% enter medical schools, 1% dental schools, and 3% law schools. Another 40% pursue careers in business and industry.

Services: Free health care, tutoring, psychological counseling, and job placement are available to all students. Career counseling and placement services are given to graduates and undergraduates.

Programs of Study: The college confers the B.A. degree and offers master's programs. Bachelor's degrees are offered in the following subjects: AREA STUDIES (American), BUSINESS (accounting, business administration, computer science), EDUCATION (elementary, secondary), ENGLISH (English, journalism, literature), FINE AND PERFORMING ARTS (art, music, music education, theater/dramatics), LANGUAGES (French, Spanish), MATH AND SCIENCES (biology, chemistry, ecology/environmental science, mathematics, physics), PHILOSOPHY (classics, philosophy, religion), SOCIAL SCIENCES (economics, government/political science, history, psychology, sociology). About 24% of the degrees conferred are in the social sciences and 14% are in the math and science fields.

Required: Students must take 6 credits in each of the following areas: humanities, natural sciences, philosophy, religious studies, and social studies. The total distribution requirement is 30 credits.

Special: Student-designed majors and overseas study programs are available.

Honors: Numerous honor societies are represented on campus; departmental honors are also available, including special independent study and research internships.

Admissions: About 53% of those who applied for the 1981–82 freshman class were accepted. The SAT scores of those who enrolled were as follows: Verbal—56% below 500, 40% between 500 and 599, 4% between 600 and 700, and 0% above 700; Math—38% below 500, 46% between 500 and 599, 15% between 600 and 700, and 1% above 700. Candidates should have completed 15 Carnegie units, have at least a 2.5 GPA, and rank in the upper 40% of their graduating class. Recommendations and advanced placement or honors courses are also important.

Procedure: All applicants must take the SAT between May and November of the senior year. There is no deadline; a rolling admissions policy is in effect. A $20 fee should accompany applications.

Special: AP and CLEP exams are accepted.

Transfer: For fall 1981, 187 students applied, 81 were accepted, and 48 enrolled. Credit for courses will be given only if they correspond to those offered at the college and if a C or better grade was achieved. There is a one-year residency requirement. Transfers must complete, at the college, 30 semester hours of the 120 necessary for the bachelor's degree. There is no application deadline; a rolling admissions policy is followed.

Visiting: Tours of the campus can be scheduled during the week through the admissions office.

Financial Aid: About 55% of all students receive some form of aid. Fifty percent work part-time on campus. Grants, loans, and campus jobs are available as well as some scholarships. The average award to freshmen from all sources is $3700. Tuition may be paid in installments. The college is a member of CSS; the FAF or FFS must be filed and applications submitted by March 15.

Foreign Students: Three percent of the full-time students come from foreign countries. The college offers these students an intensive English program and special counseling and organizations.

Admissions: Foreign students must achieve a minimum score of 500 on the TOEFL. The SAT is also required.

Procedure: Application deadlines are open; foreign students are admitted for the fall and spring semesters. All students must have a physical examination prior to entrance and carry health insurance, which is available through the college for a fee. Proof of funds adequate to cover the anticipated period of study is required.

Admissions Contact: Jerry E. Flanagan, Dean of Admissions.

SOUTHERN VERMONT COLLEGE A–6
Bennington, Vermont 05201 (802) 442-5427

F/T: 227M, 278W	Faculty: 14; IV, – –$
P/T: 93M, 113W	Ph.D.'s: 10%
Grad: none	S/F Ratio: 36 to 1
Year: tri, ss	Tuition: $3000
Appl: open	R and B: $2510
463 applied	463 accepted	170 enrolled
SAT, ACT: not required		NONCOMPETITIVE

Founded in 1926 as St. Joseph Business College, Southern Vermont College is a private liberal arts college. The library has more than 18,000 volumes.

Environment: The 371-acre campus occupies an estate in a rural area 40 miles from Albany, New York. The main campus building was constructed of stone, wood, and tile in 1912 in imitation of an English castle. Six dormitories house 170 students.

Student Life: About half of the students come from Vermont. Twenty-four percent of the undergraduates reside on campus. Dormitories are coed. Students may keep cars on campus.

Organizations: No social fraternities or sororities are available. The Old Castle Players, a professional resident theater company, is located on campus. A recreation center is available in town.

Sports: The college fields 3 intercollegiate teams for men and 3 for women. There are 2 intramural sports for men and 2 for women.

Handicapped: There are no special facilities for the physically handicapped, but the college estimates that 80% of the campus is accessible to these students. One percent of the student body are visually impaired; 1 percent have hearing impairments. A special services staff can provide guides, readers, and tapes. There are 4 special counselors available.

Graduates: The freshman dropout rate is 40%. About 15% of the students pursue advanced study after graduation. Four percent of the graduates enter law school. An estimated 60% go into business and industry.

Services: Students receive the following services free of charge: placement, career counseling, tutoring, remedial instruction, and psychological counseling. Health care is provided on a fee basis.

Programs of Study: The B.A. and B.S. degrees are offered. Associate degrees are also awarded. Bachelor's degrees are offered in the following subjects: BUSINESS (accounting, business administration, management, secretarial), ENGLISH (communications management, English), HEALTH SCIENCES (health services management, medical assisting, nursing), MATH AND SCIENCES (environmental management), SOCIAL SCIENCES (criminal justice management, government/political science, human services management, public service management). Seventy-five percent of the degrees conferred are in management programs, 12% in health sciences, and 9% in social sciences.

Special: The college offers a general studies degree and allows student-designed majors.

Admissions: For the current freshman class, all those who applied were accepted. A high school diploma or GED is required. The following factors are also considered in the admissions decision, in order of importance: recommendations by school officials, personality and intangible qualities, and impressions made during an interview.

Procedure: Neither the SAT nor ACT is required. An interview is recommended. There are no application deadlines; a rolling admissions policy is used. The application fee is $10.

Special: There are early decision, early admissions, and deferred admissions plans. The application deadline for early admission is rolling. The college uses the CLEP program.

Transfer: One D grade may transfer. All students must complete, at the college, 30 of the 120 credits required for a bachelor's degree. There are no application deadlines; transfer students are admitted in the fall, spring, and summer terms.

Visiting: Guides are available for informal visits. The best time for a visit is during the fall and spring semesters. Visitors can sit in on classes and stay overnight at the school. The admissions office should be contacted to arrange a visit.

Financial Aid: About 70% of all students receive aid, mostly in the form of loans and work contracts. About 50% work part-time on campus. The average freshman award is $1965. The college is a member of CSS. The FAF, FFS, or SFS is required. There is a rolling deadline for financial aid application.

Foreign Students: Five percent of the full-time students come from foreign countries. An intensive English course, special counseling, and special organizations are available for these students.

Admissions: Foreign students must take either the TOEFL, the University of Michigan Language Test, the Comprehensive English Language Test, or the college's own English proficiency test. On the TOEFL, a score of at least 450 is required. No college entrance exams are required.

Procedure: There are no application deadlines; foreign students are admitted in the fall, spring, and summer terms. They must present proof of funds adequate to cover 1 year of study. Health insurance is not required, but is available through the college for a fee.

Admissions Contact: Chris Langlois, Director of Admissions.

TRINITY COLLEGE A–2
Burlington, Vermont 05401 (802) 658-2471

F/T: 17M, 434W	Faculty: 30; IIB, – –$
P/T: 81M, 337W	Ph.D.'s: 43%
Grad: none	S/F Ratio: 13 to 1
Year: sems, ss	Tuition: $3655
Appl: open	R and B: $2220
253 applied	215 accepted	116 enrolled
SAT: 410V 420M		LESS COMPETITIVE

Trinity College was established in 1925 by the Sisters of Mercy of the Roman Catholic Church. Its library contains over 54,000 volumes and 39,500 microfilm items, and subscribes to more than 365 periodicals.

Environment: The 23-acre campus is located one-half mile from Burlington. The 7 residence halls accommodate 500 women.

Student Life: About 82% of the students are from Vermont; 78% of the freshmen come from public schools. Approximately 77% of the students live on campus. About 1% are minority-group members. Campus housing is single-sex. Students may keep cars on campus. The college provides day-care services to all students for a fee.

Organizations: There are no sororities. The college sponsors religious, social, and cultural events.

Sports: Five intercollegiate and intramural sports are available for women.

Handicapped: There are facilities for physically handicapped students and about 92% of the campus is accessible to them. Special facilities include wheelchair ramps, parking areas, elevators, lowered drinking fountains and telephones, and specially equipped rest rooms; special class scheduling is also provided.

Graduates: About 22% of the freshmen drop out after their first year; 60% remain to graduate. Ten percent of the students pursue advanced study after graduation; about 1% enter medical school, and about 1% law school.

Services: Free psychological counseling, tutoring, and job placement services are offered to students. Health care and remedial instruction are available for a fee. Career counseling is available to students and alumni.

Programs of Study: The college confers the B.A. and B.S. degrees. Associate degrees are also awarded. Bachelor's degrees are offered in the following subjects: AREA STUDIES (American), BUSINESS (business administration, business education, secretarial science), EDUCATION (early childhood, elementary, secondary, special), ENGLISH (English), HEALTH SCIENCES (medical technology), LANGUAGES (French, modern languages, Spanish), MATH AND SCIENCES (biology, chemistry, mathematics), PREPROFESSIONAL (social work, social work/developmental disabilities), SOCIAL SCIENCES (history, psychology, social sciences). About 46% of the degrees conferred are in social sciences and 21% are in business. Education studies lead to teacher certification.

Required: Students are required to take 24 to 32 credits to fulfill distribution quotas.

Special: Interdisciplinary degree programs include business/chemistry and modern languages (Spanish/French). Overseas study, cooperative programs with other colleges, and student-designed majors are available. It is possible to earn combined B.A.-B.S. degrees in any major.

Honors: Two national honor societies are represented on campus.

910 VERMONT

Admissions: About 85% of those who applied for the 1981–82 freshman class were accepted. The SAT scores of those who enrolled were as follows: Verbal—11% between 500 and 599 and 3% between 600 and 700; Math—79% below 500, 18% between 500 and 599, 3% between 600 and 700, and 0% above 700. Candidates should have completed 16 Carnegie units, have a 2.0 GPA in college preparatory courses, and rank in the upper half of their graduating class. Other factors of importance are advanced placement or honors courses, extracurricular activities record, and recommendations by school officials.

Procedure: Either the SAT or ACT is required. An interview is recommended. Applications should be filed as early as possible; there is no deadline. A $20 fee should accompany all applications. Freshmen are admitted both semesters.

Special: Early and deferred admissions plans are offered. AP and CLEP credit is available.

Transfer: For fall 1981, 62 transfer students applied, 47 were accepted, and 29 enrolled. Applicants should have a 2.0 GPA; D grades receive credit at the discretion of the head of the department, but will not transfer in a major. At least 30 credits, of the 120 required for the bachelor's degree, must be taken in residence. Application procedure is the same as for freshmen.

Visiting: Tours of the campus can be arranged through the office of admissions. Visitors can sit in on classes and stay overnight at the college.

Financial Aid: Scholarships, grants, loans, and student employment are all available through the college. About 74% of all students receive some form of financial assistance; 30% work part-time on campus. The financial application form and the FAF or FFS must be submitted by March 1 in order to qualify for aid; the college is a member of CSS.

Foreign Students: Fewer than 1% of the full-time students come from foreign countries.

Admissions: The TOEFL is required. College entrance exams are not necessary.

Procedure: Application deadlines are August 1 (fall) and December 1 (spring). Foreign students must have the college health form certified by a physician. Proof of funds sufficient to cover the entire program of study is required. Health insurance is not required, but is available through the college for a fee.

Admissions Contact: Jessica Brugger Meserve, Director of Admissions.

UNIVERSITY OF VERMONT A–2
Burlington, Vermont 05405 (802) 656-3371

F/T: 3107M, 4303W Faculty: 552; I, — –$
P/T: 198M, 225W Ph.D.'s: 78%
Grad: 738M, 592W S/F Ratio: 16 to 1
Year: sems, ss Tuition: $2046($5276)
Appl: Feb. 1 R and B: $2469
9000 applied 4400 accepted 1830 enrolled
SAT: 533V 577M **VERY COMPETITIVE**

The University of Vermont, founded in 1791, is a state-supported institution. Its library contains over 750,000 volumes and 180,000 microfilm items, and subscribes to more than 5200 periodicals.

Environment: The 243-acre urban campus is located on Lake Champlain with views of both the Adirondacks and the Green Mountains. There are 39 dormitories which accommodate 3000 students. Special facilities are provided for married students, and fraternity and sorority houses are also available.

Student Life: About half the student body is from Vermont; 70% of the students come from public schools. About 56% reside on campus. Almost 2% of the students are minority-group members. Campus housing is both coed and single-sex. There are visiting privileges in single-sex dorms. Students may have cars on campus. The university provides day-care services to faculty and staff only for a fee.

Organizations: There are 14 fraternities and 5 sororities on campus to which 15% of the students belong. The student government and special-interest clubs sponsor social and cultural activities.

Sports: The university has a full intercollegiate athletic program consisting of 13 sports for both men and women. There are 12 intramural sports open to men and 13 to women.

Handicapped: Special facilities for physically handicapped students include wheelchair ramps, parking areas, elevators, lowered drinking fountains and telephones, and specially equipped rest rooms.

Graduates: Only 16% of the freshmen drop out after their first year; 70% remain to graduate. Of those, 25% continue their studies, and 50% pursue careers in business and industry.

Services: Free tutoring, remedial instruction, career counseling, and job placement services are offered to students. Health care and psychological counseling are also available for a fee.

Programs of Study: The university confers the B.A., B.Ed., and B.S. degrees. Associate, master's, and doctoral degrees are also awarded. Bachelor's degrees are offered in the following subjects: AREA STUDIES (Canadian, European, Latin American, Russian/East European), BUSINESS (business administration), EDUCATION (early childhood, elementary, health/physical, industrial, secondary, special), ENGLISH (English), FINE AND PERFORMING ARTS (art education, art history, music, music education, studio art, theater/dramatics), HEALTH SCIENCES (communication science and disorders, medical technology, nursing, occupational therapy, physical therapy, speech therapy), LANGUAGES (French, German, Greek/Latin, Russian, Spanish), MATH AND SCIENCES (biology, botany, chemistry, geology, mathematics, physics, statistics, zoology), PHILOSOPHY (classics, philosophy, religion), PREPROFESSIONAL (agriculture, computer science, engineering, forestry, home economics, social work), SOCIAL SCIENCES (anthropology, economics, geography, government/political science, history, psychology, sociology).

Special: Students may study abroad, and a living-learning center curriculum is also offered. Combined B.A.-B.S. programs in certain departments are available.

Honors: There are 14 honor societies represented on campus.

Admissions: About 50% of those who applied for the 1981–82 freshman class were accepted. The SAT scores of those who enrolled were as follows: Verbal—43% below 500, 46% between 500 and 599, 10% between 600 and 700, and 1% above 700; Math—19% below 500, 49% between 500 and 599, 28% between 600 and 700, and 4% above 700. Candidates should have completed 16 Carnegie units, have a B average, and graduate in the upper two-fifths of their class. Recommendations, impressions made during an interview, and evidence of special talents are also considered.

Procedure: The SAT is required and should be taken by December of the senior year. ATs are used for placement purposes and should be taken by March. The application deadlines are February 1 for the fall term and December 1 for the spring term. Freshmen are admitted to both sessions. There is a $25 application fee.

Special: Early decision and deferred admissions plans are available. AP and CLEP credit is given.

Transfer: For fall 1981, 1633 students applied, 600 were accepted, and 330 enrolled. The last 42 credits, of the 122 usually required for the bachelor's degree, must be taken in residence. D grades do not transfer. Deadlines are April 1 for fall and December 1 for spring.

Visiting: Tours of the campus can be arranged weekdays through the office of admissions.

Financial Aid: The college, a member of CSS, requires the FAF or FFS. Tuition may be paid in installments. The deadline to apply for aid is March 1. About 40% of all students receive some form of aid; 54% of the in-state students and 36% of those from out of state work part-time on campus.

Foreign Students: Foreign students comprise less than 1% of the full-time enrollment. The university offers these students special counseling and special organizations.

Admissions: Foreign students normally achieve a score of 500 on the TOEFL. The SAT is also required.

Procedure: Application deadlines are February 1 (fall) and November 1 (spring). Proof of funds adequate to cover a minimum of 1 year of study is required. The university recommends that foreign students carry health insurance, which is available through the university for a fee.

Admissions Contact: Jeff M. S. Kaplan, Director of Admissions.

VERMONT COLLEGE OF NORWICH UNIVERSITY C–3
Montpelier, Vermont 05602 (802) 229-0522

F/T: 31M, 291W Faculty: 44; IIB, +$
P/T: 104M, 357W Ph.D.'s: 30%
Grad: 83M, 124W S/F Ratio: 14 to 1
Year: sems, ss Tuition: *
Appl: open R and B: *
452 applied 393 accepted 169 enrolled
SAT, ACT: not required **LESS COMPETITIVE**

Vermont College, a division of Norwich University, offers 3 bachelor's- and 15 associate-degree programs, and a master's program in art therapy. Since their merger in 1972, Norwich University and Vermont College have participated in a coordinated education program that allows Vermont students to share the academic, athletic, and recreational facilities of Norwich University. The Vermont library contains over 28,000 volumes and 2000 reels of microfilm, and subscribes to more than 210 periodicals.

Environment: The 25-acre campus is located in a suburban area 45 miles from Burlington. The 4 dorms house 308 students.

Student Life: About half the students are from Vermont. Seventy percent live on campus. Five percent are minority-group members. Campus housing is single-sex, and there are visiting privileges. Students may have cars on campus.

Organizations: There are no fraternities or sororities on campus. The college sponsors social and cultural activities. Among the most active groups are Big Sisters/Big Brothers, the outing club, the student nurse association, and Organization of Human Services.

Sports: Women compete in 3 intercollegiate sports. There are 4 intramural sports for both men and women.

Handicapped: There are no facilities for the handicapped.

Graduates: About 20% of the freshmen drop out during their first year; 75% remain to graduate.

Services: Free health care, career counseling, tutoring, remedial instruction, psychological counseling, and job placement services are offered to all students.

Programs of Study: The college confers the B.A. and B.S. degrees. Associate and master's degrees are also offered. Bachelor's degrees are offered in the following subjects: EDUCATION (early childhood), HEALTH SCIENCES (medical technology, nursing).

Required: All students must take freshman English and two semesters of physical education.

Special: The college offers 2 bachelor's degrees and 3 master's degrees on a low residency basis. These programs are specifically aimed at the adult learner who wishes to combine a full-time career with higher education. Study abroad is also offered.

*A comprehensive fee of $7650 covers tuition, room, board, activity fee, and infirmary fee for students in 4-year programs.

Honors: Phi Theta Kappa is offered to qualified students.

Admissions: About 87% of those who applied were accepted for the 1981–82 freshman class. Candidates should have completed 16 Carnegie units, should have a C average, and should rank in the upper 50% of their class. High school record, advanced placement or honor courses, and recommendations by school officials are also strongly considered. Preference is given to children of alumni.

Procedure: There are no application deadlines. A rolling admissions policy is in effect. A personal interview is recommended. A $20 fee must be submitted.

Special: The early decision deadline is December 1. Deferred admission is also available. AP and CLEP credit is given.

Transfer: All of the recent transfer applicants were accepted. An average of C is required, and 60 of the 120 credits required for the bachelor's degree must be taken in residence. Application deadlines are open. Transfers are admitted to the fall and spring semesters. C grades or better transfer.

Visiting: Individual visits are strongly encouraged. Visitors may sit in on classes and stay overnight at the school. Campus visits are best made weekdays from 9 A.M. to 4 P.M. The admissions office will make arrangements.

Financial Aid: About 60% of all students receive aid through the college. Thirty-eight percent work part-time on campus. There are numerous federal and state loans, work contracts, and scholarships available. The total scholarship aid available to freshmen is $85,000. The college, a member of CSS, administers $75,000 in federal loan funds and $305,800 in state loan funds. Tuition may be paid in installments. The FAF and FFS are required, as is an institutional form. Aid applications should be filed by March 1.

Foreign Students: About 1% of the full-time students come from foreign countries. The college actively recruits these students and offers them an intensive English course.

Admissions: Foreign students must achieve a score of at least 500 on the TOEFL. The SAT or ACT is not required.

Procedure: Application deadlines are March 1 (fall) and October 1 (spring). Students must complete a college-supplied form to establish proof of health. They must also carry health insurance, which is available through the college for a fee. Proof of funds sufficient to cover 1 year of study is required.

Admissions Contact: William S. Neal, Dean of Admissions.

VIRGIN ISLANDS

COLLEGE OF THE VIRGIN ISLANDS
Charlotte Amalie, U.S. Virgin Islands 00801 (809) 774-9200

F/T: 175M, 457W
P/T: 517M, 1261W
Grad: 55M, 143W
Year: sems, ss
Appl: Apr. 15
600 applied
SAT: 335V 344M

Faculty: 73; IIA, —$
Ph.D.'s: 50%
S/F Ratio: 18 to 1
Tuition: $467 ($1267)
R and B: $1267

300 accepted   162 enrolled
LESS COMPETITIVE

The College of the Virgin Islands, established in 1962, is a publicly supported coed institution. Programs are offered in the liberal arts, nursing, marine biology, business, and education. The library houses 50,000 volumes and 154,000 microfilm items.

Environment: The campus occupies 175 acres on a hill overlooking the Caribbean. The surrounding area is suburban. The air-conditioned plant includes a student center with dining and recreational facilities and an infirmary; a nursing education building containing classrooms, theater, and faculty offices; a field house; and dormitories that accommodate about 390 students.

Student Life: About 80% of the entering freshmen come from public schools. About one-third of the students live in dormitories. About 65% of the students are Protestant, 30% Catholic, 1% Jewish. About 90% of the students are minority-group members. Campus housing is coed. Students may keep cars on campus.

Organizations: There are no fraternities or sororities. However, a performing arts center on campus and the many beaches and scenic walks on the island provide opportunity for numerous cultural, social, and recreational activities.

Sports: The college does not offer an intercollegiate athletics program. There are 7 intramural sports for men and 7 for women.

Handicapped: Special facilities include some wheelchair ramps, elevators, and specially equipped rest rooms. Seventy-five percent of the campus is accessible to handicapped students.

Graduates: The freshman dropout rate is 40%; 25% remain to graduate. About 25% of the graduates pursue further education; 33% enter careers in business or industry.

Services: Placement and career counseling, tutoring, remedial instruction, and health care are available free of charge.

Programs of Study: The college offers the B.A. and B.S. degrees. Associate and master's degrees are also offered. Bachelor's degrees are offered in the following subjects: AREA STUDIES (Black/Afro-American), BUSINESS (accounting, business administration), EDUCATION (elementary), ENGLISH (English), FINE AND PERFORMING ARTS (music), HEALTH SCIENCES (nursing), LANGUAGES (Spanish), MATH AND SCIENCES (biology, chemistry, marine biology, mathematics), PREPROFESSIONAL (engineering), SOCIAL SCIENCES (social sciences, social welfare). There is also a certificate program in paralegal services.

Required: Satisfactory scores on the Undergraduate Program area tests are required for graduation. Students must also pass an English Proficiency Exam.

Special: The program in marine biology is augmented by work at the Marine Research Center on the island of St. John. Special summer courses are conducted for entering freshmen who do not fully meet entrance requirements. The college also offers a 3-2 program in engineering.

Admissions: About 50% of those who applied were admitted to the 1981–82 freshman class. Candidates must be high school graduates and must have completed 17 units. The minimum GPA accepted is 2.0. The college also considers SAT scores, class rank, and grade average, as well as advanced placement or honors courses, impres-

912 VIRGIN ISLANDS

sions made during an interview, recommendations by school officials, leadership record, and evidence of special talents.

Procedure: The SAT or ACT is strongly recommended. A placement test is given to all entrants. The college uses a rolling admissions policy. The application and a $10 fee must be submitted by April 15 for fall admission.

Special: An early admissions plan is available. AP and CLEP credit is given.

Transfer: For fall 1981, 60 transfer students applied, 50 were accepted, and 35 enrolled. A 2.0 GPA is required of transfer students; Grades of 2.5 or above transfer. Transfer applicants are considered for all classes. Preference is given to students transferring from within the Virgin Islands. A student must complete, at the college, between 30 and 36 credits, of the 120 to 122 credits required to earn a bachelor's degree. Application deadlines are the same as those for freshmen.

Visiting: There are regularly scheduled orientations for prospective students. Guides are available for informal visits. Visitors may sit in on classes but may not stay overnight at the school. Visits are best scheduled during the mid-summer program or at mid-semester. The development office should be contacted for arrangements.

Financial Aid: About 75% of all students receive financial aid, which is available in the form of scholarships, loans, and part-time campus employment; 25% of the students work part-time on campus. The average award to freshmen from all sources is $2000. Financial aid applications should be submitted by March 15. The college is a member of CSS; the FAF must be submitted.

Foreign Students: About 15% of the full-time students come from foreign countries.

Admissions: Foreign students must achieve a minimum TOEFL score of 550; no further exams are required.

Procedure: Application deadlines are April 15 for fall and November 15 for spring. Foreign students must present proof of health, and proof of adequate funds. Health insurance is available through the college.

Admissions Contact: Mario A. Watlington, Director of Admissions.

VIRGINIA

AVERETT COLLEGE D-4
Danville, Virginia 24541 (804) 793-7811

F/T: 400M, 500W	Faculty: 58; n/av
P/T: 50M, 75W	Ph.D.'s: 58%
Grad: 3M, 30W	S/F Ratio: 18 to 1
Year: 4-1-4, ss	Tuition, R and B: $4800
Appl: Aug. 15	
960 applied	760 accepted	350 enrolled
SAT: 450V 450M	ACT: 23	COMPETITIVE+

Averett College, founded in 1859, is a private, coeducational liberal arts college affiliated with the Virginia Baptist General Association. The library contains 75,000 volumes, and subscribes to 425 periodicals.

Environment: The campus is located in a residential section of Danville, a small city 45 miles from Greensboro, N.C. The 5 dormitories house 550 students.

Student Life: About 65% of the students are from Virginia, and 80% come from public schools. Approximately 45% of the students live on campus. Seventeen percent are minority-group members. About 65% are Protestant, 20% are Catholic, and 2% are Jewish. Campus housing is single-sex; there are visiting privileges. Drinking is prohibited on campus. Students may keep cars on campus.

Organizations: About 12% of the men belong to a local fraternity, and 10% of the women belong to a local sorority. Campus activities include student government, theater and choral groups, publications, films, concerts, and dances. The major social event is Spring Weekend. Recreational and cultural activities are available in the city of Danville.

Sports: The college fields intercollegiate teams in 7 sports for men and 7 for women. There are 7 intramural sports for men and 6 for women.

Handicapped: About half the campus is accessible to physically handicapped students. Special facilities include wheelchair ramps, and a special counselor is available. Fewer than 1% of the students have impaired vision, and the library has audio facilities for them.

Graduates: The freshman dropout rate is 15%; about 70% of the entering freshmen remain to graduate. Thirty percent of the graduates pursue advanced degrees, including 3% who enter medical school, 1% who enter dental school, and 8% who enter law school. About 55% of the graduates begin careers in business and industry.

Services: Placement, career counseling, tutoring, remedial instruction, and psychological counseling are provided free to students. Health care is available on a fee basis.

Programs of Study: The college offers the B.A. and B.S. degrees. Master's and associate degrees also are offered. Bachelor's degrees are offered in the following subjects: BUSINESS (accounting, aviation administration, business administration, business administration/equestrian studies, business education, management, marketing), EDUCATION (early childhood, elementary, emotionally disturbed, health/physical, learning disabilities, reading, secondary, special), ENGLISH (English, journalism, literature, speech), FINE AND PERFORMING ARTS (art, art education, art history, music, studio art, theater/dramatics), HEALTH SCIENCES (medical technology), MATH AND SCIENCES (biochemistry, biology, chemistry, equestrian studies, mathematics, natural sciences), PHILOSOPHY (philosophy, religion), PREPROFESSIONAL (dentistry, law, medicine, ministry, pharmacy, social work, veterinary), SOCIAL SCIENCES (history, psychology, social sciences, sociology). An A.S. degree is offered in secretarial studies. About 30% of the undergraduate degrees are conferred in business and 25% in education.

Required: All undergraduates must take courses in English, fine arts, mathematics or natural science, religion or philosophy, and social science.

Special: Four-year B.A.-B.S. degrees may be earned in most majors. Regular degrees may be earned in 3 years. A general studies major is offered, and students may design their own majors. Junior year abroad, independent study, and an exchange program with Anstey College of Physical Education in Warwickshire, England, also are offered.

Honors: Four national honor societies have chapters on campus.

Admissions: About 79% of those who applied for admission to the 1981–82 freshman class were accepted. The SAT scores of those who enrolled were as follows: Verbal—54% below 500, 40% between 500 and 599, 5% between 600 and 700, and 1% above 700; Math—50% below 500, 45% between 500 and 599, 4% between 600 and 700, and 1% above 700. On the ACT, 12% scored below 21, 80% between 21 and 23, 5% between 24 and 25, 2% between 26 and 28, and 1% above 28. Applicants should have completed at least 15 Carnegie units with an average of at least 2.0 and rank in the upper 60% of their class. Admissions officers also consider, in descending order of importance, advanced placement or honors courses, recommendations by school officials, impressions made during an interview, extracurricular activities, and evidence of special talents.

Procedure: Applicants must take the SAT or ACT; junior-year results are acceptable. Application deadlines are August 15 (fall), December 1 (winter), December 15 (spring), and May 15 (summer). The application fee is $15. Notification is made on a rolling basis.

Special: Early and deferred admissions plans are available. AP and CLEP credit is accepted.

Transfer: For fall 1981, 224 students applied, 187 were accepted, and 144 enrolled. A 2.0 GPA is required. D grades do not transfer. All students must complete, at the college, 30 of the 120 credits required for a bachelor's degree. There is a 1-year residency requirement. Application deadlines are the same as those for freshmen.

Visiting: Prospective students are asked to arrange visits with the admissions office in advance. "Open house" weekends are held in the fall and spring. Visits should be scheduled from September through December 15, or from February through May 20. Guides are provided, and visitors may sit in on classes and stay overnight at the school.

Financial Aid: About 70% of the students receive college-administered aid. Much of the aid is based on academic achievement. Scholarships are awarded to all high school graduates in the top 10% of their class and to all junior college graduates rated cum laude or better. Averett Scholars receive departmental awards of $1000 each. The college administers $180,000 in federal loan funds and awards work contracts to 30% of the students, including freshmen. Grants must be matched dollar for dollar with loans or job earnings. The average package of grants, loans, and work-study jobs for boarding students in 1981–82 was $2700. Tuition may be paid on the installment plan. The college, as a member of CSS, requires aid applicants to submit the FAF. Aid applications should be submitted by April 1 (summer or fall), December 1 (winter), or December 15 (spring).

Foreign Students: One percent of the full-time students come from foreign countries.

Admissions: Foreign students must achieve a minimum score of 450 on the TOEFL and must take the SAT.

Procedure: Application deadlines are June 1 (fall), November 1 (winter), December 1 (spring), and March 1 (summer). Foreign students must present proof of adequate funds.

Admissions Contact: Walt Crutchfield, Director of Admissions.

BLUEFIELD COLLEGE D-2
Bluefield, Virginia 24605 (304) 327-7137

F/T: 215M, 185W	Faculty: n/av
P/T: 15M, 15W	Ph.D.'s: 40%
Grad: none	S/F Ratio: 17 to 1
Year: 4-1-4, ss	Tuition: $1760
Appl: see profile	R and B: $1780
200 applied	180 accepted 160 enrolled
SAT: 850 (composite)	LESS COMPETITIVE

Bluefield College, founded in 1922, is a private, independent Baptist college. The library contains 48,000 volumes, and subscribes to 200 periodicals.

Environment: The 85-acre campus is located in the Appalachian Mountains, 3 miles from the town of Bluefield. The campus has 8 major buildings, including 3 dormitories that accommodate 300 students. Housing is also provided for married students.

Student Life: About 75% of the students are residents of Virginia. Approximately 65% live on campus in the single-sex dormitories. Unmarried freshmen and sophomores under 21 are required to do so. Weekly chapel attendance is compulsory. Alcohol is forbidden on campus, and there are no visiting privileges in the dorms.

Organizations: Approximately 30 college-sponsored extracurricular activities, including student government and the Baptist Student Union, are open to students. There are no fraternities or sororities.

Sports: The college fields intercollegiate or club teams in 6 sports for men and 6 for women. Intramural sports also are available.

Handicapped: About 25% of the campus is accessible to handicapped students. Facilities include special parking and wheelchair ramps.

Graduates: About 15% of the freshmen drop out by the end of the first year, and 20% remain to graduate. Of those who graduate, 25% pursue advanced degrees; 2% enter medical school, 1% enter dental school, and 2% enter law school. Another 15% begin careers in business and industry.

Services: Career counseling and placement services are available free to students.

Programs of Study: The college confers the B.A. and B.S. degrees. Associate degrees also are awarded. Bachelor's degrees are offered in the following subjects: BUSINESS (accounting, business education, business and engineering, office administration), EDUCATION (elementary, secondary), ENGLISH (English), FINE AND PERFORMING ARTS (art, music, music education, sacred music), MATH AND SCIENCES (general science), PHILOSOPHY (philosophy, religion), SOCIAL SCIENCES (history, psychology, social sciences).

Required: Students are required to take courses in physical education, health, and religion. They also must complete distribution requirements.

Honors: One honor society has a chapter on campus.

Admissions: About 90% of those who applied were accepted for the 1981-82 freshman class. The SAT scores of those who enrolled were as follows: Both parts—65% below 500, 20% between 500 and 599, 15% between 600 and 700, and 0% above 700. Candidates should have completed 13 high school units.

Procedure: Applicants must take the SAT or ACT. An interview is recommended. Students are admitted to all terms; applications should be filed at least 2 weeks before registration. The college follows a rolling admissions plan. There is a $10 application fee.

Special: AP and CLEP credit is available.

Transfer: For a recent year, 25 students applied, 20 were accepted, and 15 enrolled. An average of C is required, and a limited number of D grades may be transferred. Students must earn at least 36 credits in residence of the 126 or more required for a bachelor's degree.

Visiting: Guides are available for informal visits by prospective students. Visitors may sit in on classes. The admissions office should be contacted for arrangements.

Financial Aid: About 85% of the students receive aid. The college offers a limited number of scholarships. Loans and campus jobs are available. The average award to a 1981-82 freshman totaled $3000. The college is a member of the CSS. The FAF is required. The deadline for aid applications is June 1.

Foreign Students: About 8% of the full-time students come from foreign countries. Special counseling and special organizations are provided.

Admissions: Applicants must achieve a TOEFL score of at least 500 and must take the SAT or ACT.

Procedure: Application deadlines are open; foreign students are admitted to all terms. They must complete a health questionnaire and provide proof of funds adequate to cover 1 year. They also are required to carry health insurance, which is available through the college for a fee.

Admissions Contact: Charles R. Addington, Director of Admissions and Financial Aid.

BRIDGEWATER COLLEGE D-2
Bridgewater, Virginia 22812 (703) 828-2501

F/T: 452M, 462W	Faculty: n/av; IIB, av$
P/T: 13M&W	Ph.D.'s: 78%
Grad: none	S/F Ratio: 15 to 1
Year: 3-3-1-3, ss	Tuition, R and B:
Appl: June 1	$5600
850 applied	586 accepted 302 enrolled
SAT: 1000 (composite)	COMPETITIVE

Bridgewater College, founded in 1880, is a liberal arts institution affiliated with the Church of the Brethren. The library contains more than 100,000 volumes and about 25,000 bound periodicals.

Environment: The 35-acre campus is located in a rural area about 7 miles from Harrisonburg and 20 miles from Staunton. The campus has 17 major buildings, including a recently renovated auditorium that contains a 51-rank pipe organ. Dormitories accommodate about 800 men and women.

Student Life: About 70% of the students are residents of Virginia. Ninety-seven percent come from public schools. Ninety percent live on campus in single-sex dormitories. Full-time students under 24, who do not live with relatives, generally are required to live in the dorms. About 22% of the students are members of the Church of the Brethren. Convocation attendance twice a week is compulsory; attendance at church services is voluntary. An honor code governs student behavior.

Organizations: Extracurricular activities include student government, music and drama groups, a ski club, publications, and special-interest clubs. Religious clubs include the Fellowship of Christian Athletes, the Student Committee for Religious Activities, the Brethren Student Fellowship, and the Wesley Fellowship. There are no sororities or fraternities.

Sports: The college fields intercollegiate teams in 7 sports for men and 5 for women. Intramural sports also are available.

Graduates: About 7% of the freshmen drop out, and 60% remain to graduate. About 30% of the graduates pursue advanced degrees.

Programs of Study: The college confers the B.A. and B.S. degrees. Bachelor's degrees are offered in the following subjects: BUSINESS (business administration), EDUCATION (elementary, health/physical, secondary), ENGLISH (English), FINE AND PERFORMING ARTS (art, art education, music, music education), LANGUAGES (French, German, Spanish), MATH AND SCIENCES (biology, chemistry, general science, mathematics, physical sciences, physics), PHILOSOPHY (philosophy, religion), PREPROFESSIONAL (engineering, home economics), SOCIAL SCIENCES (economics, government/political science, history, international relations, psychology, sociology).

Required: Students must complete general education requirements, which include physical education and proficiency in a foreign language.

Special: The college offers a cooperative forestry program with Duke University and a combination degree program in engineering with Georgia Institute of Technology. Independent study projects are available. Students may spend their junior year abroad. A cooperative medical technology program also is available. Nonmajor preprofessional programs are offered in computer science, dentistry, pharmacy, law, medicine, ministry, and social work.

914 VIRGINIA

Honors: Five honor societies have chapters on campus. Juniors and seniors may register for honors independent-study projects.

Admissions: About 69% of those who applied were accepted for the 1981–82 freshman class. Applicants should rank in the top half of their graduating class and have completed 16 high school units. Applicants are accepted on the basis of their high school records, test scores, recommendations, character and personality, extracurricular activities, and impressions made during an interview.

Procedure: The SAT or ACT is required and should be taken by February of the senior year. An interview is recommended. Applications for fall admission should be filed by June 1 but will be accepted as long as there is room. Students also are admitted to other terms. Notification is made on a rolling basis. There is a $15 application fee.

Special: The college has an early admissions plan. AP and CLEP credit is accepted.

Transfer: Applicants must have a GPA of at least 2.0. D grades generally do not transfer. Students must complete at least 30 units in residence of the 123 or more required for a bachelor's degree.

Financial Aid: About 55% of the students receive aid. Scholarships, loans, and grants are available. CWS and institutional work programs are also offered. The average award to a 1981–82 freshman totaled $3400. The FAF is required. Aid applications must be filed by April 1.

Foreign Students: About 1% of the full-time students come from foreign countries. Special counseling is provided for these students.

Admissions: Applicants must take the TOEFL and the SAT.

Procedure: Foreign students are admitted to all terms; applications must be submitted at least 6 weeks before registration. Students must submit a health record before enrollment and show evidence that they have at least two-thirds of the funds required for 4 years of study. Health insurance is required and is available through the college for a fee.

Admissions Contact: Linda S. Glover, Director of Admissions.

CHRISTOPHER NEWPORT COLLEGE   F-3
Newport News, Virginia 23606   (804) 599-7015

F/T: 847M, 1084W
P/T: 917M, 1250W
Grad: none
Year: sems, ss
Appl: Aug. 15
675 applied
SAT: 453V 492M

Faculty: 112; IIB, +$
Ph.D.'s: 78%
S/F Ratio: 20 to 1
Tuition: $1120 ($1453)
R and B: n/app
500 accepted
COMPETITIVE

Founded in 1960 as a 2-year college, Christopher Newport College began offering 4-year degrees in 1969. The library houses more than 92,000 volumes, and subscribes to 545 periodicals.

Environment: The 75-acre campus is located in a suburban section of Newport News. The college's 9 buildings include a science complex, a gymnasium, and a new 4-story, 30,000-square-foot administration and faculty office building.

Student Life: Most students are Virginia residents. All commute; there are no dormitories. Ten percent of the students are minority-group members.

Organizations: Extracurricular activities include publications, special-interest clubs, and student government. About 15% of the men belong to 1 of the 3 fraternities on campus; 15% of the women are members of 1 of the 2 sororities. Colonial Williamsburg is 20 miles to the west; Virginia Beach 35 miles to the east.

Sports: The college participates in 6 intercollegiate sports. Intramural sports for men and women include basketball, volleyball, and flag football.

Handicapped: About 60% of the campus is accessible to handicapped students. Special facilities include wheelchair ramps, parking areas, elevators, lowered drinking fountains, and specially equipped rest rooms. Special class scheduling is also available. There are no special counselors. Fewer than 1% of the students have visual or hearing impairments.

Graduates: Thirty percent of the graduates pursue graduate study.

Services: Free placement services and career and psychological counseling are provided to students. Tutoring and remedial instruction are available on a fee basis.

Programs of Study: The college confers the B.A., B.S., B.S.B.A., B.S.G.A., and B.S.I.S. degrees. Bachelor's degrees are offered in the following subjects: AREA STUDIES (urban), BUSINESS (accounting, business administration, computer science, finance, management, marketing, real estate/insurance), EDUCATION (elementary, leisure studies), ENGLISH (English, journalism), FINE AND PERFORMING ARTS (art, music, theater/dramatics), LANGUAGES (French, Spanish), MATH AND SCIENCES (biology, chemistry, mathematics), PHILOSOPHY (humanistic studies, philosophy), PREPROFESSIONAL (dentistry, law, medicine, pharmacy, social work), SOCIAL SCIENCES (corrections, criminal justice, economics, government/political science, history, international relations, psychology, public management, sociology). An interdisciplinary studies major also is available. Preprofessional training is offered in some health professions.

Required: All students must fulfill distribution requirements in composition and literature, humanities, mathematics, or philosophy, natural and social science, physical education, and in some programs, foreign language.

Special: Bachelor's degrees are awarded through day and evening programs. Students may design their own majors.

Honors: Two national honor societies have chapters on campus. The college offers an honors program for all classes.

Admissions: About 74% of those who applied were accepted for the 1981–82 freshman class. The SAT scores of those who enrolled were as follows: Verbal—20% between 500 and 599, 4% between 600 and 700, and 1% above 700; Math—25% between 500 and 599, 5% between 600 and 700, and 1% above 700. Applicants should have at least a 2.0 average and rank in the top half of their high school class. The school also considers, in descending order of importance: extracurricular activities, recommendations by school officials, evidence of special talents, and advanced placement or honors courses.

Procedure: The SAT or ACT is required. Application deadlines are August 15 (fall) and December 1 (spring). Notifications are made on a rolling basis. The application fee is $10.

Special: Early decision and early admissions plans are available. AP and CLEP are accepted.

Transfer: For fall 1981, 500 students applied, and 400 were accepted. A C average is required. D grades transfer. All students must complete, at the college, 30 of the 124 credits required for a bachelor's degree. Application deadlines are August 15 (fall) and December 1 (spring).

Visiting: Campus tour programs for prospective students are scheduled regularly. Guides also are available for informal visits. Visitors can sit in on classes. Visits are best scheduled in spring. Arrangements should be made with the admissions office.

Financial Aid: About 23% of the students receive financial aid. The college awards scholarships, loans, and CWS work contracts to students with demonstrated need. The FAF should be submitted by May 1 (fall) or November 15 (spring). The college is a member of CSS.

Foreign Students: Fewer than 1% of the full-time students come from foreign countries.

Admissions: Foreign students must achieve a TOEFL score of at least 500 and must take the SAT.

Procedure: Application deadlines are July 1 (fall) and November 15 (spring). Foreign students must present proof of adequate funds and must carry health insurance.

Admissions Contact: Keith F. McLoughland, Dean of Admissions.

CLINCH VALLEY COLLEGE OF THE   C-2
UNIVERSITY OF VIRGINIA
Wise, Virginia 24293   (703) 328-2431

F/T: 326M, 352W
P/T: 77M, 140W
Grad: none
Year: sems, ss
Appl: Aug. 15
469 applied
SAT: 400V 410M   ACT: 20

Faculty: 40; IIB, +$
Ph.D.'s: 68%
S/F Ratio: 15 to 1
Tuition: $902 ($1364)
R and B: $1735
440 accepted
LESS COMPETITIVE

Clinch Valley College, founded in 1954 as a branch of the University of Virginia, is a publicly controlled liberal arts college. The library contains 90,000 volumes and 2381 microfilm items, and subscribes to 819 periodicals.

Environment: The 350-acre campus is located in a rural area 60 miles from Bristol. A student center and chapel complex have just been completed. Living facilities include dormitories, married student housing, and fraternity houses.

Student Life: Thirty percent of the students live on campus. Three percent are minority-group members. College housing is single-sex; there are visiting privileges. Students may keep cars on campus.

Organizations: About 1% of the men belong to 2 fraternities on campus; 1% of the women belong to 1 sorority. Extracurricular activities include cheerleading; chorus; student government; debating; drama; student publications; and various social, service, religious, and political clubs. The college sponsors films, lectures, plays, dances, and exhibits. Outdoor recreation areas are near the campus.

Sports: The college fields intercollegiate teams in 4 men's and 3 women's sports. There are 5 intramural sports for men and 4 for women.

Handicapped: The entire campus is accessible to physically handicapped students. Facilities include wheelchair ramps, parking areas, and specially equipped rest rooms. Special class scheduling and counselors are available. No students with impaired vision or hearing are enrolled.

Graduates: Twenty-five percent of the freshmen drop out during their first year. Forty percent remain to graduate. About 10% of the graduates continue their education, including 2% each who enter medical and law schools. About 30% of the graduates pursue careers in business and industry.

Services: Students are provided with free placement, career and psychological counseling, tutoring, and remedial instruction. Placement services are available to graduates as well as students. Health care is available on a fee basis.

Programs of Study: The college awards the B.A. and B.S. degrees. Associate degrees are also offered. Bachelor's degrees are offered in the following subjects: BUSINESS (accounting, business administration, business education), EDUCATION (early childhood, elementary), ENGLISH (English), FINE AND PERFORMING ARTS (art education, dance, music education, theater/dramatics), HEALTH SCIENCES (medical technology), LANGUAGES (French, Spanish), MATH AND SCIENCES (biology, chemistry, ecology/environmental science, mathematics), SOCIAL SCIENCES (history). Two-year transfer programs are available in nursing and forestry. Two-year certificate programs are offered in business, secretarial science, and medical secretarial science. About 35% of degrees are conferred in education and 28% in business.

Required: Freshmen in the 4-year program take a basic liberal arts curriculum, including 1 year of English composition and at least 1 semester each of mathematics and of a laboratory science.

Special: Students may design their own majors. A general studies degree is available.

Honors: Two national honor societies have chapters on campus. All departments offer graduation-with-honors programs.

Admissions: About 94% of those who applied for admission to the 1981–82 freshman class were accepted. The SAT scores of those who enrolled in a recent year were as follows: Verbal—15% between 500 and 600, 1% between 600 and 700, and 0% above 700; Math—23% between 500 and 600, 5% between 600 and 700, and 1% above 700. Applicants must have graduated from an accredited high school with an average of at least C, or have obtained a GED certificate. Besides class rank and test scores, admissions officers consider recommendations by school officials, impressions made during an interview, advanced placement or honors courses, and leadership record.

Procedure: Applicants must take the SAT or the ACT. Application deadlines are August 15 (fall) and January 15 (spring). Freshmen also are admitted to the summer sessions. Applicants are notified as soon as their applications are complete. The application fee is $15.

Special: A deferred admissions plan is available.

Transfer: For fall 1981, 80 students applied, and 73 were accepted. Applicants must have a GPA of at least 2.0 and be in good standing at their previous college. D grades do not transfer. Those with fewer than 54 transferable hours must submit their high school transcript and SAT scores. All applicants must submit college transcripts. Students must complete, at the college, at least 30 of the 122 credits needed for a bachelor's degree. The application deadline is August 15.

Visiting: The college schedules regular orientation sessions at which prospective students tour the campus and meet faculty members and administrators. Arrangements also can be made with the admissions office for informal visits in fall and spring. Guides are provided, and visitors may sit in on classes and stay overnight at the school.

Financial Aid: About 67% of all students receive aid in the form of grants, work-study jobs, and/or loans. Fifty percent of the students work part-time on campus. Average aid to freshmen from all sources covers 74% of costs. The college is a member of CSS. The FAF is required. Application deadlines are May 1 (fall) and December 1 (spring).

Foreign Students: One percent of the full-time students come from foreign countries. The college offers these students special counseling and special organizations.

Admissions: Foreign students must score at least 550 on the TOEFL. They must also take the SAT or ACT; a composite score of at least 800 is required on the SAT.

Procedure: The application deadlines are July 15 (fall) and December 7 (spring). Foreign students must complete the college's own medical form. They must also provide proof of funds adequate to cover their first year of study.

Admissions Contact: Sandy C. Birchfield, Director of Admissions.

COLLEGE OF WILLIAM AND MARY   E-3
Williamsburg, Virginia 23185   (804) 253-4223

F/T: 2122M, 2429W   Faculty: 430; I, av$
P/T: 27M, 31W   Ph.D.'s: 75%
Grad: 597M, 481W   S/F Ratio: 16 to 1
Year: sems, ss   Tuition: $1334 ($3368)
Appl: Feb. 1   R and B: $2284
5768 applied   2033 accepted   1107 enrolled
SAT: 590V 610M   HIGHLY COMPETITIVE

College of William and Mary, a state-supported institution chartered in 1693, is the second-oldest college in the United States. Besides offering undergraduate instruction, the college has schools of business administration, education, law, and marine science. The library contains 717,449 volumes and 407,787 microfilm items, and subscribes to 5073 periodicals.

Environment: The college occupies 1200 acres in a suburban area about halfway between Norfolk and Richmond. The campus borders colonial Williamsburg. Living facilities include dormitories, on-campus apartments, and fraternity and sorority houses. The college has a branch campus in Petersburg.

Student Life: About 70% of the students are from Virginia. Eighty percent live on campus. Eight percent are minority-group members. Campus housing is both coed and single-sex; there are visiting privileges in the single-sex housing. Students may keep cars on campus. The school is run on the honor system.

Organizations: About 35% of the undergraduates belong to 1 of 12 national fraternities or 10 national sororities on campus. Social, cultural, and special-interest activities are available at the college, including art galleries, a speaker series, concerts, movies, and music groups. Busch Gardens amusement park is nearby, and Williamsburg has a theater company and an orchestra.

Sports: The college participates in 15 intercollegiate sports for men and 11 for women. There are 11 intramural sports for men and 7 for women.

Handicapped: Special facilities for physically handicapped students include wheelchair ramps, parking areas, specially equipped rest rooms, and first-floor housing. Special class scheduling also is available. Fewer than 1% of the students are visually or hearing-impaired; for those students the college provides notetakers and special library resources. One special counselor is available for handicapped students, and there is an advisory committee on the needs of the handicapped.

Graduates: Fewer than 5% of the entering freshmen drop out at the end of the first year; 76% remain to graduate. Thirty percent of the graduates seek advanced degrees (5% go to medical school, 1% to dental school, and 9% to law school). Fifty percent enter business and industry.

Services: Health care, placement, and career and psychological counseling are available free to students.

Programs of Study: The college offers the B.A., B.S., and B.B.A degrees. Master's and doctoral degrees also are available. Bachelor's degrees are offered in the following subjects: BUSINESS (accounting, business administration, computer science, management), EDUCATION (elementary, health/physical), ENGLISH (English), FINE AND PERFORMING ARTS (art, art education, music, music education, theater/dramatics), LANGUAGES (French, German, Greek/Latin, Spanish), MATH AND SCIENCES (biology, chemistry, computer science, geology, mathematics, physics), PHILOSOPHY (philosophy, religion), PREPROFESSIONAL (dentistry, engineering, forestry, law, medicine, veterinary), SOCIAL SCIENCES (anthropology, economics, government/political science, history, psychology, sociology). About 33% of the degrees are conferred in social sciences, 22% in math and sciences, and 15% in business.

916 VIRGINIA

Required: Students must take courses in humanities, social sciences, and natural sciences, and demonstrate proficiency in English, a foreign language, and physical education.

Special: The college offers an Experimental Academic and Residential Program and a 3-2 program in Engineering. Students may create their own majors. Several foreign-study plans are available.

Honors: Many honor societies, including Phi Beta Kappa, have chapters on campus. Most departments also offer honors programs.

Admissions: About 35% of those who applied for admission to the 1981-82 freshman class were accepted. The SAT scores of those who enrolled were as follows: Verbal—14% below 500, 42% between 500 and 599, 39% between 600 and 700, and 5% above 700; Math—4% below 500, 35% between 500 and 599, 50% between 600 and 700, and 11% above 700. Admissions officers consider SAT scores, academic record at an accredited high school, class rank, advanced placement or honors courses, leadership record, and evidence of special talents. Children of alumni receive special consideration. There is a 30% enrollment quota on out-of-state students.

Procedure: Applicants must take the SAT and are encouraged to take 3 ATs, including English Composition and a foreign-language test. Application deadlines are February 1 (fall) and November 15 (spring). Early decision candidates for fall admission are notified about December 1, and regular candidates about April 1. The application fee is $20.

Special: Early and deferred admissions plans are available. AP credit is accepted.

Transfer: For fall 1981, 814 students applied, 173 were accepted, and 114 enrolled. D grades do not transfer. All students must complete, at the college, 60 of the 240 credits required for a bachelor's degree. Application deadlines are the same as those for freshmen.

Visiting: Information sessions and campus tours are scheduled regularly at 10 A.M. and 2:30 P.M. Monday through Friday and 10 A.M. Saturday while classes are in session. Students may sit in on classes with the instructor's permission. Arrangements should be made through the admissions office.

Financial Aid: About 22% of the students receive aid through the college. The average freshman award is $1355. Scholarships are available mainly to Virginia residents. Loans and part-time jobs are available. Applications for financial aid should be in by February 15 for priority consideration.

Foreign Students: One percent of the full-time students come from foreign countries. Special organizations are available for these students.

Admissions: Foreign students must take the TOEFL and the SAT.

Procedure: Application deadlines are February 1 (fall) and November 15 (spring). Foreign students must present proof of funds adequate to cover 4 years of study.

Admissions Contact: G. Gary Ripple, Dean of Admissions.

EASTERN MENNONITE COLLEGE D-2
Harrisonburg, Virginia 22801   (703) 433-2771

F/T: 351M, 606W   Faculty: 62; IIA, — — $
P/T: 20M, 44W   Ph.D.'s: 33%
Grad: 74M, 16W   S/F Ratio: 15 to 1
Year: qtrs, ss   Tuition: $3831
Appl: Aug. 15   R and B: $1785
356 applied   333 accepted   249 enrolled
SAT: 450V 480M   COMPETITIVE

Eastern Mennonite College, a private liberal arts institution founded in 1917, is affiliated with the Mennonite Church. Its library contains 105,847 volumes and 3734 microfilm items, and subscribes to 890 periodicals.

Environment: The 106-acre campus is located in a rural area 2 miles from Harrisonburg, a town of 15,000 people, and 120 miles from Richmond and Washington. Living facilities include dormitories, married student housing, and on-campus and off-campus apartments.

Student Life: About 28% of the students are from Virginia. More than a third come from parochial schools. About 86% reside on campus. Three percent are minority-group members. About 98% are Protestant; 65% are Mennonite. Campus housing is single-sex; there are visiting privileges. Students may keep cars on campus. Attendance at the College Assembly is required. Smoking and drinking are prohibited on campus. Curfews for men and women are 12:30 P.M. on weekdays and 1 A.M. on weekends.

Organizations: There are no fraternities or sororities on campus. Extracurricular activities include clubs, publications, music, drama, and service groups. There are Protestant religious organizations on campus.

Sports: The college fields 5 intercollegiate teams for men and 6 for women. There are 9 intramural sports for men and 8 for women.

Handicapped: Special facilities for physically handicapped students include elevators, lowered drinking fountains and telephones, and specially equipped rest rooms. Special class scheduling is also available. The campus's hillside setting, however, presents significant problems for some physically disabled students.

Graduates: Thirty percent of the graduates seek advanced degrees. Many enter church-related and service-oriented professions.

Services: Free health care, psychological counseling, tutoring, remedial instruction, career counseling, and job placement services are offered. Placement services may be used by alumni as well as students.

Programs of Study: The college grants the B.A. and B.S. degrees. Associate and master's degrees are also awarded. Bachelor's degrees are offered in the following subjects: BUSINESS (accounting, business administration, business education, management), EDUCATION (early childhood, elementary, health/physical, secondary), ENGLISH (English), FINE AND PERFORMING ARTS (art, art education, music, music education), HEALTH SCIENCES (medical technology, nursing), LANGUAGES (French, German, modern languages, Spanish), MATH AND SCIENCES (biology, chemistry, mathematics), PHILOSOPHY (Biblical studies, philosophy, religion), PREPROFESSIONAL (community development, dentistry, dietetics, home economics, law, medicine, ministry, social work, veterinary), SOCIAL SCIENCES (history, international agricultural development, psychology, sociology). About half of the degrees are conferred in education, nursing, sociology, business, and Biblical studies.

Required: All freshmen must take 7 interdisciplinary courses. B.A. candidates must take a foreign language. All students must take physical education and courses in Biblical and church studies.

Special: The college offers independent study. Students may design their own majors. Study-abroad programs are available in Mexico, Canada, Europe, Jerusalem, and Latin America.

Admissions: About 94% of those who applied were accepted for the 1981-82 freshman class. The SAT scores of those who enrolled were as follows: Verbal—42% below 500, 13% between 500 and 599, 5% between 600 and 700, and 2% above 700; Math—32% below 500, 17% between 500 and 599, 11% between 600 and 700, and 2% above 700. On the ACT, 11% scored below 21, 4% between 21 and 23, 5% between 24 and 25, 2% between 26 and 28, and 1% above 28. Candidates should have 15 Carnegie units, a C average, and a combined score of 750 on the SAT or 18 on the ACT, and should rank in the upper half of their high school class. Advanced placement or honors courses, recommendations, and impressions made during the interview are also considered important.

Procedure: The SAT or ACT is required. An interview is recommended. The application fee is $15. Application deadline for fall admission is August 15; freshmen also are admitted to winter and spring terms. Notification is made on a rolling basis.

Special: There is a deferred admissions plan. AP and CLEP credit is accepted.

Transfer: For fall 1981, 190 students applied, 141 were accepted, and 82 enrolled. An average of at least C and a combined SAT score of at least 750 are required; D grades transfer. All students must complete, at the college, 30 of the 128-136 credits required for a bachelor's degree. Application deadlines are the same as those for freshmen.

Visiting: At regularly scheduled orientations, prospective students can tour the campus and meet faculty members, admissions representatives, and financial aid officers. Guides also are available for informal visits; visitors may sit in on classes and stay overnight at the college. The admissions office should be contacted for arrangements.

Financial Aid: About 80% of all students receive financial aid. About 60% work part-time on campus. Scholarships and loans are available to freshmen. The college belongs to the CSS, and aid applicants must submit the FAF. The deadline for priority consideration of aid applications is April 1.

Foreign Students: Four percent of the full-time students come from foreign countries. Special counseling and special organizations are available for these students.

Admissions: Foreign students must achieve a TOEFL score of at least 550. No college entrance exams are required.

EMORY AND HENRY COLLEGE B-4
Emory, Virginia 24327 (703) 944-3121

F/T: 402M, 348W	Faculty: 52; IIB, av$
P/T: 24M, 15W	Ph.D.'s: 75%
Grad: none	S/F Ratio: 14 to 1
Year: terms, ss	Tuition: $2874
Appl: open	R and B: $1626
426 applied 331 accepted	211 enrolled
SAT or ACT: required	COMPETITIVE

Emory and Henry College, founded in 1836, is a private liberal arts college operated by the Holston Conference of the United Methodist Church. The library contains 140,000 volumes, and subscribes to 700 periodicals.

Environment: The 100-acre campus is located in a rural area 8 miles from Abingdon and 22 miles from Bristol. There are dormitories on campus.

Student Life: Most students are from Virginia, and about 92% come from the South. Nearly 3% of the students are minority-group members. About 90% are Protestant and 5% are Catholic. Half of the students are Methodist. Dormitories are single-sex; there are visiting privileges. About 90% of the students live on campus. Drinking on campus is prohibited. Students in good standing may keep cars on campus.

Organizations: About 50% of the students belong to 1 of 5 fraternities and 4 sororities. The college provides social and cultural events.

Sports: The college participates intercollegiately in 5 sports for men and 5 for women. There are 15 intramural sports for men and 14 for women.

Handicapped: There are no special facilities for physically handicapped students.

Graduates: About 2% of the freshmen drop out by the end of the first year, and about 60% remain to graduate. Of the graduates, 33% pursue advanced degrees; 2% enter medical school. About 30% of the graduates begin careers in business and industry.

Services: Free health care, psychological counseling, tutoring, and career counseling are available to students. Free placement services are available to students and alumni.

Programs of Study: The college awards the B.A. and B.S. degrees. Bachelor's degrees are offered in the following subjects: AREA STUDIES (Appalachian, environmental, international), BUSINESS (accounting, business administration, computer science, management), EDUCATION (early childhood, elementary, health/physical, secondary), ENGLISH (English, journalism, literature), FINE AND PERFORMING ARTS (art, art education, music, music—church, music education, radio/TV, theater/dramatics), HEALTH SCIENCES (medical technology), LANGUAGES (French, German, Greek/Latin, Spanish), MATH AND SCIENCES (biology, chemistry, ecology/environmental science, mathematics, physics), PHILOSOPHY (philosophy, religion), PRE-PROFESSIONAL (dentistry, engineering, forestry, human services, law, medicine, ministry, pharmacy, veterinary), SOCIAL SCIENCES (anthropology, economics, geography, government/political science, history, international relations, psychology, sociology).

Required: All students must take at least 1 course in religion.

Special: Students may design their own majors. Cooperative programs are offered in engineering, forestry, Chinese, and Hindi. Travel abroad and student-directed seminars are offered for credit. A non-Western studies major is available and the college is a member of the Asian Consortium.

Honors: Four honor societies have chapters on campus. Freshman seminars and honors curricula also are available.

Admissions: About 78% of those who applied were accepted for the 1981-82 freshman class. A combined SAT score of 850 to 1000 or an ACT composite of 20 to 22 is generally the minimum required. Applicants must be graduates of an accredited high school, rank in the upper half of their class, and present an average of at least 2.5. Admissions officers also consider, in descending order of importance, recommendations by school officials, extracurricular activities, leadership, and impressions made during an interview.

Procedure: Applicants must take the SAT or ACT. There is no application deadline. Freshmen are admitted to fall, winter, spring, and summer terms. The application fee is $15. Notification is made on a rolling basis.

Special: Early decision and early admissions plans are offered. AP and CLEP credit is accepted.

Transfer: For fall 1981, 99 students applied, 79 were accepted, and 59 enrolled. Applicants must have a GPA of at least 2.0. D grades do not transfer. All students must complete, at the college, 10 of the 38 credits required for a bachelor's degree. There are no application deadlines; transfer students are admitted in all 4 terms.

Visiting: New Student Days are scheduled regularly in spring for prospective students and their parents. For those who want to visit in fall or early winter, the college will provide guides and arrange overnight accommodations at the school. Visits should be scheduled with the director of admissions.

Financial Aid: About 88% of the students receive financial assistance. About 40% work part-time on campus. The average amount of aid available to freshmen from scholarships, loans, and part-time jobs is $2500. The college is a member of CSS. The FAF, FFS, or SFS and applications should be submitted by April 1.

Foreign Students: Fewer than 1% of the students come from foreign countries.

Admissions: Foreign students must achieve a TOEFL score of at least 500. No college entrance exams are required.

Procedure: There are no application deadlines; foreign students are admitted in all 4 terms. They must complete a health form and must have a physical exam, and they must present proof of funds adequate to cover 1 year of study.

Admissions Contact: Cary Bennett, Director of Admissions.

FERRUM COLLEGE C-3
Ferrum, Virginia 24088 (703) 365-2121

F/T: 800M, 700W	Faculty: 85; n/av
P/T: 50M, 50W	Ph.D.'s: 35%
Grad: none	S/F Ratio: 18 to 1
Year: sems, ss	Tuition, R and B:
Appl: open	$4390
2000 applied 1400 accepted	600 enrolled
SAT: 350V 400M	LESS COMPETITIVE

Ferrum College, founded in 1913, is a liberal arts college affiliated with the Methodist Church. Most students are enrolled in the junior college program. The library contains 60,000 volumes, and subscribes to 479 periodicals.

Environment: The 754-acre campus is located in a rural area in the foothills of the Blue Ridge Mountains, 35 miles southwest of Roanoke. Living facilities include dormitories and on-campus and off-campus apartments.

Student Life: About 85% of the students are from Virginia, and 96% come from public schools. About 85% live on campus; only married students may live off campus. Twelve percent of the students are minority-group members. Campus housing is both coed and single-sex; there are visiting privileges in the single-sex housing. Students may keep cars on campus. Drinking is forbidden on campus.

Organizations: There are fraternities on campus. More than 40 extracurricular activities, including a student government and service organizations, are available. The college schedules 2 to 5 cultural activities each week.

Sports: The college fields intercollegiate teams in 8 men's and 5 women's sports. There are 12 intramural sports for men and 7 for women.

Handicapped: The college has no special facilities for physically handicapped students, but special class scheduling is available. Fewer than 1% of the students have impaired vision or hearing.

Graduates: Ten percent of entering freshmen drop out after the first year; 70% remain to graduate. About 20% of the graduates pursue further study.

Services: Psychological and career counseling, placement services, tutoring, and remedial instruction are provided free to students. Health care is available on a fee basis.

Programs of Study: The college offers the B.A., B.S., and B.S.W. degrees. Associate degrees are also awarded. Bachelor's degrees are offered in the following subjects: BUSINESS (business administration), EDUCATION (early childhood), ENGLISH (journalism), FINE AND PERFORMING ARTS (theater/dramatics), MATH AND SCIENCES (ecology/environmental science), PHILOSOPHY (religion), PRE-

Procedure: The application deadline is August 1; foreign students are admitted in the fall, winter, and spring quarters. They must have the health form completed by a physician and must present proof of funds adequate to cover the entire period of study.

Admissions Contact: Ross D. Collingwood, Director of Admissions.

918 VIRGINIA

PROFESSIONAL (agriculture, public affairs, social work), SOCIAL SCIENCES (leisure services, psychology).

Required: All students must take courses in English, math, physical education, religion, biology, and Western civilization. Students must maintain a GPA of at least 2.0 to graduate.

Special: Students may travel on college-sponsored overseas trips or work off campus for credit. Special courses in developmental math, reading skills, writing skills, and special services are offered to freshmen.

Honors: Three honor societies have chapters on campus.

Admissions: About 70% of those who applied were accepted for the 1981-82 freshman class. Candidates should have completed 15 Carnegie units at an accredited high school. Admissions officers also consider advanced placement or honors courses, impressions made at a personal interview, recommendations by school officials, and extracurricular activities. Some preference is given to children of alumni.

Procedure: The SAT or ACT is required. There is no application deadline, but most places are filled by May. Freshmen are admitted to the fall, spring, and summer terms. A personal interview is recommended. A $15 application fee is required. Notification is on a rolling basis.

Special: The college has an Upward Bound Program for minority students. AP and CLEP credit is available.

Transfer: Applicants must be in good academic standing. D grades do not transfer. All students must complete, at the college, 87 of the 127 credits required for a bachelor's degree. There is no application deadline; transfer students are admitted in the fall, spring, and summer terms.

Visiting: Four weekend orientations for prospective students are scheduled in summer. Informal visits may be arranged with the admissions office anytime except major holidays. Visitors may sit in on classes, and guides are provided.

Financial Aid: About 60% of the students receive assistance. Freshman scholarship funds vary from year to year. Loans and work contracts also are available. About 60% of the students work part-time on campus. The college is a member of the CSS, and aid applicants must submit the FAF. Aid applications should be submitted by March 1.

Foreign Students: An intensive English course and special counseling are available for students from foreign countries.

Admissions: Foreign students must take the TOEFL and the SAT or ACT.

Procedure: There are no application deadlines; foreign students are admitted in the fall, spring, and summer terms. They must present proof of funds adequate to cover 1 year of study and must complete a health form.

Admissions Contact: F. Ross Ferguson, Director of Admissions.

GEORGE MASON UNIVERSITY   E-2
Fairfax, Virginia 22030   (703) 323-2102

F/T: 2866M, 3460W
P/T: 1675M, 2537W
Grad: 1631M, 2094W
Year: sems, ss
Appl: June 1
3267 applied
SAT: 498V 506M

Faculty: 462; IIA, av$
Ph.D.'s: 82%
S/F Ratio: 16 to 1
Tuition: $1008 ($1872)
R and B: $3070-3220
2593 accepted   1623 enrolled
COMPETITIVE

George Mason University is a state-supported university made up of the colleges of Arts and Sciences, Professional Studies, Business Administration, and Continuing Education; the School of Law; and the Graduate School. The main library contains more than 215,000 volumes and 298,000 microfilm items, and subscribes to 3000 periodicals.

Environment: The 571-acre suburban campus is located in a town 16 miles from Washington, D.C. Living facilities include dormitories and on-campus apartments. A fieldhouse, a second student union, and a second library tower are currently under construction.

Student Life: About 95% of the students live off campus, and the university maintains a list of approved housing in the area. Nine percent of the students are minority-group members. Campus housing is coed. Students may keep cars on campus. The honor system is patterned after that at the University of Virginia, once George Mason's parent institution.

Organizations: About 5% of the men belong to 1 of 5 fraternities, and 3% of the women belong to 1 of 4 sororities. Extracurricular activities include debating, publications, student government, special-interest clubs, drama and music productions, and weekly film series and dances.

Sports: The university participates in 11 intercollegiate sports for men and 8 for women. There are 13 intramural sports for men and 12 for women.

Handicapped: About 90% of the campus is accessible to physically handicapped students. Facilities include wheelchair ramps, special parking, elevators, specially equipped rest rooms, and lowered drinking fountains and telephones. Fewer than 1% of the students have impaired vision, and the university maintains large-print readers for their use. No special counselors are available.

Services: Health care, placement services, career and psychological counseling, and tutoring are available free to students. The extensive placement services, including weekly mailings of full-time job listings, may also be used by alumni.

Programs of Study: The university confers the B.A., B.S., B.S.N. B.I.S., B.M., and B.S.Ed. degrees. Master's and doctoral degrees also are offered. Bachelor's degrees are offered in the following subjects: AREA STUDIES (American, European, Latin American, Russian), BUSINESS (accounting, business administration, decision sciences, finance, management, marketing), EDUCATION (early childhood, elementary, health/physical, industrial, recreation), ENGLISH (literature, speech, writing), FINE AND PERFORMING ARTS (art education, art history, dance, music, music education, studio art, theater/dramatics), HEALTH SCIENCES (medical technology, nursing), LANGUAGES (French, German, Spanish), MATH AND SCIENCES (biology, chemistry, computer science, geology, mathematics, physics), PHILOSOPHY (philosophy), PREPROFESSIONAL (engineering—computer, engineering—electronics, fire administration and technology, law enforcement, social work), SOCIAL SCIENCES (anthropology, economics, geography, government/political science, history, international relations, psychology, public administration, sociology). About 27% of the undergraduate degrees conferred are in business and 25% in social sciences.

Required: All B.A. candidates must take 21 hours of English composition and literature, speech, and a foreign language; 3 hours of analytical reasoning; 12 hours of humanities; 12 hours of social and behavioral sciences; 8 hours of natural sciences; and 6 hours of non-Western studies. B.S. candidates in the College of Arts and Sciences must complete 12 hours of English composition and literature in addition to the major requirements.

Special: Five-year combined B.A.-B.S. degrees may be earned. George Mason is part of a consortium of 5 Northern Virginia colleges. Two courses may be taken on a nongraded basis. Students may design interdisciplinary majors through the Bachelor of Individualized Study degree program.

Honors: Nine national honor societies have chapters on campus. All departments in the College of Arts and Sciences offer honors programs. Students may earn graduation with distinction and with recognition.

Admissions: About 79% of those who applied for admission to the 1981-82 freshman class were accepted. The SAT scores of those who enrolled were as follows: Verbal—69% below 500, 25% between 500 and 599, 5% between 600 and 700, and 1% above 700; Math—48% below 500, 39% between 500 and 599, 12% between 600 and 700, and 1% above 700. Applicants must have at least a 2.5 average and rank in the top 50% of their high school class. Admissions officers also consider leadership record, impressions made during an interview, advanced placement or honors courses, and recommendations by school officials.

Procedure: Applicants must take the SAT or ACT. Application deadlines are June 1 (fall) and December 1 (spring). The application fee is $10. Candidates are notified as soon as possible after all credentials are received.

Special: An early admissions plan is available. AP and CLEP credit is accepted.

Transfer: For fall 1981, 2765 students applied, 2351 were accepted, and 1577 enrolled. Applicants must have a GPA of at least 2.0. D grades do not transfer. All students must complete, at the university, 30 of the 120 credits required for a bachelor's degree. Application deadlines are the same as those for freshmen.

Visiting: Orientations for prospective students are scheduled regularly. Students meet with faculty members and academic deans, tour the campus, and attend a reception with the university president. The admissions office will provide guides for informal visits, and students may sit in on classes. Visitors may stay overnight on campus during the summer. Visits are best scheduled for 2:30 P.M. Fridays.

Financial Aid: About 25% of all students receive aid. About 25% work part-time on campus. Scholarships, loans, grants, and part-time employment are awarded on the basis of need and academic performance. The university is a member of CSS and requires the FAF. The application deadline is April 15.

Foreign Students: Two percent of the full-time students come from foreign countries. An intensive English program, special counseling, and special organizations are available for these students.

Admissions: Foreign students must achieve a TOEFL score of at least 550 and must take the SAT or ACT.

Procedure: Application deadlines are May 1 (fall) and November 1 (spring). Foreign students must present proof of adequate funds and must carry health insurance, which is available through the university for a fee.

Admissions Contact: Patricia M. Riordan, Acting Director of Admissions.

HAMPDEN-SYDNEY COLLEGE D-3
Hampden-Sydney, Virginia 23943 (804) 223-4381

F/T: 750M	Faculty: 51; IIB, ++$
P/T: 2M	Ph.D.'s: 90%
Grad: none	S/F Ratio: 13 to 1
Year: sems, ss	Tuition: $5065
Appl: Mar. 1	R and B: $1600
589 applied	469 accepted	245 enrolled
SAT: 500V 550M		COMPETITIVE+

Hampden-Sydney College, established in 1776 and affiliated with the Presbyterian Church, is a liberal arts institution for men. Its library contains 140,000 volumes and 7100 reels of microfilm, and subscribes to 650 periodicals.

Environment: The 565-acre campus is located in a rural area 65 miles from Richmond. The college's 14 buildings of Georgian architecture include dormitories that accommodate 520 students. Living facilities also include fraternity houses and married student housing.

Student Life: Sixty percent of the students are from Virginia, and 59% come from public schools. Ninety-two percent of the students live on campus, including 15% who live in fraternity houses. Twenty percent of the students are Catholic, 71% Protestant, and 1% Jewish. Two percent of the students are minority-group members. College housing is single-sex; there are visiting privileges. Students may keep cars on campus.

Organizations: About 53% of the students belong to 1 of 10 national fraternities. Several religious clubs also are available. The student government plans social and cultural events, including plays, guest speakers, concerts, and movies.

Sports: The college fields intercollegiate teams in 11 sports. There are 11 intramural sports.

Handicapped: There are no facilities for the handicapped.

Graduates: About 8% of the freshmen drop out during the first year; 76% remain to graduate. About 60% of the graduates continue their studies; 8% enter medical school, 2% dental school, and 12% law school. About 35% pursue careers in business and industry.

Services: Free services include health care, tutoring, psychological and career counseling, placement services (available to graduates as well as to students), and remedial instruction.

Programs of Study: The college confers the B.A. and B.S. degrees. Bachelor's degrees are offered in the following subjects: ENGLISH (English), LANGUAGES (French, Greek/Latin, Spanish), MATH AND SCIENCES (biochemistry, biology, biophysics, chemical physics, chemistry, mathematics, mathematics and computer science, mathematics and natural sciences, physics), PHILOSOPHY (classics, philosophy, religion), SOCIAL SCIENCES (economics, government/political science, history, psychology). About 32% of degrees are conferred in social sciences, 30% in math and sciences, and 26% in economics.

Required: All students must take courses in humanities, social sciences, and natural sciences. They must meet proficiency requirements in English and in a foreign language.

Special: A summer "short term" provides students the opportunity to take experimental courses. A Washington semester program, an Appalachian semester program, a dual degree program in engineering, an applied chemistry cooperative program, college exchange, and foreign study are also offered.

Honors: Phi Beta Kappa and Omicron Delta Kappa are 2 of the 12 honor societies with campus chapters. Honors programs are offered for all classes. They include independent study and special courses.

Admissions: About 80% of those who applied were accepted for the 1981-82 freshman class. The SAT scores of those who enrolled were as follows: Verbal—50% below 500, 37% between 500 and 599, 10% between 600 and 700, and 2% above 700; Math—27% below 500, 46% between 500 and 599, 23% between 600 and 700, and 4% above 700. About 71% of those enrolled were in the top half of their high school class, and 36% were in the top fifth. Applicants must have completed 16 Carnegie units. The college recommends that applicants have an average of between C and B. Admissions officers also consider advanced placement or honors courses, leadership, extracurricular activities, personality, and recommendations by school officials among the important factors. Sons of alumni are given preference.

Procedure: The SAT or ACT and 2 ATs (English Composition and Math I) are required and should be taken between March of the junior year and January of the senior year. An on-campus interview is recommended. The application deadlines are March 1 (fall) and December 15 (spring). Early decision candidates should apply by November 1. Notification is usually made by mid-March. There is a $25 application fee.

Special: Early decision, early admissions, and deferred admissions plans are available. AP and CLEP credit is awarded.

Transfer: Of 55 applicants for fall 1981, 33 were accepted and 25 enrolled. D grades do not transfer. Students must complete at least 60 hours, at the college, of the 123 hours needed to receive a bachelor's degree. Application deadlines are March 1 (fall) and December 15 (spring).

Visiting: Guides are available for informal visits. Visitors may sit in on classes and spend the night at the school. Visits should be scheduled with the admissions office on weekdays from 8:30 A.M. to 4 P.M. or Saturdays from 9 A.M. to noon while classes are in session.

Financial Aid: Twenty-eight percent of the students receive financial aid. Twenty percent work part-time on campus. The average financial aid package available to a freshman, including loans, scholarships, and job earnings, totals 80% of costs. The school is a member of the CSS and requires aid applicants to submit the FAF. The deadline for aid applications is March 1.

Foreign Students: Fewer than 1% of the full-time students come from foreign countries.

Admissions: Foreign students must take the TOEFL. They must also take the SAT or ACT.

Procedure: Application deadlines are March 1 (fall) and December 15 (spring). Foreign students must present the college's own health form. They must also present proof of funds adequate to cover each year of study.

Admissions Contact: Robert H. Jones, Director of Admissions.

HAMPTON INSTITUTE F-3
Hampton, Virginia 23668 (804) 727-5328

F/T: 1311M, 1750W	Faculty: 230; n/av
P/T: 70M, 82W	Ph.D.'s: 47%
Grad: 65M, 195W	S/F Ratio: 14 to 1
Year: sems, ss	Tuition: $2925
Appl: June 30	R and B: $1410
2725 applied	1631 accepted	913 enrolled
SAT: 430V 410M		LESS COMPETITIVE

Hampton Institute is an independent college founded in 1868. The library contains more than 270,000 volumes and 210,000 microfilm items, and subscribes to 1000 periodicals. The most distinctive group of materials in the library is the Peabody Collection, composed of 14,000 items by and about black people, including 12,000 books and more than 1200 pamphlets on slavery.

Environment: The 201-acre waterfront campus, located in an urban environment, accommodates 121 buildings, staff residences, and other structures. Historical landmarks include Memorial Church, the Academy Building, and Virginia Cleveland Hall. Living facilities include dormitories and off-campus apartments.

Student Life: Attendance at worship services and involvement in campus religious activities are encouraged. About 66% of the students live on campus. Ten percent of the students are Catholic, and 82% are Protestant. Ninety-seven percent of the students are minority-group members. Institute housing is both single-sex and coed. There are visiting privileges in single-sex housing.

Organizations: The Student Government Association is the recognized governing agency for the student body and, as such, bears a relationship to all student organizations. There are many clubs and organizations on campus.

Sports: The athletic program is designed to encourage the participation of every able-bodied student. The institute competes on an inter-

920 VIRGINIA

collegiate level in 7 sports for men and 6 for women. There are 9 intramural sports for men and 7 for women.

Handicapped: There are special facilities for the physically handicapped, including wheelchair ramps, special parking, specially equipped rest rooms, and lowered drinking fountains.

Services: Students receive the following services free of charge: placement, psychological counseling, career counseling, tutoring, and remedial instruction. Health care is available on a fee basis.

Programs of Study: The institute confers the B.A., B.Arch., and B.S. degrees. Master's programs are also offered. Bachelor's degrees are offered in the following subjects: BUSINESS (accounting, business education, computer science, finance, management, marketing), EDUCATION (early childhood, elementary, health/physical, secondary, special), ENGLISH (English, journalism, speech), FINE AND PERFORMING ARTS (art, art education, film/photography, music, music education, radio/TV, theater/dramatics), HEALTH SCIENCES (nursing, speech therapy), MATH AND SCIENCES (biology, chemistry, marine science, mathematics, physics), PREPROFESSIONAL (architecture, dentistry, engineering, home economics, law, medicine, social work, veterinary), SOCIAL SCIENCES (criminal justice, economics, government/political science, history, psychology, social work, sociology).

Required: Freshmen take a common core of general education courses. At the end of the first year, students enter one of the professional divisions or departments.

Special: The pass-fail option is available for some general education courses. A general studies degree and a 2-3 engineering program are offered.

Honors: Honors programs are open to superior students in the senior year and to exceptional students in the junior year. Courses provide extensive reading and study in specific areas, to be conducted as tutorial or laboratory sessions. There are 9 national honor societies represented on campus.

Admissions: About 60% of those who applied were accepted for the 1981-82 freshman class. The SAT scores of those who enrolled were as follows: Verbal—77% below 500, 20% between 500 and 599, 3% between 600 and 700, and 0% above 700; Math—82% below 500, 16% between 500 and 599, 2% between 600 and 700, and 0% above 700. Admission is limited to recommended candidates from accredited secondary schools who rank in the upper half of their class. Candidates from unaccredited schools may qualify for admission by entrance examination. Every candidate must present satisfactory credentials as to ability, character, and health. Admission is based on secondary school record, standardized test scores, advanced placement or honors courses, recommendations of high school officials, personality, extracurricular activities, background and experience, health record, and educational objectives.

Procedure: The SAT or ACT is required and should be taken during July of the junior year, no later than March of the senior year. Applications should be filed by June 30 (fall), December 15 (spring), and June 15 (summer). Admissions are on a rolling basis. There is a $10 application fee.

Special: There are early decision, early admission, and deferred admissions plans. AP and CLEP credit is awarded.

Transfer: For fall 1981, 460 students applied, 195 were accepted, and 162 enrolled. A 2.0 GPA is required. D grades do not transfer. Thirty credits must be earned, in residence, of the 120 needed for a bachelor's degree. Application deadlines are June 30 (fall) and December 15 (spring).

Visiting: There are no regularly scheduled orientations for prospective students. Informal visits and guided tours can be arranged 5 days a week by the dean of admissions.

Financial Aid: About 67% of all students receive financial aid in the form of scholarships, grants-in-aid, loans, CWS, and part-time employment. Thirty-two percent work part-time on campus. Average aid to freshmen from all sources is $2600. All student aid is awarded on the basis of need or academic merit, and recipients are expected to maintain a high performance level. Scholarship grants awarded by the Virginia State Department of Education are available to students who are preparing to teach in the public elementary or high schools of the state. The institute is a member of CSS. The FAF is required. Aid applications should be filed by June 30.

Foreign Students: Two percent of the full-time students come from foreign countries. The institute offers these students an intensive English course, special counseling, and special organizations.

Admissions: Foreign students must score 550 or above on the TOEFL. No college entrance examination is required.

Procedure: The application deadlines are June 30 (fall) and December 15 (spring). Foreign students must present the institute's health form. They must also present proof of funds adequate to cover 1 year of study.

Admissions Contact: Ollie M. Bowman, Jr., Dean of Admissions.

HOLLINS COLLEGE C-3
Hollins College, Virginia 24020 (703) 362-6401

F/T: 825W Faculty: 70; IIB, ++$
P/T: 50W Ph.D.'s: 85%
Grad: 25M, 42W S/F Ratio: 10 to 1
Year: 4-1-4 Tuition: $5522
Appl: Mar. 1 R and B: $2600
865 applied 630 accepted 277 enrolled
SAT: 500V 500M COMPETITIVE

Hollins College is a private liberal arts college for women. Its library contains 205,000 volumes and 8500 microfilm items, and subscribes to 1200 periodicals.

Environment: The 450-acre suburban campus is located in the Blue Ridge Mountains, 2 miles from the city of Roanoke. The campus quadrangle is listed in the *National Register of Historic Places*. Students are housed in 6 dormitories, 3 houses, and an apartment complex.

Student Life: About 72% of the students are from out of state. Ninety-six percent live on campus. Three percent of the students are minority-group members. College housing is single-sex; there are visiting privileges. Students may keep cars on campus. The college operates on the honor system. Drinking is permitted in specified areas of the campus.

Organizations: There are no sororities on campus. Attendance at weekly chapel services is voluntary. Social and cultural programs are found in town or at nearby universities. The Appalachian Trail is 30 minutes away.

Sports: The college fields intercollegiate teams in 8 sports. There are 14 intramural sports.

Handicapped: Special facilities for physically handicapped students include wheelchair ramps, parking areas, elevators, lowered telephones, and specially equipped rest rooms. Special class scheduling also is available. No special counselors are available. No students with visual or hearing impairments were enrolled in 1981-82.

Graduates: Two percent of the freshmen drop out by the end of their first year; 60% remain to graduate. Of the graduates, about 30% continue their studies including 1% who enter medical school and about 3% who enter law school. About 65% pursue careers in business and industry.

Services: Health care, tutoring, remedial instruction, psychological and career counseling are provided free. Free job placement services are offered to graduates as well as to students. They include a credentials service and help in arranging interviews.

Programs of Study: The college confers the B.A. degree. Master's degrees also are available. Bachelor's degrees are offered in the following subjects: AREA STUDIES (American, ancient, Mediterranean art and archeology), ENGLISH (English), FINE AND PERFORMING ARTS (art, art history, dance, film/photography, music, music education, studio art, theater/dramatics), LANGUAGES (French, German, Greek/Latin, Spanish), MATH AND SCIENCES (biology, chemistry, mathematics, natural sciences, physics, statistics), PHILOSOPHY (classics, philosophy, religion), SOCIAL SCIENCES (economics, government/political science, history, psychology, social sciences, sociology). About 36% of undergraduate degrees are conferred in social sciences, 20% in fine and performing arts, 18% in math and sciences, and 26% in humanities.

Special: Students may design their own majors. The college offers semesters in Washington and at the U.N., undergraduate scientific research, and study abroad programs. Hollins participates in an exchange program with 6 other Virginia colleges.

Honors: Seven national honor socieites, including Phi Beta Kappa, have chapters on campus. All departments offer honors programs that may involve research, a thesis, special examinations, seminars, and/or reading programs.

Admissions: About 73% of those who applied were accepted for the 1981-82 freshman class. The SAT scores of those who enrolled in a recent freshman class were as follows: Verbal—31% between 500 and 599, 4% between 600 and 700, and 1% above 700; Math—31% between 500 and 599 and 7% between 600 and 700. Candidates should have completed 16 Carnegie units. Almost half the applicants ranked in the top 20% of their graduating class. Admissions officers also consider, in descending order of importance, recommendations by school officials, advanced placement or honors courses, impressions made during a personal interview, extracurricular activities, personality, leadership, and evidence of special talents.

Procedure: The SAT is required. Application deadlines are March 1 (fall) and December 15 (spring). A $20 fee is required.

Special: Early and deferred admissions and early decision plans are offered. AP is used.

Transfer: For fall 1981, 77 students applied, 48 were accepted, and 27 enrolled. A 2.5 GPA is recommended. D grades do not transfer. Students must spend 2 years in residence and earn 64 of the 128 credits needed to receive a bachelor's degree. The application deadlines are the same as those for freshman applicants.

Visiting: Orientations for prospective students are scheduled regularly. Visitors spend the night on campus, tour the college, attend classes and special programs, and meet faculty members. Guides also are available for informal visits, and such visitors may sit in on classes. With at least 1 week's notice, the admissions office will arrange for informal visitors to spend the night at the school. Visits are best scheduled Sunday through Thursday when classes are in session.

Financial Aid: Seventy percent of the students receive financial aid. Forty percent work part-time on campus. Average aid to freshmen from all sources is $6500. The college is a member of CSS. The FAF is required. Application deadlines are March 1 (fall) and December 15 (spring).

Foreign Students: Two percent of the full-time students come from foreign countries. The college offers these students special counseling and special organizations.

Admissions: Foreign students should score at least 550 on the TOEFL. The SAT is required if English is the student's native tongue.

Procedure: The application deadline is March 1 (fall). Foreign students must present a health certificate completed by a certified physician. They must also present proof of funds adequate to cover each year's transportation, summer vacation, and a minimum of $2000 a year toward the comprehensive fee.

Admissions Contact: Sandra J. Lovinguth, Director of Admissions.

JAMES MADISON UNIVERSITY D-2
Harrisonburg, Virginia 22807 (703) 433-6147

F/T: 3472M, 4072W	Faculty: 444; IIA, av$
P/T: 139M, 178W	Ph.D.'s: 66%
Grad: 273M, 503W	S/F Ratio: 17 to 1
Year: early sems, ss	Tuition: $1210 ($1930)
Appl: Feb. 1	R and B: $2010
7933 applied	3263 accepted 1611 enrolled
SAT: 496V 545M	VERY COMPETITIVE

James Madison University, founded in 1908, is a state-supported institution governed by a board of visitors. The library contains 369,000 volumes and 369,000 microform items, and subscribes to 3000 periodicals.

Environment: The 365-acre urban campus is located in Harrisonburg, a Shenandoah Valley town of 20,000 people about 120 miles from Richmond and Washington, D.C. The 60 buildings on campus include dormitories and undergraduate apartments. Living facilities also include fraternity and sorority houses. A major addition to the library and an 8500-seat convocation center were recently completed.

Student Life: About 80% of the students are from Virginia. Ninety-five percent come from public schools. About 65% of the students live on campus. Eighteen percent of the students are Catholic, 50% Protestant, and 2% Jewish. Four percent of the students are minority-group members. University housing is both single-sex and coed. There are visiting privileges in single-sex housing. Students may keep cars on campus.

Organizations: About 15% of the men belong to 1 of 9 national fraternities on campus, and 10% of the women belong to 1 of 7 national sororities. Extracurricular activities include a student government, publications, the Honor Council, and religious organizations for Catholic, Protestant, and Jewish students. There is a movie theater on campus. Outdoor recreation and skiing areas are nearby.

Sports: The university fields intercollegiate teams in 12 sports for men and 12 for women. There are 16 intramural sports for men and 14 for women.

Handicapped: About 35% of the campus is accessible to handicapped students. Special facilities include wheelchair ramps, parking areas, elevators, specially equipped rest rooms, and lowered drinking fountains and telephones.

Graduates: About 20% of the freshmen drop out by the end of their first year; 63% remain to graduate. Twenty percent of the graduates pursue advanced degrees, including 1% who enter medical school and 2% who enter law school. About 50% of the graduates begin careers in business and industry.

Services: Tutoring, remedial instruction, placement services, and career and psychological counseling are available free to students. Health care is available on a fee basis. Placement services also may be used by graduates.

Programs of Study: The university confers the B.A., B.S., B.F.A., B.S.N., B.B.A., B.Mus.Ed., B.Mus., B.G.S., and B.S.W. degrees. Master's degrees also are available. Bachelor's degrees are offered in the following subjects: BUSINESS (accounting, business administration, business education, computer science, finance, hotel-restaurant management, international business, management, management information systems, marketing, office administration), EDUCATION (distributive, early childhood, elementary, health/physical, home economics, industrial, special), ENGLISH (English), FINE AND PERFORMING ARTS (art, art education, art history, communication arts, dance, music, music education), HEALTH SCIENCES (community health, medical technology, nursing, speech therapy), LANGUAGES (French, German, Russian, Spanish), MATH AND SCIENCES (biology, chemistry, computer science, energy resources management, geology, mathematics, physics), PHILOSOPHY (philosophy, religion), PREPROFESSIONAL (dietetics, home economics, library science, public administration, social work), SOCIAL SCIENCES (anthropology, economics, geography, government/political science, history, psychology, social sciences, sociology). About 30% of the degrees are conferred in business, 20% in education, 15% in social sciences, and 10% in communications.

Required: All students must complete a core program of basic studies, including 15 hours in humanities, 11 in natural sciences, 3 in physical education, and 12 in social sciences.

Special: Study abroad and a general studies major are available.

Honors: Several honor societies are represented on campus.

Admissions: About 41% of those who applied were admitted to the 1981-82 freshman class. The SAT scores of those who enrolled were as follows: Verbal—52% below 500, 41% between 500 and 599, 6% between 600 and 700, and 1% above 700; Math—23% below 500, 59% between 500 and 599, 17% between 600 and 700, and 1% above 700. Applicants must have graduated from an accredited high school in the upper half of their class. Besides test scores, class rank, and grades, admissions officers consider evidence of special talents, leadership, extracurricular activities, advanced placement or honors courses, recommendations by school officials, and impressions made during an interview.

Procedure: Applicants must take the SAT between March of the junior year and January of the senior year. The application deadline for fall admission is February 1. A $15 application fee is required.

Special: An "honors admissions" plan providing early notification is available for especially meritorious students. AP and CLEP credit is accepted.

Transfer: For fall 1981, 1403 students applied, 1068 were accepted, and 621 enrolled. A 2.0 GPA is required. D grades do not transfer. Students must earn at least 32 hours, on campus, of the 128 needed to receive a bachelor's degree. The university encourages transfer applications. The deadline is February 1.

Visiting: Regular orientations are scheduled for prospective students. The admissions office also will arrange guides for informal visits on weekdays and on Saturday mornings. Visitors may sit in on classes by prearrangement.

Financial Aid: Sixty percent of the students receive financial aid. Twenty percent work part-time on campus. Average aid to freshmen from all sources is $1300. About 750 freshman scholarships, grants, and loans are awarded. Loans also are available from federal and state governments, banks, and private sources. Tuition may be paid in installments. The university is a member of CSS. Aid applicants must submit the FAF or the VFAF by March 1.

Foreign Students: Fewer than 1% of the full-time students come from foreign countries. The university offers these students special counseling.

Admissions: Foreign students must score at least 550 on the TOEFL. No college entrance examination is required.

Procedure: The application deadline is February 1 (fall). Foreign students must present proof of health and provide proof of adequate funds. They must carry health insurance.

Admissions Contact: Francis Turner, Director of Admissions.

LIBERTY BAPTIST COLLEGE   D-3
Lynchburg, Virginia 24506   (804) 237-5961

F/T: 1736M, 1505W   *Faculty:* 152; IIB, av$
P/T: 50M, 50W   *Ph.D.'s:* 38%
Grad: none   *S/F Ratio:* 21 to 1
Year: sems, ss   *Tuition:* $2270
Appl: Aug. 1   *R and B:* $2200
1511 applied   1326 accepted   994 enrolled
SAT: 404V 429M   ACT: 19   **LESS COMPETITIVE**

Liberty Baptist College, founded in 1971, is a liberal arts college affiliated with the Independent Baptist Church. Its academic program, taught within the context of fundamental Christianity, emphasizes spiritual development and the practical application of knowledge. The library contains more than 119,000 volumes and subscribes to about 550 periodicals.

Environment: The 550-acre campus is located in suburban Lynchburg, a city of 70,000 people. The college has more than 30 buildings, including 21 dormitories that house more than 2700 students. All classes are held in buildings that have been built since 1977.

Student Life: About 30% of the students are from Virginia or neighboring states. Eighty-six percent come from public schools. Seventy-two percent live on campus. All students are Protestants; weekly attendance at religious services is compulsory. About 6% of the students are minority-group members. College housing is single-sex; there are no visiting privileges. Students may keep cars on campus. Drinking on campus is prohibited.

Organizations: There are no fraternities or sororities. Among the numerous extracurricular organizations are the Youth Aflame Singers, "To People With Love," and the Student Government Association, which charters and finances student activities, runs campus visitation functions, and raises funds.

Sports: There are intercollegiate teams for men in 7 sports, and for women in 5. Intramural teams for men include 10 sports; for women, 8.

Graduates: Fifteen percent of the freshmen drop out during their first year. Fifty-two percent remain to graduate. Twenty percent of the graduates pursue graduate study. Nine percent enter careers in business and industry.

Services: The following services are available to students free of charge: placement and career counseling, psychological counseling, tutoring, and remedial instruction. Health care is available for a fee.

Programs of Study: All programs lead to the B.S. degree. Associate degrees are also granted. Bachelor's degrees are offered in the following subjects: BUSINESS (accounting, business administration, business education, secretarial science), EDUCATION (elementary, health/physical), ENGLISH (English, speech), FINE AND PERFORMING ARTS (music, music education, radio/TV, theater/dramatics), MATH AND SCIENCES (biology, mathematics), PHILOSOPHY (religion), SOCIAL SCIENCES (government/political science, history, psychology). A large number of students major in religion.

Required: Students are required to take course work in religion, humanities, math and science, social sciences, and physical education.

Special: Students may spend up to 15 months studying in Israel through the college's association with the Institute of Holy Land Studies in Jerusalem. The Office of International Studies also sponsors 10 other programs in other countries.

Admissions: About 88% of those who applied were accepted for the 1981–82 freshman class. Applicants must be high school graduates with a GPA of at least 2.0 and have 16 Carnegie units. Personality and secondary school recommendations are also considered important.

Procedure: The SAT or ACT is required. The deadlines for application are August 1 (fall), December 15 (spring), and May 15 (summer). Students are admitted on a rolling basis. There is a $25 application fee.

Special: The college has early and deferred admissions plans. AP and CLEP credit may be earned.

Transfer: For fall 1981, 405 students applied, 331 were accepted, and 250 enrolled. Transfers are considered for all classes. Applicants should be eligible to return to the previous institution. They should have a 2.0 GPA. D grades do not transfer. A student must study at the college for 1 year or complete, at the college, 32 semester hours of the 128 needed to receive a bachelor's degree. Application deadlines are the same as those for regular applicants.

Financial Aid: About 80% of the students receive some form of financial aid. Twenty-four percent work part-time on campus. Average aid to freshmen from all sources is $1146. The college awards scholarships, loans, and federal work-study grants. Athletic scholarships are also available. The college is a member of the CSS and requires the FAF. The aid application deadlines are August 1 (fall), December 1 (spring), and May 1 (summer).

Foreign Students: Three percent of the full-time students come from foreign countries. The college offers these students special counseling and special organizations.

Admissions: Foreign students must score at least 450 on the TOEFL. No college entrance examination is required.

Procedure: The application deadlines are February 1 (fall), June 1 (spring), and November 1 (summer). Foreign students must present proof of health. They must also present proof of funds adequate to cover 1 year of study. They must carry health insurance, which is available through the college for a fee.

Admissions Contact: Tom Diggs, Director of Admissions.

LONGWOOD COLLEGE   D-3
Farmville, Virginia 23901   (804) 392-9251

F/T: 700M, 1700W   *Faculty:* 143; IIB, +$
P/T: 33M, 113W   *Ph.D.'s:* 66%
Grad: 29M, 66W   *S/F Ratio:* 17 to 1
Year: sems, ss   *Tuition:* $1390 ($1890)
Appl: open   *R and B:* $1705
2429 applied   1530 accepted   711 enrolled
SAT: 430V 470M   ACT: 18   **COMPETITIVE**

Longwood College, established in 1839, is a state-supported college offering education in business, liberal arts, teaching, social work, and premedicine. Its library contains 186,600 volumes and 5802 microfilm items, and subscribes to 1420 periodicals.

Environment: The 50-acre main campus is located in a rural town of about 7000 people 60 miles from Richmond. The 24 Georgian brick buildings on campus include 10 residence halls. A $4.5-million physical education facility was completed in 1980. The college also owns the 103-acre Longwood Estate, which contains a golf course and other recreational facilities.

Student Life: Ninety percent of the students live on campus. Freshmen may live off campus only if living with parents or close relatives. About 5% of the students are minority-group members. College housing is both single-sex and coed. There are visiting privileges in single-sex housing. Students may keep cars on campus.

Organizations: About 20% of the students belong to 1 of 5 fraternities and 11 sororities on campus. Various campus organizations, including Catholic and Protestant religious groups and a student government, are available.

Sports: The college fields intercollegiate teams in 7 sports for men and 9 for women. Men can choose from 10 intramural sports, and women can participate in 9.

Handicapped: About 60% of the campus is accessible to physically handicapped students. Facilities include wheelchair ramps, special parking areas, elevators, and specially equipped rest rooms. Special class scheduling also is available. The college psychologist is the director of centralized services for special students.

Graduates: Fifteen percent of the freshmen drop out by the end of their first year. About 65% eventually graduate from Longwood. About 7% of the graduates pursue advanced degrees; fewer than 1% enter either medical or dental school, and 1% enter law school. Forty-seven percent begin careers in business and industry.

Services: Free services provided to students include health care; placement, career and psychological counseling, tutoring, and remedial instruction. Placement services also are available to alumni. Tutoring is available on a fee basis.

Programs of Study: The college awards the B.A., B.S., B.F.A., B.M., B.M.E., B.S.B.A., and B.S.B.E. degrees. Master's programs are also available. Bachelor's degrees are offered in the following subjects: BUSINESS (business administration, business education, office administration), EDUCATION (early childhood, elementary, health/physical, secondary), ENGLISH (English, speech pathology), FINE AND PERFORMING ARTS (art, art education, art history, music, music education, music performance, theater/dramatics), HEALTH SCIENCES (medical technology), LANGUAGES (foreign languages), MATH AND SCIENCES (biology, chemistry, earth science, mathematics, natural sciences, physics), PHILOSOPHY (philosophy), PRE-PROFESSIONAL (dentistry, engineering, home economics, law, medicine, pharmacy, social work), SOCIAL SCIENCES (anthropology, government/political science, history, psychology, sociology). About 30% of degrees conferred are in education and 14% are in business.

Required: All students must take basic general-education courses.

Special: Cooperative programs in prenursing, preengineering, and predietetics are offered, as is preprofessional training leading to a transfer to schools of dentistry, medicine, medical technology, pharmacy, physical therapy, occupational therapy, or veterinary medicine. Students may take courses at Hampden-Sydney College at no extra charge. Summer- and semester-abroad programs in languages and art are available.

Honors: Eleven national honor socieites have chapters on campus. All departments offer honors programs, which include special studies directed by an adviser and an honors thesis.

Admissions: The college accepted about 63% of those who applied for admission to the 1981-82 freshman class. The SAT scores of those who enrolled were as follows: Verbal—83% below 500, 14% between 500 and 599, 2% between 600 and 700, and fewer than 1% above 700; Math—63% below 500, 33% between 500 and 599, 4% between 600 and 700, and fewer than 1% above 700. Applicants must have graduated from an accredited high school with an average of at least 2.0. The college prefers that applicants rank in the top half of their class. Besides grades, test scores and class rank, admissions officers consider advanced placement or honors courses, recommendations by school officials, extracurricular activities, leadership, personality, and evidence of special talents.

Procedure: The SAT or ACT is required and should be taken between March of the junior year and January of the senior year. An interview is recommended. Freshmen are admitted to fall, spring, and summer terms. Applications are accepted as long as places remain. Applications for fall admission should be submitted by the end of February. The application fee is $15.

Special: Early and deferred admissions plans are available. CLEP and AP credit is accepted.

Transfer: For fall 1981, 363 students applied, 195 were accepted, and 128 enrolled. Applicants must have an average of at least 2.0 and present acceptable high school recommendations and SAT scores. D grades do not transfer. All students must complete at least 30 credits, at the college, of the 126 to 128 needed to receive a bachelor's degree. Application deadlines are open.

Visiting: Informal visits may be arranged with the admissions office when classes are in session. Guides are provided, and visitors may sit in on classes. Overnight accommodations at the school can be arranged if the admissions office has at least 2 weeks' notice.

Financial Aid: About 65% of all students receive aid in the form of scholarships, part-time jobs, and loans. Twenty-five percent of the students work part-time on campus. Average aid to freshmen from all sources is $1250. Virginia offers Teachers' Scholarships to residents. The college is a member of CSS. The FAF is required. Priority consideration is given to aid applications received by April 1 (fall).

Foreign Students: Fewer than 1% of the full-time students come from foreign countries.

Admissions: Foreign students must score at least 500 on the TOEFL. They must also take the SAT or ACT.

Procedure: Application deadlines are open. Foreign students must take the standard physical examination required of all students. They must also present proof of funds adequate to cover 4 academic years.

Admissions Contact: Gary C. Groneweg, Director of Admissions.

LYNCHBURG COLLEGE D-3
Lynchburg, Virginia 24501 (804) 522-8300

F/T: 689M, 965W	Faculty: 125; IIA, —$
P/T: 64M, 107W	Ph.D.'s: 58%
Grad: 231M, 278W	S/F Ratio: 14 to 1
Year: sems, ss	Tuition: $4900
Appl: July 1	R and B: $2400
1497 applied	1092 accepted	515 enrolled
SAT: 440V 480M	ACT: 20	COMPETITIVE

Lynchburg College, established in 1903, is a private coeducational liberal arts college affiliated with the Disciples of Christ. The library contains 120,589 volumes and 43,049 microfilm items, and subscribes to 597 periodicals.

Environment: The 214-acre campus is located in suburban Lynchburg, a city of 149,000 people near the Blue Ridge mountains. The buildings, of predominantly colonial design, include 6 dormitories and 42 apartments for seniors and married students. Hall Campus Center and a library expansion are recent additions.

Student Life: About 53% of the students are from Virginia, and 87% come from public schools. Seventy-nine percent of the students live on campus. Twenty-one percent of the students are Catholic, and 63% are Protestant. College housing is single-sex; there are visiting privileges. Students may keep cars on campus.

Organizations: Five percent of the men belong to 1 of 2 fraternities on campus; 7% of the women belong to 1 of the 2 sororities. The college sponsors cultural, religious, and social activities. A number of extracurricular activities are offered.

Sports: The college fields intercollegiate teams in 9 sports for men and 8 for women. Seven intramural sports are offered for men and 8 for women.

Handicapped: The college offers no special facilities for physically handicapped students.

Graduates: About 9% of the freshmen drop out during their first year. About 77% eventually graduate. Of these, about 25% pursue advanced degrees, including fewer than 1% who enter medical school, fewer than 1% who enter dental school, and 1% who enter law school. Another 35% of the graduates begin careers in business and industry.

Services: Health care, placement, and career and psychological counseling are available to students free of charge. Tutoring is available on a fee basis. Placement services also are available for alumni.

Programs of Study: The college confers the B.A., B.S., and B.S.N. degrees. Master's degrees also are available. Bachelor's degrees are offered in the following subjects: AREA STUDIES (American), BUSINESS (accounting, business administration, foreign language-business administration), EDUCATION (early childhood, elementary, health/physical, secondary, special), ENGLISH (English, journalism, literature, speech communications, writing), FINE AND PERFORMING ARTS (art, art education, art history, art-psychology, dramatic literature and history, music, music education, studio art, theater/dramatics), HEALTH SCIENCES (health sciences, life sciences, medical technology, nuclear medicine technology, nursing), LANGUAGES (French, German, Spanish), MATH AND SCIENCES (biology, chemistry, mathematics, natural history, physical sciences, physics), PHILOSOPHY (philosophy, religion), PREPROFESSIONAL (dentistry, forestry, law, medicine, ministry, pharmacy, veterinary), SOCIAL SCIENCES (economics, government/political science, history, psychology, social sciences, sociology). About 20% of the degrees are conferred in business, 14% in preprofessional fields, and 13% in English.

Special: A 3-1 nuclear medicine technology program is offered in cooperation with the University of Virginia, and a 3-2 engineering program is offered with Georgia Tech. A 4-year combined B.A.-B.S. degree can be earned in life sciences. Students may earn degrees in under 4 years by studying summers. Junior year abroad and 6-week summer study programs are offered in other countries. Internship and independent study programs are available. The college's 2-option system permits each student to select a general-education or thematic approach to liberal arts.

Honors: Six honor societies have chapters on campus.

Admissions: About 73% of those who applied for admission to the 1981-82 freshman class were accepted. The SAT scores of those who enrolled were as follows: Verbal—60% below 500, 15% between 500 and 599, 3% between 600 and 700, and 0% above 700; Math—64% below 500, 29% between 500 and 599, 4% between 600 and 700, and 1% above 700. Applicants should have earned at least 15 Carnegie units and have graduated from an accredited high school in the top half of their class. Admissions officers also consider grades, advanced placement or honors courses, recommendations by school officials, personality, and leadership.

Procedure: Applicants must take the SAT or ACT. Application deadlines are July 1 (fall), December 15 (spring), and May 10 (summer). Early decision applicants must apply by December 1 for fall admission and will be notified 2 weeks after their application is complete. Regular applicants are notified on a rolling basis. The application fee is $15.

Special: Early and deferred admissions plans are available.

Transfer: For fall 1981, 387 students applied, 239 were accepted, and 183 enrolled. Applicants must have an average of at least 2.0 and be in good standing at their last school. D grades transfer. Students must spend 4 semesters at the college. They must complete 48 of the 124 credits needed to receive a bachelor's degree. Application deadlines are the same as those for freshmen.

Visiting: Individual interviews and visits to campus may be scheduled in the fall and spring with the admissions office. Guides are provided. Students may sit in on classes and stay overnight at the school.

Financial Aid: About 35% of the students receive aid. Programs include scholarships, work opportunities, and loans. Twenty-three percent work part-time on campus. The average aid to freshmen from all sources is $3413. The college is a member of CSS. The FAF and the

924 VIRGINIA

college's application must be submitted by April 1 (fall), December 1 (spring), and May 1 (summer).

Foreign Students: The college offers foreign students an intensive English course and special counseling.

Admissions: Foreign students must take the TOEFL if their native language is not English; a score of at least 550 is required. They must also take the SAT.

Procedure: Application deadlines are July 1 (fall), December 15 (spring), and May 10 (summer). Foreign students must submit a completed health form. They must also submit a certificate of finance. They must carry health insurance, which is available through the college for a fee.

Admissions Contact: Ernest R. Chadderton, Dean of Admissions.

MARY BALDWIN COLLEGE   D-2
Staunton, Virginia 24401   (703) 885-0811

F/T: 701W	Faculty: 54; IIB, av$
P/T: none	Ph.D.'s: 67%
Grad: none	S/F Ratio: 12 to 1
Year: 4-4-1	Tuition, R and B: $6950
Appl: Mar. 15	
455 applied	421 accepted	214 enrolled
SAT: 430V 450M		LESS COMPETITIVE

Mary Baldwin College, founded in 1842, is a small liberal arts college for women, affiliated with the Presbyterian Church. Its library contains 150,000 volumes and 15,000 microfilm items, and subscribes to 400 periodicals.

Environment: The college is located in a rural Shenandoah Valley town of 25,000 people 100 miles from Richmond. The school recently purchased a military academy and plans to convert the barracks to residence halls. Living facilities include dormitories and on-campus apartments.

Student Life: About 50% of the students come from outside Virginia, and 60% are graduates of public schools. Approximately 98% live on campus. Freshmen must observe a midnight curfew during the first six weeks of the fall term. Sixteen percent of the students are Catholic, and 71% are Protestant. College housing is single-sex; there are visiting privileges. All students may keep cars on campus.

Organizations: There are no sororities on campus. Extracurricular activities include art, chorus, dance, drama, a glee club, publications, tutoring and service groups, student government, political groups, and religious organizations. The college sponsors art shows, concerts, films, lectures, and plays. Major social events include the Junior Dad's Weekend and the Sophomore Show.

Sports: The college fields intercollegiate teams in 5 sports. There are 4 intramural sports.

Handicapped: Special class scheduling can be arranged for physically handicapped students.

Graduates: About 10% of the freshmen drop out during the first year, and 75% remain to graduate. Of those, 35% continue their education. About 2% enter medical school, 1% enter dental school, and 2% enter law school.

Services: Free health care, tutoring, remedial instruction, placement, career counseling, and psychological counseling are provided for students.

Programs of Study: The college confers the B.A. degree. Bachelor's degrees are offered in the following subjects: AREA STUDIES (American, Asian), BUSINESS (management), EDUCATION (elementary, secondary, special), ENGLISH (English), FINE AND PERFORMING ARTS (art, art history, arts management, music, speech communications, studio art, theater/dramatics), HEALTH SCIENCES (medical technology), LANGUAGES (French, Spanish), MATH AND SCIENCES (biochemistry, biology, chemistry, mathematics), PHILOSOPHY (philosophy, religion), PREPROFESSIONAL (dentistry, law, medicine, pharmacy, veterinary), SOCIAL SCIENCES (economics, government/political science, history, psychology, social work, sociology). About 36% of the degrees are conferred in math and sciences, 29% in social sciences, and 20% in area studies.

Special: Students may take courses at 6 other area colleges. The 3-1 medical technology degree program is offered in conjunction with a local clinic. Students may design their own majors. Other options include pass/fail grading, summer study in England, independent study, and junior year abroad. B.A. degrees may be earned in 3 years.

Honors: Seven honor societies, including Phi Beta Kappa, have chapters on campus. The college offers an honors seminar for qualified students.

Admissions: About 93% of those who applied for admission to the 1981-82 freshman class were accepted. Of those who enrolled, the SAT scores were as follows: Verbal—81% below 500, 15% between 500 and 599, 4% between 600 and 700, and 0% above 700; Math—68% below 500, 30% between 500 and 599, 2% between 600 and 700, and 0% above 700. Applicants must have completed 16 units of high school work, and the college prefers that they rank in the top fifth of their class and present at least a B average. Admissions officers also consider advanced placements or honors courses, extracurricular activities, recommendations by school officials, personality, leadership record, and impressions made during an interview.

Procedure: The SAT is required and should be taken in November or December of the senior year. Three ATs, including English Composition and 2 of the student's choice, must be taken by January. The application deadlines are March 15 (fall) and November 15 (spring). Other applicants are notified on a rolling basis. The application fee is $20. Applicants are encouraged to schedule an interview.

Special: Early decision and deferred admissions plans are available. AP and CLEP credit is accepted.

Transfer: For fall 1981, 81 students applied, 72 were accepted, and 52 enrolled. A C average is needed. Neither D grades nor quality points transfer. Students must spend at least 2 years in residence and complete 18 of the 36 courses needed for a bachelor's degree at the college. Application deadlines are March 15 (fall) and November 1 (spring).

Visiting: Prospective students may schedule campus visits on weekdays while school is in session. Guides are provided, and visitors may sit in on classes and spend the night in the residence halls. Arrangements should be made with the admissions office.

Financial Aid: Sixty percent of the students receive financial aid. Thirty percent work part-time on campus. The average award to freshmen from all sources is $4570. The college is a member of CSS. The FAF is required. The application deadline is April 15.

Foreign Students: Two percent of the full-time students come from foreign countries. The college offers these students special counseling and special organizations.

Admissions: Foreign students must take the TOEFL or the SAT.

Procedure: The application deadlines are March 15 (fall) and November 15 (spring).

Admissions Contact: Clair Carter, Director of Admissions.

MARYMOUNT COLLEGE OF VIRGINIA   E-2
Arlington, Virginia 22207   (703) 522-5600

F/T: 5M, 860W	Faculty: 50; IIB, +$
P/T: 5M, 271W	Ph.D.'s: 75%
Grad: 85M, 168W	S/F Ratio: 12 to 1
Year: sems, ss	Tuition: $3700
Appl: open	R and B: $2300
747 applied	591 accepted	323 enrolled
SAT: 450V 430M	ACT: 20	COMPETITIVE

Marymount College of Virginia, founded in 1950, is affiliated with the Roman Catholic Church. Its library contains 55,000 volumes and 1900 microfilm items, and subscribes to 360 periodicals.

Environment: The campus is located in a suburban area of Arlington, a city 7 miles from Washington, D.C.

Student Life: Forty-five percent of the students live on campus. Freshmen may live off campus only if staying with their family. Fifty-five percent of the students are Catholic, and 35% are Protestant. Twenty-two percent of the students are minority-group members. College housing is single-sex; there are visiting privileges. Students may keep cars on campus. Day-care services are available.

Organizations: There are no fraternities or sororities on campus. College activities include clubs and service groups, cultural and social events, and student government. Museums, theaters, and other activities are close by in Washington.

Sports: The college participates intercollegiately in 4 sports. There are 6 intramural sports.

Handicapped: Half the campus is accessible to physically handicapped students. Facilities include special parking areas and elevators. Other facilities can be adapted as the need arises. Special class scheduling can be arranged. One special counselor is available. No students with hearing or visual impairments have been enrolled recently.

Graduates: Twelve percent of the freshmen drop out by the end of their first year. Eighty percent remain to graduate. Twenty-five percent pursue advanced study after graduation; 3% enter medical school, and 8% enter law school. Fifty percent of graduates enter careers in business and industry.

Services: Placement, career counseling, and tutoring are provided free to students and alumni. Health care and psychological counseling are free to full-time resident students for the first visit.

Programs of Study: The college awards the B.A., B.S., B.S.N., and B.B.A. degrees. Associate and master's degrees also are available. Bachelor's degrees are offered in the following subjects: BUSINESS (accounting, business administration, business law, economics, finance, health care administration, management, marketing, personnel), EDUCATION (early childhood, elementary, recreation and physical activities management, special), ENGLISH (communication arts), FINE AND PERFORMING ARTS (commercial art, fashion/merchandising, fashion design, interior design, studio art), HEALTH SCIENCES (nursing), MATH AND SCIENCES (mathematics), SOCIAL SCIENCES (business psychology, human services, politics/public service, psychology, research).

Required: Each major has a required liberal arts core curriculum.

Special: The junior and senior years can be completed in 12 months.

Honors: Three honor societies are represented on campus.

Admissions: About 79% of those who applied for admission to the 1981-82 freshman class were accepted. The SAT scores of those who enrolled were as follows: Verbal—50% below 500, 45% between 500 and 599, 5% between 600 and 700, and 0% above 700; Math—50% below 500, 45% between 500 and 599, 5% between 600 and 700, and 0% above 700. Applicants must have graduated from an accredited high school after completing at least 16 Carnegie units. They must present an average of at least 2.0 and rank in the top half of their class. Admissions officers also consider, in descending order of importance, advanced placement or honors courses, extracurricular activities, recommendations by high school officials, leadership, impressions made during an interview, evidence of special talents, and personality.

Procedure: Applicants must take the SAT or ACT. Application deadlines are open; new students are admitted to the fall, spring, and summer terms. Admissions decisions are made on a rolling basis. The application fee is $20.

Special: A deferred admissions plan is available.

Transfer: For fall 1981, 235 students applied, 160 were accepted, and 120 enrolled. Applicants must have a GPA of at least 2.0. D grades do not transfer. Students must complete 30 credits, at the college, of the 120 needed for a bachelor's degree. Application deadlines are open.

Visiting: The college schedules open houses for prospective students. Informal visits also may be arranged with the admissions office. Recommended times are Monday through Friday, 9 A.M. to 4:30 P.M. Guides are provided, and visitors may sit in on classes.

Financial Aid: Seventy percent of the students receive aid. Twenty-five percent work part-time on campus. Average aid to freshmen from all sources is $3500. Scholarships, loans, government grants, and CWS are available. The college is a member of the CSS. The application, the FAF, and the college's own form must be submitted by May 1.

Foreign Students: Fifteen percent of the full-time students come from foreign countries. The college offers these students an intensive English course, an intensive English program, special counseling, and special organizations.

Admissions: Foreign students must take the TOEFL or the college's own language test. They must score 500 or above on the TOEFL. They must take the college's own entrance examination.

Procedure: Application deadlines are open. Foreign students must submit a health form. They must also present proof of funds adequate to cover their entire period of study.

Admissions Contact: Kathryn B. del Campo, Director of Admissions.

MARY WASHINGTON COLLEGE   E-2
Fredericksburg, Virginia 22401   (703) 899-4681

F/T: 542M, 1715W	Faculty: 130; IIB, +$
P/T: 161M, 264W	Ph.D.'s: 82%
Grad: 15M, 28W	S/F Ratio: 16 to 1
Year: sems, ss	Tuition: $958 ($1804)
Appl: Mar. 1	R and B: $2124
2118 applied	1325 accepted 700 enrolled
SAT: 500V 507M	VERY COMPETITIVE

Mary Washington College, founded in 1908, is a state-supported liberal arts institution. Its library contains 266,736 volumes and 23,380 microfilm items, and subscribes to 1168 periodicals.

Environment: The 280-acre suburban campus is located 50 miles from Washington, D.C. The brick buildings with white pillars and neoclassical porticoes were designed in the style Thomas Jefferson established at the University of Virginia. The 17 dormitories house almost 2000 students. Some buildings are undergoing renovation.

Student Life: About 76% of the students come from Virginia, and 77% are graduates of public schools. Eighty-five percent of the students live on campus. An honor system provides a code of personal integrity; it prohibits lying, cheating, stealing, or breaking one's word of honor. Drinking is permitted in residence halls and the Student Union. Five percent of the students are minority-group members. College housing is both single-sex and coed. There are visiting privileges in single-sex housing. Residents of each dormitory determine visitation regulations. Students may keep cars on campus.

Organizations: There are no fraternities or sororities on campus. Activities include a chorus; dance; publications; a campus radio station; a student government; and science, service, and special-interest clubs. Religious organizations and counselors for Protestant, Catholic, and Jewish students are available. The college sponsors art shows, concerts, films, plays, lectures, and recitals.

Sports: The college participates in 9 intercollegiate sports for men and 12 for women. There are 13 intramural sports for men and 14 for women.

Handicapped: About 60% of the campus is accessible to physically handicapped students. The college is moving to eliminate architectural barriers. Facilities include wheelchair ramps, parking areas, and elevators. Fewer than 1% of the students have hearing or visual impairments. No special counselors are available for handicapped students.

Graduates: About 13% of the freshmen drop out during the first year. Sixty-five percent remain to graduate, and of those 20% enter graduate school; 1% enter medical school, 1% dental school, and 3% law school. About 20% of the graduates pursue careers in business and industry.

Services: Placement, career, and psychological counseling are provided free to students. Free placement services also are available to graduates. Health care is available on a fee basis.

Programs of Study: The college confers the B.A., B.S., and B.G.S. degrees. Master's degrees are also awarded. Bachelor's degrees are offered in the following subjects: AREA STUDIES (American), BUSINESS (business administration), ENGLISH (English, speech pathology and audiology), FINE AND PERFORMING ARTS (art, art history, dance, music, performing arts, studio art, theater/dramatics), HEALTH SCIENCES (medical technology), LANGUAGES (French, German, Greek/Latin, Spanish), MATH AND SCIENCES (biology, chemistry, ecology/environmental science, geology, mathematics, physics), PHILOSOPHY (classics, philosophy, religion), PREPROFESSIONAL (dentistry, law, library science, medicine, ministry, pharmacy, social work, veterinary), SOCIAL SCIENCES (economics, geography, government/political science, historic preservation, history, international relations, psychology, social sciences, sociology). About 41% of all degrees are conferred in social sciences and 17% in fine and performing arts.

Required: All students must meet basic college requirements in 5 broad subject areas—the natural world, human behavior, abstract thought, intellectual frameworks, and modes of creativity—and in 4 skill areas—physical education, laboratory science, foreign language, and writing.

Special: Students may spend their junior year abroad. Combined B.A.-B.S. degrees may be earned in psychology. Students may design their own majors. A general studies degree is available. One elective per semester may be taken on a pass/fail basis. Degrees may be earned in 3 years. A nontraditional Bachelor of Liberal Studies program is offered for students over age 23.

Honors: Seven honor societies have chapters on campus. All major departments also offer honors programs, which may include honors projects or theses.

Admissions: About 63% of those who applied for admission to the 1981-82 freshman class were accepted. The SAT scores of those who enrolled were as follows: Verbal—51% below 500, 38% between 500 and 599, 10% between 600 and 700, and 1% above 700; Math—41% below 500, 47% between 500 and 599, 11% between 600 and 700, and 1% above 700. Applicants should rank in the top half of their high school class and present a GPA of at least 2.5 and SAT scores of at least 1000. A 3.0 average is preferred. Admissions officers also consider, in descending order of importance, advanced placement or honors courses, recommendations by school officials, evidence of spe-

926 VIRGINIA

cial talents, leadership record, extracurricular activities, impressions made during an interview, and ability to finance a college education.

Procedure: The SAT is required and should be taken by January of the senior year. Application deadlines are March 1 (fall), December 1 (spring), and flexible for the summer term. The application fee is $15. Early decision applicants are notified by December 1, the rest around April 1.

Special: Early decision and early and deferred admissions plans are available. AP and CLEP credit is accepted.

Transfer: For fall 1981, 292 students applied, 159 were accepted, and 116 enrolled. A minimum GPA of 2.0 is required. D grades do not transfer. Up to 90 hours of credit may be transferred, but students must complete, at the college, 1 year and 30 of the 124 credits needed to receive a bachelor's degree. Application deadlines are March 1 (fall) and December 1 (spring).

Visiting: Information sessions and campus tours for prospective students are scheduled regularly, while the college is in session, Monday through Friday at 10:30 A.M. and 2 P.M. and Saturdays at 10:30 A.M. Visitors also may sit in on classes. Arrangements should be made with the admissions office.

Financial Aid: Thirty percent of the students receive financial aid. Twenty percent work part-time on campus. Average aid to freshmen from all sources is $1140. Scholarships, grants, loans, and part-time jobs are available. The college is a member of CSS. The FAF is required. Aid applications must be filed by March 1 (fall) and December 1 (spring).

Foreign Students: Fewer than 1% of the full-time students come from foreign countries.

Admissions: Foreign students must score 500 or above on the TOEFL. They must also take the SAT.

Procedure: Application deadlines are March 1 (fall) and October 1 (spring). Foreign students must present proof of funds adequate to cover 1 academic year. They must pay out-of-state tuition fees. They must also carry health insurance, which is available through the college for a fee.

Admissions Contact: H. Conrad Warlick, Dean of Admissions and Financial Aid.

NORFOLK STATE UNIVERSITY   F-4
Norfolk, Virginia 23504   (804) 623-8396

F/T: 2236M, 3305W	Faculty: 335; IIA, —$
P/T: 352M, 299W	Ph.D.'s: 40%
Grad: 114M, 269W	S/F Ratio: 16 to 1
Year: sems, ss	Tuition: $740 ($1658)
Appl: Aug. 1	R and B: $1488
2377 applied	2201 accepted 1492 enrolled
SAT: required	LESS COMPETITIVE

Norfolk State University, founded in 1935, offers liberal arts, vocational and technical, and preprofessional education in 2-year and 4-year, day and evening programs. Its library contains 200,000 volumes, and subscribes to 2300 periodicals.

Environment: The urban campus is located in Norfolk, a port city of 350,000 people within easy reach of oceanfront recreation areas. Campus buildings include 2 dormitories.

Student Life: Most students are Virginia residents. A majority of the students commute. About 88% are minority-group members. Campus housing is single-sex; there are visiting privileges. Students may keep cars on campus.

Organizations: There are no fraternities or sororities on campus. The city of Norfolk and recreation areas nearby provide culture and entertainment.

Sports: The university fields 6 intercollegiate teams for men and 4 for women. There are 8 intramural sports for men and 8 for women.

Handicapped: Special facilities for handicapped students include wheelchair ramps, parking areas, and elevators. Special class scheduling is available.

Graduates: Thirty-one percent of the graduates pursue advanced study after graduation.

Services: Free career counseling, placement services, tutoring, and remedial instruction are available to students. Health care is provided on a fee basis.

Programs of Study: The university confers the B.A. and B.S. degrees. Associate and master's degrees are also awarded. Bachelor's degrees are offered in the following subjects: AREA STUDIES (American, Black/Afro-American, urban), BUSINESS (accounting, business administration, business education, finance, management, marketing, real estate/insurance), EDUCATION (early childhood, health/physical, recreation, special, urban), ENGLISH (English, journalism, mass communication), FINE AND PERFORMING ARTS (art, art education, music, music education), HEALTH SCIENCES (health management, medical technology, nursing, occupational therapy, physical therapy, speech therapy), LANGUAGES (French, German, Spanish), MATH AND SCIENCES (biology, chemistry, mathematics, physical sciences, physics), PREPROFESSIONAL (home economics, law, medicine, social work), SOCIAL SCIENCES (economics, geography, government/political science, history, psychology, social sciences, sociology).

Required: All students must complete general education requirements, which include courses in humanities, social sciences, natural and physical sciences, and physical education.

Special: Programs at the University Center are open to Norfolk State students. A general studies degree is offered.

Admissions: About 93% of those who applied were accepted for the 1981–82 freshman class. Candidates must have completed 16 Carnegie units and should have a GPA of at least 2.0. High-school grades are the most important factor in determining admission. Advanced placement or honors courses, recommendations, and extracurricular activities are also considered important.

Procedure: The SAT is required and should be taken by March of the senior year. Application deadlines are August 1 (fall) and December 1 (spring). New students are admitted to both terms. The application fee is $10. Admissions decisions are made on a rolling basis.

Special: An early decision plan is available.

Transfer: D grades do not transfer. All students must complete, at the university, 30 of the 126 credits required for a bachelor's degree. Application deadlines are the same as those for freshmen.

Visiting: Guides are provided for informal visits, which should be arranged Monday through Friday, 8 A.M. to 5 P.M., with the admissions office.

Financial Aid: About 90% of the students receive aid. About 25% work part-time on campus. The university is a member of CSS. The FAF must be filed. Aid applications should be filed with admissions applications.

Foreign Students: About 4% of the full-time students come from foreign countries. Special organizations and special counseling are available for these students.

Admissions: Foreign students must take the TOEFL and the SAT.

Procedure: Application deadlines are the same as those for other students. Foreign students must present proof of health and of funds adequate to cover 1 year of study. Health insurance is required and is available through the university.

Admissions Contact: Charles W. Pleasants, Assistant Director of Admissions.

OLD DOMINION UNIVERSITY   F-4
Norfolk, Virginia 23508   (804) 440-3637

F/T: 4581M, 4395W	Faculty: n/av; IIA, +$
P/T: 1257M, 1437W	Ph.D.'s: 95%
Grad: 1626M, 1837W	S/F Ratio: 35 to 1
Year: sems, ss	Tuition: $1066 ($1882)
Appl: July 1	R and B: $2086
5065 applied	2859 accepted 1604 enrolled
SAT: 440V 490M	COMPETITIVE

Old Dominion University, founded in 1930, is a state-supported university. Its library contains 412,000 volumes and 75,000 microfilm items, and subscribes to 2745 periodicals.

Environment: The 120-acre urban campus is located in a residential section of Norfolk. The 26 buildings include a library and an expanded student center. Two dormitories house 888 students. University apartments are reserved for upperclassmen.

Student Life: About 80% of the students are Virginia residents. Thirty percent of the students live on campus. About 13% of the students are minority-group members. University housing is both single-sex and coed. There are visiting privileges in single-sex housing. Students may keep cars on campus.

Organizations: About 15% of the students belong to 1 of the 14 national fraternities and 8 national sororities on campus. Extracurricular activities include art, drama, debating, and music groups; publications; religious organizations; and service, special-interest, and departmental clubs. The university sponsors art shows, concerts, films, lectures, operas, and recitals. There is a student government, and students have a voice in the University Senate. Activities available in Norfolk include an orchestra, a ballet company, the Chrysler Art Museum, and annual waterfront and azalea festivals.

Sports: The university participates in 14 intercollegiate sports for men and 14 for women. There are 11 intramural sports for men and 9 for women.

Handicapped: About 75% of the campus is accessible to physically handicapped students. Facilities include wheelchair ramps, parking areas, elevators, specially equipped rest rooms, and lowered drinking fountains and telephones. Special class scheduling also is available.

Graduates: Five percent of the freshmen drop out by the end of their first year. Forty percent remain to graduate.

Services: Career and psychological counseling, tutoring, and remedial instruction are provided free to students. Placement services are available free to students and graduates. Health care is available on a fee basis.

Programs of Study: The university confers the B.A., B.S., B.S.B.A., B.S.Ed., and B.S.Eng. degrees. Master's and doctoral degrees also are available. Bachelor's degrees are offered in the following subjects: BUSINESS (accounting, business administration, computer science, finance, management, marketing), EDUCATION (early childhood, elementary, health/physical, leisure services, secondary, special), ENGLISH (English, speech), FINE AND PERFORMING ARTS (art, art education, art history, dance, music, music education, studio art, theater/dramatics), HEALTH SCIENCES (dental hygiene, environmental health, medical technology, nursing, physical therapy), LANGUAGES (French, German, Russian, Spanish), MATH AND SCIENCES (biochemistry, biology, chemistry, earth science, geology, mathematics, physical sciences, physics), PHILOSOPHY (philosophy), PREPROFESSIONAL (dentistry, engineering, engineering technology, library science, medicine, pharmacy, veterinary), SOCIAL SCIENCES (criminal justice, economics, geography, government/political science, history, international relations, psychology, social sciences, sociology).

Required: All students must take English, a laboratory science, social studies, mathematics, and humanities.

Special: Five-year combination B.A.-B.S. degrees are offered in economics, criminal justice, interdisciplinary studies, and music. Students may design their own majors or earn a general studies degree.

Honors: Thirty-three honor societies have chapters on campus. The history, English, biology, chemistry, physics, and psychology departments have their own honors programs.

Admissions: About 56% of those who applied for admission to the 1981-82 freshman class were accepted. The SAT scores of those who enrolled in a recent year were as follows: Verbal—10% above 540, 25% above 490, 50% above 430, 75% above 390, and 90% above 340; Math—10% above 590, 25% above 540, 50% above 480, 75% above 420, and 90% above 380. Applicants should have completed at least 15 Carnegie units with an average of 2.5 or better, and should rank in the upper half of their class. Admissions officers also consider, in descending order of importance, advanced placement or honors courses, personality, extracurricular activities, recommendations by high school officials, leadership record, impressions made during a personal interview, and evidence of special talents.

Procedure: The SAT is required and should be taken in May of the junior year or December of the senior year. Application deadlines are July 1 (fall), December 1 (spring), and April 1 (summer). The university follows the rolling admissions policy. A $20 application fee is required.

Special: Early and deferred admissions plans are available. AP and CLEP credit is granted.

Transfer: Applicants must have a GPA of at least 2.0. D grades do not transfer. Students must take at least 30 hours, at the university, of the 120 needed to receive a bachelor's degree. Application deadlines are the same as those for freshmen.

Visiting: Prospective students may meet with admissions officers and tour the campus at regularly scheduled orientation sessions. Guides also are available for informal visits. Visitors may sit in on classes by appointment and arrange to stay overnight on campus only in the summer. Campus visits are best scheduled with the admissions office Monday through Friday from 10:30 A.M. to 1:30 P.M.

Financial Aid: About 34% of the students receive aid. Scholarships and loans from federal government, state government, and private banks are available. Campus jobs are available as well. The college is a member of CSS. The FAF and the university's own application must be submitted by April 1.

Foreign Students: About 3% of the full-time students come from foreign countries. The university offers these students an intensive English course, an intensive English program, special counseling, and special organizations.

Admissions: Foreign students must take the TOEFL or the CELT. They must score 550 or above on the TOEFL for nontechnical studies and 500 for technical studies. They must take the CELT for placement purposes, or score at least 850 (combined) on the SAT.

Procedure: The application deadlines are April 1 (fall), October 1 (spring), and February 1 (summer). Foreign students must present proof of funds adequate to cover 1 year of study. They must carry an international insurance policy, and must carry health insurance, which is available through the university for a fee.

Admissions Contact: Karen Scherberger, Admissions Counselor.

RADFORD UNIVERSITY C-3
Radford, Virginia 24142 (703) 731-5371

F/T: 1539M, 3648W   Faculty: n/av; IIA, —$
P/T: 305M, 629W   Ph.D.'s: 60%
Grad: 300M, 500W   S/F Ratio: 19 to 1
Year: qtrs, ss   Tuition: $1125 ($1875)
Appl: Mar. 1   R and B: $2016
3704 applied   2494 accepted   1350 enrolled
SAT: 425V 425M   ACT: 18   COMPETITIVE

Radford University is a state-supported institution. Its library contains 175,000 volumes and 20,000 microfilm reels, and subscribes to 2153 periodicals.

Environment: The 70-acre campus is located in a residential section of the town, in a rural area 45 miles from Roanoke. Facilities include a $6.5-million recreation-convocation center. Living facilities include dormitories and fraternity and sorority houses.

Student Life: About 85% of the freshmen come from Virginia. About 82% come from public schools. Sixty-one percent of the students live on campus. Unmarried freshmen and sophomores under age 21 are required to live on campus if they do not live at home. Five percent of the students are minority-group members. University housing is both single-sex and coed. There are visiting privileges in single-sex housing. Freshmen are not allowed to have cars on campus.

Organizations: Seven percent of the students belong to 1 of 6 fraternities and 6 sororities on campus. Student organizations sponsor social and cultural activities. Outdoor recreational areas, including the Appalachian Trail, are nearby.

Sports: The university participates in 6 intercollegiate athletics for men and 7 for women. There are 9 intramural sports for men and 8 for women.

Handicapped: About half the campus is accessible to the physically handicapped. Special facilities include wheelchair ramps, parking areas, elevators, and specially equipped rest rooms and residence hall rooms. Special class scheduling also is available. One special counselor is available to handicapped students. Fewer than 1% of the students are visually or hearing-impaired, and the university has no special facilities for these students.

Graduates: About 26% of the freshmen drop out by the end of their first year. Of the remainder, about 86% graduate. About 15% of the graduates continue their education; 1% enter medical school, fewer than 1% dental school, and 2% law school. About 55% of the graduates pursue careers in business and industry.

Services: Health care, placement, remedial instruction, and career and psychological counseling are available free to students. Job placement services are available to graduates as well as students. Tutoring is available on a fee basis.

Programs of Study: The university confers the B.A., B.S., B.B.A., B.F.A., and B.M. degrees. Master's degrees also are available. Bachelor's degrees are offered in the following subjects: BUSINESS (accounting, business education, computer science, finance, general business, management, marketing, office administration, real estate/insurance, small business management), EDUCATION (early childhood, elementary, health/physical, secondary, special, speech), ENGLISH (English, journalism, speech), FINE AND PERFORMING ARTS (art, art education, dance, music, radio/TV, studio art, theater/dramatics), HEALTH SCIENCES (health, medical technology, nursing, speech therapy), LANGUAGES (French, German, Greek/Latin, Spanish), MATH AND SCIENCES (biology, chemistry, geology, mathematics, medical technology), PHILOSOPHY (religion), PREPROFESSIONAL (dentistry, home economics, law, library science, medicine, nursing, social work, veterinary), SOCIAL SCIENCES (anthropology, economics, geography, government/political science, history, psychology, social sciences, sociology). About 75% of undergraduate degrees conferred are in preprofessional fields, 14% in business, and 13% in education.

928 VIRGINIA

Required: All students must take 75 quarter hours in a core curriculum of English, history, mathematics, music and art, philosophy, health and physical education, psychology, science, social science, basic economics, and speech. B.A. candidates also must take a foreign language.

Special: Students may design their own majors.

Honors: Eighteen honor societies have chapters on campus. All academic departments offer honors programs.

Admissions: About 67% of those who applied were accepted for the 1981–82 freshman class. In a recent year, of those who enrolled, 17% scored above 500 on the Verbal SAT and 15% scored above 500 on the Math SAT. Applicants should have completed 16 Carnegie units, have earned at least a C average, and rank in the upper half of their graduating class. Recommendations, extracurricular activities, advanced placement or honors courses, and leadership record are also considered important.

Procedure: The SAT or ACT is required and should be taken between April of the junior year and December of the senior year. Application deadlines are March 1 (fall), November 1 (winter), February 1 (spring), and May 1 (summer). New students are admitted to all quarters. Admissions decisions are made on a rolling basis. A $15 fee should accompany all applications.

Special: An early decision plan is available. AP and CLEP credit is accepted.

Transfer: For fall 1981, 1127 students applied, 814 were accepted, and 555 enrolled. Applicants should have a 2.0 GPA. D grades do not transfer. Students must take at least 46 credits, in residence, of the 186 needed to receive a bachelor's degree. Application deadlines are June 1 (fall), November 1 (winter), February 1 (spring), and May 1 (summer).

Visiting: Guides are available for informal visits from 8 A.M. to 5 P.M. daily except for Christmas holidays. Visitors may sit in on classes but may not spend the night in the residence halls. The admissions office should be contacted for arrangements.

Financial Aid: About 51% of the students receive aid. Thirty-six percent work part-time on campus. The average aid awarded to freshmen from all sources is $1805. Scholarships, loans, fellowships, BEOG, and campus employment are available. The university is a member of CSS. The FAF and the university's own financial statement must be submitted by March 1.

Foreign Students: Fewer than 1% of the full-time students come from foreign countries. The university offers these students an intensive English course, special counseling, and special organizations.

Admissions: Foreign students must score 550 or above on the TOEFL. No college entrance examination is required.

Procedure: The application deadlines are March 1 (fall), November 1 (winter), February 1 (spring), and May 1 (summer). Foreign students must present proof of funds adequate to cover 1 year of study. They must carry health insurance, which is available through the university for a fee.

Admissions Contact: Drumont I. Bowman, Director of Admissions.

RANDOLPH-MACON COLLEGE D-3
Ashland, Virginia 23005 (804) 798-8372

F/T: 542M, 367W Faculty: 60; IIB, +$
P/T: 1M, 3W Ph.D.'s: 55%
Grad: none S/F Ratio: 14 to 1
Year: 4-4-1, ss Tuition: $5000
Appl: Mar. 1 R and B: $2200
933 applied 746 accepted 294 enrolled
SAT: 470V 510M COMPETITIVE

Randolph-Macon College, established in 1830, is a private liberal arts institution affiliated with the Methodist Church. Its library contains 120,000 volumes and 800 microfilm items, and subscribes to over 500 periodicals.

Environment: The 85-acre suburban campus is located 15 miles from Richmond. The 37 major buildings include dormitories, on-campus apartments, married student housing, fraternity houses, a student union building, a multi-million dollar science center, an observatory with a 12-inch reflecting telescope, and a new dining hall.

Student Life: About 64% of the students are from Virginia. About 65% come from public schools. About 95% live on campus. Twenty-one percent of the students are Catholic, 68% Protestant, and 1% Jewish. About 4% of the students are minority-group members. College housing is single-sex; there are visiting privileges. Students may keep cars on campus.

Organizations: About 50% of the men belong to 1 of 9 national fraternities; there are no sororities on campus. There are several community service, social, and religious organizations on campus. There are also a weekly newspaper, a yearbook, literary magazine, Drama Guild, Franklin Debating Society, Washington Literary Society, Mixed Chorus, and Volunteers in Action.

Sports: The college participates in 7 intercollegiate sports for men and 5 for women. Seven intramural sports are offered for both men and women.

Handicapped: About 35% of the campus is accessible to physically handicapped students. Special facilities include parking areas and elevators. Special class scheduling is available. The college employs no special counselors for the handicapped.

Graduates: About 15% of the freshmen drop out by the end of the first year, and 55% remain to graduate. Over 40% of the graduates continue their studies, including 6% who enter medical school, 4% who enter dental school, and 8% who enter law school. Another 45% of the graduates begin careers in business and industry.

Services: Health care, career and psychological counseling, job placement (available to graduates as well as students), tutoring, and remedial instruction are available free of charge.

Programs of Study: The college offers the B.A. and B.S. degrees. Bachelor's degrees are offered in the following subjects: BUSINESS (computer science, economics/business), ENGLISH (English), LANGUAGES (French, German, Greek/Latin, Spanish), MATH AND SCIENCES (biology, chemistry, mathematics, physics), PHILOSOPHY (classics, philosophy, religion), PREPROFESSIONAL (dentistry, law, medicine, ministry), SOCIAL SCIENCES (economics, government/political science, history, psychology, sociology). Most degrees are granted in the social sciences.

Required: Students must take courses in English composition, literature, mathematics, natural science, a foreign language, European history, social science, philosophy and/or religion, humanities, and physical education. May Term is required for freshmen and optional for upperclassmen.

Special: Combination degree programs in forestry and engineering are offered. There are 3-2 dual degree programs in engineering with Washington University and Columbia University. The college offers a 3-2 B.A.-M.A. program in forestry with Duke University. Major/minor options and double majors are possible. There are also internships and field study opportunities for students in all majors.

Honors: Eight honor societies are open to qualified students. New Honors Program enables superior students to participate in interdisciplinary courses and other challenging educational experiences.

Admissions: About 80% of those who applied were accepted for the 1981–82 freshman class. Of those who enrolled, the SAT scores were as follows: Verbal—67% below 500, 27% between 500 and 599, 5% between 600 and 700, and 1% above 700; Math—40% below 500, 44% between 500 and 599, 13% between 600 and 700, and 3% above 700. Applicants should be graduates of accredited high schools with an average of at least C+ in 15 units of work. The main criteria for evaluating applicants are grades, SAT scores, class rank, advanced placement or honors courses, recommendations by school officials, leadership record, impressions made during an interview, and extracurricular activities.

Procedure: The SAT is rquired. The ACT is also accepted. Early decision candidates should take it in May of the junior year; regular candidates in December or January of the senior year. An interview is recommended. ATs are used for placement only. Application deadlines are March 1 (fall), December 1 (spring), and June 14 (summer). Early decision candidates are notified around November 15, others by April 1. The application fee is $20.

Special: Early decision and early and deferred admissions plans are available. AP credit is accepted.

Transfer: For fall 1981, 62 students applied, 44 were accepted, and 23 enrolled. Applicants must have a GPA of at least 2.0. D grades do not transfer. Students must spend at least 2 years in residence and complete 56 of the 112 credits needed to receive a bachelor's degree. Application deadlines are the same as those for freshmen.

Visiting: Regular orientations for prospective students are scheduled on several Saturdays. Guides also are available for informal visits while classes are in session. Visitors may sit in on classes and, sometimes, spend the night on campus. Arrangements should be made with the admissions office.

Financial Aid: About 40% of the students receive financial aid. Twenty-two percent work part-time on campus. Average aid awarded to freshmen from all sources is $1440. Seventy-five freshman scholarships are awarded each year. Loans and campus employment also are available. The college is a member of CSS. The FAF must be filed along with the college's own form. The deadline for aid applications is February 1.

Foreign Students: One percent of the full-time students come from foreign countries.

Admissions: Foreign students must score 500 or above on the TOEFL. No college entrance examination is required.

Procedure: The application deadlines are March 1 (fall) and December 1 (winter). Foreign students must submit the Standard Health Form. They must also provide proof of funds adequate to cover each of their 4 years of study.

Admissions Contact: Charles F. Nelson, Jr., Dean of Admissions.

RANDOLPH-MACON WOMAN'S COLLEGE D–3
Lynchburg, Virginia 24503   (804) 846-7392

F/T: 750W	Faculty: n/av; IIB, +$
P/T: 15W	Ph.D.'s: n/av
Grad: none	S/F Ratio: 10 to 1
Year: sems	Tuition: $5100
Appl: Mar. 1	R and B: $2200
SAT or ACT: required	**VERY COMPETITIVE**

Randolph-Macon Woman's College, founded in 1891, is an independent liberal arts institution. The library contains 150,000 volumes and subscribes to 679 periodicals.

Environment: The 100-acre campus is located in the foothills of the Blue Ridge Mountains in suburban Lynchburg. Buildings include an art gallery and music and fine arts centers.

Student Life: Three-fourths of the students are from out of state. About 60% of the freshmen come from public schools. Almost all of the students live on campus. College housing is single-sex; there are visiting privileges. Students regulate their own curfews. Consumption of alcoholic beverages is permitted in dormitories and other designated areas.

Organizations: There are no sororities on campus. The college sponsors such cultural events as art shows, concerts, lectures, operas, and plays. Major social events include Fall Weekend, Winter Weekend, and the senior dinner-dance. Religious facilities are provided for Protestant and Catholic students; attendance is voluntary.

Sports: The college participates intercollegiately in 9 sports.

Handicapped: The college is working formally on barrier-free compliance.

Graduates: About 2% of the freshmen drop out by the end of the first year, and 70% remain to graduate. Fifty-five percent of the graduates seek advanced degrees.

Services: The following are offered free of charge to students: placement, health care, psychological counseling, career counseling, and tutoring.

Programs of Study: All programs lead to the B.A. degree. Bachelor's degrees are offered in the following subjects: AREA STUDIES (American, Asian, Latin American, Russian), ENGLISH (communications, English), FINE AND PERFORMING ARTS (art, art history, dance, music, studio art, theater/dramatics), HEALTH SCIENCES (medical technology), LANGUAGES (French, German, Greek/Latin, Japanese, Russian, Spanish), MATH AND SCIENCES (biology, chemistry, mathematics), PHILOSOPHY (classics, philosophy, religion), SOCIAL SCIENCES (economics, government/political science, history, international relations, psychology, sociology).

Required: All students must take courses in at least 4 departments each semester. Students must take at least 36 credits outside their major field.

Special: Students may design their own majors. Independent study programs are available. Students may spend a summer or their junior year abroad; the college is affiliated with the University of Reading in England, the American School of Classical Studies in Athens, the Intercollegiate Center for Classical Studies in Rome, and the Institute for Mediterranean Studies, which sponsors a summer seminar in the archaeology of the Near East. Juniors and seniors may take courses on a pass-fail basis. A cooperative program with 7 other area colleges is in effect.

Honors: Chapters of Phi Beta Kappa and Eta Sigma Phi are open to qualified students. Honors programs are available.

Admissions: About 48% of those who applied were accepted for the 1981-82 freshman class. Candidates should have completed 16 Carnegie units and have a strong high-school record as well as the recommendations of a high school counselor and 3 teachers.

Procedure: The SAT or ACT should be taken by December or January of the senior year. Three ATs, including English Composition, also are required. Applications should be in by March 1 (fall) and November 1 (spring). Students are notified as soon as their files are complete, no later than December 1 for early decision or April 15 for regular decision. The application fee is $20.

Special: Early and deferred admissions plans are available. AP and CLEP credit is offered.

Transfer: Recently, 56 students applied, 23 were accepted, and 16 enrolled. Transfers are accepted for all classes, but no more than 62 credits may be transferred. Grades lower than C– do not transfer. Students must spend the last year in residence to receive a bachelor's degree.

Financial Aid: About 50% of all students receive financial aid. Campus employment, loans, and scholarships are available. The college is a member of CSS and requires aid applicants to submit the FAF. Deadlines for application are March 1 for regular admission and November 1 for early decision.

Foreign Students: Three percent of the full-time students come from foreign countries. The college offers these students special counseling and special organizations.

Admissions: Foreign students must take the TOEFL and the SAT.

Procedure: The application deadlines are March 1 (fall) and November 1 (winter). Foreign students must present proof of health. They must also present proof of adequate funds. They must carry health insurance, which is available through the college for a fee.

Admissions Contact: Robert T. Merritt, Director of Admissions.

ROANOKE COLLEGE C–3
Salem, Virginia 24153   (703) 389-2351

F/T: 575M, 562W	Faculty: 67; IIB, +$
P/T: 115M, 90W	Ph.D.'s: 70%
Grad: none	S/F Ratio: 17 to 1
Year: 4-1-4, ss	Tuition: $4200
Appl: July 1	R and B: $1900
1175 applied	800 accepted	340 enrolled
SAT: 470V 500M		**COMPETITIVE**

Roanoke College, established in 1842, is a coeducational liberal arts college affiliated with the Lutheran Church in America. The library contains 130,000 volumes and subscribes to 637 periodicals.

Environment: The 65-acre campus is located in a suburban college town in the Shenandoah Valley, 7 miles from Roanoke. Three buildings have been designated state historical landmarks. Eight dormitories house 461 men and 416 women.

Student Life: About 50% of the students are from Virginia. Seventy percent come from public schools. Twenty-five percent of the students are Catholic, 73% Protestant, and 1% Jewish. Eighty-three percent live on campus. About 4% of the students are minority-group members. College housing is single-sex; there are visiting privileges. First semester freshmen may not keep cars on campus.

Organizations: About 35% of the students belong to 1 of 4 national fraternities and 3 national sororities with campus chapters. Campus activities include religious clubs, theater and music groups, lectures, and films. Chapel attendance is voluntary. Many students enjoy hiking and backpacking in the nearby mountains.

Sports: The college participates intercollegiately in 8 sports for men and 6 for women. There are 7 intramural sports for men and 5 for women.

Handicapped: About half the campus is accessible to physically handicapped students. Facilities include elevators, special parking areas, and specially equipped rest rooms. Special class scheduling also is available. No counselors are provided. No students with impaired vision or hearing were enrolled recently.

Graduates: Ten percent of the freshmen drop out during their first year. About 69% remain to graduate. About 35% of the graduates immediately begin graduate study, including 3% who attend medical school, 1% dental school, and 2% law school; 73% of the students eventually go on to advanced study. Another 45% of the graduates pursue careers in business and industry.

Services: Health care, placement, remedial instruction, and career and psychological counseling are available free to students. Tutoring is available on a fee basis.

930 VIRGINIA

Programs of Study: The college awards the B.A., B.B.A., and B.S. degrees. Bachelor's degrees are offered in the following subjects: BUSINESS (business administration, computer science, management), EDUCATION (early childhood, elementary, health/physical), ENGLISH (English), FINE AND PERFORMING ARTS (art, music), HEALTH SCIENCES (medical technology, radiologic technology), LANGUAGES (French, German, Spanish), MATH AND SCIENCES (biology, chemistry, mathematics, physics, statistics), PHILOSOPHY (philosophy, religion), PREPROFESSIONAL (dentistry, engineering, law, medicine, ministry, pharmacy, social work, veterinary), SOCIAL SCIENCES (economics, government/political science, history, international relations, psychology, sociology).

Required: All students must take courses or pass competency exams in English, the humanities, mathematics, natural sciences, and social sciences.

Special: There is a combination 3-1 degree program in medical technology. Some electives may be taken on a pass-fail basis. Study abroad and interdisciplinary courses are available.

Honors: A number of honor societies are represented on campus.

Admissions: About 68% of those who applied were accepted for the 1981–82 freshman class. Candidates should have completed 16 Carnegie units at an accredited high school, present at least a C average, rank in the top 50% of their graduating class, and score at least 400 on each section of the SAT. Admissions officers also consider advanced placement and honors courses, recommendations by school officials, personality, impressions made during an interview, leadership, and extracurricular activities.

Procedure: Applicants must take the SAT or ACT and are encouraged to take ATs in English, a foreign language, and mathematics. An interview also is recommended. Application deadlines are July 1 (fall), December 15 (winter), January 15 (spring), and May 15 (summer). Notification is made on a rolling basis. A $15 fee is required.

Special: Early and deferred admissions and early decision plans are available. AP and CLEP credit is accepted.

Transfer: For fall 1981, 113 students applied, 89 were accepted, and 79 enrolled. An average of at least 2.0 is required. D grades do not transfer. Sixteen units, or approximately 2 years, must be completed in residence out of the 36 units required for a bachelor's degree. The application deadlines are the same as those for freshman applicants.

Visiting: Arrangements can be made through the admissions office for informal visits. Guides are provided, and prospective students may sit in on classes and stay overnight at the school. Visits are best scheduled in spring or fall.

Financial Aid: About 48% of the students receive financial aid. Forty-seven percent work part-time on campus. Average aid to freshmen from all sources covers 45% of costs. Aid is awarded in scholarships, grants, and jobs to students who qualify on the basis of need or achievement. The college is a member of CSS. Tuition may be paid in installments. Aid applicants must submit the FAF and the college's form by April 15 (fall), November 1 (winter and spring), and April 1 (summer).

Foreign Students: Fewer than 1% of the full-time students come from foreign countries.

Admissions: Foreign students must score 500 or above on the TOEFL. No college entrance examination is required.

Procedure: The application deadlines are July 1 (fall), December 15 (winter), January 15 (spring), and May 15 (summer). Foreign students must submit a health form. They must also provide proof of funds adequate to cover 1 year of study.

Admissions Contact: William C. Schaaf, Director of Admissions.

SAINT PAUL'S COLLEGE   E-4
Lawrenceville, Virginia 23868   (804) 848-4356

F/T: 300M, 330W	Faculty:	n/av
P/T: 10M, 15W	Ph.D.'s:	41%
Grad: none	S/F Ratio:	n/av
Year: sems, ss	Tuition:	$2180
Appl: open	R and B:	$1660
600 applied	480 accepted	233 enrolled
SAT: required		COMPETITIVE

Saint Paul's, founded in 1888, is a private liberal arts college affiliated with the Episcopal Church. The library contains 55,000 volumes and more than 2000 microfilm items, and subscribes to more than 300 periodicals.

Environment: The 75-acre campus, located in a rural area 80 miles from Richmond, has been entered in the *National Register of Historic Places*. Its 30 buildings include a gymnasium, a dining hall, and 4 dormitories.

Student Life: Virginia residents make up 70% of the student body. Eighty-eight percent of the students live on campus. Dormitories are single-sex. Ninety-nine percent of the students are black. Most students are not members of the Episcopal Church. Alcohol is prohibited on campus.

Organizations: Four percent of the students belong to 1 of 3 fraternities and 3 sororities with chapters on campus. Other campus activities include a choir, art and science clubs, and publications.

Sports: The college participates on an intercollegiate level in 5 sports. Intramural sports also are offered.

Handicapped: About 25% of the campus is accessible to handicapped students. Special facilities include wheelchair ramps, special parking, elevators, and specially equipped rest rooms.

Graduates: About 20% of the freshmen drop out, and 60% remain to graduate. About 20% of the graduates pursue advanced degrees; 1% enter dental school, 1% enter medical school, and 1% enter law school.

Services: Students receive the following services free: tutoring or remedial instruction, health care, placement aid, and career counseling.

Programs of Study: The college offers the B.A., B.S., and B.S.Ed. degrees. Bachelor's degrees are offered in the following subjects: BUSINESS (business administration, business education, office administration), EDUCATION (elementary), ENGLISH (English), MATH AND SCIENCES (biology, mathematics), SOCIAL SCIENCES (government/political science, history, social sciences, sociology).

Required: Students must take a general-education program that includes courses in humanities, social science, natural sciences and mathematics, and physical education.

Special: The college offers a general-studies degree. Additional minors are offered in accounting, chemistry, and economics. Nonmajor preprofessional programs are avalailable in law, ministry, and the health professions.

Honors: Alpha Kappa Mu has a chapter on campus.

Admissions: Eighty percent of those who applied were accepted for the 1981–82 freshman class. Of those who enrolled, 9% ranked in the top fifth of their high school class and 20% ranked in the top two-fifths. Applicants should have completed 16 Carnegie units at an accredited high school, have an average of at least 2.5, and rank in the top 75% of their class. The college admits students on the basis of high school record, class rank, and SAT scores. Other important considerations are advanced placement or honors courses, recommendations, extracurricular activities, personality, and leadership record.

Procedure: The SAT is required and should be taken in December, January, or March of the senior year. Application deadlines are open. The college uses the rolling admissions procedure. There is a $10 application fee.

Special: The CRDA is observed.

Transfer: For a recent year, 40 students applied, 19 were accepted, and 15 enrolled. Transfers are accepted for all classes except the senior class. D grades do not transfer. Students must complete at least 30 hours at the college of the 120 required for a bachelor's degree.

Visiting: Guides are available for informal visits by prospective students, and regularly scheduled orientations are conducted. Visitors may sit in on classes and stay overnight at the school. The director of admissions should be contacted for arrangements.

Financial Aid: About 95% of all students receive aid. Freshman scholarships, state and federal grants and loans, and CWS are available. The average freshman aid package in 1981–82 totaled $4000. Saint Paul's is a member of the CSS; the FAF is required. The aid application deadline is July 1.

Foreign Students: Three percent of the full-time students come from foreign countries. Special counseling is provided for these students.

Admissions: Applicants must take the SAT. No English proficiency exams are required.

Procedure: Application deadlines are open; students are admitted in the fall and spring. They must submit the report of a physical examination and provide evidence of funds adequate to cover 1 year. They also must deposit enough funds with the college to pay their passage back home. Health insurance is required, and is available through the college for a fee.

Admissions Contact: L. Robert Parker, Director of Admissions and Registrar.

SHENANDOAH COLLEGE AND CONSERVATORY OF MUSIC
Winchester, Virginia 22601   (703) 667-8714   D-1

F/T: 245M, 440W	Faculty: 85; IIB, — — $
P/T: 45M, 90W	Ph.D.'s: n/av
Grad: 61M, 30W	S/F Ratio: 8 to 1
Year: sems, ss	Tuition: $4190
Appl: open	R and B: $2400
1016 applied 786 accepted	458 enrolled
SAT: 440V 480M ACT: 21	COMPETITIVE

Shenandoah College and Conservatory of Music is a four-year private liberal arts institution affiliated with the United Methodist Church. It has 4 divisions: Liberal Arts and Sciences, Allied Health, Business Administration, and Music. Its library contains 800,000 volumes and 1600 microfilm items, and subscribes to 350 periodicals.

Environment: The suburban campus is located a mile from Winchester. Dormitories are available.

Student Life: About 60% of the students live on campus. Twenty-four percent of the students are Catholic, 46% Protestant, and 10% Jewish. Twelve percent of the students are minority-group members. College housing is single-sex; there are visiting privileges. Students may keep cars on campus.

Organizations: About 20% of the men belong to 1 of 3 fraternities on campus, and 25% of the women belong to 1 of 3 sororities. Campus activities include student government, drama, music ensembles, publications, special-interest clubs, and service organizations.

Sports: The college participates in 1 intercollegiate sport for both men and women. There are 6 intramural sports for both men and women.

Handicapped: The entire campus is accessible to physically handicapped students. Facilities include wheelchair ramps, special parking areas, elevators, specially equipped rest rooms, and lowered drinking fountains and telephones.

Graduates: Eight percent of the freshmen drop out by the end of their first year. Thirty-eight percent remain to graduate. About 40% of the graduates pursue advanced degrees.

Services: Free services for students include health care, placement, career and psychological counseling, tutoring, and remedial instruction. Placement services also are available to graduates.

Programs of Study: The college confers the B.A., B.S., B.M., and B.M.T. degrees. Associate and master's programs are also offered. Bachelor's degrees are offered in the following subjects: BUSINESS (business administration), EDUCATION (elementary), ENGLISH (English), FINE AND PERFORMING ARTS (dance, music—applied, music—church, music—composition, music—jazz studies, music—piano accompaniment, music—piano pedagogy, music—piano technology, music—theater, music—therapy, music education, theater/dramatics), HEALTH SCIENCES (nursing, respiratory therapy), MATH AND SCIENCES (mathematics), PHILOSOPHY (religion), SOCIAL SCIENCES (history, psychology).

Admissions: About 77% of those who applied were accepted for the 1981–82 freshman class. Candidates should have completed 16 Carnegie units and should have a GPA of at least 2.0. An audition is required of applicants to the conservatory.

Procedure: Applicants must take the SAT or ACT. Application deadlines are open. Notification is made on a rolling basis. A $20 fee is required.

Special: Early decision and early and deferred admissions plans are offered. AP and CLEP credit is accepted.

Transfer: A C average is required. D grades transfer. Application deadlines are the same as those for freshman applicants.

Visiting: Visits can be arranged through the admissions office. Guides are provided. Students may sit in on classes. Visits are best scheduled for the regular Information Day Programs.

Financial Aid: Seventy-two percent of the students receive financial aid. Forty-two percent work part-time on campus. Scholarships are given for academic, musical, and athletic talent. CWS programs, grants, NDSL, BEOG, and bank loans also are available. The college is a member of CSS. Aid applicants should submit the FAF and the college's own application by April 1.

Foreign Students: No special services are available for students from foreign countries.

Admissions: Foreign students must score 500 or above on the TOEFL.

Procedure: For information on application procedures, the admissions office should be contacted.

Admissions Contact: Dwight D. Moore, Director of Admissions.

SWEET BRIAR COLLEGE
Sweet Briar, Virginia 24595   (804) 381-5548   D-3

F/T: 1M, 668W	Faculty: 64; IIB, + + $
P/T: 3M, 19W	Ph.D.'s: 90%
Grad: none	S/F Ratio: 8 to 1
Year: 4-1-4	Tuition: $6010
Appl: Mar. 1	R and B: $2000
611 applied 475 accepted	230 enrolled
SAT: 500V 500M	COMPETITIVE

Sweet Briar College, founded in 1901, is an independent residential college for women. Its library contains 170,000 volumes, and subscribes to 850 periodicals.

Environment: The 3300-acre campus is located in a rural area in the foothills of the Blue Ridge Mountains, 12 miles north of Lynchburg and 165 miles from Washington, D.C. Eight dormitories and 2 houses accommodate 700 students. Special areas of the campus have been designated for ecological studies. The campus includes recently constructed riding and swimming facilities.

Student Life: About 20% of the students are from Virginia, and about 50% come from public schools. Almost all students live on campus. Students live under an honor system. College housing is single-sex; there are visiting privileges. Students may keep cars on campus.

Organizations: There are no sororities on campus. Cultural activities include movies and lecture series. Many students serve as volunteers for public and private welfare agencies. Several skiing, outdoor recreation, and historic areas are nearby. Social life is augmented by men's colleges in the area, including Washington and Lee, Virginia Military Institute, the University of Virginia, and Hampden-Sydney.

Sports: The college fields intercollegiate teams for women in 9 sports. There is one intramural sport available for women.

Handicapped: Special facilities for handicapped students include elevators and specially equipped rest rooms. Special class scheduling can be arranged. No students with visual or hearing impairments are enrolled, but the college has provided tutoring for such students in the past.

Graduates: Twenty percent of the freshmen drop out during their first year. About 50% of the freshmen remain to graduate. Forty percent of the graduates pursue advanced degrees, and 34% of them do so immediately after graduation. One percent of the graduates enter medical school and 2% enter law school. Seventy-five percent of the graduates begin careers in business and industry.

Services: Health care, placement, career and psychological counseling, tutoring, and remedial instruction are provided free to students. Placement services also are available to alumni. Tutoring is also available on a fee basis.

Programs of Study: The college confers the B.A. degree. Bachelor's degrees are offered in the following subjects: ENGLISH (English, creative writing), FINE AND PERFORMING ARTS (art history, music, music in culture, studio art, theater/dramatics), LANGUAGES (French, French studies, German, German studies, Greek/Latin, Italian, Italian studies, Spanish), MATH AND SCIENCES (biochemistry, biology, chemistry, mathematics, mathematical physics, mathematical science, physics), PHILOSOPHY (classics, philosophy, religion), SOCIAL SCIENCES (anthropology, economics, government/political science, history, international relations, political economics, psychology, sociology). Prelaw, premedicine, business, and education courses are offered. Programs are also available in arts management, business management, American studies, Asian studies, European studies, and environmental studies. A dual degree program is also available. About 56% of the degrees conferred are in social sciences, 13% in math and sciences, 11% in economics, and 20% in fine and performing arts.

Required: Students must complete 1 unit each in English, social sciences, social studies, and non-Western studies, and 2 units each in physical education, literature or the arts, and math or science. All students also must demonstrate proficiency in a foreign language.

Special: Programs abroad include junior years in France and at St. Andrew's University in Scotland, and other opportunities in countries including Spain, Italy, Germany, and England. Each department offers independent study and, during the winter term, intensive courses ranging from meteorology to theater workshop. Student-teaching is offered in the campus nursery and kindergarten and in the Amherst County public schools. There are 3-2 combination degree programs in business with the University of Virginia, in engineering with the

932 VIRGINIA

Georgia Institute of Technology, and a dual engineering degree with Columbia University. Students may design their own majors.

Honors: The Theta Chapter of Phi Beta Kappa is represented on campus. All departments offer independent study under tutorial direction to qualified students. An honors program and merit scholarships are also available.

Admissions: About 78% of those who applied for admission to the 1981–82 freshman class were accepted. The SAT scores of those who enrolled were as follows: Verbal—49% below 500, 35% between 500 and 599, 5% between 600 and 700, and 1% above 700; Math—49% below 500, 43% between 500 and 599, 8% between 600 and 700, and 0% above 700. Applicants must have completed at least 16 high school units. Admissions officers consider, in descending order of importance, grades, recommendations by high school officials, SAT and AT scores, the application essay, advanced placement or honors courses, impressions made during a personal interview, leadership record, and extracurricular activities.

Procedure: Applicants must take the SAT and 3 ATs, including English Composition. An interview is preferred but not required. Application deadlines are March 1 (fall), December 1 (winter), and January 1 (spring). Applicants are notified after February 15 as decisions are made. The application fee is $20.

Special: Early decision and early and deferred admissions plans are available. Early decision applicants are notified by December 1. CLEP and AP credit is accepted.

Transfer: For fall 1981, 62 students applied, 42 were accepted, and 19 enrolled. Transfer students are accepted for all classes. A 2.5 GPA is required. D grades do not transfer. Students must spend at least 2 years at the college and earn 19 of the 38 course credits needed to receive a bachelor's degree. Application deadlines are August 15 (fall), December 1 (winter), and January 1 (spring).

Visiting: Orientation sessions for prospective students are scheduled regularly. Visitors attend classes, meet students and faculty members, stay overnight in the dormitories, and are interviewed by admissions officers. Informal visits also may be scheduled from 8:30 A.M. to 4 P.M. on Mondays through Fridays during the school year. Guides are provided. Visitors may sit in on classes and stay overnight at the school. The admissions office should be contacted for arrangements.

Financial Aid: About 65% of the students receive aid. Forty percent work part-time on campus. Average aid awarded to freshmen from all sources is $4700. Loans are available from the federal government, the college, and local banks. A deferred tuition payment plan is offered. The college is a member of CSS. Aid applicants must file the FAF and the college's aid application. Deadlines are March 1 (fall), December 1 (winter), and January 1 (spring).

Foreign Students: Four percent of the full-time students come from foreign countries. The college offers these students special counseling and special organizations.

Admissions: Foreign students must score 500 or above on the TOEFL. They must take the college entrance examination offered by their own country.

Procedure: The application deadlines are March 1 (fall), December 1 (winter), and January 1 (spring). Foreign students must present proof of health. They must also carry health insurance, which is available through the college for a fee.

Admissions Contact: Terry Scarborough, Director of Admissions.

UNIVERSITY OF RICHMOND E–3
Richmond, Virginia 23173 (804) 285-6262

F/T: 1372M, 1097W	Faculty: 200; IIA, +$
P/T: 13M, 44W	Ph.D.'s: 80%
Grad: 458M, 285W	S/F Ratio: 13 to 1
Year: sems, ss	Tuition: $4845
Appl: Feb. 15	R and B: $1815–$2020
3198 applied	1752 accepted 719 enrolled
SAT: 513V 552M	VERY COMPETITIVE

University of Richmond, founded in 1830, is a private institution affiliated with the Baptist Church. The university has 6 schools and colleges: Richmond College for men, Westhampton College for women, the Robins School of Business, the T.C. Williams School of Law, the University College, and the Graduate School. The library contains 341,645 volumes, 8662 microfilm items, 22,500 art slides, and 5000 music scores, and subscribes to 2373 periodicals.

Environment: The 350-acre wooded campus, built around a lake, is located in suburban Richmond. The 27 buildings of Gothic architecture include dormitories and on-campus apartments. Sports facilities are contained in the $10-million Robins Center.

Student Life: About 30% of the students are Virginia residents. Sixty-six percent are public school graduates. Eighty-five percent of the students live on campus. Seven percent of the students are minority-group members. University housing is single-sex; there are visiting privileges. Drinking is permitted on specified areas of the campus. All students may keep cars at the university.

Organizations: About 45% of the men belong to 1 of 11 national fraternities; there are no sororities on campus. Activities include dances, receptions, art shows, concerts, debates, recitals, films, and plays. Campus organizations include a band, a chorus, a glee club, publications, student government, and religious groups for members of the major faiths.

Sports: The university fields intercollegiate teams in 13 sports for men and 9 for women. There are 12 intramural sports for men and 10 for women.

Handicapped: Most of the campus is inaccessible to physically handicapped students. Facilities include specially equipped rest rooms and lowered drinking fountains. No students with impaired vision or hearing were registered recently.

Graduates: Sixteen percent of the freshmen drop out by the end of their first year. Seventy-five percent go on to graduate. Of those who graduate, about 34% seek advanced degrees, including 11% who enter medical school, fewer than 1% dental school, and 11% law school.

Services: Free services provided to students include health care (only to dorm students), career and psychological counseling, placement (available to students and alumni), and tutoring.

Programs of Study: The university confers the B.A., B.S., and B.M. degrees. Master's degrees are also offered. Bachelor's degrees are offered in the following subjects: AREA STUDIES (American, criminal justice, Russian, urban, women's), BUSINESS (accounting, business administration), EDUCATION (early childhood, elementary, health/physical), ENGLISH (English, journalism, speech), FINE AND PERFORMING ARTS (art, art history, music, music education, studio art, theater/dramatics), LANGUAGES (French, Greek/Latin, Italian, Spanish), MATH AND SCIENCES (biology, chemistry, mathematics, physics), PHILOSOPHY (classics, philosophy, religion), SOCIAL SCIENCES (economics, government/political science, history, psychology, sociology). Preprofessional training is offered in dentistry, law, medicine, and pharmacy. About 33% of the undergraduate degrees are conferred in business and 25% in social sciences.

Required: Most courses in the first 2 years are required; the aim is to give students a broad cultural background. All students must take 4 semesters of physical education.

Special: Summer study abroad and a general studies major are available. Students may design their own majors.

Honors: Twenty-three honor societies including Phi Beta Kappa, Omicron Delta Kappa, and Mortar Board have chapters on campus. Departmental honors programs are offered in English, history, French, German, Spanish, music, philosophy, political science, religion, and sociology. There is a University Honors Program for students selected from those who scored a combined total of at least 1200 on the SATs and ranked in the top 10% of their high school class. Distribution requirements are waived for participants.

Admissions: About 55% of those who applied for admission to the 1981–82 freshman class were accepted. The SAT scores of those who enrolled were as follows: Verbal—47% below 500, 41% between 500 and 599, 9% between 600 and 700, and 1% above 700; Math—17% below 500, 57% between 500 and 599, 22% between 600 and 700, and 1% above 700. Applicants should have completed 16 Carnegie units with at least a C average at an accredited high school. They should rank in the top third of their class. The university also considers the high school's reputation and the applicant's extracurricular activities, leadership potential, and advanced placement or honors courses. Some preference is given to children of alumni.

Procedure: Applicants must take the SAT and 3 ATs, including English Composition and Mathematics Level I or II. Application deadlines are February 15 (fall), December 1 (spring), and May 1 (summer). The application fee is $25.

Special: Early decision and early and deferred admissions plans are available. AP and CLEP credit is accepted.

Transfer: For fall 1981, 237 students applied, 83 were accepted, and 45 enrolled. They must have at least a C average to be considered and spend at least 60 hours, in residence, out of the 120 needed to receive a bachelor's degree. Application deadlines are February 15 (fall) and December 1 (spring).

Visiting: Informal visits to campus can be arranged with the admissions office for weekdays, 8:30 A.M. to 5 P.M. Guides are provided.

Visitors may sit in on classes and may stay overnight on campus on Monday through Thursday nights.

Financial Aid: Fifty percent of the students receive financial aid. Thirty percent work part-time on campus. Loans are available through government, university, and private sources. The college is a member of CSS. The FAF and the university's own financial aid form are required. The application deadline is March 15.

Foreign Students: Fewer than 1% of the full-time students come from foreign countries. The university offers these students special counseling.

Admissions: Foreign students must score 550 or above on the TOEFL. No college entrance examination is required.

Procedure: The application deadlines are February 15 (fall), December 1 (spring), and May 1 (summer). Foreign students must present proof of funds adequate to cover 4 years of study. They must also carry health insurance.

Admissions Contact: Thomas N. Pollard, Director of Admissions.

UNIVERSITY OF VIRGINIA D-3
Charlottesville, Virginia 22903   (804) 924-7751

F/T: 5614M, 5438W	Faculty: 1570; I, +$
P/T: none	Ph.D.'s: 90%
Grad: 3231M, 2123W	S/F Ratio: 11 to 1
Year: sems, ss	Tuition: $1130 ($2630)
Appl: Feb. 1	R and B: $2150
11,564 applied	4329 accepted 2574 enrolled
SAT: 570V 630M	**HIGHLY COMPETITIVE**

Since its founding in 1819, the University of Virginia has borne the impress of its creator, Thomas Jefferson, who planned its early curriculum as well as its grounds and original buildings. Today, in addition to its main campus, the university includes Clinch Valley College in Wise. The university's academic divisions are the College of Arts and Sciences and the professional undergraduate Schools of Applied Science, Architecture, Commerce, Education, Engineering, and Nursing. The library contains 2.5 million volumes and 9 million microfilm items, and subscribes to 5000 periodicals.

Environment: Located in a suburban setting 70 miles from Richmond and 110 miles from Washington, D.C., the 2000-acre campus is of prime historic interest. Newcomb Hall is the center of extracurricular, social, and cultural life on campus. A new reader's library opened in 1982. Living facilities include dormitories, on-campus apartments, and married student housing.

Student Life: Sixty-five percent of the students come from Virginia, and 35% come from other states. Seventy-four percent of entering freshmen come from public schools. Students entering directly from secondary school are required to live in a residence house during their first year. Forty-three percent of the students live on campus. Seven percent of the students are minority-group members. University housing is coed. First-year students may not have cars during the fall semester.

Organizations: Extracurricular activities include literary, political, athletic, forensic, musical, dramatic, and scientific groups, in addition to student publications, a concert band, a glee club, an orchestra, a choir, various hobby clubs, and academic clubs. Religious organizations and counselors exist for students of all major faiths. About 37% of the men belong to 1 of 33 national social fraternities; 25% of the women belong to 1 of 14 national sororities.

Sports: The university competes in 14 sports on an intercollegiate level for men and 13 for women. There are 16 intramural sports for both men and women.

Handicapped: Approximately 75% of the campus is accessible to wheelchair-bound students. Special facilities include wheelchair ramps, parking areas, elevators, lowered drinking fountains and telephones, and specially equpped rest rooms. There are special advisors available.

Graduates: The freshman dropout rate is 2%; 88% remain to graduate. Seventy percent of graduates pursue graduate study.

Services: Students receive the following services free of charge: placement, health care, psychological counseling, career counseling, and tutoring. Tutoring is also available on a fee basis. In addition, a resume service, an interview service, and internships are available.

Programs of Study: The university confers the B.A., B.S., B.S.C., B.Arch.Hist., Bachelor of City Planning, B.S.Ed., and B.S.N. degrees. Master's and doctoral degrees are also offered. Bachelor's degrees are offered in the following subjects: AREA STUDIES (Asian, Black/Afro-American, Latin American, Russian), BUSINESS (accounting, finance, management, management information systems, marketing), EDUCATION (elementary, health/physical, secondary, special), ENGLISH (English, speech), FINE AND PERFORMING ARTS (art history, music, studio art, theater/dramatics), HEALTH SCIENCES (audiology, nursing, speech therapy), LANGUAGES (French, German, Greek/Latin, Russian, Spanish), MATH AND SCIENCES (astronomy, astrophysics, biology, chemistry, ecology/environmental science, mathematics, physics), PHILOSOPHY (classics, philosophy, religion), PREPROFESSIONAL (architecture, engineering—aerospace, engineering—applied mathematics, engineering—chemical, engineering—civil, engineering—computer science, engineering—electrical, engineering—mechanical, engineering—nuclear, engineering science, engineering systems), SOCIAL SCIENCES (anthropology, economics, government/political science, history, international relations, psychology, sociology).

Required: Students in the College of Arts and Sciences must take English composition, demonstrate proficiency in a foreign language, and satisfy area requirements in the humanities, the social sciences, and mathematics or laboratory science.

Special: Student-designed majors are available. Students may take advantage of the various year-abroad programs supervised by American Colleges. A 3-year bachelor's degree program is available.

Honors: Practically all the national honor societies have chapters on campus. The Echols Scholars Program, begun in 1960, is designed to meet the needs of exceptional students in the College of Arts and Sciences. The Rodman Scholars Program is available to students in the School of Engineering. Honors theses may be done.

Admissions: Thirty-seven percent of those who applied were accepted for the 1981-82 freshman class. Of those who enrolled, the SAT scores were as follows: Verbal—18% below 500, 42% between 500 and 599, 33% between 600 and 700, and 7% above 700; Math—12% below 500, 28% between 500 and 599; 45% between 600 and 700, and 15% above 700. The majority of successful candidates rank in the upper quintile. All candidates must be graduates of accredited secondary schools and have completed 16 academic units. Preference is given to Virginia residents. The following factors are considered most heavily in the admissions decision: secondary school curriculum and record, evaluation by school officials, SAT and AT scores, extracurricular activities, leadership record, and special talents. Some preference is also given to children of alumni.

Procedure: All candidates must present the SAT and 3 ATs (English Composition, Mathematics Level I or II, and 1 in a foreign language or natural science). Tests should be taken between March of the junior year and December or January of the senior year. Application deadlines are February 1 (fall) and May 1 (summer). Admissions notification is made on April 1. There is a $20 application fee.

Special: Early decision candidates should apply by November 1; notification is made on November 15. These candidates should take the SAT no later than July. AP credit is accepted.

Transfer: For fall 1981, of the 1759 applicants, 724 were accepted, and 503 enrolled. The university requires a 3.0 GPA from transfer students. D grades do not transfer. All students must spend 2 years at the university and earn 54 to 60 of the 120 to 132 semester hours needed for a bachelor's degree. Applications for the fall semester are due by February 1.

Visiting: There are regularly scheduled orientations for prospective students. The office of admissions should be contacted for schedules. Guides are available for informal visits.

Financial Aid: Thirty-two percent of all students receive financial aid, which is available in the form of scholarships, loans, and part-time employment. About 650 freshman scholarships are awarded each year. The average aid to freshmen is $2200. Loans are available from the federal government, the state government, local banks, funds administered by the university, and private funds. The university is a member of CSS. The FAF is required. The aid application deadline is February 15 (fall).

Foreign Students: About 2% of the full-time students come from foreign countries. The university offers these students special counseling and special organizations.

Admissions: Foreign students must score 600 or above on the TOEFL. They must also take the SAT and ATs (English Composition, Math Level I or II, and 1 science or 1 language).

Procedure: The application deadline is February 1 (fall). Foreign students must present proof of health. They must also provide proof of funds adequate to cover each year of study. They must carry health insurance, which is available through the university for a fee.

Admissions Contact: John T. Casteen, III, Dean of Admissions.

VIRGINIA COMMONWEALTH UNIVERSITY   E-3
Richmond, Virginia 23284   (804) 257-0366

F/T: 3346M, 5460W   Faculty: 1607; I, − −$
P/T: 886M, 1224W   Ph.D.'s: 70%
Grad: 1665M, 2559W   S/F Ratio: 16 to 1
Year: sems, ss   Tuition: $1216 ($2186)
Appl: Aug. 1   R and B: $1860–2280
4493 applied   3580 accepted   1787 enrolled
SAT: 438V 462M   **COMPETITIVE**

Virginia Commonwealth University, founded in 1838, is a state-controlled liberal arts college that also offers professional and technical instruction. Its library contains 579,836 volumes and 98,534 microfilm items, and subscribes to 8547 periodicals.

Environment: The 54-acre campus is located in metropolitan Richmond, 100 miles from Washington, D.C. The college's 98 buildings include dormitories and on- and off-campus apartments.

Student Life: About 92% of the students come from Virginia. Ninety percent of the freshmen are from public schools. Eighteen percent of the students live on campus. About 16% of the students are minority-group members. University housing is both single-sex and coed. There are visiting privileges. Students may keep cars on campus. Day-care services are available to all students, faculty, and staff for a fee. Drinking is permitted in specified areas of the campus in compliance with state law.

Organizations: Two percent of the students belong to a fraternity or sorority. About 150 student organizations, including a radio station and a student government, are available on campus. Additional recreational opportunities can be found in the city of Richmond. Washington, Virginia Beach, and the Blue Ridge Mountains are within 100 miles.

Sports: The university participates intercollegiately in 8 sports for men and 6 for women. There are 10 intramural sports for men and 7 for women.

Handicapped: Special facilities for physically handicapped students include wheelchair ramps, elevators, and specially equipped rest rooms. The university also provides special housing features for the visually and hearing-impaired.

Graduates: Thirty-six percent of the freshmen remain to graduate. About 77% enter careers in business and industry.

Services: The university provides students with free placement, career and psychological counseling, tutoring, and remedial instruction. Placement services also are available to alumni. Health care is available on a fee basis.

Programs of Study: The university confers the B.A., B.S., B.G.S., B.F.A., B.Mus., and B.Mus.Ed. degrees. Associate, master's, and doctoral degrees also are available. Bachelor's degrees are offered in the following subjects: AREA STUDIES (urban), BUSINESS (accounting, business administration, business education, computer science, economics, marketing, office administration), EDUCATION (early childhood, elementary, health/physical, secondary, special), ENGLISH (English, literature), FINE AND PERFORMING ARTS (art, art education, art history, communication arts and design, crafts, dance, fashion design, interior design, mass communications, music—church, music—composition and theory, music—history and literature, music education, sculpture, studio art, theater/dramatics), HEALTH SCIENCES (dental hygiene, health care management, medical records, medical technology, nursing, occupational therapy, physical therapy, radiation science, radiology technology), LANGUAGES (French, Spanish), MATH AND SCIENCES (biology, chemistry, interdisciplinary science, mathematics, physics), PHILOSOPHY (philosophy, religion), PREPROFESSIONAL (pharmacy, social work), SOCIAL SCIENCES (administration of justice, anthropology, economics, government/political science, history, psychology, recreation, rehabilitation services, sociology). About 22% of the degrees are conferred in social sciences, 18% in health sciences, 16% in business, and 15% in fine and performing arts.

Special: A dual degree program is offered in physics and engineering. A D.D.S.W. and law degree is offered through T. C. Williams Law School, University of Richmond. Students may study abroad in Israel, Jordan, Egypt, France, Canada, Germany, Italy, Mexico, and Spain. A general studies major is available.

Honors: Eight national honor societies have chapters on campus. The English department also offers an honors program.

Admissions: About 80% of those who applied were accepted for the 1981–82 freshman class. The SAT scores of those who enrolled were as follows: Verbal—79% below 500, 18% between 500 and 599, 3% between 600 and 700, and 0% above 700; Math—69% below 500, 26% between 500 and 599, 5% between 600 and 700, and 0% above 700. Candidates should have completed at least 16 Carnegie units and earned at least a C average. Recommendations from high school officials and extracurricular activities also are considered. Applicants to the School of Arts must submit a portfolio.

Procedure: The SAT is required. Application deadlines are August 1 (fall) and December 1 (spring). New students are admitted to both semesters. Admissions decisions are made on a rolling basis. The application fee is $10.

Special: An early admissions plan permits exceptional high school students to enroll full time. The university also enrolls about 100 disadvantaged/minority students each year through the federally funded Special Services Program. AP and CLEP credit is accepted.

Transfer: For fall 1981, 2204 students applied, 1763 were accepted, and 1032 enrolled. Applicants must have a GPA of at least 2.0. Those with fewer than 30 semester hours must submit SAT scores. D grades do not transfer. Students must be at the university for at least 12 months and must complete 30 semester hours of those required for a bachelor's degree. The application deadlines are the same as those for freshman admissions.

Visiting: Information sessions and guided tours begin at the admissions office each Monday, Wednesday, and Friday at 11:30 A.M. Guides also are provided for informal visits. Visitors may sit in on classes but may not stay overnight at the school. The Office of Enrollment Services will handle arrangements.

Financial Aid: Seventy-five percent of the students receive financial aid. Sixty percent work part-time on campus. Average aid to freshmen from all sources is $1100. Scholarships, federal and state loans, and work-study programs are available. The university is a member of CSS and requires aid applicants to submit the FAF and the University Aid Form. The final deadline is May 1.

Foreign Students: About 9% of the full-time students come from foreign countries. The university offers these students special counseling and special organizations.

Admissions: Foreign students must score 550 or above on the TOEFL. No college entrance examination is required.

Procedure: The application deadlines are April 1 (fall) and October 1 (spring). Foreign students must present proof of funds adequate to cover 1 year of study. They must also carry health insurance, which is available through the university for a fee.

Admissions Contact: Richard Dremuk, Dirctor of Enrollment Services.

VIRGINIA INTERMONT COLLEGE   B-4
Bristol, Virginia 24201   (703) 669-6101

F/T: 123M, 470W   Faculty: 42; IV, − −$
P/T: 13M, 42W   Ph.D.'s: 30%
Grad: none   S/F Ratio: 14 to 1
Year: sems   Tuition: $3465
Appl: open   R and B: $2100
419 applied   390 accepted   298 enrolled
SAT or ACT: required   **COMPETITIVE**

Virginia Intermont College, founded in 1884, is a liberal arts institution affiliated with the Baptist Church. The library contains 55,979 volumes and 471 microfilm items, and subscribes to 403 periodicals.

Environment: The 18-acre campus is located in a residential section of Bristol, a small city of 40,000 within a metropolitan area of 300,000. A 124-acre rural tract is used for riding programs. Four dormitories house 500 students.

Student Life: About 37% of the students come from Virginia. More than 20 other states are also represented. Approximately 73% live on campus. Twenty percent of the students are Catholic, 75% Protestant, and 1% Jewish. Nine percent of the students are minority-group members. College housing is single-sex. There are limited visiting privileges. Students may keep cars on campus. Drinking is forbidden on campus. Women dormitory residents without key privileges observe a curfew.

Organizations: There are no fraternities or sororities on campus. The student government and special-interest clubs provide social and cultural entertainment. The city of Bristol and nearby outdoor recreation areas, including Bristol Caverns and South Holston Dam and Lake, provide off-campus activities. The students activities program provides mixers, dances, parties, picnics, camping trips, skiing weekends, concerts, coffee house entertainment, tours, and both modern and classic films. Students from area colleges are invited to share many of these events. There are six colleges within a 25-mile radius, and trips to other schools are popular.

Sports: The college participates in 1 intercollegiate sport for men and 4 sports for women. There are 4 intramural sports for men and 9 for women.

Handicapped: There are no facilities for the physically handicapped; and 20% of the campus is accessible to such students.

Graduates: About 30% of the freshmen drop out during the first year, and 55% remain to graduate. Ten percent of the graduates seek advanced degrees, including 1% who enter law school. Thirty-five percent pursue careers in business and industry.

Services: Health care, tutoring, remedial instruction, and psychological and career counseling are available to students. Free placement services, including a credentials service, are available to graduates as well as students.

Programs of Study: The college offers the B.A. degree. Associate degrees are also granted. Bachelor's degrees are offered in the following subjects: BUSINESS (business administration, computer science, management), EDUCATION (early childhood, elementary, secondary), ENGLISH (creative writing, English, journalism), FINE AND PERFORMING ARTS (art, art education, dance, film/photography, music, music education, studio art), HEALTH SCIENCES (medical technology), MATH AND SCIENCES (biology), PREPROFESSIONAL (law, medicine, pharmacy, social work, veterinary), SOCIAL SCIENCES (psychology, sociology). About 20% of degrees conferred are in business, 20% in fine and performing arts, and 16% in education.

Special: A 3-1 cooperative program in medical technology and a general studies degree are available. Students are allowed to design their own majors.

Honors: Three honor societies have chapters on campus.

Admissions: About 93% of those who applied were accepted for the 1981–82 freshman class. The SAT scores of those who enrolled were as follows: Verbal—65% below 500, 20% between 500 and 599, 10% between 600 and 700, and 5% above 700; Math—65% below 500, 20% between 500 and 599, 10% between 600 and 700, and 5% above 700. On the ACT, 60% scored below 21, 15% between 21 and 23, 13% between 24 and 25, 7% between 26 and 28, and 5% above 28. Candidates should have completed 15 Carnegie units with an average of at least C. The college also considers the applicant's personality, recommendations by high school officials, special talents, advanced placement or honors courses, and impressions made during the recommended personal interview.

Procedure: Either the SAT or the ACT is required. Application deadlines are open. Freshmen are admitted in the fall, spring, and summer terms. Admissions decisions are made on a rolling basis. A $15 fee should accompany all applications.

Special: Early and deferred admissions plans are available. AP and CLEP credit is accepted.

Transfer: For fall 1981, 107 students applied, 95 were accepted, and 75 enrolled. A 2.0 GPA is necessary. D grades transfer. Students must complete, in residence, the last 30 hours of the 124 needed to receive a bachelor's degree. Application deadlines are open.

Visiting: Informal visits can be arranged on weekdays through the admissions office. Visitors may sit in on classes and spend the night on campus.

Financial Aid: About 67% of all students receive aid. Forty percent work part-time on campus. Average aid awarded to freshmen from all sources is $3000. Scholarships, loans, and CWS contracts are available. The college is a member of CSS and requires that the FAF be submitted. Application deadlines are open.

Foreign Students: Four percent of the full-time students come from foreign countries. The college offers these students an intensive English course, special counseling, and special organizations.

Admissions: Foreign students must take the TOEFL. No college entrance examination is required.

Procedure: Application deadlines are open. Foreign students must present proof of health. They must also provide proof of adequate funds.

Admissions Contact: Thomas M. Hughes, Dean of Admissions.

VIRGINIA 935

VIRGINIA MILITARY INSTITUTE D–3
Lexington, Virginia 24450 (703) 463-6211

F/T: 1300M	Faculty: 105; IIB, ++$
P/T: none	Ph.D.'s: 72%
Grad: none	S/F Ratio: 13 to 1
Year: sems, ss	Tuition: $2145 ($3465)
Appl: Apr. 1	R and B: $1435
1281 applied 780 accepted	443 enrolled
SAT: 500V 548M	COMPETITIVE+

Virginia Military Institute, founded in 1839, is a state-operated military college that offers training in the liberal arts, engineering, and sciences. Its library contains 259,466 volumes and 6065 microfilm items, and subscribes to 914 periodicals.

Environment: The 134-acre campus is located in a small rural town 50 miles from Roanoke. The 23 campus buildings are situated around a parade ground. All cadets live in a barracks.

Student Life: About 50% of the students are from Virginia. More than 50% come from public schools. About 5% of the students are minority-group members. There are no visiting privileges in the barracks. Only seniors may keep cars on campus. Cadets are organized into a military regiment. The cadets administer the honor system, standards of conduct, and class privileges through elected officers. Drinking on campus is prohibited, and cadets may not marry while attending VMI.

Organizations: VMI has no fraternities, but there are more than 70 clubs and organizations. Activities include publications and social events.

Sports: The institute fields intercollegiate teams in 16 sports, and intramurals in 11 sports.

Handicapped: There are no special facilities for handicapped students.

Graduates: About 10% of the students drop out by the end of their freshman year. Sixty-six percent remain to graduate. Sixty percent of the graduates eventually pursue advanced degrees, including 3% who enter medical school, 2% dental school, and 5% law school. Eighty percent enter careers in business and industry.

Services: Free services provided to students include health care, placement, career and psychological counseling, tutoring, and remedial instruction. Placement services also are available to graduates.

Programs of Study: The institute confers the B.A. and B.S. degrees. Bachelor's degrees are offered in the following subjects: ENGLISH (English), LANGUAGES (French, German, Russian, Spanish), MATH AND SCIENCES (biology, chemistry, mathematics, physics), PREPROFESSIONAL (engineering—civil, engineering—electrical, engineering—mechanical), SOCIAL SCIENCES (economics, history). About 50% of all degrees conferred are in engineering, and 38% in liberal arts.

Required: All students must take courses in chemistry, English, history, mathematics, physical education, aerospace studies, and military or naval science.

Special: Study abroad is available.

Honors: Honor societies in economics, engineering, and physics have chapters on campus. The biology, English, and history departments offer honors programs.

Admissions: About 61% of those who applied for admission to the 1981–82 freshman class were accepted. SAT scores of those who enrolled were as follows: Verbal—47% below 500, 40% between 500 and 599, 12% between 600 and 700, and 1% above 700; Math—34% below 500, 50% between 500 and 599, 23% between 600 and 700, and 3% above 700. Applicants must have graduated from accredited high schools and completed 16 Carnegie units with an average of at least C. The institute prefers that applicants have a B+ average and rank in the top half of their class. Admissions officers also consider advanced placement or honors courses, leadership, extracurricular activities, impressions made during an interview, recommendations by school officials, and evidence of special talents. Special consideration is given to sons of alumni.

Procedure: The SAT is required and should be taken in March or May of the junior year or in November of December of the senior year. New students may enter only in the fall. Applications should be sent by April 1. Admissions decisions are made on a rolling basis. The application fee is $15.

Special: A deferred admissions plan is available. AP credit is accepted.

936 VIRGINIA

Transfer: For fall 1981, 40 students applied, 30 were accepted, and 29 enrolled. Applicants must have at least a 2.0 average and be in good standing at their last school. D grades do not transfer. Students must complete, in residence, 72 of the 144 credits needed for a bachelor's degree. The application deadline is April 1 (fall).

Visiting: Weekend orientations are scheduled regularly for accepted applicants. Interviews and tours are conducted Monday through Friday from 8:30 A.M. to 4:00 P.M. and on Saturdays from 8:30 A.M. to noon. Visits should be scheduled in fall, winter, or spring with the director of admissions.

Financial Aid: Fifty-five percent of the students receive financial aid. Ten percent work part-time on campus. The average award to freshmen from all sources is $1000. Loans are also available. The institute is a member of CSS. The FAF is required and applications should be filed by February 1.

Foreign Students: Two percent of the full-time students come from foreign countries. The institute offers these students special counseling and special organizations.

Admissions: Foreign students must score 500 or above on the TOEFL. They must also take the SAT.

Procedure: The application deadline is April 1 (fall). Foreign students must present proof of health. They must also present proof of funds adequate to cover 4 years of study. They must carry health insurance, which is available through the institute for a fee.

Admissions Contact: Col. William J. Buchanan, Director of Admissions.

VIRGINIA POLYTECHNIC INSTITUTE AND STATE UNIVERSITY C-3
Blacksburg, Virginia 24061 (703) 961-6267

F/T: 12,559M, 7705W
P/T: 745M, 575W
Grad: 2234M, 1136W
Year: qtrs, ss
Appl: Jan. 1
12,008 applied 6684 accepted 3973 enrolled
SAT: 500V 570M
Faculty: 1923; I, av$
Ph.D.'s: 80%
S/F Ratio: 11 to 1
Tuition: $1095 ($2160)
R and B: $1425
VERY COMPETITIVE

Virginia Polytechnic Institute and State University, a coeducational, state-supported institution founded in 1872, has undergraduate colleges of agriculture, architecture, arts and science, business, education, engineering, and home economics. The library contains more than 1.4 million volumes and 1.8 million microfilm items, and subscribes to 12,466 periodicals.

Environment: The 2300-acre campus is located in a rural setting 40 miles from Roanoke. Among the more than 88 buildings are dormitories that house about 8400 students.

Student Life: About 80% of the students are Virginia residents. Ninety percent have graduated from public schools. Thirty-nine percent of the students live on campus. Freshmen are required to live in dormitories unless married, over 21, veterans, or living with close relatives. University housing is both single-sex and coed. There are visiting privileges in single-sex housing. Students may keep cars on campus. Student conduct is governed by an honor system. All students taking ROTC are members of the Corps of Cadets, wear uniforms, and live under military discipline.

Organizations: About 10% of the men belong to 1 of 30 fraternities on campus; 7% of the women belong to 1 of 10 sororities. Several mountain hunting and fishing areas are near the campus.

Sports: The university fields intercollegiate teams in 12 sports for men and 8 for women. There are 18 intramural sports for men and 13 for women.

Handicapped: About 70% of the campus is accessible to physically handicapped students. Facilities include wheelchair ramps, special parking areas, and elevators. Special class scheduling and counselors also are available. The university's Office of Equal Opportunity/Affirmative Action provides for the needs of handicapped students on an individual basis. Twelve students with impaired vision or hearing were enrolled at the university in a recent year.

Graduates: About 7% of the freshmen drop out by the end of their first year. Fifty-eight percent eventually graduate. About 21% of the graduates pursue advanced degrees, including 3% who enter medical school, 1% who enter dental school, and 2% who enter law school. Sixty percent of the graduates begin careers in business and industry.

Services: Placement, career and psychological counseling, tutoring, and remedial instruction are provided free for students. Health care and tutoring are also availble on campus on a fee basis. Free placement services may also be used by graduates.

Programs of Study: The university confers the B.A., B.S., B.Arch., and B.Land.Arch. degrees. Master's, doctoral, and professional degrees are also available. Bachelor's degrees are offered in the following subjects: AREA STUDIES (urban), BUSINESS (accounting, business education, computer science, finance, management, marketing), EDUCATION (early childhood, elementary, health/physical, industrial, secondary, special), ENGLISH (English), FINE AND PERFORMING ARTS (art, art education, music, music education, theater/dramatics), LANGUAGES (French, German, Spanish), MATH AND SCIENCES (biochemistry, biology, chemistry, geology, mathematics, physical sciences, physics, statistics), PHILOSOPHY (philosophy, religion), PREPROFESSIONAL (agriculture, architecture, dentistry, engineering, forestry, home economics, law, medicine, pharmacy, social work, veterinary), SOCIAL SCIENCES (economics, geography, government/political science, history, international relations, psychology, sociology). About 27% of the undergraduate degrees are conferred in engineering, 23% in business, and 25% in arts and sciences.

Required: All students must take courses in English, mathematics, social science, and physical science.

Special: The university offers cooperative education programs in many fields; student work in industry for alternate quarters during the sophomore and junior years. Students may study abroad and create their own majors.

Honors: Forty-one honor societies have chapters on campus. Honors courses are offered by the English, math, chemistry, biology, geology, philosophy, computer science, geography, history, political science, sociology, and engineering departments. To enroll, students must have ranked in the top 10% of their high school class and have scored a combined total of 1200 on the SAT and at least 550 on each section.

Admissions: About 56% of those who applied for admission to the 1981-82 freshman class were accepted. The SAT scores of those who enrolled were as follows: Verbal—49% below 500, 37% between 500 and 599, 12% between 600 and 700, and 1% above 700; Math—19% below 500, 42% between 500 and 599, 31% between 600 and 700, and 8% above 700. Applicants must have graduated from an accredited high school with at least 18 Carnegie units. Admissions officers consider high school record and class rank, SAT scores, advanced placement or honors courses, recommendations by school officials, extracurricular activities, leadership record, evidence of special talents, personality, and impressions made during an interview. Twenty percent of the freshman class may be composed of out-of-state students.

Procedure: The SAT is required and should be taken by December of the senior year. Application deadlines are January 1 (fall), November 1 (winter), and January 1 (spring and summer). Early decision candidates must apply by November 1 for fall admission and are notified by December 1. The application fee is $10.

Special: Early decision and early admissions plans are available.

Transfer: For fall 1981, 3213 students applied, 1714 were accepted, and 1001 enrolled. Applicants must meet freshman entrance requirements, have at least a 2.0 GPA, and be in good standing at their last school. D grades do not transfer. Preference is given to applicants from other Virginia colleges. Students must spend at least a year in residence and complete, at the institute, 45 of the last 60 quarter hours (180 to 235 quarter hours are needed to receive a bachelor's degree). Application deadlines are March 1 (fall), November 1 (winter), January 1 (spring), and March 1 (summer).

Visiting: Informal visits may be scheduled with the admissions office for Monday through Friday, 8 A.M. to 5 P.M. and most Saturdays 8:30 A.M. to noon. Guides are provided. Prospective students may sit in on classes and stay overnight at the school.

Financial Aid: About 65% of all students receive aid through university-administered scholarships, loans, grants, and cooperative programs. Fifteen percent work part-time on campus. The average aid per freshman totals $1650. More than 500 scholarships are available to freshmen each year, but most are restricted to state residents. Freshman scholarships are awarded on the basis of academic achievement and character as well as need. The university participates in NDSL and CWS programs. The university is a member of CSS. The FAF is required. The application deadline is March 1.

Foreign Students: Three percent of the full-time students come from foreign countries. The institute offers these students special counseling and special organizations.

Admissions: Foreign students must score 600 or above on the TOEFL or show evidence of the successful completion of a full academic year of English at an accredited college or university. They must also take the SAT and ATs (English Composition and Math Level I or II).

Procedure: Application deadlines are January 1 (fall, spring, and summer) and November 1 (winter). Foreign students must present the results of a physical examination reported by a licensed physician. They must also present proof of funds adequate to cover 1 academic year.

Admissions Contact: Archie G. Phlegar, Director of Admissions.

VIRGINIA STATE UNIVERSITY E-3
Petersburg, Virginia 23803 (804) 520-6542

F/T: 1588M, 2010W Faculty: 218; IIA, av$
P/T: 258M, 377W Ph.D.'s: 44%
Grad: 126M, 205W S/F Ratio: 21 to 1
Year: sems, ss Tuition: $979 ($1554)
Appl: May 1 R and B: $2054
1900 applied 1655 accepted 1044 enrolled
SAT: required LESS COMPETITIVE

Virginia State University, established in 1882, is a combination land-grant, liberal arts, and education college. The library contains 197,357 volumes and 232,000 microtexts, and subscribes to 1300 periodicals.

Environment: The 210-acre main campus is located in a rural area 25 miles from Richmond. The 59 buildings include 10 dorms. The student village complex houses 490 students. The university also owns a 436-acre farm.

Student Life: About 80% of the students are from Virginia, and 46% live on campus. Ninety-four percent of the students are minority-group members. University housing is single-sex; there are visiting privileges. Students must secure permission to keep cars on campus.

Organizations: Numerous fraternities and sororities have chapters on campus. Literary, music, religious, and cultural activities are provided at the university. There is a student government, and students are represented on faculty committees.

Sports: The university fields intercollegiate teams in 8 sports for men and 3 sports for women. There are 7 intramural sports for men and 6 for women.

Handicapped: About 90% of the campus is accessible to physically handicapped students. Facilities include wheelchair ramps, special parking areas, elevators, lowered drinking fountains, and specially equipped rest rooms. One special counselor and one assistant counselor also are available.

Services: The university provides tutoring, remedial instruction, and career counseling free to students. Free job placement services are available to students and graduates. Health care and psychological counseling are also available on campus for a fee.

Programs of Study: The university confers the B.A., B.S., B.F.A., B.Mus., and Bachelor of Individualized Studies degrees. Master's programs are also available. Bachelor's degrees are offered in the following subjects: BUSINESS (accounting, business administration, business education, computer science, food industry management, food marketing, hotel and restaurant management, public administration), EDCUCATION (elementary, health/physical, industrial, special), ENGLISH (English), FINE AND PERFORMING ARTS (art education, commercial art, music, music education), HEALTH SCIENCES (nursing), LANGUAGES (French, Spanish), MATH AND SCIENCES (biology, chemistry, earth science, geology, mathematics, physics, statistics), PREPROFESSIONAL (agriculture, home economics, social work, veterinary), SOCIAL SCIENCES (economics, government/political science, history, psychology, sociology).

Required: All students must take 48 credits of general education courses in humanities, social sciences, natural sciences, and health/physical education. A GPA of C or better is required for graduation.

Special: Dual degrees are offered in mathematics and engineering in cooperation with Old Dominion University. All departments have work experience programs.

Honors: Sixteen honor societies have chapters on campus. All departments invite qualified students to participate in honors programs.

Admissions: About 87% of those who applied were accepted for the 1981-82 freshman class. Candidates should have 16 Carnegie units and a satisfactory grade average.

Procedure: Applicants must take the SAT. Applications should be submitted by May 1 (fall) and October 1 (spring). Applications will be considered if received after these dates. New students are admitted to fall, spring, and summer terms. The university follows a rolling admissions policy. The application fee is $10.

Transfer: For fall 1981, 497 students applied, 421 were accepted, and 310 enrolled. Transfer applicants must be in good standing at accredited institutions and have at least a 2.0 GPA. Transcripts of college work must be submitted; those with fewer than 30 semester hours also must submit a high school transcript and SAT scores. Students must study at the university for 1 year and complete 30 of the 120 to 128 semester hours needed for a bachelor's degree. Application deadlines are the same as those for freshman applicants.

Visiting: During the school year, informal visits to the campus can be arranged weekdays from 8 A.M. to 4 P.M. through the director of admissions. Guides are provided. Visitors may sit in on classes but may not stay overnight at the school.

Financial Aid: About 95% of all students receive aid. Scholarships, loans, and work-study jobs are available. Twenty percent work part-time on campus. Average aid to freshmen from all sources is $1858. Need is the main criterion for aid. The university is a member of CSS. The FAF is required. The application deadlines are April 30 (fall) and October 1 (spring).

Foreign Students: Two percent of the full-time students come from foreign countries. The university offers these students special counseling and special organizations.

Admissions: Foreign students must score 500 or above on the TOEFL. They must also take the SAT.

Procedure: Application deadlines are May 1 (fall) and September 1 (spring). Foreign students must present a health record form signed by a physician. They must also present proof of funds adequate to cover at least 2 years. They must carry health insurance.

Admissions Contact: Edward L. Smith, Director of Admissions.

VIRGINIA UNION UNIVERSITY E-3
Richmond, Virginia 23220 (804) 257-5600

F/T: 1218M&W Faculty: n/av; IIA, --$
P/T: 75M&W Ph.D.'s: 38%
Grad: 91M&W S/F Ratio: 15 to 1
Year: sems, ss Tuition: $2640
Appl: Aug. 1 R and B: $1756
1041 applied 830 accepted 376 enrolled
SAT: required COMPETITIVE

Virginia Union University, established in 1865, is affiliated with the Baptist Church and offers undergraduate programs in the liberal arts and sciences, education, and business. The library contains 130,000 volumes and 11,000 microfilm items, and subscribes to 600 periodicals.

Environment: The 55-acre campus is located in central Richmond and has 18 buildings, including 7 residence halls. There also are facilities for commuting students.

Student Life: About 55% of the students come from Virginia. Eighty-five percent are graduates of public schools. Half live on campus in the single-sex dorms. About 98% of the students are black; the majority are Baptists.

Organizations: About 5% of the students belong to sororities and fraternities. Other campus activities include religious organizations, music groups, special-interest clubs, drama, films, lectures, concerts, and social events.

Sports: The university fields intercollegiate teams in 4 sports. Six intramural sports are available.

Graduates: About 40% of the freshmen drop out, and 55% remain to graduate. About 20% of the graduates go on for further study.

Services: Health care, tutoring or remedial instruction, career counseling, and placement aid are offered.

Programs of Study: The university confers the A.B. and B.S. degrees. Master's degrees also are awarded. Bachelor's degrees are offered in the following subjects: AREA STUDIES (urban), BUSINESS (accounting, business administration, business education, finance, secretarial and office administration), EDUCATION (early childhood, elementary, recreation, secondary, special), ENGLISH (English, journalism), FINE AND PERFORMING ARTS (music, music education), LANGUAGES (French), MATH AND SCIENCES (biology, chemistry, mathematics), PHILOSOPHY (philosophy, religion), PREPROFESSIONAL (social work), SOCIAL SCIENCES (government/political science, history, psychology, sociology).

Required: The general-education requirement includes courses in religion, English, mathematics, science, social science, a foreign language, and physical education.

Special: Work-study, a general studies degree, exchange programs, and a dual degree program in engineering are offered. Additional minors are offered in computer science and gerontology.

VIRGINIA

Honors: An honors program is offered.

Admissions: About 80% of those who applied were accepted for the 1981–82 freshman class. A 2.0 high school average is required. The GED is accepted. Special consideration is given to disadvantaged students. Children of alumni are given some preference.

Procedure: The SAT is required. Application deadlines are August 1 (fall) and December 1 (spring). Notification is made on a rolling basis. There is a $10 application fee.

Special: Early and deferred admissions plans are offered. CLEP credit is accepted.

Transfer: About 60 transfer students enroll yearly. Good academic standing is required. D grades do not transfer. Students must complete at least 1 year in residence and earn 124 credits to receive a bachelor's degree.

Visiting: Campus tours with student guides can be arranged. Visitors may sit in on classes.

Financial Aid: About 95% of the students receive aid. The university participates in federal programs such as NDSL, BEOG/SEOG, and CWS. Other loans and freshman scholarships are offered. The average freshman aid package in 1981–82 totaled $4250. The FAF is required and should be filed by June 1 for priority consideration.

Foreign Students: Five percent of the full-time students come from foreign countries. The university offers these students special counseling and special organizations.

Admissions: Applicants must score at least 450 on the TOEFL. They also must take the SAT.

Procedure: Application deadlines are the same as those for American students. Foreign students must present a completed health form and show evidence of funds adequate to cover 1 year.

Admissions Contact: James Gunnell, Director of Institutional Planning and Research.

VIRGINIA WESLEYAN COLLEGE F-4
Norfolk, Virginia 23502 (804) 461-3232

F/T: 350M, 453W	Faculty: 46; IIB, +$
P/T: 6M, 17W	Ph.D.'s: 80%
Grad: none	S/F Ratio: 16 to 1
Year: sems, ss	Tuition: $4115
Appl: open	R and B: $2150
657 applied	470 accepted	253 enrolled
SAT: 477V 515M		COMPETITIVE

Virginia Wesleyan College, a Methodist-affiliated liberal arts institution, was founded in 1961. Its library contains 65,000 volumes.

Environment: The college is located in a suburban setting. The campus is based on the academic village concept, patterned on Thomas Jefferson's adaptation of the Oxford and Cambridge plans. Each of the 4 villages includes 4 dormitories, 2 classrooms, and a dining hall, all connected by glassed-in galleries. A centrally located science building, chapel, fine arts center, gymnasium, greenhouses, and other facilities serve all 4 villages. Living facilities also include off-campus apartments and fraternity houses.

Student Life: About 79% of the students are from Virginia. Fifty-four percent of the students live on campus. Twenty-five percent of the students are Catholic, 56% Protestant, and 1% Jewish. About 8% of the students are minority-group members. Campus housing is both single-sex and coed. There are visiting privileges in the single-sex housing. Drinking is prohibited on campus. Cars are permitted.

Organizations: About 10% of the students belong to 1 of 4 fraternities and 2 sororities on campus. Activities include publications, glee club, drama, and student government. Students have voting representatives on most administration committees. Cultural and recreational activities are available in Norfolk. Williamsburg, Yorktown, Jamestown, and Virginia Beach are within an hour's drive.

Sports: The college fields intercollegiate teams in 6 sports for men and 5 for women. There are 5 intramural sports for men and 4 for women.

Handicapped: The entire campus is accessible to handicapped students. Facilities include wheelchair ramps, special parking, elevators, and lowered telephones. Special class scheduling is available. No students with impaired hearing or vision were registered recently.

Graduates: About 26% of the freshmen drop out by the end of their first year. Thirty-five percent remain to graduate. One percent of the graduates go on to medical or dental schools.

Services: Placement, tutoring, remedial instruction, career counseling, and psychological counseling are provided free to students. Health care is available on a fee basis.

Programs of Study: The college offers the B.A. degree. Bachelor's degrees are offered in the following subjects: AREA STUDIES (American, urban), BUSINESS (business administration, computer science, management), EDUCATION (elementary, health/physical, secondary), ENGLISH (English), FINE AND PERFORMING ARTS (art, art education, music, music education, radio/TV, theater/dramatics), LANGUAGES (French, Spanish), MATH AND SCIENCES (biology, chemistry, ecology/environmental science, mathematics, marine biology, oceanography), PHILOSOPHY (philosophy, religion), PRE-PROFESSIONAL (dentistry, engineering, forestry, law, medicine, ministry, pharmacy, social work, veterinary), SOCIAL SCIENCES (government/political science, history, international relations, psychology, social sciences, sociology). About 38% of the degrees conferred are in social sciences, 13% in education, and 11% in business.

Required: All students must earn 6 credits of English, 6 credits of philosphy and religion, and 6 credits of science and mathematics.

Special: The college offers study abroad in Eastern Europe and Asia through the Association of Colleges for International-Intercultural Studies. Students are allowed to design their own majors.

Honors: The college has a chapter of the National Honor Society.

Admissions: About 72% of those who applied for admission to the 1981–82 freshman class were accepted. Of those who enrolled in a recent freshman class, 35% scored above 500 on each section of the SAT. Applicants should have completed at least 16 Carnegie units at an accredited high school and rank in the upper three-fourths of their class. They should have scored at least 400 on each section of the SAT.

Procedure: The SAT is required and should be taken in May of the junior year or December or January of the senior year. The deadlines for applications are open. Notification is made on a rolling basis. The application fee is $10.

Special: Early and deferred admissions plans are available. AP credit is accepted.

Transfer: For fall 1981, 186 students applied, 138 were accepted, and 89 enrolled. Applicants must have at least a 2.0 GPA. D grades do not transfer. Students must earn, at the college, 30 credits overall, and 15 in their major, of the 124 needed to earn a bachelor's degree. Application deadlines are open.

Visiting: Orientations for prospective students are scheduled regularly. Visitors tour the campus and have an interview with an admissions officer. Informal visits also can be arranged for weekdays, 9 A.M. to 4 P.M., with the admissions office. Guides are provided. Visitors may sit in on classes.

Financial Aid: Eighty-nine percent of the students receive financial aid. Campus employment and loans from federal and state governments, local banks, and private sources also are available. There is an automatic scholarship program for those scoring 1000 total on the SAT and who are in the top third of their high-school class. The average scholarship granted to a freshman is $1000. The college is a member of CSS. Applicants must file the FAF. The college's deadline for aid applications is open.

Foreign Students: Four percent of the full-time students come from foreign countries. The college offers these students an intensive English program and special counseling.

Admissions: Foreign students must take the TOEFL. No college entrance examination is required.

Procedure: Application deadlines are open. Foreign students must present proof of health. They must also present proof of adequate funds.

Admissions Contact: Frank S. Badger, Director of Admissions.

WASHINGTON AND LEE UNIVERSITY D-3
Lexington, Virginia 24450 (703) 463-9111

F/T: 1311M	Faculty: 150; IIB, ++$
P/T: 9M, 12W	Ph.D.'s: 82%
Grad: 247M, 100W	S/F Ratio: 11 to 1
Year: 4-4-1	Tuition: $4855
Appl: Feb. 15	R and B: $1925
1369 applied	768 accepted	388 enrolled
SAT (mean): 560V 590M		VERY COMPETITIVE+

Washington and Lee University was founded in 1749. Its library contains 390,000 volumes and 100,869 microfilm items, and subscribes to 1200 periodicals.

Environment: The 305-acre campus is located in a rural Shenandoah Valley town of 7500 people, 50 miles north of Roanoke and 135 miles from Richmond. The campus is a national historic landmark. Living facilities include dormitories, fraternity houses, married student housing, and on- and off-campus apartments.

Student Life: About 25% of the students come from Virginia. Sixty-one percent are from public schools. Fifty percent of the students live on campus. Nineteen percent are Catholic, 48% Protestant, and 2% Jewish. One percent of the students are minority-group members. University housing is single-sex; there are visiting privileges. Students may keep cars on campus. The university is run on the honor system.

Organizations: About 60% of the students belong to 1 of the 17 national fraternities on campus. Extracurricular activities include religious organizations, student government, and music, drama, and other special-interest groups. Skiing and other outdoor recreation areas are located nearby.

Sports: The university fields intercollegiate teams in 13 sports for men. There are 12 intramural sports for men.

Handicapped: About 70% of the campus is accessible to physically handicapped students. Facilities include wheelchair ramps and elevators. Special class scheduling is available. Fewer than 1% of the students have visual impairments, and there are no special facilities for them. No special counselors are available.

Graduates: About 5% of the freshmen drop out by the end of their first year. Eighty percent remain to graduate. Of the graduates, 70% pursue advanced degrees; 8% enter medical school, 1% dental school, and 15% law school. Forty-five percent pursue careers in business and industry.

Services: Health care, placement, career and psychological counseling, tutoring, and remedial instruction are provided free to students. Placement services also are available to graduates.

Programs of Study: The university confers the B.A. and B.S. degrees. The law school offers the J.D. degree. Bachelor's degrees are offered in the following subjects: AREA STUDIES (Asian), BUSINESS (accounting, business administration, public policy), ENGLISH (English, journalism), FINE AND PERFORMING ARTS (art, theater/dramatics), LANGUAGES (French, German, Greek/Latin, Romance languages, Spanish), MATH AND SCIENCES (biology, chemistry, chemistry-engineering, geology, natural sciences and mathematics, physics, physics-engineering), PHILOSOPHY (classics, philosophy, religion), SOCIAL SCIENCES (anthropology, economics, government/political science, history, psychology, sociology). About 26% of the undergraduate degrees are conferred in social sciences, 17% in business, and 19% in math and sciences.

Required: Each student must take courses from 4 academic divisions.

Special: A 3-2 or 4-2 engineering program is offered in cooperation with Columbia University, Rensselaer Polytechnic Institute, and Washington University of St. Louis. Combination degree programs also are available in other fields, including law and forestry. Study-abroad programs are offered. Students may design their own majors.

Honors: Eight national honor societies, including Phi Beta Kappa and Omicron Delta Kappa, have campus chapters. Most departments offer honors programs that involve 6 to 12 credits of independent work.

Admissions: About 56% of those who applied for admission to the 1981–82 freshman class were accepted. The SAT scores of those who enrolled were as follows: Verbal—8% below 500, 51% between 500 and 599, 34% between 600 and 700, and 7% above 700: Math—17% below 500, 57% between 500 and 599, 24% between 600 and 700, and 2% above 700. Applicants must have completed at least 16 Carnegie units. Besides grades, class rank, and test scores, admissions officers consider advanced placement or honors courses, recommendations by high school officials, leadership, and extracurricular activities.

Procedure: Applicants must take the SAT and 3 ATs, including English Composition. They should be taken between March of the junior year and January of the senior year. Early decision candidates should complete them by the July following the junior year. The application deadline is February 15 (fall). The application fee is $20.

Special: Early decision and deferred admissions plans are available. AP credit is accepted.

Transfer: For fall 1981, 88 students applied, 36 were accepted, and 24 enrolled. Applicants must have at least a 2.0 GPA. D grades do not transfer. Students must complete, in residence, 60 of the 127 credits needed to receive a bachelor's degree. Applications are due July 15 (fall) and November 15 (winter).

Visiting: Informal visits to campus can be arranged for Monday through Friday, 9 A.M. to 4 P.M., with the admissions office. Guides are provided. Prospective students may sit in on classes and, if they give sufficient notice, stay at the school.

Financial Aid: Twenty-five percent of the students receive financial aid. Twenty percent work part-time on campus. Average aid to freshmen from all sources is $4500. Scholarships, loans, grants, and part-time jobs are available. The university is a member of CSS. Applications, accompanied by the FAF, must be submitted by February 15.

Foreign Students: One percent of the full-time students come from foreign countries. The university offers these students special counseling and special organizations.

Admissions: Foreign students must score 600 or above on the TOEFL. No college entrance examination is required.

Procedure: The application deadline is February 15 (fall). Foreign students must present proof of a physical examination. They must also present proof of funds adequate to cover 1 year of study.

Admissions Contact: William M. Hartog, Director of Admissions.

WASHINGTON

CENTRAL WASHINGTON UNIVERSITY D–2
Ellensburg, Washington 98926 (509) 963-1211

F/T: 2500M, 2600W Faculty: 290; IIA, ++$
P/T: 300M, 560W Ph.D.'s: 82%
Grad: 650M, 1330W S/F Ratio: 18 to 1
Year: qtrs, ss Tuition: $942 ($3210)
Appl: open R and B: $2000
3432 applied 3087 accepted 1055 enrolled
SAT, ACT, or WPCT: required COMPETITIVE

Central Washington University is a state-supported institution which offers programs in liberal arts and teacher education. Its library contains 302,380 volumes and 527,671 reels of microfilm and microfiche.

Environment: The 350-acre campus is located in a rural area 100 miles east of Seattle. There are 52 nonresidential facilities for instruction and support. Living facilities include dormitories, on- and off-campus apartments, and married student housing.

Student Life: About 95% of the students are from the West and Northwest, with 90% coming from Washington. Single freshmen and sophomores must live in dormitories if under the age of 21. Half of all students live in dormitories. About 12% of the students are minority-group members. Campus housing is coed and single-sex; there are visiting privileges. Students may keep cars on campus.

Organizations: There are no fraternities or sororities on campus. Social groups organize activities and cultural events for all students. Popular recreational activities include skiing, river floating, hiking, and dances.

Sports: The university fields 11 intercollegiate teams for men and 8 for women. There are 8 intramural sports for men and 7 for women.

Handicapped: Special facilities for the physically handicapped are lowered drinking fountains, specially equipped rest rooms, designated parking, elevators, wheelchair ramps, and tactile room numbering. Over 90% of the campus is accessible to these students.

Graduates: The freshman dropout rate is 20%; 55% remain to graduate. Of the graduates, 35% continue their education on a higher level: 2% enter medical school, 4% enter law school, and 2% enter dental school. About 25% of the graduates enter careers in business and industry.

Services: Free health care, tutoring, remedial instruction, career and psychological counseling, and job placement services are offered to students.

Programs of Study: The university confers the B.A., B.S., and B.A.Ed. degrees. Master's programs are also available. Bachelor's degrees are offered in the following subjects: AREA STUDIES (ethnic), BUSINESS (accounting, administrative office management, business administration, business economics, business education, economics operation analysis, executive secretary, fashion merchandising, finance, management, marketing), EDUCATION (community health, distributive, early childhood, elementary, health/physical, industrial, secondary, special), ENGLISH (English, mass media, speech), FINE

940 WASHINGTON

AND PERFORMING ARTS (art, art education, graphic design, music, music education, theater/dramatics), HEALTH SCIENCES (allied health science, food science and nutrition, medical technology, occupational health and safety, paramedics, speech pathology and audiology), LANGUAGES (bilingual studies, French, German, Spanish), MATH AND SCIENCES (biology, botany, chemistry, earth science, geology, mathematics, natural sciences, physics, zoology), PHILOSOPHY (philosophy, religion), PREPROFESSIONAL (construction management technology, electronics industrial technology, flight officer, home economics, industrial distribution technology, industrial supervision, leisure services, manufacturing engineering technology, public relations), SOCIAL SCIENCES (anthropology, economics, family and consumer studies, geography, government/political science, history, law and justice, psychology, social services, sociology, studies in aging). Twenty-two percent of the degrees conferred are in business.

Required: All students must take 65 hours in basic and breadth requirements.

Special: Student-designed majors, independent study, and study abroad are possible.

Honors: The Douglas Honors College is offered to superior students. There are 5 national honorary societies represented on campus. Many departments have honors programs.

Admissions: About 90% of those who applied for the 1981-82 freshman class were accepted. Candidates should be graduates of accredited high schools and have a 2.5 G.P.A. Recommendations by school officials, impressions made during an interview, and advanced placement or honors courses are also considered important.

Procedure: The Washington Pre-College Test is required except for out-of-state students, who may substitute the SAT or ACT. The tests are used only for counseling and placement. There are no application deadlines. Freshmen are admitted for all terms. There is no application fee. The university uses a rolling admissions plan.

Special: A deferred admissions plan is available. AP credit is granted.

Transfer: For fall 1981, 1986 transfer students applied, 1562 were accepted, and 1103 enrolled. Transfer applicants need a 2.0 GPA; college-level grades receive credit. Students must earn, at the university, at least 45 of the 180 credits required to earn a bachelor's degree. There are no application deadlines.

Visiting: There are regularly scheduled orientations, and arrangements can be made through the admissions office for guided tours of the campus, classroom visits, and overnight stays.

Financial Aid: Scholarships are available, as are loans from the federal government, local banks, the university, and private funds. Many college-assigned jobs are also offered. About 25% of all students receive some form of financial assistance. The FAF must be submitted. Application for aid must be in by March 1.

Foreign Students: About 1% of the students are from foreign countries. The university offers these students an intensive English program, special counseling, and special organizations.

Admissions: A score of 500 or above is required on the TOEFL; no further exams are required.

Procedure: Application deadlines are July 1 for fall, October 1 for winter, January 1 for spring, and April 1 for summer. Foreign students must complete the university's health form and must present proof of funds adequate to cover 1 year of study. Health insurance is required and is available through the university for a fee.

Admissions Contact: Bruce Bradberry, Director of Admissions.

CORNISH INSTITUTE
Seattle, Washington 98102   C-2   (206) 323-1400

F/T: 151M, 227W   Faculty: 15; IV, --$
P/T: 36M, 91W   Ph.D.'s: n/av
Grad: none   S/F Ratio: 8 to 1
Year: sems, ss   Tuition: $3750
Appl: open   R and B: n/app
359 applied   270 accepted
SAT or ACT: required   SPECIAL

The Cornish Institute, founded in 1914, is an independent nonresidential school for students aspiring to careers in dance, design, fine arts, music, or theater. The library contains 3500 volumes and subscribes to 200 periodicals.

Environment: The 8 buildings that make up the school, which is located in urban Seattle, house studios for ceramics, printmaking, sculpture, design, and dance, as well as the Cornish Theater and a woodshop. The institute's main buildings have been designated a historical landmark. There are no living facilities on campus.

Student Life: Over 65% of the students are residents of Washington. About 85% of the freshmen come from public schools. About 13% of the students are minority-group members. All students live off campus.

Organizations: There are no fraternities or sororities. Activity on campus centers around concerts, dance performances, and gallery openings.

Sports: There is 1 intramural sport for men and 1 for women.

Handicapped: There are lowered telephones, specially equipped rest rooms, wheelchair ramps, and special class scheduling for physically handicapped students, to whom about 30% of the campus is accessible.

Graduates: About 30% of the freshmen drop out during the first year; 30% remain to graduate. Of those who graduate, 20% go on to graduate study.

Services: Free career counseling, psychological counseling, and job placement services are provided. Remedial instruction is available for a fee.

Programs of Study: The institute confers the B.F.A. degree in dance, design, music, studio art, and theater. About 20% of the students major in music, 30% in fine arts, 20% in design, 15% in theater, and 15% in dance.

Required: Music students give juried auditions and fine arts students hold thesis shows before graduation. Allied arts courses are required of all students.

Special: Performing arts students may earn credit for performances and design students may receive credit for working in Seattle-area design studios.

Honors: The Phi Beta-Performing Arts honorary society is represented on campus.

Admissions: About 75% of those who applied were accepted for the 1981-82 freshman class. Candidates should be graduates of an accredited high school or present a GED certificate. The audition or portfolio review is the single most important criterion in admissions decisions; the institute looks primarily for evidence of artistic talent.

Procedure: A personal interview is required. Students should apply to 1 of the 5 departments. Preference is given to those who apply by March 28, although there are no formal application deadlines. Freshmen are admitted for the fall and spring terms. The final notification date is August 10. Applications for midyear entrance should be filed by December 20. There is a $20 application fee. The institute uses a rolling admissions plan.

Special: A deferred admissions plan and an early admissions plan are offered.

Transfer: For fall 1981, 270 transfer students applied and 203 were accepted. The deadlines for transfer applications are the same as those for freshmen. Grades of C or better transfer. Transfer students must present a portfolio review or have an audition. Students must earn, at the institute, at least 32 of the 128 credits necessary for a bachelor's degree.

Visiting: There are regularly scheduled orientations for prospective students.

Financial Aid: Freshman scholarship funds total $25,000; the institute administers $90,000 in federal loans to 20% of the student body. About 90% of those receiving aid have work contracts. The average financial aid package awarded to a freshman consists of a $1000 scholarship, a $1000 loan, and a $1500 work contract. About 60% of all students receive some form of financial assistance; 30% of the students work part-time on campus. The FAF is required. The deadline for financial aid applications is May 15.

Foreign Students: About 4% of the full-time students come from foreign countries. These students are offered an intensive English program, special counseling, and special organizations.

Admissions: A minimum score of 500 on the TOEFL is required; no further exams are required.

Procedure: Application deadlines are August 1 for fall and December 15 for spring. Foreign students must present proof of funds adequate to cover 1 year of study. Health insurance is available through the institute for a fee.

Admissions Contact: Lois Pittenger, Admissions Officer.

EASTERN WASHINGTON UNIVERSITY E-2
Cheney, Washington 99004 (509) 359-2397

F/T: 3146M, 3194W	Faculty: 376; IIA, +$
P/T: 151M, 226W	Ph.D.'s: 65%
Grad: 529M, 616W	S/F Ratio: 17 to 1
Year: qtrs, ss	Tuition: $867 ($2910)
Appl: open	R and B: $1905
3315 applied	2582 accepted 1175 enrolled
SAT, ACT: not required	COMPETITIVE

Eastern Washington University, founded in 1882, is a publicly supported college, with emphasis on liberal arts and education. The library contains 338,000 volumes and 300,000 microfilm items, and subscribes to 4700 periodicals.

Environment: The 335-acre campus is located in a rural area 16 miles from Spokane. There are dormitories for 1750 single students; 30 units are available for married students.

Student Life: Most of the students come from the immediate area; about 5% are from outside Washington. About 30% of the students live on campus. About 27% of the students are minority-group members. Campus housing is coed; students may keep cars on campus. Day-care services are available to all students, faculty, and staff.

Sports: The university fields 12 intercollegiate teams for men and 10 for women. There are 10 intramural sports for men and 11 for women.

Handicapped: There are full facilities for physically handicapped students, to whom the entire campus is accessible.

Graduates: About 10% of the freshmen drop out during their first year; 65% remain to graduate. Of those who graduate, 14% pursue advanced degrees; 1% enter medical school, and 1% enter law school. About 47% pursue careers in business and industry.

Services: The college offers free health care, tutoring, remedial instruction, career counseling, psychological counseling, and job placement services.

Programs of Study: The university offers the B.A., B.A.Ed., B.S., B.B.A., B.F.A., and B.S.N. degrees. Master's degrees are also offered. Bachelor's degrees are offered in the following subjects: AREA STUDIES (Asian, Black/Afro-American, Latin American, Russian), BUSINESS (accounting, business administration, business education, computer science, decision science, finance, information science, management, marketing, technology administration), EDUCATION (elementary, health/physical, industrial, recreation and leisure studies, secondary, special), ENGLISH (communication studies, creative writing, English, journalism, literature, speech, writing), FINE AND PERFORMING ARTS (art, art education, art history, film/photography, music, music composition, music education, music history, music literature, music performance, music theory, radio/TV, studio art, theater/dramatics), HEALTH SCIENCES (dental hygiene, health services administration, health education, medical technology, nursing, speech therapy), LANGUAGES (French, German, Russian, Spanish), MATH AND SCIENCES (biology, chemistry, earth science, geology, mathematics, natural sciences, physical sciences, physics), PHILOSOPHY (humanities, philosophy), PREPROFESSIONAL (forestry, home economics, law, occupational safety and health, social work), SOCIAL SCIENCES (anthropology, criminal justice, economics, geography, government/political science, history, international affairs, psychology and child development, public administration, social sciences, sociology, urban and regional planning). About 33% of degrees conferred are in business, 25% in education, and 15% in health sciences.

Special: Students are allowed to design their own majors. A general studies (no major) degree is offered, as is a program in electronics technology.

Admissions: About 78% of those who applied were accepted for the 1981–82 freshman class. Candidates should have a minimum 2.5 average and rank in the top half of their graduating class.

Procedure: The Washington Pre-College Test is required as a guidance tool; it may be taken upon arrival at the campus. Deadlines for applications are open. Freshmen are admitted for all terms. There is no application fee. The university follows a rolling admissions policy.

Special: A deferred admissions plan is offered. AP credit is accepted.

Transfer: For fall 1981, 1962 transfer students applied, 1506 were accepted, and 1270 enrolled. A 2.0 GPA is required. D grades will receive credit. All students must take 45 quarter credits (1 year) at the university, of the 180 quarter credits required to earn a bachelor's degree. Deadlines are open.

Visiting: There are no regularly scheduled orientation sessions. Prospective students can arrange informal visits through the admissions office during the week. Visitors may sit in on classes, tour the campus, and stay at the university. Overnight stays cost visitors $5.00 per person per night.

Financial Aid: Assistance in the form of loans, grants, and work is available. The priority application deadline for financial aid is March 15, but applications are accepted until funds are expended. The college is a member of the CSS; the FAF is required. The only criterion for financial aid is need. About 33% of all students receive some form of financial assistance; 18% of the students work part-time on campus. The average award to freshmen from all sources is $2325.

Foreign Students: About 4% of the full-time students are from foreign countries. The college offers these students an intensive English course, an intensive English program, special counseling, and organizations especially for foreign students.

Admissions: Foreign students must achieve a score of at least 500 on the TOEFL or a score of at least 80 on the University of Michigan Language Test.

Procedure: Application deadlines are August 1 for fall, October 1 for winter, January 1 for spring, and April 1 for summer. Foreign students must present proof of funds adequate to cover 1 year of study. Health insurance is available through the college.

Admissions Contact: Glenn Fehler, Director of Admissions.

THE EVERGREEN STATE COLLEGE B-3
Olympia, Washington 98505 (206) 866-6170

F/T: 1093M, 1190W	Faculty: 127; IV, ++$
P/T: 175M, 240W	Ph.D.'s: 66%
Grad: 40M, 28W	S/F Ratio: 20 to 1
Year: qtrs, ss	Tuition: $942 ($3210)
Appl: Sept. 1	R and B: $2300
716 applied	611 accepted 266 enrolled
SAT, ACT: not required	LESS COMPETITIVE

The Evergreen State College, founded in 1971, is a state-supported liberal arts college offering an innovative, interdisciplinary program. Its library contains 185,000 volumes and 43,734 microfilm items, and subscribes to 2500 periodicals.

Environment: The 1000-acre campus is located in a rural area 5 miles from Olympia. Living facilities include on-campus apartments and married student housing.

Student Life: About 80% of the students are residents of Washington. Thirty-seven percent of the students live on campus. About 7% of the students are minority-group members. College housing is coed. Students may keep cars on campus. Day-care services are available to all students, faculty, and staff; fees are based on income.

Organizations: There are no fraternities or sororities. Extracurricular activities include the student newspaper, radio station, drama group, ballet, and various student associations.

Sports: The college competes in 6 sports for men and 5 for women on the intercollegiate level and offers 13 intramural sports for both men and women.

Handicapped: Specially equipped rest rooms, special parking, elevators, and wheelchair ramps are provided for physically handicapped students. There are no hearing or visually impaired students currently enrolled.

Graduates: Five percent of the freshmen drop out by the end of their first year. Forty percent remain to graduate. About 10% of the students who graduate pursue graduate study; 4% enter medical school, and 5% law school.

Services: Free tutoring, remedial instruction, career counseling, psychological counseling, placement services, and health care are offered.

Programs of Study: The college confers the B.A. and B.S. degrees. Master's programs are also offered. Bachelor's degrees are offered in the following subjects: AREA STUDIES (American, Russian), BUSINESS (management), EDUCATION (early childhood, elementary, secondary), ENGLISH (English, literature), FINE AND PERFORMING ARTS (art, film/photography, music, radio/TV, studio art, theater/dramatics), LANGUAGES (French, Greek/Latin, Russian, Spanish), MATH AND SCIENCES (biochemistry, biology, botany, chemistry, ecology/environmental science, mathematics, natural sciences, physical sciences, physics), PHILOSOPHY (classics, humanities, philosophy), PREPROFESSIONAL (agriculture), SOCIAL SCIENCES (anthropology, economics, government/political science, history, psychology, social sciences).

Special: All work at the college is interdisciplinary, and the programs of study change annually. The college's credit-generating options include coordinated studies and contracted studies programs. Credits

942 WASHINGTON

may be earned through cooperative learning enterprises, specific projects, research, or mastering a specific specialty. Study abroad and internship programs are also available.

Admissions: About 85% of those who applied were accepted for the 1981-82 freshman class. Candidates should be graduates of an accredited high school and rank in the top half of their graduating class.

Procedure: A personal interview is not required, but it is recommended. The deadlines for application are September 1 (fall), December 1 (winter), and March 1 (spring). The college operates on a rolling admissions plan. There is a $15 application fee.

Special: The college offers early and deferred admissions plans. AP and CLEP credit is accepted.

Transfer: For fall 1981, 1265 students applied, 1089 were accepted, and 700 enrolled. Transfer applicants should have completed 15 quarter units with a 2.0 GPA. D grades are not acceptable. There is a 1-year residency requirement. Forty-five of the 180 required credits must be completed, at the college, to earn a bachelor's degree. Application deadlines are the same as those for freshmen.

Visiting: There is no regularly scheduled orientation session. Prospective students may sit in on classes, tour the campus and stay overnight by arrangement with the admissions office.

Financial Aid: Twenty percent of the students receive financial aid. Forty-five percent work part-time on campus. Average aid to freshmen from all sources is $1200. Competitive scholarships are available to new students only and are not renewable. The college administers federal loans, bank loan funds, and college loan funds. The college is not a member of the CSS. The FAF is accepted. The deadline for financial aid applications is April 15.

Foreign Students: Fewer than 1% of the full-time students come from foreign countries.

Admissions: Foreign students must score 500 or above on the TOEFL. No college entrance examination is required.

Procedure: The deadlines for application are September 1 (fall), December 1 (winter), and March 1 (spring). Foreign students must present proof of funds adequate to cover 1 academic year. They must also pay out-of-state tuition fees.

Admissions Contact: Arnaldo Rodriquez, Director of Admissions.

GONZAGA UNIVERSITY E-2
Spokane, Washington 99258 (509) 328-4220

F/T: 1113M, 805W Faculty: 157; n/av
P/T: 90M, 110W Ph.D.'s: 72%
Grad: 156M, 82W S/F Ratio: 17 to 1
Year: sems, ss Tuition: $4040
Appl: Aug. 15 R and B: $2100
1197 accepted 500 enrolled
SAT: 470V 500M ACT: 21 COMPETITIVE

Gonzaga University, established in 1887, is an independent Roman Catholic liberal arts institution with 4 undergraduate and 2 graduate colleges. Its library contains 250,000 volumes and 25,000 microfilm items, and subscribes to 1000 periodicals.

Environment: The 75-acre campus is in a wooded, residential area near mid-Spokane. There are 13 dormitories that accommodate 550 women and 640 men.

Student Life: About 34% of the students are residents of Washington. Approximately 50% of the entering freshmen come from public schools. Fifty-nine percent of the students are Catholic, and 30% are Protestant. Fifty-five percent of the students live on campus. About 8% of the students are minority-group members. Campus housing is coed and single-sex; there are visiting privileges. Students may keep cars on campus. Day-care services are available to students, faculty, and staff at a fee.

Organizations: There are no fraternities or sororities. The college sponsors many social and cultural activities.

Sports: The university fields 9 intercollegiate teams and 4 intramural teams.

Handicapped: Special parking, elevators, and wheelchair ramps are available to handicapped students.

Graduates: Fewer than 20% of the freshmen drop out during the first year; 50% remain to graduate. Of those, 65% pursue advanced degrees.

Services: Free health care, career counseling, job placement services, tutoring, and psychological counseling are available.

Programs of Study: The university confers the B.A., B.S., B.Ed., and B.B.A. degrees. Master's and doctoral programs are also offered. Bachelor's degrees are offered in the following subjects: AREA STUDIES (American, Italian), BUSINESS (accounting, business administration, business communications, business journalism, finance, international business, management, marketing), EDUCATION (elementary, secondary, special), ENGLISH (English, journalism, literature, speech), FINE AND PERFORMING ARTS (art, music, music education, radio/TV, studio art, theater/dramatics), HEALTH SCIENCES (medical technology, nursing, speech therapy), LANGUAGES (French, Greek/Latin, Italian, Spanish), MATH AND SCIENCES (biology, chemistry, ecology/environmental science, mathematics, physics), PHILOSOPHY (classics, humanities, philosophy, religion), PREPROFESSIONAL (dentistry, engineering, law, medicine), SOCIAL SCIENCES (criminal justice, economics, government/political science, history, psychology, sociology). The nursing program is open only to registered nurses who have graduated from associate degree and diploma institutions.

Required: All students must take the university core.

Special: A 5-year program of engineering and business leads to a B.S. in engineering and an M.B.A. in industrial management. Italian Studies requires 1 year of study at Gonzaga in Florence, Italy. Interdepartmental majors are also available. Students may spend their junior year studying abroad, but this is not offered as part of the regular curriculum.

Honors: Alpha Sigma Mu and the university honors program are open to qualified students.

Admissions: The SAT scores of those who enrolled in the 1981-82 freshman class were as follows: Verbal—61% below 500, 29% between 500 and 599, 9% between 600 and 700, and 1% above 700; Math—40% below 500, 41% between 500 and 599, 18% between 600 and 700, and 1% above 700. Candidates should have completed 16 Carnegie units and have a minimum 2.5 average.

Procedure: The SAT, ACT, or Washington Pre-College Test is acceptable and should be taken by January of the senior year. The application deadlines are August 15 (fall) and December 15 (spring). There is a $15 application fee. Notification is made on a rolling basis.

Special: Early decision, early admissions, and deferred admissions plans are available. AP and CLEP credit is accepted. PEP exams are also given credit.

Transfer: For fall 1981, 561 transfer students applied. A minimum G.P.A. of 2.5 is required. Grades of C or better transfer. There is a 1-year residency requirement; 128 credits are required to earn the bachelor's degree. Deadlines are the same as those for freshmen.

Visiting: The university has a visitation program; arrangements can be made through the admissions office during the week. Prospective students may sit in on classes, tour the campus, and stay overnight.

Financial Aid: Scholarship awards are based on need as established through the university's membership in the CSS. Average aid to freshmen is $2523. About 65% of all students receive some form of financial assistance; about 25% of the students work part-time on campus. Fifty departments have work-study programs. The FAF is required. The deadline for aid applications is March 15.

Foreign Students: About 10% of the full-time students come from foreign countries. The university offers these students an intensive English program, special counseling, and special organizations.

Admissions: Foreign students must score a minimum of 500 on the TOEFL or 80 on the University of Michigan Language Test; no further exams are required.

Procedure: Application deadlines are August 15 for fall, December 15 for spring, and June 15 for summer. Foreign students must present proof of adequate funds. Health insurance is available through the university.

Admissions Contact: Marian McDonnell Horton, Associate Director of Admissions.

HERITAGE COLLEGE D-3
Toppenish, Washington 98948 (509) 865-2244

F/T: 93M, 70W Faculty: 15; n/av
P/T: 173M, 165W Ph.D.'s: 35%
Grad: 10M, 16W S/F Ratio: 8 to 1
Year: sems, ss Tuition: $2850
Appl: open R and B: n/app
SAT or ACT: required LESS COMPETITIVE

Heritage College, founded in 1982, is an Ecumenical Christian institution offering undergraduate programs in education, nursing, business, and general studies as well as graduate programs in education. It has absorbed the 4-year liberal arts degree programs of Fort Wright College.

Environment: The main campus is located in a town of 6000 people in a rural area 20 miles from Yakima. Other campuses are located in Omak (the Paschal Sherman Indian School) and in Spokane (a special campus for foreign students). The Toppenish campus maintains no student housing facilities.

Student Life: Virtually all students come from Washington, and 90% are graduates of public schools. Seventy-five percent are members of minority groups, primarily Native American and Hispanic. Students may keep cars on campus. The college was in the process of establishing day-care services in 1982.

Organizations: Students may participate in the Business Club.

Sports: The college offers no organized sports programs.

Handicapped: The entire campus is accessible to handicapped students. Facilities include wheelchair ramps.

Graduates: About 25% of the students seek advanced degrees, and 25% begin careers in business and industry.

Services: Free placement aid and career counseling are offered. Fees are charged for tutoring and remedial instruction.

Programs of Study: The college awards bachelor's, associate, and master's degrees. Bachelor's degrees are offered in the following subjects: BUSINESS (business administration, management), EDUCATION (adult, early childhood, elementary, multicultural, secondary), ENGLISH (English), HEALTH SCIENCES (nursing). Forty percent of degrees are conferred in business, 25% in education, and 25% in nursing.

Required: Students must take a core curriculum of 6 courses.

Special: Students may arrange to study abroad.

Honors: Four honor societies have chapters on campus.

Admissions: Applicants must be high school graduates.

Procedure: Students must take the SAT or the ACT unless they are over age 23. Application deadlines are open. There is no application fee. Admissions decisions are made on a rolling basis.

Special: Early decision and early admissions plans are offered.

Transfer: Students must study at the college for at least 1 year, earning 24 of the 128 units required for graduation. Application deadlines are open.

Visiting: Prospective students may arrange informal visits to the campus by contacting the director of admissions. Guides are provided, and visitors may sit in on classes.

Financial Aid: About 94% of the students receive aid through the school; 10% work part-time on campus. The college is a member of the CSS. Students must file the FAF and the college aid application; deadlines for doing so are open.

Foreign Students: About 103 students from foreign countries are enrolled at the Spokane campus. The college provides an intensive English program, special counseling, and special organizations.

Admissions: Foreign applicants must score 500 or better on the TOEFL. No college entrance exams are required.

Procedure: Foreign students are admitted to all terms; application deadlines are open. There is a special application fee of $25. Students must present proof of adequate funds. Health insurance is available through the college at no additional charge.

Admissions Contact: Bertha Ortega, Director of Admissions.

PACIFIC LUTHERAN UNIVERSITY C–2
Tacoma, Washington 98447 (206) 535-7151

F/T: 1225M, 1561W	Faculty: n/av; IIA, –$
P/T: 241M, 336W	Ph.D.'s: 70%
Grad: 168M, 121W	S/F Ratio: 14 to 1
Year: 4-1-4, ss	Tuition: $4672
Appl: June 1	R and B: $2090
1800 applied	1235 accepted 678 enrolled
SAT: 500V 520M	ACT: 24 VERY COMPETITIVE

Pacific Lutheran University, founded in 1890, is a private coeducational institution related to the Lutheran Church, offering liberal arts, professional, and preprofessional programs. The library contains 250,000 volumes and 38,860 microfilm items, and subscribes to 1281 periodicals.

Environment: The 130-acre campus is located near Puget Sound and within sight of Mt. Ranier, in a suburban setting 7 miles from Tacoma. There are 11 dormitories for 1800 students and 31 apartments for married students.

Student Life: About 60% of the students are residents of Washington. Almost all freshmen come from public schools. Approximately 50% of the students are members of the Lutheran Church. About 9% of the students are minority-group members. Chapel is offered 3 times a week, but attendance is not compulsory. Drinking is prohibited and smoking is allowed only in designated areas. Campus housing is coed and single-sex; there are visiting privileges. Cars are allowed on campus by permission only. Day-care services are available to all students, faculty, and staff.

Organizations: There are no fraternities or sororities. Extracurricular activities include service and special interest groups, opera, concerts, artist series, dances, and science exhibits.

Sports: The university fields 13 intercollegiate teams for men and 11 for women. There are 6 intramural sports for men and 6 for women.

Handicapped: Specially equipped rest rooms, elevators, special parking, and wheelchair ramps are available for physically handicapped students, to whom 75% of the campus is accessible.

Graduates: About 20% of the freshmen drop out during their first year; 60% remain to graduate. Of those who graduate, 30% go on to graduate study; 2% enter medical school, 2% enter dental school, and 3% enter law school. About 30% pursue careers in business and industry.

Services: Free health care, tutoring, remedial instruction, career counseling, psychological counseling, and job placement services are provided by the university.

Programs of Study: The university confers the B.A., B.S., B.B.A., B.F.A., B.A.Ed., B.M., B.S.N., and B.S.Med.Tech. degrees. Master's degrees are also offered. Bachelor's degrees are offered in the following subjects: BUSINESS (accounting, business administration, business education, computer science, finance, management, marketing, personnel relations), EDUCATION (early childhood, elementary, health/physical, secondary, special), ENGLISH (English, journalism, literature, speech), FINE AND PERFORMING ARTS (art, art education, art history, music, music education, radio/TV, studio art, theater/dramatics), HEALTH SCIENCES (medical technology, nursing), LANGUAGES (French, German, Norwegian, Spanish), MATH AND SCIENCES (biochemistry, biology, chemistry, earth science, geology, mathematics, physics), PHILOSOPHY (classics, humanities, philosophy, religion), PREPROFESSIONAL (agriculture, architecture, dentistry, engineering, forestry, law, library science, medicine, ministry, optometry, pharmacy, social work, veterinary), SOCIAL SCIENCES (anthropology, economics, government/political science, history, international relations, psychology, sociology).

Required: All students must take physical education, 1 course each in philosophy, fine arts, history or literature, social science, natural science, health education, English composition, and 2 courses in religion.

Special: Combination degree programs are offered in most subjects as a double major. Physics majors may participate in original research projects. The graphic arts department offers an artist-in-residence program. Study abroad and student-designed majors are also offered. During the interim session, special tours are available all over the world.

Honors: Five national honorary societies have chapters on campus. An honors program is open to qualified students, who may design their own major with the assistance of advisors and the honors council.

Admissions: About 69% of those who applied were accepted for the 1981–82 freshman class. The SAT scores of those who enrolled were as follows: Verbal—34% below 500, 49% between 500 and 599, 15% between 600 and 700, and 2% above 700; Math—31% below 500, 45% between 500 and 599, 20% between 600 and 700, and 4% above 700. Candidates should have completed 16 Carnegie units, have a 2.5 GPA, and rank in the top half of their graduating class. Extracurricular activities records and evidence of special talents are also strongly considered.

Procedure: The SAT, ACT, or WPCT is required and should be taken by January of the senior year. The university administers placement tests in foreign languages and mathematics. Application deadlines are June 1 (fall), December 15 (winter), January 15 (spring), and June 15 (summer). Notification is made on a rolling basis. There is a $25 application fee.

Special: Early decision, early admissions, and deferred admissions plans are available. AP and CLEP credit is accepted.

Transfer: For fall 1981, 700 transfer students applied, 582 were accepted, and 346 enrolled. Transfers are accepted for all classes. A

944 WASHINGTON

minimum 2.25 GPA is required. Grades of C or above transfer. Students must complete, at the university, at least 28 of the 128 credits necessary for a bachelor's degree. Deadlines are the same as those for freshmen.

Visiting: Arrangements for informal visits can be made through the admissions office when regular classes are in session. Visitors may sit in on classes, tour the campus, and stay at the school.

Financial Aid: The university has a total of $600,000 available for freshman scholarships, depending on need. Federal government loans and federally-insured loans total $1,000,000 each; university-administered loans total $20,000; loans from industrial, private and other sources total $10,000. The average scholarship is $1800; the maximum $3600; the average loan is $1000, with a maximum of $1500; campus employment income is $800 on the average, with a maximum of $1500. The average aid from all sources is $3800; the maximum is $6000. Most aid is in a package of gift, loan, and part-time employment. About 65% of all students receive some form of financial assistance; about 40% of the students work part-time on campus. Tuition may be paid in installments. The deadline for fall aid applications is March 1. The university is a member of CSS; the FAF is required.

Foreign Students: About 3% of the students are from foreign countries. The university offers these students an intensive English program, special counseling, and special organizations.

Admissions: Foreign students must achieve a TOEFL score of at least 500, or a University of Michigan Language Test score of at least 80.

Procedure: Application deadlines are June 1 for fall, December 1 for spring, and June 1 for summer. Foreign students must complete the university's medical form, and must present proof of funds adequate to cover the total proposed study period. Foreign students must carry health insurance, which is available through the university for a fee.

Admissions Contact: James Van Beek, Dean of Admissions.

SAINT MARTIN'S COLLEGE   B-3
Lacey, Washington 98503   (206) 491-4700

F/T: 361M&W	Faculty:	n/av; IIB, av$
P/T: 127M&W	Ph.D.'s:	60%
Grad: 10M&W	S/F Ratio:	15 to 1
Year: sems, ss	Tuition:	$4422
Appl: Aug. 1	R and B:	$2268
251 applied	234 accepted	107 enrolled
SAT: 437V 464M		LESS COMPETITIVE

Saint Martin's College, founded in 1895, is a small Roman Catholic college conducted by the Benedictine order, offering liberal arts, science, and selected professional programs. Its library contains 88,956 volumes and 2522 microfilm items, and subscribes to 355 periodicals.

Environment: The 400-acre wooded campus is located in a suburban area 3 miles from Olympia and 60 miles south of Seattle. There are 2 dormitories.

Student Life: Approximately 76% of the students are from Washington. Half the students are Catholic. About 44% live on campus. Campus housing is coed. Students may keep cars on campus.

Organizations: Extracurricular activities include forums, concerts, debating, plays, films, and class outings. There are religious counselors for Catholic and Protestant students.

Sports: The college fields 2 intercollegiate teams for men and 2 for women. There are 6 intramural sports for men and 4 for women.

Handicapped: Approximately 90% of the campus is accessible to the physically handicapped. Facilities include special parking, elevators, and specially equipped rest rooms.

Graduates: The freshman dropout rate is 20%; approximately 74% of the entering freshmen remain to graduate. Fifteen percent of the graduates pursue graduate study; 50% pursue careers in business and industry.

Services: Placement services, career counseling, health care, psychological counseling, tutoring, and remedial instruction are offered free of charge.

Programs of Study: The college confers the B.A., B.S., and B.S.C.E. degrees. Associate and master's degrees are also awarded. Bachelor's degrees are offered in the following subjects: BUSINESS (accounting, management), EDUCATION (elementary, secondary), ENGLISH (English), FINE AND PERFORMING ARTS (art, fine arts, music, theater/dramatics), MATH AND SCIENCES (biology, chemistry, forensic chemistry, ecology/environmental science, mathematics), PREPROFESSIONAL (dentistry, engineering—civil, law, medicine, pharmacy, veterinary), SOCIAL SCIENCES (community services, criminal justice, economics, government/political science, history, psychology, sociology). About 50% of degrees conferred are in social sciences, 16% in math and sciences, and 9% in education.

Required: One year of freshman composition is required. All undergraduates must take 1 course in philosophy, 2 courses in social science, 1 in literature, 2 credits of physical education, 1 course in fine arts, 1 course in religious studies, 1 course in natural science with a laboratory, and 1 math or science course.

Special: Combined B.A.-B.S. degrees in a 5-year curriculum are offered in many subjects. A general studies (no major) degree is also offered.

Honors: Three national honorary societies have chapters on campus.

Admissions: Approximately 93% of those who applied were accepted for the 1981-82 freshman class. Candidates should be graduates of an accredited high school, rank in the top 75% of their class, and have at least a 2.0 GPA. Results of entrance examinations are important. Other factors entering into the admissions decision are recommendations, extracurricular activities record, advanced placement or honors courses, and leadership record.

Procedure: The SAT, ACT, or WPCT is required. Application deadlines are August 1 for fall, January 1 for winter, and June 1 for summer. The college follows a rolling admissions policy. There is a $15 application fee.

Special: There are early admissions and deferred admissions plan. CLEP and AP credit is accepted.

Transfer: Recently 238 transfer applications were received, 180 were accepted, and 116 students enrolled. Transfers are accepted for all classes. A 2.0 GPA is required; D grades transfer but do not count toward graduation requirements. At least 30 semester hours must be completed at the college; between 120 and 125 credits are required for the bachelor's degree. The application deadlines are the same as those for freshman applicants.

Visiting: There is a regularly scheduled orientation for prospective students. Arrangements for a campus visit, class observation, and overnight stay can be made through the admissions office.

Financial Aid: Entering freshmen and transfer students may qualify for the Merit Scholarships, based on GPA, extracurricular activities, and college potential. Other scholarships are available to freshmen and transfer students. Loan funds are available through NDSL and GSL. Aid packages include CWS and BEOG programs. The college belongs to CSS; the FAF is required. About 65% of all students receive some form of financial assistance. The deadline for financial aid applications is March 1.

Foreign Students: Fifteen percent of the full-time students come from foreign countries. The college offers these students special counseling and special organizations.

Admissions: Foreign students must achieve a TOEFL score of at least 500; no further exams are required.

Procedure: Application deadlines are August 1 for fall, January 1 for winter, and June 1 for summer. Foreign students must present proof of funds adequate to cover the total duration of their study.

Admissions Contact: Patricia A. Connors, Director of Admissions.

SEATTLE PACIFIC UNIVERSITY   C-2
Seattle, Washington 98119   (206) 281-2021

F/T: 750M, 1250W	Faculty:	n/av; IIA, av$
P/T: 75M, 175W	Ph.D.'s:	47%
Grad: 125M, 200W	S/F Ratio:	17 to 1
Year: qtrs, ss	Tuition:	$4002
Appl: see profile	R and B:	$2190
1091 applied	759 accepted	625 enrolled
SAT: 502V 535M		COMPETITIVE+

Seattle Pacific University, founded in 1891, offers programs in liberal arts and preprofessional studies. It is operated by the Free Methodist Church. The university is made up of 9 schools. The library contains 116,000 volumes and 160,000 microfilm items, and subscribes to 900 periodicals.

Environment: The 25-acre campus is located near the center of Seattle. Seven dormitories accommodate 1200 students. The university also operates 2 island campuses in Puget Sound: Casey Campus, 130 acres on Whidley Island, and Blakely Campus, 965 acres on Blakely Island. These campuses are used for marine biology, environmental studies, and field experiences.

Student Life: About 61% of the students are residents of Washington, and 75% come from public schools. About 65% of the students live on campus. Both single-sex and coed dorms are available. Students are required to attend chapel services 3 days a week. Neither drinking nor smoking is permitted on campus. Students are expected to conduct themselves in accordance with evangelical Christian standards.

Organizations: Social and extracurricular activities include music, drama, publications, debate, religious activities, special-interest clubs, and student government. There are no fraternities or sororities.

Sports: The university competes in 11 intercollegiate sports, including 5 for women. About 25 intramural sports also are available.

Handicapped: Specially equipped rest rooms, elevators, and special parking are provided for the physically handicapped. Student assistants are available to aid handicapped students.

Graduates: About 25% of the freshmen drop out during their first year, and 52% remain to graduate. Of those who graduate, 14% pursue advanced degrees.

Services: Free health care, career counseling, and psychological counseling are offered to students. Tutoring or remedial instruction and placement services are also available.

Programs of Study: The university confers the B.A. and B.S. degrees. Master's degrees also are awarded. Bachelor's degrees are offered in the following subjects: AREA STUDIES (American, European, urban), BUSINESS (accounting, finance, management, marketing), EDUCATION (Christian, elementary, health/physical, recreation, secondary, special), ENGLISH (communication, English), FINE AND PERFORMING ARTS (art, art education, church music, music, music education, theater/dramatics), HEALTH SCIENCES (nursing), LANGUAGES (French, German, Greek/Latin, Russian), MATH AND SCIENCES (biology, chemistry, computer science, ecology/environmental science, mathematics, physics), PHILOSOPHY (humanities, philosophy, religion), PREPROFESSIONAL (clothing and textiles, engineering, engineering—engineering science, foods and nutrition, home economics, social work), SOCIAL SCIENCES (anthropology, economics, government/political science, history, marital and family therapy, psychology, sociology).

Required: All students except general honors participants must fulfill distribution requirements in fine and applied arts, language and literature, science and mathematics, and social science.

Special: The university offers a teaching internship program, an institute for research, and interterm studies. A general studies degree is also offered. Students may study abroad and design their own majors. The university offers combined study and work programs in nursing, cadet teaching, and medical technology. Preprofessional programs are offered in medicine, dentistry, dental hygiene, medical records administration, medical technology, physical therapy, and law.

Honors: The Alpha Kappa Sigma honor society is represented on campus. Qualified students may participate in the general honors program.

Admissions: About 70% of those who applied were accepted for the 1981–82 freshman class. The SAT scores of those who enrolled were as follows: Verbal—58% scored below 500, 29% between 500 and 599, 12% between 600 and 700, and 1% above 700; Math—43% scored below 500, 35% between 500 and 599, 20% between 600 and 700, and 2% above 600. Candidates should have a 2.5 GPA or better; those who do not qualify may be given qualified admission to the Developmental Assistance Program. Leadership record and personality are also considered.

Procedure: Either the SAT, the ACT, or the Washington Pre-College Test is required. Applications should be submitted at least 1 month before the start of a semester. Financial aid applicants seeking fall admission must apply by March 1. There is a $15 application fee, which may be waived at the high school counselor's request.

Special: An early admissions plan is available. AP and CLEP credit is accepted.

Transfer: For a recent year, 567 applications were received, 437 were accepted, and 216 students enrolled. D grades are given credit if offset by B grades in other courses. At least 45 quarter hours must be taken in residence of the 180 required for a bachelor's degree.

Visiting: A regularly scheduled orientation is held for prospective students. Arrangements for informal visits can be made through the admissions office during the winter quarter. Visitors may sit in on classes, tour the campus, and stay overnight at the school.

Financial Aid: About 65% of the students receive aid. The university awards scholarships based on need and academic merit. Loans and campus jobs also are available. The FAF is required. Applications should be filed by February 1.

Foreign Students: Two percent of the full-time students come from foreign countries. The university offers these students an intensive English course, an intensive English program, and special counseling.

Admissions: Applicants must score at least 550 on the TOEFL or at least 85 on the University of Michigan Language Test. No college entrance exams are required.

Procedure: Foreign students are admitted to all quarters, and application deadlines are the same as those for American students. Proof of funds adequate to cover 1 year is required. Foreign students must carry health insurance, which is available through the university for a fee.

Admissions Contact: Marj Goodwin, Director of Admissions.

SEATTLE UNIVERSITY C–2
Seattle, Washington 98122 (206) 626-5720

F/T: 1237M, 1326W Faculty: 174; IIA, –$
P/T: 403M, 490W   Ph.D.'s: 58%
Grad: 607M, 516W S/F Ratio: 14 to 1
Year: qtrs, ss   Tuition: $4275
Appl: open   R and B: $2277
1714 applied   1382 accepted   528 enrolled
SAT: 460V 520M   COMPETITIVE

Seattle University, established in 1891, is a Roman Catholic institution conducted by the Jesuit Fathers in accordance with their 400-year-old traditions. Its library contains 200,000 volumes and 67,500 microfilm items, and subscribes to 2000 periodicals.

Environment: The 43-acre urban campus is located close to the center of downtown Seattle. Dormitories accommodate 725 students.

Student Life: About 65% of the students are residents of Washington; 85% of the freshmen come from public schools. About 35% of the students live on campus. About 11% are minority-group members. Campus housing is both coed and single-sex; there are visiting privileges in the single-sex housing. Students may keep cars on campus. Day-care services are available to all students.

Organizations: There are no fraternities or sororities. Extracurricular activities include service clubs, social organizations, student publication groups, music groups, religious committees, and civic and charitable organizations.

Sports: The university fields 4 intercollegiate teams for men and 4 for women. There are 19 intramural sports for men and 19 for women.

Handicapped: Approximately 50% of the campus is accessible to the physically handicapped. Facilities include wheelchair ramps, special parking, elevators, specially equipped rest rooms, and lowered drinking fountains and telephones; special class scheduling can be arranged. Auxiliary aids are available for hearing and visually impaired students.

Graduates: Approximately 9% of the freshmen drop out during their first year. Approximately 33% of the graduates pursue advanced degrees.

Services: Free health care, tutoring, remedial instruction, career counseling, psychological counseling, and job placement services are offered.

Programs of Study: The university confers the B.A., B.S., B.Mus., B.A.Ed., B.S.N., and Bachelor of Social Science degrees. Master's and doctoral programs are also offered. Bachelor's degrees are offered in the following subjects: BUSINESS (accounting, business administration, finance, management, marketing), EDUCATION (adult, early childhood, elementary, health/physical, secondary, special), ENGLISH (English, journalism, literature), FINE AND PERFORMING ARTS (art, art education, art history, dance, music, music education, theater/dramatics), HEALTH SCIENCES (medical technology, nursing), LANGUAGES (French, German, Spanish), MATH AND SCIENCES (biology, chemistry, mathematics, natural sciences, physical sciences, physics), PHILOSOPHY (humanities, philosophy, religion), PREPROFESSIONAL (engineering), SOCIAL SCIENCES (economics, government/political science, history, psychology, social sciences, sociology). Twenty-five percent of degrees are conferred in business, 17% in health sciences, and 16% in math and sciences.

Required: All students must take a prescribed sequence of courses in English, history, social science, and mathematics or natural science. In addition, electives in philosophy and theology are required.

Special: The community services degree in social work includes field work in the senior year. A combination degree in engineering, study abroad, and a 4-year course in clinical chemistry are also offered. A 3-year program leading to the B.A. in Humanities degree is offered through Matteo Ricci College.

Honors: Six national honor societies are represented on campus. Honors programs are offered in humanities.

Admissions: About 81% of those who applied were accepted for the 1981–82 freshman class. Candidates should have completed 16 Carnegie units in academic areas including English, mathematics, history, social sciences, a lab science, and a foreign language; should have a B– average; and should rank in the top half of their graduating class. Leadership and extracurricular activities records are also considered.

Procedure: The SAT, ACT or WPCT is required, and should be taken by January of the senior year. There are no application deadlines; freshmen are admitted in all 4 terms. Notification is on a rolling basis. There is a $15 application fee.

Special: Early decision candidates are notified by November 15. An early admissions plan is also available. AP and CLEP credit is accepted.

Transfer: For fall 1981, 1351 students applied, 887 were accepted, and 447 enrolled. D grades transfer. All students must complete, at the university, 45 of the 180 credits required for a bachelor's degree. There are no application deadlines.

Visiting: There are regularly scheduled orientation sessions for prospective students. Guides are also available for informal visits; visitors may sit in on classes and stay overnight at the school. The admissions office should be contacted to arrange visits.

Financial Aid: Scholarships and loans (NDSL and local bank) are available. There are work-study programs in all university offices and departments. About 65% of all students receive some form of financial assistance. About 60% work part-time on campus. The average freshman award is $4600. Tuition is payable in installments. Applications for academic scholarships should be filed no later than March 15. The FAF, FFS, or SFS is required. Notification of awards is made by May 1.

Foreign Students: Ten percent of the full-time students come from foreign countries. Special counseling and special organizations are available for these students.

Admissions: Foreign students must achieve a TOEFL score of at least 520. No college entrance exams are required.

Procedure: Application deadlines are August 6 (fall), November 6 (winter), March 6 (spring), and April 6 (summer). Foreign students must present proof of funds adequate to cover 1 year of study and must carry health insurance, which is available through the university for a fee. There is a special $10-per-quarter fee for foreign students.

Admissions Contact: Michael Fox, Director of Admissions.

UNIVERSITY OF PUGET SOUND   C–2
Tacoma, Washington 98416   (206) 756-3211

F/T: 1229M, 1478W	Faculty:	159; IIA, av$
P/T: 128M, 230W	Ph.D.'s:	82%
Grad: 16M, 42W	S/F Ratio:	14 to 1
Year: 4-1-4, ss	Tuition:	$4860
Appl: none	R and B:	$2260
2099 applied	1788 accepted	722 enrolled
SAT (mean): 492V 527M	ACT (mean): 24	COMPETITIVE+

The University of Puget Sound is a privately endowed institution with an historical affiliation to the Methodist Church. Its library contains 300,000 volumes and 10,500 microfilm items, and subscribes to 2250 periodicals.

Environment: The 72-acre campus is located in a suburban area 5 miles from the center of Tacoma, and 35 miles south of Seattle. Living facilities include 8 residence halls, 4 A-frame cabins, 35 residential annex houses, and 8 fraternity and sorority houses. The university also sponsors off-campus apartments.

Student Life: Fifty percent of the students live on campus. Approximately half of the students are from Washington; 43 states and 20 foreign countries are represented in the student body. Twenty-seven percent of the students are Catholic, 52% Protestant, 2% Jewish. About 12% of the students are minority-group members. College housing is both coed and single-sex; there are visiting privileges. Students may keep cars on campus.

Organizations: There are 6 fraternities and 7 sororities, to which approximately 25% of the students belong. There are religious counselors and organizations for students of the Catholic, Jewish, and Protestant faiths. Extracurricular activities include forensics, drama, music, publications, student senate, and a number of scholastic and special interest clubs.

Sports: The university fields 12 intercollegiate teams for men and 11 for women. There are 16 intramural sports for men and 15 for women, as well as a sailing club and Wilderness House for students interested in outdoor recreation.

Handicapped: Approximately 22% of the campus is accessible to the physically handicapped. Facilities include special parking, and wheelchair ramps and specially equipped rest rooms in various locations; special class scheduling can be arranged. The learning skills and counseling centers provide special assistance for handicapped students. Signers are available for hearing impaired students.

Graduates: The freshman dropout rate is 14%; 45% remain to graduate. Fifty-two percent of the graduates pursue graduate study; 1% enter medical school, 3% enter law school. Eighty-three percent enter careers in business and industry.

Services: Placement services, career counseling, health care, psychological counseling, tutoring, and remedial instruction are offered free of charge.

Programs of Study: The university confers the B.A., B.S., B.M., and B.A.S. degrees. Master's and doctoral degrees are also awarded. Bachelor's degrees are offered in the following subjects: AREA STUDIES (American, Asian, urban), BUSINESS (accounting, business administration, computer science, finance, international business, management, marketing), EDUCATION (elementary, health/physical, secondary, special), ENGLISH (English, literature, writing), FINE AND PERFORMING ARTS (art, art education, music, music education, theater/dramatics), HEALTH SCIENCES (occupational therapy, physical therapy), LANGUAGES (French, German, Spanish), MATH AND SCIENCES (biology, chemistry, earth science, geology, mathematics, natural sciences, oceanography, physics), PHILOSOPHY (philosophy, religion), PREPROFESSIONAL (dentistry, engineering, law, medicine, veterinary), SOCIAL SCIENCES (economics, government/political science, history, international relations, psychology, sociology). About 38% of degrees conferred are in business, 11% in math and sciences, and 10% in fine and performing arts.

Required: A core curriculum including 11 units in skills, perspectives, and knowledge areas is required.

Special: The university has a term in England program, a junior year in the Netherlands, and every 3 years a group of students can spend 1 year on a tour of the Pacific Rim of the Asian continent. Internships, independent research, a cooperative education program, double majors, interdisciplinary studies, and independent study are also offered.

Honors: Three national honorary societies have chapters on campus. An honors program is open to qualified students from all departments.

Admissions: Approximately 85% of those who applied were accepted for the 1981–82 freshman class. The SAT scores of those who enrolled were as follows: Verbal—59% below 500, 28% between 500 and 599, 11% between 600 and 700, and 2% above 700; Math—44% below 500, 32% between 500 and 599, 20% between 600 and 700, and 4% above 700. It is preferred that candidates rank in the top one-quarter of their class and have a 3.3 GPA. The university considers test scores, class rank, GPA, advanced placement or honors courses, recommendations from significant secondary school authorities, personal essays, and evidence of special talent in evaluating candidates.

Procedure: The SAT, ACT, or WPCT should be taken by January of the senior year. New students are admitted for any term. There are no application deadlines. The university follows a rolling admissions policy. There is a $20 application fee.

Special: Early decision, early admissions, and deferred admissions plans are available.

Transfer: For fall 1981, 1050 transfer students applied, 945 accepted, and 478 enrolled. It is recommended that applicants have a 3.3 GPA and be in good academic standing at an accredited institution. All students must take, at the university, at least 90 of the 180 quarter credits required for the bachelor's degree. Grades of D or above transfer. Application deadlines are open.

Visiting: There are regularly scheduled campus days. Informal visits can be arranged through the admissions office during the week. Visitors may sit in on classes and stay at the school.

Financial Aid: The average freshman award is $4500. About 65% of all students receive some form of financial assistance; 25% of the students work part-time on campus. The FAF is required; the university is a member of CSS. A first preference date of March 1 is observed for freshmen and transfer students, although financial aid applications are accepted throughout the spring.

Foreign Students: About 2% of the students are from foreign countries. The university offers these students special counseling and special organizations.

Admissions: Foreign students must achieve a minimum TOEFL score of 520; if they are entering as freshmen, they must also take the SAT.

Financial Aid: The university is a member of the CSS. Scholarships and loans are available from university, private, and federal funds. Many departments have work-study programs. About 45% of all students receive some form of financial assistance; 20% of the students work part-time on campus. The average award to freshmen from all sources is $2000. Applications for scholarships must be filed by April 1. Applications for other types of aid must be filed by June 1. The FAF must be filed in addition to the university's own application form and the IRS 1040 form.

Foreign Students: About 6% of the students are from foreign countries. The university offers these students an intensive English course, special counseling, and special organizations.

Admissions: Foreign students must achieve a minimum TOEFL score of 520 or must take the University of Michigan Language Test; no further exams are required.

Procedure: Application deadlines are May 15 for fall and October 1 for spring. Foreign students must present proof of funds adequate to cover 1 year of study. They must also carry health insurance, which is available through the university for a fee.

Admissions Contact: Stan Berry, Director of Admissions.

WESTERN WASHINGTON UNIVERSITY C-1
Bellingham, Washington 98225 (206) 676-3440

F/T: 4190M, 4622W	Faculty: 429; IIA, +$
P/T: 176M, 228W	Ph.D.'s: 77%
Grad: 505M, 517W	S/F Ratio: 22 to 1
Year: qtrs, ss	Tuition: $867 ($2910)
Appl: Sept. 1	R and B: $1900
5400 applied	4185 accepted	1543 enrolled
SAT: 492V 504M	ACT: 23	COMPETITIVE

Western Washington University, founded in 1893, has been designated a regional university. Its 29 academic departments offer the bachelor's and master's degrees. The library contains 392,000 volumes and 400,000 units of microtext, and subscribes to 4692 periodicals. The university has an innovative division, Fairhaven College, which offers students an interdisciplinary, individualized education.

Environment: The 224-acre suburban campus is located on a hillside overlooking the city, Bellingham Bay, and many of the San Juan islands; there are 60 permanent buildings. Living facilities include dormitories and on-campus apartments. Nearby facilities include the Shannon Point Marine Center and 9 acres of property on Lake Whatcom.

Student Life: About 92% of the students are residents of Washington; 93% of the freshmen come from public schools. About 40% of the students live on campus. Four percent are minority-group members. Campus housing is both coed and single-sex; there are visiting privileges in the single-sex housing. Students may keep cars on campus. Day-care services are available to all students for a fee.

Organizations: There are no fraternities or sororities on campus. Various special-interest groups and the student government organize social and cultural events.

Sports: The university fields 8 intercollegiate teams for men and 7 for women. There are 11 intramural sports for men and 9 for women.

Handicapped: Approximately 75% of the campus is accessible to the physically handicapped. Facilities include wheelchair ramps, special parking, elevators, specially equipped rest rooms, and lowered drinking fountains and telephones. Special class scheduling and student services are also available. Visual aids, signers, and tape-recorded lectures and books are provided for students with visual or hearing impairments.

Graduates: About 30% of the freshmen drop out during the first year; 40% remain to graduate. Of those who graduate, 18% pursue advanced degrees: 1% enter medical school, 1% enter dental school, and 2% enter law school. About 60% of the graduates pursue careers in business and industry.

Services: Free tutoring, career counseling, and psychological counseling are offered. Health care and placement services are provided on a fee basis.

Programs of Study: The university offers the B.A., B.S., B.Mus., B.A.Ed., and B.F.A. degrees. Master's degrees are also awarded. Bachelor's degrees are offered in the following subjects: AREA STUDIES (American, Canadian-American, ethnic), BUSINESS (accounting, business administration, business administration/computer science, business education, computer science, office management), EDUCATION (early childhood, elementary, health/physical, human services, secondary, special), ENGLISH (creative writing, English, journalism, literature, speech), FINE AND PERFORMING ARTS (art, art education, art history, dance, interdisciplinary arts, music, music composition, music education, music history and literature, music—jazz, music performance, radio/TV, studio art, theater/dramatics), HEALTH SCIENCES (environmental health, nursing, speech pathology and audiology), LANGUAGES (French, German, Greek/Latin, Russian, Spanish), MATH AND SCIENCES (biochemistry, biology, biology/mathematics, chemistry, earth science, ecology/environmental science, environmental geology, fresh water studies, geology, geophysics, mathematics, natural sciences, physical geochemistry, physical sciences, physics, physics/astronomy, physics/mathematics, science education), PHILOSOPHY (philosophy), SOCIAL SCIENCES (anthropology, economics, economics/accounting, economics/mathematics, geography, geography/social studies, government/political science, history, history/social studies, liberal studies, political science/social studies, psychology, public policy and administration, sociology, urban and regional planning). About 16% of degrees are conferred in math and sciences, 15% in education, and 15% in business.

Special: All courses except general university requirements and major or professional work may be taken on a pass/fail basis. Study abroad, internships, and a liberal studies major are offered. Fairhaven College students design their own majors and may conduct independent studies; the curriculum is divided into 3 stages: exploration, precision and specialization, and generalization and prospectus.

Honors: Three national honor societies are represented on campus. The university honors program is open to all majors; a senior thesis is required.

Admissions: About 78% of those who applied for the 1981–82 freshman class were accepted. Candidates should have at least a 2.7 GPA and rank in the top half of their graduating class. Impressions made during the interview, recommendations, and advanced placement or honors courses are also considered important.

Procedure: Nonresidents must take the SAT or ACT; state residents must take the WPCT. Deadlines for application are September 1 (fall), December 1 (winter), March 1 (spring), and June 1 (summer). There is a $15 application fee. Notification is made on a rolling basis.

Special: A deferred admissions plan is available. CLEP credit is accepted for subject exams only.

Transfer: For fall 1981, 3133 applications were received, 2204 were accepted, and 1185 students enrolled. Applicants should be in good standing with a 2.3 GPA in the last term before transferring; a 2.7 GPA is required if fewer than 40 credits have been completed and the high school GPA is less than 2.7. D grades are accepted. All students must complete, at the university, 45 of the 180 credits required for a bachelor's degree. Deadlines are the same as those for freshman applicants.

Visiting: There is no regularly scheduled orientation program for prospective students. Arrangements for informal visits can be made through the admissions office. Visitors may sit in on classes, tour the campus, and stay overnight at the university.

Financial Aid: CWS provides on-campus part-time employment in 66 departments and offices, and off campus in 35 private and public nonprofit agencies, with total funds of over $630,000. About 43% of all students receive university-administered financial assistance; 25% earn money through part-time employment on campus. The average freshman award is $1600. The university is a member of CSS. The deadlines for financial aid applications are April 1 (fall), December 1 (winter), and March 1 (spring). The FAF with supplement and the university's application form must be filed.

Foreign Students: Four percent of the full-time students come from foreign countries. Special counseling and special organizations are available for these students.

Admissions: Foreign students must achieve a TOEFL score of at least 500, with a score of at least 50 in each subsection. No college entrance exams are required.

Procedure: The application deadline is 3 full months before any quarter. Foreign students must complete a health form and must present proof of funds adequate to cover 1 year of study. Health insurance is required and is available through the university for a fee.

Admissions Contact: Richard J. Riehl, Director of Admissions.

WHITMAN COLLEGE E-3
Walla Walla, Washington 99362 (509) 527-5176

F/T: 582M, 623W	Faculty: 80; IIB, ++$
P/T: 7M, 18W	Ph.D.'s: 72%
Grad: none	S/F Ratio: 13 to 1
Year: sems	Tuition: $5150
Appl: Mar. 1	R and B: $2210
1074 applied	825 accepted	410 enrolled
SAT: 540V 580M		VERY COMPETITIVE

950 WASHINGTON

Whitman College, chartered in 1859, is a privately endowed, coeducational, liberal arts college. Its library contains 312,174 volumes and 26,800 microfilm items, and subscribes to 1900 periodicals.

Environment: The 50-acre urban campus is in a small city 235 miles from Portland and 250 miles from Seattle. Dormitories, fraternity and sorority houses, a foreign language house, and a multiethnic house provide housing for students on and off campus.

Student Life: About 94% of the students are residents of the West and Northwest; 85% of the freshmen come from public schools. About 80% of the students live on campus. Out-of-town, unmarried, underclass students must live in residence halls. Eleven percent of the students are minority-group members. College housing is both single-sex and coed. There are visiting privileges in single-sex housing. Students may keep cars on campus.

Organizations: There are 5 national fraternities and 5 national sororities on campus, with a membership of 47% of the student body. The college sponsors concerts, lectures, films, and other social activities.

Sports: The college competes intercollegiately in 11 sports for men or women. There are 20 intramural sports for men or women.

Handicapped: There are full special facilities for physically handicapped students, to whom the entire campus is accessible. Fewer than 1% of the students currently enrolled are visually or hearing impaired. Special class scheduling can be arranged for handicapped students.

Graduates: About 2% of the freshmen drop out during the first year; 60% remain to graduate. Of those who graduate, 80% pursue advanced degrees: 10% enter medical school, 2% dental school, and 20% law school. About 60% pursue careers in business and industry.

Services: Free career counseling, psychological counseling, job placement, health care, and remedial instruction are available. Tutoring is available on a fee basis.

Programs of Study: The college awards the B.A. degree, with majors in the following subjects: AREA STUDIES (American), ENGLISH (English), FINE AND PERFORMING ARTS (art, music, theater/dramatics), LANGUAGES (French, German, Japanese, Spanish), MATH AND SCIENCES (astronomy, biology, chemistry, ecology/environmental science, geology, mathematics, physics), PREPROFESSIONAL (dentistry, engineering, forestry, law, library science, medicine, ministry, social work, veterinary), SOCIAL SCIENCES (anthropology, economics, government/political science, history, psychology, sociology). Teacher education programs lead to certification on the elementary and secondary levels. About 41% of degrees conferred are in social sciences and 27% are in math and sciences.

Special: The college offers combined B.A.-B.S. programs in engineering and applied science and a 3-2 engineering program with California Institute of Technology and Columbia University. A 3-2 forestry and environmental management program is also available through Duke University. Study abroad and Washington and Urban semesters are offered. A science research internship program is available through the Battelle Northwest Laboratories and NASA.

Honors: Three national honor societies have chapters on campus. Honors programs are available in most departments.

Admissions: About 77% of the students who applied were accepted for the 1981-82 freshman class. The SAT scores of those who enrolled were as follows: Verbal—31% below 500, 42% between 500 and 599, 22% between 600 and 700, and 5% above 700; Math—20% below 500, 35% between 500 and 599, 36% between 600 and 700, and 9% above 700. Candidates should have completed 16 Carnegie units, have a 3.0 GPA, and rank in the top half of their graduating class. Special talents and advanced placement or honors courses are also taken into consideration. Children of alumni are given some special consideration.

Procedure: The SAT, ACT, or WPCT is required, and should be taken no later than February of the senior year. Deadlines for application are March 1 (fall) and December 1 (spring). There is a $20 application fee.

Special: Early decision, early admissions, and deferred admissions plans are offered. AP credit is accepted.

Transfer: For fall 1981, 82 students applied, 52 were accepted, and 34 enrolled. Transfers must be in good academic standing. D grades do not transfer. A minimum of 2 semesters must be taken in residence. At least 34 of the 124 semester credits necessary to earn a bachelor's degree must be earned at the college. The deadlines for transfer applications are May 1 (fall) and December 1 (spring).

Visiting: There is a special visitors' day held in April. Arrangements for informal visits can be made through the admissions office during the week. Prospective students may sit in on classes, tour the campus with guides, and stay overnight at the college.

Financial Aid: Fifty percent of the students receive aid. Sixty percent work part-time on campus. Average aid to freshmen from all sources is $3400. Financial aid is awarded in the form of scholarships, grants, employment grants, and loans. Whitman is a member of the CSS. The FAF, FFS, or SFS is required. The deadline for financial aid applications is February 15.

Foreign Students: Three percent of the full-time students come from foreign countries. The college offers these students special counseling and special organizations.

Admissions: Foreign students must take the TOEFL and the SAT. They must score at least 550 on the TOEFL.

Procedure: The deadline for application is February 1 (fall). Foreign students must submit the college's own health form. They must also present proof of adequate funds. They must carry health insurance, which is available through the college for a fee.

Admissions Contact: William D. Tingley, Director of Admissions.

WHITWORTH COLLEGE C-2
Spokane, Washington 99251 (509) 466-3212

F/T: 582M, 661W	Faculty:	69; IIA, −$
P/T: 122M, 278W	Ph.D.'s:	60%
Grad: 106M, 197W	S/F Ratio:	16 to 1
Year: 4-1-4, ss	Tuition:	$4660
Appl: Sept. 1	R and B:	$2000
1000 applied	816 accepted	480 enrolled
SAT: 464V 495M	ACT: 21	COMPETITIVE

Whitworth College, a small liberal arts institution established in 1890, is affiliated with the Presbyterian Church. The library contains 80,000 volumes, 55,000 microfilm items, 975 records, and 300 cassettes and reels, and subscribes to 770 periodicals.

Environment: The 200-acre wooded campus is located 2 miles from Spokane, in a suburban atmosphere. Living facilities include dormitories and on-campus apartments.

Student Life: About 55% of the students come from out of state. About 65% live on campus. Only 35% of the students belong to the Presbyterian Church; chapel attendance is not required. Drinking on campus is not permitted. Campus housing is both coed and single-sex; there are visiting privileges in the single-sex housing. Students may keep cars on campus.

Organizations: There are no fraternities or sororities. The college regularly sponsors concerts, dances, and films.

Sports: The college competes in 7 intercollegiate sports for men and 5 for women. There are 5 intramural sports for men and 4 for women.

Handicapped: Specially equipped rest rooms and special class scheduling are available to physically handicapped students.

Graduates: About 18% of the freshmen drop out during their first year; 55% remain to graduate. About half the graduates pursue advanced degrees.

Services: Free tutoring, remedial instruction, career counseling, psychological counseling, and job placement services are offered. Health care is provided on a fee basis.

Programs of Study: The college confers the B.A. and B.S. degrees. Master's degrees are also awarded. Bachelor's degrees are offered in the following subjects: BUSINESS (accounting, business administration), ENGLISH (English), FINE AND PERFORMING ARTS (art, music, theater/dramatics), HEALTH SCIENCES (nursing), LANGUAGES (French, German, Spanish), MATH AND SCIENCES (biology, chemistry, mathematics, nutrition, physics), PHILOSOPHY (philosophy, religion), PREPROFESSIONAL (dentistry, law, medicine, ministry, pharmacy, social work), SOCIAL SCIENCES (history, international relations, psychology, sociology).

Required: All students must take a minimum of 12 courses in basic work, including 1 course of the student's choice in religion and physical education.

Special: Students are allowed to create their own majors; study abroad is offered to second-, third-, and fourth-year students. It is possible to earn combined B.A.-B.S. degrees.

Admissions: About 82% of those who applied were accepted for the 1981-82 freshman class. Candidates should have a 2.5 GPA and rank in the upper 75% of their graduating class. The college encourages students to engage in a college preparatory course of study in high school. Advanced placement or honors courses, special talent, leadership record, and extracurricular activities are also considered by the college.

Procedure: The SAT, ACT, or WPCT is required and should be taken by March of the senior year. Applications should be filed by September 1 (fall), December 1 (winter), January 1 (spring), or May 1 (summer). There is a $15 application fee. Notification is made on a rolling basis.

Special: Early decision notification is December 1. AP and CLEP credit is accepted.

Transfer: For fall 1981, 267 applications were received, 206 were accepted, and 142 students enrolled. Transfers must have a 2.5 GPA. D grades transfer. There is a minimum 1-year residency requirement; all students must complete at least 8.5 courses at the college. Application deadlines are the same as those for freshmen.

Visiting: Arrangements for campus visits can be made through the admissions office during the school year. Students receive a guided tour, sit in on classes, and may stay at the college overnight.

Financial Aid: Scholarships, grants, and loans are available. All departments have work-study programs; 45% of the students work part-time on campus. About 70% of all students receive some form of financial assistance. The average freshman award is $2000. The FAF must be filed. The aid application deadline is March 31. The college is a member of CSS.

Foreign Students: Six percent of the full-time students come from foreign countries. An intensive English course, an intensive English program, special counseling, and special organizations are available for these students.

Admissions: Foreign students must achieve a TOEFL score of at least 500 or a University of Michigan Language Test score of at least 80. No college entrance exams are required.

Procedure: Application deadlines are September 1 (fall), December 1 (winter), January 1 (spring), and April 1 (summer). Foreign students must present proof of funds adequate to cover 1 year of study and must carry health insurance, which is available through the college for a fee.

Admissions Contact: Shirlene Short, Director of Admissions.

WEST VIRGINIA

ALDERSON-BROADDUS COLLEGE C-3
Philippi, West Virginia 26416 (304) 457-1700

F/T: 254M, 493W	Faculty:	52; IIB, — $
P/T: 20M, 27W	Ph.D.'s:	40%
Grad: none	S/F Ratio:	14 to 1
Year: terms, ss	Tuition:	$3460
Appl: Sept. 9	R and B:	$1400

439 applied 429 accepted 260 enrolled
SAT: 450V 420M ACT: 19 **LESS COMPETITIVE**

Alderson-Broaddus College, a privately controlled coeducational college, offers academic programs in the liberal arts, education, and professional and technical areas. It is sponsored by the West Virginia Baptist Convention and is related to the American Baptist Convention. The library contains 88,000 volumes and 2009 microfilms, and subscribes to 390 periodicals.

Environment: The 170-acre campus is located in a rural setting 25 miles from Clarksburg. The school is self-contained. Among the 14 major buildings are a humanities and social science building, a chapel, a health sciences building, an administration center, and 4 dormitories housing 525 women and 510 men.

Student Life: About 44% of the students are from West Virginia. Seventy-five percent of the students live on campus; 45% leave the campus on weekends. There are curfews for freshmen for the fall and winter terms of the first year. Fifty-nine percent of the students are Protestant, and 14% are Catholic; weekly attendance at religious services is not required. About 9% of the students are minority-group members. College housing is single-sex, and there are visiting privileges. Freshmen may not have cars on campus.

Organizations: Thirty-five percent of the men have joined 1 of the 4 local fraternities, and about 35% of the women belong to 1 of the 5 local sororities. Campus cultural events and extracurricular activities include service clubs, concerts, dances, movies, art shows, and dramatic presentations. A variety of off-campus cultural and recreational opportunities are available in the surrounding area.

Sports: The college fields 4 intercollegiate teams for men and 2 for women. There are 8 intramural sports for men and 7 for women.

Handicapped: About 90% of the campus is accessible to the physically handicapped. Special facilities for these students include wheelchair ramps, special parking, elevators, and specially equipped rest rooms. Special class scheduling can be arranged.

Graduates: The freshman dropout rate is 3%, and 55% of the freshmen remain to graduate. Twenty-five percent of the graduates pursue advanced study; 5% enter medical school, 1% enter dental school, and 3% enter law school. Thirty-five percent enter careers in business and industry.

Services: Students receive career counseling, psychological counseling, and remedial instruction free of charge. Health care, tutoring, and placement services are available on campus for a fee.

Programs of Study: All programs lead to the B.A. or B.S. degrees. Bachelor's degrees are offered in the following subjects: BUSINESS (accounting, business administration, management, management information systems), EDUCATION (early childhood, elementary, health/physical, school library—media, secondary, special), ENGLISH (creative writing, literature, technical writing), FINE AND PERFORMING ARTS (music, music education, speech communication—broadcasting, speech communication—speech and theater), HEALTH SCIENCES (medical technology, nursing, physician's assistant, radiologic technology), MATH AND SCIENCES (biology, chemistry, mathematics/computer programming), PHILOSOPHY (Christian studies, humanities), PREPROFESSIONAL (dentistry, law, medicine, ministry, pharmacy, physical therapy, social work, veterinary), SOCIAL SCIENCES (government/political science, history, psychology, recreational leadership, recreational leadership/therapy, social sciences, social work, sociology). Of the total undergraduate degrees conferred, 49% are in health sciences, 14% in social sciences, and 12% in education.

Required: The Liberal Studies program is required as an introduction to wide areas of knowledge. Some programs require off-campus education. UP area tests are required for graduation.

Special: The college allows student-designed majors and offers a general studies degree. The student may choose among such options as independent study, travel and study in another culture (generally through the college's program in Salzburg, Austria), humanitarian service projects, and cooperative education.

Honors: The Silver Key Honorary Society has a chapter on campus.

Admissions: Ninety-eight percent of those who applied were accepted for the 1981–82 freshman class. Of those who enrolled, the SAT scores were as follows: Verbal—26% below 500, 11% between 500 and 599, 2% between 600 and 700, and 1% above 700; Math—27% below 500, 10% between 500 and 599, 3% between 600 and 700, and 0% above 700. On the ACT, 57% scored below 21, 17% between 21 and 23, 7% between 24 and 25, 6% between 26 and 28, and 3% above 28. Applicants should have completed, in an accredited high school, 4 years of English, 2 years of a foreign language (recommended), and 2 to 4 years each of mathematics and science. Students should rank in the upper half of the high school class. The college also considers the following factors: advanced placement or honors courses, evidence of special talents, recommendations by school officials, and impressions made during an interview.

Procedure: The ACT is required; students must present ACT scores prior to enrollment for placement purposes. Applications should be filed by September 9 (fall), November 30 (winter), or March 3 (spring). Notification is on a rolling basis. Applications should be submitted with a $10 fee.

Special: Early admissions and early decision plans are available. CLEP and AP credit is given.

Transfer: For fall 1981, 84 students applied, 76 were accepted, and 57 enrolled. Transfers are accepted for all years. Transferring students must have a high school diploma or the equivalent, a GPA of at least 2.0, and ACT scores; an interview is recommended. D grades transfer. Students must spend 3 full terms in residence and complete 30 of the 124 credits necessary for a bachelor's degree. Transfer application deadlines are the same as those for freshmen.

Visiting: Regularly scheduled orientations for prospective students include open house programs with tours, concerts, and interviews. Guides are also available for informal visits. Visitors can sit in on classes and stay overnight at the school. The best times for campus visits are weekdays from 8:30 A.M. to 4:30 P.M. and most Saturday mornings from 9 to 12. The admissions office should be contacted for further information.

952 WEST VIRGINIA

Financial Aid: Ninety-six percent of the students receive financial aid. Forty-eight percent work part-time on campus. Scholarships and loans are available. The college is a member of CSS and requires the FAF. Application deadlines are open.

Foreign Students: Two percent of the full-time students come from foreign countries. The college offers these students special counseling and special organizations.

Admissions: Foreign students must achieve a TOEFL score of at least 450. No college entrance exam must be taken.

Procedure: Application deadlines are open for both the fall and winter sessions. Foreign students must present proof of a physical exam and proof of adequate funds. They must also carry health insurance, which is available through the college.

Admissions Contact: Wendell Teets, Director of Admissions.

BETHANY COLLEGE C-1
Bethany, West Virginia 26032   (304) 829-7611

F/T: 477M, 371W	Faculty:	62; IIB, av$
P/T: 5M, 9W	Ph.D.'s:	62%
Grad: none	S/F Ratio:	14 to 1
Year: 4-1-4, ss	Tuition:	$5195
Appl: May 1	R and B:	$1780
934 applied	686 accepted	305 enrolled
SAT or ACT: required	ACT: 21	COMPETITIVE

Bethany College, founded in 1840, is a private liberal arts college and the oldest degree-granting institution of higher learning in West Virginia. Its library contains 143,000 volumes and 3941 reels of microfilm, and subscribes to 587 periodicals.

Environment: The 1600-acre campus is located in a rural area in the northern panhandle of West Virginia, 40 miles from Pittsburgh. There are 32 buildings on campus, including four buildings listed in the *National Register of Historical Places*. There are 21 housing units for 890 students. The college also sponsors fraternity and sorority houses.

Student Life: About 83% of the students are from out-of-state. Almost all the students live on campus. About 41% are Protestant, and 38% are Catholic. Six percent of the students are minority-group members. College housing is single-sex, and there are visiting privileges; women freshmen have a curfew. Freshmen may not have cars on campus.

Organizations: There are 7 national fraternities and 4 national sororities on campus, to which half the students belong. Special-interest groups also offer social and cultural entertainment on campus. A nearby park provides a variety of outdoor recreational activities.

Sports: The college fields 11 intercollegiate teams for men and 8 for women. There are 12 intramural sports for men and 9 for women.

Handicapped: There are no special facilities for physically handicapped students.

Graduates: The freshman dropout rate is about 15%, and 60% of the freshmen remain to graduate. Fifty percent of the graduates pursue advanced study; 4% enter medical school, 2% enter dental school, and 5% enter law school. Another 25% of the graduates enter careers in business and industry.

Services: Free health care, tutoring, career and psychological counseling, and job placement services are available to students.

Programs of Study: The college confers the B.A. and B.S. degrees. Bachelor's degrees are offered in the following subjects: BUSINESS (business/economics, communications—advertising/public relations, computer science), EDUCATION (elementary, health/physical, secondary), ENGLISH (communications—journalism, communications—speech, English), FINE AND PERFORMING ARTS (art, art education, communications—radio/TV, fine arts, music, music education, theater/dramatics), HEALTH SCIENCES (health science), LANGUAGES (French, German, Spanish), MATH AND SCIENCES (biology, chemistry, general science education, mathematics, physics, psychology), PHILOSOPHY (philosophy, religion), PREPROFESSIONAL (social work), SOCIAL SCIENCES (economics, government/political science, history, psychology, social studies education, sociology). About 25% of the degrees are conferred in social sciences, 24% in math and sciences, and 15% in business.

Required: The Bethany Plan gives students the responsibility of developing their own curriculum with the help of their advisers. All students are expected to have exposure to the areas of sciences, humanities, and social sciences. In addition, students are required to take a 1-semester course in religion, a freshman cultural course, a lecture course in interdisciplinary studies, and 4 practicums in work, citizenship, intercultural experience, and recreation.

Special: Bethany offers a 3–2 program in engineering with Columbia, Georgia Tech, Case Western Reserve, and Washington University of St. Louis.

Honors: There are chapters of 12 national honor societies on campus open to qualified students.

Admissions: About 73% of those who applied were accepted for the 1981–82 freshman class. Of those who enrolled, the SAT scores were as follows: Verbal—25% between 500 and 599, and 7% between 600 and 700; Math—53% below 500, 30% between 500 and 599, 15% between 600 and 700, and 2% above 700. The ACT scores were as follows: 45% below 21, 27% between 21 and 23, 12% between 24 and 25, 11% between 26 and 28, and 5% above 28. Admissions requirements include graduation from an accredited high school with a good reputation, completion of 15 Carnegie units, rank in the upper half of the graduating class, and a minimum grade average of 2.0. Other factors entering into the admissions decision are advanced placement or honors courses, recommendations by high school officials, personality, and impressions made during an interview.

Procedure: The SAT or ACT is required and should be taken by December. Application deadlines are May 1 for fall and November 1 for spring. Notification is on a rolling basis. A $15 application fee is required.

Special: Early and deferred admissions plans and an early decision plan are available. AP and CLEP credit is given in some departments.

Transfer: For fall 1981, 42 students applied, 37 were accepted, and 23 enrolled. A 2.0 GPA and standardized exam scores, preferably with a score of 450 on each part of the SAT, are required; an interview is recommended. D grades do not transfer. Students must spend the final year in residence and complete at least 32 of the 128 credit hours necessary for a bachelor's degree. Application deadlines are the same as those for freshmen.

Visiting: Tours of the campus can be arranged through the admissions office.

Financial Aid: About 65% of the students receive aid administered by the college. Sixty-one percent work part-time on campus. Average aid to freshmen is $4500. Assistance is given in the form of scholarships and loans. The college financial aid program, from all sources, totals $2.4 million. The college is a member of CSS and requires the FAF. The priority deadline for aid application is April 1, with a December 1 deadline for spring session if funds are available.

Foreign Students: Three percent of the full-time students come from foreign countries. The college offers these students special organizations.

Admissions: Foreign students must take the TOEFL. They must also take either the SAT or the ACT.

Procedure: The application deadline is January 1 for fall entry. Foreign students must present proof of funds adequate to cover 1 year of study. They must also carry health insurance, which is available through the college for a fee.

Admissions Contact: David J. Wottle, Director of Admissions.

BLUEFIELD STATE COLLEGE B-5
Bluefield, West Virginia 24701   (304) 325-7102

F/T: 1200M, 1200W	Faculty:	n/av; IIB, av$
P/T: 1200M, 1200W	Ph.D.'s:	n/av
Grad: none	S/F Ratio:	n/av
Year: sems, ss	Tuition:	$480 ($1480)
Appl: open	R and B:	n/app
475 applied	400 accepted	350 enrolled
ACT: 15		NONCOMPETITIVE

Bluefield State College, founded in 1895, is a publicly supported institution offering programs in business, the liberal arts, technology, and education. It is operated by the West Virginia Board of Regents. Its library contains 100,000 volumes and 110,000 reels of microfilm, and subscribes to 650 periodicals.

Environment: The 40-acre campus, located in an urban area of 16,000 persons, has 13 buildings. The college has no student housing.

Student Life: About 87% of the students are from West Virginia. Ninety-eight percent are graduates of public schools. Cars are permitted on campus.

Organizations: Eight percent of the students belong to one of 4 fraternities and 3 sororities. A student council organizes social and cultural entertainment.

Sports: The college participates in intercollegiate sports and also sponsors intramural programs.

Handicapped: There are no special facilities for handicapped students.

Graduates: About 3% of the freshmen drop out, and 25% remain to graduate. Of those, 10% seek advanced degrees; about 2% enter medical, dental, or law school. Sixty percent of the graduates pursue careers in business and industry.

Programs of Study: The college confers the B.A., B.S., and B.S.Ed. degrees. Associate degrees also are available. Bachelor's degrees are offered in the following subjects: BUSINESS (accounting, business administration, business education, management, marketing), EDUCATION (elementary, secondary, special), ENGLISH (English), FINE AND PERFORMING ARTS (art education), HEALTH SCIENCES (nursing), MATH AND SCIENCES (biology, chemistry, mathematics, natural sciences, physical sciences, zoology), PREPROFESSIONAL (architecture, engineering), SOCIAL SCIENCES (government/political science, history, psychology, social sciences, sociology).

Special: Study abroad can be arranged. The college confers the B.G.S. degree. Students may earn combined B.A.-B.S. degrees.

Admissions: About 84% of those who applied were accepted for the 1981–82 freshman class. Eight percent of those who enrolled ranked in the top fifth of their high school class; 25% ranked in the top two-fifths. Candidates are judged on their ACT scores and high school record. The GED is accepted.

Procedure: The ACT is required. New students are admitted to all terms. Application deadlines are open. No application fee is required.

Special: Early and deferred admissions plans are available. AP and CLEP credit is given.

Transfer: An open admissions policy is in effect. Transfer students are accepted for all classes. D grades transfer. Students must earn at least 32 hours at the college to receive a bachelor's degree.

Visiting: Regularly scheduled orientations are held for prospective students. Guides are available for informal visits; visitors may sit in on classes.

Financial Aid: Thirty percent of all students receive aid. Scholarships, loans, and work-study jobs are available. The college is a member of the CSS, and the FAF or FFS is required. The application deadline is April 1.

Foreign Students: About 50 students from foreign countries are enrolled. The college offers these students an intensive English program, special counseling, and special organizations.

Admissions: Applicants must score 550 or better on the TOEFL. No college entrance exams are required.

Procedure: Application deadlines are open. Foreign students must present proof of adequate funds for 1 semester.

Admissions Contact: Rick Snow, Director of Admissions.

CONCORD COLLEGE B-5
Athens, West Virginia 24712 (304) 384-3115

F/T: 760M, 967W
P/T: 183M, 452W
Grad: none
Year: sems, ss
Appl: open
848 applied 700 accepted 503 enrolled
ACT: 18 LESS COMPETITIVE

Faculty: 82; IIB, +$
Ph.D.'s: 45%
S/F Ratio: 20 to 1
Tuition: $452 ($1452)
R and B: $1902

Concord College, supported by the state of West Virginia, provides programs of liberal arts, medical technology, science, business administration, and teacher training. The library has 144,000 volumes and 16,050 microfilm items, and subscribes to 650 periodicals.

Environment: The college is located on a 95-acre site, in a rural setting, 5 miles from Princeton, West Virginia. Roanoke, Virginia, is 60 miles away. Traditional, high-rise, and coed dormitories are available on a first-come, first-served basis. The college also sponsors married student housing and sets aside specific floors for fraternities and sororities in the dormitories.

Student Life: About 80% of the students are state residents; 98% of the entering freshmen come from public schools. Sixty percent of the students live on campus. Students may have cars but must observe parking regulations. About 80% of the students are Protestant and 18% are Catholic. About 9% are minority-group members. Campus housing is coed and single-sex; there are visiting privileges.

Organizations: About one-third of the men belong to 1 of the 6 national fraternities on campus; 33% of the women are members of 1 of the 4 national sororities. Extracurricular activities include dances, parties, and social and organizational gatherings. A center for the creative and performing arts is located on campus. Nearby recreation areas provide fishing and hunting.

Sports: The college fields 6 intercollegiate teams for men and 4 for women. There are 15 intramural sports for men and 14 for women.

Handicapped: About 75% of the campus is accessible to physically handicapped students. Wheelchair ramps, special parking, and elevators are available.

Graduates: The freshman dropout rate is 20%. About 45% of entering freshmen graduate 4 years later; 20% pursue graduate study. One percent enter medical school. Thirty percent pursue careers in business and industry.

Services: Students receive the following services free of charge: placement, career counseling, health care, tutoring, and remedial instruction. There is a placement service for undergraduates.

Programs of Study: The college confers the B.A., B.S., B.S.W., and B.S.Ed. degrees. Bachelor's degrees are offered in the following subjects: BUSINESS (business administration, business education), EDUCATION (early childhood, elementary, health/physical, secondary, special), ENGLISH (English, speech/drama), FINE AND PERFORMING ARTS (art, art education, music education), HEALTH SCIENCES (medical technology), MATH AND SCIENCES (biology, chemistry, mathematics, mathematics/computer science), PREPROFESSIONAL (library science, social work), SOCIAL SCIENCES (community development and regional planning, geography, government/political science, history, psychology, sociology, travel industry management). Fifty percent of the degrees are conferred in education, 25% in business, and 10% in preprofessional studies.

Special: Concord offers a 3-1 program in medical technology. Work-study programs exist in all departments.

Honors: There are 5 honor and leadership organizations.

Admissions: Eighty-three percent of those who applied were accepted for the 1981–82 freshman class. The candidate must be a graduate of an accredited high school, have completed 17 Carnegie units of work, and rank in the upper 75% of the graduating class. Graduates in the lowest fourth may be admitted if they scored 14 or higher on the ACT.

Procedure: The SAT or ACT is required for freshmen. The deadlines for regular admission are open. Freshmen are admitted to all sessions. There is no application fee. The college uses a rolling admissions plan.

Special: The college offers advanced placement and credit through CLEP. The application deadline for advanced admission is the completion of the junior year in high school.

Transfer: For fall 1981, 471 transfer students applied, 469 were accepted, and 406 enrolled. Transfers are accepted for all classes. D grades transfer except in English and education courses. A 2.0 GPA is required. A transfer student must earn a minimum of 32 semester hours of credit in residence to receive a degree from the college; the bachelor's degree requires 128 credits. Transfer application deadlines are open. The ACT or SAT is required for transfer students with less than 30 hours of college credit.

Visiting: A 2-day orientation for students is held prior to the start of the fall semester. Guides are also available for informal visits. Visitors can sit in on classes and stay overnight at the school. The best time for campus visits is in the fall and spring. The admissions office should be contacted for further information.

Financial Aid: Financial aid is usually in the form of a package, with maximum aid to out-of-state students of $4300 and average aid to freshmen of $1500. Twenty-five percent of the students are engaged in work-study programs. The deadline for the college's financial aid application is April 15; the FAF must also be filed. The college is a member of CSS. About 55% of the students receive financial aid.

Foreign Students: Fewer than 1% of the students come from foreign countries. The college offers these students special counseling.

Admissions: Foreign students must achieve a minimum TOEFL score of 450; in addition, they must take the SAT or ACT.

Procedure: Application deadlines are open. Foreign students must present proof of health as well as proof of funds adequate to cover 1 year of study.

Admissions Contact: Dale Dickens, Director of Admissions.

954 WEST VIRGINIA

DAVIS AND ELKINS COLLEGE C-3
Elkins, West Virginia 26241 (304) 636-1900

F/T: 479M, 442W	Faculty: 56; IIB, --$
P/T: 95M, 59W	Ph.D.'s: 52%
Grad: none	S/F Ratio: 14 to 1
Year: 4-1-4, ss	Tuition: $4075
Appl: Sept. 1	R and B: $1920
691 applied	625 accepted	277 enrolled
SAT or ACT: required		LESS COMPETITIVE

Davis and Elkins College, founded in 1904 by the Presbyterian Church, is a private liberal arts college. The library has 95,000 volumes and more than 3000 microfilm items, and subscribes to 595 periodicals.

Environment: The 160-acre campus is located in a rural setting, 135 miles from Pittsburgh and 205 miles from Washington, D.C. The campus buildings include a chapel, student union, a campus center, and a science center. Six dormitories house 660 students.

Student Life: The student body is drawn from all parts of the country, with fewer than 39% from West Virginia. Ninety percent of the entering freshmen come from public schools. Over 70% of the students live on campus in the residence halls. Only students with special permission are not required to live in the dormitories. About 60% of the students are Protestant, 37% are Catholic, and 1% are Jewish. About 10% of the students are minority-group members. Campus housing is coed and single-sex; there are visiting privileges. Students may keep cars on campus.

Organizations: About 35% of the student body belong to national fraternities and sororities on campus. Popular recreational activities include hiking, fishing, hunting, and camping in the nearby hills and mountains.

Sports: The college fields 6 intercollegiate teams for men and 4 for women. There are 7 intramural sports for men and 6 for women.

Handicapped: Special facilities for the physically handicapped include some buildings with specially equipped rest rooms, wheelchair ramps, and elevators. Only 1% of the campus is accessible to these students.

Graduates: The freshman dropout rate is 25%; 52% remain to graduate, and about 38% of the graduates go on to graduate or professional school. One percent enter medical school, 2% law school, and 1% dental school. About 50% enter careers in business and industry.

Services: The following services are available to students free of charge: placement and career counseling, psychological counseling, tutoring, and remedial instruction. There are placement services for undergraduate and graduate students. Health care is available for a fee.

Programs of Study: The college awards B.A. and B.S. degrees, and also offers associate degree programs. Bachelor's degrees are offered in the following subjects: BUSINESS (accounting, business education, computer science, fashion merchandising, finance, health care administration, management, marketing, public health administration, secretarial science), EDUCATION (early childhood, elementary, health/physical, secondary), ENGLISH (English composition, literature), FINE AND PERFORMING ARTS (art, communication, theater/dramatics), HEALTH SCIENCES (medical technology, nursing), LANGUAGES (French, Spanish), MATH AND SCIENCES (biology, chemistry, ecology/environmental science, mathematics), PHILOSOPHY (philosophy, religion), PREPROFESSIONAL (dentistry, engineering, forestry, law, medicine, veterinary), SOCIAL SCIENCES (anthropology, economics, government/political science, history, psychology, social sciences, sociology, youth services).

Special: There are 3-2 combination degree programs offered in engineering and forestry, and a 3-1 program in medical technology. Off-campus projects include internships, work-study, field studies, foreign study tours, and extended study abroad. Independent study and interdisciplinary majors are offered.

Honors: Honorary societies include Alpha Phi Omega. All departments offer special honors classes to qualified students.

Admissions: About 90% of those who applied were accepted for the 1981-82 freshman class. The SAT scores of those who enrolled were as follows: Verbal—90% below 500, 2% between 500 and 599, less than 1% between 600 and 700, and 0% above 700; Math—86% below 500, 6% between 500 and 599, 3% between 600 and 700, and 0% above 700. On the ACT, 74% scored below 21, 10% between 21 and 23, 10% between 24 and 25, 7% between 26 and 28, and 0% above 28. A minimum C average is required of all entering freshmen. Graduation from an accredited high school is required, and a substantial high school program is desirable. Other factors that are considered are recommendations from a guidance counselor, evidence of special talents, impressions made during an interview, and advanced placement or honors courses.

Procedure: The SAT or the ACT is required and should be taken in the fall of the senior year. Application deadliens are September 1 for the fall term, January 1 for the winter term, February 1 for the spring term, and June 1 for the summer session. A $15 application fee is required. The college has a rolling admissions policy.

Special: The college offers early admissions, deferred admissions, and early decision plans. The notification date for early decision is 10 days after the admissions file has been completed.

Transfer: For fall 1981, 117 transfer students applied, 95 were accepted, and 61 enrolled. An average of C is required of all transfer students. Twenty-eight hours must be earned in residence; the bachelor's degree requires 124 credits. D grades transfer. Application deadlines are the same as those for freshmen.

Visiting: There are regularly scheduled orientation sessions for prospective students. Guides are provided for informal visits, which are best made weekdays. Visitors may sit in on classes and may stay overnight at the school. The admissions office will arrange such visits.

Financial Aid: About 53% of all students receive financial aid administered by the college. The deadlines for aid application are June 1 (fall), November 1 (winter), December 1 (spring), and March 1 (summer). The average award to freshmen is $3684. All departments have CWS programs; 24% of the students earn money through part-time employment. Installment financing is available. The college is a member of CSS; the FAF is required.

Foreign Students: About 4% of the students come from foreign countries. The college offers these students an intensive English course, special counseling, and special organizations.

Admissions: Foreign students must achieve a minimum TOEFL score of 450; no further exams are required.

Procedure: The application deadline for the fall is September 1. Foreign students must present the college's medical form as well as proof of funds adequate to cover 1 year of study.

Admissions Contact: David H. Wilkey, Director of Admissions.

FAIRMONT STATE COLLEGE C-2
Fairmont, West Virginia 26554 (304) 367-4141

F/T: 1470M, 1845W	Faculty: 147; IIB, +$
P/T: 821M, 1029W	Ph.D.'s: 39%
Grad: none	S/F Ratio: 22 to 1
Year: sems, ss	Tuition: $450 ($1450)
Appl: see profile	R and B: $1954
1933 applied	1933 accepted	1095 enrolled
ACT: 16		NONCOMPETITIVE

Fairmont State College is a state-supported, coeducational institution that was founded in 1867. The library has 151,000 volumes and 25,000 microfilm items, and subscribes to 700 periodicals.

Environment: The modern 80-acre campus in Fairmont (population, 30,000) is located in a suburban area 72 miles south of Pittsburgh, Pennsylvania. The campus is self-contained and includes a physical education center and basketball arena. Dormitories, on or adjacent to the campus, all under college supervision, houses 132 men and 313 women.

Student Life: Ninety-five percent of the students are state residents; 98% of the entering freshmen come from public schools. Ten percent of the students live in residence halls on campus. About 6% of the students are minority-group members. Campus housing is single-sex; there are visiting privileges. Students may keep cars on campus.

Organizations: There are 5 national fraternities and 1 local fraternity; 10% of the men belong to 1 of these organizations. About 10% of the women belong to 1 of the 4 national sororities that have chapters on campus.

Sports: The college fields 8 intercollegiate teams for men and 6 for women. There are 10 intramural sports for men and 6 for women.

Handicapped: The college offers special parking for the handicapped and estimates that 30% of the campus is accessible to these students. There are 3 special counselors.

Graduates: At the end of the freshman year, 20% drop out; another 40% remain to graduate, and 5% of these students become candidates for graduate or professional degrees. One percent enter medical school, 1% enter dental school, and 2% go on to law school.

Services: Students receive the following services free of charge: placement and career counseling, health care, tutoring, remedial instruction, and psychological counseling.

Programs of Study: The college offers the B.A. and B.S. degrees. The B.A.Ed. is granted in kindergarten, elementary, and high school education. Associate degree programs are also offered. Bachelor's degrees are offered in the following subjects: BUSINESS (accounting, business administration), EDUCATION (elementary, health/physical, secondary), ENGLISH (English), LANGUAGES (French), MATH AND SCIENCES (biology, chemistry, mathematics), PREPROFESSIONAL (dentistry, engineering, medicine, pharmacy), SOCIAL SCIENCES (history, psychology, sociology). Thirty percent of the degrees are conferred in engineering technology, 30% in business administration, and 20% in education.

Special: It is possible to earn a combined B.A.-B.S. degree.

Admissions: All of those who applied for the 1981–82 freshman class were accepted. The ACT scores of those who enrolled were as follows: 77% below 21, 10% between 21 and 23, 8% between 24 and 25, 4% between 26 and 28, and 1% above 28. To be admitted, a student must have graduated from high school and must submit the following credentials: application, ACT scores, and final high school transcript. Fairmont also recommends that a complete health form be submitted.

Procedure: The ACT is required. The suggested application deadliens are two weeks prior to the start of each semester. There is no application fee. The college follows a rolling admissions policy.

Special: Early decision, early admissions, and deferred admissions plans are available. CLEP and AP credit is given.

Transfer: Transfers are admitted to all classes. An average of C is required in previous college work; D grades are accepted. To receive a bachelor's degree, the transfer student must complete, at the college, 32 of the 128 credits required. Transfer application deadlines are the same as those for freshmen.

Visiting: Guides are available for informal visits. Visitors are not permitted to stay at the school. For further information, Blair Montgomery should be contacted.

Financial Aid: About 60% of all students receive financial aid; 30% of the students work part-time on campus. The deadline for financial aid application is March 1. About 110 freshman scholarships are offered each year, including tuition-waiver scholarships. The college participates in the BEOG program, the NDEA student loan program, the guaranteed loan program, and the work-study program. The college is a member of CSS; the FAF is required.

Foreign Students: About 2% of the students come from foreign countries. The college offers these students special organizations.

Admissions: Foreign students must achieve a minimum TOEFL score of 500; in addition, they must take the ACT.

Procedure: Applications must be submitted by March for fall, August for winter, and January for summer. Foreign students must present proof of health as well as proof of adequate funds. They should also carry health insurance.

Admissions Contact: John G. Conaway, Director of Admissions and Assistant Registrar.

GLENVILLE STATE COLLEGE C–3
Glenville, West Virginia 26351 (304) 462-7361

F/T: 668M, 590W	Faculty: 76; IIB, av$
P/T: 205M, 535W	Ph.D.'s: 38%
Grad: none	S/F Ratio: 20 to 1
Year: sems, ss	Tuition: $444 ($1444)
Appl: open	R and B: $1880
598 applied	598 accepted 367 enrolled
ACT: 17	NONCOMPETITIVE

Glenville State College is a state-controlled coeducational college of liberal arts and teacher training. The college library houses 296,000 volumes and 200,000 microfilm items, and subscribes to 116 periodicals.

Environment: The college occupies 310 acres in a rural area 60 miles from Clarksburg and consists of 10 modern buildings, including dorms for both men and women. There are 2 residence halls and 1 sorority house. The college also sponsors married student housing.

Student Life: About 88% of the students are from West Virginia. Ninety-five percent of the entering freshmen come from public schools. Resident students make up 60% of the total. About 85% of the students are Protestant and 15% are Catholic. About 8% of the students are minority-group members. Campus housing is single-sex; there are visiting privileges. Students may keep cars on campus.

Organizations: Twenty percent of the men belong to 2 national fraternities; about 20% of the women students belong to 2 national sororities. Popular recreational, cultural, and social activities include trips to nearby rural areas to visit Appalachian craft shops, skiing in the adjacent mountains, and attending blue grass music concerts and festivals.

Sports: Glenville fields intercollegiate teams in 8 sports for men and 4 for women. There are 4 intramural sports for men and 4 for women.

Handicapped: Very steep hills on the campus hinder handicapped students. Special class scheduling and special parking can be arranged for these students. Only about 25% of the campus is accessible to the handicapped.

Graduates: Of those who enter as freshmen, about 25% drop out; 35% to 40% graduate with their class. About 10% of these graduates enter graduate or professional school. One percent of the graduates enter medical school and 1% enter law school. About 15% of the students pursue careers in business and industry.

Services: The following services are available to students at no charge: placement and career counseling; tutoring; and remedial instruction.

Programs of Study: Glenville confers the B.A. and B.S. degrees. Associate degree programs are also available. Bachelor's degrees are offered in the following subjects: BUSINESS (business administration), EDUCATION (early childhood, elementary, health/physical, secondary), ENGLISH (English), FINE AND PERFORMING ARTS (art education), MATH AND SCIENCES (biology, chemistry), PREPROFESSIONAL (agriculture, dentistry, forestry, law, medicine, pharmacy), SOCIAL SCIENCES (history). About 40% of all degrees are conferred in education and 25% in business.

Special: Two-year technical programs are offered in secretarial science, forest technology, social service technology, and land surveying. Advanced placement credit is given in English, mathematics, and French. Other programs include foundation studies in reading, English, mathematics, and science.

Admissions: All of the students who applied were accepted for the 1981–82 freshman class. The ACT scores of those who enrolled were as follows: 60% below 21, 20% between 21 and 23, 7% between 24 and 25, 7% between 26 and 28, and 6% above 28. All in-state high school graduates are eligible for admission to the college. Out-of-state residents must rank in the upper half of their class. The ACT is required but is used only for placement purposes.

Procedure: The ACT is required. There are no application deadlines or application fees. A decision regarding admissions will be made immediately upon receipt of credentials. New students are admitted to all sessions.

Special: CLEP and general subject exams are accepted.

Transfer: For fall 1981, 74 transfer students applied, 74 were accepted, and 49 enrolled. Transfers are accepted for all classes. To receive a bachelor's degree, students must complete 30 hours in residence; those with less than 30 hours' work must provide a high school transcript as well as their college transcript. The bachelor's degree requires the completion of 128 credits. An average of C for transfer students is desirable; D grades transfer. Application deadlines are open.

Visiting: There are no regularly scheduled orientations for prospective students; however, informal visits to the campus are encouraged, and guides are provided. Visitors may sit in on classes and may stay overnight at the school. Weekdays are the best time for campus visits. The dean of records and admissions should be contacted to arrange such visits.

Financial Aid: About 60% of all students receive financial aid in the form of scholarships, loans, and campus employment. About 20% of the students work part-time. The average award to freshmen from all sources is $1800. The deadline for aid applications is March 1. The FAF is required.

Foreign Students: About 1% of the students come from foreign countries. The college offers these students special counseling.

Admissions: Foreign students must achieve a minimum TOEFL score of 450; in addition, they must take the ACT.

Procedure: Application deadlines are June 1 for fall and October 1 for spring. Foreign students must present proof of funds adequate to cover 1 year of study. They must also carry health insurance, which is available through the college.

Admissions Contact: Mack K. Samples, Dean of Records and Admissions.

MARSHALL UNIVERSITY
A-4
Huntington, West Virginia 25701   (304) 696-3160

F/T: 3005M, 3270W	Faculty:	n/av; IIA, −$
P/T: 1280M, 1635W	Ph.D.'s:	53%
Grad: 1145M, 1484W	S/F Ratio:	24 to 1
Year: sems, ss	Tuition:	$500 ($1500)
Appl: Aug. 15	R and B:	$2000
3400 applied	3300 accepted	2150 enrolled
ACT: 18		LESS COMPETITIVE

Marshall University, established in 1837, is a state-supported institution consisting of 5 undergraduate colleges, a graduate school, and a medical school. The library houses 300,000 volumes and 200,000 microfilm items, and subscribes to 2200 periodicals.

Environment: Located in Huntington, in an urban area 50 miles from Charleston, West Virginia, the main campus consists of 45 acres. Dormitories on campus house 2235 men and women. Housing is also available in fraternity and sorority houses adjacent to the campus. The university also sponsors married student housing. Commuter facilities include a student center.

Student Life: Most of the students are residents of the state; 14% come from other states, and a few are from foreign countries. About 45% of the students are Protestant, 18% are Catholic, and 1% are Jewish. About 5% of the students are minority-group members. Campus housing is coed. Students may keep cars on campus. Day-care services are available to all students, faculty, and staff for a fee.

Organizations: About 10% of the men and 12% of the women belong to 1 of 9 fraternities and 13 sororities with chapters on campus. There are approximately 100 student social organizations and academic groups. Popular cultural and recreational areas off campus include the civic center and a nearby park.

Sports: Marshall fields 11 intercollegiate teams for men and 8 for women. There are 20 intramural sports for men and 19 for women.

Handicapped: Marshall provides special facilities for the physically handicapped, including wheelchair ramps, special parking, elevators, and specially equipped rest rooms. Special class scheduling can be arranged. About 95% of the campus is accessible to these students. One special counselor is available for handicapped students.

Graduates: The freshman dropout rate is 29%; 51% remain to graduate. About 37% of students pursue graduate study after graduation. About 2% enter medical school, 3% law school, and 3% dental school. About 25% enter careers in business and industry.

Services: The following services are available free of charge to all students: placement and career counseling, psychological counseling, tutoring, and remedial instruction. Health care services are available for a fee.

Programs of Study: The university awards the B.A., B.S., B.F.A., and B.B.A. degrees, as well as associate, master's, and doctoral degrees. Bachelor's degrees are offered in the following subjects: BUSINESS (accounting, business administration, business education, computer science, finance, management, marketing, real estate/insurance), EDUCATION (early childhood, elementary, helath/physical, secondary, special), ENGLISH (English, journalism, literature, speech), FINE AND PERFORMING ARTS (art, art education, art history, music, music education, radio/TV, studio art, theater/dramatics), HEALTH SCIENCES (medical technology, nursing, speech therapy), LANGUAGES (French, German, Spanish), MATH AND SCIENCES (biology, botany, chemistry, geology, mathematics, natural sciences, physical sciences, zoology), PHILOSOPHY (humanities, philosophy), PREPROFESSIONAL (home economics, library science, social work), SOCIAL SCIENCES (anthropology, economics, geography, government/political science, history, international relations, psychology, social sciences, sociology). Thirty percent of all degrees conferred are in education, 29% are in math and sciences, and 29% are in English.

Special: It is possible to combine the B.S. and B.A. degrees in the sciences and education. The college also offers a general studies curriculum. Two-year preprofessional preparation (with no degree) is offered in agriculture, architecture, dentistry, engineering, forestry, law, medicine, ministry, pharmacy, and veterinary.

Honors: There are 11 honor societies presently on the Marshall campus, including Phi Delta Kappa. Honors programs are available in 20 departments, as well as on an interdisciplinary basis.

Admissions: Approximately 97% of those applying were accepted into the 1981-82 freshman class. The ACT scores of those who enrolled were as follows: 59% below 21, 23% between 21 and 23, 5% between 24 and 25, 5% between 26 and 28, and 8% above 28. Applicants must have a C average.

Procedure: The ACT is required. Students are accepted in the fall, spring, or summer terms. Application deadlines are August 15 (fall), January 1 (spring), and June 1 (summer). There is no application fee. A rolling admissions policy is in effect; notification is on a daily basis.

Special: Early admissions, deferred admissions, and early decision plans are offered. AP and CLEP credit is available.

Transfer: For fall 1981, 700 transfer students applied, 600 were accepted, and 580 enrolled. An average of C (2.0) is required of all transfer students; D grades, however, are acceptable. There is a residency requirement of 30 credits; the bachelor's degree requires 128 credits. Application deadlines are the same as those for freshmen.

Visiting: Regularly scheduled orientations are held for prospective students at 10 A.M. and 2 P.M. Monday through Friday. Saturday orientations may be arranged. There are guides for informal visits, which are best made during the week; visitors may sit in on classes. Although there is limited space, visitors may stay overnight at the school. Those interested should contact the admissions office.

Financial Aid: About 36% of all students receive financial aid, in the form of loans, grants, scholarships, and campus employment. Fifteen percent of the students work part-time on campus. Work-study programs are available in all departments. The university is a member of CSS; the FAF is required. Aid applications should be filed by March 1 (fall), November 1 (spring), or April 1 (summer).

Foreign Students: About 3% of the students come from foreign countries. The university offers these students an intensive English course, special counseling, and special organizations.

Admissions: Foreign students must achieve a score of 500 on the TOEFL or 79 on the University of Michigan Language Test; in addition, they must also take the ACT.

Procedure: Application deadlines are 3 months prior to the start of each semester. Foreign students must present proof of funds adequate to cover their entire period of study. They must also carry health insurance.

Admissions Contact: James W. Harless, Director of Admissions.

SALEM COLLEGE
C-3
Salem, West Virginia 26426   (304) 782-5336

F/T: 450M, 400W	Faculty:	54; IIB, −−$
P/T: 400M, 250W	Ph.D.'s:	25%
Grad: 43M, 31W	S/F Ratio:	14 to 1
Year: sems, ss	Tuition:	$3470
Appl: Aug. 15	R and B:	$1825
1314 applied	1013 accepted	353 enrolled
SAT: 400V 400M	ACT: 18	LESS COMPETITIVE

Salem College, founded in 1888, is a private institution offering a career-centered curriculum. Standard liberal arts and preprofessional courses are available at Salem. The college library contains 125,000 volumes and 39,000 microfilm items, and subscribes to 450 periodicals.

Environment: Located in a rural area near Salem, a small town of 3000 people, the 200-acre campus is approximately 10 miles from Clarksburg, West Virginia, the nearest major city.

Student Life: Most of the students are from New York, New Jersey, and Pennsylvania. Seventy percent of the entering freshmen come from public schools. About 25% of the students commute; there is on-campus housing for 720. Campus housing is coed and single-sex; there are visiting privileges. Students may keep cars on campus.

Organizations: About 37% of the men belong to 1 of 5 fraternities; 20% of the women belong to 1 of 3 sororities. National forests and ski resorts in the area provide recreational facilities. Campus events include Winter Weekend, the annual Heritage Arts Festival, and Special Convocation. There are extracurricular activities, special-interest groups, and department clubs.

Sports: Salem fields 7 intercollegiate teams for men and 4 for women. There are 6 intramural sports for men and 6 for women.

Handicapped: Special facilities for the physically handicapped include wheelchair ramps, special parking, elevators, specially equipped rest rooms, and lowered telephones. About 90% of the campus is accessible to these students. Tutoring is available to the handicapped, as are the services of 4 counselors and 7 assistant counselors.

Graduates: About 10% of the freshmen drop out, and 60% eventually graduate. Approximately 30% pursue graduate study after graduation. One percent enter medical school and 2% enter law school. Fifty-one percent of the graduating class pursue careers in business and industry.

Services: The following services are offered to students free of charge: placement and career counseling, tutoring, remedial instruction, psychological counseling, and health care. Placement services are available for undergraduates and alumni seeking summer, part-time, or postgraduate jobs.

Programs of Study: The college awards the B.A., B.S., B.S.W., and B.S. in Equestrian Studies degrees, as well as associate and master's degrees. Bachelor's degrees are offered in the following subjects: BUSINESS (accounting, computer science, management, marketing), EDUCATION (elementary, health/physical, industrial, secondary, special), ENGLISH (journalism, speech), FINE AND PERFORMING ARTS (art, art education, heritage arts, radio/TV), HEALTH SCIENCES (art therapy, medical media, medical technology, radiologic technology), MATH AND SCIENCES (biology, chemistry, mathematics, natural sciences), PREPROFESSIONAL (law, medicine, social work), SOCIAL SCIENCES (government/political science, psychology, sociology, youth agency). About 25% of the students receive degrees in business, 20% in social sciences, and 19% in health sciences.

Required: All students are expected to take certain basic courses, including English, social studies, science, fine arts, and physical education. Seniors must take the Undergraduate Record Exam.

Special: The college allows student-designed majors. There are work-study programs in 21 departments.

Honors: Salem College has a chapter of the Gamma Beta Phi honorary society on campus.

Admissions: About 77% of those who applied for admission were accepted into the 1981-82 freshman class. The SAT scores of those who enrolled were as follows: Verbal—85% below 500, 12% between 500 and 599, 3% between 600 and 700, and 0% above 700; Math—88% below 500, 10% between 500 and 599, 2% between 600 and 700, and 0% above 700. On the ACT, 85% scored below 21, 11% between 21 and 23, 4% between 24 and 25, 0% between 26 and 28, and 0% above 28. Applicants must have graduated from an accredited high school and are expected to be in the upper two-thirds of their class. In addition, character and potential are evaluated, and satisfactory ACT or SAT scores are essential. Sixteen high school units should have been completed. Other factors entering into the admissions decision are impressions made during an interview, advanced placement or honors courses, and recommendations by school officials.

Procedure: The application deadlines are August 15 (fall), December 15 (spring), and May 15 (summer). ACT or SAT scores are required, and an application fee of $10 must be submitted. There is a rolling admissions plan.

Special: Students may earn credit through CLEP and AP exams.

Transfer: Most applications are accepted. A minimum average of C is required, but students have the option of transferring D grades. Thirty-two hours must be completed at Salem; the bachelor's degree requires 128 credits. Application deadlines are the same as those for freshmen.

Visiting: There are regularly scheduled orientations for prospective students. Guides are provided, and visitors may sit in on classes. The best times for campus visits are during the semesters. Visitors may stay overnight at the school. The admissions office should be contacted for arrangements.

Financial Aid: About 90% of all students receive financial aid. The deadline for aid applications is April 15. Scholarship funds, loans, and grants are available. The average aid to freshmen is $1700. About 60% of the students work part-time on campus. The college is a member of CSS; the FAF is required.

Foreign Students: About 1% of the students come from foreign countries.

Admissions: Foreign students must achieve a minimum TOEFL score of 450; no further exams are required.

Procedure: Application deadlines are August 15 for fall and December 15 for spring. Foreign students must present proof of funds adequate to cover 1 year of study. They must also carry health insurance, which is available through the college for a fee.

Admissions Contact: Stephen Ornstein, Director of Admissions.

SHEPHERD COLLEGE E-2
Shepherdstown, West Virginia 25443 (304) 876-2511

F/T: 1299M, 1807W	Faculty:	110; IIB, +$
P/T: none	Ph.D.'s:	65%
Grad: none	S/F Ratio:	21 to 1
Year: sems, ss	Tuition:	$466 ($1466)
Appl: Aug. 1	R and B:	$1500
1900 applied	1200 accepted	1000 enrolled
SAT: 550V 550M	ACT: 24	COMPETITIVE+

Shepherd College, founded in 1871, is a public liberal arts and teachers' college under the control of the state of West Virginia. The library contains 230,000 volumes and 5500 microfilm items, and subscribes to 530 periodicals.

Environment: The 156-acre rural campus is located in a small town 65 miles from Washington, D.C. The campus consists of 27 buildings on 2 adjoining campuses. These buildings include 7 dormitories housing 1100 students, 8 academic buildings, a creative arts center, a modern library, and an athletic center.

Student Life: Fifty-seven percent of the student body are from West Virginia; 40% are from bordering states. About 85% of the entering freshmen come from public schools. Thirty percent of the students live on campus; the other 70% live in off-campus apartments and private homes. About 10% of the students are minority-group members. Campus housing is coed and single-sex; there are visiting privileges. Students may keep cars on campus.

Organizations: Fifteen percent of the men belong to the 1 local and 5 national fraternities on campus; 20% of the women join the 1 local and 5 national sororities on campus. A wide range of social, cultural, and recreational activities are scheduled regularly on campus. In addition, the extensive resources of the Washington, D.C., area supplement those of the college.

Sports: The college fields 7 intercollegiate teams for men and 7 for women. There are 18 intramural sports for men and 15 for women.

Handicapped: About 70% of the campus is accessible to wheelchair-bound students. A wide range of facilities, including wheelchair ramps, special parking, elevators, lowered drinking fountains, and specially equipped restrooms, are offered to the handicapped. Special class scheduling can be arranged. Special counselors are provided for handicapped students.

Graduates: The freshman dropout rate is 22%; 65% remain to graduate. Fifty percent of the graduates pursue advanced study after graduation. Five percent enter medical school, 2% enter dental school, and about 10% enter law school. Forty percent of the graduates pursue careers in business and industry.

Services: The following services are available free of charge to all students: placement and career counseling, health care, tutoring, and remedial instruction. Psychological counseling is available on a fee basis. The college provides placement services for both undergraduate students and alumni.

Programs of Study: The college awards the B.A. and B.S. degrees. Associate degrees are also available. Bachelor's degrees are offered in the following subjects: BUSINESS (accounting, business administration, business education, computer science, finance, hotel and restaurant management, management, marketing), EDUCATION (early childhood, elementary, health/physical, middle school, secondary), ENGLISH (communications, English, journalism, literature, speech), FINE AND PERFORMING ARTS (art, art education, art history, art therapy, commercial art, music, music education, music therapy, photography, studio art, theater/dramatics), HEALTH SCIENCES (medical technology, nursing), LANGUAGES (French), MATH AND SCIENCES (biology, botany, chemistry, earth science, mathematics, physical sciences, zoology), PREPROFESSIONAL (agriculture, dentistry, engineering, home economics, law, library science, medicine, pharmacy, social work, veterinary), SOCIAL SCIENCES (economics, government/political science, history, international relations, psychology, sociology). There are also programs in recreation and leisure services, and park administration. Forty percent of the degrees are conferred in business, 20% in education, and 10% in preprofessional areas.

Required: All undergraduates are required to take English, literature, music and art appreciation, speech, biology or physical science, mathematics, Western civilization, economics, political science, sociology, and physical education. In order to graduate, the student must earn 128 semester hours with at least 256 quality points and an average of 2.0-2.3 in elementary education and at least 2.5 in secondary education. Students are required to take GRE aptitude tests and GRE advanced tests for graduation.

Special: It is possible to earn a combined B.A.-B.S. degree in all areas of study. The college also offers a general studies degree. CLEP general and subject exams are accepted. Students may take courses by independent study and are permitted to participate in study-abroad programs of other institutions. Some work-study programs are offered.

Honors: Five national honor societies presently have chapters on campus. The following departments offer honors programs: Education, Home Economics, Library Science, History, and English.

Admissions: Sixty-three percent of those who applied were accepted for the 1981-82 freshman class. Candidates for admission must be graduates of an accredited high school, must have a minimum

958 WEST VIRGINIA

GPA of 2.5, and must have completed 17 Carnegie units. The minimum acceptable ACT score for in-state students is 18. Other factors in the admissions decision are impressions made during an interview, leadership and extracurricular activities records, evidence of special talents, recommendations by high school officials, and advanced placement or honors courses.

Procedure: The ACT is required and should be taken by December for fall admission. The college operates on the early semester system (August–December and January–May) and offers 2 summer sessions. Application deadlines are August 1 for the fall (February 1 for residence hall housing), December 1 for the spring, and May 1 for the summer. A rolling admissions policy is used. A personal interview is required. There is no application fee.

Special: The application deadline for Shepherd's early decision plan is November 1; May 1 is the deadline for early admission. The college also provides a deferred admissions plan.

Transfer: For fall 1981, 300 transfer students applied, 250 were accepted, and 200 enrolled. Transfer students are admitted to all classes. They are required to have a GPA above 2.0 and an acceptable social and academic record from previous institutions. To earn a degree at Shepherd, a transfer student must take 32 semester hours of credit in residence; the bachelor's degree requries 128 hours. D grades are accepted. Application deadlines are the same as those for freshmen.

Visiting: There are regularly scheduled orientations for prospective students at Shepherd. An admissions interview, a tour of the campus, and a department interview are part of the agenda of the campus visit. There are guides for informal visits. Visitors may sit in on classes. The best time for campus visits is Monday through Friday. The college admissions office should be contacted to arrange such visits.

Financial Aid: About 40% of all students receive financial aid; 20% of the students work part-time on campus. The deadline for financial aid application is March 1. Scholarships, loans, and work contracts are available to qualified students. Need, scholarship, and character of the applicant are given greatest consideration in determining aid awards. The college is a member of CSS; the FAF is required.

Foreign Students: Fewer than 1% of the students come from foreign countries. The college offers these students special counseling and special organizations.

Admissions: Foreign students must achieve a minimum TOEFL score of 500; in addition, they must also take the ACT.

Procedure: Application deadlines are May 1 for fall, August 1 for spring, and January 1 for summer. Foreign students must present a completed health form as well as proof of funds adequate to cover 1 year of study. They must also carry health insurance, which is available through the college for a fee.

Admissions Contact: Karl L. Wolf, Director of Admissions.

UNIVERSITY OF CHARLESTON B–4
Charleston, West Virginia 25304 (304) 346-1400

F/T: 310M, 463W Faculty: 78; n/av
P/T: 499M, 749W Ph.D.'s: 38%
Grad: 7M, 6W S/F Ratio: 18 to 1
Year: sems, ss Tuition: $2700
Appl: Aug. 1 R and B: $2250
653 applied 589 accepted 245 enrolled
SAT: 442V 448M ACT: 18 LESS COMPETITIVE

The University of Charleston offers undergraduate degree programs through its 5 colleges: the Morris Harvey College of Arts and Sciences, the College of Business, the College of Health Sciences, College 2000 (adults), and the American College of Rome. The university has an affiliation with Sophia University in Tokyo, Japan. Certain business majors require 1 semester in Tokyo. Its library contains 89,500 volumes and over 600 reels of microfilm, and subscribes to 450 periodicals.

Environment: The 40-acre riverfront campus is located in a suburban setting, 2 miles from Charleston. Most of the buildings have been constructed or remodeled within the last 10 years. There are residence halls for men and women.

Student Life: About 98% of the students are from the middle Atlantic and northeast areas. Ninety percent of the freshmen come from public schools. Twenty-five percent of the students live on campus. About 6% of the students are minority-group members. Campus housing is coed and single-sex; there are visiting privileges. Students may keep cars on campus.

Organizations: There are 4 national fraternities and 2 national sororities to which 15% of the students belong. The student government and social clubs provide social and cultural entertainment on campus.

Sports: The university fields 5 intercollegiate teams for men and 4 for women. There are 7 intramural sports for men and 6 for women.

Graduates: About 16% of the freshmen drop out after their first year; 48% remain to graduate. Of those, 35% continue their education and others pursue careers in business and industry.

Services: Free tutoring, career and psychological counseling, and job placement services are available to all students. Remedial instruction is available on a fee basis.

Programs of Study: The university confers the B.A. and B.S. degrees. Master's and associate degrees are also offered. Bachelor's degrees are offered in the following subjects: BUSINESS (accounting, computer science, finance, management, marketing), EDUCATION (elementary, health/physical, secondary, special), ENGLISH (English, speech), FINE AND PERFORMING ARTS (art, art education, mass communications, music), HEALTH SCIENCES (medical technology, respiratory therapy), LANGUAGES (French, Japanese), MATH AND SCIENCES (biology, chemistry, mathematics, natural sciences), PHILOSOPHY (philosophy and religion), SOCIAL SCIENCES (government/political science, history, psychology, social sciences, sociology). The majority of degrees are conferred in business and the health sciences.

Special: Associate degrees may be earned in nursing, radiologic technology, and respiratory therapy. College 2000 serves adults who have been out of school for a period of time or who have unusual specific needs.

Honors: Recommended students in English and the humanities areas are allowed to take 1 honors course per year.

Admissions: About 90% of those who applied were accepted for the 1981–82 freshman class. Candidates must have graduated from accredited high schools and should have completed 15 Carnegie units. A minimum average of C is required. Advanced placement or honors courses, recommendations by school officials, leadership record, and impressions made during an interview are also considered in the admissions decision.

Procedure: The SAT or ACT should be taken by January of the senior year. The applications should be filed by August 1 (fall), January 1 (spring), or May 1 (summer). The university follows a rolling admissions policy. There is a $15 application fee.

Special: The early admissions deadline is August 1, and an interview is required. Early decision is available: the notification date is December 15. There is also a deferred admissions plan. AP and CLEP credit is given.

Transfer: Transfers are accepted for all classes. Applicants must have a C average; D grades are acceptable. Students must take 32 semester hours in residence to earn a degree; the bachelor's degree requires 128 credits. Application deadlines are the same as those for freshmen.

Visiting: The university holds regularly scheduled orientations for prospective West Virginia students; out-of-state students are welcomed on an individual basis. Visitors may sit in on classes and may arrange to stay overnight at the school. Guides are provided for informal visits. The recommended time for visiting is Thursday through Sunday. The admissions office should be contacted for further information.

Financial Aid: Scholarships, loans, and grants are available. About 67% of the students receive some form of aid. About 24% of the students work part-time on campus and the average award to freshmen from all sources is between $2800 and $3000. The university is a member of CSS; the FAF must be filed. Applications should be in by May 1.

Foreign Students: About 2% of the students come from foreign countries. The university offers these students special counseling and special organizations.

Admissions: Foreign students must achieve a minimum TOEFL score of 500; no further exams are required.

Procedure: Application deadlines are 5 months prior to the start of each semester. Foreign students must present proof of funds adequate to cover 1 year of study. Tuition for foreign students is $3500. They should carry health insurance, which is available through the university for a fee.

Admissions Contact: June D. Williams, Director of Admissions.

WEST LIBERTY STATE COLLEGE C–1
West Liberty, West Virginia 26074   (304) 336-8077

F/T: 984M, 1112W	Faculty: n/av; IIB, +$
P/T: 127M, 331W	Ph.D.'s: 35%
Grad: none	S/F Ratio: 19 to 1
Year: sems, ss	Tuition: $470 ($1470)
Appl: see profile	R and B: $1806
824 applied	807 accepted	505 enrolled
ACT: 17		LESS COMPETITIVE

West Liberty State College, established in 1837, is a publicly controlled college offering programs in teacher education and liberal arts. The library has 170,000 volumes and 50,000 microfilm items, and subscribes to 1200 periodicals.

Environment: The 185-acre hilltop campus is located in a rural setting 10 miles northeast of Wheeling and 40 miles from Pittsburgh, Pennsylvania. Facilities include a fine arts center, a physical education building, a student union, and dormitories that accommodate 1531 students. Dormitories have separate wings for fraternities and sororities. Apartments are available for married students.

Student Life: Sixty-four percent of the students come from West Virginia. Almost 93% are graduates of public schools. About 56% of the students live in the single-sex dormitories. Religious counselors are available for Catholic, Protestant, and Jewish students. Students may keep cars on campus.

Organizations: About 23% of the men belong to the 7 fraternities on campus, and 15% of the women belong to the 4 sororities. Campus activities include departmental clubs, drama and music groups, and student government. The college is within easy driving distance of Pittsburgh, and a variety of recreational activities are available in the vicinity.

Sports: The college competes on an intercollegiate level in 9 sports for men and 4 for women. Intramural sports also are available.

Handicapped: The entire campus is accessible to handicapped students. Special facilities include wheelchair ramps, specially equipped rest rooms, and lowered telephones. Elevator keys, special parking permits, special class scheduling, and other services are provided. Readers, special hardware, tutors, and special "mini-courses" are available to students with visual or hearing impairments.

Graduates: About 20% of the freshmen drop out, and 55% remain to graduate. About 25% of the graduates seek advanced degrees; 2% enter medical, dental, or law school. Almost half of the graduates begin careers in business and industry.

Services: The college offers free career and psychological counseling, health care, tutoring, remedial instruction, and placement aid. Placement services also are available to alumni.

Programs of Study: The college confers the B.S.B.A., A.B., and B.S. degrees. Associate degrees also are available. Bachelor's degrees are offered in the following subjects: AREA STUDIES (urban), BUSINESS (accounting, administrative mathematics, administrative science, business, business education, computer science, finance, food service management, general business, management, marketing, office administration), EDUCATION (early childhood, elementary, health/physical, secondary, special), ENGLISH (communications, English), FINE AND PERFORMING ARTS (art, art education, commercial art, music education), HEALTH SCIENCES (dental hygiene, medical technology, nursing, pre-speech therapy), MATH AND SCIENCES (biology, chemistry, mathematics), PHILOSOPHY (philosophy), PRE-PROFESSIONAL (dentistry, engineering, home economics, law, medicine, optometry, pharmacy, social work), SOCIAL SCIENCES (criminal justice, economics, government/political science, history, psychology, public administration, sociology).

Special: An integrated degree program is offered in medical technology. Work-study programs are available in all departments. A B.G.S. degree is offered. Adults seeking an A.B. degree can enter the nontraditional Regents Degree Program, which gives credit for life experience and designs an individualized program for each student.

Honors: Nine national honor societies have chapters on campus. All departments participate in the honors program.

Admissions: Ninety-eight percent of those who applied were accepted for the 1981–82 freshman class. The ACT scores of those who enrolled were as follows: 60% below 21, 10% between 21 and 23, 5% between 24 and 25, 1% between 26 and 28, and 1% above 28. Applicants should rank in the upper 75% of their high school class or have a composite score of at least 14 on the ACT. Graduation from an accredited high school is required.

Procedure: Applicants must take the ACT. Freshmen are accepted for all sessions. Applications must be submitted at least 2 weeks before registration. There is no application fee. The college follows the rolling admissions plan.

Special: An early admissions plan is offered. CLEP and AP credit is accepted.

Transfer: For a recent year, 390 transfer students applied, 350 were accepted, and 211 enrolled. Transfers are accepted for all classes. The college requires evidence of an honorable withdrawal from the previous college and a 2.0 GPA in previous college work. D grades are accepted. Students must earn at least 36 semester hours in residence of the 128 required for a bachelor's degree.

Visiting: A freshman orientation is offered at the beginning of the school year, and a preregistration program is offered in summer. Guides are also available for informal visits. Visitors may sit in on classes and stay overnight at the school. The best times for campus visits are between 8:30 A.M. and 5 P.M. Monday through Friday. The Office of Student Recruitment should be contacted for information.

Financial Aid: About 75% of the students receive aid in the form of scholarships, loans, grants, and work-study jobs. The average award to 1981–82 freshmen totaled $1200. The deadline for aid applications is March 1. The FAF must also be filed.

Foreign Students: The foreign students at the college make up less than 1% of enrollment. Special counseling is offered for these students.

Admissions: Applicants must score at least 450 on the TOEFL. No college entrance exams are required.

Procedure: Application deadlines are the same as those for American students. Foreign students must submit a completed medical form and provide evidence of adequate funds for 1 year. Health insurance is required, and is available through the college for a fee.

Admissions Contact: E. Nelson Cain, Registrar and Director of Admissions.

WEST VIRGINIA INSTITUTE OF TECHNOLOGY B–4
Montgomery, West Virginia 25136   (304) 442-3167 or 3103

F/T: 1734M, 692W	Faculty: n/av; IIB, +$
P/T: 537M, 352W	Ph.D.'s: 57%
Grad: 13M	S/F Ratio: 15 to 1
Year: sems, ss	Tuition: $479 ($1479)
Appl: Aug. 15	R and B: $1950
1336 applied	1312 accepted	672 enrolled
ACT: 18		LESS COMPETITIVE

Founded in 1895, this state-supported institution provides professional training in the fields of engineering, business, education, and the arts and sciences. The library has 130,982 volumes, 869 periodical subscriptions, and over 11,000 rolls of microfilm.

Environment: The 111-acre campus is on a mountainside overlooking the small town of Montgomery and the Kanawha River. Charleston, the nearest major city, is 28 miles away. Campus buildings and facilities include 2 engineering buildings, a community and technical college building, science and physical education buildings, and high-rise dormitories housing 1153 students.

Student Life: Eighty percent of the students come from West Virginia. About 96% of the freshmen are from public schools. Fifty-seven percent live on or near the campus in dormitories, apartments, and fraternity houses. Campus housing is coed and single-sex; there are visiting privileges. Students may keep cars on campus.

Organizations: About 12% of the men belong to 1 of 5 national fraternities; 3% of the women belong to the 1 national sorority on campus. Among the cultural and recreational opportunities are whitewater rafting, attending outdoor dramas, and student activity groups.

Sports: The institute fields 8 intercollegiate teams for men and 5 for women. There are 9 intramural sports for men and 8 for women.

Handicapped: Special facilities for the handicapped include wheelchair ramps, special parking, elevators, and specially equipped rest rooms. Special class scheduling can be arranged. About 40% of the campus is accessible to these students. Two special counselors assist all handicapped students.

Services: The following services are available free of charge to students: placement and career counseling; tutoring; remedial instruction; and psychological counseling. Job placement services are available for undergraduates and alumni.

Programs of Study: The institute confers the B.A. and B.S. degrees, as well as master's degrees and associate degrees in nursing, dental hygiene, and technology. Bachelor's degrees are offered in the following subjects: BUSINESS (accounting, business administration, busi-

960 WEST VIRGINIA

ness education, computer science, management, printing), EDUCATION (health/physical, industrial, secondary), FINE AND PERFORMING ARTS (music, music education), MATH AND SCIENCES (biology, chemistry, mathematics, physics), PREPROFESSIONAL (engineering—chemical, engineering—civil, engineering—electrical, engineering—mechanical), SOCIAL SCIENCES (history, social sciences). About 39% of all students receive degrees in math and sciences, 23% in education, and 16% in business.

Special: The institute offers a general studies degree.

Honors: There are chapters of 3 national honor societies on campus.

Admissions: Approximately 98% of those who applied were accepted for the 1981–82 school year. Applicants must be graduates of an accredited high school, with 17 successfully completed Carnegie units of work, and have a minimum GPA of 2.0.

Procedure: The ACT is required. There is no application fee. The institute has a rolling admissions policy. Freshmen are admitted to all sessions. Application deadlines are August 15 (fall), January 5 (spring), and May 15 (summer).

Special: An early admissions plan is offered by the institute.

Transfer: For fall 1981, 398 transfer students applied, 388 were accepted, and 198 enrolled. Transfer students should have a 2.0 GPA to be admitted in good standing but may be admitted on academic probation with averages ranging from 1.7 to 1.95, depending on the number of hours taken. Preference is given to students transferring from colleges within the state. Transfers are accepted in all classes. D grades transfer. Thirty of the last 36 credits must be taken at Tech in order to receive a degree; the bachelor's degree requires the completion of 128 credits. Transfer application deadlines are the same as those for freshmen.

Visiting: Regularly scheduled orientations for prospective students are held at the institute. Orientation for new students begins 4 days prior to the start of classes. There are guides for informal visits. Visitors may sit in on classes and also stay overnight at the school. The admissions office should be contacted to arrange such visits.

Financial Aid: About 65% of all students receive financial aid. The deadlines for the aid application are April 1 (fall) and November 1 (spring). The FAF is required. Scholarships, loan funds, and grants are available to qualified students. Work-study programs are offered in all departments.

Foreign Students: The institute accepts foreign students and offers these students special counseling and special organizations.

Admissions: Foreign students must achieve a minimum TOEFL score of 500; in addition, they must also take the ACT.

Procedure: Applications must be submitted by March for fall, August for spring, and January for summer. Foreign students must present proof of health as well as proof of funds adequate to cover 4 years of study. They must also carry health insurance, which is available through the institute.

Admissions Contact: Robert P. Scholl, Jr., Director of Admissions.

WEST VIRGINIA STATE COLLEGE B-4
Institute, West Virginia 25112 (304) 766-3221

F/T: 1081M, 975W	Faculty:	n/av; IIB, +$
P/T: 977M, 1452W	Ph.D.'s:	37%
Grad: none	S/F Ratio:	18 to 1
Year: sems, ss	Tuition:	$499 ($1799)
Appl: open	R and B:	$2010
2281 applied	2250 accepted	1530 enrolled
ACT: 16		LESS COMPETITIVE

Established in 1891, this state-supported liberal arts college offers professional and teacher training, as well as liberal arts curricula. The library contains over 250,000 volumes and subscribes to 1200 periodicals.

Environment: The 83-acre campus is located in a suburb 10 miles from Charleston, in part of the valley of the Great Kanawha River. The following student residences are available: a high-rise for women, 1 married couples' dorm, and 2 men's dorms (1 for freshmen and sophomores, 1 for juniors and seniors). The college has a total of 30 buildings.

Student Life: About 90% of the students are from West Virginia. Seven percent of all students live on campus. About 19% of the students are minority-group members. Campus housing is single-sex; there are visiting privileges. Students may keep cars on campus. Day-care services are available to all students, faculty, and staff for a fee.

Organizations: There are 2 local fraternities on campus, 6 national fraternities, and 3 national sororities, but these organizations do not provide housing. Popular cultural and recreational areas off campus include the West Virginia Cultural Center and 2 nearby parks.

Sports: The college fields 7 intercollegiate teams for men and 5 for women. There are 5 intramural sports for men and 5 for women.

Handicapped: There are special facilities for the physically handicapped on campus, including wheelchair ramps, special parking, elevators, specially equipped rest rooms, lowered drinking fountains, and lowered telephones. The West Virginia Rehabilitation Center is adjacent to the campus.

Graduates: At the end of the freshman year, 15% of the class drop out. Most of the remainder stay to graduate; of these, 4% pursue advanced study after graduation. Two percent enter law school, and about 1% enter either medical school or dental school. About 35% of the graduates pursue careers in business and industry.

Services: The following services are available at no charge: health care, tutoring, remedial instruction, psychological counseling, and a career planning and placement office program.

Programs of Study: The college awards the B.A. and B.S. degrees. Associate degrees are also awarded. Bachelor's degrees are offered in the following subjects: BUSINESS (accounting, business administration, business education, computer science, consumer resources, finance, management, marketing), EDUCATION (early childhood, elementary, health/physical, secondary, special), ENGLISH (communications, English), FINE AND PERFORMING ARTS (art, art education, music, music education), HEALTH SCIENCES (health physics, therapeutic recreation), MATH AND SCIENCES (biology, chemistry, mathematics, physics), PREPROFESSIONAL (architectural technology, building construction technology, dentistry, industrial technology, law, medicine, recreation administration, social work), SOCIAL SCIENCES (criminal justice, economics, government/political science, history, psychology, sociology). Twenty percent of the degrees are conferred in business, 9% in social sciences, 8% in math and sciences, and 8% in education.

Special: Students may choose a general studies degree. The college allows student-designed majors.

Honors: There are 11 national honorary societies with chapters on campus.

Admissions: Ninety-nine percent of those who applied were accepted for the 1981–82 freshman class. Eligibility depends for the most part on a C average or better, high school accreditation, and the completion of 17 Carnegie high school units. West Virginia State particularly seeks students who come well recommended by a secondary school of high standing, who can present AP or honor courses, and who show leadership potential.

Procedure: The ACT or SAT is required. There are no application deadlines. Freshmen are admitted in the fall, spring, and summer. The college follows a rolling admissions policy. No application fee is required.

Special: AP and CLEP credit is given.

Transfer: About 450 transfer students enroll yearly. An average of C is required. The final 32 semester hours must be completed in residence; the bachelor's degree requires 128 credits. D grades are accepted. There are no application deadlines.

Visiting: In addition to regularly scheduled orientations for prospective students, guides are available for informal visits. Visitors can sit in on classes and stay overnight at the school. The best times for campus visits are in late spring and summer.

Financial Aid: About 35% of all students receive financial aid in the form of scholarships, federal and state loans, college loans, and loans from private funds. Campus employment may yield additional funds; about 5% of the students work part-time on campus. The deadlines for financial aid application are August 1 (fall), December 1 (spring), and May 1 (summer). The college is a member of CSS; the FAF must be filed.

Foreign Students: Fewer than 1% of the students come from foreign countries. The college offers these students special counseling and special organizations.

Admissions: Foreign students must achieve a minimum TOEFL score of 500; in addition, they must also take the SAT or ACT.

Procedure: Application deadlines are July 15 for fall, December 1 for spring, and April 15 for summer. Foreign students must present proof of health as well as proof of adequate funds.

Admissions Contact: Michael Lampros, Acting Coordinator of Admissions.

WEST VIRGINIA UNIVERSITY   C–2
Morgantown, West Virginia 26506   (304) 293-2121

F/T: 7899M, 5877W   Faculty: n/av; I, — –$
P/T: 332M, 560W   Ph.D.'s: 75%
Grad: 3165M, 3432W   S/F Ratio: 29 to 1
Year: sems, ss   Tuition: $314 ($854)
Appl: open   R and B: $2196
6054 applied   5945 accepted   3300 enrolled
ACT: 20   COMPETITIVE

West Virginia University is a university and land-grant college under state control. University divisions include the Graduate School; the colleges of Agriculture and Forestry, Arts and Sciences, Business and Economics, Creative Arts, Dentistry, Engineering, Human Resources and Education, Journalism, Medicine, Military Science and Air Force Aerospace, Mines, Nursing, Pharmacy, Physical Education, and Social Work; and the College of Law at the Evansdale campus. The library contains 930,652 volumes and 59,251 microfilm items, and subscribes to 9425 periodicals.

Environment: University campuses cover some 600 acres in Morgantown, in Evansdale (half a mile from the Morgantown campus), and at the medical center area. The main campus is located near town, in an urban setting, about 80 miles from Pittsburgh, Pennsylvania. The school provides supervised housing and off-campus private dorms and apartments.

Student Life: Most of the students come from West Virginia, but almost every state and many foreign countries are represented. There are religious facilities for Protestant, Catholic, and Greek Orthodox students. About 30% of the students live on campus. About 2% of the students are members of minority groups. Campus housing is coed and single-sex.

Organizations: About 18% of the men belong to 20 national fraternities; 11% of the women belong to 11 national sororities. Opportunities for enjoying art, music, and the theater are made possible by the many performances at the Creative Arts Center on campus. A variety of social activities take place at the Mountain Lair, the university's student union.

Sports: The university fields 9 intercollegiate teams for men and 7 for women.

Handicapped: Facilities for the physically handicapped include wheelchair ramps, special parking, elevators, and specially equipped rest rooms. Special class scheduling can be arranged. About 85% of the campus is accessible to physically handicapped students. One special counselor and 1 assistant counselor are available to help handicapped students.

Services: The following services are offered free of charge to university students: placement and career counseling, psychological counseling, and remedial instruction. Health care services are available at modest fees for full-time students. Tutoring is also available on a fee basis. Placement services for graduate and undergraduate students include placement files, interviewing within the career services center, and job placement.

Programs of Study: The university confers B.A. and B.S. degrees and offers master's and doctoral programs. Bachelor's degrees are offered in the following subjects: AREA STUDIES (Asian, Black/Afro-American, Russian), BUSINESS (accounting, business administration, computer science, finance, management, marketing), EDUCATION (early childhood, elementary, health/physical, secondary), ENGLISH (English), FINE AND PERFORMING ARTS (art, art education, dance, music, music education, radio/TV, studio art, theater/dramatics), HEALTH SCIENCES (medical technology, nursing, physical therapy, speech pathology and audiology, speech therapy), LANGUAGES (Chinese, French, German, Greek/Latin, Hebrew, Italian, Japanese, Russian, Spanish), MATH AND SCIENCES (biology, botany, chemistry, geology, mathematics, natural sciences, physical sciences, physics, statistics), PHILOSOPHY (classics, philosophy, religion), PRE-PROFESSIONAL (agriculture, architecture, dentistry, engineering, forestry, law, medicine, pharmacy, social work, veterinary), SOCIAL SCIENCES (anthropology, economics, geography, government/political science, history, international relations, psychology, social sciences, sociology).

Special: A combined B.A.-B.S. degree may be earned in 5 years. The university also offers a general studies degree, referred to as a liberal arts degree, in the College of Arts and Sciences. In addition, students may design their own majors under the interdepartmental majors program.

Honors: There are 25 national honor societies that have chapters on the West Virginia campus, including Phi Beta Kappa. There is a General Honors program, in addition to honors programs in biology, chemistry, physics, and political science.

Admissions: About 98% of those who applied were accepted into the 1981–82 freshman class. A West Virginia candidate must have a 2.0 GPA to be admitted to the college; out-of-state residents must have a 3.0 average. All candidates must have successfully completed at least 4 units of English and 2 units of algebra in their high school work.

Procedure: The ACT is required. There is no application fee at the university. Rolling admissions are used; there are no application deadlines. The notification date is within a week of application.

Special: The university offers early decision, early admissions, and deferred admissions plans. Students may earn credit through CLEP and AP exams.

Transfer: For fall 1981, 1352 transfer students applied and 1177 were accepted. A 2.0 GPA is required for transfer students. The final 30 hours must be completed in residence; the bachelor's degree requires the completion of 128 credits. Grades of C and above transfer. There are no application deadlines.

Visiting: The university provides a regularly scheduled orientation period during the summer for entering high school students. Guides are provided for informal visits. Visitors can sit in on classes. The best times for campus visits are weekdays. Although there are no formal provisions for visitors, students may stay with friends while on campus. To arrange such visits the campus tour office should be called: (304) 293-3489.

Financial Aid: About 50% of all students receive financial aid. The average award to freshmen from all sources is between $1500 and $2000. The fall deadline for financial aid application is March 1. The university is a member of CSS; the FAF must be filed.

Foreign Students: There are 863 students who come from foreign countries. The university offers these students an intensive English course and special organizations.

Admissions: Foreign students must achieve a minimum TOEFL score of 550; in addition, they must also take the ACT.

Procedure: Application deadlines are April 1 for fall, October 1 for spring, and March 1 for summer. Foreign students must present proof of funds adequate to cover 1 year of study. They must also carry health insurance.

Admissions Contact: John D. Brisbane, Dean of Admissions.

WEST VIRGINIA WESLEYAN COLLEGE   C–3
Buckhannon, West Virginia 26201   (304) 473-8510

F/T: 687M, 964W   Faculty: 121; IIB, av$
P/T: 11M, 14W   Ph.D.'s: 40%
Grad: 1M, 3W   S/F Ratio: 16 to 1
Year: 4-1-4, ss   Tuition: $3625
Appl: July 31   R and B: $2075
1206 applied   1198 accepted   627 enrolled
SAT: 424V 455M   ACT: 19   LESS COMPETITIVE

West Virginia Wesleyan College, founded in 1890, is a coeducational liberal arts institution affiliated with the United Methodist Church. It is also a teacher training college. The library houses over 135,000 volumes and 5500 microfilm items, and subscribes to 625 periodicals.

Environment: The 80-acre rural campus has 19 buildings of Georgian design, including 7 dormitories and 2 dining halls for resident and commuting students. New buildings include a dormitory/apartment complex and an art building.

Student Life: About 30% of the students are from West Virginia, 69% from other states, and 1% from abroad. Eighty percent of the entering freshmen come from public schools. About 95% of the resident students live in dormitories. There is fraternity housing but none for sorority members. About 66% of the students are Protestant, 28% are Catholic, and 2% are Jewish. About 6% of the students are minority-group members. Campus housing is single-sex; there are visiting privileges. Students may keep cars on campus.

Organizations: About 33% of the men belong to 5 national fraternities; 38% of the women belong to 4 national sororities. There are approximately 60 organizations, clubs, honor societies, and special-interest groups on campus.

Sports: The college fields 8 intercollegiate teams for men and 4 for women. There are 4 intramural sports for men and 4 for women.

Handicapped: The following special facilities are supplied for the physically handicapped: wheelchair ramps, special parking, elevators, specially equipped rest rooms, and lowered drinking fountains. About 90% of the campus is accessible to these students.

962 WEST VIRGINIA

Graduates: About 18% of the freshmen drop out; 57% remain to graduate. Sixty percent of the students pursue graduate study after graduation. Five percent of the graduates enter medical school and 2% enter dental school. Thirty-five percent of all students pursue careers in business and industry.

Services: The following services are available free of charge to all students (costs for services are included in tuition): placement and career counseling; health care and psychological counseling; and tutoring.

Programs of Study: The college grants B.A., B.S., and B.Mus.Ed. degrees. Associate and master's degrees are also awarded. Bachelor's degrees are offered in the following subjects: AREA STUDIES (American, international studies), BUSINESS (accounting, business administration, business education, management, marketing, office administration), EDUCATION (Christian, early childhood, elementary, health/physical, secondary, special), ENGLISH (communications, English, literature, speech), FINE AND PERFORMING ARTS (applied music, art, art education, music, music education, music theory, theater/dramatics), HEALTH SCIENCES (health physics technology, medical technology, nursing), LANGUAGES (Chinese, French, German), MATH AND SCIENCES (biology, chemistry, computer science, engineering physics, mathematics, physical sciences, physics), PHILOSOPHY (philosophy, religion), PREPROFESSIONAL (dentistry, dietetics, engineering, fashion merchandising, forestry, law, library science, medicine, ministry, pharmacy, social work, veterinary), SOCIAL SCIENCES (economics, government/political science, history, psychology, rehabilitation, sociology, youth services).

Required: Students must attend certain liberal arts classes. The humanities course provides an interdisciplinary experience during the freshman year.

Special: The college offers cooperative degree programs in engineering and environmental studies. Also, students have opportunities for internships, independent studies, and field study experiences through the contract learning program. Contract majors are also available.

Honors: The college has an honors program which offers honors seminars each semester.

Admissions: About 99% of the students who applied for the 1981-82 freshman class were accepted. An applicant must have completed 16 academic units of high school work, rank in the upper half of his or her graduating class, and have a 2.0 average or better. Non-high-school graduates must present a GED diploma. Other factors involved in determining admissions include advanced placement or honors courses, extracurricular activities, leadership records, and evidence of special talents.

Procedure: The SAT or ACT is required. Freshmen are admitted in the fall, at midyear, and in the summer. Application for fall admission should be made no later than July 31. There is a $25 application fee. Admissions are on a rolling basis.

Special: The college has early decision, early admissions, and deferred admissions plans. CLEP and AP credit is available.

Transfer: For fall 1981, 100 transfer students applied, 95 were accepted, and 90 enrolled. An average of C is necessary, and one year (32 semester hours) must be completed in residence. The bachelor's degree requires 128 credits. June 1 is the fall semester deadline; December 15, the spring.

Visiting: Guides are provided for informal visits, which should be made when school is in session. Visitors may sit in on classes and may stay overnight at the school. The admissions office should be contacted to make arrangements.

Financial Aid: About 76% of all students receive some form of financial aid, including scholarship and loan funds, SEOG, and work-study assistance. Campus employment is also available; about 23% of the students work part-time on campus. The FAF and the Wesleyan aid application must be filed before the March 1 deadline. The college is a member of CSS.

Foreign Students: About 2% of the students come from foreign countries. The college offers these students special counseling and special organizations.

Admissions: Foreign students must achieve a minimum TOEFL score of 450; no further exams are required.

Procedure: Application deadlines are rolling. Foreign students must present the college's health form as well as proof of funds adequate to cover 1 year of study. They must also carry health insurance, which is available through the college.

Admissions Contact: Wenrich H. Green, Director of Admissions.

WHEELING COLLEGE   C-2
Wheeling, West Virginia 26003   (304) 243-2359

F/T: 350M, 424W   Faculty: 62; IIB, av$
P/T: n/av   Ph.D.'s: 63%
Grad: 91M, 26W   S/F Ratio: 12 to 1
Year: sems, ss   Tuition: $3850
Appl: Aug. 15   R and B: $2150
635 applied   530 accepted   224 enrolled
SAT: 450V 470M   ACT: 21   COMPETITIVE

Wheeling College, founded in 1954 under Jesuit auspices, combines a liberal arts curriculum with career-oriented programs in such fields as business, nursing, communications, allied health, and criminal justice. The library has 130,000 volumes and 17,000 microfilm items, and subscribes to 599 periodicals.

Environment: The self-contained 60-acre campus is located in a suburban area 60 miles from Pittsburgh, Pennsylvania.

Student Life: Thirty-three percent of the students come from West Virginia. The remainder are from 18 other states. About 79% of the students are Catholic and 21% are Protestant. About 5% of the students are minority-group members. Campus housing is coed and single-sex; there are visiting privileges. Students may keep cars on campus.

Organizations: The college sponsors various cultural, spiritual, and scientific organizations. Nearby parks offer opportunities for a variety of outdoor recreational activities.

Sports: The college fields 5 intercollegiate teams for men and 6 for women. There are 5 intramural sports for men and 5 for women.

Handicapped: The college provides wheelchair ramps, special parking, and elevators for physically handicapped students. About 60% of the campus is accessible to these students.

Graduates: The freshman dropout rate is 20%; 60% remain to graduate. Twenty-five percent of the graduates pursue graduate study. Two percent enter medical school, 2% enter law school, and 1% enter dental school. Fifty percent of the students pursue careers in business and industry.

Services: Wheeling College offers the following services free of charge to all students: placement, career counseling, health care, tutoring, remedial instruction, and psychological counseling. Placement services for undergraduates and graduates include referral and on-campus recruiting.

Programs of Study: The A.B., B.S., and B.S.N. degrees are conferred. There are also master's degree programs. Bachelor's degrees are offered in the following subjects: BUSINESS (accounting, behavioral analysis management, business administration, finance and banking, labor and industrial relations, management, marketing, public administration), ENGLISH (communications, English), FINE AND PERFORMING ARTS (art, fine arts management), HEALTH SCIENCES (allied health, anesthesia, medical technology, nuclear medical technology, nursing, respiratory therapy), LANGUAGES (French, Spanish), MATH AND SCIENCES (biology, chemistry, mathematics, physics), PHILOSOPHY (philosophy, religion), PREPROFESSIONAL (dentistry, law, medicine, veterinary), SOCIAL SCIENCES (criminal justice, government/political science, history, psychology, social sciences, sociology). Thirty-eight percent of the degrees are conferred in business, 28% in health sciences, and 15% in humanities and letters.

Required: A liberal arts core curriculum is required of all students and includes courses in English, a foreign language, math or science, Western civilization, theology, and philosophy.

Special: The college offers a general studies degree and allows student-designed majors. There is a special concentration in computer science. Cooperative education opportunities are available. The junior year may be spent abroad in Rome, Freiburg, or Madrid. The curriculum offers internship options in business, government, and public agencies. Students may choose a 2-3 program in pre-engineering or a 3-1 program in medical technology.

Honors: Alpha Sigma Nu, the national Jesuit honor society for men and women, has a chapter on campus.

Admissions: Eighty-three percent of those who applied were accepted for the 1981-82 freshman class. The candidate should be in the top 50% of his or her high school graduating class and have a minimum GPA of 2.5. A total of 15 high school units must be presented. In addition to these qualifications the college considers the following factors, in order of importance: advanced placement or honors courses, evidence of special talents, recommendations by school officials, leadership record, and personality.

Procedure: Either the ACT or SAT is required. The deadline for regular admissions is rolling, but prospective students should apply to the college early in their senior year. Regular applications should be submitted by August 15, but applications will be considered as long as space is available. Freshmen are admitted in the fall and spring. Applications should be submitted with a $15 fee.

Special: The early admissions plan has a deadline of August 1. There is also a deferred admissions plan. CLEP and AP credit is available.

Transfer: For fall 1981, 95 transfer students applied, 82 were accepted, and 36 enrolled. Transfers are accepted for all classes. Students must have a 2.5 GPA for previous work in an accredited college. To earn a degree, the student must study a minimum of 1 year, completing at least 30 credits, at Wheeling. The bachelor's degree requires 120 credits. Grades of C or above transfer. Application deadlines are the same as those for freshmen.

Visiting: Guides are available for informal visits, which can be arranged at the student's convenience. Visitors can stay overnight at the school and sit in on classes. The admissions office should be contacted for further information.

Financial Aid: Sixty-five percent of all students receive financial aid; 33% of the students work part-time on campus. Wheeling participates in federal aid programs, including grants, loans, and jobs. In addition, there are scholarships for academically superior students. The average award to freshmen from all sources is $2700. The college is a member of CSS; the FAF must be filed. The application deadline for financial aid is March 1.

Foreign Students: About 1% of the students come from foreign countries. The college actively recruits these students and offers them special counseling.

Admissions: Foreign students must achieve a minimum TOEFL score of 500; no further exams are required.

Procedure: Application deadlines are August 1 for fall, December 1 for spring, and April 15 for summer. Foreign students must present proof of health as well as proof of funds adequate to cover 1 year of study. They must also carry health insurance, which is available through the college for a fee.

Admissions Contact: Kenneth J. Rudzki, Director of Admissions.

WISCONSIN

ALVERNO COLLEGE E-4
Milwaukee, Wisconsin 53215   (414) 647-3790

F/T: 788W	Faculty: 107; IIB, −$
P/T: 511W	Ph.D.'s: 40%
Grad: none	S/F Ratio: 16 to 1
Year: sems, ss	Tuition: $3400
Appl: Aug. 15	R and B: $1550
SAT or ACT: required	COMPETITIVE

Alverno College, established in 1936 by the School Sisters of Saint Francis, offers undergraduate programs for women in the arts and sciences, management, education, and nursing. It is affiliated with the Roman Catholic Church. Its library has nearly 78,500 books and 87,500 microfilm items, and subscribes to 734 periodicals.

Environment: The 50-acre suburban campus, approximately 20 minutes from downtown Milwaukee, has 12 buildings, including residence halls that accommodate 150 women.

Student Life: Most of the students come from Wisconsin and the Midwest. About 75% attended public schools. Fifteen percent live on campus. Sixty percent are Catholic. Attendance at religious services is not required.

Organizations: Campus activities include music and drama groups, publications, clubs, fine-arts performances, and social functions. There are no sororities.

Sports: There is a "Body Expression and Movement Fitness" approach to recreation, and a noncompetitive approach to physical activities.

Handicapped: Ramps, parking areas, elevators, lowered telephones, and specially equipped rest rooms are provided for physically handicapped students. There are 2 special counselors.

Graduates: The freshman dropout rate is about 15%, and 60% remain to graduate. Of these, 14% go on for further education and 7% begin careers in business.

Services: Career counseling, placement services, health care, psychological counseling, remedial instruction, and tutoring are free to students.

Programs of Study: The college confers the B.S., B.S.N., B.M., B.S.Ed., and B.S.Med.Tech. degrees. Bachelor's degrees are offered in the following subjects: BUSINESS (computer science, management), EDUCATION (adult, bilingual, early childhood, elementary, secondary), ENGLISH (English, professional communications), FINE AND PERFORMING ARTS (art, art education, art therapy, liturgical music, music, music education, music therapy), HEALTH SCIENCES (medical technology, nuclear medical technology, nursing), MATH AND SCIENCES (biology, chemistry, ecology/environmental science, mathematics, physics), PHILOSOPHY (humanities, philosophy, religion), PREPROFESSIONAL (dentistry, engineering law, library science, medicine, veterinary), SOCIAL SCIENCES (history, psychology, social sciences).

Required: All students must complete coursework in the humanities.

Special: A general studies major is offered. Study abroad, and weekend college and off-campus experiential learning programs are available.

Honors: Four national honor societies are represented on campus. Qualified students may earn honors at graduation.

Admissions: About 69% of those who applied for a recent freshman class were accepted. The ACT scores of those who enrolled were as follows: 41% between 20 and 23, 24% between 24 and 26, and 15% between 27 and 28. Applicants should rank in the top half of their high school class and have at least a 2.0 GPA in at least 10 high school units. Impressions made during an interview, recommendations, and personality also are considered.

Procedure: The ACT is preferred, but SAT scores are also accepted. August 15 is the fall application deadline. New students also are accepted in the spring. Applications are processed on a rolling basis. There is a $10 fee. An interview is recommended.

Special: CLEP and AP credit is accepted.

Transfer: Transfers are accepted in all departments. Application deadlines are the same as those for freshmen. A 2.0 GPA is required.

Visiting: Informal campus tours with student guides can be arranged for Mondays through Fridays when school is in session. Visitors may stay overnight at the school and attend classes. For further information contact the admissions office.

Financial Aid: About 59% of the students receive aid. The college offers freshman scholarships; various loans, grants, and jobs are available. The FAF should be filed; application deadlines are open.

Foreign Students: The foreign students enrolled full-time at the college make up about 10% of the student body. The college actively recruits such students.

Procedure: Application deadlines are the same as those for other freshman applicants.

Admissions Contact: Director of Admissions.

BELOIT COLLEGE D-5
Beloit, Wisconsin 53511   (608) 365-3391

F/T: 546M, 480W	Faculty: 83; IIB, +$
P/T: 35M, 45W	Ph.D's: 85%
Grad: 1M, 3W	S/F Ratio: 12 to 1
Year: sems, ss	Tuition: $5860
Appl: open	R and B: $1920
723 applied	647 accepted 267 enrolled
SAT: 526V 544M	ACT: 25 VERY COMPETITIVE+

Beloit College, established in 1846, is an independent institution offering undergraduate programs in the liberal arts and sciences, business, and education. Its library has over 250,000 books and 8000 microfilm items, and subscribes to more than 873 periodicals.

Environment: The 40-acre campus is located in a community of 40,000, about 75 miles from Milwaukee. There are 17 residence halls that, along with 4 fraternity houses, accommodate 880 students.

Student Life: About 18% of the students come from Wisconsin. Sixty-seven percent attended public schools. About 90% live on campus. Twenty percent of the students are Catholic, 40% are Protestant, and 20% are Jewish. Nine percent are minority-group members. Campus

964 WISCONSIN

housing is both coed and single-sex. There are visiting privileges in single-sex dorms. Students may have cars on campus.

Organizations: Four national fraternities attract 25% of the men; about 5% of the women belong to 1 of 2 sororities. Extracurriculars include dramatics, a symphony orchestra, weekly lectures and concerts, student government, religious organizations, and clubs.

Sports: There are 11 intercollegiate sports for men and 9 for women. Intramurals consist of 3 sports for both men and women.

Graduates: The freshman dropout rate is 14%; about 55% remain to graduate. Sixty percent to 70% go on for further education, and 25% enter business careers. Five percent of each graduating class enter medical school, 1% dental school, and 7% law school.

Services: Psychological counseling, remedial instruction, placement services, and career counseling are provided without cost. Health care and tutoring are available for a fee.

Programs of Study: The college confers the B.A., B.S., and B.S. Med. Tech. degrees. Master's degrees are also awarded. The bachelor's degree is offered in the following subjects: BUSINESS (business administration), EDUCATION (elementary, secondary), ENGLISH (composition, English, literature), FINE AND PERFORMING ARTS (art education, art history, music, music education, studio art, theater/dramatics), HEALTH SCIENCES (medical technology), LANGUAGES (French, German, Greek/Latin, Spanish), MATH AND SCIENCES (biochemistry, biology, chemistry, geology, mathematics, mathematics and computer science, physics), PHILOSOPHY (classics, philosophy, religion), PREPROFESSIONAL (dentistry, engineering, forestry, law, medicine, ministry, social work, veterinary), SOCIAL SCIENCES (anthropology, economics, government/political science, history, international relations, psychology, sociology). About 49% of the degrees are conferred in social sciences, 21% in math and sciences, and 13% in the arts.

Required: There is a distribution requirement.

Special: Student-designed majors, study abroad, and combination degree programs with other institutions are offered.

Honors: There are chapters of 5 honor societies on campus, including Phi Beta Kappa. Honors work is offered in all departments.

Admissions: About 89% of the applicants for the 1981-82 freshman class were accepted. The SAT scores of entering freshmen were as follows: Verbal—10% below 500, 68% between 500 and 599, 20% between 600 and 700, and 2% above 700; Math—14% below 500, 59% between 500 and 599, 25% between 600 and 700, and 2% above 700. On the ACT, 15% scored below 21, 15% between 21 and 23, 45% between 24 and 25, 20% between 26 and 28, and 5% above 28. The average high school GPA is 3.2. Applicants should rank in the upper 40% of the graduating class; preference is given to those with at least 16 units of high school work. Other important factors include recommendations, advanced placement or honors work, and impressions made during an interview.

Procedure: The SAT or ACT is required. Deadlines are open; a rolling admissions plan is used. New students are admitted to both fall and spring terms. There is a $20 application fee.

Special: There are early admissions and deferred admissions plans. AP and CLEP credit is granted.

Transfer: Of 61 applications received for the current year, 49 were accepted, and 32 students enrolled. Transfers are accepted for all classes. A 2.0 GPA is required; D grades are not accepted. Four semesters must be completed in residence, and transfers must take, at the college, 16 of the 31 courses required for the bachelor's degree. The rolling admissions policy is followed.

Visiting: There are orientation programs for new students and prospective applicants. Visitors may attend classes and stay overnight at the school. The admissions office will arrange guided tours on weekdays.

Financial Aid: About 60% of the students are receiving assistance; 52% work part-time on campus. Grants, loans, and campus employment are available. The college is a member of CSS. The FAF is required; deadlines are April 1 (fall) and December 1 (spring).

Foreign Students: Foreign students comprise about 3% of the full-time enrollment. The college, which actively recruits these students, offers them special counseling.

Admissions: Foreign students must earn a score of at least 550 on the TOEFL. The SAT or ACT is also required.

Procedure: Application deadlines are May 1 (fall) and November 15 (spring). Proof of funds adequate to cover 1 year of study is required. Foreign students must carry health insurance, which is available through the college for a fee.

Admissions Contact: John W. Lind, Director of Admissions and Financial Aid.

CARDINAL STRITCH COLLEGE E-4
Milwaukee, Wisconsin 53217 (414) 352-5400

F/T: 84M, 355W	Faculty:	43; IIA, −−$
P/T: 26M, 272W	Ph.D.'s:	35%
Grad: 55M, 333W	S/F Ratio:	12 to 1
Year: sems, ss	Tuition:	$3225
Appl: open	R and B:	$1800
398 applied	248 accepted	125 enrolled
SAT: 460V 460M	ACT: 18	COMPETITIVE

Cardinal Stritch College, established in 1937, is affiliated with the Roman Catholic Church and offers undergraduate programs in the arts and sciences, business, and education. The library has 93,461 volumes and 14,700 microfilm items, and subscribes to 479 periodicals.

Environment: The 56-acre campus is located in a suburban area near Lake Michigan, about 7 miles from downtown Milwaukee. There are 9 buildings on campus, including 3 dormitories that house 180 men and women.

Student Life: About 77% of the students come from Wisconsin. Approximately 77% attended public schools. Twenty-five percent live on campus. Sixty-nine percent of the students are Catholic, 28% are Protestant, and 1% are Jewish; attendance at religious services is not compulsory. About 13% of the students are minority-group members. College housing is coed and single-sex; students in single-sex housing have visiting privileges. Students may keep cars on campus.

Organizations: There are no fraternities or sororities. The extracurricular program includes drama and music groups, publications, and a model U.N. There are regularly scheduled social and cultural events on campus, such as mixers, concerts, films, plays, and art shows.

Sports: The college fields 3 intercollegiate teams for men and 4 for women. There are 3 intramural sports for men and 3 for women.

Handicapped: About 75% of the campus is accessible to the physically handicapped. Special facilities for these students include wheelchair ramps and parking areas. Special class scheduling can be arranged.

Graduates: The freshman dropout rate is 50%, and 45% of the freshmen remain to graduate. Almost 15% of the graduates seek advanced degrees. Another 19% pursue careers in business and industry.

Services: Free career counseling, placement, and health care services are available to students. Psychological counseling, tutoring, and remedial instruction require a fee.

Programs of Study: The college awards the B.A., B.F.A., B.S., and B.S.P.A. degrees. Associate and master's degrees are also awarded. Bachelor's degrees are offered in the following subjects: BUSINESS (business administration, computer science), EDUCATION (early childhood, elementary, secondary, special), ENGLISH (English), FINE AND PERFORMING ARTS (art, art education, music, theater/dramatics), LANGUAGES (French, Spanish), MATH AND SCIENCES (biology, chemistry, mathematics, natural sciences), PHILOSOPHY (religion), PREPROFESSIONAL (dentistry, home economics, law, medicine, veterinary), SOCIAL SCIENCES (history, psychology, social sciences, sociology).

Required: The general education requirement includes courses in religious studies, philosophy, history, science, mathematics, literature, and social and behavioral sciences.

Special: A general studies major is possible. Other special programs include independent study, double majors, study abroad, and internships.

Honors: There are chapters of 7 national honor societies on campus.

Admissions: About 62% of the applicants for the 1981-82 freshman class were accepted. Of those who enrolled, the SAT scores were as follows: Verbal—66% below 500, 34% between 500 and 599, 0% between 600 and 700, and 0% above 700; Math—66% below 500, 34% between 500 and 599, and 0% above 599. On the ACT, 55% scored below 21, 33% between 21 and 23, 0% between 24 and 25, 12% between 26 and 28, and 0% above 28. Fifteen Carnegie units, class rank in the upper half, and a high school average of 2.0 are required; an interview is recommended. Other factors considered are the results of the SAT or ACT, recommendations from school officials, advanced placement or honors courses, and personality.

Procedure: The SAT or ACT is recommended and should be taken by January of the senior year. Application deadlines are open; notification is on a rolling basis. There is a $15 application fee.

Special: There are early and deferred admissions plans. CLEP is used.

Transfer: For fall 1981, 80 students applied, 80 were accepted, and 65 enrolled. Transfer students are accepted for all years. A 2.0 GPA, a minimum SAT score of 450, and 64 credit hours are required. D grades are unacceptable. Students must spend at least one year in residence and complete 32 of the 128 credits required for a bachelor's degree. Application deadlines are open.

Visiting: There is an orientation program for prospective applicants. Visitors may have a tour of the campus, attend classes, and stay overnight in the dormitories. The director of admissions handles such arrangements.

Financial Aid: About 65% of the students are receiving aid. Seventeen percent work part-time on campus. Average aid to freshmen is $2777, which combines a scholarship or grant with a loan or employment. Freshman scholarships, various government and commercial loans, and federal and state grants are available. The college is a member of CSS. The FAF should be filed by March 1 for priority consideration.

Foreign Students: Eight of the full-time students come from foreign countries. The college offers these students special counseling.

Admissions: Foreign students must achieve a TOEFL score of at least 550. If entering as freshmen, they must also take the college's own entrance exam.

Procedure: Application deadlines are open. Foreign students must present both the report of a general health exam and proof of funds adequate to cover 1 year of study. They must also carry health insurance.

Admissions Contact: Patricia B. Ranger, Director of Admissions.

CARROLL COLLEGE
Waukesha, Wisconsin 53186   D–5   (414) 547-1211

F/T: 534M, 559W	Faculty: 77; IIB, +$
P/T: 13M, 18W	Ph.D.'s: 67%
Grad: none	S/F Ratio: 14 to 1
Year: 4-1-4, ss	Tuition: $5010
Appl: open	R and B: $1680
900 applied	792 accepted 302 enrolled
SAT: 470V 527M	ACT: 23 COMPETITIVE+

Carroll College, established in 1846, presents an undergraduate degree program with emphases in the liberal arts and sciences, business, and education. The college is affiliated with the United Presbyterian Church but is nonsectarian. Its library contains 156,000 volumes and 7836 microfilm items, and subscribes to 600 periodicals.

Environment: The 36-acre campus is located in a suburban area 17 miles from Milwaukee. An additional 60-acre tract is used for scientific experiments. Five dormitories on campus and 5 fraternity houses off campus provide housing facilities.

Student Life: Over 60% of the students come from Wisconsin. Eighty-five percent live on campus. About 8% of the students are minority-group members. College housing is coed and single-sex; students in single-sex housing have visiting privileges. Students may keep cars on campus.

Organizations: There are 2 local and 3 national fraternities, to which 30% of the men belong; there are 4 national sororities, to which 30% of the women belong. Other extracurricular activities are traditional.

Sports: The college fields 10 intercollegiate teams for men and 6 for women. There are 11 intramural sports for men and 7 for women.

Handicapped: About 30% of the campus is accessible to physically handicapped students. All new facilities have ramps and elevators. Special class scheduling may be arranged. Designated parking is available.

Graduates: The freshman dropout rate is 20%, and 62% of the freshmen remain to complete degrees. Twenty-five percent of the graduates go on for additional study; 3% enter medical school, 2% enter dental school, and 4% enter law school. Another 40% enter careers in business and industry.

Services: Career counseling, placement services, health care, and psychological counseling are offered without additional charge. Placement services for students include resume-writing workshops and on-campus interviews.

Programs of Study: The B.A. and B.S. degrees are conferred. Bachelor's degrees are offered in the following subjects: BUSINESS (accounting, business administration, computer science, finance), EDUCATION (early childhood, elementary, health/physical, secondary), ENGLISH (English, journalism, speech), FINE AND PERFORMING ARTS (art, art education, music, music education, theater/dramatics), HEALTH SCIENCES (medical technology), LANGUAGES (French, German, Spanish), MATH AND SCIENCES (biology, chemistry, mathematics, physics), PHILOSOPHY (philosophy, religion), PREPROFESSIONAL (dentistry, engineering, hospital administration, law, medicine, ministry, pharmacy, social work, veterinary), SOCIAL SCIENCES (economics, geography, government/political science, history, international relations, psychology, social sciences, sociology). About 25% of the degrees conferred are in social sciences, 21% are in business, and 19% are in math or sciences.

Required: All students must take and pass the URE.

Special: Study abroad, student-designed majors, a Washington semester, a 3-year bachelor's degree, a U.N. semester, and combination degree programs (3-2 in engineering and 3-1 in medical technology) are offered.

Honors: Seven departments offer honors work. There are 14 honor societies on campus.

Admissions: Eighty-eight percent of the applicants for the 1981–82 freshman class were accepted. Of those who enrolled, the SAT scores were as follows: Verbal—25% between 500 and 599, 8% between 600 and 700, and 5% above 700; Math—30% between 500 and 599, 23% between 600 and 700, and 4% above 700. On the ACT, 22% scored between 21 and 23, 24% between 24 and 25, 20% between 26 and 28, and 10% above 28. Applicants must rank in the upper half of their high school class; a grade average of 2.0 is suggested. In addition to the quality of the high school record, scholastic aptitude (as indicated by the SAT or ACT results) and personal qualities are major factors in the admissions decision. Recommendations, advanced placement or honors work, and the applicant's extracurricular activities record are also considered important.

Procedure: Either the SAT or the ACT is required. Deadlines are open. New students are admitted each semester. Admission and notification are on a rolling basis. There is no application fee.

Special: There are early and deferred admissions plans. AP and CLEP credit is accepted.

Transfer: For fall 1981, 106 students applied, 72 were accepted, and 41 enrolled. A 2.0 GPA and transcripts from all post-secondary institutions attended are required. D grades are not accepted. One year must be completed in residence, and the student must complete 32 of the 128 credits required for a bachelor's degree. Application deadlines are open.

Visiting: The orientation program any weekday for prospective applicants includes guided tours, a meal, class visits, and faculty and counselor interviews. Student visitors may stay overnight at the school. The admissions office handles such arrangements.

Financial Aid: The college administers aid for about 77% of the students. Thirty-three percent work part-time on campus. Average aid to freshmen is $3573. Freshman scholarships, loans (government and commercial, including NDSL), and grants are available. Need, academic potential, and scholastic achievement are the determining factors. The college is a member of CSS. The FAF should be submitted as early as possible, as applications are processed on a rolling basis.

Foreign Students: Fewer than 1% of the full-time students come from foreign countries. The college offers these students special counseling and special organizations.

Admissions: Foreign students must achieve a TOEFL score of at least 550. No college entrance exam must be taken.

Procedure: Application deadlines are open. Foreign students must present both a college health statement based on a physical exam and proof of funds adequate to cover the first year of study. They must also carry health insurance, which is available through the university for a fee.

Admissions Contact: Frank Hetherington, Dean of Admissions.

CARTHAGE COLLEGE
Kenosha, Wisconsin 53141   E–5   (414) 551-8500

F/T: 530M, 548W	Faculty: n/av; IIB, +$
P/T: 113M, 179W	Ph.D.'s: 77%
Grad: 31M, 81W	S/F Ratio: 14 to 1
Year: 4-1-4, ss	Tuition: $4211
Appl: open	R and B: $1790
736 applied	639 accepted 309 enrolled
ACT: 20	COMPETITIVE

Carthage College, established in 1847, is a private liberal arts institution affiliated with the Lutheran Church in America. Until 1962, it was

966 WISCONSIN

located in Carthage, Illinois. The library contains 179,000 volumes and subscribes to 1048 periodicals.

Environment: The 78-acre campus is located on Lake Michigan in an urban area of 85,000, 35 miles southeast of Milwaukee. All major campus buildings have been completed since 1962. Dormitories house most of the students.

Student Life: Eighty-five percent of the students come from the Midwest. Seventy-nine percent of entering freshmen come from public schools. Ninety-five percent of the students live on campus. Fifty-five percent are Protestant, and 25% are Catholic; chapel attendance is required. Fourteen percent of the students are minority-group members. College housing is coed and single-sex; students in single-sex housing have visiting privileges. Students may keep cars on campus, and alcohol is permitted.

Organizations: There are 5 fraternities and 4 sororities on campus, to which 30% of the men and 30% of the women belong. The college sponsors more than 50 student organizations, including religious groups, student government, Student Activities Board, yearbook, newspaper, and literary magazine. Other extracurricular activities include music and drama. On-campus events are supplemented by cultural facilities in nearby Milwaukee and Chicago.

Sports: The college fields 12 intercollegiate teams for men and 7 for women. There are 6 intramural sports for men and 6 for women.

Handicapped: About 90% of the campus is accessible to handicapped students. Special facilities include wheelchair ramps, parking areas, elevators, and specially equipped rest rooms. Special class scheduling is also possible.

Graduates: The freshman dropout rate is 4%, and 75% of the freshmen remain to graduate. About 20% of the graduates pursue advanced degrees; 1% enter medical school, 1% enter dental school, and 3% enter law school. Thirty percent pursue careers in business and industry.

Services: Health care and placement services are available to students free of charge.

Programs of Study: The college confers the B.A. degree. Master's degrees are also offered. Bachelor's degrees are offered in the following subjects: AREA STUDIES (Latin American), BUSINESS (accounting, business administration, business education, international business, marketing), EDUCATION (elementary, health/physical, secondary, special), ENGLISH (English, literature, speech), FINE AND PERFORMING ARTS (art, art education, art history, music, music education, studio art, theater/dramatics), HEALTH SCIENCES (medical technology), LANGUAGES (French, German, Spanish), MATH AND SCIENCES (biology, chemistry, mathematics, natural sciences, physics), PHILOSOPHY (philosophy, religion), PREPROFESSIONAL (dentistry, engineering, law, medicine, ministry, social work, veterinary), SOCIAL SCIENCES (anthropology, economics, geography, government/political science, history, psychology, social sciences, sociology).

Required: All students are required to take physical education, oral and written communications, and 2 courses in religion.

Special: A study-abroad program is available. The Spanish department conducts a study tour in Mexico; the English department in the southeastern United States. Combination degree programs are offered in engineering and medical technology. Student-designed majors are permitted.

Honors: Honors programs are offered in various departments. There are 14 honor societies on campus.

Admissions: About 87% of those who applied were accepted for the 1981–82 freshman class. Of those who enrolled, the ACT scores were as follows: 44% below 20, 41% between 20 and 24, 35% between 25 and 29, and 2% above 29. Applicants should be graduates of accredited high schools, have completed 14 units of academic work, rank in the upper half of their class, and have at least a 2.0 GPA; an interview is preferred but not required. Other considerations include personality, advanced placement or honors courses, and recommendations by school officials.

Procedure: The ACT or SAT is required (ACT preferred) and should be taken by April of the senior year. Application deadlines are open. Admissions are granted on a rolling basis. There is a $15 application fee.

Special: Early and deferred admissions plans and an early decision plan are available. CLEP and AP credit may be earned.

Transfer: For fall 1981, 70 students applied, 65 were accepted, and 64 enrolled. Transfers are accepted for all classes. A 2.0 GPA is required; the ACT and an interview are recommended. D grades are not accepted. Students must earn, at the college, at least 32 of the 126 credits necessary for a bachelor's degree. Application deadlines are open.

Visiting: Guides are available for informal campus visits. Visitors may sit in on classes and stay overnight on campus. Visits are best scheduled on weekdays or Saturday mornings. The admissions office should be contacted for arrangements.

Financial Aid: About 67% of the students receive financial aid. Twenty percent work part-time on campus. Scholarships and loans are available. The college is a member of the CSS. The FAF is required. The deadline for aid applications is March 1; notification is on a rolling basis.

Foreign Students: Five percent of the full-time students come from foreign countries. The college offers these students special counseling and special organizations.

Admissions: Foreign students must achieve a TOEFL score of at least 500. No college entrance exam must be taken.

Procedure: Application deadlines are open. Foreign students must present proof of funds adequate to cover 1 year of study. They must also carry health insurance, which is available through the college.

Admissions Contact: Kent Duesing, Director of Admissions.

CONCORDIA COLLEGE E–4
Milwaukee, Wisconsin 53208 (414) 344-3400

F/T: 188M, 229W
P/T: 88M & W
Grad: none
Year: 4-1-4, ss
Appl: Aug. 15
426 applied
SAT or ACT: required

Faculty: 36; III, — –$
Ph.D.'s: 14%
S/F Ratio: 14 to 1
Tuition: $3050
R and B: $850

LESS COMPETITIVE

Concordia College, founded in 1881, is a liberal arts and teachers' college affiliated with the Lutheran-Missouri Synod.

Environment: The 30-acre urban campus is located in Milwaukee. Living facilities include dormitories, which can accommodate 250 men and 150 women, and married student housing.

Student Life: Eighteen percent of the students are minority-group members. College housing is single-sex, and there are visiting privileges. Students may keep cars on campus.

Organizations: There are no fraternities or sororities. The cultural offerings of the city of Milwaukee are accessible to students.

Sports: The college fields 4 intercollegiate teams for men and 4 for women. There are 6 intramural sports for men and 6 for women.

Handicapped: Forty percent of the campus is accessible to the physically handicapped. Special facilities for these students include elevators and specially equipped rest rooms. No special counselors are available.

Graduates: Seventy percent of the graduates pursue careers in business and industry.

Services: Students receive the following services free of charge: placement, career, and psychological counseling and tutoring.

Programs of Study: The college confers the B.A. and B.S.N. degrees. Associate degrees are also awarded. Bachelor's degrees are offered in the following subjects: BUSINESS (business administration), EDUCATION (early childhood, elementary, secondary, special), FINE AND PERFORMING ARTS (music education), HEALTH SCIENCES (nursing), MATH AND SCIENCES (mathematics), PHILOSOPHY (humanities, religion), PREPROFESSIONAL (engineering, ministry), SOCIAL SCIENCES (social sciences).

Required: Students must achieve a minimum 2.0 GPA overall, with a 2.5 in selected studies, in order to graduate.

Special: Student-designed majors, combined B.A.-B.S. degrees, and a 3-2 engineering program with Marquette University are offered.

Admissions: Applicants must have completed 16 Carnegie units and hold a grade average of at least 2.0. Other factors considered include advanced placement or honors courses, recommendations by school officials, and evidence of special talent.

Procedure: The SAT or ACT is required. Application deadlines are August 15 (fall), December 15 (winter), and January 15 (spring). Notification is on a rolling basis. There is a $25 application fee.

Special: AP and CLEP credit is accepted.

Transfer: Applicants for transfer need a 2.0 GPA, and an interview is recommended. D grades do not transfer. Students must earn, at the college, at least 30 of the 126 credits necessary for a bachelor's degree.

Visiting: There are regularly scheduled orientations for prospective students. Guides are available for informal visits. Students may sit in on classes and stay overnight at the school. Weekday visits are recommended. Arrangements should be made through the admissions office.

Financial Aid: Eighty-five percent of the students receive aid. Scholarships, grants, and loans are available. The college is a member of CSS. The FAF is required. Application deadlines are May 1 (fall) and January 1 (winter).

Foreign Students: Three percent of the full-time students come from foreign countries.

Admissions: Foreign students must take an English proficiency exam, preferably the TOEFL, for which a minimum score of 500 is required. No college entrance exam must be taken.

Procedure: Application deadlines are August 15 (fall) and January 15 (winter). Foreign students must present both proof of health and proof of adequate funds.

Admissions Contact: William H. Ebel, Dean of Admissions.

EDGEWOOD COLLEGE C-4
Madison, Wisconsin 53711 (608) 257-4861

F/T: 100M, 350W Faculty: 53; IIB, — $
P/T: 70M, 225W Ph.D.'s: 51%
Grad: 2M, 25W S/F Ratio: 10 to 1
Year: 4-1-4, ss Tuition: $3100
Appl: Aug. 1 R and B: $1660
202 applied 161 accepted 100 enrolled
ACT: 19 COMPETITIVE

Edgewood College, founded in 1927, is a private liberal arts college affiliated with the Roman Catholic Church. Its library has 81,000 volumes and 24,500 microtexts, and subscribes to 501 periodicals.

Environment: Located in an urban area on the shore of a lake, the college has a theater, a biological research station, a student center, a gymnasium, an elementary school, and a high school on its 55-acre campus. In addition to 3 residence halls, the college sponsors on-campus apartments and married-student housing.

Student Life: The majority of students come from the Midwest. About 75% attended public schools. Fifty percent live on campus. Sixty percent are Catholic, 10% are Protestant, and 2% are Jewish. Nine percent are minority-group members. College housing is coed and single-sex; students in single-sex housing have visiting privileges. Students may keep cars on campus.

Organizations: The extracurricular program includes publications, student government, clubs, service and religious groups, and social and cultural events. There are no sororities or fraternities.

Sports: The college fields 2 intercollegiate teams for men and 2 for women. There are 3 intramural sports for men and 3 for women.

Handicapped: About 90% of the campus is accessible to the physically handicapped. Special facilities include wheelchair ramps, cross-campus walks for wheelchairs, elevators, telephones, and specially equipped rest rooms. The college was installing lowered drinking fountains in 1981-82. Two counselors provide assistance.

Graduates: The freshman dropout rate is 10%, and 65% of the freshmen remain to graduate. About 20% of the graduates continue their education: 5% enter medical, dental, or law school. Another 25% pursue careers in business and industry.

Services: Health care, tutoring, remedial instruction, career counseling, and placement aid are offered free; psychological counseling is available for a fee.

Programs of Study: The college grants the B.A. and B.S. degrees. Associate degrees are also awarded. Bachelor's degrees are offered in the following subjects: AREA STUDIES (American), BUSINESS (accounting, applied mathematics and business, business administration, computer science, management), EDUCATION (child life, early childhood, elementary, secondary, special), ENGLISH (English), FINE AND PERFORMING ARTS (art, art education, theater/dramatics), HEALTH SCIENCES (medical technology, nursing), LANGUAGES (French, Spanish), MATH AND SCIENCES (biology, mathematics, natural sciences, physical sciences), PHILOSOPHY (humanities, religion), PREPROFESSIONAL (dentistry, law, medicine, pharmacy, social work), SOCIAL SCIENCES (criminal justice, economics, government/political science, history, psychology, social sciences, sociology).

Required: The college designates area requirements which may be satisfied in several departments.

Special: Combined degrees in science and nursing, study-year abroad, field experiences, and independent study are offered. A weekend degree program is available. Students may design their own majors.

Admissions: About 80% of the 1981-82 freshman applicants were accepted. Of those who enrolled, the ACT scores were as follows: 14% scored below 21, 55% between 21 and 23, 15% between 24 and 25, 14% between 26 and 28, and 2% above 28. Applicants must have 16 Carnegie units and a 2.0 high school GPA; the college uses the ACT scores for placement purposes. Impressions made during an interview, evidence of special talent, and recommendations by school officials are also considered.

Procedure: Freshmen are required to take the ACT either before or after admission. New students are admitted to all terms. Application deadlines are August 1 (fall) and January 6 (winter). Admissions and notification are on a rolling basis. There is a $10 application fee.

Special: CLEP and AP credit is granted.

Transfer: For fall 1981, 218 students applied, 187 were accepted, and 124 enrolled. Transfers are accepted for all classes. A 2.0 GPA is required. D grades are accepted. Students must earn, at the college, at least 32 of the minimum 120 credits necessary for a bachelor's degree. Application deadlines are the same as those for freshmen.

Visiting: An orientation program is held for prospective students. Informal campus tours with student guides can be arranged. Visitors may attend classes and stay overnight at the school. Arrangements should be made through the admissions office.

Financial Aid: About 75% of the students are receiving assistance. Seventy percent work part-time on campus. Average aid to 1981-82 freshmen was $4000. Scholarships, grants (such as Pell), and government and commercial loans (including NDSL) are available. The college is a member of CSS. The FAF is required. Aid application deadlines are August 15 (fall) and January 15 (spring).

Foreign Students: Two percent of the full-time students come from foreign countries. The college offers these students special counseling and special organizations.

Admissions: Foreign students must score at least 550 on the TOEFL. No college entrance exams are required.

Procedure: Application deadlines are August 1 (fall) and January 6 (spring). Foreign students must present proof of adequate funds for their entire period of study.

Admissions Contact: Sr. Barbara Hubeny, Director of Admissions.

LAKELAND COLLEGE E-4
Sheboygan, Wisconsin 53073 (414) 565-1217

F/T: 272M, 204W Faculty: 31; IIB, — $
P/T: 190M, 92W Ph.D.'s: 67%
Grad: none S/F Ratio: 16 to 1
Year: 4-1-4, ss Tuition: $3890
Appl: open R and B: $1970
347 applied 278 accepted 139 enrolled
ACT: 17 COMPETITIVE

Lakeland College, founded in 1862, offers liberal arts and teacher training. It is affiliated with the United Church of Christ. The library houses 55,000 volumes and 23,000 microfilm items, and subscribes to 210 periodicals.

Environment: The 150-acre campus is located in a rural setting 8 miles from Sheboygan and 60 miles from Milwaukee. Thirteen buildings are used for academic and extracurricular activities. Students live in dormitories.

Student Life: More than half of the students are from Wisconsin. Eighty-eight percent of the freshmen are public school graduates. Seventy-three percent of the students live on campus. Fifty percent are Protestant and 32% are Catholic. About 10% of the students are minority-group members. College housing is coed and single-sex; students in single-sex housing have visiting privileges. Students may keep cars on campus.

Organizations: Fifteen percent of the men belong to 1 of the 4 fraternities on campus; 15% of the women belong to 1 of the 2 sororities. Protestant and Catholic organizations function at the college. The John Michael Kohler Art Center is one of the cultural attractions in the area. Recreational areas include the Lake Michigan beaches and Kettle Moraine State Forest.

968 WISCONSIN

Sports: Lakeland fields 6 intercollegiate teams for men and 4 for women. There are 6 intramural sports for men and 6 for women.

Handicapped: Special class scheduling is available for handicapped students. Parking facilities and specially equipped rest rooms are also provided.

Graduates: The freshman dropout rate is 45%, and 40% of the freshmen remain to graduate. Sixteen percent of the graduates pursue advanced degrees; 1% enter medical school, 1% enter dental school, and 2% enter law school. Another 37% pursue careers in business and industry.

Services: Psychological and career counseling are offered free to students; free placement services are available to both students and alumni. Tutoring can be obtained for a fee.

Programs of Study: The B.A. degree is conferred. Bachelor's degrees are offered in the following subjects: BUSINESS (accounting, business administration, computer science administration, specialized administration), EDUCATION (early childhood, elementary), ENGLISH (English, journalism, speech), FINE AND PERFORMING ARTS (art, music, theater/dramatics), HEALTH SCIENCES (health care administration, medical technology, mental health care administration), LANGUAGES (German), MATH AND SCIENCES (biology, chemistry, mathematics), PHILOSOPHY (philosophy, religion), PREPROFESSIONAL (dentistry, law, medicine, ministry, pharmacy, social work), SOCIAL SCIENCES (behavioral science, history, psychology, public policy administration, social sciences, sociology). Twenty-five percent of the degrees conferred are in business, 15% in health sciences, and 15% in education.

Required: Students must demonstrate competency in reading, writing, and math through exams or completion of certain courses. They must complete 3 of the 9 team-taught interdisciplinary core courses as well as basic courses in the humanities, social sciences, and natural sciences. Students also must complete a minimum of 7 courses per year.

Special: Among options open to students are self-designed majors and junior-year study abroad. During Winterim some students remain on campus to take 1 course or do individual research. Others leave campus for work-study experiences.

Honors: A college-wide honors program is based on the great books. Three national honor societies have chapters on campus.

Admissions: Eighty percent of those who applied for the 1981-82 freshman class were accepted. The ACT scores of those who enrolled were as follows: 63% scored below 21, 23% between 21 and 23, 10% between 24 and 25, 2% between 26 and 28, and 2% above 28. Candidates must be graduates of accredited high schools, have completed 15 Carnegie units, rank in the upper half of their high school class, and have a GPA of at least 2.0. Also considered are recommendations by school officials, advanced placement or honors courses, and extracurricular activities.

Procedure: Either the ACT or the SAT is required, and a campus interview is highly recommended. Application deadlines are open. Notification is made on a rolling basis up to the start of classes. There is a $15 application fee.

Special: An early admissions plan and an early decision plan are available. CLEP and AP credit is accepted.

Transfer: For fall 1981, 115 students applied, 98 were accepted, and 51 enrolled. A GPA of at least 2.0 and a dean's report of good standing are required; the SAT or ACT and an interview are recommended. D grades transfer with an associate degree only. Students must spend at least 1 year in residence, earning at least 36 of the 136 credits necessary for a bachelor's degree. Application deadlines are open.

Visiting: Guides are available for informal campus visits. Visitors may sit in on classes and stay overnight at the school. Visits are best scheduled on weekdays. The admissions office should be contacted for arrangements.

Financial Aid: Ninety percent of the students receive aid. Fifty-two percent work part-time on campus. The average aid given to freshmen in 1981-82 covered 65% of costs. Scholarships and loans are available to freshmen. The college is a member of CSS. The FAF or a federal tax return is required. Application deadlines are open.

Foreign Students: Fewer than 3% of the full-time students are from foreign countries. The college offers these students special counseling and special organizations.

Admissions: Foreign students must score at least 500 on the TOEFL or take the University of Michigan Language Test. No college entrance exams are required.

Procedure: Application deadlines are September 1 (fall), January 1 (winter), February 1 (spring), and May 15 (summer). Foreign students must present proof of adequate funds. They also must carry health insurance, which is available through the university for a fee.

Admissions Contact: Allyn A. French, Director of Admissions.

LAWRENCE UNIVERSITY   D-3
Appleton, Wisconsin 54912   (414) 735-6500

F/T: 571M, 571W   Faculty: 102; IIB, + + $
P/T: none   Ph.D.'s: 97%
Grad: none   S/F Ratio: 11 to 1
Year: tri   Tuition: $5883
Appl: see profile   R and B: $1767
1045 applied   835 accepted   300 enrolled
SAT: 525V 557M   ACT: 25   VERY COMPETITIVE+

Lawrence University, founded in 1847, is an independent, nonsectarian institution that offers programs in the liberal arts and sciences. Its library has 225,000 volumes and 110,000 microfilm units, and subscribes to 1100 periodicals.

Environment: The 72-acre campus is located in a city of 65,000 inhabitants, about 100 miles north of Milwaukee. The 28 major buildings include 7 dormitories and 6 fraternity houses that accommodate 1200 students. There is a sorority wing in one of the residence halls.

Student Life: About 43% of the students are from Wisconsin. Seventy-eight percent come from public schools. All but 1% live on campus. About 3% are minority-group members. University housing is coed. Students may keep cars on campus.

Organizations: About 25% of the students belong to the 6 national fraternities and 4 national sororities on campus. Extracurricular activities include student government, religious and service groups, clubs, publications, and performing groups. There are regularly scheduled on-campus social and cultural events.

Sports: The university fields 15 intercollegiate teams for men and 13 for women. There are more than 13 intramural sports for men and 12 for women.

Handicapped: About 85% of the campus is accessible to handicapped students. Special facilities for the physically handicapped include wheelchair ramps, parking areas, elevators, lowered drinking fountains and telephones, and specially equipped rest rooms. Special class scheduling and personnel are provided.

Graduates: The freshman dropout rate is 4%, and 80% of the freshmen remain to graduate. Thirty percent of the graduates go on for further study; 4% enter medical school, 1% enter dental school, and 4% enter law school. Another 40% enter careers in business and industry.

Services: Career counseling, placement services, psychological counseling, tutoring, and remedial instruction are offered to all students without additional charge. Health care is available on a fee basis.

Programs of Study: The university confers the B.A. and B.M. degrees. Bachelor's degrees are offered in the following subjects: AREA STUDIES (Black/Afro-American), BUSINESS (computer science), EDUCATION (elementary, secondary), ENGLISH (English), FINE AND PERFORMING ARTS (art, art education, art history, music, music education, music performance, music theory and composition, studio art, theater/dramatics), HEALTH SCIENCES (medical technology, nursing), LANGUAGES (French, German, Greek/Latin, linguistics, Russian, Slavic, Spanish), MATH AND SCIENCES (biology, chemistry, ecology/environmental science, geology, mathematics, neurosciences, physics), PHILOSOPHY (classics, philosophy, religion), PRE-PROFESSIONAL (dentistry, engineering, forestry, law, library science, medicine, ministry, pharmacy, social work, veterinary), SOCIAL SCIENCES (anthropology, government/political science, history, international relations, psychology, public policy analysis, sociology). Thirty percent of the degrees are conferred in humanities, 30% in math and sciences, and 20% in social sciences.

Required: Freshman Studies and physical education are required. Students also must fulfill general distribution requirements.

Special: Students may design their own majors. Cooperative degree programs, interdisciplinary majors, study abroad, teacher certification, and combination-degree programs are offered.

Honors: All departments offer independent study, in which projects often qualify for honors. Phi Beta Kappa and 5 other honor societies have campus chapters.

Admissions: About 80% of the 1981-82 freshman applicants were accepted. The SAT scores of those who enrolled were as follows: Verbal—33% scored below 500, 48% between 500 and 599, 18%

between 600 and 700, and 1% above 700; Math—22% scored below 500, 42% between 500 and 599, 29% between 600 and 700, and 7% above 700. On the ACT, 12% scored below 21, 18% between 21 and 23, 24% between 24 and 25, 31% between 26 and 28, and 15% above 28. Applicants should rank in the top 30% of their graduating class; a 3.0 high school GPA and an interview also are recommended.

Procedure: The SAT or ACT should be taken by January of the senior year. March 1 is the preferred fall-term application deadline. Students also are admitted in winter and spring. Admission and notification are on a rolling basis. The CRDA is observed. There is a $15 application fee.

Special: Early and deferred admissions plans are offered. AP credit can be earned.

Transfer: For fall 1981, 111 students applied, 66 were accepted, and 38 enrolled. Transfers are accepted for freshman, sophomore, and junior years and, infrequently, for the senior year. A minimum GPA of 3.0 is recommended. D grades are not accepted. Students must spend at least 2 years in residence, completing at least 18 of the 36 course credits necessary for a bachelor's degree. The application deadlines are September 1 (fall), December 1 (winter), and February 1 (spring).

Visiting: There is an orientation program for prospective applicants. Informal campus tours with student guides may be arranged during the week, when school is in session. Visitors may stay at the school and attend classes. For further information, contact the admissions office.

Financial Aid: About 52% of the students are receiving assistance. Seventy-seven percent work part-time on campus. Average aid to freshmen in 1981–82 was $5200. Aid includes scholarships, grants, and loans. The university is a member of CSS and requires either the FAF or the Lawrence University FAF. Applications should be filed by March 15.

Foreign Students: Three percent of the full-time students come from foreign countries. The university offers these students special counseling and special organizations.

Admissions: Foreign students must score at least 540 on the TOEFL. No college entrance exams must be taken.

Procedure: Application deadlines are the same as those for freshmen. Foreign students must present proof of adequate funds. Health insurance, though not required, is available through the university.

Admissions Contact: David E. Busse, Director of Admissions and Financial Aid.

MARIAN COLLEGE OF FOND DU LAC D-4
Fond Du Lac, Wisconsin 54935 (414) 921-3900

F/T: 80M, 484W Faculty: 45; IIB, −$
P/T: 17M, 70W Ph.D.'s: 26%
Grad: none S/F Ratio: 10 to 1
Year: sems, ss Tuition: $2970
Appl: Aug. 15 R and B: $1500
226 applied 211 accepted 148 enrolled
SAT: 350V 350M ACT: 22 LESS COMPETITIVE

Marian College of Fond Du Lac, established in 1936, is a liberal arts institution affiliated with the Roman Catholic Church. The library has 74,000 volumes and 80,000 microfilm items, and subscribes to 500 periodicals.

Environment: The 50-acre campus is located in a city of 36,000 inhabitants, in a rural area about 60 miles from Milwaukee. The 8 college buildings include 3 residence halls that accommodate 230 students. Women students are housed in 2 dorms; men students live in a college-owned apartment building. The college also sponsors off-campus apartments.

Student Life: About 88% of the students come from Wisconsin. Eighty percent attended public schools. About 50% live on campus. Sixty-six percent are Catholic and 2% are Protestant. About 2% of the students are minority-group members. College housing is both coed and single-sex; students in single-sex housing have visiting privileges. Students may keep cars on campus.

Organizations: On-campus events and groups include concerts, plays, dances, movies, clubs, and student government. There are no sororities or fraternities. A large lake nearby offers facilities for water sports.

Sports: The college fields 4 intercollegiate teams for men and 6 for women. There are 6 intramural sports for men and 6 for women.

Handicapped: About 90% of the campus is accessible to the handicapped. Elevators are available. There is 1 special counselor, and students are assigned to assist handicapped students.

Graduates: The freshman dropout rate is 12%, and about 70% remain to graduate. Twelve percent of the graduates go on for further study, and 8% enter careers in business and industry.

Services: Career counseling, placement services, health care, psychological counseling, and remedial instruction are offered free. Some tutoring requires a fee.

Programs of Study: The college awards the B.A., B.S., B.S.W., B.S.N., B.S.B.A., B.S.Ed., and B.S. in Radiological Technology degrees. Bachelor's degrees are offered in the following subjects: BUSINESS (business administration), EDUCATION (early childhood, elementary, secondary), ENGLISH (English), FINE AND PERFORMING ARTS (art, art education, music education), HEALTH SCIENCES (medical technology, nursing, radiological technology), MATH AND SCIENCES (biology, chemistry, ecology/environmental science, mathematics), PHILOSOPHY (philosophy, religion), PREPROFESSIONAL (dentistry, law, medicine, ministry, pharmacy, veterinary), SOCIAL SCIENCES (history, psychology, social sciences, social studies, sociology). About 50% of the degrees conferred are in health sciences.

Required: The distribution requirement includes courses in theology, English, fine arts, natural science, mathematics, social science, and philosophy. Students in the business-administration and social-work programs must successfully complete on-the-job training to receive a degree.

Special: Student-designed majors and study abroad are possible.

Honors: Two national honor societies have chapters on campus.

Admissions: About 93% of the 1981–82 freshman applicants were accepted. The SAT scores of those who enrolled were as follows: Verbal—74% scored below 500, 18% between 500 and 599, 7% between 600 and 700, and 1% above 700; Math—39% scored below 500, 36% between 500 and 599, 16% between 600 and 700, and 9% above 700. On the ACT, 30% scored below 21, 23% between 21 and 23, 34% between 24 and 25, 10% between 26 and 28, and 3% above 28. Candidates should be graduates of accredited high schools, with a GPA of 2.5 in 16 Carnegie units and a class rank in the upper 65%. An interview is recommended. Other factors considered are the test scores, leadership record, and advanced placement or honors courses.

Procedure: The SAT or ACT is required; junior-year results are acceptable. Deadlines for application are August 15 (fall), December 15 (spring), and June 15 (summer). Notification is made on a rolling basis. There is a $10 application fee.

Special: Early and deferred admissions plans and an early decision plan are available. AP and CLEP are used.

Transfer: For fall 1981, 36 students applied, 27 were accepted, and 21 enrolled. Transfers are admitted to all years except the freshman first-semester class; usually, no nursing transfers are accepted. A 2.0 GPA and a minimum score of 750 on the SAT or 16 on the ACT are required. D grades are not accepted. Students must earn in residence at least 32 of the 128 credits necessary for a bachelor's degree. Application deadlines are the same as those for freshmen.

Visiting: Informal campus tours with student guides can be arranged. Visitors may attend classes and stay overnight at the school. The recommended times for visiting are mornings and early afternoons on Mondays, Tuesdays, and Wednesdays. Arrangements can be made through the admissions office.

Financial Aid: About 70% of the students are receiving aid. Fifteen percent work part-time on campus. The college offers scholarships, federal grants (BEOG and SEOG), state grants, and loans (including NDSL). Tuition may be paid in installments. Need is the determining factor. The college is a member of the CSS and requires the FAF. Aid applications are due by April 15 for priority consideration. Final deadlines are August 15 (fall) and December 15 (spring).

Foreign Students: Fewer than 1% of the full-time students come from foreign countries. The college offers these students special counseling.

Admissions: Foreign students must score at least 450 on the TOEFL. They also must score at least 450 on each section of the SAT or 16 on the ACT.

Procedure: Application deadlines are August 1 (fall), October 15 (spring), and April 15 (summer). Foreign students must submit a completed health form and proof of adequate funds for the completion of a bachelor's degree. Half the tuition must be paid before arrival, and the other half before classes start.

Admissions Contact: Jerry Wiedmeyer, Director of Admissions.

WISCONSIN

MARQUETTE UNIVERSITY   E-4
Milwaukee, Wisconsin 53233   (414) 224-7302

F/T: 4321M, 3610W
P/T: 742M, 553W
Grad: 897M, 602W
Year: sems, ss
Appl: open
6528 applied   4935 accepted   2005 enrolled
SAT: 477V 531M   ACT: 24   COMPETITIVE+
Faculty: 568; I, —$
Ph.D.'s: 68%
S/F Ratio: 15 to 1
Tuition: $4023
R and B: $2270

Marquette University, founded in 1881, is conducted by the Society of Jesus. One of the largest Catholic universities in the nation, Marquette consists of the colleges of Liberal Arts, Nursing, Business Administration, Journalism, Speech, and Engineering; and the schools of Dentistry, Law, Education, and Graduate Study. The library contains 700,000 volumes and 200,000 microfilm items, and subscribes to 10,000 periodicals.

Environment: Located near Lake Michigan in downtown Milwaukee, the 64-acre campus includes about 40 buildings. Dormitories accommodate 3600 students.

Student Life: About 43% of the students are from Wisconsin, and 50% come from public schools. Sixty-five percent live on campus. Seventy-three percent are Catholic, 16% are Protestant, and 1% are Jewish. About 10% of the students are minority-group members. University housing is both coed and single-sex; students in single-sex housing have visiting privileges. Students may keep cars on campus.

Organizations: There are 8 fraternities and 5 sororities on campus; 10% of the men and 6% of the women belong. The 150 student organizations include publications, special-interest clubs, band, chorus, speech, and service groups. A wide range of social and cultural activities takes place on campus.

Sports: The university fields 7 intercollegiate teams for men and 5 for women. There are 12 intramural sports for men and 9 for women.

Handicapped: About 60% of the campus is accessible to handicapped students. Special facilities include wheelchair ramps, parking, elevators, specially equipped rest rooms, and lowered drinking fountains and telephones. Special class scheduling is also possible. A counselor is available to handicapped students.

Graduates: The freshman dropout rate is 14%, and 56% of the freshmen remain to graduate. About 34% of the graduates pursue advanced degrees; 1% enter medical school, 1% enter dental school, and 1% enter law school. Fifty percent pursue careers in business and industry.

Services: The following services are provided free to students: health care, psychological counseling, placement and career counseling, tutoring, and remedial instruction. Placement services also are available to alumni.

Programs of Study: The university confers the B.A., B.S., B.S.B.A., B.S.J., B.S.E., B.S.Med.Tech., B.S.N., and B.S. in Physical Therapy degrees. Associate, master's, and doctoral programs are also offered. Bachelor's degrees are offered in the following subjects: BUSINESS (accounting, business administration, business economics, finance, management, marketing), EDUCATION (elementary, health/physical, secondary), ENGLISH (English, journalism, speech), FINE AND PERFORMING ARTS (radio/TV, theater/dramatics), HEALTH SCIENCES (dental hygiene, medical technology, nursing, physical therapy, speech therapy), LANGUAGES (French, German, Greek/Latin, Spanish), MATH AND SCIENCES (biology, chemistry, mathematics, physics, statistics), PHILOSOPHY (philosophy, theology), PREPROFESSIONAL (dentistry, engineering—biomedical, engineering—civil, engineering—electrical, engineering—mechanical, law, medicine), SOCIAL SCIENCES (anthropology, economics, government/political science, history, law enforcement, psychology, social sciences, sociology). Twenty-two percent of all degrees are conferred in health sciences and 20% in business.

Required: All students must take fundamental liberal arts courses.

Special: The College of Liberal Arts conducts its own Study Center at the University of Madrid for juniors majoring in Spanish. The college also sponsors summer sessions in West Germany and France. The colleges of Business Administration and Engineering offer cooperative work-study programs. The university operates a program for economically or culturally disadvantaged students. A Legal Research Center is also located on campus. Combined B.A.-B.S. degrees may be earned in most subjects. Interdisciplinary majors are permitted.

Honors: An honors program is offered to qualified students in English, history, philosophy, and theology. Six honor societies, including Phi Beta Kappa, have chapters on campus.

Admissions: About 76% of those who applied were accepted for the 1981–82 freshman class. The SAT scores of those who enrolled were as follows: Verbal—58% scored below 500, 33% between 500 and 599, 8% between 600 and 700, and 1% above 700; Math—34% scored below 500, 40% between 500 and 599, 22% between 600 and 700, and 4% above 700. Of those who took the ACT, 14% scored below 21, 16% between 21 and 23, 25% between 24 and 25, 21% between 26 and 28, and 24% above 28. Applicants must be graduates of an accredited high school and have completed at least 15 units of high school work. School recommendations, advanced placement or honors courses, leadership record, and impressions made during an interview are also considered. Admissions criteria are flexible.

Procedure: The SAT or ACT is required and should be taken by December of the senior year. Application deadlines are open. Freshmen are admitted to all sessions. Notification is made within 3 weeks after all credentials are submitted. There is a $15 application fee.

Special: Students whose high school performance has not matched their potential, as indicated by scores on the SAT or ACT, may be admitted into the Freshman Frontiers Program, a college-level freshman course that includes guidance and tutorial assistance. CLEP and AP credit is available.

Transfer: For fall 1981, 1083 students applied, 589 were accepted, and 327 enrolled. Transfers are accepted for all classes. Applicants must have at least 12 credit hours, good standing at their previous school, and course work equivalent to that offered at Marquette; a 2.0 GPA is recommended. D grades are not acceptable. Students must spend at least 1 year in residence, earning at least 32 of the minimum 124 credits necessary for a bachelor's degree. Application deadlines are August 15 (fall) and January 15 (spring).

Visiting: There is an orientation program for prospective students. Guides are available for informal visits. Visitors may sit in on classes and stay overnight on campus. The admissions office should be contacted for arrangements.

Financial Aid: About 80% of the students receive financial aid. Twenty-five percent work part-time on campus. Average aid to freshmen in 1981–82 was $3500. Scholarships, loans, and grants are available. The university is a member of CSS. The FAF is required. Application deadlines are open.

Foreign Students: Two percent of the full-time students are from foreign countries. The university offers these students special counseling and special organizations.

Admissions: Foreign students must score at least 550 on the TOEFL. No college entrance exams must be taken.

Procedure: Application deadlines are open. Foreign students must present proof of adequate funds for the duration of their studies. They also must carry health insurance, which is available through the university for a fee.

Admissions Contact: Leo B. Flynn, Director of Admissions.

MILTON COLLEGE   D-5
Milton, Wisconsin 53563   (608) 868-2906

F/T: 171M, 54W
P/T: 99M, 291W
Grad: none
Year: sems
Appl: open
473 applied   126 accepted   59 enrolled
ACT: 16   LESS COMPETITIVE
Faculty: 18; IIB, — —$
Ph.D.'s: 25%
S/F Ratio: 12 to 1
Tuition: $3680
R and B: $1850

Milton College, founded in 1844, is an independent, nondenominational college offering undergraduate programs in the liberal arts and career-oriented majors. Its library has 65,000 volumes and 627 microfilm items, and subscribes to 273 periodicals.

Environment: The 74-acre rural campus is located in a small town about 30 miles from Madison. There are five dormitories for men and women.

Student Life: About 38% of the students come from Wisconsin. Twelve percent are minority-group members. Fifty-four percent live on campus. Campus housing is both coed and single-sex; there are visiting privileges in the single-sex housing. Students may keep cars on campus.

Organizations: There are no fraternities or sororities. Extracurricular activities include student government, clubs, religious groups, and social events. The cultural and recreational facilities of Madison and Milwaukee are within an hour's drive.

Sports: There are 4 intercollegiate sports for men and 3 for women. The college also offers 7 intramural sports for men and 6 for women.

Handicapped: There are no special facilities for physically handicapped students.

Graduates: The freshman dropout rate is 25%, and about 33% of the freshmen remain to graduate. Ten percent go on for further study; 40% enter careers in business and industry.

Services: Free remedial instruction, tutoring, placement services, and career and psychological counseling are available. Placement services also are offered to alumni.

Programs of Study: The B.A. or B.S. degree is offered in the following subjects: BUSINESS (accounting, agribusiness, human resources administration, management, marketing), EDUCATION (elementary, secondary), ENGLISH (communication arts), SOCIAL SCIENCES (criminal justice, history/political science, human services).

Special: A general studies degree is offered, as are off-campus programs in nursing (for registered nurses), criminal justice, and business management.

Admissions: About 27% of the 1981–82 applicants were accepted. On the ACT, 41% of those who enrolled scored below 21, 8% between 21 and 23, and 0% above 24. Applicants should be graduates of accredited high schools, rank in the top 60% of their high school class, and have a 2.0 GPA and 15 Carnegie units. Advanced placement or honors courses, recommendations from school officials, and impressions made during an interview also are considered.

Procedure: The SAT or ACT is required. New students are admitted each semester; application deadlines are open. The college uses the rolling admissions plan. There is a $15 application fee. An interview is recommended.

Special: AP and CLEP credit is granted.

Transfer: For fall 1981, 66 applications were received, 28 were accepted, and 26 students enrolled. Transfers are accepted for all classes. D grades are not accepted. Students must complete at least 30 credits in residence of the 120 required for a bachelor's degree. Application deadlines are open.

Visiting: There is an orientation program for prospective students. Informal campus tours with student guides can be arranged; visitors may stay at the school and sit in on classes. The admissions office handles arrangements.

Financial Aid: About 85% of the students are receiving aid. The college offers scholarships, grants, loans, and work-study; 29% of the students work part-time on campus. Government and commercial loans and federal and state grants are available. The FAF is required; the college is a member of CSS. The suggested deadlines for aid application are June 30 for fall and December 20 for spring.

Foreign Students: About 3% of the students are from foreign countries. Special counseling is available for these students.

Admissions: Foreign students must take either the TOEFL or the University of Michigan Language Test. A minimum score of 525 is required on the TOEFL. No college entrance exams are required.

Procedure: Foreign students are admitted for the fall and spring semesters; there are no application deadlines. Proof of adequate funds for 1 year is required.

Admissions Contact: Scott Pratt, In-House Counselor.

MILWAUKEE SCHOOL OF ENGINEERING E–4
Milwaukee, Wisconsin 53201 (414) 277-7200

F/T, P/T: 1400M&W
Grad: 80M&W
Year: qtrs, ss
Appl: open
800 applied 750 accepted 500 enrolled
ACT: required
Faculty: 75; n/av
Ph.D.'s: 11%
S/F Ratio: 19 to 1
Tuition: $4110
R and B: $1845
LESS COMPETITIVE

Established in 1903, Milwaukee School of Engineering is an independent institution that is privately owned by the M.S.O.E. Corporation. Its technical reference library contains over 30,000 volumes and subscribes to 371 periodicals.

Environment: Located in downtown Milwaukee, 6 blocks from Lake Michigan, the campus has 2 high-rise dormitories accommodating 850 men and women. The major building on campus is the engineering sciences facility.

Student Life: About 70% of the students come from Wisconsin. Fifty percent live in the coed residence halls, 15% in fraternity houses. All unmarried students under 21 must live in the residence halls unless living at home.

Organizations: About 10% of the men belong to 1 of the 5 local and 4 national fraternities with chapters on campus. There are no sororities. In addition to more than 25 educational, social, and professional groups, students enjoy a variety of on-campus social and cultural events.

Sports: The school fields intercollegiate teams in 3 sports. Intramural competition is offered in 9 sports.

Handicapped: About 50% of the campus is accessible to physically handicapped individuals. Ramps, elevators, lowered telephones, and special parking areas are provided. Two counselors are available.

Graduates: Nearly all of the graduates enter careers in business and industry; about 20% go on to further study.

Services: Remedial instruction, tutoring, placement and career counseling (for alumni as well as students), and psychological counseling are provided.

Programs of Study: The school offers the B.S.E.T., B.S. in E., B.I.M., B.I.S., and B.S.A.S. degrees. Associate and master's degrees also are awarded. Bachelor's degrees are offered in: BUSINESS (administrative sciences, industrial management, industrial safety), PREPROFESSIONAL (engineering—architectural and building construction engineering technology, engineering—biomedical engineering technology, engineering—electrical engineering, engineering—electrical engineering technology, engineering—manufacturing engineering technology, engineering—mechanical engineering, engineering—mechanical engineering technology). Ninety-two percent of the degrees conferred are in engineering and 6% are in business.

Admissions: About 94% of the applicants for the 1981–82 freshman class were accepted. Applicants must be high school graduates or have a GED. In addition to the academic record and ACT scores, special talents and recommendations from high school officials are also considered.

Procedure: The ACT is required. Math and science placement tests are given by the school. New students are admitted each quarter. Application deadlines are open; notification is made on a rolling basis. There is a $15 application fee.

Special: Early decision and deferred admissions plans are available. AP and CLEP credit is accepted.

Transfer: Transfer students are accepted for all classes. A 2.0 GPA is needed. D grades do not transfer. Half the program must be completed in residence. There are no application deadlines.

Visiting: The orientation program for prospective applicants includes a campus tour and an interview with a counselor. Informal campus visits and tours can be arranged. Visitors may attend classes and stay overnight in the dormitories. Arrangements can be made through the admissions office.

Financial Aid: About 81% of the students are receiving aid. The school offers freshman scholarships, various loans, and government grants. Tuition may be paid in installments. The FAF is required. The recommended due date for filing the aid application is April 30.

Foreign Students: The foreign students enrolled full-time at the school make up about 1% of the student body. Special counseling is provided.

Admissions: Applicants must score at least 485 on the TOEFL. No academic exams are required.

Procedure: New students are admitted to all terms; applications should be submitted at least 60 days before the start of the term in which the student seeks to enroll. Students must present proof of adequate funds for 1 year. Health insurance, though not required, is available through the school.

Admissions Contact: Robert Savatovic, Director of Admissions.

MOUNT MARY COLLEGE E–4
Milwaukee, Wisconsin 53222 (414) 258-4810

F/T: 701W
P/T: 426W
Grad: none
Year: sems, ss
Appl: Aug. 15
208 applied 201 accepted 123 enrolled
SAT or ACT: required
Faculty: n/av; IIB, –$
Ph.D.'s: 30%
S/F Ratio: n/av
Tuition: $2920
R and B: $1700
LESS COMPETITIVE

Mount Mary College was founded in 1913 and is affiliated with the Roman Catholic Church. It offers undergraduate programs for women in education, business, health areas, and the arts and sciences. The

972 WISCONSIN

library has 106,000 books and 2000 microfilm items, and subscribes to 692 periodicals.

Environment: The 80-acre campus is located 5 miles from downtown Milwaukee and has 6 buildings, including a new library and 1 dormitory that houses 220 women.

Student Life: About 90% of the students come from Wisconsin. Seventy-one percent attended public schools. About 7% are minority-group members. Approximately 62% are Catholic, 26% are Protestant, and 1% are Jewish. There are no religious attendance requirements. Twenty percent of the students live in the residence hall; there are visiting privileges. Freshmen observe curfew regulations. Students may keep cars on campus. Day-care services are available, for a fee, to all students, faculty, and staff.

Organizations: There are no sororities. Extracurricular activities include special-interest clubs, cultural and social events on campus, and religious groups.

Sports: Intramural competition is offered in 8 sports. There are 3 intercollegiate teams.

Handicapped: Special facilities for physically handicapped students include ramps, elevators, and lowered drinking fountains. All buildings are connected by underground tunnels.

Graduates: About 29% of the freshmen drop out; 48% remain to graduate. Ten percent of the graduates go on for further education: 1% each enter medical, dental, and law schools. About 40% begin careers in business and industry.

Services: Offered without charge are career and psychological counseling, tutoring, remedial instruction, and placement services. Health care is available for a fee.

Programs of Study: The college awards the B.A. and B.S. degrees. Bachelor's degrees are offered in the following subjects: BUSINESS (business administration, business education, computer science, marketing), EDUCATION (bilingual, early childhood, elementary, religious, secondary), ENGLISH (English), FINE AND PERFORMING ARTS (art, art therapy, fashion design, interior design, music, music education), HEALTH SCIENCES (medical technology, occupational therapy), LANGUAGES (French, German, Spanish), MATH AND SCIENCES (biology, chemistry, mathematics, physics), PHILOSOPHY (philosophy, religion), PREPROFESSIONAL (home economics, social work), SOCIAL SCIENCES (geography, history). Thirty percent of the degrees conferred are in health sciences.

Required: All students must take 12 courses in the liberal arts.

Special: Student-designed majors and study abroad are offered.

Honors: Six honor societies have chapters on campus. The college has an honors program.

Admissions: About 97% of the 1981–82 freshman applicants were accepted. The SAT scores of those who enrolled were as follows: Verbal—77% below 500, 23% between 500 and 599, and 0% above 599; Math—75% below 500, 19% between 500 and 599, 6% between 600 and 700, and 0% above 700. Applicants should have a high school GPA of at least 2.0, and should rank in the top 50% of the class.

Procedure: The SAT should be taken by January of the senior year; ACT scores are also accepted. The fall application deadline is August 15; the spring, December 15. Freshmen are also admitted in the summer. Selection and notification are on a rolling basis. There is a $10 application fee.

Special: There are early admissions and deferred admissions plans. CLEP and AP credit is accepted.

Transfer: For fall 1981, 119 students applied, 117 were accepted, and 72 enrolled. A 2.0 GPA (2.5 GPA for professional programs) is required; D grades do not transfer. Students must complete, at the college, 32 of the 128 credits required to receive a bachelor's degree. Application deadlines are the same as those for freshmen.

Visiting: There is an Open House each semester. Informal guided campus tours can be arranged. Visitors may attend classes and stay overnight in the dormitory. Arrangements can be made through the admissions staff.

Financial Aid: About 68% of the students receive aid. The aid package could consist of state and federal grants, loan funds, and campus employment. Nearly 16% of the students work part-time on campus. Merit scholarships are offered by the college. The average award to freshmen from all sources is $3122. The college is a member of CSS. The FAF and the aid application should be submitted by March 1 for fall or December 1 for spring.

Foreign Students: Four percent of the full-time students are from foreign countries. Special counseling is available for these students.

Admissions: Foreign students must achieve a TOEFL score of at least 500. College entrance exams are not required.

Procedure: Students are admitted to the fall and spring semesters. Proof of funds adequate to cover the length of the student's visa is required, and students must also carry health insurance, which is available through the college for a fee.

Admissions Contact: Mary Jane Reilly, Director of Admissions.

MOUNT SENARIO COLLEGE B-2
Ladysmith, Wisconsin 54848 (715) 532-5235

F/T: 188M, 198W	Faculty: 30; IIB, ——$
P/T: 43M, 74W	Ph.D.'s: 23%
Grad: none	S/F Ratio: 11 to 1
Year: sems, ss	Tuition: $3520
Appl: Aug. 1	R and B: $1930
251 applied	202 accepted 152 enrolled
ACT: 15	LESS COMPETITIVE

Mount Senario College, founded in 1962, is an independent, private liberal arts college. The library contains 40,000 volumes and 74 microfilm items, and subscribes to 389 periodicals.

Environment: The 130-acre rural campus is located on the Flambeau River in a small town of 5000 people, 110 miles from Minneapolis-St. Paul and 60 miles from Eau Claire. The campus consists of 3 large buildings, including a dormitory that houses 200 students.

Student Life: Seventy-five percent of the students are from Wisconsin, and 89% come from public schools. Forty-two percent live on campus, 10% live off campus in apartments, and the remainder commute from home. Thirty-eight percent of the students are Catholic and 32% are Protestant. About 30% are minority-group members, primarily Native Americans. Campus housing is coed. Students may keep cars on campus. Day-care services are available to all students, faculty, and staff.

Organizations: The college sponsors 15 extracurricular organizations, the most active of which are the ski club, the art club, and the natural interest club. Religious counselors are available for Catholic and Protestant students. There are no sororities or fraternities.

Sports: The college fields intercollegiate teams in 7 sports.

Handicapped: About two-thirds of the campus is accessible to handicapped students. Special facilities include parking areas, elevators, and specially equipped rest rooms.

Graduates: About 45% of freshmen drop out during their first year, and 33% remain to graduate. About 15% of the graduates pursue advanced study; 2% enter law school. Twelve percent enter careers in business or industry.

Services: The following services are available free to students: psychological counseling, career counseling, tutoring, and remedial instruction. Placement services are available on a fee basis.

Programs of Study: The college confers the B.A., B.F.A., and B.S. degrees. Associate degrees are also awarded. Bachelor's degrees are offered in the following subjects: BUSINESS (accounting, business administration), EDUCATION (early childhood, elementary, health/physical, secondary), ENGLISH (English), FINE AND PERFORMING ARTS (art, art education, music, music education, studio art), HEALTH SCIENCES (medical technology), MATH AND SCIENCES (biology, mathematics, natural sciences, physical sciences), PREPROFESSIONAL (engineering, forestry, law, medicine, pharmacy, social work), SOCIAL SCIENCES (criminal justice, government/political science, history, psychology, sociology).

Special: The college offers an American Indian program and independent study. Students may spend their junior year abroad on their own or participate in an established study-abroad program sponsored by another college. Special programs are available in modern dance/mime, ballet, and jazz dancing. Dual-degree programs in forestry and engineering are offered in conjunction with Michigan Tech. Students may design their own majors.

Honors: One honor society has a chapter on campus.

Admissions: About 80% of the applicants for the 1981–82 freshman class were accepted. The ACT scores of those who enrolled were as follows: 58% below 21, 28% between 21 and 23, 12% between 24 and 25, 3% between 26 and 28, and 0% above 28. High school graduation is not required. Sixteen Carnegie units are recommended. The minimum acceptable test scores are 350 Verbal and 320 Math on the SAT, or 15 on the ACT. Other factors considered are school recommendations, impressions made during an interview, and evidence of special talents.

Procedure: Either the SAT or ACT is required. Junior-year scores are acceptable. Application deadlines are August 1 (fall) and December 1 (winter). A personal interview is recommended. Admissions are granted on a rolling basis. There is a $10 application fee.

Special: CLEP general and subject exams are accepted. There is an early admissions plan.

Transfer: For fall 1981, 44 transfer students enrolled. Transfer students are accepted for all classes. A minimum GPA of 2.0 is required, and an interview is recommended. If the student has an associate degree, all credits transfer; otherwise, D grades do not transfer. Students must earn at least 32 credits in residence of the 128 necessary for the bachelor's degree. Application deadlines are the same as those for freshmen.

Visiting: A three-day orientation session is held before registration. Guides are available for informal campus visits. Visitors may sit in on classes and stay overnight at the school. The admissions office should be contacted for arrangements.

Financial Aid: About 81% of the students receive aid through the college. CWS is available in all departments; 41% of the students work part-time on campus. Tuition may be paid in installments. The student's need and academic achievement are the main considerations in determining awards. Applications are processed in order of receipt; the FAF is required.

Foreign Students: About 5% of the students are from foreign countries. The college offers these students an intensive English course and special counseling.

Admissions: Applicants must score at least 500 on the TOEFL or 80 on the University of Michigan Language Test. No college entrance exams are required.

Procedure: Application deadlines are June 1 (fall), November 1 (winter), and April 1 (summer). Proof of good health and evidence of adequate funds for each year of study are required. Health insurance also is required, and is available through the college for a fee.

Admissions Contact: Max M. Waits, Director of Admissions.

NORTHLAND COLLEGE B-1
Ashland, Wisconsin 54806 (715) 682-4531

F/T: 340M, 267W	Faculty: 40; IIB, –$
P/T: 19M, 27W	Ph.D.'s: 50%
Grad: none	S/F Ratio: 14 to 1
Year: 4-4-1, ss	Tuition: $3785
Appl: open	R and B: $1970
836 applied	703 accepted	266 enrolled
SAT: 995 V&M	ACT: 22	COMPETITIVE

Northland College, an independent institution established in 1892 and affiliated with the United Church of Christ, offers undergraduate programs in the liberal arts and sciences, business, and education. Its library has 75,000 volumes.

Environment: The 116-acre campus is located in a rural area 75 miles east of Duluth, Minnesota. Residence halls accommodate 200 women and 300 men. The college also sponsors on-campus apartments.

Student Life: About 35% of the students come from Wisconsin. Forty percent of the students are Catholic, 30% are Protestant, and 3% are Jewish. Twelve percent are minority-group members. Campus housing is coed and single-sex; there are visiting privileges in the single-sex housing. Students are permitted to keep cars on campus.

Organizations: There are 3 national fraternities and 2 local sororities to which 15% of the students belong. Extracurricular activities include student government, publications, performing groups, religious organizations, clubs, and nearby outdoor recreation, notably skiing.

Sports: The college sponsors intercollegiate teams in 4 sports for men and 3 for women. There are 7 intramural sports each for men and women.

Handicapped: About 80% of the campus is accessible to the physically handicapped. Special facilities include wheelchair ramps, designated parking, elevators, and specially equipped rest rooms. Special class scheduling can be arranged.

Graduates: The freshman dropout rate is 30%, and 50% remain to graduate. Nineteen percent of the graduates go on for further education (3% to medical school, 1% to dental school, and 4% to law school), and 45% begin careers in business and industry.

Services: Psychological counseling, health care, tutoring, remedial instruction, career counseling, and placement services are provided free.

Programs of Study: The college grants the B.A. or B.S. degree in the following subjects: BUSINESS (business administration, finance, management, marketing), EDUCATION (elementary, secondary), ENGLISH (English), FINE AND PERFORMING ARTS (art, art education, music, music education, studio art), MATH AND SCIENCES (biochemistry, biology, chemistry, earth science, ecology/environmental science, geology, mathematics, natural sciences, physical sciences, physics, zoology), PHILOSOPHY (religion), PREPROFESSIONAL (dentistry, engineering, forestry, law, medicine, ministry, pharmacy, veterinary), SOCIAL SCIENCES (anthropology, economics, geography, history, psychology, social sciences, sociology). About 47% of the degrees conferred are in sciences and mathematics and 15% are in business.

Required: Students must take courses in fine arts, philosophy, literature, natural and social sciences, writing, and physical education.

Special: A general studies degree and combined degree programs are offered. Students may design their own majors.

Honors: The college offers honors work to qualified students.

Admissions: About 84% of the 1981–82 freshman applicants were accepted. Candidates generally should rank in the upper two thirds of their graduating class. The high school record is the major criterion, but applicants with below-average records will be considered if other factors indicate a possibility of success in college.

Procedure: The SAT or ACT is required. Application deadlines are open; students are admitted in fall and winter. Admission and notification are on a rolling basis. There is no application fee.

Special: AP and CLEP credit is accepted. Early decision, early admissions, and deferred admissions plans are offered.

Transfer: For fall 1981, 124 students applied, 109 were accepted; and 64 enrolled. A minimum GPA of 2.0 is required. D grades transfer if they are not in the student's major or minor. Students must spend at least 1 year at the college, earning at least 30 of the 124 credits required for a bachelor's degree. There are no application deadlines.

Visiting: Informal campus tours can be arranged; visitors may stay overnight at the college and attend classes. The recommended months for visiting are October, November, and January through April. Arrangements can be made through the director of admissions.

Financial Aid: About 80% of the students are receiving aid. Freshman scholarships, loans, grants, and part-time jobs are available. Forty percent of the students work part-time on campus. The average freshman aid package in 1981–82 was $3400; the maximum, $5700. The FAF or FFS should be filed; application deadlines are open. The college is a member of CSS.

Foreign Students: About 3% of the students are from foreign countries. The college offers these students an intensive English course and special counseling.

Admissions: Students must score at least 500 on the TOEFL. No college entrance exams are required.

Procedure: Foreign students are admitted for the fall and winter terms; there are no application deadlines. Proof of adequate funds for 1 year is required. Health insurance, though not required, is available through the college for a fee.

Admissions Contact: James L. Miller, Dean of Admissions.

NORTHWESTERN COLLEGE
Watertown, Wisconsin 53094 (414) 261-4352
(Recognized Candidate for Accreditation)

Northwestern College is a four-year liberal arts college for men that is affiliated with the Evangelical Lutheran Synod. Its enrollment comprises 258 men.

RIPON COLLEGE D-4
Ripon, Wisconsin 54971 (414) 748-8102

F/T: 534M, 408W	Faculty: 66; IIB, ++$
P/T: 5M, 5W	Ph.D.'s: 79%
Grad: none	S/F Ratio: 12 to 1
Year: sems	Tuition: $5400
Appl: open	R and B: $1700
770 applied	664 accepted	276 enrolled
SAT: 510V 540M	ACT: 24	COMPETITIVE+

Ripon College, founded in 1851, is a privately controlled, nonsectarian liberal arts college. The library contains 120,000 volumes and 11,000 microfilm items, and subscribes to 500 periodicals.

974 WISCONSIN

Environment: The 250-acre campus is located in a rural area about 80 miles north of Milwaukee. The 35 campus buildings include a fine-arts center and East Hall, a national historic landmark. The college provides dormitories and fraternity or sorority houses.

Student Life: About 50% of the students are from Wisconsin. Eighty-five percent come from public schools. Four percent are minority-group members. Campus housing is coed and single-sex; there are visiting privileges in the single-sex dorms. Students may keep cars on campus.

Organizations: There are 7 fraternities and 3 sororities; 55% of the men and 34% of the women belong. The college offers drama and music programs, a fine-arts series, and a lecture series. Religious facilities are available for Protestant and Catholic students.

Sports: The college fields intercollegiate teams in 16 sports for men and 12 for women. There are 6 intramural sports for men and 6 for women.

Handicapped: About 85% of the campus is accessible to handicapped students. Special facilities include wheelchair ramps, elevators in some buildings, and specially equipped rest rooms. Special class scheduling is also possible. Four counselors are available for handicapped students.

Graduates: The dropout rate for freshmen is 15%, and 60% remain to graduate. Thirty percent of the graduates pursue advanced degrees; 3% enter medical school, and 6% enter law school. About 70% of the graduates pursue careers in business or industry.

Services: The following services are provided free to students: health care, psychological counseling, placement, career counseling, tutoring, and remedial instruction.

Programs of Study: The B.A. degree is conferred in the following subjects: AREA STUDIES (Latin American), BUSINESS (business administration, computer science), ENGLISH (English), FINE AND PERFORMING ARTS (art, music, theater/dramatics), HEALTH SCIENCES (medical technology, nursing), LANGUAGES (French, German, Spanish), MATH AND SCIENCES (biochemistry, biology, chemistry, mathematics, physics), PHILOSOPHY (philosophy, religion), PREPROFESSIONAL (dentistry, engineering, forestry, law, medicine, social work, veterinary), SOCIAL SCIENCES (anthropology, economics, government/political science, history, psychology, sociology). Thirty percent of the degrees are conferred in math and sciences, 20% in preprofessional areas, and 20% in business.

Required: All students must complete 6 credits each in the behavioral and social sciences, English, fine arts, language, humanities, and natural sciences, and 2 credits in physical education.

Special: Ripon has a 3-2 program with the Massachusetts Institute of Technology leading to bachelor's degrees in both arts and sciences. The college also has 3-2 engineering programs with Washington University (Missouri), University of Southern California, Rensselaer Polytechnic Institute, and a 3-2 program in forestry with Duke University. Science students may spend 1 semester at Oak Ridge National Laboratory as part-time assistants in biology, chemistry, or physics. Study-abroad programs are offered. Cooperative programs in nursing and medical technology are offered with Rush University Medical Center in Chicago. Superior students may pursue independent study and research in an off-campus semester. Students may design their own majors. The college offers a 3-year B.A. degree. Teaching certification is also offered.

Honors: Numerous honor societies, including Phi Beta Kappa, have chapters on campus.

Admissions: About 86% of those who applied were accepted for the 1981–82 freshman class. SAT scores of enrolled students were as follows: Verbal—42% below 500, 45% between 500 and 599, 12% between 600 and 700, and 1% above 700; Math—28% below 500, 42% between 500 and 599, 25% between 600 and 700, and 5% above 700. Of those who took the ACT, 12% scored below 19, 16% between 19 and 21, 26% between 22 and 24, 28% between 25 and 27, and 17% above 28. Applicants should have completed 15 Carnegie units and rank in the top half of their graduating class. Any candidate scoring lower than 425 on either section of the SAT will not receive serious consideration unless his or her class rank is uncommonly high. Other factors considered are advanced placement or honors courses, impressions made during an interview, school recommendations, and personality.

Procedure: Either the SAT or the ACT is required and should be taken by January of the senior year. There are no application deadlines. Students are admitted in fall and spring. The college uses a rolling admissions plan. Interviews are recommended. There is a $15 application fee.

Special: The college offers early and deferred admissions plans. AP credit may be earned.

Transfer: For fall 1981, Ripon received 60 transfer applications and accepted 47; 28 students enrolled. Transfers are accepted for the freshman (second semester) and sophomore years. Requirements include a good high school record and a 2.0 GPA. D grades are not acceptable. The college recommends that transfer students have a minimum score of 1000 (combined) on the SAT or 20 on the ACT. To receive a bachelor's degree, which requires 124 credits, students must complete half the requirements for their major at the college. There are no application deadlines.

Visiting: Guides are available for informal visits. Visitors may sit in on classes and stay overnight at the school. Visits are best scheduled during the academic year.

Financial Aid: About 79% of all students receive aid; 34% work part-time on campus. The average aid package to 1981–82 freshmen was $5309. Scholarships range from $100 to $3550 a year, and loans from $200 to $2000 a year. Tuition may be paid in installments. The college participates in the CSS. Applications for aid must be filed by March 1. The FAF is required.

Foreign Students: About 1% of the students are from foreign countries. Special counseling and special organizations are available.

Admissions: Students must score at least 580–600 on the TOEFL. They also must score at least 1000 (total) on the SAT or 24 on the ACT.

Procedure: Foreign students are admitted for the fall and spring semesters; application deadlines are open. Proof of adequate funds for 1 year is required. Health insurance, though not required, is available through the college for a fee.

Admissions Contact: John C. Corso, Dean of Admissions.

ST. NORBERT COLLEGE   D–3
DePere, Wisconsin 54115   (414) 337-3005

F/T: 809M, 856W Faculty: 100; IIB, +$
P/T: 28M, 40W Ph.D.'s: 66%
Grad: none S/F Ratio: 16 to 1
Year: sems, ss Tuition: $3970
Appl: April 15 R and B: $1975
1121 applied   822 accepted   485 enrolled
SAT: 460V 505M ACT: 23 COMPETITIVE+

St. Norbert College, founded in 1898, offers undergraduate programs in business, education, and the arts and sciences. It is affiliated with the Roman Catholic Church. Its library has 142,219 volumes and 14,600 microfilm items, and subscribes to 701 periodicals.

Environment: The 30-acre suburban campus is located 5 miles from Green Bay. There are 9 dormitories, including 2 apartment-style residence halls. The college also sponsors off-campus houses.

Student Life: About 52% of the students come from Wisconsin. Seventy-five percent live on campus. Half attended public schools. Eighty-five percent are Catholic and 7% are Protestant. Three percent are minority-group members. Campus housing is both coed and single-sex; there are visiting privileges in the single-sex dorms. Students may keep cars on campus.

Organizations: Social and cultural events on campus include a Winter Carnival, dances, concerts, and plays. Three local and 2 national fraternities attract 10% of the men; 10% of the women belong to 1 of 3 local sororities.

Sports: There are 9 intercollegiate sports teams for men and 8 for women. On the intramural level, men and women each compete in 5 sports.

Handicapped: About 80% of the campus is accessible to physically handicapped students. Wheelchair ramps, parking areas, and elevators are provided.

Graduates: The freshman dropout rate is 13%, and 80% remain to graduate. About 35% of the graduates go on for additional study; 2% enter medical school, 1% enter dental school, and 5% enter law school. Sixty percent begin careers in business and industry.

Services: Career counseling, placement aid, tutoring, psychological counseling, and health care are offered free to students.

Programs of Study: The college confers the B.A., B.S., B.M., and B.B.A. degrees. Bachelor's degrees are offered in the following subjects: BUSINESS (accounting, business administration, finance, management, marketing), EDUCATION (early childhood, elementary, secondary), ENGLISH (English), FINE AND PERFORMING ARTS (art, art education, music, music education), HEALTH SCIENCES (medical technology), LANGUAGES (French, Greek/Latin, Spanish), MATH AND SCIENCES (biology, chemistry, mathematics, physics), PHILOSOPHY (classics, humanities, philosophy, religion), PREPROFESSIONAL (dentistry, engineering, law, medicine, pharmacy, veterinary), SOCIAL SCIENCES (economics, government/political science, history, psychology, social sciences, sociology).

Required: Students must take 8 courses outside their major, 2 courses from each of the outside divisions (including 2 courses in philosophy or religious studies), and 2 courses in language.

Special: Study abroad, laboratory assistantships, and independent study are offered. Students may design their own majors.

Honors: Two honor societies have chapters on campus.

Admissions: About 73% of the 1981-82 freshman applicants were accepted. SAT scores of those who enrolled were as follows: Verbal—61% below 500, 23% between 500 and 599, 4% between 600 and 700, and 2% above 700; Math—48% below 500, 34% between 500 and 599, 16% between 600 and 700, and 2% above 700. Of those who took the ACT, 51% scored below 21, 23% between 21 and 23, 13% between 24 and 25, 10% between 26 and 28, and 3% above 28. Applicants should be graduates of accredited high schools and should have taken a college-preparatory program. They should rank in the top 50% of their class and have at least a 2.7 GPA. Special talents, leadership, and extracurricular activities also are considered.

Procedure: Either the SAT, ACT, or PSAT is required. There is a $15 application fee. The application deadlines are April 15 (fall) and December 1 (spring); notification is made on a rolling basis.

Special: AP and CLEP credit is granted.

Transfer: Approximately 155 applications were received for fall 1981, 76 were accepted, and 33 students enrolled. Transfers are accepted for second-semester freshman, sophomore, and junior years. D grades do not transfer. A 2.5 minimum GPA is required, and students should have a minimum of 20 credit hours earned. An interview is recommended. The college has a residency requirement of 1 year. Fall and spring application deadlines are the same as those for freshmen; the deadline for summer is June 1.

Visiting: There is an orientation program. Informal campus tours can be arranged. Visitors may attend classes and stay overnight at the college. Arrangements can be made through the admissions office.

Financial Aid: About 75% of the students receive aid, which includes freshman scholarships, government and commercial loans, grants, and campus employment (CWS included). About 33% of the students work part-time on campus. Tuition may be paid in installments. The FAF must be filed by March 1; the college is a member of CSS.

Foreign Students: About 1% of the students are from foreign countries.

Admissions: Students must score at least 500 on the TOEFL. No college entrance exams are required.

Procedure: Applications should be submitted 6 months before the start of classes for the fall or spring semester. Students must present proof of adequate funds for 4 years. They are required to carry health insurance, which is available through the college for a fee.

Admissions Contact: Matthew G. Flanigan, Dean of Admissions and Financial Aid.

SILVER LAKE COLLEGE OF THE HOLY FAMILY
E-3

Manitowoc, Wisconsin 54220   (414) 684-5955

F/T: 39M, 171W   Faculty: 28; n/av
P/T: 21M, 80W   Ph.D.'s: n/av
Grad: none   S/F Ratio: 6 to 1
Year: sems, ss   Tuition: $3200
                 ($3400 for music students)
Appl: open   R and B: $1980
89 applied   82 accepted   57 enrolled
ACT: 19   LESS COMPETITIVE

Silver Lake College of the Holy Family, founded in 1935, is a private liberal arts college under the direction of the Franciscan Sisters of Christian Charity. The library contains 60,000 volumes and subscribes to 270 periodicals.

Environment: The 30-acre campus is located in a rural area on the shores of Silver Lake, 4 miles west of Manitowoc, a city of 35,000 people. The college sponsors off-campus apartments; there are no dormitories on campus.

Student Life: Over 95% of the students are from Wisconsin. Eighty-three percent come from public schools. About 55% are Catholic. Alcohol and cars are not permitted on campus.

Organizations: The college has 1 fraternity and 1 sorority. A traditional extracurricular program is offered.

Sports: The college sponsors 1 intercollegiate team for women. There are 4 intramural sports each for men and women.

Handicapped: There are no special facilities for handicapped students.

Graduates: Three percent of the freshmen drop out during the first year, and 90% remain to graduate. About 3% of the graduates pursue advanced degrees. Twenty percent pursue careers in business or industry.

Services: Placement services, tutoring, remedial instruction, and career and psychological counseling are provided free.

Programs of Study: The college confers the B.A., B.S., and B.Mus. degrees. Associate degrees also are awarded. Bachelor's degrees are offered in the following subjects: BUSINESS (accounting, business administration, management), EDUCATION (early childhood, elementary, secondary, special), ENGLISH (English), FINE AND PERFORMING ARTS (art, art education, music, music education, studio art), LANGUAGES (French), MATH AND SCIENCES (biology, chemistry, mathematics, natural sciences, physics), PHILOSOPHY (humanities, religion), PREPROFESSIONAL (ministry), SOCIAL SCIENCES (economics, history, social sciences, sociology).

Required: Students must take courses in humanities, natural sciences, social science, physical education, philosophy, and communication arts. Two courses in theology also are required.

Special: Freshman seminars are available. Students may arrange to spend the junior year abroad. A field natural science major is available, as is a dual program of special and elementary education. Students may design their own majors.

Honors: One honor society is represented on campus.

Admissions: About 92% of those who applied were accepted for the 1981-82 freshman class. The ACT scores of those who enrolled were as follows: 48% below 21, 35% between 21 and 23, 5% between 24 and 25, 2% between 26 and 28, and 2% above 28. Applicants must be graduates of accredited high schools, rank in the upper two-thirds of their class, and have at least a 2.0 GPA and the recommendation of their high school. A minimum of 16 units of high school work must have been completed.

Procedure: Either the ACT or SAT is required. Students are admitted for both semesters and for the summer session. There are no application deadlines. Admissions decisions are made on a rolling basis. There is a $15 application fee.

Special: The college offers early decision and early admissions plans.

Transfer: For a recent year, 31 applications were received and 29 were accepted. Transfers are accepted for all classes except the senior year; D grades do not transfer. A GPA of at least 2.0 is required. Students must earn at least 30 credits in residence of the 128 necessary for a bachelor's degree. Transfer students are admitted for all semesters; there are no application deadlines.

Visiting: Regularly scheduled orientations are held for prospective students. Guides are also available for informal campus visits. Visitors may sit in on classes and stay overnight at the school. The admissions office should be contacted for arrangements.

Financial Aid: Eighty-three percent of the students receive aid; 30% work part-time on campus. The average award to 1981-82 freshmen from all sources was $3000. Tuition may be paid in installments. The FAF is required. The aid application deadline is April 15.

Admissions Contact: Mark McLaughlin, Director of Admissions.

UNIVERSITY OF WISCONSIN

The University of Wisconsin, founded in 1848, is one of the highest-ranked and most diversified university systems in the world. Originally established in Madison on a series of wooded hills overlooking Lake Mendota, a mile from the state capital, it has expanded its educational and research efforts to encompass the entire state, in a pioneering concept of public education now known as "The Wisconsin Idea."

In 1971, the University of Wisconsin was merged with the Wisconsin State Universities to form a new university system. The system now includes campuses at Eau Claire, Green Bay, La Crosse, Madison, Milwaukee, Parkside (Kenosha), Oshkosh, Platteville, River Falls, Stevens Point, Stout (Menomonie), Superior, and Whitewater. Individual profiles of these 4-year schools follow.

The university system also includes the 13 freshman-sophomore centers in the University of Wisconsin Center System, and the University of Wisconsin Extension. Preprofessional and associate-degree courses taken at center system campuses are transferable to any col-

UNIVERSITY OF WISCONSIN/ EAU CLAIRE   B-3
Eau Claire, Wisconsin 54701   (715) 836-5415

F/T: 4120M, 5302W	Faculty: 623; IIA, +$
P/T: 436M, 556W	Ph.D.'s: 48%
Grad: 177M, 372W	S/F Ratio: 15 to 1
Year: sems, ss	Tuition: $932 ($3183)
Appl: open	R and B: $1620
5887 applied	5071 accepted 2441 enrolled
SAT: 465V 521M	ACT: 21 COMPETITIVE

The University of Wisconsin/Eau Claire, founded in 1916, offers undergraduate programs in arts and sciences, business, teacher education, and nursing. The library contains 406,000 volumes and 600,000 microfilm items, and subscribes to 2400 periodicals.

Environment: The 310-acre campus is located in a city of 50,000 people about 90 miles from Minneapolis and St. Paul. The dormitories house 3600 men and women.

Student Life: About 88% of the students come from Wisconsin. Thirty-two percent live on campus. About 5% are minority-group members. Campus housing is both single-sex and coed; there are visiting privileges in single-sex housing. Students may keep cars on campus. The university provides day-care services to all students, faculty, and staff for a fee.

Organizations: About 2% of the students belong to 4 national fraternities and 3 national sororities. Extracurricular activities include religious groups for all major faiths.

Sports: The university fields 10 intercollegiate teams for men and 7 for women. There are 17 intramural sports for men and 15 for women.

Handicapped: About 86% of the campus is accessible to handicapped students. Special facilities include wheelchair ramps, parking areas, elevators, specially equipped rest rooms, and a van with a lift to transport wheelchair-bound students. The university also provides taped textbooks, readers, speech instruction, and TTYs for students with impaired vision or hearing. Three counselors are available to handicapped students.

Graduates: Thirty percent of the freshmen drop out by the end of the first year. Forty-five percent remain to graduate. Nine percent of the graduates pursue advanced degrees. Forty percent enter careers in business and industry.

Services: Health care, psychological counseling, tutoring, remedial instruction, placement aid, and career counseling are available free to students.

Programs of Study: The university awards the B.A., B.S., B.S.E.P.H., B.S.Med.Tech., B.B.A., B.S.H.C.A., B.F.A., B.Mus., B.Mus.Ed., B.S.N., and B.S.W. Master's and associate degrees are also available. Bachelor's degrees are offered in the following subjects: AREA STUDIES (Latin American), BUSINESS (accounting, business administration, business education, finance, management, management information systems, marketing, office administration), EDUCATION (communicative disorders, elementary, health/physical, secondary, special), ENGLISH (English, journalism, speech), FINE AND PERFORMING ARTS (art, art education, music, music education, theater/dramatics), HEALTH SCIENCES (environmental health, health care administration, medical technology, nursing, music therapy, speech therapy—communicative disorders), LANGUAGES (French, German, Spanish), MATH AND SCIENCES (astronomy, biology, chemistry, chemistry business, geology, mathematics, physical sciences, physics, physics/math), PHILOSOPHY (philosophy, religion), SOCIAL SCIENCES (criminal justice, economics, geography, government/political science, history, psychology, public administration, social sciences, sociology). Thirty-nine percent of the degrees are awarded in arts and sciences, 27% in education, 28% in business, and 6% in nursing.

Required: All students must take a distribution of credits in general studies courses.

Special: Cooperative education programs are offered in 17 different areas. Minors include American Indian studies, English as a second language, gerontology, writing, coaching, sports medicine, and Scandinavian studies. The university offers international studies programs in 7 different countries and will help arrange other placements. Nondegree preprofessional programs are offered in agriculture, architecture, dentistry, engineering, forestry, law, medicine, ministry, mortuary science, pharmacy, social work, and veterinary science.

Honors: Twenty-two honor societies have chapters on campus. Honors programs are available for students majoring in sociology, history, political science, and social work.

Admissions: About 86% of those who applied for admission to the 1981–82 freshman class were accepted. The SAT scores of those who enrolled were as follows: Verbal—67% scored below 500, 25% between 500 and 599, 8% between 600 and 700, and 1% above 700; Math—38% scored below 500, 39% between 500 and 599, 22% between 600 and 700, and 1% above 700. Of those who took the ACT, 33% scored below 21, 26% between 21 and 23, 15% between 24 and 25, 14% between 26 and 28, and 3% above 28. Applicants must rank in the top half of their class.

Procedure: The SAT or ACT is required and should be taken by July following the senior year. Application deadlines are open. Admissions decisions are made on a rolling basis. There is a $10 application fee.

Special: AP and CLEP credit is accepted.

Transfer: For fall 1981, 1372 students applied, 1068 were accepted, and 536 enrolled. Applicants must be in good standing at their last school. They must present a GPA of 2.0 or better or have been in the upper half of their high school class. A combined SAT score of 900 or an ACT score of 19 are also required. D grades generally transfer. Students must complete at least 1 year (32 credits) in residence of the 128 needed to receive a bachelor's degree. Application deadlines are August 15 (fall) and 5 days before registration for the spring semester.

Visiting: Orientations for prospective students are scheduled regularly. These sessions include a visit with an admissions counselor, a campus tour, and meetings with faculty members. Guides are provided for informal visits. Visitors may sit in on classes and, when space is available, stay overnight in the dormitories. The admissions office should be contacted for arrangements.

Financial Aid: Seventy-two percent of the students receive aid. Fifteen percent work part-time on campus. Average aid to freshmen from all sources in 1981–82 was $2200. Aid includes grants, scholarships, loans, and part-time jobs administered by the university. Aid applicants should file the FAF. Application deadlines are April 1 (fall), October 1 (winter), and May 15 (summer).

Foreign Students: About 1% of the full-time students come from foreign countries. The university offers these students an intensive English program, special counseling, and special organizations.

Admissions: Foreign students must score at least 550 on the TOEFL or 80 on the University of Michigan Language Test. They take the University of Michigan Language Test and the CELT for placement on arrival. No college entrance examination is required.

Procedure: Application deadlines are July 1 (fall) and December 1 (spring). Foreign students are also admitted in the summer term. Students must present a negative TB skin test or a chest X-ray. They must show evidence of adequate funds for 4 years of study. They also must carry health insurance, which is available through the university for a fee.

Admissions Contact: John L. Kearney, Director of Admissions.

UNIVERSITY OF WISCONSIN/ GREEN BAY   D-3
Green Bay, Wisconsin 54302   (414) 465-2111

F/T: 1305M, 1453W	Faculty: 179; IIA, av$
P/T: 498M, 1003W	Ph.D.'s: 90%
Grad: 145M, 132W	S/F Ratio: 15 to 1
Year: 4-1-4, ss	Tuition: $906 ($3156)
Appl: open	R and B: $1900
1588 applied	1388 accepted 773 enrolled
SAT, ACT: not required	COMPETITIVE

The University of Wisconsin/Green Bay, established in 1968, offers programs of individualized education in the arts and sciences, business, education, health fields, and preprofessional areas. Students enroll in interdisciplinary majors called concentrations, which provide a study of issues from many perspectives. Students have great flexibility in combining programs or designing their own. The library contains 285,000 volumes and 405,646 microfilm items, and subscribes to 4750 periodicals.

Environment: The 645-acre campus, located in a suburban area 7 miles from Green Bay, has 16 major buildings, including residence halls and on-campus apartment buildings.

Student Life: About 90% of the students come from Wisconsin and 88% come from public schools. About 12% of the students live on campus. Five percent are minority-group members. Sixty-three percent are Catholic and 17% are Protestant. Campus housing is coed.

Students may keep cars on campus. Day-care services are provided to all students for a fee.

Organizations: Extracurricular activities include clubs, performing groups, publications, and religious organizations. Regularly scheduled on-campus social and cultural events are offered. There are no sororities or fraternities.

Sports: The university fields intercollegiate teams in 6 sports for men and 7 for women. There are 12 intramural sports for men and 12 for women.

Handicapped: The entire campus is accessible to handicapped students. Special facilities include wheelchair ramps, parking areas, elevators, specially equipped rest rooms, and lowered drinking fountains and telephones. Special class scheduling is also possible.

Graduates: The freshman dropout rate is 36%, and 35% remain to graduate. About 21% of the graduates pursue advanced degrees; 2% enter medical school and 3% enter law school. Forty-one percent enter careers in business or industry.

Services: Health care, psychological and career counseling, placement, tutoring, and remedial instruction are offered free to students.

Programs of Study: The B.A. and B.S. degrees are conferred. Associate and master's programs are also offered. Bachelor's degrees are awarded in the following subjects: AREA STUDIES (urban), BUSINESS (accounting, business administration, finance, management, marketing), EDUCATION (early childhood, elementary, secondary), ENGLISH (English, journalism, literature, speech), FINE AND PERFORMING ARTS (art, art education, dance, music, music education, studio art, theater/dramatics), HEALTH SCIENCES (environmental health, nursing), LANGUAGES (French, German, Spanish), MATH AND SCIENCES (biology, chemistry, earth science, ecology/environmental science, mathematics, natural sciences, physical sciences, physics), PHILOSOPHY (humanities, philosophy), PREPROFESSIONAL (agriculture, architecture, dentistry, engineering, forestry, home economics, law, library science, medicine, ministry, pharmacy, social work, veterinary), SOCIAL SCIENCES (anthropology, economics, geography, government/political science, history, psychology, social sciences, sociology). About 20% of the degrees are conferred in business and 18% in math and sciences.

Special: Interdisciplinary majors, study abroad, student-designed majors, a general-studies degree, and a combined B.A.-B.S. degree in engineering are offered.

Honors: All departments offer honors work.

Admissions: About 87% of the applicants for the 1981-82 freshman class were accepted. Candidates should rank in the top 50% of their graduating class.

Procedure: Neither the SAT nor the ACT is required. There are no application deadlines. Freshmen are admitted in the fall, spring, and summer terms. Notification is made on a rolling basis. There is a $10 application fee.

Special: Early decision, early admissions, and deferred admissions plans are offered. AP and CLEP credit is available.

Transfer: For fall 1981, 601 students applied, 500 were accepted, and 367 enrolled. A 2.0 GPA is required; D grades from other University of Wisconsin schools transfer. All students must complete, at the university, 31 of the 124 credits required for a bachelor's degree. Application deadlines are August 15 (fall) and January 15 (spring).

Visiting: There is an orientation program for prospective students. Informal campus tours may be arranged. Visitors may sit in on classes. Visits are best scheduled on weekdays between 11 A.M. and 2 P.M. The admissions office should be contacted for arrangements.

Financial Aid: About 70% of the students receive aid; 25% work part-time on campus. The university offers scholarships, loans, grants, and part-time work opportunities. Scholarships range from $300 to $1200; loans from $450 to $2500. The average freshman award in 1981-82 was $2155. The university is a member of CSS. CWS is offered in all departments. The FAF must be filed by March 1.

Foreign Students: Two percent of the full-time students come from foreign countries. Intensive English courses, special counseling, and special organizations are available for these students.

Admissions: Foreign students must score at least 450 on the TOEFL. No college entrance exams are required.

Procedure: Application deadlines are July 1 (fall), December 1 (spring), and April 1 (summer). Foreign students must fill out a health form and must present proof of adequate funds for 4 years. Health insurance, though not required, is available through the university for a fee.

Admissions Contact: Myron Van de Ven, Director of Admissions and Financial Aid.

UNIVERSITY OF WISCONSIN/ LA CROSSE B-4

La Crosse, Wisconsin 54601 (608) 785-8068

F/T: 3426M, 4138W	Faculty: n/av; IIA, +$
P/T: 379M, 528W	Ph.D.'s: 70%
Grad: 207M, 272W	S/F Ratio: 19 to 1
Year: sems, ss	Tuition: $960 ($3211)
Appl: open	R and B: $1560
4610 applied	4361 accepted 2037 enrolled
ACT: 20	LESS COMPETITIVE

The University of Wisconsin/La Crosse, founded in 1906, offers undergraduate programs in the arts and sciences, business, education, and health fields. The library contains 435,000 volumes and more than 410,000 microfiche items, and subscribes to 2927 periodicals.

Environment: The 53-acre campus is located in a suburban area about 130 miles from Madison and 150 miles from Minneapolis-St. Paul. Eight of the 11 residence halls are coed.

Student Life: About 84% of the students come from Wisconsin. Ninety-five percent come from public schools. Forty-seven percent are Catholic and 42% are Protestant. About 1% are minority-group members. There are visiting privileges in the single-sex dorms. Students may keep cars on campus.

Organizations: Five percent of the men belong to the 7 fraternities on campus, and 6% of the women belong to the 5 sororities. Traditional extracurricular activities are offered. There are regularly scheduled cultural and social events on campus.

Sports: The university fields intercollegiate teams in 11 sports for men and 11 for women. There are 8 intramural sports for men and 7 for women.

Handicapped: About 90% of the campus is accessible to handicapped students. Special facilities include wheelchair ramps, parking areas, elevators, specially equipped rest rooms, and lowered drinking fountains and telephones. Special class scheduling is also possible.

Graduates: Thirty-one percent of freshmen drop out during the first year, and 40% remain to graduate. About 10% of the graduates pursue advanced degrees; 1% enter medical and dental schools, and 3% enter law school. About 65% begin careers in business or industry.

Services: Placement aid, career counseling, health care, psychological counseling, tutoring, and remedial instruction are provided free to students.

Programs of Study: The university confers the B.A. and B.S. degrees. Associate and master's degrees are also offered. Bachelor's degrees are awarded in the following subjects: BUSINESS (accounting, business administration, computer science, finance, management, marketing), EDUCATION (early childhood, elementary, health/physical, recreation and parks, secondary, special), ENGLISH (English, mass communications, speech), FINE AND PERFORMING ARTS (art, art education, music, music education, theater/dramatics), HEALTH SCIENCES (medical technology, nuclear medicine technology, physical therapy), LANGUAGES (French, Spanish), MATH AND SCIENCES (biology, chemistry, mathematics, physics), PHILOSOPHY (philosophy), SOCIAL SCIENCES (economics, geography, government/political science, history, psychology, sociology).

Required: All students must complete distribution requirements in basic studies.

Honors: Seven honor societies are represented on campus. Honors work is offered in foreign languages, and a general honors program also is available.

Admissions: About 95% of the applicants for the 1981-82 freshman class were accepted. ACT scores of those who enrolled were as follows: 53% below 21, 24% between 21 and 23, 13% between 24 and 25, 10% between 26 and 28, and 2% above 28. Applicants should rank in the upper 75% of their high school class. Recommendations by school officials also are considered.

Procedure: The ACT is required. Application deadlines are open; students are admitted to all terms. Notification is made on a rolling basis. There is a $10 application fee.

Special: An early admissions plan is available. AP and CLEP credit may be earned.

Transfer: For fall 1981, 652 students applied, 601 were accepted, and 430 enrolled. Transfers are accepted for all classes. A 2.0 GPA is recommended; D grades transfer if the student's GPA is 2.0 or

978 WISCONSIN

better. Thirty-two credits of the 130 necessary for a bachelor's degree must be completed in residence.

Visiting: An orientation program is held for prospective students. Informal campus tours may be arranged. Visitors may sit in on classes and arrange to stay overnight at the school. The admissions office should be contacted for information.

Financial Aid: About 58% of the students receive aid. The average award to freshmen from all sources in 1981–82 was $1925. The university offers scholarships, government and commercial loans, grants, and part-time jobs (including CWS). Twenty-one percent of the students work part-time on campus. The FAF or FFS should be submitted by March 1. The college is a member of CSS.

Foreign Students: Fewer than 1% of the full-time students are from foreign countries. Special counseling and special organizations are available.

Admissions: Students must score at least 500 on the TOEFL. No college entrance exams are required.

Procedure: Foreign students are admitted in the fall, spring, and summer. Application deadlines are open. Students must undergo a physical exam and carry health insurance, which is available through the university for a fee. Students also must present proof of adequate funds for 1 year.

Admissions Contact: Gale G. Grimslid, Director of Admissions.

UNIVERSITY OF WISCONSIN/MADISON   C–4

Madison, Wisconsin 53706   (608) 262-3961

F/T: 14,014M, 11,828W   Faculty: 2298; I, ++$
P/T: 1011M, 1274W   Ph.D.'s: 78%
Grad: 6522M, 4128W   S/F Ratio: 12 to 1
Year: sems, ss   Tuition: $1045 ($3632)
Appl: Mar. 1   R and B: $1711–2266
11,613 applied   9559 accepted   4863 enrolled
SAT: 510V 580M   ACT: 25   COMPETITIVE+

The University of Wisconsin/Madison consists of 3 colleges and 6 schools offering undergraduate and graduate study in almost every major field. The library contains over 3.3 million items.

Environment: The 569-acre urban campus has more than 400 buildings and is located 70 miles from Milwaukee. Twenty dormitories accommodate 6700 men and women; married-student housing is also available. There are facilities for commuting students.

Student Life: About 82% of the students come from Wisconsin, and 28% live on campus. Minority-group members made up about 5% of the 1981–82 freshman class. Campus housing is both coed and single-sex; there are visiting privileges in the single-sex dorms. Students may keep cars on campus. Day-care services are available for a fee to all students, faculty, and staff.

Organizations: The university sponsors over 400 professional, recreational, and special-interest organizations. There are 24 fraternities and 9 sororities. Extracurricular activities include student government, clubs, religious groups, publications, and music and drama groups. Many social and cultural events are scheduled.

Sports: The university fields intercollegiate teams in 14 sports for men and 12 for women. Nineteen intramural sports are offered for men and 16 for women.

Handicapped: Special facilities for handicapped students include wheelchair ramps, parking areas, elevators, specially equipped rest rooms, and lowered drinking fountains and telephones. Special class scheduling is also possible. The McBurney Resource Center is available to students with disabilities.

Graduates: The freshman dropout rate is 6%.

Services: Career counseling, placement aid, tutoring, remedial instruction, health care, and psychological counseling are offered free to students.

Programs of Study: The B.A., B.S., B.B.A., B.F.A., and B.M. degrees are conferred. Master's and doctoral programs are also offered. Bachelor's degrees are awarded in the following subjects: AREA STUDIES (American, Asian, Black/Afro-American, Latin American, urban), BUSINESS (accounting, actuarial science, business administration, business education, computer science, finance, management, marketing, quantitative analysis, real estate/insurance, transportation and public utilities), EDUCATION (adult, early childhood, elementary, health/physical, secondary, special), ENGLISH (English, journalism, literature, speech), FINE AND PERFORMING ARTS (art, art education, art history, dance, film/photography, music, music education, radio/TV, studio art, theater/dramatics), HEALTH SCIENCES (medical technology, nursing, occupational therapy, physical therapy, physician assistant, speech therapy), LANGUAGES (Chinese, French, German, Greek/Latin, Hebrew, Italian, Japanese, Polish, Portuguese, Russian, Spanish), MATH AND SCIENCES (applied math/physics, astronomy, biochemistry, biology, botany, chemistry, earth science, ecology/environmental science, geology, history of science, mathematics, natural sciences, physics, statistics, zoology), PHILOSOPHY (classics, history of culture, philosophy), PREPROFESSIONAL (agriculture, engineering, entomology, forestry, home economics, pharmacy, social work), SOCIAL SCIENCES (anthropology, economics, geography, government/political science, history, international relations, psychology, sociology).

Required: Required courses vary with individual programs.

Special: Students may design their own majors and study abroad in various countries.

Honors: An honors program is offered in most majors. The 56 honor societies represented on campus include Phi Beta Kappa.

Admissions: About 82% of the applicants for the 1981–82 freshman class were accepted. Candidates should rank in the top 50% of their graduating class.

Procedure: Neither the SAT nor the ACT is required. Freshmen are admitted to all terms. March 1 is the application deadline for fall and summer admission; for spring, the deadline is November 15. Notification is made on a rolling basis. There is a $10 application fee.

Special: CLEP and AP credit is given. An early admissions plan is available.

Transfer: For fall 1981, 5441 students applied, 3416 were accepted, and 2369 enrolled. Transfer students are considered for all classes. A 2.0 GPA is required. D grades generally transfer. Thirty credits of the 120 necessary for a bachelor's degree must be completed in residence. The application deadline is April 15 for fall and summer, and November 15 for spring; for priority consideration the deadline is February 1.

Visiting: An orientation program is held for prospective students. Informal campus tours with student guides may be arranged. Visitors may sit in on classes; a limited number of rooms are available for overnight stays. Visits are best scheduled on weekdays. The office of new-student services should be contacted for arrangements.

Financial Aid: The university offers scholarships, grants, loans (including NDSL), and part-time jobs (including CWS). About 40% of the students receive aid through the university. The average award to freshmen from all sources in 1981–82 was $2187. The university is a member of CSS; the FAF should be submitted by March 1 for priority consideration.

Foreign Students: About 7% of the full-time students are from foreign countries. An intensive English course, an intensive English program, special counseling, and special organizations are available.

Admissions: Students must score at least 500 on the TOEFL or 80–85 on the University of Michigan Language Test. They also must take the SAT or, preferably, ATs. ATs in mathematics, physics, and chemistry are recommended for applicants to the College of Engineering.

Procedure: Application deadlines are February 1 for fall and summer and November 1 for spring. Students must present proof of adequate funds for their entire period of study. Health insurance, though not required, is available through the university for a fee.

Admissions Contact: David E. Vinson, Director of Admissions.

UNIVERSITY OF WISCONSIN/MILWAUKEE   E–4

Milwaukee, Wisconsin 53201   (414) 963-4572

F/T: 6682M, 6566W   Faculty: 806; I, av$
P/T: 3854M, 4991W   Ph.D.'s: 75%
Grad: 2137M, 2433W   S/F Ratio: 20 to 1
Year: sems, ss   Tuition: $1167 ($3754)
Appl: open   R and B: $2100
5095 applied   4119 accepted   2806 enrolled
SAT: 453V 523M   ACT: 19   COMPETITIVE

The University of Wisconsin/Milwaukee, established in 1956, offers undergraduate degree programs in the arts and sciences, business, education, engineering and applied sciences, fine arts, architecture and urban planning, social welfare, and health fields. The library houses 2.7 million items.

Environment: The 90-acre urban campus is located in a residential neighborhood in the northeast corner of Milwaukee. The 56 buildings include 3 high-rise dormitories that accommodate 1780 students.

Student Life: About 94% of the students come from Wisconsin, and 83% come from public schools. About 6% live on campus. About 10% of the students are minority-group members. Campus housing is both single-sex and coed; there are visiting privileges in single-sex housing. Students may keep cars on campus. Day-care services are provided for a fee.

Organizations: There are 7 fraternities and 3 sororities; fewer than 1% of the students are members. Extracurricular activities include departmental, political, recreational, religious, performing arts, and service groups.

Sports: The university fields 11 intercollegiate teams for men and 8 for women. There are 15 intramural sports for men and 12 for women.

Handicapped: About 98% of the campus is accessible to handicapped students. Special facilities include wheelchair ramps, parking areas, elevators, specially equipped rest rooms, lowered drinking fountains and telephones, automatic doors, and a tactile map. Special class scheduling is also possible.

Graduates: Forty percent of the freshmen drop out by the end of the first year. Thirty percent remain to graduate. About 9% of the graduates pursue advanced degrees.

Services: Tutoring, remedial instruction, psychological counseling, health care, placement aid, and career counseling are offered free to students.

Programs of Study: The B.A., B.S., B.B.A., and B.F.A. degrees are conferred. Master's and doctoral programs are also offered. Bachelor's degrees are awarded in the following subjects: AREA STUDIES (Black/Afro-American, ethnic), BUSINESS (accounting, business administration, computer science, finance, industrial relations, management, marketing, real estate/insurance), EDUCATION (early childhood, elementary, health/physical, pre- and early adolescent, secondary, special), FINE AND PERFORMING ARTS (art, art education, art history, dance, film/photography, music, music education, radio/TV, studio art, theater/dramatics), HEALTH SCIENCES (medical records administration, medical technology, nursing, occupational therapy, recreation, speech therapy), LANGUAGES (French, German, Greek/Latin, Hebrew, Italian, linguistics, Russian, Spanish), MATH AND SCIENCES (biology, botany, chemistry, earth science, geology, mathematics, physics, statistics, zoology), PHILOSOPHY (classics, philosophy), PREPROFESSIONAL (architecture, engineering, medicine, social work), SOCIAL SCIENCES (anthropology, economics, geography, government/political science, history, international relations, psychology, sociology). About 17% of the degrees are conferred in business, 17% in preprofessional areas, 13% in education, and 6% in health sciences.

Required: Students must complete distribution requirements.

Special: Students may design their own majors. Study abroad and interdisciplinary majors are offered.

Honors: Thirteen honor societies have chapters on campus. The College of Letters and Science offers an honors program.

Admissions: About 81% of the applicants for the 1981–82 freshman class were accepted. The SAT scores of those who enrolled were as follows: Verbal—64% scored below 500, 29% between 500 and 599, 8% between 600 and 700, and 0% above 700; Math—33% scored below 500, 37% between 500 and 599, 24% between 600 and 700, and 6% above 700. Of those who took the ACT, 32% scored below 21, 29% between 21 and 23, 28% between 24 and 25, 5% between 26 and 28, and 3% above 28. Students should be graduates of accredited high schools, have completed 16 Carnegie units, and rank in the upper half of their graduating class.

Procedure: Neither the SAT nor the ACT is required, but satisfactory test scores may compensate for lower class rank. Although there are no formal application deadlines, the recommended filing date for fall is August 1. New students are admitted each semester. Notification is made on a rolling basis. There is a $10 application fee.

Special: Early admissions and deferred admissions plans are available. CLEP and AP credit is given.

Transfer: For fall 1981, 3568 students applied, and 3060 enrolled. A 2.0 GPA is needed. D grades sometimes transfer. Transfers are considered for all classes. Thirty credits must be completed at the university of the 120 usually required for a bachelor's degree. Students should apply one month before the start of the semester.

Visiting: An orientation program is held for admitted students. Informal campus tours may be arranged for applicants. Visitors may sit in on classes with the professor's consent. Visits are best scheduled on weekdays. The department of high school and college relations should be contacted for arrangements.

Financial Aid: Thirty-seven percent of the students receive aid. Thirty-five percent work part-time on campus. Average aid to freshmen from all sources in 1981–82 was $2879. The university offers scholarships, grants, government and commercial loans, and part-time campus jobs (including CWS). All aid awards are based on need. The university is a member of CSS. The FAF should be filed by March 9 (fall), November 1 (spring), or April 1 (summer).

Foreign Students: Five percent of the full-time students come from foreign countries. The university offers these students an intensive English course, an intensive English program, and special organizations.

Admissions: Foreign students must take the TOEFL. No college entrance examination is required.

Procedure: Applications must be filed at least 3 months before the beginning of the term in which the student seeks to enroll. Students must present proof of adequate funds for 1 year. They must carry health insurance, which is available through the university for a fee.

Admissions Contact: Benjamin Litwin, Associate Director of Admissions.

UNIVERSITY OF WISCONSIN/OSHKOSH D-4
Oshkosh, Wisconsin 54901 (414) 424-0202

F/T: 4100M, 4250W Faculty: 650; IIA, +$
P/T: n/av Ph.D.'s: 45%
Grad: 950M, 800W S/F Ratio: 17 to 1
Year: sems, ss Tuition: $931 ($3182)
Appl: open R and B: $1606
4010 applied 3500 accepted 2105 enrolled
SAT or ACT: required LESS COMPETITIVE

The University of Wisconsin/Oshkosh, established in 1871, offers undergraduate programs in the arts and sciences, business, education, and health fields. The library contains over 500,000 volumes and 15,000 microfilm items, and subscribes to 1600 periodicals.

Environment: The 165-acre urban campus has 33 buildings, including 11 residence halls. Fraternity and sorority housing also is provided.

Student Life: About 94% of the students come from Wisconsin, and 80% come from public schools. More than half the students live on campus. Dormitories are both single-sex and coed; visiting privileges are permitted in some of the single-sex dorms.

Organizations: The university sponsors on-campus social and cultural events as well as social, special-interest, and professional organizations. Three fraternities and 3 sororities have chapters on campus.

Sports: The university fields intercollegiate teams in 9 sports for women and 10 for men. Intramural sports are offered in many areas for men and women.

Handicapped: The entire campus is accessible to handicapped students. Facilities include wheelchair ramps, parking areas, elevators, specially equipped rest rooms, and lowered drinking fountains and telephones. Special class scheduling can be arranged. Counselors are available to handicapped students.

Graduates: The freshman dropout rate is 25%, and about 55% remain to graduate. About 25% of the graduates pursue advanced degrees.

Services: Career and psychological counseling, placement, health care, tutoring, and remedial instruction are provided free to students.

Programs of Study: The university confers the B.A., B.S., B.M., B.F.A., B.Mus.Ed., B.S.Ch., B.S.Med.Tech., B.S. in Elem.Ed., B.S. in Sec.Ed., B.S.N., B.B.A., B. Art Education, B. Human Services, and B.S. in Special Education degrees. Associate and master's programs are also available. Bachelor's degrees are offered in the following subjects: AREA STUDIES (urban), BUSINESS (accounting, business administration, computer science, finance, management, manpower management, marketing, operations management), EDUCATION (elementary, health/physical, human services, secondary, special), ENGLISH (English, journalism, speech), FINE AND PERFORMING ARTS (art, art education, art history, film/photography, music, music education, music therapy, radio/TV, theater/dramatics), HEALTH SCIENCES (communicative disorders, medical technology, nursing), LANGUAGES (French, German, Spanish), MATH AND SCIENCES (biology, chemistry, earth science, geology, mathematics, microbiology, natural sciences, physics), PHILOSOPHY (philosophy), PREPROFESSIONAL (library science, social work), SOCIAL SCIENCES (anthropology, criminal justice, economics, geography, government/political science, history, international relations, psychology, social sciences, sociology).

Required: All students must complete general-education requirements.

Special: Students may design their own majors. Combined B.A.-B.S. degrees are offered.

Honors: Twelve honor societies have chapters on campus. A university scholars program is offered.

Admissions: About 87% of the applicants for the 1981–82 freshman class were accepted. The ACT scores of those who enrolled were as follows: 49% below 21, 17% between 21 and 23, 4% between 24 and 25, 2% between 26 and 28, and 2% above 28. Applicants should have completed 16 high school academic units, rank in the upper 75% of their class, and present an average of 2.0 or better. Others may be accepted conditionally.

Procedure: The SAT or ACT is required. Application deadlines are open. New students are admitted each semester. Notification is made on a rolling basis. There is no application fee.

Special: There are early decision and early admissions plans. AP and CLEP credit is given.

Transfer: Transfer students are admitted to all classes. A 2.0 GPA is necessary. D grades are accepted. Thirty semester hours must be completed in residence.

Visiting: An orientation program for prospective students is provided. Campus tours with student guides may be arranged. Visitors may sit in on classes and stay overnight at the school. The admissions office should be contacted for arrangements.

Financial Aid: About 50% of the students receive aid. The university offers scholarships, grants, government and commercial loans, and CWS as well as other part-time jobs. The FAF or FFS should be filed by March 31.

Foreign Students: The foreign students enrolled full-time at the university make up nearly 2% of the student body. The university offers these students an intensive English course and special counseling.

Admissions: Foreign applicants must score 550 or better on the TOEFL. No further entrance exams are required.

Procedure: Application deadlines are open; students are admitted to all terms. Foreign students must provide a physician's statement as proof of good health. They must show evidence of adequate funds for 1 year. Health insurance is available through the university for a fee.

Admissions Contact: R. Thomas Snider, Director of Admissions.

UNIVERSITY OF WISCONSIN/PARKSIDE E–5
Kenosha, Wisconsin 53141 (414) 553-2339

F/T: 1564M, 1357W Faculty: 220; IIA, +$
P/T: 1281M, 1301W Ph.D.'s: 85%
Grad: 178M, 153W S/F Ratio: 17 to 1
Year: sems, ss Tuition: $898 ($3148)
Appl: Aug. 15 R and B: n/app
SAT, ACT: not required NONCOMPETITIVE

The University of Wisconsin/Parkside, founded in 1968, offers undergraduate programs in the arts and sciences, business, and health fields. The library contains 310,000 volumes and 500,000 microfilm items, and subscribes to 2000 periodicals.

Environment: The 700-acre campus is located in a suburban area 4 miles from Kenosha. There are 8 buildings on campus; apartment-style university-owned housing is available adjacent to the campus. Facilities also are available for commuting students.

Student Life: About 90% of the students come from Wisconsin, and 80% come from public schools. Eight percent are minority-group members. Cars are permitted on campus. Day-care services are available for a fee.

Organizations: There are no fraternities or sororities. Extracurricular activities as well as on-campus cultural and social events are offered.

Sports: The university fields 10 intercollegiate teams for men and 8 for women. Men and women compete in 6 intramural sports each.

Handicapped: The campus is completely accessible to handicapped students. Wheelchair ramps, elevators, parking areas, specially equipped rest rooms, and lowered drinking fountains and telephones are available.

Graduates: By the end of the freshman year, 25% of the students drop out. About 20% of the graduates pursue advanced degrees; 2% enter medical school, 2% enter dental school, and 3% enter law school. Another 70% begin careers in business or industry.

Services: Health care, psychological counseling, placement aid, career counseling, tutoring, and remedial instruction are offered free to students.

Programs of Study: The B.A. and B.S. degrees are conferred. Master's programs are also available. Bachelor's degrees are offered in the following subjects: BUSINESS (accounting, business administration, computer science, finance, industrial relations, management, marketing), EDUCATION (elementary, secondary), ENGLISH (English), FINE AND PERFORMING ARTS (art, communication, theater/dramatics), HEALTH SCIENCES (environmental health, nursing), LANGUAGES (French, German, Spanish), MATH AND SCIENCES (biology, chemistry, earth science, mathematics, physics), PHILOSOPHY (humanities, philosophy), PREPROFESSIONAL (architecture, dentistry, law, medicine, pharmacy, veterinary), SOCIAL SCIENCES (anthropology, economics, geography, government/political science, history, international relations, psychology, social sciences, sociology). About 33% of the degrees are conferred in business, 26% in social sciences, and 17% in math and sciences.

Special: Independent study programs and a 3-year bachelor's degree are available.

Honors: An honors program is offered.

Admissions: All the applicants for a recent freshman class were accepted. The university has an open admissions policy for high school graduates.

Procedure: Neither the SAT nor the ACT is required. Applications for the fall term should be filed by August 15, for spring, by January 10, and for summer, by June 10. Notification is made on a rolling basis. There is a $10 application fee.

Special: An early admissions plan is available. AP and CLEP credit may be earned.

Transfer: A 2.0 GPA is recommended; D grades generally transfer. Transfers are considered for all classes. Thirty credits of the 120 required for the bachelor's degree must be completed in residence.

Visiting: An orientation program is held for prospective students. Informal campus tours with student guides may be arranged. Visitors may sit in on classes. Visits are best scheduled on weekdays. The office of student development should be contacted for arrangements.

Financial Aid: About 25% of the students receive aid. The university offers commercial and government loans, part-time jobs (including CWS), grants, and scholarships. About 80% of the students work part-time on campus. Tuition may be paid in installments. The FAF should be filed by March 15.

Foreign Students: About 2% of the full-time students are from foreign countries. Special organizations are available for these students.

Admissions: Students must score at least 550 on the TOEFL. The SAT is also required.

Procedure: Application deadlines are May 1 for fall and September 1 for spring. Proof of adequate funds for 1 year is required.

Admissions Contact: John F. Elmore, Director of Student Development.

UNIVERSITY OF WISCONSIN/PLATTEVILLE C–5
Platteville, Wisconsin 53818 (608) 342-1125

F/T: 2480M, 1085W Faculty: 238; IIA, +$
P/T: 180M, 240W Ph.D.'s: n/av
Grad: 145M, 165W S/F Ratio: 18 to 1
Year: sems, ss Tuition: $1020 ($3200)
Appl: open R and B: $1900
2400 applied 2225 accepted 1296 enrolled
SAT, ACT: not required LESS COMPETITIVE

The University of Wisconsin/Platteville, established in 1866, offers undergraduate programs in the arts and sciences, agriculture, business, engineering, and education. The library holds 231,000 books and 320,000 microfilm items, and subscribes to more than 3000 periodicals.

Environment: The 360-acre campus and 400-acre experimental farm are located in a rural area 25 miles from Dubuque, Iowa. Nine residence halls accommodate 2400 students; fraternity and sorority housing also is available.

Student Life: About 82% of the students come from Wisconsin. More than 50% live on campus. Dormitories are both coed and single-sex. Freshmen and sophomores who are not married, veterans, or living with parents must live on campus.

Organizations: There are fraternities and sororities, special-interest clubs, religious and service groups, student government, performing groups, publications, and regularly scheduled social and cultural events.

Sports: The university fields 11 intercollegiate teams for men and 6 for women. Intramural sports also are available.

Handicapped: Most of the campus is accessible to handicapped students.

Graduates: The freshman dropout rate is 15% and about 35% remain to graduate. About 20% of the graduates pursue advanced degrees.

Programs of Study: The B.A. and B.S. degrees are conferred. Master's programs are also offered. Bachelor's degrees are offered in the following subjects; BUSINESS (accounting, agricultural business, business administration, computer science, occupational safety), EDUCATION (agricultural, elementary, health/physical, industrial, secondary), ENGLISH (English), FINE AND PERFORMING ARTS (art, music, music education, radio/TV), LANGUAGES (French, German, Spanish), MATH AND SCIENCES (biology, botany, chemistry, computer science, general science, geology, mathematics, physics, zoology), PHILOSOPHY (philosophy), PREPROFESSIONAL (agriculture, dentistry, engineering—agricultural, engineering—civil, engineering—industrial, engineering—mechanical, engineering—mining, industrial technology, law, light building technology, medicine, ministry, reclamation, safety, veterinary), SOCIAL SCIENCES (criminal justice, economics, geography, government/political science, history, international relations, psychology, sociology).

Required: All students must complete distribution requirements.

Special: Students may design their own majors and arrange to study abroad. Cooperative education and internship programs are offered. Minors are available in women's studies and environmental studies.

Honors: The university offers an honors program.

Admissions: About 93% of the applicants for the 1981–82 freshman class were accepted. Median SAT scores of those who enrolled were 520V and 630M. Of those who took the ACT, 9% scored below 21, 30% between 21 and 23, 40% between 24 and 25, 11% between 26 and 28, and 10% above 28. Applicants should have completed a college-preparatory program, rank in the top half of their high school class, and have a GPA of 2.0 or higher. Students who do not meet these standards may be admitted on probation.

Procedure: Neither the SAT nor the ACT is required. Application deadlines are open. Notification is made on a rolling basis. There is no application fee.

Special: AP and CLEP credit is given. Early admissions and deferred admissions plans are available.

Transfer: Applicants must have at least a 2.0 GPA. D grades are accepted. One year must be completed in residence. The application deadlines are August 1 (fall) and January 1 (spring).

Visiting: Informal campus tours with student guides can be arranged. Visitors may sit in on classes.

Financial Aid: About 63% of the students receive financial aid. The university offers scholarships, grants, government and commercial loans, and part-time jobs (including CWS). The average award to a freshman in 1981–82 totaled $1900 from all sources. The FAF must be submitted by March 1.

Foreign Students: Foreign students enrolled full-time represent about 5% of the student body. The university provides these students with special counseling and special organizations.

Admissions: Applicants must score 550 or better on the TOEFL. No college entrance exams are required.

Procedure: Application deadlines are June 1 for fall entry and November 1 for spring entry. Students must submit a completed health form, and provide evidence of adequate funds for at least 1 year and preferably 4.

Admissions Contact: Edward Deneen, Director of Admissions.

UNIVERSITY OF WISCONSIN/ RIVER FALLS
A–3

River Falls, Wisconsin 54022 (715) 425-3500

F/T: 2694M, 2450W Faculty: 264; IIA, +$
P/T: 163M, 118W Ph.D.'s: 63%
Grad: 118M, 240W S/F Ratio: 22 to 1
Year: qtrs, ss Tuition: $966 ($3217)
Appl: open R and B: $1758
2441 applied 2305 accepted 1294 enrolled
SAT, ACT: not required LESS COMPETITIVE

The University of Wisconsin/River Falls offers undergraduate programs in the arts and sciences, education, business, and agriculture. The library contains more than 180,000 volumes and 230,000 microfilm items, and subscribes to 1492 periodicals.

Environment: The 540-acre campus is located in a rural area 25 miles from St. Paul, Minnesota. The 40 buildings include 9 residence halls that accommodate 1144 men and 870 women. The university also sponsors fraternity and sorority houses. There are facilities for commuting students.

Student Life: About 65% of the students come from Wisconsin. About 45% live on campus. Three percent are minority-group members. Campus housing is both coed and single-sex; there are visiting privileges in the single-sex dorms. Students may keep cars on campus. Day-care services are available.

Organizations: There are 5 fraternities and 3 sororities. Extracurricular activities include clubs, student government, religious groups, music and drama groups, and regularly scheduled cultural and social events.

Sports: The university sponsors 14 intercollegiate teams for men and 14 for women. There are 9 intramural sports for men and 8 for women.

Handicapped: About 90% of the campus is accessible to handicapped students. Wheelchair ramps, elevators, and parking areas are provided. Special class scheduling can be arranged. A counselor is available to handicapped students.

Graduates: The freshman dropout rate is 12%; about 60% of the freshmen remain to graduate. Five percent of the graduates pursue advanced degrees.

Services: Psychological and career counseling, placement, tutoring, and remedial instruction are offered free to students. Fees are charged for health care.

Programs of Study: The university confers the B.A., B.S., and B.F.A. degrees. Master's programs are also offered. Bachelor's degrees are offered in the following subjects: AREA STUDIES (American, urban), BUSINESS (accounting, business administration, computer science), EDUCATION (early childhood, elementary, health/physical, secondary), ENGLISH (English, journalism, literature, speech), FINE AND PERFORMING ARTS (art, art education, music, music education), HEALTH SCIENCES (physical therapy), LANGUAGES (French, German), MATH AND SCIENCES (biology, chemistry, earth science, geology, mathematics, physics), PREPROFESSIONAL (agriculture, dentistry, engineering, law, medicine, pharmacy, veterinary), SOCIAL SCIENCES (economics, geography, government/political science, history, psychology, social sciences, sociology).

Required: All students must take courses in English, social science, science, psychology, physical education, speech, and fine arts.

Special: Students may design their own majors. Study abroad is offered.

Honors: Several honor societies have chapters on campus.

Admissions: About 94% of the 1981–82 applicants were accepted. Candidates should rank in the top 75% of their graduating class.

Procedure: Neither the SAT nor the ACT is required. New students are admitted each quarter. There are no application deadlines. Notification is made on a rolling basis. There is a $10 application fee.

Special: AP and CLEP credit is given. Early decision and early admissions plans are available.

Transfer: For fall 1981, 603 students applied, 508 were accepted, and 369 enrolled. A 2.0 GPA is required. D grades transfer. Students must complete, at the university, 48 of the 192 credits required for the bachelor's degree. There are no application deadlines.

Visiting: Informal campus tours with student guides may be arranged. Visitors may sit in on classes and stay overnight at the school. Visits are best scheduled on weekdays between 8 A.M. and 4 P.M. The admissions office should be contacted for arrangements.

Financial Aid: About 67% of the students receive aid. The university offers scholarships, grants, loans, and part-time jobs (including CWS). Tuition may be paid in installments. The FAF, FFS, or SFS must be filed by September 1; for priority consideration, applications should be submitted by March 1.

Foreign Students: About 120 foreign students are enrolled at the university. An intensive English course, special counseling, and special organizations are available for these students.

Admissions: Applicants must score at least 500 on the TOEFL. No college entrance exams are required.

Procedure: Foreign students are admitted to all terms; there are no application deadlines. Students must submit a completed health form

982 WISCONSIN

and must present proof of adequate funds for 4 years. Health insurance is also required.

Admissions Contact: Wilbur W. Sperling, Director of Admissions.

UNIVERSITY OF WISCONSIN/ STEVENS POINT   C-3
Stevens Point, Wisconsin 54481   (715) 346-2441

F/T, P/T: 4310M, 4314W	Faculty: 488; IIA, +$
Grad: 210M, 417W	Ph.D.'s: 60%
Year: sems, ss	S/F Ratio: 19 to 1
Appl: open	Tuition: $966 ($3217)
3902 applied 3784 accepted 1953 enrolled	R and B: $1806
SAT, ACT: not required	LESS COMPETITIVE

The University of Wisconsin/Stevens Point, established in 1894, offers undergraduate training in the arts and sciences, business, education, and technology. The library contains 260,000 volumes and 70,000 microfilm items, and subscribes to 2370 periodicals.

Environment: The 250-acre campus is located in a rural area 110 miles north of Madison. The university has 14 dormitories.

Student Life: About 90% of the students come from Wisconsin. Eighty percent come from public schools. About 40% live on campus. Five percent are minority-group members. Campus housing is both coed and single-sex; there are visiting privileges in single-sex dorms. Students may keep cars on campus. Day-care services are available for a fee.

Organizations: The 4 fraternities on campus attract 4% of the men; the 2 sororities attract 3% of the women. The university sponsors a full program of extracurricular activities, including regularly scheduled social and cultural events.

Sports: The university fields 11 intercollegiate teams for men and 9 for women. Intramural competition is offered in 19 sports for men and 15 for women.

Handicapped: About 90% of the campus is accessible to handicapped students. Facilities include wheelchair ramps, parking areas, elevators, specially equipped rest rooms, and lowered drinking fountains and telephones. One percent of the students have hearing impairments and 1% have visual impairments. A counselor is available to handicapped students.

Graduates: The freshmen dropout rate is 5%, and about 75% of the freshmen remain to graduate. Fifteen percent of the graduates pursue advanced degrees (1% each enter law, medical, and dental schools) and 40% begin careers in business and industry.

Services: The following free services are available: placement, career counseling, health care, psychological counseling, tutoring, and remedial instruction.

Programs of Study: The university confers the B.A., B.S., B.F.A., and B.M. degrees. Associate and master's degrees are also available. Bachelor's degrees are offered in the following subjects: AREA STUDIES (American, Latin American, Russian), BUSINESS (accounting, business administration, business education), EDUCATION (early childhood, elementary, home economics, health/physical, secondary), ENGLISH (English), FINE AND PERFORMING ARTS (art, art education, communication, dance, music, music—applied, music education, music literature, theater/dramatics), HEALTH SCIENCES (communicative disorders, medical technology), LANGUAGES (French, German, Spanish), MATH AND SCIENCES (biology, chemistry, mathematics, natural sciences, physics), PHILOSOPHY (philosophy), PREPROFESSIONAL (dietetics/food and nutrition, fashion merchandising, forestry, home economics, home economics in business, housing and interiors, paper science, resource management, soil science, water resources, wildlife management), SOCIAL SCIENCES (anthropology, economics, geography, government/political science, history, psychology, social sciences, sociology). About 20% of the degrees are awarded in math and sciences, and 15% in fine and performing arts.

Honors: Three honor societies have chapters on campus. There is a campus-wide honors program.

Admissions: About 97% of the applicants for the 1981–82 freshman class were accepted. Applicants should rank in the top 75% of their high school class. Other factors considered in the admissions decision include test scores, advanced placement or honors courses, impressions made during an interview, and school recommendations.

Procedure: Neither the SAT nor ACT is required. There are no application deadlines; students are admitted to all terms. Notification is made on a rolling basis. There is a $10 application fee.

Special: AP and CLEP credit is given.

Transfer: For fall 1981, 1071 students applied, 918 were accepted, and 597 enrolled. Transfers are considered for all classes. The recommended minimum GPA varies from 1.6 to 2.0, depending on the number of credits completed. D grades transfer. Students must complete at least 30 credits in residence of the 124–132 required for a bachelor's degree. There are no application deadlines.

Visiting: An orientation program is held for prospective students. Informal campus tours with student guides may be arranged. Visitors may sit in on classes and stay overnight at the school. The admissions office should be contacted for arrangements.

Financial Aid: About 60% of the students receive aid. The university offers scholarships, various loans, grants, and part-time jobs (CWS included). The FAF should be filed by March 1 for priority consideration.

Foreign Students: About 2% of the students are from foreign countries. An intensive English course, special counseling, and special organizations are available.

Admissions: A minimum score of 500 on the TOEFL is required. Students also must take the SAT.

Procedure: Application deadlines are July 15 (fall), October 15 (spring), and April 15 (summer). Students must submit a physician's statement, and must present proof of adequate funds for their entire period of study. Health insurance is also required, and is available through the university for a fee.

Admissions Contact: John A. Larsen, Director of Admissions.

UNIVERSITY OF WISCONSIN/ STOUT   B-3
Menomonie, Wisconsin 54751   (715) 232-1293

F/T: 3572M, 3351W	Faculty: 320; IIA, av$
P/T: 154M, 158W	Ph.D.'s: n/av
Grad: 287M, 248W	S/F Ratio: 22 to 1
Year: sems, ss	Tuition: $959 ($3108)
Appl: Aug. 1	R and B: $1730
3155 applied 2417 accepted 1371 enrolled	
SAT, ACT: not required	COMPETITIVE

The Stout campus of the University of Wisconsin was founded in 1893. It specializes in home economics and industrial technology. The library houses 175,000 volumes and 4400 microfilm items, and subscribes to 1914 periodicals.

Environment: The 120-acre campus is located in an urban area 60 miles east of St. Paul, Minnesota. Dormitories accommodate 2900 students. The university also sponsors off-campus apartments and married-student housing.

Student Life: About 67% of the students are from Wisconsin. Sixty percent live on campus. About 5% are minority-group members. Campus housing is coed. Students may keep cars on campus.

Organizations: Six fraternities and 5 sororities have chapters on campus. Extracurricular activities include student government, publications, special-interest clubs, and music and drama groups.

Sports: The university sponsors 11 intercollegiate teams for men and 7 for women. There are 19 intramural sports for men and 18 for women.

Handicapped: About 95% of the campus is accessible to handicapped students. Wheelchair ramps, elevators, parking areas, specially equipped rest rooms, and lowered drinking fountains and telephones are provided. Special class scheduling can be arranged. A counselor is available to handicapped students.

Graduates: About 30% of the freshmen drop out by the end of their first year, and 62% remain to graduate. Five percent of the graduates pursue advanced degrees. Sixty-six percent begin careers in business or industry.

Services: Health care, psychological and career counseling, placement aid, tutoring, and remedial instruction are provided free to students.

Programs of Study: The university confers the B.A. and B.S. degrees. Master's degrees are also awarded. Bachelor's degrees are offered in the following subjects: BUSINESS (business administration, fashion merchandising, home economics in business, hotel and restaurant management), EDUCATION (early childhood, industrial, marketing and distributive, vocational and technical), FINE AND PERFORMING ARTS (art, art education), HEALTH SCIENCES (dietetics, food service administration), MATH AND SCIENCES (mathematics), PREPROFESSIONAL (clothing and textiles, home economics, industrial technology), SOCIAL SCIENCES (psychology, vocational rehabilitation). Forty-five percent of the degrees are conferred in business and 33% in education.

Special: The university has the largest school of industry and technology in the world, and one of the top-ranking schools of home economics in the nation.

Honors: Five honor societies have chapters on campus.

Admissions: Seventy-seven percent of those who applied for the 1981–82 freshman class were accepted. Applicants must rank in the upper 75% of their high school class.

Procedure: Neither the SAT nor the ACT is required. The application deadline for fall admission is August 1. Enrollment quotas restrict the number of students allowed in each major. Notification is made on a rolling basis. There is no application fee.

Special: There are early decision and early admissions plans. CLEP subject exams are accepted.

Transfer: For fall 1981, 1369 applications were received, 1009 were accepted, and 631 students enrolled. Applicants must be in good standing at their last school. D grades do not transfer. Students must complete, at the university, 32 of the 128–133 credits necessary to receive a bachelor's degree. The application deadline is August 1.

Visiting: Regularly scheduled orientations are held for prospective students. Guides are available for informal visits. Visitors may sit in on classes and stay overnight at the school. Visits are best scheduled on weekdays. The director of high school relations should be contacted for arrangements.

Financial Aid: About 75% of the students receive aid. Scholarships, loans, and part-time jobs are available; 40% of the students work part-time on campus. The FAF is required. Applications should be submitted by June for fall, October for spring, or April for summer.

Foreign Students: About 3% of the students are from foreign countries. Special counseling and special organizations are available for these students.

Admissions: No English proficiency or college entrance exams are required.

Procedure: The application deadline for fall is August 1. Proof of good health is required, and students also must present proof of adequate funds for their entire period of study. Health insurance, though not required, is available through the university for a fee.

Admissions Contact: Donald E. Osegard, Admissions Director.

UNIVERSITY OF WISCONSIN/ SUPERIOR
Superior, Wisconsin 54880   (715) 392-8101

A–1

F/T: 1000M, 800W   Faculty: n/av; IIA, +$
P/T: 100M, 102W   Ph.D.'s: n/av
Grad: 300M, 295W   S/F Ratio: n/av
Year: qtrs, ss   Tuition: $924 ($3174)
Appl: Aug. 30   R and B: $1980
1000 applied   890 accepted   450 enrolled
SAT, ACT: not required   LESS COMPETITIVE

The University of Wisconsin/Superior, founded in 1893, is a publicly supported institution offering undergraduate programs in liberal arts and sciences, education, and business. The library contains 280,000 volumes and 2800 microfilm items, and subscribes to 400 periodicals.

Environment: The 200-acre campus is located in a suburban area, near the center of a city of 35,000 on the tip of Lake Superior. Summer and winter vacationlands, the Indian Head Country, and the Arrowhead Country are nearby. The campus has over 25 buildings. Five dormitories accommodate more than 1200 students.

Student Life: Three-fourths of the students are from Wisconsin. Campus housing is both single-sex and coed.

Organizations: There are 5 fraternities and 5 sororities; 10% of the men and 18% of the women belong. Many clubs and special-interest groups are available in such areas as music, religion, politics, drama, art, and student government. Religious organizations for the major faiths are also provided.

Sports: The university sponsors teams in 11 intercollegiate sports. There are 20 intramural sports.

Handicapped: The entire campus is accessible to handicapped students. Special facilities include wheelchair ramps, parking areas, elevators, specially equipped rest rooms, and lowered drinking fountains and telephones.

WISCONSIN 983

Graduates: About 25% of the freshmen drop out by the end of the first year, and 60% remain to graduate. About 30% of the graduates pursue advanced degrees; 10% enter medical school, 5% enter dental school, and 5% enter law school. Fifteen percent of the graduates pursue careers in business and industry.

Services: The following services are provided free to students: health care, psychological counseling, placement and career counseling, tutoring, and remedial instruction. Placement services also are available to alumni.

Programs of Study: The university confers the B.A., B.F.A., and B.S. degrees. Associate and master's degrees are also offered. Bachelor's degrees are offered in the following subjects: BUSINESS (accounting, business administration, business education, computer science, data processing, management, marketing, office administration), EDUCATION (elementary, health/physical, secondary), ENGLISH (English, speech), FINE AND PERFORMING ARTS (art, art education, music, music education, studio art, theater/dramatics), HEALTH SCIENCES (art therapy, medical technology), LANGUAGES (German, Spanish), MATH AND SCIENCES (biology, chemistry, ecology/environmental science, mathematics, physics), PREPROFESSIONAL (engineering, forestry, law, library science, medicine, pharmacy, social work), SOCIAL SCIENCES (economics, government/political science, history, psychology, social sciences, sociology).

Special: Cooperative degree programs are available in several fields. Credit may be granted for independent study abroad. Combined B.A.-B.S. degrees are offered in many areas. The B.G.S. degree is available. Students may design their own majors.

Honors: Students may earn a place on the dean's list and graduation with honors.

Admissions: Eighty-nine percent of those who applied were accepted for the 1981–82 freshman class. Applicants should be high school graduates, rank in the top three-fourths of their graduating class, and have at least a 2.0 GPA. The university also considers advanced placement or honors courses, recommendations, and leadership record.

Procedure: Neither the SAT nor the ACT is required. The deadline for fall applications is August 30. Students are also admitted for the winter, spring, and summer quarters. Notification is made on a rolling basis. There is a $10 application fee.

Special: CLEP credit is accepted on a departmental basis.

Transfer: For fall 1981, 200 students applied, 190 were accepted, and 140 enrolled. Second-semester freshmen must have a 1.8 GPA; second-semester sophomores and upperclassmen, a 2.0. Those with a lower GPA may be admitted on probation. D grades are transferable. Transfers are considered for all classes. Students must complete at least 48 credit hours in residence of the 192 required for a bachelor's degree. The deadline for applications is registration day (August 30 for fall).

Visiting: Regular orientations for prospective students include a campus tour, meetings with faculty members, and other events. Guides are also available for informal visits. Visitors may sit in on classes and stay overnight on campus. Visits are best scheduled September through October, and April through August. The admissions office should be contacted for arrangements.

Financial Aid: About 90% of the students receive aid administered by the university. Forty percent of the students work part-time on campus. Various scholarships and loans are made from a fund totaling $90,000. The average award to freshmen in 1981–82 totaled 80% of college costs. The FAF is required; applications for aid should be submitted by March 15 for fall, October 1 for winter, January 1 for spring, or April 1 for summer. The college is a member of CSS.

Foreign Students: About 3% of the students are from foreign countries. An intensive English course, special counseling, and special organizations are available for these students.

Admissions: Applicants must take either the TOEFL or the University of Michigan Language Test. Students applying for the fall quarter must score at least 500 on the TOEFL; those applying for the winter and spring quarters must score 525.

Procedure: Application deadlines are May 1 for fall, July 1 for winter, November 1 for spring, and February 1 for summer. Students must present proof of adequate funds for 1 year. There is a special application fee for foreign students. Students must carry health insurance, which is available through the university for a fee.

Admissions Contact: Lowell W. Banks, Director of Admissions and Records.

984 WISCONSIN

UNIVERSITY OF WISCONSIN/ WHITEWATER
Whitewater, Wisconsin 53190   D-5
   (414) 472-1440

F/T: 3810M, 3931W
P/T: 410M, 515W
Grad: 807M, 1160W
Year: sems, ss
Appl: open
4823 applied   4357 accepted   2194 enrolled
SAT, ACT: not required   LESS COMPETITIVE

Faculty: 524; IIA, ++$
Ph.D.'s: 56%
S/F Ratio: 19 to 1
Tuition: $940 ($3190)
R and B: $1540

The University of Wisconsin/Whitewater, founded in 1868, offers undergraduate programs in the arts and sciences, business, and education. The library contains 250,000 volumes and 9000 microfilm items, and subscribes to 1900 periodicals.

Environment: The 380-acre campus is located in a rural area 40 miles from Madison and 45 miles from Milwaukee. Fourteen dormitories house 2000 men and 2000 women. There are also facilities for commuting students.

Student Life: About 92% of the students come from Wisconsin. Ninety percent come from public schools. About 40% live on campus. About 3% are minority-group members. Housing is both single-sex and coed; there are visiting privileges in single-sex housing. Students may keep cars on campus. Day-care services are available, with fees based on ability to pay.

Organizations: The 8 fraternities on campus attract 8% of the men; the 7 sororities attract 6% of the women. Extracurricular activities include religious groups, clubs, publications, student government, and performing groups. Social and cultural events are held on campus.

Sports: The university fields intercollegiate teams in 12 sports for men and 10 for women. There are 6 intramural sports for men and 5 for women.

Handicapped: The entire campus is accessible to handicapped students. Special facilities include wheelchair ramps, parking areas, elevators, specially equipped rest rooms, and lowered drinking fountains and telephones. Special class scheduling can be arranged.

Graduates: The freshman dropout rate is 15%; 60% remain to graduate. Ten percent of the graduates pursue advanced degrees. About 40% enter business or industrial careers.

Services: Students are offered free health care, psychological counseling, career counseling, placement aid, tutoring, and remedial instruction.

Programs of Study: The B.A. and B.S. degrees are conferred. Associate and master's programs are also offered. Bachelor's degrees are awarded in the following subjects: AREA STUDIES (American), BUSINESS (accounting, business administration, business economics, business education, computer science, finance, management, marketing, secretarial studies), EDUCATION (counseling and guidance, early childhood, elementary, health/physical, secondary, special, speech correction), ENGLISH (English, journalism, speech), FINE AND PERFORMING ARTS (art education, art history, music, music education, theater/dramatics), HEALTH SCIENCES (speech pathology and audiology, speech therapy), LANGUAGES (French, German, Spanish), MATH AND SCIENCES (biology, chemistry, mathematics, physics), PREPROFESSIONAL (social work), SOCIAL SCIENCES (economics, geography, government/political science, history, international relations, psychology, public administration, social sciences, sociology). About 40% of the degrees are conferred in business, 25% in education, and 15% in social sciences.

Required: All students must complete a basic-studies program that includes courses in English, mathematics, science, history, fine arts, speech, social science, and physical education.

Special: A general studies degree is offered. Students may design their own majors. Study abroad is also possible.

Honors: A general honors program is available for freshmen.

Admissions: About 90% of the applicants for the 1981-82 freshman class were accepted. Students should rank in the top 75% of their graduating class. Recommendations, extracurricular activities, and advanced placement or honors courses are also considered.

Procedure: Neither the SAT nor the ACT is required for admissions, but one of the tests must be taken before registration. Application deadlines are open. New students are admitted to all terms. A rolling admissions policy is used. There is a $10 application fee.

Special: AP and CLEP credit is available.

Transfer: More than 700 transfer students are admitted annually. A 2.5 GPA is recommended. D grades are not accepted. Preference is given to students from other University of Wisconsin schools. Thirty credits must be completed in residence of the 120 required for a bachelor's degree. Application deadlines are June 1 (fall), November 1 (spring), and April 15 (summer).

Visiting: An orientation program is held for prospective students. Guides are available for informal visits. Visitors may sit in on classes. Visits are best scheduled on weekdays. The admissions office should be contacted for arrangements.

Financial Aid: About 40% of the students receive aid. Twenty-five percent work part-time on campus. The university offers scholarships, loans, grants, and part-time jobs (including CWS). Awards are made on a package basis. The college is a member of CSS. The FAF should be submitted.

Foreign Students: One percent of the full-time students come from foreign countries. The university offers these students special counseling and special organizations.

Admissions: Foreign students must score at least 500 on the TOEFL. No college entrance examination is required.

Procedure: Application deadlines are June 1 (fall), November 1 (spring), and April 15 (summer). Foreign students must submit a record of a physical examination. They also must present proof of adequate funds for 4 years of study. Foreign students must carry health insurance, which is available through the university for a fee.

Admissions Contact: I. A. Madsen, Director of Admissions.

VITERBO COLLEGE
La Crosse, Wisconsin 54601   B-4
   (608) 784-0040

F/T: 134M, 695W
P/T: 84M, 200W
Grad: none
Year: sems, ss
Appl: open
452 applied   334 accepted   244 enrolled
SAT: 440V 467M   ACT: 21   COMPETITIVE

Faculty: 69; IIB, -$
Ph.D.'s: 50%
S/F Ratio: 12 to 1
Tuition: $3380
R and B: $1700

Viterbo College, founded in 1931, is an independent liberal arts college affiliated with the Roman Catholic Church. The library houses 66,622 volumes and 447 microfilm items, and subscribes to 549 periodicals.

Environment: The college occupies 5 acres in a small city 140 miles from Minneapolis-St. Paul. Buildings include a nursing center, a classroom and administration building, and a fine-arts building. Dormitories and on-campus apartment buildings house 400 students.

Student Life: Eighty percent of the students are from Wisconsin. Eighty-four percent are public-school graduates. Forty-five percent live on campus. Sixty percent are Catholic; 40% are Protestant. Two percent of the students are minority-group members. College housing is single-sex, with visiting privileges. Students may keep cars on campus.

Organizations: There are no fraternities or sororities. The Viterbo Arts Center and the La Crosse Community Theatre provide cultural activities for students. There are both Catholic and Protestant organizations. Mt. La Crosse is accessible for skiing as is the Mississippi River for water sports.

Sports: The college sponsors 4 intercollegiate sports for men and 4 for women. There are 11 intramural sports for both men and women.

Handicapped: Eighty-five percent of the campus is accessible to handicapped students. Wheelchair ramps and elevators are provided.

Graduates: Twenty-five percent of the freshmen drop out by the end of the first year, and 60% remain to graduate. About 5% of the graduates pursue further study; 3% enter medical school and 2% enter dental school. Ninety percent pursue careers in business and industry.

Services: Students receive the following free services: health care, psychological counseling, tutoring, remedial instruction, and career counseling. Placement services are offered free to students and alumni.

Programs of Study: The B.A., B.S., B.Art.Ed., B.Mus., B.Mus.Ed., and B.S.N. degrees are awarded. Bachelor's degrees are offered in the following subjects: BUSINESS (accounting, art in business, business administration, computer management systems, computer science, home economics in business, management, personnel administration), EDUCATION (early childhood, elementary, secondary), ENGLISH (English, journalism), FINE AND PERFORMING ARTS (art, art education, art history, arts administration, music, music education, theater/dramatics), HEALTH SCIENCES (community medical dietetics, medical records administration, medical technology, nursing), MATH AND SCIENCES (biochemistry, biology, chemistry), PHILOSOPHY (religion), PREPROFESSIONAL (dentistry, engineering, home economics, law, medicine, ministry, pharmacy, veterinary), SOCIAL SCIENCES (human services, psychology, social sciences, sociology). Fifty-nine percent of the degrees are conferred in the health sciences.

Required: Students must take a basic-studies program that includes English, history, science, philosophy, theology, fine arts, and sociology or psychology.

Special: Viterbo offers a general studies degree. Juniors may spend the year abroad on their own or as participants in a study-abroad program sponsored by another college. Students may design their own major.

Admissions: Seventy-four percent of those who applied were accepted for the 1981–82 freshman class. Sixteen Carnegie units must be completed. Applicants must rank in the upper half of their graduating class and have a minimum GPA of 2.0. Other factors include advanced placement or honors courses, recommendations by school officials, evidence of special talents, extracurricular activities, and impressions made during an interview.

Procedure: The ACT is required. The application deadlines are open; students are admitted to all terms. The college uses a rolling admissions plan. A personal interview is recommended. A $10 fee must accompany the application.

Special: CLEP and AP credit is available.

Transfer: For fall 1981, 119 students applied, 88 were accepted, and 54 enrolled. A 2.0 GPA is essential. D grades do not transfer. Students must earn at least 30 credits in residence of the 128 needed for a bachelor's degree. Application deadlines are the same as those for freshmen.

Visiting: Regularly scheduled orientations for prospective students are held. Guides are available for informal tours. Visitors may stay overnight at the school and sit in on classes. Individual visits may be scheduled by phoning or writing the admissions office one week in advance.

Financial Aid: Eighty-seven percent of all students receive aid. Average aid from all sources available to a freshman in 1981–82 was $3900. Federal work-study funds are available in all departments. Loans are also available. Tuition may be paid in installments. The college is a member of CSS. The FAF, FFS, or SFS are accepted. Application deadlines are open.

Foreign Students: Three percent of the full-time students come from foreign countries. The college offers these students special counseling and special organizations.

Admissions: Foreign students must score at least 500 on the TOEFL. They also must take the SAT or ACT.

Procedure: Application deadlines are August 15 (fall) and December 15 (spring). Foreign students must submit a completed health form and evidence of adequate funds for 4 years of study. They must carry health insurance, which is available through the college.

Admissions Contact: M. Ray Duvall, Director of Admissions.

WISCONSIN CONSERVATORY OF MUSIC
E–4

Milwaukee, Wisconsin 53202 (414) 276-4350
(Recognized Candidate for Accreditation)

F/T: 53M, 36W	Faculty: 11; n/av
P/T: 8M, 4W	Ph.D.'s: 5%
Grad: 4M, 9W	S/F Ratio: 8 to 1
Year: sems, ss	Tuition: $3480
Appl: Aug. 1	R and B: n/app
91 applied 54 accepted	42 enrolled
SAT, ACT: not required	SPECIAL

The Wisconsin Conservatory of Music, founded in 1899, offers undergraduate and graduate programs in several areas of music. The library contains more than 30,000 volumes and subscribes to 12 periodicals.

Environment: The 2-building campus is situated in downtown Milwaukee, overlooking Lake Michigan. There is no student housing on campus.

Student Life: Ninety percent of the students come from Wisconsin. Twenty-two percent are minority-group members.

Organizations: The cultural offerings of Milwaukee are easily accessible.

Sports: The school offers no athletic program.

Handicapped: About 25% of the campus is accessible to handicapped students. Special facilities include lowered drinking fountains. Two counselors are available to handicapped students.

Graduates: Twenty percent of the freshmen drop out by the end of their first year, and 20% remain to graduate. About 40% of the graduates pursue advanced degrees. Sixty percent pursue careers in business and industry.

Services: Career counseling, tutoring, and remedial instruction are provided free to students.

Programs of Study: The B.Mus. degree is offered. Master's programs are also available. Bachelor's degrees are offered in: FINE AND PERFORMING ARTS (composition, performance, studio teaching, theory). Most students major in performance.

Special: Emphasis for the bachelor's degree may be in either jazz or classical music.

Admissions: Fifty-nine percent of those who applied were accepted for the 1981–82 freshman class. Applicants must be high school graduates. An audition, impressions made during an interview, personality, and recommendations are considered in the admissions decision.

Procedure: Neither the SAT nor the ACT is required. Application deadlines are August 1 (fall), December 15 (spring), and May 15 (summer). A rolling admissions policy is used. There is a $25 application fee.

Special: A deferred admissions plan is available. CLEP credit may be earned.

Transfer: For fall 1981, 24 students applied, 14 were accepted, and 8 enrolled. Good standing at the previous college and a 2.0 GPA are required. D grades are not acceptable. Students must spend at least 1 year in residence, earning 30 of the 130 credits needed for a bachelor's degree. Application deadlines are the same as those for freshman applicants.

Visiting: Guides are available for informal campus visits. Visitors may sit in on classes. Visits are best scheduled on weekdays. The admissions office should be contacted for arrangements.

Financial Aid: Seventy-five percent of the students receive financial aid. Nine percent work part-time on campus. The average award to freshmen from all sources in 1981–82 covered 60% of college costs. Scholarships are determined by audition and based on ability and achievement. All other aid is based on need. Loans and work contracts (including CWS) are also available. Tuition may be paid in installments. The conservatory is a member of CSS. The FAF is required. The deadline for aid applications is March 15.

Foreign Students: Two percent of the full-time students come from foreign countries. The conservatory offers these students special counseling.

Admissions: Foreign students must take the TOEFL or the University of Michigan Language Test. A score of at least 450 on the TOEFL is required. Foreign students also must audition.

Procedure: Application deadlines are August 1 (fall), December 15 (spring), and May 15 (summer). Foreign students must present proof of adequate funds for 1 year.

Admissions Contact: Gregory P. Fish, Registrar and Director of Admissions.

WYOMING

UNIVERSITY OF WYOMING
Laramie, Wyoming 82071
D-4
(307) 766-5160

F/T: 4069M, 3054W	Faculty: n/av; I, +$
P/T: 257M, 398W	Ph.D.'s: 90%
Grad: 1090M, 767W	S/F Ratio: 11 to 1
Year: sems, ss	Tuition: $616 ($2076)
Appl: July 15	R and B: $2152
3404 applied	3028 accepted 1625 enrolled
ACT: 21	NONCOMPETITIVE

The University of Wyoming, established in 1886, is a state-supported institution. Its library has 900,000 volumes and 140,000 reels of microfilm, and subscribes to 6500 periodicals.

Environment: The 735-acre rural campus is located on the eastern border of the historic Laramie plains, 135 miles from Denver, Colorado. Six dormitories house 3400 students and 424 married couples. Fraternities and sororities also offer housing.

Student Life: About 67% of the students are residents of Wyoming. Nearly 6% are members of minority groups. Campus housing is both coed and single-sex; there are visiting privileges in single-sex dorms. Students may keep cars on campus. Day-care services are available to full-time students.

Organizations: There are 9 fraternities and 6 sororities, to which 5% of the students belong. Besides the student government association, there are 145 special-interest and departmental clubs and organizations.

Sports: The university competes in 11 intercollegiate sports for men and 9 for women. Seventeen intramural sports are offered for men and 13 for women.

Handicapped: Ninety percent of the campus is accessible to physically handicapped students. Special facilities include wheelchair ramps, parking areas, elevators, lowered drinking fountains and telephones, and specially equipped rest rooms. Special class scheduling can be arranged. A staff of 6 counselors and 4 assistants is provided. Additional services for specific disabilities are available.

Graduates: About 35% of the freshmen drop out during their first year, and 49% remain to graduate. Of those graduates who apply, 65% are admitted to medical school and 90% to dental school. About 13% of the graduates begin careers in business and industry.

Services: Free health care, tutoring, remedial instruction, career and psychological counseling, and placement services are offered to all students.

Programs of Study: The university confers the B.A., B.S., B.Mus., and B.F.A. degrees. Master's and doctoral degrees are also awarded. Bachelor's degrees are offered in the following subjects: AREA STUDIES (American), BUSINESS (accounting, agribusiness, business administration, business education, computer science, farm/ranch management, finance, industrial relations, international agriculture, management, management information systems, marketing, office administration), EDUCATION (early childhood, elementary, health/physical, industrial, secondary), ENGLISH (agricultural communications, communication theory, English, journalism), FINE AND PERFORMING ARTS (art, art education, dance, music, music education, radio/TV, theater/dramatics), HEALTH SCIENCES (medical technology, nursing, speech therapy), LANGUAGES (French, German, Greek/Latin, Russian, Spanish), MATH AND SCIENCES (animal science, astronomy, astrophysics, biochemistry; biology, botany, chemistry, crop science, entomology, food science, geology, mathematics, microbiology, natural sciences, physical sciences, physics, range management, soil science, statistics, wildlife conservation and management, zoology), PHILOSOPHY (humanities, philosophy), PREPROFESSIONAL (agriculture, architecture, engineering—bioengineering, engineering—agricultural, engineering—architectural, engineering—chemical, engineering—civil, engineering—computer, engineering—construction, engineering—electrical, engineering—mechanical, engineering—petroleum, home economics, law, library science, pharmacy, social work), SOCIAL SCIENCES (administration of justice, agricultural economics, anthropology, economics, geography, government/political science, history, international relations, psychology, social sciences, sociology). About 18% of the degrees conferred are in education, 13% are in business, and 13% are in math and sciences.

Special: Nonmajor preprofessional programs include occupational therapy, physical therapy, dentistry, forestry, medicine, and veterinary science. The university offers a general-studies degree.

Honors: Twenty-five national honor societies are represented on campus.

Admissions: About 89% of those who applied were accepted for the 1981–82 freshman class. The ACT scores of those who enrolled were as follows: 49% below 21, 21% between 21 and 23, 14% between 24 and 25, 13% between 26 and 28, and 3% above 28. All graduates of accredited Wyoming high schools are eligible. Out-of-state residents must have at least a 2.5 average and rank in the upper half of their graduating class. State residents receive preference. Special talents and advanced placement or honors courses also are considered.

Procedure: The ACT is required of nonresident students. New students are admitted to both semesters and the summer session. Applications are due July 15 (fall), December 15 (spring), and May 15 (summer). There is no application fee.

Special: Students may earn credit through AP, CLEP, and university departmental exams.

Transfer: For fall 1981, the university received 1419 applications, accepted 1184, and enrolled 698 students. Transfers are accepted for all classes. A minimum average of C is required. D grades are acceptable for admission but may not fulfill degree requirements. At least 30 semester hours of the 120–164 necessary for the bachelor's degree must be taken at the university. Application deadlines are the same as those for freshmen.

Visiting: The university holds seven 2-day orientation sessions in July for entering students. These include meetings with faculty, tours of the campus, and preregistration. Arrangements for informal visits, guided tours, classroom visits, and overnight stays can be made through the admissions office.

Financial Aid: About 80% of the students receive aid. Scholarships, loans, and grants are available. The average award to freshmen was $1100 in 1981–82. There are work-study programs in 60 departments, and approximately 70% of the students earn money through part-time employment. The university is a member of CSS. The application deadline is February 15.

Foreign Students: Nearly 4% of the full-time students are from foreign countries. Special counseling and special organizations are available.

Admissions: Students must score at least 525 on the TOEFL. They also must take the SAT.

Procedure: The application deadline for fall, the only semester to which undergraduates are admitted, is March 1. Students must present proof of adequate funds for at least 1 year. Health insurance is required, and is available through the university for a fee.

Admissions Contact: Arland L. Grover, Director of Admissions.

CANADA AND MEXICO

About five percent of the undergraduate students enrolled in Canadian colleges and universities come from the United States and other foreign countries. All Canadian universities admit foreign students—although some have a quota on the number they will accept—and will give interested students information on how their academic qualifications are equated with Canadian requirements.

Canada has sixty-five non-theological colleges and universities, twelve of which are affiliated with, and grant degrees through, larger institutions. Almost all Canadian colleges are coeducational. Of the sixty-five, six use French as the language of instruction, six use both French and English, and the rest primarily use English. This section contains individual profiles for the nine largest English-language universities in Canada, those that enroll more than 10,000 students. Affiliated with each of these universities is a number of general, theological, or residential colleges, which also have been listed here. The names and addresses of the three French-speaking colleges with enrollments of more than 10,000 may be found at the end of this introduction.

Admissions requirements vary much more among Canadian universities than among American schools, and the amount of time it takes to earn degrees also varies more widely.

Each Canadian province has its own pattern of elementary and secondary education; provinces may require eleven, twelve, or thirteen years of schooling. Universities generally base admissions requirements on the educational pattern of the province in which they are located. Therefore, foreign students may have to complete a year or more of college-level work before some universities will consider their applications. Students also may be required to take special courses in specific subject areas at some point during their college careers.

Some universities require American students to submit SAT and AT scores, but most rely primarily on high school performance in determining admission. Students from British Commonwealth countries may have to pass appropriate A- or O-level exams. Students whose native language is not English generally are required to take the TOEFL, the University of Michigan English Language Test, the University of Cambridge Certificate of Proficiency in English, or some other test of competency in English. Some universities also require English-speaking students to take English tests at the start of their freshman year to determine whether a student needs remedial instruction.

Universities also usually ask foreign students to submit, along with their high school records, a notarized translation of those records into English or French. However, no Canadian university requires students to be fluent in both languages.

Once a student is accepted, he or she must obtain a student visa from a Canadian diplomatic mission in his or her home country. The mission will ask the student to provide evidence of university admission and proof of adequate funds to pay all expenses in Canada as well as the cost of the journey home. Visas are good only for a specific program at a specific institution for a specific period of time, and cannot be changed once the student is in Canada. Except in special cases, a student visa prohibits its holder from obtaining a job in Canada.

All students in Canada, including those from foreign countries, must be covered by a public or private hospital and medical insurance program.

Canadian universities, like those in the United States, grant three levels of degrees: bachelor's or first professional, master's, and doctoral. Earning the first degree can take three to five years. A general, or unspecialized, program leading to a Bachelor of Arts or Bachelor of Science usually can be completed in three years. An honors degree, earned in a specialized program, usually requires four years. Students must meet more rigorous requirements to enter an honors-degree program and must maintain high grades to remain in it. But students who enter graduate programs with a general degree usually must study a year longer than those with honors degrees. First professional degrees in some fields may take more than four years to earn, and students may be required to spend two or three years in general academic study before enrolling in the professional program.

Virtually all universities have organizations for foreign students, and sponsor international student centers and advisers. There also are national organizations that aid foreign students, including the World University Service of Canada and the Canadian Bureau for International Education, which arranges for representatives to meet foreign students arriving at Canadian airports.

Universities and colleges are heavily subsidized by provincial and federal governments, and tuition fees actually cover less than fifteen percent of university operating costs. Canadian colleges charge different fees for different programs, unlike American institutions, which charge the same tuition regardless of a student's major. Each profile lists the range of tuitions, which may or may not include student fees. Some universities have higher fees for foreign students, and where that is the case, the profile includes just the higher fee. In all cases, you should check with the university in which you are interested to obtain the most up-to-date information about tuition and room-and-board charges.

Special financial-aid programs are available to foreign students, including the Commonwealth Scholarship and Fellowship Plan. Agencies that provide aid to foreign students include the Canadian International Development Agency, the Social Sciences and Humanities Research Council, the Association of Universities and Colleges of Canada, and several cultural-exchange programs in effect between Canada and other countries. Students interested in applying for aid should contact a Canadian diplomatic mission in their home country and, for information on cultural exchange programs, their own nation's education department or ministry.

Students who would like information on the three largest universities in which French is the language of instruction should write directly to the schools and request the booklet *Livret à l'usage des étrangers et non-quebécois* (Handbook for Foreign and Non-Quebec Applicants). The schools and their addresses and telephone numbers are:

Université Laval
Cité universitaire
Québec (Québec) Canada G1K 7P4
(418) 656-2131

988 CANADA AND MEXICO

Université de Montréal
Case postale 6128
Montréal (Québec) Canada H3C 3J7
(514) 343-6111

Université du Québec
2875 boulevard Laurier
Ste-Foy (Québec) Canada G1V 2M3
(418) 657-3551

Students interested in more information on studying in Canada can write to the following sources:

Association of Universities and Colleges of Canada
151 Slater Street
Ottawa, Ontario, Canada K1P 5N1
(publications include *Notes for Foreign Students, A Survey of Facilities for Physically and Visually Handicapped and Deaf Students at Canadian Universities, Directory of Canadian Universities*)

Canadian Bureau for International Education
141 Laurier Avenue West, Suite 809
Ottawa, Ontario, Canada K1P 5J3
(publications include *Guide to Foreign Student Authorizations for Canada* and *Funding Sources*, a handbook on financial aid for foreign students)

Canadian Consulate General
1251 Avenue of the Americas
16th Floor (Library)
New York, New York 10020
(212) 586-2400

Canadian Employment and Immigration Commission
Ottawa, Ontario, Canada K1A OJ9
(publications include *Studying in Canada: Facts for Foreign Students*)

Canadian International Development Agency
Place du Centre 200, Promenade du Portage
Hull (Québec) Canada K1A OG4

Social Sciences and Humanities Research Council
255 Albert Street
P.O. Box 1610
Ottawa, Ontario, Canada K1P 6G4

Statistics Canada
Education, Science, and Culture Division
R.H. Coats Building, 16th Floor
Holland and Scott Streets
Ottawa, Ontario, Canada K1A OT6
(publications include *Tuition and Living Costs at Canadian Universities*, updated annually)

World University Service of Canada
880 Wellington Street
Suite 99
Ottawa, Ontario, Canada K1R 6K7

The Mexican schools presented in this section are the only two accredited by a regional accrediting association in the United States. Both are accredited by the Southern Association of Colleges and Schools. For information on applying to Mexican schools and on immigration regulations, American students can write or call:

Mexican Consulate
8 East 41st Street
New York, New York 10017
(212) 689-0456

McGILL UNIVERSITY
Montreal, Québec, Canada H3A 2T5   (514) 392-4311

F/T:	11,803M&W	Year:	sems, ss
P/T:	3333M&W	Appl:	Mar. 1
Grad:	4100M&W	F/T Faculty:	1545
Tuition:	$50 p/c	R and B:	$2080–2470

McGill University, founded in 1821, is a private, nondenominational institution that grants undergraduate, graduate, and professional degrees. The 23 libraries contain more than 3.9 million volumes and 27,400 microfilm items, and subscribe to 16,100 periodicals.

Environment: The 80-acre campus, located on the slopes of Mount Royal in the city of Montreal, includes approximately 75 buildings, including a student center, a gymnasium, and a concert hall. A second campus, Macdonald College, is located in Ste-Anne-de-Bellevue, 25 miles from Montreal, and houses the Faculty of Agriculture. On the main campus, 4 coed residence halls house 816 students and 1 women's residence houses 257 students. The university also maintains apartments for married students.

Student Life

Organizations: The more than 250 student groups include student government; international, religious, and political clubs; drama and music societies; a campus radio station; and a student newspaper. Seven fraternities and 4 sororities have chapters on campus.

Sports: The university fields intercollegiate teams in 11 sports for men and 7 for women. Intramural sports also are available.

Services: The university provides free placement aid, career and psychological counseling, and health services. Fees are charged for tutoring or remedial instruction.

Programs of Study: The university awards the following undergraduate degrees: B.Sc. (agriculture), B.Sc. (agricultural engineering), B.Sc. (architecture), B.Arch., B.A., B.Ed., B.Eng., B.Sc. (food science), B.Com., B.Mus., B.Sc. (nursing), B.Sc. (occupational therapy), B.Sc. (physical therapy), B.Th., B.Sc., and B.S.W. Special programs are offered in African studies, Jewish studies, North American studies, Middle East studies, environmental studies, and humanistic studies. Associate, master's, and doctoral degrees also are available, as are professional degrees in law, dentistry, and medicine.

Admissions: American students must be high school graduates (at least 1 year of further preparation is required of applicants to programs in architecture, physical or occupational therapy, or social work). They must also take the SAT and, possibly, ATs. Students from Great Britain and other Commonwealth countries must pass appropriate A- or O-level exams. Students from other foreign countries should submit SAT and AT scores, and must take the TOEFL if their native language is not English.

Procedure: Applications must be submitted by March 1 for fall admission and November 1 for spring admission.

Affiliated: Montreal Diocesan Theological College (Anglican), Presbyterian College of Montreal (Presbyterian, theology), United Theological College of Montreal (United Church, theology).

UNIVERSITY OF ALBERTA
Edmonton, Alberta, Canada T6G 2E5   (403) 432-3111

F/T:	16,176M&W	Year:	sems, ss
P/T:	2307M&W	Appl:	July 1
Grad:	2633M&W	F/T Faculty:	1790
Tuition:	$621–895	R and B:	$1890–2340

The University of Alberta, founded in 1908, is a privately supported institution offering undergraduate and graduate instruction. The library system contains over 2 million volumes, 500,000 documents, and 980,000 microfilm items, and subscribes to 15,000 periodicals.

Environment: The 154-acre campus is located on the North Saskatchewan River in a city of 491,000 people. The campus includes 35 academic buildings, 2 swimming pools, a year-round ice rink, 3 student residences, a student apartment complex, and married-student housing.

Student Life

Organizations: Campus activities include the student government and a semiweekly student newspaper.

Sports: Intercollegiate, intramural, and recreational sports are available. There are facilities for gymnastics, handball, ice sports, racquetball, squash, swimming, tennis, weight lifting, wrestling, and other sports.

Services: Academic and personal counseling, and health care are available to students.

Programs of Study: The university confers the B.A., B.Comm., B.Ed., B.F.A., B.Mus., B.O.T., B.P.E., B.P.T., B.Sc. (medical laboratory science), B.Sc. (food science), B.Sc. (medicine), and B.Sc. (home economics) degrees. Bachelor's degrees are awarded in agriculture, agricultural engineering, forestry, food science, pre-veterinary medicine, liberal arts, business, education, engineering, fine arts, home economics, medical laboratory science, music, nursing, pharmacy, physical education, recreation administration, physical and occupational therapy, speech pathology and audiology, sciences, and theology. Bilingual programs are available. Associate, master's and doctoral degrees are also awarded.

Admissions: Foreign applicants must have completed coursework equivalent to that of grade 12 in Alberta. The SAT and ATs are recommended. U.S. applicants must have undertaken full academic high school programs and show satisfactory SAT and AT scores. Students who have studied English as a second language must present a TOEFL score of at least 600.

Procedure: Applications must be submitted by July 1. New students are admitted only to the winter session, which begins in September.

Affiliated: Camrose Lutheran College (Lutheran), Canadian Union College (Seventh-day Adventist), Concordia Lutheran College (Lutheran), St. Joseph's College (Roman Catholic), St. Stephen's College (United Church, theology).

UNIVERSITY OF BRITISH COLUMBIA
Vancouver, British Columbia,   (604) 228-2211
Canada V6T 1W5

F/T:	17,198M&W	Year:	see profile
P/T:	3853M&W	Appl:	Apr. 30
Grad:	3293M&W	F/T Faculty:	1817
Tuition:	$688–1043	R and B:	$1851–2012

The University of British Columbia, established in 1908, is a province-supported institution offering undergraduate, graduate, and professional degrees. The library holds more than 4 million volumes and microfilm items.

Environment: The 1000-acre campus is located on the Point Grey peninsula in the city of Vancouver. The more than 200 buildings include a student union, gymnasiums, residence halls for single students, and married-student housing.

Student Life

Organizations: Campus activities include student government, a student newspaper, groups for international students, and more than 150 clubs that cover a range of interests from Chinese literature to skydiving. A number of fraternities and sororities have chapters on campus.

Sports: The university fields intercollegiate teams in 11 sports for men and 8 for women. Intramural sports include softball, basketball, cricket, cross country, fencing, golf, hockey, karate, rugby, skiing, soccer, swimming, tennis, volleyball, and wrestling.

Services: Health care, placement aid, and academic and career counseling are provided.

Programs of Study: The university awards the following undergraduate degrees: B.Sc. (agriculture), B.Land Arch., B.Arch., B.A., B.F.A., B.Com., B.Ed., B. Applied Sc. (engineering), B.Sc. (pharmacy), B.P.E., B. Recreational Ed., B. Home Ec., B.Med.Lab.Sc., B.Mus., B.S.N., B.S. Rehabilitation, B.Sc., and B.S.W. Associate, master's, doctoral, and professional degrees also are awarded. The winter session lasts from September through April. Spring and summer sessions are available.

Admissions: Foreign students must have completed coursework equivalent to that of Canadian secondary schools. They must demonstrate an adequate knowledge of English by passing a language test administered by the university.

Procedure: Non-Canadian students must submit applications by April 30. New students generally are admitted only in the fall. Evidence of adequate funds is required.

Affiliated: Carey Hall (Baptist, men), Regent College (theology), St. Andrew's Hall (Presbyterian, men), St. Mark's College (Roman Catholic, men), Vancouver School of Theology.

UNIVERSITY OF MANITOBA
Winnipeg, Manitoba, Canada R3T 2N2   (204) 474-8880

F/T:	11,166M&W	Year:	see profile
P/T:	5576M&W	Appl:	see profile
Grad:	2298M&W	F/T Faculty:	1264
Tuition:	$630–855	R and B:	$1652–2149

The University of Manitoba, founded in 1877, is a publicly supported institution that grants undergraduate, graduate, and professional degrees. The university libraries contain more than 1.1 million volumes, 16,000 audiovisual items, and 540,000 microfilm items, and subscribe to 13,100 periodicals.

Environment: The 685-acre campus is located in the suburb of Fort Garry, 7 miles from the center of Winnipeg. The campus includes 35 classroom buildings, 2 gymnasiums, 2 recreation halls, and an ice rink. Agricultural facilities are located on this campus and on an 1100-acre experiment station at Glenlea, 26 kilometers away. The schools of medicine, dentistry, medical rehabilitation, and dental hygiene are located near the Winnipeg Health Sciences Center. The Fort Garry Campus has 6 dormitories that house 1100 students.

Student Life

Organizations: Campus activities include student government; debating, drama, choral, and instrumental groups; a radio station; publications; and a film society.

Sports: The university fields intercollegiate teams in 10 sports for men and 10 for women. Intramural sports include softball, basketball, fencing, field hockey, football, gymnastics, golf, ice hockey, karate, lacrosse, skiing, soccer, swimming, tennis, and track.

Services: Academic and psychiatric counseling, health care, and placement services are available to students.

Programs of Study: The university confers the B.A., B.Comm., B.Int. Design., B.S.Ag., B. Environmental Studies, B.Ed., B.Sc. (engineering), B.F.A., B. Home Ec., B.O.T., B.P.T., B.Mus., B.Nursing., B.Sc.Pharm., B.P.E., B.Sc., and B.S.W. Associate, master's and doctoral degrees also are available, as are professional degrees in medicine, dentistry, and law.

Admissions: Applicants from the United States must be high school graduates with an average of at least C and must submit SAT scores. Students from other foreign countries must present certificates equivalent to those required of Canadian applicants. All non-Canadian students whose native language is not English must score at least 550 on the TOEFL.

Procedure: Applications for programs in medicine must be submitted by January 5; for dentistry, by February 14; for law and pharmacy by March 1; for social work, commerce, administrative studies, integrated home economics/education program, dental hygiene, engineering, environmental studies, fine arts, interior design, music, nursing, and physical education, by May 1; and for all other programs, by June 1.

Affiliated: Collège universitaire de Saint-Boniface (French), St. John's College, St. Paul's College, Canadian Mennonite Bible College (theology, sacred music), Canadian Nazarene College (theology, sacred music), St. Andrew's College (Ukranian Greek Orthodox ministry).

CANADA AND MEXICO

UNIVERSITY OF OTTAWA
Ottawa, Ontario, Canada K1N 6N5   (613) 231-3311

F/T:	10,455M&W	Year:	sems, ss
P/T:	6518M&W	Appl:	see profile
Grad:	2662M&W	F/T Faculty:	944
Tuition:	$1744	R:	$844–992

The University of Ottawa, founded in 1848, is a bilingual, private institution subsidized by the government of Ontario. The university grants undergraduate, graduate, and professional degrees. The main undergraduate library holds more than 1 million volumes and 850,000 manuscripts and audiovisual items, and subscribes to 11,940 periodicals.

Environment: The 42-acre campus, located in the Sandy Hill distict of Ottawa, includes 17 instructional buildings and 4 residence halls that house a total of 1268 students.

Student Life

Organizations: Campus activities include student government, a radio station, 2 bimonthly newspapers, and a variety of special-interest clubs.

Sports: Intercollegiate and intramural sports are available.

Services: The university provides health services, career and personal counseling, and placement aid.

Programs of Study: The university confers the following bachelor's degrees: B. Administration, B.Comm., B. Management Sci., B.P.A., B.A., B.Mus., B. Canon Law, B.Ed., B. Applied Sc. (engineering and engineering management), B.P.E., B.Sc. (kinanthropology), B.Sc. (nursing), B.Sc., B. Social Sciences, and B.Th. Associate, master's, and doctoral degrees also are available, as are professional degrees in law and medicine.

Admissions: American students must be high school graduates and have completed an additional year of study comparable to the fifth year of Ontario secondary schools. They may have to meet additional requirements for the specific program in which they seek to enroll. All foreign students must demonstrate fluency in either English or French. Those whose native language is neither are required to take the TOEFL, the university's Test of French as a Second Language, or a similar test.

Procedure: Application deadlines vary with the major. Students should contact the university for information.

Affiliated: Saint Paul University (Roman Catholic—theology and cannon law).

UNIVERSITY OF TORONTO
Toronto, Ontario, Canada M5S 1A1   (416) 978-2011

F/T:	28,017M&W	Year:	sems, ss
P/T:	11,394M&W	Appl:	see profile
Grad:	9489M&W	F/T Faculty:	2756
Tuition:	$1650 (foreign students)	R and B:	$1675–1970

The University of Toronto, founded in 1827, is a province-supported university that offers undergraduate, graduate, and professional degrees. The library system contains 4.5 million volumes and 1.1 million microtexts, and subscribes to 27,000 periodicals.

Environment: The main section of the university, the St. George Campus, is located in downtown Toronto. The Scarborough Campus and the Erindale Campus are each 33 kilometers from the main campus. The university also owns a dentistry building in the city's hospital district, a 20,000-acre forest north of the city, and the David Dunlap Observatory. Together, the campuses provide residence facilities for 1919 single students and a married-student complex housing 710 families.

Student Life

Organizations: Campus activities include student government, 2 student newspapers, and a number of special-interest clubs.

Sports: The university fields intercollegiate teams in 18 sports for men and 14 for women. Intramural sports include basketball, field and ice hockey, lacrosse, rugby, skiing, soccer, and volleyball.

Services: The university provides health care, career and psychological counseling, placement services, and shuttle buses among the campuses.

Programs of Study: The university offers the following undergraduate degrees: B.Arch., B.Land.Arch., B.A., B.Comm., B.Sc. Dentistry (dental hygiene), B.Ed., B. Applied Sc. (engineering), B.Sc.F., B.Sc. (occupational therapy), B.Sc., (physical therapy), B.Mus., B.Sc. Nursing, B.Sc. Pharmacy, B.Phys.Hlth.Ed., and B.Sc. Master's and doctoral degrees also are available, as are professional degrees in law, dentistry, and medicine.

Admissions: American students must have completed a year at an accredited university, although high school graduates with excellent grades and AP scores will be considered. The Arts and Science Faculty will consider American high school graduates with an average of 600 or better on the SAT and 3 ATs. Students from other foreign countries may be asked to present at least 1 year of university-level work. Those whose native language is not English may be required to take TOEFL or a similar test.

Procedure: Applications for applied science and engineering, forestry and landscape architecture, music, nursing, pharmacy, and physical and health education programs must be filed by April 1. Applications for arts and science programs are due by June 30. Students interested in other programs should contact the university for application deadlines.

Affiliated: Emmanuel College of Victoria University (theology), Knox College (Presbyterian, theology), Regis College (Roman Catholic, theology), University of St. Michael's College, University of Trinity College, Victoria University, Wycliffe College (Anglican, theology), Royal Conservatory of Music, Ontario Institute for Studies in Education, Massey College (graduate residential), Pontifical Institute of Medieval Studies (graduate).

UNIVERSITY OF WATERLOO
Waterloo, Ontario, Canada N2L 3G1   (519) 885-1211

F/T:	13,108M&W	Year:	sems
P/T:	4497M&W	Appl:	July 1
Grad:	1705M&W	F/T Faculty:	730
Tuition:	$897–946		
(regular) $537–561 (co-op)		R and B:	$1810–2100

The University of Waterloo, founded in 1957, is a publicly supported institution that awards undergraduate and graduate degrees. It also offers an extensive cooperative education program. The libraries hold 1.5 million volumes and microfilm items.

Environment: The 1000-acre campus is located in Waterloo. The twin cities of Waterloo and Kitchener have a total population of more than 170,000. All campus buildings are accessible to handicapped students. Housing is available on campus through the church colleges affiliated with the university, and married-student apartments are provided.

Student Life

Organizations: Campus activities include student government, a radio station, a newspaper, an arts board that sponsors drama and music productions, special-interest and political groups, and ethnic-student clubs.

Sports: The university fields intercollegiate teams in 17 sports for men and 11 for women. Intramural sports include softball, basketball, hockey, football, golf, sailing, skiing, soccer, swimming, tennis, track, and volleyball.

Services: Health care, placement services, and psychological counseling are available.

Programs of Study: The university confers the following undergraduate degrees: B. Environmental Studies, B.Arch., B.A., B. Applied Sc. (engineering), B.Sc. (kinesiology and health studies), B.A. (recreation), B.Sc. (dance), B.A. (dance), B.Math., and B.Sc. Students may design their own integrated-studies programs. Master's and doctoral degrees are also available, as are professional degrees in optometry. In the cooperative study program, students alternate terms of full-time study with terms of full-time work in their career fields. Students spend 8 academic terms of 4 months each in study, and 6 terms working in business, industry, or education. Some departments offer only cooperative education programs, others only standard college programs, and some offer a choice.

Admissions: American students must be high school graduates and have completed an additional year of study comparable to the fifth year of Ontario secondary schools. Students from other foreign countries also may be required to complete some college work. Applicants whose native language is not English may be required to take the TOEFL; the university generally requires a minimum score of 600. Students seeking to enroll in cooperative programs must gain landed-immigrant status before applying and must demonstrate to the admissions committee that they can perform satisfactorily during their work terms.

Procedure: Foreign students should apply by July 1 for priority consideration.

Affiliated: Renison College (Anglican-supported), St. Paul's College (United Church), Conrad Grebel College (Mennonite), University of St. Jerome's College (Roman Catholic).

THE UNIVERSITY OF WESTERN ONTARIO
London, Ontario, Canada N6A 3K7   (519) 679-2111

F/T:	14,775M&W	Year:	sems, ss
P/T:	4347M&W	Appl:	Aug. 1
Grad:	2436M&W	F/T Faculty:	1298
Tuition:	$1714 (foreign students)	R and B:	$1887–2157

The University of Western Ontario, chartered in 1878, is a public institution that confers undergraduate, graduate, and professional degrees. The library contains 1.4 million volumes and 1.1 million reels of microfilm, and subscribes to 11,000 periodicals.

Environment: The 402-acre campus is located on the shore of the Thames River. The 72 buildings include a health-sciences center, an observatory, and residence halls that house over 2400 students. Four hundred apartment and townhouse units are provided for married students.

Student Life

Organizations: Campus activities include student government; a biweekly newspaper and other periodicals; and academic, debating, music, drama, political, and art clubs. About 2% of the students belong to the 8 fraternities and 3 sororities with chapters on campus.

Sports: The university fields intercollegiate teams in 22 sports. Intramural sports include soccer, touch football, lacrosse, cross country, tennis, hockey, softball, basketball, volleyball, squash, and racquetball.

Services: Free placement assistance, career and psychological counseling, health care, and tutoring or remedial instruction are available.

Programs of Study: The university awards the following undergraduate degrees: B.A., B.F.A., B.A. (business), B.Ed., B.Eng.Sc., B.Sc. (communicative disorders), B.Sc. (occupational therapy), B.Sc. (physical therapy), B.Mus., B.Mus. Arts, B.Sc. Nursing, B.A. (physical education), B.Sc., B.S.H.E., B.A. (secretarial and administrative studies), B.A. (administrative and commercial studies), B.Min., and B.S.W. Associate, master's and doctoral degrees also are offered, as are professional degrees in law, medicine, dentistry, and ministry.

Admissions: American students must have graduated from an accredited high school with an A average. Additional academic courses may be required in some majors. Students from other foreign countries generally must show education equivalent to that required of Canadian students and may be required to have completed at least 1 year of university study.

Procedure: Applications must be filed by August 1 for fall admission.

Affiliated: Brescia College (Roman Catholic, women), Huron College, King's College (Roman Catholic).

YORK UNIVERSITY
Downsview, Ontario, Canada M3J 1P3   (416) 667-2100

F/T:	10,174M&W	Year:	sems, ss
P/T:	10,045M&W	Appl:	see profile
Grad:	2476M&W	F/T Faculty:	1033
Tuition:	$1740 (foreign students)	R and B:	$1736–1913

York University, founded in 1959, is a province-supported institution that awards undergraduate, graduate, and professional degrees. The libraries contain more than 1 million volumes and an equivalent number of microfilm items and audiovisual materials.

Environment: The 570-acre main campus, located on the edge of metropolitan Toronto, houses most academic buildings and athletic facilities, a religious center, and an observatory. The nearby 82-acre Glendon Campus houses Glendon College, a largely residential undergraduate college affiliated with the university. Apartments and residence halls on the main campus accommodate 2759 students, and residence halls at the Glendon Campus house 427 students.

Student Life

Organizations: Campus activities include student government, a radio station, publications, and special-interest clubs. Jewish and Christian religious groups are available.

Sports: The university fields intercollegiate teams in 17 sports for men and 13 for women. Intramural sports include softball, basketball, cross country, fencing, hockey, football, karate, rugby, soccer, swimming, tennis, volleyball, and wrestling.

Services: Free health care is available to all students, and free legal aid is available to those with low incomes. Psychological and career counseling is provided, as is special counseling for handicapped students. Placement services are also available.

Programs of Study: The university awards the following undergraduate degrees: B.B.A., B.A., B.Ed., B.F.A., B.Sc., B.A. (administration), and B.S.W. Master's, doctoral, and law degrees also are available.

Admissions: American students must be high school graduates and submit SAT scores. All foreign students must present certificates of education equivalent to that required of Canadian students. Those whose native language is not English must present evidence of fluency in English.

Procedure: Application deadlines can be obtained from the university admissions office.

Affiliated: Joseph E. Atkinson College (evening, part time), Glendon College (bilingual), Osgoode Hall Law School.

INSTITUTO TECHNOLOGICO Y DE ESTUDIOS SUPERIORES DE MONTERREY
Monterrey, Mexico

F/T, P/T, Grad:		Year:	sems, ss
	13,155M&W	Appl:	July 15
		F/T Faculty:	295
Tuition:	$925	R and B:	$850

Instituto Technologico y de Estudios Superiores de Monterrey, a privately controlled institution, emphasizes technology and science but also offers programs in the liberal arts. The library contains more than 100,000 volumes and subscribes to 21,000 periodicals.

Environment: The 239-acre campus is located in a large city in the Sierra Madres, about 120 miles from the Texas border and 140 miles from Laredo. Thirteen dormitories accommodate about 1200 students.

Student Life

Organizations: Extracurricular activities include student government, drama, concerts, films, lectures, a student newspaper, radio and television stations, and music ensembles.

Sports: Intercollegiate and intramural sports include football, basketball, soccer, softball, baseball, tennis, track, swimming, and gymnastics.

Services: The institute provides counseling and health care for students and placement services for graduates.

Programs of Study: The institute grants degrees equivalent to the B.A. and B.S. Master's and doctoral degrees are also available.

Admissions: Students are selected on the basis of high school grades and scores on entrance examinations. Applicants should have a C average or better. Recommendations from high school officials are required.

Procedure: The SAT is required and must be taken by May of the senior year. The application deadline for fall admission is July 15. Notification is made on a rolling basis beginning in May.

UNIVERSIDAD DE LAS AMERICAS
Puebla, Mexico

Universidad de las Americas is a private university that offers programs leading to bachelor's and master's degrees. It has a total enrollment of 2097 students, 60% of whom are men.

Information on Canadian schools from *Directory of Canadian Universities* is used by permission of the Association of Universities and Colleges of Canada.

COLLEGES WITH SPECIAL PROGRAMS

RELIGIOUS

Included here are four-year, regionally accredited institutions and candidates for accreditation whose specialized programs of study prepare students for the clergy or for other church-related vocations. In general, the admissions requirements are not based primarily on academic criteria, but on evidence of special interest or religious commitment. Many other colleges and universities offer religious programs in addition to regular academic curricula. These are included in the regular section of this book. Any liberal arts programs offered by the schools listed here are limited in scope. Regionally accredited religious schools that offer a bachelor's degree program beginning with the junior or senior year of undergraduate study are included in the Upper Division list in this book.

CALIFORNIA

CHRIST COLLEGE IRVINE D-5
Irvine, California 92715 (714) 752-6222

F/T: 105M, 107W	Appl: Aug. 15
P/T: 10M, 4W	Faculty: 32
Grad: none	Tuition: $2790
SAT: 450V 467M	R: $975

Christ College Irvine, founded in 1972, is a liberal arts institution affiliated with the Lutheran Church—Missouri Synod. The B.A. degree is offered with majors in Christian education, pre-deaconess, pre-law, pre-ministry, social welfare, teacher education, and general liberal arts. Associate degrees are also conferred.

PACIFIC CHRISTIAN COLLEGE D-5
Fullerton, California 92631 (714) 879-3901

F/T: 122M, 144W	Appl: July 31
P/T: 53M, 50W	Faculty: n/av
Grad: 26M, 6W	Tuition: $2670
SAT: required	R & B: $1650–3280

Pacific Christian College, founded in 1928, is affiliated with the Christian Churches/Church of Christ. The college serves to assist young men and women in preparation for a consecrated, dynamic, and educated ministry for the church and for about 40 other occupations. The B.A. degree is conferred in child development, children's ministry, Christian education, diversified general studies, English, management, missions, music, preaching, psychology, social science, youth education, and other fields. Associate and master's degrees are also awarded.

PATTEN COLLEGE B-3
(Formerly Patten Bible College)
Oakland, California 94601 (415) 533-8300

F/T: 20M, 35W	Appl: open
P/T: 40M, 45W	Faculty: 20
Grad: none	Tuition: $2006
SAT or ACT: required	R & B: $1930

Patten College, founded in 1945, is affiliated with the Christian Evangelical Churches of America. The college offers 2- and 4-year liberal arts and ministerial training programs; associate and B.A. degrees are offered. Areas of emphasis for B.A. degrees are Christian education, ministerial, pre-seminary, and an elective sequence of study. Applicants must be able to testify to a definite experience of conversion and be living a separated Christian life.

ST. JOHN'S COLLEGE C-4
Camarillo, California 93010 (805) 482-4697

F/T: 86M	Appl: Aug. 1
P/T: none	Faculty: 12
Grad: none	Tuition, R & B:
SAT: 400V 400M	$2400

St. John's College, founded in 1927, is controlled by the Vincentian Fathers. St. John's is a liberal arts college that prepares students for the Roman Catholic priesthood. The college confers the B.A. degree in scholastic philosophy. This program is followed by a 4-year program in theology.

ST. PATRICK'S COLLEGE B-3
Mountain View, California 94042 (415) 967-9501

F/T: 99M	Appl: open
P/T: none	Faculty: n/av
Grad: none	Tuition: $2080
SAT: required	R & B: $750

St. Patrick's College, established in 1898, is a small liberal arts college for men. It is under private control and is affiliated with the Roman Catholic Church under the direction of the Sulpician Fathers. The purpose of the college is to train young men for the Catholic priesthood. The college confers the B.A. degree in humanities, philosophy, and religious studies.

CONNECTICUT

HOLY APOSTLES COLLEGE C-2
Cromwell, Connecticut 06416 (203) 635-5311

F/T: 40M&W	Appl: Aug. 1
P/T: 75M&W	Faculty: 8
Grad: 60M&W	Tuition: $2000 (residents)
SAT or ACT: not required	$77 p/c (nonresidents)
	R & B: $2200

Holy Apostles College, founded in 1956, is a Roman Catholic institution that essentially prepares men for the priesthood; it also provides a liberal arts curriculum for both adult men and women seeking degrees in specialized fields. There is on-campus housing for men only. The college grants the B.A. degree in the following major fields: English, philosophy, psychology, religious studies, and sociology. The Master of Divinity and Master of Arts in Theology are also offered.

SAINT ALPHONSUS COLLEGE C-1
Suffield, Connecticut 06078 (203) 668-7393

F/T: 64M	Appl: Aug. 1
P/T: none	Faculty: 11
Grad: none	Tuition: $2900
SAT: 460V 470M	R & B: $1800

Saint Alphonsus College was established in 1963 for the purpose of educating young men who aspire to be Roman Catholic priests or brothers in the Congregation of the Most Holy Redeemer. It is strictly residential and offers a B.A. in philosophy.

FLORIDA

BAPTIST BIBLE INSTITUTE B-1
Graceville, Florida 32440 (904) 263-3261
(Recognized Candidate for Accreditation)

F/T: 275M, 40W	Appl: open
P/T: 14M, 40W	Faculty: 13
Grad: none	Tuition: $833
SAT or ACT: not required	R: $370

Baptist Bible Institute, founded in 1943, is affiliated with the Southern Baptist Church. The purpose of the institute is to train adults who are preparing to serve in the pastoral, music, educational, evangelistic, youth, and missionary ministries of Southern Baptist churches. Bachelor's degrees are offered in church music, religious education, and theology.

CLEARWATER CHRISTIAN COLLEGE D-4
Clearwater, Florida 33519 (813) 544-2836
(Recognized Candidate for Accreditation)

F/T: 83M, 95W Appl: Aug. 15
P/T: 10M, 18W Faculty: 13
Grad: none Tuition: $1738
SAT or ACT: not required R & B: $2000

Clearwater Christian College, founded in 1966, is a nondenominational college whose purpose is to train students for Christian leadership. Bachelor's degrees are offered in Biblical literature, elementary education, special education, secondary education, physical education, English education, humanities, music education, psychology, social studies, buisness administration, and business education. Associate degrees are also awarded.

MIAMI CHRISTIAN COLLEGE E-5
Miami, Florida 33167 (305) 685-7431
(Recognized Candidate for Accreditation)

F/T: 76M, 57W Appl: July 15
P/T: 86M, 37W Faculty: 11
Grad: none Tuition: $2430
ACT: 20 R & B: $1920

Miami Christian College, founded in 1949, provides leadership in church-related vocations. The B.A. and B.S. degrees are offered, with majors in Bible, Biblical languages, communications, church ministry, elementary education, pre-ministry, psychology/counseling, and sacred music.

ST. JOHN VIANNEY COLLEGE SEMINARY E-5
Miami, Florida 33165 (305) 223-4561

F/T: 53M Appl: open
P/T: none Faculty: 12
Grad: none Tuition: $1770
SAT or ACT: required R & B: $1625

St. John Vianney College Seminary, founded in 1959, provides an undergraduate education for men whose objective is to serve the Roman Catholic Church in the priesthood, and enriches their spiritual and intellectual formation within an Anglo-Hispanic billingual, bicultural setting to prepare these students for bilingual ministries. The B.A. degree is awarded in philosophy.

WARNER SOUTHERN COLLEGE D-4
Lake Wales, Florida 33853 (813) 638-1426

F/T: 141M, 133W Appl: Sept. 1
P/T: 12M, 24W Faculty: 15
Grad: none Tuition: $2850
SAT: 395V 394M R & B: $1500

Warner Southern College, founded in 1968, is a liberal arts college operated by the Church of God. The college places a strong emphasis on Christian commitment and on the preparation of men and women for church-related and service occupations. The college grants the B.A. degree in the following areas: Biblical studies; business administration; Christian education; church ministries—missions, music, music/youth, pastoral ministries, youth work/Christian education; communications/English; missions/Bible; psychology/counseling; sociology/social services; and education—elementary, music, secondary in English/speech and biology. Associate degrees are also awarded.

GEORGIA

EMMANUEL COLLEGE SCHOOL OF CHRISTIAN MINISTRIES C-2
Franklin Springs, Georgia 30639 (404) 245-7226

F/T: 37M, 13W Appl: Sept. 12
P/T: 1M Faculty: 2
Grad: none Tuition: $1740
SAT or ACT: not required R & B: $1550

Emmanuel College School of Christian Ministries, founded in 1973, provides a professional program, terminal in nature and designed to equip graduates for immediate full-time service as pastors or Christian education directors in local churches. The school is affiliated with the Pentecostal Holiness Church and offers the B.A. and B.S. degrees in pastoral ministry and Christian education.

INDIANA

ST. MEINRAD COLLEGE B-5
St. Meinrad, Indiana 47577 (812) 357-6520

F/T: 183M Appl: July 30
P/T: 5M Faculty: 12
Grad: none Tuition: $2148
SAT: required R & B: $2450

St. Meinrad College, established in 1861, is a private Roman Catholic liberal arts college conducted by the Order of St. Benedict for students interested in the priesthood as a vocation. The college confers the B.A. and B.S. degrees with majors in biology, chemistry, classical language, English, history, philosophy, psychology, and Spanish.

IOWA

DIVINE WORD COLLEGE E-2
Epworth, Iowa 52045 (319) 876-3354

F/T: 91M Appl: Aug. 1
P/T: 3W Faculty: 20
Grad: none Tuition: $3000
SAT: 385V 423M ACT: 15 R & B: $1200

Divine Word College, founded in 1912, is a privately controlled Roman Catholic liberal arts seminary college. It seeks to provide the proper atmosphere, guidance, and opportunities for the growth and development of the modern missionary priest or brother. The college confers the B.A. and B.S. degrees in philosophy, humanities, social science, and general science.

KANSAS

ST. JOHN'S COLLEGE D-3
Winfield, Kansas 67156 (316) 221-4000

F/T: 100M, 156W Appl: Aug. 15
P/T: 10M, 25W Faculty: 28
Grad: none Tuition: $2550
ACT: 19 R & B: $1650

St. John's College, founded in 1893, is affiliated with the Lutheran Church. The college provides instruction for church-related careers, liberal arts, nursing, and business-related fields. The B.A. degree is awarded in pre-seminary study, the B.S. in elementary education and business. Associate degrees are also conferred.

KENTUCKY

SEMINARY OF SAINT PIUS X D-1
Erlanger, Kentucky 41018 (606) 371-4448

F/T: 76M Appl: Aug. 15
P/T: none Faculty: 6
Grad: none Tuition: $2835
SAT: 400V 400M ACT: 18 R & B: $1700

The Seminary of Saint Pius X was founded in 1955 "to provide the student who wishes to dedicate his life to God in the service of the Catholic priesthood with the spiritual, moral, and academic formation necessary for entrance into a school of theology." The seminary is conducted by the Diocese of Covington and confers the B.A. degree in philosophy.

994 RELIGIOUS

LOUISIANA

ST. JOSEPH SEMINARY COLLEGE D-3
St. Benedict, Louisiana 70457 (504) 892-1800

F/T: 110M	Appl: open
P/T: 1W	Faculty: 30
Grad: none	Tuition: $1800
ACT: required	R & B: $2000

St. Joseph Seminary College is a small liberal arts college affiliated with the Roman Catholic Church. The college is dedicated to the purpose of educating young men for the priesthood on the undergraduate level. St. Joseph grants the B.A. degree in English, history, philosophy, psychology, and religion.

MARYLAND

BALTIMORE HEBREW COLLEGE D-2
Baltimore, Maryland 21215 (301) 466-7900

F/T: 12M, 30W	Appl: open
P/T: 18M, 76W	Faculty: n/av
Grad: 25M, 66W	Tuition: $55 p/c
SAT: required	R & B: n/app

Baltimore Hebrew College, founded in 1919, offers undergraduate and graduate study in Hebrew and Judaic learning. The college confers the B.A. degree with a major in Jewish studies and the Bachelor of Hebrew Literature. Master's and doctoral degrees are also awarded.

MASSACHUSETTS

HEBREW COLLEGE D-2
Brookline, Massachusetts 02146 (617) 232-8710

F/T: 63M, 51W	Appl: open
P/T: 36M, 39W	Faculty: 9
Grad: 28M, 41W	Tuition: $810
SAT or ACT: not required	R & B: n/app

Hebrew College, founded in 1926, provides Hebrew teacher training and knowledge in areas of Jewish history and literature. The college confers the Bachelor of Jewish Education and Bachelor of Hebrew Literature degrees, with programs available in Hebrew language, history, literature, education, and rabbinics. Associate and master's degrees are also offered.

ST. HYACINTH COLLEGE AND SEMINARY B-3
Granby, Massachusetts 01033 (413) 467-7191

F/T: 55M	Appl: June
P/T: none	Faculty: 10
Grad: none	Tuition: $3050
SAT: 420V 450M	R & B: $2000

St. Hyacinth College and Seminary, established in 1927, is a Roman Catholic institution supported by the Order of Friars Minor Conventual. The college seeks to prepare young men for the priesthood and the religious way of life within the Franciscan community. It grants the B.A. degree in philosophy and offers special programs in preparation for further study at a theological seminary for those men who have received a bachelor's degree without sufficient philosophical background.

ST. JOHN'S SEMINARY E-2
Brighton, Massachusetts 02135 (617) 254-2610

F/T: 84M	Appl: open
P/T: none	Faculty: 11
Grad: 112M	Tuition: $2000
SAT: required	R & B: $2000

St. John's Seminary, established in 1884, is a Roman Catholic institution which serves to prepare men for the priesthood. The B.A. is conferred in philosophy; the M.A. and Master of Divinity degrees are also offered.

MICHIGAN

GRAND RAPIDS BAPTIST COLLEGE AND SEMINARY D-4
Grand Rapids, Michigan 49505 (616) 949-5300

F/T: 337M, 367W	Appl: May 1
P/T: 50M, 53W	Faculty: 46
Grad: 237M, 31W	Tuition: $3160
ACT: 18	R & B: $2150

Grand Rapids Baptist College and Seminary is a privately controlled institution offering liberal arts programs and graduate seminary training. The B.A., B.Mus., and B.Rel.Ed. degrees are conferred with majors in Bible, biology, business administration, Christian education, English, history, missions, music, pastoral studies, physical education, psychology, religion, sociology, speech, and teacher education. The Master of Divinity, Master of Religious Education, and Master of Theology degrees are also offered, as are associate degrees.

MICHIGAN CHRISTIAN COLLEGE E-4
Rochester, Michigan 48063 (313) 651-5800

F/T: 135M, 164W	Appl: open
P/T: 13M, 9W	Faculty: 15
Grad: none	Tuition: $2300
ACT: required	R & B: $1850

Michigan Christian College, founded in 1959, is affiliated with the Churches of Christ. The college seeks to provide a liberal arts education in an atmosphere that upholds Christian principles and includes study of the Bible in the normal curriculum. Most students are enrolled in associate-degree liberal arts programs. However, the school also offers the Bachelor of Religious Education with majors in Christian ministry and Biblical and related studies.

SACRED HEART SEMINARY COLLEGE E-5
Detroit, Michigan 48206 (313) 868-2700

F/T: 38M	Appl: Aug. 15
P/T: 89M, 45W	Faculty: 9
Grad: none	Tuition: $2600
SAT: 416V 470M	R & B: $1200

Sacred Heart Seminary College, established in 1919, is affiliated with the Roman Catholic Archdiocese of Detroit. The purpose of the seminary is to provide a liberal arts education for candidates preparing for the Roman Catholic priesthood in Michigan, for candidates for the permanent diaconate, and for students preparing for the various other ministries within the Church. The seminary confers the B.A. degree in English, history, philosophy, and interdisciplinary studies. Associate degrees are also awarded.

MINNESOTA

DR. MARTIN LUTHER COLLEGE C-4
New Ulm, Minnesota 56073 (507) 354-8221

F/T: 223M, 551W	Appl: open
P/T: 1M, 2W	Faculty: 70
Grad: none	Tuition: $1620
ACT: 21	R & B: $1270

Founded in 1884, Dr. Martin Luther College is a church-affiliated college which trains elementary teachers for the Christian day schools of the Wisconsin Evangelical Lutheran Synod. The college confers the B.S. degree in elementary education.

ST. PAUL BIBLE COLLEGE
Bible College, Minnesota 55375 (612) 446-1411

F/T: 267M, 344W	Appl: open
P/T: 17M, 26W	Faculty: 32
Grad: none	Tuition: $2300
SAT: 470V 440M ACT: 18	R & B: $1920

St. Paul Bible College, founded in 1916, is affiliated with the Christian and Missionary Alliance. The college professionally prepares men and women for church-related ministries. The B.A., B.S., and Bachelor of Religious Education degrees are offered in Bible and theology, history, music, Christian education, missiology, communications, elementary

MISSISSIPPI

WESLEY COLLEGE C-4
Florence, Mississippi 39073　　　　　　(601) 845-2265

F/T: 58M, 56W	Appl: July 15
P/T: 8M, 9W	Faculty: 12
Grad: none	Tuition: $1090
ACT: 15	R & B: $1400

Wesley College is affiliated with the Congregational Methodist Church and offers undergraduate training in religious areas. The college confers the B.A. and B.S. degrees in fine and applied arts, music, religious education, and theology.

MISSOURI

CARDINAL GLENNON COLLEGE D-2
St. Louis, Missouri 63119　　　　　　(314) 644-0266

F/T: 95M	Appl: July 30
P/T: none	Faculty: 26
Grad: none	Tuition: $1265
ACT: 23	R & B: $800

Cardinal Glennon College is the college division of the St. Louis Roman Catholic Theological Seminary. The purpose of the college is to provide the student preparing for ordination with a sound liberal education along with the spiritual formation required for the priest in today's world. The college confers the B.A. in philosophy.

CONCEPTION SEMINARY COLLEGE A-1
Conception, Missouri 64433　　　　　　(816) 944-2218

F/T: 74M	Appl: open
P/T: 12M, 5W	Faculty: 21
Grad: none	Tuition: $1740
ACT: 21	R & B: $2240

Conception Seminary College, founded in 1886, is a Roman Catholic seminary college conducted by the Order of St. Benedict and devoted principally to the formation of young men for the Roman Catholic priesthood. It provides the broad intellectual, cultural, and religious foundation requisite for specialized and professional training in a graduate school of theology. Integrated knowledge of the humanities and social and natural sciences is emphasized. The college confers the B.A. degree in philosophy, theology/religion, and social sciences.

HANNIBAL-LaGRANGE COLLEGE D-2
Hannibal, Missouri 63401　　　　　　(314) 221-3113

F/T: 143M, 180W	Appl: Sept. 10
P/T: 62M, 53W	Faculty: 25
Grad: none	Tuition: $2344
ACT: required	R & B: $1320

Hannibal-LaGrange College, founded in 1858, is affiliated with the Southern Baptist Church. The college offers B.A. and B.S. degrees in accounting, business, religious education, sacred music, secondary education, and theology. Associate degrees are offered in a variety of liberal arts disciplines.

ST. MARY'S SEMINARY COLLEGE E-3
Perryville, Missouri 63775　　　　　　(314) 547-6533

F/T: 60M	Appl: July 15
P/T: none	Faculty: 14
Grad: none	Tuition: $2907
SAT: 405V 457M	R & B: $1750

St. Mary's Seminary College is a Roman Catholic seminary conducted by the Vincentian Fathers and operated exclusively for the training and education of candidates for the Roman Catholic priesthood. It grants the B.A. in philosophy.

NEW JERSEY

DON BOSCO COLLEGE D-2
Newton, New Jersey 07860　　　　　　(201) 383-3900

F/T: 83M	Appl: open
P/T: none	Faculty: 8
Grad: none	Tuition: $2860
SAT: 435V 470M	R & B: $1925

Don Bosco College, founded in 1928, is a private, liberal arts college conducted by the Salesians of St. John Bosco. Through a well-balanced educational program in the liberal arts, the college seeks to develop its students intellectually, spiritually, socially, and physically. The college offers a B.A. degree in philosophy.

NORTHEASTERN BIBLE COLLEGE E-3
Essex Fells, New Jersey 07021　　　　　　(201) 226-8272

F/T: 132M, 80W	Appl: open
P/T: 73M, 52W	Faculty: 18
Grad: none	Tuition: $2930
SAT: 427V 468M	R & B: $1900

Northeastern Bible College, founded in 1950, is an independent, non-denominational, professional theological college. The baccalaureate programs develop 3 major areas simultaneously: Biblical, professional, and general education. The college awards the B.A., the Bachelor of Sacred Music, and the Bachelor of Theology degrees, with programs available in ministerial studies, Christian education, elementary education, counseling/psychology, and missions. An associate degree in religious arts and a 1-year Bible diploma are also conferred.

NEW YORK

CATHEDRAL COLLEGE OF THE IMMACULATE CONCEPTION D-5
Douglaston, New York 11362　　　　　　(212) 631-4600

F/T: 110M	Appl: July
P/T: none	Faculty: 20
Grad: none	Tuition: $3300
SAT: 426V 423M	R & B: $2000

Cathedral College of the Immaculate Conception, founded in 1914, is a Roman Catholic liberal arts college that prepares men for graduate studies in theology with a view toward their ordination as priests. The B.A. degree is conferred in English, history, philosophy, psychology, and sociology.

WADHAMS HALL SEMINARY-COLLEGE C-2
Ogdensburg, New York 13669　　　　　　(315) 393-4231

F/T: 63M	Appl: Aug. 1
P/T: none	Faculty: n/av
Grad: none	Tuition: $2280
SAT: 490V 500M ACT: 24	R & B: $2100

Wadhams Hall Seminary-College is a Roman Catholic seminary college that educates men for the priesthood. It offers independent study to those who need the assistance of philosophical study and spiritual formation prior to acceptance to a theologate. The institution grants the B.A. degree in philosophy with concentrations in behavioral sciences, English, history, languages, literature, and religious studies.

NORTH CAROLINA

JOHN WESLEY COLLEGE D-2
High Point, North Carolina 27260　　　　　　(919) 889-2262

F/T: 33M, 10W	Appl: Aug. 15
P/T: 14M, 7W	Faculty: 7
Grad: none	Tuition: $1574
SAT or ACT: recommended	R & B: n/app

John Wesley College is a small Protestant Bible college. It confers the B.A., B. Theology, and A.A. degrees. Majors offered include Bible, Christian education, Christian counseling, church history, general Christian ministries, pastoral ministries, and pre-seminary.

OHIO

THE ATHENAEUM OF OHIO A-5
Cincinnati, Ohio 45230 (513) 231-2223

F/T: 10M, 26W	Appl: open
P/T: 1M, 6W	Faculty: 29
Grad: 88M, 27W	Tuition: $1910
SAT or ACT: not required	R & B: $1510

The Athenaeum of Ohio, founded in 1829, is affiliated with the Roman Catholic Church. The school serves to prepare men for ordained ministry in the Catholic Church and to prepare men and women for lay ministry in the Church. The B.A. degree is offered in theology. Master's programs are also available.

BORROMEO COLLEGE OF OHIO D-1
Wickliffe, Ohio 44092 (216) 585-5900

F/T: 90M	Appl: Aug. 1
P/T: 7M, 10W	Faculty: 15
Grad: none	Tuition: $2700
SAT: 460V 440M	R & B: $1350

Borromeo College, founded in 1954, is a liberal arts college controlled by the Roman Catholic Diocese of Cleveland. Emphasis is placed on philosophical and theological preparation for graduate school. The college confers the B.A. degree in classical languages, history, English, philosophy, and social and behavioral science. Students trained at the college will eventually engage in educational and social work in the northern Ohio area.

THE PONTIFICAL COLLEGE JOSEPHINUM C-3
Columbus, Ohio 43085 (614) 885-5585

F/T: 96M	Appl: Aug. 15
P/T: none	Faculty: 19
Grad: 99M, 11W	Tuition: $2373
SAT: 455V 462M ACT: 22	R & B: $1868

The Pontifical College Josephinum is a Roman Catholic liberal arts seminary college geared to preparing young men for the study of theology toward ordination in the Roman Catholic priesthood. The college grants the B.A. degree in American studies, English, history, Latin American studies, philosophy, and religious studies. Master's degrees are also awarded.

OKLAHOMA

SOUTHWESTERN COLLEGE OF CHRISTIAN MINISTRIES D-3
(Formerly Oklahoma City Southwestern College)
Bethany, Oklahoma 73008 (405) 787-9609

F/T: 40M, 22W	Appl: open
P/T: 16M, 4W	Faculty: 5
Grad: none	Tuition: $1675
ACT: required	R & B: $1440

Southwestern College of Christian Ministries, founded in 1946 under a different name, is affiliated with the Pentecostal Holiness Church. The college offers B.A. and B.S. degrees in Christian education, missions, pastoral ministry, church music, and Biblical studies.

OREGON

COLUMBIA CHRISTIAN COLLEGE B-2
Portland, Oregon 97220 (503) 255-7060

F/T: 118M, 155W	Appl: Apr. 1
P/T: 18M, 25W	Faculty: n/av
Grad: none	Tuition: $2877
SAT: 400V 440M ACT: 17	R and B: $1962

Columbia Christian College, founded in 1956, is a liberal arts college operated by members of the Church of Christ in order to maintain and conduct an educational institution in which students will be encouraged to become responsible citizens. The college grants the B.A. degree in Biblical studies, business, counseling education, education, interdisciplinary studies, music, music education, and psychology. Associate degrees are also awarded.

MOUNT ANGEL SEMINARY B-2
Saint Benedict, Oregon 97373 (503) 845-3030

F/T: 50M	Appl: Aug. 15
P/T: none	Faculty: 20
Grad: 57M	Tuition: $2125
SAT: required	R & B: $1750

Mount Angel Seminary, established in 1887, is a Roman Catholic liberal arts college conducted by the Benedictine Monks of the Mount Angel Abbey. The seminary has complete residential preprofessional and professional programs which lead toward ordination to the priesthood or to a Master of Divinity or M.A. degree in Theology. The B.A. degree is awarded in philosophy, or in liberal arts with a concentration in history, literature, philosophy, or social science.

NORTHWEST CHRISTIAN COLLEGE B-2
Eugene, Oregon 97401 (503) 343-1641

F/T: 129M, 84W	Appl: open
P/T: 17M, 23W	Faculty: 11
Grad: none	Tuition: $3019
SAT or ACT: required	R & B: $1755

Northwest Christian College, established in 1895, is a private, church-related institution supported by the Christian Church/Church of Christ. The college aims at preparing students for a career in the ministry, and it offers the B.A., B.S., and B. Theology degrees with majors in Biblical studies, educational ministries, missions and outreach ministry, pastoral ministries, and church music. Associate degrees are also awarded.

WESTERN BAPTIST COLLEGE B-2
Salem, Oregon 97301 (503) 581-8600

F/T: 172M, 150W	Appl: Sept. 1
P/T: 25M, 12W	Faculty: 16
Grad: none	Tuition: $3564
SAT or ACT: required	R & B: $2100

Western Baptist College, founded in 1936, blends a Bible college curriculum with that of a Christian liberal arts college. The college confers B.A. and B.S. degrees, with majors offered in Bible, business management, elementary and secondary education, missions, music, pastoral ministries, psychology, social science, and theology. Associate degrees are offered in a number of fields.

PENNSYLVANIA

THE ACADEMY OF THE NEW CHURCH COLLEGE F-3
Bryn Athyn, Pennsylvania 19009 (215) 947-4200

F/T: 61M, 71W	Appl: Mar. 15
P/T: 8M, 19W	Faculty: n/av
Grad: none	Tuition: $1437
SAT: 450V 490M	R & B: $1476

The Academy of the New Church College is a liberal arts college and theological training institution of the General Church of the New Jerusalem (Swedenborgian). The B.S. degree is conferred in elementary education and the B.A. degree in religion and interdisciplinary studies. The B. Theology is conferred at the end of the theological program as a first professional degree. Associate programs are also offered.

BAPTIST BIBLE COLLEGE AND SCHOOL OF THEOLOGY E-2
Clarks Summit, Pennsylvania 18411 (717) 587-1172
(Recognized Candidate for Accreditation)

F/T: 321M, 388W	Appl: Aug. 1
P/T: 41M, 54W	Faculty: 30
Grad: 62M	Tuition: $2783
SAT or ACT: required	R & B: $1672

Baptist Bible College and School of Theology, founded in 1932, is affiliated with the General Association of Regular Baptists. The purpose of the school is to train young people for the Gospel ministry and other lines of Christian ministry vocations, such as pastors, missionaries, local church Christian education workers, teachers for Christian schools, and church musicians. The school awards the Bachelor of Religious Education and the Bachelor of Sacred Music degrees. Bachelor's degrees are offered in pastoral studies, general missions, minister of Christian education, youth minister, youth and music, campus ministry, elementary Christian school teacher education, secondary Christian school teacher education, music education Christian school teacher, church music, pre-seminary, Bible teaching, and children's worker. Associate and master's degrees are also conferred.

GRATZ COLLEGE F-3
Philadelphia, Pennsylvania 19141 (215) 329-3363

F/T: 37M, 77W Appl: Sept. 10
P/T: 43M, 87W Faculty: 5
Grad: 8M, 17W Tuition: $375
SAT: not required R & B: n/app

Gratz College, founded in 1895, is the oldest Hebrew teachers' college in the western hemisphere. The college confers the B. of Hebrew Literature degree (both by itself and with a Hebrew teacher's diploma) and the B.A. in Jewish Studies degree. A joint education program is available with Temple University. Gratz also confers the Master of Hebrew Literature and the Master of Arts in Jewish Music.

LANCASTER BIBLE COLLEGE E-3
Lancaster, Pennsylvania 17601 (717) 569-7071
(Recognized Candidate for Accreditation)

F/T: 182M, 129W Appl: open
P/T: 45M, 49W Faculty: 18
Grad: none Tuition: $3200
ACT: 19 R & B: $1888

Lancaster Bible College, founded in 1933, is an independent institution dedicated to the teachings of the Bible, and to training people for full-time Christian work. The college confers the B.S. degree in Bible.

PHILADELPHIA COLLEGE OF BIBLE F-3
Langhorne, Pennsylvania 19047 (215) 752-5800

F/T: 250M, 233W Appl: Aug. 15
P/T: 47M, 41W Faculty: n/av
Grad: none Tuition: $2800
SAT or ACT: required R & B: $1940

Philadelphia College of Bible, founded in 1913, is a denominationally unaffiliated, coeducational professional school that prepares students for Christian church-related vocations. The college confers the B.S., B.S.W., and B.Mus. degrees with professional emphases in Christian education, communications, music, missions, pastoral studies, and social work. The B.S.W. and B.Mus. programs are 5-year curricula.

SAINT CHARLES COLLEGE SEMINARY F-3
(formerly Saint Charles Borromeo Seminary)
Philadelphia, Pennsylvania 19151 (215) 839-3760

F/T: 69M Appl: Aug. 1
P/T: 9M Faculty: n/av
Grad: none Tuition: $2615
SAT or ACT: required R & B: $2400

Saint Charles College Seminary, founded in 1832, is a 4-year liberal arts college that prepares seminarians to enter the seminary theologate. The seminary is owned and operated by the Roman Catholic Archdiocese of Philadelphia. The college offers the bachelor's degree in philosophy. The School of Religious Studies offers evening and summer classes for men and women leading to a B.A. in religious studies.

UNITED WESLEYAN COLLEGE E-3
Allentown, Pennsylvania 18103 (215) 439-8709
(Recognized Candidate for Accreditation)

F/T: 199M, 55W Appl: open
P/T: 15M, 9W Faculty: 6
Grad: none Tuition: $2700
SAT: 391V 424M R & B: $1800

United Wesleyan College, founded in 1921, is affiliated with the Wesleyan Church. The college was established to prepare students for full-time occupations within church organizations. Bachelor's degrees are offered in Christian education, ministry, and sacred music. Associate degrees are also available.

SOUTH CAROLINA

COLUMBIA BIBLE COLLEGE C-3
Columbia, South Carolina 29230 (803) 754-4100
(Recognized Candidate for Accreditation)

F/T: 278M, 197W Appl: Aug. 15
P/T: 21M, 36W Faculty: 27
Grad: 199M, 108W Tuition: $2380
SAT: 430V 460M R & B: $1755

Columbia College, founded in 1923, is an independent, interdenominational college offering bachelor's degrees in Bible studies, Bible teaching, Christian education, church music, elementary education, missions, pastoral studies, and pre-seminary. Associate and master's programs are also available.

TENNESSEE

JOHNSON BIBLE COLLEGE E-3
Knoxville, Tennessee 37920 (615) 573-4517

F/T: 212M, 155W Appl: open
P/T: 10M, 21W Faculty: 16
Grad: none Tuition: $1440
SAT or ACT: required R & B: $1950

Johnson Bible College, founded in 1893, is a specialized church school that educates individuals for careers in the Christian ministry, church school teaching, church music, and church administration. The college offers the B.A. and B.S. degrees with majors in church music, Christian education, Christian communications, elementary education, youth ministry, missions, preaching, and secretarial science. Associate degrees are also awarded.

TEXAS

GULF-COAST BIBLE COLLEGE E-3
Houston, Texas 77270 (713) 862-3800

F/T: 160M, 140W Appl: Aug. 15
P/T: 40M, 20W Faculty: 22
Grad: none Tuition: $2000
ACT: required R & B: $1250

Gulf-Coast Bible College was founded in 1953 for the training and preparation of men and women for the Christian ministry. It is affiliated with the Church of God, Anderson, Indiana. The college grants the B.A. and B.S. degrees in the fields of behavioral science, elementary education, ministry, music, and professional ministries. Associate and master's degrees are also awarded.

SOUTHWESTERN ASSEMBLIES OF GOD COLLEGE D-2
Waxahachie, Texas 75165 (214) 937-4010

F/T: 282M, 253W Appl: open
P/T: 37M, 23W Faculty: 16
Grad: none Tuition: $1652
ACT: 17 R & B: $1890

Southwestern Assemblies of God College, founded in 1927, is a coeducational liberal arts and Bible college affiliated with the Assemblies of God Church. The college confers B.A. and B.S. degrees in Christian education, missions, pastoral ministry and evangelism; the Bachelor of Sacred Music degree is also granted. Associate degrees are offered in Bible, education, psychology, and other subjects.

ROTC 998

WASHINGTON

NORTHWEST COLLEGE OF THE   C-2
ASSEMBLIES OF GOD
Kirkland, Washington 98033   (206) 822-8266

F/T: 386M, 304W	*Appl:*	Aug. 1
P/T: 39M, 32W	*Faculty:*	46
Grad: none	*Tuition:*	$1920
SAT or ACT: required	*R & B:*	$1583

Founded in 1934, Northwest college is affiliated with the Assemblies of God Church and offers programs of study leading to work in service to the church. The B.A. degree is conferred with majors in Christian education, sacred music, religion, and theology.

WISCONSIN

HOLY REDEEMER COLLEGE   D-5
Waterford, Wisconsin 53185   (414) 534-3191

F/T: 51M, 1W	*Appl:*	Aug. 1
P/T: 9M, 15W	*Faculty:*	11
Grad: none	*Tuition:*	$1860
ACT: 18	*R & B:*	$1620

Holy Redeemer College, founded in 1965, is a liberal arts college affiliated with the Roman Catholic Church and dedicated to preparing young men to be priests or brothers of the Redemptorist Congregation. The college confers the B.A. degree in philosophy.

ROTC

AIR FORCE

In the Air Force ROTC program, young men and women may earn commissions by participating in 2- and 4-year programs while attending college. Options such as scholarships and flight training are available. The amount of academic credit given for Air Force ROTC varies from school to school.

In the 4-year program, students spend their first 2 years in the General Military Course, studying the function and operation of the Air Force in 1 hour of instruction and 1 hour of laboratory or drill each week. Students may register for this as they register for any other course, and incur no military obligation. After 2 years, they may compete for entry into the Professional Officer Course on the basis of standardized tests, their major and grade-point average, a physical examination, an interview, and a recommendation from a professor of aerospace science (ROTC instructor). This course involves 3 hours of classes a week in aerospace studies, leadership, and defense policy; a leadership laboratory; and a 4-week field-training course between the sophomore and junior years.

The 2-year program, for students with junior standing and above, allows direct entrance into the Professional Officer Course, but students must complete a 6-week field-training course instead of the 4-week course.

All cadets enrolled in the Professional Officer Course receive a nontaxable subsistence allowance of $100 a month during the school year. They also are paid during field training. The Air Force provides all uniforms and textbooks required for the program.

Four year scholarships are available on a competitive basis to high school seniors who plan to major in certain science and engineering fields. Many of these students become pilots, navigators, or missile-launch officers. A limited number of these scholarships are available to students who enroll in nontechnical programs such as business administration. The scholarships provide tuition, instructional fees, textbooks, and a $100-a-month subsistence allowance. The application deadline for these scholarships is December 15. Selections are made on the basis of scores on the SAT or ACT and on the Air Force Officer Qualifying Test, academic record, an interview with an Air Force officer, extracurricular activities record, and recommendations from high school officials.

Scholarships for 4, 3½, 3, 2½, and 2 years also are available for students already in college. Special scholarships are available through the Pre-Health Professions Program for students in premedical programs. There are also 2-year nursing scholarships.

Students accepted for flight training during their last year of Air Force ROTC receive a ground-school course and up to 25 hours of flight training at Air Force expense.

Cadets in the Professional Officer Course agree to serve 4 years on active duty if assigned to non-flying duties. Pilots must serve at least 6 years after completion of training and navigators must serve 5 years; training generally takes 1 year. Those in the Health Professions Program must serve 7 or 8 years, depending on the length of their training. After leaving active duty, officers may be required to serve in the Air Force Reserve.

Applicants for Air Force ROTC must be U.S. citizens in good physical condition and meet Air Force physical requirements (which are more rigorous for flight-training candidates). Applicants for the General Military Course must be at least 14 years old, or at least 17 to qualify for a scholarship. Further information can be obtained from the professor of aerospace studies at any institution offering Air Force ROTC, or from the Air Force ROTC Office of Public Affairs, Maxwell Air Force Base, Alabama 36112.

The following list shows the colleges and universities included in this book that either host Air Force ROTC or offer it through cross registration with another school.

ALABAMA

Alabama State University
Auburn University
Auburn University at Montgomery
Birmingham-Southern College
Huntingdon College
Miles College
Samford University
Troy State University System
Tuskegee Institute
University of Alabama
University of Alabama in Birmingham
University of Montevallo

ARIZONA
Arizona State University
Grand Canyon College
Northern Arizona University
University of Arizona

ARKANSAS
University of Arkansas at Fayetteville

CALIFORNIA
Biola University
California Institute of Technology
California Lutheran College
California State Polytechnic University/Pomona
California State University/Chico
California State University/Dominguez Hills
California State University/Fresno
California State University/Fullerton
California State University/Hayward
California State University/Long Beach
California State University/Los Angeles
California State University/Northridge
California State University/Sacramento
Chapman College
Cogswell College
Dominican College of San Rafael
Golden Gate University
Holy Names College
Loyola Marymount University
Mills College
Mount St. Mary's College
Northrop University
Occidental College
Pepperdine University
Point Loma College
Saint Mary's College of California
San Diego State University
San Jose State University
Stanford University
University of California/Berkeley
University of California/Davis
University of California/Irvine
University of California/Los Angeles
University of California/Riverside
University of Redlands
University of Santa Clara
University of Southern California

COLORADO
Colorado State University
Metropolitan State College
Regis College
University of Colorado at Boulder
University of Colorado at Denver
University of Denver
University of Northern Colorado

CONNECTICUT
Central Connecticut State College
Eastern Connecticut State College
University of Connecticut
University of Hartford
Western Connecticut State College

DISTRICT OF COLUMBIA
American University
Georgetown University
George Washington University
Howard University
Trinity College

FLORIDA
Barry University
Bethune-Cookman College
Biscayne College
Embry-Riddle Aeronautical University
Florida Agricultural and Mechanical University
Florida Memorial College
Florida State University
Rollins College
University of Central Florida
University of Florida
University of Miami
University of South Florida

GEORGIA
Agnes Scott College
Clark College
Georgia Institute of Technology
Morehouse College
Southern Technical Institute
Spelman College
University of Georgia
Valdosta State College

HAWAII
Chaminade University of Honolulu
University of Hawaii at Manoa

IDAHO
University of Idaho

ILLINOIS
Chicago State University
Elmhurst College
Illinois Institute of Technology
Lewis University
McKendree College
Northeastern Illinois University
Northwestern University
Parks College of St. Louis University
Saint Xavier College
Southern Illinois University at Carbondale
Southern Illinois University at Edwardsville
University of Illinois at Chicago
University of Illinois at Urbana-Champaign

INDIANA
Butler University
Depauw University
Indiana State University
Indiana University at South Bend
Indiana University/Bloomington
Indiana University Southeast
Marian College
Purdue University/West Lafayette
Saint Joseph's College
Saint Mary's College
Taylor University
University of Notre Dame

IOWA
Drake University
Grand View College
Iowa State University
University of Iowa

KANSAS
Baker University
Kansas State University
University of Kansas
Washburn University of Topeka

KENTUCKY
Bellarmine College
Georgetown College
Northern Kentucky University
Spalding College
Thomas More College
Transylvania University
University of Kentucky
University of Louisville

LOUISIANA
Louisiana State University and Agricultural and Mechanical College
Louisiana Tech University
Our Lady of Holy Cross College
Southern University and A&M College
Southern University in New Orleans
Tulane University
University of New Orleans
University of Southwestern Louisiana

MAINE
Husson College
University of Maine at Orono

MARYLAND
Johns Hopkins University
Towson State University
University of Maryland/Baltimore County
University of Maryland/College Park
Western Maryland College

MASSACHUSETTS
Amherst College
Anna Maria College
Assumption College
Bentley College
Boston University
Central New England College
Clark University
Hampshire College
Harvard University/Harvard and Radcliffe Colleges
Holy Cross College
Massachusetts Institute of Technology
Mount Holyoke College
Tufts University
University of Lowell
University of Massachusetts at Amherst
Wellesley College
Western New England College
Worcester Polytechnic Institute
Worcester State College

MICHIGAN
Concordia College
Eastern Michigan University
Ferris State College
Michigan State University
Michigan Technological University
University of Michigan/Ann Arbor
University of Michigan/Dearborn
Wayne State University

MINNESOTA
Augsburg College
Bethel College
College of St. Catherine
College of St. Scholastica
College of St. Thomas
Concordia College/Moorhead
Macalester College
Moorhead State University
University of Minnesota/Duluth
University of Minnesota/Twin Cities

MISSISSIPPI
Delta State University
Millsaps College
Mississippi State University
Mississippi University for Women
Mississippi Valley State University
University of Mississippi
University of Southern Mississippi
William Carey College

MISSOURI
Columbia College

1000 ROTC

Harris-Stowe State College
Saint Louis University
Southeast Missouri State University
Stephens College
University of Missouri/Columbia
University of Missouri/Rolla
University of Missouri/St. Louis
Washington University

MONTANA

Montana State University

NEBRASKA

Bellevue College
College of Saint Mary
Concordia Teachers College
Creighton University
Nebraska Wesleyan University
University of Nebraska at Omaha
University of Nebraska/Lincoln

NEW HAMPSHIRE

Daniel Webster College
Franklin Pierce College
Keene State College
Nathaniel Hawthorne College
New Hampshire College
Notre Dame College
Plymouth State College
St. Anselm College
University of New Hampshire

NEW JERSEY

College of Saint Elizabeth
Monmouth College
Montclair State College
New Jersey Institute of Technology
Princeton University
Rutgers University/College of Engineering
Rutgers University/College of Nursing
Rutgers University/College of Pharmacy
Rutgers University/Cook College
Rutgers University/Douglass College
Rutgers University/Livingston College
Rutgers University/Mason Gross School of the Arts
Rutgers University/Newark College of Arts and Sciences
Rutgers University/Rutgers College
Rutgers University/University College—Newark
Rutgers University/University College—New Brunswick
Seton Hall University
Stevens Institute of Technology
Trenton State College
William Paterson College of New Jersey

NEW MEXICO

New Mexico State University
University of Albuquerque
University of New Mexico

NEW YORK

Clarkson College of Technology
Colgate University
College of Mount Saint Vincent
College of Saint Rose
Columbia University/Columbia College
Cornell University
Daemen College
Eisenhower College of Rochester Institute of Technology
Ithaca College
Le Moyne College
Manhattan College
Mercy College
New York Institute of Technology
Polytechnic Institute of New York
Rensselaer Polytechnic Institute
Russell Sage College
St. Thomas Aquinas College
State University of New York at Binghamton
State University of New York/College at Cortland
State University of New York/College at Potsdam
Syracuse University
Union College
Utica College of Syracuse University
Wells College

NORTH CAROLINA

Belmont Abbey College
Bennett College
Duke University
East Carolina University
Fayetteville State University
Greensboro College
Guilford College
High Point College
Johnson C. Smith University
Meredith College
North Carolina Agricultural and Technical State University
North Carolina Central University
North Carolina State University
Pembroke State University
Shaw University
University of North Carolina at Chapel Hill
University of North Carolina at Charlotte
University of North Carolina at Greensboro

NORTH DAKOTA

North Dakota State University

OHIO

Ashland College
Bowling Green State University
Capital University
Cedarville College
The Defiance College
Franklin University
Heidelberg College
Hiram College
Kent State University
Miami University
Ohio Dominican College
Ohio Institute of Technology
The Ohio State University
Ohio University
Ohio Wesleyan University
Otterbein College
University of Akron
University of Cincinnati
University of Dayton
University of Toledo
Wilberforce University
Wittenberg University
Wright State University

OKLAHOMA

Oklahoma Christian College
Oklahoma City University
Oklahoma State University
University of Oklahoma

OREGON

Concordia College
Oregon State University
Portland State University
University of Portland
Willamette University

PENNSYLVANIA

Allentown College of St. Francis DeSales
Bloomsburg State College
Carlow College
Carnegie-Mellon University
Chatham College
College Misericordia
Drexel University
Duquesne University
East Stroudsburg State College
Grove City College
King's College
Kutztown State College
Lafayette College
La Roche College
Lehigh University
Marywood College
Moravian College
Muhlenberg College
Pennsylvania State University/University Park Campus
Point Park College
Robert Morris College
Saint Joseph's University
Saint Vincent College
Slippery Rock State College
Temple University
University of Pennsylvania
University of Pittsburgh
University of Pittsburgh at Bradford
University of Pittsburgh at Greensburg
University of Scranton
Villanova University
West Chester State College
Wilkes College

PUERTO RICO

University of Puerto Rico/Mayaguez

RHODE ISLAND

Roger Williams College

SOUTH CAROLINA

Baptist College at Charleston
Benedict College
Central Wesleyan College
The Citadel
Clemson University
South Carolina State College
University of South Carolina

SOUTH DAKOTA

South Dakota State University

TENNESSEE

Belmont College
Christian Brothers College
David Lipscomb College
Fisk University
Knoxville College
LeMoyne-Owen College
Memphis State University
Middle Tennessee State University
Southwestern at Memphis
Tennessee State University
Trevecca Nazarene College
University of Tennessee/Knoxville

TEXAS

Angelo State University
Baylor University
East Texas State University
Lamar University
North Texas State University
Paul Quinn College
St. Edward's University
Southern Methodist University
Southwest Texas State University
Texas A&M University
Texas Christian University
Texas Lutheran College

Texas Tech University
Texas Wesleyan College
Trinity University
University of Dallas
University of Mary Hardin-Baylor
University of Texas at Arlington
University of Texas at Austin
University of Texas at El Paso
University of Texas at San Antonio

UTAH

Brigham Young University
University of Utah
Utah State University
Weber State College
Westminster College

VERMONT

Lyndon State College
Norwich University
Saint Michael's College
Trinity College
University of Vermont
Vermont College of Norwich University

VIRGINIA

University of Virginia
Virginia Military Institute
Virginia Polytechnic Institute and State University

WASHINGTON

Central Washington University
Pacific Lutheran University
Saint Martin's College
Seattle University
University of Puget Sound
University of Washington
Washington State University

WEST VIRGINIA

Fairmont State College
Shepherd College
West Virginia University

WISCONSIN

Edgewood College
University of Wisconsin/Madison
University of Wisconsin/Superior
Viterbo College

WYOMING

University of Wyoming

ARMY

The Army Reserve Officers' Training Corps offers college students a chance to earn a commission in the Army, the Army National Guard, the Army Reserve, or the Army Nurse Corps. ROTC cadets may take either a 2-year or a 4-year program. Those who attend schools that do not host ROTC programs may participate in ROTC through cross-enrollment with a school that does. Most institutions give academic credit for ROTC.

The 4-year program is divided into a Basic Course and an Advanced Course. During the Basic Course, students study management and military science. They incur no military obligation and may withdraw at any time. When they register for the Advanced Course, cadets agree to complete the program, to accept a commission, and to serve 3 months to 3 years on active duty. (Scholarship recipients agree to serve 4 years on active duty and 2 years in the Reserve.) The Advanced Course includes further study of military management and tactics, and a 6-week Advanced Camp during the summer after the junior year, at which cadets put into practice the theory they have learned.

In the 2-year program, cadets enter directly into the Advanced Course, but must complete a 6-week Basic Camp the summer before they enroll.

ROTC cadets receive a living allowance of up to $1000 a year while they are enrolled in the Advanced Course, and they are paid during Advanced Camp and Basic Camp. In addition, cadets may apply for 2-, 3-, and 4-year ROTC scholarships that pay full tuition, textbook costs, lab fees, and a living allowance of up to $1000 a year. Scholarship recipients must be U.S. citizens, at least 17 years old, and expect to be under 25 on June 30 of the year they complete their college degree and receive their commission. The Army must approve their academic major.

Applications for 4-year scholarships must be requested by November 15 from Army ROTC, P.O. Box 9000, Clifton, New Jersey 07015. Students must take the SAT or the ACT by December of the year they apply. Information on 2- and 3-year scholarships may be obtained from a professor of military science at any college or university that offers ROTC. The 2- and 3-year scholarships also are available to enlisted men and women on active duty.

Through the Simultaneous Membership Program, students can combine ROTC service with service in the Army Reserve or National Guard. Under this plan, students can complete the Advanced Course and become officers in their Guard or Reserve units after 2 years in college, and can earn up to $6500 during their college careers.

Further information on the Army ROTC program is available from Army ROTC, Fort Monroe, Virginia 23651.

The following list shows the colleges and universities included in this book that either host Army ROTC or offer it through cross registration with another school.

ALABAMA

Alabama Agricultural and Mechanical University
Auburn University
Auburn University at Montgomery
Birmingham-Southern College
Huntingdon College
Jacksonville State University
Judson College
Miles College
Mobile College
Spring Hill College
Stillman College
Tuskegee Institute
University of Alabama
University of Alabama in Birmingham
University of Alabama in Huntsville
University of North Alabama
University of South Alabama

ALASKA

University of Alaska/Fairbanks

ARIZONA

Arizona State University
Northern Arizona University
University of Arizona

ARKANSAS

Arkansas State University
Arkansas Tech University
The College of the Ozarks
Henderson State University
Hendrix College
Oachita Baptist University
Southern Arkansas University
University of Arkansas at Fayetteville
University of Arkansas at Little Rock
University of Arkansas at Monticello
University of Arkansas at Pine Bluff
University of Central Arkansas

CALIFORNIA

Biola University
California Institute of Technology
California Lutheran College

1002 ROTC

California Polytechnic State University
California State College/San Bernardino
California State Polytechnic University/ Pomona
California State University/Chico
California State University/Dominguez Hills
California State University/Fresno
California State University/Fullerton
California State University/Hayward
California State University/Long Beach
California State University/Los Angeles
California State University/Northridge
California State University/Sacramento
The Claremont Colleges/Claremont McKenna College
The Claremont Colleges/Harvey Mudd College
The Claremont Colleges/Pitzer College
The Claremont Colleges/Pomona College
The Claremont Colleges/Scripps College
Dominican College of San Rafael
Golden Gate University
Holy Names College
Mills College
Mount St. Mary's College
Northrop University
Occidental College
Pepperdine University
Point Loma College
Saint Mary's College of California
San Diego State University
San Francisco State University
San Jose State University
Stanford University
University of California/Berkeley
University of California/Davis
University of California/Los Angeles
University of California/Riverside
University of California/Santa Barbara
University of Redlands
University of San Francisco
University of Santa Clara
University of Southern California
Westmont College

COLORADO
Colorado College
Colorado School of Mines
Colorado State University
Colorado Technical College
Mesa College
Metropolitan State College
University of Colorado at Boulder
University of Colorado at Colorado Springs
University of Colorado at Denver
University of Denver
University of Southern Colorado

CONNECTICUT
Central Connecticut State College
Eastern Connecticut State College
Sacred Heart University
University of Bridgeport
University of Connecticut
University of Hartford
University of New Haven
Western Connecticut State College
Yale University

DELAWARE
University of Delaware
Wilmington College

DISTRICT OF COLUMBIA
American University
Catholic University of America
Georgetown University
George Washington University
Howard University

FLORIDA
Bethune-Cookman College
Biscayne College
Eckerd College
Edward Waters College
Embry-Riddle Aeronautical University
Flagler College
Florida Agricultural and Mechanical University
Florida Institute of Technology
Florida Southern College
Florida State University
Jacksonville University
Saint Leo College
Stetson University
University of Central Florida
University of Florida
University of Miami
University of South Florida
University of Tampa
Webber College

GEORGIA
Albany State College
Armstrong State College
Augusta College
Berry College
Clark College
Columbus College
Emory University
Fort Valley State College
Georgia College
Georgia Institute of Technology
Georgia Southern College
Georgia Southwestern College
Georgia State University
Kennesaw College
LaGrange College
Mercer University
Morehouse College
North Georgia College
Paine College
Piedmont College
Savannah State College
Southern Technical Institute
Spelman College
University of Georgia

GUAM
University of Guam

HAWAII
Brigham Young University/Hawaii Campus
Chaminade University of Honolulu
Hawaii Pacific College
University of Hawaii at Manoa

IDAHO
Boise State University
Idaho State University
Northwest Nazarene College
University of Idaho

ILLINOIS
Bradley University
Chicago State University
De Paul University
Eastern Illinois University
Illinois Benedictine College
Illinois State University
Knox College
Loyola University of Chicago
Monmouth College
Mundelein College
Northeastern Illinois University
Northern Illinois University
Olivet Nazarene College
Southern Illinois University at Carbondale
University of Illinois at Chicago
University of Illinois at Urbana-Champaign
Western Illinois University
Wheaton College

INDIANA
Anderson College
Ball State University
Butler University
Depauw University
Franklin College
Indiana Central University
Indiana Institute of Technology
Indiana State University
Indiana University at South Bend
Indiana University/Bloomington
Indiana University-Purdue University at Fort Wayne
Indiana University-Purdue University at Indianapolis
Marian College
Purdue University/West Lafayette
Rose-Hulman Institute of Technology
Saint Joseph's College
Saint Mary-of-the-Woods College
Saint Mary's College
Taylor University
University of Notre Dame
Wabash College

IOWA
Coe College
Dordt College
Drake University
Iowa State University
University of Dubuque
University of Iowa
University of Northern Iowa
Upper Iowa University

KANSAS
Baker University
Benedictine College
Emporia State University
Fort Hays State University
Kansas State University
Pittsburg State University
University of Kansas
Wichita State University

KENTUCKY
Bellarmine College
Centre College of Kentucky
Cumberland College
Eastern Kentucky University
Georgetown College
Kentucky State University
Morehead State University
Murray State University
Northern Kentucky University
Thomas More College
Transylvania University
Union College
University of Kentucky
Western Kentucky University

LOUISIANA
Centenary College of Louisiana
Dillard University
Grambling State University
Louisiana College
Louisiana State University and Agricultural and Mechanical College
Louisiana State University/Shreveport
Loyola University/New Orleans
McNeese State University
Nicholls State University

Northeast Louisiana University
Northwestern State University
Southeastern Louisiana University
Southern University and A & M College
Southern University in New Orleans
Tulane University
University of New Orleans
Xavier University of Louisiana

MAINE

Bates College
Husson College
Nasson College
University of Maine at Orono
University of Southern Maine

MARYLAND

Bowie State College
College of Notre Dame of Maryland
Coppin State College
Frostburg State College
Johns Hopkins University
Loyola College
Morgan State University
Mount St. Mary's College
Salisbury State College
Towson State University
University of Maryland/Eastern Shore
Washington College
Western Maryland College

MASSACHUSETTS

American International College
Amherst College
Assumption College
Boston University
Bridgewater State College
Central New England College
Clark University
College of Our Lady of the Elms
Fitchburg State College
Framingham State College
Hampshire College
Harvard University/Harvard and Radcliffe Colleges
Massachusetts Institute of Technology
Mount Holyoke College
Nichols College
Northeastern University
Salem State College
Simmons College
Smith College
Springfield College
Stonehill College
Suffolk University
Tufts University
University of Massachusetts at Amherst
University of Massachusetts at Boston
Wellesley College
Wentworth Institute of Technology
Western New England College
Westfield State College
Worcester Polytechnic Institute

MICHIGAN

Adrian College
Alma College
Central Michigan University
Eastern Michigan University
Lake Superior State College
Lawrence Institute of Technology
Madonna College
Michigan State University
Michigan Technological University
Nazareth College
Northern Michigan University
University of Detroit
University of Michigan/Ann Arbor
University of Michigan/Dearborn

Wayne State University
Western Michigan University

MINNESOTA

Bemidji State University
College of St. Benedict
Concordia College/Moorhead
Concordia College/St. Paul
Gustavus Adolphus College
Mankato State University
Moorhead State University
Saint John's University
Saint Mary's College
University of Minnesota/Twin Cities
Winona State University

MISSISSIPPI

Alcorn State University
Delta State University
Jackson State University
Millsaps College
Mississippi College
Mississippi State University
Mississippi Valley State University
Rust College
Tougaloo College
University of Mississippi
University of Southern Mississippi
William Carey College

MISSOURI

Central Missouri State University
Columbia College
Drury College
Evangel College
Fontbonne College
Lincoln University
Maryville College
Missouri Southern State College
Missouri Western State College
Northeast Missouri State University
Northwest Missouri State University
Saint Louis University
Southwest Missouri State University
Stephens College
University of Missouri/Columbia
University of Missouri/Rolla
University of Missouri/St. Louis
Washington University
Westminster College
William Woods College

MONTANA

Eastern Montana College
Montana State University
University of Montana
Western Montana College

NEBRASKA

Bellevue College
College of Saint Mary
Concordia Teachers College
Creighton University
Doane College
Nebraska Wesleyan University
University of Nebraska/Lincoln

NEVADA

University of Nevada/Las Vegas
University of Nevada/Reno

NEW HAMPSHIRE

Dartmouth College
Keene State College
Nathaniel Hawthorne College
New Hampshire College
Plymouth State College
St. Anselm College
University of New Hampshire

NEW JERSEY

College of Saint Elizabeth
Fairleigh Dickinson University (Florham-Madison campus)
Glassboro State College
Jersey City State College
Monmouth College
Montclair State College
Princeton University
Rider College
Rutgers University/College of Engineering
Rutgers University/College of Nursing
Rutgers University/College of Pharmacy
Rutgers University/Cook College
Rutgers University/Douglass College
Rutgers University/Livingston College
Rutgers University/Mason Gross School of the Arts
Rutgers University/Newark College of Arts and Sciences
Rutgers University/Rutgers College
Rutgers University/University College—Newark
Rutgers University/University College—New Brunswick
Saint Peter's College (Jersey City campus)
Seton Hall University
Stevens Institute of Technology
Trenton State College
Upsala College

NEW MEXICO

Eastern New Mexico University
New Mexico State University

NEW YORK

Albany College of Pharmacy
Alfred University
Canisius College
City University of New York/Herbert H. Lehman College
City University of New York/John Jay College of Criminal Justice
Clarkson College of Technology
College of Saint Rose
Columbia University/Columbia College
Cornell University
Dominican College of Blauvelt
D'Youville College
Eisenhower College of Rochester Institute of Technology
Elmira College
Fordham University/College at Lincoln Center
Fordham University/College of Business Administration
Fordham University/Fordham College
Hofstra University
Houghton College
Iona College
Ithaca College
Le Moyne College
Long Island University/Brooklyn Center
Medaille College
Molloy College
Nazareth College of Rochester
Niagara University
Polytechnic Institute of New York
Pratt Institute
Rensselaer Polytechnic Institute
Roberts Wesleyan College
Rochester Institute of Technology
Russell Sage College
St. Bonaventure University
St. Francis College
St. John Fisher College
St. John's University
St. Lawrence University
Siena College
State University of New York at Albany

1004 ROTC

State University of New York at Binghamton
State University of New York/College at Brockport
State University of New York/College at Buffalo
State University of New York/College at Cortland
State University of New York/College at Fredonia
State University of New York/College at Geneseo
State University of New York/College at Oswego
State University of New York/College at Potsdam
Syracuse University
Union College
United States Military Academy
Utica College of Syracuse University
Wagner College
Wells College

NORTH CAROLINA

Appalachian State University
Belmont Abbey College
Bennett College
Campbell University
Davidson College
Duke University
Elon College
Greensboro College
Guilford College
High Point College
Johnson C. Smith University
Lenoir-Rhyne College
Meredith College
Methodist College
North Carolina Agricultural and Technical State University
North Carolina State University
Pembroke State University
Pfeiffer College
Sacred Heart College
Saint Augustine's College
Shaw University
University of North Carolina at Chapel Hill
University of North Carolina at Charlotte
University of North Carolina at Greensboro
University of North Carolina at Wilmington
Wake Forest University
Western Carolina University
Wingate College
Winston-Salem State University

NORTH DAKOTA

Jamestown College
North Dakota State University
University of North Dakota
Valley City State College

OHIO

Bowling Green State University
Case Western Reserve University
Cedarville College
Central State University
Cleveland State University
The Defiance College
Franklin University
Hiram College
John Carroll University
Kent State University
Muskingum College
Notre Dame College of Ohio
Ohio Dominican College
Ohio Northern University
The Ohio State University
Ohio University
Rio Grande College
University of Cincinnati
University of Dayton
University of Toledo
Wilberforce University
Wittenberg University
Wright State University
Xavier University
Youngstown State University

OKLAHOMA

Bethany Nazarene College
Cameron University
Central State University
East Central Oklahoma State University
Northeastern Oklahoma State University
Northwestern Oklahoma State University
Oklahoma Christian College
Oklahoma City University
Oklahoma Panhandle State University
Oklahoma State University
Southwestern Oklahoma State University
University of Oklahoma
University of Science and Arts of Oklahoma
University of Tulsa

OREGON

Eastern Oregon State College
Oregon Institute of Technology
Oregon State University
Western Oregon State College

PENNSYLVANIA

Allentown College of St. Francis DeSales
Beaver College
Bloomsburg State College
Bryn Mawr College
Bucknell University
California State College
Carlow College
Carnegie-Mellon University
Chestnut Hill College
Cheyney State College
Clarion State College
College Misericordia
Dickinson College
Drexel University
Duquesne University
East Stroudsburg State College
Edinboro State College
Franklin and Marshall College
Gannon University
Gettysburg College
Indiana University of Pennsylvania
King's College
Kutztown State College
Lafayette College
La Roche College
La Salle College
Lehigh University
Lincoln University
Lock Haven State College
Lycoming College
Mansfield State College
Marywood College
Mercyhurst College
Millersville State College
Moravian College
Muhlenberg College
Pennsylvania State University/Behrend College
Pennsylvania State University/University Park Campus
Philadelphia College of Pharmacy and Science
Point Park College
Robert Morris College
Saint Joseph's University
Shippensburg State College
Slippery Rock State College
Spring Garden College
Susquehanna University
Temple University
University of Pennsylvania
University of Pittsburgh
University of Pittsburgh at Bradford
University of Pittsburgh at Greensburg
University of Scranton
Villa Maria College
Washington and Jefferson College
Waynesburg College
West Chester State College
Westminster College
Widener College
Wilson College
York College of Pennsylvania

PUERTO RICO

Caribbean University College
Catholic University of Puerto Rico
Inter-American University of Puerto Rico/Metropolitan Campus
Turabo University
University of Puerto Rico/Cayey University College
University of Puerto Rico/Mayaguez

RHODE ISLAND

Barrington College
Bryant College
Providence College
Rhode Island College
Roger Williams College
Salve Regina—The Newport College
University of Rhode Island

SOUTH CAROLINA

Central Wesleyan College
The Citadel
Claflin College
Clemson University
College of Charleston
Converse College
Erskine College
Francis Marion College
Furman University
Lander College
Presbyterian College
South Carolina State College
University of South Carolina
University of South Carolina at Spartanburg
University of South Carolina/Coastal Carolina College
Voorhees College
Winthrop College
Wofford College

SOUTH DAKOTA

Black Hills State College
Dakota State College
Mount Marty College
National College
Northern State College
South Dakota School of Mines and Technology
South Dakota State University
University of South Dakota
University of South Dakota at Springfield
Yankton College

TENNESSEE

Austin Peay State University
Belmont College
Carson-Newman College
David Lipscomb College
East Tennessee State University
Fisk University
King College
Knoxville College

Memphis State University
Middle Tennessee State University
Milligan College
Tennessee Technological University
Trevecca Nazarene College
University of Tennessee at Chattanooga
University of Tennessee at Martin
University of Tennessee/Knoxville
Vanderbilt University

TEXAS

Abilene Christian University
Bishop College
Dallas Baptist College
Hardin-Simmons University
Houston Baptist University
Huston-Tillotson College
Incarnate Word College
Lubbock Christian College
McMurry College
Midwestern State University
Our Lady of the Lake University of San Antonio
Pan American University
Prairie View A&M University
Rice University
St. Edward's University
St. Mary's University
Sam Houston State University
Stephen F. Austin State University
Tarleton State University
Texas A&I University
Texas A&M University
Texas Christian University
Texas College
Texas Southern University
Texas Tech University
Texas Wesleyan College
Texas Woman's University
Trinity University
University of Houston/Central Campus
University of Houston/Downtown Campus
University of St. Thomas

University of Texas at Arlington
University of Texas at Austin
University of Texas at El Paso
University of Texas at San Antonio
West Texas State University

UTAH

Brigham Young University
University of Utah
Utah State University
Weber State College
Westminster College

VERMONT

Norwich University
University of Vermont
Vermont College of Norwich University

VIRGINIA

Christopher Newport College
College of William and Mary
Ferrum College
George Mason University
Hampden-Sydney College
Hampton Institute
Hollins College
James Madison University
Longwood College
Lynchburg College
Mary Baldwin College
Norfolk State University
Old Dominion University
Radford University
Randolph-Macon College
Saint Paul's College
University of Richmond
University of Virginia
Virginia Commonwealth University
Virginia Military Institute
Virginia Polytechnic Institute and State University
Virginia State University

Virginia Union University
Washington and Lee University

WASHINGTON

Central Washington University
Eastern Washington University
Pacific Lutheran University
Seattle University
University of Washington
Washington State University
Whitworth College

WEST VIRGINIA

Fairmont State College
Marshall University
Salem College
University of Charleston
West Virginia Institute of Technology
West Virginia State College
West Virginia University
West Virginia Wesleyan College

WISCONSIN

Cardinal Stritch College
Edgewood College
Marian College of Fond Du Lac
Marquette University
Milton College
Ripon College
St. Norbert College
University of Wisconsin/Green Bay
University of Wisconsin/La Crosse
University of Wisconsin/Madison
University of Wisconsin/Milwaukee
University of Wisconsin/Oshkosh
University of Wisconsin/Platteville
University of Wisconsin/Stevens Point
University of Wisconsin/Whitewater
Viterbo College
Wisconsin Conservatory of Music

WYOMING

University of Wyoming

NAVY

The Naval Reserve Officers Training Corps gives young men and women an opportunity to earn commissions in the Navy and the Marine Corps while attending college. Two types of NROTC programs are available: a scholarship program of 2, 3, or 4 years, and a non-subsidized program.

Under the scholarship program, which is highly competitive, students are granted full costs of tuition, fees, and textbooks, and receive a subsistence allowance of $100 per month for up to 40 months and pay for summer training periods. Scholarship recipients agree to major in engineering, science, or another field "of interest to the Navy or Marine Corps," and to serve 4 years of active duty and 2 years of Reserve duty after graduation.

In the nonsubsidized program, called the College Program, students undergo the same training as scholarship students, but attend college at their own expense. During their junior and senior years, they receive $100 per month for up to 20 months. College Program students also receive uniforms and books required for naval-science courses. Students may take a 2-year or 4-year College Program. Those in the 4-year program incur no military obligation until they start the advanced course in their junior year. Juniors and seniors may enter the advanced course directly, but must complete a 6-week paid Naval Science Institute program in the summer before their junior year to catch up. Graduates of the College Program agree to serve on active duty for 3 years.

In addition to their normal studies, students take courses in naval science and management and participate in drills. Scholarship students also participate in 3 summer training programs of 4 to 6 weeks each, conducted between the academic years. College Program students participate in 1 summer training program between the junior and senior years.

Applicants for 4-year scholarship programs must take the SAT or ACT before December 1 and have their scores released to the NROTC scholarship program. Those who qualify as finalists will be notified. For 1983, the minimum scores required to ensure qualification as a finalist were: Navy—SAT verbal 430 and math 520, or ACT English 18 and math 24; Marines—SAT composite of 1000 or ACT math and English total of 45. Navy and Marine selection boards will make the final choices on the basis of academic achievement, test scores, demonstrated leadership ability, extracurricular activities, and aptitude for service. Some of those not selected for 4-year scholarships will receive guarantees of 3-year scholarships to start the following year. Students seeking 2-year scholarships for their third or fourth years of college should write to the Navy Opportunity Information Center, P.O. Box 5000, Clifton, N.J. 07012 for further information.

Admissions for the College Program are handled by the professor of naval science at each school. Those who apply for NROTC must be United States citizens between the ages of 17 and 21, possess a high school diploma or equivalency certificate, and meet standards of physical fitness, height, and weight. Further information on NROTC and initial application forms for NROTC scholarships are available from high school guidance offices, colleges and universities that offer NROTC, Navy and Marine Corps processing stations, and the Naval Recruiting Command, Code 314, 4015 Wilson Boulevard, Arlington, Virginia 22203.

The following list shows the colleges and universities included in this book that either host NROTC or offer it through cross registration with another school.

ALABAMA
Auburn University

CALIFORNIA
California Institute of Technology
California State University/Chico
California State University/Fullerton
California State University/Hayward
California State University/Los Angeles
California State University/Northridge
Holy Names College
Menlo College
Mills College
Mount St. Mary's College
Northrop University
Saint Mary's College of California
Stanford University
University of California/Berkeley
University of California/Los Angeles
University of La Verne
University of San Diego
University of Southern California

COLORADO
University of Colorado at Boulder

FLORIDA
Florida Agricultural and Mechanical University
Florida State University
Jacksonville University
University of Florida
Webber College

GEORGIA
Armstrong State College
Clark College
Emory University
Georgia Institute of Technology
Morehouse College
Savannah State College
Southern Technical Institute
Spelman College

IDAHO
University of Idaho

ILLINOIS
Chicago State University
Illinois Institute of Technology
Northwestern University
University of Illinois at Chicago
University of Illinois at Urbana-Champaign

INDIANA
Indiana University at South Bend
Purdue University/West Lafayette
Saint Mary's College
Taylor University
University of Notre Dame

IOWA
Iowa State University

KANSAS
Baker University
University of Kansas

KENTUCKY
Thomas More College

LOUISIANA
Louisiana State University and Agricultural and Mechanical College
Southern University and A & M College
Tulane University
University of New Orleans

MAINE
Bates College
Maine Maritime Academy

MARYLAND
Western Maryland College

MASSACHUSETTS
Assumption College
Boston University
Central New England College
Clark University
Harvard University/Harvard and Radcliffe Colleges
Holy Cross College
Massachusetts Institute of Technology
Massachusetts Maritime Academy
Tufts University
Wellesley College
Worcester Polytechnic Institute
Worcester State College

MICHIGAN
Eastern Michigan University
University of Michigan/Ann Arbor
University of Michigan/Dearborn

MINNESOTA
University of Minnesota/Twin Cities

MISSISSIPPI
University of Mississippi

MISSOURI
Columbia College
Stephens College
University of Missouri/Columbia

NEBRASKA
Concordia Teachers College
Nebraska Wesleyan University
University of Nebraska/Lincoln

NEW JERSEY
College of Saint Elizabeth
Rutgers University/College of Nursing
Rutgers University/Newark College of Arts and Sciences
Rutgers University/University College—Newark

NEW MEXICO
University of Albuquerque
University of New Mexico

NEW YORK
College of Saint Rose
Cornell University
Ithaca College
Nazareth College of Rochester
Rensselaer Polytechnic Institute
Roberts Wesleyan College
Rochester Institute of Technology
Russell Sage College
St. John Fisher College
State University of New York/College at Cortland
State University of New York/Maritime College
Union College
University of Rochester
Wagner College
Wells College

NORTH CAROLINA
Bennett College
Duke University
Guilford College
Shaw University
University of North Carolina at Chapel Hill

OHIO
The Defiance College
Miami University
Ohio Dominican College
The Ohio State University

OKLAHOMA
Oklahoma City University
University of Oklahoma

OREGON
Oregon State University

PENNSYLVANIA
Carnegie-Mellon University
Drexel University
Pennsylvania State University/University Park Campus
Saint Joseph's University
Temple University
University of Pennsylvania
Villanova University

SOUTH CAROLINA
The Citadel
University of South Carolina

TENNESSEE
Belmont College
David Lipscomb College

Fisk University
Trevecca Nazarene College
Vanderbilt University

TEXAS
Houston Baptist University
Prairie View A&M University
Rice University
St. Edward's University
Texas A&M University
Texas Southern University

University of Houston/Central Campus
University of St. Thomas
University of Texas at Austin

UTAH
University of Utah
Westminster College

VIRGINIA
University of Virginia
Virginia Military Institute

WASHINGTON
Gonzaga University
Seattle University
University of Washington
Washington State University

WISCONSIN
Marquette University
University of Wisconsin/Madison
Viterbo College
Wisconsin Conservatory of Music

UPPER DIVISION

The following institutions offer bachelor's degree programs that begin with the junior or senior year of undergraduate study. To enter such a program, the student must have completed one or two years (generally 30 or 60 semester hours) at another institution. Included are upper division schools that are accredited by a regional accrediting association or are candidates for such accreditation.

ALABAMA
Athens State College
Athens, AL 35611

ARIZONA
University of Phoenix
Phoenix, AZ 85004

CALIFORNIA
California College of Podiatric Medicine
San Francisco, CA 94115
Consortium of the California State
  Universities and Colleges
Long Beach, CA 90802
Dominican School of Philosophy and
  Theology
Berkeley, CA 94709
Holy Family College
Mission San Jose, CA 94538
John F. Kennedy University
Orinda, CA 94563
Melodyland School of Theology
Anaheim, CA 92802
Monterey Institute of International Studies
Monterey, CA 93940
Naval Postgraduate School
Monterey, CA 93940
Otis Art Institute of Parsons School of
  Design
Los Angeles, CA 90057
Pacific Oaks College
Pasadena, CA 91105
Southern California College of Optometry
Fullerton, CA 92631
University of California/San Francisco
San Francisco, CA 94143
University of Judaism
Los Angeles, CA 90024
University of West Los Angeles
Culver City, CA 90230

COLORADO
Naropa Institute
Boulder, CO 80302
Saint Thomas Seminary
Denver, CO 80210
University of Colorado Health Sciences
  Center
Denver, CO 80262

DISTRICT OF COLUMBIA
Oblate College
Washington, DC 20017

FLORIDA
Florida Atlantic University
Boca Raton, FL 33431
Florida International University
Miami, FL 33199
Seminary of Saint Vincent de Paul
Boynton Beach, FL 33435
University of North Florida
Jacksonville, FL 32216
University of West Florida
Pensacola, FL 32504

GEORGIA
Mercer University/Southern School of
  Pharmacy
Atlanta, GA 30312

HAWAII
West Oahu College
Aiea, HI 96701

ILLINOIS
Forest Institute of Professional Psychology
Des Plaines, IL 60018
Governors State University
Park Forest South, IL 60466
Illinois College of Optometry
Chicago, IL 60616
National College of Chiropractic
Lombard, IL 60148
National College of Education/Lombard
  Campus
Lombard, IL 60148
Rush University
Chicago, IL 60612
Sangamon State University
Springfield, IL 62708
University of Health Sciences/The
  Chicago Medical School
Chicago, IL 60664
University of Illinois at the Medical Center
Chicago, IL 60680

LOUISIANA
Louisiana State University Medical Center/
  New Orleans
New Orleans, LA 70012

MARYLAND
Saint Mary's Seminary and University
Baltimore, MD 21210
Sojourner-Douglass College
Baltimore, MD 21205
University of Baltimore
Baltimore, MD 21205
University of Maryland at Baltimore
Baltimore, MD 21201

MASSACHUSETTS
New England College of Optometry
Boston, MA 02115

MICHIGAN
Cranbrook Academy of Art
Bloomfield Hills, MI 48013
Walsh College of Accountancy and
  Business Administration
Troy, MI 48084

MINNESOTA
Metropolitan State University
St. Paul, MN 55101
Saint Paul Seminary
St. Paul, MN 55105

NEW HAMPSHIRE
University of New Hampshire/School of
  Lifelong Learning
Durham, NH 03824

NEW YORK
SUNY/College of Environmental Science
  and Forestry
Syracuse, NY 13210
SUNY/College of Technology
Utica, NY 13502
SUNY/Downstate Medical Center
Brooklyn, NY 11203

OHIO
Medical College of Ohio at Toledo
Toledo, OH 43699

OREGON
University of Oregon Health Sciences
  Center/School of Nursing
Portland, OR 97201

PENNSYLVANIA

Hahnemann College of Allied Health
  Professions
Philadelphia, PA 19102

Pennsylvania State University/Capitol
  Campus
Middletown, PA 17057

Thomas Jefferson University/College of
  Applied Health Sciences
Philadelphia, PA 19107

PUERTO RICO

University of Puerto Rico/Health
Sciences Campus
San Juan, PR 00936

TENNESSEE

Scarritt College for Christian Workers
Nashville, TN 37203

University of Tennessee for the Health
  Sciences
Memphis, TN 38103

TEXAS

American Technological University
Killeen, TX 76541

Corpus Christi State University
Corpus Christi, TX 78412

East Texas State University at Texarkana
Texarkana, TX 75501

Laredo State University
Laredo, TX 78040

University of Houston at Clear Lake City
Houston, TX 77058

University of Houston at Victoria Center
Victoria, TX 77901

University of Texas Health Science Center
  at San Antonio
San Antonio, TX 78284

University of Texas Medical Branch
Galveston, TX 77550

University of Texas of the Permian Basin
Odessa, TX 79762

University of Texas at Tyler
Tyler, TX 75701

VERMONT

School for International Training
Brattleboro, VT 05301

WASHINGTON

City College
Seattle, WA 98104

Griffin College
Seattle, WA 98121

ALPHABETICAL INDEX OF COLLEGES

Abilene Christian University, TX, **857**
Adams State College, CO, **94**
Adelphi University, NY, **531**
Adrian College, MI, **390**
Agnes Scott College, GA, **150**
Alabama Agricultural and Mechanical University, AL, **1**
Alabama State University, AL, **1**
Alaska Pacific University, AK, **16**
Albany College of Pharmacy, NY, **532**
Albany State College, GA, **150**
Albertus Magnus College, CT, **107**
Albion College, MI, **390**
Albright College, PA, **726**
Alcorn State University, MS, **436**
Alderson-Broaddus College, WV, **951**
Alfred University, NY, **532**
Allegheny College, PA, **727**
Allentown College of St. Francis de Sales, PA, **728**
Alliance College, PA, **729**
Alma College, MI, **391**
Alvernia College, PA, **729**
Alverno College, WI, **963**
Amber University, TX, **858**
American International College, MA, **347**
American University, DC, **123**
Amherst College, MA, **348**
Anderson College, IN, **226**
Andrews University, MI, **392**
Angelo State University, TX, **858**
Anna Maria College, MA, **349**
Antillian College, PR, **795**
Antioch College, OH, **657**
Appalachian State University, NC, **622**
Aquinas College, MI, **392**
Arizona State University, AZ, **19**
Arkansas College, AR, **24**
Arkansas State University, AR, **25**
Arkansas Tech University, AR, **25**
Armstrong College, CA, **34**
Armstrong State College, GA, **151**
Arnold and Marie Schwartz College of Pharmacy and Health Sciences, NY, **533**
Art Center College of Design, CA, **35**
Asbury College, KY, **289**
Ashland College, OH, **657**
Assumption College, MA, **350**
Atlanta College of Art, GA, **152**
Atlantic Christian College, NC, **622**
Atlantic Union College, MA, **350**
Auburn University/Auburn, AL, **2**
Auburn University/Montgomery, AL, **3**
Augsburg College, MN, **416**
Augusta College, GA, **152**
Augustana College, IL, **184**
Augustana College, SD, **825**
Aurora College, IL, **184**
Austin College, TX, **859**
Austin Peay State University, TN, **834**
Averett College, VA, **912**
Avila College, MO, **446**
Azusa Pacific University, CA, **36**

Babson College, MA, **351**
Baker University, KS, **273**
Baldwin-Wallace College, OH, **658**
Ball State University, IN, **226**
Baptist College at Charleston, SC, **808**
Barat College, IL, **185**
Barber-Scotia College, NC, **623**
Bard College, NY, **534**
Barrington College, RI, **801**
Barry University, FL, **132**
Bartlesville Wesleyan College, OK, **700**
Bates College, ME, **318**
Bayamon Central University, PR, **795**

Baylor University, TX, **860**
Beacon College, DC, **124**
Beaver College, PA, **730**
Belhaven College, MS, **436**
Bellarmine College, KY, **290**
Bellevue College, NE, **477**
Belmont Abbey College, NC, **623**
Belmont College, TN, **834**
Beloit College, WI, **963**
Bemidji State University, MN, **417**
Benedict College, SC, **809**
Benedictine College, KS, **274**
Bennett College, NC, **624**
Bennington College, VT, **901**
Bentley College, MA, **351**
Berea College, KY, **291**
Berklee College of Music, MA, **352**
Berry College, GA, **153**
Bethany Bible College, CA, **36**
Bethany College, KS, **275**
Bethany College, WV, **952**
Bethany Nazarene College, OK, **700**
Bethel College, IN, **227**
Bethel College, KS, **275**
Bethel College, MN, **418**
Bethel College, TN, **835**
Bethune-Cookman College, FL, **133**
Biola University, CA, **37**
Birmingham-Southern College, AL, **3**
Biscayne College, FL, **133**
Bishop College, TX, **860**
Black Hills State College, SD, **826**
Blackburn College, IL, **186**
Bloomfield College, NJ, **498**
Bloomsburg State College, PA, **731**
Bluefield College, VA, **913**
Bluefield State College, WV, **952**
Blue Mountain College, MS, **437**
Bluffton College, OH, **659**
Boise State University, ID, **179**
Boricua College, NY, **535**
Boston College, MA, **353**
Boston Conservatory of Music, MA, **353**
Boston State College, MA. See University of Massachusetts at Boston, MA.
Boston University, MA, **354**
Bowdoin College, ME, **319**
Bowie State College, MD, **331**
Bowling Green State University, OH, **660**
Bradford College, MA, **355**
Bradley University, IL, **186**
Brandeis University, MA, **355**
Brenau College, GA, **154**
Brescia College, KY, **291**
Briar Cliff College, IA, **254**
Bridgeport Engineering Institute, CT, **108**
Bridgewater College, VA, **913**
Bridgewater State College, MA, **356**
Brigham Young University, UT, **897**
Brigham Young University/Hawaii Campus, HI, **176**
Brooks Institute, CA, **38**
Brown University, RI, **802**
Bryan College, TN, **835**
Bryant College, RI, **803**
Bryn Mawr College, PA, **731**
Bucknell University, PA, **732**
Buena Vista College, IA, **255**
Burlington College, VT, **902**
Butler University, IN, **228**
Cabrini College, PA, **733**
Caldwell College, NJ, **499**
California Baptist College, CA, **38**
California College of Arts and Crafts, CA, **39**
California College of Pediatric Medicine, CA, **39**
California Institute of Technology, CA, **39**

California Institute of the Arts, CA, **40**
California Lutheran College, CA, **41**
California Maritime Academy, CA, **41**
California Polytechnic State University/San Luis Obispo, CA, **42**
California State College, PA, **733**
California State College/Bakersfield, CA, **43**
California State College/San Bernardino, CA, **43**
California State College/Stanislaus, CA, **44**
California State Polytechnic University/Pomona, CA, **45**
California State University/Chico, CA, **45**
California State University/Dominguez Hills, CA, **46**
California State University/Fresno, CA, **47**
California State University/Fullerton, CA, **48**
California State University/Hayward, CA, **48**
California State University/Humboldt, CA. See Humboldt State University, CA.
California State University/Long Beach, CA, **49**
California State University/Los Angeles, CA, **50**
California State University/Northridge, CA, **50**
California State University/Sacramento, CA, **51**
California State University/San Diego, CA. See San Diego State University, CA.
California State University/San Francisco, CA. See San Francisco State University, CA.
California State University/San Jose, Ca. See San Jose University, CA.
California State University/Sonoma, CA. See Sonoma State University, CA.
Calumet College, IN, **228**
Calvin College, MI, **393**
Cameron University, OK, **701**
Campbellsville College, KY, **292**
Campbell University, NC, **625**
Canisius College, NY, **535**
Capital University, OH, **661**
Capitol Institute of Technology, MD, **331**
Cardinal Newman College, MO, **446**
Cardinal Stritch College, WI, **964**
Caribbean University College, PR, **796**
Carleton College, MN, **418**
Carlow College, PA, **734**
Carnegie-Mellon University, PA, **735**
Carroll College, MT, **471**
Carroll College, WI, **965**
Carson-Newman College, TN, **836**
Carthage College, WI, **965**
Case Western Reserve University, OH, **661**
Castleton State College, VT, **902**
Catawba College, NC, **625**
Catholic University of America, DC, **124**
Catholic University of Puerto Rico, PR, **796**
Cedar Crest College, PA, **736**
Cedarville College, OH, **662**
Centenary College, NJ, **499**
Centenary College of Louisiana, LA, **304**
Center for Creative Studies, MI, **394**
Central Connecticut State College, CT, **108**
Central Methodist College, MO, **447**
Central Michigan University, MI, **394**
Central Missouri State University, MO, **448**
Central New England College, MA, **357**
Central State University, OH, **663**
Central State University, OK, **701**
Central University of Iowa, IA, **255**
Central Washington University, WA, **939**
Central Wesleyan College, SC, **809**
Centre College of Kentucky, KY, **293**
Chadron State College, NE, **477**
Chaminade University of Honolulu, HI, **176**
Chapman College, CA, **52**
Chatham College, PA, **736**
Chestnut Hill College, PA, **737**
Cheyney State College, PA, **738**

INDEX

Chicago State University, IL, **187**
Christian Brothers College, TN, **837**
Christian Heritage College, CA, **53**
Christian University College of the Americas, PR, **797**
Christopher Newport College, VA, **914**
Citadel, The, SC, **810**
City University of New York/Bernard M. Baruch College, NY, **536**
City University of New York/Brooklyn College, NY, **537**
City University of New York/City College, NY, **537**
City University of New York/College of Staten Island, NY, **538**
City University of New York/Herbert H. Lehman College, NY, **539**
City University of New York/Hunter College, NY, **539**
City University of New York/John Jay College of Criminal Justice, NY, **540**
City University of New York/Medgar Evers College, NY, **541**
City University of New York/Queens College, NY, **541**
City University of New York/York College, NY, **542**
Claflin College, SC, **810**
Claremont Colleges/Claremont McKenna College, The, CA, **53**
Claremont Colleges/Harvey Mudd College, The, CA, **54**
Claremont Colleges/Pitzer College, The, CA, **55**
Claremont Colleges/Pomona College, The, CA, **56**
Claremont Colleges/Scripps College, The, CA, **57**
Clarion State College, PA, **738**
Clark College, GA, **154**
Clarke College, IA, **256**
Clarkson College of Technology, NY, **543**
Clark University, MA, **357**
Clemson University, SC, **811**
Cleveland Institute of Art, OH, **664**
Cleveland Institute of Music, OH, **664**
Cleveland State University, OH, **665**
Clinch Valley College of the University of Virginia, VA, **914**
Coe College, IA, **257**
Cogswell College, CA, **57**
Coker College, SC, **812**
Colby College, ME, **320**
Colby-Sawyer College, NH, **489**
Colegio Universitario Metropolitano, PR, **797**
Colgate University, NY, **543**
College for Human Services, NY, **544**
College Misericordia, PA, **739**
College of Charleston, SC, **812**
College of Great Falls, MT, **472**
College of Idaho, ID, **180**
College of Insurance, NY, **544**
College of Mount Saint Joseph on the Ohio, OH, **666**
College of Mount Saint Vincent, NY, **545**
College of New Rochelle, NY, **546**
College of Notre Dame, CA, **58**
College of Notre Dame of Maryland, MD, **332**
College of Our Lady of the Elms, MA, **358**
College of St. Benedict, MN, **419**
College of St. Catherine, MN, **420**
College of Saint Elizabeth, NJ, **500**
College of St. Francis, IL, **188**
College of St. Joseph the Provider, VT, **903**
College of Saint Mary, NE, **478**
College of Saint Rose, NY, **547**
College of St. Scholastica, MN, **420**
College of Saint Teresa, MN, **421**
College of St. Thomas, MN, **422**
College of Santa Fe, NM, **525**
College of Steubenville, OH. See University of Steubenville, OH.

College of the Atlantic, ME, **320**
College of the Holy Cross, MA. See Holy Cross College, MA.
College of the Ozarks, The, AR, **26**
College of the Southwest, NM, **526**
College of the Virgin Islands, VI, **911**
College of William and Mary, VA, **915**
College of Wooster, OH, **666**
Colorado College, CO, **95**
Colorado School of Mines, CO, **95**
Colorado State University, CO, **96**
Colorado Technical College, CO, **97**
Columbia College, IL, **188**
Columbia College, MO, **448**
Columbia College, SC, **813**
Columbia Union College, MD, **333**
Columbia University/Barnard College, NY, **547**
Columbia University/Columbia College, NY, **548**
Columbia University/School of Engineering and Applied Science, NY, **549**
Columbia University/School of General Studies, NY, **550**
Columbus College, GA, **155**
Columbus College of Art and Design, OH, **667**
Combs College of Music, PA, **740**
Concord College, WV, **953**
Concordia College, IL, **189**
Concordia College, MI, **395**
Concordia College, NY, **550**
Concordia College, OR, **713**
Concordia College, WI, **966**
Concordia College/Moorhead, MN, **422**
Concordia College/St. Paul, MN, **423**
Concordia Teachers College, NE, **478**
Connecticut College, CT, **109**
Conservatory of Music of Puerto Rico, PR, **797**
Converse College, SC, **814**
Cooper Union for the Advancement of Science and Art, The, NY, **551**
Coppin State College, MD, **333**
Cornell College, IA, **257**
Cornell University, NY, **552**
Cornish Institute, WA, **940**
Covenant College, TN, **837**
Creighton University, NE, **479**
Culver-Stockton College, MO, **449**
Cumberland College, KY, **293**
Curry College, MA, **358**

Daemen College, NY, **552**
Dakota State College, SD, **827**
Dakota Wesleyan University, SD, **827**
Dallas Baptist College, TX, **861**
Dana College, NE, **480**
Daniel Webster College, NH, **490**
Dartmouth College, NH, **491**
David Lipscomb College, TN, **838**
Davidson College, NC, **626**
Davis and Elkins College, WV, **954**
Defiance College, The, OH, **668**
Delaware State College, DE, **120**
Delaware Valley College of Science and Agriculture, PA, **740**
De Lourdes College, IL, **190**
Delta State University, MS, **437**
Denison University, OH, **668**
De Paul University, IL, **190**
Depauw University, IN, **229**
De Vry Institute of Technology, AZ, **20**
De Vry Institute of Technology, GA, **155**
De Vry Institute of Technology, IL, **191**
De Vry Institute of Technology, TX, **861**
Dickinson College, PA, **741**
Dickinson State College, ND, **652**
Dillard University, LA, **305**
Doane College, NE, **480**
Dominican College of Blauvelt, NY, **553**
Dominican College of San Rafael, CA, **58**
Dordt College, IA, **258**
Dowling College, NY, **554**
Drake University, IA, **258**

Drew University/College of Liberal Arts, NJ, **501**
Drexel University, PA, **742**
Drury College, MO, **449**
Duke University, NC, **627**
Duquesne University, PA, **742**
Dyke College, OH, **669**
D'Youville College, NY, **555**

Earlham College, IN, **230**
East Carolina University, NC, **627**
East Central Oklahoma State University, OK, **702**
Eastern College, PA, **743**
Eastern Connecticut State College, CT, **109**
Eastern Illinois University, IL, **191**
Eastern Kentucky University, KY, **294**
Eastern Mennonite College, VA, **916**
Eastern Michigan University, MI, **395**
Eastern Montana College, MT, **472**
Eastern Nazarene College, MA, **359**
Eastern New Mexico University, NM, **526**
Eastern Oregon State College, OR, **714**
Eastern Washington University, WA, **941**
Eastman School of Music, NY, **555**
East Stroudsburg State College, PA, **744**
East Tennessee State University, TN, **839**
East Texas Baptist College, TX, **862**
East Texas State University, TX, **863**
Eckerd College, FL, **134**
Edgewood College, WI, **967**
Edinboro State College, PA, **745**
Edward Waters College, FL, **135**
Eisenhower College of Rochester Institute of Technology, NY, **556**
Elizabeth City State University, NC, **628**
Elizabethtown College, PA, **745**
Elmhurst College, IL, **192**
Elmira College, NY, **557**
Elon College, NC, **629**
Embry-Riddle Aeronautical University, AZ. See Embry-Riddle Aeronautical University, FL.
Embry-Riddle Aeronautical University, FL, **135**
Emerson College, MA, **360**
Emmanuel College, MA, **360**
Emory and Henry College, VA, **917**
Emory University, GA, **156**
Emporia State University, KS, **276**
Erskine College, SC, **814**
Eureka College, IL, **193**
Evangel College, MO, **450**
Evergreen State College, The, WA, **941**

Fairfield University, CT, **110**
Fairleigh Dickinson University, NJ, **501**
Fairmont State College, WV, **954**
Fashion Institute of Technology, NY. See State University of New York/Fashion Institute of Technology, NY.
Fayetteville State University, NC, **629**
Felician College, NJ, **502**
Ferris State College, MI, **396**
Ferrum College, VA, **917**
Findlay College, OH, **670**
Fisk University, TN, **839**
Fitchburg State College, MA, **361**
Flagler College, FL, **136**
Flaming Rainbow University, OK, **703**
Florida Agricultural and Mechanical University, FL, **137**
Florida Institute of Technology, FL, **137**
Florida Memorial College, FL, **138**
Florida Southern College, FL, **139**
Florida State University, FL, **139**
Florida Technological University, FL. See University of Central Florida, FL.
Fontbonne College, MO, **451**
Fordham University/College at Lincoln Center, NY, **558**
Fordham University/College of Business Administration, NY, **558**

INDEX 1011

Fordham University/Fordham College, NY, 559
Fort Hays State University, KS, 277
Fort Lewis College, CO, 97
Fort Valley State College, GA, 159
Framingham State College, MA, 362
Francis Marion College, SC, 815
Franklin and Marshall College, PA, 746
Franklin College, IN, 230
Franklin Pierce College, NH, 491
Franklin University, OH, 670
Freed-Hardeman College, TN, 840
Fresno Pacific College, CA, 59
Friends University, KS, 278
Frostburg State College, MD, 334
Furman University, SC, 816

Gallaudet College, DC, 125
Gannon University, PA, 747
Gardner-Webb College, NC, 630
General Motors Institute, MI, 397
Geneva College, PA, 748
George Fox College, OR, 715
George Mason University, VA, 918
Georgetown College, KY, 294
Georgetown University, DC, 126
George Washington University, DC, 127
George Williams College, IL, 193
Georgia College, GA, 157
Georgia Institute of Technology, GA, 158
Georgia Southern College, GA, 159
Georgia Southwestern College, GA, 159
Georgia State University, GA, 160
Georgian Court College, NJ, 503
Gettysburg College, PA, 749
Glassboro State College, NJ, 503
Glenville State College, WV, 955
Goddard College, VT, 903
Golden Gate University, CA, 60
Goldey Beacom College, DE, 120
Gonzaga University, WA, 942
Gordon College, MA, 362
Goshen College, IN, 231
Goucher College, MD, 335
Grace College, IN, 232
Graceland College, IA, 259
Grambling State University, LA, 305
Grand Canyon College, AZ, 21
Grand Valley State Colleges, MI, 397
Grand View College, IA, 260
Green Mountain College, VT, 904
Greensboro College, NC, 630
Greenville College, IL, 194
Grinnell College, IA, 260
Grove City College, PA, 749
Guilford College, NC, 631
Gustavus Adolphus College, MN, 424
Gwynedd-Mercy College, PA, 750

Hamilton College, NY, 560
Hamline University, MN, 424
Hampden-Sydney College, VA, 919
Hampshire College, MA, 363
Hampton Institute, VA, 919
Hanover College, IN, 233
Harding University, AR, 27
Hardin-Simmons University, TX, 863
Harris-Stowe State College, MO, 451
Hartwick College, NY, 561
Harvard University/Harvard and Radcliffe Colleges, MA, 364
Hastings College, NE, 481
Haverford College, PA, 751
Hawaii Loa College, HI, 177
Hawaii Pacific College, HI, 178
Heidelberg College, OH, 671
Hellenic College and Holy Cross Greek Orthodox School of Theology, MA, 365
Henderson State University, AR, 27
Hendrix College, AR, 28
Heritage College, WA, 942
High Point College, NC, 632

Hillsdale College, MI, 398
Hiram College, OH, 672
Hobart and William Smith Colleges/Hobart College, NY, 561
Hobart and William Smith Colleges/William Smith College, NY, 562
Hofstra University, NY, 563
Hollins College, VA, 920
Holy Cross College, MA, 365
Holy Family College, PA, 751
Holy Names College, CA, 61
Hood College, MD, 335
Hope College, MI, 399
Houghton College, NY, 564
Houston Baptist University, TX, 864
Howard Payne University, TX, 865
Howard University, DC, 128
Humboldt State University, CA, 61
Huntingdon College, AL, 4
Huntington College, IN, 233
Huron College, SD, 828
Husson College, ME, 321
Huston-Tillotson College, TX, 865

Idaho State University, ID, 181
Illinois Benedictine College, IL, 195
Illinois College, IL, 195
Illinois Institute of Technology, IL, 196
Illinois State University, IL, 197
Illinois Wesleyan University, IL, 197
Immaculata College, PA, 752
Incarnate Word College, TX, 866
Indiana Central University, IN, 234
Indiana Institute of Technology, IN, 235
Indiana State University/Evansville, IN, 236
Indiana State University/Terre Haute, IN, 235
Indiana University/Bloomington, IN, 238
Indiana University/Kokomo, IN, 237
Indiana University Northwest, IN, 239
Indiana University of Pennsylvania, PA, 753
Indiana University-Purdue University at Fort Wayne, IN, 240
Indiana University-Purdue University at Indianapolis, IN, 240
Indiana University/South Bend, IN, 237
Indiana University Southeast, IN, 241
Instituto Technologico y de Estudios Superiores de Monterrey, MEX, 991
Inter-American University of Puerto Rico/Arecibo Regional College, PR, 797
Inter-American University of Puerto Rico/Metropolitan Campus, PR, 797
Inter-American University of Puerto Rico/San German, PR, 798
International Institute of the Americas of World University, PR, 798
Iona College, NY, 565
Iowa State University, IA, 261
Iowa Wesleyan College, IA, 261
Ithaca College, NY, 565

Jackson State University, MS, 438
Jacksonville State University, AL, 4
Jacksonville University, FL, 140
James Madison University, VA, 921
Jamestown College, ND, 652
Jarvis Christian College, TX, 867
Jersey City State College, NJ, 504
Jewish Theological Seminary of America, The, NY, 566
John Brown University, AR, 29
John Carroll University, OH, 672
Johns Hopkins University, MD, 336
Johnson C. Smith University, NC, 632
Johnson State College, VT, 905
Judson College, AL, 5
Judson College, IL, 198
Julliard School, The, NY, 567
Juniata College, PA, 754

Kalamazoo College, MI, 400

Kansas City Art Institute, MO, 452
Kansas Newman College, KS, 278
Kansas State University, KS, 279
Kansas Wesleyan University, KS, 280
Kean College of New Jersey, NJ, 505
Kearney State College, NE, 482
Keene State College, NH, 492
Kendall College, IL, 199
Kennesaw College, GA, 161
Kent State University, OH, 673
Kentucky State University, KY, 295
Kentucky Wesleyan College, KY, 296
Kenyon College, OH, 674
Keuka College, NY, 567
King College, TN, 841
King's College, PA, 754
King's College, The, NY, 568
Knox College, IL, 199
Knoxville College, TN, 841
Kutztown State College, PA, 755

Lafayette College, PA, 756
LaGrange College, GA, 162
Lake Erie College for Women, OH, 675
Lake Forest College, IL, 200
Lakeland College, WI, 967
Lake Superior State College, MI, 400
Lamar University, TX, 867
Lambuth College, TN, 842
Lander College, SC, 817
Lane College, TN, 842
Langston University, OK, 703
La Roche College, PA, 757
La Salle College, PA, 757
Lawrence Institute of Technology, MI, 401
Lawrence University, WI, 968
Lebanon Valley College, PA, 758
Lee College, TN, 843
Lehigh University, PA, 759
Le Moyne College, NY, 568
LeMoyne-Owen College, TN, 844
Lenoir-Rhyne College, NC, 633
Lesley College, MA, 366
Le Tourneau College, TX, 868
Lewis and Clark College, OR, 715
Lewis-Clark State College, ID, 181
Lewis University, IL, 201
Liberty Baptist College, VA, 922
Limestone College, SC, 817
Lincoln Memorial University, TN, 844
Lincoln University, CA, 62
Lincoln University, MO, 452
Lincoln University, PA, 760
Lindenwood Colleges, The, MO, 453
Linfield College, OR, 716
Livingston University, AL, 6
Livingstone College, NC, 634
Lock Haven State College, PA, 760
Loma Linda University, CA, 63
Long Island University/Arnold and Marie Schwartz College of Pharmacy and Health Sciences, NY. See Arnold and Marie Schwartz College of Pharmacy and Health Sciences, NY.
Long Island University/Brooklyn Center, NY, 569
Long Island University/C. W. Post Center, NY, 570
Long Island University/Southampton College, NY, 571
Longwood College, VA, 922
Loras College, IA, 262
Loretto Heights College, CO, 98
Los Angeles Baptist College, CA, 63
Louisiana College, LA, 306
Louisiana State University and Agricultural and Mechanical College, LA, 307
Louisiana State University/Shreveport, LA, 308
Louisiana State University/University of New Orleans, LA. See University of New Orleans, LA.
Lousiana Tech University, LA, 308

1012 INDEX

Louisville School of Art, KY, 296
Loyola College, MD, 337
Loyola Marymount University, CA, 64
Loyola University/New Orleans, LA, 309
Loyola University of Chicago, IL, 201
Lubbock Christian College, TX, 869
Luther College, IA, 263
Lycoming College, PA, 761
Lynchburg College, VA, 923
Lyndon State College, VT, 905

Macalester College, MN, 425
MacMurray College, IL, 202
Madonna College, MI, 401
Maharishi International University, IA, 264
Maine Maritime Academy, ME, 322
Malone College, OH, 675
Manchester College, IN, 241
Manhattan College, NY, 572
Manhattan School of Music, NY, 572
Manhattanville College, NY, 573
Mankato State University, MN, 426
Mannes College of Music, NY, 574
Mansfield State College, PA, 762
Marian College, IN, 242
Marian College of Fond Du Lac, WI, 969
Marietta College, OH, 676
Marion College, IN, 243
Marist College, NY, 574
Marlboro College, VT, 906
Marquette University, WI, 970
Marshall University, WV, 956
Mars Hill College, NC, 634
Martin Center College, IL, 243
Mary Baldwin College, VA, 924
Mary College, ND, 653
Marycrest College, IA, 264
Marygrove College, MI, 402
Maryland Institute/College of Art, MD, 338
Marylhurst Education Center, OR, 717
Marymount College, NY, 575
Marymount College of Kansas, KS, 280
Marymount College of Virginia, VA, 924
Marymount Manhattan College, NY, 576
Maryville College, MO, 454
Maryville College, TN, 845
Mary Washington College, VA, 925
Marywood College, PA, 763
Massachusetts College of Art, MA, 366
Massachusetts College of Pharmacy and Allied Health Sciences, MA, 367
Massachusetts Institute of Technology, MA, 367
Massachusetts Maritime Academy, MA, 368
Mayville State College, ND, 653
McGill University, CAN, 988
McKendree College, IL, 203
McMurry College, TX, 869
McNeese State University, LA, 310
McPherson College, KS, 281
Medaille College, NY, 577
Medical College of Georgia, GA, 162
Memphis Academy of Arts, TN, 846
Memphis State University, TN, 846
Menlo College, CA, 65
Mercer University, GA, 163
Mercer University in Atlanta, GA, 163
Mercy College, NY, 577
Mercy College of Detroit, MI, 403
Mercyhurst College, PA, 763
Meredith College, NC, 635
Merrimack College, MA, 369
Mesa College, CO, 99
Messiah College, PA, 764
Methodist College, NC, 636
Metropolitan State College, CO, 99
Miami University, OH, 677
Michigan State University, MI, 403
Michigan Technological University, MI, 404
Mid-America Nazarene College, KS, 281
Middlebury College, VT, 907
Middle Tennessee State University, TN, 847

Midland Lutheran College, NE, 482
Midwest College of Engineering, IL, 203
Midwestern State University, TX, 870
Miles College, AL, 6
Millersville State College, PA, 765
Milligan College, TN, 848
Milliken University, IL, 204
Millsaps College, MS, 439
Mills College, CA, 65
Milton College, WI, 970
Milwaukee School of Engineering, WI, 971
Minneapolis College of Art and Design, MN, 427
Minot State College, ND, 654
Mississippi College, MS, 439
Mississippi Industrial College, MS, 440
Mississippi State University, MS, 440
Mississippi University for Women, MS, 441
Mississippi Valley State University, MS, 442
Missouri Baptist College, MO, 454
Missouri Institute of Technology, MO, 455
Missouri Southern State College, MO, 455
Missouri Valley College, MO, 456
Missouri Western State College, MO, 457
Mobile College, AL, 7
Molloy College, NY, 578
Monmouth College, IL, 204
Monmouth College, NJ, 505
Montana College of Mineral Science and Technology, MT, 473
Montana State University, MT, 474
Montclair State College, NJ, 506
Moore College of Art, PA, 766
Moorhead State University, MN, 427
Moravian College, PA, 766
Morehead State University, KY, 297
Morehouse College, GA, 164
Morgan State University, MD, 338
Morningside College, IA, 265
Morris Brown College, GA, 165
Morris College, SC, 818
Mount Holyoke College, MA, 370
Mount Marty College, SD, 828
Mount Mary College, WI, 971
Mount Mercy College, IA, 265
Mount St. Clare College, IA, 266
Mount Saint Mary College, NY, 579
Mount St. Mary's College, CA, 66
Mount St. Mary's College, MD, 339
Mount Senario College, WI, 972
Mount Union College, OH, 678
Mount Vernon College, DC, 129
Mount Vernon Nazarene College, OH, 678
Muhlenberg College, PA, 767
Mundelein College, IL, 205
Murray State University, KY, 297
Museum Art School, OR. See Pacific Northwest College of Art, OR
Muskingum College, OH, 679

Nasson College, ME, 322
Nathaniel Hawthorne College, NH, 493
National College, SD, 829
National College of Education, IL, 206
National University, CA, 67
Native American Educational Services, IL, 207
Nazareth College, MI, 405
Nazareth College of Rochester, NY, 579
Nebraska Wesleyan University, NE, 483
Neumann College, PA, 768
Newberry College, SC, 818
New College of California, CA, 67
New College of the University of South Florida, FL, 141
New England College, NH, 493
New England Conservatory of Music, MA, 371
New Hampshire College, NH, 494
New Jersey Institute of Technology, NJ, 507
New Mexico Highlands University, NM, 527
New Mexico Institute of Mining and Technology, NM, 527
New Mexico State University, NM, 528

New School for Social Research/Seminar College, NY. See Seminar College, NY.
New School of Music, PA, 769
New York Institute of Technology, NY, 580
New York University, NY, 581
Niagara University, NY, 510
Nicholls State University, LA, 310
Nichols College, MA, 371
Norfolk State University, VA, 926
North Adams State College, MA, 372
North Carolina Agricultural and Technical State University, NC, 636
North Carolina Central University, NC, 637
North Carolina School of the Arts, NC, 637
North Carolina State University, NC, 638
North Carolina Wesleyan College, NC, 639
North Central College, IL, 207
North Dakota State University, ND, 655
Northeastern Illinois University, IL, 208
Northeastern Oklahoma State University, OK, 704
Northeastern University, MA, 372
Northeast Louisiana University, LA, 311
Northeast Missouri State University, MO, 457
Northern Arizona University, AZ, 21
Northern Illinois University, IL, 208
Northern Kentucky University, KY, 298
Northern Michigan University, MI, 406
Northern Montana College, MT, 474
Northern State College, SD, 830
North Georgia College, GA, 165
Northland College, WI, 973
North Park College, IL, 209
Northrop University, CA, 68
North Texas State University, TX, 871
Northwestern College, IA, 267
Northwestern College, MN, 428
Northwestern College, WI, 973
Northwestern Oklahoma State University, OK, 705
Northwestern State University, LA, 312
Northwestern University, IL, 210
Northwest Missouri State University, MO, 458
Northwest Nazarene College, ID, 182
Northwood Institute, MI, 406
Norwich University, VT, 907
Notre Dame College, NH, 495
Notre Dame College of Ohio, OH, 680
Nova University, FL, 141
Nyack College, NY, 582

Oakland City College, IN, 244
Oakland University, MI, 407
Oakwood College, AL, 7
Oberlin College, OH, 680
Occidental College, CA, 68
Oglethorpe University, GA, 166
Ohio Dominican College, OH, 681
Ohio Institute of Technology, OH, 682
Ohio Northern University, OH, 682
Ohio State University, The, OH, 683
Ohio State University at Lima, The, OH, 684
Ohio State University at Mansfield, The, OH, 684
Ohio State University at Marion, The, OH, 685
Ohio State University at Newark, The, OH, 686
Ohio University, OH, 686
Ohio Wesleyan University, OH, 687
Oklahoma Baptist University, OK, 705
Oklahoma Christian College, OK, 706
Oklahoma City University, OK, 707
Oklahoma Panhandle State University, OK, 707
Oklahoma State University, OK, 708
Old Dominion University, VA, 926
Olivet College, MI, 408
Olivet Nazarene College, IL, 211
Oral Roberts University, OK, 708
Oregon College of Education, OR. See Western Oregon State College, OR.
Oregon Institute of Technology, OR, 718
Oregon State University, OR, 718
Ottawa University, KS, 282

Otterbein College, OH, **688**
Ouachita Baptist University, AR, **29**
Our Lady of Angels College, PA. See Neumann College, PA.
Our Lady of Holy Cross College, LA, **312**
Our Lady of the Lake University of San Antonio, TX, **871**

Pace University/College of White Plains, NY, **583**
Pace University/New York Campus, NY, **583**
Pace University/Pleasantville/Briarcliff, NY, **584**
Pacific Lutheran University, WA, **943**
Pacific Northwest College of Art, OR, **719**
Pacific Union College, CA, **69**
Pacific University, OR, **720**
Paine College, GA, **167**
Palm Beach Atlantic College, FL, **142**
Pan American University, TX, **872**
Park College, MO **458**
Parks College of St. Louis University, IL, **212**
Parsons School of Design, NY, **585**
Paul Quinn College, TX, **873**
Peabody Conservatory of Music, MD, **340**
Pembroke State University, NC, **639**
Pennsylvania State University/Behrend College, PA, **769**
Pennsylvania State University/University Park Campus, PA, **770**
Papperdine University, CA, **70**
Peru State College, NE, **484**
Pfeiffer College, NC, **640**
Philadelphia College of Art, PA, **770**
Philadelphia College of Pharmacy and Science, PA, **771**
Philadelphia College of Textiles and Science, PA, **772**
Philadelphia College of the Performing Arts, PA, **772**
Philander Smith College, AR, **30**
Phillips University, OK, **709**
Piedmont College, GA, **167**
Pikeville College, KY, **299**
Pine Manor College, MA, **373**
Pittsburg State University, KS, **283**
Plymouth State College, NH, **495**
Point Loma College, CA, **71**
Point Park College, PA, **773**
Polytechnic Institute of New York, NY, **585**
Polytechnic University of Puerto Rico, PR, **799**
Portland School of Art, ME, **323**
Portland State University, OR, **720**
Post College, CT, **111**
Prairie View A&M University, TX, **873**
Pratt Institute, NY, **586**
Presbyterian College, SC, **819**
Prescott College, AZ, **22**
Princeton University, NJ, **507**
Principia College, IL, **212**
Providence College, RI, **803**
Purdue University/Calumet, IN, **245**
Purdue University/West Lafayette, IN, **245**

Queens College, NC, **641**
Quincy College, IL, **213**
Quinnipiac College, CT, **111**

Radford University, VA, **927**
Ramapo College of New Jersey, NJ, **508**
Randolph-Macon College, VA, **928**
Randolph-Macon Woman's College, VA, **929**
Reed College, OR, **721**
Regis College, CO, **100**
Regis College, MA, **374**
Rensselaer Polytechnic Institute, NY, **587**
Rhode Island College, RI, **804**
Rhode Island School of Design, RI, **805**
Rice University, TX, **874**
Rider College, NJ, **509**
Ringling School of Art and Design, FL, **142**
Rio Grande College, OH, **689**
Ripon College, WI, **973**

Rivier College, NH, **496**
Roanoke College, VA, **929**
Robert Morris College, PA, **773**
Roberts Wesleyan College, NY, **588**
Rochester Institute of Technology, NY, **588**
Rochester Institute of Technology/Eisenhower College, NY. See Eisenhower College of Rochester Institute of Technology, NY.
Rockford College, IL, **214**
Rockhurst College, MO, **459**
Rockmont College, CO, **100**
Rocky Mountain College, MT, **475**
Roger Williams College, RI, **806**
Rollins College, FL, **143**
Roosevelt University, IL, **215**
Rosary College, IL, **215**
Rose-Hulman Institute of Technology, IN, **246**
Rosemont College, PA, **774**
Russell Sage College, NY, **589**
Rust College, MS, **442**
Rutgers University/Camden College of Arts and Sciences, NJ, **509**
Rutgers University/College of Engineering, NJ, **510**
Rutgers University/College of Nursing, NJ, **511**
Rutgers University/College of Pharmacy, NJ, **512**
Rutgers University/Cook College, NJ, **512**
Rutgers University/Douglass College, NJ, **513**
Rutgers University/Livingston College, NJ, **514**
Rutgers University/Mason Gross School of the Arts, NJ, **515**
Rutgers University/Newark College of Arts and Sciences, NJ, **516**
Rutgers University/Rutgers College, NJ, **516**
Rutgers University/University College — Camden, NJ, **517**
Rutgers University/University College — Newark, NJ, **518**
Rutgers University/University College — New Brunswick, NJ, **519**

Sacred Heart College, NC, **641**
Sacred Heart University, CT, **112**
Saginaw Valley State College, MI, **408**
St. Ambrose College, IA, **267**
St. Andrews Presbyterian College, NC, **642**
St. Anselm College, NH, **497**
Saint Augustine's College, NC, **643**
St. Bonaventure University, NY, **590**
St. Cloud State University, MN, **429**
St. Edward's University, TX, **874**
Saint Francis College, IN, **246**
St. Francis College, NY, **591**
Saint Francis College, PA, **775**
St. John Fisher College, NY, **591**
St. John's College, MD, **340**
St. John's College, NM, **529**
Saint John's University, MN, **429**
St. John's University, NY, **592**
Saint Joseph College, CT, **112**
Saint Joseph's College, IN, **247**
St. Joseph's College, ME, **323**
St. Joseph's College, NY, **593**
Saint Joseph's University, PA, **776**
St. Lawrence University, NY, **593**
Saint Leo College, FL, **144**
St. Louis College of Pharmacy, MO, **460**
St. Louis Conservatory of Music, MO, **460**
Saint Louis University, MO, **461**
St. Martin's College, WA, **944**
Saint Mary College, KS, **284**
Saint Mary of the Plains College, KS, **284**
Saint Mary-of-the-Woods College, IN, **248**
Saint Mary's College, IN, **249**
Saint Mary's College, MI, **409**
Saint Mary's College, MN, **430**
Saint Mary's College of California, CA, **71**
St. Mary's College of Maryland, MD, **341**
St. Mary's Dominican College, LA, **313**
St. Mary's University, TX, **875**
St. Michael's College, VT, **908**

St. Norbert College, WI, **974**
St. Olaf College, MN, **431**
Saint Paul's College, VA, **930**
Saint Peter's College, NJ, **519**
St. Thomas Aquinas College, NY, **594**
Saint Vincent College, PA, **776**
Saint Xavier College, IL, **216**
Salem College, NC, **643**
Salem College, WV, **956**
Salem State College, MA, **374**
Salisbury State College, MD, **342**
Salve Regina — The Newport College, RI, **807**
Samford University, AL, **8**
Sam Houston State University, TX, **876**
San Diego State University, CA, **72**
San Francisco Art Institute, CA, **73**
San Francisco Conservatory of Music, CA, **73**
San Francisco State University, CA, **74**
San Jose State University, CA, **75**
Sarah Lawrence College, NY, **595**
Savannah College of Art and Design, The, GA, **168**
Savannah State College, GA, **168**
School of the Art Institute of Chicago, IL, **217**
School of the Ozarks, The, MO, **461**
School of Visual Arts, NY, **595**
Seattle Pacific University, WA, **944**
Seattle University, WA, **945**
Seminar College, NY, **596**
Seton Hall University, NJ, **520**
Seton Hill College, PA, **777**
Shaw College at Detroit, MI, **410**
Shaw University, NC, **644**
Sheldon Jackson College, AK, **17**
Shenandoah College and Conservatory of Music, VA, **931**
Shepherd College, WV, **957**
Shimer College, IL, **217**
Shippensburg State College, PA, **778**
Shorter College, GA, **169**
Siena College, NY, **596**
Siena Heights College, MI, **410**
Sierra Nevada College, NV, **487**
Silver Lake College of the Holy Family, WI, **975**
Simmons College, MA, **375**
Simon's Rock of Bard College, MA, **376**
Simpson College, CA, **75**
Simpson College, IA, **268**
Sioux Falls College, SD, **830**
Skidmore College, NY, **597**
Slippery Rock State College, PA, **779**
Smith College, MA, **376**
Sonoma State University, CA, **76**
South Carolina State College, SC, **820**
South Dakota School of Mines and Technology, SD, **831**
South Dakota State University, SD, **831**
Southeastern Louisiana University, LA, **314**
Southeastern Massachusetts University, MA, **377**
Southeastern Oklahoma State University, OK, **710**
Southeastern University, DC, **129**
Southeast Missouri State University, MO, **462**
Southern Arkansas University, AR, **30**
Southern California College, CA, **77**
Southern Connecticut State College, CT, **113**
Southern Illinois University/Carbondale, IL, **218**
Southern Illinois University/Edwardsville, IL, **219**
Southern Methodist University, TX, **877**
Southern Missionary College, TN, **848**
Southern Oregon State College, OR, **722**
Southern Technical Institute, GA, **170**
Southern University and A & M College, LA, **314**
Southern University/New Orleans, LA, **315**
Southern Utah State College, UT, **897**
Southern Vermont College, VT, **909**
Southwest Baptist University, MO, **463**
Southwestern Adventist College, TX, **877**
Southwestern at Memphis, TN, **849**

1014 INDEX

Southwestern College, KS, **285**
Southwestern Oklahoma State University, OK, **711**
Southwestern University, TX, **878**
Southwest Missouri State University, MO, **463**
Southwest State University, MN **432**
Southwest Texas State University, TX **879**
Spalding College, KY, **299**
Spelman College, GA, **170**
Spertus College of Judaica, IL, **219**
Spring Arbor College, MI, **411**
Springfield College, MA, **377**
Spring Garden College, PA, **779**
Spring Hill College, AL, **9**
Stanford University, CA, **77**
State University of New York at Albany, NY, **598**
State University of New York at Binghamton, NY, **599**
State University of New York at at Buffalo, NY, **600**
State University of New York at Stony Brook, NY, **601**
State University of New York/College at Brockport, NY, **601**
State University of New York/College at Buffalo, NY, **602**
State University of New York/College at Cortland, NY, **603**
State University of New York/College at Fredonia, NY, **604**
State University of New York/College at Geneseo, NY, **605**
State University of New York/College at New Paltz, NY, **605**
State University of New York/College at Old Westbury, NY, **606**
State University of New York/College at Oneonta, NY, **606**
State University of New York/College at Oswego, NY, **607**
State University of New York/College at Plattsburgh, NY, **608**
State University of New York/College at Potsdam, NY, **609**
State University of New York/College at Purchase, NY, **609**
State University of New York/Empire State College, NY, **610**
State University of New York/Fashion Institute of Technology, NY, **610**
State University of New York/Maritime College, NY, **611**
State University of New York/Regents External Degree Program, NY, **612**
State University of New York/Upstate Medical Center, NY, **612**
Stephen F. Austin State University, TX, **879**
Stephens College, MO, **464**
Sterling College, KS, **286**
Stern College for Women, NY. See Yeshiva University, NY.
Stetson University, FL, **144**
Stevens Institute of Technology, NJ, **521**
Stillman College, AL, **10**
Stockton State College, NJ, **521**
Stonehill College, MA, **378**
Strayer College, DC, **130**
Suffolk University, MA, **379**
Sul Ross State University, TX, **880**
Susquehanna University, PA, **780**
Swain School of Design, MA, **380**
Swarthmore College, PA, **781**
Sweet Briar College, VA, **931**
Syracuse University, NY, **612**
Syracuse University/Utica College, NY. See Utica College of Syracuse University.

Tabor College, KS, **286**
Talladega College, AL, **10**
Tarkio College, MO, **465**
Tarleton State University, TX, **881**

Taylor University, IN, **249**
Temple University, PA, **781**
Tennessee State University, TN, **849**
Tennessee Technological University, TN, **850**
Tennessee Wesleyan College, TN, **851**
Texas A&I University, TX, **881**
Texas A&M University, TX, **882**
Texas A&M University at Galveston, TX, **883**
Texas Christian University, TX, **883**
Texas College, TX, **884**
Texas Lutheran College, TX, **885**
Texas Southern University, TX, **885**
Texas Tech University, TX, **886**
Texas Wesleyan College, TX, **886**
Texas Woman's University, TX, **887**
Thiel College, PA, **782**
Thomas A. Edison State College, NJ, **522**
Thomas Aquinas College, CA, **78**
Thomas College, ME, **324**
Thomas More College, KY, **300**
Tift College, GA, **171**
Toccoa Falls College, GA, **171**
Tougaloo College, MS, **443**
Touro College, NY, **613**
Towson State University, MD, **342**
Transylvania University, KY, **300**
Trenton State College, NJ, **522**
Trevecca Nazarene College, TN, **851**
Tri-State University, IN, **250**
Trinity Christian College, IL, **220**
Trinity College, CT, **114**
Trinity College, DC, **130**
Trinity College, IL, **220**
Trinity College, VT, **909**
Trinity University, TX, **888**
Troy State University System, AL, **11**
Tufts University, MA, **380**
Tulane University, LA, **315**
Turabo University, PR, **799**
Tusculum College, TN, **852**
Tuskegee Institute, AL, **11**

Union College, KY, **301**
Union College, NE, **485**
Union College, NY, **614**
Union University, TN, **853**
Union University/Albany College of Pharmacy, NY. See Albany College of Pharmacy, NY.
United States Air Force Academy, CO, **101**
United States Coast Guard Academy, CT, **114**
United States International University, CA, **79**
United States Merchant Marine Academy, NY, **615**
United States Military Academy, NY, **615**
United States Naval Academy, MD, **343**
Unity College, ME, **325**
Universidad de las Americas, MEX, **991**
University of Akron, OH, **689**
University of Alabama, AL, **12**
University of Alabama/Birmingham, AL, **13**
University of Alabama/Huntsville, AL, **14**
University of Alaska/Anchorage, AK, **18**
University of Alaska/Fairbanks, AK, **18**
University of Alaska/Juneau, AK, **19**
University of Alberta, CAN, **989**
University of Albuquerque, NM, **529**
University of Arizona, AZ, **23**
University of Arkansas/Fayetteville, AR, **31**
University of Arkansas/Little Rock, AR, **32**
University of Arkansas/Monticello, AR, **32**
University of Arkansas/Pine Bluff, AR, **33**
University of Bridgeport, CT, **115**
University of British Columbia, CAN, **989**
University of California/Berkeley, CA, **79**
University of California/Davis, CA, **80**
University of California/Irvine, CA, **81**
University of California/Los Angeles, CA, **82**
University of California/Riverside, CA, **82**
University of California/San Diego, CA, **83**
University of California/Santa Barbara, CA, **84**
University of California/Santa Cruz, CA, **84**
University of Central Arkansas, AR, **34**

University of Central Florida, FL, **145**
University of Charleston, WV, **958**
University of Chicago, The, IL, **221**
University of Cincinnati, OH, **690**
University of Colorado/Boulder, CO, **102**
University of Colorado/Colorado Springs, CO, **103**
University of Colorado/Denver, CO, **104**
University of Connecticut, CT, **116**
University of Dallas, TX, **889**
University of Dayton, OH, **691**
University of Delaware, DE, **121**
University of Denver, CO, **104**
University of Detroit, MI, **412**
University of Dubuque, IA, **269**
University of Evansville, IN, **251**
University of Florida, FL, **146**
University of Georgia, GA, **172**
University of Guam, GU, **175**
University of Hartford, CT, **116**
University of Hawaii at Hilo, HI, **178**
University of Hawaii at Manoa, HI, **179**
University of Houston/Central Campus, TX, **889**
University of Houston/Downtown Campus, TX, **890**
University of Idaho, ID, **183**
University of Illinois/Chicago, IL, **222**
University of Illinois/Urbana-Champaign, IL, **223**
University of Iowa, IA, **269**
University of Kansas, KS, **287**
University of Kentucky, KY, **302**
University of La Verne, CA, **85**
University of Louisville, KY, **303**
University of Lowell, MA, **381**
University of Maine at Farmington, ME, **325**
University of Maine at Fort Kent, ME, **326**
University of Maine at Machias, ME, **327**
University of Maine at Orono, ME, **327**
University of Maine at Presque Isle, ME, **328**
University of Manitoba, CAN, **989**
University of Mary Hardin-Baylor, TX, **891**
University of Maryland/Baltimore County, MD, **344**
University of Maryland/College Park, MD, **344**
University of Maryland/Eastern Shore, MD, **344**
University of Massachusetts at Amherst, MA, **382**
University of Massachusetts at Boston, MA, **383**
University of Miami, FL, **147**
University of Michigan/Ann Arbor, MI, **412**
University of Michigan/Dearborn, MI, **413**
University of Michigan/Flint, MI, **414**
University of Minnesota/Duluth, MN, **432**
University of Minnesota/Morris, MN, **433**
University of Minnesota/Twin Cities, MN, **434**
University of Mississippi, MS, **443**
University of Missouri/Columbia, MO, **465**
University of Missouri/Kansas City, MO, **466**
University of Missouri/Rolla, MO, **467**
University of Missouri/St. Louis, MO, **467**
University of Montana, MT, **475**
University of Montevallo, AL, **14**
University of Nebraska/Lincoln, NE, **486**
University of Nebraska/Omaha, NE, **485**
University of Nevada/Las Vegas, NV, **488**
University of Nevada/Reno, NV, **489**
University of New England, ME, **329**
University of New Hampshire, NH, **497**
University of New Haven, CT, **117**
University of New Mexico, NM, **530**
University of New Orleans, LA, **316**
University of North Alabama, AL, **15**
University of North Carolina at Asheville, NC, **644**
University of North Carolina at Chapel Hill, NC, **645**
University of North Carolina at Charlotte, NC, **646**
University of North Carolina at Greensboro, NC, **647**

University of North Carolina at Wilmington, NC, 647
University of North Dakota, ND, 655
University of Northern Colorado, CO, 105
University of Northern Iowa, IA, 270
University of Notre Dame, IN, 252
University of Oklahoma, OK, 711
University of Oregon, OR, 723
University of Ottawa, CAN, 990
University of Pennsylvania, PA, 783
University of Pittsburgh, PA, 784
University of Pittsburgh/Bradford, PA, 785
University of Pittsburgh/Greensburg, PA, 785
University of Pittsburgh/Johnstown, PA, 786
University of Portland, OR, 723
University of Puerto Rico/Bayamon Technological University College, PR, 799
University of Puerto Rico/Cayey University College, PR, 799
University of Puerto Rico/Humacao, PR, 800
University of Puerto Rico/Mayaguez, PR, 800
University of Puerto Rico/Rio Piedras, PR, 800
University of Puget Sound, WA, 946
University of Redlands, CA, 86
University of Rhode Island, RI, 807
University of Richmond, VA, 932
University of Rochester, NY, 616
University of Rochester/Eastman School of Music, NY. See Eastman School of Music, NY.
University of St. Thomas, TX, 891
University of San Diego, CA, 87
University of San Francisco, CA, 87
University of Santa Clara, CA, 88
University of Science and Arts of Oklahoma, OK, 712
University of Scranton, PA, 786
University of South Alabama, AL, 16
University of South Carolina, SC, 820
University of South Carolina at Aiken, SC, 821
University of South Carolina at Spartanburg, SC, 822
University of South Carolina/Coastal Carolina College, SC, 823
University of South Dakota, SD, 832
University of South Dakota at Springfield, SD, 832
University of Southern California, CA, 89
University of Southern Colorado, CO, 106
University of Southern Maine, ME, 329
University of Southern Mississippi, MS, 443
University of South Florida, FL, 147
University of Southwestern Louisiana, LA, 317
University of Steubenville, OH, 692
University of Tampa, FL, 148
University of Tennessee at Chattanooga, TN, 853
University of Tennessee at Martin, TN, 854
University of Tennessee/Knoxville, TN, 855
University of Texas at Arlington, TX, 892
University of Texas at Austin, TX, 893
University of Texas at El Paso, TX, 894
University of Texas at San Antonio, TX, 894
University of the District of Columbia, DC, 131
University of the Pacific, CA, 90
University of the Sacred Heart, PR, 706
University of the South, The, TN, 855
University of Toledo, OH, 692
University of Toronto, CAN, 990
University of Tulsa, OK, 713
University of Utah, UT, 898
University of Vermont, VT, 910
University of Virginia, VA, 933
University of Washington, WA, 947
University of Waterloo, CAN, 990
University of Western Ontario, The, CAN, 991

University of Wisconsin/Eau Claire, WI, 976
University of Wisconsin/Green Bay, WI, 976
University of Wisconsin/La Crosse, WI, 977
University of Wisconsin/Madison, WI, 978
University of Wisconsin/Milwaukee, WI, 978
University of Wisconsin/Oshkosh, WI, 979
University of Wisconsin/Parkside, WI, 980
University of Wisconsin/Platteville, WI, 980
University of Wisconsin/River Falls, WI, 981
University of Wisconsin/Stevens Point, WI, 982
University of Wisconsin/Stout, WI, 982
University of Wisconsin/Superior, WI, 983
University of Wisconsin/Whitewater, WI, 984
University of Wyoming, WY, 986
Upper Iowa University, IA, 271
Upsala College, NJ, 523
Urbana College, OH, 693
Ursinus College, PA, 787
Ursuline College, OH, 694
Utah State University, UT, 899
Utica College of Syracuse University, NY, 617

Valdosta State College, GA, 173
Valley City State College, ND, 656
Valparaiso University, IN, 252
Vanderbilt University, TN, 856
Vandercook College of Music, IL, 224
Vassar College, NY, 618
Vermont College of Norwich University, VT, 910
Villa Maria College, PA, 788
Villanova University, PA, 789
Virginia Commonwealth University, VA, 934
Virginia Intermont College, VA, 934
Virginia Military Institute, VA, 935
Virginia Polytechnic Institute and State University, VA, 936
Virginia State University, VA, 937
Virginia Union University, VA, 937
Virginia Wesleyan College, VA, 938
Viterbo College, WI, 984
Voorhees College, SC, 823

Wabash College, IN, 253
Wagner College, NY, 619
Wake Forest University, NC, 648
Walla Walla College, WA, 947
Walsh College, OH, 694
Warner Pacific College, OR, 724
Warren Wilson College, NC, 649
Wartburg College, IA, 271
Washburn University of Topeka, KS, 288
Washington and Jefferson College, PA, 789
Washington and Lee University, VA, 938
Washington College, MD, 346
Washington International College, DC, 131
Washington State University, WA, 948
Washington University, MO, 468
Wayland Baptist College, TX, 895
Waynesburg College, PA, 790
Wayne State College, NE, 487
Wayne State University, MI, 415
Webber College, FL, 149
Webb Institute of Naval Architecture, NY, 619
Weber State College, UT, 900
Webster College, MO, 469
Wellesley College, MA, 383
Wells College, NY, 620
Wentworth Institute of Technology, MA, 384
Wesleyan College, GA, 174
Wesleyan University, CT, 118
Wesley College, DE, 122
Westbrook College, ME, 330
West Chester State College, PA, 791
West Coast University, CA, 91
Western Carolina University, NC, 650

Western Connecticut State College, CT, 118
Western Illinois University, IL, 224
Western International University, AZ, 24
Western Kentucky University, KY, 303
Western Maryland College, MD, 346
Western Michigan University, MI, 415
Western Montana College, MT, 476
Western New England College, MA, 385
Western New Mexico University, NM, 530
Western Oregon State College, OR, 725
Western State College, CO, 106
Western Washington University, WA, 949
Westfield State College, MA, 385
West Georgia College, GA, 174
West Liberty State College, WV, 959
Westmar College, IA, 272
Westminster Choir College, NJ, 524
Westminster College, MO, 469
Westminster College, PA, 791
Westminster College, UT, 900
Westmont College, CA, 91
West Texas State University, TX, 895
West Virginia Institute of Technology, WV, 959
West Virginia State College, WV, 960
West Virginia University, WV, 961
West Virginia Wesleyan College, WV, 961
Wheaton College, IL, 225
Wheaton College, MA, 386
Wheeling College, WV, 962
Wheelock College, MA, 387
Whitman College, WA, 949
Whittier College, CA, 92
Whitworth College, WA, 950
Wichita State University, KS, 288
Widener College, PA, 792
Wilberforce University, OH, 695
Wiley College, TX, 896
Wilkes College, PA, 793
Willamette University, OR, 725
William Carey College, MS, 445
William Jewell College, MO, 470
William Paterson College of New Jersey, NJ, 524
William Penn College, IA, 273
Williams College, MA, 387
William Woods College, MO, 470
Wilmington College, DE, 122
Wilmington College, OH, 696
Wilson College, PA, 793
Wingate College, NC, 650
Winona State University, MN, 435
Winston-Salem State University, NC, 651
Winthrop College, SC, 824
Wisconsin Conservatory of Music, WI, 985
Wittenberg University, OH, 696
Wofford College, SC, 824
Woodbury University, CA, 93
Worcester Polytechnic Institute, MA, 388
Worcester State College, MA, 389
World College West, CA, 93
World University/International Institute of the Americas, PR, 706
Wright State University, OH, 697

Xavier University, OH, 698
Xavier University of Louisiana, LA, 317

Yale University, CT, 119
Yankton College, SD, 833
Yeshiva University, NY, 621
York College of Pennsylvania, PA, 794
York University, CAN, 991
Youngstown State University, OH, 699

Notes

Notes

Notes

Notes

Notes

Notes

: **Notes**

ORDER FORM

Please send the following titles:

COLLEGE GUIDES

QTY

___ PROFILES OF AMERICAN COLLEGES, VOL. 1 (Descriptions)
___ paper (2459-1) $11.95
___ cloth (5449-0) $25.95
___ PROFILES OF AMERICAN COLLEGES, VOL. 2 (Index)
___ paper (2460-5) $9.95
___ cloth (5450-4) $17.95
___ REGIONAL EDITION: THE NORTHEAST (2467-2) $5.75
___ REGIONAL EDITION: THE SOUTH (2469-9) $5.75
___ REGIONAL EDITION: THE MIDWEST (2470-2) $5.75
___ REGIONAL EDITION: THE WEST (2468-0) $4.95
___ GUIDE TO THE MOST PRESTIGIOUS COLLEGES (2499-0) $5.95
___ GUIDE TO THE BEST, MOST POPULAR, MOST EXCITING COLLEGES (2500) $5.95
___ COMPACT GUIDE TO COLLEGES (2288-2) $2.95
___ GUIDE TO THE TWO-YEAR COLLEGES, VOL. 1 (Descriptions)
___ paper (2315-3) $6.95
___ cloth (5408-3) $11.00
___ GUIDE TO THE TWO-YEAR COLLEGES, VOL. 2 (Index)
___ paper (2317-4) $6.95
___ cloth (5409-1) $11.95
___ MONEY FOR COLLEGE (2348-x) $3.95

TEST PREPARATION

QTY

___ VERBAL APTITUDE WORKBOOK FOR COLLEGE ENTRANCE EXAMINATIONS (2074-x) $4.75
___ MATH WORKBOOK FOR COLLEGE ENTRANCE EXAMINATION (0654-2) $6.95
___ HOW TO PREPARE FOR THE TEST OF STANDARD WRITTEN ENGLISH (2095-2) $5.95
___ HOW TO PREPARE FOR THE ACT (2495-8) $7.95

HOW TO PREPARE FOR COLLEGE BOARD ACHIEVEMENT TESTS

QTY

___ AMERICAN HISTORY/SOCIAL STUDIES (0489-2) $6.50
___ BIOLOGY (2328-5) $6.95
___ CHEMISTRY (2069-3) $6.95
___ ENGLISH (2282-3) $5.95
___ FRENCH (0941-x) $7.95
___ GERMAN (0977-0) $4.95
___ EUROPEAN HISTORY/WORLD CULTURES (0656-9) $6.95
___ LATIN (0125-7) $4.50
___ MATH LEVEL 1 (2344-7) $6.95
___ MATH LEVEL 2 (0325-x) $7.95
___ PHYSICS (2065-0) $6.95
___ SPANISH (978-9) $8.95
___ HOW TO BEAT TEST ANXIETY AND SCORE HIGHER ON THE SAT (2583-0) $3.95
___ STRATEGIES FOR TAKING TESTS (2565-2) $7.95

OTHER VALUABLE STUDY AIDS

___ BETTER GRADES IN COLLEGE WITH LESS EFFORT (0415-9) $3.95
___ GETTING READY FOR COLLEGE (2080-4) $3.50
___ HOW TO WRITE THEMES AND TERM PAPERS (2266-1) $4.95
___ STUDENT SUCCESS SECRETS (2589-x) $3.95
___ STUDY TACTICS (2590-3) $4.95
___ TYPING THE EASY WAY (2284-x) $6.95

BARRON'S
113 Crossways Park Drive
Woodbury, NY 11797

Please include 10% postage and handling ($1.50 minimum) on all orders. N.Y. residents add sales tax. If not satisfied, return books within 30 days for a full refund.

I enclose $ _____ in total payment.
Bill my _____ Visa _____ MasterCard
_____ American Express
($10.00 minimum charge order)

Acct. # _____ Exp. Date ____ / ____ / ____

Signature _____

PLEASE PRINT

Name: _____

Address: _____

City: _____ State: _____ Zip: _____

All prices subject to change without notice.

BARRON'S TEST PREPARATION MATERIALS FOR THE TOEFL

Test of English as a Foreign Language

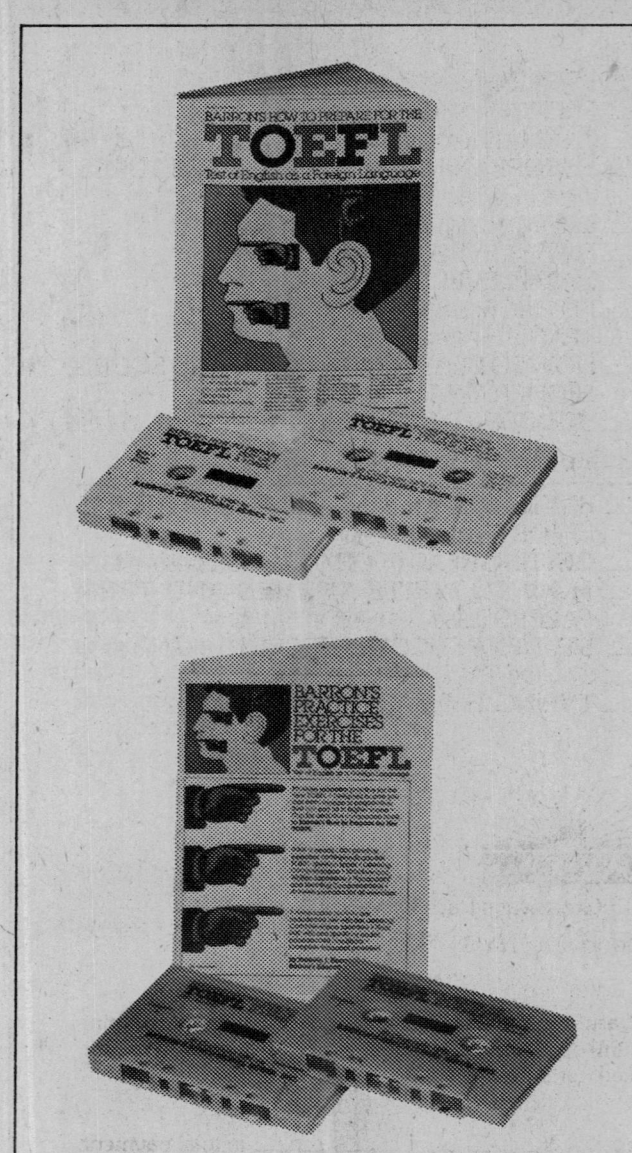

Barron's How to Prepare for the TOEFL • Includes six records covering listening comprehension portions of Model Tests 1-3. (#2115-0) $8.95

How to Prepare for the TOEFL — Listening Comprehension Cassette 1 • Covers listening comprehension portions of Model Tests 1-3. (#2488-5) $7.95

How to Prepare for the TOEFL — Listening Comprehension Cassette 2 • Covers listening comprehension portions of Model Tests 4-6. (#2170-3) $7.95

Barron's Practice Exercises for the TOEFL • Includes six records covering listening comprehension exercises 1-12. (#2164-9) $8.95

Practice Exercises for the TOEFL — Listening Comprehension Cassette 1 • Covers listening comprehension exercises 1-12. (#2489-3) $7.95

Practice Exercises for the TOEFL — Listening Comprehension Cassette 2 • Covers listening comprehension exercises 13-19. (#2490-7) $7.95

BARRON'S EDUCATIONAL SERIES, INC., 113 Crossways Pk. Dr., Woodbury, N.Y. 11797

Canadian orders and inquiries should be addressed to:
BARRON'S
BOOK WAREHOUSE/CANADA
125 Bermondsey Road, Toronto, Ontario M4A 1X3

UK orders and inquiries should be addressed to:
BARRON'S BIBLIOS
Glenside Industrial Estate
Partridge Green, Horsham, West Sussex, RH13 8RA

Please send me the following titles:

Quan.		PRICE: U.S.	Can.	U.K.
____	HOW TO PREPARE FOR THE TOEFL (#2115)	$8.95	$11.95	£6.50
____	CASSETTE 1, Listening Comprehension for Model Tests 1-3 (#2488)	$7.95	$9.95	£5.50
____	CASSETTE 2, Listening Comprehension for Model Tests 4-6 (#2170)	$7.95	$9.95	£5.50
____	PRACTICE EXERCISES FOR THE TOEFL (#2164)	$8.95	$10.50	£5.95
____	CASSETTE 1, Listening Comprehension for practice exercises 1-12 (#2489)	$7.95	$9.95	£5.50
____	CASSETTE 2, Listening Comprehension for practice exercises 13-19 (#2490)	$7.95	$9.95	£5.50

I am enclosing a check for $_____ which includes applicable sales tax, plus 10% transportation charges

Charge to my ☐ MasterCard ☐ Visa ☐ American Express

Account # _____ Expiration Date _____

Signature _____

Name _____

Address _____

Please return book within 15 days if not satisfied for a full refund.

Other Helpful BARRON'S Guides for College-Bound Students

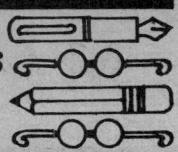

Practical, legitimate tips on remembering more of what you have read, writing better papers in less time, calmly taking—and passing—exams. Provides a sure way to enjoy more of college. $3.50 paper

A step-by-step guide: from selecting the topic and deciding on the type of theme, to writing an effective conclusion. How not to begin a paragraph; cliches to be avoided; the best ways to end a paragraph, more. $4.95 paper

This pocket-sized guide identifies many sources of public and private financial aid programs and provides detailed guidelines on the application process. Includes information on aid for minorities and a listing of college costs, resource material, and specialized programs $3.95 paper

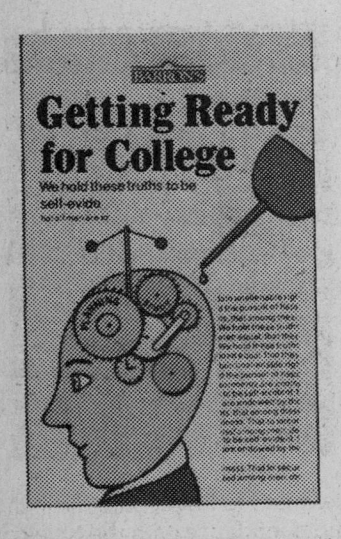

Valuable pointers on getting oriented to college and developing study skills that lead to success. How to plan ahead, make use of time, and other helpful techniques. Don't leave for college without it! $3.50

In-depth preparation for an important part of the SAT. Includes thorough review of English grammar and usage, a diagnostic test, and 5 full-length practice exams, all with explained answers. $5.95 paper

Designed to boost test scores by acquainting you with the 18 basic question types that appear on standardized exams, then showing you how to answer them. Includes a model exam with explained answers. $7.95 paper

All prices are in U.S. dollars and subject to change without notice. At your local bookseller, or order direct adding 10% postage (minimum charge $1.50) plus applicable sales tax.

BARRON'S Barron's Educational Series, Inc., 113 Crossways Park Drive, Woodbury, N.Y. 11797

Other BARRON'S Study Aids You Should Know About

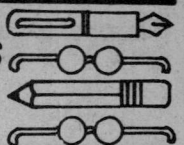

This reassuring book will help nervous test-takers gain skill and confidence. The authors reveal how test-taking skills can be learned; how basic preparation techniques can reduce anxiety and improve performance. Includes 14 rules for higher SAT scores. Essential reading. $3.95

A dynamic approach to better grades and improved self-confidence, using positive thinking techniques. Among the topics covered: Lack of Motivation—the #1 Problem, Success Habits, Attack Plan for Studying, Using Your Memory More Effectively, Word Power, How to Take Tests. Includes cartoons and charts. $3.95

A strategic plan for mastering the skills essential to academic success: reading, writing, test-taking, organizing study time, and more. Solid traditional approach; filled with wisdom and helpful advice. $4.95

The ideal course for non-secretarial students who want to learn typing. The basic skills can be mastered in 30 days; the sturdy "easel" binding lets you practice directly from the book. Part of Barron's new "Easy Way" series. $6.95

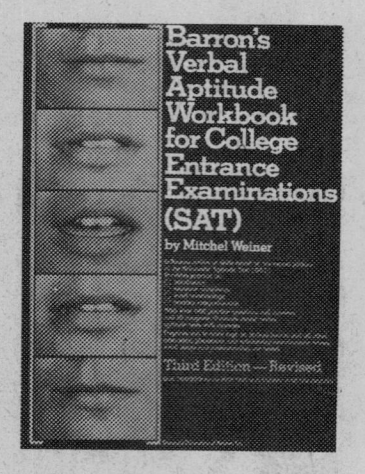

Intensive practice in the verbal question types found on the SAT and other college entrance exams: sentence completion, analogies, vocabulary, and reading comprehension. Includes 1000 practice questions and a battery of 10 verbal aptitude tests with explained answers. $4.75

Designed to help you build skill and confidence with the types of math problems found on college entrance exams. Contains 185 drill exercises, over 650 word problems, and 20 aptitude tests with complete solutions. $6.95

All prices are in U.S. dollars and subject to change without notice. At your local bookseller, or order direct adding 10% postage (minimum charge $1.50) plus applicable sales tax.

BARRON'S Barron's Educational Series, Inc., 113 Crossways Park Drive, Woodbury, N.Y. 11797

Barron's How to Prepare for College Board Achievement Test Series

This series can be used to supplement textbooks, clear up difficult areas, highlight significant facts, diagnose weak spots, and test progress. The model tests, with answers fully explained, prepare the student on subject matter and test-taking techniques.

- ☐ AMERICAN HISTORY/ SOCIAL STUDIES, $6.95
- ☐ BIOLOGY, $6.95
- ☐ CHEMISTRY, $6.95
- ☐ ENGLISH, $5.95
- ☐ FRENCH, $7.95
- ☐ GERMAN, $4.95
- ☐ EUROPEAN HISTORY AND WORLD CULTURES, $6.95
- ☐ LATIN, $4.50
- ☐ MATH LEVEL I, $6.95
- ☐ MATH LEVEL II, $7.95
- ☐ PHYSICS, $6.95
- ☐ SPANISH, $8.95

All prices subject to change without notice.

Prevent your dream school from turning into a four-year nightmare

If you're deciding on the college of your choice for next year, the chances are excellent you'll make the wrong decision.

In fact last year, quite a few students began their sophomore year at a different school.

Obviously a lot of bright, well-intentioned kids just didn't know what they were getting into. And their lack of information proved disastrous.

Barron's College Profiles in-Depth Series begins where most college catalogs leave off.

In every one of our studies we work directly with students. So the things that are often left unsaid are laid on the line.

You might find out that your first choice of schools pours on the pressure. Or your third choice has a new interdisciplinary program that turns you on. Or the majority of classes have huge enrollments. Or a modern, co-ed dorm has just been built. Or the kids don't have much to say about how things are run.

Naturally we include the usual stuff: costs, admission policies and academic programs.

So if the literature you have on the college of your choice just skims the surface, send for our in-depth studies. They might prevent your dream school from turning into a four year nightmare.

☐ Adelphi University (1000)
☐ Alfred University (1001)
☐ American University (1170)
☐ Barnard College (1006)
☐ Bennington College (1340)
☐ Boston University (1010)
☐ Brown University (1014)
☐ Bucknell University (1015)
☐ City College (CUNY) (1020)
☐ Claremont Colleges, (1021)
  Claremont Men's College
  Harvey Mudd College
  Pitzer College
  Pomona College
  Scripps College
☐ Clark University (1177)
☐ Colby College (1024)
☐ Colgate University (1025)
☐ Coll of William & Mary (1026)
☐ Cornell University (1030)
☐ Dartmouth College (1031)
☐ Denison University (1032)
☐ Drew University (1227)
☐ Duke University (1339)
  Fairleigh Dickinson Univ.
☐ Madison Campus (1230)
☐ Rutherford Campus (1040)
☐ Teaneck Campus (1229)
☐ Fashion Inst. of Technology (1330)
☐ Franklin & Marshall College (1211)
☐ George Washington Univ. (1043)
☐ Georgetown University (1044)
☐ Gettysburg College (1046)
☐ Harvard & Radcliffe Colls (1054)
☐ Howard University (1061)
☐ Johns Hopkins University (1065)
☐ Lehigh University (1070)
☐ Lehman College (CUNY) (1335)
☐ Manhattan College (1294)
☐ Mass. Inst. of Tech. (1073)
☐ Mercy College (1334)
☐ Middlebury College (1076)
☐ Montclair State College (1288)
☐ Muskingum College (1302)
☐ Northeastern University (1184)
☐ Ohio University (1255)
☐ Penn State University (1167)
☐ Princeton University (1091)
☐ Purdue University (1093)
☐ Rutgers, State Univ. of N.J. (1099)
☐ St. John Fisher College (1312)
☐ St. Lawrence University (1226)
☐ Seton Hall University (1106)
☐ Smith College (1109)
☐ Southampton College (1333)
☐ Stanford University (1110)
☐ SUC/Brockport (1277)
☐ SUC/Cortland (1278)
☐ SUC/Geneseo (1280)
☐ SUC/New Paltz (1281)
☐ SUC/Oswego (1284)
☐ SUC/Potsdam (1286)
☐ SUNY/Binghamton (Harpur) (1052)
☐ SUNY/Stony Brook (1111)
☐ Swarthmore College (1113)
☐ Syracuse University (1114)
☐ Tufts University (1119)
☐ U.S. Coast Guard Academy (1225)
☐ U.S. Mil. Acad. (West Point) (1338)
☐ University of Bridgeport (1125)
☐ University of Calif., L.A. (1168)
☐ University of Cincinnati (1128)
☐ University of Connecticut (1129)
☐ University of Denver (1132)
☐ University of Miami (1138)
☐ University of Michigan (1139)
☐ University of Pennsylvania (1142)
☐ University of Rochester (1144)
☐ University of Utah (1326)
☐ Vassar College (1148)
☐ Villanova University (1149)
☐ Washington University (1164)
☐ Washington & Lee University (1150)
☐ Wesleyan University (Conn.) (1153)
☐ West Virginia University (1305)
☐ Wheaton College (Mass.) (1299)
☐ Williams College (1156)
☐ Yale College (1159)

Barron's Educational Series, Inc., 113 Crossways Park Drive, Woodbury, New York 11797

A minimum order of 4 Profiles in-Depth at $2.50 each is required. Please add 10% postage and handling charges on all orders. New York State residents please add applicable sales tax.

Name _____ Address _____
City _____ State _____ Zip _____

Barron's College Profiles In-Depth